Britannica
Book of the Year

Britannica
World Data

INDEX

1986
Britannica
Book of the Year

Encyclopædia Britannica, Inc.
Chicago
Auckland/Geneva/London/Manila/Paris/Rome
Seoul/Sydney/Tokyo/Toronto

THE UNIVERSITY OF CHICAGO

*The Britannica Book of the Year is published with the editorial advice
of the faculties of the University of Chicago.*

CONTENTS

CALENDAR 1986

JANUARY

1 New Year's Day

1 Emancipation Proclamation (1863), Pres. Abraham Lincoln's historic edict declaring that all slaves in the Confederate States were free

1 27th anniversary of the revolution that ended the rule of Gen. Fulgencio Batista in Cuba and brought Fidel Castro to power

12 Tenth anniversary of the death of Dame Agatha Christie, British author best known for her immensely popular detective stories and plays

15 15th anniversary of the inauguration of the Aswan High Dam in Egypt. For the first time in history, man was able to control the flow and distribution of the waters of the Nile River

19 250th anniversary of the birth of James Watt, a Scotsman whose invention of the steam engine contributed significantly to the Industrial Revolution

20 U.S. federal holiday honouring the Rev. Martin Luther King, Jr., a civil rights activist

26 Australia Day (1788)

26 Republic Day in India (1950)

FEBRUARY

3 20th anniversary of the first soft landing of a spacecraft on the Moon. It was achieved by Luna 9, a Soviet probe

4 Independence Day in Sri Lanka (1948)

9 Chinese New Year's Day, ushering in the Year of the Tiger

11 Mardi Gras, traditional boisterous celebrations on the day before Lent; the most flamboyant affairs are in Rio de Janeiro, Brazil, and in New Orleans, La.

11 Revolution Day in Iran (1979). The Islamic fundamentalist supporters of Ayatollah Ruhollah Khomeini won control of the country when the Army declared its neutrality and the prime minister resigned

12 Ash Wednesday, first day of Lent in Western Christian churches

14 Valentine's Day in the U.S.

17 Official U.S. observance of George Washington's birthday (Feb. 22, 1732)

24 Bicentennial of the birth of Wilhelm Carl Grimm, coauthor with his brother of *Grimm's Fairy Tales*

27 Independence Day in the Dominican Republic (1844)

MARCH

6 150th anniversary of the fall of the Alamo. Davy Crockett and James Bowie were among the Texas volunteers who died when Mexican troops led by Gen. Antonio López de Santa Anna captured the mission

13 Halley's Comet, which was first sighted at least 2,200 years ago, will be studied from less than 485 km (300 mi) by the Giotto spacecraft. The comet probe, carrying television cameras and an array of sensors, was launched by the European Space Agency in July 1985

16 250th anniversary of the death, at age 26, of Italian composer Giovanni Pergolesi

17 St. Patrick's Day

21 180th anniversary of the birth of Benito Juarez, Mexican national hero and president (1861–72)

24 Tenth anniversary of the death of Montgomery of Alamein, British field marshal, who was one of the great Allied commanders in World War II

25 165th anniversary of Greek independence

30 Easter in Western churches

APRIL

1 April Fool's Day in the U.S.

3 Opening of an exhibition in London to commemorate the 900th anniversary of the Domesday Book. The precious manuscript is an extraordinary record of such things as who owned what lands and farm animals and how many slaves and freemen resided in each region. The detailed nature of the survey, which was ordered by William the Conqueror, amazes even modern statisticians

5 Ch'ing Ming, Chinese Tomb Sweeping Day honouring the deceased

12 25th anniversary of man's first space flight. Yury A. Gagarin circled the Earth in the Soviet Vostok 1 spacecraft and reached a maximum altitude of 301 km (187 mi)

21 60th birthday of Queen Elizabeth II of Britain

24 Jewish feast of Passover

29 85th birthday of Hirohito, emperor of Japan

30 Queen's Day in The Netherlands. Queen Beatrix ascended the throne in 1980 after Queen Juliana, her mother, abdicated

MAY

1 May Day, observed as International Labour Day, especially in Communist countries

4 Easter in Eastern churches

4 Centenary of the Haymarket Riot, a milestone in the history of the U.S. labour movement. When workers gathered in Haymarket Square in Chicago to protest the deaths of six persons the previous day, an unidentified person threw a dynamite bomb that killed seven policemen

8 Centenary of Coca-Cola, which was introduced to the public at Jacob's Pharmacy in Atlanta, Ga. That same year Dr. Pepper also went on the market in Waco, Texas

11 Mother's Day in the U.S.

11 Projected date of the first day of Ramadan, the ninth month in the Islamic calendar

19 450th anniversary of the beheading of Anne Boleyn, second wife of King Henry VIII of England and mother of Queen Elizabeth I

26 U.S. observance of Memorial Day

29 250th anniversary of the birth of Patrick Henry, gifted orator and a major figure of the American Revolution

JUNE

11 Dragon Boat Festival, one of the liveliest of Chinese celebrations. It recalls the futile search for the body of Qu Yuan (Ch'ü Yüan), a celebrated 3rd-century BC poet who, overcome by despair, drowned himself in the Mi-lo River after his career as a trusted counselor was destroyed by slander

12 Independence Day in the Philippines. The islands were ceded to the U.S. after the Spanish-American War of 1898. Although the present republic was formally established on July 4, 1946, independence was later backdated to June 12, 1898

13 20th anniversary of the U.S. Supreme Court's "Miranda decision," which required that policemen advise criminal suspects of certain basic rights before interrogating them

14 Official birthday celebration for Queen Elizabeth II of Britain

15 Father's Day in the U.S.

17 Establishment of the Republic of Iceland (1944), which had been united to Denmark

26 150th anniversary of the birth of C.-J. Rouget de Lisle, composer of "La Marseillaise," France's national anthem

JULY

1 Canada Day (1867)

1 20th anniversary of Medicare, a U.S. government-sponsored health insurance program that benefits all recipients of Social Security

4 210th anniversary of the Declaration of Independence (1776). The U.S., however, did not elect its first president until 1789

5 15th anniversary of Pres. Richard Nixon's certification of the 26th Amendment to the U.S. Constitution, which lowered the voting age to 18

6 15th anniversary of the death of Louis ("Satchmo") Armstrong, great jazz trumpeter

12 450th anniversary of the death of Desiderius Erasmus, a Dutch Humanist regarded as one of the greatest scholars of the northern Renaissance

14 Bastille Day in France, a national holiday commemorating the start of the French Revolution of 1789

28 Tenth anniversary of the devastating earthquake in Tangshan (T'ang-shan), China; an estimated 800,000 people were killed

31 100th anniversary of the death of Hungarian composer and piano virtuoso Franz Liszt

AUGUST

3 Fifth anniversary of the U.S. air traffic controllers strike; though warned that a violation of the no-strike contract would mean permanent dismissal, few at the time believed it would actually come to that

6 Hiroshima Peace Festival, an annual commemoration of the dropping of the first atomic bomb

12 25th anniversary of the Berlin Wall. The original barricade, constructed overnight with barbed wire, was later replaced by a concrete wall. Its height was raised to three metres (ten feet) in 1970 to discourage continued defections to the West

13 20th anniversary of China's Great Cultural Revolution, which disrupted the country and was later officially condemned. The movement, led by Chairman Mao Zedong (Mao Tse-tung), aimed to consolidate the dictatorship of the proletariat, to prevent the restoration of capitalism, and to build socialism

17 Independence Day in Indonesia (1945), the most populous Muslim country in the world

SEPTEMBER

1 Labor Day in the U.S. and Canada

3 Centenary of the surrender of Apache Indian chief Geronimo to U.S. government forces in Arizona. The event, in effect, ended the American Indian wars

5 Islamic New Year's Day

11 15th anniversary of the death of Nikita Khrushchev, a Ukrainian who replaced Georgy Malenkov as leader of the Soviet Union in 1953 but was ousted in 1964 and denied a state funeral when he died in 1971

14 150th anniversary of the death of Aaron Burr, vice-president of the U.S. during the administration of Thomas Jefferson. During Burr's stormy career, he killed his chief political rival, Alexander Hamilton, in a duel in 1804 and was arrested for treason in 1807 but was acquitted

18 Chusok, a Korean national festival dating back to antiquity. Fresh fruits, rice cakes, and wine are placed before ancestral shrines at home, then carried to the grave sites. After fitting rituals, the food is consumed during an all-day picnic characterized by lively songs and dances

OCTOBER

4 Rosh Hashana, Jewish New Year's Day

12 Columbus Day, celebrated in Spain and in many lands visited by the great explorer. U.S. observance is on the 13th

13 Thanksgiving Day in Canada

13 Jewish observance of Yom Kippur, the Day of Atonement. The day is marked by prayer, fasting, and mutual requests for and acceptances of forgiveness for offenses

24 United Nations Day (1945)

28 Centenary of the dedication of the Statue of Liberty. A gift to the U.S. by the people of France, it was designed by sculptor Frédéric Auguste Bartholdi and built in a Paris workshop under the supervision of Gustave Eiffel, who designed the Eiffel Tower

31 Reformation Day, commemoration of the day in 1517 when Martin Luther nailed his 95 Theses to the door of All Saints Church in Wittenberg, Germany. This act was subsequently regarded as the first step in the development of Protestantism

31 Halloween, which in some places is joined to an appeal to aid the United Nations Children's Fund

NOVEMBER

7 Anniversary of the Bolshevik Revolution (1917), which brought Lenin to power as head of a Soviet state. Eight months later the deposed emperor, Nicholas II, his wife, Alexandra, and their young children were murdered

11 Veterans Day in the U.S. The armistice signed on Nov. 11, 1918, ended World War I hostilities between Germany and the Allied powers. On this day many nations honour those who died fighting for their countries

12 70th anniversary of the death of Percival Lowell, U.S. astronomer who predicted the existence of the planet Pluto and in 1905 initiated a search that led to its discovery in 1930

23 50th anniversary of the first issue of *Life* magazine

27 Thanksgiving Day in the U.S. It was first celebrated in 1621 when William Bradford, governor of the first permanent colony in New England, invited neighbouring Indians to join the Pilgrims at Plymouth for a three-day festival to express gratitude for the season's bountiful harvest. Pres. Abraham Lincoln made it a national holiday in 1863

DECEMBER

4 Tenth anniversary of the death of Benjamin Britten, acclaimed Britain's finest operatic composer since Henry Purcell (d. 1695)

14 75th anniversary of Roald Amundsen's unprecedented trek to the South Pole. The intrepid Norwegian explorer undertook the last leg of the trip with four companions and 52 dogs. Amundsen lost his life trying to rescue an explorer friend who had crashed in a dirigible in the Arctic

20 Tenth anniversary of the death of Richard J. Daley, longtime mayor of Chicago and the last unchallenged boss of a major U.S. city political machine

25 Christmas Day

25 60th anniversary of the reign of Japanese Emperor Hirohito, the 124th direct descendant of Jimmu, Japan's legendary first emperor

26 Boxing Day

27 Jewish festival of Hanukka, also called the Feast of Lights and the Feast of Dedication, commemorates the rededication in 165 BC of the Second Temple of Jerusalem after its desecration three years earlier by Antiochus IV Epiphanes, the Syrian king

9

The New Asia-Pacific Era

A Perspective from an International Nation Building for the 21st Century

BY YASUHIRO NAKASONE

When I first entered the Japanese Diet in 1947, I was 28 years old. My country was still in ruins from the total defeat of World War II, a disaster brought upon us by the arrogance of our militarists and our shortsightedness in following them. I shall never forget threading my way to the corridors of the National Diet in Tokyo, past the rubble and the black-market peddlers outside. Large areas of Tokyo, like most of our cities, remained blackened moonscapes, with people still digging in the ruins. But even at that time I was encouraged by the vigour and resilience of our people. Freed at last from military imperatives and long constraints on their liberties, they set out from their makeshift shacks to rebuild a country based on the ideals of a shared culture and dedicated to the welfare of all.

Through almost 40 years since then, I have been honoured to serve Japan's people as a Diet representative from my home prefecture of Gumma and, in addition, to have had the privilege of holding Cabinet office. I first entered the Cabinet, as minister of state for science and technology, at the age of 41. Through most of these years I was caught up with my fellow citizens in the work of rebuilding a peaceful, prosperous, and democratic Japan. I shared the excitement and sense of achievement in our country as we grew into the world's second-largest economic power. But in the midst of our affluence, newly found and hard won, I was worried and concerned that our very zeal to "catch up" with the world's economic leaders would distort our view of the future. As early as 1957, after a visit to Europe, Southeast Asia, and the Middle East, I wrote: "If we are complacent and leave things as they are, the time will surely come when we shall be criticized for building a new economic empire to replace our military empire of the war years."

Since I became prime minister in November 1982, I have dedicated myself not merely to furthering Japan's own peace and prosperity but to contributing positively to the peace and well-being of other nations and the construction of an abiding world order. These are not merely laudable goals for Japan; they are necessities. There are no options among them. For today a vast gap still exists between the Japanese reality and what the rest of the world expects of Japan. Japan is no longer "catching up." We have, as they say, arrived. There were times when Japanese merely adopted a low posture in the face of outside criticism. That attitude is no longer possible for us. We must make policy, not merely reflect the policy of others. We must see that our enormous economic strength is more effectively displayed and mobilized.

The shell of Hiroshima's old city hall is preserved as a peace monument in the heart of the vibrant new city that has grown up since World War II.

PHOTOGRAPH, TOM HALEY—SIPA/SPECIAL FEATURES

Much of the criticism directed at Japan today is unfair. But fair or unfair, it demands our concern, our reflection, our action. The world balance of power has shifted. This is true not merely in a narrow economic sense. That is why one of the first things I did on coming to office was to address the Japanese people on Japan's need to become an *"international* nation"; that is to say, a nation that must bear a heavy share of international responsibilities, in keeping with its international position.

Just as life was hard for us Japanese in the immediate postwar days, it has become rather easy for us today—too easy, one might say, in the sense that it is easy for prospering people to avoid thinking of their responsibilities. I consider it my role, as prime minister, to communicate to the Japanese people our goals and challenges. In a democracy, without good communication, leadership is ineffective. As I once said about my own government's reform program: To announce a new and difficult program in a democracy is rather like launching a glider. As long as the winds of public opinion and mass media blow, it can fly. If the supporting winds diminish, the glider will stall and crash. Thus, when we advocate a program, it must be made easily understandable. We must communicate directly and graphically—with charts, pictures, with whatever aids to understanding our advanced information society can provide—for true popular consensus in Japan is not lightly achieved.

It is in this spirit that I set forth an outline of Japan's policy as an international nation, as well as some guidelines on how our domestic structure must also change, both to better our own condition and the better to play our international role.

A Foreign Policy for Tomorrow. For Japan's foreign policy to be effective, it should have a basic philosophy, which we might express as follows:

The Active Pursuit of World Peace. This is not the mere abstract expression that it may seem. To maintain and secure world peace, nations as well as individuals must actively work at it. Thus Japan pledges itself to a national policy of supporting nuclear nonproliferation and working for the ultimate elimination of all nuclear weapons. We must work for the reduction of conventional armaments as well. Japan's own armament is purely defensive and will remain so. We do not wish to be thought of as a menace to any other country.

The Advancement of Science and Technology. The accomplishments that man has registered in this area must be used to extend prosperity and to enhance human dignity on this planet. The dramatic betterment of communications and information distribution, in particular, should encourage constant dialogue among the nations. International disputes should be discussed and solved, in a cooperative spirit, by democratic means.

11

In October U.S. ambassador to Japan Mike Mansfield helped kick off a two-month campaign, sponsored by the Japanese government, aimed at encouraging Japanese consumers to buy more imported goods.
HITOSHI FUGO

Aid to the Developing Nations. It is still not so long since Japan's sobering defeat in World War II. We should remember also that Japan has only recently—as history's slow clock reckons—risen from the status of a developing nation to rank with the industrially advanced powers. Therefore, we shall endeavour to contribute to the welfare of international society by helping the developing nations.

Planning for the 21st-Century World. We see a new vision of this world. We shall do everything in our power to bring it to reality. For almost a century Japan has worked to bring about a fusion of Eastern and Western civilization. We feel that our country is uniquely situated to promote cooperation between the Pacific and the Atlantic regions in a spirit of harmony.

Japan can best further these objectives by dealing with several pressing global issues in a practical, realistic, and constructive way.

First, Japan will do its collective best to combat protectionist tendencies, wherever they may occur, by strengthening the free trade system and enlarging the perimeters of world trade. In the course of my administration we have already enacted a series of "market-opening" initiatives and have made a great effort for the promotion of the new round of multilateral trade negotiations. Whatever difficulties this may cause our own producers at home, I am determined to continue on this course until all vestiges of past protectionist thinking among us have been erased.

Second, Japan will seek to prevent war by our commitment to the concept of deterrence and the balance of power. Under present conditions these are the best guarantees of peace. In addition, we will work toward reducing the present level of armaments, nuclear armaments in particular.

Finally, Japan hopes to enhance peace by promoting a spectacular increase in the exchange of both people and information across international borders. The more exchanges we have, the further the world can move in the direction of a truly international culture.

The prospects for world peace are, of course, influenced by developments in the Soviet Union. Since Mikhail Gorbachev assumed the leadership in Moscow, we have heard much speculation about new or altered policies. Without seeming to be too optimistic, I believe that a Gorbachev regime is worth watching very closely, for several reasons.

In the first place, it is obvious that Soviet policy is stagnating, not only in the domestic area but also in international relations. Gorbachev is under heavy pressure to take some action. The Soviets have observed with keen interest the policy reorientation of China, where a general opening of the market, economic liberalization, and the widespread appointment of younger leaders have taken place under a Communist Party leadership.

As a young leader himself, Gorbachev must inevitably regard older "classic" Communists as outdated—almost medieval—people. He seems to be paying more attention to long-range strategic considerations in his planning, as well as showing a talent for a more flexible handling of problems. This is, after all, in the Leninist tradition. The key factor here is age. Compare his age with that of Andrey Gromyko, for example. He may well stay in power for 20 years. Thus he has enough time to introduce innovations in Soviet Communism—in the short, the intermediate, and the long term. For any significant kind of innovation, however, he needs peace. That is what makes me think that nuclear arms negotiations between the Soviet Union and the United States will make some partial progress.

Japan must reexamine and establish a policy toward the Soviet Union in the light of this analysis. We may have before us an excellent opportunity to promote nuclear disarmament, thereby expediting the improvement of East-West relations in general. For this policy to succeed, however, it is of paramount importance to consolidate further the unity of the West. It is Western unity that has, thus far, brought about the amelioration of relations with the Soviet bloc.

This statement may sound paradoxical. It is quite logical and understandable, however, in view of the Soviet Union's international political activity, as it has unfolded over the years. The Soviets, as a matter of consistent policy, have tried recurrently to drive a wedge between the Western allies, as witness their recent unsuccessful efforts to mobilize Western European opinion against the United States. It is only when such efforts are shown to have failed that the Soviets seem more amenable to peaceful discussion and constructive negotiation.

The key role in building Western security is played by the United States, and we must take into account Japan's long-standing ties with the United States as we formulate our policy. It is no exaggeration to say that the relationship

with the United States—an alliance in every sense of the word—is the cornerstone of Japan's foreign policy. The Mutual Security Treaty between the United States and Japan is a key pillar in the global strategy of the free nations. To implement the goals of the treaty properly, Japan must, on its own, build up a defense capability sufficient to discourage any hostile action against us. By assuming its fair share of the burden for the defense of the free world, Japan will be the more readily recognized as a full partner of the alliance, able to offer advice when it is desirable to do so. Another stabilizing influence, particularly in an Asian context, is the U.S. presence on the Korean Peninsula. Strengthening the present cooperation between Japan, the Republic of Korea, and the United States is another indispensable condition for keeping the peace in East Asia.

Let me make one additional point about Asia. The security of Asia is not merely a matter of pacts and defense commitments, important though these are. Asia is different from Europe. Rich in their diversity, its peoples nonetheless share a common heritage. There are many cultural common denominators among the Asian peoples. Not least among these is a bent toward mysticism and the transcendental that gives Asians the patience to wait for events, in a sense, even as we are moving them. This is in contrast to the legal and determinedly historical mind-set of the West.

These differences of viewpoint and tradition inevitably affect even such concrete matters as our requirements for security and defense. Europe is divided between the NATO alliance and the Warsaw Pact in a geometric balance, so to speak. Europe is like an oil painting with no portion of the canvas unpainted. Asia, by contrast, is like a *sumie* (black ink) picture, which has a great deal of white space. This is partly due to Asia's poverty and the widely different stages of development among Asian nations, but it is also due to Asia's "nongeometric" way of thinking.

Asian psychology is different. In Asia it is common practice to contain water that overflows riverbanks in a pond or makeshift reservoir and to leave the water there until it recedes or eventually dries up. We have time. We do not try to expedite this process. Much the same is true of Asian attitudes toward strategy and diplomacy. Unlike Europeans, Asians do not put a high priority on adversarial discussion or military threat. This produces confrontation, even when

it is used only as a bargaining counter. Asians prefer to use dialogue, whether direct or indirect, as a means of easing tension. One might call this a tactic of "wait and see and talk." The style of "wait and see and talk" may seem, in the short run, time-consuming. Some Westerners may feel that such diplomacy by dialogue wastes time. It blurs the edges of controversy and reduces the sharp opposition of issues. Yet this is often not a bad thing. It often prevents the aggravation of disputes and indeed can work toward their settlement.

Trade Friction: Prosperity Versus Protectionism. On some economic problems, however, pressing decisions must be made. The postwar world economy owes much to the open and outward-looking policies developed within the framework of the International Monetary Fund and the General Agreement on Tariffs and Trade (GATT). In this climate, the free-market economies achieved an unprecedented level of material wealth. Serious economic dislocation, however, has become manifest in recent years. We have had a growth recession, fiscal deficits, high interest rates, unemployment, and inflation. Under pressure to solve these thorny problems, many nations are tempted to adopt the inward-looking policies of protectionism.

Protectionism is the most direct threat to a stable and growing global economy. If unchecked in time, it may bring down the entire postwar economic order. We must put new life into the free-market economic system for the 21st century, therefore, by continually expanding free economic exchange.

At their meetings in London (1984) and Bonn (1985), the leaders of the seven major industrialized democracies did not merely reaffirm their resistance to protectionist pressures. They also acknowledged the importance of the open multilateral trading system to the economies of both developed and developing nations. They agreed to consult with their partners in GATT on beginning a new round of multilateral negotiations for trade liberalization.

At this point, I would like to refer briefly to the trade friction that is currently disturbing our relations with the United States and the EC. Since Japan lacks natural resources, we must import the essential sinews of industry—our energy and key raw materials—as well as food in great quantities. To pay for these vital imports, we must export a variety of manufactured goods. Otherwise, we cannot feed the 120 million people on this densely crowded, narrow

Scenes in Tokyo's Tsukiji wholesale market (above) and Yokohama's dockyards (left) illustrate the making of a favourable balance of trade: raw materials and commodities, such as fruit from the U.S., New Zealand, and the Philippines, in; manufactured goods, such as electronics components bound for New York, out.

The competitiveness of Japanese goods in the world market has relied more and more on Japan's leadership in research and development, both in primary industries, such as the Hitachi-built experimental hydrogen fusion power plant (left), and in consumer goods, such as Honda's computerized automobile navigation system (above).

MILT & JOAN MANN—CAMERAMANN INTERNATIONAL; (ABOVE) EIJI MAYAZAWA—BLACK STAR

archipelago, which is smaller than France or the single U.S. state of California.

In 1984, however, our export surplus with the United States amounted to $36.8 billion (nearly one-third of the total U.S. import excess). That with the EC amounted to $10.8 billion. Such large surpluses are both unnecessary and undesirable. They have brought on a storm of criticism from America and Europe, giving rise to a fierce outbreak of protectionist sentiment. The U.S. Congress, in particular, has become highly emotional on this issue. Its members have put intense pressure on the White House to move against Japan. Only the statesmanship of Pres. Ronald Reagan has thus far kept the so-called trade war under control. For my part, I have done my best to cope with the situation by instituting the series of sweeping market liberalization measures already mentioned. I will continue my earnest efforts to eradicate all traces of any so-called unfair practices in Japan. Nothing is more derogatory to the national honour of Japan than to be accused of being unfair.

Ultimately, I am optimistic about alleviating trade frictions. Economic disputes, however sharp, are generally amenable to solution, provided the parties concerned keep mutual goodwill alive. The United States and Japan are the largest and the second-largest economies in the free world. Together we account for over one-third of the total world gross national product. We are each other's largest overseas trading partner. In a way, we are responsible for the economic welfare of mankind. The importance of our relationship, however, lies not only in the economic dimension but also in our shared values of freedom and democracy. The twin pillars of stability in the Pacific edifice cannot afford to fall out. If we indulge in recriminations, it would only please our political antagonist, the Soviet Union, which is constantly scheming to separate us.

As the world moves toward a postindustrial society, it behooves Japan, as a leading industrial power, to contribute toward shaping a reformed international order, economic and monetary, to serve the requirements of the 21st century.

A New Asia-Pacific Era. One often hears predictions that the 21st century will be the Japanese century. While such predictions may be flattering to my country, I would prefer to think of these decades just ahead of us as the Pacific century, the advent of a new Asia-Pacific era. History teaches us that civilizations not only expand their frontiers but tend to produce new civilizations and cultures on what were once the peripheries of the old. European civilizations

constantly extended their frontiers, from Greece to Rome, from Rome to England, France, and Germany, and from Europe itself toward the American colonies. Gradually the compass needle of history swung from Mediterranean civilization to Atlantic civilization. Now it is pointing toward the Pacific.

The Pacific region, as we know, is endowed with rich natural resources and vigorous peoples. Once remarkable for its sheer diversity, the Pacific region has been drawn together—in part by the rapid development of communications, transportation, and shared technology—so that what was once thought of as an oceanic Great Divide has become a Great Connector. The Pacific peoples also share a faith in the market economy. We now see an interplay of aggressive free-enterprise economies in this area.

The French historian Fernand Braudel wrote eloquently about how Western capitalism was nurtured first in the Mediterranean Basin, then moved outward to the Atlantic. In the Pacific we are witnessing the birth of a new kind of capitalism. Here the vigour and competitiveness of Western—particularly American—capitalism has been enriched by the Asian cultural heritage, in a life-style that values harmony over adversarial procedures, conciliation over confrontation, and circumspection over assertion. We might call this our Confucian heritage. It is, I believe, an extremely useful shock absorber for a modern society with its tendencies toward division and conflict.

Yet Asian free enterprise has shown itself capable of fostering a competitive dynamism of its own. The distinguishing mark of the Pacific Basin countries has been their commitment to free enterprise economics. The past growth record of the newly industrialized countries (NICs)—the Republic of Korea, Taiwan, Hong Kong, and Singapore—has been quite extraordinary. The ASEAN countries—Thailand, Malaysia, Singapore, the Philippines, Indonesia, and Brunei—have forged a unique and harmonious community, also dedicated to a free market system. The developed countries in the Pacific area—the United States, Canada, Australia, New Zealand, and Japan—have welcomed their increasingly important trading partners. And, indeed, trading patterns among the industrial nations have shifted correspondingly. By 1979 the United States' trade with the Pacific already surpassed its Atlantic trade, and this trend has continued. The ASEAN countries as a group have become the fifth-largest trading partner of Canada and the United States.

The growth records bear eloquent testimony to the vitality of the Pacific Rim nations. For the past two decades,

14

Pacific area growth has averaged 6.7% per year, as compared with 3.7% for the European Communities (EC), for example.

The future also looks promising. According to a study (dated July 24, 1985) conducted by Japan's Economic Planning Agency, real economic growth for the 15-year period 1985–2000 is estimated as follows: world at large 3%; EC 2.5%; Pacific region 4%; Japan 4%; U.S., Canada, Australia 3%; China 7%. Among the ASEAN countries, Malaysia, Thailand, and Indonesia are expected to reach 7%, which is equal to the growth rate of NICs like the Republic of Korea and Taiwan. Such expansion in the Pacific region economy cannot help but have a salutary effect on the rest of the world.

Since assuming the office of prime minister, I have shaped our policies to further enhance Japan's economic cooperation with the nations of the Pacific Basin. We are mutually dependent. There can be no security and prosperity for Japan without security and prosperity for the other Pacific nations, and vice versa.

To render constructive assistance to the nation building of Pacific developing countries, Japan has been expanding our official development assistance (ODA), despite an extremely tight fiscal situation. In 1984 Japan's ODA amounted to $4,319,000,000, an amount inferior only to that spent by the United States. Following our new medium-term target, our government aims to provide total ODA during the seven years starting in 1986 of more than $40 billion, ultimately doubling the annual amount. The ASEAN countries, in particular, will remain the highest priority area for our assistance efforts.

The transfer of industrial technology and the dissemination of managerial know-how are of the utmost importance in promoting productivity in the developing nations. As such transfers are primarily undertaken by private enterprise, it is necessary to make full use of the initiative and vitality of our private sector.

Japan participates in a wide variety of international cooperative enterprises in science and technology. We want to share the fruits of such international research with other Pacific countries as much as possible. When I visited the ASEAN nations in the spring of 1983, for example, I ventured a suggestion that we begin consultations for the promotion of Japan-ASEAN science and technology cooperation. The ASEAN leaders responded favourably to my suggestion. In areas like agriculture, engineering, and medicine, such consultations have now become routine.

My government has long stressed the importance of personal contacts with other Asian countries. In my address at Kuala Lumpur, Malaysia, on May 9, 1983, I proposed to invite a total of 3,750 young people in education and other fields from the ASEAN countries to Japan over the next five years. An increasing number of Japanese youth will visit the ASEAN countries for similar opportunities and experiences. When these people take their rightful places at the centres of their respective societies, the amicable relations between Japan and the ASEAN countries will be truly consolidated.

In 1984 "human resources development" projects were agreed upon anew at the ASEAN ministerial meeting with the "dialogue countries"—Australia, New Zealand, the United States, Canada, and Japan. Recently, the same partners chose 32 urgent projects to bring together specialists for the promotion of trade, the construction and management of industrial ports, airport and highway construction, maritime training, and other areas. Of these, Japan will take part in 15. As the idea of human resources development was originally advanced by Japan, we shall do our

The Jieitai, or Self-Defense Force, is the only military force permitted by Japan's constitution. It includes army, navy, and air force components and comprises some 245,000 personnel.
TOSHI MATSUMOTO—SYGMA

best to ensure its success. Such joint ventures will provide the countries concerned with social infrastructures that will serve them as master keys, so to speak, in exploiting their potential.

In this and other areas, notably international investment and the development of energy and communications resources, Japan has participated with enthusiasm in the meetings of groups from the 12 nations represented in the Pacific Economic Cooperation Conference. Here Japan and the United States play consistently supportive—although not the leading—roles.

The success of such activities justifies U.S. Secretary of State George Shultz's comment that "a sense of Pacific Community is emerging." The growing awareness of the approaching Pacific era not only excites our imagination; it calls upon us to refine our global perspective as an Asian nation. For example, Japan must be prepared to change its industrial structure to meet the requirements of Asian solidarity. As the NICs enlarge their trade volume, they shift the content of *their* exports from primary products to manufactured goods. The challenge that confronts the industrialized nations is to accept increased imports from the NICs. This necessitates sometimes painful domestic adjustments. Yet, unless the nations of the North accept their exports, we can hardly expect the developing nations of the South to contribute to our own export growth. Nor, in the absence of expanding two-way trade, can other heavily indebted NICs (such as Brazil, Mexico, and Argentina) earn enough money to repay their debts and thus preserve the viability of the financial institutions on which both North and South rely.

Unfortunately, I must mention one discordant note in the chorus of Pacific collaboration: the Vietnamese occupation of Kampuchea. Japan has supported the proposal put forward by ASEAN for a negotiated solution of the Kampuchean problem. That proposal is based on the restoration of Kampuchea's sovereignty and the right of its people to choose their own government, free of Vietnamese occupation. So far Vietnam refuses to respond, but Japan will continue its efforts to develop a climate conducive to a political settlement.

The Broader Pacific Perspective. We must bear in mind that Pacific cooperation should not acquire too political a character. In particular, it should not develop a militaristic posture. I once proposed the concept of a Pacific Economic and Cultural Enclave (PEACE). In that proposal, I stressed the wisdom of enlarging cooperation in the economic and

cultural spheres, on the assumption that our interests converged most obviously in these fields.

It is 30 years since the historic conference of Asian-African nations was held in Bandung, Indon., in 1955. Eighty-two nonaligned nations participated in a ceremonial commemoration of the conference in April 1985 and reaffirmed the original Bandung Declaration. The first Bandung Declaration was proposed by the Japanese delegation. Its ten points are still valuable in regulating the international conduct of nations. It was therefore natural that participants in the 1985 ceremony pledge adherence to them.

Let me add one caution on the Pacific relationship, however. We should not perceive this as the establishment of an exclusive regional bloc. The dynamic Pacific Basin economy should serve as a stimulus to the global economy. We should on no account think in terms of the Pacific *versus* the Atlantic, or Asia *versus* Europe. It is not a question of confrontation, one arrayed against the other. Far from it. We should look forward to an era of Atlantic-Pacific collaboration. It is my earnest hope that cooperation between the Atlantic and Pacific, a strong Europe and a developing Asia-Pacific linked together, will inspire mankind in the coming century.

Already the trilateral consultations of North America, Western Europe, and Japan have scored great successes. They demonstrate the truth that the industrialized democracies, sharing the common values of freedom and democracy, can combine their genius for the common good. My visit of July 1985 to Western European countries convinced me anew that there exists among the people of Europe an untapped reservoir of goodwill toward Japan, despite the current trade friction. With Great Britain, our historic ally, we have revived a particularly close relationship. The many new Anglo-Japanese business ventures underline this fact.

Finally, in advancing Pacific cooperation, we should work to develop overall interdependence and mutual reliance. It remains the role of the more advanced nations to respect and support fully the initiatives of other countries in establishing a foundation for regional cooperation. I think "realistic gradualism"—to borrow a phrase from Prime Minister Robert Hawke of Australia—is a good principle to guide the Pacific adventure. My visit to Oceania in January 1985, incidentally, served to reinforce the growing friendship that binds Japan with Australia and New Zealand.

A Vital Power Balance. The peace and stability of Asia are maintained by the balance of four major powers: Japan, the United States, the Soviet Union, and China. Of these, only Japan is a lightly armed, nonnuclear nation. In the old days of rampant power politics, such a balance would have been unthinkable. Military force alone counted. That Japan, although militarily vulnerable, is now regarded as a major stabilizing force attests to the decreasing influence of mere military strength. This is a welcome trend for Japan, since we are determined to remain militarily small but economically great.

If other powers followed Japan's example, the world would become a much safer place. Not only would humanity be freed from the nightmare of a nuclear holocaust, but we would also all be spared the burden of military expenditures. It is estimated that all nations, great and small, spend roughly $800 billion a year on armaments. Think what we could achieve if this money were diverted to peaceful uses.

I would like to examine Japan's relations with the United States, the Soviet Union, and China. We cannot overstate the vital importance of the United States for Japan. A

decade has passed since the United States withdrew from Vietnam in April 1975. A period of drift and debate over the American role in Asia followed, but now the United States is reasserting its presence as a Pacific power, renewing its commitment to the peace of the Pacific region. The U.S. military presence is the great deterrent to Soviet encroachment.

Over the past 20 years, the Soviets have continued a relentless military buildup, nuclear and conventional, far surpassing the legitimate needs of self-defense. This buildup is particularly notable in the Asia-Pacific region. The Pacific Fleet, the largest of the Soviet Union's four fleets, has grown steadily since the mid-1960s, from about 50 major surface combat vessels to over 80, including two carrier task forces. Soviet submarine forces are also impressive. Moreover, the Soviets have deployed a number of missile systems with the capability of reaching targets in much of Asia. The mobile SS-20s, deployed since 1977, now number around 170. Soviet ground forces are also formidable. Totaling some 50 active divisions, they are mainly deployed along the Sino-Soviet border.

Evidently, the Kremlin calculates that if the Soviets are perceived as enjoying military superiority, any enemy can be intimidated without firing a shot. They are adept at employing military force as an instrument of coercion. The buildup of forces on Japan's Northern Territories—the four islands off the northeastern coast of Hokkaido which the Soviet Union occupies illegally—is a case in point. This Soviet military presence in Asia, however, has not been translated into political or economic gains. This is due, I think, to the renewed commitment of the United States to its allies and friends. Our mutually supporting positions on major international issues ensure peace, the prerequisite of prosperity.

This is especially apparent with regard to Japan, which the United States regards as the cornerstone of its Asian policy. Indeed, the United States now treats Japan as a major partner in world politics. Our relationship has doubtless been strengthened by the personal trust which President Reagan and I have established since early 1983, when I first visited the White House immediately after becoming prime minister. I would like to take this opportunity to express my admiration for the president's vision and leadership, stating also my deep gratitude for the warm kindness he so generously bestowed on me. "Ron" and "Yasu" will see to it that our two nations continue to work in unison as the vanguard of peace in Asia and elsewhere.

It was under President Reagan's guidance that the U.S. Defense Department took a firm position not to link the trade and defense issues. Japan's sole rationale for increasing defense capability is to maintain effective deterrence against military attack. The failure of an increasingly prosperous Japan to assume greater defense responsibilities, however, is inexcusable. We should do more for our self-defense not because the United States demands it but because we deem it necessary. What counts, above all, is the national will to defend our own fatherland. Unless we demonstrate this will, our allies and antagonists will not respect our independence.

I have already mentioned the Soviet attitude toward Asia. Although it is difficult to ascertain the ultimate design of the Soviet leadership, I am inclined to think that, generally speaking, the Soviet posture is defensive toward Europe and offensive toward Asia. In the West the Soviet Union wants to preserve the status quo by maneuvering the NATO nations into recognizing and respecting the postwar boundaries bequeathed to it at Yalta. In the East,

(continued on page 18)

Japan's Presidential Prime Minister

Rarely has a nation needed a spokesman as badly as pre-21st-century Japan, the economic superpower whose extraordinary postwar achievement has been almost canceled out by the chronic inability (or unwillingness) of its political and business leaders to tell the rest of the world what the Japanese are up to. In Yasuhiro Nakasone they have finally found one. Since he took office in November 1982, Japan's 15th postwar prime minister has used every means available to him—high visibility summit meetings with his international peers, a tireless round of overseas visits and a barrage of books, well-hyped public relations events and TV interviews—to describe his mission and dramatize a new role for his island country: as a responsible, active leader in the world's political as well as economic decision making.

Japanese newspapers have called Nakasone—less than half admiringly—their "presidential" prime minister. In fact, his ringing statements, keen sense of showmanship, and highly developed personal style represent a sharp break from Japan's postwar tradition of bureaucrat-politicians. Nakasone has not hesitated to go to the people over the heads of his own faction-ridden majority party. He has jolted Japan's complacency on, among other things, the idea of restricting defense expenditures to a token level while relying on U.S. protection. He has appealed, bluntly and forcefully, for Japanese to import more and build up their domestic economy, instead of relying on exports for so much of their growth. And at home he has tackled major sociopolitical problems like educational reform.

For all his nagging about their responsibilities—perhaps because of this—the Japanese like him. Over his first two two-year terms in office, he has done better in the public opinion polls than any of his predecessors. A handsome activist who gives out an air of youthful dynamism belying his 68 years, Nakasone embodies a happy combination of internationalism and homely "Japanese" virtues. An enthusiastic painter in the Western mode, he also enjoys Japanese brush painting and gives samples of his calligraphy to his friends and political supporters. Well traveled and widely read—and, typically, a graduate of Tokyo University's Law Faculty—he is also a small-town boy whose father was a lumber merchant in the mountain-girt prefecture of Gumma. While he manages to get in his weekly tennis game every Saturday, he also spends an hour or two each weekend in Zen meditation. Nakasone's favourite recreation away from the political pits is writing the elliptical, impressionistic, intensely private, and archetypically Japanese haiku verses—an interesting characteristic in a man given to blunt language.

Nakasone's inability to suffer fools gladly has made him many enemies among his own consensus-loving party faithful. A man of scholarly tastes, he has a lively mind capable of digesting complex issues quickly. He is a good listener, with an unceasing curiosity. The titles of the 16 books he has written—covering topics from revisionist capitalism to the creation of a postwar culture—suggest the almost bewilderingly wide range of his interests.

In a most immediate way, Nakasone has lived the history of his generation. In April 1941, a newly

arrived bureaucrat in the Home Ministry, he volunteered for the Navy. When war broke out with the United States, he was a junior lieutenant aboard the cruiser *Aoba*. In August, four years later, he saw the strange mushroom cloud over Hiroshima from the nearby naval base at Kure. He did his first campaigning for the Diet on a bicycle, pedaling through the rubble of a devastated countryside.

The difference, however, between Nakasone and his thoughtful contemporaries elsewhere is that he has spent virtually all of the past four decades in public office. Thanks to the almost continuous rule of Japan's majority Liberal-Democratic Party, he has accumulated the sort of political experience only rarely enjoyed by politicians in a working democracy. With 14 terms as a member of the lower house behind him, he has served, variously, as head of the Defense Agency and the Science and Technology Agency, minister of transport, minister of international trade and industry, and secretary-general of the Liberal-Democratic Party. An incurable traveler, he has negotiated with Andrey Gromyko, visited with Jawaharlal Nehru and Zhou Enlai (Chou En-lai), started a close "Ron and Yasu" friendship with Ronald Reagan in English, and greeted the president and people of Japan's closest neighbour with a few well-chosen words in Korean.

In Japan he played the game of Liberal Party politics rather well. It is not for nothing that he has been called the "Weathervane" (*Kazamidori*). For no Japanese politician could ever hope to climb to political power without long experience in faction-mending, opposition-placating, and teahouse power brokering. What is distinctive about Nakasone still, however, is a kind of engaging brashness and personal assertiveness. The present-day proponent of "easy to understand politics," who dramatizes the trade imbalance by TV shopping expeditions for foreign goods, is the same man who shocked Douglas MacArthur by sending him a 7,000-word memorandum on what he was doing wrong during the U.S. occupation.

After almost four years in the top job, Nakasone's self-confidence remains massive. Whether his party will allow him a third term as prime minister—against recent precedent—remains to be seen. A veteran of political rough-and-tumble, he has already taken more than his share of opposition. But whether or not he remains in office, Yasuhiro Nakasone has already changed the nature of that office, possibly permanently. The concept of the presidential prime minister is there to stay. More important than that, beneath his assertiveness and showmanship, Nakasone has given to his fellow-Japanese a coherent view of their nation's character and role, a sense of leadership and mission, as it were, that the Japanese have not known for a long time.　　　　　　　　(FRANK GIBNEY)

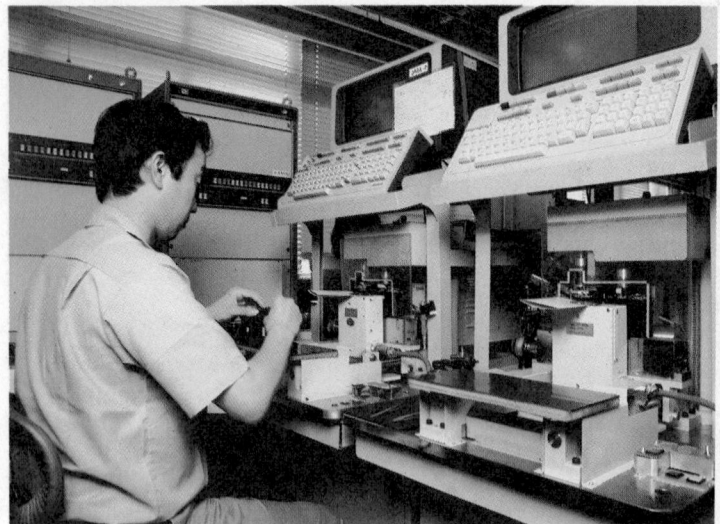

U.S. products in the Japanese market: at left, a computer designed by Hewlett-Packard is used to test and adjust Nikon cameras as they come off the assembly line; at right, a familiar American design figures prominently in a Tokyo display of telephone equipment.

(LEFT) MILT & JOAN MANN—CAMERAMANN INTERNATIONAL; (RIGHT) TOSHI MATSUMOTO—SYGMA

(continued from page 16)

however, it tries to expand the Soviet sphere of influence by challenging the status quo. Confrontation with China—although mitigated recently—is one, but not the only, reason for an aggressive Soviet policy. The massing of Soviet military forces in the Far East is clearly beyond the requirements of normal defense.

The menace of the Soviet forces has not been felt sufficiently by the Japanese people. This is because the Japan-U.S. Mutual Security Treaty, concluded in 1960 to replace the former Security Treaty of 1951, has functioned so effectively. Accustomed to the protection they have long received from the United States, the Japanese take it for granted that they need not worry about the security of their country. There is nothing so dangerous, however, as this kind of *self-deception*.

As I noted earlier, I am not at all pessimistic about the possibility of improving relations with the Soviet Union. Indeed, I am quite hopeful that the U.S.S.R. will eventually see the wisdom of friendly coexistence with Japan. We have a prior condition, however, for any such rapprochement: the Soviet Union must return the Northern Territories, which it has occupied forcibly. This will be a proof of the Kremlin's repeatedly avowed desire to promote neighbourly relations with Japan. If the Soviet Union demonstrates its sincerity through deeds, not words, then a peace treaty can finally be concluded. In that event, Japan's cooperation in developing Siberian economic resources will also be forthcoming, to the immense benefit of the Soviets.

As for China, that giant country is in the throes of a bold industrial and social experiment known as the Four Modernizations, intended to push China's economy to the front rank. The goal is to raise per capita income from $250 in 1978 to $1,000 by the end of the century. Over a decade has elapsed since the late Premier Zhou Enlai (Chou En-lai), a statesman of great vision, enunciated this policy in 1975. After many trials and tribulations, the present leadership under Deng Xiaoping (Teng Hsiao-p'ing) is confidently carrying out the task. In Deng's words: "The purpose of revolution, after all, is to liberate and develop the productive forces of a country." In implementing his unprecedented plans, Deng has sought the cooperation of the developed countries, notably Japan and the United States. (*See* WORLD AFFAIRS [East Asia]: *China:* Special Report.)

We in Japan have pledged to extend our utmost help. Japan and China both face formidable challenges as we lay the foundations for the 21st century. We must strive together to achieve our goal of ensuring common peace and prosperity.

On my visit to China in March 1984, I was overwhelmed by the enthusiastic welcome accorded me by its government and people. I took this as a token of goodwill toward Japan. During my sojourn, I again met Premier Zhao Ziyang (Chao Tzu-yang) and General Secretary Hu Yaobang (Hu Yao-pang) and reaffirmed the principles that guide our relationship: (1) peace and friendship; (2) equality and reciprocity; (3) long-term stability; and (4) mutual trust. I suggested the addition of this fourth principle, to which the general secretary wholeheartedly agreed. In this way this statement is a compass that will guide us through all weather, fair or foul.

It was to symbolize this newfound harmony between China and Japan that the two countries have inaugurated the Japan-China Friendship Committee for the 21st Century. It is my conviction that the development of a friendly, peaceful relationship between Japan and China is vital not only to both countries but also to the peace of Asia and the whole world. Improvement of relations, now evident, between China and the United States adds to the stability of the Pacific region. The United States justly regards a nonaligned, secure China striving for modernization and pursuing an independent policy as a stabilizing factor in Asia. Thus, the United States is cooperating with China in selected defense areas.

Three Major Domestic Initiatives. Japan must act upon all these pressing issues if we are to realize our aim of building a new "international nation." Yet we cannot succeed without a most intensive review of our domestic policy. The people of Japan have seen major changes not only in their economy but in their thought, their life-style, their social patterns. People want spiritual enrichment and the satisfaction of achievement as well as the externals of a stable society. In short, we must prepare for the 21st century here at home.

To this end I have dedicated myself to making Japan a nation of resilient culture and welfare. What do I mean

by "resilient"? I mean a society that can absorb change without succumbing to it, that can leave itself open to all outside influences without losing its inner harmony and integrity—a society that can teach and contribute as much as and more than it has learned.

Thus we are working on three major areas: administrative, fiscal, educational.

Administrative. I came to office pledged to review thoroughly Japan's whole administrative structure. This includes reviewing and rationalizing the organization of government ministries and agencies, in accordance with guidelines set for us by a distinguished national commission. During the high-growth years, Japan's body politic managed to accumulate a good bit of excess administrative fat. We are now, of necessity, slimming down. Many functions that government performed for us during our rise to a higher stage of economic development now seem better given into the hands of private business.

We have already reorganized two large institutions that were government monopolies, the Nippon Telegraph and Telephone Public Corporation (NTT) and the Japan Tobacco and Salt Public Corporation. They are now private joint stock companies. Plans for separating, streamlining, and ultimately privatizing the huge network of the Japanese National Railways are now well advanced. We feel that new operating methods and private ownership will get at the root causes of JNR's massive deficits.

Administratively, our government is tightening its belt. And the drive toward privatization should surprise those foreign critics of a mythical creature called Japan, Inc., who believe everything in Japan is run by the government.

Fiscal. Our government has worked intensively to reduce government spending. By consistent cost cutting and better planning, we have set out to escape from our dependency on deficit-financed government bonds, which now amount to some 40% of Japan's gross national product! Income and residence taxes have been cut, while we seek to gain revenue from other forms of taxation.

But the goal of fiscal reform is not merely to balance the government's books. Here also we seek a wider objective. By reviewing the modalities of government finance, we hope to respond better to emerging economic and social trends. In so doing we will forge new relationships between the national and local governments and between the public and private sectors. This whole process will stimulate the private sector and take full advantage of its vitality. It is the same with our administrative reforms. With NTT's privatization, for example, more competitors will appear, involving many smaller businesses in related fields. Such changes will generate substantial private demand. They should have a wide-ranging "ripple effect" on the entire economy.

Education. Of all these renewal projects, education is the most important in the long run. Nothing matters more to the Japanese public. Of course I am not underrating the progress already made. Japan's prosperity to date can be said to represent the achievement of our outstanding educational system. More than a century ago education was the imperative on which Japan's modernizing Meiji Restoration based its success. Our grandfathers built schools before they built steel mills, with a keen sense of priorities. The uniform system of education we developed was designed for the "catch-up" era in Japan's development and best suited to it.

Now, however, we are entering an age of higher technology. We are living in an information society that demands questing and creativity from its students. Education is the foundation of the nation's future. Thus I believe the time has come for sweeping reforms across the entire educational spectrum, in preparation for the 21st century.

Postwar education, I believe, has been too narrowly and exclusively dependent on the basic school curricula. We have tended to neglect the importance of comprehensive education from a broader perspective, including family and social education. This imbalance lies behind the explosive increase in juvenile delinquency and violence in our schools, problems that in past years were of no consequence. Thus educational reform cannot be content with education of the intellect alone. We must aim at education of the whole person by making our curricula more diverse and flexible. We must expand freedom of choice for people seeking education; we must emphasize home and social education and make more practical, hands-on training available outside the school.

I intend to push for discussion and reform in a broad range of fields. We must review educational theory, teacher education, preschool education, language instruction, education for Japanese nationals overseas, as well as the whole system of entrance examinations. To do this we have set up a special council on educational reform. And I am asking for the advice of people from all walks of life and the cooperation of all political parties.

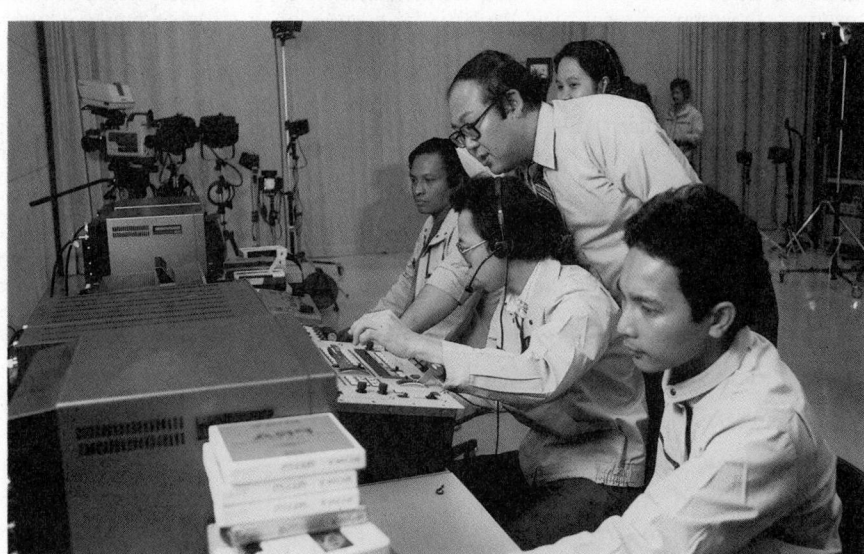

JAPAN INTERNATIONAL COOPERATION AGENCY

As part of Japan's growing involvement with its Asian Pacific neighbours, trainees from Indonesia, Singapore, and the Philippines study audio visual engineering at the Okinawa International Centre.

The Meika school is the oldest public primary school in Tokyo, but it has been a leader in introducing new and informal teaching methods, as in this language class. Much is hoped for in moving away from rigidly traditional methods and curricula.

In a spirit of public morality, we should seek a humanism that will foster respect for the individual. We wish also to internationalize education in Japan, in a way befitting the people of a truly international state. To that end, incidentally, we have set up a joint study group of the Japanese Ministry of Education and the U.S. Department of Education to examine the educational systems of both countries and to make recommendations, each in its home country, for improvement. This study grew out of a conversation between President Reagan and myself two years ago about the urgency of educational problems in both our countries. It is a good example of a new kind of international cooperation.

Japan's Role in a 21st-Century World. In these pages I have been advocating the concept of Japan as an international nation. This means, as I have said, that we shift from a passive attitude of merely responding to events to an active effort to influence events positively. We have been a beneficiary of peace. We must become a creator of peace. As we move into the information society, not only Japan but most of the world's nations are in the midst of a search for new identities. It is at this crucial point that we hold the Tokyo summit in May 1986. In the past these summit meetings of the industrial powers have focused primarily on economic issues but, inevitably, economic and political issues are linked. Recent international developments have again made clear the need for preserving and ensuring our common security as the basis for economic prosperity.

It is hard to foresee the extent of our conversations—or the problems that may suddenly come upon us. As a famous Japanese political leader once noted, "In politics, one inch ahead of you it is pitch dark." But at least, on the eve of the Tokyo summit, I would like to offer some thoughts about our future goals.

The most important thing in our world today is for all peoples and nations to affirm some common principles and premises for establishing the 21st-century world and to discuss concrete means for attaining them. These tasks must be shared among the nations, depending on their circumstances, so that while we cope with today's problems, we can build our hopes for tomorrow's world.

We are passing another milestone in 1986. On April 29 we shall celebrate the 85th birthday of Emperor Hirohito and the 60th year of his reign. The first 20 years of this reign were extremely turbulent. While the emperor endeavoured strenuously to save peace, he could not avert war. Finally, in August 1945, he took the momentous decision to terminate hostilities by accepting the Potsdam Declaration. On that day, the emperor composed the following poem:

> Entirely regardless of what may happen to myself, I commanded the cessation of hostilities. Thinking only of my people who were dying in that conflict.

We are all grateful to the emperor for his courage in that dark hour of our history.

All nations are trying to cope with a variety of grave problems. They should share these burdens as much as possible, relying not merely on themselves but on the work of the United Nations and of various regional and functional world organizations. We should urge the existing organizations to invite all the members of the international community to a global discussion on the theme of "A Better World in the 21st Century." Such a discussion should draw up a blueprint for the world culture and the world environment that we seek.

These should be items for such a discussion:

· How to preserve human dignity in an era of rapid scientific progress.

· Amelioration of East-West and North-South relations.

· The reduction of nuclear and conventional armaments; population policy; environmental policy.

· The exchange of cultures, of peoples, of information.

· Policy for handling youth problems, drug addiction, and terror.

This is not a complete list, but it is to grapple with such major problems and to solve them that mankind must bend its concerted efforts. Such problems transcend national boundaries and cultures. The efforts of all nations, united, are required if we are to hope for solutions.

The Soviet Union Under Gorbachev

BY ARKADY N. SHEVCHENKO

For the U.S.S.R. it is the best of times and the worst of times. Both aspects of this paradox bear importantly on what the Western world can anticipate from the first leader of the Soviet Union born after the Bolshevik Revolution, Mikhail S. Gorbachev.

It is the best of times for the Soviet military, which has developed the mightiest war machine in history. For the first time, Soviet armed forces have overcome the challenge of trying to catch up with the West. The Soviet Union has now achieved its long-cherished dream of strategic nuclear parity with the United States and has firmly secured superpower status. The conventional forces of the United States and NATO combined are inferior to those of the U.S.S.R. In certain categories of its nuclear arsenal, particularly in heavy, land-based ICBM (intercontinental ballistic missiles), the Soviet Union is superior to the United States. Deployment of the newest medium-range SS-20 missiles has drastically altered the military balance in Europe in favour of the U.S.S.R.

The Soviet military buildup has been attained, however, at the expense of the civilian economy. The emphasis on the military has created structural economic imbalances that preclude development and modernization of civilian industries, services, agriculture, and general technological innovation. It has become increasingly obvious that, in addition to old economic and social ills, new and more serious ones have appeared.

The U.S.S.R. is at a crossroads. If pressing economic and social problems are not alleviated in the near future, further erosion in its economic system is inevitable, thus endangering, in the long term, its very survival. Gorbachev and his followers in the Kremlin understand the urgent need to mitigate the worst of the Soviet Union's domestic problems better than their predecessors. I say "mitigate" and not "solve" because many of the worst of these problems are beyond solution, barring a radical departure from the present Soviet economic model.

Typically, Gorbachev has blamed his predecessors for the U.S.S.R.'s current economic and social ailments and has promised a new beginning. Although there is nothing new in his tactics, there is some truth to Gorbachev's recriminations. For many years the ancient Kremlin oligarchs promoted a doctrine of "continuity and stability." In fact, their main purpose was a futile attempt to hold back the clock—to retain power as long as possible. Because the Soviet political structure is conservative in the extreme, for a time they actually appeared to accomplish their goal, but at great cost to the nation. Their *après nous le déluge* philosophy led to stagnation and worse.

Gorbachev has definitely initiated a new style; he is dynamic and relatively young. Barring unforeseen crises, he could remain in power for a long time. But whether his stewardship will open a new era for the U.S.S.R. remains to be seen. Even if he should receive the goodwill and cooperation of all his subordinates, he faces problems that are almost insurmountable, given the U.S.S.R.'s economic system. And that is the crux of the Soviet dilemma.

The Agriculture Gap. As Gorbachev himself has stated publicly and repeatedly, both the old and new problems afflicting the Soviet Union are tremendous. Soviet agri-culture remains a perennial disaster. Food shortages are worse than they were in the 1960s, even in Moscow, except for the very heart of the city, where such a situation would be too embarrassing to tolerate. Supplies of milk and dairy products, meat and meat products, and other staple foods are always meagre to nonexistent. In many provincial regions of the Soviet Union, food rationing has been established, as it was during World War II.

The catastrophic failure of Soviet agriculture is a direct result of the collective farm plan so long celebrated in Soviet propaganda. It simply does not work. Considerable human resources and machinery were allocated to the collective farming experiment and squandered on the theory's doctrinaire application. The Soviet Union, finally, had to rediscover that incentives borrowed from capitalism could move farmers to produce and market crops, while Marxist theory and Stalinist enforcement could only breed agricultural failures.

Even in the U.S.S.R. there is no denial of the fact that the minuscule private sector of Soviet farming, which utilizes something like 3 to 4% of the land under cultivation, produces more than half of the country's vegetables, fruit, and meat. But not many Soviet citizens can afford to shop in the private market, where prices run from 2 to 20 times the official prices set for the same items in government-run

21

food stores. The Catch-22 to this situation is, of course, that the government stores rarely, if ever, have such items as grapes, melons, peas, or lettuce.

In many areas, not just in their eating habits, the Soviet people are denied the ordinary accompaniments to living that most people in the West take for granted. In any country of the West, you can buy literally anything you want, as long as you can pay for it. In the Soviet Union you cannot. Money is not enough; one must belong to the ruling class, the party and government elite, to obtain the luxuries that in the West are mundane conveniences.

In typical Soviet farming country, where the best land may be little better than marginal, living conditions border on the primitive. Houses typically lack running water and other modern facilities. Public transportation, generally adequate in Moscow and Leningrad, is sporadic at best outside these cities, inadequate in many parts of the country. Cars and trucks are in short supply. There is almost no public entertainment, and life is dull. But as people have become better educated, they are less and less satisfied with the farmer's lot. Young people move to the cities as soon as they are old enough.

The Economy's Clogged Arteries. The entire Soviet economy lags far behind what its leaders call "normal international standards." By this they mean the way all the rest of the industrialized world lives. The U.S.S.R. is behind in heavy industry, in light industry, and in every aspect of the consumer economy across the board, from vital medicines to children's toys. In all they aspire to, except in military strength, the Soviets trail the United States, France, Japan, West Germany, the United Kingdom, and other industrialized countries.

The balance of achievements is lower than all expectations. The population is frustrated over unfulfilled promises of abundance and high living standards; a lack of incentive has led to apathy. There is a lot of truth in the old joke that there is no unemployment in the Soviet Union but nobody works. The leadership simply cannot ignore the situation any longer. Soviets are long-suffering but not infinitely so.

Soviet industry desperately needs modernization. In many factories one can still see machine tools of '20s and '30s vintage. Rigid central planning, poor management, the absence of competition, and artificial pricing policies make inefficiency the norm rather than the exception. Labour productivity is far below any Western standards. Factory workers' salaries and standards of living are the lowest among the industrialized nations. But the workers' lack of initiative cannot be overcome unless the existing egalitarian salary system is abandoned. For example, a man who wants to make extra money may work overtime, but no matter how many additional hours he puts in, he is paid no more than 5 to 10% above his regular salary. Therefore, in order to make more money, he resorts to "moonlighting," selling or trading his skills according to what others are willing to pay. This creates, in effect, an underground free market system operating in the same way as do the private farmers' markets.

Another problem vitally affecting all economic sectors is transportation. There is no general network of paved highways, such as exist in Western Europe or the United States. In a country much less than half the size of the Soviet Union, the United States has nearly seven times as much paved highway. The absence of a first-class road system helps explain why Soviet trucks are out of service almost half the time. Vehicles are worked for long periods at a time, and routine maintenance is often neglected.

The Soviet Union has no advanced passenger railway system comparable to those of Western Europe. The ordinary Soviet citizen must often wait for weeks even to buy a ticket to go anywhere in the country. This is a permanent condition of Soviet life, true at any time of the day or year, but during rush hours or holiday seasons the difficulty is compounded. Except, of course, for the upper elite, the *nomenklatura,* who can get tickets easily at any time. Railroad trains have special cars for them where no one else may enter, even if only one member of the ruling class—or no one at all—is using these accommodations.

Rail freight facilities suffer from maintenance problems, equipment shortages, heavy use, and the vast distances of the country. The United States, with only 42% of the area of the Soviet Union, has twice the railroad track. But Soviet freight trains haul two and one half times as much freight.

Soviet airliners fly about two-thirds of the passenger-kilometres and not quite one-third as much freight as those in the United States, but fewer than 50 Soviet airports have scheduled flights, as against more than 12,500 in the U.S. Soviet airliners have the equivalent of first-class sections, and these, like the first-class railroad cars, are for the elite. (Naturally, special hotels cater only to the same class.)

Westerners accustomed to dialing an area code and a number and almost instantly talking with the desired party, even in some distant state or country, would find it difficult to believe what the ordinary Soviet citizen must put up with in the way of telephone service. In many areas Soviet telephone exchanges are operated just as they were a half century ago in the advanced countries of the West.

On a wheat farm near Stavropol in Mikhail Gorbachev's native region, mechanization of agriculture is still rather primitive, compared with that of the United States and other Western industrialized nations.

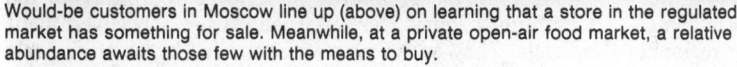

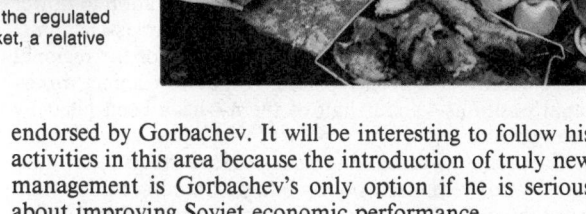

Would-be customers in Moscow line up (above) on learning that a store in the regulated market has something for sale. Meanwhile, at a private open-air food market, a relative abundance awaits those few with the means to buy.

PHOTOGRAPHS, WALLY MCNAMEE—WOODFIN CAMP & ASSOCIATES

It is frustrating enough to telephone within a city; intercity calls take hours or days to complete.

The latest economic woes are those regarding energy conservation (oil production has begun to drop) and, even more important, the widening gap between East and West in the field of high technology. The U.S.S.R. has not yet mastered the production of high technology that is now largely yesterday's news in the West. In computers, microprocessors, fibre optics, robots, ceramics, and many other elements of advanced technology, the Soviet Union is so far behind Japan and the West that the spectre of losing the economic competition with them is beginning to haunt the Kremlin leadership.

Facing the Problems. Gorbachev's first statements as general secretary of the Communist Party of the Soviet Union vividly reflected this concern. He hinted at substantial changes to come regarding policy in this area. Indeed, some experiments in planning and management in industry and agriculture have been initiated during his first year as Soviet leader, but most of these moves were not really innovative. In somewhat different form, similar measures have been tried in the past. As of now, Gorbachev's "reforms" are essentially palliatives, not cures, for the economy. More recently, his policy emphasis has shifted from the idea of "restructuring the economy," and he has fallen back on the tired techniques of sloganeering about the need to increase the role of party organizations in supervising economic management, the introduction of strict working discipline, the replacement of inefficient personnel, and a vigorous campaign against alcoholism. Each and every one of these measures has been called for by the last several leaders, with little effect on overall economic performance. I am sure Gorbachev realizes that even strict adherence to these exhortations cannot substantially improve the situation. I am just as sure that he realizes what the real problem is and that he recognizes that not much can be done about it without changing the economic system that keeps him and many others in power.

Gorbachev elucidated his ambitious economic blueprint in the documents "Basic Guidelines for the Next Five-Year Plan and Beyond to the Year 2000" and in the "Food Program," announced under Leonid Brezhnev and endorsed by Gorbachev. It will be interesting to follow his activities in this area because the introduction of truly new management is Gorbachev's only option if he is serious about improving Soviet economic performance.

Why, then, has he not launched such new methods immediately? There is no single answer to this question. I would like to emphasize that Gorbachev's numerous recent statements on economic problems and other matters leave no doubt that he is a product of the Soviet system or, more precisely, of the Communist Party apparatus. It would be totally wrong to conclude that he would want to alter the existing system substantially or to ease ideological indoctrination of the people. Gorbachev was selected as the new Kremlin leader not to change the system but to make it function better.

It is also certain that the inert but still powerful old men of the party and government elite would resist absolutely any meaningful changes in the U.S.S.R. Gorbachev and the Soviet mass media do not even try to hide the fact of that resistance.

Finally, Western speculation that Gorbachev has already solidified his power and authority to the point where he has assumed the mantle of the autocratic and infallible Kremlin ruler are considerably exaggerated. In my opinion, Gorbachev has not achieved the level of authority among his peers that either Nikita Khrushchev or Brezhnev had in his heyday. Things simply do not move that quickly in Soviet politics.

Gorbachev needs more time to consolidate his power, a power that he now shares with other members of the Politburo and party Secretariat. He must enlarge his base of support at the regional level. One reason the misunderstanding in the West about Gorbachev's authority came about was that he began weeding out aging bureaucrats from high party and government ranks so swiftly that it surprised Western analysts of Soviet affairs. I would caution those who follow Soviet affairs not to inflate Gorbachev's gifts and effectiveness too quickly. The old party apparatchiks he removed from the bureaucracy would have left soon anyway, for natural causes if for no other. It is also important to remember that Gorbachev, unlike his predecessors, did not have very strong rivals to overcome

in the final contest for the post of party leader. Grigory Romanov, the former party chief of Leningrad—young by Politburo standards at 62—and considered a possible rival for the top post, has been easily and unceremoniously retired by Gorbachev. That, however, was not a true test of strength; Romanov did not have enough time to consolidate an effective support base among leading Moscow politicians. Nor did he enjoy the necessary support of the majority in the Politburo.

The New Generation. The most important thing Gorbachev has done to solidify his authority has been his policy of replacing the old party and government cadres by new party apparatchiks. These functionaries are men of Gorbachev's generation who have been waiting a long, long time for their turn at higher posts. They can and will resist serious reforms in the U.S.S.R., but there is no doubt about their hearty enthusiasm for Gorbachev's cadre policy. Well before I broke with the Soviets, I knew that influential elements of the party and government elite were increasingly concerned about the need to infuse fresh blood into the ruling gerontocracy.

Gorbachev is rapidly bringing a new generation to power with him. The composition of the Politburo is changing. More than one-third of the first secretaries of the regional party bodies have been replaced. About 40 Cabinet ministerial positions—about half of them—have been filled by younger men.

Gorbachev is dismissing many older bureaucratic managers, who were often poorly educated and conspicuously unqualified for their jobs, with better educated and abler, younger technocrats who have more imagination and ingenuity. He is also firing some of the most corrupt elements of the elite.

Bureaucratic corruption is endemic in the Soviet Union. There is an unwritten law that the perquisites of the ruling class must be enjoyed discreetly; they must not be flaunted before the working class, and they must not be traded for money, goods, or favours. Over the years many in Brezhnev's elite coterie violated this rule openly, lulled into complacency by the longevity of Brezhnev's tenure. Gorbachev is now making an example of the more profligate abusers.

Replacements in the ranks of the elite should not be viewed as a new party purge, however. Neither are they in any way meant to undermine or curtail the dominant status and privileges of the party and government apparatus. There is no indication that Gorbachev is trying to encroach on the perquisites and prerogatives of the *nomenklatura* class. He, himself, is the embodiment of that class and is, above all, the representative of its interests. The *nomenklatura* elite will continue as the ruling class isolated from the people.

Gorbachev is merely attempting to eliminate the worst excesses committed by some. It should be clearly understood that he does not want to change one of the fundamental cornerstones of the Soviet system. Moreover, even if he should wish to do so, the *nomenklatura* elite would never permit anything to undermine its power, and it has the power to prevent anything it opposes from happening. At the moment, however, it is a good political move, as a sop to the people, that the elite should suffer some inconveniences for a while as it relearns the necessity for circumspection in exercising its privileges.

To revitalize economic performance, Gorbachev must first of all convince the apparatchiks and managers that their jobs are not necessarily lifetime sinecures. That pernicious belief has fostered laziness and an arrogant confidence that they may behave with impunity in any matter.

The illusion of lifelong security as a matter of right in matters of position and privilege was primarily a legacy of Brezhnev's rule. And what Gorbachev is doing now is not something new in Soviet history. The *nomenklatura* have experienced troubles many times in the past. During my time as a member of the elite, I remember that we were much more afraid of being removed from our positions than were ordinary workers, because with loss of position would come loss of privilege. Under the *nomenklatura* system, emoluments are attached to the job, not the person. At the same time, the elite views these partial losses of fortune and favour as the inevitable price it must render periodically for its advantages.

Changes in top Kremlin leadership and in the party and government apparatus under Gorbachev have had only a marginal effect on the power structure's essential character or on the Soviet system in general. I am sure that Gorbachev has never considered making any changes whatever regarding the latter. The Soviet government is not a government of the people; power in the U.S.S.R., as in the past, is concentrated in the hands of a small group composed of members of the Politburo, the Central Committee of the Communist Party Secretariat, and a few top government officials. They are in no way controlled by or answerable to the people or even to the party's rank and file. In the U.S.S.R. there are no free elections at any level, no freedom of religion, speech, or the press; Soviet people have no right to assemble freely, nor do they have free access to information available to all in the West. If the people do not like such conditions, it is of no consequence, for they also have no right to emigrate, nor do they have the right to be properly protected from injustice. Gorbachev would be the last man in the U.S.S.R. one might expect to contemplate bringing democracy to the Soviet people. To control a people it can no longer inspire, the Kremlin under Gorbachev continues to rely upon security police and informers, coercion and intimidation.

Like each of his predecessors, Gorbachev has utilized the support of the KGB and the Army to gain the pinnacle of Soviet power. To obtain military secrets and advanced technology it cannot develop efficiently at home, Gorbachev's leadership continues to employ KGB and GRU (military intelligence) espionage abroad. One should not, however, overestimate the influence of the KGB and the Army in the Soviet Union, as some Westerners are prone to do. While their influence is important, they are only the instruments of the ruling party group. Gorbachev's policy line in this connection is clear: firm control by the party apparatus over the Army and the KGB.

The Military Paradox. As things stand in the Soviet government and the Communist Party, the military establishment, for all its strength of arms, is perhaps at its weakest point politically. There are several reasons for this. One is the depth and scope of the modernization and buildup that went on during the 1970s. That was so effective that the Soviet Union now has the strongest military structure on Earth. No longer can Soviet marshals demand new weaponry to "catch up with America." In fact, the buildup was so successful that, to some degree, it immobilized the military politically. In addition, the critical economic problems facing the country make heavy military spending impossible without enormous and possibly intolerable effort.

Finally, all the great Soviet military heroes, such as the late Marshal Georgy Zhukov, are dead. There are none left who are universally known and respected and whose voice for military spending would carry compelling weight. The current Soviet defense minister, Marshal Sergey Sokolov,

is, at 74 years of age, an obscure figure, little known even in the Soviet Union and without substantial political importance. Unlike his two immediate predecessors, he is not even a full Politburo member but only a nonvoting candidate member.

The relative political impotence that characterizes the military is to an extent true also of the KGB. Although Gorbachev has made the KGB chairman, Viktor M. Chebrikov, a full Politburo member, he is still a bureaucrat, not a politician. The difference between being a politician and a bureaucrat in the Soviet Union is that the former has a base of support that allows him to exert some political weight. A bureaucrat is usually someone who has no such support beyond his immediate circle in his own branch of the government and may, therefore, be dismissed by the leadership with no repercussions. Chebrikov is 62 years old and has spent his entire career in the KGB, where he was deputy chairman under Brezhnev, Yury Andropov, and Konstantin Chernenko.

Western Illusions. In recent times, some Western Soviet watchers have predicted an imminent collapse of the Soviet system, followed by the fall of the Soviet empire within a few years. The "problems" fueling such predictions are, in fact, exaggerated. For example, the dissident movement in the U.S.S.R. has been decapitated. It now represents no serious threat to the Soviet regime. In the same vein, suggestions that rising ethnonationalism and the burgeoning population in Soviet Central Asia (much exceeding the growth of the Slavic population) will soon cause destabilizing effects for the future of the U.S.S.R. are also overstated. It is true that there have been protests against the denial of national rights in the Baltic republics; in fact, Lithuania, Latvia, and Estonia would probably secede from the U.S.S.R. if they could. There has also been protest and discontent for the same reason in parts of the Ukraine and among the Crimean Tatars. These are problems of concern for the Kremlin, and Soviet leaders do not deny the existence of nationally related prejudices, tensions, and other difficulties. But the Soviet state with its enormous arsenal of coercive, organizational, and ideological resources is capable of dealing with any demonstrations of nationalistic fervour that might become too vociferous.

The Central Asian republics—and others—have quite a number of devoted Communist Party members, for there has been considerable economic and social progress there under Soviet rule. The standard of living in some of the non-Slavic Soviet republics is higher than it is in central Russia. The women of Soviet Asia, though many of them are Muslims, are not in the position of women in much of the Arab world. They have opportunities for education and work, and they no longer wear the veil.

As to population growth in Soviet Central Asia and some other parts of the U.S.S.R., the Russians will still rule the roost for a long time to come. In a total population of some 270 million, there are almost 140 million Russians and more than 50 million Ukrainians and Byelorussians. The Central Asians will not soon lose their minority status.

The Soviet government has tried since 1917 to eradicate religion, and if eradication is the test, the effort has failed. Diligent antireligious propaganda and atheist indoctrination in the schools were not without effect, however. The majority of Soviet citizens have no religion, and so to that extent the effort to root out religion has succeeded.

During World War II the Russian Orthodox Church did a great deal to rally patriotism and the determination to fight the Nazi invader, and this, coinciding as it did with a wartime upsurge in religious faith, greatly slowed the antireligious campaign, at least for Orthodoxy. Out of this wartime détente emerged an accommodation between state and church. The Orthodox leadership pledged that it would not engage in any political activity whatever. In return, Stalin agreed to the restoration of some churches that had been closed and allowed the clergy to work more or less openly among the population. This agreement was honoured by Stalin's successors and describes the general situation today. The Russian Orthodox leaders became active in the World Council of Churches and especially in its peace initiatives, which coincided precisely with Soviet foreign policy. But the Kremlin has consistently refused cooperation with Roman Catholicism, whose spiritual leadership came from Rome instead of Moscow, as well as various other religions with connections abroad.

Islam has been more or less tolerated in Soviet Central Asia, primarily because it is not as militant and fanatical as the Ayatollah Khomeini's brand of Shi'ah. As its part of the unwritten arrangement with its Muslims, the government allowed restoration of some of the mosques that were converted to movie theatres in the early days of antireligious zeal under Lenin.

Two decades of military modernization and buildup starved the civilian and consumer economies of the Soviet Union. Can Gorbachev shift gears?

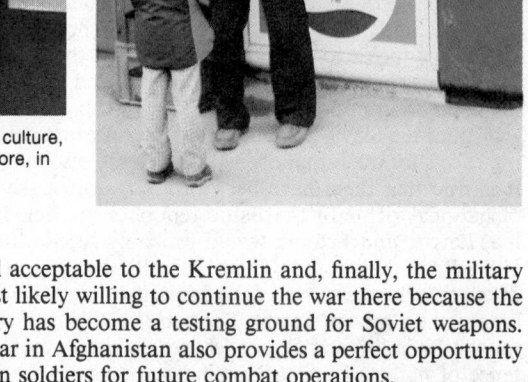

However decadent it may be in Marxist theory, the West—its political traditions, its culture, and its consumer society—is a powerful presence that the Soviet Union cannot ignore, in the schoolroom or in a Moscow park.

The situation of Jews in what is now the Soviet Union has been a troubled one since the days of the tsars. Anti-Semitism has been a fact of Russian life, and it has never eased significantly. Gorbachev recently asserted that Jews fare better in the Soviet Union than outside it, but this is ridiculous nonsense.

When the state of Israel was established, the Soviet Union was the first nation to recognize it. Any friendly implications of this move quickly turned sour when it became apparent that many Soviet Jews wanted to immigrate to the new Jewish homeland. Party leaders were suspicious of any Soviet citizens who wanted to leave the country. Even Jewish members of the Communist Party, and there were quite a few at that time, wanted to go to Israel. At times Jews have been allowed to leave for various reasons, political or economic. When the situation of Soviet Jews became an issue in international politics, the Soviets found they could sometimes trade Jewish exit visas for advantages in trade or economic deals with the West.

Outside the Soviet Union, its six-year-old aggression in Afghanistan is a nagging problem for the Kremlin. For the West this situation, sometimes referred to rather smugly as the Soviets' Vietnam, is another frequently misunderstood situation. Embarrassing and frustrating as this seemingly endless war is for the Kremlin, it is not a Soviet Vietnam. For one thing, the United States in Vietnam had major problems of logistics and transport fighting a war on the other side of the world. The Soviet transport problem is trivial by contrast; the war is next door. In Vietnam the U.S. war effort was finally undermined and disabled by hostile American public opinion. There is, of course, no informed public opinion in the Soviet Union. Public perception of the war is whatever the leadership tells it: "Our troops are helping the friendly government against the bandits." Soviet casualties in Afghanistan are apparently still at a level acceptable to the Kremlin and, finally, the military is most likely willing to continue the war there because the country has become a testing ground for Soviet weapons. The war in Afghanistan also provides a perfect opportunity to train soldiers for future combat operations.

Afghanistan is not the only headache facing the U.S.S.R. beyond its borders. There are even more difficulties and troubles in Poland and other parts of the Soviet bloc, as well as in the Kremlin's relations with pro-Moscow regimes in the third world. Nevertheless, to any careful scholar, it is obvious that the Soviet empire is far from collapse.

Foreign Policy Leadership. Gorbachev's appointment of Andrey A. Gromyko (76), the venerable former Soviet foreign minister, to the largely ceremonial post of chairman of the Presidium of the Supreme Soviet (the nominal chief of state), as well as his replacement as foreign minister by Eduard A. Shevardnadze (57), surprised most Soviet analysts. At the time of Gorbachev's elevation to party leader, Gromyko was solidly entrenched as master of Soviet foreign policy. As a senior and most powerful member of the Politburo and one of the few Soviet statesmen of international as well as domestic repute, he nominated Gorbachev for the post of general secretary of the party. Gorbachev needed Gromyko's assistance because the latter could deliver the support of the older leaders (they still held the majority in the Politburo at the time of Gorbachev's selection). Without his aid, Gorbachev might well have had difficulty in winning the power struggle.

Although Gromyko no longer directs the Foreign Ministry, it is unlikely that he has lost Gorbachev's confidence, nor is it likely that he has been shunted away from the inner group of Kremlin policymakers. Gromyko is a man whose experience and expertise are invaluable. His advice is sure to be sought and respected in Gorbachev's Politburo.

Gromyko is no longer foreign minister, but he played the leading role in Soviet foreign affairs for so long, enjoying prominence under so many Soviet leaders, that he became an institution, acquiring a degree of independence that is all but unique in the U.S.S.R. Gromyko would not easily accede to Gorbachev's bidding if he did not agree with it. He, probably alone among Soviet leaders, would be capable of taking Gorbachev by the arm and saying: "No, you're wrong!" This the new leader would not be likely to countenance. Naturally, Gorbachev would not want a stern and patronizing personality like Gromyko permanently intervening in the conduct of foreign policy. Yet Gromyko certainly has not disappeared. He is quite aware of his influence, and although he probably misses his former role, in sum, it is likely that he is pleased with his new appointment. His health is not the best, and for that reason he has had to reduce his accustomed work load drastically in recent years.

It is significant that Gorbachev's party and government housecleaning left Foreign Ministry officials practically untouched. Except for a few new faces, most Soviet diplomatic personnel, both in Moscow and abroad, remain the same as before. It is quite possible that experienced Foreign Ministry experts have even more influence now than in the past.

Eduard A. Shevardnadze is Gorbachev's choice to succeed Gromyko as foreign minister. Shevardnadze spent most of his career in Georgia, where he was first secretary of the Georgian party's Central Committee for many years. Earlier he had been a Komsomol (Young Communist League) leader there, and he is an old friend of Gorbachev, who is a native of the neighbouring territory of Stavropol. Gorbachev saw to it that Shevardnadze was quickly made a full voting member of the Politburo, and he has joined the group of key personalities in the new Kremlin leadership.

Faces in the Politburo. Unlike Gromyko, Shevardnadze came up through the Communist Party ranks instead of the government bureaucracy. Gorbachev also found his way to power through a party career. It is true that he came from a peasant family, that he worked on a collective farm for several years in his youth, and that he took a correspondence course from an agricultural institute at Stavropol—after he had earned his law degree at Moscow University. But it was his party credentials (including membership in the Komsomol from 1946 and the CPSU since 1952) and his later service as a party apparatchik, both in Stavropol and in Moscow, that made it possible for him to become the general secretary.

One of the most significant replacements of the old guard is that of Nikolay A. Tikhonov (80) by Nikolay I. Ryzhkov. As chairman of the Council of Ministers, Tikhonov was the oldest member of the Politburo. Ryzhkov is an ethnic Russian, 56 years of age, with an impressive executive career in industry but without any conspicuous party background. In 1982 he joined the Secretariat of the Central Committee as secretary for economic affairs. Ryzhkov is obviously a close ally of Gorbachev's since his new position puts him in charge of implementing the leader's economic programs and plans for technological innovation. With little visibility either at home or abroad, Ryzhkov was rapidly advanced over more senior party officials and has become one of the most powerful figures in the new leadership.

Yegor K. Ligachev, a 65-year-old Russian and a Gorbachev appointee to voting membership in the Politburo, is another party apparatchik who is one of the leader's closest associates. Ligachev is, in fact, number two man in the Central Committee Secretariat. He deals with ideological affairs and with cadre policy in the party apparatus.

Ligachev provides Gorbachev a useful link with the older generation of party elite, who may still harbour suspicions about Gorbachev's intentions.

Vitaly I. Vorotnikov (60), a voting member, is also considered close to Gorbachev. He is chairman of the Council of Ministers of the Russian Soviet Federated Socialist Republic (R.S.F.S.R.), the largest of the 15 republics, which stretches from the Baltic Sea to the Bering Strait.

Another voting member of the Politburo who predates Gorbachev (he was brought in under Andropov) is Geidar A. Aliyev (62), a non-Russian from the Azerbaijan Soviet Socialist Republic. He is first deputy chairman of the Council of Ministers of the U.S.S.R. and is responsible for managing major segments of Soviet industry. Although he was once considered a rising star with prime ministerial potential, Aliyev's influence has apparently faded.

Mikhail S. Solomentsev (72) is chairman of the Party Control Committee. He is one of the older Politburo members and also predates Gorbachev.

Vladimir V. Shcherbitsky (67), the Ukrainian party chief and a professional apparatchik, is also one of the older Politburo members. Dinmukhamed A. Kunayev (74), another non-Russian, is party secretary of the Kazakh Soviet Socialist Republic, the largest of the Central Asian republics and a major agricultural region. Kunayev, like Shcherbitsky, has little involvement in foreign affairs. Both men go to Moscow infrequently, spend most of their time in their republics, and, although they are both voting members, do not attend all Politburo meetings.

Viktor V. Grishin (71), another of the older generation, was retired at the end of 1985 from his important post as Moscow party boss. He will inevitably lose his Politburo membership in the near future.

Among several candidate (nonvoting) members of the Politburo, Boris N. Ponomarev (80) deserves special attention. He is a longtime party secretary and chief of the Central Committee's International Department. Ponomarev is responsible for the guidance and oversight of Communist parties in capitalist countries. He is also in charge of liaison with the Social Democrat parties. He oversees the World Peace Council and a number of similar movements.

Further personnel changes in the top Kremlin leadership and in the provinces were expected at the Communist Party congress scheduled for February 1986. This would be the first congress under Gorbachev. A revised party program and statute was expected to win approval, along with Gorbachev's economic plan.

The Struggle with Capitalism. To implement the present economic program, the Soviet leadership needs, first and foremost, a climate of international stability and normal relations with Western industrialized nations. Only this will allow Gorbachev to devote proper attention to the U.S.S.R.'s pressing domestic problems. At the same time, such an atmosphere will facilitate Soviet economic cooperation and trade with the West. Gorbachev's only real option in this respect, if he is to begin the massive efforts required to keep the U.S.S.R. from sinking further into its economic morass, is to avoid any major confrontation with the West in the near future.

But the revised party program, along with a number of Gorbachev's speeches—most of which have drawn amazingly little attention—indicates with absolute clarity that his calls for normalization or détente with the West are merely tactical maneuvers and do not represent a change in strategic policy.

In no way will this latest Gorbachev tactic supersede the Marxist-Leninist idea of final victory through a worldwide

(continued on page 29)

Shevchenko

Arkady Nikolaevich Shevchenko, the Soviet ambassador then serving as under secretary-general of the United Nations for political and Security Council affairs, startled the world when, in April 1978, he made public his decision to seek asylum in the United States. He was (and is to date) the highest ranking Soviet official ever to defect from the U.S.S.R., and he had reached his high government position at the age of 42 after one of the most rapid series of career advances in Soviet history.

Shevchenko was born on Oct. 11, 1930, in Gorlovka, Ukrainian S.S.R. His father, a well-connected physician, moved the family in 1935 to the Crimean resort town of Yevpatoriya on the Black Sea, where he managed a hospital. Arkady grew up there in circumstances that were, except during World War II, generally comfortable.

Upon his graduation from secondary school in 1949, his father's political influence helped win him an appointment to the Moscow State Institute of International Relations, a much-coveted prize that was considered the gateway to a life of luxury and foreign travel. When he graduated in 1954, he was offered a job with the KGB. He declined in favour of graduate studies and remembers being surprised that there were no repercussions.

One of Shevchenko's fellow graduate students was Anatoly Gromyko, the son of the redoubtable Soviet foreign minister, whom Arkady first met when he and Anatoly were preparing a paper for joint publication and young Gromyko asked his father to read it and comment.

On the completion of his graduate work in 1956, Shevchenko was posted to the department of United Nations and disarmament affairs in the Foreign Ministry. In 1958, having been a faithful Komsomol member throughout his youth, he joined the Communist Party—a prerequisite to entertaining any hope of career advancement and foreign assignments. Before long he was given assignments as a staff member at a London disarmament conference and for three months as a disarmament specialist with the Soviet UN delegation. There, despite the brevity of his visit and his constant strict surveillance by the KGB, he

GLOGAU STUDIO

was greatly impressed by the openness of U.S. society.

When Nikita Khrushchev visited the United States in September 1960, Shevchenko was a member of the Soviet leader's party, and the visit and the sea voyage afforded an invaluable opportunity to become well acquainted with him. Three years later the rising young diplomat was assigned to the Soviet UN Mission as chief of its Division of Security Council and Political Affairs.

A few months before the maximum time that Soviet diplomats were allowed to spend in foreign posts was to expire for Shevchenko in 1970, Andrey Gromyko offered to make him his personal political adviser, with the rank of ambassador. The experience of regular meetings at the side of the powerful Gromyko enormously increased Shevchenko's familiarity with the very top level of Soviet leadership. One of the realizations this exposure brought him was the isolation of the ruling class—the *nomenklatura*—from the Soviet people. In December 1972 Gromyko told Shevchenko that the job of under secretary-general at the UN would be vacated and that he could have it. He accepted promptly.

The job was no bed of roses. Like all Soviet UN staff members, he was ordered to consider himself at all times an agent of the Soviet government and to turn every opportunity to Soviet advantage. His top assistant and his chauffeur were both KGB agents. A number of Soviet employees on the UN staff were too busy as KGB operatives to do the UN's work. Also like all other Soviet UN personnel, he was required to kick back a substantial portion of his generous UN salary to the Soviet mission. All this added to Shevchenko's growing disaffection with his government.

Throughout his meteoric rise in the Foreign Ministry, he had been oppressed by the fundamental contradiction between theory and practice at the top of the Soviet hierarchy, which condemned Western consumerism while immersing itself in luxury. He considered resigning and going home to fight the system from within but quickly realized that such a step would take him to prison or a mental institution for the rest of his life.

Although his wife made it evident that she would not defect, and although it probably meant never seeing his son and daughter again, he concluded that he could not continue his life of hypocrisy. Through an American acquaintance he trusted, Shevchenko sent word of his intentions in 1975. He was then contacted by the U.S. Central Intelligence Agency, at whose urging he agreed to stay in place for a time and supply information that could enable U.S. analysts to understand Gromyko's thought processes, how Soviet policies are arrived at, and the like.

He remained in his difficult double role until April 1978, when he was suddenly summoned home for consultations, a message he was sure meant that he had come under suspicion. After his defection he used his unique experience to further Western understanding of Soviet objectives and methods. He now resides in Washington, D.C., and is a consultant and lecturer on Soviet affairs. He is the author of the recent bestselling memoir *Breaking with Moscow.*

(BRUCE L. FELKNOR)

(continued from page 27)
Soviet-style revolutionary process. Although the Kremlin is committed to the ultimate vision of a world under its control, the leaders are realistic enough to understand that at the present time this is impossible. But they are patient and take the long view. They wait and work toward a clear goal. To be sure, the notion held by some in the West that the Soviet leaders have a secret master plan, a timetable for conquering the world's nations one by one, is pure fiction; but while no such specific plan exists on paper, the idea of expanding Soviet power to the point of world domination is a fundamental long-range aspiration. Whether through ideology, diplomacy, force, or economics, Soviet leaders believe that eventually they will be supreme—not necessarily in this century but certainly in the next—in the competition between socialist and capitalist systems, and that such a struggle will be progressively intensified and is historically inevitable. In other words, those goals cannot be comprehended as the mere continuation of historical Russian imperialist designs or as simple power politics. They are much broader and are deeply ideological.

It is essential to understand the nature of this international struggle that is so central to our time, and to which Gorbachev is as committed as were any of his predecessors.

In the West, unfortunately, not only do some of the general populace trust the Kremlin's repeated protestations that it wants only to coexist peacefully with the West, but there are also quite a few politicians, Kremlinologists or Sovietologists, and journalists who place their hopes before considerable evidence to the contrary. Of course, such voices carry weight and are therefore often profoundly misleading to the public. Such wishful thinking on the part of many otherwise hardheaded realists in the West flows from confusion about Soviet tactics and strategy.

To be sure, the Soviet tactic is to avoid any reference to the general, ultimate objectives of world Communism. Addressing the West, Soviets deliberately create the impression that they no longer believe in certain old goals left over from Marx. The Soviet leadership does not hesitate to employ mendacity in its efforts to gull the Western public. I remember a meeting at which both Brezhnev and Gromyko reminded us that it was advisable to avoid any direct references to "inevitable socialist revolutions" in our conversations with people in the West. But inside the U.S.S.R. Soviet leaders and ideologists have never tried to hide their true convictions. In his speeches in the Soviet Union, Gorbachev boldly declared: "Capitalism has no future. . . . We are convinced that social progress cannot be stopped, that the historic process of mankind's transition to socialism cannot be impeded."

It is an old message that has been restated at every party congress, but perhaps because it is old it does not strike the ear as forcefully or as alarmingly as it did earlier in the century. Nevertheless, it is meant today as it was meant in 1917. Some of the methods and styles of implementation have changed, but the underlying desire of the Soviet Union's leaders to dominate the Earth remains ever fresh. For our survival, we in the West must understand that, despite our intention to live peacefully together forever, the Soviet intention is to conquer.

In order to widen their zone of control or influence, Soviet leaders are focusing their attention on support of various national liberation movements in Asia, Africa, and Latin America while pursuing subversive activities in the West through Communist parties and other organizations. They provide matériel and military help, training, and ideological indoctrination.

For the time being, the Soviet Union needs the West. It has used détente successfully before to get what it wanted: amicable relations with the United States and Europe, trade credits, and substantial economic aid. The U.S.S.R. realizes that it can obtain that assistance only from the West. How would the leadership provide bread for its citizens if not for American and other nations' grain sales? Where else can the Soviets secure advanced technology that they are incapable of producing in sufficient quantity or of adequate quality for themselves? In this connection, it does indeed seem that Lenin was right: capitalists are willing to fight for the privilege of selling Communists the rope that the Communists will use to hang them.

But I believe that Gorbachev and his followers, like the former leaders of the Kremlin, do not intend to achieve victory by resorting to nuclear war with the United States and its allies. As long as the United States' strategic nuclear deterrent is strong enough, nuclear war is something Soviet leaders might contemplate only in the most extreme circumstances, if they were absolutely convinced that the country was in mortal peril and they could see no alternative. They consider the prospect of worldwide nuclear war unthinkable, to be avoided at all costs, even at the expense of Soviet prestige. All Soviet leaders, the old as well as the new generation, understand perfectly that nuclear world war could bury Communism and capitalism in the same grave.

Soviet political and military chiefs also realize that, even if the U.S.S.R. were to launch a preemptive nuclear strike, the American second-strike capability could still virtually wipe out most of the heart and brain of the Soviet Union. The Soviets cannot accept such a risk. At the same time, however, by projecting its military might over the globe, the U.S.S.R. does invite the risk that conventional conflicts and confrontations with the West could escalate out of control. Among the militant ideologues and the military, there are those who are willing to take such a gamble.

Gorbachev and the West. As far as the new Kremlin's foreign policy direction under Gorbachev is concerned, one can arrive at only one conclusion: except for style and some active tactical maneuvering, Gorbachev will essentially continue the foreign policy line of his forerunners. Since World War II Soviet-U.S. relations have occupied a special place in Soviet foreign policy. They were and are not just dealings between two powerful states but complex ties between the two poles of power in the world, between the mightiest forces of two opposite and competing sociopolitical systems.

K. MURADOV—TASS/SOVFOTO

Students at Turkmen State University in Ashkhabad exemplify the general satisfaction with Soviet life in the Central Asian republics.

Gorbachev and his Politburo, pictured along a boulevard in downtown Moscow: some old, some new, all facing serious problems but deeply reluctant to initiate thoroughgoing reforms.

Gorbachev appears to have embraced broadly Gromyko's attitude in this regard, which was that Soviet-U.S. relations are central and crucially important. I disagree with some Western analysts' assertions that Gorbachev is shifting the focus of foreign policy to relations with Europe and the third world. Those areas have been highly important centres of Soviet foreign affairs activity for a long time. Gorbachev's latest gambits in those regions do not represent something substantially new. There are also strong indications that Gorbachev, like Gromyko, assesses the United States in terms of its might and its potential as a Soviet rival in world affairs. It is likely that he believes the United States to be not only the Soviet Union's main adversary but also its partner as long as the interests of both nations—whether temporarily or in the long term—are parallel or coincide.

In October 1985 Gorbachev said that the Soviet leadership is "firmly committed to returning Soviet-American relations to a normal track, back onto the road of mutual understanding and cooperation."

During the early 1980s, when superpower relations went from bad to worse, the Kremlin lost more than it anticipated or could afford. Soviet leaders want to avoid the risk of nuclear catastrophe. They are concerned about U.S. military programs. They have also had to adjust to the reality of the deployment of U.S. Pershing II and cruise missiles in Western Europe. They understand that poor relations with Washington have backfired in Western Europe, created strains among the Warsaw Pact countries, and given China a trump card to play against Moscow.

All these things have led the Kremlin leadership back to the necessity of resuming arms control negotiations with the United States and of adopting a somewhat more flexible position in those talks. The Soviet leaders have also indicated more willingness to compromise on some other issues, and they agreed to the summit meeting held in November 1985 in Geneva. That meeting was disappointing to many because no substantial agreements were reached. But resumption of such meetings after a long interval is in itself a success. If nothing else, the summits seem to help these partner/adversaries avoid misunderstandings that could bring on dangerous confrontations.

The joint statement of Pres. Ronald Reagan and General Secretary Gorbachev that emerged from the Geneva summit to the effect that nuclear war must never be initiated and their recognition that there can be no winner in such a war constitute a positive step toward preventing the possibility of a nuclear holocaust. The two leaders also agreed that neither side would seek military superiority.

Is the Soviet declaration that the Kremlin is not now seeking military superiority over the United States credible? My own experience tells me that, at least for the time being, Soviet leaders understand that, even if they should wish such superiority, it is beyond their ability because of their domestic economic problems, as well as the present U.S. administration's determination not to permit it. I remember Gromyko once telling me that if in the past one or another American president did not have such resolve, another would work to revitalize American strength.

The Kremlin feels comfortable with the present strategic nuclear balance. Soviet political leaders as well as military chiefs have openly expressed their satisfaction with the current state of affairs. Obviously, the Kremlin's paramount aim is to preserve the existing balance before embarking on any agreements about reducing nuclear arsenals. That is why it vehemently opposes the U.S. Strategic Defense Initiative (SDI), dubbed "Star Wars." But the U.S.S.R. is the only nation that has an operational ABM (antiballistic missile) system in place (the Galosh around Moscow) that can possibly stop over half of any incoming missiles. Despite U.S. assurances that the SDI design is purely defensive, Soviets portray it as a weapon meant to be used for a first-strike attack. At the Geneva summit and afterward, Gorbachev continued his vigorous campaign against SDI, stressing that pursuit of that program might wreck the fresh start in U.S.-Soviet relations and that it "will not only lead to a further arms race but it will mean that all restraints will be blown to the wind."

Strategic parity has cost the Kremlin dearly in the course of a relentless and unprecedented military buildup that has continued for many years. It is true that the SDI program, if it is possible to implement—and if some important elements of it can be carried out before the Soviet Union can follow suit—would drastically alter the balance between the two superpowers to U.S. advantage. The Soviet Union's greatest fear is that it will be left behind in an uncontrollable competition for more and more technologically sophisticated strategic and, particularly, space-based weaponry. Moscow is alarmed over the astronomical expenses that would be inevitable in a new armaments-in-space race. Such expenditures would strain the U.S.S.R.'s economic resources more than ever at a time when Gorbachev is desperately trying to improve Soviet economic performance.

In the United States there is heated debate on all sides regarding SDI. However, if we talk not about the deployment of strategic defensive systems but about research in this field, we should understand that research is essential

for national security. It is also inevitable, since the Soviet Union has been engaged in the very same kind of research for a long time. If the U.S. curtails its SDI research, we might face a situation in which the Soviet Union secretly continued its own SDI program while we did nothing. The West and the United States cannot simply watch what might happen; we must proceed with SDI research. Gorbachev's ability to charm the people should not encourage the West to trust the Soviet Union. While the Soviets are not at present becoming more aggressive, they assuredly are not becoming less aggressive.

The U.S. and the Soviet Union seem to be moving to a new period in their relations in the aftermath of the Geneva summit, but it will be quite different from the détente of the Nixon and Carter years. Although a Soviet-U.S. dialogue at the highest level is to be resumed, with Gorbachev scheduled to visit the U.S. in 1986 and Reagan set to go to the U.S.S.R. in 1987, the present administration has no doubts about the nature of the Soviet system. The administration's key policymakers realize that many basic Soviet-U.S. differences are irreconcilable and will remain so. In his address to a joint session of Congress upon his return from Geneva, President Reagan stated: "The United States cannot afford illusions about the nature of the U.S.S.R. We cannot assume that their ideology and purpose will change. This implies enduring competition." Similarly, Gorbachev declared that "our differences [with the United States] are tremendous."

Yet both President Reagan and General Secretary Gorbachev agreed in Geneva that the search for arms control agreements must be accelerated. Arms control is a complex matter, and the protracted deadlock in the Geneva talks will not be easy to break.

Gorbachev's Kremlin will certainly continue to attempt to split NATO and put the president, the Congress, and the American people at odds on this issue. Soviet leaders know that negotiations tend to have a calming effect. In the West there are already demands to stop some or all military programs because some people believe that we

The International Festival of Youth and Students, the 12th of its kind, opened in Moscow in July 1985. The festival ran heavily to political and ideological propaganda aimed chiefly at persuading the world of the Soviet Union's dedication to peace.
SIPA/SPECIAL FEATURES

have to make unilateral concessions even before coming to the negotiating table. This theory is dangerous; it is the wrong way to approach the Kremlin. Moscow sees this attitude very clearly and has become expert at playing upon fears that feed, so naturally, upon other fears. On the other hand, we should not be discouraged or misled by Soviet attacks against U.S. policy in arms reduction. Regarding foreign policy generally and disarmament in particular, the Soviet Union has always taken a double-track approach: propaganda bluster on the one hand, coupled with realistic talks on the other.

The 1985 proposals from the U.S.S.R. to reduce U.S. and Soviet nuclear arms capable of reaching each other's territory by 50%, along with Gorbachev's new plan to elim-

APN/GAMMA/LIAISON

On the other side of the propaganda coin, the May Day festival in Moscow featured signs pinning the blame for the arms race and international tensions on the United States and its NATO allies.

In the battle for world opinion and the political advantage it may bring, Mikhail Gorbachev has displayed a grasp of public relations and a talent for gaining favourable media coverage that his predecessors conspicuously lacked.

M. PHILIPPOT—SYGMA

inate nuclear weapons by the end of the century, should be welcomed. But is the Soviet Union serious in suggesting complete elimination of nuclear arsenals?

For a long time the Kremlin has publicly espoused the ultimate elimination of such weapons. However, I am sure that the Soviet leadership does not consider that goal achievable or even desirable. There should be no illusions that the Kremlin would agree to liquidate all nuclear weapons. Without them the U.S.S.R. would cease to be a real superpower capable of influencing world developments as it now does. Moscow enjoys the deference power invariably fosters and would never voluntarily strip itself of the cornerstone of that power. Beyond that, the Soviets would never trust their adversaries in the "imperialistic camp." There is also the matter of China. The Soviets would never be willing to rely solely on conventional forces in case of military confrontation with Beijing (Peking). Gorbachev once pointed out that: "While attaching great significance to the normalization of relations with the United States and to honest talks with it on all the topical problems of international life, at the same time, we never forget for a minute that the world is not limited to that country alone, but is a much bigger place."

Nevertheless, Kremlin interest in reducing the risk of nuclear war and the enormous burden of the arms race should not be underestimated. An unrestricted arms race and new weapons technology could introduce new instabilities and uncertainty. There is also the urgent necessity of reallocating resources from the military to the civilian economy if there is to be any hope of improving the civilian economy's performance. In proportion to its gross national product, the U.S.S.R. spends more than the U.S. does on its military machine. Therefore, under Gorbachev's leadership, the Soviet Union might eventually be willing to go further in nuclear arms reduction and make more serious concessions than many people in the West are inclined to believe. Any chance to achieve that—and there are such opportunities now—should not be missed.

Dealing with the Kremlin. The West must deal with the Soviet Union, like it or not. There is more than enough rationale for this: the Soviet Union and the United States occupy unique positions of power that will inevitably affect mankind's future. Although East and West apply different rules of the game to their competition, it is imperative, if we are to avoid cataclysm, to maintain a dialogue with the U.S.S.R. to seek reasonable and practical accommodations—even cooperation—where our interests are in alignment. This cooperation is essential to resolving global problems, such as preventing accidental nuclear war and nuclear proliferation, reducing the level of military threat, and achieving progress in arms control. It is required to handle the crisis situations that will inevitably appear from time to time, irrespective of the status of Soviet-U.S. relations.

The faltering economy and other afflictions besetting the Soviet Union should not mislead anyone about the durability of its regime. There is no doubt that the U.S.S.R. is experiencing serious domestic and other difficulties, but it has overcome worse troubles in the past. It has both tremendous natural wealth and vast human resources. In their ability to withstand centuries—not decades—of hardship and privation and yet persevere, the Soviet people are unmatched by any nation on Earth, with the possible exception of the Chinese.

The West, therefore, should not delude itself by focusing its attention exclusively on Soviet flaws and shortcomings. There have also been successes. It is premature to predict the imminent decline of the U.S.S.R. and its empire; matters must worsen considerably before this idea can be entertained realistically.

The United States sometimes lacks the steadiness needed to deal persuasively with the Soviets. Its policy toward the Soviet Union seems to jump from extreme to extreme. Yet I have never doubted that America's strength makes it the one power capable of forcing Moscow to restrain itself. This is something that can be achieved if American leaders do not forget an old and still true lesson: what the men in the Kremlin understand best is military and economic might, energetic political conviction, strength of will. If the West cannot confront the Soviets with equal determination, Moscow will continue to play the bully around the globe.

Major Revisions from the 1986 *Macropædia*

The purpose of this section is to introduce to continuing *Book of the Year* subscribers selected *Macropædia* articles or portions of them that have been completely revised or written anew. It is intended to update the *Macropædia* in ways that cannot be accomplished fully by reviewing the year's events or by revising statistics annually, because the *Macropædia* texts themselves—written from a longer perspective than any yearly revision—supply authoritative interpretation and analysis as well as narrative and description.

Three wholly new articles have been chosen from the 1986 printing: ETHICS, printed here in part; The Forms of GOVERNMENT; and HUMANISM. Each is the work of a distinguished scholar, and each represents the continuing dedication of the *Encyclopædia Britannica* to bringing such works to the general reader. New bibliographies accompany the articles as well for readers who wish to pursue certain topics. A more general bibliographical updating of the *Macropædia* begins on page 62.

Ethics

How should we live? Shall we aim at happiness or at knowledge, virtue, or the creation of beautiful objects? If we choose happiness, will it be our own or the happiness of all? And what of the more particular questions that face us: Is it right to be dishonest in a good cause? Can we justify living in opulence while elsewhere in the world people are starving? If conscripted to fight in a war we do not support, should we disobey the law? What are our obligations to the other creatures with whom we share this planet and to the generations of humans who will come after us?

Ethics deals with such questions at all levels. Its subject consists of the fundamental issues of practical decision making, and its major concerns include the nature of ultimate value and the standards by which human actions can be judged right or wrong.

The terms ethics and morality are closely related. We now often refer to ethical judgments or ethical principles where it once would have been more common to speak of moral judgments or moral principles. These applications are an extension of the meaning of ethics. Strictly speaking, however, the term refers not to morality itself but to the field of study, or branch of inquiry, that has morality as its subject matter. In this sense, ethics is equivalent to moral philosophy.

Although ethics has always been viewed as a branch of philosophy, its all-embracing practical nature links it with many other areas of study, including anthropology, biology, economics, history, politics, sociology, and theology. Yet, ethics remains distinct from such disciplines because it is not a matter of factual knowledge in the way that the sciences and other branches of inquiry are. Rather, it has to do with determining the nature of normative theories and applying these sets of principles to practical moral problems.

This article is divided into the following sections:

The origins of ethics

MYTHICAL ACCOUNTS

When did ethics begin and how did it originate? If we are referring to ethics proper—*i.e.,* the systematic study of what we ought to do—it is clear that ethics can only have come into existence when human beings started to reflect on the best way to live. This reflective stage emerged long after human societies had developed some kind of morality, usually in the form of customary standards of right and wrong conduct. The process of reflection tended to arise from such customs, even if in the end it may have found them wanting. Accordingly, ethics began with the introduction of the first moral codes.

Virtually every human society has some form of myth to explain the origin of morality. In the Louvre in Paris there is a black Babylonian column with a relief showing the sun god Shamash presenting the code of laws to Hammurabi. A more familiar example of the same type of myth is the Old Testament account of God giving the Ten Commandments to Moses on Mt. Sinai. In Plato's *Protagoras* there is an avowedly mythical account of how Zeus took pity on the hapless humans, who, living in small groups and with inadequate teeth, weak claws, and lack of speed, were no match for the other beasts. To make up for these deficiencies, Zeus gave humans a moral sense and the capacity for law and justice, so that they could live in larger communities and cooperate with one another.

Notion of divine origin

That morality should be invested with all the mystery and power of divine origin is not surprising. Nothing else could provide such strong reasons for accepting the moral law. By attributing a divine origin to morality, the priesthood became its interpreter and guardian, and thereby secured for itself a power that it would not readily relinquish. This link between morality and religion has been so firmly forged that it is still sometimes asserted that there can be no morality without religion. According to this view, ethics ceases to be an independent field of study. It becomes, instead, moral theology.

There is some difficulty, already known to Plato, with the view that morality was created by a divine power. In his dialogue *Euthyphro,* Plato considered the suggestion that it is divine approval that makes an action good. Plato pointed out that if this were the case, we could not say that the gods approve of the actions because the actions are good. Why then do the gods approve of these actions rather than others? Is their approval entirely arbitrary? Plato considered this impossible and so held that there must be some standards of right or wrong that are independent of the likes and dislikes of the gods. Modern philosophers have generally accepted Plato's argument because the alternative implies that if the gods had happened to approve of torturing children and to disapprove of helping one's neighbours, then torture would have been good and neighbourliness bad.

A modern theist might say that since God is good, he could not possibly approve of torturing children nor disapprove of helping neighbours. In saying this, however, the theist would have tacitly admitted that there is a standard of goodness that is independent of God. Without an independent standard, it would be pointless to say that God is good; this could only mean that God is approved of by God. It seems therefore that, even for those who believe in the existence of God, it is impossible to give a satisfactory account of the origin of morality in terms of a divine creation. We need a different account.

There are other possible connections between religion and morality. It has been said that even if good and evil exist independently of God or the gods, only divine revelation can reliably inform us about good and evil. An obvious problem with this view is that those who receive divine revelations, or who consider themselves qualified to interpret them, do not always agree on what is good and what is evil. Without an accepted criterion for the authenticity of a revelation or an interpretation, we are no better off, so far as reaching moral agreement is concerned, than we would be if we were to decide on good and evil ourselves with no assistance from religion.

Traditionally, a more important link between religion and ethics was that religious teachings were thought to provide a reason for doing what is right. In its crudest form, the reason was that those who obey the moral law will be rewarded by an eternity of bliss while everyone else roasts in hell. In more sophisticated versions, the motivation provided by religion was less blatantly self-seeking and more of an inspirational kind. Whether in its crude or sophisticated version, or something in between, religion does provide an answer to one of the great questions of ethics: Why should I do what is right? As will be seen in the course of this article, however, the answer provided by religion is by no means the only answer. It will be considered after the alternatives have been examined.

PREHUMAN ETHICS

Can we do better than the religious accounts of the origin of morality? Because, for obvious reasons, we have no historical record of a human society in the period before it had any standards of right and wrong, history cannot tell us the origins of morality. Nor is anthropology able to assist because all human societies studied have already had, except perhaps during the most extreme circumstances, their own form of morality. Fortunately there is another mode of inquiry open to us. Human beings are social animals. Living in a social group is a characteristic we share with many other animal species, including our closest relatives, the apes. Presumably, the common ancestor of humans and apes also lived in a social group, so that we were social beings before we were human beings. Here, then, in the social behaviour of nonhuman animals and in the evolutionary theory that explains such behaviour, we may find the origins of human morality.

Social life, even for nonhuman animals, requires constraints on behaviour. No group can stay together if its members make frequent, no-holds-barred attacks on one another. Social animals either refrain altogether from attacking other members of the social group, or, if an attack does take place, the ensuing struggle does not become a fight to the death—it is over when the weaker animal shows submissive behaviour. It is not difficult to see analogies here with human moral rules. The parallels, however, go much further than this. Like humans, social animals may behave in ways that benefit other members of the group at some cost or risk to themselves. Male baboons threaten predators and cover the rear as the troop retreats. Wolves and wild dogs bring meat back to members of the pack not present at the kill. Gibbons and chimpanzees with food will, in response to a gesture, share their food with others of the group. Dolphins support sick or injured animals, swimming under them for hours at a time and pushing them to the surface so they can breathe.

Apparent altruistic behaviour among nonhuman animals

It may be thought that the existence of such apparently altruistic behaviour is odd, for evolutionary theory states that those who do not struggle to survive and reproduce will be wiped out in the ruthless competition known as natural selection. Research in evolutionary theory applied to social behaviour, however, has shown that evolution

need not be quite so ruthless after all. Some of this altruistic behaviour is explained by kin selection. The most obvious examples are those in which parents make sacrifices for their offspring. If wolves help their cubs to survive, it is more likely that genetic characteristics, including the characteristic of helping their own cubs, will spread through further generations of wolves.

Less obviously, the principle also holds for assistance to other close relatives, even if they are not descendants. A child shares 50 percent of the genes of each of its parents, but full siblings too, on the average, have 50 percent of their genes in common. Thus a tendency to sacrifice one's life for two or more of one's siblings could spread from one generation to the next. Between cousins, where only 12½ percent of the genes are shared, the sacrifice-to-benefit ratio would have to be correspondingly increased.

When apparent altruism is not between kin, it may be based on reciprocity. A monkey will present its back to another monkey, who will pick out parasites; after a time the roles will be reversed. Reciprocity may also be a factor in food sharing among unrelated animals. Such reciprocity will pay off, in evolutionary terms, as long as the costs of helping are less than the benefits of being helped and as long as animals will not gain in the long run by "cheating"—that is to say, by receiving favours without returning them. It would seem that the best way to ensure that those who cheat do not prosper is for animals to be able to recognize cheats and refuse them the benefits of cooperation the next time around. This is only possible among intelligent animals living in small, stable groups over a long period of time. Evidence supports this conclusion: reciprocal behaviour has been observed in birds and mammals, the clearest cases occurring among wolves, wild dogs, dolphins, monkeys, and apes.

In short, kin altruism and reciprocity do exist, at least in some nonhuman animals living in groups. Could these forms of behaviour be the basis of human ethics? There are good reasons for believing that they could. A surprising proportion of human morality can be derived from the twin bases of concern for kin and reciprocity. Kinship is a source of obligation in every human society. A mother's duty to look after her children seems so obvious that it scarcely needs to be mentioned. The duty of a married man to support and protect his family is almost equally as widespread. Duties to close relatives take priority over duties to more distant relatives, but in most societies even distant relatives are still treated better than strangers.

If kinship is the most basic and universal tie between human beings, the bond of reciprocity is not far behind. It would be difficult to find a society that did not recognize, at least under some circumstances, an obligation to return favours. In many cultures this is taken to extraordinary lengths, and there are elaborate rituals of gift giving. Often the repayment has to be superior to the original gift, and this escalation can reach such extremes as to threaten the economic security of the donor. The huge "potlatch" feasts of certain American Indian tribes are a well-known example of this type of situation. Many Melanesian societies also place great importance on giving and receiving very substantial amounts of valuable items.

Many features of human morality could have grown out of simple reciprocal practices such as the mutual removal of parasites from awkward places. Suppose I want to have the lice in my hair picked out and I am willing in return to remove lice from someone else's hair. I must, however, choose my partner carefully. If I help everyone indiscriminately, I will find myself delousing others without getting my own lice removed. To avoid this, I must learn to distinguish between those who return favours and those who do not. In making this distinction, I am separating reciprocators and nonreciprocators and, in the process, developing crude notions of fairness and of cheating. I will strengthen my links with those who reciprocate, and bonds of friendship and loyalty, with a consequent sense of obligation to assist, will result.

This is not all. The reciprocators are likely to react in a hostile and angry way to those who do not reciprocate. Perhaps they will regard reciprocity as good and "right" and cheating as bad and "wrong." From here it is a small

Concern for kin and reciprocity

step to concluding that the worst of the nonreciprocators should be driven out of society or else punished in some way, so that they will not take advantage of others again. Thus a system of punishment and a notion of desert constitute the other side of reciprocal altruism.

Although kinship and reciprocity loom large in human morality, they do not cover the entire field. Typically, there are obligations to other members of the village, tribe, or nation even when these are strangers. There may also be a loyalty to the group as a whole that is distinct from loyalty to individual members of the group. It may be at this point that human culture intervenes. Each society has a clear interest in promoting devotion to the group and can be expected to develop cultural influences that exalt those who make sacrifices for the sake of the group and revile those who put their own interests too far ahead of the interests of the group. More tangible rewards and punishments may supplement the persuasive effect of social opinion. This is simply the start of a process of cultural development of moral codes.

Before considering the cultural variations in human morality and their significance for ethics, let us draw together this discussion of the origins of morality. Since we are dealing with a prehistoric period and morality leaves no fossils, any account of the origins of morality will necessarily remain to some extent speculative. It seems likely that morality is the gradual outgrowth of forms of altruism that exist in some social animals and that are the result of the usual evolutionary processes of natural selection. No myths are required to explain its existence.

ANTHROPOLOGY AND ETHICS

It is commonly believed that there are no ethical universals—*i.e.*, there is so much variation from one culture to another that no single principle or judgment is generally accepted. We have already seen that such is not the case. Of course, there are immense differences in the way in which the broad principles so far discussed are applied. The duty of children to their parents meant one thing in traditional Chinese society and means something quite different in contemporary Anglo-Saxon society. Yet, concern for kin and reciprocity to those who treat us well are considered good in virtually all human societies. Also, all societies have, for obvious reasons, some constraints on killing and wounding other members of the group.

Beyond that common ground, the variations in moral attitudes soon become more striking than the similarities. Man's fascination with such variations goes back a long way. The Greek historian Herodotus relates that Darius, king of Persia, once summoned Greeks before him and asked them how much he would have to pay them to eat their fathers' dead bodies. They refused to do it at any price. Then Darius brought in some Indians who by custom ate the bodies of their parents and asked them what would make them willing to burn their fathers' bodies. The Indians cried out that he should not mention so horrid an act. Herodotus drew the obvious moral: each nation thinks its own customs best.

Variations in morals were not systematically studied until the 19th century, when knowledge of the more remote parts of the globe began to increase. At the beginning of the 20th century, Edward Westermarck published *The Origin and Development of the Moral Ideas* (1906–08), two large volumes comparing differences among societies in such matters as the wrongness of killing (including killing in warfare, euthanasia, suicide, infanticide, abortion, human sacrifices, and duelling); whose duty it is to support children, the aged, or the poor; the forms of sexual relationship permitted; the status of women; the right to property and what constitutes theft; the holding of slaves; the duty to tell the truth; dietary restrictions; concern for nonhuman animals; duties to the dead; and duties to the gods. Westermarck had no difficulty in demonstrating tremendous diversity in all these issues. More recent, though less comprehensive, studies have confirmed that human societies can and do flourish while holding radically different views about all such matters.

As noted earlier, ethics itself is not primarily concerned with the description of moral systems in different societies.

That task, which remains on the level of description, is one for anthropology or sociology. In contrast, ethics deals with the justification of moral principles. Nevertheless, ethics must take note of the variations in moral systems because it has often been claimed that this knowledge shows that morality is simply a matter of what is customary and is always relative to a particular society. According to this view, no ethical principles can be valid except in terms of the society in which they are held. Words such as good and bad just mean, it is claimed, "approved in my society" or "disapproved in my society," and so to search for an objective, or rationally justifiable, ethic is to search for what is in fact an illusion.

One way of replying to this position would be to stress the fact that there are some features common to virtually all human moralities. It might be thought that these common features must be the universally valid and objective core of morality. This argument would, however, involve a fallacy. If the explanation for the common features is simply that they are advantageous in terms of evolutionary theory, that does not make them right. Evolution is a blind force incapable of conferring a moral imprimatur on human behaviour. It may be a fact that concern for kin is in accord with evolutionary theory, but to say that concern for kin is therefore right would be to attempt to deduce values from facts. As will be seen later, it is not possible to deduce values from facts in this manner. In any case, that something is universally approved does not make it right. If all human societies enslaved any tribe they could conquer, some freethinking moralists might still insist that slavery is wrong. They could not be said to be talking nonsense merely because they had few supporters. Similarly, then, universal support for principles of kinship and reciprocity cannot prove that these principles are in some way objectively justified.

This example illustrates the way in which ethics differs from a descriptive science. From the standpoint of ethics, whether human moral codes closely parallel one another or are extraordinarily diverse, the question of how an individual should act remains open. If you are thinking deeply about what you should do, your uncertainty will not be overcome by being told what your society thinks you should do in the circumstances in which you find yourself. Even if you are told that virtually all other human societies agree, you may choose not to go that way. If you are told that there is great variation among human societies over what people should do in your circumstances, you may wonder whether there can be any objective answer, but your dilemma has still not been resolved. In fact, this diversity does not rule out the possibility of an objective answer either: conceivably, most societies simply got it wrong. This, too, is something that will be taken up later in this article, for the possibility of an objective morality is one of the constant themes of ethics.

ANCIENT ETHICS

The first ethical precepts were certainly passed down by word of mouth by parents and elders, but as societies learned to use the written word, they began to set down their ethical beliefs. These records constitute the first historical evidence of the origins of ethics.

The Middle East. The earliest surviving writings that might be taken as ethics textbooks are a series of lists of precepts to be learned by boys of the ruling class of Egypt, prepared some 3,000 years before the Christian Era. In most cases, they consist of shrewd advice on how to live happily, avoid unnecessary troubles, and advance one's career by cultivating the favour of superiors. There are, however, several passages that recommend more broadly based ideals of conduct, such as the following: Rulers should treat their people justly and judge impartially between their subjects. They should aim to make their people prosperous. Those who have bread are urged to share it with the hungry. Humble and lowly people must be treated with kindness. One should not laugh at the blind or at dwarfs.

Why then should one follow these precepts? Did the ancient Egyptians believe that one should do what is good for its own sake? The precepts frequently state that it will

profit a man to act justly, much as we say that "honesty is the best policy." They also emphasize the importance of having a good name. Since these precepts are intended for the instruction of the ruling classes, however, we have to ask why helping the destitute should have contributed to an individual's good reputation among this class. To some degree the authors of the precepts must have thought that to make people prosperous and happy and to be kind to those who have least is not merely personally advantageous but good in itself.

The precepts are not works of ethics in the philosophical sense. No attempt is made to find any underlying principles of conduct that might provide a more systematic understanding of ethics. Justice, for example, is given a prominent place, but there is no elaboration of the notion of justice nor any discussion of how disagreements about what is just and unjust might be resolved. Furthermore, there is no probing of ethical dilemmas that may occur if the precepts should conflict with one another. The precepts are full of sound observations and practical wisdom, but they do not encourage theoretical speculation.

The same practical bent can be found in other early codes or lists of ethical injunctions. The great codification of Babylonian law by Hammurabi is often said to have been based on the principle of "an eye for an eye, a tooth for a tooth," as if this were some fundamental principle of justice, elaborated and applied to all cases. In fact, the code reflects no such consistent principle. It frequently prescribes the death penalty for offenses that do not themselves cause death—*e.g.,* for robbery or for accepting bribes. Moreover, even the eye-for-an-eye rule applies only if the eye of the original victim is that of a member of the patrician class; if it is the eye of a commoner, the punishment is a fine of a quantity of silver. Apparently such differences in punishment were not thought to require justification. At any rate, there are no surviving attempts to defend the principles of justice on which the code was based.

The Hebrew people were at different times captives of both the Egyptians and the Babylonians. It is therefore not surprising that the law of ancient Israel, which was put into its definitive form during the Babylonian Exile, shows the influence both of the ancient Egyptian precepts and of the Code of Hammurabi. The book of Exodus refers, for example, to the principle of "life for life, eye for eye, tooth for tooth." Hebrew law does not differentiate, as the Babylonian law does, between patricians and commoners, but it does stipulate that in several respects foreigners may be treated in ways that it is not permissible to treat fellow Hebrews; for instance, Hebrew slaves, but not others, had to be freed without ransom in the seventh year. Yet, in other respects Israeli law and morality developed the humane concern shown in the Egyptian precepts for the poor and unfortunate: hired servants must be paid promptly, because they rely on their wages to satisfy their pressing needs; slaves must be allowed to rest on the seventh day; widows, orphans, and the blind and deaf must not be wronged, and the poor man should not be refused a loan. There was even a tithe providing for an incipient welfare state. The spirit of this humane concern was summed up by the injunction to "love thy neighbour as thyself," a sweepingly generous form of the rule of reciprocity.

The famed Ten Commandments are thought to be a legacy of Semitic tribal law when important commands were taught, one for each finger, so that they could more easily be remembered. (Sets of five or 10 laws are common among preliterate civilizations.) The content of the Hebrew commandments differed from other laws of the region mainly in its emphasis on duties to God. In the more detailed laws laid down elsewhere, this emphasis continued with as much as half the legislation concerned with crimes against God and ceremonial and ritualistic matters, though there may be other explanations for some of these ostensibly religious requirements concerning the avoidance of certain foods and the need for ceremonial cleansings.

In addition to lengthy statements of the law, the surviving literature of ancient Israel includes both proverbs and the books of the prophets. The proverbs, like the pre-

Code of Hammurabi

Hebrew proverbs and the books of the prophets

cepts of the Egyptians, are brief statements without much concern for systematic presentation or overall coherence. They go further than the Egyptian precepts, however, in urging conduct that is just and upright and pleasing to God. There are correspondingly fewer references to what is needed for a successful career, although it is frequently stated that God rewards the just. In this connection the Book of Job is notable as an exploration of the problem raised for those who accept this motive for obeying the moral law: How are we to explain the fact that the best of people may suffer the worst misfortunes? The book offers no solution beyond faith in God, but the sharpened awareness of the problem it offers may have influenced some to adopt belief in reward and punishment in another realm as the only possible solution.

The literature of the prophets contains a good deal of social and ethical criticism, though more at the level of denunciation than discussion about what goodness really is or why there is so much wrongdoing. The Book of Isaiah is especially notable for its early portrayal of a utopia in which "the desert shall blossom as the rose . . . the wolf also shall dwell with the lamb . . . . They shall not hurt or destroy in all my holy mountain."

India. Unlike the ethical teaching of ancient Egypt and Babylon, Indian ethics was philosophical from the start. **The Vedas** In the oldest of the Indian writings, the Vedas, ethics is an integral aspect of philosophical and religious speculation about the nature of reality. These writings date from about 1500 BC. They have been described as the oldest philosophical literature in the world, and what they say about how people ought to live may therefore be the first philosophical ethics.

The Vedas are, in a sense, hymns, but the gods to which they refer are not persons but manifestations of ultimate truth and reality. In the Vedic philosophy, the basic principle of the universe, the ultimate reality on which the cosmos exists, is the principle of *Ritam,* which is the word from which the Western notion of right is derived. There is thus a belief in a right moral order somehow built into the universe itself. Hence, truth and right are linked; to penetrate through illusion and understand the ultimate truth of human existence is to understand what is right. To be an enlightened one is to know what is real and to live rightly, for these are not two separate things but one and the same.

The ethic that is thus traced to the very essence of the universe is not without its detailed practical applications. These were based on four ideals, or proper goals, of life: prosperity, the satisfaction of desires, moral duty, and spiritual perfection—*i.e.,* liberation from a finite existence. From these ends follow certain virtues: honesty, rectitude, charity, nonviolence, modesty, and purity of heart. To be condemned, on the other hand, are falsehood, egoism, cruelty, adultery, theft, and injury to living things. Because the eternal moral law is part of the universe, to do what is praiseworthy is to act in harmony with the universe and accordingly will receive its proper reward; conversely, once the true nature of the self is understood, it becomes apparent that those who do what is wrong are acting self-destructively.

The basic principles underwent considerable modification over the ensuing centuries, especially in the *Upaniṣad*s, a body of philosophical literature dating from 800 BC. The Indian caste system, with its intricate laws about what members of each caste may or may not do, is accepted by the *Upaniṣad*s as part of the proper order of the universe. Ethics itself, however, is not regarded as a matter of conformity to laws. Instead, the desire to be ethical is an inner desire. It is part of the quest for spiritual perfection, which in turn is elevated to the highest of the four goals of life.

During the following centuries the ethical philosophy of this early period gradually became a rigid and dogmatic system that provoked several reactions. One, which is uncharacteristic of Indian thought in general, was the **The Cārvāka** Cārvāka, or materialist school, which mocked religious ceremonies, saying that they were invented by the Brahmans (the priestly caste) to ensure their livelihood. When the Brahmans defended animal sacrifices by claiming that the sacrificed beast goes straight to heaven, the members of the Cārvāka asked why the Brahmans did not kill their aged parents to hasten their arrival in heaven. Against the postulation of an eventual spiritual liberation, Cārvāka ethics urged each individual to seek his or her pleasure here and now.

Jainism, another reaction to the traditional Vedic outlook, went in exactly the opposite direction. The Jaina **Jaina philosophy** philosophy is based on spiritual liberation as the highest of all goals and nonviolence as the means to it. In true philosophical manner, the Jainas found in the principle of nonviolence a guide to all morality. First, apart from the obvious application to prohibiting violent acts to other humans, nonviolence is extended to all living things. The Jainas are vegetarian. They are often ridiculed by Westerners for the care they take to avoid injuring insects or other living things while walking or drinking water that may contain minute organisms; it is less well known that Jainas began to care for sick and injured animals thousands of years before animal shelters were thought of in Europe. The Jainas do not draw the distinction usually made in Western ethics between their responsibility for what they do and their responsibility for what they omit doing. Omitting to care for an injured animal would also be in their view a form of violence.

Other moral duties are also derived from the notion of nonviolence. To tell someone a lie, for example, is regarded as inflicting a mental injury on that person. Stealing, of course, is another form of injury, but because of the absence of a distinction between acts and omissions, even the possession of wealth is seen as depriving the poor and hungry of the means to satisfy their wants. Thus nonviolence leads to a principle of nonpossession of property. Jaina priests were expected to be strict ascetics and to avoid sexual intercourse. Ordinary Jainas, however, followed a slightly less severe code, which was intended to give effect to the major forms of nonviolence while still being compatible with a normal life.

The other great ethical system to develop as a reaction to the ossified form of the old Vedic philosophy was Buddhism. The person who became known as the Buddha, which means the "enlightened one," was born about 563 BC, the son of a king. Until he was 29 years old, he lived the sheltered life of a typical prince, with every luxury he could desire. At that time, legend has it, he was jolted out of his idleness by the "Four Signs": he saw in rapid succession a very feeble old man, a hideous leper, a funeral, and a venerable ascetic monk. He began to think about old age, disease, and death, and decided to follow the way of the monk. For six years he led an ascetic life of renunciation, but finally, while meditating under a tree, he concluded that the solution was not withdrawal from the world, but rather a practical life of compassion for all.

Buddhism is often thought to be a religion, and indeed over the centuries it has adopted in many places the trappings of religion. This is an irony of history, however, because the Buddha himself was a strong critic of religion. He rejected the authority of the Vedas and refused to set up any alternative creed. He saw religious ceremonies as a waste of time and theological beliefs as mere superstition. He refused to discuss abstract metaphysical problems such as the immortality of the soul. The Buddha told his followers to think for themselves and take responsibility for their own future. In place of religious beliefs and religious ceremonies, the Buddha advocated a life devoted **The teachings of the Buddha** to universal compassion and brotherhood. Through such a life one might reach the ultimate goal, Nirvāṇa, a state in which all living things are free from pain and sorrow. There are similarities between this ethic of universal compassion and the ethics of the Jainas. Nevertheless, the Buddha was the first historical figure to develop such a boundless ethic.

In keeping with his own previous experience, the Buddha proposed a "middle path" between self-indulgence and self-renunciation. In fact, it is not so much a path between these two extremes as one that draws together the benefits of both. Through living a life of compassion and love for all, a person achieves the liberation from selfish cravings sought by the ascetic and a serenity and satisfaction that are more fulfilling than anything obtained by indulgence in pleasure.

It is sometimes thought that because the Buddhist goal is Nirvāṇa, a state of freedom from pain and sorrow that can be reached by meditation, Buddhism teaches a withdrawal from the real world. Nirvāṇa, however, is not to be sought for oneself alone; it is regarded as a unity of the individual self with the universal self in which all things take part. In the Mahāyāna school of Buddhism, the aspirant for Enlightenment even takes a vow not to accept final release until everything that exists in the universe has attained Nirvāṇa.

The Buddha lived and taught in India, and so Buddhism is properly classified as an Indian ethical philosophy. Yet, Buddhism did not take hold in the land of its origin. Instead, it spread in different forms south into Sri Lanka and Southeast Asia, and north through Tibet to China, Korea, and Japan. In the process, Buddhism suffered the same fate as the Vedic philosophy against which it had rebelled: it became a religion, often rigid, with its own sects, ceremonies, and superstitions.

China. The two greatest moral philosophers of ancient China, Lao-tzu (flourished *c.* 6th century BC) and Confucius (551–479 BC), thought in very different ways. Lao-tzu is best known for his ideas about the Tao (literally "Way," the Supreme Principle). The Tao is based on the traditional Chinese virtues of simplicity and sincerity. To follow the Tao is not a matter of keeping to any set list of duties or prohibitions, but rather of living in a simple and honest manner, being true to oneself, and avoiding the distractions of ordinary living. Lao-tzu's classic book on the Tao, *Tao-te Ching*, consists only of aphorisms and isolated paragraphs, making it difficult to draw an intelligible system of ethics from it. Perhaps this is because Lao-tzu was a type of moral skeptic: he rejected both righteousness and benevolence, apparently because he saw them as imposed on individuals from without rather than coming from their own inner nature. Like the Buddha, Lao-tzu found the things prized by the world—rank, luxury, and glamour—to be empty, worthless values when compared with the ultimate value of the peaceful inner life. He also emphasized gentleness, calm, and nonviolence. Nearly 600 years before Jesus, he said: "It is the way of the Tao . . . to recompense injury with kindness." By returning good for good and also good for evil, Lao-tzu believed that all would become good; to return evil for evil would lead to chaos.

The lives of Lao-tzu and Confucius overlapped, and there is even an account of a meeting between them, which is said to have left the younger Confucius baffled. Confucius was the more down-to-earth thinker, absorbed in the practical task of social reform. When he was a provincial minister of justice, the province became renowned for the honesty of its people and their respect for the aged and their care for the poor. Probably because of its practical nature, the teachings of Confucius had a far greater influence on China than did those of the more withdrawn Lao-tzu.

Confucius did not organize his recommendations into any coherent system. His teachings are offered in the form of sayings, aphorisms, and anecdotes, usually in reply to questions by disciples. They aim at guiding the audience in what is necessary to become a better person, a concept translated as "gentleman" or "the superior man." In opposition to the prevailing feudal ideal of the aristocratic lord, Confucius presented the superior man as one who is humane and thoughtful, motivated by the desire to do what is good rather than by personal profit. Beyond this, however, the concept is not discussed in any detail; it is only shown by diverse examples, some of them trite: "A superior man's life leads upwards . . . . The superior man is broad and fair; the inferior man takes sides and is petty . . . . A superior man shapes the good in man; he does not shape the bad in him."

One of the recorded sayings of Confucius is an answer to a request from a disciple for a single word that could serve as a guide to conduct for one's entire life. He replied: "Is not reciprocity such a word? What you do not want done to yourself, do not do to others." This rule is repeated several times in the Confucian literature and might be considered the supreme principle of Confucian ethics. Other

duties are not, however, presented as derivative from this supreme principle, nor is the principle used to determine what is to be done when more specific duties—*e.g.*, duties to parents and duties to friends, both of which were given prominence in Confucian ethics—should clash.

Confucius did not explain why the superior man chose righteousness rather than personal profit. This question was taken up more than 100 years after his death by his follower Mencius, who asserted that humans are naturally inclined to do what is humane and right. Evil is not in human nature but is the result of poor upbringing or lack of education. But Confucius also had another distinguished follower, Hsün-tzu, who said that man's nature is to seek self-profit and to envy others. The rules of morality are designed to avoid the strife that would otherwise follow from this nature. The Confucian school was united in its ideal of the superior man but divided over whether such an ideal was to be obtained by allowing people to fulfill their natural desires or by educating them to control those desires.

Ancient Greece. Early Greece was the birthplace of Western philosophical ethics. The ideas of Socrates, Plato, and Aristotle, who flourished in the 5th and 4th centuries BC, will be discussed in the next section. The sudden blooming of philosophy during that period had its roots in the ethical thought of earlier centuries. In the poetic literature of the 7th and 6th centuries BC, there were, as in the early development of ethics in other cultures, ethical precepts but no real attempts to formulate a coherent overall ethical position. The Greeks were later to refer to the most prominent of these poets and early philosophers as the seven sages, and they are frequently quoted with respect by Plato and Aristotle. Knowledge of the thought of this period is limited, for often only fragments of original writings, along with later accounts of dubious accuracy, remain.

Pythagoras (*c.* 580–*c.* 500 BC), whose name is familiar because of the geometrical theorem that bears his name, is one such early Greek thinker about whom little is known. He appears to have written nothing at all, but he was the founder of a school of thought that touched on all aspects of life and that may have been a kind of philosophical and religious order. In ancient times the school was best known for its advocacy of vegetarianism, which, like that of the Jainas, was associated with the belief that after the death of the body, the human soul may take up residence in the body of an animal. Pythagoreans continued to espouse this view for many centuries, and classical passages in the works of such writers as Ovid and Porphyry opposing bloodshed and animal slaughter can be traced back to Pythagoras.

Ironically, an important stimulus for the development of moral philosophy came from a group of teachers to whom the later Greek philosophers—Socrates, Plato, and Aristotle—were consistently hostile: the Sophists. This term was used in the 5th century to refer to a class of professional teachers of rhetoric and argument. The Sophists promised their pupils success in political debate and increased influence in the affairs of the city. They were accused of being mercenaries who taught their students to win arguments by fair means or foul. Aristotle said that Protagoras, perhaps the most famous of them, claimed to teach how "to make the weaker argument the stronger."

The Sophists, however, were more than mere teachers of rhetorical tricks. They saw their role as imparting the cultural and intellectual qualities necessary for success, and their involvement with argument about practical affairs led them to develop views about ethics. The recurrent theme in the views of the better known Sophists, such as Protagoras, Antiphon, and Thrasymachus, is that what is commonly called good and bad or just and unjust does not reflect any objective fact of nature but is rather a matter of social convention. It is to Protagoras that we owe the celebrated epigram summing up this theme, "Man is the measure of all things." Plato represents him as saying "Whatever things seem just and fine to each city, are just and fine for that city, so long as it thinks them so." Protagoras, like Herodotus, was an early social relativist, but he drew a moderate conclusion from his relativism. He

Lao-tzu

The teachings of Confucius

Pythagorean school of thought

The Sophists

argued that while the particular content of the moral rules may vary, there must be rules of some kind if life is to be tolerable. Thus Protagoras stated that the foundations of an ethical system needed nothing from the gods or from any special metaphysical realm beyond the ordinary world of the senses.

The Sophist Thrasymachus appears to have taken a more radical approach—if Plato's portrayal of his views is historically accurate. He explained that the concept of justice means nothing more than obedience to the laws of society, and, since these laws are made by the strongest political group in their own interests, justice represents nothing but the interests of the stronger. This position is often represented by the slogan "Might is right." Thrasymachus was probably not saying, however, that whatever the mightiest do really is right; he is more likely to have been denying that the distinction between right and wrong has any objective basis. Presumably he would then encourage his pupils to follow their own interests as best they could. He is thus an early representative of Skepticism about morals and perhaps of a form of egoism, the view that the rational thing to do is follow one's own interests.

It is not surprising that with ideas of this sort in circulation other thinkers should react by probing more deeply into ethics to see if the potentially destructive conclusions of some of the Sophists could be resisted. This reaction produced works that have served ever since as the cornerstone for the entire edifice of Western ethics . . . .

APPLIED ETHICS

The most striking development in the study of ethics since the mid-1960s has been the growth of interest among philosophers in practical, or applied, ethics; *i.e.,* the application of normative theories to practical moral problems. This is not, admittedly, a totally new departure. From Plato onward moral philosophers have concerned themselves with practical questions, including suicide, the exposure of infants, the treatment of women, and the proper behaviour of public officials. Christian philosophers, notably Augustine and Aquinas, examined with great care such matters as when a war was just, whether it could ever be right to tell a lie, or if a Christian woman did wrong to commit suicide in order to save herself from rape. Hobbes had an eminently practical purpose in writing his *Leviathan,* and Hume wrote about the ethics of suicide. Practical concerns continued with the British Utilitarians, who saw reform as the aim of their philosophy: Bentham wrote on an incredible variety of topics, and Mill is celebrated for his essays on liberty and on the subjection of women.

Nevertheless, during the first six decades of the 20th century moral philosophers largely isolated themselves from practical ethics—something that now seems all but incredible, considering the traumatic events through which most of them lived. There were one or two notable exceptions. The philosopher Bertrand Russell was very much involved in practical issues, but his stature among his colleagues was based on his work in logic and metaphysics and had nothing to do with his writings on topics such as disarmament and sexual morality. Russell himself seems to have regarded his practical contributions as largely separate from his philosophical work and did not develop his ethical views in any systematic or rigorous fashion.

The prevailing view of the period was that moral philosophy is quite separate from "moralizing," a task best left to preachers. What was not generally considered was whether moral philosophers could, without merely preaching, make an effective contribution to discussions of practical issues involving difficult ethical questions. The value of such work began to be widely recognized only during the 1960s, when first the U.S. civil rights movement and subsequently the Vietnam War and the rise of student activism started to draw philosophers into discussions of the moral issues of equality, justice, war, and civil disobedience. (Interestingly, there has been very little discussion of sexual morality—an indication that a subject once almost synonymous with the term morals has become marginal to our moral concerns.)

The founding, in 1971, of *Philosophy and Public Affairs,* a new journal devoted to the application of philosophy to public issues, provided both a forum and a new standard of rigour for these contributions. Applied ethics soon became part of the teaching of most philosophy departments of universities in English-speaking countries. Here it is not possible to do more than briefly mention some of the major areas of applied ethics and point to the issues that they raise.

Applications of equality. Since much of the early impetus for applied ethics came from the U.S. civil rights movement, such topics as equality, human rights, and justice have been prominent. We often make statements such as "All humans are equal" without thinking too deeply about the justification for the claims. Since the mid-1960s much has been written about how they can be justified. Discussions of this sort have led in several directions, often following social and political movements. The initial focus, especially in the United States, was on racial equality, and here, for once, there was a general consensus among philosophers on the unacceptability of discrimination against blacks. With so little disagreement about racial discrimination itself, the centre of attention soon moved to reverse discrimination: Is it acceptable to favour blacks for jobs and enrollment in universities and colleges because they had been discriminated against in the past and were generally so much worse off than whites? Or is this, too, a form of racial discrimination and unacceptable for that reason?

Inequality between the sexes has been another focus of discussion. Does equality here mean ending as far as possible all differences in the sex roles, or could we have equal status for different roles? There has been a lively debate—both between feminists and their opponents and, on a different level, among feminists themselves—about what a society without sexual inequality would be like. Here, too, the legitimacy of reverse discrimination has been a contentious issue. Feminist philosophers have also been involved in debates over abortion and new methods of reproduction. These topics will be covered separately below.

Many discussions of justice and equality are limited in scope to a single society. Even Rawls's theory of justice, for example, has nothing to say about the distribution of wealth between societies, a subject that could make acceptance of his maximin principle much more onerous. But philosophers have now begun to think about the moral implications of the inequality in wealth between the affluent nations (and their citizens) and those living in countries subject to famine. What are the obligations of those who have plenty when others are starving? It has not proved difficult to make a strong case for the view that affluent nations, as well as affluent individuals, ought to be doing much more to help the poor than they are generally now doing.

There is one issue related to equality in which philosophers have led, rather than followed, a social movement. In the early 1970s, a group of young Oxford-based philosophers began to question the assumption that while all humans are entitled to equal moral status, nonhuman animals automatically have an inferior position. The publication in 1972 of *Animals, Men and Morals: An Inquiry into the Maltreatment of Non-humans,* edited by Roslind and Stanley Godlovitch and John Harris, was followed three years later by Peter Singer's *Animal Liberation* and then by a flood of articles and books that established the issue as a part of applied ethics. At the same time, these writings provided the philosophical basis for the animal liberation movement, which has had an effect on attitudes and practices toward animals in many countries.

Environmental ethics. Environmental issues raise a host of difficult ethical questions, including the ancient one of the nature of intrinsic value. Whereas many philosophers in the past have agreed that human experiences have intrinsic value and the Utilitarians at least have always accepted that the pleasures and pains of nonhuman animals are of some intrinsic significance, this does not show why it is so bad if dodos become extinct or a rain forest is cut down. Are these things to be regretted only because of the loss to humans or other sentient creatures? Or is there

The application of normative theories to practical moral problems

Questions related to racial discrimination

more to it than that? Some philosophers are now prepared to defend the view that trees, rivers, species (considered apart from the individual animals of which they consist), and perhaps ecological systems as a whole have a value independent of the instrumental value they may have for humans or other sentient creatures.

Issue of obligations to future generations

Our concern for the environment also raises the question of our obligations to future generations. How much do we owe to the future? From a social contract view of ethics or for the ethical egoist, the answer would seem to be: nothing. For we can benefit them, but they are unable to reciprocate. Most other ethical theories, however, do give weight to the interests of coming generations. Utilitarians, for one, would not think that the fact that members of future generations do not exist yet is any reason for giving less consideration to their interests than we give to our own, provided only that we are certain that they will exist and will have interests that will be affected by what we do. In the case of, say, the storage of radioactive wastes, it seems clear that what we do will indeed affect the interests of generations to come.

The question becomes much more complex, however, when we consider that we can affect the size of future generations by the population policies we choose and the extent to which we encourage large or small families. Most environmentalists believe that the world is already dangerously overcrowded. This may well be so, but the notion of overpopulation conceals a philosophical issue that is ingeniously explored by Derek Parfit in *Reasons and Persons* (1984). What is optimum population? Is it that population size at which the average level of welfare will be as high as possible? Or is it the size at which the total amount of welfare—the average multiplied by the number of people—is as great as possible? Both answers lead to counterintuitive outcomes, and the question remains one of the most baffling mysteries in applied ethics.

War and peace. The Vietnam War ensured that discussions as to the justness of a war and of the legitimacy of conscription and civil disobedience were prominent in early writings in applied ethics. There was considerable support for civil disobedience against unjust aggression and against unjust laws even in a democracy.

With the cessation of hostilities in Vietnam and the end of conscription, interest in these questions declined. Concern about nuclear weapons in the early 1980s, however, has caused philosophers to argue about whether nuclear deterrence can be an ethically acceptable strategy if it means using civilian populations as potential nuclear targets. Jonathan Schell's *Fate of the Earth* (1982) raised several philosophical questions about what we ought to do in the face of the possible destruction of all life on our planet.

Abortion, euthanasia, and the value of human life. A number of ethical questions cluster around both ends of the human life span. Whether abortion is morally justifiable has popularly been seen as depending on our answer to the question "When does a human life begin?" Many philosophers believe this to be the wrong question to ask because it suggests that there might be a factual answer that we can somehow discover through advances in science. Instead, these philosophers think we need to ask what it is that makes killing a human being wrong and then consider whether these characteristics, whatever they might be, apply to the fetus in an abortion. There is no generally agreed upon answer, yet some philosophers have presented surprisingly strong arguments to the effect that not only the fetus but even the newborn infant has no right to life. This position has been defended by Jonathan Glover in *Causing Death and Saving Lives* (1977) and in more detail by Michael Tooley in *Abortion and Infanticide* (1984).

Such views have been hotly contested, especially by those who claim that all human life, irrespective of its characteristics, must be regarded as sacrosanct. The task for those who defend the sanctity of human life is to explain why human life, no matter what its characteristics, is specially worthy of protection. Explanation could no doubt be provided in terms of such traditional Christian doctrines as that all humans are made in the image of God or that all humans have an immortal soul. In the current debate, however, the opponents of abortion have eschewed religious arguments of this kind without finding a convincing secular alternative.

Somewhat similar issues are raised by euthanasia when it is nonvoluntary, as, for example, in the case of severely disabled newborn infants. Euthanasia, however, can be voluntary, and this has brought it support from some who hold that the state should not interfere with the free, informed choices of its citizens in matters that do not cause others harm. (The same argument is often invoked in defense of the pro-choice position in the abortion controversy; but it is on much weaker ground in this case because it presupposes what it needs to prove—namely, that the fetus does not count as an "other.") Opposition to voluntary euthanasia has centred on practical matters such as the difficulty of adequate safeguards and on the argument that it would lead to a "slippery slope" that would take us to nonvoluntary euthanasia and eventually to the compulsory involuntary killing of those the state considers to be socially undesirable.

Philosophers have also canvassed the moral significance of the distinction between killing and allowing to die, which is reflected in the fact that many physicians will allow a patient with an incurable condition to die when life could still be prolonged, but they will not take active steps to end the patient's life. Consequentialist philosophers, among them both Glover and Tooley, have denied that this distinction possesses any intrinsic moral significance. For those who uphold a system of absolute rules, on the other hand, a distinction between acts and omissions is essential if they are to render plausible the claim that we must never breach a valid moral rule.

Distinction between killing and allowing to die

Bioethics. The issues of abortion and euthanasia are included in one of the fastest growing areas of applied ethics, that dealing with ethical issues raised by new developments in medicine and the biological sciences. This subject, known as bioethics, often involves interdisciplinary work, with physicians, lawyers, scientists, and theologians all taking part. Centres for research in bioethics have been established in Australia, Britain, Canada, and the United States. Many medical schools have added the discussion of ethical issues in medicine to their curricula. Governments have sought to deal with the most controversial issues by appointing special committees to provide ethical advice.

Several key themes run through the subjects covered by bioethics. One, related to abortion and euthanasia, is whether the quality of a human life can be a reason for ending it or for deciding not to take steps to prolong it. Since medical science can now keep alive severely disabled infants who a few years ago would have died soon after birth, pediatricians are regularly faced with this question. The issue received national publicity in Britain in 1981 when a respected pediatrician was charged with murder, following the death of an infant with Down's syndrome. Evidence at the trial indicated that the parents had not wanted the child to live and that the pediatrician had consequently prescribed a narcotic painkiller. The doctor was acquitted. The following year, in the United States, an even greater furor was caused by a doctor's decision to follow the wishes of the parents of a Down's syndrome infant and not carry out surgery without which the baby would die. The doctor's decision was upheld by the Supreme Court of Indiana, and the baby died before an appeal could be made to the U.S. Supreme Court. In spite of the controversy and efforts by government officials to ensure that handicapped infants are given all necessary lifesaving treatment, in neither Britain nor the United States is there any consensus about the decisions that should be made when severely disabled infants are born or by whom these decisions should be made.

Major issues of bioethics

Medical advances have raised other related questions. Even those who defend the doctrine of the sanctity of all human life do not believe that doctors have to use extraordinary means to prolong life, but the distinction between ordinary and extraordinary means, like that between acts and omissions, is itself under attack. Critics assert that the wishes of the patient or, if these cannot be ascertained, the quality of the patient's life provides a more relevant basis for a decision than the nature of the means to be used.

Another central theme is that of patient autonomy. This arises not only in the case of voluntary euthanasia but also in the area of human experimentation, which has come under close scrutiny following reported abuses. It is generally agreed that patients must give informed consent to any experimental procedures. But how much and how detailed information is the patient to be given? The problem is particularly acute in the case of randomly controlled trials, which scientists consider the most desirable way of testing the efficacy of a new procedure but which require that the patient agree to being administered randomly one of two or more forms of treatment.

The allocation of medical resources became a life-and-death issue when hospitals obtained dialysis machines and had to choose which of their patients suffering from kidney disease would be able to use the scarce machines. Some argued for "first come, first served," whereas others thought it obvious that younger patients or patients with dependents should have preference. Kidney machines are no longer as scarce, but the availability of various other exotic, expensive lifesaving techniques is limited; hence, the search for rational principles of distribution continues.

New issues arise as further advances are made in biology and medicine. In 1978 the birth of the first human being to be conceived outside the human body initiated a debate about the ethics of in vitro fertilization. This soon led to questions about the freezing of human embryos and what should be done with them if, as happened in 1984 with two embryos frozen by an Australian medical team, the parents should die. The next controversy in this area arose over commercial agencies offering infertile married couples a surrogate mother who would for a fee be impregnated with the sperm of the husband and then surrender the resulting baby to the couple. Several questions emerged: Should we allow women to rent their wombs to the highest bidder? If a woman who has agreed to act as a surrogate changes her mind and decides to keep the baby, should she be allowed to do so?

The culmination of such advances in human reproduction will be the mastery of genetic engineering. Then we will all face the question posed by the title of Jonathan Glover's probing book *What Sort of People Should There Be?* (1984). Perhaps this will be the most challenging issue for 21st-century ethics.

BIBLIOGRAPHY

General works: For an introduction to the major theories of ethics, the reader should consult RICHARD B. BRANDT, *Ethical Theory: The Problems of Normative and Critical Ethics* (1959), an excellent comprehensive textbook. WILLIAM K. FRANKENA, *Ethics,* 2nd ed. (1973), is a much briefer treatment. Another concise work is BERNARD WILLIAMS, *Ethics and the Limits of Philosophy* (1985). There are several useful collections of classical and modern writings; among the better ones are OLIVER A. JOHNSON, *Ethics: Selections from Classical and Contemporary Writers,* 5th ed. (1984); and JAMES RACHELS (ed.), *Understanding Moral Philosophy* (1976), which places greater emphasis on modern writers.

Origins of ethics: JOYCE O. HERTZLER, *The Social Thought of the Ancient Civilizations* (1936, reissued 1961), is a wide-ranging collection of materials. EDWARD WESTERMARCK, *The Origin and Development of the Moral Ideas,* 2 vol., 2nd ed. (1912–17, reprinted 1971), is dated but still unsurpassed as a comprehensive account of anthropological data. MARY MIDGLEY, *Beast and Man: The Roots of Human Nature* (1978, reissued 1980), is excellent on the links between biology and ethics; and EDWARD O. WILSON, *Sociobiology: The New Synthesis* (1975), and *On Human Nature* (1978), contain controversial speculations on the biological basis of social behaviour. RICHARD DAWKINS, *The Selfish Gene* (1976, reprinted 1978), is another evolutionary account, fascinating but to be used with care.

History of Western ethics: HENRY SIDGWICK, *Outlines of the History of Ethics for English Readers,* 6th enlarged ed. (1931, reissued 1967), is a triumph of scholarship and brevity. WILLIAM EDWARD HARTPOLE LECKY, *History of European Morals from Augustus to Charlemagne,* 2 vol., 3rd rev. ed. (1877, reprinted 1975), is fascinating and informative. Among more recent histories, VERNON J. BOURKE, *History of Ethics* (1968, reissued in 2 vol., 1970), is remarkably comprehensive; while ALASDAIRE

MACINTYRE, *A Short History of Ethics* (1966), is a readable personal view. . . .

Applied ethics: Many of the best examples of applied ethics are to be found in journal articles, particularly in *Philosophy and Public Affairs* (quarterly). There are many anthologies of representative samples of such writings. Among the better ones are JAMES RACHELS (ed.), *Moral Problems,* 3rd ed. (1979); JAN NARVESON (ed.), *Moral Issues* (1983); and MANUEL VELASQUEZ and CYNTHIA ROSTANKOWSKI, *Ethics, Theory and Practice* (1985). There are also books and collections on specific topics. MARSHALL COHEN, THOMAS NAGEL, and THOMAS SCANLON (eds.), *Equality and Preferential Treatment* (1977), is a collection of some of the best articles on equality and reverse discrimination; while ALAN H. GOLDMAN, *Justice and Reverse Discrimination* (1979), is a book-length treatment of the issues. Some of the more philosophically probing discussions of feminism are JANET RADCLIFFE RICHARDS, *The Sceptical Feminist* (1980, reprinted with corrections, 1982); MARY MIDGLEY and JUDITH HUGHES, *Women's Choices: Philosophical Problems Facing Feminism* (1983); and ALISON M. JAGGAR, *Feminist Politics and Human Nature* (1983). The moral obligations of the wealthy toward the starving are discussed in the anthology *World Hunger and Moral Obligation,* ed. by WILLIAM AIKEN and HUGH LAFOLLETTE.

The ethics of the treatment of animals has given rise to much philosophical discussion. Books arguing for radical change include STANLEY GODLOVITCH, ROSLIND GODLOVITCH, and JOHN HARRIS (eds.), *Animals, Man, and Morals: An Enquiry into the Maltreatment of Non-Humans* (1971); PETER SINGER, *Animal Liberation: A New Ethics for Our Treatment of Animals* (1975); STEPHEN R.L. CLARK, *The Moral Status of Animals* (1977, reissued 1984); and TOM REGAN, *The Case for Animal Rights* (1983). R.G. FREY, *Interests and Rights: The Case Against Animals* (1980), and *Rights, Killing, and Suffering: Moral Vegetarianism and Applied Ethics* (1983), resist some of these arguments. MARY MIDGLEY, *Animals and Why They Matter* (1983), takes a middle course.

Essays dealing with ethical issues raised by concern for the environment are collected in ROBERT ELLIOT and ARRAN GARE (eds.), *Environmental Philosophy* (1983); and K.S. SHRADER-FRECHETTE, *Environmental Ethics* (1981). Useful full-length studies include JOHN PASSMORE, *Man's Responsibility for Nature: Ecological Problems and Western Tradition,* 2nd ed. (1980); and H.J. MCCLOSKEY, *Ecological Ethics and Politics* (1983). For specific problems of future generations, see R. SIKORA and BRIAN BARRY (eds.), *Obligations to Future Generations* (1979). A difficult but fascinating discussion of the problem of optimum population size in an ideal world can be found in DEREK PARFIT, *op. cit.*

MICHAEL WALZER, *Just and Unjust Wars* (1977), is a fine study of the morality of war; RICHARD A. WASSERSTROM (ed.), *War and Morality* (1970), is a valuable collection of essays. NIGEL BLAKE and KAY POLE (eds.), *Objections to Nuclear Defence* (1984), and *Dangers of Deterrence* (1984), are collections of philosophical writings on nuclear war.

There is an immense amount of literature on abortion, though of various philosophical depth. MICHAEL TOOLEY, *Abortion and Infanticide* (1983), is a penetrating study. For contrasting views, see GERMAIN G. GRISEZ, *Abortion: The Myths, the Realities, and the Arguments* (1970); and BARUCH A. BRODY, *Abortion and the Sanctity of Human Life: A Philosophical View* (1975). Another notable treatment is L.W. SUMNER, *Abortion and Moral Theory* (1981). JOEL FEINBERG (ed.), *The Problem of Abortion,* 2nd ed. (1984), is a good collection of essays. For a discussion of sanctity of life issues in general, including both abortion and euthanasia, see JONATHAN GLOVER, *Causing Death and Saving Lives* (1977); and PETER SINGER, *Practical Ethics* (1979). The specific problem of the treatment of severely handicapped infants is discussed in HELGA KUHSE and PETER SINGER, *Should the Baby Live?* (1985).

For a comprehensive textbook on bioethics, see TOM. L. BEAUCHAMP and JAMES F. CHILDRESS, *Principles of Biomedical Ethics,* 2nd ed. (1983). Anthologies of essays on diverse topics in bioethics include SAMUEL GOROVITZ *et al.* (eds.), *Moral Problems in Medicine,* 2nd ed. (1983); and JOHN ARRAS and ROBERT HUNT (comp.), *Ethical Issues in Modern Medicine,* 2nd ed. (1983). JAMES F. CHILDRESS, *Who Should Decide?* (1982), deals with paternalism in medical care; while PETER SINGER and DEANE WELLS, *The Reproduction Revolution: New Ways of Making Babies* (1984), focusses on the new reproductive technology. For the philosophical issues underlying genetic engineering and other methods of altering the human organism, see JONATHAN GLOVER, *What Sort of People Should There Be?* (1984).

(PETER SINGER)

The Forms of
Government: Their Historical Development

Most of the key words commonly used to describe governments, words such as monarchy, oligarchy, and democracy, are of Greek or Roman origin. They have been current for more than 2,000 years and have not yet exhausted their usefulness. This suggests that mankind has not changed very much since they were coined; but such verbal and psychological uniformity must not be allowed to hide the enormous changes in society and politics that have occurred. The earliest analytical use of the term monarchy occurred in ancient Athens, chiefly in Plato's dialogues, but even in Plato's time the word was not self-explanatory. There was a king in Macedon and a king in Persia, but the two societies, and therefore their institutions, were radically different. To give real meaning to the word monarchy in these two instances, it would be necessary to investigate their actual political and historical contexts. Any general account of monarchy required then, and requires today, an inquiry as to what circumstances have predisposed societies to adopt monarchy, and what have led them to reject it. So it is with all political terms.

This article is divided into the following sections:

PRIMITIVE GOVERNMENT

Agricultural society. So long as humankind were few, there was hardly any government. The division of function between ruler and ruled occurred only, if at all, within the family. The largest social groups, whether tribes or villages, were little more than loose associations of families, in which every elder or family head had an equal voice. Chieftains, if any, had strictly limited powers; some tribes, no doubt, did without chieftains altogether. This prepolitical form of social organization may still be found in undeveloped regions of the world, such as the Amazonian jungle in South America or the Upper Nile Valley in Africa.

Pre-political societies

The rise of agriculture began to change this state of affairs. In the land of Sumer (modern Iraq) the invention of irrigation necessitated grander arrangements. Control of the flow of water down the Tigris and Euphrates rivers had to be coordinated by a central authority, so that downstream fields could be watered as well as those further up. It became necessary also to devise a calendar, so as to know when the spring floods might be expected. As these skills evolved, society evolved with them. In early Sumer, it is reasonable to assume, the heads of the first cities, which were little more than enlarged villages, only gradually assumed the special attributes of monarchy, the rule of one; and the village council only gradually undertook a division of labour, so that some specialized as priests and others as warriors, farmers, or tax gatherers (key figures in every civilized society). As organization grew more complex, so did religion: an elaborate system of worship was necessary to propitiate the quite elaborate family of gods who, it was hoped, would protect the city from attack, from natural disaster, and from any questioning of the political arrangements deemed necessary by the ruler group.

Unfortunately, but inevitably, the young cities of Sumer quarrelled over the distribution of the rivers' water, and their wealth excited the greed of nomads outside the still comparatively small area of civilization. War, perhaps the most potent of all forces of historical change, announced its arrival, and military leadership became at least as important an element of kingship as divine sanction. It was to remain so throughout the long history of monarchy: whenever kings have neglected their military duties they have endangered their thrones. The wars of Sumer also laid bare another imperative of monarchy—the drive for empire, arising from the need to defend and define frontiers by extending them, and the need to find the means to pay for troops and weapons, whether by the plunder of an enemy or by the conquest of new lands.

Military and imperial imperatives

The spread of civilization. The history of Old World monarchy, and indeed of civilization, was to consist largely of variations on these patterns for four or five millennia. Trade contacts carried the principles of civilization to Egypt and to India (China seems to have evolved independently); and everywhere, once the social order was established, the problem of defending it became paramount. For although the broad zone of civilization spread steadily, so that by the reign of the Roman emperor Trajan (AD 98–117) there was a continuous band of civilized societies from Britain to the China Sea, it was always at risk from the barbarian nomads who roamed the great steppelands of central Eurasia. These nomads had retained the loose and simple institutions of humanity's infancy, but they had in other ways evolved as rapidly and successfully as the cities themselves (and partly under the cities' influence). The steppe was horse country, and, armed with bows and arrows, the barbarians of all epochs were marvelously swift and deadly light cavalry. They fought constantly among themselves for pasturage, and the losers were forever being driven west, south, and east, where they all too often overcame such defenses as the farms and cities of civilization could muster against them.

The nomads' military challenge was never sufficient to overturn civilization entirely. Either the invaders would overrun the settled lands and then adopt civilized customs, or the frontier defenses would prove strong enough to hold them off. There were even long periods of peace, when the barbarian threat was negligible. It was at such times that the spontaneous ingenuity of mankind had greatest play, in politics as in everything else. But it is noteworthy that, in the end, what may be described as the ancient norm always reasserted itself, whether in Europe, the Middle East, India, or China. Military crises—civil war or barbarian invasion or both—recurred and necessitated the strengthening of government. The effort to secure a measure of peace and prosperity required the assertion of authority over vast distances, the raising of large armies, and the gathering of taxes to pay for them. These requirements in turn fostered literacy and numeracy and the emergence of what later came to be called bureaucracy, government

by official. Bureaucratic imperialism emerged again and again and again and spread with civilization. Barbarian challenge occasionally brought it low but never for very long. When one city or people rose to hegemony over its neighbours, it simply incorporated their bureaucracy with its own. Sumer and Babylon were conquered by Assyria; Assyria was overthrown by the Medes, in alliance with Babylon and nomad Scythians; the empire of the Medes and Persians was overthrown by Alexander of Macedon; the Macedonian successor states were conquered by Rome, which was in due course supplanted in the Middle East and North Africa by the Islāmic Caliphate of Baghdad. Conquerors came and went; life for their subjects, whether peasants or townsmen, was not much altered by anything they did, so long as the battles occurred at safely remote sites.

Bureau-
cratic
monarchy

Nevertheless, from time to time experiments were made, for no monarchy commanded the resources to rule all its subjects directly. So long as they paid tribute punctually, local rulers and local communities were perforce left very much to govern themselves. Even if they did not pay, the effort required to mount a military operation at a distance from the imperial centre was so great that only in exceptional circumstances would it be undertaken, and even then it might not succeed, as the kings of Persia found when they launched punitive expeditions against mainland Greece at the beginning of the 5th century BC. So, in normal times, the inhabitants of the borderlands had extensive freedom of action.

Although civilization, as its advantages became clear, spread west and northwest out of Asia, bureaucratic monarchy could not easily follow it, for the sea was becoming a historical factor as important as the steppe and the great irrigable rivers. Tyre and Sidon, maritime cities of Phoenicia, had long exploited their coastal situation, not only to remain independent of the landward empires but also to push across the sea, and beyond the Strait of Gibraltar, in quest of trade. Their daughter-cities, Carthage, Utica, and Cádiz, were the first colonies, but primitive communications made it impossible for Phoenicia to rule them from afar.

GREECE

The city-state. The Phoenician example was followed by the Greeks. The Greeks were originally Indo-European nomads, who gradually made their way down to the Aegean and there took to the sea. They built on the achievements of earlier peoples, even taking over the first bureaucratic monarchy to appear on European soil: the Minoan civilization of the island of Crete, which succumbed to the invaders about 1450 BC. Continuing invasions from the north overthrew the mainland kingdoms of Mycenae, Tiryns, and Pylos in about 1200 BC. The so-called dark ages of Greece that then began lasted until the 8th century BC, by which time the Greeks had not only recovered literacy, by adapting the Phoenician alphabet, and begun to found overseas colonies, but had also brought the city-state to something near maturity. This form of government was the great political invention of classical antiquity.

Mediterranean geography is such that every little fishing village had to be able to defend itself against attack from land or sea, for outside help could not reach it easily. A man's dependence on his community, for physical as well as economic survival, was therefore obvious and complete. The city (*polis*) had first claim on his labour and loyalty, a claim that was usually freely recognized. It was this reality that led Aristotle (who himself came from just such a small commonwealth, Stageira, or Stagirus) to define man as a political animal.

The *polis*

Coastal mountain ranges made it difficult for any community to dominate more than a few square miles of land. They also for a long time deterred the rise of an empire to federate and control all the cities. If a few of these centres nevertheless rose to imperial greatness, like Tyre and Sidon before them, it was in the main because, like their Phoenician predecessors, they traded across the sea successfully. Athens, for example, exported olive oil, silver, and pottery. The profits of this trade enabled it to build a great navy and formidable city walls. Athenian

ships defeated Persia (480 BC) and won a small empire in the Aegean Sea; the combination of ships and walls enabled Athens long to defy, and nearly to defeat, its chief rival among the Greek cities, Sparta. Even after Sparta's triumph at the end of the Peloponnesian War (404 BC), Athens remained an independent sovereign state until its defeat by Philip of Macedon at the battle of Chaeronea (338 BC). In short, during the period of its prime Athens was free to make what experiments it liked in the realm of government, and to that period are owed not just the first example of successful democracy in world history but also the first investigations in political thought.

Monarchy, oligarchy, democracy. No Athenian believed that he had anything to learn from the bureaucratic monarchies of the East, which were incompatible with Greek notions of citizenship. All monarchies, indeed, seemed bound to deteriorate into such tyrannies. Self-defense necessitated that every adult male be required, and indeed be willing, to fight when called on; in return he had to be given some measure of respect and of personal autonomy—in a word, freedom. To protect that freedom, government was necessary; anarchy had no attractions for any Greek. The central question of politics, then, was the distribution of power among the citizens. Was Greek freedom best preserved and defined by the rule of the few or by that of the many? On the whole the great names favoured aristocracy, the rule of the best. Plato believed that the object of politics was virtue, and that only a few would ever thoroughly understand the science by which virtue could be attained. These trained few, then, should rule. Aristotle, his pupil, seems to have put the cultivation of the intellect highest among human goods; and he believed—quite reasonably, given the limited resources then available—that this fruit of civilization could be reaped only among a leisure class supported by the labours of the many. In return for their leisure the gentry would agree to sacrifice some of their time to the tedious business of governing, which only they would be sufficiently disinterested and well informed to do successfully. Neither of these apologies for oligarchy had any success in practice. The democrats carried the day, at any rate in Athens and its allied cities. In return for playing their parts as soldiers or sailors, ordinary Athenians insisted on controlling the government.

Views of
Plato and
Aristotle

The result was impressive. The people were misled by demagogues; they were intolerant enough to put Plato's master, Socrates, to death; they were envious of all personal distinction; and of their three great wars (against Persia, Sparta, and Macedon), they lost two. Furthermore, passionate devotion to the idea that Athens was the greatest of all cities, the school of Greece, and the wonder of civilization, misled them into basing their society in large part on slave labour, into wanton imperial adventure abroad, and into denying Athenian citizenship to all who were not born to it (even Aristotle), however much they contributed to the city's greatness and however much more they might have done. The foundations of Athenian democracy were narrow and shallow and fragile. But to say all this is only to say that the city could not entirely shake off the traditions of its past. Its achievement was the more remarkable for that. Seldom since has civilized humanity equalled democratic Athens, and until the last the city was satisfactorily governed by law and by popular decision. It owed its fall less to any flaw than to the overwhelming force that was mounted against it.

For to the north of Hellas proper a new power arose. Greek civilization had slowly trained and tamed the wild men of Macedon. Their king Philip forged them into a formidable army; he and his son Alexander then seized the opportunity open to them. History and geography made it impossible for the Greek cities to unite, and so they hanged separately. It seemed as if the city-state had been but a transient expedient. Henceforward Athens and Sparta would take their orders from the Great King.

ROME

The republic. As it turned out, the city-state had barely begun to display its full political potential. To the west, two non-Greek cities, Carthage and Rome, began to strug-

gle for mastery, and after the defeat of Hannibal at Zama (202 BC) Rome emerged as the strongest state in the Mediterranean.

The Roman *res publica*

The Greeks did not know how to classify Rome. The Greek historian Polybius, who chronicled Rome's rise, suggested that its constitution was such a success because it was a judicious blend of monarchy, aristocracy, and democracy. The Romans, a conservative, practical people, showed what they thought of such abstractions by speaking only of an unanalyzed "public thing"—*res publica*—and thus gave a new word to politics. With this focus the patriotism of the city-state reached its greatest intensity. The Romans were deeply attached to their traditions, and these traditions all taught the same lesson. For example, the legendary hero Mucius Scaevola gave his right hand to the flames to prove that there was nothing a Roman would not endure for his city. This passionate devotion to Rome's survival was tested again and again in war. All the tales of early Rome turn on battle. With dour persistence the peasants who had gathered for self-protection on the seven hills resisted every invader, fought back after every defeat, learned from all their mistakes, and even, however reluctantly and belatedly, modified their political institutions to meet the new needs of the times as they arose. Polybius was right: power in Rome was indeed shared among the people, the aristocracy, and the consuls, the executive officers of the republic who had replaced the kings. The claims of the many and of the few were fought out at election time, when the world's first clearly identifiable political parties appeared. Until Rome's late decadence, the results of elections were universally respected, and the triumphant alliance of the few and the many against the world was proclaimed in the letters blazoned on the city's buildings and battle standards: SPQR, for Senatus Populusque Romanus, the Senate and the people of Rome.

Like Athenian democracy, this system worked well for a surprisingly long time, and if the chief Athenian legacy was the proof that politics could be understood and debated logically and that under the right conditions democracy could work, Rome proved that the political process of competition for office and public discussion of policy was a valuable thing in itself.

Nevertheless, the Roman republic had been forged in a grim world. Its power had gradually extended over Italy in wars, always supposedly of self-defense. It is not surprising that what impressed the world most about the city was its military strength rather than its political institutions, even though the two were intimately related. As the weakness of Rome's neighbours became apparent, the Romans began to believe in their mission to rule, "to spare the conquered and war down the proud," as the poet Virgil put it. Military strength, in short, led to military adventurism. By the 1st century BC, Rome, having become a naval power as well as a military one, had conquered the whole Mediterranean basin and much of its hinterland. The strains of empire building made themselves felt. The Roman armies, no longer composed of citizens temporarily absent from the plow or the workshop but of lifetime professionals, were now loyal to their generals rather than to the state; and these generals brought on civil war as they competed to turn their foreign conquests into power at home. The population of Rome swelled, but economic growth could not keep pace, so that many citizens became paupers dependent on the public dole. The aristocrats appointed to govern the provinces saw their postings merely as opportunities to get rich quickly by pillaging their unfortunate subjects. The republic could not solve these and other problems and was in the end superseded by the monarchy of Caesar Augustus.

The empire. The bedrock of Augustus' power was his command of the legions, but he himself was a much better politician than he was a general, and he knew quite well that naked political power is as unstable as it is expensive. He reduced the military establishment as much as was prudent, laboured to turn the revolutionary faction that had supported his bid for power into a respectable new ruling class, and proclaimed the restoration of the republic. But not even Augustus could make the restoration real. With the safety of the state, questions of war and

The Augustan state

peace, and most of the business of governing the empire in the hands of a monarch, there was not enough for the Senate to do, and Augustus never went so far as to restore genuinely free elections or the organs of popular government. He kept the crowd happy with chariot races, gladiatorial contests, and the dole of bread. Nevertheless, he could not give up the attempt to legitimize his regime. Like earlier monarchs elsewhere, he called in the aid of religion, even though the religion of Rome was as republican as its constitution. Later emperors made their own divinity a tenet of the public faith.

For four centuries the resemblance between Rome and the bureaucratic eastern monarchies steadily increased. Roman nationalism, Roman traditionalism, and Roman law survived as legacies that posterity would one day claim; and if nobody much believed in the constitutional shams of Augustus' day, the example of his constitutional monarchy was to prove potent at a much later period.

The age of the city-state was at last drawing to a close. The emperor Caracalla extended Roman citizenship to all subjects of the empire, but that was merely so that he could tax them more heavily. The demands of the imperial administration began to bankrupt the cities, which had previously prospered as the local organs of government under Rome. New barbarian attacks threw the empire onto the defensive, and in AD 410 Rome fell to the Visigoths.

THE MIDDLE AGES

Dissolution and instability. Seen against the background of the millennia, the fall of Rome was so commonplace an event that it is almost surprising that so much ink has been spilt in the attempt to explain it. The Visigoths were merely one among the peoples who had been dislodged from the steppe in the usual fashion. They and others, unable to crack the defenses of Sāsānian Persia or of the Roman Empire in the east (though it was a near thing), probed farther west and at length found the point of weakness they were seeking on the Alps and the Rhine.

What really needs explaining is the fact that the western empire was never restored. Elsewhere the universal throne was never vacant for long. In China, after every time of troubles, a new dynasty received "the mandate of Heaven," and a new Son of Heaven rebuilt order. For instance, in AD 304 the Huns had invaded China, and a long period of disruption followed; but at the beginning of the 7th century the T'ang dynasty took charge and began 300 years of rule. The Europeans failed to emulate this story. Justinian, the greatest of the eastern Roman emperors, reconquered large portions of the West in the 6th century, though the destruction wreaked by his soldiers made things worse rather than better. In 800, Charlemagne, king of the Franks, was actually crowned emperor of the West by the Pope. In later centuries the dynasties of Hohenstaufen and Habsburg tried to restore the empire; so, as late as the 19th century, did Napoleon Bonaparte. None of these attempts succeeded. Probably the chance was only real in the earliest period, before Europe had got used to doing without an overlord. But at that time there was never a long enough breathing space for society to regain its stability and strength. Most of the barbarian kingdoms, successor states to Rome, succumbed to later assailants. Britain fell away from the empire in the 5th century; the little kingdoms of the Angles and Saxons were just coming together as one kingdom of England when the Viking invasions began. In the 7th century the Arabs conquered North Africa, and in the 8th they took Spain and invaded Gaul. Lombards, Avars, Slavs, Bulgars, and Magyars poured into Europe from the East. Not until Otto I's victory over the Magyars at Lechfeld in 955 did these incursions cease, and not until the late 11th century was Latin Christendom more or less secure within its borders; and by then it had been without an effective emperor for more than 600 years.

Feudalism. Various institutions had emerged to fill the gap. The church, against enormous odds, had kept the light of religion and learning alive and spread what was left of Roman civilization into Ireland, England, Central Europe, and Scandinavia. It also provided a reservoir of literacy against the day when professional government

Attempts at restoration

should be possible again. The kings of the barbarians, of whom Charlemagne was the greatest, had provided military leadership and tried to acquire some of the prestige and governmental machinery of the Roman emperors. But the troublous times ensured that effective power fell to a military aristocracy. Its members called themselves *nobiles* in the Roman fashion and appropriated various late imperial titles such as *comes* (count) and *dux* (duke). But this was mere decoration. The new kings, lacking the machinery for imperial taxation, could not pay for standing armies. Besides, this was the age in which the heavily armoured cavalryman (*chevalier* in French; knight in English) dominated war. He was an independent force and thus a much less dependable instrument than a Roman legionary had been. Legally, the new masters of the soil were liegemen of the various kings (it was a maxim that every man had a lord), but in practice they could usually ignore royal claims. Europe thus fell under the rule of armoured lords; and the course of the next few hundred years gave everyone reason to wonder whether the democrats of Greece had not been right to distrust the very idea of oligarchy, for the tonic note of noble rule seemed to be almost incessant warfare.

Even at their height the military aristocrats never had it all their own way. Strong monarchies gradually developed in England, France, and, a little later, in the Iberian Peninsula. During the heyday of the papacy (*c.* 1050–1300) the Roman Catholic Church was able to modify, if not control, baronial behaviour. Trade gradually revived and brought with it a revival of the city-state in Italy, the Rhineland, and the Low Countries, for the newly prosperous burghers could now afford to build stout walls around their towns, and it became difficult for the nobility to muster the force to besiege them successfully. Even the peasants from time to time made themselves felt in bloody uprisings. The nobility itself was far from a homogeneous or united class.

The rise of law and the nation-state. Medieval Europe, in short, was a constantly shifting kaleidoscope of political arrangements; to the extent that it ever settled down, it did so on the principle that since everybody's claim to power and property was fragile and inconsistent with everybody else's, a certain degree of mutual forbearance was necessary. This explains the great importance attached to custom or (as it was called in England) common law. Disputes were still often settled by force, especially when kings were the disputants, but the medieval European became almost as fond of litigation as he was of battle. Every great estate was hung about with quasi-permanent lawsuits, and the centralization of the church on the papal courts at Rome ensured yet more work for lawyers, the greatest of whom began to merge with the military nobility into an aristocracy of a new kind. Rights, titles, and privileges were forever being granted, revoked, and reaffirmed. Parchment deeds came to regulate men's political, social, and economic relationships at least as much as the sword did. In these ways the idea of the rule of law was reborn. By the beginning of the early modern period, legally demonstrable privileges had become the universal cement of European society. The weak were thus enabled to survive alongside the strong, and Europe, where everyone knew to which order of society he belonged, thus took on a faint resemblance to India, where the caste system was so strong as to make many of the usual functions of government quite unnecessary.

But there was a dynamism in European society that prevented it from setting permanently into this or any other pattern. This evolving Europe of privileged orders was also the Europe of rising monarchies. With many setbacks the kings clawed power to themselves; by 1500 most of them presided over bureaucracies (initially staffed by clerics) that would have impressed any Roman emperor. But monarchy could no longer claim universality. The foundations of the new monarchies were purely territorial. The kings of England, France, and Spain had enough to do to enforce their authority within the lands they had inherited or seized and to hammer their realms into some sort of uniformity. This impulse explains the wars of the English against the Welsh, Scots, and Irish; the drive of the French

Influence of knighthood

The common law

kings toward the Alps, the Pyrenees, and the Rhine; and the rigour of the Spanish kings in forcing Catholicism on their Jewish and Moorish subjects. Uniformity paved the way for the most characteristic governmental form of the modern world, the nation-state.

EMERGENCE OF THE MODERN WORLD

The failure of absolutism. That evolution was not easy, for kings or anybody else. The invention of gunpowder enabled kings to overbear their turbulent nobles, for cannon were exceedingly effective at demolishing the castles in which rebellious barons had formerly been quite safe. But artillery was cruelly expensive. This fact underlies the rise and persistence of the greatest political discovery of the later Middle Ages: the principle of representation. A sufficient revenue had always been one of the chief necessities of monarchy; none of the great European kingdoms had ever succeeded in securing one for long. The intractable complexities of medieval society permitted very little coercion of taxpayers; for the rest, money could be secured only by chicanery, or by selling offices or crown lands (at the price of a long-term weakening of the monarch), or by robbing the church, or by a lucky chance, such as the acquisition of the gold and silver of Mexico and Peru by the king of Spain, or by dealing, on a semi-equal footing, with parliaments (or estates, as they were more generally known).

Yet the principle of parliamentary representation was of slow and uncertain growth, except perhaps in England, where the folly of the Stuart kings ensured its survival. Before then, three great occurrences, the Renaissance, the Reformation, and the discovery of America, had transformed Europe.

The impact of the Renaissance defies summary, even if its political consequences are all that need be considered. The truest symbol of its importance is the printing press. For one thing, this invention enormously increased the resources of government. Laws, for example, could be circulated far more widely and more accurately than ever before. But more important still was the fact that the printing press increased the size of the educated and literate classes. Renaissance civilization thus took a quantum jump, acquiring deeper foundations than any of its predecessors or contemporaries by calling into play the intelligence of more individuals than ever before. But the catch (from a ruler's point of view) was that this development also brought public opinion into being for the first time. Not for much longer would it be enough for kings to win the acquiescence of the nobility and the upper clergy; a new force was at work, as was acknowledged by the frantic attempts of all the monarchies to control and censor the press.

The Reformation was the eldest child of the press; it, too, had diffuse and innumerable consequences, the most important of which was the destruction of the Roman Church's claim to universality. It had always been a somewhat fraudulent claim: the pope had never actually been accepted by all the Christian bodies, even all the orthodox ones; but after Martin Luther and John Calvin, the scope of his commands was radically reduced. In the long run the consequence was the secularization of politics and administration and the introduction of some measure of religious toleration. Gradually the way became clear for rational, utilitarian considerations to shape government.

The discovery of the Americas opened a new epoch in world history. The Spanish overthrew the monarchies of the Aztecs and the Incas, thanks partly to the superior weapons that they brought with them and partly to the diseases. It was a spectacular episode, the first to proclaim that the old struggle between the steppe and the sown had been bypassed: from now on the drama of history would lie in the tension between the oceans and the land. The globe was circumnavigated for the first time; European ships, bearing explorers, traders, pirates, or men who were something of all three, penetrated every sea and harbour; and although the ancient civilizations of Islām, India, China, and Japan saw no need to alter their customs to take account of European innovations, the signal had been given for their fall.

The principle of representation

Portuguese and Spanish explorations gave far-flung overseas empires to both countries, and perhaps as many difficulties as benefits. Other countries—France, England, the Netherlands, Sweden, Denmark—thought it both undesirable and unsafe not to seek empire themselves; the Iberian monarchies were thus involved in a perpetual struggle to defend their acquisitions. This entailed incessant expenditure, more, in the end, than the kingdoms' revenues could match. Financial weakness was one of the chief causes of the ultimate decline of Spain. But by then the inadequacies of the monarchical system had been cruelly exposed in such episodes as the revolt of the Netherlands, the defeat of the Spanish Armada by England, and, worst of all, the snail's-pace development of the colonies in the New World. Charles V and Philip II were as able as all but a few monarchs in history; but they could not overcome the structural weaknesses of hereditary monarchy. There was no mechanism by which they could devolve their most crushing duties on their ministers, so government moved slowly, if at all. As lawful sovereigns they were bound by the customs of their numerous realms, which frequently blocked necessary measures. They were unable to guarantee that their heirs would be their equals. The same difficulties eventually ruined the French monarchy. The only remedy discoverable within the system was for the king in effect to abdicate in favour of a chief minister. Unfortunately a man equal to the task was seldom found, and anyway no minister, however great, was ever safe from the constant intrigues and conspiracies of disgruntled courtiers. Problems tended to accumulate until they became unmanageable.

Weaknesses of monarchy

Representation and constitutional monarchy. Meanwhile, in England, the rise of Parliament introduced a republican, if not a democratic, element into the workings of one of Europe's oldest kingdoms.

The republican tradition had never quite died out. The Dutch had emerged from their long struggle against Catholic Spain clinging triumphantly to their new religion and their ancient constitution, a somewhat ramshackle federation known as the United Provinces. Switzerland was another medieval confederation; Venice and Genoa were rigidly oligarchical republics. What set England apart was that everywhere else in monarchical Europe the medieval representative institutions—the États-Généraux in France, the Cortes in Spain, the various diets of the Germanic countries—fell into oblivion. In England alone the expense of naval war, the incompetence of the kings, the exhaustion of all other sources of finance, and the absence of a standing army brought about the continuance and strengthening of Parliament. The climax came under William III, a Dutchman who was quite content to let Parliament take an unprecedentedly large share in government so long as it voted money for his war against Louis XIV of France. He conceded, in short, full power of the purse to the House of Commons, and before long it became a maxim of the dominant Whig Party that no man could be legally taxed without his own consent or that of his representatives. A radically new age had dawned.

The Whig system was called constitutional monarchy. Disputes about the right and legal way of governing England had raged throughout the 17th century. Civil wars and revolutions had been accompanied, perhaps in part caused, by endless rummaging through old manuscripts and a nearly ceaseless war of printed pamphlets. The increasingly rationalist temper of the times, exemplified in the works of John Locke, finally buried some of the more blatantly mythological theories of government, such as that of the divine right of kings; and after the flight of King James II in 1688, Parliament finally settled the issues that had so vexed the country by passing a series of measures that gave England a written fundamental law for the first time. Henceforth the country was to be ruled by a partnership between King and Parliament (in practice, between the king and an oligarchy of country gentlemen who controlled most parliamentary elections); and if many Englishmen looked with distaste on the squabbles of party politics, which were the sordid result of this arrangement, few could propose a plausible alternative. Tories drank toasts to the King over the water; republicans published

Rise of the British Parliament

more pamphlets; and Sir Robert Walpole ruled for 21 years as the first British prime minister.

The secret of Walpole's strength lay in his ability simultaneously to please the King, to give the country sound government finances, and to command a majority in the houses of Parliament. He performed this last trick partly by giving out sinecures, salaries, and titles to his supporters, partly by his superiority in debate, and partly by exploiting Whig fears of Tories and Roman Catholics. These three elements—party interest, practical decision making, and party ideology—have in one form or another come to dominate most modern political systems where brute force is at a discount.

Even after Walpole's fall his arrangements continued. They were vindicated by the Seven Years' War (1756–63), when Britain defeated both the French and Spanish empires and emerged predominant in every ocean and (especially) in North America. Immediately afterward republican ideology found its classical expression.

The American and French republics. The limited British monarchy found it little easier to govern a sea-borne empire than did the kings of France and Spain. If Britain's American colonies were to grow in population and riches, so as to become sources of strength to the empire, not military and financial liabilities, they had to be given a substantial measure of religious, economic, and political independence, and the gift could not be revoked. Once British policy had created a chain of more or less self-governing communities along the Atlantic seaboard of North America—communities much like the city-states of old—it could not undo its own work, even when it found its clients unreasonable, small-minded, and recalcitrant. Thus, when the British government attempted to impose tighter rule from London, the old empire broke down in bickering about taxation and, in riot, rebellion, and civil war—in short, in the American Revolution. From 1775 to 1783 the Anglo-Americans fought with determination and good luck against their former overlord, King George III; and in 1776 their leaders determined to be free of him and the British Parliament forever. The principles on which they meant to found a new commonwealth were expounded in the Declaration of Independence:

The Declaration of Independence

> . . . We hold these truths to be self-evident, that all men are created equal, that they are endowed by their Creator with certain inalienable Rights, that among these are Life, Liberty and the pursuit of Happiness. —That, to secure these rights, Governments are instituted among Men, deriving their just powers from the consent of the governed. . . .

The application of these principles was more difficult than their enunciation, and it took the Americans 12 years to get themselves a suitable form of government. When they did adopt a new constitution it served them so well that it is still operative. This durability is not unconnected with the fact that the Constitution opened the door to modern liberal democracy. "The consent of the governed" was agreed to be the key to governmental legitimacy, and in practice the phrase rapidly came to mean "the consent of the majority." The principle of representation was embodied in the Constitution (the first article of which was entirely devoted to the establishment of Congress, the American parliament); this implied that there was no limit to the potential size of a successful republic. From Plato to Rousseau, theorists had agreed that democracies had to be small, because by definition all their citizens had to be able to give their consent in person. This restriction was alone almost sufficient to explain the recurrent failures of republican government down the ages. Now it had been evaded.

Yet its example might have had little effect on Europe but for the French Revolution of 1789. The French had helped the Americans to beat the British, but the effort had been too much in the end for the monarchy's finances. To avert state bankruptcy the États-Généraux were summoned for the first time in 175 years, and soon the whole government had been turned upside down. The French repudiated the divine right of kings, the ascendancy of the nobility, the privileges of the Roman Catholic Church, and the regional structure of old France, and, in the end, they set up a republic and cut off the former king's head.

Unfortunately for peace, in destroying the monarchy the Revolution also crowned its centuries-old labours. The kings had created the French state; the Revolution made it stronger than ever. The kings had united their subjects in the quest for glory; now the nation made the quest its own. In the name of rationality, liberty, and equality (fraternity was not a foremost concern), France again went to war. The Revolution had brought the new invention, the nation-state, to maturity, and soon it proved capable of conquering the Continent, for everywhere French armies went the revolutionary creed went, too.

In all this the French Revolution was giving expression to a general longing for government devoted to the greatest happiness of the greatest number. But there was also considerable resistance, which increased as time went on, to receiving the benefits of modern government at the hands of the French. Besides, the facts of demography began to tilt against the Revolution, as population growth in Britain and Germany accelerated and that of France slowed down. The century that began with the victories of Marengo, Austerlitz, and Jena ended with the Third Republic nervously on the defensive and French society still bitterly at odds with itself.

Yet, on the whole, the work of the French Revolution survived. However many changes of regime France endured (seven between 1814 and 1870), its institutions had been thoroughly democratized, and the underlying drift of events steadily reinforced this achievement. By mid-century universal manhood suffrage had been introduced, putting France in this respect on the same footing as the United States. Britain, pursuing its own historical logic, evolved in much the same way; its oligarchs slowly and ungraciously consented to share political power with other classes, rather than lose it altogether. By the end of the century manhood suffrage was clearly at hand in Britain, too, and women would not much longer be denied the vote. Smaller European countries took the same course. And everywhere (in America as well as western Europe) the representative principle combined with the necessity of government to produce the modern political party. Elections could only be won by organized factions; politicians could only attain or retain power by winning elections. Permanent parties resulted. The Industrial Revolution and continuing population growth made an elaborate state apparatus more and more necessary. The spread of education and prosperity made more and more citizens feel fully equal to taking part in politics, whether as voters or statesmen. Modern government in the West thus defined itself as a blend of bureaucracy, party politics, and passionate individualism, the whole held together by the cement of an equally passionate nationalism.

Nationalism and imperialism. The kingdom of Prussia and the empires of Austria and Russia readily learned from the French Revolution that it was necessary to rationalize government. They had been struggling along that path even before 1789. Carrying out the necessary changes proved exceedingly difficult (Russia, which in some ways was more like ancient Egypt than a modern country, made far too few changes until far too late), but gradually they were managed. Meanwhile the libertarian and egalitarian components of the revolutionary legacy were rigidly resisted. The great dynasts, and the military aristocracies that supported them, had no intention of admitting their obsolescence. Though they were forced to make limited concessions to the liberal spirit between 1789 and World War I, the autocratic citadel of their power was never surrendered. Instead, the myth of the nation was adopted to reinforce the authority of the state.

Nationalism intensified the competitiveness that had always been a part of the European state system. Peoples, it emerged, could be as touchy about their prestige as monarchs. But for a hundred years an uneasy peace prevailed in Europe, leaving the powers free to pursue interests in other parts of the world. Asia and Africa thus came to feel the full impact of European expansion, as the Americas had felt it before. Only the Japanese proved to have the resources to adapt successfully to the new ways, taking what suited them and rejecting the rest. They kept their millennial sacred monarchy but modernized the armed

forces. In 1895 they fought and won a war against China, which was sliding into chaos, and in 1905 they defeated a great power, Russia. But Japan was wholly exceptional. Elsewhere, European power was irresistible. Britain gave up the attempt to govern overseas settlements of its own people directly—the experiment had proved fatal in America and nearly so in Canada—but retained indirect authority over them, in part through the useful device of its own sacred monarchy. And it had no scruple about assuming direct rule over more and more non-British peoples. France, Germany, and the United States eagerly followed the example; The Netherlands, Spain, and Portugal clung to what they had, though the last two suffered great imperial losses as Mexico, Brazil, and others shook off colonial rule. It seemed that before long the whole world would be ruled by half a dozen powers.

It did not turn out so, or not for long. The problem of governmental legitimacy in central, eastern, and southern Europe was too explosive. The obstinate conservatism of the dynasts proved fatal to more than monarchy. There were too many who regarded the empires as unacceptable, either because they were the instruments of class oppression, or because they embodied foreign rule, or both. And the romantic tradition of the French Revolution—the fall of the Bastille, the Reign of Terror, the Jacobin dictatorship—helped to drive many of these critics into violent rebellion, permanent conspiracy, and corrosive cynicism about the claims of authority. Authority itself, corrupted by power and at the same time gnawingly aware of its own fragility, embarked on more and more risky militarist adventures. The upshot was the war of 1914, the revolutions that followed it, and the new model government that emerged in Russia at the end of the period.

20TH-CENTURY MODELS

The Soviet state. In theory the Soviet Union was and is a democracy. In practice it has proved to be one of the most effective oligarchies in history. Lenin and his followers won power in the turmoil of revolutionary Russia because they were abler and more unscrupulous than anyone else. They retained and increased their power by force, but they argued that the social theories of Karl Marx, as developed by Lenin, are of universal, permanent, and all-sufficient validity; that the leadership of the Communist Party has a unique understanding of these theories; and that its will can never legitimately be resisted. All institutions of the Soviet state are devised primarily to assure the untrammelled power of the party, and no methods have been spurned, from mass starvation to the suppression of works of art, in furthering this aim. Even the extraordinary economic and military achievements of the regime have been secondary to its overall purpose.

From the first the Soviet model found many imitators. Lenin's strictly disciplined revolutionary party, the only morality of which was unswerving obedience to the leader, was a particularly attractive example to those intent on seizing power in a continent much weakened by the war. Benito Mussolini of Italy modelled his Fascist Party on the Leninists; Adolf Hitler of Germany copied Mussolini. Both men won power, which they criminally abused, in conditions of social and political chaos like those Lenin had exploited. In the Soviet Union itself, Lenin's successor and disciple, Joseph Stalin, outdid his master in building up his power by mass terror and party discipline. Between them these three dictators brought about World War II, after which Stalin was able to extend the Soviet model directly to the eastern European countries that victory enabled him to dominate. Since his death in 1953 his empire has lurched from crisis to crisis, never resolving its basic dilemma. The terror, the lies, the regimentation are less insistent than they were in the 1930s and '40s, but the regime dares not dispense with them altogether; yet while they persist there can be no rational and effective program for tackling the Soviet Union's many problems, of which all-pervasive corruption is probably the worst.

Liberal democracy. Government in the West has evolved along more reassuring lines. The democratic dogma is everywhere in the ascendant and has brought with it greater influence for the working classes, for women, for

The nation-state

Political parties

Legitimacy and upheaval

Stalinist totalitarianism

non-European races, and for small states. Liberalism has a unique claim to its credit: no Western democracy has ever fought a war against another. The muddled processes of open debate and decision have produced an economic order that has proved vastly more productive than the command economies of the East and has brought greatly improved living standards for almost all. Free elections have meant that bad, or at any rate unpopular, governments have been regularly dismissed by the voters with historically unparalleled ease and peacefulness. But Western democracy, however perfect its forms (and nowhere are they entirely consistent with its principles), always has problems on its hands that may prove too much for it. It could not avert the outbreak of two world wars, and a third has been averted so far more through terror of nuclear weapons than by democratic wisdom. Class conflicts are muted rather than resolved. Nationalism still distorts voters' judgments in matters of foreign policy; greed misleads them over economic policy. Demagogues are as much a menace as they ever were in ancient Athens, and many politicians are personally corrupt.

The great experiment of European imperialism has collapsed. The two world wars robbed the powers of the will and the means to maintain overseas rule. Unfortunately the empires have not been succeeded by new governmental forms fully capable of dealing with the problems of technologically backward, overpopulated, culturally premodern societies. In the Muslim world the idea of the Islāmic republic has arisen. In Iran it amounts to an attempt to wed church and state, religion and government, as indissolubly as they were in the age of the first caliphs, only now the religion is to be Shi'ah Islām, and the state a modern republic. If the experiment proves a success it may well have as widespread an impact within the Muslim world as Leninist Communism has had on revolutionaries everywhere; but by the nature of the case it cannot spread outside regions of Islāmic dominance. In India a regime of more or less democratic nationalists endeavours to overcome a pervasive regionalism and social stratification that have been part of the subcontinent for more than 2,000 years. China, which during the lifetime of Mao Tse-tung wholeheartedly followed the Leninist model, began after his death to draw back. Japan has adapted to Western notions of capitalism and parliamentarism without contributing any fresh ideas. Elsewhere in the world the commonest expedient adopted has been dictatorship, usually military, in which the ancient tradition of autocracy reasserts itself; but it is autocracy without its ancient stability, and of all current political forms it seems by far the least likely to deal effectively with the universal enemies: hunger, war, poverty, disease, waste, violence. Some thinkers believe that only a form of world government can make decisive headway against these evils, but no one has yet suggested either how world government can be set up without a world war or how, if such a government did somehow come peacefully into existence, it could be organized so as to be worthy of its name. Even effective cooperation among national governments often seems unattainable, as the story of such international bodies as already exist demonstrates all too sadly.

For the time being the world exists in uneasy equipoise. The United States and the Soviet Union, dedicated rivals, are too big and willful to subordinate themselves to international organizations. The nation-state has, with few exceptions, become the political norm. The issues that once made the distinctions between monarchies and republics so important have withered into insignificance. Everywhere the growing complexity of life has necessitated, and technology has made possible, an immense expansion of the state, so that it seems at times almost as if the Italian economist and sociologist Vilfredo Pareto, who believed that all government is but a facade for oligarchy, was right. But even if so, problems still remain for which mere oligarchy is no answer. The incompatible claims of the city-states ruined ancient Greece; the modern world may yet be ruined by the incompatible claims of the nations. If man, the political animal, is to save himself and his civilizations, he cannot yet rest from seeking new forms of government to meet the ever-new needs of his times.

The Islāmic republic

BIBLIOGRAPHY. Classical texts on governmental forms are widely available in numerous editions. They include PLATO, *The Republic;* ARISTOTLE, *Politics;* NICCOLÒ MACHIAVELLI, *The Prince* and *The Discourses;* THOMAS HOBBES, *Leviathan;* JOHN LOCKE, *Second Treatise of Government;* MONTESQUIEU, *The Spirit of Laws;* JEAN-JACQUES ROUSSEAU, *The Social Contract;* THOMAS JEFFERSON, *Declaration of Independence;* ALEXANDER HAMILTON, JAMES MADISON, and JOHN JAY, *The Federalist;* EDMUND BURKE, *Reflections on the Revolution in France;* THOMAS PAINE, *Rights of Man;* ALEXIS DE TOCQUEVILLE, *Democracy in America;* WALTER BAGEHOT, *The English Constitution;* JAMES BRYCE, *The American Commonwealth;* FRIEDRICH ENGELS, *The Origin of the Family, Private Property, and the State;* V.I. LENIN, *The State and Revolution.*

For a subject of this nature, a solid background in world history is absolutely necessary, and WILLIAM H. MCNEILL, *A World History,* 3rd ed. (1979), is an excellent introduction. GORDON CHILDE, *What Happened in History,* rev. ed. (1954, reprinted 1982), is a classic survey of the contribution of archaeology to our understanding of prehistory and the ancient world. For the development of governmental forms in Greece see *The Cambridge Ancient History,* 3rd ed. (1970–); and N.G.L. HAMMOND, *A History of Greece to 332 B.C.,* 2nd ed. (1967, reprinted 1981). A.H.M. JONES, *Athenian Democracy* (1957, reprinted 1975), is indispensable, particularly as a corrective to Plato, Aristotle, and Thucydides. The most exciting work about the Romans written since Gibbon is RONALD SYME, *The Roman Revolution* (1939, reprinted 1974); those wanting more general accounts of the Romans may turn to J.P.V.D. BALSDON (ed.), *The Romans* (1966); and H.H. SCULLARD, *From the Gracchi to Nero,* 5th ed. (1982). A.H.M. JONES, *The Later Roman Empire,* 2 vol. (1964), is the most authoritative account of the fall of the empire.

The best introduction to the medieval papacy is WALTER ULLMANN, *A Short History of the Papacy in the Middle Ages* (1972). The same author's *Growth of Papal Government in the Middle Ages,* 3rd ed. (1970), links ideas and institutions but makes few concessions to beginners. MARC BLOCH, *Feudal Society* (1961, reissued 1974; originally published in French, 1939), is an indispensable study of its subject.

The development of political thought from the Renaissance to the 19th century is well presented in JOHN P. PLAMENATZ, *Man and Society,* 2 vol. (1963, reprinted 1972–74). An attempt to trace modern government back to its origins is demonstrated in BARRINGTON MOORE, JR., *Social Origins of Dictatorship and Democracy* (1966). See also PERRY ANDERSON, *Lineages of the Absolutist State* (1974); and FRANCO VENTURI, *Utopia and Reform in the Enlightenment* (1970; originally published in Italian, 1970).

Works on governmental forms of a general, comparative nature include A. GOODWIN (ed.), *The European Nobility in the Eighteenth Century,* 2nd ed. (1967); A. LAWRENCE LOWELL, *Governments and Parties in Continental Europe,* 2 vol. (1896, reissued 1970); EUGENE N. ANDERSON and PAULINE R. ANDERSON, *Political Institutions and Social Change in Continental Europe in the Nineteenth Century* (1967); MICHAEL OAKESHOTT (ed.), *The Social and Political Doctrines of Contemporary Europe* (1939, reissued 1949); and S.E. FINER, *Comparative Government* (1970, reissued 1974).

Useful studies of particular states include J.H. PLUMB, *The Growth of Political Stability in England, 1675–1725* (1967, reissued 1980; U.S. title, *The Origins of Political Stability, England, 1675–1725);* and ÉLIE HALÉVY, *A History of the English People in the Nineteenth Century,* 6 vol. (1924–34; originally published in French, 5 vol., 1913–32); for France, C.B.A. BEHRENS, *The Ancien Régime* (1967, reissued 1976); GEORGE LEFEBVRE, *The French Revolution,* 2 vol. (1962–64; originally published in French, 1930); and D.W. BROGAN, *The French Nation from Napoleon to Pétain* (1957, reissued 1961); for Germany, HANS ROSENBERG, *Bureaucracy, Aristocracy, and Autocracy: The Prussian Experience, 1660–1815* (1958, reprinted 1968); A.J. NICHOLLS, *Weimar and the Rise of Hitler,* 2nd ed. (1979); FRANZ NEUMANN, *Behemoth,* 2nd ed. (1944, reissued 1963); and MARTIN BROSZAT, *The Hitler State: The Foundation and Development of the Internal Structure of the Third Reich* (1981; originally published in German, 1969); for Italy, DENIS MACK SMITH, *Italy: A Modern History,* new rev. ed. (1969); and S.J. WOOLF (ed.), *The Nature of Fascism* (1968); for the Soviet Union, JEROME BLUM, *Lord and Peasant in Russia: From the Ninth to the Nineteenth Century* (1961, reprinted 1971); LEONARD SCHAPIRO, *The Origin of the Communist Autocracy: Political Opposition in the Soviet State, First Phase 1917–1922,* 2nd ed. (1977); and DEREK J.R. SCOTT, *Russian Political Institutions,* 4th ed. (1969); and for the United States, RICHARD HOFSTADTER, *The American Political Tradition and the Men Who Made It* (1948, reprinted 1974), and *The Idea of a Party System: The Rise of Legitimate Opposition in the United States, 1780–1840* (1969).

(HUGH BROGAN)

Humanism

The word *humanism* has been freely applied to a variety of beliefs, methods, and philosophies that place central emphasis on the human realm. Most frequently, however, the term is used with reference to a system of education and mode of inquiry that developed in northern Italy during the 14th century and later spread through Europe and England. Alternately known as "Renaissance humanism," this program was so broadly and profoundly influential that it is one of the chief reasons why the Renaissance is viewed as a distinct historical period. Indeed, though the word *Renaissance* is of more recent coinage, the fundamental idea of that period as one of renewal and reawakening is humanistic in origin. But humanism sought its own philosophical bases in far earlier times and, moreover, continued to exert some of its power long after the end of the Renaissance.

This article is divided into the following sections:

ORIGIN AND MEANING OF THE TERM "HUMANISM"

The ideal of humanitas. The history of the term *humanism* is complex but enlightening. It was first employed (as *humanismus*) by 19th-century German scholars to designate the Renaissance emphasis on classical studies in education. These studies were pursued and endorsed by educators known, as early as the late 15th century, as *umanisti:* that is, professors or students of classical literature. The word *umanisti* derives from the *studia humanitatis,* a course of classical studies that, in the early 15th century, consisted of grammar, poetry, rhetoric, history, and moral philosophy. The *studia humanitatis* were held to be the equivalent of the Greek *paideia.* Their name was itself based on the Latin *humanitas,* an educational and political ideal that was the intellectual basis of the entire movement. Renaissance humanism in all its forms defined itself in its straining toward this ideal. No discussion, therefore, of humanism can have validity without an understanding of *humanitas.*

The studia humanitatis

Humanitas meant the development of human virtue, in all its forms, to its fullest extent. The term thus implied not only such qualities as are associated with the modern word *humanity*—understanding, benevolence, compassion, mercy—but also such more aggressive characteristics as fortitude, judgment, prudence, eloquence, and even love of honour. Consequently the possessor of *humanitas* could not be merely a sedentary and isolated philosopher or man of letters but was of necessity a participant in active life. Just as action without insight was held to be aimless and barbaric, insight without action was rejected as barren and imperfect. *Humanitas* called for a fine balance of action and contemplation, a balance born not of compromise but of complementarity. The goal of such fulfilled and balanced virtue was political in the broadest sense of the word. The purview of Renaissance humanism included not only the education of the young but also the guidance of adults (including rulers) via philosophical poetry and strategic rhetoric. It included not only realistic social criticism but also utopian hypotheses, not only painstaking reassessments of history but also bold reshapings of the future. In short, humanism called for the comprehensive reform of culture, the transfiguration of what humanists termed the passive and ignorant society of the "dark" ages into a new order that would reflect and encourage the grandest human potentialities. Humanism had an evangelical dimension. It sought to project *humanitas* from the individual into the state at large.

The wellspring of *humanitas* was classical literature. Greek and Roman thought, available in a flood of rediscovered or newly translated manuscripts, provided humanism with much of its basic structure and method. For Renaissance humanists, there was nothing dated or outworn about the writings of Plato, Cicero, or Livy. Compared with the typical productions of medieval Christianity, these pagan works had a fresh, radical, almost avant-garde tonality. Indeed, recovering the classics was to humanism tantamount to recovering reality. Classical philosophy, rhetoric, and history were seen as models of proper method—efforts to come to terms, systematically and without preconceptions of any kind, with perceived experience. Moreover, classical thought considered ethics qua ethics, politics qua politics: it lacked the inhibiting dualism occasioned in medieval thought by the often conflicting demands of secularism and Christian spirituality. Classical virtue, in examples of which the literature abounded, was not an abstract essence but a quality that could be tested in the forum or on the battlefield. Finally, classical literature was rich in eloquence. In particular (since humanists were normally better at Latin than they were at Greek) Cicero was considered to be the pattern of refined and copious discourse. In eloquence humanists found far more than an exclusively aesthetic quality. As an effective means of moving leaders or fellow citizens toward one political course or another, eloquence was akin to pure power. Humanists cultivated rhetoric, consequently, as the medium through which all other virtues could be communicated and fulfilled.

The role of the classics

Humanism, then, may be accurately defined as that Renaissance movement which had as its central focus the ideal of *humanitas.* The narrower definition of the Italian term *umanisti* notwithstanding, all the Renaissance writers who cultivated *humanitas,* and all their direct "descendants," may be correctly termed humanists.

Other uses. It is small wonder that a term as broadly allusive as *humanism* should be subject to a wide variety of applications. Of these (excepting the historical movement described above) there are three basic types: humanism as classicism, humanism as referring to the modern concept of the humanities, and humanism as human-centredness. Accepting the notion that Renaissance humanism was

simply a return to the classics, some historians and philologists have reasoned that classical revivals occurring anywhere in history should be called humanistic. St. Augustine, Alcuin, and the scholars of 12th-century Chartres have thus been referred to as humanists. In this sense the term can also be used self-consciously, as in the New Humanism movement in literary criticism led by Irving Babbitt and Paul Elmer More in the early 20th century.

The word *humanities,* which like the word *umanisti* derived from the Latin *studia humanitatis,* is often used to designate the nonscientific scholarly disciplines: language, literature, rhetoric, philosophy, art history, and so forth. Thus it is customary to refer to scholars in these fields as humanists and to their activities as humanistic.

Humanism and related terms are frequently applied to modern doctrines and techniques that are based on the centrality of human experience. In the 20th century the pragmatic humanism of Ferdinand C.S. Schiller, the Christian humanism of Jacques Maritain, and the movement known as secular humanism, though differing from each other significantly in content, all show this anthropocentric emphasis.

Not only is such a large assortment of definitions confusing, but the definitions themselves are often redundant or impertinent. There is no reason to call all classical revivals humanistic when the word classical suffices. To say that professors in the many disciplines known as the humanities are humanists is to compound vagueness with vagueness, for these disciplines have long since ceased to have or even aspire to a common rationale. The definition of humanism as anthropocentricity or human-centredness has a firmer claim to correctness. For obvious reasons, however, it is confusing to apply this word to classical literature.

BASIC PRINCIPLES AND ATTITUDES

Underlying the early expressions of humanism were principles and attitudes that gave the movement a unique character and would shape its future development.

Classicism. Early humanists returned to the classics less with nostalgia or awe than with a sense of deep familiarity, an impression of having been brought newly into contact with expressions of an intrinsic and permanent human reality. Petrarch, the acknowledged founder of the humanistic movement, dramatized his feeling of intimacy with the classics by writing "letters" to Cicero and Livy. Coluccio Salutati remarked with pleasure that possession of a copy of Cicero's letters would make it possible for him to talk with Cicero. Niccolò Machiavelli would later immortalize this experience in a letter that described his own reading habits in ritualistic terms:

The pursuit of reading

> Evenings I return home and enter my study; and at its entrance I take off my everyday clothes, full of mud and dust, and don royal and courtly garments; decorously reattired, I enter into the ancient sessions of ancient men. Received amicably by them, I partake of such food as is mine only and for which I was born. There, without shame, I speak with them and ask them about the reason for their actions; and they in their humanity respond to me.

Machiavelli's term *umanità* ("humanity") means more than kindness; it is a direct translation of the Latin *humanitas.* Machiavelli implies that he shared with the ancients a sovereign wisdom of human affairs. He also describes that theory of reading as an active and even aggressive pursuit that was common among humanists. Possessing a text and understanding its words were not enough; analytic ability and a questioning attitude were necessary before a reader could truly enter the councils of the great. These councils, moreover, were not merely serious and ennobling; they held secrets available only to the astute, secrets the knowledge of which could transform life from a chaotic miscellany into a crucially heroic experience. Classical thought offered insight into the heart of things. In addition, the classics suggested methods by which, once known, human reality could be transformed from an accident of history into an artifact of will. Antiquity was rich in examples, actual or poetic, of epic action, victorious eloquence, and applied understanding. Carefully studied and well employed, classical rhetoric could implement enlightened policy, while classical poetics could carry enlightenment into the very souls of men. In a manner that might seem paradoxical to more modern minds, humanists associated classicism with the future.

Realism. Early humanists shared in large part a realism that rejected traditional assumptions and aimed instead at the objective analysis of perceived experience. To humanism is owed the rise of modern social science, which emerged not as an academic discipline but rather as a practical instrument of social self-inquiry. Humanists avidly read history, taught it to their young, and, perhaps most importantly, wrote it themselves. They were confident that proper historical method, by extending across time their grasp of human reality, would enhance their active role in the present. For Machiavelli, who avowed to treat of men as they were and not as they ought to be, history would become the basis of a new political science. Similarly, direct experience took precedence over traditional wisdom. Leon Battista Alberti's dictum that an essential form of wisdom could be found only "at the public marketplace, in the theatre, and in people's homes" would be echoed by Francesco Guicciardini:

History and experience

> I, for my part, know no greater pleasure than listening to an old man of uncommon prudence speaking of public and political matters that he has not learnt from books of philosophers but from experience and action; for the latter are the only genuine methods of learning anything.

Renaissance realism also involved the unblinking examination of human uncertainty, folly, and immorality. Petrarch's honest investigation of his own doubts and mixed motives is born of the same impulse that led Giovanni Boccaccio in the *Decameron* to conduct an encyclopaedic survey of human vices and disorders. Similarly critical treatments of society from a humanistic perspective would be produced later by Erasmus, More, Castiglione, Rabelais, and Montaigne. But it was typical of humanism that this moral criticism did not, conversely, postulate an ideal of absolute purity. Humanists asserted the dignity of normal earthly activities and even endorsed the pursuit of fame and the acquisition of wealth. The emphasis on a mature and healthy balance between mind and body, first implicit in Boccaccio, is evident in the work of Giannozzo Manetti, Francesco Filelfo, and Paracelsus; it is embodied eloquently in Montaigne's final essay, "Of Experience." Humanistic tradition, rather than revolutionary inspiration, would lead Francis Bacon to assert in the early 17th century that the passions should become objects of systematic investigation. The realism of the humanists was, finally, brought to bear on the Roman Catholic Church, which they called into question not as a theological structure but as a political institution. Here as elsewhere, however, the intention was neither radical nor destructive. Humanism did not aim to remake humanity but rather to reform social order through an understanding of what was basically and inalienably human.

Critical scrutiny and concern with detail. Humanistic realism bespoke a comprehensively critical attitude. Indeed, the productions of early humanism constituted a manifesto of independence, at least in the secular world, from all preconceptions and all inherited programs. The same critical self-reliance shown by Coluccio Salutati in his textual emendations and Boccaccio in his interpretations of myth was evident in almost the whole range of humanistic endeavour. It was cognate with a new specificity, a profound concern with the precise details of perceived phenomena, that took hold across the arts and the literary and historical disciplines and would have profound effects on the rise of modern science. The increasing prominence of mathematics as an artistic principle and academic discipline was a testament to this development.

The emergence of the individual and the idea of the dignity of man. These attitudes took shape in concord with a sense of personal autonomy that first was evident in Petrarch and later came to characterize humanism as a whole. An intelligence capable of critical scrutiny and self-inquiry was by definition a free intelligence; the intellectual virtue that could analyze experience was an integral part of that more extensive virtue that could, according to many humanists, go far in conquering fortune. The

emergence of Renaissance individualism was not without its darker aspects. Petrarch and Alberti were alert to the sense of estrangement that accompanies intellectual and moral autonomy, while Machiavelli would depict, in *The Prince,* a grim world in which the individual must exploit the weakness of the crowd or fall victim to its indignities. But happy or sad, the experience of the individual had taken on a heroic tone. Parallel with individualism arose, as a favourite humanistic theme, the idea of the dignity of man. Backed by medieval sources but more sweeping and insistent in their approach, spokesmen such as Petrarch, Manetti, Valla, and Ficino asserted man's earthly preeminence and unique potentialities. In his noted *De hominis dignitate oratio* ("Oration on the Dignity of Man"), Giovanni Pico della Mirandola conveyed this notion with unprecedented vigour. Humanity, Pico asserted, had been assigned no fixed character or limit by God but instead was free to seek its own level and create its own future. No dignity, not even divinity itself, was forbidden to human aspiration. Pico's radical affirmation of human capacity shows the influence of Ficino's recent translations of the Hermetic writings. Together with the even bolder 16th-century formulations of this position by Paracelsus and Giordano Bruno, the *Oratio* betrays a rejection of the early humanists' emphasis on balance and moderation; it suggests the straining toward absolutes that would characterize major elements of later humanism.

Active virtue. The emphasis on virtuous action as the goal of learning was a founding principle of humanism and (though sometimes sharply challenged) continued to exert a strong influence throughout the course of the movement. Salutati, the learned chancellor of Florence whose words could batter cities, represented in word and deed the humanistic ideal of an armed wisdom: that combination of philosophical understanding and powerful rhetoric which alone could effect virtuous policy and reconcile the rival claims of action and contemplation. In *De ingenuis moribus et liberalibus studiis* ("On the Manners of a Gentleman and Liberal Studies"), a treatise that influenced Guarino Veronese and Vittorino da Feltre, Pietro Paolo Vergerio maintained that just and beneficent action was the purpose of humanistic education; his words were echoed by Alberti in *Della famiglia* ("On the Family"):

> As I have said, happiness cannot be gained without good works and just and righteous deeds. . . . The best works are those that benefit many people. Those are most virtuous, perhaps, that cannot be pursued without strength and nobility. We must give ourselves to manly effort, then, and follow the noblest pursuits.

Matteo Palmieri wrote that

> the true merit of virtue lies in effective action, and effective action is impossible without the faculties that are necessary for it. He who has nothing to give cannot be generous. And he who loves solitude can be neither just, nor strong, nor experienced in those things that are of importance in government and in the affairs of the majority.

Palmieri's philosophical poem, *La città di vita* ("The City of Life"), developed the idea that the world was divinely ordained to test human virtue in action. Later humanism would broaden and diversify the theme of active virtue. Machiavelli saw action not only as the goal of virtue but also (via historical understanding of great deeds of the past) as the basis for wisdom. Baldassare Castiglione, in his highly influential *Libro del cortegiano* (*Book of the Courtier*), developed in his ideal courtier a psychological model for active virtue, stressing moral awareness as a key element in just action. François Rabelais used the idea of active virtue as the basis for anticlerical satire. In his profusely humanistic *Gargantua,* he has the active hero Friar John save a monastery from enemy attack, while the monks sit uselessly in the church choir, chanting meaningless Latin syllables. John later asserts that, had he been present, he would have used his manly strength to save Jesus from crucifixion, and he castigates the Apostles for betraying Christ "after a good meal." Endorsements of active virtue, as will be shown, would also characterize the work of English humanists from Sir Thomas Elyot to John Milton. They typify the sense of social responsibility, the instinctive association of learning with politics and moral-

ity, that stood at the heart of the movement. As Salutati put it, "One must stand in the line of battle, engage in close combat, struggle for justice, for truth, for honour."

EARLY HISTORY

The influence of Petrarch (Francesco Petrarca, 1304–74) was profound and many-sided. As the most prominent man of letters of the 14th century, he promoted the recovery and transcription of classical texts, providing the impetus for the important classical researches of Boccaccio and Salutati. He threw himself into controversies in which he defined a new humanism in contradistinction to what he considered to be the barbaric influence of medieval tradition. He carried on an energetic correspondence that established him as a cultural focal point and would provide, if all his other works were lost, an accurate index of his views and their development. As a theologian (he was an ordained priest) he advanced the view, held by many humanists to follow, that classical learning and Christian spirituality were not only compatible but also mutually fulfilling. As a political apologist, he gave hearty support to Cola di Rienzo's brief revival of the Roman Republic (1347). As a poet, he was the first Renaissance writer to produce a Latin epic (*Africa*), but he was even more important for his compositions in the vernacular. His *Canzoniere* provided the model on which the Renaissance lyric was to take shape and the standard by which future productions would be judged. His work established secular poetry as a serious and noble pursuit. His eloquent and forceful presence made him a personal symbol of his own ideas. Crowned with laurel, favoured by rulers, legates, and scholars, he became the human focus for the new interest in classical revival and literary artistry.

It was, however, as a philosophical spokesman that Petrarch exerted his greatest influence on the history of humanism. In his prose works and letters he established many of the positions that would be central to the movement and broached many of the issues that would be its favourite subjects for debate. His idea of the poet as a philosophical teacher and thus as a champion of culture would inspire humanists from Boccaccio to Sidney. His endorsement of the study of rhetoric and his underlying notion of language as an informing principle of the individual and society would become crucial subjects of humanistic discussion and debate. His view of classical culture, not as an undifferentiated element of the past but as an authentic alternative to his own medieval society, was of equal historical importance. Petrarch broke with the past and helped to reestablish the Socratic tradition in Europe by specifying self-knowledge as a primary goal of philosophy. This attitude and his unfailing insistence on moral autonomy were early and important signs of the individualism that would become a Renaissance hallmark. He emphasized human virtue as opposed to fortune, thus setting the stage for numerous famous treatments of this theme. He struggled repeatedly with the dilemma of action versus contemplation, establishing it as a favourite topic for humanistic debate. Petrarch did not invent these subjects, nor does he usually treat them with overwhelming power. His preeminence lies in the fact that he was the first writer since antiquity to assert that they and other human matters were valid issues for philosophical inquiry in and of themselves, and in the energy and eloquence with which he made his work their forum.

Petrarch's influence was immediately apparent in the work of two major Florentine humanists, Giovanni Boccaccio and Coluccio Salutati. A close friend and devoted supporter of Petrarch, Boccaccio (1313–75) not only enlarged upon his preceptor's ideas but also made important humanistic contributions of his own. His *Teseide* was the first classical epic to have been written in the vernacular and influenced the more famous Italian epics of Ariosto and Tasso. His *De genealogia deorum gentilium* ("On the Genealogy of the Gods of the Gentiles"), a scholarly interpretive compendium of classical myth, was the first in a long line of Renaissance mythographies; it includes a celebrated defense of poetry as a medium of hidden truth, a stimulant to virtue, and a source of mental health. His most memorable contribution to humanism, however, was

Armed wisdom

Rabelais's Gargantua

Petrarch's greatest influence

Boccaccio's *Decameron* probably the famous *Decameron*. Ostensibly this work is no more than a collection of 100 tales about love. But subjected to the interpretive scrutiny that Boccaccio himself recommends in *De genealogia deorum gentilium*, the *Decameron* takes on a far more serious tone. The opening phrase "*Umana cosa è*" ("It is a human thing") is deeply thematic, reminding us that the author structured his work on Dante's spiritual epic, *La divina commedia*. A close reading of the *Decameron* suggests that in it Boccaccio is trying to establish for the human realm the same sort of comprehensive understanding that Dante established for the life of the spirit. Through moral fable and direct address to the reader, he undertakes a reinterpretation of human experience based not on traditional doctrine but rather on perceived reality. Appealing repeatedly to reason and nature, and constantly implying the superiority of awareness to innocence (which he equates with ignorance), he calls for a moral order built fairly and solidly on the potentialities of human nature. His 10 storytellers, who leave the plague-ravaged and chaotic city of Florence and reestablish themselves at a delightfully landscaped villa, suggest the remaking of culture through disentanglement with the past, unprejudiced analysis, and enlightened imagination. Rightly considered to be the wellspring of Western realism, the *Decameron* is also a monument to humanism. Though it makes little mention of classical thought, Boccaccio's great work rings with a tone that was even more basic to the humanistic movement: an emphasis on the human capacity for self-knowledge and willed renewal.

Coluccio Salutati Other humanistic elements implicit in Petrarch's thought were developed in the life and work of Coluccio Salutati (1331–1406). Like Petrarch, Salutati collected manuscripts, wrote on morality and politics, and carried on a voluminous correspondence. He was an aggressive and scientific philologist, instrumental in establishing principles of textual criticism that would become key elements of the humanistic method. He was a forceful apologist for the active life, and his theories bore fruit in his own career as chancellor of the Florentine republic. His use of classical eloquence in the service of his state was an early documentation of the humanistic faith in the political power of rhetoric; it led a bitter enemy, Gian Galeazzo Visconti of Milan, to say that a thousand Florentine horsemen had hurt him less than the letters of Coluccio. Salutati was succeeded in the Florentine chancellorship by two scholar-statesmen who reflected his influence, first Leonardo Bruni (1369–1444) and then Gian Francesco Poggio Bracciolini (1380–1459). Bruni was a pioneer in the advocacy of humanistic education, holding that the *studia humanitatis* shape the perfected man and that the goal of this perfected virtue is political action. His theory of education stressed the importance of practical experience (implicit in the work of Boccaccio) and put heavy emphasis on historical studies. His history of Florence is considered to be the first work of modern historiography; and, under the influence of Emmanuel Chrysoloras (1368–1415), a Byzantine teacher who had lectured at Florence and Pavia, he produced Latin translations of Plato and Aristotle that broke with medieval tradition by reproducing the sense of the Greek prose rather than following it word by word. Poggio, the foremost recoverer of classical texts, was also a moralist, a historian, a brilliant correspondent, and an early scholar of architectural antiquities. His long career, which included service to both church and state and friendships with Salutati, Bruni, Niccolò Niccoli, Guarino, Nicholas of Cusa, Donatello, and Cosimo de' Medici, exemplifies the scope and vitality of Italian humanism. Together these Florentine chancellors, whose active lives spanned almost a century, strengthened and consolidated the humanistic program. Moreover, their leadership strongly influenced the cultural developments that would make 15th-century Florence the most active intellectual and artistic centre in Europe.

As one proceeds with the history of humanism, the following major points about its development in the 14th century ought to be kept in mind. Humanism received its crucial imprint from the work of a single man and thence developed among men who maintained close touch with each other and acknowledged a shared mission. Humanism was not originally an academic movement but rather a program defined and promoted by statesmen and men of letters. Its proclaimed goal was widespread cultural renewal; therefore, it chose its subjects for consideration from the phenomena of human life as lived and adopted the Ciceronian model of philosopher as citizen in preference to the contemplative ideal. The heavy emphasis on civic action is connected with the fact that humanism developed in a republic rather than a monarchy.

By the turn of the 15th century, all of the key elements that came to define humanism were in place except for two: its detailed educational system and what might be called its Greek dimension. The founders of the first humanistic schools were Vittorino da Feltre (1373–1446) and Guarino Veronese (Guarino da Verona, 1374–1460). Vittorino and Guarino were fellow students at the University of Padua at the turn of the century; they are said later to have tutored each other (Guarino as an expert in Greek, Vittorino in Latin) after Guarino had opened the first humanistic school (Venice, *c.* 1414). Vittorino taught in both Padua (where he was briefly professor of rhetoric) and Venice during the early 1420s. In 1423 he accepted the invitation of Gianfrancesco Gonzaga, marquis of Mantua, to become tutor to the ruling family. At this post Vittorino spent the remaining 22 years of his life. His school, held in a delightful palace that he renamed "La Giocosa," had as its students not only the Gonzaga children (among them the future marquis, Ludovico) but also an increasing number of others, including sons of Poggio, Guarino, and Filelfo. The eminent humanist Lorenzo Valla studied there, as did Federico da Montefeltro, who later promoted humanistic institutions as duke of Urbino. Vittorino's school in Mantua was the first to focus the full power of the humanistic program, together with its implications in other arts and sciences, upon the education of the young. Latin literature, Latin composition, and Greek literature were required subjects of study. Heavy emphasis was placed on Roman history as an educational treasury of great men and memorable deeds. Rhetoric (as taught by Quintilian) was a central topic, not as an end in itself but as an effective means of channeling moral virtue into political action. Vittorino summed up the essentially political thrust of humanistic education as follows: **The humanistic schools**

> Not everyone is called to be a physician, a lawyer, a philosopher, to live in the public eye, nor has everyone outstanding gifts of natural capacity, but all of us are created for the life of social duty, all are responsible for the personal influence that goes forth from us.

Other studies at Mantua included music, drawing, astronomy, and mathematics. The meadows around La Giocosa were turned into playing fields. Vittorino's educational policy spoke at once to mind and body, to aesthetic enjoyment and moral virtue. His work embodied a more comprehensive appeal to human perfectibility than had been attempted since antiquity. Humanists were not unaware of the originality and ambitiousness of this project. With reference to a similar program of his own, Guarino's son Battista remarked that "no branch of knowledge embraces so wide a range of subjects as that learning that I have now attempted to describe."

Guarino had learned his Greek in Constantinople under the influence of Chrysoloras, whose dynamic presence had done much to foster Greek studies in Italy. During the course of the 15th century, which saw the famous council of Eastern and Western churches (Ferrara–Florence, 1438–45) and later the fall of Constantinople to the Turks (1453), Italy received as welcome immigrants a number of other eminent Byzantine scholars. George Gemistus Plethon (1355–1450) was a major force in Cosimo de' Medici's foundation of the Platonic Academy of Florence. George of Trebizond (Georgius Trapezuntius, 1395–1484), a student of Vittorino, was a formidable bilingual stylist who wrote important handbooks on logic and rhetoric. Theodore Gaza (*c.* 1400–75) and Johannes Argyropoulos (1410–90) contributed major translations of Aristotle. John (originally Basil) Bessarion (1403–72), who became a cardinal in 1439, explored theology from a Platonic perspective and sought to resolve apparent conflicts between Platonic and Aristotelian philosophy; his large collection **Byzantine influence**

of Greek manuscripts, donated to the Venetian senate, became the core of the notable library of St. Mark. This infusion of Byzantine scholarship had a profound effect on Italian humanism. By making Greek texts and commentaries available to Western students, and by acquainting them with Byzantine methods of criticism and interpretation, the teachers from Constantinople enabled Italian humanists to explore the bases of classical thought and to appreciate its greatest monuments, either in the original or in accurate new Latin translations.

THE 15TH CENTURY

As Italian humanism grew in influence during the 15th century, it developed ramifications that connected it with every major field of intellectual and artistic activity. Moreover, the advent of printing at mid-century and the contemporaneous upsurge of publication in the vernacular brought new sectors of society under humanistic influence. These and other cultural impetuses hastened the export of humanistic ideas to the Low Countries, France, England, and Spain, where significant humanistic programs would be in place by the early 16th century. Even as these things were happening, however, other changes were deeply and permanently affecting the character of the movement. The concerns of many major humanists were narrowed by inevitable historical processes of specialization, to the extent that, in a large number of cases, humanism lost its comprehensive thrust and became a predominantly academic or literary pursuit. The political élan of humanism was weakened by the decline of republican institutions in Florence. Ambiguities and paradoxes implicit in the original program developed into open conflicts, dividing the movement into camps and depleting much of its original integrity. But before considering these developments, one might do well to appreciate three 15th-century examples of humanism at its height: the career of Leon Battista Alberti and the humanistic courts at Florence and Urbino.

Leon Battista Alberti. The achievement of Leon Battista Alberti (1404–72) testifies to the formative power and exhaustive scope of earlier Italian humanism. He owed his boyhood education to Gasparino da Barzizza (1359–1431), the noted teacher who, with Vergerio, was influential in the development of humanism at Padua. Alberti attended the University of Bologna from 1421 until 1428, by which time he was expert in law and mathematics and so adept at humanistic literary skills that his comedy *Philodoxeos* was accepted as the newly discovered work of an ancient author. In 1428 he became secretary to Cardinal Albergati, bishop of Bologna, and in 1432 he accepted a similar position in the papal chancery at Rome. His service to the church soon brought him incomes that permanently secured his livelihood, and he spent the remainder of his life at a variety of literary, philosophical, and artistic pursuits so dazzling as to challenge belief. He was a poet, essayist, and biographer. His moral and philosophical works, especially *Della famiglia, De iciarchia* ("On the Man of Excellence and Ruler of His Family"), and *Momus,* are humanistic statements that nonetheless bear the mark of a unique individual. He wrote a rhetorical handbook and a grammatical treatise, the *Regule lingue Florentine,* which bespeaks his strong influence on the rise of literary expression in the vernacular. He contributed an important text on cartography and was instrumental in the development of ciphers. A prominent architect (*e.g.,* the Tempio Malatestiano in Rimini and the facade of Sta. Maria Novella in Florence), he was also an eminent student of all artistic ideas and practices. His three studies—*De pictura* (*On Painting*), *De statua* (*On Sculpture*), and *De re aedificatoria* (*Ten Books on Architecture*)—were landmarks in art theory, powerful in developing the theory of perspective and the idea of "human" space. His theoretical and practical reliance on mathematics (which he considered to be the basic, unifying element of all science) is rightly seen as an important step in the early development of modern method.

Behind these achievements was a man of startling physical prowess and inexhaustible sanguinity. He said outright that an individual could encompass whatever project he truly willed, and his own life bore witness to this radical

thesis. In the 19th century Jacob Burckhardt would write of him as a "universal man" of the Renaissance, while his own contemporary Politian described him with wonderment: "It is better to be silent about him than not to say enough." Alberti's theory and practice bore an undeniably humanistic stamp. His passion for mathematics was in all likelihood an outgrowth of the educational program at Padua (Vittorino, himself an avid mathematician, was also a student of Barzizza). His omnivorous pursuit of knowledge recalls Barzizza's conviction that *humanitas* was the unifying principle of many arts. An advocate of classical erudition in art and architecture as well as in literary activity, he extended into his artistic studies the same sense of precision and specificity that earlier humanists had applied to philology. His sense of human dignity, evident in all his productions, was supported and indeed justified by a strenuous realism. His advocacy of the vernacular disturbed a number of more doctrinaire humanists, who favoured total Latinity. But this predisposition, rather than a divergence from humanistic principle, was a direct outgrowth of its evangelistic thrust. In short, Alberti uniquely fulfilled the humanistic aspiration for a learning that would comprehend all experience and a philosophical heroism that would renew society.

The Medici and Federico da Montefeltro. The 15th century saw the rise of the Platonic Academy of Florence and the great humanistic courts. Close ties between Poggio and the Medici helped make that ruling family of Florence the new custodians of the humanistic heritage. Cosimo de' Medici (Cosimo the Elder, 1389–1464), who had personally lured the great council of churches from Ferrara to Florence in 1439, became so enamoured of Greek learning that, at the suggestion of Gemistus Plethon, he decided to found a Platonic academy of his own. He amassed a great collection of books, which would form the nucleus of the Laurentian Library. He generously supported the work of scholars, in particular encouraging the brilliant Marsilio Ficino (1433–99) to undertake a complete Latin translation of Plato. Other notable members of the academy were Politian, Cristoforo Landino (1424–1504), and Ficino's own student, Giovanni Pico della Mirandola (1463–94). The Medici family was equally notable in its patronage of the arts, supporting projects by a list of masters that included Brunelleschi, Michelangelo, and Cellini. Cosimo's famous grandson Lorenzo (Lorenzo the Magnificent, 1449–92) was of a thoroughly humanistic disposition. Lorenzo's versatile and energetic nature lent itself equally to politics and philosophy, to martial arts and music. He wrote poetry and literary commentary and formed close ties with Ficino, Pico, and other leading scholars of the academy. He continued his grandfather's lavish patronage of art and learning and was said to have spent half of his city's revenues on the purchase of books alone. Active in many fields, he nonetheless acknowledged the preeminence of the life of the mind. When chided by a friend for sleeping late and not going out to work, Lorenzo replied, "What I have dreamed in one hour is worth more than what you have done in four."

The influence of humanism was evident in many 15th-century Italian courts, including Rome itself, which boasted, in Pius II (Enea Silvio Piccolomini, also known as Aeneas Sylvius Piccolomini, 1405–64), a humanist pope. It manifested itself strikingly at Urbino, where Federico da Montefeltro (1422–82) turned an isolated hill town into a treasury of Renaissance culture. Schooled by Vittorino in Mantua, Federico chose warfare as his calling. As a mercenary he gained a reputation for winning his battles and keeping his word, and the fortune he accumulated in fees and prizes became the medium for his city's renewal. He brought architects, artists, and scholars to Urbino and built a great palace whose unadorned exterior concealed magnificent chambers, a graceful courtyard, and a secret garden. Federico was enthusiastically devoted to the collection and preservation of books. His library, described by Vespasiano Bisticci as being even more complete than that of the Medici, contained an army of 30 to 40 scribes who were constantly at work. His own virtues were so notable and diverse as to mark him as a possible model for Rabelais's humanistic giant, Gargantua. Mighty at

Alberti's writings

The Medici patronage

Federico's library

arms, he was also conscientious in religious observances; supremely powerful, he was nonetheless a modest and courteous companion. Beneath the ivied tranquility of his secret garden stretched an indoor equestrian arena. He commissioned paintings by Piero della Francesca and was the object of humanistic dedications by Poggio, Landino, and Ficino. He kept two organists at court and maintained five men to read the classics aloud at meals. Federico's intellectual accomplishments were impressive. His skill at mathematics shows the influence of Vittorino. He was a good Latinist and as a student of classical history was able to hold his own in conversation with the erudite Pius II. At philosophy Federico was even more astute. Vespasiano wrote that

> he began to study logic with the keenest understanding, and he argued with the most nimble wit that was ever seen. After he had heard (Aristotle's) *Ethics* many times, comprehending it so thoroughly that his teachers found him hard to cope with in disputation, he studied the *Politics* assiduously.... Indeed, it may be said of him that he was the first of the Signori who took up philosophy and had knowledge of the same. He was ever careful to keep intellect and virtue to the front, and to learn some new thing every day.

Federico's balance and versatility made him, even more than Lorenzo, an example of the humanistic program in action. Baldassare Castiglione, perhaps the most thoughtful of the later Italian humanists, would speak of him as "the light of Italy; there is no lack of living witnesses to his prudence, humanity (*umanità*), justice, intrepid spirit, (and) military discipline." Castiglione described Federico's residence as seeming to be less a palace than "a city in the form of a palace"; one might say as well that this structure, with its elegant accommodation for every creative human activity, was an architectural image of the humanistic mind.

LATER ITALIAN HUMANISM

The achievement of Alberti, Federico, and the Medici up to Lorenzo may be seen as the effective culmination of Italian humanism, the ultimate realization of its motives and principles. At the same time as these goals were being achieved, however, the movement was beginning to suffer bifurcation and dilution. Even the enthusiastic Platonism of the Florentine academy was, in its idealism and emphasis on contemplation, a significant digression from the crucial humanistic doctrine of active virtue, and Pico della Mirandola himself was politely admonished by a friend to forsake the ivory tower and accept his civic responsibilities. The conflicting extremes to which sincere humanistic inquiry could drive scholars are nowhere more apparent than in the fact that the arch-idealist Pico and the arch-realist Machiavelli lived in the same town and at the same time. Castiglione, who had belonged to the court of Federico's son Guidobaldo, would be saddened by its decline and shocked when another of his patrons, the "model" Renaissance prince Charles V, ordered the sack of Rome. To a large extent, the cause of these and other vicissitudes lay in the nature of the movement itself, for that boundless diversity which nourished its strength was also a well of potential conflict. Humanists' undifferentiated acceptance of the classical heritage was also in effect an appropriation of the profound controversy implicit in that heritage. Rifts between Platonists, monarchists, and republicans; positivists and skeptics; idealists and cynics; and historians and poets came to be more and more characteristic of humanistic discourse. Some of these tensions had been clear from the start, Petrarch having been ambiguous in his sentiments regarding action versus contemplation, and Salutati having been not wholly clear about whether he preferred republics to monarchies. But the 15th century, bringing with it the irreconcilable heterogeneity of Greek thought, vastly multiplied and deepened these divisions. Of these schisms, the two that perhaps most deeply influenced the course of humanism were the so-called *res-verbum* ("thing-word") controversy and the split between Platonic idealism and historical realism.

Things and words. Simply put, the *res-verbum* controversy was an extended argument between humanists who believed that language constituted the ultimate human reality and those who believed that language, though an important subject for study, was the medium for understanding an even more basic reality that lay beyond it. The origin of the controversy lay in the debate in the 5th–4th century BC between the Socratic school, which held that language was an important means of understanding deeper truths, and the Sophistic-rhetorical school, which held that "truth" was itself a fiction dependent on varying human beliefs and therefore that language had to be considered the ultimate arbiter. Petrarch, who had no direct contact with the works of Plato and little detailed knowledge of his ideas, drew on Cicero and St. Augustine in his development of a Christian-rhetorical position, holding that "it is more satisfying (*satius*) to will the good than to know the truth" and espousing rhetoric as the effective means of convincing people "to will the good."

This assertion would critically shape the character of humanism through the Renaissance and beyond. It was never effectively challenged by Renaissance Platonists because, for reasons discussed below, Renaissance Platonists, though strong in Platonic idealism, were weak in Platonic analytical method. The enthronement of language as both subject and object of humanistic inquiry is evident in the important work of Lorenzo Valla (1407–57) and Politian (Angelo Poliziano, 1454–94). Valla spoke of language as a "sacrament" and urged that it be studied scientifically and historically as the synthesis of all human thought. For Valla, the study of language was, in effect, the study of humanity. Similarly, Politian held that there were in fact two dialectics: one of ideas and one of words. Rejecting the dialectic of ideas as being too difficult and abstruse, he espoused the dialectic of words (*i.e.*, philology and rhetoric) as the proper human study. This project would bear fruit in the intensive linguistic-philosophical researches of Mario Nizolio (1498–1575). Though anticipated by Petrarch, the radical emphasis on the primacy of the word constituted a break with the teaching of other early humanists, such as Bruni and Vittorino, who had strongly maintained that the word was of value only through its relationship to perceived reality. Nor did the old viewpoint lack later adherents. In an epistolary debate with Ermolao Barbaro (1454–93), Pico asserted the preeminence of things over words and hence of philosophy over rhetoric: "But if the rightness of names depends on the nature of things, is it the rhetorician we ought to consult about this rightness, or is it the philosopher who alone contemplates and explores the nature of everything?" Appeals of this sort, however, were not to win the day. Philosophical humanism declined because, though rich in conviction, it had failed to establish a systematic relationship between philosophy and rhetoric, between words and things. By the 16th century, Italian humanism was primarily a literary pursuit, and philosophy was left to develop on its own. Despite significant challenges, the division between philosophical and literary studies would solidify in the development of Western culture.

Idealism and the Platonic Academy of Florence. The idealism so prominent in the Florentine academy is called Platonic because of its debt to Plato's theory of Ideas and to the epistemological doctrine established in his *Symposium* and *Republic*. It did not, however, constitute a complete appreciation or reassertion of Plato's thought. Conspicuously absent from the Florentine agenda was the analytic method (dialectic), which was Socrates' greatest contribution to philosophy. This major omission cannot be explained philologically, at least after Ficino's work had made the complete Platonic corpus available in clear Latin prose. The explanation lies rather in a specific cast of mind and in a dramatically successful forgery. The major Platonists of the mid-15th century, Plethon, Bessarion, and Nicholas of Cusa (Nicholaus Cusanus, 1401–64), had all concentrated their attention on the religious implications of Platonic thought; and, following them, Marsilio Ficino (1433–99) sought to reconcile Plato with Christ in a *pia philosophia* ("pious philosophy"). The transcendental goals of these philosophers left little room for the painstaking dialectical method that sifted through the details of perception and language, even though Plato himself had repeatedly alleged that transcendence itself was impos-

Origin of the *res-verbum* controversy

Diversification and erosion

sible without this method. Along with Plato, moreover, Ficino had translated into Latin the works of the so-called Hermes Trismegistos. These books, which also emphasized transcendence at the expense of method, laid claim to divine authority and to an antiquity far greater than Plato's. They were, in fact, forgeries from a much later period, and are in many ways typical of the idealized and diluted versions of Plato that are called Neoplatonic. But the academy, and for that matter all the other Platonists of the 15th century, bought them wholesale. The result of these factors was a Platonism sans Platonic method, a philosophy that, straining for absolutes, had little interest in establishing its own basis in reality. Near the end of *The Book of the Courtier,* Castiglione puts a speech typical of Florentine Platonism in the mouth of his friend, the Platonist Pietro Bembo (1470–1547). As Bembo finishes his oration, a female companion tugs at the hem of his robe and says, "Take care, Master Pietro, that with such thoughts your soul does not forsake your body."

Machiavelli's realism. Niccolò Machiavelli (1469–1527), whose work derived from sources as authentically humanistic as those of Ficino, proceeded along a wholly opposite course. A throwback to the chancellor-humanists Salutati, Bruni, and Poggio, he served Florence in a similar capacity and with equal fidelity, using his erudition and eloquence in a civic cause. Like Vittorino and other early humanists, he believed in the centrality of historical studies, and he performed a signally humanistic function by creating, in *La Mandragola,* the first vernacular imitation of Roman comedy. His characteristic reminders of human weakness suggest the influence of Boccaccio; and like Boccaccio he used these reminders less as satire than as practical gauges of human nature. In one way at least, Machiavelli is more humanistic (*i.e.,* closer to the classics) than the other humanists, for while Vittorino and his school ransacked history for examples of virtue, Machiavelli (true to the spirit of Polybius, Livy, Plutarch, and Tacitus) embraced all of history, good, evil, and indifferent, as his school of reality. Like Salutati, though perhaps with greater self-awareness, Machiavelli was ambiguous as to the relative merits of republics and monarchies. In both public and private writings (especially the *Discorsi sopra la prima deca di Tito Livio* ["Discourses on the First Ten Books of Livy"]) he showed a marked preference for republican government, while in *The Prince* he developed, with apparent approval, a model of radical autocracy. For this reason, his goals have remained unclear.

His methods, on the other hand, were coherent throughout and remain a major contribution to social science and the history of ideas. Like earlier humanists, Machiavelli saw history as a source of power, but, unlike them (and here perhaps influenced by Sophistic and Averroistic thought), he saw neither history nor power itself within a moral context. Rather he sought to examine history and power in an amoral and hence (to him) wholly scientific manner. He examined human events in the same way that Alberti, Galileo, and the new science examined physical events: as discrete phenomena that had to be measured and described before they could be explained and evaluated. To this extent his work, though original in its specific design, was firmly based in the humanistic tradition. At the same time, however, Machiavelli's achievement significantly eroded humanism. By laying the foundations of modern social science, he created a discipline that, though true to humanistic methodology, had not the slightest regard for humanistic morality. In so doing, he brought to the surface a contradiction that had been implicit in humanism all along: the dichotomy between critical objectivity and moral evangelism.

The achievement of Castiglione. Though Italian humanism was being torn apart by the natural development of its own basic motives, it did not thereby lose its native attractions. The humanistic experience, in both its positive and negative effects, would be reenacted abroad. Baldassare Castiglione (1478–1529), whose *Book of the Courtier* affectionately summed up humanistic thought, was one of its most powerful ambassadors. Alert to the major contradictions of the program, yet intensely appreciative of its brilliance and energy, Castiglione wove its

various strains together in a long dialogue that aimed at an equipoise between various humanistic extremes. Ostensibly a treatise on the model courtier, *The Book of the Courtier* is more seriously a philosophically organized pattern of conflicting viewpoints in which various positions—Platonist and Aristotelian, idealist and cynic, monarchist and republican, traditional and revolutionary—are given eloquent expression. Unlike most of his humanistic forebears, Castiglione is neither missionary nor polemical. His work is not an effort at systematic knowledge but rather an essay in higher discretion, a powerful reminder that every virtue (moral or intellectual) suggests a concomitant weakness and that extreme postures tend to generate their own opposites. The structure of the dialogue, in which Bembo's Platonic ecstasy is balanced by Bibbiena's assortment of earthy jests, is a testament to this intention. While Castiglione's professed subject matter would epidemically inspire European letters and manners of the 16th century, his more profound contribution would be echoed in the work of Montaigne and Shakespeare. His work suggests a redefined humanism, a virtue matured in irony and directed less toward knowledge than toward wisdom.

Tasso's Aristotelianism. In 16th-century Italy, humanistic methods and attitudes provided the medium for a kaleidoscopic variety of literary and philosophical productions. Of these, the work that perhaps most truly reflected the original spirit of humanism was the *Gerusalemme liberata* of Torquato Tasso (1544–95). New humanistic translations of Aristotle during the 15th century had inspired an Aristotelian Renaissance, and the attention of literary scholars focused particularly on the *Poetics.* In constructing his epic poem, Tasso was strongly influenced by Aristotle's views regarding the philosophical dimension of poetry; loosely paraphrasing Aristotle, he held (in his *Apologia*) that poetry, by incorporating both particulars and universals, was capable of seeking truth in its perfect wholeness. As a vehicle for philosophical truth, poetry consequently could provide moral education, specifically in such virtues (reinterpreted from a Christian perspective) as Aristotle had described in the *Nichomachean Ethics.* The Aristotelian Renaissance thus facilitated the revival of one of the chief articles in the original humanistic constitution: the belief in the poet's role as renewer of culture.

NORTHERN HUMANISM

Though humanism in northern Europe and England sprang largely from Italian sources, it did not emerge exclusively as an outgrowth of later Italian humanism. Non-Italian scholars and poets found inspiration in the full sweep of the Italian tradition, choosing their sources from Petrarch to Castiglione and beyond.

Desiderius Erasmus. Erasmus (*c.* 1466–1536) was the only other humanist whose international fame in his own time compared with Petrarch's. While lacking Petrarch's polemical zeal and spirit of self-inquiry, he shared the Italian's intense love of language, his dislike for the complexities and pretenses of medieval institutions both secular and religious, and his commanding personal presence. More specifically, however, his ideas and overall direction betray the influence of Lorenzo Valla, whose works he treasured. Like Valla, who had attacked biblical textual criticism with a vengeance and proved the so-called Donation of Constantine to be a forgery, Erasmus contributed importantly to Christian philology. Also like Valla, he philosophically espoused a kind of Christian hedonism, justifying earthly pleasure from a religious perspective. But he was most like Valla (and indeed the entire rhetorical "arm" of Italian humanism) in giving philology prominence over philosophy. He described himself as a poet and orator rather than an inquirer after truth. His one major philosophical effort, a Christian defense of free will, was thunderously answered by Luther. Though his writings are a well of good sense, they are seldom profound and are predominantly derivative. In Latin eloquence, on the other hand, he was preeminent, both as stylist and theorist. His graceful and abundant Ciceronian prose (whose principles he set down in *De copia verborum et rerum*) helped shape the character of European style. Perhaps his most original work is *Moriae encomium* (*The Praise of*

*Machia-
velli's
writings*

*The Book
of the
Courtier*

*The Praise
of Folly*

Folly), an elegant combination of satire and poetic insight whose influence was soon apparent in the work of More (to whom it was dedicated) and Rabelais.

The French humanists. Erasmus' associates in France included the influential humanists Robert Gaguin (1433–1501), Jacques Lefèvre d'Étaples (*c.* 1455–1536), and Guillaume Budé (Guglielmus Budaeus, 1467–1540). Of these three, Budé was most central to the development of French humanism, not only in his historical and philological studies but also in his use of his national influence to establish the Collège de France and the library at Fontainebleau. The influence of Francis I (1494–1547) and his learned sister Margaret of Angoulême (1492–1549) was important in fostering the new learning. The diversity and energy of French humanism is apparent in the activities of the Estienne family of publishers; the poetry of Pierre de Ronsard (1524–85), Joachim du Bellay (*c.* 1522–60), and Guillaume du Bartas (1544–90); the political philosophy of Jean Bodin (1530–96); the philosophical methodology of Petrus Ramus (Pierre de la Ramée, 1515–72); and the dynamic relationship between humanistic scholarship and church reform (see below, *Humanism and Christianity*). Hampered by religious repression and compressed more severely in time, the French movement lacked the intellectual fecundity and the programmatic unity of its Italian counterpart. In François Rabelais and Michel de Montaigne, however, the development of humanistic methods and themes resulted in unique and memorable achievement.

François Rabelais (c. 1490–1533). Rabelais ranks with Boccaccio as a founding father of Western realism. As a satirist and stylist (in his hands French prose became a free, poetic form), he influenced writers as important as Jonathan Swift, Laurence Sterne, and James Joyce and may be seen as a major precursor of modernism. His five *Gargantua* books concerning the deeds of the giant princes Gargantua and Pantagruel constitute a treasury of social criticism, an articulate statement of humanistic values, and a forceful, if often outrageous, manifesto of human rights. Rabelaisian satire took aim at every social institution and (especially in Book III) every intellectual discipline. Broadly learned and unflaggingly alert to jargon and sham, he repeatedly focused on dogmas that fetter creativity, institutional structures that reward hypocrisy, educational traditions that inspire laziness, and philosophical methodologies that obscure elemental reality. His heroes, Gargantua and his son and heir Pantagruel, are figures whose colossal size and appetites (Rabelais's etymology for *Pantagruel* is "all-thirsty") symbolize the nobility and omnivorous curiosity that typified the humanistic scheme. The multifarious educational program detailed in *Gargantua* is reminiscent of Vittorino, Alberti, and the Montefeltro court; and the utopian Abbey of Thélème, whose gate bears the motto "Do as you please," is a tribute to enlightened will and pleasure in the manner of Valla, Erasmus, and More. Characteristically overstated and never wholly free of irony, Rabelais's work is a far cry from the earnest moral and educational programs of the early humanists. Rather than rebuild society, he seeks to amuse, edify, and refine it. His qualified endorsement of human dignity is based on the healthy balance of mind and body, the sanctity of all true learning, and the authenticity of direct experience.

Michel de Montaigne (1533–92). Montaigne's famous *Essays* are not only a compendious restatement and reevaluation of humanistic motives but also a milestone in the humanistic project of self-inquiry that had been originally endorsed by Petrarch. Scholar, traveler, soldier, and statesman, Montaigne was, like Machiavelli, alert to both theory and practice; but while Machiavelli saw practice as forming the basis for sound theory, Montaigne perceived in human events a multiplicity so overwhelming as to deny theoretical analysis. Montaigne's use of typical humanistic modalities—interpretation of the classics, appeals to direct experience, exclusive emphasis on the human realm, and universal curiosity—led him, in other words, to the refutation of a typical humanistic premise: that knowledge of the intellectual arts could teach one a sovereign art of life. In an effort to make his inquiry more inclusive and unsparing, Montaigne made himself the subject of his book, demonstrating through hundreds of personal anecdotes and admissions the ineluctable diversity of a single human spirit. His essays, which seem to move freely from one subject or viewpoint to another, are often in fact carefully organized dialectical structures that draw the reader, through thesis and antithesis, stated subject and relevant association, toward a multidimensional understanding of morality and history. The final essay, grandly titled "Of Experience," counsels a mature acceptance of life in all its contradictions. Human dignity, he implies, is indeed possible, but it lies less in heroic achievement than in painfully won self-knowledge. In this sense Montaigne's attitude toward the humanistic tradition is generally similar to that suggested in the work of Castiglione and Rabelais. While effectively taking issue with a number of the more extreme humanistic contentions, he retained and indeed justified the basic attitudes that gave the movement its form.

"Of Experience"

The English humanists. English humanism flourished in two stages: the first a basically academic movement that had its roots in the 15th century and culminated in the work of Sir Thomas More, Sir Thomas Elyot, and Roger Ascham, the second a poetic revolution led by Sir Philip Sidney and William Shakespeare.

Though continental humanists had held court positions since the days of Humphrey of Gloucester, English humanism as a distinct phenomenon did not emerge until late in the 15th century. At Oxford William Grocyn (*c.* 1446–1519) and his student Thomas Linacre (*c.* 1460–1524) gave impetus to a tradition of classical studies that would permanently influence English culture. Grocyn and Linacre attended Politian's lectures at the Platonic Academy of Florence. Returning to Oxford, they became central figures in a group that included such younger scholars as John Colet (1466/67–1519) and William Lily (1468?–1522). The humanistic contributions of the Oxford group were philological and institutional rather than philosophical or literary. Grocyn lectured on Greek and theology; Linacre produced several works on Latin grammar and translated Galen into Latin. To Linacre is owed the foundation of the Royal College of Physicians; to Colet, the foundation of St. Paul's School, London. Colet collaborated with Lily (the first headmaster of St. Paul's) and Erasmus in writing the school's constitution, and together the three scholars produced a Latin grammar (known alternately as "Lily's Grammar" and the "Eton Grammar") that would be central to English education for decades to come.

In Sir Thomas More (1478–1535), Sir Thomas Elyot (*c.* 1490–1546), and Roger Ascham (1515–68), English humanism bore fruit in major literary achievement. Educated at Oxford (where he read Greek with Linacre), More was also influenced by Erasmus, who wrote *The Praise of Folly* (Latin *Moriae encomium*) at More's house and named the book punningly after his English friend. More's famous *Utopia*, a kind of companion piece to *The Praise of Folly,* is similarly satirical of traditional institutions (Book I) but offers, as an imaginary alternative, a model society based on reason and nature (Book II). Reminiscent of Erasmus and Valla, More's Utopians eschew the rigorous cultivation of virtue and enjoy moderate pleasures, believing that "Nature herself prescribes a life of joy (that is, pleasure)" and seeing no contradiction between earthly enjoyment and religious piety. Significantly indebted both to classical thought and European humanism, the *Utopia* is also humanistic in its implied thesis that politics begins and ends with humanity: that politics is based exclusively on human nature and aimed exclusively at human happiness. Sir Thomas Elyot chose a narrower subject but developed it in more detail. His great work, *The Book Named The Governor,* is a lengthy treatise on the virtues to be cultivated by statesmen. Born of the same tradition that produced *The Prince* and *The Courtier, The Governor* is typical of English humanism in its emphasis on the accommodation of both classical and Christian virtues within a single moral view. Elyot's other contributions to English humanism include philosophical dialogues, moral essays, translations of ancient and contemporary writers (including Isocrates and Pico), an important Latin-English dictionary, and a highly popular health manual. He served

Utopia

Elizabeth I

his country as ambassador to the court of Charles V. Finally, the humanistic educational program set up at the turn of the century was vigorously supported by Sir John Cheke (1514–57) and codified by his student Roger Ascham. Ascham's famous pedagogical manual, *The Schoolmaster,* offers not only a complete program of humanistic education but also an evocation of the ideals toward which that education was directed.

Ascham had been tutor to the young princess Elizabeth, whose personal education was a model of humanistic pedagogy and whose writings and patronage bespoke great love of learning. Elizabeth I's reign (1558–1603) saw the last concerted expression of humanistic ideas. Elizabethan humanism, which added a unique element to the history of the movement, was the product not of pedagogues and philologists but of poets and playwrights.

Sidney and Spenser. Sir Philip Sidney (1554–86) was, like Alberti and Federico da Montefeltro, a living pattern of the humanistic ideal. Splendidly educated in the Latin classics at Shrewsbury and Oxford, Sidney continued his studies under the direction of the prominent French scholar Hubert Languet and was tutored in science by the learned John Dee. His brief career as writer, statesman, and soldier was of such acknowledged brilliance as to make him, after his tragic death in battle, the subject of an Elizabethan heroic cult. Sidney's major works, *Astrophel and Stella,* the *Defence of Poesie,* and the two versions of the *Arcadia,* are medleys of humanistic themes. In the sonnet sequence *Astrophel and Stella,* he surpassed earlier imitators of Petrarch by emulating not only the Italian humanist's subject and style but also his philosophical bent and habit of self-scrutiny. The *Defence of Poesie,* composed (like Erasmus' *Praise of Folly*) in the form of a classical oration, reasserts the theory of poetry as moral doctrine that had been articulated by Petrarch and Boccaccio and revived by the Italian Aristotelians of the 16th century. The later or "new" *Arcadia* is an epic novel whose theoretical concerns include the dualities of contemplation and action, reason and passion, and theory and practice. In this ambitious and unfinished work, Sidney attempts a characteristically humanistic synthesis of classical philosophy, Christian doctrine, psychological realism, and practical politics. Seen as a whole, moreover, Sidney's life and work form a significant contribution to a debate that had been smoldering since the decline of political liberty in Florence in the 15th century. How, it was asked, could humanism be politically active or "civic" in a Europe that was almost exclusively monarchic in structure? Many humanists had counseled retirement from active life, while Castiglione had seen his learned courtier rather as an advisor than as a leader. Sidney and his friend Edmund Spenser (1552/53–1599) sought to resolve this dilemma by creating a form of chivalric humanism. The image (taken on personally by Sidney and elaborated upon by Spenser in *The Faerie Queene*) of the hero as questing knight suggests that the humanist, even if not empowered politically, can achieve a valid form of activism by refining, upholding, and representing the values of a just and noble court. Spenser's poetic development of this humanistic program was even more specific than Sidney's. In his famous letter to Raleigh, he asserts that his purpose in *The Faerie Queene* is "to fashion a gentleman or noble person in virtuous and gentle discipline" and describes a project (never to be completed) of presenting his idea of the Aristotelian virtues in twelve poetic books. As with Sidney, however, this moral didacticism is neither self-righteous nor pedantic. The prescriptive content of *The Faerie Queene* is qualified by a strong emphasis on moral autonomy and a mature sense of the ambiguity of experience.

Chapman, Jonson, and Shakespeare. The poetry and drama of Shakespeare's time were a concourse of themes, ancient and modern, continental and English. Prominent among these motives were the characteristic topics of humanism. George Chapman (1559?–1634), the translator of Homer, was a forthright exponent of the theory of poetry as moral wisdom, holding that it surpassed all other intellectual pursuits. Ben Jonson (1572–1637) described his own humanistic mission when he wrote that a good poet

was able "to inform young men to all good disciplines, inflame grown men to all great virtues, keep old men in their best and supreme state, or, as they decline to childhood, recover them to their first strength" and that the poet was "the interpreter and arbiter of nature, a teacher of things divine no less than human, a master in manners." Jonson, who sought this moral goal both in his tragedies and in his comedies, paid tribute to the humanistic tradition in *Catiline,* a tragedy in which Cicero's civic eloquence is portrayed in heroic terms.

Less overtly humanistic, though in fact more profoundly so, was William Shakespeare (1564–1616). Thoroughly versed (probably at his grammar school) in classical poetic and rhetorical practice, Shakespeare early in his career produced strikingly effective imitations of Ovid and Plautus (*Venus and Adonis* and *The Comedy of Errors,* respectively) and drew on Ovid and Livy for his poem *The Rape of Lucrece.* In *Julius Caesar, Antony and Cleopatra,* and *Coriolanus* he developed Plutarchan biography into drama that, though Elizabethan in structure, is sharply classical in tone. Shakespeare clearly did not accept all the precepts of English humanism at face value. He grappled repeatedly with the problem of reconciling Christian doctrine with effective political action, and for a while (*e.g.,* in *Henry V*) seemed inclined toward the Machiavellian alternative. In *Troilus and Cressida,* moreover, he broadly satirized Chapman's Homeric revival and, more generally, the humanistic habit of idolizing classical heroism. Finally, he eschewed the moralism, rationalism, and self-conscious erudition of the humanists and was lacking as well in their fraternalism and their theoretical bent. Yet on a deeper level he must be acknowledged the direct and natural heir of Petrarch, Boccaccio, Castiglione, and Montaigne. Like them he delighted more in presenting issues than in espousing systems and held critical awareness, as opposed to doctrinal rectitude, to be the highest possible good. His plays reflect an inquiry into human character entirely in accord with the humanistic emphasis on the dignity of the emotions, and indeed it may be said that his unprecedented use of language as a means of psychological revelation gave striking support to the humanistic contention that language was the heart of culture and the index of the soul. Similarly, Shakespeare's unparalleled realism may be seen as the ultimate embodiment, in poetic terms, of the intense concern for specificity— be it in description, measurement, or imitation—endorsed across the board by humanists from Boccaccio and Salutati on. Shakespearean drama is a treasury of the disputes that frustrated and delighted humanism, including (among many others) action versus contemplation, theory versus practice, *res* versus *verbum,* monarchy versus republic, human dignity versus human depravity, and individualism versus communality. In treating of these polarities, he generally proceeds in the manner of Castiglione and Montaigne, presenting structures of balanced contraries rather than syllogistic endorsements of one side or another. In so doing, he achieves a higher realism, transcending the mere imitation of experience and creating, in all its conflict and fertility, a mirror of mind itself. Since the achievement of such psychological and cultural self-awareness was the primary goal of humanistic inquiry, and since humanists agreed that poetry was an uncommonly effective medium for this achievement, Shakespeare must be acknowledged as a preeminent humanist.

One cannot leave Shakespeare and the phenomenon of English humanism without reference to a highly important aspect of his later drama. Throughout his career, Shakespeare had shown a keen interest in the concept of art, not only as a general idea but also with specific reference to his own identity as dramatist. In two of his final plays, *The Winter's Tale* and *The Tempest,* he developed this concept into dramatic and thematic structures that had strongly doctrinal implications. Major characters in both plays practice a moral artistry—a kind of *humanitas* compounded of awareness, experience, imagination, compassion, and craft—that enables them to beguile and dominate other characters and to achieve enduring justice. This special skill, which is cognate with Shakespeare's own dramatic art, suggests a hypothetical solution to many of

Shake-speare

the dilemmas posed in his earlier work. It implies that problems unavailable to political or religious remedy may be solved by creative innovation and that the art by which things are known and expressed may constitute, in and of itself, a valid field of inquiry and an instrument for cultural renewal. In developing this idea of the sovereignty of art, Shakespeare made the final major contribution to a humanistic tradition that will be discussed in the two sections that follow.

HUMANISM AND THE VISUAL ARTS

Humanistic themes and techniques were woven deeply into the development of Italian Renaissance art; conversely, the general theme of "art" was prominent in humanistic discourse. The mutually enriching character of the two disciplines is evident in a variety of areas.

Realism. Humanists paid conscious tribute to realistic techniques in art that had developed independently of humanism. Giotto di Bondone (c. 1266–1337), the Florentine painter responsible for the movement away from the Byzantine style and toward ancient Roman technique, was praised by Vasari as "the pupil of Nature." Giotto's own contemporary Boccaccio said of him in the *Decameron* that

> there was nothing in Nature—the mother and ruling force of all created things with her constant revolution of the heavens—that he could not paint with his stylus, pen, or brush or make so similar to its original in Nature that it did not appear to be the original rather than a reproduction. Many times, in fact, in observing things painted by this man, the visual sense of men would err, taking what was painted to be the very thing itself.

Boccaccio, himself a naturalist and a realist, here subtly adopts the painter's achievement as a justification for his own literary style. So Shakespeare, at the end of the Renaissance, praises Giulio Romano (and himself), "who, had he himself eternity and could put breath into his work, would beguile Nature of her custom, so perfectly he is her ape" (*The Winter's Tale*). It should be noted that neither Vasari, Boccaccio, nor Shakespeare endorses realistic style as a *summum bonum:* realism is rather the means for regaining touch with the sovereign creative principle of Nature.

Classicism. Like the humanists, Italian artists of the 15th century saw a profound correlation between classical forms and realistic technique. Classical sculpture and Roman painting were emulated because of their ability to simulate perceived phenomena, while, more abstractly, classical myth offered a unique model for the artistic idealization of human beauty. Alberti, himself a close friend of Donatello and Brunelleschi, codified this humanistic theory of art, using the fundamental principle of mathematics as a link between perceived reality and the ideal. He developed a classically based theory of proportionality between architectural and human form, believing that the ancients sought "to discover the laws by which Nature produced her works so as to transfer them to the works of architecture."

Anthropocentricity and individualism. Humanism and Italian art were similar in giving paramount attention to human experience, both in its everyday immediacy and in its positive or negative extremes. The religious themes that dominated Renaissance art (partly because of generous church patronage) were frequently developed into images of such human richness that, as one contemporary observer noted, the Christian message was submerged. The human-centredness of Renaissance art, moreover, was not just a generalized endorsement of earthly experience. Like the humanists, Italian artists stressed the autonomy and dignity of the individual. High Renaissance art boasted a style of portraiture that was at once humanely appreciative and unsparing of detail. Heroes of culture such as Federico da Montefeltro and Lorenzo de' Medici, neither of whom was a conventionally handsome man, were portrayed realistically, as though a compromise with strict imitation would be an affront to their dignity as individuals. Similarly, artists of the Italian Renaissance were, characteristically, unabashed individualists. The biographies of Giotto, Brunelleschi, Leonardo, and Michelangelo by Giorgio

Vasari (1511–74) not only describe artists who were well aware of their unique positions in society and history but also attest to a cultural climate in which, for the first time, the role of art achieved heroic stature. The autobiographical writings of the humanist Alberti, the scientist Gerolamo Cardano (1501–76), and the artist Benvenuto Cellini (1500–71) further attest to the individualism developing both in letters and in the arts; and Montaigne dramatized the analogy between visual mimesis and autobiographical realism when he said, in the preface to his *Essays,* that given the freedom he would have painted himself "*tout entier, et tout nu*" ("totally complete, and totally nude").

Art as philosophy. Italian Renaissance painting, especially in its secular forms, is alive with visually coded expressions of humanistic philosophy. Symbol, structure, posture, and even colour were used to convey silent messages about humanity and nature. Renaissance style was so articulate, and the Renaissance sense of the unity of experience so deeply ingrained, that even architectural structures could be eloquently philosophical. Two features of Federico's palace at Urbino exemplify the profound interrelationship between humanistic principle and Renaissance art. The first feature is architectural. On the ground floor of the palace two private chapels, of roughly the same dimensions, stand side by side. The chapel at the left is a place of Christian worship, while that at the right is dedicated to the pagan Muses. Directly above these chapels is a study, the walls of which are covered with representations (in intarsia) of assorted humanistic heroes: Homer, Plato, Aristotle, Cicero, Virgil, Seneca, Boethius, St. Augustine, Dante, Petrarch, Bessarion, and Federico's revered teacher Vittorino, among others. The message conveyed by the positioning of the three rooms is hard to ignore. Devotion to the opposed principles of Christianity and earthly (pagan) beauty is rendered possible by a humanistic learning (represented by the study) so generous and appreciative as to comprehend both extremes.

The second feature is iconographic—a portrait of Federico and his son Guidobaldo (probably by Pedro Berruguete) that occupies a central position on the wall of the study. It depicts the Duke, his full coat of armour partly covered by a courtly robe, sitting and reading. The son stands beside his father's chair, gazing out of the picture toward the viewer's left. An abbot's mitre rests on a shelf in the upper left, while the Duke's helmet sits on the floor in the lower right. Here also a typically humanistic message is evident. The Duke's scholarly attitude and curious attire suggest his triple role as warrior, ruler, and humanist. The two main axes of the picture—the line between mitre and helmet and the line between father and son—converge at the book, symbolizing the central role of humanistic learning in reconciling the concerns of church and state and in conveying humanistic virtue from generation to generation. The boy's outward gaze implies the characteristic direction of humanistic learning: into the world of action. The scope and organic wholeness of Federico's humanistic iconography are so striking as to rival great expressions of religious faith. The private heart of his palace concealed, like a genetic code, the principle that had given shape to the edifice and informed the state.

HUMANISM, ART, AND SCIENCE

It is impossible to speak knowledgeably about Renaissance science without first understanding the Renaissance concept of art. The Latin *ars* (inflected as *artis*) was applied indiscriminately to the verbal disciplines, mathematics, music, and science (the "liberal arts"), as well as to painting, sculpture, and architecture; it also could refer to technological expertise, to magic, and to alchemy. Any discipline involving the cultivation of skill and excellence was de facto an art. To the Renaissance, moreover, all arts were "liberal" arts in their capacity to "free" their practitioners to function effectively in specific areas. The art of rhetoric empowered the rhetorician to convince; the art of perspective empowered the painter to create visual illusion; the art of physics empowered the scientist to predict the force and motion of objects. "Art," in effect, was no more or less than articulate power, the technical or intellectual analogy to the political power of the monarch and

Giotto

Biography and autobiography

The "liberal arts"

the divine power of the god. The historical importance of this equation cannot be overestimated. If one concept may be said to have integrated all the varied manifestations of Renaissance culture and given organic unity to the period, it was this definition of art as power. With this definition in mind, one may understand why Renaissance humanists and painters assigned themselves such self-consciously heroic roles: in their artistic ability to delight, to captivate, to convince, they saw themselves as enfranchised directors and remakers of culture. One may also understand why a humanist-artist-scientist like Alberti would have seen no real distinction between the various disciplines he practiced. As profoundly interconnected means of understanding nature and humanity, and as media for effective reform and renewal, these disciplines were all components of an encompassing art. A similar point may be made about Machiavelli, who wrote a book about the "art" of warfare and who used history and logic to develop an art of government, or about the brilliant polymath Paracelsus, who spent his whole career perfecting an art that would comprehend all matter and all spirit. With the equation of art and power in mind, finally, one may understand why a revolutionary scientist like Galileo (1564–1642) put classical and medieval science through a winnowing fan, keeping only such components as allowed for physically reproducible results. Since every Renaissance art aimed for a dominion or conquest, it was completely appropriate that science should leave its previously contemplative role and focus upon the conquest of nature.

Humanism benefited the development of science in a number of more specific ways. Alberti's technological applications of mathematics, and his influential statement that mathematics was the key to all sciences, grew out of his humanistic education at Padua. Vittorino, another student at Padua, went on to make mathematics a central feature of his educational program. Gerolamo Cardano, a scholar of renowned humanistic skills, made major contributions to the development of algebra. In short, the importance of mathematics in humanistic pedagogy and the fact that major humanists like Vittorino and Alberti were also mathematicians may be seen as contributing to the critical role mathematics would play in the rise of modern science. Humanistic philology, moreover, supplied scientists with clean texts and clear Latin translations of the classical works—Plato, Aristotle, Euclid, Archimedes, and even Ptolemy—that furthered their studies. The richness of the classical heritage in science is often underestimated. Galileo, who considered Archimedes his mentor, also prized the dialogues of Plato, in particular the *Meno*. The German philosopher Ernst Cassirer has demonstrated the likelihood that Galileo was fond of the *Meno* because it contained the first statement of the "hypothetical" method, a modus operandi that characterized Galileo's own scientific practice and that would come to be known as one of the chief principles of the New Science. Humanism may also be seen as offering, of itself, methods and attitudes suitable for application in nonhumanistic fields. It might be argued, for example, that the revolutionary social science of Machiavelli and Juan Luis Vives (1492–1540) was due in large measure to their application of humanistic techniques to fields that lay outside the normal purview of humanism. But most of all it was the general spirit of humanism—critical, questing, ebullient, precise, focused on the physical world, and passionate in its quest for results—that fostered the development of the scientific spirit in social studies and natural philosophy.

The classical heritage in science

HUMANISM AND CHRISTIANITY

Though much humanistic activity was specifically Christian in intention, and though the majority of humanists made firm avowals of faith, the relationship between Christianity and humanism is complex and not wholly untroubled. First, humanists from Petrarch onward recognized that the classical (pagan) direction of humanism necessarily constituted, if not a challenge to Christianity, at least a breach in the previous totality of Christian devotion. The Christian truth that had been acknowledged as comprehending all phenomena, earthly or heavenly, now had to coexist with a classical attitude that was overwhelmingly directed toward earthly life. Humanistic efforts to resolve the contradictions implied by these two attitudes were, if one may judge by their variety, never wholly successful. In particular, the extent to which humanistic inquiry led scholars toward the secular realm, and the extent to which humanistic pedagogy concentrated on secular subjects, suggest erosions of the domain of faith. Coluccio Salutati, who urged the young Poggio not to let humanistic enthusiasm take precedence over Christian piety, thereby acknowledged a dualism implicit in the humanistic program and never wholly absent from its historical development.

Implicit dualism

Second, the humanistic philology that meticulously compared ancient sources and "cleaned up" the texts of important Christian writings was a serious challenge to the authority of the church. With new authorities or refined texts in hand, humanists found fault with established commentaries and questioned traditional interpretations. Valla's arraignment of the Donation of Constantine and Bessarion's discovery that the supposed Dionysius the Areopagite (later called Pseudo-Dionysius) had borrowed some of his material from Plato exemplify the uneasy relationship between humanism and Catholic dogma. Third, the independent and broadly critical attitude innate to humanism could not but threaten the unanimity of Christian belief. Intellectual individualism, which has never been popular in any church, put particular stress on a religion that encouraged simple faith and alleged universal authority. Finally, humanism repeatedly fostered the impulse of religious reform. The humanistic emphasis on total authenticity and direct contact with sources had, as its religious correlative, a desire to obliterate the medieval accretions and procedural complexities that stood between the worshiper and his god. The reform-mindedness of such humanists as Petrarch, Boccaccio, Erasmus, and Rabelais was balanced on the religious side by reformers such as Calvin and Melanchthon, who employed humanistic techniques in their own cause. And the reform movement, while it may have modernized and thus preserved Christianity, rang the death knell for a medieval culture whose essential characteristic had been participation in a universal church.

The impulse of reform

LATER FORTUNES OF HUMANISM

Shakespeare may be seen as the last major interpreter of the humanistic program. Sir Francis Bacon and John Milton, though formidably adept at humanistic techniques, diverged in their major work from the central current of humanism, Bacon toward natural science, Milton toward theology. If Bacon's rationalism may be seen as a link between humanism and the Enlightenment, his strong emphasis on nature (rather than humanity) as subject matter presaged the permanent separation of the sciences from the humanities. In Milton's theocentricity, on the other hand, lay the Christian distrust (going back, perhaps, to Luther) of humanistic secularism. These epochal divergences, moreover, were complemented by a series of rifts and ramifications within the humanistic movement. The split between philosophy and letters was, over future generations, to be compounded by the development of countless discrete specialties within both fields. Philosophers came more and more to define themselves within narrow boundaries. Creative writers and "critics" took up distinct positions and assumed adversarial relationships. The profound loss of coherence in humane letters was furthered by the gradual decline of Latin as the lingua franca of European intellectuals and the consequent separation of national traditions.

By the 19th century, humanism was such a lost art as to have to be reassembled, like a disjointed fossil, by careful historians. Of course there were exceptions. Jonathan Swift (1667–1745) reasserted humanistic values in a broad-based attack on contemporary institutions, and in Gottfried Wilhelm Leibniz (1646–1716) can be found the serious intention and multifarious curiosity that characterized humanism at its best. Strong humanistic motives may be found in Germany at the turn of the 19th century, particularly in the work of Gotthold Ephraim Lessing (1729–81), Friedrich von Schiller (1759–1805), and Georg Wilhelm

Goethe

Friedrich Hegel (1770–1831); while Johann Wolfgang von Goethe (1749–1832) was perhaps the last individual whose breadth of achievement and sense of the unity of experience lived up to the ideal established by Alberti.

More recently, the mode of inquiry and interpretation developed by the political philosopher Leo Strauss (1899–1973) showed strong signs of the humanistic spirit. But in general the traces of the original program have been scattered. To the modern mind, a "humanist" is a university scholar, walled off from the interdisciplinary scope of the original humanistic program and immune to the active experience that was its basis and its goal. This decline is easy enough to explain. Had there been nothing else, one external factor would have made the cultivation of *humanitas,* as originally practiced, more and more difficult from the beginning of the 16th century on. The proliferation of published work in all fields, and the creation of many new fields, made increasingly impracticable the development of the comprehensive learning and awareness that were central to the original program. In 1500 the major texts constituting a humanistic education, though numerous, could still be counted; by 1900 they were legion, and people had long ceased agreeing about exactly which ones they were. But problems implicit in the movement were equally responsible for its demise. The characteristic emphases on rhetoric and philology, which gave the humanistic movement vitality and made it available to countless students of moderate gifts, also betokened its im-

The lack of method

permanence. Weak in dialectic or any other comprehensively analytic method, the movement had no instrument for self-examination, no medium for self-renewal. By the same token, neither had humanism any valid means of defense against the attackers—scientists, fundamentalists, materialists, and others—who camped in ever larger numbers on its borders. Lacking an integral method, finally, humanism in effect lacked a centre and became prey to an endless series of ramifications. While eloquent humanists rambled through Europe and spread the word about the classics, the method that might have unified their efforts lay, available but unheeded, in texts of Plato and Aristotle. Given this core of rigorous analysis, humanism might (all other challenges notwithstanding) have retained its basic character for centuries. But ironically it might also have failed to attract followers.

CONCLUSION

Though lacking permanence itself, humanism in large measure established the climate and provided the medium for the rise of modern thought. An impressive variety of major developments in literature, philosophy, art, religion, social science, and even natural science had their basis in humanism or were significantly nourished by it. Important spokesmen in all fields regularly made use of humanistic eloquence to further their causes. More generally, the so-called modern awareness—that sense of alienation and freedom applied both to the individual and to the race—derives ultimately, for better or worse, from humanistic sources. But with humanism, as with every other historical subject, one should beware lest valid concern about changes, crises, sources, and influences obscure the even more important issues of human continuity and human value. Whatever its weaknesses and inner conflicts, the humanistic movement was heroic in its breadth and energy, remarkable in its aspirations. For human development in all fields, it created a context of seldom-equaled fertility. Its characteristic modalities of thought, speech, and image lent themselves to the promptings of genius and became the media for enduring achievement. Its moral program formed the basis for lives that are remembered with admiration.

BIBLIOGRAPHY

General treatments: The three general studies most helpful in approaching humanism are EUGENIO GARIN, *Italian Humanism: Philosophy and Civic Life in the Renaissance,* trans. from the Italian (1965, reprinted 1975); PAUL OSKAR KRISTELLER, *Renaissance Thought and Its Sources* (1979); and CHARLES TRINKAUS, *The Scope of Renaissance Humanism* (1983). Other valuable readings include HANS BARON, *The Crisis of the Early Italian Renaissance: Civic Humanism and Republican Liberty*

in an Age of Classicism and Tyranny, rev. ed. (1966); QUIRINUS BREEN, *Christianity and Humanism: Studies in the History of Ideas* (1968); JACOB BURCKHARDT, *The Civilization of the Period of the Renaissance in Italy: An Essay* (1878; originally published in German, 1860), available in later English-language editions; DOUGLAS BUSH, *The Renaissance and English Humanism* (1939, reprinted 1972); ERNST CASSIRER, *The Individual and the Cosmos in Renaissance Philosophy* (1964, reprinted 1972; originally published in German with appendices, 1927); JACK D'AMICO, *Knowledge and Power in the Renaissance* (1977); MYRON P. GILMORE, *The World of Humanism, 1453–1517* (1952; reprinted 1983); DENYS HAY, *The Italian Renaissance in Its Historical Background,* 2nd ed. (1977); PAUL OSKAR KRISTELLER, *Renaissance Concepts of Man, and Other Essays* (1972); EDWARD P. MAHONEY (ed.), *Philosophy and Humanism* (1976); ROBERT MANDROU, *From Humanism to Science, 1480 to 1700* (1979; originally published in French, 1973); HEIKO A. OBERMAN and THOMAS A. BRADY, JR. (eds.), *Itinerarium Italicum: The Profile of the Italian Renaissance in the Mirror of Its European Transformations* (1975); CHARLES B. SCHMITT, *Studies in Renaissance Philosophy and Science* (1981); JOHN ADDINGTON SYMONDS, *Renaissance in Italy,* 7 vol. (1875–86, reprinted 1971–72); GUISSEPPE TOFFANIN, *History of Humanism* (1954; originally published in Italian, 1933); BERTHOLD L. ULLMAN, *Studies in the Italian Renaissance,* 2nd ed. (1975); and ROBERTO WEISS, *The Spread of Italian Humanism* (1964). For classical and medieval backgrounds, see ERNST ROBERT CURTIUS, *European Literature and the Latin Middle Ages* (1973; originally published in German, 1948); MOSES HADAS, *Humanism: The Greek Ideal and Its Survival* (1960, reprinted 1972); and WERNER JAEGER, *Paideia: The Ideals of Greek Culture,* 2nd ed., 3 vol. (1965; originally published in German, 1934).

Specific topics: T.W. BALDWIN, *William Shakspere's Small Latine and Lesse Greeke* (1944, reprinted 1966); HANS BARON, *From Petrarch to Leonardo Bruni: Studies in Humanistic and Political Literature* (1968); GENE BRUCKER, *Renaissance Florence* (1969, reprinted 1983); ERNST CASSIRER, "Galileo's Platonism," in M.F. ASHLEY MONTAGU (ed.), *Studies and Essays in the History of Science and Learning,* pp. 277–297 (1946; reprinted 1975); JOAN GADOL, *Leon Battista Alberti* (1969); EUGENIO GARIN, *Science and Civic Life in the Italian Renaissance* (1969, reissued 1978; originally published in Italian, 1965; 4th Italian ed., 1980); PAUL OSKAR KRISTELLER and PHILIP P. WIENER (eds.), *Renaissance Essays* (1968); LAURO MARTINES, *The Social World of the Florentine Humanists, 1390–1460* (1963); JAMES J. MURPHY (ed.), *Renaissance Eloquence: Studies in the Theory and Practice of Renaissance Rhetoric* (1983); IRWIN PANOFSKY, *Renaissance and Renascences in Western Art,* 2 vol. (1960, reissued in 1 vol, 1969); J.H. PLUMB (ed.), *Renaissance Profiles* (1965); PASQUALE ROTONDI, *The Ducal Palace of Urbino: Its Architecture and Decoration* (1969; originally published in Italian in 2 vol., 1950–51); CHARLES B. SCHMITT, *Aristotle and the Renaissance* (1983); CHARLES TRINKAUS, *In Our Image and Likeness: Humanity and Divinity in Italian Humanist Thought,* 2 vol. (1970), and *The Poet as Philosopher: Petrarch and the Formation of Renaissance Consciousness* (1979); BERTHOLD L. ULLMAN, *The Humanism of Coluccio Salutati* (1963); WILLIAM HARRISON WOODWARD, *Vittorino da Feltre and Other Humanist Educators* (1897, reissued 1970), and *Studies in Education During the Age of the Renaissance, 1400–1600* (1906, reissued 1967); and G.F. YOUNG, *The Medici,* 2 vol. (1909, reissued in 1 vol., 1933).

Works of the humanists: Works by the later humanists and the English poet-humanists mentioned in the article are readily available in many modern English editions. For the writings of the earlier humanists, see LEON BATTISTA ALBERTI, *The Family in Renaissance Florence,* trans. by RENÉE NEU WATKINS (1969); GIOVANNI BOCCACCIO, *The Decameron,* trans. by MARK MUSA and PETER BONDANELLA (1982), and *Boccaccio on Poetry,* 2nd ed., ed. and trans. by CHARLES G. OSGOOD (1956, reprinted 1978), a translation of the preface and books 14 and 15 of his *De genealogia deorum gentilium;* biographies of Dante by Boccaccio and Leonardo Bruni in *The Earliest Lives of Dante,* trans. by JAMES ROBINSON SMITH (1901, reprinted 1976); letters by Poggio Bracciolini in *Two Renaissance Book Hunters,* trans. by PHYLLIS WALTER GOODHART GORDAN (1974); and works by Petrarch, including *The Life of Solitude,* trans. by JACOB ZEITLIN (1924, reprinted 1978); "On His Own Ignorance and That of Many Others," trans. by HANS NACHOD in ERNST CASSIRER, PAUL OSKAR KRISTELLER, and JOHN HERMAN RANDALL, JR. (eds.), *The Renaissance Philosophy of Man* (1948, reprinted 1971); and *Petrarch's Secret; or, The Soul's Conflict with Passion,* trans. by WILLIAM H. DRAPER (1911, reprinted 1978). WILLIAM HARRISON WOODWARD, *op. cit.,* contains valuable translations of works by Vergerio, Bruni, Aeneas Sylvius Piccolomini (Pius II), and Battista Guarino.

(ROBERT GRUDIN)

Bibliography: Recent Books

The following list encompasses some 100 recent books that have been judged significant contributions to learning and understanding in their respective fields. Each citation includes a few lines of commentary to indicate the general tenor of the work. The citations are organized by subject area, using the ten parts of the *Propædia* as an outline.

Matter and Energy

Rodney Cotterill, *The Cambridge Guide to the Material World* (1985), an informative exposition of the theory that the atomic structure of a material determines its properties. The book is written in clear nonmathematical language.

Steven Weinberg, *The Discovery of Subatomic Particles* (1983), an exploration of the beginnings of modern physics, with explanations of many crucial 20th-century experiments and their place in the historical perspective.

Harald Fritzsch, *The Creation of Matter: The Universe from Beginning to End* (1984; originally published in German, 1983), an authoritative, nontechnical introduction to present-day concepts of physics, astronomy, and cosmology.

David R. Owen, *A First Course in the Mathematical Foundations of Thermodynamics* (1984), a sound, instructive introduction to new developments in the application of thermodynamics.

John R. Pierce, *The Science of Musical Sound* (1983), a concise analysis of the psychoacoustics of musical sound, with an emphasis on sound-wave generation by computer.

Richard Morris, *Time's Arrows: Scientific Attitudes Toward Time* (1984), an introduction to the modern understanding of time and the development of the concept of time.

Nigel Henbest and Michael Marten, *The New Astronomy* (1983), a lavishly illustrated appraisal of the use of new technology in optical astronomy.

Guy Ottewell, *Astronomical Calendar 1985* (1984), a familiar reference source of excellent quality that this time includes a wealth of information on Halley's Comet.

James Elliot and Richard Kerr, *Rings: Discoveries from Galileo to Voyager* (1984), an account of studies of the planetary ring systems, by a participant of many discoveries in the field and a well-known science writer.

Gary W. Kronk, *Comets: A Descriptive Catalog* (1984), chronologically arranged reference information about 700 comets.

The Earth

DeVerle P. Harris, *Mineral Resources Appraisal: Mineral Endowment, Resources, and Potential Supply: Concepts, Methods, and Cases* (1984), a discussion of methods of quantitative estimation of undiscovered mineral resources.

Heinrich D. Holland, *The Chemical Evolution of the Atmosphere and Oceans* (1984), a comprehensive treatment of current information on the topic.

Paul R. Ehrlich *et al.*, *The Cold and the Dark: The World After Nuclear War* (1984), an analysis by participants in the 1983 Conference on the Long-Term Worldwide Biological Consequences of Nuclear War.

George Deacon, *The Antarctic Circumpolar Ocean* (1984), an authoritative survey of Antarctic exploration and its results, with an analysis of environmental issues.

Stephen H. Schneider and Randi Londer, *The Coevolution of Climate and Life* (1984), an analysis of climatic history, the nature of climatic change, and the social impact of climate.

Stan Gibilisco, *Violent Weather: Hurricanes, Tornadoes, and Storms* (1984), a scientifically accurate study of bad weather.

N. Eyles (ed.), *Glacial Geology* (1983), an authoritative study of the field, with analysis of engineering practices in glacial areas.

R. J. Blong, *Volcanic Hazards: A Sourcebook on the Effects of Eruptions* (1984), a comprehensive outline of social aspects and humanitarian concerns, and a study of technological methods of diminishing hazardous effects.

Farouk El-Baz (ed.), *Deserts and Arid Lands* (1984), an overview of new technologies for exploration of specific areas.

Heinrich D. Holland and A. F. Trendall (eds.), *Patterns of Change in Earth Evolution* (1984), an exploration of changes in geological processes and physical and chemical environments of nonliving matter.

Life on Earth

Kenneth D. Johnson, David L. Rayle, and Hale L. Wedberg, *Biology* (1984), a well-organized, comprehensive introduction.

Friedrich G. Barth, *Insects and Flowers: The Biology of a Partnership* (1985; originally published in German, 1982), an impressively illustrated exploration of pollination biology and of the intricate mutual influences of plants and pollinators.

J. R. Napier and P. H. Napier, *The Natural History of the Primates* (1985), a well-illustrated description and classification of primates, with surveys of habitats and behaviour.

The Conservation Foundation, *State of the Environment: An Assessment at Mid-Decade* (1984), a detailed overview of contemporary environmental problems and policies.

Burke K. Zimmerman, *Biofuture—Confronting the Genetic Era* (1984), an introduction to genetic engineering, based on a case study of the recombinant-DNA controversy.

Anthony K. Lee and Andrew Cockburn, *Evolutionary Ecology of Marsupials* (1985), a survey of contemporary ecological research on this unusual group of animals.

Christian de Duve, *A Guided Tour of the Living Cell*, 2 vol. (1984), an introduction to cell biology by a qualified author.

Douglas H. Boucher (ed.), *The Biology of Mutualism: Ecology and Evolution* (1985), essays on interactions between species.

John Elkington, *The Poisoned Womb: Human Reproduction in a Polluted World* (1985), a thoughtful though polemical examination of the threat that chemical pollution of the environment poses to genetic stability.

Norman Myers, Uma Ram Nath, and Melvin Westlake, *Gaia, an Atlas of Planet Management* (1984), a comprehensive, detailed description of current ecological conditions on Earth and the phenomenon of homeostasis, with a discussion of some resource-management solutions.

R. M. Laws (ed.), *Antarctic Ecology*, 2 vol. (1984), an exhaustive survey of both marine and nonmarine habitats.

Catherine Caufield, *In the Rainforest* (1985), a thorough and impassioned look at the negative impact of human activities on tropical forests and the disruption of their ecological role.

Norman Myers, *The Primary Source: Tropical Forests and Our Future* (1984), an exploration of catastrophic consequences of destruction of the forests, with analysis of alternatives.

Human Life

Bernard Campbell, *Human Ecology* (1985), an examination of human adaptation and cultural evolution.

James R. Brennan, *Patterns of Human Heredity: An Introduction to Human Genetics* (1985), an informative discourse on present knowledge in the field of general genetics.

G. J. V. Nossal, *Reshaping Life: Key Issues in Genetic Engineering* (1985), a concise work on new concepts in molecular biology, written for the lay reader.

Eugene D. Robin, *Matters of Life and Death: Risks vs. Benefits of Medical Care* (1984), an analysis of physician-patient relations in view of the limitations of medicine.

Marie Haug and Bebe Lavin, *Consumerism in Medicine: Challenging Physician Authority* (1983), a review of changing attitudes to medical care and of the social implications of consumer awareness in medicine.

D. Gareth Jones, *Brave New People: Ethical Issues at the Commencement of Life* (1984), a critical but evenhanded conservative Christian view of contemporary biomedical progress in a particularly sensitive field.

Ellen Grant, *The Bitter Pill: How Safe is the "Perfect Contraceptive"?* (1985), a polemical examination of uncertainties and long-term implications of the pill.

Walter Sneader, *Drug Discovery: The Evolution of Modern Medicines* (1985), a readable historical study.

Allan M. Brandt, *No Magic Bullet: A Social History of Veneral Disease in the United States Since 1880* (1985), an informative study of social attitudes and their role in the success or failure of medical efforts.

Henry J. Aaron and William B. Schwartz, *The Painful Prescription: Rationing Hospital Care* (1984), an analytical comparison of the health care systems in the U.S. and Britain and their ability to cut costs.

Joel Aronoff and John P. Wilson, *Personality in the Social Process* (1985), a scholarly work on social interaction and situational behaviour.

G. E. Zuriff, *Behaviorism: A Conceptual Reconstruction* (1985), an analysis of the critical concepts of behavioural philosophy and science.

Human Society

Gena Corea, *The Mother Machine: Reproductive Technologies from Artificial Insemination to Artificial Wombs* (1985), a polemical discussion of reproductive alternatives and their political and social implications, with an informative reference apparatus.

Thomas H. Murray, Willard Gaylin, and Ruth Macklin (eds.), *Feeling Good and Doing Better: Ethics and Nontherapeutic Drug Use* (1984), an analysis of moral, social, legal, and health issues connected with recreational use of drugs.

Robert N. Bellah *et al.*, *Habits of the Heart: Individualism and Commitment in American Life* (1985), a study of civic values of contemporary Americans, based on interviews and concluding that there is an imbalance between private and public values.

David L. Altheide, *Media Power* (1985), an exploration of the influence of media on social developments, through analysis of both format and contents and discussion of crucial moral and political implications.

Peter F. Cowhey, *The Problems of Plenty: Energy Policy and International Politics* (1985), a study of international management strategies in consumption and distribution of energy.

Norman Macrae, *The 2025 Report: A Concise History of the Future, 1975–2025* (1984), an optimistic forecast of technological, political, and social developments.

Benjamin R. Barber, *Strong Democracy: Participatory Politics for a New Age* (1984), a polemical discussion of the fate of the democratic political system, accompanied by a presentation of a hypothetical program for reform in democratic government.

Hedley Bull and Adam Watson (eds.), *The Expansion of International Society* (1984), an important collection of essays on the traditional European state system and its development under the emerging new international order.

Thomas M. Franck, *Nation Against Nation: What Happened to the U.N. Dream and What the U.S. Can Do About It* (1985), an exhaustive and critical study of the development and current state of the United Nations.

Roberta Achtenberg (ed.), *Sexual Orientation and the Law* (1985), a treatise sponsored by a grant from the National Lawyers Guild to provide information support to legal practitioners on issues involved in homosexuality.

Charles A. Perfetti, *Reading Ability* (1985), a comprehensive examination of the development of reading skills, and of other related issues including reading instruction.

Barbara Miller Solomon, *In the Company of Educated Women: A History of Women and Higher Education in America* (1985), a comprehensive scholarly survey of the period from 1776 to 1985, with a detailed analysis of attitudes and controversies.

John H. Bunzel (ed.), *Challenge to American Schools: The Case for Standards and Values* (1985), a collection of views of prominent educators on the decline in the quality of public education, with evaluations of approaches to reform.

Art

Moshe Barasch, *Theories of Art: From Plato to Winckelmann* (1985), a scholarly analysis of theoretical developments in Western art from antiquity to the beginning of the 18th century.

David Best, *Feeling and Reason in the Arts* (1985), a well-referenced study of the role of art and aesthetics of creativity in the life of society, and of their place in social theory.

Derek Elley, *The Epic Film: Myth and History* (1984), an illustrated analysis of the genre, with informative filmography and bibliography.

Robert B. Ray, *A Certain Tendency of the Hollywood Cinema, 1930–1980* (1985), a study of American film since the advent of sound, based on thorough research.

Ada Louise Huxtable, *The Tall Building Artistically Reconsidered: The Search for a Skyscraper Style* (1984), an examination of the place of the skyscraper in urban design and in contemporary architecture as a whole.

Kenneth Laws, *The Physics of Dance* (1984), an exploration of physiological aspects of ballet from the point of view of physics, with scholarly appendixes and glossaries.

Claude Marks, *World Artists, 1950–1980* (1984), a source on 312 mainstream modern European and American artists.

Curtis Roads (ed.), *Composers and the Computer* (1985), a discussion of the new sound-production technology and of the problems that composers of modern music confront.

Mark Roskill, *The Interpretation of Cubism* (1985), a useful analysis of the theory and history of Cubism and of events and attitudes inside the movement.

Heinrich Schwarz, *Art and Photography: Forerunners and Influences: Selected Essays,* ed. by William E. Parker (1985), an examination of the place of photography in the aesthetic and historical framework of art in general.

Henry James, *Literary Criticism,* 2 vol. (1984), a scholarly edition of critical writings by the great novelist, embracing an impressive range of works about one-third of which appear in book form for the first time.

Martin Seymour-Smith, *The New Guide to Modern World Literature,* 3rd rev. ed. (1985), a massive, informative reference work by an author who reads primary sources in about 20 languages, and whose strong, candid, often controversial opinions may save many interesting names from oblivion.

J. Michael Walton, *The Greek Sense of Theatre: Tragedy Reviewed* (1984), a modern study of the ancient tradition of the interdependence of the playwright, the actor, and the audience, and its relation to other art forms.

Roland John Wiley, *Tchaikovsky's Ballets: Swan Lake, Sleeping Beauty, Nutcracker* (1985), a well-researched discussion of original productions of the famous ballets, with the study of audiences, performers, conventions, and social life of the time.

Technology

David A. Hounshell, *From the American System to Mass Production, 1800–1932: The Development of Manufacturing Technology in the United States* (1984), an informative history of manufacturing technology and industrial leadership.

Charles Perrow, *Normal Accidents: Living with High-Risk Technologies* (1984), a study of technological accidents in different industrial, transportation, and research environments and of methods of controlling them.

Diana Schumacher *et.al.*, *Energy: Crisis or Opportunity?* (1985), an objective historical study of the consumption, conservation, and renewability of energy resources.

J. H. Fremlin, *Power Production—What Are the Risks?* (1985), a comparative review of the risks of nuclear and other tech-

nologies of power generation, by an acknowledged expert in the field of applied radioactivity.

R. Paul Singh and Dennis R. Heldman, *Introduction to Food Engineering* (1984), an informative and well-illustrated text on principles of food-producing technologies.

G. B. Bleazard, *Introducing Satellite Communications* (1985), an overview of the history of satellite communications, coding systems, and signal-channeling techniques.

J. L. Alty and M. J. Coombs, *Expert Systems: Concepts and Examples* (1984), an introduction to computer applications in medical diagnostics, data analysis, and problem solving.

Tom Forester (ed.), *The Information Technology Revolution* (1984), an anthology of writings on developments in modern technology and their sociological implications.

Donald Michie and Rory Johnston, *The Knowledge Machine: Artificial Intelligence and the Future of Man* (1985), a comprehensive overview of the applications and social impact of artificial intelligence and its harbinger, the computer.

James Everett Katz (ed.), *Arms Production in Developing Countries* (1984), a survey of the arms industries of Argentina, Brazil, China, Egypt, India, and Israel.

Stephanie Yanchinski, *Setting Genes to Work: The Industrial Era of Biotechnology* (1985), a broad study of biotechnology as it has evolved from industrial microbiology, with evaluation of accompanying economic factors.

Religion

Rodney Stark and William Sims Bainbridge, *The Future of Religion* (1985), a theory postulating a dynamic balance between secularization, on the one hand, and schism, sect, and cult formation on the other, in American culture.

Hugh Montefiore, *The Probability of God* (1985), a readable and perceptive discussion of religious aspects of evolution, by the bishop (Church of England) of Birmingham.

Letty M. Russell (ed.), *Feminist Interpretation of the Bible* (1985), an exposition of feminist perspective in hermeneutics in a collection of essays by writers representing the American Academy of Religion and the Society for Biblical Literature.

Martin E. Marty, *Pilgrims in Their Own Land: 500 Years of Religion in America* (1984), a biographical history of American religion since the colonial times.

Helen Hardacre, *Lay Buddhism in Contemporary Japan* (1984), an informative study based on four years of documented fieldwork and emphasizing the complexity of the social and psychological structure of Japanese life.

Darrell J. Fasching (ed.), *The Jewish People in Christian Preaching* (1984), essays on Jews in Christian theology.

Kurt Aland, *A History of Christianity: From the Beginnings to the Threshold of the Reformation* (1985; originally published in German, 1980), a sophisticated interpretative study with informative chronological tables and a thorough index.

John L. Esposito, *Islam and Politics* (1984), a historical survey of Islam as a political and social force in the Arab countries, Iran, and Pakistan, and their relationship with the West.

William S. Hatcher and J. Douglas Martin, *The Baha'i Faith* (1984), a comprehensive introduction to the history, philosophy, and practices of one of the world's youngest religions.

David Robinson, *The Unitarians and the Universalists* (1985), an informative analysis of these denominations, with a series of biographical outlines and a bibliography.

The History of Mankind

Erich S. Gruen, *The Hellenistic World and the Coming of Rome*, 2 vol. (1984), an original, thoroughly researched study of the role of Roman expansion in ancient culture.

J. Alberto Soggin, *A History of Ancient Israel* (1985; originally published in Italian, 1984), a modern historical critical study by a noted biblical scholar.

Jesse D. Jennings (ed.), *Ancient North Americans* (1983), and *Ancient South Americans* (1983), a well-illustrated and referenced collection of research material on American prehistory.

Edward Reynolds, *Stand the Storm: A History of the Atlantic Slave Trade* (1985), a comprehensive study of African society and slavery in the 18th century.

William R. Keylor, *The Twentieth-Century World: An International History* (1984), a broad, though analytical, survey of this century's political and economic events.

Raymond L. Garthoff, *Détente and Confrontation: American-Soviet Relations from Nixon to Reagan* (1985), an exhaustively researched and detailed treatment of the topic.

Elim Papadakis, *The Green Movement in West Germany* (1984), a survey of the influential movement active in the areas of pacifism, feminism, ecology, and participatory democracy.

Peter Lane, *Europe Since 1945: An Introduction* (1985), an overview of European events and their influence on contemporary international relations.

Ludmilla Alexeyeva, *Soviet Dissent: Contemporary Movements for National, Religious, and Human Rights* (1985; originally published in Russian in the U.S., 1984), a comprehensive collection of data with some analysis of events.

Andrew H. Malcolm, *The Canadians* (1985), a well-researched and illustrated treatment of the economy, the people, geography, and problems of regionalism and national identity.

Lester D. Langley, *Central America: The Real Stakes: Understanding Central America Before It's Too Late* (1985), a historical study of policy disagreements between Latin-American governments and the U.S.

Alan Riding, *Distant Neighbors: A Portrait of the Mexicans* (1985), a country study with analyses of political, cultural, economic, and social phenomena and profiles of major figures.

Lloyd G. Reynolds, *Economic Growth in the Third World, 1850–1980* (1985), a historical study of economic progress in 41 major developing countries.

Gwendolen M. Carter and Patrick O'Meara (eds.), *African Independence: The First Twenty-Five Years* (1985), a collection of analytical essays providing a broad coverage of the topic.

The Branches of Knowledge

Georges Ifrah, *From One to Zero* (1985; originally published in French, 1981), a fascinating study of the development of numeric notation throughout the world, illustrated with the author's engaging drawings.

Derek Gjertsen, *The Classics of Science: A Study of Twelve Enduring Scientific Works* (1984), a case study of major works pertaining to astronomy, biology, geology, and mathematics, with an analysis of their place in the history of science.

Evelyn Fox Keller, *Reflections on Gender and Science* (1985), a historical examination of scientific activity since Plato presented from the standpoint of feminism.

Martin Goldstein and Inge Goldstein, *The Experience of Science: An Interdisciplinary Approach* (1984), an informative and highly readable exploration of science from its cultural roots to its role in humanitarian causes.

Maclyn McCarty, *Transforming Principle: Discovering That Genes Are Made of DNA* (1985), a history of one of the greatest scientific discoveries of this century and the people behind it; written by one of the three original discoverers.

Daniel J. Kevles, *In the Name of Eugenics: Genetics and the Uses of Human Heredity* (1985), a readable scholarly analysis of the controversial history of eugenics, with discussions of major figures associated with the field.

Martin S. Pernick, *A Calculus of Suffering: Pain, Professionalism, and Anesthesia in Nineteenth-Century America* (1985), a history of the development of anesthesia and an analysis of its impact on medical opinion and the social environment.

Daniel N. Robinson, *Philosophy of Psychology* (1985), an examination of issues seldom discussed in the literature.

Walter A. McDougall, *The Heavens and the Earth: A Political History of the Space Age* (1985), an examination of the moral and intellectual implications of technological progress.

Donald K. Grayson, *The Establishment of Human Antiquity* (1983), a thorough exposition of research that made human prehistory a legitimate part of the science of man.

Kenneth Neill Cameron, *Marxism, the Science of Society* (1985), a good though uncritical introduction to Marxism and to the Marxist interpretation of contemporary social phenomena, written from the traditional Marxist point of view.

(Opposite) Photograph, Larry Downing—Woodfin Camp and Assoc.

Chronology of 1985

JANUARY

2 Japan and U.S. discuss trade imbalance. Japanese Prime Minister Yasuhiro Nakasone arrived in Los Angeles to discuss bilateral trade and other issues with U.S. Pres. Ronald Reagan. The unresolved problem of Japan's huge trade surplus with the U.S. had become a burning issue because U.S. congressmen and businessmen were publicly demanding that the Reagan administration adopt strong measures to counter what were termed unjustifiable barriers keeping U.S. goods out of Japanese markets.

3 Ethiopian Jews resettled in Israel. The Israeli government publicly confirmed rumours that some 10,000 Ethiopian Jews had been secretly flown to Israel in recent years, but it would give no details of the operation. An additional 10,000–15,000 black Jews were believed to be still living in Ethiopian villages and Sudanese refugee camps. The rescue operation apparently began in 1977, two years after Israel's Sephardic chief rabbi ruled that the Ethiopians were descendants of the tribe of Dan and were, therefore, true Jews. As such, they were eligible for immediate Israeli citizenship. Ethiopia denounced the exodus as illegal trafficking in Ethiopian citizens.

4 Shenuda resumes papacy. Shenuda III returned to Cairo to resume his duties as patriarch of Egypt's Coptic Church. In September 1981 Pres. Anwar as-Sadat, hoping to end violent confrontations between Muslims and Christians, had ordered the arrest of some 1,500 persons on charges of contributing to the seemingly endless turmoil. Most of those rounded up were Muslim fundamentalists, Copts, journalists, and political opponents of Sadat. Shenuda was ordered to leave the capital and took up residence in the Western Desert.

5 Colombia turns over drug dealers. Four Colombians accused of international drug trafficking and money laundering were flown to the U.S. to face federal charges. This first-ever extradition of Colombian citizens to the U.S. was in effect a declaration by Pres. Belisario Betancur that he fully intended to continue prosecuting the war initiated by the minister of justice before he was murdered by members of the drug underworld in May 1984.

Mubarak visits Jordan. Egyptian Pres. Hosni Mubarak met with King Hussein in Jordan to discuss problems of the Middle East. They agreed that an international conference, attended by U.S. and Soviet representatives as well as by Arabs and Israelis, held the greatest promise for a comprehensive settlement of the area's many problems. Syrian Pres. Hafez al-Assad, however, denounced Hussein as an agent of Zionism because he was dealing with Egypt, which had signed a separate peace treaty with Israel at Camp David, Md., in 1978.

7 Vietnamese attack Kampucheans. An estimated 4,000 Vietnamese in occupied Kampuchea launched a tank, artillery, and infantry attack against the non-Communist Khmer People's National Liberation Front (KPNLF) force of about 5,000 near the Thai border. The successful assault on Ampil, the largest concentration of KPNLF troops, occurred on the sixth anniversary of Vietnam's victory over the former Khmer Rouge government. The Vietnamese then moved against other rebel strongholds, causing tens of thousands of civilians and resistance fighters to seek refuge in Thailand.

8 Arms control talks to resume. U.S. Secretary of State George Shultz and Soviet Foreign Minister Andrey Gromyko concluded two days of talks in Geneva after agreeing on the format, content, and objectives of arms control negotiations that were expected to get under way in a month or two. It was the first meeting between top officials of the two superpowers in more than a year.

10 Daniel Ortega takes office. In a ceremony attended by only one foreign head of state, Cuban Pres. Fidel Castro, Daniel Ortega Saavedra took the oath of office as president of Nicaragua. He had been a member of the ruling junta ever since the overthrow of Pres. Anastasio Somoza Debayle in July 1979. The presidential inauguration followed by one day the installation of a new National Assembly, which had been elected in November 1984. The Assembly was firmly under the control of the Sandinista National Liberation Front, which held 61 of the 96 seats.

14 Israelis to leave Lebanon. The Cabinet of Israeli Prime Minister Shimon Peres voted 16–6 in favour of a Defense Ministry timetable for the withdrawal of Israeli troops from Lebanon. Foreign Minister Yitzhak Shamir, head of the right-wing Likud bloc and Peres's predecessor, led the opposition. The three-stage pullout was expected to begin in about five weeks and to conclude in six to nine months. Implementation of the plan would depend in part on conditions within Lebanon but not on the willingness of either the UN or the Lebanese government to cooperate.

U.S. indicts protectors of aliens. The U.S. Department of Justice announced the indictments of 16 persons on charges of smuggling Central American aliens into the U.S. or giving them refuge after their arrival. Among those named in the 71-count indictment were a Presbyterian minister, two Roman Catholic priests, and three nuns. The U.S. government contended that most of those illegally entering the U.S. from Central America did not qualify for political asylum because they were

CLAUDE URRACA—SYGMA

Cuban Pres. Fidel Castro (left) arrived unannounced for the inauguration of Daniel Ortega Saavedra as president of Nicaragua. Castro was the only foreign head of state to attend the ceremony.

trying to escape poverty, not persecution. Activists involved in what was called the Sanctuary Movement insisted that those they were helping faced persecution and possible death at the hands of death squads in El Salvador and Guatemala.

15 **Brazil gets new president.** Brazil's 686-member electoral college overwhelmingly elected Tancredo de Almeida Neves the nation's first civilian president in 21 years. Neves told a jubilant nation that he would introduce "real, effective, daring, and irreversible changes," including the drafting of a new constitution. He also hoped to arrange a new presidential election in 1988 so that Brazilians would choose their president directly. Gen. João Baptista de Oliveira Figueiredo, the outgoing president, said he would turn over the reins of government on March 15.

Ershad dismisses Cabinet. Lieut. Gen. Hossain M. Ershad, president of Bangladesh, dismissed his Council of Ministers and announced that the first parliamentary elections in six years would be held on April 6. Ershad was responding to demands from a 22-party opposition coalition called Movement for the Restoration of Democracy. The group had campaigned long and hard for an end to martial law, the release of political prisoners, new parliamentary elections, the restoration of political freedoms, and the installation of a caretaker government.

18 **India uncovers spy ring.** Indian Prime Minister Rajiv Gandhi told Parliament that "certain employees in sensitive positions" had been arrested for "activities detrimental to the national interest." The following day the news media reported that photocopies of secret military information were among many incriminating documents found in the homes of government officials. It quickly became apparent that an extensive and well-placed spy ring had been operating for some time. The mastermind was said to have been Coomar Narain, an employee of SLM-Maneklal, a company representing Western European industrial-equipment manufacturers that had received government military contracts. Other suspects included a private secretary and a personal assistant in the prime minister's secretariat, the senior assistant to the president's press secretary, a senior assistant in the Department of Economic Affairs, and a personal assistant in the office of the secretary for defense production. Shortly after the story broke, Alain Bolley, an aviation expert serving as deputy military attaché in the French embassy, was reportedly ordered to leave India on the first available flight. French officials, however, said Bolley had simply been called home. There were also reports that the U.S. Central Intelligence Agency was involved.

U.S. defies World Court. The U.S. government formally announced it would participate no further in proceedings initiated against it by Nicaragua in the International Court of Justice because the issue was "an inherently political problem that is not appropriate for judicial resolution." The suit charged the U.S. with

An Ethiopian Jew, one of some 10,000 secretly flown to Israel in recent years, visits the Wailing Wall in Jerusalem.
MOSHE MILNER—SYGMA

illegally supporting paramilitary attacks by rebels in Nicaragua and mining its harbours; it also sought millions of dollars in reparations. The U.S. contended that the real issue was regional, not bilateral, because it arose from the threat Nicaragua posed to much of Central America, exemplified by Nicaragua's "huge buildup of Soviet arms and Cuban advisers, its cross-border attacks and promotion of insurgency within various nations of the region."

19 **Mitterrand visits New Caledonia.** French Pres. François Mitterrand made a 12-hour visit to New Caledonia, a French territory in the South Pacific, to urge an end to violence and acceptance of a referendum to determine the island's political future. During the visit he spoke privately with both sides in the dispute. Opponents of independence, including most whites and some Asians and Polynesians, staged a demonstration during the visit to urge that the wishes of "pro-Soviet" elements not prevail. On January 20, during a televised address in Paris, Mitterrand said France intended to protect its strategic interests in the area by keeping out "whatever foreign power" might try to set up a presence on the island. He also indicated that France's military base in New Caledonia would be strengthened.

20 **Reagan takes oath of office.** In a brief private ceremony, Ronald W. Reagan was sworn in for his second four-year term as president of the United States. At 73 he was the oldest man ever elected to the nation's highest office. After a public swearing-in ceremony the following day (Monday), Reagan delivered his inaugural address. He called on Republicans and Democrats to work together in the months ahead because the nation faced hard decisions that would prove to be turning points in its history. He also reiterated his call for less government spending and for a freer economy.

Cyprus peace talks fail. Spyros Kyprianou, the Greek president of Cyprus, and Rauf Denktash, leader of the Turkish Cypriots, ended several days of discussions at UN headquarters in New York City without agreeing on a plan to reunite the country. When UN Secretary-General Javier Pérez de Cuéllar brought the two together for the first time in five years, hopes were high because separate preliminary discussions appeared to have established common ground for a settlement of basic differences. Kyprianou, however, was dissatisfied with certain proposals and agreed only to resume talks sometime in the future.

23 **Suspects in Aquino murder named.** A panel of three government-appointed prosecutors announced in Manila that they had found ample evidence to charge 26 persons with involvement in the August 1983 assassination of Benigno Aquino, Jr., a leader of the opposition to Philippine Pres. Ferdinand Marcos. Arrest warrants were expected to be issued the following day. The prosecutors, in effect, sided with four of the five civilian investigators who a few months earlier, after intense interrogations and study of the evidence, had found sufficient grounds to indict all 26. The accused included Gen. Fabian C. Ver, chief of staff of the armed forces and a close personal friend of Marcos; Maj. Gen. Prospero A. Olivas, head of metropolitan Manila's constabulary; and Brig. Gen. Luther Custodio, who had been in charge of airport security when Aquino was gunned down on the tarmac moments after he returned from self-imposed exile in the U.S.

24 **Verdict reached in Sharon libel trial.** A federal jury in Manhattan reached a final verdict in the $50 million libel suit filed against *Time* magazine by Ariel Sharon, Israel's former defense minister. The trial focused on a paragraph in *Time*'s Feb. 21, 1983, cover story that portrayed Sharon as indirectly responsible for the massacre of hundreds of Palestinian refugees by Lebanese Phalangist militiamen. Judge Abraham D. Sofaer ordered the jury to decide three separate issues: whether the *Time* article was defamatory; whether it was false; and whether it was published with reckless disregard for its truth or falsity. After agreeing that the article was both defamatory and false, the jury found *Time* innocent of reckless disregard for the truth. Without a finding of malice, Sharon could not collect monetary damages. The jury, however, severely reprimanded *Time* for negligence and carelessness.

26 **Pope visits South America.** Pope John Paul II arrived in Venezuela to begin a 12-day apostolic journey that would also carry him to Ecuador and Peru and then to Trinidad and Tobago, off the coast of Venezuela. It was the pope's 25th foreign trip since his elevation to the papacy in 1978. As the pope's plane was taxiing to a stop in Lima, Peru, guerrillas blew up several towers that supplied electricity to the city. Moments later hillside lanterns formed a hammer and sickle, the symbol of the Shining Path Maoist guerrillas.

FEBRUARY

2 **Chile extends state of siege.**
Gen. Augusto Pinochet, president of Chile's military government, ordered a 90-day extension of the state of siege that he had imposed on Nov. 6, 1984. The presidential decree, which noted that the country was still experiencing internal convulsions, was issued over the objections of several members of the Cabinet. The state of siege gave the government authority, among other things, to hold suspected dissidents without charge. It also extended the ban on specific publications, unauthorized gatherings, and political activities.

4 **Lange closes port to U.S. destroyer.** The U.S. State Department announced that the ANZUS naval exercises scheduled for March had been canceled because Prime Minister David Lange would not permit a U.S. Navy destroyer to visit New Zealand unless the U.S. first certified that the ship carried no nuclear weapons. As a matter of policy, the U.S. never revealed the type of weapons carried by the ships of its fleet. The Reagan administration said Lange's decision was a matter of grave concern to the United States because it jeopardized the future of the ANZUS (Australia, New Zealand, U.S.) alliance (formerly the Pacific Security Treaty). Though Lange insisted that New Zealand would remain a member of ANZUS, the U.S. was considering retaliatory measures to express its displeasure.

Italy tries 251 suspected gangsters. The trial of 251 suspected gangsters or their accomplices got under way in Naples, Italy, under extraordinarily tight security. Police believed that virtually all of the defendants were associated with a faction of the Nuova Camorra crime syndicate controlled by Raffaele Cutolo, currently in prison. The 153 defendants who chose to be present at the initial proceedings were confined in 20 metal cages in a specially constructed windowless courtroom. Two of the cages were reserved for those who had turned state's evidence. Nearly 400 other suspected Neapolitan gangsters would be tried in two separate trials, to be held at a later date. All those currently in police custody had been rounded up in June 1983 during a massive crackdown on organized crime.

Yugoslav dissidents sentenced. After a highly publicized public trial, three Yugoslavs were found guilty of disseminating propaganda hostile to the state. The sentences they received were relatively light: 24 months, 18 months, and 12 months; the latter was the minimum allowed by law. Far harsher terms would have been mandated had the judge not reduced the charge from counterrevolutionary conspiracy to spreading hostile propaganda. One of those found guilty viewed the outcome of the trial as a compromise between hardliners and soft-liners in the government. In a separate trial, a fourth dissident was found guilty of antistate activities and sentenced to an 18-month prison term.

5 **Libya frees four Britons.** Four Britons, taken hostage in Tripoli after Britain broke diplomatic ties with Libya in April 1984, were released after eight months of captivity. Col. Muammar al-Qaddafi, leader of Libya, expressed a hope that Britain would respond favourably by normalizing diplomatic relations and releasing Libyans held in British jails. Four had just gone on trial, charged with bombing attacks against anti-Qaddafi Libyans living in Great Britain. The British government had severed diplomatic ties with Libya after a 25-year-old British policewoman was shot and killed by Libyan students firing automatic weapons from inside the Libyan People's Bureau (embassy) in London. In addition, ten Libyans, demonstrating against Qaddafi outside the embassy, were wounded by the gunfire. Because all those inside the embassy claimed diplomatic immunity, they were allowed to leave the country without incident.

Access to Gibraltar restored. Spain officially removed all restrictions on travel to and from Gibraltar, the tiny British enclave on the southern tip of Spain. Gen. Francisco Franco had closed the border a decade and a half earlier, but limited pedestrian traffic had continued. In November 1984 Britain and Spain agreed that the time had come to initiate talks on the political future of the territory, which Britain had occupied since 1704. Working out details for the transfer of sovereignty and other matters was expected to take several years, but in the meantime Spaniards would be allowed to seek work and buy property in Gibraltar.

7 **Polish police convicted of murder.** A five-judge tribunal in Torun, Poland, found four security policemen guilty of abducting and murdering the Rev. Jerzy Popieluszko, an outspoken supporter of Solidarity. The two senior officers were given 25-year sentences; the

two other men were ordered to prison for 15 and 14 years. Before the beginning of the 25-day trial, three of the four had admitted their roles in the October 1984 crime. One defendant testified that his superior had ordered the kidnapping and murder, but no evidence was presented to support the allegation. The trial was believed to have been the first instance of a Communist government publicly prosecuting members of its own security force for killing a dissident.

8 **Kim Dae Jung returns home.**
After spending two years in the U.S., South Korean dissident Kim Dae Jung returned to Seoul accompanied by two U.S. congressmen and other supporters. Tempers flared at the Kimp'o International Airport when policemen tried to separate Kim from those around him. After a scuffle with Kim's supporters, police drove the 59-year-old politician to his home, where he was placed under virtual house arrest. After losing the 1971 presidential election to Park Chung Hee, Kim had become internationally known as a critic of South Korea's authoritarian rulers. He was sentenced to death for sedition following the 1980 Kwangju riots, but his sentence was commuted to life imprisonment and then further reduced to 20 years. In December 1982 Kim was released, ostensibly so he could obtain medical treatment in the U.S.

10 **Mandela rejects offer of freedom.** Nelson Mandela, the leader of South Africa's banned African National Congress, refused a government offer of freedom even though he had already been jailed for more than 20 years. The government had insisted that Mandela renounce violence as a condition for his release. Mandela's 23-year-old daughter quoted her father as saying: "Let him [Pres. P. W. Botha] renounce violence. Let him say that he will dismantle apartheid. Let him unban the people's organization, the

GIANSANTI—SYGMA

Some of the more than 250 suspected gangsters being tried in Naples, Italy, observe the proceedings from a specially built cage in the high-security courtroom.

African National Congress. Let him free all who have been imprisoned, banished, or exiled for their opposition to apartheid. Let him guarantee free political activity so that the people may decide who will govern them." With neither side prepared to accept the conditions of the other, no immediate resolution of the impasse seemed possible.

12 **South Korea elects Assembly.** In elections for South Korea's National Assembly, the opposition New Korea Democratic Party (NKDP) surprised virtually everyone by winning 50 of the 184 contested seats. The ruling Democratic Justice Party (DJP) captured 87 seats, and the Democratic Korea Party 26. Of the remaining 21 contested seats, 15 went to the Korea National Party and 6 to others. Though the DJP won 35.3% of the popular vote and the NKDP 29.2%, the DJP was defeated in several major cities. In Seoul the NKDP won 14 seats, the DJP 13. In Pusan the NKDP captured 6 seats to 3 for the DJP. In the 276-seat Assembly the DJP would still hold an absolute majority with its 148 seats, but leaders of the NKDP hoped its 67 representatives would become a potent force in the Assembly.

Dikko kidnappers convicted. Three Israelis and one Nigerian were convicted in a London court of kidnapping and drugging Umaru Dikko, Nigeria's former transport minister, in July 1984. Their prison sentences ranged from 14 to 10 years. All four had pleaded guilty to the charges. Dikko had been sought by Nigerian authorities for allegedly amassing millions of dollars while serving in the Cabinet of deposed president Alhaji Shehu Shagari.

15 **Uruguay's legislature revived.** After 12 years of military rule, Uruguay moved a step closer to democracy with the convening of a new Parliament. The legislature, which was elected on Nov. 25, 1984, consisted of 30 senators and 99 deputies. Julio María Sanguinetti Cairolo, who replaced Gen. Gregorio Conrado Álvarez Armelino as president on March 1, faced the immediate and delicate task of satisfying demands for the release of political prisoners without thereby angering the military officers who had imprisoned them.

16 **Israeli troops leave Sidon.** Some 300 Israeli troops initiated the first stage of Israel's withdrawal from Lebanon by pulling out of the battered city of Sidon after 32 months of occupation. The Lebanese Army forces that took over control of the area south of the Awali River were welcomed by the local populace with great rejoicing. The Israeli soldiers appeared equally happy to be vacating the region. Members of the South Lebanon Army, which supported Israel, had left the city earlier. On February 17 Pres. Amin Gemayel, a Maronite Christian, visited Sidon, but the following day armed Shi'ah fundamentalists—mainly members of the Party of God—poured into the city aboard hundreds of cars, buses, and trucks. They denounced Gemayel as the "shah of Lebanon" and called for the establishment of an Islamic state.

18 **Westmoreland drops suit against CBS.** Attorneys for Gen. William C. Westmoreland announced that the former commander of U.S. forces in Vietnam had withdrawn his $120 million libel suit against CBS. In a televised documentary, CBS had asserted that the general's command had deliberately underreported the number of enemy troops before their devastating Tet offensive of January 1968. The out-of-court settlement made both parties responsible for their own legal fees and did not require CBS to pay damages or retract any part of its report. Westmoreland stated that he was satisfied with what he termed a CBS "apology." The company said it "never intended to assert, and does not believe, that General Westmoreland was unpatriotic or disloyal in performing his duties as he saw them."

20 **Ireland seizes IRA funds.** The Irish High Court, acting in accordance with a law passed by both houses of Parliament the previous day after banking hours, seized more than $1.6 million said to belong to the outlawed Irish Republican Army. The minister of justice said the account represented extortion money obtained by threatening to kidnap or murder.

Thatcher addresses U.S. Congress. British Prime Minister Margaret Thatcher told a joint session of the U.S. Congress that she firmly endorsed President Reagan's plan

to develop a space-based missile defense capability. "Let us be under no illusions," Thatcher said. "It is our strength, not their good will, that has brought the Soviet Union to the negotiating table in Geneva."

25 **Pakistan elects National Assembly.** Pakistani voters, generally ignoring a call from leaders of banned political parties to boycott the election, cast ballots for a new National Assembly. Pres. Mohammad Zia-ul-Haq, however, did not receive the broad support most observers had expected. Five members of his Cabinet and some 30 other supporters all lost the Assembly seats to which Zia had named them. The mere fact that an election had been held served to lend respectability to Zia's government, even though hundreds of the president's critics had been arrested before the election and candidates not backed by the government had to run as individuals rather than as representatives of a political party. It was not known how much power Zia would transfer to the new Assembly.

26 **U.S. indicts alleged Mafia bosses.** In a 15-count indictment filed in a Manhattan federal court, nine men were accused of belonging to a crime commission that ruled five Cosa Nostra families in New York City. The crime syndicates were said to control a wide range of illegal operations that included drug trafficking, loansharking, gambling, labour racketeering, and extortion. The Mafia commission was also accused of sanctioning the 1979 murders of Carmine Galante and four of his crime family associates. The indictment was more than ordinarily significant because, for the first time, the commission itself, rather than individuals, was the focus of attention.

28 **IRA guerrillas kill nine.** Members of the Irish Republican Army (IRA) killed nine constables when one of nine mortar shells they fired at a police base in Newry, Northern Ireland, hit a crowded cafeteria. It was the deadliest such attack since violence first erupted in 1969. Though the stated purpose of the IRA was to unite Northern Ireland with the Republic of Ireland, the Irish government had publicly condemned the IRA's guerrilla tactics.

MARCH

3 **U.K. coal miners end strike.** After three hours of heated debate, union representatives of Britain's coal miners decided in a close vote to end the strike that had kept miners out of pits for almost a year. The union was never able to work out a settlement with the National Coal Board, which insisted to the end that unprofitable coal mines had to be closed, even if it meant the loss of thousands of jobs. Though some miners were as determined as ever to continue the strike, union leaders appeared to have no choice but to call off the strike because thousands of miners, hard-pressed for money, had recently returned

to work without the union's approval. A spokesman for the government, addressing one of the miners' prime concerns, said he wanted to make it absolutely clear that although some of the 700 miners dismissed during the strike might be rehired, no one "guilty of crimes of violence or serious damage against the industry" would be reinstated.

6 **South Korea removes political bans.** The government of South Korean Pres. Chun Doo Hwan, noting that a new political climate "born of a harmonizing blend of freedom and order" had settled over the nation,

announced that the political bans still affecting 14 politicians were being removed. Kim Dae Jung and Kim Young Sam, both internationally known dissidents, were among this last group to be pardoned. In November 1980, after Chun seized power, a total of 567 politicians had been blacklisted. Though Kim Dae Jung was freed from house arrest, he would still be forbidden to join or organize a political party because he remained under a suspended 20-year sentence for sedition. Kim Young Sam, generally viewed as more moderate in his political opinions, had directed the surprisingly successful campaign of the New Korea Democratic

Party in the February 12 elections for the National Assembly.

U.S. drug agent murdered in Mexico. The decomposed bodies of a U.S. drug enforcement agent and his Mexican pilot were discovered on a ranch about 110 km (70 mi) southeast of Guadalajara, Mexico, four days after a shootout in which one Mexican federal policeman and five suspected drug traffickers had been killed. Enrique Camarena Salazar and Alfredo Zavala Avelar had been kidnapped separately on February 7, then brutally beaten and murdered. On March 14 the Mexican attorney general's office reported that it had taken 13 suspects into custody, 7 of whom were judicial police officers. One had reportedly confessed to his part in the abduction of Camarena. On April 4 Rafael Caro Quintero, a major figure in Mexico's illegal drug trade and a prime suspect in Camarena's murder, was arrested in Costa Rica; he was deported to Mexico the following day. On April 8 police arrested Ernesto Fonseca Carillo in Puerto Vallarta; he was reported to be the king of Mexican drug dealers.

10 **Chernenko dies in Moscow.** Konstantin U. Chernenko, general secretary of the Communist Party of the Soviet Union and chairman of the Presidium of the Supreme Soviet (president), died in Moscow after a long, debilitating illness. The 73-year-old leader had replaced Yury Andropov as head of the Communist Party in February 1984. The official announcement of Chernenko's death was made on March 11, the same day 54-year-old Mikhail Gorbachev was named to succeed him as party secretary. On March 13 Chernenko was laid to rest during an elaborate ceremony attended by many heads of government or by their high-ranking stand-ins. After the funeral U.S. Vice-Pres. George Bush and Gorbachev met for the first time. Both expressed a desire to improve relations between their two countries. Other world leaders also took the opportunity to discuss issues of special interest.

12 **Arms control talks begin in Geneva.** Soviet and U.S. officials came together in Geneva for their first formal arms control negotiations in 15 months. The seriousness of the talks was underscored by the fact that the Soviet Union did not ask for a postponement when news of Konstantin Chernenko's death on March 10 was announced to the world. After nearly three hours of discussing basic issues, the two sides agreed to meet again in two days. Viktor P. Karpov, head of the Soviet delegation, told reporters he did not intend to return to Moscow for Chernenko's funeral because it would upset the schedule of arms talks. He also confirmed that there was no need to confer with the new leader of the Soviet Union, Mikhail Gorbachev, because he had presided over the meeting of the Politburo less than a week earlier when it formulated the policy to be followed in the negotiations.

15 **Military rule ends in Brazil.** With Brazil's 75-year-old President-elect Tancredo Neves critically ill, José

In March Konstantin Chernenko, who had held the general secretaryship of the Communist Party for just over a year, became the third Soviet leader to die in 28 months.

NOGUES—SYGMA

Sarney was sworn in as the country's new vice-president and assumed responsibility for the government as interim president. The ceremony brought to an end 21 years of military rule in the largest country in South America. The civilian government's most urgent task was to find a way to solve the country's severe economic problems. Despite slow economic growth in 1984, the inflation rate for the year was 224%. Some analysts feared that democratic rule would be short-lived unless Brazil's economic situation improved substantially.

17 **Reagan travels to Quebec.** Canadian Prime Minister Brian Mulroney announced in Quebec that he and President Reagan had, after brief consultation, appointed members to a joint team that would study ways of solving the problem of acid rain. "We have broken a three-year deadlock," he said, "by agreeing to our common and shared responsibility to preserve our common environment." Acid rain, the airborne transfer of oxides of sulfur and nitrogen, had caused friction between the two countries. Factories and power plants in the Midwestern United States were in large part responsible for fossil-fuel emissions that were believed to be harming marine and plant life in both Canada and the northeastern region of the United States.

18 **Capital Cities to buy ABC.** Leonard Goldenson, chairman and chief executive officer of ABC, one of three major television networks in the U.S., publicly acknowledged that he had accepted an offer from Capital Cities Communications Inc. to buy ABC. The deal, worked out with Thomas S. Murphy, the chairman and chief executive officer of Capital Cities, involved more than $3.5 billion. It thus became the largest business acquisition in U.S. history outside the oil industry. Murphy, who had already

worked out the basic financing, would offer ABC stockholders a very attractive $118 for each share of stock purchased. In addition, ABC stockholders would receive warrants allowing them to purchase stock in Capital Cities. The new organization would be called Capital Cities/ABC Inc.

Court rejects limit on PAC spending. The U.S. Supreme Court in a 7–2 vote upheld a lower federal court decision by ruling that the limit of $1,000 on the amount of money a political action committee (PAC) could spend on behalf of a presidential candidate in a general election was a violation of constitutionally guaranteed freedom of speech and association. The court viewed such expenditures by PACs as "independent" because they are not made "at the request of or in coordination with" a candidate's campaign election committee. U.S. citizens, the court insisted, have a fundamental right to promote, within the limits of the law, the candidacy of any person whose ideology they espouse. The justices further believed that there was little likelihood that PAC money would lead to political corruption or even the appearance of corruption, and even if that likelihood did exist, limiting independent expenditures to $1,000 would be "a fatally overbroad response to that evil."

20 **Belgium accepts U.S. missiles.** By a vote of 116 to 93, Belgium's Parliament approved the government's decision to deploy cruise missiles as part of its commitment to NATO. Prime Minister Wilfried Martens said his coalition Cabinet had made its decision out of an intense sense of duty. Some eight months earlier The Netherlands had announced that it would accept 48 cruise missiles if the Soviet Union deployed additional SS-20 missiles in Eastern Europe by November 1985. Belgium's decision, however, appeared to increase the likelihood that The Netherlands, sometime

before the end of the year, would become the last of the NATO allies who had originally agreed to deploy the missiles to endorse the decision.

21 **South African blacks killed.** In one of South Africa's most violent racial incidents in many years, police shot and killed 19 blacks near Uitenhage, an industrial area northwest of Port Elizabeth. Black activists in the region were among the strongest supporters of the outlawed African National Congress, but the shooting had no direct link to that organization. Tensions rose when several thousand blacks marching in a funeral procession refused to obey orders to disperse. In effect, they were denying the legitimacy of a recent government prohibition against large gatherings in Uitenhage and several other places that authorities judged to have a higher than normal potential for violent confrontation. In giving their version of the shooting, police said they had been attacked by the crowd and had fired their weapons in self-defense. On March 22 the government ordered a judicial inquiry to determine what actually provoked the shootings. These latest killings in South Africa brought the death toll to nearly 250 in just over a year.

28 **Honduras faces political crisis.** The Congress of Honduras defied Pres. Roberto Suazo Córdova by dismissing five justices of the Honduran Supreme Court on the grounds that they had distorted election laws to benefit the president's faction of the ruling Liberal Party. The following day Congress swore in five new justices. Suazo, describing developments as a "technical coup," informed the head of the armed forces that a "rupture of constitutional order" had occurred and ordered him to deploy troops around the presidential residence and around the buildings used by the Congress and Supreme Court. Later that day the new chief justice was arrested, and one day later he was formally charged with treason. The four other justices, similarly charged, had apparently gone into hiding. The crisis, which revolved

around efforts by factions within each of the two leading political parties to control the nomination of presidential candidates before the November election, centred on the Supreme Court because it had the power to name the key fifth, tiebreaking member of the Supreme Electoral Tribunal, which settles party disputes.

MX missiles get final approval. In their second and final vote on the issue, members of the U.S. House of Representatives approved, 217–210, President Reagan's request for 21 additional MX missiles at a cost of $1.5 billion. The Senate had already twice voted 55–45 to fund the program. There was, however, serious doubt that the president's request for 48 more missiles the next year would receive similar backing. Many legislators apparently felt that limited production of the MX would strengthen the U.S. bargaining position at the Geneva arms control talks and would demonstrate bipartisan support for the president's policies. One Democrat also noted that a negative vote at this time would have provided Republicans with a "first-strike capability" before the next congressional elections. In 1983 Congress had approved the first batch of 21 MX missiles, which were still under construction.

29 **Greek Parliament chooses president.** The Greek Parliament, meeting in special session, elected Supreme Court Justice Christos Sartzetakis president of the republic with the absolute minimum 180 required votes. The opposition immediately claimed the results were invalid because, they said, the acting president did not have the right to cast a ballot. Sartzetakis, the candidate of the ruling Panhellenic Socialist Movement (Pasok) headed by Prime Minister Andreas Papandreou, needed the votes of every Communist parliamentarian to garner the 180 votes. The new head of state replaced Konstantinos Karamanlis, who had resigned in anger on March 10 after Papandreou withdrew a promise he had made to support him in his bid for reelection. Karamanlis's entire statement read:

"In view of the projected developments, in which I cannot possibly participate, as of today I terminate my service as president of the republic, resigning from the rest of my term."

Spain and Portugal to join EC. After a marathon bargaining session in Brussels, representatives of the European Communities (EC) announced that Spain and Portugal had agreed to become the 11th and 12th members of the organization on Jan. 1, 1986. The main issues during the negotiations involved Spain's large fishing industry, the marketing of agricultural products, and access to EC markets for wine produced by both Spain and Portugal. Formal acceptance of the agreement was subject to ratification by the parliaments of all ten current members and by the EC itself. There was some uncertainty about Greece, which had threatened to veto the admission of Spain and Portugal if it did not receive some $2 billion in special agricultural subsidies. On March 30 Greece was persuaded to settle for $1.4 billion in aid and withdrew its threat of a veto.

31 **Duarte's party wins election.** The Christian Democratic Party (CDP) of José Napoleón Duarte, president of El Salvador, claimed an unexpected victory in elections for the National Assembly and local offices. Initial results indicated that for the first time the CDP had won an absolute majority in the Assembly and had captured about 54% of the popular vote. On April 3 the Central Election Council, which arbitrates all election disputes, unanimously rejected a demand from right-wing parties, headed by Roberto d'Aubuisson's Nationalist Republican Alliance, to void the election results on the grounds that they were fraudulent. The council, however, promised to investigate specific charges of irregularities involving, among other things, members of the military. Duarte himself issued a call for national unity, urging all "to participate in the democratic process and the process of confronting the crisis in which we live."

APRIL

2 **Lebanese prisoners taken to Israel.** The Israeli Army announced that it had moved about 1,100 "violent" Lebanese prisoners from the Ansar detention camp in southern Lebanon to Israel so they could not disrupt the orderly withdrawal of Israeli troops from Lebanon. Israel was quickly accused of violating international law (the 4th Geneva Convention of 1949) because the persons moved from one country to another were technically civilians and not recognized by Israel as prisoners of war. Israel sought to mute such criticism by announcing that 750 other prisoners would be released as a gesture of goodwill. Those scheduled to be set free were described as "members of various terrorist organizations" who "did not personally or actively participate in attacks" against the Israeli Defense Forces or Israeli citizens.

6 **Sudanese president ousted.** Gaafar Nimeiry, president of The Sudan, was overthrown in a military coup led by Gen. 'Abd ar-Rahman Siwar ad-Dahab, commander in chief of the armed forces and minister of defense. Nimeiry had named him to both posts just three weeks earlier. The military said it had seized power because of "the worsening situation in the country and the political crisis, which worsens continuously." Just hours after Nimeiry left for a visit to the U.S. on March 27, demonstrators took to the streets in Khartoum to denounce Nimeiry and the U.S. and to protest against a 33% increase in prices for essential commodities. The situation worsened on April 4 when a general strike brought the country to a virtual standstill. After seizing power, Siwar ad-Dahab promised to institute political, economic,

and social reforms; he also guaranteed freedom of the press, of religion, and of political organizations. Egypt, however, was especially anxious to learn how the new Sudanese regime would align itself politically because the two countries had formerly been of one mind in opposing the policies of Col. Muammar al-Qaddafi, the leader of Libya. Qaddafi had openly called for Nimeiry's overthrow and immediately recognized Siwar ad-Dahab's government. On April 24 The Sudan reciprocated by announcing it would resume diplomatic relations with Libya.

8 **India sues Union Carbide.** The government of India filed suit in a Manhattan Federal District Court charging Union Carbide Corp. with responsibility for the gas leak at its plant in Bhopal, India, on Dec. 3, 1984.

At least 1,700 people were killed and 200,000 more were injured. In addition to compensation for victims of the disaster, India was seeking punitive damages "in an amount sufficient to deter Union Carbide and any other multinational corporation from the willful, malicious and wanton disregard of the rights and safety of the citizens of those countries in which they do business."

9 **Japanese urged to buy foreign goods.** In a nationally televised address, Japanese Prime Minister Yasuhiro Nakasone urged his fellow countrymen to buy foreign goods even though certain local industries would "suffer pain" as a consequence. He warned his audience that failure to resolve Japan's foreign trade surplus could affect "the life and death of our country," because Japan could not survive without free trade. Nakasone conceded that some of Japan's import regulations had limited foreign access to Japanese markets. He then pointed out that both the U.S. Senate and the House of Representatives had debated the issues and then overwhelmingly authorized President Reagan to restrict Japanese imports. But Nakasone also said the U.S. shared blame for the present crisis. Among other things, he called attention to the high quality of Japanese products, their relatively low cost to American consumers, the strength of the U.S. dollar, and the fact that Japanese doing business in the U.S. speak English, "but do the Americans who come to Japan [to market U.S. products] speak Japanese? I haven't met any American salesmen who are fluent in Japanese." The prime minister asked every Japanese to spend $100 on foreign goods.

Verdicts rendered in Liu murder case. A three-judge panel in Taiwan convicted Ch'en Ch'i-li, the reputed head of an underworld syndicate called the Bamboo Union gang, of scripting the murder of a Chinese-American author and critic of the Taiwanese government, Henry Liu, in California in October 1984. His accomplice Wu Tun, who confessed to being one of the gunmen, was also convicted. Both were sentenced to life imprisonment. A third suspect was still at large. In a separate trial before a military tribunal, Vice-Adm. Wong Hsi-ling, who had headed the military intelligence bureau, was sentenced on April 19 as a "joint offender, or for assisting, in a homicide." During the trial Ch'en testified that Wong had ordered Liu's murder. Wong acknowledged that he had provided Ch'en with Liu's picture and address but insisted he had said only that Liu had to be "taught a lesson." Two of Wong's deputies were convicted of being accessories to the murder. Wong was given life imprisonment; the two others each received sentences of two and a half years. Although Henry Liu had written a biography critical of Pres. Chiang Ching-kuo, head of the Nationalist Chinese government in Taiwan, the ultimate reason for murdering Liu was never publicly revealed.

11 **Hoxha dies in Albania.** Enver Hoxha, Albania's 76-year-old Communist leader, died after a long, debilitating illness. As a World War

Armed with charts and graphs, Japan's Prime Minister Yasuhiro Nakasone presented a detailed analysis of U.S.-Japanese trade in a televised address to his countrymen in April.

II Communist guerrilla he had fought Italian and German occupation forces in his country, which had been annexed by Italy in 1939. After the war he established a Stalinist government, which he headed for 40 years. During that period Albania became more and more isolated, especially after Nikita Khrushchev denounced Stalin's "intolerance, brutality, and abuse of power" in 1956. Hoxha also found fault with China's decision to move back into the mainstream of world events. Pres. Ramiz Alia was expected to succeed Hoxha as first secretary of the Albanian (Communist) Party of Labour. He had assumed many responsibilities during Hoxha's illness and appeared to want to move the country toward normal relations with the rest of the world.

15 **South Africa abolishes racial sex laws.** The South African government announced that it had accepted the recommendations of a special parliamentary committee and would abolish laws that forbade marriage and sex between whites and nonwhites. The minister of cooperation and development said the decision "represents the dismantling of the negative aspects of apartheid." Conservatives in the government called the change a "pathetic" rejection of "one of the cornerstones of separate development." Although many welcomed the announcement, antiapartheid activists said it was merely cosmetic, a minor concession since blacks were still not allowed to exercise any political power. Many questions remained unanswered, such as where couples of different races could live, what schools their children could attend, and which hospitals and theatres would be available to them. Two days earlier some 60,000 persons attended a funeral ceremony in Kwanobuhle township near Uitenhage for 27 blacks killed during riots in the past month in black townships.

17 **Discrimination outlawed in Canada.** The antidiscrimination section of Canada's three-year-old

federal constitution became the law of the land even though many local laws had not yet been rewritten to conform to the principles laid down in the new Charter of Rights and Freedoms. The charter, which forbids discrimination on grounds of sex, colour, race, ethnic origin, religion, or mental or physical disability, was hailed by feminists as a great victory. It also constituted a milestone for the disabled, whose rights, it was believed, had never before been spelled out in the constitution of any nation.

19 **China to trim armed forces.** During a visit to New Zealand, Hu Yaobang (Hu Yao-pang), general secretary of the Chinese Communist Party, told reporters that China would cut about one million troops from its army by the end of 1986. The reduction would affect about 25% of those now in military service. Deng Xiaoping (Teng Hsiao-p'ing), China's paramount leader, believed that the nation's economy could not support the current military organization if China hoped to realize its goal of modernization. The fact that China's present leadership felt sufficiently confident to make such an announcement was seen as an important victory for Deng because diehard Maoists in the military had long opposed any erosion of their power. Deng's judicious military appointments, however, had systematically undermined opposition to his plans.

21 **Brazil's president-elect dies.** Tancredo Neves, Brazil's 75-year-old president-elect, died after intestinal surgery in São Paulo. On March 15 Vice-Pres. José Sarney had taken his oath of office and assumed the duties of president because Neves was hospitalized in critical condition. Sarney, who automatically became head of the government when Neves died, would be Brazil's first civilian president after five successive military regimes that held power for 21 years. He promised to implement the programs that Neves had advocated

during the campaign, including a vigorous attack on corruption in government On May 8 the Brazilian Congress approved a constitutional amendment that deprived the electoral college of the power to elect the president and transferred that right to the general electorate.

23 Violence continues in Gujarat. At least 15 persons were believed killed and about 100 injured as rival Hindu castes continued to clash in the state of Gujarat, India. In the industrial city of Ahmadabad, where much of the violence occurred, at least 55 persons had been killed in riots during the preceding two months. The latest violence was blamed in part on police who, on April 22, had deserted their posts and gone on a rampage through Ahmadabad. The minister of home affairs said the officers were bent on taking revenge for the brutal killing of a police sergeant, but other sources claimed the police had attacked newspaper offices and reporters to protest against stories charging them with brutality. The intercaste troubles had begun after state authorities announced that nearly half of government-controlled positions would be reserved for lower caste Hindus, who up to that time had been allotted 31% of such jobs.

24 Pope names 28 new cardinals. The Vatican revealed the names of 28 persons Pope John Paul II had chosen to elevate to the rank of cardinal. The group represented 19 different countries. Five of the appointees were from Italy; two cardinals each were named from the U.S., France, Poland, Canada, and West Germany. The list also included one new cardinal from each of the following countries: Austria, Belgium, Chile, Czechoslovakia, Ethiopia, India, The Netherlands, Nicaragua, Nigeria, the Philippines, Spain, and Venezuela. In addition, one new cardinal from the Soviet Union would represent Ukrainian Eastern Rite Catholics both inside and outside the U.S.S.R. The new appointments would increase membership in the College of Cardinals to 152, 60 of whom had been named by John Paul II. Only 120 cardinals were under the age of 80 and thus still eligible to vote in a papal election. Formal installation of the new cardinals was scheduled to take place in Rome on May 25.

25 Peruvian leftists concede election. After a three-hour meeting Peru's United Left coalition of Socialist and Communist parties decided to concede a scheduled runoff election between its Marxist candidate, Alfonso Barrantes Lingan, and Alan García Pérez, whose 46% of the popular vote in the April 14 presidential election was nearly twice that garnered by Barrantes though still short of the required 50%. García was expected to take his oath of office on July 28. It would be the first time in 40 years that one elected Peruvian president had turned over the duties of his office to another elected chief executive.

Nonaligned nations meet in Indonesia. Representatives from more than 80 nations ended a two-day meeting in Bandung, Indon., that commemorated the 30th anniversary of the founding of the nonaligned movement. In an official declaration the delegates stated that the world was "beset by pervasive tensions, violence, and growing insecurity" making the global situation more perilous than it had been in 1955, when 29 less developed African and Asian nations agreed not to become embroiled in the cold war being waged by the U.S. and the Soviet Union. One of many policy statements at that time was an evenhanded condemnation of "colonialism in all its manifestations." At both conferences China affirmed its intention to remain part of the nonaligned world. Only 29 Asian and African countries had attended the original Bandung Conference, although they had represented over half the world's population.

26 Warsaw Pact nations renew alliance. Representatives of Bulgaria, Czechoslovakia, East Germany, Hungary, Poland, Romania, and the Soviet Union signed a 20-year extension of their Warsaw Pact treaty. The agreement also provided an option that would renew the treaty for an additional 10 years after the 20 years had elapsed. The ceremony, presided over by Mikhail Gorbachev, the new leader of the Soviet Union, was held in the royal palace in Warsaw where the military alliance had first been formalized 30 years earlier.

MAY

2 Witness says she saw Aquino shot. Rebecca Quijano, a 32-year-old businesswoman, testified in a Manila courtroom that she was a passenger on the same plane that took Benigno Aquino, Jr., back to the Philippines in August 1983 and that she "saw a soldier holding a gun aimed at the back of Senator Aquino's head, and simultaneously I heard a gunshot." Quijano was the first person to swear in court to having been an eyewitness to the assassination, but defense attorneys chose not to cross-examine her. The dramatic testimony supported the conclusion reached earlier by an independent civilian panel of investigators, implicating the 26 persons standing trial.

3 Economic conference opens in Bonn. An international economic conference got under way in Bonn, West Germany, with little hope that all seven nations would agree on what steps should be taken to attack various problems. The participants included West German Chancellor Helmut Kohl, the host of the conference, Canadian Prime Minister Brian Mulroney, French Pres. François Mitterrand, British Prime Minister Margaret Thatcher, Italian Prime Minister Bettino Craxi, Japanese Prime Minister Yasuhiro Nakasone, and U.S. Pres. Ronald Reagan. Mitterrand alone opposed Reagan's proposal to begin, in 1986, worldwide negotiations to remove barriers to free trade. He also refused to endorse U.S. plans to develop defensive space weapons. Illegal traffic in drugs was discussed, but no specific program was adopted to curtail drug abuse. There was praise for U.S. efforts to negotiate an arms control agreement with the U.S.S.R. but dissatisfaction with the trade embargo Reagan had imposed on Nicaragua on May 1. The final communiqué noted that the international monetary system needed to be made more stable and effective.

5 Reagan visits Nazi cemetery. President Reagan, ignoring the pleas of Jewish organizations, protests by U.S. veterans' groups, and the advice of numerous congressmen, paid a brief visit to a military cemetery in West Germany in the company of Chancellor Helmut Kohl. When news spread that Reagan had accepted Kohl's request that they visit the cemetery, a heated controversy had arisen because 49 Nazi SS graves were among the 2,000 graves of German soldiers in the Bitburg cemetery. Reagan, insisting that his trip to Bitburg was "morally right," said his action was meant to symbolize "the great reconciliation" that had taken place between the U.S. and Germany since the end of World War II. The fact that Reagan and Kohl first went to the Bergen-Belsen concentration camp, where some 50,000 victims of Nazi atrocities lay buried in mass graves, did little to mute criticism of his visit to Bitburg.

U.S. Pres. Ronald Reagan and West German Chancellor Helmut Kohl stroll through the Bitburg cemetery; protests were sharp but short-lived.

WALKER—GAMMA/LIAISON

10 Indian Sikhs escalate attacks. Sikh extremists killed at least 70 persons and injured about 150 others in terrorist attacks in New Delhi and the states of Haryana, Uttar Pradesh, and Punjab. Most of the casualties occurred in New Delhi, the nation's capital, where a series of explosions was set off, apparently by remote control. Some people lost their lives when two buses were blown up in a crowded bus terminal. Prime Minister

Rajiv Gandhi called an emergency meeting of his Cabinet to discuss ways of preventing an immediate escalation of the violence, especially by angry Hindus seeking revenge. Although some 1,500 Sikhs were taken into custody and police patrols were increased, bombings continued.

11 **Salvadoran rebels attack mayors.** Leftist guerrillas in El Salvador acknowledged in a radio broadcast that they had made mayors their new target because local government officials had become part of "counterinsurgency plans financed by the United States." In recent weeks Salvadoran rebels had burned more than 30 offices of mayors, killed two newly elected mayors, and kidnapped at least eight others. The guerrillas had also resorted to more assassinations in San Salvador, the capital, and the killing of civilians. Such tactics were thought to be a desperate response to the government's antiguerrilla military operations, which had been considerably more successful during the past year and had contributed to the success of Pres. José Napoleón Duarte's Christian Democratic Party in the March elections.

14 **Violence spreads in Sri Lanka.** The Sri Lankan government reported that Tamil separatists disguised as soldiers had carried out several terrorist attacks in Anuradhapura, about 165 km (105 mi) north of Colombo, the capital. It was the first Tamil attack in an area heavily populated by Sinhalese. Most of the nearly 150 victims were waiting at a bus stop or congregated beneath a tree sacred to Buddhists. They included numerous women and children. The Hindu Tamils, who reportedly obtained weapons from India, sought independence from the mostly Buddhist Sinhalese, who comprised more than 70% of the island republic's population. After the attacks the government ordered a 16-hour curfew, but Sinhalese bent on revenge killed at least ten Tamils and burned as many homes. In another incident, one of many reported from other areas of Sri Lanka, more than 40 Tamils, including women and children, were reportedly hacked to death on a ferry boat off Jaffna. There was no indication that either group was prepared to set aside its animosities and reach a peaceful accommodation. On May 24 Sri Lankan Pres. J. R. Jayawardene said he intended to establish martial law courts to counter the "breakdown of law and order."

16 **Israel offers to return krytrons.** Officials at the Israeli Defense Ministry refused to comment on the U.S. federal grand jury indictment of Richard Smyth, who was accused of illegally supplying some 800 krytrons to Israel between 1979 and 1983. Nonetheless, Israel offered to return all its unused krytrons if the U.S. so requested. Most were reportedly still in storage. The high-speed timing devices could be used, among other things, to control nuclear explosions. During the course of the grand jury investigation, a U.S. agent was sent to Israel but obtained very little information from either the government or the importers because traffic in krytrons violated no Israeli law.

Sri Lankan soldiers surround the wreckage of a train derailed by Tamil separatist guerrillas.
SANDRO TUCCI—GAMMA/LIAISON

17 **Japanese women win job equality.** The Japanese Diet (parliament) approved a bill that opened up new job opportunities for women by removing certain restrictions on the time of day and number of hours they could work. Starting in 1986 employers were expected to begin adopting new policies to eliminate sex discrimination in hiring, promoting, and assigning jobs. Some women's groups were unhappy with the equal employment bill because employers who chose to ignore it faced no sanctions. Others objected that the proposed new employment practices would upset the Japanese way of life. Still others feared that many women would be forced against their will to work overtime. The greatest potential benefits would accrue to women executives, who could now legally put in the extra hours expected of most persons in managerial positions.

19 **Muslims battle in West Beirut.** Lebanese Shi'ah Muslim militiamen, mostly members of Amal, began a fierce battle to drive Palestinian forces out of three refugee camps—Sabra and Shatila in West Beirut and Burj al-Brajneh, south of the city. The Palestinians were mostly Sunni Muslims from dissident factions of the Palestine Liberation Organization and from the Marxist-oriented Democratic Front for the Liberation of Palestine. On May 23 more than 200 persons were reported to have been killed as both sides fought furiously with rocket-propelled grenades, mortars, antiaircraft guns, automatic and recoilless rifles, machine guns, and handguns. On May 31 the Shi'ahs claimed to be in control of Sabra and Shatila, but they acknowledged there was still stiff resistance at Burj al-Brajneh.

20 **U.S. Navy men arrested as spies.** John A. Walker, a retired U.S. Navy chief warrant officer, was arrested by agents of the Federal Bureau of Investigation and charged with spying for the Soviet Union. Walker reportedly had in his possession classified documents passed to him by his 22-year-old son, Michael, a yeoman third class, who was subsequently arrested aboard the aircraft

carrier USS *Nimitz* and returned to the U.S. A substantial quantity of classified materials was allegedly found near his bunk aboard ship. On May 29 Arthur Walker, a retired navy lieutenant commander and brother of John, was arrested and charged with espionage. Navy officials were quoted as saying they believed the case would prove to be one of the most serious breaches of security in U.S. Navy history.

Israel releases 1,150 prisoners. Under the supervision of International Red Cross officials, Israel released 394 guerrillas in Geneva and an additional 756 other prisoners in the Middle East in exchange for the last three Israeli soldiers still held by the Palestinians. Bruno Kreisky, former chancellor of Austria, played a key role in negotiating the exchange. Even though the nation as a whole rejoiced that the last Israeli prisoners of war had been released, the government was severely criticized by those who felt the nation had compromised its policy of never capitulating to terrorists. Defense Minister Yitzhak Rabin, however, said there was no other alternative because the three men were being held in Syria and could not be rescued. Others expressed outrage that convicted Arab terrorists had been set free but not Israelis convicted of similar crimes against Arabs. Japan, too, was upset because Israel had ignored a specific request not to release Kozo Okamoto, a member of the Japanese Red Army. He had been part of a three-man team of assassins who in 1972 killed 26 persons at the Lod Airport in Israel.

Strike in Sweden settled. Sweden's 265,-000-member civil servants' union accepted a government offer of a 2% pay increase effective in December, thereby ending an 18-day-old strike that had, among other things, closed down airports and crippled rail transportation. The union had already been granted a 5% increase through centralized negotiations with other unions, but members of the civil servants' union asked for an additional 3.1% to keep them on a par with peers who were employed by private businesses. A highly effective selective strike begun on May 2 by 20,000 civil servants had led to a lockout of an

additional 80,000 government workers, including 55,000 secondary school teachers.

21 **Pope visits Low Countries.** Pope John Paul II returned to Rome after completing a spiritual pilgrimage to Luxembourg, The Netherlands, and Belgium. The Netherlands stop was newsworthy because, for the first time during his papacy, John Paul was publicly mocked, ridiculed, and by many ignored. The visit to Utrecht was especially unpleasant because marchers carried an antipope banner and hurled rocks, bottles, and smoke bombs at the police and pelted the pope's car with eggs and other objects. The surprisingly small crowds that attended many of the public functions appeared to indicate that many of the most liberal-minded among the Dutch Roman Catholics had given up hope that the pope would ever modify the church's traditional stand on such things as homosexuality, abortion, and the ordination of women.

23 **Korean students stage sit-in.** About 70 South Korean university students began a peaceful occupation of the second-floor library of the U.S. Information Service Building in downtown Seoul. There was no effort to take hostages or restrict access to other parts of the building. The students demanded that the U.S. government apologize for its alleged role in suppressing the 1980 political upheaval in Kwangju that claimed some 200 lives. Because the commanding officer of U.S. troops in South Korea also served as the operational commander of most of South Korea's armed forces, the students accused the U.S. of complicity in violently suppressing political dissent. The U.S., however, had contended that the U.S. commander did not authorize any military action in Kwangju. On May 26 the students left the building carrying a South Korean flag and chanting "Down with the military dictatorship of Chun Doo Hwan" (president of South Korea). On May 28 the government arrested 25 of the protesters; if they were found guilty of the charges placed against them, they could be sentenced to prison for up to seven years.

25 **Cyclone ravages Bangladesh.** As many as 40,000 people in Bangladesh were believed drowned when a killer cyclone swept across the Bay of Bengal and drove a one-story-high wall of water across small inhabited islands in the delta of the Ganges River. Accurate figures on the number of those who lost their lives would probably never be known. When the fury subsided, countless human bodies were seen floating in the bay or strewn across the muddy terrain. The fate of thousands more was still unknown, but in just one area the homes of 50,000 families were destroyed. According to one radio report, 80% of the croplands suffered severe damage, and perhaps half a million head of cattle were killed or missing.

28 **Reagan proposes new tax system.** President Reagan, in a nationally televised address, set forth his proposals for a new federal income tax plan that would be "clear, simple, and fair" and would "reduce the tax burdens on the working people of this country." The new tax code, which would have to be enacted into law by Congress, would among many other things eliminate local and state taxes as deductible items but would substantially increase personal exemptions. Mortgage interest payments on a principal residence would still be deductible, but certain types of business expense deductions would be eliminated or reduced. According to White House calculations, 79% of individual U.S. taxpayers would have either lower or unchanged tax bills, with an overall reduction of 7%. On the other hand, corporations would on average pay 9% more. Rep. Dan Rostenkowski of Illinois, the Democratic chairman of the House Ways and Means Committee, which handles all revenue measures, wholeheartedly endorsed Reagan's initiative but stated that he viewed the specific proposals as merely a starting point for discussions.

JUNE

2 **Socialists win Greek election.** Incomplete election returns indicated that the Panhellenic Socialist Movement (Pasok) of Prime Minister Andreas Papandreou had won a majority of the seats in Greece's 300-member Parliament, but its percentage of the popular vote was somewhat less than in 1981. The conservative New Democracy Party, which finished in second place, received about 5% more of the popular vote than it had in the previous election. Papandreou called the election results "a victory for the people and a defeat for reaction." During the campaign the prime minister promised again to close down four U.S. military bases in Greece, but he conspicuously made no mention of an earlier pledge to withdraw from NATO and the European Communities.

Jayawardene confers with Gandhi. During a visit to New Delhi, Sri Lankan Pres. J. R. Jayawardene discussed with Indian Prime Minister Rajiv Gandhi Sri Lanka's difficulties in quelling the escalating ethnic conflicts between Sinhalese and the minority Hindu Tamils, some of whom seemed determined to gain independence through violent means. India was believed to hold the key to a peaceful settlement because it was thought that the Tamil insurgents in Sri Lanka obtained their arms, and possibly military training, in the Indian state of Tamil Nadu. One peace proposal reportedly under consideration included the establishment of a provincial council in territory dominated by the Tamils; they might also be given limited authority over local police.

3 **Vatican and Italy ratify concordat.** The Vatican and Italy exchanged documents ratifying a concordat that replaced the Lateran Treaty of 1929 and significantly reduced the privileges the church had previously enjoyed in Italy. The new treaty no longer recognized Roman Catholicism as the state religion or Rome as a sacred city, but it affirmed the independence of Vatican City. Tax exemptions for religious institutions would henceforth be more strictly interpreted, and state subsidies for the clergy would be phased out by 1990. Other provisions ended compulsory Catholic instruction in public schools and abrogated Vatican ownership of the Jewish catacombs.

8 **Hungarian independents score victories.** In elections to the 352-seat Hungarian Parliament, 25 of 71 independent candidates waged successful campaigns. All were first obliged to pledge in writing that, if elected, they would not challenge the socialist structure of the government. Since 1949, when Hungary held its first election under Communist rule, only one candidate had been elected to Parliament without the endorsement of the (Communist) Patriotic People's Front.

10 **Israel completes Lebanon pullout.** Israel completed its three-stage withdrawal of combat troops from Lebanon but left an unannounced number of patrols, advisers, and observers in the "security zone" it had established in Lebanon along Israel's northern border. The Israelis who remained in Lebanon would assist the Christian-led

A hooded hijacker sits directly behind John Testrake, pilot of the TWA jetliner that was held for over two weeks in Beirut in June.
GAMMA/LIAISON

South Lebanon Army, which had accepted responsibility for defending the area with Israeli-supplied equipment. The feeling in Israel was one of general relief that the nation's three-year direct military involvement in Lebanon had ended.

11 **Spy exchange takes place in Berlin.** On a bridge linking East Germany and West Berlin, the U.S. released four Eastern Europeans serving prison terms for spying in exchange for 25 Western agents held in East Germany and Poland. The agreement included family members who wanted to enter

West Berlin. Two of the 25 preferred, for personal reasons, to remain behind, but they were allowed two weeks to reconsider their decisions. Although no U.S. citizens were involved in the exchange, the Justice Department conceded that some of those being returned to the West were "of interest" to the U.S. During the three years of negotiations, the U.S. had sought in vain to have Soviet dissidents Andrey Sakharov and Anatoly Scharansky included among those released, but the U.S.S.R. reportedly refused even to consider it.

Karen Ann Quinlan dies. Karen Ann Quinlan died in Morris Plains, N.J., at the age of 31. After she became irreversibly comatose on April 14, 1975, her parents urged the doctors to disconnect the respirator so that their daughter could die "with grace and dignity." When the doctors refused, the Quinlans took the matter to court. A Superior Court judge sided with the doctors, but he was later overruled by the New Jersey Supreme Court, which decided in a unanimous opinion that the father had the right to seek out doctors who would remove the life-supporting systems. The courts, in an unprecedented statement, also ruled that no one could be held criminally liable for such an action because resultant death "would not be homicide, but rather expiration from existing natural causes." After the respirator was removed, Quinlan continued to breathe on her own.

12 **Contras to get U.S. aid.** The U.S. House of Representatives voted 248–184 to allocate $27 million in nonmilitary aid to Nicaraguan *contras* fighting to overthrow the country's Sandinista government. The bill stated that neither the Pentagon nor the Central Intelligence Agency could distribute the money, which would be dispersed over a period of nine months. Since the Senate had not ruled out CIA involvement in its version of the bill and had defined nonmilitary aid in broader terms than the House had, members of both branches of Congress would have to resolve these and other differences before submitting the bill to the president for his signature. After the House voted against aid to the *contras* in April, Nicaraguan Pres. Daniel Ortega traveled to Moscow to seek Soviet assistance. This and other considerations apparently caused certain congressmen to have second thoughts about totally abandoning the rebels.

14 **Terrorists seize TWA plane.** Two Shi'ah Muslims, said to be members of Islamic Jihad ("Islamic Holy War"), hijacked a Trans World Airlines plane after it left Athens on a scheduled flight to Rome. Of the 153 passengers and crew aboard, 104 were Americans. The pilot was forced to fly to Beirut, then to Algiers, then back to Beirut, where one of the passengers, 23-year-old U.S. Navy diver Robert Stethem, was brutally beaten and then shot to death. About a dozen other soldiers that were members of the more mainstream Shi'ah Amal militia then joined the original two gunmen. Israel, which was not directly involved in the affair, said it would not consider acceding to the hijackers' demand

Argentines wait patiently in long lines at a Buenos Aires bank to exchange their pesos for the new currency, australs.

VILLALOBOS—GAMMA/LIAISON

that it free the more than 700 prisoners (mostly Shi'ah) it had captured in Lebanon unless the U.S. made a public request that it do so. The U.S. declined to do so. Finally, on June 30, the 39 hostages who had not been among those released in stages during the 17-day crisis were driven from Beirut to Damascus, Syria, where they boarded a flight to West Germany. Though Israel released 31 prisoners on June 24, it insisted that the decision was in no way connected with the hijacking since it had long intended to release the prisoners in groups.

Argentina discards peso. Argentine Pres. Raúl Alfonsín went on national television to explain new steps the government was taking to implement "a profound reform of our economic system with the objective of reconstructing and modernizing Argentina." A new currency called the austral would have a fixed value of $1.25, approximately 1,000 times more than the peso that it replaced. Salaries would be frozen as of July 1, and prices would not be allowed to rise above the level in effect on June 13. In addition, the government would no longer resort to deficit spending or to indexing as a way to keep pace with inflation, which had been running at an annual rate in excess of 1,000%. Many Argentines believed the plan could work if the government did not capitulate to pressure, especially from labour unions, but there were also worries that the severity of the measures could lead to political and social unrest.

Poland sentences three activists. Three political activists were sentenced to prison in Gdansk, Poland, after being found guilty of fomenting civil disorder. They had been accused of planning a nationwide 15-minute strike, which never took place, to protest against increases in food prices. Less than a year earlier, the defendants had been freed in a general amnesty along with some 600 other defenders of Solidarity. The three men were sentenced to prison terms of 42 months, 30 months, and 24 months. Lech Walesa, who testified during the trial, told foreign reporters,

who had not been permitted to enter the courtroom, that he told the judge, "I know three innocent people are sitting in the dock."

15 **Lebanese free 21 UN troops.** Gen. Antoine Lahd, the Christian commander of the South Lebanon Army (SLA), ordered the release of 21 Finnish soldiers who had been seized on June 7. All were members of the ten-nation United Nations Interim Force in Lebanon. Lahd agreed to set the Finnish hostages free after the International Red Cross assured him that the Finns had turned over 11 members of the SLA to Amal, the Shi'ah Muslim militia, only because the men wanted to defect. Each SLA member had given the Red Cross a written statement affirming his desire to sever connections with the SLA and join fellow Shi'ah farther north.

17 **Namibia given limited autonomy.** South Africa named a new multiracial administration in South West Africa/Namibia but retained the right to defend the country and dictate its foreign policy. In 1978 South Africa had attempted to defuse political unrest in Namibia by installing a surrogate regime, but when the plan collapsed in 1983, South Africa resumed direct control over the former German colony. A definitive settlement was hampered by the presence of Cuban troops in neighbouring Angola, a Marxist state, and by repeated attacks against Namibia by the South West Africa People's Organization (SWAPO) based in Angola. By June 19 the UN Security Council had issued a weak statement calling for "appropriate measures" against South Africa if it did not respond to UN efforts to grant Namibia full independence. On June 30 South African troops once again clashed with SWAPO in Angola, reportedly killing 16 guerrillas.

20 **Electricity towers bombed in Chile.** After a series of antigovernment protests and the arrest of demonstrators in various parts of the country, five electricity transmitting

towers were damaged by bombs in Chile's central valley. The saboteurs, who cut off power to some nine million people, were not identified. However, on May 24 the Manuel Rodríguez Patriotic Front, a leftist guerrilla organization, had claimed responsibility for a similar bombing of Chile's largest power station. Although Pres. Augusto Pinochet Ugarte had recently lifted the state of siege he had imposed on the country, a state of emergency, which restricted personal freedoms and broadened the powers of the police, was still in force.

Bombings reported in Nepal. Terrorists detonated five bombs in Kathmandu, the capital of Nepal, in separate attacks on the royal palace, government buildings, and a hotel. Seven people were reported killed and 24 wounded in what was believed to be the first terrorist incident in the Himalayan kingdom. Though no one claimed responsibility for the bombings, suspicions centred on political opponents of King Birendra Bir Bikram Shah Deva, who were clamouring for a return to

multiparty government. Leaflets were also found in Kathmandu streets that said a group called the United Liberation Army took responsibility for the attacks. King Birendra told the National Assembly that the Nepalese had a duty to oppose those who tried to destabilize a system freely chosen by the people themselves. In a 1979 national referendum, voters had approved the present government structure by a narrow margin.

Norwegian guilty of spying. Seven judges of the Norwegian Crown Court convicted Arne Treholt, a 42-year-old former diplomat, of espionage and sentenced him to 20 years in prison. Treholt was also ordered to turn over nearly $150,000, most of which represented money he had received for espionage. Treholt was found guilty of passing classified or sensitive information to agents of the Soviet Union from 1974 until his arrest in January 1984. When taken into custody he was carrying 66 documents that authorities said were to have been handed over to a Soviet agent in Vienna. Besides purely

military information, Treholt also had provided the Soviets with details of private meetings between Norwegian officials and important foreign dignitaries, including Lord Carrington of Great Britain, Helmut Schmidt of West Germany, and Henry Kissinger of the U.S.

21 **Mengele's remains identified.** An international team of forensic experts announced in São Paulo, Brazil, that the exhumed remains of a man who had reportedly drowned in 1979 were in fact those of Josef Mengele, the notorious Nazi doctor. On June 11 Mengele's son had issued a statement in West Germany saying he had no doubt that the grave in Embu, which bore the name Wolfgang Gerhard, contained his father's remains. He also claimed to have gone to Brazil in 1979 to confirm the circumstances of his father's death. Mengele had sent tens of thousands of men, women, and children to their deaths at the Auschwitz-Birkenau extermination camp in Poland and had personally selected others, especially twins, as subjects for his medical experiments.

JULY

1 **Shevardnadze joins Politburo.** Eduard A. Shevardnadze was made a full member of the Soviet Communist Party Politburo, the fourth such appointment made by Mikhail Gorbachev since he came to power in March. Grigory V. Romanov's resignation from the Politburo was reportedly tendered for reasons of health. He was once regarded as Gorbachev's chief rival for the Soviet leadership. Gorbachev had also made three appointments to the Communist Party Secretariat, thus guaranteeing that his domestic and foreign policies would have strong support. On July 2 Shevardnadze replaced Andrey Gromyko as foreign minister. Gromyko, who was 75 years old, had been honoured with the title of president of the Soviet Union after years of dedicated service.

6 **Mugabe's party wins election.** The Zimbabwe African National Union-Patriotic Front won 63 of 79 contested seats allotted to blacks in Zimbabwe's 100-seat Parliament. Voting in one constituency was postponed because one of the candidates had died. Prime Minister Robert Mugabe interpreted the victory as a mandate to do away with the British-drafted constitution, which reserved 20 seats for whites, who comprised less than 2% of the population. Mugabe's victory, however, did not extend to all parts of the country as he had hoped. The party of his chief political rival, Joshua Nkomo, won 15 seats in Matabeleland. That pocket of opposition was expected to make it more difficult for the prime minister to unite the country, as he had planned, under "one political umbrella."

7 **Guinea rebels to be shot.** Brig. Gen. Lansana Conté, president of Guinea, told a cheering crowd in the capital city of Conakry that the leader of a failed coup had just been captured

Killing, looting, and burning became commonplace in Kampala, Uganda, in the days following the July coup that overthrew Pres. Milton Obote.

and that he and his collaborators would be tried and shot. Col. Diara Traoré, a former prime minister, had attempted to seize power while Conté was out of the country attending a meeting in Togo of the Economic Community of West African States. Traoré had taken part in the 1984 coup that followed the death of Pres. Ahmed Sékou Touré and brought Conté to power.

OPEC still at odds over prices. The 13 oil ministers of the Organization of Petroleum Exporting Countries (OPEC) ended a three-day meeting in Vienna without agreeing on any change in the price or production level of oil. With OPEC production at the lowest level in 20 years and such nations as Mexico threatening to undercut OPEC prices even further, the OPEC ministers faced a difficult task in trying to recover their previous share of the world market. During the past ten years OPEC's share of the market had dropped from 53 to 30%, mainly because of competition from Great

Britain, Norway, and Mexico. Toward the end of the month the oil ministers met again, this time in Geneva. In a 10–3 vote they agreed to reduce some oil prices moderately, but Algeria, Libya, and Iran refused to endorse the decision of the majority.

8 **Egypt curbing fundamentalism.** Egyptian Pres. Hosni Mubarak's ban on religious bumper stickers went into effect without significant opposition. Mubarak, who had become increasingly concerned about the spread of Islamic fundamentalism throughout the region, reportedly outlawed the stickers because they had become part of a campaign to turn Egypt into an Islamic state. In an earlier move to curb the influence of fundamentalists, the Ministry of Religious Affairs had appointed its own sheikh to preach in the Noor mosque, a stronghold of Islamic fundamentalism in Cairo, where Sheikh Hafez Salama had been demanding that Egypt be governed

by Islamic law. On July 13 Salama and 13 of his supporters were arrested on charges of sedition. Other "agitators" were also arrested in other parts of the country.

9 **Stockman resigns Cabinet post.** David Stockman announced that he would resign on August 1 as director of the Office of Management and Budget for the Reagan administration. Stockman, who had fought tirelessly to control federal budget deficits by reducing government spending, had exercised exceptional power during his tenure. Friends and foes alike conceded that his mastery of facts and figures and his understanding of the federal bureaucracy were the main factors in his success. Most of those who challenged his policies did so on philosophical principles or to protect their own interests. Stockman's announcement dismayed some members of a joint House-Senate committee struggling to work out a federal budget for the next fiscal year. They had planned on having Stockman's advice until the task was completed.

10 **Greenpeace ship sunk.** Two explosions aboard the *Rainbow Warrior,* a ship belonging to an environmental group called Greenpeace, sank the 49-m (160-ft) vessel while it was moored to a wharf in Auckland, N.Z. A Portuguese-born photographer with Dutch citizenship was killed. The ship had been scheduled to sail to the South Pacific to disrupt French nuclear tests. On July 11 Auckland's detective superintendent reported that preliminary evidence indicated sabotage because an examination of the hull showed that an explosive device had been placed on the outside of the ship near the engine room. On July 23 a man and a woman carrying Swiss passports were arrested as suspects in the case. They were later identified as French external security agents.

13 **Reagan undergoes surgery.** President Reagan underwent major abdominal surgery at the Bethesda (Md.) Naval Medical Center to remove a polyp found growing in his large intestine. Though the surgeons reported there was no visual evidence of cancer, a biopsy later revealed that the growth was malignant. Before the operation Reagan temporarily transferred his presidential powers to Vice-Pres. George Bush in accordance with the 25th Amendment to the Constitution. Some eight hours later Reagan reclaimed the powers of his office. On July 20 the president returned to the White House looking remarkably fit. Doctors expressed confidence that the timely surgery had prevented cancer cells from migrating to any other part of the president's body.

14 **Bolivians vote in general election.** Bolivians cast ballots in a national election that some feared would be nullified by a military coup or invalidated because of fraud. Early returns indicated that 59-year-old Hugo Banzer Suárez, candidate of the Nationalist Democratic Action (ADN) party and a retired general who had ruled Bolivia after a 1971 military coup, would win a plurality. His closest rival was 77-year-old Víctor Paz Estenssoro, a former president

representing the Revolutionary Nationalist Movement (MNR). When a final tally showed that no candidate had received 50% of the popular vote, which was needed for outright victory, the newly elected Congress exercised its right by naming Paz Estenssoro president on August 5. The MNR had won 59 seats in the Congress and the ADN 51. With inflation rising at an astronomical rate and the country in a deep financial crisis, there would be no easy way for Paz Estenssoro to solve the country's economic problems.

15 **UN holds women's conference.** A 12-day women's conference opened in Nairobi, Kenya, to mark the end of the United Nations Decade for Women. The meeting was called to assess the achievements and failures of the past 10 years and to set goals for the next 15 years. More than 2,000 official delegates came from nearly 160 nations, 8 of which were not members of the UN. Women's issues, however, were repeatedly shunted aside when various delegates introduced such topics as international terrorism, conflicts and disagreements between nations, and problems in the Middle East. On one occasion Arab delegates walked out when an Israeli delegate spoke. Later the U.S. and Israeli delegations threatened to walk out if the final conference document equated Zionism with racism. The phrase was deleted. In its final form the conference statement dealt mostly with nonpolitical problems faced by women and suggested long-term approaches to solve them. Even so, Maureen Reagan, the chief U.S. delegate and the daughter of the president, called the conference "an orgy of hypocrisy" and said the U.S. should carefully consider whether it should participate in future meetings.

17 **Japan's election system denounced.** The Japanese Supreme Court ruled that the 1983 elections to the Diet (parliament) were invalid because inequities in the procedures made some votes worth more than others and thus violated the constitution. The court, however, did not invalidate the results because, it said, it would not be in the public interest to do so. The ruling, which was the third such declaration since 1976, increased the likelihood that a special session of the Diet would be called to consider reapportionment. Politicians agreed that any shift of farm votes to the constantly expanding metropolitan areas would adversely affect the long-ruling Liberal-Democratic Party.

18 **South Korean students arrested.** The South Korean government announced that 56 student activists had been arrested in recent weeks and that 20 others were still being sought; all were said to belong to the organization that planned the May 23 sit-in at a U.S. government building in Seoul. Korean officials said the group was "a pro-Communist organization serving the cause of the enemy." The government had freed some student dissidents the previous year after announcing that the police would not disrupt campus demonstrations unless university authorities requested intervention. That policy was reviewed

New Soviet Foreign Minister Eduard A. Shevardnadze (right) greets U.S. Secretary of State George Shultz in Helsinki, Finland, in July.

F. LOCHON—GAMMA/LIAISON

and changed after protests against the government of Pres. Chun Doo Hwan became more violent.

20 **OAU ends conference in Ethiopia.** The Organization of African Unity ended a three-day meeting in Addis Ababa, Eth., with a declaration that most African nations were on the brink of economic collapse. While acknowledging the existence of "some domestic policy shortcomings," the delegates placed most of the blame for Africa's problems on "an unjust and inequitable economic system." In wide-ranging discussions they condemned the secret removal of African Jews to Israel and warned the U.S. against any involvement in the internal affairs of Angola. They also discussed the composition of a Pan-African anthem, cooperation between African and Arab states, and ways to control a disease that had been attacking cattle. Special attention was paid to improving agriculture and to the continent's huge foreign debts.

22 **Jewish terrorists sentenced.** An Israeli court sentenced 15 Jews to prison for crimes committed against Palestinian Arabs on the West Bank. On July 10 a panel of three judges had found the suspects guilty of a number of crimes, including murder, membership in a terrorist organization, and plotting to blow up Islam's holiest shrine in Jerusalem. Three of the 15 who stood trial were sentenced to life imprisonment; the 12 others received sentences ranging from three to ten years. Israeli Pres. Chaim Herzog, an outspoken critic of Jewish terrorism, was the only person who had authority to grant amnesty to the men, who were viewed by some as heroes and by others as dangerous extremists. He said he would judge each case brought before him on its individual merits.

23 **Chinese president visits U.S.** President Reagan, in an abbreviated ceremony, welcomed Chinese Pres. Li Xiannian (Li Hsien-nien) to the White House to mark the beginning of an official state visit. Li, a specialist in economics, was named president in 1983 when the office was restored after an interval of eight years. The most

important event during Li's visit was the signing of a nuclear agreement between the U.S. and China. China would receive U.S. nuclear equipment and technology with the understanding that they would be used exclusively for peaceful purposes.

24 **Gandhi and Sikh leaders reach accord.** Indian Prime Minister Rajiv Gandhi told a surprised Parliament that an agreement had been reached with moderate Sikh leaders that was designed to lessen hostility toward the central government. Concessions included the enlargement of Punjab's boundaries to increase the Sikh population within the state and thus enhance Sikh political power in the area; Sikhs who had been arrested during riots over the past three years would be accorded more lenient treatment; and greater compensation would be given to victims of the 1984 anti-Sikh riots. The following day two militant Sikh groups denounced the accord as a betrayal of Sikh rights. Other Sikh leaders, however, welcomed the settlement.

27 **Ugandan president overthrown.** Ugandan Pres. Milton Obote was overthrown in a military coup led by Brig. Basilio Olara Okello. Obote had seized power in 1966, four years after becoming prime minister when Uganda gained independence from Great Britain. He was ousted by Idi Amin in 1971 but was reelected president in a controversial election in 1980. The latest coup appeared to be the result of rivalry between two northern tribes within the Army, the Acholi represented by Okello and the Langi represented by Obote. On July 29 Lieut. Gen. Tito Okello, who was not related to the leader of the coup, was sworn in as interim head of state.

28 **García takes over in Peru.** Alan García Pérez, the 36-year-old leader of the Alianza Popular Revolucionaria Americana, replaced Fernando Belaúnde Terry as president of Peru. García had become president-elect on June 1 when the National Election Board ruled that no runoff election needed to be held because Alfonso Barrantes Lingan, runner-up in the April 14 election, had withdrawn from the race. In his inaugural speech García reaffirmed a campaign promise that Peru would not allocate more than 10% of its export profits to service its $14 billion foreign debt. He also confirmed his intention to deal directly with Peru's creditors rather than with the International Monetary Fund, which García claimed shared responsibility for many of Peru's current financial problems.

30 **Helsinki talks underscore differences.** The foreign ministers of 35 nations met in Helsinki, Fin., to mark the tenth anniversary of the signing of the Helsinki accords on security and cooperation in Europe. U.S. Secretary of State George Shultz used the occasion to accuse the Soviet Union of violating human rights; the new Soviet foreign minister, Eduard Shevardnadze (who had replaced Andrey Gromyko after his elevation to the presidency), denounced the U.S. for building up its military arsenal. Shultz also chided the U.S.S.R. for its policies regarding such things as religion, labour unions, and emigration. Shevardnadze countered that his country had eliminated poverty, unemployment, homelessness, and racial discrimination and should serve as a model for other countries. The two men later met to discuss plans for the scheduled November meeting between Soviet leader Mikhail Gorbachev and President Reagan.

AUGUST

1 **U.S. Congress passes budget.** After months of haggling, the U.S. Senate and House of Representatives approved the basic outline for a 1986 federal budget that would trim $55.5 billion from the projected deficit and $276.2 billion from deficits over the next three years. Some members of Congress believed the latter projection was overly optimistic. The 1986 budget set spending at $967.6 billion, revenues at $795.7 billion, and the resultant deficit at $171.9 billion. Revenue sharing with the states was the only major federal program eliminated.

5 **South African blacks go on trial.** The trial of 16 black leaders, all charged with treason, got under way in Pietermaritzburg, South Africa. The accused were members of the United Democratic Front, which opposed the government of Pres. P. W. Botha. The trial was being compared to one in 1964 when Nelson Mandela was sentenced to life imprisonment; this time, however, the defendants could be given death sentences. The nonjury trial was being conducted by a white judge who had power to rule on points of law and by two assessors, one Indian and one black, who could overrule the judge on points of fact. In a detailed 587-page indictment, the defendants were accused of forming an alliance with the outlawed African National Congress, which was based in Zambia and was committed to overthrowing the white government of South Africa. Twenty-two other blacks were facing charges of treason in a separate trial.

FALN terrorists convicted. Four members of a Puerto Rican terrorist group called the Armed Forces of National Liberation (FALN) were convicted of seditious conspiracy in a Chicago Federal District Court. Alejandrina Torres, Edwin Cortés, and Alberto Rodríguez had described themselves as "armed combatants" waging war for Puerto Rican independence. As "prisoners of war" they claimed immunity from prosecution. A fourth person facing trial, José Rodríguez, pleaded innocent. The FALN had taken responsibility for some 120 bombings in U.S. cities between 1974 and 1983. Five persons had been killed and many buildings severely

MATSUMOTO—SYGMA

Airborne troops carried in by helicopter were the first rescue workers to reach the site of August's Japan Air Lines crash.

damaged. In the Chicago area 28 such incidents occurred between 1975 and 1979. On October 4 Torres, Cortés, and Alberto Rodríguez were all sentenced to 35 years in prison. José Rodríguez, who was judged to have been only peripherally involved, was placed on probation for five years.

6 **President of Guyana dies.** Forbes Burnham, president of the South American republic of Guyana, died at the age of 62 after undergoing surgery. He was succeeded by Prime Minister Desmond Hoyte, who had served as a senior Cabinet minister for more than a decade. Burnham had hoped to make the former British colony self-sufficient regarding basic needs, but the nation's economy began to sag with falling prices for its chief exports—rice, sugar, and bauxite.

7 **Arab League meets in Morocco.** King Hassan II of Morocco opened an emergency meeting of the Arab League hoping that frank discussions of issues that divided Arab nations, including all aspects of the "Palestinian question," would revitalize the organization. Algeria, Lebanon, Libya, South Yemen, and Syria boycotted the conference and only 10 of the 16 nations in attendance were represented by heads of state. In a final communiqué, the participants "took note" of the Jordanian-Palestinian plan for peace talks with Israel, thereby satisfying both those who supported such talks and those who opposed them.

10 **Ugandan leaders to meet rebels.** Gen. Tito Okello, appointed interim head of state after a suc-

cessful military coup in Uganda on July 27, announced that the new government would hold talks with the rebel National Resistance Army (NRA) in the hope of finally terminating decades of political upheaval. Though the NRA was not the only antigovernment force causing unrest, its cooperation was considered essential in working out a lasting peace settlement. Okello spoke in a public square in Kampala, where more than 1,000 political prisoners, jailed by the ousted government, were released. Many had been held in maximum-security prisons for years, and some had been detained under security laws even after they had been acquitted of the charges leveled against them.

12 **Airliner crashes in Japan.** A Japan Air Lines jumbo jet crashed in central Japan after the pilot lost control of the disabled aircraft. Only 4 of the 524 persons aboard were found alive when rescue teams finally reached the site of the crash. It was the worst single plane disaster in the history of aviation. On August 13 a navy ship retrieved part of the plane's tail in waters some 130 km (80 mi) from where the plane went down, but it was not possible to determine without careful investigation what caused the accident.

13 **Attempt to impeach Marcos fails.** The Philippine National Assembly's Committee on Justice, Human Rights, and Good Government rejected a motion to impeach Pres. Ferdinand Marcos for alleged graft and corruption, violations of the constitution, and other "high crimes." Sixteen of the 25 members of the committee belonged to the ruling New Society Movement (NSM). One member of the opposition remarked: "If this motion is overruled, it will not be by the merits of the case but by the tyranny of numbers." Members of the NSM, however, described the opposition's efforts at impeachment as "nothing more than a product of unsubstantiated news reports, irresponsible speculations and gossips, and baseless conclusions motivated by petty partisan intentions."

14 **Hanoi returns U.S. dead.** The government of Vietnam turned over to U.S. officials what were said to be the remains of 26 Americans killed during the Vietnam war. The remains were then flown to Honolulu, where experts would attempt to make positive identifications. Although Vietnam had previously handed over the remains of 99 other persons, an additional 2,464 U.S. servicemen and civilians were still unaccounted for in Indochina, more than half of them in Vietnam. A Vietnamese deputy foreign minister told reporters that his government would also permit U.S. officials to enter Vietnam to discuss the entire issue of Americans still listed as missing in action. He also pledged that Vietnam would exert every effort to find the remains of all MIAs within the next two years so that the matter could finally be put to rest.

15 **Botha takes tough stand.** South African Pres. P. W. Botha, in a speech many hoped would signal

The death toll, particularly among young blacks, arising from continued unrest in South Africa mounted throughout the year.
CHIASSON—GAMMA/LIAISON

a historic change in the country's system of apartheid, told an audience of 1,800 whites in Durban that he was "not prepared to lead white South Africans and other minority groups on a road to abdication and suicide." He later added: "The violence of our enemies is a warning to us. We who are committed to peaceful negotiation also have a warning to them. Our warning is that our readiness to negotiate should not be mistaken for weakness. . . . Don't push us too far." For those who had expected Botha to make greater concessions to the black majority than those set forth in his speech, the address was both disappointing and discouraging. The following day Bishop Desmond Tutu, the 1984 recipient of the Nobel Peace Prize, said he felt, after hearing Botha's speech, that the nation was "on the brink of a catastrophe."

Gandhi moves to resolve Assam conflict. Indian Prime Minister Rajiv Gandhi announced that plans had been approved for ending the violence that had periodically flared up in the state of Assam between native Hindus and illegal immigrants, most of whom were Muslims from Bangladesh. The worst riots had occurred during the 1983 state elections, when some 5,000 people lost their lives. The prime minister said that new elections would be held in the near future, but no immigrant who had arrived in Assam after 1965 would be allowed to vote. In addition, the hundreds of thousands of illegal immigrants who had entered Assam after 1971 would be deported, although no one was sure that mass deportation was practical.

20 **Sikh leader assassinated.** Sant Harchand Singh Longowal, president of the moderate Sikh party Akali Dal, was shot and killed by fellow Sikhs in Punjab. Two of the alleged assassins were quickly captured, but two others who managed to escape were being sought by police. On July 24 Longowal and Indian Prime Minister Rajiv Gandhi had signed an accord that both hoped would end violence between Sikhs and Hindus in the state of Punjab and would quiet demands of Sikh extremists for total independence from India.

Car bomb kills 44 in Tripoli. A car bomb detonated in Saddun Square in Tripoli, Lebanon, killed 44 persons and wounded 90. It was the fifth such explosion in Lebanon in a week and raised the cumulative death toll to about 150. In the latest incident the bomb-laden car had been parked near the home of Sheikh Kenaan Naji, the leader of the Soldiers of God. The group was a Sunni Muslim fundamentalist militia backed by the Palestine Liberation Organization (PLO). Because the Soldiers of God had been fighting the Syrian-supported Arabian Knights for control of the city, there was speculation that Syria may have instigated the bombing. On August 17 at least 50 people had been killed when a car bomb was detonated in a Christian suburb of East Beirut. Two days later 29 persons died when a similar explosion took place in the Muslim section of the city.

23 **West German spy scandal grows.** West Germany reported that Hans J. Tiedge, who had been missing since August 19, had defected to East Germany. He had held sensitive posts in West Germany's counterintelligence agency for two decades and knew the identities of numerous contact persons in East Germany. It seemed likely, therefore, that Tiedge had been at least partly responsible for the apprehension of scores of West German agents during the previous 18 months. After a flurry of sudden disappearances and arrests, the spy story took a distinctly different turn on August 25 when it was learned that the East German chargé d'affaires in Buenos Aires, Arg., had defected to West Germany.

27 **Crocker Bank heavily fined.** The U.S. Treasury Department announced that it had fined the Crocker National Bank of San Francisco $2,250,000 for failing to report some $3.9 billion in cash transactions over a period of four years. This was the most severe penalty ever imposed under the Banking Secrecy Act, designed to help trace money involved in crime. The law applied only to sums of $10,000 or more. A Treasury spokesman said there was no evidence that bank employees had deliberately

laundered money, even though the bank had unquestionably been used for that purpose by drug dealers from Mexico and the Far East. If an Internal Revenue investigation found evidence of criminal activity, the case would be turned over to the Federal Bureau of Investigation.

31 **Thousands of South African blacks attend mass funeral.** An estimated 70,000 South African blacks gathered in the small township of Duncan Village for a mass funeral of 18 persons who had been killed in recent violence. It was believed to have been the largest funeral procession since widespread violence began to sweep across the country 12 months earlier. The gathering also disregarded provisions of the state of emergency that Pres. P. W. Botha had declared in July. A similar demonstration was expected to take place in Cape Town, where 29 persons had lost their lives in recent days. On August 9 officials had reported that 32 people had been killed in the Cape Town area in just 24 hours.

Bolivian miners strike. Bolivian authorities, concerned about possible violence, ordered a police alert as miners began a 48-hour strike to protest steps the government had taken to curb inflation. Earlier in the year labour unions had organized a 16-day general strike when the government devalued the peso by 82%. This time the new government of Pres. Víctor Paz Estenssoro floated the peso, thereby effectively devaluing it by 95%. Other measures included the freezing of salaries until December, the raising of gasoline prices by 1,000%, and the resetting of the official exchange rate twice a week. Exporters would thus be encouraged to increase production because they would be paid realistic prices for their goods.

SEPTEMBER

1 **Titanic wreck found.** A team of U.S. and French marine explorers positively identified the wreck of the luxury liner *Titanic*, which sank some 150 km (95 mi) off the coast of Newfoundland in 1912 with the loss of more than 1,500 lives. Using underwater robots, television cameras, sonar, and other equipment, the crew was able to locate and then photograph the ship, which was remarkably well preserved and sitting upright on the ocean floor about 4 km (2.5 mi) below the surface of the sea. It did not appear likely that any effort would be made to bring the ship to the surface.

2 **Pol Pot said to retire.** The Khmer Rouge announced that Pol Pot was retiring as leader of the Communist organization. He had ruled Kampuchea for four years until Vietnam invaded the country in 1979. As many as two million people were believed to have been killed during Pol Pot's reign of terror. In recent years the Khmer Rouge had been associated with the non-Communist Khmer People's National Liberation Front led by Son Sann and with the followers of Prince Norodom Sihanouk. The unlikely alliance was based on shared opposition to Vietnamese occupation of Kampuchea. Sihanouk was one of many who tended to doubt that Pol Pot was relinquishing power, except perhaps in name.

6 **Cape Town schools closed.** The South African government announced the closing of 454 schools for students of mixed race in the Cape Town area because, it said, violence threatened the safety of those attending classes. Some 360,000 students were affected. On September 5 mixed-race youths had attacked a white suburb outside Cape Town and had been driven off by gunfire. Two days earlier a strike for higher wages by some 60,000 coal and gold miners had ended after just three days. The general secretary of the National Union of Mine Workers said the "intensity of intimidation was a lot higher than we expected."

8 **Norwegians go to polls.** Norwegians began two days of voting to decide if the conservative-led coalition of Prime Minister Kåre Willoch would remain in power or be replaced by a socialist coalition dominated by the Labour Party and its leader, former prime minister Gro Harlem Brundtland. Though the popular vote favoured the socialist coalition, Willoch's supporters won 78 seats in Parliament to 71 for the Labour Party and 6 for its closest ally, the Socialist Left Party. With the guaranteed support of two Progressive parliamentarians, whose party had lobbied for lower taxes, less government, and tighter controls over welfare programs, Willoch was assured of another term in office.

9 **Riots erupt in Britain.** White and black youths began rampaging through the Handsworth area of Birmingham, Britain's second largest city, after firemen arrived to extinguish a blaze in an abandoned building. The area's population contained a high proportion of unemployed youths and drug users. The looting and arson, which were directed especially against Asians, continued the following day as police tried to protect themselves against rocks, bottles, and gasoline (petrol) bombs and attempted to prevent the turmoil from spreading farther into nearby neighbourhoods. Officials said it was the worst such incident since 1981. There seemed to be no simple or clear reason why rioting of such proportions should have erupted at this specific time. On September 28 similar rioting broke out in Brixton, south London, after police shot a black woman during an early morning search for her son.

Coup fails in Thailand. Some 400–500 soldiers, many said to have acted out of loyalty to former colonel Manoon Roopkachorn, initiated an early morning coup in Bangkok, Thailand, while the prime minister was in Indonesia and the head of the armed forces was in Europe. Troops loyal to the government ended the rebellion about ten hours after it began. At least four persons were killed, including two members of an NBC News television crew. Manoon, who had attempted to overthrow Gen. Prem Tinsulanond during his first term as prime minister, reportedly fled first to Singapore and then to West Germany.

10 **Duarte's daughter kidnapped.** The eldest daughter of José Napoleón Duarte, president of El Salvador, was kidnapped, together with a female companion, outside a university on one of the main streets of San Salvador. One of her bodyguards was killed and another wounded in the attack. Though police

ALON REININGER—CONTACT PRESS IMAGES

Although an estimated 20,000 died as a result of earthquakes in Mexico, it was the rescue efforts, and especially the rescue of several infants from the rubble, that captured the world's attention.

began an immediate and intense search for Inés Guadalupe Duarte Durán, no trace was found. On September 17 government officials revealed that on September 13 and 14 an anonymous caller, claiming to represent the little-known Pedro Pablo Castillo Front, had said his group was holding the woman. A tape recording had also reportedly been sent to the president to prove that his daughter, the mother of three children, was still alive. One caller demanded freedom for certain imprisoned rebels and an end to government military operations against the guerrilla forces.

EC pressures South Africa. The foreign ministers of nine full members and two future members of the European Communities (EC) approved sanctions against South Africa in the hope that such action would induce the government to end its policy of apartheid. President Reagan had announced U.S. sanctions the previous day. On September 13 Canada followed suit. Britain, which had postponed its decision in order to study more fully the ramifications of sanctions, lined up with its EC partners on September 25. Though none of the sanctions was considered severe, South Africa was put on notice that even friendly nations supported the demands of South Africa's blacks for an end to apartheid.

11 **Argentine leaders face trial.** Nine military officers who ruled Argentina during six years of extraordinary violence went on trial in Buenos Aires. They were charged with murder, torture, and kidnapping involving more than 9,000 citizens who "disappeared" during that period. The trial, one of the most sensational in the nation's history, had been ordered by Raúl Alfonsín shortly after he was elected president in December 1983. In his opening statement the chief prosecutor said that in its fight against leftist guerrillas, the government had been "ferocious, clandestine, and cowardly" and had resorted to the same tactics used by the insurgents but on a much greater scale.

12 **KGB agent defects in Britain.** The British government announced that Oleg A. Gordiyevsky, a high-ranking member of the Soviet intelligence agency (KGB), had defected in London and that 25 Soviet spies, identified by Gordiyevsky, had been ordered to leave the country for activities "totally incompatible with their status and declared tasks." One report from Denmark claimed that Gordiyevsky had been a double agent since the 1970s. On September 17 West Germans learned that a secretary in Chancellor Helmut Kohl's office had defected to East Germany with her husband. The first revelation that Soviet spies had been operating at high levels in the West German government had occurred in August, when a top West German counterintelligence officer defected to East Germany. Toward the end of September one senior Soviet military intelligence officer defected to the U.S., and it was also confirmed that another had defected to Greece in May. The former claimed that several employees of the CIA were engaged in espionage for the Soviet Union.

15 **Social Democrats win in Sweden.** The Social Democratic Party of Prime Minister Olof Palme retained power in national elections even though it lost 7 of the 180 seats it had held in the 349-seat Riksdag (parliament). The Communist Party lost one of its six seats but provided Palme with enough additional votes to keep him in power. The Social Democrats, who won 45% of the popular vote, were especially pleased that the Conservative Party's 21.4% of the popular vote showed that it had lost considerable support. The nonsocialist party had campaigned vigorously for reductions in taxes, cuts in welfare spending, and an end to state control of health services, education, and television.

16 **China promotes younger leaders.** The Chinese Communist Party announced that 10 of the 24 members of the Politburo were retiring to make room for younger persons. China also confirmed that 64 of the 340 members of the Central Committee, which appoints members to the Politburo, were also being replaced. The new appointees, whose average age was 50, were generally better educated than their predecessors and less doctrinaire. An additional 56 persons were named to the Central Advisory Commission and 31 to the Central Commission for Party Discipline Inspection. All replaced aging functionaries. Chen Yun (Ch'en Yün), one of the chief architects of China's new economic reforms, remained in government even though he had openly criticized the speed and extent of some of the changes initiated by Deng Xiaoping (Teng Hsiao-p'ing), China's preeminent leader.

19 **Quakes devastate Mexico City.** The first of two powerful earthquakes hit central and southwestern Mexico, causing huge buildings to crumble in ruins. The death toll, which was especially high in Mexico City, could not be immediately assessed because thousands of people were trapped alive beneath the rubble. In many cases the rescue teams, which included experts from other countries, did not dare use heavy equipment for fear it would cause massive blocks of concrete and steel to crush the very persons the workers were trying to save. Several times newly born babies were rescued alive from the ruins of a hospital, but it was later estimated that more than 20,000 people had died.

20 **French defense minister resigns.** French Prime Minister Laurent Fabius accepted the resignation of Defense Minister Charles Hernu and fired Adm. Pierre Lacoste as head of the French intelligence agency as evidence mounted that top government officials had been involved in sabotaging a ship belonging to the environmentalist group Greenpeace that had been tied up at the New Zealand port of Auckland. The *Rainbow Warrior* had been part of a flotilla that planned to sail to South Pacific waters to disrupt nuclear tests being conducted by the French government. On September 22 the government officially acknowledged that intelligence agents, acting under orders, had planted the explosives that sank the

ship on July 10. New Zealand Prime Minister David Lange called the attack "a sordid act of international state-backed terrorism" and said he would demand millions of dollars in damages from the French government. A Portuguese-born photographer with Dutch citizenship was killed by the explosives.

Korean families reunited. For the first time since the Korean War ended in 1953, small contingents of North and South Koreans were allowed to cross the demilitarized zone to visit relatives they had not seen in at least 32 years. During emotional reunions the following day, many learned for the first time that parents of other relatives had died during the years of separation. Red Cross officials had been trying for years to arrange such an exchange. The success of this largely symbolic act of cooperation raised hopes that both governments might now be ready to begin discussions to resolve their major differences.

21 **Filipinos rally to air grievances.** Tens of thousands of people in Manila and other cities of the Philippines marked the 13th anniversary of the imposition of martial law (which had been lifted in 1981) by holding antigovernment rallies. To minimize the impact of such demonstrations, the government had once again declared September 21 a holiday to celebrate "the birth of the new society that saw the implementation of sweeping reforms under President Marcos." The previous day sugar farmers and workers in the province of Negros Occidental had held rallies to call attention to food shortages and low wages. When they clashed with riot police, 20 were killed and 27 others injured.

26 **Tunisia cuts ties to Libya.** The Tunisian government notified Libya that it was severing diplomatic relations. The rupture followed a bitter dispute over Libya's expulsion of some 30,000 Tunisian migrant workers from Tripoli and accusations that four Libyan diplomats had mailed more than 100 letter bombs to Tunisian journalists. During August Tunisia had expelled more than 250 Libyans who were said to be spies.

27 **Soviet premier retires.** Nikolay A. Tikhonov, the 80-year-old chairman of the Council of Ministers (premier) of the Soviet Union, retired for reasons of health. His post was immediately filled by Nikolay I. Ryzhkov, a member of the Politburo and one of the ten members of the Communist Party Secretariat. He had earlier been given the responsibility of carrying out the new economic policies of Mikhail Gorbachev, who had become general secretary of the Communist Party, and thus leader of the Soviet Union, after the death of Konstantin Chernenko in March.

28 **Panama's president resigns.** Panamanian Pres. Nicolás Ardito Barletta tendered his resignation after less than one year in office. He claimed not to have sufficient political and military support to solve the nation's economic problems. There were indications, how-

ever, that the Army had in fact forced Ardito Barletta to resign in order to impede a possible investigation of the torture and decapitation two weeks earlier of Hugo Spadafora, a prominent critic of the Army. Vice-Pres. Eric Arturo Delvalle took the oath of office as Ardito Barletta's successor.

29 **D'Aubuisson quits party post.** Roberto d'Aubuisson, leader of El Salvador's far right Nationalist Republican Alliance (Arena), resigned his position during a national party convention. After Arena suffered a severe setback in elections to the National Assembly on March 31, the party was weakened by internal policy disputes and financial difficulties. D'Aubuisson had reportedly decided that in such circumstances he could no longer lead the party effectively.

30 **Soviet diplomats seized in Beirut.** In two separate incidents, four members of the Soviet embassy staff were kidnapped by unidentified gunmen in West Beirut, Lebanon. The terrorists later said they would kill all four hostages if Soviet- and Syrian-backed leftist militiamen continued to attack the northern Lebanese city of Tripoli, which was held by Sunni Muslim fundamentalists. On October 2, following an anonymous tip, the body of Arkady Katakov, a secretary at the embassy, was found in an empty lot. He had been shot in the head. Another caller warned the Soviets that their embassy would be blown up unless all personnel left the country.

OCTOBER

1 **Israel attacks PLO base in Tunisia.** Israeli military aircraft flew some 2,400 km (1,500 mi) across the Mediterranean to Tunisia, where they virtually obliterated the headquarters of the Palestine Liberation Organization (PLO) near Tunis. Some 60 persons were reported killed, but Yasir Arafat, chairman of the PLO, was not present at the time of the raid. Israel said the bombing raid was undertaken to avenge the murders of three Israelis who were gunned down by Palestinians in Larnaca, Cyprus, on September 25. Though Egypt and Jordan joined other nations in condemning the attack, they promised to continue efforts to work out a Middle East peace settlement with Israel. On October 10 the bodies of two Israeli sailors were found in Barcelona, Spain. An anonymous caller said the "Zionists" had been slain by Palestinians on October 5.

2 **Bolivian miners end strike.** The Bolivian Workers Central reached a settlement with the government of Pres. Víctor Paz Estenssoro to end the monthlong strike that had shut down some of the country's largest silver and tin mines. The government had promised to release 97 detained union members if the 27,000 miners returned to work the following day.

3 **Gorbachev visits France.** Mikhail Gorbachev, leader of the Soviet Union, told about 50 members of the French National Assembly that the time had come for the U.S.S.R., France, and Great Britain to negotiate their own separate arms agreement. "Security in Europe," he said, "can be achieved only on the road to peaceful coexistence, relaxation of tension, disarmament, strengthening of trust, and development of international cooperation." In a reference to the U.S., Gorbachev also called for a prohibition on weapons in outer space. During a news conference the following day, French Pres. François Mitterrand rejected Gorbachev's proposal for separate negotiations on arms reductions. Sir Geoffrey Howe, Britain's foreign secretary, said in London that no direct negotiations with the U.S.S.R. were possible until the Soviet Union and the U.S. had signed a strategic arms agreement.

6 **Portuguese elect new Parliament.** The centrist Social Democratic Party (PSD) under the leadership

Egyptian soldiers occupy the quay in Port Said after the Italian cruise ship *Achille Lauro* was freed from the Palestinian terrorists who had hijacked it and murdered a passenger.
BISSON—SYGMA

of Aníbal Cavaço Silva fell far short of winning a majority of the seats in Portugal's Parliament, but its victory over the Socialist Party (PSP) of Prime Minister Mário Soares guaranteed that the nation would have a new government. With about 90% of the vote counted, the PSD appeared to have won at least 85 seats along with 30% of the popular vote. The PSP, which had captured over 36% of the popular vote in the previous election and held 101 seats in Parliament, was supported this time by only 21% of the voters. After discussing the outcome with political leaders, a constitutional requirement, Pres. António Ramalho Eanes was expected to ask Cavaço Silva to form a government.

7 **Palestinians seize Italian ship.** Four Palestinian terrorists hijacked the Italian cruise ship *Achille Lauro* after it departed Alexandria, Egypt, for Port Said with 400 persons aboard. The terrorists threatened to blow up the ship unless 50 Palestinians were released from Israeli jails. The following day, while the ship was off the coast of Syria, the gunmen shot and killed a 69-year-old American, then ordered his body and wheelchair dumped into the sea. The drama appeared to have ended when the terrorists surrendered to the Palestine Liberation Organization in Port Said on October 9. During the next 36 hours or so, the news media tried to reconstruct events and determine who had organized the hijacking and for what purpose. Reporters, however, could not even find out with certainty where the gunmen were being held. Then, on October 10, unscheduled news bulletins interrupted television and radio programs to announce that U.S. F-14 fighters had intercepted an Egyptian plane over the Mediterranean and had ordered it to land at a NATO base in Sicily. Intelligence agents had learned that the four hijackers of the *Achille Lauro* were aboard the aircraft and were being secretly flown to Tunisia. Hosni Mubarak, president of Egypt, expressed outrage that the U.S., a close ally, had "committed piracy"—especially after Egypt had been asked to act as a mediator in the crisis and had negotiated the safe release of hundreds of people, none of whom was Egyptian. U.S. relations with Italy were also strained when Italian officials refused to detain an Arab who, the U.S. said, was suspected of having organized the hijacking.

11 **Nicaraguan rebels get U.S. aid.** A U.S. State Department official acknowledged that nearly $1 million worth of nonlethal supplies had been flown to an undisclosed location in Central America to aid rebels fighting the Sandinista government of Nicaragua. The shipment, which consisted mainly

of shoes, clothing, and medicines, was the first consignment of $27 million in supplies finally approved by the U.S. Congress in July. Though Congress had strictly forbidden the shipment of military supplies, the arrival of clothes and medicines would permit the rebels to use more of the money they had from other sources to satisfy their military needs.

Antinuclear group gets Nobel Prize. The Norwegian Nobel Committee announced that the 1985 Prize for Peace had been awarded to a group called International Physicians for the Prevention of Nuclear War. The five-year-old Boston-based organization had been cofounded by Yevgeny I. Chazov, a Soviet physician and high-ranking member of the Communist Party, and Bernard Lown, a cardiologist at the Harvard School of Public Health. The group, which claimed a membership of 135,000 in 41 countries, advocated an unequivocal end to all nuclear explosions.

13 **Martens retains power in Belgium.** Early general election returns indicated that Belgium's centre-right coalition, which was headed by the Flemish Christian Democratic Party of Prime Minister Wilfried Martens, not only would remain in power but would add two seats to the 113 it had controlled in the 212-seat Parliament before the election. The campaign had focused on Martens's economic austerity policies and on his decision to deploy up to 48 U.S. cruise missiles on Belgian soil. The Flemish Socialist Party, somewhat surprisingly, made substantial gains by strongly criticizing Martens for deploying the missiles. Missiles, consequently, did not appear to be an overriding issue in the minds of the voters.

15 **Lebanon takes step toward peace.** Syria announced that Lebanese Christian, Druze, and Shi'ah Muslim militias—the principals in Lebanon's civil war—had for the first time reached basic agreement on a plan to end the decade of mutual slaughter that had taken more than 100,000 lives. Previous settlements had been ineffectual because the politicians who drew them up had no control over the militias. Syria became directly involved in 1976 when the Arab League asked it to send troops into Lebanon to keep the peace.

Japan to spur economic growth. The Japanese government of Prime Minister Yasuhiro Nakasone adopted a series of measures to stimulate the nation's economic growth and, it was hoped, curb its huge trade and capital surpluses. According to one estimate, the new policy would increase Japanese imports during 1986 by $2 billion. Some economists were less optimistic because the program included neither tax cuts nor substantial increases in government spending.

16 **Reagan envoy visits Marcos.** U.S. Sen. Paul Laxalt held the first of several frank discussions with Philippine Pres. Ferdinand Marcos in Manila. Laxalt had delivered a written message from President Reagan, who, it was widely reported, expressed grave con-

cern over economic, social, political, and military developments in the Philippines and the need to take prompt action to avert an impending disaster. The U.S. was especially concerned about reports that the Communist insurgents were rapidly gaining strength and could eventually endanger two strategically important U.S. bases near Manila: Clark Air Force Base and the Subic Bay naval station. One pro-government Manila newspaper greeted Laxalt with the headline: "Another Meddler from U.S.," and it announced the senator's departure with the words: "Good Riddance." Marcos himself, in later interviews with U.S. reporters, continued to downplay his nation's problems, but he seemed more concerned than previously about U.S. criticism of his regime.

21 **Peres makes new peace proposals.** Israeli Prime Minister Shimon Peres, in a speech delivered before the UN General Assembly, appeared to be willing to accept the notion of an international conference if that appeared essential for Middle East peace negotiations involving King Hussein of Jordan. Israel, however, would insist that the Soviet Union first restore diplomatic relations with Israel if it wanted to participate in the negotiations along with the four other permanent members of the UN Security Council. Though some members of the Israeli coalition government were clearly upset by Peres's remarks, such opposition did not jeopardize his government.

24 **Duarte's daughter released.** Salvadoran Pres. José Napoleón Duarte's eldest daughter, Inés Guadalupe Duarte Durán, was released by terrorists 44 days after she and a female companion were kidnapped in San Salvador. The exchange was part of a complicated agreement that included the release of 22 political prisoners and safe passage out of the country for 96 leftist guerrillas who had been disabled during the war. The rebels released the two women and more than 20 mayors of small towns who had been abducted. Red Cross officials, diplomats of various nations, and clergymen were all involved in the "delicate operation."

Arms sales to Jordan delayed. The U.S. Senate, with but one dissenting vote, approved a bill that prohibited the sale of advanced military equipment to Jordan before March 1, 1986. There was a proviso, however, that the proposed sale of up to $1.9 billion in jet fighters and air defense systems could proceed if Jordan began "direct and meaningful peace negotiations with Israel." The House of Representatives had not yet debated and voted on the matter. King Hussein had held numerous but inconclusive discussions with Yasir Arafat, the chairman of the Palestine Liberation Organization. The two men, however, were unable to agree on basic principles before entering into negotiations with Israel.

UN celebrates 40 years. The United Nations commemorated its 40th anniversary without being able to agree on a declaration to mark the special occasion. Numerous dignitaries from all over the

world traveled to New York to address the General Assembly, but despite a shared hope that the ceremonies at the UN would help revitalize the organization, old animosities surfaced. One diplomat described the atmosphere as testy. When President Reagan addressed the Assembly, he cited five countries where, he said, Communism was at war with the people: Afghanistan, Angola, Cambodia, Ethiopia, and Nicaragua.

25 **Argentina under state of siege.** Argentine Pres. Raúl Alfonsín imposed a 60-day state of siege, presumably to facilitate government efforts to combat violence believed to be instigated by right-wing advocates of amnesty for the former military leaders on trial for murder, torture, and kidnapping. On October 22 a judge had ruled that the government had violated the constitution by arresting 12 persons suspected of being involved in a series of bombings. Under a state of siege, such arrests would have been legal.

26 **France conducts nuclear tests.** France carried out its second nuclear test in three days at Mururoa Atoll in the South Pacific. New Zealand scientists, who monitored the explosions from the Cook Islands, estimated the yield to be between 12 and 14 kilotons. On October 24 French commandos seized a sailboat belonging to the Greenpeace environmentalist group and arrested all seven members of the crew; none resisted. The crew was accused of disregarding warnings that the test area had been temporarily declared off-limits to all but authorized personnel. The crew denied that their boat had entered the restricted area.

27 **Tanzania gets new leader.** An estimated seven million Tanzanian voters cast ballots to approve or disapprove the selection of Ali Hassan Mwinyi as successor to Pres. Julius K. Nyerere, who announced his retirement in July after 20 years in office. Though Mwinyi won approval by a wide margin, he would have a difficult time improving the lot of his fellow countrymen, who were considered among the poorest in the world.

30 **Kidnapped Soviets set free.** Three diplomats from the Soviet embassy in Beirut, Lebanon, were freed unharmed one month after they were kidnapped by Muslim fundamentalists. A fourth member of the embassy staff had been shot and killed two days after being kidnapped. On October 4 the U.S.S.R., reacting to threats against its citizens, evacuated all nonessential embassy personnel. After the kidnappings, the Islamic Liberation Organization (ILO) had demanded that the Soviet Union use its influence with Syria to end attacks against the Sunni Muslims who were occupying the northern city of Tripoli. A truce was arranged about two weeks later, but the kidnapped Soviets were not released. They were set free only after the chief of Syrian intelligence operations had concluded extensive talks in West Beirut with representatives of the ILO.

NOVEMBER

2 South Africa curtails press. The government of South Africa imposed broad restrictions on journalists, which forbade them, without explicit approval, to "make, take, record, manufacture, reproduce, publish, broadcast or distribute, or take or send to any place within or outside the Republic, any film . . . or any photograph, drawing or other representation, or any sound recording" that dealt with such things as public disturbances, riots, strikes, killings, and property damage. Violators could be imprisoned for up to ten years and fined $8,000. South Africa's minister of law and order said that the presence of television and camera crews in areas of unrest had "proved to be a catalyst to further violence." The new regulations applied only to the 38 magisterial districts that had been placed under a state of emergency.

3 KGB agent redefects to U.S.S.R. Vitaly Yurchenko, who was said to be a high-ranking Soviet KGB agent, astonished U.S. government officials by announcing that he wanted to return to the U.S.S.R. During a news conference held at the Soviet embassy in Washington, Yurchenko told reporters he had been kidnapped in Rome three months earlier and then transported in a drugged state to the U.S., where he was held prisoner by the Central Intelligence Agency. The bizarre case left many unanswered questions. Some believed Yurchenko had been a double agent all along. There were also reports that Yurchenko had been emotionally involved with the wife of a Soviet diplomat in Canada. According to some reports, the woman rebuffed Yurchenko during a secretly arranged reunion in Ottawa. After the U.S. was satisfied that Yurchenko had freely decided to return home, he was allowed to depart by plane on November 6.

Marcos agrees to early election. During a live television interview transmitted by satellite to the U.S. from Manila, Philippine Pres. Ferdinand Marcos surprised his audience by saying he was willing to support a "snap" presidential election in mid-January provided members of his New Society Movement party approved. The constitution, however, would have to be modified to permit Marcos to run in a special election without first resigning. On

November 14 representatives of various political factions agreed that the election would not be held until some time in February at the earliest.

Guatemala chooses president. Large numbers of Guatemalans cast ballots to decide which of the presidential candidates would become the nation's first civilian leader in 30 years. Incomplete returns showed that Marco Vinicio Cerezo Arevalo, a Christian Democrat, had won about 40% of the popular vote but not the absolute majority needed for outright victory. His closest rival, Jorge Carpio Nicolle of the National Union of the Centre, had received only half as many votes, but he appeared unwilling to concede that a run-off election in December would simply confirm the people's preference for Cerezo.

6 Jaruzelski elected head of state. Poland's newly formed Sejm (parliament) elected Gen. Wojciech Jaruzelski chairman of the Council of State (president); he replaced Henryk Jablonski, who had held the post since 1972. The Parliament then unanimously approved Jaruzelski's choice for premier, Zbigniew Messner. By taking over the post Jaruzelski had vacated, Messner accepted the responsibility for solving the nation's dire economic problems. Jaruzelski, however, was expected to remain the country's most powerful political figure because he still held the top post in the Polish United Workers' (Communist) Party. There was also speculation that he intended to become directly involved in policy-making by restoring that power to the Council of State. In another move, Foreign Minister Stefan Olszowski, who reportedly had strong Soviet support, lost his position on the Politburo.

7 Colombian judges die in siege. Government troops and police in Bogotá, Colombia, virtually destroyed the Palace of Justice in an assault against leftist guerrillas of the April 19 Movement who had seized control of the five-story building the previous day and taken dozens of judges and government workers hostage. When the fighting was over, the president of the Supreme Court and 11 other judges were among the hundred persons who had lost their lives. In the initial attack on November 6, soldiers

shot their way into the building, gained control of the three lower floors, and freed more than 100 persons. On November 11 a memorial service for those who had died was boycotted by 12 surviving judges to protest the government's handling of the affair.

9 Soviet seaman defector changes mind. Miroslav Medved, a 25-year-old Ukrainian seaman, left Reserve, La., aboard a Soviet freighter after declaring to the satisfaction of U.S. officials that he had changed his mind about defecting to the West. On October 24 the seaman had jumped into the Mississippi River in an apparent attempt to defect. Though the man was interviewed on shore several times, some charged that U.S. authorities had badly mishandled the case. There were even charges that the person last interviewed was not the same person who had originally tried to escape.

11 Arrest warrants issued in *Achille Lauro* case. Italian authorities issued arrest warrants for 16 Palestinians, all thought to have been directly involved in planning or carrying out the hijacking of the cruise ship *Achille Lauro* on October 7. The suspects were said to be members of the Palestine Liberation Front (PLF), one of several factions of the Palestine Liberation Organization. On November 18 four of the Palestinians were convicted in Genoa of illegally possessing guns and explosives and sentenced to prison for four to eight years. They would later stand trial for hijacking and murder. On November 19 authorities confirmed that Muhammad Abbas, the leader of the PLF, was one of those being sought. He had been detained earlier but was released.

12 U.S. spy gets life imprisonment. Arthur Walker, a retired U.S. Navy lieutenant commander, was sentenced to life imprisonment in Norfolk, Va., after pleading guilty to charges of espionage. Walker, who was also fined $250,000, had been recruited by his brother to gather classified information.

Coup fails in Liberia. Liberian Pres. Samuel Doe went on radio to inform the nation that he was still in full command of the government despite an attempt by

 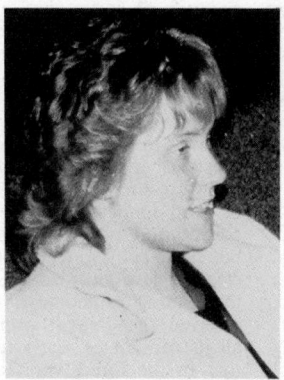 

A rash of spy cases kept government and intelligence circles stirred up. Among those implicated in spying on the U.S. were (left to right) Jonathan Pollard, his wife, Anne Henderson-Pollard, and Larry Wu-tai Chin.

former general Thomas Quiwonkpa to seize power by force. In a predawn attack, rebel forces captured the radio station and moved against other predetermined targets, but by nightfall it was clear they had lost the battle to overthrow Doe.

13 Colombian volcano kills thousands.
The Nevado del Ruiz volcano, which had been dormant for nearly 400 years, came to life late at night with a violent explosion. An estimated 25,000 were killed as raging waters and a sea of mud swept through surrounding valleys and obliterated entire villages. The catastrophic mud slides, known as lahars, often destroy everything in their paths as they race downhill at speeds so fast that flight is impossible. The snow-capped volcano was located 135 km (85 mi) northwest of the capital city of Bogotá. Although rescue teams began work immediately, it was soon evident that most of those who had disappeared would never be found alive.

17 Churchman meets Beirut kidnappers.
Terry Waite, a special envoy of the archbishop of Canterbury, returned to London after telling reporters in Beirut, Lebanon, that he had succeeded in meeting the captors of four kidnapped Americans, whose release he was seeking to arrange. Waite, who was presumed to be negotiating with members of Islamic Jihad ("Islamic Holy War"), said the situation was "critical and dangerous." The captors had reportedly demanded the release of 17 of their companions who had been jailed in Kuwait after being convicted of several bombings that occurred in December 1983. On November 24 Waite arrived in the U.S. to discuss the situation with Reagan administration officials.

19 U.S.-Soviet summit begins in Geneva.
For the first time in six years, the leaders of the world's two most powerful nations met face to face in Geneva. The initial meeting between President Reagan and Soviet leader Mikhail Gorbachev was expected to be a brief personal encounter held behind closed doors. It continued for two hours, far longer than anyone had expected. A second session later in the day also lasted two hours. The following day the two men continued to discuss U.S.-Soviet differences. When the summit concluded the next day with a joint appearance, both leaders acknowledged that the meetings had been important and successful inasmuch as both sides had spoken frankly and left with a better understanding of each other's point of view. There was little if any progress in resolving such fundamental issues as arms control, human rights, U.S. plans to develop a space-based defense system, and regional conflicts that in various ways involved both countries, but the two men agreed to meet again in the U.S. in 1986 and in the Soviet Union in 1987.

22 New Zealand jails French agents.
Sir Roland Davison, the highest ranking judge in New Zealand, sentenced two French agents to ten years in prison for their roles in blowing up and sinking the *Rainbow Warrior*

while it was at berth in Auckland Harbour. A photographer aboard the ship, which belonged to the environmental organization Greenpeace, was killed by the explosions. Prosecutors had dropped charges of murder, conspiracy, and arson when the agents agreed to plead guilty to manslaughter and willful damage to the ship. On November 22 France's defense minister said he hoped the two would be quickly returned to France, but three days later New Zealand's Prime Minister David Lange said the agents would not be deported while he remained in office.

23 Egyptian plane hijacked to Malta.
An Egyptian Boeing 737 airliner, on a night flight from Athens to Cairo, was hijacked by terrorists who forced the pilot to land on the Mediterranean island of Malta. (It was the same aircraft that U.S. F-14 fighter planes had intercepted on October 10 when it was carrying the four hijackers of the Italian cruise ship *Achille Lauro* to safety in Tunisia.) The latest hijackers demanded that the plane be refueled, but Maltese authorities refused to comply until all the hostages were released, even though two passengers had already been killed and their bodies dumped on the tarmac. When there appeared to be no hope of resolving the impasse, Egyptian commandos stormed the plane about 8:15 the next evening. Of the original 98 passengers and crew, 57 died in the gunfight and subsequent fire. The one hijacker who had not died was taken unconscious to a hospital. The hijacking was believed to have been organized by Abu Nidal, a pro-Libyan Palestinian.

24 Pope opens synod in Rome.
Pope John Paul II opened an Extraordinary Synod of Bishops in St. Peter's Basilica in Rome. The 165 prelates invited to take part had been called to the Eternal City to evaluate the results of the Second Vatican Council, which began in 1962 and formally ended on Dec. 8, 1965. During the following 20 years the church had undergone great changes ranging from the use of vernacular, rather than Latin, in the liturgy to the adoption by some priests and nuns of liberation theology, especially in Latin America. On several occasions the pope had warned that the adoption of Marxist analysis as a means of attaining social justice perverted true liberation theology and was inimical to Catholic teaching. Many Catholics were also known to disagree with the church's absolute prohibition against such things as artificial birth control and abortion. Bishops attending the synod had only the right to advise the pope, not the authority to make binding decisions.

Honduras elects president. Honduran voters went to the polls to elect a successor to Pres. Robert Suazo Córdova, but no one knew for sure which of two methods would be used to determine the outcome. The constitution stipulated that the president be elected by direct vote, but a new election law awarded the presidency to the leading candidate of whatever party received the greatest overall support for all its candidates. Early returns indicated that in the direct vote Rafael Leonardo

Callejas of the opposition National Party would come out far ahead of any of the eight other candidates, but the ruling Liberal Party, whose leading candidate was José Azcona Hoyo, appeared certain to win a larger total share of all the votes that were cast. In that case, Azcona Hoyo would become president, provided the court definitively ruled in favour of the new election law.

27 Suspected U.S. spies appear in court.
Jonathan Pollard, a U.S. Navy counterintelligence analyst, appeared in a Washington, D.C., court after admitting he had provided Israel with huge quantities of classified military documents. The judge ordered Pollard held without bail. His wife had also been arrested and charged with espionage. In a separate hearing in Baltimore, Md., Ronald Pelton, a former communications specialist at the National Security Agency, was also denied bond after being accused of spying for the Soviet Union. In a third court hearing the same day, this one in Alexandria, Va., Larry Wu-tai Chin, a retired analyst with the Central Intelligence Agency, was ordered to remain in custody until he stood trial on charges of spying for China. Despite the extraordinary series of arrests, a government official said more suspected spies would be apprehended as soon as sufficient evidence was marshaled against them.

Britain approves Ulster pact. The British House of Commons voted 473–47 in favour of giving Ireland a consultative role and official presence in Northern Ireland. It was hoped that such concessions would eventually end the bloodshed and sectarian violence that had plagued that part of the United Kingdom for many years. Following the vote, the Rev. Ian Paisley led a planned phased withdrawal of Ulster Unionists, who represented Ulster's Protestant majority in Parliament. British Prime Minister Margaret Thatcher and Irish Prime Minister Garret FitzGerald had signed the pact in Hillsborough, Northern Ireland, on November 15. The agreement acknowledged that the political status of the territory would remain unchanged until the majority of the people "clearly wish for and formally consent to the establishment of a united Ireland." Meanwhile, an intergovernmental council would, among other things, meet regularly to discuss political, social, and legal matters, including the administration of justice.

29 South African blacks form new union.
During a meeting in Durban, South African black union leaders formed a union of some 500,000 workers, the largest such organization since labour unions were first sanctioned in 1979. Organizers of the Congress of South African Trade Unions, however, disagreed on what policies the group should follow to translate labour strength into political power. Because the new congress welcomed the support of whites who backed the fight to end the government's policy of apartheid, it excluded black unions that espoused "black consciousness" to the point of refusing to ally themselves with whites sympathetic to their cause.

DECEMBER

2 **Manila court acquits all 26 on trial for Aquino's murder.** A three-judge court appointed by Philippine Pres. Ferdinand Marcos acquitted Gen. Fabian Ver and all of the other 25 defendants standing trial for involvement in the assassination of opposition leader Benigno Aquino, Jr., in August 1983. The judges totally rejected the conclusions of an independent panel of civilian investigators who had determined, after months of testimony, that there was convincing evidence that military personnel were involved in the murder. A spokesman for the U.S. State Department said, in words that were clearly carefully chosen, that it was "very difficult" to reconcile the verdict with the findings of the investigators. Immediately after the verdict was rendered, Marcos reinstated Ver as chief of staff of the armed forces. The next day Corazon C. Aquino, the widow of the slain politician, announced that she would oppose Marcos in the presidential election scheduled for Feb. 7, 1986. On December 19 the Philippine Supreme Court, in a split decision, ruled that the election, which some believed would be unconstitutional unless Marcos first resigned as president, could be held as planned.

South Korean students seize U.S. office. Six male and three female students, some carrying gasoline bombs, took over the office of the director of the U.S. Culture Office in Kwangju, South Korea. Nine hours later, after negotiations failed, the police moved in. This incident was but the latest in a long series of protests that had taken place in recent months against the government of Pres. Chun Doo Hwan and, in some cases, against U.S. policies. In late June police had arrested 65 students in nine different universities for "unlawful activities"; similar arrests were made in mid-July. On October 2, 20 college students were given prison sentences for taking over the U.S. Information Office in Seoul in May. On October 29, 26 present or former students of Seoul National University were taken into custody and charged with violating the National Security Law. On November 18, 191 students took control of the ruling Democratic Justice Party's training institute. All 191 were arrested as "prime criminals"; on December 19 four of the 81 indicted for acts of violence and obstruction of official duties were also charged with arson.

Voters oust Parti Québécois. Voters in the Canadian province of Quebec overwhelmingly backed candidates of the Liberal Party running for seats in the provincial National Assembly. The victory meant that 52-year-old Robert Bourassa, the leader of the Liberals, would once again head the provincial government even though he appeared to have lost the race for his district seat. He could, however, become a member of the legislature by winning a by-election in a different district. Outgoing Premier Pierre-Marc Johnson interpreted the election results as a clear desire for "profound change." When René Lévesque defeated Bourassa in 1976, Lévesque began a campaign to separate Quebec from the rest of Canada because, he said, it was the only viable way to guarantee and preserve the rights of the minority French-speaking Canadians.

3 **Dutch limit role in NATO's plans.** Jacob de Ruiter, the Dutch defense minister, informed fellow members of NATO during a meeting in Brussels that his government was adhering to its earlier decision to deploy cruise missiles on its soil, but it would not accept two wartime tasks its NATO allies wished to assign it, namely, that Dutch pilots man F-16s to deliver nuclear weapons and that they also fly Orion aircraft carrying nuclear depth charges to be dropped on enemy submarines.

4 **Jaruzelski visits Paris.** Gen. Wojciech Jaruzelski, Poland's head of state, met with French Pres. François Mitterrand for more than an hour in Paris. It was the first visit Jaruzelski had made to a Western capital since Poland suppressed Solidarity, the federation of trade unions, and placed the country under martial law in 1981. The meeting represented a clear political risk for Mitterrand because members of his Socialist Party had been ardent supporters of Solidarity and backed the demands its members had made that their human and political rights be respected. Opposition to the visit was so rife in France that even Prime Minister Laurent Fabius felt compelled to inform members of the National Assembly that Jaruzelski's visit troubled him deeply.

6 **U.K. joins "Star Wars" project.** The U.S. approved an agreement whereby Great Britain would have an active role in research projects linked to the development of a U.S. space-based missile defense system. Although details of the agreement were classified, it appeared that Britain would be awarded contracts to pursue specific intermediate goals that were considered vital to the overall success of the project.

8 **Guatemala chooses president.** Marco Vinicio Cerezo Arévalo, candidate of the centre-left Christian Democratic Party, defeated Jorge Carpio Nicolle of the National Union of the Centre in a runoff election for the presidency of Guatemala. Cerezo, who captured two-thirds of the popular vote, would be the country's first nonmilitary president in years. The historical importance of the election was underscored by Carpio, who was gracious in defeat and confident that—after years of turmoil, poverty, social injustices, and repression—Guatemala had "found its way" to a more hopeful future by embracing democracy.

Oil price structure collapses. During a meeting in Geneva, the 13 oil ministers of OPEC agreed in effect that repeated efforts to maintain oil prices by curtailing production had been futile. Instead, OPEC would attempt to recapture its share of the world market by cutting prices as circumstances required. The decision was an acknowledgement that members of OPEC had not adhered to assigned quotas and were selling oil below the price that had been officially established. Nations that imported oil were expected to profit substantially from the new policy, but oil-producing nations in financial difficulties were certain to be adversely affected.

9 **Argentina's ex-leaders found guilty.** A civilian court in Buenos Aires concluded that five members of two military juntas that ruled Argentina during the 1970s were guilty of serious crimes committed during their campaigns against urban guerrillas. During that period approximately 9,000 people disappeared and were never heard from again. Gen. Jorge Videla, who headed the junta that seized power after Isabel Martínez de Perón was overthrown in 1976, and Adm. Emilio Massera, a member of that same government, were both given life sentences. Gen. Roberto Eduardo Viola, president of the second junta, was sentenced to 17 years in prison. Adm. Armando Lambruschini, a member of the second junta, and Brig. Gen. Orlando Agosti, a member of the first junta, were sentenced to 8- and 4¹⁄₂-year terms, respectively. Four other members of the military were acquitted. The trial, ordered by Pres. Raúl Alfonsín, was unprecedented in modern Latin-American history.

Pres. François Mitterrand of France (right) created controversy for himself by receiving Gen. Wojciech Jaruzelski of Poland (left) at the Elysée Palace.

12 **U.S. soldiers die in plane crash.** A chartered DC-8 aircraft operated by Arrow Air of Miami, Fla., crashed as it took off from the international airport at Gander, Newfoundland. All 256 persons aboard were killed. The victims included 248 U.S. soldiers from the 502nd Infantry of the 101st Airborne Division who were returning home for Christmas after serving a six-month tour with the 11-nation peacekeeping force in the Sinai. A spokesman for the U.S. military confirmed that chartered flights were commonly used to transport troops in such situations. Investigators at the scene of the crash had no immediate explanation for the tragedy and said there were no obvious indications that the aircraft had been sabotaged.

17 **Ugandan factions sign peace accord.** Gen. Tito Okello, who became the leader of Uganda after a successful military coup in July, and Yoweri Museveni, leader of the rebel National Resistance Army, signed a peace accord that, it was hoped, would finally end decades of political strife. Museveni's forces were not the only antigovernment units operating within the country, but without their cooperation no peace was possible. Some observers doubted that the cease-fire would hold even though Okello had promised to give the insurgents, who were mostly Bantus from the south, important posts in the government, which was dominated by members of the northern Nilotic tribe. The peace ceremony took place in Kenya at the invitation of Pres. Daniel arap Moi, who also signed the document.

20 **Nigerian coup foiled.** The Nigerian minister of defense reported that an attempted coup against the four-month-old government of Maj. Gen. Ibrahim Babangida had been foiled while it was still being organized. There was no information on the number of persons arrested, but those taken into custody were said to come from all branches of the armed forces. The rebels reportedly were dissatisfied with some of Babangida's appointments, including his retention of some personnel who had served in the previous administration.

21 **Winnie Mandela defies government.** Armed police forcefully removed Winnie Mandela from her home in Soweto, a black township in South Africa, when she refused to promise to observe new but less-restrictive limits on her movements. The next day she was arrested for slipping back into Soweto during the night. Eight days later she was arrested again while attempting to return to Soweto. Under the Criminal Procedures Act, she could be held for 48 hours without being charged. After being banished to Brandfort eight years earlier, Mandela had complied with government orders until her home was gasoline bombed in September 1985. She then began to taunt officials openly and defy government regulations. Her husband, Nelson, who had been imprisoned since 1964, had rejected a recent offer of freedom because it included a promise that he would not resort to violence after his release.

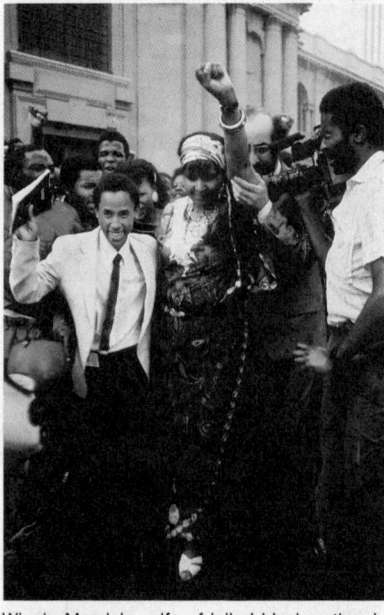

Winnie Mandela, wife of jailed black nationalist leader Nelson Mandela, continued to defy the South African government's attempts to restrict her movements.
GAMMA/LIAISON

Haitians continue protests. Thousands of protesters in various cities and towns of Haiti continued to defy army troops by marching through the streets to demand an end to the dictatorial rule of Pres. Jean-Claude Duvalier. The unprecedented demonstrations were all the more remarkable because they continued even after several young protesters had been killed. Government officials were said to be worried about a possible escalation of violence; they also reportedly feared the U.S. would cut back its annual financial aid because it "would have difficulty" certifying that the Haitian government's record on human rights was showing improvement. Haiti, which was considered one of the most impoverished nations in the Western Hemisphere, had been ruled by the Duvalier family since 1957.

23 **Reagan signs farm bills.** President Reagan signed into law two agriculture bills that together constituted the most fundamental change in U.S. government farm policy in half a century. The long-range purpose of the first bill was to make it more profitable and more necessary for U.S. farmers to compete for world markets because they would not be able to rely on generous federal income and price supports. Huge government food surpluses would also be reduced as a result of the new legislation. The second bill, which reorganized the Farm Credit System, would permit a new agency to take over billions of dollars of delinquent loans and then resolve each case either by renegotiating the loans or by foreclosing.

24 **South African tribesmen clash.** For reasons that were not immediately clear, several thousand Zulus engaged in a bloody battle with a larger number of Pondo tribesmen near Durban, South Africa. Reports from the

area indicated that 53 persons had been killed with spears, knives, and possibly firearms. The number of fatalities was far larger than in previous violent engagements between the two rival tribes.

27 **Palestinians attack Rome and Vienna airports.** In virtually simultaneous attacks, Palestinian gunmen hurled hand grenades and fired automatic weapons indiscriminately at civilian passengers congregated near El Al Israel Airlines counters at Leonardo da Vinci Airport in Rome and Schwechat Airport in Vienna. The seven terrorists, four in Rome and three in Vienna, killed 18 persons and wounded at least 110 others before four of their number were killed by security guards and the other three wounded and subdued. One of the gunmen was taken alive in Rome and the other two in Vienna. Evidence gathered from the belongings of the terrorists and from interrogations indicated that the men were members of a Palestinian group headed by Abu Nidal, who had broken away from the al-Fatah faction of the Palestine Liberation Organization (PLO) headed by Yasir Arafat. A note found in one of the terrorist's pockets said the suicide attacks were in reprisal for the destruction of the PLO headquarters near Tunis, Tunisia, by Israeli bombers on October 1. Experts on Middle East terrorism suspected the terrorists had been trained in Iran and had the backing of Libyan leader Col. Muammar al-Qaddafi.

30 **Zia ends martial law.** Mohammad Zia-ul-Haq ended eight and a half years of martial law in Pakistan, but he remained in power as president of the civilian government, and he retained his post as army chief of staff. The expected announcement, which was made before a joint session of the Senate and National Assembly, included a warning that any attempt to disrupt peace and order could lead to a resumption of military rule. Some aspects of martial law had been incorporated into the civil code before Zia's announcement and the official return to democratic rule. In 1977 Zia led a successful military coup against Prime Minister Zulfikar Ali Bhutto, who was executed in April 1979.

31 **Hussein and Assad hold talks.** Jordan's King Hussein ended a two-day visit to Damascus during which he and Syrian Pres. Hafez al-Assad exchanged views face to face for the first time in six years. No communiqué was issued at the end of the talks, and no details of the discussions were made public, but it was taken for granted that the two Arab leaders discussed regional problems and Arab cooperation. Hussein was known to look favourably on direct peace negotiations with Israel, but Assad opposed any such dealings with the Jewish state. Hussein, moreover, supported Iraq in its war with Iran, while Assad backed Iran. Still another point of disagreement centred on Yasir Arafat, chairman of the Palestine Liberation Organization, who had of late been working closely with Hussein but was anathema to Assad because Arafat now appeared willing to compromise with Israel in order to achieve peace.

People of 1985

BIOGRAPHIES

Alexander, Lincoln

On Sept. 20, 1985, Lincoln Alexander was installed as the 24th lieutenant governor of Ontario. Thus he became the first black person to hold a vice-regal office in Canada. Upon assuming the position, he was entitled to a 15-gun salute as the chief executive officer of Ontario and the representative of H.M. Queen Elizabeth II in the province.

Alexander began his career in public office in 1968, when, in the face of the Liberal Party's sweep of that year's general election, he became the first black member of the Canadian Parliament and the only member of the Progressive Conservative Party to be elected from an Ontario urban centre. As member of Parliament for Hamilton West, he earned a reputation for honesty and directness. In the House of Commons he served his party as spokesman on such subjects as housing, labour, manpower, unemployment, immigration, and welfare. He was also designated observer to the UN (1976, 1978). When the Conservatives formed a government after the 1979 general election, Prime Minister Joe Clark appointed him minister of labour in his short-lived Cabinet.

Born Jan. 21, 1922, in Toronto, Lincoln MacCaulay Alexander served as a radio operator in the Royal Canadian Air Force during World War II. In 1949 he received his B.A. from McMaster University in Hamilton, Ont. After his graduation from Osgoode Hall Law School in Toronto (1953), Alexander practiced as a criminal lawyer in Hamilton. In 1965 he was given the honorary title of queen's counsel by the Ontario government. His law partners helped engender in him an interest in politics that led to his running for Parliament.

In 1980 Alexander resigned his parliamentary seat to become chairman of the Ontario Workers' Compensation Board. He received the Man of the Year Award from the Ethnic Press Council of Canada in 1982, and the following year he was made a Commander of the Order of St. John. As lieutenant governor, Alexander became the chief of state of the province of Ontario. His duties included summoning and dissolving the provincial legislature, giving assent to legislative bills, and reading the speech from the throne at the opening of each legislative session.

(DIANE LOIS WAY)

Alia, Ramiz

Two days after the death on April 11, 1985, of Enver Hoxha (see OBITUARIES), first secretary of the Albanian (Communist) Party of Labour since 1943, Ramiz Alia was confirmed as chairman of the Presidium of the People's Assembly (president) at the plenary session of the party's Central Committee and was also appointed to succeed Hoxha as first secretary. At Hoxha's funeral on April 15, Alia solemnly committed himself to follow the road laid out by his comrade and patron.

Ramiz Alia was born on Oct. 18, 1925, at Shkoder into a poor Muslim family. Under King Zog I he took part in the patriotic youth movement. During the Italian occupation in World War II, he joined the National Liberation Movement, organized by Hoxha and controlled by the Albanian Communist Party, which in November 1948 became the Albanian Party of Labour. After World War II Alia went to Moscow for ideological training. His loyalty to Hoxha secured his election to the party Central Committee (1948) and to the People's Assembly (1950). By 1961 he was a member of the party Secretariat and a full member of the Politburo.

When on Dec. 18, 1981, Radio Tirane announced that Mehmet Shehu, Albanian premier since 1954, had committed suicide, Hoxha, having the succession in mind, appointed Adil Carcani chairman of the Council of Ministers (premier) and chose Alia to replace Haxhi Leshi as chairman of the Presidium of the People's Assembly. It was obvious that Alia was Hoxha's choice to succeed as party leader because on Albanian television the two began appearing together, and in new volumes of Hoxha's memoirs Alia was often described as "my dear friend." From 1984, as Hoxha's health failed, Alia's responsibility for day-to-day affairs of state increased.

(K. M. SMOGORZEWSKI)

Archer, Jeffrey Howard

A millionaire author of popular thrillers, Jeffrey Archer made a surprising return to politics in 1985 when he was appointed by U.K. Prime Minister Margaret Thatcher to be deputy chairman of the Conservative Party. As an Oxford undergraduate Archer (born April 15, 1940, in Weston-super-Mare, Somerset) excelled chiefly as an athlete, winning "blues" for both gymnastics and athletics and breaking the university record for the 100-yd sprint. After graduation he soon gained success as a politician. He was elected the youngest member ever of the Greater London Council in 1966 and in 1969 became a member of Parliament by winning a by-election in the safe Conservative seat of Louth.

This promising career was quickly in ruins. Financial difficulties led to his resignation from Parliament in 1974. Faced with bankruptcy, he turned his hand to

RICHARD OPEN—CAMERA PRESS, LONDON

writing, and his first novel, published in the next year as *Not a Penny More, Not a Penny Less,* became an international bestseller. From that day he never looked back financially. Best-seller followed best-seller, including *Shall We Tell the President?* (1977) and *First Among Equals* (1984), but Archer continued to hanker after a political career.

It was as "famous writer" that he became a popular star on the Conservative speaking circuit. The exact circumstances of his appointment to a senior position at the Conservative Central Office were not clear. It was thought that Margaret Thatcher took a special fancy to him as a self-made man of wealth. His popularity with party workers seemed to make him an ideal surrogate for the new chairman, Norman Tebbit (*q.v.*), who, as the result of his wife's grave injury in the Brighton bombing of 1984, had to restrict his travel and speaking engagements.

Archer got off to another fast start in his new career. In a radio interview on the eve of the Conservative Party conference, he made unsympathetic remarks about the unemployed that jarred badly with the softer tone that the prime minister was adopting. Other Archer miscues followed. However, a deputy chairmanship of the Conservative Party was not normally a frontline office, and by the end of 1985 it looked as if Archer had been reminded that his task was to be seen widely but heard only by the Tory faithful.

(PETER JENKINS)

Babangida, Ibrahim

Nigeria's sixth military coup, on Aug. 27, 1985, brought to power a very different soldier from his predecessor, the austere and remote Mohammed Buhari. Maj. Gen. Ibrahim Babangida was a tough character, with a reputation for personal courage and decisiveness, who enjoyed the respect and loyalty of the soldiers who were the basis of his power. He played a vital role in suppressing the attempted coup of Feb. 13, 1976, when, unarmed, he walked into the rebel-held radio station. During the 30-month civil war he distinguished himself as an able frontline soldier.

Babangida was born on Aug. 17, 1941, at Minna in Niger State and went to Bida school. He underwent military training at Kaduna and then at the Indian Military Academy; later he took training courses in Britain and the U.S. After holding various commands, in 1975 he was sworn in as a member of Murtala Mohammed's Supreme Military Council (SMC). Babangida was generally credited with masterminding the coup that overthrew Pres. Alhaji Shehu Shagari at the end of 1983, and he supported Buhari as the new head of state. Under Buhari he was chief of army staff and a member of the SMC.

On assuming chairmanship of the SMC in 1985, Babangida made a virtual clean sweep of the old faces, retaining only six of Buhari's ministers. He told his new Cabinet ministers that they had been selected on their merits and not for regional or tribal reasons and stated that he intended to run "a government of action committed to a program with clear economic and social goals." He insisted that it had to be an open government; ministers did not know all the answers, and they should be ready to consult with others. He was also determined to defend human rights, and one of his first actions was to release political detainees. Babangida thus brought a different, more open style to running his troubled country; the problems he faced were enormous, and whether the style would survive remained to be seen.

(GUY ARNOLD)

Bacon, Francis

A major retrospective held at London's Tate Gallery during May–August 1985 provided ample opportunity to study the art of Francis Bacon, widely considered one of the finest and most relevant artists of the mid-20th century, perhaps even the greatest living painter. Bacon's timeless, haunting, anguished images were totally individual yet firmly within the tradition of Michelangelo, Rembrandt, and Velázquez.

Bacon's paintings, whether portraits or religious or literary subjects, were characterized by a vivid central image, rendered often with a thick impasto of paint and in minute detail, set against a bleak background that isolated the image from its surroundings. This formal juxtaposition, combined with the often-disturbing central image, reinforced the sense of alienation. The images themselves were recognizable yet somehow disjointed and disturbing—familiar elements were distorted and recombined in frightening yet vivid ways. The screaming mouth, the bloody carcass, or the haunted veiled visage were characteristic Bacon images; few artists had man-

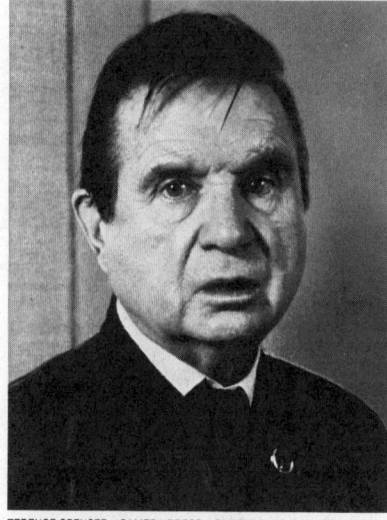

TERENCE SPENCER—CAMERA PRESS, LONDON

aged to convey such a powerful message of horror and decay.

Bacon was born in Dublin on Oct. 28, 1909, the son of an English horse trainer working in Ireland. Lacking formal schooling, he moved to London in 1925 and a few years later traveled to Berlin and Paris, where he was impressed by the work of Picasso and inspired to start drawing and painting. For a few years he worked as an interior decorator and designer of furniture. In 1929 he began, entirely self-taught, to paint in oils, and by 1931 he had begun to concentrate exclusively on painting. His first major work was "Crucifixion 33," which gained public attention when it was published in critic Sir Herbert Read's *Art Now* (1933). In 1934 he had his first one-man show in London.

After 1962, when Bacon had his first major Tate Gallery retrospective, his work was widely shown in Europe and the U.S. Themes to which he frequently returned included portraits of popes, the crucifixion, and portraits of friends. His central images were usually human or animal.

(SANDRA MILLIKIN)

Baker, James

In February 1985 Donald Regan (*q.v.*) succeeded James Baker as chief of staff at the White House, and Baker succeeded Regan as secretary of the treasury. In their new roles both men continued to be influential in the administration of Pres. Ronald Reagan. Baker, a respected political strategist who had never before worked intensively in finance, remained a designated member of the National Security Council. In April President Reagan instructed heads of departments and other ranking officials to meet as the Economic Policy Council, with Baker as chairman, whenever economic policies were to be formulated.

In June, at a meeting in Tokyo of officials of 11 of the most economically important non-Communist nations, Baker successfully advocated floating exchange rates for national currencies. But later, on September 22, Baker, never a free-trade ideologue, met officials of four of those same nations in New York City and secured from them promises of help in reducing the exchange rate of the U.S. dollar.

In October, at a meeting of the Inter-

national Monetary Fund in Seoul, South Korea, Baker presented a plan to help the heavily indebted governments of several less developed countries. The plan called for the Fund to offer assistance, for the World Bank to guarantee private loans, and for the assisted governments to follow free-market policies.

Baker was born in Houston, Texas, on April 28, 1930. In 1952 he received a B.A. from Princeton University. After serving as a lieutenant in the U.S. Marine Corps from 1952 to 1954, he received a law degree from the University of Texas in 1957 and joined the law firm of Andrews, Kurth, Campbell & Jones in Houston. In 1970 he worked on George Bush's campaign for the U.S. Senate from Texas and first publicly declared himself a Republican. He became an undersecretary in the Department of Commerce in 1975. In 1976 he resigned that job, worked on Gerald Ford's campaign for the presidency, and then rejoined Andrews, Kurth, Campbell & Jones.

In 1980 Baker managed George Bush's presidential campaign and then campaigned for the Reagan-Bush ticket. As chief of staff to President Reagan from 1981 to 1985, he ran the White House staff in close collaboration with two longtime aides to Reagan, Michael Deaver, the deputy chief of staff, and Edwin Meese, counselor to the president.

(CHARLES JOHNSON TAGGART)

Ballard, Robert

At two o'clock in the morning on Sept. 1, 1985, in the North Atlantic some 900 km (560 mi) south of Newfoundland, the U.S. Navy research ship *Knorr* slowly cruised the dark swells. Almost 4,000 m (13,000 ft) beneath the *Knorr,* tethered to it by a thick steel cable and skimming the ocean bottom in icy darkness, was a 5-m (16-ft) submersible robot sled christened *Argo.* Suddenly *Argo*'s video cameras, working in the glare of searchlights, sent to television screens aboard the *Knorr* images of the greatest shipwreck of all time. Resting upright on the edge of a submarine canyon, shorn of its stern and two of its four smokestacks yet otherwise beautifully preserved after 73 years, lay the ocean liner *Titanic.* Robert Ballard's search was over.

As head of the Deep Submergence Laboratory of the Woods Hole (Mass.) Oceanographic Institution, Ballard designed *Argo* and was in charge of testing it for the Navy. He chose the *Titanic* as his goal because it had sunk in a depth ideal for testing the deep-sea explorer. Teaming up with the French vessel *Le Suroit,* which until late June conducted its search for the ocean liner by towing an unmanned submersible equipped with side-scanning sonar for mapping the ocean bottom, the *Knorr* began combing the site of the disaster in early August. After *Argo*'s cameras picked up pictures of a large riveted metal cylinder (a *Titanic* boiler), the *Titanic* was located by the *Knorr*'s 25-year-old sonar system. *Argo* and an older Woods Hole sled, *Angus,* snapped 12,000 colour photos. Mission accomplished, Ballard and his team returned home to worldwide acclaim.

Robert Duane Ballard was born in Wichita, Kan., on June 30, 1942. In 1966, a year after graduating with a degree in chemistry and geology from the University of California at Santa Barbara, he joined the U.S.

Navy and was assigned as liaison officer for the Office of Naval Research at Woods Hole. He became a civilian researcher there three years later, at first working with *Alvin,* a three-man submersible. In 1973–75 he dived 2,750 m (9,000 ft) in *Alvin* and in a French submersible to explore the Mid-Atlantic Ridge. In 1976 he took *Alvin* 3,660 m (12,000 ft) down into the Cayman Trench in the Caribbean, and in 1977 and 1979 he joined an international team exploring hydrothermal vents in the Galápagos Rift and the East Pacific Rise.

(ROBERT CURLEY)

Batmunkh, Zhambyn

On Dec. 12, 1984, Zhambyn Batmunkh was elected chairman of the Presidium of Mongolia's Great People's Hural, thus becoming head of state in succession to Yumzhagiyen Tsedenbal, who had held that office since 1974. Tsedenbal had been removed from his post in August 1984 at an extraordinary session of the Central Committee (CC) of the Mongolian People's Revolutionary (Communist) Party, when he was replaced by Batmunkh as first secretary of the party. Batmunkh had previously been chairman of the Council of Ministers (premier) since 1974. Tsedenbal's poor state of health was said to be the reason for the change of leadership.

Batmunkh was born on March 10, 1926, in the Khyargas district of the Ubsa-Nur region of Mongolia. He graduated from the Mongolian State University and from the Academy of Social Sciences of the Communist Party of the Soviet Union (CPSU). Joining the Mongolian party in 1948, he was elected a CC candidate member in 1971 and a full member three years later, when he also became a member of the Politburo. Batmunkh lectured at the State University and Pedagogical Institute during 1951–52 and was then rector of the Higher Party School (1952–58) and of the Higher School of Economics (1962–67). He then served six years as vice-rector and later rector at the State University. In 1973 Batmunkh was made head of the CC department of science and education. The following year he was appointed deputy chairman and then chairman of the Council of Ministers, thus taking over the premiership from Tsedenbal, who became head of state.

One of Batmunkh's first functions after taking over as head of state was to welcome CPSU General Secretary Mikhail Gorbachev to Ulan Bator in August. Replying to Gorbachev's toast at a state banquet, Batmunkh proclaimed Mongolia a faithful ally of the Soviet Union and a partner in joint efforts to maintain peace and security in the Far East.

(K. M. SMOGORZEWSKI)

Becker, Boris

He looked reckless, dashing and diving around the tennis court. But Boris Becker became the darling of professional tennis in 1985 by coolly channeling that energy, imposing Björn Borg's self-control on John McEnroe's fury. "He never thinks about the pressure," said Henri LeConte, whom Becker defeated in the Wimbledon quarterfinals. "He just plays, hits the ball, wins, says 'Thank you' and 'goodbye.'"

Becker won the Wimbledon final 6–3, 6–7, 7–6, 6–4 over Kevin Curren. He thus became the first West German, the first unseeded player, and, at 17 years, 7 months, the youngest male to win Wimbledon in its 99 years. He was the youngest to win any Grand Slam tournament. Becker's style made his youth all the more remarkable. Tennis's precocious children most often are conservative baseline players, but Becker was a serve-and-volley man. He served 21 aces against Curren.

Becker was born Nov. 22, 1967, in Leimen, West Germany, a bedroom community of 17,300 near Heidelberg. His father, architect Karl-Heinz Becker, designed and built the tennis centre where Boris learned the game. He was 12 when he chose to forgo his promise in soccer and concentrate on tennis. He was 16 when his long-time coach Gunther Bosch introduced him to manager Ion Tiriac.

That summer, 1984, Becker won his third consecutive West German junior championship. He won 11 of 22 matches in 13 tournaments, climbing from 200th to 65th in the world rankings. Tiriac put him on a rigorous winter training program, ignoring advice that it would wear out the youngster. Becker responded by vaulting to sixth in the rankings at the end of 1985.

Becker won his first professional tournament the week before Wimbledon, the Queen's Club men's grass court championship in London. After his Wimbledon triumph he defeated third-ranked Mats Wilander for the Association of Tennis Professionals championship and led his country past the United States to the Davis Cup final. There he did well—again beating Wilander—although his team lost to Sweden 3–2.

(KEVIN M. LAMB)

Berri, Nabih

Minister of state for southern Lebanon and justice minister in Lebanon's national unity government formed in April 1984, Nabih Berri was better known as the leader since 1980 of Amal (the Movement of Hope), a militia organization representing the Shi'ah community in Lebanon (about 40% of the nation's population). Its role in the 1985 hijacking of a Trans World Airlines aircraft and Berri's role in the negotiations to release hostages propelled Amal into international prominence. Amal was

considered a more moderate organization than more fundamentally religious Shi'ah groups such as Hizballah ("Party of God") and Islamic Amal (influenced by the Islamic regime in Iran).

Born about 1938 in Sierra Leone, then a British colony, Berri was the son of a Lebanese merchant there. He moved to Lebanon as a boy, studied law at the Lebanese University in Beirut (graduating in 1963), and subsequently studied in France. He practiced as a lawyer in Beirut and joined Amal when it was formed in 1974. Four years later he became its leader. His first wife was a U.S. citizen, and he held a "green card" entitlement to residence in the U.S., enabling him to visit his children there.

Berri became known for his moderate secular views. His influence on Amal changed it from a relatively obscure movement to a structured politico-military group. Amal was opposed to the partition of Lebanon, urging greater civil rights for the Shi'ah, who saw themselves as the most deprived sect in the nation. As a minister in the government, Berri participated in talks aimed at persuading Israel to withdraw from Lebanon in 1985, although many Shi'ah believed that Lebanon should not even talk to Israel. He and his Amal militia helped to secure the release of one American and a Frenchman kidnapped by extremists in early 1984.

Under Berri's leadership Amal was involved in armed clashes with Israeli forces, Maronite Christians, Palestinians, Sunni Muslims, and even the Druse, with whom Amal was allied. Despite his credentials as a moderate, Berri was forced to take responsibility and criticism for the radical actions of his militia. His contacts with Western diplomats resulted in his becoming a valued intermediary on Lebanon's increasingly unstable political scene.

(JOHN WHELAN)

Blaize, Herbert A.

After 17 years out of office, Herbert Blaize became prime minister of Grenada on Dec. 4, 1984, after a general election that restored parliamentary rule following the U.S.-led intervention that finally ended the era of the People's Revolutionary Government (1979–83). During 1985 Blaize followed a policy based on close economic, political, and military ties with the U.S. and aimed at encouraging overseas private investment and containing any revival of left-wing forces.

Blaize was born on Carriacou on Feb. 26, 1918. After attending the Grenada Boys Secondary School, in 1937 he joined the civil service in the Treasury Department. In 1944 he immigrated to Aruba to work as a clerical officer and English teacher in the oil refinery. He returned to Grenada in 1952 and the next year founded the Grenada National Party (GNP) as a rival to the Grenada United Labour Party headed by Eric Gairy. After taking a Law Society correspondence course, Blaize became a solicitor.

Entering Parliament in 1957, Blaize became minister of trade and production. In 1960 he became chief minister, but he was defeated by Gairy in the 1961 election. He took office again a year later, after Gairy had been removed by the British government following accusations of corruption.

During Blaize's five-year term, Grenada achieved internal self-government as an associated state. Gairy regained power in 1967 and oversaw a controversial move to independence in 1974. The GNP briefly joined forces with the New Jewel Movement (NJM) in an unsuccessful attempt to defeat Gairy in the 1976 election. When the NJM seized power in 1979, Blaize retired to Carriacou.

He came out of retirement to head a coalition of the GNP and other centre-right parties under the name New National Party. During 1985 reports surfaced of factional fighting within the coalition; Blaize, who also held the portfolios of finance, planning, trade, industrial development, home affairs, Carriacou affairs, information, and national security, was criticized by some of his colleagues for being uncommunicative and authoritarian. In October he spent four weeks in a U.S. military hospital in Washington, D.C., undergoing radiology treatment.   (ROD PRINCE)

Boesak, Allan Aubrey

With most leading black nationalist politicians under detention or in exile, two South African church leaders assumed an increasingly important role in the struggle against apartheid (racial separation). Protected both by their religious calling and by their high international standing, Bishop Desmond Tutu, the 1984 Nobel Peace Prize winner, and the Rev. Allan Boesak were able to establish themselves as two of the most influential spokesmen of nonwhite South Africans. In 1982 Boesak became president of the World Alliance of Reformed Churches (WARC),

ALLAN TANNENBAUM—SYGMA

which spoke for 70 million Protestants around the world. He was also patron of the United Democratic Front (UDF), which he helped establish. A loose federation of several hundred social, political, civic, and religious associations, the UDF tried to fill the vacuum in national politics caused by the banning of the black political parties.

Ordained in 1968, Boesak was a clergyman in the Dutch Reformed Church (DRC), which was closely identified with the apartheid system. Racially, he was himself classified as Coloured, a person of mixed-race descent. Boesak was persuaded that he could be more effective by

remaining within the DRC. Having influenced the WARC (with which the DRC was affiliated) to denounce apartheid as a heresy, Boesak tried to persuade the DRC to endorse this stand. His career in the church was briefly threatened when the police leaked documents alleging that he was engaging in extramarital relations with a white church worker; however, he was cleared by the church authorities. He was arrested in August 1985 when he attempted to lead a mass march to Pollsmoor Prison near Cape Town to protest against the continued detention of Nelson Mandela (q.v.). He was released on bail, and his passport was later withdrawn.

Boesak was born in 1946 in Kakmas, an isolated village in arid northwestern Cape of Good Hope, the seventh of eight children. His father was a teacher and his mother a seamstress. With the help of scholarships he was able to complete his theological studies at the Calvinist theological seminary in Kempen, Neth. As a student he was inspired by the anti-Nazi German theologian Dietrich Bonhoeffer, by Martin Luther King, Jr., and by the dissident DRC Afrikaner clergyman the Rev. W. C. Beyers Naude.   (COLIN LEGUM)

Boff, Leonardo

Father Leonardo Boff, a Brazilian Franciscan, was "silenced" by the Vatican on March 11, 1985. He was allowed neither to publish nor to lecture. This decision came from the Sacred Congregation for the Doctrine of the Faith (formerly the Holy Office), whose head, Joseph Cardinal Ratzinger, explained that "some of Boff's opinions were such as to endanger the sound doctrine of the faith."

Boff had said some harsh things about the church: "The drive for security was much stronger than that for truth and authenticity. Tensions were, and frequently are, suffocated through a repression that often violates basic human rights." Yet it was liberation theology that was at the heart of the dispute. That had been the subject of Boff's "colloquy" with Ratzinger in Rome on Sept. 7, 1984. They discussed Boff's collection of essays called *Church: Charism and Power.* Boff felt no great anxiety, for he was accompanied to Rome by two Brazilian prelates (both, as it happened, Franciscans), who defended him stoutly. That made it difficult for critics to say that he had invented a "popular church" at odds with the hierarchy. Ratzinger even hinted that Boff's contribution to a promised "positive" document on liberation theology might be welcomed.

The silencing, only six months later, came as a surprise to many. Boff accepted the ban, which was described as "indefinite," presumably one year. There were many ironies in the case, the chief of which perhaps was that liberation theology, which had often claimed to be "the voice of those who had no voice," now had lost its principal voice. (*See* WORLD AFFAIRS [Latin America and the Caribbean]: *Latin-American Affairs:* Special Report: Sidebar.)

Boff was born in Concordia, Brazil, in 1938, ordained a priest in 1964, and awarded a theology doctorate at Munich, West Germany. Until 1985 he was editor of the leading Brazilian theological review and had written many books.

          (PETER HEBBLETHWAITE)

Botha, P(ieter) W(illem)

A miscued speech by Pres. P. W. Botha in August 1985 tumbled South Africa into an unprecedented financial crisis during which the value of its rand currency was cut in half. His speech had been given a lengthy buildup, leading Western governments and international bankers, as well as domestic critics of apartheid (the policy of racial separation), to expect a major pronouncement about a program of reforms that would bring hope of peaceful political change in South Africa and restore international confidence in its long-term future.

Explaining later why he made the kind of speech that he did, Botha said that he was determined to show that he would not be "pushed around" (one of his favourite phrases) by his critics. Throughout a long political career spanning over half a century, Botha had invariably reacted negatively and aggressively to any action or suggestion that he believed to be hostile. Prickly and choleric, he was, nevertheless, a formidable politician—unquestionably the strongest white leader in South Africa.

Botha was committed to phasing out apartheid laws and to a policy of negotiating with representative black leaders about a new constitution for South Africa, but in implementing those policies he found himself trapped between two opposing forces: conservative elements within the Afrikaner (majority white) electorate who were totally opposed to abandoning apartheid, and an increasingly militant black opposition, angry and frustrated by the failure to move faster toward ending the discredited system. Even such a skillful politician as Botha found it difficult to steer his way between those conflicting forces.

Botha was born in a village in the Orange Free State on Jan. 12, 1916. After college he became an organizer of the Cape Province National Party at the age of 20. Twelve years later he entered Parliament with an established reputation as a shrewd party organizer. After holding several Cabinet posts, he became defense minister in 1966 and set about building his power base. He became known as the spokesman for the Army, and under his leadership the South African Defence Force grew into what might be the strongest and best armed in Africa. He became prime minister in 1978 and was elected executive president in September 1984.   (COLIN LEGUM)

Brown, Michael Stuart

As fellow interns at Massachusetts General Hospital in Boston, Michael Brown and Joseph Goldstein (q.v.) began a friendship that eventually developed into a close, lasting, and unusually successful scientific collaboration. Their discoveries about the metabolism of cholesterol were recognized in 1985 by the Nobel Prize for Physiology or Medicine. In the words of David Baltimore, an earlier winner of the Nobel Prize, "They changed a whole way of thinking about how cells and blood interact" by showing that a high concentration of cholesterol in the bloodstream is a sign of a defect in the cells rather than the blood.

Brown was born on April 13, 1941, in New York City. He attended the University of Pennsylvania, receiving a bachelor's degree in 1962 and a doctorate from the

School of Medicine in 1966. After spending two years at Massachusetts General, he and Goldstein moved to Bethesda, Md., to join different components of the National Institutes of Health. Brown became affiliated with the National Institute of Arthritis and Metabolic Diseases and the laboratory of biochemistry of the National Heart Institute; he concentrated on gastroenterology and the functions of the enzymes involved in the digestion of food. As he and Goldstein gained clinical experience with patients suffering from disorders of cholesterol metabolism, they began to formulate a program in which their complementary skills could be brought to bear on the study of these ailments.

In 1971 Brown accepted an appointment to the faculty of the Southwestern Medical School of the University of Texas at Dallas. In 1977 he was named Paul J. Thomas professor of genetics and director of the Center for Genetic Diseases at the university's Health Science Center. When Brown and Goldstein were reunited in Dallas in 1972, they set their plans in motion. Within a year they were able to announce a major discovery: that the process by which the cells absorb cholesterol from the bloodstream depends on the presence of specific receptors on the cell surface, and that the absence of those receptors results from a genetic defect. In children inheriting this defect from both parents, the cells are almost completely incapable of removing cholesterol from the blood. During the first few years of life the circulation to the heart can become so severely impaired that the child suffers a crippling or fatal heart attack.   (JOHN V. KILLHEFFER)

Buthelezi, Gatsha Mangosuthu

As the leader of six million Zulus—much the largest of all the ethnic communities in the country—Chief Gatsha Buthelezi was one of South Africa's most significant politicians. He was also one of its most controversial figures, increasingly out of step with most other black and white leaders except for the Progressive Federal Party. As chief minister of the KwaZulu homeland from 1972, he continued to defy the union government by refusing the kind of independence it offered, despite acceptance of similar terms by four other homelands. As leader of Inkatha, a movement claiming about one million members (almost exclusively Zulus), he tenaciously fought the government over its constitutional reform introducing a tricameral parliament (excluding blacks) and campaigned for a fully democratic constitution based on universal suffrage.

Buthelezi also quarreled with most other black political movements, especially the African National Congress (ANC). Two serious points of conflict concerned his campaign against economic sanctions and his criticism of armed struggle and other forms of political violence.

Buthelezi was born Aug. 27, 1928, at Mahlabatini, where his father was chief of the Shenge tribe. Through his mother he was a descendant of the Zulu royal line. His grandfather, King Dinizulu, had founded Inkatha as a Zulu cultural movement in 1924. Buthelezi revived it in 1974 as a mass political movement open to all Africans, but few non-Zulus joined. He therefore established the South African

JAN KOPEC—CAMERA PRESS, LONDON

Black Alliance, to which nonwhite political groups other than Inkatha could belong. However, when its important affiliate, the Labour Party, agreed to support the tricameral parliament, the Alliance declined in importance.

While still a student at the University College of Fort Hare, where he graduated in history and native administration, Buthelezi showed himself to be a rebel. As a member of the ANC Youth Wing, he was expelled during his final year in 1950 over his boycott of a visit by the governor-general (South Africa was then a Commonwealth of Nations dominion). At the age of 25 he was made acting chief of his tribe and in 1957 full chief.
          (COLIN LEGUM)

Cauthen, Steve

Steve Cauthen won his second British jockeys' championship in 1985. During the previous season he had become the first U.S.-born champion since Danny Maher in 1913, but his score was a modest 130, the lowest winning total since 1967. In 1985, however, he was truly champion with 195 winners. He held a good chance, almost to the final day of the season, of reaching 200, a feat previously achieved only by Fred Archer, Tommy Loates, and Sir Gordon Richards. But any disappointment that Cauthen may have felt could well be dissipated in 1986, because he had forged an excellent relationship with Henry Cecil, champion trainer in Britain six times in the last ten years. Cauthen replaced Lester Piggott as Cecil's retained jockey at the start of the 1985 season, and together they won four of the five British classics, with Oh So Sharp and Slip Anchor.

Cauthen, born May 1, 1960, in Covington, Ky., was a champion in the U.S. before he ever went to Europe. He took his first mount in a race at Churchill Downs in Kentucky on May 12, 1976, just 12 days after attaining the legally required age of 16, and rode his first winner, Red Pipe, on May 17 at River Downs, an Ohio track at which his father was working as a blacksmith. His mother and more than one of his uncles were horse trainers, and this background in the sport gave him a maturity beyond his years, enabling him to

cope with overnight success. By November 1976 he was in New York, where he soon started to break all records. It took him only to February 14 to ride 100 winners in 1977, and his total that year was 487 for then record earnings of more than $6 million.

Cauthen had formed a productive association with the leading two-year-old, Affirmed, and in 1978 he rode that colt to become the youngest jockey ever to win the Triple Crown. But luck turned against him early in 1979. A sequence of 110 losers included two defeats on Affirmed, and he lost the mount. His career appeared in ruins, and he accepted an invitation to ride in Britain. There, though he won the 1979 Two Thousand Guineas on Tap on Wood, he was not an immediate success. It took him several years to adapt his style and method to the requirements of European courses, but he revealed a champion's confidence on many occasions in 1985.
          (ROBERT W. CARTER)

Chiyonofuji

In the fifth of Japan's six annual sumo *basho* (tournaments), *yokozuna* (grand champion) Chiyonofuji ("Chiyo") won his 13th title in September with a perfect 15–0 record. It was the third straight victory for Chiyo in Kokugikan, the new sumo stadium that opened in Tokyo in January. When he won his fourth title of the year in November, Chiyo tied Wajima, a retired *yokozuna,* for third place on the list of all-time winners. In June the 30-year-old *rikishi* won the Pres. Ronald Reagan Cup during a tournament in New York City's Madison Square Garden. Chiyo was one of 38 wrestlers who participated in the rugged three-day event. He also performed *dohyoiri,* the impressive *yokozuna* ring-entering ritual, before members of the U.S. Department of State. Chiyo was featured in an advertisement that read "The Biggest Thing to Ever Hit New York," even though he was only 1.83 m (6 ft) tall and weighed 120 kg (264 lb); the tallest *rikishi* in competition was 1.99 m (6 ft 6½ in) and the heaviest 230 kg (506 lb). It was Chiyo's speed and skill that set him apart. He was also noted for his intense prefight stare and swift attack that earned him the nickname "Wolf." In a sport where fat is beautiful, he had manly good looks. When Chiyo married in September 1982, he may have lost some of his female supporters, but his earnings continued to climb steadily. In 1984 he reportedly earned more than 80 million yen (about $320,000). His monthly salary later reached 750,000 yen (about $3,750), but he earned extra money with each victory and advertising contract.

Chiyonofuji was born Mitsugu Akimoto on June 1, 1955, in the district of Matsumae, Hokkaido. As a boy he swam, played baseball, and ran track, but he did not wrestle. When he was 15 he graduated from junior high school and, encouraged by a retired *yokozuna* from Hokkaido, joined a sumo stable. In September 1970 he made his sumo debut and four years later became *juryo,* a full-fledged wrestler. By his fifth year Chiyo had reached the *makuuchi* division. He won his first *basho* in January 1981 with a 14–1 record and was promoted to *ozeki* (champion). After winning his second title in July, he was promoted to *yokozuna.* His trainer be-

lieved Chiyo could win five more championships before competition from younger men forced him to retire. Wolf promised only to try to win as many *basho* as he could.   (CHRISTINE PATTON CHAPMAN)

Cosby, Bill

For black comedian Bill Cosby, star and executive producer of the hit television series "The Cosby Show," comedy need not always be a laughing matter. Unlike his contemporaries Richard Pryor and Eddie Murphy, Cosby eschewed aggressive humour—the kind that leaves audiences shaking with laughter. Instead, Cosby's comedy was indirect and gentle; his wry observations on life coaxed audiences into knowing smiles.

In 1985 his television series induced so many smiling faces that it regularly ranked number one in the Nielsen ratings. The show featured the humorous adventures of the Huxtables, an upper-middle-class black family that closely resembled Cosby's real-life clan. Appropriately, Cosby played father: the witty, wise, and sometimes harried obstetrician, Heathcliff Huxtable. Cosby kept the show free of the conventions of television comedy; as he put it, "I told the writers I don't want sit-com jokes. I don't want jokes about behinds, or breasts, or pimples." The series also avoided racial stereotypes. In developing the story line, Cosby explained, his guiding philosophy "is to be true rather than funny." This serious approach to comedy won him major honours: a People's Choice award, a Golden Globe award, and first place on the TVQ index, the industry's most important measure of a star's popular appeal.

Cosby, who was born in Philadelphia on July 12, 1937, first became recognized as a comedian in the sixth grade. His teacher wrote, "William is an alert boy who would rather clown than study." Those words proved prophetic. In 1962 Cosby quit his studies at Temple University to tell jokes for $60 a week at the Gaslight Cafe in New York City's Greenwich Village. He soon graduated to such clubs as The Flamingo in Las Vegas and Mr. Kelly's in Chicago and to guest appearances on "Tonight" and "The Jack Paar Show."

Cosby's act impressed producer Sheldon Leonard, who in 1965 cast the comedian as CIA agent Alex Scott in "I Spy," the first television series to feature a black costar. In "I Spy" Cosby showed he could be funny in a serious milieu; he received Emmys for that effort in 1966 and 1967. He later starred as teacher Chet Kincaid in "The Bill Cosby Show," costarred in such films as *Uptown Saturday Night* (1974) and *Let's Do It Again* (1975), performed in concert halls across the U.S. and Canada, and appeared in numerous television commercials, including those that offered viewers "a Coke and a smile"—Cosby style, of course.   (MICHAEL AMEDEO)

Cossiga, Francesco

Francesco Cossiga was inaugurated as Italy's eighth president on July 9, 1985. At 56 he was the youngest person ever to be chosen head of the Italian state. He was also the first man to occupy the Quirinale Palace since World War II who had played no role in the resistance movement during the German occupation. In fact, Cossiga's career had been devoted almost exclusively

to his Christian Democrat Party since his university days. He was elected on June 24 by the combined houses of Parliament on the first ballot, something that had not happened since the election in 1946 of Enrico de Nicola, Italy's first (provisional) president. The message to the nation was that the two major parties, Cossiga's Christian Democrats and the Italian Communist Party (PCI), had come to an agreement beforehand, and the smaller parties fell into line. At the time of his election Cossiga was serving his second year as chairman of the Italian Senate. To that post, the second highest in the country, he had also been elected on the first ballot by the senators.

Cossiga was a Sardinian, born July 26, 1928, in Sassari. He was a second cousin of Enrico Berlinguer, leader of the PCI until his death in 1984. Cossiga joined the Christian Democrat Party in 1945 and three years later gained a law degree at Sassari. After holding minor party offices, he was elected to Parliament for the first time in 1958.

In 1976 Prime Minister Aldo Moro offered Cossiga the post of minister of the interior. "But I am a man of doubts," was the reserved Sardinian's response. "Precisely why I thought of you," said Moro; "doubts and imagination are necessary for the job." Two years later Cossiga had the sad challenge of supervising the state police when Moro was kidnapped by terrorists. A few hours after Moro's body was found, Cossiga resigned his Cabinet post. He was later called by his party to be prime minister in two successive Cabinets in 1979–80, for a total of 418 days.

Before being sworn in as president, Cossiga visited his native Sardinia, had a private audience with the pope, and formally resigned from the Christian Democrat Party. The last gesture was without precedent, and its message was understood and applauded throughout Italy.

(GEORGE ARMSTRONG)

Delvalle, Eric Arturo

When Eric Arturo Delvalle was sworn in as Panama's president on Sept. 28, 1985, there were serious doubts about his ability to remain in power for long. Not only had the country gone through three presidents in so many years, but its economic and political situation had become critical. With a $3.6 billion external debt and a stagnant economy, Panama was compelled in June to refinance $603 million in foreign payments due in 1985–86. Moreover, the mysterious murder in September of Hugo Spadafora—a controversial former minister of health—created a political scandal that was largely responsible for the resignation, on September 28, of Pres. Nicolás Ardito Barletta Vallarina, a move that opened the way for then vice-president Delvalle to assume the presidency.

The new president's moderate Republican Party was the smallest partner in the ruling coalition led by the left-of-centre Revolutionary Democratic Party (PRD), which immediately after the presidential transition dictated a series of economic policies that would have led inevitably to a confrontation with the nation's foreign creditors. The National Guard, Panama's defense force—which clearly played a major role in the "easing out" of Ardito Barletta—seemed willing enough to let Del-

valle try to solve the country's economic problems, especially after some opposition politicians claimed there was a link between the military and the Spadafora murder. Still, a coup was a possibility should the economy deteriorate further.

Eric Arturo Delvalle was born in Panama City on Feb. 2, 1937, and educated at Louisiana State University. A wealthy businessman with interests in sugar, real estate, and industry, in 1968 he was elected congressman and became vice-president of the National Assembly. He was chosen president of the Republican Party in 1983 and was later nominated vice-presidential candidate by the PRD-led coalition that narrowly—and disputedly—triumphed in the 1984 elections.

President Delvalle showed from the beginning that he intended to maintain an independent course. He rebuffed the PRD's policy demands when he informed the nation's creditors that he would continue the moderate economic policies of his predecessor. He also appointed Héctor Alexander as his finance minister. But even the best economic management might not be sufficient if general business conditions did not improve soon.   (SERGIO SARMIENTO)

Ditka, Mike

At Mike Ditka's first team meeting as the Chicago Bears' coach, he talked about going to the Super Bowl. It was a pipe dream no one had dared mention in recent years. Four years later, with two-thirds of the roster changed and the youngest team in the National Conference of the National Football League (NFL), the Bears beat New England in the 1986 Super Bowl 46–10. It was the highest score and biggest winning margin in the game's 20 years. Ditka was voted NFL coach of the year for 1985.

Ditka had always regarded the Bears with special pride. Even during Ditka's 13 seasons with the Dallas Cowboys, including 9 as an assistant coach, Cowboys coach Tom Landry told him he was a Bear at heart. He had played with the Bears in 1961–66 but left after saying owner-coach George Halas "tossed nickels around as if they were manhole covers." Halas forgave him and rehired Ditka in 1982 to restore the Bears to their prominence of the 1930s and 1940s. Ditka's comparative inexperience made him a surprising choice, but he did what Halas wanted. He convinced the Bears that they had as much right as anyone to win and that they should play harder simply because they were Bears.

Ditka was an all-star tight end for five of his six Bears seasons. He was NFL rookie of the year in 1961 and set a professional football record with 75 catches at tight end in 1964. He battled opponents to the last inch and challenged teammates who were not living up to his lofty standards. As coach he told the players, "Put a chip on your shoulder in July, and don't take it off until January."

Ditka designed an imaginative offense around the Bears and did not interfere with an innovative defense that threatened to revolutionize the game. After a 3–6 strike-shortened season in 1982 and a 3–7 start in 1983, the Bears won 30 of their next 38 regular-season games, including their first 12 in the 15–1 1985 season. They won division championships in 1984 and 1985, their first since 1963.

Michael Keller Ditka was born Oct. 18, 1939, in Carnegie, Pa., and grew up nearby in the steel-mill town of Aliquippa. His high-school coach had to talk him out of quitting because he thought he was too small. That problem solved, he became an All-America college player at nearby Pittsburgh and a first-round NFL draft choice.

(KEVIN M. LAMB)

Fisher, Mel

On July 20, 1985, Mel Fisher's diving crew found a treasure hunter's dream; stacked on a reef 15 m (50 ft) underwater, in the Straits of Florida 65 km (40 mi) west of Key West, lay hundreds of silver bars. They were from the cargo of the *Nuestra Señora de Atocha,* a galleon bound for Spain that sank with several sister ships in a hurricane on Sept. 6, 1622. Colonial records indicated that the *Atocha* had gone down with about 1,200 silver ingots weighing 31.5 kg (70 lb) each, 160 small gold bars and disks, and more than 250,000 silver coins. Long sought by colonial Spanish as well as modern American hunters, the trove was finally discovered after a 19-year effort by Fisher's own firm, Treasure Salvors, Inc. Often near bankruptcy and locked in legal disputes, Treasure Salvors was little more than a tourist museum and a fleet of second-hand tugs, barges, and pleasure boats. But if estimates of the find's value proved true (anywhere between $200 million and $400 million), Fisher, his crew, and the investors in his enterprise would be rich.

Melvin A. Fisher was born Aug. 21, 1922, in Gary, Ind. He graduated from Purdue University and served in the Army Corps of Engineers during World War II. In 1950 he moved to California to work on his parents' chicken farm, but his love of underwater exploring led him to open a scuba shop. In 1963 he moved to Florida, where he incorporated Treasure Salvors the next year. During the next 20 years his firm found more than 100 shipwrecks.

In 1966 Fisher began to search the Florida Keys for the *Atocha* fleet, using such devices as high-speed magnetometers, side-scanning sonar, and his own invention, called the "mailbox"—a pipe that blows away sand cover by directing jets

SYGMA

of water from the boat's screws to the seafloor below. In 1971 his crew found the *Atocha*'s anchor. In 1980 they came across a sister ship, the *Santa Margarita,* and began salvaging an estimated $20 million in gold chain and bullion, much of which was distributed to outside investors. Then, following a trail of scattered gold and debris, they worked back to where the *Atocha* lay, eight kilometres (five miles) from where they had found the anchor.

The riches came at a great cost to Fisher and his family (his wife and children all dived for the firm); in 1975 his eldest son and daughter-in-law drowned with another crewman while searching for the *Atocha.*

(ROBERT CURLEY)

Fontaine, André

Associate editor of *Le Monde* since 1969, André Fontaine on Jan. 18, 1985, became the fourth director and editor in chief of France's premier newspaper of record since it was established in 1945. At the age of 63 he took over as successor to *Le Monde*'s founder Hubert Beuve-Méry, Jacques Fauvet, and André Laurens, who had resigned on Dec. 20, 1984.

Fontaine was elected managing director by 890 of the 1,000 shareholders' votes in the company. The choice came as no surprise to those who had known him for many years and admired his professionalism, his wide culture, his expertise in foreign affairs, and his intellectual honesty. He matured with the newspaper and was certain to carry on the tradition of independence that was the pride of its journalists. Moreover, he appeared to be the only person able to remedy a situation that had deteriorated in recent years to the point where the newspaper's survival seemed in jeopardy. On January 21 a plan was put into effect involving financial restructuring and measures to reform the company (salary reductions, increases in charges for sales and advertising, and economies in personnel and production).

The establishment of a "Society of Readers of *Le Monde*" allowed the floating of new shares in the *Le Monde* limited company following an increase in the amount of registered capital. On the editorial side, *Le Monde* became more readable, with more compact articles and clearer layout. Scoops like the one on September 17 that exposed the French government's involvement in the "Greenpeace affair" proved profitable, bringing an increase of 11% in sales throughout the week, compared with the corresponding period in 1984. Long under threat, *Le Monde* had made a fresh start.

Born on March 30, 1921, in Paris, Fontaine gained an arts degree and postgraduate qualification in public law and political economy. His career in journalism began at *Temps Présent* (1946–47). Joining *Le Monde* in 1947, he became the head of its foreign service in 1951 and associate editor in 1969. He was the author of several books, including *Histoire de la guerre froide* (1969), *Un Seul Lit pour deux rêves* (1981), and in 1985 a work written with Pierre Li, *Sortir de l'Hexagonie.*

(JEAN KNECHT)

Fox, Michael J.

In 1985 many people in the United States continued to protest the country's trade

policy, but at least one import proved beyond criticism: the subcompact Canadian actor Michael J. Fox, who became an American superstar. The 24-year-old, 1.6-m (5-ft 4-in) Fox won recognition as both a matinee idol and a talented comic for his work in "Family Ties," a television series that climbed to the number two spot in the Nielsen ratings, and *Back to the Future,* a film that outgrossed every other 1985 release, including *Rambo.*

The keys to Fox's success lay in his slight build, apple-pie face, and engaging, laid-back manner, which together gave him the look of a pleasantly ordinary American teen. In his role as 18-year-old Alex Keaton in "Family Ties," Fox's conventionality took on an additional twist: he played the ultraconservative son of two fortyish liberals, both former flower children. In *Back to the Future* Fox became the hip, small-town youth Marty McFly, who journeys 30 years into the past, meets his parents as teenagers, and accidentally changes the course of their lives. To capitalize on his new fame, Fox in 1985 also starred in *Teen Wolf,* a low-budget comedy in which he breaks out with something more unfortunate than acne: werewolf hair.

Fox was born in Edmonton, Alta., on June 9, 1961. The son of an army man, he moved often—changing schools, friends, and personalities as often as he changed addresses. In high school Fox studied drama and discovered he could look and act younger than his years. During a screen test for the Canadian Broadcasting Corporation, the 15-year-old Fox struck officials as the brightest ten-year-old they had ever seen. A star was in the making.

Despite appearing with Art Carney in *Letters from Frank* (1979), a film made in Vancouver, B.C., Fox soon concluded that he faced a dim future as an actor in Canada, so he accepted jobs in the United States, eventually appearing in the 1980–81 television series "Palmerstown, USA," the movie *Midnight Madness* (1980), and then "Family Ties" (September 1982). Reflecting on his move, Fox said that "the only way to success for a young person in Canada is to be a hockey player." And though he enjoyed playing his country's national sport, he preferred to make people laugh, a service in great demand in a humour-hungry United States.

(MICHAEL AMEDEO)

García Pérez, Alan

The conclusive victory won by Alan García Pérez in the April 14, 1985, presidential election was widely seen to mark a watershed in modern Peruvian history. García narrowly missed winning outright with 48% of the vote, but the runner-up, Alfonso Barrantes Lingán of the Marxist Izquierda Unida party, conceded defeat, thus saving a second round of voting. García, who was sworn in on July 28, became the first elected president to succeed another democratically chosen candidate in Peru in more than 40 years. He was also the first Alianza Popular Revolucionaria Americana (APRA) leader to take office as president, despite APRA's being the country's oldest political party.

Alan García, born May 23, 1949, in Lima, had risen fast. A lawyer educated in Lima and in Spain and France, he won his first political victory in 1980 when

he gained a seat in the lower house of Congress. Two years later he became general secretary of APRA. His opponents criticized his lack of political experience, and certainly he had no experience of governing. To his supporters, however, this very weakness became a strength, and certainly he did not bow to the customary pressures of the military and (more recently) the international bankers.

An imposing figure (heavily built and 1.9 m [6 ft 4 in] tall), García was compared to Spain's Prime Minister Felipe González Márquez as one who wanted to put ideology to one side and aimed to make politics practical. After taking office García became extremely visible both at home and abroad. In his maiden speech to the UN General Assembly, he was critical of the role that the wealthy industrialized world (especially the U.S.) played in relation to less developed debtor countries. This outspokenness won him many supporters at home but served to raise eyebrows internationally.

Probably the most politically destabilizing problem that García faced was that of the Maoist Sendero Luminoso (Shining Path) guerrilla movement. One of his most fervent campaigns was to alter the imbalance between Lima and the rest of Peru because he believed that this would be the way to cut off support for Sendero and also would slow the uncontrolled migration to the cities. García's strongest impact, however, was to change the demoralized mood of the country to one of tentative hope.

(INGRID IVERSEN)

Geldof, Bob

Bob Geldof, pop star in decline, was prompted by television reports of the famine in Ethiopia in October 1984 to turn crusader in the cause of reawakening the pop music world's social conscience. He established the Band Aid charity, which in turn inspired USA for Africa in the U.S., to raise money for famine victims. He then employed his energies in organizing the hugely ambitious and successful Live Aid concert, which took place in London and Philadelphia on July 13, 1985. In its wake Geldof was nominated for the Nobel Peace Prize.

At intervals he trained the spotlight of his obsessive candour on governments and institutions. In October, during a tour of six sub-Saharan countries to assess their need for famine relief, he did not flinch from asking African leaders embarrassing questions about corruption and repression in their countries. On his return he castigated members of the European Parliament for the existence of food surpluses in Europe in the face of extreme need in Africa.

Robert Frederick Xenon Geldof was born on Oct. 5, 1951, at Dun Laoghaire, County Dublin, Ireland. After leaving school he held a succession of jobs, ranging from bulldozer operator to pop-music journalist. In 1975 he and several friends formed a "new-wave" pop group called the Nightlife Thugs, soon renamed the Boomtown Rats; their performances involved releasing live rats among the audience. In 1976 the group moved to London, where it enjoyed a heady but brief success. Two singles—"Rat Trap" and "I Don't Like Mondays"—topped the record charts in Britain in 1979 and 1980, respectively. The

group failed to make an impact in the U.S., though the latter song, which concerned a real-life shooting incident in San Diego, Calif., brought notoriety by being banned.

At a time when pop lyrics were largely preoccupied with the deprivation of unemployment, Geldof made enemies when he accused the punk movement of hypocrisy. Nevertheless, his sincerity silenced suggestions that his fund-raising efforts were aimed at reviving his own career. In fact, the record-buying public continued to all but ignore the Boomtown Rats, while Geldof's film career—he had taken starring roles in *Pink Floyd—The Wall* (1982) and *Number One* (1985)—was no more than moderately successful.

(LOUISE WATSON)

Goizueta, Roberto

In April the Coca-Cola Co. announced that it was scrapping its 99-year-old soft-drink formula and was coming out with a new Coke. A mere three months later, feeling as though he had been under siege with no pause to refresh, Roberto Goizueta, the company's chairman and chief executive officer, capitulated to consumer pressure and brought back the old formula under the name Coca-Cola Classic; the new drink remained on the market. In spite of his being the man who had presided over the transformation of the undisputed leader of the $25 million soft-drink industry into a $7.4 billion giant, Goizueta's idea for a recipe change appeared to many business analysts to have been the marketing blunder of the decade.

Goizueta, the son of a wealthy Cuban sugar-plantation owner, moved to the United States when he was 16. Though he entered the exclusive Cheshire Academy unable to speak English, he graduated valedictorian of his class. In 1955 he received a degree in chemical engineering from Yale University and then returned to Cuba to work in Coca-Cola's research laboratories. Four years later Fidel Castro seized power in Cuba, and Goizueta and his wife and their three children fled to the U.S., settling in Miami, Fla. Goizueta continued to work for Coca-Cola, commuting to The Bahamas and administering the firm's chemical research facilities there. He began to acquire a reputation as an astute and efficient manager and by 1965 had been transferred to company headquarters in Atlanta, Ga.

Goizueta was named chief executive officer in 1981, and after that time Coca-Cola underwent significant changes. The name Coke, which for decades had been jealously reserved for the original-formula drink, was applied in July 1982 to Diet Coke, which in less than three years became the third-largest-selling soft drink in the U.S. By 1985 the name was on five other soft drinks, as well as on a line of clothing. Under Goizueta, Coca-Cola employed enterprising financing methods and advertising campaigns and in 1982 purchased Columbia Pictures Industries Inc. for $700 million in cash and stock. In June 1985 Coca-Cola acquired the television producers Embassy Communications and Tandem Productions in a $400 million deal. Such departures from Coke's former conservative, close-to-the-vest style, moving the firm into the ranks of major players on the acquisitions scene, seemed

mere tactical feints next to the decision to throw out the real thing.

(BONNIE OBERMAN)

Goldstein, Joseph Leonard

Of people suffering heart attacks before they were 60 years old, about one in 20 had a disorder called familial hypercholesterolemia, or FH. Two medical geneticists, Joseph L. Goldstein and Michael S. Brown (*q.v.*), made striking progress toward understanding FH; their discoveries earned them the Nobel Prize for Physiology or Medicine in 1985.

Most of the cholesterol in the blood is present in low-density lipoprotein (LDL), which exists in the form of tiny globules. These are coated with a detergentlike compound that keeps them suspended in the watery blood serum. The rest of the surface is occupied by a specific protein by which the LDL attaches itself to a complementary protein on the cells of the body in the first step in the transfer of cholesterol from the blood into the cells. The structure of the receptor protein is controlled by a single gene, and any of several defects in the gene leads to failure of the cells to absorb LDL.

About 500,000 U.S. residents, the victims of FH, carry one such gene; these people have about twice the normal concentration of LDL in their blood, and many of them fall prey to heart disease before they are 35 years old. The identification of the LDL receptors by Goldstein and Brown in 1973 led to a radical change in the way biologists viewed the interaction between cells and blood. It opened the way toward a series of further discoveries by the two Nobel laureates about the fate of LDL within the cell and rational methods for influencing the course of FH.

Goldstein was born in Sumter, S.C., on April 18, 1940, and graduated from Washington and Lee University, Lexington, Va., in 1962. He received his M.D. from Southwestern Medical School of the University of Texas in Dallas in 1966, then spent two years as an intern and resident at Massachusetts General Hospital in Boston, where he and Brown became close friends. They both went next to the National Institutes of Health (NIH) at Bethesda, Md., where Goldstein became a clinical associate in the laboratory of biochemical genetics of the National Heart Institute. In 1972 Goldstein returned to Dallas and the University of Texas as a member of its faculty, which Brown had joined a year earlier.

(JOHN V. KILLHEFFER)

Gooden, Dwight

When Dwight Gooden had two strikes on a batter, the stands started buzzing and the K signs started dancing. K is the baseball scorecard symbol for strikeout, and to the fans in the stands, Gooden was the 1.9-m (6-ft 3-in), high-kicking New York Mets right-hander who had struck out more batters at a younger age than any other pitcher in major league history. But to opponents in the dugouts Gooden's 155-km/h (96-mph) fastball and nearly 129-km/h (80-mph) curve were only the beginning. They marveled at his poise, at the way he controlled his pitches and knew how to use them. Chicago Cub manager Jim Frey called Gooden "the best pitcher I've ever seen at his age."

MICHAEL BONZINI—FOCUS ON SPORTS

In 1984 he was the youngest ever to be voted rookie of the year; the youngest to play in an All-Star game, where he struck out his first three batters; and the youngest to lead a league in strikeouts. He led both leagues with a rookie-record 276. In 1985 he was the youngest to win 20 games and the youngest to win the Cy Young Award, which he received the week of his 21st birthday.

"Things have moved pretty rapidly in my career," Gooden said. "You just try to do a little bit better each year." After his rookie year he went to the Instructional League, usually for minor leaguers, to develop a change-up pitch and improve his pick-off move. He had rarely needed to hold runners on base during high school and 1½ seasons in the minor leagues because batters rarely had reached base against him.

Dwight Eugene Gooden was born Nov. 16, 1964, the youngest of four children, in a predominantly black, working-class section of East Tampa, Fla. His father, Dan, played semipro baseball and started taking him to games when he was three. By the time he was 14 Gooden was so superior to his contemporaries that a local writer nicknamed him "Doc," explaining that "what Dr. J is to basketball, Dwight Gooden is to baseball." The nickname became "Dr. K" in Gooden's rookie year. His 11.39 strikeouts per nine innings shattered the previous major-league record of 10.71. His 32 strikeouts in two consecutive games tied a National League record. His won–lost record was 17–9, with a 2.60 earned run average that ranked second in the majors.

In 1985 Gooden led both leagues with a 1.53 earned run average, 268 strikeouts, and 24 wins (against 4 defeats). He won 18 of his last 19 decisions and kept his team in the pennant race until the last weekend. Perhaps most amazing was the scarcity of walks he allowed: 3.01 per nine innings as a rookie and 2.24 in 1985.

(KEVIN M. LAMB)

Gorbachev, Mikhail Sergeyevich

Before his December 1984 visit to the U.K. as leader of a Soviet parliamentary delegation, few people in the West knew anything of importance about Mikhail Gorbachev. Eleven months later, however, he was U.S. Pres. Ronald Reagan's opposite number at the summit meeting that opened in Geneva on Nov. 19, 1985. The extraordinary rapidity of Gorbachev's progress was due, first, to the unusual mortality that between November 1982 and March 1985 claimed three Soviet leaders and, second, to his personality and his disciplined intellect.

When Konstantin Chernenko died on March 10, there was little doubt either in the Kremlin or in Western foreign ministries that Gorbachev would succeed him. However, when the Politburo of the Communist Party of the Soviet Union (CPSU) met the following day, Grigory Romanov, an adversary of Gorbachev, proposed that Viktor Grishin succeed Chernenko—as the latter had himself proposed in a deathbed message to the Politburo. But no one seconded Romanov's motion, and so Andrey Gromyko proposed Gorbachev to the CPSU Central Committee (CC), which unanimously elected him as CPSU general secretary.

Gorbachev's most urgent task was to reinforce his position within the Politburo. Six weeks after he became the most powerful man within the Soviet Union, the CC elected as Politburo members Viktor Chebrikov, head of the State Security Committee (KGB); Yegor Ligachev, responsible for cadres in the party Secretariat; and Nikolay Ryzhkov (q.v.), who on September 27 was appointed chairman of the Council of Ministers (premier). On July 1 Eduard Shevardnadze (q.v.) became a full member of the Politburo and the following day was appointed foreign minister. Also on July 1 the CC accepted the "request of Comrade Romanov to be freed from the duties of a Politburo member." Then in October former premier Nikolay Tikhonov retired from the Politburo, which now had 12 members, on 8 of whom, at the very least, Gorbachev could rely for support.

Gorbachev was born March 2, 1931, at Privolnoye, Stavropol territory, into a peasant family. After working on a state farm, as a promising Komsomol (Young Communist League) member he was sent to Moscow State University, where he graduated in law. A CPSU member from 1952, he advanced steadily in the Stavropol city and territorial party organizations. In 1971 he was elected to the CC, in 1979 to candidate membership of the Politburo, and in 1980 to full Politburo membership.

(K. M. SMOGORZEWSKI)

Gower, David Ivon

When the England cricket team regained the Ashes by defeating Australia 3–1 in the six-test series in 1985, England captain David Gower was named man of the series in recognition of his outstanding performance with the bat, which included a match-winning innings of 215 in the fifth test. The enthusiastic applause for Gower drowned out the memory of calls for his resignation earlier in the season, when his own and his team's poor performance raised memories of England's humiliating defeat at the hands of West Indies in 1984, Gower's first season as captain.

Born April 1, 1957, in Tunbridge Wells, Kent, England, David Ivon Gower spent his early years in East Africa, where his father was in the colonial service. The family returned to England in 1963 after Tanganyika (now Tanzania) became independent. Gower attended King's public school, Canterbury, where, the story goes, his apparent indolence provoked a master to upbraid the 15-year-old, asking him where he thought he would be in ten years' time. "Captain of England," came the reply. His forecast was optimistic by only two years.

When approached by Leicestershire County Cricket Club in 1975, Gower had little hesitation in deciding to abandon his law studies at University College, the University of London, in favour of a full-time career in cricket. Within three years he had made his debut for England, and in 1982 he was appointed England vice-captain under Bob Willis. He became captain of both his county and his country in the same season (1984).

In the opinion of some, perhaps including Gower himself, his elevation to the England captaincy had come too soon. His style of leadership was by nature undemonstrative, while his blond curls and angelic countenance resembled more than anything the seemingly innocent choirboy who delights in the antics of his more openly rebellious companions. However, following his baptism by fire against West Indies, his captaincy acquired a new assurance in 1985, while his batting regained the touch that, most believed, would set him among the greatest batsmen of all time. An accomplished stroke-maker who batted left-handed, Gower possessed a finely tuned technique that left little margin for error. In his own words, "If you hit a four without moving your feet they say it is effortless; if you get out then it is a fault in your game."   (LOUISE WATSON)

Gregory, Cynthia

On June 4, 1985, American Ballet Theatre (ABT) accorded Cynthia Gregory an unusual honour for an individual dancer—a gala—to celebrate her 20 years with the company. One feature of the gala was "Memories," in which Gregory illustrated her outstanding versatility and brilliant technique in excerpts from several of the 70 works she had performed with ABT, works that ranged from the classical Swan Lake to contemporary solos created for her by Alvin Ailey (The River), Eliot Feld (At Midnight), and Twyla Tharp (Bach Partita). The exhilarating program carried a sense of poignancy, too, for the evening was dedicated to the memory of John Hemminger, her husband of nine years, who had died within the previous year.

Gregory was born July 8, 1946, in Los Angeles. She began her study of ballet at the age of five and was on the cover of Dance magazine at seven. In 1961 she enrolled at the San Francisco Ballet School. She officially joined the San Francisco Ballet in late 1961 and was promoted to soloist a few months later.

In 1965 she and Terry Orr, another soloist, moved to New York City and auditioned for ABT. Orr was accepted immediately, but Gregory was thought too tall—at 1.68 m (5 ft 6 in) tall, she stood nearly 1.8 m (6 ft) on pointe—and had to audition three times before she was accepted. She and Orr were married in 1966.

Gregory advanced rapidly in the company. She was promoted to soloist in 1966 and to principal dancer in 1967. The role that brought her to prominence was that of Odette/Odile in Swan Lake, which she first danced in the summer of 1967. She continued to work on the dramatic nuances of the role and made her interpretation one of the most memorable in ballet his-

tory. Other notable roles were in Antony Tudor's *Undertow* and *Lilac Garden,* José Limón's *The Moor's Pavane,* and Birgit Cullberg's *Miss Julie.* In 1975 she won a *Dance* magazine award.

There were, as she put it, "some rough spots along the way"—the two times she resigned from ABT. The first time, in 1975, followed her divorce from Orr, and she stayed away nearly a year. In 1979 she left ABT for six months, during which she made guest appearances around the world. The rough spots were far outnumbered by the triumphs, however, and she continued to dazzle audiences with her daring and her ability to bring new dimensions to familiar roles.   (BARBARA WHITNEY)

Hauptman, Herbert Aaron

When the three winners of the Nobel Prize for Physics in 1979 were announced, many commentators found it remarkable that two of them, Sheldon Glashow and Steven Weinberg, had been members of the same college class (Cornell University, 1954). Eyebrows rose even higher when Herbert Hauptman and Jerome Karle (*q.v.*) won the Prize for Chemistry in 1985; not only had they both graduated in 1937 from City College (now City University) of New York, but a third member of their class, Arthur Kornberg, had shared the Prize for Physiology or Medicine in 1959.

Hauptman and Karle were the principal architects of the most general procedure yet introduced for deducing the molecular structure of crystalline chemical compounds from the patterns formed on photographic plates when narrow beams of X-rays strike the crystals and give rise to secondary beams. The directions and intensities of those beams are strictly governed by the regular spacing of the atoms in the crystal, but the relationship is complicated, and no method had been devised for the direct translation of the X-ray patterns to crystal structures. Hauptman and Karle developed a procedure for dealing with this problem, publishing their first results by 1950. It required extensive calculations but only a single treatment of the experimental data.

Hauptman was born in New York City on Feb. 14, 1917. After completing his undergraduate education, he went on to Columbia University, also in New York City, to obtain a master's degree in 1939. He worked as a statistician for the U.S. Bureau of the Census in 1940–42 and served two two-year terms as a radar instructor in the U.S. Army Air Forces before beginning his scientific career as a physicist at the Naval Research Laboratory, Washington, D.C., in 1947. While at the laboratory Hauptman collaborated with Karle in developing a new technique for interpreting X-ray diffraction patterns. He also studied advanced mathematics at the University of Maryland and was awarded a Ph.D. in 1955.

In 1970 Hauptman moved to Buffalo, N.Y., taking a position as mathematician at the Medical Foundation, a small private organization specializing in endocrine research, and also accepting a research professorship in biophysical sciences at the State University of New York. In 1972 he was named director of research and vice-president of the Medical Foundation.
    (JOHN V. KILLHEFFER)

Howard, John Winston

On Sept. 5, 1985, John Howard became leader of the Liberal Party of Australia during an extraordinary and unexpected crisis in confidence caused by mistrust in the relationship between Howard and his chief, Andrew Peacock. Peacock, who, in the words of the Australian Broadcasting Commission, turned himself from a rooster to a feather duster in two hours, caused his own ouster by demanding from Howard an unrealistic assurance that he would in no circumstances challenge for the position of party leader. Misjudging the mood of his party, Peacock called a special meeting to settle "once and for all" the leadership question. Unconvinced by Howard's protests of loyalty, Peacock put the matter to the vote and was dumbfounded to find that the outcome was that the parliamentary party (*i.e.,* Liberal Party members of Parliament) chose Howard to lead them, at the same time moving the Liberal Party's power base back to Sydney from Melbourne. Howard, who was called back from a skiing holiday to face his leader's wrath, was magnanimous in victory and allowed Peacock to pick the shadow portfolio of his choice—that of foreign affairs.

Howard posed a considerable new threat to Prime Minister Bob Hawke's Australian Labor Party (ALP), which, despite successes with labour relations and the unemployment problem, failed to check inflation or contain the decline in the value of the Australian dollar. Howard's expertise and parliamentary reputation stemmed from his relative success as federal treasurer in Malcolm Fraser's Liberal Party–National Party coalition. With public opinion polls presaging a Liberal victory in the event of a federal election, Howard thus seemed a likely successor to the post of prime minister.

John Howard, born July 26, 1939, in Sydney, was a law graduate of the University of Sydney and practiced as a solicitor to the Supreme Court of New South Wales. He moved through the Liberal Party machine as a member of the party executive (1963–74) and vice-president (1972–74) of the New South Wales division of the party. In 1974 he was elected to the House of Representatives as member for Bennelong, New South Wales. He held several portfolios in the previous conservative administration, being minister for business and consumer affairs (1975–77), minister for special trade negotiations (1977), and, most importantly, federal treasurer from 1977 until the Fraser ministry fell in March 1983. He then became deputy leader of the opposition.   (A. R. G. GRIFFITHS)

Hoyte, Hugh Desmond

The sudden death of Pres. Forbes Burnham (*see* OBITUARIES) of Guyana on Aug. 6, 1985, thrust Hugh Desmond Hoyte, previously the country's prime minister and first vice-president, into the role of executive president at a time when Guyana was undergoing a prolonged economic and social crisis. Burnham died shortly after his ruling People's National Congress (PNC) had embarked on talks with the opposition People's Progressive Party (PPP) with a view to achieving a national unity formula to deal with the country's problems.

While confirming his willingness to continue the dialogue, Hoyte also announced that a general election would be held on December 9. Responding to criticisms of previous elections as fraudulent, he agreed to certain reforms. Nonetheless, conduct of the election, which returned the PNC to power with an increased majority, was widely criticized for irregularities, and Hoyte's chances of achieving a national reconciliation were thereby diminished.

Born on March 9, 1929, Hoyte was educated at St. Barnabas Anglican School and the Progressive High School before studying law at the University of London (1957–60). He returned to Guyana to practice law, becoming secretary (1962–66) and vice-president (1967–68) of the Guyana Bar Association.

Hoyte entered Parliament as a PNC member in 1968 and was appointed home affairs minister in 1969, moving to finance in 1970, works and communications in 1972, and economic development in 1974. From then on he concentrated on economic affairs. Following the December 1980 election he became one of five vice-presidents, with responsibility for economic planning, finance, and regional development. In August 1984 he was made first vice-president and prime minister. A retiring personality, but reputed to have a hot temper, Hoyte suffered a severe personal loss in April 1985 when his two teenage daughters were killed and his wife was seriously injured in a car crash.
    (ROD PRINCE)

Hughes, Ted

When Ted Hughes was appointed Britain's poet laureate in 1984, he announced: "For me the crown is the symbol of the unity of the tribe." This was different from the rather shy, unashamedly suburban respect for the British monarchy that had been expressed by his predecessor, Sir John Betjeman. The use of the word tribe provoked another poet, Tom Paulin, to parody Hughes's statement with a verse written in a sort of pidgin English. Undeterred, Hughes published a long, exuberant poem about the force of water, rainstorms, and swollen rivers of West Britain, to celebrate the christening of Prince Harry, under the title "Rain-Charm for the Duchy." This too was quickly parodied by a British poet; but an American critic, David Bromwich,

THOMAS VICTOR

was rather "impressed by the dexterity" with which the poem brought "a subject of state" into the precincts of Hughes's work, drawing from the elemental world of nature "a pleasant, handsome, rousing compliment to a Prince."

The open-air world of nature, in its most harsh and challenging aspects, had long been dominant in Hughes's work, ever since *The Hawk in the Rain* (1957), his first volume of verse. Edward James Hughes was born Aug. 16, 1930, at Mytholmroyd, Yorkshire. Long industrialized, although in its time a part of the last Celtic kingdom to fall to the invading Angles, Mytholmroyd inspired a sort of mythic tribalism. As a youth, son of a local shopkeeper, Hughes was much influenced by the mythology of Robert Graves's *The White Goddess*. When he went to Pembroke College, University of Cambridge, after his military service, he studied archaeology and anthropology, interests that were reflected in his works. A naturalist and an enthusiastic fisherman, Hughes took his son to Alaska in 1980 to fish for giant salmon. The experience inspired some of the poems in his most recent volume, *River* (1983).

Hughes married the American poet Sylvia Plath in 1956; the couple had two children. They were already separated when, in 1963, Plath committed suicide. For nearly three years after her death, Hughes stopped writing poetry. When he returned to it, his verse was not autobiographical or confessional, but it was recognized that in such laments as "The Howling of Wolves," in such books as *Wodwo* (1967; named after an old English "wild man of the woods"), and in the sinister *Crow* poems of 1970–71, an element of dark autobiography might be discerned. Energy, violence, and perhaps even cruelty were often recognized as disconcerting elements in his work. He edited *Sylvia Plath: Collected Poems* (1981), and his own *Selected Poems 1957–81* appeared in 1982. In 1977 he was made an Officer of the Order of the British Empire.

(D. A. N. JONES)

Jobs, Steven Paul

Steven Jobs, who cofounded Apple Computer, Inc., in his parents' garage in 1975, almost single-handedly promoted the personal computer and built Apple into a multimillion-dollar corporation. On Sept. 17, 1985, Jobs resigned as chairman of Apple; it was the end of an era and a symbol of the growing conservatism in the personal computer industry.

Steven was adopted in February 1955 by Paul and Clara Jobs. The family moved from Mountain View, Calif., to Los Altos, Calif., because of Steven's problems in school. In Los Altos young Jobs, always a loner, showed more interest in studying electronics at Hewlett-Packard Corp. in nearby Palo Alto than in attending high school. While working summers at Hewlett-Packard he met Stephen Wozniak, who was applying his engineering wizardry to his own electronic gadgets. Jobs briefly attended Reed College in Portland, Ore., and then worked on video games at Atari, Inc., before traveling to India in 1974. In 1975 he was reunited with Wozniak. Jobs was intrigued by the marketing possibilities of the gadgets that Wozniak had developed and encouraged him to design a

small computer for home use. While Jobs sought marketing strategies and financing from his bedroom office, Wozniak worked in Jobs's garage to build the prototype computer that was to become the Apple I. Jobs's name for the new company was inspired by a summer job he held in an Oregon orchard; he insisted that the new computer be lightweight and user friendly.

In 1977 Jobs and Wozniak introduced the improved Apple II, and in 1980, when the company went public, it had sales of more than $130 million. Later products failed to do as well, however, and after IBM's entry into the field with its IBM PC, Jobs's belief that Apple's computers should remain incompatible with IBM's further eroded company prospects.

In 1983 Jobs lured John Sculley, then president of Pepsi-Cola USA, to Apple to solve the marketing problems. In May 1985 (shortly after Wozniak left Apple) Sculley reorganized the firm so that Jobs continued to have creative input but had no say in daily company operations. Jobs, increasingly dissatisfied, resigned in September, announcing that he would form a new, small company. A week later Apple filed suit against its former chairman, alleging that he had "secretly schemed" to steal Apple employees as well as proprietary information on Apple's future developments.

(MELINDA SHEPHERD)

Johnson, Don, and Thomas, Philip Michael

When "Miami Vice" made its television debut in September 1984, many people dismissed it as an extended rock video. Within a year, however, the show had converted most of its critics, garnered 15 Emmy award nominations (it won four), and brought fame and fortune to its two stars, Don Johnson and Philip Michael Thomas.

Filmed entirely on location in Florida, "Miami Vice" was in some ways a morality play about undercover police—more concerned with nuance than dialogue and emphasizing atmosphere over plot. The show's real originality lay in its innovative use of techniques rarely seen in a television series, including night filming, wide-angle and distance shots, and slow motion. The gritty—if vividly imagined—world of drug dealers, smugglers, and organized crime contrasted sharply with the Art Deco beauty of Miami, the Italian silk and linen designer wardrobes for the stars, and the overwhelming use of pastel, ice-cream colours such as pink and turquoise (no earth tones allowed). The original rock music, which cost as much as $10,000 per episode, frequently served to advance the plot or comment critically on the action rather than as simple background music.

Don Johnson (Detective James ["Sonny"] Crockett) was born on Dec. 15, 1949. His father, a farmer in Flat Creek, Mo., moved the family to Wichita, Kan., where Johnson began acting in high school. He attended the University of Kansas on a drama scholarship for two years before joining the American Conservatory Theater in San Francisco. He starred in Sal Mineo's Los Angeles production of *Fortune and Men's Eyes*, but he chose not to go to New York City with the play in order to star in the film *The Magic Garden of Stanley Sweetheart* (1970). During the

NBC PHOTO

next 15 years Johnson made many television appearances and several unsuccessful films, including *The Harrad Experiment* (1973) and *A Boy and His Dog* (1975), which later became a science-fiction cult classic. With the success of "Miami Vice" and of a new television production of *The Long, Hot Summer* (based on William Faulkner stories), Johnson was one of the hottest actors of 1985.

Philip Michael Thomas (Detective Ricardo Tubbs) was born in Columbus, Ohio, on May 26, 1949, but his family soon moved to southern California. He studied theology at the Oakwood Theological Seminary in Huntsville, Ala., and philosophy at the University of California before joining the road company of the musical *Hair* in San Francisco. He made his Broadway debut in 1971 in *No Place to Be Somebody* and then appeared in *The Selling of the President* (1972). He made several movies, notably *Sparkle* (1976), and television appearances until success struck with "Miami Vice." In 1985 he released an album of his own music, *Living the Book of My Life.*

(MELINDA SHEPHERD)

Johnson, Pierre-Marc

In the first party leadership election in Canadian history in which all party members could vote directly for the candidates, Pierre-Marc Johnson was chosen leader of the Parti Québecois on Sept. 29, 1985. He replaced René Lévesque, one of the founders of the party, who was retiring from politics after nine years as premier of Quebec. Johnson, who always described himself as a *bleu* (conservative), was able to transform the Parti Québécois platform of separatism from a direct, immediate goal to a long-term ideal. Described as having a perfect political image—charming, intelligent, pragmatic—Johnson was sworn in as Quebec's 24th premier on Oct. 3, 1985.

First elected to the National Assembly of Quebec in 1976 to represent the Montreal riding of Anjou, Johnson joined Lévesque's Cabinet in 1977 as minister of labour and manpower. A man who liked to delegate authority, Johnson relied upon experienced government conciliators to solve labour conflicts. As a Cabinet minister he had a painstaking and cautious approach, attempting to avoid controversy. Late in

1980 he became minister of consumer affairs, cooperatives, and financial institutions. Less than half a year later he was made minister of social affairs. In the latter office he had the unpleasant task of cutting the amount the government spent for social services. When the Quebec physicians went on strike in 1982, Johnson brought in legislation to force them back to work. In 1984 he was appointed minister of justice and minister responsible for Canadian intergovernmental affairs.

Born July 5, 1946, in Montreal, Johnson was educated in law at the University of Montreal and in medicine at the University of Sherbrooke. He chose medicine because he felt that it was closer to life and reality than was law. For five months after his election to the National Assembly, he worked an emergency medical shift once a week because he liked the unpredictable nature of the work.

Three weeks after assuming the office of premier, Johnson called a general election. His campaign was based on realism and frankness, with no expensive promises. On Dec. 2, 1985, the Liberal Party, led by former Quebec premier Robert Bourassa, won a landslide victory, taking 99 of the 122 seats in the National Assembly. Johnson was reduced to the position of leader of the small opposition.

(DIANE LOIS WAY)

Johnston, Lynn

First appearing in 1979, the comic strip "For Better or for Worse" was an instant success and soon became a fixture in the comic sections of more than 500 newspapers around the world. The family of Elly Patterson, a bewildered modern housewife, made Lynn Johnston, Elly's creator and alter ego, one of Canada's most popular cartoonists. Johnston based the Pattersons on her own family. Her dentist husband, Rod Johnston, who fired her imagination by giving her useful one-liners for the strip, was the model for Elly's husband, John.

"For Better or for Worse" originated in a series of cartoons that Lynn Johnston drew for her obstetrician during her first pregnancy. The doctor badgered her to have the cartoons published. They appeared in 1973 as the book *David, We're Pregnant!* This was followed by another book of cartoons, *Hi Mom! Hi Dad!* (1975). Universal Press Syndicate saw Johnston's third book, *Do They Ever Grow Up?* (1977), and asked her to create some sample characters for a continuing series. The result was a ten-year contract to detail the life of the Patterson family.

Born Lynn Beverley Ridgway in Collingwood, Ont., on May 28, 1947, Lynn Johnston grew up in Vancouver, B.C. Her earliest inspiration as a cartoonist came from the work of Len Norris, whose cartoons appeared on the *Vancouver Sun*'s editorial page. After attending the Vancouver School of Art (1964–67), Johnston began her artistic career as a medical illustrator at McMaster University in Hamilton, Ont. She also illustrated two books by *Toronto Star* columnist Gary Lautens, *Take My Family . . . Please!* (1980) and *No Sex Please, We're Married* (1983).

After her second marriage in 1977, she moved to her husband's hometown of Lynn Lake, Man.—a community she described as "eight hundred miles from ev-

UNIVERSAL PRESS

erywhere." There she created the saga of the Patterson family. Never a person to do only one thing at a time, she also started Lynn Johnston Productions, a contact and resource agency for northern Canadian touring performers, and was a contributor to the *Canadian Children's Annual,* a yearly collection of original stories and poems for children.

Johnston was always serious about art and considered her job as a medical illustrator as the best position she had had. Her true delight, however, was making people laugh. The title of the 1984 National Film Board of Canada documentary about her, *See You in the Funny Papers,* would seem to describe Johnston's greatest ambition. Through the Patterson family, she succeeded in amusing and delighting a worldwide audience.   (DIANE LOIS WAY)

Kampelman, Max

Appointed in January 1985 by Pres. Ronald Reagan as the chief U.S. arms control negotiator and leader of the delegation discussing with the Soviets strategic defense systems and space-based weapons, Max Kampelman was a Democrat who strongly supported the president's research program on missile defense but did not advocate the use of weapons in space. He had impressed the Reagan administration in 1983 when he worked out an especially difficult agreement with the U.S.S.R. at the 35-nation conference convened in Madrid to review compliance with the 1975 Helsinki Accords.

Kampelman was born in New York City on Nov. 7, 1920. He graduated from New York University in 1940 and received a law degree there in 1945. During World War II, a conscientious objector, he volunteered to be part of an experiment at the University of Minnesota studying the effects of semistarvation on humans. When the war was over, Kampelman continued his education, earning a master's degree and a doctorate in political science at Minnesota. He then became politically active for Hubert Humphrey. Kampelman served as legal counsel for Senator Humphrey in Washington from 1949 to 1955. His strong ties to Humphrey and to Democratic conservatives led to his participation in the formation of the Committee on the Pres-

ent Danger, a group organized to warn against what it considered to be a growing Communist threat. In 1956 Kampelman became a partner and Washington director for a law firm based in New York City.

At the three-year Madrid conference Kampelman was credited with managing an extremely delicate compromise with the Soviets regarding human rights. Not long thereafter, demonstrating what was described as his ability to cut to the realistic core, he denounced the Soviets for their human rights abuses.

Acknowledging the difficulty of the ongoing Geneva arms control talks, Kampelman insisted that there was a formula to be found under which the U.S. and the Soviet Union could "live together in dignity." The first round of negotiations, held in March, was a "first step" forward in the abolition of nuclear weapons. The second round of talks began at the end of May.

(BONNIE OBERMAN)

Karle, Jerome

Co-winner with Herbert Hauptman (*q.v.*) of the Nobel Prize for Chemistry in 1985, Jerome Karle, with Hauptman, devised a general method for deducing the three-dimensional structure of crystalline chemical compounds from the patterns formed on photographic plates when narrow beams of X-rays strike the crystals and generate secondary beams. Their method required extensive calculations but only a single treatment of the experimental data and, with later improvements, made it possible to carry out an X-ray crystallographic analysis in a day or two instead of the period of several years that was formerly required.

Karle was born in New York City on June 18, 1918, and graduated from City College of New York in the class of 1937, which also produced Hauptman and Arthur Kornberg, two other Nobel Prize winners. Karle undertook postgraduate study at Harvard University, receiving a master's degree in 1938, and at the University of Michigan, where he earned a second master's degree in 1942 and a Ph.D. in physical chemistry in 1943.

Karle joined the Chicago research staff of the Manhattan Project, which developed the atomic bomb, and then that of a U.S. Navy project at the University of Michigan. In 1946 he moved to Washington, D.C., and a position at the Naval Research Laboratory; in 1967 he became chief scientist of its laboratory for the structure of matter. From 1951 to 1970 he also served as a professor at the University of Maryland in College Park.

(JOHN V. KILLHEFFER)

Kasparov, Garry

On Nov. 9, 1985, in the final game of their 14-month-long contest, Garry Kasparov defeated the defending champion, Anatoly Karpov, to become the world champion of chess. At 22 Kasparov was the youngest person ever to win the title.

The first phase of the competition between the two Soviet grand masters began in late 1984 in Moscow, with the first man to win six games to be crowned champion. Karpov quickly took a 5–0 lead, easily dominating his young challenger. But Kasparov rallied and by February 1985, after 48 games, had narrowed the gap to 5–3.

At that point the head of the International Chess Federation called off the match on the grounds that both players were too exhausted to continue. Kasparov protested that the decision was made to benefit Karpov, who appeared to be tiring.

The contest resumed in September under new rules. The previous score was canceled, and a 24-game match was established. One point was to be awarded for a victory, and ½ point was to be given to each player for a draw; the first player to score 12½ points would be the winner.

Karpov again took an early lead, but Kasparov fought back. Going into the final match Kasparov led 12–11 and needed only a draw to win the title. Karpov attacked aggressively, but Kasparov was equal to the challenge and won the game and the championship. At the year's end Karpov challenged the new champion to a rematch in 1986. Kasparov responded that such an early resumption of their competition would be "nonsense," but Karpov was supported by the chess federation.

Kasparov was born Garry Weinstein on April 13, 1963, in Baku, U.S.S.R., to a Jewish father and an Armenian mother. His father died when Kasparov was seven, and he was later persuaded to drop the name Weinstein and replace it with a Russianized version of his mother's name.

Kasparov demonstrated his remarkable chess-playing ability at an early age. In 1980 he won the world junior championship, and during the next year he took the Soviet title. He defeated veteran grand masters Viktor Korchnoi and Vassily Smyslov in 1983 and 1984 to earn the right to challenge Karpov.

(HARRY GOLOMBEK)

Keillor, Garrison

With *Lake Wobegon Days,* his second book, Garrison Keillor brought the upper Midwest into the great tradition of American regionalist humour. A fictional reminiscence of growing up in the small town of Lake Wobegon, Minn., the book jumped to the top of best-seller lists within a month of publication in September 1985.

Keillor's success in print capped the rising popularity of his radio show, "A Prairie Home Companion," broadcast live from St. Paul, Minn., on Saturday evenings over American Public Radio. Since 1974 he had presented a motley assemblage of folk music, ragtime, short skits, and comic monologues, stopping the music once each evening to deliver, with deadpan sincerity, the latest news from "the little town that time forgot and the decades cannot improve." The charm of Keillor's news reports, and of his book as well, lay in his obvious affection for Lake Wobegon's 900 souls and their local institutions: their monument, the Statue of the Unknown Norwegian; their churches, Lake Wobegon Lutheran and its Roman Catholic counterpart, Our Lady of Perpetual Responsibility; their watering holes, the Sidetrack Tap and the Chatterbox Cafe; and their market, Ralph's Pretty Good Grocery ("If you can't find it at Ralph's, you can probably get along without it").

Gary Edward Keillor was born Aug. 7, 1942, in Anoka, Minn. (He invented the pen name Garrison in the eighth grade when submitting poems to the school paper.) As a schoolboy he had two ambitions, radio and writing, and at the University of Minnesota (1960–66) he edited the college literary magazine and worked at the campus radio station. In 1968 he became an announcer for Minnesota Public Radio, and in 1970 he began a long association with *The New Yorker,* which published many of his humorous sketches and tales. During that period, as host of a morning show on a public radio station in a small town near St. Cloud, Minn., Keillor introduced Lake Wobegon as the location of the show's "sponsors." The idea for a live show, modeled after the Grand Ole Opry and the classic radio programs of the pretelevision era, came to him in 1974. On July 6 of that year, the first performance of "A Prairie Home Companion" was broadcast over Minnesota Public Radio. By 1985 its national audience had grown to an estimated 2.5 million. Keillor's blend of nostalgia and wry humour won the show a George Foster Peabody Broadcasting Award in 1981. His first book, *Happy to Be Here* (1982), is a collection of magazine pieces. (ROBERT CURLEY)

Kim Dae Jung

One of the milestones of South Korean politics in 1985 was the homecoming in February of leading dissident Kim Dae Jung from the U.S. after two years of exile. Timed just four days before elections to the National Assembly, Kim's move helped galvanize support for the newly formed oppositionist New Korea Democratic Party (NKDP). Later, under the combined behind-the-scenes leadership of Kim Dae Jung and Kim Young Sam, the country's other top opposition leader, the NKDP merged with the older Democratic Korea Party to create a formidable parliamentary opposition bloc that commanded 102 of the National Assembly's 276 seats. Although in March the government formally lifted its ban on Kim's participation in politics, he was still prevented from taking part in such activities by virtue of his being under a 20-year suspended jail sentence for sedition.

After the parliamentary elections Kim Dae Jung and Kim Young Sam shared the leadership of a broad coalition of opposition forces. That significantly furthered the cause of the opposition, but signs had emerged by July of a renewal of the personal rivalry between the two Kims. Suggesting that Young Sam and himself "divide their political roles," Dae Jung said that the pair should agree on a running-mate formula for the presidential elections promised by Pres. Chun Doo Hwan for 1988. The proposals, seen as an attempt by Dae Jung to gain an advantage over his rival, were widely criticized, and Kim withdrew them.

Kim Dae Jung was born in 1924 in the port of Mokpo, southwestern Korea. During the Korean War he was jailed as a "reactionary" by Communist forces after they took Mokpo. He escaped and joined the resistance. Before his 40th birthday he had gained a reputation as one of the country's most polished orators and charismatic politicians. He narrowly lost the 1971 presidential election to Park Chung Hee. His kidnapping in 1973 by South Korean intelligence agents while he was in self-exile in Tokyo dealt a heavy blow to relations between Japan and South Korea. Kim became a leading presidential contender after Park's assassination in 1979. However, when General Chun came to power after a military coup in 1980, Kim was arrested and later sentenced to death for sedition. The penalty was subsequently commuted.

(THOMAS HON WING POLIN)

Klitzing, Klaus von

After a lapse of 22 years, the Nobel Prize for Physics returned to Germany in the hands of Klaus von Klitzing, director of the Max Planck Institute for Solid State Physics in Stuttgart, West Germany. He was recognized for his discovery that under appropriate conditions the resistance offered by an electrical conductor to the passage of current is quantized; that is, it varies by discrete steps rather than smoothly and continuously. The size of these steps is directly related to one of the fundamental quantities of atomic physics, the so-called fine structure constant.

The significance of Klitzing's discovery, made in 1980, was immediately recognized. His experiments were repeated and refined in many laboratories, not only in studies of the properties of semiconductors and other solid materials but also in determining the precise value of the fine structure constant and establishing convenient standards for the measurement of electrical resistance.

Klitzing was born on June 28, 1943, in Schroda in the province of Posen, a part of Poland that had been annexed to Germany during World War II. (The region later reverted to Poland, and the Polish spellings Sroda and Poznan were restored.) At the end of the war Klitzing was taken by his parents to West Germany. He attended the Technical University of Brunswick, graduating in 1969, and then earned a doctorate in physics at the University of Würzburg in 1972. In 1980, when he made his prizewinning discovery, he was a Heisenberg fellow teaching at Würzburg. Later in 1980 Klitzing was appointed to a professorship at the Technical University of Munich. He also taught at the University of Marburg before being named director of the institute at Stuttgart at the beginning of 1985.

Klitzing's research dealt with the Hall effect, named for the U.S. physicist who first

CAMERA PRESS

observed it in 1879. It denotes the voltage that develops between the edges of a thin current-carrying ribbon placed between the poles of a strong magnet. The ratio of this voltage to the current is called the Hall resistance. When the magnetic field is very strong and the temperature very low, the Hall resistance varies only in the discrete jumps first observed by Klitzing.

(JOHN V. KILLHEFFER)

Kohl, Helmut

Public opinion in 1985 gave poor marks to Helmut Kohl for his performance as West German federal chancellor. The polls found him to be the least esteemed of all the country's senior politicians, his standing having declined steadily since the federal election in March 1983. His style of political leadership—to sit out problems until they somehow solved themselves—had many critics in his own party, the Christian Democratic Union (CDU), and was especially lamented by its Bavarian sister party, Franz-Josef Strauss's Christian Social Union (CSU).

Factors contributing to this downward slide were the spy scandal that erupted in August with numerous defections to East Germany (including a member of Kohl's personal staff) and the backlash of the "Bitburg affair" in May, when Kohl induced U.S. Pres. Ronald Reagan to lay a wreath at a cemetery that contained graves of soldiers of the Waffen SS, which had administered Hitler's concentration camps. In the election for the state parliament of North Rhine-Westphalia soon after the Bitburg ceremony, the share of the vote won by the CDU fell almost seven percentage points, to 36%. The Social Democratic Party (SPD) won a remarkable 52% of the vote, and subsequent opinion polls showed that the SPD in the country as a whole had not been so popular for 13 years.

Kohl was born in Ludwigshafen on April 3, 1930, and studied at the Universities of Frankfurt and Heidelberg. He was prominent in the youth organization of the CDU and was elected to the state parliament of his native Rhineland-Palatinate in 1959. He became state chairman of his party in 1966 and three years later was elected state minister president (premier), a position he held with considerable success for seven years. He was elected to the Bundestag (federal parliament) in Bonn in 1976.

Kohl contested the chancellorship in the 1976 federal election, losing to the SPD's Helmut Schmidt, and at the 1980 election he was forced to hand over the chancellor candidature to Strauss, who lost to Schmidt decisively. The decision of the Free Democratic Party to switch coalition partners in midterm brought Kohl to power in October 1982. The switch gave him the opportunity to become chancellor on a parliamentary vote, and this was confirmed by the 1983 federal election.

(NORMAN CROSSLAND)

Leonard, Elmore John

Elmore ("Dutch") Leonard had been called "the finest thriller writer alive," and in 1985, after 23 novels, dozens of short stories, and several screenplays, he finally gained the recognition that had eluded him for more than 30 years. Although Leonard's crime fiction was often called "hard-boiled," it bore little resemblance to most other detective novels. Leonard rarely used the same character in more than one book, and his protagonists were frequently "good guys" only in the sense that they were more nearly ethical than their enemies. He never planned his complicated plots in advance, preferring to watch them grow out of his characters. That, combined with his uncanny ear for dialogue, his effective use of sometimes grisly violence, and his unforced use of satiric wit and ironic plot twists, gave his books a natural sense of reality. "If it sounds like writing," he once said, "I rewrite it."

Leonard was born in New Orleans, La., on Oct. 11, 1925. His father, who worked for General Motors, moved the family repeatedly until they settled in 1935 near Detroit, where Leonard remained. An avid athlete in high school, he was nicknamed for Dutch Leonard, a pitcher for the Washington Senators. Leonard served in the U.S. Navy during World War II, received his Ph.D. from the University of Detroit (1950), and then went to work for a Detroit advertising agency, where he wrote copy for Chevrolet trucks. He wrote Western stories for pulp magazines in his spare time and then began writing novels. He quit advertising after his fifth novel, *Hombre* (1961), was published, but he earned extra money writing educational films for Encyclopædia Britannica, Inc.

With the release of the film version of *Hombre* (1967), Leonard could finally devote himself to fiction. He wrote several novels and screenplays for *The Moonshine War* (1970), *Joe Kidd* (1972), and *Mr. Majestyk* (1974) before switching to urban crime novels in the mid-1970s. In the 1980s he shifted his locales from Detroit to the seamier side of Miami. With *Stick* and *LaBrava* (both 1983) Leonard began to gain notice. The film version of *Stick* (1985) was a critical and box-office failure, a fact that Leonard blamed on its divergence from his original screenplay. *Glitz*, his 1985 novel based mainly in Puerto Rico and Atlantic City, was a best-seller almost from its publication, however.

(MELINDA SHEPHERD)

Li Peng

Li Peng (Li P'eng) became prominent in 1985 as one of the young Chinese leaders obviously being groomed to succeed such aging veterans as Deng Xiaoping (Teng Hsiao-p'ing) and Chen Yun (Ch'en Yün), whose roles in party and government were inevitably coming to an end. Elected to the Secretariat of the Central Committee of the Communist Party and the ruling Politburo, Li was being prominently mentioned as a potential successor to Premier Zhao Ziyang (Chao Tzu-yang). Li traveled to Moscow in March 1985 to represent China at Konstantin Chernenko's funeral and was well received by the new general secretary of the Soviet Communist Party, Mikhail Gorbachev. The meeting attracted much attention and was said to have resulted in a better understanding between the two Communist giants. His July visit to the U.S., during which he toured major industrial plants and energy complexes and held extensive discussions with leading industrialists and economic experts, received equal attention.

Li Peng was born in Chengdu (Ch'engtu), Sichuan (Szechwan) Province, in 1928.

A foster son of the late premier Zhou Enlai (Chou En-lai), Li joined the Communist Party in 1945. During 1946–48 he held several minor posts in factories in northeastern China. In 1948 he went to Moscow, where he attended the Moscow Power Institute and became president of the Chinese Students' Association. After his return to China in 1955, he held posts with electric power agencies in the northeast until his transfer in 1966 to Beijing (Peking), where he was named to similar positions. His rapid rise began in 1979 when he was appointed vice-minister of China's power industry. Elected to the party's Central Committee in 1982, he became vice-premier in 1983 and chairman of the State Education Commission in 1985. With responsibility for education, energy, transportation, and economic development, Li continued to grow in power and prestige. A technocrat known for his pragmatic approaches to China's domestic problems, Li appeared destined to play an important role in the post-Deng era.   (WINSTON L. Y. YANG)

Lightner, Candy

When an automobile swerved out of control and took the life of her 13-year-old daughter in May 1980, Candy Lightner discovered the nightmare of losing a child. Soon she also discovered that she had to do something about the drunk-driving problem in the United States, where every year 28,000 Americans were being killed by intoxicated drivers. Clarence Busch, the 46-year-old cannery worker who had killed Cari Lightner in Fair Oaks, Calif., had a long arrest record for drunk driving and indeed only the week before had made bail on an intoxicated driving charge after a hit-and-run accident.

On the eve of Cari's funeral, Lightner learned of Busch's record and how unlikely it was that he would spend time in jail for killing her daughter. Infuriated, the 33-year-old divorced real-estate agent resolved to change the way drunk driving was handled by courts. She had in mind no programs or methods, only an unstoppable determination to get drunks off U.S. highways.

Lightner's first step was to urge Gov. Jerry Brown of California to appoint a task force to deal with the problem. At first Brown refused to meet with her, but her repeated visits to his office attracted newspaper coverage of her crusade, eventually persuading him to appoint a task force that included her. Thus was Mothers Against Drunk Drivers (MADD) officially launched.

Within a year after MADD's establishment, California had passed tough new legislation that included mandatory imprisonment for repeat offenders and initial fines of $375. (Clarence Busch eventually served 21 months in jail for killing Cari Lightner.) By 1985 all 50 states had tougher laws against drunk driving, and in July 1984 Lightner was at the side of U.S. Pres. Ronald Reagan when he signed into law a bill reducing federal highway grants to states that failed to raise the legal drinking age to 21.

Lightner's goals included establishing an indemnity fund and bill of rights for victims as well as automatic imprisonment in every state for repeat offenders. However, late in 1985 she was stripped of much

of her power in MADD, losing her titles of chairman and chief executive officer though remaining as president and chief spokesperson. Critics of her administration said that it had placed too much emphasis on fund-raising and not enough on programs.   (BONNIE OBERMAN)

McTaggart, David

Among the founders of the environmentalist group Greenpeace was David McTaggart, the organization's chief spokesman and chairman of Greenpeace International since 1979. The Canadian businessman had become involved with the issue of French atmospheric nuclear weapons testing in New Zealand in 1971, and his life was tied to environmental issues from then on.

McTaggart was born in Vancouver, B.C., on June 24, 1932. As a youth he was an outstanding athlete. Moving to California in the 1960s, he became a successful building contractor and developer. He was deeply affected when two of his employees were seriously injured in an explosion at a resort lodge built by his firm. In 1971, emotionally recovered and with a new political focus, he helped found Greenpeace International in New Zealand. The group's purpose was to campaign for a "green peace," working with rather than against natural forces, carrying out peaceful but uncompromising actions in defense of the environment.

The following year McTaggart attracted attention by sailing his 12.6-m (38-ft) sailboat, formerly the *Vega* and renamed *Greenpeace III,* to French Polynesia, where, near Mururoa Atoll, France was about to conduct another in a series of atmospheric nuclear tests that had been occurring since 1966. *Greenpeace III* observed international law in establishing its anchor position, and the presence of the single small boat forced the French government to halt the testing. A French Navy vessel eventually rammed the boat to end the embarrassing situation. McTaggart repaired his boat and returned a year later, this time with an escort composed of antinuclear members of the Australian and New Zealand Labour parties. He was physically beaten by French military personnel, who denied the charge, claiming that Mc-

ALAIN NOGUES—SYGMA

Taggart's ship had already left the area. Published photographs of the battered environmentalist, however, ultimately proved them to be lying.

McTaggart entered into lengthy litigation against the French. In 1977 he began organizing new support throughout Europe for Greenpeace, by then established in 17 countries and headquartered in Lewes, England, where McTaggart lived. The growth of the organization was hampered by internal disputes, but McTaggart resolved these problems in 1979 and was elected chairman of the newly established International Greenpeace Council.

In July 1985 another Greenpeace vessel, the *Rainbow Warrior,* a 48.8-m (160-ft), 30-year-old converted trawler, sailed toward Mururoa Atoll to protest once again against the French. While moored in Auckland [N.Z.] Harbour, the rainbow-painted ship was ripped apart by an explosion, causing it to sink and killing a Greenpeace photographer. Two persons arrested in connection with the blast proved to be members of the French secret service. They were tried by a New Zealand court and convicted in November, while in France the affair was acutely embarrassing to the government, which dismissed two high-ranking officials in an effort to limit the political fallout.   (BONNIE OBERMAN)

Mamet, David

Perhaps the most successful U.S. playwright during the last decade, David Mamet brought to the stage a unique intellectual sensibility that enabled him to explore the working-class world through the mind of the average man. The 37-year-old Pulitzer Prize-winning Mamet was fascinated by the male psyche, and he wrote in an inimitable stark style, playing variations on the theme of exploitation. Indeed, though writing in another genre, it was remarked by many critics that Mamet bore a deep resemblance to Ernest Hemingway.

Mamet was born in Chicago on Nov. 30, 1947, to Jewish parents who divorced when he was ten. The playwright seemed to have been profoundly affected by his broken home. Although he moved to the suburbs when he was 13, Mamet often spent weekends in Chicago on his own, unconsciously gathering material for the poignant dramas he would eventually create. During his late teens he worked at Second City, Chicago's well-known comedy club. He attended Goddard College in Vermont and later taught there and at New York University.

An aspiring actor, Mamet at 20 began writing scenes for himself and his friends to act out together. Within four years, he had formed a Chicago theatre company, the St. Nicholas, and installed himself as the resident playwright. He was self-taught and initially had no clear or fixed ideas about writing technique or philosophy. It was perhaps for this reason that Mamet emerged as a popular and prolific author of plays that were characterized by their calculated use of stage action and stark, uncomplicated dialogue.

By 1975 Mamet had written and produced, to critical acclaim, *Sexual Perversity in Chicago* and *American Buffalo.* He followed those early successes with such highly regarded dramas as *The Water Engine, Edmond,* and *Glengarry Glen Ross*

and the screenplay for *The Verdict.* For *Glengarry Glen Ross* he won both the Pulitzer Prize and the New York Drama Critics Circle Award for the best play of 1984.   (BONNIE OBERMAN)

Mandela, Nelson Rolihlahla

During the 21 years he had served as a life prisoner, Nelson Mandela had become black South Africa's folk hero. Opinion polls showed that 70% of the country's 23.9 million blacks regarded him as their leader. His importance in the republic's changing political system was recognized by Pres. P. W. Botha when he offered to release Mandela provided he first renounced violence. As the initiator of the armed struggle, Mandela refused the offer of personal freedom. However, when the British human rights campaigner Lord Bethell was allowed to visit him in Pollsmoor Prison, Mandela said he was ready to call a truce in the armed struggle if the authorities would "legalize us, treat us like a political party, and negotiate with us."

Mandela was given his life sentence in 1964 after admitting responsibility for having started Umkonto We Sizwe (Spear of the Nation) to wage an armed struggle against South Africa's system of apartheid (racial separation). While in prison he was elected president-general of the banned African National Congress (ANC), the country's oldest black nationalist organization, founded in 1912. His wife, Winnie, also gained prominence by her defiance of the authorities despite a banning order restricting her to Brandfort, a small village in the Orange Free State.

Nelson Mandela was born in July 1918 at Umtata in Tembuland, Transkei. After completing his education at a Methodist missionary school in Transkei, he took an arts degree at the black University College (now University) of Fort Hare, the nursery of black nationalist politicians. In 1941 he hurriedly left home to avoid a traditionally arranged marriage; instead, he began to study law at the University of the Witwatersrand in Johannesburg. After qualifying he entered into a law partnership with Oliver Tambo (*q.v.*), and both founded the ANC Youth League in 1944.

The Sharpeville shootings in 1960 followed by the banning of the ANC and the Pan-African Congress led to Mandela's decision to break with the ANC's traditional policies of nonviolent resistance. He clandestinely went abroad in 1962 to seek support elsewhere in Africa and in Britain. On his return home he was arrested, and in November 1962 he was sentenced to five years in prison for subversive activity and leaving the country illegally. While still in jail he was prosecuted along with other ANC leaders in the celebrated Rivonia trial of 1963–64, which led to his life sentence.   (COLIN LEGUM)

Mifsud Bonnici, Carmelo

Sworn in as Malta's prime minister on Dec. 22, 1984, Carmelo Mifsud Bonnici succeeded Dom Mintoff in that office and also as leader of the Malta Labour Party. A relative newcomer to politics, Mifsud Bonnici was elected deputy leader of the party in 1980 and designate leader to succeed Mintoff in 1982. The following year, upon the resignation of a government member, he was co-opted as a member of Parlia-

ment by the House of Representatives and held the portfolios first of labour and social services and then of education before rising to the premiership. He had yet to contest a general election.

As minister of education, Mifsud Bonnici led the government's campaign for free education in private schools (mainly run by the church), which after a harsh battle resulted in a phasing-out agreement with the Vatican in early 1985. Under his leadership the ruling Labour government did not change any of its hard-line policies, although he adopted a somewhat different approach. He continued his predecessor's intransigent attitude toward the opposition Nationalist Party but endeavoured to woo the hostile private commercial and industrial sector and to mend Malta's fences with Western Europe, the U.S., and the Commonwealth. At the same time, he maintained Malta's strong ties with Communist countries and strengthened relations with Libya.

Born July 17, 1933, at Cospicua, Malta, Mifsud Bonnici was a bachelor and by profession a lawyer. He was something of an enigma in that he was born into a staunch Roman Catholic and Nationalist family (his brother was an opposition Nationalist MP) and was active within Roman Catholic Church organizations in his youth and especially in the 1960s, when a battle raged between the church and the Malta Labour Party. In 1969 he became legal adviser to Malta's largest trade union, which fused with the Labour Party ten years later. He was for some years a lecturer in industrial and fiscal law at the University of Malta.   (ALBERT GANADO)

Milingo, Emmanuel

Emmanuel Milingo, Roman Catholic archbishop of Lusaka, Zambia, was mysteriously summoned to Rome in 1982 for what was described as "a period of theological study and quiet reflection, as well as to seek medical aid from the doctors." The reference to "medical aid" meant that Milingo's sanity was in doubt. Although he came safely through the psychological tests, he never returned to his diocese and was, in effect, deposed and exiled. A nominal desk job in the Pontifical Commission for Pastoral Care for Migrants and Tourism was all that could be found for him.

It was not easy to determine exactly what had happened. Milingo, born in 1930, was ordained priest in 1958 and became archbishop of Lusaka in 1969 when he was only 38. Early in his ministry he became convinced that he had healing powers. He hesitated to use them at first. On visits to Europe and the U.S. he consulted leading theologians, who encouraged him to make use of his gift; the charismatic movement had produced a revival of interest in healing and the laying on of hands. Finally Milingo was persuaded of the complete orthodoxy of Christian healing.

The needs were great. When uprooted from tribal life, African women, especially, suffered from psychosomatic complaints that were susceptible to the healing ministry. Milingo began to make exorcism a regular part of his services. There was much weeping, screaming, gnashing of teeth, and writhing on the floor, which disconcerted those unfamiliar with such practices. Milingo was denounced by missionaries, who alleged that he was behaving more like a medicine man than a bishop. He had taken "africanization" too far.

By 1980 these reports were being taken sufficiently seriously in the Vatican for Milingo to be forbidden to hold healing services. He did his best to comply but had to go into hiding to escape from the more importuning members of his flock. By this paradoxical route Milingo became the best-known African prelate. Hauled from obscurity onto the world scene, in 1985 he was celebrating well-attended weekly charismatic services in Rome. He did not believe that he had to choose between being a Christian and being an African.

(PETER HEBBLETHWAITE)

Milne, Alasdair David Gordon

The banning of a British Broadcasting Corporation (BBC) documentary program about Northern Ireland by the BBC governors, after the intervention of the home secretary, caused an international furor in August 1985 and presented a critical personal challenge to the broadcasting system's professional leader, Alasdair Milne. Director general of the BBC since 1982, Milne had been faced principally with difficult matters of financing and of policy on the new media, but the affair of "Real Lives: At the Edge of the Union" was widely seen as a grave constitutional issue in which the principle of the BBC's independence was at stake.

At the moment the crisis arose, with Home Secretary Leon Brittan writing to the BBC governors protesting against the portrait of sectarian extremists in Northern Ireland (which he had not yet seen), Milne was on holiday on a ship off Scandinavia. The program had been withdrawn by the time he could return, and it took more than a month before the governors reversed their position. The film was finally shown in October with minor changes, and one outcome was that Milne appeared to have strengthened his personal authority in the running of the BBC.

Milne was born in Scotland on Oct. 8, 1930. A classical and modern languages graduate of New College, University of Oxford, he joined the BBC in 1954. He was one of a group of young men who pioneered a vigorous new style of current affairs journalism with "Tonight," which he edited in 1961–62, and went on to create the classic live satirical show "That Was the Week That Was." He left the BBC in 1965 but returned two years later to become controller of BBC Scotland (1968–72), director of programs (1973–77), managing director of BBC TV (1977–82), and deputy director general (1980–82).

Milne's advance to the director generalship did not come at a favourable time for his talents as a leader. The license fee levels allowed by the government were constricting budgets, and difficult compromises had to be found if aims for expanding services were to be achieved. In this context it seemed that the "Real Lives" crisis could have the benefit of enabling the independent-minded Milne to establish the importance of programs at the top of the BBC agenda.   (PETER FIDDICK)

Mitterrand, François Maurice

As 1985 drew to a close and the legislative elections to be held in France in March 1986 loomed closer, the time had come to take stock of what Pres. François Mitterrand had accomplished as chief of state since 1981. The year had been a testing one, marked in particular by the "Greenpeace affair" and later in the year by Prime Minister Laurent Fabius's public disavowal of his president's decision to receive the Polish leader, Gen. Wojciech Jaruzelski, at the Elysée Palace. Nevertheless, at year's end Mitterrand projected a confident image in defending the record of his Socialist government.

Certainly mistakes had been made in the first year of the president's seven-year term: too many reforms in too little time, the complete nationalization of several major private concerns, the 39-hour workweek with a fifth week of paid vacation, and the mishandling of a dispute over education. However, by appointing Fabius prime minister in 1984, Mitterrand made restraint the new central theme of his policy, asserting then that modernization of the economy was the top priority. While unemployment had not fallen during the five-year period, inflation was going down and at the end of 1985 reached 5%, the average for members of the European Communities. At the same time, the franc was strong and the stock market flourishing.

Mitterrand was the first president of the Fifth Republic to have reached the presidency directly from the leadership of a major political party. The contradictions of the man, with his right-wing culture and his left-wing conscience, made for a rich and complex personality. He might well be inclined to accept a sharing of responsibilities that would allow "cohabitation" between a left-wing president and a right-wing parliamentary majority—something that had never occurred before but might well come about after the 1986 elections. Tested in power, Mitterrand had given priority to realism and had undertaken the modernization of the left and of society.

Born into a bourgeois family on Oct. 26, 1916, at Jarnac (Charente), Mitterrand trained as a lawyer in Paris and in 1946 was elected deputy for the Nièvre. A member of several governments under the Fourth Republic, he became first secretary of the Socialist Party in 1971. Thenceforth he devoted himself to making the Socialists, at the expense of the Communists, the majority party of the left. (JEAN KNECHT)

Modigliani, Franco

Citing the practical applications of his work as well as his enormous influence in the field of corporate finance, a five-member selection committee awarded the Nobel Memorial Prize in Economic Science to Franco Modigliani, a professor at the Massachusetts Institute of Technology. The 67-year-old laureate economist pioneered research both in the analysis of household savings and in the determination of the effects of various types of national pension programs.

At the news conference announcing the prestigious prize, Modigliani wasted no time in criticizing the United States' "disastrous" federal deficit, stating that the debt "offsets savings by people and leaves less money for investment." The MIT professor called on Pres. Ronald Reagan to raise taxes and reduce defense spending.

Modigliani was born in Rome on June

18, 1918. While a law student at the University of Rome, he entered an essay contest on the topic of price controls. After he won first prize, the contest judges urged him to consider a career in economics. After he earned his law degree, he and his wife fled Italy's Fascist regime, arriving in New York in 1939. Modigliani enrolled at Manhattan's New School for Social Research, where he received his Ph.D. in social sciences in 1944. After teaching at several colleges he went to MIT in 1962.

Modigliani's research in the area of savings was first published in 1954 and was labeled his life-cycle theory. It linked household savings to demography, economic growth, and individual behaviour, holding that people save for their retirement and not to pass savings on to offspring. He and a colleague then went on to develop the theory that a company's market value is unrelated to the size and structure of its indebtedness; that, rather, stock market values are basically determined by a business's expectations of future earnings. While this had become conventional 1980s wisdom in economics classrooms, on Wall Street, and in corporate boardrooms, when it was first presented in 1958, little attention was paid to the idea that investors should focus on the future. "His work in the late '50s provided the basis for modern corporate finance," according to one Nobel committee member.

(BONNIE OBERMAN)

Momoh, Joseph Saidu

When 80-year-old Siaka Stevens finally stood down on Nov. 28, 1985, after 14 years as president of Sierra Leone (and 3 years before that as prime minister), he was succeeded by 48-year-old Maj. Gen. Joseph Saidu Momoh after a carefully arranged single-candidate election in which Momoh received 99.85% of the votes cast. Momoh was expected to bring a very different style to running troubled Sierra Leone.

He came to power on a wave of euphoria; the country wanted change, and he was seen to be the man to provide it. Confident and outgoing, he appeared to have few illusions as to the tasks he faced. His first act after taking office was to reshuffle the Cabinet, reducing it from 30 to 20 members. He himself took charge of defense and state enterprises.

Momoh's career had been a conventional one. Born Jan. 26, 1937, in Bombali district, Northern Province, he went to the Wilberforce Rural School and then the West African Methodist Collegiate secondary school, from which he graduated in 1955. He took a government clerk's course at the Technical Institute and then joined the civil service. In 1958 he left the civil service to join the Royal West African Frontier Force and had his initial cadet training at Teshi in Ghana. Subsequently, he attended courses in Nigeria and England and then again at Kaduna in 1962, when he received the baton of honour as the outstanding cadet. He repeated this performance at Mons Officer Cadet School in England, where he received the sword of honour as the outstanding overseas cadet.

Back in Sierra Leone in 1963, Momoh enjoyed rapid promotion, becoming captain in 1965 and major in 1966. Then in 1968, following the coup that restored constitutional government, he was arrested and spent seven months in detention. On his release he returned to the Army. He advanced to colonel in 1970 and in 1971 was made an Officer of the Order of the British Empire. He was promoted to brigadier in 1973, and the following year President Stevens nominated him a member of Parliament and made him a minister of state in the Cabinet. In 1983 he was promoted to major general.

(GUY ARNOLD)

Morishita, Yoko

Prima ballerina Yoko Morishita was slower to achieve recognition in Japan than abroad, but on Oct. 14, 1985, Prime Minister Yasuhiro Nakasone honoured her with a special commendation for improving the status of Japanese women. Morishita had been an inspiration through her dedication to classical dance and her success as Japan's only international ballet star. In 1971 she won the prestigious gold medal in the Varna International Competition in Bulgaria, and within two years she was dancing all over the world. *Giselle, Sleeping Beauty, Romeo and Juliet, The Nutcracker, Swan Lake,* and *Don Quixote* were included in her repertoire, as well as modern works by Maurice Béjart and George Balanchine. Partnered by Rudolf Nureyev, Fernando Bujones, Jorge Donn, or her husband, Tetsutaro Shimizu, Morishita gave about 100 performances a year in Japan and abroad. In 1985 she performed with Nureyev in the tenth Nureyev Festival in London. The two appeared together again in Greece and Japan dancing *Swan Lake* and *Don Quixote.*

The 37-year-old ballerina began dancing at age three in Hiroshima, where she

SANKEI SHINBUN

was born on Dec. 7, 1948. In 1956 she went to Tokyo to train with dance pioneer Akiko Tachibana. At 13 she performed in *Coppelia;* at 15 she danced Odette/Odile in *Swan Lake.* After studying for a year in the U.S. when she was 20 and after dancing with the American Ballet Theatre, she returned to Japan via Europe. Though she was invited to join the Stuttgart (West Germany) Ballet and Maurice Béjart's Ballet of the Twentieth Century in Brussels, she declined. She joined Tokyo's Matsuyama Ballet in 1970 determined to make her career in the company that was directed by her father-in-law.

Because Morishita was only 1.5 m (5 ft) tall, she had to develop elegance without the advantage of height. "It all depends on how you use your muscles," she once explained. She believed she possessed a sensitivity and delicacy that was unique among Japanese ballerinas. She called it "the beauty of tranquillity," and with her subtle acting skills she astounded audiences and charmed the critics. Terry Trucco, one such critic, spoke for many when he called attention to the ballerina's "elegant line, inherent musicality, and formidable technique." Morishita said that a ballerina's physical strength declines after 40, but she insisted she wanted to continue dancing for 20 more years.

(CHRISTINE PATTON CHAPMAN)

Mwinyi, Ali Hassan

Sworn in on Nov. 5, 1985, Ali Hassan Mwinyi succeeded Julius Nyerere to become Tanzania's second president. Nyerere, a passionate egalitarian socialist, had led the former British colony of Tanganyika into independence and had been in office for 24 years (the last 21 as president of the united republic of Tanganyika and Zanzibar, or Tanzania) when he decided it was time to retire. Mwinyi, an islander from Zanzibar, was not well known on the mainland. Although he had held ministerial office since 1970, he was always in Nyerere's shadow, working for most of the time in the president's personal Cabinet. In 1984 he was lifted out of relative political obscurity to become chairman of the Zanzibar government at a time when the previous incumbent had lost control over a movement demanding the island's secession from the mainland. He showed political skill and moderation in dealing with the situation.

Mwinyi resembled Nyerere in a number of ways. Like him, he began life as a teacher and was a strong believer in consensus politics. Unlike his predecessor, though, Mwinyi was not a committed ideologist. While he shared Nyerere's faith in socialism, he was likely to be more of a pragmatist. He came to office at a difficult time following years of drought and economic collapse due to a variety of causes that included the steep rise in oil prices, the downturn in world demand and prices for some of its agricultural exports, and the cost of the war to bring down Uganda's tyrant, Idi Amin.

That Mwinyi, an islander and a Muslim in a predominantly Christian country, came to be president testified to the success of Nyerere's policies in eliminating tribalism and religion as divisive factors in the nation's politics. Although Mwinyi was born (May 8, 1925) on the mainland at Kivure, he was taken as a young child by his parents to Zanzibar, where he later was trained as a teacher. He completed his education at colleges in Newcastle upon Tyne and Hull in England in the mid-1950s. After his return home he became principal at Zanzibar's Teacher Training College. In 1964 he entered the public service, in the Ministry of Education. A year later, after the island's revolution, he was given a senior post in the State Trading Corporation, where he was discovered by Nyerere in 1970.

(COLIN LEGUM)

Okello, Tito

Gen. Tito Okello became Uganda's head of state in July 1985 after the Army toppled Pres. Milton Obote for the second time. Okello had remained loyal to Obote during their exile in Tanzania following Gen. Idi Amin's takeover of power in 1971. In 1979 Okello led the Uganda National Liberation Army (UNLA), which, with the support of the Tanzanian military, succeeded in ending Amin's rule. He was made commander of the Ugandan armed forces, an ill-disciplined body composed mainly of untrained volunteers with a stiffening of the old professional army that had gone into exile with Obote and Okello.

Though well past retirement age and no longer physically fit, Okello was retained in his post by Obote because of his past loyalty, his army seniority, and the fact of his being from the Acholi tribe, which made up at least half of the Army's strength. Okello was one of the very last men whom Obote would have suspected of being disloyal to him. However, after the Acholi soldiers—dissatisfied over recent army promotions—decided to mutiny under the leadership of Brig. Basilio Okello, Tito Okello (no relation to Basilio) was invited to take over the country's leadership. His role, however, was largely symbolic, resembling that of Gen. Muhammad Naguib when Col. Gamal Abdel Nasser's Free Officers staged their coup in Egypt in 1952. Okello's failure to consolidate his position after Obote's ouster was demonstrated by the success of the rival faction, led by Yoweri Museveni, whose National Resistance Army forced Okello to grant the rebels a major share of power in the government.

Tito Okello was born at Namukora in northern Uganda in 1914. He received only a primary education and never achieved fluency in English, Uganda's national language. He joined the King's African Rifles in 1940 and served as a corporal with the colonial forces in Somaliland during World War II. After the Somaliland campaign he underwent further military training in Kenya. Promoted to the rank of sergeant, he went to Burma at the close of the war. He finally returned to Uganda in 1955 and was given officer's rank when the country became independent seven years later. After independence he enjoyed rapid promotion and became army chief of staff in 1970. When Amin seized power Okello immediately went into exile and, with Obote, played a major role in keeping alive the opposition to Amin's rule.

(COLIN LEGUM)

Paz Estenssoro, Víctor

Víctor Paz Estenssoro took office as president of Bolivia for the fourth time on Aug. 6, 1985. The general elections held in July had produced no outright winner, and so Congress was required to choose between the main contenders, Paz and Gen. Hugo Banzer Suárez. Despite winning 29% of the popular vote against Paz's 26%, Banzer was defeated in the congressional ballot by 94 votes to 51.

Paz, who had played a prominent role in Bolivian politics for 40 years, was born on Oct. 2, 1907, in Tarija, southwestern Bolivia. A law graduate of the University of San Andrés, La Paz, in 1932 he became an official in the ministry of finance. As a noncommissioned officer he took part in the Chaco War of 1932–35 between Bolivia and Paraguay. Elected to Congress as deputy for Tarija in 1938 and again in 1940, Paz was professor of economic history at his old university during 1939–41. He was one of the founders, in 1941, of the Movimiento Nacionalista Revolucionario (MNR). In 1952 the MNR ousted the military junta then in power, and Paz became president.

In his first term (1952–56) Paz instigated major changes in the structure of Bolivian society through agrarian reform and was instrumental in the nationalization of the country's mines. From 1957 to 1960 he served as ambassador to the U.K. His second term as president, which began in 1960, saw a move toward the political right. Reelected in 1964, Paz was ousted later that year by a military coup. He went into exile in Peru, where he became professor of economics at the University of Lima. In 1971 he returned to support Banzer in his overthrow of the left-wing government of Juan Torres Gonzáles.

Paz gained his 1985 victory with the backing of the leftist elements in Congress who were eager to keep Banzer out and felt that Paz would be more likely to represent their interests. However, after taking office Paz broke with the left and in October formed a pact with Banzer and his far-right Acción Democrática Nacionalista party. Paz declared his intention to reach a speedy agreement with the International Monetary Fund in order to enter negotiations with Bolivia's foreign creditors, and the resultant austerity measures were not expected to increase his popularity with the workers. Many Bolivians felt that he had broken completely with the ethos of the 1952 revolution, and it was doubtful whether the left would have supported him in the election had they known the direction he was to take. (INGRID IVERSEN)

Pendleton, Clarence

Clarence Pendleton attracted few friends during his tenure as the first black chairman of the U.S. Commission on Civil Rights—but he drew a wealth of new labels. The media variously called him "controversial," "irrepressible," "outspoken," "combative," and "sharp-tongued" for his statements antagonizing civil rights leaders. In 1985 Pendleton seemed determined to live up to every last adjective; he called upon civil rights advocates to "drop their divisive, unpopular, and immoral insistence" on quotas; he accused black leaders of fostering a "new racism" with their demands for "preferential treatment" for blacks; and he advised black leaders to petition Congress for "reparations" if they believed the U.S. owed a debt to blacks for past injustices.

Ironically, Pendleton's early history resembled that of a civil rights leader. Born on Nov. 10, 1930, he grew up in a Washington, D.C., ghetto. He overcame that environment to graduate from Howard University in 1954 and later served as a swimming coach and gym instructor there. In 1968, because of a strong belief in government help for blacks, he became recreational coordinator for Baltimore's Model Cities program, a federally funded effort to revive poor, mainly black neighbourhoods. In 1972 Pendleton moved to the West

UPI/BETTMANN NEWSPHOTOS

and veered to the right. As director of the Model Cities program in San Diego, Calif., he found that hope for progress for blacks lay with private industry rather than in public assistance, a discovery encouraged by two new friends, Republican Mayor Pete Wilson and Edwin Meese, a confidante of then-governor Ronald Reagan. With their backing he became head of the San Diego Urban League, where he initiated business development projects that, according to Pendleton, created 8,000 jobs for the poor. Some critics later contended that his programs for economic progress came at the expense of social service programs.

In 1981, wanting a conservative to head the U.S. Commission on Civil Rights—an advisory body that monitored the enforcement of civil rights laws—President Reagan gave the job to Pendleton. Three years later Pendleton joined other Reagan appointees in ending the commission's long-standing support for racial quotas. Under Pendleton's leadership the commission also opposed the concept of "comparable worth," which would require employers to pay equally for different jobs judged to be similar by various criteria. Pendleton outraged some women's groups by calling the concept of comparable worth "the looniest idea since 'Looney Tunes' came on the scene." (MICHAEL AMEDEO)

Perry, William

After William Perry's rookie season turned into a living cartoon show, his Chicago Bears coach explained why he used the 138.5-kg (305-lb) defensive tackle as an offensive fullback. "Morale," said coach Mike Ditka. The poor guy was not getting to play on defense, so Ditka put him on the goal-line offense to make him feel more a part of the team. "I never intended to make him a national hero," Ditka said.

But he did. By the time Perry scored his fourth touchdown of the season in the Bears' Super Bowl victory, he may have been the most adored athlete in the world. He made U.S. football a booming fad in England. In the United States, people who barely followed football were suddenly fascinated by "The Refrigerator." He was on

the covers of national newsmagazines and the couches of nightly talk shows. He did commercials for a car, a fast-food restaurant, a soft drink, even a brokerage house. His likeness was sold on everything from T-shirts to drinking glasses. In a word, Perry was big.

"Every underdog in America identifies with him," Ditka said. "And everyone who's two or three pounds overweight." Perry was at once a hero and a national pet. He might have come off as a bully when his block bent 102.5-kg (226-lb) Green Bay linebacker George Cumby backward like a sapling on his first goal-line play, but Perry was too clearly a nice, gentle, innocent country kid who turned the big city on its ear.

William Perry was born Dec. 16, 1962, in Aiken, S.C., the tenth of 12 children. He weighed 6.1 kg (13½ lb). "I was big when I was little," he said. He weighed 100 (220) in seventh grade and 143 (315) as a college freshman at Clemson University, when teammate Ray Brown saw him fill an elevator door, decided he was as big as a refrigerator, and called him G.E. As a senior, he led the country with 27 tackles behind the line and was Atlantic Coast Conference player of the year.

The Bears drafted him in the first round and were promptly criticized for gambling on someone who had weighed 168 kg (370 lb). "We'd rather have him for us than against us," personnel director Bill Tobin said. The team's defensive coordinator, Buddy Ryan, called him "a waste of money and a wasted draft pick" after he showed up at training camp out of shape. But he trained hard, lost weight, and finished the season playing defense fairly well; he was a starter from the eighth game on and sacked five quarterbacks, a thrill he preferred even over scoring touchdowns.

Perry first carried the ball in the sixth game. He scored a touchdown and blocked for two more in the seventh game, against Green Bay. Two weeks later he caught a touchdown pass. When he was not scoring, he kept Fridge Fever alive by trying to lift a teammate into the end zone and lumbering 59 yd with a recovered fumble. The

incongruity of it all was a refreshing delight in a league so preoccupied with pretentious dignity. "The publicity and success he's had is unbelievable," Ditka said. "The one thing that shows above all others is the kid is one heck of an athlete."

(KEVIN M. LAMB)

Peterson, David

When David Peterson was sworn in as the 20th premier of the province of Ontario on June 26, 1985, he became the first leader of the Liberal Party to hold that office since 1943. Following the provincial election of May 2, 1985, the Progressive Conservative Party held a tenuous four-seat plurality in the legislature. The Liberal Party and the New Democratic Party (NDP) then joined forces to topple the minority government of Premier Frank Miller and, with the support of the NDP, David Peterson formed a government.

Born Dec. 29, 1943, in Toronto, David Robert Peterson was raised in London, Ont., where his family owned an electronics distributing firm. After obtaining his B.A. in political science and philosophy from the University of Western Ontario in London (1964), Peterson attended the University of Toronto Law School, graduating in 1967. Although called to the bar in 1969 and given the honorary title of queen's counsel by the Ontario government in 1981, Peterson never practiced law. He preferred instead to work as president of his family's business, for which he obtained the lucrative exclusive national distributorship rights for Japanese-made Sharp electronic equipment. As a businessman, Peterson established a solid record of community service. He was a member of the London Chamber of Commerce and the honorary patron of the 1984 Free Olympiad. The youngest president of the London Canadian Club, he was also the first to admit women as members.

The Petersons were a political family. David Peterson's father was a city alderman in London, and his brother Jim was a member of the Canadian Parliament. Peterson's wife, the former Shelley Matthews (whom he married in 1974), was the daughter of a former national president of the Conservative Party.

Although he was successful in his business, Peterson too was interested in a political career. In 1975 he was elected to the Ontario legislature, where he was made Liberal Party finance critic. Running on a reform platform, Peterson was elected leader of the Ontario Liberal Party in February 1982. He proved his reputation for organizing and fund-raising skills when he succeeded in raising $350,000 toward the party's debt in only three months. In the 1985 election he ran a methodical and carefully planned campaign. As premier, Peterson vowed to conduct an open and accessible government, sealing this promise by becoming the first premier of Ontario to take the oath of office in a public, outdoor ceremony. (DIANE LOIS WAY)

Pickens, T(homas) Boone, Jr.

In 1985 the biggest story in U.S. business was corporate takeovers. The most successful and controversial of the "corporate raiders" involved in these takeovers was T. Boone Pickens, the founder, president, and chairman of the board of Mesa

Petroleum Co. During 1982–85 Pickens led Mesa Petroleum in several takeover battles with oil companies many times larger than Mesa. In every case Pickens lost the takeover attempt while gaining enormous profits. Pickens's critics accused him of applying corporate "greenmail" (buying a block of stock to force a buyout without a genuine desire to acquire the target company). Pickens, however, claimed to be "the champion of the small stockholder," and his supporters contended that his targets were poorly managed companies with undervalued stock and entrenched managements.

Pickens was born into the oil business on May 22, 1928, in Holdenville, Okla., where his father worked for Phillips Petroleum and speculated in oil leases. After receiving a degree in geology from Oklahoma State University in 1951, he worked for Phillips Petroleum until 1955, when he launched Petroleum Exploration (incorporated as Mesa Petroleum in 1964). During the 1960s and '70s he built Mesa into a thriving exploration and production firm, but in 1979 he created Mesa Royalty Trust to divest Mesa Petroleum of its production properties. His seemingly unerring instincts led him to sell Mesa holdings in Canada and the North Sea just before the industry in those regions slumped.

In 1982 Pickens made his first takeover assault, on Cities Service. When Occidental Petroleum bought out Cities Service instead, Pickens and Mesa made a pretax profit of more than $30 million. He lost out to Phillips Petroleum in a bid for General American Oil in 1983 for a profit of more than $43 million. Similar attacks on Superior Oil, Gulf Petroleum, and Phillips itself led to other financially advantageous "losses." In 1985 Pickens took on Unocal Corp., which put up the toughest fight yet, with lawsuits, proxy fights, and other antitakeover measures. Once again, Mesa's "loss" resulted in a pretax profit. Pickens announced in late 1985 that Mesa would soon be converted into a limited partnership with himself as the largest general partner, allowing him more time and money to pursue his raids.

(MELINDA SHEPHERD)

Ponting, Clive

The trial of British civil servant Clive Ponting that began on Jan. 28, 1985, was one of the most highly publicized and controversial for many years. In July 1984 Ponting had passed to an opposition member of Parliament information concerning the circumstances in which the British naval task force sank the Argentine cruiser *General Belgrano* during the 1982 Falkland Islands/Islas Malvinas conflict. Once identified as the source of the "leak," Ponting did not deny his actions. His concern, he maintained, had been to reveal the efforts of ministers at the Ministry of Defence (MOD) to conceal the full facts of the case from Parliament. Charges were brought under Sec. 2 of the Official Secrets Act, which forbids government servants from disclosing "official information," whether classified or not, to unauthorized persons. The case was not about secrecy but about whether the duties of a civil servant lay with the government of the day or with Parliament.

On February 11, in defiance of the

judge's summing-up, which virtually directed them to convict, members of the jury returned a unanimous verdict of not guilty. Ponting had been suspended from duty in August 1984 and resigned from the civil service a week after the trial ended.

Born April 13, 1946, in Bristol, England, he attended Bristol Grammar School and read history at the University of Reading before entering the civil service in 1970. As a principal at the MOD he was involved in a review, initiated by Prime Minister Margaret Thatcher's Conservative Party government when it took office in 1979, that was designed to cut waste within the civil service. His study of food supplies to the armed forces, in which he documented widespread inefficiency, was said to have won praise from Thatcher herself. Ponting was made an Officer of the Order of the British Empire in 1980 and was promoted to assistant secretary the following year.

Although the outcome of the trial was to make him the hero of the champions of more open government, Ponting was not a political radical. In *The Right to Know* (1985), his own account of the events and issues of the trial, he detailed the disillusionment that had set in as he witnessed the failure of Whitehall to act upon suggested reforms and the complacency of the Conservative government in its dealings with civil servants.   (LOUISE WATSON)

Reagan, Ronald Wilson

Inaugurated for a second term as president of the United States on Jan. 20, 1985, Ronald Reagan celebrated his 74th birthday on February 6 with an optimistic state of the union message to Congress. Later in the year his optimistic attitude served him well as he faced severe criticism for certain travel plans and underwent major surgery. He remained outwardly undaunted by the inability of Congress to act on the budget or on his proposal to reform the federal income tax and by indications of economic problems in the future.

In January Reagan's itinerary for a trip to Europe in May was released. A projected trip to the Nazi prison camp at Dachau was excluded a few weeks later, and in April plans made with West German Chancellor Helmut Kohl to lay a wreath at a cemetery for German soldiers of World Wars I and II near Bitburg, West Germany, were announced. Organizations of Jews and of war veterans objected vehemently to the choice of the cemetery because members of the Waffen SS, the group that operated Nazi Germany's prison camps, were buried there. On May 5 Reagan visited both the site of a Nazi prison camp at Bergen-Belsen and the cemetery near Bitburg.

On July 13 Reagan transferred all of his authority to Vice-Pres. George Bush and underwent surgical removal of more than half a metre of his colon. A polyp in the removed tissue was found to be cancerous, but physicians saw no threat to his life. Released from the hospital on July 20, Reagan jauntily joked about sending his surgeon "up to Capitol Hill to do some cutting." A patch of skin removed from Reagan's nose on July 30 was also found to be cancerous but not threatening.

On November 19 in Geneva Reagan for the first time met an incumbent general secretary of the Communist Party of the Soviet Union, Mikhail Sergeyevich Gorbachev. By November 21 the two leaders had agreed to plan future meetings and to work to reduce their arsenals of strategic nuclear weapons by 50%.

Ronald Reagan was born in Tampico, Ill., on Feb. 6, 1911. He received a B.A. from Eureka College in 1932 and then became a broadcaster in Iowa. In 1937 he became an actor under contract with Warner Brothers. He served as president of the Screen Actors Guild from 1947 to 1952 and 1959 to 1960 and was a host of dramatic television shows from 1954 to 1965. He was governor of California from 1967 to 1975 and was inaugurated for his first presidential term in 1981.

(CHARLES JOHNSON TAGGART)

Reeves, The Most Rev.
Sir Paul Alfred

When Paul Alfred Reeves, Anglican bishop of Auckland, was elected by the General Synod of the Church in 1980 as primate and archbishop of New Zealand, he said he was prepared to live with two possibilities as a 47-year-old facing a long and unique appointment: that he should give it a term and get out or stay and see out his useful life in the job. He also said he would not dismiss the possibility that "God may say one day, 'Reeves, I want you to do something else.' " God apparently did call again, in 1985, to ask him to represent his temporal leader, Queen Elizabeth II, as governor-general of New Zealand.

His excellency the Most Rev. Sir Paul Reeves (he was knighted in the queen's birthday honours) succeeded Sir David Beattie at Government House, Wellington, in November. He was the first clergyman and the first New Zealander of Maori descent to be so appointed. Reeves was born Dec. 6, 1932, the son of a Wellington tram (streetcar) driver. His Maori blood derived from his maternal grandmother. Reeves saw no significance in that background during his upbringing in one of Wellington's less pretentious suburbs and his primary schooling at Wellington South. He went on to Wellington College and then to the Victoria University of Wellington.

Reeves supported himself through his university years with vacation work in a wool store, on the wharves, in the Post Office, and as a waiter at a mountain resort. With a master of arts degree he changed course from training for teaching to theology. He had cause to appreciate his Maori background when the Maori Affairs Department assisted him to a scholarship at St. Peter's College, University of Oxford, England. He had already been ordained a deacon in the diocese of Waikato and had been curate in the timberland town of Tokoroa. He served as curate in English parishes and was ordained priest by the bishop of Oxford in 1960—the year after he married Beverley Watkins, a Wellington schoolteacher who was to bear him three daughters.

Back in New Zealand as vicar (1964–66) of St. Paul, Okato, on the Taranaki coast from which his Maori grandmother came, Reeves became aware of this part of his heritage and of Maori grievances. He started to identify with Maoris and their causes and went on to develop some notoriety as a commentator on social issues. During 1966–69 he lectured on church history at St. John's College, Auckland, was then director of Christian education (1969–71) for the Auckland diocese, and later was chairman (1974–76) of New Zealand's Environmental Council.

(JOHN A. KELLEHER)

Regan, Donald Thomas

In February 1985, when James Baker (*q.v.*) succeeded Donald Regan as U.S. secretary of the treasury, Regan succeeded Baker as chief of staff to Pres. Ronald Reagan. Regan, who had a strong background in both administration and finance, quickly assumed control of the staff in the White House. Baker, more of a political strategist than an administrator, had cooperated closely with Michael Deaver, the deputy chief of staff, and Edwin Meese, counselor to the president. The departure from the White House of Meese (who became attorney general in February) and of Deaver (who returned to the private sector) left Regan alone at the staff's apex. In April the president instructed department heads and other ranking officials to meet as the Economic Policy Council, with Baker as chairman, when formulating economic policy and as the Domestic Policy Council, with Meese as chairman, when formulating noneconomic domestic policy. As the official liaison between the president and the two councils, Regan was in a position to influence the final form of all domestic policies. In May, after a public-relations debacle involving the president's visit to a German cemetery that contained graves of elite Nazi troops, Regan also assumed full control over the president's schedule.

Regan was born in Cambridge, Mass., on Dec. 21, 1918. He graduated from Harvard University (1940) and entered Harvard Law School but left to join the U.S. Marine Corps as an officer candidate. In 1946, after service in the Pacific, he retired from the military and became a stockbroker trainee for Merrill Lynch, Pierce, Fenner, & Beane. He worked in the firm's offices in Washington, Philadelphia, and New York City, becoming its president in 1968 and serving as chairman of the board and chief executive officer from 1971 to 1980. In 1973 he assumed the same titles at Merrill Lynch and Co., Inc., a holding company formed as a result of his diversification program. A strong believer in the free market system, he defended his company's increasing competition with banks and persuaded the directors of the New York Stock Exchange to abolish fixed fees for brokers.

Appointed secretary of the treasury by President Reagan in 1981, Regan favoured deregulation of banking. In 1984 he proposed a plan to reform the federal income tax by reducing the number of brackets and abolishing most deductions. The Reagan administration continued to advocate a modified version of his plan in 1985.

(CHARLES JOHNSON TAGGART)

Riddles, Libby

The Iditarod Trail dogsled race had been a 1,826-km (1,135-mi) endurance test, dedicated to masochism and machismo. It went from Anchorage to Nome, Alaska, across two mountain ranges, a river, and two time zones, retracing the main winter supply route to Nome during the turn-of-the-century gold rush, a monument to a time when men were men. But on March

20, 1985, Libby Riddles drove the first dogsled across the finish line at Nome's tavern-lined Front Street. She was the first woman winner in the race's 13 years, finishing 2½ hours ahead of runner-up Duane Halverson. She had raced the Iditarod only twice before, finishing 18th in 1980 and 19th in 1981.

Fifteen of the 61 entrants already had dropped out. One was Susan Butcher, a two-time runner-up who had been the only woman to finish in the top five. A moose

had torn through her team, killing two dogs. Other hazards in the frozen wilderness were frostbite, hypothermia, icy trails, fatigue-induced hallucinations, and blinding blizzards. Conditions were worse than usual for the 1985 race. It lasted 18 days, compared with the record of a little more than 12. Winds were 70 knots, leaving trail markers virtually invisible, when Riddles crossed the ice of Norton Sound for her stretch run. "I just decided I was going to go out and try it," she said. When she won, Riddles added, "I'm just pretty glad to have it over with."

Elizabeth Nell Riddles was born April 1, 1956, in Madison, Wis. She moved to Alaska in 1974 after living in Bellingham, Wash., where she fell in love with the ocean and mountains and surmised, "Alaska would be the same, only more so. I was ready for an adventure." She settled in Teller, on the Seward Peninsula, and began dogsledding after a year in Alaska. Dogsled racers spend as much as $20,000 on their sport, mostly buying and caring for the dogs. Riddles raised $7,000 by sewing and selling fur hats and garments and trained by demonstrating sledding to tourists. "I thought I had the team to do it," she said of her 15 mixed-breed huskies, 13 of which finished the race. First prize was $50,000. Riddles's plans? "Maybe Hawaii," she said. "And a box of dog biscuits for each of the dogs." (KEVIN M. LAMB)

Robinson, Eddie

While others counted his victories, Eddie Robinson never lost sight of what counted most. "I don't want to wake up any morning and feel that breaking the record

is more important than the people with whom you're working," he said shortly before becoming the most winning coach in college football history. Robinson broke Paul ("Bear") Bryant's record on Oct. 5, 1985, with his 324th victory in 43 seasons at Grambling State College, a 27–7 win over Prairie View A&M in Dallas.

Many of Robinson's former players were there. So far in his career he had sent two on to the Pro Football Hall of Fame, 211 to the National Football League. In 1949 a Robinson protégé, Tank Younger, became the first NFL player from a predominantly black college. Now the San Diego Chargers' assistant general manager, Younger said, "I don't know what I would have done with my life had I not met Eddie Robinson at an early age." Robinson did more than mold great football players. He coaxed them through classes at a remarkable 80% graduation rate. He taught them how to speak in public, how to behave like gentlemen. When he thought of them on his record-setting night, he cried and said, "I'm the luckiest man in the world."

Edward Gay Robinson was born Feb. 13, 1919, a sharecropper's son in Baker, La. He started dreaming of coaching football in third grade. He played quarterback at nearby Leland College, but he had no coaching experience when Louisiana Negro Normal and Industrial Institute in Grambling, La., hired him in 1941 to coach its football team for $63.75 a month. He had no assistants and no budget even for replacing equipment. He did everything himself, from mowing the field to taping ankles to coaching the drill team. His wife, Doris, was expecting their first child, so he delivered ice and worked on a coal truck to make more money. "We didn't have much to look ahead to, but even less to look back on," he said much later.

The school would change names but not coaches. Robinson had just three losing seasons, and two were wiped out by World War II. In 1966 he was honoured nationally as "the man who has done the most for college football in the last 25 years." He ended 1985 with 329 victories against 109 defeats and 15 ties; the team's season record was 9–2, and the team ranked eighth in the country's highest division for small colleges. It was the Tigers' seventh conference championship, along with eight ties, in 25 years. It was their 26th consecutive winning season, including 16 with no more than two defeats. They had won seven National Negro Championships under Robinson.

Robinson was uncomfortable with the media attention to his record. He defended the legend of Bryant, a good friend whose funeral in 1983 he reached by driving 640 km (400 mi) through the night. He did not deny the handicaps of racial segregation and small budgets, but he emphasized his pride in being an American. He was a willing example to black Americans, but he was more than that. "I don't want them to think black," he said. "I want them to think coach." (KEVIN M. LAMB)

Rogers, Richard George

As the new stainless steel-clad headquarters of Lloyd's of London in the City of London neared completion, its designer, architect Richard Rogers, was awarded architecture's coveted 1985 Royal Gold Medal

of the Royal Institute of British Architects. The sophisticated and distinctive design of the Lloyd's building combined an ingenious structure and the high technology of the late 20th century with an old-fashioned romantic architectural excitement. It had evolved from Rogers's Pompidou Centre (Centre National d'Art et de Culture Georges Pompidou—the Beaubourg) in Paris.

Richard Rogers was one of Britain's most talented architects, with an international reputation. Rogers himself described architecture as a social art that could and should enrich the lives of those who lived and worked in his buildings. These were characterized by a richness of silhouette created by exploiting the decorative possibilities of necessary structural elements such as elevator towers, staircases, and service pipes and ducts.

Born July 23, 1933, in Florence, Italy, where he spent the first three years of his life, Rogers was educated at the Architectural Association School of Architecture in London and as a graduate student at the Yale University School of Architecture. In 1963 he returned to Britain and went into private practice with Norman Foster. Rogers and Foster and their wives practiced as Team 4 Architects until 1968. The Reliant Controls electronics factory in Swindon, which was later to be seen as one of the seminal structures of high-tech architecture, was Team 4's most important building.

In 1970, with Renzo Piano, Rogers entered the international design competition for the Pompidou Centre in Paris. Their design was selected from among some 680 entries and was built between 1971 and 1977. It became perhaps the most visited new building in Europe, and its colourful tube-encrusted silhouette dominated its quarter of the French capital. From 1977 Rogers practiced as Richard Rogers and Partners, and in 1978 he won the competition for the Lloyd's headquarters. Other important buildings and projects by Rogers included the controversial Coin Street redevelopment project for the South Bank of London (1979–83) and the Inmos microprocessor factory, Newport, Wales (1982). (SANDRA MILLIKIN)

Rose, Pete

Pete Rose always played baseball with enough energy to light up Cincinnati. In 23 seasons his energy lit up more hit signs on the scoreboard than any other major-league player. He broke Ty Cobb's legendary record of 4,191 hits on Sept. 11, 1985, after a national countdown. The Cincinnati Reds' player-manager finished the season with 4,204 and was aiming for 4,300. The 1986 season would begin shortly before his 45th birthday, April 14.

When he was the National League's rookie of the year in 1963, Rose was regarded as a marginally talented switch-hitter who got the most out of his ability. He was an instant fans' favourite, running to first base on walks and sliding head-first, but players nicknamed him "Charlie Hustle" with a sneer. Like Cobb, Rose was vilified for his exuberant play, but unlike Cobb, Rose became a grand old man, not a bitter one.

He set 34 major and National League (NL) records. He was the NL most valu-

able player in 1973, the World Series most valuable player in 1975, and the *Sporting News* NL player of the decade for the 1970s. He played in six World Series, was an All-Star 16 times, and led the league in batting average three times. He was 37 when he had hits in 44 consecutive games in 1978, a modern NL record. The next year he had 200 hits for the tenth time, a major league record.

HEINZ KLEUTMEIER/SPORTS ILLUSTRATED

Rose's record sparked controversy as people defended Cobb's unrivaled .367 average in 24 seasons, .063 higher than Rose's. Rose always gave him his due. In 1984 he named his baby son Tyler, the modern version of Cobb's Tyrus. Many Cincinnatians never forgave the Reds for letting Rose get away in a salary squabble in 1979, and they savoured his return as player-manager on Aug. 16, 1984, after stints in Philadelphia and Montreal. The city renamed a street Pete Rose Way for the hero who grew up on the West Side. Peter Edward Rose eclipsed the legend of his father, Harry, who played semipro football until he was 42.

He broke the career hitting record 57 years to the day after Cobb's last at bat, with a first-inning single to left against San Diego pitcher Eric Show. After the cheers subsided, Rose raised his index finger, looked toward heaven, and said he saw his father there, with Cobb right behind him. Then, as his 15-year-old son Petey ran to join him, Rose put his head on the shoulder of first-base coach Tommy Helms and cried.   (KEVIN M. LAMB)

Rostenkowski, Daniel

On May 28, 1985, he came on national television with a friendly growl, looking and sounding like a real-life version of Tony the Tiger, the popular cartoon character from TV commercials. But the burly political animal, Daniel Rostenkowski, was not selling cereal but offering a horse trade; if Americans pledged their support, his House Ways and Means Committee would pass a version of Pres. Ronald Reagan's tax-reform program. Rostenkowski's offer drew tens of thousands of enthusiastic letters. The Democratic congressman from Illinois then faced the hard part of

his political bargain—maneuvering tax reform past 35 independent-minded committee members and countless privilege-seeking interest groups.

Rostenkowski approached that challenge with skills shaped by years of experience in Chicago's political jungle. He was born on Jan. 2, 1928, the son of a Polish-American family on the city's Near Northwest Side. His father long dominated the neighbourhood as alderman and ward committeeman. During the 1950s, while serving in the Illinois legislature, the young Rostenkowski nurtured a close relationship with Mayor Richard Daley, the boss of Chicago's political machine; in 1958, with Daley's help, he won election to the U.S. House of Representatives, where he became known as a forceful wheeler-dealer who unabashedly spent all his time seeking aid for Chicago and tax breaks for its businesses. Rostenkowski's efforts pleased his largely ethnic, middle-class constituents, who reelected him each term by a large majority.

But the same kind of political brashness that impressed so many Chicagoans almost ended his climb to power in the House. At a tumultuous session of the 1968 Democratic convention, Rostenkowski mortified Chairman Carl Albert by stripping the gavel from his hand and quickly restoring order. Albert never forgave him and, as speaker of the House in 1970, Albert opposed Rostenkowski's bid to become majority whip.

Rostenkowski's next chance for a major promotion did not come until 1980, when Democratic leaders persuaded him to assume the chairmanship of the Ways and Means Committee. A year and a half later the *Washington Post* accused the new chairman of taking long golfing vacations that were paid for by groups having an interest in bills before his committee. But that allegation failed to tame Rostenkowski and his fierce ambition. He later indicated that he would still pounce on the chance to become speaker of the House or mayor of Chicago.   (MICHAEL AMEDEO)

Ryzhkov, Nikolay Ivanovich

In September 1985 Nikolay Ryzhkov replaced 80-year-old Nikolay Tikhonov as chairman of the Council of Ministers (premier) of the U.S.S.R. A technocrat who had spent more than three decades in the Urals engineering industry, Ryzhkov was elected in 1982 secretary of the Central Committee of the Communist Party of the Soviet Union (CPSU) to take charge of the Central Committee's economics department. In April 1985 he was elected a full member of the Politburo.

Ryzhkov was born on Sept. 28, 1929, into a Russian family. A graduate of the Urals Polytechnical Institute, he began his working life in 1950 as a shift foreman at the Ordzhonikidze heavy machinery plant in the Urals. A member of the CPSU from 1956, he advanced steadily to become chief engineer at the plant in 1965, manager in 1970, and then director general of the Uralmash production amalgamation, with particular responsibility for the armaments industry. He was appointed first deputy minister of heavy and transport engineering in 1975 and, four years later, first deputy chairman of the State Planning Commission (Gosplan) of the U.S.S.R. He

was twice elected to the Supreme Soviet, in 1969 and 1979, and in 1981 he became a member of the Central Committee.

Ryzhkov owed his appointment to head the Central Committee's economics department to Yury Andropov, who after becoming CPSU general secretary in 1982 set about rejuvenating the party cadres. Mikhail Gorbachev continued this drive when he came to power and secured Ryzhkov's election to the Politburo. Although during his time as economics secretary Ryzhkov had made no striking pronouncements on the subject of economic reform, the appointment of a man with his background to the premiership might be taken to herald a more modern approach. In a speech in June he called for "an organic symbiosis" between the "strengthening of democratic centralization" and the "extension of autonomous management."
          (K. M. SMOGORZEWSKI)

St. John, (Harold) Bernard

As deputy to Prime Minister J. M. G. ("Tom") Adams (*see* OBITUARIES) of Barbados, Bernard St. John was the automatic successor when Adams died of a heart attack on March 11, 1985. St. John, who had held the key portfolios of trade and tourism since 1976, was immediately confronted with the task of negotiating a solution to the complex problems of intra-Caribbean Community trade and payments, which were adversely affecting the Barbadian economy.

St. John quickly established himself as a blunt and forthright spokesman for his government's position. His threat at the beginning of September to take reprisals against Trinidad and Tobago if the latter did not implement the Nassau agreements on intraregional trade was followed by apparently constructive conversations with Trinidad Prime Minister George Chambers at the Commonwealth heads of government meeting in Nassau, The Bahamas, in October. It was subsequently announced that Chambers would visit Barbados in January 1986—an indication that matters were on the mend.

Born Aug. 16, 1931, St. John was educated at Harrison College before studying law at University College, the University of London. He became a barrister in the Inner Temple and a queen's counsel in 1969. A member of the Barbados Labour Party (BLP) since 1959, he sat in the Senate from 1964 to 1966. Elected to the House of Assembly in 1966, he lost his seat in 1971 and returned to the Senate for five years. He was reelected to the House in 1976.

The new prime minister was faced with a weak tourist industry, a stagnant manufacturing sector, and a worrying unemployment rate. With elections due in 1986, St. John would face a strong challenge from the opposition Democratic Labour Party. Although he had no difficulty establishing himself as undisputed leader of the BLP, some infighting within the party was reported during the year, which St. John sidestepped by declining to appoint a deputy prime minister.   (ROD PRINCE)

Sanguinetti Cairolo, Julio María

On Nov. 25, 1984, Julio María Sanguinetti Cairolo, representing the Colorado Party, was elected president of Uruguay for a five-year-term. The inauguration of his ad-

ministration on March 1, 1985, marked the end of 12 years of military rule. He succeeded Pres. Gen. Gregorio Conrado Álvarez Armelino in a peaceful transfer of power.

Sanguinetti was born in Montevideo on Jan. 6, 1936. He joined the Colorado Party at an early age and started a journalistic career in the party's local weekly in 1953. Later he was sent abroad as a correspondent on three occasions. After graduating as a lawyer from the University of Montevideo in 1961, he entered political life as a deputy for the department of Montevideo in 1962, a seat he continued to hold through congressional elections of 1966 and 1971. During this period he was also a member of several delegations and commissions, and he was appointed to the Ministry of Industry and Trade in 1969–71 and the Ministry of Education in 1972. He also continued his career as a journalist. He was the political editor of the evening paper *Acción* from 1965 until it was shut down by the military in 1973 and then of the daily *El Día* from 1973 to 1981, when he founded and edited the political weekly *Correo de los Viernes.*

In a 1980 editorial in *El Día,* Sanguinetti strongly opposed the armed forces' intention to legalize their control of power through a plebiscite. This action quickly boosted his political standing, and in 1982 he became secretary-general of the Colorado Party, following his appointment the previous year as leader of "Unidad y Reforma," the largest faction within the party. Sanguinetti also played a leading role in the negotiations for the country's return to democracy. He led his party to victory in the November 1984 elections by defeating his immediate opponent, Alberto Zumarán of the National Party, with 39% against 33% of the vote. None of the parties, however, achieved an overall majority in Congress. Within the framework of a social democratic philosophy, Sanguinetti favoured the establishment of a nationalistic, though moderately reformist, government based on consensus. He rejected Latin-American populism.

(ALEXANDER JOHNS CAMPBELL)

Santiapichi, Severino

Severino Santiapichi was the judge who in 1981 sentenced Mehmet Ali Agca to life imprisonment after the young Turk had admitted shooting and trying to kill Pope John Paul II in May of that year. Agca had claimed to have acted alone, but in his sentence Santiapichi said that "Agca was only the visible point of a conspiracy, which, though impossible to define, was widespread and menacing." Persons unknown were behind the "complex machination." The judge's words heralded the inquiries into what later came to be known as the "Bulgarian connection." Agca, one year after the shooting, began telling the authorities that Bulgarian officials, and others, had hired him to shoot the pope. Judge Santiapichi presided over the trial of three Bulgarians and four Turks, this trial having Agca as the sole accuser and prime witness. The trial opened in Rome in May 1985 and was expected to conclude early in 1986.

Santiapichi's patience in dealing with Agca, who changed his testimony almost daily, and who claimed to be Jesus Christ among other things, was deemed exemplary. Under British or U.S. procedures a judge might have been tempted to dismiss the charges since they were based almost exclusively on the word of a now confirmed liar. However, Santiapichi did not have that option open to him. The trial had to continue until all witnesses had been heard and the verdict rendered. Previously, in 1979, Santiapichi had presided at Italy's first big terrorist trial. He was also the judge in the trial of Red Brigades members accused of the 1978 kidnapping and murder of Christian Democrat Party leader Aldo Moro.

Santiapichi was born in 1925 in Scicli, near Ragusa, Sicily. Obtaining a law degree from Syracuse University, he became a magistrate after entering a national competition in 1952. Eight years later he was sent to Mogadishu, Somalia, to be an appeals court judge there, as part of the UN-sponsored trusteeship agreement between Italy and Somalia. The six years he spent there enabled him to cite the Qur'an to Agca and the other Muslim defendants in the 1985 trial.   (GEORGE ARMSTRONG)

Sarney, José

On April 22, 1985, the day after the death of President-elect Tancredo de Almeida Neves, José Sarney was sworn in as Brazil's president. He had been elected vice-president by an electoral college on January 15, and because of Neves's illness he was sworn in as acting president on March 15. Sarney was expected to remain at his post until March 1989, when the winner of direct presidential elections in November 1988 would succeed him. (*See* WORLD AFFAIRS [Latin America and the Caribbean]: *Brazil.*)

Born on April 30, 1930, Sarney was one of 14 children in a middle-class family in Maranhão State, which forms the division between the Amazon region and the Northeast. Qualifying as a lawyer, he entered politics in 1950 as assistant to the state governor; he switched political party allegiance three times during his career. He first represented his state in Congress when he was 26, and he was reelected in 1958 and 1962. He was associated with congressional reformist groups during the late 1950s and early 1960s and was always considered a liberal despite active participation in military-backed governments between 1964 and 1985.

Sarney served as governor of Maranhão from 1965 to 1970. His record was one of encouraging modernization, sponsoring literacy programs, and building roads, bridges, and sewerage and water systems. He was elected state senator for Maranhão in 1970 under the banner of the progovernment National Renewal Alliance (Arena) party, which changed its name to the Social Democratic Party (PDS) after political reforms in 1979. As PDS president, during 1981–84 Sarney tried to reorganize the party to help it gain increased popular support. When this failed, he became leader of the PDS faction that broke with the government in June 1984 to ally itself with the main opposition grouping, the Brazilian Democratic Movement (PMDB), and form the Liberal Party. The Liberals' votes were considered essential for Neves's victory in the electoral college, and consequently they demanded concessions, one of which was that Sarney should become vice-president. A member of the Brazilian Academy of Letters, Sarney published three books of poetry and prose.

(ROBIN CHAPMAN)

Sartzetakis, Christos

Christos Sartzetakis, a respected Supreme Court judge, was installed as president of Greece on March 30, 1985, for a five-year term following his election by the Greek Parliament. He succeeded Pres. Konstantinos Karamanlis, the conservative statesman who resigned after the Panhellenic Socialist Movement (Pasok) majority, in a surprise move, withdrew its support for his reelection. Sartzetakis was elected on the third round with the help of the Communist Party. The conservative New Democracy Party challenged the legality of the election, but after Pasok's victory in the June 2 general elections, the defeated conservatives withdrew their reservations.

Sartzetakis was born in Salonika, northern Greece, in 1929, the son of a Cretan gendarmerie officer. After law studies at the local university he was called to the bar in 1954 and became a justice of the peace in 1955. It was while serving as a judge of first instance that he first achieved prominence. Appointed magistrate to investigate the death of left-wing deputy Gregorios Lambrakis in Salonika in May 1963, he disproved the police version that it had occurred in a traffic accident and boldly exposed collusion between the police and right-wing hooligans in a political assassination. His courage, integrity, and determination inspired the novel *Z* by Vasilis Vasilikos, which later became a prizewinning film.

After the military coup in Greece in 1967, Sartzetakis, who was in Paris for postgraduate studies, was recalled and posted to Volos, in central Greece, as a misdemeanours judge. Barely a year later he was dismissed from the judiciary during a wholesale liquidation of senior judges hostile to the military regime. He was twice arrested and held without charge. He himself said he was tortured during his detention. He was set free during an amnesty in 1971 and, after the restoration of democracy in 1974, was reinstated and promoted to appeal court judge. In 1982 he was elected to the Supreme Court.

(MARIO MODIANO)

Shahani, Leticia

Among the highest ranking women in the United Nations Secretariat and a 23-year career diplomat, Leticia Shahani in 1985 faced her greatest professional challenge when she served as secretary-general for the official three-week Decade for Women Conference held in Nairobi, Kenya, in July. She skillfully steered documents for the conference, outlining the political, economic, and social needs of women to the year 2000, through their lengthy preparations.

Leticia Ramos Shahani was born in Lingayen in central Luzon, Philippines, on Sept. 30, 1929. Her upper-middle-class household was deeply involved in politics. Her father was a journalist and lawyer who became Philippine foreign minister in 1965. After attending a local high school, she earned a comparative literature degree in 1951 from Wellesley (Mass.) College.

She also received a master's degree from Columbia University, New York City, and a doctorate from the University of Paris. In 1962 she married Indian writer and journalist Rangee Shahani, and they moved to New York City. She became an attaché in the Philippines mission to the UN and two years later entered the UN Secretariat as a researcher in the human rights division and the Bureau of Social Affairs.

In 1966 Shahani began her involvement in women's social and economic issues as a researcher for the UN Commission on the Status of Women, which she eventually chaired. Her decision to seek a serious diplomatic career in order to be independent enough to raise a family was fortuitous, for in 1969 her husband died suddenly and she was left with three small children. Her commitment to remaining in the male-dominated diplomatic arena proved firm, and six years after being widowed she represented the Philippines at the kickoff Decade for Women Conference in Mexico City; she did so again at a conference in Copenhagen in 1980.

From 1981 Shahani was chief of the Vienna-based UN Centre for Social Development and Humanitarian Affairs, an agency dealing with problems of young people, criminals, the disabled, and the elderly. These responsibilities offered her the opportunity to lead the 1985 International Youth Year, and in August, following her participation in the Nairobi women's conference, she served as secretary-general of the seventh UN Crime Congress.

(BONNIE OBERMAN)

Shevardnadze, Eduard Amvrosiyevich

When, in July 1985, Andrey Gromyko was elected president of the Presidium of the Supreme Soviet—chief of state of the Soviet Union—the man appointed to replace him as foreign minister was Eduard Shevardnadze. Whereas Gromyko had held the post since 1957 and had been in the Soviet diplomatic service for many years before that, Shevardnadze was an apparatchik from Georgia with no previous experience of foreign affairs and was virtually unknown outside the Soviet Union. His appointment was taken as an indication that Mikhail Gorbachev (*q.v.*), the new general secretary of the Communist

UPI/BETTMANN NEWSPHOTOS

Party of the Soviet Union (CPSU), intended to play the leading role in foreign affairs himself.

Shevardnadze was born on Jan. 25, 1928, in the Mamati Lauchkhutsky region of Georgia, into a well-to-do family. Educated at the school of the Central Committee of the Communist Party of Georgia and at the Kutaisi Pedagogical Institute, he joined the Georgian Komsomol (Young Communist League) in 1946 and the CPSU in 1948. He held various posts in the Komsomol administration, advancing to first secretary (1957–61). Subsequently, he was first secretary (1961–63) of the Mtskheta district committee of the Communist Party of Georgia.

In 1964 Shevardnadze moved to the Georgian capital, Tbilisi, as first secretary for Pervomaysky district. The same year he was appointed first deputy minister and the following year minister of internal affairs of the Georgian S.S.R. In 1972 he was elected first secretary of the Tbilisi city committee and of the Central Committee of the Georgian party. As internal affairs minister he gained firsthand knowledge of high-level corruption and, as head of the Georgian party apparatus, he applied himself to the task of putting the house in order.

Shevardnadze became a member of the CPSU Central Committee in 1976 and two years later a candidate member of the Politburo and a deputy to the Supreme Soviet. His close association with Gorbachev secured his July 1985 election to full membership of the Politburo and his appointment as foreign minister. Shevardnadze's first appearances on the international scene outside the Soviet bloc were at the Helsinki meeting (July 30–August 1) marking the tenth anniversary of the Helsinki Accords, when he met U.S. Secretary of State George P. Shultz, and at the UN in September and October.

(K. M. SMOGORZEWSKI)

Shinto, Hisashi

When the Nippon Telegraph & Telephone Public Corporation (NTT) went private on April 1, 1985, its 320,000 employees made it the largest company in Japan. Directing this transformation from public to private ownership was Hisashi Shinto, who had been brought to NTT in 1981 as the representative of business and industry to revitalize the Japanese telecommunications industry. He was known as "Dr. Gorika" (Dr. Modernization) and lived up to the name. He welcomed competitors to the race to develop Japan's future information society and opened the doors to foreign suppliers. The so-called NTT family companies resented these moves because they had been exclusive bidders on NTT's fat purchasing accounts. Consequently, when the time came to select a president for NTT, these companies, together with their allies in politics and in the influential Ministry of Post and Telecommunications, backed Yasuda Kitahara. Shinto, however, won the battle. Known as a plainspoken man who did not shy away from confrontations, he strengthened the international orientation of NTT and frustrated more conservative colleagues by entering into agreements with AT&T and IBM.

Hisashi Shinto was born in Kurume, Fukuoka Prefecture, on July 21, 1910. Af-

YASUNORI IKEZOE/ZAIKAI MAGAZINE

ter graduating from the Imperial University of Kyushu in the field of naval architecture, he joined the Harima Shipbuilding Co. In 1951 he was transferred to National Bulk Carriers, a venture that U.S. shipping magnate Daniel K. Ludwig was setting up with Harima to build bulk carriers at the former navy dockyards in Kure, Hiroshima Prefecture. When Harima merged with Ishikawajima Heavy Industries (IHI) in 1960, Shinto returned as the shipping business department chief. His appointment had been secured by the president of IHI, Toshio Doko, a towering figure in Japanese business. In 1972 Shinto succeeded Doko as president and held the post until 1979.

Shinto's philosophy was always to give equal consideration to the customers, the employees, and the enterprise itself. In a personal memoir he recounted how he once turned down a request to build a luxury yacht for the Greek shipping tycoon Aristotle Onassis. Shinto snapped that he was willing to build ships to promote economic prosperity but not to accommodate the idle rich. Nonetheless, he still got Onassis's order for supertankers.

(GERD LARSSON)

Simon, Claude

In awarding the Nobel Prize for Literature to 72-year-old Claude Simon of France, the Swedish Academy emphasized his novels' "deepened awareness of time in the depiction of the human condition." Although Simon was a leading writer in the genre known as the new novel, or *nouveau roman,* he was not well known outside literary circles. The term new novelist is applied to a wide spectrum of writers who develop their novels unconventionally, moving away from continuous plot and character development and drawing instead on narrative techniques not unlike those of William Faulkner and James Joyce.

Varied reactions to the announcement regarding Simon emerged. A former Nobel literature prizewinner, commenting on the unorthodoxy of Simon's style, predicted that "in the future, all the so-called experiments will disappear. All those books which tell a story and describe character

will remain alive." On the other hand, another well-known author called the choice one of the "best in years," saying that Simon was a bold writer who had "forged" his own style. Simon himself was said to be very moved by the award, but he issued no public statement.

Claude-Eugène-Henri Simon was born on Oct. 10, 1913, in Tananarive, Madagascar. He grew up in Perpignan, a town in the south of France, where he still resided. His early education was in Paris, followed by brief periods of study in England. As a young man he tried his hand at painting and traveled extensively. He fought in the Spanish Civil War on the Republican side but became disillusioned with that cause. As a cavalryman in World War II he was taken prisoner in May 1940. He managed to escape and joined the French Resistance. It was during the war that he wrote his first novel, *Le Tricheur* ("The Trickster").

None of Simon's first four novels was translated into English. The turning point in his career, according to the Swedish Academy, was the publication of *Le Vent* (1957; *The Wind,* 1959) and *L'Herbe* (1958; *The Grass,* 1960). With these two novels he won critical acceptance of his idiosyncratic and sometimes difficult narrative style. In 1967 his novel *Histoire* (*History,* 1968) won the Prix de Medicis.

(BONNIE OBERMAN)

Siwar ad-Dahab, 'Abd ar-Rahman

Within a month of being appointed commander in chief of The Sudan's armed forces and defense minister, Gen. 'Abd ar-Rahman Muhammad al-Hassan Siwar ad-Dahab headed a military coup in April 1985 that overthrew Pres. Gaafar Nimeiry. By all accounts he was a reluctant coup leader but, faced with a popular upsurge against Nimeiry, who was in the U.S. at the time, he agreed that the Army should take power. However, as chairman of the Transitional Military Council he promised that the Army would stay for only one year to allow time to arrange for the country's return to civilian rule. His actions after taking power indicated that he intended to stand by that pledge.

Self-effacing, courteous, and prematurely gray, Siwar ad-Dahab was in every respect a different military character from the extroverted, ideological Nimeiry to whom he owed his rise in the Army. He was born in Omdurman in 1934, entered military college at the age of 20, and graduated as a second lieutenant four years later. His subsequent military training took him through army schools in Jordan, the U.S., and the U.K., as well as the High Military Academy in The Sudan. In 1970 he headed the cease-fire committee in Jordan and also served in Qatar. Returning to The Sudan in 1975, he subsequently commanded military operations in the southern region against the forces of the Sudan National Liberation Movement.

(COLIN LEGUM)

Springsteen, Bruce

A gold album and cover photos on two of the U.S.'s major news magazines ten years earlier did not bring Bruce Springsteen the kind of spectacular fame he achieved in 1985. With 13 million copies of *Born in the USA* sold throughout the world (the best seller in Columbia Records' history), "The Boss" became the most popular U.S. rock star since Elvis Presley. A 15-month tour completed in October took him to 62 cities around the world with every show sold out.

Springsteen was born in Freehold, N.J., on Sept. 23, 1949. A quiet and independent boy, he developed in his early teens an infatuation with the guitar and joined his first band when he was 14. He took a few courses at Ocean County (N.J.) Community College, but despite pressure from family, school, and church to abandon a musical career, he knew what he wanted to do with his life. He signed a contract with Columbia Records in June 1972, but it was not until autumn 1975 with *Born to Run* that Springsteen first received popular and critical attention.

A fuller sound than most bands of the 1970s plus Springsteen's high level of energy contributed to the enormous success of the album. On tour he made certain that no two performances were the same, offering an element of freshness and surprise to each audience.

But there were drawbacks to the extensive publicity of 1975. Springsteen saw himself becoming a commodity rather than a talent—he saw the danger of people not hearing his messages about faith and hope in a better world and the value of friendship. As he had said publicly many times, rock music brought purpose to his life, and he considered the trappings of fame to be distractions.

In the early 1980s Springsteen released *Nebraska,* an album that was described as a history lesson, a social outcry, a recognition of the anguish of the human spirit.

AP/WIDE WORLD

Much of this sense of desperation also emerged in *Born in the USA.* The album's title song, about hopes put on hold, has a chorus that many took, out of context, to be a statement of pride in America. One music critic described this phenomenon as a classic case of people hearing what they wanted rather than what was really being said.

(BONNIE OBERMAN)

Stallone, Sylvester

In 1985, in movie theatres across the United States, Americans refought the war in Vietnam—and won. Their designated warrior was actor-writer Sylvester Stallone, whose Vietnam veteran in *Rambo: First Blood Part II* rescues American soldiers from a Vietnamese prison while shooting and slashing his way through hundreds of enemy troops. The film, appealing to a public that was increasingly receptive to rethinking the Vietnam experience, grossed more money in its first two weeks than any other R-rated film ever released. It succeeded despite negative reviews; a *Washington Post* critic compared *Rambo* to the Nazi cinema of the 1920s and 1930s, remarking, "Here's a movie that wears its brown shirt on its sleeve." That failed to perturb Stallone, who said, "I'm not political. . . . I stand for ordinary Americans, losers a lot of them."

Stallone belonged to that group of ordinary Americans in 1975, when, with $106 in the bank and a pregnant wife, a starving dog, and an unpaid landlord hovering around him, he sat down to write *Rocky.* Three and a half days later he completed the script, and by early 1977 *Rocky* had catapulted him into elite company; he joined Charlie Chaplin and Orson Welles as the only artists ever to win Oscar nominations for both best screenwriter and best actor. Though Rocky resembled a typical Hollywood underdog—the tenderhearted, down-and-out boxer who unexpectedly gets the chance to compete for the title—critics praised Stallone for the energy and freshness he brought to the role. He later directed himself in *Rocky II* (1979), *Rocky III* (1982), and *Rocky IV* (1985).

In 1982 he first appeared as John Rambo in the original *First Blood.* Coscripted by Stallone, the film focuses on an unappreciated war hero who is goaded into laying waste an Oregon town. Stallone played Rambo as a mumbling, musclebound warrior, a cross between Marlon Brando and Arnold Schwarzenegger.

Stallone was born in New York City on July 6, 1946. He was a sickly child but as a teenager took up weight lifting. He studied drama at the University of Miami, but the aspiring actor could never have imagined what lay ahead: that by late 1985 he would be fighting the cold war on the big screen, saving ordinary Americans from a runaway Soviet boxer in *Rocky IV.*

(MICHAEL AMEDEO)

Takakura, Ken

One of Japan's most popular film stars, Ken Takakura marked his 30th year in movies in 1985. The handsome actor, whose close-cropped hair was his trademark, gained fame playing *yakuza* (gangster) roles during the 1960s. He generally portrayed outlaws whose impatience with hard luck finally drives them to seek revenge. Because they dared to attack the establishment, Takakura's characters were doomed to die or to rot in prison.

For audiences, emotional identification with Takakura's characters was more important than the films' message that society cannot tolerate vindictive outlaws. Moviegoers seemed to respond when the characters defied convention or manifested *giri* (obligation to the group) or *gaman* (stoic endurance). Takakura's riveting eyes, his stoic features, and his preference for silence over words seemed to strike a responsive chord in the hearts of those who also had to endure in silence.

TOHO

Takakura became a cult hero to student radicals, notably those who occupied the Tokyo University campus buildings in 1969, because his movie roles had made him the *yakuza* par excellence of that era. When Japanese gangster films began to lose their box-office appeal in the early 1970s, Takakura joined U.S. film star Robert Mitchum in the Tokyo-Hollywood production *The Yakuza* (1974). In 1976 Takakura left the Toei Motion Picture Co., his home since 1955, to become a freelance actor. Characteristically, he was generally cast as a loner with a complicated past, in search of love and peace; he combined masculine toughness with equally believable tenderness. A series of successful films, including *The Yellow Handkerchiefs of Happiness* (1977) and *A Story of the Antarctic* (1983) proved that durable tough guys finish first. Takakura won the Japan Academy Award for outstanding male actor in both 1980 and 1981 for two other films in this same tradition: *The Call of Distant Mountains* and *Station*.

Takakura was born Goichi Oda in Kita-Kyushu City in Fukuoka Prefecture on Feb. 16, 1931. His mother was a schoolteacher, his father a mining company employee. He graduated from Meiji University, Tokyo, in 1954 and in 1956 made his first film. Takakura once confided to director Yoji Yamada that he felt uneasy when he first became an actor. Having to wear a costume and makeup made the macho star from Kyushu worry that acting was not a proper job for a man.

(CHRISTINE PATTON CHAPMAN)

Takeshita, Noboru

One of the strongest contenders for the post of prime minister of Japan when Yasuhiro Nakasone's term expired in late 1986 would almost certainly be his minister of finance, Noboru Takeshita, whose surprisingly bold political moves served to obliterate his former image as a baby-faced lightweight in the ruling Liberal-Democratic Party (LDP). Polls, nonetheless, indicated that Takeshita faced an uphill battle for the party presidency, which had long been a guarantee of the prime ministership. Shintaro Abe, Japan's foreign minister, and Kiichi Miyazawa, chairman of the LDP executive council, were both considered potent rivals.

Some critics accused Takeshita of making a career out of avoiding commitments that could turn against him. Others, however, pointed out that under the iron rule of Kakuei Tanaka, the long-time strongman of Japanese politics and the leader of the pivotal LDP faction to which Takeshita belonged, the finance minister had little opportunity to assert himself. Events, however, took a dramatic turn in February 1985 when Takeshita inaugurated his own study group, Soseikai. Although this same ploy had previously been used by Tanaka to establish a personal power base within the ranks of the Sato faction, Takeshita's move reportedly infuriated Tanaka and, some speculated, brought on the stroke he suffered in February 1985; the perennial power broker was out of action thereafter.

Takeshita's outspoken support for currency intervention at a meeting of five leading industrial nations in New York City in September 1985 was also uncharacteristically bold. He also promoted more liberal financial policies, but he chose to project the image of a team player by insisting there was no such thing as an independent Takeshita policy. The only political policy the aspiring party leader had clearly set forth was a call for speedier development of the backward countryside, a policy long espoused by his political mentor Tanaka.

Takeshita's links to rural Shimane, a poor mountainous area where he was born Feb. 26, 1924, remained strong. Before being elected to the lower house of the Diet (parliament) at the age of 34, Takeshita served seven years on the Shimane prefectural council. He appeared to have upset the political balance within the LDP and said he believed that when the votes for party president were tallied, personal relationships and political luck would prove to have been decisive factors in the outcome.

(GERD LARSSON)

Tambo, Oliver

Nelson Mandela (*q.v.*) and Oliver Tambo began their professional careers as partners in a law firm in Johannesburg, South Africa, in the early 1950s. They had previously been students together at the black University College (now University) of Fort Hare and were founders of the Youth League of the African National Congress (ANC). Both were Pondos from the Transkei, but whereas Mandela was a member of the royal family, Tambo came from humble parentage. Both became recognized leaders of the ANC, generally regarded as a key factor in the political transition to a postapartheid South Africa. Their importance was recognized by a delegation of prominent South African businessmen who defied their government to engage in talks with Tambo and other ANC leaders in Zambia in September 1985. At a press conference in London the next month, Tambo criticized Prime Minister Margaret Thatcher for her reluctance to apply sanctions against South Africa.

Tambo was appointed secretary-general of the ANC in 1955. Arrested on treason charges in 1956, he was released the following year and in 1958 became ANC deputy president. In 1960 he went into exile to lead the ANC's campaign. Tambo kept out of the limelight until developments in South Africa in 1985 forced him at the age of 67 into international promi-

nence. His speeches were free of rhetoric and ideology and reflected the thoughtful and serious mind of a family lawyer. He was himself a devoted family man.

Born Oct. 27, 1917, at Bizana, Transkei, Tambo was brought up as an Anglican and left his tribal homeland at the age of 17 to become a boarder at the Anglican school of St. Peter's in Johannesburg. His modest fees were paid by an elder stepbrother and two Englishwomen. The Transkei Tribal Council later gave him a scholarship to go to Fort Hare. After completing his degree he taught for a time as a science master at his old school but soon decided that his future lay in law and nationalist politics.

(COLIN LEGUM)

Tebbit, Norman Beresford

On being appointed chairman of the Conservative Party in 1985, Norman Tebbit was widely seen to have become heir apparent to Britain's Prime Minister Margaret Thatcher as party leader. His task was to pilot the Conservatives out of their midterm trough to a third election victory in 1987 or 1988, but there were many within the party who wondered whether a chairman cast in the image of the leader herself was exactly what was required at a moment when a more conciliatory and centrist approach might be in order.

Tebbit was a Conservative very much in the Thatcher mold. She came from a family of shopkeepers, and his father was a shop assistant who during the 1930s became unemployed. His response, according to Tebbit, was to "get on his bike" and find himself another job. Tebbit passed on this exemplary advice at a Conservative Party conference to the delight of his supporters and the fury of his political opponents.

Tebbit was born in the North London suburb of Edmonton on March 29, 1931. It was a commission as a flying officer in the Royal Air Force during his national service in 1949–51 that set him on his middle-class way. During 1953–70 he was a civil airline pilot and became an officer of the British Airline Pilots Association. Tebbit was a Tory throughout his trade union career and was elected to Parliament in 1970. He showed his political colours in 1973 when he resigned a junior position as parliamentary private secretary for rea-

RICHARD OPEN—CAMERA PRESS, LONDON

sons that included opposition to Edward Heath's change of policy and, in particular, to what he saw as a too indulgent line toward the unions. When Margaret Thatcher deposed Heath as party leader in 1975, Tebbit soon became one of her most vocal supporters in the House of Commons.

Following the advent of the Conservative government in 1979, Tebbit held two junior posts before becoming secretary of state for employment in September 1981. In October 1983 he moved to the Department of Trade and Industry but had made little mark in the job when, in October 1984, he was severely injured in the Irish Republican Army bombing of the Grand Hotel in Brighton. Tebbit nevertheless determined to continue in his political career.   (PETER JENKINS)

Thatcher, Margaret Hilda

In 1985 Britain's Prime Minister Margaret Thatcher celebrated her tenth anniversary as leader of the Conservative Party and at the same time indicated in a newspaper interview that she had "about another five years" to go "before someone else will carry the torch." She became prime minister in 1979, the first woman to hold the office, and in a landslide victory in 1983 became the first incumbent since World War II to win a second election after a full term. Throughout her terms of office she exercised an unusual dominance over her Cabinet colleagues, the governmental machine, and the public, but in 1985 opinion polls for the first time reported her to be less popular than the leaders of the three opposition parties.

With the defeat of the miners' strike that had begun in the previous year, she might have expected to have been buoyed to new heights as she had been following Britain's victory in the Falklands Islands/Islas Malvinas conflict of 1982. But instead it was the Labour Party and its leader Neil Kinnock who benefited chiefly from the ending of the strike. After the government had done badly in local elections in May and had lost an important by-election in the Welsh seat of Brecon and Radnor in July, it became the widely held view that Thatcher, temporarily at least, had become an electoral liability to her party. The government softened the tone of its pronouncements and so did she; she even softened her hairstyle. By the end of the year, both the government's popularity and her own personal standing appeared to be recovering.

Born Oct. 13, 1925, in Grantham, the daughter of a shopkeeper, Thatcher won her way to the University of Oxford, where she studied chemistry. She later became a lawyer, was elected to Parliament in 1959, became a Cabinet minister under Edward Heath in 1970, and seized the party leadership from him in 1975. Her career was a mixture of persistent hard work and bold opportunism. As prime minister she personified the virtues of self-help and enterprise—the roots of a free-market philosophy nearer to that of classical Liberalism than to traditional Toryism. Her ambition, she declared, was to save Britain once and for all from socialism.   (PETER JENKINS)

Thomas, Philip Michael

See JOHNSON, DON.

Tian Jiyun

When Tian Jiyun (T'ien Chi-yün) was elected to both the Secretariat of the Central Committee of the Chinese Communist Party and the Politburo in September 1985, he became a potential successor to such aging leaders as Deng Xiaoping (Teng Hsiao-p'ing) and Li Xiannian (Li Hsiennien). An economic specialist and chief deputy to Premier Zhao Ziyang (Chao Tzu-yang), Tian became involved in foreign affairs and in the implementation of practical reforms designed to achieve China's goal of modernization.

Born in Feicheng (Fei-ch'eng) County, Shandong (Shantung) Province, in 1929, Tian received little formal education and joined the Communist Party in 1945. In the late 1940s he was involved in violent Communist-led land reforms. After the People's Republic was founded in 1949, he held a number of middle-level financial posts in Guizhou (Kweichow) Province, where he remained until his transfer to Sichuan (Szechwan) Province in 1969. In the late 1970s he assisted Zhao Ziyang, then governor of Sichuan, in carrying out experimental economic and agricultural reforms in the province. As Zhao's right-hand man, Tian played an important role in bold and flexible programs that deviated from Marxist principles but significantly increased industrial output and agricultural production. These results were achieved through such innovative policies as rewarding workers on the basis of work rather than need and providing incentives based on free enterprise and market forces rather than on rigid quotas established by central authorities. In addition, factory managers were given much greater autonomy, and peasants were allowed to benefit from individual initiative.

These approaches soon attracted national attention, and both Zhao and Tian were transferred to Beijing (Peking), where they were appointed premier and deputy secretary-general of the State Council (Cabinet), respectively, in 1980. After being elected to the party's Central Committee in 1982, Tian became an important member of a team that successfully introduced to the entire nation Zhao's Sichuan reforms, which markedly speeded up China's economic development, especially in the agricultural sector. For these achievements Tian was promoted to vice-premier and secretary-general in 1983. Capable, energetic, and self-taught, Tian was noted for his down-to-earth approaches to China's agricultural and economic problems. An efficient administrator, he demonstrated his organizational ability by coordinating various agencies in China's massive bureaucracy.   (WINSTON L. Y. YANG)

Tjibaou, Jean-Marie

Head of the Front de Libération Nationale Kanake et Socialiste (FLNKS), the militant independence movement of the Kanaks (Melanesians) of the French overseas territory of New Caledonia, Jean-Marie Tjibaou was the precise opposite of a rebel leader or a politician. He was rather almost the stereotype of the quiet man. No great orator, he spoke softly and slowly, weighing every word.

Born in 1937 in Hienghène, a small parish on the east coast of New Caledonia,

ROBERT COHEN—AGIP/PICTORIAL PARADE

Tjibaou attended the Catholic seminary in Paita and was ordained a priest in 1965. In 1970, feeling that the priesthood confined him to a "mysticoreligious ghetto," he left and devoted himself primarily to social work, without, however, ceasing to believe and practice the faith. In 1977 he was elected mayor of Hienghène and vice-president of the Union Calédonienne, the main independence party. He was elected vice-premier in the government of New Caledonia in 1982. A moderate, concerned chiefly with economic and social affairs, Tjibaou emerged on Nov. 18, 1984, in Hienghène, as a deeply determined supporter of "the active boycott policy adopted by the FLNKS." A few days later he was confirmed as the political leader of the independence movement.

During 1984–85 New Caledonia was the scene of violent confrontations between the Kanaks of the FLNKS and the *caldoches,* those of European descent. The French government decided to institute a "transitional regime" that would allow the groups concerned to express their views on the future of the country. Four regions were set up, and regional elections were held in September 1985. In October, as expected, Tjibaou, Léopold Jorédié, and Yéiweiné Yéiweiné, all three members of the Union Calédonienne, were elected premiers of the three regions where the independence movement had won the elections.

In theory, a referendum was to take place before Dec. 31, 1987, on New Caledonia's progress toward "independence in association with France." Meanwhile, Tjibaou stated that the division of the country into regions would allow the independence faction to "organize independence at the grassroots," a kind of "creeping independence."   (JEAN KNECHT)

Turner, Tina

Literally bouncing her way back to fame, Tina Turner underwent a revival in 1985 like no other rock star in recent memory. She rose to the top of the entertainment industry during the year with a multiplatinum album, *Private Dancer;* two Grammy awards for the gold single *What's Love Got to Do with It?* and one for the single *Better Be Good to Me;* and a leading role opposite Mel Gibson in the motion picture *Mad Max: Beyond Thunderdome.* Long known

as one of entertainment's most spectacular performers, she created a unique persona through her youthful appearance, her kinetic energy, and her strongly individual taste in clothing and hairstyle.

Born Annie Mae Bullock in Nutbush, Tenn., on Nov. 26, 1938, to a cotton plantation manager and his wife, she dreamed as a girl of transcending the plight of a poor rural black family and becoming a Hollywood entertainer. As a schoolgirl she sang and danced in every available talent show. In the 1950s, after moving to St. Louis, Mo., she and her sister frequented nightclubs; in 1956 they met Ike Turner and his band in one of the clubs. After hearing Annie sing, Turner used her occasionally in band engagements. In 1959 she filled in for a vocalist at a recording session, and the result was Ike's 800,000-seller entitled "A Fool in Love." Ike named his new lead

AP/WIDE WORLD

singer Tina and transformed his band into the slick Ike and Tina Turner Revue, with a female dance and vocal backup trio and a nine-piece instrumental section. Ike and Tina married and launched the first of many cross-country tours. They created a unique blend of country, gospel, rock and roll, and blues that by 1969 had filled 15 albums and 60 single recordings.

But the rewards of success for Tina Turner were overshadowed by her husband's sometimes brutal domination of her life. In July 1976 she left him. Independent for the first time, she slowly began to develop her own style and to rebuild her career. In 1983 her single "Let's Stay Together" earned her the prestigious British Silver Disc Award. A 1984 tour with Lionel Richie cemented her comeback.

(BONNIE OBERMAN)

Ullmann, Liv Johanne

True to her reputation as the world's most noted Scandinavian actress after Garbo and Ingrid Bergman and also as a caring mother who was actively concerned for the wellbeing of the Earth's suffering and starving millions, Liv Ullmann in 1985 was one of the many artists and writers who signed an appeal to the signatories of the 1975 Helsinki Accords at the tenth anniversary Conference on Security and Cooperation in Europe to "construct a cultural bridge across all conceivable borders." Five years earlier the United Nations Children's Fund

RICHARD OPEN—CAMERA PRESS, LONDON

(UNICEF) had appointed Ullmann as its "goodwill ambassador" to tour the third world countries most seriously affected by famine and allied scourges. What she saw affected her profoundly, as she revealed in an impassioned talk on the BBC's "The Light of Experience" series, transmitted at the end of the UNICEF 1985 World Children's Week.

Liv Ullmann was born on Dec. 16, 1939, in Japan to Norwegian parents, who took her first to Canada and then home to Norway and sent her to drama school in Britain at the age of 17. Some 30 years later, in 1985, she returned to London for her British stage debut, in a highly acclaimed revival of Harold Pinter's *Old Times.*

Since 1957, the year of her first Norwegian film, Ullmann had made 32 largescreen or TV films, the best of them with Swedish director Ingmar Bergman. Her stage debut was in Stavanger, Norway (in *Anne Frank*), in 1957, but her breakthrough performance was in Peter Palitzsch's 1960 production of Bertolt Brecht's *The Caucasian Chalk Circle* at the New Norwegian Theatre in Oslo. She was seen in Jean Cocteau's monodrama *The Human Voice* in Australia and in New York, both on stage and in a Public Broadcasting Service TV special. Ullmann's Broadway parts ranged from her 1975 debut as Nora in Ibsen's *A Doll's House* to the lead role in the 1979 musical *I Remember Mama.* The youngest person to receive the Order of St. Olav from the king of Norway, she also held six honorary doctorates from U.S. universities as well as numerous acting and other awards. She wrote two volumes of autobiography, *Changing* (1976) and *Choices* (1984), the first revealing her personal dilemmas and the second her public concerns. (OSSIA TRILLING)

Walker, John

The espionage activities of John Walker were described by some officials as among the gravest security breaches in the history of the U.S. Navy. Walker, a private detective and retired navy communications officer, was arrested by the FBI on May 20, 1985, on a charge of attempting to pass classified documents, mostly navy reports on movements of Soviet submarines

and surface ships, to unidentified agents of the Soviet Union. Walker had obtained the documents from his brother, Arthur, a retired navy lieutenant commander, and from his son, Michael, a navy petty officer assigned to the aircraft carrier USS *Nimitz.* During most of his 21-year naval career John Walker had had access to detailed information about the movements of both U.S. and Soviet fleets.

John Anthony Walker, Jr., was born in 1937 in Washington, D.C. His family was a troubled one. John dropped out of St. Patrick's Roman Catholic high school in West Scranton, Pa., during his junior year after attempting a burglary. He was threatened with jail unless he joined the armed forces.

Walker was assigned to the submarine *Simon Bolivar* between August 1965 and April 1967. In March 1967 he was promoted to warrant officer. Federal prosecutors said that he began selling secrets to the Soviets in 1968. Walker was stationed in California in the late 1960s and 1970s between cruises on the *Andrew Jackson,* a nuclear-powered submarine on which he served as a radioman. That assignment allowed him access to large amounts of navy sensitive material.

Walker's son, Michael, was arrested on May 22 on charges of passing navy secrets to Soviet agents. Arthur Walker admitted that in September 1980 he had begun turning secret documents over to his brother, knowing their destination.

In October Walker indicated his willingness to cooperate with military officials in their investigation of the espionage operation. In return for a reduced sentence for Michael, John agreed to plead guilty and to provide a detailed accounting of the material passed by him to the Soviets. He received a life sentence, his son 25 years, and his brother the stiffest penalty of all— a $250,000 fine and life imprisonment.

(BONNIE OBERMAN)

Walters, Vernon Anthony

On May 16, 1985, the U.S. Senate confirmed Pres. Ronald Reagan's nomination of Vernon A. Walters to be the country's chief delegate and ambassador to the United Nations. Walters acknowledged the appointment as the greatest honour in his long career of military and diplomatic service. As chief delegate he was expected to be less outspoken than his sometimes controversial predecessor, Jeane Kirkpatrick.

Walters was born in New York City of British parents on Jan. 3, 1917. He was educated abroad, becoming fluent in several European languages, but, because of family financial problems, he was unable to finish high school. He enlisted in the U.S. Army as a private in 1941, and the following year, because of his language skills, he was accepted in Officers Candidate School. During the 1943–44 military campaign in Italy, Walters was promoted to major. He served as an aide to Lieut. Gen. Mark W. Clark and as liaison to a Brazilian unit under Clark's command. From 1945 to 1948 he was assistant military attaché to Brazil.

Assigned to the Paris headquarters of NATO in 1951, Walters was reassigned to a NATO post in Washington, D.C., in 1954 after being severely injured in a skiing accident. During his long recovery he served as an interpreter for Pres.

VIOUJARD—GAMMA/LIAISON

Dwight D. Eisenhower at Geneva (1955) and for Vice-Pres. Richard M. Nixon on his 1958 tour of South America. During the Nixon presidency, Walters made the arrangements for Henry Kissinger's many secret trips to Paris during negotiations to end the Vietnam war.

Between 1960 and 1971 Walters advanced from colonel to major general. In 1972 he was promoted to the rank of lieutenant general and became deputy director of the CIA. At the request of presidential assistant H. R. Haldeman, Walters advised the FBI not to investigate the burglary that was at the heart of the Watergate affair, on the grounds that it would jeopardize a CIA operation. Later, convinced that Haldeman had deceived him, Walters refused to interfere with the FBI inquiry. He retired from the Army and resigned from the CIA in 1976.

In his autobiography, *Silent Missions* (1978), Walters denied that when he was with the CIA he had taken part in any attempts to overthrow governments that posed a threat to the United States. He also expressed his belief that Communist governments are more dangerous to U.S. interests than are right-wing dictatorships.

(CHARLES JOHNSON TAGGART)

Williams, Lynn

As president of the United Steelworkers of America, Lynn Williams became the first Canadian to head a major U.S.-based international union. International secretary of the union since 1977, Williams was named temporary acting president by the union's executive board in November 1983, following the death of Pres. Lloyd McBride. On March 29, 1984, Lynn Williams was elected president in his own right by the members of the union. Since Williams joined the Steelworkers in 1947, his career had been a steady climb from organizer to president.

Born in Springfield, Ont., on July 21, 1924, Lynn Russell Williams was the son of a United Church minister. Early in life he was attracted to the labour movement, seeing it as an expression of the social-gospel ideal of service. He attended McMaster University in Hamilton, Ont., and obtained a B.A. in liberal arts in 1944. Discovering that the only way to enter the labour movement was by working in a factory, Williams took a blue-collar job

in Toronto and joined the Steelworkers in 1947.

From 1947 to 1973 Williams pursued a career as a successful union organizer. He was an integral part of the Steelworkers' biggest success in Canada, in the late 1960s when the United Steelworkers of America replaced the Mine, Mill, and Smelter Workers as bargaining agent for the Sudbury, Ont., employees of International Nickel. Williams headed the Steelworkers' first bargaining team at Inco, and this led, in 1971, to his coordinating the first World Nickel Conference, attended by unions from nine countries.

Williams believed in political action by the labour movement. In 1956 he made an unsuccessful bid for a seat in the Canadian Parliament. He was one of the founders of the New Democratic Party in Canada and served on its Ontario executive. In 1973 he was appointed to the Ontario Economic Council.

In 1973 Lynn Williams was elected director of District 6 of the Steelworkers, based in Toronto. Elected international secretary in 1977, he moved to Pittsburgh, Pa. Upon assuming the presidency, Williams determined to use his organizing skills to rebuild union membership, which had fallen by half since 1979. As a Canadian, winning the office was important to him, since it affirmed that the United Steelworkers of America was an international union in which both nations could play a role. (DIANE LOIS WAY)

Young of Graffham, David Ivor Young, Baron

A year after his meteoric rise to the Cabinet, Lord Young was further promoted in the reshuffle of September 1985 to the senior position of secretary of state for employment. With unemployment the most contentious issue in British party politics, it was doubly unusual for such a senior ministerial responsibility to be given to a member of the House of Lords. The Department of Employment subsequently was given a second minister of Cabinet rank, to answer for it in the House of Commons. This arrangement was a measure of Prime Minister Margaret Thatcher's high regard for Lord Young.

David Young was born (Feb. 27, 1932) and educated in Thatcher's North London constituency of Finchley. He became a lawyer but soon ceased his practice to make his career, and fortune, in property development. After the 1979 election he became an adviser to Secretary of State for Industry Sir Keith Joseph. When Joseph was transferred to the Department of Education in September 1981, Young continued to advise him while at the same time maintaining his connection with the Department of Industry.

These two interests, industry and education, made Young an appropriate candidate for the chairmanship of the Manpower Services Commission, a governmental agency responsible for labour market policies and training. There he set about the reform of industrial training in the belief that the only solution to unemployment lay in improvement in the workings of the labour market.

In September 1984 Young was taken into the government and straight into the Cabinet as minister without portfolio but

with special responsibility for deregulation and the promotion of small businesses. He became known as the minister in charge of cutting red tape. As he was not a member of Parliament, his appointment to the government required his elevation to the House of Lords as a life peer. His promotion a year later to head the Department of Employment was the result of three considerations. One was his high place in the prime minister's favour as a go-getting self-made man after her own heart. Another was the unsatisfactory position of a minister without portfolio in the British system of government, especially if he was a businessman with little previous experience of government. But the chief reason was the need to counter accusations that the government was not doing enough to reduce the high level of unemployment.

(PETER JENKINS)

Yurchenko, Vitaly Sergeyevich

On Aug. 1, 1985, Vitaly Yurchenko, a Soviet diplomat who was in Rome on what was purportedly an assignment for the Soviet Ministry of Foreign Affairs, walked away from his colleagues, saying that he wanted to see the museums in the Vatican. Yurchenko never rejoined the group. Soviet officials in Rome apparently searched for him for an entire week before asking Italian authorities to investigate his disappearance.

On September 25 the *Washington Times* reported that Yurchenko had defected to the U.S. and was being debriefed in a suburb of Washington, D.C., by the CIA. The *Times* said that Yurchenko's job at the ministry was a cover for his real position as a high-ranking agent of the KGB in charge of espionage operations in the United States and Canada.

On November 2, while visiting Washington, D.C., Yurchenko quietly walked away from the U.S. intelligence official accompanying him. Two days later he called a press conference at the Soviet embassy in Washington and said that CIA agents had kidnapped him in Rome, drugged him, and held him prisoner for "three horrible months." The CIA denied the accusations, maintaining that Yurchenko had come to them voluntarily. After the press conference, State Department officials interviewed Yurchenko with no Soviet officials present; the U.S. authorities reported they were satisfied that Yurchenko had chosen freely to return to the U.S.S.R. He immediately flew to Moscow, where he repeated his accusations against the CIA.

Yurchenko was born on May 2, 1936. Before a stint as a security officer at the Soviet embassy in Washington, D.C., he served in the Soviet Navy. At the time of his defection in Rome, he was counselor to the Ministry of Foreign Affairs.

Yurchenko's return to the Soviet Union stirred a number of speculations: that he had become concerned for the safety of family members left behind; that his defection in Rome had been staged so he could accuse the CIA of kidnapping, thus embarrassing the U.S. on the eve of a major East-West summit conference; and that a love affair with a Soviet woman living in Canada had gone sour. Whatever the truth, his accusations against the CIA could deter other Soviets from trying to defect.

(CHARLES JOHNSON TAGGART)

BRITANNICA AWARDS

A program of awards has been established by Encyclopædia Britannica, Inc., to recognize exceptional excellence in the dissemination of learning for the benefit of mankind. The Britannica Award will be presented to as many as five persons each year, beginning in 1986.

Although the recipients may well have made major contributions to knowledge, that is not the achievement that the Britannica Awards celebrate. Rather, they are given for skill in the communication of knowledge and a passion for the dissemination of learning. The persons honoured by these awards will have demonstrated, in lectures or writings, exceptional ability to make a special field of knowledge or area of learning intelligible and accessible to the widest possible audience.

The Britannica Awards embrace the whole spectrum of knowledge. Candidates for the award are nominated by members of Britannica's Board of Editors and its Editorial Advisory Committees drawn from the faculties of great universities in the United States, Canada, Japan, Australia, the United Kingdom, and Europe. Final selections are made by a Britannica committee consisting of the chairmen of the corporation's Board of Directors and its Board of Editors, its president, and its editor in chief. The award consists of a gold medal, the sum of $15,000, and an allowance for the expenses of attending the presentation and subsequent lectures. Each award will be presented at a celebratory banquet in the recipient's country, and each recipient is invited to address one or two subsequent forums in other countries.

The recipients of the first Britannica Awards are Prof. Dame Leonie Kramer of the University of Sydney; Prof. Malcolm Sim Longair, astronomer royal of Scotland; U.S. Sen. Daniel Patrick Moynihan of New York; Dr. Lewis Thomas, president emeritus of the Memorial Sloan-Kettering Cancer Center in New York City; and John Tuzo Wilson, professor emeritus of geology at the University of Toronto. Biographical sketches of the recipients follow.

Kramer, Dame Leonie Judith

In 1968 the University of Sydney created the world's first chair in Australian literature and awarded it to the preeminent scholar in that field, Leonie Judith Kramer, who thereby became the first woman professor at Australia's oldest university. She had already compiled a number of other firsts, and she went on to become the first woman to head the Australian Broad-

casting Commission (ABC) and the first woman to sit on the board of directors of an Australian bank. She is an authority on and a biographer of the great Australian woman novelist Henry Handel Richardson (1870–1946). In 1976 she was made an Officer of the Order of the British Empire, and in 1983 she was made a Dame of the Order of the British Empire.

Leonie Kramer was a member of the ABC from 1977, but her tenure at its helm in 1982 and 1983 was stormy. Named chairman by the last Liberal (conservative) Party prime minister, Malcolm Fraser, she also served during the Labor Party regime of Robert Hawke, and she did not shrink from battle with either party. She remains a staunch supporter of the ABC, whose quality she wishes governments appreciated more fully and funded more adequately.

Her conspicuous accomplishments have not won her much support in Australia's women's movement. Leonie Kramer considers herself a feminist in a sense, but she has no patience with the notion that people should be given jobs or appointments for any reason other than their own merit. This attitude and her conservative political outlook have made her a frequent if undaunted target of women's liberationists. Meanwhile, she continues to exert her influence toward improving the quality of education (she is a cofounder and vice-president of the Australian Council for Educational Standards). As teacher, author, and literary and dramatic critic, she radiates her lifelong love and respect for the English language, whose wholesale abuse worries her. She notes with irritation that people tolerate mistakes in English that may obfuscate their meaning, while they will not tolerate mistakes in mathematics.

Dame Leonie was born Leonie Judith Gibson on Oct. 1, 1924, at Melbourne. Her father, a bank clerk, and mother read widely and avidly, and she grew up in suburban Kew surrounded by books. She attended Presbyterian Ladies College at Melbourne and the University of Melbourne, where she earned a B.A. in 1945. After tutoring and lecturing there for several years, she went on to the University of Oxford, where she received her D.Phil. in 1953. At Oxford she met and married a South African physician, Harold Kramer. The couple settled in Melbourne, where they had two daughters, now a lawyer and a physician. Her books include *Henry Handel Richardson* (1967) and three other volumes dealing with the novelist's work, plus several anthologies. In 1981–82 she was visiting professor of Australian studies at Harvard University.

Longair, Malcolm Sim

For only the second time since the post was created by King William IV in 1834, the astronomer royal for Scotland is a Scot, and indeed a native of Dundee like the first (Thomas Henderson). Malcolm Sim Longair was made astronomer royal in 1980. With that job went two added titles and responsibilities: regius professor of astronomy at the University of Edinburgh, and director of the Royal Observatory on Edinburgh's Blackford Hill.

The optical telescopes at the observatory are both small and obsolescent and thus no longer suited to modern astronomical observation. The significant astronomical work directed from the Royal Observatory actually goes on at British installations in Australia, Hawaii, and The Netherlands. Longair has converted the old equipment to educational uses and part of the building to a visitors centre where schoolchildren from all over Scotland, as well as curious adults, may see, touch, and understand. Since the government's budget for the observatory funds only scientific missions, the astronomer royal organized the establishment of a trust to support the public education mission he developed there.

Longair was born in Dundee on May 18, 1941, and was educated there at Morgan Academy and Queens College of the University of St. Andrews, where he received a B.Sc. degree with first-class honours in electronic physics. He went on to the University of Cambridge, where he was a research student in the Mullard Radio Astronomy Observatory and a member of Trinity College. He received his M.A. and Ph.D. there in 1967 and became a fellow, later praelector, of Clare Hall at Cambridge. In 1968–69, as a Royal Society exchange fellow to the Soviet Union, he worked at the P. N. Lebedev Institute.

In the 1970s Longair taught physics at Cambridge, with interruptions in 1972 and 1978 for visiting professorships at the California Institute of Technology and the

Institute for Advanced Study at Princeton, N.J., respectively. On several occasions in the late 1970s he returned to the U.S.S.R. on exchange visits to the Space Research Centre at Moscow. By 1980 his reputation as a scholar, a lucid teacher, and an outstanding lecturer had led to the Scottish appointment.

Among Longair's interests are architecture and music. His wife, Deborah Howard, lectures in art history at the University of Edinburgh, and the two collaborated on a study of Palladio's use of harmonic proportion in the ground plans of his *Quattro libri*. Longair's own publications include *High Energy Astrophysics* (1981), *Theoretical Concepts in Physics* (1984), and *Alice and the Space Telescope* (1986).

Moynihan, Daniel Patrick

Daniel Patrick Moynihan has successfully blended the careers of scholar and statesman ever since he joined the U.S. Department of Labor at the request of Pres. John F. Kennedy in 1961 (becoming as-

sistant secretary of labour two years later). Although he has not been a full-time professor since 1969, when he went from the Harvard University faculty to a U.S. Cabinet post under Pres. Richard M. Nixon, he has never quit either teaching or studying. While retaining his Harvard affiliation as professor of government, he has served successively as U.S. ambassador to India (1973–75), U.S. delegate to the UN (1975–76), and U.S. senator from New York (since 1977).

BOB ISEAR

Moynihan was born on March 16, 1927, in Tulsa, Okla., where his father was a newspaperman. The family moved to New York City a few months later and not long afterward was abandoned by his father. Pat Moynihan and his brother grew up scrambling to get out of poverty, and after graduating from his school in Harlem he matriculated at New York City College, launching an academic career that, interrupted by U.S. Navy service (1944–47), included studies at Tufts University (B.A., 1948), the Fletcher School of Law and Diplomacy (M.A., 1949; Ph.D., 1961), and the London School of Economics and Political Science.

His political career began in the gubernatorial administration of W. Averell Harriman of New York, and he has been at or near the forefront of Democratic Party politics virtually all his adult life except while serving in the administrations of Republican Presidents Nixon and Gerald Ford. His only electoral failure was in 1965 in the general election for president of the New York City Council. His election to a second term in the U.S. Senate in 1982 was a historic landslide.

Moynihan's writing first brought him to national attention in a landmark study of New York's ethnic groups that he wrote with the sociologist Nathan Glazer, *Beyond the Melting Pot* (1963). His writings have cemented his reputation as a penetrating social observer and critic and an influential diagnostician of societal ills who never hesitates to unmask unpleasant truths and expose shibboleths. He was a central figure in the emergence of neoconservatism in the United States and is a member of the publications committee of *The Public Interest*.

Thomas, Lewis

After nearly a half century of medical practice, teaching, research, and administration, Lewis Thomas does not think of himself as an author. But authors think of him as one of the great prose stylists of our time, a master of the art of the essay, who uses the language of poetry "to communicate human truths too mysterious for old-fashioned common sense" (Joyce Carol

Oates). Sir Peter Medawar compares him to Oliver Wendell Holmes.

Thomas's writing, which seems effortless and apparently is, found its own way into popular print. Writing down his observations and reflections on an ancient typewriter came to be his custom, and in the early 1970s an old friend, teacher, and colleague, Franz Inglefinger, urged him to submit some of those essays to the *New England Journal of Medicine*. There they appeared as a series under the general title "Notes of a Biology Watcher." They were subsequently collected as *The Lives of a Cell*, which greatly bemused Thomas by winning the 1975 National Book Award in Arts and Letters. Through most of his career Thomas has been noted by colleagues for what one described as "his care and feeding of the young scientists who flocked to him for his enthusiastic and sustained support . . . and his unflagging willingness to help others."

Thomas was born (on Nov. 25, 1913, at Flushing, N.Y.) to a medical career. His father was a physician and surgeon who took young Lewis along on house calls, and his mother was a nurse who had been supervisor of nurses at Roosevelt Hospital. He matriculated at Princeton University at 15 and then attended Harvard Medical School, graduating in 1937. After internship at Boston City Hospital, a residency at the Neurological Institute of New York, and service in the U.S. Navy Medical Corps, he taught at Johns Hopkins and Tulane universities and the University of Minnesota Medical School. In 1954 he

DOUGLAS WETZSTEIN

moved to New York University School of Medicine, which he left as dean in 1969 to teach and chair the pathology department at Yale. In 1973 he took the presidency of the Memorial Sloan-Kettering Cancer Center, becoming president emeritus in 1984.

He is at present adjunct professor at Rockefeller University, university professor at the State University of New York at Stony Brook, and visiting professor of neuropathology at the Yale Medical School. His writing continues as well, and to continuing acclaim. *The Medusa and the Snail* (1979) won the American Book Award in 1981 and was followed by *The Youngest Science* and *Late Night Thoughts on Listening to Mahler's Ninth Symphony* (both 1983).

Wilson, John Tuzo

Ontario schoolchildren remember him as the man who promoted the "touch it, push the button" approach to the provincial science museum. Assiduous map readers can find his mother's name on British Columbia's Mt. Tuzo and his own on

Antarctica's Wilson Mountains and an extinct volcano on the floor of the Pacific off the Canadian coast. Geophysicists honour him as the man who, some 25 years ago, rescued the theory of plate tectonics from the scrap heap by supplying a sort of missing link: the realization that drifting continents could slide over or under one another as well as just collide, an essential addition that permitted the theory to become almost universally accepted.

ONTARIO SCIENCE CENTER

J. Tuzo Wilson is a man of many careers, the current one as chancellor of York University. Probably the one that gave him the most fun was the director generalship of the Ontario Science Centre from 1974 until his recent retirement. He suspects the prime minister put him into the museum job because he wanted a certified academic running what may have seemed more of a fun house for schoolchildren than a serious museum.

Wilson was born on Oct. 24, 1908, at Ottawa, the son of a distinguished Scottish engineer who became Canada's director of civil aviation and a vigorous and enthusiastic mountaineer *née* Henrietta Tuzo. As a boy he worked in a forestry camp and later in the Canadian Geological Survey. When he entered the University of Toronto, he undertook a double major in physics and geology. After winning his B.A. (1930), he pursued physics and geology, with mathematics added, at the University of Cambridge for another B.A. (1932). He then went to Princeton for a Ph.D. in geology (1936), taking time out to become the first to scale 3,760-m (12,328-ft) Mt. Hague in Montana. He returned to Cambridge for an M.A. (1940) and later a D.Sc. (1958). After service in the Canadian Army as an engineer (1939–46) Wilson became professor of geophysics at the University of Toronto, where he taught for 29 years.

Wilson's work mapping the glaciers of the Canadian North in the 1950s and '60s, along with his studies of orogeny (mountain building) and mineral occurrence, made his international reputation as a geophysicist. In 1965 he published what is widely regarded as his most important contribution to the discipline, his discovery of an entirely new class of geological faults, transform faults, and an explanation of their bearing on continental drift.

He is an Officer of the Order of the British Empire and a Companion of the Order of Canada. Among his books are *Physics and Geology* (in part; 1959, 1973), *One Chinese Moon* (1959), *I.G.Y., The Year of the New Moons* (1961), and *Unglazed China* (1973). He edited the collections *Continents Adrift* (1973) and *Continents Adrift and Continents Aground* (1976).   (BRUCE L. FELKNOR)

OBITUARIES

Abruzzo, Ben, U.S. balloonist (b. June 9, 1930, Rockford, Ill.—d. Feb. 11, 1985, Albuquerque, N.M.), was a wealthy land developer turned daredevil who captured the imagination of the world when on Aug. 17, 1978, together with Maxie Anderson and Larry Newman, he completed the first crossing of the Atlantic Ocean in a balloon after piloting the *Double Eagle II* 4,800 km (3,000 mi) in six days from a clover field in Presque Isle, Maine, to a barley field in Miserey, France. Abruzzo and Anderson once cleared Pikes Peak, Colorado, by only 6 m (20 ft), and in September 1977 the two made their first transatlantic flight attempt, but the pair were rescued from the sea off the coast of Iceland four days after taking off from Massachusetts. In 1981 Abruzzo again made history as the captain of the *Double Eagle V,* which crossed the Pacific Ocean in a 8,500-km (5,300-mi) flight from Nagashima, Japan, to northern California, where it crash-landed. Abruzzo, Newman, and two others thus became the first people to cross the Pacific in a balloon. Abruzzo was killed when the twin-engine plane he was piloting crashed moments after takeoff; his wife and four others also perished.

Adams, John Michael Geoffrey Manningham, Barbadian politician (b. Sept. 24, 1931, Spooners Hill, Barbados—d. March 11, 1985, Bridgetown, Barbados), as prime minister and minister of finance and planning of Barbados (1976–85), aroused controversy in 1983 when he supported the U.S. intervention in Grenada. The son of Sir Grantley Adams, who was a former premier of Barbados (1954–58) and prime minister of the West Indies Federation (1958–62), "Tom" Adams studied at the University of Oxford and worked for the BBC before being called to the bar. After returning to Barbados in 1962, he combined legal practice with political activity in the Barbados Labour Party, which he led from 1971, restoring the party's fortunes after the electoral disaster of that year and taking it to victory in 1976. His economic austerity measures proved successful, and his party was returned to office in 1981. A moderate politician, as prime minister he concentrated on improving education and social services and on building new roads as well as encouraging the development of industry. He was deeply concerned by the events in Grenada in 1983 and won the assent of the parliamentary opposition for his call to the U.S. and Jamaica to assist and maintain the security of the region and for his subsequent support for the U.S. military intervention.

Aitken, Sir (John William) Max(well), British newspaper executive (b. Feb. 15, 1910, Montreal, Que.—d. April 30, 1985, London, England), as son and successor to the first Lord Beaverbrook, was chairman of Beaverbrook Newspapers (1968–77). He had a long struggle to escape his father's overbearing domination and to exorcise his shadow. Aitken, who contributed to the sport of ocean racing as both patron and participant, launched the prestigious annual British Boat Show and inaugurated the Cowes-Torquay powerboat races. He was a member of the British team that won the Admiral's Cup (1963). Educated at Westminster School and Pembroke College, University of Cambridge, he went into his father's newspaper business but also joined (1935) the Royal Auxiliary Air Force, and as a pilot in World War II he flew 161 sorties during the Battle of Britain (1940). He commanded a night fighter squadron (1941–42) and the Strike Mosquito Wing, Norwegian Waters (1943–45). He was Conservative member of Parliament for Holborn, London (1945–50). When his father died in 1964, Aitken succeeded him and renounced the barony but not the baronetcy. The Beaverbrook press empire was already in decline, and in 1977 it was taken over by Trafalgar House, under which Aitken was president of the renamed group, Express Newspapers, from 1978.

Alexander, Kelly Miller, Sr., U.S. civil rights leader (b. Aug. 18, 1915, Charlotte, N.C.—d. April 2, 1985, Charlotte), was a pioneering organizer of the Charlotte, N.C., chapter of the National Association for the Advancement of Colored People (NAACP) and a fearless force in recruiting members and starting new chapters in the state during the late 1940s; in 1983 he was named national chairman of the board of the NAACP. Alexander, who earned the nickname "Mr. NAACP" for his relentless fieldwork and his championship of the organization to elected officials, was widely admired for his tenacity in the face of adversity. In 1965 his family narrowly escaped injury when his home was bombed. As a result of his recruiting efforts, North Carolina's NAACP chapter boasted some 27,000 members who contributed some $100,000 each year. As board chairman he reorganized the leadership within the NAACP and was a steadying force who expertly and calmly resolved disputes within the organization's hierarchy.

Allen of Fallowfield, Alfred Walter Henry Allen, BARON, British trade unionist (b. July 7, 1914, Bristol, England—d. Jan. 14, 1985, Sale, Cheshire, England), was general secretary (1962–79) of the Union of Shop, Distributive and Allied Workers (USDAW) and, as a member of the general council of the Trades Union Congress (TUC), played a prominent part in union negotiations with Labour and Conservative governments during the 1960s and '70s. Strongly opposed to the Industrial Relations Act, which became law in 1971 under the Conservative government headed by Edward Heath, Allen was TUC chairman (1973–74) during the miners' strike that brought about Heath's downfall in February 1974. Allen, who began work at age 16 as a store clerk, served in the Royal Air Force during World War II and became a USDAW official in 1951. A member (1963–79) of the National Economic Development Council, he was a firm believer in incomes policy as an essential factor in a planned economy. He was a member of the Industrial Arbitration Board from 1973 and of various committees concerned with labour-management relations, and he was also a governor (1976–82) of the BBC. He was made a Commander of the Order of the British Empire in 1967 and a life peer in 1974.

Ashley, Laura, British fashion designer (b. Sept. 7, 1925, Dowlais, Glamorgan, Wales—d. Sept. 17, 1985, Coventry, England), founded the internationally famous soft furnishings and women's clothing empire that by 1985 had an annual turnover of more than £100 million. Using Victorian-type prints on natural fabrics, she produced flowing feminine garments that flattered the middle-aged and the young alike.

The daughter of a civil servant, and brought up as a strict Baptist, Laura Mountney worked as a secretary before her marriage (1949) to Bernard Ashley, a City of London businessman. Her first sales were scarves that had been designed and printed on the kitchen table (1953); thereafter demand rocketed and expansion was so rapid that her husband took over the business side of her venture. Company headquarters were established at Carno, Wales (1963), and eventually there were factories at nearby Newtown and in The Netherlands. The first shop was opened in Kensington, London, in 1967, followed by numerous outlets overseas including shops in Canada and Australia and later in continental Europe and the U.S. In recent years, as a tax exile, Laura Ashley lived in Brussels and at a château in France.

Bacchelli, Riccardo, Italian novelist (b. April 19, 1891, Bologna, Italy—d. Oct. 8, 1985, Monza, Italy), was a prolific and versatile writer whose work, traditionalist in its approach, was underestimated by critics during the latter part of his life. He would be remembered in particular for his historical novels, notably the family cycle *Il mulino del Po* (*The Mill on the Po*), published during 1938–40 and covering the history of a family from the Napoleonic period to the end of World War I. He began to publish poetry and stories during the 1920s, including the satire on fascism *Lo sa il tonno* (1923), and achieved his first success with *Il diavolo al Pontelungo* (1927; *The Devil at the Long Bridge,* 1929), centring on the attempts of the anarchist Mikhail Bakunin to start a revolution in Italy. Bacchelli's style, at first consciously classical, varied considerably during his long career but remained attached to traditional form. He wrote psychological novels (*Una passione coniugale,* 1939), poetry, plays, travel books, and essays on various topics, marked by sardonic humour and fantasy. Another notable novel was *Il figlio di Stalin* (1953; *Son of Stalin,* 1956).

Bailey, Sir Donald Coleman, British civil engineer (b. Sept. 15, 1901, Rotherham, England—d. May 5, 1985, Bournemouth, England), originated the bridge design that bears his name and that played an important role in the Allied advance through Europe toward the end of World War II. Bailey studied at the University

of Sheffield and worked with the London Midland and Scottish Railway and Sheffield City Engineer's Department before joining the War Office as a civilian staff engineer in 1928. At the War Office he designed military equipment, and from 1936 he worked on the concept of a sectional bridge, which later became known as the Bailey Bridge. After tests on a tubular design failed and Bailey's design proved successful, mass production of parts began in a large num-

ber of small workshops, for security purposes. The welded units of the bridge could each be handled by six men and assembled in different ways according to need. Besides making a vital contribution to the Allied war effort, the bridge was also useful in less developed countries after the war. Bailey was knighted in 1946, and two years later he was awarded £12,000 for his invention. From 1962 to 1966 he served as dean of the Royal Military College of Science.

Baker, John Fleetwood Baker, BARON, British engineer (b. March 19, 1901, Wallasey, England—d. Sept. 9, 1985, Cambridge, England), was professor of mechanical sciences and head of the department of engineering at the University of Cambridge from 1943 to 1968 and, as the designer of the Morrison air-raid shelter in 1940, was instrumental in establishing Britain's civil defense program during World War II. The shelter was the product of his work on the design of steel-frame buildings. At Cambridge, after the war, he built up an outstanding department and played a major role in academic engineering. Baker studied at Clare College, Cambridge, before becoming a research assistant at University College, Cardiff, Wales, where his work on airship design led him in 1925 to the Royal Airship Works at Cardington. He returned to Cardiff as a lecturer in civil engineering until 1928 before joining the Steel Structure Research Committee (1931–36), where he did much of his research into the theory of elastic structures. From 1933 he was professor of civil engineering at the University of Bristol and from 1939 undertook civil defense research with the Ministry of Home Security. He was a member (1939–48) of the Civil Defence Research Committee. In 1941 Baker was made an Officer of the Order of the British Empire for his invention of the Morrison shelter, and he was knighted in 1961 and made a life peer in 1977. His books included *The Steel Skeleton* (2 vol., 1954–56) and *Enterprise Versus Bureaucracy* (1978).

Balogh, Thomas Balogh, BARON, Hungarian-born British political economist (b. Nov. 2, 1905, Budapest, Hung.—d. Jan. 20, 1985, London, England), was economic adviser (1964–67) to the Labour governments during the 1960s and to Harold Wilson personally (1968) and served as minister of state for energy (1974–75). He helped to establish the British National Oil Corporation and was its deputy chairman (1976–78). After studying law and economics at the Universities of Budapest, Berlin, and Harvard, he worked in banking and moved to England in 1931. Balogh was lecturer in economics (1934–40) at University College, London, and he was attached (1938–42) to the National Institute of Economic and Social Research. In 1940 he became lecturer at Balliol College, Oxford, and in 1945 he became a fellow. There he helped to establish the university's Institute of Statistics and served as university reader in economics (1960–73). Balogh was involved in overseas financial affairs and was consultant to the Reserve Bank of Australia (1942–64) and to the central banks of Greece (1962), Mauritius (1962–63), Algeria, and The Sudan. He was deputy chief of a UN Relief and Rehabilitation Administration mission to Hungary (1946) and economic adviser to the governments of India (1955, 1960, 1971), Malta (1955–57), and Jamaica (1956, 1961–63), to the Food and Agriculture Organization of the UN (1957–58), and to the Economic Commission for Latin America (1960). He also favoured Wilson's establishment (1964) of a Department of Economic Affairs to take over the planning responsibilities of the Treasury. Balogh was created a life peer in 1968. His books included *Labour and Inflation* (1970) and *The Irrelevance of Conventional Economics* (1982).

Baxter, Anne, U.S. actress (b. May 7, 1923, Michigan City, Ind.—d. Dec. 12, 1985, New York, N.Y.), best remembered for her portrayals of seemingly sweet yet conniving women, won an Academy Award for best supporting actress as the tragic Sophie in *The Razor's Edge* (1946)

and was again nominated for best actress in 1950 for her role as the smiling schemer bent on replacing an aging star (played by Bette Davis) in *All About Eve.* Baxter, the granddaughter of Frank Lloyd Wright, made her Broadway debut at the age of 13 in *Seen but Not Heard* and in 1940 made her motion picture debut in *Twenty Mule Team.* She also gave memorable performances in *The Magnificent Ambersons* (1942), *Guest in the House* (1944), *You're My Everything* (1949), *I Confess* (1953), *The Blue Gardenia* (1953), *The Ten Commandments* (1956), and the epic Western *Cimarron* (1961). In 1960 Baxter stunned Hollywood when she moved to the Australian outback with her husband, cattle rancher Randolph Galt. She later returned (1963) to the limelight and penned a critically acclaimed book, *Intermission: A True Story* (1976), which recounted the isolation and loneliness she experienced and her final disillusionment. Since 1983 she had been most visible on television as the wealthy hotelier Victoria Cabot in the weekly series "Hotel."

Bayer, Herbert, Austrian-born graphic artist, painter, and architect (b. April 5, 1900, Haag, Austria—d. Sept. 30, 1985, Montecito, Calif.), exerted a powerful influence on the visual arts, especially advertising, as one of the masters of the Bauhaus school of art and design. Though Bayer was initially trained as an architect, he entered (1921) the Weimar Bauhaus, where he studied under Wassily Kandinsky and Moholy-Nagy until 1923. He then taught (1925–28) typography and graphic design at the Dessau Bauhaus before moving (1928) to Berlin, where he began an intense involvement with photography and worked variously in advertising, painting, exhibition design, and typography. After fleeing the Nazis in 1938, he settled in the U.S., first in New York City, where he concentrated on advertising. There he designed and coedited the exhibition catalog for the Museum of Modern Art's "Bauhaus 1919–1928" show of 1938 and the museum's "Road to Victory" and "Airways to Peace" World War II exhibitions. In Colorado (1946) he served as chairman of the department of design of the Container Corporation of America and was renowned for his contributions to their "Great Ideas of Western Man" campaign. As design consultant and architect for Aspen Development, he designed the Aspen Institute for Humanistic Studies (1962) and the Museum Tent (1965) used during the annual festival of the arts. Best known for his avant-garde art, including such techniques as photomontage and "photoplastics" (constructed still lifes of bones and geometric solids), Bayer was also an innovator in "earth art." He designed (1955) a grass-walled ring of earth to decorate the grounds of the Aspen Institute. His credits included more than 100 exhibitions of paintings, sculpture, tapestries, and photographs. *Herbert Bayer: The Complete Work* was published in 1984.

Beard, James Andrews, U.S. gastronome and author (b. May 5, 1903, Portland, Ore.—d. Jan. 23, 1985, New York, N.Y.), was a culinary expert who took an epicurian delight in the preparation and digestion of food that was personified in his corpulence (1.9 m tall, 125 kg [6 ft 3 in, 275 lb]) and evidenced in his more than 20 best-selling cookbooks. Beard acquired his appreciation of food from his mother, who owned a hotel and served only the finest cuisine. His first foray, though, was into acting, and he studied drama at the Carnegie Institute of Technology in Pittsburgh, Pa. In 1922 he made his first trip abroad and sampled the fare of restaurants in Paris and in Soho in London. After returning to the U.S. he performed on stage in *Cyrano de Bergerac* and *Othello* and landed a job on radio in San Francisco as an announcer of food commercials. In 1937 his acting prospects dimmed, and Beard moved to New York City, intent on establishing a reputation as a food expert. The following year Beard and his business partner, William Rhode, opened Hors d'Oeuvre, Inc., a catering business, and in 1940 he published his

AP/WIDE WORLD

first book, *Hors d'Oeuvre and Canapes.* Intense rivalry between the two partners led Beard to leave the business, and he published his second book, *Cook It Outdoors* (1941), the first book ever to appear on that subject, before briefly serving (1942–43) in the Army. From 1945 to 1946 he appeared on "Elsie Presents," the first commercial food program to be televised in the U.S., and established a reputation as a connoisseur of fine food. Beard organized his cooking school in 1955, and in 1960 he converted part of his newly acquired Greenwich Village town house into a kitchen classroom. The foremost champion of American cooking, Beard himself possessed an eclectic palate; he savoured such dishes as sauerkraut and sausages, pork, and even hot dogs. The bon vivant of food and drink also published *The Fireside Cookbook* (1949), *The Complete Cookbook for Entertaining* (1954), *How to Eat Better for Less Money* (1954), *The James Beard Cookbook* (1959), and *Beard on Bread* (1973).

Beeching, Richard Beeching, BARON, British business executive (b. April 21, 1913, Sheerness, Kent, England—d. March 23, 1985, East Grinstead, Sussex, England), was chairman of British Railways in 1963 and responsible for the "Beeching Report" of that year advocating massive cuts in the rail network. The controversy around his proposals and subsequent government action became a focus for the debate on the role of the nationalized industries. Beeching, who studied physics and obtained his Ph.D. at the Imperial College of Science and Technology, University of London, worked at the Ministry of Supply during World War II. He joined Imperial Chemical Industries (ICI) in 1948 and was vice-president of ICI (Canada) Ltd. in 1953. In 1961 he was called in by Conservative Minister of Transport Ernest Marples to reorganize the British railway system. His report, *The Reshaping of British Railways,* was designed to "make the railways pay" by eliminating 8,000 km (5,000 mi) of track (nearly one-third of the total network), nearly half the existing stations, and 70,000 jobs. Two years later another report called for rail traffic to be concentrated on only 4,800 km (3,000 mi) of track. Both reports aroused considerable hostility from the public and the trade unions, and the arrival of a Labour government in 1964 meant that Beeching faced a party that interpreted the term economic in a wider sense than that of mere profit and loss and was ideologically committed to supporting the nationalized industries. Despite this conflict major cuts were made, and British Railways saw a decline in its losses and in its staff. In 1965 Beeching left British Railways to become a life peer and deputy chairman of ICI.

Beldon, Eileen, British actress (b. Sept. 12, 1901, Bradford, England—d. Aug. 3, 1985, England), was a skilled exponent of Shakespearean and Shavian roles and spent her formative years under the tutelage of Barry Jackson at the Birmingham Repertory Company. She played in many

of the modern-dress Shakespearean productions of the 1920s but first attracted attention as Imogen in *Cymbeline* in 1923. She also appeared in Shaw's *Back to Methuselah* and *Heartbreak House.* Beldon was with Jackson at London's Royal Court Theatre as Petronel in Eden Phillpotts's *The Farmer's Wife* (1924–27) and as Katharina in *The Taming of the Shrew* (1928). At Jackson's Malvern festivals she portrayed Lysistrata in Shaw's *The Apple Cart* (1930), Elizabeth's maid in Rudolph Besier's *The Barretts of Wimpole Street* (1932), Lady Would-be in Jonson's *Volpone* (1935), Begonia in Shaw's *Geneva* (1938), and Nell Gwyn in Shaw's *In Good King Charles's Golden Days* (1937; and in London in 1940). She played Sally Pratt in J. B. Priestley's *I Have Been Here Before* (London, 1937; New York, 1938). Beldon was Paulina in *A Winter's Tale* and Juno in Sean O'Casey's *Juno and the Paycock* at Birmingham (1944–45), later returning there as a guest star (1961–64). One of her last theatrical appearances was in *King John* at Stratford in 1970.

Blake, Eugene Carson, U.S. religious leader (b. Nov. 7, 1906, St. Louis, Mo.—d. July 31, 1985, Stamford, Conn.), was a dominant figure in U.S. Protestantism during the 1950s and 1960s and a towering leader in the ecumenical movement. Blake, who graduated from Princeton Theological Seminary in 1932, served as pastor of Presbyterian churches in New York City, Albany, N.Y., and Pasadena, Calif., where he gained a reputation as a dynamic administrator and a staunch defender of civil and human rights. In 1951 Blake was elected stated clerk, or chief executive officer, of the Presbyterian General Assembly, the United Presbyterian Church's highest position; he served in that post until 1966. He effectively used his position of leadership to champion such causes as civil rights and to speak out against McCarthyism, the Vietnam war, and the anti-Catholic sentiments prevalent when John F. Kennedy served as U.S. president. In his fight for the unification of Protestant denominations, he proposed (1960) that his own denomination merge with the Methodist and Episcopal churches and the United Church of Christ. In 1983 Blake's national denomination combined with a predominately southern body to form Presbyterian Church (U.S.A.), which boasted some 3.1 million members. Blake also served as president of the National Council of Churches (1954–57) and as general secretary of the World Council of Churches (1966–72). After his 1972 retirement he continued to preach and lecture and remained active in such organizations as Bread for the World.

Boland, Frederick Henry, Irish diplomat (b. Jan. 11, 1904, Dublin, Ireland—d. Dec. 4, 1985, Dublin), was ambassador to Britain (1950–56), his country's permanent representative at the UN (1956–63), and president of the UN General Assembly (1960). He studied classics and law at Trinity College, Dublin, and at the King's Inns there before taking up a Rockefeller research fellowship in social sciences at Harvard University and the University of Chicago (1926–28). In 1929 he returned to the Irish Free State and joined its still nascent foreign service as third secretary in the Department of External Affairs. He became first secretary at the Irish embassy in Paris (1932) and principal officer in the Department of Industry and Commerce (1936) before returning to the Department of External Affairs as assistant secretary (1938). During World War II he mitigated the anglophobia of Permanent Secretary Joseph Walshe, whom he succeeded in 1946. Boland helped build departmental morale by promoting juniors rather than bringing in outsiders. In London he faced the difficulties of Ireland's having recently (1949) left the Commonwealth; nevertheless, he succeeded in arranging a cordial meeting between Eamon de Valera and Sir Winston Churchill. At the UN he improved his country's standing, and as president he showed great ability in controlling the turbulent scenes created by visiting Soviet leader Nikita Khrushchev.

Böll, Heinrich Theodor, West German novelist (b. Dec. 21, 1917, Cologne, Germany—d. July 16, 1985, Hürtgenwald-Grosshau, West Germany), was one of the two leading literary figures in West Germany (the other being Günther Grass) and was internationally respected for his Catholic humanism and his democratic and conscientious stands on public issues. When Böll was awarded the 1972 Nobel Prize for Literature, he was recognized as the conscience of a country preoccupied with the consumerist and capitalist post-World War II boom. Though less experimental than Grass, Böll combined plain realism with humour, and his poetry lifted his best work outside mere literature of political commitment. After military service in World War II he returned to Cologne, where he attended the university and produced his first book, *Der Zug war pünktlich* (1949; *The Train Was on Time,* 1956). In 1950 Böll joined the Gruppe 47 writers, who strove to restore German literature to its pre-Nazi traditions. From then until his death he produced novels, short stories, radio plays, journalism, and translations that reflected the changes taking place in his country and the dilemmas of coming to terms with its immediate past. In his best works he managed to sum up in a symbolic image or a metaphor the irony and tragedy of his generation. In such novels as *Ansichten eines Clowns* (1963; *The Clown,* 1965) and *Ende einer Dienstfahrt* (1966; *End of a Mission,* 1968), he explored the Christian conscience and individual and national history, always directly or indirectly haunted by the shadow of Nazism and the collective amnesia that he portrayed in *Billard um halb zehn* (1959; *Billiards at Half-Past Nine,* 1961). The late 1960s brought a more general disillusionment to the country, and the student unrest, followed by the urban terrorism of the early 1970s, confronted Böll with further personal dilemmas. He found himself under attack from the right-wing press and political parties, as well as from the Soviet Union—he had consistently expressed his support for dissident writers in Eastern Europe. Appealing for a fair hearing for members of the Baader-Meinhof Gang, he was accused in the popular press of instigating terrorism. In 1974 he published one of his most passionate indictments of German capitalism, *Die verlorene Ehre der Katherina Blum* (*The Lost Honour of Katharina Blum,* 1975). This story of an ordinary woman hounded to death by the press was written in documentary style and would probably be remembered as his outstanding achievement; it was filmed in 1977. More ambitious was *Gruppenbild mit Dame* (1971; *Group Portrait with Lady,* 1973). He later became a father figure to the ecological party, the Green Party, and campaigned as a pacifist and nuclear disarmer.

Boulting, John Edward, British film producer and director (b. Nov. 21, 1913, Bray, Berkshire, England—d. June 17, 1985, Warfield Dale, Berkshire), codirected with his twin brother, Roy, such satirical comedies as *Private's Progress* (1956) and *I'm All Right, Jack* (1959). He entered the film industry as an office boy in the 1930s before serving with the International Brigade in the Spanish Civil War. In 1937 Boulting and his brother founded Charter Film Productions Ltd. and served as managing directors for the company. They directed and produced short features before *Pastor Hall* (1940) and *Thunder Rock* (1942) secured their reputation. After World War II they scored a number of successes including *Brighton Rock* (1947), *The Guinea Pig* (1948), and *The Magic Box,* which was the official film of the Festival of Britain in 1951. The Boulting brothers' comedies of the 1950s introduced a new flavour to British cinema by satirizing such social institutions as the Army (*Private's Progress,* 1956), industry (*I'm All Right, Jack,* 1959), and the church (*Heavens Above!,* 1963). Their comedies were also particularly entertaining because they served as vehicles for such stars as Ian Carmichael and Peter Sellers. The brothers' later films included *The Family Way* (1966) and *There's a Girl in My Soup* (1970). John Boulting served as a member of the board (1958–72) and managing director (1966–72) of British Lion Films.

Boyle, William Anthony ("Tony"), U.S. union leader (b. Dec. 1, 1904, Bald Butte, Mont.—d. May 31, 1985, Wilkes-Barre, Pa.), as the notorious president (1963–72) of the United Mine Workers (UMW), committed fraud and embezzlement and served three consecutive life sentences for masterminding the shooting deaths in 1969 of his rival Joseph A. ("Jock") Yablonski and his wife and daughter. Boyle, the handpicked successor of labour giant John L. Lewis, was a coal miner before entering into the union hierarchy as assistant to Lewis. After Lewis retired in 1960, Thomas Kennedy, then ill, assumed the union presidency, though Boyle, as vice-president, wielded most of the actual power. When Kennedy died three years later, Boyle claimed the presidency and ruled the UMW with an iron fist. When Yablonski challenged Boyle for the union leadership in 1969, Boyle won the election by a 2–1 margin; however, Yablonski told federal officials that Boyle had won by fraud, and he threatened to seek a new vote. Three weeks later Yablonski and his family were murdered in their Clarksville, Pa., home. In 1972 Boyle lost the UMW presidency to Arnold R. Miller and was charged with and convicted of embezzling union funds for political use. The following year Boyle was indicted for the Yablonski murders, and in 1974 he received three consecutive life sentences, which he began serving after his prison term for embezzlement ended in 1976. Granted a retrial in 1977, he was again found guilty, given the same sentence, and returned to prison in 1978.

Brambell, Wilfrid, British actor (b. March 22, 1912, Dublin, Ireland—d. Jan. 18, 1985, London, England), was best known for his role in "Steptoe and Son," a BBC television comedy series that attracted a huge following during the 1960s and '70s. The series, about a father and son in the rag-and-bone trade, featured Brambell as the curmudgeonly, possessive father and Harry H. Corbett (d. 1982) as his son. After a three-year run from 1962, the series was revived in 1970 for another four years; NBC's "Sanford and Son" (1972) was based on it. During World War II Brambell, a journalist before taking to the stage, toured with ENSA (Entertainments National Service Association; an organization that provided entertainment for troops on active service). After the war he played in repertory in the provinces, making his London debut in 1950. He also appeared in films, notably the Beatles' *A Hard Day's Night,* in which he portrayed Paul McCartney's grandfather, and in two adaptations of the "Steptoe" series.

Braudel, Fernand, French historian (b. Aug. 24, 1902, Luméville-en-Ornois, Meuse, France—d. Nov. 28, 1985, Savoie, France), was one of the most prominent exponents of the method of historical study developed in the French journal *Annales d'Histoire Économique et Sociale,* which focused on all social and cultural events and not solely on political events. This was best illustrated in his work on the Mediterranean world, *La Méditerranée et le monde méditerranéen à l'époque de Philippe II* (1949), an attempt to encompass all aspects of the history of the region in the 16th century. He also published a sweeping study of economic and social history in Europe from the 15th to the 18th century, describing the development of capitalism and the sources of the Industrial Revolution. Braudel studied at the Sorbonne and taught in Algiers before becoming a teacher at the Lycée Condorcet in Paris in 1932. He also taught for a time in Brazil. In 1937 he became director of the École Pratique des Hautes Études and, during World War II as a prisoner of war, wrote from memory the text of his doctoral thesis on the Mediterranean world at the time of Philip II. Meanwhile, his thinking had been influenced by the founders of the *Annales* school, Marc Bloch and Lucien Febvre. The original French

edition achieved success in the wake of a much-praised English translation. The second edition appeared in 1967, when he also published *Les Structures du quotidien,* the first part of his work on European capitalism, which once again achieved critical success in England as well as in France. An admirer of Marx as a predecessor in the construction of historical models, Braudel was not a doctrinaire historian and remained conscious, above all, of the diversity of factors influencing historical events. Braudel was elected to the French Academy in 1984.

Brooks, Louise, U.S. actress (b. Nov. 14, 1906, Cherryvale, Kan.—d. Aug. 8, 1985, Rochester, N.Y.), was a strikingly beautiful star of the silent screen who evoked a sensual eroticism with her smoldering countenance and helmet of bobbed brunet hair, which became her trademark. Brooks made her motion picture debut in *The American Venus* (1926) and became the embodiment of the disdainful flapper in such films as *Love 'Em and Leave 'Em* (1926), *A Girl in Every Port* (1928), and *Beggars of Life* (1928). She reached the pinnacle of her career, however, in German director G. W. Pabst's silent-film classics *Pandora's Box* (1929) and *Diary of a Lost Girl* (1929), starring as Lulu

in the former. When she returned to the U.S., she won only minor film roles because of her disagreements with Hollywood executives. She appeared in *It Pays to Advertise* (1931), *God's Gift to Women* (1931), and *The Public Enemy* (1931) before her career declined. Her last film was a Western, *Overland Stage Riders* (1938). In 1983 she published her memoirs, *Lulu in Hollywood.*

Brown, Carter (ALAN GEOFFREY YATES), British-born thriller writer (b. Aug. 1, 1923, London, England—d. May 5, 1985, Sydney, Australia), wrote over 270 books in different genres, some under other pseudonyms. Soon after immigrating to Australia in 1948, Brown launched his writing career. He achieved his greatest successes with thrillers featuring hard-boiled private eyes and cops. The adventures, including *Nemesis Wore Nylons* (1954), *Baby, You're Guilt-Edged* (1956), *Sinner, You Slay Me* (1957), *Lament for a Lousy Lover* (1960), and *Blonde on a Broomstick* (1966), followed a similar formula, mixing sex and violence in predictable quantities. Brown also penned science fiction and Westerns. His thrillers were translated into several languages, and his books sold 55 million copies.

Bryant, Sir Arthur Wynne Morgan, British historian (b. Feb. 18, 1899, Dersingham, Norfolk, England—d. Jan. 22, 1985, Salisbury, England), as a well-known author of over 30 books of English history and biography, aroused popular interest in history. Bryant wrote with perception and literary flare and was meticulous in his documentary research. Educated at Harrow School and, after service in France during World War I, at Queen's College, University of Oxford,

he became lecturer in history to the University Delegacy for Extra-Mural Studies (1925–36) at Oxford. He was educational adviser (from 1929) to Bonar Law College, Ashridge, Buckinghamshire, and later its chairman (1946–49). He was Watson professor of American history at the University of London (1935), and from 1936 until his death he contributed the feature "Our Note Book" for the *Illustrated London News.* His second book, *King Charles II* (1931), won him widespread acclaim, and the succeeding trilogy on Samuel Pepys—*The Man in the Making* (1933), *The Years of Peril* (1935), and *The Saviour of the Navy* (1938)—established his reputation even among academics. An enthusiastic patriot, during World War II he chronicled his country's struggles in the Napoleonic Wars with *The Years of Endurance* (1942) and *Years of Victory* (1944). He dealt with contemporary history in *Dunkirk* (1943), *The Turn of the Tide* (1957), and *Triumph in the West* (1959). Other works included *English Saga* (1940), *The Age of Elegance* (1950), and biographies of Nelson (1970) and Wellington (1971). He was knighted in 1954.

Brynner, Yul, U.S. actor (b. July 11, 1920?, Sakhalin Island, U.S.S.R.—d. Oct. 10, 1985, New York, N.Y.), became a romantic sex symbol with his magnificent performances as the virile, baldheaded, pompous yet lovable potentate in *The King and I,* the hugely successful Broadway musical that was made into a motion picture in 1956. Brynner, who prided himself on his exotic origins (his father was Swiss-Mongolian, his mother a Gypsy), delighted in obscuring the year of his birth, variously proclaiming it to be in 1915, 1917, 1920, and 1922. He spent his childhood in Beijing (Peking) and Paris before becoming a trapeze artist with the circus, but a serious accident in which he sustained 47 fractures ended his career as an acrobat. In 1934 Brynner joined a French acting troupe, and he arrived in the U.S. in 1941. He made his Broadway debut in *Lute Song* (1946), but it was as the king of Siam on Broadway (1951–54) that he became a star. Brynner garnered a Tony award for his performance and earned an Academy Award for best actor for his 1956 motion picture portrayal. He also had major film roles in *The Ten Commandments* (1956), *Anastasia* (1956), and *The Magnificent Seven* (1960), but he would forever be identified with his role as the king, which he performed 4,625 times, the last on June 30, 1985.

Bull, Hedley Norman, Australian specialist in international relations (b. June 10, 1932, Sydney, Australia—d. May 18, 1985, Oxford, England), was professor of international relations at the University of Oxford from 1977 and the author of *The Control of the Arms Race* (1961), a major analysis of nuclear arms control. He studied at the University of Sydney, then at Oxford, before joining the London School of Economics and Political Science, where he was reader from 1963. *The Control of the Arms Race* was published after Bull attended the 1960 conference of the International Institute for Strategic Studies; the volume established his reputation as a leading authority in the field. He was made director of the Arms Control and Disarmament Research Unit at the British Foreign Office in 1964 and engaged in a controversial attack on the behaviourist school of international relations. From 1967 to 1977 he served as professor at the Australian National University, and he also was research director (1968–73) at the Australian Institute for International Affairs. Following a year in India (1974–75) he turned to the study of third world affairs, which preoccupied him for the remainder of his career. He also wrote *The Anarchical Society* (1977) and (with Adam Watson) *The Expansion of International Society* (1984).

Bunting, Basil, British poet (b. March 1, 1900, Scotswood, Northumberland, England—d. April 17, 1985, Hexham, Northumberland), was a disciple of the American poet Ezra Pound and

gained little critical regard until the 1960s, when he published his best-known work, the long autobiographical poem *Briggflatts* (1965). He was educated at a Quaker school and at the London School of Economics and Political Science, and during World War I he was imprisoned as a conscientious objector. He spent some time in Paris in the early 1920s, acting as assistant editor for Ford Madox Ford's *Transatlantic Review,* and was the music critic for *The Outlook* in London. He then lived in Italy until 1933 and later in the U.S. After World War II he acted as foreign correspondent in Persia for *The Times* of London and, returning to his much-loved native countryside, became a subeditor for the *Newcastle Evening Chronicle.* He wrote poetry throughout his life but before 1965 published only *Redimiculum Matellarum* (Milan, 1930) and *Poems* (Texas, 1950). In 1965, besides *Briggflatts,* he published (all in London) *Loquitur* and *The First Book of Odes,* followed by *Collected Poems* (London, 1966), *What the Chairman Told Tom* (U.S., 1967), and *Descant on Rawthey's Madrigal* (U.S., 1968). Bunting's work showed his profound knowledge of musical form and influences of Greek, Roman, and Persian poetry. He was president of the Poetry Society (1972–76) and of Northern Arts (1973–76).

Burnet, Sir (Frank) Macfarlane, Australian virologist (b. Sept. 3, 1899, Traralgon, Victoria, Australia—d. Aug. 31, 1985, Melbourne, Australia), made important contributions to knowledge about viruses and was joint winner (with Peter Medawar) of the 1960 Nobel Prize for Physiology or Medicine for the discovery of acquired immunological tolerance to tissue transplants. Developing Ernest Goodpasture's discovery that viruses could be grown in developing embryos, he cultured many viruses, notably increasing knowledge of those causing influenza and showing that several different types produce poliomyelitis. He brought nearer the conquest of diseases such as Q-fever. He also developed a method for identifying bacteria by the bacteriophages that attack them. Educated at Geelong College and the University of Melbourne, Burnet was Beit fellow for medical research at the Lister Institute in London (1926–27) and worked at the National Institute for Medical Research at Hampstead (1932–34). From 1928 he was assistant director and from 1944 director of the Walter and Eliza Hall Institute for Medical Research in Melbourne, drawing to it students from all over the world. He was professor of experimental medicine at the University of Melbourne (1946–65). His books included *Biological Aspects of Infectious Disease* (1940; 4th ed., 1972), *Viruses and Man* (1953), *The Clonal Selection Theory of Acquired Immunity* (1959), and *Immunity, Aging and Cancer* (1976). His autobiography, *Changing Patterns,* appeared in 1968. Burnet was elected a fellow of the Royal Society in 1942, knighted in 1951, and awarded the Order of Merit in 1958.

Burnham, Linden Forbes Sampson, Guyanese politician (b. Feb. 20, 1923, Kitty, East Demarara, British Guiana—d. Aug. 6, 1985, Georgetown, Guyana), while serving as prime minister (following independence in 1966) and then president (from 1980) of Guyana, gained a reputation for ruthlessness; his Socialist Cooperative government was charged frequently with election abuses and suppression of democratic freedoms. Burnham was educated in England as a lawyer, and in 1948 he returned to then British Guiana to help form (1949) the People's Progressive Party, led by Cheddi Jagan, an ethnic Indian. The two men split in 1957, and Burnham founded the People's National Congress (PNC), the party that brought him to power as prime minister in 1964 when the party defeated the Marxist government of Jagan. As prime minister and president, Burnham retained a modicum of support for his repressive policies by tempering them with small social gains. But the 800,000 civilians under his rule had recently experienced a drastic fall in living standards when prices of Guyana's basic commodities—sugar, rice, and bauxite—fell sharply in international markets and a financial crisis made it difficult to import necessary supplies of basic foodstuffs. A heavy smoker, drinker, and a diabetic, Burnham died after having minor throat surgery.

Burroughes, Hugh, British aviation engineer (b. Dec. 22, 1883, Cley-next-the-Sea, Norfolk, England—d. Oct. 3, 1985, High Wycombe, England), founded the Gloster Aircraft Co. with A. W. Martyn in 1917 and remained a powerful figure in British aviation until his retirement from the board of Hawker Siddeley Aviation in 1966. He trained at Manchester School of Technology and became a technical assistant at the Army Balloon Factory, Farnborough, in 1909 before his appointment as general manager of Airco, Hendon, in 1914 to build Farman aircraft under license. He supervised production of de Havilland-Airco aircraft during World War I until he formed his own company. By 1923 Burroughes was producing the Gloster Grebe for the Royal Air Force (RAF), followed by the Gamecock, the Gauntlet, and the Gladiator. In 1935 Gloster was merged into the Hawker Siddeley group, of which Burroughes became deputy managing director. During World War II Gloster built many leading RAF planes including the Gloster Whittle, the first British jet aircraft. His company was later responsible for the production of Meteor and Javelin planes until 1961. Although Burroughes was instrumental in the development of the British aircraft industry from the earliest days to the postwar period, he received little general recognition.

Burrows, Abe (ABRAM SOLMAN BOROWITZ), U.S. writer and director (b. Dec. 18, 1910, New York, N.Y.—d. May 17, 1985, New York), as the coauthor of such Broadway smash hits as *Guys and Dolls* (1950), *Can-Can* (1953), and *How to Succeed in Business Without Really Trying* (1961), for which he won a Pulitzer Prize, was one of the pioneers of musical comedy. Burrows worked variously as a runner on Wall Street, an accountant, and a maple syrup salesman before finding his niche writing comedy material for such radio shows as the "Texaco Star Theater" and "Duffy's Tavern." From 1947 to 1948 he was the host of his own radio show, "The Abe Burrows Show," on which he delighted listeners with his lampoons of Tin Pan Alley music. Some of his most famous compositions included "The Girl with the Three Blue Eyes," "I Looked Under a Rock and I Found You," and "Green Christmas." After appearing on "Breakfast with Burrows" he turned to Broadway and began a fruitful association with composer-lyricist Frank Loesser and librettist Jo Swerling. Some of Burrows's other Broadway credits included *Silk Stockings* (1955), *Say, Darling* (1958), and *Cactus Flower* (1965). In 1980 the witty raconteur published his memoirs, *Honest, Abe: Is There Really No Business like Show Business?*

Caldwell, Taylor (JANET MIRIAM TAYLOR HOLLAND CALDWELL), U.S. writer (b. Sept. 7, 1900, Manchester, England—d. Aug. 30, 1985, Greenwich, Conn.), was the indomitable and prolific author of 33 best-selling novels, including *Dynasty of Death* (1938), *Testimony of Two Men* (1968), *Great Lion of God* (1970), *Captains and the Kings* (1972), and *Answer as a Man* (1981). Caldwell, who had been totally deaf since 1967 and had suffered a paralyzing stroke that left her speechless in 1980, nonetheless continued to pen her sombre novels, which showcased her flair for melodrama. Her characters usually climbed from rags to riches but experienced little personal happiness. Caldwell also turned out books on such historical figures as Richelieu and Genghis Khan, and three of her books, including *Dear and Glorious Physician* (1959), were among the best-selling religious novels of all time. Two of her novels, *Captains and the Kings* and *Testimony of Two Men,* were later made into successful television miniseries, and though her books were not critically acclaimed, they were so popular among readers that they were translated into 11 languages.

Calvino, Italo, Italian novelist (b. Oct. 15, 1923, Santiago de las Vegas, Cuba—d. Sept. 19, 1985, Siena, Italy), was a prominent figure in post-World War II Italian fiction with tales that combined fantasy, humour, and irony. Perhaps his greatest achievement was to have crossed the divide between experimental literature and the traditional novel. Forced to join the Young Fascists during World War II, he went over to the Resistance in 1943 and became a member of the Communist Party, in which he remained until 1957. After studying at Turin University, he worked for the publisher Einaudi, having in 1947 published his first novel, *Il sentiero dei nidi di ragno (The Path to the Nest of Spiders,* 1957). The growing element of fantasy in his work was evident by the time of his trilogy, *I nostri antenati* (1960; "Our Ancestors"), and in his *Fiabe italiane* (1956, rev. ed., 1971; *Italian Folktales,* 1980). He continued to demonstrate his inventiveness in such works as *Il castello dei destini incrociati* (1973; *The Castle of Crossed Destinies,* 1977), *Le città invisibili* (1972; *Invisible Cities,* 1974), and *Se una notte d'inverno un viaggiatore* (1979; *If on a Winter's Night a Traveller,* 1981), the last parodying various fictional styles. Calvino's interest in science and his ability to incorporate contemporary scientific philosophical and linguistic concerns into his work, illustrated in *Le cosmicomiche* (1965; *Cosmicomics,* 1968), led him to be compared to the French 18th-century writer Voltaire. He was awarded the Premio Riccioni and the Premio Feltrinelli per la Narrativa.

Cameron, (Mark) James Walter, British journalist (b. June 17, 1911, London, England—d. Jan. 26, 1985, London), was considered by many to be one of the most distinguished and controversial correspondents of his day. His work was a combination of brilliant and intuitive writing with an outstanding integrity and a preoccupation with the human condition. In the words of Lord Beaverbrook, Cameron wrote "the grim hard truth from the heart." Cameron, the grandson of a Scottish Highland minister and son of a writer of serial stories, was educated at various small schools, mostly in France. He began work as an office boy in Salford and as a reporter in Dundee and Glasgow. During World War II he was a subeditor for the London *Daily Express* but became a foreign correspondent when the war was over. One of his earliest assignments (and for him probably the most seminal) was coverage of the Bikini atom bomb explosion (1946); as a result he became a founding member of the Campaign for Nuclear Disarmament. Cameron resigned (1950) from the *Daily Express* in protest against a sensation-mongering attack by Beaverbrook newspapers on a government minister, John Strachey. Cameron joined the celebrated weekly *Picture Post* but again became involved in a conflict of principles when the proprietor Edward Hulton refused publication of Cameron's exposé on the treatment of prisoners in South Korea's Syngman Rhee regime. He then moved to the *News Chronicle,* but after its collapse in 1960 he worked as a free-lancer. From 1973 until three months before his death he contributed a weekly column to *The Guardian.* His curiosity and compassion took him to many of the world's trouble spots; in 1965 Cameron became the first Western correspondent to tour North Vietnam after the saturation bombing by U.S. forces began there. It was while traveling to war-torn East Pakistan (1971) that he was so severely injured in an automobile accident that his heart required a pacemaker; the experience gave rise to his play *The Pump* (1973; television production, 1980), which won the 1973 Prix Italia. He began to use his journalistic skills for television; his work included BBC2's "Cameron Country" (1967–68) and "James Cameron: Once Upon a Lifetime" (1984), a showcase of the most memorable events he had covered. His books included *Witness* (1966; U.S. title, *Here Is Your Enemy*), *Point of Departure* (autobiography, 1967), *An Indian Summer* (1974), and *The Best of Cameron* (1981).

Cameron of Balhousie, Neil Cameron, BARON, British air force officer (b. July 8, 1920, Perth, Scotland—d. Jan. 29, 1985, London, England), rose from the ranks to become marshal of the Royal Air Force (RAF), chief of air staff (1976–77), and chief of defense staff (1977–79). Cameron enlisted in the RAF volunteer reserve in 1939 at age 18 and flew fighter and fighter-bomber aircraft throughout World War II. Commissioned in 1941, he was twice decorated and after the war accepted a permanent commission. After passing through the RAF Staff College in 1949, he served on its directing staff (1952–55). He then successively served as principal staff officer to the deputy supreme commander, Supreme Headquarters, Allied Powers, Europe, in Paris (1964); chairman of the Programme Evaluation Group at the Ministry of Defence (1965–66); and deputy commander, RAF Germany (1972–73). As chief of defense staff Cameron frequently sounded warnings against Soviet military preparedness, and after retiring in 1979 he continued to interest himself in defense matters through the activities of the British Atlantic Committee. In 1980 he became principal of King's College, University of London, and in 1983 was created a life peer.

Caton-Thompson, Gertrude, British archaeologist (b. Feb. 1, 1889, London, England—d. April 18, 1985, Broadway, Worcestershire, England), contributed substantially to the knowledge of East African prehistory through her excavations in Rhodesia (now Zimbabwe) and at Saharan oasis sites; she also worked in the South Arabian Hadhramaut. She was privately educated and during World War I worked in the Ministry of Shipping (1915–19). Caton-Thompson was a student at the British School of Archaeology in Egypt (1921–26) and, under the tutelage of Sir Flinders Petrie, undertook excavations at Abydos and Oxyrhynchus (1921–22) and in Malta (1921 and 1924). Her first excavation alone was of an Egyptian predynastic village; she published her findings in *The Badarian Civilisation* (1928; with Guy Brunton). Caton-Thompson's excavations in the Fayyum Desert produced evidence of two hitherto unknown Neolithic cultures—later linked with finds at Khartoum (*The Desert Fayum,* 1935). In Rhodesia (1929) she proved that the monuments there were the product of an indigenous Bantu civilization of around 700–900 AD (*The Zimbabwe Culture,* 1931). Her work (1930–32) at Saharan oasis sites produced *Kharga Oasis in Prehistory* (1952). In 1937–38 she excavated the Moon Temple and various shrines and tombs at al-Huraydhah, dated to the 5th–4th century BC (*The Tombs and Moon Temple of Hureidha* [*Hadhramaut*], 1944). Caton-Thompson, who helped found the British Institute of the History and Archaeology of East Africa, received the Huxley Medal (1946)

and Burton Medal (1954) of the Royal Asiatic Society. Her autobiography, *Mixed Memoirs,* appeared in 1983.

Chagall, Marc, Russian-born painter (b. July 7, 1887, Vitebsk, Russia—d. March 28, 1985, Saint-Paul-de-Vence, Alpes-Maritimes, France), was one of the most original and most outstanding figures in 20th-century art. His work, nourished by Jewish tradition and by childhood memories of Russian village life, had a unique quality of naive poetry. His father worked for a fishmonger in a suburb of Vitebsk, where Chagall took his first lessons in painting before going to the Imperial School of Fine Arts in St. Petersburg (now Leningrad) in 1907. Three years later he went to Paris, where he found a brilliant artistic community at a moment of revolutionary experimentation. Though influenced by Cubism, Fauvism, and Surrealism, Chagall adapted their discoveries to suit his own imaginative vision, which was characterized by a range of colours and subject matter drawn from Jewish folklore, Hasidic mysticism, and peasant life. He returned to Russia in 1914. In 1915 he married, and his love for his wife, Bella, provided the inspiration for many paintings. After the revolution he became a district commissar for fine art, working contemporaneously with Kazimir Malevich and El Lissitzky. But his individual style was not, in the long run, compatible with their styles or with that advocated by the state; in Moscow his murals and other paintings are still not publicly exhibited. In 1922 Chagall left for Berlin, after which he went to Paris, where he created some notable illustrations for editions of Gogol's *Dead Souls* and La Fontaine's *Fables.* He published his au-

KARSH OF OTTAWA—CAMERA PRESS, LONDON

tobiography in 1929. The deteriorating situation in Europe brought a new theme, that of the Crucifixion, into his work, with Christ's suffering as a symbol of Jewish martyrdom. With the outbreak of World War II he went to Provence and then to the U.S., where his work reflecting the horror of the war years was relieved by commissions for theatre design. After returning to France in 1948, Chagall found an opportunity to work in stained glass, on windows in Metz and Reims and in 1962 on 12 windows for the Hadassah Medical Centre of Hebrew University in Jerusalem. Two years later he was commissioned to paint the ceiling of the Paris Opéra, and he also worked in ceramics, mosaic, and tapestry. Major retrospectives of Chagall's work were held from 1946 in New York, Paris, Amsterdam, Basel, and London; the last during his lifetime opened in London in 1985. He continued to paint until the end of his life, and his last works exhibited the same vitality and highly personal imaginative vision evident in his earlier paintings.

Charlotte of Luxembourg, GRAND DUCHESS (b. Jan. 23, 1896, Berg Castle, Luxembourg—d. July 9, 1985, Fischbach Castle, Luxembourg), succeeded her sister Grand Duchess Marie-Adelaide on Jan. 15, 1919, and reigned over the duchy until she abdicated in favour of her son Prince (now Grand Duke) Jean on Nov. 12, 1964. Her sister had abdicated under popular pressure, and Charlotte was chosen to succeed by an 80% majority in a national referendum. The next 20 years were spent bringing up her family and ensuring Luxembourg's identity as a sovereign state. In 1940 the country was invaded by Germany, despite its neutrality, and Charlotte went into exile, first in Portugal, the U.S., and Canada and from 1943 in Britain, from where she made daily morale-boosting broadcasts to her people. On her return in 1945 to an enthusiastic welcome, she set about rebuilding the country, acting as guarantor of its democratic system and its independence and, among other achievements, securing its founder-membership in the European Communities. By the time of her abdication, after a reign of 45 years, she was recognized as a key figure in the country's history, and she continued to play a role in its political life, though her official appearances became increasingly rare.

Chase, James Hadley (RENÉ BRABAZON RAYMOND), British thriller writer (b. Dec. 24, 1906, Ealing, London, England—d. Feb. 6, 1985, Corseaux-sur-Vevey, Vaud, Switz.), established his reputation in 1939 with the publication of his first novel, *No Orchids for Miss Blandish,* and went on to write some 80 thrillers under various pseudonyms. Chase's experience working for a bookseller demonstrated to him that there was a public demand for tough, American-style thrillers. *No Orchids for Miss Blandish* found that market and was an immediate success, though the sadistic violence and the American slang in this story of the kidnapping of a millionaire's daughter were all secondhand. Chase, a retiring man who enjoyed classical music, visited the U.S. for the first time in 1965. His critical reputation was greater in France than in England. The publisher Gallimard created the series "Carré Noir" for his books, admired for their unconscious probing of sadistic themes and for the creation of a mythical underworld that, in translation, was better able to withstand comparison with the works of Raymond Chandler and James Cain. Chase lived in France, then in Switzerland, perfecting the formula established in his first novel. Several films were made from his works, including two versions of *No Orchids* and Joseph Losey's *Eva* (1965).

Chernenko, Konstantin Ustinovich, Soviet chief of state (b. Sept. 24, 1911, Bolshaya Tes, Krasnoyarsk region, Siberia—d. March 10, 1985, Moscow, U.S.S.R.), served as general secretary of the Communist Party of the Soviet Union (CPSU) from Feb. 13, 1984, and as chairman of the Presidium of the Supreme Soviet from April 11, 1984, until his death. The son of peasants, Chernenko worked as a farm labourer as a youth. A member of the Komsomol (Young Communist League) from 1926, he joined the CPSU in 1931 and became a party official in Krasnoyarsk region in 1933, advancing to regional secretary in 1941. After a period as party secretary in Penza region, in 1948 he became head of the propaganda department in Moldavia, where he formed a close relationship with Leonid Brezhnev (first secretary of the Moldavian party, 1950–52), who became his mentor and helped him advance within the party. Moving to Moscow in 1956, Chernenko became Brezhnev's chief aide in 1960 when the latter assumed the chairmanship of the Presidium of the Supreme Soviet. Chernenko was elected a member of the CPSU Central Committee (CC) in 1971 and of the Politburo in 1978. He traveled with Brezhnev to the Helsinki Conference on Security and Cooperation in Europe in 1975 and to the signing of the SALT II agreement in Vienna in 1979. He also attended Communist party congresses in East Germany, Denmark, Greece, Cuba, and France. On the death of Mikhail Suslov in January 1982, Chernenko succeeded him as CC secretary in charge of ideology. When Brezhnev died in Novem-

ber 1982, Chernenko had high expectations of succeeding his patron but was outmaneuvered by Yury Andropov. Following the latter's death 15 months later, Chernenko was unanimously elected CPSU general secretary, and two months later the Supreme Soviet elected him chairman of its Presidium—titular chief of state.

Chevalier, Haakon, U.S.-born academic and writer (b. Sept. 10, 1901, Lakewood, N.J.—d. July 4, 1985, Paris, France), became a victim of McCarthyism as a result of being named in 1947 by J. Robert Oppenheimer, director of the Los Alamos atomic bomb project during World War II, as a possible security risk. The two had been friends and fellow faculty members during the 1930s at the University of California at Berkeley, where Chevalier held the chair of French literature. Following Oppenheimer's denunciation of him, later withdrawn at a 1954 Senate investigation, Chevalier (son of a French father and Norwegian mother) was forced to abandon his U.S. academic career. In 1950 he left for France, where he took up permanent residence. Chevalier wrote studies of French literature such as *The Ironic Temper: Anatole France and His Time* (1933) and translated works by André Malraux and Louis Aragon. His novel *The Man Who Would Be God* (1959), with a physicist as hero, reflected his relationship with Oppenheimer, as did *Oppenheimer: The Story of a Friendship* (1965).

Cilento, Sir Raphael West, Australian physician and barrister (b. Dec. 2, 1893, Jamestown, South Australia—d. April 15, 1985, Queensland, Australia), was director (1946) of the refugees division of the UN and then of the UN division of social activities (1947–50); he was considered a leading expert on tropical medicine. Cilento was educated at the University of Adelaide and served with the Army Medical Corps during World War I. He then joined the Colonial Medical Service in the Federated Malay States before further study at the School of Tropical Medicine in London. He was director (1922–28) of the Australian Institute of Tropical Medicine and director (1924–28) of public health in New Guinea. From 1934 to 1945 he was director general of health and medical services for Queensland. Having served with the League of Nations during the 1920s, Cilento was appointed director of the UN Relief and Rehabilitation Administration in the British Zone of Germany in 1945 and in the following year moved to the UN in New York City, where his responsibilities included relief for the Palestinian refugees. He was the author of a number of books on tropical diseases.

Claire, Ina (INA FAGAN), U.S. actress (b. Oct. 15, 1892, Washington, D.C.—d. Feb. 21, 1985, San Francisco, Calif.), was a bubbly comedienne who specialized in sophisticated comedy featuring well-bred, bad-mannered characters whose spiteful behaviour gave her ample opportunity to showcase her quicksilver wit. The blond, hazel-eyed actress first graced the

FRED FEHL

vaudeville stage with her impersonations of famous stage performers and was featured in the *Ziegfeld Follies* of 1915 and 1916. She starred in *The Gold Diggers* (1919) for nearly two years and gained critical acclaim in the title role of a young adventuress in *Polly with a Past* (1920). Some of her most famous roles were the sly thief in the 1925 play *The Last of Mrs. Cheyney* and Greta Garbo's nemesis in the 1939 classic film *Ninotchka*. Claire, who appeared in only nine motion pictures, was more at home on Broadway, where she starred in *Biography* (1932), *Ode to Liberty* (1934), and *The Confidential Clerk* (1954), her farewell stage performance. The second (1929–31) of her three marriages was to the silent screen idol John Gilbert.

Clark, William Donaldson, British journalist and international official (b. July 28, 1916, Haltwhistle, Northumberland, England—d. June 27, 1985, Cuxham, Oxfordshire, England), worked tirelessly on behalf of the third world as founder (1960) and director (1960–68) of the Overseas Development Institute, vice-president for external relations of the World Bank (1974–80), and from 1980 president of the International Institute for Environment and Development. He had been (1946–49) London editor of *Encyclopædia Britannica*. Educated at Oundle School and Oriel College, University of Oxford, Clark was a Commonwealth fellow at the University of Chicago (1938–40). He worked in Chicago for the British Ministry of Information (1941–44) and was press attaché to the British embassy in Washington, D.C. (1945–46). Clark worked for *The Observer* (London) newspaper as diplomatic correspondent (1950–55) and as foreign correspondent for Africa and India (1958–60). In 1955 he became public relations officer for Prime Minister Sir Anthony Eden but resigned over the Suez Canal crisis (1956). He served the World Bank as director of information and public affairs (1968–73). Clark's writings included *Less than Kin* (1957), *What Is the Commonwealth?* (1958), and two novels—*Cataclysm: The North-South Conflict of 1987* (1984) and *Number 10* (1966).

Clarke, Kenny ("KLOOK"; KENNETH SPEARMAN CLARKE), U.S. jazz drummer (b. Jan. 9, 1914, Pittsburgh, Pa.—d. Jan. 25, 1985, Paris, France), was a gifted jazz innovator who as the foremost drummer in the development of bebop during the 1940s was credited with breaking the traditional four-beat rhythm from the bass drum to the cymbal, thereby permitting the use of the bass and snare drums for independent counterrhythms in support of improvising soloists. Clarke—who participated in the seminal jam sessions at Minton's Playhouse in New York City together with trumpeter Dizzy Gillespie, guitarist Charlie Christian, pianist Thelonius Monk, and, later, saxophonist Charlie Parker—was also a founding member of the Modern Jazz Quartet, in which he collaborated from 1952 to 1955. The following year Clarke moved to France, where in 1960 he organized a big band with Belgian pianist-composer Francy Boland. He later enjoyed a six-year engagement (1961–67) at the Blue Note nightclub in Paris and tours of major European cities. Clarke's compositions include "Salt Peanuts" (with Gillespie) and "Epistrophy" (with Monk). Some of his recordings were *One O'Clock Jump* (with Sidney Bechet) and *Stompin' at the Savoy* (with Charlie Christian).

Cochrane, Robert Greenhill, British leprologist (b. Aug. 11, 1899, Beidaihe (Pehtaiho), Hebei (Hopeh) Province, China—d. Aug. 3, 1985, Norristown, Pa.), worked in India and Africa on the treatment of leprosy and was identified particularly with the introduction of sulphone therapy for the disease. He was the son of missionaries (his father founded the Union Medical College in Beijing [Peking]) and was a practicing Christian. He studied at the University of Glasgow and in London at St. Bartholomew's Hospital and the School of Tropical Medicine before training in leprology in Calcutta. He worked in

Bihar and in 1929 was appointed secretary to the British Empire Leprosy Relief Association. Returning to India in 1933, he became chief medical officer at the Leprosy Sanatorium in Chingleput, Madras, and from 1944 to 1948 was principal of the Christian Medical College at Vellore. From then until 1966 he worked in England, where he founded the Leprosy Research Fund, advised the Ministry of Health, and served from 1961 as consultant at the Tropical Diseases Hospital. He spent two years in India before joining the Africa Inland Mission in Tanzania. Cochrane did much to break down prejudice against leprosy within the medical profession and to encourage diagnosis and treatment of the disease and related injuries. He wrote standard textbooks on the subject and was awarded the Kaisar-i-Hind medal first class for his work in India. Cochrane was made a Companion of the Order of St. Michael and St. George in 1969.

Cole, Lester, U.S. screenwriter (b. June 19, 1904, New York, N.Y.—d. Aug. 15, 1985, San Francisco, Calif.), was the prolific writer of 36 scripts, including *The House of Seven Gables* (1940), *None Shall Escape* (1944), *Objective Burma!* (1945), and *High Wall* (1947), before being branded one of the "Hollywood Ten"—writers and directors who refused to testify before the House Committee on Un-American Activities and were sentenced to a year in prison. After his release Cole was unable to find work as a screenwriter and held a variety of jobs before helping to write the screenplay for *Born Free* in 1965 under the name Gerald L. C. Copley. He later used his talents to teach screenwriting at the University of Southern California at Berkeley, where he taught until 1984. He was one of the founders (1933) of the Screen Writers Guild.

Condie, Richard P., U.S. conductor (b. July 5, 1898, Springville, Utah—d. Dec. 22, 1985, Salt Lake City, Utah), as the eminent maestro (1957–74) of the Mormon Tabernacle Choir, led the ensemble to international prominence with 850 weekly radio concerts for "Music and the Spoken Word," 15 national tours, 50 record albums, and a hit single, "The Battle Hymn of the Republic." Condie's musical background included studies at Brigham Young University, Provo, Utah; the New England Conservatory of Music, Boston; and the Fontainebleau (France) Conservatory. He was also a gifted leading tenor with the Sebastiani Opera Company in Italy and the Salt Lake City Civic Opera before launching his career as a choral conductor at Utah State University in 1932. He was remembered, however, as the longtime director of the Mormon Tabernacle Choir.

Cowles, Gardner ("Mike"), U.S. publisher (b. Jan. 31, 1903, Algona, Iowa—d. July 8, 1985, Southampton, N.Y.), as the architect of a publishing empire, founded *Look* in 1937, a highly successful monthly (then biweekly in 1940) picture magazine that folded in 1971 when national advertising revenue was channeled toward television. Cowles, who graduated from Harvard University, launched his career in the 1920s as city editor of the *Des Moines Register and Tribune*, which was owned by his father. During the 1930s Cowles and his brother, John, acquired radio stations, and the family purchased the *Minneapolis Star* newspaper. After World War II, in which Cowles served as deputy director of the Office of War Information, he moved to New York City to oversee *Look*, which had moved there in 1940. He also retained the title of president of the Des Moines Register and Tribune Co. During the 1950s Cowles purchased such unsuccessful magazines as *Quick, Flair,* and *Venture* and a daily newspaper, the *Suffolk Sun*. But he also scored a number of triumphs: he founded (1959) Puerto Rico's first English-language daily, the *San Juan Star*, which won a Pulitzer Prize its first year; he bought *Family Circle*, the popular supermarket magazine; and he bought a number of radio stations and newspapers, predominantly in Florida. Though

Cowles valiantly tried to save *Look*, the magazine continued to lose revenue, and he was forced to cease publication. From 1971 to 1974 he served as director of the New York Times Co., and in 1978 he dissolved Cowles Communications. During the last years of his life Cowles was active administering the $11 million Cowles Charitable Trust.

Cruz Uclés, Ramón Ernesto, Honduran lawyer and politician (b. Jan. 4, 1903, San Juan de Flores, Honduras—d. Aug. 6, 1985, Honduras), served two years (1971–72) of his six-year term as president of Honduras before being ousted in a coup engineered by Gen. Osvaldo López Arellano. Cruz, an expert on international law, earned a law degree from the Central University of Honduras and became a member of the nation's Supreme Court in 1949. From 1958 to 1960 Cruz defended his country's territorial rights in a border dispute with Nicaragua before the International Court of Justice at The Hague, Neth.; the court upheld the boundaries between the two countries. In the 1963 presidential election, Cruz was the National Party candidate, but López was brought to power by a military coup. When Cruz was elected president in 1971, he became the first president of the country to serve under the new national unity system, in which the National and Liberal parties shared congressional seats, Cabinet posts, and judicial positions. Though the system was endorsed by outgoing president López, who remained commander of the armed forces, the military overthrew Cruz in 1972 and reinstated López.

Cushman, Robert Everton, Jr., general (ret.), U.S. Marine Corps (b. Dec. 24, 1914, St. Paul, Minn.—d. Jan. 2, 1985, Fort Washington, Md.), was commandant of the U.S. Marine Corps (1972–75) and deputy director of the CIA (1969–72) in the Nixon administration. Cushman served valiantly during World War II by leading (1943) a crumbling battalion of the 9th Marines on Guam, an action that earned him the Navy Cross, the nation's second highest medal, and during the final years of the Vietnam war, he was awarded the largest troop command (more than 160,000 men) ever held by a Marine officer. Cushman, who graduated from the U.S. Naval Academy tenth in a class of 442, served with distinction during World War II, earning the Bronze Star, the Legion of Merit, and the Navy Cross. In 1935 Cushman was commissioned a second lieutenant, and in 1941 he assumed command of the battleship *Pennsylvania*, which was attacked at Pearl Harbor on Dec. 7, 1941. During the war he repeatedly led his battalion into combat in the Pacific—on Bougainville, Guam, and Iwo Jima. Cushman joined the CIA in 1949 and was promoted to colonel the following year. His friendship with Richard Nixon was viewed as a boon to his career, and in 1969 Nixon appointed him deputy director of the CIA. It was in this position, though, that Cushman was implicated in the Watergate scandal. A transcript of a recorded conversation between E. Howard Hunt, an engineer of the burglary, and Cushman revealed that Cushman gave initial approval to CIA participation in the White House burglary of the office of antiwar activist Daniel Ellsberg's psychiatrist, though the agency never took part in the break-in. As commandant of the Marine Corps (1972–75), Cushman was known for his rigorous adherence to a strict military structure.

D'Oyly Carte, Dame Bridget, British theatre and hotel director (b. March 25, 1908, London, England—d. May 2, 1985, Shrubs Wood, Chalfont St. Giles, Buckinghamshire, England), for over 30 years successfully carried on her family's presentation of the Gilbert and Sullivan comic operas, in the U.S. and Canada as well as in Britain. Educated privately and at Dartington Hall, Totnes, where she studied dance and drama, she was briefly married (1926–31) but reverted (1932) to the use of her maiden name. After her only brother was killed in an accident, she prepared to manage as well as

inherit the family businesses, and she served as her father's assistant at the Savoy Hotel (1933–39). When her father, Rupert D'Oyly Carte, died (1948), she became managing director of the D'Oyly Carte Opera Company and a director of Savoy Hotel Ltd. and Savoy Theatre Ltd. In 1961 her family's performing rights in the Gilbert and Sullivan operas ran out. However, since there was still a strong popular demand for the operas, she was advised to continue to present them, and for that purpose she founded and endowed the D'Oyly Carte Opera Trust and became chairman and managing director of Bridget D'Oyly Carte Ltd. The last London presentation was made in 1982. She was made a Dame Commander of the Order of the British Empire in 1975.

Davies of Leek, Harold Davies, BARON, British politician (b. July 31, 1904, Glamorgan, Wales—d. Oct. 28, 1985, Stoke-on-Trent, England), was Labour member of Parliament for Stafford Leek constituency from 1945 to 1970 and parliamentary private secretary to Prime Minister Harold Wilson from 1967 to 1970. His trip to Hanoi in 1965 on behalf of the government caused some controversy; he was well known as a left-winger in the Wilson government and was chosen to lead the peacemaking mission because of his links with the North Vietnamese. Davies worked as a schoolteacher and lecturer before standing for Parliament in 1945. He soon established his reputation as a figure on the left of the Labour Party and was appointed parliamentary secretary at the Ministry of Pensions and National Insurance after the Labour victory in 1964. His "secret" mission to Hanoi in the following year, which was apparently disclosed to the press by a leak from the right wing of the Cabinet, proved unsuccessful. He lost his seat in 1970 and was made a life peer.

De Guillebon, Jacques, French army officer (b. Oct. 13, 1909, Lunéville, Meurthe-et-Moselle, France—d. Feb. 25, 1985, Paris, France), was Gen. Philippe Leclerc's chief of staff in the Free French forces during World War II. He studied at the École Polytechnique and served with the artillery in Chad (then part of French Equatorial Africa), holding the rank of captain on the outbreak of war. He at once rallied to Gen. Charles de Gaulle and the Free French, joining Leclerc in North Africa to help recapture the oasis of Koufra, Libya, from the Italians. With Leclerc's 2nd Armoured Division he went on to the liberation of Paris and the advance of the Allied forces across France into Germany. De Guillebon accompanied Leclerc to Indochina after the war, was then military attaché in Bern, Switz., and, after an unsuccessful attempt to enter politics in de Gaulle's Rassemblement du Peuple Français, held a command in southern Tunisia. In 1957 he was appointed commander of the École Polytechnique and in 1965 director of the Institut des Hautes Études de Défense Nationale. De Guillebon was Grand Officer of the Légion d'Honneur and Companion of the Liberation.

De Quay, Jan Eduard, Dutch politician (b. Aug. 26, 1901, s' Hertogenbosch, Neth.—d. July 4, 1985, Beers, Neth.), was prime minister of The Netherlands from 1959 to 1963, a period that was marked by conflict with Indonesia over the future of Netherlands New Guinea and that ended with the territory's incorporation into Indonesia as Irian Barat (now Irian Jaya). De Quay, who from 1934 served as professor of business and psychology at Tilburg Roman Catholic University, began his political career during World War II when in 1940, under the German occupation, he helped form the Netherlands Union. The main objective of this short-lived movement was to prevent the formation of a Dutch National Socialist government, even if some cooperation with the occupying power was needed to achieve that end. However, the movement was banned by the Germans in 1941, and de Quay was imprisoned during 1942–43. In 1945 he became minister of war

in the postwar interim government and then provincial governor (1946–59) of Nordbrabant. As prime minister following the 1959 election, he presided over a coalition of his own Catholic People's Party with Liberals, Anti-Revolutionaries, and Christian-Historicals, with the Socialists in opposition. De Quay, who was chairman of Royal Dutch Airlines (KLM) from 1964 to 1972, withdrew from politics in 1969.

Diplock, (William John) Kenneth Diplock, BARON, British lawyer (b. Dec. 8, 1907, Croydon, Surrey, England—d. Oct. 14, 1985, London, England), recommended the controversial "Diplock" courts set up in Northern Ireland after 1972 to try terrorist cases without a jury. The intention of these courts was to prevent reported threats to and interference with juries. His name was also associated with some notable judicial inquiries. He was educated at University College, Oxford, practiced as a barrister, and was secretary to Sir Leslie Scott, master of the rolls, before serving in the Royal Air Force during World War II. He became a king's counsel in 1948, was recorder of Oxford from 1951 to 1956 and judge of the High Court until 1961, then was lord justice of appeal until 1968. He also developed an advisory practice, particularly in Commonwealth countries, where he was consulted on constitutional matters; in 1955 he appeared for the kabaka of Uganda. From 1968 Diplock was a member of the judicial committee of the House of Lords and became renowned for his powers of analysis and incisiveness of judgment, though his manner was often aloof. From 1971, as chairman of the Security Commission, he dealt with some notorious cases, including the investigation of Earl Jellicoe and Lord Lambton, two government ministers who were involved with prostitutes, to discover whether this represented a security risk. He exonerated the late Sir Roger Hollis, a former head of military intelligence accused of spying. During 1980–81 he was appointed to monitor authorized communications interception by the police, customs, and security forces and pronounced that such measures were necessary to maintain law and order. He renounced his seniority in 1984 but continued to serve as a lord of appeal.

Donghia, Angelo R., U.S. interior designer (b. March 7, 1935, Vandergrift, Pa.—d. April 10, 1985, New York, N.Y.), specialized in unusual combinations of patterns and textures and was especially noted for his signature gray flannel fabric, with which he covered walls and upholstered overstuffed chairs. Donghia, who created bold and innovative interiors for such clients as Diana Ross, Ralph Lauren, Halston, and Steve Martin, was one of the first designers to mass market his products, including furniture, fabrics, sheets, and china. After graduating from the Parsons School of Design in 1959, he joined Yale Burge Interiors, and when he became a partner in 1966, the firm's name was changed to Burge-Donghia Interiors. In 1976 Donghia opened his own showroom in Los Angeles and gained a reputation for his eclectic approach to interior design, combining, for example, bleached-wood floors, gray flannel overstuffed furniture, and shiny lacquered walls. Some of his corporate commissions included PepsiCo's world headquarters in Purchase, N.Y., the Intercontinental Hotel in New Orleans, La., and the Omni International Hotel in Miami, Fla. In 1982 Donghia Companies grossed $67.5 million.

Douglas-Home, Charles Cospatrick, British journalist (b. Sept. 1, 1937—d. Oct. 29, 1985, London, England), was editor of *The Times* of London from 1982 until his death from cancer. He had previously worked as the newspaper's defense correspondent, as editor in various departments, and as deputy editor to Harold Evans. Douglas-Home was educated at Eton, then commissioned in the Royal Scots Greys before becoming aide-de-camp to the governor of Kenya. Turning to journalism, he worked as a general reporter on the *Scottish Daily Ex-*

THE TIMES/CAMERA PRESS, LONDON

press and from 1961 to 1964 was military, then political and diplomatic correspondent for the London *Daily Express.* Moving to *The Times* in 1965 as defense correspondent, he traveled widely, covering the Arab-Israeli war in 1967 and the Soviet invasion of Czechoslovakia in 1968. He published *The Arabs and Israel* (1968), *Britain's Reserve Forces* (1969), and biographies of Field Marshal Erwin Rommel and Sir Evelyn Baring. In 1970 he was appointed features editor, then home editor and foreign editor, before Harold Evans made him deputy editor in 1981. The paper had recently been taken over by the Australian media tycoon Rupert Murdoch and was experiencing internal upheavals as well as financial difficulties. Evans left after only a year as editor and Douglas-Home was appointed to succeed him. He immediately attracted new readers by expanding the features pages while imposing a more right-wing tone on the editorial content. Douglas-Home was admired by his staff for his relaxed but determined style of leadership and for his courageous fight against the disease that was diagnosed within a year of his taking charge of the paper. He introduced *The Times* Portfolio, a stocks and shares game, and saw the circulation rise from under 300,000 to nearly 500,000.

Dubuffet, Jean, French painter (b. July 31, 1901, Le Havre, France—d. May 12, 1985, Paris, France), created powerful and naive images through the use of various materials in his paintings and constructions, which he classified as *art brut.* Characteristic early works show figures executed with apparently childlike outlines moving across a surface where the addition of glass, sand, and other materials to the paint exhibits Dubuffet's delight in textures. He studied at the Académie Julian in Paris but then largely abandoned painting to manage his father's wine business and to travel in South America. In 1942 he finally devoted himself to painting, and he held his first exhibition in 1944. Traveling in North Africa during the late 1940s, he made a series of landscapes influenced by the emptiness of the desert, but he returned to the depiction of the human form in 1950 with the series "Corps de dames." Dubuffet took inspiration from Surrealism and the work of Paul Klee, as well as the art of the mentally disturbed, and his paintings increasingly drew attention to the materials of which, in a form of collage, they were constructed. His growing reputation led to exhibitions in London in 1955, Paris in 1960, and New York City in 1961, but he remained a controversial figure, sometimes dismissed as a mere trickster or a sensation seeker. A commission for the Renault car factory was turned down, but New York purchased his "Quatre arbres," and his "Monument à la bête debout" was inaugurated on the plaza of the State of Illinois Center in Chicago in 1984. In 1967 his collected manifestos and pamphlets were published as *Écrits de Jean Dubuffet.*

Duffy, Terence, British trade unionist (b. May 3, 1922, Wolverhampton, England—d. Oct. 1, 1985, London, England), was president of the Amalgamated Union of Engineering Workers (AUEW) from 1978 and a noted figure on the right wing of the British trade union movement. Duffy, a tenacious negotiator, was respected for his forthright approach. He came from a Catholic family and served in the Army throughout World War II. He joined the Norton motorcycle factory and became a shop steward, later moving to Lucas Aerospace. Although he had no particular political ambitions, he was persuaded in 1969 to run for the post of AUEW divisional officer and, as a "moderate," to try for the national executive against a left-winger, Bob Wright. He won, despite Wright's apparently strong position, and the two men met again in 1978 in the contest for the presidency. Duffy was elected and in 1980 reelected by a large majority. However, the AUEW was weakened by economic recession in the industry and by its political leanings, and Duffy sought to make alliances with other groups, in particular the electricians' union. He had been elected by postal ballot and came into conflict with the Trades Union Congress over his acceptance of government funds for such ballots. A staunch anti-Communist, he also used the influence of his union to work against the left on the Labour Party national executive and disguised a considerable measure of political cunning under a guileless exterior.

Eisenhower, Milton Stover, U.S. diplomat and educator (b. Sept. 15, 1899, Abilene, Kan.—d. May 2, 1985, Baltimore, Md.), was an astute and levelheaded adviser to six U.S. presidents, including his brother Dwight, and served as president of Kansas State College (1943–50), Pennsylvania State University (1950–56), and Johns Hopkins University (1956–67 and 1971–72). Eisenhower, the youngest of seven brothers, graduated from Kansas State in 1924. Two years later he entered government service as an assistant to the secretary of agriculture, and in 1928 he became director of information for the Department of Agriculture, a post he held until 1940. As a presidential adviser he served as a troubleshooter for refugee and relief problems in North Africa for Franklin D. Roosevelt, helped Harry S. Truman reorganize the Agriculture Department, was special ambassador to Latin America and his brother Dwight's most trusted adviser, negotiated with Fidel Castro for John F. Kennedy, headed the National Commission on the Causes and Prevention of Violence for Lyndon B. Johnson following the assassinations of Robert F. Kennedy and the Rev. Martin Luther King, Jr., and headed study groups for Richard M. Nixon. The distinguished diplomat, who penned *The President Is Calling* (1974), recounting his accomplishments in various administrations, was president emeritus of Johns Hopkins and in recent years worked actively for the Eisenhower Foundation.

Enders, John Franklin, U.S. microbiologist (b. Feb. 10, 1897, West Hartford, Conn.—d. Sept. 8, 1985, Waterford, Conn.), shared the 1954 Nobel Prize for Physiology or Medicine with Thomas H. Weller and Frederick C. Robbins for their work on the cultivation of the poliomyelitis viruses in tissue culture. This research laid the foundation for the development of an effective polio vaccine and led to the isolation of many other viruses and to the development of new diagnostic methods. Enders, who earned (1922) an M.S. in English literature at Harvard University, later turned to the study of bacteria and earned (1930) a Ph.D. in microbiology there. Two years later he was named instructor in the Harvard Medical School's bacteriology and immunology department. His research shed new light on problems associated with tuberculosis, pneumococcal infections, and resistance to bacterial diseases. In 1946 Enders was invited to establish and head a laboratory at Children's Medical Center, Boston, where, together with fellow Harvard researchers, he conducted

pioneering studies on the polio virus. In the late 1950s Enders, Weller, and Robbins collaborated on the production of a vaccine against the measles virus that led to the development of a licensed vaccine in 1963. The same year Enders was awarded the Medal of Freedom by Pres. John F. Kennedy.

Erlander, Tage Fritiof, Swedish politician (b. June 13, 1901, Ransäter, Värmland, Sweden—d. June 21, 1985, Stockholm, Sweden), was prime minister of Sweden from 1946 to 1969. A Social Democrat, he headed a series of coalition governments, but in 1968 his party won an overall majority in the Riksdag's (parliament's) lower house. In foreign policy he promoted Sweden's traditional stance of neutrality; his keeping the country out of NATO resulted in heavy expenditures on defense. Erlander encouraged active participation in the UN, and Sweden was a member of various nonmilitary European institutions. At home he gave impetus to a program of economic and social development; nationalization of industry was accelerated after his 1968 victory. The son of a teacher, Erlander was educated in local schools at Karlstad and graduated (1928) in economics and political science at the University of Lund. He then worked (1928–38) on the editorial staff of the Swedish encyclopaedia *Svensk Uppslagsbok.* He was elected to Lund City Council in 1930 and entered national politics in 1933, sitting in the Riksdag's lower chamber (1933–44 and 1949–70), in its second chamber (1945–48), and in the new unicameral Riksdag (1971–73). After working on the Employment Commission in the mid-1930s, he became an assistant at the Ministry of Social Welfare (1937) and its under secretary of state (1938). He was minister without portfolio (1944) and minister of education (1945), becoming prime minister on the sudden death of Per Albin Hansson. Erlander was the author of several volumes of memoirs.

Ervin, Samuel James, Jr., U.S. politician (b. Sept. 27, 1896, Morganton, N.C.—d. April 23, 1985, Winston-Salem, N.C.), was a crusty Democratic senator from North Carolina (1954–74) who as an expert on the U.S. Constitution achieved national prominence in 1973–74 while presiding as chairman of the Senate Select Committee on Presidential Campaign Activities, popularly known as the Senate Watergate committee. A self-styled "ole country lawyer," Ervin graduated from Harvard Law School in 1922 and was active in North Carolina politics before serving in the U.S. House of Representatives in 1946 and 1947. The following year he was named to the North Carolina Supreme Court, and in 1954 he was appointed to fill the Senate seat of the deceased Sen. Clyde Hoey. An old-fashioned conservative politician, the jowly Ervin opposed civil rights legislation and the Equal Rights Amendment. He fervently supported civil liberties and the Vietnam war. His conservatism coupled with his reputation as a strict interpreter of the Constitution made him an ideal chairman of the Watergate hearings, in

which former top officials in the White House and in Pres. Richard Nixon's reelection committee were questioned about the 1972 burglary and bugging of the Democratic National Committee's headquarters. Ervin, who conducted a dogged investigation that was broadcast on national television, became a moral folk hero with such pronouncements as, "There has been murder and larceny in every generation, but that hasn't made murder meritorious or larceny legal," and "Freedom is a fluid, intangible condition of our society. . . . It is lost not all at a time, but by degrees." Ervin retired in 1974.

Espriu, Salvador, Catalan poet (b. 1913, Santa Coloma de Farnés, Spain—d. Feb. 22, 1985, Barcelona, Spain), was the most outstanding Catalan writer of his generation and one of the few in the language to achieve an international reputation. At the age of 16 he published *Israel,* a book of prose stories, and in 1931 his first novel, *El doctor Rip.* Espriu studied law and ancient history at the University of Barcelona and wrote *Les hores,* a collection of poems on the Spanish Civil War. His treatment of such universal themes as death and the human condition were drawn from his knowledge of the Bible and of ancient Egypt as well as from his own Catalan tradition. His tragedy *Antígona* was written in 1939 but could not be published until 1955. *Cementiri de Sinera* (1946), another collection of poems, appeared clandestinely; the mythical Sinera (an anagram of his boyhood home, Arenys de Mar) was featured in later works as a place of reconciliation between the different peoples and ideologies of Spain, and his remarkably consistent vision united hope and a sombre perception of human fate. Espriu won the Montaigne Prize in 1971 and was several times nominated for the Nobel Prize.

Fender, Percy George Herbert, British cricketer (b. Aug. 22, 1892, Balham, London, England—d. June 15, 1985, Exeter, Devon, England), made the fastest century (100 runs in an innings) in first-class cricket and, though he never captained the English team, was one of the most respected players in the history of the game. His failure to reach the captaincy of the national side was ascribed to his unorthodox approach to the game and, alternatively, to his Jewish background. Fender played for Sussex during his last year at St. Paul's School in 1910, and he was a noted county player. When World War I broke out, he joined the Royal Fusiliers, later transferring to the Royal Flying Corps. He also served with the Royal Air Force during World War II and retired with the rank of wing commander. Fender reached his peak as a cricketer in the 1920s; he joined the English tour in Australia in 1920 and a year later was appointed captain of Surrey. He played in 13 test series and in his career scored 19,034 runs, including 21 centuries, and took 1,894 wickets and 558 catches. His record-breaking century was made in 35 minutes (though he claimed 34) in 1920. An original and entertaining player, he was one of the great characters of the game, though his unorthodox views on and off the field sometimes brought him into conflict with its authorities. He published a number of books, including the semiautobiographical *ABC of Cricket* (1937). A wine merchant, he also headed his own company, Herbert Fender & Co., from 1922 to 1977.

Ferron, Jacques, Canadian physician and author (b. 1921, Louiseville, Que.—d. April 22, 1985, Longueuil, Que.), was the witty founder of the satirical Rhinoceros Party, a quasi-political party that was established in the 1960s to ridicule the lack of policies of the candidates in the federal election of that year. The name of the party was fashioned after an election held in Rio de Janeiro, where voters elected a rhinoceros city councillor to show their disdain for the official candidates. Ferron received his M.D. degree from Laval University and practiced medicine in a suburb of Montreal. He was also a prolific author of plays, short

AP/WIDE WORLD

stories, and novels, including such works published in English as *Tales from the Uncertain Country* (1972), *Dr. Cotnoir* (1973), *The Saint Elias* (1975), and *The Juneberry Tree* (1975). In 1970 Ferron made headlines when Paul and Jacques Rose and Francis Simard (who were being hunted as the kidnappers and killers of Quebec labour minister Pierre Laporte) were trapped in a cellar by police and requested that Ferron be appointed their negotiator. Ferron successfully negotiated their peaceful surrender. Known for his biting wit, Ferron was once asked what his Rhinoceros Party candidates would do if elected. He replied, "The same as yours—nothing." Some of the party's most outrageous campaign promises included the repeal of the law of gravity, paying off Canada's public debt with an American Express credit card, and nationalizing hockey star Guy Lafleur. After Ferron died the Rhinoceros Party was disbanded by its president, who remarked that Ferron had "taught us the power of positive absurdity in the face of absolute idiocies."

Fetchit, Stepin (LINCOLN THEODORE MONROE ANDREW PERRY), U.S. actor (b. May 30, 1902, Key West, Fla.—d. Nov. 19, 1985, Los Angeles, Calif.), delighted motion picture audiences in the 1920s and '30s with his comic portrayals, usually as a shuffling, lazy, and easily frightened servant, a role that made him both a millionaire and the first black performer to attain featured billing with such stars as Shirley Temple and Will Rogers. Stepin Fetchit was a name he borrowed from a racehorse that had won him some money before he went to Hollywood. He became a sensation with his motion picture debut in *In Old Kentucky* (1927). A string of hits followed, including *The Tragedy of Youth* (1928), *The Ghost Talks* (1928), *The Big Fight* (1930), *Stand Up and Cheer* (1934), *Charlie Chan in Egypt* (1935), *Dimples* (1936), and *Miracle in Harlem* (1947). In the last year, Fetchit, who had adopted a luxurious life-style, employing 16 Chinese servants and owning 12 cars, notably a pink Rolls-Royce, filed for bankruptcy. In later years his comic roles were characterized as insulting stereotypes of the American Negro, a charge that prompted Fetchit to sue (1970) CBS television for $3 million because he complained that the network's 1968 documentary "Of Black America" depicted him as "the white man's Negro, the traditional lazy, stupid, crap-shooting, chicken-stealing idiot." The suit was dismissed in 1974 because a federal judge ruled that the comments were directed at his role, not at Fetchit himself. After a two-decade absence, Fetchit returned to the screen in *Amazing Grace* (1974). From 1977 he resided at the Motion Picture and Television Country House in Woodland Hills, Calif.

fforde, Sir Arthur Frederic Brownlow, British lawyer, educationist, and public servant (b. Aug. 23, 1900, India—d. June 26, 1985, Wonersh, Surrey, England), was headmaster of Rugby School (1948–57) and chairman of the board of governors of the British Broadcasting Corporation (1957–64) during a time of fierce competition from commercial television. He was influential in the planning of the BBC's second channel, BBC II. Educated at Rugby and Trinity College, University of Oxford, fforde qualified as a solicitor (1925) and joined his uncle as a partner (1928) in a firm of City of London solicitors. During World War II he worked at the Ministry of Supply (1941–43) and was transferred to the Treasury, serving as an under secretary (1944–45) and dealing mainly with supply contracts. He returned briefly to his legal partnership before accepting the invitation to Rugby; his appointment there was controversial since he lacked experience in the scholastic world, but he brought to the school administrative and financial expertise. He was an enthusiastic lay preacher and chairman (1960–65) of the Church of England's Board of Finance. Knighted in 1946, he was made a Knight Grand Cross of the Order of the British Empire in 1964.

Flory, Paul John, U.S. physical chemist (b. June 19, 1910, Sterling, Ill.—d. Sept. 9, 1985, Big Sur, Calif.), was awarded the 1974 Nobel Prize for Chemistry for his investigations of synthetic and natural polymers, substances composed of very large molecules that are multiples of simpler chemical units. Flory revolutionized his field by discovering that polymers could be compared once they were dissolved in a suitable solvent. His work demonstrated the importance of understanding the sizes and shapes of these flexible molecules in establishing relationships between their chemical structures and their physical properties. His studies also led to the introduction of such commercially successful polymers as nylon and synthetic rubber. Flory earned a Ph.D. from Ohio State University in 1934 and worked for such companies as Standard Oil and Goodyear Rubber before joining the faculty at Stanford University in 1961. A towering figure in the field of science, Flory was also an outspoken campaigner for human rights, and he used his Nobel Prize to gain publicity for worldwide social issues.

Fraser, Sir Robert Brown, British television administrator (b. Sept. 26, 1904, Adelaide, Australia—d. Jan. 20, 1985, London, England), was director-general of Britain's Independent Television Authority (ITA) from its formation in 1954 until 1970. The ITA was a public body set up under the Television Act 1954 to control commercial television (which the act legalized); as its chief executive under successive chairmen (the first of whom was Sir Kenneth Clark), Fraser exerted considerable influence on the development of commercial programming in competition with the British Broadcasting Corporation—the public, noncommercial system that had hitherto exercised a monopoly. After graduating from the University of Melbourne, Fraser left Australia for England, earned a degree at the University of London, and in 1930 joined the *Daily Herald* newspaper as a writer. In 1939 he joined the Ministry of Information, where he became director of publications (1941–45) and controller of production (1945–46). When the Central Office of Information superseded the ministry in 1946, Fraser became its director-general and retained that post until his appointment to the ITA. After retiring from the ITA he was chairman (1971–74) of Independent Television News. Created an Officer of the Order of the British Empire in 1944, he was knighted in 1949. He was also a recipient of the gold medal of the Royal Television Society.

Fujiyama, Aiichiro, Japanese politician and business executive (b. May 22, 1897, Tokyo, Japan—d. Feb. 22, 1985, Tokyo), symbolized "big business" in Japan as president of Dai Nippon Sugar Manufacturing Co. and executive officer of Nitto Chemical Industry Co. and used his influence to help bring about the fall of Prime Minister Hideki Tojo in 1944. After Japan's World War II surrender, Fujiyama was imprisoned without a trial for three years as a suspected war criminal. After his release he represented Japan at the 1951 Unesco meeting in Paris. As Japan's foreign minister (1957–60) he headed Japan's first delegation to the UN (1957), helped revise the U.S.-Japanese security treaty (1960), and promoted the restoration of diplomatic relations between Japan and China. Fujiyama was elected to Parliament in 1957 and was reelected five times. He also served as director of Japan's Economic Planning Agency.

Gardiner, Muriel, U.S. psychoanalyst (b. Nov. 23, 1901, Chicago, Ill.—d. Feb. 6, 1985, Princeton, N.J.), specialized in the treatment of disturbed children but was better known for her activities as a member of the socialist underground movement in Vienna during her student years there (1934–38). Gardiner, who used the code name "Mary," joined the movement after witnessing Nazis hurl Jewish students from the windows of schools. She supplied false passports, concealed dissidents in her apartment, and then helped smuggle them to freedom. Born

into an immensely wealthy family (her paternal grandfather founded Chicago's Union Stockyards, and her maternal grandfather launched the Swift meat-packing empire), Gardiner graduated from Wellesley (Mass.) College and then attended Oxford University (1923–25) before deciding to attend medical school at the University of Vienna. She recounted her underground activities in the 1983 memoir *Code Name Mary,* and Gardiner's publisher claimed that she was the model for the title character in the movie *Julia,* based on Lillian Hellman's 1973 memoir *Pentimento,* but Hellman denied any connection. During her later years Gardiner was active in establishing a Sigmund Freud museum in the house in Hampstead, England, where he had lived with his daughter Anna. The museum was scheduled to open in 1986.

George-Brown, George Alfred George-Brown, BARON, British politician (b. Sept. 2, 1914, London, England—d. June 2, 1985, Cornwall, England), served as deputy leader of the Labour Party (1960–70), secretary of state for economic affairs (1964–66), and foreign secretary (1966–68). The son of a truck driver, George Brown became full-time organizer in north London for the Transport and General Workers' Union and, as its nominee, won (1945) the parliamentary seat of Belper, Derbyshire. After serving as parliamentary secretary to the Ministry of Agriculture and Fisheries (1947–51), he became minister of works (1951). Despite defeating Harold Wilson in the 1961 and 1962 elections for the party's deputy leadership, George Brown lost to Wilson when a new leader was chosen after Hugh Gaitskell's death (1963). Heading the newly created (and short-lived) Department of Economic Affairs (DEA), he faced balance of payment problems and hostility from the Treasury, on whose ground the DEA impinged. Brown's position became untenable when in a 1966 crisis Wilson took Treasury rather than DEA advice. As foreign secretary Brown made a strenuous but unsuccessful effort (1967) to achieve for Britain membership in the European Communities. He resigned on an impulse when he was not consulted on an urgent decision. He lost his House of Commons seat in 1970 and was created a life peer, changing his surname from Brown to George-Brown by deed poll. He resigned from the Labour Party in 1976 and was a founder-member (1981) of the Social Democratic Party. His memoirs, *In My Way* (1971), exhibited the injudicious temper that had marred a career of great potential promise.

Gernreich, Rudi, Austrian-born U.S. avant-garde fashion designer (b. Aug. 8, 1922, Vienna, Austria—d. April 21, 1985, Los Angeles, Calif.), a revolutionary in the fashion world, shocked the U.S. populace when he introduced the topless bathing suit in 1964. Among Gernreich's other innovations were the use of psychedelic colours and the popularization of sportswear, miniskirts, safari suits, see-through blouses, and tank suits. In 1938 he immigrated to the U.S., and five years later he became a citizen. He was a dancer (1942–48) with the Lester Horton Dance Theatre troupe before free-lancing as a designer (1948–51). In 1959 Gernreich formed his own fashion house, and it was at this time that his own fashion statements began to evolve. His use of easy-to-care-for, inexpensive, and comfortable designs—especially his knitwear—and of bold, daring colour became a turning point in U.S. fashion and left an indelible impact on the fashion industry. In 1968, at the height of his popularity, he left fashion, but he continued to dabble in furniture design, ballet costumes, and clothes for television. In 1967 Gernreich was inducted into the Fashion Hall of Fame.

Gilels, Emil Grigoryevich, Soviet pianist (b. Oct. 19, 1916, Odessa, Ukraine, Russia—d. Oct. 14, 1985, Moscow, U.S.S.R.), was professor at the Moscow Conservatory from 1952 and considered the outstanding Soviet pianist of his generation, acquiring an international reputation through both recordings and concert tours in

Europe, the U.S., and Japan. He was noted in particular for his interpretations of Beethoven's later piano works. Gilels studied at the Odessa and Moscow conservatories, gaining first prize in the Soviet All-Union Musicians' Contest in 1933. A precocious student who made his debut at the age of 13, Gilels was unable to tour abroad until after World War II. His virtuosity was immediately recognized. He broadened his repertoire to include such composers as Bach, Mozart, Bartok, and Prokofiev and showed great skill in interpreting a range of moods and styles combining technical dexterity with fluency and sensitivity. Gilels's recordings of Beethoven and Brahms attracted particular critical acclaim. He was made a People's Artist of the U.S.S.R. in 1954, awarded the Order of Lenin twice, and gained the Lenin Prize in 1962.

Gordon, Ruth (RUTH GORDON JONES), U.S. actress (b. Oct. 30, 1896, Quincy, Mass.—d. Aug. 28, 1985, Edgartown, Mass.), was a vivacious and determined personality who used her boundless energy to help write such successful screenplays as *A Double Life* (1948), *Adam's Rib* (1949), and *Pat and Mike* (1952) and to perform onstage and in motion pictures, notably *Rosemary's Baby* (1968), for which she won an Academy Award for best supporting actress for her spooky portrayal of a devil worshipper. Gordon, who was discouraged by her teachers in her pursuit of an acting career, ignored their advice and became one of the silver screen's most endearing eccentrics. Gordon made her Broadway debut as Nibs in *Peter Pan* (1915) and appeared onstage in *The Matchmaker* before securing her reputation with *Ethan Frome* (1936), starring as Mattie Silver. She later received rave reviews for her Nora in *A Doll's House* (1937), but from 1940 to 1943 she pursued a film career, appearing in *Abe Lincoln in Illinois* (1940), *Two-Faced Woman* (1941), and *Edge of Darkness* (1943). During the next 23 years she left the glamour of Hollywood for other activities, but when she returned to the screen in 1966 she reveled in the challenge of entertaining new and younger audiences. At the age of 72 she garnered her Oscar for *Rosemary's Baby*, and thereafter she gained a cult following for her roles in *Where's Poppa?* (1970), as the kooky mother who eats Lucky Charms cereal drenched in Pepsi-Cola, and in *Harold and Maude* (1971), as an old woman who takes a 19-year-old lover. She was at her comic best as Clint Eastwood's shotgun-toting mother in *Every Which Way But Loose* and *Any Which Way You Can*. Gordon was also the recipient of an Emmy award for a 1979 television appearance on "Taxi." Her books included *Myself Among Others* (1971) and *My Side* (1976). At the time of her death the veteran character actress had four films pending release.

Gould, Chester, U.S. cartoonist (b. Nov. 20, 1900, Pawnee, Okla.—d. May 11, 1985, Woodstock, Ill.), as the creator of "Dick Tracy"—a hawk-nosed square-chinned detective whose adventures pitted him against such rogues as Flattop, the Mole, Mumbles, B-B Eyes, Pruneface, and the Brow—introduced crime and violence to the comic strip pages. Gould worked as an artist for newspapers and commercial art studios while trying to persuade Joseph Patterson, head of the Chicago Tribune-New York Daily News Syndicate, to buy his comic strips. He finally succeeded when Patterson purchased "Plainclothes Tracy" and renamed the strip "Dick Tracy." The embattled detective, who was run over by cars, stabbed, gassed, chloroformed, pressurized, depressurized, maimed, blinded by acid, and shot countless times, made his debut on Oct. 4, 1931, in the short-lived *Detroit Daily Mirror*. Tracy's adversaries, who usually had a life span of about three months, were disposed of in grisly fashion—Flattop drowned wedged in underwater pilings; the Midget was scalded to death in a Turkish bath; and the Brow was impaled on a flagpole. Tracy's family, including his sweetheart and wife, Tess Trueheart, adopted son, Junior, and daughter, Bonny Braids, were also victims of crimes. The comic strip spawned a television program, "Dick Tracy" (1950–51), such motion pictures as *Dick Tracy's Dilemma* and *Dick Tracy Meets Gruesome*, starring Ralph Byrd in the title roles, and such paraphernalia as Dick Tracy two-way wrist radios, Tess Trueheart and Sparkle Plenty dolls, and Tracy clothes, including snap-brim hats. Gould's *The Celebrated Cases of Dick Tracy, 1931–1951* was published in 1970. Gould retired in 1977 after masterminding the strip for 46 years.

Graves, Robert Ranke, British man of letters (b. July 24, 1895, Wimbledon, London, England—d. Dec. 7, 1985, Deyá, Majorca, Spain), a writer of immense versatility, received the greatest acclaim for his poetry but was generally best known for his historical novels, of which *I, Claudius* and *Claudius the God* (both 1934) achieved the widest renown after they were brilliantly adapted for television in 1976.

After Graves was educated at Charterhouse School, Godalming, he was immediately commissioned in the Royal Welch Fusiliers, serving in France during much of World War I. Twice mentioned in dispatches, he was so severely wounded (1916) that he was reported killed. Taking up a classical scholarship at St. John's College, Oxford, he lived outside the city with his first wife, Nancy. He was appointed (1926) lecturer in English at Cairo University but stayed there only three months. His financial position became assured, however, through his official biography of his friend T. E. Lawrence, *Lawrence and the Arabs* (1927), and his immensely successful autobiography, *Goodbye to All That* (1929). He parted from Nancy in 1929 and, with the American poet Laura Riding, who had resided with them since 1926, went to live at Deyá in Majorca. Rejected by the Army in World War II, he settled in Devonshire with Beryl Pritchard, who became his second wife; his relationship (long platonic only) with Riding had ended in 1939. He returned to Deyá, with his family, in 1946. Books written during the 1940s included *Sergeant Lamb of the Ninth* (1940), *The Golden Fleece* (1944), the controversial *King Jesus* (1946), and *The White Goddess* (1948). Later books were numerous but less outstanding. His poetry, for which he won a number of awards, appeared in a series of collections, spanning the years 1948 to 1975. He also wrote critical essays and made translations of Greek and Latin classical works. He was Clarke lecturer at Trinity College, Cambridge (1954), and professor of poetry at the University of Oxford (1961–66).

Greene, Richard, British film and television actor (b. Aug. 25, 1918, Plymouth, England—d. June 1, 1985, Norfolk, England), began his film career in 1938 as a supporting actor but achieved his greatest success in the 1950s starring on British television in the title role of "The Adventures of Robin Hood." Greene performed in repertory theatre before his film debut in John Ford's *Four Men and a Prayer* (1938). After appearing in other Hollywood films, he served with the British Army during World War II but was given a medical discharge. After the war he returned to Hollywood and appeared in several films, but his career declined until he was picked for the "Robin Hood" series. He appeared in 143 episodes of the series, which made his fortune. He later became a leading horse breeder and continued to appear on the stage and on television.

Grigson, Geoffrey Edward Harvey, British poet and critic (b. March 2, 1905, Pelynt, Cornwall, England—d. Nov. 25, 1985, Broad Town, Wiltshire, England), was most widely known as a literary journalist and a poetry anthologist, although his own poetry had a distinctive style. As a critic he held strong views and expressed them forcefully, with equally marked enthusiasms and dislikes (the latter including the poetry of Dylan Thomas). He was particularly drawn to natural history and the English countryside, contributing to the Shell guides and editing the nature poets John Clare and William Diaper (an 18th-century poet whom he rediscovered). He was educated at the University of Oxford and during the 1930s was literary editor of the *Morning Post* and founder and editor (1933–39) of the influential *New Verse*. His *Collected Poems* appeared in 1963, and a later compilation, for 1963–80, was published in 1984. As a free-lance writer after World War II, he was a regular contributor to *The Times Literary Supplement* and other periodicals and edited several anthologies, including the *Penguin Book of Ballads* (1975), the *Oxford Book of Satirical Verse* (1980), and books of popular verse, love poems, and nonsense verse for the publishers Faber & Faber.

Grimes, Burleigh, U.S. baseball player (b. Aug. 18, 1893, Clear Lake, Wis.—d. Dec. 6, 1985, Clear Lake), was the last professional baseball pitcher to throw a legal spitball in the major leagues. He had a 19-year career (1916–35) with such teams as the Pittsburgh Pirates, Brooklyn Dodgers, St. Louis Cardinals, Chicago Cubs, and New York Yankees. When Grimes broke into organized baseball, his spitball, moistened with slippery elm, was a legal pitch. In 1920, however, the joint rules committee outlawed it but permitted 17 active major leaguers, including Grimes, to continue to throw the pitch. He did so until he retired at the age of 42. During his career Grimes had a record of 270 wins and 212 losses and was a 20-game winner five times. During the 1937–38 baseball season he served as manager of the Brooklyn Dodgers but was fired following the 1938 season. Grimes, who was inducted into the Hall of Fame in 1964, was a scout for the Yankees and the Baltimore Orioles until 1970.

Guarnieri, Johnny, U.S. jazz pianist (b. March 23, 1917, New York, N.Y.—d. Jan. 7, 1985, Livingston, N.J.), as a virtuoso keyboard specialist, was one of the foremost jazz pianists of the swing era and was credited with the first jazz harpsichord solos. Guarnieri, a descendant of Italy's famous Guarnerius family of violin makers, began studying classical piano at the age of ten. His first important engagement was in 1939 with Benny Goodman's band, and in the following year he joined Artie Shaw's orchestra and its offshoot, the Gramercy Five; with the latter he produced his original jazz harpsichord solos. A leading exponent of Fats Waller's Harlem stride style, Guarnieri was also influenced by Teddy Wilson and Count Basie. Guarnieri also performed with Jimmy Dorsey and Raymond Scott in the 1940s and later performed in Hollywood at the Plaza Hotel and the Tail of the Cock. A prolific composer, Guarnieri produced such recordings as "The Duke Again," "Breakthrough," "Superstride," and such tribute pieces as "Basie English" and "Salute to Fats." Guarnieri performed in jazz concerts throughout his career.

Hamilton, Margaret, U.S. actress (b. Dec. 9, 1902, Cleveland, Ohio—d. May 16, 1985, Salisbury, Conn.), rode to fame on a broomstick with her frightening portrayal of the green-skinned, cackling Wicked Witch of the West, who terrorized Dorothy and her dog, Toto, in the 1939 motion picture classic *The Wizard of Oz*. She was a superb character actress whose sharp-featured looks marked her for such roles as stern spinsters, pushy town gossips, and puritanical aunts. A former kindergarten teacher who loved children, Hamilton launched her acting career in 1927 as a member of the Cleveland Play House. In 1932 she appeared on Broadway in *Another Language*, and she made her motion picture debut the following year when she reprised her role for the screen. Hamilton appeared in some 75 motion pictures including *My Little Chickadee* (1940) as a prudish busybody, *Johnny Come Lately* (1943) as a dour newspaper office worker, *George White's Scandals* (1945) as a reproving spinster, *State of the Union* (1948) as a political boss's maid, and *Brewster McCloud* (1970) as an ill-tempered

AP/WIDE WORLD

dowager. She was, however, best remembered as the ghastly Wicked Witch of the West. Hamilton was also popular on television in such series as "Ethel and Albert," "The Patty Duke Show," "The Addams Family," and "Search for Tomorrow." Millions of television viewers also came to recognize her on commercials as Cora, the New England storekeeper, who recommended Maxwell House coffee.

Hampson, Frank, British comic-strip cartoonist (b. Dec. 22, 1918, Audenshaw, Manchester, England—d. July 8, 1985, Epsom, Surrey, England), created Dan Dare, one of the most successful cartoon characters, and until 1962 was the chief artist of *Eagle,* Britain's leading children's comic during the 1950s. After a long period of neglect, Hampson was rediscovered in the mid-1970s and recognized as the outstanding comic-strip artist of his generation. Hampson, who left school at 14 to work for the Post Office, at the same time contributed cartoons to magazines and took evening classes in art. During World War II he was commissioned in the Royal Army Service Corps but failed to obtain a transfer to the Royal Air Force; this frustrated ambition eventually found an outlet in the character of space pilot Dan Dare. In 1946 Hampson obtained a grant to continue studying art and met the Rev. Marcus Morris. In 1950 Morris found a publisher for the first *Eagle,* a new kind of children's comic, designed as an alternative to imported crime and horror comics. Hampson designed the layout of the paper and drew the main strips, including "Dan Dare—Pilot of the Future"; drawn with obsessive attention to detail, its hero (more formally, Col. Daniel MacGregor Dare, chief pilot of the Interplanet Space Fleet and leader of the Venusian Expedition of 1996) incorporated Christian and sportsmanlike virtues. Hampson's artwork, making full use of new colour printing techniques, was admired by connoisseurs of the genre as well as by *Eagle's* schoolboy readers. The magazine was an immediate success until the publishers, Hulton, sold it in 1960. Two years later Hampson left and continued freelance illustration while working as a graphics technician at Ewell College. In 1975, forgotten in Britain, he was invited to the International Festival of Comics in the Italian town of Lucca and gained the top award.

Hanley, James, British novelist (b. Sept. 3, 1901, Liverpool, England—d. Nov. 11, 1985, London, England), was a prolific and gifted writer whose critically acclaimed work was compared to that of Joseph Conrad, yet Hanley remained largely unknown. As a boy he ran away to join the merchant marine and jumped ship in New Brunswick. During World War I he falsified his age and went to France with the Canadian Expeditionary Force. After working as a deckhand, he became a railway porter (1924) and began to study writing and music. Later he lived in a small Welsh village. His first novel, *Drift*

(1930), about a son's struggle to break parental ties, was followed by *Men in Darkness* (1931), a collection of short stories about seamen. *Boy* (1931), a story of shipboard sexual assault, was published in England only in an expurgated edition. Titles of other novels showed his predominant settings: *Hollow Sea* (1938), *The Ocean* (1941), and *The Closed Harbour* (1952). He also wrote a five-volume family saga (completed in 1958) and a few plays, of which *Leave Us Alone* (1972) was produced in London. His last play for television was *A Walk in the Sea* (1966).

Harlech, William David Ormsby Gore, 5th Baron, British politician and diplomat (b. May 20, 1918, London, England—d. Jan. 26, 1985, near Shrewsbury, Shropshire, England), served as British ambassador in Washington, D.C. (1961–65), president of the British Board of Film Censors from 1965, and founder and chairman of the independent company Harlech Television. Educated at Eton and at New College, University of Oxford, he served in the Army and the Phantom reconnaissance unit during World War II before taking a course in business management. As Conservative member of Parliament (1950–61) for Oswestry, Shropshire, from 1951, he held various Foreign Office posts, ending as minister of state for foreign affairs (1957–61), in which capacity he was involved in

CAMERA PRESS, LONDON

nuclear test ban negotiations. In Washington he established a close relationship with Pres. John F. Kennedy, reportedly exercising a restraining influence during the Cuban missile crisis (1962). He succeeded his father in the peerage (1964) and was deputy leader of the (Conservative) opposition in the House of Lords (1966–67). He was deputy chairman of the commission (1972) sent to sound out Rhodesian opinion on a possible settlement of the independence problems and in 1979 again visited Salisbury (Harare) as a prelude to the decisive Lancaster House conference. He was a trustee (1971–78) of London's Tate Gallery and chairman (1976–84) of the National Committee for Electoral Reform. He died as a result of injuries sustained in an automobile accident.

Harris, Patricia Roberts, U.S. lawyer and educator (b. May 31, 1924, Mattoon, Ill.—d. March 23, 1985, Washington, D.C.), was a dynamic civil rights activist and the first black woman to hold a Cabinet post or serve as a U.S. ambassador. Harris, the determined daughter of a Pullman-car waiter, graduated first in a class of 94 from George Washington University National Law Center in 1960. Since 1943 she had participated in civil rights sit-ins in Washington, and she became a political figure in 1965 when Pres. Lyndon B. Johnson appointed her ambassador to Luxembourg. During Pres. Jimmy Carter's administration she served as the secretary of housing and urban development (1977–79) and then as the secretary of health, education, and welfare (1979–80); she continued in the latter post (1980–81) after the department

AP/WIDE WORLD

was renamed health and human services. She was characterized as a resolute administrator and an unwavering proponent of government intervention to solve social problems. Harris later became dean of the law school at Howard University, a post she resigned in 1969. In 1981 she returned to her alma mater as a full-time professor.

Hathaway, Henry (Henri Leopold de Fiennes), U.S. motion picture director (b. March 13, 1898, Sacramento, Calif.—d. Feb. 11, 1985, Los Angeles, Calif.), as a master of suspense, turned out such thrillers as *The House on 92nd Street* (1945), *Kiss of Death* (1947), *Call Northside 777* (1948), and *The Desert Fox* (1951). Hathaway, a child actor in one-reel Westerns directed by Allan Dwan, later became a prop boy and assistant to directors Josef von Sternberg and Victor Fleming. In 1932 he made his debut as a director with a series of low-budget Westerns including *Heritage of the Desert* and *Wild Horse Mesa.* Though he was nominated only once for an Academy Award—for his superb adventure saga *The Lives of a Bengal Lancer* (1935)—Hathaway was highly regarded for his consistently superior craftsmanship. Some of his other motion picture credits in his more than 60 films include *The Black Rose* (1950), *The Sons of Katie Elder* (1965), *Nevada Smith* (1966), and *True Grit* (1969), which earned actor John Wayne his only Oscar.

Hoffmann, Heinz, East German army officer and politician (b. Nov. 28, 1910, Mannheim, Germany—d. Dec. 2, 1985, East Berlin), was from 1960 defense minister of the German Democratic Republic and his country's representative in the supreme command of the Warsaw Treaty Organization. He was instrumental in making the East German Army one of the most reliable in the Warsaw Pact. He was also responsible for the Moscow-prompted building of the Berlin Wall (1961). He was an official in the Communist Youth Organization (1926–30) and joined the German Communist Party in 1930. He immigrated to the U.S.S.R. (1935), where he attended the Internationale Leninschule (1935–37). Hoffmann fought with the International Brigade in the Spanish Civil War but later returned to the U.S.S.R. and fought in World War II. He went to Germany (1946), working for the Sozialistiche Einheitspartei Deutschlands (SED; Socialist Unity Party) in Berlin (1946–49). He was a member of the Volkskammer of the newly formed Democratic Republic from 1950, a member of the SED's Central Committee from 1952, and a member of its politburo from 1973. He served as lieutenant-general of the People's Police and as deputy minister of the interior (1952–55) and as lieutenant-general of the National People's Army (1956–59), becoming minister of defense in 1960. He attained the rank of general in 1961. His memoirs, *Mannheim Madrid Moskau,* were published in 1981.

Hornsby-Smith, (Margaret) Patricia Hornsby-Smith, BARONESS, British politician (b. March 17, 1914, East Sheen, Surrey, England—d. July 3, 1985, London, England), was parliamentary secretary to the Ministry of Health (1951–57) and joint parliamentary under secretary to the Home Office (1957–59) and to the Ministry of Pensions and National Insurance (1959–61). At the time of her first appointment, Hornsby-Smith was the youngest woman ever to hold government office in Britain. She was educated at Richmond County School, and at the age of 17 she showed her interest in politics by working for the Conservatives in the general election of 1931. During World War II she was principal private secretary to the minister of economic warfare and was elected to run the borough council of Barnes in West London (1945). At that time Hornsby-Smith was chairman of the Surrey Young Conservatives. Chosen to contest Chistlehurst in Kent in the 1950 general election, she won the seat from Labour, further increasing her majority in 1951, 1955, and 1959. She lost the seat in 1966 but was reelected in 1970. Following boundary changes that partially merged her constituency with that of Prime Minister Edward Heath, Hornsby-Smith withdrew from the area for the 1974 election, unsuccessfully contesting a Midlands seat instead. Created a Dame of the Order of the British Empire in 1961, she was made a life peer in 1974.

Horrocks, Sir Brian Gwynne, British army officer (b. Sept. 7, 1895, Ranikhet, India—d. Jan. 4, 1985, West Sussex, England), as a corps commander during World War II, used his tactical skill and qualities of leadership to help defeat the Germans in North Africa and Western Europe. The son of a colonel in the Royal Army Medical Corps, Horrocks was educated at Uppingham School and the Royal Military College, Sandhurst. Commissioned in 1914 at the outset of World War I, he was posted to France and taken prisoner. Repatriated in 1918, the following year he took part in the Allied intervention in Russia against the Bolsheviks, was wounded, and was awarded the Military Cross. Horrocks spent the interwar years in England as a staff captain, brigade major, and (from 1938) instructor at the Staff College, Camberley. During April–June 1940 he was a battalion commander and then brigadier in France. In August 1942 Lieut. Gen. Bernard Montgomery, newly appointed to command the 8th Army in the Western Desert, chose Horrocks as commander of the Army's XIII Corps and later of X and IX Corps. For the vital role he played in the defeat of Gen. Erwin Rommel's Afrika Corps, Horrocks, seriously wounded at Tunis as the campaign ended in May 1943, was made a Companion of the Order of the Bath (1945) and of the Distinguished Service Order. After a year in a hospital, in August 1944 he again joined Montgomery, who now headed the British-Canadian 21st Army Group in Normandy, and as commander of XXX Corps was in the forefront of the Allied drive across France and the Low Countries into Germany. After the war Horrocks was appointed commander in chief of the British Army of the Rhine, but he retired early in 1949, still suffering from the effects of his wounds. King George VI then appointed him Gentleman Usher of the Black Rod in the House of Lords, an office he retained until 1963. During the 1950s and '60s Horrocks wrote and presented three television documentary series for the BBC—"Great Captains," "Men of Action," and "Men in Battle"—which enjoyed considerable popularity. His autobiography, *A Full Life,* appeared in 1960 (2nd ed., 1974). He was created a Knight Commander of the Order of the British Empire in 1943.

Hoxha, Enver, Albanian Communist Party leader (b. Oct. 16, 1908, Gjirokaster, Albania—d. April 11, 1985, Tirana, Albania), was for 42 years the dominant personality in his country. After secondary education at the French school at Korce, in 1930 he received a scholarship to

the University of Montpellier, France, which he forfeited a year later for neglecting his studies. Moving to Paris, he joined the French Communist Party and published pseudonymously a series of articles in the party newspaper, *L'Humanité,* attacking King Zog I's reign in Albania. Later he was employed as secretary by the honorary Albanian consul in Brussels, and at the same time he studied law at Brussels University but without graduating. In 1936 Hoxha returned to Albania and became a teacher at his old school at Korce. After the partition of Albania by Germany and Italy in 1941, Hoxha formed under Yugoslav guidance the Albanian (Communist) Party of Labour. In 1943 he was elected secretary-general of its Central Committee by the first party congress. In 1944 Hoxha became prime minister. After World War II

Albania became a Communist republic under Yugoslav protection. In 1946 Hoxha became minister of foreign affairs and minister of defense. He used the enmity between Josip Broz Tito and Joseph Stalin to break with Yugoslavia in 1948, maintaining good relations with the U.S.S.R. until Stalin's death. In 1954 Hoxha relinquished his government posts, reverting to the party first secretaryship. After 1960 Albanian-Soviet relations deteriorated, and by December 1961 all contacts had ceased. Meanwhile, Hoxha sought to strengthen his country's ties with China. However, in 1977 Hoxha castigated the "three worlds" theory put forward by China's new leaders to justify better relations with the U.S., and the following year China ceased its economic and military aid to Albania. During the last decade of Hoxha's tenure in power, there were numerous purges within the party leadership.

Hu Feng, Chinese writer (b. 1903, I-tu, Hupeh [Hubei] Province, China—d. June 8, 1985, China), was a left-wing critic, poet, and essayist who followed Marxist theory in political and social matters but insisted on individual freedom to foster creativity in literature. In the mid-1950s, during the drive against intellectuals, his unorthodox views were squelched; Hu was publicly denounced, stripped of his posts, and imprisoned for several years. He later lived in Sichuan (Szechwan) Province until his rehabilitation in 1981, when he was named to a 200-member committee organized to commemorate the centenary of the birth of his mentor, the writer Lu Hsün (Lu Xun). In the same year, one of Hu's poems was published in *Chinese Literature* magazine.

Hudson, Rock (b. ROY SHERER, JR.; later adopted surname of his stepfather, Wallace Fitzgerald), U.S. actor (b. Nov. 17, 1925, Winnetka, Ill.—d. Oct. 2, 1985, Beverly Hills, Calif.), was a tall, dark, and handsome Hollywood superstar who became a matinee idol with his romantic melodramas of the 1950s and his bubbling sex comedies of the 1960s, many featuring co-star Doris Day. Hudson held a variety of odd jobs before his persistent agent secured him a

small role in *Fighter Squadron* (1948), but it was his performances in two melodramas with Jane Wyman, *Magnificent Obsession* (1954) and *All That Heaven Allows* (1955), that vaulted him to stardom. In 1956 he earned an Academy Award nomination for his role as an imperious Texas rancher in *Giant,* and he starred in *Written on the Wind* (1956) and *The Tarnished Angels* (1957) before exhibiting his flair for comedy in *Pillow Talk* (1959), *Lover Come Back* (1961), *Man's Favorite Sport?* (1963), and *Send Me No Flowers* (1964). Included in his 62 motion picture credits were also the science-fiction thriller *Seconds* (1966), the adventure romp *Ice Station Zebra* (1968), and *Avalanche* (1978). During the 1970s Hudson was best identified with his title role in the romantic mystery television series "McMillan and Wife." His last role as an actor was on television's "Dynasty." Hudson, who was hastily married to his agent's secretary in 1955 when a scandal sheet threatened to expose his homosexuality, was divorced three years later. In July 1985 he made headlines when he flew to Paris seeking experimental treatment for AIDS (acquired immune deficiency syndrome), a disease that primarily afflicts hemophiliacs, drug users, and homosexuals. The implication that he was homosexual and the publicity generated by the disclosure led to an AIDS benefit, which raised more than $1 million, and helped secure an increase in congressional appropriations for AIDS research.

Ingersoll, Ralph McAllister, U.S. journalist, author, and publisher (b. Dec. 8, 1900, New Haven, Conn.—d. March 8, 1985, Miami Beach, Fla.), helped nurture U.S. journalism in the mid-20th century as the first managing editor (1925–30) of *The New Yorker* magazine, as managing editor (1930–35) of *Fortune* magazine, as a founder (1936) of *Life* magazine, and as founder (1940) and editor (until 1946, except during his army service from 1943 to 1945) of *PM,* a New York tabloid, published until 1948, that printed no comics or advertisements. Ingersoll, who earned a degree in mining engineering from Yale University in 1921, spent two years as an engineer before launching his writing career as a reporter for the *New York American.* An intense personality who thrived in the fast-paced publishing industry and took an active interest in the people and events that shaped the news, he provided much of the news coverage in Europe during World War II. Ingersoll was instrumental in executing a secret plan that deceived the Germans into believing the Allied invasion of Europe would take place at Calais instead of the Normandy coast. From the mid-1950s until his semiretirement in 1975, Ingersoll ran a string of small-town newspapers in the northeastern U.S. In 1982 he formally retired from Ingersoll Publications. He was the author of nine books, the best known including *Top Secret* (1946), *The Great Ones* (1948), *Wine of Violence* (1951), and *Point of Departure* (1961), his autobiography.

Jankélévitch, Vladimir, French philosopher (b. 1903, Bourges, France—d. June 6, 1985, Paris, France), adopted a broadly existentialist position in writings characterized by tolerance and a concern with practical questions of morality. As professor at the Sorbonne from 1951 to 1978, he was an inspiring and brilliant lecturer. A man of wide culture, he wrote extensively on music with a profound understanding of the works of Fauré and Debussy, about whom he wrote *Debussy et le mystère de l'instant.* After studying at the École Normale Supérieure, Jankélévitch taught in Prague, Czech., and in Caen, Lyon, and Toulouse, France. He published his first book, a study of the philosopher Henri Bergson, in 1931. During World War II he was wounded (1940) and, because of his Jewish background, was dismissed from the forces by the Vichy regime. He then joined the Resistance. After the liberation he taught at the University of Lille and then at the Sorbonne. Jankélévitch's best known works were reflections on irony and on death; explanations of his views on traditional morality and Marxism; and explorations of the

frontiers of thought, as in *Le je-ne-sais-quoi et le presque-rien* (1957).

Jeans, Isabel, British actress (b. Sept. 16, 1891, London, England—d. Sept. 4, 1985, London), was one of the most admired and most versatile stars of the English theatre during the 1920s and 1930s. She played walk-on parts at His Majesty's Theatre from 1909 to 1913 before being given her first speaking role. Her serious acting career began during a U.S. tour with Harley Granville-Barker's company in 1915–16. In 1919 Jeans played in the musical *Kissing Time* and during the next decade showed her talents in a variety of modern and classical roles, including Zélie in *The Rat* in 1924 and roles by Shakespeare and Shaw. During the 1930s Jeans triumphed in *The Beggar's Opera, Full House,* and *The Happy Hypocrite.* She went briefly to Hollywood but returned to play in Shaw's *Heartbreak House,* in Oscar Wilde's *Lady Windermere's Fan* and *A Woman of No Importance,* and in T. S. Eliot's *The Confidential Clerk.* After taking a ten-year break from the theatre, she resumed her career and appeared in comedies by Wilde, Sheridan, and Anouilh from 1966 until her retirement in 1971. Her films included *Gigi* (1958), and she appeared in a 1955 television production of *The Confidential Clerk.*

Jones, Jo (JONATHAN JONES), U.S. drummer (b. Oct. 7, 1911, Chicago, Ill.—d. Sept. 3, 1985, New York, N.Y.), was the heartbeat of the Count Basie band from 1935 to 1948 and a major innovator who revolutionized jazz percussion with his steady four-beat rhythm on the high-hat cymbal. Jones, also known as Kansas City Jo Jones and Papa Jo Jones, was sometimes confused with jazz drummer Philly Joe Jones. Jones studied piano, saxophone, and trumpet before mastering the drums, and when he joined Basie's band in 1935, he contributed a new light, graceful rhythm to the otherwise heavy jazz beat, shifting the pulse from the bass drum to the high-hat. In 1957 Jones toured Europe with Ella Fitzgerald and Oscar Peterson, and when he returned to the U.S., he led his own combos and performed with such Basie alumni as Buck Clayton, Buddy Tate, and Joe Newman. The influential Jones also appeared in several films, including *Jammin' the Blues* (1944), *The Unsuspected* (1947), *Born to Swing* (1973), and *Last of the Blue Devils* (1979).

Jones, Philly Joe (JOSEPH RUDOLPH JONES), U.S. drummer (b. July 15, 1923, Philadelphia, Pa.—d. Aug. 30, 1985, Philadelphia), was one of the greatest hard bop drummers of all time and gave the influential 1950s Miles Davis quintet its distinctive sound with his combination of deep-toned tom-tom and bass drums with subtle swirls of cross-rhythm on cymbals. After his stint (1952–58) with Davis, Jones worked as a bandleader and a sideman with saxophonists John Coltrane, Johnny Griffin, Art Pepper, and Jackie McLean; trumpeter Lee Morgan; and pianist McCoy Tyner, before living (1967–72) in Europe, where he taught drums. He returned to the U.S. in 1972 and later led his own jazz-rock band, with which he toured the U.S. Jones, who helped make the transition from prewar big band sounds to postwar "cool" jazz, contributed to more than 500 record albums.

Karas, Anton, Austrian musician (b. July 1, 1906, Vienna, Austria—d. Jan. 10, 1985, Vienna), achieved fame through a fortuitous encounter with the British film director Carol Reed, who took him to England to compose a theme song for his film *The Third Man* (1949) after hearing Karas play the zither in a tavern in Vienna's Grinzing district. Karas had trained as a locksmith but found an old zither, took lessons, and soon became an accomplished player. Although he was unaccustomed to composition, his haunting Harry Lime theme music contributed much to the film's great success. Homesick, Karas soon returned to Vienna and acquired his own tavern in Grinzing, where he played regularly to its patrons.

Kerans, John Simon, British naval officer (b. June 30, 1915—d. Sept. 11, 1985, Oxted, Surrey, England), became a national hero in 1949 when the ship HMS *Amethyst* was trapped by the Chinese authorities in the Chang Jiang (Yangtze River) and he managed to sail it down the river and escape to Hong Kong after three months of fruitless negotiation. Kerans was trained at the Royal Naval College, Dartmouth, and had served in China before World War II. After serving as an intelligence officer in Hong Kong, he was transferred to Nanjing (Nanking) in 1949 as naval attaché. When the *Amethyst* was shelled by Communist forces and its commanding officer and 16 other crew members were killed, Kerans went on board to take command of the marooned ship. Although the Chinese authorities allowed food to be delivered, conditions on board were appalling, with the crew suffering from the heat and from rats and mosquitoes. On July 30, after the ship had been camouflaged to make it look like a passenger craft, Kerans piloted the *Amethyst* 225 km (140 mi) down the river and, despite shelling, succeeded in reaching the open sea, where he was able to refuel and eventually make for Hong Kong. For this daring exploit he was made a Companion of the Distinguished Service Order (DSO). He returned to naval intelligence, was retired in 1958, and served as a Conservative member of Parliament (1959–64) and then as a civil servant (1969–80).

Kertész, André, U.S. photographer (b. July 2, 1894, Budapest, Hung.—d. Sept. 27, 1985, New York, N.Y.), as one of the most influential lyrical photojournalists of the century, inspired such photographers as Henri Cartier-Bresson, Robert Capa, and Brassaï with his pioneering use of the small hand-held 35-mm camera. He first gained renown with his black and white pictures, in which he recorded the street life of Paris and Greenwich Village for more than 50 years. Kertész began capturing images while working as a clerk at the Budapest Stock Exchange (1912–14), and during World War I he photographed his comrades while serving in the Hungarian Army until he was severely wounded. Many of his photographs were lost during the 1918 Hungarian Revolution. In 1925 he went to Paris to work as a free-lance photographer for such European magazines as *Vu, Art et Médecine,* the London *Sunday Times,* and *UHU.* His work received critical acclaim, and he held his first one-man show in 1927. In 1936 he accepted a position in the U.S. working for Keystone Studios in New York City. When World War II broke out he was unable to return to Europe, and he began (1937) accepting commercial (largely fashion) photography assignments for such magazines as *Look, Harper's Bazaar, Vogue,* and *Town and Country.* He became a U.S. citizen in 1944. It was not until late in his life, though, that he again began (1963) devoting himself to personal creative photography and earned the recognition he had eagerly sought for decades. Kertész, who worked in a variety of modes including portraits, still lifes, the distortion nude, and photo reportage, consistently captured the essence of the moment. Some of his most famous photographs, including "Sur le Quai de la Seine" (1926), "Satiric Dancer" (1926), "Meudon, France" (1928), "Relaxation" (1943), and "West 23rd Street" (1970), were showcased in such books as *Day of Paris* (1945), *Andre Kertész: Sixty Years of Photography* (1972), and *Distortions* (1976). A major exhibition of his work by the Metropolitan Museum of Art opened in December 1985.

Kimball, Spencer W., U.S. religious leader (b. March 28, 1895, Salt Lake City, Utah—d. Nov. 5, 1985, Salt Lake City), as the 12th "prophet, seer and revelator" of the 5.8 million-member Church of Jesus Christ of Latter-day Saints, the Mormons, instituted such momentous changes as allowing blacks to hold the Mormon priesthood (a decree that struck down the church's 148-year-old policy excluding black men from full participation in the church), retiring elderly church leaders, adding the first non-Americans to the modern church hierarchy, and consolidating all Sunday church meetings into a three-hour block. Kimball, the son of a missionary, was an Arizona banker and insurance executive before serving as a high-ranking spiritual leader and church administrator. Kimball acceded to the First Presidency of the Mormon Church on Dec. 30, 1973, and his appointment was approved by a symbolic raising of hands of thousands of Mormons at a meeting in Salt Lake City on April 6, 1974. During Kimball's 12-year ministry, the Mormon church nearly doubled its membership, 51 missions were created overseas, 968 new stakes (or dioceses) were founded, and the number of church temples increased from 16 to 31. Despite ill health since 1957, and his infirmity and frailty in his final years, Kimball's boundless energy served as an inspiration to millions who were propelled to greater efforts by embracing his motto, "Lengthen your stride."

Knight, G(eorge Richard) Wilson, British literary critic (b. Sept. 19, 1897, Sutton, Surrey, England—d. March 20, 1985, Exeter, Devon, England), achieved distinction as a Shakespearean scholar whose own experience in the theatre as an actor, producer, and dramatist gave him a particularly keen insight into the theatrical dimension of Shakespeare's work. He was professor (1931–40) at the University of Toronto and, during 1946–62, reader and then professor of English at the University of Leeds. He studied at St. Edmund Hall, University of Oxford, making his name with such works as *Myth and Miracle* (1929), *The Wheel of Fire* (1930), and *Principles of Shakespearian Production* (1936). His approach to literature was original, even eccentric, with its emphasis on the spiritual and magical dimensions of the writer's craft. He was particularly attracted to the figure of the writer John Cowper Powys and wrote two exceptional studies of Byron—*Lord Byron: Christian Virtues* (1952) and *Lord Byron's Marriage* (1957). His many other published works included a biography of his brother, the classical scholar W. Jackson Knight.

Koopmans, Tjalling Charles, Dutch-born economist (b. Aug. 28, 1910, 's-Graveland, Neth.—d. Feb. 26, 1985, New Haven, Conn.), was a scholarly theoretician who in 1975 shared the Nobel Prize for Economics with Leonid Kantorovich of the Soviet Union for their contributions to the theory of optimum allocation of resources. Koopmans and Kantorovich independently developed what became known as activity analysis (a method for allocating resources in such a way that a given economic objective was achieved at the lowest cost); the system had practical importance to both collective and free-enterprise economic systems. Koopmans was educated in The Netherlands at the universities of Utrecht and Leiden; he received a Ph.D. in economics at the latter in 1936. Four years later he settled in the U.S., working for the British Merchant Shipping Mission and the Combined Shipping Adjustment Board in Washington, where he devised a system of equations that minimized the total cost of transporting goods from various ports in the U.S. to specified destinations in Britain. After World War II Koopmans joined the Cowles Commission for Research in Economics at the University of Chicago. When the commission was moved to Yale University in 1955 and renamed the Cowles Foundation for Research in Economics, he became professor of economics at Yale; he was director of the foundation from 1961 to 1967, when he became Alfred Cowles professor of economics. He also extended his studies and became one of the originators of econometrics, the statistical and mathematical analysis of economic relationships. Koopmans also wrote a widely read book on the methodology of economic analysis, *Three Essays on the State of Economic Science* (1957). He retired from Yale in 1981 and thereafter was professor emeritus.

Kuznets, Simon (Smith), Ukrainian-born economist (b. April 30, 1901, Kharkov, Ukraine—d. July 8, 1985, Cambridge, Mass.), won the 1971 Nobel Prize for Economics for his use of sophisticated statistical analysis to compute the gross national product (GNP), total market value of the final goods and services produced by a nation's economy during a specific period of time, computed before allowance is made for the depreciation or consumption of capital used in the process of production. Kuznets immigrated to the U.S. in 1922 and earned his Ph.D. from Columbia University, New York City, in 1926. He then worked as a fellow of the Social Science Research Council before joining the staff of the National Bureau of Economics, where he conducted pioneering studies of business cycles. From 1930 to 1954 he taught at the University of Pennsylvania, with an interruption during World War II to serve as associate director of the War Production Board's Bureau of Planning and Statistics. In 1954 he moved to Johns Hopkins University, Baltimore, Md., and six years later he joined the faculty at Harvard University, where he served as George F. Baker professor of economics until his retirement in 1971. Kuznets's extensive research on the economic growth of nations was detailed in his classic two-volume work, *National Income and Its Composition, 1919 to 1938*, which was published in 1941 and ushered in the era of quantitative economics.

Kyser, Kay (JAMES KING KERN KYSER), U.S. radio and film personality (b. June 18, 1906, Rocky Mount, N.C.—d. July 23, 1985, Chapel Hill, N.C.), delighted radio listeners as the amiable host of "Kay Kyser's Kollege of Musical Knowledge" (1938–49), which featured a blend of swing music, comedy routines, and quiz questions for contestants, who could earn cash for answering the "kollege brainbuster question." Kyser graduated from the University of North Carolina in 1928 and became a hit when he and his band started broadcasting from the Blackhawk in Chicago in 1933. Though he never learned to read music or play an instrument, Kyser became a star as the host and self-styled "old professor," who donned academic cap and gown to enhance the "kollege" theme. Kyser's band enjoyed fame with such hits as "Three Little Fishes," "Praise the Lord and Pass the Ammunition," and "Who Wouldn't Love You?"; one of its members, the trumpeter Merwyn Bogue, became especially popular with his novelty songs, his comic haircut (bangs), and the unforgettable stage name Ish Kabibble. Kyser's 60-minute variety show premiered in 1938, was trimmed to 30 minutes in 1946, and was last heard in 1949. At the height of his popularity, Kyser starred in several Hollywood films. After his retirement, Kyser became a teacher and practitioner of Christian Science, and his trademark down-home style ensured his popularity on the lecture circuit.

La Guma, Alex (JUSTIN ALEXANDER LA GUMA), South African writer (b. Feb. 20, 1925, Cape Town, South Africa—d. Oct. 11, 1985, Havana, Cuba), found in the oppression of the black man in his native country the material for a bleak vision of the plight of individuals in society; but despite its universal implications, his work had a clear political message. Educated at the Cape Technical College and at the London School of Journalism, he worked at various jobs and was already politically active when the writer Ulli Beier discovered the manuscript of his first short novel, *A Walk in the Night* (1962). This was published in Nigeria by Beier's Mbari Press and was followed by short stories and such novels as *And a Threefold Cord* (1964) and *The Stone Country* (1967). Meanwhile, La Guma had been twice detained in solitary confinement and in 1966 left South Africa to live in London, then in Cuba, where he represented the African National Congress. He was a member of the editorial board of the Afro-Asian Writers' Bureau and deputy secretary-general of the Afro-Asian Writers' Association. His work, banned

in South Africa, drew on his experiences in the townships and in prison and achieved a visionary quality with *Time of the Butcherbird* (1979). He won the Afro-Asian Lotus Award in 1969.

Lander, Toni, Danish ballerina (b. June 19, 1931, Gentofte, Den.—d. May 19, 1985, Salt Lake City, Utah), achieved international fame as a dancer with the American Ballet Theatre, the London Festival Ballet, and the Royal Danish Ballet. Probably her finest and most exacting role was in Harald Lander's *Études*. Born Toni Petersen, she entered the Royal Danish Ballet School (1939) and made her debut (1947) in August Bournonville's *The King's Volunteers of Amager*. She danced her first solo role in 1950, the same year she married the Danish choreographer Harald Lander. In 1951 the Landers left the Royal Danish Ballet, and Toni Lander performed with the Paris Opéra. She was a soloist with the Original Ballet Russe in London (1951–52) and starred in the London Festival Ballet (1952 and 1954–59). Lander was with the Grand Ballet du Marquis de Cuevas (1953)

FRED FEHL

and created (1958) the leading role in John Taras's version of Françoise Sagan's *Le Rendez-vous manqué*. She was a leading dancer with the American Ballet Theatre (1960–71) and returned to the Royal Danish Ballet (1971–76) as dancer and teacher, making her farewell performance in *The Moor's Pavane*. After a divorce from Lander, she married (1966) the American dancer Bruce Marks. In 1976 Lander and Marks joined Ballet West in Salt Lake City, Utah, where Lander was appointed principal teacher, and Marks served as artistic director. Just several months before she died, Lander mounted a reconstruction of the 1855 Bournonville ballet *Abdallah* for Ballet West.

Langer, Susanne Knauth, U.S. philosopher and educator (b. Dec. 20, 1895, New York, N.Y.—d. July 17, 1985, Old Lyme, Conn.), assigned unprecedented importance to signs, symbols, and feelings in her philosophical approach to such things as language, art, and psychoanalysis. In *Philosophy in a New Key: A Study in the Symbolism of Reason, Rite, and Art* (1942), she rejected the premise that language is the only means of articulating thought and that everything that is not speakable thought is feeling. After earning a Ph.D. (1926) from Harvard University, she served as a tutor in the philosophy department from 1927 to 1942. She also taught philosophy (1954–62) at Connecticut College in New London. As an undergraduate at Radcliffe College, Cambridge, Mass., she had studied under the noted philosopher Alfred North Whitehead and was deeply influenced by him, as well as by the philosopher Ernst Cassirer. Langer recorded her views in such books as *The Practice of Philosophy* (1930), *Feeling and Form* (1953), and her three-volume opus *Mind: An Essay on Human Feeling* (1967, 1972, 1982).

Larkin, Philip Arthur, British poet (b. Aug. 9, 1922, Coventry, Warwickshire, England—d. Dec. 2, 1985, Hull, England), produced only five small collections of poetry but became recognized by critics as perhaps the most gifted living English poet and as a result enjoyed considerable popularity. He was educated at King Henry VIII School, Coventry, and at St. John's College, Oxford, where he gained a first-class degree in English language and literature (1943). He worked as a librarian throughout his adult life, at Wellington in Shropshire (1944–46), at the University College of Leicester (1946–50), at the Queen's University of Belfast (1950–55), and from 1955 at the Brynmor Jones Library, University of Hull. His first two volumes of poems, *The North Ship* (1945) and *XX Poems* (1951), were printed at his own expense, as were his novels *Jill* (1946) and *A Girl in Winter* (1947). The poems in *The Less Deceived* (1955) were the first to receive interested notice from some critics; *The Whitsun Weddings* (1964) had much greater success, while his collection *High Windows* (1974) sold 6,000 copies in only three weeks. He won the Queen's Gold Medal for Poetry (1965) and in that year was asked to edit *The Oxford Book of Twentieth Century Verse* (1973). Unmarried, and shunning publicity, he was nevertheless able to express what many felt but could not themselves say. Another of his interests was jazz; his critical pieces written for the *Daily Telegraph* in the 1960s were collected in *All What Jazz* (1970). He published a book of essays, *Required Writing*, in 1983. Larkin, who many had expected would succeed Sir John Betjeman as poet laureate, was made a Companion of Honour in 1985.

Lehmann, Hermann, German-born British biochemist (b. July 8, 1910, Dresden, Germany—d. July 13, 1985, Cambridge, England), was professor of clinical biochemistry at the University of Cambridge from 1967 to 1977 and made important contributions to the study of hemoglobins. Educated in Germany and Switzerland, he conducted research in biochemistry in Heidelberg (1934–36) and at Cambridge (1936–42). During World War II he served with the Royal Army Medical Corps and, after two years of research in Uganda, became reader in chemical pathology at the University of London. Lehmann specialized in the study of abnormal hemoglobins, with particular attention to their genetic aspects. His work led to the discovery of different types of hemoglobin and to a better understanding of genetically inherited abnormalities, notably in human anemia. In 1963 he was appointed university biochemist at Addenbrooke's Hospital, Cambridge, and was made honorary director of a special unit for research into abnormal hemoglobins. He was joint author of *Man's Haemoglobins* (1966) and of *Human Haemoglobin Variants and Their Characteristics* (1976). From 1972 he was a member of the Royal Society, and in 1980 he was appointed Commander of the Order of the British Empire.

Lewis, Saunders, Welsh poet and playwright (b. Oct. 15, 1893, Wallasey, England—d. Sept. 1, 1985, Cardiff, Wales), was an outstanding figure in modern Welsh literature and a founder-member of the Welsh Nationalist Party (Plaid Cymru). Lewis's literary and political activities gave him a unique status in Welsh cultural life. His radio broadcast *Tynged yr Iaith* ("The Fate of the Language," 1962) inspired the founders of Cymdeithas yr Iaith Gymraeg, the militant Welsh language society, and his insistence that "the language is more important than self-government" did much to determine the course of the struggle for a national identity in his country. But as a Catholic whose best work was written in dramatic form, he was an exception in a traditionally Nonconformist culture in which poetry was the dominant literary form. The son of a Nonconformist minister, Lewis studied at the University of Liverpool and served in France during World War I. He was a founder and president (1925–35) of the Welsh Nationalist Party but steered it away

from the Fascist tendencies evident elsewhere in Europe, outlining his beliefs in *Principles of Nationalism* (1926). In 1936 he was involved with D. J. Williams and the Rev. Lewis Valentine in an arson attack on a Royal Air Force bombing range. After giving themselves up, the three were tried in Caernarvon, then, when the jury failed to reach a verdict, at a second trial in London, where they were sentenced to nine months' imprisonment. Lewis lost his post as lecturer in Swansea and, under the patronage of BBC Wales, turned to writing and plays. His works, including *Gymerwch chi sigaret?* (1956), *Siwan a Cherddi Eraill* (1956), *Brad* (1958), and *Esther* (1960), dealt with such themes as medieval legend, religious history, and contemporary literature, emphasizing the influence of European literature, especially the drama of ideas. His works were translated into several languages and helped establish the basis of the modern Welsh dramatic repertory. Lewis also wrote two novels and some notable poetry. He worked as a school inspector until reappointed to a university post in 1952.

Lightwood, Reginald, British pediatrician (b. Jan. 28, 1898, Croydon, Surrey, England—d. May 26, 1985, Ticehurst, Sussex, England), was largely responsible for the establishment of pediatrics as an important branch of medicine in Britain. He achieved an international reputation for his work. He was educated at Monckton Coombe School, Bath, served in the Royal Artillery during World War I, and then studied medicine at King's College Hospital, London. After becoming a physician in 1924, he worked as a general practitioner for three years before being elected (1933) to the honorary staff at the Westminster Hospital, London, and (1935) serving as honorary consultant at the Hospital for Sick Children, Great Ormond Street, London. Lightwood was appointed (1939) the first honorary consultant pediatrician to St. Mary's Hospital, London, and during World War II he worked in a number of outer London hospitals. When the National Health Service was established in 1948, he realized the urgent need to train more pediatricians and helped to establish the seminal Academic Unit of Paediatrics at St. Mary's Medical School. After his retirement (1963) he held posts abroad—in Beirut, Lebanon (1964–65), Rhodesia (1966–69), Los Angeles, Calif. (1969), and Newfoundland (1970–71). With Wilfrid Gaisford he edited *Paediatrics for the Practitioner* (1953); earlier he had taken over authorship and continued to produce new editions of Donald Paterson's textbook *Sick Children.*

Littler, Sir Emile, British theatrical producer and impresario (b. Sept. 9, 1903, Ramsgate, Kent, England—d. Jan. 23, 1985, Ditchling, Sussex, England), during his career put on more than 200 pantomimes in London and the provinces and achieved outstanding successes with such productions as *The Song of Norway* (1945), *Lilac Time* (1949), and *Zip Goes a Million* (1951). He was born into a family connected with theatrical management, was educated at Stratford-on-Avon, and first worked at the Royal Artillery Theatre, Woolwich, which was run by his parents. In 1922 he became an assistant stage manager at Southend-on-Sea, but in 1925 he moved to the Birmingham Repertory Theatre. After working in the U.S. (1927–31) for the Shubert brothers and Charles Hopkins, he returned to the Birmingham theatre as manager and licensee. From 1934 he worked independently, staging pantomimes and organizing provincial tours of successful London productions. During World War II Littler staged revivals at the London Coliseum of a number of musical comedies, including *The Maid of the Mountains* (1942) and *The Quaker Girl* (1944), as well as mounting many original productions, such as *Claudia* (1942). At the London Casino Littler produced (1947) a British-cast version of *Annie Get Your Gun,* and in 1958 he staged Eugene O'Neill's *The Iceman Cometh* (1958). He was knighted in 1974.

Lodge, Henry Cabot, U.S. politician and diplomat (b. July 5, 1902, Nahant, Mass.—d. Feb. 27, 1985, Beverly, Mass.), was a Boston aristocrat who served (1937–44 and 1947–53) as a three-term Republican senator from Massachusetts, as longtime delegate to the UN (1953–60) during the cold war, and as ambassador to South Vietnam (1963–64 and 1965–67). Lodge, whose patrician family boasted six U.S. senators, a governor of Massachusetts, a secretary of state, and a secretary of the navy, graduated cum laude from Harvard University in 1924. In 1932 he was elected to the lower chamber of the Massachusetts state legislature, and four years later he was elected to the U.S. Senate. He resigned from the Senate in 1944 to serve in the Army and was later reelected. As a senator, Lodge was immensely proud of his sponsorship of the Lodge-Brown Act, legislation that led to the formation of the Hoover Commission, which scrutinized the operations of the executive branch of the government and resulted in savings in excess of $3 billion. Like his grandfather, Sen. Henry Cabot Lodge (1850–1924), he was an iso-

AP/WIDE WORLD

lationist but, following the outbreak of World War II, Lodge broke with family tradition and became an internationalist. In 1952 Lodge lost his Senate seat to John F. Kennedy, presumably because he was so active in promoting Dwight D. Eisenhower's presidential campaign. The following year Eisenhower rewarded Lodge with a permanent UN post. There he earned a reputation for toughness in confrontations with the Soviets. During a UN Security Council debate concerning an American U-2 intelligence plane that was shot down over the U.S.S.R., Lodge created a sensation when he disclosed that the Soviets had bugged a plaque—a gift to the U.S. ambassador—that had hung for years in the U.S. embassy in Moscow. Lodge held his UN post longer than any other U.S. delegate—for seven years and eight months. In 1960 Lodge ran unsuccessfully as Richard M. Nixon's vice-presidential running mate. John F. Kennedy won the election, and he shrewdly appointed Lodge ambassador to South Vietnam to maintain Republican support for U.S. policy there. He was later ambassador to West Germany (1968–69), chief negotiator at the talks in Paris on peace in Vietnam (1969), and special envoy to the Vatican (1970–77). His books include *Cult of Weakness* (1932), *The Storm Has Many Eyes* (1973), and *As It Was* (1976).

Lon Nol, Kampuchean army officer and politician (b. Nov. 13, 1913, Kampong Leon, Prey Veng Province, Cambodia—d. Nov. 17, 1985, Fullerton, Calif.), was a prime architect of the March 1970 coup that overthrew Prince Norodom Sihanouk and from then until 1975 was one of his country's most prominent leaders, serving as premier (until 1972) and then as president of the Khmer Republic (1972–75). Educated at Chasseloup Laubat High School in Saigon, Vietnam, and at the Cambodian Royal Military Academy, he entered the French colonial service (1937), becoming a magistrate, then

governor of Kratie Province (1945) and head of the national police (1951). He joined the Army (1952) and fought against the insurgent Viet Minh as an area commander. He was governor of Battambang Province (1954) and became army chief of staff (1955) and commander in chief (1960) under the premiership of Sihanouk. He was deputy premier (1963) and premier (1966–67), resigning because of injury in an automobile crash. He returned to the Cabinet as minister of defense (1968) and one year later regained the premiership. Lon Nol's five years of U.S.-aided ascendancy (sharing real power in an uncertain degree with Prince Sisowath Sirik Matak and with Long Boret) was an unhappy period for his country; the Vietnam war increasingly impinged on Cambodian territory, with consequent economic collapse and internal unrest. He finally left Cambodia (April 1, 1975) and doomed a U.S. attempt to establish in Phnom Penh a regime that could negotiate with the approaching Khmer Rouge forces. He lived first in Hawaii but moved to California in 1979.

London, George (GEORGE BURNSTEIN), Canadian-born opera singer (b. May 30, 1920, Montreal—d. March 24, 1985, Armonk, N.Y.), used his rich and sonorous bass-baritone voice together with his commanding stage presence to convey the malevolence of Mephistopheles in *Faust* and Scarpia in *Tosca* and to portray Boris Godunov and Don Giovanni in the operas of the same name. He was the son of Russian-American parents. He made his U.S. debut in *La Traviata* at the Hollywood Bowl in 1942. After touring in 1947 with Mario Lanza and Frances Yeend as the Bel Canto Trio, London made his European opera debut in 1949 with the Vienna State Opera as Amonasro in *Aida.* He also won critical acclaim for his debuts at the Metropolitan Opera in 1951 as Amonasro and at La Scala in 1952 as Pizarro in *Fidelio.* London, who was best known for his roles in works by Mozart (*The Marriage of Figaro*), Wagner (*The Ring*), and Mussorgsky (*Boris Godunov*), in 1960 became the first American to perform Boris at Moscow's Bolshoi Theatre. In 1967 his career was cut short by a paralyzed vocal cord, and in the following year he was named music administrator of the John F. Kennedy Center for the Performing Arts in Washington, D.C. He was serving as general director of the Washington Opera when a heart attack left him disabled in 1977.

Longowal, Sant Harchand Singh, Indian Sikh priest (b. 1928, Laungowal, Punjab, India—d. Aug. 20, 1985, Sherpur, Punjab), as a moderate leader of the Sikh political party, the Akali Dal, was assassinated by Sikh extremists resentful that he had signed an agreement with India's Prime Minister Rajiv Gandhi. Agitation for Sikh autonomy in the Punjab had built up through the 1980s, culminating (1984) in the storming by Indian troops of the Sikhs' Golden Temple

PATRICE HABANS—SYGMA

at Amritsar and the consequent assassination by Sikhs of Prime Minister Indira Gandhi. After Amritsar, Longowal surrendered to the Indian Army and was imprisoned until July 1985, when he signed a memorandum of settlement, by which the Indian government met most of the Sikh demands and the question of autonomy was referred to a commission. In return, Longowal agreed that elections should be held in September 1985. He was supported by 80% of his followers but was felt by extremists to have betrayed their cause. Joining the Akali Dal in 1944, Longowal adopted Mahatma Gandhi's tactics of nonviolent civil disobedience and was several times arrested during peaceful protests in the 1950s and 1960s. He became president (1964) of his local Akali Dal branch and in 1980, as a compromise candidate, president of the party. He launched a civil disobedience campaign (1982) but was hindered by the activities of the extremists, notably of Jarnail Singh Bhindranwale, who was killed in the Golden Temple battle.

López Bravo, Gregorio, Spanish politician (b. Dec. 19, 1923, Madrid, Spain—d. Feb. 19, 1985, near Bilbao, Spain), played an important government role as minister of industry (1962–69) and foreign minister (1969–73) during the later years of Gen. Francisco Franco's dictatorship. After studying naval architecture in both Spain and the U.S., López Bravo quickly made his mark in shipbuilding and by the age of 30 had become a director of two shipyards in northern Spain. Favouring contemporary European, rather than Falangist, theories of management, he became useful to the government when Franco was seeking to adopt a less doctrinaire stance. He was appointed director general of the Department of Trade (1959) within the Ministry of Commerce, moving (1960) to become head of the Institute of Foreign Currency in the Ministry of Finance. As minister of industry (1962) with a seat in the Cabinet, he encouraged private investment, which prompted speedy economic growth. In foreign affairs López Bravo continued established policies, attempting to increase Spain's trading links with the European Communities, the U.S.S.R. and Eastern Europe, Latin America, and the Arab states. His dismissal (1973) followed his failure to extract from Britain any promises regarding the future status of Gibraltar. He returned to private industry but after Franco's death (1975) was a member (1977–79) of the Cortes (parliament) elected under the Political Reform Law. He was killed in an air crash.

Lule, Yusufu Kirolde, Ugandan academic and politician (b. April 10, 1912, Kampala, Buganda, Uganda—d. Jan. 21, 1985, London, England), became president of Uganda in 1979 after the downfall of Pres. Idi Amin but held office for less than ten weeks. A graduate of Fort Hare University College, South Africa, and of the University of Edinburgh, Scotland, Lule became the first African lecturer at Makerere University College, Uganda. From 1955 he was one of three African ministers in the colonial government, and in 1962 he became chairman of the Uganda Public Service Commission. In 1964 he became principal at Makerere, by then a constituent college of the University of East Africa. In 1970 Makerere became an independent university under the direct control of Pres. Milton Obote, with whom Lule had political differences. Lule left Uganda for England, where he served as assistant secretary-general in charge of education on the Commonwealth Secretariat for two years. He then spent seven years as secretary-general of the Association of African Universities. In March 1979 he became the head of the Uganda National Liberation Front, a coalition of forces opposed to Ugandan dictator Idi Amin. Following the Tanzanian-backed invasion of Uganda and Amin's overthrow, Lule was chosen to lead a provisional administration. Sworn in as president on April 13, he soon encountered difficulties because of his refusal to include supporters of Obote in his government

and his failure to consult with others. After a vote of no confidence by the National Consultative Council, he resigned and was replaced on June 20 by Godfrey L. Binaisa. He returned to exile in London. After Obote became president again in December 1980, Lule was an outspoken opponent of Obote's government. In 1981 he became chairman of the National Resistance Movement, the political wing of the National Resistance Army, which was engaged in guerrilla operations in Uganda.

Lyons, Sir William, British industrialist (b. Sept. 4, 1901, Blackpool, England—d. Feb. 8, 1985, Wappenbury, Warwickshire, England), as inventor and producer of Jaguar cars made a notable contribution to automobile development in Britain. He was the son of a piano dealer. He began (1922) to manufacture sidecars for motorcycles, and his "Swallow Sidecars" proved so successful that he soon also produced coachwork for automobiles and brought out his own first car, the "SS" (Swallow Sports), in 1931. He launched (1933) SS Cars Ltd., which went public in 1935, the year in which the name Jaguar was first used. The company's name was changed to Jaguar Cars Ltd. in 1945, and it soon achieved major export successes, notably with its XK120, 140, and 150 models. During the 1950s Jaguar entered sports-car racing, winning the Le Mans 24-hour race five times. By 1959 the annual production topped 20,000, and in 1961 the E-type and Mark X models were introduced. Despite well-planned expansion (Lyons acquired companies such as Daimler and Coventry Climax Engines during the early 1960s), Jaguar was obliged (1966) to merge with the British Motor Corporation (the Austin-Morris group). Although Lyons regretted the subsequent amalgamation into British Leyland (1968), he remained on the board, concerning himself with Jaguar cars and introducing the XJ saloon range. He officially retired in 1972 but remained honorary president of Jaguar. In 1984 he saw the company returned to the private sector. British Leyland was taken under government control in 1975. Lyons was knighted in 1956.

MacInnes, Helen Clark, U.S. novelist (b. Oct. 7, 1907, Glasgow, Scotland—d. Sept. 30, 1985, New York, N.Y.), was dubbed "the queen of international intrigue" as the best-selling author of 21 spy novels, notably *Above Suspicion* (1941), *Assignment in Brittany* (1942), *The Venetian Affair* (1963), and *The Salzburg Connection* (1968), all of which were made into motion pictures. While on her honeymoon in Bavaria with Gilbert Highet, a classics scholar, the couple encountered Nazi activities; her observations became her inspiration for a series of books featuring honest, sensitive individuals who combated Communists and Nazis. Her tried-and-true formula mixed suspense, espionage, and romance. Her books, which sold more than 23 million copies in the U.S. alone, were translated into 22 languages. Her last novel, *Ride a Pale Horse,* appeared in 1984.

McKell, Sir William John, Australian politician (b. Sept. 26, 1891, Pambula, New South Wales, Australia—d. Jan. 11, 1985, Sydney, New South Wales, Australia), served as governor-general (1947–53) of Australia and premier (1941–47) of New South Wales (NSW). At age 13 McKell became a dockyard apprentice and later was an official of the Boilermaker's Union before entering politics. He became a Labor Party member of the NSW legislative assembly in 1917 and served as minister of justice (1920–22) in the state government. He then studied law, was admitted to the NSW bar in 1925, and became a king's counsel in 1945. McKell was a member of the NSW Labor governments of 1925–27 and 1930–32 and was elected party leader in 1939 during Labor's seven years in opposition. He became premier when Labor won the 1941 election and remained in office when his government was returned in 1944. McKell's appointment as governor-general while an ac-

tive politician was controversial, but he always maintained the strict impartiality that befitted the monarch's representative in Australia. In private life McKell, a keen footballer and boxer in his youth, was a successful sheep farmer. He was knighted in 1951.

Maltz, Albert, U.S. screenwriter (b. Oct. 28, 1908, Brooklyn, N.Y.—d. April 26, 1985, Los Angeles, Calif.), won two Academy Awards for the documentary films *Moscow Strikes Back* (1942; an adaptation of the Soviet war propaganda film *The Defeat of the German Armies near Moscow*) and *The House I Live In* (1945) before gaining notoriety as one of the Hollywood Ten (one producer-director-writer, one producer-writer, one director, and seven screenwriters), who refused to answer questions posed to them by the House Committee on Un-American Activities. The ten were convicted of contempt of Congress, fined $1,000, given one-year prison sentences, and, after their release, blacklisted by the U.S. motion picture industry. Maltz also wrote the classic thriller *This Gun for Hire* (1942), such patriotic films as *Destination Tokyo* (1944) and *Pride of the Marines* (1945), and *The Naked City* (1948), the last film credited to him before his blacklisting. After his release from prison, Maltz lived in Mexico until 1962 and wrote U.S. films under pseudonyms. When the blacklisting was ending in the early 1960s, he returned to Hollywood and resumed his work under his own name. His most recent works included *Two Mules for Sister Sara* (1970) and *Scalawag* (1973). His short story "The Happiest Man on Earth" won the O. Henry Memorial Prize in 1938.

Maris, Roger Eugene, U.S. baseball player (b. Sept. 10, 1934, Hibbing, Minn.—d. Dec. 14, 1985, Houston, Texas), was an exceptional defensive outfielder and a powerful hitter who in 1961 surpassed Babe Ruth's 1927 season home run record of 60 by slamming 61 homers for the New York Yankees; because Maris's one-season total was accumulated during a 162-game schedule and Ruth's was accrued during a 154-game season, the baseball commissioner, Ford C. Frick, ruled that Maris had not broken Ruth's record. Maris earned an asterisk in the record books and was booed roundly by Yankee fans who would have preferred Mickey Mantle to accomplish the feat. Maris broke into the major leagues with the Cleveland Indians in 1957 and was traded to the Kansas City Athletics in 1958. He joined the New York Yankees in 1960 and was awarded the most valuable player award for the American League in 1960 and 1961. Maris appeared in seven World Series and played with the St. Louis Cardinals in 1967 and 1968 before retiring with 275 home runs, 851 runs batted in, and a lifetime batting average of .260.

Marks, Johnny, U.S. composer (b. Nov. 10, 1909, Mount Vernon, N.Y.—d. Sept. 3, 1985, New York, N.Y.), was the prolific writer of 175 published tunes but was best known for the Christmas classic "Rudolph the Red-Nosed Reindeer," first performed by singer Gene Autry (1949). He also wrote such all-time favourites as "I Heard the Bells on Christmas Day" (1956, Bing Crosby), "Rockin' Around the Christmas Tree" (1960, Brenda Lee), and "A Holly, Jolly Christmas" (1963, Burl Ives). Marks began writing songs at the age of 13 but did not become a professional songwriter until 1935, after graduating with a B.A. from Colgate University and studying music in Paris. Some of his other songs included "Address Unknown," "Who Calls?," "She'll Always Remember," and "Don't Cross Your Fingers, Cross Your Heart," but "Rudolph the Red-Nosed Reindeer" assured his immortality with sales of more than 150 million records and 8 million sheet-music copies.

Marriott, J(ohn) Willard, U.S. hotelier (b. Sept. 17, 1900, Marriott, Utah—d. Aug. 13, 1985, Wolfeboro, N.H.), parlayed his nine-stool Washington, D.C., root beer stand into a food and

lodging empire that boasted an airline-catering service, 143 hotels, and some 1,400 restaurants worldwide. Marriott, who graduated from the University of Utah in 1926, opened his first stand, the Hot Shoppe (1927), after his father's fledgling sheep business went bankrupt. By 1932 Marriott was operating seven Hot Shoppes in Washington and had begun expanding outside the capital. In 1957 he opened his first motel, the Marriott Twin Bridges Motor Hotel in Washington, and ten years later the Hot Shoppes Corp. became the Marriott Corp., with widespread chains of restaurants (primarily Big Boy and Roy Rogers), hotels and resorts in 95 cities, and 90 flight kitchens serving 150 airlines worldwide. Marriott, a devout Mormon, was also known for his support of the Republican Party. In 1972 Marriott turned over active management of the company to his first son, J. Willard, Jr., but at the time of his death he was still serving as chairman of the board of the Marriott Corp., which had sales totaling over $3.5 billion in 1984.

Martin, John Joseph, U.S. dance critic (b. June 2, 1893, Louisville, Ky.—d. May 19, 1985, Saratoga, N.Y.), fostered the development of modern dance in the U.S. by promoting the new art form's importance in his dance critiques for the *New York Times* (1927–62) and later also became a leading exponent of U.S. ballet. Martin, who had an abiding love for theatre, was active in Chicago's Little Theatre before directing the Chautauqua Theater at Swarthmore, Pa. When he was given the job of dance critic for the *New York Times,* he had the distinction of being the first critic to write full-time on dance for a major U.S. publication. He was able to exert a profound influence on dance because of his unique position. Martin, who was considered the dean of U.S. dance critics, was widely quoted for his precept that "the modern dance is not a system, it is a point of view." Some ballet enthusiasts took Martin to task for championing modern dance and neglecting ballet, but in 1939 he set forth a course to renew the essence of ballet, urging choreographers to concentrate on the dance element as "an end in itself," rather than on the art form's athletic or dramatic potentialities. His suggestions were realized most eloquently in the plotless neoclassical works of George Balanchine. Some of Martin's books included *The Modern Dance* (1933), *Introduction to the Dance* (1939), and *World Book of Modern Ballet* (1952). After his retirement from the *New York Times* he became lecturer in dance at the University of California at Los Angeles.

Mayer, Sir Robert, German-born British philanthropist and centenarian (b. June 5, 1879, Mannheim, Germany—d. Jan. 9, 1985, London, England), as a profound lover of music used the fortune he accumulated to promote concerts for children. Educated at the Mannheim Conservatoire, he went to England when his father moved there in the 1890s. Mayer was naturalized, and he traded in nonferrous metals both in London and in the U.S. and was already wealthy at the outbreak of World War I, during which he served in the British Army. Mayer, impressed by concerts given in the U.S. by Walter Damrosch, founded (1923), together with his wife, the soprano Dorothy Moulton, the Robert Mayer Children's Concerts. These were given in provincial centres as well as in London and continued annually except during World War II. From 1974 they were produced by the BBC. Mayer also founded Youth and Music (1954) for a slightly older age-group, emulating the continental Jeunesses Musicales movement. He was cofounder, with Sir Thomas Beecham, of the London Philharmonic Orchestra. Other projects attracting his interest and support included the International Student Service, the Elizabeth Fry Fund, and the Anglo-Israel Foundation. Knighted in 1939, he was made a Companion of Honour in 1973. He published *Young People in Trouble* (1945) and his autobiography, *My First Hundred Years* (1979).

Médici, Emílio Garrastazú, Brazilian army officer and politician (b. Dec. 4, 1905, Bagé, Rio Grande do Sul, Brazil—d. Oct. 9, 1985, Rio de Janeiro, Brazil), as president of Brazil from 1969 to 1974, led the country's phenomenal "economic miracle" by instituting such measures as incentives to those who invested in underdeveloped areas, the promotion of exports, and huge investments in electric power production, road construction, and port facilities. During his tenure as president, the country recorded an average annual growth rate of better than 9%. Médici, who was propelled from the military to the presidency when the then president, Gen. Artur da Costa e Silva, became ill, ruled the country with an iron hand. His dictatorial government reportedly killed or tortured some 170 government opponents. He left office in 1974 after naming his successor, Gen. Ernesto Geisel, but continued to advise military and political leaders throughout his life.

Mihalovici, Marcel, Romanian-born composer (b. Oct. 22, 1898, Bucharest, Rom.—d. Aug. 12, 1985, Paris, France), composed five symphonies and five operas, including *Phèdre* (1949), but was probably best known for his chamber works. Structurally a traditionalist, he was recognizably modern in his experiments with atonality, as in his awareness of popular music. He studied in Bucharest before going to Paris in 1919 to attend the Schola Cantorum, where he taught from 1959 to 1962. Trained as a violinist and married to the pianist Monique Hass, he took French nationality in 1955 and, like Bohuslav Martinu, became one of a notable group of foreign musicians practicing in France. *Phèdre* was considered his masterpiece, but his chamber works were frequently performed and revealed his concern for form and his admiration for Brahms within an idiom that was, nonetheless, distinctively original. In 1979 he was awarded the Grand Prix de la Société des Auteurs, Compositeurs et Éditeurs de Musique.

Miller, Arnold Ray, U.S. labour leader (b. April 25, 1923, Cabin Creek, S.C.—d. July 12, 1985, Charleston, W.Va.), helped dismantle the autocratic and corrupt union leadership of W. A. ("Tony") Boyle and, by campaigning on an anticorruption platform and calling for greater mine safety and better pension benefits, was elected in 1972 the 12th president of the United Mine Workers (UMW) in an upset victory (70,373 to 56,334) over Boyle. Boyle had been convicted of fraud and embezzlement and was later found guilty of ordering the 1969 New Year's Eve murder of his chief rival, Joseph A. ("Jock") Yablonski, and his family. Miller, a partly disabled coal miner who suffered from black lung disease (caused by constant exposure to coal dust), left the mines in 1969 but emerged as a public figure when he became a spokesman for a wildcat strike by 40,000 miners protesting against the union's failure to control excess coal dust in the mines. The West Virginia legislature responded by making those suffering from black lung disease eligible for worker's compensation. As president of the UMW Miller negotiated huge contract increases in 1974 and 1978, but a 111-day national strike in 1978 led to factional power struggles and rank-and-file dissension. In failing health, he retired from the UMW presidency in late 1979, just a few days before the executive board planned to oust him.

Mitchell, James Alexander Hugh, British publisher (b. July 20, 1939, Great Hallingbury, Essex, England—d. March 12, 1985, London, England), founded with John Beazley the publishing firm of Mitchell Beazley, specializing in best-selling nonfiction works. Educated at Winchester and Trinity College, University of Cambridge, he worked for publishers Constable & Co. and then Thomas Nelson, where he met Beazley. In 1969, with backing from George Philip, an educational publisher noted for geographical works, they brought out *The Moon Flight Atlas.* Exploiting new printing techniques, excellently designed and illustrated, it was an outstanding success and was followed by other similar publications. In 1972 they published Alex Comfort's *The Joy of Sex,* which sold seven million copies, and between 1977 and 1978 Mitchell himself edited *The Joy of Knowledge Encyclopaedia* in ten volumes. This was translated into many languages and reached a total of 28 editions in various countries. Following Beazley's early death, Mitchell explored the potential of video and later of hardback publications. From 1980 to 1983 the firm was controlled by American Express Co., with Mitchell as chairman.

Mitchell, Leslie, British television and newsreel commentator (b. Oct. 4, 1905, Edinburgh, Scotland—d. Nov. 23, 1985, London, England), was involved in the launching of BBC Television (1936) and of the commercial company Associated Rediffusion (1955). He was also a commentator for British Movietone News, and it was his voice that was often heard with the many clips of (especially World War II) newsreel still shown on television. Educated at King's School, Canterbury, and at Chillon College in Switzerland, he began his career on the stage. He toured in Edgar Wallace's *Flying Squad* (1928) but was prevented by a serious road accident from appearing when the play opened in London. He toured South Africa in R. C. Sherriff's *Journey's End* (1928) and later understudied for leading roles in London. He became a dance band radio commentator (1932), joining the BBC as a general announcer and variety producer (1934). He was appointed senior announcer (1936) for BBC Television, and his was the first voice heard when transmission began. He had already acted as a commentator for British Movietone News, and he joined them full time (1939–46) while re-forming a connection with BBC radio and presiding over the popular "Brains Trust" sessions. He was with Associated Rediffusion (1955–58). In demand for his recollections of early times, he celebrated BBC TV's 25th (1961; with Richard Dimbleby) and 40th (1976) anniversaries and presented for Tyne-Tees Television his own series, "Those Wonderful TV Times" (1976–78).

Moch, Jules, French politician (b. March 15, 1893, Paris, France—d. Aug. 1, 1985, Cabris, Alpes-Maritimes, France), was minister of the interior from 1947 to 1950, then minister of defense (1950–51), delegate (1953–60) to the UN Disarmament Committee, and once more minister of the interior for a few dramatic days in May 1958. His career was marked by his commitment to Socialism and his hostility to Communism; when he finally resigned from the Socialist Party (SP) in 1974, it was in protest against its alliance with the French Communist Party—the "union of the left" entered into by SP leader François Mitterrand in 1972. Moch studied at the École Polytechnique and served with the artillery in World War I before working in industry. Elected député in 1928, he became minister for public works in the Popular Front government ten years later. After the fall of France in 1940, he voted against Marshal Philippe Pétain, was interned, was freed in 1941, and joined the Resistance, then Gen. Charles de Gaulle's Free French Forces in England. Returning to the Ministry of Public Works after World War II, he later became minister of the interior, where he helped to build up the Compagnies Républicaines de Sécurité (CRS; a special police unit used to combat civil disturbance). His opposition to the European Defense Community Treaty brought conflict within his own party; he turned to the study of disarmament questions and participated actively in the creation of Pugwash, the international movement for world peace. On May 14, 1958, favouring a centre-left government, he returned to the Ministry of the Interior under Premier Pierre Pflimlin to confront an expected invasion by parachutists of the disaffected French Army units in Algeria. He resigned on May 31. He was among the Socialists who voted for the return of de Gaulle, became a member of

the bureau of the French section of the Workers' International, and spent much of his time writing memoirs, books on disarmament, and a study of the Popular Front. Moch summed up his attitude to Mitterand's "union of the left" in the title of his book *Le Communisme, jamais!* ("Communism, Never!"; 1978).

Moncreiffe of that Ilk, Sir (Rupert) Iain Kay, 11TH BARONET, Scottish genealogist (b. April 9, 1919, Hampton Court, Middlesex, England—d. Feb. 27, 1985, London, England), was a notable eccentric whose books on genealogy brought him international fame. He was, from 1961, Albany Herald in the court of Scotland's Lord Lyon King of Arms. Educated at Stowe School and at Heidelberg and Oxford universities, he served in the Scots Guards during World War II and was wounded in Italy. After a brief period (1946) as attaché at the British embassy in Moscow, he studied Scots law at the University of Edinburgh; he was admitted (1950) to the

Scottish Faculty of Advocates and in 1980 became a queen's counsel (Scotland). His serious study of genealogy and heraldry began with his doctoral thesis on the Scots law of succession to peerages. Moncreiffe served in the court of Lord Lyon as Falkland Pursuivant (1952–53), Kintyre Pursuivant (1953–55), and Unicorn Pursuivant (1955–61). An expert on genealogies as recondite as those of Byzantine noblemen, he also wrote a number of books on subjects more likely to interest British and North American readers, including *Blood Royal* (1956), *The Highland Clans* (1967; rev. ed., 1982), and *Royal Scotland* (1983). He succeeded his cousin to the baronetcy (created 1685) in 1957.

Monro, Matt (TERRY PARSONS), British popular vocalist (b. 1930, London, England—d. Feb. 7, 1985, London), achieved success in the late 1950s on radio and reached the peak of his career in 1965, the year in which "Born Free" won him an Academy Award for best song in a motion picture and he was voted the best male singer in England. After national service he worked as a truck driver, milkman, and bus driver while trying to launch a career as a singer with dance hall orchestras. He succeeded with the help of pianist Winifred Atwell and by the late 1950s was a popular performer on Radio Luxembourg. Monro's first recording success came with producer George Martin, and in all he sold more than 20 million records, notably of theme music from films, including "From Russia with Love." He won second place in the 1964 Eurovision Song Contest and, after his last hit, "Yesterday" in 1965, he turned increasingly to cabaret in Britain and the U.S. His records continued to sell consistently, and he was admired for the quality of his baritone voice and for his phrasing.

Monsen, Per, Norwegian journalist (b. May 4, 1913, Hamar, Norway—d. Aug. 26, 1985, Oslo, Norway), was director of the International Press Institute in Zürich, Switz. (1964–68), and gen-

eral manager and chief editor (1970–80) of the Norwegian News Agency. He entered journalism in 1932, working on various provincial papers including *Sörlandet* (1932–37). He was secretary to Leon Trotsky while the latter was in Norway (1935–36) and covered the Spanish Civil War for a number of Norwegian newspapers. Monsen was on the staff of *Bergens Arbeiderblad* (1937–39) and joined the Oslo newspaper *Arbeiderbladet* (1939). When this paper was closed by the Nazis (1940), Monsen edited clandestine newspapers for a few months until he was arrested and imprisoned. He escaped to Sweden (1941) and worked for the Norwegian Government Information Service in Stockholm and (from 1943) in London, where he broadcast on the BBC's Norwegian service. Returning to Norway (1945), he worked as parliamentary correspondent for *Arbeiderbladet* and was press attaché on the Norwegian military mission in Berlin (1948–49). He was *Arbeiderbladet*'s political editor and deputy editor in chief (1952–64) and its editor in chief (1968–70). Monsen was chairman of the Norwegian Press Federation (1954–58). His book *Detta är Gestapo* appeared in Sweden in 1944 under a pen name.

Morante, Elsa, Italian novelist (b. Aug. 18, 1918, Rome, Italy—d. Nov. 25, 1985, Rome), won critical acclaim for both her short stories and her novels, including *L'isola di Arturo* (1957; *Arthur's Island,* 1958), which probed the mind of a boy and the myths he constructed as a defense against the world. Her most ambitious novel was *La storia* (1974; *History: A novel,* 1977), but its attempts to reconcile Christianity and Marxism failed to convince the critics, although the book sold well. The daughter of a Sicilian schoolteacher, Morante was brought up in a working-class district in Rome and remained aware in her work of both this Sicilian heritage and the vigour of Roman popular life. She published her first book, *Il gioco segreto* (*The Secret Game*), in 1941 and in the same year married novelist Alberto Moravia. In 1943, when Moravia was wanted by the police for his anti-Fascist activities, they had to go into hiding. The marriage was dissolved in 1963, but his influence was evident in some of her work, especially in her first novel, *Menzogna e sortilegio* (1948; *House of Liars,* 1951), which won the Viareggio Prize. Her other works included a children's book, which she started to write at the age of 13, published in two versions in 1942 and 1959. She was also well known as a journalist and in later years became something of an eccentric figure, devoted to her cats and to the company of young people. She was a devout Roman Catholic, and her work reflected this, as well as her attachment to myth and to elements in the human mind beyond the reach of reason; it was these hidden depths that her idiosyncratic prose style was best able to reveal.

Mota Pinto, Carlos Alberto, Portuguese politician (b. July 25, 1936, Pombal, near Coimbra, Port.—d. May 7, 1985, Coimbra), was prime minister of Portugal from November 1978 to June 1979, heading a politically nonaligned government. In 1974 he helped to found the Social Democratic Party (PSD) and, after leaving it in December 1975 because of a personality clash, he returned to lead it in 1983. Mota Pinto graduated in law from Coimbra University (1958) and, apart from a period of military service in Portuguese Guinea, thereafter taught there, becoming professor of civil law. Following the revolution of April 1974 he was elected (April 1975) a Social Democratic deputy to the Legislative Assembly and participated in the drafting of the new constitution. In the first constitutional government he served as minister of commerce and tourism (July 1976–December 1977), under Mário Soares. As prime minister, appointed by Pres. António Eanes in an attempt to avoid political infighting, Mota Pinto set out to tackle Portugal's economic problems, but his administration was eventually defeated by a combination of Communist and Socialist deputies. He remained active in politics and

became deputy prime minister and minister of defense in a coalition of his party with the Socialists (1983). Following disagreements within the PSD he resigned his seat in the Assembly (February 1985), but he was planning to reenter politics when he died of a heart attack. He also published a number of books on law and political science.

Muller, Hilgard, South African lawyer and politician• (b. May 4, 1914, Potchefstroom, Transvaal, South Africa—d. July 10, 1985, Pretoria, South Africa), was minister of foreign affairs (1964–77) in governments headed by H. F. Verwoerd and B. J. Vorster. Previously he was high commissioner (1961) then, following South Africa's withdrawal from the Commonwealth, ambassador (1961–64) in London. Muller studied classics at the universities of Pretoria and Oxford, receiving a Ph.D. from the former, and he then earned a law degree at the University of South Africa. In 1947 he started a law practice in Pretoria and served as a city councillor (1951–57) and mayor (1953–55). Muller was elected to Parliament as National Party member for Pretoria East in 1958. As ambassador to the U.K. and then minister of foreign affairs, Muller encountered problems resulting from South Africa's increased isolation following its change of status from Commonwealth member to republic and its rigid enforcement of apartheid policies.. Though he remained largely a background figure, he played an influential role in formulating policies governing relations with black African countries. Muller, who withdrew from politics in 1977, was the author of several books, including an abbreviated Afrikaans translation of the *Illiad.*

Mungo, Van Lingle, U.S. baseball player (b. June 8, 1911, Pageland, S.C.—d. Feb. 12, 1985, Pageland), as a colourful right-handed pitcher for the Brooklyn Dodgers (1931–41) and New York Giants (1942–45), earned notoriety on and off the field with his powerhouse fastball, unusual name, and fiery temperment. Mungo, who compiled a lifetime record of 120 victories, 115 losses, and an earned run average of 3.47 during his 14 years as a professional baseball player, never quite fulfilled the promise of his professional debut—a two-hit shutout of the Boston Braves with 12 strikeouts. Mungo became infamous for his altercations with opponents, teammates, and even the front office. By his own estimate he accrued a total of $15,-000 in fines. After retiring he briefly managed a minor league team in Clinton, N.C., and then operated a movie theatre, dry goods business, and a trucking line in his hometown. His name briefly regained prominence in 1970 as the title of a popular song, also known as "Dodger Blues," with lyrics consisting entirely of names of old-time baseball players.

Naipaul, Shivadhar Srinivasa, West Indian writer (b. Feb. 25, 1945, Port-of-Spain, Trinidad—d. Aug. 13, 1985, London, England), was not overshadowed by, but had yet to match the achievement of, his elder brother, the novelist V. S. Naipaul. His first novel, *Fireflies* (1970), depicting Hindu society and problems in Trinidad, won him an impressive array of literary awards, including the Royal Society of Literature's Winifred Holtby Memorial Prize, the Jock Campbell New Statesman Award, and the John Llewellyn Rhys Memorial Prize. Born into the Hindu community in Trinidad, he was educated in Port-of-Spain at Queen's Royal College and St. Mary's College and in England at University College, Oxford, where he studied Chinese. His second novel, *The Chip-Chip Gatherers* (1973), also set in Trinidad, won the Whitbread Literary Award but achieved less impact than his first and was tinged with bitterness. It was ten years before he returned to the novel with *A Hot Country* (1983; U.S. title, *Love and Death in a Hot Country* [1984]). In the interim he wrote stories and essays (*The Adventures of Gurudeva,* 1976); a travel book, *North of South: An African Journey* (1978); and

TARA HEINEMANN—CAMERA PRESS, LONDON

Black and White (1980; U.S. title, *Journey to Nowhere: A New World Tragedy* [1981]), an account of the mass suicide (1978) by members of the San Francisco People's Temple at Jonestown, Guyana. His last published work, *Beyond the Dragon's Mouth* (1984), a collection of essays and stories, offered mordant comment on many topics.

Nash, Clarence ("DUCKY"), U.S. vocal impressionist (b. 1904, Watonga, Okla.—d. Feb. 20, 1985, Burbank, Calif.), created the squawking voice of the irascible Donald Duck and served as the cartoon character's only spokesman for over 50 years in more than 150 cartoons and motion pictures. Nash, who once had ambitions to become a doctor, by his own admission became the nation's leading quack. In addition to Donald he supplied the voices for nephews Huey, Dewey, and Louie, girlfriend Daisy, and such other cartoon characters as Jiminy Cricket (after the death of Cliff Edwards), a bullfrog in *Bambi*, dogs in *101 Dalmations*, and occasionally Mickey Mouse. Though Nash officially retired from Disney studios in 1971, he was in constant demand. Perhaps Nash's greatest challenge occurred when Donald's cartoons were dubbed in French, Spanish, Portuguese, Japanese, Chinese, and German and Nash had to learn to quack in those languages. In 1984 Nash was an honoured guest at Donald's 50th birthday party (b. June 9, 1934), and Nash also received a special plaque from President and Mrs. Ronald Reagan commemorating his unique niche in family entertainment.

Nelson, Rick (ERIC HILLIARD NELSON), U.S. rock star (b. May 8, 1940, Teaneck, N.J.—d. Dec. 31, 1985, De Kalb, Texas), personified the ideal teenager on his family's television program, "The Adventures of Ozzie and Harriet" (1952–66), and became a sleepy-eyed teen idol after singing his rendition of "I'm Walking" and "A Teenager's Romance" on the show in 1957. Nelson joined his parents' radio show at age eight, and after the program made the transition to television, he became known as Ricky, a clean-cut 11-year-old who eventually became a singing idol and matured into a 25-year-old husband. Nelson scored a string of hits as a rock singer, including "Poor Little Fool," "It's Late," "Hello Mary Lou," and "Travelin' Man." In 1961 he shortened his name to Rick, and about a decade later he formed a country-rock group, the Stone Canyon Band. His fans, though, resisted the change, and when Nelson attempted to perform his new music during an oldies concert at New York's Madison Square Garden, he was booed off the stage. His autobiographical song "Garden Party," which recounted that incident, skyrocketed him back onto the charts and earned him a gold record. During the 1980s he toured county fairs and was interested in resuming work in television. Nelson, his fiancée, and the five members of his band were killed when their plane crashed en route to a concert.

Nemon, Oscar, Croatian-born British sculptor (b. March 13, 1906, Ogijek, Austria-Hungary—d. April 13, 1985, Oxford, England), became internationally famous as a portrait sculptor, perhaps best known for his depictions of Sir Winston Churchill. Educated in Belgium and Paris, he rapidly achieved fame, exhibiting in many European capitals. He moved to Britain in the 1930s. Nemon executed both busts and full-length sculptures; his subjects included Queen Elizabeth II, Queen Elizabeth the Queen Mother, Lord Beaverbrook, Margaret Thatcher, and Sir Max Beerbohm. Nemon made sculptures of Sir Winston Churchill for the Houses of Parliament, for the City of London Guildhall, and at St. Margaret's Bay in Kent. A double portrait, with Lady Churchill, now at Blenheim Palace, showed his skill in capturing private emotion.

Neves, Tancredo de Almeida, Brazilian politician (b. March 4, 1910, São João del Rei, Minas Gerais, Brazil—d. April 21, 1985, São Paulo, Brazil), as the first elected (Jan. 15, 1985) civilian president of Brazil in 21 years, sparked hope among the populace of returning the country to democracy and economic stability. A series of seven operations, however, the first on the eve of his inauguration (March 15), prevented him from taking the oath of office. Neves, one of 12 children, studied in the state capital of Belo Horizonte before returning home to practice law in 1932. He soon became involved in local politics, and in 1951 he moved to Rio de Janeiro to become a federal legislator. In 1953 Pres. Getulio Vargas appointed Neves justice minister, but the following year Vargas committed suicide and Neves returned to Congress. After serving as head of the state-owned Banco do Brasil during the late 1950s, he was again elected to Congress in 1961 and in the same year was appointed to the newly created post of prime minister by Pres. João Goulart. When the military took power in 1964, Neves became a respected leader in opposition circles and a popular centrist politician. In 1983 he became governor of his home state, and though he was not particularly innovative, his moderate and conciliatory stance made him the perfect presidential candidate; Neves united the opposition and was acceptable to the departing military government. On Jan. 15, 1985, Neves was overwhelmingly chosen by Brazil's 686-member electoral college to become the first civilian president in 21 years and return the country to democracy. Although Neves died of complications following intestinal surgery before being sworn in as president, he was buried with the presidential sash.

Nolan, Lloyd Benedict, U.S. actor (b. Aug. 11, 1902, San Francisco, Calif.—d. Sept. 27, 1985, Los Angeles, Calif.), was a reliable character actor who portrayed secondary gangsters and tough policemen. Though he turned in impressive performances in such films as *A Tree Grows in Brooklyn* (1945) and *The House on 92nd Street* (1945), he did not win recognition for his

UPI/BETTMANN NEWSPHOTOS

accomplishments until he starred as the neurotic Captain Queeg in the stage and television versions of *The Caine Mutiny Court Martial.* In 1955 he won an Emmy, his only national award, for his sterling portrayal of Queeg in a television adaptation of the play. Nolan, who made his Hollywood debut in *Stolen Harmony* (1935), appeared in more than 70 films, including *Bataan* (1943), *Guadalcanal Diary* (1943), *A Hatful of Rain* (1957), *Peyton Place* (1957), *Ice Station Zebra* (1968), and *Earthquake* (1974). From 1968 to 1971 he played the role of Dr. Morton Chegley on television's "Julia." He made his last film, *The Private Files of J. Edgar Hoover,* in 1978.

O'Brien, Edmond, U.S. actor (b. Sept. 10, 1915, New York, N.Y.—d. May 9, 1985, Inglewood, Calif.), specialized in portrayals of tough guys in such films as *The Killers* (1946), *A Double Life* (1948), *D.O.A.* (1950), *The Great Imposter* (1961), and *Birdman of Alcatraz* (1962) and garnered an Academy Award as best supporting actor for his role as the venal Hollywood press agent in *The Barefoot Contessa* (1954). O'Brien, who appeared on stage during the 1930s and '40s in such productions as *Hamlet* and *Romeo and Juliet,* began his film career in 1939 as the poet Pierre Gringoire in *The Hunchback of Notre Dame* (1939). It was not until 1949, however, when O'Brien played the tough, cool federal agent who infiltrated James Cagney's gang in *White Heat,* that his extraordinary talents were recognized. Though he played a mixture of leading and supporting roles, his jowly cheeks and stocky build eventually marked him for character roles. He also turned in notable performances in *1984* (1955), in *The Man Who Shot Liberty Valance* (1962) as the frontier newspaper editor, in *The Wild Bunch* (1969) as a grizzled old man and the only gang member to survive, and in *Seven Days in May* (1964) as an aging, alcoholic senator. For the latter role he was nominated for an Academy Award. From 1962 to 1963 O'Brien also appeared on television as the tough attorney Sam Benedict in the show of the same name.

Oppenheimer, Frank Friedman, U.S. nuclear physicist (b. Aug. 14, 1912, New York, N.Y.—d. Feb. 3, 1985, Sausalito, Calif.), conducted pioneering research on radiation, notably cosmic radiation, but his career was overshadowed by the achievements of his brother, J. Robert Oppenheimer ("father of the atomic bomb"); the two also worked on the top-secret Manhattan Project. Oppenheimer, who earned a Ph.D. in physics in 1939 from the California Institute of Technology, served as a research associate (1940–47) in the radiation laboratory at the University of California at Berkeley and as an associate professor of physics (1947–49) at the University of Minnesota. In 1949, after Oppenheimer testified before the House Un-American Activities Committee that he had been a member of the American Communist Party before World War II, he was blacklisted; his brother later lost (1954) his government security clearance, in part because of Frank's Communist associations. He raised cattle on a ranch in Colorado for ten years before returning to academia as professor of physics at the University of Colorado. One of his most well-known contributions to science was the founding (1969) of San Francisco's Exploratorium, a unique science museum featuring exhibits that visitors could touch and manipulate in order to discover scientific principles for themselves.

Ormandy, Eugene (JENO BLAU ORMANDY), Hungarian-born conductor (b. Nov. 18, 1899, Budapest, Hung.—d. March 12, 1985, Philadelphia, Pa.), as the principal conductor of the Philadelphia Orchestra from 1938 until his retirement in 1980, was credited with elevating the ensemble to one of the finest symphonies in the world, with a repertoire that featured Late Romantic and early 20th-century works. He was a musical prodigy and at the age of five became the youngest pupil to enter the Budapest Royal

Academy. A violinist, he started giving concerts at the age of 7, graduated from the academy at 14, and became a violin teacher at 17. With the promise of a recital tour, Ormandy immigrated to the U.S. in 1921; he became a U.S. citizen in 1927. The tour, however, never materialized, and Ormandy found himself playing violin in the orchestra pit at the Capitol Theatre movie palace in New York City. He made his conducting debut there in 1924 when the regular orchestra leader fell ill. Ormandy scored a coup in 1931 when he substituted for Arturo Toscanini with the Philadelphia Orchestra, and from 1931 to 1936 he was conductor of the Minneapolis Symphony. In the latter year he returned to Philadelphia as coconductor with Leopold Stokowski, and two years later he became the sole conductor of the orchestra. During his 44-year tenure (the longest music directorship in U.S. history), Ormandy developed the lush, velvety quality that epitomized the "Philadelphia sound." A dedicated craftsman who eschewed flamboyance, he elicited a high degree of technical proficiency and polish from the orchestra and reveled in the famous sound that only he could evoke. One of many highlights of Ormandy's career came in 1973, when he and the orchestra made a historic visit to China. His last concert was on Jan. 10, 1984, at Carnegie Hall, where once again he took up his baton and conducted the Philadelphia Orchestra in a program of works by Beethoven and Bartok.

Osijchuk, Hryhorij, U.S. prelate of the Ukrainian church (b. Jan. 7, 1898, Vollina, Kiev, Ukraine—d. Feb. 13, 1985, Chicago., Ill.), as archbishop and primate of the Ukrainian Orthodox Autocephalous Church in the U.S., served as the spiritual leader for 150,000 Ukrainians with parishes in the U.S., Britain, and Australia and tirelessly worked to free his church from the Russian Orthodox Church. Osijchuk, who attended the Missionary Theological School in Zhitomir, Ukraine, became a priest in 1919 and during the 1920s was active in the antisectarian movement and in the Ukrainianization of parishes. He also translated all of the church's liturgical books to Ukrainian from the Slavonic used by the Russian church. Osijchuk was consecrated bishop of Zhitomir on May 17, 1942, was elected archbishop Oct. 16, 1947, and was elevated to the rank of metropolitan Dec. 25, 1971. From 1945 to 1950 he organized parishes in displaced-persons camps in West Germany. In 1950 he went to Chicago, where he founded St. Pokrova's Ukrainian Cathedral.

Oudin, Jacques, French immunologist (b. May 15, 1908, Dreux, Eure-et-Loir, France—d. Oct. 15, 1985, Paris, France), was head of the immunology department at the Institut Pasteur from 1959 and a research director at the Centre National de la Recherche Scientifique (CNRS) from 1964. He was one of the founders of the science of immunology, and his identification of the concepts of allotypes and idiotypes paved the way for the discoveries of César Milstein, Georges Köhler, and Niels Jerne, whose work on antibodies gained the Nobel Prize for Physiology or Medicine in 1984 (an honour that some thought Oudin should have shared). He studied at the University of Paris, then at the Hospital Pasteur, gaining Ph.D.'s in medicine and science. In 1946, at the Institut Pasteur, he developed a method of immunological analysis; this was followed by his discovery of allotypes in 1956 and of idiotypes in 1963, showing the variation of antibodies in the individual and its association with the laws of genetics. Oudin was a member of many scientific bodies, including the French and U.S. academies of science. His many distinctions included the Paul Ehrlich Prize in 1960, the gold medal of the CNRS in 1972, and the grand prix of the City of Paris in 1977.

Parry, Sir Thomas, British university principal (b. Aug. 14, 1904, Carmel, Caernarvonshire, Wales—d. April 22, 1985, Bangor, Wales), was a prominent figure in Welsh academic and literary circles. As principal (1958–69) of the University College of Wales, Aberystwyth, he presided over its fortunes at a time of great expansion, both of student numbers and of buildings; he was librarian (1953–58) and president (1969–77) of the National Library of Wales; and he contributed notably to the study of Welsh literature. Parry was educated at the University College of North Wales, Bangor, studying Welsh and Latin. He was assistant lecturer (1926–29) in these subjects at University College, Cardiff, before returning to Bangor to lecture in Welsh language and literature, succeeding to the chair in 1947. Parry was vice-chancellor of the University of Wales (1961–63 and 1967–69) and president of the Honourable Society of Cymmrodorion (1978–82). His published works, all in Welsh, include a history of Welsh literature to 1900 (1944; Eng. trans., 1955), a scholarly edition of the works of the 14th-century Welsh poet Dafydd of Gwilym (1952), and a translation (1949) of T. S. Eliot's *Murder in the Cathedral.* He was editor of *The Oxford Book of Welsh Verse* (1962). A fellow of the British Academy from 1959, he was knighted in 1978.

Pène du Bois, Raoul (RAOUL-HENRI-CHARLES PÈNE DU BOIS), U.S. costume and scenic designer (b. Nov. 29, 1914, New York, N.Y.— d. Jan. 1, 1985, New York), produced magnificent costumes and theatrical sets and earned two Tony awards, one in 1953 for set design for *Wonderful Town* and the other in 1971 for costume design in the Broadway production of *No, No Nanette.* Pène du Bois, who was privately educated, designed his first Broadway show when he was 16, an edition of the *Garrick Gaities.* He designed costumes for such revues and musicals as *Life Begins at 8:40, Carmen Jones,* and *The Firebrand of Florence* and created both sets and costumes for such shows as the 1934 and 1936 editions of the *Ziegfeld Follies, Du Barry Was a Lady, Panama Hattie, Call Me Madam,* and *New Faces of 1952.* His film credits included *Louisiana Purchase, Lady in the Dark,* and *Kitty.* His genius was also showcased in his designs for ballets, ice shows, costumes for the Rockettes at Radio City Music Hall, and the production of *Jumbo* staged at the Hippodrome in New York City. His last costume commission was for the Broadway show *Sugar Babies,* which opened in 1979 and enjoyed an extended tour.

Penn Nouth, Samdech, Kampuchean politician (b. April 1, 1906, Phnom Penh, Cambodia— d. May 18, 1985, Paris, France), was prime minister of Cambodia (Kampuchea) five times between 1948 and 1969 and from 1970 to 1976 of Prince Norodom Sihanouk's alternative government, at first in exile in Beijing (Peking) but from April 1975 in Phnom Penh. Trained for the French colonial service at the Cambodian School of Administration, he worked in the Paris Ministry of Colonies (1938) before returning home as assistant to the minister of the palace (1940). He served as acting minister of finance (1945), governor of Phnom Penh (1946–48), and ambassador to France (1958–60). Penn Nouth was prime minister (September 1948–January 1949, 1952–55, 1958, 1961–62, and 1968–69) under Prince Sihanouk (at first king of Cambodia and from 1960 head of state). His adherence to Sihanouk's policies continued after the latter's exile in 1970, but he had increasing reservations about Sihanouk's association with the Khmer Rouge insurgents.

Pereira, William Leonard, U.S. architect (b. April 25, 1909, Chicago, Ill.—d. Nov. 13, 1985, Los Angeles, Calif.), designed such landmark buildings as the pyramid-shaped Transamerica Tower (1972) in San Francisco, Marineland of the Pacific (1954) in Palos Verdes, Calif., and the master-planned community of Irvine, Calif. (1960). Pereira, who studied (1926–30) at the University of Illinois School of Architecture, established (1931) a private practice in Los Angeles, where he gained a reputation for theatre designs. He was commissioned to erect a Hollywood studio for Paramount Pictures and for a time he became enamoured of the motion picture industry. In 1942 he shared an Academy Award for special effects for his work on the film *Reap the Wild Wind.* Seven years later he returned to architecture and established (1950) a partnership with Charles Luckman. Together they designed CBS Television City (1952) in Hollywood, Los Angeles International Airport (1962), the rocket-launching installations at Cape Canaveral, jet bases in California, and the Santa Barbara campus of the University of California. From 1958 Pereira served as principal and chairman of William L. Pereira Associates.

Phillips, Marjorie Acker, U.S. art patron and painter (b. Oct. 25, 1894, Bourbon, Ind.—d. June 19, 1985, Washington, D.C.), cofounded with her husband, Duncan Phillips, the first major museum of modern art in the U.S., the Phillips Collection, which from the time of their marriage in 1921 was housed in their home in Washington, D.C. As their collection increased, the couple moved out and converted the mansion into a museum, which they opened to the public. The Phillips Collection boasted some 2,500 exquisite paintings and sculptures by such late 19th- and 20th-century masters as Cézanne, Matisse, Daumier, Bonnard, Klee, Rothko, and Renoir, whose oil "Luncheon of the Boating Party," purchased in 1923 for $125,000, was considered the cornerstone of the collection. Phillips was herself an accomplished painter, and many of her more than 400 paintings and drawings were ensconced in museum collections. One of her most famous works, titled "Night Baseball," depicts Joe DiMaggio at the plate during his last season with the New York Yankees. Phillips, who served as associate director of the museum from 1922 to 1966, became director when her husband died in 1966, and she remained in that post until she retired in 1972 in favour of her son, Laughlin Phillips.

Phoumi Nosavan, Laotian army officer (b. Jan. 7, 1920, Savannakhet, South Laos—d. Nov. 3, 1985, Bangkok, Thailand), as deputy prime minister in Laos (1960–65), was especially powerful during the right-wing government of Prince Boun Oum (1960–62) and remained a forceful figure in the confused politics of the immediately succeeding years. After a varied early career, in which he had been a Buddhist monk and an amateur boxing champion and had trained as a teacher, he joined (1945) the forces of Prince Souphanouvong in the struggle to expel the French. He became chief of staff, but when Souphanouvong began to deal more closely with the Communist North Vietnamese, Nosavan left his service (1949) and entered the Royal Lao Army, becoming its inspector general. Later he moved more fully into politics and was secretary of state for national defense and veteran affairs in the Phoui Sananikone Cabinet (1959) and minister of national defense and veteran affairs under Kou Abhay Og Long (early 1960). Struggles between neutralist, right-wing, and Communist factions became more pronounced in 1960, and Nosavan joined the Boun Oum government set up in Savannakhet. Although U.S. support for Boun Oum ended in 1962, Nosavan remained influential until 1965, when Prince Souvanna Phouma initiated a reshuffle of army command that would have demoted Nosavan. He attempted a coup (February 1), but it failed, and he then went into exile in Thailand.

Pitman, Sir (Isaac) James, British publisher and politician (b. Aug. 14, 1901, London, England— d. Sept. 1, 1985, London), was Conservative member of Parliament for Bath (1945–64) and chairman (1934–66) of Sir Isaac Pitman and Sons Ltd., the publishing and business studies firm founded by his grandfather, but was best known for his extensive efforts to promote use of the Initial Teaching Alphabet (i.t.a.). Educated at Eton College and at Christ Church College, Oxford, he was a notable athlete, winning the public schools middleweight boxing championship (1919), running and skiing for

the University of Oxford (1922), and playing rugby for Oxford (1921), England (1922), and later for the Harlequins. He went into business, but during World War II he served in the Royal Air Force (1940–43) and became director of organization and methods in the British Treasury (1943–45). He was a director of the Bank of England (1941–45). Always interested in commercial education—he was vice-president of the British Association for Commercial and Industrial Education—he became increasingly preoccupied with the problems of teaching children to read and published *The Ehrhardt Augmented (40-Sound, 42-Character) Lower-Case Roman Alphabet* (1959). This alphabet, which became the i.t.a., was designed to provide a series of symbols more closely linked to actual sound than the letters of the traditional alphabet. Pitman also sat on a number of committees set up to implement George Bernard Shaw's proposals for a new British alphabet. He was knighted in 1961.

Plomley, (Francis) Roy, British broadcaster and writer (b. Jan. 20, 1914, Kingston upon Thames, England—d. May 28, 1985, London, England), originated and presented the British Broadcasting Corporation's longest-running radio program, "Desert Island Discs." In each program he invited one well-known person to be interviewed and to choose eight records he or she would like to have if cast away on a desert island. The first interview was broadcast in January 1942, with the comedian Vic Oliver as the castaway. The program was so popular that 43 years later, on May 11, 1985, Plomley interviewed his 1,791st prospective shipwreck victim. During that time his desert island had been inhabited by personalities from all walks of life, including royalty (Princess Margaret), politics (Margaret Thatcher), and the theatre (Sir Ralph Richardson). The series was terminated only by Plomley's illness and death. Plomley was educated at King's College School, London, and first worked as a copywriter for an advertising agency but soon became a radio announcer (1936). He worked in France for such commercial stations as Radio Normandie and Poste Parisien. Plomley won other contracts from the BBC (in television as well as radio) and became host of such programs as "We Beg to Differ" (1949; television 1951), "Round Britain Quiz" (1961), and "My Favourite Things" (1985). He wrote 16 plays, a novel, two books related to the "Desert Island Discs" theme, and an account of his early experiences in radio, *Days Seemed Longer* (1980).

Porter, Rodney Robert, British biochemist (b. Oct. 8, 1917, Newton-le-Willows, Lancashire, England—d. Sept. 6, 1985, Newbury, Berkshire, England), as Whitley professor of biochemistry at the University of Oxford (1967–85), was, with the U.S. physician Gerald M. Edelman, joint winner of the 1972 Nobel Prize for Physiology or Medicine for notable research into the chemical structure of antibodies. Porter, who received a degree in biochemistry at the University of Liverpool in 1939, served during World War II with the Royal Engineers, mainly in the Mediterranean zone. He was appointed (1945) to the department of biochemistry at the University of Cambridge, where he worked under Frederick Sanger on the structure of proteins. Porter worked at the National Institute for Medical Research in north London (1949–60) and was Pfizer professor of immunology at London's St. Mary's Hospital, Paddington (1960–67). At Oxford he became honorary director of a new Medical Research Council's immunology unit. He had developed (1958) a system of employing enzymes to split antibodies and succeeded (1960) in determining the peptide chains in antibody molecules. He eventually propounded the concept of a four-chain structure in antibodies and facilitated an understanding of the relation between different classes of antibody, including those produced in both normal and malignant tissue. Porter was elected a fellow of the Royal Society in 1964.

Pritikin, Nathan, U.S. nutritionist (b. Aug. 29, 1915, Chicago, Ill.—d. Feb. 21, 1985, Albany, N.Y.), was a best-selling author who in such books as *Live Longer Now* (1974) and *The Pritikin Program for Diet & Exercise* (1979) advocated a controversial low-cholesterol, low-fat diet to reverse the symptoms of heart disease, hypertension, and diabetes. Pritikin, a successful inventor who used his ingenuity to develop ideas for such companies as General Electric, Corning Glass, Bendix, and Honeywell, held more than two dozen patents in chemistry, physics, and electronics. He dropped out of the University of Chicago after his freshman year, and when at the age of 40 he was diagnosed as suffering from heart disease, he became a self-taught nutritionist and developed a diet that banned sugar, salt, oils, caffeine, and alcohol but encouraged dieters to exercise and to consume mainly vegetables, fruits, whole grains, and small amounts of fish and poultry. Though medical studies confirmed that his program had favourable short-term benefits, long-term studies had not yet confirmed that his regimen helped patients live longer. In 1976 Pritikin founded his first longevity centre in Santa Barbara, Calif. (later moved to Santa Monica, Calif.), and he also established others in Downingtown, Pa., and Surfside, Fla. The health and fitness guru, a longtime leukemia patient, took his own life when the disease suddenly recurred after a long remission.

Ramgoolam, Sir Seewoosagur, Mauritian physician and politician (b. Sept. 18, 1900, Belle Rive, Mauritius—d. Dec. 15, 1985, Le Reduit, Mauritius), was chief minister of Mauritius from 1961 and, after independence was granted (1968), prime minister (1968–82). Educated at Royal College, Mauritius, he qualified in medicine at University College and Hospital, London. Returning to Mauritius, he entered local politics, becoming mayor of Port Louis (1958). Ramgoolam built up the Labour Party, supported largely by Mauritians of Indian descent, and was a member of the Legislative Assembly from 1948. He held executive positions as liaison officer for education (1951–56) and as ministerial secretary to the Treasury (1958); he was leader of the House (1960). His party won the first elections (1959) held on universal suffrage. While he was head of government, he also held other portfolios; he was minister of finance (1960–68), minister of defense and internal security (1968–82), minister of information and broadcasting (1969–80), and minister of foreign affairs (1974–76). His long term of premiership was maintained after 1976 by skillful coalitions with other parties. He was knighted in 1965.

Redgrave, Sir Michael Scudamore, British actor (b. March 20, 1908, Bristol, England—d. March 21, 1985, Denham, Buckinghamshire, England), was a superb actor on both stage and film and was noted in particular for his intelligence and for his extraordinary portrayals of strong characters fatally flawed. In his best performances, on stage as Uncle Vanya in 1962 or on film as the schoolmaster in *The Browning Version* (1951), he achieved a tragic poignancy that was enhanced by his regal bearing and sonorous voice. The son of two actors, he was educated at Magdalene College, University of Cambridge, and taught languages in a public school until he joined the Liverpool Playhouse at the age of 26. In 1936 he went to the Old Vic, then to the Queen's Theatre, where he was strongly influenced by producer Michel Saint-Denis. He also starred in Alfred Hitchcock's *The Lady Vanishes* (1938). After a medical discharge from the Royal Navy in 1942, Redgrave began a brilliant period as a classical stage actor, starting with *Macbeth* in 1947 and culminating in the title role in *Hamlet* in 1958. In between, in 1953, he had played Antony and King Lear and at the same time developed his talent with performances in modern works and films. His portrayal of the ventriloquist in *Dead of Night* (1945) was a chilling revelation of his ability to suggest

JANE BOWN—CAMERA PRESS, LONDON

depths of violence and unease behind a polished exterior. His early literary ambition found fulfillment in books that included a novel, *The Mountebank's Tale* (1959), an adaptation of *The Aspern Papers* (1959), and his autobiography, *In My Minds I* (1983). His wife, the actress Rachel Kempson, and their children, Vanessa, Corin, and Lynn, all had successful acting careers. By the mid-1960s he was already suffering the first symptoms of Parkinson's disease, but he continued to act, though in an increasingly limited range of parts, until his final 1979 appearance as a wheelchair-bound stroke victim in *Close of Play*. Redgrave was knighted in 1959.

Riboud, Jean, French industrialist (b. Nov. 15, 1919, Lyon, France—d. Oct. 21, 1985, Paris, France), was from 1965 to 1985 president of Schlumberger Ltd., a world-renowned specialist in oil prospecting and drilling through electronic logging. His left-wing political sympathies and his friendship for Pres. François Mitterrand made him one of the most influential figures in French industry under the Socialist government; he turned down an offer of the ministerial portfolio of industry and research in 1983 because he believed that more energetic measures were needed to bring down inflation. Riboud studied law in Lyon and at the École des Sciences Politiques in Paris. Arrested as a member of the Resistance in 1943, he spent two years in Buchenwald. In 1946 he went to New York, and in 1951 he joined Schlumberger, becoming director of its company for oil prospecting in 1957 and president of Schlumberger Ltd. in 1965. The company was spectacularly successful, particularly during the 1970s, gaining a reputation as one of the best-managed companies in the world. Riboud was recognized as a determined and perhaps arrogant administrator, with wide cultural interests. He helped to set up the Magnum photographic agency, was a director of the Compagnie Luxembourgeoise de Télédiffusion and of the newspaper *Le Provençal*, as well as a member of the Fondation Express, publishers of *L'Express* magazine.

Richards, Frances, British artist (b. Aug. 1, 1901, Burslem, England—d. Feb. 14, 1985, London, England), as a specialist in design, was skilled in a wide variety of media, including engraving and embroidery. Many of her works were of biblical subjects. Born into a family of professional potters, Frances Clayton studied at the Burslem School of Art; while still a pupil there she became a designer for the Paragon China Co. After winning a national scholarship to the Royal College of Art, London, she concentrated on design and studied the fresco and tempera techniques of early Renaissance Italian artists. There she met and married (1929) the artist Ceri Richards (d. 1971), and during the following 30 years she combined her own work with teaching, preponderantly at London's Chelsea and Camberwell schools of art. Among her more notable works were a series of copper engravings of subjects taken from the Acts of the Apostles, one of which appeared in the

seventh issue (1930) of the typographer Stanley Morison's *The Fleuron* (the entire group was published in 1980). Richards provided lithographic illustrations for editions of *The Book of Revelations* (1931) and of Arthur Rimbaud's *Illuminations* (1979). She also illustrated the Book of Lamentations in *The Illustrated Bible* (1969), issued by the Oxford University Press. Many of her embroideries were exhibited in one-woman shows in 1945, 1949, and 1954.

Richter, Charles Francis, U.S. seismologist (b. April 26, 1900, near Hamilton, Ohio—d. Sept. 30, 1985, Pasadena, Calif.), in 1935, together with Beno Gutenberg, developed the scale of earthquake magnitude that became known as the Richter scale, a measure of the movement of the Earth as recorded on seismographs. Richter studied physics at Stanford University and earned a Ph.D. in theoretical physics in 1928 at the California Institute of Technology, where he spent his entire professional career (1927–70). A fanatic about earthquakes, he devoted more than half a century to plotting their origins and analyzing the forces that caused them. He even installed a seismograph in his living room, and during his final hospital confinement he monitored developments on the giant September 19–20 earthquake that devastated Mexico City. Richter's scale, which was absolute and in logarithmic terms, was devised so that an increase of one unit in magnitude implied a tenfold increase in ground motion. Richter and Gutenberg also wrote the basic textbook on seismology, *Seismicity of the Earth,* which was revised in 1954 and published under the title *Seismicity of the Earth and Associated Phenomena.* He retired in 1970 but continued to pore over seismographic data at the Caltech laboratory.

Rivière, Georges-Henri, French museologist (b. June 5, 1897, Paris, France—d. March 24, 1985, Louveciennes, Yvelines, France), founded the Musée des Arts et Traditions Populaires in 1937, originally as part of the Musée de l'Homme in the Palais de Chaillot in Paris but from 1968 independently housed in the Bois de Boulogne. His intense interest in popular and rural culture also made him a leading figure in the establishment of rural museums and in the creation of Le Creusot and other *écomusées,* which link the concept of ecology to the environment. Trained as an organist, Rivière went on to study at the École du Louvre and, as a journalist on *Cahiers d'Art,* was invited by Paul Rivet to help set up the museum of popular arts and traditions. He was a director of the Conseil National des Musées and in 1966 founded the Centre d'Éthnologie Française. His pioneering work on the study of rural France was honoured in 1979 by the award of the Grand Prix National du Patrimoine. Rivière was permanent adviser and served as first director of the International Council of Museums, which was founded in 1946.

Robert, Louis, French archaeologist (b. Feb. 15, 1904, Laurière, Haute-Vienne, France—d. May 31, 1985, Paris, France), was a specialist in Greek archaeology and an outstanding expert on inscriptions. With his wife he edited the *Bulletin épigraphique,* and he was professor of Greek epigraphy and antiquities at the Collège de France from 1939 to 1974. Earlier Robert had worked (1927–1932) at the École Française d'Athènes. His many archaeological journeys to Greece and Turkey brought his broad scholarship to bear on the interpretation of inscriptions. His contribution to Hellenic studies was considerable, and his standards were high; he was unsparing in his criticism of slipshod work by colleagues and, while he inspired great admiration, he lost many potential friends because of the ferocity of his attacks on their shortcomings.

Robins, Denise, British romantic novelist (b. Feb. 1, 1897, London, England—d. May 1, 1985, Haywards Heath, Sussex, England), was a best-selling writer of romantic novels that were translated into many languages. Her work, written in the Barbara Cartland mold, followed a predictable pattern: love always won out, and there was little mention of its usual sexual manifestations. In a writing career that spanned over 60 years, she produced some 200 books; at one time she penned some 10,000 words daily. When Robins was four years old, her father, a music teacher, left her novelist mother and took his daughter to the U.S.; later Robins returned to her mother's care and was educated in a convent school in South London. She wrote her first story, for the children's section of *The Lady* magazine, at the age of 12 and learned to type acceptable copy in preparing stories that her mother contributed to *Weekly Welcome.* Robins began working on the *Dundee Courier* at age 18 but soon became a free-lance writer of serials and short stories. Her first novel appeared in 1924. Some of her books include *The First Long Kiss* (1953), *Do Not Go, My Love* (1959), and *Dark Corridor* (1974). With Roland Pertwee she wrote a play, *Heat Wave,* which ran in London's West End (1929). Her autobiography, *Stranger than Fiction,* appeared in 1965.

Romulo, Carlos P(eña), Philippine diplomat (b. Jan. 14, 1899, Camiling, Phil.—d. Dec. 15, 1985, Manila, Phil.), was a towering figure in international politics who gained prominence as a journalist, soldier, educator, diplomat, and statesman. He was the last survivor of the 51 founding fathers of the UN and the first Asian to serve as president of the UN General Assembly (1949–50), and he thrice served as chairman of the UN Security Council. In 1931 Romulo was named editor in chief of a chain of newspapers called TVT Publications, and in 1937 he became publisher of another newspaper group. When Japan attacked the Philippines in 1941, Romulo became press aide to U.S. Gen. Douglas MacArthur on Corregidor Island, where Romulo made broadcasts as the "Voice of Freedom." After Japan captured the island, Romulo went with MacArthur to Australia and then joined his country's wartime government-in-exile, headed by Pres. Manuel Quezon in Washington, D.C. Romulo was awarded the Pulitzer Prize in journalism in 1942 for his series of articles on Japan's military resurgence in Asia. In 1945 he returned to the Philippines with U.S. forces, and in 1950 he became secretary of foreign affairs. He was named ambassador to the U.S. in 1952–53 and again in 1955–62, and in 1953 he ran for the presidency of the Philippines on a third-party ticket but abandoned his aspirations in order to serve as campaign manager for the successful Nacionalista Party candidate, Ramon Magsaysay. Romulo was also president (1962–68) of the University of the Philippines, secretary of education (1966–68), secretary of foreign affairs (1968–78), and minister of foreign affairs from 1978 until his retirement in 1984. His autobiography, *I Walked with Heroes,* appeared in 1961.

Rougemont, Denis de, Swiss writer (b. Sept. 8, 1906, Neuchâtel, Switz.—d. Dec. 6, 1985, Geneva, Switz.), was a keen and dedicated proponent of the idea of a federal Europe and was founder and from 1950 director of the European Cultural Centre at Geneva. Educated at the Universities of Neuchâtel, Vienna, and Geneva, where he studied the history of literature, Rougemont went to Paris (1930) and worked as a journalist. He soon became a contributor to many periodicals in Europe and the Americas, spreading the existentialist ideas of Søren Kierkegaard. He was lecturer in French literature at the University of Frankfurt am Main (1935–36), returning to Paris as chief editor of *Nouveaux Cahiers* (1936). During the early years of World War II he served in the Swiss Army; he was cofounder of the Ligue de Gothard, an organization set up to oppose support for Nazism in Switzerland. He went to the U.S (1941) as professor of literature at the Free School of Higher Studies in New York and became chief editor of the French-language "Voice of America" radio transmissions. He re-

turned to Switzerland and was chairman of an executive committee of the Congress for Cultural Freedom (1951–66) and of the European Association of Music Festivals (1951–83). From 1963 he was a professor at the Institute for European Studies at Geneva. He wrote more than 30 books, mainly on philosophy and the European ideal, most of which were widely translated.

Rowley, Charles Dunford, Australian social scientist (b. Oct. 12, 1906, Dunedoo, New South Wales, Australia—d. Sept. 18, 1985, Canberra, Australia), became an influential champion of the rights of Aboriginals in Australia as director (1964–68) of the Aboriginal Research Project of the Australian Academy of the Social Sciences and as chairman (1975–80) of the Aboriginal Land Fund Commission set up to buy back land for them. Two of his books, *The Destruction of Aboriginal Society* (1970) and *Outcasts in White Australia* (1971), did much to publicize the Aboriginals' plight and created a climate of opinion that facilitated the return to them of the Ayers Rock National Park in October 1985. Rowley was educated at Mudgee and Cowra high schools and at the University of Sydney. He became a secondary school teacher (1928–38) and lectured at the Sydney Teachers' College. In World War II he served with the Australian Army Education Service in New Guinea. While principal (1950–64) of the Australian School of Pacific Administration at Sydney, he visited Indonesia, the Philippines, and a number of mainland Asian countries, such as Thailand, in connection with the Unesco Adult Education Service. Rowley served as professor of political studies at the University of Papua New Guinea from 1968 to 1974.

Roy, Maurice Cardinal, Canadian prelate of the Roman Catholic Church (b. Jan. 25, 1905, Quebec, Canada—d. Oct. 24, 1985, Montreal, Que.), served as archbishop of Quebec (1947–81) and primate of Canada (1956–81) after gaining distinction as chief of chaplains of the Canadian Armed Forces during World War II. Roy, who was ordained a priest in 1927, was regarded as a brilliant theologian and served on the commission for the revision of the code of canon law. As military vicar he was a decorated hero after traversing the battlefields of North Africa and Europe during World War II. When he was named archbishop of Quebec in 1947, he became one of the youngest archbishops in the church and presided over the oldest Roman Catholic see in North America. In 1965 Pope Paul VI named Roy a cardinal and two years later appointed him head of two Vatican agencies, the Council for the Laity and the Pontifical Commission for Justice and Peace, positions he held until 1977. Roy retired from his religious posts in 1981 because of ill health.

Ryan, the Most Rev. Dermot, Irish prelate of the Roman Catholic Church (b. June 27, 1924, Dublin, Irish Free State—d. Feb. 21, 1985, Rome, Italy), served as archbishop of Dublin and primate of Ireland (1972–84) and in 1984 was appointed to the Vatican office of prefect of the Congregation for the Evangelization of Peoples. The first Irishman to attain very high rank in the Vatican, he shared Pope John Paul II's concern for traditional Catholic theology while remaining aware of the social problems of third world Catholic countries. He was the son of a physician. He was educated for the priesthood at University College, Dublin, and at St. Patrick's College, Maynooth, before being sent to Rome, where he attended the St. John Lateran and Gregorian universities and the Pontifical Biblical Institute. Ordained in 1950, he served as a convent and hospital chaplain before being appointed (1955) professor of fundamental dogmatic theology at Holy Cross College, Clonliffe. He became professor of Eastern languages (1957) and of Semitic languages (1969) at University College, Dublin. Ryan was thus known for his teaching rather than for his pastoral work, and although he was the choice of

the local clergy, he remained little known to the general public. The most obvious monument of his archiepiscopate was the large number of new churches built in Dublin to accommodate a rapidly increasing population.

Ryder, Loren L., U.S. sound engineer (b. March 9, 1900, Pasadena, Calif.—d. May 28, 1985, Carmel, Calif.), was a pioneering motion picture sound technician who garnered six Academy Awards for such innovations as the development of fine-grain emulsions for variable-density sound recording (1941), the construction and use of the first dial-controlled step-by-step sound channel lineup and test circuit (1945), the development and application of the supersonic playback and public address system (1949), the first studiowide application of magnetic sound recording for motion picture production (1950), and the invention of a projection film index to establish proper framing for various aspect ratios (1955). Ryder, who was nominated for 12 Oscars, won his first in 1938 for his recording of a pig's squeal that he reproduced backward to create the sound of an ice avalanche in *Spawn of the North.* Ryder served as sound director and chief engineer for Paramount studios from 1936 to 1957 and oversaw the sound for such films as *The Great Victor Herbert, Northwest Mounted Police, Double Indemnity, Rear Window,* and *The Ten Commandments.* He also developed the VistaVision wide-screen process and during World War II muffled the noises made by Gen. George Patton's tanks during the Battle of the Bulge so that the Germans thought that trucks, not tanks, were approaching.

Ryskind, Morrie, U.S. playwright and newspaper columnist (b. Oct. 20, 1895, Brooklyn, N.Y.—d. Aug. 24, 1985, Crystal City, Va.), shared the 1932 Pulitzer Prize for drama with George S. Kaufman and Ira Gershwin for the Broadway musical *Of Thee I Sing* and showcased his comic writing talents as a collaborator on such classic Marx Brothers films as *Coconuts* (1929), *Animal Crackers* (1930), and *A Night at the Opera* (1935). Ryskind, who was expelled (1917) from the Columbia University School of Journalism six weeks prior to graduation for referring to the university president, Nicholas Murray Butler, as "Czar Nicholas" in *The Jester,* the university's humour magazine, nonetheless landed a job as a reporter for *The World.* He penned skits for the Garrick Gaieties in 1924 before teaming up with Gershwin and Kaufman to write such musical comedies as *Strike Up the Band* and *Let 'em Eat Cake.* In 1935 Ryskind launched his Hollywood career as a screenwriter and the following year was nominated for an Academy Award for *My Man Godfrey.* In 1937 he was again nominated for an Academy Award as co-writer of *Stage Door.* Some of his other credits included *Room Service* (1938), *Man About Town* (1939), *Penny Serenade* (1941), and *Heartbeat* (1946). After testifying (1947) before the House Committee on Un-American Activities about Communist infiltration in the screenwriters' guild, Ryskind claimed he was ostracized in Hollywood. He later became involved in conservative politics and served as one of the original directors of *The National Review.* From 1960 until his retirement in 1978, he wrote for Los Angeles newspapers.

Sarkis, Elias, Lebanese politician (b. July 20, 1924, Ash Shabaniyah, Lebanon—d. June 27, 1985, Paris, France), as president of Lebanon from 1976 to 1982, attained his modest ambition of leaving the country in no worse state than he found it, despite the Israeli invasion around the time of his departure. A Maronite Christian and a graduate of the Jesuit Université Saint Joseph in Beirut, he was legal adviser to different Lebanese governments, president (1967) of the Intra Bank, and governor (1968–76) of the Bank of Lebanon before standing for the presidency in 1970, when he lost by one vote to Suleiman Franjieh. In May 1976, as a recognized moderate, he was elected by a Parliament

under Syrian "protection" at the height of the civil war. Franjieh refused at first to leave office; when Sarkis finally took power four months after his election, he faced the hopeless task of establishing his authority over a country internally divided and under constant threat from its neighbours. His successor, Bashir Gemayel, was assassinated on Sept. 14, 1982, before taking office, and Israeli forces entered West Beirut. Sarkis eventually handed over power to Bashir Gemayel's brother, Amin, after obtaining the entry of a multinational peacekeeping force to the Lebanese capital.

Sattar, Abdus, Bangladeshi lawyer and politician (b. March 1, 1906, Birbhum, India—d. Oct. 5, 1985, Dhaka, Bangladesh), was president of Bangladesh from 1981 to 1982. His brief period of democratic rule ended with the coup led by Lieut. Gen. Hossain Mohammad Ershad. Trained as a lawyer, he became an advocate in the Calcutta High Court in 1941 and continued his legal career after the independence of Pakistan, eventually becoming, in 1968, a judge of the Supreme Court. In 1954 Sattar was elected to the second Constituent Assembly, and in 1956 he served as minister for the interior and education. In 1975, after the independence of Bangladesh, he was minister of law and parliamentary affairs and special adviser to the president. He was vice-president (1977–81), and he became acting president after Pres. Ziaur Rahman's assassination, then president following the 1981 elections. But ill health, combined with the country's daunting economic and political troubles, led to a gradual loss of control, and in March 1982 effective power was assumed by General Ershad as chief martial-law administrator, with Abdul Fazal Mohammad Ahsanuddin Choudhury replacing Sattar as president. Sattar continued as a leading figure in the opposition coalition, but its strength was never tested in elections during his lifetime.

Scott, Francis Reginald, Canadian poet, lawyer, and politician (b. Aug. 1, 1899, Quebec City, Que.—d. Jan. 31, 1985, Montreal, Que.), was a distinguished member of the Montreal group of poets in the 1920s and used his creative genius to help shape Canadian constitutional law and to draft the Regina Manifesto, the founding document of the Co-operative Commonwealth Federation (CCF) party (which merged with the labour movement in 1961 to form the New Democratic Party). Scott, a Socialist, was a Rhodes scholar at Oxford (1920–23) and later studied law at McGill University in Montreal, where he served as professor (1928–61) and dean of the Law School (1961–64). His poetry celebrated the Canadian experience and ranged from social and political satire to nature, love, and metaphysical poems and translations from the French. Some of his poetic volumes include *Overture* (1945), *Events and Signals* (1954), *The Eye of the Needle: Satires, Sorties, Sundries* (1957), and *The Dance Is One* (1973). Scott was an expert on constitutional law and established his reputation as an advocate of civil liberties and minority rights before the Supreme Court of Canada by winning the Roncarelli case and convincing the court that the Quebec Padlock Act was invalid. As a man of letters he was a mentor to aspiring Canadian poets and was the founder of several poetry magazines. Scott won the first of his two Governor General's Awards in 1977 for *Essays on the Constitution* and the second in 1981 for *Collected Poems.*

Scourby, Alexander, U.S. actor and narrator (b. Nov. 13, 1913, Brooklyn, N.Y.—d. Feb. 22, 1985, Boston, Mass.), was a seasoned stage performer and motion picture character actor who excelled in villainous roles but was most famous for his mellow voice. He made his stage debut as a Shakespearean actor but became better known for his resonant voice, which was heard on radio commercials, public service messages, and offscreen narration of films and television documentaries, most notably the television series "Victory at Sea," first shown in 1952. For

the blind he recorded more than 400 of the world's great works of literature, including such classics as the complete King James Version of the Bible, *War and Peace,* and *Ulysses.* He appeared in such films as *The Big Heat* (1953), *Giant* (1956), and *The Executioner* (1970), and for the two seasons before his death, he was host for the Metropolitan Opera's "Live from the Met" broadcasts on public television.

Segal, Walter, Swiss-born architect (b. May 15, 1907, Ascona, Switz.—d. Oct. 27, 1985, London, England), was influential in his profession and a pioneer in building low-cost nonprofessionally assembled houses. He was also known for his severe and now vindicated criticism of high-rise tower blocks put up by British housing authorities after World War II. The son of Arthur Segal, an architect associated with Dadaism, he studied at Delft, Neth., Berlin, and Zürich, Switz., gaining his diploma in 1932. After practicing in Switzerland, he spent a year as excavations architect with the Cairo Museum, and he went to England in 1936. He became a naturalized British subject (1939) and during World War II worked for the Ministry of Supply designing workers' hostels. Afterward he set up in private practice but taught at the Architectural Association in London (1944–48) and at the Bartlett School of Architecture, University College, University of London (1973); from 1976 he lectured at the Thames Polytechnic. He was a visiting professor at the University of Pennsylvania (1978). His prototype house, a bungalow, was built for only £800 in the early 1960s; he cut costs by calculating quantities, using modern materials in standard production measurements, and eliminating the use of professional builders. He worked mainly for private clients, but in the 1960s he provided for the London borough of Lewisham an interesting group of assemble-it-yourself houses. His views were forcefully expressed in his book *Home and Environment* (1948).

Selke, Frank Joseph, Canadian sports executive (b. 1893, Berlin [now Kitchener], Ont.—d. July 3, 1985, near Montreal, Que.), together with Conn Smythe was instrumental in the erection of Toronto Maple Leafs Garden (opened Nov. 12, 1931) and helped create two National Hockey League (NHL) dynasties. The Toronto Maple Leafs, the league's first legitimate dynasty, had Stanley Cup victories in 1947, 1948, 1949, and 1951, and the Montreal Canadiens under Selke's orchestration captured, beginning with the 1955–56 season, five consecutive Stanley Cups, a feat that had never been equaled. Selke, an electrician by trade, worked for the University of Toronto and also coached their hockey teams before Smythe brought him into the NHL. Selke also participated in negotiations that led to the construction of the Hockey Hall of Fame, which was opened in 1961, and he was inducted into the hall the following year for his contributions to the game. At the age of 71 Selke retired as managing director of the Montreal Canadiens, and he resigned from the board of the Hockey Hall of Fame at the age of 85 when deafness plagued him.

Sessions, Roger Huntington, U.S. composer (b. Dec. 28, 1896, Brooklyn, N.Y.—d. March 16, 1985, Princeton, N.J.), was an important modern composer of orchestral, vocal, chamber, and instrumental works and had been influential since the 1920s in the development of serious American music both as a teacher of composition to such students as Milton Babbitt, Leon Korchner, and David Diamond and as a composer of his own complex works. Sessions graduated (1915) from Harvard University at age 18 and then studied composition at Yale University with Horatio Parker. Sessions, who credited Ernst Bloch as his greatest influence, studied with him and served as his assistant at the Cleveland Institute of Music. Early in his career Sessions adopted the neoclassical style of Stravinsky, but in the mid-1950s he incorporated the serialism that Arnold

Schoenberg and his followers had developed, first embracing the 12-tone style with the *Violin Sonata* (1953). Sessions's works, considered difficult both to perform and to listen to, sometimes waited years for their premieres because of their complexity. Relegated to obscurity by the general public, Sessions's music was widely admired by academicians, who bestowed many honours upon him. He was named to the National Institute of Arts and Letters in 1938 and to the American Academy of Arts and Sciences in 1961. A gifted teacher, he taught at Princeton University (1935–45 and 1953–65) and at the Juilliard School of Music from 1965 until shortly before his death. Among his most important works are *The Black Maskers* (1923; symphonic suite 1928), eight symphonies (1927, 1946, 1957, 1958, 1964, 1966, 1967, 1968), the Violin Concerto (1935), and the operas *The Trial of Lucullus* (1947) and *Montezuma* (1941–63). His later works include the cantata *When Lilacs Last in the Dooryard Bloom'd* (1970) and *Rhapsody* (1970) for orchestra. Sessions was awarded a Pulitzer Prize in 1974 for the body of his work and a second in 1981 for *Concerto for Orchestra*. Sessions was also a prolific author and published such works as *The Intent of the Artist* (1941), *Harmonic Practice* (1951), and *Roger Sessions on Music* (1979).

Sharp, Evelyn Adelaide Sharp, BARONESS, British civil servant (b. May 25, 1903, Ealing, Middlesex, England—d. Sept. 1, 1985, Lavenham, Sussex, England), as permanent secretary, Ministry of Housing and Local Government (1955–66), became the first woman in Britain to attain the highest executive rank in a government department. She was credited with helping to improve channels of communication between central and local government. Educated at St. Paul's Girls' School, London, and at Somerville College, University of Oxford, she showed comparatively little early academic promise, being notable at school for athletic prowess and at college for friendliness. She entered the administrative class of the Home Civil Service (1926), working first in the Board of Trade but quickly transferring to the Ministry of Health. During World War II she was seconded to the Treasury, where her outstanding abilities were first clearly recognized. She became deputy secretary (1946) in Prime Minister Clement Attlee's newly created Ministry of Town and Country Planning and later deputy at the Ministry of Housing and Local Government, where she spearheaded the successful drive (1951–54) of the minister, Harold Macmillan (later Lord Stockton), to build 300,000 new houses each year. After her retirement she was a member of the Independent Broadcasting Authority (1966–73). Created a Dame of the British Empire (1948), she was made Dame Grand Cross of the Order of the British Empire (1961) and a life peer (1966).

Shook, Karel, U.S. ballet master, dancer, and author (b. Aug. 8, 1920, Renton, Wash.—d. July 25, 1985, Englewood, N.J.), appeared in several Broadway musicals, danced with the Ballet Russe de Monte Carlo (1939–40 and 1950–52) and the New York City Ballet (1949), but probably made his most significant contribution to dance as a teacher and mentor to such gifted black dancers as Arthur Mitchell, Alvin Ailey, and Geoffrey Holder. Shook began teaching ballet in 1952 and in 1954 opened Studio Dance Arts in New York City, where he taught and encouraged black dancers and choreographers. He served on the faculty of the June Taylor School from 1957 to 1959, when he became ballet master of the Dutch National Ballet in The Netherlands. Shook returned to the U.S. in 1968 to cofound with Mitchell the Dance Theatre of Harlem, a classical ballet company for black dancers. He choreographed for stage, film, and television and scored successes with *Jazz-Nocturne* and *Alceste*. Shook's writings include articles for *Dance Magazine* and his 1977 book, *Elements of Classical Ballet Technique*. In 1980 he received the U.S. Presidential Award for "Excellence and Dedication in Education."

Shore, Edward W. ("EDDIE"), Canadian-born hockey player (b. Nov. 25, 1902, Fort Qu'Appelle, Sask.—d. March 16, 1985, Springfield, Mass.), as (1926–39) the aggressive National Hockey League (NHL) defenseman for the Boston Bruins professional hockey team, became notorious for his devastating body checks during an explosive career in which he scored 105 goals and 179 assists. His rough style earned him a total of 978 stitches and resulted in the permanent retirement of Ace Bailey, who underwent delicate brain surgery after Shore flattened him to the ice with a savage body check. Shore repeatedly brought hockey fans to their feet with his exciting play, and he was honoured with the Hart Trophy in 1932, 1934, 1935, and 1937 as the league's most valuable player. He also starred as a member of the Boston Bruins teams that won the Stanley Cup in 1929 and 1939. In 1939 Shore was traded to the New York Americans, but he soon retired and purchased the Springfield Indians of the American Hockey League. He sold the team in 1976. Shore was inducted into the Hockey Hall of Fame in 1945.

Signoret, Simone, French actress (b. March 25, 1921, Weisbaden, Germany—d. Sept. 30, 1985, Eure, France), matured from the young star of *Casque d'Or* (1952) to an actress with the potential to play women with the warmth and courage evident in her private life. As a political activist, with her husband, the actor Yves Montand, she was close to the Communist Party during the immediate post-World War II years and remained steadfastly committed to the defense of left-wing and humanitarian causes. She studied at the Sorbonne and took a number of small parts before achieving stardom in 1952. In the previous year, after divorcing her first husband, the director Yves Allegret, she had married Montand. Together they campaigned against the execution of the Rosenbergs, the Vietnam war, and the Algerian war, attracting at times violent hostility in France. Events in Hungary in 1956 disillusioned them with Communism and, as she recounted in her autobiography, *La Nostalgie n'est plus ce qu'elle était* (1976), they made no secret of their feelings to Soviet leader Nikita Khrushchev when they visited the Soviet Union. Signoret achieved another acting success in the British film *Room at the Top* (1958), for which she received an Oscar in 1960. Though she was established as a fine character actress, her fading beauty may have been partly responsible for a decline in her career, but she returned during the 1970s

AP/WIDE WORLD

with some fine performances on film, including *L'Aveu* (1970) and *La Vie devant soi* (1976). She also appeared in some successful television series. Signoret won critical acclaim for her best-selling books, including her second novel, *Adieu, Volodia,* which appeared in 1985. Signoret remained committed to the left despite Montand's move to the right in 1983, but their marriage survived this difference, and they were recognized as key figures in French cultural life. ·

Silvers, Phil, U.S. comedian (b. May 11, 1912, New York, N.Y.—d. Nov. 1, 1985, Los Angeles, Calif.), endeared himself to millions of television viewers as the blustering, conniving, and goldbricking Master Sergeant Ernie Bilko in the hit comedy "You'll Never Get Rich," which was rechristened "The Phil Silvers Show" (1955–59). The series, which garnered three Emmy awards, featured Silvers as a master con artist barking orders at a ragtag platoon. Silvers, who launched his career in vaudeville, achieved stardom on Broadway in *High Button Shoes* (1947) and *Top Banana* (1951) and appeared in such films as *Hit Parade of 1941, Cover Girl* (1944), *It's a Mad Mad Mad Mad World* (1963), and *A Funny Thing Happened on the Way to the Forum* (1966). After a stroke in 1972, he published an autobiography, *This Laugh Is on Me* (1973), and made numerous cameos on television and in films.

Simone, Madame (PAULINE BENDA PORCHÉ), French actress (b. April 3, 1877, Paris, France—d. Oct. 18, 1985, southwest France), had a joint career as actress and author, making her stage debut in 1902 and publishing her highly acclaimed first novel, *Le Désordre,* in 1930. Pauline Benda studied psychology at the Sorbonne and married the actor Charles Le Bargy, who persuaded her to go on the stage; her career, in a profession for which she expressed "profound indifference," lasted 30 years and established her as a leading interpreter of the works of Edmond Rostand and Luigi Pirandello. Simone later married Claude Casimir-Perier, but in 1912 she met the writer Alain-Fournier, and their relationship, until his death two years later in the first Battle of the Marne in World War I, was the greatest love of her life. Her third marriage, to the dramatist François Porché in 1923, led to a second career as a writer. *Le Désordre* was a considerable success and was followed by other novels and plays, including *Un Roi, deux dames, un valet* (1934; in collaboration with her husband), *Émily Brontë* (1953), and *En attendant l'aurore* (1954). Her autobiographical works, published between 1957 and 1970, were highly praised as the record of a brilliant mind and an acute sensibility, particularly alive to suffering. In 1960 she was awarded the Grand Prix de Littérature of the Académie Française. She was president of the Prix Femina jury and a Commander of the Légion d'honneur. Toward the end of her life she launched a new career as a radio and television presenter, demonstrating her gifts as a conversationalist.

Simpson, (Cedric) Keith, British pathologist (b. July 20, 1907, Hove, Sussex, England—d. July 21, 1985, London, England), was the first professor of forensic medicine (1962–72) at the University of London and for some 40 years, as a Home Office pathologist, was involved in some of the most outstanding criminal cases of the period, including the 1949 "acid bath murders" (*R* v. *Haigh*). After qualifying as a doctor at Guy's Hospital Medical School, University of London, in 1930, he specialized in pathology and lectured at Guy's in pathology (1932–37) and forensic medicine (1937–47). He also lectured in forensic medicine at the University of Oxford (1961–73). In 1947 he published a standard textbook, *Forensic Medicine,* which was reedited nine times and awarded a prize by the Royal Society of Arts. His other publications included many scientific articles and a variety of books, including *Modern Trends in Forensic Medicine* (1953), *The Investigation of Violence* (1978), and an autobiography, *Forty Years of Murder* (1978). He was among the first to recognize the "battered baby" syndrome, and in 1983 he aroused controversy with his refusal to perform a postmortem on a suspected victim of acquired immune deficiency syndrome (AIDS). He was a founder-member of the British Association in Forensic Medicine and served as its president in 1966–67. Simpson was appointed Commander of the Order of the British Empire in 1975.

Sims, Zoot (JOHN HALEY SIMS), U.S. saxophonist (b. Oct. 29, 1925, Inglewood, Calif.—d. March 23, 1985, New York, N.Y.), was the renowned swinging tenor saxophonist with big bands led by Benny Goodman and Stan Kenton and was one of the legendary "Four Brothers" who made up the saxophone line with Stan Getz, Herbie Steward, and Serge Chaloff in Woody Herman's Second Herd band. During the 1950s, though, Sims struck out on his own and made worldwide circuits of nightclubs and festivals, recruiting sidemen along the way. Sims began his musical career performing with a family band on drums and later clarinet. At the age of 16 he went on the road, which became his lifelong preference. He also played an elegant soprano saxophone but was better known for his buoyant tenor saxophone. Sims's more than 40 recordings include *Jive at Five, Zootcase, Joe & Zoot,* and *Soprano Sax.*

Smith, Samantha, U.S. peace advocate (b. June 1972, Maine—d. Aug. 25, 1985, Auburn, Maine), captured the imagination of the world when, as an 11-year-old schoolgirl, she wrote a letter to Soviet Pres. Yury V. Andropov expressing her fear of nuclear war. She achieved international celebrity status when she accepted Andropov's unexpected invitation to visit the Soviet Union for an all-expenses-paid trip. Smith struck a nerve when she wrote and asked Andropov, "Why do you want to conquer the whole world, or at least our country?"; she was accorded VIP treatment when she visited the Soviet Union in 1983. Her trip symbolized hopes for peace, though she never met An-

dropov. After her highly publicized two-week tour, she became a public figure and appeared on several television talk shows to recount her experience. Smith was killed, together with her father and six others, when their plane crashed and exploded on their return trip to Manchester, Maine, from London, where she had been filming a new television series, "Lime Street," starring Robert Wagner. Her death was mourned both in the United States and in the Soviet Union.

Sondergaard, Gale (EDITH HOLM SONDERGAARD), U.S. actress (b. Feb. 15, 1899, Litchfield, Minn.—d. Aug. 14, 1985, Woodland Hills, Calif.), launched her motion picture career by winning the Academy Award for best supporting actress for her first film, *Anthony Adverse* (1936). During the 1930s and '40s she specialized in villainous roles, terrifying Bob Hope in *The Cat and the Canary* (1939) and Shirley Temple in *The Blue Bird* (1940) and, without ever speaking a word, menacing Bette Davis in *The Letter* (1940). Sondergaard's dark, sultry looks and trademark sinister smile also earned her the sleek role of the Spider Woman in two films. Some of her other credits included *The Life of Emile Zola* (1937), *The Mark of Zorro* (1940), *Gypsy Wildcat* (1944), and *Anna and the King of Siam* (1946), for which she was nominated for an Academy Award. During the

early 1950s her career was interrupted when she refused to testify before the House Committee on Un-American Activities; she did not return to the screen until 1969 in *Slaves,* followed by *The Return of a Man Called Horse* (1976) and *Echoes* (1983), her last film.

Sparkman, John Jackson, U.S. politician (b. Dec. 20, 1899, Morgan County, Ala.—d. Nov. 16, 1985, Huntsville, Ala.), was an Alabama Democrat who served 42 years in Congress, first in the U.S. House of Representatives (1937–46) and then in the U.S. Senate (1946–79), reaching the pinnacle of his career when he was chosen as Adlai E. Stevenson's running mate in the 1952 U.S. presidential election. Sparkman, who earned a law degree from the University of Alabama in 1923, worked in private practice before he was elected to the House in 1936. He resigned from the House to fill a Senate vacancy created when John H. Bankhead died. During his long-time tenure in the Senate, Sparkman advocated public housing while serving as chairman (1967–74) of the Senate Committee on Banking, Housing, and Urban Affairs. As chairman (1975–79) of the Senate Foreign Relations Committee, he campaigned for presidential (as opposed to congressional) power to shape foreign policy. As the Democratic vice-presidential nominee, Sparkman did not have enough influence in the South to prevent Dwight D. Eisenhower from winning Florida, Virginia, Tennessee, and Texas and capturing 34 million out of the 61.5 million votes that were cast.

Spender, Sir Percy Claude, Australian lawyer, diplomat, and politician (b. Oct. 5, 1897, Sydney, Australia—d. May 3, 1985, Sydney), as minister of external affairs from 1949 to 1951 played a major role in the establishment of ANZUS, the security treaty involving Australia, New Zealand, and the U.S., and the Colombo Plan for Cooperative Economic Development in South and Southeast Asia, originally known as the Spender Plan. He served as ambassador (1951–58) to the U.S. and as a member (1958–64) and president (1964–67) of the International Court of Justice at The Hague. Though he started work as a clerk, he went to night school for a degree and later studied law. He was made king's counsel in 1935 and in 1937 was elected to the House of Representatives as an independent. Spender joined the United Australia Party in 1938 and was minister for the army in 1940–41 and a member of the Advisory War Council (AWC). He remained an opposition member of the AWC (1941–45) under the succeeding Labor government. When Sir Robert Menzies returned to power, Spender became minister for external affairs and territories. He went to the U.S. as vice-president of the Japanese peace treaty conference in 1951. After conversations in Canberra with John Foster Dulles, who became U.S. secretary of state under Pres. Dwight Eisenhower, he developed the concept of the ANZUS treaty. Spender, who was knighted in 1952, led the Australian delegation to the second Suez Conference in 1966. He was the author of several books on law and international affairs.

Springer, Axel, West German publisher (b. May 2, 1912, Altona, Germany—d. Sept. 22, 1985, West Berlin), as the owner of 18 newspapers and magazines, including the radio and television magazine *Hör Zu* and the mass-circulation newspaper *Bild Zeitung,* created post-World War II Germany's largest press empire. The Axel Springer publishing group's "quality" daily *Die Welt* enshrined Springer's belief in conservative democracy and advocated his causes of German reunification, anti-Communism, and support for Israel. He launched his career in his father's printing works and later served as a reporter. In 1945 Springer's knowledge of English helped him to gain permission from the British Control Commission to publish *Hör Zu.* He rapidly increased its circulation so that in 1952 he was able to found *Bild* as a sensation-seeking popular illustrated daily. In the following year

he bought *Die Welt,* establishing it as a leading right-wing newspaper. The group continued to expand during the 1950s, bringing out Sunday editions of its two main dailies, acquiring the Ullstein group, and, in a largely symbolic gesture, moving its headquarters to Berlin. By the 1960s, with *Bild*'s circulation above four million, the papers and Springer began to attract hostility. *Bild* had a taste for scandal that it used, in particular, in pursuit of political ends; student protesters in 1968 claimed that its campaign against Rudi Dutschke was indirectly responsible for the attempt to assassinate him. In time, Springer's conservatism on such issues as the development of better relations with East Germany put him increasingly out of step with the mood of the country. After the suicide of his son in 1980, Springer tried to merge with the Burda group, but this was vetoed under monopoly laws.

Stein, John ("JOCK"), Scottish soccer team manager (b. Oct. 5, 1922, Blantyre, Scotland—d. Sept. 10, 1985, Cardiff, Wales), managed Scotland's national soccer team from 1978 until his death. He was a miner but became a professional footballer at the age of 27, playing with Albion Rovers, Llanelli, and Celtic. Stein was captain of Celtic when he was forced to retire because of injury, and he went on to manage Dunfermline (1960–64), Hibernian (1964–65), and then Celtic (1965–78); he led Celtic to many successive victories in the Scottish and League cups. An expert on international competition, he made Celtic the first British club to win the European Cup, in 1967; they reached the final again in 1970. After managing Leeds United, Stein returned to Scotland in 1978 as manager of the national side, helping it to qualify for the 1982 World Cup finals. A tough and inspiring leader, he enjoyed enormous popularity with his team and its supporters.

Sterling, J(ohn) E(wart) Wallace, Canadian-born educator and historian (b. Aug. 6, 1906, Linwood, Ont.—d. July 1, 1985, Woodside, Calif.), was the visionary president of Stanford University from 1949 to 1968, during which time he built the institution into one of the world's leading research centres and presided over its rapid expansion, including a 170% increase in the faculty and a 40% increase in the student body. Sterling, who earned a B.A. in history at the University of Toronto and an M.A. at the University of Alberta, was a natural athlete who excelled in rugby football and basketball. In 1938 Sterling received a Ph.D. from Stanford and then moved to the California Institute of Technology, where he subsequently became head of the history department (1944–46). He also gained repute as a television news analyst from 1942 to 1948. As president of Stanford he was instrumental in attracting quality faculty members and even raided other campuses to acquire top-notch teachers. His phenomenal fund-raising drives (1960–64 and 1972–77) raised a total of $400 million for the university. Sterling's contributions to education were recognized with more than 20 honorary degrees; in addition, in 1976 he was awarded an honorary knighthood by Queen Elizabeth II, and in 1978 he won Stanford University's "Degree of Uncommon Man," its highest honour. After his retirement as Stanford's president in 1968, he was named university chancellor for life.

Stewart, Potter, U.S. judge (b. Jan. 23, 1915, Jackson, Mich.—d. Dec. 7, 1985, Hanover, N.H.), as associate justice of the U.S. Supreme Court (1958–81) served as the crucial "swing vote" on close court decisions involving the exercise of government powers during the Warren Court era (1953–69); he then became a centrist when the more conservative Burger Court assumed power in 1969. After graduating from Yale University's law school, he worked in New York City as a lawyer before settling in Cincinnati, Ohio, where he became involved in Republican politics as a member of the city council

and as vice-mayor. In 1954 Pres. Dwight D. Eisenhower appointed him to the U.S. Court of Appeals for the 6th District, and in 1958 Stewart was elevated to the U.S. Supreme Court to succeed Harold H. Burton. As Supreme Court justice, Stewart was hailed for his succinct opinions. In *Shelton* v. *Tucker* he wrote the majority opinion holding unconstitutional a law requiring teachers to reveal the names of all associations to which they belonged. He also wrote a number of memorable dissents in cases involving individual freedom, including *Engel* v. *Vitale, Griswold* v. *Connecticut,* and *Miranda* v. *Arizona.* In *Ginzburg* v. *United States,* Stewart warned that "government by big brother" was near. He was also the lone dissenter on the 1962 court decision striking down compulsory school prayer. Some of Stewart's notable judicial one-liners included his pronouncement in *Katz* v. *U.S.* that "the Constitution protects people, not places" and his 1964 opinion that he could not define pornographic material, "but I know it when I see it." In his 1972 concurring opinion when the Supreme Court struck down capital punishment, he wrote, "The death sentences are cruel and unusual in the same way that being struck by lightning is cruel and unusual." In 1973, when the court ruled that a debtor could be denied access to bankruptcy court because he lacked a $50 filing fee, Stewart quipped, "The Court today holds that Congress may say that some of the poor are too poor even to go bankrupt. I cannot agree." In 1980 Stewart cast the deciding vote in *Harris* v. *McRae,* ruling that legislatures need not include abortion funding in medical benefits. When Earl Warren retired as chief justice in 1969, Stewart amazed colleagues by personally advising Pres. Richard M. Nixon not to elevate him to that post. He further surprised his peers when he retired in 1981 at the age of 66.

Stewart, Msgr. Richard Louis, British prelate of the Roman Catholic Church (b. Oct. 22, 1926, Woodford, Essex, England—d. July 30, 1985, Worthing, West Sussex, England), played a key role in the development of the Roman Catholic Church's relationship with the Anglican Communion and with world Methodism. The son of a Catholic publisher, he was educated at a diocesan seminary, completing his studies for the priesthood at the English College in Rome (then, during World War II, in Britain) and at the Vatican's Gregorian University. Ordained in 1950, he taught at St. Peter's School, Guildford, before becoming lecturer in theology at St. John's Seminary, Wonersh, Surrey. Stewart became involved in ecumenical work through membership in the pioneer joint committee established by the Roman Catholic archbishop and the Anglican bishop of Southwark, under the stimulus of the Second Vatican Council (1962–65). In 1970 he became secretary of the Ecumenical Commission of the Bishops' Conference of England and Wales and had the delicate task of improving relations with the British Council of Churches while still retaining only observer status. In 1979 he moved to Rome and became cosecretary of the new Anglican-Roman Catholic International Commission.

Taniguchi Masaharu, Japanese religious leader (b. 1893, Hyogo Pref., Japan—d. June 17, 1985, Nagasaki, Japan), was the founder of Seicho-no-Ie ("House of Growth"), a religious organization that boasted some 3.5 million followers and espoused the principles of Buddhism, Christianity, and Shintoism. After leaving school in 1914 Taniguchi became disillusioned with his long and arduous labour as a foreman in a spinning mill. He was inspired by Momozo Kurata and sought repose in spiritualism and psychotherapy. Taniguchi joined the religious organization Omoto-kyo. His literary flair brought him to prominence, but he resigned after the 1921 suppression. All of these influences prompted Taniguchi to found Seicho-no-Ie, which adhered to psychic methods of treatment. He elaborated on the movement in 20 volumes, which had a seven million-copy printing. Some of his works

included *Shinri* ("Truth"; 10 vol.) and *Seimei-no-nazo* ("Enigma of Life").

Thuy, Xuan, Vietnamese politician (b. Sept. 2, 1912, near Hanoi, French Indochina—d. June 18, 1985, Hanoi, Vietnam), served as vice-speaker and secretary-general of Vietnam's National Assembly but became internationally known when he was the North Vietnamese foreign minister (1963–65) and his country's chief delegate (with Le Duc Tho, who negotiated separately with Henry Kissinger) at the Paris peace talks that ended U.S. involvement in Vietnam. He had joined (1926) the League of Young Revolutionaries founded by Nguyen Ai Quoc (afterward Ho Chi Minh) and was twice arrested (1928, 1929). As a member of the Indochina Communist Party he was imprisoned (1939–45) throughout the period of Japanese occupation and Vichy French rule. On his release (March

1945) he became editor in chief of the Viet Minh's official newspaper, *Cuu Quoc* ("National Salvation"). When the Democratic Republic of Vietnam (North Vietnam) was formed (1946), he was elected as a deputy to its National Assembly and became a member of the governing Central Committee. He represented North Vietnam at the Geneva conference that ended (1954) the French Indochina war and in 1962 was deputy chairman of a North Vietnamese delegation to a conference on Laos. In 1965 he became head of the foreign relations department of the Workers' Party Central Committee.

Tillstrom, Burr, U.S. puppeteer (b. Oct. 13, 1917, Chicago, Ill.—d. Dec. 6, 1985, Palm Springs, Calif.), delighted millions of television viewers, children and adults alike, as the creator and voice of a gallery of puppets whose antics were showcased on the "Kukla, Fran, and Ollie" television program. The members of his Kuklapolitan Theatre puppet group included Kukla, the bald-headed, round-nosed, gently mocking clown, Oliver J. Dragon (Ollie), a scatterbrained, one-toothed dragon, Beulah the Witch, Madam Ooglepuss, Colonel Crockie, Cecil Bill, Dolores Dragon, Mercedes Rabbit, and Fletcher Rabbit. The character of Fran was played by Fran Allison, the only visible human member of the troupe. Though Tillstrom attended the University of Chicago, he was more at home manipulating his puppets. In 1947 "Kukla, Fran, and Ollie" debuted in Chicago, and in 1949 it became a major national hit. The show was canceled in 1957 but was later syndicated. The multitalented Tillstrom gained five Emmy awards, two Peabody Awards, and more than 50 other honours for his imaginative work.

Trevelyan, Humphrey Trevelyan, BARON, British diplomat (b. Nov. 27, 1905, Hindhead, Surrey, England—d. Feb. 8, 1985, London, England), was ambassador to Egypt at the time of the 1956 Suez crisis and ambassador to the U.S.S.R. (1962–65). Educated at Lancing College and Jesus College, University of Cam-

bridge, he joined the Indian Civil Service in 1929. After Trevelyan was transferred (1932) to the Political Department, he worked successively in the central princely states, in Delhi, Gwalior, Mysore, and Bahawalpur, and in the southern Rajputana states before being sent (1944) to Washington, D.C., as secretary to the agent-general for India. He returned to Delhi (1946) as joint secretary in the External Affairs Department but left when India achieved independence (1947). Trevelyan successively served as counsellor in Baghdad (1948–51), economic and financial adviser at the U.K. High Commission for Germany (1951–53), British chargé d'affaires at Beijing (Peking; 1953–55), and ambassador to Egypt (1955–56). He went as under secretary to the UN in 1958 but soon resigned to become ambassador to Iraq (1958–61). He was deputy under secretary of state at the Foreign Office in London (1962) before going to Moscow. Trevelyan retired in 1965 but was sent by Prime Minister Harold Wilson as high commissioner in Southern Arabia (1967) during the troubles in Aden that preceded the establishment of independent Yemen (Aden; South Yemen). Trevelyan's books include *The Middle East in Revolution* (1970), *The India We Left* (1972), and his autobiography, *Public and Private* (1980). Knighted in 1955, he was created a life peer in 1968.

Turner, Big Joe (JOSEPH VERNON TURNER), U.S. blues singer (b. May 18, 1911, Kansas City, Mo.—d. Nov. 24, 1985, Englewood, Calif.), helped usher in the era of rock and roll as the "blues shouter" of such classic rhythm and jump songs as "Shake, Rattle and Roll," "Corrina, Corrina," and "Flip, Flop and Fly." Turner, who was dubbed the "Boss of the Blues," was widely imitated by a string of white performers including Bill Haley and the Comets, who scored a smash hit by recording his "Shake, Rattle and Roll" with censored lyrics. Turner launched his career as a teenager singing in jazz clubs in Kansas City before teaming up with boogie-woogie pianist Pete Johnson and appearing in the 1938 "From Spirituals to Swing" concert at Carnegie Hall. The pair then became popular entertainers at New York City nightclubs, and they recorded such songs as "Roll 'em Pete" and "Cherry Red" before Turner went (1941) to Hollywood to appear in Duke Ellington's Hollywood revue *Jump for Joy.* Turner returned to New York in 1951 with Count Basie and produced (1951–54) a string of hits including such top-selling rhythm-and-blues records as "Chains of Love," "Sweet 16," and "Honey, Hush." Turner continued to play and record, and in 1980 he appeared in the documentary *The Last of the Blue Devils.*

Uhlman, Fred, German-born writer (b. 1901, Stuttgart, Germany—d. April 12, 1985, London, England), was forced to flee Germany in 1933 because of his Jewish background and encapsulated the atmosphere of Nazism in a short novel, *Reunion,* published in English in 1977. A lawyer, belonging to an "integrated" Jewish family, he was unaware of the danger of Hitler's coming to power until a friend warned him to flee. He went to Paris, began to paint, and won the Paul Guillaume Prize (though it was not awarded because of his German nationality). In 1938 he went to London, where he founded a Free German League of Culture for refugee intellectuals before his internment as an enemy alien in 1940. After World War II he remained in England. His autobiography, *The Making of an Englishman,* was published in 1960. Uhlman's masterpiece, *Reunion,* records the experience of a German refugee in the U.S. who, after the war, discovers the fate of a school friend under Nazi tyranny.

Visser't Hooft, Willem Adolph, Dutch clergyman (b. Sept. 20, 1900, Haarlem, Neth.—d. July 4, 1985, Geneva, Switz.), as general secretary of the World Council of Churches (WCC) from its provisional formation (1938) until his retirement (1966), was probably the most influ-

ential individual in the movement. After studying theology at the University of Leyden, he was ordained into the Dutch Reformed Church, becoming secretary of the World Committee of the Young Men's Christian Association (1924) and general secretary of the World Student Christian Federation (1931). He attended decisive conferences (Stockholm, 1925, and Oxford, 1937) of the Life and Work ecumenical movement and the conference (Edinburgh, 1937) of the Faith and Order movement and played a vital role in the merging of these two groups to form the WCC. Its character was defined at a meeting in Utrecht, Neth. (1938), when Visser't Hooft was appointed its general secretary. After the WCC established headquarters in Geneva, he provided communication between the Dutch Resistance and the exiled government in London during World War II. He was confirmed in office at the Amsterdam WCC Assembly (1948), and his achievements included bringing the Russian Orthodox Church into full WCC membership (1961) and the establishment (1965) of a permanent joint working committee with the Vatican. He wrote nearly 20 books, including his *Memoirs* (1973).

Voegelin, Eric (HERMAN WILHELM), German-born political philosopher (b. Jan. 3, 1901, Cologne, Germany—d. Jan. 19, 1985, Palo Alto, Calif.), devoted his energies to formulating a comprehensive philosophy of man, society, and history and expressed his ideas most extensively in his four-volume *Order and History* (1956–74). Voegelin, who earned a Ph.D. from the University of Vienna in 1922, fled Austria during World War II after the Nazis annexed the country. He became a U.S. citizen in 1944 and taught at Harvard University, the University of Alabama, and Louisiana State University. From 1958 to 1969 he taught political science at the University of Munich, but he returned to the U.S. to serve as distinguished research scholar at the Hoover Institution on War, Revolution and Peace in Stanford, Calif. Some of Voegelin's other books included *Der Autoritäre Staat* (1936), *The New Science of Politics* (1952), and *From Enlightenment to Revolution* (1975).

Wahlen, Friedrich Traugott, Swiss politician (b. April 10, 1899, Gmeis, near Mirchel, Bern Canton, Switz.—d. Nov. 7, 1985, Bern), was best remembered as architect of the Wahlen Plan to organize and safeguard Swiss food supplies during World War II; he served as federal president in 1961. Educated at the Federal Institute of Technology, Zürich, he gained a diploma in agricultural engineering and was an assistant at the Institute (1920–22). He went to Canada, where he was supervising analyst at the Dominion Seed Laboratory, Quebec, and then chief analyst at the Dominion Department of Agriculture, Ottawa. He returned to Switzerland (1929) to become director of an experimental agricultural station at Oerlikon, Zürich. Wahlen was professor of agronomy at the Federal Institute of Technology (1943–49), and throughout World War II he worked in the War Food Office as chief of the section of Agricultural Production and Home Economics. He was also a member of the Swiss Council of States (1942–49). Wahlen was director of the Agricultural Division of the UN Food and Agriculture Organization (FAO), located in Washington (1949–50) and in Rome (1951–57); he became the FAO's deputy director general (1957–58). Returning to Switzerland, he held federal office as councillor in charge of justice and police (1959) and of public economy (1960). He was minister of foreign affairs (1961–65) and in 1967 became chairman of a committee set up to revise the Swiss constitution.

Walding, Joseph Albert, New Zealand politician (b. June 18, 1926, Christchurch, New Zealand—d. June 4, 1985, London, England), was a prominent member of the New Zealand Labour Party and as minister of overseas trade (1972–75) successfully negotiated continued access to New Zealand's traditional British market for its dairy produce after Britain joined the European Communities (1973). Walding was educated at Wellington and Dunedin, and he joined the merchant navy, serving during World War II in the Pacific and the Atlantic. He established a canning business at Palmerston North, where he became a city councillor and in 1967 the town's member of Parliament. Walding became (1972) minister of the environment, of recreation and sport, and of overseas trade. He also shared with Prime Minister Norman Kirk the foreign affairs portfolio. Walding took a lead in New Zealand's recognition of China (1972) and spearheaded campaigns against South Africa's apartheid (racial separation) policy in sports and the presence in New Zealand territorial waters of warships carrying nuclear weapons. He masterminded David Lange's successful campaign for a Labour victory in the July 1984 general election and was sent to London as high commissioner in February 1985.

Walker, Robert Milnes, British surgeon (b. Aug. 2, 1903, Wakefield, Yorkshire, England—d. Aug. 25, 1985, Kintbury, Berkshire, England), a notable specialist in surgery of the liver, lungs, and heart, was professor of surgery at the University of Bristol and surgeon to the Bristol Royal Hospital from 1946 to 1964. Educated at University College Hospital, London, Walker was consultant at the Royal Hospital, Wolverhampton, from 1931 and began an outstanding career in teaching while practicing as a surgeon. His most striking contribution to surgery involved his shunt operation for portal hypertension, which gained him an international reputation. He was vice-president (1966–68) of the Royal College of Surgeons (RCS) and was awarded its gold medal in 1972. After retirement he served as director (1968–71) of surgical studies at the RCS and, as master of the Worshipful Company of Barbers, jointly wrote a history of the company (*Barbers and Barber-Surgeons of London*, 1978).

Wallace-Hadrill, John Michael, British historian (b. Sept. 29, 1916, Bromsgrove, Worcestershire, England—d. Nov. 3, 1985, Cassington, Oxfordshire, England), served as Chichele professor of modern history at All Souls College, University of Oxford (1974–83), and was a distinguished early medievalist whose main field of study was the Franks, although he was also concerned with aspects of Anglo-Saxon history. Educated at Cheltenham College, he won a scholarship (1935) at Corpus Christie College, Oxford, and later began research on the Charlemagne legends under the supervision of F. M. Powicke. During World War II he served in military intelligence. He returned to Corpus Christie College as a fellow (1945–47), moving to Merton College as fellow and tutor (1947–55). Wallace-Hadrill went to the University of Manchester as professor of medieval history (1955–61) but returned to Merton as senior research fellow (1961–74), serving the college as subwarden (1964–66). He was editor (1965–74) of the *English Historical Review* and publications secretary (1978–81) of the British Academy, of which he had been made a fellow in 1969. His first book, *The Barbarian West, 400–1000* (1952), was followed by *The Long-Haired Kings* (1962), a study of the Merovingian royal dynasty, and *Early Germanic Kingship* (1971). His latest published book was *The Frankish Church* (1983).

Watt, William, British scientist (b. April 12, 1912, Edinburgh, Scotland—d. Aug. 11, 1985, Alton, Hampshire, England), joined the Royal Aircraft Establishment (RAE), Farnborough, during the 1930s and from 1944 conducted pioneering research into graphites and carbon fibres, which earned him a number of awards for technical innovation. He started work in 1928 as a laboratory assistant in the Edinburgh College of Agriculture before studying chemistry at Heriot-Watt College (now University), Edinburgh, and at the University of London. In 1944, as an assistant at the RAE, he began the study of high-temperature nonmetallic materials, which led him to develop a new method for production of high-density graphites. By 1963, as a senior principal scientist at the RAE, he was investigating the production of stiff and lightweight materials for carbon-based textile fibres and in the following year was able to patent his invention. With two colleagues he was given the Wolfe Award (1968), and he personally obtained the Royal Aeronautical Society's Silver Medal (1969). Watt was appointed Officer of the Order of the British Empire in 1969. After retirement from the RAE he joined (1975) the University of Surrey as senior research fellow in the department of materials and science.

Welch, Robert Henry Winborne, Jr., U.S. right-wing activist (b. Dec. 1, 1899, Chowan County, N.C.—d. Jan. 6, 1985, Winchester, Mass.), was a wealthy candy manufacturer who in 1958 founded the John Birch Society, an ultraconservative, staunchly anti-Communist organization that exerted its greatest influence during the mid-1960s. The society then boasted an $8 million annual budget, more than 100,000 members, two monthly magazines, a weekly radio program, and some 400 bookstores. Welch himself was best known for his preposterous accusations; he called Pres. Dwight D. Eisenhower "a dedicated conscious agent of the Communist conspiracy" and claimed that Secretary of State John Foster Dulles and CIA Director Allen W. Dulles were members of the Communist underground. While presiding over the society (named for an obscure U.S. intelligence officer who was killed by the Chinese Communists ten days after the end of World War II and was believed to be the first casualty of the cold war), Welch advocated "a militant form of Americanism" and promoted "less government, more individual responsibility and a better world." The society also demanded U.S. withdrawal from the UN, the abolition of the North Atlantic Treaty Organization, a severing of all ties to the U.S.S.R., the impeachment of Chief Justice Earl Warren, major restrictions on collective bargaining, and an end to all civil rights programs. When Welch retired as president of the society in 1983, he was named chairman emeritus.

Welles, (George) Orson, U.S. director, producer, screenwriter, and actor (b. May 6, 1915, Kenosha, Wis.—d. Oct. 10, 1985, Los Angeles, Calif.), was a maverick genius "boy wonder" whose extraordinary artistic talents included those of actor, director, producer, and filmmaker. His classic *Citizen Kane* (1941) came to be considered a cinematic masterpiece and possibly the greatest film ever made, although at the time of its release it was a box-office flop. A child prodigy, Welles received an informal education except for five years (1926–31) at the private Todd School in Woodstock, Ill. He made his professional stage debut at the Gate Theatre in Dublin at the age of 16. He made his Broadway debut playing Tybalt in *Romeo and Juliet* with Katherine Cornell before he was 20. In 1937, together with John Houseman, he

MARTINE PECCOUX—GAMMA/LIAISON

founded the Mercury Theatre, which boasted such performers as Joseph Cotten and Agnes Moorehead and became famous for its original, bold productions and cunning use of sound effects. The group created a sensation on radio on Oct. 30, 1938, with their vivid dramatization of H. G. Wells's *War of the Worlds,* which, with its innovative news bulletins from the fictional scene of the New Jersey Martian invasion, persuaded panic-stricken listeners that the broadcast was authentic. Just a few weeks earlier, at the age of 23, Welles had been dubbed the "Wonder Boy" by *Time* and featured on the magazine's cover.

In the theatre Welles created a powerful new sensibility with his all-black "voodoo" version of *Macbeth* for the Negro People's Theatre in 1936, a part of the Federal Theatre Project, and with his 1937 production of the leftist opera *The Cradle Will Rock,* which was closed down by federal officials, who locked the theatre. Welles, the cast, and 2,000 members of the audience marched several blocks to a rented theatre to stage the show. Before his Mercury Theatre disbanded in 1939, they had presented a novel modern-dress version of *Julius Caesar.*

On the strength of his theatre credits, Welles was given complete artistic control over production of the seminal *Citizen Kane,* a story of a powerful and greedy newspaper magnate (loosely based on the life of William Randolph Hearst). The film opened new avenues in American filmmaking with Welles's use of deep-focus photography, high-contrast black-and-white film stock, and innovative narrative and sound techniques. The film was a box-office failure; it received only one Academy Award, for best screenplay; and Welles never again enjoyed complete artistic control over a film, though several films—including *The Magnificent Ambersons* (1942), *Journey into Fear* (1943), *The Lady from Shanghai* (1948), and *Touch of Evil* (1958)—were considered masterpieces. After the latter film Welles went to Europe, where he directed *Le Procès* (1962; *The Trial*) and *Campanadas a Medianoche* (1966; *Falstaff,* or *Chimes at Midnight*). In 1975 he wrote, directed, and acted in the magical *F for Fake.* Some films in which he appeared as an actor include *Jane Eyre* (1944), *The Third Man* (1949), *The Long Hot Summer* (1958), *A Man for All Seasons* (1966), and *Crossed Swords* (1978). In later years the gifted raconteur appeared on television talk shows and in commercials. His sonorous voice, once heard on radio in the role of Lamont Cranston in the mystery series "The Shadow," was also familiar to millions from countless films and documentaries. In 1975 Welles received the Life Achievement Award from the American Film Institute.

Whillans, Don, British mountaineer (b. 1933, Salford, Lancashire, England—d. Aug. 4, 1985, Oxford, England), pioneered many classic climbs in Britain, in the Alps, in the Himalayas, and in South America. He was noted for his daring yet cautious approach and for his belief that mountaineering was not reserved for an athletic elite. Whillans worked as a plumber and began climbing as a hobby with Joe Brown as his partner. They started rock climbing on British faces, and together the two men opened some classic new routes before turning to the Alps, where during the 1950s they made the first British ascent of the west face of the Dru and the first ascents of the Blaitière and the central pillar of Fréney. Whillans also five times attempted the north wall of the Eiger, with Chris Bonnington, and continued to climb in Europe throughout his life. During the 1970s he climbed the south face of Annapurna, reaching the summit with Dougal Haston, and was a member of expeditions to Everest. Recognized by this time as a climber of international status, he was a popular lecturer and a much-loved figure, in part perhaps because of his approachability.

White, E(lwyn) B(rooks), U.S. essayist and stylist (b. July 11, 1899, Mount Vernon, N.Y.—d. Oct. 1, 1985, Brooklin, Maine), was universally admired for his simple yet witty and concise writing style and was especially lauded as an essayist for *The New Yorker* magazine and as the cherished author of the beloved children's classic *Charlotte's Web* (1952), the story of Wilbur the pig and how he was saved by the heroic weaving skills of Charlotte the spider. After graduating from Cornell University in 1921, White worked as a reporter and free-lance writer before joining *The New Yorker* in 1927, where for the remainder of his life he helped shape the character and flavour of the weekly with his lucid essays that explored everything from politics to modern manners. With James Thurber, White collaborated on *Is Sex Necessary?* (1929), a spoof of the then-current sex manuals, and from 1938 to 1943 he also contributed a monthly column to *Harper's* magazine. One of White's most enduring contributions, *The Elements of Style* (1935; with William Strunk, Jr.), became a standard work on American English usage; it was revised several times and sold millions of copies. His other children's books include the delightful *Stuart Little* (1945), the story of a mouse born to a human family, and *The Trumpet of the Swan* (1970), the story of a swan who realized he had no voice and compensated by learning to play the trumpet. Some of White's other memorable works include *Points of My Compass* (1962), *The Second Tree From the Corner* (1954), *Letters of E. B. White* (1976), and *Poems and Sketches of E. B. White* (1981). In 1978 the custodian of a storehouse of enchantment was awarded a special Pulitzer Prize for the body of his work.

White, Errol Ivor, British paleontologist (b. June 30, 1901, London, England—d. Jan. 11, 1985, Wallingford, England), was a leading world authority in the study of fossil fish. His most influential work was in connection with ostracoderms found in Old Red Sandstone rock; his technique, using these fossils to age and correlate rock, was adopted by geologists in Europe and North America. Educated at Highgate School and King's College, University of London, he studied geology, specializing in petrology. In 1922 White was appointed to the staff of the fossil fish department of the British Museum (Natural History), where he studied and described fossils from the Old Red Sandstone rocks of Hertfordshire and Wales. In 1934, with his assistant Ashley Toombs, he found the first complete specimens of the ostracoderm *Pteraspis,* and his paper on it in the *Philosophical Transactions* of the Royal Society (1935) secured his reputation. He became deputy keeper (1938) and keeper (1955–66) of the Department of Geology (later renamed Palaeontology). White was a member of the joint Anglo-Scandinavian scientific expedition to Spitsbergen (1939). Author of some 130 scientific papers, he was elected a fellow of the Royal Society in 1956.

Wilkinson, (Lancelot) Patrick, British classical scholar (b. June 1, 1907, Broughty Ferry, Angus, Scotland—d. April 23, 1985, Cambridge, England), was reader in Latin literature (1967–69) and in classics (1969–74) at the University of Cambridge, and through his writings he endeavoured to keep Latin letters and the values of Roman society before a public increasingly unaware of Europe's classical heritage. Educated at Charterhouse School and at King's College, Cambridge, he gained a double first in the classical tripos and undertook postgraduate research in Munich and Rome before returning to King's as a fellow (1932). During World War II he was attached to the Foreign Office cipher unit at Bletchley Park. He was vice-provost of King's (1961–65) and university orator (1958–74). His works include *Horace and His Lyric Poetry* (1945), *Letters of Cicero* (1949), and *Ovid Recalled* (1955). In *The Roman Experience* (1975) and *Classical Attitudes to Modern Issues* (1979) he wrote more widely on the classical ethos, while in *Golden Latin Artistry* (1963) he explored the resonances of Latin poetry and prose. He produced a critical study (1969) of Virgil's *Georgics* and a translation (1982) for the Penguin Classics series. Wilkinson also wrote (1963) the Latin text for Benjamin Britten's *Cantata Misericordium.*

Williams, Cootie (CHARLES MELVIN WILLIAMS), U.S. trumpeter (b. July 24, 1908, Mobile, Ala.—d. Sept. 15, 1985, New York, N.Y.), was identified by his growling, muted horn and, as the last surviving member of the classic Duke Ellington bands of the 1920s and '30s, played a key role in maintaining the inflections and nuances of the original band. Williams, who performed with the Chick Webb and Fletcher Henderson orchestras before moving to Ellington's band, played with the latter until 1940, when he joined Benny Goodman's ensemble. Williams formed his own band a year later but returned

in 1962 to the Ellington orchestra, where the veteran trumpeter resumed his role as one of the ensemble's most exciting soloists until ill health forced him to retire in 1983. Some of the pieces Ellington wrote exclusively for Williams included "Concerto for Cootie" (with lyrics, "Do Nothin' till You Hear from Me"), "Echoes of Harlem," and "The Shepherd Who Watches over the Night Flock." Major albums included "Carnegie Hall Jazz Concert," "Together 1957," and "The Big Challenge."

Wilson, Sir (Leslie) Hugh, British architect (b. May 1, 1913, London, England—d. July 20, 1985, London), was prominent in the planning of new towns and pioneered the concept of separate pedestrian walkways from which motorized traffic was excluded. An assistant architect, first in private practice (1933–39) and then for Canterbury City Council (1939–45), he became Canterbury's city architect and planning officer (1945–56). He was chief architect (1956–62) for the new town of Cumbernauld near Glasgow, where he first designed an exclusively pedestrian precinct. Wilson was technical adviser on urban development to the Ministry of Housing and Local Government (1965–67), part-time director of the Department of the Environment's Property Services Agency (1973–74), and a member of the Economic Development Committee for Building of the National Economic Development Office (1976–77). He planned the new towns of Northampton, Redditch, Skelmersdale, and Irvine (near Kilmarnock), advised on city centre plans for Exeter, Brighton, Oxford, Lewes, and Cardiff, and was involved in the redevelopment of the London docklands area (1977–84). Wilson was president of the Royal Institute of British Architects (1967–69) and a member from 1971 of the Royal Fine Arts Commission. He was knighted in 1967.

Wirkkala, Tapio, Finnish designer (b. June 2, 1915, Hangö, Fin.—d. May 19, 1985, Espoo, Fin.), was well known as a sculptor and as a designer for the Iittala glassworks. Until the outbreak of World War II he worked in advertising, and after the war he won a prize offered

by the Iittala works and the first two prizes in a competition to redesign the Finnish bank notes. He began to specialize in glassware, porcelain, and household objects, including the "puukko" knives that were among the most widely used of his designs. At the same time, he continued to work as a sculptor, winning the Gran Premio at the Milan Triennale in 1951 for objects in laminated wood. He also designed wood relief for the Finnish pavilion at the Montreal Expo 67 and worked on large-scale glass sculptures. Wirkkala's work was exhibited in permanent collections in museums throughout the world.

Wolfenden, John Frederick Wolfenden, BARON, British educationist (b. June 26, 1906, Halifax, Yorkshire, England—d. Jan. 18, 1985, Guildford, England), was a notable headmaster, vice-chancellor (1950–63) of Reading University, and chairman (1963–68) of the University Grants Committee. But his name became best known in connection with the government's Departmental Committee on Homosexual Offences and Prostitution (1954–57), of which he was chairman. The committee's report was published in 1957, but its recommendations were not acted upon until 1967, when the Sexual Offences Act legalized homosexual practices between consenting adults in private. Educated at Wakefield Grammar School and at Queen's College, University of Oxford, where he studied classics and philosophy, Wolfenden spent a year at Princeton University before returning to Oxford as fellow and tutor at Magdalen College (1929). In 1934 he was appointed headmaster of Uppingham School, moving in 1944 to Shrewsbury School. In both schools he updated the curriculum while preserving essential traditions. He was chairman of the Ministry of Education's Youth Advisory Council (1942–45) and during World War II organized the Air Training Corps. Often regarded as the best committee chairman in England, he served frequently in that capacity, notably with the Secondary School Examinations Council and the National Council of Social Service. He was also director of the British Museum (1969–73). Knighted in 1956, Wolfenden was created a life peer in 1974. His publications include *The Public Schools To-Day* (1952) and his memoirs, *Turning Points* (1976).

Woodruff, Robert Winship, U.S. business executive (b. Dec. 6, 1889, Columbus, Ga.—d. March 7, 1985, Atlanta, Ga.), as the cigar-chomping head of the Coca-Cola Co. from 1923 to 1955, built the faltering one-product soda fountain business into an international financial empire with at least 250 other products and introduced such innovations as the six-pack carton, the king-size bottle, and the soft-drink vending machine. In 1923 when Woodruff was vice-president and general manager of a trucking company, he was elected president of the debt-ridden cola company that his father had purchased four years earlier. With bold moves such as offering Coke for five cents to all servicemen during World War II, Woodruff made Coke one of the most popular soft-drink beverages in the world. After his retirement in 1955, Woodruff served as director and chairman of the finance committee of the board of directors, and from 1981 until 1984 he was chairman emeritus. Woodruff donated, often anonymously, millions of dollars to educational and cultural institutions.

Wormser, Olivier Boris, French diplomat (b. May 29, 1913, Jouy-en-Josas, France—d. April 16, 1985, Paris, France), was governor of the Bank of France from 1969 to 1974 and one of the architects of Gaullist diplomacy as ambassador to the Soviet Union and later West Germany. After obtaining his Ph.D. in law he joined (1933) the staff of the French embassy in Rome and was later a member of various Cabinets under the Popular Front government. Wormser joined the Free French forces in London during World War II and held important posts in the French Liberation Committee. During the postwar period he was director of economic and financial affairs in the Foreign Ministry and played a significant role in the European recovery program and in the creation of the European Communities. After serving as ambassador to Moscow from 1966 to 1968, he produced a major report on the reform of monetary policy and became an independent-minded governor of the Bank of France. In 1974, during the presidential election campaign, he aroused the hostility of Valéry Giscard d'Estaing because of his policy on inflation. Replaced after Giscard's victory, he was appointed ambassador to Bonn, where he remained until 1977. After his retirement Wormser became a director of the Royal Dutch/Shell Group.

Wüster, Hans-Otto, West German physicist (b. 1927, Wuppertal, Germany—d. June 30, 1985, Burcot, Oxfordshire, England), played an important role in the construction of the 400-GeV Super Proton Synchrotron at the European Laboratory for Particle Physics (CERN) in Geneva and was director of the Joint European Torus (JET) project at Culham, England. He obtained his Ph.D. in physics at Cologne University and spent seven years at the Institute of Theoretical Physics in Cologne before joining the Deutsches Elektronen Synchrotron laboratory in Hamburg in 1956. His wide understanding of physics, combined with exceptional management abilities, took him to senior posts in the organization, which he left in 1971 to become deputy to the director general of CERN, becoming a member of its directorate five years later. In 1978 he was made director of JET and headed an international team researching the feasibility of obtaining energy from nuclear fusion. The project's success, recognized on its completion and formal opening by Queen Elizabeth II in 1984, was a tribute to his abilities as a leader, as well as to his scientific expertise.

Xia Nai (HSIA NAI), Chinese archaeologist (b. 1916, Yangjia, [Yang-chia], Zhejiang [Chekiang] Province, China—d. June 19, 1985, Beijing [Peking], China), served as director general of the Chinese Institute for Archaeology (1958–82) and, as one of his country's most notable archaeologists, was responsible for the recent major advances in archaeology in China. After working (1934) under Li Ji (Li Chi) on excavations at An-yang, he went to Britain to train as an Egyptologist under Sir Flinders Petrie. Xia excavated at Maiden Castle in Dorset under Mortimer Wheeler's direction and (1937–38) at Armant in Egypt and Tell ed-Duweir (the ancient Lachish) in Palestine (now in Israel). Returning to China (1940), he worked at the National Central Museum in Sichuan (Szechwan) Province, moving later to the Institute of History and Philology, Academia Sinica. Xia conducted excavations in Sichuan, at cemeteries near Dunhuang (Tun-huang) and Wuwei (both in Gansu [Kansu] Province), and at sites on the Dao (Tao) River. As second associate director of the Institute of Archaeology and (from 1954) as associate director, he excavated at Hui Xian (Hui-hsien) in Henan (Honan) Province and at Changsha (Ch'ang-sha) in Hunan. He also took part in work on the tomb of the 16th-century Ming emperor Wanli (Wan-li). Xia wrote a number of papers, mainly on Byzantine and Sassanian coin finds on Chinese sites and on the history of the ancient silk trade. He was responsible for planning the great Chinese archaeological exhibition mounted in Paris and London in 1972.

Yutkevich, Sergey Iosifovich, Soviet film and stage director (b. Dec. 15, 1904, St. Petersburg [now Leningrad], Russia—d. April 23, 1985, Moscow, U.S.S.R.), was the director of a series of films on Lenin, *The Man with a Gun* (1938), *Stories About Lenin* (1958), *Lenin in Poland* (1964), and *Lenin in Paris* (1981); a highly acclaimed *Othello,* for which he won the best director award at the Cannes International Film Festival (1956); and some 30 other films. He studied art and helped found the Ambulant Theatre Studio. From 1921 he worked with Sergey Eisenstein on set design. As an assistant to Abram Room, he made his first major film, *The Traitor,* in 1926. He also assisted Room in making the silent comedy *Bed and Sofa* (1927) before experiencing difficulties with the authorities over some of his work during the 1930s. In 1947 his film *Light over Russia* was banned, and two years later he was dismissed for a time from his post at the All-Union State Institute of Cinematography. Nevertheless, he made some of his finest films after 1950, including an animated cartoon/live action/puppet version of Vladimir Mayakovsky's *The Bathhouse* and the last two parts of his Lenin series. Yutkevich also helped to restore some of Eisenstein's classic works, and he pursued a career in the theatre with notable productions of Karel Capek's *Mother,* J. B. Priestley's *An Inspector Calls,* and Bertolt Brecht's *Resistible Rise of Arturo Ui.*

Zafrulla Khan, Sir (Chaudhri) Muhammad, Pakistani statesman (b. Feb. 6, 1893, Sialkot, Punjab, India—d. Sept. 1, 1985, Lahore, Pakistan), was Pakistan's first foreign minister (1947–54), president of the UN General Assembly (1962–63), and president of the International Court of Justice, The Hague (1970–73). He was educated at Government College, Lahore, before studying law at King's College, University of London; he was called to the bar by Lincoln's Inn (1914). Returning to India, he practiced in Sialkot and in Lahore. Zafrulla became a member of the Punjab legislature (1926) and was a delegate to the round table conferences held in London (1930, 1931, 1932) on a proposed new constitution. He was president of the All-India Muslim League (1931) and the Muslim representative on the viceroy's council (1936), and he was sent (1942) to China as the Indian government's agent general to establish relations with the Kuomintang. As Pakistan's foreign minister he was deeply involved in the disputes with India over Kashmir and the waters of the Indus, presenting his country's case at the UN. Zafrulla was a judge of the International Court, The Hague (1954–61 and 1964–73), and Pakistan's permanent representative at the UN (1961–64). Author of *Islam: Its Meaning for Modern Man* (1962), he belonged to the Ahmadiyah sect, which was declared non-Muslim by the Pakistan National Assembly (1974); thereafter he lived in England, visiting Pakistan only infrequently.

Zimbalist, Efrem Alexandrovich, Russian-born violinist (b. April 9, 1890, Rostov-na-Donu, Russia—d. Feb. 22, 1985, Reno, Nev.), was a violin virtuoso whose unhurried tempos and refined performances were underscored by an emotional understatement and high technical polish; he was also an important composer of songs and chamber music and from 1941 to 1968 headed Philadelphia's Curtis Institute. Zimbalist, who started his violin studies with his father, Aaron Zimbalist (orchestra conductor of the Rostov Opera), later continued his education under the tutelage of Leopold Auer at the St. Petersburg Conservatory. Upon his graduation in 1907 he received the conservatory's gold medal and the Anton Rubinstein Prize. Zimbalist made his professional debuts that same year in Berlin and London and his U.S. debut in 1911 in Boston. His resounding success during his tour prompted him to settle in the U.S. During the early years of his career he also recorded extensively; he made the first recording, with Fritz Kreisler, of Bach's Concerto for Two Violins in D Minor in 1915. Zimbalist was married twice, first (1914 until her death in 1938) to the soprano Alma Gluck, with whom he toured in joint recital until her retirement in 1925, and then to Mary Louis Curtis Bok (1945 until her death in 1970), founder of the Curtis Institute. Some of his compositions include an opera, *Landara* (1956); a symphonic poem, *Portrait of an Artist* (1945); and concertos, chamber music, and solo violin music. Though Zimbalist gave his formal farewell recital in 1949, he emerged from retirement in 1952 to give the premiere performance of Gian Carlo Menotti's Violin Concerto, which was dedicated to him.

Events of 1985

Agriculture and Food Supplies

The year 1985 was one of generally bountiful harvests throughout the world. Famine still stalked much of Africa after a succession of poor crops. Massive distribution of food aid helped alleviate the disaster, and recovery of crops around most of the region was beginning to cause attention to be turned to the rehabilitation of stricken areas. The availability of large supplies of agricultural products in the developed and exporting countries depressed the prices of many agricultural commodities and contributed to further trade confrontations. The U.S. agricultural sector faced a severe financial crisis just as the U.S. Congress enacted new basic farm legislation for the next five years.

Production. World agricultural and food production in 1985 increased somewhat over 1% from the previous year according to preliminary estimates of the U.S. Department of Agriculture's Economic Research Service. The strongest gains in output occurred in the less developed countries, especially those in Africa and western Asia. Harvests were better in the Soviet Union, and China consolidated most of the exceptionally large gains made in 1984. Although agricultural production fell in the European Communities (EC) and was only slightly larger in the United States, both regions faced problems of surpluses for many commodities. Per capita world food production was unchanged from that in 1984. It was little changed in the developed nations, while gains in the less developed countries and the U.S.S.R. were offset by losses in China and Eastern Europe. The most heartening increases were in Africa south of the Sahara, where per capita food production rose about 2%.

African Food Emergency. Images of hunger and death poignantly conveyed the nature of the food situation in much of Africa during the last three years. Large-scale relief operations and generally favourable harvests throughout most of the continent brought substantial improvement in Africa's food situation in 1985. Of the 21 African countries on the "danger list" of the United Nations Food and Agriculture Organization (FAO) in 1984, only 6 remained there by the end of 1985. Despite a substantial recovery in food production, The Sudan remained on the list, as did Ethiopia, where growing conditions were improved in parts of the country. Elsewhere in East Africa average to above-average crops were harvested, and food supplies returned to normal. Total cereal production rose 50% in the seven previously afflicted countries of West Africa. All of the countries of the Sahel region (just south of the Sahara) except Cape Verde enjoyed above-average or record large

Table I. Selected Indexes of World Agricultural and Food Production
(1976–78 average = 100)

Region or country	Total agricultural production						Total food production						Per capita food production					
	1980	1981	1982	1983	1984	1985¹	1980	1981	1982	1983	1984	1985¹	1980	1981	1982	1983	1984	1985¹
Developed countries	105	108	110	102	112	113	105	108	110	103	113	113	103	105	106	99	107	107
United States	102	113	113	92	109	114	103	113	114	94	110	115	99	108	108	88	102	106
Canada	103	113	118	114	110	113	103	113	119	114	110	113	99	108	112	106	101	103
Western Europe	112	110	113	110	119	115	112	110	113	110	119	116	111	109	111	108	117	114
EC	113	112	114	111	119	116	113	112	114	111	119	116	112	111	113	109	117	114
Japan	90	92	94	94	100	101	91	92	94	94	100	102	88	89	90	90	95	96
Oceania	98	106	97	116	114	114	96	104	95	116	112	111	93	100	89	108	103	101
South Africa	107	119	107	94	101	109	106	120	107	92	101	108	99	109	94	79	84	89
Centrally planned economies	101	103	110	115	120	120	101	102	109	113	118	118	98	98	103	106	109	109
U.S.S.R.	95	92	98	102	101	105	94	91	97	102	102	105	91	87	93	96	95	98
Eastern Europe	95	95	100	103	105	106	97	102	104	104	111	109	95	100	101	101	107	104
China²	118	125	138	149	163	160	118	123	135	145	154	153	113	117	126	134	141	139
Less developed countries	107	112	113	116	121	125	107	112	114	117	121	125	100	102	101	101	102	103
East Asia³	109	116	119	124	131	134	109	117	120	125	132	135	102	107	107	110	114	114
Indonesia	120	132	129	139	148	153	120	133	131	140	150	154	111	120	116	121	127	128
South Korea	91	97	102	109	118	119	92	99	103	111	119	120	88	92	95	101	107	106
Malaysia	117	120	129	124	133	141	126	131	143	135	150	162	111	120	116	121	127	128
Philippines	108	113	111	111	106	107	108	113	110	110	106	107	100	101	97	95	89	87
Thailand	111	118	119	131	132	133	110	118	118	131	131	132	103	109	106	116	114	113
Vietnam	113	118	126	132	140	143	113	118	126	132	140	143	106	108	112	115	119	119
South Asia	103	111	108	121	123	124	102	110	108	123	123	124	96	101	97	107	105	104
Bangladesh	110	110	114	116	116	121	112	112	116	119	120	124	102	99	100	99	97	98
India	102	111	108	123	125	126	101	110	107	124	124	126	95	101	96	109	107	105
Pakistan	113	122	124	120	129	130	109	119	118	123	120	122	100	105	101	102	97	96
West Asia	103	103	111	112	113	118	104	105	114	113	115	120	96	94	99	96	95	96
Iran	88	89	96	94	90	97	89	89	97	94	91	98	81	79	83	78	73	76
Turkey	105	108	114	113	114	113	107	112	117	116	117	117	100	102	105	101	100	97
Sub-saharan Africa⁴	108	111	113	107	111	118	108	112	113	107	111	117	99	100	98	90	91	93
Ethiopia	111	110	121	113	113	112	113	111	126	113	109	115	109	105	116	101	96	100
Nigeria	113	112	114	100	114	117	113	113	115	101	114	117	103	99	98	84	94	93
The Sudan	93	109	99	100	92	110	97	116	96	92	81	101	87	100	80	75	64	75
North Africa	110	105	114	112	118	127	109	104	115	113	119	128	100	92	99	95	97	102
Morocco	107	86	111	104	107	114	108	86	111	105	108	115	99	78	98	90	91	94
Egypt	111	112	115	116	119	127	109	111	116	118	122	128	99	98	99	98	99	100
Latin America	112	116	116	115	124	128	112	115	117	115	121	125	104	105	104	100	103	104
Argentina	99	103	111	107	118	120	100	106	113	110	121	123	95	99	104	99	107	107
Brazil	119	124	120	120	138	149	117	118	120	115	126	133	108	106	106	99	105	108
Colombia	120	123	120	119	122	121	120	122	120	119	123	122	108	106	106	99	105	104
Mexico	118	120	114	120	116	115	119	122	117	124	118	119	110	110	103	106	98	97
Venezuela	112	110	118	117	123	137	113	110	120	118	124	137	102	96	102	97	99	107
World	104	108	111	110	117	119	105	107	111	110	117	118	99	100	102	100	104	104

¹Preliminary. ²Represents about two-thirds of all field crops (includes all major field crops) but excludes livestock products. ³Excludes Japan. ⁴Excludes South Africa.
Source: USDA, Economic Research Service, International Economic Division, December 1985.

Table II. World Cereal Supply and Distribution
In 000,000 metric tons

	1982–83	1983–84	1984–85	1985–86[1]
Production				
Wheat	479	491	514	505
Coarse grains	779	685	808	845
Rice, milled	286	308	319	317
Total	1,544	1,484	1,642	1,668
Utilization				
Wheat	468	487	501	494
Coarse grains	754	758	778	793
Rice, milled	290	308	316	315
Total	1,511	1,552	1,594	1,603
Exports				
Wheat	99	103	108	91
Coarse grains	90	92	101	94
Rice, milled	12	13	11	11
Total	200	207	220	196
Ending stocks[2]				
Wheat	96	101	114	125
Coarse grains	139	66	97	149
Rice, milled	17	17	21	23
Total	252	184	232	297
Stocks as % of utilization				
Wheat	20.6%	20.7%	22.8%	25.3%
Coarse grains	18.4%	8.7%	12.4%	18.7%
Rice, milled	6.0%	5.6%	6.7%	7.3%
Total	16.7%	11.9%	14.5%	18.5%
Stocks held by U.S. in %				
Wheat	42.7%	37.8%	34.0%	37.9%
Coarse grains	70.3%	48.1%	52.2%	69.4%
Rice	13.3%	8.7%	9.5%	11.3%
Total	55.9%	38.8%	39.4%	51.6%

[1] Forecast.
[2] Does not include estimates of total Chinese or Soviet stocks but is
adjusted for estimated changes in Soviet stocks.
Source: USDA, Foreign Agricultural Service, December 1985.

crops. The fact that it was too early to forecast the size of the crops that were to be harvested beginning in April 1986 in southern Africa partly explained the continued presence on the danger list of Angola, Botswana, and Mozambique.

The FAO estimated in December that the 21 African countries that were on its danger list in 1984 would require total cereal imports of 6.6 million tons in 1985–86, 5.6 million tons less than the amount needed during the previous year. It estimated the total food-aid needs of those countries to be 3.4 million tons in 1985–86, compared with 7 million in 1984–85. Donor pledges and allocations through December totaled 2.7 million tons, including 1.2 million tons that arrived too late to be distributed in 1984–85. The FAO believed that additional financial aid was needed to move surplus grain from some African countries with bumper crops to food-deficit areas on the continent or to build up national and regional reserves. Surpluses totaling 1.8 million tons were estimated to be held in Zimbabwe, Kenya, Malawi, and parts of West Africa. The FAO saw some danger of such surpluses and late-arriving food aid flooding some markets and removing incentives for increased local production in 1986.

Desertification increased in the Sahel, although most studies indicated that it was unlikely to be so extensive as to reduce food production significantly. Restocking of livestock was expected to be a problem there. Across the Sahel about one-fifth of the population were dependent upon herding. In Niger and Chad, for example, losses of livestock were estimated at more than 50%. Immediate efforts to rehabilitate agriculture in most of those countries were expected to require additional assistance to provide credit, seed, fertilizer, and other production inputs. The FAO estimated that the international community had supplied about $250 million in seeds, fertilizer, and other nonfood aid to African farmers since 1984 and called upon aid donors to increase such contributions substantially.

Grains. World stocks of wheat were expected (as of December) to increase in 1985–86 for the fifth year in a row despite a decline in world wheat production. The reduction in output was concentrated in the major wheat-exporting

countries except for Canada, which registered a small increase. Extensive participation in the acreage-adjustment programs in the U.S. during 1985 helped reduce the harvested area, but good weather kept yields high.

Wheat production either rose or was close to 1984–85 levels in most of the major importing countries except Eastern Europe, and this was expected to result in sharply reduced trading of wheat in 1985–86. Soviet wheat output reached an estimated 83 million tons, 10 million above 1984–85. Wheat imports by the U.S.S.R., therefore, might be 11 million tons smaller than the record-setting 28 million tons imported in 1984–85 (one-quarter of the world wheat trade). Reduced import demand for wheat and the expectation that world stocks of wheat could reach one-quarter of total utilization by the end of 1985–86 helped push wheat prices down in 1985. The U.S. was expected to account for nearly all the growth in wheat stocks.

During the 1970s global trade in wheat increased 5.5% annually, but this growth stagnated during the 1980s, in part because of substantial agricultural progress in certain of the former major wheat-importing countries. In the 1970s consumption outside the United States, the U.S.S.R., and China exceeded production by an average of 20 million tons a year. This gap recently narrowed to an average of five million tons. China and India made perhaps the strongest advances in production. Soviet import demand, however, grew rapidly in the late 1970s as production there failed to regain the levels achieved earlier, and wheat imports tended to steady, averaging over 18 million tons annually since 1981–82. The rest of the world's imports of wheat had increased about two million tons (about 3%) a year since 1980.

As of 1985 China had increased its wheat production 60% since 1980, almost entirely by improving yields per unit of land; China thus became the world's leading wheat producer. Some of the steps China took to provide greater producer incentives included the introduction of a household contract system in 1979 that tied a farmer's household income to farm output, a doubling of fertilizer supplies, a more than 55% rise since 1978 in the price received for grain, and the introduction of 15-year land contracts that gave farmers incentives to improve the land. As a result China's wheat imports fell from nearly 14 million tons in 1980 to about half that in the mid-1980s. The gains may have exceeded even the expectations of China's planners.

USDA/APHIS

Grasshoppers, seconded by Mormon beetles (a species of cricket), hatched in record numbers for the second year running, causing serious concern to farmers in several Western states of the U.S. Mild winter weather followed by a hot, dry spring was blamed.

The financial plight of at least some U.S. farmers was a topic of continuing concern and debate. It proved impossible to achieve consensus even on the terms and dimensions of the problem, while the search for a solution was bound up inextricably with the question of the federal budget deficit.

J.-P. LAFFONT—SYGMA

China had signed long-term agreements for delivery of wheat with all five major wheat exporters during the past five years but had failed to make the required minimum purchases from several of these suppliers in recent years.

India, the world's largest wheat importer in the 1960s, had moved steadily toward self-sufficiency in cereals by quadrupling wheat production over the past 20 years. The Indian gains resulted from a near doubling of both yields and planted area, supported by higher government procurement prices, lower prices for fertilizer, steady expansion of irrigation, and the introduction of high-yielding

wheat varieties that would grow abundantly outside of the traditional wheat-producing areas.

Estimates early in the season indicated large rice crops throughout the world for the third year in a row. Most rice was consumed where it was produced, and the small and stagnating international rice market was strongly affected by the steady increase in stocks since 1983–84. Prices of rice in world trade continued their five-year decline to their lowest level, in real terms, since the mid-1960s.

A strong expansion in world output of coarse grains was forecast for 1985–86, primarily because of a record-large 221 million-ton U.S. corn (maize) crop (14% above 1984) that resulted both from a large increase in plantings and from good weather. Aided by the continuing decline in international prices for coarse grains, the world use of these cereals continued to expand moderately, but production was likely to exceed total use substantially for the second year in a row. The result was expected to be a very large buildup in stocks. A strong contraction in world trade of coarse grains, especially of U.S. exports, seemed a likely prospect because of a probable ten million-ton reduction from 1984–85 in Soviet imports. World stocks of coarse grains were expected to grow 50% during 1985–86. The U.S. was likely to absorb all the net increase in stocks and by the end of 1985–86 could hold almost 70% of the world total, an amount roughly equal to annual world trade in coarse grains.

Cassava. World output of cassava was expected (as of October) to rise about 2% in 1985, thanks largely to improved weather conditions in Africa, according to the FAO. The increased use of biological controls and the introduction of pest-resistant high-yielding varieties through the International Institute of Tropical Agriculture in such countries as Zaire, Nigeria, and Cameroon also helped. The recent severe droughts in Africa led some governments to encourage output because of cassava's drought-resistant characteristics.

In Asia ample rice supplies probably reduced cassava's direct use as food and led to greater feed and industrial uses, particularly in Taiwan, Indonesia, Japan, and South Korea. In Brazil the competition from cash crops, such as sugarcane for producing ethanol, constrained the cultivation of cassava for food.

Table III. World Production of Oilseeds and Products

In 000 000 metric tons

	1983–84	1984–85[1]	1985–86[2]
Production of oilseeds	164.8	188.1	196.7
Soybeans	82.6	91.1	98.8
U.S.	44.5	50.6	57.9
China	9.8	9.7	9.5
Argentina	7.0	6.5	7.3
Brazil	15.2	17.2	16.2
Cottonseed	26.1	33.6	31.3
U.S.	2.8	4.7	5.0
U.S.S.R.	4.8	4.8	5.0
China	7.9	10.6	8.9
Peanuts	18.6	19.8	19.7
U.S.	1.5	2.0	1.9
China	4.0	4.8	5.6
India	7.3	6.5	5.6
Sunflower seed	15.4	17.8	18.6
U.S.	1.5	1.7	1.5
U.S.S.R.	5.0	4.5	5.2
Argentina	2.2	3.4	3.2
Rapeseed	14.2	16.7	18.6
Canada	2.6	3.4	3.4
China	4.3	4.2	5.5
India	2.6	2.9	3.0
Flaxseed	2.1	2.3	2.6
Copra	3.8	4.7	5.0
Palm Kernel	2.0	2.2	2.3
Crushings of oilseeds	136.8	149.4	151.5
Soybeans	71.1	73.0	74.8
Ending stocks of oilseeds	15.5	19.5	28.9
Soybeans	13.3	16.4	25.0
World production[3]			
Total fats and oils	54.1	58.1	58.9
Edible vegetable oils	40.1	44.3	45.2
Animal fats	11.8	11.8	11.7
Industrial and marine oils	2.2	2.0	2.1
High-protein meals[4]	89.7	95.9	97.4

[1] Preliminary.
[2] Forecast.
[3] Processing potential from crops in year indicated.
[4] Converted, based on product's protein content, to weight equivalent
to soybeans of 44% protein content.
Source: USDA, Foreign Agricultural Service, August and December 1985.

Table IV. Livestock Numbers and Meat Production in Major Producing Countries[1]

In 000,000 head and 000,000 metric tons (carcass weight)

Region and country	1984	1985	1984	1985
	Cattle		Beef and veal	
World total	965.5	963.9	41.97	42.47
Canada	11.0	10.6	1.00	0.99
United States	109.8	107.0	10.93	10.88
Mexico	33.9	33.7	1.32	1.38
Argentina	58.8	57.9	2.57	2.70
Brazil	94.7	95.2	2.30	2.40
Uruguay	9.9	10.6	0.30	0.25
Western Europe	92.6	91.4	8.53	8.47
Eastern Europe	37.7	37.6	2.50	2.47
U.S.S.R.	120.8	120.4	7.20	7.40
Australia	23.0	23.7	1.25	1.33
India	271.4	275.3	0.33	0.35
	Hogs		Pork	
World total	706.1	701.2	51.79	52.96
Canada	10.9	10.8	0.86	0.88
United States	54.0	52.0	6.72	6.71
Mexico	12.3	13.1	0.94	0.86
Western Europe	104.7	105.2	12.28	12.57
U.S.S.R.	77.8	76.5	5.80	5.60
Japan	10.7	10.5	1.43	1.49
China	306.8	303.6	14.45	15.51
	Poultry		Poultry meat	
World total	...	...	24.07	24.81
United States	...	...	7.44	7.75
Brazil	...	...	1.40	1.47
EC	...	...	4.26	4.28
U.S.S.R.	...	...	2.64	2.70
Japan	...	...	1.33	1.37
	Sheep		Sheep, goat meat	
World total	687.0	690.1	4.44	4.62
			All meat	
Total	...	...	122.27	124.85

[1] Preliminary livestock numbers at year's end. Consists of 47 countries for beef and veal, 38 for pork, 42 for poultry meat, and 30 for sheep and goat meat; roughly the same coverage for animal numbers includes nearly all European producers, the most significant in the Western Hemisphere, and scattered coverage elsewhere.
Source: USDA, Foreign Agricultural Service, September 1985.

Table V. World Production and Stocks of Dairy Products[1]

Region	1983	1984	1985[2]
	In 000,000 metric tons		
North America	80.9	77.0	80.1
United States	63.4	61.4	65.0
South America	19.1	19.1	19.4
Brazil	10.7	10.8	10.4
Western Europe	135.0	132.6	129.7
EC	111.8	109.1	106.2
France	27.9	27.6	27.0
West Germany	26.9	26.0	25.0
Italy	10.6	10.2	10.1
Netherlands, The	13.2	12.8	12.3
United Kingdom	17.3	16.6	15.9
Other Western Europe	23.2	23.6	23.5
Eastern Europe	41.8	43.2	42.4
Poland	16.1	16.8	16.3
U.S.S.R.	96.5	97.9	100.0
China	1.8	2.2	2.8
India	16.0	17.1	18.5
Australia/New Zealand[3]	12.6	13.8	14.0
Japan/South Africa	9.6	9.6	9.8
Total	413.3	412.6	416.6

Product/Region	Production		Year-end stocks	
	1984	1985[2]	1984	1985[2]
	In 000 metric tons			
Butter	6,767	6,692	1,667	1,649
EC	2,108	1,944	1,197	1,191
U.S.	500	563	135	109
Cheese	9,266	9,580	1,478	1,479
EC	3,782	3,859	595	630
U.S.	2,120	2,295	482	454
Nonfat dry milk	4,296	4,243	1,523	1,221
EC	2,089	1,875	629	375
U.S.	527	640	559	504

[1] Based on 38 major producing countries. Those not shown individually include (North America) Canada and Mexico; (South America) Argentina, Brazil, Chile, Peru, and Venezuela; (EC) Belgium-Luxembourg, Denmark, Greece, and Ireland; (Other Western Europe) Austria, Finland, Norway, Portugal, Spain, Sweden, and Switzerland; and (Eastern Europe) Czechoslovakia, East Germany, and Yugoslavia.
[2] Preliminary.
[3] Year ending June 30 for Australia and May 31 for New Zealand.
Source: USDA, Foreign Agricultural Service, November 1985.

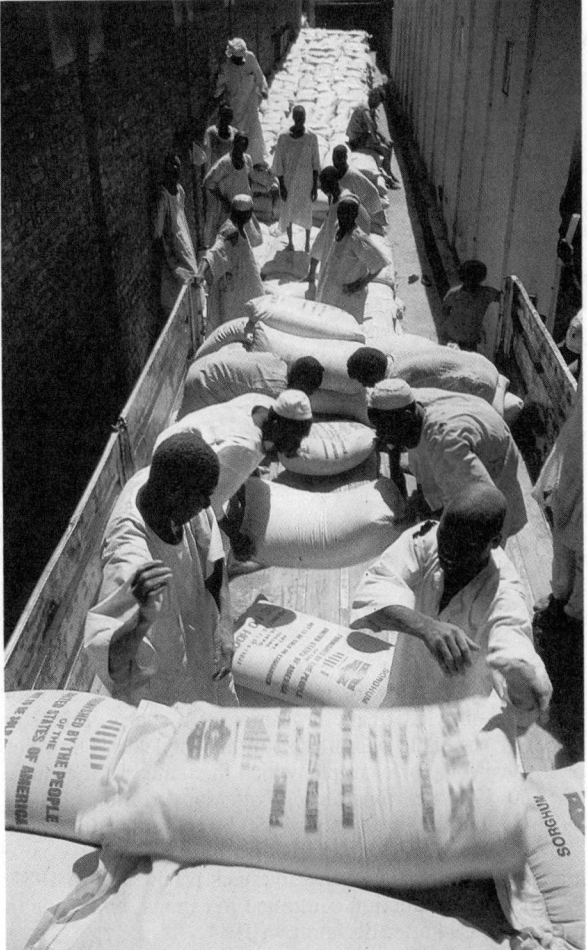

The outpouring of food aid to drought-stricken nations in Africa from more fortunate agricultural regions of the world continued through the year, but frail transportation networks, bad weather, and political stresses frequently hampered delivery of food to the starving.
S. FRANKLIN—SYGMA

World trade of tapioca (processed cassava) was forecast to rise 5% in 1985 to 7.6 million tons (product weight), 75% of it in the form of hard pellets, which are easier to handle and transport. Thailand usually accounted for more than 90% of all tapioca exports. EC imports of tapioca in 1985 again probably fell 500,000 tons short of the six million allowed under its voluntary restraint agreement. Large stocks of cassava held by exporters helped drive international prices for tapioca cassava products near their ten-year lows, making their combination with soybean meal in compound feeds particularly attractive.

Oilseeds. Despite only a small increase in plantings, world oilseed production was expected (as of December) to rise sharply in 1985–86, largely because of record-high soybean yields in the U.S. The demand for oilseed products was slackening, and stocks were expected to expand nearly 50% during 1985–86.

Generally slower growth in the livestock industry throughout the world was expected to result in world consumption of oilseed meals expanding much less than the 8% achieved in 1984–85. The price of soybean meal (c.i.f., Rotterdam), which at the end of the 1983–84 season had been about $170 a ton, slid to about $140 per ton in the summer of 1985 but had regained the lost ground by November, when it became apparent that the Southern Hemisphere soybean harvest in early 1986 was not likely to increase by much.

Production was increasing most strongly for oilseeds that have a higher oil content than soybeans, such as rapeseed, reflecting the stronger prices for vegetable oils relative to meals during 1984–85. This, together with expanded

Table VI. World Production of Centrifugal (Freed from Liquid) Sugar

In 000,000 metric tons raw value

Region	1983–84	1984–85	1985–86[1]
North America	8.6	8.8	9.0
United States	5.3	5.2	5.4
Mexico	3.2	3.4	3.5
Caribbean	10.1	9.7	8.5
Cuba	8.3	8.1	7.0
Central America	1.8	1.8	1.8
South America	14.4	14.7	13.2
Argentina	1.6	1.5	1.2
Brazil	9.4	9.3	8.2
Europe	19.8	21.6	21.1
Western Europe	14.2	15.8	15.4
EC	11.9	13.6	13.4
France	4.2	4.6	4.5
West Germany	2.7	3.2	3.3
Eastern Europe	5.6	5.7	5.7
Poland	2.1	1.9	1.8
U.S.S.R.	8.7	8.6	8.9
Africa and Middle East	9.1	10.2	10.0
South Africa	1.5	2.5	2.4
Turkey	1.8	1.7	1.5
Asia	20.5	21.2	21.8
China	3.8	4.6	5.2
India	7.0	7.1	7.3
Indonesia	1.8	1.8	1.9
Philippines	2.4	1.6	1.4
Thailand	2.3	2.6	2.7
Oceania	3.7	4.0	3.9
Australia	3.4	3.5	3.5
Total	96.7	100.7	98.0

[1]Preliminary.

Source: USDA, Foreign Agricultural Service, November 1985.

crushings of oilseeds for meal and dampened demand for vegetable oils, led to the beginning of a sharp decline in prices of vegetable oils in the summer of 1985. The price of soybean oil, for example, which fluctuated in the range of $630–$700 per ton (f.o.b., Rotterdam) during most of 1984–85, had fallen to about $450 by November.

Meat and Livestock. Large world supplies of coarse grains at low prices favoured livestock production in 1985. World meat production continued to expand, and trade in meat increased after declining in 1984.

World beef production picked up in 1985 after several years of stagnation, finally regaining the peak of about 42.5 million tons (carcass weight equivalent) achieved in 1977. Static demand for beef resulted in falling world beef prices in 1985 and in declining numbers of cattle, particularly in most of the major beef-exporting countries.

The EC continued to be the leading world exporter of beef (800,000 tons in 1985), followed by Australia (660,-000) and Brazil (510,000), which together accounted for about 55% of world beef trade. The EC subsidized beef exports in order to reduce large and costly government inventories of meat, estimated at more than one million

tons at the end of 1985, acquired in operating its price-support program. EC policies aimed at curbing milk production also led to increased slaughtering of dairy cows in 1984 and 1985. EC beef consumption had increased only about 4% since the early 1970s, while production had risen about 30%.

Australia's cattle herd was increasing slowly after a period of slaughtering that resulted from a series of devastating droughts. In the United States droughts in 1983 and 1984, together with financial problems in recent years on many farms and ranches, contributed to a reduction in cattle numbers. The U.S. remained the largest importer of beef but bought less than 900,000 tons annually in the 1980s after exceeding one million tons per year during the late 1970s. A 5,000-ton limit on imports of EC beef, voluntary limitations on exports by other beef exporters, and regulations to protect against the spread of foot-and-mouth disease held down imports.

Both world production and consumption of pork continued to climb slowly in 1985. In August 1985 the U.S. ruled that a countervailing duty on imports of hogs from Canada would be applied because such sales were subsidized and damaging to U.S. hog producers. However, no duties were imposed upon subsidized imports of fresh, chilled, or frozen pork because such imports were determined not to cause "material injury" to the U.S. industry.

World poultry production and consumption also continued to grow but much more slowly than during the rapid expansion of the 1970s. World trade in poultry continued to decline as a result of the expansion of domestic output in poultry-importing countries, especially in the Middle East and the U.S.S.R.

Dairy Products. World production of milk from cows was estimated (as of November) to have increased 1% in 1985, led by a nearly 6% rise in U.S. output. The U.S. increase was stimulated by low feed prices and price incentives under the U.S. dairy-support program, and it contributed to a substantial rise of government stocks of dairy products. The EC further reduced its milk output in 1985, aided by reductions in dairy herds growing out of the continuation of its restrictive marketing quotas. The EC had no success in reducing its stocks of butter, which could supply the region for a year. It was considering compensating milk producers who were willing to get out of milk production permanently. Similar measures were authorized by new U.S. farm legislation.

Substantial sales of dairy products in a competitive market by the EC, New Zealand, and Australia contributed to a

ROPER—GAMMA/LIAISON

Capitalizing on the success of a similar event that raised money for African relief, a number of country- and rock-music stars staged the Farm Aid concert in Champaign, Illinois, and drew some 78,000 people. Proceeds of the concert fell far short of the organizers' early hopes.

further decline in international prices for butter and butter oil in 1985. Prices of cheese in international markets were relatively stable but remained below those in 1983. The rapid expansion of trade in cheese was checked in 1985 as the EC and New Zealand exported less. Exports of nonfat dry milk rose, largely because of increased shipments of food aid, particularly by the U.S. and the EC.

Dairy industries in the developed countries faced not only the problem of disposing of current surpluses but also that of coping with further increases in dairy production as a result of rapidly emerging technological advances. For instance, the U.S. Food and Drug Administration (FDA) approved in 1984 the commercial use of "isoacids" in feed supplements. When fed to cows, this mixture of four fatty acids, found naturally in the rumen of cows, increases their concentration in a cow's digestive system and makes possible the more efficient use of feed. The isoacids increase both the bacteria that ferment feed in the rumen and those that synthesize protein out of nonprotein feed compounds.

Another process boosts milk production by increasing the flow of blood through the mammary gland, aided by injection of a bovine growth hormone that raises a cow's rate of metabolism. The hormone—once expensively extracted from the pituitary glands of slaughtered cattle—could now be produced cheaply in large quantities. The new process used bacteria to grow the hormone after transfer of the gene responsible for the hormone's production to a bacterial culture. The FDA approved the sale of milk from research herds using the hormone but as of the end of 1985 had not yet approved it for general commercial use.

Such hormones and other feed supplements were made even more effective by the use of computerized feeding equipment that allowed cows to serve themselves with the specific amount of feed appropriate to their potential for milk production. Such systems were also being used to detect health problems among cows.

Sugar. World prices for freely traded sugar remained depressed despite a forecast (in November) decline in world sugar production in 1985–86 brought about by smaller crops in Brazil and Cuba. World stocks by the end of 1984–85 grew to an estimated 45.7 million tons—about 47% of world sugar consumption. They were expected to increase further during 1985–86 because of stagnating sugar consumption. The price (International Sugar Agreement world price) of freely traded sugar, which averaged about 8.5 cents a pound in 1983, fell to 5.2 cents in 1984 and ranged between 3 and 5 cents during most of 1985. According to a commonly used rule of thumb, prices were not likely to strengthen until stocks declined to 25–30% of consumption.

Despite low prices producers generally did not respond by lowering production. They either were influenced by high domestic price supports or received more favourable prices under special arrangements. The U.S. Department of Agriculture (USDA) estimated that of the 24.3 million tons of net exports of sugar in 1984, 11.6 million were traded at an average price of just over five cents per pound. The rest was shipped under long-term agreements and preferential arrangements at an average of 21 cents per pound. These included Cuban exports to the Soviet Union (5,550,000 tons at 30 cents per pound), exports to the U.S. under quota (3,010,000 tons at 18 cents), and exports to the EC under the Lomé Convention (1,570,000 at 16 cents). Thus, the average for all sugar exported was 13.5 cents per pound. Sugar was also being traded increasingly under barter arrangements.

World sugar consumption increased about 1% in 1984–85 to 96.8 million tons and was expected to rise less in 1985–86. Increased consumption of sugar in the less developed countries was offset by a decline in the developed nations, where other sweeteners were being substituted for cane and beet sugar. For instance, high-fructose corn syrup would be used almost exclusively in soft drinks (other than diet drinks) in the U.S. in 1985–86 as the result of decisions made by beverage companies in November 1984.

Coffee. World coffee production increased slightly in 1984–85, except in South America, where Brazilian output failed to increase and Colombia's crop was smaller than expected because its growers sharply pruned back coffee groves. Colombia wanted to reduce its coffee stocks, in 1985 the world's largest and totaling more than the country's annual output, and also pressed for a larger quota under the International Coffee Agreement (ICA).

Expectations of a larger 1985–86 world coffee crop pushed the ICA's indicator price, which averaged $1.41 per pound in 1984, to $1.20 by the third quarter of 1985. Prices began to strengthen, however, when Brazil in mid-December temporarily suspended export sales of coffee while assessing the potential damage to its 1986 harvest caused by drought in southern Brazil. The ICA's global export quota was set at 60,155,500 bags (60-kg [132-lb] each) for 1984–85, but it was reduced by one million bags in July 1984 when the price fell to $1.31 per pound.

The reason that prices were not lower despite the existence of stocks of coffee beans equal to at least one-half of annual coffee consumption could be explained partly by problems of logistics, timing of harvests, and the quality of the stocks. Some coffee-consuming nations also claimed that some producers attempted to manipulate prices in quota markets by undershipping during parts of the year. The consumers maintained that producers were obligated

Table VII. World Green Coffee Production
In 000 60-kg bags

Region	1983–84	1984–85[1]	1985–86[2]
North America	15,791	19,904	16,257
Costa Rica	2,070	2,516	2,013
El Salvador	2,600	2,700	2,600
Guatemala	2,340	2,703	2,530
Honduras	1,310	1,500	1,400
Mexico	4,530	4,250	4,480
South America	47,130	42,252	50,009
Brazil	30,000	27,000	33,000
Colombia	13,000	11,000	12,500
Ecuador	1,380	1,500	1,600
Africa	17,640	20,578	21,765
Cameroon	1,000	2,100	1,900
Ethiopia	3,990	2,600	3,150
Ivory Coast	1,420	4,900	5,000
Kenya	2,232	1,525	2,170
Uganda	3,200	3,300	3,000
Zaire	1,350	1,503	1,540
Asia and Oceania	9,488	10,623	10,616
India	1,667	2,917	2,334
Indonesia	5,500	5,400	5,750
Total	90,049	90,357	98,647

[1]Preliminary.
[2]Forecast.
Source: USDA, Foreign Agricultural Service, December 1985.

Table VIII. World Cocoa Bean Production
In 000 metric tons

Region	1983–84	1984–85	1985–86[1]
North and Central America	97	100	103
South America	426	583	556
Brazil	308	415	395
Ecuador	55	100	90
Africa	861	1,041	981
Cameroon	109	120	120
Ghana	159	173	190
Ivory Coast[2]	415	540	500
Nigeria[3]	123	155	115
Asia and Oceania	158	175	205
Malaysia	90	100	125
Total	1,542	1,898	1,846

[1]Forecast.
[2]Includes some cocoa marketed from Ghana.
[3]Includes cocoa marketed through Benin.
Source: USDA, Foreign Agricultural Service, October 1985.

to spread shipments evenly by quarters throughout the year, while producers claimed a right to ship whenever they pleased.

The problem of undershipment was not dealt with conclusively at the April meeting of the ICA, but action was taken to constrain exports to nonmembers. The members agreed that they would not sell coffee to nonmembers at a price lower than to members and that such exports would be limited "to a quantity which would ensure compliance" with the price limit and with "the need to provide sufficient coffee to quota markets." Nonmembers of the ICA accounted for an estimated 14% of all coffee imports in 1984–85.

Cocoa. Another large (although somewhat smaller than the previous year's) world cocoa bean harvest was forecast (in October) for 1985–86. Grindings of cocoa beans were expected to exceed the 1,750,000 tons in 1984–85 but again to be smaller than total production. The increase was influenced by lower prices for cocoa beans and strengthened demand that resulted from continuing economic recovery in importing countries, particularly the United States. Cocoa bean prices fluctuated in the range of $0.91–$1.02 per pound during the first nine months of 1985, after averaging $1.06 per pound in 1984. World stocks of cocoa were expected to increase during 1986 by nearly one-half the 134,000-ton increase recorded in 1985. Stocks would then approximate a 3½-month supply.

The 1980 International Cocoa Agreement (ICCA), due to expire in September 1985 after a one-year extension, was extended for another year at a July meeting of the ICCA after members failed to draft a new agreement. The two-cent-per-pound contribution for maintenance of the ICCA buffer stock was to be continued during the extension. One key to the success of a negotiating conference scheduled to resume in Geneva in February 1986 was whether two observer nonmembers—Ivory Coast (the world's largest producer) and the U.S. (the largest importer)—would this time join the ICCA. The U.S. and other importers wanted the agreement to operate within a lower price band than the $1.06–$1.46 per pound specified in the current agreement. Other issues involved concerned the allocation of export quotas and the management of national and international cocoa stocks.

Cotton. A large world harvest in 1984 and slow growth in consumption led to the accumulation of record world stocks of cotton during 1984–85 that, at 42.2 million bales (216 kg [480 lb] each), were equal to 60% of annual cotton consumption. World output of cotton was estimated (in December) to have declined substantially in 1985–86, largely because of production controls adopted by China aimed at reducing the nation's surpluses of cotton and improving its quality. Nevertheless, cotton stocks were forecast to grow another ten million tons by the end of 1985–86, with China holding about 50% and the U.S. 25% of the total. These large stocks overhanging the market led international prices of raw cotton, which averaged 69.2 cents per pound (Northern Europe Outlook "A" Index) in 1984–85, to fall below 48 cents by November 1985.

Cotton exports to East Asian countries that manufactured and exported textiles were slowing in 1985, partly because of growing textile import restrictions by the developed countries. Rapid economic growth in East Asia also led to a diversification of industry away from labour-intensive industries such as textiles. Those countries—particularly Hong Kong, South Korea, Taiwan, and Japan—also exported high-quality textile products whose sales were most sensitive to changes in income in the importing countries. Exports of less expensive textiles by such countries as Pakistan and Turkey were less affected by overall economic trends.

In the United States cotton textiles began to recover some of the ground lost to synthetic fibres. Lower cotton prices relative to polyesters and a shift in consumer preferences toward natural fibres, including also wool, were responsible. The increasing popularity of "natural" blend (60% cotton and 40% polyester) pants and shirts and heavyweight 100% cotton denim were factors in this shift.

U.S. Farm Crisis. U.S. farmers at the end of 1985 were facing an accelerating crisis that approached the severity of that experienced during the Great Depression in the 1930s. At the year's end the U.S. Congress enacted new basic farm legislation intended to provide the ground rules for the nation's agriculture through 1990.

Prices received by farmers for all commodities fell by about 10% in 1985, the worst annual decline since 1953. Prices received for crops declined 13% in response to near-record production and stagnant domestic and foreign demand. The resulting huge carryover stocks for many commodities indicated little prospect for higher prices in 1986. Prices for grains, soybeans, and cotton fell to a level that triggered the government loan program to come to the aid of those commodities. Without a recovery of prices in 1986, this raised the possibility that government-owned stocks of these commodities could exceed even those that prompted the controversial PIK (payment-in-kind) program in 1983.

The lower prices were reflected in a decline in net farm income from $34.5 billion in 1984 to an estimated $25 billion–$29 billion in 1985. Real farm income (deflated to adjust for inflation) in recent years had been far below its peak of $20.3 billion (1972 prices) in 1975 and for 1985 was estimated at $10.8 billion–$12.6 billion.

The volume of farmers' debt in relation to assets had been rising steadily since 1979. It may have reached as high as 25% in 1985, compared with 23.2% in 1984 and 17% as recently as 1980. A USDA survey of 1.7 million of the country's 2.3 million farms found that 12%—214,000 farms—began 1985 unable to pay the previous year's bills. Of commercial farms—those with annual sales in excess of $40,000, which represent one-third of all farms but 90% of all farm commodities sold—one in five had negative cash flow and a debt-to-asset ratio of over 40%.

Farmers were not just worse off in terms of lower current income and rising debt. In 1985, for the fifth year in a row, the total net worth of farmers fell, to $595 billion–$653 billion from $657 billion in December 1984. From 1980 to 1984 farmers' equity fell $180 billion, $100 billion alone in 1984. The average value of farm assets fell from a peak of $823 per acre in 1982 to $679 in 1985.

Table IX. World Cotton Production
In 000,000 480-lb bales

Region	1983–84	1984–85	1985–86
Western Hemisphere	14.2	21.6	20.5
United States	7.8	13.0	13.8
Mexico	1.0	1.2	0.8
Brazil	2.6	4.2	3.0
Europe	0.8	1.0	1.2
U.S.S.R.	12.1	11.9	12.3
Africa	5.6	5.6	6.0
Egypt	1.9	1.8	2.1
The Sudan	1.0	0.9	1.0
Asia and Oceania[1]	35.0	47.2	41.1
China	21.3	28.7	24.0
India	6.1	7.9	7.2
Pakistan	2.2	4.6	4.3
Turkey	2.4	2.7	2.4
Total	67.6	87.2	81.1

[1]Includes Middle East.
Source: USDA, Foreign Agricultural Service, December 1985

A decline in land values was the principal cause of the loss of farmers' equity. About three-quarters of farm real estate assets were land. Average values of farmland fell 12% between April 1984 and April 1985. The largest single-year losses—between 14 and 29%—were recorded in the Midwestern states. Iowa, Nebraska, Illinois, and South Dakota all lost more than one-quarter of their farm values in 1985 alone. Adding to the above list Texas, Ohio, Indiana, Minnesota, and Missouri would give those states whose land had depreciated between one-third and one-half since 1981. For all the states together, land values declined 19% between their peak in 1981 and 1985.

The drop in land values also endangered the farm banking system and led to new congressional legislation in December that reorganized the system and placed it under closer federal surveillance. The shrinkage of land values reduced sharply the value of bank assets that were based on loans to farmers with land as collateral. Banks also had less money to lend because many farm families had to withdraw personal and household savings to meet living expenses and farm debt payments. These circumstances made it increasingly difficult for the banks to refinance overdue farm debt. An American Bankers Association midyear survey estimated that 3.8% of all farmers filed for bankruptcy in 1985, compared with 0.7% in June 1982.

Origins of the Crisis. Vigorous growth in foreign demand for agricultural products in the 1970s accompanied by strong commodity prices led to a rapid expansion of U.S. agriculture. At that time the U.S. captured the lion's share of growth in agricultural exports. But the onset of a worldwide recession in 1980 reduced the ability of foreign consumers to purchase agricultural products.

Furthermore, rapid inflation in the late 1970s had led the U.S. and other industrialized countries to adopt restrictive monetary policies, which contributed to a strong rise in interest rates. The U.S. budget deficit began to grow rapidly in the 1980s and was financed by greatly expanded borrowings. According to some estimates, each $50 billion of structural deficit in the fiscal budget causes real interest rates to rise one to two percentage points. Thus, both monetary and fiscal policy acted to push up interest rates.

At home, U.S. farmers felt this first as an increased cost in the credit that they used to buy or rent land, equipment, and supplies such as fertilizer and pesticides. Modern agriculture is a highly capital-intensive industry, and the USDA estimated that total farm production expenses increase $2 billion each time the average interest rate on outstanding farm debt rises one percentage point. By 1984 interest on farm debt represented 19% of all costs to farmers, compared with 13% in 1979.

Overseas, many less developed countries had already begun to cut back on imports because of the large expansion of their foreign debt during the 1970s. Higher interest payments on both their old and new debt quickly and sharply reduced their ability to finance agricultural imports. Over the longer term their need to reduce imports that fuel economic growth also dampened the growth of consumer income, the source of demand for agricultural imports.

High interest rates also attracted a flow of foreign investment into the U.S. that contributed to an appreciation of the U.S. dollar relative to foreign currencies. The USDA estimated that the value of the dollar rises 5–10% for each 1% increase in the difference between U.S. and foreign real interest rates. This made U.S. agricultural products more expensive for foreign buyers.

By reducing the foreign demand for U.S. agricultural exports, all these factors contributed to the growth of U.S. farm surpluses, which depressed both agricultural prices

Falling demand, along with large supplies of such competitive products as pork and poultry, pushed down prices for fattened steers in the spring. As prices fell past the break-even point for ranchers, they began culling their herds, further depressing prices.
ROBERT MULHERIN

and farm income. The impact was severe because the output of 30% or more of U.S. cropland was devoted to the production of commodities for export. In 1980 more than half of all U.S. wheat, rice, and cotton, 40% of the soybeans, and 37% of the corn was exported.

Many economists argued that U.S. agricultural policies embodied in the 1981 farm bill also contributed to the weakening of U.S. agricultural exports during the 1980s by stimulating production and exports by U.S. competitors. They claimed that loan rates in the 1981 farm bill were set too high in the expectation that world import demand would continue to grow as rapidly as it had during the 1970s. (The loan rate acts as a domestic support price. For instance, in 1985 the government pledged its readiness to loan a farmer who signed up for the program $3.30 on each bushel of wheat he produced. That farmer had the option of waiting for the price of wheat to rise and then paying off the loan plus interest before selling his wheat on the open market. But he could also choose not to repay the loan and turn his wheat over to the government.)

When world agricultural trade failed to expand as rapidly in the 1980s as in the 1970s, these economists claimed, the U.S. loan rate created an "umbrella" that actually protected foreign producers. In the absence of the loan rate, export prices would have been expected to fall because of weak foreign demand. Less efficient producers would, they argued, have cut back their output. The U.S., as an efficient producer, would have been better able at the lower price to maintain or even increase the share of the world market that it had won in the 1970s. But when import demand weakened, prices fell only to a level roughly corresponding to the U.S. loan rate. Competitors could export all their excess production by pricing their grain just under the U.S. price umbrella. Furthermore, foreign producers had the incentive to maintain or even increase production because they knew that U.S. farmers were unlikely to sell much grain into the world market at a price lower than they could get at home as determined by the loan rate.

New Farm Bill. The Food Security Act of 1985, signed into law on December 23, was characterized by the chairman of the Senate Agriculture Committee as "the begin-

ning of a slow, but decisive, transition to market-oriented farm policy." The act aimed at gradually reducing various large direct and indirect income aids to farmers while more rapidly allowing loan rates to fall as low as necessary to clear markets and make U.S. exports fully competitive. It also provided tools to promote agricultural exports, including several intended to reduce government stocks of surplus commodities. The eventual aim was for agriculture to respond more than it had in the past to prices determined by the basic balance between supply and demand rather than to government price and income programs.

During this transition, government seemed destined to play a very large role, one in which it would have considerable discretionary powers. The transition was also expected to be costly. For instance, the projected cost of the commodity programs administered by the Commodity Credit Corporation was about $52 billion for fiscal years 1986–88. A major uncertainty connected with the act was how it might be affected should the Gramm-Rudman Act mandating a balanced federal budget be invoked to curb federal expenditures.

The major measure adopted for protecting farm income was the freezing of target prices for specified commodities at 1985 levels for the first one or two years; after that, reductions by the secretary of agriculture would be permitted within the following limits:

	1986	1987	1988	1989	1990
Wheat per bu	4.38	4.38	4.29	4.16	4.00
Corn per bu	3.03	3.03	2.97	2.87	2.75
Cotton per lb	0.810	0.794	0.770	0.745	0.729
Rice per cwt	11.90	11.66	11.30	10.95	10.71

In addition, the support price for sugar was set at 18 cents per pound for the entire five years.

Farmers who entered the commodity programs received direct deficiency payments for the difference between the target price and the price at which they sold their commodities. They were obligated to accept acreage restrictions—many at the secretary of agriculture's discretion—that involved various combinations of mandatory or voluntary, unpaid or paid, removals of land from production. In the case of dairy farming a partially producer-funded program was authorized under which the government would buy entire dairy herds from farmers who were willing to quit milk production. Such production restraints would be necessary to keep output from rising and adding to surpluses as long as support payments remained far above world prices.

The provisions dealing with loan rates were complicated. For grains the rates were to be based on a historical aver-

age of grain prices with reductions of up to 5% permitted each year. However, the secretary of agriculture could under various conditions decide to operate under alternative provisions that permitted him to cut loan rates as much as an additional 20% in order to compete in world markets. Associated with these options were various payment-in-kind schemes.

Some of the provisions that were designed to promote agricultural exports included a bonus export program to use $2 billion in surplus commodities over the next three years to counter subsidies and unfair foreign trade practices; a minimum of $5 billion annually in short-term export credit guarantees; and $500 million annually in intermediate export credit guarantees through 1988 and up to $1 billion in 1989.

Other provisions included continuation of the farmer-owned grain reserve, limited to 30% of the wheat and 15% of the corn used domestically or exported in a year. Another created a 40 million–45 million-ac long-term conservation reserve to shift fragile cropland to less intensive use.

Trade and Aid Developments. The EC and the U.S. continued to skirmish over agricultural trade in 1985 as both regions attempted to ease burgeoning supplies of agricultural products by moving them into export markets. The U.S. announced an Export Enhancement Program (EEP) in May that committed $2 billion of U.S. government inventories of agricultural products to be used as bonuses to U.S. exporters over the next three years to expand sales of specified commodities. Sales were to be "targeted to markets identified as those taken over by competing nations with the use of unfair trade practices." The first sale under the program was wheat to Algeria, where the EC had recently made inroads upon the U.S. market share.

The EC in November increased its export refunds for wheat exports to the Mediterranean region by about 30% to protect what it regarded as its traditional market and to match U.S. prices in its subsidized sale of 500,000 tons of wheat to Egypt. The EC threatened to file a complaint against the EEP in the GATT (General Agreement on Tariffs and Trade), where a U.S. complaint against EC wheat export subsidies was already under consideration.

In the same month, the U.S. raised its import duties on certain pasta products after a GATT panel recommended that the EC remove the discrimination against imports of U.S. oranges and lemons resulting from preferential treatment given to Mediterranean citrus fruits. The EC retaliated by increasing its duties on imports of U.S. lemons and walnuts. Another dispute was averted when the U.S. International Trade Commission in October rejected a claim by U.S. grape growers that the U.S. industry had been materially injured (or threatened with injury) by subsidized or "less-than-fair-value" wine imports from the EC.

In this contentious atmosphere, and after prolonged and difficult negotiations, the members of the GATT agreed in late November to establish a preparatory committee "to determine the objectives, subject matter, modalities for and participation in" a new round of multilateral trade negotiations (MTN). The committee would have to prepare by mid-July 1986 recommendations for adoption at the GATT ministerial meeting scheduled for September 1986. Arguments about the need for a "standstill" in initiating new trade restrictions, a "rollback" of old restrictions, or special treatment for less developed countries as preconditions for the MTN appeared to have been left for resolution by the committee. The EC opposed any negotiating framework that would question the basic goals and mechanisms of its common agricultural policy (CAP). A major U.S. policy objective in the MTN was to eliminate those agri-

Table X. Shipments of Food Aid in Cereals

In 000 metric ton grain equivalent

	Average 1980–81, 1982–83	1983–84	1984–85[1]	1985–86[1]
Australia	401	460	480	400
Canada	681	817	943	900
EC	1,476	1,890	2,468	1,580
By members	675	866	1,209	...
By organization	801	1,024	1,259	...
Japan	646	445	330	300
Sweden	100	83	80	80
United States	5,309	5,655	7,512	7,200
Others[2]	480	480	676	450
Total	9,094	9,830	12,489	10,910
Percentage to low-income food-deficit countries[3]	82%	89%	86%	87%

[1]Partly estimated.
[2]Includes Argentina, Austria, China, Finland, India, Norway, OPEC Special Fund, Saudi Arabia, Spain, Switzerland, Turkey, and World Food Program, but not necessarily for all years.
[3]Per capita incomes under $790 in 1984.
Source: FAO, *Food Outlook*, December 1985.

cultural trade measures employed in support of the CAP that it regarded as unfair.

The combination of acute food shortages in Africa and large grain supplies in the exporting countries resulted in total food aid in cereals in 1984–85 exceeding for the first time the ten million-ton target set at the World Food Conference in 1974. Of the total, more than 60% was supplied by the U.S. The target was also likely to be achieved in 1985–86. As of November 1985, pledges by 29 countries to the International Emergency Food Reserve administered by the World Food Program (WFP) exceeded the target of 500,000 tons of cereals by 265,000 tons. The U.S. contributed one-third of the total. Other foods contributed totaled 56,000 tons, compared with 45,000 tons of noncereals and 620,000 tons of cereals in 1984.

The WFP as of November had allocated $179 million for emergency operations to 30 countries in Africa, 10 in Asia, 3 in the Middle East, and 5 in Latin America in 1985. Of this total, 60% was directed to refugees, displaced persons, and victims of war and civil disturbances. The countries of sub-Saharan Africa were the recipient of 64% of the emergency allocations.

Pledges by 82 donor countries to the regular resources of the WFP for the 1985–86 biennium represented 73% of the $1,350,000,000 target. Pledges for the 1983–84 biennium by 99 donors amounted to 81% of the $1.2 billion target. The Committee on Food Aid Policies and Programs, which provided policy guidance to the WFP, established a pledging target for the 1987–88 biennium of $1.4 billion, comprised of an estimated 3,250,000 tons of food aid (if bought at current prices) and $405 million in cash to be used for distribution costs.   (RICHARD M. KENNEDY)

See also Gardening.

This article updates the *Macropædia* article The History of AGRICULTURE.

FISHERIES

The entry into the European Communities (EC) of Spain and Portugal, scheduled for Jan. 1, 1986, would have far-reaching repercussions, touching most fishing nations in some way in the years ahead. The Spanish fishing fleet almost equaled the combined EC fleets in size. Of its approximately 13,000 vessels, 11,000 were relatively small, but the remainder included many large ocean-ranging freezer trawlers and tuna boats, some of which fished as far south as the Falkland Islands. With the EC fleet virtually

Crew members of a Japanese whaling ship, just returned to Tokyo from the Antarctic whaling grounds, clench their fists and shout in protest on learning that the Japanese government had agreed to close the whaling industry by 1988.
AP/WIDE WORLD

doubled, it would represent one of the world's largest fish-catching forces. At the same time, with the addition of Spain—a major seafood importer—the EC would constitute a single market of considerable size. Together, these two factors would enable the EC to exercise considerable influence at the international level. Also, Spain had become highly specialized in setting up joint ventures with other countries worldwide. These would become increasingly integrated into the EC, and already Spain was offering its joint-venture expertise to its new partners.

Meanwhile, during 1985 EC fishing countries continued to adjust to the combined effect of high fuel prices, excess catching capacity, the 200-mi exclusive economic zone (EEZ), and their own recently formulated common fisheries policy. Aid was provided by the European Commission for 442 fishery projects at a cost of 35.5 million ECUs (European currency units), with Italy the main benefactor. However, the cost of fuel was gradually becoming more closely related to income, and fleets were being tailored toward shorter trips to less distant grounds. Scrapping subsidies had failed to achieve a dramatic effect on fleet size, but restrictions in licensing had caused some vessels to be laid up and created a brisk market for licensed second-hand vessels.

There was also a move toward improving the quality of landed fish as a means of winning the high prices needed to compensate for smaller catches. The proportion of fish and shellfish undergoing processing before sale continued to rise. Food technologists were forecasting that most fish would eventually be sold as reformed mince, often utilizing those species less favoured on the market, such as blue whiting and Norway pout. Whole fish and fillets would then fetch premium prices on the more discriminating market. It was seen as a sign of the times that the hard-to-please Spanish consumer was now accepting frozen crab and lobster.

There was a repeat of the 1973 fisheries exhibition at Vigo, Spain—Europe's largest fishing port. Organized once again by the British journal *World Fishing,* it was seen by both Spain and Portugal as a launching pad for the future. The Spanish government chose the occasion to mount a conference, to which some 30 fisheries ministers and high officials were invited, to discuss aid to third world countries' fisheries. China was also the venue for a fisheries exhibition and conference—an indication of that country's

Area and country	Fin whale	Sei/ Bryde's whale	Hump-back whale	Minke whale	Sperm whale	Killer whale	Total	Percentage assigned under quota agreement[1]
Antarctic pelagic (open sea)								
Japan	—	—	—	3,027	—	—	3,027	49.99
U.S.S.R.	—	—	—	3,028	—	—	3,028	50.01
Brazil	—	—	—	—	—	—	—	—
Total	—	—	—	6,055	—	—	6,055	100.00
Outside the Antarctic								
Japan	—	536	—	290	393	—	1,219	
U.S.S.R.	—	—	—	—	—	—	169[2]	
Brazil	—	—	—	625	—	—	625	
Peru	—	149	—	—	—	—	149	
Iceland	144	100	—	204	—	3	451	
Spain	120	—	—	—	—	—	120	
Norway	—	—	—	1,869	—	—	1,869	
Korea, South	—	—	—	485	—	3	488	
Others	13	3	—	—	21	—	37	
Total	277	788	—	3,473	414	6	5,127	

Table XI. Whaling: 1983–84 Season (Antarctic); 1983 Season (Outside the Antarctic)
Number of whales caught

[1]Minke; Southern Hemisphere only.
[2]Represents gray whales; figure is included in both vertical and horizontal totals.
Source: The Committee for Whaling Statistics, *International Whaling Statistics.*

Table XII. World Fisheries, 1983[1]
In 000 metric tons

Country	Catch		Trade	
	Total	Inland	Imports	Exports
Japan	11,250.0	230.0	1,215.8	667.9
U.S.S.R.	9,756.7	796.5	320.0	501.7
China	5,213.3	1,840.8	—	104.3
U.S.	4,142.5	75.8	1,116.1	526.5
Chile	3,978.1	0.3	—	842.9
Norway	2,822.3	23.0	39.7	828.7
India	2,520.0	961.7	—	83.0
South Korea	2,400.4	46.9	77.3	443.9
Thailand	2,250.0	150.0	58.6	336.1
Indonesia	2,112.2	520.3	99.3	91.1
Denmark	1,862.1	24.6	277.2	735.4
Philippines	1,836.9	565.4	24.9	53.4
North Korea	1,600.0	90.0	—	24.1
Peru	1,486.8	24.6	50.7	256.6
Canada	1,337.2	50.0	100.6	479.7
Spain	1,250.0	23.0	268.7	199.7
Mexico	1,070.0	20.7	23.8	37.2
Brazil	844.5	198.5	43.0	58.2
Iceland	839.2	0.4	1.3	329.0
United Kingdom	811.0	6.9	706.2	364.5
France	784.0	...	531.0	177.5
Malaysia	741.1	15.2	161.4	117.0
Poland	735.1	30.4	93.8	140.4
Bangladesh	728.5	584.5	—	14.1
Vietnam	710.0	205.0	—	11.9
South Africa	600.0	0.8	51.3	63.0
Burma	585.8	142.9	—	1.7
Turkey	567.3	40.4	—	14.1
Nigeria	515.2	124.9	317.1	0.6
The Netherlands	503.3	3.9	362.3	466.4
Italy	478.4	41.3	404.2	114.3
Morocco	440.0	1.4	—	157.5
Argentina	416.3	14.6	10.9	183.7
Pakistan	343.4	60.4	—	18.9
South West Africa/ Namibia	341.0	[2]	...	...
Faeroe Islands	330.0	—	4.0	124.3
Ecuador	307.3	—	—	76.8
West Germany	305.6	22.8	916.1	321.7
Tanzania	272.5	237.0	1.0	0.1
Sweden	265.5	10.0	207.5	135.0
Portugal	246.5	...	98.1	54.7
Romania	242.5	51.3	49.4	—
East Germany	239.9	22.3	40.0	...
Ghana	228.0	43.0	19.6	22.4
Venezuela	226.9	20.0	17.7	10.2
Other	5,933.3	...	...	...
World	76,470.6	8,859.3[3]	10,167.0	10,780.0

[1]Excludes whaling.
[2]Less than 50 metric tons.
[3]Includes unspecified amounts in Other category.
Source: United Nations Food and Agriculture Organization,
Yearbook of Fishery Statistics, vol. 56 and 57.

policy of expanding and modernizing its fishing industry and moving its fleets farther into international grounds. China was also exporting its undoubted expertise in multiple-species fish farming. In 1983 one-third of China's fish harvest had come from inland waters.

Japan continued to lead the world, both in size of catch and in fish and shellfish imports. Japan was also one of the nations taking an increased interest in fishing off the Falkland Islands—in this case for squid—and there were again demands in Britain for a 200-mi or similar EEZ around the Falklands that would enable stocks to be managed more efficiently. Peru was still recovering from the loss of the shoals of anchoveta that once brought the country more than ten million metric tons of raw material for its fishmeal plants. El Niño, the warm Pacific current that was blamed for the disaster, appeared to have subsided, and Peru's catch was climbing to three million metric tons—double the 1983 figure—20% of which consisted of food fish. Chile's catch rose 11% to 4.5 million metric tons. Mexico was still having problems marketing its shrimp, while U.S. shrimpers accused it of selling into a free U.S. market while maintaining its own high tariff barriers.

The U.S. industry took an upturn as the popularity of seafood rose on dietary grounds and the campaign for improved quality took effect. Stocks of frozen cod that had been jamming cold storage began to move, and imports of lobster, shrimp, scallop, and clams increased. On the U.S. West Coast fishermen were learning to diversify their catch

and catching methods and were landing fish to foreign vessels under joint-venture agreements. Fresh optimism was demonstrated in orders for new boats, and the U.S. was at last getting tough with foreign vessels in order to support the newly burgeoning industry. Japan, the U.S.'s largest joint-venture partner, was told that it had to buy more U.S.-produced *surimi* fish mince if it wished to keep its present quota of Alaska pollack. A new crab-stick plant, to be built in Seattle, Wash., would cut U.S. imports from Japan. Squid stocks off the northwest coast were also being exploited by the U.S., with 400 metric tons landed in three months at Oregon—yet another sign of increased versatility among traditionally conservative U.S. fishermen. A massive vote of confidence in the industry was the decision to build a new fish terminal in Brooklyn, N.Y.

Iceland and Norway were learning new skills in order to exploit newly discovered beds of small scallops, known as "queenies" to the Scottish fleet. Several Icelandic vessels installed processing equipment that enabled them to land shucked, clean, frozen, and packaged scallops, bearing out forecasts of an increasing trend toward on-board processing. Iceland was emerging as an innovative nation, increasingly competent and independent in modern technology and now an exporter of marine and electronic hardware to world markets. It was also among the nations seeking new uses for the organic polymer, known as chitosan, extracted from shrimp and crab waste; this substance had already proved valuable as an antiflocculant and an antifungus treatment for seed crops, and its use for disposable contact lenses had been suggested.

Norwegian shipyards experienced a welcome return of orders, and in Scotland builders of fishing vessels were having a busy time as the fisheries successfully adapted to the EC common fisheries policy. Scotland was now the U.K.'s largest supplier of fish and shellfish, to an annual value of £300 million. An increasing percentage of Scottish landings were being processed before sale, and new processing plants were proliferating. Scottish fishermen contrived to live in uneasy peace with North Sea oil. At a meeting in Aberdeen, concern was expressed over the extent of oil industry debris littering the seabed, to the detriment of fishing operations. There were also warnings of rising pollution levels in the North Sea, which could affect fishing.

In the Far East a lull in the conflict between Tamils and Sinhalese enabled Sri Lankan fishermen to get back to sea after restrictions on movement that had caused some hardship to fishing communities were lifted. India faced continuing problems in its attempts to build a deep-sea fleet. Small-boat fishermen claimed that big trawlers were less efficient than smaller craft and more heavily subsidized and that they were destroying inshore grounds. Indian shipyards complained that red tape, inefficiency, and import restrictions made it impossible to compete with imported vessels. Of a promised 600 trawlers, only 120 had materialized, and of these 80 were imported. Indonesia announced a $50 million development plan, aided by a loan from the Asian Development Bank. There were increasing indications that future developments in both fisheries and aquaculture would be centred in Southeast Asia.

According to a study by a U.S. team, export prospects for the Far East looked promising. The team forecast an increase in consumption that could not be satisfied by existing fishing grounds in the West. Fish farming in Europe could help to fill the gap, provided higher prices were obtained for currently less popular species that were good subjects for farming. The U.S. study also forecast greater use of fish-based products made from extruded fish mince, with flavours such as crab, lobster, and scampi superim-

posed by additives. There were even hints of a fish-based substitute for the morning rasher of bacon.

The Netherlands continued to build powerful double-rig beam trawlers that towed a matrix of heavy chain to "dig out" the valuable flatfish. There was revived interest in a method of towing two nets with one boat (quotas were allocated by the boat, not the net). The new purpose-built fishing port of Lauwersoog, Neth., was proving a success and attracting foreign landings. It was visited by the research team responsible for the future New York terminal. In Denmark the new North Sea Centre at Hirtshals was also proving to be a valuable focal point for fisheries research and development.

More economical methods of propulsion continued to be sought. The first purpose-built sail-assisted tuna long-line vessel was built in Japan, though many other ships had been converted. Another experimental rig came from France; Jacques Cousteau's new semicatamaran research vessel *Alcyone,* which had twin vertical cylinders in place of sails, successfully crossed the Atlantic on its maiden voyage.

The U.S. antiwhaling lobby continued to seek support for commercial pressures to force Japan to reduce or abandon whaling activities, although some nations—notably Norway—continued to catch minke whales despite protests by the International Whaling Commission. The Soviet Union was also threatened with a reduction or even cessation of U.S. fish imports if minke whaling continued. By the end of the summer it was announced that Japan was prepared to stop whaling by 1988, having decided that the loss of U.S. fishing concessions would be a greater disaster than the loss of the whale catch. (*See* ENVIRONMENT: *Wildlife.*)

(H. S. NOEL)

This article updates the *Macropædia* article Commercial FISH-ING AND MARINE PRODUCTS.

FOOD PROCESSING

Nutrition and Health. Western consumers were becoming more and more preoccupied with their health and the effects of what they eat. Additives were increasingly under attack, and the trend toward "natural" foods continued to gain momentum. In the U.S. sales of diet foods and beverages were growing at triple the rate for all foods, and it was estimated that by 1990 the market would be worth over $40 billion. Women aged 25–44 were the prime tar-

gets for reduced calorie and low-fat foods, while those over the age of 45 were the main consumers of low-sodium, low-cholesterol, decaffeinated, high-fibre, and other special dietary foods. Products using low-calorie sweeteners were an important part of this market, with low-calorie soft drinks, iced tea, and cocoa mixes sweetened with aspartame becoming hundred-million-dollar businesses. Newer sweeteners such as polydextrose and acesulfame K were also expected to have an impact; the first product sweetened with acesulfame K appeared on the U.K. market during the year. Interest in the physiological effects of fibre in the diet was growing, and work at the Flour Milling and Baking Research Association in the U.K. tended to support the theory that fibre helps to prevent various diseases of the gastrointestinal tract.

Legislation. In the U.K. proposals for fat content labeling were issued following the publication in 1984 of a report from the Committee on Medical Aspects of Food Policy (COMA), which identified the high intake of fat in the British diet as a main cause of the country's abnormally high mortality rate from heart disease. The U.K. National Dairy Council expressed concern that fat had been singled out for statutory treatment.

After many years of discussion, the text of a new European Communities directive on containers of liquids for human consumption was published during the year, giving member states until July 1987 to comply with its provisions. The directive aimed to reduce energy consumption in the manufacture, and environmental impact in the disposal, of glass, metal, or plastic beverage containers. Draft proposals were put forward by the European Commission during the year for legislation to control the designation of milk and milk products. The need for such regulation grew out of the increase in the number of products in which part or all of the fat and milk proteins were replaced by vegetable fats and proteins. The proposals aimed to restrict descriptive terms associated with milk, such as "cream," "butter," and "cheese," to products containing only ingredients derived from milk.

Processing Technology. A new preservation technology was being commercialized by a Belgian joint venture company formed between the Sud-Lait cooperative of Luxembourg and Oleofina, a subsidiary of the Petrofina Group. It involved the extraction of two naturally occurring bacteriocides from milk for use in infant foods and as a

JOSÉ MORÉ/CHICAGO TRIBUNE

The largest outbreak of salmonella food poisoning in U.S. history—some 16,000 cases reported—was traced to two faulty valves in this dairy in Melrose Park, Illinois.

preservative in other food products. The first factory was commissioned in June at Recogne in Luxembourg. The technology was the result of research work carried out by the two parent companies.

Advances in genetic engineering and enzyme technology were providing new opportunities for food processors. Imperial Biotechnology of the U.K. developed a process for accelerating the ripening of cheese. Using enzymes extracted from selected strains of microorganisms, it could reduce the ripening time of cheddar cheese, normally nine months, to three months. A study by the market analysts Frost & Sullivan published during the year estimated that the U.S. industrial enzyme market would grow at the rate of 6.5% a year, to a value of $255 million by 1988, with three-quarters of the market accounted for by the needs of the food industry. Enzymatically produced high fructose corn syrup, for example, was already replacing sugar as the prime sweetener in prepared foods and soft drinks in the U.S., and enzymes obtained from maize (corn) were making inroads in cheese making, meat tenderizing, brewing, and the manufacture of fish protein concentrates, where processors were increasingly turning away from traditional fermentation agents. In Europe, however, such developments were inhibited by punitively high levies on imports of maize products.

Enzyme technology was also making headway in the analytical field. Conventional procedures for detecting certain substances, such as trace contaminants, in foods were giving way, in certain circumstances, to techniques in which specific enzymes were made to react with the substances. Such enzymes are known as biosensors. In the U.K. workers at Cranfield Institute of Technology and at Imperial College, University of London, developed biosensors that rely on a direct interaction between the enzyme and an electrode. Such biosensors are immune from chemical interference, would be cheap to manufacture, and could be incorporated in compact, inexpensive instruments.

Cranfield Biotechnology Centre developed a direct biosensor for glucose, which would soon be on the market for use by diabetic patients. The Leatherhead Food Research Association, with financial support from the British government, was working on a collaborative project with Cranfield to develop biosensors for process and quality control in the food industry. It was envisaged that, as a result of this project, instruments would be designed to predict the shelf life of food products. These instruments would assess the microbial state or the progress of rancidity in a food well before spoilage, and an assay could be carried out in minutes.

A butter-making plant opened in June in Wales by the U.K. Milk Marketing Board used computer-controlled equipment supplied by a West German company. The plant processed some half-million litres (l; 1 l = 1.057 qt) of milk a day, operating around the clock with a minimal work force. Another automatic plant commissioned during the year was that of Macphie & Co. of Scotland for making an imitation cream containing nondairy fat. The product had an extended shelf life and only half the fat content of whipped dairy cream. It was being made in two forms: one for manufacturing and catering use packed in 10- and 25-l bag-in-box packs, and the other for retail sale packed in 200-ml (6.8-oz) aseptic cartons. The manufacturing and catering pack won an award during the year for technical innovation. The plant, which cost over £1 million, was the first totally microprocessor-controlled plant to be installed in the U.K. by the Swedish company Alfa-Laval. The aseptic bag-in-box technology was developed in collaboration with a subsidiary of the U.K. packaging company

British Cellophane Ltd. Another Swedish company, Tetra Pak, supplied the aseptic cartons in which the product was packed for retail sale and also provided the filling machines and associated equipment.

Packaging Developments. The Coloreed bag-in-box packaging system used for Macphie's nondairy cream, which had been developed specifically for low-acid and nonacid products, used a new patented packaging principle that was said to eliminate the risk of product contamination and to provide improved operating efficiencies. Although Macphie was filling 10- and 25-l packs, the technique could handle packs of any size between 2 and 50 l, and similar systems were expected to find wide use in dairy-related industries for such products as milk, yogurt, cream, and soups.

Considerable publicity was given to the introduction by the U.K. company Crosse & Blackwell during the year of a line of shelf-stable soups in aseptic cartons. These were the first products of this type to be produced by the high-temperature short-time (HTST) process widely used for milk and fruit juices. According to the makers, the soups had a fresher and more natural taste than equivalent soups prepared by canning. The process also made it possible to prepare highly specialized and delicate soups in the gourmet category that would normally be impaired by the long cooking times involved in canning.

Within a few years, aseptic packaging had grown from relative obscurity into a billion-dollar industry. Its future looked bright, especially in the U.S., where, after a slow start, use of the technique was expanding at a faster rate than anywhere else in the world. Among the containers being used for aseptic packaging were paperboard cartons, plastic cups and bottles, and bag-in-box. During the year Tetra Pak opened its second factory in North America, in Toronto, complementing its factory in Denton, Texas, opened in 1984. The company claimed to be making 35,-000,000,000 cartons annually worldwide, or six cartons for every man, woman, and child on the Earth.

More than 40% of U.S. homes now had microwave ovens. However, most food processors had not kept up with the trend and were having trouble developing "dual ovenable" products; that is, products that could be cooked in either a conventional or a microwave oven. The main difficulty was that because microwave ovens work through induction and not radiant heating, food cooked in them does not brown or crisp and sometimes has an unappetizing appearance. The Pillsbury Co. introduced a special package for a pizza product that overcame this difficulty. The package contained a "susceptor" to aid browning—a layer of powdered aluminum laminated under plastic. The aluminum absorbs the microwave energy and raises the temperature on the surface of the pizza sufficiently to brown and crisp the crust.

Following the explosive growth in recent years of PET (polyethylene terephthalate) plastic bottles for soft drinks, especially in the U.S., such bottles, previously restricted in size to between one and two litres, had been getting both larger and smaller. The three-litre size made its appearance during the year in the U.K. At the other end of the size scale, miniature single-portion-size PET bottles of spirits were introduced, particularly for airline use. It was estimated that if all the liquor carried on an average jumbo-jet flight were to be packed in PET bottles instead of glass, the weight saving would be equivalent to two passengers and their luggage.

New Products. These continued to be introduced at an ever increasing rate. Ranks Hovis McDougall's mycoprotein food ingredient based on microbial protein appeared on the retail market in a U.K. consumer product. Fish and

fish products were growing in popularity; major U.S. and Japanese food processors were flooding North American supermarkets with products made from *surimi,* a fish paste of Japanese origin. *Surimi* products could be flavoured, shaped, and textured to resemble shrimp, lobster, and a host of other seafood products.   (ANTHONY WOOLLEN)

See also Environment; Health and Disease; Industrial Review: *Beverages; Textiles; Tobacco.*

This article updates the *Macropædia* article FOOD PROCESSING.

Anthropology

Examining the effects of apartheid (the policy of racial separation) in South Africa; working with tribal people displaced by hydroelectric development in Malaysia, India, and Canada; studying planned social change in Bulgaria; or reevaluating such basic concepts as culture and kinship; anthropologists continued to engage in a wide variety of research projects in 1985. Scholarly activity within the profession was stimulated by modest increases in research funding, growing graduate enrollments, and slightly improved employment opportunities.

Declining undergraduate enrollments, persistently high unemployment rates, and increasing underemployment (large numbers of academically employed anthropologists were hired on a part-time or temporary basis) continued to be major problems. Fundamentalist Christian groups pressing for the teaching of the biblical version of creation as scientific fact in U.S. schools continued to challenge the legitimacy of anthropology as part of their effort to discredit evolutionary theory. Despite these problems the high level of scholarly activity maintained by anthropologists throughout the world testified to the vigour and vitality of the discipline.

Reexamination of basic anthropological concepts and renewed interest in humanistic aspects of the discipline were among the important theoretical developments in anthropology in 1985. Anthropologists had long debated the validity of such standard categories as culture, tribe, religion, government, and economics. Inspired by renewed interest in the concept of culture in anthropology and other disciplines, a group of ethnologists formed the Society for Cultural Anthropology. The society planned to provide an interdisciplinary forum for cultural studies in its forthcoming journal, *Cultural Anthropology.*

A new debate on another fundamental anthropological concept was sparked by the publication of David Schneider's *A Critique of the Study of Kinship.* Schneider claimed that uncritical assumptions based upon Western ideas of the nature of society had distorted the study of kinship since the 19th century. Noting that the Western concept of kinship was not shared by other cultures, he suggested abandoning the category as a cross-cultural construct.

Anthropology had long regarded itself as a social science. At the same time, anthropologists had never lost sight of their humanistic traditions. As Jacob Pandian pointed out, "Data may be produced by the scientific method, but it is the humanist who analyzes the data in relation to the quality and value of human life." Renewed interest in this aspect of the discipline led to the recent formation of the Society for Humanistic Anthropology. The society planned to sponsor symposia, organize meetings, and publish a newsletter and journal.

Small-Group Studies. The large number of papers devoted to applied, medical, urban, and political anthropology and the anthropology of development and education presented at the 1985 American Anthropological Association meeting vividly highlighted the growing emphasis upon practical applications of anthropological theory and method. Much of this effort was directed toward small-scale societies. Taking the traditional role of participant-observer, most anthropologists worked to study objectively the effects of change upon tribal people. Increasing numbers of field-workers, however, were taking a more active role. Malaysian anthropologists, for example, worked for three years to minimize the disruptions suffered by Iban tribespeople who had been displaced by the construction of the Batang Ai hydroelectric project on their lands. Other anthropologists, such as those working with Survival International, assisted tribespeople in their resistance to development projects in India, South West Africa/ Namibia, Venezuela, and Brazil and to military repression in Nicaragua and Chile.

Anthropological research also influenced the work of others studying tribal societies. Anastasia Shkilnyk, a policy adviser to the Canadian government, skillfully used anthropological methods to assess the effects of relocation,

IRVEN DEVORE—ANTHRO-PHOTO

A plan by the South African government to create a nature preserve in the Kalahari Desert in South West Africa/Namibia was seen by some anthropologists as a threat to the traditional culture of the region's Bushmen, most of whom would be resettled.

alcoholism, and the actual and potential losses caused by mercury pollution upon the Ojibwa of Grassy Narrows, Ont. Documenting the demoralization and disorientation of the Grassy Narrows community in her book *A Poison Stronger than Love,* Shkilnyk showed that the problems of violence, illness, family breakdown, child abuse, and drug and alcohol abuse were not unique to the Ojibwa at Grassy Narrows or to other Canadian Indian groups but could be the common fate of all communities undergoing extraordinary change.

Effects of Modernization. Growing numbers of anthropologists also were turning their attention toward large-scale modern societies. In the United States June Nash studied the effects of the changeover from consumer-oriented heavy industry to production of high-technology equipment in Pittsfield, Mass. Susan Bourque and Kay Warren examined the ways in which the establishment of male-dominated cooperatives was causing rural Peruvian women to seek better economic opportunities as workers in provincial cities.

Problems associated with the rapid urbanization of a formerly rural agricultural population in Bulgaria were examined by Eleanor Smollett. Smollett's research traced the economic development of the country from pre-World War II peasant holdings to the establishment of present-day agro-industrial complexes and settlement systems, which integrated highly mechanized cooperative agriculture and industry in closely connected urban and rural areas. In this way Bulgarian social scientists and planners hoped to balance the attractions of village life with those of the city. If successful, those programs would enable Bulgaria to avoid the many problems associated with massive migration from the countryside to the city.

In his recent study *Waiting,* Vincent Crapanzano examined another society's efforts to deal with problems of modernization. Interested in the effect of domination on the people who dominate, Crapanzano conducted research in a small South African village in the Cape of Good Hope just before the recent declaration of a state of emergency. He studied attitudes of liberal (by South African standards) whites toward Coloureds (those of mixed race), blacks, and Asians. Interviewing both Afrikaners and other whites, he continually found "signs of anxiety, helplessness, vulnerability, and rage." Encountering a society simultaneously seeing itself as besieged and omnipotent, Crapanzano demonstrated how the stress of waiting while black unrest intensified affected every aspect of life in white South Africa.

Other changes associated with modernization were profoundly affecting the conduct of anthropological inquiry. Microcomputers were quickly becoming essential research and teaching tools. Computerized instruction programs were being adopted by growing numbers of instructors. Currently available packages ranged in complexity from simple administrative and testing programs to complex simulations allowing students to make decisions based upon knowledge of other cultural systems. The recent development of *World Cultures,* the first electronic journal for anthropologists, made the vast body of cross-cultural coded information contained in the Human Relations Area Files and other sources available on microcomputer diskettes.

Anthropology thus continued to experience vigorous growth in the 1980s. Reexamining old concepts in new ways and using time-tested methods and models in new settings, scholars were widening the scope of anthropological inquiry. Interdisciplinary ties were growing as scholars from diverse fields came together to solve common prob-

lems. Increasing numbers of anthropologists were taking a more active role in issues bearing upon their skills and expertise. Combining basic research with practical application, anthropology appeared likely to exert an ever increasing impact upon public policy in the coming years.

(ROBERT S. GRUMET)

See also ARCHAEOLOGY.

This article updates the *Macropædia* article SOCIAL SCIENCES: *Cultural Anthropology.*

Archaeology

Eastern Hemisphere. Archaeologists were active in the Old World during 1985 except in those regions where fieldwork was impossible because of political unrest. More than the usual amount of archaeological news came from China, and a joint U.S.-U.S.S.R. excavation took place in central Asia. In Turkey there was surprising new evidence of the cultural acceleration that took place about 8,000 BC once a basic food-producing pattern of subsistence was established.

Various breakthroughs were reported as to new techniques for the recovery of information. Underwater archaeological survey efforts were being aided by side-scan sonars, magnetometers, and acoustical devices called "pingers" or "boomers." The microscopic examination of blood residues on ancient flint tools in order to identify the animals on which the tools had been used was employed increasingly often during the year. There also was new evidence, especially from Venice, that the shift from wood and coal to oil as fuel may well be the factor in air pollution most destructive to ancient stone buildings and sculpture.

Pleistocene Prehistory. Perhaps the rather surprising lack of archaeological news from Africa during the year reflected the degree of political unrest there. In southern Turkey excavations resumed at the important site of Karain, where test excavations several years earlier had revealed a long "paleolithic" sequence. In France artifacts of "classic Acheulean" type, dating to about 350,000 years ago, were recovered in the Pas-de-Calais/Somme region. L. G. Straus published an important summary on recent work in northern Spain, covering the period from about 125,000 to 6,000 years ago. The recovery on the Lena River in Siberia of traces of an encampment with evidence of fire, judged to be more than a million years old, was reported, but few details were available.

Late Prehistoric Europe. Reports of settlement clearances in western Europe in the late Mesolithic to early Neolithic period (about 5000 to 3000 BC) came from France, Belgium, and Switzerland. In the latter country there was an

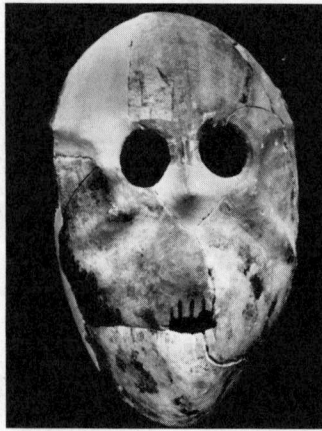

DAVID HARRIS/TIME MAGAZINE

In April the Israel Museum of Jerusalem displayed Neolithic artifacts from a cave near the Dead Sea, including the oldest painted mask ever found, a limestone human face decorated in red and green.

exhaustive modern field examination of what appeared to have been one of the classic "Swiss lake-dwelling" types of littoral border sites.

Middle East. The traditional archaeological activity in Egypt—the clearing, cleaning, and restoration of above-surface buildings and of tombs and the copying of inscriptions—proceeded, with archaeologists from an increasing number of nationalities being involved. There was interest in a new suggestion that the place of the missing (second) "solar boat" near the pharaoh Khufu's pyramid had been located. The first such boat was found in 1954, in a well-sealed pit. There was special interest in the possibility that, should this second example be likewise well sealed, it might yield uncontaminated samples of 4,600-year-old air for environmental analysis.

Archaeological activity continued to increase in northern Yemen, previously an unknown region archaeologically, but at the year's end there was not much material earlier than the 1st millennium BC. Both Israeli and foreign archaeologists were busy in Israel. A remarkable find, of approximately 9,000-year-old traces of cloth and a painted stone head, which had occurred in 1983 in a cave, Nahal Hemar, in the Negev, was put on display. Various biblical sites were being excavated, both in the Philistine (coastal) region and in the interior. A new excavation by the Oriental Institute, Chicago, was undertaken at Ashqelon. Fieldwork was also continued, by both local and foreign excavators, in Jordan, and a new joint French-Jordanian effort at Tell Abu Hamid in the Jordan Valley began.

In southern Turkey, northern Syria, and northern Iraq salvage efforts continued in regions where the flood pools behind new dams would soon form. Unfortunately, salvage archaeology has to be done hurriedly before the floodwaters rise, and large and time-consuming exposures often cannot be made. Nevertheless, the rough outlines of the cultural history of still-unknown areas could not otherwise be recovered. In both Syria and Iraq the governmental antiquity services made generous concessions and even provided financial aid for foreign participants in their salvage programs.

Both the Syrian and Iraqi governments were undertaking clearance and restoration around important old buildings in such towns as Aleppo, Damascus, Baghdad, and Mosul. In spite of the Iran–Iraq war, some brief fieldwork continued in southern Iraq.

In Turkey the joint Turkish-U.S.-West German expedition at Cayonu reported the final exposure of a nondomestic building of formal plan dating to about 9,500 years ago. It was the third such formally planned structure encountered, and it contained the burned skulls of some 50 humans. Built at a time when an effective food-producing way of life had only recently been developed, it suggested that the pace of cultural acceleration, given an assured food supply, was much faster than had been anticipated. The Turkish Antiquities Service began excavations at Harran, once visited by the biblical Abraham, and the long-range excavations by the Italians, West Germans, and Americans at Arslan Tepe, Bogazkoy, and Elmali continued.

The Greco-Roman World. Perhaps one of the most important events for Greek archaeology was the appearance of a thoughtful introduction to a description of new surface survey efforts in Boeotia. In it J. L. Bintliff and A. M. Snodgrass (*Journal of Field Archaeology* 12:123–61) assessed the future effects on archaeological research of the steadily increasing pace of urban and rural development with the consequent widespread use of bulldozers and other earth-moving equipment. They urged that, before it was too late, broad-ranging archaeological surface surveys receive more attention than the traditional concentration on individual large city sites with their often repetitious yields of well-known artifacts.

Otherwise, in Greece and in Rome the various national "schools" proceeded with their long-range excavations on large sites with familiar names. There were a few exceptional finds. In European Turkey (Thrace) near Tekirdag a rich 2nd-century BC tomb was found. In Athens the replica of a Greek sailing vessel (wrecked off Cyprus around 300 BC) was completed and launched. At Paestum in southern Italy a University of Michigan expedition recovered new evidence of the secret women's cultic rites of the goddess known as Bona Dea.

Roman remains continued to be recovered in western Europe. New clearances in London indicated that in Roman times the city had been not a carefully laid out garrison town (like Colchester, for example) but a fast-growing boomtown. In France detailed air photographs revealed the remains of an ancient theatre in the Argonne region. For post-Roman times, around AD 800, the town of Dorestad in The Netherlands yielded evidence of a much better human dietary pattern, with good protein content, than had ever been assumed.

Southern and Eastern Asia. A joint Soviet-U.S. team cleared portions of Sarazm, a 4th–3rd-millennium BC site about 45 km (28 mi) east of Samarkand, but details of the yield were not available. The Pakistan antiquities service reported that significant progress had been made in stopping the degeneration of the building remains of the great site of Mohenjo Daro (about 2500 BC). The increase of groundwater with heavy salt concentration had been an acute problem. In Thailand, at the copper-mining site of Phulong, a University of Pennsylvania group examined the tracks of very early copper recovery and processing.

The Chinese reported that the capital of the Shang Dynasty (about 1700 to 1100 BC) may have been found, in Yenshih (Yanshi), Henan (Honan) Province. It was reported as probable that the tomb of the Emperor Ch'in Shih Huang-ti (Qin Shihuangdi) himself (near the great subsurface find of terra-cotta warriors, horses, and chariots, attributable to him) might be intact. The massive terra-cotta find (about 210 BC) had been discovered in 1974. More than a thousand Han Dynasty (206 BC–AD 220) figurines were accidentally recovered at Suchow (Xuzhou) 1,100 km (700 mi) southeast of Beijing (Peking). The Chinese also reported that they planned to rebuild and restore the 13 tombs of the Ming emperors (AD 1368–1644) north of Beijing, already a great tourist attraction.

(ROBERT J. BRAIDWOOD)

Western Hemisphere. Archaeology in 1985 was noteworthy for a series of discoveries, both legitimate and not so legitimate. While treasure hunters announced the discovery of sunken ships and buried treasure, the media, both written and electronic, heralded the discovery of a not-so-lost city in the Peruvian jungle. In a less sensational vein, research during the year in North, Central, and South America highlighted the long-term nature and often unspectacular process of actual archaeological research. Finally, the application of new instrumentation to old archaeological problems provided critical radiocarbon dates in cases where samples had been too small for earlier techniques.

North America. Underwater investigations by a joint team of salvagers and archaeologists provided conclusive evidence that the sunken "treasure ship" found by private salvage divers in 1983 off the coast of Cape Cod was in fact the lost pirate ship *Whydah,* which sank with all hands after being commandeered in 1717, a year after its

This 9,500-year-old stone building uncovered in Cayonu, Turkey, provided evidence of rapid cultural progress following the introduction of agriculture in the ancient Middle East. The discovery of some 50 burned human skulls presented scholars with an intriguing puzzle.

ROBERT J. BRAIDWOOD

maiden voyage. A joint team of divers and archaeologists coordinated plans with Massachusetts state archaeologists to excavate and stabilize the wealth of discovered materials, valued at $10 million–12 million.

The potential archaeological value of the offshore waters of the east coast of the U.S. was further highlighted in 1985 by a find in New York's East River. In September a group of salvagers reported the discovery of a sunken Revolutionary War frigate, the 26-gun *Hussar,* which sank in 1780. Although cold water and the depth of the find in 30 m (100 ft) of murky water prevented further investigation, available documents indicated that the British ship also contained 80 chained American prisoners of war and a payroll in gold now estimated to be worth millions of dollars.

In addition to these rather spectacular finds, ongoing work by U.S. archaeologists at the site of George Custer's last battle with Sioux and Cheyenne warriors at the Little Bighorn River in Montana Territory was causing scholars to reassess the events and tactics that took place at the battle. After carefully considering the identity and location of artifacts at the site, the archaeologists, led by Douglas Scott of the U.S. National Park Service, announced that the battle was lost both because of errors of strategy on Custer's part and because of the vastly superior numbers of both fighters and arms on the side of the Indians. Instead of attacking en masse, as had often been assumed, the Indians, according to the archaeologists, cautiously crouched and picked off the soldiers from at least six positions before finally annihilating them. The excavated battle debris also suggested that the Indians were equipped with large numbers of some of the most advanced weapons of the period, including at least 60 new 16-shot, lever-action rifles, while the U.S. soldiers were equipped with only army-issue single-shot Springfield carbines and Colt revolvers.

Mexico. Although the devastating effects and loss of life suffered due to the September earthquake in Mexico City represent a catastrophic national disaster, this event also highlights the potential role of ancient disasters in shaping the continuity and changes that are documented in Mexican archaeology. While past excavations in the southern highlands have shown how whole regions and archaeological culture areas were rendered uninhabitable by the effects of volcanic eruptions, the magnitude and effects of the recent quake and more ancient examples suggest that natural disasters could have played a critical role in affecting the continuity and survival of cultures in the region. However,

despite the impact of natural disasters, it unfortunately had to be reported that this area was still suffering the effects of illegal looting and treasure hunters. Although recent agreements between the U.S. and Mexico shifted the flow of antiquities from a north-south axis to an international one focused on European recipients, the looting was both leading to the destruction of unstudied archaeological sites and, when interrupted in time, to the unscientific discovery of previously undocumented archaeological sites.

The vigilance of local inhabitants in the mountains of Guerrero in western Mexico who reported to authorities looting activities at an unstudied site resulted in one of the most important archaeological discoveries in that region in recent years. Located in the northern part of the state, inland from the resort of Acapulco, the site of Copalillo (currently being excavated under the auspices of the National Institute of Anthropology and History) contained on the surface a large platform and three large stone monoliths, each 1.5 m (5 ft) high, with Olmec designs inscribed on them. Ongoing excavations suggested that the site dates to between 2400 and 600 BC, that it is of Olmec cultural affiliation, and, at least tentatively, that this early Mexican civilization, previously thought to have developed on the country's east coast, may in fact have evolved simultaneously on both shores; such an interpretation would cause a drastic revision of old assumptions concerning the sources and direction of Mesoamerican culture.

Farther south, in the former Mayan territory of Belize, a husband-wife team, Arlen and Diane Chase of the University of Central Florida at Orlando, announced through the U.S. National Science Foundation the discovery of two intact late postclassic Mayan tombs at the coastal site of Santa Rita Corozal. The first tomb contained elaborately decorated pottery and ornaments and the body of what was interpreted to be a king. The second tomb contained two individuals, one of whom had Aztec ear ornaments manufactured in central Mexico and the other consisting only of the remains of an undecorated skeleton that was riddled with sting-ray spines and a copper needle, associations in Mayan culture indicative of ritual bloodletting practices.

Untouched by looters, these unusual discoveries indicated that, contrary to current thinking that Mayan culture declined sometime after AD 600–900, Mayan rule in this region instead continued for hundreds of years with high-status nobility controlling large territories until just before the arrival of the Spaniards in the early 16th century.

South America. The archaeology of Ecuador and of the Cauca River valley of Colombia had long been famous for the beautiful gold and ceramic artifacts of the highly publicized but poorly studied Quimbaya culture. Although the culture was well represented in private and museum collections, most pieces came from looted sites. Mostly by guesswork, it was estimated that they were made between AD 400 and 800, several thousand years after the appearance of the first gold technology in the south-central Andes of Peru. In 1985, however, long-overdue controlled archaeological excavations by John Isaacson of the University of Illinois at a small highland site near Quito yielded radiocarbon determinations from stylistically similar Quimbaya pottery that dated these artifacts at 600–1500 BC. These dates implied that both the elaborate Quimbaya pottery and cast gold pieces developed at about the same time as the first extensive "high" style of Peru, the Chavin culture of the 1st millennium BC, and that the highlands of Ecuador were culturally and technologically advanced much earlier than had been assumed.

In Peru the availability of new dating techniques provided solid confirmation for the antiquity of South Ameri-

ca's earliest evidence of textiles and food plants. Previously excavated in 1968 by Thomas Lynch from the highland Peruvian site of Guitarrero Cave, the textile and plant remains were thought to be early but remained in doubt because of uncertainty over the validity of the radiocarbon dates that were then available. Lynch, working in conjunction with scientists at the University of Oxford's Research Laboratory for Archaeology and the History of Art, utilized a new tandem electrostatic accelerator that was capable of returning dates from minute, previously inadequate, carbon samples. The new dates, clustered in time between 9,500 and 10,000 years before the present with the earliest being 12,500 years old, suggested that the associated preceramic textiles, basketry, beans, local tubers (potatolike plants), and a tomatolike plant all date back to the epoch close in time to the first human presence in the New World.

Events in South America of relevance to archaeology were overshadowed by a triumph of the Indiana Jones mystique over the conservatism of proper scientific data discovery and presentation. At a news conference the University of Colorado announced to a well-prepared media crowd the discovery of a pre-Inca city located on an eastern slope of the Peruvian Andes, and two faculty members, Tom Lennon and Jane Wheeler, explained their plans to study the site. News of the discovery was reported by many major media outlets, including the *Washington Post,* the television networks, and the wire services. The site was, however, not new and not unknown. Gran Pajaten had been explored by a Peruvian expedition in 1964 and by a U.S. explorer, Gene Savoy, in 1965; it was listed in the *South American Handbook,* was noted on current road maps, had been featured in a 1970 CBS documentary, and had been reported by Peruvian scientists and archaeologists in the national scientific literature over a 20-year period.

(JOEL W. GROSSMAN)

See also Anthropology.

Architecture

What is the architect's role in designing a new building for an existing historic and familiar site? To what extent should new buildings blend in with old? Is it better to create a building distinctly of its own time, a recognizable

masterpiece perhaps of its architect, than to conserve and refurbish existing buildings of lesser individual aesthetic merit? During 1985 controversy continued to swirl around these questions and the other considerations relating to the battle between modernism and conservationism that has been one of the leading concerns of those interested in architecture for at least the past decade. Many of the current issues had been aired in the planning inquiry held in the summer of 1984 in the City of London to determine whether a tower block designed by Ludwig Mies van der Rohe in 1967 should be built in the heart of the City. In May 1985 the U.K. secretary of state for the environment announced that permission would not be granted to property developer Peter Palumbo for his Mansion House Square project, which included the Mies structure.

The Mies design was rejected primarily because it would be in extreme conflict with its neighbours, being too tall and too bulky for its particular site. (In 1984 Prince Charles had described it as "another giant glass stump better suited to downtown Chicago than the City of London.") In July Palumbo selected James Stirling to prepare a new scheme for the site. The appointment was widely welcomed, Stirling being one of the leading names in British architecture. It was hoped that he would produce a design that would be suitable for the future needs of the City but would also harmonize with and respect the older structures in the area.

Similar controversy raging in New York City over the planned extension to the Whitney Museum of American Art, designed originally in the 1960s by Marcel Breuer, focused on many of the same considerations. The Whitney had become a familiar and loved cultural landmark in the city, and any proposed alteration to its character attracted attention and comments. Breuer's design presented an uncompromisingly brutal face to Madison Avenue. The extension, designed by Michael Graves, a leading exponent of "postmodernism," was very much larger and totally different in character from the existing building, although Graves had been concerned to ensure that the new extension harmonized with the old. The difficulty was that one person's harmony is another person's disharmony, and the controversy centred very much on this point.

Graves's design featured a massive wing joined to the original building by a curved element, both old and new structures being capped by an enormous stepped-back formal attic that totally altered the scale of the original Breuer

PASCHALL/TAYLOR

No stranger to controversy, architect Michael Graves provoked more of the same with his design for an addition to—or perhaps an enclosure for—the Whitney Museum in New York City. The original structure, designed by Marcel Breuer, comprises the lower left portion of this model.

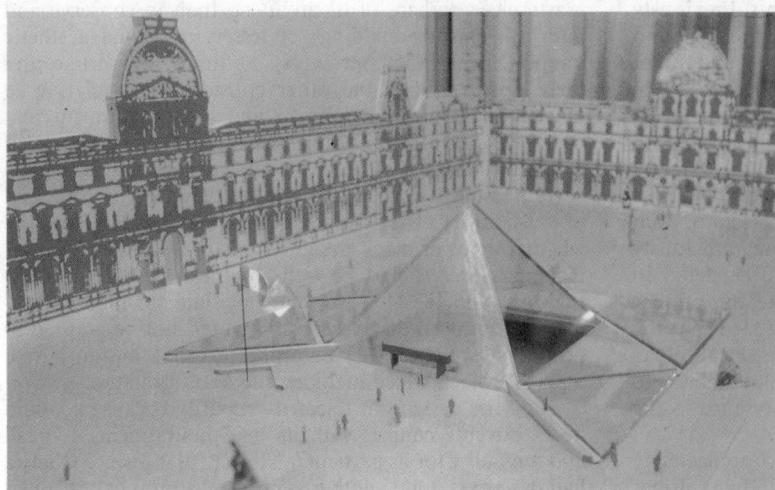

Controversy both aesthetic and political surrounded I. M. Pei's plan for a 20-metre (70-foot)-high glass pyramid for the Cour Napoleon of the Louvre in Paris.
VIOUJARD—GAMMA/LIAISON

building. Graves's design was geometric and formalist, and historical in reference, although uncompromisingly modern in concept. The addition would increase the height of the museum and extend it south at a cost of $37.5 million, adding 12,060 sq m (134,000 sq ft), of which 3,600 sq m (40,000 sq ft) would be exhibition space. The site itself was part of the Upper East Side Historical District. The new extension was to be clad in a grayish pink granite intended to harmonize with the dark gray granite of the older building. Those who opposed the scheme argued that, the suitability of the design aside, they were not convinced that a large-scale extension to the Whitney, which had always been one of the more manageable museums in terms of size and scale, was wholly desirable.

Yet another highly controversial project in which the same considerations were relevant was I. M. Pei's proposed modernization of the Louvre in Paris. Pei's plan featured a two-story underground central service and reception area with an entrance through a 20-m (70-ft)-high glass pyramid to be situated in the middle of the Cour Napoleon. The plan caused demands for a referendum and for a full-size model to be produced so that people could decide for themselves on its merits. In France the struggle seemed to be not only one between the conservationists and modernists but also a political controversy, as political conservatism was associated with conservationism in architecture whereas modernism was linked with socialism. Thus, a vigorous campaign against the scheme was mounted by the conservative newspaper *Le Figaro*.

Perhaps one of the reasons so many had become disillusioned with modern architecture and modernism in particular was that some of the landmarks of the early post–World War II period did not appear to be wearing well. A notable example of this was one of the early highly praised buildings by James Stirling, the History Faculty building at the University of Cambridge. The building, completed in 1967 at a cost of £3 million, had won numerous awards and commendations and was generally regarded as one of the most significant postwar modern structures in Britain. But by 1984 serious defects, including leaks, overheating, and the peeling of external tiling and rendering, caused the university to consider demolition. In 1985, however, the decision was made to repair and refurbish the building at a cost of £1.4 million. Urgent repair work was estimated at £629,000. It appeared that demolition and rebuilding were rejected mainly on financial grounds rather than because of any particular affection for the building or satisfaction with how well it fulfilled its function.

Also in England, it was announced that the Ronan Point housing towers in east London would be demolished. In 1968 a gas explosion in one 23-story tower had led to the progressive collapse of 18 adjoining floors, with the loss of five lives. Attention was focused on the design problems of high-rise residential units of this nature, and investigations continued into the causes for the building's failure. It seemed possible that some of the criticisms voiced at the time had not been fully taken into account, and further demolitions were expected.

Cultural Buildings. Design competitions remained popular in 1985, and a number of notable ones were under way. These were increasingly seen as useful exercises for fund-raising and publicity as well as encouragements for quality architecture. Landscapes as well as buildings provided subject matter, as for instance in Bellevue, Wash., where a competition was staged to provide a central park on a 7.1-ha (17.5-ac) midtown site. The winning design, by Beckley/Myers of Milwaukee, Wis., featured a central space within which would be an informal meadow.

The first prize in a competition funded by the National Endowment for the Arts to provide a master plan for Jacob's Pillow in the Berkshire Hills of Massachusetts, the site of a well-known summer dance festival, went to architects Stephen Furnstahl and Kenneth Warriner, Jr. Their plan featured a two-story arcade uniting the various areas of the site, including some historic structures that dated back nearly 200 years. A competition sponsored by the San Francisco Museum of Modern Art for a Napa Valley winery, intended to create a "landmark to viticulture," was won by Graves and artist Edward Schmidt. The site components included an operating winery, exhibition space for an art collection owned by the proprietors, a sculpture garden, an open-air theatre, and a residence.

Twelve internationally known architects were invited to compete for a contemporary arts and media centre— the Médiathèque—planned for Nîmes, France. Architects preparing projects included Jean Nouvel of France, Alvaro Siza of Portugal, Cesar Pelli and Frank Gehry of the U.S., Aldo Rossi of Italy, and Norman Foster of the U.K. The winner was Foster, whose design included a porticoed entrance and stepped base with horizontal glass bands beneath stone strips. Second prize went to Jean Nouvel for his centre sunk below a huge lake of glass. The Foster design was to be modified to incorporate a colonnade, which was all that remained on the site of the city's 19th-century opera house.

A plan for the extensive redevelopment of downtown

Los Angeles would create a proposed Library Square including renovation and expansion of the city's 1926 Art Deco central library. Hardy Holzman Pfeiffer Associates were architects for the renovation and expansion of the library. Two linked commercial developments opposite the library site would provide the financing. They included a $315 million office tower designed by I. M. Pei and Partners and a $337 million tower by Philip Johnson and John Burgee. Pei's would be the city's tallest building when completed. The Johnson/Burgee design featured a historicist roofline with finials and a mansard roof. Two public spaces, one a garden for the library and the other the Bunker Hill Steps, would provide outdoor relaxation areas. Even in a city as young as Los Angeles, harmony with surrounding structures was a point of wide general concern among architects, planners, and those wishing to preserve the city's unique character.

Richard Meier was chosen to design the $100 million J. Paul Getty Fine Arts Center in west Los Angeles. The prestigious complex was to include a museum, an arts and humanities centre, and a conservation institute. Construction was due to start in 1987, with completion planned for 1991. Also in the Los Angeles area, the new Filmcorp Center in Culver City would be a ziggurat-inspired terraced eight-story structure, designed by Maxwell Starkman Associates. An internal atrium lobby would rise 27 m (90 ft) to a sloping skyline. The exterior featured bands of light and dark granite alternating with gray solar glass. The project included offices, screening rooms, bars, restaurants, a library, and other facilities, totaling 37,000 sq m (400,-000 sq ft).

Gwathmey Siegel & Associates were commissioned to design a six-story addition to the annex of Frank Lloyd Wright's Guggenheim Museum in New York City. The addition would provide extra gallery space, offices, and a restaurant, with a $9 million budget provided. Completion was scheduled for 1987.

Commercial Buildings. Towers were the most prevalent form of commercial office space in most modern developments throughout the world. Naturally enough, the U.S. led the way. Philip Johnson's American Telephone and Telegraph Co. (AT&T) Building in New York City continued to provide inspiration for roofline interest, as evidenced by the Johnson/Burgee building at 190 S. La Salle Street in Chicago. A 40-story office tower perched on a red granite base was crowned by steep and ornate gables, with arched vertical bays articulating the main block. The references to the famous Chicago buildings of Louis Sullivan were unmistakable.

The Civic Opera House in Chicago was the inspiration for some of the historical allusions in another Chicago office tower, this one on Wacker Drive and designed by Perkins & Will of Chicago. The building featured an arcaded granite base and a pyramided top with a standard curtain-walled central area. Completion was projected for 1986. Skidmore, Owings & Merrill were designers of the 70-story Dearborn Center in Chicago, a building whose components seemed to be made up of various vertically stacked "segments," each with a separate "ground floor" and atrium; the building also featured multiple bay windows and large lower areas of skylit retail space. The same architects designed a 55-story office tower in Dallas, Texas, this time featuring a curved roofline punctuated by a six-story "window" or open space. A pedestrian plaza at street level was featured, and the sheathing was of the increasingly popular red granite, similar to that in the AT&T Building in New York.

The future of a 1.4-ha (3½-ac) tract at the southwest corner of Central Park in New York City, known as the Coliseum site, was decided in 1985 when it was sold to the developer Boston Properties in a complex deal. The site itself was claimed to be the most important piece of its size to come on the New York market in 50 years. The development would provide retail, office, hotel, and residential space, and the design was by architects Moshe Safdie & Associates. There would be two granite towers of 57 and 72 stories, respectively, and a curved retail galleria. Features included setback structures with five-story prismatic greenhouses at the setback points. These glass "capsules" would provide gardens for apartment dwellers and office workers. A 9-m (30-ft)-high slot opening between the towers on the 59th Street axis was another visual feature. The towers were described by one critic as "expressionistic icebergs."

Many of the major commercial developments under way were multiuse projects. One of these was Skidmore, Owings & Merrill's design for Rowe's and Foster's Wharf on the Boston waterfront. Situated south of the Quincy Market area, the project featured a huge rotunda and a large plaza with housing built on piers jutting into the bay. The blocking of the view of the waterfront caused by the buildings was criticized by many, who felt that Boston's waterfront was a visual amenity that should be easily accessible to all residents, workers, and visitors and not just to the favoured few who could afford waterside housing or office space.

Another high-class multiuse complex was Camelback Esplanade in Phoenix, Ariz., a development providing 216,000 sq m (2.4 million sq ft). Designed by the Zeidler Roberts Partnership in association with Cornoyer-Hedrick, the complex was reminiscent in form and material of Pueblo Indian adobe architecture; this was particularly emphasized by the use of pink granite. The project included four office towers, two condominium apartment buildings, a hotel area, and a retail galleria.

In Jakarta, Indon., a mixed-use complex designed by Pacific Associates Planners & Architects of San Diego, Calif., seemed to refer to traditional Balinese structures for inspiration. The developments, called Tanah Abang, were to feature a public courtyard surrounded by bank and residential towers and "shop-houses," the Asian equivalent of the apartment over the store. In Japan the Fujisawa Municipal Sports Centre, some 50 km (30 mi) from Tokyo, of steel and reinforced concrete, was completed at the end of 1984 and was hailed as one of the most ambitious new Japanese buildings in years. The architect was Fumihiko Maki. The huge gymnasium complex took on a helmet-like form when seen from the air. The roof was covered with enormous stainless steel shingles, and the interior was reminiscent of an aircraft hangar in size. The exterior of the building was clad in gray porcelain tiles.

A sports stadium for a site in Queens, New York City, was planned to occupy the air rights above rail yards in the Long Island City neighbourhood. Stephen Lepp Associates' design featured an 85,000-seat cable-supported domed stadium called the Appledome. The central portion of the dome would be removable during good weather to provide open-air sports facilities. An adjacent area, to be known as New York Garden, would provide an arena for ice hockey, basketball, indoor track, and boxing. The dome itself would be of semirigid construction supported by cables that would, in turn, be suspended from concrete pylons. The garden area would be built of open steel trusswork.

The U.S. received its first example of the British "high-tech" style as made famous in particular by architect Richard Rogers (see BIOGRAPHIES). This was the PA Technology Facility near Princeton, N.J., for which Kelbaugh

& Lee were collaborating architects. The lightweight roof structure was suspended to provide a column-free interior space and—the usual Rogers trademark—mechanical services were hidden in brightly coloured outer pipes. The cost of the building was high, $110 per square foot, and it would be interesting to see whether this mode of building would gain in popularity in the U.S. as it had done in Europe.

Awards. Richard Rogers received the Royal Institute of British Architects (RIBA) Gold Medal for 1985. The American Institute of Architects (AIA) awarded its 1985 Gold Medal posthumously to William Caudill, a founder of CRS (formerly Caudill Rowlett Scott) of Houston, Texas. This, the 45th Gold Medal, was only the fourth to be awarded posthumously, previous such winners having been Louis Sullivan, Eero Saarinen, and Richard Neutra. CRS was a leading U.S. designer of schools and hospitals during the 1960s, and in the 1970s the firm took the lead in Middle Eastern projects resulting from the oil boom. Caudill was praised for his work as a designer, teacher, and researcher in the field of architecture. The International Union of Architects awarded its first Gold Medal for outstanding architectural achievement to Egyptian architect Hassan Fathy, whose best known work was the New Gourna large-scale village relocation project in Luxor, begun in 1946.

AIA Honor Award winners in 1985 included Michael Graves's San Juan Capistrano (Calif.) Library; Richard Meier & Partners' Atheneum, in New Harmony, Ind.; and the Volvo Corporate Headquarters at Göteborg, Sweden, designed by Mitchell/Giurgola Architects. In England Foster Associates won the *Financial Times* Architecture at Work award (for outstanding industrial and commercial architecture) for the Renault Centre in Swindon. *The Times* of London and RIBA announced a jointly sponsored new annual award for community architecture projects, with Prince Charles as patron. The first award was to be made in 1986.   (SANDRA MILLIKIN)

See also Engineering Projects; Historic Preservation; Industrial Review.

This article updates the *Macropædia* article The History of Western ARCHITECTURE.

Art Exhibitions and Art Sales

Given the ever increasing cost of acquiring new works of art and the prohibitive sums needed for transport and insurance for loan exhibitions, in 1985 many museums and galleries concentrated resources on improving their own buildings and facilities and making their own collections available by way of special exhibitions. As always, however, there were notable extravaganzas. The National Gallery of Art in Washington, D.C., was host to one of the biggest, most complex, and most expensive shows ever to leave Britain. "The Treasure Houses of Britain," sponsored by the Ford Motor Co. and organized by the British Council, opened on November 3 and continued through the winter. Its theme was 500 years of private patronage and collecting as exhibited by individual treasures collected from country houses in Britain. Included were some 750 objects lent by 220 different British castles and stately homes, listed in a catalog that ran to over 600 pages.

Many organizations were involved in the planning and execution of the show, which was expected to bring a record million visitors to the National Gallery. The publicity was such that it sometimes appeared to be more an

Patrons of the "Treasure Houses of Britain" exhibit at the National Gallery of Art in Washington, D.C., were Charles and Diana, the prince and princess of Wales, who viewed the show during their visit to the city in November.

J. SLOAN—GAMMA/LIAISON

advertisement for Britain and the country-house way of life than an exhibition chosen for the merit of its objects. Nonetheless, the quality of the objects displayed was of the highest. They included tapestry and armour, along with family portraits, silver, jewelry, and furniture. Although the tiara that the princess of Wales wore at her wedding was not lent, a diamond-studded tiara worn by the duchess of Westminster at hers was on view. The logistics involved in such an exhibition were overwhelming. Most of the items traveled on 16 separate scheduled flights. Exhibits had to be collected from locations as far apart as Cornwall and Scotland, and of course they would have to be returned after the exhibition ended.

Decorative items of painting, silver, porcelain, textiles, ivories, and furniture were included in an exhibition entitled "Baroque Splendours of Mexico" at the Denver (Colo.) Art Museum. The exhibition concentrated on the art of Mexico in its period of greatest cultural achievement—the 17th and early 18th centuries. Many of the items were drawn from the museum's own holdings, but others were lent from private and public collections. An exhibition in Paris devoted to the work of one of the leading artisans of the Art Deco period, Charlotte Perriand, was held at the Musée des Arts Décoratifs. It was the first such retrospective of the work of this designer, who spent ten years working in the studio of Le Corbusier and was a leading designer of furniture and interiors throughout the 1920s and '30s. She was a pioneer particularly in the use of metal in furniture.

As always, Paris played host to a number of important art exhibitions. One of the most interesting was a show devoted to Daniel-Henry Kahnweiler, the major avant-garde Paris art dealer of the first decade of the 20th century. The Kahnweiler exhibition was held at the Beaubourg (Pompidou Centre) and was in two parts, the first part illustrating his career by means of photographs, books, and letters, and the second displaying his fine art collection, which included works by his major patrons and friends, such as Picasso, Matisse, and Braque. It was an exhibition devoted to the history of collecting and taste as well as to a display of fine paintings.

At the Galerie Marigny the first major Parisian exhibition of miniatures since 1906 was mounted. On display were 200 portrait miniatures borrowed from more than 20

French private collections. Many of these were of considerable historical interest, among them a rare miniature of a child, "Blue Boy" by Horace Vernet. The centenary of the birth of Robert and Sonia Delaunay, pioneers of the early 20th-century Orphic style of Cubism, was celebrated with a show of paintings, drawings, watercolours, and artifacts at the Musée d'Art Moderne de la Ville de Paris.

Exhibitions devoted to French art and artists were shown in many other parts of the world. The theme of one at the National Gallery of Ireland in Dublin was 17th-century French classicism. It assembled works borrowed from the Louvre and other important French museums, and lesser known artists of the period were represented, as well as Claude and Poussin. "Master Drawings by Géricault," organized by the International Exhibitions Foundation, was shown first at the Morgan Library in New York City and later at the San Diego (Calif.) Museum of Art and the Museum of Fine Arts, Houston, Texas. Many of the drawings by the important 19th-century French Romantic artist were lent from foreign collections and had not been seen previously in the U.S. "Edgar Degas: The Painter as Printmaker" was shown at the Hayward Gallery in London from May to July. Organized by the Museum of Fine Arts, Boston, and first shown there in 1984 to mark the 150th anniversary of Degas's birth, it displayed an aspect of his work less well known than his oils and pastels but one in which he was equally proficient. The chief aim was to show as many as possible of the stages of each lithograph and etching.

The 1985 Edinburgh International Festival had a French theme, and several of the art exhibitions echoed it. "Colour Since Matisse," an exhibition of exclusively French painting of the 20th century, focused on the use of colour in painting, illustrated by the works of Bonnard and Delaunay and other artists up to those of the present day. The National Gallery of Scotland concentrated on a display of French art from its own fine collections, with works from the late 16th to the late 19th century. At the Scottish National Gallery of Modern Art, French art up to 1960 was the subject, with a survey of the work of the School of Paris. At the Royal Scottish Museum, "French Connections: Scotland and the Arts of France" focused on Scottish collections of French art, including the Hamilton Palace collection. Among the manuscripts, ivories, sculpture, furniture, and ceramics on show was a silver gilt tea service that had belonged to Napoleon.

At the Hayward Gallery in London, an exhibition devoted to the ever popular works of Auguste Renoir was mounted in the spring. With more than 90 paintings on display, it was the first important retrospective of Renoir's work to be seen in Europe since the show organized by the Arts Council of Great Britain for the Edinburgh International Festival and the Tate Gallery, London, in 1953. The show offered an opportunity to assess the works of this artist on several levels and to examine his achievement, his contribution to Impressionism, and his place in the European figurative and landscape traditions. The range of colour and light was extraordinary. Organized in collaboration with the Réunion des Musées Nationaux, Paris, and the Museum of Fine Arts, Boston, the exhibition later traveled to the Grand Palais in Paris, where it was one of the year's major events, and to Boston.

The Royal Academy in London was the venue for the first major retrospective devoted to the work of Marc Chagall (*see* OBITUARIES) to be seen in England since 1948. The exhibits, borrowed from collections worldwide, included theatre designs, stained glass, oil paintings, and drawings. The show later traveled to the Philadelphia Museum of

Art. Selections from the Cone Collection, Baltimore, Md., which included many fine French works, formed a traveling show seen at the Kimbell Art Museum, Fort Worth, Texas, and at the Los Angeles County Museum of Art. The Cone Collection, given to the Baltimore Museum of Art in 1949, was especially rich in paintings by Matisse, with Picasso, Cezanne, Renoir, and Gauguin also represented.

Italian Renaissance paintings and paintings of the 17th century were the theme of another group of 1985 art exhibitions. An exhibition of 87 Renaissance drawings from the Biblioteca Ambrosiana, Milan, Italy, was shown at the Los Angeles County Museum of Art from late January to the end of March. Included were works by Leonardo da Vinci and Pisanello, as well as other masters of the 15th and 16th centuries in Italy. At the Prado in Madrid a winter exhibition featured three manuscripts by Leonardo, exhibited together for the first time in 400 years. They included the Codex Hammer (owned by Armand Hammer, the eminent U.S. collector; formerly the Codex Leicester), a scientific manuscript entitled *On the Nature, Weight and Movement of Water,* consisting of 36 folios dating from 1506 to 1510. The other two manuscripts belonged to the Biblioteca Nacional, Madrid.

"Baroque Portraiture in Italy: Works from North American Collections," organized by the John and Mable Ringling Museum of Art, Sarasota, Fla., was shown in the spring at the Wadsworth Atheneum, Hartford, Conn. Portraits in every medium including sculpture and portrait medallions were included among the works by 48 artists. "The Age of Caravaggio" was shown at the Metropolitan Museum of Art, New York City, and later at the Museo e Gallerie Nazionali di Capodimonte, Naples, Italy. It comprised 40 pictures either by or after Caravaggio, together with 60 paintings by artists who preceded him, followed him, or competed with him. Thus the exhibition was neither a monograph devoted only to Caravaggio nor solely a collection of works from his period. It afforded remarkable opportunities for visitors to compare and contrast Caravaggio with his contemporaries and his forerunners and also to study his very considerable influence on later artists. The show was sophisticated and thought-provoking.

Another exhibition at the Metropolitan Museum of Art, this time at the museum's Costume Institute, was entitled "Man and the Horse." This unique and entertaining show, organized by fashion authority Diana Vreeland, contained 150 equestrian costumes, together with riding accessories, harness, and objects depicting horse and rider. Folding

This vigorous watercolour from Rajasthan *c.* 1800 was one of some 300 pieces in the "India!" exhibit at the Metropolitan Museum of Art in New York City. The exhibit was part of a two-year Festival of India, sponsored by the Indian government, that also featured handicrafts and the performing arts.

screens were the theme of "The Folding Image" at the Yale University Art Gallery, a show that focused on screens made by American and European artists from about 1870 to the present day. A large exhibition devoted to the works of Vincent van Gogh at the Metropolitan Museum of Art, containing many of his best oils and a large selection of his drawings, showed particularly how strongly this artist was influenced by the Japanese tradition. The influence was especially noticeable in the brown ink drawings, less frequently seen and reproduced than some of the paintings.

To mark the Festival of India, which began in June in the U.S., the Metropolitan Museum of Art mounted a comprehensive show of the art of India from the 14th to the 19th century. About 350 works including paintings, jewelry, and tapestries were lent by collections in India, Europe, the U.S., and the Middle East. Indian shows were also held at the Asia Society in New York City and at the Cleveland (Ohio) Museum of Art. At the Fogg Art Museum at Harvard University, master drawings from the Woodner Collection were exhibited. Included were several recent acquisitions, notable among them a sheet of drawings by the 16th-century Italian artist and critic Giorgio Vasari. The sheet was from his *Libro dei Disegni* and was formerly in the collection of the duke of Devonshire at Chatsworth House, England.

At the Rijksmuseum, Amsterdam, an important exhibition of Rembrandt drawings from the museum's own collection was on show. It comprised the Print Room's entire collection of Rembrandt drawings, which were constantly being assessed, examined, and reattributed by experts. Sixty of the drawings were definitely attributed to Rembrandt. An exhibition in Siena, Italy, devoted to Simone Martini (*c.* 1284–1344) was mounted at the Pinacoteca Nazionale and showed 28 works, mostly panel paintings but also a few detached frescoes. Items from Martini's workshop and entourage were included. Among the masterpieces on display was the Blessed Agostino Novello altarpiece from S. Agostino in Siena. The Canadian artist John O'Brien (1831–91), best remembered as Canada's first native marine artist, was the subject of an exhibition organized by the Art Gallery of Nova Scotia. The 28 paintings of this largely self-taught artist traveled to the National Gallery of Canada in Ottawa and later to other Canadian galleries. Both in the U.S. and in Canada, works by native artists continued to attract the attention of collectors and museums.

A number of important and thought-provoking exhibitions were mounted in London. One held at the British Museum in early spring, entitled "The Golden Age of Anglo-Saxon Art: 966–1066," was jointly organized with the British Library. Many of the items, some of which had not been in England since the Middle Ages, were borrowed from foreign collections. The exhibition commemorated the 1,000th anniversary of the death of St. Aethelwold, bishop of Winchester, a key figure in the monastic reform movement out of which emerged the splendid illuminated manuscripts, ivories, and metal objects that dominated the show. The great quality and range of this period of art were well illustrated. At the other end of the spectrum was Judy Chicago's "The Dinner Party," shown in London at The Warehouse in the spring. This work of art consisted of a large open triangle that formed a banquet table with 39 place settings, each with its own embroidered runner and large ceramic dinner plate. Each place setting honoured an eminent woman, including such figures as Sappho, Boadicea, and Georgia O'Keefe. The work was an intense feminist statement, executed over five years with the help of more than 400 individuals, and provided gallery goers with an unforgettable theatrical experience.

The Tate Gallery in London mounted a retrospective exhibition devoted to the works of the artist Francis Bacon (*see* Biographies), probably the most important living English painter, to celebrate 40 years of his work since 1944. The show, dominated by Bacon's powerful, tormented expressionistic images, was later shown in Stuttgart, West Germany, and West Berlin. It was the second Tate retrospective of Bacon's work, the first having been in 1962. The centrepiece of the show was the display of 18 large triptychs completed since 1962. An exhibition of 36 paintings drawn from the Dulwich College Picture Gallery, London, entitled "Collection for a King," was sent to the U.S. and shown at the National Gallery of Art in Washington and later at the Los Angeles County Museum of Art. It was the first such display to travel from this gallery in some 40 years. "The Vital Gesture," a retrospective of the American Abstract Expressionist Fritz Kline, was mounted by the Cincinnati (Ohio) Art Museum.

There was a discernible increase of interest in the Expressionistic artists of the earlier 20th century. "Munch and the Workers," a major loan exhibition from the Munch-Museet in Oslo, consisting of over 100 works by the Norwegian Expressionist Edvard Munch, was shown at the City of Edinburgh Art Centre and later at the Barbican in London. The summer exhibition at the Museum of Fine Arts in Basel, Switz., was devoted to the same artist and entitled "Edvard Munch: His Work in Swiss Collections." It assembled paintings and graphics of the artist drawn from Swiss public and private collections, making many major works accessible to the public for the first time. Also in Switzerland, two major loan exhibitions were devoted to German Romantic painting. At the Kunstmuseum, Bern, "Traum und Wahrheit" included 290 paintings, watercolours, and drawings from collections in East Berlin, Leipzig, Weimar, and Dresden. At the Kunsthaus, Zürich, a group of 43 paintings by Caspar David Friedrich, K. F. Schinkel, and Carl Blechen was lent by the Nationalgalerie, West Berlin; 120 German Romantic drawings from the National Gallery, Oslo, were also exhibited.

"German Art in the 20th Century," which opened at the Royal Academy, London, in October, traced the development of German art from the pre-World War I Expressionist groups Die Brücke and Der Blaue Reiter through the satirical realism of the pre-Hitlerian Neue Sachlichkeit to the post-World War II Neo-Expressionism of the Neue Wilden. Finally, on a sombre note, the Museum of Modern Art, Oxford, marked the 40th anniversary of the dropping of the atomic bomb on Hiroshima with "Hiroshima: Paintings by Survivors." (SANDRA MILLIKIN)

ART SALES

Market Trends. The strong dollar made for a surge in European auction prices in late 1984 and early 1985 as U.S. dealers and collectors crossed the Atlantic looking for bargains, but prices were not sustained as the exchange rate weakened during the summer. There was a higher than normal proportion of unsold lots in auctions in Europe and the U.S. as owners' expectations were not met. Expensive pictures were particularly hard hit, with nearly half the pictures in the major Impressionist and modern picture sales failing to find buyers.

This trend also reflected the growing impact of the U.S. marketing techniques pioneered by Sotheby's under its new ownership. Special, highly promoted sales could bring prices far above normal market levels, and the publicity such prices attracted raised the expectations of all auction vendors. Sotheby's admitted to having spent $1 million on promoting the sale of Impressionist and modern pictures

from the collection of the late Florence J. Gould as part of its contract with her executors. This was the biggest "hype" of the year and secured a record total for a single collection of $32.6 million.

Where big money was concerned, U.S. private collectors were the dominating force in nearly every field. The special emphasis on furniture and pictures that could be used to decorate homes underlined the social element in the new U.S. collecting boom. For Christie's, the U.S. connection resulted in an end-of-season nightmare. Evidence submitted in a court action revealed that Christie's had purposely misled the press after a 1981 auction by announcing that a van Gogh and a Gauguin had been sold at $2.1 million and $1.3 million, respectively, when they were, in fact, bought in against the owner's reserve. After an investigation by the New York City Consumer Affairs Department, David Bathurst, who had been president of Christie's in New York in 1981 and the auctioneer at the sale, resigned as chairman of Christie's in London and from the company's main board. He also had his license to sell in New York suspended for two years.

Works of Art. Andrea Mantegna's "The Adoration of the Magi" was sold for £8.1 million at Christie's in April on behalf of Lord Northampton, setting a new auction price record for a painting. It was bought by the J. Paul Getty Museum, Malibu, Calif., but the issuance of an export license from Britain was delayed for six months to give the National Gallery of Scotland time to try to match the purchase price so the painting could be kept in Britain. The Getty paid another top price, at least $6 million, for a Flemish Old Master painting in January when it bought an "Annunciation" by Dirck Bouts from a consortium of dealers. There was considerable controversy over the suggestion made by Alain Tarica, a New York dealer, that the picture was a 20th-century fake. Such high prices led Christie's to accept a collection of 23 Old Masters, formed by Samuel T. Fee of Oklahoma, for sale in New York with very high reserves. The result was a major failure, with only seven pictures sold for a total of $3,179,000 where $11 million had been looked for.

Other outstanding prices for old pictures included £1.4 million paid by the London National Gallery at Christie's in November 1984 for Joseph Wright of Derby's "Mr. and Mrs. Thomas Cottman About to Set Out on a Ride"; F 6.9 million paid for a portrait of the duchesse de Gramont-Caderousse in Paris; and $742,000 paid by the Los Angeles County Museum of Art for "Danae" by the Dutch Mannerist Hendrik Goltzius, also in November.

The Gould sale in April was the event of the year in the Impressionist field, with a van Gogh landscape at $9.9 million and Toulouse-Lautrec's "La Clownesse" at $5,280,-000. Although 2,000 people attended the sale, the bidding was slow, and many pictures sold below estimate, reflecting a turn in the market. There was a similar slowdown in the markets for 19th-century paintings and contemporary art, although some new landmark prices were set. Willem de Kooning's "Two Women" set a new auction price record for a work by a living artist at $1,980,000 in November 1984, and Grant Wood's "Arbor Day" of 1932 made $1,375,000 in June 1985. "An Intercepted Correspondence, Cairo" by J. F. Lewis set a new auction price record for a Victorian painting of $1,265,000 at Sotheby's much publicized sale of Oriental paintings from the Coral Petroleum collection in May.

High-profile promotion also paid off in the applied arts field. A Rolls-Royce painted with psychedelic patterns by John Lennon and a mystic friend was the most astonishing example. The $2.2 million it fetched at Sotheby's in July,

The highest price ever paid for a painting— £8.1 million ($10.4 million)—was fetched by "The Adoration of the Magi" by the 15th-century northern Italian artist Andrea Mantegna. The J. Paul Getty Museum made the record bid at Christie's in London.
CHRISTIE'S

multiplying the presale estimate by ten, made the $1.7 million paid by Malcolm Forbes in June for a Fabergé Easter egg seem modest. A medal cabinet attributed to Adam Weisweiler, made for Louis XVI on the eve of the French Revolution, became the most expensive piece of furniture ever sold at auction when it fetched F 16,650,000 in Monte Carlo in November 1984. French, English, and American furniture secured very high prices at auction throughout the year, mainly selling to private collectors in the United States. A pair of Philadelphia Chippendale drop-leaf tables of around 1770 which fitted together to form a three-metre (ten-foot) dining table secured $583,000 at Sotheby's in February 1985. The previous high for a dining table was $100,000. Art Nouveau, Art Deco, and Modernist design continued to make big prices. A Tiffany bronze floor lamp with a magnolia pattern shade made an impressive $528,-000 at Christie's in December 1984, setting a new auction record both as an Art Nouveau design and as a 20th-century artifact. American designer pieces were particularly sought after; a copper urn designed by Frank Lloyd Wright sold for $93,500.

Books. The new U.S. marketing techniques pioneered by Sotheby's resulted in a very erratic market. Heavily publicized auctions brought prices sometimes two or three times higher than was paid for the same book at other auctions in the same week or month. The Elizabeth Craham collection of books on food and drink, sold for $874,505 by Sotheby's in New York in October 1984, was a case in point; the first dated edition of the first printed cookbook, B. Platina's *De Honesta Voluptate et Valetudine* of 1475, sold for $39,600 against an estimate of $5,000 to $7,000. Similarly, at the sale of the Paul Francis Webster collection of English literature in April 1985 (where a first folio edition of Shakespeare made $638,000), a fragment of the manuscript of Charles Dickens's *Pickwick Papers* fetched $26,400 (estimate, $5,000 to $8,000).

The new era at Sotheby's was marked in July by an immensely complex settlement of the case brought against it by the New York attorney general over the disputed ownership of a Hebrew library sold for $2 million a year before. It had belonged to a Berlin seminary and was smuggled out of Nazi Germany by the consignors, Dr. and Mrs. Alexander Guttmann, who were paid $900,000 by Sotheby's under the settlement. All the manuscripts had to

be returned to Sotheby's by their purchasers for redistribution to suitable Jewish institutions. An auction price record for a Hebrew manuscript was set in December 1984 when Sotheby's sold a Spanish Bible of 1312 for $825,000.

Decorative natural history and travel books were much in demand. The earl of Caledon's copy of Audubon's *Birds of America* made $1,716,660 at Sotheby's in January 1985. Private collectors were taking a new interest in manuscript material. Verdi's libretto for *Ernani* was sold for £77,000 by Sotheby's in May, and a three-page Beethoven letter went for £55,000. A notebook used by the poet W. B. Yeats between 1930 and 1933 made £275,000 in Sotheby's July sale, which also included the papers of the 18th-century connoisseur Charles Townley at £187,000.

Ader et Picard secured outstanding prices in their Paris and Monte Carlo sales. The copy of Charles Baudelaire's *Les Fleurs du mal* (1857) that he gave to the artist Delacroix made F 1.3 million in March, and an 1833 first edition of Georges Sand's *Lélia,* with a dedication to her lover, F 830,000. In a June sale H. P. Kraus of New York paid F 5 million for a 13th-century illuminated Psalter on behalf of the Getty. Americana remained popular, with Malcolm Forbes paying $297,000 for the Emancipation Proclamation of 1863, a one-page broadside signed by Pres. Abraham Lincoln, at Sotheby's in October 1984.

(GERALDINE NORMAN)

This article updates the *Macropædia* articles The History of Western PAINTING; The History of Western SCULPTURE.

Astronomy

Solar System. The year 1985 would be remembered, astronomically speaking, as the year of the comets. From the metaphorically "astronomical" scientific and popular interest surrounding the approach of Halley's Comet (*see* Sidebar) to the first encounter of a man-made space probe with a comet (named Giacobini-Zinner), these normally cool and icy objects added much heat (and even some light) to a scientific understanding of their origin and evolution and even of their possible effects on life on Earth.

The year began with continued heated debate over the possible role that a terrestrial cometary or asteroidal impact 65 million years ago might have had in causing the disappearance of 75% of the living species on Earth, including the dinosaurs. The debate was initially triggered in 1980 by the discovery of an unusually high level of the element iridium in terrestrial rock strata between the Tertiary and Cretaceous (C-T) geological periods and the suggestion that the material was brought here by a cometary or asteroidal collision with the Earth, which then led to widespread extinctions. In late 1983 researchers claimed to find evidence for periodic extinctions occurring roughly every 26 million years during the last 250 million years.

Throughout 1985 the proposed explanations for the periodicity were all challenged, the periodicity supposedly present in the extinction record itself was called into question, and even the idea of a sharp end to the dinosaurs at the C-T boundary was criticized by some paleontologists. Nonetheless, the possibility of some sort of major impact on the Earth about 65 million years ago coincident with the C-T boundary gained further geological support, including evidence for massive firestorms that swept the planet at that time (*see* EARTH SCIENCES: *Geology and Geochemistry*). By year's end the impact-induced demise of the dinosaurs and its possible similarity to the nuclear-winter scenarios predicted to follow a thermonuclear war remained intriguing speculations.

Earth Perihelion and Aphelion, 1986	
Jan. 2	Perihelion, 147,099,000 km (91,403,000 mi) from the Sun
July 5	Aphelion, 152,105,000 km (94,513,000 mi) from the Sun

Equinoxes and Solstices, 1986	
March 20	Vernal equinox, 22:30[1]
June 21	Summer solstice, 16:30[1]
Sept. 23	Autumnal equinox, 07:59[1]
Dec. 22	Winter solstice, 04:02[1]

Eclipses, 1986	
April 9	Sun, partial (begins 4:10[1]), visible in eastern Indonesia, New Guinea, Australia, southern New Zealand, and part of Antarctica.
April 24	Moon, total (begins 10:05[1]), visible in western half of North America; central, eastern, and southeast Asia; Australia, New Zealand, and most of Antarctica; Pacific and Indian oceans.
Oct. 3	Sun, total (begins 16:57[1]), visible in extreme northeastern Asia; North America except extreme southwest; Arctic regions, Greenland, Iceland; north of South America.
Oct. 17	Moon, total (begins 16:20[1]), visible in Australia, New Zealand, Asia, Africa, Europe, Iceland, Greenland; eastern Antarctica; Atlantic, Indian, and western Pacific oceans.

[1]Universal time.
Source: *The Astronomical Almanac for the Year 1986* (1985).

Although the U.S. had not proposed a dedicated mission to visit Halley's Comet, a scientist at NASA-Goddard Space Flight Center in Maryland, Robert W. Farquhar, realized that a satellite already in orbit might be redirected to the comet in 1986. That satellite, the International Sun-Earth Explorer 3, had been launched in 1978 with the aim of monitoring the properties of the solar wind near the Earth. Farquhar showed through an elaborate set of calculations that the satellite's rockets could be fired several times to direct it through repeated loops of the Earth and the Moon and then away from the Earth toward the comet. It turned out, however, that its radio transmitters were too weak to send data back from Halley, so it was aimed at the earlier arrival in 1985 of Comet Giacobini-Zinner (G-Z). The satellite, renamed the International Cometary Explorer (ICE) for its new mission, did not carry photographic equipment but had a variety of magnetic-field, space-plasma, and other detectors aboard.

Surprises began when ICE was still 1.7 million km from G-Z, where the comet's outgasing particles were first detected (1 km = 0.62 mi). Strangely the sharp bow shock that had been predicted showed up only very close to the comet. It appeared, instead, that the outgasing molecules from the comet "cushioned" the incoming solar wind, leading to a more gentle perturbation of the solar-wind/magnetic-field stream. On September 11 ICE passed through the tail of G-Z about 10,000 km from the nucleus and found the tail to be about 10,000 km wide, compared with the 1–10-km size of the nucleus. No dust particles ripped through the spacecraft, a feared possibility that might have terminated the mission instantly, but some dust was detected. Most of the outgasing material appeared to be water ice with a small admixture of carbon monoxide.

The solar system contains four giant planets—Jupiter, Saturn, Uranus, and Neptune—three of which were known to have rings. Saturn's rings were discovered through Galileo's telescope three centuries ago. Uranus's rings were found indirectly in 1977 by the occultation of a star as it passed behind the rings. Jupiter's thin ring was found in 1979 by the Voyager 1 flyby space probe. Since that time scientists had been trying to detect a ring around Neptune as well. In 1985 two groups independently reported such a discovery. On July 22, 1984, as a relatively bright star passed nearly behind Neptune, a team headed by Andre Brahic of the University of Paris, working at the European Southern Observatory in Chile, detected a brief

reduction in the star's light. A team from the University of Arizona led by William Hubbard, working at the Cerro Tololo Inter-American Observatory in Chile, also detected this dimming. By early 1985 the combined observations pointed to a partially obscuring ring, no wider than 10–20 km, lying some 76,000 km from the planet. In addition, since only one occultation event was recorded by each group, the ring appeared either to have breaks in it or to vary in optical depth from place to place. If a ring were to be confirmed, it would make rings around gas giants the rule rather than the exception they had been prior to 1977.

Stars. When is a planet a star? When is a star a planet? When it is Van Biesbroeck 8B (VB 8B), the companion to the star Van Biesbroeck 8. Perhaps the best term for this new class of object, previously only speculated to exist, is a brown dwarf, an object intermediate in mass between a planet and a nuclear burning object, which is usually called a star. The discovery had its roots in 1983, when Robert S. Harrington and colleagues at the U.S. Naval Observatory in Flagstaff, Ariz., found that VB 8 showed a small "wiggle" in its motion, indicating the presence of a low-mass companion object. The binary system, lying some 21 light-years from Earth, is quite dim. Nonetheless, in late 1984 Donald McCarthy, Jr., and colleagues at the Steward Observatory in Arizona managed to detect the companion at infrared wavelengths with the four-metre Kitt Peak telescope. VB 8B appeared to be about the same size as the planet Jupiter but 10–80 times more massive and to be some 100,000 times dimmer in the optical region of the spectrum than its stellar companion, orbiting it at a distance of about 6.5 astronomical units, which is comparable to the separation between the Sun and Jupiter. According to most theoretical calculations VB 8B is too dim and too low in mass to be supporting nuclear reactions in its interior, so it is not a normal star. On the other hand, it has a surface temperature of about 2,000 K (3,140° F) and a density much higher than that of Jupiter; hence its intermediate designation as a brown dwarf. If VB 8B eventually proved to be a planet, it would be the first discovered outside the solar system.

X-ray binary stars are co-orbiting stellar systems in which mass is transferred from a normal nuclear burning star to a collapsed stellar companion, giving rise to a variety of X-ray phenomena. Some X-ray binaries emit regular periodic pulsations at X-ray wavelengths and sometimes at other wavelengths as well. Some produce flarelike activity or transient X-ray bursts. In 1985 astronomers found a new class of X-ray sources, quasiperiodic objects (QPOs), which emit strings of pulses having varying periods. The first example to be found, GX5-1, was discovered by the European Space Agency's EXOSAT satellite and reported by a large team headed by Michiel van der Klis of ESA. No sooner had quasiperiodicity been found in this object than the same phenomenon was reported in two long-studied and well-known X-ray sources—Scorpio X-1, the brightest X-ray source in the sky, and Cygnus X-2. The explanation for such variability was not certain but might involve a kind of beat phenomenon between the precise underlying rotation period of the accreting neutron star in the binary system and the precession of an accretion disk of material surrounding the neutron star.

More exciting still, if true, were new observations concerning the X-ray source Cygnus X-3. In 1983 this system was reported to be emitting gamma rays having energies higher than a thousand million million (10^{15}) electron volts per photon—millions of times higher than previously detected from any other X-ray source. This object has a periodicity, observed at various wavelengths, of 4.8 hours.

After the energetic gamma-ray discovery, cosmic-ray research groups around the world searched their data to see if they also could detect the object. In mines under Mont Blanc in France and in the Soudan Mine in Minnesota, scientists had set up large detectors to look for the predicted decay of protons. While such decays had not been seen as of late 1985, these same detectors were being constantly bombarded by particles called muons, which are produced by the collision of cosmic rays of various types with the Earth's atmosphere. During the year three different groups reported muon signals coming from the direction of Cygnus X-3 and all having a 4.8-hour period. These remarkable observations, if interpreted correctly, implied that Cygnus X-3 is producing extremely energetic particles that are long-lived and electrically neutral and that interact strongly with the Earth's atmosphere. No such particle fitting these criteria was known, however, leading scientists to suggest either a new type of matter (a quark nugget was one proposal) or an entirely new type of elementary particle (possibly photinos or gluinos). By year's end none of these observations was certain enough to instigate a revolution in physics, but they were tantalizing enough to make them perhaps the most exciting news in astronomy.

Galaxies. For at least a decade the centre of the Milky Way Galaxy had been known to be a site of energetic astronomical phenomena. Radio, infrared, and X-ray radiation in excess of that expected from normal stars had been detected. Since the galactic centre is enshrouded by dust, however, it was difficult to observe optically what lurks there. In 1985 K. Y. Lo and collaborators at the California Institute of Technology observed the region at radio frequencies using a technique called very-long-baseline interferometry, which permitted the region to be studied at the unprecedentedly small angular scale of 0.002 seconds of arc. At the distance to the galactic centre this angular measurement corresponds to a size of some 20 astronom-

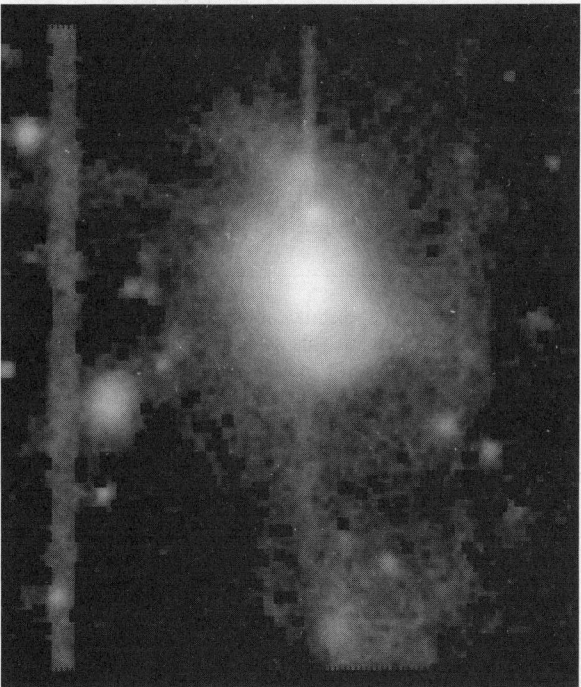

Using a charge-coupled device on the 4-metre (13-foot) Mayall telescope at Kitt Peak National Observatory in Arizona, astronomers obtained this electronic image of the compact galaxy II Zwicky 23. The irregular extensions around the galaxy were believed to be regions of active star formation.

At Halley's Comet's last appearance in 1910, the 36-inch refracting telescope at Lick Observatory in California was one of the most advanced tools available to astronomers. In 1986 the comet was to be inspected at close range by a variety of space probes, including Planet-A, developed by Japanese scientists.

(LEFT) CULVER PICTURES; (RIGHT) THE INSTITUTE OF SPACE AND ASTRONAUTICAL SCIENCE, JAPAN

The Coming of Halley's Comet

For at least the past 2,200 years Halley's Comet has swung into the inner solar system every 76 years or so. On Oct. 16, 1982, astronomers working with the Hale telescope atop Palomar Mountain spotted the comet once again, the first sighting since its last rendezvous with the Earth in 1910. This time it was due to make its closest approach to the Sun on Feb. 9, 1986.

Throughout 1985 growing popular excitement over Halley's coming manifested itself in the publication of at least 50 new books and thousands of articles about the comet, as well as the merchandising of Halley T-shirts, jewelry, posters, slide sets, stamps, coins, computer programs for orbital calculations, and the "proper" telescopes and binoculars. For those who could afford not to miss the best view of Halley, from the Southern Hemisphere, specially organized tours and cruises awaited. For the stay-at-homes there would be comet parties and other festivities, both indoors and under the stars.

Scientific excitement also swelled as a veritable armada of spacecraft sped to intercept the comet in the spring of 1986. First to be launched, in December 1984, were two Soviet spacecraft, Vega 1 and 2, whose dual mission comprised a visit to Venus in June 1985 and a rendezvous with Halley on March 6 and March 9, 1986. Japan launched the Sakigake spacecraft in January 1985 and another called Planet-A in August; the former was to fly into the comet's tail, the latter closer to the nucleus. In July 1985 the European Space Agency launched its Giotto space probe (named for the 14th-century painter who included the 1301 apparition of Halley's Comet in a Nativity scene). Giotto would pass within 500 km (310 mi) of the nucleus of the comet to provide the first pictures of how a comet really looks. The U.S., having no probe going directly to Halley, would observe the comet from a space shuttle orbiter. That country was also headquarters for the worldwide International Halley Watch, set up to help coordinate the ground-based observations planned and being carried out by more than a thousand professional and amateur astronomers.

(KENNETH BRECHER)

ical units, about the distance between the Sun and the planet Uranus. Even on this scale the investigators could not discern the structure of the central radiation source, implying an object that is both energetic and small. They suggested that only a black hole with a mass more than a million times that of the Sun, accreting matter from the surrounding region, could fill the bill.

While massive black holes may represent the end point of galactic evolution, observations made in 1985 also seemed to show processes occurring in galaxies at the beginning of their evolution. Studying the object called II Zwicky 23, a blue elliptical compact galaxy lying at a distance of some 500 million light-years from the Earth, William C. Keel of Kitt Peak National Observatory in Arizona found evidence for very recent star formation in this object. His observations of moving filaments of gas near the galaxy suggested the appearance of roughly 35 new stars per year for perhaps the past 100 million years. In cosmological terms the object is a veritable baby, allowing scientists to witness galaxy formation processes that, for the most part, took place at much earlier epochs in the history of the universe.

Peering into the deepest reaches of space Stanislaus Djorgovski and Hyron Spinrad of the University of California at Berkeley reported the discovery of the most distant galaxy known. At a distance of about 14,500,000,000 light-years, such an object indicated the gradual evolution of galaxies over time. The existence of galaxies lying at distances comparable to those of the most distant quasars should help establish answers to a number of cosmological questions, including the nature of quasars and whether the universe will stop its present expansion and begin to collapse.

(KENNETH BRECHER)

See also Space Exploration.
This article updates the *Macropædia* articles EXPLORATION: *Space Exploration*; GALAXIES; The PHYSICAL SCIENCES: *Astronomy and Astrophysics*; The SOLAR SYSTEM; STARS AND STAR CLUSTERS.

Botanical Gardens and Zoos

Botanical Gardens. Increasing awareness of the need to address world-scale problems such as plant utilization for food was galvanizing the more forward-looking gardens into action. National and international policies were slowly being formulated to increase the degree of cooperation between gardens, and there was significant activity on this front. In October 1984 the Royal Australian Institute of Parks and Recreation published a report on the collection of native plants in Australian botanical gardens and arboretums. The report emphasized the need to ensure that Australian flora were preserved and protected for posterity. One way to do this was to set aside in cultivation, in professionally designed and managed botanical gardens, a collection of indigenous Australian plants. The report, submitted to the federal and state governments, recommended a national network of 39 botanical gardens and arboretums and asked for $A92 million to fund capital works over ten years. A program of assistance to smaller supporting gardens was also recommended, with a national committee, made up of heads of major state botanical gardens, to coordinate joint programs.

The European and Mediterranean Regional Group of the International Association of Botanic Gardens (IABG) held its second meeting, in Durham, England, during September 1985. The main theme of the meeting was botanical gardens in the 21st century. Inadequate funding and lack of coordination—both nationally and internationally—were identified as the major constraints on development. Clearly defined objectives related to specific research and educational programs were recognized as being of immediate priority. In this context the cooperation between the Utrecht, Leiden, and Wageningen botanical gardens in The Netherlands and within the newly formed Ibero-Macronesian Association exemplified the successful utilization of common resources.

In November 1985 the International Union for the Conservation of Nature and Natural Resources sponsored a conference entitled "Botanic Gardens and the World Conservation Strategy," held at Las Palmas, Gran Canaria (Spain). The objective of the conference was to review the involvement of botanical gardens in complementing world conservation strategy, in particular by considering their function as centres of information and education and their capacity to carry out both ex situ and in situ conservation. Recommendations were made to enable botanical gardens to formulate arguments for additional funding to meet essential commitments in the field of conservation activity.

The introduction into Europe of many exotic species during the 18th and 19th centuries led to the construction of large conservatories and greenhouses. However, many of these structures were now in urgent need of renovation. The palm house in Göteborg, Sweden, was one of those currently being restored. Built in 1878 and situated in a municipal park in the city centre, it was a building of considerable architectural importance, and the restoration specification had to be carefully drafted to ensure that the integrity of the original structure was preserved. Completion was scheduled for 1986. At the Royal Botanic Gardens, Kew, England, restoration of the world-renowned Palm House dating from 1848 proceeded. A large new development nearing completion at Kew was a 4,500-sq m (48,600-sq ft) display complex that would provide ten separate compartments to grow extensive collections of tender herbaceous plants such as ferns, orchids, cacti, and succulents. Of contemporary design, the structure reflected the form of the original greenhouses it replaced, but modern materials and up-to-date technology were being used to create environments that would satisfy the most demanding plant groups. (REGINALD IAN BEYER)

Zoos. One of the major justifications for keeping animals in zoos was to promote the conservation of species. Not only could they be used to demonstrate the need for conservation, particularly of species liable to become extinct in the rapidly diminishing wild, but they could also be used as the nucleus of reintroduction programs.

There was encouraging news of the 1984 reintroduction of the golden lion tamarin (*Leontopithecus r. rosalia*) to a reserve in Brazil; by 1985 there had been three births, all from animals bred in zoos and released in 1983, and in July a further two family groups from zoos were sent for release into a neighbouring area. Other current examples of reintroduction projects that were under way or planned included: Przewalski horse (*Equus przewalskii*) from collections in the U.S. and U.K. to reserves in Mongolia and, possibly, Kazakhstan, U.S.S.R.; Père David's deer (*Elaphurus davidianus*) from Whipsnade Zoo and Woburn Park, England, to reserves in China; scimitar-horned oryx

ROYAL BOTANIC GARDENS, KEW

A striking new display complex was nearing completion at the Royal Botanic Gardens at Kew, England. It would house a wide variety of herbaceous plants requiring special environments.

(*Oryx dammah*) from collections in Britain to a national park in Tunisia; Jamaican hutia (*Geocapromys browni*) from Jersey Zoological Park (Channel Islands) to private estates in Jamaica; European otter (*Lutra l. lutra*) from the Otter Trust, Bungay, Suffolk, to reserves in East Anglia, England; Somali ostrich (*Struthio camelus molybdophanes*) from Oklahoma Zoo to the Shaumari Wildlife Reserve in Jordan; eastern sarus crane (*Grus antigone sharpii*) from the International Crane Foundation, Baraboo, Wis., to the Bang Phra Wildlife Sanctuary in Thailand; cheer pheasant (*Catreus wallichi*) eggs from the World Pheasant Association, Basildon, England, to a reserve in Pakistan; white-headed duck (*Oxyura leucocephala*) eggs from the Wildfowl Trust, Slimbridge, England, to a reserve in Hungary; Philippine crocodile (*Crocodylus mindorensis*) from Silliman University, Dumaguete City, Phil., to the Calauit Wildlife Sanctuary in northern Busuanga Island, Calamian Group, Philippines.

Reintroduction programs needed the cooperation of zoos and conservation bodies. Careful planning and monitoring were essential; so was the availability of scientific data on zoo animal populations and on individual animals not only for reintroduction projects but also for many aspects of zoo animal management, husbandry, and breeding. In 1985 three conferences underlined and endorsed these needs: the International Union of Directors of Zoological Gardens and the Captive Breeding Specialist Group both met in Calgary, Alta., and the American Association of Zoological Parks and Aquariums met in Columbus, Ohio.

Further progress was reported in the use of artificial breeding techniques. The Zoological Society of London announced the successful birth in June of a zebra foal to a domestic pony. This birth was the result of work involving the nonsurgical collection of an embryo and transfer to a surrogate mother. In March the New York Zoological Society reported from its breeding facilities on St. Catherine's Island the first birth of a gemsbok (*Oryx g. gazella*) following artificial insemination. In June, Ueno Zoo in Tokyo announced the birth of a giant panda (*Ailuropoda melanoleuca*) after artificial insemination, and in November the official Chinese news agency reported the birth, to a twice-artificially inseminated panda, of seven cubs, five of which survived. Notable among more straightforward breedings were the first captive breedings of a Commerson's dolphin (*Cephalorhynchus commersoni*) at Sea World, San Diego, Calif.; the false gharial (*Tomistma schlegelii*) at the Bronx (N.Y.) Zoo; Papuan pythons (*Liasis papuanus*) at Knoxville (Tenn.) Zoological Park; and twin giant pandas (one survived) in Chapultepec Zoo, Mexico City.

Recent new zoo buildings and exhibits included "Jungle World" at Bronx Zoo; Asian elephant breeding facilities at San Diego Wild Animal Park; "Alaska Tundra" at Washington Park Zoo, Portland, Ore.; "Wings of Asia" at Metrozoo, Miami, Fla.; "The Predators" at Birmingham (Ala.) Zoo; "Great Cat Complex" at Perth (Western Australia) Zoo; and "The Ark" at Paignton (England) Zoo.

(P. J. OLNEY)

See also Environment; Gardening.

Chemistry

Organic Chemistry. Spurred by the successful introduction of aspartame as a commercial sweetener in the early 1980s, interest in the chemistry of sweet-tasting substances remained high during 1985. Scientists at the Research Triangle Institute in North Carolina, supported by the U.S. National Institute of Dental Research, synthesized D,L-

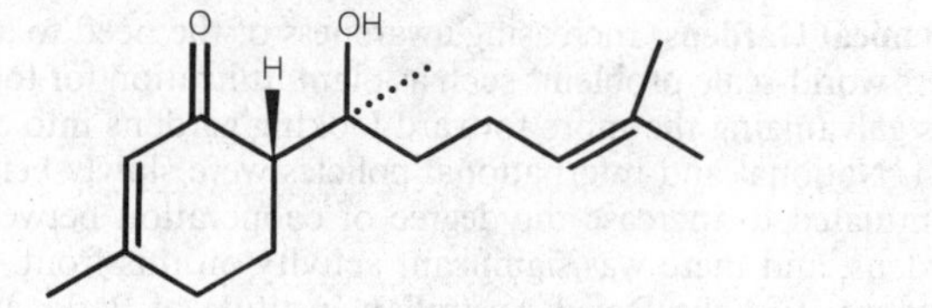

1 hernandulcin

2 punaglandin 3

amino malonyl-D-alanine isopropyl ester. This substance is nearly 60 times as sweet as sugar, although only half as sweet as aspartame. At the weakly acidic conditions found in many soft drinks (pH 3.5) the new compound showed no degradation over a 36-day period. Under the same conditions 50% of a sample of aspartame degraded.

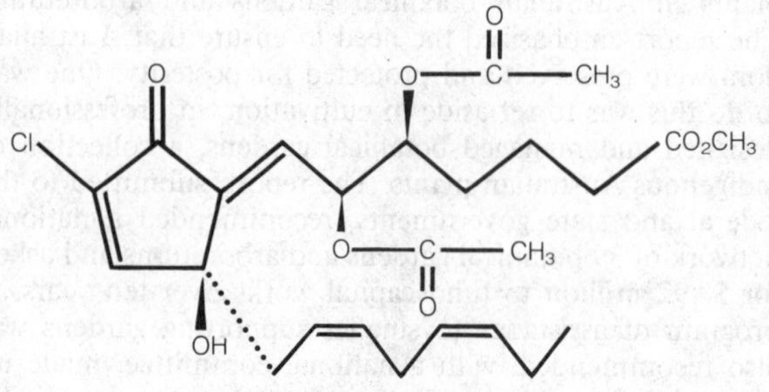

A natural compound about 1,000 times sweeter than sugar was discovered through a search of old texts and was then made synthetically. In a late 16th-century work on the natural history of New Spain by the physician Francisco Hernández, Cesar M. Compadre and colleagues at the University of Illinois, Chicago, found an account of a sweet-tasting herb used by the Aztecs. From the description they were able to identify it as *Lippia dulcis,* from which they extracted the new sweet compound, which they called hernandulcin (1).

New methods of organic synthesis appeared. In recent years many of these had aimed at improving the stereochemistry of organic syntheses; *i.e.,* the ability to control the spatial arrangement of the atoms in the molecular products. Chemists at the Massachusetts Institute of Technology developed chiral boranes (boranes having left- and right-handed mirror-image forms, or stereoisomers) that convert olefins into alcohols with high specificity for left- or right-handed products. Saturo Masamune and his colleagues used *trans*-2,5-dimethylborolanes to convert both *cis*- and *trans*-1,2-dialkylethenes and 1,1,2-trialkylethenes into chiral alcohols. As an example of the power of this new reagent, Masamune synthesized the macrolide antibiotic 6-deoxyerythronolide B in 23 stages, with an overall yield of 5.7%, of which 85% was the desired stereoisomer. An earlier synthesis involved 49 steps and gave an overall yield of 0.3%, of which only 46% was the desired stereoisomer.

Chemists continued to investigate marine life as a potential source of new drugs. During the year eicosanoids called punaglandins were isolated from the coral *Telesto riisei.* One of them, punaglandin 3 (2), has potent antileukemic activity. Punaglandin 3 slightly resembles the prostaglandins, molecules found widely in the body and exerting many different effects upon it.

In the 1980s chemotherapy was still in its infancy in the treatment of viral diseases. Although there had been some successes, there was intense pressure for further advances, particularly in view of the worldwide attention being focused on acquired immune deficiency syndrome (AIDS), known to be caused by a retrovirus. In September the pharmaceutical company Burroughs Wellcome announced that it was starting clinical trials with 3-azido-3-deoxythymidine, a compound discovered at its Research Triangle Park, N.C., laboratories. This substance is converted into a triphosphate in the body, and the phosphorylated compound interferes with one of the enzymes needed by the AIDS virus for replication.

Physical Chemistry. The effects of near-zero gravity on chemical experiments were further explored. In August an orbiting U.S. space shuttle served as the laboratory for experiments by the 3M Co. on the physical vapour transport of organic solids. Shuttle astronauts operated equipment designed to grow crystals, in the form of thin films, from the vapours of materials that either do not dissolve or cannot exist in a molten state and that are impossible to combine by some alternate method in the gravity field of Earth. If manufactured as ordered thin films deposited on suitable substrates, they could have applications in optics and electronics. General Motors also planned space experiments to see whether nylon 6, one of nylon's most widely used forms, could be formed from caprolactam in the form of larger, more nearly perfect crystals than those obtainable on Earth. The physical and mechanical properties of such space crystals could have special advantages.

Catalysis interested many chemists because it helped them understand how molecules react and because it had enormous commercial potential. Most modern industrial chemical processes would be impracticable without catalysts. Richard Smalley and co-workers at Rice University, Houston, Texas, studied the catalytic behaviour of small clusters of metal atoms produced by laser vaporization. They found that the size of the cluster affects its reactivity, although the reason was not yet known. With cobalt, for example, clusters of 3 to 5 atoms and 10 or more (but not 16) all react strongly with hydrogen. Single atoms of cobalt and clusters of two or six to nine atoms do not.

Robert E. Sievers of the University of Colorado explored the use of gold as a catalyst in reactions between nitrogen dioxide and organic compounds. One such reaction is the oxidation of alcohols to aldehydes. Many oxidizing agents, which do their work by removing electrons from a reactant, do not stop at this intermediate step but oxidize the alcohols to acids. Using gold—precipitated onto glass beads as gold chloride and then reduced with hydrogen to the free metal—and nitrogen dioxide, Sievers obtained a rapid and complete reaction without any significant by-products.

It would be useful for many purposes to be able to predict the solubility of one substance in another from basic principles. Mortimer J. Kamlet and Ruth M. Doherty of the Naval Surface Weapons Center, White Oak, Md., together with Michael Abraham of the University of Surrey, England, and Robert W. Taft of the University of California at Irvine, devised a universal equation for this purpose. The equation involves three different terms: a cavity term representing the energy required to make a hole in the solvent into which a molecule of solute can fit, a dipole interaction term, and a hydrogen-bonding term. This attempt to produce such an equation differed from predecessors in its use of the hydrogen-bonding term to replace terms based on acidity (proton transfer). Its usefulness in specific fields awaited the collection of sufficient data to establish meaningful coefficients.

Inorganic Chemistry. Life on Earth owes its existence to the tremendous combining ability of carbon atoms, which can link together into large molecules by means of both single (two-electron) bonds and stable multiple bonds. At one time it was thought that life elsewhere in the universe might be based on silicon, the abundant element that occurs directly below carbon in the periodic table. Silicon atoms, however, ordinarily are unable to form multiple bonds with one another. In recent years compounds had been made with silicon-silicon double bonds, but the molecules had to include bulky organic substituents to help hold the multiple bonds together. In 1985 scientists at the University of Frankfurt, West Germany, reported the first silicon-nitrogen triple bond. Heating of a triazidosilane compound gave an aromatic compound that appeared, from photoelectron spectroscopy, to contain a nitrogen atom attached by a single bond to one of the carbons in a benzene ring and by a triple bond to a silicon atom. The compound was isolated at a temperature near absolute zero; on warming it formed an insoluble polymer.

By contrast, the first stable compound containing a germanium-phosphorus double bond was isolated at Paul Sabatier University, Toulouse, France. Germanium falls directly below silicon in the periodic table and is therefore in the same family as carbon. This compound, isolated as orange crystals, had its double bond protected by bulky organic groups attached to both the germanium and the phosphorus atoms.

Another interesting inorganic compound reported was the phosphorus analogue of benzene. Benzene is one of the commonest organic compounds, consisting of a six-membered ring of carbon atoms, to each of which is attached a hydrogen atom. The peculiar characteristic of benzene is the sharing of bonding electrons around the ring to form hybrid bonds that are intermediate between double and single bonds, an arrangement that confers particular stability on the compound. Chemists working at the University of Kaiserslautern, West Germany, prepared a six-membered phosphorus ring by stabilizing it with two atoms of molybdenum, each of which was linked to a pentamethylcyclopentadienyl ion (3).

Analytical Chemistry. Sievers, whose work with gold catalysts is related above, was also exploring their potential for a new detection system in gas chromatography (GC), a technique used widely to separate complex mixtures. The

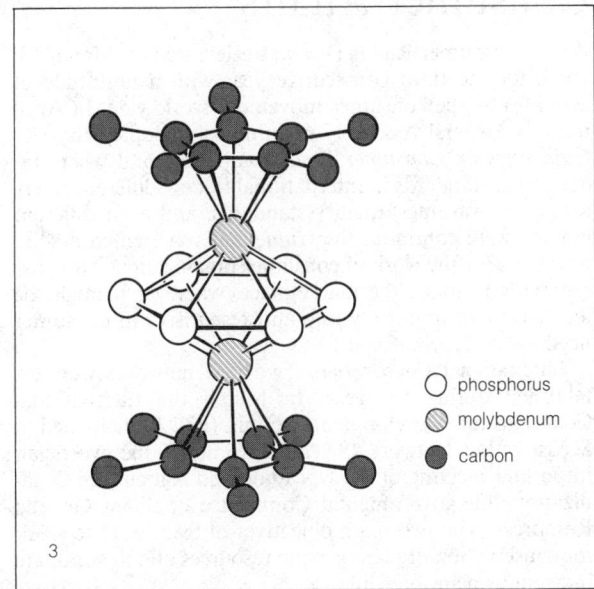

3

○ phosphorus
◐ molybdenum
● carbon

key to successful GC is a suitable detector. The flame ionization detector had proved effective for many years, but it could not detect some types of compounds. Sievers's gold catalysts, used in a device called a redox chemiluminescence detector, induced such compounds to react with nitric oxide as they came out of the chromatographic column. Detection was based on a light-emitting reaction between the residual nitric oxide and ozone. Although the new procedure involved more steps than a conventional detector, it was highly specific. For example, when a flame ionization detector was used to find the antioxidant butylated hydroxytoluene (BHT) in aviation fuel, to which it is added at levels of about ten parts per million, the hydrocarbons in the fuel swamped any signal from the BHT. Sievers's system did not respond to hydrocarbons and showed the BHT clearly.

The uses of nuclear magnetic resonance (NMR) spectroscopy, which derives information from the way hydrogen, phosphorus, and certain other atoms respond to radio waves in the presence of a strong magnetic field, further expanded during 1985. Nino Yannoni and colleagues at IBM's research laboratory in San Jose, Calif., picked up an idea first mooted in the late 1940s as the basis for a new variation of NMR that could work out bond lengths between atoms in solids, such as powders, that have no long-range order. Nutation NMR used what was effectively a continuous field of radio waves rotating perpendicular to the applied magnetic field in an NMR machine. This arrangement had the effect of canceling out signals from various interactions among the atoms while emphasizing others, and it allowed bond lengths to be determined within 1%. The new technique did not apply to liquid or gaseous states. Nevertheless, it should prove useful as a research tool. For example, it was possible to show that the polymerization of acetylene catalyzed by molybdenum occurs via a mechanism different from that which operates with titanium catalysts.   (MARTIN A. SHERWOOD)

This article updates the *Macropædia* articles Physical and Chemical ANALYSIS AND MEASUREMENT; CHEMICAL COMPOUNDS; CHEMICAL REACTIONS; DRUGS AND DRUG ACTION; ENERGY CONVERSION; Principles, Methods, and Instruments of MEASUREMENT AND OBSERVATION; MOLECULES; The PHYSICAL SCIENCES: *Chemistry.*

Consumer Affairs

World Consumer Rights Day was celebrated on March 15, 1985, for the third consecutive year with a multitude of activities by the consumer movement worldwide. In April the UN General Assembly unanimously adopted the UN *Guidelines on Consumer Protection.* In a world where inconsistent standards in international trade—different safety measures, warnings, quality standards, and even different ethics—were common, the *Guidelines* represented a solid new basis for the work of consumer organizations and governments to make the marketplace, wherever it might be located, more uniformly safe and responsive to consumer needs. (*See* Special Report.)

International Cooperation. Two new networks were established during the year. In March the International Coalition for Development Action (ICDA) launched a Seeds Action Network (SAN) in Rome on the eve of an important meeting of the UN Food and Agriculture Organization Intergovernmental Committee on Plant Genetic Resources. The two main objectives of SAN were to work for conservation of plant genetic resources and to stimulate indigenous plant breeding.

A month earlier a "No more Bhopals" network had been launched in Nairobi, Kenya, headquarters of the UN Environment Program. The new network was part of an action plan formulated at a meeting on environment and development for nongovernmental organizations (NGOs) on February 4–8. NGOs were encouraged to hold a "Bhopal Day" to mobilize global opinion on the prevention of future industrial disasters and to focus attention on the continuing plight of the victims of the December 1984 toxic-gas leak at Bhopal, India. In September the International Organization of Consumers Unions (IOCU) published its own response to the tragedy, *The Lessons of Bhopal—A Community Action Resource Manual on Hazardous Technologies.*

In December 1984 the UN General Assembly voted to continue to publish and expand a directory listing 500 potentially dangerous products that were banned, were restricted, or had failed to win approval in any of 60 countries. With the exception of the U.S., all UN members gave their backing to the consolidated list, which was promoted through IOCU's Consumer Interpol Program. As of 1985 the latter numbered some 62 correspondents in 43 countries; its concerns ranged from the safety of consumer products to issues relating to the transfer and use of hazardous technologies.

During 1985 the IOCU's campaign to curb tobacco promotion—Action Groups to Halt Advertising and Sponsorship of Tobacco (AGHAST)—laid the foundation for strong support within the consumer movement and reached out to other antismoking groups. Aimed not at the smoker—the victim—but at the tobacco industry, the campaign was designed to promote the adoption of smoking control measures at the national level and to encourage consumer organizations to focus their efforts at that level.

Drugs and World Health, a major consumer policy paper on medicines, set the scene for much of the year's work on pharmaceuticals. The report linked the problem of drug overconsumption in the developed world with its mirror image—chronic shortages of essential medicines in the third world. In response to consumer pressure, Ciba-Geigy Corp. withdrew Tandearil (oxyphenbutazone) and further restricted the recommended uses for Butazolidin (phenylbutazone). The company's decision followed a meeting in London—the first time that a multinational pharmaceutical company had met with consumer representatives to discuss how to deal with "problem" drugs it was marketing.

Regional Developments. In July 1985, after ten years of discussion, debate, and argument, the European Communities (EC) Council of Ministers adopted a product liability directive. This instrument, which had to be implemented by EC member states within three years, would make producers and importers throughout the Community strictly liable for damage caused by unsafe products. In September a new coalition of European and international consumer groups published *Cleared for Export,* a report examining the EC's pharmaceutical and chemical trade. The new coalition marked renewed, vigorous efforts to act against dangerous exports from European countries.

The Australian government increased its funding to the Australian Federation of Consumer Organizations (AFCO) by 41.6%, thus reflecting its growing commitment to consumer affairs generally. AFCO was closely involved in the collection of national statistics on injuries and deaths associated with consumer products. The data would be used to target areas where government action, such as banning or recalling products, was needed to protect the health and safety of consumers.

(continued on page 183)

Consumer Activism and Corporate Responsibility

BY BRIJ KHINDARIA

Because of events that are gradually forcing them to accept a greater degree of public responsibility, multinational companies face unprecedented challenges in coming years. A key element in this change is the growing realization by the multinationals that they cannot apply lower standards of corporate behaviour in less developed countries than they do in developed countries. A primary reason for this newly developed sense of conscience is the fear of litigation in their home countries, which could result in penalties of hundreds of millions of dollars. Another important consideration is the growing realization that corporate responsibility extends not only to consumers of the company's product but also to others in the countries or localities where the company operates.

Reinforcing the fear of litigation is the concern that huge liability claims could undermine stock prices and encourage takeover bids by corporate rivals. The loss of public confidence may be particularly damaging if company officials appear to have placed lesser value on human health and life in poorer nations than in rich ones. Whatever the excellence of a company's operating record, what remains in the public perception after a disaster such as that at Bhopal, India, in December 1984 is the image of human suffering. In the wake of such an event even the most thoughtful legal or technical arguments run the risk of being dismissed as apologetics for the careless pursuit of profit, regardless of the human cost.

The notion that a corporation must be accountable for its products and policies has become fairly widely accepted, particularly since the rise of the kind of consumer activism pioneered by Ralph Nader in the U.S. What is new is that this accountability transcends national frontiers. Multinationals now face regulation by international bodies designed to restrict their activities in foreign countries. The prospect of such limitations may be particularly daunting in view of the cumbersome domestic laws already forced upon companies in response to local consumer movements in the U.S. and Western Europe.

The International Consumer Movement. No fewer than 25 international bodies are currently active in designing codes and rules to protect consumers—especially those in less developed countries—against what these bodies deem irresponsible behaviour on the part of multinational corporations. The most prominent of these groups are the European Communities, the Organization for Economic Cooperation and Development, and various UN agencies. Entire industrial sectors, rather than individual companies, are the targets of such international regulation. The lobby

Brij Khindaria is a Geneva-based specialist in relationships among multinational companies, consumer activists, and international regulatory bodies.

in favour of regulation consists of a variety of highly articulate, if somewhat disorganized worldwide consumer protection groups, which get sympathetic hearings from the governments of many less developed countries and a number of international agencies.

These lobbying groups usually focus their efforts on specific practices, such as the aggressive marketing of unnecessary pharmaceuticals, harmful pesticides, infant formulas and breast milk substitutes, and tobacco and alcohol products. Other groups are more ideologically motivated; for example, those that have brought shareholder pressure to bear upon multinational companies and banks operating in South Africa, forcing them to speak out against apartheid (racial separation).

One of the best known worldwide consumer groups is the Hague-based International Organization of Consumers Unions (IOCU), which has, among its many activities, established a transnationals monitoring network to monitor the practices of transnational companies everywhere in the world. The network's aim is to identify "inappropriate practices" and to force their elimination through pressure on governments and companies. The global popularity of the consumer protection movement is illustrated by the IOCU's rapid expansion from a five-nation Western group at its founding in 1960 to its current status as an international organization representing more than 120 consumer unions in 50 countries, including many less developed nations. The focus of the organization's work has also shifted from the West to the third world.

One of the most successful recent consumer protection campaigns was mounted by the International Baby Foods Action Network (IBFAN), an IOCU affiliate. Working in cooperation with another group that sponsored a boycott against some Nestlé products, IBFAN was partially responsible for adoption in 1981 by the World Health Organization (WHO) of a code representing the minimum requirements for the framing of national regulations on the promotion of breast-milk substitutes. The purpose of the code is to prevent advertising and marketing strategies that discourage women from breast-feeding their infants.

Harmful Products, Harmful Practices. Another worldwide consumer activist network, Health Action International, is lobbying strongly for a code of behaviour for multinational pharmaceutical companies to prevent them from aggressively marketing a variety of costly, sophisticated drugs that are rarely needed in less developed

IOCU, THE HAGUE

One of the most popular and effective activities undertaken by national consumers' unions is the publication of magazines and pamphlets guiding consumers through the thicket of competing goods and conflicting claims that are hallmarks of market economies.

On the first anniversary of the toxic-gas disaster at Bhopal, India, in December, police surrounded the closed Union Carbide plant to protect it from thousands of protesters.
AP/WIDE WORLD

countries. Partly in response to pressure from consumers and governments, the International Federation of Pharmaceutical Manufacturers Associations has established a voluntary code of behaviour for the industry, with the aim of demonstrating that supplementary regulations imposed by outsiders are unnecessary.

Reflecting consumer concerns about the harmful effects of pesticide residues in food and the damage to soil fertility, the Food and Agriculture Organization of the UN has developed an *International Code of Conduct on the Distribution and Use of Pesticides.* In a separate effort another IOCU affiliate, the Pesticide Action Network, is trying to win support for special measures limiting the use of 12 of the most toxic pesticides. The UN Environment Program has also prepared a list of hazardous and dangerous chemicals to serve as an information base for third world governments planning safety measures.

The UN has drawn up a separate set of worldwide guidelines on consumer protection designed to curb business practices that adversely affect consumers and to encourage consumer protection legislation in less developed countries. The WHO, in cooperation with several other UN agencies, is currently mounting campaigns to reduce smoking and alcohol consumption. The IOCU has made the curbing of ads that promote smoking a major focus of its program for the next three years.

Predictably, most of the above-mentioned international efforts met with opposition from industry federations and, in some cases, from the U.S. government. But while consumer protection regulations may circumscribe the business environment of multinational companies, the real bite comes from stockholder pressure and consumer litigation in response to industrial accidents.

Bhopal and After. Union Carbide Corp., a respected U.S. chemicals manufacturer, is currently entangled in lawsuits seeking more than $100 billion in compensation for victims of one of the worst industrial disasters in history. The claims were made on behalf of the more than 1,700 people who were killed and about 200,000 others who were injured during a toxic gas leak at a small factory (operated by the Indian subsidiary of Union Carbide) outside the provincial Indian city of Bhopal on Dec. 3, 1984. Indian investigators later alleged that the security system in the plant was not sophisticated enough to provide adequate protection against such an accident.

Although negligence by Union Carbide has not been proved in the Bhopal case, the company did accept the responsibility for the toxic-gas leak of Aug. 11, 1985, at its plant at Institute, W.Va., in which 135 people received hospital treatment for minor ailments. The leak at the West Virginia plant occurred in spite of the most sophisticated security measures available. Lawsuits claiming about $88 million in compensation were filed by the victims of the latter incident.

In addition to claims for compensation—which could take several years to settle—such accidents have other costs. Apart from legal and public relations fees, Union Carbide committed $120 million for environmental protection and safety measures in 1985, and another $100 million was similarly earmarked for 1986. At the same time, Carbide was also fighting to defend itself against a takeover bid by another company.

Accidents, particularly in the chemical industry, reinforce the worst fears of consumer activists. Frequently they also furnish ammunition to others who argue that multinationals treat human lives in less developed countries with less respect than they accord to those in developed countries. Several governments of less developed countries are lobbying for a UN code to ensure the safety of chemical technology transfers by Western multinationals.

The Lesson and the Choice. It would be dangerous to draw simplistic lessons from such events as the Bhopal disaster, with their complex technical and legal ramifications. One thing is clear, however—despite the best technology available, the nightmare of large industrial accidents cannot be totally eradicated. Certain kinds of technical mishaps and human miscalculations cannot be guarded against. Yet the products of this same modern technology are often as necessary as safety itself, and reconciling the two is not always possible.

Nonetheless, it is possible to reduce the potential for human injury in industrial accidents and to guard against marketing practices that encourage the consumption of unnecessary or potentially harmful products. These goals can be achieved if companies take it upon themselves to voluntarily assume greater responsibility for the direct and indirect effects on people of their actions. Given the growth of an active international consumer movement, however, the assumption of social responsibility may not long remain a matter of choice.

(continued from page 180)

In China the first consumer council was established in Guangzkou (Canton). Its main functions would be handling complaints, undertaking surveys and tests, and educating consumers. Subsequently a central consumer council was set up in Beijing (Peking).

In Latin America the consumer movement continued to grow stronger. Brazil passed a consumer protection law, and Argentina and Uruguay had similar bills before their legislative bodies.   (RUTH VERMEER)

The safety of air travel was a major focus of attention in the U.S. as the crashes of several large scheduled airliners around the world made 1985 the worst year in civil aviation history. (*See* DISASTERS.) These accidents raised growing concern about the effect of deregulation on the airline industry, lending support to the notion that deregulation had resulted in cost cutting that placed strains on airline equipment and personnel. The Federal Aviation Administration (FAA) held to its contention that aviation was still the safest mode of transportation, but congressional critics questioned whether the FAA was doing everything possible to keep the skies safe. Inspectors' reports confirmed the FAA findings that the great majority of U.S. airlines were operating within the safety rules; however, the reports did reveal serious problems among the smaller regional and commuter carriers, which flew millions of passengers a year. In January 1985 consumer advocate Ralph Nader accused the FAA of underreporting the number of near collisions in the nation's airways. Nader said a spot check of documents from regional FAA offices revealed that more than 100 airborne close calls had not been included in official FAA data. In June 1985 the FAA issued a revised report, stating that there had been 592 near collisions of U.S. airliners in 1984, 293 more than the previous estimate.

In March and April six midwestern states were hit with an outbreak of salmonella food poisoning described as the worst of its kind in U.S. history. Altogether some 16,000 reported cases were traced to contaminated milk produced at a suburban Chicago dairy. Two valves had evidently allowed tainted raw milk to mix with pasteurized milk, thus causing the contamination. In July California state agencies ordered grocers to destroy more than ten million watermelons after reports of over 180 cases of sickness caused by watermelons treated with the pesticide aldicarb. The Environmental Protection Agency subsequently published a report stating that aldicarb would be banned because it is highly carcinogenic.

The closing in March of 71 Ohio savings institutions whose deposits were insured by a state-affiliated fund was thought to have been the most drastic action of its kind since the Great Depression. The decision to close the banks was made after the failure of a Cincinnati-based financial institution undermined the stability of the state's deposit insurance fund. Following the passage of emergency legislation requiring that these banks apply for federal insurance, several were allowed to reopen, and a feared run on state-insured savings banks in four other states was averted. Nonetheless, concern persisted about the financial stability of savings and loan associations in general. A federal government report revealed that one-third of the 3,200 U.S. thrift institutions had liabilities that exceeded their tangible assets. Many thrifts reported positive net worths (assets minus liabilities) by using special accounting techniques. The financial condition of the nation's thrifts posed questions about the stability of the Federal Savings and Loan Insurance Corporation (FSLIC), the unit of the Federal Home Loan Bank that insured thrift institutions.

In August the Manville Corp. offered to pay $2.5 billion

Chemists at the state agriculture department in Oregon began testing watermelons for pesticide residues in the wake of an outbreak of illness in California attributed to use of the pesticide aldicarb on that state's watermelon crop.
AP/WIDE WORLD

to victims of asbestos-related health problems in the largest health-related settlement ever made by a U.S. company. Manville offered to set up a fund to which shareholders would surrender half the value of their stock and the company would give up a large part of its projected earnings for the next 25 years. For this offer to become effective, it would have to be accepted by shareholders, claimants, and the bankruptcy court.

A. H. Robins, manufacturer of the birth control device known as the Dalkon Shield, set up a $615 million reserve fund to settle legal claims from women who suffered injuries from the device. More than 12,000 users of the Dalkon Shield had already sued Robins. In 1984 the company had settled 8,300 claims for $314.6 million, but new lawsuits were being filed at an average of 300 a month. Robins asked for a federal court decision to consolidate all the suits into a single class action suit to determine the company's total liability.

In February, SmithKline Beckman Corp. was sentenced to two years' probation and ordered to spend $100,000 to establish a child abuse prevention program and to perform 500 hours of community service for having delayed reporting adverse side effects of Selacryn, a drug to control high blood pressure. It was the first time the U.S. Department of Justice had prosecuted a violator of reporting requirements under provisions of the Food, Drug, and Cosmetic Act.

(EDWARD MARK MAZZE)

See also Economic Affairs: *World Economy;* Industrial Review: *Advertising.*

Crime, Law Enforcement, and Penology

Violent Crime. *Terrorism.* With numbing frequency the world's media were dominated in 1985 by news of terrorist attacks. During one ten-day period alone, reports flowed in of an airplane hijacking near Athens, a bombing at the Frankfurt, West Germany, international airport, a possibly sabotaged jumbo jet falling in pieces into the Atlantic Ocean, and an explosion at Tokyo's Narita Airport.

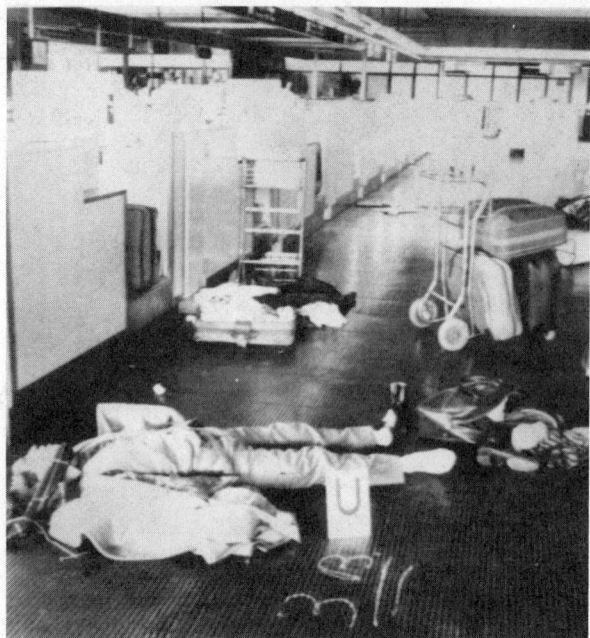

The bodies of two terrorists lie amid the litter in the aftermath of a grenade and machine-gun attack at Rome's Leonardo da Vinci Airport. This and a simultaneous attack in Vienna in December left 18 dead and more than 100 wounded.
AP/WIDE WORLD

For the passengers and crew aboard Rome-bound TWA Flight 847, a terrifying ordeal began on June 14 when the jet was hijacked shortly after takeoff from Athens. Seized initially by two gunmen, believed to be members of a militant pro-Iranian Shi'ah Muslim group, the plane shuttled for many hours between Beirut, Lebanon, and Algiers. Women, children, and elderly passengers were released, but the gunmen also beat and shot to death one passenger, Robert Stethem, a U.S. Navy diver. Eventually landed in the Lebanese capital and dispersed through the Muslim sector of the city to foil rescue efforts, Flight 847's remaining 39 passengers and crew became the subject of prolonged and tense negotiations for their release in exchange for more than 700 prisoners, mostly Shi'ah, held in Israeli prison camps. Negotiations proved successful, and the 39 hostages regained their freedom on June 30.

On June 19 a powerful bomb blast ripped through the international departure hall at Frankfurt's airport, killing two children and an adult and injuring 42 people. A terrorist cell calling itself the Arab Revolutionary Organization claimed responsibility. On June 23 an Air-India Boeing 747, bound for Bombay from Canada, disintegrated in midair and crashed into the sea 145 km (90 mi) off the coast of Ireland. All 329 people aboard, including 279 Canadians, perished in the worst airline disaster at sea to that date. On the same day, halfway around the globe, an explosion in a luggage container being unloaded at Tokyo's Narita Airport from a Canadian Pacific Air 747 just arrived from Vancouver, B.C., killed two baggage handlers and injured four others. Investigators began to explore the possibility that unidentified terrorists, from a base in North America, had planned to blow up two jumbo jets. Responsibility for planting explosives aboard the Air India jet was claimed by two Indian terrorist organizations. However, the cause of the crash was still unconfirmed at year's end.

In the violence-racked Middle East three middle-aged Israelis were murdered on their yacht in the harbour of Larnaca, Cyprus, in September. A group calling itself Force

17 said it was responsible and claimed the Israelis were spies monitoring the movement of vessels carrying Palestine Liberation Organization (PLO) fighters from Cyprus to Lebanon. The same terrorist group was believed to have been involved in the hijacking on October 7 of the Italian liner *Achille Lauro.* The ship, with more than 400 passengers and crew aboard, was seized by four gunmen in the eastern Mediterranean. The gunmen, who demanded the release of Palestinians held prisoner by the Israelis, eventually surrendered to Egyptian authorities in Port Said after allegedly murdering a crippled U.S. citizen, Leon Klinghoffer. (*See* WORLD AFFAIRS [Western Europe]: *Italy.*) An Egyptian airliner was hijacked on November 23 by terrorists, thought to be Palestinians, and taken to Valletta airport in Malta. After two passengers were killed, Egyptian commandos, with the permission of the Maltese government, stormed the plane in a rescue attempt, but 57 of the 98 passengers and crew on board died in the gunfight and subsequent fire; one of the hijackers survived. In nearly simultaneous attacks at the Rome and Vienna airports on December 27, travelers at the counters of the Israeli airline El Al and others nearby were raked with machine-gun fire and grenades. Fifteen people (including 3 terrorists) were killed and 74 wounded at Rome, and 3 (including 1 terrorist) were killed and 47 wounded at Vienna. A PLO splinter group claimed responsibility.

Terrorism took an unexpected twist with the sinking on July 10 in New Zealand of the *Rainbow Warrior,* flagship of the international conservation group Greenpeace. The *Rainbow Warrior,* which was to have led a flotilla to Mururoa Atoll in the South Pacific to protest French nuclear weapons tests, sank in Auckland Harbour after mines ripped holes in its hull. A photographer aboard the vessel was killed. New Zealand authorities quickly arrested a man and a woman believed to be members of the General Directorate for External Security (DGSE), France's foreign intelligence agency. Despite initial denials by the French government, the *Rainbow Warrior* affair escalated into a major political scandal. In September Prime Minister Laurent Fabius placed the blame for the sinking on the defense minister, Charles Hernu, who resigned, and on the chief of the DGSE, Adm. Pierre Lacoste, who was removed from office. Further revelations were anticipated at the murder trial of the two suspects in New Zealand,

LENTZ—VISIONS

As part of a U.S.-funded $26 million program to control the flow of cocaine from Peru to the United States, Peruvian workers uprooted and burned coca plants in the Huallaga Valley. Although growers were reimbursed, the program was suspended for a time after 19 workers were murdered.

but the proceedings ended when they pleaded guilty to the lesser charges of manslaughter and sabotage. (*See* WORLD AFFAIRS [Oceania]: *Oceanian Affairs.*)

In Rome what was billed as "the trial of the century" opened on May 27: three Bulgarian and four Turkish citizens were charged with having assisted in a Bulgarian plot to assassinate Pope John Paul II. Principal witness for the prosecution was Mehmet Ali Agca, the man convicted of shooting the pope in May 1981. Agca's initial testimony included a claim that he was Jesus Christ.

Murder and Other Violence. In the U.S. the FBI's Crime Index figures showed a 3% decline in serious crime during 1984. This was the third consecutive year in which the overall Crime Index had moved downward, although this encouraging news was tempered by the release in July of a U.S. Justice Department study that claimed the Crime Index, based on voluntary reports by approximately 15,000 law-enforcement agencies, was seriously flawed. The study proposed a number of reforms. Another study, *American Violence and Public Policy,* conducted by the Eisenhower Foundation, claimed that despite the continuing improvement in crime rates since 1982, as reported by the FBI, the level of violent crime in the U.S. remained at "astronomical" levels compared with other industrialized countries. Fear of crime in U.S. cities, said the study, was just as intense in 1985 as in the 1960s.

The case of Bernhard H. Goetz, the so-called subway vigilante, illustrated how anger and frustration about crime could affect city dwellers. On Dec. 22, 1984, four black youths (all of whom had criminal records) approached Goetz on a New York subway car and asked him for money. Goetz produced a .38-calibre pistol and shot each of the four, injuring one very seriously, before fleeing. He later surrendered to police. He was hailed as a vigilante hero by many New Yorkers and by the tabloid press, and a grand jury refused to indict him on charges of attempted murder or manslaughter, agreeing only to proceed against him for weapons violations. However, public sympathy for Goetz began to erode when it was revealed that, after shooting the four youths, he shot one again. Brought before a second grand jury in March, Goetz was indicted for attempted murder. (*See* Sidebar.)

During the summer citizens of California were terrified by a serial killer, dubbed the Night Stalker, who was believed responsible for murdering as many as 16 people and gravely assaulting at least 21 others. In virtually every case the Night Stalker entered his victims' homes through unlocked doors and windows, killing men in their sleep and then raping women. The attacks were extraordinarily vicious. On August 31 Richard Ramirez was apprehended by angry citizens after he had tried to steal a car in a Mexican-American neighbourhood of Los Angeles. Los Angeles police subsequently identified Ramirez as the man they believed to be the Night Stalker. The veracity of confessed serial killer Henry Lee Lucas came under question after two reporters from a Dallas, Texas, newspaper contended in April that his claims to have committed as many as 600 slayings between 1975 and 1983 were a hoax intended to delay his transfer to death row. Police in 26 U.S. states were said to have closed more than 200 homicide cases on the basis of his confessions.

In another troubling criminal case, an Illinois rape victim recanted testimony given originally at the trial of her alleged rapist in 1979. Cathleen Crowell Webb, now 23, claimed that in 1977 she had falsely accused Gary E. Dotson, now 28, of raping her because of fears that she was pregnant by her boyfriend. Dotson was convicted of the crime and sentenced to 25 to 50 years in prison. Deciding eventually to commute Dotson's sentence, Illinois Gov. James Thompson said he still believed Webb had been raped and Dotson properly convicted. Some observers feared the case could provoke a backlash against measures taken over the past decade to protect sexual assault victims.

Nonviolent Crime. *Political Crime.* A meeting of Commonwealth heads of government held in mid-October in Nassau, The Bahamas, focused international attention on

---

Reflections on the Bernhard Goetz Case

At a press conference shortly after his arrest, Bernhard Goetz was asked how it felt to be a celebrity, to have people interested in what he stood for. Goetz paused, then asked pointedly, "What *do* I stand for?" The precise answer to this question is still unclear. Perhaps of greater ultimate importance to society, however, are the insights that the case provided into the shortcomings of the criminal justice system and into some unfortunate aspects of media sensationalism.

That an act of vigilantism could garner such public support demonstrates the almost universal frustration with a system of criminal justice that is generally regarded as, at best, ineffective. Furthermore, the media took advantage of the situation, capitalizing on the feelings of many New Yorkers that crime was running rampant. Goetz was billed as a hero, a man who "finally decided to fight back." The perceived unresponsiveness of the police, prosecution, and courts only added to the outpouring of sympathy for him.

Interestingly, while Goetz was hailed as a man who justifiably had taken the law into his own hands, the mayor and other officials joined in the applause. Goetz was indicted only for illegal possession of a gun and was released on bail. Subsequently, however, additional information came to light. Goetz apparently had been prepared to fire in the face of questionable provocation. At later press conferences, he appeared somewhat unbalanced. The mayor and other officials withdrew their support; black leaders denounced Goetz's actions and the failure to prosecute as racist acts. A grand jury was reconvened and presented with "new" evidence. This time Goetz was indicted for attempted murder, aggravated assault, reckless endangerment, and illegal possession. Inevitably, questions were raised. Had the first indictment been a result of racist attitudes? Was the new indictment a pandering to the evident reversal of public opinion?

Had the Goetz case created a sustained media interest in solving the problems of the criminal justice system, the sensationalism and the injury to public confidence in the system might have been worthwhile. However, no such journalistic initiative has been forthcoming, and public anxiety about the court system is undiminished. Thus, unless the system itself takes corrective measures, society will have to cope with more vigilante justice, more media hype, and constantly frightened citizenry.

(ROBERT P. PATTERSON, JR.; EDWARD REDLICH)

that Caribbean nation's involvement in massive drug-smuggling operations. Sir Lynden Pindling, The Bahamas prime minister, and members of his government faced continuing accusations of large-scale corruption linked to the island's role as a transit point for cocaine and marijuana sent from Latin America to the U.S. In March, in Miami, Norman Saunders, chief minister of the Turks and Caicos Islands, a British dependency south of The Bahamas, and three others were indicted on charges involving a plot to use the island group as a staging point for drug shipments bound for the U.S.

In August Otto Lambsdorff, former economics minister in the West German government, went on trial in Bonn with two other defendants accused of corruption in connection with a payoff scandal. Lambsdorff, the first West German Cabinet minister to be indicted while in office, was alleged to have accepted $50,000 between 1977 and 1980 from Flick, a giant German corporation, in exchange for granting lucrative tax waivers. The trial was expected to last at least a year.

White Collar Crime and Theft. In the U.S. a wave of revelations concerning white collar crime touched some of the nation's largest business and financial institutions, including more than 40 of the top military suppliers. In May the nation's third largest defense supplier, General Dynamics, suffered the cancellation of two contracts worth more than $22 million and the suspension of two of its divisions from obtaining fresh contracts until it repaid $75 million in cost overruns and installed a new code of ethics for its staff. In December the company, three of its officers, and James Beggs, a former officer and currently administrator of the National Aeronautics and Space Administration, were indicted on seven counts of defrauding the Army. The charges involved illegal billings for cost overruns on the Sergeant York antiaircraft gun, which was eventually dropped as unworkable. Earlier, General Electric, the sixth largest U.S. military contractor, pleaded guilty to defrauding the Air Force of $800,000 in 1980 on a Minuteman missile project. The company agreed to pay fines and penalties of more than $2 million.

Also in May, Wall Street's largest stockbroking firm, E. F. Hutton, pleaded guilty to a fraud that had bilked some 400 banks out of at least $8 million between 1980 and 1982. The firm agreed to pay a fine and court costs of $2,750,000 and to repay the banks, but no individual executives were prosecuted. The settlement was strongly criticized by congressmen and others who alleged that federal authorities were showing undue leniency toward corporate offenders. In marked contrast, former deputy secretary of defense Paul Thayer and a codefendant were sentenced to a four-year prison term and fined $5,000 after pleading guilty to obstruction of justice charges relating to an insider trading investigation by the federal Securities and Exchange Commission.

In August Crocker National Bank of San Francisco, the 11th largest U.S. bank, was fined $2,250,000 for failing to report almost $4 billion in foreign currency transactions. Federal authorities hoped the penalty, the most severe ever imposed under the U.S. Banking Secrecy Act, would ensure that law-enforcement officials received information required to trace laundered money involved with organized crime, drug deals, or corruption.

Chinese officials revealed in August that naval aircraft, and possibly ships, had been involved in a major profiteering scandal on the southern Chinese island of Hainan. Motor vehicles, video cassette recorders, television sets, and other highly prized consumer goods were said to have been shipped by the military from Hainan, an "open port,"

Senior members of Yamaguchi-gumi, the largest organization of *yakuza* (gangsters) in Japan, arrive for the funeral of their boss, Masahisa Takenaka, who with his aides was ambushed by members of a rival gang in Osaka. Some 1,000 *yakuza* attended the funeral.
AP/WIDE WORLD

to the mainland for resale at double or triple the original price.

Maritime fraud cost the international shipping industry more than $13 billion per year, according to a report presented in August by the UN Conference on Trade and Development (UNCTAD) to the seventh UN Crime Congress in Milan, Italy. The largest fraud in shipping history, according to UNCTAD, occurred when an empty supertanker, the *Salem,* was scuttled in 1980 off the coast of Senegal as part of an elaborate scheme to cover up the theft of its original cargo of oil and to obtain $80 million in insurance. In April a Greek court sentenced a shipping agent to 11 years in prison and four seamen to up to 4 years each for their complicity in the *Salem* fraud.

Law Enforcement. The importance of international cooperation in the fight against crime was underscored in March when President Reagan and Canadian Prime Minister Brian Mulroney signed a treaty designed to expedite criminal investigations involving their two countries. A key provision required the establishment in both nations' justice departments of central clearinghouses for cross-border evidence, witnesses, and fugitives.

U.S. relations with Mexico were strained following the kidnapping and murder of a U.S. Drug Enforcement Administration (DEA) agent, Enrique Camarena Salazar. Camarena Salazar was abducted at gunpoint in February outside the U.S. consulate in Guadalajara. His body, and that of a Mexican pilot working for the DEA, were found several weeks later near Villahermosa. Suspicions by DEA officials that these murders could have occurred only with the knowledge and assistance of corrupt Mexican law-enforcement officials were confirmed late in March when six members of the Jalisco state police and a number of civilians were arrested by Mexican authorities in connection with the crimes.

The FBI announced in August that audits conducted in a dozen U.S. states indicated that at least 12,000 invalid or

inaccurate reports on suspects wanted for arrest were transmitted each day to federal, state, and local law-enforcement agencies. The audits also brought to light problems with about 7,000 reports transmitted each day concerning stolen vehicles and license plates. The information, supplied to the bureau's National Crime Intelligence Centre, was intended to give police officers speedy notice of whether a person stopped for a traffic offense was wanted on a criminal charge or whether a particular car had been reported stolen.

Law-enforcement officials in Pennsylvania were the subject of extensive investigations following a disastrous fire on May 13 that erupted after police dropped a bomb from a helicopter on a house in Philadelphia. The drastic action was taken by police in an attempt to end a two-day siege of the heavily fortified house occupied by members of a bizarre radical cult known as Move. The explosion set off an inferno that killed 11 people, 5 of them children, in the Move house and destroyed or damaged more than 60 surrounding houses.

In Poland, following an unprecedented public trial, four members of the secret police were convicted in February of the abduction and murder of a well-known Polish activist priest, Father Jerzy Popielusko. (*See* WORLD AFFAIRS [Eastern Europe and the U.S.S.R.]: *Poland:* Sidebar.) Police in Belgium faced censure for failing to take adequate security precautions in the aftermath of a riot during a soccer game in Brussels that left 38 spectators dead and as many as 200 persons injured. (*See* SPORTS AND GAMES: *Football:* Sidebar.)

Severe street rioting occurred in a number of British cities during the summer. In Brixton, a London suburb that was also the scene of major riots in 1981, the disturbances were sparked when police accidentally shot a black woman during a raid on her house. A police officer was also killed during the rioting, leading to suggestions by police union leaders that their members be allowed to fire rubber bullets to disperse rioters—a crowd-control measure frequently used by British authorities in Northern Ireland. The continuing sectarian conflict in Northern Ireland produced more casualties, including the deaths in March of 9 police officers in a mortar attack on a police station in Newry; 37 others were injured.

A report prepared by researchers at the University of Cape Town's Institute of Criminology gave further credence to long-standing allegations of the use of physical and psychological torture by South African police. The study, which was supported by funds from the U.S.-based Ford Foundation, included interviews with 176 former political detainees, 83% of whom reported suffering some form of physical torture while in custody, and almost all of whom said that they had been subjected to psychological abuse. Police subsequently denied the allegations, although the South African government was known to have made an undisclosed number of out-of-court settlements with former detainees or their families who had brought civil legal proceedings.   (DUNCAN CHAPPEL)

Prisons and Penology. The swing in emphasis from reformation to punishment, now called "the new realism" by European penologists, continued and accelerated in 1985. In his state of the union speech, U.S. Pres. Ronald Reagan noted that, despite a fall in the crime rate, there were record numbers in U.S. prisons. Popular support for tough treatment of criminals was shown by the acclaim given Bernhard Goetz for shooting four youths who he thought were mugging him in the New York subway. (*See* Sidebar.) In the U.K., where prison numbers also broke records, Prime Minister Margaret Thatcher called for sterner sen-

In September nearly 100 prisoners of the Spike Island minimum-security prison in Cork, Ireland, rioted and took control of the grounds. They then escaped after having set fire to the building. Most of the escapees were recaptured nearby within hours.
AP/WIDE WORLD

tences for violence and proposed legislation allowing the Court of Appeal to review overlenient sentences. From Islamic countries there were continued reports of floggings, the chopping off of fingers and hands, public hangings, and beheadings. In Teheran, Iran, a woman whose husband had blinded her was allowed by judicial order to cut out his eyes. The Ministry of Justice in China claimed that its new policy of harsh punishment had helped to reduce the number of reported serious crimes from 800,000 to 500,000.

Graeme Newman's book *Just and Painful: A Case for the Corporal Punishment of Criminals* advocated the punishment by electric shock of men, women, and children convicted of crime. Susan Jacoby's *Wild Justice: The Evolution of Revenge* considered the legitimacy of vengeance as an element in judicial punishment. While both books attracted as much censure as praise, their significance for Western penology lay in opening up for discussion ideas thought scarcely mentionable for many decades. Penal reformers in the U.S. advocated compensation for people imprisoned pending trial and subsequently acquitted; this was available in most European countries but not generally in Britain or the U.S. British government proposals to extend compensation for victims of crime seemed to arouse greater support.

In November 1984 Greece, in legislation required by the constitution of 1975, formally prohibited the torture of prisoners. It was the first country to do so.

Capital Punishment. Amnesty International reported worldwide growth in the number of executions. It had documentary evidence of 1,500 in 40 countries in 1984 but thought the real total to be many times higher. In the U.S. individual executions became less newsworthy, attracting widespread public attention only when they were particularly macabre. Abolitionists began to focus less on individual executions and more on the broad social and moral issues involved in capital punishment; for example, that it discriminated against black people: 42% of the 1,400

Private Means to Public Ends

During the early 1980s, few proposals in the field of corrections stimulated as sharply divided opinions as the prospect of contracting with the private sector for the management of prison and jail facilities. Some saw a chance to introduce efficiency and innovation to a field labouring under the burden of outmoded facilities, unprecedented population increases, and declining resources. Others feared that the profit motive would interfere with professional corrections practice and questioned whether it was appropriate to make the administration of justice a market for economic enterprise.

The propriety of delegating matters of social control proved to be the most controversial issue. In a facility operated by the private sector, a range of quasi-judicial functions would be delegated to the contractor. The deprivation of liberty, the administration of discipline, the capacity to use restraining or deadly force, control over decisions that could affect how much time an inmate served and the conditions of his or her confinement—all would be transferred to managers in the private sector. Those who questioned the propriety of such a shift argued that the administration of justice is a raison d'être of government and neither can nor should be delegated.

In this view, imprisonment serves broad social interests; to the extent that private purposes are superimposed, justice is compromised. The compromise might take many forms. Economic motives might conflict with the need to provide decent conditions of confinement. Private contractors might skim off the cream of the inmate crop, leaving the public corrections system with the most expensive inmate-management problems. Paid on the basis of the number of inmates housed, contractors might maintain high occupancy rates, even in the absence of demonstrated need.

In rebuttal, others argued that policy development—and not the execution of policy—is the central role of government. In this view, private motives would conflict with the public interest only if public-sector managers failed to establish appropriate performance standards and closely supervise their contractors. Indeed, because a private vendor would be under competitive pressure to perform, the quality of privately provided services would probably be superior to the same services dispensed in the monopolistic environment of government. Left unanswered was whether there would be sufficient market pressure to sustain any improvements over the long term or whether competition would be stifled—either because few providers were attracted to the field or because it was impractical to turn contracts over often enough to maintain competition.

Questions of efficiency also remained largely unanswered. After considering all the hidden costs of contracting (including the burden of contractor supervision), would proprietary facilities save the government money? Many public-sector prisons and jails were underfunded in relation to the number of offenders in custody. Was it really possible for the private sector to provide more for less? Or would time simply reveal that more prisoners require more resources and that, if public-sector managers could negotiate the same deal, they might do just as well?   (JOAN MULLEN)

people on "death row" in 1984 were black, according to the American Civil Liberties Union, whereas blacks constituted only 12% of the general U.S. population. Supporters of capital punishment, meanwhile, protested strongly when the California Supreme Court overturned four death sentences in June 1985; the court had already overturned 29 and affirmed only 3 since the reinstatement of capital punishment in the U.S. in 1976.

In the U.K. those favouring restoration of the death penalty found support for their cause in Home Office figures showing that 33 people had been convicted of a second homicide between 1973 and 1983, and that an estimated 4,000 to 5,000 convicted killers were at large in England and Wales in 1985. In Ireland the government announced its intention to abolish capital punishment.

Prisons. In many countries, including the U.S. and the U.K., the trend to severer sentencing led to greater prison overcrowding, often producing squalid physical conditions. Sharp rises in the number of juveniles in custody, despite the decline of this age group in the general population, caused particular concern, as did the growing practice reported from the U.S. of incarcerating "difficult" juveniles in hospital "secure units" at the expense of insurance companies and without court hearings. Fear of AIDS (acquired immune deficiency syndrome) added new terrors to life in prisons, where homosexual behaviour is common. When a homosexual prison chaplain died from AIDS in February at Chelmsford, England, movements in and out of prisons were restricted, known homosexual prisoners were threatened, and the Prison Department was blamed for employing the chaplain. Most Western countries also reported growing drug problems in prisons. Alcohol and heroin were said to be so readily available in British prisons that attempts at treatment were useless. Serious rioting in protest against prison conditions occurred in many countries. At Spike Island, Ireland, a new prison modeled on Alcatraz, inmates drove the staff and their families off the island and destroyed all the buildings. Prisoners at Belo Horizonte, Brazil, began the regular killing of inmates, chosen by lot, as a protest against conditions.

Unprecedented prison overcrowding, public pressure for more and longer prison sentences, and general opposition to increased public spending combined to present governments and prison authorities with a dilemma. One solution tried in the U.S. was "privatization." (*See* Sidebar.) More traditional penal reformers sought the solution in reduced prison numbers. The National Association for the Care and Resettlement of Offenders, London, demonstrated that, relative to populations, the U.S. imprisoned about twice as many people as the U.K., the U.K. twice as many as France, and France twice as many as Portugal. Reformers also urged reduction in the use of pretrial detention, which accounted for half the prison population in Italy and France. French Minister of Justice Robert Badinter announced his government's intention to restrict examining magistrates' power to remand in custody. Another attempt to reduce prison numbers was by the "tracking" of offenders set at liberty. In New Mexico surveillance was effected by nonremovable bracelets transmitting radio signals.

Notable prison escapades in 1985 included the escape of three men at Bogotá, Colombia, by dynamiting a hole in a prison wall. Convicts at a new maximum-security prison in Sydney, Australia, using sophisticated prison workshop equipment, forged $A20 notes, marriage certificates, drivers' licenses, and other documents for a year before being detected. In Surrey, England, two robbers escaped from custody in an ambush of the prison van transferring them between prisons. Bernard Welch, notorious for burglaries

and the killing of a prominent doctor in Washington, D.C., escaped with a fellow prisoner from the Metropolitan Correctional Center in Chicago, where he had been invited to advise the prison authorities on possible escape plans. A trusted prisoner at the San Jose (Calif.) prison succeeded in altering his release date by breaking the prison's computer code; he was foiled when the fellow inmate to whom he boasted of his exploit informed the authorities.

During the year many European countries, the U.S., and Canada signed the Council of Europe's Convention on the Transfer of Sentenced Prisoners, allowing prisoners to serve or complete sentences in their home countries. The convention did not extend to African, Arab, Asian, or South American countries. (C. R. M. DAVIES)

See also Law.

This article updates the *Macropædia* articles CRIME AND PUNISHMENT; POLICE.

Dance

North America. In a year dense with new productions and imports, the dance community in 1985 was beset with losses and changes that underscored the field's instability. In the U.S. three regional ballet companies (Los Angeles, Baltimore [Md.], and Connecticut) and American Ballet Theatre's second company (ABT II) were shut down. New York City lost critical rehearsal and teaching space (including the Harkness Center and Richard Thomas Studio) to real estate interests. On the positive side, new initiatives—among them the National Choreography Project, the National Performance Network, and the public television series "Alive from Off-Center"—addressed the need to bring innovative programming to audiences.

It was the year of the full-length story ballet, with rival first U.S. productions of John Cranko's *Romeo and Juliet* (Joffrey Ballet) and Sir Kenneth MacMillan's version of the same romantic tale at ABT; Ballet West's "20th-century world premiere" of August Bournonville's 1855 work, *Abdallah;* and the first regional productions of George Balanchine's *A Midsummer Night's Dream* (Pacific Northwest and San Francisco).

At ABT, director Mikhail Baryshnikov pursued his commitment to the new by commissioning David Gordon's first ballet, *Field, Chair, and Mountain.* Debate over the decline of the star system continued even as ballerina Cynthia Gregory (*see* BIOGRAPHIES) was given an old-fashioned gala commemorating her 20th year with the company. Alessandra Ferri was recruited from the Royal Ballet to dance with Baryshnikov, but knee surgery curtailed his appearances. In its 45th year, ABT drew fire for casting unripe dancers in major classical roles, giving short shrift to its Antony Tudor heritage—a revival of *Dim Lustre* was

roundly criticized—and dismantling its school and junior company.

At the New York City Ballet (NYCB), Darci Kistler, Kyra Nichols, and Suzanne Farrell stole the season—Kistler in an exultant return as Titania, Nichols for her moody reverie in Peter Martins's trio *Poulenc Sonata,* and Farrell for transcendent artistry in Jerome Robbins's elegiac *In Memory of . . .,* to Alban Berg's *Violin Concerto.* NYCB's major Balanchine revival, after 20 years, was *Gounod Symphony;* the novelty was Martins's charity ballet for Ethiopian famine relief, *We Are the World.* Helgi Tomasson's *Menuetto* entered the repertory, and Tomasson himself retired, dancing his ardent signature role in the *Divertimento* from *Le Baiser de la Fée.* Later, following Michael Smuin's stormy departure, Tomasson was appointed artistic director of the San Francisco Ballet.

Ballet West's artistic coup restoring Bournonville's charming, opulent *Abdallah* was tempered by the untimely death of Toni Lander (*see* OBITUARIES), who, with director Bruce Marks, had staged the reconstruction and whose impeccable coaching brought forth authentic results. Marks was appointed artistic director of the Boston Ballet; former Royal Ballet principal John Hart was named to succeed him at Ballet West.

Karel Shook (*see* OBITUARIES), cofounder/director of the Dance Theatre of Harlem, died following the company's successful debut at the Metropolitan Opera House featuring David Gordon's companionate *Piano Movers.* Frederic Franklin took over as acting director of the Cincinnati/New Orleans Ballet following the death in late 1984 of director David McLain.

The Joffrey Ballet's first repertory season at Lincoln Center included a respectful 80th birthday celebration for Sir Frederick Ashton and impassioned dancing by James Canfield and Patricia Miller as Romeo and Juliet (the two subsequently left Joffrey and joined a small company in Oregon).

The Pennsylvania Ballet produced Peter Martins's modernized *La Sylphide* and commissioned Merce Cunningham's spare *Arcade.* Eliot Feld's new ballets included three to Steve Reich scores exploring motion on inclined surfaces. Feld's company performed ballets by Paul Taylor dancer David Parsons and the first New York City production of Bronislava Nijinska's landmark *Les Noces.*

Other notable revivals included the Kansas City Ballet's staging of the Balanchine-Haieff *Divertimento* (last seen in 1952); George Verdak's versions of Balanchine's "lost" *Le Bal* and *Barabau* in Indianapolis, Ind.; Oakland (Calif.) Ballet's *Lynchtown* (Weidman); Louisville (Ky.) Ballet's *La Fête Étrange* (Andrée Howard) and Meredith Monk's *Quarry.*

Former Olympic figure skater John Curry's most recent ice dances proved him to be a true innovator in the field.

JACK MITCHELL

Ballet West revived August Bournonville's *Abdallah,* which had not been performed for 127 years, with the aid of original costume designs, musical score, and notations on choreography discovered in the Royal Library in Copenhagen.

David Gordon's *Field, Chair, and Mountain* at the American Ballet Theatre featured Martine van Hamel and Clark Tippet in the lead roles and had a set designed by Santo Loquasto.
MARTHA SWOPE

The American Ballroom Theater brought the essence of couples dancing to the concert stage, and new Pilobolus repertory veered toward dance theatre. On Broadway, Twyla Tharp directed and choreographed *Singin' in the Rain,* and Peter Martins choreographed *Song and Dance.* Baryshnikov and jazz tap virtuoso Gregory Hines won rave notices costarring in the Hollywood feature *White Nights.*

Alvin Ailey's company became the first modern dance troupe to visit China. Season highlights were his jazz dance tribute to Charlie Parker, *For Bird—With Love,* and Bill T. Jones and Arnie Zane's *How to Walk an Elephant,* a postmodern gloss on *Serenade.*

Merce Cunningham's emotionally resonant *Native Green* was among the year's masterworks. Paul Taylor celebrated his 30th anniversary with contrasting premieres—the romantic *Roses* (Richard Wagner) and the apocalyptic *Last Look* (Donald York/Alex Katz). Martha Graham unveiled *Song,* sensual and poetic, with Romanian folk music and spoken biblical text. Among numerous new works by David Gordon, *My Folks* and *Beethoven and Boothe* were outstanding. Mark Morris, the year's most sought-after choreographer, rekindled the spirit and audacity of early modern dance. Trisha Brown marked her 15th anniversary with *Lateral Pass,* a complex collaboration with composer Peter Zummo and artist Nancy Graves. Kenneth King's 20th anniversary concert was typically brain-teasing and mysterious. There was exciting new work from Karol Armitage ($-p=dH/dq$), Deborah Hay (a three-hour version of *Tasting the Blaze,* with composer Pauline Oliveros in Austin, Texas), and Dana Reitz (collaborating with light artist James Turrell on *Severe Clear* at Radcliffe College, Cambridge, Mass.). Los Angeles-based Rudy Perez helped the Dance Theater Workshop celebrate its 20th anniversary in his first New York appearance in a decade.

At the Brooklyn Academy of Music's (BAM's) third annual trend-setting Next Wave Festival, Nina Wiener collaborated with the Miami, Fla., architectural firm Arquitectonica and composer Richard Landry, and Laura Dean premiered works with commissioned scores by Steve Reich and Anthony Davis.

From abroad came an influx of dance of all kinds. The Grand Kabuki brought its largest touring ensemble to three U.S. cities. *Tango Argentino,* offering an intense exploration of the genre, had an extended Broadway run. Pina Bausch's neoexpressionist Tanztheater Wuppertal drew throngs of admirers and detractors in a second BAM engagement. The Festival of India brought assorted classical and folk artists. From West Berlin the Deutsche Oper Ballet's production of Roland Petit's *The Blue Angel,* starring Petit and Natalia Makarova, was disappointing. Gerhard Bohner's reconstruction of Oskar Schlemmer's Bauhaus *Triadic Ballet,* with its fantastic costumes, intrigued historians.

Merce Cunningham and Paul Taylor were the first choreographers to receive six-figure MacArthur Foundation fellowships. Cunningham was also a Kennedy Center honouree. Lincoln Kirstein and Martha Graham were among the first recipients of the Presidential National Medal of Arts. Other awards were the Astaire (to Jerome Robbins), American Film Institute Life Achievement (Gene Kelly), Capezio (Doris Hering), and Scripps (Alwin Nikolais). The second annual "Bessie" awards honoured 29 experimental artists and collaborators.

Deaths in the dance world included those of John Martin (*see* OBITUARIES), the influential first dance critic (1927–62) of the *New York Times;* dance benefactor Ben Sommers of the Capezio Foundation; "legomania" dancer Hal Le Roy; jazz/tap revivalist Leon Collins; Al Minns of the famous lindy team Minns and James; and ballet and Broadway dancer Harold Lang. In a tragic performance ac-

cident in Seattle, Wash., Yoshiuki Takada of the Japanese Butoh group Sankaijuku fell to his death.

Proving the Canada Council's contention that dance was the fastest-growing art in that country, the year was rife with new work, festivals, and tours. The major event was Montreal's first Festival International de Nouvelle Danse. Eight Canadian companies were joined by six from the U.S., Japan, Belgium, England, and West Germany. Merce Cunningham's pure movement pieces—not seen in Canada in two decades—contrasted with the prevailing trend toward dance theatre and expressive content.

Four rising choreographers contributed large-scale dramatic works. *Stella,* Jean-Pierre Perrealt's stark two-hour manifesto on women's regimentation, provoked controversy in Montreal. James Kudelka's *Dracula* for Les Grands Ballets Canadiens offered Margie Gillis a plum role. On tour, Edouard Lock's assaultive *Human Sex* (La La La Human Steps) combined punk rock, laser technology, and high-voltage scrimmages. Robert Desrosiers's surreal fantasy *Blue Snake* was a departure for the National Ballet of Canada (NBC). NBC director Erik Bruhn also commissioned contemporary work from David Earle, produced Constantin Patsalas's revised *Piano Concerto,* and took the company to Europe.

The peripatetic Royal Winnipeg Ballet premiered Sandra Neels's *The War Collection* and broke ground for a permanent home. Les Grands Ballets Canadiens, under new codirection of Jeanne Renaud and Linda Stearns, premiered a half-dozen works and performed at the Spoleto and Athens festivals. Les Ballets Jazz toured Africa and Central America, and a dozen smaller troupes made important debuts in the U.S. and Europe.

(SALI ANN KRIEGSMAN)

The Feld Ballet staged *Les Noces,* created by Bronislava Nijinska in 1923 and re-created for the Feld and the Pittsburgh Ballet by her daughter, Irina Nijinska. The elder Nijinska was enjoying a revival that inspired a traveling exhibit on her life and works.

Europe. Britain's Royal Ballet came under attack at the beginning of 1985 for apparent decline in standards of performance. Inadequate training and rehearsal were alleged, and there was criticism of a new company policy regarding design, which promoted the involvement of artists without dance or theatre experience. Choreographer Michael Corder set a precedent in wrestling a management concession that two of five scheduled performances of his work, *Number Three,* should be performed at Covent Garden with the dancers clad entirely in white rather than in the patterned tights that had been designed by New York artist Helen Frankenthaler. Royal Ballet director Norman Morrice, absent several months owing to illness, accepted blame for any shortcomings that might have been thought justified. Speculation about his and the company's future was allayed by an announcement that principal dancer Anthony Dowell would succeed Morrice as director as of the 1986–87 season. They would share responsibility during the 1985–86 season.

After a successful spring European tour (Budapest, Hung.; Dresden, East Germany; East Berlin; Barcelona, Spain; and Lisbon), the company returned much encouraged and in better shape. Its associated company, Sadler's Wells Royal Ballet, took Western classical ballet to Bombay, India, for the first time, on a tour that also included performances in New Zealand and South Korea. These travels illustrated an increasingly complex web of international touring. With no language barriers to hinder them, classical and modern-dance companies were regularly placed in the forefront of cultural exchange, especially between East and West. This trend was further exemplified during the year by the visit of the Bolshoi Ballet to West Germany and that of the Stuttgart Ballet to the Soviet Union, while the Leningrad Kirov Ballet appeared at the Athens Festival, and Britain's modern-dance troupe Ballet Rambert was welcomed in Poland.

Several European countries received visits from overseas companies: the National Ballet of Canada went to Luxembourg, West Germany, Switzerland, Italy, and The Netherlands; Les Grands Ballets Canadiens to Greece and Italy; the Ballets de Montreal and the Merce Cunningham company and several smaller U.S. groups to Britain and elsewhere; and the Martha Graham Dancers to Paris, where their celebrated founder, still creating new works at age 90-plus, received the French capital's highest civic award, the *Médaille de vermeil.*

The escalating costs of such intercontinental tours required increasing support from public funds, often involving the host country as well as the home base. Lack of financial support in some cases prevented other much-desired tours from taking place. However, Japan's well-established Matsuyama Ballet from Tokyo traveled to London to demonstrate—in association with Rudolf Nureyev as guest principal—how such Western classics as *Swan Lake* and *Giselle* could acquire an Oriental tinge while preserving their choreographic character.

Nureyev took time off from his continuing directorship of the Paris Opéra Ballet to make this and several other guest appearances abroad, prompting a certain concern about his absences from Paris. Reports nevertheless indicated that the leading French classical company was maintaining the high standards and reputation of recent years. The same could not be said about its experimental wing, the Groupe de Recherche Chorégraphique de l'Opéra de Paris, on the evidence of performances at the Edinburgh (Scotland) International Festival.

Maurice Béjart's innovative Ballet of the Twentieth Century, dividing seasons between its Brussels base and

Maria and Carlos Rivarola were among the 30 performers in *Tango Argentino,* an unusual and exciting program of tango music and dancing devised by Claudio Segovia and Héctor Orezzoli that was a popular and critical success in New York City.
BEATRIZ SCHILLER

Paris, chose the latter to premiere *Le Concours,* Béjart's much-acclaimed spoof of international ballet competitions. He took his company to Stuttgart to premiere *Operette,* in which Marcia Haydée, the Stuttgart Ballet's Brazilian-born ballerina-director, personified varied characters from street cleaner to revue star in a work described as Béjart's tribute to West Germany's equally innovative choreographer, Pina Bausch.

Bausch and her Wuppertaler Tanztheater continued their idiosyncratic modern-dance idiom with a new *Tanzabend II,* Bausch again melding dance and drama in her own highly original way. Instances multiplied in many European centres of choreographic styles that continuously crossed and even obliterated the traditional boundaries between classical and modern dance, theatrical drama and revue. The Frankfurt (West Germany) Opera Ballet's adventurous first season under the direction of U.S.-born William Forsythe culminated in ostentatious audience walkouts from his *LDC,* a work described as "a futuristic fairytale about the present" from which "every last vestige of classical dance vocabulary [had] disappeared."

John Neumeier, also from the U.S., renewed his contract to direct the Hamburg (West Germany) Ballet until 1996. Neumeier retained much classical technique while expanding its theatrical possibilities. His *Hamlet* for the Royal Danish Ballet, which reopened Copenhagen's Royal Theatre in November after a two-year renovation, followed his Hamburg productions of *Themes from Mozart and "As You Like It"* and a new *Othello,* reflecting a continuing use of Shakespeare as a source of inspiration for European

dance. *Othello* also served as a vehicle for Britain's Northern Ballet Theatre, and *A Midsummer Night's Dream* did so for the National Ballet of Finland. An adaptation of *Macbeth* as "total dance theatre" was mounted in Prague, Czech., and yet more and varied versions of *Romeo and Juliet* continued to proliferate on European stages.

Among the latter was the reconstruction after 40 years, for London Festival Ballet, of Sir Frederick Ashton's *Romeo and Juliet,* created originally for the Royal Danish Ballet and long thought to be lost. Danish-born Peter Schaufuss, giving new heart to the London company in his first season as director, restaged the ballet with the help of his father (who had danced the role of Mercutio, while his mother had been Ashton's first Juliet) and other diverse sources, including the 80-year-old Ashton himself, who aided in rehearsal and approved the final product. Never before given in London, the Ashton ballet showed a more lyrical than dramatic approach to storytelling, more dance than mime, more poetry than drama. Besides Schaufuss as Romeo, the work featured the 16-year-old U.S.-born Katherine Healy as a wonderfully assured Juliet, followed a few weeks later by the Spanish-born Trinidad Sevillano, performing her first Juliet on her 17th birthday.

Britain's leader of "postmodern" dance, Michael Clark, undertook his first major European tour with his small group and made new programs for festivals in Brussels and Edinburgh. His irreverent mix of sexual allusion, fashion design, and rock music with movement derived from classical technique was seen by critics as increasingly repetitious and lacking in any corresponding development in imagination. Natalia Makarova, after her stint in *On Your Toes* in London and New York City, returned to classical ballet, including a debut as Tatiana in the London Festival Ballet production of John Cranko's *Onegin.* She also appeared in Roland Petit's *The Blue Angel,* premiered by the Deutsche Oper Ballet in West Berlin and taken later to New York City.

Makarova appeared as *commère* (French: godparent) for the first Modern-Dance Gala, with the Royal Opera House, Covent Garden, as host, given to benefit the London School of Contemporary Dance. Visitors ranged from a New York City break-dance company to former Paris revue star Zizi Jeanmaire, returning to the stage she had first trod 38 years before. The program ended with the London Contemporary Dance Theatre's demonstration work, *Class,* by its founder-director, Robert Cohan. Cohan's major creation for the year, in association with composer Geoffrey Burgon, was *A Mass for Man,* commissioned by BBC Television.

Among the year's directorial changes, Frank Andersen took charge of the Royal Danish Ballet (of which he had been a longtime member), Uwe Scholz went to Zürich, Switz.; Youry Vamos went to Dortmund, West Germany; and Vassily Vassiliev was named to succeed Rosella Hightower at La Scala, Milan, Italy, in 1986. Another Soviet dancer, Maris Liepa, went to the Bulgarian State Ballet, Sofia.

Among the deaths that occurred during the year were those of Stanley Judson, first leading male dancer of the embryonic Royal Ballet in the 1930s; Kathleen Gordon, educator and former director of Britain's Royal Academy of Dancing; Lisa Ullmann, educator and proponent of the expressionistic techniques of Laban, Jooss, and Leeder; and Barry Kay, Australian-born artist and designer.

(NOËL GOODWIN)

See also Music; Theatre.
This article updates the *Macropædia* article The History of Western DANCE.

Disasters

The loss of life and property from disasters in 1985 included the following:

Aviation

January 1, Near La Paz, Bolivia. A Boeing 727 jetliner slammed into the snow-covered Illimani Mountain while trying to make its descent to the La Paz airport; all 29 persons aboard were killed.

January 18, Jinan (Chi-nan), China. A twin-engine turboprop Antonov-24 crashed while attempting to land at Jinan airport; 38 persons aboard were killed in the crash.

January 19, Near San José de las Lajas, Cuba. A Cuban jetliner that was apparently experiencing engine trouble crashed shortly after takeoff; all 40 persons aboard were killed.

January 21, Reno, Nev. A four-engine Lockheed Electra charter airliner carrying 71 persons crashed moments after takeoff from Reno; the craft was returning to Minneapolis after a gambling junket. Three persons survived the crash.

January 22, Off the coast of Honduras. A U.S. C-130A military transport plane carrying 21 U.S. soldiers crashed into the sea near Trujillo, the intended destination; all aboard were presumed drowned.

January 23, Between Neiva and Cali, Colombia. An airplane owned by Aires Co. was reported missing in a remote mountain area; all 17 persons aboard were feared dead.

January 23, Northwest Colombia. A Twin Otter plane crashed in a remote mountain area some 95 km (60 mi) west of Medellín; all 23 persons aboard perished in the crash.

February 1, Near Minsk, U.S.S.R. A Soviet TU-134 crashed shortly after takeoff; though no official casualty figures were released, the 80 to 90 passengers believed aboard were presumed dead.

February 19, Near Durango, Spain. A Spanish jetliner crashed into a mountain after striking a television relay tower some 29 km (18 mi) from the airport in Bilbao; all 148 persons aboard were killed.

February 22, Near Timbuktu, Mali. An Air Mali AN-24 turboprop passenger plane crashed and exploded over the Sahara shortly after takeoff; 50 of 51 persons aboard were killed, and the lone survivor was in critical condition.

March 13, Ft. Bragg, North Carolina. A U.S. Army helicopter nose-dived and crashed in the woods while flying in formation on a routine training mission; all 12 soldiers aboard were killed in the fiery crash.

March 28, Near San Vicente de Caguán, Colombia. A twin-engine turboprop commercial airliner slammed into a fog-shrouded mountain; all 40 persons aboard were killed.

March 29, Near Edmonton, Alta. Two C-130 Hercules transport planes collided in midair during a ceremonial flight over a military base; ten persons died in the crash.

April 4, Balikesir, Turkey. A Turkish F-104 Starfighter caught fire on a routine flight and crashed into a coffeehouse; 14 persons were killed, including one of the two pilots, and 21 others were injured.

April 9, Rampura Maphi, Uttar Pradesh, India. An Indian Air Force MiG jet fighter plane crashed into a village and killed 15 villagers; the pilot, who was on a routine training flight, ejected from the cockpit.

April 26, Vrelo, Yugos. A Yugoslav Air Force plane crashed into three houses while making a routine training flight; nine villagers and the pilot were killed.

May 3, Lvov, U.S.S.R. A Soviet airliner and a small military plane collided and crashed while approaching Lvov airport; 80 persons were reported dead.

May 6, Off the coast of Yakushima, Japan. A U.S. military heavy-duty, twin-engine helicopter fell into the ocean after experiencing engine trouble on a routine flight; all 17 marines aboard were killed.

June 23, Near Diamintino, Brazil. A twin-engine turboprop airplane carrying 13 persons exploded while trying to make an emergency landing; all aboard were killed.

June 23, Off the coast of Ireland. An Air-India Boeing 747 carrying 329 persons dived into the ocean, apparently after a bomb exploded aboard the aircraft; the crash, which claimed the lives of all aboard, was the worst disaster at sea in aviation history and the third worst aviation disaster to date.

July 10, U.S.S.R. A plane believed to have been carrying some 150 persons crashed between Karshi and Leningrad; all aboard perished.

July 24, Near Leticia, Colombia. A Colombian Air Force DC-6 carrying 79 persons crashed in the jungle; there were no signs of life near the wreckage.

August 2, Dallas-Fort Worth, Texas. A Delta Air Lines jumbo jet attempting to land at Dallas-Fort Worth Airport suddenly nosedived and struck several cars on Highway 114 (decapitating one driver) before crash landing, breaking in half, and bursting into flames; 135 of the 162 persons aboard perished. Experts believed that wind shear, a sudden shift in wind direction and velocity, was responsible for the crash.

August 12, Gumma Prefecture, Japan. A Boeing 747SR Japan Air Lines jumbo jet, carrying 524 persons, crashed into Mt. Osutaka after the pilot reported that the right rear cabin door had broken and that he had lost control of the airliner; there were only 4 survivors in the worst single-plane disaster in aviation history.

August 22, Manchester, England. A Boeing 737 jetliner, carrying 137 persons, burst into flames after an engine caught fire and exploded; 54 persons were killed in the inferno.

September 6, Milwaukee, Wis. A twin-engine DC-9 jetliner crashed and burned moments after takeoff; all 31 persons aboard perished.

September 23, Weyers Cave, Virginia. A twin-engine commuter airplane carrying 14 persons slammed into the side of a mountain enveloped with clouds; all aboard perished.

September 29, Jenkinsburg, Ga. A single-engine plane carrying a pilot and 16 skydivers who were preparing to jump in formation nose-dived onto a rural road shortly after takeoff; the crash killed all aboard.

October 15, Off the coast of North Carolina. A CH-46D helicopter carrying 19 marines on maneuvers crashed into Onslow Bay off the coast of Jacksonville, N.C.; there were 4 survivors.

December 12, Gander, Newfoundland. A DC-8 jetliner carrying 248 U.S. soldiers and 8 crew members crashed and exploded moments after taking off from a refueling stop; all aboard perished.

December 31, Nelson Island, Antarctica. A twin-engine plane, carrying eight U.S. sightseers who were preparing to spend the New Year's holiday in Antarctica, crashed and killed all aboard including the pilot and copilot.

Fires and Explosions

January 9, Grandvilliers, France. A fire erupted at an old people's home after severe cold caused water pipes to burst, thus causing electrical wiring to short-circuit; 24 residents died in the blaze.

February 13, Manila, Phil. An eight-hour raging fire at the luxurious Regent of Manila Hotel claimed the lives of 27 persons.

March 6, Ceara, Brazil. The explosion of a steam boiler in a cashew nut plant resulted in the deaths of 12 persons; 40 others were injured.

April 12, Madrid, Spain. A bomb exploded in a restaurant housed in a three-story building, killing 24 persons and injuring 82 others; the blast, which caused the entire structure to collapse, was believed to be the work of Basque separatist guerrillas.

April 18, Harbin, China. A fire, which swept

An aerial view shows battered and derailed passenger cars after a collision between two trains in central Portugal on September 11.

through the top stories of a newly built hotel, claimed the lives of ten persons and injured seven others.

April 21, Tabaco, Phil. A fire in a theatre complex on the second floor of a three-story building claimed the lives of 44 persons, most of them teenagers who were trampled to death when the audience panicked and rushed to the exits; 53 others were also injured, 20 of them seriously.

April 26, Saavedra, Arg. A three-hour blaze confined to the top two floors of a six-story mental hospital claimed the lives of at least 78 persons and injured 150 others.

May 11, Bradford, England. A flash fire in four minutes incinerated a 79-year-old wooden grandstand packed with some 3,500 soccer fans; 56 persons were killed, and 44 persons were in need of plastic surgery following the blaze.

May 20, Beaver Township, Ohio. An explosion in a shed housing illegal fireworks claimed the lives of nine persons and left two huge craters in the ground.

June 25, Hallett, Okla. Three major explosions leveled a legal fireworks factory; 21 persons were killed in the blast.

June 27, Chongqing (Chungking), China. An explosion in a 396-m (1,300-ft) sewage pipe claimed the lives of at least 24 persons and injured 92 others on a crowded street; 80 homes were destroyed and 130 others were damaged by the blast.

August 3, Chandernagore, India. An explosion at a fireworks factory claimed the lives of 18 persons and injured 4 others.

September 8, Lamego, Port. A raging forest fire claimed the lives of 14 volunteer firemen who were overcome by smoke and burned to death.

October 13, Lala, Phil. A hand grenade exploded at a cock-fighting arena; ten persons lost their lives.

December 16, Glenwood Springs, Colo. A two-story gas company building was razed when a propane tank was accidentally ignited by a welding torch; 12 persons were killed and 15 others were injured.

Marine

January 12, Northeastern Peru. The 55-ton *Rosita* sank in the Amazon River some three hours after leaving Iquitos; 50 persons were missing and feared dead.

February 8, North Sea. A Polish freighter carrying a cargo of steel rolled over and sank minutes after the load shifted during a storm; only one of the 25 crewmen aboard was rescued.

February 12, Indian Ocean. A luxury cruise ship was damaged by a fire presumably caused by a short circuit in an air-conditioning duct; 34 persons perished in the blaze.

March 23, Near Dhaka, Bangladesh. An overcrowded ferry capsized in the Buri Ganga River apparently after colliding with dredging machinery during a storm; at least 100 passengers were feared dead.

March 28, Off the coast of Guandong (Kwangtung) Province, China. A ferry carrying 228 persons capsized apparently after being buffeted by heavy winds; 77 persons lost their lives.

April 9, Saran district, Bihar, India. A boat capsized on the Ganges River, and 75 persons were feared drowned.

April 24, Near Huancayo, Peru. A ferry sank in the Mantaro River, and 20 persons were feared drowned.

May 5, Sichuan (Szechwan) Province, China. A boat slammed into a rock in the Jinsha (Chinsha) River, and 54 persons drowned.

May 20, Near Morgan City, La. An oil rig, under tow to a new location, capsized in calm waters for no apparent reason; 11 of the 22 persons aboard were killed.

May 26, Off Algeciras, Spain. Two explosions ripped through two tankers moored next to each other, killing 33 seamen; the first blast occurred aboard the *Petragen-One,* which was unloading a cargo of highly flammable naphtha, and the second explosion rocked the Spanish tanker *Camponavia,* which was taking on fuel

at a refinery located across from the Rock of Gibraltar.

May 26, Near Morena, India. An overcrowded boat carrying 90 passengers capsized in the middle of the Chambal River; 74 persons drowned.

Early June, Atlantic Ocean. An overloaded boat traveling from Ivory Coast to Ghana capsized and sank; 40 of the 75 persons aboard drowned.

Mid-August, Off the coast of The Bahamas. A rickety fishing boat loaded with Haitian refugees was found beached on a barren Bahamian island; seven refugees reported that smugglers had tossed at least 100 Haitians overboard, and they were feared drowned.

August 18, Near Harbin, China. An overcrowded ferry capsized after passengers ran to one side of the vessel to witness a brawl by two drunken riverboat pilots; 174 persons were feared drowned.

September 10, Bay of Bengal. Some 100 Bangladeshi crewmen were feared drowned after Thai fishermen threw them overboard and confiscated their catch, which presumably was going to be shared by the two nations.

October 5, Karnaphuli River, Bangladesh. A ferry carrying 200 persons split in half and sank after colliding with a fishing trawler; 100 persons were feared dead, trapped inside the boat's hull or swept away by the strong current.

October 17, Near Pointe-à-Pierre, Trinidad. An explosion aboard a barge that was commissioned to repair a broken oil main on the seabed in the Gulf of Paria occurred when oil fumes escaped and ignited; ten men were known dead, and four others were missing and presumed dead.

December 14, Off the coast of Ciudad del Carmen, Mexico. A ship that serviced offshore oil rigs sank in the wind-whipped Gulf of Mexico; 32 of the 71 persons aboard were missing and feared dead.

December 17, South China Sea. A boat carrying some 80 Vietnamese refugees was attacked by pirates; 50 refugees were slain and 10 women were raped.

December 18, Off the coast of Mindoro Island, Philippines. A ferry transporting some 200 persons between Palawan Island and Manila sank in the shark-infested China Sea; only 85 persons were rescued.

Mining

February 25, Forbach, France. An explosion, possibly caused by firedamp, a combustible gas given off by coal, blasted through an underground coal mine; 22 miners were killed in the explosion, and 103 others were either injured or overcome by fumes.

April 24, Off the coast of Nagasaki, Japan. An explosion in a coal mine on a small island killed 11 of the 501 workers in the mine at the time of the blast.

May 17, Hokkaido, Japan. An explosion in a coal mine, probably triggered by methane gas, killed 36 miners and injured 22 others, 7 of them seriously.

July 12, Guangdong (Kwangtung) Province, China. An explosion in a coal mine, possibly triggered by a gas leak, killed at least 47 miners; 8 others were missing and presumed dead in the blast, which blocked a tunnel entrance with some 2,000 tons of coal.

Late October, Diat and Diwata, Phil. Landslides at two gold mines buried some 300 to 400 prospectors; at least 150 miners and their families were missing and feared dead.

Miscellaneous

February 7, Castellaneta, Italy. A six-story apartment building housing some 70 persons collapsed after extensive water seepage weakened the foundation; 34 persons were found dead in the rubble, and 8 others were injured.

Late March-Early April, Somalia. A cholera epidemic, first detected at the Gannet refugee camp in northwestern Somalia, claimed the lives of more than 1,500 persons.

May 9, Uster, Switz. The roof of a public swimming pool collapsed, killing 13 persons and injuring 5 others; there was no apparent reason why the ten-year-old structure caved in.

May 26, St.-Cyr-sur-Mer, France. A 27-m (90-ft) concrete wall collapsed onto a crowded Mediterranean seaside campsite while most of the campers were sleeping; the structure's foundation apparently eroded away after heavy rains, and 11 persons were killed and 6 others were seriously injured in the crush.

May 26, Mexico City, Mexico. An unruly mob of soccer fans tried to force their way into a Mexican soccer championship, and ten persons were trampled to death in the stampede.

May 29, Brussels, Belgium. A group of drunken British soccer fans supporting the Liverpool team initiated a brawl with rival Italian fans supporting Juventus before the start of the European Champions' Cup soccer final; as the British fans attacked spectators, a concrete retaining wall collapsed and 39 persons were killed, 32 of them Italians.

Mid-June, California and Texas. An outbreak of listeria monocytogenes, linked to a Mexican-style cheese manufactured by Jalisco Mexican Products, claimed the lives of 62 persons, including at least 20 infants, some of whom were stillborn.

July 19, Stava, Italy. An earthen dam collapsed and sent a wall of mud and water cascading into an Alpine valley resort; some 250 persons died as three hotels were totally destroyed, a fourth was partially demolished, and some two dozen homes were leveled.

Late July, Dipayal Panchayat, Nepal. An outbreak of gastroenteritis claimed the lives of 13 children.

August 13, Bombay, India. An overcrowded

Only a burned-out hulk remained after the engine of a British charter jet caught fire and ignited the plane's fuel tanks during takeoff at Manchester on August 22.

three-story building in a slum collapsed during heavy monsoon rains; 52 persons were killed and 56 others were injured.

September, London, Ont. A deadly outbreak of *E. coli* bacteria at an Extendicare nursing home claimed the lives of at least 15 elderly residents during the month and affected 69 others.

October 15, Dhaka, Bangladesh. Heavy rains generated by a fierce storm in the Bay of Bengal caused the roof of the Dhaka University assembly hall to cave in on hundreds of students viewing a popular television soap opera; 71 persons were known dead and 300 others were injured.

Natural

January, Shaanxi (Shensi) Province, China. Two months of heavy rain precipitated thunderous landslides that buried entire villages; some 60 persons were killed.

January, Southern Brazil. Monthlong rains caused extensive flooding that claimed the lives of at least 71 persons and left thousands of others homeless.

Early January, Western Europe. A ten-day Arctic weather blast gripped France, Spain, Italy, and Portugal; some 200 deaths were attributed to the extreme cold.

January 5, Eastern Algeria. Relentless storms caused severe flooding that left 3,000 families homeless, blocked roads, and damaged power lines; 26 persons were known dead.

January 6, Rangpur, Bangladesh. A cold wave claimed the lives of 17 persons.

January 15, Near Vitória, Brazil. Torrential rains triggered a predawn rockslide that obliterated shacks in a hillside shantytown; at least 26 persons were killed.

January 22, Viti Levu, Fiji. Cyclones Eric and Nigel inflicted serious damage to crops, housing, communications, and transport; 23 persons were killed.

Late January, U.S. A nationwide cold wave set record low temperatures in the East and Southeast, severely damaged Florida citrus crops, and was blamed for at least 128 deaths.

January 30–February 2, U.S. A widespread storm system that set record low temperatures from Michigan to Texas and dumped snow from the Southwest to New England was blamed for the deaths of 24 persons.

February 14, Czechoslovakia. A series of avalanches in the High Tatra mountain range killed ten persons.

February 16, Omi, Japan. Melting snow precipitated a landslide that destroyed several homes and buried ten persons.

February 17, Eastern Peru. Heavy rain triggered a mud slide, killing at least 13 persons.

February 21, Lombok and Java, Indonesia. Monsoon rains triggered a landslide on Lombok that killed at least 11 persons, and severe flooding in central and eastern Java was blamed for the deaths of 10 persons.

March 3, Chile. A powerful earthquake that measured 7.8 on the Richter scale at its epicentre near the village of Algarrobo shook an area stretching more than 1,600 km (1,000 mi) along the country's mountainous coast both north and south of Santiago; at least 177 persons were known dead, 2,000 others were injured, and some 150,000 persons were left homeless in the wake of the quake, which damaged some 60,000 buildings and knocked out communications.

March 3, Switzerland. A thundering avalanche claimed the lives of 11 persons in the Alps, just north of the Italian border.

March 3, Zimbabwe. A violent electrical storm produced bolts of lightning that struck and killed 15 persons.

Late March, Bangladesh. Early season monsoon storms flattened villages in northwestern and western Bangladesh with gigantic hailstones that took hours to melt; 750 persons succumbed and some 10,000 others were left homeless.

Mid-April, Northeastern Brazil. Heavy rainstorms precipitated severe flooding that drove some one million people from their homes; torrents of muddy river water swirled through 181 municipalities and claimed 27 lives.

Gander, Newfoundland, was the site of a crash that killed 248 U.S. servicemen on their way home for Christmas from peacekeeping duty in the Sinai Peninsula.

STEVE LISS—GAMMA/LIAISON

April 18, Yunnan Province, China. An earthquake measuring 6.3 on the Richter scale killed at least 22 persons and injured 300 others; the temblor also destroyed many homes and schools.

May 25, Bay of Bengal, Bangladesh. A devastating cyclone accompanied by 3–5-m (10–15-ft) tidal waves struck a cluster of islands at the mouth of the Ganges River, including Sandwip Island, North Hatia Island, South Hatia Island, Maiskhal Island, Bhola Char, Urrir Char, Char Clark, and Kutubdia Island; the storm's high winds reportedly swept thousands of people out to sea. Though the official death toll was placed at 2,540, some feared that as many as 11,000 people had perished.

May 30–31, Buenos Aires, Arg. A record 29 cm (11.4 in) of rain inundated the city; at least 14 persons were killed (some were struck by lightning, some drowned, and others were electrocuted when power lines fell on flooded streets), and more than 90,000 others were forced from their homes.

May 31, Pennsylvania, Ohio, New York, Ontario. A 483-km (300-mi) frontal system spawned a pack of killer tornadoes that left a swath of death and destruction; at least 88 persons were known dead, hundreds were injured, and whole towns were virtually wiped out by the roaring twisters. Hardest hit were such Pennsylvania towns as Albion, Atlantic, Cherry Tree, Wheatland, and Beaver Falls.

Early June, Bihar, India. A scorching heat wave claimed the lives of 40 persons, most of them children.

June 6, Guangxi (Kwangsi) and Hunan provinces, China. Heavy rains sparked severe flooding that killed 64 persons and left thousands of others stranded.

June 16, Peru. A massive landslide near the Ucayali River in the Hoyada region killed scores of people.

Late June, Western India. Four days of monsoon storms battered the country, triggering landslides and heavy flooding; at least 46 persons were known dead, 50 others were injured, and 25,000 people were left homeless.

Late June, Northern Philippines. Monsoon rains precipitated three days of flooding that left at least 65 persons dead and more than 100,000 others homeless.

July 1, Japan. Destructive Typhoon Irma struck Numazu City before passing through

Tokyo and caused widespread damage; 19 persons were known dead.

Mid-July, Punjab, India. Rising monsoon floodwaters claimed the lives of 87 persons and submerged at least 20 villages.

July 30, Zhejiang (Chekiang) Province, China. A deadly typhoon struck the country's eastern coast; 177 persons were known dead and at least 1,400 others were injured.

Late July–Early August, Near Dandong (Tantung), China. Two weeks of torrential rains caused raging floodwaters to slam through dikes along the China-North Korea border and the Yalu River to overflow its banks; two villages were swept away in the flood; 64 persons lost their lives, and thousands of others were left homeless.

Early August, China. Savage hailstorms, torrential rains, typhoons, and rampaging floodwaters killed more than 500 persons and left 14,000 others homeless.

August 2, Cheyenne, Wyo. A brutal thunderstorm, accompanied by damaging winds and hail, in less than four hours dumped 15 cm (6 in) of rain and precipitated heavy flooding; 12 persons were known dead and 70 others suffered minor injuries.

August 6–7, Western Europe. Raging storms battered Europe from the French Mediterranean coast to Denmark with heavy rain, high winds, snow, and funnel clouds; 23 deaths were attributed to the storm.

August 23, Western China. A major earthquake measuring 7.4 on the Richter scale struck the sparsely settled agricultural Xinjiang Uygur (Sinkiang Uighur) autonomous region; 63 deaths were reported and about 16,000 people were left homeless.

August 30, Kyushu, Japan. Deadly Typhoon Pat, packing winds of up to 200 km/h (124 mph), claimed 15 lives; 11 others, mostly fishermen, were still missing.

September 19–20, Mexico City. Twin earthquakes, the first measuring 8.1 on the Richter scale and the second, the following day, measuring 7.5, reduced much of the city to rubble; more than 20,000 persons were killed, at least 40,000 were injured, and 31,000 others were left homeless.

September 30, Minas Gerais, Brazil. A freak hailstorm caused houses to collapse under the weight of hailstones and left a thick layer of ice on roads; 22 persons died in the storm.

A jumble of stones in a churchyard in Santiago, Chile, bears witness to the powerful earthquake that shook that nation on March 3.

CARRION—SYGMA

October 7, Ponce, P.R. A two-day tropical deluge triggered a massive mud-and-rock slide that buried some 150 persons in their tin and wood shacks built on the hillside in the shantytown of Mameyes.

October 13, Tadzhik S.S.R. A powerful earthquake, measuring 6.1 on the Richter scale, devastated a factory employing 5,600 persons in Kayrakkum; 29 persons were killed, more than 80 were injured, and some 8,000 were left homeless.

Mid-October, Thailand. Two typhoons triggered flash floods that killed 16 persons.

October 16–17, Bangladesh. Successive typhoons killed 12 persons in a two-day period.

October 18–19, India. Severe flooding, precipitated by raging storms, claimed the lives of 78 persons.

October 19, Luzon, Phil. Devastating Typhoon Dot battered the island and virtually demolished the capital city of Cabanatuan, destroying 90% of the buildings and causing an estimated $5.3 million in damages; 63 persons were known dead.

October 21, Monkayo, Phil. A landslide, precipitated by a week of heavy rains, unleashed an avalanche of mud on a gold mine and mining town huts; at least 30 persons were killed, 20 others were missing, and 30 were injured.

Late October, Louisiana. Tropical Storm Juan caused four days of flooding, $1 billion in damages, and at least seven deaths; eight other persons were missing and feared dead.

Early November, West Virginia, Virginia, Maryland, and Pennsylvania. A staggering 50 cm (20 in) of rainfall in a 12-hour period caused swollen rivers to overflow their banks, thereby destroying thousands of homes and killing at least 49 persons; property damage in the Virginias alone was estimated at half a billion dollars.

November 13, Armero, Colombia. The long-dormant snowcapped volcano known as Nevado del Ruiz came to life with a double eruption that melted the mountain's icecap and sent a liquid avalanche (lahar) of dirty water, gray ash, and mud cascading down its slopes, thereby burying the sleeping town of Armero; thousands were injured, 60,000 persons were left homeless, and more than 25,000 people were feared dead in one of the ten worst volcanic disasters in history.

Mid-November, Northwestern U.S. A winter snowstorm was blamed for the deaths of at least 33 persons.

November 19–21, Cuba and Florida. Hurricane Kate pounded the northern coast of Cuba,

the Florida Keys, and northern Florida with high winds and heavy rain; at least 24 persons were killed in the hurricane, which was believed to have been the most powerful November storm in U.S. history.

Early December, Midwestern U.S. An early winter snowstorm pummeled Michigan, South Dakota, Iowa, Minnesota, and Wisconsin with heavy snow and high winds that created blizzardlike conditions; 19 deaths were attributed to the storm.

Late December, Northwestern Saudi Arabia. Heavy rains precipitated severe flooding that killed at least 32 persons in the areas of Tabuk, Abu Raka, Zeba, and al-Wajh; another 31 persons were missing and feared dead.

Railroads

January 13, Near Awash, Eth. A five-car passenger train derailed while traveling over a bridge and plunged into a ravine apparently because the engineer, who was later arrested, had failed to slow the train as it rounded a curve; 392 persons were known dead and nearly 400 others were injured.

January 13, Bangladesh. A fire that started on the Samanta Express shortly after the train left the Puradaha station burned for more than an hour before the train stopped; at least 27 persons were killed.

January 19, Near Kilinochchi, Sri Lanka. A train was blown up presumably by Tamil separatist rebels; 33 persons were killed and 44 others were injured in the blast, which ripped through 11 cars.

February 19, Near Sabuk, South Korea. A coal train derailed and rammed into a village; 13 persons were killed and 14 others were injured.

February 23, Near Raipur, India. A predawn fire aboard a packed passenger train claimed the lives of 50 persons, including a honeymoon couple and 18 members of their wedding party.

March 11, Near Rio de Janeiro, Brazil. Two passenger trains collided head-on when railroad signals malfunctioned; 10 persons were killed and at least 87 others were injured in the crash.

April 5, Uttar Pradesh state, India. A number of people who were riding free on top of the coaches of two trains were swept off as the trains passed under scaffolding on a Ganges River bridge; 35 persons were killed and 20 others were listed in serious condition.

April 19, Near Mexico City, Mexico. Two passenger trains collided; 18 persons were killed and 80 others were injured.

June 11, Near Haifa, Israel. An express passenger train slammed into a school bus at an

unguarded railroad crossing; 21 persons were killed, including 17 children.

June 13, Agra, India. A passenger train and a freight train collided head-on near the Taj Mahal; 37 persons died in the crash.

June 17, Isna, Egypt. A passenger train and a freight train collided head-on, and 10 of the 13 cars of the passenger train erupted in flames; 30 persons were killed in the crash.

July 24, Kywebwe, Burma. A passenger train derailed when rebels set off a land mine under the tracks; 67 persons were known dead and 112 others were injured.

August 3, Flaujac-Gare, France. A four-car passenger train and a local two-car "autorail" collided head-on apparently after the station-master gave the go-ahead for both trains to move toward each other on the same track; 35 passengers were killed and 165 others were injured in the crash.

August 31, Near Argenton-sur-Creuse, France. A speeding passenger train, traveling in a repair zone at nearly three times the speed limit, derailed and then collided with a mail train traveling in the opposite direction; 49 persons were killed and nearly 100 others were injured.

September 11, Near Viseu, Port. An express train bound for France slammed into a local passenger train after both trains apparently were directed to use the same track; more than 100 persons perished in the blazing wreckage.

October 2, Bahr al-Ghazal, The Sudan. A train carrying famine relief supplies derailed, killing 129 persons; the accident was attributed to poor maintenance of tracks.

Traffic

January 26, Near Harare, Zimbabwe. A bus was pushed off a low-level bridge by swirling floodwaters from the swollen Mukwadzi River; 18 persons were known dead, and 10 others were missing and feared dead.

January 28, Nagano, Japan. A bus carrying a party of skiers plunged into an icy reservoir; 25 persons were killed, and 8 of the 20 others who were rescued were injured.

March 27, Near Johannesburg, South Africa. A double-decker school bus ran out of control presumably after a tire blowout, crashed through a fence, and plunged into the Westdene Dam reservoir; 39 high school students drowned and 28 others were injured, 5 of them critically.

July 1, Near Accra, Ghana. A bus carrying members of Ghana's Cocoa Marketing Board collided with a seven-ton truck while returning from a meeting in Breman Asikua; 21 persons died in the crash.

September 1, Northern Pakistan. A speeding bus carrying 76 persons went out of control and plummeted into a mountain ravine in the remote Malakand region; 40 persons were killed and the others aboard were injured.

September 5, Near Adana, Turkey. A minibus plunged 90 m (300 ft) down a cliff and killed 16 of the 17 passengers aboard.

September 14, Ekumfi-Ekotsi, Ghana. A bus slammed into the retinue of a newly installed junior chief as they danced across a road; 26 persons including the chief were killed.

September 28, Uttar Pradesh, India. A bus carrying Hindu pilgrims to the Badrinath temple swerved off of a sharp bend on a mountain road and plunged into a gorge; 27 persons were killed and 22 others were injured.

October 21, Near Lancaster, England. An 11-vehicle collision claimed the lives of 13 persons and injured 36 others; the accident was Britain's worst highway disaster to date.

November 1, Tadola, India. A fuel truck exploded after the driver stopped to inspect a leaky cargo tank, and 25 persons were killed and 70 others injured; the accident apparently occurred after someone in a crowd of villagers dropped a lighted cigarette that ignited the gasoline.

November 21, Java, Indonesia. A truck carrying construction workers swerved to avoid a motorcycle, fell off a bridge, and plunged into a river in the southeastern district of Kepanjeng; 45 persons were killed and 13 others were injured.

Earth Sciences

GEOLOGY AND GEOCHEMISTRY

In 1985 the Deep Sea Drilling Project and its research drilling ship *Glomar Challenger* were succeeded by the Ocean Drilling Program (ODP) and a new vessel, the *JOIDES Resolution*. Leg 100, the first cruise of the ODP, tested the drilling systems and the scientific laboratories on board. Results from Leg 101, in the Bahama archipelago, favoured the theory that isolated areas like The Bahamas are remnants of a vast carbonate platform, extending from Mexico to the eastern U.S., that was disrupted in the mid-Cretaceous Period (about 100 million years ago) over the theory that the topography formed much earlier when the African and North American continents were rifted apart 160 million years ago.

The recently proposed idea that clay minerals might serve as templates capable of self-replication and that these inorganic protoorganisms were the forerunners of later biomolecules, the primitive genes, found support in the discovery that clay has the ability to absorb, store, and transfer energy, which would be necessary for chemical reactions involving organic life. Energy storage in clays, perhaps achieved by capturing photons of light in lattice defects, was revealed by the slow emission of ultraviolet light when the clays were wetted, fractured, or irradiated.

The hypothesis that an event triggered by the collision of some astronomical body with the Earth caused the extinction of many life forms at the Cretaceous-Tertiary boundary, 65 million years ago, gained strength and supporters. Remarkable new evidence was reported in 1985 by Edward Anders and colleagues of the University of Chicago. They discovered concentrations of sooty carbon in the sediment layer corresponding to the time of impact that were 10,000 times higher than in sediments above and below. They concluded that the carbon came from global firestorms ignited by the fireball spreading out from the impact site.

The idea that an earlier, larger impact on the Earth might

The *JOIDES Resolution* made its first working cruise in 1985. The vessel featured a six-story laboratory area and a drilling derrick 60 metres (200 feet) high. It could drill in water up to 8,200 metres (27,000 feet) in depth.

have formed the Moon was discussed at the 16th Lunar and Planetary Science Conference in 1985. According to the new impact-trigger hypothesis, a giant object perhaps as large as Mars smashed obliquely into the Earth near the end of its accretion period, after the core had formed and while the mantle was at least partly molten. The impact caused ejection of material from both the Earth and the other body, which subsequently aggregated in orbit around the Earth to form the Moon. Geochemists agreed that the mantles of the Earth and Moon have similar compositions and that most of the geochemical differences between the two are understandable in terms of the large-impact hypothesis. Dynamic and thermal modeling of the processes of impact, ejection, and aggregation supported the hypothesis, while dynamicists mounted strong arguments against the three classical hypotheses for origin of the Moon; *i.e.,* that it was a part of the Earth ripped away by tidal forces, that it was an independent body captured by the Earth's gravity, or that it formed in orbit around the Earth at the time of the origin of the solar system.

The large-impact origin requires a totally molten Moon to begin with, an idea consistent with the concept of a magma ocean that had been formulated to explain the origin of lunar rocks. The geochemical approaches, however, had not yet resolved the question of whether the magma ocean was confined to the outer several hundred kilometres or whether the Moon had been totally molten. In fact, some petrologists were abandoning the concept of a magma ocean in favour of a solid Moon, a position that appeared difficult to defend against the results of dynamic and thermal modeling.

The concept of a magma ocean was carried from the Moon to the Earth with a proposition that, if the density of magma at depth were higher than that of mantle rock, a layer of magma might remain below the lithosphere. The first relevant measurements were reported in a paper on "Densities of Liquid Silicates at High Pressures," which in 1985 earned the Newcomb-Cleveland Prize for the best paper in the periodical *Science* for S. Rigden, T. J. Ahrens, and E. M. Stolper of the California Institute of Technology (Caltech). The experiments were conducted in a shock-wave apparatus in which high-speed projectiles were fired for the first time at molten targets instead of solid material, and they permitted determinations of the density of the liquid at pressures equivalent to a depth of 700 km (435 mi). The results indicated that magmas that are formed by partial melting of mantle rock at depths greater than 250–350 km (155–215 mi) indeed may be more dense than the solid. Therefore, if melts formed in the Earth at these depths, they would sink rather than rise. Furthermore, they would carry with them the heat-producing radioactive elements uranium and potassium-40, which were generally considered to be concentrated into the Earth's crust by rising magmas and volcanism. This process would require significant revision of interpretations of the geochemical and thermal evolution of the Earth and of other planetary bodies.

The classical approach of interpreting the geochemistry of basaltic and other lavas to provide information about the source rocks in the mantle from which they were derived, one of the most active areas in geochemistry, appeared to be on the verge of revision. The idea had been that the concentrations of elements in magmas are a simple function of the degree of partial melting and the partitioning of elements between liquid and the minerals present. Discrepancies in geochemical interpretations had been resolved by appealing to metasomatism (chemical alteration) of the mantle source rocks or to contamination by crustal

rocks. During the year M. J. O'Hara of the University College of Wales published an article in the periodical *Nature* dealing with theoretical calculations on different degrees of partial melting in different zones of a mantle volume and the subsequent migration and coalescence of the magma before or during uprise. The geochemical product of this process, however, would yield quite erroneous conclusions if interpreted in the classical way. Variable partial melting of a volume of mantle was certainly a more realistic physical picture than the batch production of a fixed percentage of magma, and it was evident that, in order to understand the geochemistry of magmas, scientists also needed to understand the physics of the processes.

The Columbia Glacier, an ice mass 4.8 km (3 mi) wide near Valdez, Alaska, began to retreat in 1978 after at least 80 years of stability. Two years later the U.S. Geological Survey predicted on the basis of mathematical models that the glacier would begin to retreat more rapidly. The prediction was confirmed by 1985 when the glacier experienced a drastic retreat, with accelerating breakup. The models had successfully incorporated, for the first time, the effect of loss of ice due to calving from the glacier. Over the next 30–50 years the glacier could retreat as much as 30 km (19 mi). The models might be useful in evaluating ice streams in west Antarctica.

Elsewhere in Alaska the Variegated Glacier experienced a forward surge in 1982–83, with an increase in flow speeds from about 0.2 m (0.7 ft) per day to as much as 65 m (213 ft) per day. The observation of this surge culminated a multiyear program of field measurements by Barclay Kamb of Caltech and co-workers. They explained the cause and mechanism of surging, a central unsolved problem in glacier mechanics, in terms of a physical model in a 1985 publication. Their measurements showed that the surge motion was due to rapid sliding at the base of the glacier, caused by high basal water pressure. In the nonsurging state water is transported by way of a few large basal tunnels, whereas in the surging state the tunnels are destroyed and water transport takes place through a linked-cavity system between the ice sole and the glacier bed. The role of water pressure is similar to its role in overthrust faulting of rocks and in landsliding. The advance of the surge front involves the development of a succession of thrust faults and folds in the ice, analogous to the imbricated (overlapping) structures in tectonic fold-and-thrust belts.

(PETER JOHN WYLLIE)

GEOPHYSICS

Along the southwest coast of Mexico the Cocos Plate, a massive slab of the Earth's crust, is sliding under the North American Plate at a rate of five to ten centimetres (two to four inches) per year. This subduction causes a very high level of seismic activity including frequent large earthquakes. In the late 1970s scientists discovered a gap, or locked section, of this boundary where seismicity was much lower than that of adjacent sections. Named the Michoacán Gap, it was postulated to be the most likely site for the next major earthquake. Accordingly the region was extensively instrumented with seismographs.

On the morning of Sept. 19, 1985, the long vigil produced results when an earthquake of magnitude 8.1 occurred at 18.2° N, 102.6° W, a few kilometres onshore. The nearest coastal cities and the towns and villages of the eastward mountains suffered some damage and a few fatalities, but minutes later, when the train of shock waves reached the alluvial lake bed upon which most of downtown Mexico City is built, about 370 km (230 mi) from the epicentre, a major disaster resulted. Of the wide range of frequencies in the train that passed through the alluvium, certain of them were attuned to the physical configuration of the lake bed, causing resonance and great amplification of the motion. When these movements were transmitted to the buildings, similar resonant vibrations were induced. As a result more than 100 buildings collapsed in the centre of the city, and many more were either damaged beyond repair or rendered unsafe for habitation. Then, on the following day, amid massive rescue efforts, a very large aftershock of magnitude 7.5 endangered rescue workers and added to the destruction. Near the year's end the death toll was estimated at more than 20,000, and many hundreds were still missing.

Seismicity elsewhere during the year included several earthquakes of magnitude greater than 7.0 that resulted in death and property damage. One, of magnitude 7.8, occurred on March 3 near the coast of central Chile and was followed on April 9 by another shock, of magnitude 7.2, in the same area. An earthquake of estimated magnitude 7.4 occurred in the Hindu Kush on July 29, triggering avalanches in the epicentral area and in Tadzhikistan and northern India. On August 23 an earthquake of magnitude 7.5 struck near the Xinjiang-Kirgiz (Sinkiang-Kirgiz) Sino-Soviet border; the Wuqia-Shufu (Wu-ch'ia-Shu-fu) area of China and the Andizhan-Fergana-Namangan region of the U.S.S.R. were the most affected. At least eight other earthquakes, all of moderate size, also caused fatalities.

The first official earthquake prediction to be endorsed by the U.S. National Earthquake Prediction Evaluation Council and its California counterpart was issued during the year. Its forecast, that a shock between magnitude 5.5 and 6.0 would occur near Parkfield, Calif., before 1993, was based on the historical regularity of Parkfield earthquakes. Shocks had been reported in the vicinity in 1857, 1881, 1901, 1922, 1934, and 1966, with an average interval of 22 years. The council's panel members agreed that the potential existed for the next earthquake to be larger than magnitude 6.0 and for fault rupture to extend to the adjacent segment of the San Andreas Fault, but the data were insufficient to include these factors in the prediction.

One of the worst volcanic disasters in history took place on November 13 when Nevado del Ruiz, a 5,400-m (17,-700-ft) peak in central Colombia, violently erupted, melting part of the mountain's ice cap and sending a flood of mud, ash, and stones down its flanks. The deluge poured into several river valleys at the base of the mountain and buried almost all of the town of Armero on the Lagunilla River. Several other towns were also badly damaged. The Colombian government estimated the death toll at more than 25,000, with many thousands injured and homeless.

Nevado del Ruiz, about 140 km (90 mi) west of Bogotá, lies at the northern end of a chain of two dozen active volcanoes along the Andean Cordillera Central. It was believed to have erupted at least six times in the past 3,000 years, including one in 1595 that was recorded by Spanish explorers and another in 1845 that produced mudslides and killed 1,000. In December 1984 the volcano began emitting large quantities of sulfurous gases, and in ensuing months seismographs detected numerous small tremors within the mountain. On September 11 a small explosion produced steam and ash. As a result the Colombian government, with the help of volcanologists from Costa Rica, Ecuador, and the U.S., began to monitor the volcano and to prepare warning and evacuation plans. Before these plans could be implemented, however, the disaster struck.

The November 13 eruption took the form of two directed blasts on the northeast side of the volcano. These explosions dissolved a portion of the ice cap and sent mud and ash hurtling down the Azufrado riverbed on the

A lahar of volcanic ash mixed with water from the melting ice cap produced a torrent and then a lake of mud after the eruption of Nevado del Ruiz in Colombia in November.
BARR—GAMMA/LIAISON

eastern slope at speeds estimated at 30–50 km/hr (20–30 mph). The mudflow then pushed into the Lagunilla River, burst through a natural dam just upstream of Armero, and inundated the town. On the western side of the mountain, a second mudslide surged over hundreds of homes and killed as many as 1,000 in the town of Chinchiná. Heroic rescue efforts began immediately under the most difficult circumstances. Hundreds of victims were saved after being entombed alive in the mud, some for as long as a week.

In the early morning of December 25, Mt. Etna on the island of Sicily erupted, sending several rivers of lava down its flanks. Earthquakes triggered by the activity caused the collapse of a resort hotel on the mountain's slope, killing one person.

Following the designation by the U.S. in 1983 of an Exclusive Economic Zone (EEZ) extending 320 km (200 mi) from its shores, the U.S. Geological Survey (USGS) developed an important program, EEZ-SCAN, designed to map this zone systematically using long-range side-scan sonar equipment. The heart of the EEZ-SCAN program, in which the USGS was cooperating with the Institute of Oceanographic Sciences (IOS) in the U.K., was the Geological Long-range Inclined Asdic, the GLORIA II. The GLORIA II, developed by the IOS, was a two-ton side-scan sonar device, 8 m (26 ft) in length, which was towed behind the research ship at a depth of 50 m (165 ft). It could be towed at ten knots and could scan a swath of sea bottom 60 km (37 mi) wide. A row of 30 transducers on each side of the device emitted sonar pulses of 6.5 KHz. Return signals were recorded digitally and displayed visually as they were received for monitoring purposes.

By September 1984 the British research ship *Farnella* had completed four cruises with the GLORIA II and had mapped 650,000 sq km (250,000 sq mi) of Pacific seafloor between the Mexican and Canadian borders. This high-resolution system provided more intricate detail of submarine structures and much more thorough coverage than previously attainable. The data were being processed using adaptations of computer-enhancement techniques developed by the USGS for space and planetary science programs. An atlas of these interpretations consisting of 33 maps at a scale of 1:150,000 was scheduled for publication in early 1986. After several months of planning and preparation, the *Farnella* set sail in August 1985 to map the coast of the Gulf of Mexico.   (RUTLAGE J. BRAZEE)

HYDROLOGY

The effects of the African drought remained widespread in 1985 despite rains in some areas. The Niger River was reported to be at its lowest level in more than 60 years; the surface area of Lake Chad (located in Chad, Cameroon, Niger, and Nigeria) diminished significantly; and Egyptian authorities were increasingly concerned with the low discharge of the Nile River from Lake Nasser. Large numbers of people dislocated by religious, ideological, and political conflicts were being forced to move into environmentally fragile areas where water and other resources were scarce. Social and economic problems were exacerbated by destructive land-use practices, such as overgrazing and deforestation, that encouraged desertification. An evaluation of this problem was made by the UN Environment Program, Desertification Branch, and reported in *General Assessment of the Progress in the Implementation of the Plan of Action to Combat Desertification, 1978–84.*

A five-year drought in nine states of Brazil's northeastern region was followed in April by devastating floods that left more than a million people homeless and caused widespread destruction of crops, highways, and other structures.

In much of the U.S., streamflow remained normal or above normal during the year but was significantly lower than in 1984. The combined flow of the Mississippi, St. Lawrence, and Columbia rivers, which drain more than half of the coterminous U.S., was 11% above the long-term average although 9% less than in 1984. Below-normal streamflows occurred in two large areas. One was along the East Coast from Maine to Florida and included parts of the Ohio River basin and eastern Gulf Coast states, and the other encompassed much of the Columbia and Missouri river basins. Below-normal streamflow also was evident in parts of Iowa, Missouri, Kansas, Texas, New Mexico, California, Oregon, and Hawaii. In April drought emergencies affecting about 21 million people were declared in New Jersey, eastern Pennsylvania, and New York City. The Delaware River had record low flows in April, and reservoir levels were also at record lows. Above-normal flows were seen in south-central Texas, in an area extending from North Dakota to Wisconsin (including parts of the lower peninsula of Michigan), in Utah and New Mexico, in parts of Alaska, and in Puerto Rico. Flooding

was severe in Michigan, Ohio, and New York in February; in northwestern Illinois in March; and in Flint, Mich., in September.

Utah's Great Salt Lake rose 1.5 m (5 ft) from September 1983 to July 1984, the second largest seasonal rise for this lake since record collection began in 1847. The continued increase in the lake area resulted in extensive damage to roads, railroads, wildlife-management areas, recreational facilities, and industrial installations that were built on the lakebed. In 1985 state officials were considering several measures, including pumping lake water into the desert, to decrease the lake level.

During the year one of the longest environmental controversies in the U.S. ended with the signing of a compromise plan to dramatically reduce the size of the Garrison Diversion, one of the largest federal irrigation projects ever proposed. Conceived in the 1940s as a solution to problems caused by drought in North Dakota, the project had become a major environmental battleground and was opposed by conservationists, hunters, and the Canadian government. The compromise plan would convert a planned $1.1 billion dam and attendant irrigation projects into a project providing less irrigation water and more drinking water for towns and rural areas.

Three years of collaborative effort by personnel of the U.S. Geological Survey and the Saudi Arabian Ministry of Agriculture and Water culminated in the publication of a water atlas of Saudi Arabia. The work included 77 maps and diagrams, numerous photographs, descriptive text, and feature articles on weather, climate, geology, and water resources of the kingdom as well as on water utilization, demand, development, management, and conservation. It was published in both Arabic and English.

Since World War II China had devoted much effort to the investigation of groundwater resources. By 1985 regional hydrogeological mapping had been completed for most of the country, and total groundwater resources were estimated at 872,000,000,000 cu m (6.5 trillion gal). Intensive exploration had been done to develop irrigation and urban supplies. Limestone aquifers, widespread in China, were regarded as an important source of irrigation supply. The use of groundwater was found to have created problems such as groundwater pollution, subsidence, and saltwater intrusion into coastal aquifers.

The UN International Drinking Water Supply and Sanitation Decade (1981–90) approached its midpoint. The UN secretary-general's official progress report on the first three years of the decade, published in April 1985, indicated that some progress toward the goal of reasonable access to safe drinking water and adequate sanitation services had been made.   (JOHN E. MOORE)

METEOROLOGY

Hurricanes dominated the weather scene in 1985. Six hurricanes and two tropical storms made landfall along the U.S. coast, giving that country its most active hurricane season since 1916. Two of the hurricanes, Elena and Gloria, were major storms that caused evacuation of an estimated two million people from the Gulf of Mexico and Atlantic coastlines. The death toll was held to four in Elena and nine during Gloria's sweep up the heavily populated East Coast.

The year's first hurricane, Bob, briefly reached hurricane force before moving inland across South Carolina on July 25. Hurricane Danny reached a maximum strength of 145 km/hr (90 mph) near the time of landfall on August 15 along a sparsely populated coastal region of Louisiana.

Elena formed off Cuba on August 28 and finally went ashore at Biloxi, Miss., on September 2 with winds as high as 200 km/hr (125 mph). Its exceptionally erratic movement in the Gulf of Mexico had it going first toward the northwest, then east; then it stalled off the western coast of Florida and finally moved to the west, threatening the Florida panhandle for the second time in a week. Before it was over, about 1.5 million residents had been safely evacuated (some of them twice) in communities along the coast of Florida, Alabama, Mississippi, and Louisiana. Damage was estimated as high as $1 billion in the four-state area.

Hurricane Gloria reached hurricane status on September 22. Three days later, when it hung 240 km (150 mi) east of The Bahamas, it was the most intense hurricane in recent history. Its central pressure was measured at 929 millibars (27.43 in) with winds up to 240 km/hr (150 mph). The entire coastal area from just south of Charleston, S.C., to Eastport, Maine, came under a hurricane warning. A half million residents were evacuated to safety. Gloria skirted the coastline, brushing Cape Hatteras, but its most dangerous core remained offshore. When it made landfall in Long Island and Connecticut, it did so at low tide, minimizing the feared death and destruction. Damage was estimated at $350 million.

Two tropical storms, Henri and Isabel, also affected the U.S. coast but inflicted little damage and no deaths in the U.S. The tropical wave that later developed into Isabel

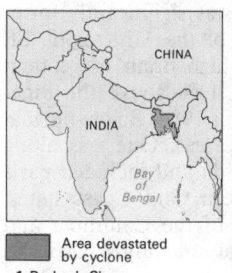

Area devastated by cyclone

1 Darbesh Char
2 Bhola Char
3 North Hatia Island
4 Lakshmi Char
5 Char Jabbar
6 Bata Char
7 Urrir Char
8 Char Clark
9 Sandwip Island
10 Daulatkhan Char
11 Manpura Char
12 South Hatia Island
13 Kutubdia Island
14 Maiskhal Island

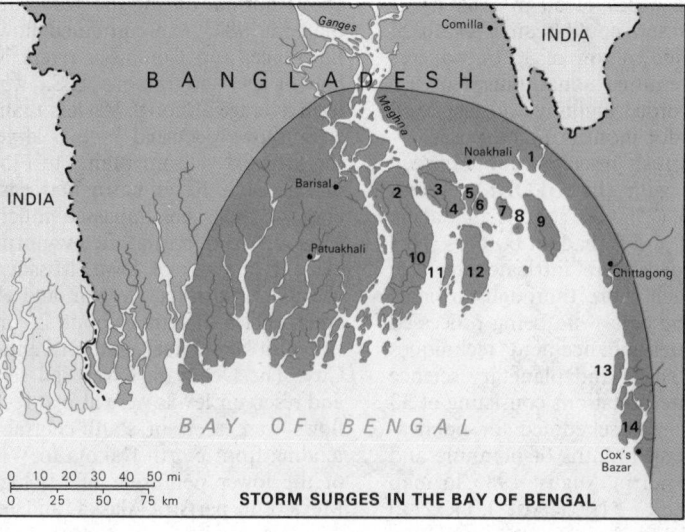

STORM SURGES IN THE BAY OF BENGAL

Cyclone-driven tidal waves in the Bay of Bengal on May 25 devastated about 7,770 square kilometres (3,000 square miles) of coastal Bangladesh, affecting about 5.5 million persons. Heaviest hit were the *chars,* tiny shifting dots of land formed by rich silt deposits from streams of the Meghna estuary and tidal channels (*khals*). About 400 such *chars* in the Ganges River delta were inhabited by farmers who had migrated from the country's overpopulated mainland. The raging cyclone left over 11,000 people dead in the coastal districts of Barisal, Chittagong, Noakhali, and Patuakhali.

Hurricane fans in Clinton, Connecticut, enjoyed a spectacular surf and considerable relief as Hurricane Gloria proved less of a threat than they had feared.
STEVE LISS

dumped as much as 380 mm (15 in) of rain in Puerto Rico, causing major flooding and landslides on the south central coast and killing at least 180 people. Damage was estimated at $500 million.

A late-season hurricane, Juan, created havoc in southern Louisiana. It moved inland southwest of New Orleans on October 29, was downgraded to a tropical storm, moved back to the central Louisiana coast on October 30, looped into the Gulf, and made landfall a second time just west of Pensacola, Fla., on October 31. Between 230 and 330 mm (9 and 13 in) of rain fell in southern Louisiana, causing extensive flooding. At least seven people died, and damages neared the $1 billion mark.

Just when it seemed the hurricane season was over, Kate formed north of Puerto Rico on November 16. It passed near The Bahamas, crossed the northern coastline of Cuba leaving at least ten dead, sideswiped the Florida Keys, and then burst into the Gulf of Mexico with winds of 185 km/hr (115 mph). Kate made landfall in the Florida panhandle between Panama City and Apalachicola on November 21. More than 100,000 residents heeded the advanced warning and again evacuated. Seven people were reported dead as a result of Kate's passage. During the 1985 hurricane season parts of every coastal state from Texas to Maine received hurricane warnings.

On May 25 a tropical cyclone (hurricane) struck Bangladesh's eastern delta region with a huge storm surge that left 2,540 dead by one official estimate; some believed as many as 11,000 died. It was the world's deadliest storm since 300,000 drowned in that same area in the 1970 cyclone. There were also numerous typhoons (hurricanes) in the western Pacific in 1985, which caused widespread flooding and damage in China, Japan, and the Philippines.

Drought continued to afflict Africa in 1985, especially the nations along the southern border of the Sahara known as the Sahel. Its extreme severity marked it as one of the most significant climatic events of modern times. While patterns of alternating wet and dry episodes are typical of most semiarid regions of Africa, it was the long-term variations such as those affecting the Sahel that concerned global meteorologists. A turn toward more arid conditions in the Sahel had been observed for the past three decades, and some scientists speculated that a deterioration might have been under way there for as long as a century. Some climatologists were concerned that it could be an early indication of the global effects of rising carbon dioxide in the atmosphere.   (RICHARD E. HALLGREN)

This article updates the *Macropædia* article CLIMATE AND WEATHER.

OCEANOGRAPHY

In the early morning of April 15, 1912, the ocean liner *Titanic* sank about 900 km (560 mi) south of Newfoundland after striking an iceberg. At the same location and at nearly the same time of day on Sept. 1, 1985, video images sent by the underwater search vehicle *Argo* to researchers on the U.S. research vessel *Knorr* showed a boiler with three fire doors. The wreck of the *Titanic* had been found.

The successful search, led by Robert D. Ballard of the Woods Hole (Mass.) Oceanographic Institution (*see* BIOGRAPHIES), was a joint undertaking between U.S. and French researchers using very different techniques. The French ship *Le Suroit* towed a high-resolution acoustic scanner in a regular pattern about the search site—chosen on the basis of the estimated position of the *Titanic* when it sank and of the ships that came to its aid—continuously imaging the seafloor. U.S. researchers made use of a remotely controlled underwater search vehicle developed jointly by Woods Hole and the U.S. Navy. About the size of a large automobile, this vehicle was outfitted with powerful lights and sensitive video cameras and sent television images via cable to observers in a tender ship overhead.

The wreck lay at a depth of about 4,000 m (13,100 ft). The hull had evidently broken in two, and debris was scattered over an area hundreds of metres on a side. Returning to a site this small for further study would not be difficult with modern navigational techniques, although it would have been impossible a decade or two earlier.

The Strait of Gibraltar is a narrow (13-km; 8-mi) and shallow (about 300-m; 1,000-ft) passage, bounded by Spain and Morocco, through which the Mediterranean Sea and the Atlantic Ocean exchange water. Because insolation and evaporation are high in the Mediterranean, its water is saltier than that of the open Atlantic. Between one million and two million cubic metres per second of this saline water spill out of Gibraltar along the bottom of the strait into the north Atlantic. Although the flow rate is only 1–2% of that of a major ocean current such as the Gulf Stream, the resulting increase in salinity of the intermediate and deep waters of the Atlantic was believed to lead to important differences in the subsurface circulations of the Atlantic and the Pacific. In spite of the importance of this flow, scientists did not know what determines its rate or how it fluctuates.

In late 1985 scientists from the U.S., Spain, Morocco, Canada, and France began a year-long study of the flow in the strait. Moored current meters, to be maintained in the strait for an entire year, would measure the flow directly, while repeated research cruises would observe the temperature and salinity of the water in the strait from shipboard. Although these measurements would describe the flow over the year of the experiment, they were too costly and time-consuming for monitoring the flow over longer periods. Hence, an array of bottom-mounted pressure sensors as well as an array of coastal sea-level (tide) gauges were also being maintained. These devices were easier to operate over long periods, and their ability to monitor the flow and its variations could be carefully evaluated by comparison with the results of the current-meter array and the shipboard observations. If they proved able to monitor the flow, then it also was possible that existing tide-gauge records contained useful information about the variation of the flow in past years.

Other measurements in the strait would use acoustic signals reflected from marine organisms and debris in the water to identify locations of intense vertical motion; in theoretical studies these are locations at which the geometry of the strait is decisive in fixing the flow rate. At these sites repeated profiles of temperature capable of resolving details only centimetres in height would indicate how much mixing occurs between the deep, salty outflowing water and the fresher surface water flowing in from the Atlantic. The age of the outflowing water would be estimated by measuring its content of chlorofluorocarbons (CFCs, or freons) and of tritium.

Global measurements of CFCs and of tritium would be an important part of the World Ocean Circulation Experiment (WOCE), the first truly global survey of ocean circulation, for which planning took place in 1985. Interest in WOCE was sparked by the fact that far less was known about the circulation of the southern oceans than of the northern oceans, and hardly anything was known about the variability of basinwide circulation in either hemisphere. WOCE necessarily would be a many-year effort lasting into the 1990s. By then satellites dedicated to oceanographic research should be in orbit, and in 1985 it was not possible to foresee what studies would then be undertaken. But powerful new techniques for observing the circulation directly were being developed; their global application would be an important part of WOCE.

WOODS HOLE OCEANOGRAPHIC INSTITUTION

The 5-metre (16-foot)-long cagelike *Argo*, towed from the research ship *Knorr*, was used to locate the hulk of the *Titanic* in September. The *Argo* was equipped with sonar, strobe lights, and cameras.

One such was the measurement of CFCs and of tritium in the oceans. Chlorofluorocarbons F-11 and F-12 have no natural sources. They have entered the ocean primarily from the atmosphere since the mid-1930s, when F-12 became industrially important in refrigeration; F-11 was introduced later but in greater quantity. The ratio of F-11 to F-12 in ocean water was thus a sensitive indicator of when in the past few decades the water was last in contact with the atmosphere. Tritium is a by-product of atmospheric nuclear-weapons testing. It entered the ocean from the atmosphere in the Northern Hemisphere and was being spread throughout the deep ocean by the processes WOCE was intended to study. Both CFCs and tritium were unusual tracers of water motion because scientists expected to see their global distribution change measureably in a few decades and so directly see the deep circulation at work.

Other new techniques included the possibility of constructing "pop-up" floats. These would follow the deep circulation at a preset depth for a period of weeks or months, pop up to the surface to report their position to a satellite, and then descend to the preset depth for another period of deep movement. Oceanographers recently began following surface floats from satellites, and they also tracked floats ballasted to remain at depths of 1,000–3,000 m (3,300–9,850 ft) from acoustic listening stations. The pop-up float combined both of these capabilities into a new instrument for describing the deep circulation.

(MYRL C. HENDERSHOTT)

See also Disasters; Energy; Life Sciences; Mining and Metallurgy; Space Exploration; Sports and Games: *Spelunking.*

This article updates the *Macropædia* articles ATMOSPHERE; The EARTH; EARTHQUAKES; The EARTH SCIENCES; GEOCHRONOLOGY; Principles, Methods, and Instruments of MEASUREMENT AND OBSERVATION; OCEANS; PLATE TECTONICS; RIVERS; VOLCANISM.

Economic Affairs

World economic growth during 1985 slowed significantly in comparison with 1984. During that year member countries of the Organization for Economic Cooperation and Development (OECD) recorded a gain in gross domestic product (GDP) of 4.5%. However, in 1985 business activity became weaker in most countries, and the latest available information suggested that growth for the full year was unlikely to exceed 3%. Some deceleration in growth also occurred in the principal oil-exporting and the less developed countries, although the extent of this could not be estimated meaningfully owing to the unavailability of up-to-date statistical information.

The principal reason for 1985's relatively poor performance was the loss of momentum in the U.S. economy. In 1984 GDP in the U.S. rose by 6.8%, outperforming just about every comparable country. In 1985, however, growth was thought to have fallen back to about 2.7%. This was in spite of a relatively relaxed fiscal and monetary policy and a steady downward trend of interest rates. Inevitably, a slowdown of this magnitude in the world's most powerful economy could not but have an adverse effect on the performance of other countries. For example, Japan, which in recent years had increased its reliance on overseas demand as a source of domestic growth, saw its growth rate fall from 5.8 to about 5%; France appeared to have declined from 1.6 to 1.3%; West Germany may have just equaled its 1984 GDP gain of 2.5%; but the smaller OECD countries were heading for an increase of only 2.3%, as against 2.7% during the preceding year. The one exception to the rule was the U.K., where the growth in GDP was put at about

3.5% for 1985, compared with 2.6% in the preceding year. Much of this acceleration, however, was the result of the ending of the yearlong strike in the mining industry in the spring; if one allows for this distortion, the 1985 performance was broadly similar to that in 1984.

Private consumption accounted for the largest single component of the expenditure on gross domestic product in all developed as well as most other countries. In 1984 private consumption was relatively sluggish everywhere except in the U.S. In 1985 the case was reversed, with consumers' expenditure growth slowing from 5.3 to about 3.5% in the U.S. but accelerating a little in Japan, West Germany, and the U.K. In Japan and the major European countries, stockbuilding was also a strong positive factor as producers attempted to rebuild inventories that had fallen to historically low levels during the previous year. In the U.S., however, demand as a result of stockbuilding was relatively poor, with the latest estimates suggesting that net additions to inventories for the year would be less than half of the figure recorded for 1984.

Investment activity, which was generally buoyant in 1984, was considerably more sluggish in 1985. Under the impact of increasing business confidence and good corporate profitability, a major investment boom took place in the U.S. in 1984. By early 1985 concern about future growth and the potential problems associated with the huge fiscal and external payments deficit weakened business confidence and thus caused a reduction in the growth of investment expenditures for the year as a whole to less than one-third of that achieved in 1984. Partly because of a change in the tax treatment of corporate investments, the U.K. also experienced a slower growth in this area, although it was some consolation that manufacturing investments, essential for future growth in output and productivity improvement, held up relatively well. The same was true of other Western European countries; in fact, in West Germany machinery and equipment investments may have grown some four to five times as fast as in 1984. Japanese spending on new plant and equipment, however, grew at less than half the previous year's rate, although—because of government measures to ease the availability of housing finance—residential construction activity grew by some 5%, as against a 1% decline in the preceding year.

A common feature of the world's economies during 1985 was a spectacular deterioration in foreign trade performance. On the basis of incomplete data, it was estimated that world trade, as measured by world exports, grew by approximately 4% in volume terms, compared with a gain in excess of 8% in 1984. It appeared that hardly any country enjoyed an increase in export sales and that a significant number faced a massive decline in the volume of merchandise sold abroad. Thus, Japanese exports, which were affected adversely by the weakness of the U.S. market, an increase in protectionist sentiments, and a strong appreciation in the external value of the yen, grew by some 8–9%, as against an increase of 16% in 1984. Exports by the U.S. rose by about 3–4%, as against more than 7% in the previous year, partly because the rapid rise in the value of the dollar to February 1985 made U.S. products less competitive. Oil-producing countries were confronted with reduced demand for energy in the industrialized world and therefore experienced a cutback in exports of about 4%. As in other areas of economic achievement, the larger European countries seemed to do relatively well, with both the U.K. and West Germany experiencing a decline of only some 2% from their 1984 growth rates to 6.5 and 7%, respectively.

Exports from the non-oil less developed countries ap-

peared to be weaker in 1985 than in 1984. However, a development of even greater consequence for those countries was the weakness of commodity prices. Harvests and/or crop prospects were generally good in both 1984 and 1985. As a result both food commodities and agricultural raw materials were in good supply at a time when the slowdown in the developed world's growth created a weakness in demand. The result was a significant decline in prices (estimated at 13% in the case of food and 8–9% in the case of agricultural raw materials), which had an adverse effect on the foreign exchange earnings of the producing countries. Lower oil consumption and the reduction in the developed world's oil stocks caused a further decline of about 2% in the price of oil, but metal prices appeared to have suffered little or no decline. The effect of declining commodity prices on less developed countries was aggravated by the fall in value of the dollar (which raised the price of manufactured products in dollar terms) and resulted in a massive shift in the terms of trade in favour of the industrialized world.

In 1985, as in the previous year, the world financial scene was dominated by the massive fiscal and foreign payments deficits of the U.S. and the large surpluses of Japan and West Germany. Consequently, the U.S. remained a significant net importer of capital, making it more difficult for the weaker economies of the world, many of which faced problems in meeting their debt repayment and servicing schedules, to finance their deficits. Unlike 1984, however, most of 1985 was characterized by a gradual fall in the external value of the dollar. This was partly a result of the gradual decline in the level of U.S. interest rates as well as concerted action by the U.S. and other major industrial countries to force the dollar down to more realistic levels. As a result the trade-weighted value of the U.S. dollar in terms of the world's leading currencies was some 18% lower in early December than at the start of the year.

A noticeable difference in emphasis between the fiscal and monetary policies being pursued in the U.S. and Europe became apparent in 1985. Although there was growing concern with the large (approximately $200 billion) U.S. budget deficit, the U.S. authorities resisted suggestions for a significant reduction in expenditures so as not to undermine the already less than satisfactory growth in

Table I. Real Gross Domestic Products of Selected OECD Countries

% change seasonally adjusted at annual rates

| Country | \multicolumn{5}{c}{Change from previous year} |
	1981	1982	1983	1984	1985*
United States†	2.3	−2.1	3.7	6.8	3.25
Japan†	4.0	3.3	3.4	5.8	5.25
West Germany†	0.2	−1.0	0.3	2.6	2.50
France	0.2	2.0	0.7	1.7	1.25
United Kingdom	−2.0	2.3	3.1	2.4	3.25
Canada†	3.8	−4.4	3.3	4.7	3.25
Italy†	−0.2	−0.5	−0.4	2.6	2.25
Total major countries†	1.8	−5.0	4.1	8.4	3.25
Australia	4.1	0.7	0.5	6.2	3.75
New Zealand	4.0	−0.8	3.8	4.9	0.25
Austria	0	1.0	2.1	2.2	2.75
Belgium	−1.8	1.1	0.4	2.2	1.75
Denmark	0.1	3.0	2.0	4.1	2.75
Finland	1.3	2.8	2.9	2.9	3.75
Greece	−0.4	−0.2	0.3	2.4	2.0
Ireland†	1.1	−1.3	0.7	2.5	2.0
Netherlands, The	−1.2	−1.7	0.5	2.2	1.75
Norway	0.8	−1.0	3.2	4.3	1.75
Spain	0.3	1.2	2.3	2.2	2.0
Sweden	−0.6	−0.8	2.5	3.0	2.75
Switzerland	1.9	−1.1	0.7	2.4	2.75
Total OECD countries	1.6	−4.4	3.6	7.8	3.2

*OECD projection.
†GNP.
Sources: OECD, *Economic Outlook*, July 1985; National Institute of Economic Review.

the economy. Monetary policy was also generally accommodating, with a fairly relaxed attitude about both the growth of monetary aggregates and interest rates as means of boosting domestic growth and cutting back the inflow of funds in an attempt to weaken the dollar.

On balance, the approach to government spending and monetary policy was more restrictive in Europe. In France the relatively tight fiscal policies adopted in 1984, involving restrictions on public spending as well as wage and price controls, remained in force, although there was a modest decline in interest rates as the year went on. In West Germany the Lombard rate was unchanged until August, when there was a token reduction of 0.5%. The target for monetary growth was, however, reduced by 1%, and the budget adopted for 1985 pointed to a modest tightening of fiscal policy. Monetary growth targets were also reduced (but subsequently exceeded) in the U.K. and, although interest rates fell between March and July, this could not be considered a relaxation in policy because there was a substantial and sudden rise in the banks' base rate from 9.5% in December 1984 to 14% in January 1985. In Japan the official discount rate was raised from 5 to 5.5% in November 1985.

Inflation remained under control in 1985. In fact, consumer prices in the OECD area were estimated to have risen by about 4.5%, representing a considerable slowdown from the gain of 5.3% recorded in 1984. As in 1984, inflation rates varied from country to country, with Japan and West Germany registering increases of only about 2% but with Italy and the smaller OECD countries producing rises of 8–9%. With the exception of the U.K., most countries experienced a slowdown in inflation rates. U.S. consumer prices rose by only about 3.5%, as against 4.3% in 1984; Canada achieved a slowdown from 4.3 to 3.9%; France cut the rise in the retail price index from 7.4 to about 6%; and Italian consumer prices rose 9%, as against 10.8% in 1984. Inflation in the U.K., on the other hand, gained strength from 5 to 6%; this was largely due to higher mortgage rates and increases in indirect taxation early in the year, but by late 1985 the trend was firmly downward. Apart from the generally cautious fiscal and monetary policies, the weakness of world commodity prices and the strengthening exchange rates helped to slow inflation in Europe and Japan.

Despite the slowdown in economic growth, there was a further, though relatively small, drop in the level of unemployment. On the basis of ten-month figures for the larger OECD countries, it was estimated that for the OECD as a whole the number of unemployed expressed as a percentage of the labour force would be 8%. This compared with 8.2% in 1984 and 8.6% in 1983. As in 1984, a significant part of the improvement was provided by the U.S., where the unemployment rate was believed to have declined from 7.4% in 1984 to just under 7.2%. Canada also seemed to have achieved a modest reduction in the rate from 11 to 10.5%, but France, West Germany, Italy, and the U.K. were heading for a modest increase. In most European countries the trend was stable and slightly downward during the second half of the year, giving rise to cautious hopes that, assuming continued economic growth at about 4%, the number out of work in Europe would decline in 1986 for the first time in at least five years.

NATIONAL ECONOMIC POLICIES

Developed Market Economies. *United States.* U.S. economic performance during the first half of 1985 was worse than most forecasters had projected at the start of the year. Expectations were raised by the robust growth in the GNP in the final quarter of 1984 (4.9% annual rate) that the economy had recovered from the summer slowdown. However, real GNP rose by a disappointing 0.3% annual rate during the first quarter of 1985 and by 1.9% in the second. Thus, the economy expanded by only 2% during the first half of 1985, compared with the same period a year earlier. A much faster than expected rebound in the economy pushed up the GNP growth rate in the third quarter to 4.3%. In the absence of clear economic indicators, however, expectations about the final quarter varied. The administration's view was that the economy had entered into a new growth phase, while many private economists and analysts believed that the underlying trend was still sluggish and that in the final quarter the growth rate would slip back to the 2.5–3% range. Even if the economy did not falter in the closing quarter, the GNP growth for 1985 as a whole would not exceed 2.7%, a far cry from the 6.8% registered in 1984.

The lacklustre performance of the economy during the first half of the year hid the fact that real domestic demand

A four-year-long and almost uninterrupted rise in the exchange value of the dollar continued well into 1985, and only late in the year did the trend begin to yield to efforts to reverse it.

In November Sen. Bill Bradley (left; Dem., N.J.) and Rep. Jack Kemp (right; Rep., N.Y.) sponsored a two-day U.S. Congressional Summit on Exchange Rates and the Dollar, at which some 400 international financial experts agreed that wide fluctuations in world currencies were a serious problem requiring more attention.

MICHAEL EVANS/TIME MAGAZINE

was quite strong during that period. Personal consumption rose by 4%, fixed domestic investment by 6.8%, and government expenditure by 5.5%. The reason that the strength of the domestic demand was not fully translated into real GNP growth was the sharp deterioration in net exports and a deceleration in stockbuilding. Imports in the first half of 1985 rose by 11.3% over the same period of 1984, while exports on the same basis registered a decline of 2.5%.

It was not surprising that industrial output slowed dramatically during 1985 under the onslaught of cheap imports and the increased uncompetitiveness of U.S. exports in the world markets. At the beginning of 1984, industrial production stood 15% higher than at the beginning of 1983, but by the end of 1984, it was only 6.8% higher and the growth by August 1985 had all but evaporated to 1%. Growth in industrial production when measured against 1984 was expected to become negative before the end of 1985. New orders by manufacturers were affected by the same insidious process of domestic demand leaking out of the economy. After a poor performance during 1984, manufacturers' new orders rose by only 0.8% during the first ten months of 1985. Until the value of the dollar declined appreciably, no change in the state of the order books was expected.

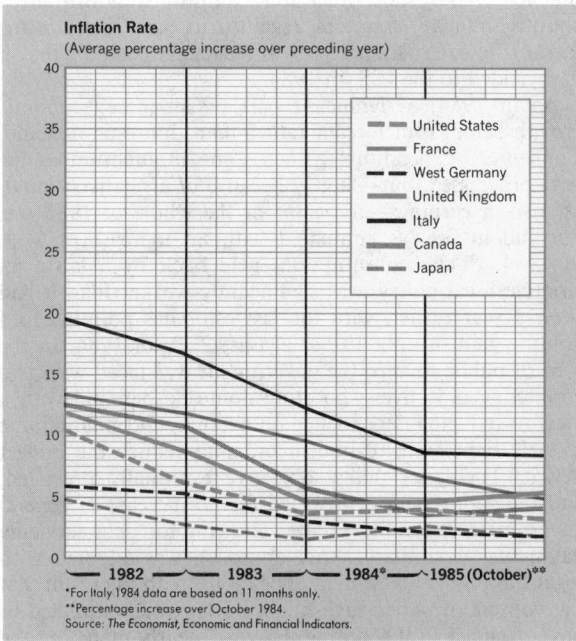

Inflation Rate
(Average percentage increase over preceding year)

Legend:
- United States
- France
- West Germany
- United Kingdom
- Italy
- Canada
- Japan

1982   1983   1984*   1985 (October)**

*For Italy 1984 data are based on 11 months only.
**Percentage increase over October 1984.
Source: *The Economist, Economic and Financial Indicators.*

The underlying personal income growth remained at a healthy rate of 0.3–0.4% per month for most of the year. This on its own would have maintained a reasonable momentum of retail sales, but it was reinforced by a sharp decline in the percentage of income that was saved as consumers reacted positively to price-cutting campaigns. In August, for instance, this savings ratio sank to 2.8%, the lowest level since the panic buying during the Korean War. However, the hectic growth pace of 8.3% in retail sales during the first nine months of 1985 was not expected to be maintained during the closing quarter of the year.

Unemployment experienced a significant reduction in 1983 and 1984 in response to the economic upswing, a success story not repeated in the other developed countries. The rapid decline gave way, however, to a static unemployment rate during 1985 at just over 7%. The rate of unemployment remained unchanged at 7.3% from February to July. Then it declined to 7% in August before climbing back up to 7.1% in October. Stable unemployment was facilitated by the generation of new jobs in service industries that matched the increase in job seekers. Employment in service industries increased at a monthly average of 350,-000, while employment in manufacturing fell by about 20,000 a month.

Consumer price inflation remained remarkably stable throughout 1985 at about 3.5%. In fact, during the second half of the year it even managed a slight reduction to 3%. Strong competition from cheap imports, which, in turn, was buoyed by the strong dollar, was the main reason for these low inflation figures. These competitive pressures caused the prices of manufactured goods to rise by less than 1%, while services, which are not prone to foreign competition, registered much higher price rises. Because services have a much larger share in the consumer price index, virtually all of the consumer price increase in 1985 was attributed to rising prices in services.

The continued strength of domestic demand and the resilience of the dollar fueled an inexorable rise in imports, while exports stagnated. After trade deficits of $69.4 billion in 1983 and $123.3 billion in 1984, based on the figures available until September a record deficit of $150 billion for 1985 appeared inevitable. However, thanks to a moderation in the trade deficit during the final quarter, brought about by the unexpectedly large decline in the value of the dollar in November, a smaller deficit (perhaps as low as $138 billion) seemed probable. Inevitably the current account deficit widened and was expected to be in the region of $120 billion, nearly 20% higher than in 1984 and three times as high as the deficit in 1983. The ever rising current

account deficit was financed largely by capital inflows from abroad attracted by high interest rates and the strength of the dollar.

In September the United States became a debtor nation for the first time since World War I. Foreign ownership of U.S. assets exceeded U.S. ownership of foreign assets by about $30 billion. Given the continually deepening trade deficit, it was not surprising that protectionist sentiment increased alarmingly. No fewer than 200 protectionist bills were brought before Congress in the autumn. Because many of them were designed specifically to reduce foreign competition rather than to open up foreign markets to U.S. exports, they conflicted with the administration's free-trade principles. The possibility of a presidential veto of such bills threatened a huge rift between the president and the Congress. The only long-term solution to the massive trade imbalance of the U.S. would be a lower exchange rate.

An agreement in September between the Group of Five—the five major industrial countries (U.S., Japan, West Germany, U.K., and France)—to step up their efforts to intervene in the foreign exchange market was another attempt to engineer a decline in the value of the dollar. In the short term this had the desired effect, and by December the dollar had depreciated by 20% against the yen, 14% against the Deutsche Mark, and 10% against the pound sterling.

While the decline in the value of the dollar marked the beginning of the correction of one of the imbalances in the economy, the trade deficit, by the year's end there was no real progress toward closing the federal deficit. Fiscal policy during 1985 remained expansionary. Increased defense spending and higher interest payments on the national debt reversed the previous year's trend.

Compared with a deficit of $175 billion during fiscal 1984 (ended Sept. 30, 1984), fiscal 1985 registered a deficit of $210 billion, nearly 5.4% of the GNP. The administration's budget proposals introduced in February envisioned reducing the budget deficit to $180 billion, or 4.5% of the GNP. Initially, the president proposed a 12.6% increase in defense expenditure. Apart from debt servicing, most other programs were to be either frozen or cut back. Based on an economic growth rate of 4% per year, the president's proposals envisioned a decline in the budget deficit to $144 billion, or 2.9% of the GNP, by the end of President Reagan's term. In the ensuing budget battle with the Congress, it was effectively agreed to freeze defense spending and not provide for indexation of Social Security in 1986.

When the economy entered into a growth recession in the second half of 1984, the Federal Reserve Board (Fed) relaxed its monetary stance to avoid sending the economy into an outright recession. The monetary growth targets announced at the beginning of 1985, while slightly lower than the previous year, were sufficiently high to accommodate an inflation rate of 3–3.5% and a similar growth rate without undue upward pressure on interest rates. In the opening months of the year, when monetary aggregates grew much faster than the upper limit of the target range, the response of the Fed was a modest tightening of its monetary growth policy; this led to slightly higher interest rates.

Later, as the economy was stunned into a growth recession by the strong expansionary forces generated by the huge budget deficit (which kept domestic demand growth strong) and the contractionary forces released by the overvalued dollar, the Fed shifted its policy to accommodate faster monetary growth. By adopting a policy of lower interest rates against a background of relatively fast monetary growth, it hoped to foster a downward trend in the value of the dollar. Although this policy was only moderately successful in the summer, it was perhaps instrumental in underpinning the flagging economy. After the September meeting of the Group of Five, however, the continuation of an accommodating monetary policy together with concerted intervention in the foreign exchange markets appeared to have been more successful in putting greater downward pressure on the dollar.

Japan. Partial evidence at the end of 1985 suggested that the year as a whole recorded a gain of about 5% in real GDP. While this was somewhat smaller than the increase of 5.8% achieved during the previous year, it was broadly in line with expectations and was probably faster than that achieved by most other non-Communist industrialized countries. Japan, therefore, regained its usual place at the top of the international growth league, a position that it had yielded to the U.S. in 1984.

As in 1984, a significant part of Japanese economic growth came from foreign rather than domestic demand. Consumers' expenditure gained some momentum as the year progressed, but—largely because of a relatively modest rise in earnings—the gain for the whole of 1985 was only about 3%, as compared with an increase of 2.7% in 1984. Public consumption, held back by a fairly restrictive fiscal policy, was significantly weaker than it had been a year earlier, with the last estimates pointing to a volume gain of only 1%, as against 2.2% in 1984. In the area of public finance the government was faced with two conflicting objectives—boosting domestic demand with a view to reducing dependence on exports, and maintaining a fairly tight fiscal regime in order to reduce the budget deficit. The latter policy objective eventually prevailed, and the spring budget provided for no increase in general government expenditures after allowing for debt servicing payments. A similarly strict approach was adopted with regard to public investment allocations, with the result that the volume of public investment outlays was estimated to have declined by 1% during the year, nearly matching the

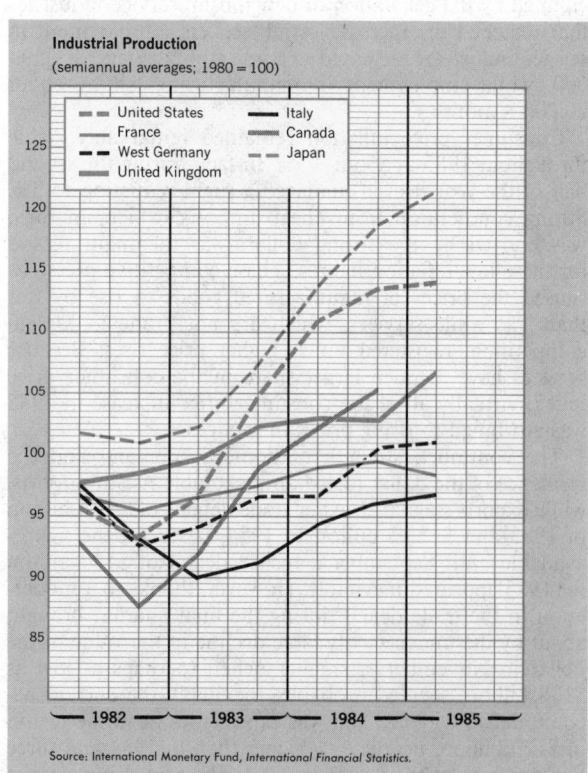

Industrial Production

(semiannual averages; 1980 = 100)

United States
France
West Germany
United Kingdom
Italy
Canada
Japan

125

120

115

110

105

100

95

90

85

— 1982 — 1983 — 1984 — 1985 —

Source: International Monetary Fund, *International Financial Statistics.*

Table II. Percentage Changes in Consumer Prices in Selected OECD Countries

Country	1980	1981	1982	1983	1984	1985*
United States	13.5	10.4	6.1	3.2	4.3	3.2
Japan	8.0	4.9	2.7	1.9	2.2	1.4
West Germany	5.5	6.3	5.3	3.3	2.4	1.8
France	13.6	13.4	11.8	9.6	7.4	5.0
United Kingdom	18.0	11.9	8.6	4.6	5.0	5.4
Italy	21.2	17.8	16.6	14.6	10.8	8.6
Canada	10.2	12.5	10.8	5.9	4.3	4.2
Austria	6.4	6.8	5.4	3.3	5.6	2.9
Belgium	6.6	7.6	8.7	7.7	6.3	4.6
Denmark	12.3	11.7	10.1	6.9	6.3	3.9
Finland	11.6	12.0	9.6	8.3	7.1	5.1
Greece	24.9	24.5	21.0	20.2	18.5	20.1
Iceland	57.5	51.6	49.1	86.7	18.1	31.1
Ireland	18.2	20.4	17.1	10.5	8.6	5.5
Luxembourg	6.3	8.1	9.4	8.6	5.6	3.1
Netherlands, The	6.5	6.7	6.0	2.8	3.3	2.3
Norway	10.9	13.6	11.3	8.4	6.2	5.8
Portugal	16.6	20.0	22.4	25.5	29.3	20.1
Spain	15.5	14.6	14.4	12.1	11.3	7.4
Sweden	13.7	12.1	8.6	8.9	8.0	6.7
Switzerland	4.0	6.5	5.6	3.0	2.9	2.5
Turkey	94.3	37.6	32.7	28.8	45.6	43.4
Australia	10.2	9.6	11.1	10.1	4.0	6.7
New Zealand	12.9	10.5	7.8	5.3	5.3	4.3

*Twelve-month rate of change (not directly comparable with annual changes). Sources: OECD, *Economic Outlook*, July 1985; OECD, *Main Economic Indicators*.

decline of 1.5% in 1984. In contrast, private investment activities were fairly buoyant. Private housing expenditure rose by about 5%, partly in reaction to a decline of 1% during the preceding year. At the same time, private plant and equipment investments were thought to have risen by about 10%, approximately equaling the previous year's gain of 11.1%. Such investments did well because of good corporate profitability and a strong upward trend in industrial production. The index of industrial output, supported to a large extent by the strength of overseas demand, was characterized by a strong but moderating growth throughout the year and was thought to have registered an overall gain of between 6 and 7%.

In general, domestic demand was not significantly more buoyant than in 1984. As a result, a substantial part of the year's economic growth came from exports; in late 1985 it was estimated that the volume of overseas sales would record an increase of 12% for the year, faster than any other component of GDP. Although this represented a marked slowdown from the runaway export growth of 18% in 1984, the expansion of imports—at some 5%, as against 12.5% in 1984—experienced an even greater deceleration. The net result was that, just as in the previous year, an unduly high proportion of the country's GDP gain was generated by overseas demand; consequently, the trade and balance of payments surpluses again increased dramatically. During the first nine months of 1985, the current account surplus amounted to $36 billion, as against $23 billion in the corresponding period of the previous year. Historically, Japan had faced a substantial deficit in invisible transactions (such as shipping, tourism, profits, dividends remitted to and from other countries); this had had the effect of blunting the consequences of its strong trade performance in overall balance of payments terms. However, because of the rapid rise in Japanese foreign investments in recent years, profits remitted from abroad were making significant inroads into the invisible deficit, thereby making the problem of the large external payments surplus more acute.

Not surprisingly, Japan's principal trading partners, headed by the U.S., remained highly critical of the Tokyo government's failure to reduce the country's external payments imbalance despite several previous assurances that it would do so. Most countries contended that official policies were not sufficiently stimulatory for domestic demand,

that more should be done to open up the Japanese market to foreign exporters, and that the relatively low external value of the yen had the effect of boosting exports and reducing imports. The latter message was addressed by the government fairly early in the year. Partly as a result of official pressure, the steadily weakening value of the yen in comparison with the dollar that characterized 1984 was reversed in the second quarter of 1985. After that time the yen appreciated, partly as a result of an agreement in September by the finance ministers of the Group of Five to combine efforts to weaken the U.S. dollar. As a result the value of the yen rose from 258 yen per dollar in the first quarter of 1985 to 214 yen per dollar by October, although it was widely suggested that the rate would have to rise even further in order to make a significant and early dent in Japan's huge trade surplus with the U.S.

The Tokyo government was thought to be reluctant to see the rate rise to below 200 yen per dollar. In October, however, it was forced to make a further gesture to its overseas critics by introducing a package of measures designed to boost domestic demand as well as to encourage imports. This was greeted by a mixture of qualified approval and skepticism on the part of Japan's trading partners, skepticism because demand-boosting measures of this nature had been a standard feature of Japanese economic policy for the last decade and approval because the measures were expected to have some positive effect on the growth of domestic demand. Although the measures came too late to have more than a marginal influence on domestically generated growth in calendar 1985, the government claimed, on the basis of some questionable assumptions, that over a 12-month period they would boost GDP by 1.3%.

Monetary policy during the period under review was fairly relaxed. Although there were fears that the authorities would have to raise interest rates as part of the campaign to strengthen the yen, up to late November the central bank resisted pressures to do so on the grounds that this would have an adverse effect on domestic demand. The official discount rate, therefore, remained at 5% throughout the first 11 months of the year. As was usually the case, unemployment was no problem. During the first two quarters of 1985, approximately 2.5% of the labour force was on the unemployment register (compared with 2.7% for the whole of 1984), and subsequent months pointed to a further improvement in the situation. In OECD terms Japan's unemployment rate was among the lowest, little more than one-quarter of the OECD average of about 8%.

United Kingdom. A rapid growth in the economy took place in 1985 but, contrary to expectations, this was coupled with a further, significant rise in the level of unemployment. The volume of GDP was estimated to have risen by some 3.5% during the year, compared with a gain of only 2.6% in 1984. However, much of this acceleration was the result of the decision of the National Union of Mineworkers to end its yearlong strike in March 1985. Without this boost to output, the underlying growth rate during the year would have been approximately the same as in 1984. Nevertheless, this was widely acknowledged to be a satisfactory performance for two reasons: the underlying growth recorded by the U.K. in 1985 was in line with that achieved in Western Europe as a whole, and it represented a continuation of an already unusually long period of upturn in the economy. Thus, by the end of 1985 the British economy had been on an upward path for nearly five years, longer than any other period of growth for the last 25 years.

Most principal sectors of the economy contributed to growth during 1985. Consumers' expenditure and retail

Table III. Standardized Unemployment Rates in Selected OECD Countries

% of total labour force, seasonally adjusted

Country	1980	1981	1982	1983	1984	1985*
Canada	7.4	7.5	10.9	11.8	11.2	11.0
United States	7.0	7.5	9.5	9.5	7.4	7.1
Japan	2.0	2.2	2.1	2.6	2.7	2.7
Australia	6.0	5.7	7.1	9.9	8.9	8.3
France	6.4	7.3	8.1	8.3	9.7	10.0
West Germany	3.0	4.4	6.1	8.0	8.6	8.6
Italy	7.5	8.3	9.0	9.8	10.2	10.0
Sweden	2.0	2.2	3.1	3.5	3.1	3.0
United Kingdom	6.9	10.6	12.3	13.1	13.2	13.1

*Partially estimated.
Source: OECD, *Economic Outlook*, July 1985.

sales were strong because of a rapid rise in disposable incomes. These were boosted by an increase in average earnings considerably in excess of the rate of inflation and some tax concessions provided by the budget. In fact, consumer expenditure became increasingly buoyant as the year progressed and by late 1985 was heading for an annual volume gain of 2.5%, compared with one of only 1.7% in 1984. In contrast, fixed investments started off strongly but declined sharply in the second half of the year. This was largely the result of the expected reduction in the level of investment expenditure in the oil and natural gas industry as well as a further cutback in public-sector investment activities. Total fixed investment, therefore, grew by only about 3% during 1985, as against a gain of more than 8% in 1984. However, fixed investment in the manufacturing sector—underpinned by a strong improvement in business confidence and a rapid rise in corporate profitability—rose by more than 11%, only 2–3% points below the increase seen in the preceding year.

Exports were buoyant during the period under review. In part this was the result of the strong economic expansion in most of Britain's principal trading partners as well as an improvement in the country's export competitiveness. By the beginning of 1985 relative export prices in the U.K. were some 6.5% lower than they had been 12 months earlier. This gave a strong boost to overseas sales and, although some of this advantage was lost because of a higher sterling exchange rate as the year went on, the volume of exports for 1985 recorded a gain of 7.5%, compared with an increase of 7% in 1984. At the same time, the resumption of normal working in the coal industry led to a cut in fuel purchases from abroad, and the volume of imports rose by only 4.5%, as against an increase of 9.4% in 1984.

Partly as a result of the developments described above, the balance of payments improved significantly, with the current account surplus rising from just under £1,000 million in 1984 to an estimated £3,000 million. Some of this improvement, however, was attributable to the strong recovery in the external value of sterling during the last three quarters of the year. Sterling lost ground steadily in 1984 and in the first few months of 1985, with the result that by the opening quarter of the year its effective rate was 12% below the figure for the corresponding period of 1984. The downward trend, however, was reversed sharply in March 1985, and by October of that year the rate was back to the level of early 1984.

Industrial production rose by approximately 4.5% during the year. Although this represented a marked improvement over the previous year's growth rate of 1.2%, much of the gain came from the resumption of full-scale coal output in March 1985. In fact, the performance of manufacturing industry did not improve as fast as in 1984; the gain for the year was estimated at only some 2.5%, compared with 3.8% a year earlier. This was regarded as one of the few

unsatisfactory features of the economy, together with a slowdown in the growth of output per person employed. During 1984 this had risen by 5.8%, but partial statistics for 1985 suggested that the improvement for the year as a whole would not exceed 3%. Together with the relatively rapid rise in average earnings—approximately 8.5% for the whole year—this had an adverse effect on labour costs per unit of output; in 1984 these rose by only about 3.5%, but during the first two quarters of 1985 the increase was 5.9%. Combined with the strengthening of sterling from March 1985 onward, the net effect was a loss of international competitiveness during the second half of the year.

Inflation also accelerated during the period under review. During the last few months of 1984, there had already been an acceleration in the rate of retail price inflation, a trend that gained further momentum in the first three quarters of 1985. The principal reasons for this included a substantial rise in mortgage interest rates in the spring, a rise in taxes on alcoholic drinks and tobacco announced in the March budget, and the (normally) delayed adverse import price effect of the external weakness of sterling in 1984 and early 1985. Nevertheless, because of the change in sterling's fortunes in the spring, inflation was beginning to lose momentum toward the end of the year, and it was estimated that for 1985 as a whole the retail price index would rise by 5.5%, only a relatively modest advance over the 4.8% recorded a year earlier.

By far the least satisfactory feature of the year was the failure to make any significant inroads into unemployment. This was even more discouraging because toward the end of 1984 there had appeared to be a flattening in the previously consistent upward curve of unemployment, giving rise to cautious hopes of a modest cut in the numbers out of work during 1985. Despite the relative strength of the economy, however, these hopes were not realized; during the first nine months of the year, an average of just under 13.1% of the labour force was out of work (calculated on a seasonally adjusted basis). This compared with a figure of 12.6% for 1984, which reinforced the view that—given the

Table IV. Changes in Output in the Less Developed Countries, 1980–84

In %

Area	Annual average 1967–76	Change from preceding year				
		1980	1981	1982	1983	1984
All less developed countries	5.8	3.4	2.4	1.6	1.5	3.7
Oil-exporting countries	5.6	−1.0	1.2	−0.2	−0.8	2.0
Non-oil less developed countries						
Africa	4.8	3.7	0.9	0.1	−0.2	2.2
Asia	5.0	4.7	5.8	5.1	7.1	6.4
Europe	5.5	1.6	2.5	2.2	1.3	2.5
Middle East	9.2	−1.8	−0.7	0.3	0.6	2.3
Western Hemisphere	6.6	5.3	1.0	−1.0	−3.1	2.4

Sources: Adapted from IMF, *Annual Report 1985*, and World Bank, *Annual Report 1985*.

Table V. Changes in Consumer Prices in the Less Developed Countries, 1980–84

In %

Area	Annual average 1967–76	Change from preceding year				
		1980	1981	1982	1983	1984
Less developed countries	13.8	27.3	26.1	24.7	33.0	37.7
Oil-exporting countries*	7.9	15.9	16.4	18.0	25.5	20.1
Non-oil less developed countries*	15.9	32.2	30.6	28.0	36.9	47.1
Africa	8.5	16.6	21.4	13.4	19.0	17.8
Asia	9.4	13.1	10.6	6.2	6.6	6.9
Europe	9.0	37.9	24.0	23.8	23.2	28.0
Middle East	8.7	15.6	12.7	12.7	12.7	16.5
Western Hemisphere	24.5	54.0	58.6	65.5	100.5	119.8

*Weighted average.
Source: Adapted from IMF, *Annual Report 1985*.

The annual summit conference of the seven leading industrial democracies, held at the Schaumburg Palace in Bonn, West Germany, in May, was cordial but failed to reach accord on the question of a new round of world trade talks.

FRANCIS APESTEGUY/CHIP HIRES—GAMMA/LIAISON

present structure of the British economy—a growth rate well in excess of 3% would be required to reduce the level of joblessness. As the year drew to a close, however, there were signs that unemployment was past its peak, and a real improvement was expected in 1986.

The government's cautious fiscal and monetary stance remained unchanged during the year. The 1985–86 budget, submitted by the chancellor of the Exchequer in March, provided for some modest income-tax concessions as well as additional expenditure on youth training programs and a reduction in some national insurance contributions. However, much of the cost of these measures was offset by increases in indirect taxation, and so the overall effect of the budget was only marginally expansionary. At the same time, the authorities' monetary policy was broadly in line with the previously announced medium-term financial strategy. Thus, the target range for monetary growth—as defined by the M3 series—was set at 3–7%, as against 4–8% during the previous year. The public sector borrowing requirement (PSBR) was set at £7,000 million, compared with a 1984–85 outturn—incorporating £3,000 million in overspending as a result of the miners' strike—of £10,000 million. Late in 1985 the indications were that these targets would be exceeded. During the first nine months of the year, M3 grew by some 14% but, largely because of the gradual loss of confidence in this measure as an indicator of the economic well-being of the country, the government was not unduly concerned. Of more importance was the fact that the PSBR was also heading for an increase of some £1,500 million over the target of £7,000 million, but there was no sign that the government was rethinking its overall strategy to get back to the desired figure. Interest rates rose rapidly in the first quarter of the year but fell back a little in subsequent months. In an attempt to protect the weak sterling, the London clearing banks' base rate was raised from 9.5% in December 1984 to 14% in February 1985. This was, however, followed by a percentage point drop

a month later, and by September the rate was down to 11.5%.

France. During 1985 the French economy remained under the influence of the restrictive policies introduced in 1983 to correct the twin imbalances affecting the economy: large current account deficits and high inflation. This austerity program was fairly successful. The inflation rate was halved from the 1982 level, and a near balance was achieved in the current account. Moreover, the adjustment was achieved without completely sacrificing economic growth. Following a real growth of 1.6% in GDP during 1984, based on incomplete data for 1985 the economy was expected to post a growth rate of just under 1.5%.

Most of the growth resulted from private consumption and stockbuilding. Household consumption started strongly, increasing by 1.5% in the first quarter. A sluggish period followed, but there was a good recovery by the third quarter, and consumption was expected to remain buoyant during the closing months as the income-tax reductions and stable inflation rate boosted the purchasing power of consumers. Investment by large companies, especially industrial investment, rose strongly in the last half of the year. There was also a modest contribution from stockbuilding. Most sectors of industry benefited from the stronger demand. The index of industrial production, which rose by 0.8% in the second quarter, grew by 1.1% in the third. Although the year was expected to close on a strong note, the industrial production index would still be below the 1979 level.

Despite the remarkable improvement in the current account balance in 1984 (and to a lesser extent in 1983), the economy's structural weakness in this area remained. Thus, any spurt in growth was accompanied by a rise in imports. On a seasonally adjusted basis the trade deficit for the first nine months was F 18.7 billion. The government's own forecasts put the expected deficit for the year at about F 2.5 billion, similar to the overall deficit in 1984.

Table VI. Balances of Payments on Current Account, 1980–84

In $000,000,000

Area	1980	1981	1982	1983	1984
Industrial countries	−38.8	3.1	1.2	2.2	−34.2
Fuel-exporting countries	100.1	34.7	−23.4	−17.0	−5.7
Non-fuel-exporting countries	−77.5	−91.0	−76.2	−53.6	−38.2
Africa	−5.3	−25.2	−24.4	−15.5	−10.9
Asia	−21.8	−23.4	−19.8	−16.3	−7.9
Europe	−12.5	−10.5	−6.7	−5.3	−3.3
Middle East	−91.6	−45.8	−6.5	−21.7	−16.3
Western Hemisphere	−29.3	−43.1	−42.1	−11.7	−5.5
Total	−190.1	−56.0	−95.8	−63.5	−71.4

Source: Adapted from IMF, *Annual Report 1985.*

In contrast to the disappointing trade balance figures, the current account showed more promise during 1985. From a substantial deficit position in the opening quarter of the year, it moved to surplus in the third quarter, leading to hopes that for the year as a whole there could be a small surplus; a large surplus on tourist accounts was one of the main contributing factors.

Perhaps the most encouraging development in the French economy during the year under review was progress made on the inflation front. The prices and incomes policy, reinforced by a tight fiscal and monetary stance, succeeded in bringing down the inflation rate to 5.5% by November 1985. It was the first time since 1972 that France's inflation rate had fallen below 6%. Though at this level it was nearly 3.2% above that of West Germany, it was in line with the European Communities (EC) average.

Tight monetary and fiscal policies adopted in the spring of 1983 were not relaxed during 1985 despite the approaching general election and the obvious temptation of any government to boost its electoral popularity beforehand. The economic goals of the government were the reduction of inflation to less than 5% and the maintenance of stability on the balance of payments account. As in 1984 these were tackled by a mixture of wage and price controls, control over public spending, and tight monetary policies. However, despite the government's commitment to maintaining the public sector deficit at 3% of GDP, a little slippage occurred, pushing the initial estimated budget deficit from F 125.8 billion to F 138.9 billion. Encouraged by the apparent success of its budget strategy of using cuts in public spending to make way for modest reductions in personal and corporate taxes while keeping unchanged the budget deficit as a percentage of GDP, the Mitterrand government in its 1986 budget (announced in September 1985) stuck to the same strategy. It promised income-tax cuts of 3% after the 5% implemented in 1985, and a 5% reduction in company profits reinvested. To finance these and an expected steep rise in interest payments on public debt, certain types of government expenditure were sharply cut back. Consequently, total budget spending was projected to rise by 3.6%, well under the government's forecast of a 6.1% increase in nominal GDP and a 4% increase in inflation. The budget deficit at F 145.2 billion was projected at 3% of GDP, unchanged from 1983–84.

While monetary policy was also fairly restrictive, a slight slippage in curbing money growth rates was evident. The money growth targets were set at a range of 4–6% (down from 5.5–6.6% in 1984). Relatively buoyant bank lending for consumer purchases, home buying, and modest inflows of foreign currency caused the target range to be exceeded slightly. However, success achieved in controlling the growth of domestic credit and in reducing the inflation rate enabled interest rates to decline modestly. The Bank of France discount rate, for instance, was lowered from 10.75% at the beginning of 1985 to 9.5% in November. However, the lending rates by the state banks, at about 10.5% at the end of the year, remained relatively high in real terms.

West Germany. The West German economy bounced back strongly in the second half of 1984 following the settlement of a strike by the metalworkers, and the GNP registered a real growth rate of 2.6%, double the 1983 result. This strong underlying trend was widely expected to continue in 1985; therefore, it seemed like a minor disaster when in the first quarter the economy declined by 0.8% (from the previous quarter). Most of the setback, however, was attributed to the effects of the very cold weather, a view largely confirmed by the impressive 2% growth achieved in the second quarter. The improved trend held for the remainder of the year, and the GNP was likely to have achieved a growth rate of 2.5%, largely unchanged from the previous year.

Unlike the previous year, when strong export performance was the main engine of economic growth, the economy during 1985 was also spurred by an investment surge and an improvement in private consumption. The strength of new investment was all the more remarkable because it took place against a background of continuing uncertainty in such important planning variables as exchange rates and interest rates. There were also clear signs that it was broadening from the modernization type of investment into areas of new technology. Gross fixed investment during 1985 was likely to have expanded by more than 3%, double the previous year's growth rate. Thanks to the unexpectedly low inflation rate, real wages rose by some 1%. During the first half of the year, most of this additional income was saved by wage earners, but a gradual shift occurred in the second half, as reflected by a recovery in retail sales led by sales of automobiles and other durable goods.

The timing of the recovery in domestic demand coincided nicely with the downturn in orders for imports. While foreign orders during the first half of the year rose by nearly 12% from the same period in 1984, the trend on a month-to-month basis was slightly down; this became more pronounced in the second half of the year, reflecting the strength of the Deutsche Mark against the dollar and EC currencies. However, the decline in the growth pace of exports did not prevent West Germany from heading for a record surplus on the visible account in 1985. During the first ten months of the year, the cumulative trade surplus rose to a record DM 58.3 billion (DM 40.9 billion in the same period of 1984), lending support to forecasts of an annual surplus of about DM 72 billion. The performance of the current account, which included service transactions and transfer payments, was even more spectacular. Between January and October 1985 the surplus more than tripled to DM 27.4 billion from DM 8.3 billion during the same period of 1984. Expectations for the full year were about DM 42 billion.

Missing from this otherwise cheerful economic picture was a sharp increase in employment levels. In each of the first seven months of 1985, the unadjusted unemployment figure was higher than in the equivalent month of the preceding year. The seasonally adjusted figures were only marginally better. The number of unemployed remained at about 2.2 million, or 9.3% of the work force. Although in the closing months of the year West German unemployment eased a little, reducing the unemployment figure to 9%, unemployment nonetheless had remained above the politically sensitive level of two million people for exactly three years. Unemployment thus became a major issue for political debate in the country, but the government refused

Representatives of the 90 member nations of the General Agreement on Tariffs and Trade convened in Geneva in September; in November they voted to begin a new round of trade liberalization talks, the eighth since World War II, in September 1986.
AP/WIDE WORLD

repeated demands from the unions to reflate the economy to provide more jobs.

After achieving a record low for the post-oil crisis period of 2.4% in 1984, the inflation rate headed for another record in 1985. During the first ten months of the year, inflation averaged 2.3% and, in the absence of any inflationary pressures in the economy, it was expected to remain at that level.

Against a background of record low inflation, a quickening pace of economic activity, and a rise in the central money stock (CBM) well within the target range, the Bundesbank at the beginning of 1985 decided to reduce the CBM growth target by 1% to 3–5%. The Bundesbank did not regard the lowering of the target range as necessarily signifying a tightening of monetary policy. It claimed that this was consistent with a likely growth of 2.5–3% in real terms and inflation of just over 2%. Early in the year, as the U.S. dollar hit a 13-year peak of DM 3.45 to $1, the Bundesbank raised the Lombard rate by a token 0.5% to defend its currency. While the dollar eased from the spring onward and the CBM growth remained within the target range, the authorities remained cautious, and it was not until August that the discount rate and the Lombard rate were each reduced by 0.5%. As in other EC countries, the real interest rates remained high throughout the year, at about 5%, compared with an inflation rate of less than 2.5%.

The budget for 1985 signaled a slight tightening of fiscal policy but with the promise of a relaxation in 1986 as the first phase of income-tax reductions were due to become effective. The federal budget deficit for 1985 was voted at DM 23.9 billion (under 1.5% of GNP), compared with the actual deficit of DM 28.3 billion for 1984. The expected figure of about DM 25 billion, based on incomplete data, was likely to be slightly above the official target owing to a mixture of factors, including a rebate on surcharges on high income earners, lower than expected tax receipts, and higher than expected social security payments. In spite of the DM 20 billion tax-cut package, announced as early as December 1984 and to be implemented in two stages in January 1986 and January 1988, the outline budget for 1986 indicated a target deficit of about DM 25 billion.

Less Developed Countries. After three years of indifferent performance, the level of economic activity increased appreciably in the less developed countries in 1984 and 1985. A rapid economic growth rate in the U.S. and to a lesser extent in the other industrialized nations was the main stimulus, coupled with earlier measures taken by

some countries to enhance economic efficiency. Encouraging as was the quickening pace of economic growth, many less developed countries were constrained by protectionist attitudes and measures among their industrialized trade partners. High borrowers were also burdened by the relatively high international interest rates.

Output. According to International Monetary Fund (IMF) and World Bank estimates, during 1984 (the latest year available) the GDP of the less developed countries in real terms expanded by 3.8%, compared with about 2% in the preceding two years. Growth was led by a sharp rise in exports, thanks to a strengthening of import demand in the U.S. Although this stimulus weakened during 1985 as the U.S. economy slowed down, import markets in the industrial world remained sufficiently buoyant. Thus, the modest recovery in the less developed countries was expected to continue during 1985, further strengthening their balance of payments positions.

While 1984 was a good year for the less developed countries, regional performances varied considerably. The strongest took place in Asia. According to the World Bank, China registered an impressive increase in GDP, thanks to economic reforms instituted earlier. Good weather conditions and a strong export performance helped, too. India, South Korea, Malaysia, and Singapore all registered rapid growth rates, mainly led by growth in exports. Indonesia, though burdened by a large debt and stagnant oil prices, achieved good growth in GDP. By contrast, the Philippines suffered a reversal because of measures taken to correct a severe balance of payments problem.

Southern Europe, North Africa, and the Middle East posted modest economic growth rates in real terms. The oil-exporting countries did better than the others despite a decline in the dollar price of oil. This was counterbalanced by a rise in export volumes and by an appreciation in the value of the dollar, thus increasing their purchasing power for nondollar imports.

After two consecutive years of decline, the GDP in Latin-American countries increased by 2.4%. However, because the economic expansion rate was only marginally above the increase in population, the impact on overall economic standards was negligible. Indeed, unemployment increased sharply in many countries in this region. In part this was attributable to the fact that Latin-American countries needed to use the additional resources to cover interest payments and build up reserves rather than to channel it to domestic consumption and investment.

In the drought-stricken sub-Saharan African region,

GDP declined by 0.6%, bringing the cumulative decrease since 1980 to 16%. Worst affected were large parts of East Africa. Middle-income African countries suffered from low commodity prices, slow growth in exports, and financing constraints. The GDP in those nations fell by 1.9% in 1984.

The recovery in the rate of economic activity in 1984 coincided with a change in the fiscal policies in the less developed countries. The fiscal deficits of central governments, which had risen from 1.25% of GDP in 1980 to 5.5% in 1983, declined to 4.5% in 1984. The IMF observed that the largest improvements in fiscal deficits were among countries that had previously experienced debt-servicing problems. This was paralleled by an improvement in the overall savings ratio of the less developed countries. Investment spending appeared to have been a casualty of this external adjustment.

Consumer Prices. The progress achieved on the economic growth front was not matched in the field of price performance. The inflation rate for the less developed countries as a whole rose to nearly 38% in 1984, up from 33% in 1983. However, the average was disproportionately affected by the extremely adverse performance of a few countries. The median rate of inflation, which had stabilized at about 10% since 1982, remained largely unchanged during 1984. The IMF considered it disquieting that virtually no progress had been made in reducing the inflation rate since 1982. By contrast the industrial countries during the same period cut their inflation rates by more than a third. Once again the highest rates of inflation occurred in Latin America and Israel, while Asia enjoyed the lowest inflation rate.

Balance of Payments, Debt, and Financing. A further improvement in the external accounts of the less developed countries took place in 1984. Many countries took advantage of the strong growth in demand in industrial countries and increased their exports in volume terms. The total increase during 1984 was 8%, compared with 0.9% the year before. Latin-American and East Asian countries, which traditionally served the U.S. market, took full advantage of the opportunities. African countries experienced a much slower growth in exports, as import demand in their European markets was not as strong as in the U.S. Most African countries continued to rely on a few primary commodities, demand for which was fairly inelastic.

Against this favourable external background, the combined current account deficit of the less developed countries continued to improve. During 1984 it fell by more than $20 billion to $35.6 billion. Between 1981 and 1983 the reduction in the current account deficit from $105 billion to $57 billion was achieved entirely by a severe cutback in imports. Over the same period export revenue fell by $19 billion, and interest payments increased by $5.4 billion. Of the $33 billion increase in export revenues during 1984, only $3 billion was used for financing additional imports. The rest went to service interest payments and to build up depleted reserves.

Import cutting and other adjustment policies adopted by the major oil-exporting countries in the face of their sharply deteriorating current account position between 1981 and 1982 continued to have beneficial effects during 1984. Their current account deficit in 1984 narrowed to just under $6 billion, compared with $17 billion in 1983. A further modest improvement during 1985 was likely despite the sluggish global demand for oil and the high value of the dollar.

The aggregate deficit of the non-oil-exporting countries declined to $38 billion in 1984 (from a peak of $91 billion in 1981), representing 9% of exports of goods and services. These countries, not having the cushion of previous years' current account surplus that the oil exporters enjoyed, had to adopt stabilizing policies as early as 1982. Their economic policies during 1985 were still largely dominated by restrictive measures and import compression.

Centrally Planned Economies. The 40th session of the Council for Mutual Economic Assistance (Comecon) was held in Warsaw during June 25–27, 1985. The session was attended by the premiers, or their deputies, of all member countries: Bulgaria, Czechoslovakia, Cuba, Hungary, East Germany, Mongolia, Poland, Romania, Vietnam, and the Soviet Union. Delegates from Yugoslavia also attended, as did delegates with observer status from Afghanistan, Angola, Ethiopia, Laos, Mozambique, Nicaragua, and Yemen (Aden). The head of the Polish delegation, Gen. Wojciech Jaruzelski, chaired the session.

The first part of the debates was devoted to political issues. The session took note of the 40th anniversary of the victory over Germany and Japan and stressed the role "in liberating mankind from fascist captivity" that had been played by the Soviet Union. The session also acknowledged, with satisfaction, the fact that the host country, Poland, "had successfully resisted imperialist plotting."

The second part of the session was devoted to the economic and technical problems of Comecon. Emphasis was placed on improvements in economic efficiency, with the achievements being attributed to the growing role and importance of the economic, scientific, and technological cooperation between the member countries. In the discussion on the implementation of decisions adopted at the June 1984 Comecon summit, it was agreed that priority had to be given to certain areas of cooperation, mainly in engineering and electronics. Industrial specialization and cooperation in production had already brought significant improvements in supplying machinery and electronic equipment throughout the member nations. Currently, there was cooperation in planning the production of industrial robots. During the 40th session a general agreement was signed on multilateral cooperation in the development of automated production systems.

The delegates at the 40th session stated that the fuel, energy, and raw material bases of all member countries had been strengthened through the tapping of those countries' own resources. In the Soviet Union the construction of

Table VII. Output of Basic Industrial Products in Eastern Europe, 1984
In 000 metric tons unless otherwise stated

Country	Anthracite (hard coal)	Lignite (brown coal)	Natural gas (000,000 cu m)	Crude petroleum	Electric power (000,000 kw-hr)	Steel	Sulfuric acid	Cement
Bulgaria	240	32,124	...	...	44,580	2,868	908.4	5,712
Czechoslovakia	26,424	105,168	25,404	96	78,108	14,832	1,246.8	10,536
East Germany	...	296,340	...	...	110,100	7,572	884.4	11,556
Hungary	2,568	22,476	249,552	2,004	26,232	3,744	549.6	4,140
Poland	191,592	50,376	210,408	264	135,300	16,536	2,769.6	16,656
Romania	...	36,000	...	12,504	...	...	...	...
U.S.S.R.	484,320	153,000	20,468,640	612,228	1,493,004	153,996	25,296.0	130,056

Source: UN, *Monthly Bulletin of Statistics.*

a mining complex at Krivy Rog, which would eventually supply 13 million tons of iron ore to member countries, was well under way. Also in the Soviet Union the construction of the first one million-kw generating unit at the Khmielnicka nuclear power station was near completion.

The session considered the coordination of the national economic plans of the Comecon countries for the years 1986 to 1990. This decision, made at the summit meeting in 1984, was being implemented. The member countries agreed in principle on the delivery quotas of goods during the next five-year period. Moreover, the Comecon countries signed 17 agreements concerning the development of economic, scientific, and technological cooperation that would be valid until the year 2000. The Comecon member nations also agreed to provide economic assistance to Cuba, Mongolia, and Vietnam, as well as to other nonmember less developed countries.

The session stated that in 1984 the national income of the Comecon countries increased by 3.6%, as compared with 1983, while industrial output expanded by 4.4% and agricultural production by 3%. Foreign trade by Comecon countries in 1984 increased 9.7% over 1983.

Dealing with political and economic relations with the West, the session declared that these were pursued under conditions of international tension "caused by the policy of confrontation and the imperialistic circles' attempts to obtain military supremacy." The session claimed that "the rapid growth of military expenditure and of the deficit of the United States budget" was disturbing the normal development of world trade. The session reaffirmed, however, its intention to establish formal relations between Comecon and the European Economic Community.

In spite of many promises and expectations, the coordination of national economic plans was not completed at the 40th session, and the joint program for technological advancement was still in the planning stage. In fact, no grand plan for economic integration emerged. There were several reasons for the lack of progress. One was that member countries of Comecon tended strongly to defend their own particular interests. Another reason was the fact that there was no unified price-forming system within Comecon, thus making it impossible to calculate the profitability of any transaction. Also there were significant differences in the ways the nations planned and managed their economies, with Hungary relying more on market mechanisms and the Soviet Union, as well as most other Comecon countries,

adhering more to a "command economy" controlled by central planning.

The slow progress of implementing decisions taken at Comecon sessions prompted leaders of Comecon countries to involve national Communist parties in Comecon planning. In May 1985 an unprecedented meeting took place in Moscow in which party secretaries responsible for economic affairs took part. The objective of the meeting was to assess the implementation of decisions made at the 1984 summit meeting, especially those relating to economic integration and cooperation in technological advancement.

INTERNATIONAL TRADE

During 1985 economic growth in OECD member countries was estimated at 2.75%, representing a marked deceleration from the rise of 4.9% achieved a year earlier. In the same period, however, the slowdown in the growth of world trade was much more pronounced. At the end of 1985 it was estimated that the volume of world exports for the entire year would register a gain of 4–5%, as against a rise of 8% in 1984. By far the most important reason for this was the unexpectedly large cutback in oil imports. Mainly because of continued energy conservation, aided by several years of heavy investment in energy-saving equipment, Western industrialized countries used significantly less oil in 1985 than in 1984. During the first six months of 1985 oil usage was approximately 3% below that of the corresponding period of the preceding year, and the estimated outcome for the whole of 1985 was a reduction of some 2.5%. At the same time, oil stocks were depleted in anticipation of a further weakening of oil prices.

The effect of these developments was reflected in OPEC (Organization of Petroleum Exporting Countries) exports. In volume terms these were believed to have declined 4%, compared with an increase of 1.6% in 1984. Another reason for the relatively slow growth in world trade was the weakness of commodity prices. This had an adverse effect on foreign exchange earnings and, therefore, on the ability to afford imports of a number of less developed countries. As 1985 drew to a close, only partial statistics were available, but the initial estimates suggested that imports by the less developed countries would grow by only some 4.5%, as against just over 5% in 1984.

The cutback in OPEC exports had a marked adverse effect on imports by OPEC members. These were believed to have fallen by 5% in 1985, as against a cutback of 3% during the preceding year. This decline, which weakened the import capacity of the non-oil less developed countries, had a significant effect on the exports of the industrialized world. Thus, total exports from the OECD area were estimated to have risen by only about 5.5%, compared with a gain of 9.5% in 1984. Most OECD members faced a deceleration in their export growth, with West Germany and the U.K. losing comparatively little momentum but with Japan and the U.S. experiencing less than half their 1984 growth rates. Although the centrally planned economies appeared to have maintained their import growth at about the 1984 level, their exports were heading for an increase of little more than 5%, as compared with 7.5% in 1984. This was the result of the generally lower level of economic activity in the world's principal markets as well as a reduction in exports of Soviet fuel.

During 1985 the terms of trade moved sharply in favour of the industrialized countries. Despite a cutback in OPEC oil production in response to reduced world demand, the average price of crude oil declined by about 2% in the wake of a 4% decline in 1984. At the same time, non-

(continued on page 216)

Table VIII. Soviet Trade with Eastern European Countries
In 000,000 rubles, current prices

Country	Exports			Imports		
	1982	1983	1984	1982	1983	1984
Bulgaria	4,884.6	5,510.8	6,124.4	4,288.1	5,053.3	5,608.0
Czechoslovakia	5,047.5	5,871.6	6,590.8	4,731.9	5,420.4	6,016.5
East Germany	6,419.6	6,797.8	7,481.4	5,776.2	6,595.7	7,367.2
Hungary	3,707.2	4,058.0	4,320.8	3,746.4	4,007.0	4,434.4
Poland	4,812.9	5,274.3	6,069.2	4,097.0	4,786.7	5,296.8
Romania	1,423.6	1,639.6	1,807.2	1,683.4	1,665.3	1,755.2

Source: U.S.S.R. Foreign Trade Statistics/Moscow.

Table IX. Soviet Crude Petroleum and Products Supplied to Eastern Europe
In 000 rubles

Country	1982	1983	1984
Bulgaria	1,546,132	1,784,757	2,020,887
Czechoslovakia	2,067,504	2,433,526	2,746,953
East Germany	2,414,248	2,740,140	3,124,839
Hungary	1,120,233	1,156,062	1,396,398
Poland	1,889,191	2,185,268	2,520,403
Romania	66,314	185,201	283,586

Source: U.S.S.R. Foreign Trade Statistics/Moscow.

The Case Against Protectionism: A U.S. View

BY SENATOR CHARLES McC. MATHIAS, JR.

The issue of trade protectionism has gathered political force in many countries beset with continuing economic problems. It is proving increasingly difficult to craft sound national and international trade policies at a time of low or uneven global economic growth. The seemingly simple solution of restricting imports to protect certain domestic workers and industries has had considerable appeal to politicians unable or unwilling to act decisively with respect to fundamental economic problems. Yet the prospects for stimulating and perpetuating economic growth in the future will be jeopardized by trade-restricting measures under consideration in many capitals.

The United States has led and benefited from the tremendous growth in global commerce in the last 30 years. In 1950 U.S. exports and imports of goods and services constituted only about 9% of the nation's gross national product. By 1985 this had grown to 21%. The U.S. is the world's largest importer and exporter. Annual U.S. merchandise exports are in excess of $200 billion. One in every five dollars of U.S. manufacturing output is exported, along with roughly 30% of U.S. grain production. The economy benefits, as well, from imports that hold down costs and so stimulate economic growth and inhibit inflationary pressures.

The GATT Regime. Current sentiment favouring trade protectionism flies in the face of the dominant direction of informed opinion in free-market economies since World War II. This opinion has advocated, and political leaders have sought, reductions in the barriers to the free flow of goods across international borders. The framework for this effort has been the General Agreement on Tariffs and Trade (GATT).

The GATT was first negotiated in 1947. The sorry experience with trade restrictions during the Great Depression of the 1930s provided the impetus for implementing tariff reductions and establishing orderly trade arrangements. The GATT contains a list of negotiated tariff schedules and principles and rules governing the trade of the signatory countries. These elements have been modified in seven rounds of trade negotiations since the 1940s, most notably the Kennedy Round, concluded in 1967, which greatly reduced tariff schedules, and the Tokyo Round, concluded in 1979, which sought to address issues of nontariff barriers to trade. The unifying concept governing the GATT system is the most-favoured-nation principle holding that contracting parties will conduct their commercial relations with each other on the basis of nondiscrimination.

Annual world merchandise exports reached $2 trillion

in the 1980s, aided by a generally receptive global trading environment and a framework of accepted rules. Nonetheless, the 1980s have witnessed a significantly lessened commitment in the U.S. and elsewhere to expanding the free-trade system. In part, this is because the evolution in the GATT has not kept up with the evolution in the global economic environment.

The global economy has changed significantly since the first GATT negotiations took place in the 1940s. Trade in goods has been swamped by short-term financial flows ($2 trillion versus approximately $40 trillion annually). Floating exchange rates have disrupted the exchange markets. The debt crisis of the 1980s has exacerbated the uncertainties in the global economy. Lowered growth in industrialized countries has focused greater attention on persistent unemployment problems.

Moreover, GATT member governments have not fully subscribed to the nontariff barrier agreements or codes established during the Tokyo Round. Successful tariff negotiations have exposed nontariff barriers to trade. Significant areas of global trade are not covered by GATT. And there are a rising number of bilateral agreements and understandings, such as voluntary restraint agreements, that circumvent GATT rules.

The New Wave of Protectionism. More important, in terms of the U.S. commitment to free-trade principles, has been the emergence in recent years of three economic factors that, together, have sent the U.S. trade deficit to unprecedented heights and weakened opposition to import restrictions. These factors are the global debt crisis, the appreciation of the U.S. dollar, and faster U.S. economic growth relative to other major economies.

The Latin-American debt crisis has been a disaster for U.S. exporters. In 1981 U.S. exports south of the border totaled $42 billion; two years later this figure had dropped to $25.5 billion. But, if the Latin Americans could not buy, others would not buy because an overvalued U.S. dollar made U.S. products uncompetitive abroad. By March 1985, when the value of the dollar peaked, it had risen 98% in less than five years against a trade-weighted average of ten major currencies. Finally, relatively greater U.S. economic growth in 1983 and 1984 helped to bid up the value of the dollar and attracted imports.

These factors merged to drive the U.S. trade deficit from a modest $25 billion in 1981 to a projected $150 billion in 1985, with no end in sight. The U.S. current account went from a positive $6.3 billion in 1981 to a negative $101.6 billion in 1984. The trade balances of virtually every U.S. industry have deteriorated since 1980. The free-trade community in the U.S. has retreated in the face of a rising chorus of voices favouring protectionist measures of one sort or another. The benefits to the U.S. economy from imports, such as lowered inflation, have been submerged by the distress of the exporting sectors and of industries competing with imports.

Inevitably, the issue of trade protectionism has become politically charged. It arises at a time of difficult transition for certain U.S. industries and their workers. The understandable political reaction to the pain experienced by U.S. textile and steel workers is to seek to protect them from the pressures of imports. Moreover, there is an understandable tendency to see their problems as resulting from the unfair practices of others. In response to these pressures, numerous trade-restricting bills have been introduced into both houses of Congress. Much of this legislation is based on unilateral reciprocity, discrimination, and threats of retaliation that fly in the face not only of U.S. GATT obligations but of economic good sense as well.

Charles McC. Mathias, Jr., served as U.S. senator from Maryland from 1969 and as U.S. representative (1961–69).

The protectionist analysis of U.S. trade problems is faulty, and therefore the proposed remedy of restricting imports is incorrect and ultimately dangerous. The root of the problem is that Americans do not save enough. There is a gap between what they save as a nation and what they invest. That gap is being filled through foreign borrowing. But this means that foreigners are purchasing dollars, thus keeping the value of the dollar high, and investing these dollars in the U.S. market. In the process U.S. exports stagnate and imports soar.

Much has been made of the so-called "Japan problem." The U.S. trade deficit with Japan continues to worsen, rising from $15.8 billion in 1981 to an annual rate of over $45 billion in 1985. Some in the U.S. point to Japanese barriers to imports. Barriers exist, but no one argues that the increase in the trade deficit between the two countries is due to an increase in Japanese restrictions on imports. Even if all the barriers were removed, a sizable trade deficit would exist, the result of comparative U.S.-Japanese rates of productivity and unit labour costs as well as comparative savings rates. The Japanese, quite simply, produce more, for less money, and save more and consume less than Americans.

Dealing with the Trade Deficit. In order to deal with the trade deficit, the U.S. must deal with its saving-investment problem. It must reduce the federal budget deficit, which is maintaining upward pressure on U.S. interest rates and increasing the need to borrow abroad. Productivity must be increased. Domestic savings must be encouraged. Furthermore, the U.S. must encourage growth in other countries that will strengthen their currencies and raise their demand for imports.

The U.S. must do so because self-interest demands it. A nation must export to grow. Moreover, others look to the U.S. for leadership in this area. The prime minister of Singapore, Lee Kuan Yew, in addressing a joint session of the United States Congress on Oct. 9, 1985, made this point: "Putting up barriers to America's markets would halt the economic advancement of the free-market-oriented developing countries. It would send a signal that the model provided by the countries of East and Southeast Asia is no longer an available option. It could set off a chain reaction which would result in a downward spiral of the world economy."

Protectionists want tariffs. They argue that not only would domestic workers and industries be protected from unfair competition but revenue would be raised to put against the budget deficit and so reduce pressure on U.S. interest rates. These benefits must be weighed against the costs of tariffs, which would include:

- Higher prices and, therefore, reduced national output;
- Reduced economic activity for countries exporting to the U.S., including major debtor nations;
- Possible retaliation against U.S. exports;
- Increases in the dollar exchange rate and therefore lower U.S. exports.

These costs argue not for more barriers to trade but for fewer. The needs of workers in vulnerable industries should be met by retraining, not by putting workers in other industries on the unemployment rolls. The U.S. should also seek negotiated reductions in the remaining barriers to trade. This means a new round of GATT negotiations.

The obstacles likely to be encountered in another round, however, are formidable. As in the past, the U.S. would have to be the moving force behind a new round of negotiations. However, the U.S. no longer dominates the global economy as it once did. Nor is there a consensus about what should be achieved in a new round and what the U.S.

Talked about nearly as much in 1985 as they had been in 1930: Willis Hawley (left), chairman of the Ways and Means Committee of the U.S. House of Representatives, and Reed Smoot, head of the Senate Finance Committee, whose names became a byword for self-destructive trade protectionism.
UPI/BETTMANN NEWSPHOTOS

should be prepared to give up. High U.S. unemployment in key industries such as textiles and steel, whose products might be subject to negotiation, complicates the task of consensus building. The administration, in seeking authority from Congress to proceed, would have to indicate both what it wants to obtain in a new round and what it might be prepared to give up.

Other countries have reservations with respect to a new round. France has maintained that priority should be placed on international monetary reform. The European Communities, though on record in support of a new round, would be hesitant to move on agricultural issues that might jeopardize the EC's common agricultural policy. Though Japan is supportive of a new round, there are those who maintain that the "Japan problem" should be one of its main topics. The major debtor nations express concern that easing of import restrictions in their countries could ignite a fresh debt crisis. Brazil and India have led the opposition of the less developed countries.

Furthermore, in many ways, the easy issues have been tackled by previous GATT negotiations. Tariffs have been significantly lowered in successive GATT rounds. Now the less visible barriers to trade remain—at a time of lowered global economic growth, excess capacity in key industrial sectors, and chronic unemployment.

There are numerous agendas for a new round in circulation. Generally they seek to (1) reverse the trend to protectionism, (2) involve less developed countries in the process, and (3) deal with nontariff barriers. Ideally, a new round would strengthen the existing trading system by dealing more substantively with agriculture, textiles, and steel. It would extend GATT to new areas, including trade in services, high tech, investment, and intellectual property. Beyond that, it would improve the existing safeguard system intended to provide troubled industries with temporary relief from import competition through protection implemented on an evenhanded basis against all foreign suppliers. Further, the process of dispute settlement in the GATT system would be improved. The subsidies, government procurement, and standards codes negotiated during the Tokyo Round need to be fully implemented, enforced, and extended as well.

These efforts should constitute the priorities of wise U.S. trade policy, not erecting dangerous barriers to trade.

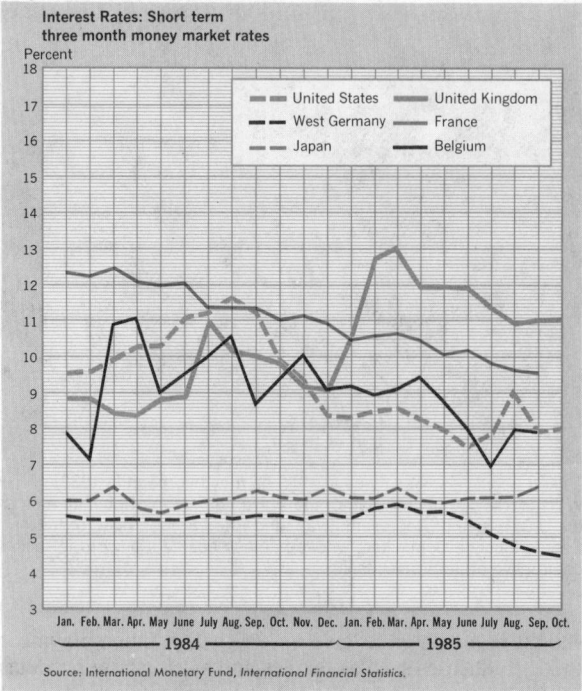

Interest Rates: Short term three month money market rates

Percent

Legend:
— United States
— United Kingdom
— West Germany
— France
— Japan
— Belgium

Jan. Feb. Mar. Apr. May June July Aug. Sep. Oct. Nov. Dec. | Jan. Feb. Mar. Apr. May June July Aug. Sep. Oct.
1984 · 1985

Source: International Monetary Fund, *International Financial Statistics.*

(continued from page 213)

oil commodity prices did even worse, recording a fall of 9–10%, as compared with a modest gain of 1% in 1984. The weakest area was food. As a result of good harvests in 1984 for most food crops, 1985 opened with weakening prices and fairly large supplies. During the year output (and crop prospects) remained strong, and prices declined rapidly. At the end of the year the average fall in the price of the principal food commodities—grains, sugar, coffee, tea, and cocoa—was about 13%, as against an increase of 5% in 1984. A substantial decline, perhaps about 8–9%, was also registered in prices of agricultural raw materials such as wool, cotton, and rubber. This compared with a decline of only 2% for those goods in 1984 and was the result of the high level of output in both 1985 and the preceding year. By contrast, the trend of metal prices was comparatively encouraging. Although these exhibited (the customary) widespread fluctuations from period to period and product to product, it seemed that on average they lost no significant ground in 1985, after declining about 6% in 1984.

The figures available at the end of 1985 suggested that the trade deficit of the OECD area could total some $50 billion for the year. This was about $10 billion more than the deficit recorded in 1984 ($41.3 billion) but more than double the shortfall in 1983. Just as the 1984 explosion was the result of a severe deterioration in U.S. foreign trade performance, the unexpected increase in 1985 owed much to U.S. developments. In 1984 a rapidly appreciating dollar made imports relatively cheap and exports expensive for the U.S. Combined with a rapid growth in domestic demand, this resulted in a massive 24% gain in the volume of imports and a relatively modest rise of 7% in exports. This pushed the U.S. trade balance into deficit to the tune of $123 billion, compared with $69 billion in 1983. Although the dollar continued to strengthen during the first quarter of 1985, it weakened markedly against most other currencies during the remainder of the year. This reduced the attraction of foreign products, which, together with weaker demand for oil and a less buoyant growth in the economy, led to a cutback in the rise of imports to about

7–8%. Nevertheless, although the weaker dollar also made U.S. exports more competitive, it was not possible to gain the full benefit of this in view of the slowdown in world economic growth and the weakening of import demand in the oil-producing nations and, to a lesser extent, in the non-oil less developed countries. As a result the volume of U.S. exports during 1985 was estimated to have risen by only some 3–4% and, combined with the fall in the external value of the dollar, the net effect of those developments was a further, but relatively modest, increase in the U.S. trade deficit. On the basis of the figures for the first three quarters of 1985, the outcome for the year was projected to be a deficit of around $135 billion, representing an increase of some 10% over the 1984 figure.

In sharp contrast to the U.S., Japan experienced an additional rise in its already excessive trade surplus, although the rate of increase slackened as the year went on and was not as pronounced as in 1984. During that year the volume of Japanese exports rose by just over 16% as a result of a weak yen and little growth in domestic demand. During 1985, however, partly in response to growing foreign criticism of Japanese trade and economic policies, the yen appreciated sharply and domestic demand rose somewhat. This had a marked effect on the volume growth of Japanese merchandise sales overseas, with the latest available projections pointing to an increase of only some 8–9%. Unfortunately, and unexpectedly, there was also a significant slowdown—from 10.8% in 1984 to perhaps 6% in 1985—in the volume growth of imports, with much of the weakness coming from goods supplied by the U.S. and OPEC. The net result was a further rise in the trade surplus to an estimated $50 billion, an increase of approximately 12% over the preceding year. The Tokyo government, therefore, remained under considerable international pressure to take effective steps to reduce this imbalance by restraining the growth of Japanese exports and by enhancing domestic demand, in combination with further measures to open up its markets to overseas exporters.

The foreign trade performance of the United Kingdom improved markedly during the year under review. Largely because of a weakening in the external value of sterling and a decline in unit labour costs in manufacturing to the first quarter of 1985, U.K. export competitiveness improved significantly. As a result, following a strong growth of some 9% in export volume in 1984, there was an increase of nearly 10% in the first six months of 1985. However, with sterling appreciating from the spring onward, export growth became a little weaker in the second half of the year. Nevertheless, 1985 as a whole was still expected to produce an overall gain of 7%, a slowdown of less than two percentage points from the advance of the preceding year. At a time when the volume of OECD exports as a whole increased less than half as much as in 1984, this was widely considered to be a creditable achievement. Imports, on the other hand, fully shared in the slowdown in growth experienced by the developed countries. As in the case of the U.S., this was partly the result of lower imports of oil, which was particularly marked in the wake of the resumption of work in the country's coal mines in March 1985. For the year as a whole, merchandise imports rose by about 4.5%, approximately half as fast as in 1984. Together with the strengthening in the value of sterling, these trends combined to produce a dramatic reduction in the country's trade deficit from £4,100 million in 1984 to approximately £1,800 million in 1985.

Other important OECD countries followed a somewhat different course. Although West Germany's overall economic growth may have slackened a little in 1985, the

STEVE SACK; REPRINTED WITH PERMISSION FROM THE MINNEAPOLIS STAR

volume of overseas purchases remained relatively high, and the final figures for the year were expected to show a gain of around 4.5%, as against one of 5.2% a year earlier. Exports, on the other hand, registered an overall advance of 7%, about 2% slower than a year earlier but still well in excess of the rise in imports. The result was a strong increase in the trade surplus, from $22 billion to $24 billion. Like West Germany, France did not manage an acceleration in the rate of economic growth during 1985. In contrast to the West German experience, however, the volume of French imports rose faster than in the previous year, by approximately 3.5%, as against 2.3% in 1984. This was regarded as a disappointing performance, betraying some

structural weakness in the economy. Also, after a relatively good start, the rate of growth in exports slackened, and expectations were that the trade deficit would increase.

While there was some increase in OECD trade between 1984 and 1985, the current account of the balance of payments deteriorated somewhat. This was the result of a significant increase in the deficit on invisible transactions—shipping, tourism, receipts, and remittances of profits on foreign investments—from $24 billion in 1984 to approximately $33 billion in 1985. The main reason for this was the trend in the U.S., where there were indications of a substantial decline in the traditional invisible surplus as a result of a cutback in the net inflow of investment income. In Japan, however, the position appeared to be the reverse. Japanese business had been investing large sums abroad in recent years as a means of reducing the country's external surplus and thus lessening protectionist sentiment among its trading partners. As a result profits earned from foreign investments rose rapidly, offsetting an increasing proportion of the traditional deficit in such invisible items as transportation and tourism. The last available forecast suggested that the 1984 invisible deficit of $9.3 billion might have been cut back by about $1 billion in 1985. Most other major members of the OECD performed as they had in 1984; West Germany and Canada recorded large but broadly unchanged deficits, while the U.K., France, and Italy earned modest surpluses.

For the OECD as a whole, the visible and invisible trade developments gave rise to a current account deficit of about $83 billion. This represented an increase of some 33%, compared with the gain of 160% in 1984. In relative terms, therefore, the 1985 performance represented a significant improvement, although the absolute level of the deficit was more than three times as high as the 1982–83 average. As has already been pointed out, this was entirely due to the U.S. performance; in fact, apart from the U.S., with a deficit of around $120 million, the only major member of the OECD recording a current account deficit was Italy, where the total was estimated at around $4 billion. In contrast, Japan and West Germany were heavily in surplus, and small positive balances were also earned by the U.K., France, Spain, The Netherlands, and Canada.

On the basis of incomplete figures available in late 1985, OPEC countries seemed to have secured an improvement

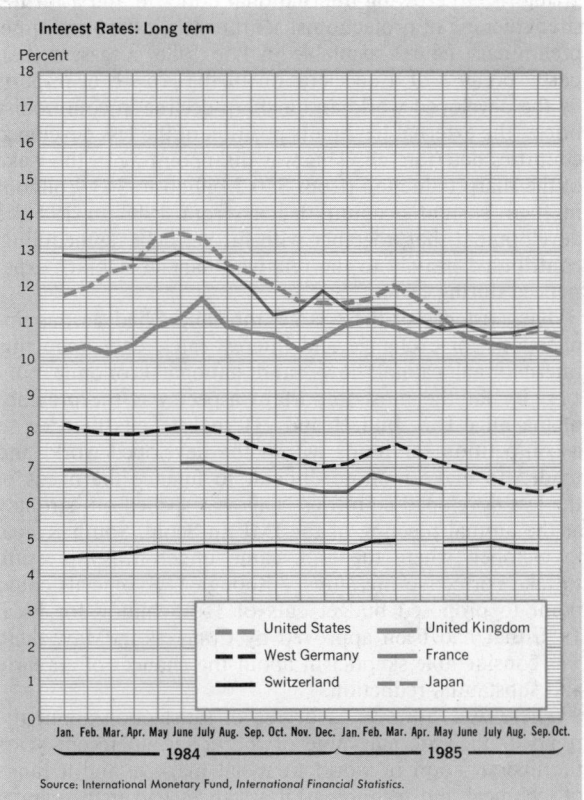

Interest Rates: Long term

Percent

United States
West Germany
Switzerland
United Kingdom
France
Japan

Jan. Feb. Mar. Apr. May June July Aug. Sep. Oct. Nov. Dec. Jan. Feb. Mar. Apr. May June July Aug. Sep. Oct.
— 1984 — — 1985 —

Source: International Monetary Fund, *International Financial Statistics.*

in their external payments position. Although both the price of and the demand for oil were weak in 1985, OPEC countries cut back their imports and managed to enlarge their trade surplus from $55 billion to $60 billion. As in the past, however, this was more than offset by the deficit incurred on invisible transactions, and the current account was heading for a net deficit of about $5 billion. This, however, represented a marked improvement over 1984, during which the deficit was $10 billion; in 1983 it had been $20 billion. In contrast, the non-oil less developed countries faced a deterioration in their external payments position, reversing the steady improvement they had made between 1980 and 1984. Their overall current

deficit was expected to reach $30 million, as against $24 million, partly because of weaker demand for their products and a significant shift in the terms of trade in favour of the industrialized countries. There was little up-to-date information about the external accounts of the centrally planned economies, but the early expectations were that there would not be a significant change in 1985 from the current account surplus of $9.6 billion achieved in 1984.

INTERNATIONAL EXCHANGE AND PAYMENTS

Contrary to the fears expressed toward the end of 1984, a relatively stable world financial climate characterized 1985. In spite of a slowdown in the growth of the world economy, a marked deceleration in the rise of world trade, a sharp fall in commodity prices, and continuing concern about the volume and nature of deficit financing in some countries, the problems of the principal debtors remained under control, and there were no crises of significant international proportions. This, to a large extent, was a tribute to the degree of cooperation between the major financial powers as well as to the efficiency and sophistication of both national and international financial institutions in managing a potentially troublesome situation. In terms of solving the underlying problems of world finance, however, only limited progress was made.

As in 1984, the international financial scene was characterized by major imbalances. The U.S. administration continued to run a huge budget deficit and, despite some attempts to reverse the trend, there was a further increase in the current account deficit from approximately $102 billion to an estimated $120 billion. Furthermore, as in the previous year, a very large part of the U.S. deficit was financed by an inflow of foreign funds, making it more difficult for other, less powerful economies to cover their funding requirements. By contrast, a significant rise in their trade and current account surpluses took place in Japan and West Germany, with the performance of the former giving rise to growing international criticism and a further strengthening of protectionist sentiment. At the same time, preliminary figures available in late 1985 suggested that, partly because of a deceleration in the growth of imports by the developed world and a sharp decline in commodity prices, the external payments position of the less developed countries deteriorated. This was disappointing in the wake of the sharp reduction (from $70.5 billion to $43.9 billion) in their current account deficits from 1983 to 1984, a development that, together with further debt rescheduling, contributed heavily to the relative financial stability experienced during 1984.

The existence of these large imbalances had serious implications for exchange and interest rates, debt financing, international capital flows, and national economic policies. By far the most important aspect was the presence of the huge U.S. budget and external deficits that led to a competition for funds within the developed world and tended to make it more difficult to finance the needs of the less developed countries. This was spelled out strongly at the annual meeting of the IMF in Seoul, South Korea, in October, where the U.S. came under heavy pressure to take corrective measures. Although U.S. officials could point to proposed budget cuts of $55.5 billion for fiscal 1986 that had been approved by Congress in May, there was considerable skepticism about the chances of an early and substantial reduction.

There was, however, a degree of satisfaction about the trend of the external value of the dollar. In recent years the liberalization of world financial markets and a range of technical and technological advances had made capital

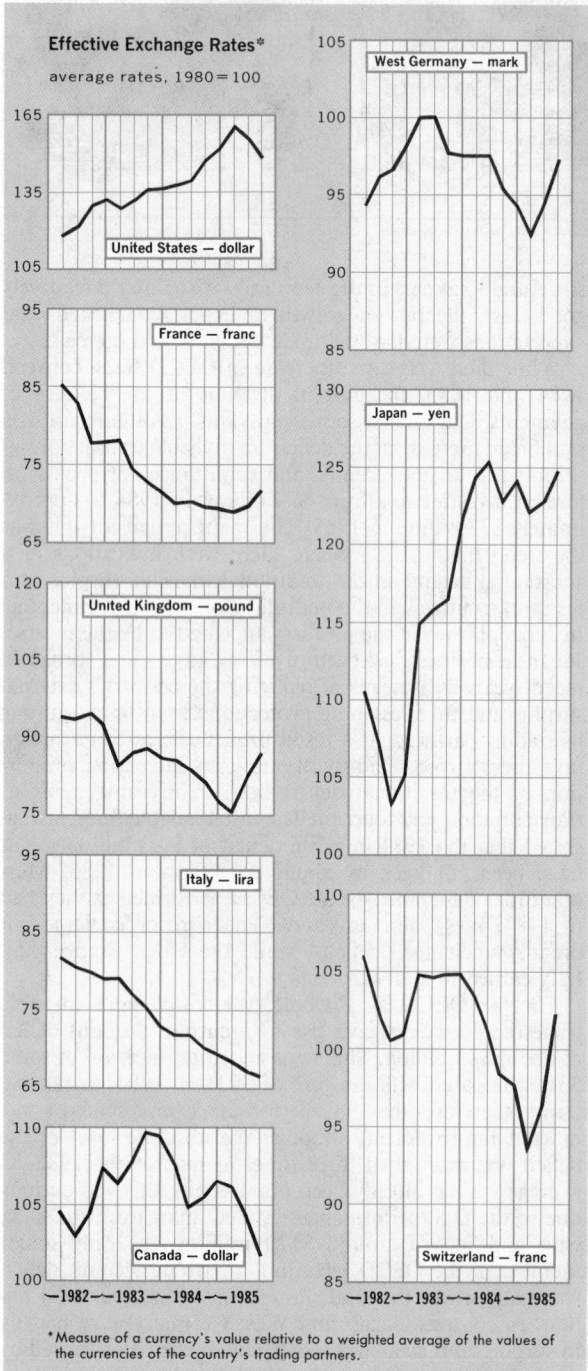

Effective Exchange Rates*

average rates, 1980 = 100

United States — dollar

France — franc

United Kingdom — pound

Italy — lira

Canada — dollar

West Germany — mark

Japan — yen

Switzerland — franc

—1982— —1983— —1984— —1985

*Measure of a currency's value relative to a weighted average of the values of the currencies of the country's trading partners.

Source: International Monetary Fund, *International Financial Statistics.*

flows from country to country considerably easier. The result was that, unlike the situation in the age of strict national controls on external capital transactions, it became relatively simple for countries to attract external finance in order to cover their deficits as long as they provided a sufficiently high reward/risk ratio to foreign holders of capital. This created a situation in which the traditional weapons of dealing with national deficits—deflation, currency devaluation, and restrictions on the outflow of capital—became less relevant. On the contrary, as long as a sufficient flow of funds from abroad was maintained, it was possible to run large external deficits and at the same time ensure an appreciation in the currency.

Such an appreciation, however, made imports cheaper and exports more expensive, and this in turn tended to make the achievement of external equilibrium more difficult. The recent U.S. experience was a case in point. Under the impact of relatively high interest rates, continued confidence in the growth prospects of the economy, and fears about the financial stability of some less developed countries, a strong flow of international capital to the U.S. had taken place during the past few years. This not only financed the huge U.S. budget and external deficits but also resulted in a significant appreciation in the external value of the dollar during 1984 and the first two months of 1985, tending to impair U.S. trade performance even further. From February 1985, however, the underlying trend in the dollar was in a downward direction, largely as a result of a reduction in interest-rate differentials as well as an increasing degree of national and international intervention in foreign exchange markets aimed at pushing the U.S. currency down to more realistic levels. As a result, by the second quarter of 1985 the trade-weighted value of the dollar was 2.7% below the average for the previous three-month period. This was followed by a further significant depreciation in the wake of the September agreement reached by the Group of Five to take further steps to push the dollar down. As a result, the average for the July–September quarter revealed a further decline of 4.8% from the preceding quarter. The downward trend was confirmed in October and November, and it was widely anticipated that by the end of the year the external value of the dollar would be some 20% lower than in January 1985. Nevertheless, many observers believed that even at that level the dollar was overvalued and that a further reduction would be required to make significant inroads into the large U.S. trade deficit.

In terms of the dollar, most major currencies appreciated significantly. The most spectacular increase occurred in the dollar value of sterling, which was some 32% higher in November 1985 than in February of the same year. Between February and October the value of the West German Deutsche Mark rose by some 20% and that of the Japanese yen by 24%. As the year drew to a close, the trend was still upward, although in some countries, notably the U.K., there were growing fears that a further appreciation would have a serious adverse effect on exports.

Currencies within the European Monetary System (EMS) achieved a high degree of stability against each other. This was largely because of a broad convergence of their economic policies that were aimed at restricting inflation and reducing government deficits. Nevertheless, Italy experienced considerably higher inflation than most other European countries, and in July 1985 the lira's central parity within the EMS was devalued by 6% while the other members' parities were revalued by 2%. Other developments of interest during the period under review included the decision in March 1985 to allow the New Zealand dollar to float in an attempt to bring the exchange-rate policy in line with the gradual liberalization of the country's financial sector that had begun halfway through 1984.

As pointed out above, one of the reasons for the gradual depreciation in the external value of the U.S. dollar was the narrowing of that nation's interest-rate differentials with respect to other major countries. Nevertheless, as 1985 drew to a close, U.S. interest rates were still appreciably higher than in other major OECD members except for the U.K. The U.S. federal funds rate started to decline from its high point of 11.6% in August 1984, and by the beginning of 1985 it was down to 8.3%. A modest strengthening took place during the next two months, but the downward trend was resumed in March and by September the rate was down to 7.9%. Short- and long-term yields followed a largely similar pattern, with the rate on 91-day Treasury bills falling from 7.8% in January 1985 to 7.1% in September. Japanese interest rates, by contrast, were largely stable. The Bank of Japan's official discount rate was raised by 0.5% to 5.5% in November in order to ensure a further rise in the value of the yen against the dollar. However, interest-rate differentials with the U.S. remained significant although not quite as pronounced as in the second half of 1984. The same was true of West Germany, where the Lombard rate was reduced from 6 to 5.5% in August 1985. French interest rates also moved downward, reflecting the government's preoccupation with boosting domestic economic activity. Between the first and third quarter of the year, the money market intervention rate dropped from 10.75 to 9.38%, a trend that was reflected in three-month interbank rates. In spite of this, French rates were still somewhat above those in the U.S. at the end of 1985. The same was also true of the U.K. During 1984 U.K. base rates tended to be slightly higher than the U.S. federal fund rate. In January 1985 the base rates were hiked to 14% in an attempt to underpin sterling, and although they had fallen back to 11.5% by July, this was well in excess of comparable U.S. rates of about 7.9%. It was largely due to the existence of this wide gap that the dollar value of sterling appreciated 32% between January and November 1985.

During 1984–85 the IMF confirmed its efforts to ease the problems of weaker debtor countries by rescheduling their debts and mobilizing support from commercial banks and other nongovernmental sources. The most important agreements negotiated during this period included a major multiyear rescheduling plan for Mexico that involved a total of $49 billion, the stretching of repayment over 14 years, and an improvement in the terms of the loan. Another $21 billion agreement was reached with Venezuela, and progress was also made with other smaller rescheduling agreements. However, although these and other similar steps helped to defuse a number of particularly difficult and potentially dangerous situations, the underlying problem of the huge debts incurred by the less developed countries was not solved.

With the downturn in the growth of world trade and the weakening in commodity prices, many debtor nations were likely to face renewed problems and display growing resistance to the inevitable economic sacrifices involved in meeting IMF requirements. During 1985 Peru failed to comply with the IMF's terms and called for the debt-servicing terms of a less developed country to be related to its export performance. Brazil, too, failed to meet its obligations and declared a 140-day moratorium on debt repayments, while Pres. Fidel Castro of Cuba called for the unilateral repudiation of the debts of the less developed countries. Another difficulty was South Africa's inability to meet its debt obligations, and while this was regarded

Years of hyperinflation, devaluation, and currency changes created new kinds of money consciousness in Argentina, as evidenced by these three-year-old bills on sale as curiosities in a Buenos Aires antique shop.
REUTERS/BETTMANN NEWSPHOTOS

as a problem of a less fundamental nature, it served to underline the potentially destabilizing effects of adverse economic and political development for countries with large debts.

It was feared that one consequence of this situation would be a growing reluctance on the part of commercial banks to adopt a flexible approach to countries with debt problems and to the granting of new credit. This, in turn, could restrain the growth of the comparatively poor and unstable economies, which not only would affect growth in the rest of the world but might force those poorer nations to take extreme steps detrimental to world financial stability. Recognizing these dangers, the October IMF conference held in Seoul devoted considerable attention to the problem of world debt.

In addition to agreeing (as it always did) to the key importance of rapid economic growth in the industrialized world, to the rejection of protectionism, and to continuing efforts to increase the volume of investable savings generated within less developed countries, the conference also discussed a specific proposal put forward by the U.S. Known as the Baker Plan (after U.S. Secretary of the Treasury James Baker), this would provide some $20 billion over three years, largely through commercial banks, to the large debtor countries, including Mexico, Brazil, Argentina, and Yugoslavia. The plan would also provide for additional lending of $9 billion by the World Bank and regional development banks over and above the $18 billion that would, under present policies, have been lent anyway.

At the same time, it was suggested that the bulk of the repayments due to the IMF Trust Fund should be re-lent to particularly poor countries with serious external payments difficulties. Both the president and the managing director of the IMF gave strong support to the plan, although commercial bankers, already overexposed in terms of lending to the third world, greeted the proposals with a distinct lack of enthusiasm.   (IEIS)

This article updates the *Macropædia* articles BANKS AND BANKING; ECONOMIC GROWTH AND PLANNING; GOVERNMENT FINANCE; INTERNATIONAL TRADE.

STOCK EXCHANGES

Stock exchanges throughout the world generally staged broad-based advances in 1985. All of the major stock price indexes except one registered gains (*see* TABLE X),

with many reaching new all-time highs. World commodity prices also experienced gains but remained well below their record highs set in 1980.

Stock price movements are generally determined by a mixture of economic developments and psychological factors. In 1985 the favourable conditions outweighed the negative influences. Real GNP in most countries was modest but on the upswing. Corporate profits were rising, and consumer confidence about the outlook for world peace was generally high. Moreover, substantial surpluses existed worldwide in manufacturing capacity; wage costs were stabilizing; and new wage settlements were down significantly from the early 1980s. In an environment of relatively slow economic growth and subdued inflation, both short- and long-term interest-rate levels tended to enhance the relative attractiveness of equity securities and reduce the appeal of investing in tangible assets, such as precious metals, stamps, rare coins, and art.

The widespread bullish performance of stock prices throughout the industrialized world in 1985 was also influenced by growing economic and political conservatism and by the apparent success of the private sector in adjusting to the structural imbalances caused by the long and painful process of moving from inflation to disinflation. The adoption of policies and programs by major industrial nations to give higher priority to increasing productivity and boosting corporate profits began to bear fruit. The new entrepreneurial spirit and profit-oriented business philosophy was reflected not only in the trend toward the sale of state-owned assets, public distribution of the shares of denationalized enterprises, and increased incentives for equity investment but also in a greater willingness by the electorate and their representatives to accept relatively high unemployment in return for slow and consistent economic performance. Moreover, the extensive restructuring efforts undertaken by many companies improved earnings prospects and enhanced their competitive standings. Indeed, the growing worldwide trend toward restructuring played an important role in the boom in corporate mergers, acquisitions, and divestitures.

As 1985 drew to a close, the constant flow of positive economic and political news produced a salutary environment for equity investment. Yet the outlook for the world economy was clouded by uncertainties over potential turmoil in currency exchange markets, the mounting debt burden of third world countries, high levels of bankrupt-

cies, rising protectionist sentiment, and the effects of the precipitous drop in selected commodity prices.

(ROBERT H. TRIGG)

United States. The stock market posted the most profitable year in its history in 1985. The value of common stocks rose $462 billion, with most of the gain in the final quarter. The Dow Jones Industrial Average rose irregularly during the first three quarters of the year before achieving a dramatic record-breaking spurt in the fourth quarter. From a low of 1,184.96 at the beginning of 1985, the index reached an all-time high of 1,553.10 in December. Volume on major exchanges reached record levels, with 50,200,000,000 shares changing hands, as compared with 39,600,000,000 in 1984. The bull market also boosted trading in stock index options, while volume on individual equity options was little changed from 1984 levels. In the bond market, prices soared as interest rates on fixed-income securities dropped to their lowest levels in six years.

Investor uncertainty about economic prospects at the beginning of the year gave way to a growing perception that high interest rates and the threat of inflation were gone and, as interest rates fell, increasing numbers of investors began shifting funds into the stock market. After the September 22 Group of Five finance ministers' meeting took action to reduce the value of the dollar, a record-breaking rally began.

The stock market rally was fueled by a growing conviction among investors that corporate profits would rise because of lower interest rates and controlled inflation. A declining dollar, growth in the money supply, takeovers, corporate buyouts and stock repurchases, steady economic growth, an improved profit outlook, falling oil prices, and an influx of Individual Retirement Account funds into the market were all bullish factors. Analysts were more cautious in their forecasts because of continuing uncertainty about the course of interest rates, high consumer debt, possible defaults on some bonds, major changes in Federal Reserve policy, and a surplus of confidence by investors.

Corporate mergers and buyouts were among the major stock market developments in 1985. RCA was acquired by General Electric Co. in a $6.2 billion deal; Beatrice Companies Inc. agreed to a leveraged buyout by Kohlberg Kravis Roberts & Co. for a similar amount; Royal Dutch Shell purchased 30.5% of Shell Oil Co. for $5.7 billion; General Foods Corp. was acquired by Philip Morris Inc. for $5.6 billion; and Hughes Aircraft was bought by General Motors Corp. for $5 billion. Texaco Inc., which attempted to intervene in a Getty Oil Co. acquisition by Pennzoil Co., was sued successfully, with Pennzoil obtaining a judgment for $11.1 billion, the largest such judgment in history. (*See* INDUSTRIAL REVIEW: *Special Report.*)

Salomon Brothers Inc. was the leading underwriter of securities sold by U.S. issuers in 1985, with 20% of the volume. They managed more than $34 billion of underwritten public offerings by U.S. issuers worldwide. Drexel Burnham Lambert Inc. managed 56% of the "junk bonds," high-yielding bonds issued in leveraged buyouts and corporate takeovers. The total of taxable securities underwritten was $138,530,000,000, breaking the previous record of $97,280,000,000 set in 1983.

The prime rate began the year at 10.75%, fell to 10.5% in January, to 10% in May, and to 9.5% in June, its lowest level in many years. On May 20 the discount rate was cut by the Fed to 7.5 from 8%, the lowest since August 1978. Interest rates generally fell throughout the year with few interruptions. The consumer price index rose only 3.5%, down from 4.3% in 1984. The unemployment rate declined from 7.5% in 1984 to 7.1% in 1985. The dollar dropped

18.5% for 1985 against all major world currencies, its lowest level in 2½ years. Real economic growth, as measured by GNP, was the slowest since 1982 according to the U.S. Department of Commerce.

Volume on the New York Stock Exchange (NYSE) rose 19% in 1985, with a turnover of 27,510,706,353 shares, as compared with 23,071,031,447 a year earlier. The number of stock issues traded was 2,332 in 1985, slightly less than the comparable figure of 2,351 in 1984. The most active issues on the NYSE were American Telephone & Telegraph Co. with a turnover of 406,014,000 shares; International Business Machines Corp., 305,969,200; Phillips Petroleum Co., 301,165,700; Unocal Corp., 213,377,800; and Exxon Corp., 205,181,700. The NYSE reported that a seat was sold in 1985 for $480,000, up $5,000 from the previous sale in 1984. At the end of the year the current market for a seat was $475,000 bid and $500,000 offered. A survey estimated the number of Americans owning stock at 47 million, up 12% from 1983. Most of the growth was among stock mutual funds, which accounted for 30.3% of the total number of shareholders in 1985. Bond sales totaled $9,046,453,000 in 1985, a rise of 30% from the $6,982,291,000 achieved in 1984.

The NYSE averaged close to 115 million shares a day traded in 1985, up from 92 million in 1984. Among industry groups the best performers in 1985 were savings and loans, up 859% in earnings; oil service companies, up 188%; leisure-time, up 90%; real estate, up 70%; and drugs, up 59%. The worst performers were electronics, down 29%;

New York Stock Exchange Common Stock Index Closing Prices
Stock prices (Dec. 31, 1965 = 50)

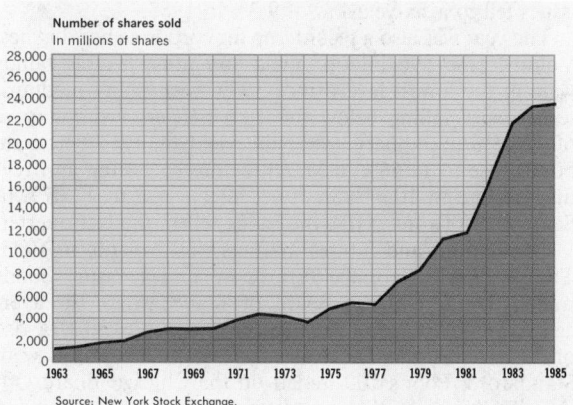

Number of shares sold
In millions of shares

Source: New York Stock Exchange.

automotive products, down 21%; general machinery, down 18%; and conglomerates, down 16%. A study group was set up in June to examine the creation of a common trading system that could lead to broad trading ties with the London Stock Exchange.

Turnover on the American Stock Exchange (Amex) totaled 2,100,860,000 shares in 1985, up 36% from the 1984 figure of 1,545,010,000 shares. Daily volume on the Amex averaged a record 8.3 million shares, compared with 6.1 million shares in 1984. The number of traded issues rose from 924 in 1984 to 936 in 1985, with 74 new companies being listed for a total of 941. Bond trading on the Amex rose to $645,182,000 in 1985, an increase of 73% over the prior-year figure of $371,990,000. Options trading volume totaled 45 million contracts in 1985, compared with 40 million in 1984. In September the Amex became the first exchange to open two-way trading with a foreign market when it linked up with the Toronto Stock Exchange. Volume on the Midwest Exchange rose 27% for the year, while the Pacific Stock Exchange boosted its volume by 35% to a level of 1,361,368,015 shares traded.

Mutual fund sales in 1985 totaled $110.5 billion, compared with the previous record of $45.9 billion in 1984. Sales were bolstered by the rising stock market as well as by keen investor interest in high-yielding funds. Total assets of mutual funds in 1985 were $495 billion, a 34% increase over the $370,680,000,000 in 1984. The return on mutual funds was 27.45%, compared with 4.88% in 1984.

The Standard & Poor's Index of 500 stocks climbed 26.3% in 1985, with a total return of 31.57%, compared with 6.10% in 1984. The high for the year was 212.02 and the low 163.68. During January the average jumped from the 1984 year-end level of 164.48 to 171.61; it then moved to 180.88 in February, slid briefly in March, and moved ahead in April to 180.62, peaking by July at 192.54 (TABLE XI). Railroad stocks were well ahead of 1984 levels after January 1985, as were the industrial issues and the public utilities. Stock price averages gained across the board, with the industrials leading the other stock groups with a rise of 25.86%. The average price-earnings ratio on the S & P 500 was 13.69 at mid-December, compared with 10.09 a year earlier.

While short-term interest rates were stable in 1985, with three-month Treasury bills trading between 7 and 7.3% and Federal Funds trading within a narrow range of 8%, the Treasury bond yield on 30-year bonds dropped from 11.7% in January to 9.5% by year-end. U.S. government long-term bond yields (TABLE XII) in 1985 were well below the levels of 1984. From 11.15% in January they rose to 11.78% in March, drifted lower to 10.36% in June, and then remained in a narrow range before declining below 10% in December. Bond yields on the long-term Treasury issues fell to a six-year low of 9.3% in 1985.

The year was also a record one for corporate bond issues. Volume rose $96 billion. Yields on most taxable bonds were at the lowest levels since 1979, with many medium-term issues falling below the 10% barrier. From a level of 12.08% in January 1985, the yield on U.S. corporate bonds rose to 12.56% in March before beginning an irregular decline to 10.94% in June; after a rise to 11.07% in September (TABLE XIII), the index fell in the last quarter.

The options and futures markets were volatile in 1985. The year's most popular futures were in Treasury bonds traded on the Chicago Board of Trade, where the average daily volume of 154,592 contracts represented a rise of 29% over 1984. The year's most popular options were Standard & Poor's 100 traded on the Chicago Board Options Exchange, with an average daily volume of 347,791

contracts for a gain of 30% over 1984. Seat prices on most U.S. commodity exchanges fell during 1985 because of competition from the stock market and a glut of failures and consolidations among futures brokerage firms.

The securities industry recorded its second best year in earnings, with $3.5 billion in pretax profits, because of rising stock prices and falling interest rates. Fees from corporate takeovers contributed at least $425 million.

The Securities and Exchange Commission stepped up its inspection of financial advisers and investment companies in 1985 with a well-publicized campaign against insider trading and financial fraud. A major development was the decision by the SEC to extend its regulatory scope over the stock-brokerage activities of approximately 2,000 banks. The SEC took the position that the stock-brokerage activities of banks should be subject to the same rules as any brokerage firm.

Canada. Canadian stock prices rose to record highs in 1985 on unprecedented volume based upon favourable economic conditions. Canada's stocks were boosted by the lowest interest rates since 1978, economic growth above 4% for the year, low inflation, and record levels of exports. The Toronto Stock Exchange 300 composite index gained 21%, closing at a record 2,900.60. Except for a brief retreat in the fall, the market was strong throughout the year, with retailing, gold mining, and banking stocks leading the way. Volume on the Toronto Stock Exchange was 3,170,000,000 shares, 50% above 1984. Total dollar value of shares traded rose 57% to Can$41,790,000,000. Both measures topped records set in 1983. Stock prices on other Canadian exchanges also rose sharply, with Montreal Exchange share prices up 18% overall and volume up 60% to 643 million shares. Share prices on Vancouver's more speculative market rose 59% as volume increased 22% to 2,750,000,000 shares.

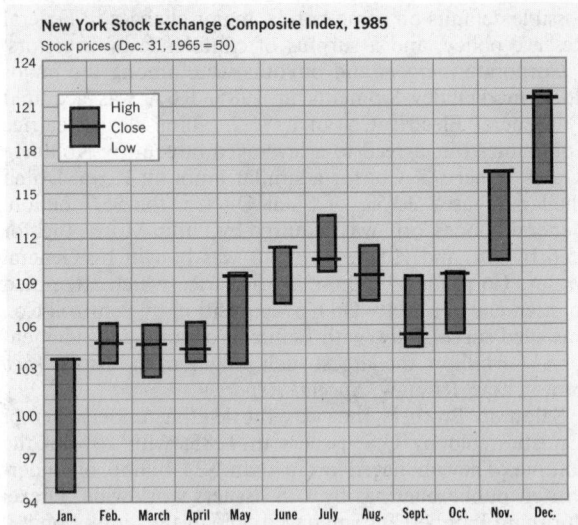

New York Stock Exchange Composite Index, 1985
Stock prices (Dec. 31, 1965 = 50)

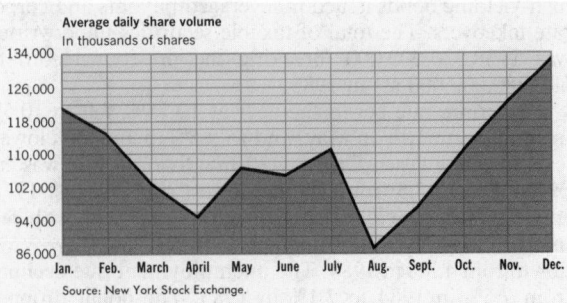

Average daily share volume
In thousands of shares

Source: New York Stock Exchange.

Canada's economic performance in 1985 was surprisingly good. In January, because they were probably disappointed at the relatively small 1984 improvement in the still-high unemployment rate, the authorities attempted to reduce interest rates without regard to U.S. levels of rates. This sent the Canadian dollar to a record low level against its U.S. counterpart, prompting a sudden firming of Bank of Canada policy. The prime rate fell to 10% from a prior-year level of 11.25%, and yields on bellwether bonds fell sharply. Canada 11.25%/1989 bond yields fell from 10.91% in 1984 to 9.47% in 1985. The Canada 10.25%/2004 bond yields fell from 11.61 to 9.92% by the end of 1985.

On a year-to-year basis the gains recorded in Canadian securities were impressive. The Toronto Stock Exchange 300 rose 20.9%. Meanwhile, among selected groups of stocks cable television rose 130.6%; clothing stores, 67.9%; lodging and food service, 64.7%; food stores, 63.9%; insurance, 62%; merchandising, 53.2%; and gold, 50.5%. On the downside, machinery company shares declined on average by 19%.

The Canadian stock market outlook at the end of 1985 was cautious because of uncertainties with respect to the value of the dollar combined with lacklustre economic prospects. The linkage of markets between the Toronto Stock Exchange and the American Stock Exchange was a major structural development in 1985. (IRVING PFEFFER)

Western Europe. Stock markets throughout Western Europe were uniformly strong during 1985. Gains in the U.K., France, the Scandinavian countries, and Belgium were comparatively modest, while sharply higher stock prices prevailed in Austria, Italy, West Germany, and The Netherlands. In Switzerland stock prices were also strong.

The stock market in Great Britain rose for the sixth year in a row. The *Financial Times* index of 30 industrial issues traded on the London Stock Exchange increased almost 19% from the end of 1984 to the end of 1985. The index topped 1,000 for the first time in mid-January, but government moves to defend the British pound in international currency markets ended the rally. In late January the pound's exchange rate against the U.S. dollar sank to a record low of $1.11, more than 8% lower than its value had been in early December. In response, interest rates were raised two percentage points to 14%, the highest level in three years. The major factor contributing to the slide of the pound sterling was the deteriorating price of North Sea oil and the market's perception that Britain's economy could be vulnerable to lower oil prices. However, investor worries about the adverse effects of higher interest rates on the domestic economy were counterbalanced by the realization that a tighter monetary policy would tend to dampen the inflation rate. Moreover, the profitability of British firms was improving sharply.

While stock prices traded within a relatively narrow range of 100 points or so during the next eight months, British interest rates fell several percentage points as the nation's economic recovery showed signs of losing some of its steam and the value of sterling in currency exchange markets recovered to nearly $1.50, its highest level since early 1984. The ensuing rally in equity prices was also boosted by the government's commitment to continue the battle against state intervention in the economy, by its announced intention to increase the pace of sales of state assets to the private sector, and by its willingness to take a laissez-faire attitude toward the record number of mergers and acquisitions of companies listed on the London Stock Exchange. In October the industrial share index surged through the 1,000 level, and stock prices moved decisively up once that psychological barrier had been pierced. As a result stock prices finished the year a fraction below their all-time high and 24% above the lows recorded in January.

In France the Paris Bourse staged a vigorous advance in 1985 as the nation's economic recovery continued to show progress. The success of the Socialist government's austerity program, begun in 1982, was reflected in a decline in the annual inflation rate to below 5%, its lowest level since the 1960s. Moreover, the structural rigidities that were introduced when Pres. François Mitterrand came to power in 1981 were beginning to crumble. Not only were moves

Table X. Selected Major World Stock Price Indexes*

Country	1985 range† High	1985 range† Low	Year-end close 1984	Year-end close 1985	Percent change
Australia	1,052	715	726	1,004	+ 38.3
Austria	122	58	59	120	+103.4
Belgium	2,986	2,091	2,126	2,943	+ 38.4
Denmark	238	158	167	237	+ 41.9
France	266	181	181	266	+ 47.0
West Germany	1,952	1,112	1,108	1,952	+ 76.2
Hong Kong	1,763	1,221	1,200	1,752	+ 46.0
Italy	460	229	230	457	+ 98.7
Japan	13,129	11,545	11,543	13,083	+ 13.3
Mexico	2,795	1,042	1,158	2,686	+132.0
Netherlands, The	243	148	145	243	+ 67.6
Norway	413	288	287	393	+ 36.9
Singapore	853	596	813	620	− 23.7
South Africa	1,068	767	935	1,068	+ 14.2
Spain	138	101	100	135	+ 35.0
Sweden	1,751	1,285	1,354	1,738	+ 28.4
Switzerland	588	389	386	588	+ 52.3
United Kingdom	1,147	911	952	1,131	+ 18.8

*Index numbers are rounded and limited to countries for which at least 11 months' data were available on a weekly basis.
†Based on daily closing price.
Sources: *The Economist, Financial Times, Barron's, the New York Times.*

Table XI. U.S. Stock Market Prices

Month	Railroads (6 stocks) 1985	Railroads (6 stocks) 1984	Industrials (400 stocks) 1985	Industrials (400 stocks) 1984	Public utilities (40 stocks) 1985	Public utilities (40 stocks) 1984	Composite (500 stocks) 1985	Composite (500 stocks) 1984
January	111.65	112.90	191.64	187.50	75.83	68.50	171.61	166.39
February	120.18	102.29	202.13	177.14	78.14	66.25	180.88	157.25
March	114.15	103.41	200.42	177.85	78.89	65.25	179.42	157.44
April	113.56	103.58	201.13	178.57	81.25	64.34	180.62	157.60
May	117.19	100.93	204.83	177.60	83.60	64.94	184.90	156.55
June	121.48	94.36	208.50	174.20	86.90	64.00	188.89	153.12
July	130.00	90.53	212.90	171.70	87.22	64.66	192.54	151.08
August	125.85	100.83	209.40	186.86	83.21	68.11	188.31	164.42
September	123.58	103.03	205.15	188.10	81.46	69.71	184.06	166.11
October	...	101.35	...	185.44	...	72.02	...	164.82
November	...	101.47	...	186.57	...	73.58	...	166.27
December	...	102.16	...	183.62	...	74.43	...	164.48

Sources: U.S. Department of Commerce, *Survey of Current Business;* Board of Governors of the Federal Reserve System, *Federal Reserve Bulletin.* Prices are Standard & Poor's monthly averages of daily closing prices, with 1941–43 = 10.

Table XII. U.S. Government Long-Term Bond Yields

Month	Yield (%) 1985	Yield (%) 1984	Month	Yield (%) 1985	Yield (%) 1984
January	11.15	11.29	July	10.51	12.82
February	11.35	11.44	August	10.59	12.23
March	11.78	11.90	September	10.67	11.97
April	11.42	12.17	October	...	11.66
May	10.96	12.89	November	...	11.25
June	10.36	13.00	December	...	11.21

Source: U.S. Department of Commerce, *Survey of Current Business.* Yields are for U.S. Treasury bonds that are taxable and due or callable in ten years or more.

Table XIII. U.S. Corporate Bond Yields

Month	Yield (%) 1985	Yield (%) 1984	Month	Yield (%) 1985	Yield (%) 1984
January	12.08	12.20	July	10.97	13.44
February	12.13	12.08	August	11.05	12.87
March	12.56	12.57	September	11.07	12.66
April	12.23	12.81	October	...	12.63
May	11.72	13.28	November	...	12.29
June	10.94	13.55	December	...	12.57

Source: U.S. Department of Commerce, *Survey of Current Business.* Yields are based on Moody's Aaa domestic corporate bond index.

undertaken to denationalize state-owned enterprises and to modernize the nation's financial markets and promote competition, but the government also announced plans to decontrol key industrial prices. Stock prices ended the first half of 1985 about 24% higher than they began the year and 146% higher than they had stood at the end of 1981.

However, nearly half of the year's gain was wiped out by profit taking in the period between early July and early October. Stock prices then rallied, and by early November they had regained all of the earlier losses. The collapse of a nine-day strike in October by one of France's largest labour unions reflected the decline of militant union power and the increasing economic realism among workers in regard to the relationship between corporate profits and job security. On the bearish side the approach of national elections in March 1986 caused jitters among investors who feared the threat of political turmoil if five years of Socialist rule were brought to an end. Stock prices continued strong throughout the final weeks of 1985, with the Paris stock-market index hitting an all-time high on the last trading day of the year, some 47% above the 1984 close.

Among the Scandinavian countries Denmark enjoyed a larger increase (+42%) than either Norway (+37%) or Sweden (+28%). The rise in industrial stock prices in Denmark, which followed a 22% decline in 1984, occurred despite the country's first major labour strike in 12 years. In Norway stock prices rose for the third consecutive year as merger fever or takeover battles contributed to a surge in trading volume. Prices on the Oslo Stock Exchange ended the year nearly 5% below the record high of November 12 but almost three times higher than at the beginning of 1983. The Swedish stock market also set a new all-time high, although gains were tempered by slowing economic growth and a relatively high annual inflation rate of 8%.

The stock market in Belgium traced out a pattern similar to that of Norway. Prices on the Brussels Stock Exchange increased 38% in 1985, with more than two-thirds of the gain coming during the last six months of the year. Equity investors correctly anticipated that the centre-right coalition government of Prime Minister Wilfried Martens would win the October general election. Prior to the election, reflecting the growing conservatism of the country, the head of the Socialist Party endorsed extending beyond Dec. 31, 1985, the tax breaks given to Belgian investors for buying shares in Belgian companies.

Beginning with the first trading session of 1985, the stock market in Austria entered an upward phase of considerable proportions. From year-end 1984 to year-end 1985, prices on the Vienna Stock Exchange rose 103%. As with other investors, the Austrians not only enjoyed the fruits of economic recovery but also benefited from a number of government initiatives to encourage savings and investment. Proposals included tax incentives to make it more attractive for Austrians to buy stocks and own their homes and also included the elimination of double taxation on dividends. In addition, for the first time since 1973 the government allowed Austrian companies to pay stock dividends; this tended to promote investment in stocks. In November the Creditanstalt-Aktien index of shares traded on the Vienna Stock Exchange exceeded its all-time high, set in October 1962, and closed the year at more than double its January 24 low.

Stock prices also followed a bullish pattern in Italy. Prices on the Milan Stock Exchange in 1985 jumped 99%, after rising 20% in 1984 and 15% in 1983. The uptrend in equity values gathered strength from the first trading day of the new year, and by mid-February stock prices had risen 23%. The technical correction that followed caused prices to backtrack nearly 7% before the advance resumed in early April. The ensuing upswing recorded even stronger gains throughout the summer, and by mid-October prices had surged 79% above the 1984 close. After some mild profit taking the rally resumed, with the market finishing the year only three points below its all-time high. The driving forces behind the bull market were the continued restructuring of both private and state-owned Italian companies, which tended to lower costs and boost profits; new attitudes toward wage increases, which were reflected in voter approval of cuts in indexed wages; and an estimated annual flow into mutual funds of $2 billion from the savings of Italian investors.

In West Germany the stock market sustained the impressive momentum evidenced since the fourth quarter of 1981. The Commerzbank index of 60 issues traded on the Frankfurt Stock Exchange topped 1,800 for the first time. The West German inflation rate, at about 2%, was among the lowest in Western Europe. At the same time, real GNP was expected to increase 2½% in 1985, while forecasts for 1986 were as high as 4%. After a strong start the stock market did not encounter profit taking until early July. But by that time equity values had increased 34%. The market's retreat, however, was relatively modest, with the entire decline having been retraced by the first week of September. The subsequent upswing lasted throughout the fall. The prospects that West Germany's largest private concerns would transform themselves into public companies raised investors' hopes that the government would give priority to free-market policies and to lightening the corporate tax burden. Offsetting these bullish developments was the fear that the Social Democrats might return to national power in 1987. A flurry of stock buying enabled the Commerzbank index to close at a new high of 1,952.

The Netherlands also experienced a strong bull market, with stock prices rising 68% from the end of 1984 to the end of 1985. The demand for stocks was influenced largely by the increase in industrial production and the trend toward lower interest rates. The level of unemployment, although relatively high by post-World War II standards, fell markedly.

In Switzerland stock prices on the Zürich Stock Exchange rose 52% in 1985. The Swiss Bank Corporation's General Index was up about 8% by the end of February. In March the Index surpassed its previous peak, set in

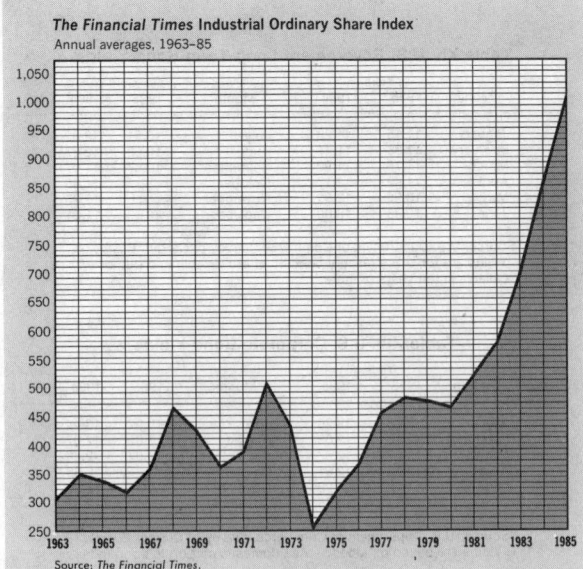

The Financial Times Industrial Ordinary Share Index
Annual averages, 1963–85

Source: The Financial Times.

September 1972. The upward momentum of stock prices accelerated in May, and before the end of October the 500 level of the Index had been breached for the first time, leaving equity values more than 30% higher than at the end of 1984. With trends in Swiss corporate profits and long-term interest rates both favourable, equity investors were bullish, allowing the Swiss stock market to close the year at the best level it had ever recorded.

Other Countries. The stock market in Mexico enjoyed the largest increase (+132%) among the world's major indexes. Despite a Mexican economy deeply troubled by a combination of a 60% inflation rate, increasing government deficits, an inability to service the interest costs on foreign debt, and escalating wage demands from militant labour unions, the general index of shares traded on the Bolsa Stock Exchange experienced a triple-digit gain as Mexicans tried to protect themselves against declines in purchasing power by pouring their savings into the stock market. As 1985 drew to a close, the Mexican economy continued to be under the influence of the severe economic crisis that had begun in 1982, when world oil prices started falling.

After rising 12% in 1983 and 37% in 1984, stock prices in Hong Kong added another 46% to equity values but failed to surpass the all-time high they had reached in 1981. Although investors were concerned about the health of the financial services industry, largely because of the failure of some small local banks, the real-estate sector experienced speculator gains as land prices showed dramatic increases. Also fueling the bullish mood were improved corporate profits, lower interest rates, and continued strong interest in Hong Kong equity securities by foreign investors.

The broad trend of stock prices in Australia was also up in 1985. Share prices on the Sydney Stock Exchange jumped 38% after falling 6% in 1984. The plunge in the value of the Australian dollar to 68.3 cents in December from 82.7 cents at the end of 1984 amounted to a 17.4% de facto devaluation, which tended to enhance the competitiveness of Australian exports.

In Japan the Nikkei average of leading industrial shares gained 13% in 1985 to reach its highest level ever recorded. The strength of the Japanese bull market, which had begun in 1977, continued to be propelled by relatively strong growth in economic activity, a record trade surplus, and improved corporate earnings. Although the value of the yen against the U.S. dollar increased approximately 25% in 1985, the bulk of the rise came after the September Group of Five meeting at which the decision was made to drive down the value of the dollar. However, the sharp rise in Japanese interest rates toward the end of 1985 raised fears that the contraction of Japan's domestic economy might more than offset the long-term favourable effects of yen appreciation on the global economy.

Economic, political, and social turmoil in South Africa during 1985 did not deter the stock market. After falling 3% in 1984, industrial share prices on the Johannesburg Stock Exchange increased 14%. A tumbling currency, widespread unrest in the mining industry, a debt moratorium, and the implementation of a number of disinvestment programs by nations concerned about the government's apartheid (racial separation) policies were offset and absorbed by tight monetary and fiscal policies that tended to slow the rate of inflation, a relatively large current-account surplus, and a low debt-service ratio.

Singapore's stock market, which usually reflected equity price trends in Hong Kong, followed a divergent pattern in 1985. In fact, the *Singapore Straits Times* Industrial Index experienced the only decline (−24%) among the world's major indexes. After rising more than 8% in 1984, real

gross material product was expected to fall by 2% in 1985. In addition to economic woes, the Singapore Stock Exchange was forced to suspend trading for the first time in its history for three days in December owing to the collapse of a major industrial company that threatened bankruptcy for several brokerage firms. As a result stock prices ended the year near their lowest level, some 42% below the record high set Feb. 8, 1984.

Commodity Markets. Relatively narrow fluctuations characterized the broad-based international commodity price indexes during 1985. For the year as a whole, the broad trend of major world commodity price indexes revealed small gains. *The Economist*'s commodity index, which measured spot prices in terms of the U.S. dollar for 28 internationally traded foodstuffs, nonfood agricultural products, and metals, climbed 5% from the end of 1984 to the end of 1985. That left *The Economist*'s dollar index 6% above its October 1982 low and more than 21% below its 1980 peak.

The two major sectors of *The Economist*'s index of dollar commodity prices experienced divergent patterns. The average 1985 price level of the food index gained nearly 14%, while industrial raw materials declined nearly 3%. Within the industrial materials component, nonfood agricultural products fell almost 6% and metals lost nearly 4%. The price index of foodstuffs finished the year at its highest level, having gained 5% from its July lows. The rebound in commodity prices in the fall was a reflection of the September accord reached by major industrialized nations to depress the international value of the U.S. dollar. A declining dollar tended to increase the demand for commodities priced in dollars. However, a permanent reversal of the downtrend in commodity prices would likely require a world economy growing fast enough to absorb excess commodity supplies.

The big news in international commodity markets in 1985 was the tin crisis that threatened the existence of the 108-year-old London Metal Exchange. The inability of the International Tin Council's chief trader to meet his obligation to dealers on the Exchange forced the suspension of trading in tin on October 24. Amid fears of a price collapse in tin that could spill over to other metals' markets, the Exchange announced that it would remain closed until Jan. 13, 1986. In fact, after the prices of nickel and zinc dropped 4 and 8%, respectively, following the halt in tin trading, the major producers of those commodities asked the London Metal Exchange to suspend trading in the hope that it would stem the sharp decline in their prices.

The price of gold, an inflation bellwether, reflected the disinflationary psychology that had plagued the precious-metals markets since 1980. During the first two months of 1985, news of plunging crude-oil prices in both spot and futures markets and the strength of the U.S. dollar against the Deutsche Mark and pound sterling in currency exchange markets triggered a selling wave that caused the price of gold in the London market to fall from $309 per ounce to below $290 during the last week of February. The subsequent rebound carried gold's price back to $330, but by the end of June it had fallen below $315. From the end of July to the end of December, the price of gold generally fluctuated between $320 and $330, and at the end of the year, it closed at $325. This indecision reflected uncertainty over the outlook for inflation and the growing belief that a gradual decline in the value of the U.S. dollar against other currencies could be offset by a fall in oil prices resulting from OPEC's decision in December to abandon price supports. (ROBERT H. TRIGG)

This article updates the *Macropædia* article MARKETS.

Education

Teachers' pay and conditions of service, always a significant educational issue, dominated the headlines in 1985 in countries as diverse as the U.K., Ireland, Australia, and Israel. In Scotland, where teachers were demanding not less than a 10% pay rise, the dispute over remuneration threatened to disrupt examination reform in 1986. In England and Wales the teachers' unions dug in their heels, and negotiations dragged on through the year. The teachers claimed that the major gains made in teachers' salaries some ten years earlier had been eroded, and to recover the position an increase of some 34% was necessary across the board. The government, on the other hand, advocated a decrease in public spending on education, both on economic grounds and because school enrollments were declining. In the U.S., in contrast, schools opened in September on a rather peaceful note. The largest strike, which affected Chicago's 431,000 students, ended after only two days. Strikes of varying duration were called in other Illinois districts and in Rhode Island, Ohio, Pennsylvania, Michigan, Vermont, New York, and Washington.

The prolonged dispute in Britain had a serious effect on teacher morale, and this was not helped by the government's growing interest in some form of teacher appraisal linked with teachers' pay. A working group was established under the chairmanship of the director of education for Suffolk, Duncan Graham, to look into the whole question of teacher appraisal, notably in the U.S., where the issue of merit pay had received considerable attention. The Graham Report (issued in July 1985) concluded that experience in both Britain and the U.S. failed to support the view that there was any advantage in linking pay with appraisal. Nevertheless, where appraisal was practiced, there was an improvement in professional skills and commitment of teachers. Indeed, the Graham Report advocated appraisal of the teaching achievements of whole schools.

The effect of all the talk about appraisal on the British teachers' unions was to increase their suspicions of the government's motives, but in the U.S. the president of the National Education Association, Mary H. Futrell, urged her group to drop its longtime opposition to the testing of new teachers to assure that they had mastered both subject matter and professional competences. Albert Shanker, president of the American Federation of Teachers, declared that improved status for teachers could come only through a national examination that would limit entrance into teaching, student choice of schools they wanted to attend, evaluation of teachers by veteran teachers who could help to weed out incompetents, "career ladders" to permit experienced teachers to supervise novices, and encouragement of the brightest young persons to enter the teaching profession. In a Gallup Poll, conducted in cooperation with an education fraternity, Phi Delta Kappa, teachers reported that the main problems facing schools were parental indifference, limited financial support, lack of student interest, overcrowded classrooms, and discipline.

A number of reports on education were issued during the year, including two on the education of ethnic minorities, *Education for All* (the Swann Report) in the U.K. and *Equality and Excellence* in the U.S. (*See* Sidebar.) In Japan Prime Minister Yasuhiro Nakasone's Ad Hoc Advisory Council on Education Reform issued its first report. The council had an all-embracing mandate to look into ways of reforming Japan's educational system, notably how to provide for the needs of the 21st century and how to deal with what the Japanese regarded as rising school violence,

delinquency, and truancy. The council put forward the idea of establishing six-year specialist state secondary schools alongside the present three-year lower- and upper-level institutions. Critics argued that such schools would be used to prepare an elite for entry into prestigious universities and could threaten the legally enshrined principle of equal compulsory education for all up to age 15. They might also have the effect of pushing selection down from the secondary to the primary level, thus exacerbating the great pressure on Japanese schoolchildren. The Japan Teachers' Union deplored the report's failure to deal with industry's influence over the educational system but supported its call for greater emphasis on individuality.

Another major report emerged from Prime Minister Rajiv Gandhi's new government in India. Called *Challenge of Education—Policy Perspective,* it proposed a restructuring of the whole educational system. The document anticipated an ambitious fourfold increase in state spending on education between 1980 and 1990, leading to a demand for an additional 2,250,000 teachers (on top of approximately 2 million in 1980). The report argued that a top-heavy bureaucracy killed the teachers' creativity and pointed out that 80% of spending on education went for administration and teachers' salaries and relatively little for teaching aids. It did not add to the credibility of education in India that there were more illiterates in 1981 (437 million) than at independence in 1947 (300 million).

One of the remedies put forward by the Indian report was to introduce a vocational dimension into secondary schools and junior colleges. This emphasis on the vocational side emerged strongly in many countries in 1985, fueled by continuing high unemployment among young people. Thus in Britain the Manpower Services Commission, concerned with 16–19-year-olds, brought in a two-year Youth Training Scheme. At the same time, it reinforced its support for the schools through the Technical and Vocational Education Initiative, which gave extra money to schools that introduced innovative technological topics into the curriculum. Like the Indian government's report—which favoured a moratorium on the expansion of traditional liberal arts colleges in favour of institutions with a strong vocational bias—the U.K. government, in a Green Paper, advocated a relentless movement to technology in the universities. The Green Paper caused considerable bitterness among the academic community, which saw it not only in terms of a spending cut but as demeaning the role of the universities.

In the Soviet Union the reform program initiated in 1984 seemed intended to reorient the system more toward what the Soviets called labour training. According to an article in the *Literaturnaya Gazeta* by M. Kondakov, president of the U.S.S.R.'s prestigious Academy of Pedagogical Sciences, the intention was to create a labour-training syllabus that would develop appropriate habits in schoolchildren, familiarize them with industrial materials, and teach them to use basic tools. The curriculum included work experience. Behind this was a desire to raise the prestige of labour, presumably following the line initiated by the late Yury Andropov to improve standards of labour discipline in the Soviet Union.

But it was in China, with its centuries-long tradition of reverence for book learning and scholarship, that the biggest shift was in evidence. This emerged from the major announcement in July that the Ministry of Education was to be replaced by a State Education Commission, directly under the State Council and headed by a vice-premier, 56-year-old Li Peng (Li P'eng). In effect, this was an upgrading of the Ministry of Education. The context of the reform,

as outlined by Chinese leader Deng Xiaoping (Teng Hsiao-p'ing), was that China's economy should approach the level of the developed nations by the year 2049. To that end, by 1990, 70% of senior middle school students (aged 15–18) would receive a vocational education instead of the present purely academic curriculum. Currently some 95% of Chinese children went through the primary-school stage (ages 6–12), but there were places for only some two-thirds of them in junior middle schools (ages 12–15). An essential ingredient of the reform was that a nine-year school system should be compulsory for all. Working conditions and teachers' pay should be improved, and there should be a much greater emphasis on the opening up of new fields of knowledge and the promotion of independent thinking.

The country that had moved furthest toward raising the prestige of vocational education was Hungary, and considerable interest in its system was expressed in 1985. The Hungarian minister of education, for example, visited England and Wales, among other countries. In a vigorous attempt to revitalize the Hungarian economy, the government had almost reversed the conventional system of monetary rewards, giving skilled manual workers and those in similar occupations the highest wages. Pupils in the secondary schools were allowed to opt for the vocational side at age 15, and a large majority of boys chose that route, resulting in what the Hungarians called "the feminization of intellectual professions." The government was not wholly satisfied with this outcome, but it was proving exceedingly difficult to remedy.

Primary and Secondary Education. There were heartening accounts of progress in primary education from some parts of the world. From Brazil came the example of the Centros Integrados de Educacao Publica (CIEPs). Housed in simple, cheap, but highly distinctive buildings designed by the Brazilian architect Oscar Niemeyer, they were part of a program that aimed eventually to provide schooling for 300,000 children in the Rio de Janeiro area. The plan, strongly supported by the state governor, Leonel Brizola, was intended to tackle the interlinked problems of lack of schooling, juvenile delinquency, and malnutrition. The CIEPs provided not only full-time schooling from 7:30 AM to 5 PM but also three meals a day, clothing, and school materials. In an effort to revitalize teaching methods, a "cultural animator" was employed to incorporate popular culture into the curriculum, and dance and music were used extensively.

Another example was the Hills Area Education project (HAE), a nonformal primary school curriculum being used in the hills of northern Thailand. Some 400,000 people lived in this area near the borders with Burma and Laos, leading a migrant life and practicing shifting cultivation. The curriculum combined the traditional emphasis on the Thai language and mathematics with other subjects having some local relevance. There were signs that HAE, started as a pilot program with U.S. aid, would become a permanent program.

Such attempts at innovation seemed in curious contrast to the situation in France. When François Mitterrand's Socialist government took office in 1981, the emphasis in French primary schools was on stimulating motivation and developing the child's personality. After the humiliation of the French government in 1984 over its measures to incorporate parochial schools into the state system, the minister of education resigned and was replaced by Jean-Pierre Chevènement, whose attitude to schooling found more favour with his right-wing opponents than with his Socialist supporters. A paperback guide for schools issued in September 1985 emphasized the "transmission of knowl-

In April Theresa Knecht Dozier of Columbia, South Carolina, received from Pres. Ronald Reagan the golden apple signifying her selection as 1985 National Teacher of the Year. The award is sponsored by the Encyclopædia Britannica Companies, *Good Housekeeping* magazine, and the Council of Chief State School Officers.
AP/WIDE WORLD

edge" and listed seven subjects that were to take up a total of 27 hours a week in primary schools: French, mathematics, history and geography (always taught together), art, music, and physical activities. In addition, there was to be one hour a week of "civic education," and "the meaning of effort and work well done" and respect for property and other people were to be emphasized.

Similar beliefs were voiced by William J. Bennett, the new U.S. secretary of education, who became an active spokesman for conservative views on the federal role in education and on education itself. He called for higher academic standards on all levels, firmer school discipline, more teaching of traditional morals and ethics, and greater emphasis on the humanities. A number of Bennett's pronouncements provoked controversy during the year, among them his recommendation that federal guidelines on bilingual education be eased. Current federal policy dictated that basic subjects be taught in the native language of children who speak little or no English. Bennett wanted local schools to determine the instructional methods to be used for such children, and he wanted the goal to be mastery of English. The federal government had provided some $1.7 billion to fund bilingual programs since legislation on the subject was passed 20 years earlier. The largest group in bilingual programs was the Hispanics. Hispanic youth were described as "wasted" by a national study commission, which found that they had a 45% dropout rate.

Venturing into the delicate area of public aid to private schools, Bennett suggested that the federal remedial program aiding students with special learning problems be changed to a voucher system that would permit parents to

A concerted effort in Brazil to bring children of the slums, who might not otherwise attend, into the schools achieved considerable success by the use of food—breakfast, lunch, snacks—as a lure.
AP/WIDE WORLD

select the school of their choice. This would enable parents to send their children to either a public or a private school. The recommendation was made after the U.S. Supreme Court ruled that public school teachers could not conduct special education classes in parochial schools. A Gallup Poll showed that Americans were divided on the subject, with 45% favouring government aid to parochial schools and 47% opposing it. In another decision upholding the "wall of separation" between church and state, the Supreme Court continued its mandate against Bible reading and prayer in public schools. An Alabama law authorizing a minute of silence "for meditation or voluntary prayer" was struck down because prayer was specifically mentioned as an option, though the court indicated that other approaches to the period of silence might be acceptable. Twenty-six states had "silence" laws in some form. Meanwhile, Congress passed a bill guaranteeing religious groups the same access to school property after school hours given to other groups that used school space for their meetings. In a move that might have far-reaching consequences, the California Board of Education rejected all the science textbooks submitted for possible use in the seventh and eighth grades on the grounds that they "watered down" instruction on evolution. In doing so, the board bypassed objections by fundamentalists that the books overemphasized evolution at the expense of biblical creationism. Because California represented a large share of the national textbook market, the move could affect science textbooks nationwide.

In a case involving a student whose purse had been searched for cigarettes, the Supreme Court gave school officials authority to tailor Fourth Amendment provisions on searches and seizures to school settings if there was a reasonable suspicion that a law or school rule was being violated. Attorney General Edwin Meese began to consider ways to increase the powers of school staffs to fight violence in the schools, a common topic in Pres. Ronald Reagan's speeches about education. The Justice Department also eased legal standards for determining whether a school district could be released from court-imposed busing and other antidiscrimination plans. The new guidelines permitted school districts to be released from court orders if they could show that they had taken "good faith" steps to eliminate discrimination and had avoided segregation.

Media attention to some cases of child abuse in day-care centres and schools created considerable interest in new federal guidelines for child-care workers. While welcomed, the guidelines were criticized by some observers for not going beyond employment screening to keep out criminals and child abusers. Experts advocated efforts to improve staff and program quality. Interest in child care had grown as more and more mothers went to work and the number of child-care facilities increased to meet the demand. Other social concerns also reached into the schools. Controversy arose over the question of how to treat children with acquired immune deficiency syndrome (AIDS). Although the number of school-age children with AIDS was small, and experts insisted that the disease could not be spread by casual contact, the public's fear of the fatal ailment forced many school districts to establish policy on the issue. There was no consensus among districts. Los Angeles, for example, barred AIDS victims from the schools, while New York City admitted them on a case-by-case basis after an expert panel had made recommendations. The decision to admit one such student to a school in Queens led to a school boycott. (*See* HEALTH AND DISEASE.) In a Maine court case, a judge ruled that school officials were within their rights in canceling a speech by a lesbian student. The judge determined that homosexuals have no special protection under the law.

President Reagan's proposed tax reforms were seen by some critics as a threat to local and state school financing. Specifically under fire was the provision that would eliminate local and state taxes as federal income-tax deductions. The value of the deductions was estimated at $16.5 billion per year, constituting a form of federal subsidy. Without the deductions, it was feared, voters might revolt against school taxes, further hurting school districts already affected by declining federal dollars. Supporters of the president's reform believed that the effect would not be great, since only about one-third of taxpayers itemize deductions, and that, in any case, proposed reductions in the federal tax rate would free up more local tax dollars. They also claimed that polls showed that the public was willing to support the schools. The U.S. Department of Education, for example, released figures indicating that two-thirds of the people would pay higher taxes to raise teacher salaries

and standards, increase teacher training, and lower class size. The survey sample was considered balanced except for the disproportionate number of college graduates among those responding.

The states were increasing their control over education, according to Terrel Bell, secretary of education during Reagan's first term. Bell noted that the states' share of school funding had exceeded the local share during the past five years and that hundreds of state laws regulating local schools had been passed. Much of this legislative activity had been inspired by the critical reports on U.S. public schools issued during the past few years and the resulting emphasis on excellence in education. The states were having a greater say about such matters as high school graduation requirements, testing, and teacher standards. Some states, however, were becoming very specific in their regulations; for example, by fixing the number of times announcements could be made over a school's public address system.

The Census Bureau released figures showing that the U.S. school-age population overall had declined 5.3% over four years, to 44.8 million in 1984, but there was a 9% increase in preschool-age children during the 1980–84 years. There were 17.8 million preschool children in 1984, and the population under the age of five was the highest since 1968. The Census Bureau attributed the increase to the larger number of mothers of childbearing age rather than to an increase in fertility rates. A Gallup Poll showed that the level of public confidence in the schools had risen 11% and that 42% of Americans believed the schools were getting better. Achievement levels for U.S. elementary and secondary students improved again in 1985. Average scores on the Scholastic Aptitude Test, widely used as an admissions tool by colleges, rose for both verbal and mathematical skills. The Census Bureau found that U.S. children averaged more than an hour of homework per day, with white girls and all black students putting in more time than white boys.

The Education of Ethnic Minorities

The educational needs of blacks and other ethnic minorities have been the subject of growing concern in many Western countries, whether their minorities are of long standing or the result of recent immigration. Two important reports on this topic appeared in 1985, one in the U.S. (*Equality and Excellence: The Educational Status of Black Americans*) and the other in the U.K. (*Education for All*). The latter was widely known as the Swann Report, after Lord Swann, the chairman of the committee that produced it.

The U.S. report, prepared for the College Entrance Examination Board of New York by sociologist Linda Darling-Hammond, had a narrower focus than the Swann Report. It recognized that U.S. blacks had made great gains in education since the early 1960s, but since 1975 there had been some erosion of those gains, and the report even suggested that the movement toward educational equality was threatened with reversal. College attendance and completion rates for blacks had declined since 1975, and black participation in postgraduate education had declined since the early 1970s. All along the educational pipeline, from primary school to bachelor's degree, blacks had been losing ground relative to nonblacks. Furthermore, all minority students were disproportionately placed in vocational courses or low-track classes where they were not intellectually challenged and where teachers' expectations were low.

In part, this resulted from policy. Education was underfinanced because of federal aid cuts, the economic recession, and the property-tax revolt of the late 1970s. Also a factor was the decline in the morale and occupational prestige of the teaching profession. But there were also disturbing changes in the structure of black families that must provide part of the explanation. In the past decade the percentage of black households headed by females had risen from 28 to 41%, partly because of higher divorce rates and partly because of increases in the number of never-married mothers. Nearly one-half (47.6%) of all black children 18 years and under lived in households below the poverty line in 1982, compared with 17% of white children. The real median income of black families

had been decreasing, both in absolute terms and as compared with whites.

In Britain the immigrant population was too recent for such trends to emerge so starkly. Moreover, the immigrants fell chiefly into two rather different groups—those from the Caribbean, and those from the Indian subcontinent. The first had what appeared on the surface to be a more flamboyant, extroverted culture; the second was more self-contained and, above all, Muslim. The stereotype of the Asian pupils was that they were well motivated, had strong parental support, and were relatively successful. In fact, the Swann Report found that children of Bangladeshi origin, in particular, were not doing at all well. The other stereotype was that the West Indian children were not achieving as might be expected, but it seemed that they were doing better (although there was still a great deal of room for improvement). The report rebutted the argument that some ethnic groups are innately less intelligent than others.

There is another side to this argument—namely, that racism itself affects educational performance (a point the U.S. report did not tackle directly). Could it be that poor performance at school is a result of being at the receiving end of prejudiced attitudes? There are many examples of groups who have triumphed over such attitudes, educationally at least. Nonetheless, as the U.S. report amply confirms, where racism can affect work, housing, and similar factors, the quality of life is affected, and there must be a correlation between such conditions and school performance.

Perhaps the most important issue on which the U.S. and British reports found common ground was that education in a democracy must mean "education for all"—the Swann Report title. George Hanford, the College Board president, echoed this in his preface to the U.S. report: "The unique promise of the United States has been its commitment to extend opportunities to *all*—not just some—of its children. Since its earliest days, this nation has been dedicated to the principle that each generation deserves a fair start, and acting on this principle has served not only justice but the national well-being."   (TUDOR DAVID)

Teachers in North Little Rock answer questions intended to demonstrate their competency in reading, writing, and mathematics in March as Arkansas became the first U.S. state to require testing in basic skills for practicing public school teachers.
AP/WIDE WORLD

In Australia the first primary school for Aborigines opened in South Australia amid some controversy. There were accusations of segregation, countered by arguments that the Aborigines were underachievers and needed special primary schooling. A movement toward segregated schools was apparent among Muslims in several countries. In Turkey there was evidence of a significant growth of Islamic schools basing their teaching on the Qur'an. Official figures suggested a 10% increase in such schools in 1985, but this did not include unrecognized Muslim schools run by Islamic sects, which were acknowledged to be multiplying. There were also strong moves for separate Muslim schools in Malaysia, but the demand was being resisted by the Ministry of Education. In England demands for Muslim schools established with government support were stimulated by one or two well-publicized examples of hostility toward immigrant children by head teachers.

In Zimbabwe five years of independence had seen a remarkable expansion of both primary and, more especially, secondary schools, but—in a legacy of the colonial past— the whole emphasis in secondary schools was on passing an examination identical with that taken in England and Wales. This examination was devised to be passed by some 20% of the age cohort, and putting the entire age cohort into the exam meant certain failure for between 70 and 80%. Strenuous efforts were made by educators in Zimbabwe to persuade teachers to relate their teaching to practical needs. A science kit was produced in the hope of encouraging a more creative approach, but—though it was widely praised and, indeed, adopted by other black African countries—it did not appear to be wholly successful at home. The teachers, more than three-quarters of them virtually untrained, remained wedded to rote learning and the copying of textbooks.

In South Africa, where education was seriously disrupted by civil strife, there appeared to be some slight movement on the part of the white government to recognize the blacks' demand for reforms. Gerrit Viljoen, the minister of cooperation, development, and education, said that black education ought to be depoliticized by meeting the "reasonable political demands" of blacks in Africa. There was no indication, however, that the government would accede to the blacks' key demand for a single Ministry of Education and an end to separate educational systems. The situation was exacerbated by the fact that enrollment in white schools was diminishing while black schools were experiencing a population explosion. It was claimed that the enrollment figures in black schools were increasing at a rate of 250,000 a year, and the department in charge of black education had to provide for about six million pupils. The average pupil–teacher ratio in white schools was recorded as 20 to 1; in black secondary schools, 36 to 1; and in black primary schools, 52 to 1. It was estimated that the South African government spent seven times more on a white child's education than on that of a black child.

Higher Education. In keeping with the general upgrading of education in China, the Communist Party announced sweeping changes in higher education, some of which seemed to suggest a moving away from socialist ideals. An example was the introduction of a scholarship system linking grants to academic performance. Universities and colleges were to have greater autonomy in spending their funds, making appointments, and designing courses. It was also proposed to let universities select their own research projects, allowing them to engage in commercially profitable undertakings. As in the lower schools, there was emphasis on steering teaching away from the academic mold and toward the acquisition of practical skills for employment. Higher education in China had expanded from 400 higher education institutions with 584,000 students in 1977 to 800 institutions with 1,250,000 students in 1985.

In Kenya the pressure on higher education places, especially in the University of Nairobi and Moi University, led to passage of a Universities Act designed to discourage Kenyans from going elsewhere for their higher education. It also led to the setting up of a national commission to rationalize higher education, with the possibility of opening a private university. Denmark, the country with the longest university degree course in Europe, again attempted to shorten the traditional seven- to ten-year requirement. This was in the context of a 3% cut in university spending for 1985–86. Australia also set about curbing spending on institutions of higher learning. The Tertiary Education Commission, an advisory body, issued a highly critical report on the lack of coordination in Australian higher education. In neighbouring New Zealand a Maori study centre was established in Victoria University of Wellington.

In the U.S. a proposed administration plan to cut $2.3 billion from college aid programs raised fears that many students could no longer afford to attend private colleges. Tuition at many colleges already exceeded the total a student could receive through a combination of federal grants, guaranteed loans, and work-study programs. Officials estimated that one million students would be affected by the changes. Meanwhile, federal officials claimed that student defaults on federally guaranteed loans administered by colleges had reached excessive levels.

The suspense over the appointment of a professor of parapsychology in the University of Edinburgh, Scotland, was ended. This chair, endowed in the will of the author Arthur Koestler, was given to Robert Morris, a research coordinator in computer and information sciences at Syracuse (N.Y.) University. Asked whether he would look for Koestler's ghost, Morris explained that "ghost" was not a word he approved of.   (JOEL L. BURDIN; TUDOR DAVID)

See also Libraries; Motion Pictures.

This article updates the *Macropædia* articles History of EDUCATION; TEACHING.

Energy

In 1985, for the third consecutive year, oil prices remained persistently weak. The Organization of Petroleum Exporting Countries (OPEC) remained incapable of coping with the situation or of enforcing internal discipline on its members, and the cumulative effect of events throughout the year threatened its very existence.

At the January meeting of OPEC, 9 of the 13 members agreed to a cut in official prices, the second such action in the organization's history. Non-OPEC exporters such as Mexico and Egypt promptly followed suit. In March it was announced that the British National Oil Corporation, the state trading concern handling one-half of all British North Sea oil production, would be abolished. This meant that from that time on, all such oil would be sold at spot market prices. This action occurred almost simultaneously with the ending of the British coal strike (*see* below), which removed a significant portion of the world demand for the heavy fuel oil that had been substituted for coal in British electric power generators.

Market conditions worsened during the summer as oil production in non-OPEC countries (except for the U.S.S.R.) continued to increase by small but nevertheless significant amounts while demand continued to decline. Mexico cut its price a second time, as did OPEC. All members except for Saudi Arabia, however, continued to give hidden discounts from official prices and to produce in excess of their quotas. Saudi Arabia became increasingly dissatisfied with this state of affairs as it persisted alone in rigid adherence to official prices, producing well below its quota and very far below capacity; this caused the nation to incur increasingly large trade and budget deficits.

At the July OPEC meeting the Saudis threatened openly to increase their production, no matter what the effect would be on prices. The representatives at the meeting took no action, and neither did the Saudis. In September, however, they announced that henceforth they would no longer abide by official prices and were, in fact, signing new contracts for increased sales at prices determined by the market. Even this ominous development was not sufficient to produce agreement among the OPEC members. An OPEC meeting in October accomplished nothing.

The Saudi action raised fears among world oil producers of a price war that could lead to total market collapse. The immediate prospect of such an event was averted by a sudden flare-up of hostilities in the Iran-Iraq war. In a series of air raids Iraq seriously damaged Iran's only large oil-export facility, at Kharg Island in the Persian Gulf, and severely curtailed Iran's export capability. The general consensus was, nevertheless, that the possibility of collapse had only been postponed and that everything would depend on whether world economic growth in 1986 would revive demand sufficiently to offset the normal spring decline at the end of the heating season.

In December the OPEC oil ministers, meeting in Geneva, agreed to abandon the strategy of defending a set oil price and to concentrate on defending the cartel's market share, cutting prices if this proved necessary. A six-nation committee was set up to work out details. The new strategy, in effect, gave official recognition to the unofficial practice of most OPEC members.

In November the United States Department of Energy held its first test sale of crude oil from the Strategic Petroleum Reserve, as had been directed by the U.S. Congress in July. The purpose of the 1.1 million-bbl sale was to test the maximum rate at which oil could be drawn from the Reserve. At the time of the test the Reserve contained 490 million bbl, equivalent to approximately six months of crude oil imports.

In Canada the year was notable for governmental decisions affecting the petroleum industry. The federal government reached agreement with the province of Newfoundland on the management of offshore oil production, settling a 15-year dispute. In the so-called Western Accord reached with the provinces of Alberta, Saskatchewan, and British Columbia on March 28, the federal government agreed to the abolition of oil price controls and certain oil taxes, and the provincial governments reduced their royalties. The effect was a sharp stimulus to the Canadian oil and gas industries. By coincidence, the first commercial delivery of crude oil from the Canadian Arctic Islands to a Montreal refinery was made in September. In October the federal government completed the deregulation of oil and gas prices by abolishing controls on the domestic and export prices of natural gas. This action freed Canadian gas producers to compete in the decontrolled U.S. gas market.

JEREMY NICHOL

Coal miners in Great Britain return to work in the pits after a year-long strike that split their union, apparently permanently, cost them an average of more than $8,000 in wages, and left the National Coal Board free to close uneconomic mines.

A new record water depth for oil production was set by a well drilled in 750 m (2,470 ft) of water in the Mediterranean Sea off Spain. In April North Sea oil production exceeded that of Saudi Arabia for the first time. In the United States the Environmental Protection Agency announced a new rule further reducing the lead content of gasoline to 0.1 g per gal by the end of the year, with all lead to be removed by 1988. The European Communities announced that it had agreed to require all members to introduce lead-free gasoline by 1989. No date was fixed for the elimination of lead from gasoline, however.

In natural gas matters the major events of the year in the United States concerned regulation. On January 1 price controls on some 70% of natural gas sales were ended, under the provisions of the Natural Gas Policy Act of 1978. Owing to a general oversupply of gas, however, the effect on natural gas prices in general was negligible. In October the Federal Energy Regulatory Commission announced policy changes in the regulation of natural-gas pipelines. The new policies were designed to lower prices by giving consumers the chance to buy directly from producers.

Elsewhere, the United Kingdom ended several years of negotiations with Norway by declining to buy gas from the Sleipner field in the Norwegian North Sea, on the grounds that increased domestic reserves made the commitment unnecessary. Negotiations of several years between Australia and Japan, in contrast, were successful. Agreement was reached in 1985 to begin the export to Japan of liquefied natural gas from one of the world's largest gas fields, located off the northwest coast of Australia, by 1990. Fulfillment of the commitment would require completion of the largest resource project ever undertaken in Australia. Switzerland began producing its first natural gas, from a small field at Finsterwald. The Soviet Union announced the first commercial gas discovery on the Kamchatka Peninsula near the Sea of Okhotsk.

The most noteworthy event in coal was the ending of the British coal strike in March. Almost exactly a year in duration, it was the longest major national strike in British history. The strike was called in response to the National Coal Board's (NBC's) announcement that it intended to close 20 pits that were losing money. The strike was never fully effective, and when it ended the NCB was free to carry out its original intention. In the United States coal continued in general oversupply, with the market in the doldrums. Alaska, on the other hand, marked a notable event with the beginning shipment of coal to South Korea, the first export ever of Alaskan coal. The South Korean contract was expected to result in an eventual doubling of Alaskan coal production.

Electric utilities in four northeastern states were severely crippled by Hurricane Gloria in September. Although not an especially severe hurricane, the storm downed many power lines in Long Island, Connecticut, Massachusetts, and Rhode Island. At the storm's peak almost 2.5 million people were without electric power. Restoration of service took more than a week in some areas.

Other developments in the electric power industry concerned nuclear power. In October Three Mile Island Unit 1 in Pennsylvania began to produce power after being shut down for more than $6\frac{1}{2}$ years. At the time of the accident to its sister unit in 1979, it was inoperative because of refueling; since that time all attempts to obtain permission to restart it had been vehemently opposed on the grounds that it was no safer than its ill-fated sister. Permission was granted for restarting after opponents had exhausted all avenues of litigation and the U.S. Supreme Court had refused to review the final decision. On the adverse side for nuclear power, the U.S. government announced that it was closing its original uranium-enrichment plant at Oak Ridge, Tenn., putting it on standby, and halting construction on a second plant near Portsmouth, Ohio. The announcement was part of a restructuring of U.S. enrichment facilities in the face of worldwide overcapacity and the development of a new, more efficient enrichment technology using lasers.

In the United Kingdom a public hearing on the proposal to build a pressurized water reactor next to an existing gas-cooled reactor came to an end in March after 340 days of hearings and an estimated 16 million words of transcript. The Sizewell B public inquiry, as it was known, constituted the longest such inquiry in British history. (*See Electricity,* below.) A report on the findings was expected in 1986. The first high-temperature gas reactor in West Germany began operation in October; the 300-MW plant was located near Düsseldorf. In France the world's largest fast-breeder reactor, the "Superphénix," was activated in September. The 1,200-MW unit was built with the participation of five other Western European countries.

Developments in the field of unconventional energy resources were both positive and negative. The largest commercial solar power plant, rated at 14.7 MW, began operation at Daggett, Calif. The largest geothermal power project, at the Geysers in central California, celebrated its 25th anniversary with the addition of two new units, bringing the total capacity of the project to 1,360 MW. Also in California the world's first commercial-size binary geothermal power plant began operation. Located in the Imperial Valley near Heber, the 45-MW unit uses geothermal brine at less than the boiling point to vaporize a second fluid that drives a turbine.

A French research ship completed successful testing of a "turbosail" wind-propulsion system. Large hollow cylinders, like smokestacks, are equipped with fans at the bottom. The fans draw air through the side of the cylinder to produce an effect, like an airplane wing, that moves the ship forward. The system was designed to supplement conventional screw propulsion and to save fuel. A research institute in the United States announced the successful production of synthetic methane (a constituent of natural gas) from water and carbon dioxide. This was the first synthesis of methane from inorganic compounds and was described as a significant first step toward the ultimate commercial production of the gas from such sources.

The world's first fully commercial plant to convert natural gas to gasoline began operation during the year at Motunui, N.Z. (A similar plant in the United States built soon after World War II never achieved reliable operation.) The plant was designed to satisfy one-third of New Zealand's gasoline needs.

On the negative side were two project abandonments. Failure to receive sufficient subsidy caused sponsors of the Great Plains coal gasification plant at Beulah, N.D., to turn ownership of the plant over to the federal government. Completed in 1984 at a cost of $2 billion, the plant was intended to demonstrate the feasibility of large-scale gasification of lignite, processing 12,600 metric tons (14,000 short tons) per day to produce 3.5 million cu m (125 million cu ft) of synthetic gas a day. The plant continued operation under federal ownership while the government pondered whether to shut it down. In Israel the government stopped all work on a project to generate electricity by carrying water from the Mediterranean to the Dead Sea. The 400-m (1,300-ft) drop to the Dead Sea would have been harnessed in an 800-MW power plant, at a cost of $1.5 billion. Lower than expected prices for crude oil made the project uneconomic.   (BRUCE C. NETSCHERT)

COAL

Although coal consumption generally continued to grow in 1984, reflecting the economic recovery (especially that of the steel market), future prospects appeared so uncertain during 1985 that major producers set up a promotional body for the fuel. Fifteen of the world's major coal-producing companies, operating in four continents and producing more than 400 million metric tons a year (all absolute figures given below are in metric tons), founded the International Coal Development Institute. This was "a non-profit-making organization dedicated to the continuance and extension of the use of coal as the most abundant long-term fossil fuel source adaptable to the widest possible energy requirements." Other hard-coal producers were invited to become members.

The UN Economic Commission for Europe (ECE) reported that in 1984 solid fuel consumption in European Communities countries—excluding the U.K., where a strike affected about two-thirds of the normal output—grew by 6.8%, while oil use declined by 2.3%; Eastern European countries slightly increased their consumption, though there was a small decrease in the U.S.S.R. In the U.S. solid fuel consumption rose by 7.6%. Worldwide, energy policy continued to be generally directed toward substituting other energy sources for oil when possible.

To meet demands resulting from these trends, world production of hard coal in 1984, at 3,067,000,000 tons, showed an increase of 4.7 million tons compared with the previous year. The European share fell; those of North America, Asia, and Oceania increased; and that of Latin America remained the same. The largest individual decline in output (57.1%) was in the U.K., a result of the strike that lasted almost a year and cost the nation about 70 million tons, part in 1984 and the remainder in 1985; the largest rise was 27.8% in Canada.

Brown coal production also increased, by 5.4% to 1,141,000,000 tons. This was made up of increases in most parts of the world where it was produced—the largest again being in Canada (27%). It is difficult to assess the relative significance of coal production when the products vary so widely in calorific value, moisture, and ash—particularly in the case of brown coal. To resolve the difficulty the ECE report included a new section based on a standardized metric ton of coal equivalent (tce), applying conversion coefficients used in the main UN *Energy Statistics Yearbook* for 1983. When countries did not supply their own such coefficients, it was assumed that 1 ton of hard coal equals 0.9 tce and 1 ton of brown coal equals 0.3 tce. On this basis, for 1984 the 3,067,000,000 tons of hard coal equaled 2,527,000,000 tce and the 1,141,000,000 tons of brown coal corresponded to only 437 million tce. This made the world total equivalent to 2,964,000,000 tce and the overall increase 4.6%—all on the standardized basis.

Reverting to absolute figures, hard coal trade totaled 304.7 million tons in 1984, 14.5% above 1983 and split fairly equally between coking coal and steam coal. For the first time Australia became the largest exporter with 75.8 million tons, increasing its exports by more than 25% compared

with the previous year. Next in order of quantity were the U.S., Poland, and South Africa. Stabilization and even some increase in coal prices also took place during the year. Only 3.4 million tons of brown coal were traded internationally.

The ECE saw prospects for the future as mixed. There were increases in industrial demand during 1984, but in the near future, in the industrialized economies, coal would have to compete "with the surge of nuclear power in Western Europe." In addition, no expansion in industrial capacity in North America was foreseen. Trends in the centrally planned economies were uncertain.

Environment. To meet growing criticism of harmful effects to the environment caused by the burning of coal, the Coal Research section of the International Energy Agency (IEA) made this area a "major strand in its work." Research concentrated on improving coal preparation, flue gas desulfurization, methods of containing nitrogen oxide emissions, and the role of sulfates in acid deposition. In Sweden the National Institute of Environmental Medicine investigated effects of emissions from coal-fired power stations; the researchers found that emissions often annoyed nearby residents but caused no extra acute symptoms of the respiratory tract.

The continuing furor about damage to trees and lakes alleged to be due to acid rain led many European countries (including the U.S.S.R. but excluding the U.K.) to agree to cut annual sulfur emissions 30% from the 1980 levels by 1993 at the latest. At the ninth symposium on flue gas desulfurization (FGD), held in mid-1985 in the U.S., it was reported that FGD systems in operation in the U.S. were purifying gases emitted from 50,000 MW of electrical generating capacity (about 17% of coal-fired capacity). It was estimated that 100,000 MW would be converted by 1991 and 175,000 MW by the late 1990s.

Coal-Liquid Mixtures. In the conversion of coal to a form that could be used in oil-handling equipment, emphasis shifted from coal-oil mixtures to the less viscous and less expensive coal-water mixtures (CWM). These mixtures typically contained about 70% by weight of (preferably high volatile) coal. The energy density of about 30 gigajoules (GJ) per cubic metre was intermediate between that of bulk coal at 25 GJ per cu m and oil (42 GJ per cu m).

An IEA study on CWM as a competitor to heavy fuel oil found conversion economically attractive if boiler utilization was higher than overall industrial averages. The second European conference on coal-liquid mixtures was heavily devoted to CWM, and the U.K.'s National Coal Board was planning a consortium with industrial companies to construct a plant that would produce 50,000 tons a year of CWM for market assessment.

Coal Conversion. A mixed picture emerged during the year in regard to coal conversion. The U.S. federal program for energy was severely cut from more than $6 billion in 1981 to less than one-third of that figure for 1985. The IEA, in its latest international review, covering 1983, found overall a 25% decline in spending on coal research by its 21 member countries compared with the previous year. The agency termed this "a disturbing trend, against the

background of an anticipated increase in the use of coal and the need to develop technologies to use that coal more cleanly." Among positive features Eastman Kodak, whose plant (using 1,800 tons of coal a day) for making acetic anhydride from coal gasification came on stream in late 1983, planned to manufacture other chemicals from coal. In Sweden two groups, AGA and A. Johnson, agreed to build the world's largest coal gasification plant, to become operational late in 1989. It would produce 450,000 tons a year of ammonia, mainly for use in fertilizers, and a sulfur-free fuel gas. Surplus heat would be delivered to a district heating project in Stockholm.

Krupp-Koppers in West Germany started a feasibility study for a large-scale coal gasification plant based on the Prenflo process, by which coal is ground and treated with oxygen and then steam at a pressure of 30 bar and at temperatures between 1,350° C (2,462° F) and 1,600° C (2,912° F). Satisfactory results were obtained on a pilot plant handling 150 tons a day, and the main plant was to come into operation in 1990. It would handle all kinds of coal, yielding a sulfur-free gas containing 95% of carbon monoxide with hydrogen, available for chemical synthesis or fuel purposes.

Meanwhile, the first stage of an Australian project to produce synthetic petroleum from brown coal was expected to start operating late in 1985. The pilot plant was designed to convert 50 tons a day of dry coal. Full-scale operation was not expected until the next century, but the aim was to produce 100,000 bbl a day of synthetic petroleum. In Canada TransAlta, the largest privately owned electric power utility in that country, commissioned a design study for a coal gasification combined-cycle plant. The design included a cleanup of hot gas to remove sulfur, particulates, and other impurities. Using a combustion turbine generating unit, the prototype plant was expected to produce 70 MW(e), while the combined cycles would provide much higher thermal efficiency.

The IEA continued to warn that the expectation of cheaper oil prices had "blunted the drive" for energy research and development, despite the prospect of declining oil production in the next 20 years. In a study entitled *Energy Technology Policy,* the IEA therefore called for more international collaboration to reduce costs, spread risks, and yield faster results.

(ISRAEL BERKOVITCH)

ELECTRICITY

Electricity continued to be the most favoured form of energy everywhere because of its flexibility and ease of use, and because it could be made available over wide areas from central generating stations or utilities. Its use was on the increase in almost every country. The biggest user was the U.S. with up to 2,700,000,000 MW-hr a year, followed by the U.S.S.R. with about 1,400,000,000 MW-hr. Japan's consumption was approaching 600 million MW-hr, while the main Western European countries averaged less than half that. When considered in terms of electrical energy consumption per capita of the population, the picture was different. Even though industry uses much more than householders, these figures serve as a

Electrical Power Production of Selected Countries, 1984
By source

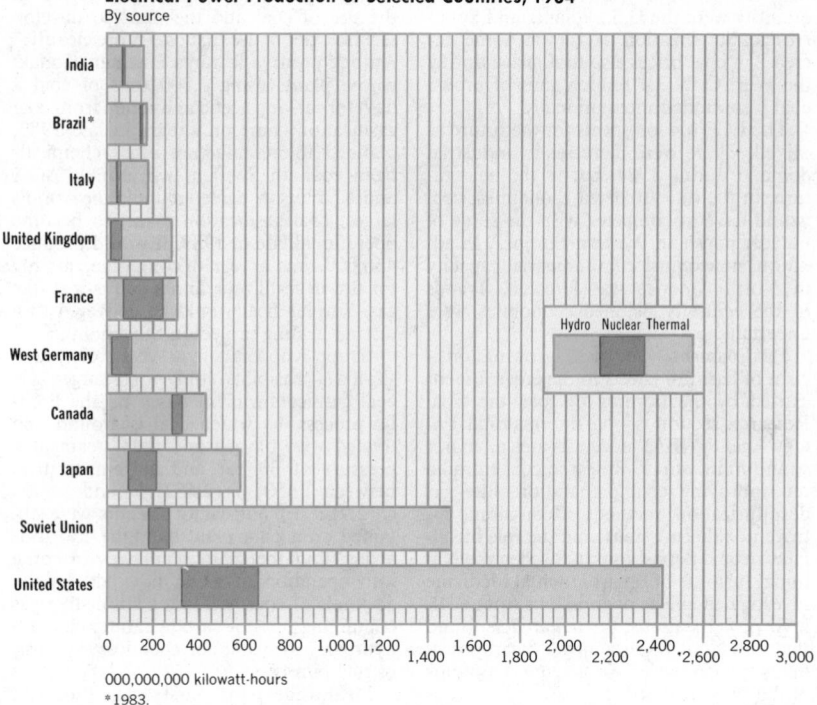

000,000,000 kilowatt-hours
*1983.

Sources: U.S. Department of Energy, 1984 International Energy Annual;
United Nations, Monthly Bulletin of Statistics.

comparative measurement. Canada stood out as the most electrified country in the world, with some 20 MW-hr per capita per year. The second in this imagined table was the U.S. with a figure of 12. Japan, the U.S.S.R., and European countries fell variously between 4 and 7.

The comparative figure for China was well down, at about 0.5 MW-hr per capita per annum. In that country, whether owing to its size and huge population or to ideologically inspired neglect, electricity had so far been of little importance. This was changing. Plans were under way to add another 50 million MW-hr a year to the available electrical energy supply. Negotiations with Britain and France on the construction of a $4 billion, 1,800-MW pressurized-water reactor (PWR) nuclear plant in southern China were in progress during the year. A total nuclear generating capacity of more than 10,000 MW was planned to be in operation by the year 2000, when it would amount to 5% of the country's total predicted generating capacity. Consequently, U.S. nuclear plant manufacturers were also looking to China for orders.

Most of the new projects in China were for hydroelectric plants. Hydroelectric generation can be used only where the geography is suitable—as, for example, in the Scandinavian countries—but electricity produced in this way was the cheapest of all. Some of the world's largest hydroelectric projects were in Brazil; the first phase of the Tucurui project in the north of the country would have a generating capacity of 3,960 MW that would be operational by 1989, to be increased to 7,900 MW in the planned second phase. In the U.S. it was predicted that hydroelectric utilities would in the future supply some 16% of the nation's electricity. Scandinavia got most of its electricity in the same way, as did a small part of Africa.

For countries not endowed with ample water power, the energy for transformation into electricity had to be produced by the burning of coal, oil, or gas or by nuclear fission. In the countries of the European Communities the use of coal decreased during the year by nearly 15%, while that of oil-based products increased by nearly 24%. These changes were temporary and due to the long miners' strike in the U.K. They did not occur elsewhere. The U.S., for example, produced some 69% of its electricity from coal and other fossil fuels, and that proportion was expected to be maintained with little change in years to come. In the U.K. the proportion in normal years was just over 80%. At what would be the biggest coal-fired power station in Western Europe—the Drax station in North Yorkshire—2,000 MW of additional capacity was added to the national grid during the year. No new oil-fired utilities were planned in the U.S. or the U.K. or, in fact, anywhere else.

The only serious challenge to coal or other fossil fuels as a source of heat to create steam to drive turbo generators was from nuclear fission. In this field there was worldwide activity. By the end of 1984 there were 345 nuclear power stations in operation, and 180 more were under construction. Construction was expected to start on 11 more in 1985. Although no new ones were ordered in the U.S. during the year, that nation still had more nuclear power stations than any other country. The advantages were obvious; nuclear power contributed nothing to air pollution or acid rain, and it was less expensive. Estimates made by the European Commission of the relative costs of coal-fired and nuclear electricity generation for power sta-

tions coming into service in EC countries in 1990 indicated that even where the difference was least (Italy), coal-fired generation cost about 30% more than nuclear generation; in France, with its extensive nuclear power network, the corresponding figure was 88%.

In the U.S., where nuclear power development had come to a standstill, the Nuclear Regulatory Commission authorized the reopening of the Three Mile Island, Pa., plant, closed down since the 1979 accident there. In the U.K. the long public inquiry into whether permission should be given for the Central Electricity Generating Board (CEGB) to build a nuclear power station at Sizewell in Suffolk, using the PWR system for its reactor, came to an end. Most of the world's power stations (including that at Three Mile Island) were based on this type of reactor. All nuclear plants in the U.K., however, had so far been based on the graphite-moderated air-cooled system, which was used in the world's first nuclear power station of commercial size at Calder Hall, still in operation after nearly 30 years. An improvement on this was the advanced gas-cooled reactor (AGR). The report of the inquiry's findings would not be available until 1986. One outcome, however, apart from the environmental protest aroused, was a long debate between the CEGB, which operated only for England and Wales, and the South of Scotland Electricity Board (SSEB). The latter supported the AGR against the PWR. The debate was important in that an export market could perhaps be found for the British-invented AGR. The CEGB claimed that the PWR was cheaper, but the SSEB said that this would not be so if the latest AGR designs were used. Furthermore, the nuclear fuel for an AGR could be changed on load, whereas a PWR had to be closed down for more than a month every year in order to change fuel. The operating staff of an AGR was exposed to less radiation, said the SSEB, which also pointed to the shorter construction time for its Torness AGR plant compared with PWRs in Europe. It attributed bad experience with the Dungeness B AGR plant to a bad design.

The enticing view that renewable energy from the Sun or wind or sea waves or tides should be used to produce electricity was still being supported. However, in this area many problems had still to be overcome, not least that of making outputs comparable with those of coal-fired and nuclear stations. For industrial countries the generation of a few kilowatts was of interest only as export potential to isolated communities. In the U.K. the CEGB was proceeding carefully with wind machines. All those in use were experimental, although some had already been joined to the national grid. Plans for erecting a multi-MW wind turbine remained in abeyance. In West Germany a 3-MW wind machine was being scrapped with a loss of some $32 million. In Denmark, however, the production of high-technology windmills, mainly for export to the U.S., was a thriving industry.

Solar energy was in a similar stage of development. Solar cells were expensive, usable only in satellites where cost was not the prime consideration. However, small solar-driven pumps and refrigerators were feasible, as one British firm demonstrated.

Scores of windmills on the Kahua Ranch in Hawaii utilize the regular trade winds that blow out of the northeast to produce two megawatts of electrical power for the island's grid.
WALTER SULLIVAN/THE NEW YORK TIMES

As for other renewable sources of energy, such as waves and tides, the outlook was not encouraging, although valiant efforts were still being made by enthusiasts. A 270-kw experimental tidal power installation on the island of North Uist, Scotland, underwent trials during the year.

Electricity was being increasingly used in transportation. In this connection work continued on the development of new rechargeable chemical cells, with the sodium-sulfur type likely to be in commercial production in the near future; batteries of this type would increase the range of electric-powered vehicles to 240 km (150 mi) without the need for recharging. A more fundamental approach in research at the U.K. Atomic Energy Research Establishment at Harwell promised a revolutionary new type of completely dry cell with an immense packing density.

(C. L. BOLTZ)

NATURAL GAS

The world's proven reserves of natural gas continued to increase, reaching an estimated 96,197,000,000,000 cu m (96,197 billion cu m or bcm) as of Jan. 1, 1985. This represented a 6.5% increase in proven reserves over the 1984 estimate and an increase of 30% over the estimate for 1980. New discoveries more than kept pace with world gas consumption. Commercial production in 1984 was 1,686 bcm, and so proven reserves were equivalent to 57 years of production at that rate.

Reserves, however, were unevenly distributed. The U.S.S.R. had easily the world's largest supply, which grew by 1,500 bcm to 37,500 bcm, 39% of the world's total. An additional 30% of the total was in the Middle East and North Africa, notably in Iran (13,550 bcm), Qatar (4,280 bcm), Algeria (3,087 bcm), and Abu Dhabi (2,650 bcm). The U.S. had reserves of 5,670 bcm (though later estimates were lower), and Canada had 2,660 bcm. The total for Western Europe was 5,511 bcm.

As well as having the largest reserves, the U.S.S.R. was also easily the largest gas producer, supplying not only domestic demand but also much of Eastern and Western Europe. Soviet gas production rose to 587 bcm in 1984. The U.S. produced 487 bcm, Canada 78 bcm, The Netherlands 75 bcm, and the U.K. 40 bcm. The U.S.S.R.

and the U.S. were also the world's largest gas consumers, using 523 and 510 bcm, respectively, in 1984.

When the U.S. Department of Energy published its annual figures for proven reserves in the U.S., it estimated a figure for the end of 1984 of 197.5 trillion cu ft—equivalent to 5,593 bcm—a decline of 79 bcm compared with its 1983 figure and the lowest level since such estimates were first made in 1960. New discoveries were failing to keep pace with production. About half of the U.S. gas production was affected by the deregulation of prices that took effect in January 1985. It remained to be seen whether the restructuring of the U.S. gas industry proposed by the Federal Energy Regulatory Commission would lead to lower prices by encouraging competition between pipelines, as its proponents predicted. New rules on gas transportation were to take effect in November 1985, but the crucial rules on the prices that pipeline companies would be allowed to charge to

gas distributors were not expected to be settled until 1986.

The Canadian government gave its approval to lower prices for gas exports in order to maintain competitiveness in the U.S. market. This helped to boost Canadian exports, which might increase further should plans to pipe gas from Alberta and from a large Nova Scotia offshore field to New England succeed. On the other hand, the planned export of liquefied natural gas (LNG) from British Columbia to Japan was put in doubt when one of the five Japanese utility customers withdrew from the project.

Western Europe was a buyers' market, with the U.S.S.R., Algeria, and The Netherlands all cutting the prices of their exports. The Netherlands succeeded in negotiating ten-year extensions to its major contracts with West Germany, France, and Belgium, while the U.S.S.R. cut prices to France and deferred the date at which deliveries would reach their full rate. France

AP/WIDE WORLD

Robert O. Anderson, chairman of Atlantic Richfield (ARCO), and Qin Wencai, president of the China National Offshore Oil Corporation, signed an agreement in September by which ARCO undertook to spend up to $500 million to develop a natural gas field near Hainan (Hai-nan) Island. It was China's largest foreign-investment deal to date.

then sought a price reduction for its Algerian imports. Algeria finally settled its dispute with Spain, after several years during which Spain had taken much less than the contracted quantity. A project for Algerian LNG to be exported to Brazil met with opposition in Brazil, where gas discoveries were reported both onshore and offshore.

In the Middle East, talk of Iranian gas exports revived. Such plans had been shelved following the Iranian revolution. In 1985 Iran and Turkey began studies of piping gas from Iran to Europe via Turkey. Qatar's North Field, discovered as long ago as 1972 and estimated to contain as much as 4,250 bcm, moved another step toward development with reports that a Japanese company had taken a stake in the project and would market LNG in Japan. Whether or not any gas was actually sent to Japan, Qatar now seemed set on beginning development to meet domestic needs and to feed a gas grid linking six Gulf states.

South Africa, which five years earlier had had no proven gas reserves, was planning to press ahead with development of the Mossel Bay gas field off its southeastern coast. This would be South Africa's first indigenous source of gas or oil. The gas would probably be converted into gasoline or diesel fuel. South Africa was also considering development of a field off the coast of South West Africa/Namibia, discovered in 1974 but left unexploited.

Exports to Japan from Australia moved closer to reality with the drilling of the first well for the export phase of the North West Shelf development. Eight Japanese companies signed agreements to buy LNG for 20 years beginning in 1989. Taiwan seemed set to join the ranks of LNG importers with plans for new port facilities to handle imports from Malaysia, beginning in 1991. Malaysia was not restricting its plans to LNG; its government was considering plans to build the world's first middle-

distillate synthesis plant in Sarawak, to convert natural-gas liquids into transport fuels and kerosene. (RICHARD J. CASSIDY)

PETROLEUM

OPEC was once more in the spotlight on the oil scene in 1985, the year of its 25th anniversary. Its lower marker price of $28 per barrel and a production ceiling of 16 million bbl a day were under threat because of weakening demand for crude oil in the major industrialized markets of Western Europe, Japan, and North America. OPEC production declined nearly 14% in the first half of 1985 and that of the Middle East by nearly 17%, but world production was down only 3.5%. There was a modest 2% increase in Latin America, nearly 4% in Western Europe, and a rise of just over 1% in the U.S. The greatest single downward change was in Saudi Arabia, by one-third. The Soviet Union and Eastern Europe registered a decline of just over 3.5%.

Most of OPEC's troubles resulted from three major developments: (1) a 6% reduction in energy consumption during 1979–84; (2) the introduction of oil-conservation and oil-substitution programs; and (3) production increases of 20% by non-OPEC countries during 1979–84 at the same time that OPEC output was falling by more than 50%. Moreover, OPEC revenues dropped from $280 billion in 1979 to $125 billion in 1984. The situation was complicated by differing political priorities and economic factors in the member countries. The collapse predicted by some was averted because Saudi Arabia largely absorbed the strain of declining production by producing below its allocated level. At a series of OPEC conferences in Geneva at the end of 1984 and in January and July 1985, moves to enforce production and price standards met with limited success. On September 22 King Fahd of Saudi Arabia, while hoping for "continued harmony and solidarity

within OPEC," reserved the right to conclude arrangements to restore output from 2.1 million bbl a day in August up to the permitted ceiling of 4,350,000 bbl a day. At a conference in Vienna on October 3–4, maintenance of the OPEC production quota of 16 million bbl a day was accepted, and an agreement was reached to postpone any redistribution of that figure. There was growing understanding of the need for price flexibility in order to take account of market conditions rather than reliance on the application of fixed pricing. At a December meeting in Geneva, OPEC agreed in principle to stop trying to defend the $28 a barrel price and to concentrate on protecting its market share, cutting prices if necessary

Reserves. By the end of 1984 the absolute level of world recoverable "published proved" reserves increased from 677,700,-000,000 bbl in 1983 to 707,200,000,000 bbl. Western Hemisphere reserves, 17.9% of the total, were much the same as in the previous year, with 11.8% in Latin America. Middle East reserves increased again to 56.4% of the total, with a reserves/production (r/p) ratio of 93.8 years. African and Western European reserves remained steady at, respectively, 8 and 3.5% of the total. Soviet reserves were unchanged from the previous year, but the share of the total was down from 9.3 to 8.8%. Also unchanged were the reserves of China (19,-100,000,000 bbl) and the U.S. (34,500,-000,000 bbl). There was a minor increase in OPEC reserves to 476,300,000,000 bbl from 448,300,000,000 bbl, 67.2% of the total from 66.1%, with an r/p ratio of 72 years. The largest reserves for a single country were in Saudi Arabia with 169,-000,000,000 bbl, 23.9% of the world total and an r/p of over 100 years.

Production. World oil production increased by 2.1% in 1984 to 57.8 million bbl a day, compared with 56,705,000 bbl

AP/WIDE WORLD

This methanol plant in Jubail, Saudi Arabia, one of the world's largest, was just part of that nation's emergence as a major force in the petrochemicals industry.

a day in 1983, but the share of the Middle East continued to fall, to 11,735,000 bbl a day; this was 20.3% of the world total and only a little more than half the 1977 amount of 22,545,000 bbl. Saudi Arabia had the greatest drop in volume, 4,690,000 bbl a day from 5,225,000 bbl, for 8.1% of the world total, 39% of the Middle East's, and 25% of OPEC's. Iran's production fell 10.7% to 2,195,000 bbl a day from 2,465,000 bbl, but the country remained the second largest producer in the Middle East with 3.9% of the total share. The Middle East share was below that of the U.S.S.R. (21.7%), just above that of North America (20.1%), above that of the U.S. (16.1%), more than three times that of Western Europe, and more than twice that of Africa. Among individual Middle Eastern countries there were large increases in Qatar (36.8%; 425,000 bbl a day) and the Kuwait Neutral Zone (35.5%; 420,000 bbl a day) and smaller increases in Kuwait (9.5%; 985,000 bbl a day) and Dubai (5.3%; 365,000 bbl a day). There was a small decrease in Abu Dhabi (2.3%; 840,000 bbl a day). Iraqi production rose 6.3% to 1,170,000 bbl a day, 2% of the world total.

Latin-American production was up 3.7% to 6,705,000 bbl a day, 11.9% of the world share. Mexico contributed 3,010,-000 bbl, almost half the total, followed by Venezuela (1,875,000 bbl a day). Brazil's 495,000 bbl a day represented a 36.8% increase. Colombia's 170,000 bbl a day was 9% above the preceding year. Only Argentina's production fell, by 2.5% to 465,-000 bbl a day.

Western Europe registered the largest regional rise in production, 9.1% to 3.8 million bbl a day and 6.5% of the total. The U.K.'s production was largest, up 9.6% to 2,580,000 bbl a day and 4.5% of the world total. Norway's production increased by 15% to 710,000 bbl a day, and France's by 16.3% to 60,000 bbl a day. Elsewhere, Austria declined by 4.2%, Turkey 4.7%, West Germany 2.9%, and Yugoslavia 4.2%.

In Africa the continued rise in Egyptian production was noticeable, 18% to 915,000 bbl a day, roughly comparable with Algeria's 990,000 bbl a day; in 1974 Egypt's production had been 230,000 bbl a day, compared with Algeria's 1,010,000 bbl. Nigeria's production increased 13.9% to 1,405,000 bbl a day, while that of Libya dropped 1.8% to 1,115,000 bbl a day, well below its 1979 peak of 2,090,000 bbl.

Production in Asia and Australia at 42,-685,000 bbl a day, 5.8% of the world total, increased by 2.6% over 1983. Indonesia was the largest single producer in the area with 1,440,000 bbl a day, an increase of 7.2%. Malaysian production showed a modest rise to 300,000 bbl a day, its highest ever. Production in China rose 8.1% to 2.3 million bbl a day, 4.1% of the world total, whereas Soviet production fell slightly from 12,520,000 bbl to 12,415,000 bbl a day, 21.7% of the world total.

Consumption. After five consecutive years of declining consumption, a small increase of 1.5%, worldwide, to 58,870,-000 bbl a day took place in 1984. In Western Europe, as the economic situation improved slightly, there was a minimal increase of 0.8% to 12,335,000 bbl a day, 20.8% of the world total. West Germany remained the largest consumer with 2,340,-

John Zaozirny, energy minister of Alberta, and Pat Carney, federal energy minister, meet with the press after signing the "Western Accord" that effectively ended Canada's National Energy Program enacted in 1980 and traded abolition of federal price controls and some taxes for a lowering of provincial royalties to Alberta, British Columbia, and Saskatchewan.
GREG KINCH

000 bbl a day, followed by the U.K. with a 19.5% increase to 1,835,000 bbl a day, due mainly to the national coal strike. France's consumption fell slightly to 1,820,000 bbl a day and Italy's to 1,735,000 bbl a day. Consumption fell in Austria, Belgium, Denmark, Ireland, The Netherlands, Portugal, Spain, Sweden, and Switzerland; it increased in Finland, Greece, Iceland, Norway, Turkey, and Yugoslavia.

Consumption in the U.S., after dropping for two years, rose 2.7% to 15,150,000 bbl a day, 25.5% of the world total. Canadian consumption fell 1% to 7.7% of the world total. Elsewhere there were mostly increases. Japan remained the third largest consumer after the U.S. and the Soviet Union, with consumption rising 3.6% to 4,550,000 bbl a day, 7.5% of the world total. Southeast Asia consumed 4.1% of the total, up 2.7% to 2,350,000 bbl a day. Middle Eastern consumption rose 4.9% to 1,890,000 bbl a day, 3.3% of the world total. African consumption increased 3.9% to 1.7 million bbl a day, a 2.9% share of the world total. Consumption in China was up a little, to 1,720,000 bbl a day, whereas that of the Soviet Union fell slightly to 9,040,000 bbl a day, 19.7% of the world total.

Refining. World refining capacity fell for the fourth year in succession in 1984, by 2.2% to 74,690,000 bbl a day, although refinery throughput increased slightly, by 1.7% to 56,165,000 bbl a day. Once again the greatest regional decline took place in Western Europe, down 7.1% to 15,815,000 bbl a day, 21.1% of the world total. Italy's capacity remained the largest in the region despite an 18.4% drop to 2,745,000 bbl a day. Similar declines occurred in France (2,190,000 bbl a day) and West Germany (2,105,000 bbl a day).

In the U.S., refining capacity fell by 4.6% to 15,135,000 bbl a day, 20.3% of the world total. In Latin America as a whole there was a decline of 3.2% to 7,940,000 bbl a day. Mexico had the largest refinery capacity, 1,525,000 bbl a day, followed by Brazil (1,305,000 bbl) and Venezuela

(1,225,000 bbl). In the Middle East there was a small increase of 1.9% in refinery capacity to 3,630,000 bbl a day. Saudi Arabia led with 865,000 bbl a day, followed by Kuwait with 590,000 bbl. Iranian capacity dropped to its lowest in a decade, 530,000 bbl a day, but that of Iraq reached its highest, 300,000 bbl a day.

Japanese capacity, third after the U.S. and the Soviet Union, remained unaltered at 4,975,000 bbl a day, 6.6% of the world total, as did Singapore's (1,020,000 bbl a day). Indonesia's capacity increased by 19.1% to 905,000 bbl a day. Australian capacity remained constant at 815,000 bbl a day, as did the Soviet Union's at 12 million bbl a day, 16.1% of the world total. China's capacity increased 4.9% to 2,150,-000 bbl a day, 2.5% of the world total.

Tankers. In 1984, for the seventh successive year, the world tanker fleet declined in size by 4.8%, to 269 million tons deadweight (dw). Ownership by flag remained much the same, with Liberia first at 71.8 million tons dw, 26.6% of the world total, followed by Japan (24.9 million tons dw), Greece, supplanting Norway as third (19.1 million tons dw), Norway (15.7 million tons dw), the U.S. (15.6 million tons dw), Panama (14.9 million tons dw), and the U.K. (13.3 million tons dw).

Tankers between 200,000 and 320,000 tons dw amounted to 41.4% of the world tanker fleet size, followed by 17.1% for those of 65,000 to 125,000 tons dw, 10.7% for 125,000 to 200,000 tons dw, and 10.5% for 320,000 tons dw and over. Only 4.7% were in the 10,000- to 25,000-tons-dw range. Tanker tonnage scrapped in 1984 amounted to 17.6 million tons dw, 63.1% of which was accounted for by tankers of 160,000 tons dw and more. In 1984 some 24,750,000 bbl of oil a day were transported by tankers, a small rise over 1983.

(R. W. FERRIER)

See also Engineering Projects; Industrial Review; Mining and Metallurgy; Transportation.

This article updates the *Macropædia* articles ENERGY CONVERSION; FOSSIL FUELS.

Engineering Projects

Bridges. Work started in 1985 on building the second bridge across the Bosporus. A suspension bridge, its main span of 1,090 m (1 m = 3.3 ft) would be the fifth longest in the world when completed. Sited about five kilometres (three miles) north of the first Bosporus bridge (main span 1,075 m), it would form a vital section of a second peripheral road around Istanbul that would provide the main route for traffic moving between Europe and Asia. It would be a toll bridge with the single toll plaza located on the European side and, if traffic grew as fast as it did when the first bridge was opened in 1973, would pay for itself within three years of its scheduled completion in 1988. The bridge was being built by a consortium of major Japanese firms and an Italian organization. The Japanese were currently the most experienced builders of major bridges, but this would be the first really long-span suspension bridge they had built. It would provide the essential experience required to tackle the Akashi Kaikyo suspension bridge, the main span of which would exceed 1,700 m and which would form an essential part of the third crossing being built between the Japanese islands of Honshu and Shikoku.

Railway bridges present special problems to the engineer. China completed a steel box structure described as the longest of its type in the world. The deck box was a continuous girder 304 m long; the two end spans were 56 m long, and the central 192 m was supported at the third points by raking A-frames. It was an interesting, elegant, and economical design and was built of high-strength steel made in China and having good welding characteristics.

The Italian government announced that construction of a suspension bridge across the Strait of Messina would begin in 1988. The bridge, which would join the toe of Italy to Sicily in a single leap, would have a main span of 3,300 m, more than twice that of England's Humber Bridge (1,410 m), currently the longest bridge span in the world, and nearly three times the span of the Mackinac (Mich.) Bridge (1,158 m). The main girder of the Messina bridge would be a long steel box essentially triangular in cross-section, wide at the top and narrower below. Three traffic decks were planned to be inside the box, protected from the immediate effects of the wind. The top deck would carry four traffic lanes for road vehicles, the second deck two tracks for bicycles, and the third a single rail track. The structure would be massive, with the towers 380 m high. Each of the two main cables would measure 1,600 mm (62 in) in diameter and contain 45,000 5-mm (0.2-in)-diameter high-tension steel wires. Triangulated hangers, as used on the Humber Bridge, would be used to dampen any tendency of the bridge girder to oscillate; extensive tests in wind tunnels showed that the design could cope with gusts of up to 225 km/h (140 mph).

Although big bridges attracted public attention, the great majority of bridge engineers were primarily concerned with the very much smaller spans required at frequent intervals along highways. Those responsible for new bridges were continuously seeking new materials and design details that would lengthen the life of the structure and, at the same time, reduce the maintenance required. One such "new" material (although it had been in use by the building industry for some 15 years) was glass-fibre reinforced cement (GRC). It was being used increasingly in the construction of concrete bridges. GRC bonded well with the concrete and, since it was basically the same material, the GRC skin was compatible with the concrete core, reacting similarly to temperature changes. Since it was a microreinforced

cement product, GRC had a very smooth finish that could be fully exploited in the architectural styling of the bridge.

Engineers responsible for older bridges that were now being called upon to carry traffic loads undreamed of when the bridges were built were faced with finding methods of determining the load capacity of these old structures in order to ensure safety and, equally, to avoid imposing unnecessarily conservative limits. Tests conducted by Britain's Transport and Road Research Laboratory showed that the ultimate load capacity of masonry arch bridges of the kind commonly built in the 19th century, many of which were still in use, was considerably higher than established estimates had suggested. It was possible that load restrictions placed on some of those bridges might be relaxed, thereby relieving traffic congestion in the area. The possibility was also raised that engineers designing future short-span bridges might revert to the structural form and construction methods of earlier days, since those older bridges often had a better record than did newer ones.

(DAVID FISHER)

Buildings. Industry's demand for high-quality accommodations for manufacturing led to the continued development of medium-span structures with advanced environmental services. Construction of this type was reflected in the new laboratory facility for PA Technology in New Jersey. The building took the form of a central linear circulation zone with an approximately 24-m span of usable area on each side. The main structural support was a row of A-frames spanning the circulation zone; from the apex of the row ran ties that were divided at a lower level to provide end and intermediate supports to the roofs. Within the A-frame at the second-floor level was a continuous platform that supported the equipment for environmental services. Exposed ducting hung below the platform and dropped into the building just inside the circulation zone.

Similarly, at Cambridge, England, an advanced test station facility for Schlumberger Ltd. was completed. In this case the designers utilized Teflon-coated fibreglass fabric to form a row of three marquee-like enclosures of an approximately 24-m span. Instead of being supported on poles like

OMRANIA; PHOTOGRAPH, CRISPIN BOYLE PHOTOGRAPHY & ASSOCIATES

A model of the Diplomatic Club in Riyadh, Saudi Arabia, illustrating the architect's oasislike plan, was displayed at the Royal Academy in 1984. The completed structure, opened in 1985, made innovative use of fabric with concrete and stone.

a tent, however, the tops of the enclosures were suspended by cables from a system of columns, the tops of which were themselves stayed by cables. Along each side of the row was a single-story block of offices and laboratories, the roof of which was suspended from external trusses. The main framing of the central portion likewise displayed its truss-type structural form.

The Diplomatic Club in Riyadh, Saudi Arabia, was an example of fabric used with concrete and stone as opposed to fabric with steel. A relatively narrow three-story structure, snakelike in plan, enclosed an open oasis of gardens and palm trees. The Teflon-coated fibreglass fabric roof was supported by a radial tension cable system with anchor blocks at the perimeter. The reinforced concrete work was clad in stone, the roughness of which contrasted with the smoothness of the fabric roof. The completed building contained 24,000 sq m (258,000 sq ft) of floor area including a banquet hall, restaurants, an auditorium, and areas for sports.

On a smaller scale and using modern fabrication methods, a pair of houses in Hollywood, Calif., attracted considerable interest. In the development of their design, efficiency was the key word. The designs centred on a 1,200-mm (4-ft) standard sheet module and used precut stud-framed walls in the North American tradition. The roof and floors were supported on light composite steel and timber trusses; plywood-sheathed timber decking provided the floor and ceiling and also braced the trusses. The stud walls were clad in plywood with fibreglass insulation and had metal sidings as exterior sheathing. Standard aluminum windows and doors fitted neatly into the modular grid.

As the stock of existing buildings aged, the question as to whether to refurbish them or replace them with new construction arose. As part of redeveloping a school in Fleet, England, a novel upgrading of an ailing 1960s building was carried out. The three-story structure had a flat roof, flat facades, and a considerable amount of glass. The roof and the timber-framed cladding were deteriorating, and the internal environment was too hot in summer and too cold in winter. A new light external steel frame was constructed outside the existing cladding. This supported a new shallow pitched roof of insulated steel panels extending out 1.2 m beyond the facade to keep rain off the cladding. To reduce the heat from the Sun, sloping shades of translucent corrugated plastic at the first and second floors extended similarly to 1.2 m from the facade. The result was a simple and effective means of improving the environment and extending the life of the building.

Repairs to the (West) Berlin Congress Hall were under way following its collapse in 1980, when one of the inclined arches carrying the suspended roof failed. The new arch beams would have the same two-metre-square section but would be made of prestressed lightweight concrete and would not rely on the roof tendons to provide support. The roof itself, while suspended as before, would be lighter in weight. A similar roof in Milan, Italy, over the 126-m-diameter Palazzo dello Sport stadium, sustained comparable damage in January 1985. At the time, the roof was covered with some 750 mm (30 in) of snow, greatly in excess of the 100-mm (4-in) depth normally expected. The damage occurred when three 2.5-m-long sections of steel box-girder ring beam crushed. This caused the roof to sag some ten metres at the centre. The tragic collapse of the concrete ceiling at the Uster, Switz., swimming pool in May, killing 13 people, illustrated the need for constant vigilance to attain necessary standards of quality in building engineering.   (GEOFFREY M. PINFOLD)

Dams. A recent UN report claimed that by 1990 more than 1,200,000,000 people would be without water supplies and that in the early 1980s some 345 million people benefited from new water projects. The less developed countries continued to plan water resource developments, even at the risk of creating enormous debts, in the firm belief that such developments were essential for their survival. For example, Thailand was placing its hopes on the development of the lower Mae Ping project, which would supply 875 million cu m (1 cu m = 1.3 cu yd) of water for irrigation as well as 215 MW of generating capacity to meet power shortages. Ethiopia was planning a large dam on the Albera River, designed to irrigate 300,000 ha (1 ha = 2.5 ac) in the Gambela Valley. Nigeria started construction of the $90 million Jibiya Dam on the Gada River, which was designed to provide drinking water for 200,000 people and to irrigate their farms.

Algeria announced a five-year plan to build 18 dams with an investment of $20 billion. This would double the domestic water supplies and irrigate more than 100,000 ha. Somalia started a 75-m-high concrete dam to irrigate 220,000 ha at a cost of $350 million. Angola, in need of a dam and hydroelectric plant but short of funds, arranged to have Brazil build the $1 billion Capana Dam on the Cuanza River in exchange for oil. Iran began work on a dam across the Abu Fares River at Ramhormoz. It was designed to provide irrigation for 1,500 ha, while another dam across the Marun River at Behbehan would irrigate 13,000 ha. Four dams were completed during 1985: the 63-m-high earth dam in the Baluchistan region, the 133-m-high Tiroft arch dam in Kerman Province, and the 65-m-high Toroq and Kabo dams in Khorasan Province.

The Soviet Union built four dams in Uzbekistan on the Amudarja River. The capacity of the four reservoirs formed by the dams totaled 7,000,000,000 cu m of water, enough to irrigate one million hectares of the Kara-Kum Desert.

In the interest of saving construction time and reducing costs, engineers continued to search for new technology. The introduction in the early 1980s of roller-compacted concrete (RCC) placed in the body of the dam won acceptance, and many more such dams were being built. A 45-m-high dam in the eastern U.S. built of RCC was completed for $12 million, compared with an estimated $17 million cost for a comparable earth dam.

The U.S.S.R. continued its interest in trying to blast the banks of a river to form a dam. Soviet engineers applied this technology to create a 16 million-cu m reservoir on the Alindzha River in the Nachicevan Republic.

While the development of new technology is important, the need to improve the safety of existing dams was demonstrated by several accidents during the year. In Brazil the Santa Helena Dam, a 17-m-high earthfill dam completed in 1979 on the Jacuipe River in Bahia State, failed by overtopping and released 240 million cu m of water. Fortunately, an early warning system permitted the evacuation of more than 10,000 people to safety, with no loss of life. In Italy two "tailings" dams failed, with heavy loss of life. While properly engineered dams were considered relatively safe, the dams made up of tailings from mines, which are mine-waste dumpings heaped to form a barrier, often were not scientifically engineered and, therefore, were unsafe. The two tailings dams in Italy were each 20 m high, one located above the other. Following a heavy rain, the dams gave way, releasing about 250,000 cu m of mud that swept down the Fiemme Valley, flooding the resort towns of Stava and Tesero, where approximately 250 people lost their lives.

Major World Dams Under Construction in 1985[1]

Name of dam	River	Country	Type[2]	Height (m)	Length of crest (m)	Volume content (000 cu m)	Gross reservoir capacity (000 cu m)
Altinkaya	Kizilirmak	Turkey	E,R	195	604	2,600	5,763,000
Ataturk	Euphrates	Turkey	E,R	184	746	85,000	48,700,000
Bakun	Balui	Malaysia	A	204	1,092	3,900	43,800,000
Boruca	Terraba	Costa Rica	E,R	267	700	43,000	14,960,000
Bureya	Bureya	U.S.S.R.	G	139	810	3,561	20,900,000
Casa de Piedra	Rio Colorado	Argentina	E	56	10,000	16,500	4,000,000
Chapeton	Paraná	Argentina	E,G	35	224,000	296,200	60,600,000
Corpus Posadas	Paraná	Argentina/Paraguay	E,G	65	8,474	18,200	13,000,000
Dabaklamm	Dorferbach	Austria	A	220	332	1,000	235,000
Dongjiang	Laishui	China	A	157	438	940	8,120,000
Dorna	Lerez	Spain	G	151	163	68	27,500
El M'Jara	Ouergha	Morocco	E	87	1,600	25,000	4,000,000
Gallito Ciego	Jequetepeque	Peru	E,R	112	750	15,000	400,000
Garabi	Uruguay	Argentina/Brazil	E,G	60	3,960	18,740	10,974,000
Grand Maison	Eau d'Oile	France	E,R	160	550	12,500	140,000
Guavio	Guavio	Colombia	E,R	243	390	17,755	1,020,000
Guri (Raúl Leoni)	Caroni	Venezuela	E,R,G	162	11,409	77,971	138,000,000
Hrusov-Dnakiliti	Dunaj	Czechoslovakia	E,G	29	31,500	18,340	199,000
Ilha Grande	Paraná	Brazil	E,G	29	7,060	11,573	30,000,000
Ingapata	Paute	Ecuador	G	166	430	1,600	413,000
Karakaya	Euphrates	Turkey	A	173	462	2,000	9,580,000
Kishau	Tons	India	E,R	253	360	18,400	2,400,000
Kouilou	Kouilou	Congo	A	137	345	390	35,000,000
La Vueltosa	Caparo	Venezuela	E	118	1,200	15,000	5,300,000
Lhakwar	Yamuna	India	G	192	440	2,000	580,000
Lower Tunguska	Lower Tunguska	U.S.S.R.	E,G	200	6,200	23,000	45,000,000
Lower Usuma	Usuma	Nigeria	E	49	1,350	93,000	100,000
Maqarin	Yarmuk	Jordan	E,R	164	700	21,000	486,000
Menzelet	Ceyhan	Turkey	E,R	151	425	8,000	19,500,000
Michihuao	Limay	Argentina	E	70	6,700	29,840	5,860,000
Naramata	Naramata	Japan	E,R	158	520	12,300	90,000
Oosterschelde	Vense Gat Oosterschelde	The Netherlands	E,G	50	9,000	50,000	2,780,000
Pati	Paraná	Argentina	E,G	36	174,900	230,180	38,000,000
Piedra del Aquila	Limay	Argentina	G	174	795	2,764	12,800,000
Planicie Banderita	Neuquen	Argentina	E	35	350	1,194	43,000,000
Porto Primavera	Paraná	Brazil	E,G	38	11,385	8,441	18,500,000
Potrerillos	Mendoza	Argentina	E	146	550	17,120	860,000
Rogun	Vakhsh	U.S.S.R.	E	335	660	75,500	13,300,000
Rocandor	Uruguay	Brazil/Argentina	E,R	78	1,598	9,940	33,580,000
San Roque	Agno	Philippines	E	210	1,130	43,150	990,000
São Felix	Tocantins	Brazil	E,R	160	1,950	34,000	55,200,000
Sardar Sarovar	Narmada	India	G	163	1,199	7,472	9,500,000
Tehri	Bhagirathi	India	E,R	261	570	22,750	3,539,000
Thein Dam Ranjit	Ravi	India	E,R	160	565	16,187	3,280,000
Upper Wainganga	Wainganga	India	E	43	181	6,290	50,700,000
Urra II	Sinu	Colombia	R	170	275	23,500	34,300,000
Warna	Warna	India	E,G	91	1,580	15,310	964,000
Yacyreta-Apipe	Paraná	Paraguay/Argentina	E,G	42	82,000	61,200	21,000,000
Zillergründl	Ziller	Austria	A	186	506	1,355	90,000

Major World Dams Completed in 1984 and 1985[1]

Name of dam	River	Country	Type[2]	Height (m)	Length of crest (m)	Volume content (000 cu m)	Gross reservoir capacity (000 cu m)
Bath County, Upper	Back Creek	U.S.	E,R	143	731	18,000	43,790
Canales	Genil	Spain	R	158	340	1,217	70,700
Colbun	Maule	Chile	E	116	550	15,000	1,478,000
El Cajon	Ulua	Honduras	A	234	382	1,600	7,085,000
Gura Apelor Retazat	Riul Mare	Romania	E,R	168	450	9,020	225,000
Itaparica	São Francisco	Brazil	E,R	105	4,150	16,530	10,700,000
Kenyir	Trengganu	Malaysia	E,R	155	800	16,800	13,500,000
Khudoni	Inguri	U.S.S.R.	A	201	545	1,475	365,000
Longyangxia	Huang He	China	G	172	342	1,750	24,700,000
Los Leones	Los Leones	Chile	E	179	510	9,200	106,000
Ozkoy	Gediz	Turkey	E,R	180	420	11,251	940,000
Ray Roberts (Aubrey)	Trinity	U.S.	E	43	4,561	15,475	986,000
Revelstoke	Columbia	Canada	E,R,G	153	1,620	13,000	5,180,000
Salvajina	Cauca	Colombia	E,R	160	360	3,500	904,000
Tres Irmaos	Tiete	Brazil	E,G	67	3,700	15,000	3,450,000
Tucurui	Tocantins	Brazil	E,G	93	10,677	64,300	43,000,000

[1] Having a height exceeding 150 m (492 ft); or having a volume content exceeding 15 million cu m (19.6 million cu yd); or forming a reservoir exceeding 14,800 × 10^6 cu m of capacity (12 million ac-ft).
[2] Type of dam: E = earth; R = rockfill; A = arch; G = gravity.

(T. W. MERMEL)

The voices of environmentalists were heard during the year. India's Sardar Sarovar Dam, representing an ultimate investment of $5 billion, faced a restudy of the impact of relocating about 85,000 people. Dams on the Danube River in Europe were also being delayed because of objections of environmentalists to the possible loss of rare plants and animals in the floodplain. (T. W. MERMEL)

Roads. Construction began on a segment of Interstate 80 (I-80) in Utah. When completed in 1986, it would provide the final link of the first intercontinental interstate highway in the U.S. Other major road projects begun during 1985 in the U.S. included the $1.3 billion, 11.2-km (1 km = 0.62 mi) segment of I-90 through Seattle, Wash., including a floating bridge, a conventional bridge, and 1 tunnel; a 21.5-km segment of I-595 in Florida, with three four-level interchanges, costing $1.2 billion; the 29-km Century Freeway in Los Angeles, at $1 billion; and a 321-km segment of I-49 in Louisiana, also costing $1 billion.

Mexico planned to spend $1.6 billion on its current highway infrastructure program, which focused on trunk road modernization and the reconstruction and maintenance of rural roads. Chile was building 320 km of roads and upgrading 245 km of existing roads to serve regions in the south that previously were accessible only by air or sea. Construction started in 1985 on a 650-km highway from Puerto Lopez to Puerto Carreno in Colombia, linking the central mountain region with the Venezuelan border.

A Transport and Communications Decade was announced for Asia and the Pacific by the UN Economic and Social Council. The ten-year program was designed to focus public attention on the specific problems of roads and road transport, which accounted for 80% of all freight carried in the region. More than 900 km of toll highways, including the longest road bridge in Asia, were being built in Malaysia. The major segment was the 773-km North–South Inter-Urban Toll Expressway from the Thai-

land frontier to the Singapore Causeway. The motorway (expressway) system of Bangkok, Thailand, was to be extended at a cost of $370 million, with financing expected to come from Japan. South Korea announced a $1.6 billion program to improve its existing roads, improve highway maintenance, and reduce the traffic accident rate. During 1985 Indonesia initiated a massive $385 million plan to rehabilitate and upgrade its entire system of national and provincial roads and bridges, with financial assistance from the World Bank. The World Bank was also helping China modernize its highway design and construction specifications. China now had 900,000 km of roads, 11 times more than in 1949. Some 500 km of India's national highway system in six states were undergoing a massive repair and rehabilitation program at a cost of $425 million.

The Hume Highway between Sydney and the New South Wales border in Australia was being widened at a cost of $330 million, providing a four-lane highway between Australia's two largest cities, Sydney and Melbourne. A new five-year plan to guarantee road funding went into effect in Australia on July 1, 1985.

The United Nations Economic Commission for Africa initiated an African Highway Master Plan Study, which was to be completed in 1986. As of 1985 more than 3,000 km of the 6,399-km Trans-African Highway were in service, with the entire highway scheduled for completion in the 1990s. It would link Nigeria, Cameroon, the Central African Republic, Zaire, Uganda, and Kenya.

More than 1,700 km of the Trans-European Motorway were in service, with 500 km under construction. The 11,-000-km system was planned to run through ten European countries. Also in Europe, Britain planned to renew and improve 112 km of motorways in the 1985–86 fiscal year at a total cost of $182 million.

Denmark's expressway from the West German-Danish border in the south to Vejle in the north was completed with the opening in 1985 of the 23-km segment from Skovby to Christianfeld. Road tunnels under the Pyrenees Mountains were being considered to improve communication between Toulouse (France) and Barcelona (Spain) and to open up the landlocked nation of Andorra.

Construction contracts were signed in 1985 for a 650-km, $500 million toll road across Turkey from the Bulgarian border to Ankara. The highway was intended to carry heavy traffic in and out of Iran and Iraq.

(HUGH M. GILLESPIE)

Tunnels. Transport-related tunneling continued to feature prominently among the world's major underground projects. Work on mass transit systems in Singapore; Lyon, France; Antwerp, Belgium; Washington, D.C.; Vancouver, B.C.; Seoul, South Korea; and Taipei, Taiwan, continued, while other large cities such as Los Angeles, Istanbul, and Shanghai were actively pursuing evaluations of the possible use of such systems.

In Western Europe, notably in West Germany and Switzerland, work on many road and rail tunnels continued or began during the year. The Sonnenberg mountain road tunnel near Luzern, Switz., was equipped as a nuclear shelter for 21,000 people, complete with communal living facilities, hospital, police station, and bank. Austria adopted a $1,180,000,000 plan to divert all foreign truck transport onto railway transporter trains, thus relieving the heavy traffic on the national road network; the scheme would involve major enlargement of many rail tunnels and construction of new sections.

The 3,200-km Baikal-to-Amur railway in the U.S.S.R. became operative in 1985, having been officially inaugurated in 1984. This new trans-Siberian line had taken some

Officials of a consortium of French and British organizations display artists' renderings of their proposed fixed link between the two countries. The proposal involves two 9-kilometre (5.6-mile) bridges from land to artificial islands that would be linked by a 19-kilometre (11.8-mile) tunnel under the English Channel.
AP/WIDE WORLD

ten years to complete. The greatest difficulties occurred in some of the nine tunnel sections, which totaled 30 km in length and where such diverse problems as permafrost, hot-water springs, and highly unstable geologic conditions had to be overcome or, in some cases, avoided. The Seikan Tunnel in Japan, whose pilot bore was completed in 1983 after some 19 years of construction, neared the final phase of conversion into a rail tunnel and service tunnel capable of accommodating the Shinkansen Bullet Train. An interesting revelation was that seismic observatories had recorded an earthquake registering 7.7 on the Richter scale in the vicinity of the tunnel, and no damage had occurred.

The British and French governments agreed to receive proposals for a commercially financed fixed link between their countries across the Strait of Dover. From a tunneling point of view, the most appealing proposal publicized was one that envisioned a system of rail shuttle transporter trains carried in twin tunnels of 7.3-m diameter, with an additional 4.5-m-diameter service tunnel. The total tunneled length would be 150 km, and the intensive program necessary for early completion of the $3 billion project could result in the need for up to 12 tunnel-boring machines working simultaneously during peak program activity. Another proposal utilized a combination of bridges, artificial islands, and immersed-tube elements laid in a seabed trench and would also involve inland tunnels on the British coast. To supplement this road link, there would be a separate conventional passenger and freight train railway tunnel bored under the seabed between Dover and Calais. The cost of the total scheme was estimated at about $6.5 billion. A bigovernmental decision and approval for a fixed link was expected early in 1986.

Sweden's Atlas-Copco company announced the arrival of its multipurpose Foro boring machine. Described as a "quantum leap forward" in tunneling technology, the new machine was said to be capable of excavating either vertical or inclined shafts (raise bores) or horizontal rock tunnels. It was computer controlled from a remote operator position and guided by the latest in inertial guidance systems of the type used in nuclear submarines. A major breakthrough in operational use made it possible for cutter head excavation to be sustained virtually continuously by means of a large number of automatic gripper pads that provided a balancing side thrust against shaft or tunnel walls at all times.

(GEOFFREY J. NOBLETT)

This article updates the *Macropædia* articles BUILDING CONSTRUCTION; PUBLIC WORKS.

Environment

Acid rain continued to be a dominant issue in 1985, especially in Europe. Reports from West Germany of apparently accelerating damage to forests were accompanied by increasing pressure on Britain to join those countries pledged to reduce their emissions of sulfur dioxide. The relationship between damage to trees and acid deposition remained controversial, however, and new theories were proposed to account for the "acid rain" phenomena.

After long and difficult negotiations, European Communities (EC) environment ministers agreed in June on emission standards for vehicle exhausts. When implemented, these would reduce discharges of carbon monoxide, oxides of nitrogen, and hydrocarbons and might be more effective in limiting acid rain damage in forests than further reductions in sulfur dioxide emissions.

Concern increased over the so-called greenhouse effect—climatic warming induced by carbon dioxide emissions. A slight warming in the middle latitudes of the Northern Hemisphere, detected over a five-year period by British scientists, was consistent with greenhouse effect predictions, and U.S. scientists reported on the atmospheric accumulation of other gases that might increase the warming.

Opposition to nuclear testing in the Pacific, spearheaded by the environmental protest group Greenpeace, attracted international attention in July when the group's vessel *Rainbow Warrior* was sunk by saboteurs in Auckland Harbour, New Zealand. The incident caused a political crisis in France, which admitted responsibility for the sinking. Greenpeace continued its campaign, sending other vessels to protest the French nuclear tests at Mururoa Atoll near Tahiti. (*See* WORLD AFFAIRS [Western Europe]: *France;* [Oceania]: *Oceanian Affairs.*)

INTERNATIONAL COOPERATION

At the economic summit held in Bonn, West Germany, in April, heads of government from Britain, Canada, Italy, Japan, West Germany, and the U.S. agreed to support a two-year study that would lead to the devising of internationally acceptable standards for measuring environmental changes, starting with the identification of areas where the scientific basis of assessment was weak. The study would concentrate on atmospheric pollution, toxic and radioactive wastes, marine pollution, pollution of soils and fresh water, appropriate land husbandry, and climatic change. The agreement followed a meeting of environment ministers from the participating countries held in London in December 1984, which discussed these matters and also problems relating to acid rain, the ozone layer, the greenhouse effect, and the transfer of hazardous substances to third world countries.

United Nations. A treaty to protect the eastern Indian Ocean was signed at UN Environment Program (UNEP) headquarters in Nairobi, Kenya, in June by the eight countries most concerned: Comoros, France (for Réunion), Kenya, Madagascar, Mozambique, Seychelles, Somalia, and Tanzania.

The UN Consultative Committee on the Ozone Layer met in Geneva in October 1984. Chlorofluorocarbons (CFCs) were regarded as a continuing threat, accumulating at a rate of at least 7.5% a year; methane was also accumulating, probably from rice paddies growing high-yielding varieties and from the draining of swamps. The committee called for more research into atmospheric chemistry, since it could devise no policy on the basis of the conflicting information available to it. In March, 49 countries agreed

In response to reports from various private sources of acidification in a number of lakes high in the Rocky Mountains, scientists from the U.S. Environmental Protection Agency, aided by the U.S. Forest Service, launched a $5 million study of the problem in September.
AP/WIDE WORLD

on a UN convention to protect the ozone layer but not on ways in which this might be achieved. Some countries, including the Scandinavian group and the U.S., favoured a ban on nonessential uses of CFCs; others, including the EC, preferred a limit to CFC production. Japan objected to both, and third world countries feared that a production ceiling would prevent them from building more refrigeration plants.

By the December 1984 deadline for signing the treaty establishing the Law of the Sea convention, promulgated by the third UN Conference on the Law of the Sea in 1982, 159 nations and organizations had signed and 14, mostly in Africa and the Caribbean region, had ratified it. West Germany joined Britain and the U.S. in opposing the treaty.

European Communities. Opposition by Britain, Greece, Ireland, and Italy at a meeting of EC environment ministers held in Brussels on Dec. 6, 1984, prevented the introduction on Jan. 1, 1985, of a directive setting uniform emissions standards for sulfur dioxide, nitrogen oxides, and dust from generating plants with a capacity of 50 MW or more. At the meeting it was agreed that by 1989 a single grade of lead-free petrol (gasoline), probably at around 95 octane, would have to be on sale throughout the Community. All new cars would have to be able to run on lead-free petrol from Jan. 1, 1989, and the petrol would have to be on sale by October 1 of that year. Discussions during 1985 concentrated on the limitation of exhaust emissions from vehicles.

The aim was to set limits to emissions of carbon monoxide, hydrocarbons, and nitrogen oxides. Disagreement centred on the control methods to be used and the design of the test cycle used to measure emissions. West Germany sought to make it compulsory for all cars to be fitted with catalytic converters, with tax relief for drivers when they complied, but France and Britain objected, the British favouring the "lean-burn" engine. Since EC manufacturers depended on exports to the U.S., consideration was given to the U.S. emissions test cycle, which measures emissions under U.S. driving conditions. A test cycle developed by

the EC was not directly comparable, and this caused further difficulty.

The environment ministers met in February and March and finally in June in Luxembourg, where, after 21 hours of unbroken negotiation, they reached agreement on June 28. The standards would not be based on the U.S. test cycle, and hydrocarbon and nitrogen oxide emissions would be considered together. Standards would come into force on October 1 of the year in question and would be (in grams per test): for vehicles of more than 2-litre cylinder capacity, carbon monoxide 25, hydrocarbons and nitrogen oxides 6.5 (of which nitrogen oxides were not to be more than 3.5), applied in 1988 to new models and in 1989 to new cars; for vehicles of 1.4 to 2 litres, carbon monoxide 30, hydrocarbons and nitrogen oxides 8, applied in 1991 to new models and in 1993 to new cars. For vehicles of less than 1.4 litres, standards would be imposed in two stages, the first being carbon monoxide 45, hydrocarbons and nitrogen oxides 15 (of which nitrogen oxides were not to exceed 6), applied in 1990 to new models and in 1991 to new cars. Stage two was to be agreed on in 1987 for implementation by 1992 and 1993.

Council of Europe. At the October 1984 plenary session of the Standing Conference of Local and Regional Authorities of Europe, a resolution was adopted calling for measures to increase public awareness of air pollution and for local authorities to reduce pollution. This would be achieved by controlling traffic, substituting public for private transport where feasible, creating traffic-free areas, and by encouraging nonpolluting methods for the combustion of wastes. In June 1985 the second International Conference on Action to Combat the Dying-Off of Forests and Atmospheric Pollution was held in Strasbourg, France. It called for the establishment of an international tribunal to monitor air quality, a directory of damage to forests, and an assessment of all damage from air pollution. It favoured an antipollution tax and the introduction of cleaner industrial technologies and clean, cheap transport.

Organization for Economic Cooperation and Development. The OECD published its *State of the Environment* report in July. It found strong public support for environmental protection and pointed out that, although economic policies might affect the environment, environmental protection had little effect on economies.

Marine Pollution. The dumping of radioactive wastes at sea was the main issue at the ninth consultative meeting of the Convention on the Prevention of Marine Pollution by Dumping of Wastes and Other Matter (generally referred to as the London Dumping Convention), held in London in September. The 25 members voted in favour of a Spanish resolution to continue a moratorium on such dumping. Six countries voted against, including Britain, which said it would ignore the resolution and resume dumping provided its own study, the results of which were expected by year's end, found that to be the best means of disposal. Britain had agreed in December 1984 to halt its dumping in the northeastern Atlantic for nine months. According to the U.S. State Department, the report on radioactive waste dumping from the International Council for Scientific Unions scientific review panel estimated that past dumping would cause about one human death in every 100 billion over the next 10,000 years, or 1,000 deaths in all.

A report on UNEP-sponsored research published in January showed that each year between 5,000 and 30,000 metric tons of lead reached the Mediterranean in rain and a further 2,200 to 3,100 tons entered the sea from rivers. This produced lead concentrations in the Mediterranean ten times higher than those found in the open ocean. The World Health Organization (WHO) sponsored a workshop meeting in Venice, Italy, on June 10–14 at which 30 engineers and scientists from 18 countries bordering the Mediterranean discussed the discharge of industrial effluents into the sea.

In May Saudi Arabia became the fourth state to ratify the Regional Convention for the Conservation of the Red Sea and Gulf of Aden. The convention, which came into force in July, established an organization to monitor, prevent, and control pollution issuing from Saudi Arabia, Yemen (San'a'), Yemen (Aden), Jordan, Sudan, and Somalia into the Red Sea, Gulf of Aqaba, Gulf of Suez, Suez Canal, and Gulf of Aden.

NATIONAL DEVELOPMENTS

Acid Rain. Throughout the year the British government resisted pressures to order power stations to fit flue-gas desulfurization equipment to reduce sulfur dioxide emissions. The pressure came from the House of Commons Select Committee on the Environment, other EC members, and

GIL HANLY—SYGMA

The converted trawler *Rainbow Warrior*, belonging to the environmentalist group Greenpeace, sank in four minutes in Auckland (New Zealand) Harbour after a bomb explosion opened the hull and killed a photographer aboard.

voluntary groups, all of which urged Britain to join those countries pledged to reduce sulfur dioxide emissions by 30% over a ten-year period or to accept the EC proposal to reduce sulfur dioxide emissions by 60% and nitrogen oxides by 40% by 1995. The government view was supported by the Central Electricity Generating Board and the National Coal Board. The Forestry Commission reported in March that widespread damage to conifers observed in 1984 was due mainly to harsh weather during the previous winter, not to acid rain. On August 21 the commission published *Forest Health and Air Pollution: 1984 Survey,* which found no clear evidence of acid rain damage in British forests.

When U.S. Pres. Ronald Reagan met Canadian Prime Minister Brian Mulroney in Quebec in March, acid rain was the main item on the agenda. The final agreement called for more research but not for controls. Canada continued to take unilateral action aimed at reducing wet sulfur deposition in the eastern provinces to 20 kg per ha (18 lb per ac) per year in a series of steps that would be completed in 1994. This would bring emissions of nitrogen oxides from cars and light trucks into line with U.S. standards by September 1987. Acting under a court order, the U.S. Environmental Protection Agency (EPA) issued rules in November 1984 that would reduce sulfur dioxide emissions from power stations, mainly in the Ohio Valley. The regulations reduced the maximum permitted height for stacks and thus compelled power stations to burn low-sulfur fuel or install scrubbers if they were to meet ambient air quality standards.

In West Germany the third annual Forest Damage Inventory, published in November 1984, showed that 50% of forests were affected by acid rain, compared with 34% in 1983. There were no reports of forest tracts in which all the trees were dead, but damage to broad-leaved species had increased. In August 1985 Otto Kandler of the Botanical Institute of the University of Munich suggested that disease might be responsible for the damage. He said several epidemics affected German forests, each with a cycle of peaks and troughs, and the "acid rain" phenomenon might be due to the coincidence of several peaks accompanied by a new disease that had not been diagnosed. A virus causing damage similar to that seen in Germany had been isolated in Czechoslovakia. Chemists from the Institute of Ecological Chemistry in Munich advanced yet another theory in September, suggesting that certain unsaturated hydrocarbon compounds produced by the trees themselves

could react with ozone to form substances able to destroy tree cells and enzymes.

In November 1984 acid rain was reported from two widely separated sites in the Northern Territories of Australia. Much less acid than rains in the Northern Hemisphere, the acidity in Australia was due to formic, acetic, and other weak acids. In September 1985 the U.S. government began a major survey of western lakes. Private researchers claimed to have found evidence of acidification in high-altitude lakes in the region.

The "Greenhouse Effect." Scientists at the Climatic Research Unit, University of East Anglia, England, reported in March that the period from 1979 to 1984 was the warmest since 1851 over the land masses of the Northern Hemisphere, reversing the cooling trend observed between 1950 and 1970. Accumulating carbon dioxide was held to be the most plausible explanation, although in relation to natural climatic changes the warming was not sufficient to make this certain. A team at the National Center for Atmospheric Research, Boulder, Colo., led by Ralph Cicerone, warned in May that nitrous oxide and methane were also accumulating in the atmosphere at rates that could double the warming effect from carbon dioxide.

The Ozone Layer. Guy Brasseur and A. de Rudder of the Belgian Institute for Space Aeronomy reported in February that any threat to the ozone layer was sufficiently distant to allow time for further scientific evaluation. They calculated that if CFC emissions increased by 3% annually there might be some ozone depletion by the year 2034, but that if emissions were restricted the amount of ozone would increase. Further doubt was cast on the threat from CFCs in May when David Harper of Queen's University, Belfast, Northern Ireland, published his calculations of the rate at which chloromethane, similar chemically to a CFC, is released naturally by the common wood-rotting fungus *Phellinus pomaceus.* The fungus emits about 5 million metric tons of chloromethane annually, compared with an estimated release of 26,000 tons of industrial CFCs. He argued that if free chlorine were a genuine threat, the ozone layer should have been destroyed millions of years ago. In July, however, S. Lal, R. Borchers, P. Fabian, and B. C. Kruger, all of the West German Max-Planck-Institut, warned that bromine may catalyze the destruction of ozone more efficiently than chlorine. CFCs containing bromine, used mainly in fire extinguishers, release some 3,000 metric tons of bromine a year.

SYGMA

A humpback whale nicknamed Humphrey frustrated scientists, environmentalists, and well-wishers for over three weeks in October after it swam into San Francisco Bay and up the San Joaquin and Sacramento rivers. The whale, member of an endangered species, ignored all efforts to drive it back to the safety of salt water but finally succumbed to recorded sounds of humpbacks feeding.

Photographs taken of the same spot in the Harz Mountains in West Germany in 1970 (left) and 1985 illustrate dramatically the severity of the forest damage that had become a matter of great concern in that nation. Acid rain was blamed for the damage, although the link between industrial effluents and the destruction of trees had so far not been demonstrated.

PHOTOGRAPHS, REGIS BOSSU—SYGMA

Marine Pollution. Part Two of Britain's Control of Pollution Act 1974 came into force on January 31. It gave water authorities wide powers to deal with agricultural pollution of inland waters, discharges into coastal waters, and accidental pollution at sea.

The quality of water at bathing beaches gave cause for concern. EC standards—a maximum 10,000 coliform bacteria or 2,000 fecal bacteria per 100 ml of water—were due to be imposed in December, but few British beaches would meet them. Exemptions until 1990 were sought for especially contaminated beaches at Scarborough, Margate, and Ryde, Isle of Wight, but in May government research showed that one-third of the 85 beaches examined failed to meet EC standards and a further third barely did so. These figures were confirmed in June, when the Coastal Anti-Pollution League published its findings. Of 690 beaches it examined, only 130 would meet EC requirements by the December deadline. By declaring that the EC directive applied only to beaches where on at least one day in summer more than 1,000 people bathed at the same time on a one-kilometre stretch, the government reduced the number of beaches to be monitored from more than 600 to 27, compared with 1,500 in France and 3,300 in Italy; under pressure from the Royal Commission on Environmental Pollution and the European Commission, the number was increased in July to about 200.

In a report published in June, the Fisheries Research Laboratory of the U.K. Ministry of Agriculture, Fisheries, and Food warned that a scheme to treat sewage before discharging it into the Mersey estuary could cause serious heavy metal contamination of sediments in the Liverpool Bay area of the Irish Sea. Solids and heavy metals were being removed from sewage before its discharge into the estuary, but the residue was being dumped as a sludge in the bay some 20–30 km (12–18 mi) offshore. Metal residues had increased from 220 parts per million in 1976 to 1,000 parts per million in 1980 as the sewage treatment plants came into operation.

In Poland it was reported in June that beaches at ten Baltic coast resorts near Gdansk were to be closed for the summer because of industrial pollution that could cause skin diseases.

Freshwater Pollution. July 18 was the deadline for the introduction of EC standards for drinking water, but as it approached several water authorities in the U.K. appealed for exemption or more time. Some used aluminum salts to treat water from acid peat moorland, and the aluminum content of the resulting water was very slightly higher than the EC limit. Others could not meet nitrate standards, and in July the government announced a three-year extension during which nitrate concentrations would be allowed to exceed the EC limit by 60 to 100% at 52 supply points serving 900,000 people.

There were fears of contamination of underground aquifers by chlorinated solvents when the contents of an unpublished Department of the Environment report were released in September. Engineers from the Imperial College of Science and Technology, University of London, who carried out the survey for the government, warned that 10% of aquifers could contain trichloroethylene and tetrachloroethylene in amounts exceeding limits recommended by the WHO.

In May the Ganga Authority, whose nine-member committee was headed by India's Prime Minister Rajiv Gandhi, was given the five-year task of cleaning the Ganges. The river was polluted from the point where it enters Uttar Pradesh, at Hardwar, all the way to Calcutta, and some of the Ganges Basin was infertile because of salinity and metal contamination. The basin received one-third of all the fertilizer used in India and 3,000 metric tons of pesticides a year; 80% of the river pollution was caused by the discharge of sewage from 100 cities along the banks, and 20% from untreated effluent, cattle, farm fertilizers and pesticides, and incompletely cremated human corpses, hundreds of which floated in the river every day. A £180 million scheme to produce methane for fuel, fertilizer, and irrigation water from sewage was planned to reduce pollution by 75% in its first stage, which would treat sewage from the largest cities. The second stage would provide similar facilities for the smaller towns.

A report issued in January said contamination of drinking water by supposedly "clean" high-tech industries may have contributed to high rates of birth abnormalities and miscarriages in Los Paseos, in California's "Silicon Valley." In 1980–81 there were 41 miscarriages in the town, compared with 23 in a control area, 13 birth defects compared with 5, and 30% of pregnancies ended in either miscarriage or a birth defect. In 1981–82 the proportion of Los Paseos children with congenital heart deformities was more than twice that in the county as a whole. The report suggested the cause was water contamination due to a leakage of 250,000 litres (55,000 gal) of 1,1,1 trichloroethane and dichloroethylene, both of which are degreasing agents, from storage tanks at a semiconductor factory 600 m (1,970 ft) from Los Paseos.

According to a policy statement issued by the Japanese

A cloud of thick smoke containing toxic hydrogen chloride rises from a burning plastic dome over a disused water pollution control plant in Cedar Rapids, Iowa, in July; some 10,000 people were evacuated from the path of the cloud.

AP/WIDE WORLD

Environment Agency in June, the migration of large numbers of people into new satellite cities with inadequate infrastructures was causing severe pollution of rivers and lakes. The pollution was said to be spreading to groundwater, which supplied 30% of Japan's drinking water.

Air Pollution. In its report *Urban Air Pollution 1973–80,* published in October 1984, the Global Environment Monitoring System of the WHO listed the cities with the most polluted air. Measured in micrograms per cubic metre, and with a recommended limit of 60, sulfur dioxide was most serious in Milan, Italy (242), Teheran, Iran (160), Prague, Czech. (154), Santiago de Chile (137), and São Paulo, Brazil (135), while Helsinki, Fin., Glasgow, Scotland, and Warsaw and Wroclaw, Poland, were seriously polluted in winter. Measured in the same units, and also with a recommended limit of 60, smoke was worst in Teheran (222), Madrid (196), Bogotá, Colombia (120), Cairo (105), and Havana (101). Total particulate matter was worst in Lahore, Pak. (690), Baghdad, Iraq (563), Delhi (535) and Calcutta (462), India, Accra, Ghana (398), Jakarta, Indon. (275), and Athens (235).

On Sept. 16, 1985, Justice Minister Elizabeth Kopp announced that from October 1986 Switzerland would impose the strictest car emission controls in Europe. Only vehicles using lead-free petrol and fitted with catalytic converters would be able to comply. The regulations, aimed at reducing carbon monoxide emissions by 91%, would not apply to old cars or motorcycles but would come into force for vehicles other than passenger cars on Oct. 1, 1988.

On January 17 a stage-two smog alert was imposed in North Rhine-Westphalia, West Germany. Private cars were banned during the morning and evening rush hours, and power stations were required to burn only light oil. For most of January 19 a stage-three alert caused a virtual shutdown of factories and a ban on all private cars in several cities, including Düsseldorf, Essen, Duisburg, Bottrop, Gelsenkirchen, and Oberhausen. Police were drafted to man smog barriers closing roads into the cities. The

stage-two alert was lifted on January 20, but a stage-one alert remained in force. Citizens were asked to keep use of private cars to a minimum, and people with respiratory complaints were advised to remain indoors.

In the U.S. a survey of emissions from 80 of the country's largest chemical companies, made by the House Health and Environment Subcommittee, chaired by Rep. Henry Waxman (Dem., Calif.), reported on March 26 that hazardous substances were being released in more places and in larger amounts than had been suspected. Companies admitted discharging more than 200 substances they themselves classed as "hazardous," including acrylonitrile, ammonia, chloroform, vinyl chloride, ethylene oxide, and hydrochloric acid. Only asbestos, benzene, vinyl chloride, mercury, beryllium, and radionuclides were regulated federally, and the subcommittee was working on legislation that would require the EPA to produce regulations on a specific list of substances.

Land Conservation. The scheme to build a tunnel linking the Mediterranean with the Qattara Depression in northern Egypt was abandoned in November 1984. The tunnel would have provided hydroelectric power, but there were fears that subsurface rocks would crack, contaminating fresh water and possibly triggering earthquakes. Despite opposition from environmentalists and an announcement in February that work had been halted, in August the Hungarian government decided to proceed with the construction of the Gabcikovo-Nagymaros hydroengineering project on the Danube. Opposition was based on fears that the "Danube Bend," a popular resort area for residents of Budapest, would be flooded, fears of the consequences for Budapest in the event of an earthquake, and doubts about the effects on wildlife of diverting 25 km (15.5 mi) of the river and its bayous through a concrete channel. The project would also divert the main navigational channel marking the border between Hungary and Czechoslovakia, leaving it inside Czechoslovak territory.

Nikolay Basilyev, the Soviet minister for land reclamation and water resources, announced on June 5 that the plan to divert the Irtysh and Ob rivers was essential to Soviet food production and would proceed. The scheme called for a 2,400-km (1,500-mi) canal and would reduce water flow into the Arctic, but Basilyev said scientists had concluded that any environmental effects would be merely local.

The year was an exceptionally bad one for brush and timber fires in the western U.S. and Canada, where two years of dry weather had produced tinderbox conditions. During one period of high heat and humidity in the summer more than a million acres of 11 western states were ablaze, and fire fighters were brought in from as far away as Alaska. Electrical storms that produced lightning but little rain set off many of the fires, including most of those in wilderness areas, but arson was blamed for some of the blazes in California, where more than 170 homes were destroyed.

Radioactive Wastes. The trial of British Nuclear Fuels Ltd. (BNFL) began on June 5 at Carlisle Crown Court. BNFL faced six charges of contravening the Radioactive Substances Act 1960 and the Nuclear Installation Act 1965, arising from the accidental release of materials into the Irish Sea in November 1983. The company admitted one charge of failing to keep adequate records, and on July 9 the judge instructed the jury to acquit BNFL of two charges: failing to keep adequate records of radioactive materials stored on site, and failing to control material so it could not escape. The trial ended after eight weeks with the conviction of BNFL, although the judge stressed that

the breaches of safety rules had not caused a discharge of material in excess of the authorized limits and there had been no risk to the public. Fines, costs, and legal expenses cost BNFL about £30,000.

Toxic Chemical Wastes. Following the disaster at Bhopal, India, in December 1984 resulting from the leaking of highly toxic methyl isocyanate from a pesticide plant owned by the Indian subsidiary of Union Carbide Corp., the neighbourhood was left deserted. By Jan. 10, 1985, the 16 tons of methyl isocyanate remaining in the factory had been processed into insecticides and so rendered safe, and people began to return. By July 11, when the factory was finally closed, the official death toll stood at 1,745, and an estimated 10,000 people were suffering from serious lung complaints that in about 20% of cases would require treatment for up to ten years. Preliminary hearings in the lawsuits arising from the incident began in New York in April. It was estimated that if damages were awarded at U.S. rather than Indian levels they could amount to $1 billion.

Tanks at Union Carbide plants in West Virginia leaked twice in 1985, on August 11 at Institute and on August 13 at South Charleston. The first leak, caused by failure to contain a runaway reaction similar to that at Bhopal, released aldicarb oxime gas, and 135 people received hospital treatment as a result. Following the Bhopal accident, the Institute plant had been modified to convert methyl isocyanate to the less dangerous aldicarb before it was transported across the country to make the finished pesticide Temik. The South Charleston incident released 1,900 litres (418 gal) of polyalkaline glycol (hydraulic brake fluid), isopropanol (solvent), and sulfuric acid into the Kanawha River. The chemicals were foul-smelling, but no one was injured.

In June the U.S. Economic Development Commission reported that exposure to toxic wastes in California would probably cause about 2,500 deaths annually for the next decade, and the cost of cleaning up the state would be about $4 billion a year. The oil refining, petrochemical, aerospace, defense, electronics, and agriculture industries,

which were producing the wastes, also provided half the total employment in manufacturing in the state and 25% of state income. According to the head of the commission, Leo McCarthy, for every dollar invested, two more were spent managing toxic chemicals. The treatment of cancer caused by exposure to toxic wastes cost the state $1.3 billion a year; company lawsuits cost $2.7 billion a year; and replacing contaminated drinking water cost $32 million a year. The commission proposed seven immediate steps to deal with the problem, along with a five-year plan, based largely on treating wastes rather than dumping them.

In Britain the Hazardous Waste Inspectorate reported in June that many of the tips (dumps) receiving the 4.4 million metric tons of waste produced annually in England and Wales were badly managed and potentially dangerous. The report also warned of a shortage of incineration capacity for certain wastes, including polychlorinated biphenyls (PCBs). Britain was the only Western European country to rely on the private sector for industrial waste disposal, and many of the companies were in financial difficulties. The tips were licensed by local authorities, however, and in July the government told the county councils it expected better monitoring of the toxic waste tips they would inherit following abolition of the metropolitan counties. Re-Chem International, one of the companies equipped to incinerate PCB, opened community relations centres at Pontypool and Fawley but failed to appease the public. Complaints of illness with symptoms similar to those previously reported from Bonnybridge, Scotland, were made by people living near the Fawley, Southampton, plant. Two scientific investigations reported in February that nothing unusual had been found in the health of humans or animals in the Bonnybridge area and that there was no evidence of high levels of PCB, dioxins, or furans near Bonnybridge or Pontypool.

In January a transformer containing insulation made from PCB exploded in the basement of an apartment building in Reims, France. The PCB burned to yield dioxins and furans. In August 343 people were told they had been contaminated, although no symptoms of injury had

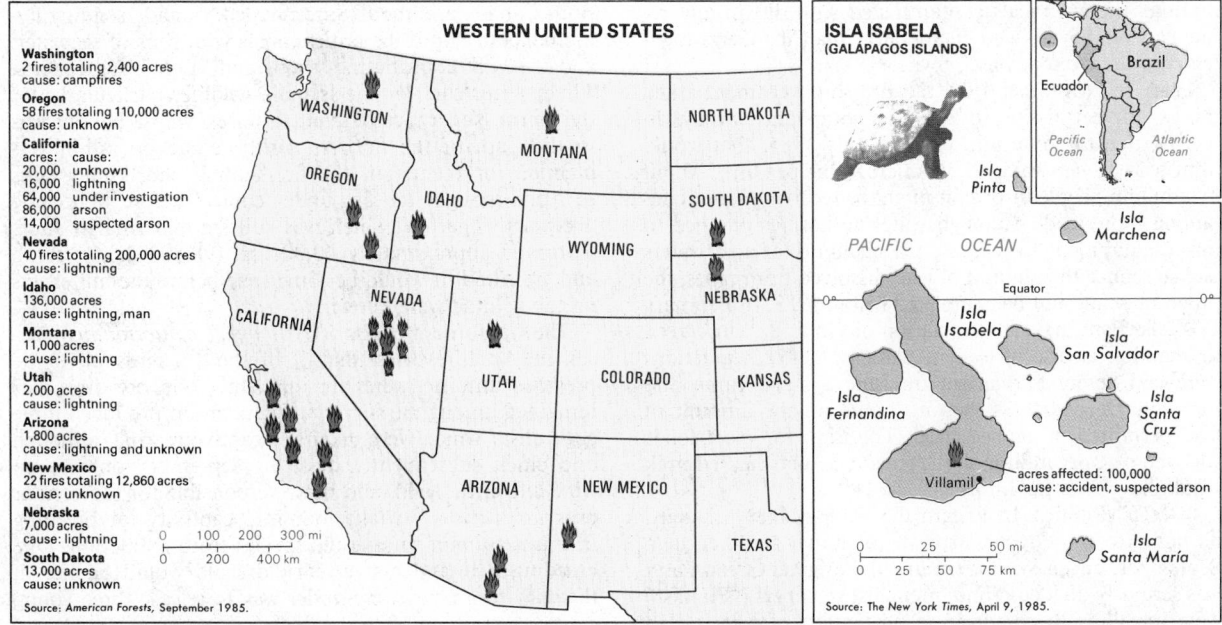

Wildfires in the American West and on Isla Isabela of the Galápagos Islands group caused heavy short- and long-term damage. Erosion and sedimentation were the most immediate problems, while a reduced water supply, altered soil characteristics, and loss of wildlife habitats posed longer-range threats. On Isla Isabela fires destroyed the food supply for a subspecies of the nearly extinct giant Galápagos tortoise (*Geochelone elephantopu*).

As a frightening footnote to the previous year's disaster at Bhopal, India, this Union Carbide chemical plant at Institute, West Virginia, experienced an uncontrolled leak of toxic gas in August. Although the plant processes methyl isocyanate, the gas spilled at Bhopal, the Institute accident involved a less toxic chemical.

ALLAN TANNENBAUM—SYGMA

been reported. Bernard Paringaux, head of a waste disposal firm, was fined and sentenced to 18 months' imprisonment in June for receiving and concealing dioxin waste from Seveso, Italy (where an explosion at the Icmesa chemical plant in 1976 had caused widespread dioxin poisoning).

On May 14 a Milan appeal court reversed the convictions of five defendants on the most serious charges arising from the Seveso case. All charges were dropped against Guy Waldvogel, chairman of Icmesa, Fritz Moeri, head of Icmesa planning, and Giovanni Radice, Icmesa technical director. Jörg Anton Sambeth, technical director of Givaudan, the Swiss parent company, and Herwig von Zwhel, another Icmesa technical director, were given suspended prison sentences. At Seveso it was reported in June that the Icmesa factory site was being made into a park. Also in June, the chemicals contaminated with dioxin and removed from Seveso were incinerated in a Ciba-Geigy high-temperature oven at Basel, Switz.

Lead. In November 1984 the British government asked the EC for permission to waive its compliance with a directive, due to come into force in July 1985, that would limit lead in tap water to 50 micrograms per litre. About five million people in Britain might be receiving water containing more lead. Although water authorities planned to install equipment to increase the alkalinity of acid waters and so reduce the amount of lead dissolved from pipes, the program would not be completed before 1989. In February 1985 the Paintmakers Association of Great Britain agreed to abandon all use of lead in paint by 1987. Regulations were laid before Parliament on June 24, and came into force on December 31, setting limits on the amount of lead permitted in canned food. The limit for most foods was one part per million, but corned beef and canned milk would have separate limits.

"Green" Politics. In Britain the Ecology Party changed its name to the Green Party at its annual conference in September, but in West Germany the original Green Party was seriously divided. Fundamentalist members ("Fundis") were unwilling to compromise on matters of principle in order to form coalitions with other parties, but others, nicknamed "Realos" (realists), were prepared to do so. The party was divided over its relationship to the Social Demo-

cratic Party (SPD), with the fundamentalists maintaining that by supporting SPD governments Greens compromised their principles. Nor was there agreement over the rotation of seats in the Bundestag (parliament), whereby elected Greens were replaced between elections. The Greens failed to increase their share of the vote significantly in the Saarland elections in March or in the North-Rhine Westphalia elections in May, and their support seemed to be waning. However, in October they entered a state government for the first time, forming a coalition with the SPD in Hesse.

Pani Panchayat, India's first "green" party, which contested the Purandhar state election in March, was based on cooperatives of small farmers and aimed principally to help them irrigate their land and supply water to local people.

(MICHAEL ALLABY)

WILDLIFE CONSERVATION

On Jan. 13, 1985, ornithologists counted 1,350 great white cranes (*Grus leucogeranus*) at Poyang Lake Bird Sanctuary in China, which was established in 1983. It was believed to be the largest flock of cranes in the world. Also in January, China reported a survey revealing 700 black-necked cranes (*Grus nigricollis*) in the country; previously there were thought to be only 300–400 left in the wild. Efforts were made in Ladakh, India, to protect 14–16 pairs of black-necked cranes by placing armed guards at the breeding areas. Chicks were ringed in order to locate the wintering area of the Indian flock, believed to be in China or Bhutan. In North America the whooping crane (*Grus americana*) conservation program suffered a setback at the end of 1984 when seven members of the captive flock of 37 birds died of eastern equine encephalitis. This left 148 whooping cranes alive, including captive birds.

A fire broke out on Isabela, the largest island in the Galápagos archipelago, on February 26. It was started accidentally by farmers burning diseased coffee bushes and spread into the national park, where it burned intensely, fueled by the abnormally heavy growth of vegetation induced by the 1983 El Niño current and dried by the 1984 drought. Ecuador mobilized soldiers and local residents to fight the fire and in March appealed for international aid. Both Canada and the U.S. responded, Canada sending flying boats to bomb the critical areas with tons of seawater, and the U.S. contributing troops and fire-fighting experts. There were fears for the island's wildlife, particularly for the Sierra Negra race of giant tortoises, whose habitat was in the path of the fire. An airlift rescue operation was planned for them, but the fire-fighting efforts and rains in April brought the fire under control before it became necessary. The fire, which was still smouldering in June, destroyed approximately 40,000 ha (98,800 ac) of scrub and grassland. It would be some time before the full effects on the wildlife were known.

The Californian condor (*Gymnogyps californianus*) census in April revealed that 7 of the 15 birds alive the previous autumn were missing. Only one breeding pair remained among the surviving eight, and it produced three eggs, all of which were taken for captive rearing, although one chick subsequently died. In September only seven were left in the wild, and those responsible for the condor program decided to take four into captivity for breeding in a last attempt to save the species from extinction. One breeding pair and a five-year-old male would be left in the wild, and plans were under way to release three young captive females in 1986.

The white-tailed sea eagle (*Haliaeetus albicilla*) reintroduction project on the Scottish island of Rhum had a success in 1985 when the first bird to be bred in the wild

in Britain for 70 years took flight. Thailand reintroduced sarus cranes (*Grus antigone*) to the Bang Phra Wildlife Sanctuary after receiving three pairs from the U.S.-based International Crane Foundation. In New Zealand a new population of the world's heaviest parrot, the kakapo (*Strigops habroptilus*), was discovered; only about 50 kakapos were known to exist. In the New Zealand Parliament the death was announced of "Old Blue," a female Chatham Island black robin (*Petroica traversi*), which was, in 1980, among the last five of the species. All but 2 of the 30 black robins alive at the end of 1984 were Old Blue's direct descendants.

The parties to the Convention on International Trade in Endangered Species of Wild Fauna and Flora (CITES) assembled in Buenos Aires, Arg., in April for their fifth biennial conference. The resolutions approved included one, put forward by 12 South American countries, to reject all wildlife shipments originating in Bolivia until that country reorganized its permit system. Bolivia had been strongly criticized early in the meeting for exporting large quantities of specimens taken illegally in other countries, in contravention of the CITES. Another resolution approved establishment of a special Ivory Unit to scrutinize the trade in African elephant ivory more closely; the proportion of poached ivory entering the trade was estimated at up to 80% in recent years. The meeting decided to relax controls on trade in Nile crocodile hides for those countries able to demonstrate that they had healthy crocodile populations and the means of controlling the trade effectively.

The International Whaling Commission (IWC) held its 37th annual meeting in Bournemouth, England, in July, the last meeting before the indefinite moratorium on commercial whaling due to begin at the end of 1985. The U.S.S.R., Japan, and Norway remained formally opposed to the moratorium, but the U.S.S.R. announced that it would halt Antarctic whaling in 1987. The meeting voted to give full protection to Norway's severely depleted stock of minke whales in the northeast Atlantic, making it unlikely that Norway would continue whaling. Japan showed no signs of ceasing whaling. In the 1984–85 season it took 400 sperm whales in defiance of the IWC's zero quota. The U.S., required by law to impose sanctions on nations contravening IWC decisions, privately agreed with Japan not to impose sanctions if Japan promised to cease whaling by 1988. In late 1984 conservationists had taken the U.S. government to court over this agreement. A district court ruled that the government had acted illegally, and the ruling was confirmed in August by the Federal Court of Appeals. The government appealed the decision to the Supreme Court. Iceland and South Korea did not formally oppose the moratorium but announced their intention to take 200 whales each year for the next four years, using an IWC clause that allowed governments to grant themselves special permits to take any number of whales for purposes of scientific research.

In February hundreds of white whales (*Delphinapterus leucas*), trapped in the Bering Sea by ice since mid-December, were freed by a Soviet icebreaker, which broke open a 19-km (11.8-mi) channel and lured them through it into open water by playing classical music through a loudspeaker.

Plans to breed Sumatran rhinos (*Dicerorhinus sumatrensis*) in captivity were announced in August. With fewer than 800 individuals in existence, this rhino was one of the 12 animals identified by the International Union for Conservation of Nature and Natural Resources (IUCN), at its general assembly in Madrid in November 1984, as among the world's most endangered species. As part of an IUCN-coordinated project, an agreement was made between Indonesia and the U.K. under which two pairs of the rhinos would be captured and taken to two British zoos for captive breeding. The status of rhinos in parts of Africa became critical in 1985. Kenya decided to round up its last black rhinos to keep them in heavily guarded sanctuaries. Rhinos in Zimbabwe's Middle Zambezi Valley, once considered safe because of their remoteness, became the latest target of armed poaching gangs, which killed 18 rhinos in early 1985 alone.

On September 27 the ban on imports of baby harp and hooded seal skins to the EC, imposed in 1983 and due to expire on Oct. 1, 1985, was extended for four years.

(JACQUI M. MORRIS)

See also Agriculture and Food Supplies; Botanical Gardens and Zoos; Energy; Historic Preservation; Life Sciences; Transportation.

This article updates the *Macropædia* article CONSERVATION OF NATURAL RESOURCES.

Fashion and Dress

During the winter of 1984–85 that Japanese tendency to make all silhouettes, male or female, look alike still prevailed. Loose and slouchy jackets with broad, squared-off shoulders, borrowed from "Big Brother," were worn over fully gathered skirts that descended to below the calf, effectively camouflaging the body. This androgynous appearance was emphasized by the new cropped haircut. Previously, boy and girl had worn the same long, fluffy curls, but now, with hair closely trimmed over ears and neck, they were even more difficult to identify from the back. In the more extreme cases there was, at the top of the head, a sort of flat, closely cropped platform, reminiscent of a clothes brush, or a stand-up effect like a cutoff bunch

(continued on page 251)

VINCENZO GIACO—A.R.T. FOTO

Byblos, one of Italy's most talented and iconoclastic design studios, showed their facetious new menswear collection in Milan in July. Although clearly in tune with trends in Italian design, the two designers responsible for the look are actually English.

The Street Scene—Pop, Glam, Androgyny

BY SUZY MENKES

Street style over the past decade has spawned many important fashion trends—the "retro" clothing revivals, deliberately torn, crumpled, and distressed clothes, androgyny, oversize. Where streetwise youth has led, mainstream fashion has followed, the ideas grasped, absorbed, and rehashed by dress manufacturers eager for profit. The concept of youth style was born out of the optimistic post-World War II years when a rising teenage generation was given its own cultural and commercial identity. The 1980s style was part of a harsher world in which unemployment and international upheaval bred insecurity. Against this background clothes became a form of tribal identity—a uniform in which to fight the generational war, a chance to escape, in the pleasure of dressing up, from too much reality.

Street fashion itself became the height of fashion by the spring of 1985, when established international designers declared the streets an inspiration. In Milan the Paris-based designer Karl Lagerfeld made a high-fashion fur collection in homage to wild street fashion, and Jean-Paul Gaultier in Paris re-created London street looks at couture prices.

The strongest single influence on the street scene as a manifestation of youth culture was pop music. With the growth of the pop video, identification of a singer and group with a particular clothing image reflected back on their fans. Many of the young British designers, products of a unique art college training system, were linked to the pop music world, so its stars now had personal image makers. The politically committed pop star expressed his ideals in clothes as well as lyrics; thus designer Katharine Hamnett

created slogan T-shirts that were co-opted by Frankie Goes to Hollywood, and the streets were instantly beaming out messages like "Protest and Survive," "Frankie Say Arm the Unemployed," and "Save the Whales." Other designers captured the fragmented sequences of the pop video with visual disturbance prints, some in graphic patterns resembling computer printouts.

Androgyny was the fashion buzz word in 1985. Women were taking control of their own lives and taking over the male wardrobe with its aggressive wide shoulder line and trousers. The most persistent street motif was the hanging shirttail, worn by both sexes. It was a conspicuous kind of dishabille, the tails negligently but deliberately on show under a tailored, formal jacket—often bought from the flea market or thrift shop, both important sources of street fashion.

Gender-bending, as Boy George showed, is a two-way street, and 1985 was also the year of the peacock male. Shiny and transparent fabrics revealing the male torso were a new interpretation of a theme familiar in women's clothes. Vivid colours and prints, often in floral and traditionally feminine patterns, made the young man more colourful than he had been since the 1960s. Cheeks contoured with blusher, discreet foundation, and subtle eye colour (but not lipstick) were all seen among young men during the early part of 1985, but the identification of male makeup with the gay community discouraged the cosmetic companies from backing the trend.

The swinging '60s were now an inspiration to the children of the decade. The skinny rib polo neck, the miniskirt

JOHN VOSS/THE TIMES

JOHN VOSS/THE TIMES

(continued from page 249)
of carrots. Some spiky hairdos were tipped with yellow, orange, green, or purple, but that imitation of Chewbacca the Wookie now looked passé.

On the Establishment side, ponchos and reversible lamb-skin coats did little to delineate the silhouette. However, the general look was livened by a great display of patterned stockings. Heavy black lace was the favourite and so important that boots were practically eliminated, except for short bootees. The low-heeled shoe, laced up the front and with side cutouts, soon became the hit for town wear. Black in winter, it turned white in the spring. Long, bright-coloured, plain wool scarves replaced shawls. Gloves, now part of the wardrobe, had a second purpose: protecting rings from street snatchers. Hats were mainly the pull-on soft felt cloche type. From under the brim glittered heart-shaped diamond ear clips or swinging gold metal hoops—the larger the better.

Discarding the androgynous look, fashion turned to a new gentleness in the spring of 1985. This was achieved mainly through rounded instead of square padding at the shoulders, gathers and pleating at the sleeve tops on dresses and blouses, and very deep batwing armholes on everything including knitwear. Hemlines were a decision every woman made for herself. The very young, who had nothing to hide, jauntily paced the streets in tubelike skirts at mid-thigh level, preferably in black leather or knitwear. Others, no less young, yielded to the winsomeness of the 1920s. In London the inspiration came from the Bloomsbury group—Virginia Woolf and, particularly, Vita Sackville-West, whose style was reputed to be outstanding. Long strands of pearls to hip level, in twos or threes, worn straight or nonchalantly slung over one shoulder, put the finishing touch to a slinky line with narrow hips, skirts to below calf or longer, and heels low, flat or small. Another influence came from the "flappers" of the '20s, revived in the film *The Cotton Club,* where the girls wore huge bows at hem or hip and at the side of the head. Another way of putting the accent on hips was to add a softly draped sash all around or to drape the lower part of a separate top to one side above a slim skirt. In this case the skirt could reach knee level or well below the calf.

A great display of colour heralded the coming of spring. It started with pale apricot or melon, for everything from knitwear to knife-pleated crêpe skirts. Then came bright red, even for shoes. There followed a range of sherbet colours, pale pink, green, or yellow, before the all-white look took over for full summer. For town wear, white was worn with black accessories—bag, shoes, and jewelry, including jet eardrops and innumerable bracelets.

After "The Raj Quartet" on television, David Lean's film *A Passage to India,* and the visit to Paris of India's Prime Minister Rajiv Gandhi, an Indian influence on fashion was inevitable. Flowing garments in "White for Liberty" after Mahatma Gandhi, "Red for Joy" in fitted Nehru coats, as well as embroidered raja jackets, all put their mark on summer clothes. Paisley prints were used for blouses, skirts, pants, or whatever part of the wardrobe they could be fitted into. Straight from the home furnishing department came the large floral prints usually selected for sofas and armchairs, now seen on fitted jackets, jodhpurs, and pants, as well as low-heeled pumps and handbags. Similar floral designs, but in jacquard weave, conveyed a tapestry look to cardigans and sweaters. Most of them were on a black or dark background, with combinations of royal blue and emerald green or purple and fuchsia.

On the summer beaches, there were no more strings. Swimsuits were all in one piece, with shoulder straps,

in moderation, op art and geometric patterns were all exuberantly rehashed. The trawl through times and closets past also brought back the ski-pant trouser (now for both sexes) and nostalgic re-creations of Grace Kelly's Capri pants, Audrey Hepburn's hooded headscarf, pointed pumps, and wrap sunglasses. Ray-ban glasses were the cult eyewear. Day-Glo colours lit up the street as sherbet-coloured socks and accessories switched in and out of fashion like neon lights. Plastic sandals walked on and off just as rapidly. The dishabille look reached its zenith in the summer, with baggy oversize cottons and even silks, all deliberately crumpled and wrinkled. Yet at the same time, there was movement back toward the body, a rejection of natural fibres (the preoccupation of mainstream fashion), and a new emphasis on stretchy, clinging synthetics. Body-hugging leggings replaced the shirttail as a badge of style.

Both fashion and pop have a voracious appetite for change, and under the spotlight of media attention the street redefined its style by redefining gender. Pop heroes Michael Jackson, George Michael of Wham!, and Simon Le Bon of Duran Duran all turned elegantly tailored backs on hanging shirts and tailcoats. A strong return to tailoring was followed (or maybe led) on the streets, where 16-year-old boys wore for pleasure the smart suits their fathers had abandoned in favour of casual wear. At the same time, Madonna in the pop world and the TV stars of "Dynasty" suggested a new image for young women, in total contrast to the man-size collarless tweed jackets and overcoats, the straight pants and heavy boots of androgynous style. The sexist woman—tight black leather skirt and spiky high heels—had been a part of punk. In her new manifestation she was less aggressive, more overtly glamorous, in the pop tradition of glam rock.

Suzy Menkes is fashion editor of The Times *of London.*

rounded neckline, and bare back. Swooping cutouts at the side, baring thighs nearly up to the waistline, turned them into real knockouts.

The best image of this was the poster for the latest James Bond film, *A View to a Kill,* showing the hero, Roger Moore, back to back with his partner, Grace Jones, who wore one of these cutout suits and the mannish hairdo with the clothes-brush effect on top. In the same direction was the swimsuit line designed by Princess Stephanie of Monaco: same cutouts at thigh level, same choice of plain colours rather than prints, as well as many high-necked models and scooped-out armholes. Thigh-baring cutouts were also applied to lingerie for all-in-one "bodies" in lace or plain stretch material with lace trimming. Abbreviated boxer shorts were the pick of all the youngsters, who fell for the imaginative prints. Borrowed from lingerie and revived from the 1950s were the "bustiers" or boned *guê-pières,* with or without straps, worn on the beaches with tight miniskirts or boxer shorts. They topped long, fully gathered skirts for dancing in the evening.

The big, rounded shoulder line introduced in the spring pursued its natural course for autumn and winter. Contrasting with the pin-size head, top volume was the rule. Waists were belted or well defined. Shape was reinstated. Skirts were generally straight, but hemlines varied a great deal—from mini or mid-thigh to long and very long. In the autumn, colours switched to deeper, richer shades, as a counterpoint to black. A dark, inky blue was often the choice for the first autumn buy, the three-quarter-length jacket with deep armholes, large lapels or shawl collar, to be worn with a slim black skirt. The same deep blue was selected for blouses, sweaters, and wool scarves and again worn with black. Purple was also in the colour race but more closely combined with black in weave or in print.

Short, narrow skirts put the emphasis on shoes and tights. Shoes were dressed up with bows—neat flat bows, pageboy style, or large draped bows over a covered instep and pointed toes. Heels were sometimes wide and flat, sometimes small or medium size, only occasionally really high, as for fancy sandals with draped straps. Tights were responsible for the big colour splash and the touch of humour in winter fashion. With the miniskirt they either matched in plain colour or contrasted in black. Lace patterns, dating from the previous winter in black or from the summer in white, were set aside. A multitude of jacquard patterns featuring plaids, checks, or light specks were suggested for daytime. There were also many pretty prints, such as allover paisley, feather, or marble effects or flowers.

AP/WIDE WORLD

Issey Miyake, a leading exponent of the so-called Japanese look, struck a characteristically bold note in his 1986 collection of ready-to-wear clothes for women.

A scattering of rose bouquets was effective on black, as were rows of sequins for a very special evening.

The colour outburst in fashion was bound to influence makeup. The cheeks were brushed with pastel pink and the eyelids with smoky gray; lipstick was blueish red. The technicolour effect really began at night, with focus on the eyes. Eye shadow, eyeliner, and mascara for eyelashes all drew on parakeet yellow, green, blue, and red.

(THELMA SWEETINBURGH)

Men's Fashions. Designs and designers of fabrics and fashions were the key words in menswear in 1985. New patterns in natural and man-made fibres were largely the outcome of skillful variations of one or more standard weaves. In woolens and worsteds, these new and more colourful cloths, mostly in the now universally accepted lighter weights, provided international clothing designers with the foundations for their new fashions. The National Wool Textile Export Corporation in Britain, in conjunction with British and Scottish banks, presented trophies for prizewinning designs in menswear cloths.

Individual and avant-garde designers in Paris dominated the Salon International de l'Habillement Masculin exhibitions in the spring and autumn. Groups of adventurous designers, notably the Swiss Syndicate for Avant-garde Fashion Trends at the International Men's Fashion Week in Cologne, West Germany, and the English Menswear Designer Collections at the Menswear Association of Britain (MAB) 1985 exhibition in London, created outfits that had a refreshing novelty appeal. They were in sharp contrast to the more conservative styles seen on exhibitors' stands at these and other menswear trade fairs held in Amsterdam and Madrid.

Throughout the year unconventional and avant-garde outfits became even more unconventional. This trend was summarized in the phrase "Mix but don't match" at the MAB '85 exhibition, where the emphasis continued to be on leisure clothes with bigger and bulkier jackets and shirts, as well as "baggy" trousers. Conventionally styled suits, sports jackets, and topcoats, on the other hand, became even more conventional, with U.S. and British tailored and ready-to-wear fashions providing the classics for business and formal wear. The division between the conventional and the unconventional was also seen in footwear, where traditional full and semibrogue Oxford styles were worn for formal and business occasions, only to be replaced by the colourful track and running shoes for leisure and pleasure.

The "layered" looks of the previous year continued in both sports shirts and summer knitwear, much of it in cotton and some with blends of linen. Among younger men, the fashion of wearing the shirt outside the trousers led to many new lines of shirts especially designed for this purpose, with a short, squared front and a much longer, rounded shirttail at the back.   (STANLEY H. COSTIN)

See also Industrial Review: *Furs.*

This article updates the *Macropædia* article DRESS AND ADORNMENT.

Gardening

Weather had a strong impact on U.S. gardening in 1985. With a late spring-summer drought in many sections, lack of rainfall reduced soil moisture, and growth of woody plants and seedlings was hampered. Water levels in civic reservoirs were down, and restrictions on water use made browned-off lawns the summer's norm. This was a significant problem for property owners; the Lawn Institute estimated that of the 83 million households in the United

The fruit of 13 years' labour by Adam Purple, the "Garden of Eden" in a burned-out area of New York City's Lower East Side was destroyed in September to make way for a low-income housing project. Purple had declined offers to move the garden because it was, he said, the centre of the universe.

STEVEN FERRY—GAMMA/LIAISON

States, 53 million had lawns. Each lawn was about 371 sq m (about 4,000 sq ft) in size—about 2 million ha (nearly 5 million ac) of land, equivalent to six times the land area of the state of Rhode Island. Other weather factors also took their toll. Hurricane Gloria struck the northeastern coastal midsection with near 145 km/hr (90-mph) winds, causing extensive property damage in eastern Long Island and into New England. Many heritage trees were lost.

But in spite of discouraging weather, the American Association of Nurserymen said that the garden market was growing rapidly, with a projected increase in sales of between 23 and 28%. The growth of the market was attributed to increased confidence in the economy as well as to homeowners' having more disposable income. The latter was evidenced during the year in a larger volume of residential landscaping contracts, plus higher sales for patio plants and vegetable garden seeds and seedlings. The effect of these trends was particularly marked in the post-World War II baby boom population, now centring between ages 34 and 44. Members of this group spent more than the average consumer on "self-help" products, including gardening tools and plants.

Tomatoes remained at the top of the vegetable popularity poll of crops grown at home. Next in popularity were peppers, green beans, cucumbers, and onions. Least popular with the U.S. gardener was the parsnip. Among flowers, petunias yielded first place to impatiens. Other popular flowers sold as seedlings at garden centres included marigolds, geraniums, sweet alyssum, and zinnias.

The national rose testing organization, All-America Roses, set an unusual precedent by giving its awards for the year exclusively to the hybrid tea class of roses. The three hybrid tea prizewinners, which were to be available for planting early in 1986, were Touch of Class (pink, shaded coral, and cream), Broadway, a bicolor (red-pink and yellow), and Voodoo (a blend of yellow, peach, and orange blushing to scarlet).

Indoor greenery remained a significant part of the U.S. life-style. At least 90% of homeowners surveyed by the Society of American Florists said that they had at least one plant in their homes, and of these, 57% said they had at least five plants. These same people said they preferred live plants to fresh-cut flowers.

An increased awareness of the effect of environmental stress on the nation's plant heritage was underscored by a new federal policy to eliminate the plant designation "rare" species, replacing it with the term "threatened" species. A threatened species is one that is likely to become endangered within the foreseeable future; an endangered species is one that is in danger of extinction throughout all or a significant portion of its range. Wildlife experts estimated that of the approximately 25,000 species of plants native to the U.S., one out of every eight—about 3,000—was currently rare or endangered. With these statistics in mind, the National Center for Plant Conservation was founded, made up of 20 national botanic gardens. The organization not only would monitor wild plant populations but would seek means to propagate the rarest species.

Eighty percent of British homes had gardens—the highest percentage in Europe. Not surprisingly, the garden market had continued to grow and now had an estimated value of £700 million. Garden visiting continued to be a major reason for a day's excursion, and the numbers visiting gardens, both private and public, was still increasing. Garden openings in aid of charities made up a large proportion of the opportunities for such outings. At the end of 1985 the activities of the two main charities in this field in England and Wales were amalgamated. Another "marriage" in 1985 was that of two weekly gardening magazines: *Popular Gardening,* which had been published for more than 80 years, was combined with *Amateur Gardening.*

New varieties of flowers that won awards after trials during the year included Summer Showers, an ivy-leaved geranium for raising from seed. The roses that received gold medals from the Royal National Rose Society were both hybrid tea types, as yet unnamed, and among certificate winners were Polar Star, another hybrid tea, raised in West Germany, and Princess Alice, a polyantha rose raised in Britain.

Two events that were of significance in the restoration of historic gardens were a large grant from English Heritage and the National Heritage Memorial Fund for the reclamation of the mid-18th-century landscape garden at Painshill, Surrey, and the opening of the walled garden at the royal palace at Apeldoorn in The Netherlands. The 17th-century garden at Apeldoorn, made for King William in the French style of the period, was the first of what are, in England, now called Dutch gardens. During the year the world-famous British nurseryman Sir Harold Hillier died. His chief legacies to gardeners were his arboretum, now in the care of Hampshire County Council, and his "Manual," which lists and describes most of the trees and shrubs that can be grown in Britain and similar climates.

(JOAN LEE FAUST; ELSPETH NAPIER)

See also Agriculture and Food Supplies; Environment; Life Sciences.

This article updates the *Macropædia* article GARDENING AND HORTICULTURE.

Health and Disease

The health and medicine news in 1985 was dominated largely by the acquired immune deficiency syndrome (AIDS). It was the fourth year since the disease had been recognized and named, and the number of AIDS victims had at least doubled in each subsequent year. By December 1985 nearly 16,000 AIDS cases had been reported in the U.S.; more than 8,000 Americans had died from AIDS, and an estimated 50,000–100,000 showed possible early signs of the disease—the "AIDS-related complex," or ARC. In March the U.S. Food and Drug Administration (FDA) licensed a test to be used to screen all blood donors for the AIDS virus (HTLV-III, also called LAV). It was estimated that as many as one million people in the U.S. had antibodies to AIDS in their blood, an indication that they had been exposed to the virus. According to the U.S. Centers for Disease Control (CDC), 5 to 10% of homosexual men who had positive blood tests for viral antibodies would develop the full-blown disease within three to five years. By this sort of calculation, 100,000 people in the U.S. alone might come down with AIDS in the next five years. The campaign to find better treatment methods and, ultimately, a vaccine to prevent AIDS was given tremendous added impetus by the death in October of film star Rock Hudson (*see* Obituaries), the first celebrity to become an acknowledged victim of the disease.

The spread of AIDS in Great Britain and other parts of Europe paralleled the earlier development of the epidemic in the U.S. As the epidemic spread, it was becoming clear that the disease was not confined to homosexual men, intravenous drug users, and hemophiliacs and other recipients of blood or blood products—the first major groups to be identified. The disease was also appearing in children of AIDS patients and persons at risk and in sexual partners of patients and people in high-risk groups. Several studies indicated that the prevalence of AIDS antibodies in female prostitutes—many of whom are also drug abusers—was considerably higher than in the general population. A study conducted by the U.S. Army identified a number of cases of AIDS in military personnel in which heterosexual contact was the sole identifiable risk factor. The possibility that the virus could be transmitted through heterosexual relations was further substantiated by reports from Africa, which showed almost equal numbers of men and women affected by the disease.

Several findings published during the year further extended the scientific knowledge about AIDS. One of the discoverers of the AIDS virus, Robert Gallo, and his colleagues found the virus in the tears of one out of seven AIDS patients tested. The investigators concluded that although no transmission of disease had been traced to this source of virus, professionals concerned with eye care and treatment should minimize direct contact with tears. Researchers at several institutions reported the discovery of virus in the cerebrospinal fluid and brain tissue of AIDS patients. These findings raised the prospect that the virus can infect cells other than lymphocytes (the type of white blood cell characteristically attacked by the virus).

Although medical investigators and government health officials emphasized that AIDS is not a casually transmitted disease and that it is spread through contact with a patient's body fluids, fear of the disease gripped portions of the U.S. public. The Pentagon announced that it would begin testing all military personnel for antibodies to the AIDS virus. For the first time, parents and school boards grappled with the problem of whether to allow children

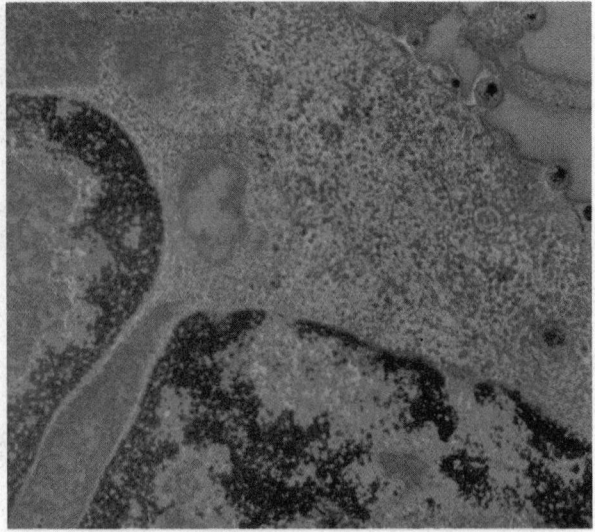

The AIDS virus, a retrovirus known as human T-cell lymphotropic virus type III, or HTLV-III (shown in this photomicrograph as spheres with dark nuclei), suppresses the body's immune system, leaving it open to attack by infection and cancer.
SIPA-SPECIAL FEATURES

with AIDS to attend regular classes in public schools. In New York City a decision by officials to allow a seven-year-old AIDS victim to attend classes led to a boycott involving some 12,000 students. Other school boards reached varying decisions on how to treat children with AIDS—some decided to bar them from the schools; others agreed to consider the question on a case-by-case basis.

Public concern in Great Britain also spurred government action. New regulations enacted during the year gave British magistrates increased authority to protect the public from AIDS. These included the power for local authorities to order an AIDS patient to be hospitalized if necessary to prevent a risk to others in the community and the power to prevent the relatives of a deceased AIDS victim from taking possession of the body.

In the U.S. one consequence of public awareness of the AIDS threat was that people were apparently changing their behaviour to avoid exposure. The most profound change was among homosexual men, more and more of whom were reportedly using condoms, avoiding multiple sexual relationships, and avoiding bathhouses and other sites of casual encounters. Many heterosexuals also seemed to be reevaluating their attitudes toward casual sex, and the incidence of venereal disease among both homosexuals and heterosexuals declined during the year.

In July U.S. Pres. Ronald Reagan was operated on for colon cancer. During a routine physical exam in March, Reagan's physicians had found a noncancerous polyp in the lower portion of his colon. Four months later, during what was expected to be routine surgery to remove that growth, doctors, using a colonoscope (a flexible fibre-optic viewing device), examined the president's entire large intestine. They found another, larger growth in the cecum, the junction between the large and small intestines. In a subsequent operation this tumour, along with 46 cm (18 in) of intestine, was removed. The excised tissue showed some microscopic evidence of cancer. Nonetheless, the president's doctors were optimistic, predicting that he had a 95% chance of being cancer-free five years from the date of the operation.

Although the surgery was considered successful, Reagan's physicians were criticized by some for not having been more diligent in their routine examinations. Despite

a family history of colon cancer and two earlier tests that had shown blood in his stool, Reagan had not undergone any of the more definitive diagnostic procedures (barium X-rays, colonoscopy) that might have revealed the tumour at an earlier stage.

The artificial heart was a centre of controversy in 1985 as researchers and medical ethicists began to question the high incidence of complications in recipients of the device. By year's end, surgeon William C. DeVries of the Humana Heart Institute in Louisville, Ky., had implanted permanent artificial hearts in four patients, all of whom had suffered from complications involving bleeding and blood clots. A Swedish man who had been making remarkable progress in the six months since he had been given a Jarvik-7 heart (the same kind used by DeVries) suffered a stroke in September and subsequently died.

Despite these setbacks, supporters of the artificial heart argued that it might at least prove useful as a temporary device to keep a patient alive until a human heart could be found. Critics said that unless the problems could be resolved, even this use would remain questionable. In late August physicians at the University Medical Center in Tucson, Ariz., implanted an artificial heart in a 25-year-old man, Michael Drummond, to tide him over until a suitable human heart could be found. Drummond subsequently suffered a series of strokes that impaired his speech and led his doctors to speed up the search for a human heart; he received a transplanted human heart within ten days of the implantation of the artificial heart.

As a result of Drummond's experience, however, researchers thought they had discovered one cause of the problems with the artificial device. After examining the heart removed from Drummond, Donald Olsen of the University of Utah concluded that a plastic connection between the artificial heart and Drummond's artery was the source of the clotting problems that may have caused strokes in the artificial heart patients. Olsen planned to begin testing a new connecting system in animals, and Robert Jarvik, inventor of the Jarvik-7, the most widely used artificial heart, said he was considering some design changes in the device. In October a man awaiting human heart transplantation received a temporary implant from doctors at the Pennsylvania State University Medical Center. The device used in this case—a slightly different model known as the "Penn State heart"—functioned satisfactorily for the 11 days that elapsed before a suitable human heart was found, but the patient died several days after receiving the transplanted human organ.

Several major studies concluded during the year extended the knowledge of coronary heart disease and its prevention. An analysis of middle-aged men in Boston and Ireland showed that those who for 20 years had been consuming a diet high in saturated fats and cholesterol were more likely to have suffered a fatal heart attack during the intervening period. The influence of diet on heart disease was confirmed by several other studies. In one, the Leiden Intervention Trial, 39 patients with stable angina pectoris (chest pain) and evidence of an arteriosclerotic lesion were monitored over a two-year period during which they ate a vegetarian diet low in cholesterol and high in polyunsaturated fats. Eighteen of the 39 experienced no worsening of the arteriosclerosis.

The health value of fish received considerable attention during the year. Investigators in The Netherlands and the U.S. suggested that people could reduce their risk of succumbing to heart attack by increasing their intake of fish oils. Even the consumption of only one or two servings of fish per week might confer a protective effect. The 1985

Nobel Prize for Physiology or Medicine was awarded to Joseph L. Goldstein and Michael S. Brown, U.S. researchers whose work over the past two decades had significantly advanced the understanding of cholesterol metabolism. (*See* BIOGRAPHIES.)

The results of a study from the Multicenter Post-Infarction Research Group in the U.S. contradicted some earlier theories about the adverse effects of so-called type A behaviour (characterized by easily aroused hostility and high-pressure dedication to achievement) on cardiovascular health. Among 516 heart attack victims monitored for one to three years after the event, survival and long-term outcome were not related to the factors associated with type A personality. On the other hand, a British study of 192 test subjects judged to be at risk for heart disease (because of high blood cholesterol, heavy smoking, or severe hypertension) showed that a combination of relaxation training, breathing exercises, and medication reduced the individual's chances of developing coronary disease.

The year saw considerable progress in methods of prenatal detection of serious congenital conditions. One such advance was based on the use of extremely pure monoclonal antibodies (artificially produced antibodies with particular ability to target specific tissues). David Brock and colleagues at the Western General Hospital, Edinburgh, employed one monoclonal antibody to reveal neural tube defects such as spina bifida in the early fetus. The new technique had two important advantages over current methods: it was more reliable, and it required less technical skill to perform. Later in the year Brock's group announced a similarly successful method for the prenatal diagnosis of cystic fibrosis.

There were also major developments in genetics based on the application of DNA probes—short pieces of DNA (the material that carries the genetic code) that are capable of identifying other pieces of DNA by sticking to them

AP/WIDE WORLD

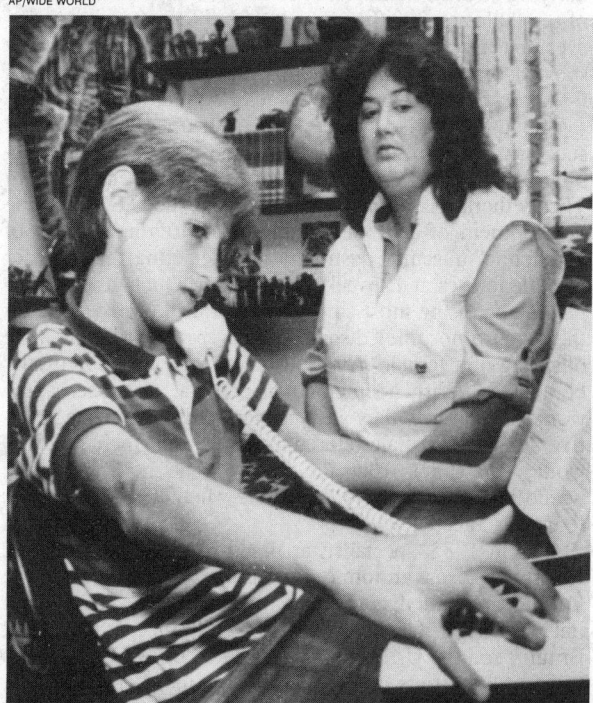

Ryan White, who contracted AIDS through a blood transfusion, was refused admittance to a Kokomo, Indiana, school in August. A special telephone line was installed to allow him to take part in his seventh-grade classes, but neither he nor his mother thought it an adequate substitute for the classroom.

Septuplets born to Patricia and Samuel Frustaci in Orange, California, in May constituted the largest multiple birth on record in the United States. The infants all weighed less than 900 grams (2 pounds) at birth; three of the seven, a girl and two boys, survived.
AP/WIDE WORLD

very specifically. Geneticists in Sardinia reported success in using a DNA probe to identify the particular genetic mutation responsible for most local cases of β-thalassemia, a hereditary anemia fairly common in Mediterranean countries. The technique could not be applied universally because any of a number of mutations can cause the underlying error in hemoglobin synthesis that is characteristic of the thalassemias. By using several different probes, however, a team from the University of Oxford subsequently showed that they could identify the majority of cases of β-thalassemia in two Mediterranean populations.

The use of DNA probes was instrumental in several successful attempts at prenatal diagnosis of hereditary disorders. International collaboration among geneticists in The Netherlands, Canada, England, and the U.S. led to the development of a probe capable of identifying carriers of Duchenne muscular dystrophy and detecting the disorder in male fetuses at 12 weeks of gestation. Duchenne dystrophy is one of the most common sex-linked (i.e., carried on the X chromosome) disorders. Fifty percent of the male offspring of a female carrier of the disease may potentially be affected. With no method of prenatal diagnosis, some women who knew they were carriers had relied upon selective abortion of male fetuses to ensure that their children would not suffer from the disease. The new technique would enable parents to determine whether or not a male fetus was affected.

Also in 1985, specialists at Baylor College of Medicine, Houston, Texas, announced the creation of a DNA probe for the prenatal diagnosis of phenylketonuria, a congenital enzymatic deficiency. Groups in France, Italy, Great Britain, and the U.S. reported success in using DNA probes to identify carriers of classical hemophilia (hemophilia A, also known as factor VIII deficiency) and to detect the disease in a fetus during the first trimester of pregnancy.

What was hailed as a major triumph in helping women who experienced repeated spontaneous abortion was accomplished by a team at St. Mary's Hospital Medical School, London. Their technique was to immunize female patients by injecting them with purified white blood cells from their male partners. Of 22 women so treated, 17 proceeded to enjoy a successful pregnancy immediately after undergoing the procedure. Scientists were not entirely certain how the method worked. One theory was that the man's white blood cells can induce antibodies that, in turn, protect parts of the fetus that would otherwise be attacked by the maternal immune system. However, 10 of 27 women injected with their own white cells also had normal pregnancies, suggesting the possibility of a placebo effect.

The adverse effect of cigarette smoking on fertility was highlighted by a survey of more than 17,000 women conducted at the Radcliffe Infirmary, Oxford. Five years after stopping contraception, 10.7% of women who smoked more than 20 cigarettes a day still had not given birth; among nonsmokers, the rate of infertility was only 5.4%.

Drug treatment of infertility was a subject of some controversy during the year. In May, Patricia Frustaci, a California woman who had been treated with the fertility drug Pergonal, gave birth to septuplets. Although the birth was 12 weeks premature and one of the infants was stillborn, the parents were initially buoyant. However, three of the remaining six babies died within weeks. In October, only a few days after bringing the last of the three surviving babies home from the hospital, Frustaci and her husband filed a lawsuit charging the doctor and clinic with prescribing "excessive and inappropriate dosages" of fertility drugs. The surviving infants had multiple medical problems that might require years of costly treatment.

The possible link between aspirin and Reye's syndrome was the source of another lawsuit during the year. In January 1985 the results of a small pilot study on the association between aspirin use and Reye's syndrome were released by the CDC, spurring a demand by consumer groups for warning labels on aspirin bottles. Reye's syndrome is a potentially fatal viral illness that may be accompanied by vomiting, fever, convulsions, and coma. The pilot study, which was to precede a larger scale investigation, showed that youngsters who were given aspirin when they were suffering from flu or chicken pox ran a sharply increased risk of developing Reye's syndrome, compared with similar patients not treated with aspirin. Margaret Heckler, U.S. secretary of health and human services, requested that aspirin manufacturers voluntarily put warning labels on their products, and while many proceeded to comply, in the summer of 1985 the first suit was filed against a drug company by parents of a child who had developed Reye's syndrome.

The year 1985 saw the conclusion of two major U.S. cancer studies that helped to resolve professional disagreements about the most appropriate surgical treatment for breast cancer. Both were conducted at U.S. hospitals under the auspices of the National Surgical Adjuvant Breast Project. One study compared ten-year survival rates in mastectomy patients whose tumours had not spread to the axillary (underarm) lymph nodes. The results showed that simple removal of the breast was as effective as the more extensive and disfiguring surgical procedure known as radical mastectomy. The other survey, based on five years' experience, revealed equally satisfactory results from the even more limited segmental mastectomy. Together, these studies indicated that breast cancer could be dealt with by much less mutilating surgery than was thought necessary in the past.

A trial organized by the Swedish National Board of Health and Welfare demonstrated the benefits of mass

screening for breast cancer using the technique of mammography. The results of a study initiated in 1977 showed a 31% reduction in mortality from the disease and a 25% reduction in stage 2 (more advanced) breast cancer among women offered screening every two or three years, compared with those who were not offered screening.

Two other important cancer studies reported during the year yielded largely negative results. One was a detailed analysis of the 3,373 deaths among 39,546 employees of the U.K. Atomic Energy Authority over a period of 23 years. The study had been carried out because of concern that people exposed to low levels of ionizing radiation might have an above-average risk of contracting malignant disease; overall mortality figures for the group, however, proved to be lower than those for England in general. Of all causes of death, mortality rates from only four types of cancer—leukemia, non-Hodgkin's lymphoma, and thyroid and testicular cancers—were higher than the national average, but even these numbers were close to the boundaries of statistical significance.

Negative findings also emerged from an investigation conducted at the Mayo Clinic, Rochester, Minn., to confirm or refute earlier claims that high doses of vitamin C have a beneficial effect on people suffering from advanced cancer. In a double-blind study, 100 patients with large colorectal tumours were given considerable quantities of either vitamin C or a placebo; results showed that the vitamin treatment had no effect on patient survival and did not limit the progression of the disease.

Every year the U.S National Institutes of Health (NIH) sponsored consensus panels—meetings in which a panel of experts determined medical advice that established a national standard of care. In 1985 one such panel, considering cancer treatment, recommended hormonal therapy for certain postmenopausal breast cancer patients whose disease had spread to the lymph nodes. Taximofen—a hormonal therapy that blocks the actions of estrogens—should be given, the panel said, if tests of the cancerous tissue showed that it would be responsive to the drug.

Two NIH panels focused on nutrition-related topics. The first recommended that the entire U.S. population strive to lower blood cholesterol levels by reducing consumption of saturated fats and cholesterol. The panel endorsed a diet similar to the one proposed by the American Heart Association, which emphasized fresh fruits and vegetables, restricted egg yolks to no more than two a week, and specified lean meat, skim milk, and low-fat cheeses. Another panel, considering the "Health Implications of Obesity," attempted to define obesity and to consider its influence as a risk factor in relation to other conditions such as hypertension and diabetes. The 14-member panel concluded that any level of obesity increased health risk, but it identified a level of 20% or more above "desirable" body weight as the threshold for medical intervention.

In June Karen Ann Quinlan, 31, died after ten years in a coma. Quinlan was the focus of a 1975 "right-to-die" lawsuit that altered the way decisions to withdraw medical care were made. In a precedent-setting decision, the New Jersey Supreme Court held that, since the medical authorities saw "no reasonable possibility" that Quinlan would recover, it was permissible to honour her parents' request that life-sustaining mechanical equipment be disconnected. Although artificial life support was withdrawn, Quinlan lived, continuing to breathe on her own although comatose and receiving food and antibiotics through a nasogastric tube. Her death was attributed to respiratory failure following a series of lung infections.

(BERNARD DIXON; GINA KOLATA)

MENTAL HEALTH

Continued efforts to break down the barriers segregating the mentally ill were symbolized by two developments in Great Britain. First, a report from the Institute of Psychiatry in London showed that recent years had seen an unprecedented movement of psychiatric specialists away from hospitals and into community-based services. Nearly one-fifth of 811 psychiatrists and psychotherapists questioned in the survey said they now spent at least some time working with physicians in general practice. Second, a pioneering experiment at Amersham General Hospital (Buckinghamshire, England) showed that children with psychiatric disorders could be treated successfully in a general ward, rather than being relegated to facilities for the mentally disturbed. All of the children admitted over a period of four years, with conditions ranging from psychoses to anorexia, improved appreciably and were later discharged.

The growth of drug addiction caused increasing concern to physicians and politicians alike. Official statistics in Great Britain showed that the number of addicts notified to the Home Office was about 7,400. Although probably a considerable underestimate of the total magnitude of the problem, this figure was the highest ever recorded and represented a 50% increase over the previous year. There was particular anxiety about the increasing number of young people addicted to the sniffing of volatile substances.

A report from Lee Salk and colleagues at Cornell University Medical College in New York City and other research centres threw light on previously unsuspected influences on suicide among adolescents: their condition at birth and their mothers' health during the course of pregnancy. When the Cornell group compared the records of 52 teenagers who had taken their own lives with those of matched "controls," they discovered three factors clearly linked with suicide—respiratory distress for more than an hour at birth, lack of antenatal care before 20 weeks of pregnancy, and chronic disease of the mother during pregnancy. Although Salk was unable to discern the mechanisms behind these relationships, he pointed out that the identification of specific risk factors offered new opportunities for prevention.

Alcoholism continued to be a burgeoning health challenge for most Western countries and for the U.S.S.R. and some other members of the Eastern bloc as well. Collaborative research between Columbia University, New York City, and the Royal Perth Hospital in Australia confirmed that brain shrinkage occurs in chronic alcoholics. Such

C. STEELE PERKINS—MAGNUM

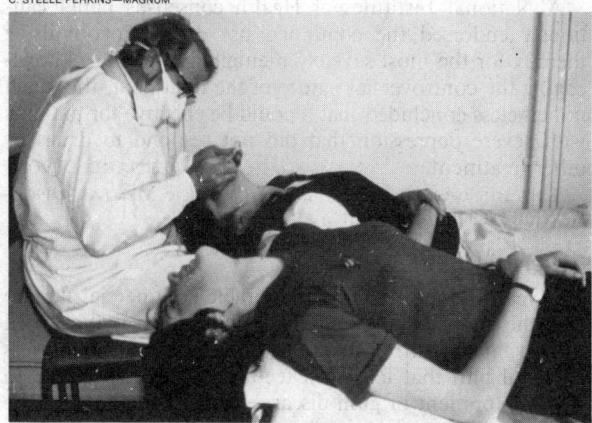

Volunteers are given nose drops, some only saline solution and some containing live cold virus, at the Common Cold Unit, a pioneering research facility near Salisbury, England. Researchers there found that introverts tend to have worse colds than extroverts.

individuals had long been known to run the risk of developing Korsakoff's syndrome, a form of brain damage that results in severe memory failure. Studies at the University of Modena, Italy, showed that memory is affected even in drinkers without detectable brain damage. Men who had been consuming at least two litres of wine per day for five years or more performed poorly in memory tests, compared with a control group of individuals who drank no more than two glasses each day.

The year was notable for developments that forged new links between psychiatric practitioners and physicians concerned with physical illnesses, as evidence accumulated to establish that personality and state of mind have an important influence on vulnerability to disease. Researchers at Ohio State University studied the effects of stress on the activity of natural killer (NK) cells—an important component of the immune system. In blood tests of medical students, activity of NK cells was significantly lower the day after final exams than at times when the students were more relaxed. Because these cells normally help to repel viruses and other invading pathogens, a diminution of their activity could account for the fact that people seem to be more susceptible to colds and other infections during stressful periods in their lives.

Further evidence of the link between psychological factors and disease came from a study conducted at Britain's Common Cold Unit, near Salisbury, England. Over a period of 21 months, subjects volunteering in the project were given personality questionnaires and inoculated with cold viruses. Although the clinicians assessing the volunteers' symptoms had not seen the psychological findings, the results were dramatically clear: the introverts suffered much worse colds than did the extroverts.

Although the subject of cancer and mental outlook remained highly controversial, research at King's College School of Medicine and Dentistry, London, supported the theory that an individual's mental approach may have a pronounced influence on the outcome of malignant disease. Studies of women with breast cancer, ten years after the initial diagnosis, showed that significantly more deaths had occurred among those who had responded with feelings of helplessness or hopelessness than among those who reacted either with a fighting spirit or by denying that they had the disease. Work at the University of California School of Medicine suggested that endorphins, natural opiumlike substances in the brain, may affect the body's immune system and thus function as the mechanism by which the mind can affect the course of physical illness.

A National Institutes of Health consensus panel cautiously endorsed the continued use of electroconvulsive therapy for the most severely mentally ill. While acknowledging the controversial nature of the treatment, the panel nonetheless concluded that it could be effective for patients with severe depression that did not respond to drugs or other treatment.   (BERNARD DIXON)

This article updates the *Macropædia* article MENTAL DISORDERS and Their Treatment.

DENTISTRY

The year was marked by considerable commercial fanfare over the introduction of oral hygiene products that claimed to prevent or control dental plaque—the sticky, colourless bacterial film that forms on teeth and that was linked to the development of gum disease. While it remained to be seen whether any such products would be proved effective, the value of one simple hygienic measure, toothbrushing, was reaffirmed in 1985. University of Michigan dental researchers found that brushing alone actually reduces gingivitis, the early stage of gum disease. Students from two public schools in Ann Arbor, Mich., who had shown signs of early gum disease were clinically examined for levels of gingivitis and plaque. The students were given toothbrushes and nonfluoridated toothpaste for use at least once daily. A nonfluoride toothpaste was chosen to avoid any possible effects of fluoride on plaque control. Results showed a significant reduction in both plaque and gingivitis.

Synthetic tooth roots made of a bonelike plastic material could be good news for denture wearers. Surgically implanted tooth replacements of hydroxylapatite—an inert material chemically similar to bone and tooth enamel—can prevent much of the bone loss that typically accompanies tooth loss, according to researchers at the Tulane University of Louisiana School of Dentistry, New Orleans. In a study of 49 patients, hydroxylapatite root implants preserved about twice as much bone as was retained at "control" sites on opposite sides of patients' mouths. Patients and dentists also observed that the hydroxylapatite roots, implanted shortly after tooth extractions, seemed to reduce the oral discomfort normally associated with extractions.

The two most potent weapons against tooth decay—fluoride and plastic sealants—were brought together for the first time to yield anticavity protection that was potentially twice as strong as either substance alone. Scientists at the National Institute of Dental Research, Bethesda, Md., blended the anticavity capabilities of fluorides and sealants into a fluoride-releasing coating that could eventually provide children with invincible armour against decay. Like the sealants already in use, the new fluoride-releasing shield physically seals teeth from the oral bacteria that cause decay. But the new sealant goes a step further; it continuously releases trace amounts of fluoride, thus offering a significant extra measure of protection against decay. Like conventional sealants, the fluoride-releasing covering would be applied primarily to pits and fissures on the biting surfaces of teeth, where most decay occurs; the new sealants might also be used to shield tiny predecay spots in other parts of the tooth as well.   (LOU JOSEPH)

VETERINARY MEDICINE

As levels of competition in racing and show jumping events became steadily more intense, it became increasingly important to detect signs of potential lameness in horses. However, surprisingly little was known about the effects on bone of training, fatigue, concussion, and trauma. At the University of Melbourne, Australia, L. B. Jeffcott and R. N. McArtney looked for ways of assessing how the biomechanical stress to which horses are subjected affects the structure of bone. They developed a relatively simple technique that used ultrasound to measure the velocity of sound through bone, which made it possible to assess the variations that occur with age and to evaluate different types of lameness. It was found that as young horses mature, the velocity of sound passing through the bone increases, reflecting the fact that the soft cartilaginous part of the bone becomes harder with age. However, when the technique was applied to horses that had sore shins, damaged tendons, or hairline fractures, the velocity fell below that normally found in healthy animals. The new technique, which was simple to use in the stable or paddock, offered considerable potential for assessing bone quality and could make it possible to demonstrate changes in bone density or elasticity that warned of impending lameness or reduced racing performance.

The value of comparative studies in veterinary and human medicine was recently exemplified when studies of a

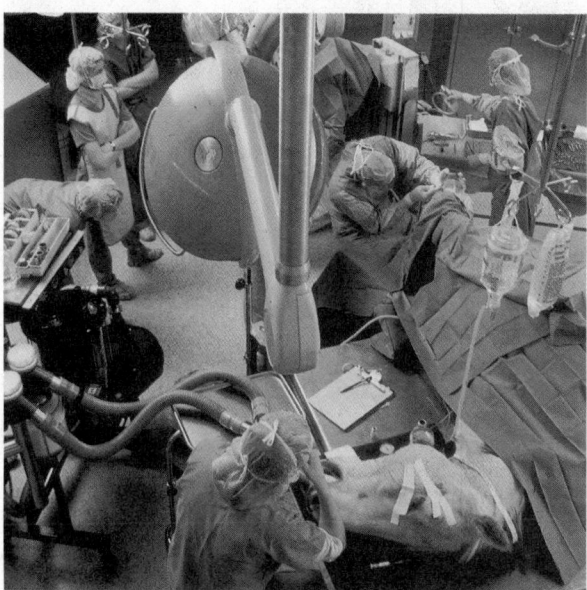

A number of innovative approaches to the treatment of injured horses were developed at the School of Veterinary Medicine of Tufts University in Grafton, Mass., including the use of large operating rooms equipped much like those used for human surgery.

JOHN DOMINIS/DISCOVER MAGAZINE

disease in cats, feline leukemia, threw significant light on the nature of the virus that causes AIDS. Feline leukemia was first identified as a new disease in the 1960s by a research team at the University of Glasgow (Scotland) Veterinary School and Hospital. Further investigation established that the disease was caused by a rare type of virus called a retrovirus. The Glasgow workers went on to devise experimental vaccines against feline leukemia, which were developed commercially in the U.S. In 1984 researchers in France and the U.S. discovered that AIDS was also caused by a retrovirus. This discovery paved the way for the initiation of an attempt to produce a vaccine against AIDS, based on knowledge gained in developing the feline leukemia vaccine.   (EDWARD BODEN)

See also Life Sciences; Populations and Population Movements; Social Security and Welfare Services.

This article updates the *Macropædia* articles DISEASE; MEDICINE.

Historic Preservation

The fifth General Assembly of nations that were parties to the International Convention Concerning the Protection of the World Cultural and Natural Heritage met in November 1985 in Sofia, Bulg., in conjunction with Unesco's 23rd General Conference. The latest adherents to the convention were the Dominican Republic, Hungary, and Sweden, bringing to 87 the total number of countries that had ratified or accepted it. Subsequently, in December, the convention's World Heritage Committee held its ninth session in Paris. After careful evaluation of national recommendations, 30 properties were added to the World Heritage List, bringing the total to 216 sites in 55 countries.

Additions to the list included the royal palaces of Abomey (17th–19th century) in Zou Province, Benin; the historic centre of Salvador (16th–18th century), Bahia state, Brazil; the Thracian tomb of Sveshtari (3rd century BC), Razgrad Province, Bulg.; the historic area of Quebec City (17th–19th century), Canada; the painted churches of the Troodos region (a selection of nine representative churches from the 12th–15th century, notable for the quality of their Byzantine and post-Byzantine paintings), Nicosia and Limassol districts, Cyprus; the "Pont du Gard" (the Nîmes aqueduct, 1st century BC), département of Gard, France; the remains of the Parthian fortified city of Hatra (c. 1st–3rd century), near Mosul, Iraq; the archaeological site of Petra (ancient capital of the Nabataeans, 4th century BC to 2nd century AD), district of Ma'an, Jordan; the medina of Marrakech (12th–19th century), Morocco; the rock drawings of Alta Fjord (4200–500 BC), Finnmark County, Norway; the Altamira cave (prehistoric wall paintings of the Solutrean and Magdalenian periods), near Santander, Cantabria, Spain; the historic district of Segovia (primarily medieval and Renaissance periods) and the Roman aqueduct (1st–2nd century), Segovia, Spain; the historic district of Santiago de Compostela (11th–18th century), Galicia, Spain; the Punic town of Kerkuane (c. 6th–3rd century BC), Nabeul governorate, Tunisia; and the Great Mosque and Hospital of Divrigi (built by the architect Khurramshad of Ahlat, 13th century), eastern Anatolia, Turkey.

As well as studying nominations to the list and making decisions for or against inclusion, the World Heritage Committee played an important role by ensuring that action was taken at the national level to protect the monuments and sites listed. When adding a new entry, the committee often at the same time made recommendations on the safeguarding or restoration of the site. This procedure helped to make the convention an effective instrument for the protection of the common heritage. Moreover, the committee tried to ensure that the World Heritage List was as representative as possible of different types of cultural and natural property.

Closely related to these activities for the protection of immovable cultural properties was the recent Unesco publication in English of a two-volume compendium of extracts from national legislation governing the protection of movable properties in 45 countries. The aim was to make known the legal status of such properties in order to expose and combat theft, clandestine excavations, and illicit traffic on both national and international levels. Unesco also recently published a series of booklets that presented the full texts of national legislation regarding such protection in 16 countries. In support of such activities, the fourth session of the Intergovernmental Committee for Promoting the Return of Cultural Property to Its Countries of Origin or Its Restitution in Case of Illicit Appropriations took place in April in Greece. Resolutions were passed regarding the "Sandstone Panel of Tyche with the Zodiac" (request submitted by Jordan) and the Elgin Marbles from the Parthenon in Athens (held by the British Museum since 1816, but whose return was being sought by Greece).

Two international campaigns to safeguard the cultural heritage were launched by the director general of Unesco in 1985. The first, in Bangladesh, was for the restoration and preservation of two sites, Paharpur and Bagherhat, which were also inscribed on the World Heritage List in 1985. The monastic site of Paharpur was perhaps the largest Buddhist monastic complex south of the Himalayas. The Somapura Mahavihara ("great monastery") became a renowned intellectual centre, attracting monks, scholars, and pilgrims from the 8th until the 17th century. From Paharpur, monks were also sent to Central Asia and the Far East. The monastery was notable for its monumental architectural organization, which influenced later Buddhist architecture in Burma, Java, and Cambodia, and for its carved stone bas-reliefs and terra-cotta panels. The Bagherhat remains, dating from the first half of the 15th century, included a re-

Petra (located in present-day Jordan), capital of the Nabataeans from the 4th century BC to the 2nd century AD, is renowned for its rock-cut tombs and monuments, including the Treasury Tomb (above); the site was placed on the World Heritage List in 1985.

HAROLD C. KINNE—PHOTO RESEARCHERS

markable number of Islamic religious monuments such as the mausoleum of the founder, the Turkish general Ulugh Khan Jahan, and the Shait Gumbad mosque, renowned for its large prayer room divided into 7 longitudinal aisles and 11 deep bays. More than 50 monuments were identified for preservation and restoration.

The second Unesco campaign, for the restoration of the architectural heritage of Guatemala, was aimed particularly at providing assistance for Spanish colonial structures damaged by the earthquake of Feb. 4, 1976. However, an integral part of the campaign was also the preparation of a detailed inventory of Guatemala's architectural patrimony. This would assist in the protection of Maya monuments and sites such as Tikal, Quirigua, Kaminaljuyu, and Iximche. (JOHN POPPELIERS)

See also Architecture; Environment; Museums.

Human Rights

Human rights may be defined either narrowly or broadly. In the usage of the information media and of major "human rights organizations" such as Amnesty International, the primary denials of human rights are those that punish individuals by imprisonment, torture, execution, exile, or travel restrictions for their nonviolent expression of opinion or organizational activities. Torture for any reason is, of course, opposed by all human rights advocates. Human rights as defined in United Nations documents, and especially in a growing academic literature on human rights,

include a wide variety of "rights" to organize, to express opinion, to cultural choice, as well as to specified levels of nutrition, health, and education. The denial of human rights may be by governments, societies, or dissidents, but the struggle for human rights is primarily a struggle against the unjustified expression of the power of the state.

A survey of the year's record in human rights will necessarily concentrate on those areas that have received greatest attention in the press. Still, the denials of human rights that are reported most frequently should be regarded as symptoms of institutionalized systems of oppression that affect whole societies rather than the particular individuals or groups whose problems are reported by the news services. Human rights violations in countries where the mechanisms of repression are most thoroughly established are infrequently reported. Countries where the result of the struggle for human rights continues to be in doubt have their human rights violations most fully exposed.

Communist Societies. For the purpose of assessing human rights performance, Communist societies may be divided into traditional Marxist-Leninist societies, including the U.S.S.R., Cuba, Vietnam, North Korea, and Albania, and evolving Communist societies, such as China, Poland, Hungary, and Yugoslavia. In the traditional Communist societies, there is no assumption of individual rights against the state. In such states there are thousands of prisoners of conscience, and the least hint of dissent or of organizational independence from the regime is severely punished. The traditional Communist denial of the cultural and religious rights of selected peoples was exemplified in 1985 by reports of a Bulgarian campaign to forcibly change the names of all citizens of Turkish background.

In the evolving Communist states, alongside the maintenance of many repressive Marxist-Leninist practices, governments allow individual activity and criticism greater scope. Polish society, for example, shows a somewhat higher degree of pluralism.

Latin America. Many Latin-American countries persevered in their attempt to institutionalize respect for human rights. The trial in Argentina of military leaders for their part in torturing and executing thousands of citizens reached its conclusion. (*See* WORLD AFFAIRS [Latin America and the Caribbean]: *Argentina.*) Similar investigations of former military rulers began in Brazil and Uruguay, although not on the same scale. Peru managed a fair election amid staggering economic and security problems; the new government moved quickly to reassert civilian control over counterinsurgency forces. Elections in El Salvador confirmed civilian control and were followed by a reduction in the brutal killings attributed to the right wing.

Mexico and Chile failed to follow the trend to greater democracy among the larger countries of the hemisphere. Mexican elections were reported to have been more questionable than ever, while Chile's Gen. Augusto Pinochet Ugarte resisted the society's desire to return to democracy with detention, internal exile, and murder. The murder of those thought to be opposed to the system continued in Guatemala, much of it attributable to security forces; nevertheless, there was a partial return to electoral democracy. In Nicaragua there was strong evidence that the Sandinista government was carrying out a clandestine policy of executing suspected opponents, and toward the end of the year a pretext was found for the further reduction of the civil liberties of the internal opposition. Institutionalized repression continued in Cuba, Haiti, and Paraguay.

Middle East. In the Middle East violence and terror—by both governments and their opponents—were the order of the day in many societies. An attempt to set up a human

rights organization in relatively moderate Algeria was met by imprisonment of its leaders, but even the attempt would have been impossible in half of the countries of the region. In Lebanon, where contestants appeared to have decided that only weapons could be decisive, there could be little expectation of respect for human rights. The Kurdish people's right to self-determination continued to be denied by Turkey and Iraq—Iran denied Kurdish rights within its borders but supported them within those of its neighbours. The quest for Arab self-government in territories occupied by Israel helped to keep the region in ferment. There were positive trends, however, in Jordan, Egypt, and Kuwait.

Executions of political opponents, violent and nonviolent, were once again reported to be common in Iran. Women of the Middle East continued to fight a losing battle against their second-class citizenship. New and revised laws in Algeria and Pakistan reinforced discrimination in family life and court testimony. In Egypt a legislative attempt to cancel gains achieved in the Sadat era was only partially blocked.

Africa South of the Sahara. In sub-Saharan Africa many governments again failed to meet their elementary responsibilities to serve the interests of their starving and uneducated peoples. Most flagrant was the willingness of the Ethiopian government to put the suppression of dissident peoples and the celebration of the new Communist Party ahead of famine relief. Many parts of the continent, such as Chad, southern Sudan, and much of Uganda, relapsed during the year into general anarchy.

Human rights violations in Africa commonly result when peoples from one ethnic or racial background oppress peoples from a different background. Persistent examples of such oppression were blacks by Arabs in The Sudan, Chad, and Mauritania; the Baganda by the northern tribes in Uganda; the Hutu by the minority Tutsi in Burundi; and the Ndebele by the Shona in Zimbabwe. The denial of equal rights to people of a different ethnic, religious, or racial group that claimed major international attention in 1985 occurred in South Africa. In an effort to meet the rising tide of internal and external criticism, the South African government, over the past few years, had enacted reforms in petty apartheid—marriage laws, residence rights, constitutional change. Real power remained with the whites, however, and reforms only served to fan the flames of dissent, which in 1985 broke out in sustained riots, boycotts, demonstrations, and the inevitable violent police reactions. This crisis was not caused by increased denials of human rights—in many ways the denials had been marginally eased—but by the buildup in South Africa of the struggle for equal rights that had taken place over many years. (*See* WORLD AFFAIRS [Africa South of the Sahara]: *South Africa:* Special Report.)

Asia. In Asia, India moved effectively to overcome the challenging problem represented by the demand of many Sikhs for greater self-determination. (*See* WORLD AFFAIRS [South Asia]: *India.*) The minority problem in Sri Lanka seemed more intractable. Government forces continued to kill civilians in revenge for attacks against its forces, and Tamil rebels replied in kind. Authoritarian regimes in the Philippines and Taiwan continued to repress the legitimate opposition. In the Philippines the problem was compounded by the existence of revolutionary Communist forces. Killing and torture by security forces and by fanatic outlaw gangs allied with them had become an escalating part of the human rights problem in the Philippines, although the country continued to have strong and well-organized groups campaigning for fair elections and other human rights. In Indonesia suppression of the East Ti-

In Udon Thani, Thailand, a billboard illustrates the wrong—conical, Vietnamese-style, marked by an X—and the right—traditional Thai, marked by a check mark—kinds of hats. An adjacent sign urges the claims of Thai political and cultural nationalism and denounces Thais who adopt Vietnamese habits.
JIM WILSON/THE NEW YORK TIMES

morese was most often in the news, but the government's suppression of the people of West Irian represented a more serious violation of the right to self-determination. The Melanesian peoples of the province were in danger of being submerged in a tide of Javanese settlement.

Western Democracies. Against this background, the continuing human rights problems of the Western democracies appeared less significant. Aside from the continuing and intractable case of Northern Ireland, the most obvious problems concerned immigrants and aliens, problems that now affected nearly all industrialized democracies. The U.S. struggled with an inconsistent immigration policy that allowed easy entry for people from countries whose governments the administration did not like, such as Iran or Poland, but severely limited entry from countries it wished to support, such as El Salvador or Guatemala. In Great Britain continued rioting in areas of recent immigration pointed up the difficulty of accommodating people from quite different cultural backgrounds.

The development and expression of human rights concerns appeared to be growing in many countries. The annual report of the U.S. State Department on human rights conditions in all countries continued its year-by-year improvement. "Helsinki watch" groups brought out a number of reports on human rights issues associated with the Helsinki process; these same issues were considered at an "experts meeting" of the Helsinki Accords countries in Ottawa, Ont. The Inter-American Commission on Human Rights of the Organization of American States became more active during the year, preparing several detailed studies of human rights problems in the hemisphere. Amnesty International continued its well-publicized campaigns, emphasizing its commitment to ending the practice of torture by issuing reports on torture occurring in the U.S.S.R., Mozambique, Turkey, and other countries.

(RAYMOND DUNCAN GASTIL)

See also Race Relations.
This article updates the *Macropædia* article HUMAN RIGHTS.

A Field Guide to Corporate Mergers

BY ALAN J. AUERBACH

The heightened level of merger activity that began in the U.S. in 1984 continued into 1985, amid calls for increased regulation of the behaviour of the corporations involved. Many attributed the increase in mergers to the liberalized antitrust position taken by the Justice Department under the Reagan administration, but there have been many other explanations as well, ranging from changes in industrial structure to innovations in the methods of financing acquisitions and changes in tax law.

Though there had been "merger waves" in the past, most recently in the late 1960s, many aspects of the current boom in corporate combinations made it different from and more controversial than those of earlier times. Chief among them were the enormous scale of the largest mergers, the spirited tactics adopted by managements in defending against hostile takeover attempts, the financial innovations that allowed small firms to gain control of much larger ones, and the potential tax benefits derived from merging. Particular attention focused on certain industries rife with mergers and takeovers. Members of Congress and other observers debated whether the current mergers were in the interest of the shareholders of the companies involved and whether the common good more generally was being served.

Mergers: Good or Bad? When two firms merge, is this good or bad? Orthodox economic theory says it is probably good for the owners of the firms concerned, or at least the owners believe it is. Evidence suggests that the combined value of the shares of stock in merging firms increases with the merger.

A merger may also be good for society as a whole, if synergy leads to innovation or increased production efficiency. Traditionally, the important policy question involving mergers has been whether these gains to the firms involved and, perhaps, to the economy as a whole, might be outweighed by the damage done through increased industrial concentration and reduced competition. This was the focus of "trust-busting" in the early years of the century and of the hearings conducted by the late Sen. Estes Kefauver in the 1950s.

With the increase in *conglomerate mergers* in the late 1960s, by which companies in unrelated businesses combined, the policy emphasis shifted from concern about reduced competition to the role of the corporate manager in serving the interests of shareholders. Some theories of corporate structure argue that the power of stockholders is diffuse, so when the interests of top-level managers diverge from those of the shareholders, the managers may have the ability to steer a course for the firm that is in their own favour. Such a course will involve preserving the existing power and influence of management and increasing it

---

Alan J. Auerbach, Professor of Economics at the University of Pennsylvania, is the author of The Taxation of Capital Income.

when the opportunity arises. Two types of behaviour often held to support this view are the acquisition of other firms, at large premiums over their prior stock market value, even when there are few evident economic reasons for the firms to be joined, and resistance to attempts by others to acquire the firm, even when the price offered for the firm's shares is well above the going market price.

Recent merger activity has been characterized by increased sophistication, both in the mounting of takeover attempts and in the resistance to such attempts. It also has included several extremely large mergers that increased industrial concentration.

The Rise in Hostile Takeovers. A merger occurs when two firms combine to form a new one; in a takeover, one firm absorbs another. While the distinction is often unimportant, it is crucial when corporate managements disagree about the course the companies should follow. This situation gives rise to the hostile takeover attempt, with one corporation seeking to purchase the shares of another in order to gain voting control and displace the target corporation's management. The hostile takeover has become much more a part of the merger scene than it was in the past, and it has spawned a series of defensive maneuvers used by the managements of target corporations to fend off unwanted takeover attempts.

Managements adopting such tactics argue that they are necessary to protect shareholders from being pressured to tender their shares at too low a price or to a purchaser who might harm the company. Critics contend that the primary aim of such behaviour is the entrenchment of the firm's current managers, regardless of how poorly they are operating the corporation.

A glossary of the terms for some of these defensive tactics indicates the bases for such arguments:

> *Greenmail.* An agreement to purchase the outstanding shares of the pursuer at a price in excess of the market price of the shares. An example of this practice occurred when takeover specialist Saul Steinberg gave up his shares in the Walt Disney empire, at a substantial profit.
>
> *Poison Pill.* A provision intended to make the company valueless in the event of a takeover, such as giving shareholders the right to purchase additional shares in the firm at a substantial discount should the contesting corporation succeed in gaining a controlling interest in the company. An example of this type of activity was provided when Unocal Corp. successfully fought off the tender offer of T. Boone Pickens (*see* BIOGRAPHIES). Unocal threatened to dissipate a substantial fraction of its net worth by purchasing its own shares at an elevated price from shareholders *other than* Pickens.
>
> *Golden Parachutes.* Large severance benefits to be paid to corporate managers in the event of their displacement via takeover. In 1984 Congress introduced tax penalties on the use of such payments.
>
> *Supermajority Rules.* When two-thirds or even 80% of all shareholders of a target corporation must approve a takeover.
>
> *Fair Price Provisions.* When the use of other defensive tactics (such as a supermajority rule) is threatened unless all shareholders in the target company receive the same price for their shares in the event of a takeover.

In many cases, legal battles are part of the takeover process. Because so many U.S. corporations call the state home, Delaware's Supreme Court is often at the centre of such activity. Its decisions, such as that in the Pickens–Unocal fight, have been watched carefully by those on both sides for portents of the future. In the current climate, corporate managements have a relatively free hand to take any defensive actions that have been sanctioned by a vote of their shareholders.

Giant Mergers: Oil Leads the Way. Merger activity in 1984 proceeded at a much faster pace than it had in earlier years. Well over $100 billion of corporate assets changed hands through merger activity in that year, more than double the level for 1983. Nearly $43 billion of this activity was in the oil industry. The year's three largest mergers each involved one oil company taking over another (Standard Oil of California–Gulf, Texaco–Getty, and Mobil–Superior). One reason was weak demand for petroleum, which led to depressed share values for firms in the industry. This gave firms the opportunity to "purchase" oil reserves at a cost below that of drilling for them by taking over another company and its oil fields. This was seen by some as an efficient contraction of an industry facing the need to reduce capacity. Others viewed it as an increase in the concentration of an already noncompetitive industry.

Other industries also played an important role in the current merger wave. Deregulation in the financial area helped spur mergers in banking and brokerage. Many airlines were in financial trouble, and mergers often were associated with attempts to reduce operating costs.

Junk Bonds and Leveraged Buyouts. One of the largest mergers of 1985 was the sale of the American Broadcasting Cos. to Capital Cities Communications for several billion dollars. Ted Turner tried to take over CBS, a company much larger than his own, but was rebuffed and turned elsewhere. The ability of Turner and others to mount such "David–Goliath" takeover attempts was attributable in part to the use of borrowed money. A small company may borrow substantial amounts to purchase a larger company, perhaps with the target company's assets used to back the loans. Such loans have frequently been termed *junk bonds* because of their riskiness.

An even more extreme case of borrowing to finance an acquisition is known as the *leveraged buyout,* in which a small group of investors, usually including the company's top management, purchases the stock of all the other shareholders and "takes the company private." When this is done, the company's shares are no longer traded publicly on a stock exchange, and no public reports on its operations need be issued. In 1984 approximately one quarter of all mergers and acquisitions over $1 million in value were leveraged buyouts.

Many voiced concern over the increased use of junk bonds and leveraged buyouts, arguing that it has a destabilizing influence on the country's financial structure. An additional fear about leveraged buyouts is that managers engaging in them might be using inside information about their companies to take advantage of the shareholders whose stock they are buying.

The Tax Motive. Many companies involved in mergers and acquisitions have tax deductions and credits they cannot use because of insufficient profits. By merging, they can effectively "sell" these benefits to other corporations. Especially after it liberalized the corporate tax law in 1981, Congress evinced concern that the trading of such tax benefits provided undue incentives for corporations to merge at the taxpayer's expense. Hearings were held in 1985 to determine whether the trading of tax benefits by merging should be curtailed.

This problem hit close to home in 1985, with the Department of Transportation's proposed sale of Conrail, the government-controlled railroad system, to the Norfolk Southern Corp. It was estimated that the sale could bring the acquiring corporation additional tax benefits worth nearly the entire purchase price to be paid to the government.

Industrial Review

Manufacturing activity grew relatively rapidly in 1984. Output in the Western world rose by 7%; the most important contribution to this high rate of growth came from the advanced industrial countries, whose manufacturing production rose by 6.5%, the highest rate since 1976. Output in the less industrialized countries rose by 8.5%. The manufacturing industries in the centrally planned economies also raised their output, but at a more moderate rate of about 3.5%.

Table I. Index Numbers of Production, Employment, and Productivity in Manufacturing Industries
1980 = 100

Area	Relative importance[1] 1975	1980	1984	Production 1983	1984	Employment 1983	1984	Productivity[2] 1983	1984
World[3]	1,000	1,000	1,000	100	107	...	...	...	...
Industrial countries	868	861	849	99	105	...	...	...	...
Less industrialized countries	132	139	151	107	116	...	...	...	...
North America[4]	315	282	291	99	110	...	...	...	...
Canada	27	22	21	95	103	108	104	88	99
United States	288	260	270	101	112	91	96	111	117
Latin America[5]	74	79	71	92	96	...	...	...	...
Argentina	15	12	10	89	93	...	...	...	...
Brazil	27	26	19	75	79	...	...	...	...
Mexico	12	18	17	96	101	94	...	102	...
Asia[6]	159	183	210	110	122	...	...	...	...
India	11	11	12	115	121	106	...	108	...
Japan	109	131	151	105	117	104	107	101	109
South Korea	...	6	10	139	160	...	...	...	...
Europe[7]	416	422	396	97	100	...	...	...	...
Austria	8	9	9	99	104	91	89	109	117
Belgium	14	13	12	98	102	...	...	...	...
Denmark	6	5	5	106	117	94	97	113	121
Finland	6	6	6	107	112	98	97	109	115
France	80	75	68	95	96	93	...	102	...
West Germany	115	114	106	96	99	90	89	107	111
Greece	3	4	4	93	95	100	100	93	95
Ireland	1	2	2	110	125	89	86	124	145
Italy	43	54	49	90	95	...	...	...	...
Netherlands, The	18	14	14	99	105	87	84	114	125
Norway	6	5	6	96	118	91	89	105	133
Portugal	4	3	3	105	106	...	...	...	...
Spain	24	23	22	99	100	88	...	113	...
Sweden	17	13	13	103	110	87	90	118	122
Switzerland	13	13	12	94	97	92	91	102	107
United Kingdom	50	58	55	97	100	83	82	117	122
Yugoslavia	11	10	10	105	111	110	...	95	...
Rest of the world[8]	36	34	32	...	...	...	...	...	...
Oceania	18	15	13	95	96	...	...	...	...
Australia	15	13	11	92	93	98	98	94	95
South Africa	7	8	8	96	101	99	99	97	102
Centrally planned economies[9]	...	...	...	110	113	...	...	...	...

[1] The 1975 and 1980 weights are those applied by the UN Statistical Office; those for 1984 were estimated on the basis of the changes in manufacturing output since 1975 in the various countries.
[2] This is 100 times the production index divided by the employment index, giving a rough indication of changes in output per person employed.
[3] Excluding Albania, Bulgaria, China, Czechoslovakia, East Germany, Hungary, Mongolia, North Korea, Poland, Romania, the U.S.S.R., and Vietnam.
[4] Canada and the United States.
[5] South and Central America (including Mexico) and the Caribbean islands.
[6] Asian Middle East and East and Southeast Asia; including Japan, Israel, and Turkey.
[7] Excluding Albania, Bulgaria, Czechoslovakia, East Germany, Hungary, Poland, Romania, and the U.S.S.R.
[8] Africa and Oceania.
[9] These are not included in the above world total and consist of the European countries listed in note 7 above.

Table II. Pattern of Output, 1981–84
Percent change from previous year

	World[1]				Developed countries				Less developed countries				Centrally planned economies[2]			
	1981	1982	1983	1984	1981	1982	1983	1984	1981	1982	1983	1984	1981	1982	1983	1984
All manufacturing	0.5	−2	4	6	0	−4	3	7	1	2	4	9	2	3	5	3
Heavy industries	0.8	−3	4	8	0.3	−5	3	9	−0.2	1	3	11	3	4	5	4
Base metals	−1	−10	3	7	−1	−13	3	8	−2	3	2	9	0.7	0.5	4	2
Metal products	2	−2	3	9	1	−4	3	10	−3	−3	2	7	4	4	6	5
Building materials, etc.	−2	−3	3	4	−4	−5	2	4	2	0.5	−0.7	6	2	2	5	3
Chemicals	0.6	−1	5	6	−0.2	−2	6	7	2	5	5	10	2	3	3	3
Light industries	0	−0.5	4	4	−0.7	−1	3	4	3	2	5	7	0	2	5	2
Food, drink, tobacco	2	2	3	3	1	1	2	3	6	5	4	5	0.4	3	6	3
Textiles	−1	−2	2	2	−3	−3	2	2	−0.2	−1	4	2	0.9	−0.6	1.6	1
Clothing, footwear	0.3	−1	1	2	−2	−2	0.9	3	8	0.8	5	9	2	0.6	1.6	1
Wood products	−3	−4	7	4	−4	−5	7	4	−0.8	0.6	8	3	1	3	5	4
Paper, printing	0.1	−0.3	5	6	−0.1	−0.6	5	6	2	2	2	5	2	3	5	4

[1] Excluding centrally planned economies. [2] Excluding China.
Source: UN, *Monthly Bulletin of Statistics.*

The high growth rate in the industrial countries was the result of different developments in the three main manufacturing areas of the world: booming conditions in the North American and Japanese industries and a much weaker advance in Western Europe. The recovery in the U.S. had already started in 1983 and, although the level of manufacturing stopped rising after the summer of 1984, the year-on-year change indicated an expansion in manufacturing of more than 10% in 1984. Japanese growth was of the same order. Among the large Western European countries West Germany, Italy, and the U.K. raised manufacturing output by some 3.5%, while in France the increase was barely 1%.

During the first half of 1985 growth in manufacturing activity slowed significantly. Output in Europe continued to grow at about the same rate as in 1984, but manufacturing in the U.S., having reached its peak in the third quarter of 1984, moved ahead hardly at all to the middle of 1985. The speed of progress slowed appreciably in Japan as well.

Apart from higher domestic demand in most countries, the record level of international trade helped to raise manufacturing activity in 1984. In the ten years to 1983 the volume of total world exports of manufactures rose, on average, by 4% a year; in 1984, however, it rose by 10.5%. This was an important factor in helping the manufacturing industries to emerge from the 1982–83 recession.

In contrast with the two preceding years, in 1984 the heavy industries raised their output twice as fast as the light industries. This trend occurred in all areas. Products of the metal-using industries grew at the fastest rate; within this wide category, generally benefiting from higher investment activity, the electronic, instrument, and office machinery industries (the latter including data processing equipment) were the prime movers; the aerospace and automotive industries also experienced a fairly good year, while shipbuilding and heavy electrical equipment lagged. The chemical industries had their best year since 1980, as did building materials, although continued restraint in construction activity prevented the latter from registering more than moderate growth. Among light industries the paper-printing-publishing trades were the leaders, apart from the very rapid growth of the clothing-footwear industries in less developed countries.

Much of the higher investment activity aimed at applying new technology, particularly microprocessors, in many branches of the manufacturing industries in such forms as automated systems, robotics, and computerized quality and stock control. Advanced production methods and controls contributed to the increase in labour productivity. The growth of output itself, the highest in the past ten years in the market economies, positively influenced productivity per head, which rose by more than 10% in the U.S. and relatively rapidly in most other industrial countries. Productivity per hour worked in manufacturing rose fastest in Japan, by 9%; it increased by 4–6% in France, Italy, and the U.K. and by about 3% in West Germany and the U.S.

Manufacturing activity in the centrally planned economies (comprising the U.S.S.R. and Eastern Europe but not China) also increased in 1984 but at a rate that was moderate by their own historical standards and also as compared with the advances in the market economies. Though for almost the whole post-World War II period industry in the centrally planning countries grew faster than in the market economies, in 1984 the reverse was the case.

(G. F. RAY)

Table III. Annual Average Rates of Growth of Manufacturing Output, 1973–84
Percent

Area	1973–78	1978–81	1981–82	1982–83	1983–84
World[1]: market economies	2.2	1.4	−3.5	3.3	7.0
Industrial countries	1.7	1.0	−4.4	3.2	6.7
Less industrialized countries	5.8	3.6	1.7	3.6	8.7
Centrally planned economies[1]	7.6	3.2	2.8	4.6	3.5

[1] For definition see Table I.
Source: UN, *Monthly Bulletin of Statistics.*

Table IV. Output per Hour Worked in Manufacturing
1980 = 100

Country	1978	1979	1981	1982	1983	1984
France	92	98	101	105	109	114
West Germany	96	100	102	103	110	113
Italy	88	96	104	104	106	112
Japan	91	97	100	100	103	112
U.K.	101	101	105	110	117	122
U.S.	95	98	104	107	113	116

Source: National Institute, *Economic Review.*

Table V. Manufacturing Production in the U.S.S.R. and Eastern Europe[1]
1980 = 100

Country	1981	1982	1983	1984
Bulgaria[2]	105	110	115	...
Czechoslovakia	102	104	107	112
East Germany[2]	105	108	112	117
Hungary	103	105	107	109
Poland	86	84	89	94
U.S.S.R.	104	108	113	...

[1] Romania not available.
[2] All industries.
Source: UN, *Monthly Bulletin of Statistics.*

ADVERTISING

After 99 years the Coca-Cola Co. announced in April 1985 that it was changing the formula for Coke. Industry experts believed the move was an attempt to counter Pepsi Cola's growing popularity. Coca-Cola had 21.8% of the $23 billion U.S. soft-drink market, compared with 17% for Pepsi, but Pepsi's share had been increasing. Coca-Cola had spent four years on research and development of the new beverage. However, strong consumer and bottler discontent forced it to reintroduce the original formula, and in July board chairman Roberto Goizueta (see BIOGRAPHIES) announced that the reformulated drink would be sold as new Coca-Cola and the original as Coca-Cola Classic. Early figures suggested that Classic was leading new Coca-Cola in sales.

The reversal was viewed as one of the most dramatic turnarounds in U.S. marketing history. Pepsi, meanwhile, took advantage of the situation with ads suggesting that it did not need to change. It was estimated that Pepsi's ads using such figures as Michael Jackson and former vice-presidential candidate Geraldine Ferraro gained it close to $3 million in free exposure because of those personalities' publicity value.

In May the U.S. Supreme Court upheld the right of a lawyer to present truthful newspaper and magazine advertising, including legal advice, to solicit clients on specific legal problems. The high court ruled 5–3 that the legal advice, as long as it is truthful and not deceptive, is protected by the guarantee of freedom of speech in the First Amendment to the Constitution. The case involved a lawyer whose ads advised women that they might be able to sue the manufacturer of the Dalkon Shield if they had been injured by the birth-control device. The decision overturned an Ohio state court ruling that the ads violated rules against offering unsolicited legal advice and against recommending oneself as a lawyer.

Each year *Advertising Age* publishes a list of the 100 leading national advertisers in the U.S. In 1984 these advertisers spent $22.5 billion, an increase of 16% over the $19.4 billion spent in 1983. Procter & Gamble was the biggest spender, followed by General Motors, Sears, Beatrice, and R. J. Reynolds Industries. With the merger of R. J. Reynolds and Nabisco Brands in 1985, however, Procter and Gamble might lose its perennial number one position.

The five leading users of network television in 1984 were Procter & Gamble, AT & T, General Motors, General Foods, and American Home Products. Network television accounted for $6,460,000,000 of advertising spending by the 100 largest national advertisers. Procter & Gamble spent $412.7 million, or 47% of its advertising budget, on this medium. Government spending was 26th on the list, accounted for mainly by a $46 million program to raise money for the Olympics through the sale of coins. General Motors was the largest user of newspaper advertising, while R. J. Reynolds was the largest magazine advertiser. With an increase of 71% over the previous year, AT & T moved to first place in expenditures for network radio advertising.

Advertising revenues were expected to increase by about 9% in 1985, but sales of network television time were expected to grow by only 3% because of advertiser dissatisfaction. In 1985 the average prime-time network television commercial cost $180,000, about three times more than in 1975, but only 7% more households were watching. Spending for ads on cable television was expected to rise by 20% in 1985, and advertisers were also turning to other types of media. Anheuser-Busch placed advertising on billboard-size video screens at sports stadiums. Packaged goods companies advertised on shopping carts at thousands of supermarkets. Campbell Soup placed ads in church bulletins and on parking meters, and companies such as Lever Brothers and General Foods paid fees starting at $50,000 to get their products used in movies.

In April the U.S. Federal Trade Commission (FTC) denied a request from 29 organizations to restrict the advertisement of alcoholic beverages. The groups had complained about advertisements directly associating drinking with driving and about company-sponsored beer-drinking contests on college campuses. A ban on beer and wine advertisements would cost broadcasters about $700 million a year. The National Association of Broadcasters (NAB) introduced public-service announcements for its members pointing out that driving and drinking do not mix. The FTC planned to review the alcoholic beverage industry's advertising and marketing practices on a case-by-case basis.

In October more than six million households in Western Europe began to receive the "official" pan-Europe station of the European Communities (EC), a satellite-to-cable television channel broadcasting public service programming and advertisements in four languages—Dutch, English, German, and Portuguese. Ten percent of air time was being devoted to commercials, with advertising sales expected to reach about $9 million a year. The station competed with the private commercial satellite channels that had gained large audiences in Europe with entertainment-oriented English-language programs.

The Japanese government launched a major advertising campaign using television, newspapers, and posters to encourage its citizens to buy foreign products. The advertising effort was the result of U.S. pressure to allow more foreign products into the Japanese market. The TV ads reminded viewers that it was their responsibility to buy foreign products to maintain a free trade system.

The Spanish government introduced legislation in April to ban misleading, unfair, or irrational advertising. Misleading advertising was defined as including all advertising where any relevant information on the product is omitted, and according to the Spanish advertising industry, this would cover most ads for analgesics, cars, and computers as well as hard-sell, price-oriented advertisements. The bill would also regulate the use of testimonials, comparative advertising, and material that is offensive to the dignity of women or fails to respect the rights of children.

(EDWARD MARK MAZZE)

AEROSPACE

A succession of serious accidents in 1985 marred what had been a decade of steadily improving air safety. While not a single life was lost in a Western-built passenger jet during the first half of 1984, no fewer than 639 perished during the corresponding period of 1985. Worse was to follow: during August another 715 were killed, 520 of them in a single accident, the world's worst disaster in the air. There was no common factor, but two of the accidents involved Boeing 747s, an airliner that up to then had enjoyed an excellent safety record. Another 747 earlier in the year had a miraculous escape after falling uncontrolled from 11,285 m (37,000 ft) to 2,898 m (9,500 ft) with 273 people on board. Later, a DC-8 carrying U.S. soldiers home for the Christmas holidays crashed at Gander, Newfoundland, killing 256 passengers and crew. (*See* DISASTERS.)

In Seattle, Washington, Gay Mullins founded the Old Cola Drinkers of America to help ensure that what Coca-Cola hoped would be a marketing coup would come a cropper instead. Mullins compared his right to choose "old Coke" to the Declaration of Independence.

Meanwhile, business continued to improve in the international air transport industry. Traffic maintained its upward trend, though profits were still weak. Nevertheless, recovery was sufficient to accelerate production rates among the major aircraft manufacturers. Boeing inevitably led the way and by the end of the year's third quarter had sold 184 new transports, more than all 1984 sales. In Europe demand for the Airbus A320 (the only completely new airliner) continued; PanAm placed orders for 28 A310s and A320s, enhancing their credibility in the U.S. market. Recovery was also marked by the brisk trade in used aircraft, and by the year's end stocks of popular models such as the Boeing 727 had rapidly diminished. A notable reason for this was the falling price of oil; a gallon of fuel costing $1 in January 1982 could be bought for only 72 cents three years later, making the less fuel-efficient but much cheaper secondhand airplanes increasingly attractive.

The same anticipated increases in oil prices that in the late 1970s had launched a new generation of fuel-efficient transports also spurred a new development in propulsion technology known as the prop-fan. Essentially sophisticated multiblade propellers, prop-fans were seen by U.S. and European manufacturers as promising huge fuel savings even over the efficient existing high-bypass turbine engines. Others were not so sure, arguing against the greater technical risk and likely much higher initial cost of the prop-fans. First seen at the Farnborough Air Show in 1984, they were promoted to a much greater extent at the 1985 Paris International Air Show. The airlines themselves—the potential customers—were taking little interest in them, however, being too occupied with the slow climb back to profitability. The Paris show was also notable for the first appearance of the U.S.S.R.'s huge, 400-ton Antonov An-124 military transport, closely matching the U.S.'s Lockheed C-5 Galaxy in size. It was powered by the first Soviet high-bypass fan engines, disclosing that the U.S.S.R. was 20 years behind Western technology in this field.

The tiny Concorde fleet of Britain and France continued to service the two or three routes approved for the supersonic jetliners. Increasing demand, and the rise of the charter trade, prompted British Airways to bring out of mothballs its seventh Concorde, an encouragement to potential investors currently analyzing the airline's prospects as it headed for private ownership. In the U.S. the National Aeronautics and Space Administration (NASA) and a few enthusiastic research groups among the manufacturers continued to extol the virtues of supersonic or even hypersonic (five times the speed of sound) transport. They continued to be ignored by the airlines, put off by Europe's huge struggle to build just 16 Concordes.

In June the Douglas DC-3 reached its 50th birthday. For its contribution to aviation, the DC-3/C-47/Dakota was widely acknowledged the outstanding airplane of all time, and more than 700 continued to earn their keep around the world. Longevity had also become a characteristic of military aircraft, and words such as "updating," "enhancement," and "improvement" described the most important activities in this field. The most widely used combat aircraft were 15–25 years old, and even the newer types such as the F-16 Falcon and F/A-18 went back more than a decade. The time had long since gone when a new engine or weapon could justify the expense of a completely new aircraft, especially since progress in electronics was so rapid that the performance of equipment doubled every few years. Thus, entire fleets of such aircraft as F-111s, F-4 Phantoms, A-7 Corsairs, and even venerable B-52s were being reequipped with more capable black boxes or better and more reliable engines.

While the 30-year-old B-52 continued to be extensively updated, its successor, the B-1, reached the beginning of its service career; the first of a planned fleet of 100 aircraft was handed over to the U.S. Air Force in June. The B-1 had been canceled by U.S. Pres. Jimmy Carter in 1977 as part of a unilateral arms-reduction move, but it was reinstated by Pres. Ronald Reagan in 1981. Meanwhile, in the greatest secrecy, U.S. industry accelerated work on new "stealth" aircraft, the visibility of which to radar beams would be greatly reduced by the application of advanced electronic and structural techniques. However, there was considerable argument as to whether the money would be better spent on more B-1s.

V/STOL (vertical/short takeoff and landing) credibility received a boost when, in the 25th year since the first flight of an operational V/STOL fighter, its second-generation successor, the AV-8B/Harrier II, entered squadron service. Masterminded now by McDonnell Douglas, this much-improved close-support fighter was being operated by the U.S. Marines and the Royal Air Force. Some 400 were being built by the U.S. company and by British Aerospace, the original designers. A much larger program, that for the U.S.

Air Force's new Advanced Tactical Fighter (ATF), passed a significant milestone when in October invitations to submit bids were issued to industry. ATF would be one of the handful of really large Western military aircraft programs of the mid-1990s and, not surprisingly, every major U.S. manufacturer was working on proposals.

The long-running struggle among European countries to agree upon a common fighter finally bore fruit. In August Britain, West Germany, and Italy voted to launch the program without France, which had sought to dominate design. In October Spain also joined the consortium, and in November France had second thoughts and agreed to participate.

(MICHAEL WILSON)

AUTOMOBILES

World automobile and truck output in 1984, at 41,282,000 vehicles, was 4.4% higher than in 1983 but still fell some 600,000 vehicles short of the record set in 1978. World car production, at 30,237,000, rose 2.2% from 1983 but fell short of the 1978 peak of 30,910,000. Commercial vehicle production hit a new high of 11,045,000 (1978, 10,982,000) and was 11% over 1983.

Major gains in both automobile and commercial vehicle output in North America largely offset losses elsewhere. The biggest increases were recorded in both cars and commercial vehicles in Canada and the U.S., with the latter regaining the world automobile production lead from Japan for the first time since 1979. U.S. car output in 1984 was 7,773,000, up from 6,781,000 in 1983, and U.S. commercial vehicle output rose from 2,444,000 to 3,151,400. In Canada car output rose from 969,000 in 1983 to 1,022,000, and commercial vehicle production increased from 545,500 to 808,000.

Japan continued its domination of world commercial vehicle production, rising to a new high of 4,392,000 from 3,960,000, but car output there dipped slightly from 7,152,000 in 1983 to 7,073,000. In the six vehicle-producing countries of the EC, total car and commercial vehicle output declined. Car output slipped from 9,645,000 to 9,172,000 and commercial vehicles from 1,124,000 to 1,086,000. The only major European producer to increase both car and commercial vehicle output was Italy, while West Germany, France, and the U.K. all had declines in both categories.

Spain continued its strong growth in cars (a record 1,177,000), consolidating its seventh place in the world behind the U.S., Japan, West Germany (3,790,000),

The competition for General Motors's new Saturn plant, expected to employ 6,000 people, was fierce and complex, involving a variety of tax, financing, training, real estate, and other inducements. None of these contestants won.

France (2,713,000), Italy (1,439,000), and the U.S.S.R. (1.3 million). Canada (1,022,000) filled eighth place in 1984, relegating the U.K. (909,000) to ninth. The world's largest percentage gain in automobile output for the year was South Korea, up from 122,000 to 159,000, while South Korean commercial vehicle output rose from 99,000 to 107,000; both were new records. In Australia car output rose from the depressed 1983 figure of 317,000 to 370,000 and commercial vehicle production from 22,000 to 29,000; the latter included substantial numbers of vehicles assembled from virtually complete imported kits.

Total new car sales were higher in 1984 than in 1983 only in Italy, Sweden, Australia, and North America among the major motoring nations. Japan, West Germany, Belgium, France, and Spain all recorded lower 1984 car sales, and France, West Germany, and Spain also had lower commercial vehicle sales.

Europe and Australia. A major and unusual feature of the European automotive scene in 1984 was the longest industrial strike ever in West Germany, causing the direct loss to West German manufacturers of some 360,000 cars over seven weeks. Such was the importance of the West German industry and so interdependent had the European manufacturers become that the strike also contributed to production losses in Spain, Belgium, the U.K., and, to a lesser degree, in each of the other European manufacturing nations.

For Britain's three large-volume manufacturers—Austin Rover, Ford Motor Co., and General Motors Corp. (Vauxhall/Bedford)—there were also production losses because of strikes after two years of much improved labour relations. In Britain overall sales held up to near the 1983 record levels, as customers increasingly bought imported vehicles when the home product was unavailable. The U.K. market was also buoyed up, in volume if not profit terms, by the continuing market support activities of General Motors in its bid to boost market share almost regardless of immediate financial cost. Both Ford (the U.K. market leader) and Austin Rover lost market share to General Motors. GM and Austin Rover both fell further into the red in their accounts.

Smaller prestige British manufacturers, including Jaguar, Rolls-Royce, TVR, and Lotus, all increased production and world sales, especially to North America, which also proved a rich market for West Germany's highly successful BMW, Mercedes-Benz, and Porsche. The strong U.S. dollar and expanding U.S. market proved both profitable and beneficial for European manufacturers.

Australia prepared for the introduction of unleaded fuel in mid-1985 and its compulsory use, together with catalytic converters, in all new cars from January 1986. The Australian importers and manufacturers forecast higher than ever car sales for at least the first nine months of 1985 as buyers rushed to buy the precatalytic/unleaded cars; sales figures for the first half of 1985 bore out this forecast.

United States. In the U.S. 1985 was the year of Saturn as 38 states made presentations to General Motors Corp. in an attempt to win a new assembly plant. In July GM announced that tiny Spring Hill,

The surprise of the year in the U.S. auto market was the success of the Yugo, priced under $4,000. Yugoslav labour rates, lower even than those in South Korea, whose Excel, from Hyundai, also appeared in 1985, were the chief advantage.
AP/WIDE WORLD

Tenn., with a population of fewer than 1,000, would be the site of the plant to build 400,000 to 500,000 units annually of a new line of small cars starting with the 1989 model year.

The intent of the Saturn plant was to build small cars for less money in order to compete more effectively with Japanese producers. GM said that it hoped to reduce the cost of producing a car by $2,000.

While GM planned a new U.S. plant to combat imports, several of the importing firms announced plans either to build U.S. assembly plants or to enter into joint ventures with U.S. producers to build cars in that country. Chrysler Corp. and Mitsubishi Motors Corp. of Japan chose a site outside the neighbouring cities of Bloomington and Normal in central Illinois as the site of a plant to produce jointly from 180,000 to 240,000 subcompact cars annually starting in the 1989 model year.

Ford Motor Co. and Mazda Motors Corp. of Japan announced that Mazda would begin building a new line of luxury compact cars in the 1988 model year at a former Ford plant in Flat Rock, Mich. Mazda would build 200,000 cars a year and sell half of that output to Ford, which owned an equity interest in Mazda. Ford would sell the car under the Mustang nameplate.

Meanwhile, Honda, which was already building compact Accords in the U.S. in Marysville, Ohio, said that it would add production of its subcompact Civic to Marysville in 1986 and boost output of the two car lines from 150,000 to 300,000 annually within two years. Nissan, which had been producing compact pickup trucks in Smyrna, Tenn., began in 1985 producing its subcompact Sentra car at Smyrna as well.

Despite the unprecedented flurry of planned new plants, the industry hinted at even more activity in the near future as Ford announced that it had reached agreement with Kia Industries of South Korea to supply it with a new line of minicars for 1988. Also, GM's Pontiac Division said that Daewoo of South Korea would supply it with a minicar for the 1987 model year.

Yamaha of Japan and Ford reached agreement for Yamaha to sell high-performance engines to Ford for the 1988 models. Chrysler and Samsung Group of South Korea agreed that Samsung would supply

Chrysler with parts and other components for the late 1980s. Chrysler and Maserati of Italy entered into an agreement whereby Maserati would design and build a two-seat roadster for Chrysler for 1987 using Chrysler engines and transmissions.

All these future production plans were made amid a good sales year for the automakers. During the 1985 model year, ended Sept. 30, 1985, U.S. automakers sold 8,380,000 cars, a 6% increase from the 7.9 million sold in the 1984 model year. This was the highest total since 8.6 million cars were sold in 1979. Imports, meanwhile, accounted for record sales of 2,670,000 cars, an 11.7% increase from the 2.4 million sold in the 1984 model year. Domestic and import sales combined reached 11,050,000 units, a 7% increase from the 10.3 million sold in 1984 and the highest total since 11,090,000 in 1983.

GM sold 4.7 million cars in the 1985 model year, up only slightly from the 4.6 million sold in 1984 but still its highest tally since selling 5.1 million cars in 1979. Ford sold 2,160,000 cars, a 13% increase from the 1.9 million sold in 1984 and its highest total since 2.2 million were sold in 1979. Chrysler sold 1,140,000 cars, up 21% from the 946,575 sold in 1984 and its best year since selling 1,180,000 cars in 1977. Chrysler had not sold one million cars in a single year since 1979, when it sold 1,120,000.

Honda laid claim to being the industry's fourth best-selling producer with sales of 147,674 units, a 24% increase from the 119,336 units sold in 1984. American Motors Corp. sold only 137,493 cars, a 32% decline from the 201,275 sold in 1984 and its lowest total since selling 99,300 in 1982. Volkswagen sales of cars made in the U.S. fell 17% to 71,884 units from 86,600 a year earlier, while in its first year in the U.S. Nissan sold 21,077 Sentras built in Smyrna.

Of the major imports—all Japanese—Toyota remained the top seller with sales of 456,561 units, a 10% increase from the 413,781 sold a year earlier. Nissan was second with sales of 407,733 units, up 11% from 367,029 in 1984.

Truck sales set a record at 4,591,578 units, up from 3,935,369 sold in 1984 and also above the previous high of 4,225,500 sold in 1978. Car and truck sales com-

bined totaled 15.6 million units, topping the previous combined record of 15.3 million in 1978.

Individually, the best-selling vehicle in the industry in 1985 was the F-series Ford pickup truck with sales of 581,767 units. The Chevrolet C/K pickup truck was second with sales of 498,525 units.

The best-selling car was the subcompact Chevrolet Cavalier with sales of 422,927 units. The subcompact Ford Escort was second at 410,978 units, and the midsize Chevrolet Celebrity was third at 360,167 units.

Rounding out the top ten were the Oldsmobile Cutlass Ciera in fourth with sales of 315,569; the Ford Tempo in fifth at 297,656; the Honda Accord in sixth at 259,937 (domestically produced and imported models combined); the Chevrolet Impala/Caprice seventh at 251,693; the Buick Century eighth with 239,570; the Oldsmobile Cutlass Supreme ninth at 234,242; and the Oldsmobile 88 tenth at 213,833.

Sales of all cars benefited from incentive programs undertaken by the manufacturers. These incentives for the most part were discounted automobile loan rates varying from 9.9 to 7.5%. The discount rates were offered by each automaker's financing subsidiary. The effect of the incentives was that new car sales rose sharply when the loans were offered but declined sharply when the programs ended.

For the new model year GM raised prices an average of $400, Ford by $350, Chrysler by $320, American Motors by $208, Volkswagen by $107, Nissan by $50, and Honda by $562 on its only U.S. model, the Accord.

With the 1986 model year came a variety of new cars, both domestic and imported. At GM the automaker's downsizing campaign continued with the introduction of a smaller Buick LeSabre and Oldsmobile 88 along with conversion of those cars from rear- to front-wheel drive. Both cars were built on 110.8-in wheelbases, 5.1 in shorter than on the previous rear-drive models, and were 196.2 in long overall, 22 in shorter than in 1984. Curb weight dropped by 400 lb.

GM also unveiled new downsized versions of the Cadillac Eldorado and Seville, Buick Riviera, and Oldsmobile Toronado. The wheelbases were shrunk 6 in to 108 in, and overall length was reduced 19 in to 187.2 in. The Cadillac models offered a 4.1-litre V-8 engine, but the others dropped V-8s and went to a 3.8-litre V-6 powerplant only.

Among some new gimmicks Buick began offering a cathode-ray-tube screen in the dashboard of the Riviera in which controls for radio, air conditioning, and the like were activated by touching words on the screen. And the Pontiac STE added a second set of radio controls in the steering wheel hub.

At Ford the midsize, rear-wheel-drive Ford LTD and Mercury Marquis were replaced by a pair of front-wheel-drive cars called the Ford Taurus and Mercury Sable. They were offered in four-door sedan and station-wagon body styles. Both featured aerodynamic rounded body lines. In an unusual move Ford introduced the cars on December 26 rather than in the fall. Late in the summer Ford also introduced

as a 1986 model the Aerostar minivan, a rear-wheel-drive van to compete with Chrysler's front-wheel-drive Dodge Caravan and Plymouth Voyager.

Chrysler added a new engine, a 2.5-litre four-cylinder, which took the place of a 2.6-litre four-cylinder that it had been importing from Mitsubishi of Japan. The 2.5-litre was used in cars only, while the 2.6-litre was still offered in vans.

American Motors unveiled a new compact pickup truck in both two- and four-wheel-drive versions. Named the Comanche, it was based on the same platform as the Jeep Cherokee utility vehicle.

Among the imports Toyota redesigned its subcompact Celica sports model and converted it to front-wheel drive. Nissan restyled its 300ZX sports model and added a four-wheel-drive Stanza to its compact station-wagon lineup. Honda restyled its compact Accord and lengthened the body by five inches. Mazda renamed its former GLC (Great Little Car) the 323 and put a larger engine under the hood.

Audi added four-wheel antiskid brakes to its 5000 Turbo Quattro; Mercedes-Benz restyled its 300 series of midsize cars; and Porsche introduced a turbocharged version of its 944 and reintroduced the 911 to the U.S. Rolls-Royce made cellular phones standard in its Silver Spur and Silver Spirit, while Volkswagen offered a four-wheel-drive version of its Vanagon van.

Perhaps the car that captured the most interest during the year was the Yugo, a tiny car imported from Yugoslavia that went on sale in August for only $3,990. By year's end more than 8,000 had been sold, but the company had orders for four times that many. Yugo America, Inc., distributors, said it would import 60,000 Yugos during the full 1986 calendar year.

When the new cars appeared, they did so under a new set of federal fuel economy laws. The U.S. government, under its Corporate Average Fuel Economy (CAFE) regulations begun in the 1978 model year, had mandated that each automaker's fleet of cars obtain 27.5 miles per gallon (mpg) fuel economy in the 1985 model year and thereafter. However, after arguments by GM and Ford that demand for big cars by new car buyers was upsetting their CAFE and threatened to limit output of those models in order to conform to the law, the government rolled back the standard to 26 mpg for the 1986 model year. The automakers asked that 26 mpg be kept as the standard for at least two to three years, but the government did not respond immediately.

In the annual fuel economy ratings by the Environmental Protection Agency, the Chevrolet Sprint E/R was the most fuel-efficient car with a city rating of 55 mpg. Sprint was built by Suzuki of Japan, in which GM owned an equity interest, and was sold through the Chevrolet dealer network.

The only car in the top ten that was made in the U.S. was the subcompact Ford Escort FS with a 41-mpg city rating. However, Ford obtained the four-cylinder diesel engines for that car from Japan.

At the low end of the mileage ratings was the Rolls-Royce Silver Spur limousine, rated at 8 mpg in the city. The only U.S.-made cars in the bottom ten were the Chevrolet Caprice and Pontiac Parisi-

enne station wagons, rated at 15 mpg in city driving.

Chrysler chairman Lee Iacocca continued to deny speculation that he eventually would like to run for the office of president of the United States. Iacocca did take on a new job, however, as a columnist for the *Los Angeles Times* syndicate under a one-year contract. While taking on a column, Iacocca said that he would not write a second book. His first, *Iacocca: An Autobiography,* topped two million in sales.

Japan. During the year Toyota continued to be Japan's corporate giant. According to its financial statement for the year ended June 1985, Toyota sold a record 3,530,000 cars, trucks, and buses, amounting to 6,060,000,000,000 yen ($27.5 billion) with a sales profit of 505 billion yen.

Car production in Japan for 1985 was expected to achieve a record of 7.5 million units, up from 7,073,000 in 1984. This was mainly due to a large increase in exports to the U.S., where Japan's voluntary restriction quota was raised by 24% to an annual level of 2.3 million units beginning in April.

In the Tokyo motor show held during the autumn, Toyota, Nissan, and other major manufacturers displayed models featuring various new concepts for the next generation. High maneuverability and computerization were the highlights, and the future models were equipped with such technological advances as full-time four-wheel drive and four-wheel steering and were notable for their use of microchips for many purposes.

(JAMES L. MATEJA; JOHN R. WEINTHAL)

BEVERAGES

Beer. Estimated world production of beer in 1984 was 954 million hectolitres (hl; 1 hl = 26.4 U.S. gal), a decrease of 0.4% from 1983. Brewing in the Americas showed a marginal increase, almost entirely attributable to a revival of output in Mexico following a slump in 1983. The relatively new brewing nations of Africa and Asia continued to develop their industries with technical aid from Western Europe. The West German brewer Erste Kulmbacher (EKU) contracted to build breweries at Libreville and Lambaréné, Gabon, during the year. EKU already brewed 900,000 hl a year in Togo and also had a brewery in the Solomon Islands. The Belgian contractors Unibra signed a BF 225 million deal to supply brewing plant and fermentation equipment to the Five Stars Brewery in Beijing (Peking), due to begin operation in 1987. China continued to emerge as a growing force in world brewing and in 1985 introduced its first variety of domestically bred hops. Its output added to the international surplus of hops resulting from three successive excellent harvests in Europe.

The 20th international European Brewery Convention congress, held in Helsinki, Fin., attracted 1,200 delegates from 35 countries. The year marked the 50th anniversary of canned beer. The first beer in cans appeared in January 1935 from the Krueger Brewery in Richmond, Va. Since then, the U.S. alone had produced 610,000,000,000 cans. In the U.S. beer market, canned beers reigned supreme, accounting for 62% of all beer consumed. In Great Britain, where the first can appeared in December 1935 from the Felinfoel Brewery in

South Wales, only about 12% of beer was currently packaged in this way. The U.S. also retained the distinction of being the world's biggest consumer of foreign beer, importing over 8.3 million hl (220 million gal) in 1984, but imports still represented less than 4% of total consumption. The Netherlands remained the largest exporter of beer, with over 25% of its national output being sold abroad.

In the U.S.S.R., as part of the government's clampdown on alcohol abuse, the price of yeast was doubled to discourage illegal home brewing.

(MICHAEL D. RIPLEY)

Spirits. Although the Scotch whisky market, which had peaked in 1979, again showed some growth in 1985, uncertainty prevailed over future sales in two key markets. Success in Western Europe was overshadowed by an impending increase in the U.S. federal excise tax and the ascendancy in Japan of *shochu*, a cheap, home-produced white spirit taxed at a preferential rate.

The increase in U.S. tax, due early in 1986, was expected to be substantial and particularly damaging to spirits at a time when Americans were turning increasingly to table wine and lower-strength liqueurs and cocktails. It would be a severe setback for the Scotch Whisky Association (SWA), which had been spending heavily on generic advertising for the past three years. The problem of parallel exports of whisky still affected the Japanese market, and the SWA urged the EC to step up efforts to obtain a fairer duty and tax structure in Japan. Scotch's performance in its home market and in France, where the product was fashionable among younger drinkers, was encouraging. A notable development during the year was the successful Guinness bid for Arthur Bell & Sons, Britain's leading whisky producers. The deal cost Guinness £370 million, and the priority would now be to develop sales in the U.S.

France, Italy, the U.S., Japan, West Germany, and the U.K. together accounted for 50% of world spirit sales. The U.S. domi-

Keizo Saji (centre), chairman of the Japanese distilling and brewing company Suntory, sports a "Penguin Boy" tie at a display of Suntory products bearing the highly successful promotional character, who has turned up in hit songs, on T-shirts, and even on teacups.
MATSUMOTO—SYGMA

nated with consumption at 1,613,000,000 litres in 1984, ahead of Japan at 1,071,-000,000 l. Only France and Japan had increased the volume of spirit sales since 1980. National drinks generally accounted for the majority of sales; for example, *pastis* in France, brandy in West Germany, and grappa in Italy. Whisky still accounted for about 50% of the U.K. market, and white spirits like vodka and white rum enjoyed massive sales in the U.S.

(ANTONY C. WARNER)

Wine. The 1985 European harvest, which had seemed threatened by winter frosts and a dry summer, appeared not to have suffered as much as had been feared. French production was estimated at 68 million hl, including 16.5 million hl of *appellation contrôlée* wines. In Italy, where the winter was unusually severe, production was down, especially in Veneto and Emilia-

Romagna, possibly 10,000–20,000 hl below the 1984 total of 70.2 million hl. West German production suffered much more; its estimated 4.8 million hl was only half the average of recent years. In Spain a harvest of between 28 million and 31 million hl was forecast, compared with 35.5 million hl in 1984. Portugal's estimated production of 9.7 million hl was up nearly 15%, while that of Greece, 4.5 million hl, was only slightly below the 1984 level. Austrian viticulture was hard hit by the year's adulteration scandal. (*See* WORLD AFFAIRS [Western Europe]: *Austria.*)

The projected overall decline in production in the EC countries, combined with a reduction in the area given to viticulture, would to some extent balance reduced exports and lower consumption in some of the producing countries, notably France and Italy. With the entry of Spain and

Table VI. Estimated Consumption of Beer in Selected Countries			
In litres[1] per capita			
Country	1982	1983	1984
East Germany	147.0	146.7	...
West Germany	147.9	148.7	144.4
Czechoslovakia	146.3	147.8	140.1
Denmark	128.59	133.97	129.74
Belgium	132.7	128.0	126.3
Luxembourg	120.5	121.8	120.6
Ireland	115.0	121.0	120.0
New Zealand	121.1	114.1	115.3
Australia[2]	121.6	117.8	115.0
United Kingdom	109.5	110.5	110.1
Austria	108.5	109.4	107.7
United States	92.0	92.0	90.7
Hungary	89.7	88.8	87.0
Netherlands, The	81.96	87.53	83.43
Canada[3]	85.7	83.5	83.1
Venezuela	75.3	71.8	...
Switzerland	71.9	70.3	68.6
Bulgaria	59.5	61.2	60.0
Spain	56.9	58.4	59.0
Finland	55.96	57.37	56.65
Yugoslavia	47.8	50.0	...
Norway	47.07	45.32	46.82
Romania	45.0	45.0	...
Colombia	50.0	45.0	45.0
Sweden	46.6	44.7	44.5

[1] One litre = 1.0567 U.S. quart = 0.8799 imperial quart.
[2] Years ending June 30.
[3] Years ending March 31.

Table VII. Estimated Consumption of Spirits in Selected Countries			
In litres[1] per capita			
Country	1982	1983	1984
Luxembourg	8.25	8.0	6.75
Hungary	4.76	4.80	5.10
East Germany	4.8	4.8	...
Poland	4.2	4.1	4.2
U.S.S.R.	3.3	3.3	3.3
Czechoslovakia	3.56	3.32	3.28
Bulgaria	3.05	3.04	3.0
Finland	2.82	2.83	2.87
United States	2.93	2.86	2.81
Spain	3.0	3.0	2.8
Canada[2]	3.25	3.06	2.79
Netherlands, The	2.57	2.63	2.36
West Germany	2.53	2.46	2.32
Cyprus	2.1	2.3	2.3
Yugoslavia	2.3	2.3	...
France[3]	2.42	2.38	2.22
Iceland	2.12	2.10	2.21
Switzerland	2.21	2.15	2.11
Japan	1.97	2.16	2.1
Sweden	2.45	2.26	2.10
Romania	2.0	2.0	2.0
Belgium	2.04	2.17	1.91
New Zealand	2.0	1.69	1.72
United Kingdom	1.58	1.63	1.61
Denmark	1.64	1.55	1.50

[1] One litre = 1.0567 U.S. quart = 0.8799 imperial quart.
[2] Years ending March 31.
[3] Including aperitifs.

Table VIII. Estimated Consumption of Wine in Selected Countries			
In litres[1] per capita			
Country	1982	1983	1984
Italy	91.4	91.4	90.5
Portugal	78.4	89.1	84.2
France	88.0	85.0	82.0
Argentina	73.8	71.1	66.3
Luxembourg	48.3	53.6	62.5
Switzerland	49.3	48.3	49.9
Spain	57.0	57.0	45.0
Greece	35.3	44.1	43.9
Austria[2]	35.3	37.4	36.4
Chile	54.7	39.1	35.0
Hungary	31.8	29.6	30.7
Uruguay	25.0	30.0	...
Yugoslavia	29.0	30.0	...
Romania	28.0	29.0	...
West Germany	24.8	26.5	25.7
Belgium	21.7	21.7	22.9
Bulgaria	24.8	22.6	22.5
Australia[2]	19.7	20.4	21.3
Denmark	17.35	18.86	18.86
Czechoslovakia	14.6	14.6	15.6
Netherlands, The	14.15	13.87	15.22
New Zealand	13.2	12.8	13.9
U.S.S.R.	12.9	12.9	12.7
Cyprus	11.1	11.1	11.9
Sweden	10.43	10.8	11.61

[1] One litre = 1.0567 U.S. quart = 0.8799 imperial quart.
[2] Years ending June 30.

Source: Produktschap voor Gedistilleerde Dranken, *Hoeveel alcoholhoudende dranken worden er in de wereld gedronken?*

Portugal in 1986, the EC's share of world wine production would be around 46%. Increasing competition among the producing countries was foreseen.

Despite initial doubts, vintages of good quality were expected almost everywhere in Europe. In Italy forecasts for the wines of Abruzzi, the Marches, Trentino-Alto Adige, and Umbria were excellent, while in Tuscany an exceptionally fine Chianti was expected. In France vintages in Champagne (where production was down 40% because of winter frosts), Bordeaux, and Burgundy promised to be of very high, even exceptional quality.

Algeria, Morocco, and Tunisia all had good harvests. South Africa's production was somewhat below the previous year. Argentina's production fell again, to 15.7 million hl, while that of the U.S. recovered somewhat, to 17.8 million hl. U.S. consumers continued to show a marked preference for light white wines of low alcoholic content.

(MARIE-JOSE DESHAYES-CREUILLY)

Soft Drinks. Soft drink sales, which had maintained a fairly steady growth rate of 3 to 4% over the last several years, accelerated considerably in 1985. Strong competition within the industry, including advertising and marketing support, bolstered the unprecedented spate of new product and new product category introductions begun in 1984. Most of the industry growth was absorbed by the major franchise companies and larger manufacturers. The attempt to change the formula of Coca-Cola generated headlines. (See *Advertising,* above.)

Increased health consciousness among consumers continued to affect beverage consumption. Juice-added soft drinks, introduced nationwide in 1984, quickly captured a strong following, and in 1985 the trend evolved even further with the national introduction of a vitamin-fortified diet soft drink. One result was a blurring of the lines distinguishing different types of beverage, as soft drink companies produced juices and related beverages and conglomerates specializing in food extended into soft drinks.

Some of the increased market share being gained by soft drinks was at the expense of the stronger alcoholic beverages, which were experiencing a decline, attributable in large part to the emphasis on health and nationwide campaigns against drunk driving and alcoholism. The health trend was also reflected in the continued growth of the sugar-, caffeine-, and sodium-free soft drink categories.

Product development was backed up by technical progress in packaging. A new four-litre plastic bottle was introduced. Aseptic packages for still beverages grew in popularity, although they were not yet suitable for carbonated drinks. An aluminum-topped plastic soft drink can for single servings, introduced in a U.S. test market, represented a significant technical breakthrough. Formerly, the carbonation-retaining properties of plastic were not sufficient for soft drinks in smaller containers.   (FREDERICK L. WEBBER)

BUILDING AND CONSTRUCTION

In the U.S. in 1985, higher dollar outlays for construction continued to provide support for the national economy. Despite concern over the economic future,

the continued lower rate of inflation and lower interest rates contributed to stronger consumer interest in housing and to investment in nonresidential building construction. The high level of residential construction was a major factor in the ongoing recovery in the construction industry, which had started in early 1983.

On a seasonally adjusted annual rate basis, the value of new construction put in place in June 1985 was $343,837,000,000, according to the U.S. Department of Commerce. Monthly figures for the first nine months of 1985 indicated that the value of new construction put in place would reach a new record for the entire year of over $340 billion. Outlays in 1984, the previous peak year, had totaled $312,988,-000,000. Throughout the first nine months the Composite Construction Cost Index of the Department of Commerce fluctuated between a low of 166.2 (1977 = 100) and a high of 169.3, compared with an annual average of 163.7 in 1984. All the producer price indexes of materials used in building construction indicated that the rate of inflation in construction in 1985 was low.

Mortgage interest rates had edged upward in 1984 until the last quarter of the year, when they turned down slightly, and these lower levels continued throughout 1985. The average effective commitment interest rate for 25-year conventional mortgages (75% loan-to-price ratio) was 11.75% in June 1985, compared with an average rate of 13.13% in 1984. The median sales price of a new home sold in July 1985 was $82,100, and it appeared that the median for the year would be slightly higher. The median in 1984 was $79,900.

In Canada it was expected that the increase in the gross national product (GNP)

BRIAN SMITH

would approach 3% in 1985, followed by a smaller increase in 1986. Consumer spending rose in early 1985, and housing investment was up sharply, but there was little change in business investment. In April and May, housing starts, responding to the fall in interest rates, were 20% higher than in the corresponding months of 1984. However, it did not appear that construction activity would improve further in the last half of the year.

Private investment in housing in Great Britain had fallen sharply in the last half of 1984. It increased in the first quarter of 1985, but this was attributable mainly to improvements made in existing housing, while investment in new housing continued to fall. Housing starts, which declined throughout 1984, rose sharply in the second quarter of 1985, but it appeared that neither private nor public investment in housing would increase during the remainder of the year. The French economy showed little vitality in 1985, and construction activity declined sharply in the cold winter months. Improvements in corporate profits during the year suggested that investments would rise, but with gross domestic product (GDP) growing at only a little over 1%, building and construction were expected to continue at low levels.

In West Germany the severe winter of 1984–85 had an adverse effect on construction. The industry had also experienced difficulty in 1984, when its contribution to GNP fell significantly. Despite large increases in orders for capital goods in mid-1985, the outlook for consumer spending was not good, and the overall outlook for the construction industry was unfavourable. Japan experienced an increase in residential construction in 1985, bolstered by a predicted growth of about 5% in GNP, stable prices for construction materials, and lower mortgage rates. A survey by the Bank of Japan indicated that nonresidential construction would also grow in 1985 and 1986 because of planned business expenditures on plant and equipment.   (CARTER C. OSTERBIND)

CERAMICS

The strength of the U.S. economy in 1984 both helped and hurt U.S. ceramic companies. Low inflation and interest rates helped to keep costs low, but the value of the dollar in overseas markets hurt U.S. exports and favoured foreign imports.

U.S. ceramic sales for 1984 were about $28 billion, up from $26 billion in 1983. Glass sales accounted for 63% of the market, porcelain enamel 15%, and advanced ceramics 14%. Whiteware sales, including ceramic tile, dinnerware, and artware, represented 8% of the total.

In the glass industry, containers accounted for 26% of all sales. However, volume was dropping steadily, primarily because of competition from plastics and legislation requiring the return of empty containers. Sales of flat glass, particularly for windows and doors, were 27% of all glass sales. They benefited from strong housing and automobile markets but were hurt by the energy-saving emphasis on smaller autos and fewer windows in buildings. The remaining glass sales were in fibreglass (18%), lighting (13%), consumer glassware (6%), cathode-ray tubes for television sets and computers (6%), and several smaller areas.

The porcelain enamel industry recorded sales of $4 billion in 1984, riding the crest of good sales of housing and appliances. There were strong indications, however, that appliance enamels, 91% of all porcelain enamel sales, might suffer as appliance manufacturers turned to cheaper, more energy-efficient coating processes.

Advanced ceramic sales in the U.S., representing a wide variety of high-technology applications, totaled $3.8 billion in 1984 and appeared poised for great future growth. Low-voltage insulators, primarily automotive spark plugs, represented 24% of U.S. sales in this category. Capacitors and electronic ceramic packages represented another 24%. Capacitor sales rose 31% over 1983 levels, with multilayer ceramic chip capacitors making particularly strong advances. The engineering ceramic segment, including heat-, wear-, and corrosion-resistant components; cutting tools; and bioceramics accounted for 18% of all U.S. advanced ceramic sales. Ferrites (12%), optical fibres (8%), high-voltage insulators (5%), and other electrical and electronic ceramics (9%) accounted for the remainder. Whitewares, including bathroom fixtures, floor and wall tile, artware, and dinnerware, maintained their sales level in the U.S. at $2.3 billion. However, U.S.-made products faced extremely strong competition from imports.

Forecasts for future worldwide ceramic sales were bright, especially for advanced ceramics. In this area growth estimates by the Japanese Ministry of International Trade and Industry and by A. R. C. Westwood of Martin Marietta Corp. suggested worldwide sales of $25 billion–$30 billion by the year 2000. Charles River Associates, in a report prepared for the National Bureau of Standards, predicted growth rates of 12–14% per year throughout the 1990s for some electronic ceramics to as much as 40% per year in the heat engine and integrated optics areas.

Japanese ceramic producers continued their strategy of early commercialization to assure a major share in future markets. They appeared willing to forgo early profits in exchange for the long-term advantages of high-volume production. During the year Toshiba introduced a spectrum analyzer that for the first time used integrated optic circuits based on advanced ceramics. Toshiba's unit appeared to be based on a U.S. (Westinghouse Corp.) design, but U.S. companies had been unwilling to sell the product without further development.

Japanese firms were also pursuing low-technology applications for advanced ceramics. For example, they began marketing, in the form of ceramic scissors, knives, and ballpoint pen tips, advanced ceramics that might be used in a few years in automotive engine parts.

The importance of these future advanced ceramic markets stirred action in Europe. In the U.K. two "clubs" consisting of companies that had agreed to pursue specific advanced ceramic applications cooperatively were formed. One was pursuing advanced ceramics for turbines and the other for reciprocating engines. In Sweden a group of companies was cooperatively emphasizing the application of hot isostatic pressing technology developed by the Swedish company ASEA.

(NORMAN M. TALLAN)

CHEMICALS

The recovery of most of the major chemical industries of the world continued through 1984 and into the first half of 1985. Some indications in the fourth quarter of 1985, however, were that the recovery was losing momentum.

In the U.S. the value of chemical shipments in 1984, according to the U.S. Department of Commerce, totaled $211,833,000,000, an 11.4% increase over 1983. During the first six months of 1985 the value of shipments was $110,133,000,000, 6.6% higher than it was during the same period of 1984.

Chemical production in the U.S. in 1984 rose 6.8% as measured by the Federal Reserve Board's index of chemical production, which went from 114 (1977 = 100) in 1983 to 121.7 for 1984. During the first half of 1985 the index moved up slowly and steadily—except for a slight dip in May—to reach 127.6 on a seasonally adjusted basis in June.

As a result of increased production and sales, profits for the U.S. chemical industry grew at a healthy rate, despite only relatively modest increases in prices. The Bureau of the Census reported that profits of companies in the chemicals and allied products industry rose 18.8% in 1984 to $13,833,000,000. Producer prices for chemicals and allied products, as reported by the U.S. Department of Labor, rose 2.7%; its index of producer prices, which averaged 293 (1967 = 100) in 1983, rose to 300.8 for 1984. During the first half of 1985 the seasonally adjusted index inched up in a sawtooth pattern from 322.9 in January to 324.7 in July.

The chemical industry faced a number of problems in 1985. An accident on Dec. 3, 1984, at the Bhopal, India, plant of Union Carbide India Ltd., which was 50.9% owned by the Union Carbide Corp. of the U.S., resulted in the deaths of at least 1,700 and probably more than 2,000 nearby residents. Called the worst industrial accident ever, it led to a number of investigations as well as several initiatives aimed at preventing the recurrence of such an event.

Another concern during the year in the U.S. was the nation's still strong, but shrinking, positive chemical trade balance. The problem had arisen partly because of the strength of the U.S. dollar against the currencies of the nation's major trading partners. In 1983 the U.S. Department of Commerce reported that the country exported $19,751,000,000 worth of chemicals and posted net chemical exports of $8,972,000,000. In 1984 chemical exports rose to $22,336,000,000, but imports grew even faster to reach $13,694,000,000. As a result the favourable balance of trade dropped from $8,971,000,000 in 1983 to $8,639,000,000 in 1984. During the first six months of 1985 the value of chemical exports was $11,138,000,000 while that for imports was $7,540,000,000, producing a net chemical export figure of $3,597,000,000. That was 17.8% lower than the figure for the first half of 1984.

In Japan chemical sales in 1984, according to preliminary figures, reached $84.5 billion, an increase of 4.8% over the $80,604,000,000 reported by the European Council of Chemical Manufacturers' Federation (CEFIC) for 1983. Early in 1985 Japan was hoping for a 2.9% increase over 1984.

Japan had been posting a negative trade balance in chemicals, but in the first half of 1984 it managed to bring chemical imports into balance with exports. By 1985 Japanese chemical exports were running approximately $500 million ahead of imports.

In general 1984 was a good year for Japanese chemical makers, and industry leaders were optimistic about 1985. Thirty leading chemical makers increased their aggregate sales 5.1% in 1984 to $37,525,000,000. Their earnings on those sales rose 98.7% to $638 million. The optimism was evidenced in a survey by Japan's Ministry of International Trade and Industry (MITI), which showed that in 1985, 65 of Japan's petrochemical makers planned to boost their capital spending 20.3% to $700 million.

West German chemical sales in 1984 increased to $45 billion according to the Association of the German Chemical Industry. Over half that, $25 billion, was accounted for by exports. The country imported $14.8 billion, and so net exports were $10.2 billion.

During the first quarter of 1985 West Germany's sales totaled $12.2 billion. Despite an increase in chemical production of only 0.5%, the sales figure represented an increase of 5% over the fourth quarter of 1984. That was a respectable increase, but it was far below the 15% growth that was attained in the first quarter of 1984.

The West German chemical industry was traditionally export minded, but industry leaders in the nation began to realize that, although a large trade balance was desirable, a heavy reliance on exports was somewhat risky. Exports could drop off suddenly should importing countries build their own chemical plants. Furthermore, a number of factors, such as sudden currency changes or balance of payments problems, could affect the importing countries' ability to pay.

One West German strategy to cope with such possibilities was to build up chemical operations in other countries, particularly in the U.S. During the first three quarters of 1985 five West German chemical companies bought sizable operations in the U.S., one of which was worth $1 billion.

In France the restructured chemical industry became profitable in 1984, far sooner than had been expected. Chemical sales reached an estimated $27.4 billion, and the country posted a $3.4 billion favourable balance of trade in chemicals. Early in 1985 the industry was expecting the recovery to flatten out and to show only modest growth.

For the U.K. 1984 proved to be a good year. Sales increased 10% from 1983, to $24.9 billion, and record profits were made. Chemical production was 4.5% higher than in 1983, and the country had a $2.2 billion favourable balance of trade in chemicals.

The outlook for 1985 early in the year was for a slower rate of growth. Chemical sales were expected to increase 7.5% to $26.8 billion, according to an economist with the U.K. Chemical Industry Association. The general expectation was that chemical output during the year would rise 2%.

(DONALD P. BURKE)

ELECTRICAL

The low level of investment by electrical utilities during the last several years had caused many changes in the business activities of most firms in the electrical industry, but even so, some unexpectedly radical decisions were made in 1985. For example, Westinghouse Electric Corp. stopped making high-voltage circuit breakers. One of the pioneers in producing transmission switchgear at the highest voltages, Westinghouse scheduled the closing of its Trafford, Pa., plant by early 1986. The company announced that it would market a line of circuit breakers through a joint venture with Mitsubishi of Japan, but its domestically produced product line had become "extremely unprofitable." The reasons for this included the shrinking U.S. transmission equipment market, increased foreign competition, and the strong U.S. dollar.

Prior to the Westinghouse announcement General Electric Co. (GE) decided to donate its huge Project UHV (ultrahigh voltage) research facility at Lenox, Mass., to the Electric Power Research Institute, Inc., a body funded by the U.S. electric utilities. In 1978 a three-phase 1,500-kv alternating-current (ac) line had been erected as part of the project. But since the mid-1970s the utilities had grown at a lower rate than predicted, and this, coupled with right-of-way problems, caused UHV hopes to fade.

GE's corporate strategy was to be leaner and more agile. In 1984 it sold several businesses, including its domestic electrical appliances business to Black & Decker Mfg. Co. In its six core businesses (lighting, major appliances, motors, turbines, transportation equipment, and construction equipment), GE improved earnings over 1983–84 by 39%. Much of the $1,038,-000,000 spent by the firm on research and development in 1984 ($919 million in 1983) was devoted to GE's high-tech businesses, including industrial control and automation. GE's total earnings in 1984 were $2,280,000,000, a 13% increase from 1983; sales totaled $27,950,000,000, 4% above 1983.

Westinghouse was also restructuring its heavy electrical businesses. Prior to pulling out of circuit-breaker manufacturing, it resized its power transformer activities and sold its Sturtevant industrial and utility fans division. Sales in 1984 were $10,264,-000,000; operating profit, at 5.9% of sales, showed a 28% improvement over 1983. Net income totaled $449 million.

In October 1985 West Germany's car and truck manufacturer Daimler-Benz AG bought a controlling share in the country's second largest electrical company, AEG-Telefunken AG (AEG). Only three years earlier AEG had been saved from bankruptcy by a major rescue operation mounted by 24 West German banks. Its chief executive, Heinz Dürr, quickly slimmed down the company's loss-making consumer-goods division and steered AEG into the new technology sector—communications, electronics, and energy production by solar cells—a similar exercise to that mounted by GE and Westinghouse. In AEG's case this meant a turnaround from a DM 932 million loss in 1982 to a DM 100 million profit in 1984. It was this successful high-tech development that attracted Daimler.

The £1,500 million cash mountain built up by the U.K.'s General Electric Co. (GEC) provided £34 million needed to buy a major British shipyard involved in warships. About half the cost of a modern warship was related to its electrical and electronic equipment. GEC's pretax profits for the year ended March 31, 1985, rose by 8% over the previous year to £725 million; the turnover of £5,976,000,000 was an almost 8% increase over 1983–84. As with the two U.S. giants, GEC lost money on high-voltage switchgear.

Siemens AG of West Germany reported a 16% increase in sales for the year ended Sept. 30, 1984, to DM 45,819,000,000 and a 33% increase in net income to DM 1,066,000,000. One of the main reasons for the company's success was that 50% of its sales came from advanced products developed during the preceding five years. Another reason was the company's attention to the continuing education of its skilled and professional work force; in 1983–84 Siemens training programs cost the company DM 225 million.

The Swedish electrical manufacturer ASEA AB claimed in its 1984 annual report that it had become the world's largest manufacturer of industrial robots. During 1984 ASEA sold 1,500 robots and tripled its robot exports to Japan. ASEA also built up a worldwide reputation for high-voltage DC transmission equipment and early in 1985 won the order for the first high-voltage DC system in India; rated at 500 MW, it would link the country's northern and eastern 400-kv AC grids.

In Japan Toshiba Corp. recorded a 33% increase in sales of heavy electrical apparatus to 964.5 billion yen ($3,858,100,000). Sales of factory automation equipment and general-purpose industrial electrical apparatus rose because of an increase in domestic capital equipment expenditure.

(T. C. J. COGLE)

FURNITURE

Retail household furniture sales in the U.S. reached a record $23.4 billion in 1985, an increase of 4.2% over the previous year. Adjusted for inflation, however, the rate of growth was only 1.3%, the lowest in four years. Reasons for the slowdown were high interest rates in the first half of the year and poor economic conditions in some areas of the country. Housing starts and sales of existing homes are key factors in home furnishings sales, and the U.S. Department of Commerce reported a three-year low of 1.7 million starts in the first quarter of 1985. However, the outlook had improved by year's end.

Wholesale domestic wood furniture shipments in the U.S. totaled $6.8 billion in 1985, representing a real (adjusted for inflation) growth rate of 3.1% over 1984, according to the American Furniture Manufacturers Association. Upholstered furniture sales rose 4.6% to a total of $4,727,-000,000, while the smallest increase was shown by metal furniture—1%, to $2,392,-000,000.

U.S. manufacturers of household furniture, particularly wood bedroom and dining room furniture and occasional tables, lost ground to imports from the Far East and Europe as the strong U.S. dollar gave a competitive advantage to foreign manufacturers. Another factor was the aggressive marketing of furniture manufacturers from Taiwan, Singapore, and Hong Kong. The International Tariff Commission reported that furniture imports into the U.S., the world's largest home furnishings market, reached $2.5 billion in 1985, representing 10.6% of the U.S. market, at wholesale. The expected drop in the value of the U.S. dollar on international exchanges would increase the price of imports. It was not, however, expected to diminish the interest of European and Far Eastern furniture makers in the lucrative U.S. market, where they had gained a foothold during 1983–85.

One of the most significant long-term trends in the household furniture industry was consumer acceptance of Scandinavian designs, featuring contemporary styling in rosewood, teak, and birch. Despite the implication that most of the furniture was made in Sweden, Denmark, and Norway, much of the product was manufactured in the U.S. and Canada for merchandising through Scandinavian specialty stores. Another growth area was ready-to-assemble furniture, known in the trade as RTA. The product was sold as parts, both wood and metal, that could be assembled in the consumer's home. The advantages were that it

AP/WIDE WORLD

While the rest of the world marveled at the speed with which a liberalizing China adopted Western technology and products, one Chinese entrepreneur, a custom upholsterer, displayed a flair for innovative marketing by staging a parade of sofas and chairs to mark the new year.

was compact, was easy to ship, required reduced retail floor space, and was relatively inexpensive. RTA furniture had been popular in Europe for many years, and much of it was manufactured there. In 1985 the Ready to Assemble Furniture Manufacturers Association was formed in the U.S.

The upholstered furniture market in the U.S. and Canada was experiencing growth in "motion seating," not to be confused with the conventional recliner, which had been on the market for half a century. Motion seating combined a sofa with a recliner-like mechanism, known as an incliner, that permitted the seated person to adjust the back and footrest. The incliner unit was positioned at either end of the sofa.

Lacquered wood finishes, which had been popular since 1983, remained a staple in many wood furniture lines, but the trend appeared to be toward natural finishes. Oak remained the most favoured species. Poplar, a plentiful hardwood long used for interior parts such as rails and drawer sides, was finding increasing acceptance for exterior surfaces. Other woods in heavy use included rosewood, birds-eye maple, and elm burls. (ROBERT A. SPELMAN)

FURS

Fur fashions continued to increase in popularity in 1985, most noticeably in the Western industrialized nations. U.S. retailers recorded another banner year, the 14th consecutive year of sales increases. Trade estimates toward the end of 1985 put volume for the year at approximately $1.7 billion. One reason was the development of relatively inexpensive garment production in third world countries and other low-wage areas, bringing furs within reach of consumers of modest means, the majority of whom had never owned a fur before.

The important retail markets in Western Europe showed some improvement in 1985, although business in such centres as West Germany and Italy was still far below the levels of earlier years. An important reason was the high value of the U.S. dollar, the currency in which most furs are sold internationally. When the dollar began to recede around midyear, there was a noticeable resurgence in fur purchases by Europeans. Prices of pelts generally declined about 10% in 1985, partly because of the strong dollar but also as a result of slack demand from Europe and Japan. The latter had been growing rapidly as a fur market, reaching $1.2 billion in 1984, but an unseasonably warm winter caused many Japanese retailers to carry over heavy inventories the following year.

Although the U.S. was still the largest producer of fur garments in the world, its imports from other countries—principally the Far East—soared by about 40% in 1985 to more than $400 million. The main sources were South Korea, Hong Kong, and Canada. Hong Kong lost its duty-free status under the Generalized System of Preferences for less developed nations (as Korea had the year before), and its merchandise became dutiable at the rate of 6.9%.

World production of ranched mink rose to about 32 million pelts for the 1985–86 marketing season, compared with 30 million the previous season. Scandinavia accounted for over 13 million. In 1985 the

two principal U.S. ranching groups united in a single marketing association called American Legend—The Mink Source, with about 1,200 members.

Antifur groups made some gains in such countries as West Germany, Switzerland, Belgium, The Netherlands, and the U.K., where mink and fox farms were vandalized and huge outdoor billboards condemned the wearing of furs. In the U.S. antifur actions were mainly confined to legislative attempts to ban the use of steel leghold traps. (SANDY PARKER)

GAMES AND TOYS

There was a continuing decline in 1985 in world demand for video and electronic games and an increasing call for basic toys. Plush toys—especially teddy bears—dolls, and other traditional items returned to favour, and there was a rise in the shipment of board games. The previous year's success of "GoBots," produced by the Bandai Co. of Japan, and Hasbro Bradley's "Transformers"—robot figures that can be transformed into vehicles—had encouraged some U.S. and European manufacturers to make parallel items, while a number of import firms placed orders with factories in the Far East for similar products. Consequently, at the U.S. and European trade fairs at the beginning of 1985, there was an explosion in the availability of those toys.

The enormous popularity of Coleco Industries' "Cabbage Patch" dolls and Hasbro Bradley's "My Little Pony," both of which were launched in 1983, influenced other leading U.S. toymakers to develop their own characters. Lewis Galoob Toys, Inc., and Mattel Inc. both chose to produce new action toys for girls. Galoob introduced "Golden Girl and the Guardian of the Gemstones," a concept of fantasy-adventure figures and accessories, while Mattel produced "She-Ra," a sister for "He-Man" of the "Masters of the Universe" series. Coleco introduced a line of fantasy dolls called "Sectaurs," and L.J.N. Toys Ltd. decided to capitalize on the popularity of televised professional wrestling by making a series of action figures based on the wrestlers.

The penetration of Western markets by toys manufactured in the Far East continued to increase in 1985. Hong Kong strengthened its position as the world's

When Mattel Inc. invited its best customers—kids—to come up with designs for its popular "Masters of the Universe" toy line, Nathan Bitner of Naperville, Ill., and 44,000 others responded. Nathan's design, for a character he called "Fearless Photog," was one of four finalists in the competition.

WALTER NEAL/CHICAGO TRIBUNE

leading toy exporter, increasing its total in 1984 by 30%. The U.S. absorbed 58% of Hong Kong's total export figure of $1,447,-000,000. As of late 1985, there were 2,600 toy factories in Hong Kong, employing 56,000 workers. The toy and other industries were given stimulus by the signing in December 1984 of the Sino-British accord over the future of the crown colony's economy after it reverted to China in 1997. However, there was some speculation about the amount of manufacturing that would continue in Hong Kong. During the last five years labour costs had increased, and there was the tempting prospect of a vast amount of cheaper labour available in China. Some forecasters believed that international business agencies and design consultants would continue to operate in Hong Kong but that much labour-intensive production would move to China.

The subject of counterfeiting dominated the 11th annual meeting of the International Committee of Toy Industries, held at Windsor, England, in May and attended by representatives from eight national toy manufacturers' associations. U.S. manufacturers, who asked for the subject to be placed on the agenda, claimed to be the main victims of counterfeiting, and according to their representative the chief offending countries were Taiwan, South Korea, and Hong Kong. The Toy Manufacturers of America (TMA) decided to make 1985 a year of action against counterfeits. A declaration was to be written into exhibitors' contracts at the American International Toy Fair in New York City to the effect that immediate action would be taken against items found to be counterfeit. The Consumer Product Safety Commission (CPSC) was to be informed by the TMA of all counterfeit products; the CPSC had reported that 65% of calls it received on its hotline arose from counterfeit toys that failed to meet safety standards. At the Congress of the European Toy Institute, held in Edinburgh, Scotland, in June, the subject of counterfeiting was also discussed at length by delegates of European manufacturers. Their main complaint was against the activities of importers and retail buyers who took European-designed toys to the Far East to be copied.

A new Toy Safety Act became law in the U.S. at the end of 1984. The act amended the Federal Hazardous Substances Act and

gave the CPSC the authority to notify the public and immediately recall potentially hazardous toys. According to the TMA, the previous recall procedures used by the CPSC were too time-consuming.

Toys "R" Us, the giant U.S. toy retail chain, opened the first five of its European megastores in the U.K. in the autumn of 1985. In the U.S. the chain had 14% of the retail toy market, and its entry into the U.K. was viewed with understandable concern by independent toy retailers, whose share of this national market had declined from 35% in 1975 to 22% in 1984. Each of the five new stores occupied a 0.4-ha (one-acre) site and carried 19,000 product lines, a stock far in excess of the capability of the majority of specialist toy retailers in the U.K. In 1986 Toys "R" Us planned to open a number of megastores in West Germany.   (THEODORE V. THOMAS)

GEMSTONES

There was little change during 1985 as regards coloured stones, although argument persisted over whether heat treatment should be disclosed when coloured stones known to have been treated are sold. Closely linked with the question of colour enhancement was that of country of origin, which once meant just that but had become an indication of type of colour. The gem trade laboratories in general were not happy about being asked to state country of origin, preferring to certify qualities in a stone that could be proved. Lack of nomenclature standardization meant that no appraiser could base market value on previous designations of a particular stone insofar as colour was concerned. This applied particularly to coloured diamonds. In discussing the use of spectrophotometers to grade stones for colour, the point was made that the instrument does not see colour as the eye does.

In the U.S. the tight control exerted by the Internal Revenue Service over tax-shelter donations badly affected the once steady flow of gem donations to major collections, particularly that of the National Museum of Natural History at the Smithsonian Institution in Washington, D.C. Most blamed the tax abusers who wrote inflated appraisals during the gem investment boom years of the 1970s and early 1980s. Many dealers felt that legitimate ends were being defeated in too harsh a crackdown on gifts. Working groups, including dealers and museum officials, were trying to set effective standards to clear up this difficult situation, but no progress was reported during the year.

In the diamond world, Indian production threatened to undercut traditional sources, with stones offered to the U.S. at bargain prices. This could be a serious threat to the Israeli diamond industry in the market for good-quality stones. Demand in the U.S. was moving to better quality grades, and it was said that De Beers had encouraged Indian cutters to invest in higher quality equipment. The first Indian bourse, situated in Bombay, opened in February 1985, but as of midyear it had not yet been recognized by the World Federation of Diamond Bourses.

Diamond and gemstone production showed little change from previous years. The Aredor field in Guinea was producing 95% gem-quality diamonds, after some delays caused by boulders and clay deposits that hindered mining operations.
          (MICHAEL O'DONOGHUE)

GLASS

The recession in the major Western economies continued to affect most sections of the glass industry at the start of 1985 as a result of reduced demand for glass from such major sectors of the economy as building, automobile production, and food and drink packaging. Important glass manufacturing concerns in the U.S. (Thatcher Glass) and Belgium (Verlipack) went bankrupt during the year, and the Verrerie Ouvrière d'Albi in France was restructured in order to rescue the company after substantial losses in 1984. The problem of overcapacity remained, particularly in the flat-glass and container-glass sectors, but during the year demand started to pick up. Some sectors, like glass fibres, optical and special glasses, and parts of the domestic glassware market continued to grow at a high rate, particularly when associated with such developing technologies as telecommunications.

In the flat-glass industry the main current trends were the continued development of low-emissivity glass for heat insulation and solar control and the development of laminated glass for architectural use for security purposes. The major development in the container glass industry was the announcement of new research to develop stronger, lighter glass for packaging. International Partners in Glass Research (IPGR) was set up as a cooperative venture by six glassmakers and a manufacturer of glassmaking machinery (ACI International of Australia, Brockway Inc. of the U.S., Consumers Glass of Canada, Rockware Glass of the U.K., Wiegand Glas of West Germany, Yamamura of Japan, and Emhart Corp. of Switzerland) with the aim of developing a container glass ten times stronger and half the weight of that currently used. An initial budget of $5 million would support basic research at universities in several countries. In a parallel development Owens-Illinois Inc. donated $120,000 to the new Institute for Glass Science and Engineering at Alfred (N.Y.) University, also for work on developing stronger and lighter glass.

New work on glass production methods focused on reduction in energy consumption, the costliest element of production. Better control of furnace and process temperatures by microprocessors was now widespread; other new developments included a Japanese gas monofuel combustion-type glass crucible furnace incorporating a heat insulator that was resistant to very high temperatures and automatic regulation of furnace pressure. This enabled higher thermal efficiency to be achieved with a 50% reduction in fuel consumption. The French company Rhône-Poulenc developed a process called "Crisver" whereby a prepared liquid mix for lead crystal glass enabled producers of handmade crystal glass to produce glass of a consistent quality at a temperature 200° C lower than by traditional methods.

In the high-technology area of optical fibres, developments included a breakthrough in the ability to transmit large amounts of data over long distances by a new kind of monomode "dispersion shifted" glass fibre that allowed very simple lasers to be used. Plessey Research of the U.K. reported that this method enabled the equivalent of 16,000 simultaneous telephone calls per second to be transmitted without error over 107 km (66.4 mi). Developments in other special glasses included controlled release glasses for pest control, medicine and surgery, agrochemical, and materials protection uses; new glass capillary membranes for the separation of liquids; open-pored sintered glasses that operate like sponges for filtration purposes; and glass ceramics for astronomical telescopes.   (ALLEN F. BROBYN)

INSURANCE

Worldwide insurance premiums in 1985 continued above the $500 billion level of recent years. However, business was largely unprofitable in many insurance markets, as price increases and high interest earnings were more than offset by rapidly rising losses. Insurance capacity shrank as many insurers severely restricted their writing of business liability exposures, and some stopped insuring high-loss classes such as satellites and professional malpractice.

In the EC liability insurance costs were likely to rise as a result of directives requiring the addition of property damage liability to automobile insurance contracts. In addition, laws taking effect within the next three years would impose strict liability for defective products, under which the injured person would have to show only negligence rather than fault of the manufacturer. The World Bank announced the support of its 148 members for a new Multilateral Investment Guarantee Agency, which would provide war and political risks insurance for new private investments in less developed countries.

In the U.K. annual premiums of British insurance companies by 1985 were in excess of £11,000 million for general insurance lines and £14,000 million for long-term (principally life) business. Growth of 17 and 23%, respectively, in these areas was achieved, despite record crime and fire losses and the discontinuance of tax relief on life insurance premiums. Lloyd's of London, which operates on a three-year accounting basis, reported a 1982 global profit, including investment income, of £57 million. Marine, aviation, and automobile insurance showed profits, but large losses occurred in nonmarine risks, particularly in U.S. liability business. Notwithstanding unfavourable immediate prospects, individual underwriting memberships of Lloyd's rose to 26,000 by early 1985. Nearly half of the members added deposits to increase their underwriting capacity, and the Central Fund earmarked £60 million to provide for the liabilities of nearly 200 suspended members.

Four U.K. insurance company market associations merged at midyear into a new Association of British Insurers. Tariff rates set for some industrial fire insurance classes were discontinued. The government came under heavy criticism for proposing the elimination of earnings-related supplements to basic social security retirement pensions.

Assets of U.S. insurance companies reached a record $1 trillion during 1985, three-fourths of which was held by life and health insurers. According to the Life Insurance Marketing and Research Associ-

ation, new ordinary life insurance premiums rose to slightly less than $10 billion, a gain of 14%, compared with 21% the previous year. Approximately 40% of the new premiums in about 18 million new policies issued were from replacements of older contracts. Universal life policies, which combine renewable term insurance and flexible premiums with current earnings on a cash fund, exceeded expectations by reaching 43% of annualized premiums. Variable, adjustable, and current-assumption whole life contracts also remained popular. Insurers disagreed on how best to adapt traditional underwriting questions and other practices to cope with the spread of acquired immune deficiency syndrome (AIDS). (*See* HEALTH AND DISEASE.)

Higher prices and more restrictive policies characterized the U.S. property and liability insurance business in 1985. Although total premiums were up more than 15% to $68 billion for the first six months, underwriting losses were at a record $11.5 billion. Operating losses, including investment returns, were predicted at nearly $5 billion for 1985. These losses would exceed by 70% those of 1984, the first year that investment income failed to offset underwriting losses.

Liability insurance was a major source of these losses, especially in the areas of product liability and medical malpractice. Punitive damages, unique to the U.S. legal system, frequently added large amounts to liability payments. Many policy forms scheduled to be used after Jan. 1, 1986, would provide only "claims-made" coverage, eliminate or restrict other liability protection (such as liquor and pollution liability), and perhaps even require separate

limits for the costs of defense. More and more frequently, brokers and risk managers who could not find or could not afford traditional insurance coverages were considering retention or self-insurance plans. An example was bankers' blanket bonds, where high rates and a small market caused the American Bankers Association to consider forming a "captive" insurer to insure its members.

Expansion into financial services networks continued as Metropolitan Life purchased Century 21 Real Estate Corp. In health insurance, health maintenance organizations (HMOs) and preferred provider organizations (PPOs) increased competition in many urban markets. Despite the industry's problems, insurance stocks rose an average of 30% during the first half of 1985. Several large insurers raised additional capital through stock issues; Firemen's Fund raised more than $900 million in one of the largest initial public offerings ever made.   (DAVID L. BICKELHAUPT)

IRON AND STEEL

The improvement in world steel activity that began in late 1983 continued and broadened in 1984. Output for 1984 was about 710 million metric tons, which represented a gain of 7% over 1983 and 10% compared with the exceptionally low level in 1982. Moreover, this advance was experienced in all regions, including the large traditional non-Communist producing areas (Japan, the European Coal and Steel Community [ECSC], and the U.S.), whose share of the world total rose to 44% from 42% in 1983.

The welcome recovery in 1984 had to be seen in perspective, however. World output

in that year was no more than at the start of the decade, before the severe downturn of 1982, and was only marginally higher than in 1974. Thus an entire decade of growth anticipated before the first oil crisis had failed to materialize. On the other hand, not only did investment plans made by established producers in the earlier, more buoyant era come to fruition in due course, but many countries also began steel production or greatly expanded it during the decade. The latter development, however, was expected to exacerbate the problem of structural excess capacity with which the steel industry had been confronted in recent years.

By late 1984 the recovery in production had lost momentum, and output in 1985 was likely to be little changed or might indeed be lower. That was certainly expected to be the case with the U.S., where production in the first three quarters of 1985 was more than 8% less than during the corresponding period in 1984. This decline, together with the strength of the U.S. dollar, increased the pressure for protection of the U.S. market, which had been a persistent and increasingly critical factor on the world steel scene in recent years.

Recent U.S. steel import protective measures centred on the presidential decision of Sept. 18, 1984, on the import relief case brought by U.S. steel producer and steel labour union interests earlier in the year. The U.S. trade representative was charged by the president with reaching voluntary restraint arrangements with main supplying countries in order to reduce the total import share of the U.S. market from about 24% at that time to 18.5%. In subsequent months eight such arrangements were con-

Table IX. World Production of Crude Steel
In 000 metric tons

Country	1980	1981	1982	1983	1984	1985 Year to date	No. of months	Percent change 1985/84
World	716,210	707,660	644,870	663,200	710,320			
U.S.S.R.	147,930	148,520	147,150	152,510	155,000*	49,550	4	−4.5
Japan	111,400	101,680	99,550	97,170	105,580	79,320	9	+0.8
U.S.	101,460	109,590	67,640	76,760	84,500	60,000	9	−8.2
West Germany	43,840	41,610	35,880	35,730	39,390	30,710	9	+3.6
China	37,120	35,600	37,020	40,020	43,360	†		
Italy	26,500	24,780	24,010	21,670	24,030	17,820	9	−1.0
France	23,180	21,260	18,400	17,610	19,010	14,160	9	+0.7
Poland	19,490	15,720	14,790	16,240	16,300*	6,510	5	−7.0
Canada	15,900	14,810	11,870	12,830	14,720	10,530	9	−5.4
Brazil	15,310	13,230	13,000	14,660	18,390	15,030	9	+9.7
Czechoslovakia	14,930	15,270	14,990	15,020	15,160*	5,120	4	−1.2
Romania	13,180	13,030	13,060	12,590	13,750*	†		
Spain	12,640	12,900	13,150	12,730	13,490	10,350	9	+4.3
Belgium	12,420	12,380	9,990	10,160	11,300	8,020	9	−4.8
United Kingdom	11,280	15,570	13,710	14,990	15,200	11,870	9	+4.6
India	9,510	10,780	11,000	10,310	10,510*	8,160	9	+3.7
South Africa	9,070	9,010	8,200	7,000	7,710	6,170	9	+7.4
South Korea	8,560	10,750	11,760	11,920	13,030	10,010	9	+3.2
Australia	7,590	7,640	6,370	5,610	6,210	4,700	9	+1.2
East Germany	7,310	7,470	7,170	7,220	7,220*	3,230	5	+4.5
Mexico	7,160	7,660	7,060	6,920	7,480	5,250	9	−6.5
North Korea*	5,800	5,500	5,800	5,900	6,500*	†		
Netherlands, The	5,270	5,470	4,350	4,480	5,740	4,160	9	−2.9
Luxembourg	4,620	3,790	3,510	3,290	3,990	2,930	9	−0.5
Austria	4,620	4,660	4,260	4,410	4,870	3,490	9	−4.2
Sweden	4,240	3,770	3,900	4,210	4,710	3,500	9	+4.1
Hungary	3,770	3,650	3,700	3,620	3,700*	1,550	6	−6.4
Yugoslavia	3,630	3,980	3,840	4,140	4,220	3,420	9	+9.9
Taiwan	3,420	3,160	4,150	5,020	5,010	3,780	9	−3.8
Argentina	2,690	2,530	2,910	2,940	2,630	2,080	9	+6.8
Bulgaria	2,570	2,480	2,590	2,800	2,800*	1,410	6	+0.2
Turkey	2,540	2,430	2,840	3,800	4,300	3,510	9	+12.0
Finland	2,510	2,430	2,410	2,420	2,630	1,840	9	−5.2
Venezuela	1,980	2,030	2,280	2,320	2,750	2,330	9	+16.8
Iran	1,200*	1,200*	1,200*	1,200*	1,200*	†		
Switzerland	930	930	840	840	840	†		
Greece	870	910	930	870	880*	580	8	+3.6
Norway	860	850	780	900	880*	700	9	+6.8

*Estimated. †1985 figures not yet available.
Sources: International Iron and Steel Institute; United Nations.

Table X. World Production of Pig Iron
In 000 metric tons

Country	1980	1981	1982	1983	1984
World	506,480	495,570	450,320	453,510	490,480
U.S.S.R.	107,280	107,770	106,720	110,450	112,000*
Japan	87,040	80,050	77,660	72,940	80,400
U.S.	62,340	66,740	39,280	44,210	47,030
China	38,020	34,170	35,510	37,380	40,000
West Germany	33,870	31,880	27,620	26,600	29,910
France	18,680	16,960	14,720	13,500	14,730
Brazil	12,690	10,760	10,800	10,720	13,750
Italy	12,150	12,260	11,540	10,310	11,630
Poland	11,380	8,870	8,110	9,470	9,540*
Canada	10,890	9,740	8,000	8,570	9,640
Belgium	9,990	9,810	7,830	8,030	8,970
Czechoslovakia	9,820	9,900	9,530	9,450	9,480*
Romania	9,100	8,860	8,640	8,180	9,560*
India	8,510	9,470	9,670	9,160	9,460
South Africa	7,200	7,370	6,760	5,220	5,530
Australia	6,980	6,740	5,950	5,060	5,330
Spain	6,370	6,560	5,990	5,430	5,340
United Kingdom	6,260	9,470	8,330	9,480	9,500
South Korea	5,580	7,930	8,440	8,020	8,760
North Korea	5,400	5,000	5,250	5,300	5,750*
Netherlands, The	4,330	4,600	3,620	3,750	4,930
Mexico	3,640	3,770	3,590	3,540	3,870
Luxembourg	3,570	2,890	2,590	2,320	2,770
Austria	3,490	3,480	3,120	3,320	3,750
East Germany	2,450	2,420	2,140	2,210	2,200*
Yugoslavia	2,440	2,820	2,700	2,840	2,750
Turkey	2,440	2,820	2,700	2,840	2,750
Sweden	2,380	1,770	1,780	2,010	2,210
Hungary	2,210	2,210	2,200	2,060	2,100*
Finland	2,020	1,970	1,940	1,900	2,040
Taiwan	1,720	1,610	2,700	3,420	3,360
Bulgaria	1,540	1,520	1,560	1,640	1,640*
Argentina	1,040	920	1,020	910	900
Chile	650	600	450	540	590
Norway	620	570	480	570	550
Venezuela	500	420	210	170	330

*Estimated.
Source: International Iron and Steel Institute.

cluded with major supplying countries, including Japan, to run to October 1989. These arrangements were estimated potentially to involve some three million metric tons of finished steel imports into the U.S. The displacement of such a large tonnage would clearly have appreciable effects on other markets.

Treated somewhat apart from the above arrangement were imports to the U.S. from the ECSC. These had been subject, in the case of most general steel products, to the U.S.-ECSC General Steel Arrangement concluded in October 1982 to run to the end of 1985. In the early part of 1985 a parallel arrangement was reached on tubes and pipes, and in August a similar agreement was concluded on so-called consultation products, a range of steel products referred to in the October 1982 arrangement but not made subject to licensed quotas thereunder.

During autumn 1985 the U.S. and EC authorities were engaged in negotiations for the extension of the October 1982 arrangement to embrace also the "consultation products," stainless steel products currently subject to a range of separate unilateral U.S. import restraints, and semifinished steel. Agreement was reached in early December on a new arrangement to run to September 1989 covering most products except semis, on which the U.S. authorities announced unilateral restrictions.

In the EC the end of 1985 marked a watershed in the development of special measures to combat the long steel crisis. First, the Steel State Aids Code, defined in its existing form in August 1981, expired. Under its terms EC governments were permitted to make public funds available to steel companies, to an extent authorized by the European Commission, in return for capacity reductions to total 26.7 million metric tons of hot rolled products for the ECSC as a whole by the end of 1985 from a 1980 baseline. At a meeting of the ECSC Council of Ministers on Oct. 29,

1985, the terms by which state funds could be made available to steel firms for an additional three years were unanimously agreed upon. These were stringent: essentially for research and development and for environmental protection measures on the same basis as for other industries within the EC, and for certain direct costs involved in further plant closing. At the same meeting agreement was also reached on extension of the quota system for another two years to the end of 1987. This was to be on a modified basis, with certain products taken out of the system. More products were likely to be freed from quotas at the end of 1986.

The statutory minimum price system that had applied to a range of products since the beginning of 1984 was to be suspended from Jan. 1, 1986. The EC was expected to decide before the end of November 1985 on the 1986 regime of voluntary restraint arrangements for imports of steel into the ECSC from the principal supplying countries. The agreed-upon tonnages would almost certainly be increased to some extent. However, any long-term strengthening of the world steel market was rendered uncertain by a continuing excess of capacity.

(TREVOR J. MACDONALD)

MACHINERY AND MACHINE TOOLS

Worldwide machine-tool production was estimated to have totaled $20 billion in 1984. This was up slightly from $19.4 billion in 1983 but below the high of $26.5 billion reached in 1980. In 1984 Japan accounted for $4.5 billion of the total, while the Soviet Union ranked second with production estimated at nearly $3 billion. Third was West Germany with production of $2.8 billion, while the United States was fourth with $2.4 billion.

The U.S. total was down from the high of $5.1 billion in 1981 but up from the $2.1 billion of 1983. Orders for U.S.-built

machine tools in 1984, as contrasted to shipments, totaled $2.9 billion. This included $1.9 billion in orders for metal-cutting machines such as lathes, milling machines, and drilling machines and $1 billion for metal-forming machines such as brakes, presses, and shears. Total orders and exports of U.S.-built machine tools in the first half of 1985 remained at about the same levels as for the first half of 1984, but shipments were up about 10% and imports rose 48%.

Imports of machine tools to the U.S. during the first half of 1985 totaled $880 million and were supplied principally by Japan, West Germany, Taiwan, and the United Kingdom in that order. Imports from Japan in that period totaled $450 million, up 50% from the first half of 1984. Imports from West Germany during the first half of 1985 reached nearly $120 million, an increase of more than 40% over the first half of 1984. Imports from Taiwan rose over 60% from 1984 to $78 million. U.S. imports from the United Kingdom during the first half of 1985 rose about 33% from the prior year's level, to nearly $48 million.

Exports of U.S.-built machine tools during the first half of 1985 had a total value of approximately $200 million and were primarily to Canada, Mexico, the United Kingdom, Japan, Singapore, and China. Exports to Canada, exceeding $38 million, accounted for nearly 20% of the total. Exports to Mexico were 12% of the total, while the United Kingdom and Japan each accounted for 8%.

The technology of machine tools had advanced considerably during recent years with the advent of better metal-cutting materials, the use of less vibration-prone machine-tool structures designed by computers, the use of advanced servomechanisms to control the relative positions of tools and workpieces, and the development of techniques for efficient integration and common control of machine

Keeping ahead of the competition forced Chaparral Steel Co. to invest heavily in overhauling this minimill even though it was only ten years old. As a result Chaparral was able to produce steel in the U.S. with 22% less labour than its Japanese rivals.

tools, tool-changing mechanisms, material-handling systems, and workpiece inspection equipment. These advances in the design and technology of computers and factory communications systems allowed many machine tools to be combined into commonly controlled cells and systems, and these, in turn, allowed the concept of the unattended or nearly unattended manufacturing facility to become a reality.

(JOHN B. DEAM)

MICROELECTRONICS

The year 1985 was one of extremes for the microelectronics industry. Economically, it was one of the worst in the 40-year history of the industry. But from a technological standpoint the year was a ringing success.

After two years of tremendous growth—in 1984 United States semiconductor sales totaled $25.9 billion—1985 sales tumbled 25% to $19.5 billion.

Part of the slump was due to overordering of semiconductors by such customers as personal computer makers, who also saw the market for their products crash in 1985. Another reason for the poor results was the downward pressure on prices of such items as dynamic random-access memories (DRAMs) and erasable programmable read-only memories (EPROMs). Japanese companies were selling these memories at such low prices that three major U.S. semiconductor houses asked the International Trade Commission to levy a dumping tax on eight Japanese companies. (Dumping is the illegal selling of products below the cost of manufacturing them.)

The U.S. was not alone, however, in suffering from a frigid economic climate. In Europe growth was a minuscule 2%, and in Japan it was even less.

In regard to technological development, major strides were made during the year in both the memory and logic segments of the microelectronics industry. One-megabit (one million bits) dynamic RAMs were announced by both Japanese and U.S. companies; some even had samples to deliver. This led some analysts to believe that the life of the 256-kilobit (256,000-bit) DRAMs would be short. But the one-megabit RAMs presented their designers with testing problems that they had not encountered with memories of lower capacity. Until those problems were solved, mass production could not begin, and the 256-kilobit generation might after all have a long life.

Both U.S. and Japanese companies announced or were delivering small quantities of 256-kilobit static RAMs. Static RAMs differ from DRAMs in that they do not need to be continually refreshed (or recharged) in order to retain the data that they hold. Thus, if a battery is designed into a system with static RAMs, then the memories can keep the data even when the power is shut down.

A new kind of memory, a hierarchical RAM, was developed in 1985. It combined both dynamic and static features; the cells were dynamic, but the memory was addressed as though it were static.

The workhorse of microelectronics remained the microprocessor. During 1985 all of the major firms introduced 32-bit processors; such processors took instructions and processed data in chunks that were 32 characters (or bits) wide.

The 32-bit processors, coupled with the high-capacity memory chips, produced powerful but inexpensive desktop computer systems. Just ten years earlier, systems with comparable processing power cost millions of dollars and were so large and power hungry that they needed to be kept in special air-conditioned rooms.

A British firm introduced what it called a transputer. Essentially a system on a chip, the transputer consisted of a 32-bit microprocessor, four communications links, memory, and a memory interface on one chip. Unlike computers, which process instructions one at a time, the transputer executed a number of instructions simultaneously. (STEPHEN M. ZOLLO)

NUCLEAR INDUSTRY

The most commonly used type of nuclear reactor in the world was the pressurized light-water reactor (PWR), accounting for over half of all reactor types. The PWR enjoyed a significant improvement in average performance in 1984 as judged from figures for 1984 published during 1985. The average capacity factor (energy produced as a percentage of the maximum possible) for all PWRs in 1984 was 68.9%, compared with 61.9% for the previous year. The rise in average performance figures for the PWR had, with some minor variations, occurred steadily each year since 1979, and by 1985 average PWR performance exceeded that of other reactor types.

Performance figures for pressurized heavy-water reactors (PHWRs) for the year dropped considerably, to 62.1% in 1984, compared with 72.2% in 1983. The decline was due mainly to the shutdown for replacement of the pressure tubes in two of the reactors at Pickering, Ont. Boiling-water reactors (BWRs) had annual capacity factors of 64.1% in 1984, compared with 60.1% the previous year.

Two Canadian Candu PHWRs achieved the best individual annual performances of the 263 reactors worldwide (rated at 150 MW or more and excluding those in Soviet-bloc countries). They were followed by a Japanese PWR. Two Canadian PHWRs also headed the lifetime performance list, followed by a Swiss PWR.

The total operating nuclear power capacity in the world at the beginning of 1985, based on International Atomic Energy Agency (IAEA) figures for 1984, was 220,407 MW, and a further 175,729 MW of plant was under construction. Under a new agreement with the Soviet Union, IAEA inspectors, including those from Western countries, began inspection of Soviet PWR installations during the year. However, the inspection agreement did not cover the U.S.S.R.'s water-cooled graphite-moderated reactors, which produce high-quality plutonium, or that nation's fuel-fabrication facilities. Later in the year the Chinese delegation to the IAEA general conference pledged to place some of its civilian nuclear installations under IAEA safeguards "at an appropriate time."

Both the Soviet Union and China proposed operating a service to dispose of a nation's nuclear waste in return for hard cash. The Chinese included the offer in negotiations with West Germany as part of a possible reactor sale. Kraftwerk Union, the West German nuclear reactor vendor, signed a memorandum of understanding with the Chinese government on the possible supply of four 1,000-MW PWRs to China.

Negotiations were protracted as bids were reviewed for the first nuclear power projects of several nations. Egypt continued discussions with a number of vendors for its first PWR. Turkey made a novel proposition to the international nuclear industry for financing the Akkuyu project on its southern Mediterranean coast. The successful bidder would be asked to take a majority share in the nuclear station, to operate it, and to sell the electricity produced to the Turkish state electricity authority in competition with other power sources. The power station would be turned over to Turkey after 15 years. Two bidders remained under consideration when this plan was announced, Atomic Energy of

Canada Limited and Kraftwerk Union. The Canadian company was chosen for the final negotiations.

The international 1,200-MW Superphénix fast-breeder reactor project in France underwent a shaky start in its run up to power, suffering from vibration in some of the components in the liquid sodium cooling system. It achieved the initial sustained chain reaction toward the end of the year.

In the U.S., with the cancellation of the Clinch River fast-breeder project, the Department of Energy began letting development contracts for advanced breeder concepts. The department invested $14 million during the year in design work by General Electric Co. and Rockwell International Corp. for small fast-breeder reactors that could be assembled to suit the overall rating required.

The British government gave its support to a new nuclear fuel reprocessing plant at Dounreay in the north of Scotland. It was intended to service the British fast-breeder development program and to establish a European centre for the reprocessing of fast-breeder reactor fuel. The public inquiry into Britain's proposed first PWR project at Sizewell finally came to an end after more than two years. The inspector, Sir Frank Layfield, was expected to report his recommendations to the government early in 1986.

DWK, a West German reactor-fuel-cycle company, placed a letter of intent for the construction of a new irradiated fuel-reprocessing plant at Wackersdorf in Bavaria. A partial construction license was issued late in the year.

A number of independent studies investigating the possible effects of the most serious conceivable breach of containment after a nuclear power accident reported that the release of radioactive material into the environment would be much less than had been supposed in earlier studies on which modern safety standards were based. During the accident at the Three Mile Island nuclear plant in Pennsylvania in 1979, for example, the release of radioactive material to the outside environment was so small that no detectable health effects were ever expected to result from it. The reason for this was that the main contaminants tended either to be trapped inside the reactor or the surrounding structures by natural adhesion or to simply dissolve in water. Several other reports came to similar conclusions, including those by Idcor, Battelle, and Stone & Webster in the United States, the CEA in France, and the KfK Research Centre in West Germany.

At the Loss-of-Fluid-Test facility in Idaho, a reactor that was due to be decommissioned underwent a test in which the Three Mile Island accident was almost duplicated. After a simulated break in the primary coolant circuit, the reactor was left operating with no emergency cooling for some 30 minutes. Fuel began to melt, releasing fission products inside the reactor, and temperatures of over 4,000° C were reached. Emergency cooling supplies were then introduced, and the fuel began cooling within 15 seconds. Control rods and melted fuel slumped to the bottom of the reactor, as happened at Three Mile Island. The test was being used to verify computer models that had been developed

In addition to running a simulation of the 1979 Three Mile Island accident, the Loss-of-Fluid-Test facility in Idaho also completed a series of simulated cooling system accidents that would benefit nuclear reactor operations in ten nations.
UPI/BETTMANN NEWSPHOTOS

to predict releases from reactors under the most severe accident conditions.

Early in October, after several legal battles, appeals, court orders, and a ruling by the U.S. Supreme Court, the unharmed Unit 1 at Three Mile Island finally resumed operation. The Tennessee Valley Authority, one of North America's largest electricity utilities, applied a self-imposed shutdown of its nuclear plants because of inadequate record keeping relating to some aspects of safety procedures. The utility blamed this on poor management and shut down its nuclear plant while new management training was carried out.

Nuclear power had a clear cost advantage over coal in Western Europe, according to reports presented to the International Union of Electricity Producers (Unipede) and by the Organization for Economic Cooperation and Development's Nuclear Energy Agency. This advantage applied even if loadings of the nuclear plant were as low as 3,000 hours a year, and even if nuclear costs rose substantially. The Unipede report, compiled by an international team, found a wide variation in capital costs between the countries studied. In North America the west coasts of Canada and the U.S. still could obtain coal-fired electricity at prices lower than from nuclear power. In the U.S. this was due mainly to the increasing costs of nuclear power, brought about by a decade of growing project delays, high interest rates, and inflation.

In a review of energy development to the year 2000, the International Energy Agency forecast a "massive expansion" of nuclear power in each of the 21 member countries. Nuclear power generation was predicted by member governments to grow from the thermal equivalent of 156.8 million tons oil equivalent (mtoe) in 1983 to 460 mtoe by 2000, representing 25% of all fuels used for electricity generation.

(RICHARD A. KNOX)

PAINTS AND VARNISHES

Among Western countries the U.S. paint industry produced the best results in 1985. Volume was running 5.3% ahead of the previous (also successful) year, while value was ahead 13.2%. In Western Europe, by contrast, several countries reported volume losses. West Germany was 2% below the previous year, although value was up slightly. The French industry achieved a 5.7% advance in value from 0.1% less volume. The U.K. situation was relatively healthy, with gains of 1.8% by volume and 7.2% by value, but no European country matched the 7–8% volume growth achieved in Japan and China.

European paint makers were hit by the rising costs of raw materials as the chemical suppliers made determined efforts to widen their margins. Most materials were affected, but frequent increases in the price of titanium dioxide caused the greatest concern to companies using large amounts in their decorative paints. Overcapacity in the paint industry made it difficult for many companies to reflect these cost increases in their selling prices.

Two new leaders in the U.K. paint industry emerged during the year, Kalon and West Germany's BASF (Bayerische Anilin-und-Soda Fabrik). Kalon, a British group formerly known as Silver Paint and Lacquer Co., acquired Leyland Paints to become the third largest decorative paint manufacturer. BASF acquired Inmont U.K. as part of a deal with its U.S. parent, United Technologies. U.S. interest in the British paint industry was shown by PPG's acquisition of the automotive business of International Paint and Sherwin-Williams's approach to Ault and Wiborg.

Powder coatings continued to be the fastest growing sector of the coatings industry. U.S. sales were rising at some 10% per quarter and, more significantly, sales

of application equipment showed quarterly growth exceeding 30%. This boom was largely due to the fact that powder coatings involved no solvents and so were regarded as friendly to the environment. The largest European producer of thermosetting powders was West Germany with 16,317 metric tons in 1984. Next were Italy (12,900 tons), France (10,500), and the U.K. (8,300).

An area with bright prospects for development of paint manufacture seemed to be Southeast Asia. Indonesia was currently the biggest market, consuming about 110 million litres a year, followed by Malaysia (48 million l), Thailand (40 million l), and Singapore (34 million l).

(LIONEL BILEFIELD)

PHARMACEUTICALS

Manufacturers of brand-name prescription drugs in the U.S. made a last-ditch effort to stave off generic competitors during 1985, but a steady stream of Food and Drug Administration (FDA) approvals of Abbreviated New Drug Applications (ANDAs) for generic versions of some of the leading prescription drugs made the exercise rather futile. The primary spur to the approval of generic drugs was the Waxman-Hatch Act (more properly, the Drug Price Competition and Patent Term Restoration Act), signed into law in September 1984. This cleared the way for FDA approval of generic versions of post-1962-approved drugs in exchange for extending the patent on drugs whose viable patent life had been curtailed by the time-consuming FDA approval process.

The brand-name manufacturers appeared to accept the consequences of Waxman-Hatch until it became clear that some key companies would lose more to generic competition than they would gain from patent extensions. They then began a series of delaying tactics that included petitions to the FDA pointing out that conventional bioavailability comparisons might not be sufficient to determine the efficacy of generic versus brand-name drugs. Despite these maneuvers, generic versions of Inderal, Valium, Motrin, Diabenese, Darvon, Orinase, and a dozen or so other frequently prescribed drugs were approved and appeared to be receiving a warm welcome from hospitals and other institutions, senior citizens, and third-party payment plans.

There were some benefits during the year for brand-name manufacturers, namely, a higher rate of FDA approvals of new drugs and some indications that the process for extending patents was operating well. There also seemed to be sentiment in Congress for a proposed new law that would allow drug manufacturers to export nonapproved drugs overseas. This would enable brand-name manufacturers to compete more effectively in third world countries.

In Europe there were strong pressures to reduce drug costs under national health plans. The British government removed some 1,800 products from the Approved List that physicians use to prescribe under the National Health Service. As part of a plan to decrease the cost of social programs, the Italian government proposed to reduce drug spending by a third, and France already had imposed a similar plan designed to save $177 million a year in

"nonessential" drug payments. These measures encouraged the expansion of large European drug companies into the still healthy U.S. market, either by acquisition or by expanding their manufacturing facilities there.

India continued to experience shortages of some essential drugs as its government wrestled with a series of ongoing problems, stemming in part from attempts to reduce foreign ownership in multinational company branches operating there. The FDA counterpart in India, the Drug Controller of India Registration, exacerbated the problem by holding up approval of at least 35 drugs for many months because of legal challenges to its rule requiring that all new single-ingredient drugs be marketed under generic rather than brand names.

(DONALD A. DAVIS)

PLASTICS

In the plastics industry, overall growth—modest but real—in 1985 was of the same order as that experienced in 1984, and the downturn in the world business cycle that many expected did not occur. Competition was especially fierce in commodity plastics, and Western Europe continued to be the most critical area. Polyvinyl chloride (PVC) consumption, and consequently prices, rose during the year, giving a measure of relief to its hard-pressed suppliers, and polystyrene (PS) business stayed generally stable. The situation with low-density polyethylene (LDPE) was more turbulent. Early in 1985 a remarkable coincidence of ethylene plant failures in European locations ranging from Italy to Sweden created an unexpected shortage of LDPE. Prices weakened sharply later in the year, however, as normal supplies were resumed in a period of slack seasonal demand, exacerbated by some loss of exports.

The completion of large petrochemical and plastics plants in the Middle East (especially Saudi Arabia), based on cheap and abundant supplies of petroleum-associated gas that previously went to waste, had long been feared by manufacturers in less favoured areas. In 1985 the threat became a reality, so far almost entirely in the form of linear low-density polyethylene (LLDPE). The Organization for Economic Cooperation and Development estimated that exportable surpluses of ethylene derivatives such as LLDPE from the Middle East to the two most vulnerable areas, Europe and Japan, might amount to 3–3.5% of their total consumption by 1990, with the remainder going largely to less developed countries. This nevertheless represented a considerable tonnage of extra material in saturated markets. The first LLDPE that arrived in Europe helped to create downward pressure on LDPE prices as a whole because these two varieties of polyethylene were largely in competition.

This situation underlined the urgent need for further restructuring in the European industry, generally recognized since 1980 but never sufficiently implemented. A number of important intercompany deals were announced in the second half of 1985. Imperial Chemical Industries (ICI) of the U.K. and Enichem of Italy revealed that they were considering collaboration in the PVC field. The combined capacities of these two producers amounted to over 1.3 million metric tons a year, which,

even allowing for the shutdown of older plants, would make this the largest European PVC enterprise. Similarly, Borg-Warner Chemicals of the U.S. and CdF Chimie of France said they were planning to merge their European acrylonitrile-butadiene-styrene (ABS) plastics businesses. Hoechst of West Germany, having sold its PS facilities in the U.S. to Huntsman Chemical, discussed the disposal of its share in a joint PS manufacturing venture in The Netherlands to its partner, Shell. Also under discussion was the acquisition by Shell of an ICI LDPE plant in France.

Polypropylene (PP) and, to a lesser extent, high-density polyethylene (HDPE) continued to fare better than the other commodities. ABS also had a good year, largely because of further expansion in the automotive, telecommunications, electronics, and appliance fields. Manufacturers continued to seek high-priced specialty plastics that might profitably replace or supplement less attractive commodity business, and interest in the products of new chemistry intensified. For instance, liquid crystal polymers with self-reinforcing properties were shown for the first time in Europe by Celanese Corp. at the Interplas 85 exhibition. (ROBIN C. PENFOLD)

PRINTING

The personal computer brought change to printing production techniques. In typesetting, PCs were linked to sophisticated phototypesetting systems to merge word processing and type production. Quantel's Paintbox introduced television technology to colour-picture generation and brought

BRIAN R. WOLFF

One very popular new application for ABS plastics was in watches, such as these Swiss models that even have plastic rivets.

finer resolution to the video image. Advision in London linked advanced electronic colour page-composition systems to the video display unit (VDU) screen to allow a reproducer to display the outcome of electronic page generation via telephone link on the VDUs of clients in remote locations. Similarly, Vista colour editing systems linked print design offices in Hamburg, West Germany, with printers Roto-Smeets in The Netherlands.

R. R. Donnelley, the largest printing group in the U.S., created a worldwide satellite link to transmit pages of colour magazines via London to printing facilities in Singapore, Hong Kong, and Tokyo. *Time* magazine expanded its network allowing direct page transmission for printing in nine U.S. locations to include Hong Kong and other locations overseas. Taiwan's *United Daily News* set up satellite printing editions in Paris and San Francisco. Japan's *Asahi* transmitted pages to London, while another group sent colour reproductions from London to Saudi Arabia, where magazine pages compiled in Washington, D.C., were combined for printing.

Proofing of pages to check colour before platemaking went electronic. Dr.-Ing. Rudolf Hell in West Germany presented a fully electronic system that could double as an origination station. MacDonald Dettwiler in Canada worked with Scitex to develop an Instant Fire colour proofing station using electronic signals to proof on instant Polaroid material. Dainippon Printing in Japan introduced a colour preproofing system working onto thermal paper to provide low-cost, rapid proofing.

Integration of electronic colour pagemakeup systems with budget-priced outside systems, like DNP Micropage, offered publishers access to the large systems installed by their printers. In Australia the *Herald* started a project to electronically integrate full colour and text newspaper pages with a Crosfield Series 800 system in which automatic electronic masking allowed integration of colour and text components onto one film. Web offset speeds increased. Harris Graphics's M-1000B, Baker Perkins, and Mitsubishi offered printing of 50,000 copies an hour on 16-page presses.

In the bindery, complete robot automation of paper-handling operations began at Dainippon Printing, using Toshiba presses coupled to Tokyo Kikai Seisakusho signature-handling equipment. A Kolbus Systems bindery line was linked to the world's largest 3,200-mm (10-ft)-wide Miller-Nohab Bookomatic web offset press at Chuo Seihan in Japan to permit integrated manufacture of books from paper reel to bound copy. (W. PINCUS JASPERT)

RUBBER

Tire plant closings in the U.S. and reductions in the work forces of tire factories in Europe made headlines in the rubber industry in 1985. Severe overcapacity coupled with increased imports brought about most of the plant closings that had occurred in the U.S. since 1980. Firestone and B. F. Goodrich scheduled plant closings, and Armstrong threatened to shut one down.

Firestone, the world's third largest rubber company by sales, announced it was shutting down its Albany, Ga., tire facility and eliminating passenger- and truck-tire production at its Des Moines, Iowa, plant. Firestone had closed nine manufacturing facilities between 1978 and 1981. Goodrich, as part of a restructuring move, closed tire plants in Miami, Okla., and Oaks, Pa., and announced it was selling its tire service stores and would quit the markets for farm, heavy-duty-truck, and off-the-road tires. Armstrong said it would close its Hanford, Calif., radial passenger- and light-truck-tire manufacturing plant in 1986 if contract concessions could not be obtained from the United Rubber Workers Union. Contract language with the URW specified that a company must give six months' notice of its intent to close a facility. Tire capacity was also reduced in Europe, with Michelin cutting its U.K. work force by 28% and laying off 1,000 Italian workers.

Changes in ownership included Continental of West Germany's purchase of 75% of Semperit of Austria's tire subsidiary for $15.3 million and the leveraged buyouts of Dunlop Tire America and Uniroyal. The management of Dunlop America bought the company from BTR p.l.c. Uniroyal, faced with an unfriendly takeover attempt by corporate raider Carl Icahn, arranged a buyout by top management together with investment firms, making the eighth largest rubber company a privately held firm. In other transactions, Uniroyal sold its Malaysian natural rubber plantations to a local concern; Dow Chemical bought Upjohn Chemical's worldwide urethane business; and Stepan Chemical bought the polyurethane and polyol business of Reichhold Chemicals.

There was no relief in pricing in 1985 for the natural rubber producers, as they saw their product's price fall even lower than in 1984. The low prices forced more stockpile buying by the International Natural Rubber Organization's buffer stock manager. The buffer stock level surpassed the 300,000-metric-ton limit, forcing a crisis meeting of both producer and consumer nations that resulted in a 3% price cut. The situation left many of the producing nations wondering whether the INRO agreement was workable, and Malaysia, the largest natural rubber producer, asked for a suspension of the agreement to let the market find its own level. Later, however, Malaysia agreed to continue with the pact pending further study.

Rubber consumption in 1985 was running behind that of 1984 by a little more than 4%. Natural rubber consumption was increasing by 1.5%, and its share of the U.S. market was rising from 28.5 to 30.2%. Worldwide consumption increased by 2% for all rubber in 1984, with natural rubber consumption reaching 4,070,000 tons and synthetic accounting for 8,750,000 tons. Significant increases in 1984 were registered in the U.S. (+5.5%), Japan (+3.8%), and South Korea (+8%).

Styrene butadiene rubber (SBR) remained the most consumed of the synthetics because of its importance in tire manufacturing, but usage had declined steadily following the introduction of radial tires and the downsizing of automobiles by the major car manufacturers. SBR consumption in 1985 was running 6% behind the preceding year. Most of the other major synthetic rubbers—nitrile, polybutadiene, Butyl, poly-chloroprene, and polyisoprene—were also showing a decline in consumption. Ethylene-propylene rubber was the one major synthetic to post an increase (5.7%) in 1985, thanks to its popularity as a roofing material.

The U.S. was the leading consumer of both natural and synthetic rubber, followed by Japan, West Germany, and France. Malaysia was the top natural-rubber-producing country, accounting for 36% of world output. Indonesia accounted for 27.5%, followed by Thailand, China, India, and Sri Lanka.

The U.S. accounted for approximately 25% of the world's synthetic rubber production, followed by Japan, France, and West Germany. In rankings by sales, the leading rubber product companies in the world were Goodyear (U.S.), Michelin (France), Firestone (U.S.), Pirelli (Switzerland), B. F. Goodrich (U.S.), Bridgestone (Japan), GenCorp (U.S.), Uniroyal (U.S.), Dunlop Holdings (U.K.), Dunlop Olympic (Australia), Continental (West Germany), Gates (U.S.), Yokohama (Japan), and the Freudenberg Group (West Germany). Goodyear had 1984 sales of $10.2 billion, and Michelin's sales were just over $5 billion. (DONALD SMITH)

SHIPBUILDING

Gross overcapacity within the world shipbuilding industry continued to make survival difficult for shipyards. Although few yards were closed down, there was a vast reduction in the number of people employed in ship construction. With no recovery in shipbuilding demand in sight and the productivity level within existing yards constantly improving, there appeared to be little hope of reversing the decline in European shipbuilding unless shipbuilding capacity in the Far East was drastically reduced. For most of 1985 the world total of new orders for ships remained at the same low level as in the corresponding period of 1984. Only 14% of the new orders went to European shipyards, while Japan took 44% and South Korea 16%.

The Association of West European Shipbuilders pointed to the cheap credits offered by the Export-Import Bank of Japan that had attracted many orders, while South Korean yards had been accepting new orders at well under realistic prices. Although there were moves throughout the European Communities to make member governments reduce the level of subsidies to either shipbuilders or shipowners, it became clear that European governments were not in general prepared to see their industries driven out of the market. It appeared that subsidies to European yards would not be reduced until Japanese and South Korean shipyards quoted what the Europeans would consider to be fair prices.

At mid-1985 the tonnage of new ships on order was 47,749,261 tons deadweight (dw), compared with 58.5 million tons dw at the same time in 1984. By the autumn the figure had fallen again to 46,-990,304 tons dw. At midyear bulk carriers led the list of new tonnage with 444 vessels totaling 25,727,724 tons dw, followed by 284 tankers totaling 12,972,882 tons dw. Dry cargo ships (not bulk carriers) totaled 3,092,638 tons dw and container-ships 3,956,285 tons dw.

Japan continued to gain the bulk of the

Even the Hyundai shipyards in Ulsan, South Korea, considered among the world's most efficient, were forced into heavy layoffs by the slump in the market for new bottoms.

IAN STEEL

new orders at 19,449,570 tons dw (down from the 1984 figure of 26.3 million tons dw), followed by South Korea with 9,009,-188 tons dw (10 million tons dw in 1984); Brazil retained third place with 2,395,437 tons dw. There was a surprising rise in the amount of new tonnage won by shipyards in Taiwan, which secured 2,016,900 tons dw and went into fourth place, followed by China with just over 1.5 million tons dw. Poland took sixth place with 1,332,660 tons dw. Seventh and eighth were Yugoslavia with 980,846 tons dw and Spain with 845,300 tons dw. During the year several yards closed in Western European countries, particularly France and The Netherlands.

Orders for large and sophisticated cruise liners were again a feature of world shipbuilding activity, and by the end of the summer there were nine passenger liners on order totaling 314,000 gross registered tons (grt), with orders for at least three more to come. One of the largest orders, placed in July by Norway's Royal Caribbean Cruise Line, was for a 70,000-grt vessel costing some $170 million and with a capacity of 2,500 passengers. Earlier in the year the same line had ordered two 40,000-grt cruise liners at a total cost of $200 million; each of these ships would carry 990 passengers. Contessa Cruise Line placed an order for two 18,000-grt passenger vessels with Marine P. & E. Inc.—one of the very few orders for merchant ships to be won by a U.S. shipyard. The Soviet Union broke ground by ordering four 20,000-grt cruise liners from a Polish shipyard.

There were signs by midyear that prices for new building had bottomed out and were very slowly moving upward and that contracting activity was beginning to improve. Despite the prevailing low prices, however, shipowners were not tempted to order in any strength because the market outlook appeared to be uncertain and financing had become more difficult to obtain. One result of the uncertainty was a move by owners to delay delivery of ordered vessels or even to try to negotiate

an alteration in price because of a change in design. Shipyards strongly resisted such moves. (W. D. EWART)

TELECOMMUNICATIONS

In 1985 both telecommunications developers and users had a mixed year. The makers of the equipment that transmits voice and data around the world enjoyed some successes, such as the slow but continuing evolution of the International Telegraph and Telephone Consultative Committee's integrated services digital network (ISDN). And they enjoyed the advances in widebandwidth fibre-optics technology. Cellular telephony also continued to grow.

On the other hand, insurance firms balked at backing communications satellites that seemed to have more than their fair share of launch aborts, and local network technology was further saddled with a host of offerings that left buyers confused as to which system to purchase. Indeed, users continued to be confused by a variety of

new offerings for their every voice and data telecommunications need. These were not always dependable; for example, private branch exchange manufacturers went in and out of business as they attempted the complex job of simultaneously handling voice and data. Adding to the problems for all involved, as in the previous year, government and standards agencies had the most influence in determining who built what equipment and what services consumers would have from which organizations.

In the long run ISDN would replace the still mostly analog worldwide telecommunications network with a digital technology-based network that would provide voice, television, videotext, data, and a host of other telecommunications services to users in a home, office, and factory world that would be wired together. Necessary to the success of this idea was that users would control their ISDN interface and select the services they needed from a catalog of offerings. While some circuits were designed and some products were made available in 1985, the massive undertaking was expected to require additional years of development.

A bright spot on the local network scene was the rapid progress of the factory network standard known as manufacturing automation protocol (MAP). Unique in that it was a network standard promoted by users of communications and computer equipment rather than by equipment manufacturers, MAP was enjoying rapid development. One reason for the rapid pace was the economic strength of its main backers, such as General Motors Corp.

MAP was based on the International Standards Organization's work in defining how computers should communicate in both local and global networks. ISO's standards for software and hardware to allow easy communication enjoyed success in 1985. For example, several major communications and computer firms in the U.S. and Europe announced that their products would be ISO-compatible by late 1985 or 1986.

U.S. telecommunications users continued to suffer with AT&T as that firm endured

FRED PROUSER

Bell Telephone Co. of Pennsylvania began an experiment in Harrisburg involving telephones that display the phone numbers from which incoming calls originate, allowing subscribers to decide not to receive unwanted calls.

its second year as a deregulated activity. Continued layoffs plagued AT&T as it persisted in its attempts to enter the computer industry and strengthen its position in the telecommunications industry with the introduction of several new products. Also using its great strength in telecommunications, the firm made new local network and service offerings in such fields as teleconferencing and videotext. AT&T also continued to lead in the use of fibre-optic technology in both local and global networks, although Japanese firms were a close second if not equal. The goal of this work was to adapt the hair-thin glass fibres to ever more uses in transmitting telecommunications signals with minimal attenuation and, compared with any other technology, with a maximum number of different signals on one cable. Both the U.S. and Japan were also active in using new kinds of single-mode fibre that introduced less distortion to the signals being transmitted.

Fibre was so cost-effective that it could compete with satellites for transatlantic telecommunications coverage. And in 1985 the possibility of laying fibre cable under the ocean rather than launching communications satellites by rocket or space shuttle got a boost when several such satellites were lost, causing insurance carriers to raise their premium rates and thereby introducing a major new cost factor into satellite communications. Even the comparatively inexpensive Ariane rocket used in Europe for launches suffered failures and financial reverses.

Other worldwide telecommunications developments of interest in 1985 included the continuing debate over who should control the data that flow from country to country and continent to continent at ever increasing rates over satellite and telephone links. The Europeans, with their national boundaries separated by comparatively short distances, paid particular attention to this area, and legislation to maintain control continued to evolve. In Japan the government sought ways to bring that nation's AT&T counterpart, the giant Nippon Telegraph & Telephone, into the new deregulated environment.

(HARVEY J. HINDIN)

TEXTILES

A growing trend throughout the textile industries of industrialized countries was the appearance of numerous small organizations that, rather than manufacturing massive volumes of low-priced goods, sought to provide goods with a high added value and at prices that generated good profit margins. There were fewer very large factories employing perhaps several thousand operatives, and the organizations of this kind that did survive were concentrating on increasing automation, with the aim of achieving faster production and better quality with much less labour.

The new smaller concerns—often family owned—specialized in specific areas. In Britain, for example, one newly established company was producing very high quality fine worsteds, but it was using yarns from Japan because a competitive alternative was not available from other sources. In the cotton sheeting trade, another British company depended on Egyptian sources for its very fine count 100% cotton yarns.

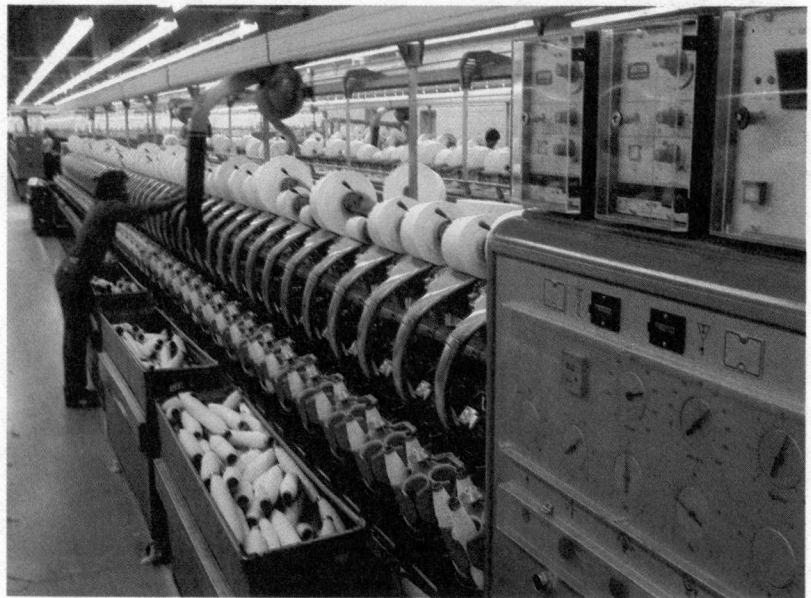

To cope with a growing flood of imports—which doubled between 1980 and 1984 and continued to grow—U.S. textile firms were investing heavily in technology.
NANCY PIERCE/U.S. NEWS & WORLD REPORT

There was also a major revival of the flax (linen) trade, with manufacturers selling linens to such markets as cruise liners, where price was of less importance than excellence. The so-called management buy-back or buyout was an effective method of making a small company out of a large one, reducing labour and overhead and enabling it to compete on more favourable terms. (PETER LENNOX-KERR)

Wool. World currency changes in 1985 were the dominant force in governing wool prices. Normal market forces were distorted, and floor prices were effectively raised or lowered for overseas buyers. In Australia, the leading producer of internationally traded wool, a strong currency coupled with a firmly maintained floor price led to an increase in the Australian Wool Corporation stockpile in the first half of the 1984–85 season, from over 1,144,000 bales in July 1984 to a peak of 1.6 million bales in January 1985. A subsequent rapid and substantial depreciation in the Australian dollar meant lower prices for major buying countries, causing a reduction in the stockpile to 936,000 bales in June 1985.

Extreme and erratic currency weakness in South Africa disrupted trading conditions there in the first half of the 1985–86 season. On the other hand, New Zealand's relatively strong currency, together with floor-price support, meant that its coarse crossbred wool was overpriced, and Wool Board stocks rose.

Despite currency-related problems, a reasonable long-term supply-demand balance was maintained. Finer merinos showed outstanding price strength in 1984–85 because of fashion demand and limited supply, but otherwise there were no market reasons sufficient to lift the price level substantially above floor prices. Consumption by the main wool-textile industries continued on an upward trend in 1984 but, despite a year-on-year increase of 1.5% in the first quarter of 1985, the U.K. Commonwealth Secretariat identified "a marked

slackening in the pace of the upturn" in manufacturing performance. World production of wool in the 1984–85 season was 1,668,000 metric tons clean, compared with 1,646,000 tons in 1983–84. The forecast for 1985–86 was 1,670,000 metric tons clean. (H. M. F. MALLETT)

Cotton. World cotton production in the 1984–85 season totaled nearly 84 million bales (a bale = 217.7 kg or 480 lb), compared with only 68 million bales in the previous growing season. China led with nearly 28 million bales, followed by the U.S. with 13 million and the U.S.S.R. with 12 million. Among other important growing countries, though with much lower production, were Egypt (1,791,000 bales) and The Sudan (860,000 bales), both noted for their excellent long-staple-fibre cottons.

New highly sophisticated, high-speed spinning processes were appearing in various parts of the world, and machine builders warned cotton growers that as a result there was likely to be a growing demand from textile manufacturers for finer cottons, and that, in anticipation of this, they should start now to breed new strains of cotton that would provide the necessary fineness. Man-made fibre producers were already offering exceedingly fine regenerated and synthetic fibres for blending with cotton, which were better suited for such processes as open-end spinning. If the cotton growers were to avail themselves of the advantages of providing the natural component for blending into such yarns, they would have to introduce superior cottons. However, the breeding of new strains of cotton would take time. Research establishments and breeding stations would have to pay attention to these probable future demands if cotton growers were not to suffer the fate of jute growers, who were decimated by the emergence of polypropylene for such uses as twines, carpet backings, and sackings. (PETER LENNOX-KERR)

Silk. During 1984–85 the silk industry was dominated by fluctuating exchange rates and the strength of the dollar. In

the spring of 1984 China decided to base its silk export prices on the dollar. At the time, this appeared logical, but as the dollar strengthened, the silk price was artificially inflated, causing strong buyer resistance. Considerable pressure was brought on the Chinese to revise this policy, and by the autumn Canton Fair they had succumbed, in some cases offering friendly rates and discounts and in others agreeing to sell in currencies other than the dollar. This revived demand during the winter of 1984–85.

Meanwhile, consumption in Western European countries held up well as the strong dollar enabled them to increase their exports of high-quality fabric and garments to the U.S. Because of fashion as well as U.S. customs regulations, demand for silk blended with other fibres such as wool continued, creating a shortage of silk tops, noils, and spun silk yarn. Prices soared, with the inevitable consequence that during the autumn stocks in the Far East grew and buyers held off, anticipating a fall in price. Only small reductions were forthcoming, however. Chinese silk fabrics containing silk waste also were in short supply. Prices rose but demand appeared to remain unsatisfied.

Japan continued to suffer decreasing demand, and steps were taken to reduce the mountain of government-held silk. Raw silk prices were reduced on Nov. 16, 1984, by 2,000 yen per kilogram, the first such step in 26 years. The quality of silk from Brazil improved, but its export sales were adversely affected by the strength of the dollar. Hong Kong began to obtain world recognition as an important silk market, consuming about as much raw silk as the Western European market.

During 1983 world production of raw silk totaled 54,551 metric tons, with China producing 28,169 tons and Japan 12,456 tons. Consumption was greatest in Japan, at 13,222 tons. Silk of Chinese origin accounted for 90% of the international silk trade.   (ANTHONY H. GADDUM)

Man-Made Fibres. Excess capacity in the man-made fibre industries of several countries was somewhat reduced in 1985, although few plants were working to capacity. As in other sectors of textile manufacture, fibre producers were concentrating on expensive specialities, and increasing numbers of modified fibres were appearing. In the U.S. and Japan there was a move toward an elastic form of polyester fibre. The U.S. effort was directed toward the use of this fibre in fabrics such as stretch denim, while in Japan the new polyesters—of which there were at least five—were being used for all manner of action wear.

The aerospace industry was laying down very strict flammability rules, and this was forcing the creation of "fire blocking" materials, often based on carbon fibres or mixes with aramids, glass, or even ceramic fibres. The objective was to enable a fire to be extinguished or at least retarded before it reached the foam fillings, which release toxic fumes when they burn. Weight for weight, aramid fibres were stronger than steel. Now some even stronger fibres based on polyethylene were being produced. Much of the initial research and development had been in The Netherlands, although the fibres were currently being

evaluated in the U.S. and Japan. These fibres had certain specific advantages, but compared with the aramids they had a much lower melting point. However, this would not hinder their use, for example, as plastic reinforcements or in marine applications such as ropes, cordage, and sailcloths.   (PETER LENNOX-KERR)

TOBACCO

World consumption of tobacco, taxed and denounced as never before, went on rising in 1985. Sales of cigarettes, the mode of tobacco intake preferred by more than 80% of the world's smokers, edged up to a record of about 4,835,000,000,000. Typical cigarettes became longer, more flavourful despite being mild, a little lower in tar content, and more glamorous in packaging imagery. U.S. and British blends were briskly ousting traditional black-tobacco formulas in France, Spain, and those less developed countries where people displayed their use of international brands as status symbols.

In 1985 some three million farmers grew 6,320,000,000 kg (13,904,000,000 lb) of leaf. That, once again, was more than the world needed, especially as surplus stocks from previous crops were already spilling out of warehouses in the U.S., Greece, and elsewhere. Accordingly, prices to farmers drifted down. They seemed set to decline further in 1986, under the lead of a bold plan to restructure the U.S. price-support program and regain for U.S. export tobacco some of the international markets lost to competitors such as Zimbabwe and Brazil.

Since world leaf prices depended on U.S. prices, poor countries could suffer from such a decline. Costs of production were given urgent, critical study in the unmechanized, labour-intensive third world, whose yields per hectare were half or less those of the most efficient producers, such as the U.S., Canada, Japan, and Italy. Less developed countries pointed out that inputs such as fertilizer and crop-protection chemicals often had to be imported at high international prices. The idea was gaining ground that the low productivity of the less developed countries resulted more from lack of know-how than from tobacco not being ideally suited to their soils and climates.

Meanwhile, a more spirited world economy lifted international cigarette trade slightly. Domestic markets for branded products in North America and Western Europe were flat, but economy and generic products, and the materials for making roll-your-own cigarettes, were doing well. Cigar sales remained depressed. Major manufacturers continued to invest their tobacco profits into diversified enterprises, most recently on a huge scale in the food industry and financial services.

(MICHAEL F. BARFORD)

TOURISM

According to World Tourism Organization (WTO) estimates, international travel and tourist volume in 1985 increased by 4% to a new record of 325 million arrivals. Dollar receipts were worth $105 billion, an increase of 4% over 1984. Although high unemployment in many countries acted as a brake on leisure and holiday travel, business travel boomed. The strength of the U.S. dollar early in the year did much to stimulate Americans' foreign

travel plans. Western European countries welcomed 15% more U.S. visitors than in 1984. These 6.6 million tourists spent a record of over $5 billion. But although U.S. resident travel grew by 9% in the first half of 1985, Americans cut back 6% on their travel plans for the second half of the year, partly in response to the later weakening of the dollar's international value.

Spain retained its preeminent position in world tourism. Although arrivals at 42.9 million were roughly equal to the 1984 total, visitors from abroad spent 4% more in dollar terms. A record eight million visitors traveled in Spain in August alone— more than some leading countries received in the entire year. Italian arrivals rose strongly, and U.S. arrivals improved by 16%. Spain also remained the premier destination for tour operators, though other countries experienced faster growth rates. British tourists, however, perhaps deterred by reports of crime and terrorism in tourist areas, stayed away from Spain until an unprecedentedly wet British summer prompted a flurry of late bookings.

Along with Tunisia and Yugoslavia, Greece reported a boom in inclusive tours, although the luxury hotels in Athens suffered a drop in bookings following U.S. State Department warnings about airport security after the TWA hostage crisis in June. London welcomed 8.8 million overseas visitors in 1985 as well as 15 million from Britain itself. The British Tourist Authority expected a 10% growth in arrivals and a 25% jump in receipts to reach £6,000 million for the year. But soaring hotel prices worried operators, and the British government moved to introduce simplified planning procedures to promote new accommodations and leisure projects. In Sweden 29-year-old tennis star Björn Borg signed a contract with the Swedish Tourist Board to market Sweden as a travel destination.

Table XI. Major Tourism Spenders and Earners in 1984

Major spenders	Expenditure
United States	$15,805,000
West Germany	13,910,000
United Kingdom	6,142,000
Japan	4,639,000
France	4,271,000
Canada	3,883,000
Netherlands, The	3,016,000
Austria	2,607,000*
Switzerland	2,288,000
Italy	2,098,000
Australia	1,970,000
Belgium/Luxembourg	1,955,000
Sweden	1,653,000
Norway	1,474,000
Denmark	1,220,000
Spain	840,000

Major earners	Receipts
United States	$11,426,000
Italy	8,595,000
Spain	7,760,000
France	7,598,000
United Kingdom	5,546,000
West Germany	5,479,000
Austria	5,029,000†
Switzerland	3,171,000
Canada	2,829,000
Belgium/Luxembourg	1,676,000
Netherlands, The	1,532,000
Greece	1,309,000
Denmark	1,292,000
Australia	1,228,000
Sweden	1,073,000
Yugoslavia	1,054,000
Portugal	959,000

*Includes international fare payments.
†Includes earnings from international fares.
Source: World Tourism Organization, 1985.

YES, OUR TRIP TO PARIS WAS LOVELY, AND WITH THE INCREDIBLY STRONG U.S. DOLLAR WE PICKED UP SOME BARGAINS YOU WON'T **BELIEVE!**...

STEVE SACK; REPRINTED WITH PERMISSION FROM THE MINNEAPOLIS STAR AND TRIBUNE

Portugal reported strong growth in tourism with 20% more West Germans and Britons and 26% more travelers from Spain. Italy's excellent summer weather helped that country enjoy a good season. Austria promoted Vienna as the "lively capital" and planned to act as host to the first World Cup ski race in 1986. Austria's traditional winter tourism remained highly successful, but a 12% drop in overnight stays had taken place between 1980 and 1984.

In Eastern Europe Hungary offered possibly the widest choice of international hotels in Budapest, where the Spring Festival was helping to lengthen the tourist season. Hungary's state tour operator handled 724,000 foreign visitors in 1985 alone. Israel's $300 per person travel tax seriously affected outgoing tourism in 1985, with a 30% drop in departures in the early part of the year. The tax was lowered to $100 in October.

China received more than 50,000 European tourists in 1985. With 89% hotel occupancy in 1984, Hong Kong expected its boom in visitors to run out of steam in late 1985 owing to tight capacity and a strong currency. Sri Lanka's dependence on leisure travel (88% of arrivals) explained the 17% drop in total arrivals by July in the face of continuing political unrest. In Japan a hotel boom was under way with 82 new hotels offering 20,300 rooms due to open between 1985 and 1987; the aim was to strengthen Japan's position as a convention destination.

Theme parks were a popular tourist attraction, and 400,000 visitors were expected to visit New Zealand's Heritage Park in the year following its formal opening by Prime Minister David Lange in December 1984. In Africa, Mauritius expected a 15% increase in arrivals from the 140,000 recorded in 1984. A new hotel and conference centre opened in Zimbabwe's capital, Harare, in October 1985. In the Caribbean, Cuba embarked on a five-year program intended to double tourist accommodations.

During the year there were moves to improve Europe's communications networks. Oct. 31, 1985, was the date fixed for submission of bids to build a "fixed link" between Britain and France. British Prime Minister Margaret Thatcher and French Pres. François Mitterrand affirmed their commitment to the project, but a decision on the form the project would take—a tunnel, a bridge, or a combination of these—would not be announced before 1986. European railways looked forward to an extension of the high-speed network of 250-km/h (155-mph) passenger trains. The French railways' Train à Grand Vitesse (TGV) Atlantic project was expected to cut journey times from Paris to the Spanish frontier to four hours by 1990.

(PETER SHACKLEFORD)

WOOD PRODUCTS

The world timber market in 1985 was largely dominated by exchange rates. European demand was well below supply, and softwood, hardwood, and sheet materials producers were able to provide most requirements on a short-term basis. In the U.S. and Canada demand was reasonably good. U.S. housing starts hovered around the 1.8 million rate, and the American Plywood Association predicted a rate of 1,850,000 by the end of the year. For most of the year there was debate as to whether Canadian softwood lumber imports into the U.S. should be restricted, but no decisions were reached. The U.S. accounted for about 10,000,000,000 bd-ft of Canadian production, wood that Canada would have difficulty selling elsewhere.

Lumber production in North America reached 57,704,000,000 bd-ft in 1984, and production capacity was not shrinking. Sales to Europe in 1985 were hampered by the strength of the dollar, as was trade in North Africa and the Middle East. Prices and volumes in Japan also fell, but they started to pick up again toward the fourth quarter.

Building activity in Europe was depressed all year, with the U.K. providing the most active market. Although French importers placed more Soviet wood than in 1984, the Soviets, like their Scandinavian counterparts, found it hard to sell in Europe. However, sales to Algeria and Egypt to some extent offset a drop of about 20% in sales to Europe as a whole. In spite of severe cold at the start of the year, which caused production cutbacks of about 15% in Sweden and Finland, mills' stocks there became unwieldy.

Short-term buying also prevailed on the hardwood market. Sales from the U.S. were badly hit by the exchange rate, and domestic consumption, although good, was not enough to maintain stability. Components manufacturers were struggling to compete with cheaper imports from Taiwan in particular. Hardwood producers in the Far East encountered depressed demand in virtually all of their world markets, and prices tumbled. Toward the end of the third quarter, demand in Europe improved to some extent, putting pressure on the Philippines and Brazil, where mills had cut back log buying and lumber production to counter falling prices. The International Tropical Timber Organization, linking almost 90 producers and consuming countries, was well supported in principle, but the logistics of setting it up were proving exceedingly complex, and headquarters had yet to be chosen.

The U.S. and Canada competed for a share of the European coniferous plywood market and were finding growing interest in this area in China. In Indonesia, by far the largest producer in the Far East, plywood production for 1985 was targeted at 4.1 million cu m (144.8 million cu ft), increasing to 4,640,000 cu m (163.9 million cu ft) in 1986. The Indonesian plywood producers' association envisaged a static market share in the U.S. and Europe, further leveling out in the Middle East, and growing sales to China and Japan. Exports in 1985 accounted for more than 80% of total production.

The decimation of the world's tropical rain forests came under attack from the Friends of the Earth (FoE), particularly in the U.K. There, the Timber Trade Federation was quick to join forces with the FoE to attain the same aim—the proper management of tropical forests around the world. Further research was carried out on acid rain, but a new school of thought, spearheaded by West Germany, was that the tree damage ascribed to acid rain was in fact due to an airborne virus.

(JEAN CLARK CAMERON KLOOS)

See also Agriculture and Food Supplies; Consumer Affairs; Economic Affairs; Energy; Information Processing and Information Systems; Labour-Management Relations; Mining and Metallurgy; Photography; Television and Radio; Transportation.

This article updates the *Macropædia* articles BEVERAGE PRODUCTION; ELECTRONICS; ENERGY CONVERSION; FORESTRY AND WOOD PRODUCTION; FURS, LEATHERS, AND HIDES; INDUSTRIAL GLASS AND CERAMICS; Chemical Process INDUSTRIES; Extraction and Processing INDUSTRIES; Manufacturing INDUSTRIES; Textile INDUSTRIES; INSURANCE; MARKETING AND MERCHANDISING; PRINTING, TYPOGRAPHY, AND PHOTOENGRAVING; TELECOMMUNICATIONS SYSTEMS; TOOLS.

Information Processing and Information Systems

Virtually without warning the computer business was rocked by a deep, prolonged slump in 1985. Manufacturers' inventories soared, resulting in the layoff of thousands of workers in all sectors of the business, from mainframes to microcomputers to semiconductors. Earnings of virtually every major vendor plunged, at times into the red, as even industry leader IBM Corp. struggled to avert its first earnings decline in four years. Nor did the immediate future seem very promising as corporate computer users, who purchased 80% of the output of the computer industry in the United States, began questioning whether the billions of dollars they had poured into computerized information systems over the years were really worth the investment. However, through the gloom of the year there were glimmers of promise on the technology front as breakthroughs in software and semiconductors pointed toward future generations of very powerful computers whose applications could be mastered by computer novices.

Business. The computer industry slump of 1985 had two major causes, one being a pronounced downturn in corporate capital spending and the other a situation in which too many computer vendors were chasing too few buyers of equipment. U.S. government figures showed that the overall growth in the computer industry crawled ahead at an annual rate of under 2% during the first six months of the year, compared with annual growth of 15% in 1984 and 25% in 1983. Industry studies throughout the year bore witness to a continuing erosion in the confidence of computer users in their own systems' capabilities. The conclusion reached in a study of 200 major banks worldwide by the accounting firm of Touche Ross & Co. was that many banks had invested heavily in high technology during the late 1970s and 1980s, but no bank had emerged with a competitive advantage as a result. An annual report conducted by the International Data Corp. on user spending on data processing showed a slowing of computer-related spending by major corporations for the second consecutive year. Even the federal government contributed some bad news, blaming long delays in the processing of income tax return checks on a modernization of the Internal Revenue Service computer system.

Hardest hit by the slump were the semiconductor companies, whose silicon chips formed the processing and storage hearts of all computers and related equipment. The Semiconductor Industry Association, to which most semiconductor makers belonged, labeled the downturn the worst in the history of the business. In the third quarter of 1985 alone, National Semiconductor Corp. lost $53 million as sales plummeted more than $100 million, compared with the same quarter a year earlier. Intel Corp. posted its first quarterly loss in several years, cut the pay of its 14,500 U.S. workers by 4 to 8%, laid off some 1,850 workers throughout the year, and furloughed remaining employees for various periods. The semiconductor factory of Motorola Inc. announced layoffs that were to exceed 1,200 workers by the year's end, and Advanced Micro Devices Inc., another semiconductor maker, issued its first unscheduled furloughs. Japan's production of semiconductors in 1985 also was likely to fall short of the preceding year's level for the first time in a decade.

Also hard hit were the minicomputer companies as the U.S. market for midsized systems turned particularly soft. Wang Laboratories Inc., which had enjoyed several con-

One particularly fruitful line of development in the burgeoning field of artificial intelligence was the creation of "expert" systems, by means of which computers were being applied to such difficult and diverse tasks as engineering controls, medical diagnosis, and (above) aircraft navigation.
BEN MARTIN/TIME MAGAZINE

secutive years of 30%-plus growth in both sales and profits, felt the sting of a $109 million quarterly loss during the second quarter of the year. The company trimmed its employment rolls by 5%, or 1,600 workers, and witnessed the departure of its president and chief operating officer and the return of founder An Wang as its de facto leader. Data General Corp. was hit with its first quarterly loss, $16 million, and first dismissal of workers, 7% of the total, or 1,300 in all. And AT&T, which just a year earlier had entered the computer market with a host of minicomputer offerings, announced plans to lay off 24,000 workers from its Information Systems group.

Mainframe makers, which had been immune from most downturns in the past, also fell victim to the slump. Even industry giant IBM saw its profits decline 15% through the first three quarters of the year, citing weak mainframe sales and even softer minicomputer sales as the reasons. Sperry Corp., Burroughs Corp., and Honeywell Inc. each posted declining profit figures, while Control Data Corp. canceled a $300 million bond offering at the last minute in the face of mounting losses in its computer unit that were expected to top $100 million by the year's end.

Microcomputer companies, those making home computers in particular, were also affected by the slump. Apple Computer Inc., second only to IBM in microcomputer sales, laid off 1,200 workers and completely overhauled its corporate structure, losing company founder Steven Jobs (see BIOGRAPHIES) in the process. Commodore International Ltd., which boasted the largest installed base of computers in the world, posted a staggering $124 million third-quarter loss and laid off 700 workers in the face of a projected $80 million loss in the fourth quarter.

One glimmer of hope came from IBM, which unveiled critical elements of its long-term strategy to sell communications products capable of linking dozens of computers and peripherals in a cohesive network called a token ring local area network. The product ignited activity in literally dozens of communications product companies that sought to piggyback new product offerings onto IBM's network, even though IBM's announcement dealt only with the networking of microcomputers. However, the company held out the promise of more comprehensive network products for minicomputers and mainframes.

Technology. A technology that attracted considerable attention was that of reduced instruction set computer (Risc) architectures. Computers designed using these architectures contained relatively complex instructions within

(continued on page 287)

The Homeless Computer

BY R. L. ASHENHURST

The Computer Moves In
*By the millions, it is beeping its way
into offices, schools and homes*

WILL SOMEONE PLEASE TELL ME, the bright red advertisement asks in mock irritation, WHAT A PERSONAL COMPUTER CAN DO? The ad provides not merely an answer, but 100 of them. A personal computer, it says, can send letters at the speed of light, diagnose a sick poodle, custom-tailor an insurance program in minutes, test recipes for beer. Testimonials abound. . . .
Time, Jan. 3, 1983, cover story
"Machine of the Year"*

The Computer Revolution can be dated from 1946, when the first electronic computer, the ENIAC, was completed. The growth of the computer industry since then is a remarkable phenomenon. The Microcomputer Revolution, a sort of "revolution within a revolution," essentially dates from 1975, when the Altair personal computer was introduced by the MITS company.

The size and price of that original personal computer (PC) made it possible for many people to envision having one in the home. Both size and price have diminished considerably since 1975, and the PC is now an established part of the information processing scene. Its role in "everyday life," however, remains a bit ambiguous.

It seems best to think of the "personal" aspect of a PC as meaning that one controls the machine on a personal level, whether in a business, professional, recreational, or other context, rather than as connoting the usual "personal versus business" dichotomy. Personal computers can in principle be used by a variety of people for many different purposes: by executives to do quick planning without recourse to their corporate data-processing departments; by managers of athletic teams to support playing-field decisions; by independent brokers to keep track of their clients, their portfolios, or both; by office workers to allow them to do a certain amount of their work at home; and by family members to play games and keep track of their Christmas lists and their household accounts.

The PC Marketplace. As anyone who has dabbled in computer stocks in the 1980s knows, a great many companies whose focus is the personal computer industry have sprouted, bloomed, and in some cases died, or at least withered, during the first years of the decade. In trying to analyze the computer industry, however, one should distinguish between the hardware and the software marketplaces; this distinction is ignored at one's peril. Some hardware companies started literally in a garage, but today it takes a substantial manufacturing and marketing setup for such a firm to be competitive. Software development can still be entrusted to the "superkid" working away back in the hills, but there, too, effective marketing is necessary. Liberal doses of venture capital are appropriate in either case.

When buying hardware, one must think not only about its compatibility (with various peripheral devices and software) but also about whether the particular model or brand contemplated has a reasonable chance for survival, and thus will be supported by service facilities and software developers. Computers designed by one company to be functionally indistinguishable from those of another company are called "clones." Computers that belong to discontinued product lines, perhaps of defunct vendors, are called "orphans."

The compatibility problem also confronts the consumer who is acquiring software, but it pales beside the problem of determining, from among a bewildering number of possibilities, which software program is the best for the envisioned application.

Computer Literacy. With the proliferation of computers there has developed the notion that they should be worked into the educational process at all levels—primary, secondary, college, and graduate.

From the beginning there has been confusion as to the best way to proceed and even as to what exactly is to be the subject of instruction. On the one hand, computers can be used as tools in the learning process and adapted to any subject matter whatever; on the other hand, one can learn about computers themselves and how to use them. The former use often is described as computer-assisted instruction. The latter must be considered on several levels, depending on the intended objective. The minimal objective, to impart "what every citizen should know" about computers, has come to be known as computer literacy, although the implied analogy to learning the rudiments of reading and writing becomes less appropriate as the subject unfolds.

Courses designed to impart computer literacy have been characterized (not always kindly) by the term "computer appreciation." The usual course tends to contain a little technical information (components of a computer, etc.),

a little elementary programming (the computer language BASIC was developed with just this idea in mind), and a little about the wonderful world of applications (existing and potential). Missing is much of a sense of the complexity of modern computer configurations of hardware/software and, consequently, of the complexity involved in developing "real" applications on them. Also not included in such courses is the revelation that, in a commercial or scientific setting, the end users and the system developers are two different sets of people, a fact that is largely responsible for many problems that arise.

Computer Competency. It is most useful to approach the subject of education about computers, and learning to deal with computers generally, as problems in achieving computer competency. Sidestepping the question of how college and graduate-school students should be prepared for the use of computers in business or a profession, and how grammar- and high-school students should be prepared to deal with computers in the workplace, one can instead look at the question of what a person needs to know to make reasonable use of a PC in the home.

Competition in the marketplace has resulted in considerable emphasis on the supposed simplicity of use of a PC. The popular term for such simplicity is "user-friendly." This can mean a variety of things, such as responses by computer with messages in English instead of in cryptic code and the inclusion of a great amount of "canned software" (already programmed applications), which allows a person to use a computer without knowing how to program. Much of this software has been written to ensure compatibility; that is, so that program X will run on both computers Y and Z, and on others as well. This requires the user to "tell" the software about the hardware on which it is going to operate.

Adapting a variety of packages to one's PC therefore requires remembering a lot of seemingly nit-picking rules of procedure, which must be brought into play whenever one is starting up or switching from one application to another. There is also the matter of files, remembering on which "diskette" one has stored this or that set of data. All of this, of course, takes place after the initial task of selecting the software that one will buy from among the aforementioned bewildering array of possibilities.

The effect of these complexities is to make the "casual" user of a home computer just that. After such an owner fiddles around with the PC for awhile, setting up a spreadsheet or two and seeing what there is in the games department, the computer often is left to sit in the corner until its owner can get around to working up something really serious. This results in a "homeless" computer. On the other hand, the person (the writer, the broker) who acquires a PC for one main purpose quickly finds that "logging in" becomes second nature. He or she soon is using the computer regularly.

Computer manufacturers are somewhat aware of this situation, and they have responded by trying to combine several different functions in one user-friendly package. However, these new "integrated" products (with such names as Symphony and Framework) have been somewhat slow to catch on. Evidently there must be a further period of accommodation before the occasional user feels sufficiently at home with the PC to set up housekeeping.

Robert L. Ashenhurst, a professor in the Graduate School of Business at the University of Chicago, is the author of many articles and research papers on computers and information systems.

(continued from page 285)

them relative to conventional computers, which often had many complex subroutines built into them. This simpler design characteristic of the Risc architectures made it possible for computers to execute certain applications much more quickly and efficiently than could conventional machines, which had to deal with more intricate architectures to execute programming instructions. Such new firms as Pyramid Technology Corp. and Ridge Computers unveiled computers based on Risc concepts. But the biggest boost for the concept came from Hewlett-Packard Co., which announced that it would base its future-generation computers around Risc architectures. Yet for all its promise, Risc architecture appeared destined to take a back seat to future computer designs built upon standard microprocessors, or single-chip computers, which, when stacked one atop another, promised quantum leaps in computing power at dramatically reduced prices.

One of the biggest breakthroughs in microprocessor design came from Intel Corp., which announced its 80386 microprocessor chip. Intel's 8086, 8088, and 80286-series microprocessors powered the entire line of microcomputers from IBM, which owned 20% of Intel. Breaking performance barriers, the 80386 32-bit chip could process three million to four million instructions per second. Moreover, the chip offered system developers, such as IBM and the makers of IBM-compatible computers, the ability to support multiple users performing separate tasks with one microcomputer, a performance domain reserved in the past for minicomputers and mainframes. The chip also allowed system developers to build machines that would run the thousands of programs already designed for the existing line of IBM and IBM-compatible microcomputers, only much faster. Introduction of the chip placed Intel in heated competition with Motorola and National Semiconductor, both of which had previously introduced high-speed, 32-bit microprocessors.

Amdahl Corp. enlarged its family of so-called supercomputers, machines designed almost solely for mathematics-intensive applications. Amdahl's supercomputer additions, produced by Japan's Fujitsu Ltd., which owned controlling interest in Amdahl, included the model 1400, capable of performing an astounding 1,000,000,000 arithmetic operations per second. IBM also entered the supercomputer arena with its first so-called vector processing machine, although its entry was not nearly as powerful as Amdahl's or those of industry leader Cray Research, Inc.

In the market for home computers, the spotlight turned to two veterans of the home computer wars, Commodore International Ltd. and Atari Corp., owned and headed by former Commodore chief executive Jack Tramiel. Both companies began shipping new and technologically advanced microcomputers designed for both home and business use. Commodore's Amiga, priced at about $1,200, showcased features never before seen on a computer of that price, including advanced graphics capabilities based on a separate microprocessor designed to manage these graphics on the screen so as not to overtax the machine's basic microprocessor. However, early sales of the machine, greeted by industry watchers as a truly innovative and unique computer, were slowed by the reluctance of software developers to write programs for it. Atari's machine, the 520-ST, began arriving in stores in midsummer with very little software to run on it. Nonetheless, the machine, priced at only $700, had many features of computers costing twice as much and more.

In software, advances in artificial intelligence began to move that concept out of the laboratory and into main-

stream data processing environments. Ansa Software, Inc., a California-based company, unveiled its Paradox data base management system, which offered microcomputer users the ability to query vast data bases and extract complex data with relatively simple English language commands.

(WILLIAM E. LABERIS)

Hitachi Ltd. announced in July that it would join with the Chinese government to develop Chinese-language computer software that would run on Hitachi's 16-bit personal computer, the B16/EX. The Tokyo firm planned to export 30,000 units of the PC to China in two years to July 1987. Ascii Corp., a Tokyo software developer, unveiled in May an enhanced version of the MSX software, an international unified standard for personal computers developed in 1983 by Ascii and its partner Microsoft Corp. of the U.S. Sony, Matsushita, and 13 other Japanese concerns were marketing MSX-based personal computers.

Bravice International Inc., a software firm in Tokyo, developed a Japanese-to-English machine translation system based on a personal computer. The software sold in Japan for less than one million yen. Oki Electric Industry Co. announced the development of a Japanese-to-English translation system based on a workstation. Oki planned to start selling the system in early 1986.

NEC Corp. won three orders totaling 12 billion yen for its supercomputer, the SX-2, featuring a processing speed of 1,400,000,000 floating operations per second. Nippon Telegraph and Telephone Corp., which became a private firm on April 1, announced that it would purchase a Cray XMPI supercomputer. (YASUSHI YUGE)

This article updates the *Macropædia* article INFORMATION PROCESSING AND INFORMATION SYSTEMS.

Labour-Management Relations

In 1985 few of the industrialized market economies were without massive, or at least high, unemployment. While modest economic growth was achieved generally, in most of those countries somewhat austere economic policies continued to be judged necessary. The feeling grew, in Europe particularly, that lack of competitiveness owed much to rigidities in both industrial structure and the labour market. Comparison between economic and employment performance in the U.S. and Japan and in Europe reinforced the feeling that in Europe payroll taxes and constraints relating to employment, working conditions, and working practices had made many industries uncompetitive. Hence, interest grew in ways to increase labour market flexibility without sacrificing social benefits.

One of the most interesting developments in the move toward greater flexibility was a change in attitudes toward working time. From the Industrial Revolution onward, standard industrial practice, often reinforced by legislation, had been based on fairly rigid notions of the workweek. The idea of individual flexibility of working hours (within controlled limits) gained ground in the 1970s, but there was no radical change in practice. Later, reductions in weekly working time were undertaken in some countries with a view to creating jobs, but the results were disappointing. In 1985 the emphasis—notably in West Germany, Belgium, The Netherlands, and France—was on accompanying reductions with an easing of legislative and collectively bargained constraints on the arrangement of hours. The objective was to increase plant operating time in order to pay for shorter time for workers, thereby achieving higher

efficiency as well as increasing the number of jobs available.

Since the late 1940s most of the world's national trade union bodies had been associated with one or another of the three international trade-union groupings—in the centrally planned economies the (Communist) World Federation of Trade Unions (WFTU), and in the market economies the International Confederation of Free Trade Unions (ICFTU) or the smaller World Confederation of Labour (WCL). There was little cooperation between the Communist and non-Communist bodies at any level, and the Communist organizations had few affiliates in the market economies. The long-standing balance was disturbed in September 1985 when the British National Union of Mineworkers (NUM) joined with the Communist mining unions (acting as a group), the small Australian mineworkers' union, and some left-wing unions from third world countries to form a new International Mineworkers Organization, with headquarters in Paris and the NUM's Arthur Scargill as president.

United Kingdom. The long-running strike in the coal mines gradually crumbled until more than half of the nation's miners were working. The NUM called off the strike, without any last-minute attempt to achieve an agreement, and work was resumed on March 5, almost a year after the stoppage began. Miners in some areas where dissatisfaction with the way the strike had been called was particularly great decided to break away from the NUM. In October miners in Nottinghamshire and South Derbyshire, with some Durham miners, voted to create the Union of Democratic Mineworkers, which gained recognition from the National Coal Board and the government-appointed certification officer for trade unions. The NUM, meanwhile, at a national delegate conference in July, had strengthened the powers of its executive body, thus further antagonizing the dissidents.

A dispute that dragged on throughout the year concerned teachers' pay. Feelings ran high among the teachers about the erosion, over several years, of the levels of their real pay. The employers, however, were in no position to find the money to meet the claim, and the government remained generally unsympathetic, though it did agree to contribute an extra £1,250 million for restructuring teachers' salaries, with the proviso that the teachers should agree to a modernized redefinition of their work. The teachers' unions refused to accept a coupling of pay and responsibilities and rejected the pay offers that were made as inadequate. In support of their claim, the teachers waged a campaign that included selective strikes and refusal to help with school meals, cover for absent colleagues, or undertake school activities outside basic school hours.

The provisions of the Trade Union Act 1984 requiring a ballot to be held before a strike if legal immunity was to be retained were tested on numerous occasions and proved more successful than expected. Unions became increasingly hesitant about calling a strike without a ballot.

United States and Canada. Collective bargaining in the U.S. continued to reflect the competitive pressures on employers to increase efficiency. In numerous cases employers negotiated concessions from their workers. Two-tier arrangements (the hiring of new employees on less generous terms than those for existing employees) were the source of several disputes. In general, however, the volume of strikes continued to decline. In February the AFL-CIO approved a statesmanlike report entitled *The Changing Situation of Workers and Their Unions*. Labour-management cooperation generally was much in the news during the year, assisted by a major Department of Labor-sponsored program.

The United Auto Workers of Canada achieved independent status in March, and six months later the union led in demanding substantial gains in a new contract with Chrysler, which had won concessions from labour during the automaker's financial crisis of 1979–82.
CANAPRESS

The United Auto Workers (UAW) union entered into an agreement with General Motors setting out radically new terms of employment to be adopted in GM's plant for its new Saturn model, scheduled to become operative in the late 1980s with an expected labour force of 6,000. As had been expected, the 120,000-strong Canadian branch of the UAW seceded from the Detroit-based union to form an autonomous Canadian autoworkers' union.

In March U.S. Secretary of Labor Raymond Donovan, who faced legal charges arising from a contract made by his construction company before he took office, resigned from the Cabinet. He was succeeded in May by William E. Brock.

Continental Western Europe. In France, although the 1984 negotiations on labour market flexibility were not resumed, flexibility was very much in the air, especially in relation to working time. New legislation established a framework for voluntary agreements under which retraining of laid-off workers could be assisted by the National Employment Fund. It also relaxed constraints on part-time work, fixed-term contracts, and temporary layoffs.

The climate of French industrial relations remained generally calm, although the Communist-inclined Confédération Générale du Travail (CGT) made a sustained effort to stimulate industrial action. In June, after workers had been evicted from an 18-month occupation of the Swedish-owned SKF ball-bearing factory at Ivry, near Paris, a CGT commando team fought an unsuccessful battle with police in an effort to reoccupy the premises. In October the CGT failed to bring about a major stoppage at the Renault car firm. A "day of action" called by the CGT for October 24 was not widely followed.

In West Germany legislation effective May 1 sought to create new jobs by making the labour market more flexible. On September 6 Chancellor Helmut Kohl met union and employer leaders together—the first such tripartite talks since 1977—to discuss the employment situation. It was agreed to carry out studies concerning training, the long-term unemployed, and overtime work in the public sector. In Italy the long-running saga of the wage indexation system, or *scala mobile,* continued. A motion sponsored by the Italian Communist Party to annul a 1984 decree limiting the operation of the system went to a national referendum, after a decision by the Constitutional Court.

Annulment would have been damaging to the government's counterinflation policy, but in the event 54.3% of the votes were cast against the motion.

In Belgium new legislation authorized the lifting of restrictions on working time provided the limits on annual hours of work were observed and the arrangement was covered by a collective agreement, extended the period of probationary employment, and relaxed obligations to establish health and safety committees. Denmark's highly centralized collective bargaining system broke down in March; at the peak of the disturbances, some 300,000 workers were on strike or locked out. The government rushed an incomes policy measure through the Folketing (parliament) legally blocking further strikes and lockouts. The imposed settlement provided for modest wage increases over the next two years and a reduction of the workweek by one hour at the end of 1987. In Sweden a central framework agreement for manual workers was reached in February, but a dispute in the public sector was resolved only after personal intervention by Prime Minister Olof Palme.

Israel. The 1984 wage freeze was superseded by a comprehensive wage and price accord in January. Economic difficulties continued, however, and on July 1 Prime Minister Shimon Peres announced a stern austerity program, to which the central trade union, Histadrut, responded by calling a 24-hour general strike. Under a tripartite agreement reached on July 16, the program was softened somewhat. In October the Knesset (parliament) agreed to continue several of the austerity provisions until June 1986.

South Africa. The climate of industrial relations was disturbed and sometimes violent. There were numerous disputes, though what threatened to be the largest, in the coal and gold mines, petered out after three days at the beginning of September. In an important judgment, the Industrial Court ordered a mining company to reinstate union members dismissed after the (legal) September strike. On December 1 more than 30 unions, claiming some 500,000 members, came together to form the Congress of South African Trade Unions, a multiracial but mostly black grouping that would be by far the largest of the country's union federations.

Australia. The government successfully negotiated with the unions for a two-year extension of the 1983 national pay and prices accord. The year's major dispute was in the electricity supply industry in Queensland and involved a confrontation between Premier Sir Johannes Bjelke-Petersen and the union. The Hancock Committee on Australian Industrial Relations Law and Systems, which reported in May, proposed modest changes, including the establishment of a labour court.   (R. O. CLARKE)

The views expressed in this article are the author's and should not be attributed to any organization with which he may be connected.

See also Economic Affairs: *World Economy;* Industrial Review.
This article updates the *Macropædia* article WORK AND EMPLOYMENT.

Law

Court Decisions. In 1985 the various judicial tribunals throughout the world decided a number of important cases, most of which involved civil rights, criminal law, and business matters.

Religious Freedom. Three cases handed down by the U.S. Supreme Court, regarded by scholars as that court's most important decisions during the year, clarified the meaning of the "establishment of religion clause" of the

First Amendment to the U.S. Constitution. That clause prevents states and the federal government from establishing an official religion in the U.S. *Wallace* v. *Jaffree* involved a challenge to the constitutionality of an Alabama statute that authorized a one-minute period of silence in all public schools "for meditation or voluntary prayer." The court held that the purpose of the statute was to endorse religion rather than some secular interest; that the establishment clause requires the government to pursue a course of complete neutrality toward religion, including the right of individuals to select any religious faith or none at all; and that, therefore, the statute was unconstitutional.

For similar reasons, the "Community Education and Shared Time" program adopted by the city of Grand Rapids, Mich., was held unconstitutional in *Grand Rapids School District* v. *Ball.* The program provided classes to nonpublic school students at public expense and was intended to supplement the core curricula of the private schools so that their students could meet the requirements of an accredited school program, as mandated by the state of Michigan. Among the subjects offered were remedial and enrichment mathematics and reading, art, music, and physical education. Most of the nonpublic schools involved in the programs were sectarian religious schools. The court held that these programs impermissibly involved the government in the support of sectarian religious activities and thus violated the "establishment clause" of the First Amendment.

In *Aguilar* v. *Felton,* the Supreme Court also struck down, on "establishment clause" grounds, a program developed by New York City that was similar in a number of respects to that of Grand Rapids.

Freedom of Speech. Significant cases on freedom of expression were handed down by the European Court of Human Rights (ECHR) and the U.S. Supreme Court. In *Lingens* v. *Austria,* the ECHR held that a conviction for defamation of the Austrian chancellor interfered with freedom of expression as guaranteed by Art. 10 of the European Convention for the Protection of Human Rights and Fundamental Freedoms.

In *Barthold* v. *Germany,* a veterinarian had been enjoined from making statements to the press favouring night service for vets on the grounds that this gave him a professional advantage over those who confined their practice to normal working hours, as required by professional rules of conduct. A newspaper article had carried a story indicating that the vet in question had treated animals outside of normal working hours and that he advocated a change of the professional rules on this matter. The injunction prohibited him from repeating similar statements in the press. The ECHR held that the injunction violated freedom of expression and thus should be dissolved. The court indicated that an injunction could be had to prohibit the violation of professional rules, but it could not prohibit members of the profession or others from debating in public the wisdom of those rules. In addition, if such an injunction were permitted, it could hamper the press in its tasks as "purveyor of information and as public watchdog."

Federal Election Commission v. *National Conservative Political Action Committee* entangled the U.S. Supreme Court in a political fight between the Republican and Democratic parties concerning campaign financing through political action committees, known familiarly as "PACs." A federal law offered presidential candidates the option of receiving public financing for their general election campaigns, but it provided that, if the candidate elected such financing, it was a criminal offense for an independent political committee to expend more than $1,000 to further

the candidate's election. Believing that a particular PAC intended to violate this law on the grounds that it was invalid, the Democratic Party brought an action to have it declared constitutional. The court found the statute unconstitutional as a violation of free speech guaranteed by the Constitution.

Harper & Row v. *National Enterprises* attracted worldwide interest, though scholars tended to agree that it had little legal significance. The case involved the theft and publication of portions of former U.S. president Gerald Ford's unpublished memoirs, including his account of the pardoning of former president Richard Nixon. The unauthorized publication was held to be a violation of the copyright laws.

Criminal Law. Anderston v. *Ryan,* decided by the House of Lords, the highest court in the Commonwealth, fascinated criminal law experts throughout the common law world. The case dealt with the criminal law of "attempt," generally defined as any overt act that is done with the intent to commit a crime but is prevented from commission by the interference of some independent cause. Unanswered by this definition is the question: Can one with criminal intent "criminally attempt" to do something that is lawful? The House of Lords said no. The case involved the buying of a video recorder by a person who erroneously believed it was stolen. The court said this could not be a crime because the factual circumstances made the intended offense incapable of fulfillment, contrary to the defendant's mistaken belief.

For the same reason, the court opined, sexual intercourse with a woman who had reached the age of majority could not be statutory rape, even though the man thought she was only 15. But what about the thief who puts his hand into an empty pocket? This, said the court, does involve a "criminal attempt." Buying goods and sexual intercourse are not illegal, standing alone. When these activities are done in connection with an "illegal" intention, no crime occurs. But putting one's hand into another's pocket is illegal and, when this activity is combined with a criminal intention, a crime occurs, even though the intended result of the act was impossible from the start. In view of the doctrinal importance of *Anderston* v. *Ryan* to common law countries, including the U.S., scholars were eagerly awaiting possible clarification from the House of Lords through a pending case dealing with a person convicted of "smuggling" tea leaves in the belief that they were a controlled drug.

In *Winston* v. *Lee,* the Supreme Court held that a person could not be required to undergo surgery in order to produce evidence of his guilt or innocence of a crime. A shopkeeper had been wounded during an attempted robbery but, being armed with a gun, wounded his assailant in the left side. The assailant then ran from the scene. Police officers found the accused eight blocks away from the shooting suffering from a gunshot wound to his left chest area. He was arrested, and the state moved for an order directing him to undergo surgery to remove a bullet lodged under his left collarbone, asserting that the bullet would provide evidence of his guilt or innocence. The court held that the proposed surgery would violate the accused's right to be secure in his person and that, consequently, the proposed "search" was unreasonable and in violation of the Fourth Amendment to the Constitution.

The ECHR finally got an opportunity to pass on the validity of the Italian criminal law system of trying "fugitives" in absentia (known as trying the "empty chair"). Surprising some scholars, the court held that trials in absentia did not per se violate the fair trial concept embraced by Art. 6(1)

of the European Convention on Human Rights. It found, however, that such a trial must afford the defendant a means to obtain a "fresh determination" of the case on the merits once he or she becomes aware of the fact of the trial. In this connection, the court said the Italian procedure of "late appeal" did not satisfy the requirements of the convention.

Tennessee v. *Garner* was concerned with whether the use of deadly force could be employed by police to prevent the escape of an apparently unarmed felon. The U.S. Supreme Court held that it could not, because such activity is proscribed by the Fourth Amendment to the Constitution. The court concluded that such force may not be used unless it is necessary to prevent the escape of the suspected felon and the officer has probable cause to believe that the suspect poses a significant threat of death or serious physical injury to the officer and others.

Business Matters. Banking law in the U.S., almost from the start, was dominated by the idea that a bank in one state, whether chartered by the federal or state government, could not conduct business in another. This idea was threatened by the emergence of bank holding companies, separate corporate entities that acquired banks in many states. To deal with this threat, the "Douglas Amendment" was passed in 1956. Under it, the Federal Reserve Board was charged with approving or disapproving bank holding companies and, significantly, a holding company located in one state was prohibited from acquiring a bank in another state unless such acquisition was specifically authorized by the laws of that state. Beginning with Massachusetts in 1982, several states enacted laws lifting the Douglas Amendment ban on a reciprocal basis within geographic regions, and these laws had spawned an impressive literature as to their legality and constitutionality. One such law, enacted by most New England states, permits holding companies to establish banks in their states provided that other New England states accord reciprocity. This kind of law, passed by Massachusetts, was attacked by New York banks and others as discriminatory. In *Northeast Bancorp, Inc.* v. *Board of Governors,* a case of major importance to the U.S. economy and the banking community, the Supreme Court sustained the Massachusetts statute. In this opinion, Justice William Rehnquist established guidelines for interstate banking that, in the view of many experts, would dominate for the remainder of the century.

Because many important arbitrations involving international commercial transactions are conducted in London by agreement of the parties, a case from the English Court of Appeal was deemed noteworthy in the worldwide commercial community. England, like many other countries, has required that an agreement to arbitrate be in writing and be specific, since the general feeling is that arbitration is a substitute for judicial proceedings to be used only where the parties have indicated unequivocally that it is their preferred method of resolving disputes. In the past the English courts had been considered somewhat formalistic in their application of this concept, so *Excomm Ltd.* v. *Ahmed Abdul-Qawi Bamaodah* caused some surprise. In this case, the Court of Appeal held that an arbitration agreement need not be signed by the parties or contained in one document, apparently contrary to some past decisions. The court held, however, that the arbitration agreement must be "written" in the sense that there is some documentary evidence that the parties want to resolve disputes by arbitration. (WILLIAM D. HAWKLAND)

International Law. *Sovereignty Violations.* The nature of world violence took a new turn in 1985, although the signs had been visible in previous years. Whereas in the past breakdowns in international law and order were localized in wars, interventions, and traditional border incursions, there now emerged a broader willingness on the part of major powers to disregard the territorial sovereignty of other states and, as a matter of deliberate policy, to place military or police expediency above compliance with international law. This applied not only to the improper use of force and to unauthorized incursions by state instrumentalities (military ships and aircraft) into the territory of foreign friendly states but also to the extended exercise of criminal or quasi-criminal jurisdiction, and the application of domestic criminal law, against foreign nationals living in their own country and in respect of acts carried out there. These trends began to raise the question of whether the basic concept of classic international law as a system governing relations between independent sovereign states was beginning to dissolve as greater regional and global interdependence and the increasingly hegemonic attitudes of the two superpowers diluted the old concept of the nation-state.

The most dramatic example of this trend involved a very complex legal situation. An Italian cruise liner in the Mediterranean, the *Achille Lauro,* was seized by four Palestinian terrorists and held to ransom for the release of 50 Palestinians held in an Israeli prison camp. This was the first extension of aerial hijacking to the sea, and there was dispute among lawyers as to whether the law of piracy would apply in such a case; some still restricted the crime of piracy to robbery at sea, thus excluding acts of violence for political purposes. While in control of the ship, the captors murdered a U.S. passenger. The Egyptian president negotiated the release of the ship, and the captors, having been promised transport to "neutral" territory, embarked on an Egyptian civil aircraft for Tunis. U.S. Navy fighter aircraft then approached the Egyptian plane in international airspace off Crete and compelled it to fly under escort to the NATO air base at Sigonella in Italy. There the Palestinians were taken into Italian custody, after an attempt to keep them in U.S. military custody had been disallowed. Although the U.S. action had some similarity to a classic "intervention," it was the first example of such a seizure on the high seas or in international airspace outside a contiguous zone or in the absence of a state of war and in an area remote from the territory of the seizing state.

A similar extension of the intervention concept had taken place a week earlier when Israeli war planes breached Tunisian airspace 2,400 km (1,500 mi) away and bombed the headquarters of the Palestine Liberation Organization near Tunis. In July French government agents, using explosives, clandestinely sank the ship *Rainbow Warrior,* belonging to the environmental organization Greenpeace, in Auckland Harbour, New Zealand. The ship had been about to lead a demonstration against French nuclear weapons tests at Mururoa Atoll in the Pacific. The French agents breached New Zealand territorial sovereignty as well as engaging in unlawful violence against a British-registered ship. The accidental death of a photographer in the explosion ensured that the affair would become a major diplomatic incident, which led to the resignation of the French minister of defense. In a sense, these events represented an escalation of traditional border raids, which in themselves are illegal unless involving hot pursuit. Such raids (both punitive and aggressive) continued throughout the year and included Israeli raids on villages in southern Lebanon, South African military action in Angola, border incidents between Pakistan and Afghanistan, and cross-border shelling by Vietnamese troops in Kampuchea into Thailand.

As controversy between Italy and the U.S. over the handling of the hijackers of the *Achille Lauro* continued, the four terrorists were taken by van from Sicily to Spoleto, one of four cities that claimed jurisdiction in the case.

ARAL—SIPA/SPECIAL FEATURES

Less dramatic was the extension of breaches of territorial waters and airspace by foreign submarines and military aircraft. In October a Czechoslovak fighter fired on a U.S. military helicopter, the 17th violation of West German airspace by Warsaw Pact aircraft in six months; in April a U.S. helicopter had been buzzed by Soviet fighters after itself crossing into Czechoslovak airspace. In the Aegean, Greece protested vigorously against multiple violations of its airspace by U.S. and Turkish aircraft during a military exercise. A new, accidental, but potentially worrying type of air violation occurred at the turn of the year when a Soviet cruise missile (unarmed), launched from a submarine in the Barents Sea, unlawfully crossed Norwegian territory into Finland, where it crash-landed; the Soviet government apologized.

Scandinavian maritime boundaries were also the site of two incidents. In the Barents Sea a Norwegian seismic research ship had its cable cut deliberately by a Soviet naval vessel 50 km (30 mi) within the Norwegian boundary. In the eastern Baltic the U.S.S.R. had long claimed that the border with Sweden should follow the median line between the two coasts, while Sweden had claimed that the line should be calculated from the coast of the island of Gotland (not from the Swedish mainland). In the resulting disputed area, Soviet fishery-protection vessels boarded and expelled numerous Swedish, Danish, and West German fishing boats. A more serious incident occurred in October when a Soviet minesweeper collided with a Swedish electronic surveillance ship, the *Orion,* which was monitoring signals from a Soviet Kilo-class submarine; this took place not in the disputed zone but on the high seas.

Boundary Disputes. In addition to the Soviet-Swedish and Soviet-Norwegian disputes, a main area of active disagreement over maritime boundaries concerned the British islet of Rockall in the northeastern Atlantic. It was argued that, being uninhabitable, it could have territorial waters but no appurtenant continental shelf or fishery zone, following the rules in the Law of the Sea Convention (which the U.K. did not sign). Consequently, both Iceland and Denmark put in claims during the year for a continental

shelf/exclusive economic zone covering the sea plateau on which Rockall stands, thus bringing the total number of claimants to four (Ireland and the U.K. being the other two). Discussions were proceeding on the drafting of an arbitration agreement between the U.K. and Ireland to settle the matter between them. Farther west, Canada in September drew a straight baseline around the whole of its Arctic archipelagic territory, thus affirming that all the sea between the islands constituted internal waters and was under the complete sovereignty of Canada. This followed a voyage made through the Northwest Passage by the U.S. Coast Guard icebreaker *Polar Sea* without first obtaining the permission of the Canadian government, pursuant to U.S. policy, which regarded the Northwest Passage as an international strait.

The most noteworthy boundary settlement during the year was the agreement between Chile and Argentina on their boundary in the Beagle Channel, following lengthy mediation by the Vatican. The two countries exchanged instruments of ratification in May. Guinea-Bissau and Senegal agreed to submit their maritime boundary dispute to arbitration, after a similar dispute between Guinea-Bissau and Guinea resulted in an arbitration award in February. In December 1984 Australia and Papua New Guinea signed a treaty settling their mutual boundary in the Torres Strait. The UN preparatory commission for the future International Sea-Bed Authority reached a compromise agreement on the delimitation of the seabed exploitation areas between the U.S.S.R. and Japan; no agreement could be reached, however, on the more complex dispute between the U.S.S.R. and France, since 80% of their claims overlapped. The U.S., the U.K., and West Germany were unable to take part in such proceedings because they had refused to sign the Law of the Sea Convention.

Boundary treaties were concluded between North Korea and the U.S.S.R.; Algeria and Mauritania; France and Spain (an adjustment of the Treaty of the Pyrenees of 1659 resulting in the transfer of 300 sq m [3,230 sq ft] of the town of Agullana and 600 of its inhabitants from Spain to France); Italy and Switzerland (border adjustments agreed

on in 1981 but not ratified or entering into force until January 1985); and Sweden and Finland (the boundary in the Torne River, affecting fishing rights). Relaxation of border controls was agreed on between Italy and France and Italy and Austria; the Albania-Greece border was at last opened; and a commission was set up under the auspices of the Contadora Group (Colombia, Mexico, Panama, and Venezuela) to establish the Costa Rica-Nicaragua border.

International Adjudication. A new president, Judge Nagendra Singh (India), and a new vice-president, Judge Guy Ladreit de Lacharrière (France), were appointed to the International Court of Justice. For the first time in its history, the court would also include a woman member, Mme Suzanne Bastid; she was nominated as judge ad hoc by Tunisia to sit on its application for revision and interpretation of the court's February 1982 judgment in its continental shelf dispute with Libya. In December the court rejected Tunisia's application. In June the court delivered another judgment in a similar dispute between Libya and Malta, but it excluded from the ruling areas to which Italy might have a claim (thus ensuring that its refusal the previous year to let Italy intervene in the case would not prejudice any future claim it might make). The award was based on the median line between the two opposite coasts of Malta and Libya (disregarding an uninhabited Maltese island, Filfla), but because Libya had a much longer coastline, the court shifted the final boundary 18′ north of the true midline.

The decision of the International Court in November 1984 to accept jurisdiction in Nicaragua's action against the U.S., alleging interventionist acts against Nicaraguan territory, had two consequences. The U.S., which bitterly disputed the correctness of the judgment, withdrew its acceptance of the "optional clause" as from April 1986, since continued acceptance of the court's compulsory jurisdiction would be "contrary to our commitment to the principle of the equal application of the law, and would endanger our vital national interests." Second, the U.S. refused to participate further in the proceedings brought by Nicaragua. Oral argument took place in September, but in the absence of U.S. representatives. However, the U.S. was not boycotting the court as such, and it reached an agreement with Italy to submit to the court a dispute involving Italian subsidiaries of two U.S. companies.

The Iran-U.S. Claims Tribunal resumed sittings early in the year, after its work had been interrupted by an assault by two Iranian judges on a neutral Swedish colleague. The two were recalled and replaced. The Swedish judge retired from the tribunal later in the summer, as did a Dutch judge, and a West German lawyer, Karl-Heinz Boekstiegel, was appointed as the new president. The Council of Europe set up a new European Tribunal on Matters of State Immunity to resolve problems arising from divergent state practice and to improve the position of individuals. It would consist of judges from the European Court of Human Rights sitting in public in chambers of seven members. The London Court of International Arbitration adopted new rules from the beginning of the year, aimed at speeding procedure and making arbitration more congenial to disputants. The new rules took fully into account the UN Commission on International Trade Law's Model Law on International Commercial Arbitration as representing prevailing contemporary international opinion.

(NEVILLE MARCH HUNNINGS)

See also Crime, Law Enforcement, and Penology; World Affairs: *United Nations.*

This article updates the *Macropædia* articles CONSTITUTIONAL LAW; INTERNATIONAL LAW.

Libraries

Libraries continued to suffer from the effects of the world recession. In general, resources were being stretched ever more thinly to provide a greater range and depth of service, and the purchase of books and journals had to compete with progress toward automation.

Widespread disillusionment with education—at least in European countries—was affecting the finances of university and college libraries. Librarians were being asked to provide ever more effective and efficient services, often with fewer resources. This frequently resulted from a lack of national library and information policies, which were difficult to formulate in developed countries where diverse agencies had grown up over the past 50 or more years. In less developed countries the major problems were the scarcity of hard currency and of adequate professional training. Lack of books continued to plague African countries in particular; efforts were being made to help through charities like the Ranfurly Library Service, Books for Development, and recent initiatives of the Nordic countries to provide works in science and technology.

In spite of current difficulties, new library buildings were being constructed. Examples in Britain were those at the University of Newcastle upon Tyne (with an overall program of automation) and at the City of Birmingham Polytechnic. In Kenya new library buildings were completed, under construction, or planned for all three of the country's universities. In Sri Lanka the National Library building neared completion, while several new library buildings were under construction in Brazil. China also was building new university libraries.

The international aspects of librarianship and information work were also under duress. UNESCO's General Information Program (PGI—Programme général d'information) and Book Promotion Program were suffering from that organization's general financial problems. PGI was nevertheless effective in promoting collaboration in the establishment of information systems in Asia, Africa, and Latin America and in promoting education and training programs throughout the third world. Recent initiatives included information science departments at Addis Ababa (Eth.) University and the University of Ibadan, Nigeria. UNESCO operated not only through its own staff but also through nongovernmental organizations such as the Fédération Internationale de Documentation (FID), the International Federation of Library Associations and Institutions (IFLA), and the International Council of Archives (ICA). In association with UNESCO, the Council for Libraries, the British Library, and the West German National Library, IFLA continued to develop its Universal Bibliographical Control (UBC) program.

IFLA also turned its attention to the problems of transborder information flow and to another new preoccupation of librarians, conservation. While greater and better provision of books had been called for during recent decades, little account had been taken of the state of the books themselves. These, made for the past century or so of chemical papers and for the past 30 years bound in impermanent bindings, were in imminent danger of disintegrating. Conservation had therefore become a pressing concern, particularly of librarians dealing with collections of major national importance.

Library automation and on-line services for bibliographical information continued to play an increasing part in library development. Malaysia, for instance, had a shared cataloging program involving the national and university

A patron at the New York Public Library consults the new computerized catalog from one of 50 terminals in the system. The electronic system was to replace some ten million cards and the nearly 9,000 drawers that contained them and greatly shorten the time it took to thumb through them in search of a book.

JOHN MCGRAIL/TIME MAGAZINE

libraries. There were now nearly 3,000 data-base services, covering most disciplines. (P. HAVARD-WILLIAMS)

In the U.S. strong local and state funding brightened the public-library picture. The Miami-Dade County, Fla., public library system opened a new 18,600-sq m (200,000-sq ft) central library in a Mediterranean-style cultural plaza in Miami on July 19; the Los Angeles City Council approved a $110.4 million, 18,600-sq m expansion and rehabilitation of the landmark 1926 central library; the Atlanta-Fulton (Ga.) Public Library won a $38 million bond referendum in October for new library buildings and improvements; and the New York Public Library began converting its ten million-card catalog into book and on-line formats and began renovating its main library facade as part of a $45 million restoration program. Major library renovations were under way or announced in Baltimore, Md., Chicago, and Boston. In general, however, according to 1984 figures reported in mid-1985, public libraries were struggling with an 11.5% rise in expenses.

School libraries, still limited to some $4.62–$6.41 per pupil for books, according to a University of North Carolina survey, got moral support from the first National School Library Media Month, designated in a joint congressional resolution introduced by Sen. Daniel P. Moynihan (Dem., N.Y.) and celebrated April 1 on the U.S. Capitol steps. Biennial statistics from the Association of College and Research Libraries showed members' interlibrary lending up 21% and borrowing up 28%, reflecting the current emphasis on cooperative activity among academic and research libraries. A showcase on-line catalog system at the University of Illinois at Urbana began operation in April, giving users quick access not only to the university's holdings but, through interlibrary loan, to the collections of 25 other Illinois libraries.

Three presidential library projects moved forward, amid controversy. In February, Stanford University trustees approved an 8-ha (20-ac) site on campus for a Ronald Reagan library. The Jimmy Carter library was under construction in Atlanta, and fund-raising proceeded for a Richard Nixon library on an approved site in San Clemente, Calif.

Among current trends, job vacancies for children's librarians were going unfilled in several regions and public libraries were lending large numbers of videocassettes—for example, some 100,000 loans a year at the Thousand Oaks, Calif., and Findlay-Hancock, Ohio, libraries. Robert Wedgeworth stepped down as director of the American Library Association after 13 years and was succeeded by Thomas J. Galvin, formerly dean of the University of Pittsburgh library school. During Wedgeworth's tenure, ALA membership climbed from 31,580 to 42,017. The National Commission on Libraries and Information Science estimated the number of U.S. libraries at 103,774, including the 70,854 school libraries counted in 1978.

(ARTHUR PLOTNIK)

This article updates the *Macropædia* article LIBRARIES AND LIBRARY SCIENCE.

Life Sciences

ZOOLOGY

Technological developments in the field and laboratory offered opportunities for zoological advances during 1985, from understanding the ecological genetics of disappearing species to the discovery of new life forms in the ocean's abyssal zone. Fossil evidence suggesting new interpretations of the origins of vertebrates, from reptiles to humans, was gathered at key sites in Asia, Africa, and North America.

Rare and endangered species continued to occupy the interests of scientists worldwide. To date more than 1,000 species of animals had been officially declared as threatened or endangered. Some notable species, such as the California condor, were nearing extinction. According to the U.S. Fish and Wildlife Service, the number of condors in the wild dwindled to seven during the year. Included among the world's endangered animals were most members of the cat family, including the cheetahs of Africa. Using the technique of protein electrophoresis to separate the components of the genetic material, a team of scientists led by Stephen O'Brien of the U.S. National Cancer Institute reported that genetic diversity in South African cheetahs was extremely low. Skin grafting experiments further confirmed that the cheetahs in the study population were more genetically identical than researchers had anticipated. A possible explanation given was that in the past the cheetah populations of southern Africa had become greatly reduced in number. Inbreeding followed, resulting in both wild and captive descendants having low genetic variability due to the elimination of many alleles (*i.e.,* alternative genetic traits) from the natural populations. The researchers emphasized the importance of maintaining genetic variation in species and populations by demonstrating that South African cheetahs have high juvenile mortality and are more susceptible to certain diseases, presumably because of genetic homogeneity.

Further support for considering genetic variability in the management of endangered species was given by Robert C. Vrijenhoek (Rutgers University, New Brunswick, N.J.), Michael E. Douglas (Oklahoma State University), and Gary K. Meffe (Savannah River Ecology Laboratory, Aiken, S.C.). In electrophoretic studies of the Gila topminnow, a small fish of desert hot springs, they discovered that the widespread and abundant populations of Sonora, Mexico, had high genetic variability, compared with that of the isolated populations in Arizona, along the northern margin of the species' geographic range. The Gila topminnow was recognized as an endangered species in the U.S., and management practices included habitat protection and

restocking from hatchery populations. However, these researchers pointed out that present hatchery populations were derived from wild stocks having low genetic diversity and low rates of reproduction. They recommended that the fish used for restocking be chosen from more genetically variable wild populations, so that endangered populations would be better equipped genetically to respond to variable environmental conditions. These studies of cheetahs and topminnows suggested that serious attention be paid to the genetic variability existing within populations of any species destined for management and manipulation.

The use of protein electrophoresis had dominated the study of ecological genetics in recent years, but another genetics technique—analysis of mitochondrial DNA—promised to provide an informative approach for some zoological questions. Some DNA (the material carrying the genetic code) is housed within the cell's respiratory organelles, or mitochondria. This mitochondrial DNA has an unusual mode of inheritance, being transmitted by the female parent to her offspring through egg cytoplasm. In 1985 knowledge of this process of maternal transmission across generations enabled scientists to apply mitochondrial DNA analysis to a specific problem in ecological genetics. Trip Lamb and John C. Avise of the University of Georgia examined populations of two frog species—green tree frogs and barking tree frogs—that had undergone extensive hybridization. Although the two species may breed at the same aquatic sites, they do not normally hybridize, presumably because male green tree frogs issue mating calls from shoreline shrubs and trees, whereas male barking tree frogs call to their females from the water itself. At the hybrid sites habitat maintenance practices had eliminated shoreline vegetation so that most green tree frogs called from the bare ground. It was suggested, therefore, that most mismatings resulting in hybrids would involve green tree frog males that intercepted barking tree frog females en route to the water to breed with their own males. Lamb and Avise confirmed this prediction by demonstrating that the mitochondrial DNA pattern in each hybrid was identical to that of the barking tree frog, indicating the maternal role in hybrid events. The results of this study demonstrated how the rigid mating behaviours characteristic of many animals can control genetic structure; even minor environmental perturbations might cause biologically significant changes.

While certain life-forms were disappearing from the Earth and natural habitats were being eliminated or modified, modern technologies were leading to discoveries of previously unknown animal species and environments. In 1977 a new habitat and its associated animal community were discovered within the abyssal zone of the Pacific Ocean at a depth of 2,500 m (8,200 ft). The area is a major fissure between plates making up the Earth's crust. The gradual separation of the plates and the underlying volcanic activity result in ultracold seawater percolating downward, encountering hot rocks, and emerging onto the seafloor. These hydrothermal vents support formerly unknown deep-sea communities. The animals of these communities dwell far below the depth of light penetration; chemosynthetic bacteria, rather than plants, form the base of the food chain. Animals found in hydrothermal vent communities include previously unknown species of clams, mussels, jellyfish, worms, and fishes. In many species population density and body size are greater than those normally found at such depths.

During the year oceanographic scientists using manned deep-sea vessels extended the known distribution of abyssal-zone vent communities and of the animals that inhabit them. C. K. Paull of the Scripps Institution of Oceanography, La Jolla, Calif., and colleagues discovered vent communities in the Gulf of Mexico that apparently use sulfide seepage areas on the ocean floor as a chemical energy source. Notably, it was found that water temperatures in the Gulf communities are near normal for the deep-sea environment, a distinct contrast to the volcanically heated vents of the Pacific.

At the U.S. National Oceanic and Atmospheric Administration, Miami, Fla., Peter Rona and associates confirmed the existence of additional deep-sea vents in the Atlantic Ocean, and the Canadian American Seamount Expedition reported the discovery of a hydrothermal vent with more than a dozen new kinds of vent animals in the Pacific Ocean, off the coast of Vancouver, more than 4,830 km (3,000 mi) from the earliest known vent. A joint project of French and Japanese scientists reported colonies of giant clams and tube worms in the Japan trench at depths of more than 5,000 m (16,400 ft). J. Frederick Grassle of the Woods Hole (Mass.) Oceanographic Institution noted that vent communities from numerous sites in the Pacific and the Gulf of Mexico were strikingly similar in species composition. Although vent communities have existed on Earth for more than 200 million years, any particular vent lasts for only a few decades at most. With the eventual disappearance of its chemical energy source, the animal community cannot survive. Grassle suggested, however, that vent species displayed rapid individual growth and had reproductive capabilities that ensured widespread dispersal of larval forms in the ocean environment, thus increasing the opportunities for successful colonization of new vent sites.

Fossil finds and interpretations continued to add new spirit to inquiries about the origins and evolution of humans, apes, and other vertebrates. In Wyoming, at an Eocene Epoch site estimated to be 50 million years old, fossil vertebrates were examined by Leonard Krishtalka

A hybrid tree frog makes his mating call from dry ground, as do green tree frogs, rather than from the water, which is preferred by barking tree frogs. Analysis of hybrids' DNA confirms that they are typically crosses involving male green and female barking parents.

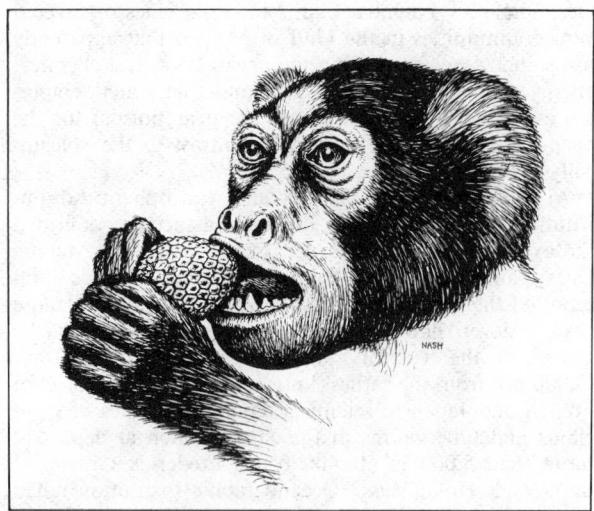

Researchers' conception of *Amphipithecus mogaungensis,* developed from the reconstruction of jawbones and teeth found in Burma in 1978. *Amphipithecus* was nominated as the common ancestor of Old and New World monkeys, apes, and humans.

RECONSTRUCTION BY STEPHEN NASH AND RUSSELL CIOCHON, STATE UNIVERSITY OF NEW YORK AT STONY BROOK

and Richard Stucky of the Carnegie Museum of Natural History, Pittsburgh, Pa. They had identified more than a dozen previously undescribed animal species, including primates similar to lemurs and tarsiers. The material from this site was expected to reveal much about the origin of modern mammals.

In the Old World, fossil evidence relating to human origins continued to accumulate. At a site in Kenya investigators from the National Museums of Kenya and Johns Hopkins University in Baltimore, Md., reported the unprecedented finding of a nearly complete human skeleton estimated to be 1.6 million years old. They concluded that the skeleton would further establish the modern human as a direct descendant of *Homo erectus.* Members of the team also reported the discovery of 18 million-year-old bones of *Proconsul africanus* on an island in Lake Victoria. The fossils revealed that *Proconsul,* regarded as a prehuman form of ape, was tailless. Because the remains of several individuals were excavated, the find should provide additional information about the biology of the species.

Perhaps the most significant scientific find relating to the early origin of prehumans was made by Russell L. Ciochon of the State University of New York at Stony Brook and colleagues, who reported that a 40 million-year-old Burmese fossil primate, *Amphipithecus mogaungensis,* may be the oldest known common ancestor of monkeys, apes, and humans. The report was controversial in that the area of origin of the prehuman line had generally been thought to have been Africa rather than Asia. These investigators suggested that the higher primates evolved in Asia and later migrated to Africa and South America.

(J. WHITFIELD GIBBONS)

Entomology. The Royal Entomological Society of London (RESL), Britain's premier association of entomologists, celebrated the 100th anniversary of its royal charter (and the 152nd anniversary of the society's foundation) by mounting what was probably the most ambitious entomological expedition ever undertaken. Project Wallace, located in the Indonesian island of Celebes (Sulawesi), was named after Alfred Russel Wallace, the celebrated naturalist and former RESL president (1870–71) who established Wallace's Line, a hypothetical boundary between the Oriental and Australasian zoogeographical regions. The

boundary runs adjacent to a group of islands, including Celebes, collectively named Wallacea by zoogeographers; the region provides ecologists with an opportunity to observe the interpenetration of two faunas, probably first brought together by the abutment of the Oriental and Australian tectonic plates.

With the cooperation of the Indonesian Institute of Sciences and logistic support from a training team from the British Army, Project Wallace allowed more than 150 scientists from 19 countries to investigate one of the world's significant remaining areas of undisturbed rain forest, the Dumoga-Bone National Park, a cachement area for developing agricultural projects in the Dumoga and the Bone valleys. Directed by W. J. Knight of the British Museum (Natural History), the current RESL secretary, the expedition generated data that would take many years to evaluate and to follow up.

In Celebes, as in other remaining rain forest regions, farms encroaching into and surrounded by natural forest were, to an extent, screened from pest attacks; H. van Emden of the University of Reading, England, leader of the agricultural entomology program, expected that the project would provide an ideal opportunity to study the ecology of the invasion of pests—such as *Niloparvata* and other leafhoppers that attack rice—into virgin areas. It should also provide baseline data for studies on reforestation techniques.

An illustration of the interpenetration of fauna in Wallacea was provided by the work of Lance Durden of Vanderbilt University, Nashville, Tenn. Investigating the ectoparasites of mammals in the Dumoga-Bone National Park, Durden discovered a number of pygiopsyllid fleas, including a giant 5-mm (0.2-in) species, on the endemic rodents; in Australia related fleas were commonly found on marsupials but not on rodents.

Ilka Hanski of the University of Helsinki, Fin., made a special study of the fate of excrement and carrion on the forest floor. He found that *Geotrupes* beetles—which, in other parts of the world, specialize in rolling and burying dung—feed on subterranean fungi in Celebes. Flies, ants, and beetles of other species compete for excrement or carrion. Blowflies are usually first on the scene—they may arrive at fresh excrement within 30 seconds of its deposition—but their larvae are subject to destruction by those of later arriving sarcophagid flies. Ants generally are not the first scavengers to reach a dead body, but when they do arrive first, they prevent other insects from gaining access to the carcass. Silphid beetles counter the tactics of competitors by rapidly burying the carcass, while *Gymnopleurus,* a scarab beetle, attempts to roll away and bury small lumps of carrion in the same way other dung beetles deal with excrement. Meanwhile, the scavengers are preyed upon by a variety of carnivorous beetles, and all the insects attracted to the site may be eaten by lizards.

In the rain forest of Celebes almost every fallen log and many branches on trees are infested by termites, which are continually under attack by ants. Both, in turn, may fall prey to phorids, minute black flies, most of which are parasites. Henry Disney, a research fellow of Britain's Field Studies Council, had not yet had time to identify or name all the species he had investigated but meanwhile had coined names to describe them. Small, wingless "gallery phorids" inhabit ant and termite nests, although probably they feed only on fungus. "Squatter ants" take over termite nests in trees, and once the nests are broken open (*e.g.,* when rotten branches fall), "spear-gun phorids" dart in and stab the ants with spring-loaded ovipositors; in contrast, "highwayman phorids" run alongside or behind

squatter ants and stab them. "Con flies" gain the attention of termites by butting them in the rear, then attract them with scent; once the termite has been lured into isolation, an egg is laid in it. The ovipositing secretion first paralyses the termite, then keeps it fresh after death, long enough for the phorid larva to mature in ten days or so. Some termites have a special soldier caste called nasutes. The nasute repels the attacks of other insects, including phorids, by spraying a sticky chemical from a nozzlelike gland on its head.

The hardship of the continuing drought in much of central and southern Africa was exacerbated in East Africa especially by a new and potentially devastating pest of maize (corn)—the staple for much of the African population. *Prostephanus truncatus,* a grain-boring beetle that originated in Central America, gained entry to Tanzania probably some six years ago. By 1985 it had spread to Kenya and Burundi, had threatened Zambia and Malawi, and had most recently been found on the other side of the continent in Togo. In America it was preyed upon by a carnivorous beetle and was not considered a particularly significant pest, but in Africa it had so far avoided major enemies and had already caused average losses of 9% of grain stores. *Prostephanus* was easily controlled with pyrethroid insecticides, but African subsistence farmers generally could not afford chemical control.

(PETER W. MILES)

This article updates the *Macropædia* article INSECTS.

Ornithology. During the decade since the end of the Cultural Revolution, there had been a resurgence of ornithological activity in China. Birdbanding was begun in 1983, and some 3,000 birds had been marked by the end of 1984. Bar-headed geese and brown-headed gulls were caught in considerable numbers at a breeding site on the Tibetan plateau. The biology of the white-rumped swift was under investigation in Shanghai.

In an imaginative experiment in economic ornithology, azure-winged magpies were trained by the forestry authorities in Shantong (Shantung) Province as "tree doctors"; the trees were suffering from the overattentions of the pine moth. First, nestling magpies were brought into captivity and reared to the fledgling stage. The birds were reared on a diet of adult moths or pupae (caterpillars), and every time a meal was made available, a whistle was blown. After three years' training, the birds were taken to an infested part of the forest and released, and the whistle was blown. The birds were attracted to the vicinity of their trainer and at once began searching for the injurious insects. After 20 days, 18 birds had eaten 8,000 larvae, 1,700 pupae, and a number of full-winged adult moths.

By 1985 the five-year-old Ornithological Society of China had attracted 342 members. The new standard work on the birds of the republic listed 1,186 species, 20 of them new to China since 1976. Special attention was being paid to members of the pheasant family, no fewer than 16 of which were endemic to China. In Sichuan (Szechwan) the vocabulary of the brown-eared pheasant was extensively taped. A British ornithological expedition to China established a temporary observatory on the coast of the Yellow Sea during March–June 1985 and observed no less than half the world's population of Siberian cranes on migration from the Chang Jiang (Yangtze) marshes south to their breeding grounds in the U.S.S.R.

In the Soviet Union itself the first ornithological society was formed, with branches in even the most remote republics. Surprisingly, there were no fewer than 1,000 full-time ornithologists active in the U.S.S.R. Some notable studies, such as those of E. Panov on the wheatears

(thrush species common to Eurasia), were outstanding in their excellence.

The theory that migratory birds from Europe and Soviet Asia fly nonstop across the Mediterranean and the Sahara in one "hop" en route to their winter quarters in Central Africa was disproved by researchers of the Max Planck Institute for Behavioural Physiology, Seewiesen, West Germany. After more than three months in the Libyan desert, investigator Herbert Biebach established that the genetically predetermined migration program of such birds as the spotted flycatcher is affected by climatic, ecological, and physiological factors. He set up two research camps in the desert, about 300 km (186 mi) south of the Mediterranean and 180 km (112 mi) west of the Nile; one camp was at an oasis, the other in the arid desert. At both camps Biebach spread mist nets. Many insectivorous migratory birds travel at night, and each dawn Biebach netted an average of 80–90 birds. For each specimen, body temperature and amount of subcutaneous fat were measured and recorded. Some birds were given blood tests to establish the level of their water reserves. They were then divided by species and weight. Biebach found that all desert-resting birds remained still for only 12 hours, from dawn till dusk, finding whatever shade they could. Significantly, the body weight of these birds was, on average, 10% higher than that of oasis-resting birds. No underweight birds landed in the desert; they flew on, presumably until they found food and water. At the oasis site, too, most birds stayed only for the day, but a significant proportion remained longer, some for weeks. These were predominantly underweight birds, who used the oasis to replenish their fat supplies and were prepared to interrupt their flight program to do so. The research emphasized that because there were very few oases in the Sahara to accommodate the estimated 5,000,000,000 land birds that crossed the Mediterranean and Sahara each year, it might be assumed that the overwhelming majority were forced to rest in the desert proper; in fact, however, only well-fed birds were found to do so. These findings were confirmed in the laboratory during simulated migration flights.

In *A Dictionary of Birds* (1985), edited by Bruce Campbell and Elizabeth Lack, 300 authors synthesized the current state of the science. Among the very recent discoveries published there for the first time, one of the more surprising was the slowness with which birds fly. The so-called swift was shown to be capable of only 40 km (24.8 mi) per hour. The fastest bird known to science (level flight, still air) was the eider duck, timed by radar at 72 km (44.7 mi) per hour.

(JEFFERY BOSWALL)

This article updates the *Macropædia* article BIRDS.

MARINE BIOLOGY

Studies of marine picoplankton estimated that 25–90% of total biomass in parts of the ocean might be attributable to these small single-celled organisms of less than ten-micrometre size. Cyanobacteria (*Synechococcus*) in this community, deep in the water column, were shown to absorb light specifically in the blue and green regions of the spectrum. This observation necessitated the raising of estimates of primary production at depth, which hitherto had underestimated picoplankton abundance. Previous estimates had also been based on total light penetration and had ignored the filtering effect of seawater, which allows blue and green light to penetrate to greatest depths. The inability of existing laboratory instruments to distinguish between different organisms of similar size had limited researchers' ability to count small organisms. During 1985, however, the technique of flow cytometry, which detects

The coral reef exists like an oasis in the midst of this marine desert. The highest rates of primary productivity measured anywhere on earth occur in water from the open ocean flowing over the reef. To find out why, scientists travel to reefs to conduct experiments. As a result of these experiments, scientists have been able to re-create in the laboratory this living reef, which also serves as a tool for further research.

One of the Smithsonian Institution's new coral reef "microcosm" exhibits emphasizes the coral reef's ecological status as something of an oasis of life in the midst of the relative lifelessness that is characteristic of tropical oceans.

SMITHSONIAN; PHOTOGRAPH, CHIP CLARK

different fluorescence patterns, made possible the accurate counting of such organisms.

New Australian studies emphasizing the relationship in zooplankton between metabolic rates, body mass, and temperature could lead to critical reassessments of previous estimates of zooplankton community activity. Over the past three decades, Continuous Plankton Recorder surveys of the Northeast Atlantic had revealed a quasilinear downward trend in abundance of phyto- and zooplankton. Since 1980, however, this downward movement had appeared to be reversing, but the effect of such factors as climate changes and fisheries had yet to be evaluated.

Ultraviolet light inhibits the growth of bryozoans and tunicates but not of corals on shallow Australian reefs; recent studies indicated that the corals have an ultraviolet blocking agent that might have potential as a sunscreen agent in paints and plastics. Studies of Caribbean reefs resulted in the construction of several coral reef "microcosms" at the Smithsonian Institution, Washington, D.C., which mimicked to an unusually successful degree the complexity and function of a natural coral reef and its lagoon. There were new insights into long-standing questions about the methods by which geologically recent and isolated coral reefs, such as those of the Hawaiian archipelago, had been colonized. One possible method might be via floating colonies of corals on logs, coconuts, and volcanic pumice. Another might be by mechanisms such as that described in *Pocillopora;* the planulae (free-swimming larvae), newly settled and metamorphosed, are able to re-form as secondary distributive planulae if subjected to stress within three days of settlement.

Extensive three-dimensional measurements of herring and mackerel shoals in large sea cages confirmed earlier

predictions that fish in schools choose neighbours of similar body size. Juveniles of the solitary Red Sea blenny (*Meiacanthus nigrolineatus*) were found to possess a colour pattern resembling that of various cardinal fish among shoals of which the blenny is often found; this discovery was the first example of school-oriented mimicry in a fish. Winter flounders (*Pseudopleuronectes americanus*) in North America cope with subzero temperatures by synthesizing blood-borne antifreeze peptides, which appear at different times of the year in different genetic races of fish, depending on local water temperatures. Juvenile menhaden (*Brevoortia*) in the eastern U.S., which feed on plants growing in coastal marshes, were shown to readily digest cellulose and other vascular plant material with 75% efficiency, thus providing the first example within a food web of a direct link from marsh-plan primary production to fishery use without intermediate steps involving microbial decomposition. A reduction of a giant kelp canopy off southern California from an area of 63 sq km (24.3 sq mi) in 1982 to 6 sq km (2.3 sq mi) in 1984 was attributed to temperature stress and nutrient starvation associated with the recent activities of El Niño, the periodic warming of the Pacific Ocean off the coasts of Peru and Ecuador. In 1982 and 1983 this increase in temperature was the most intense ever recorded.   (ERNEST NAYLOR)

This article updates the *Macropædia* articles CRUSTACEANS; FISHES; MOLLUSKS; etc.

BOTANY

In addition to the five groups of identified plant hormones (auxins, gibberellins, cytokinins, ethylene, and abscisic acid), there exists an array of chemical substances—referred to collectively as plant growth regulators, or PGRs—that affect plant growth and development. A PGR is a group of molecules that is chemically diverse and includes synthetically manufactured substances as well as natural products isolated from various plant tissues. These substances are useful in agriculture for a variety of purposes. Some PGRs act as dwarfing agents, allowing crop plants such as peanuts to be planted in closer rows, which results in increased yields. Others enhance storage quality of certain fruits such as apples, prevent sprouting of onions and potatoes, act as chemical hybridizing agents in wheat, or facilitate mechanical harvesting of crops such as cotton and potatoes.

In spite of the wide range of effects that both hormones and PGRs elicit in plants and the importance of PGRs in agriculture, discovery of their mode of action had been elusive—in part because application of PGRs to plants seemed to influence several developmental events at once. Furthermore, some aspects of development seemed to require the presence of more than one PGR, the right pH (degree of alkalinity or acidity), and other contributing substances as well.

Recently, however, a new group of molecules with perhaps more direct effects on morphogenesis was discovered. Surprisingly, this group includes naturally occurring carbohydrates, called oligosaccharins, that are components of plant cell walls. Oligosaccharins are short-chain sugars that can act as regulators of developmental processes. These substances were being studied for their ability to control a number of plant processes, including the production of phytoalexins (toxins that kill invading pathogens) and the control of certain symbiotic associations.

Most recently, experiments demonstrated the ability of oligosaccharins to control a number of developmental effects in tobacco tissue culture systems; for example, the promotion of both shoot and root development in undifferentiated tissue cultures and the regulation of the de-

velopment of either flowers or vegetative buds. Previously these developmental processes had been shown to be influenced only by adjustment of the concentrations of auxin and cytokinin in the tissue culture medium. The demonstration of control of morphogenesis by molecules that are derived from the cell walls led investigators to suggest that the oligosaccharins may be in situ regulators of plant development.

Several toxic or carcinogenic compounds were known to persist in the environment as pollutants for extended periods of time, presumably because microorganisms either were unable to degrade them or did so only very slowly. Some of these compounds, such as DDT, also showed a tendency to accumulate in the body fat of animals high in the food chain. It was recently shown that a common white rot fungus can be induced to secrete an enzyme that breaks down lignin, a complex component of plant cell walls. Because the complex lignin molecule contains structures similar to molecules of DDT, dioxin, and PCB (polychlorinated biphenyl), researchers decided to test the lignin-degrading enzyme against these substances and found it to be active in degrading them as well. While it was too early to determine the potential impact of this finding on the task of cleaning up contaminated environments, the investigators did suggest that inoculation of waste treatment water with the fungus that secretes the lignin-degrading enzyme might prevent the environmental accumulation of certain toxic wastes.

Efforts continued during the year to develop genetically engineered bacteria that would be beneficial to the plants on which they lived. Such symbiotic relationships had long been known in nature—for example, the association of nitrogen-fixing bacteria with the roots of certain plants. At least three newly engineered bacteria had been produced.

THOMAS KUSTER, U.S. FOREST PRODUCTS LABORATORY

An enzyme dubbed lignase, secreted by the common white rot fungus *Phanerochaete chrysosporium,* attacks lignin molecules in a pine-wood cell. The enzyme, whose structure had not been determined, also proved effective in degrading DDT, dioxin, and PCB.

One conferred frost resistance to the infected host; another produced an endotoxin that protects the host plant from invading insects; and a third conferred resistance to herbicide damage. However, as some doubt remained about the long-term effects of releasing genetically engineered organisms into the environment, the U.S. Environmental Protection Agency was continuing to evaluate the results of these experiments.   (PHILIP D. REID)

MOLECULAR BIOLOGY

Hemorrhagic Shock and the Oxygen Paradox. When large volumes of blood are lost as a result of trauma, the blood pressure falls and the blood flow to many tissues is curtailed, leaving them short of oxygen (hypoxic). If the lost blood is promptly replaced by transfusion, the blood pressure rises to within the normal range and remains there. In contrast, if the transfusion is delayed, the subsequent rise in blood pressure is only transient, and death ensues. This apparently irreversible situation, which develops when blood pressure and, therefore, blood flow are inadequate for an hour or two, is called hemorrhagic shock. It appears to be due to damage to the small blood vessels, which allows fluid and dissolved components of the blood to leak from the vessels and pool in the tissues. Hemorrhagic shock is of great concern to physicians who treat the victims of civilian or military accidents; the cause of this condition is now beginning to be understood.

The effects of temporary ischemia (insufficient blood flow) can also be seen on the scale of a single organ or even part of an organ. Thus, when the blood supply to a loop of intestine, or to part of the heart, is diminished by blockage of an artery, even for only an hour or two, the affected tissue suffers extensive and apparently irreversible damage. The same thing can happen in an organ that is being transplanted from a donor to a recipient. Conventional wisdom has stated that such damage was due to hypoxia imposed during the period of ischemia; it was thought that the only way to lessen such damage was to chill the tissue to reduce its oxygen needs and to reestablish blood flow as quickly as possible. According to this view, hypoxic cells are unable to meet their needs for the energy-rich compound adenosine triphosphate (ATP) and without ATP are unable to maintain proper ionic concentrations inside and outside the cell, synthesize new macromolecules, or repair damage to existing macromolecules, such as DNA.

Recent studies have demonstrated that the situation is at once more complicated and more easily controlled or remedial than previously believed. Much of the damage caused by a temporary cessation of blood flow occurs not during the period of ischemia-hypoxia but rather during the period of reperfusion-reoxygenation, when blood flow is restored. Temporary lack of oxygen makes the affected cells more susceptible to the toxicity of oxygen; this is the "oxygen paradox," and it can be prevented. Oxygen toxicity is largely due to reactive metabolic intermediates produced by partial reduction of oxygen. It can be lessened either by prevention of the production of these substances or by elimination of them as quickly as they are produced. Both of these ends can be achieved, and it is thus possible to sharply decrease the damaging consequences of temporary ischemia.

Xanthine dehydrogenase, ATP, and a calcium-activated proteinase are the components whose interactions lead to the oxygen paradox. Xanthine dehydrogenase is the enzyme that catalyzes the conversion of the metabolic product hypoxanthine to xanthine and of xanthine to uric acid. These conversions are oxidations; *i.e.,* they entail loss of electrons. Xanthine dehydrogenase readily transfers

the electrons, removed from its substrates (the specific molecules upon which the enzyme acts), to a coenzyme but not to oxygen.

Xanthine dehydrogenase can be converted into xanthine oxidase by hydrolysis (breaking) of just a few of the thousands of peptide bonds that hold its component amino acids together. Enzymes that catalyze such hydrolyses are called proteinases. Xanthine oxidase transfers electrons to molecular oxygen (O_2), both singly and in pairs, concomitantly reducing the oxygen to the superoxide radical (O^-_2) and to hydrogen peroxide (H_2O_2), which are reactive entities and damaging to living cells. The conversion of xanthine dehydrogenase to xanthine oxidase can, therefore, have serious consequences. It occurs during ischemia-hypoxia and is the first factor in the oxygen paradox.

Adenosine triphosphate, or ATP, serves as a source of readily available chemical energy in all living cells. It drives energy-requiring processes as diverse as muscle contraction and the pumping of ions across membranes. When it powers such processes, ATP loses phosphate and is converted to adenosine diphosphate (ADP), which, in turn, can lose another phosphate, yielding more energy plus adenosine monophosphate (AMP). There is a great deal of ATP in cells, ordinarily kept in this form by active resynthesis from AMP and ADP. Since the breakdown of ATP gives up energy, its resynthesis requires energy. In mammalian cells chemically useful energy is made available primarily during the transfer of electrons to oxygen in a process called oxidative phosphorylation. This process requires the presence of molecular oxygen. During hypoxia, when the oxygen supply fails, ATP synthesis cannot keep pace with ATP breakdown, and the ATP is degraded, first to ADP and then to AMP and ultimately to hypoxanthine and other products. Hypoxanthine, which is a substrate for xanthine oxidase, will thus accumulate in ischemic-hypoxic tissues. This is the second factor in the oxygen paradox.

Normal cells contain a calcium-activated proteinase. Under ordinary conditions, when the ATP level is high, the activity of this proteinase is limited because the calcium level is very low. The concentration of calcium in the cytosol (the fluid portion of the cytoplasm) of cells is usually kept low by the active pumping of calcium into subcellular organelles and out across the cell envelope. This active pumping of calcium requires energy and is driven by ATP. A decrease in the supply of ATP, such as that imposed by hypoxia-ischemia, will prevent the outpumping of calcium, and calcium concentration in the cytosol will rise. This is the third factor in the oxygen paradox.

A chain of adverse events is set in motion by ischemia. The lack of oxygen puts a virtual stop to the production of ATP, but the use of ATP continues. The ATP is degraded first to ADP and AMP, then to ammonia, ribose, and hypoxanthine. Hypoxanthine thus accumulates in the cells. The lack of ATP stops the active pumping of calcium; calcium accumulates in the cytosol, triggering activation of the calcium-dependent proteinase. The proteinase, in turn, modifies the xanthine dehydrogenase, converting it to xanthine oxidase. This sequence of events, occurring during the period of oxygen deficiency, sets the stage for the oxygen paradox. When blood flow is reestablished it provides oxygen, which allows the xanthine oxidase to act upon the accumulated hypoxanthine and to produce large quantities of superoxide and hydrogen peroxide, to the detriment of the cell membranes and macromolecules.

This destructive process can be stopped at two points. The first is the conversion of hypoxanthine by xanthine oxidase, which can be inhibited by the presence of allopurinol. This compound, which is another substrate of xanthine oxidase and which competes successfully for its activity, has been used for many years to inhibit the production of uric acid by xanthine dehydrogenase/oxidase and thus to ameliorate the symptoms of gout. Treatment with allopurinol prior to reperfusion should—and does—protect against the oxygen paradox.

The second point of intervention is during the appearance of superoxide and hydrogen peroxide. Small amounts of the two species are always produced in aerobic cells, but the enzymes superoxide dismutase and catalase protect against their deleterious effects by catalyzing their conversion to the harmless products water and oxygen. If the oxygen paradox is due to enhanced production of superoxide radical and hydrogen peroxide, then the enzymes superoxide dismutase plus catalase should protect against the toxic effects of oxygen if injected prior to reperfusion. In fact, they have been found to do so very effectively.

Amelioration of the oxygen paradox would improve the outlook for victims of heart attack caused by lodgement of a blood clot in a coronary artery. Such clots could be dissolved by introducing the enzyme plasmin into the vicinity of the clot via a catheter. However, dissolution of the clot and the reestablishment of blood flow expose the affected part of the heart to the potential of damage caused by the toxic effects of oxygen. Allopurinol, with superoxide dismutase plus catalase, could now be used to avoid this complication. In 1985 genetic engineering companies were producing large amounts of human superoxide dismutase, and clinical trials were under way, with promising results.

(IRWIN FRIDOVICH)

A New Way to Turn Genes Off. For any cell or any organism the process of living and growing depends upon the continuous and carefully regulated expression of its genetic material. Genes, which are composed of DNA, encode the information necessary for making all of the working parts of a cell. The expression of this information allows cells to grow and divide, to replace worn-out parts, and to adjust to changing environmental conditions. The expression of genes, in the form of their ultimate products, often proteins, is a complicated process involving many steps. The possibilities for regulation of this process are therefore also manifold. Recent investigations revealed a novel mechanism of regulation that not only seemed to function in living cells but that might also have significant impact on biological research and on the possibilities for corrective gene therapy.

To appreciate the regulation of a process, one must first understand the process itself. Although gene expression involves many steps, these steps can be grouped into two major categories: transcription and translation. Transcription, which occurs in the nucleus of higher cells, involves the synthesis of RNA from a corresponding DNA template. Once the mature RNA "message" has been transported from the nucleus to the cytoplasm of the cell, it may be used to direct the assembly of amino acids to make a specific protein. Because this process involves a change of "language"—from information encoded as a sequence of purine and pyrimidine bases in the RNA to that same information encoded as a sequence of amino acids in the protein—it is called translation.

Perhaps the best understood of the regulatory mechanisms governing gene expression work at the level of transcription. Of the factors known to regulate this process, all are proteins. Because transcription of DNA into RNA is the first step of gene expression, many regulatory mechanisms operate at this basic level. To turn something on, one must start at the beginning, and the most efficient

(continued on page 303)

Animal Rights

BY BENEDICT A. LEERBURGER
AND MICHAEL ALLABY

The belief that animals are endowed with certain rights is not a new concept. However, when England enacted legislation in 1822 "to prevent cruel and improper treatment of Cattle," it became the first country to codify and define not only what rights animals possessed but which animals possessed them. Perhaps more important, the act established the authority of government to regulate the treatment of privately owned animals. The animal rights movement, in Britain as in most other Western countries, grew out of fears that working farm animals and circus animals were being ill-fed and that livestock destined for slaughter were being subjected to needless suffering. Until the completion of the British railway network, sheep and cattle were driven to market, often for hundreds of miles, and people saw them being openly whipped. Throughout the 20th century new laws were enacted to protect specific types of animals—livestock, race horses, zoo animals, wildlife—and to cover specific circumstances—transportation, caging, pet keeping. But while certain abuses were being dealt with by statute, new practices, not covered by existing law, were arousing the anger of animal protectionists. Thus public concern today focuses primarily on inhumane treatment of animals in intensive livestock husbandry and laboratory experimentation, illegal hunting practices, and the callous neglect inflicted in private by some pet owners. In the U.S. more than 400 groups with two million dues-paying members are involved in protesting these practices.

Animals in Service to Man. Perhaps the greatest source of anger to all animal rights groups is the treatment received by animals in scientific tests and experiments. It is estimated that in the United States alone up to 70 million animals are employed in research each year. Although the vast majority of these are specially bred mice and rats, the use of other animals—including rabbits, primates, bovids (cattle, sheep, and related animals), and impounded cats and dogs—has spurred animal rights organizations to take action. To dramatize their point of view, one group, the Animal Liberation Front, was involved on Dec. 25, 1983, in the theft of several dogs that were being used in medical research at a Los Angeles hospital.

One of the prime goals of many animal rights groups is the replacement of experimental animals with alternatives such as tissue cultures and computer models. The Draize test, a procedure widely used by drug and cosmetic manufacturers, is frequently cited by these groups as a typical instance of the needless suffering to which laboratory animals are subjected. In the Draize test, the chemical under scrutiny is dropped into the eyes of rabbits to measure its potential for causing irritation. An even more contro-versial procedure is the "Lethal Dose 50" (LD50) test, which measures the toxicity of a substance by determining the dose lethal to half of the animals in any test group. This process was designed in 1927 to standardize drug potency. Until 1983 federal agencies, including the U.S. Food and Drug Administration, demanded LD50 testing prior to accepting certain substances—including such household products as oven cleaners—as "safe." In 1984, however, several research groups developed a substitute procedure using computer models to predict toxicity.

The Mobilization for Animals (MFA), an international network representing several hundred animal-protectionist organizations, makes a particularly strong attack on the use of "higher" animals, especially primates, in various forms of psychological experimentation. The MFA states that "Of all experiments [using animals], those conducted in psychology are the most painful, pointless and repulsive." The MFA and other animal advocacy groups have alleged that animals are given "intense, repeated electric shocks . . . are deprived of food and water . . . and are mutilated to produce behavioral changes." However, a study by Rockefeller University psychologists D. Caroline Coile and Neal E. Miller takes issue with these charges. Coile and Miller evaluated each of the 608 articles involving studies in which animals were used that appeared over a five-year period in the journals of the American Psychological Association. They concluded that none of the MFA claims could be supported, noting that while unreported acts of cruelty may have occurred, "it is extremely misleading to imply that they are typical of experimental psychology."

Those who support the use of higher animals in experimental programs contend that psychological studies require the observation of the whole animal and its relationship to the environment. They claim that behaviour problems cannot be observed in tissue cultures and do not lend themselves to computer models. Further, they point out that each year ten million dogs are destroyed by pounds, animal shelters, and humane societies, organizations often funded by animal protectionist groups. These scientists point out that in the U.S. there are existing mechanisms to ensure that research animals are treated in a humane

---

Benedict A. Leerburger is an editorial consultant and science writer whose articles have appeared in many popular publications, among them Look *and* Science News.

Michael Allaby is a free-lance writer and lecturer and a regular contributor to the Britannica Book of the Year.

A group called People for the Ethical Treatment of Animals staged a sit-in demonstration at a National Institutes of Health facility in Bethesda, Maryland, in July and succeeded in winning a suspension of a research project that involved inflicting head injuries on baboons.
AP/WIDE WORLD

way. Such mechanisms include the federal Animal Welfare Act, periodic inspection of all animal-research facilities by the Department of Agriculture, and personal inspections by representatives of federal agencies that fund animal research. In addition, most universities and research institutes have special committees that monitor animal research and care.

The Movement in Britain. The British animal welfare organizations fall into three main groups. There are those like the Royal Society for the Prevention of Cruelty to Animals that have a broad concern for all animals. They accept the need for some use of animals in scientific experimentation but seek to tighten controls over such procedures, to reduce the number of animals necessary, and, wherever possible, to adopt alternative techniques. Others, such as the Research Defense Society, the Humane Trust, and the other members of the so-called Moderate Coalition, concentrate on encouraging the development of laboratory procedures that eliminate the need for test animals.

The third group takes a more extreme position. They regard humans and nonhumans as moral equals and view all exploitation of animals as unjust. They would not permit the keeping of animals for meat, milk, or eggs, much less for furs, and they would ban all animal experimentation. One such organization is the British Union for the Abolition of Vivisection, which supports other "animal liberation" groups as well. It does not advocate violent protest but, like the Animal Liberation Front in the U.S., it supports those who enter premises illegally to destroy equipment and remove animals. In February 1985 its prosecution of the Royal College of Surgeons succeeded despite the fact that evidence produced by the union had been obtained illegally. The case, in which the college was found guilty of cruelty to a macaque monkey, was under appeal at year's end.

The Controversy over Hunting. Perhaps the question "To hunt or not to hunt?" best illustrates the controversy between advocates of animal rights and those who believe it is essential to permit limited killing. U.S. experts in wildlife management have urged the selective hunting of white-tailed deer to prevent overpopulation of the species.

Biologists estimate that one square mile of range can support no more than 25 deer; when this number is exceeded, the food supply diminishes and, in turn, the herd's physical condition is directly altered. With hunting being either limited or curtailed, deer populations are increasing at an alarming rate, according to these authorities. Today, for example, more deer roam the state of Pennsylvania than existed in the entire country at the turn of the century. Mississippi's herd has grown from about 1,500 in the 1930s to a current size of about a million.

In early 1985 state and federal wildlife managers agreed to open selected state and national preserves to limited deer hunting to thin the herds. Opposing this action is the Fund for Animals, which proposed instead a program of mass birth control—the implantation of time-release capsules that would prevent ovulation for several years. Although a similar method is used by zoos, it proved unsuccessful when tried in the wild on Angel Island, California, in the early 1980s. Says animal rights advocate Priscilla Cohn, "A lot of people say that hunting is as American as apple pie. But we're not living on the Plains with herds of buffalo anymore." Spokesmen for hunting organizations term such comments "Bambi hysteria."

The Fund for Animals is also one of the leading animal rights organizations opposed to the killing of baby harp seals, which are "harvested" by Canadian Eskimos for their highly desirable downy-white fur. Even following a ban on the importation of "white-coat" pelts by the European Communities in 1983, it was estimated that in 1984, 143,-000 seal pups were slaughtered. Although the Canadian government has imposed a limit of 186,000 seal pups per year, various animal rights organizations, including the International Fund for Animal Welfare and Greenpeace, have urged a U.S. boycott of Canadian fish to protest that government's policy of allowing the killing of any baby seals.

The direct killing of animals is only one aspect of hunting objected to by animal rights groups. It has been estimated that each year U.S. hunters deposit some 3,000 tons of lead pellets in lakes, ponds, and marshes. Waterfowl accidentally ingest these pellets while feeding, and this has led to increased mortality from lead poisoning. According to *Sports Illustrated,* "The mortality rate from lead poisoning is thought to be 2 to 3% of the fall population of all species, and that means that between 1.6 and 2.4 million ducks die each year."

A Growing Movement. In the U.S. those supporting a general policy of humane treatment of all animals have made significant inroads by their lobbying efforts with state and national lawmakers. Legislation now exists in many states governing the treatment and sale of pets. In some states, for example, rabbits and baby chickens—once bought in great numbers as Eastertime novelties—can no longer be sold as pets. And despite the guidelines issued by the U.S. Department of Agriculture for the humane raising and slaughter of domestic animals, animal protectionists continue to protest the abuses of "factory" farming, including the overcrowded caging of calves, hogs, and chickens. The international movement to assure the rights of all animals is active on all continents. Australian philosopher Peter Singer, author of *Animal Liberation,* observes that "we treat animals as if they were things to be used as we please, rather than as beings with lives of their own to live." If the advocates of animal rights are successful in their campaign, the lives of animals will be regarded with increased respect, and those who deal with animals, from pets to prey, will be increasingly subject to oversight and regulation.

(continued from page 300)

way to turn something off is to "nip it in the bud." Sometimes, however, speed rather than efficiency is the key issue. The fastest way to halt production of a gene product is to interfere with the terminal step of production. The terminal step, translation of protein from messenger RNA (mRNA), is in fact the stage at which this newly described form of regulation appears to function. What is more, the regulatory factor is not a protein but an RNA molecule.

The observation that a factor inhibiting the translation of specific mRNAs is itself a molecule of RNA is striking because it immediately suggests a mechanism of action: base pairing. To understand why, one must consider the structure of RNA; it is a linear arrangement of four types of ribonucleotides, each of which may contain either adenine (A), uracil (U), guanine (G), or cytosine (C). Each of these four bases may form stabilizing hydrogen bonds to another base. The formation of such stabilizing bonds is called base pairing because bases associate with each other not randomly but in an orderly way: A pairs only with U, and G pairs only with C.

One can imagine that the most stable association for two strands of RNA, then, would involve a pattern in which each base found itself directly opposite a base with which it could pair. Such strands exist and are called complementary. The following example illustrates two complementary strands of RNA that have associated with one another by the pairing of their bases. Such association is called hybridization. The dotted lines denote the hydrogen bonds formed between complementary bases.

—A—A—U—C—C—A—G—C—

—U—U—A—G—G—U—C—G—

Why should one strand of RNA inhibit translation of its complementary strand? This is a complicated question, and in 1985 the answer was not yet known; there were, however, several possibilities under consideration.

The process of translation involves a close association between the RNA being translated (mRNA) and subcellular particles known as ribosomes. These ribosomes, which are the cell's protein-making machinery, must bind to the mRNA, along with several other factors, and then move along the mRNA sequence while assembling the corresponding chain of amino acids. The mRNA must be single-stranded in order to accommodate the ribosome. Were the cell to produce another strand of RNA that was complementary to all or even to a part of a particular mRNA, it could combine with the first strand, by hydrogen bonding of the bases, to form a stable double-stranded structure. Because translation of mRNA depends upon its remaining single-stranded, hybridization with a complementary RNA might prevent translation of the mRNA. At the State University of New York at Stony Brook, Masayori Inouye and his colleagues recently confirmed that the production of RNA strands complementary to particular mRNAs functions within cells as a means of regulating gene expression.

It was also possible that any strand of mRNA that is bound by its complementary strand might simply be more susceptible to degradation than its single-stranded counterparts. In 1985 data were still sparse on this topic, and it remained difficult to draw definite conclusions. Preliminary evidence suggested that double-stranded RNA is found only in the nucleus of the cell (where RNA is transcribed from DNA), not in the cytoplasm (where translation takes place). These data suggested that the block in gene expression caused by the formation of complementary RNA may occur prior to the step of translation.

What is so special about this form of regulation that makes it useful for biologic research? Classically, scientists have studied the function of particular gene products by observing what happens to cells in their absence. If cells with a certain gene are able to make a particular product while cells lacking that gene also lack that product, the logical conclusion is that the gene under study has something to do with the formation of the product in question. The problem is finding those cells that lack a particular gene but in which all other genes are intact. Because genes mutate to inactivity at a small but finite frequency in nature, the isolation of cells lacking particular functional genes can be accomplished by selecting those cells from amid a large population of nonmutated cells. This can be very difficult. An alternative method involves the introduction into cells of RNA that is complementary to the gene under study. Experiments conducted by Harold Weintraub and colleagues at the Fred Hutchinson Cancer Research Center, Seattle, Wash., showed that the presence of this "antisense" RNA, as it is called, drastically reduces the expression of the related gene. Hence, the cell can be studied as though it carried a crippling mutation in that gene. Furthermore, the antisense RNA can be introduced into cells in a way such that it is inducible—that is, made or not made, depending on the conditions under which the cells are maintained. This means, in essence, that the complementary gene may be turned off ("mutated") or turned back on ("restored to function") at will. The impact of such technical possibilities on future biologic research could be profound.

What about the application of this biologic research to the field of medicine? When people think of corrective gene therapy, they often think of replacing mutated genes with functional ones. Numerous examples exist of diseases caused by mutated genes—sickle-cell anemia, phenylketonuria, and β-thalassemia, to name a few.

Individuals suffering from sickle-cell anemia, for example, carry a single mutation in one of the genes coding for hemoglobin, the blood protein that carries oxygen from the lungs to the rest of the tissues. Victims of sickle-cell anemia carry a defective gene that codes for the production of an aberrant type of hemoglobin, which functions poorly, leading directly to the symptoms of the disease. The obvious therapy for this disease is the replacement of the mutated gene with a normal one. Replacement involves two steps: introduction of a normal gene product and suppression of the mutant form. Techniques for introducing genes into cells were currently available and were being improved. The use of antisense RNA technology might facilitate suppression of the aberrant gene product by inhibiting the expression of the mutant gene.

In addition, the ability to selectively suppress gene products from cells might prove relevant to the battle against cancer. It was becoming increasingly apparent that the introduction of specific gene products into cells could make them cancerous. If this was true, reasoning suggested that the removal of those gene products might cause cancerous cells to behave normally again. The possibilities for medical applications of the control of gene expression were numerous and exciting.   (JUDITH L. FRIDOVICH-KEIL)

See also Earth Sciences; Environment.

This article updates the *Macropædia* articles Animal BEHAVIOUR; BIOCHEMICAL COMPONENTS OF ORGANISMS; THE BIOLOGICAL SCIENCES; CANCER; CIRCULATION AND CIRCULATORY SYSTEMS; ECOSYSTEMS; ENDOCRINE SYSTEMS; THE PRINCIPLES OF GENETICS AND HEREDITY; BIOLOGICAL GROWTH AND DEVELOPMENT; ORGANS AND ORGAN SYSTEMS; REPRODUCTION AND REPRODUCTIVE SYSTEMS.

Literature

The 1985 Nobel Prize for Literature was awarded to the French novelist Claude Simon. (*See* BIOGRAPHIES; *French: France,* below.) He was remembered as a representative of the *nouveau roman* ("new novel") mode of the 1950s, a method of writing without regular construction or punctuation to give the impression of a stream of consciousness. As this technique had never been widely admired or emulated in the English-speaking world, there was a reaction of surprise at the Stockholm committee's decision and a feeling that, if it was France's turn for the prize, Marguerite Yourcenar, the first woman elected to the Académie Française, might well have been the recipient.

In France the Prix Goncourt went to Yann Queffélec for his novel *Les Noces barbares,* the story of a young boy hated by his mother. Another story of adult hostility to a child won the Booker McConnell Prize in Britain; this was *The Bone People,* written by the New Zealand feminist Keri Hulme. The runner-up in this London contest was a long novel about 40 years of life in Australia, *Illywhacker,* by Peter Carey; it presented the tamed inhabitants of a Sydney pet shop as a tragicomic picture of what had happened in Australia. Another Australian, Julian Croft, joined Lauris Edmond, a New Zealander, among the winners of the British Airways Poetry Prize, promoted by the Commonwealth Institute. The newly created $50,000 Ritz Paris Hemingway Award, commemorating Ernest Hemingway's long association with the Paris Ritz Hotel, went to Mario Vargas Llosa of Peru for *Guerra del fin del mundo* (*The War of the End of the World*).

In Eastern Europe, Hungarian writers challenged the state with a paradoxical appeal *for* censorship. "Give us censorship," said Istvan Eorsi. "Give us one office which is clearly and officially denoted as the Censors'. Specify its powers." The Hungarian predicament was described in a New York journal by Timothy Garton Ash, foreign editor of the London *Spectator,* who attended an official literary conference in Budapest and also an unofficial parallel conference, where the participants were not certain if their proceedings were permitted. Garton Ash urged Western writers to pay attention to the plight of their Hungarian counterparts. Comparable problems in Czechoslovakia were illustrated in two fine novels. One was *The Engineer of Human Souls,* a long and complicated study by Josef Skvorecky, a Czech exiled in Canada. The other was Philip Roth's *The Prague Orgy,* a neater, slicker tale that came to remarkably similar conclusions.

Claude Simon

ENGLISH

United Kingdom. It was a good year for dead authors, seen as solid investments. Fiction best-sellers, good or bad, became a Stock Exchange attraction as investors sought a share of the profits made by commercial publishers, rationalizing the industry through a series of takeovers. Paul Hamlyn took over William Heinemann (with books by Conrad, Kipling, Lawrence, Stevenson, and Wells) to add to the strength of his Octopus group; Associated Book Publishers acquired Routledge & Keegan Paul; Penguin took over Hamish Hamilton and Michael Joseph. Much of the financial success of these maneuvers came from the use of novels by dead authors to make films for television or the cinema, among them E. M. Forster's *A Passage to India,* Paul Scott's *The Raj Quartet,* and J. B. Priestley's *Lost Empires.* The director of the Publishers' Association told the London *Daily Telegraph* that the takeovers were "part of the transformation of book publishing into big business. People are looking for companies that have a good list of titles." Dead authors, he meant. A *Daily Telegraph* writer applauded the book trade for "catching up, belatedly, with other forms of big business" but was worried that this rationalization might mean that "those in the seat of power will be people who can add up rather than read. Authors may feel that they will be handled like pieces of merchandise." Live authors, he meant.

Encyclopaedic books about dead authors proliferated. Margaret Drabble compiled a new edition of the *Oxford Companion to English Literature.* Pat Rogers, editor of the forthcoming *New Oxford Illustrated History of English Literature,* wrote with great enthusiasm of Peter Conrad's *Everyman History of English Literature.* Rogers remarked that this book was more academic than the original Everyman series, which had offered reference books for mythology and historical atlases but did not expect readers to want a history of literature. The original Everyman literary introductions, said Rogers, had been "confident and untechnical—Chesterton on Dickens, Saintsbury on Balzac—making the classics appear accessibly classical." Another compendium, *Guide to Modern World Literature,* was compiled by Martin Seymour-Smith, giving aggressive critical accounts of fiction and poetry in English and no fewer than 32 other languages. John Carey, professor of English literature at the University of Oxford, wondered why the "ferociously industrious and scathing" Seymour-Smith had performed this task. He surmised that such critics could "reconcile their love of literature with their hostility and suspicion only by criticizing."

The centenary of the birth of D. H. Lawrence was celebrated with a Lawrence Poetry Prize sponsored by the East Midlands Gas Board and with films and plays about his affair with Frieda Weekley. In Eastwood, his Nottinghamshire birthplace, there was a move to rename a school after Lawrence, but the proposal was opposed by Councillor Ernest Chambers, a relative of Lawrence's earlier girlfriend, Jessie Chambers. "Lawrence hated the place," said the councillor. "When he left with Frieda he literally dusted his boots on the tram. I don't want Eastwood to prostitute itself for Lawrence."

Fiction. Among the most ambitious and impressive novels of the year were three historical romances, all of them expressing or implying strong views about the 20th century. *Gentlemen in England,* by the often mordant and morbid A. N. Wilson, expressed a real affection for the year 1880, which he found preferable to the present day. "Gentlemen in England now a-bed," he began (quoting *Henry V*), "Shall think themselves accurs'd they were not here"—

in 1880. The hero of the story was Lionel Nettleship, a young man striving to become a priest in the Church of England, against the will of his atheistic father, a learned geologist. Arguments and eccentricities within the church and its Catholic Revival combined with tales of 19th-century painting, courtship, and simple gossip to present an agreeable and historically credible reconstruction.

With *A Maggot* John Fowles offered a historical mystery about the disappearance of a dissident, visionary young nobleman while traveling with a prostitute, a mute manservant, and two men of the London theatre in the year 1736. The manservant is found hanged, prompting a legal inquiry into his death. Much of the book was presented in the form of an 18th-century report of a lawyer's interrogation, credibly imitated by the author. The title referred to the archaic use of the word maggot to mean a whim or a quirk. Nevertheless, the word maggot was used in at least two different senses in the book, helping *A Maggot* to take on a persuasively occult or metaphysical authority.

Also set in the 18th century, for the most part, was Peter Ackroyd's eerie mystery *Hawksmoor,* concerning a 20th-century policeman of that name (which was also the name of an 18th-century church architect) investigating a series of child murders that somehow relate to the satanic activities of another 18th-century church architect. This complex, unhinging story gave many readers horrid but pleasurable thrills, and it was one of the winners of the important Whitbread Prize.

Among the unsuccessful contenders for the Booker McConnell Prize were two senior novelists whom the jury perhaps considered too successful and well established to win the competition. Doris Lessing, after five volumes of science-fiction fantasy, returned to the real-life world of left-wing politics in *The Good Terrorist,* castigating not only the inequalities of the social system but also the childish folly of some of those in rebellion against it. "A bunch of canting cronies who term themselves the Communist Centre Union," wrote the critic Peter Kemp, with relish. "They are people in whom virulent political propaganda has taken festering hold of a personality already weakened by psychological and emotional maladies."

Iris Murdoch, with *The Good Apprentice,* offered a novel about another group of confused people, unsure about the meaning and use of the words good and evil in a world without God. The godless ones, wrote Victoria Glendinning, "all want to worship, to confess . . . and they turn to spiritualism, . . . or to sex, romantic love, drugs or psychiatry. . . . Stuart, who wants to be good without recourse to any such devices, operates in a sterile vacuum until he realizes that he can't begin to be good without recognizing his capacity for evil. Stuart is the good apprentice who, like Doris Lessing's 'good terrorist,' has got it all a bit wrong." This was a novel with relevance to Murdoch's work as a scholarly philosopher.

Discovered in the archives of Metro-Goldwyn-Mayer was a novel by Graham Greene, written in 1944 as the draft for a film script. It was published as *The Tenth Man,* with a preface by Greene, who was surprised to find "this forgotten story very readable—indeed I prefer it in many ways to *The Third Man.*" It was the story of a Frenchman called Charlot (the French name for Charlie Chaplin), held as a hostage during the Nazi occupation, making a disgraceful bargain to save his life and finally making a good death. The pressure of Roman Catholicism in the story disconcerted many critics but did not detract from its appeal to the general reader.

Lives, Letters. To commemorate the career of Earl Mountbatten, assassinated by Irish terrorists in 1979, Philip

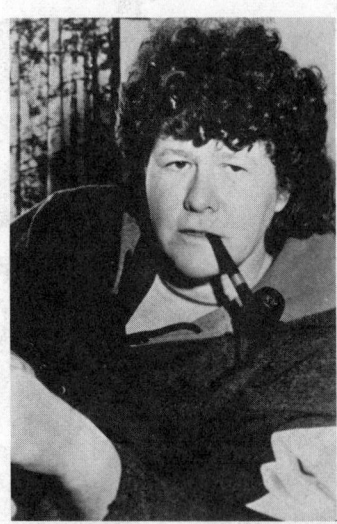

Keri Hulme

Ziegler offered *Mountbatten: The Official Biography.* The author, sometimes irritated by Mountbatten's ways, remarked that he had kept upon his desk a notice reading: Remember, in spite of everything, he was a great man. Roy Jenkins, a former home secretary, shed doubt on this evaluation but admitted that "Mountbatten, for good or ill, was decisive in replacing the old, fairly tight-knit white family with the loose new multi-racial Commonwealth."

Other statesmen reconsidered were Sir Austen Chamberlain, of whom Winston Churchill said, "He always played the game and always lost it," and the half-forgotten Hugh Dalton, a powerful member of Clement Attlee's government, brought back to life in Ben Plimlott's admired biography. Churchill himself, inevitably, was prominent again in *The Fringes of Power,* diaries kept between 1939 and 1955 by his secretary, Sir John Colville. The published diaries of poet Stephen Spender also had a strong political tinge, taking him from his pro-Communist youth in prewar Germany through his work for the anti-Communist journal *Encounter* and his international campaigning against political censorship. Another long diary, kept by the Scottish left-wing historical novelist Naomi Mitchison during World War II as a contribution to the "Mass Observation" experiment in sociology, was edited, published, and admired under the Burns-inspired title *Among You Taking Notes.*

There were new lives of two British cardinals of the Roman Catholic Church, Henry Manning and Arthur Hinsley, two composers, Schubert and Schumann, and two Victorian prophets, Charles Darwin and John Ruskin. Tim Hilton's *John Ruskin: The Early Years, 1819–1859* was especially admired. With *Chaplin: His Life and Art* David Robinson added a weighty tome to the library of books about the great man. Robinson's book looked like the definitive biography, the end of the whole story, but immediately after its publication some long-lost reels of old Chaplin movies were discovered, thus adding new material for future writers. Another distinguished actor, Sir Alec Guinness, presented his memoirs as *Blessings in Disguise,* with characteristic elegance and mysterious self-effacement.

Among the new series of feminine biographies was "Lives of Modern Women," which got off to a good start with four books (all by women) about the novelists Jean Rhys and Rebecca West, the singer Bessie Smith, and the intrepid traveler and Arabist Freya Stark. The collected letters of Dylan Thomas were published and mocked by Kingsley Amis for their "lyric flights of imitation pathos

Graham Greene
GAMMA/LIAISON

and real cadging," reminding readers of a good, new, Amis-like novel about Thomas-haunted Swansea, *Banana Cat* by Christopher Hood. A remarkable new study of Byron by Louis Crompton, called *Byron and Greek Love,* developed the story of his amours into an account of homosexual behaviour in the Regency period, with references to the impressive liberalism of Jeremy Bentham at a time when such behaviour was a capital offense.

Poetry. Sir Stephen Spender published, as well as his diaries, a new version of his *Collected Poems,* much trimmed and refined, and his translation, as a stage version, of three plays by Sophocles to be performed together in one evening. Ted Hughes (*see* BIOGRAPHIES), the new poet laureate, published two poems of public statement and national concern. One addressed the issue of conservation, supporting Prince Philip's argument that to "preserve" game birds for shooting parties was a reputable and coherent policy. The other, "For the Duration," concerned an old soldier whose grim silence about his wartime exploits combined with his nighttime shouting during nightmares to suggest that "his war was more unbearable than anybody else's."

Basil Bunting died in the spring at the age of 85 (*see* OBITUARIES). A north-country poet and music critic, he was almost unknown in Britain (although respected in the U.S.) until the mid-1960s, but he ended his long life with a high reputation for his original, difficult work, constructed in accordance with his ideas of musical form, influenced by Ezra Pound, his prewar friend, and by Wordsworth, his fellow north-countryman. In the winter three other senior poets died, all of them remarkably independent and influential: Robert Graves, Geoffrey Grigson, and Philip Larkin. (*See* OBITUARIES.) Graves was 90 and had published several novels, essays, and translations, as well as his memorable poems, some brilliantly waspish, some gaily scornful about death, many at once clever and ecstatic about love between men and women. The versatile Grigson was 80 when he died. Best known as an editor and ferociously severe critic of poetry, he also had a following

for his terse, refined verses, the last of which was published in December. Philip Larkin was only 63, and so his death was mourned with great regret. Although he was quite formidably witty and sturdy as a man, his poems often expressed a stoical contemplation of his own frailty and diffidence. One of the last, "Aubade," sternly evoked a fear of death, but some of his mourners preferred to remember his beautiful poem about dying, "Cut grass lies frail."

(D. A. N. JONES)

United States. *Fiction.* Perhaps the most notable literary event in the United States during 1985 was the appearance of a new novel by William Gaddis. *Carpenter's Gothic* was his first since *JR,* which won the National Book Award in 1976, and only his third in a 30-year literary career. Although considerably briefer than its massive predecessors, *Carpenter's Gothic* certainly approached them in artfulness and originality.

While it was not among his best work, the appearance of Ray Bradbury's first novel in more than 20 years was also a welcome event. *Death Is a Lonely Business,* an affectionate pastiche of the hard-boiled detective novel, was full of allusions not only to Dashiell Hammett and Raymond Chandler but also to Bradbury's own stories and to his early years as a writer.

Among the most enthusiastically praised fiction of the year was Anne Tyler's tenth novel, *The Accidental Tourist.* Set in her now familiar literary landscape of middle-class Baltimore, Md., Tyler's crisply written comedy of manners once again displayed her brilliant gift for rendering dialogue and the details of domestic life. Ann Beattie, another writer who had marked out a fictional territory, in her case the world of the upwardly mobile members of the baby-boom generation, returned to it in her third novel, *Love Always.* As adept as Tyler at amusing dialogue and relentless in amassing sharply observed details of everyday life among the yuppies, Beattie was less successful in making use of these gifts to delineate convincing character, and *Love Always* degenerated into self-parody.

Two of American literature's foremost practitioners of black comedy produced notable examples of the genre during the year. In *Stanley Elkin's The Magic Kingdom* the author employed his idiosyncratic prose style to brilliant comic effect on what would seem an impossible subject, a trip to Disneyland for a group of terminally ill children. *Galápagos,* the best of Kurt Vonnegut's recent novels, returned to one of his familiar themes, apocalypse. An account of the founding of a colony on one of the Galápagos Islands by the survivors of a sunken luxury liner in the wake of various planetary disasters, Vonnegut's new novel was typically inventive, digressive, and funny.

Gloria Naylor's first book, *The Women of Brewster Place,* a powerfully written series of connected short stories about the black inhabitants of a poor neighbourhood, won the 1983 American Book Award for first fiction. In her ambitious and effective novel *Linden Hills,* she moved up the social ladder to explore the stressful world of upper-middle-class black professionals. *Betsey Brown,* a second novel by poet and playwright Ntozake Shange, was a vivid account of the life of a black middle-class family in St. Louis, Mo., in 1959—the year that city began to integrate its schools—seen through the eyes of its 13-year-old heroine. Full of the lyrical passages that marked her first novel, *Sassafrass, Cypress & Indigo,* it was more conventional in its storytelling than her eccentric earlier book.

The latest American writer to emerge from the confines of genre fiction and into the awareness of a larger public was Elmore Leonard, whose 19th crime novel, *Glitz,* was widely and extravagantly praised by the reviewers and

spent many weeks on the best-seller list. Science-fiction writer Ursula K. Le Guin's latest novel, *Always Coming Home,* was an intriguing multimedia experiment. The entire ethnography of the Kesh, a people dwelling in the far-distant future, including everything from their myths to their recipes, was accompanied by a cassette containing the music of the Kesh, the work of composer Todd Barton.

The new celebrity among U.S. humorists was radio monologist Garrison Keillor (*see* BIOGRAPHIES), whose eminence was confirmed by his appearance on the cover of *Time* magazine. Keillor demonstrated a broad range of comic tone in *Lake Wobegon Days,* his account of the doings of the stoic locals in a small Minnesota town, from the poignant absurdity of the sad tale of the rise and fall of local baseball great Wally ("Hard Hands") Bunsen to the epigrammatic daffiness of his description of a religious neighbour who "thought cards were okay so long as you didn't play with a full deck." *Crows,* a fine second novel by Charles Dickinson, author of the much-praised *Waltz in Marathon,* demonstrated the same strengths as his first book—convincing, attractive, well-drawn characters, a strong pictorial quality, a droll humour, and considerable stylistic resource. His affection for the engaging eccentrics of Mozart, Wis., was as appealingly obvious as that of Keillor for Lake Wobegon, Minn.

Carolyn Chute's impressive first novel, *The Beans of Egypt, Maine,* an account of life in the rural slums of the Northeast, was an extraordinary mixture of poverty, squalor, violence, and hilarity. Louise Erdrich's first novel, *Love Medicine,* forcefully employed multiple narrators in the creation of the fictional tapestry blending past and present with which Erdrich expressed contemporary Native American life; it won the National Book Critics Circle's award for fiction. *In Country,* a first novel by Bobbie Ann Mason, dealt movingly with the legacy of the Vietnam war and confirmed the high reputation established by her first book, *Shiloh and Other Stories.*

There was continuing evidence of the revival of interest in short fiction. E. L. Doctorow's sixth book was a collection of short fiction. *Lives of the Poets: Six Stories and a Novella* contained some of the best writing Doctorow had done. Philip Roth appended a brilliant comic novella, *The Prague Orgy,* as an epilogue to a new, single-volume edition of his three Zuckerman novels. The American Book Award for fiction went to Ellen Gilchrist's collection of short stories, *Victory over Japan.* Tobias Wolff's brief, brilliant first novel, *The Barracks Thief,* won the year's PEN/Faulkner award for fiction.

Explaining the popularity of the short story with younger writers, David Leavitt observed that it was "a form they seem to find most appropriate to the age of shortened attention spans, fractured marriages, and splintering families in which they grew up." Several of the members of this new literary generation, some in their late 20s and early 30s, published their first collections of short fiction during the year. Among the most highly praised were Leavitt's own collection, *Family Dancing,* Amy Hempel's *Reasons to Live,* and Lorrie Moore's *Self-Help.* The stories in Tobias Wolff's second collection, *Back in the World,* displayed the narrative strength, well-defined characterization, and moral subtlety that marked those in his superb first volume, *In the Garden of the North American Martyrs.* With *Greasy Lake and Other Stories,* his first collection of short fiction since the brilliant and eccentric tales of *Descent of Man* in 1979, T. Coraghessan Boyle once again demonstrated his black-comic virtuosity.

History, Biography, and Belles Lettres. The revival in popularity of narrative history continued during the year.

The figures of Theodore Roosevelt and Woodrow Wilson dominated the seventh volume of Page Smith's *People's History of the United States. America Enters the World: A People's History of the Progressive Era and World War I* was a comprehensive, highly readable narrative of two critical decades during which the U.S. emerged as a world power. Well-handled narrative also dominated *The Workshop of Democracy,* the second volume of *The American Experiment,* James McGregor Burns's projected three-volume history of the U.S., which covered the period from the Civil War to the early years of the Great Depression.

Having extensively studied World War II "from the rarefied perspective of the Supreme Commander" in producing his definitive biography of Dwight D. Eisenhower, historian Stephen E. Ambrose felt the desire to get closer to the action "because at Ike's level one did not hear the guns, see the dead, feal the fear, know any combat." The result of the desire was an interesting essay in narrative history, *Pegasus Bridge: June 6, 1944,* a skillful minute-by-minute account of a single military operation, the seizure of a critical bridge in Normandy by British gliderborne troops who were the first Allied soldiers to touch French soil on D-Day. Another well-written account of World War II combat was *Iwo Jima: Legacy of Valor* by Bill D. Ross. Far larger in scope than *Pegasus Bridge,* Ross's book exhaustively considered both the background and the impact of one of the bloodiest campaigns in U.S. military history.

Perhaps the most debated book of the year was *Losing Ground: American Social Policy 1950–1980* by neoconservative intellectual Charles Murray. A compelling if tendentious piece of revisionism, it detailed its author's view that the liberal social programs that had shaped U.S. domestic politics for the last several decades had had a perverse effect. Focusing his study on American blacks, Murray amassed a great deal of data to demonstrate that, despite the fact that welfare spending was 20 times greater in 1980 than in

Ursula Le Guin

Garrison Keillor
JIM BRANDENBURG

1950, the same period had also seen enormous increases among blacks in unemployment, crime, and illegitimacy and decreases in educational levels and family stability. Another absorbing study of the unintended consequences of liberal social programs was J. Anthony Lukas's *Common Ground,* a brilliantly written account of what happened in Boston between 1968 and 1978 as a result of court-ordered busing to integrate the city's schools.

Hemingway: A Biography by Jeffrey Meyers was only the second full-scale life of the writer to have appeared since his death in 1961. While in no way replacing Carlos Heard Baker's massively detailed 1969 volume, *Ernest Hemingway: A Life Story,* Meyers's book was generally well done and did contain revealing new material. Peter Griffin's study, *Along with Youth: Hemingway, the Early Years,* dealt in an interesting way with the writer's childhood and youth and carried its account of Hemingway forward to the time of his first marriage. Griffin's book included five previously unpublished short stories by the young Hemingway. *Dateline: Toronto,* edited by William White, was an interesting collection of articles written by Hemingway for the *Toronto Star* between early 1920 and late 1924. Norman Mailer, whom Jeffrey Meyers termed "the hip-pocket Hemingway of our time," was himself the subject of a huge, gossipy biography by Peter Manso. *Mailer: His Life and Times* was an inevitably intriguing patchwork pieced together from the tape-recorded recollections of scores of the writer's friends and enemies.

James Baldwin's *The Price of the Ticket: Collected Nonfiction, 1948–1985,* which included such polemical classics as his book-length essay from 1963, *The Fire Next Time,* gave powerful testimony to his stature as a literary stylist and social critic. Perhaps the most eloquent discussion

of literature to appear during the year was *Enlarging the Change: The Princeton Seminars in Literary Criticism, 1949–1951,* by the late Robert Fitzgerald, who died January 16. A fascinating presentation of conversations involving such figures as John Berryman, Delmore Schwartz, R. P. Blackmur, Erich Auerbach, Jacques Maritain, Mark Schorer, and Allen Tate, *Enlarging the Change* was based on Fitzgerald's original transcriptions, which had lain forgotten in his files for 30 years. John McPhee's *Table of Contents* and Stephen Jay Gould's *The Flamingo's Smile* confirmed both writers' high reputations as essayists on scientific topics. The English language lost a staunch defender and able practitioner with the death of E. B. White (*see* OBITUARIES).

Poetry. Certainly the major event in American poetry during the year was the appearance of Allen Ginsberg's *Collected Poems 1947–1980,* which both fully displayed his evolution and achievement as a poet and offered substantial evidence of the importance of his role in the literary and political history of the last several decades. James Merrill's *Late Settings,* his tenth collection of poetry and his first since his highly regarded metaphysical epic *The Changing Light at Sandover* in 1982, was more relaxed in its virtuosity but confirmed his reputation as one of America's foremost poets. Galway Kinnell's new collection, *The Past,* dealt strongly with his most persistent theme, the transience of existence. In his fourth book, *Black Hair,* Gary Soto continued his examination of the experience of being Mexican in the U.S., but the tone of his latest verse was far less bleak than that of his earlier work. John Updike's fifth collection of poetry, *Facing Nature,* demonstrated once again his mastery of, among many other things, light verse.

Literary Awards. Pulitzer Prizes were awarded in 1985 for work published in 1984. The winners included: fiction—Alison Lurie, *Foreign Affairs;* history—Thomas K. McCraw, *The Prophets of Regulation;* biography—Kenneth Silverman, *The Life and Times of Cotton Mather;* general nonfiction—Studs Terkel, *"The Good War": An Oral History of World War Two;* poetry—Carolyn Kizer, *Yin;* drama—Stephen Sondheim and James Lapine, *Sunday in the Park with George.* The 1985 Bollingen Prize in Poetry was awarded jointly to John Ashbery and Fred Chappell. Both were honoured for the body of their work. Pamela Alexander's *Navigable Waterways* was a somewhat controversial choice for Volume 80 of the prestigious Yale Series of Younger Poets. The Library of Congress named Gwendolyn Brooks as poetry consultant for 1985–86.

(FITZGERALD HIGGINS)

Canada. It was exciting to see how Canada's social and cultural mosaic was increasingly reflected in the works of new writers. In 1985, for example, there were *Digging Up the Mountains: Selected Stories* by Neil Bissoondath, with stories set in the West Indies, Canada, and anonymously violent countries throughout the world; a different slant on the experience of West Indians in Canada in the eight stories comprising Austin Clarke's *When Women Rule;* and *Darkness* by Bharati Mukherjee, another collection of short stories, in which the cruelty of some Canadians toward people from Pakistan and India is incised on the reader's consciousness with ironic precision. Books dealing with the experiences of European immigrants in Canada included *My Harp Has Turned to Mourning,* Al Reimer's poignant exploration of the ways in which Mennonites adapted—or did not adapt—to their new lives.

Other significant prose works published during the year were Janette Turner Hospital's third novel, *Borderline,* in which two strangers, meeting at the Canadian border,

Robertson Davies
PAUL ORENSTEIN

create an international incident out of a flurry of misunderstandings; Margaret Atwood's *The Handmaid's Tale,* a grim fable of the puritanical theocratic dictatorship that could develop if certain current trends were taken to one of their possible logical extremes; and Ann Ireland's *A Certain Mr. Takahashi,* winner of the 1985 Seal First Novel Award. There were also new works by Hugh Hood, a collection of short stories and a novella entitled *August Nights;* David Donnell, *The Blue Ontario Hemingway Boat Race,* in which the protagonist of a series of linked stories is based on Hemingway during the 1920s when he worked on the *Toronto Star;* Mavis Gallant, *Overhead in a Balloon: Stories of Paris;* Robert Harlow, *Felice: A Travelogue,* which on one level recounts a woman's private encounter with the sorrows of Poland and on another considers "a woman's place" in contemporary Canadian society; and Edna Alford, *The Garden of Eloise Loon,* a familiar place viewed from a strange angle.

Also deserving of mention were Scott Symons's celebration of the many incarnations of love in *Helmet of Flesh;* George Ryga's *In the Shadow of the Vulture,* based on a real incident in which a truckload of illegal Mexican immigrants were left to die when their importers panicked and fled; *Night Studies* by Constance Beresford-Howe, which uses the device of an adult education program to assemble several diverse characters for dramatic effect; *Inland Passage* by Jane Rule, through which she plumbs the deeps of human nature; and the *Lost and Found Stories of Morley Callaghan,* as well as his *Our Lady of the Snows,* a novel-length extension of his novella *The Enchanted Pimp.* A posthumously published collection of stories by Marian Engel, *The Tattooed Woman,* was a stylish pursuit of the will-o'-the-wisp irrationality as it flashes its fateful light into the lives of her characters. Robertson Davies was back at what he did best in *What's Bred in the Bone,* following a boy from small-town Ontario into the devious world of art forgery, while Katherine Govier in *Fables of Brunswick Avenue* and Carol Shields in *Various Miracles* reflected the complexities of modern life.

Notable new poetry collections included Phyllis Webb's *Water and Light: Ghazals and Anti Ghazals,* an imaginative gambol through the rigours of poetic form; Doug Fetherling's *Variorum: New Poems and Old, 1965–1985,* dissecting his subjects with a critical eye and a manic tongue; *Silk Trail* by Andrew Suknaski, contrasting the high sheen of Chinese culture with the harsher aesthetic of the West; P. K. Page's *The Glass Air: Poems Selected and New,* containing eight of her drawings as well; *A Linen Crow—A Caftan Magpie,* in which Patrick Lane provides much lyrical material for thought; Anne Marriott's explorations of connections from both psychic and physical distances in *Letters from Some Island;* Joy Kogawa's haunting evocations of the primitive within each of us in *Woman in the Woods;* and Joe Rosenblatt's *Poetry Hotel: Selected Poems 1963–1983,* containing some of his best and most whimsical works. Robert Kroetsch fearlessly continued to give *Advice to My Friends,* while Erin Mouré waxed incandescent on love in *Domestic Fuel.* In bill bissett's *Canada Geese Mate for Life,* the great white light of urban consciousness is refracted through the poet's crystal of introspection. Lorna Crozier creates an equally brilliant scene in *The Garden Going On Without Us.*

Anthologies and collaborations included Dennis Lee's *The New Canadian Poets,* presenting 45 poets born between 1940 and 1955; *The Three Roberts on Childhood,* competitive and complementary excursions by the Roberts Priest, Sward, and Zend; and *The Transparence of November/Snow* by Roo Borson and Kim Maltman.

(ELIZABETH WOODS)

FRENCH

France. While no one would begrudge Marguerite Duras the 1984 Goncourt, it had to be admitted that she did not represent the fresh young talent that the prize was originally intended to foster. The emphasis in 1985 shifted to a younger generation, indeed to the second generation, children of well-known writers taking both major prizes. Yann Queffélec, son of the Breton novelist Henri Queffélec, won the Prix Goncourt for his second novel, *Les Noces barbares,* the story of a boy's retreat into the world of his imagination and of his tortured relationship with his mother. The Prix Renaudot went to Raphaele Billetdoux, daughter of playwright François Billetdoux, for *Mes Nuits sont plus belles que vos jours.* This story of a tragic love affair was considered self-indulgent and overwritten by some critics but marked a stage in the development of a consistently interesting novelist. Earlier in the year, the Académie Française gave its Grand Prix du Roman to Patrick Besson for *Dara,* and Claude Simon, veteran of the *nouveau roman* tradition, became the 12th Frenchman to accept the Nobel Prize for Literature from the Swedish Academy, Jean-Paul Sartre having refused it in 1964.

Studies of Sartre, including a biography by Annie Cohen-Solal, continued to gush from an apparently inexhaustible well, and literary scholarship was encouraged by some important anniversaries. The centenary of the death of Victor Hugo, the poet, novelist, and playwright whose generous output spanned 19th-century literature from Romanticism onward, was the impetus for conferences, criticism, and biographies. In honour of the 100th anniversary of the

birth of the novelist François Mauriac, Claude Mauriac published a biography of his father, an earlier Nobel Prize winner. There was no such obvious excuse, however, for the attention paid to Louis-Ferdinand Céline (1894–1961), whose work was the subject of several books, including a comprehensive bibliography by Jean-Pierre Dauphin and Pascal Fouché and the second volume of François Gibault's biography, covering the period 1932–44. There were other notable biographies: Jean Lacouture continuing his study of Charles de Gaulle, Claude Schopp on Alexandre Dumas, Yves Courrière on Joseph Kessel, and lives of the publishers Michael and Calmann Lévy (by Jean-Yves Mollier) and Gaston Gallimard (by Pierre Assouline). French Prime Minister Laurent Fabius published *Moderniser et rassembler* and Jacques Chaban-Delmas a historical study, *Les Compagnons de la Libération.*

The autumn lists saw the publication of more than 200 new novels. In the year as a whole, several established writers confirmed earlier tendencies. Françoise Sagan's *De Guerre lasse* was a triangular love story in which the World War II German occupation formed a background counterpointing the relationships of the central characters; Pierre-Jean Rémy, constructing *La Vie d'un héros* around Mozart's *Magic Flute,* showed his taste for opera and the baroque; after *Femmes,* Philippe Sollers published *Portrait du joueur,* a further installment in his part-erotic, part-poetic autobiography. J.-M. G. Le Clezio in *Le Chercheur d'or* recalled the Mauritanian origins of his family in a fable set in the early part of the century, and Andrée Chédid's *La Maison sans racines* dealt with Lebanon in 1975.

There were new novels, too, from Patrick Modiano (*Quartier perdu*), Serge Bramly (*Un Poisson muet surgi de la mer*), and Alain Robbe-Grillet (*Le Miroir qui revient*), and from Catherine Rihoit, whose *Soleil* elevated the material of popular romance to the status of myth. A conventional passion was given similarly unconventional treatment in Antoine Compagnon's short novel *Ferragosto.* Other writers made use of more unusual themes. Bernard Waller, in *Les Portes gigognes,* evoked a crisis in the life of a middle-aged man; Jean Bloch-Michel (*L'Évanouie*) and the Argentine writer Hector Bianciotti (in his first novel in French, *Sans la miséricorde du Christ*) investigated the inner lives of two older women from the circumstances of their deaths. Bianciotti was awarded the Prix Femina for his book. The Prix Médicis went to Michel Braudeau for his novel *Naissance d'une passion.*

Two figures well known in other fields published their first novels, the actress Simone Signoret (*see* OBITUARIES) with *Adieu Volodia* and the poet Jacques Roubaud, whose *La Belle Hortense* was a tribute to the work of the French writer Raymond Queneau. There was experiment with narrative viewpoints in Gilbert Toulouse's *L'Imposteur,* and René-Victor Pilhes returned to the novel with the first part of what promised to be a massive investigation—undisciplined and densely written—into the late 20th century. Like Roubaud's novel, it made use of elements from detective fiction, a genre that, in literature and in cinema, the French had frequently adapted to their own ends while conserving a particular admiration for the classic American thrillers of Raymond Chandler and Dashiell Hammett.

French readers' continuing respect for their cultural heritage ensured the success of historical studies and the memoirs of well-known writers such as Sollers, Duras (*La Douleur*), and Julien Cracq (*La Forme d'une ville*). Michel Leiris, in *Langage, tangage,* went beyond autobiography to investigate the nature of language and the self. Notable in the field of historiography was Paul Veyne and Georges Duby's *Histoire de la vie privée.*

Daniel Boulanger, the outstanding exponent of the short story in French, showed in *Les Noces du merle* his mastery in creating atmosphere and a unique gallery of characters. The poet Alain Bosquet ironically explored family relationships in the stories of *Un Homme pour un autre.* The poetry Goncourt was awarded to Claude Roy. Gilbert Lély, poet and biographer of the marquis de Sade, was among the writers who died during the year.   (ROBIN BUSS)

Canada. To speak about the literary history of Quebec in 1985 was first to recall the deaths of Jacques Ferron (*see* OBITUARIES) and Michel Beaulieu. With more than 30 books to his credit, not to mention his plays, Ferron was unquestionably the most brilliant intellect of French Canadian literature. Beaulieu, author of, among other works, *Oracle des ombres, Visages,* and *Kaléidoscope,* was a poet who did not often make the headlines of the literary pages, but he played a dominant role in shaping the views of young Quebec poets, to whom he knew how to communicate notions of taste, knowledge, and culture and concern about writing.

Among new publications, *Une Enfance à l'eau bénite* by Denise Bombardier was the object of violent criticism, although this seemed to have more to do with the author's personality than with the novel itself. It tells of the childhood of a girl brought up in the suffocating atmosphere of religion. On the other hand, *Les Lilas fleurissent à Varsovie* by Alice Parizeau, a history of Poland from 1945 to 1980 told through the lives of three women and the men around them, was compared by some to *Gone with the Wind.*

La Tentation de dire by Madeleine Ouellette-Michalska is a clear, vibrant journal, full of a solemn and tender sense of humour. Superbly written and polished, the text leads the reader to the heart of personal reflections. In *La Paix et la folie* by Claude Péloquin, both content and form display the provocative style of this controversial writer. With caustic words he achieves a realistic and almost hopeless vision of the existence of modern man. Parts of the book would move the most insensitive. In a different vein, *Les Signes s'envolent* by Louis Francoeur treats the theory of the action of the language.   (ROBERT SAINT-AMOUR)

GERMAN

West Germany, Austria, Switzerland. The death of Heinrich Böll (*see* OBITUARIES), the very symbol of post-World War II German literature, was a melancholy landmark of 1985. His final, posthumous novel, *Frauen vor Flusslandschaft,* included appropriate reminders of a past that Böll, above all, had been concerned to exorcise. Told in dialogue, a new departure for its author, it was set in the prosperous milieu of Bonn politicians and industrialists and included an attack on the usurpation of Germany's cultural heritage by the rich and unscrupulous. Siegfried Lenz's *Exerzierplatz* was another popular success on a not dissimilar topic. This story of a simple-minded man whose selfless devotion to his master and his garden is rewarded with dismissal by the heirs was an allegory on the exploitation of nature and man and had strong political connotations in the context of postwar German developments. Other writers dealt with more personal crises. Waltraud Mitgutsch's *Die Züchtigung* was an impressive account of a mother and daughter relationship. Elisabeth Plessen's *Stella Polare* describes a marital crisis from the woman's standpoint. Joseph Zoderer's *Lontano* and Bernard Hüttenegger's *Der Glaskäfig* were both studies in existential alienation.

A preoccupation with sensuality was a keynote of the contemporary scene. Karl Krolow's Proustian evocation of a North German childhood, *Geschonte Kindheit,* was a

kind of *éducation sensuelle* mainly in touch and smell. But the success of the year was undoubtedly Patrick Süskind's *Das Parfüm,* a virtuoso rendering into words of the most subtle scents. Set in 18th-century France, it told of a man who had a sense of smell so acute that he could detect the slightest odour. For Süskind human personality is defined by smell—his hero, being odourless, is not only inconspicuous but also totally amoral.

Süskind's novel was traditional narrative. Other authors rejected such conventions. Friederike Mayröcker's *Reise durch die Nacht* was a lyrical montage of fragments from a stream of consciousness, relating the theme of the journey to the process of aging. Even more radical in its rejection of the fictional plot was *Hessmers Gedanken,* Martin Walser's most melancholy book to date, consisting of aphorisms and meditations on personality, responsibility, and death. The title of Gerhard Roth's *Landläufiger Tod* underlined his preoccupation with mortality; over 795 pages Roth presented disparate scenes from contemporary Austrian life told by a dumb 20-year-old in modes varying from the journal to the fairy tale.

Other authors used elements of the fantastic. Michael Köhlmeier's witty *Moderne Zeiten* mingled generations and centuries in parodying some of the conventions of the realist novel. Ulla Berkewicz's *Michel, sag ich* was an allegory of the destruction of the student movement, set in a distant, mythological age after some unspecified catastrophe. An impressive debut was Barbara Strohschein's *Die Reisen der Gerda Seidenwinkel,* 21 surreal episodes from the life of a young woman who, like so many of her male contemporaries, failed to find "connection." More ambitious was Peter Sloterdijk's much-discussed *Der Zauberbaum,* which traced the development of psychoanalysis to the death of theology in the late 18th century.

Other notable events of the year included the posthumous publication of Uwe Johnson's earliest novel, *Ingrid Babendererde* and, ironically enough, the latest novel from Ernst Jünger, who was celebrating his 90th birthday and with whom Böll had frequently taken issue. Under the guise of the detective story, *Eine gefährliche Begegnung* was a series of brilliant if clinically cold character sketches from fin-de-siècle Paris. The only slightly younger Elias Canetti (winner of the 1981 Nobel Prize for Literature) produced the third volume of his autobiography, *Das Augenspiel,* on the years 1931–37.

Among the many collections of lyric poetry that appeared during the year were Ludwig Fels's *Der Anfang der Vergangenheit,* George Forestier's *Hätt ich das Wort,* Ulla Hahn's *Freudenfeuer,* and Johannes Schenk's *Café Americain.*

East Germany. The outstanding work was Volker Braun's latest variation on his favourite theme, the *Hinze-Kunze-Roman.* Braun used the adventures of Hinze the chauffeur and Kunze his master to draw some delightfully ironic pictures of life in East Germany, and in the manner of his model Diderot he included the intervention of a narrator with his own controversial ideas on the nature of fiction. Hans Weber's *Alter Schwede,* the story of an orphan and his fantasies, also contained satirical passages at the expense of journalism and petty bourgeois materialism. With *Wie ein Vogel im Schwarm,* Helmut Sakowski produced a nicely open-ended account of small-town tensions between professional and working-class people, older and younger generations. Dorothea Kleine's *Das schöne bisschen Leben* was a more serious examination of a writer's personal crisis—a heart operation, her professional dissatisfaction, the estrangement of her husband. Erik Neutsch delivered the third volume of *Der Friede in Osten,* his monumental

historical novel on the development of East Germany since World War II, here dealing with events surrounding the building of the Berlin Wall in 1961. (J. H. REID)

SCANDINAVIAN

Denmark. Some interesting thematic innovations appeared during the year. Charlotte Strandgaard's *En fugl foruden vinger* wove a complex intrigue around surrogate motherhood. Roger Poole and Henrik Stangerup produced a novel, *Dansemesteren,* about Søren Kierkegaard, consisting entirely of quotations extracted from Kierkegaard's writings. Klaus Rifbjerg's *Falsk forår* (1984) demonstrated another kind of ingenuity by portraying two relationships, one in 1945 between a Danish girl and an English officer, the other in 1983 between the daughter resulting from this liaison and an unemployed fisherman. Anders Bodelsen's *Domino* (1984) was a political thriller, written with Bodelsen's usual sense of construction. There were also political overtones in Rifbjerg's *Harlekin Skelet,* centred on a fantastic attempt by a representative of a Marxist state to prove the superiority of his system by "saving" a drug addict. Still more fantastic was Sven Åge Madsen's *Af sporet er du kommet* (1984) about Fegge, who helps create an imaginary person and furnishes him, via a computer, with all the papers needed for modern life.

Martha Christensen's *Tusindfryd* (1984) portrays a group of mentally handicapped housed together in a vain attempt to reintegrate them into the local community, while Dea Trier Mørch's *Morgengaven* (1984) is about the relationship between two artists and the problems arising when she is more successful than he. Hanne Marie Svendsen's *Guldkuglen* is a series of interrelated short stories about the inhabitants of a mythical island, juxtaposing patriarchal, selfish men with gentler but stronger women.

On his 70th birthday, Halfdan Rasmussen published *Fremtiden er forbi;* with grimmer humour than usual he reviews his life and the problems of aging. Bo Green Jensen continued his seven-volume suite with *Stedernes mening,* wide-ranging but marked by a pronounced melancholy. Less melancholy was Henrik Nordbrandt's *Violinbyggernes by,* though it, too, questioned the meaning of life. Erik Knudsen, in *Digte siden sidst,* was less questioning in his left-wing view, while Jess Ørnsbo in *Hjertets søle* was only slightly less to the left and just as biting in his criticism of the superficiality of modern life.

Thorkild Bjørnvig published the second volume of his memoirs, *Månehuset. Erindringer 1934–1938* (1984). Henrik Nordbrandt was awarded the Critics' Prize, and William Heinesen received the prestigious Sonning Prize.

(W. GLYN JONES)

Norway. Pride of place among the year's literary output had to go to Johannes Heggland for an outstanding description of childhood, *Seglet og vinden. Syllfest,* set in a fishing and farming community in western Norway in the second half of the 19th century. A humorous and penetrating analysis of the frustrated life-style of the average Norwegian in the 1980s was provided by Dag Solstad in *Forsøk på å beskrive det ugjennomtrengelige.* Mona Lyngar's extremely well-written novel *Fasadeklatrerne* was a merciless X-raying of the bankrupt inner world of socially successful Oslo suburbia. In *Scribe,* Odd Winger presented the sad, pathetic, and yet amusing final stages of the failed life of a retired sports journalist. The conflict between reality and art was the main theme in Finn Carling's *Under aftenhimmelen.* Similar problems were humorously dealt with in Tom Lotherington's *Den tredje tjeneren.* Cosmopolitan in the extreme was Ola Bauer's *Metoden,* where the violent action was motivated by tensions between

Johannes Heggland
GYLDENDAL NORSK FORLAG

an authoritarian shipowner and his two sons. Tor Åge Bringsværd's *Gobi. Barndommens måne* was a strangely fascinating, fragmented poetic novel about a member of the 13th-century German and French Children's Crusade who, as an escaped slave in the Gobi Desert, writes down childhood reminiscences in the light of his subsequent encounter with the mysticism of the East.

Shifting personal relationships formed the centre of Karsten Alnæs's cosmopolitan novel *Øy*. Profound insight into the Russian soul characterized Jahn Otto Johansen's *Russland, Russland* . . . . Hard-boiled realistic scenes in a cardiology operating theatre in *Hjertelag*, published under the pen name Jan Bersari, were not for the squeamish. Sad aspects of sexuality were presented with humour in Bjørg Vik's short stories *En gjenglemt petunia*, and a retrospective selection of her short stories, *Når en pike sier ja*, showed her as the undisputed master in this genre. Bisexuality was dealt with in Elin Brodin's *Den krydrede vin*, rape in Frederick Skagen's *Voldtatt*, and prostitution in Lars Saabye Christensen's *Blodets bånd*. In a class of its own was Michael Grundt Spang's spy-thriller *Spionen som lengtet hjem. Moderne norsk lyrikk. Frie vers 1890–1980* was a comprehensive survey of modernistic poetry.

The poet, novelist, and distinguished translator André Bjerke died in January 1985.   (TORBJØRN STØVERUD)

Sweden. Most of Sweden's leading novelists published works in 1985, the majority being continuations or culminations of fictional worlds built up over many years. With one exception they dealt with a historical past, as though their authors wished to analyze the roots of the present. In *Järnkronan* Sara Lidman ended her chronicle of the coming of the railway to a Norrland seen as a colonized and plundered province. With *Maria ensam*, Sven Delblanc concluded the re-creation of his family history through three generations of adversity. In 1975 Lars Gyllensten's *I skuggan av Don Juan* featured the famous libertine; a decade later his novel *Skuggans återkomst* presented the aging penitent in a text balancing ironic ambivalence with philosophical speculation. Christian Marxist Birgitta Trotzig's vision in *Dykungens dotter* was, as in her earlier works, of a world in which divine love exists but cannot undo the cruelty of man and society toward the defenseless.

P. O. Enquist gained an international reputation with his documentary novel *Legionärerna* in 1968, but much water had flowed under Swedish literary bridges since the politically committed Vietnam period. His new novel, *Nedstörtad ängel*, centred on a marital tangle involving murder and suicide, juxtaposed with a dream of a Mexican circus freak. All these new works used narrative modes far removed from straight social realism; only Karl Rune Nordkvist practiced it gently in *Slaktarens hus*, although in other respects (action set in the past, characters reappearing from earlier works) his book had much in common with those of his colleagues.

Among younger writers, Torbjörn Lindhe's novel *Utställningen* (set in Paris) proved that fantasy was fashionable, featuring as it did a young man's thoughts about the relationship between art and life, with (yet another!) circus freak in a central role. In Peter Nilson's *Guldspiken*, biblical diction and mythical elements merge with realism in a poor boy's visions of heaven and hell. Lars Åke Augustsson readably explores political and personal treachery and class barriers in *Vapenmakt* and *Fjärrförbindelser*, respectively, while Lars Ardelius's *Större än störst* tells of ordinary people's realizable kindness.

Folke Isaksson's prose poems *Skiftningar i en väv* gained critical acclaim, as did Lars Lundkvist's poems in *Korn*.

(KARIN PETHERICK)

ITALIAN

After 20 years of almost complete silence, Vasco Pratolini published *Il mannello di Natascia*, a collection of autobiographical verse and occasional prose written during 1930–80 that reviewed with unspoiled freshness some of Italy's recent historical crises. Another welcome return was that of the old Neapolitan writer Domenico Rea, who published *Il fondaco nudo*, a collection of short stories in his characteristic neorealist register. Alberto Moravia's new novel, *L'uomo che guarda*, dealt as skillfully as ever with his usual concern for sexual relationships, the crisis of the bourgeois family, and the conflict between generations with the interesting underlying theme of the nuclear threat.

Rather disappointing was Natalia Ginzburg's *La città e la casa*, an epistolary novel in which a group of middle-aged friends exchange letters, mainly to tell each other whom they have fallen in or out of love with. More complex and ambitious, and more widely praised, was Carlo Sgorlon's *L'armata dei fiumi perduti*, an imaginative dramatization of a little-known and tragic episode of World War II, when the Cossack army, together with its women, children, and animals, was temporarily resettled by its Nazi allies in Friuli, in northeastern Italy. Another historical novel was Mario Biondi's *Gli occhi d'una donna*, a long chronicle, seen through the eyes of a woman, of the rise and fall of two Italian families, one aristocratic, the other industrial bourgeois, from 1914 to 1982. Susanna Agnelli fully confirmed her narrative gifts with *Addio, addio, mio ultimo amore*, in which she effectively describes her ten-year experience as mayor of Argentario in Tuscany.

Several works by new or recently emerged writers were more compelling. Gesualdo Bufalino's loosely autobiographical novel, *Argo il cieco ovvero i sogni della memoria*, punctuated his past quest for happiness with a subtly ironic commentary in the present, and again his imaginative style worked magic. One of the year's best books was *La notte della cometa* by Sebastiano Vassalli, a biography of the poet Dino Campana, who died in a mental asylum in 1932. In a relentless series of short chapters, Vassalli reconstructs Campana's tormented life and the incomprehension that greeted him and his poetic genius.

Narratori delle pianure, Gianni Celati's collection of 30 short stories, was somewhat curious and unsettling. His stories read more like summaries of themselves and even

then sound paradoxical and inconclusive, with characters ostensibly plain and simple, yet bizarre, submerged in a world of mingled barbarity and high technology: a bleak view of a landscape, once familiar and now estranged from its inhabitants. Equally arresting, though formally much more conventional and confident about the powers of literature, was *Notturno indiano* by another young author, Antonio Tabucchi, who also published a collection of fine short stories, *Piccoli equivoci senza importanza.* By contrast, Andrea De Carlo's third novel, *Macno,* relied too much on cliches and too little on imaginative originality. De Carlo's cinematic eye was considered the strength of his first two novels; in *Macno,* however, the reader was led to look not through, but too much at, the camera.

Finally, the year's revelation was Roberto Pazzi's first novel, *Cercando l'imperatore,* which concentrates in alternating chapters on the last days of the Russian imperial family, imprisoned at Yekaterinburg, and on the vicissitudes of the tsar's favourite regiment. While the Romanovs dream in captivity, the regiment, cut off from the rest of the world, wanders through Siberia for months on end seeking to bring help to the tsar. Slowly but inevitably it is decimated by sickness, desertions, the weather, and a creeping madness. The drama of the minds, involved in the awesome and quasi-religious mystery of the abolition of power, is handled by Pazzi with remarkable sensitivity and superb control.

Elsewhere on the literary scene the most successful book was *Impariamo l'italiano* by Cesare Marchi. This witty but rigorous Italian grammar seemed to demonstrate with its popularity that Italians thought they did not yet know their national language. Almost as successful were two books by well-known journalists, Luca Goldoni's *Viaggio in provincia* and Camilla Cederna's *Vicino e distante:* reflections, often amusing and perceptive, on the quirks of Italian society, past and present. Altogether more demanding were Mario Luzi's *Discorso naturale,* a book on the nature of poetry by one of Italy's foremost poets, and critic Alberto Asor Rosa's *L'ultimo paradosso,* philosophical meditations on the problems of human existence.

The deaths of the novelists Italo Calvino and Riccardo Bacchelli occurred during the year (*see* OBITUARIES).

(LINO PERTILE)

SPANISH

Spain. In mid-December 1984 the Spanish Ministry of Culture gave the highest award in Hispanic letters, the Miguel de Cervantes Prize, to the Argentine novelist and outspoken social critic Ernesto Sábato. Sábato's notoriety as head of the commission appointed to investigate recent human rights violations in Argentina and as principal author of that body's horrific "Sábato Report" (published in Spain as *Nunca más*) superseded his literary prestige as author of the existentialist classic *El túnel* (1948) and only two other novels. While some critics thus questioned this award, the event itself underscored an important cultural phenomenon in Spain's literary world: the increasing presence, both personal and editorial, of major Latin-American writers, many of whom published new work first in Spain.

Paralleling this internationalist trend, the translator, literary historian, and poet Ángel Crespo published *Parnaso confidencial* (1971–), a five-part verse collection on wide-ranging extraterritorial themes; and the publisher Plaza y Janés gave its newly established International Novel Prize to the young Spanish writer Ángel García Roldán for *Las Cortes de Coguaya,* set in tropical Latin America. By contrast, the steadily increasing attention being paid to "regional" authors was conspicuously marked by the

publication of the fourth and final bilingual volume of *Obras completas, narrativa* by the Catalan novelist-poet Salvador Espriu (1913–85) and by the award, late in 1984, of the National Spanish Letters Prize to Josep Vincenç Foix, whose voluminous work, mainly poetry and all written in Catalan, was now certain to be widely translated into Spanish. In 1985 the same prize went to the Catalan symbolist poet Joan Vinyolí (1914–84) for his eighth book of poems, *Passeig d'aniversari,* published shortly before his death.

With his latest novel, *100 años de honradez,* Fernando Vizcaíno Casas, the ultraconservative chronicler of Franco-regime society and values, continued to defy predictions of the decline of his extraordinary popularity. At the opposite extreme, the perennially best-selling pop journalist Francisco Umbral added to his enormous output with two more collections of stylish essays, *Mis queridos monstruos,* consisting of lively interviews with well-known Spanish intellectuals, artists, and politicians, and *Fábula del falo,* a meditation on modern sexuality. By one vote, Umbral's novel *Pio XII, la escolta mora y un general sin un ojo* lost in the important Planeta Prize competition to Juan Antonio Vallejo-Nájera's *Yo, el Rey,* a first-person psycho-narrative of Joseph Bonaparte's seizure of the Spanish throne in 1808.

Established serious writers were also active. Juan Benet published the second volume of his *Herrumbrosas lanzas* cycle; Camilo José Cela promised a modern sequel to his famous *Viaje a la Alcarria* (1948) and a new novel, *Madera de boj,* set in Galicia, as was his *Mazurca para dos muertos,* which won the National Prize for Literature late in 1984. New novels by Vázquez Montalbán (*El pianista*), Torrente Ballester (*La rosa de los vientos*), and Juan Goytisolo (*Coto vedado*) earned critical acclaim.

Timed to coincide with the centenary of Leopoldo Alas's *La Regenta* (1884–85), John Rutherford's translation made this masterpiece novel available (1984) for the first time in English. (ROGER L. UTT)

Latin America. The major writers to publish books during the year were the Mexicans Carlos Fuentes and Gustavo Sainz, the Peruvian Mario Vargas Llosa, the Argentine Jorge Luis Borges, and the Chilean Antonio Skármeta. Best-selling novels among established writers included *La casa de los espíritus* (originally published in 1982; *The*

Ernesto Sábato

House of the Spirits, 1985) by Isabel Allende, *El hombre que hablaba de Octavia de Cádiz* by the Peruvian Alfredo Bryce Echenique, and *No te duermas, no me dejes* by the Argentine Marta Lynch.

The two outstanding novels of the year in Mexico were Fuentes's *Gringo viejo* and Sainz's *Paseo en trapecio. Gringo viejo* is Fuentes's novelistic projection of what might have happened to the American writer Ambrose Bierce when he crossed into Mexico during the Mexican Revolution (1910–20) and disappeared. Fuentes once again demonstrates his mastery of characterization. Sainz's sixth novel, *Paseo en trapecio,* is the intensely autobiographical and fantastic story of an individual who returns to Mexico City. The novel's narrative technique is both demanding and sophisticated. Another successful experimental novel, with three lines of plot development, was Daniel Leyva's *Una piñata llena de memoria.* Other noteworthy Mexican novels were Sergio Pitol's *El desfile de amor* (late 1984), Arturo Azuela's *El don de la palabra,* Angeles Mastretta's *Arráncame la vida,* Severino Salazar's *Donde deben ser las catedrales* (late 1984), Sergio Galindo's *Los dos ángeles* (late 1984), and Francisco Prieto's fourth and best novel, *Si Llegamos a diciembre.*

Colombia did not produce a large number of novels. Alberto Duque López published his third and most accessible work, a story of a crime, titled *El pez en el espejo.* Alonso Aristizábal, an accomplished short-story writer, published his first novel, *Una y muchas guerras.* Like his stories, it deals with historic violence in the state of Caldas. Several important Colombian novels appeared in late 1984: Héctor Sánchez's *Entre ruinas,* Roberto Burgos Cantor's *El patio de los vientos perdidos,* Albalucía Angel's *Las andariegas,* and Juan José Hoyo's *Tuyo es mi corazón.*

In the Southern Cone, writing flourished in Argentina and Uruguay, whereas most of Chile's major figures continued to work abroad. The venerable Jorge Luis Borges brought out a book of poems, *Los conjurados.* Back in Argentina after several years of exile, Antonio Di Benedetto published *Sombras, nada más,* a novel about exile. Nicolás Casullo wrote an experimental novel, *El frutero de los ojos radiantes.* One of Uruguay's most prolific young writers, Cristina Peri Rossi, published the novel *La nave de los locos,* and *Yod,* an experimental novel, was written by Carlos Pelegrino. Two important volumes of poetry in Uruguay were Eduardo Espina's *El corazón con razón* and Maresa Di Giorgio's *Mesa de esmeraldas.* One of the best novels of the region was the Chilean Antonio Skármeta's *Ardiente paciencia,* a fascinating and superbly written account of the Chilean experience of the early 1970s and the life of the late poet Pablo Neruda.

The Peruvian Mario Vargas Llosa received the first Ritz-Hemingway Prize and published a novel about the political left in Peru during the 1950s and today, *Historia de Mayta.* The Argentine novelist and essayist Ernesto Sábato was awarded the Miguel de Cervantes Prize. (See *Spain,* above.) Alberto Esquivel, a young and previously unknown writer, won the Plaza y Janés National Novel Prize in Colombia with *Acelere.* José Luis Garcés, author of novels and stories, received the second prize in Colombia with *Entre la soledad y los cuchillos.* The venerable novelist Juan Carlos Onetti was awarded the National Prize for Literature in Uruguay.   (RAYMOND L. WILLIAMS)

PORTUGUESE

Portugal. The commemoration of the 50th anniversary of Fernando Pessoa's death ended with an official ceremony in the Hyeronomite monastery in Lisbon, where his body now lay alongside that of Lúis de Camões. By coincidence, José Saramago's novel *O Ano da Morte de Ricardo Reis* came out before the commemoration and became an instant literary success. Ricardo Reis is one of the imaginary poets created by Pessoa, who wrote poems in totally different styles, expressing different and even contradictory ideas and sentiments. Pessoa went so far as to provide biographical profiles of these imaginary authors, keeping up this illusion all through his life.

In Saramago's novel, Reis, the politically conservative and solitary aesthete, returns to Lisbon from his self-imposed exile in Brazil in the year of Pessoa's death and is immediately plunged into the claustrophobic atmosphere of the city under Salazar's dictatorship at the time of the Spanish Civil War. Reis's aloofness, so often shown in his verses, is shaken by the simple fact of his daily existence, and this forces him to question himself and the nature of his own poetry. Extremely subtle, funny, ironic, reflective, deeply moving at times, this was a work that confirmed Saramago's reputation as one of the most stimulating writers of his time.

Another remarkable novel was Lídia Jorge's *Notícia da Cidade Silvestre,* a pungent tale of the human condition caught up in the strains of modern urban life and its frustrations. One of the most distinguished authors of the 1970s, Jorge here discarded her earlier experimental style for straightforward narrative. The narrator replies to the writer's implicit questions and inquiries, a device that effectively reveals the mysteries and tensions of a friendship between two women whose conflicting experience finally sets them apart. The sham, self-deception, and ambiguity of the male characters are matched by the weakness of their female counterparts, thus preventing the book from becoming a feminist novel.   (L. S. REBELO)

Brazil. In 1985 a new democratic government faced Brazil's worst economic crisis, but the book industry began to thrive. Indeed, the political situation seemed to help. The most successful publication of the year was *Brasil: Nunca Mais,* an account of the "disappeared" during the height of the military regime's persecutions.

Tocaia Grande, Jorge Amado's newest novel, narrates the comic-epic existence of a mythical town in his native

Antônio Callado

state of Bahia. It delicately unifies the social themes of his early career with the techniques and character types of his post-1960 fiction. Another important contribution was Antônio Callado's *Concerto Carioca.* Callado's deep concern for the Brazilian Indian as the nation's greatest moral problem is highlighted here through Jaci, the uprooted, symbolic Indian who, upon arriving in Rio, turns the city into his own private kingdom. Works by younger writers of note were João Gilberto Noll's *Bandoleiros,* set in Boston and Brazil, and Sônia Nolasco Ferreira's *Moreno como Vocês,* which focuses on the moral/emotional dilemma of Brazilians who have chosen self-exile in the never-never land of New York City. Other notable fiction included Ignácio de Loyola Brandão's *O Beijo Não Vem na Boca,* comparing contemporary Brazil to post-World War II Berlin; Roberto Drummond's *Hitler Manda Lembranças,* which also invokes that war and its influence on the life of a Brazilian worker; Nélida Piñón's *A República dos Sonhos,* tracing a Spanish family's roots in Brazil from a feminist perspective; and Fernando Sabino's first foray into detective fiction, *A Faca de Dois Gumes.*

The noted short-story writer Dalton Trevisan wrote his first novel, *A Polaquinha,* and a novelist, Oswaldo França Junior, published his first collection of short (mini) stories. Wander Piroli's new stories, *Minha Bela Putana,* are much less ironic than his previous writings. Julieta de Godoy Ladeira presented an interesting view of Brazilian life in *Era Sempre Feriado Nacional.*

Carlos Drummond de Andrade, Brazil's poet laureate, published six volumes during his 82nd year (from late 1984 through 1985), including new poetry, memoirs, "chronicles," and a volume of children's literature. *Corpo* sold over 40,000 copies, probably as a result of the poet's unusually strong social statement. *Cocktails* by Luís Aranha, a member of the Brazilian Modernist group, was finally published. Other interesting works of poetry included Ledo Ivo's *Calabar,* Sérgio Sant'Anna's off-beat *Junk Box,* Haroldo de Campos's *Galáxias,* and Carlos Nejar's *Livro de Gazéis.*

Contributions in the area of criticism included Fernando Peres's new biography of the 17th-century poet Gregório de Matos Guerra and Décio de Almeida Prado's biography of the late Brazilian actor Procópio Ferreira. José Mauro de Vasconcellos, an extremely popular novelist of the 1960s, died.   (IRWIN STERN)

RUSSIAN

Soviet Literature. The civic spirit in Soviet fiction was on the increase in 1985. Foremost authors responded to burning issues at home and abroad and directly influenced public opinion. Writers received ever more media attention, and the link between artistic and ethical quests and real-life events and processes—a link always typical of Soviet prose, poetry, and drama—became even more visible. In their analyses of such recent novels as Yury Bondarev's *Gamble,* Anatoly Kurchatkin's *Evening Twilight,* Zoya Boguslavskaya's *Relatives,* and Sergey Aleksayev's *Word;* such novellas as Valentin Rasputin's *Fire,* Sergey Yesin's *An Imitator,* and Irina Grekova's *Pheasant;* or the short stories of Viktor Astafyev, Vladimir Krupin, and Vladimir Makanin, critics centred their attention on their social topicality, profound analytical quality, and the authors' preoccupation with topics and heroes literature once used to ignore.

The trend toward writing about public issues was apparent not only in works about contemporary life but also in historical ones. Prominent were novels, stories, plays, and poems about the Great Patriotic War (World War II) marking the 40th anniversary of victory over fascism.

Yury Bondarev
K. TARUSOV—TASS/SOVFOTO

They included Ivan Stadnyuk's major novel *Moscow in '41,* Yury Semyonov's thrillers, and novels by Vyacheslav Kondratyev, Anatoly Genatullin, Vsevolod Alekseyev, and Mikhail Godenko. Also noteworthy was the Belorussian journalist Svetlana Aleksevich's *The Last Witnesses*—a collection of eyewitness accounts of wartime horrors made by people who were children at the time, with the author's comments. The best books on significant events in Russian and world history included the final part of Sergey Zalygin's major novel *After the Storm,* about Siberia in the early 1920s; Boris Bursov's *Pushkin's Fate;* and Igor Volgin's *Dostoyevsky's Last Year.*

Among the most read works of the year was Yevgeny Yevtushenko's long poem *Fookoo,* a broad panorama of the century's political history, imbued with antifascist spirit; it was an impassioned meditation on the relations between art and power, the state and the individual, art and the public. A well-defined civic stand also characterized Aleksandr Mezhirov's *Prose in Verse* cycle of poems and the latest works appearing both in book form and in periodicals by Andrey Voznesensky, Oleg Chukhontsev, Vladimir Leonovich, Yunna Moritz, Robert Rozhdestvensky, and other Soviet poets.

Literary criticism flourished. Books and essays by Lev Anninsky, Igor Dedkov, Yevgeny Sidorov, Igor Zolotussky, Vladimir Gusev, and Stanislav Rassadin, to name but a few, won great popularity among fellow writers and readers at large. Extensive publication of Aleksandr Tvardovsky's *Letters on Literature* and of letters and other documents from the archives of Konstantin Simonov, Anna Akhmatova, Mikhail Zoshchenko, Mikhail Prishvin, and Yury Trifonov were also notable events in Soviet literary life.

(SERGEY CHUPRININ)

Expatriate Russian Literature. The year saw the publication of the English translation of a major work of postwar Russian literature—Vasily Grossman's *Life and Fate* (Collins Harvill, London, and Harper & Row, New York). Had the book been published when it was written, in 1960, "it would have been a literary sensation of worldwide importance," according to the Russian novelist Vladimir Voinovich, speaking at the Frankfurt Book Fair

to introduce the German edition of the book. But *Life and Fate* was never published in Russia; instead, the KGB confiscated every copy of the manuscript they could lay their hands on, taking even the author's carbon papers and typewriter ribbon. The chief party ideologist, the late Mikhail Suslov, told Grossman that his novel could not be printed for "at least 200 years." Nevertheless, a copy did get smuggled out of the Soviet Union by Voinovich when he immigrated to West Germany in 1981. Another important literary event was the publication, in the original Russian, of Varlam Shalamov's life story told in a series of sketches of life in a labour camp, *Voskreshenie listvinnitsy* ("Resurrection"; YMCA Publishers, Paris).

Possev in Frankfurt am Main, West Germany, brought out Vladimir Rybakov's *Tiski* ("Pressures"), a collection of stories about life in the Soviet Army with an introduction by the exiled novelist Georgy Vladimov. Overseas Publishers in London published Yury Lyubimov's stage adaptation of Mikhail Bulgakov's novel *The Master and Margarita.* Although the stage version ran successfully for seven years at Lyubimov's Taganka Theatre in Moscow, the text was never published in the U.S.S.R. The book includes the director's account of the circumstances of the production.

Vasyl Stus, the Ukrainian poet, died in a labour camp in September at the age of 47. He was the third writer to die in a Soviet labour camp within the year, the others being Yury Litvin and Oleksa Tykhy. In his annual report, Michael Scammell, the chairman of the PEN Writers in Prison Committee, listed the Soviet Union as one of five countries causing the most concern (Cuba, Iran, Turkey, and Vietnam were the others), with a total of 68 writers recorded as being in either prison, labour camp, psychiatric hospital, or internal exile. The Ukrainian poet Mykola Horbal—a monitor of adherence to the Helsinki Accords on human rights—was sentenced on April 9 to a further 11 years in labour camp and exile for "anti-Soviet agitation and propaganda" in songs and verse. Horbal, age 44, had already spent 12 years in prison.   (GEORGE THEINER)

EASTERN EUROPEAN LITERATURE

"The writer must have the right to express views that are at variance with the offical view. Let authors' works be printed just as they were written. And let writers not be persecuted because they had written them. A writer needs no higher authority to decide about his works, nor to permit or forbid him to travel abroad. It is time that the state stopped treating us like unruly children—it is absurd that we should be afraid because we write." With these words the Hungarian novelist Gyorgy Konrad opened the unofficial writers' symposium organized by the International Helsinki Federation for Human Rights in Budapest in October 1985. The two-day session was held to coincide with the inauguration of the official Budapest Cultural Forum, at which delegations from the 35 nations that signed the Helsinki Accords of 1975 met to discuss cultural problems and cooperation.

The unofficial event, a unique undertaking in a Warsaw Pact country, was meant to demonstrate that literature and the arts are the province not of governments and official institutions but of the writers and artists, their readers and audiences. Apart from Konrad, the ten-member panel included Susan Sontag (U.S.), Per Wästberg (Sweden), Amos Oz (Israel), Danilo Kis (Yugoslavia), François Bondy (Switzerland), Timothy Garton Ash (U.K.), Alain Finkielkraut (France), Hans Magnus Enzensberger (West Germany), and Jiri Grusa, the Czech novelist and poet now living in exile in West Germany. Konrad's *Anti-Poli-*

tics, which, like several of his previous books, had not been published in Hungary, was published by Quartet Books in London in an English translation earlier in the year.

The Romanian writer Dorin Tudoran, who had been writing about such delicate topics as chauvinism, anti-Semitism, and corruption in public life since he broke with the Ceausescu regime four years earlier, was allowed to immigrate to the United States after going on a hunger strike in April. In Poland Tadeusz Konwicki brought out yet another novel, *Rzeka podziemna* ("Underground River"), in a samizdat (literary underground) edition. Having been refused a passport on several previous occasions, Konwicki was allowed to visit Australia, the U.S., London, and Paris. The historian Adam Michnik, released from detention in the amnesty of July 1984, was rearrested and, at a trial in Gdansk on June 14, sentenced to two and a half years' imprisonment.

In Czechoslovakia Eva Kanturkova and Zdenek Urbanek were the joint recipients of the first Tom Stoppard Prize for new and original writing. The prize was to be awarded annually by a panel consisting of banned writers living in Czechoslovakia. Kanturkova, who was appointed one of the three Charter 77 (a reference to the Czechoslovak human rights manifesto of 1977) spokesmen for 1985, won the prize for her book *Pritelkyne z domu smutku* ("Friends from the House of Sorrow"), which was based on her prison experiences.

Prometheova jatra ("Prometheus's Liver") by the Czechoslovak poet and artist Jiri Kolar was among the most interesting books published during the year by émigré publishers. Banned in his native country since the 1950s, Kolar, who now lived in Paris, had won international recognition for his paintings and collages. Ivan Klima's book of seven short stories, *My Merry Mornings,* was published in English by Readers International, who also brought out *Poland Under Black Light,* by the young Polish writer Janusz Anderman.

The exiled Serbian poet Milan Milenkovic, whose works had hitherto appeared only in newspapers and periodicals, brought out his first collected volume of verse, *Slovo za glasove* ("A Word for Voices"). Published privately in Paris, it dealt with the injustices and violence suffered by the Serbian people in present-day Yugoslavia and with the life of an émigré. The book was described as "a valuable addition to the growing body of Serbian poetry abroad" by Vasa D. Mihailovich in *World Literature Today.* The same journal announced the publication, by the Serbian Heritage Academy in Toronto, of *Letters* by Ivo Andric (1892–1975), the only Yugoslav writer to win the Nobel Prize (1961). The correspondence, edited and translated by Zelimir B. Juricic, throws interesting light on the writer's private life as well as on his relationships with other writers and Yugoslav officials.   (GEORGE THEINER)

JEWISH

Hebrew. The literary highlights of the year included the appearance of significant additions to continuing novelistic projects. David Shahar published *Kayits Bederekh haNevi'im,* the latest installment in his "Palace of Shattered Vessels" series, and Moshe Shamir penned *Hinumat Kala,* the second volume of a family trilogy. Other distinctive works were *Lustig* by Adam Barukh, *Keheres haNishbar* by Shulamit Lapid, *Miba'ad La'avotot* by Netiva Ben-Yehuda, a volume of short stories, *Kavim Levanim,* by Dorit Peleg, and the autobiographical novel *Mem* by Matti Megged. Engaging works of fiction were published by the veteran writers Natan Shaham, Yehoshua Bar-Yosef, and Yonat and Alexander Sened and by the new or younger

authors Mishka Ben-David, Tamar Harsagur, Yigal Lev, Iris Mor, and Moshe Hacohen. Amalia Kahana-Carmon was awarded the prestigious Brenner Prize for her fiction.

The world of Israeli poetry mourned the passing of David Rokeah and Yona Wollach. Wollach's collection *Tsurot* appeared just before her death. Two significant volumes of poetry were published posthumously, Zelda's *Shirei Zelda* and Amir Gilboa's *haKol Holekh*. A definitive edition of Rachel's poetry, letters, and other pieces was edited by Uri Milstein, and Natan Alterman's early poetry was featured in *Shirim 1931–1935*. Also published were Haim Gouri's *Mahbarot Elul*, Avner Treinin's *Euclidom*, Ory Bernstein's collection of selected works, Maia Bejerano's *Shirat haTsiporim*, David Avidan's *Sefer haEfsharuyot*, and Peretz Banai's *Keshet Vekhidon*. The younger poets Zeli Gurevitz, Sigalit Davidovitch, and Alon Alteres also published new collections, as did the well-known poets Aharon Amir and Moshe Dor. Avot Yeshurun's *Homograph* volume was added to his list of distinctive publications.

Two new periodicals were established: *Shufra*, edited by Ilan Sheinfeld, and *Makom*, which featured a new group of younger poets. The journal *Akhshav* celebrated its 50th issue. Among noteworthy works of criticism published during the year were Avraham Sha'anan's study of Saul Tchernichovsky, Hillel Barzel's monograph on Amir Gilboa, for which he was awarded the Bialik Prize, Nurit Govrin's study of turn-of-the-century Hebrew fiction, and Nissim Kalderon's analysis of poetry and politics in the early 1960s.   (WARREN BARGAD)

Yiddish. The 1985 Yiddish literary scene was stimulating, with new entries in most genres. Literary nonfiction—memoirs, documentaries, and criticism—flourished. Writers themselves were the subjects of two valuable volumes of criticism. Itskhak Janosowicz penned a collection of analytical essays about Yiddish writers, *Faces and Names*. Avrom Lis discussed several poets and novelists in his *Conversation in Written Form*. In a second collection, *Discovered Treasures*, the Soviet scholar Leyb Vilsker examined the interest Jews have had in Pushkin and translations of his work into Hebrew and Yiddish.

A compelling work of fiction set in Israel, Yosl Birshteyn's novel about a financier, *The Collector*, integrates belles lettres and satire in a masterful unfolding of fantasy and reality. Avrom Karpinovitsh's *On Foot in the Land of Israel* offers a retrospective look at life, strife, and heroism in Europe and the Middle East. Yisroel Kaplan's documentary novel *Last Spring* tells of the rise of independent Lithuania after World War I and of the contribution and role of Jews in that enterprise. Yishayahu Spiegel's *The Heavens After the Storm* is a fictive account of the Lodz Ghetto during the years 1941–43. Volf Tambur's *Listen to a Story* offers a multidimensional view of his life and times in contemporary Eastern Europe.

Two autobiographical volumes throw light on significant episodes in modern Jewish history. French Communist Party member Khaym Sloves's *A Mission to Moscow* relates his negotiations with the Soviet authorities about the revival of Jewish cultural life. Hersh Smoliar deals with Belorussian Jewry, the struggle of the inhabitants of the Minsk Ghetto, and the aid provided to them by the partisans in *Fences in the Ghetto*.

The 100th volume of Shmuel Rozhansky's *Exemplary Editions* appeared in Buenos Aires, Arg., completing a series that began publication in 1957. This major undertaking embraces the panoramic scope of Yiddish literature from its beginnings to the present day. The editor's introductions give biographical and bibliographical data about each writer and work. Meyer Segal's second collection, a

philosophical meditation, is entitled simply *Poems*. Shaye Tanenbaum's memoir *Ash and Fire Is Your Crown*, a series of cameo portrayals of painters, sculptors, and musicians, was awarded the Workman's Circle Prize. Itche Goldberg's *Essays* received the Manger Prize.

(THOMAS E. BIRD; ELIAS SCHULMAN)

CHINESE

China. There were contradictory literary developments in China in 1985: frequent calls for ideological and political conformity and repeated statements, such as that by Communist Party leader Hu Qili (Hu Ch'i-li) at a congress of artists and writers, on the need for creative freedom. While rejecting past restrictions on artistic freedom and urging efforts to restore China to the forefront of world culture, the Chinese leadership stressed the necessity for broad ideological constraint and the social responsibility of writers and artists. In evaluating literary works, some critics attacked the principle of "political standard first and artistic standard second." The dismissal of Deng Liqun (Teng Li-ch'ün) as the party's propaganda chief had paved the way for the increasingly evident trend toward more liberalization but with proper self-restraint.

Nevertheless, Wang Beikung's (Wang Pei-k'ung's) play *We*, which launched a fierce attack on the corruption associated with the Communist Party both before and after Mao Zedong's (Mao Tse-tung's) death in 1976, was banned, despite its immense popularity. Liu Binyan's (Liu Pin-yen's) "The Second Type of Loyalty," in which the author ruthlessly exposes the dark side of China, ran into trouble because of his rejection of "blind" loyalty to Communist authorities.

The party, however, tolerated Zhao Huan's (Chao Huan's) play *Marx in London*, which, in line with the current Communist view, reduced Marx to a mortal whose outdated theory could no longer provide solutions to all China's problems. Also tolerable to the Communist leadership was the "opaque poetry" of Shu Ding (Shu Ting) and others, which, in sharp contrast to works by the more established poets of the earlier generation, was highly personal, ambiguous, and sometimes downright obscure. Chong Acheng's (Ch'ung A-ch'eng's) *Chess King*, which stressed the importance of human dignity and traditional

EASTFOTO

Liu Binyan

Chinese culture, was widely read. Also attracting considerable attention in China was Nieh Hua-ling, a Chinese woman writer residing in the U.S., whose *The River Flows Beyond Thousands of Mountains* presented sharp contrasts between Chinese and American ways of life, values, and cultures.

Taiwan. Despite the commercial success of a number of literary works, few achieved artistic distinction. An exception was Li Chiao's *Trilogy of Cold Nights,* which traced the lives of an ethnic group in Taiwan, the Hakka, and revealed a keen sense of history and political and social sensitivity. Another exception was Wang T'o's *Taipei! Taipei!,* a realistic portrayal of the lives of idealistic youths, students, workers, and intellectuals in Taiwan in the 1970s, especially their awakening, struggles, criticism, disappointments, frustration, disillusionment, searches for answers to Taiwan's future, and their debates on such issues as nationalism, socialism, Taiwan's independence, and the reunification of Taiwan and China.

Another popular novel was Li Ang's *Killing of the Husband,* which presented a powerful attack on the male chauvinist attitude toward women prevalent in Taiwan. Equally popular was Liu K'e-hsiang's poetic anthology *The Homeland of the Wandering Bird,* in which the author used "the wandering bird" to symbolize himself, one of the "lost and rootless generation" in search of a "homeland."

(WINSTON L. Y. YANG)

Haruki Murakami

JAPANESE

There were several signs that a "new wave" in Japanese writing might be emerging. One was the awarding of the prestigious Tanizaki Prize to Haruki Murakami's novel *The End of the World and the Hard-boiled Wonderland.* Murakami, still in his 30s, was exceptionally young to receive this prize, and his work was a definitely new type of novel by Japanese standards—a sophisticated combination of science fiction and light, witty comments on contemporary civilization. The novel combines two separate stories or "worlds"—the actual and the fantastic, hard-boiled action and a "wonderland" atmosphere. One of the protagonists visits a new office on business and is tempted into a

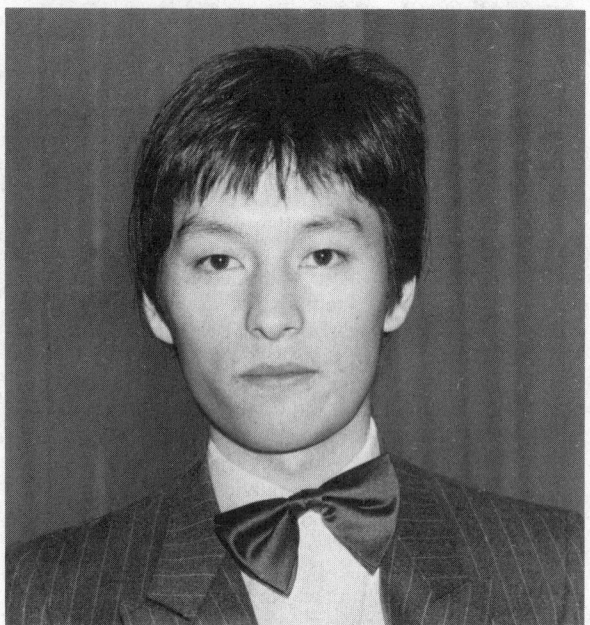

Masahiko Shimada

secret underground room, where an old biologist informs him of the danger of a subterranean monster. The fantastic story could be enjoyed for its own sake, but its symbolic significance was somewhat unclear and the integration of the two "worlds" not entirely convincing. The Tanizaki Prize jurors were said to have been divided.

Another bright young novelist was Masahiko Shimada, who received the Noma Prize for New Writers as a university student. In *Heaven Descends,* his third book, the young protagonist, obsessed with a passion for freedom, commits scandalous actions one after another and finally is driven to suicide, but he leaves more than 30 rolls of tape recording as his testament. In his successful moments, Shimada reminds the reader of the late Yukio Mishima. One of the most remarkable young women writers was Agata Hikari, whose novelette *One Room* provides a refreshing insight into some aspects of urban life in Tokyo. Two established novelists issued impressive new works during the year. Hideo Takubo's elaborately constructed *The Sea-chart* explores the relationship between father and daughter in sensitive, imaginative vignettes. Tetsuro Miura published a moving family chronicle, *Those Who Travel Through White Night.*

Two remarkable collections of poems were issued. Taro Naka's *Diary of Kuga Sanbo* succeeds as stylistic experiment by juxtaposing hard, factual *kanbun* prose (full of Chinese characters) with soft, sonorous, evocative passages. Shozo Kajima's poems are light and casual in tone but still convey a mature poet's sense of self-liberation. Notable in the field of literary criticism were the first two volumes of Jinichi Konishi's *History of Japanese Literature,* Saiichi Maruya's controversial *What Is Chushingura?,* a new approach to the traditional Kabuki play, and Shoichi Saeki's *U.S. and Japan: Literary Relationship,* focusing on the stormy years before the Pacific War (World War II).

(SHOICHI SAEKI)

See also Art Exhibitions and Art Sales: *Art Sales;* Libraries; Publishing.

This article updates the *Macropædia* article The History of Western LITERATURE and articles on the literatures of the various languages.

Mathematics

In 1985 the symbiosis of computing and mathematics moved rapidly toward becoming a dominant theme in mathematical research. Many areas of investigation were involved; *e.g.,* numerical modeling of complex scientific phenomena, graphical representation of images ranging from molecules to movie animations, and analysis of nonlinear physical systems in transition from order to turbulence. The new emphasis on parallel-processing computers stimulated major work in all fields in which mathematics and computing overlapped.

During the year particular progress was made in the art of factoring numbers, a specialized branch of mathematics often considered somewhat out of the mainstream of research. Factoring is often pursued primarily for the joy of discovery, but it also is of immense practical value in cryptography. In the 1980s many of the most secure codes used for transmission of financial and military information relied on a scheme of "public keys" that everyone can know but only authorized persons can use.

These cryptographic systems work because the public keys are large numbers that have only two factors chosen so as to be very difficult to find. But an authorized person, who knows one factor, can easily determine the other. Hence, someone who is able to factor large numbers could break these codes. For this reason much of the current work on factoring was done at the U.S. National Security Agency, Ft. Meade, Md., the premier federal agency for cryptographic and communications security and intelligence.

Traditional methods of factoring rely on clever "sieves," schemes for rapidly eliminating layer after layer of potential factors. The oldest such method, attributed to the Greek mathematician Eratosthenes of Cyrene, is used as a systematic means of finding prime numbers: eliminate from a list of numbers the multiples of 2, then the multiples of 3, then the multiples of 5, then of 7, then of 11, etc. What remain will be numbers that have no factors other than 1 and themselves—the primes. Numbers having factors will be "caught" by this sieve, together with at least one of the factors.

Modern methods for factoring specific numbers are based on this sieve but employ more sophisticated mathematical theory. In the mid-1970s, with the best methods at the time on the fastest computers, the hardest numbers that could be factored in reasonable amounts of time were those with about 40 digits. By 1985 advances in hardware, software, and especially in mathematical theory had moved this limit to nearly 80.

For nearly two centuries all theories of factoring were based on the properties of certain quadratic equations introduced by Carl Gauss in the late 18th century. But during the year Hendrik W. Lenstra, Jr., of the University of Amsterdam devised a method of factoring based on so-called elliptic curves, equations of the form $y^2 = x^3 + ax + b$. The behaviour of these curves, supported by the extensive theory of algebraic geometry, made it possible to factor large numbers that had resisted all other methods.

Lenstra's algorithm is especially useful for numbers having two factors that are far apart in size—unfortunately, not the ones most often encountered in cryptographic work. Typical large numbers have lots of factors, usually many that are small and easy to find. In the middle range are numbers having only a few factors, each large. The hardest and rarest are those with just two factors that are approximately the same size. It is these rare numbers that

code makers select to keep their codes secure. Lenstra's algorithm, therefore, would help number theorists fill in their charts of factors and of known primes but would not be particularly useful for breaking public-key codes.

Factoring was also under attack by computer scientists from two quite different perspectives. One line of attack made use of the new, very powerful parallel-processing computers. Such machines could carry out many calculations simultaneously rather than sequentially. The challenge in this approach was to adapt an algorithm designed for step-by-step solution to work well with many calculations taking place at the same time. To cite an analogy, if one person can build a house in a thousand days, can a thousand people build the same house in one day? Only with very careful planning can the task be done.

The other approach was through specially designed computers whose sole purpose was factoring. Often the design of such computers was limited to numbers of a certain type; matching hardware to classes of numbers was sometimes more efficient than trying to write software that made up for a mismatch between the machine and the problem.

One common strategy is to increase the word size from the 8, 16, or 32 bits used on standard computers to sizes as high as 256. On a 16-bit machine, numbers larger than 16 binary digits (2^{16}, approximately 64,000) must be broken up into separate pieces that each require separate processing. By changing the architecture of the machine to handle larger words, one can treat each number used in the factoring algorithm as a whole. A machine with 256-bit words could handle numbers of about 75 digits at one time.

Theory guarantees, however, that even as the techniques of factoring improve, more numbers will remain to be factored. Euclid proved that there are an infinite number of prime numbers. No one can ever find the last one.

(LYNN ARTHUR STEEN)

This article updates the *Macropædia* articles CRYPTOLOGY and NUMBER THEORY.

Military Affairs

U.S. Pres. Ronald Reagan's surprisingly successful summit meeting with Soviet leader Mikhail Gorbachev during November 19–21 in Geneva was the most important defense event of 1985. It symbolized the limited adversarial relationship between the two military superpowers that had dominated international affairs since World War II ended in 1945.

The competition between the two nations had been constrained by their possession of nuclear weapons and by the emergence of an increasingly stable balance of nuclear deterrence. Despite the acquisition by the U.S.S.R. of superior nuclear as well as conventional forces in the 1970s, Soviet leaders continued to believe that the potential costs of a nuclear war outweighed the potential gains. Significantly, the balance of nuclear deterrence between the U.S.S.R. and the three smaller nuclear powers—Britain, France, and China—also remained stable.

The result was an international system that was, in military terms, divided between the balances of nuclear deterrence and the balances of conventional deterrence. The nations within the nuclear balances were deterred by the threat of nuclear war from using force, nuclear or conventional, directly against one another. However, the emergence of the Soviet Union as a global military power, able to project its forces anywhere it wished, added a Soviet-U.S. dimension to the many existing regional conflicts, particularly in the Middle East. This increased

In September the U.S. Air Force successfully tested an antisatellite weapon consisting of a heat-seeking missile fired from an F-15 fighter plane. The missile destroyed an aging satellite at an altitude of 470 kilometres (290 miles) over the Pacific Ocean.
AP/WIDE WORLD

the dangers that such conflicts could escalate or expand, dragging the superpowers into a conflict that neither had intended or wanted. The danger of international conflict was also increasing with the spread of nuclear weapons to other countries, now thought to include Israel, South Africa, India, and Pakistan. The proliferation of chemical and biological weapons (CBW) had also begun with their use in the continuing Iran-Iraq war.

The overriding defense problem facing the U.S. and Soviet leaders, therefore, was how to manage their competition in such a way as to prevent its leading to a major nuclear war through miscalculation. Their objectives were, however, very different. President Reagan, like his predecessors, wanted to contain the Soviets within the areas they already controlled, including Eastern Europe, and maintain the independence of the three other major power centres in the world—Western Europe, Japan, and China. By contrast, Gorbachev, like his predecessors, sought to expand the areas under direct and indirect Soviet control with the eventual objective of gaining control of one or more of those three power centres.

The Geneva summit was successful because the two leaders were able to discuss their differing interests honestly and to agree to meet again in Washington (1986) and Moscow (1987). This suggested that their competition would continue but would be controlled. The superpower relationship would thus remain a limited adversarial one.

UNITED STATES

U.S. all-volunteer armed forces (AVF) in 1985 totaled 2,151,600 personnel (200,400 women). Retention rates remained high, as did personnel quality. The defense budget for fiscal 1985 was $258.2 billion, some 7.4% of 1983 gross domestic product (GDP) and about 30% of the federal budget.

Modernization of U.S. strategic and intermediate-range nuclear forces (S/INF) continued. In the Strategic Air Command (SAC) the first squadron of Rockwell B-1B strategic bombers was becoming operational. The aging B-52 bomber force had been reduced to 151 B-52Gs and 90 B-52Hs (first deployed in 1959 and 1962, respectively). Of the B-52Gs, 90 carried 12 AGM-86B air-launched cruise missiles (ALCM) each, and 61 were used in a nonnuclear antishipping role with Harpoon missiles. SAC also had 56 FB-111A medium-range nuclear bombers. Development of the advanced technology (stealth) bomber and of the advanced cruise missile continued.

The vulnerability of the U.S. land-based fixed-silo intercontinental ballistic missile (ICBM) force remained a problem without a solution. At the end of 1985 this force comprised 1,000 silos containing Minuteman II and III ICBM. Only the 550 Minuteman IIIs were modernized missiles, each carrying three multiple independently targetable reentry vehicles (MIRV). The 450 Minuteman II missiles were nearly 20 years old. The last of the 26 Titan II missiles were scheduled to be retired.

Intense political debate continued on replacements for this force. Production of 48 MX Peacekeeper ICBM was approved. These were large missiles, each weighing about 88,000 kg (195,000 lb) and carrying ten MIRV. Tests of the MX Peacekeeper in 1985 were successful, but the Peacekeepers were to be deployed in existing Minuteman silos, which could not survive a Soviet attack.

Development of the small (weighing about 11,350 kg [25,000 lb]) single-warhead Midgetman ICBM was continuing. Deployment modes being considered included a land-mobile version carried in armoured vehicles.

The ballistic missile nuclear submarine (SSBN) force rose to 37, carrying 640 submarine-launched ballistic missiles (SLBM). Six new Ohio-class SSBN each carried 24 Trident I/C-4s, which were to be replaced by the Trident II/D-5 SLBM in 1988–89. Older SSBN comprised 12 of the Franklin class (192 Trident I/C-4s) and 18 of the Lafayette class (288 Poseidon C-3s).

Deployment of submarine-launched nuclear cruise missiles continued with four nuclear cruise-missile submarines (SSGN) so equipped. A total of 700 BGM-109A Tomahawk sea-launched cruise missiles (SLCM) was planned. An additional 2,300 conventionally armed Tomahawk SLCM were being deployed so that each vessel would carry a mix of nuclear and conventionally armed missiles. Dispersing the nuclear SLCM would enhance their survivability.

North American Aerospace Defense Command matériel remained minimal, with only 72 U.S. F-15 Eagle and 38 Canadian CF-18D (F-18) Hornet modern interceptors. To balance the Soviet antisatellite (ASAT) system, the U.S. was developing an ASAT system carried by F-15. It was successfully tested in September, destroying a target satellite. Development continued on the components of the Strategic Defense Initiative (SDI) announced by President Reagan in his March 23, 1983, television address. Although SDI was popularly known as "Star Wars," only some components would be space-based.

The U.S. Navy continued building toward a 600-ship goal, with 213 major surface combatants, 91 nuclear-attack submarines (SSN), and personnel totaling 568,800. These provided 13 carrier battle groups (to rise to 15), each with an attack wing of 70–95 aircraft plus escorting surface vessels and SSN. The modern (post-1955) aircraft carrier fleet of 11 comprised 4 nuclear and 7 conventionally powered carriers. Modern aircraft included 300 F-14A Tomcat interceptors, 166 A-6 Intruder and 84 F/A-18A Hornet strike planes, and 82 F-2C electronic warfare/airborne electronic warning aircraft. A third World War II battleship, *Missouri,* was being recommissioned with Tomahawk SLCM. The 9 nuclear and 20 conventionally powered guided weapons (GW) cruisers included three new Ticonderoga-class ships with the Aegis fleet air defense missile/radar system. Other major surface combatants included 37 GW and 31 gun/antisubmarine warfare (ASW) Spruance-class destroyers, plus 48 GW and 53 gun frigates.

The Marine Corps, with 198,200 personnel, formed with the Navy the main U.S. power-projection force. It was organized in three divisions, each with its integral air wing. Modern aircraft included 92 F-18 Hornet interceptor/strike

aircraft, 69 A-6 Intruder, and 52 AV-8A/C Harrier vertical/short takeoff and landing (V/STOL) interceptor strike aircraft. The amphibious warfare ships carrying the Corps included five Tarawa and seven Iwo Jima helicopter/Harrier/troop carriers.

The 603,900-strong Air Force had approximately 7,000 combat aircraft. Modern types included F-15 Eagle interceptors, F-16 Fighting Falcon fighter-bombers, and 34 E-3A/8 Sentry airborne warning and control systems. Among older types were 570 F-4 Phantom fighter-bombers/reconnaissance, 230 F-111A/D/E/F medium bombers, and 288 A-10A Thunderbolt ground-support aircraft.

The Army, with 780,800 personnel, formed 16 divisions (18,500 men each): 4 armoured, 6 mechanized, 3 infantry, 1 light infantry, 1 air assault, and 1 airborne. In addition, five new light infantry divisions were being formed. They were to be smaller (about 10,000 men each) and easier to transport. As part of the Rapid Deployment Force (RDF), they were intended for use outside NATO-Europe.

Armour included 2,833 M-1 Abrams tanks, 2,150 M-2/3 Bradley mechanized infantry combat vehicles (MICV), some 9,000 M-60A1, M-60A2, and M-60A3 Patton tanks, and 12,300 M-113 armoured personnel carriers (APC). Missile systems included multiple-launch rocket systems and Patriot surface-to-air missiles (SAM). Secretary of Defense Caspar Weinberger canceled the Sergeant York divisional air defense system (DIVAD) as ineffective. The Army manned the two new INF systems, the Pershing II intermediate-range ballistic missile (IRBM; range 1,800 km [800 mi]) and the BGM-109A Tomahawk ground-launched cruise missile (GLCM; range 2,500 km [1,100 mi]).

U.S.S.R.

The Soviet military machine remained the most powerful in the world. Personnel totaled 5.3 million (including 1.3 million command and general support personnel) plus 25 million in the reserves. Defense spending remained high at about $295 billion, 12–17% of gross national product (GNP).

The Strategic Rocket Forces had 300,000 troops and continued to increase their superiority over U.S. and NATO S/INF in missile and warhead numbers and warhead yields and accuracy. As of 1985 the Soviets had a first-strike capability that the U.S. would not have during the rest of the 20th century. The figures shown in Table I underestimate the Soviet advantage because the U.S.S.R. also deployed 1,000–3,000 reload missiles for their ICBM, IRBM, and SLBM launchers. New systems being tested and deployed included two ICBM, the SS-X-24 and SS-X-25 (both mobile); five long-range cruise missiles, three similar to the U.S. Tomahawk—the SS-NX-21 SLCM, the SSC-X-4 GLCM, and the AS-X-15 ALCM (all in the 3,000-km [1,400-mi] range)—plus two long-range G/SLCM; and the SS-NX-23 SLBM carried in the DIV SSBN. The three new Typhoon-class SSBN, each carrying 20 SS-N-20 MIRVed SLBM, were the world's largest, displacing 23,000 tons.

The strategic aviation force comprised the new Blackjack A, larger than the U.S.'s B-1B; 125 older Bears plus resumed production of the Bear H as an ALCM launcher; and 130 Tu-22M Backfire B/Cs. Additional medium-range bombers included 130 Tu-22 Blinder A/Bs, 220 obsolete Tu-16 Badgers, and 450 Su-24 strike aircraft.

Soviet strategic defensive forces were also large. The Soviet National Air Defense Troops (APVO) formed a separate service with some 635,000 personnel, 1,200 interceptors, and 9,600 SAM launchers at 1,200 fixed sites. The latest SAM, the SA-X-12, had a tactical antiballistic missile (T-ABM) capability. Soviet upgrading of the ABM

Table I. U.S./NATO–Soviet Strategic and Intermediate Nuclear Force Balance, July 1985

Weapons systems	Range (km)	Payload[1] (000 lb)	Warheads, yield[2]	CEP[3]	Speed (Mach)	Number deployed
UNITED STATES Strategic Forces						
Intercontinental ballistic missiles (ICBM)						1,000
Titan II	15,000	8.3	1 × 9 mt	1,300	...	26[4]
Minuteman II	11,300	1.6	1 × 1.2 mt	370	...	450
Minuteman III Mod 1	14,800	2.2	3 × 170 kt	350	...	250
Mod 2	12,900	2.4	3 × 335 kt	220	...	300
Submarine-launched ballistic missiles (SLBM; in 37 nuclear submarines)						640
Poseidon C-3	4,600	3.3	10 × 50 kt or 14 × 100 kt	450	...	304
Trident I/C-4	7,400	3.0+	8 × 100 kt	450	...	312
Manned bombers and air-launched cruise missiles (ALCM)						
B-52G	12,000	70	...	...	0.95	90
B-52H	16,000	70	...	...	0.95	90
FB-111A	4,700	37.5	...	...	1.5	56
AGM-86B ALCM	2,400	0.66	200 kt	60	0.7	1,100
U.S./NATO Intermediate Nuclear Forces[5] (Total: 702 weapons, 342 delivery systems)						
Intermediate-range ballistic missiles (IRBM)						
U.S. Pershing II	1,800	...	5–50+ kt	45	...	48
Manned bombers and ground-launched cruise missiles (GLCM)						
U.S. F-111 E/F	4,700	28	3	...	2.5	250[6]
U.S. Tomahawk GLCM	2,500	0.27	10–50 kt	20	0.7	64
BRITAIN (Strategic and INF)[7]						
Submarine-launched ballistic missiles (SLBM; in 4 nuclear submarines)						
Polaris A-3	4,600	1.5	3–6 × 200 kt	900	...	64
Strike aircraft						
Tornado	2,800	16	...	...	1.5	123
FRANCE (Strategic and INF)[7]						
Submarine-launched ballistic missiles (SLBM; in 5 nuclear submarines)						
MSBS M-20	3,000	...	1 × 1 mt	...	...	64
MSBS M-4	4,400+	...	6 × 150 kt	...	...	16
Intermediate-range ballistic missiles (IRBM)						
SSBS S-3	3,500	...	1 × 1 mt	...	...	18
Strike aircraft						
Mirage IVA	3,200	2.2	1 × 60 kt	...	1.0	22
Mirage IIIE	2,400	1.8	2 × 15 kt	...	1.5	30
Super Etendard	1,500	1	2 × 15 kt	...	1.0	36
SOVIET UNION Strategic Forces						
Intercontinental ballistic missiles (ICBM)						c. 1,600+
SS-11 Mod 1	10,500	2	1 × 1 mt	1,400	...	} 520
Mod 2/3	8,800	2.5	3 × 100–300 kt	1,100	...	
SS-13 Savage	10,000	1	1 × 750 kt	2,000	...	60
SS-16	9–10,000	...	3 × 150 kt	...	...	200[8]
SS-17 Mod 1	10,000	6	4 × 750 kt	450	...	
Mod 2	11,000	3.6	1 × 6 mt	450	...	} 150
Mod 3	10,000	...	4 × 20 kt	...	...	
SS-18 Mod 4	16,700	16.7	10 × 500 kt	300	...	308
SS-19 Mod 3	10,000	8	6 × 550 kt	300	...	360
Submarine-launched ballistic missiles (in 63 nuclear plus 14 diesel submarines)						c. 1,000
SS-N-5 Serb	1,400	...	1 × 1–2 mt	2,800	...	39
SS-N-6 Mod 1,2	3,000	1.5	1 × 1 mt	900	...	
Mod 3	3,000	1.5	2 × 500 kt	900	...	} 336
SS-N-8 Mod 1	7,800	1.5	1 × 1 mt	1,300	...	
Mod 2	9,100	8	1 × 800 kt	900	...	} 292
SS-N-17	3,900	2.5	1 × 1 mt	1,500	...	12
SS-N-18 Mod 1	6,500	5	3 × 200 kt	1,400	...	
Mod 2	8,000	3.6	1 × 450 kt	600	...	} 224
Mod 3	6,500	...	7 × 200 kt	600	...	
SS-N-20	8,300	...	9–12 × 200 kt	...	...	60
Manned bombers						c. 380
Tu-95 Bear B/C	12,800	40	3–5	...	0.78	125
Mya-4 Bison	11,200	20	4	...	0.87	45
Tu-26 Backfire B	8,000	17.5	4	...	2.5	230
Soviet INF (Total: c. 4,823 warheads, c. 1,423 delivery systems)						
Variable/intermediate/medium-range ballistic missiles (V/I/MRBM)[9]						
SS-4 Sandal	2,000	3	1 × 1 mt	2,300	...	120
SS-20 Mod 1	5,000	1.2	1 × 1.5 mt	...	...	
Mod 2	5,000	...	3 × 150 kt	c. 400	...	} c. 1,269
Mod 3	7,400	...	1 × 50 kt	...	...	
Medium/short-range ballistic missiles and ground/sea-launched cruise missiles[10]						
SS-22 MRBM	c. 1,000	...	1 × 500 kt	300	...	c. 100
SS-N-12 G/SLCM	1,000	2.2	1 × 350 kt	...	...	c. 100
Manned bombers[11]						745
Tu-16 Badger	4,800	20	2	...	0.8	220
Tu-22 Blinder	4,000	12	2	...	1.5	130

[1] Payload refers to a missile's throw weight or a bomber's weapons load.
[2] For MIRV and MRV the figure to the left of the multiplication sign gives the number of warheads and the figure to the right is the yield per warhead. For bombers, weapons per bomber are given.
[3] Circular Error Probable: the radius (in metres) of a circle within which at least half of the missile warheads aimed at a specific target will fall.
[4] Obsolete systems being withdrawn; excluded from number deployed.
[5] INF systems are missiles with ranges or aircraft with unrefueled combat radii of 1,000–5,499 km; combat radii are about one-third or less of the range.
[6] Total deployed worldwide; 150 is the inventory normally based in Europe, or within striking range of Europe.
[7] British nuclear forces are under national control but may be assigned to NATO. French nuclear forces are controlled and targeted independently of NATO.
[8] Mobile SS-16 ICBM reported deployed, based on SS-20 V/IRBM.
[9] Total deployed against both NATO and China theatres; two-thirds are thought to be deployed against NATO. Three missiles per launcher for SS-20.
[10] Although not always classified as Soviet INF, Soviet M/SRBM and G/SLCM could hit targets in Western Europe and are therefore shown for illustrative purposes.
[11] Total deployed worldwide. Of these, about half are allocated to Soviet Naval Aviation (some 160 Tu-16, 35 Tu-22, and 100 Tu-26). Two-thirds of the remaining strike bombers and ASM carriers are considered deployed against NATO. Tu-26 Backfire is now counted as strategic.

Sources: International Institute for Strategic Studies, *The Military Balance 1985–1986;* and *Aviation Week and Space Technology.* Figures for Soviet forces, especially INF, can only be estimates.

system around Moscow, plus the construction of other ABM radars, would enable the U.S.S.R. to field a nation-wide ABM system.

The two million-strong Army was organized into 51 tank, 141 motor rifle (mechanized), 16 artillery, and 7 airborne divisions (10,500–12,500 men each). Equipment remained at much higher levels than for the U.S., its NATO allies, and China. It included 52,600 tanks (the modern types comprising 9,800 T-72/-80s and 9,300 T-64s, plus 33,500 older T-54/-55/-62s); 70,000 armoured fighting vehicles; and 33,000 artillery pieces, including new self-propelled 203-mm, 152-mm, and 122-mm guns.

Deployment of the Soviet Army forces was roughly two-thirds against NATO-Europe and one-third against China. There were three Strategic Theatre Commands (GTVD), plus a central strategic reserve military district with 16 divisions. The Western GTVD controlled 28 Soviet divisions (14 tank, 12 motor rifle) and 45 non-Soviet divisions in Central and Eastern Europe, plus 62 divisions (31 tank, 29 motor rifle, 2 airborne) in the European U.S.S.R. The Southern GTVD controlled 30 divisions, mainly motor rifle, including some 115,000 troops occupying Afghanistan. The Far Eastern GTVD controlled 53 divisions (7 tank, 45 motor rifle). Large overseas deployments were in Syria (7,000), Vietnam (7,000), and Cuba (9,000), with smaller ones of 500–2,500 troops each in Algeria, Angola, Ethiopia, Iraq, Laos, Libya, Yemen (San'a'), and Yemen (Aden).

WARSAW PACT

The continuing strong support in Poland for the illegal Solidarity trade union movement underlined the political uncertainties in Eastern Europe about the degree of non-Soviet Warsaw Pact support for a possible Soviet invasion of Western Europe. Soviet forces included 20 divisions in East Germany, 2 in Poland, and 4 in Hungary. Poland maintained the largest military forces of the Eastern European nations, totaling 319,000 personnel and including a 210,000-strong Army with 3,450 T-54/-55/-72 main battle tanks and a 91,000-strong Air Force with 675 combat aircraft (400 MiG-21/-21U/-23 interceptors). Czechoslovakia's 203,300-strong forces, the second largest, comprised an Army of 145,000 with 3,500 T-54/-55/-72 tanks and an Air Force of 58,000 with 474 combat aircraft (275 MiG-21/-21U/-23 interceptors).

East Germany's armed forces totaled 174,000, mainly an Army of 120,000 with 1,500 T-54/-55/-72 tanks (plus 1,600 in storage) and an Air Force of 39,000 with 380 combat aircraft, including 300 MiG-21F/MF/PF/U/-23 interceptors. Hungary's armed forces, with 106,000 personnel, included an Army of 84,000 with about 1,200 T-54/-55/-72 tanks and an Air Force of 22,000 with 145 MiG-21/-23 interceptors. All four countries allocated much lower proportions of their GNPs to defense than did the U.S.S.R.; 1983 figures were 5.7% for East Germany, 3.8% for Czechoslovakia, 2.7% for Poland, and 2.2% for Hungary.

NATO

The five-year crisis caused by NATO's 1979 decision to deploy 572 new INF (108 Pershing II IRBM and 464 GLCM) was finally resolved by a decision in favour of deployment by the last two members who had promised to do so, Belgium and The Netherlands. Britain, Italy, and West Germany continued deployment. Although protests against deployment still occurred, they had become negligible by the end of 1985.

A new issue facing the NATO alliance was whether its members should participate in the U.S. SDI program.

Those governments and groups opposing SDI argued that it was potentially destabilizing and threatened to leave NATO-Europe exposed to Soviet nuclear weapons while the U.S. sheltered behind its strategic shield. Those favouring SDI argued that it would be stabilizing because it would balance Soviet strategic defenses and would provide a shield for NATO-Europe as well as the U.S. The December 1985 U.S.-U.K. agreement that Britain would participate in SDI was a major advance in alliance cooperation. Canada, Denmark, and Norway decided that their governments would not participate but that private firms could do so.

NATO's major long-term problem remained its lack of political will to fund the emerging conventional weapons technologies, dubbed ET, needed to offset the buildup of the Soviet/Warsaw Pact forces. On the crucial Northern/Central Front, stretching from Norway to West Germany, the balance of forces was, in terms of total divisions (or equivalent) war-mobilized, for NATO, 54 divisions (19 tank, $19\frac{1}{3}$ mechanized, and $15\frac{2}{3}$ other) with 8,800 main battle tanks and, for the Warsaw Pact, $113\frac{1}{3}$ divisions ($72\frac{1}{3}$ Soviet) comprising 43 tank, 55 mechanized, and $5\frac{1}{3}$ other with 24,200 main battle tanks. This gave the Soviet/Warsaw Pact forces an advantage of about 2:1 in divisions and 2.5:1 in battle tanks.

This military imbalance was accentuated by the imbalance in sharing the burden of military expenses. As Table II shows, U.S. defense spending as a percentage of 1983 GDP was, at 7.4%, approximately twice that of France and West Germany (4.2 and 3.4%) and three times that of Canada, Denmark, and Italy. Only Britain's burden, at 5.5% of GDP, was comparable to that of the U.S.

UNITED KINGDOM

Defense expenditure for 1983–84 was $21,401,000,000 (5.5% of 1983 GDP). The all-volunteer forces were efficient but relatively small and short of modern equipment. The Army of 163,000 had 130 new Challenger and 900 Chieftain main battle tanks plus 2,338 MICV/APC. The Royal Air Force (RAF) had 93,500 personnel and about 600 combat aircraft. About 123 of the new Tornado GR-1 multirole combat aircraft were being deployed in fighter, ground-attack, and reconnaissance models, replacing 150 Phantom fighters. Other modern aircraft included 53 Harrier GR-3/T-4 V/STOL, 96 Jaguar GR-1 ground-attack fighters, 24 Jaguar GR-1 reconnaissance planes, and 28 Nimrod MR-1/-1A/-2 maritime reconnaissance aircraft. The Royal Navy was among the world's largest with 70,600 personnel. It had 28 attack submarines (13 nuclear), 60 major surface combatants including 4 ASW carriers with Sea Harriers, 15 GW destroyers, and 39 general-purpose frigates. Royal Marine personnel totaled 7,800.

The major overseas deployment was the British Army of the Rhine with 55,288 army and 10,440 RAF personnel. An additional 2,400 personnel manned the Falkland Islands base. Modernization of Britain's national nuclear forces (NNF) continued with the construction of four SSBN carrying 64 U.S. Trident II SLBM with U.K. nuclear warheads.

FRANCE

Defense spending in 1985 was estimated at $15,859,000,-000. Modernization of France's NNF continued, with five SSBN operational, two being refitted, and one under construction. Replacement of the M-20 SLBM with the M-4 was beginning. Medium-range and tactical nuclear forces were also being increased, including the ASMP nuclear air-to-surface missile (ASM).

Military personnel totaled 476,560 (300,000 in the Army), but this was to be reduced to 439,000 by 1988. There were 1,260 AMX-30 and 169 new AMX-30B2 main battle tanks, 780 AMX-10P/PC Milan MICV, and about 3,000 APC. These were organized in six armoured, two light armoured, and two motor rifle divisions, plus a Rapid Action Force for overseas intervention consisting of one parachute, one air portable marine, one light armoured, one alpine, and one air mobile division. The Air Force of 96,550 personnel had 475 combat aircraft, the newer models including 120 Mirage F-1C and 30 Mirage 2000C interceptors plus 30 Mirage 5F and 135 Jaguar A ground-attack fighters. The 67,710-strong Navy's 47 major surface combatants included 2 light and 1 helicopter carriers, 19 destroyers, and 25 frigates; the Navy also had 18 attack submarines (2 SSN). Approximately 28,000 personnel from all services were deployed overseas, with an additional 48,-500 in West Germany.

The Mitterrand government was politically embarrassed by the discovery of the French security service's responsibility for the destruction of the Greenpeace organization's ship *Rainbow Warrior* in a New Zealand harbour in an attempt to stop Greenpeace's protests against continued French nuclear tests at Mururoa Atoll. (*See* WORLD AFFAIRS [Oceania]: *Oceanian Affairs.*) The tests in 1985 apparently included French neutron (enhanced-radiation) weapons.

WEST GERMANY

West Germany's defense budget totaled $15,740,000,000 in 1985. Standing armed forces totaled 478,000, more than half of them volunteers, rising to 1,250,000 on mobilization, plus 20,000 paramilitary forces. The 335,600-strong Army totaled 12 divisions organized in 5,000-man brigades, of which 66 were tank, 62 armoured infantry, 32 armoured artillery, 12 parachute, 4 mountain, and 11 armoured reconnaissance. Armour included 1,280 new Leopard 2 and 2,437 Leopard 1 main battle tanks, plus 2,546 MICV and 3,357 APC. Artillery, antiaircraft guns and missiles, and antitank guns and guided weapons were also deployed in large numbers.

The Air Force had 106,000 personnel with 586 combat aircraft. These included 137 new Tornados, 60 older F-4 Phantoms, 90 obsolete F-104G and 173 Alpha Jet ground-attack fighters, plus 60 F-4F interceptors and 58 RF-4E reconnaissance planes. The 36,200-strong Navy was designed for coastal warfare in the Baltic Sea, with 40 fast-attack craft equipped with guided missiles plus 7 GW destroyers, 6 GW frigates, and 24 coastal submarines. The naval air arm consisted of 122 combat aircraft, including 47 Tornados and 29 F/TF-104G attack planes.

ARMS CONTROL AND DISARMAMENT

The declining importance of arms control negotiations and agreements was dramatized by the expiration of the unratified 1979 Salt II Treaty on Dec. 31, 1985. No replacement agreement was in sight. The Reagan administration was unlikely to extend the Salt II limits on U.S. forces because the Soviets had not observed them. A particularly blatant violation by the Soviets was their testing of two, instead of the one permitted, new ICBMs, the SS-X-24 and SS-X-25. Additional Soviet violations were detailed in the U.S. Department of Defense's November 1985 report.

Arms control attention was thus focused in 1985 on the future of the 1972 ABM treaty, the last major agreement of the 1970s still in force, and on the possibility of other limits on the deployment of strategic defensive systems. Soviet presummit propaganda had focused on stopping President

The new SS-X-24 intercontinental missile (shown here in an illustration based on intelligence photographs), equipped with ten nuclear warheads and launched from mobile carriers, was expected to become an operational component of the Soviet Union's strategic forces during 1986.
AP/WIDE WORLD

Reagan's SDI, claiming that this was a precondition for progress in superpower relations. But the president had insisted he would not sacrifice SDI, and the Soviets had accepted this, though reluctantly. No agreement limiting strategic defenses or ASAT systems was expected. Soviet violations of the ABM Treaty, particularly the continued construction of an illegal ABM radar at Krasnoyarsk, made it doubtful that the treaty could last indefinitely, as intended.

In light of these developments, the continued U.S.-U.S.S.R. negotiations in the talks covering strategic offensive forces (START), weapons in space, and INF were not expected to produce effective results. The proposals put forward by both sides, particularly the Soviet offer in September/October of a 50% reduction in strategic forces, seemed designed for propaganda purposes.

No progress was made in the other arms control negotiations, including the Vienna talks on mutual and balanced force reductions (MBFR) and the Stockholm Conference on Disarmament in Europe (CDE).

MIDDLE EAST

The Middle East remained the most militarily unstable area in the world. Its sharp divisions on economic, political, racial, and religious issues were reflected in the high relative levels of defense spending and large military forces of the major regional powers. The Iran-Iraq war entered its sixth year with no end in sight. Lebanon remained divided. Israel's 1982 intervention had started the expulsion from Lebanon of the Palestine Liberation Organization that was later completed by Syria to ensure its unchallenged control over Lebanon north of the Awali River. South of the river Israel ended an increasingly costly and unpopular occupation but continued to strike against terrorist bases.

Syria's Pres. Hafez al-Assad remained the regional strongman with massive Soviet aid. Syrian armed forces personnel totaled 402,500, with an Army of 270,000 forming five armoured and three mechanized divisions. Equipment included 1,100 new T-72 and 3,100 T-54/-55/-62 main battle tanks plus 2,200 BMP/BTR-series MICV/APC.

The separate Air Defense Command had 60,000 personnel manning 63 batteries with Soviet SA-2/-3/-5/-6 SAM. The 70,000-strong Air Force had some 500 combat aircraft, including 30 MiG-25 Foxbat E, 70 MiG-23 Flogger E, and 180 MiG-21 PF/MF interceptors, plus 50 MiG-23

Table II. Approximate Strengths of Regular Armed Forces of the World

Country	Military personnel in 000s			Warships[1]			Jet aircraft[3]		Tanks[4]	Defense expenditure as % of 1983 GNP[5]
	Army	Navy	Air Force	Aircraft carriers/cruisers	Submarines[2]	Destroyers/frigates	Bombers and fighter-bombers	Fighters/reconnaissance		
I. NATO										
Belgium	67.2	4.6	19.8	—	—	4 FFG	119 FB	44, 18 R	334	3.3
Canada[6]	34.4	18.9	28.7	—	3	4 DDG, 19 FF	101 FB	42 F	114	2.1
Denmark	17.0	5.7	6.9	—	4	5 FFG, 5 FF	71 FB	16,16 R	208	2.4
France[7]	300.0	67.7	96.5	2 CV, 1 CVH, 1 CG	16, 2 SSN, 5 SSBN	19 DDG, 25 FFG	28 B, 288 FB	186, 53 R, 42 MR	1,429	4.2
Germany, West	335.6	36.2	106.0	—	24	7 DDG, 6 FFG, 3 FF	534 FB	60, 87 R, 14 MR	4,662	3.4
Greece	158.0	19.5	24.0	—	10	14 DD, 2 FFG, 5 FF	167 FB	100, 35 R, 16 MR	1,611	6.9
Italy	270.0	44.5	70.6	1 CVH, 2 CAH	10	4 DDG, 12 FFG, 4 FF	306 FB	29 R, 14 MR	1,770	2.6
Luxembourg	0.7	—	—	—	—	—	—	—		0.9
Netherlands, The	67.0	16.7	16.8	—	5	2 DDG, 16 FFG	200 FB	18 R, 15 MR	1,146	3.3
Norway	20.0	7.6	9.4	—	14	5 FFG	86 FB	7 MR	100	3.1
Portugal	45.7	13.9	13.4	—	3	17 FF	50 FB	—	66	3.5
Spain	230.0	57.0(8)	33.0	1 CVH	8	11 DD, 11 FFG	43 FB	114, 17 R, 6 MR	779	2.4
Turkey	520.0	55.0	55.0	—	14	12 DD, 1 FFG, 5 FF	308 FB	32, 35 R	2,922	4.9
United Kingdom	163.0	70.6[8]	93.5	3 CVH	15, 13 SSN, 4 SSBN	15 DDG, 39 FFG	285 FB	321, 27 R, 28 MR	1,030	5.5
United States	780.8	767.0[8]	603.9	2 BBG, 4 CVN, 10 CV, 9 CGN, 20 CG, 5 LHA, 7 LPH, 14 LPD, 24 LSD/T	91 SSN, 36 SSBN, 4 SSGN,	37 DDG, 31 DD, 48 FFG, 53 FF	300 SB, 230 B, 2,110 FB	2,330, 270 R, 380 MR/ASW	14,140	7.4
II. WARSAW PACT										
Bulgaria	105.0	8.5	35.0	—	2	2 FFG	100 FB	80, 36 R	1,860	3.2
Czechoslovakia	145.0	—	58.0	—	—	—	152 FB	275, 37 R	3,500	3.8
Germany, East	120.0	15.0	39.0	—	—	2 FFG	59 FB	300, 18 R	1,500	5.7
Hungary	84.0	—	22.0	—	—	—	—	120	1,230	2.2
Poland	210.0	19.0	91.0	—	3	1 DDG	220 FB	400, 55 R, 10 MR	3,450	2.7
Romania	150.0	7.5	32.0	—	—	—	130 FB	224, 18 R	1,380	1.5
U.S.S.R.	3,315.0	460.0[8]	1,625.0[9]	4 CV, 2 CVH, 2 CGN, 27 CG, 8 CA	131, 72 SSN, 65 SSBN, 14 SSB, 49 SSGN, 17 SSG	47 DDG, 22 DD, 32 FFG, 35 FF	400 SB, 615 B, 2,940 FB	3,560, 660 R, 135 MR	52,600	12–17
III. OTHER EUROPEAN										
Albania	30.0	3.2	7.2	—	3	—	—	100	100	...
Austria	50.0	—	4.7	—	—	—	32 FB	—	170	1.4
Finland	30.9	2.7	2.9	—	—	—	—	61	c. 100	1.6
Ireland	11.9	1.0	0.9	—	—	—	—	—		1.8
Sweden[10]	47.0/800.0	9.6	9.0	—	12	1 DD	115 FB	216, 54 R	770	3.2
Switzerland[10]	20.0/1,100.0	—	3.0/45.0	—	—	—	139 FB	140, 16 R	860	2.1
Yugoslavia	191.0	13.0	37.0	—	7	2 FFG	200 FB	150, 35 R	920	3.7
IV. MIDDLE EAST AND MEDITERRANEAN; SUB-SAHARAN AFRICA; LATIN AMERICA[11]										
Algeria	150.0	8.0	12.0	—	—	3 FF	150 FB	113, 6 R	700	1.8
Egypt	320.0	20.0	105.0	—	14	3 DDG, 4 FFG	176 FB	164, 38 R	2,160	8.7
Iran[12]	250.0	20.0	35.0	—	—	3 DDG, 4 FFG	75 FB	20 F, 7 R	1,000	13.3
Iraq[12]	475.0	4.5	40.0	—	—	—	17 B, 181 FB	285	3,750	33.7
Israel[10]	104.0/400.0	10.0/10.0	28.0/37.0	—	3	—	532 FB	13 R	3,600	29.8
Jordan	62.7	0.3	7.2	—	—	—	68 FB	35	795	13.7
Kuwait	10.0	1.1	2.0	—	—	—	30 FB	34	240	6.7
Lebanon[13]	16.0	0.3	1.0	—	—	—	—	3	50	13.3
Libya[14]	58.0	6.5	8.5	—	6	1 FFG	9 B, 204 FB	285, 7 R	2,800	...
Morocco	130.0	6.0	13.0	—	—	1 FFG	77 FB	—	120	9.8
Oman	16.5	2.0	3.0	—	—	—	40 FB	—	33	25.6
Qatar	5.0	0.7	0.3	—	—	—	17 FB	8	24	2.6
Saudi Arabia	35.0	3.5	14.5	—	—	4 FFG	65 FB	80	450	18.2
Sudan, The	53.0	0.6	3.0	—	—	—	34 FB	—	170	3.4
Syria	270.0	2.5	130.0	—	—	2 FF	193 FB	280	4,200	14.3
Tunisia	30.0	2.6	2.5	—	—	1 FF	12 FB	—	68	5.3
United Arab Emirates	40.0	1.5	1.5	—	—	—	3 FB	30	136	8.8
Yemen, North	35.0	0.6	1.0	—	—	—	—	76	664	17.9
Yemen, South	24.0	1.0	2.5	—	—	—	67 FB	36	450	...
Angola[15]	36.0	1.5	2.0	—	—	—	98 FB	30	445	...
Ethiopia[16]	210.0	3.0	4.0	—	—	—	150 FB	—	900	10.4

Flogger F and 40 Su-20 fighter-bombers. Defense spending totaled $3,312,000,000 in 1985.

Israel remained the region's strongest military power, especially in the quality of its weapons. Its defense spending burden was increasingly difficult to support, even with massive U.S. aid; reaching $3,621,000,000 in 1985, defense had consumed 29.8% of GNP in 1983. From a population of only 4.3 million, Israel raised standing armed forces of 142,000 that would rise to 512,000 on mobilization. The Army of 104,000 formed 11 armoured divisions and 33 armoured, 5 mechanized infantry, 5 parachute, and 15 artillery brigades. There were some 3,600 main battle tanks plus 4,000 MICV/APC. The 28,000-strong Air Force had 684 combat aircraft, including 46 U.S. F/TF-15 Eagles, 75 U.S. F-16A/B Falcons, 150 Israeli Kfir C1/C2/C7s, and 131 U.S. F-4E Phantom interceptor/fighter-bombers.

Egypt's armed forces totaled 445,000, with defense spending estimated at $4,143,000,000 in 1985–86. The nation's conversion from Soviet to Western equipment was continuing, most of the Soviet equipment being in reserve. The Army of 320,000 had 659 U.S. M-60A3 and 500 effective Soviet T-54/-55/-62 main battle tanks. The 25,000-strong Air Force's effective aircraft comprised 33 F-4E Phantoms and 54 Mirage 5SDE2 fighter-bombers plus 32 F-16A and 100 MiG-21 interceptors. Jordan's small but effective Army (62,750 personnel) had 795 main battle tanks, and the Air Force (7,200) had 68 F-5E/F and 35 Mirage F-1C/E fighter-bombers.

The Iran-Iraq war continued as a World War I-type conflict of attrition between entrenched infantry supported by artillery and limited quantities of armour. Casualties were heavy and much equipment was destroyed, causing the figures in Table II to be rough estimates. Iraq continued air strikes on oil tankers in the Persian Gulf to limit Iranian

Country	Military personnel in 000s			Warships[1]			Jet aircraft[3]			Defense expenditure as % of 1983 GNP[5]
	Army	Navy	Air Force	Aircraft carriers/cruisers	Submarines[2]	Destroyers/frigates	Bombers and fighter-bombers	Fighters/reconnaissance	Tanks[4]	
Kenya	13.0	0.6	—	—	—	—	12 FB	—	76	4.8
Madagascar	20.0	0.6	0.5	—	—	—	12 FB	—	—	2.3
Mozambique[17]	14.0	0.8	1.0	—	—	—	18 FB	—	300	…
Nigeria	80.0	5.0	9.0	—	—	1 FFG	42 FB	—	75	2.1
Somalia	60.0	0.5	2.0	—	—	—	21 FB	39	215	9.7
South Africa[10]	76.4/404.5	9.0	13.0	—	3	—	12 B, 102 FB	40	250	3.4
Tanzania	38.5	0.85	1.0	—	—	—	—	28	30	…
Zaire	22.0	1.5	2.5	—	—	—	—	7	50	…
Zimbabwe	41.0	—	1.0	—	—	—	5 B, 14 FB	—	30	…
Argentina	55.0	36.0[8]	17.0	1 CV	3	6 DDG	8 B, 73 FB	73 R 5 MR	230	8.9
Brazil	183.0	48.0[8]	45.0	1 CV	7	10 DD, 6 FFG	38 FB	14, 28 MR	—	0.6
Chile	57.0	29.0	15.0	1 CA	3	4 DDG, 2 DD, 2 FFG	48 FB	11, 6 MR	171	8.4
Colombia	53.0	9.0	4.2	—	2	4 FFG	12 FB	—	—	1.2
Cuba	130.0	13.5	18.0	—	3	—	51 FB	200	850	8.6
El Salvador	38.6	0.6	2.3	—	—	—	28 FB	—	—	4.3
Mexico	100.0	23.6[8]	5.5	—	—	2 DD, 4 FF	—	12 F, 8 MR	—	0.4
Nicaragua	60.0	0.8	2.0	—	—	—	…	—	120	9.8
Peru	85.0	27.0[8]	16.0	2 CA	12	10 DD, 4 FFG	15 B, 64 FB	13 MR	250	8.7
Venezuela	34.0	10.0	5.0	—	2	6 FFG	20 B, 13 FB	46	80	1.4
V. FAR EAST AND OCEANIA[11]										
Afghanistan[18]	40.0	—	7.0	—	—	—	135 FB	—	450	…
Australia	32.0	18.0	22.7	—	6	3 DDG, 10 FFG	24 FB	58, 12 MR	103	3.2
Bangladesh	82.0	6.5	3.0	—	—	3 FF	16 FB	10	50	2.0
Burma	170.0	7.0	9.0	—	—	—	—	—	25	3.8
China	2,973.0	350.0[8]	490.0	—	107, 3 SSN, 1 SSBN	16 DDG, 23 FFG, 5 FF	800 B, 500 FB	4,600, 130 R	11,450	n.a.
India	100.0	47.0	113.0	1 CV	8	3 DDG, 10 FFG	281 FB	400, 25 R, 8 MR	2,500	3.4
Indonesia	216.0	40.0[8]	25.0	—	2	4 FFG, 5 FF	30 FB	16	—	3.5
Japan	155.0	44.0	44.0	—	14	28 DDG, 3 DD, 3 FFG, 16 FF	50 FB	200, 16 R, 84 MR	1,070	1.0
Korea, North	750.0	35.0	53.0	—	20	4 FF	80 B, 410 FB	220	3,275	9.6
Korea, South	520.0	45.0[8]	33.0	—	—	7 DDG, 4 DD, 2 FFG, 5 FF	260 FB	65	1,200	5.7
Laos	50.0	1.7	2.0	—	—	—	—	20	30	…
Malaysia	90.0	9.0	11.0	—	—	2 FFG, 1 FF	40 FB	3 MR	—	7.1
Mongolia	33.0	—	3.5	—	—	—	—	12	650	10.9
New Zealand	5.6	2.8	4.4	—	—	4 FFG	25 FB	5 MR	—	1.9
Pakistan	450.0	15.2	17.6	—	6	7 DDG	108 FB	200, 10 R, 3 MR	1,506	6.9
Philippines	70.0	28.0[8]	16.8	—	—	7 FF	24 FB	22	—	1.8
Singapore	45.0	4.5	6.0	—	—	—	68 FB	26, 13 R	—	4.8
Taiwan	329.0[8]	38.0	77.0	—	2	24 DD, 9 FF	377 FB	19, 8 R, 29 MR	309	6.5
Thailand	160.0	32.2[8]	43.1	—	—	6 FF	14 FB	39, 7 R, 10 MR	390	4.1
Vietnam	1,027.0	12.0[8]	15.0	—	—	8 FF	70 FB	200	1,600	…

Note: Data exclude paramilitary, security, and irregular forces. Naval data exclude vessels of less than 100 tons standard displacement. Figures are for July 1984.

[1]Aircraft carrier (CV); aircraft carrier, nuclear (CVN); helicopter carrier (CVH); general purpose amphibious assault ship (LHA); amphibious transport dock (LPD); amphibious assault ship (helicopter) (LPH); dock/tank landing ship (LSD/T); battleship (BBG); heavy cruiser (CA); guided missile cruiser (CG); guided missile cruiser, nuclear (CGN); helicopter cruiser (CAH); destroyer (DD); guided missile destroyer (DDG); frigate (FF); guided missile frigate (FFG); N denotes nuclear powered.
[2]Nuclear-powered attack submarine (SSN); ballistic missile submarine (SSB); guided (cruise) missile submarine (SSG); coastal (C); N denotes nuclear powered.
[3]Bombers (B), fighter-bombers (FB), strategic bombers (SB), reconnaissance fighters (R); maritime reconnaissance (MR). Data include jet combat aircraft from all services including naval and air defense. MR also includes propeller drive ASW and ECM aircraft; data exclude light strike/counter-insurgency (COIN) aircraft.
[4]Main battle tanks (MBT), medium and heavy, 31 tons and over.
[5]Figures for NATO members are for GDP.
[6]Of Canada's other military personnel, approximately 49,000 are not identified by service.
[7]French forces were withdrawn from NATO command structure in 1966, but France remains a member of NATO.
[8]Includes marines.
[9]Figure includes the Strategic Rocket Forces (300,000) and the Air Defense Force (635,000), both separate services.
[10]Second figure is fully mobilized strength.
[11]Sections IV and V list only those states with significant military forces.
[12]Losses in Iran-Iraq war made remaining force estimates uncertain.
[13]Figures approximate, given Lebanon's civil war and division.
[14]Some advanced Libyan aircraft are maintained and manned by Soviet/Warsaw Pact crews.
[15]Plus 30–35,000 Cubans and 500 East Germans serving with Angolan forces.
[16]Ethiopia also has 7,000 Soviet, Cuban plus other Soviet bloc troops, and a 150,000-strong People's Militia.
[17]Plus Cuban, Warsaw Pact, and Chinese advisers and technicians.
[18]Figures approximate, given Soviet occupation of Afghanistan. Excludes about 115,000 Soviet occupation troops, plus 5,000 Cubans/Czechs.

Sources: International Institute for Strategic Studies, 23 Tavistock Street, London, *The Military Balance 1985–1986, Strategic Survey 1984–85.*

earnings from oil exports that were used to buy military supplies. The very small strike forces available to Iran and Iraq limited damage to shipping to tolerable levels, avoiding a spread of the conflict. Libya's forces remained large, totaling 73,000 personnel with 2,800 main battle tanks and 535 combat aircraft.

SOUTH, EAST, AND SOUTHEAST ASIA

The continued Soviet occupation of Afghanistan and the growing number of border incidents between Afghanistan and Pakistan made Soviet military strikes into the Baluchistan area of Pakistan increasingly likely. This necessitated more U.S. military aid to Pakistan. Despite this aid, Pakistan's armed forces totaled only 482,800 personnel, mainly an Army of 450,000 with 1,506 main battle tanks (mostly Type-59). The Air Force consisted of 17,600 personnel and 375 combat aircraft, including 30 F-16 Falcon

and 50 Mirage 5PA3 fighter-bombers. The defense budget in 1985–86 was $2,059,000,000.

India's armed forces in 1985 totaled some 1,260,000 personnel. The 1.1 million-strong Army had 2,500 main battle tanks, including 300 new T-72s. The Air Force of 113,000 had 846 combat aircraft, including 90 MiG-23 Flogger H and 68 Jaguar GR-1 fighter-bombers. Defense spending was $6,126,000,000 in 1985–86.

China's forces remained strong in manpower (3.9 million) but weak in modern equipment. China's nuclear stockpile was small, with limited numbers of comparatively old, vulnerable delivery systems. These included about 6 ICBM (DF-4/-5), 60 DF-3 IRBM, and 50 DF-2 medium-range ballistic missiles, along with 120 H-6 (Tu-16) medium bombers. Two Xia-class SSBN with 12 CSS-NX-4 SLBM (modified DF-3s) were operational. The Army had 2,973,-

(continued on page 329)

Intervention and Defense in Central America and the Caribbean

BY ROBIN RANGER

The continuing guerrilla wars in El Salvador and Nicaragua symbolized the problem of defense and military preparedness that has plagued much of Central America and the Caribbean region. In El Salvador the U.S. supported Pres. José Napoleón Duarte's democratically elected government against Soviet- and Cuban-backed guerrillas. In Nicaragua the U.S. assisted, with nonmilitary aid, guerrillas (*contras*) trying to overthrow the Sandinista government of Pres. Daniel Ortega Saavedra, a close Soviet ally. The basic problem was simple, although there was no simple solution to it: the weakness of the regional powers made them vulnerable to small military forces. Historically, these forces had been used by external powers or indigenous groups to seize and hold militarily and economically valuable resources. More recently, since 1962, the vulnerability of the governments has been exacerbated by Soviet and Cuban intervention to replace existing regimes with pro-Soviet revolutionary ones. The U.S. has tried to counter this intervention.

Central America is composed of small nations (populations less than nine million) with small armies (fewer than 50,000 personnel, except for Nicaragua). To the north, Mexico also maintains surprisingly small armed forces (129,100 personnel) for its size (population 79 million). To the south, the Andes Mountains largely cut off Central from South America. The neighbouring Caribbean thus forms, with Central America, a single geopolitical entity, one that also includes five South American countries: Colombia, Venezuela, Guyana, Suriname, and French Guiana. They also have small armed forces relative to their size and population. Only Colombia and Venezuela have armed forces with more than 10,000 personnel (66,200 and 49,000, respectively).

The Caribbean consists of even smaller nations, apart from Cuba and the Dominican Republic. Their armed forces in 1985 were either minimal (10,000 personnel or fewer) or nonexistent. The exception was Cuba's 161,500 military personnel.

Small military forces (about 1,000 to 3,000 personnel) have been the traditional means of seizing and holding control of governments in Central America. The Somoza regime in Nicaragua gained control in 1933 because Anastasio Somoza García commanded the loyalty of the National Guard. His son, Anastasio Somoza Debayle, lost control (and later his life) in 1979 because his forces could not defeat the revolutionary guerrillas. Such guerrilla

Robin Ranger is associate professor, Defense and Strategic Studies Program, School of International Relations, at the University of Southern California

forces have been an equally traditional feature of regional politics because of the low level of economic and social development.

Soviet and Cuban Intervention. The new ingredient in 1979 was the presence of a revolutionary faction (the Sandinistas) that was strongly supported by the Soviets and Cubans and that consequently was able first to help overthrow the Somoza government and second to seize control of the Nicaraguan revolution. The U.S.S.R. had turned Cuba into a major military and political asset because of the U.S.-Soviet bargain ending the 1962 Cuban missile crisis. At that time U.S. Pres. John Kennedy committed the U.S. not to intervene directly to overthrow the government of Cuban Prime Minister Fidel Castro, while the Soviets withdrew the medium/intermediate-range ballistic missiles that they had been attempting to install in Cuba. But Kennedy's promise gave the U.S.S.R. an invulnerable outpost in the Caribbean. Supported by Soviet arms, Cuban military and intelligence forces began to assist revolutionary groups in other nations in their efforts to overthrow existing governments and replace them with pro-Soviet ones.

From a Soviet perspective such intervention could secure both positive and negative defense objectives. Positively, the Soviets could gain control of geographically valuable states in a traditional imperialistic fashion. Negatively, they could tie down U.S. defense forces and political attention in a region that was of vital interest to the U.S. but not to the U.S.S.R. The Soviets committed only limited quantities of military equipment, advisers, and political prestige; the actual fighting was done by Cubans and local revolutionaries.

The first Soviet/Cuban offensive was launched after Castro seized control of the 1959 revolution in Cuba that overthrew Pres. Fulgencio Batista. In the early 1960s Cuba attempted to overthrow the governments of the Dominican Republic and Venezuela. This led to Cuba's expulsion from the Organization of American States (OAS) in 1962 and, in 1965, to U.S. counterintervention in the Dominican Republic. U.S. military assistance, especially with counterguerrilla warfare training and equipment, helped South American governments to defeat this offensive. But these countermeasures were often repressive. The Cuban revolutionary Che Guevara was killed after fighting with Bolivian guerrillas in 1967, becoming a left-wing folk hero. Soviet concerns that Cuba was pushing this offensive too far and too fast led to a rift between the two countries from 1967 to 1969.

Then, between 1972 and 1974, the two launched a second South American offensive, paralleling one that they were undertaking in Africa. Both offensives took advantage of U.S. military and political weaknesses in the aftermath of the Vietnam war and the Watergate scandal. In Africa this offensive enabled the Soviets to gain control of Angola and Mozambique (1975–76) and Ethiopia (1977). In each case about 20,000 Cuban troops directed by Soviet generals were used, supported by 1,000–2,000 Warsaw Pact technical/security forces, all transported and supplied by Soviet/Warsaw Pact air-/sea-lift forces.

Revolutionary groups received Soviet and Cuban support in many parts of South and Central America. From the Soviet viewpoint this support was partially successful if it increased the political polarization in these societies, destroying the moderate centre and pitting the military against the people. In Chile Pres. Salvador Allende's Marxist, pro-Soviet policies led the previously apolitical military to overthrow him in 1973. The Argentine military government's campaign against the increasingly active revolu-

tionary groups led to the so-called secret war (1976–82), in which many innocent civilians were killed. In Central America the first major Soviet/Cuban victory took place in Nicaragua in 1979. The two nations then aimed, apparently, to repeat this triumph by overthrowing the governments of El Salvador, Honduras, and others in the region and then taking control of their revolutionary forces. The ultimate objective was the establishment of a pro-Soviet government in Mexico.

In the Caribbean the first Soviet/Cuban victory was in Grenada, where the New Jewel Movement seized power in 1979. Covert Soviet/Cuban intervention in Jamaica seemed likely to bring about similar developments there in the late 1970s, but the plan was defeated by indigenous political groups.

As a map of the region shows, the Soviets were pursuing traditional geopolitical objectives. They sought control of the Caribbean islands that in turn control the sea lines of communication, particularly the choke points through which shipping has to pass. In a major war the Soviets would be able to cut off such sea lines needed by the U.S., including important oil shipments, thereby forcing the U.S. and its allies to divert forces needed elsewhere to neutralize that threat.

Military Strengths. The vulnerability of both regions to Soviet/Cuban intervention is shown by the Table II in the accompanying article, which gives the military strengths of the local armed forces. Cuba and Nicaragua are the regional military superpowers, with forces totaling 161,500 and 62,850 personnel. The Cuban forces in Nicaragua, esti-

mated at 8,000–10,000 personnel, equal about one-quarter of El Salvador's armed forces of 41,650 personnel. Neighbouring Honduras has only 16,600 armed forces, Panama and Costa Rica have about 12,000 and 8,000 each, and Guatemala has 31,700.

These figures underestimate the military weakness of the region. Traditionally, its armies (plus small air and naval units) have been internal security forces. The rank-and-file soldiers were usually poorly equipped, trained, and led. The officers saw a military career as a route to personal wealth and political power. Such forces were adequate to deal with the traditional peasant revolts, but they could not deal with revolutionaries trained and equipped by the Soviets and advised by Cubans. The Soviets/Cubans could direct these revolutionaries because they badly needed the military supplies the Soviets/Cubans controlled.

The U.S. Response. For the U.S., Soviet/Cuban intervention in Central America and the Caribbean posed major new defense problems. After the Vietnam war U.S. military and political leaders were determined not to commit U.S. forces to ground combat if they could avoid doing so. U.S. military leaders, many of whom had fought as junior officers in Vietnam, believed that they had won a military victory over North Vietnam in the 1968 Tet offensive only to suffer political defeat. The Joint Chiefs of Staff, the president's military advisers, thus strongly opposed any military intervention except under conditions where a rapid political and military victory could be achieved. Even when those conditions existed, they were still reluctant to commit U.S. forces, as in Grenada.

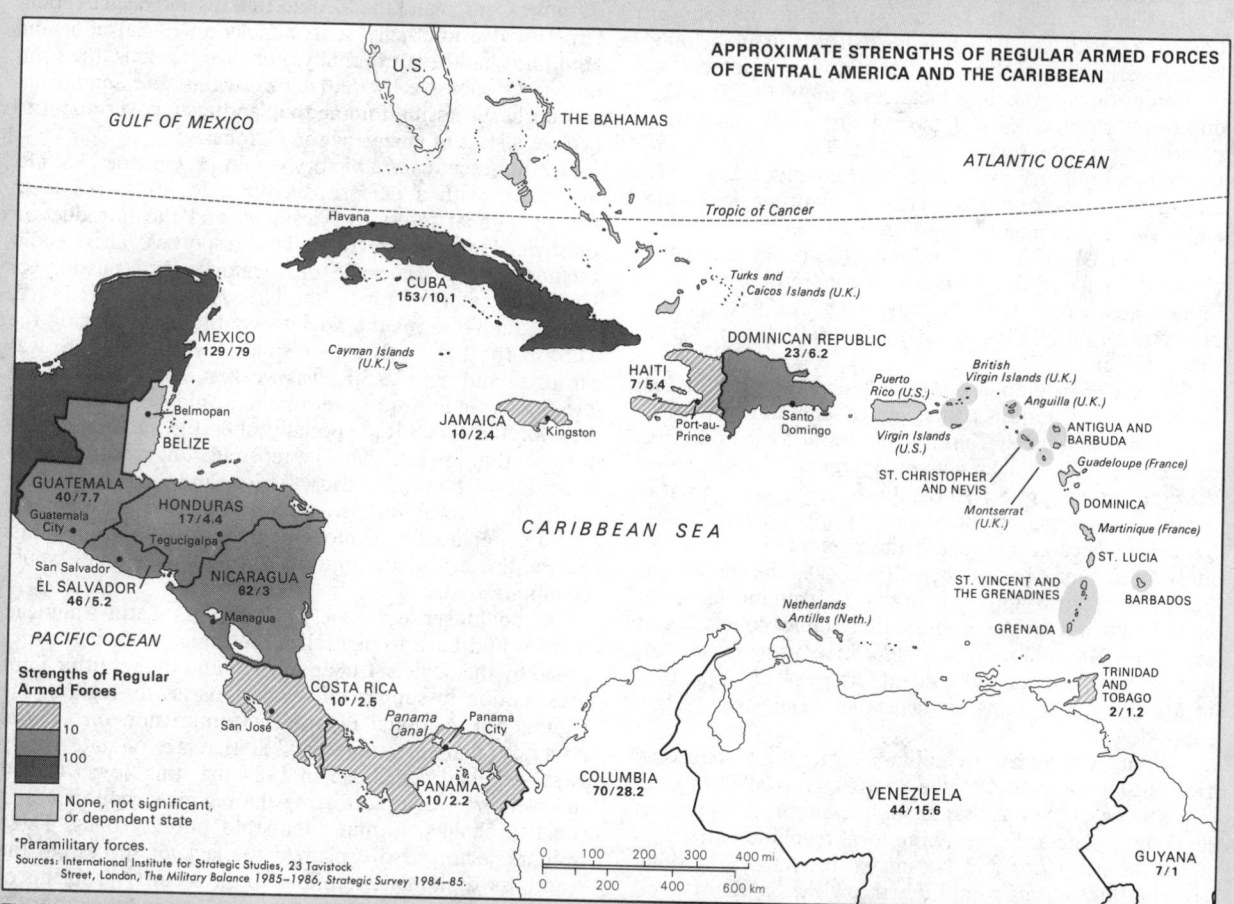

The first figure shown for each nation represents the approximate strength of that nation's armed forces in thousands; the second figure represents the approximate population in millions. Thus, Mexico had armed forces numbering approximately 129,000 out of a total population of approximately 79 million.

This reluctance to intervene was shared by Presidents Jimmy Carter and Ronald Reagan, the U.S. Congress, and the American people. Yet the U.S. could not allow the Soviets and their Cuban allies to destabilize the region's governments at will.

Under President Carter the U.S. tried to work with, rather than against, the region's revolutionary groups, seeing these as the irreversible forces of progressive social change. Accordingly, the U.S. denied military aid to the Somoza government but offered economic aid to the Sandinista revolutionaries, only to discover that a repressive right-wing military dictatorship had been replaced by a repressive left-wing military dictatorship with much larger and better-equipped forces.

Under President Reagan the U.S. was trying to formulate a balanced and effective solution to these problems. The administration recognized that the military, political, and economic threat posed by Soviet/Cuban support for revolutionaries had to be neutralized. But it also recognized the basic truth that the U.S. could help regional powers help themselves but could not solve their security problems for them. The Reagan administration accordingly provided military and economic aid (in a ratio of one to three) in El Salvador but only 55 military advisers. Continued aid was made contingent on El Salvador's Army becoming an effective fighting force.

Although faulted by critics on the left and the right for intervening too much or too little, the Reagan administration's overall strategy seemed to be succeeding in El Salvador. President Duarte's forces were containing and wearing down the guerrillas. This strategy was supported by the Congress and the electorate. In other nations in Central America the U.S. was also successful in helping local governments to contain Soviet/Cuban attempts to overthrow them by aiding local revolutionaries. But the direct and indirect costs of these efforts were significant, particularly for the local populations. The region's existing minimal military forces had to be expanded. Guerrilla attacks on their economies increased, retarding economic and social development. These problems were marked in El Salvador's neighbour Honduras. There, the U.S. had obtained the government's reluctant consent to establish a series of temporary bases through which U.S. forces could be brought in if Nicaragua's attacks on El Salvador led to full-scale war.

This situation emphasized the basic limitation of the Reagan administration's strategy of containing Soviet/Cuban intervention in Central America: it forced the U.S. to react to their attacks without removing the source of the problem, the pro-Soviet Sandinista government in Managua. For this reason the administration supported anti-Sandinista Nicaraguan rebels, the *contras*. This was the most controversial part of the U.S. policy in the region. But the U.S. Congress approved nearly $27 million for 1985 nonmilitary aid to the *contras* after initial doubts about approving $14 million. A key factor in securing this authorization was Nicaraguan President Ortega's April 1985 visit to Moscow, underlining his dependence on Soviet/Cuban support.

Military Outcomes. In military terms there were only two possible outcomes to the Soviet-U.S. conflict in Central America. One was that it would continue at its present level or escalate as Soviet aid to local revolutionaries, funneled through Cuba and Nicaragua, increased. The other was that the *contras* would overthrow the Sandinistas, establishing an independent democratic government allied with the U.S.

On balance the latter outcome seemed more likely. By

A contingent of Cuban military advisers is welcomed home to Havana from a tour in Nicaragua in May. Some 700 others remained on duty, assisting the Sandinista regime. The two nations were the most heavily militarized in Central America and the Caribbean.
AP/WIDE WORLD

the end of 1985 the Sandinista government had alienated most of its former supporters. Its attacks on the Roman Catholic Church and the Miskito Indians had been as counterproductive internally as its attacks on El Salvador and Honduras had been externally. For these reasons, the summer 1985 offensive by the *contras* against the Sandinistas was fairly successful, forcing the Sandinista government to declare a state of emergency in October.

An imminent *contra* victory would present the U.S.S.R. and Cuba with a defense dilemma. Major increases in Cuban combat forces in Nicaragua and the introduction of Soviet forces would trigger U.S. responses. These could include a naval blockade of Nicaragua and possibly of Cuba and intervention by the U.S. Army and Air Force. In geographic terms the Soviets would be challenging the U.S. in the latter's own hemisphere, where the U.S. was strongest and the U.S.S.R. was weakest. Yet the fall of the pro-Soviet Sandinista government would be a significant loss for the U.S.S.R., especially after the successful U.S. intervention in Grenada. The repercussions would be considerable in South America, Africa, and Asia, suggesting that other Soviet-imposed or Soviet-backed governments could be replaced by democratic ones. Militarily, the limits on the Soviet/Cuban ability to support their allies would be emphasized.

In the longer term the U.S. and its Latin-American allies would have to neutralize the threat to their security posed by the Soviets' Cuban outpost and the resulting joint intervention in support of revolutionaries throughout the region. The National Bipartisan Commission on Central America, chaired by former U.S. secretary of state Henry Kissinger, had concluded in 1984 that this Soviet/Cuban intervention was exacerbating the regime's economic and social problems, turning them into military ones. These military factors also explained the lack of success in the search for diplomatic solutions to the security problems of Latin America, such as that by the Contadora group of nations (Colombia, Mexico, Panama, and Venezuela) in the Nicaragua-El Salvador conflict.

The U.S. Navy's seventh Trident-missile submarine is christened *Alaska* in Groton, Connecticut, in January. The commissioning of the *Alaska* was accompanied by scrapping of the old Poseidon-missile submarine *Sam Rayburn*, a tradeoff required to keep the U.S. in compliance with the SALT II treaty limits on nuclear weapons.
AP/WIDE WORLD

(continued from page 325)

000 personnel, to be reduced by 25%, but only 11,450 main battle tanks (mostly T-59/-69s), while the 490,000-strong Air Force's 5,300 combat aircraft were modifications of old Soviet models, including 3,000 J-6/MiG-19 fighters.

In Southeast Asia the largest active military power was Vietnam, with armed forces, mostly Army, totaling 1,027,-000. The Army had about 1,600 main battle tanks. The 15,000-strong Air Force had approximately 270 combat aircraft. Deployment of occupation forces abroad included 160,000 in Kampuchea and 40,000 in Laos. Evidence of illegal Vietnamese use of Soviet-supplied chemical and biological weapons, especially against the Hmong people of Laos, continued to mount.

Although North Korea's forces were larger than those of South Korea, they remained inadequate for invasion purposes. The balance was 838,000 personnel, 3,275 main battle tanks, 1,100 APC, and 800 combat aircraft (mostly older types) for the North versus 598,000 personnel, 1,200 main battle tanks, 700 APC, and 451 combat aircraft (mostly modern types) for the South.

Despite U.S. pressure Japan still refused to spend more than 1% of GNP on defense; its 1985–86 total was $12,-471,000,000. Japan's armed forces personnel totaled 243,-000, including an Army of 155,000 with 1,070 main battle tanks. The Air Force and Navy had 44,000 personnel each. Equipment included 50 Japanese-made F-1 fighter-bombers, 60 F-15J/DJ Eagle and 110 F-4/EJ Phantom fighter-bombers, 31 destroyers (23 GW), 18 frigates, and 14 submarines. Taiwan's armed forces, totaling 444,000, continued to provide a credible defense against China. The Army, with 290,000 personnel, had 309 main battle tanks, and the 77,000-strong Air Force had 567 combat aircraft, including 256 F-5E/F fighter-bombers. Defense spending in 1985–86 was $3,948,000,000.

AFRICA SOUTH OF THE SAHARA

The major conflicts in sub-Saharan Africa remained those between South Africa and Angola and between the white and nonwhite populations of South Africa. South Africa continued to be the dominant military power in the region, with armed forces totaling 106,400, rising to 423,400 on mobilization. Equipment included 250 main battle tanks, 1,500 Ratel MICV, and 356 combat aircraft. These were extremely effective forces with considerable combat experience. Defense spending was estimated at $2,147,000,000 for 1985–86.

South Africa's conflict with Mozambique had been partly settled by negotiation, leaving Angola as the main opponent. The latter's armed forces, of poor quality, totaled 49,500 plus 26,000 Cubans and 700 Soviet advisers. South Africa and Angola were both trying to ensure the presence of a friendly government in South West Africa/Namibia when and if that territory became independent. At the same time, South Africa was supporting the National Union for the Total Independence of Angola (UNITA), which was trying to overthrow the Angolan government. The resulting conflicts were mostly low-level guerrilla operations but occasionally involved division-sized units (15,000 troops). A 1984 cease-fire agreement between South Africa and Angola failed to end guerrilla activity.   (ROBIN RANGER)

See also Space Exploration.

This article updates the *Macropædia* article The Technology of WAR.

Mining and Metallurgy

In many respects experience in the mining industry worldwide was quite uniform during 1984 and 1985. Market pressures to obtain the lowest price possible for raw materials required mine operators to seek every economy of operation they could identify, including reduction of costs for labour, energy, transportation, and processing and concentrating activities. Furthermore, marketing arrangements, currency movements, and research and development to identify new product applications, as well as accommodation of conservation, environmental, and safety legislation without loss of profits, all demanded attention if a particular company or mineral sector expected to remain healthy. For many countries, however, constraints of capital, manpower, extent and geologic implacement of resources, energy costs, and aging physical plant meant loss of traditional markets or of market share to new producers, inability to fully exploit certain kinds of operations, or inability to undertake new operations to succeed those no longer profitable.

Exploration. As was the case in 1983, exploration and development projects in 1984 and 1985 concentrated heavily (to the extent of perhaps a third of all new properties) on gold-mining operations. Some of the more active areas included the Casa Berardi locality in northern Quebec, the Milot area of Haiti, and Obenemase, Ghana; and there were extensions of existing properties in Australia, Canada, and South Africa. Even Czechoslovakia, which had ceased gold mining some 20 years earlier, announced plans to reopen its Celina Mokrsko facility and to develop new facilities by 1990 at Slate Hory in Moravia.

Of particular interest in the U.S. Geological Survey's report for fiscal 1984 were the descriptions provided of several new instrumental techniques for exploration (a coaxial-loop, extra-low-frequency electromagnetic sounder, for locating sulfide mineral deposits as deep as 850 m [2,790

ft]), mapping (the APT, or Aerial Profiling of Terrain, System, a laser terrain profiler with extraordinary capacity for detail), and interpretation of potential mineralization via analysis of paleothermal anomalies (identifying ancient heating events with mineralizing potential by identification of fluid inclusions, fission tracks, and alteration of organic materials).

Mine Operations. The coal miners' strike in the U.K. that had begun in March 1984 was settled partially by a return to work on March 5, 1985, but the fundamental issues of mine closures on economic grounds remained unresolved. The year-long strike was among the most bitter, divisive (among Britain's labour unions), and destructive in that nation's history. (*See* WORLD AFFAIRS [Western Europe]: *United Kingdom.*)

In South Africa the mines were one of the principal centres of labour and social unrest during the year. Repercussions included, from the South African side, threats by authorities to consider means of repatriating jobs, especially those in the mines, held by expatriate workers (from Lesotho, Botswana, Swaziland, and the black states that South Africa had declared independent) and, from abroad, the imposition of additional economic pressure by countries outside South Africa to force movement away from apartheid (racial separation). Among these measures were the banning of Krugerrand sales in the U.S. by Pres. Ronald Reagan from October 11 and the announcement by France late in the year that contracts for coal purchases from South African producers would not be renewed.

New Caledonian mine properties were attacked during the year by Kanak (indigenous Melanesian) militants attempting to disrupt nickel mining operations at Thio by blockades (beginning in November 1984) and sabotage. By the year's end this violence had reduced production targets for 1985 by more than 40%.

Safety. Two elements of the overall problem of mine safety gained attention in 1985. In July the collapse of two tailings dams holding fluid wastes from a fluorite mine in the Dolomite Mountains above Stava, Italy, caused the loss of some 250 lives when 1.5 million cu m (53 million cu ft) of water and tailings destroyed the village, a tourist-oriented centre with many hotels. The responsibility of the Italian government and Trentino provincial authorities to inspect and of the mine owners to build and maintain such structures properly all came into question, but by year's end no clear assignment of culpability had taken place.

The first International Conference on the Health of Miners, held in Pittsburgh, Pa., June 2–7, drew speakers from 15 nations and more than 200 representatives of union, government, industry, and health groups. Problems discussed included occupational injury and exposure to toxic substances, dust, heat, noise, and a variety of other factors that were serious enough concerns in those countries having worker protection laws but were far more destructive in countries with child labour, endemic ill health among workers, or a lack of protective legislation. Health problems related to mining were said to be as bad in the third world in the 1980s as they were in Europe during the Industrial Revolution.

Business and Markets. A World Bank study, *The Outlook for Primary Commodities, 1984 to 1995,* released in 1985, provided a long-term analysis and forecast of prices, production, demand, and trade patterns for some 30 commodities, about a third of which were minerals, either metals or fertilizers. These forecasts were developed within the framework of a set of general economic assumptions of a relatively unsanguine nature: an inflation rate for the U.S. dollar of 6% per annum during the period, no

United Mine Workers members stage a demonstration in Lobata, West Virginia, as part of their protracted strike against the A. T. Massey Co., which was resisting the union's demand for a single umbrella contract covering all the company's divisions and affiliates.
AP/WIDE WORLD

growth in much of the third world except Asia (principally China and India), and a rise in energy prices by about 4% annually after 1990. Prices for a group of metals (copper, lead, tin, zinc, nickel, iron ore, bauxite, manganese, and aluminum) were forecast to show steady growth within a high, medium, and low set of assumptions.

Although the study took account of the considerable overcapacity of many mineral industries currently and of elements like changing consumption patterns, substitution of materials, conservation, and energy constraints, it seemed to give too little attention to irrational market and cost elements like government intervention in production and trade, currency and trading elements, political elements, and the like to make the exercise much more than a modeling report where prices were concerned. Predictions of production, consumption, and trade appeared to be more realistic, or at least to permit assumptions about more rational use of capacity, economic optimization in the world market, and changes in regional shares of world production. Most of these share changes were not dramatic, but the overall trend showed the industrialized and centrally planned economies losing market share to the less developed countries for all commodities except tin and manganese.

Both price activity and trade patterns continued to reflect the strong U.S. dollar of 1984–85. For most commodities the effect was to make non-U.S. producers more competitive in U.S. markets (for many metals, the major consumer), giving many of these nations an economic lift but leaving U.S. producers in the doldrums. The precious metals market, especially for coinage, underwent substantial realignment in 1985 as banning by the U.S. of imports of the South African Krugerrand led to considerable increases in sales of coins like the Canadian maple leaf and Chinese "grand gold panda," as well as to planned U.S. and Australian issues of gold coinage.

Technology. The relatively small contribution of the U.S. to worldwide technological innovation in mining was troubling to many. Research and development investment did not suffice either to gain ground on other nations or to maintain position in fields of past importance. Computerization, artificial intelligence, and robotics were prominent examples. Japanese and Western European advances in such areas as mechanization of dangerous tasks, safety monitoring equipment (especially rapid analysis and warning systems), work scheduling and process control (using fifth-

Indexes of Production, Mining and Mineral Commodities

(1980 = 100)

	1980	1981	1982	1983	1984	1985 I	1985 II
Mining (total)							
World[1]	100.0	92.9	84.8	81.8	82.3	84.0	...
Centrally planned economies[2]	100.0	99.4	102.3	104.2	106.2	...	...
Developed market economies[3]	100.0	103.2	98.6	97.6	100.9	107.2	100.3
Less developed market economies[4]	100.0	84.5	72.0	66.7	65.0	63.1	...
Coal							
World[1]	100.0	100.3	102.1	101.5	99.7	103.2	...
Centrally planned economies[2]	100.0	98.4	102.5	104.5	106.3	...	...
Developed market economies[3]	100.0	101.2	101.1	98.1	92.8	94.2	89.9
Less developed market economies[4]	100.0	109.3	112.2	115.1	123.4	142.4	...
Petroleum							
World[1]	100.0	89.4	78.7	74.6	74.6	76.8	...
Centrally planned economies[2]	100.0	102.1	104.5	106.6	109.2	...	...
Developed market economies[3]	100.0	105.8	101.3	99.5	104.9	117.2	103.3
Less developed market economies[4]	100.0	81.3	67.0	61.7	59.1	56.5	...
Metals							
World[1]	100.0	100.4	94.2	91.2	93.4	94.1	...
Centrally planned economies[2]	100.0	88.7	89.9	92.9	93.6	...	...
Developed market economies[3]	100.0	100.0	90.6	92.7	97.3	100.1	100.9
Less developed market economies[4]	100.0	102.0	97.9	89.6	89.9	88.5	...
Manufacturing (total)	100.0	100.5	98.4	101.8	108.4	111.7	...

[1] Excluding Albania, China, North Korea, Vietnam.
[2] Bulgaria, Czechoslovakia, East Germany, Hungary, Poland, Romania, U.S.S.R.
[3] North America, Europe (except centrally planned), Australia, Israel, Japan, New Zealand, South Africa.
[4] Caribbean, Central and South America, Africa (except South Africa), Asian Middle East, East and Southeast Asia (except Israel and Japan).
Source: UN, *Monthly Bulletin of Statistics* (November 1985).

generation artificial-intelligence systems), and new mining technologies (especially for the developing field of ocean-floor mining) were both aggressive in scope and long-term in outlook.

The Mining '85 exhibition held in Birmingham, England, June 10–14 displayed many examples of advanced or new technology for mine work. Equipment shown included several advanced submersible pumps for mine drainage; slurry pumps, including a gravel pump; alignment, orientation, and remote-control systems for large equipment like shearers, both to control working of the mine face and to permit operations in dangerous areas; and support equipment capable of remote operation.

Production. The most significant trend visible in the United Nations overall indexes of mining production for 1984 and the first two quarters of 1985 (see TABLE) was the exceptional effort made by the less developed countries to substitute coal for more expensive imported hydrocarbon fuels. The concomitant drop in petroleum output among these same countries could probably be attributed to conservation efforts at a time when world oil prices made it inexpedient to put increasingly valuable supplies on the market. In the metals sector the ability of the developed countries' mining sectors to regain production levels of 1980 by 1985 represented the culmination of half a decade's efforts to obtain every efficiency possible in production to offset the generally higher labour costs. The failure of the less developed countries to maintain production levels was probably in part a consequence of their debt situation, which made new investment capital difficult to obtain.

Worldwide, production of mineral commodities enjoyed few areas of strong growth other than the recovery of previous production levels. The base metals generally showed production levels during 1984 and 1985 within ±4% of the previous year, copper, lead, and zinc all gaining modestly. The principal exception was tin, where unrealistic price- and export-control policies by the International Tin Council had finally begun to exact their toll both on member countries' domestic industries and on world markets. One of the few areas of strong growth was among the nonmetals; perhaps the most significant was phosphate rock, which showed a 15% gain. The light metals (especially aluminum, manganese, and titanium) showed moderate to good growth during 1984 and 1985, mostly on the strength of increased demand and new technological applications,

although energy costs remained a constraint on future development.

The U.S. mining sector reported a total value of some $22,672,000,000 in 1984, a strong 7% improvement over the previous year. The value of the minerals after processing rose to an estimated $253 billion, a 14% gain over 1983. The metals sector showed only a 3% gain (actually a loss when adjusted for inflation). The nonmetals rose, however, by some 9% to an estimated value of $16,714,000,000.

Aluminum. World production of bauxite, the principal ore of aluminum, was estimated by the U.S. Bureau of Mines to have risen by about 3.7% during 1984, from 76,016,000 metric tons in 1983 to approximately 78.8 million tons the following year. The major producer, again Australia with some 25 million tons, was followed by Guinea, at about 12 million tons; the next rank of producers included Jamaica, Brazil, and, probably, the U.S.S.R. Australia's share remained relatively constant at just under a third of world production; Jamaica and Brazil both showed strong growth over 1983, at 14.7 and 37.3%, respectively. Output of alumina, the concentrated intermediate stage in the production of aluminum metal, was estimated by the International Primary Aluminium Institute to have risen very strongly, about 18.4%, to 27,628,000 tons. Australia continued to lead producers with 8,433,000 tons. Production of aluminum metal showed lesser growth against 1983, rising only about 0.5% to an estimated total of 18,740,000 tons, about 31% of this being produced by the U.S.

Antimony. After four straight years of decline, world production levels of antimony finally showed a gain in 1984 of some 6½% against the previous year for a total of 53,662 metric tons. China, thought to be the largest producer, at about 15,000 metric tons, was followed either by Bolivia, at 9,765 tons, or by the U.S.S.R., at an estimated 9,700 tons. South Africa was probably the fourth leading producer. Mexico, in fifth place at 3,064 tons, gained some 21% against 1983. World market prices rose temporarily during 1985 because of uncertainty about the dependability of supplies from China, but they returned to more basic levels as sales of stocks from the U.S. National Defense Stockpile continued monthly.

Cement. World output of cement during 1984 was estimated to have risen only about 1% over 1983, to approximately 889 million metric tons. Production levels of individual countries changed substantially, however, except for the U.S.S.R., which led at approximately 130,050,-000 tons. Among lesser producers were China, at 121.1 million tons (up 14.4%); Japan, 78,850,000 tons (down 2.5%); and the U.S., 70,490,000 tons (up 10.3%). Foreign ownership of U.S. production capacity continued to rise during 1984, reaching almost 30% of clinker capacity.

Chromium. World mine output of chromite, the principal ore of chromium, was estimated by the U.S. Bureau of Mines to have grown by about 2.6% during 1984 to a total of 8.3 million metric tons. The leading producer was South Africa, with a reported 3,006,000 tons; the U.S.S.R. was estimated to be in second place at approximately 2,450,000 tons and was followed by Albania at about 900,000 tons. Very strong gains had been shown by South Africa (up almost 35%) and by several middle-rank producers, including Finland (up 71% to some 420,000 tons) and Turkey (up 27% to about 520,000 tons).

Copper. Mine output of copper was thought to have risen by just under 1% during 1984 to an estimated world total of 8,120,000 metric tons. If reflected in final figures, this would represent one of the few areas of strength in base metals during the 1980s, although prices were

by no means as stable as production levels. Major producers were Chile at 1,290,000 tons, up about 2.6% over 1983; the U.S. at 1,087,000 tons, up 4.7% over 1983; and the U.S.S.R. at approximately 1 million tons. Such stability as did return to world markets during 1984–85 was largely a result of continued low production levels in the U.S., where, as a result of the strong dollar, many export markets had been lost and much capacity remained underutilized or on standby. (Data for blister copper production [smelter output of semirefined metal] and refined metal production on a worldwide basis were unavailable from the U.S. Bureau of Mines as a consequence of a general reduction in government statistical output.) United Nations estimates of copper metal showed a slight decline during 1984, down 0.2% to about 8,589,000 tons. The U.S.S.R. was probably the leading smelter and refinery producer at some 1,280,000 and 1.5 million metric tons, respectively; following it was the U.S. with 1,200,188 metric tons (smelter) and 1.5 million metric tons (refined), up slightly over 1983. Japan, normally the third leading producer, was off about 15% in both smelter production and refinery output as Japanese producers were forced to cut back both because of scarcity of supplies and because of the high prices of stock that actually became available.

Gemstones. World mine production of both gem and industrial diamonds was virtually unchanged against 1983, at some 21,040,000 and 36 million carats, respectively. In terms of combined production Zaire outdistanced its competitors for a second year, but in 1984 by more than 50% over its closest competitors (Botswana and South Africa) on the basis of new smuggling regulations (rather than increased production), which raised visible 1984 output to 18.5 million carats. Botswana, principally from output at its Jwaneng mine, increased its production again, to 12.9 million carats (up more than 20%), replacing South Africa as second leading producer for a second year.

Gold. World mine production of gold appeared to have risen for the sixth straight year in 1984, reaching an estimated total of some 45,573,000 troy ounces (1,723 metric tons). The leading producer, South Africa, held production levels almost constant with 1983, with output of about 827 metric tons in 1984, more than twice the estimated output of the second leading producer, the U.S.S.R., at 350 tons, perhaps 1% higher than 1983. Among lesser producers the strongest gains were shown by Colombia (up 22%) and Canada (up 10%). U.S. output, most of which was extracted as a by-product of copper mining, rose above two million troy ounces (77.8 tons) for the first time since 1950, representing about 4.2% of world output. Market analysts during 1985 were somewhat surprised by an apparent weakening toward the end of the year in the usual inverse relationship between the value of the U.S. dollar and the price of gold, as both appeared to be declining simultaneously.

Iron. Iron ore was estimated to have recovered somewhat against the losses of recent years, showing a 2% gain to approximately 689 million tons in 1984. The Soviet Union's share of the world total rose slightly to about 36%, or approximately 246,450,000 tons, little changed from the previous year. China, the second leading producer, showed a gain of about 7% in reaching a new high of 121.9 million tons. Brazil ranked third in terms of published output (108,160,000 tons) but probably ranked second in terms of metal contained in ores extracted, as its ores were about 68% iron, while those of China were only about 50%. Australia, in fourth place at 88.7 million tons, remained at production levels as much as 17% below those of the early 1980s. The U.S. industry, next at 54.8 million tons, remained at levels 37% below those of the late 1970s, and U.S. domestic production during the first eight months of 1985 was almost 10% below the comparable period in 1984. Output of pig iron gained about 2% during 1984, totaling some 504 million metric tons worldwide. The U.S.S.R. remained the leading producer at 110.5 million metric tons, virtually unchanged from the previous year. Japan showed a 10% improvement over 1983's poor results, with some 80,403,000 tons. The U.S., China, and West Germany followed at 46,476,000, 41,160,000, and 30,360,000 tons, respectively.

Lead. World mine output of lead in 1984 was unavailable on a worldwide basis, but Australia was certainly the leading Western (and probably world) producer at approximately 440,825 metric tons. Despite a 28% loss in 1984 against the previous year, the U.S. remained the second leading Western producer with 321,897 tons. Following it were Canada at 259,402 tons (off 4.6%), Peru at 205,000 tons (off 3.8%), and Mexico at 183,314 tons (up 9.5%). The loss in U.S. production levels was a consequence of a number of strikes, which were settled by December 1984. Refined metal output suffered similar declines as loss of feedstocks from nearby mine output curtailed production in the U.S., which nevertheless remained the leading producer with 395,577 metric tons, off 23% from 1983 levels. Following much more closely than in earlier years were West Germany with 373,000 tons, Japan with 331,000 tons, and the U.K. with 269,000 tons.

Magnesium. World mine output of magnesite, a principal source of refractories for the steel industry, was estimated to have risen about 2.6% during 1984, to a total of some 10,843,000 metric tons, an uncertain figure since the chief producers were all socialist countries, which normally withheld production data. The three chief producers were probably the U.S.S.R. at 2,180,000 tons, China at 2 million tons, and North Korea at 1.9 million tons. The U.S. remained the primary producer of magnesium metal at 144,430 metric tons, representing about 47% of a world total of 304,000 tons. The U.S. figure also represented a 38% increase over 1983, although it was derived by inference from North American totals published by the International Magnesium Association, an exact U.S. figure having been withheld for reasons of confidentiality. Although the metal usually is produced from brines or seawater, an energy-efficient process was developed to extract it from magnesite, and pilot developments were under way during the year.

Manganese. World mine production of manganese was estimated to have remained virtually unchanged with respect to 1983, at 22.6 million metric tons. The U.S.S.R. accounted for almost half of this output, with some 10.5 million tons as estimated by the U.S. Bureau of Mines. Among lesser producers in the West, South Africa led with some 3,049,000 metric tons, off almost 50% from 1980 levels, following the fortunes of the steel industry. Gabon, at 2,093,000 tons, was almost unchanged from 1983. Brazil, China, and Australia were probably closely matched with outputs between 1.7 million and 1.9 million tons.

Mercury. World mine production of mercury in 1984 totaled approximately 174,500 34.5-kg (76-lb) flasks, down slightly from 1983. The U.S.S.R. and Spain continued to account for about 60%, Soviet production being estimated at 64,000 flasks and Spanish output at about 40,000, both representing continuations of 1983 production levels. U.S. output, probably third worldwide, was 19,048 flasks and was probably on a par with that of China. U.S. production dropped more than 20% below that of the previous year, although imports more than doubled consumption availability; of the 54,600 flasks consumed, about 54% was used in battery manufacture during 1984.

Molybdenum. Recovering with improved U.S. output, world mine production of molybdenum rose almost 45% to some 92,430 metric tons. Virtually all of the increase came from U.S. output, which reached 47,022 tons, still short of early 1980s levels but approaching a more normal figure. Chilean production rose about 10% to approximately 16,860 tons. Two socialist countries, Bulgaria and the U.S.S.R., were thought to occupy similar ranks at about 11,000 tons. Mexican production dropped more than 30% to 4,054 tons in 1984, although most other producers were believed to have achieved results similar to those of 1983. Closure of many facilities in the U.S. and Canada, sale of major stocks (especially that of Anaconda's Tonopah, Nev., inventory), and limitation of sales by producers all combined to create a strong price basis at the beginning of 1985, significantly at a time when consumption, especially in moly steels, was also rising.

Nickel. World output of nickel was estimated by the U.S. Bureau of Mines to have risen by about 1% during 1984, to approximately 697,000 tons, according to preliminary data; these data underestimated Canadian output, however, by almost 40,000 tons, making it likely that final figures would reveal both a substantially higher world total and a restored position for Canada, replacing the U.S.S.R., as the world's leading producer. Canadian output in 1984 was 174,195 tons, just ahead of the 172,000 tons estimated for the U.S.S.R. The Canadian figure represented almost a 40% increase over 1983, although it just failed to regain 1980 production levels. Among other leaders Australia attained a total of 76,889 tons, maintaining production levels of recent years. Output in New Caledonia declined for a fourth year, to some 40,000 tons, little more than half of 1980 production levels.

Phosphate Rock. Another year of strong growth worldwide (almost 6%) in production levels was led by the U.S., which raised its 1984 output to 49.2 million metric tons. This figure, representing an increase of more than 15% over 1983, accounted for a 34% share of the world total, some 143 million tons. Despite interruptions and uncertainties caused by the war between Polisario Front guerrillas and Morocco in the Western Sahara, output there maintained levels comparable to those of the previous year, with some 21 million tons, third in the world, according to U.S. Bureau of Mines estimates, after the U.S.S.R. at about 27.5 million tons. China's output amounted to an estimated 13 million tons. Despite output levels, prices during 1985 were poor and were expected to remain so for the rest of the decade, as production capacity appeared likely to exceed demand by more than 40% by 1990.

Platinum-Group Metals. World mine production of the platinum-group metals (platinum, iridium, palladium, osmium, rhodium, and ruthenium) was thought to have advanced during 1984, although for platinum only figures for supply (up 19%) and demand (up 24%) were available. The principal supplier, South Africa, released some 60 metric tons of platinum during 1984, up almost 10% and representing more than three-quarters of known supply. Canadian output rose nearly 56% to 10.8 tons of platinum-group metals, returning nearly to output levels of 1981. Though prices remained weak, considerable expansion of South African capacity was under way during 1984–85, based on increased demand from the automotive, jewelry, chemical processing, electronics, and precious-metal investment industries.

Silver. World silver production rose slightly during 1984, according to estimates by the Silver Institute, to approximately 408.3 million troy ounces (12,698 metric tons). Mexico and Peru retained their first and second positions with 63,874,000 and 56,521,000 troy ounces, respectively; Soviet output was just behind Peru, at about 52.4 million. The U.S. and Canada retained their 1983 positions as fourth and fifth leading producers, with the U.S. up 2.3% at 44,440,000 troy ounces and Canada declining by about the same amount to 38,484,000. Some market analysts foresaw a declining position for silver as a precious metal in the long term, anticipating that oversupply, especially by Latin-American nations with debt problems, would keep prices depressed.

Tin. World mine output of tin declined for a third year, by about 6% against 1983 to approximately 162,000 metric tons in the market-economy countries. This drop was partly a consequence of the strong export controls imposed by the International Tin Council (ITC) on members in its efforts to maintain price levels on the world market and partly a foreshadowing of the collapse of tin trading on the London Metal

Exchange (LME) in October 1985, when efforts by the ITC's buffer stock manager to support prices failed. The details of the collapse laid some responsibility at the door of the ITC's buffer stock manager, who had for some time been selling ITC tin for cash on an immediate basis and repurchasing it on a three-month basis at a fixed price while at the same time arranging to sell an equivalent amount to an industrial consumer, also on a three-month basis but at a price to be determined at the delivery date. While tin prices rose (in part because of the decline of the British pound against ITC prices denominated in Malaysian currency tied to the U.S. dollar), this strategy worked, but when the pound began to rise against the dollar, the buffer stock manager was left with three-month purchase commitments at fixed prices against sales commitments at declining prices. Liabilities were estimated at $900 million when LME trading ceased.

Titanium. World production of both ilmenite and rutile concentrates rose in 1984, by about 7.5 and 10%, respectively; ilmenite concentrates reached some 3,875,000 metric tons, and rutile 358,000 tons. Australia was the major supplier of each, with 1,143,000 tons of ilmenite (about 29% of the world total) and 182,000 tons of rutile (51% of world output). A 27% increase in output of rutile, to 91,289 tons, was recorded in Sierra Leone, where about a quarter of world production came from a single mine, the world's largest. Production of titanium sponge (unconsolidated refined metal) was thought to be up nearly 25% during 1984, with substantial increases in all three major producing countries: the U.S.S.R. (41,700 tons), the U.S. (22,068, a 75% increase), and Japan (16,000 tons).

Tungsten. World mine production of tungsten ores (principally wolframite and scheelite) was estimated to have risen by about 11% during 1984, reaching some 43,200 metric tons (of contained metal). About half this total originated in China and the U.S.S.R., for which firm production data were not available. Among Western producers Canada increased its share of the world total to more than 10%, raising output by some 284% to 4,328 tons. Nevertheless, deliveries of increasing amounts of ammonium paratungstate to North America by China and South Korea were having a negative effect on North American producers and prices. Efforts by the UN Conference on Trade and Development's Committee on Tungsten to establish a basis for producer-consumer agreement on prices continued during 1984 and 1985 without success.

Zinc. Production of zinc ore was estimated to have risen about 2% during 1984 worldwide and about 4% among market-economy Western producers, where output reached 4,979,000 metric tons. Canada and Australia were the major producers in the West at 1,022,000 tons (20.5% of output) and 864,000 tons (17.4%), respectively. Mexico, the U.S., and Japan comprised the next rank of producers, at 290,000, 252,768, and 252,700 tons, respectively; only the Mexican and U.S. production represented substantial changes in output level, a rise of 12.7% for Mexico and a drop of 8.2% for the U.S. A number of strikes at U.S. mines during 1985 were expected to reduce output by almost a sixth against 1984, based on the first nine months. World output of refined metal remained almost identical with that of 1983, rising only slightly to some 6,079,000 tons. Canada and Japan remained the major producers at about 685,000 tons each.   (WILLIAM A. CLEVELAND)

Metallurgy. During the year one of the most academically interesting and, initially, controversial observations was published by a team of researchers from the U.S. National Bureau of Standards (NBS)—the observation of a rapidly solidified metallic material having fivefold symmetry. When a molten material is cooled to a solid at rates that exceed 10,000 K (17,500° F) per second, it is generally considered to have undergone rapid solidification. Rapid solidification techniques, which were developed in the early 1960s, have proved to be very useful for producing unique microstructures unattainable with slower freezing rates, including amorphous metallic glasses (metal alloys lacking a regular crystal structure) and superior engineering alloys.

In their paper the NBS investigators published several electron diffraction patterns from a rapidly solidified alloy of aluminum (Al) and manganese (Mn). In a diffraction pattern the observed symmetry is indicative of the symmetry of the atoms in the structure. The patterns from the Al-Mn alloy exhibited icosahedral symmetry; *i.e.*, they corresponded to a regular geometric solid called an icosahedron. A regular icosahedron is polyhedron with 12 vertices, 20 faces, and 30 edges. Such a figure has three types of rotation axes: 6 fivefold axes, 10 threefold axes, and 15 twofold axes. In the past there had been reports of fivefold symmetry in other materials, such as intermetallic aluminum-iron compounds, although it was later determined that the fivefold symmetry observed in those materials was the result of twinning, the intergrowth of two crystal grains

having different orientations. Twinning, however, appeared not to be responsible for the fivefold symmetry found by the NBS team.

The primary reason for the excitement involved the requirement that a crystalline material must possess translational symmetry; that is, once the smallest repeat unit cell of a crystal is defined, a simple translation, or shifting through space, of that unit cell in three dimensions is enough to completely describe the entire crystal structure. The resultant crystalline lattice generated by the translations is completely space-filling. In addition to translational symmetry, a crystal may also possess rotational symmetry. For example, connecting rectangles along their edges would result in a pattern that has twofold symmetry; that is, rotating a portion of the lattice by 180° reproduces the original lattice.

When combined with the translational symmetry, the requirements of space-filling permit only one-, two-, three-, four-, and sixfold axes of rotations, which correspond to 360°, 180°, 120°, 90°, 60° rotations, respectively. The list excludes fivefold rotational symmetry, which corresponds to 72° rotations. Attempting to construct a lattice having fivefold rotational symmetry, for example, by connecting arrays of pentagons along their edges, gives a two-dimensional lattice that does not completely fill space.

Because the combination of fivefold rotational symmetry and translational symmetry is forbidden for ordinary crystalline solids, a new class of material represented by the Al-Mn alloy, called a quasicrystal, was proposed during the year. A quasicrystal does not exhibit periodic long-range translational symmetry, but it may exhibit rotational symmetry. Simply speaking, the dimensions of the smallest repeat unit are the size of the quasicrystal itself. There are numerous organic molecules and biologically significant molecules that could be considered quasicrystals, but the aluminum-manganese alloy was the first example of a quasicrystal in a metallic system.

In the two-element Al-Mn system the quasicrystalline phase was observed in alloys with a manganese content ranging from 10 to 25% (by numbers of atoms). Increasing the manganese content increased the volume fraction of the quasicrystalline phase. Attempts to add a third alloying element such as silicon resulted in samples in which the structure was predominately quasicrystalline. In industrial metallurgy the primary reason for adding such elements as manganese to aluminum in large quantities is to produce alloys having relatively stable structures at elevated temperatures and higher elastic modulus (stiffness) than conventional aluminum alloys. Conventional ingot-casting techniques result in alloys that are extremely brittle owing to the distribution of coarse intermetallic phases. The presence of such large particles concentrates stress, thereby reducing ductility and toughness. Rapid solidification processing, however, makes it possible to achieve finely divided microstructures that have adequate tensile ductility. Since ductility and fracture toughness are important properties, use of rapidly solidified alloys would be precluded until control of the volume fraction of coarse particles could be achieved. Consequently, from a commercial standpoint the presence of quasicrystals in a rapidly solidified microstructure could be detrimental, although an understanding of the nature of the phase and how it forms would be of fundamental scientific importance.

(THOMAS H. B. SANDERS, JR.)

See also Earth Sciences; Energy; Industrial Review: *Gemstones; Iron and Steel.*

This article updates the *Macropædia* articles Extraction and Processing INDUSTRIES; MATTER: *Solid State.*

Motion Pictures

English-Speaking Cinema. *United States.* Hollywood production in 1985 seemed to be principally aimed at a teenage market, with a proliferation of comedies, romances, gory horrors, and even science fiction (John Hughes's *Weird Science*) set in colleges and high schools. This apparently wholesale surrender to those under 18 caused *Variety,* the venerable show-business journal, to declare: "When the causes of the Decline of Western Civilization are finally writ, Hollywood will surely have to answer why it turned one of man's most significant art forms over to the self-gratification of high-schoolers."

Undoubtedly the tastes of this same youthful audience dictated the box-office winners of the year: boisterous comedies like the execrable *Police Academy 2* and *Pee-Wee's Big Adventure;* comedy-dramas such as John Hughes's *The Breakfast Club;* and fantasies like Robert Zemeckis's *Back to the Future,* the top commercial success of 1985, in which a time machine carries a teenager, played by Michael J. Fox (*see* BIOGRAPHIES), back to the 1950s and his parents' own teenage days. The popularity of films in which violent, unconquerable, fabulous heroes commit wholesale slaughter, in defense of American values, against enemies within and without—Sylvester Stallone (*see* BIOGRAPHIES) in *Rambo: First Blood Part II* and Chuck Norris in *Missing in Action* and *Invasion U.S.A.*—seemed to be connected to the same teenage phenomenon.

The taste for fantasy, whether set in the future or in the past, strongly marked the year's films; Ridley Scott's *Legend* was an example of a sophisticated fairy tale picture, showing off the work of special-effects experts, while Richard Donner's *Ladyhawke* was one of the better examples of the "sword and sorcery" genre. There were attempts to revive older Hollywood styles. Bruce Beresford's return to biblical spectacular in *King David* failed to excite audiences, but Clint Eastwood's *Pale Rider* and Lawrence Kasdan's *Silverado* showed that the traditional Western maintained its appeal.

Few of the older major Hollywood directors were in evidence, though 78-year-old John Huston had a major success with his suave and ironic reading of Richard Condon's comic novel about a Mafia family, *Prizzi's Honor.* Woody Allen, too, made one of his most inspired comedies, *The Purple Rose of Cairo,* a fantasy about a sad, movie-crazed waitress of the Depression era and a screen character who comes to life, walking out of the film to woo her. Martin Scorsese's black comedy of paranoia in New York City, *After Hours,* was about a bored young man who one night strays from his Manhattan apartment to SoHo and becomes involved with a series of bizarre characters and nightmarish situations.

Of the newer directors, Ron Howard followed *Splash* with *Cocoon,* another modern fable, about a group of elderly citizens who find a fountain of youth. Susan Seidelmann also scored at the box office with *Desperately Seeking Susan,* a fast-paced farce set in New York City about a young, repressed suburban housewife who loses her memory and becomes convinced that she is Susan, an eccentrically dressed free spirit. In his second feature film Wayne Wang achieved success with *Dim Sum—A Little Bit of Heart,* which related the small adventures, hopes, and fears of a Chinatown family and neighbourhood.

Among foreign directors working for major U.S. film companies, the Australian Peter Weir made *Witness,* a stylish movie about the events that ensue after a small boy from an Amish community witnesses a murder. For *The Emerald Forest,* an adventure story with a touch of Tarzan and a strong ecological message, the English director John Boorman led a film expedition into the fast-vanishing rain forests of Brazil.

Unusual in the Hollywood context, Paul Schrader's *Mishima* was a stylized, impressionistic biography of the controversial Japanese writer Yukio Mishima, made in Japan in the Japanese language. Another exceptional exercise in film biography was Peter Bogdanovich's *Mask,* a dramatized account of the life and death of Rocky Dennis, a lively, intelligent California boy who battled to overcome the handicaps of a severely disfiguring disease. The popular success of the film was a tribute to Bogdanovich's management of sentiment without mawkishness.

Many films were released near the end of the year. Among the most notable were Steven Spielberg's *The Color Purple,* from the novel by Alice Walker about the hard lives of southern rural blacks some 50 and 60 years ago; Sydney Pollack's *Out of Africa,* based on the experiences of the Danish author Isak Dinesen; Jonathan Lynn's *Clue,* based on the popular board game; Lewis Teague's *Jewel of the Nile,* a sequel to the 1984 hit *Romancing the Stone;* Sir Richard Attenborough's adaptation of the hit Broadway musical *A Chorus Line;* Sylvester Stallone's latest in his series about the boxer Rocky Balboa, *Rocky IV;* and Taylor Hackford's cold-war drama with dancing, *White Nights.*

A notable development of the year was a rise in feature-length documentaries, aimed at the ever growing international television market. Among the most distinguished were Fred Wiseman's *Racetrack;* Martin Bell's *Streetwise,* about runaway children in Seattle, Wash.; Christine Noschese's *Metropolitan Avenue,* about the battle of an inner-city community in Brooklyn to retain its identity; and Lee Grant's *What Sex Am I?,* about transsexuals.

At the annual awards ceremony of the Academy of Motion Picture Arts and Sciences in Hollywood in March, *Amadeus* received awards for best film, best director (Milos Forman), best actor (F. Murray Abraham), best screenplay adaptation (Peter Shaffer, from his own play), art direction, sound, and makeup. Sally Field was adjudged best actress, for *Places in the Heart,* which also won the award for best original screenplay (Robert Benton). Dame Peggy Ashcroft's performance in *A Passage to India* earned her the Oscar for best supporting actress. Haing S. Ngor was best supporting actor, for his role in *The Killing Fields,* a British film that also received Oscars for cinematography and editing. The best feature documentary was Robert Epstein's *The Times of Harvey Milk.* The Swiss *Dangerous Moves* was the best foreign-language film.

Great Britain. The best British productions during the year were to be found among low- and medium-budgeted features, many of them partly or wholly funded by television networks. Several of the best of these were comedies, including *Letter to Brezhnev,* a first film by Chris Bernard, which inaugurated an authentic regional and popular cinema. Describing the troubled romance of an unemployed girl who falls in love after a brief encounter with a Soviet sailor, it managed at once to be richly comic and to treat vital topics of the social and political life of contemporary Britain. Hanif Kureishi's fine script for Stephen Frears's *My Beautiful Laundrette* touched upon issues of race, sex, ambition, and racketeering in contemporary Britain. *Brazil,* directed by Terry Gilliam of Monty Python fame, was an imaginative, futuristic comedy featuring elements of *1984* and traditional theatrical satire with a screenplay written, in part, by Tom Stoppard.

The past continued to preoccupy British filmmakers. Mike Newell's *Dance with a Stranger* returned to the 1950s

to reconstruct the story of Ruth Ellis, the last woman to be hanged in Britain for murder. Gavin Millar's inventive *Dreamchild* portrayed, as an old lady, the Alice that inspired *Alice in Wonderland,* reflecting on her relationship with the complex Rev. Charles Dodgson, alias Lewis Carroll. In *The Assam Garden,* a promising debut by Mary McMurray, the odd friendship of an elderly widow and an Indian woman immigrant afforded insights into Britain's colonial past. U.S. history figured in Nicolas Roeg's *Insignificance,* based on Terry Johnson's metaphorical play, imagining a New York City encounter, one night in the early 1950s, between Albert Einstein, Marilyn Monroe, Sen. Joseph McCarthy, and Joe DiMaggio.

Australia and New Zealand. Australia's major commercial successes of the year were *Mad Max: Beyond Thunderdome,* directed by George Miller and George Ogilvie, the third in a series of dynamic and visually inventive films picturing a future world of violent punk subcivilization, and Graeme Clifford's *Burke and Wills,* a spectacular, well-researched epic about the disastrous expedition of the two Australian explorers in 1860. Among other interesting productions, *Unfinished Business,* a witty romantic comedy about middle-aged people, marked the directorial debut of the screenwriter Bob Ellis. John Hughes's *Traps* was an essay on the decline of parliamentary democracy, combining news film with a fictional framing story. Dennis O'Rourke's *Half Life* was a distinguished feature-length documentary about the effects of the 1954 hydrogen-bomb tests on the Marshall Islanders.

Two of New Zealand's most gifted directors attempted new styles: John Reid's *Leave All Fair* starred Sir John Gielgud in the role of the aged John Middleton Murry, returning to France in quest of memories of his wife, Katherine Mansfield; Geoff Murphy's *The Quiet Earth* was a science fiction fantasy about three people left alone on an Earth devastated by nuclear catastrophe.

Canada. While the hopes of many Canadian filmmakers were set on breaking into the U.S. market with low-budget horror films and youth comedies, one or two films of indigenous character emerged. Two of these were comedies: Giles Walker's sophisticated and funny *Ninety Days,* about the problems of a shy suitor and a mail-order bride, and John Paizs's debut feature *Crime Wave,* which dealt with a man suffering a creative block. Mort Ransen's appealing *Bayo* set its story of the friendship of a seastruck boy and his crusty grandfather on the Newfoundland coast.

Western Europe. *France.* Commercial production continued to be dominated by comedies and police thrillers. Of the latter, one of the most engaging was Jacques Deray's *On ne meurt que deux fois.* Two major directors tried variations on that genre, Jean-Luc Godard with the perverse and whimsical *Détective* and Maurice Pialat with *Police,* a realistic account of a none-too-upright detective.

Agnès Varda's *Sans toit ni loi,* an unsparing study of the last days of an uncommunicative runaway girl ending with death in a country ditch, won the Golden Lion of the Venice Film Festival. This festival also screened two marathon French productions: a painfully static version of Paul Claudel's *Le Soulier de satin,* directed by the Portuguese veteran Manoel de Oliveira, and *Shoah,* a nine-and-a-half-hour documentary on the Holocaust, directed by Claude Lanzmann.

The novelist-director Marguerite Duras, in collaboration with Jean-Marc Turin and Jean Mascolo, made a whimsical-absurdist essay on the human condition, *Les Enfants,* about a seven-year-old (played by a grown man) who announces that he will leave school because they teach him only what he does not know. Jacques Rivette made

Hurlevent, an adaptation of *Wuthering Heights* transposed to France of the 1930s, while Claude Chabrol directed a rural murder mystery, *Poulet au vinaigre.*

Italy. The Italian film industry pinned its hopes on future government aid to stave off impending crisis. In less than ten years the movie audience had declined by 50%; film exports had shrunk dramatically; and foreign films—mainly U.S.—earned more than three-quarters of the box-office revenue. Meanwhile, production was sustained at about 100 feature films a year, though the majority of these were quickly made movies in the horror, science fiction, soft-core sex, and comedy or regional comedy genres. A new factor in Italian cinema repertory was the feature film cut down from a television miniseries. The best of these during the year was Luigi Comencini's adaptation of the Edmondo De Amicis novel *Cuore,* about children growing up in the years before World War I.

Two box-office hits of the year were *Non ci resta che piangere,* directed by Massimo Troisi and Roberto Benigni, a comedy about two men transported back to 1492 and desperately trying to prevent Columbus from discovering America, and Dino Risi's *Scemo di guerra,* a dark, moralistic comedy about a psychopathic military commander in the desert. Three promising debuts took place during the year. Loredana Dordi's *Fratelli* was an uncompromising film about a man trying to penetrate his beloved brother's mental illness; Nicola de Rinaldo's *L'Amara Scienza* was an equally sombre tale of the humiliations of three young people trying to raise money to save their family home; and Gianfranco Fiore Donati successfully avoided the morbid or mawkish in *Blu cobalt,* a surprisingly cheerful description of life in a cancer ward.

West Germany. The phenomenon of the year was the overwhelming box-office success of *Otto—Der Film,* directed by Xaver Schwarzenberger and starring a popular comedian, Otto Waalkes. Clearly, comedy was in demand, and another hit of the season was Christian Rateuke and Dieter Hallervorden's *Didi und die Rache der Enterbten,* starring Hallervorden. Art and "authors'" films were

PRIZZI'S HONOR © 1985 ABC MOTION PICTURES, INC.

Kathleen Turner and Jack Nicholson starred as rival professional killers who become lovers in *Prizzi's Honor,* an unconventional comedy directed by John Huston.

eclipsed at the box office by comedies and thrillers, though Percy Adlon's *Zuckerbaby,* a whimsical romantic comedy about a mortuary attendant and a subway driver, was well received. The 40th anniversary of the end of World War II produced a crop of documentaries, including Irmgaard von zur Mühlen's *Es liegt an uns, diesen Geist Lebendig zu erhalten,* Manfred Vosz's *Goethe in D,* and Gertrud Pinkus's strange fiction-documentary reflection on Resistance days, *Duo Valentianos.*

Belgium. A new film by Belgium's most distinguished feature director, André Delvaux, gained a special distinction by receiving its funding from the national lottery as a 50th-anniversary celebration of the lottery. The film, *Babel Opéra, ou la Répétition de Don Juan,* was a finely crafted mood piece in which people on the periphery of the opera play out their real life roles as if they were characters on the opera stage.

Spain. Reflections on the Franco era dominated the year in Spain. The veteran Luis Garcia Berlanga realized a 20-year-old script about a group of Republicans in 1938 attempting to steal a bull from a village behind Nationalist lines, *La Vaquilla.* Francesco Betriu's *Requiem por un campesino español* was a moving story of the life and death of a peasant in the 1930s, which pointed to the church's passive collaboration with the state. José Luis Sánchez's *La corte de faraon* was a comedy about a theatre company tried by the censors for performing a zarzuela of 1910. In *Los paraísos perdidos* the director Basilio Martín Patino reflected on his own years of exile.

Switzerland. The most distinguished Swiss film of the year, and the Swiss entry in the Venice Film Festival, was Alain Tanner's *No Man's Land,* a metaphorical drama of people living in the unclaimed space between the Swiss and French borders. The success of the West German marathon *Heimat* seemed to have revived the genre of "Heimatfilm" (movies that affirm domestic culture) in Europe; two Swiss examples were Francis Reusser's *Derborence,* a mystical tale of death and rebirth set among majestic mountain scenery, and *Hohenfeuer,* a sombre drama about isolated lives and incest in remote mountain vastnesses.

Scandinavia. Swedish production resources were given a considerable boost by an increase in the film industry's share of home video profits, and several major productions were in preparation for 1986 release. However, the Scandinavian films that attracted most international attention during the year were Norwegian. They included Ola Solum's cold war thriller *Orion's Belt,* about Norwegian tourist boat operators who accidentally come upon a Soviet listening operation in Norwegian territory, and Gianni Lepre's *Øye for Øye* ("An Eye for an Eye"), a highly professional thriller.

Greece. The outstanding film of the year, a condensed version of a television series, was Pantelis Voulgaris's *Petrina Chronia—The Stone Years,* a harrowing tale of a leftwing couple during the troubled decades from 1954 to 1974. A more elusive study in political history was Andreas Pantzis's *The Rape of Aphrodite,* which related the tragedy of Cyprus in highly stylized terms.

Eastern Europe. *U.S.S.R.* There were signs in 1985 of a more relaxed atmosphere for Soviet cinema. Sergey Paradjanov, after years of inactivity and imprisonment, completed a strange and visionary epic, *Legend of the Suram Fortress.* Eldar Shengelaya made a witty satire about bureaucrats in a crumbling state publishing house, *The Blue Mountains.* Nikolay Gubenko's *Love, Life and Tears,* set in an old peoples' home, was a sharp attack on uncaring bureaucracies. The outstanding film of the year, well timed for the 40th anniversary of the end of World War II, was

Elem Klimov's *Go and See,* an epic tragedy of the Nazi massacre of a Belorussian village in 1943.

Poland. Gradual relaxation led to the release of films that had been shelved since the introduction of martial law, and new films were increasingly outspoken. Krzysztof Kieslowski's *Without End* dealt allegorically with events of recent years, describing a woman's efforts to continue her dead husband's support of illegal labour movements. Wieslaw Saniewski's *Custody,* shown in 1985 after being shelved since 1981, exposed the unproductive inhumanity of the prison system through the story of a young woman condemned to life in prison for petty embezzlement in the 1970s. Radoslaw Piwowarski's *Yesterday* was a melancholy anecdote of the crushed dreams of youth and, incidentally, an homage to the Beatles era.

Hungary. Hungarian cinema offered fewer highlights than in most recent years, though Istvan Szabo's *Colonel Redl,* a coproduction with West Germany, enjoyed major international success. As in *Mephisto,* Szabo brought his own imaginative interpretation to historical events—in this case an army scandal that shocked Imperial Vienna during the last years of the Austro-Hungarian Empire. Gyula Gazdag's *Package Tour,* a remarkable cinéma vérité about a group of elderly Jewish Holocaust survivors revisiting the Nazi death camps, was a powerful commentary on that sombre piece of history.

Yugoslavia. The emergence of an innovative new generation was underlined by the award of the Cannes Festival Grand Prix to Emir Kusturica (whose *Do You Remember Dolly Bell?* took the Venice Golden Lion in 1981). His winning film, *When Father Was Away on Business,* treated a previously taboo era of Yugoslavian history, the imprisonment of Stalinists in the early years of Yugoslavia's breakaway from Soviet domination, viewing it from the standpoint of the six-year-old son of a small-town family. The Grand Prix of the Mannheim Festival went to Filip Robar-Dorin's *Sheep and Mammoths,* an ebullient comic essay on nationalist prejudice in a multinational state. Bora Draskovic's *Life Is Beautiful* was a vivid but more elusive film metaphor set in a country inn where travelers who provide a microcosm of an entire society are stranded by a train that, mysteriously, refuses to proceed.

Middle East and North Africa. Youssef Chahine directed Egypt's most ambitious production to date, *Adieu, Bonaparte,* a spectacular but somewhat muddled account of Napoleon's Egyptian campaign and the cultural interaction of the French and Egyptians. In Morocco Moumen Smihi adopted an imaginative approach to more recent history in *44 ou les récits de la nuit,* an assemblage of elliptical sketches, shot with great visual flair and illuminating the fate of Morocco as a European protectorate between 1912 and 1956. Among an indifferent year's production in Israel, Nissim Dayan's *On a Narrow Bridge* was exceptional for its seriousness and courage in tackling a deeply controversial subject, the love story of a young Israeli lawyer and a West Bank Arab woman.

In Turkey several former assistants and associates of the director Yilmaz Guney, who died in 1984, were active, concentrating their films on social issues. Serif Goren's *The Escape* was a drama about the disasters that befall a woman who kills the husband she discovers is a bigamist. Turkish machismo was explored in Bilge Olgac's tragicomedy *The Wedding Chamber,* which described the aftermath of an explosion in which all but one of the eligible females of a village are killed.

Latin America. Peru enjoyed an international success with Francisco J. Lombardi's *The City and the Dogs,* adapted from a novel that uses a military college as a

The Girl in the Red Shirt won China's coveted Golden Rooster award in 1985.

NEW CHINA PICTURES CO./AUTHENTICATED NEWS INTERNATIONAL

microcosm of a corrupt society. A Franco-Venezuelan coproduction, *Oriana*—an atmospheric story about the memories that haunt an old country house—also achieved an international market.

Rapidly recovering from the years of the generals, when major talent was blacklisted, the Argentine cinema was immeasurably helped in its efforts at renascence by the worldwide success of María Luisa Bemberg's *Camila* in 1984 and of Luis Puenzo's *La historia oficial* in 1985. For her role in the latter film, which tells how a liberal-minded housewife and history teacher gradually recognizes the extent to which she had been implicated in the events of the bad years, Norma Aleandro won the best actress prize at the Cannes Festival in May.

Brazilian production was undergoing both economic and artistic crisis. Growing political censorship tended to drive filmmakers to find outlets in eroticism, and the resulting proliferation of pornography proved bad for the box office. The best film of the year, Hector Babenco's *Kiss of the Spider Woman*, succeeded in combining political and sexual motives. Based on a story by Manuel Puig, it told of the mutually enlightening relationship that develops between a homosexual and a political prisoner sharing a prison cell.

The most striking film to emerge from Cuba during the year was a coproduction with Italy and Spain, Fernando Birri's *Mi hijo el "Che"*. This was a 60-minute portrait of the aged but still sprightly father of "Che" Guevara, through whose memories and old home movies emerges an impression of his son, not as a legend but as a vital, likable, idealistic young man.

Asia. *Japan.* The major event of the year was Akira Kurosawa's spectacular *Ran* (*Chaos*), which translated *King Lear* to 16th-century Japan and changed the monarch's daughters to sons. The film opened the Tokyo Film Festival, promised great commercial success, and, according to the 75-year-old director, was the renascence of his career. Another veteran, Kon Ichikawa, remade his 30-year-old classic *The Burmese Harp*, but colour could not recapture the poetic qualities of the original. Masaki Kobayashi's *The Empty Table* related the disastrous effects upon an ordinary middle-class family when the eldest son becomes a terrorist. Kobayashi also completed *The Tokyo Trial*, a remarkable 265-minute compilation on the International

Military Tribunal for the Far East of 1946–48. The actor Juzo Itami made his directorial debut with *The Funeral*, a brilliant black comedy about the rituals and commerce of Japanese funerals.

China. Political relaxation was reflected in the enlarged range of subjects; China even embarked on martial arts films with Tsui Siu Ming's *The Holy Robe of the Shaolin Temple*. The outstanding production of the year, however, was Chen Kaige's *Yellow Earth*, a film of classic style, about a Communist soldier traveling in Shaanxi (Shensi) Province in the 1930s and befriending poverty-stricken peasants who are enmeshed in restrictive ancient traditions.

(DAVID ROBINSON)

Nontheatrical Motion Pictures. Probably the best U.S. short-subject film of the year featured sports and daring plus magnificent cinematography. Such a winning combination was *Up*, produced by Mike Hoover. Besides winning an Academy Award in Hollywood, it won the grand prize at the Budapest Festival.

At the American Film Festival in New York City, a number of films on famous artists were winners. The highest honour, the Emily Award, went to *He Makes Me Feel like Dancin'*, featuring Jacques d'Amboise, formerly a principal dancer of the New York City Ballet. Produced by Emile Ardolino, it told the story of d'Amboise's involvement in teaching schoolchildren to dance, culminating in a grand finale with 1,000 children participating.

The youth film of the year was *Divided We Fall* by two University of Southern California students, Kevin Meyer and Jeff Burr. Their story is of two southern brothers during the Civil War who grew up with divided opinions on the issue of slavery. In Japan the Hiroshima Amateur Festival gave it the grand prize. It took top honours at Christchurch in New Zealand, at St. Hubert in Canada, and at the Huy Festival in Belgium. It also garnered a CINE Golden Eagle award for amateur films.

Another CINE Golden Eagle film, *The Stone Carvers*, won the Academy Award as the best documentary short feature. It told the story of the craftsmen who built the National Cathedral in Washington, D.C.

(THOMAS W. HOPE)

See also Photography; Television and Radio.
This article updates the *Macropædia* article MOTION PICTURES.

Museums

Administration and Facilities. Money and how to raise it continued to preoccupy many museum administrations in 1985. In Britain a consultation paper issued by the Office of Arts and Libraries in the autumn was designed to give the institutions greater incentives for raising cash from the public. This was thought by some to point toward eventual privatization of museums. Admission charges were again a controversial subject as the Victoria and Albert Museum in London introduced "voluntary" charges in November. The V & A also announced the formation of a merchandising company whose purpose would be fund-raising. Following the example of a number of U.S. museums, the new company would produce and sell consumer goods based on objects in the museum's collection. The National Gallery of Art in Washington, D.C., announced that its Patrons Permanent Fund, which solicited small donations, had exceeded $50 million. The Art Institute of Chicago became the first U.S. cultural institution to issue short-term demand bonds.

The financial future of the National Gallery, London, seemed more secure following the announcement of a gift of £50 million by J. Paul Getty II. The gift would help to fund acquisitions, perhaps keeping treasures in Britain that otherwise might have gone abroad (for example, to the Getty Museum in Malibu, Calif.). A gift of some £20 million was intended to finance the planned extension to the gallery.

In London's East End the Whitechapel Gallery reopened after having been closed more than two years for renovation. The Prado in Madrid opened its recently doubled floor space with an exhibition of Neapolitan paintings. The exhibition was the first to be held in the Villahermosa Palace, formerly a bank headquarters, acquired for the Prado by the Ministry of Culture. More than 12 years after the artist's death, the Picasso Museum in Paris was completed and opened to the public in September. It was housed in the 17th-century Hôtel Sâlé in the Marais district, restoration of which had cost F 80 million. At the British Museum the Wolfson Galleries of Classical Sculpture and Inscriptions were opened formally in April. The renovated area comprised eight basement-level galleries, including the Duveen Gallery displaying the Elgin Marbles. In Scotland a major new museum complex was formed by the amalgamation of the Royal Scottish Museum and the National Museum of Antiquities of Scotland in Edinburgh, to be known as the Royal Museum of Scotland.

At the Virginia Museum of Fine Arts in Richmond, a new $22 million west wing would hold the modernist decorative arts and paintings from the Mellon and Lewis collections. The National Building Museum, housed in the Pension Building in Washington, D.C., opened its exhibition galleries. Perhaps the most active museum in the U.S., the Whitney Museum of American Art in New York City, opened its fourth satellite branch in the lower floors of the Equitable Life Assurance Society Building. The Whitney also revealed plans for a controversial expansion, a block-long, $37.5 million, ten-story addition by the postmodernist architect Michael Graves, which would engulf its main structure. Another mid-Manhattan expansion was announced by the Guggenheim Museum, which planned to build an 11-story, $9 million extension to its present 4-story annex in a style sympathetic to its famous Frank Lloyd Wright structure. The Isamu Noguchi Garden Museum, endowed by the sculptor and featuring his works, opened in Long Island City, N.Y.

The voluntary admission charge at the Victoria and Albert Museum in London provoked an angry demonstration. Colin Welland, an actor, said, "I do not believe I should be charged to see what is essentially mine."
JONATHAN PLAYER/TIMES NEWSPAPERS LTD.

The planned move of the International Museum of Photography from Eastman House in Rochester, N.Y., to the Smithsonian in Washington, D.C., was halted by a public outcry and subsequent refunding. The Kodak Co. donated property valued at $15 million to form an endowment for the museum. In Dallas, Texas, the Museum of Art unveiled its new 1,395-sq m (15,000-sq ft) decorative arts wing, which would house the Reeves Collection of 1,400 works. B. Gerald Cantor established an outdoor garden at Stanford University in which to display the 19 large sculptures of Auguste Rodin that he had given the university.

New Acquisitions. At Colmar, France, the "Isenheim Altarpiece," with panels by Matthias Grünewald and sculptures by Nicholas de Haguenau, was reassembled and went on view at the Musée d'Unterlinden. The sculptures had been purchased by the Badisches Landesmuseum, Karlsruhe, West Germany, in 1977 and after years of negotiations had finally returned to Colmar. The National Gallery, London, purchased a major painting by Van Dyck, "Charity." The V & A acquired the Rodney Searight Collection of watercolours, drawings, prints, and illustrated travel books depicting the Middle East as it appeared to travelers of the past. The British Museum raised £200,000 for the purchase of a Samuel Palmer watercolour, "Moonlight with Evening Star." The painting had been sold to a U.S. buyer, but an export license was refused.

The J. Paul Getty Museum, with its huge endowment, bought two of the year's most expensive paintings: an "Adoration of the Magi" by the 15th-century Italian master Andrea Mantegna, for £8.1 million; and "The Annunciation" by Dirck Bouts, a later 15th-century Flemish artist, for at least $6 million. Other purchases, while not so spectacular, involved significant works. The Museum of Art in Philadelphia acquired 43,000 European Old Master and 19th-century prints through purchase and exchange with the Pennsylvania Academy of the Fine Arts. The Toledo (Ohio) Museum of Art displayed a small portion of a recent gift of 1,100 modern illustrated books given by Molly and Walter Bareiss.

A robbery in October at the Musée Marmottan in Paris resulted in the disappearance of one of the most important pictures in the history of modern art: Claude Monet's celebrated "Impression, Soleil Levant," from which the Im-

pressionist movement derived its name. In an even more spectacular robbery, some 140 priceless pre-Columbian artifacts were stolen from the National Museum of Anthropology in Mexico City on Christmas Eve.

(JOSHUA B. KIND; SANDRA MILLIKIN)

See also Art Exhibitions and Art Sales.

This article updates the *Macropædia* article MUSEUMS.

Music

Classical. A year of contrasts, 1985 witnessed the birth of a strange dichotomy, unknown since the 1950s, whereby the Western world's promoters and orchestra managers scratched their heads and wondered where the next season's funding was coming from, while the record companies (courtesy of the "CD," the laser-read compact disc) waxed prosperous in a manner undreamed of as recently as 1982. The boom in live music making was, it seemed, drawing to a close. Music in the home, by comparison, enjoyed a renaissance not seen since the introduction of the long-playing record in the late 1940s.

Widely celebrated in 1985 were the tercentenaries of the births of Bach and Handel. (*See* Sidebar.) The year also marked the tercentenary of the birth of Italian keyboard composer Domenico Scarlatti. Other birthdays celebrated as the year progressed included those of baritone Dietrich Fischer-Dieskau and composer-conductor Pierre Boulez, who both reached 60 (the latter completing a new work, his *Third Mallarmé Improvisation,* for the occasion), while Chile-born, U.S.-domiciled pianist Claudio Arrau celebrated his 82nd birthday by accepting France's prestigious order of Commander of the Legion of Honour. British composer Sir Michael Tippett's recently completed Fourth Piano Sonata was premiered by Paul Crossley to mark the occasion. The 100th anniversaries of the births of composer Alban Berg and conductor Otto Klemperer were recognized by extensive critical reappraisals and a quantity of book and record issues (a number of the latter on CD).

At 69, New York City-born master violinist Yehudi Menuhin accepted British nationality and thus formally became "Sir" Yehudi (having received an honorary knighthood in 1965). In France the trinket-infested, fantastically imagined house that formed the Musée Maurice Ravel near Paris, and that had served as the composer's home, reopened after essential renovations.

Losses to the world of music in 1985 included composers Marcel Mihalovici and Roger Sessions; conductors Eugene Ormandy and Nelson Riddle; pianists Stefan Askenase, Emil Gilels, and Eugene List; violinist Efrem Zimbalist, Sr.; zither player Anton Karas; and music patron Sir Robert Mayer. (*See* OBITUARIES.)

Symphonic Music. The year's single most important symphonic premiere was that in Manchester, England, of British composer Peter Maxwell Davies's sinuously powerful Third Symphony. A BBC commission designed to mark the 50th anniversary of the BBC Northern Orchestra (since renamed the BBC Philharmonic), the symphony had been inspired by certain principles of Renaissance architecture. Its London premiere (at the Henry Wood Promenade concerts) confirmed earlier impressions of a work of striking potency and creative vigour. Other important firsts (both of which took place in Paris) were of Boulez's revised *Notations,* in which the composer directed the Paris Orchestra, and of Karlheinz Stockhausen's *Katinka's Song.*

Further premieres (of a sort) came in the shape of a performance and subsequent recording, at the small town of Odense in Denmark, of what might (or might not—

scholars remained divided) be a previously unknown symphony by the young Mozart, the orchestral parts for which had been discovered in the Odense Symphony's library by orchestra archivist Gunnar Thygesen; and a concert performance at Bristol, England, under the baton of Carl Davis of a suite of incidental music written in 1967 by Sir William Walton for the film *The Battle of Britain* but subsequently jettisoned by producer Harry Saltzman. Andrew Lloyd Webber's sugary *Requiem* enjoyed worldwide popularity but divided critical opinion, many reviewers finding the work a pale imitation of Benjamin Britten's *War Requiem* (one English wit asked "when we might now look forward to Mr. Lloyd Webber's Crucifixion?").

Principal interest in the U.S. centred on the Paris Orchestra's visit (their sixth to date) with chief conductor Daniel Barenboim and the spectacular progress of the previously shabby-sounding St. Louis Symphony under the increasingly impressive charge of Leonard (son of Felix) Slatkin. A European tour had yielded plaudits from even the most seasoned critics, the orchestra's freshly signed long-term contract with RCA appearing richly deserved.

Also in the U.S., Lorin Maazel succeeded André Previn as principal conductor with the Pittsburgh Symphony, Previn having returned full time to Britain and a rapidly improving Royal Philharmonic Orchestra. Herbert Blomstedt took charge of the San Francisco Symphony from Edo de Waart (who had traveled home to assume control of the troubled Netherlands Opera). In Canada exiled Soviet conductor Rudolf Barshai was appointed principal conductor of the Vancouver Symphony, at the same time retaining a similar post with England's Bournemouth Symphony. Mstislav Rostropovich and the Washington National Orchestra scored a particular triumph in Paris, as did Sir Georg Solti and the Chicago Symphony in London.

Paris (along with provincial Rouen) played host to the legendary Leningrad Philharmonic under assistant conductor Arvid Yansons (the orchestra's principal conductor, Yevgeny Mravinsky, being unwilling to travel outside the Eastern bloc). Yansons's son Mariss was appointed principal conductor of Norway's Oslo Philharmonic with results that rapidly proved to be wholly beneficial. A blistering series of Tchaikovsky symphony performances augured well for the future.

John Conklin and Thomas Munn designed striking sets, costumes, and lighting for the San Francisco Opera's highly successful productions of *Das Rheingold* and the other three parts of the *Ring* cycle.

U.S.-born James Conlon succeeded Hans Vonk as conductor in chief of The Netherlands' Rotterdam Philharmonic, Dutchman Vonk moving sideways with his appointment as music director of both the Dresden (East Germany) State Opera and Staatskapelle Orchestra. British conductor-scholar Norman del Mar replaced Ole Schmidt as principal at Denmark's Aarhus Symphony.

In Britain the English Chamber Orchestra appointed, in physician-turned-musician Jeffrey Tate, the first principal conductor ever to be formally recognized as such in the orchestra's 25-year history. The 26-year-old Finn Esa-Pekka Salonen stepped up (to mixed critical reactions) as deputy conductor at London's Philharmonia, while German-born Gunter Wand was appointed assistant conductor at the BBC Symphony Orchestra. The Bournemouth Symphony found itself threatened with uprooting from its sleepy seaside watering place to Bristol, western England's industrial and shipping centre. Similar plans to resite the capital's Royal Philharmonic in Leeds, Yorkshire, were, however, scrapped.

Opera. The biggest operatic news in the U.S. was perhaps the San Francisco Opera's lavish staging of Wagner's *The Ring* tetralogy (an event heavily advertised and promoted as far away as London and Paris). Principal singers included sopranos Helga Dernesch, Gwyneth Jones, and Eva Marton; contralto Hanna Schwarz; tenors Peter Hofmann and René Kollo; and basses Walter Berry and Thomas Stewart. Departing San Francisco Symphony music director Edo de Waart was the conductor.

The New York City Metropolitan Opera's season included a new production of *Khovanshchina* (the Shostakovich version), with Dernesch, in her Met debut, as Martha, Martti Talvela as Dositheus, Aage Haugland as Khovansky, Wieslav Ochman as Golitsin, and Alan Monk as Shaklovity. Among concert opera performances the Philadelphia Orchestra (conductor, Riccardo Muti) presented *Rigoletto* at Carnegie Hall in New York City, using Martin Chusid's new interpretation of the score. In the name part was Renato Bruson; Cecilia Gasdia made her U.S. debut as Gilda, and the Duke was Michael Myers.

At the Bayreuth Festival in West Germany it proved to be conductor Giuseppe Sinopoli's year, with a strikingly sombre new production (by Wolfgang Wagner) of Wagner's *Tannhäuser* and the customary *Ring* cycle, in which soprano Hildegard Behrens's assumption of the role of Brunnhilde was considered to be one of the most impressive, vocally, of recent years. The 1985 Bayreuth Festival witnessed also the last scheduled stagings of Harry Kupfer's fiery *The Flying Dutchman* production.

In Britain the Royal Opera House at Covent Garden in London crossed its fingers and hoped for the best with productions of such curiosities as Stockhausen's untranslatable *Donnerstag aus Licht,* produced by the National Theatre's Michael Bogdanov and conducted by Boulez protégé Peter Eotvos; and Alexander von Zemlinsky's *The Birthday of the Infanta* and *Florentine Tragedy,* adapted from Oscar Wilde and produced in association with the West German Hamburg State Opera. The English National Opera's characteristically innovative season showcased, among more familiar fare, Handel's *Xerxes,* Sir Michael Tippett's *The Midsummer Marriage,* and (an increasing rarity in the unsentimental 1980s) the sweetly saccharine nonsense of

The Bach-Handel Tercentenaries

Many music lovers still tend to think of composers as falling neatly into pairs. In the case of Johann Sebastian Bach and George Frideric Handel, such conveniences carry more than a grain of truth. Both men were born in what later became Germany, Bach at Eisenach and Handel at Halle; and both were born in the same year of 1685, Handel on February 23 and Bach on March 21.

Both Bach and Handel (who never met) suffered certain of fortune's more outrageous slings. Until Mendelssohn rediscovered and performed (in 1829) the *St. Matthew Passion,* the pedagogues of the day had dismissed Bach as a mere "powdered wig, stuffed with learning." As recently as the first decade of the present century, the composer's six great unaccompanied cello suites lay neglected and forgotten.

By the same token, Handel remained best known for various of the religious epics so beloved of our

Bach

Handel

Victorian forebears, among them the great oratorio *Messiah.* The chamber music, the secular cantatas, and Handel's magnificent series of operas were resolutely ignored. The tercentenary celebrations could thus be seen as marking a watershed in appreciation of both composers' work. Festivals abounded. The major Handel summer festival, organized in London as part of European Music Year, brought forth such rarities as the operas *Alcina, Teseo* (also performed at the 1985 Boston Early Music Festival), and *Theodora* and the cantata *Clori, Tirsi and Fileno* and included a four-day Handel conference.

Of particular interest to Handelians was the discovery, in the attic of a Victorian house in Manchester, England, of manuscript fragments of a setting by the composer of the *Roman Carmelite Vespers,* last heard in Rome in 1715. The important discovery at Yale University's library of what proved to be a series of mature Bach chorale preludes was consolidated when they were premiered and subsequently recorded by U.S. harpsichordist Joseph Payne.

Perhaps the greatest kudos for "Old Father Bach" came with two issues of records originating in West Germany. In the first of these (issued by Laudate in ten boxes of ten discs each), Helmut Rilling conducted the first complete recording of all Bach's surviving cantatas; in the second, Deutsche Grammophon marked both Bach's tercentenary and the rising ascendancy of the laser-read CD with a 26-CD Bach edition that ran the gamut of the composer's output.

(NICHOLAS HARPER)

Gounod's *Faust*. Other operatic delights enjoyed by Londoners in 1985 included productions of two rarities of Puccini's youth, *Le Villi* ("The Spirits") and *Edgar*, at the Bloomsbury Theatre and, at the Camden Festival, even more offbeat offerings, among them Caccini's *Euridice*, Boito's *Nerone*, and Richard Strauss's *Friedenstag*.

Across the English Channel the first French performances of Luciano Berio's *The True Story* (in the La Scala, Milan, staging) and a rare opportunity to sample César Franck's dust-laden *Stradella* took place in Paris. Pomp and pageant were added to the Paris Opéra's season by Meyerbeer's inflatedly gorgeous *Robert le Diable*. Further afield Strasbourg's Opéra du Rhin chimed in with a rarity in the shape of Tchaikovsky's *The Queen of Spades*, and Nancy chanced its luck (with variable success) in a full-dress staging of Prokofiev's flag-waving concert piece, the *October Cantata*.

Albums. After many seasons of recession, 1985 ranked as the audio and record industry's most important year in decades. CD came of age, consolidating throughout the Western world the previous three years of progress; in Europe and especially in the U.S. the new medium made its mark to the extent that current world production capacity (calculated at some 50 million units annually) proved inadequate, and demand began steadily to outstrip supply. As a result, the recording industry took on an almost jaunty air for the first time in more than a decade, a state of affairs reflected in RCA's sudden reemergence from its slumbers and subsequent lightning takeover of France's Erato.

Of particular interest to classical collectors was the quantity of back-catalog material already finding its way (by means of some highly sophisticated digital remastering techniques) onto compact discs. Classics such as Benjamin Britten's composer-conducted *War Requiem* (London-Decca), Karl Böhm's 1966 Bayreuth *The Ring* (Philips), Otto Klemperer's Beethoven symphony cycle (Angel-EMI), Sir Georg Solti's Richard Strauss *Salomé* (London-Decca), and many Wilhelm Furtwängler (Angel-EMI Japan) and Bruno Walter (Columbia-CBS Japan) reissues found their way (to spectacular effect) onto CD.

Under the circumstances the standard microgroove LP disc was obliged to take something of a back seat. Significant developments continued in this area, however. PRT (Precision Records and Tapes) unlocked in England a particularly valuable collection of reissues that returned to the catalog at budget prices a treasure trove of material that featured such figures as conductors Sir Adrian Boult and Sir John Barbirolli, cellist André Navarra, and pianist Bela Siki. Transfer and pressing quality were of a high order, as they were in Angel-EMI France's "Références" series. The latter continued to provide valuable material from the Angel-EMI lists, much of it unavailable for half a century.

Important first recordings included Bizet's *The Fair Maid of Perth* (Angel-EMI); Leonard Bernstein's complete *West Side Story,* conducted by the composer (Deutsche Grammophon); complete cycles of Bizet and Mussorgsky piano music (both Melodiya); Rutland Boughton's *The Immortal Hour* and Holst's *The Dream City* (both Hyperion); Francesco Cavalli's *Xerxes* (Harmonia Mundi); Gottfried von Einem's *Danton's Death* (Orfeo); Elgar's early cantata *King Olaf* (Angel-EMI); Ferenc Erkel's *Hunyadi László* and Respighi's *The Flame* (both Hungaraton); Josef Förster's *Eva* (Supraphon); Philip Glass's *Satyagraha* (Columbia CBS); Kalomiris's *Mother's Ring* (Concert Athens); a complete five-disc set of Sibelius songs (London-Decca); Richard Strauss's *Guntram* (Columbia-CBS); Tchaikovsky's *Iolanthe* (Erato); and the collected symphonies of Eduard Tubin. (NICHOLAS HARPER)

Jazz. The year 1985 was one in which the proliferation and viability of styles and trends within jazz had to be weighed against the grievous loss of many great musicians, some still in their creative prime. On balance, the pool of promising new talent and the continued vitality of the jazz tradition boded well for the future.

The most striking young player to become visible in 1985 was guitarist Stanley Jordan, 26, whose unorthodox approach to his instrument (he tapped the strings rather than plucking them) found favour with the public. His debut album, *Magic Touch* (Blue Note), was the year's best-selling jazz LP and also placed on the pop charts.

A new sextet, OTB (for "Out of the Blue"), made up of gifted players in their 20s, was launched by Blue Note, a label reactivated with much fanfare and a marathon New York concert featuring many of the luminaries associated with it in the 1950s and 1960s. It quickly assumed a leading position in the field.

Trumpeter Wynton Marsalis repeated his astonishing feat of 1984 by winning Grammy awards as best instrumental soloist in both the jazz and classical categories. No new classical record by Marsalis was issued in 1985, but his jazz album *Black Codes (from the Underground)* (Columbia) was hailed as his best yet.

While Marsalis separated his jazz and classical careers, some notable "crossing over" took place between these musics. The San Francisco-based Kronos String Quartet recorded music by Thelonious Monk (for Landmark Records) and premiered, at New York City's Carnegie Recital Hall, new works by Muhal Richard Abrams, Anthony Braxton, Leroy Jenkins, and Leo Smith, noted composer-instrumentalists who all emerged from Chicago's AACM (Association for the Advancement of Creative Musicians) in the 1960s. An opera by composer and pianist Anthony Davis, "X" (based on the life of Malcolm X), was presented in Philadelphia in October and was scheduled for full-scale production at the New York City Opera in 1986. Classical and jazz works by Ornette Coleman were performed at a week-long event in his honour in Hartford, Conn.

Two of the most respected saxophonists in modern jazz, Sonny Rollins and Wayne Shorter, made news in 1985. Rollins gave the first solo concert of his long career at New York City's Museum of Modern Art. It was recorded (by Fantasy) and was a milestone in the annals of unaccompanied jazz performances. Shorter, to the delight of his many admirers, detached himself from Weather Report, the successful jazz-fusion band he had led with Joe Zawinul since 1970, and toured with his own quartet in the wake of the release of his first album as a leader in a decade (*Atlantis;* Columbia).

In the field of big-band jazz, trumpeter-composer-arranger Thad Jones was appointed leader of the Count Basie Orchestra. Though best known as coleader (with drummer Mel Lewis) of one of the most innovative big bands of the 1960s and '70s, Jones declared himself proud to perpetuate Basie's legacy, which also was celebrated by the publication of *Good Morning Blues,* Basie's posthumous autobiography, as told to essayist, novelist, and jazz historian Albert Murray. One of the few surviving stars of the golden age of big bands, Benny Goodman, resumed active performing after a lengthy layoff. At the helm of a big band borrowed from a young tenor saxophonist, Loren Schoenberg (which itself made its recording debut in 1985), Goodman led a tribute to Fletcher Henderson at Waterloo Village in New Jersey and gave a concert at Yale University. With the band, and such noted alumni as Teddy Wilson, Red Norvo, and Slam Stewart, he also

taped a television special. On drums for that occasion was Louie Bellson, whose own big band was among the several active in Los Angeles.

Among other veteran jazz performers, Joe Williams had an outstanding year. The singer won his first Grammy award; saw the publication of his biography, *Every Day* (by Leslie Gourse); and joined the cast of the nation's most popular television series, "The Cosby Show," portraying Bill Cosby's father-in-law. Also conspicuously active was Benny Carter. A mere 78, the saxophonist, trumpeter, and arranger toured Europe and the U.S. and made his first album as a leader since 1976 (*A Gentleman and His Music,* Concord Jazz).

Previous attempts at organizing the jazz community had not been notably effective, but some promising developments occurred in 1985. The formation of the National Jazz Service Organization, based in Washington, D.C., and supported by the National Endowment for the Arts, was announced in the spring. It was to function as a national advisory centre and planned to establish a permanent jazz repertory ensemble and an archive. Also formed during the year was the American Federation of Jazz Societies, dedicated to setting up a national touring network for jazz performers and to the general promotion of jazz.

Three of the foremost jazz drummers died in 1985: Jo Jones, famed for his seminal work with the original Count Basie Band; Kenny Clarke, a founding father of bebop; and Philly Joe Jones, a leading post-bop stylist. Other deaths included trombonists Benny Morton and Dicky Wells, veterans of the Basie and Fletcher Henderson bands; the trumpeter Cootie Williams, one of the great Duke Ellington stars; pianist Johnny Guarnieri, who pioneered the use of the harpsichord in jazz; and bassist George Duvivier, not well known to the public but considered by his peers as the greatest all-round bassist in jazz. Big Joe Turner, the famous blues singer, also died, as did blues pianists Little Brother Montgomery and Blind John Davis and such younger musicians as trumpeters Lonnie Hillyer and Richard Williams and alto saxophonist Chris Woods. (*See* OBITUARIES.)   (DAN M. MORGENSTERN)

Popular. In 1985 pop musicians rediscovered an idealism, and even an unlikely political power, that had been dormant on the music scene since the heady 1960s days of civil rights and Vietnam protests. It was, as a result, a year in which the music itself often seemed secondary to the causes to which it was allied.

The biggest pop music event of the year—indeed, the most spectacular event in the entire history of pop—was very much a triumph of this new idealism. On July 13, 72,000 people packed Wembley Stadium in London, and a further 90,000 packed the JFK Stadium in Philadelphia, for a 16-hour concert that took place on both sides of the Atlantic and was televised live around the world. In all, it was watched by over 1,500,000,000 people. More remarkable still was the fact that this was a charity concert, at which all performers and technicians gave their services free, to raise money for the Band Aid fund to combat starvation in Africa. The two Live Aid shows raised over $71.5 million from viewers around the world. The extraordinary event had been arranged by Bob Geldof (*see* BIOGRAPHIES), the singer with the Boomtown Rats, who immediately became an international celebrity.

Live Aid, along with the earlier Band Aid appeal in Britain and USA for Africa in the U.S., showed that musicians could still be as socially concerned as they had been in the 1960s; now, however, they were better organized and more powerful as a result. After Live Aid, musical benefits for different causes began to spring up in Britain and the U.S. After turning their thoughts to those suffering abroad, U.S. musicians began to concentrate on those suffering at home. Bob Dylan had commented on the plight of U.S. farmers during Live Aid, and Willie Nelson later organized his own Farm Aid concert. Meanwhile, Bruce Springsteen (*see* BIOGRAPHIES), undoubtedly the most successful U.S. pop musician of the year, went from publicizing the plight of the Vietnam veterans to publicizing the problems of hunger in the U.S., promoting Food Bank programs and donating money to them in towns where he performed.

Along with the social concern came political involvement. In Britain a year-long miners' strike ended in March. Many musicians had been politicized by the strike, giving benefit shows for the miners, and this in turn led to musical support for Britain's Labour Party. Soloist Billy Bragg invited members of Parliament from the Labour Party to his "Jobs for Youth" tour in March and later started an organization called Red Wedge, pledged to win youth votes for Labour at the next election. Renewed interest in international politics helped organizations in Britain and the U.S. fighting apartheid (racial separation) in South Africa. In Britain Robert Wyatt and Jerry Dammers from The Specials collaborated with students from South West Africa/Namibia on the *Wind of Change,* a record that became a minor hit and raised money for the South West Africa People's Organization. In the U.S. a whole set of musicians—Dylan, Miles Davis, Springsteen, and Bobby Womack, along with such British artists as Pete Townshend and Ringo Starr—collaborated in an even more commercial antiapartheid fund-raiser, *Sun City.*

While the musical causes of 1985 were easy to spot, the musical trends that went with them were not so obvious, as must have been clear to anyone watching the Live Aid concert. On show, after all, were grand old bands from the 1960s, like The Who, alongside newer, established superstars like U2 and Simple Minds or brand new contenders like Madonna. One of the stars of Live Aid was Phil Collins, who flew by Concorde across the Atlantic during the show and so managed to appear in both London and Philadelphia. His enormous success during the year with the album *No Jacket Required* reflected one clear trend—for well-known performers with a particular band to go off on a solo career of their own. Mick Jagger (who sang solo and with Tina Turner [*see* BIOGRAPHIES] at Live Aid) released his first solo album during the year, to only moderate critical acclaim. He then returned to recording with the Rolling Stones. Sting, the lead singer with The Police, also went solo during the year with an album, *The Dream of the Blue Turtles,* and a world tour. He was accompanied on both by musicians from the black American jazz scene and reflected the new socially concerned trend in music with songs about miners and the arms race.

The year's best-sellers in the U.S. came mostly from these well-established artists, along with other veterans such as John Fogerty, who was once the leader of Creedence Clearwater Revival. The most successful black U.S. artists were also mostly well-established performers, including Tina Turner and Stevie Wonder; the latter contributed to the antiapartheid trend with one of the songs on his album *In Square Circle.*

New developments on the white American rock scene included the continued resurgence of guitar bands like R.E.M., while the most inventive U.S. album of the year was Tom Waits's *Raindogs,* a mixture of blues, Kurt Weill, and Broadway. Newcomers who did well in the U.S. ranged from the British duo Tears for Fears, who sold more than six million copies of their album *Songs from the Big Chair,* to a new U.S. rock queen, Madonna. An

Over 72,000 people jammed the Live Aid concert in Wembley Stadium, London, and 90,000 filled John F. Kennedy Stadium in Philadelphia as international pop stars raised money for African famine relief.

G. DEKEERLE—GAMMA/LIAISON

established British group that enjoyed a big success in the U.S. was Dire Straits with *Brothers in Arms.*

In the far more fluid and volatile British home market, there was no one clear trend. Favourites of previous years like Frankie Goes to Hollywood and Culture Club slipped from favour, and in their place came everything from the mournful self-pitying balladry of The Smiths to the cool soulful balladry of Sade or the far more chaotic but exhilarating blend of punk and Irish traditional styles offered by The Pogues, one of the more unexpected successes in a colourful year.   (ROBIN DENSELOW)

See also Dance; Motion Pictures; Television and Radio; Theatre.

This article updates the *Macropædia* article The History of Western MUSIC.

Philately and Numismatics

Stamps. There was further improvement in the market for rare stamps and postal history material during 1985, but dealing at the general collector and junior level remained quiet. In the U.S. the Postal Service worked closely with the Council of Philatelic Organizations to stimulate interest among the general public, especially children. In the U.K. the Stamp Collecting Promotion Council became part of the British Philatelic Federation (BPF).

Among the large number of internationally famous one-country collections sold at auction for high totals were the Benwell Barbados, £67,000; Dunstan Uganda, £117,300; and Crabb Tristan da Cunha, £60,000. The postponed (second) sale of surplus archival material held at London's National Postal Museum proved disappointing, and the third sale was incorporated in a Phillips auction of Great Britain stamps from various owners, an experiment that improved realizations.

A Boston collector discovered the 16th example of the Falkland Islands 1964 6d stamp featuring HMS *Glasgow*

in error for HMS *Kent.* The original sheet of 60 had been broken up and distributed as a normal new issue before the error was discovered. Newly discovered errors were colour trials of the Australian 1982 60-cent humpback whale stamp accidentally included in the printers' delivery to the Australian Post Office. Argyll Etkin Ltd. of London began handling the Ishikawa collection of U.S. classic stamps valued at £11.4 million ($16 million), the most valuable private collection of these issues ever marketed. The Philatelic Foundation of New York discovered more than 200 fakes of its Expert Committee certificates. Charges were brought against an employee of the foundation and three others.

Several rare stamps and covers made record realizations: Western Australia 1854 4d deep blue "inverted swan" error, £60,000 (estimate, £35,000); Bermuda 1861 "Perot" postmaster provisional, one of five now known and the only unused example, £33,000 (£20,000); India 1854 4 annas (cut to shape) error "inverted head," used, a new find, £12,000 (£7,500); U.S. 1918 24-cent airmail error, inverted centre, $88,000 (estimated to $100,000); Confederate States cover with a pair of the Livingston, Ala., 5-cent blue, $176,000 (estimate, $160,000); Baden, Germany, 1851 9-kreutzer black on blue-green colour error (only three known), on cover, £615,000; Tristan da Cunha cover with ½d and 1d King George V Great Britain with typed overprint, £12,000 (£6,000); Great Britain 1840 2d blue, Plate 1, mint marginal block of four, £20,350.

The BPF congress was held in Oxford for the first time. Three collectors signed the Roll of Distinguished Philatelists: Carl Richard Brühl (West Germany), author of a newly published two-volume history of philately; Roberto M. Rosende (U.S.), a leading authority on Cuban philately; and W. Raife Wellsted (Great Britain), an internationally known postal historian and curator of the National Postal Museum. The BPF Congress medal was awarded to A. Herbert Grimsey, honorary secretary of the BPF and collector of musical philately.

The major Fédération Internationale de Philatélie (FIP) international stamp exhibition of the year was held in Tel Aviv, Israel, in May. The FIP Grand Prix d'Honneur was awarded to Jochen Heddergott (West Germany) for a collection of classic Indian stamps; the Grand Prix National to "Manuela" (Italy) for Holy Land Forerunners; and the Grand Prix International to L. Kapiloff (U.S.) for U.S. postal history of 1847.   (KENNETH F. CHAPMAN)

Coins and Paper Money. In October U.S. Pres. Ronald Reagan banned the importation of South African Krugerrands, the world's most widely traded gold coin. The ban was one of several economic sanctions imposed on the government of South Africa for its racial policies. Some other nations also prohibited—or considered a prohibition of—Krugerrand imports during 1985. South Africa first minted the one-ounce Krugerrand in 1967, and by 1971 it had become the dominant gold coin on international bullion markets. In 1984 the Krugerrand accounted for about two-thirds of all bullion coins sold in the world, compared with 27% for its nearest rival, the Canadian maple leaf. However, many bankers and metal dealers thought the maple leaf might emerge as the world's top seller in 1985. On December 17 President Reagan signed legislation authorizing the issuance of four U.S. bullion gold coins ($5, $10, $15, and $50) to compete with the Krugerrand. The Australian government made plans to issue a bullion gold coin during 1986.

On Oct. 18, 1985, the U.S. Mint began striking three different coins to commemorate the Statue of Liberty's 100th anniversary in 1986. Coin sales to collectors could raise as much as $137.5 million for repairs to the statue

Bans by various nations against trade in or import of Krugerrands, occasioned by opposition to South Africa's racial policies, raised the possibility that the Canadian maple leaf coin, first introduced in 1979, might emerge as the leading bullion coin in world trade.

CANAPRESS

and to the old immigration facilities on nearby Ellis Island in New York Harbor. The U.S. Olympic coin program, which ended in January 1985, netted $72 million.

Throughout 1985 the U.S. Treasury continued to study ways to protect paper money from would-be counterfeiters operating improved colour copying machines, which were expected to be widely available later in the decade. Under serious consideration was the use of watermarks or thin metal security threads in the paper, as well as other subtle changes. The Bank of England distributed new £20 notes with a revised watermark and other changes in an effort to thwart counterfeiters. Also, the bank quit printing one-pound notes on Jan. 1, 1985, forcing British citizens to use a one-pound coin introduced in 1983. Officials said the move would lower the cost of producing money because each coin should remain in circulation for about 40 years, while the typical note lasted ten months.

Australia continued to replace its $A1 notes with a $A1 coin first minted in 1984, and the Canadian government studied the feasibility of making a new Can$1 coin and eliminating the Can$1 bill. In September, Canada unveiled the first two silver coins of a ten-piece set commemorating the 1988 Winter Olympics in Calgary, Alta. Many other countries also issued new types of coins and currency in 1985, especially nations with high inflation. The Bank of Israel released into circulation new shekel notes worth 1,000 times the old notes.

Rare coin prices increased 11.5% in the 12 months ended June 1, 1985, according to a Wall Street securities firm, putting them fourth on a list of 14 investment vehicles. Nonetheless, the values of many old coins remained below the highs set during the market boom of 1979 and 1980. Two U.S. rarities brought impressive prices at a 1985 auction; one of five known 1913 Liberty nickels sold for $385,000, and an 1804 silver dollar fetched $308,000.

(ROGER BOYE)

This article updates the *Macropædia* article COINS AND COINAGE.

Photography

Among the most important technical developments in photography during 1985 was the introduction by Minolta of a new autofocus system for interchangeable-lens 35-mm cameras. Although that company's sales reaped the immediate benefits, this newest convenience feature promised to help rekindle popular interest in single-lens-reflex (SLR) cameras and increase lagging sales across the board as other manufacturers brought out their own autofocus designs. On the cultural side, 1985 was a vintage year for photographic exhibitions and books, many of which emphasized photojournalistic, documentary, and humanistic work.

Photo Equipment. Among new designs for 35-mm SLRs, Minolta decisively led the way with its new Maxxum line. Not since Canon introduced its landmark AE-1 in 1976 did an SLR have such an impact on the photographic industry and marketplace. The Maxxum 7000 established its commanding position by being the first production-line interchangeable-lens 35-mm camera to provide fast, accurate automatic focusing at even relatively low light levels by incorporating electronic distance detectors and a focusing motor within the camera body rather than within individual lenses. To function with these components, Minolta designed a family of new dedicated lenses that coupled to the shaft of the built-in motor and supplied focal-length and *f*-stop data to the camera via five gold contacts. Twelve A-mount autofocusing lenses having focal lengths from 24 mm to 300 mm were introduced initially, with more to come.

The Maxxum 7000 offered a variety of other convenient, high-technology features including multimode, multiprogrammed exposure automation, optional manual operation, automatic film loading, automatic setting of ISO (International Standards Organization) film speeds based on Kodak's DX cartridge and film coding system, LCD (liquid-crystal-display) function readouts on the camera deck, a variety of pushbutton controls, and motorized film transport and rewind. Also available was a Maxxum 2800 AF flash unit, which focused in the dark by infrared light.

Later in the year the company introduced a second, professional model, designated the 9000 in the U.S. Whereas the original Maxxum had a top shutter speed of 1/2,000 second, the professional Maxxum provided a 1/4,000 second. Other features unique to the 9000 included an automatic-exposure metering system that allowed the photographer to choose among a centre-weighted average reading, a conventional spot reading, a spot highlight reading (plus 2¼ stops) or a spot shadow reading (minus 2¾ stops). While the 7000 model allowed the shutter to be tripped only when the subject was in focus, the 9000 permitted this option with an FP (focus-priority) setting.

A new 35-mm SLR from Olympus, the OM-PC, offered a novel feature called ESP (for electro-selective-pattern) metering. When the ESP button was set, the camera's metering system automatically compensated for difficult lighting situations such as backlighting or a very light or very dark background. Otherwise the user could choose conventional centre-weighted average metering. The OM-PC offered three exposure modes: program, aperture-priority, and full manual control. A DX-capable camera, it had a top shutter speed of 1/1,000 second.

Models of compact 35-mm "auto-everything" cameras continued to proliferate. The Olympus Quick Flash was the first compact to use a new cartridge-packaged six-volt lithium battery to power the camera's various electronic functions. The lithium cells provided an estimated five years of performance with ordinary use, gave rapid flash-recycling time, and, unlike earlier types, could be replaced easily by the user. To increase picture-taking versatility some manufacturers of compact cameras introduced dual-lens models. For example, the Fuji TW-300 allowed the user to switch between a 38-mm $f/3.5$ and a 65-mm $f/5.6$ telephoto, while the Minolta AE-Tele provided, at the flip of a switch, a choice between a 38-mm $f/2.8$ and a 60-mm $f/4.3$.

A number of new colour-printing papers were introduced, including an Agfacolor Type 8 for making prints from negatives and Agfachrome Color Reversal Paper for prints from colour slides. Eastman Kodak delivered Ektacolor Professional Paper as a replacement for Ektacolor 74 (and also celebrated the 50th anniversary of Kodachrome film). Fuji Photo Film introduced Fujicolor Paper Type 02 (prints from negatives) and Fujichrome Paper Type 33 (prints from colour slides).

The new series of autofocus A-mount lenses for the Minolta Maxxum was the most innovative development in consumer camera lenses during the year. Added to the 12 models mentioned above was a giant 600-mm $f/4$ apochromat telephoto with internally focusing elements that quickly and efficiently responded to the small motor built into the Maxxum's body. Camera manufacturers and independent lens makers introduced numerous new zoom lenses, especially in the popular range covering wide-angle (28-mm or 35-mm) to moderate telephoto (70-mm to 135-mm). An even longer range was offered by some models, including the 35–200-mm $f/3.5$–4.8 Soligor one-touch zoom and Vivitar's 28–200-mm $f/3.8$–5.6.

None of the prototype all-electronic still cameras previously demonstrated reached the production stage as the year ended. Kodak, however, began test marketing two new photo/video still-image systems. One, the Color Video Imager, enabled the user to select a scene from a videocassette recorder, video camera, or computer or TV monitor and make a 1/10-second exposure of it on Kodak Trimprint film, which produced a fully developed colour print in less than two minutes. Kodak's second system comprised two parts: a photo-laboratory-based transfer station that stored the images of 50 35-mm colour negatives (converting them to colour positives in the process) on a video floppy disc and a home player/recorder unit that displayed the positive images on a standard colour television set.

Cultural Trends. Many of the year's major photographic exhibitions and books displayed the work of journalistic, documentary, and humanistic photographers. Some observers speculated that the subjective, inward-looking, and formalist bent of contemporary photography, which had dominated the art world in recent years, had peaked. Whether a significant trend or not, during 1985 the art and museum establishment did recognize a more reportorial and content-oriented variety of photography.

"André Kertész: Of Paris and New York," a major retrospective exhibition of the Hungarian-born master photographer's work, opened at the Art Institute of Chicago and later at the Metropolitan Museum of Art in New York City. (Concurrently a book with the same title was published.) Kertész, at age 91, was present at the Chicago opening but did not live to see the New York premiere. Kertész was highly regarded in Paris during the 1920s and 1930s as a creative artist and a photojournalist, but after moving to the U.S. in 1936 he felt that he was misunderstood and unappreciated. From the 1960s on, however, he received much recognition and eventually was showered with honours. (*See* OBITUARIES.)

The Amon Carter Museum in Fort Worth, Texas, displayed two documentary exhibitions. One was a selection of work by former *Life* staffer Carl Mydans during his years with the U.S. Farm Security Administration and as a combat photographer in World War II. The second was the result of an unusual project in which the museum assigned fashion photographer Richard Avedon to document the people of the western U.S., which he proceeded to do with an 8×10-in view camera over a period of six years. The exhibition, "In the American West" (also the title of a book published concurrently), was a deromanticized record of harsh aspects of life and work among ranchers, miners, oil-field hands, carnival people, and drifters. The larger-than-life-size prints had visual power, but some viewers criticized Avedon for exploiting his subjects to create his own myth of the West.

The International Center of Photography in New York City displayed the work of Robert Capa in a retrospective that ranged from his early photojournalism in Paris to the last frame he exposed moments before being killed by a land mine in Vietnam in 1954. Two books were published in conjunction with the exhibition: *Robert Capa Photographs,* edited by Cornell Capa and Richard Whelan, and *Robert Capa: A Biography,* by Richard Whelan. The Philadelphia Museum of Art showed "W. Eugene Smith: 'Let Truth Be the Prejudice'," with 250 master prints on loan from the Center for Creative Photography of the University of Arizona. A book was published under the same name with a biography of Smith by Ben Maddow.

Coinciding with the run of the Tsukuba World Expo '85, a large photo exhibition was held in nearby Tsukuba City, Japan, from March 9 to September 16. Although not permanent in character, it was heralded as a significant event in view of the fact that there were so few photo museums in Japan. The exhibition presented 450 original prints by 170 well-known photographers from Japan and elsewhere.

At the 42nd Pictures of the Year competition sponsored by the National Press Photographers Association and the

The big news in 35-mm single-lens-reflex cameras, the most popular type among consumers, was Minolta's Maxxum line, premiered in the highly sophisticated 7000 model.

André Kertész (right) attended the opening of a retrospective showing of his work at the Art Institute of Chicago, where he was greeted by the institute's curator of photography, David Travis.
UPI/BETTMANN NEWSPHOTOS

University of Missouri School of Journalism, Fred Comegys of the *Wilmington* (Del.) *News Journal* was named Newspaper Photographer of the Year; Steve McCurry of *National Geographic* was named Magazine Photographer of the Year; and Stan Grossfeld of the *Boston Globe* received the Canon Photo Essayist Award. The 1985 Pulitzer Prize for spot news photography went to the staff of the *Santa Ana* (Calif.) *Register* for "Olympic Games." The Pulitzer for feature photography was given to Stan Grossfeld for "Famine in Ethiopia" and "Illegal Aliens from the Mexican Border" and to Larry C. Price of the *Philadelphia Inquirer* for "War-Torn Inhabitants of Angola and El Salvador."

The World Press Photo of the Year Award went to Pablo Bartholomew of Gamma agency. In Japan Keiichi Tahara received the tenth Ihei Kimura prize for his "Eclat" and other aesthetic works. The W. Eugene Smith Memorial Grant in Humanistic Photography was split between Donna Ferrato for "Domestic Violence" and Letizia Battaglia for "The Mafia in Sicily." The Hasselblad Award for photography given by the Hasselblad Foundation in Göteborg, Sweden, went to Irving Penn.

(ARTHUR GOLDSMITH)

See also Motion Pictures.
This article updates the *Macropædia* article PHOTOGRAPHY.

Physics

Over many years physicists have refined their techniques for producing very thin, high-quality, single-crystal samples of metals, semiconductors, and insulators. By the 1980s their progress had been such that studies of the samples were leading to the discovery of totally new physical phenomena. Essential to these advances has been the ability to grow successive layers of materials whose atoms are perfectly aligned from one layer to the next.

Until very recently some of the quantum electronic properties expected of these defect-free materials, wherein the behaviour of the electrons results from their being allowed only certain discrete, or quantum, energy levels, were treated as academic exercises with no practical reality. In 1985, however, they were being observed and studied in the laboratory as a result of the development of heterostructures and superlattices. Heterostructures consist of thin, single-crystal films of different materials layered one on top of the other, while superlattices comprise numerous alternating heterostructure layers. It is important for achieving the desired properties that the lattices of the different materials have the same symmetry and similar interatomic spacing so that their atomic arrangements match each other as closely as possible. Heterostructures and superlattices offer opportunities for novel, useful devices, making them of worldwide interest.

The fabrication of ultrathin films and heterostructures is carried out by molecular beam epitaxy (MBE). Epitaxy is the phenomenon by which the crystallinity and orientation of a growing crystalline layer is determined by the lattice of the substrate on which it is being grown. In MBE materials for the growing layers are supplied by hot beams of atoms or molecules directed at the substrate, which is maintained at an appropriate temperature under very high vacuum. The whole process takes place in a clean stainless-steel environment. Under these conditions growth occurs very slowly, allowing the deposition of layers only a single atom in thickness. A further advantage of MBE is that the deposited atoms attach themselves preferentially to the sides of any depressions in the surface. Consequently, films can be produced that on an atomic scale are smoother than the original substrate.

If a heterostructure is made of a layer of gallium arsenide and one of gallium aluminum arsenide, then the interface between these two nearly perfect, lattice-matched semiconductors will be extremely smooth and abrupt. At temperatures near absolute zero such a structure gives rise to a sheet of electrons, mobile only in two dimensions and localized at the interface. The heterostructure thus provides a two-dimensional electron gas readily available for experimentation. Since the electron gas exists in a semiconductor, one of the first studies physicists wish to make is on the Hall effect. This fundamental property of semiconductors gives information about the carriers of electric current and their mobility.

The Hall effect manifests itself when an electric current is passed through a conductor (or semiconductor) at right angles to an applied magnetic field. It is evidenced by the appearance of a voltage, called the Hall voltage, across the conductor and perpendicular to both the current flow and the field. In 1980 the Hall resistance, defined as the Hall voltage divided by the current, was measured in a two-dimensional electron gas formed in a heterostructure. When the magnetic field was made very high, the Hall resistance showed distinct plateaus, the values being described in terms of h/ve^2, in which h is Planck's constant, e is the charge on the electron, and v is a quantum number having values 1, 2, 3, etc. The precision with which these quantized steps occur for the different quantum numbers allowed the universal constant h/e^2 to be determined to the amazing accuracy of one part in ten million. This behaviour was soon explained by many theoreticians in terms of a standard quantum mechanical treatment of the electrons. For discovering the quantized Hall effect, West German researcher Klaus von Klitzing (*see* BIOGRAPHIES) received the 1985 Nobel Prize for Physics.

In 1983, when these experiments were extended to yet lower temperatures and higher magnetic fields, more plateaus in the resistivity were observed. What was totally unexpected, however, was that they occurred for fractional quantum numbers; *e.g.*, when v was $1/3$, $2/3$, $2/5$, $4/5$, or $2/7$. This was the first time such fractional quantum effects had been reported, and in 1985 theoreticians were still busy

trying to explain the behaviour. It was thought that the phenomena could be understood by considering the two-dimensional electron gas to be acting like a condensed electron liquid.

In addition to revealing some exciting fundamental physics, the ability of MBE to tailor-make heterostructures was leading to tremendous opportunities for creating novel devices. Diodes, transistors, photodetectors, and lasers all were benefiting from this advance.

As an example, a diode laser can be constructed from a heterostructure consisting of alternating layers of gallium indium arsenide and aluminum indium arsenide. If the thickness of the former layer is varied from 0.8 micrometres (millionths of a metre) to 10 micrometres, then the laser wavelength changes from 1.5 to 1.7 micrometres. Such tunability in the infrared region of the spectrum is ideal for fibre-optic communication systems.

In the heterostructures described above, the two different materials are chosen to have the same lattice constants, leading to lattice-matched structures. Obviously the range of possibilities would be much increased if nonmatched materials could be joined without dislocations, which reduce their usefulness as electronic devices. Recently physicists found that if the layers of dissimilar materials are made sufficiently thin, then the mismatch leads to strains in the two layers without actual dislocations at the interface. The technique, known as strained-layer epitaxy, was allowing silicon, the most popular of all semiconductor materials, to be introduced in superlattices. Both nickel-silicon and germanium-silicon compounds can be interfaced with silicon without generating dislocations.

Heterostructures and two-dimensional crystals were not solely of interest to the semiconductor physicist. Epitaxial techniques were being exploited by workers in magnetism to extend their understanding of the fundamental interactions that produce the atomic ordering seen in magnetic materials, whose atoms behave like tiny bar magnets, or dipoles. Studies of rare-earth metals such as gadolinium and dysprosium might help to answer questions concerning the range of this magnetic interaction. Does a single atom really have a magnetic influence on its neighbours that extends over perhaps ten atomic planes as other experiments would indicate? Measurements of dysprosium samples one atom thick, two atoms thick, and so on would be most enlightening. Similar questions concerned the nature of magnetism in the transition metals: is the magnetism localized on the atoms or ions, or is it associated with the mobile conduction electrons and thus allowed to have more freedom?

Some of these questions were being attacked, for example, with investigations on very thin films of nickel and cobalt. Recent work showed that a layer of nickel one or two atoms thick is not magnetic. As further planes are added, its atoms order magnetically but only at low temperatures. It is only when the film is six planes thick that the temperature at which magnetic order appears approaches that of nickel in bulk. Cobalt, on the other hand, becomes ferromagnetically ordered (the atomic dipoles are all aligned parallel to each other) when it is only one atom thick and has an ordering temperature above room temperature when it is two planes thick. A theoretical interpretation of these contrasting phenomena was eagerly awaited. Theory and experiment did come together for chromium; both agreed that the atoms in a monolayer of the metal are strongly magnetic but that adding a second layer of metal atoms quenches the magnetism. The addition of subsequent atomic layers allows the magnetism to develop again.

Perhaps the most interesting discovery came from heterostructures made of the rare-earth metal dysprosium layered with yttrium. In the bulk state dysprosium orders antiferromagnetically at about −90° C (−130° F). In other words, in a particular plane the dipoles are all parallel to one another; on moving up a plane the dipoles are again all parallel, but this direction has rotated by an angle, say θ, from the first plane; in the third plane the dipoles have rotated by 2θ from the first plane; and so on. The result is a helical or spiral magnetic structure having no resultant magnetism in bulk. In a prepared heterostructure material in which seven planes of dysprosium are separated by a monolayer or two of yttrium, the dysprosium is again ordered helically. The spiral, however, does not continue coherently across the intervening yttrium layer, and the seven steps in each "spiral staircase" do not quite cancel each other since the spiral has done only approximately half a turn. The resulting magnetism, which is coming from an almost perfect single-crystal structure, strangely mimics that of an amorphous (noncrystalline) rare-earth alloy.

(S. B. PALMER)

This article updates the *Macropædia* articles ELECTRICITY AND MAGNETISM; ELECTRONICS; MATTER: *Solid State;* The PHYSICAL SCIENCES: *Physics.*

Populations and Population Movements

DEMOGRAPHY

World population stood at 4,842,042,000 at mid-1985, according to the latest estimate of the UN Population Division, up 79 million from 4,763,004,000 at mid-1984. The annual growth rate was expected to decline from 1.7 to 1.5% by the year 2000, but because of the growing base population, 89 million would then be added annually. The UN projected world population at 6,127,000,000 in 2000 and 8,177,000,000 in 2025. Between 1985 and 2025, 93% of world population growth would occur in the less developed countries of Africa, Asia (minus Japan), and Latin America. These countries would account for 83% of world population in 2025, compared with 76% in 1985. The proportion of population living in urban areas in 1985 was

World's 25 Most Populous Urban Areas[1]

Rank	City and Country	City proper Population	Year	Metropolitan area Population	Year
1	Tokyo, Japan	8,362,000	1985 estimate	29,002,000	1981 estimate
2	New York City, U.S.	7,164,742	1984 estimate	17,807,100	1984 estimate
3	Mexico City, Mexico	8,831,079	1980 census	17,321,800	1985 estimate
4	Osaka, Japan	2,631,000	1985 estimate	16,224,000	1983 estimate
5	São Paulo, Brazil	10,036,900	1985 estimate	15,143,000	1985 estimate
6	Los Angeles, U.S.	3,096,721	1984 estimate	12,372,600	1984 estimate
7	London, England	6,756,000	1984 estimate	12,231,200	1983 estimate
8	Cairo, Egypt	5,881,000	1983 estimate	12,001,000	1983 estimate
9	Shanghai, China	6,320,872	1982 census[2]	11,940,000	1983 estimate
10	Rhine-Ruhr, W.Ger.	[3]	[3]	10,984,000	1982 estimate
11	Paris, France	2,149,900	1984 estimate	10,210,059	1982 census
12	Buenos Aires, Arg.	2,924,000	1984 estimate	9,677,200	1981 census
13	Beijing, China	5,597,972	1982 census[2]	9,541,000	1983 estimate
14	Seoul, South Korea	[4]	[4]	9,501,413	1984 estimate
15	Calcutta, India	3,305,006	1981 census	9,194,018	1981 census
16	Rio de Janeiro, Brazil	5,090,700	1980 census	9,014,274	1980 census
17	Moscow, U.S.S.R.	8,275,000	1984 estimate	8,537,000	1984 estimate
18	Bombay, India	[4]	[4]	8,243,405	1981 census
19	Chicago, U.S.	2,992,472	1984 estimate	8,035,000	1984 estimate
20	Nagoya, Japan	2,112,000	1985 estimate	7,968,000	1981 estimate
21	Tianjin, China	5,142,565	1982 census[2]	7,880,000	1983 estimate
22	Jakarta, Indonesia	[4]	[4]	7,585,000	1985 estimate
23	Manila, Philippines	1,725,500	1983 estimate	6,914,581	1985 estimate
24	Chongqing, China	2,673,200	1982 census	6,511,100	1983 estimate
25	Istanbul, Turkey	3,017,940	1985 estimate	5,758,743	1985 estimate

[1]Ranked by population of metropolitan area.
[2]Preliminary figures.
[3]An industrial conurbation within which no single central city is identified.
[4]City proper not identified by reporting countries.

estimated at 41% for the world as a whole, 32% in less developed countries, and 72% in more developed countries. Regionally, Asia's population was the least urbanized (28%) and Europe's the most (73%).

According to the U.S. Census Bureau, the U.S. population (including armed forces overseas) was 238,816,000 on July 1, 1985, an increase of 2,135,000 over a year earlier. About 1.6 million of this was due to natural increase (excess of births over deaths), and the remainder (about 500,000) was accounted for by legal immigration. Illegal immigration added more to the U.S. population each year, but that figure was unknown. In 1985 the urban proportion of the U.S. population was 74%.

Birth Statistics. The National Center for Health Statistics reported that 3,697,000 births occurred in the U.S. in 1984, 2% more than in 1983. The birthrate was 15.7 live births per 1,000 population, and the fertility rate was 66 births per 1,000 women aged 15–44, both 1% higher than the rates for 1983. The increase continued into 1985. For the 12-month period ended in May, there were 2% more births than in the same period a year earlier. This trend was attributed to increases in birthrates of older women. Detailed data showed that birthrates were stable for women aged 15–29 from 1975 to 1982 but rose 23% for women aged 30–34. During this period the proportion of all births occurring to women age 30 and older increased from 17 to 22%. The rate of first births for women aged 30–34 more than doubled between 1972 and 1982.

In 1982 the total fertility rate, which indicates the average number of lifetime births per woman if current fertility rates were to continue, was 1.8 births for all women, 1.7 for white women, and 2.2 for black women. For U.S. women as a group, this rate had been below the "replacement" level of 2.1 births per woman since 1972. There were 715,227 births to unmarried women in 1982, 4% more than in 1981. Almost 20% of all births occurred to unmarried women, and the birthrate per 1,000 unmarried women aged 15–44 was 30, the highest ever recorded. In 1982, 12% of white births, 57% of black births, and 51% of all births to adolescents under age 20 were to unmarried mothers.

Although the overall U.S. birthrate was low, the Alan Guttmacher Institute reported that adolescent women in the U.S. had higher rates of pregnancy, abortion, and childbearing than adolescent women in 37 developed countries studied, and the U.S. was the only developed country where adolescent pregnancy (though not fertility) had increased in recent years. Details from six countries showed that in 1981 the pregnancy rate per 1,000 women aged 15–19 was 96 overall and 83 for whites in the U.S., compared with 45 in England and Wales, 44 in Canada, 43 in France, 35 in Sweden, and 14 in The Netherlands.

Recent estimates reported by the Population Reference Bureau put the world birthrate at 27 per 1,000 population in 1985, down from 28 a year earlier. The average was 31 in less developed countries and 15 in more developed countries. Africa had the highest regional rate, 45, and Kenya the highest country rate, 54. The regional rates were 31 in Latin America, 28 in Asia, 15 in North America (Canada and the U.S.), and 13 in Europe. Total fertility rates continued to fall in most parts of the world except sub-Saharan Africa, but slowdowns in the decline were observed in several less developed countries. China reached the replacement level in 1983, but there were reports that it was easing its one-child-per-family policy. The total fertility rate for less developed countries about 1985 was estimated at 4.2, on average, with Kenya highest at 8. For developed countries, the estimated average was 2.

According to the "State of World Population 1985" report of the UN Fund for Population Activities, which focused on women to mark the end of the UN Decade for Women, the total fertility rate in less developed countries would fall only to 3.2 by 2000 and would still be as high as 5.8 in Africa. At the world conference ending the women's decade, held in Nairobi, Kenya, in July 1985, 153 official delegations called on governments to strengthen family planning and maternal and child health programs and to ensure women a free choice in family-size decisions, and they urged efforts to raise the age of entry into marriage "in countries in which this age is still quite low" and to provide adolescents with adequate family planning information and education.

Death Statistics. Provisional estimates put deaths in the U.S. at 2,047,000 in 1984 and the death rate at 8.7 per 1,000 population, 1% more than the rate of 8.6 in 1983. The leading causes of death in 1984 were:

	Causes of death	Estimated rate per 100,000 population
1.	Diseases of the heart	324.4
2.	Malignant neoplasms	191.6
3.	Cerebrovascular diseases	65.6
4.	Accidents and adverse effects	40.1
5.	Chronic obstructive pulmonary diseases	29.8
6.	Pneumonia and influenza	25.0
7.	Diabetes mellitus	15.6
8.	Suicide	12.3
9.	Chronic liver disease and cirrhosis	11.3
10.	Atherosclerosis	10.4
11.	Nephritis, nephrotic syndrome, and nephrosis	8.5
12.	Homicide and legal intervention	8.3
13.	Conditions of the perinatal period	8.0
14.	Septicemia	6.4
15.	Congenital anomalies	5.6

Heart disease, cancer, and stroke accounted for over two-thirds (67.1%) of all deaths. Between 1983 and 1984, death rates rose for cancer and declined for heart disease and stroke.

Worldwide, the death rate averaged 11 per 1,000 population, unchanged from the previous two or three years. Death rate declines offset birthrate declines in many less developed countries, so natural increase remained at relatively high levels. In eastern Africa, for example, a death rate of 17 and a birthrate of 48 resulted in an annual increase of 3.1%. At that rate a population would double in 23 years. In Western Europe, by contrast, the death rate was 11 and the birthrate 12, resulting in an annual increase of 0.1%. These countries would take more than 1,000 years to double if this rate continued. Deaths exceeded births in Denmark and East and West Germany.

Infant Mortality. The infant mortality rate in the U.S. in 1984 was the lowest ever recorded: 10.6 deaths of infants under one year per 1,000 live births. Detailed data for 1982 showed that the mortality rate for black infants was almost twice that of white infants, as it had been 20 years earlier.

Recent estimates put infant mortality rates at 81 per 1,000 live births worldwide, 18 in more developed countries and 90 in less developed countries—all lower than previous estimates. The rates were lowest in Finland (6), Japan (6.2), Sweden (7), and Iceland (7.1). The rate for Africa, although declining, remained regionally the highest at 119.

Life Expectancy. Average life expectancy in the U.S. in 1984 was the same as the record high set in 1983—an estimated 74.7 years for the total population. New highs were recorded in 1984 for white women (78.8 years), white men (71.8), and black men (65.5). Life expectancy for black women declined slightly, from 74 to 73.7.

Worldwide, life expectancy was estimated at 62 years, a slight improvement over recent years, but there was still a gap of 15 years between the estimated average for less

developed countries (58 years) and that of more developed countries (73). Japan claimed to have set a world record with a life expectancy of 80.18 years for girls born in 1984, the first time the 80-year mark had been topped by so large a major population group. Japan also claimed the highest rate for males born in 1984, 74.54 years. The UN reported that life expectancy remained higher for females than for males in all regions of the world except southern Asia. Africa had the lowest life expectancy (50 years).

Marriage and Divorce Statistics. The number of marriages in the U.S. rose 2%, from an estimated 2,444,000 in 1983 to a record 2,487,000 in 1984. Because population also increased, the marriage rate per 1,000 population was the same in both years, 10.5. The median age at first marriage in 1982 was 22.3 for brides and 24.1 for grooms, compared with 20.6 and 22.5, respectively, in 1970. About 45% of marriages in 1982 were remarriages for one or both partners, up from 31% in 1970.

The number of divorces in the U.S. in 1984, 1,155,000, marked the third consecutive annual decline since the historic high of 1,213,000 in 1981. The divorce rate of 4.9 per 1,000 population in 1984 was the lowest since 1975. Final figures for 1982 showed that the median duration of marriages ending in divorce was seven years. The number of children involved in divorce declined from 1,180,000 in 1981 to 1,108,000 in 1982.

Surveys. Findings reported by the National Center for Health Statistics from the latest U.S. national fertility survey revealed that in 1982 contraception was used by 55% of all U.S. women aged 15–44, including 68% of currently married women, 54% of previously married women, and 35% of never-married women. Sterilization was the leading contraceptive method, used by 33% of all who practiced some form of contraception (22% female sterilization; 11% male sterilization), followed by the pill (29%).

The World Fertility Survey of 1972–84 completed its program in 42 less developed countries with publication of several country reports from sub-Saharan Africa. In seven of ten sub-Saharan African countries surveyed, fertility had increased in the 15 to 20 years before the surveys (conducted in the late 1970s and early 1980s). The proportion of married women using contraception ranged from 1% in Ivory Coast and Mauritania to 10% in Ghana. Overall, the average number of children the women said they would like to have was eight.   (JEAN VAN DER TAK)

See also World Data.

INTERNATIONAL MIGRATION

The determination of the governments of the richer countries to control immigration from the poorer ones remained unshaken during 1984–85. In France and West Germany immigration restriction was reinforced by offers of money to encourage unwanted foreign workers and their families to return to their countries of origin. These policies were accompanied by increasing levels of anti-immigrant agitation, notably in the French right-wing press.

In Britain the Commission for Racial Equality (CRE) reported that immigration policy placed an "excessive" emphasis on "detecting and preventing evasion and abuse." This overrode the "interests and welfare of those with a rightful claim to come to the U.K." and exacted "an unacceptable cost to genuine families and to race relations generally." These conclusions were given added weight by the leak of a confidential Home Office briefing to ministers, which stated that long lines of people claiming a legal right to enter Britain from the Indian subcontinent were maintained deliberately to regulate numbers. The number of clearance officers dealing with the demand for entry was "the primary regulator of the number of husbands, wives, children, and male fiancés admitted from the Indian sub-

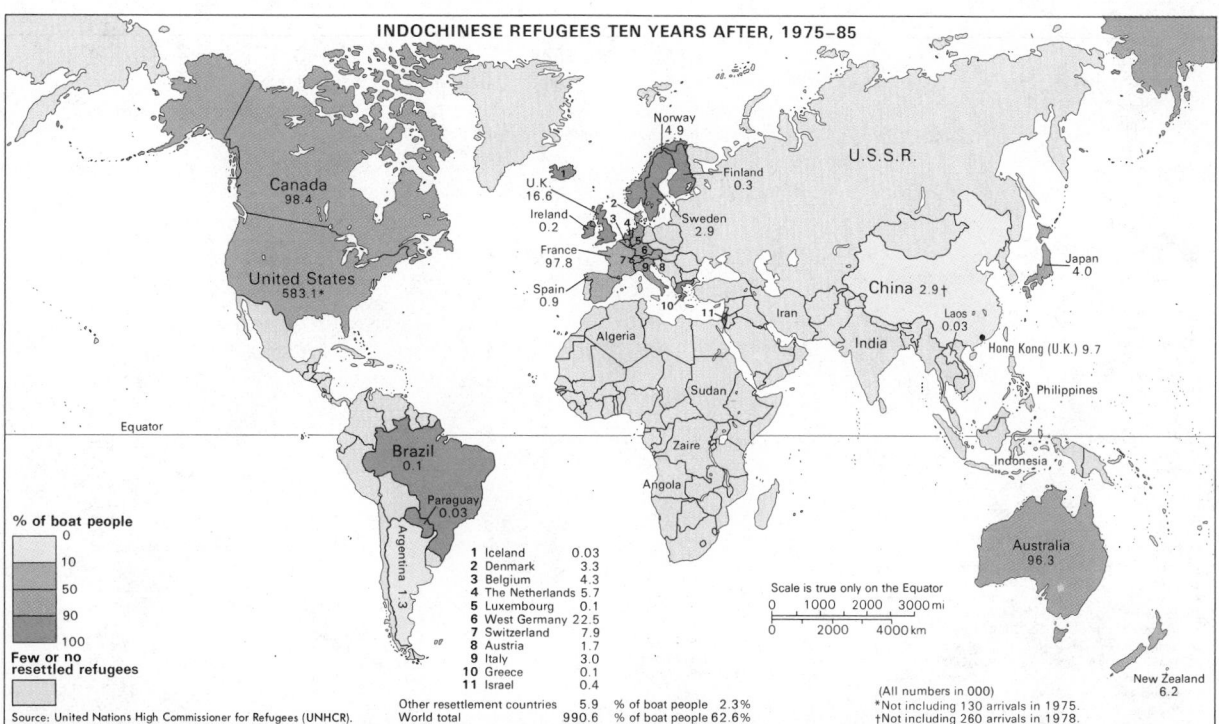

The plight of Indochinese refugees since 1975, and the tragedy of Vietnamese boat people in particular, prompted an agreement in May 1979 between the UNHCR and the Socialist Republic of Vietnam to establish the Orderly Departure Program (ODP). With the implementation of the ODP, aided by the Intergovernmental Committee for Migration (ICM), the plan overcame controversy and a painfully slow start. By 1985 the ODP had successfully resettled a significant number of refugees. In spite of the ODP, however, the influx of boat people in Hong Kong, Thailand, Indonesia, the Philippines, and Singapore continued, growing from a trickle in 1975 to the hundreds of thousands in 1985.

continent in any one year." This led to waiting times in 1984 of 22 months for those applying from Bangladesh, 11 months for Pakistanis, and 12 months for Indians. As a result, there were 19,400 women and children in the subcontinent waiting to join family members already in Britain.

The number of immigrants allowed to settle in the U.K. in 1984—51,000—was the lowest since statistics were first compiled in 1962 and 2,500 below the 1983 figure. The number of people accepted from the New Commonwealth (nonwhite Commonwealth) and Pakistan fell for the eighth successive year to 24,800—2,750 fewer than in 1983. The refusal rate for applicants from the Indian subcontinent was one in three.

British immigration rules were again declared unlawful in a unanimous ruling by the European Court of Human Rights on May 28, 1985. The court found that the rules introduced by the Conservative government in 1980, which denied to foreign women with full residency rights in the U.K. the right to bring in their husbands or fiancés (a right allowed to men), violated Art. 13 of the European Convention on Human Rights because they discriminated against women. The British government responded to the court's ruling on July 10 by amending the restrictions on entry to include foreign wives and fiancées, thus ending sex discrimination but extending the already long waiting lists for entry certificates. These applications would be considered as nonpriority cases, and the applicants would have to prove that "immigration is not the primary purpose of the marriage." In the past this requirement had led to a rejection rate of 45% of husbands and fiancés from the Indian subcontinent, and it was feared that wives and fiancées would also have problems in this area.

Chris Hurford, the Australian minister for immigration and ethnic affairs, announced on June 3 a series of changes in Australian immigration policy to take effect on July 1.

The number of immigrants targeted to settle in Australia in 1985–86 was increased to 84,000 from the 80,000 targeted for 1984–85; this was a significant increase from the 70,000 expected to be granted permanent residence in 1984–85. A major feature of the new program was a doubling in admissions of migrants with business and professional skills—for example, nurses—from the estimated 9,000 visas issued in 1984–85 to a target of 18,500.

In the U.S. there was continuing controversy over immigration, particularly from the Western Hemisphere and Asia, and an increase in violence directed against Asian immigrants. During the 1985 legislative session, Congress debated the Simpson-Rodino bill, which represented another attempt to pass a comprehensive immigration statute. On September 19 the Senate passed the immigration bill, which included an amendment establishing a "guest worker" program allowing up to 350,000 aliens into the U.S. to harvest perishable fruit and vegetable crops, on the grounds that there was a shortage of domestic farm workers. This argument was challenged in testimony by Dolores Huerta, vice-president of the United Farm Workers, who pointed out that more than 14% of domestic farm workers were unemployed—twice the national unemployment rate.

Refugees from Central America and their supporters continued to protest the U.S. administration's refusal to grant political asylum to Salvadoran and Guatemalan refugees; the rate for Salvadorans was 3% of those applying. Refugees at the El Centro detention camp in California carried out a hunger strike in protest against mistreatment and U.S. immigration policy, beginning on Memorial Day, May 27, and ending on June 4. Lawyers acting for refugee children won a legal victory in a Los Angeles federal court when, on September 20, U.S. District Judge Edward Rafeedie ruled that deporting minors without allowing them to contact a parent, relation, friend, or lawyer was unconstitutional. (*See* Sidebar.)   (LOUIS KUSHNICK)

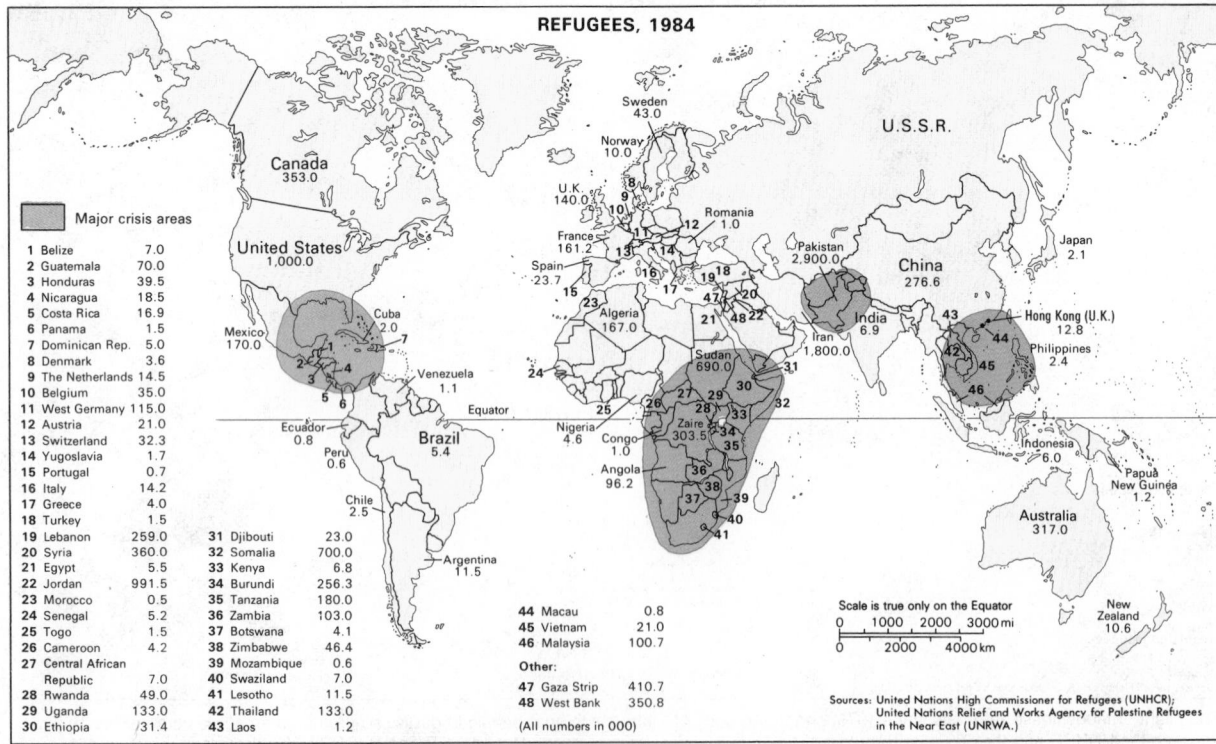

Refugees covered by the UNHCR and the UNRWA mandates numbered an estimated ten million people in 1984. Standards of treatment and of protection of refugees varied widely; while in some areas prospects for repatriation or integration into host societies were improving, in others camps were frequently under threat of military attack.

The Sanctuary Movement

On Oct. 22, 1985, 11 clergy and laity, indicted on more than 50 felony counts of conspiracy, smuggling and transportation, concealing, harbouring, and shielding, as well as encouraging the entry of illegal aliens into the U.S., went on trial in federal court in Tucson, Ariz. There had been two prior court proceedings against activists of the Sanctuary Movement, but it was the Tucson case that attracted national attention to Sanctuary's efforts to assist refugees from El Salvador and Guatemala in finding a haven in the United States.

The number of undocumented Salvadorans and Guatemalans in the U.S. was unknown but, whatever the actual figures, the reach of the Sanctuary Movement was limited to a small fraction of them. However, its impact far exceeded its scope, as reflected in the endorsements it received from national religious bodies or their affiliates. A denominational breakdown of Declared Sanctuaries as of Dec. 1, 1985, prepared by the Chicago Religious Task Force on Central America, listed 259 church facilities, of which 44 were Roman Catholic, 43 under Quaker auspices, 40 Unitarian/Universalist, 26 Presbyterian, 15 Jewish, 13 United Church of Christ, 11 Lutheran, 11 Methodist, and 10 Mennonite. They were located in 33 states, with the heaviest concentration (98) in California.

Officially, the movement began on March 24, 1982, when the Southside Presbyterian Church of Tucson declared itself a Public Witness Sanctuary and so advised the Immigration and Naturalization Service. Clandestine transport of refugees across the Mexican border had been going on since 1981. By moving into the open, Sanctuary meant to publicize its work, challenge the administration, and, as was freely acknowledged, influence U.S. policy in Central America. The Justice Department at first refrained from entering churches to search for illegal aliens. It was unclear why this policy was abandoned or why undercover agents and informers were infiltrated into the movement, since its activities were quite open.

In practice, the Sanctuary Movement did not reach out to exiles from all of Central America but only to those from El Salvador and Guatemala. The position of the government was that, with a few exceptions, the Salvadorans and Guatemalans entering from Mexico were economic migrants rather than political refugees, victims not of persecution but of poverty. And as economic migrants they could not be fitted into the legal guidelines controlling the granting of asylum. Echoing the finding of the UN High Commissioner for Refugees that some people who might not meet the definition of the UN Convention on Refugees were leaving their countries of origin to escape severe internal upheavals or armed conflict and, therefore, should not be returned to areas where they might be exposed to danger, the Sanctuary Movement advocated the granting of extended voluntary departure (EVD) to Salvadorans and Guatemalans. EVD is an administrative remedy previously granted to nationals of several countries who were permitted to remain and work in the U.S. until conditions in their home countries returned to normal.

The Sanctuary Movement did not admit or accept the consequences of deliberate defiance of legal authority. In this sense its stated rationale was not civil disobedience. It nevertheless was within the tradition of conscientious objection to laws perceived as oppressive and in conflict with religious and ethical imperatives.

(CHARLES STERNBERG)

REFUGEES

Hopes that 1985 could be a year for the consolidation of attempts to achieve durable solutions for refugee problems were dashed by the dramatic crisis in Africa, where over a million persons were displaced by unprecedented drought and famine as well as civil and political disturbances. UN High Commissioner for Refugees Poul Hartling had launched his first Africa Emergency Appeal in November 1984 for $8 million, but as UNHCR found itself obliged to organize a vast emergency relief operation—at the expense of its ongoing programs—in the Central African Republic, Djibouti, Ethiopia, Somalia, and The Sudan, successive appeals raised the target by the end of 1985 to $107 million. While the crisis was largely brought under control, it stretched the financial and human resources of UNHCR and had serious repercussions on the organization's ability to push forward with durable solutions in Africa and elsewhere in the world. In addition, contributions made by the international community to the African emergency came at the expense of UNHCR's general programs, with the result that UNHCR entered the last quarter of 1985 in the midst of an unprecedented financial crisis. At the end of October it faced a shortfall of $40 million in its reduced program budget of $319 million.

Elsewhere in Africa, the voluntary repatriation of Ugandans took place from Rwanda, The Sudan, and Zaire, and UNHCR participated in negotiations between Rwanda and Uganda to find a solution to the problem of some 40,000 displaced persons and asylum-seekers who crossed from Uganda to Rwanda in 1982. A major new influx from Angola into Zaire's Shaba Province began in late 1984 and continued throughout the first half of 1985; by midyear UNHCR was assisting over 60,000 refugees in the area. The highlight of the year was the handing over to the government of Tanzania in July of the rural refugee settlement of Mishamo; this marked the achievement of a durable solution to at least one refugee problem in the troubled continent.

In Southeast Asia resettlement remained the main durable solution for refugees in camps, though an increasing number of Indochinese "long-stayers" awaiting resettlement caused concern. The Orderly Departure Program from Vietnam maintained a rate of over 2,000 legal emigrants a month, which made it likely that the milestone of 100,000 orderly departures would be reached by year's end. Progress was also made in the areas of rescue-at-sea and antipiracy activities, though pirate attacks on boat people continued. The Anti-Piracy Program concluded with Thailand was renewed in June.

In Latin America, while progress toward durable solutions was recorded in Mexico and to some extent in Costa Rica, the situation in Honduras remained difficult, particularly for refugees from El Salvador. Efforts to relocate refugees away from the border were planned; similar efforts were successful in Mexico, where some 45% of the 45,000

A Haitian refugee is carried from a Coast Guard plane after he and three others needing medical care were airlifted to Florida from a remote island in The Bahamas; more than 125 refugees had been stranded there for over a week in August.

AP/WIDE WORLD

Guatemalan refugees assisted by UNHCR were relocated in new agricultural settlements. Large numbers of refugees returned to Argentina, Bolivia, and Uruguay following the restoration of democratic forms of government in those countries.

In Europe the increasingly negative public reaction to the arrival of larger numbers of refugees and asylum-seekers from other continents, some of them by irregular means, prompted UNHCR to convene intergovernmental consultations on the problem in May. The discussions at this meeting were widely seen as a useful basis for further action.

The year marked the end of the second term of office of High Commissioner Hartling, who had first been elected to the post in December 1977.   (UNHCR)

This article updates the *Macropædia* article POPULATION.

Publishing

The epidemic of mergers and takeovers that was a feature of 1985 affected publishing as much as any other branch of industry, with many long-established imprints and mastheads changing hands during the year. Among deals too numerous to list, Penguin Books celebrated the 50th anniversary of the publication of the first Penguin paperbacks with the acquisition of five imprints from the International Thomson Organisation, and in its 60th year *The New Yorker* magazine was bought by publishing tycoon Samuel I. Newhouse, Jr.

Freedom of information (*see* Special Report) continued to be a leading issue. It was highlighted by events in South Africa, by the media coverage given to hijacking and other terrorist activities in Lebanon and elsewhere, and, in the U.K., by the trial of an official accused of leaking information to the press (*see* BIOGRAPHIES: *Ponting, Clive*) and moves to ban a television program about Northern Ireland. In France investigative journalism gained prominence with

Le Monde's revelation of the French government's role in the "Greenpeace affair." In Eastern Europe Hungary became the first Warsaw Pact country to allow Western newspapers to be sold to the general public. In the Soviet Union there were indications that under Mikhail Gorbachev freer media criticism of official actions, economic waste, and corruption might be countenanced.

Worldwide, journalists faced increasing danger to life and limb. In 1984, 23 journalists were killed, 81 wounded, 205 jailed, and 50 expelled from the countries in which they were working. In December 1985 a meeting took place in Amsterdam with the aim of devising procedures to protect journalists at risk.

Newspapers. At a ten-minute ceremony in New York City in September, Rupert Murdoch, the Australian-born publisher whose holdings included more than 80 newspapers and magazines on three continents, became a U.S. citizen. Murdoch took that unusual step to complete a deal he had made earlier in the year to purchase six television stations from Metromedia Inc., a major U.S. broadcasting firm. U.S. Federal Communications Commission regulations barred foreigners from holding more than 20% of a broadcast license. At the same time, other FCC rules prohibited simultaneous ownership of a TV station and a daily newspaper in the same city, and so it appeared that Murdoch would have to dispose of two major dailies he owned in cities with Metromedia outlets: the *New York Post* (circulation 930,000) and the *Chicago Sun-Times* (circulation 650,000).

Even before the Metromedia purchase, however, Murdoch had sold another of his newspapers, the *Village Voice* (circulation 164,000), a leftist weekly published in New York City. The buyer was Leonard Stern, president of Hartz Mountain Industries, manufacturers of products for pet animals, and the purchase price was slightly more than $55 million. Murdoch had acquired the paper in 1977, when he bought *New York* and *New West* magazines. Though the publisher would not have been required to dispose of the *Voice* under FCC rules, it was widely assumed that he sold it to raise cash to buy the Metromedia stations.

In any case, the *Village Voice* sale and the prospect that the *Post* and the *Sun-Times* would soon change hands

AP/WIDE WORLD

Tony Heard, editor of the *Cape Times*, leaves Magistrates' Court in Cape Town after being arrested for publishing quotes attributed to Oliver Tambo, a leader of the African National Congress and a "banned" person.

Editorial employees of the *Des Moines Register* await word of the paper's fate in January. The highly regarded *Register* and three small sister papers were bought by the Gannett Co. for $200 million.

AP/WIDE WORLD

made 1985 a busy year for newspaper buying and selling. Much of it was done by a single firm, Gannett Co., the nation's sixth largest media company (86 daily newspapers, 6 television stations, and 14 radio stations). Gannett bought the respected *Des Moines* (Iowa) *Register* (circulation 238,000) and three sister papers for $200 million from the Des Moines Register and Tribune Co. Then Gannett spent $42 million for *Family Weekly,* a magazine supplement inserted in the Sunday editions of more than 300 newspapers that had a combined circulation of more than 12 million. The supplement was subsequently renamed *USA Weekend,* prompting many subscriber newspapers to stop carrying it. The papers objected that the redesigned supplement was too similar to Gannett's three-year-old national daily, *USA Today* (circulation 1,247,000), which many of the papers considered a direct competitor. In perhaps the biggest newspaper transaction of the year, Gannett acquired the Evening News Association, parent firm of the *Detroit News* (circulation 656,000), which had been controlled by the Scripps family for 112 years. The price was $717 million and included lucrative television stations in six cities. Under FCC rules, Gannett could keep all of the stations only if it disposed of several newspapers, most notably the *Tucson* (Ariz.) *Citizen* (circulation 61,000).

Newspaper readership and advertising revenues had another record-breaking year in 1984. Average daily circulation hit an all-time high of 63,081,740 according to the 1985 *Editor & Publisher International Year Book.* That represented an increase of 437,137 over 1983. A preliminary report of the Newspaper Advertising Bureau revealed a 15% increase in advertising dollars spent in newspapers.

An exact comparison with the previous period was difficult to make because 1985 was the first full year in which column inches replaced agate lines in the U.S. as the standard unit for measuring newspaper advertising. An overwhelming majority of U.S. dailies agreed to the change, which was the first such move toward standardization since 1820, when the agate line was first adopted.

Despite the industry's evident prosperity, the number of daily newspapers in the U.S. declined in 1985 to 1,688, a net loss of 13. Nineteen dailies switched to morning publication, bringing the total of morning papers to 458 and total morning circulation to 35,424,418. The number of evening papers dropped to 1,257, and evening circulation declined to 27,657,322.

In Canada average circulation rose in 1984 by 78,969 copies, or about 1½%, to 5,339,712. Morning circulation increased by 85,014 to 2,574,174, while evening distribution dropped by 6,045 to 2,765,538. The number of dailies declined by one, to 114.

The gold medal for public service, most prestigious of the Pulitzer Prizes, went to the *Fort Worth* (Texas) *Star-Telegram* for a series by its Defense Department reporter, Mark Thompson, about defects in U.S. Army helicopters that had been cited as a cause in 67 crashes and had killed nearly 250 servicemen. The medal was especially gratifying to journalists at the paper, which had been the target of an advertising boycott organized by the Fort Worth-based firm that manufactured the helicopters.

None of the usual Pulitzer-winning papers—the *New York Times,* the *Washington Post,* and the *Wall Street Journal*—won a prize in 1985. Instead, the *Philadelphia Inquirer* and Long Island's *Newsday* each took home two Pulitzers. In addition, Jon Franklin of the *Baltimore* (Md.) *Evening Sun* received an award in the newly created category of explanatory journalism for his seven-part series on molecular psychiatry. Alice Steinbach of the *Baltimore Sun,* the *Evening Sun*'s sister paper, won a Pulitzer for feature writing. Thomas Knudson of the *Des Moines Register* was cited for a six-part series on the occupational hazards of farming, while Lucy Morgan and Jack Reed of the *St. Petersburg* (Fla.) *Times* won a prize for their investigation of alleged corruption in a local sheriff's office.

In other Pulitzer awards Jeff MacNelly, political cartoonist for the *Chicago Tribune,* received his third prize; Studs Terkel was cited for his nonfiction book *"The Good War": An Oral History of World War Two;* Alison Lurie won a prize for her novel *Foreign Affairs;* and *Sunday in the Park with George,* with music by Stephen Sondheim and book by James Lapine, was awarded the Pulitzer for drama.

(DONALD MORRISON)

In the last quarter of 1985 ownership of 5 of Britain's 17 national newspaper titles changed hands, the staff on three others agreed to cuts of up to one-third in manpower levels, and a long-awaited change in printing union attitudes to the less labour-intensive new technologies seemed well under way. One of the most important catalysts in this ferment of change was the arrival on the national newspaper scene of Eddie Shah, publisher of a small chain of free newspapers in northwestern England. He had first come to prominence in 1983 by means of a long industrial confrontation and legal battle with the printing union, the National Graphical Association, that had ended with the union's being heavily fined for contempt of court under new trade union legislation. Early in 1985 Shah announced his intention of setting up a new national daily newspaper, which by printing outside London would escape the union rules on manpower and use of electronic technology that had made the "Fleet Street" nationals so unprofitable and slow to change. This gave existing owners both reason and excuse for speeding technological change and forced the printing and journalists' unions to negotiate seriously with national newspapers over the changes of method already being accepted in the regional and local press.

Each publisher took a different approach, but most involved investing in new production facilities away from the

traditional central London area of Fleet Street. The most ambitious of these plans ended the reign, with dramatic swiftness, of one of the oldest remaining Fleet Street proprietors, the Berry family, who in December had to yield a controlling interest in the Telegraph group to a newcomer, Canadian businessman and publisher (through his Argus group) Conrad Black. The *Daily Telegraph,* although by far the biggest-selling and most profitable of the serious dailies, with a circulation of about 1.2 million, had been under pressure during the past five years from an aging readership profile, slipping sales, and newly aggressive competition from *The Times* under Rupert Murdoch's ownership. In June Lord Hartwell, 74-year-old chairman and editor in chief of the group, announced a bold and massive plan to build a new printing centre in the rejuvenated East London dockland, at a capital cost of £105 million. Most of the funding would come from banks and institutions, but for the final £10 million, a 14% share, Hartwell was introduced to Black, who came in on condition that he would have first right to any future share disposals. By October it was clear that the current financial position of the *Daily Telegraph* and its sister *Sunday Telegraph* was straitened and that more capital was needed; Black, exercising his option, put in an additional £20 million and achieved control.

The Guardian, which had shared printing facilities in London with *The Times,* was building its own centre on the Isle of Dogs in London's East End. Murdoch's News Group sought to activate its Wapping centre, which had been mothballed for several years because of a failure to agree on terms with the unions, by announcing another new title, the *London Post,* planned as an evening paper but with 24-hour capacity. The *London Post* had as editorial director Charles Wilson, but he returned to *The Times* in November, as editor, on the death of Charles Douglas-Home (*see* OBITUARIES).

The other change of ownership was to be seen in the context of the international wave of takeovers and mergers. United Newspapers, primarily publishers of British regional newspapers (*The Yorkshire Post*) and magazines (*Punch*), had under a new chief executive, David Stevens, already shown its ambitions with the purchase of a U.S. publishing chain (Miller Freeman Publications), but in 1985 it bid to take over Fleet Holdings (the *Daily Express, Sunday Express, Daily Star,* and Morgan-Grampian magazines), run by Lord Matthews since he had masterminded the Trafalgar House buyout of Lord Beaverbrook's heirs seven years earlier. A bitter battle left Matthews in retirement and Stevens in Fleet Street.

Robert Maxwell continued his own style of management, threatening to close down Mirror Group Newspapers, which he bought in 1984, if massive economies were not achieved. In December he announced that the union had agreed that as many as 2,000 jobs would be eliminated, one-third of the total, but the details remained unclear. This was seen as yet another sign of the urgency with which the newspaper industry as a whole was facing the need for change.

In France *Le Monde,* having reached new depths of financial and editorial crisis at the end of 1984, entered 1985 with a new editor in chief and director, André Fontaine (*see* BIOGRAPHIES). Fontaine's rescue plan involved cutting jobs by one-sixth, selling the prestigious building near L'Opéra, and reducing the number of pages in each issue. During the year sales and advertising both rose; a F 22 million trading loss in 1984 became a F 10 million profit, debts were wiped out, and, in a notable coup, in December a F 15 million stock offer to readers was subscribed within ten days.

There were many instances during the year of tighter controls and pressures on the media and journalists. In South Africa Anthony Heard, editor of the *Cape Times,* was arrested after publishing an interview with Oliver Tambo, "banned" president of the African National Congress, in November. Heard faced a maximum three-year prison sentence if convicted under the Internal Security Act. South Africa's leading liberal newspaper, the 83-year-old *Rand Daily Mail,* closed in April. (PETER FIDDICK)

Magazines. Court cases dominated magazine news during the year. In 1979 *The Nation* had published an article based on the memoirs of former U.S. Pres. Gerald Ford, which were copyrighted by the book publisher Harper & Rowe. In 1985 the U.S. Supreme Court ruled that *The Nation* had infringed the copyright law, thus overturning a Court of Appeals ruling that the use by *The Nation* of 300 words from the memoirs constituted "fair use." *The Nation* claimed that public officials had no right to withhold public information for profit, but the court said that what was being protected was Ford's own personal viewpoint.

Time scored only a partial victory over Gen. Ariel Sharon. The end of the trial found that the magazine was guilty of "false and defamatory" accusations against the former defense minister of Israel but was innocent of libel. Soon after General Sharon lost his $50 million libel suit, a second general, William Westmoreland, dropped his $120 million suit against CBS.

The thousands of investment newsletters apparently need not worry about libel. Where no malice is intended, a newsletter may advise someone not to invest in a particular stock, bond, or other financial instrument. This was the ruling by a federal judge, who said that negative ratings by the *Hulbert Financial Digest* were not libelous.

The continuing headache of policing fair use of journal material took another turn in 1985 when six journal publishers brought a class action suit against Texaco Inc. The lawsuit was an effort to ensure payment to the publishers through the Copyright Clearance Center. Established in 1978, the Center represented more than 1,000 publishers

(continued on page 357)

Ariel Sharon speaks to reporters outside the U.S. Federal District Court Building in New York City after a jury found that *Time* magazine had published false and defamatory statements about him.

Freedom of Information

BY HAROLD EVANS

Tension between government and press is a healthy commonplace in all the political democracies. Terrorism has given it a new twist. Both the British and U.S. governments accuse television of sustaining terrorists with the oxygen of publicity. In the U.S. the Reagan administration condemned the television interviewing of American hostages held by Lebanese Shi'ah in Beirut in 1985 as "terribly harmful" in the negotiations. In Britain shortly afterward, Prime Minister Margaret Thatcher's government intimidated the lay governors of the BBC into banning a documentary program featuring a leader of the Irish Republican Army.

The issues of public policy that provoke charges of irresponsibility and countercharges of censorship are similar in all the political democracies, but the grounds of the debate, and the consequences of it, are very different. The difference is notable between the U.S. and the two European countries most closely associated with the early republic, Britain and France. It is greatest between the U.S. and Britain, which are thought to share a common heritage of law and language.

Free Debate Versus Free Inquiry. Europeans go to the barricades for the right to free speech. Americans talk more often of "the right to know." The insufficiently appreciated distinction between these two ideas is at the heart of the matter. It is a distinction between opinion and fact. The coercive power of the state and the law is seldom brought to bear against the utterance of an opinion. The teachings of Milton, Locke, and Mill are embedded in everyone's consciousness. In Britain a beaming policeman protects speakers at Hyde Park Corner, within earshot of Buckingham Palace, who incite the violent overthrow of the monarchy. In the U.S. the lawns opposite the White House are frequently ablaze with banners denouncing the administration. Nothing is sacred in Voltaire's France; debate there is more catholic than in the U.S., where Constitution, church, and capitalism are secure from satire. But this tolerant convergence on free speech does not apply to free inquiry. U.S. law obliges government agencies to disclose official information. The law of Britain punishes disclosure. The French leave it to custom and practice, which is usually just as restrictive.

The differences are apparent at once in the nomenclature. The relevant statute in the U.S. is the Freedom of Information (FOI) Act; in Britain it is the Official Secrets Act. The Freedom of Information Act, 20 years old in 1986, lays it down that all records in the possession of the executive branch of the federal government must be provided to anyone on request unless they can be withheld

by one or more of nine specific tests (concerning mainly national defense, privacy, privileged or confidential trade secrets, or the regulation of financial institutions). The Official Secrets Act, betraying its origins as a weapon against espionage in World War I, threatens jail or heavy fine for officials who give information without approval and for receivers of it.

In two recent cases the British prosecuted officials for revealing information that was politically embarrassing but, on the government's own admission, no threat to national security. A junior clerk in the Ministry of Defence was jailed for six months for passing a document to *The Guardian* newspaper discussing how the government proposed to handle public relations for the deployment of cruise missiles. A senior civil servant (*see* BIOGRAPHIES: *Ponting, Clive*) was prosecuted for sending a document to a member of Parliament that showed how Parliament had been deceived by ministers during the Falklands war about the sinking of the Argentine cruiser *General Belgrano.* The jury acquitted, though the judge instructed the jury to convict on the grounds that the interests of the state and of the government of the day are one and the same.

The authoritarian overtones of this view were widely criticized, but the British political and legal establishment places high value on confidentiality and secrecy in government and business. There has been talk about freedom of information legislation since the Fulton Report in the '60s, through the Franks Report, Labour manifesto promises, draft Civil Service codes, private members' bills, and an abandoned Conservative Party measure entitled *The Protection* (author's italics) *of Official Information Bill;* a new all-party campaign for a freedom of information act was launched in 1982. All these efforts have foundered on two things: a genuine belief in Lord Salisbury's dictum that government must be private to be good; and an anxiety to do nothing to disturb the paramountcy of Parliament. Even the sovereign body of Parliament is restricted in the right to know. Successive administrations have refused to answer questions from members of Parliament on rent for government offices, telephone tapping, Cabinet committees, forecasts of future trends in incomes, the names of nonmedicinal and cosmetic products containing hexachlorophene, and many more such subjects remote from any question of national security.

Opinion Versus Information. The roots of the striking difference between Britain and the U.S. go back further than 1966, for the U.S. Freedom of Information Act is no more than a legislative embodiment of the prescription of James Madison: "A people who mean to be their own governors, must arm themselves with the power knowledge gives. A popular government without popular information or the means of acquiring it, is but a prologue to a farce or a tragedy or both." This was the logic of the First Amendment to the Constitution that "Congress shall make no law . . . abridging the freedom of speech, *or of the press*" (author's italics). The emphasis on popular sovereignty was, of course, a reaction to the suppressions of the British crown. In Britain itself there was nothing to disturb the assumption of the classical philosophers that free speech was underpinned by a free flow of facts.

The assumption that the facts on which to base an opinion were available was tolerable in a society with very small conglomerations of power and a ruling elite, certainly as tolerable as the assumption of the classical economists that there was a free flow of goods and services in a perfect market. But in Britain the citizen's access to knowledge failed to keep pace with the vast expansion of state and corporate power. Two attitudes seem to underlie the re-

Editor of The Sunday Times *(1963–66) and* The Times *(1981–82) of London, Harold Evans is currently editorial director of* U.S. News and World Report, *Washington, D.C. The recipient of several awards for journalism, he has written a number of books on newspaper publishing, including* Good Times, Bad Times.

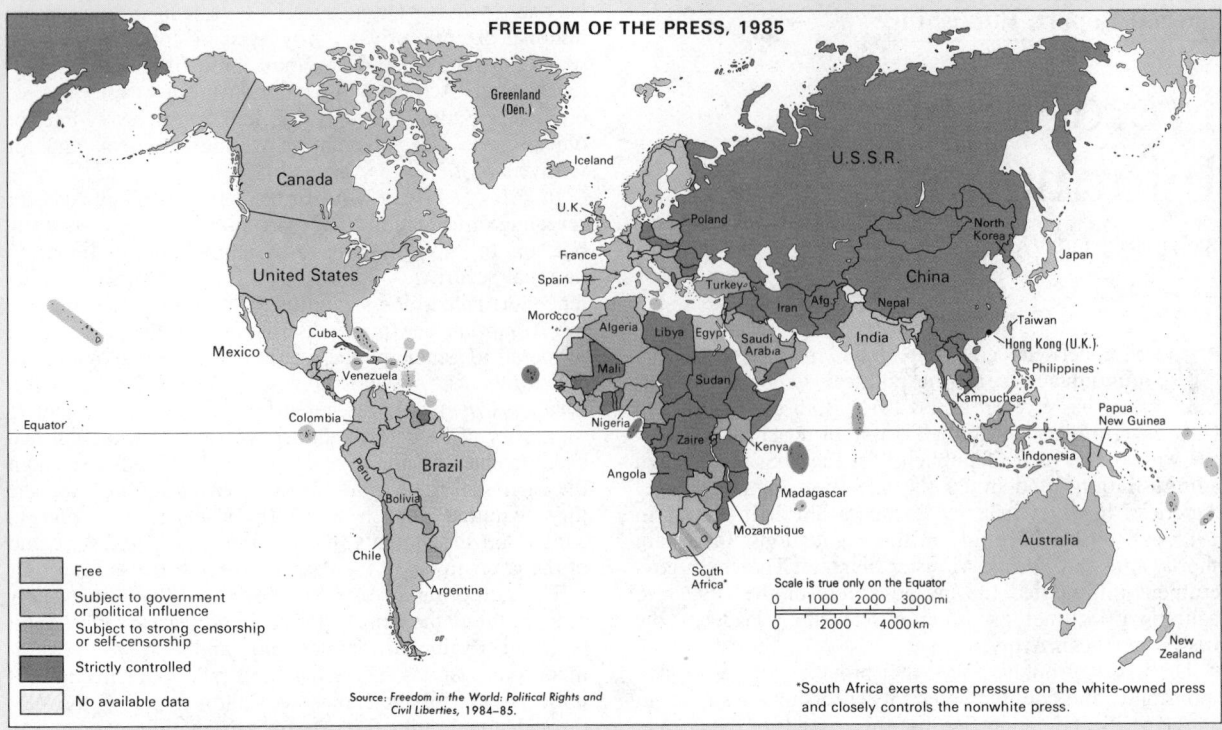

Free

Subject to government
or political influence

Subject to strong censorship
or self-censorship

Strictly controlled

No available data

Source: *Freedom in the World: Political Rights and
Civil Liberties, 1984–85.*

Scale is true only on the Equator

0   1000   2000   3000 mi

0   2000   4000 km

*South Africa exerts some pressure on the white-owned press
and closely controls the nonwhite press.

While some countries such as Argentina moved toward a free press, worldwide the press was for the most part subjected to varying degrees of governmentally or politically induced censorship. The independence of the print medium and its relationship to the respective country's government formed the basis for assessing freedom of the press on a country-by-country basis.

striction of freedom of information. First, information is frequently referred to by judges and politicians as if it were the property of the government and not of the people. This lends substance to Thomas Jefferson's conviction that in Britain the Tory or Norman concept of rights is dominant: that they are grants from the crown, as distinct from the Whig or Saxon concept that they are natural to the people and the crown has no powers except those expressly granted. Second, in cases where free publication has been challenged, the British courts have fallen back on common law precedents rooted in the rights of property. There is no Bill of Rights to put personal rights into the balance, and a Bill of Rights is rejected on the grounds that it would limit the supremacy of Parliament.

The Right to Know.   The First Amendment has been the principal bulwark against censorship in the U.S., but the right to publish is not the same as access to official information, a concept that seems to have originated in Scandinavia. Though the principle of freedom of information has long been accepted in the U.S., it took many years of campaigning by press, lawyers, and members of Congress to gain the Freedom of Information Act. Before 1966 the American citizen had to prove his right to look at governmental records. The revolution of the Freedom of Information Act was to shift the burden of proof from the individual to the government. Congress enacted a series of amendments in 1974 that encouraged even more disclosure. Inquiries have run around 150,000 a year. They have uncovered an astonishing diversity of information of public importance, from illegal FBI harassment of domestic political groups to congressional and executive abuse of travel funds. As a result of news reports based on FOI information, legislation and court rulings have brought about the overhaul of the nursing home industry, the removal of unsafe drugs from market shelves, and a closer examination of defense contracting.

The Reagan administration has sought to reverse this process, by seeking lifetime secrecy pledges from government employees, by lobbying in Congress for amendment of the act, and by discretionary executive action that has made exploitation of the act much more costly and time-consuming. Delays of 6 to 9 months have become common, 14 months with the CIA. The federal courts, with an increasing number of Reagan appointees, also have cut down on the availability of information. Recent decisions have allowed officials to remove records from agency files, thereby precluding access under the act; permitted the director of the CIA to protect any intelligence source or method without any showing of harm to national security; and made all documents that are privileged in civil litigation unavailable under FOI. A comprehensive package of 40 amendments has been proposed by Sen. Orrin Hatch (Rep., Utah), principally on the grounds of enabling business to protect its commercial secrets and preventing access by organized crime. The Reporters' Committee for the Freedom of the Press in Washington says the package will increase delays and costs still further.

In its efforts to curb the flow of information, the philosophical approach of the Reagan administration, contrary to the American tradition, is that government information is government property. There is an echo of the dominant attitude in Britain and France (though not in Denmark or Sweden, or in Canada, Australia, and New Zealand, where Conservative administrations have brought in freedom of information legislation). The Reagan campaign has had limited success, but the proven value of openness, the robustness of the judiciary, the existence of the First Amendment, and the spirit of the country seem likely to sustain the U.S. as the most open of the democracies, convinced still, in the words of Justice Louis Brandeis, that "sunlight is the best of disinfectants and electric light the most efficient policeman."

(continued from page 354)

and some 10,000 copyrighted scientific and technical journals. Users paid for photocopies through the Center.

Considered by many to be the world's best general magazine, *The New Yorker* had its 60 years of independence cut short when it was bought in 1985 by Samuel I. Newhouse, Jr., for $142 million. The arbiter of good taste and superior fiction was guaranteed continued freedom by the new owner, and its well-known editor, William Shawn, was retained. Among other major sales was the $362 million purchase of the Ziff-Davis Publishing Co. by CBS. The magazine titles that CBS thus acquired included *Car and Driver, Modern Bride, Stereo Review,* and *Yachting.*

Most magazines reporting to the Audit Bureau of Circulation noted circulation increases for the second half of 1984 and continued gains in 1985. Subscription gains were posted by 65% of the magazines, but 53% reported declines in single-copy (at the newsstand) sales.

In the 1985 National Magazine Awards, *American Heritage* and *The Washingtonian* magazine led the ten winners. *The Washingtonian* won for public service and for an article on medical care. *American Heritage* won for general excellence and the best single-topic issue, on medicine. Among the other winners were *Time* and *American Health* for general excellence, *Texas Monthly* for reporting, and *Life* for photography.

Essence, the first magazine for black women, celebrated its 15th birthday in 1985. With a circulation of more than 800,000, it covered such subjects as fashion, beauty, food, health, and child care from a black perspective.

Among the new entries of the year were *Manhattan, inc.,* the first magazine in the U.S. published expressly for yuppies (young urban professionals). It told those with an income of at least $50,000 how to dress for success and make the right connections. Among the failures during the year was *GEO,* a glossy rival to *National Geographic* and *Smithsonian* brought to the United States in 1979 by a German publisher. After six years it ceased publication because of heavy costs and persistent inability to gain U.S. readers.

For the second year in a row, *McCall's* was the best place for a free-lance writer to place an article. According to a *Writer's Digest* poll, the magazine paid a minimum of $1.25 a word, compared with *Redbook,* which paid a minimum of 25 cents but a maximum of $2. Among other top markets were *Reader's Digest,* the *New York Times Magazine, Travel & Leisure,* and *Sports Afield.*

(WILLIAM A. KATZ)

The British magazine market continued to ride a wave of activity, and several new titles were introduced in 1985. There were some notable failures, too, and the year ended with a clear indication of strain as International Publishing Corp. (IPC) Magazines, the biggest publisher in the market, announced a package of economies including a list of specialist titles to be eliminated or offered for staff buyout. This confirmed the trend in which smaller energetic publishing operations were scoring greater successes than the giant created in the 1960s; one of IPC's new titles, *The Hit,* aimed at the teenage male market, ceased publishing after six weeks.

The main centre of activity continued to be the younger woman. IPC and the D. C. Thomson group launched new titles aimed at teenage girls, *Mizz* and *Etcetera,* respectively. Each made respectable debuts, but the star continued to be East Midlands Allied Press's (EMAP's) *Just Seventeen,* launched in 1983 as a fortnightly with spectacular success and switched to weekly publication in February 1985 without denting its upward sales graph. In September

EMAP introduced *Looks,* aimed at picking up the sister magazine's readers as they grew out of it.

Publishers had been awaiting a decision from official regulatory bodies that had been considering the practice whereby the British Broadcasting Corporation (BBC) and Independent Television (ITV) could claim a copyright on their schedules, thereby protecting their own *Radio Times* (BBC) and *TV Times* (ITV) as the largest and most profitable magazines in the country. Several contenders hoped to have the chance to run an equivalent of the U.S.'s *TV Guide.* However, the networks' copyright was upheld.

She celebrated its 30th anniversary and *The Lady* ("A Journal for Gentlewomen") its 100th, while the 143-year-old *Illustrated London News* was bought from International Thomson Publishing Ltd. by U.S. businessman James Sherwood. A famous French title spread its wings. *Elle,* the Paris-based fashion magazine published by Hachette, introduced English-language editions in the U.S. and the U.K. through a deal with the Murdoch empire.

In West Germany Gerd Heidemann and Konrad Kujau were convicted on charges arising from the 1983 "Hitler Diaries" fraud perpetrated on *Stern* magazine. They received prison sentences of more than four years but were released pending appeal. (PETER FIDDICK)

Books. After posting a broad economic recovery in 1983 and the early months of 1984, U.S. book publishers turned in a mixed performance late in the year that resulted in modest forecasts for the industry's short-term future. The Association of American Publishers estimated total sales for 1984 at $9,120,000,000, a 6.2% increase over the previous year. By comparison, in 1983 the industry achieved a 9.5% increase. Overall bookstore trade sales rose 6.3% to $1.7 billion, compared with a 17% rise in 1983. Sales of children's books rose almost 10% in 1984, but adult hardcovers and mass-market paperbacks made only slight gains—3.2 and 3.8%, respectively. The Book Industry Study Group (BISG), which monitored sales performances month by month, reported erratic figures early in 1985, with the first half of the year showing a 6.6% increase in total industry dollar volume over 1984. School textbook sales posted the largest sales gain—18%—and both adult hardcovers and trade paperbacks were up about 12% for the six-month period; however, mass-market sales declined 3.6% on a 12% drop in units sold. A five-year industry forecast by the U.S. Department of Commerce predicted only 3.5% growth through 1989, while the BISG, covering the same period, drew an even gloomier picture—with the exception of a 10% gain for trade books, no growth at all.

The big publishing conglomerates tended to become

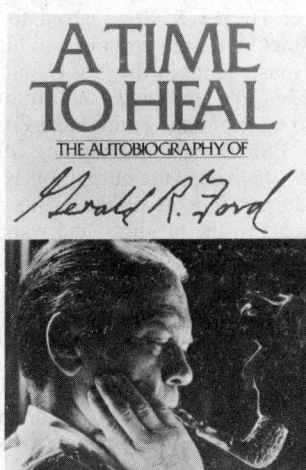

HARPER & ROW

The U.S. Supreme Court ruled that *The Nation* exceeded the bounds of fair use in printing extensive quotations from former president Gerald Ford's memoirs.

even bigger in 1985 as major mergers and acquisitions, a trend of the past 15 years, continued unabated. As the year began, the talk of book publishing was the purchase by Gulf and Western Industries in December 1984 of Prentice-Hall Inc., the nation's leading college textbook publisher, for $718 million. Gulf and Western, which already owned Simon & Schuster, thus became the nation's largest book publisher by a wide margin. (McGraw Hill Inc. had previously been ranked first.) In March Macmillan Inc., which bought the Scribner Book Co. in 1984, vaulted to fifth place among U.S. publishers by acquiring Bobbs-Merrill and six other companies from ITT. One month later Macmillan dissolved the 157-year-old Bobbs-Merrill in the name of business efficiency. Another venerable house, Dial Press, met the same fate when it was absorbed into the Doubleday corporate fold.

Grove Press, an often avant-garde and controversial publisher, was sold in March for $2 million to the Wheatland Corp., headed by Ann Getty, wife of an heir to the Getty oil fortune, and George Weidenfeld, a British publisher. Barney Rosset, Grove's founder and publisher, was to remain at the helm. In June Lord Weidenfeld inaugurated a second Wheatland publishing venture in the U.S., Weidenfeld & Nicholson.

The line separating hardcover and paperback houses, once quite distinct, blurred even further in 1985. New American Library (NAL), a leader in paperbacks, acquired E. P. Dutton to complement its own hardcover imprint started in 1980. The move was part of a trend, born of high auction prices for reprint rights, in which paperback houses bought rights for both the hardcover and softcover editions of a book. The strategy seemed to have had the intended effect; rights auctions were generally lacklustre in 1985. One of the biggest was Knopf's sale of *The Accidental Tourist* by Anne Tyler to Berkley for $962,500.

Paperback publishers were not the only ones to gain by eliminating the middleman. Best-selling authors realized larger profits, since by selling all rights to a single house they no longer had to split paperback revenues with the hardcover publisher. NAL granted the biggest deal of all when it guaranteed Stephen King, who topped the year's fiction lists with two titles, *Skeleton Crew* and *Thinner* (by the pseudonymous Richard Bachman), $10 million for a hardcover/paperback package on two novels due in 1987. Bantam made a similar deal for *Destiny* by the little-known British writer Sally Beauman, paying just over $1 million.

Memoirs and the prospect of memoirs made news repeatedly. Lee Iacocca's *Iacocca* sold more than two million copies in hardcover and shared the top spot on the nonfiction lists with Chuck Yeager's *Yeager*. In September Harper & Row agreed to pay $2 million for David Stockman's remembrance of his years in the Reagan White House. Later in the year Geraldine Ferraro's million-dollar *My Story* appeared, and Simon & Schuster was reported to be negotiating with Fidel Castro for his story.

Publishing's faltering love affair with the computer was not revived. Title output was reported down 43% for 1985; Harper & Row disbanded its software division after two years in the business; and what had been one of the more successful specialty houses in the field, dilithium Press, filed for bankruptcy.

Free-speech guarantees were confirmed in the first test of a new kind of antipornography law. In Indiana a federal district court ruled unconstitutional an Indianapolis ordinance construing pornography as a violation of women's civil rights. Judges in Colorado and Virginia also struck down laws limiting minors' access to pornography.

In an unprecedented case a government effort to bring fraud charges against Antoni Gronowicz, author of *God's Broker*, a suspect biography of Pope John Paul II, was aided by a Court of Appeals ruling that Gronowicz had to obey a subpoena of his notes. The same court earlier had ruled that the author's notes were protected by the First Amendment. An appeal to the Supreme Court was expected.

There was an unexpected development in an antitrust suit brought by the Northern California Booksellers Association against Avon Publishers for granting preferential wholesale discounts to chain stores. As a result of a cost study undertaken to bolster its case—and without waiting for a verdict—Avon dropped 1,742 bookstore accounts that it deemed did too little business to justify the cost of service.

Meanwhile, chain stores were having their own battles over discounting. Waldenbooks, the nation's largest chain, entered the retail-discount wars with its Reader's Market outlets offering 35 and 25% off *New York Times* bestsellers and 15% off other titles. Crown Books responded by raising its discount rates. A February Gallup Poll revealed that 24% of paperbacks and 37% of hardbacks were bought at a discount. (GEORGE BLOOSTON)

Takeovers were the main feature of British book publishing in 1985. Associated Book Publishers bought Routledge & Keegan Paul; Century Publications merged with Hutchinson; Penguin acquired Thomson Books; Longmans took over Pitman; and Macdonald & Evans and Heinemann were absorbed into the new giant Heinemann-Octopus group. The realities of publishing now obviously favoured the big battalions, both in terms of economies of scale and in securing an integrated line from hardcover into paperback rights.

The sales impact of the main literary prizes, and most particularly the Booker-McConnell Prize, was spreading significantly overseas and in 1985 became a subject of interest and promotion in Australia, New Zealand, and North America. It was also gaining ground in Europe, and in 1986 a major Booker promotion was planned for The Netherlands.

The announcement by the U.K. chancellor of the Exchequer in his budget speech that the government had no intention of levying a value-added tax on books was regarded as a major triumph throughout the world book trade. In New Zealand, however, a threatened goods and services tax was almost certain to apply to books. New Zealand publishers and booksellers were deeply concerned with the likely impact on general book sales and were lobbying hard for additional educational budgets to cover the inevitable increased prices. Educational sales in the U.K. continued to suffer from government pressure on local-authority expenditures.

The British government also announced that it intended to introduce a new copyright bill in the 1986–87 parliamentary session. The copyright industries in the U.K. were currently estimated to account for approximately 6% of total U.K. output, and the bill could thus have a major economic impact. Two of the issues that would have to be covered by the new act were refinements to the law relating to computer software and the problem of private copying of works without the permission of the copyright holder—particularly photocopying and audio copying.

Developments with regard to copyright overseas included a revision of Taiwan's copyright law to allow the possibility of the registration of foreign copyrights for protection; the British government processed an Order in Council in November that offered reciprocal recognition to Taiwanese works in the U.K. to make this possible. The

most outstanding copyright event of the year, however, was the long-awaited judgment in the Singapore case, in which it was ruled that the U.K. 1911 act did apply in Singapore. Copyright protection was thus granted in that country to foreign works. Late in 1985 first applications for compulsory reprint rights were made under India's 1984 legislation.

The Frankfurt Book Fair, in its second year in new premises, separated the British and U.S. contingents for the first time. British publishers reported less aisle traffic but far more serious business as a result. Altogether 6,400 publishers from 77 countries exhibited 3,200 titles in an open area of 93,000 sq m (1 million sq ft).

(ANTHONY A. READ)

See also Literature.
This article updates the *Macropædia* article PUBLISHING.

Race Relations

More than 90 church leaders from Belgium, Britain, and The Netherlands signed a declaration in 1985 acknowledging that, in their view, racial prejudice and racist practices were to be found in all parts of Europe and admitting that "the churches have failed to resist this evil adequately." The evidence of continuing racial discrimination and racist violence lent added weight to this declaration. In the U.S., according to the National Urban League, progress made by the black community during the 1960s had peaked in the 1970s and declined since then. On the other hand, international condemnation of apartheid—institutionalized racism—in South Africa gathered force during the year; but some Western governments, notably that of the U.K., refrained from bringing to bear on South Africa the economic pressure called for by apartheid's most vocal opponents. (*See* WORLD AFFAIRS [Africa South of the Sahara]: *South Africa:* Special Report.)

Great Britain. The Policy Studies Institute found that at least one-third of employers discriminated against black job applicants, the same proportion found in a previous study in 1974. John Cordrey of the Commission for Racial

Leading a 20th anniversary commemoration of the celebrated march from Selma to Montgomery, Alabama, were the Rev. Jesse Jackson (left) and the Rev. Joseph Lowery (right); Coretta Scott King, widow of the 1965 march's leader, was also present.

Equality (CRE) said that throughout the country, "The whole of the recruitment situation . . . is riddled with discrimination." The CRE found that Asians were twice as likely to be refused a mortgage as were whites, and a number of studies on public housing documented racist practices. Studies of the government's Youth Training Scheme found extensive discrimination against black youths. A number of establishment figures, including judges and the president of the Royal College of Physicians, reported racial discrimination in the legal and medical professions. The report of the committee headed by Lord Swann, on the education of ethnic minority children, found racism to be a major factor in the poor showing of black and Asian pupils. (*See* EDUCATION: Sidebar.) In the face of this evidence and of specific policy recommendations, the government continued its opposition to strengthening the enforcement powers of the CRE, to the establishment of affirmative-action and contract-compliance procedures, and to increased expenditures.

In September and October 1985 major outbreaks of violence took place in a number of British cities with large nonwhite communities: the Handsworth district of Birmingham; Toxteth in Liverpool; and Brixton, Peckham, and Tottenham in London. All of these areas suffered from high levels of unemployment, urban blight, and homelessness. Relations with the police had deteriorated in the wake of charges of lack of police protection of the black communities against an increasing incidence of racist violence, combined with what was seen as an increasing level of victimization by the police. Each of the riots was triggered by a police-community interaction, including the shooting of a black woman in a dawn raid on her home by police in Brixton and the death of another black woman (apparently of a heart attack) after a police search of her home in Tottenham. After the Brixton violence nine Brixton Anglican priests issued a public statement in which they declared: "We deplore the conditions of life which have persisted and worsened in Brixton since the 1981 riots. We deplore the fact that no effective steps have been taken by the government in the past four years to alleviate unemployment."

Continental Western Europe. In November an all-party committee of the European Parliament reported a rise of racism and neofascism throughout Europe. The evidence cited for this conclusion included instances of violence against members of ethnic minorities, the revival of "scientific" racist theories, and growing support for ultraright and neofascist political parties.

In France the National Front (NF) gained 10.4% of the vote in constituencies in which its candidates campaigned in the first round of the March 1985 cantonal elections. They gained their highest votes in Toulon (31%), Marseille (30%), Cannes (26%), and Seine St. Denis (17%). Pres. François Mitterrand's suggestion in April that France's four million immigrants be given the right to vote in local elections was denounced by the NF and other opposition parties.

The increase in racist violence against "guest workers" in Denmark was such that Queen Margrethe referred to the problem directly in her 1985 New Year speech. In Geneva a right-wing group, the Vigilance Party, based its campaign on the repatriation of foreign workers and won 19 seats in the cantonal parliament in the October 1985 elections, tying for first with the Liberals.

South Africa. The South African Institute of Race Relations calculated in November 1985 that 834 people had died in racial violence in the 14 months since the arrests on charges of treason of the leaders of the United Demo-

Blazing automobiles block an intersection in the Brixton district of London during the October riots there.

T. STODDART—GAMMA/LIAISON

cratic Front in September 1984. On July 21, 1985, the South African government imposed a state of emergency that led to a doubling of the number of deaths. Police and army activity accounted for more than 50% of the deaths. More than 6,000 antiapartheid activists had been interned without trial by mid-October 1985.

Pres. P. W. Botha's control over the white minority was challenged in 1985 on a number of fronts. Large numbers of white students took part in demonstrations against the state of emergency and following the hanging of the black activist and poet Benjamin Moloise, convicted of complicity in the 1982 murder of a policeman, on October 18. Seven of South Africa's leading white businessmen and newspaper editors defied President Botha and met with the leaders of the outlawed African National Congress (ANC) in Zambia on September 13. The government subsequently had to withdraw the passports of a number of white student and church leaders to prevent them from meeting with ANC leaders. On November 4 the *Cape Times* published an interview with ANC leader Oliver Tambo (*see* BIOGRAPHIES) despite the risk of prosecution and imprisonment of its editor, Tony Heard. Along with the protests, however, there was an increase of more than 200% in support for two ultraright parties in the October "mini election" in five constituencies. In Sasolburg the Herstigte Nasionale Party (HNP) won its first parliamentary seat ever on a platform of opposition to all reforms and concessions to the country's black majority. Louis Stofberg, the Sasolburg victor and general secretary of the HNP, declared that his victory "heralded the resurrection of the Afrikaner nation as a free and independent entity."

Botha's reforms had apparently frightened some sections of white Afrikanerdom, but he continued to resist demands for a fundamental overthrow of apartheid, legalization of the ANC, and the release of Nelson Mandela (*see* BIOGRAPHIES) and other ANC leaders from prison. In a major address in August he declared that he "could not accept the principle of one man, one vote. That would lead to the domination of one [race] over the others." Faced with an increasingly serious sanctions campaign throughout the world, a sharp drop in the value of the rand and a major threat to the South African banking system, and an increasingly determined militant African majority, Botha announced on November 1 the prohibition of the televising, photographing, recording, or even drawing of conflict situations in the 38 magisterial districts covered by the state of emergency except with the permission of the commissioner of police.

United States. Pres. Ronald Reagan's administration continued to focus attention on civil rights programs and laws of the 1960s. On Sept. 26, 1985, Secretary of Education William Bennett declared that over the last two decades federal policies concerning bilingual education had become "confused as to purpose and overbearing as to means." He claimed that $1.7 billion had been wasted and proposed new legislation to allow local school districts virtually complete autonomy in deciding how to teach children whose first language was not English.

Also undergoing reconsideration were affirmative-action programs that set specific targets and guidelines for black and other minority employment. The Department of Justice filed a brief supporting white teachers who were appealing against a layoff plan adopted by the school board of Jackson, Mich., that gave preference to members of minority groups over whites with more seniority. In its brief in *Wygant* v. *Jackson* the department asked the U.S. Supreme Court to hold that all governmental preferences based on race were unconstitutional, whether they benefited blacks, whites, or others. U.S. Attorney General Edwin Meese III triggered a storm of controversy when, in a speech on September 17, he likened supporters of racial quotas to Americans who once argued "that slavery was good not only for the slaves but for society." In another case before the Supreme Court, *Thornburg* v. *Gingles,* the Department of Justice supported North Carolina in its appeal against a lower court ruling that the state's 1982 redistricting plan violated the rights of black voters. This was the first major test of the 1982 amendments to the Voting Rights Act. These actions reinforced the gulf between the administration and the black community and illustrated the divergence of views that led Urban League president John Jacob to describe President Reagan's record on civil rights as "deplorable."

Despite a drop of just under one percentage point in the poverty rate from 15.3% in 1983 to 14.4% in 1984, the poverty rate for blacks remained nearly three times the white rate—33.8% to 11.5%. Of the 404,000 families who moved over the poverty-line definition, more than one-quarter were black.   (LOUIS KUSHNICK)

See also Human Rights.

Religion

The day before he was scheduled to go on trial, a defiant Denis Hurley, Roman Catholic archbishop of Durban, South Africa, told a cheering crowd in his cathedral that "the Gospel is political." Hurley, accused by the South African government of making unlawful remarks about alleged police atrocities in neighbouring Namibia, was acquitted in February 1985, but this dispute was only one of many clashes between religious and government leaders during the year.

The competing claims of the "sacred" and "secular" spheres were drawn most sharply in South Africa, the scene of massive protests against the government's apartheid (racial separation) policy. (*See* WORLD AFFAIRS [Africa South of the Sahara]: *South Africa.*) Church leaders were in the forefront of the struggle. Among the most radical and visible was Allan Boesak (*see* BIOGRAPHIES), president of the World Alliance of Reformed Churches. Boesak, classified by the government as "Coloured," was detained, then arrested after he called for black boycotts of white businesses and the withdrawal of foreign investments from the country. He also was accused of participating in public gatherings defined as illegal by the nation's strict security laws.

Allied with Boesak was black Anglican Bishop Desmond Tutu, winner of the 1984 Nobel Peace Prize. As a peacemaker, Tutu often was caught in the middle, most dramatically in July when he saved the life of a black man about to be burned alive by black militants who regarded him as a government informer. In August Tutu drew criticism when he refused to join other South African religious leaders in a meeting with Pres. P. W. Botha. After a five-day trip to South Africa, Jerry Falwell, fundamentalist leader of the Moral Majority in the U.S., said that "if Bishop Tutu maintains he speaks for the black people of South Africa, he's a phony." Falwell later softened his accusations but remained opposed to the many religious leaders who were active in antiapartheid protests. At an emergency meeting in Harare, Zimbabwe, in December, the World Council of Churches called for church pressure and economic sanctions against South Africa.

In the U.S. the so-called wall of separation between church and state was the site of many battles. One of the most protracted resulted from the decision by more than 200 churches and synagogues to provide "sanctuary" for illegal aliens from Central America whom they regarded as victims or potential victims of persecution in their homelands. In Brownsville, Texas, Lorry Thomas, a Sanctuary leader, was sentenced to prison after telling a judge she would continue violating federal immigration laws. In Tucson, Ariz., 11 persons—including a Protestant minister, 2 Roman Catholic priests, and a nun—faced federal charges of transporting and concealing illegal aliens. Before the trial opened in October, the defendants accused the government of violating their constitutional right to freedom of religion by having agents infiltrate their churches. (*See* POPULATIONS AND POPULATION MOVEMENTS: *Sidebar.*)

Several church-state issues were on the docket of the U.S. Supreme Court. In two 5–4 decisions, the court ruled that public school officials in New York City and Grand Rapids, Mich., should not permit public school teachers to lead special education classes in parochial schools. In other rulings the court invalidated a Connecticut law that gave employees an unqualified right to observe their Sabbath as a day off from work and struck down an Alabama law that allowed a moment of silence for prayer in public schools.

Such decisions prompted William J. Bennett, the U.S. secretary of education, to accuse the court of displaying a "fastidious disdain for religion." Throughout the year the Cabinet official became a magnet for praise and blame as he lashed out at those he held responsible for "a new aversion to religion."

The battle lines on church-state issues were drawn in a different way when Sun Myung Moon, head of the Unification Church of America, was released from a federal prison where he had served a term for income tax evasion. The church, regarded by many as a questionable cult, launched a lavish public relations campaign to convince Americans that the Korean-born evangelist was the victim of "selective prosecution." One newspaper ad stated: "When [Moon] went to prison, our religious freedom went with him. If you don't stand up now, who will be next?" The ad was signed by several religious leaders, liberal and conservative, who disagreed with Moon's theological views but supported his contention that the state had interfered in the internal affairs of his church.

Some public policy issues not only drove a wedge between church and state but also created divisions within the church. In Pennsylvania an activist Lutheran minister incurred the wrath of both civil and religious authorities. After serving a jail term for contempt of court, D. Douglas Roth was defrocked by an ecclesiastical court convened by the Lutheran Church in America. The church court decided that Roth had acted in "willful disregard and violation" of church law when he refused to obey his bishop's order to vacate his pulpit. Roth's congregation in Clairton, Pa., was divided over the role the radical minister played in an ecumenical campaign to combat the causes of unemployment in the steel mill area.

Debate over the proper role of the church in the public arena divided ranks in the Roman Catholic Church. Following precedents set down in the early days of his pontificate, Pope John Paul II continued to insist that priests and nuns stay out of public office. In February four priests in Nicaragua lost their priestly status, on orders from the Vatican, when they refused to give up their prominent positions in that nation's Marxist-oriented Sandinista government. In other ways, however, Catholic leaders, from the pope on down, tried to influence political decisions by vigorously articulating the church's teaching on abortion, nuclear warfare, birth control, human rights, and economic justice. During a 12-day trip to Latin America in January and February, John Paul went out of his way to visit regions of extreme poverty. Wherever he went, he championed the cause of "authentic liberation" that leads to social justice without resorting to violence. On the eve of his departure in August for a 12-day trip to Africa, he condemned apartheid. In May, however, during his 26th trip abroad, sparse crowds and hostile street demonstrations marred his visit to The Netherlands, where there was strong opposition to his strict orthodox views.

In Rome, John Paul took several steps to put his own "household of faith" in order. His most decisive step resulted in the convening of an Extraordinary Synod of Bishops. In the months prior to the 13-day meeting in November and December, Catholic leaders anticipated the event with a combination of hope and dread. In particular, progressive Catholics feared that the Synod would set in motion policies that would roll back the reforms of the Second Vatican Council (Vatican II). By the time the Synod ended, however, a synthesis of views was achieved that enabled both progressives and conservatives to go home with the feeling that at least some of their views had been incorporated into the final document. Far from

Pope John Paul II's visit to The Netherlands in May was marred by demonstrations, riots, and public lectures on toleration and pluralism from various political and religious figures. This demonstration in Utrecht turned particularly ugly.

LOCHON—GAMMA/LIAISON

being dismissed as a historical aberration, Vatican II was hailed as a "gift of God to the church and to the world," and champions of "collegiality" were gratified that regional and national bishops' conferences were endorsed as "useful, even necessary." Conservatives and progressives came together to support the development of a "universal catechism" of official Catholic teaching. In his closing homily, John Paul declared that "at the end of the 2nd millennium, the church truly deserves to be the church in the modern world."

The pope continued to meet resistance from members of religious orders, especially women's orders in the U.S. A focus of controversy was a December 1984 decree by the Vatican's Congregation for Religious and Secular Institutes that threatened to expel from their orders 24 nuns who signed a newspaper ad stating that "a diversity of opinions regarding abortion exists among committed Catholics." The contest of wills simmered throughout 1985. The pontiff deepened his personal imprint on the church by naming 28 new members of the College of Cardinals. All the appointees echoed in their own statements the pope's conservative theological views. Many of the new cardinals were distinguished chiefly by their opposition to Marxist regimes or by their outspoken denunciation of Christians who, in the Vatican's judgment, had compromised their faith by capitulating to the secular "spirit of the times." (See *Roman Catholic Church,* below.) Outside the Vatican walls, the Italian Chamber of Deputies ratified a concordat that brought to an end Roman Catholicism's status as the official religion of the state.

Jewish feelings were roused in the spring when U.S. Pres. Ronald Reagan carried out his controversial plan to visit a West German cemetery at Bitburg, the burial site for 2,000 German soldiers, including 49 members of the Waffen SS, which was responsible for the deaths of Jews in World War II concentration camps. Reagan pictured the visit as an act of reconciliation designed to close the book on German-American tensions left over from World War II, but many Jews believed that Reagan had failed to take seriously the depth of Jewish feelings about the horrors of the Holocaust. In the White House to receive an award, author Elie Wiesel, a Holocaust survivor, told Reagan that his proper place was not at Bitburg but "with the victims of the SS." (See *Judaism,* below.)

Relationships between blacks and Jews in the U.S. continued to be somewhat strained, despite efforts by leaders on both sides to rebuild the "coalition of goodwill" forged during the civil rights campaigns of the 1960s. In Los Angeles black Muslim leader Louis Farrakhan inflamed Jewish feelings when he hold Jews: "Don't push your 6 million [Holocaust victims] when we lost 100 million [in slavery]." Farrakhan's remarks drew a stern rebuke from Tom Bradley, Los Angeles' black mayor. The controversy intensified a short time later when Farrakhan, addressing 25,000 supporters in New York's Madison Square Garden, accused his critics of aiming to murder him.

Insurgency in the ranks of Orthodox Jews aggravated tensions within the Jewish community. In Israel the Knesset (parliament) narrowly defeated a bill that would have recognized as Jews only those converts to Judaism instructed by an Orthodox rabbi. The bill was strongly opposed by Reform and Conservative rabbis, and Prime Minister Shimon Peres pleaded with the legislature to turn its attention to other, "more weighty problems."

Elsewhere, other religious convictions also fueled political passions. In India attempts to resolve tensions between Sikhs and the Hindu majority received a serious setback in August when the moderate Sikh leader Sant Harchand Singh Longowal (*see* OBITUARIES) was slain. Shortly before, he had signed an agreement with Prime Minister Rajiv Gandhi that proposed giving more power to Sikhs but stopped short of granting them autonomy. The conflict had reached its bloodiest level in 1984 when Indian troops stormed the Golden Temple in Amritsar, the holiest shrine of the Sikh religion, which had been turned into an armed fortress by Sikh extremists, and Prime Minister Indira Gandhi was assassinated by her Sikh bodyguards. (See *Hinduism,* below.)

In Lebanon Hizbollah, the "Party of God," an Islamic fundamentalist movement with strong ties to Iran, was believed to be chiefly responsible for the hijacking of a Trans World Airlines jet. (*See* WORLD AFFAIRS [Western Europe]: *Italy.*) Meanwhile, Egyptian Pres. Hosni Mubarak took steps to curb the activities of Islamic fundamentalists. One phase of Mubarak's campaign called for drivers whose vehicles carried religious bumper stickers to be fined and subject to having their licenses revoked for a year. In another effort to control social unrest, Mubarak released Shenuda III, leader of Egypt's Coptic Church, from house arrest. (See *Eastern Non-Chalcedonian Churches,* below.)

At a troubled time in Mormon history, Ezra Taft Benson, 86, a Cabinet member in the Eisenhower administration, became president of the Church of Jesus Christ of Latter-day Saints. The origins of the movement had been called into question by publication of the so-called White Salamander letter, which suggested that Joseph Smith, the church's founder, was involved with early 19th-century superstitions at the time he discovered the "golden tablets" that led to the birth of Mormonism. Also during the year, a series of pipe bomb attacks in Salt Lake City, Utah, resulted in the deaths of two persons and injuries to others who had been involved in the sale or purchase of Mormon documents.

Christian fundamentalists continued to play a major role in American religion. In Dallas, Texas, hard-line fundamentalists clung to control of the Southern Baptist Convention (SBC), the nation's largest Protestant denomination, when Charles Stanley was reelected SBC president. (See *Baptist Churches,* below.) One of the few religious liberals who made news was Edmond Lee Browning, the bishop of Hawaii, elected to a 12-year term as presiding bishop of the Episcopal Church.   (ROY LARSON)

PROTESTANT CHURCHES

Anglican Communion. During 1985 the issue of women's ordination provoked renewed debate and conflict throughout the communion. In the U.S. the bishops of the Episcopal Church announced during the church's General Convention in September that they did not intend to withhold consent to the election of a woman as bishop if that time came. In Australia the church's Appellate Tribunal handed down decisions indicating that there were no constitutional barriers to the ordination of women, and shortly afterward the Australian General Synod rejected by only two votes a motion that would have opened the priesthood to women. Several bishops believed that the tribunal's decisions authorized them to act unilaterally in ordaining women, but it was thought likely that they would await the outcome of a special General Synod, which would discuss the question again in two years' time.

In the Church of England, which was preparing legislation to allow women in the priesthood, some Anglo-Catholics and Evangelicals formed a group to defeat the process. The bishop of London, Graham Leonard, issued a stern warning that ordaining women might split the church in two, and the whole subject played a major part in the General Synod elections.

The Anglican-Roman Catholic International Commission, meeting in New York City in August, embarked on its first serious discussion of the ordination of women and the implications for Christian unity. No immediate conclusions were reached. Earlier in the year the Anglican-Orthodox Joint Doctrinal Commission reported that a wide measure of agreement had been reached despite some difficulties, the ordination of women being one.

The church in South Africa found itself heavily involved in the urgent search for

BART BARTHOLOMEW—BLACK STAR

Edmond Lee Browning, bishop of the small and relatively remote diocese of Hawaii, was chosen presiding bishop of the Episcopal Church in September. Browning, who had been prominent in the liberal wing of the church, was to lead the church until 1997.

reconciliation and political reform amid the serious unrest there. The archbishop of Canterbury, Robert Runcie, warned the South African government not to lay hands on Bishop Desmond Tutu of Johannesburg. Four years after extricating a group of British missionaries held in Iran, the archbishop's special envoy, Terry Waite, took home four Britons who had been detained in Libya. Late in the year he began an effort to obtain the release of Americans being held hostage in Lebanon.

New Zealand's primate, Paul Reeves (*see* BIOGRAPHIES), was named in March as the country's next governor-general. In the U.S. the bishop of Hawaii, Edmond Lee Browning, was elected in September as the new presiding bishop of the Episcopal Church.   (SUSAN YOUNG)

Baptist Churches. At a conference sponsored by the Anti-Defamation League of B'nai B'rith at the Interchurch Center in New York City, Georgy Vins, Baptist leader exiled from the Soviet Union in 1979, charged that the KGB was infiltrating Western Christian organizations in general and had targeted the Baptist World Alliance (34 million members worldwide) in particular. In response, Denton Lotz, the BWA's associate secretary for evangelism and education, noted that the concept of religious freedom in the West is quite different from that in the East and defended Aleksey Bychkov, the new general secretary of the All-Union Congress of Evangelical Christians-Baptists in the Soviet Union, as a "very committed Baptist." In March, reflecting Lotz's confidence in Bychkov, nearly 1,000 persons attended the Soviet Baptist Union's 43rd congress. Bychkov reported that "about 40,000 souls" had been converted in the last five years and 268 new congregations had been registered.

In January leaders of the Baptist Convention of Nicaragua sent a letter to President Reagan appealing for a halt in the aggressive attitude reflected in U.S. policy toward that country. The letter charged that U.S. policies had already been responsible for 7,000 deaths. The American Baptist Churches in the U.S.A. (Northern Baptists), meeting in their biennial session in Portland, Ore., in June, passed a statement of concern in which they supported their brothers and sisters in Nicaragua and took a stand against the Reagan administration's policies.

Southern Baptists met in convention session in Dallas in June, with twice the usual number of messengers (delegates). The 45,000-strong assembly arrived ready to continue the seven-year battle between fundamentalists and moderates, with control of the denomination's boards and seminaries at stake. The large attendance made podium logistics difficult at best, resulting in considerable frustration for many of those present. Fundamentalist Charles Stanley of Atlanta, Ga., was reelected president of the more than 14 million-member denomination. The meeting ended with some moves toward reconciliation, which in the course of the convention had appeared highly unlikely.

The Divinity School of Shaw University, Raleigh, N.C., awarded an honorary degree to Sun Myung Moon, founder of the Unification Church. The action by the largely black school generated denunciation from some alumni and the black General Bap-

tist State Convention of North Carolina, which went on record as "vehemently viewing with disdain" both the giving of the degree and the acceptance of Moon's $30,000 gift to the school.

(NORMAN R. DE PUY)

Christian Church (Disciples of Christ). The ecumenically oriented Disciples became the first American church body to name persons from other denominations as full voting members on its central board. The Disciples elected representatives of the Christian Methodist Episcopal Church, the United Church of Christ (UCC), the United Church of Canada, and the Presbyterian Church (U.S.A.) to their 180-member General Board. The church's General Assembly followed up action by the UCC approving a new "ecumenical partnership" between the three million members of the two bodies. The partnership would involve increasing joint mission, shared theological studies, and common worship.

The Disciples ended a 25-year reorganizational period in which they had sought to develop a "church" from a collection of loosely affiliated congregations, agencies, and individuals. The architect of the restructuring, Kenneth L. Teegarden, retired as general minister and president and was succeeded by John O. Humbert of Ohio. An ordained Disciples minister, Sang Jung Park of South Korea, was elected general secretary of the Christian Conference of Asia, based in Singapore. Trevor Banks of Australia was named by Disciples to head their world ecumenical consultative council.   (ROBERT LOUIS FRIEDLY)

Churches of Christ. Over $8 million was given for African aid during the year. Fourteen thousand people were being fed daily, and medical assistance was provided in programs under the leadership of Bread for a Hungry World of Richland Hills, Texas; Manna International of Redwood City, Calif.; and Whites Ferry Road Church in Louisiana.

Growing interest in publications was evident in the launching of two new national magazines in the U.S., *Christian Woman* and *Image.* The circulation of the newsmagazine *Christian Chronicle* expanded by 100,000. Biblical scholarship received strong impetus through the founding of the College of Biblical Studies at Abilene Christian University in Texas and the Biblical Research Institute at Pepperdine University in Malibu, Calif.

A total of 691 persons were baptized in evangelistic campaigns in Ghana and Nigeria and 101 in a campaign in Guyana held in conjunction with the World Bible School. The church was recognized in Yugoslavia and given permission to hold public meetings after 14 years of meeting in homes. A two-hectare (five-acre) site worth $3 million was given in Nairobi, Kenya, for constructing a church building and a vocational school.   (M. NORVEL YOUNG)

Church of Christ, Scientist. Plans for expanding the broadcasting activities of the *Christian Science Monitor* were announced by John H. Hoagland, Jr., manager of the Christian Science Publishing Society, at the denomination's annual meeting in Boston in early June 1985. "Monitoradio," broadcast over National Public Radio, was expanded from a weekly to a daily schedule. A monthly television news and feature program was launched in August in the

U.S., and during the spring an hour-long weekly *Monitor* program over Radio Luxembourg was initiated.

A worldwide videoconference, beamed from Boston and London at the close of 1984, was attended by Christian Scientists in 140 cities on four continents. Its theme, "To Live for All Mankind," was taken from the writings of church founder Mary Baker Eddy. In August 1985 about 2,500 student and faculty members of Christian Science organizations at colleges and universities gathered at the Mother Church in Boston. Students from 35 countries attended the three-day conference, which focused on the theme "Individual Spirituality and the Future of Mankind."

Robert H. Mitchell of Edinburgh, Scotland, was named to the one-year post of church president. (NATHAN A. TALBOT)

Church of Jesus Christ of Latter-day Saints. Spencer Kimball (*see* OBITUARIES), president of the church since Dec. 30, 1973, died November 5 and was succeeded by Ezra Taft Benson.

Effective July 1985 much of the work of the church was decentralized and directed by area presidencies, many of whom moved from church headquarters in Salt Lake City to their assigned areas. By that time the church was established in 96 nations and 18 colonies, territories, and possessions.

The international thrust of the church was also reflected during late 1984 and 1985 in the dedication of temples in Freiberg, East Germany, the first in a Communist country; Santiago, Chile; Sydney, Australia; Manila; Taipei, Taiwan; Guatemala City; Stockholm; and in Dallas, Atlanta, and Glenview, near Chicago. By the end of 1985 the church had 35 operating temples.

Continued interest in the early history of the church was highlighted by the discovery of a letter of Joseph Smith to J. W. Stowell, written in 1825, the earliest handwriting of the founding prophet; the disclosure of an 1830 letter from Martin Harris to W. W. Phelps, describing the finding of the plates from which the Book of Mormon was written; the acquisition by a private collector of the so-called Papyrus No. 2, part of which was translated by Joseph Smith and is in the Book of Abraham; the location of the papers of William McLellin, an early LDS apostle; and the uncovering of an early manuscript history of the church by Oliver Cowdery, ostensibly written in 1830–31. (See *Introduction,* above.)

The church increasingly joined with other religious groups in extending relief to Ethiopia ($6 million); in fighting pornography, alcoholism, and drug abuse; and in sponsoring or assisting with the Special Olympic Games.

(LEONARD J. ARRINGTON)

Jehovah's Witnesses. Believing in the inerrancy of the Bible, in the necessity for Christians to conform their lives to its standards, and in the primary importance of their commission to preach the good news of God's Kingdom, Jehovah's Witnesses continued their evangelizing work in over 200 lands during 1985. A series of "Integrity Keepers" conventions were held in the U.S. during the summer and then around the world.

At the conventions a new Watch Tower Society publication entitled *"Life—How Did It Get Here? By Evolution or by Creation?"* was released in a first edition of two million copies. The publication, which discusses the theory of evolution and examines the evidence in the fossil record and in the structures of the animate and inanimate world, expounds and upholds the biblical account of the origins and purpose of life.

An annual growth rate of about 7% brought worldwide membership to a new peak of more than 2.8 million. This rapid expansion stimulated development of a new method of building the Kingdom Halls, or places of worship, whereby large teams of volunteers constructed an entire finished building, often over a single weekend. The system was being used in many countries. (FREDERICK W. FRANZ)

Lutheran Communion. The Lutheran World Federation (LWF), chief global expression of the Lutheran communion, ended the year with a new general secretary (chief executive officer). Gunnar Staalsett, a priest of the (Lutheran) Church of Norway and most recently general secretary of the Norwegian Bible Society, began his work at LWF headquarters in Geneva on September 1. He succeeded Carl Mau, a pastor of the American Lutheran Church, who held the post for almost 11 years.

At its annual meeting, the LWF executive committee, which governs the LWF between its worldwide assemblies, adopted statements on peace and justice and on the situation in South Africa. The former opposed "further militarization of outer space" and the spread of nuclear weapons and urged church people to lobby governments to divert money from armaments to the alleviation of world hunger. The South Africa statement endorsed disinvestment and other economic sanctions as a means of opposing the country's system of apartheid. It also voiced "solidarity and support" for those "under foreign occupation in Namibia," the neighbouring territory controlled by South Africa. About half the Namibian population is counted as Lutheran.

Ecumenical relations were also on the LWF agenda, especially with Roman Catholics and Anglicans. Mau said it was time for Lutherans and Roman Catholics to think about "appropriate forms of visible unity," perhaps following the model of U.S. Anglicans (Episcopalians) and Lutherans, who had approved "interim sharing of the eucharist." At Staalsett's request, the LWF was to have two new assistant general secretaries, one for ecumenical affairs, the other for international affairs and human rights. The number of church bodies in the LWF increased to 104 with the addition of denominations in Bangladesh, Botswana, El Salvador, Venezuela, and Zaire.

In North America plans to bring together two-thirds of the 8.8 million Canadian and U.S. Lutherans in new denominations in each country moved forward. The Evangelical Lutheran Church in Canada (a merger of the Evangelical Lutheran Church of Canada and the Canada Section of the U.S.-based Lutheran Church in America) held its constituting convention in May, with operations to begin officially on Jan. 1, 1986. The new U.S. denomination, yet to be named, was to unite three church bodies in 1988.

The presiding bishops of the federations of regional Evangelical (Lutheran, United, and Reformed) churches in East and West Germany, where nearly 40% of the world's 70 million Lutherans live, issued a joint statement marking the defeat of Nazi Germany and the end of World War II in Europe. (THOMAS HARTLEY DORRIS)

Methodist Churches. Plans were concluded for the 15th World Methodist Council (WMC) and Conference to be held in Nairobi in July 1986. The theme was to be "Christ Jesus, God's 'Yes' for the World." The Social and International Affairs Committee reported on the Consultation in Barbados on the subject of "North-South Dialogue and Solidarity with the Poor." Concern was expressed that Methodists often seemed to have lost their historical identity with the poor, and there was need for increased dialogue and encounter between North and South and a fresh evaluation of the philosophy and program of Mission Boards. A call was made for a simpler life-style for many Methodists.

A World Peace Conference held in London in July was planned to coincide with the 40th anniversary of the dropping of the first atomic bomb on Hiroshima. Delegates from 29 countries issued a message inviting "people everywhere to join us in a new commitment to peace-making, and to Jesus Christ, the Prince of Peace." The message emphasized that peace is a gift from God, not achieved by human effort alone, but is effected by God through men and women. It called for a freeze on further nuclear weapons and for a nuclear-free Pacific, and it urged Methodists to participate imaginatively in the International Year of Peace designated by the UN for 1986.

The "Making Disciples" program initiated by the Evangelism Committee continued to thrive, particularly in some Eastern countries. Korean Methodism grew to a membership of 900,000, and in Indonesia the goal of 10,000 new members a year was being attained. Church membership in Nigeria increased by 55,000, and in Kenya annual growth was reckoned at 17%. Churches everywhere were invited to participate in a program of "Simultaneous Local Mission" during Lent.

In the U.S. the United Methodist Church elected two women as bishops. Bishop Leontine Kelly, appointed to San Francisco, became the first black woman bishop. Bishop Judith Craig was appointed to Detroit. The British Methodist Conference received a report recommending that, in order to avoid conflicting loyalties, Methodists not become Freemasons; the final decision, however, was left to the individual. The Methodist Church of Southern Africa continued to campaign for the end of apartheid. Under the state of emergency proclaimed in South Africa, many Methodists, including a former church president, Abel Hendricks, were arrested.

(PETER H. BOLT)

Pentecostal Churches. David du Plessis, widely known as "Mr. Pentecost," was honoured by Fuller Theological Seminary, Pasadena, Calif., when the David J. du Plessis Center for Christian Spirituality was dedicated on Feb. 7, 1985, the veteran leader's 80th birthday. Fuller also experienced a growing controversy over the teaching methods and theology of John Wimber and Peter Wagner, whose classes

were deemed too "charismatic" by some members of the school of theology. The school of world missions, however, supported the two teachers.

In July the 14th World Pentecostal Conference convened in Zürich, Switz. Since the first such conference was held there in 1947, the number of Pentecostals in the world had risen from fewer than 10 million to 60 million, making up one of the largest families of Protestants in the world.

In August the Assemblies of God elected Raymond Carlson as general superintendent. He succeeded Thomas Zimmerman, who had served since 1960. The sessions of the General Council were carried on three nationwide television networks. A featured speaker at the Council was John D. Ashcroft, newly elected governor of Missouri. A member of the Assemblies of God, he was the first Pentecostal to be elected governor of a U.S. state.

Also in August, the Pentecostal Holiness quadrennial General Conference, meeting in Richmond, Va., adopted a 15-year church growth strategy called Target 2000. The plan called for the church to grow from its present 1.5 million members to 6.5 million members worldwide by the end of the century. (VINSON SYNAN)

Reformed, Presbyterian, and Congregational Churches. The World Alliance of Reformed Churches (WARC) maintained its witness for peace and justice and commended its "Covenant for Peace and Justice" to other Christian communions; a consultation on this theme took place in March 1985. WARC published *Testimonies of Faith,* a collection of letters and poems from prison in Taiwan. C. M. Kao, general secretary of the Presbyterian Church of Taiwan, who had been serving a seven-year sentence, was released. In Peru six members of the National Presbyterian Church in Callqui were murdered by marines as they worshiped.

The Uniting Church in Australia raised its voice on behalf of the Aboriginals. The WARC Executive Committee published a statement on the occasion of the widely marked 350th anniversary of the revocation of the Edict of Nantes. Many WARC members endorsed the judgment of the 1982 General Council in Ottawa that apartheid is a sin and the theological justification of it a heresy. WARC president Allan Boesak (*see* BIOGRAPHIES), a leading opponent of apartheid, was placed under severe restriction in South Africa.

WARC's theological contacts increased. The international dialogue with the Roman Catholic Church continued, and the results of conversations with the Mennonites were to be published. A booklet, *Reformed and Disciples of Christ in Dialogue,* was issued in preparation for an international consultation between the two communions. The first WARC-World Methodist Council meeting produced a statement and a plan of further work. Work began on the theme "Reformed Theology and the Jewish People," and a consultation on "Theological Explorations into Cultures" was held in Bali, Indon., in connection with the WARC study program "Called to Witness to the Gospel Today."

Many churches responded to the appeal of the Presbyterian Church of Vanuatu when that island was hit by Hurricane Nigel in January. The third meeting of the International Congregational Fellowship was held near Boston under the title "Joy in Christ." The Cumberland and the Second Cumberland Presbyterian churches in the U.S. and the Presbyterian Church of Canada published new confessions of faith. Similar actions were under consideration in North India, Taiwan, and elsewhere.

Among prominent Reformed churchmen who died during the year were Istvan Juhasz (Romania), Norman Goodall (U.K.), W. A. Visser't Hooft (The Netherlands), and E. Carson Blake (U.S.). (*See* OBITUARIES.) (ALAN P. F. SELL)

Religious Society of Friends. An event of great significance for the rising generation of Quakers was the World Gathering of Young Friends, which drew 300 young people aged 18 to 35, including many from East Africa and Latin America, to Guilford College, Greensboro, N.C., in July 1985.

In August a more seasoned international gathering, the 16th triennial meeting of Friends World Committee for Consultation (FWCC), was held at Oaxtepec, Mexico. Besides discussing questions of theology and worship, FWCC mirrored the current concerns of the worldwide Society of Friends, among them disarmament, North-South problems, South Africa, and women's issues.

In Britain many Friends supported demonstrations at nuclear missile sites at Greenham Common and Molesworth and joined the attempts of Quakers in many countries to withhold and divert taxes from military expenditure to peaceful purposes. A particular protest—the withholding of income tax on behalf of staff at Friends House, London—came to a head when the two clerks of Meeting for Sufferings (the employing body) were taken to court by the Inland Revenue and ordered to pay. An appeal was dismissed and appeal to the House of Lords refused. Payment was made, since the intention had been to test the law, not to break it. (DAVID FIRTH)

Salvation Army. During 1985 the Army was officially recognized in Angola. The first full-time officers there were appointed in October. As part of its involvement in International Youth Year, the Salvation Army held an International Youth Congress at Western Illinois University, Macomb, attended by 5,000 delegates. Each of the 85 countries where the Army was at work was represented.

The Army's international leader, Gen. Jarl Wahlström, led a pilgrimage to the Holy Land in the spring. There was no recognized Salvation Army work in Israel, but 1,500 Salvationists, representing 23 countries, attended the ten-day congress, which included religious meetings and visits to places of biblical significance. A special feature was the dedication of a "William Booth Grove" of trees planted by delegates in the Judean hills.

Col. William Layton, chief secretary of the Salvation Army in Britain since 1982, retired and was succeeded by Col. John Hounsell. On July 2 General Wahlström laid the foundation stone of an extension to the William Booth Memorial Training College in South London. The college, built in 1929 when the majority of students for officer training were single, now received many married couples. The new wing would provide accommodation for these families. (ROB GARRAD)

Seventh-day Adventist Church. In 1985 the Adventist Development and Relief Agency (ADRA) stepped up its efforts to provide food and self-help programs for African countries. ADRA was conducting relief projects in 20 countries of Africa, 21 in the Latin America/Caribbean area, and 15 in the Asia/Pacific region.

The 54th world conference of the church convened in New Orleans, La., June 27–July 6, with 1,853 delegates from throughout the world in attendance. A report on the major evangelistic thrust entitled "One Thousand Days of Reaping" stated that the goal of adding more than one million new members had been exceeded by a large margin. As 1985 closed, world membership approached five million.

The 66-member commission appointed by the 1984 Annual Council to study the role of women in the Adventist Church urged church leadership to adopt an "affirmative action" plan for the involvement of women in the work of the church. It was voted that the matter of women's ordination be studied carefully during the next five years and that further recommendations be considered by the 1990 General Conference Session.

For the first time in the history of the North American Division, a Camporee was held for junior youth from all of the U.S. and Canada. A total of 16,023 Pathfinders (the Adventist equivalent of Boy and Girl Scouts) attended the week-long event at Camp Hale, Colo. The theme, "Adventure in Service," was designed to lead the Pathfinders into greater activity for God.

H. M. S. Richards, founder of the international radio broadcast "The Voice of Prophecy," died April 24 at the age of 90. (KENNETH H. WOOD)

Unitarian (Universalist) Churches. Unitarian Universalist Association (UUA) delegates numbering 1,299 from all over North America elected the youngest president in the association's history, 35-year-old William F. Schulz, during the 1985 annual General Assembly, held June 17–22 in Atlanta. A former president of the UU Women's Federation, Natalie W. Gulbrandsen, was elected moderator, traditionally the highest lay office in the denomination. Resolutions were passed on a number of current issues, including apartheid, sanctuary, the status of blacks, nuclear arms, poverty, and U.S. intervention in Central America.

There were 129 women and 96 men studying for the ministry in the U.S. in 1985, and approximately 250 of the 1,088 ordained UU ministers were women. The UUA registered a small net growth in membership during 1984–85, while the Annual Program Fund set new records and met its goal for the seventh consecutive year. North American Unitarian Universalists gave final approval to a new statement of UUA Principles and Purposes.

British Unitarians, at their 57th annual General Assembly, April 9–11, at Dundee, Scotland, appointed Sydney H. Knight president for 1985–86. The Council was instructed to prepare a revised Statement of Objects which would move by stages toward final confirmation at the 1990 annual meeting. The Canadian Unitarian Council held its 24th annual meeting in London, Ont., May 17–20, and elected Kathleen Corlett as its executive director.

Lajos Kovacs, bishop of the Unitarian Church in Romania, and Josef Ferencz, bishop of the Unitarian Church in Hungary, visited the U.S. during the year. Bishop Kovacs reported a current membership of 80,000 in 120 organized congregations led by as many clergy. Half of the 10,000 Unitarians in Hungary reside in the Greater Budapest area. Nikkyo Niwana, founding president of Japan's Rissho Kosei-kai, retired as president of the International Association for Religious Freedom and was succeeded by Roy Smith of Great Britain.   (JOHN NICHOLLS BOOTH)

The United Church of Canada. The year was one of celebration for Canada's largest Protestant denomination as its 60th birthday was observed in congregations across the country. On June 10, 1925, representatives of Methodist, Congregational, most Presbyterian, and Local Union (in western Canada) churches met in a skating rink on Toronto's Mutual Street and approved the Basis of Union. (The Evangelical United Brethren joined in 1968.) On June 9, 1985, services celebrating the historic event were held in two Toronto locations: the Terrace—the renamed Arena—and the Metropolitan United Church, often called "the cathedral of Methodism." At the end of the service at the Terrace, church members walked in procession behind military bands to nearby Metropolitan Church to join the one thousand worshipers already there.

Moderator Robert Smith told the congregation that their church was in danger of failing its mandate as a "united and uniting" church. There were no official union talks in sight, and he saw a threat to the unity of the church itself in the deep divisions between the Gospel imperative to strive for justice and traditional personal salvation. But Smith also saw "signs of hope and signs of excitement and signs of challenge." For instance, the denomination's stewardship education program Ventures in Mission had achieved its minimum objective of $40 million and was slowly moving toward its second-level objective of $50 million; one of the early beneficiaries was a new church in Portugal Cove, Newfoundland, dedicated on anniversary Sunday. At the other end of the country, First United Church in Vancouver, B.C. (Presbyterian before union), was holding a vigil to protest injustices to the poor.

Injustice to the poor was also the subject of a Division of Mission presentation to a federal government committee: "It is immoral for the U.S. to consider spending up to $1 trillion on [the Strategic Defense Initiative] when there are millions of sick and starving people in the world."
     (NORMAN K. VALE)

United Church of Christ. At the 15th General Synod of the UCC, held in Ames, Iowa, June 27–July 2, 1985, the 700 delegates declared an ecumenical partnership with the Christian Church (Disciples of Christ) with a focus on common worship, mission, and theological agreements; called for full divestment of all financial resources from corporations doing business with South Africa by all entities of the UCC; affirmed the UCC as a just peace church; adopted a coordinated program of health and welfare ministries; determined to continue a vigorous program of church

development with a goal of 15 new and renewed churches each year for the next ten years; sealed a mission partnership with the Pentecostal Church of Chile; and adopted the UCC response to the World Council of Churches document on "Baptism, Eucharist and Ministry." By vote of the Synod, two new priorities, Spiritual Renewal and Justice and Peace, were added to the current priorities of Family Life and Youth and Young Adult Ministries.

Elected to new terms as officers of the church were Avery D. Post, president, and Charles H. Lockyear, director of finance and treasurer. Kenneth P. Stewart of Wichita, Kan., was elected moderator. David W. Stowe completed 15 years as executive vice-president of the United Church Board for World Ministries on January 31 and was succeeded by Scott S. Libbey. After 19 years as executive director of the UCC's Commission for Racial Justice, Charles E. Cobb announced his retirement.

Succeeding *A.D.*, a UCC/United Presbyterian magazine that terminated in 1983, was the monthly *United Church News*, published for the church by the Office of Communications.

Ben Mohr Herbster, first president of the UCC, died on Dec. 16, 1984. He served as president from 1961 to 1969.
     (AVERY D. POST)

ROMAN CATHOLIC CHURCH

The year was given shape by Pope John Paul II's surprise announcement on Jan. 25, 1985, that there would be a two-week Extraordinary Synod ending on December 8, exactly 20 years after the conclusion of Vatican II. Subsequent events were interpreted in the light of the hopes or anxieties aroused by this announcement. The fact that Joseph Cardinal Ratzinger, prefect of the Sacred Congregation for the Doctrine of the Faith, was the chief thinker of the pontificate seemed to confirm the theory that Vatican II was to be revoked. Ratzinger gave a series of interviews in which he talked about the need for the "restoration of preconciliar values" and showed himself to be deeply pessimistic about the postconciliar church. These were Ratzinger's personal views, but they came from the same source as the official ones. In his official capacity Ratzinger had presided over the declaration condemning liberation theology, tried to get the Peruvian bishops to denounce Gustavo Gutiérrez, known as "the father of liberation theology," and in March silenced his old pupil, Leonardo Boff (*see* BIOGRAPHIES), the leading Brazilian liberation theologian, indefinitely. (*See* WORLD AFFAIRS [Latin America and the Caribbean]: *Latin-American Affairs:* Sidebar.)

The year's papal visits seemed to confirm that Ratzinger's pessimism about Vatican II was congenial to the pope. The visit to The Netherlands (May 11–15) acquired additional symbolic importance, for that was the country where (in one view) Vatican II had gone to people's heads and produced catastrophe. For others it was a sign of hope. Pope John Paul went there to attempt to restore order. No one could claim the Dutch visit was a great success. Yet it showed that a subtler principle was at work. The question was not simply whether Vatican II was a good thing but whether the various interpretations of it

were legitimate. There was certainly room for debate about that: with no new ordained priests forthcoming, there had been a tendency to blur if not abolish the distinction between the ordained ministry and other ministries. Edward Schillebeekx, The Netherlands' best-known theologian, was moving in this direction and attracted the attention of Ratzinger's office.

In June and July the 101 national or regional episcopal conferences worked on their "reports" on the effects of Vatican II in preparation for the Synod. Most were extremely positive. Basil Cardinal Hume of Westminster, whose role was important because he was also president of the European bishops' council, said in Paris that it was not that Vatican II had failed, but that it had been failed. This was echoed in the report of the English and Welsh bishops, published in July, and in the U.S. report, which came in September. Other reports were not published, but it might safely be said that the vast majority of those consulted thought Vatican II had had positive effects in deepening Catholic interest in and knowledge of the Bible, encouraging lay participation in the ministries and worship of the church, and breaking down the barriers that had existed between clergy and laity.

By the end of the year it was clear that Ratzinger had made a bad tactical move. In his various interviews he had explained that episcopal conferences had "no theological status." In his opinion, bishops were important only as individuals in their dioceses or when gathered together, as in a council. Intermediate bodies (like the U.S. national conference) had no authority or mandate to teach. Ratzinger first made this point in connection with the U.S. bishops' peace pastoral, and it did not endear him to bishops. Nearly all the reports to the Synod were anti-Ratzinger in tone. The English and Welsh asserted authority for an episcopal conference on the grounds that it did in the modern world what a "patriarchate" did in the ancient world: adapt the gospel to the local culture. The Americans said that the authority of the bishops was enhanced if they showed themselves capable of working together, as they were now doing on a statement on the economy. These theological debates were part of a power struggle that focused on the notion of "collegiality," Vatican II's idea that all the bishops of the world shared with the pope in his concern for the universal church.

The pope's African visit in August—the third of the pontificate—showed the importance he attached to a continent that was expected to have 100 million Catholics by the year 2000. The pope put a question mark against "africanization" and upset the Kenyan government by his vigorous denunciation of artificial birth control. But he had a spectacular success in Casablanca, Morocco, when he addressed 80,000 cheering Muslim youths gathered by King Hassan II. The rest of the Arab world said Hassan was unrepresentative.

John Paul showed that he intended to take charge in Italy, too, by ignoring the voting of the Italian bishops and appointing the vicar of Rome, Ugo Cardinal Poletti, president of their episcopal conference, thus turning the Italian church into a department of the Roman Curia. This last move

was attributed to the growing influence of Opus Dei, the conservative Spanish movement, aided by Communion and Liberation, its Italian cousin. Opus Dei opened a theological institute in Rome, hoping to rival and eventually eclipse the great Jesuit and Dominican universities.

So the year moved toward the Synod, which reached a prudent compromise. (See *Introduction,* above.) Ecumenism marked time, although the English and Welsh bishops pronounced the report of the Anglican-Roman Catholic International Commission satisfactory. The "Ostpolitik" of the Vatican made little progress. An encyclical, *Slavorum Apostoli* ("Apostles of the Slavs"), commemorated the 1,100th anniversary of the death of St. Methodius, who with his brother Cyril evangelized the Slav peoples in the 9th century. Demonstrations were held at Velehrad in Slovakia, tomb of Methodius, and cries of "We want the pope!" were heard. But the pope did not appear, and most foreign bishops who tried to go were refused visas. (See WORLD AFFAIRS [Western Europe]: *Vatican City State.*)   (PETER HEBBLETHWAITE)

THE ORTHODOX CHURCH

Against the tragic background of events in Lebanon, the activities and travels of Patriarch Ignatius IV of Antioch represented a significant element of sobriety and Christian concern. Under his leadership, the Orthodox community, the largest non-Muslim religious group in Syria and the second largest in Lebanon (after the Maronites), had so far avoided any direct involvement in violence and had gained accordingly in moral prestige. The Western-educated patriarch, residing permanently in Damascus, was also one of the six presidents of the World Council of Churches. In June he presided over the fourth General Assembly of the Middle Eastern Council of Churches in Nicosia, Cyprus. Following a pastoral visit to communities of his jurisdiction in South America (September–November 1984), he traveled to the U.S. in May–August 1985, spurring concern for the survival of Christianity in the Middle East but also expressing his support for Orthodox unity in America.

The year was marked by celebrations on the occasion of the 1,100th anniversary of the death of St. Methodius, one of the two missionaries who took Christianity from Constantinople to the Slavs. Festivities and international symposia were held in Thessaloniki, Greece; Sofia, Bulg.; and Prague, Czech. In Yugoslavia there were some confrontations and press polemics between government authorities and the Orthodox Church of Serbia, whose leadership complained about government restrictions of religious freedom. However, compared with other Communist countries, the situation of the Serbian church was clearly more favourable. Among episcopal consecrations was that of Amfilochije Radovich to the see of Banat. The new bishop was a theologian noted for his intellectual authority.

In Romania the outspoken Orthodox priest Gheorghe Calciu was released in August 1984 and allowed to immigrate to the U.S. a year later. In the Soviet Union, although the Orthodox Patriarchate was allowed to continue restoration of the large monastery of St. Daniel in Moscow, several bishops known for their popularity and pastoral activities (Cyril of Vyborg, Chrysostom of Kursk) were transferred to less prominent positions. A new, younger official was appointed as head of the State Council for Religious Affairs, replacing the official who had presided over the violent antireligious pressures of the 1960s. The policies and attitude of the new appointee had not yet been clearly manifested.

In the U.S. two new American-born bishops assumed pastoral responsibilities: Bishop Nathaniel Popp, as bishop of Detroit and head of the Romanian Episcopate within the autocephalous (independent) Orthodox Church in America, and Bishop Nicholas Smisko, as titular bishop of the Greek see of Amissos and head of the Carpatho-Russian diocese under the ecumenical patriarchate. Metropolitan Philaret, primate of the Russian Orthodox Church Outside Russia, with headquarters in New York, died November 21. A pan-Orthodox theological conference was held at Hellenic College, Brookline, Mass., June 1985, to study the document on "Baptism, Eucharist and Ministry" prepared by the World Council of Churches, which required an official response of the Orthodox Church.   (JOHN MEYENDORFF)

EASTERN NON-CHALCEDONIAN CHURCHES

The "pope" of the Coptic Church of Egypt, Shenuda III, was allowed by President Mubarak to leave the desert monastery of Amba-Bishoi, where he had resided in forced isolation since 1981 by order of the late Pres. Anwar as-Sadat. No formal conditions were set for the release, but Shenuda did make a public declaration of his intention to remain out of politics.

As leader of seven million Egyptian Christians, the outspoken prelate had previously provoked anti-Christian outbursts from fanatic Muslims. His liberation was demanded by many Christian leaders of the West. In September 1985 Metropolitan Theodosius, head of the Orthodox Church in America, paid a visit to Patriarch Shenuda in Cairo.

(JOHN MEYENDORFF)

JUDAISM

Judaism, the worldview and way of life of the religious sector of the Jewish people wherever they live, unfolds in close relationship to the history of all Jews as a group. That interplay between history and religion, which brought the prophets to comment on public affairs, calls attention, in considering the state of Judaism, to political and not only synagogal or other religious events.

President Reagan's brief and symbolic visit to the Bitburg cemetery in West Germany, along with his moving pilgrimage to the memorial of the concentration camp at Bergen-Belsen, once more brought deeply Judaic religious concerns into the headlines. (See *Introduction,* above.) While regretting the president's visit to a German military cemetery, Kenneth Bialkin, chairman of the Conference of Presidents of Major American Jewish Organizations, stated: "We do not accuse the President of ill will." Bialkin said the rejection of collective guilt, which Jews do not impute to the German people, "does not involve forgiveness of or reconciliation with the Nazi movement or those who consciously or willfully advanced it. For them there can be no forgiveness from us." That statement of the requirement of both justice and mercy represented in practical terms a well-established position of Judaic theology. The conception of total forgiveness for unrepentant Nazis never found a hearing in the Judaic world.

The Public Broadcasting System's portrayal of Judaism's history, "Heritage: Civilization and the Jews," which aired in 1984, came under severe criticism from Orthodox Judaism. Various Orthodox groups

AP/WIDE WORLD

Shenuda III, patriarch of the Coptic Church, is greeted by fellow Egyptian Christians as he returns to Cairo in January from four years' exile in a desert monastery. The patriarch's release was one of several actions by Pres. Hosni Mubarak intended to quiet religious unrest in Egypt.

At a February news conference at the Jewish Theological Seminary of America in New York City, Amy Eilberg discussed her pending ordination as the first woman Conservative rabbi. She was ordained in May.

WILLIAM E. SAURO/THE NEW YORK TIMES

rejected the TV series for portraying Judaism as a historical, not a supernatural religion. The representation of the Hebrew Scriptures ("Old Testament") as the work of man, basically beginning after the exile of ancient Israel to Babylonia in 586 BCE, drew particular opprobrium among the Orthodox groups. Abba Eban, who narrated "Heritage," defended the series, saying, "We did not create this program to appeal to Orthodox rabbis, but rather to say something to millions of assimilated Jews who know little about their heritage. We also wanted to reach the non-Jewish world." Still, versions of the series shown overseas, particularly in the State of Israel, contained reworked passages framed to meet the Orthodox complaints. The Orthodox protest aside, some critics found the program dull and diffuse, but the series did draw the attention of millions to the history of Judaism and its role in world civilization.

One issue internal to the Jewish community that came under discussion in 1985 involved the moral status of the Jewish men arrested for alleged terrorist activities against Arabs in the State of Israel. The defendants were charged with forming a Jewish terrorist organization and were indicted for various acts of violence. In a spirited debate, Ariel Simon, an Orthodox Jew and an Israeli, described the group as a messianic sect, proposing to hasten the coming of the Messiah "by provoking a war between Israel and its Arab neighbours." Simon pointed out that Ariel Sharon, Israeli minister of defense at the time of the Lebanon war, had said, "No people in the world has a moral right to question our actions." On this matter Simon commented, "I believe we ourselves have the right and obligation to question our actions. You cannot use the Holocaust as a carte blanche to do whatever you want." Taking a more positive view of the same group, Avraham Weiss, a rabbi in Riverdale, N.Y., rejected violence but

held that the group had aimed at defending Jewish lives. A person has a right of self-defense of others "if the person to be killed is engaged in wrongful conduct . . . for which the person is legally culpable, or if killing the person will save the victim."

In May 1985 the first woman to be ordained a rabbi in Conservative Judaism, Amy Eilberg, wife of a Conservative rabbi, was ordained by the Jewish Theological Seminary of America (JTSA). Chancellor Gerson D. Cohen of JTSA emphasized that congregations in the Conservative movement are not obligated to accept a woman rabbi. He explained to the movement, in a letter of March 11, 1985: "It does mean that such a choice falls within the limits of Jewish law as interpreted by the Conservative Movement. . . ." Cohen maintained: "Our movement has always accepted pluralism. The final decision is left to the individual rabbi."

At the same time, Cohen, in an interview in a number of newspapers, affirmed the possibility of abrogating the principle that the status of the mother as a Jew alone defines the status, as to Judaism, of the child. Thus, if the mother is Jewish and the father not, the child is Jewish. Cohen was reported to have suggested that the status of the father alone might also serve. At year's end the matter remained in doubt. Some Conservative rabbis, organized in a League for Traditional Judaism, found the questioning of the matrilineal principle difficult to accept. Many now expressed concern that the ordination of women, strongly opposed by a sizable minority of Conservative rabbis, might prove to be the beginning of the division of Conservative Judaism between Orthodoxy and Reform movements in America.

(JACOB NEUSNER)

BUDDHISM

The mood of Buddhists in 1985 could be characterized as one of remembrance and hope. Thirty years earlier, Buddhist leaders, notably U Nu of Burma and Prince Norodom Sihanouk of Cambodia (now Kampuchea), were among the heads of 29 Asian and African nations who met in Bandung, Indon. Buddhists hoped then to gain a voice in world affairs. They also hoped that the departure of U.S. forces from Vietnam 20 years later would remove the last vestige of colonialism. Both of those hopes had been disappointed. The unity of Bandung had become a thing of the past, and Southeast Asia continued to struggle with anti-Buddhist Communism. Borobudur, an important Buddhist shrine in Indonesia, was bombed by terrorists.

Among the traditional Buddhist nations, Sri Lanka had become the bloody scene of renewed violent conflict between the Hindu Tamil minority in the north and the Buddhist Sinhalese majority. (See WORLD AFFAIRS [South Asia]: Sri Lanka.) Kampuchea in Southeast Asia was occupied by Vietnamese forces, and Prince Sihanouk, one-time advocate of Buddhist socialism, had become the titular head of anti-Vietnamese groups. In the Far East, the Beijing (Peking) regime was busy restoring Buddhist temples, more as art objects and tourist attractions than for piety's sake. The year 1985 marked the 20th anniversary of the formal incorporation of Tibet as an autonomous region of China, and the

regime was eager to lure the Dalai Lama to Tibet, even for a short visit. The Dalai Lama was reluctant, however. He believed that of 7,000 monasteries and temples in Tibet prior to 1950, all but 30 had been destroyed.

As in prior years, the West, especially the U.S., promised great hope for Buddhism. The Buddhist-promoting Foundation in Tokyo announced the establishment of visiting chairs at the University of California and elsewhere. In May 1985 the Chuang Yen Monastery was dedicated on a 190-ha (475-ac) tract in Kent, N.Y., by a layman, C. T. Shen, vice-president of the Buddhist Association of the United States. Meanwhile, the National Council of the Buddhist Churches of America, meeting in San Francisco, adopted a resolution opposing the effort to legalize prayer in the public schools.   (JOSEPH M. KITAGAWA)

HINDUISM

Tension and violence between Hindu and Sikh communities in India continued into 1985. Prime Minister Rajiv Gandhi pursued the initiatives of his late mother, Indira Gandhi, in attempting to reach accord with leaders of the Sikh community. In July Gandhi and Sant Harchand Singh Longowal (see OBITUARIES), president of the major Sikh political organization, the Akali Dal, achieved an agreement that promised an end to nearly three years of bloody strife, but scarcely a month later Longowal was assassinated by Sikh extremists. The murder did not deter Gandhi from carrying out the terms of the agreement, including election of a popular government in the Sikh-dominated Punjab and of state representatives to the Lok Sabha (parliament). The Sant's assassination, however, did indicate that strife between the communities would persist. (See WORLD AFFAIRS [South Asia]: India.)

In the state of Gujarat violence marked the disagreement within the Hindu community over the state government's plan to increase the number of places reserved for members of the lowest castes in government positions and educational institutions. The policy of "reservation," coupled with promotion in government employment along caste lines, had been instituted in India as a way to break down traditional boundaries between lower and upper castes and to increase educational and employment opportunities for the "backward" (lowest) castes. Detractors of the policy insisted that it only intensified caste distinctions. In Gujarat the discord led to bloody riots with over 300 deaths, and the Army was brought in to restore law and order in major cities.

The summer of 1985 began "Festival of India" celebrations in the U.S. and France, which in part highlighted Hindu art and thought. In India the festival occasioned controversy over the risks involved in exporting priceless pieces of religious iconography for exhibition in the U.S. As part of the Festival of India in the U.S., a Rathayatra, or car festival, was held on Fifth Avenue in New York City on September 15 to mark the opening of a special exhibition of Indian art at the Metropolitan Museum of Art. The great Rathayatra of Lord Jagannath was observed in the Indian city of Puri in mid-June with thousands of devotees pulling the great chariots holding

images of the deities Balarama, Subhadra, and Jagannatha.

In Jaipur a new marble temple, replicating traditional Rajasthani designs, was dedicated in February to the deity Lakshmi Narayan. In the state of Haryana rare images of Hindu deities, including the elephant-headed god, Ganesa, were found near Panipat, one of the richest yields of medieval stone sculpture in recent years.

Outside India, the religious community of Bhagwan Shree Rajneesh in Oregon broke up when its founder returned to India. After the defection of the Bhagwan's chief adviser, Ma Anand Sheela, and several other followers, the Bhagwan was arrested on immigration charges as he prepared to leave the country. Under a plea-bargaining arrangement, he was permitted to depart after pleading guilty to arranging sham marriages that allowed his foreign-born disciples to stay in the U.S.

(H. PATRICK SULLIVAN)

ISLAM

Two trends evident in recent years continued in 1985: political violence, including terrorism, and religious conservatism. Frequently the two were linked. Riots in Indonesia continued through January and February, when President Suharto further developed his campaign for a unifying national ideology by emphasizing secularist laws combined with a humanist belief in an unnamed god. Islamic fundamentalists found these moves objectionable. In April more than a hundred persons died in Gombe in northern Nigeria in clashes between the Army and a banned Muslim fundamentalist sect. A principal cause of the coup that overthrew Pres. Gaafar Nimeiry in the Sudan in April appeared to be his policy of imposing traditional Islamic legal practices.

In Lebanon militant Shi'ah groups became stronger and more prominent, as evidenced in the role played by one of them in the hijacking of a TWA airliner in June. Some were alleged to be under the influence of Iranian religious authorities, although there was little direct evidence of this. Their principal strongholds were in the traditional Shi'ah locations in Lebanon, namely the larger cities and the southern interior. In the early spring the government of Iran increased pressure against groups deemed hostile or antirevolutionary. In February Baha'is once again were placed under heavy restrictions. In April, however, Pres. Sayyed Ali Khamenei ordered a halt to public harassment of persons accused of improper behaviour or dress.

In Egypt increasing pressure was exerted by strong fundamentalist groups that had been agitating to repeal secularist laws enacted in recent years. In May the People's Assembly agreed to review many of the laws and to revise those deemed not in accord with the Shari'ah (Islamic religious law). However, members rejected a call for immediate full imposition of the Shari'ah. Continuing the conservative trend, the Egyptian Supreme Court struck down the 1979 law pertaining to women's rights; thus Egyptian law still recognized the practice of polygamy. A fundamentalist demonstration was attacked by the police in July, and 45 persons were arrested. Egypt's problems illustrated the difficulty of finding a viable means for accommodating both the strong tide of Muslim fundamentalism and contemporary life-styles and international influences.

Banks in Pakistan changed to Islamic principles of operation; by June no more interest charges could be assessed. China announced a $7 million grant to build an Islamic centre, thus continuing moves there toward increasing freedom of religious expression. In the U.S. the former Black Muslim movement, which had separated into two parts, was again in the news. The American Muslim Mission, which had become more traditionally Islamic, announced its dissolution in May and aimed to unify its followers with Muslims elsewhere. Meanwhile, the Nation of Islam headed by Louis Farrakhan, which had maintained the call for black separatism, received a loan of $5 million from Pres. Muammar al-Qaddafi of Libya for the announced purpose of providing economic assistance to American blacks.

(REUBEN W. SMITH)

WORLD CHURCH MEMBERSHIP

Reckoning religious adherence is a precarious exercise. Where minorities are persecuted, dissimulation and deception become survival tactics. Different religions vary greatly in their methods of counting and reporting. Some simply depend on government population statistics. For others, "numbering the people" is forbidden. Some count only adult males and heads of families; others count adults, children, servants, and retainers. Some count contributors; others estimate communicants.

Different procedures are followed even within the same religion. Quite reliable statistics are available on the mission fields and for renewal movements in Islam, Buddhism, Hinduism, and Christianity. Where a religion has been established for centuries (e.g., Christianity in Europe, Hinduism in India), whole national populations may be counted as adherents, a practice that has become highly problematic with the decline of religious observance and the rise of antireligious ideologies. It is difficult to get satisfactory estimates for populations controlled by governments hostile to traditional religions.

The traditional listing of religions makes no provision for several religions or faiths now numerous and/or influential; e.g., Baha'i, Ch'ondokyo, Umbanda, the Unification Church, the religions of the Sikhs and Jains (usually, and erroneously, subsumed under "Hinduism"). Taoism and Confucianism are now so blended in many areas that it is becoming common to refer to "Chinese folk-religion."

The reader is advised to reflect carefully upon the statistics reported and to refer to articles discussing the different countries and religions when pursuing the subject in depth. (FRANKLIN H. LITTELL)

This article updates the *Macropædia* articles The Buddha and BUDDHISM; CHRISTIANITY; EASTERN ORTHODOXY; HINDUISM; Muhammad and the Religion of ISLAM; JUDAISM; PROTESTANTISM; The Study and Classification of RELIGIONS; ROMAN CATHOLICISM; and *Micropædia* entries on the various denominations.

Estimated Membership of the Principal Religions of the World

Religions	North America[1]	South America	Europe[2]	Asia[3]	Africa	Oceania[4]	World
Total Christian	262,870,400	195,431,000	329,380,000	106,230,000	149,200,200	18,600,000	1,061,711,600
Roman Catholic	143,850,000	185,100,200	177,140,200	58,100,200	59,700,000	5,100,200	628,990,900
Eastern Orthodox	5,320,400	330,400	43,430,300	2,800,000	6,700,200[5]	370,000	58,951,100
Protestant[6]	113,700,000	10,000,400	108,809,500	45,329,800	82,800,100[7]	13,129,800	373,769,600
Jewish	7,630,000	720,200	3,800,100	4,480,200	227,500	74,000	16,932,000
Muslim[8]	1,820,300	390,100	20,400,000	381,700,800	150,300,000	89,000	554,700,200
Zoroastrian	2,700	2,600	14,000	230,000	1,500	—	250,800
Shinto[9]	48,000	—	—	32,000,000	—	—	32,048,000
Taoist	30,000	11,000	12,000	20,000,000	—	3,000	20,056,000
Confucian	100,000	56,000	410,000	150,400,000	—	18,000	150,984,000
Buddhist[10]	350,200	248,000	210,000	246,740,300	15,000	24,000	247,587,500
Hindu[11]	380,000	615,200	390,000	461,300,000	800,000	325,000	463,815,200
Totals	273,231,600	197,474,100	354,616,100	1,403,081,300	300,544,200	19,138,000	2,548,085,200
Population[12]	400,802,000	268,825,000	775,310,000	2,819,081,000	553,210,000	24,820,000	4,842,048,000

[1]Includes Central America and the West Indies.
[2]Includes the U.S.S.R. and other countries with established Marxist ideology where continuing religious adherence is difficult to estimate.
[3]Includes areas in which persons have traditionally enrolled in several religions, as well as China with a Marxist establishment.
[4]Includes Australia and New Zealand as well as islands of the South Pacific.
[5]Includes Coptic Christians, of restricted status in Egypt and precariously situated under the Marxist junta in Ethiopia.
[6]Protestant statistics vary widely in style of reckoning affiliation. See accompanying article on "World Church Membership."
[7]Includes a great proliferation of new churches, sects, and cults among African Christians.
[8]The chief base of Islam is still ethnic, although missionary work is now carried on in Europe and America. In countries where Islam is established, minority religions are frequently persecuted and accurate statistics are rare.
[9]A Japanese ethnic religion, Shinto declined rapidly after the Japanese emperor surrendered his claim to divinity (1947); a revival of cultic emphasis in recent years has had chiefly literary significance. Shinto does not survive well outside Japan.
[10]Buddhism has produced several renewal movements in the last century that have gained adherents in Europe and America. Although persecuted in Tibet and sometimes elsewhere in Asia, it has shown greater staying power than other religions of the East. It also transplants better.
[11]Hinduism's strength in India has been enhanced by its connection with the national movement, a phenomenon also observable in the world of Islam. Modern Hinduism has developed several renewal movements that have won some adherents in areas outside traditional Hindu territory.
[12]United Nations, Department of International Economic and Social Affairs; data refer to midyear 1985. (FRANKLIN H. LITTELL)

As the "New Religions" Grow Older

BY MARTIN E. MARTY

When Minister Louis Farrakhan filled Madison Square Garden in New York City in the early autumn of 1985, he drew attention to the Nation of Islam, a group that had split off from the American Muslim Mission. Controversy over his anti-Semitic remarks tended to obscure awareness that he led a small, intense religious group of the sort that several years earlier would have been called a "cult." When, in November, the Oregon commune of Rajneeshpuram announced plans to dissolve after its founder, Bhagwan Shree Rajneesh, left the country, it appeared that another such group would soon vanish.

Where Have They Gone? Such events as these occasionally kept the issue of "cults" and "the occult" before the public. For the larger part they had slipped from view, or at least from the attention they had commanded in the media 15 years earlier. Almost a generation had passed since 1969, when a California professor, Theodore Roszak, had described *The Making of a Counter Culture*, a youthful movement that provided the context for the "cults." A year later another California professor, Jacob Needleman, called his book on Meher Baba, Subud, Transcendental Meditation, and the like *The New Religions*, even though some of them had ancient roots. In the United States they were new, and they were news.

Fifteen years later, despite the occasional front-page story, it had become appropriate to ask, "Whatever happened to the 'New Religions' in America?" The Evangelical magazine *Christianity Today* consulted counsellors who deal with members of these groups. They contended that the groups were as strong as ever. A scholarly conference in April at the University of Nebraska attracted scores of researchers who found plenty of groups to study. But something *had* happened. By 1985 attention focused more on the legal rights of "cults" than on their promise, more on how to study them objectively than on what to study.

Hard evidence on cultural trends such as these is always difficult to amass; much of it comes from impression. Thus campus bulletin boards, once crowded with notices about Eastern religious groups and their meetings, now usually had only a few yellowing placards on the subject. Visual images of saffron-clad young people on street corners and in airports were dimming as the surviving members of the groups donned business suits or disappeared. Suburban conversations about young family members "lost" to intense religious groups were less frequent. Had the groups risen to a crest, only to decline and begin to slip away?

Such a question is hard to answer because it could be that the media and the public simply take the once-new phenomena for granted. It could also be that a different sort of expertise was now needed to cope with stories on the subject. Thus legal experts and reporters had to cover the news when the Rev. Sun Myung Moon, founder of the Holy Spirit Association for the Unification of World Christianity, the "Unification Church," was released in August from a Danbury, Conn., prison where he had served time for federal tax violations. At the time of his release some reporters noted that his church claimed 45,000 members. Many observers thought it numbered only 5,000 to 15,000.

The Numbers Game. In 1974 psychiatrist Harrison Pope, Jr., in *The Road East* admitted that it was hard to count the New Religious population in general. Yet Nichiren Shoshu Buddhism then claimed 100,000 American practitioners; followers of the Guru Maharaj Ji were said to be approaching 100,000; and Transcendental Meditation listed 232,118 initiates by 1973. In 1981 James Ogilvy and Philip Kohlenberg in *Religion and Values* cited a Gallup Poll that found six million in Transcendental Meditation, four million in Yoga, and a million interested in other Asian traditions. "These statistics reveal a mass movement toward Eastern thought." By the mid-'80s there was no more talk of such a mass movement, and suspicion about inflated statistics became widespread.

To the direct question "How many Americans are members of New Religion groups?" the answer is clear: "No one knows and no one can know." The U.S. Census dare not ask detailed questions about religion. Churches and religious movements need not release figures about membership. The New Religions do not report to the *Yearbook of American and Canadian Churches*. Only Transcendental Meditation released accurate statistics, and they revealed a drastic drop in initiates in the 1980s.

Leaders of the groups have good reason to inflate statistics. It gives them encouragement, suggests that they are to be reckoned with, and hints that joining them is the thing to do. Enemies of the groups organized in the Anti-Cult Movement (ACM), made up in part of parents who "lost" children to "cults," have reasons to suggest that huge numbers are involved. Such statistics would impel others to regard cults as threats to their families and country. Scholars of New Religions, many of them fair-minded in their researches and not a few of them empathic with and even congenial to New Religions, might be expected to work with inflated statistics to show that their subject matter is important.

Despite all this, more and more experts now take low membership figures seriously. In *The Cult Experience* (1982), J. Gordon Melton and Robert L. Moore, two not unfriendly scholars, suggested, on the basis of the best available data, that the two largest New Religions, Scientology and the Unification Church, seemed to have each not "much more than 5,000 and certainly than 8,000 to 10,000 active members (*i.e.*, persons who would consider themselves Scientologists or Unificationists)." They note that many mainline Christian congregations are larger than the largest of these movements. In 1978 the Church of Satan claimed 10,000 members, but "fewer than 2,000 seem to have been active at any given time," and by 1979 only three "grottoes" (congregations) remained at all active. "By the best estimates several hundred thousand persons could be considered members of alternative religions."

The Gallup Poll had gone wrong, Willa Appel contended in 1983 in *Cults in America*, for "puzzling" reasons, partly because it had to count not only members but

---

Martin E. Marty is Fairfax M. Cone distinguished service professor of history of modern Christianity at the University of Chicago and senior editor of The Christian Century.

also those peripherally involved. She phoned a Hare Krishna employee about the 1978 Gallup Youth Survey projection of 250,000 teenagers in the group. After some hesitation the employee estimated 5,000 full-time members in the United States. Scientologists had an accountable membership not of three million but of about 6,500.

End of a Phase. No one knows, one must repeat, how many are involved, but one can now speak of the rise of the New Religions as an episode in one stage of American culture. Many of the new groups arrived in the late 1960s, when the youth culture was large, when the "counterculture" of drugs, hippies, and experimenters with "alternative life-styles" thrived in the midst of economic prosperity. In the early 1970s the New Religions had grown, established themselves, and become lures for many searching young people.

In the course of the 1970s many things changed. Most scholars list several reasons for the arrested growth of the movements. First, faddism. Joining became no longer the thing to do. Second, the economy. Recession in the 1970s removed the luxury of experiment, and young people lined up straight and square, as it were, in college, there to pursue careers that might assure them prosperity in harder times. Esoteric religions became a luxury and a distraction. Third, there was a documentable high attrition or "dropout" rate, so the groups did not hold the converts whose arrival they advertised.

Later in the decade other factors became significant. The mass suicide of 913 emigrants at Jonestown, Guyana, made "People's Temple" a term with which to stigmatize cults and drive people off. Sometimes declining groups were drastically altered and became less noticeable. Thus the Transcendental Meditation movement put its energies chiefly into its university in Fairfield, Iowa, and impressed townspeople as being generally respectable, though nationally the group was suspect for claiming that initiates could or did "levitate." Others, like the Children of God, faced decline and criticism by moving to Africa and Europe.

One trend, as New Religions turned old, was that old religions turned new. They cut into what some scholars call the recruiting "market." Born-again Christians, Catholic Pentecostals, and Hasidic Jews reached for enthusiastic and exuberant forms that were congenial with home-grown religious traditions. Young people, without ranging so far, could have intense experiences, find new authorities in their lives, gain an identity in a group.

The most publicized among recent New Religions was that of the Bhagwan Shree Rajneesh, who was better known to the public for his collection of Rolls Royces than for his theology. Rajneeshpuram, the sect's commune in Oregon, was wracked by dissent and legal problems and finally dissolved in 1985.
M. NAYTHONS—GAMMA/LIAISON

It would be foolish to predict the disappearance of the New Religions. They meet the needs of too many citizens for that. They have a way of reappearing in new guises when old ones no longer attract. They are likely to remain a permanent part of the religious scene. It is not easy to picture a nation of 240 million people all of whom would be "secular" on the one hand or satisfied with conventional religion on the other. But clearly one stage of New Religion, one episode, is passing.

One might picture the movement as a glacier that moves on. It leaves a moraine, an altered landscape. In this case, the altered landscape alerts observers to at least one grand theme: people and cultures are more diverse and complex than most analysts of 20 years ago had thought. Not all are satisfied with a world in which signals of the sacred are said to disappear, or in which they are channeled into routine institutions. Such seekers will continue to search for outlets, in the New Religions grown older or the Old-Time Religions striving to be renewed.

CAROL BERNSON

Once a familiar sight on street corners and particularly at airports, where they provoked reactions ranging from amusement to outrage as they solicited contributions and distributed literature about their beliefs, the Hare Krishnas were becoming scarce.

Social Security and Welfare Services

The tendency to cut back on social security expenditure remained in evidence during 1985. The motives of governments were in part economic, in part ideological. In countries such as Spain, where the issue was approached mainly from an economic perspective, the authorities succeeded in securing a large measure of popular support for reforms designed to moderate the growth in expenditure. In the U.K., where government proposals appeared to be inspired primarily by ideological considerations, measures aimed at reforming the social security system met stiff opposition.

National Developments in Social Security. Some countries managed to improve their systems. Finland, for example, passed legislation making retirement age more flexible under both the national pensions scheme and the earnings-related pension scheme for private-sector employees. "Occupation-based early retirement pensions" were to be payable from 1986 onward to persons aged 55 or over whose working capacity had deteriorated to such an extent that they could not reasonably be expected to continue working in their normal occupation. The new benefit would be payable at the same rate as the full disability pension. A second innovation contained in the Finnish legislation was that old-age pensions might now be drawn up to five years before the standard pension age of 65, subject to a permanent reduction in benefit of 6% per annum. The pension might also be deferred, as was already the case prior to 1986, and a supplement was then payable equal to 12% per annum. Finally, it was indicated that part-time pensions for employees aged 60 and over covered by the earnings-related pension scheme would be introduced in 1987 on the basis of legislation expected to be passed in 1986. Such pensions, which avoided an abrupt transition from work to retirement, had proved very popular in Sweden.

In France a new benefit was introduced for parents who stopped work or reduced their working hours by half following the birth of a child, when that birth brought the total number of dependent children to three or more. This measure reflected the government's belief that encouraging families to have a third child was crucial in order to raise the birthrate. The benefit was approximately F 1,000 per month (or F 500, if the beneficiary continued to work half-time) and was payable until the child was aged three to parents of either sex who had worked for 24 out of the previous 30 months.

Earnings-related unemployment benefits were introduced in Portugal. Until 1985 all that had been provided for the unemployed were flat-rate, means-tested benefits introduced in 1977. The new benefit was paid at the same rate as sickness benefit (60% of previous earnings) and was payable for six months to unemployed workers who had been in employment for at least three years. The duration of benefit was one month greater for each additional year of previous employment, and unemployed workers who were 62 years old by the time their benefit entitlement was exhausted qualified for an early retirement pension. The existing unemployment assistance scheme would continue to provide lower benefits for agricultural wage earners, as long as they were not covered by the general social security scheme, as well as other unemployed workers who had exhausted their rights under the contributory scheme.

In most other countries, governments attempted with varying degrees of success to reduce their social security commitments. As part of an austerity program introduced in May, the government of Chile announced a freeze on old-age pensions that continued to be paid under the pre-1981 social security system and cut unemployment benefits by half. In Italy, where a reform to cut the costs of social security remained high on the government's list of priorities, a report to Parliament by the minister of labour revealed that the Italian social security system was being defrauded by employers on a large scale. More than 43% of the businesses visited by labour inspectors during the previous year had been found to have irregularities in the payment of their social security contributions. As a result of the inspections, more than 805 billion lire were recovered, 269 billion of which were deemed to be intentional fraud.

In Japan a major pension reform was enacted in April, for implementation in April 1986, designed to reduce the rise in social security costs expected to take place over the next 40 years because of the aging of the population and the maturing of the country's system. The accrual rate for earnings-related pensions for employees would decrease gradually from 1 to 0.75% of covered earnings per year; the accrual rate for flat-rate pensions, both for employees and for the rest of the population, would also decrease, so that it would take 40 years rather than 25 years to earn a full pension. The retirement age for employed women would be increased gradually from 55 to 60, the age applying to men. Finally, all wives would be compulsorily covered by

CHARLES HIGGINS, JR./THE NEW YORK TIMES

More than one-third of all persons labeled poor in a U.S. Census Bureau study were children, and a similar proportion were from single-parent homes. Of minority children under six years of age, over half were considered poor.

the National (flat-rate) Pension Program. These measures would be phased in over a period of 20 years. It was also the government's intention to increase the retirement age to 65, but no date for this was specified in the 1985 reform.

Social security benefits in The Netherlands were further reduced in the course of 1985. At the beginning of the year, unemployment and disability insurance benefits, which had amounted to 80% of previous earnings until the end of 1983, were lowered to 70%, and in May sickness benefits were cut from 80 to 75% of earnings, with a further reduction to 70% planned for January 1986. Legislation was passed making the duration of unemployment benefit dependent on age. At a later stage, benefit duration would be related not only to age but also to the duration of previous employment.

Legislation was passed in Spain reforming the country's pension system with a view to reducing expenditure in years to come. Pensions, previously based on average covered earnings in the best two of the last seven years of employment, were to be based on average earnings in the last eight years, the first six of these being revalued in line with the consumer price index; the new formula would be phased in over a four-year period. The minimum period of insured employment required to establish eligibility for an old-age pension was increased from 10 to 15 years. The 12 contribution categories used previously were abolished, so that contributions and benefits would now be based on actual earnings. It was expected that as a result pensions would ultimately be reduced by between 8 and 10%.

In the U.K. a government review of social security declared that the system had "lost its way" and proposed the phasing out of the State Earnings Related Pension Scheme, established with the agreement of all parties in 1978. The proposal elicited an overwhelmingly hostile reaction not only from the trade unions and poverty pressure groups but also from the Confederation of British Industry, whose members believed that it would increase total employment costs and create instability in the pension system. As a result, the government backed down on its abolition proposal while leaving the way open for some cost-cutting modifications.

A second major proposal contained in the U.K. social security review was to replace the supplementary benefit system by a new system of income support, under which benefits would be determined by age and family responsibilities. Single payments made under the existing regulations to persons lacking clothing, furniture, and other necessities would be abolished and replaced by discretionary payments from a social fund. In October an important change took place in the financing of the British social security system. The contributions ceiling, previously fixed at earnings of £265 per week, was abolished as far as employers' contributions were concerned, and the extra revenue was used to reduce the contributions payable by low-paid employees and their employers.   (ROGER A. BEATTIE)

An old social program and two relatively new ones shared the spotlight in the U.S. in 1985, while the debate over poverty and how to deal with it became more acrimonious. The old program was Social Security, which celebrated its 50th anniversary in apparently solid financial and political shape. Total income for the year for the Social Security system was expected to be $199.5 billion, with disbursements (benefit payments and administrative costs) of $193.2 billion. After years of concern over the future, the system was said to be fiscally sound for at least the next half century. According to Census Bureau estimates, beneficiaries would more than double by the year 2035—from 36,683,000 in 1985 to 79,843,000—and disburse-

ments were expected to increase 25-fold, to more than $5 trillion. However, assets were also expected to soar during those 50 years, from $35.6 billion to $11,428,700,000,000, although critics claimed that this projection was far too optimistic.

In the political arena, Congress moved to make the Social Security Administration more independent and to free its old-age and disability trust funds from future budget battles. Efforts to freeze the annual cost-of-living adjustments (COLAs) failed, as the House of Representatives and the Reagan administration prevailed over the Senate. As a result, Social Security beneficiaries would receive a 3.1% cost-of-living increase as of Jan. 3, 1986, raising the monthly benefit from $464 to $478 for the average retired worker and from $788 to $812 for the average couple. The maximum benefit for a person who retired in 1985 at age 65 would be $739. To finance the increase, Social Security taxes would go up in 1986 to 7.15% on the first $42,000 of a worker's salary, compared with 7.05% on the first $39,600 in 1985.

In another victory for beneficiaries, the Reagan administration announced that it would generally follow court precedents requiring the payment of Social Security disability benefits. The government in recent years had tried to cut monthly disability payments to almost half a million people, usually on grounds that they were no longer too ill or injured to work. The courts, however, had ruled in thousands of cases that the benefits were ended improperly.

As Social Security reached middle age, two relatively new social experiments gained attention. One of these was "workfare," which tied welfare benefits to work. It had been tried on a small scale in the 1960s and 1970s with the federal Work Incentive Program and in California when Ronald Reagan was governor. As president, Reagan proposed a national mandatory work requirement for welfare recipients in 1981, but Congress rejected the idea in favour of state programs. By the end of 1985, at least 23 states were experimenting with the idea on a limited basis. Programs varied from state to state, but most offered participants help in finding jobs or getting job training before requiring them to work for their monthly assistance. Although the number of participants was still only a small proportion of the total welfare rolls, it was growing. The nation's two most populous states, New York and California, initiated mandatory workfare programs in 1985. New York's plan, considered the most comprehensive of its kind in the U.S., would require an estimated 220,000 welfare recipients (mothers with children under age six were exempted) to take a job or enter a job-training program or have their benefits reduced.

The second stepped-up program was the crackdown on parents—almost all of them fathers—who failed to pay child support. A federal law that was enacted in 1984 and went into effect Oct. 1, 1985, required states to go after delinquent child-support payments or face the loss of up to 5% of their federal welfare funds. The law ordered states to provide for mandatory wage withholding as soon as an absent parent fell 30 days behind in payments. States would also have to arrange to withhold tax refunds from parents who were delinquent in payments and place liens on their property. As of October 1, 21 states had already adopted the required regulations. A Census Bureau study said that half of the four million parents who were legally entitled to child support from an absent spouse in 1983 did not receive the full payment.

Meanwhile, the debate over poverty and what to do about it intensified. The Census Bureau reported that the

(continued on page 376)

Urban Poverty and Homelessness

BY PETER HALL

Preparations were under way during 1985 for the International Year of Shelter for the Homeless in 1987, designated by the UN General Assembly with the aim of improving the housing of the poor. In many third world cities projects were being undertaken to achieve the UN's objective: that by 1987 at least some poor people would enjoy better shelter and upgraded neighbourhoods. In this context there was no little irony in the fact that a mere three blocks from the UN's New York headquarters, in one of the richest cities in the world, scores of homeless people were sleeping each night on the floors and in the telephone booths of Grand Central Terminal.

A Growing Problem. During the first half of the 1980s, homelessness—especially big-city homelessness—had become a major focus of U.S. media attention and public concern. In December 1982, and again in January and May 1984, the House of Representatives Subcommittee on Housing and Community Development had received expert testimony on the subject, with the most graphic coming from the victims of homelessness themselves. Committee members heard of people sleeping under freeways, in tent cities and makeshift shanties, in their cars, even—on the evidence of a Salvation Army major from Cleveland, Ohio—in the boxes maintained by the Army to receive donations of discarded clothing. They heard from the mayors of some of the nation's leading cities, and from Gov. Mario Cuomo of New York, that the problem was becoming much worse.

Just how many homeless there were was the subject of fierce controversy. *Homelessness in America: A Forced March to Nowhere,* a widely publicized report by Mary Ellen Hombs and Mitch Snyder of the Community for Creative Non-Violence, based on interviews with local experts, put the figure at 2.2 million nationally. The federal Department of Housing and Urban Development (HUD) commissioned its own study, which used a variety of methods to produce a range of from 192,000 to 586,000 on any one night in early 1984; within that range, the consultants thought the most reliable estimates were between 250,000 (quoted by local observers) and 350,000 (from operators of shelters). HUD Secretary Samuel R. Pierce used his department's report to cast doubt on the Hombs-Snyder figure. In turn, at the House subcommittee hearing, Rep. Barney Frank (Dem., Mass.) condemned the HUD report as "intellectually shoddy, methodologically lacking, morally incredibly callous."

If there was no consensus on figures, there was at least some agreement on causes. The HUD investigators confirmed the testimony of many local observers before the House subcommittee: within the homeless population, certain groups—the mentally ill, alcoholics and drug abusers, ethnic minorities, young single men—were overrepresented. They differed from much congressional evidence, however, in finding that most homeless persons had been on the fringes of society for some time. Congressional witnesses had suggested a recent sharp upswing in homelessness among the "new poor": families, especially those belonging to ethnic minorities, who had lost their homes as a result of unemployment or the steady erosion in the supply of low-rent homes and cheap hotels. Their numbers, the witnesses suggested, were augmented by two other groups: mental patients discharged from hospitals under deinstitutionalization programs, accounting for perhaps 30–40% of the total, and some 350,000 people taken off disability assistance rolls during 1981–83 because of more stringent eligibility rules.

The response to the problem was varied, and some witnesses argued strongly that it was inadequate. Coping with homelessness in the U.S. is strictly a matter for the cities themselves. In general, state law gives little guidance, although in New York a legal action of 1979 led to the signing of a consent decree that, in effect, committed the city to providing shelter. In any case, most U.S. cities can do little more than furnish emergency shelter, because their stocks of low-rent public housing are so limited.

PATRICK AVENTURIER—GAMMA/LIAISON

The rise in the number of urban homeless was a growing concern of a great many nations, developed and less developed alike. During a January cold snap, this French train station became a refuge.

As part of an outreach project administered by Gouverneur Hospital in New York City, a worker offers lunch to a man who lives in a box in Battery Park. The program's chief frustration was the large number of mentally ill homeless who refused help.

KEVIN MEYERS/THE NEW YORK TIMES

Britain's Homeless. At first sight, the situation in Britain would appear to be very different. In 1983, despite sales of some 500,000 units of public housing to the occupiers in the previous three years, 32% of all households still rented from local authorities or other public bodies. This meant that while the typical low-income U.S. household had to find private rental housing, often in bad condition and at rents that were high in relation to income (resulting in a constant risk of eviction for nonpayment of rent), its British counterpart would be housed in fairly modern public housing, with all the necessary amenities, at a subsidized rent, and with a considerable degree of security against eviction.

The most notable difference, however, is that Britain, unlike the U.S., has national legislation to provide for homeless people. The Housing (Homeless Persons) Act, 1977 (in England and Wales; the equivalent Scottish act dates from 1978), requires borough or district authorities with responsibilities for housing to take specific action to help the homeless. For certain groups considered to be in "priority need"—those with dependent children, pregnant women, the aged or handicapped, victims of disasters—the local housing authority has a responsibility to find secure accommodation.

Some limitations were written into the act by Parliament. The most important is that if a person becomes homeless "intentionally," through something he or she did or failed to do, the authority must provide advice but does not have to find housing. However, a Code of Guidance, which accompanies the act, specifically states that certain cases— mortgage arrears, marital disputes leading to violence on a wife, simple lack of money—do not fall under the category of "intentional." Although the code is not legally binding, it is fairly clear that in many—though by no means all— cases the courts regard it as such. In the early years of the act's operation, only 3–4% of applicants were declared intentionally homeless.

The number of those accepted as homeless under the act has increased steadily year by year, from 57,200 in 1979 to 83,190 in 1984. Furthermore, these figures represent only about half of those who apply; the majority of single homeless people and couples without children have no right to permanent accommodation under the act, although they may get temporary shelter. The voluntary housing organization Shelter argues that the official figures represent only "the tip of the iceberg" because they ignore those who do not apply but are living with relatives or friends, or in poor conditions. Shelter points out that there are more than one million people on the waiting lists for public housing, and that many authorities will not entertain applications from single people or childless couples.

Mainly because of this, nearly half the households accepted under the act are placed not in local authority housing but in temporary bed-and-breakfast type accommodations, sometimes for long periods. There have been numerous accounts in the media of poor conditions and huge profits accruing to some proprietors of cheap hotels. Yet local authorities are understandably reluctant to place homeless families in public housing immediately, ahead of others who may have been on the waiting list for months or years.

Once rehoused, the former homeless still must pay the rent for their new accommodations. If they qualify on the basis of low income, they will receive help from the unified housing benefit introduced by the British government in 1982. This is not paid by the Department of the Environment, the department responsible for local housing policies, but by the Department of Health and Social Security, and it is administered by local authorities. It has been the subject of considerable criticism on the grounds of complexity, delay, and the financial worries of tenants whose allowance has not arrived.

Britain, then, has not solved the problem entirely and, indeed, a perfect solution may be impossible in an imperfect bureaucratic world. Urban poverty and homelessness in Western societies spring from deeper economic and social conditions—unemployment, especially among the unskilled, marital breakdown, drug dependence. Housing policies, however well intentioned and economically administered, cannot cure these ills, and as long as they continue to fester, so will the housing problem. If public expenditures are cut as a reaction to economic recession, even greater human suffering will be the sure result.

Peter Hall is a specialist in urban studies and has joint appointments as professor in the department of geography of the University of Reading, England, and professor in the department of city and regional planning at the University of California at Berkeley. His publications include The World Cities, Great Planning Disasters, *and* The Inner City in Context.

(continued from page 373)

nation's poverty rate dropped to 14.4% in 1984 from 15.3% in 1983, the largest one-year decline in more than a decade. A total of 33.7 million Americans lived below the poverty level ($10,609 for an urban family of four). The Census Bureau attributed the drop to economic recovery and low inflation. While applauding the decline, skeptics pointed out that the percentage of poor was still at its highest level since 1966, except for 1982 and 1983, and that the gains registered in 1984 were uneven. For example, the poverty rate for black children under age six rose slightly, to 51.1%. More than one-third of the poor were children, and 35% were from one-parent homes.

At the heart of the policy debate was a book by conservative analyst Charles Murray, *Losing Ground: American Social Policy 1950–1980.* Murray argued that government assistance programs launched by the War on Poverty in the mid-1960s had done more harm than good by encouraging many of the poor to remain poor. He recommended elimination of most programs for the able-bodied poor of working age. Both Murray's facts and his conclusions were questioned by liberal critics, who contended that he failed to consider important factors and research findings. Also joining in the dialogue was the National Conference of Catholic Bishops, which issued the second draft of its pastoral letter on the U.S. economy. The bishops reiterated their concern for the poor and, while acknowledging that government cannot solve many of the problems, said the U.S. has a moral obligation to ensure that no one is hungry, homeless, or unemployed.

Congress took a middle ground. Its first fiscal 1986 budget resolution provided funding that would allow most programs for the poor to keep pace with inflation. A report from the House Ways and Means Committee indicated that the value of combined food stamp and welfare benefits for a family of four with no other income fell 22% nationwide between 1972 and 1984. The main reason, according to the committee, was that cash welfare payments failed to keep up with inflation.   (DAVID M. MAZIE)

See also Education; Health and Disease; Industrial Review: Insurance.

This article updates the *Macropædia* article SOCIAL WELFARE.

Space Exploration

On Nov. 29, 1984, a pioneer of the U.S. space program died. She was Miss Baker, a squirrel monkey. The little simian had flown into space in the nose cone of a Jupiter ballistic missile on May 28, 1959. At her death the Peruvian-born monkey was an estimated 27 years old. Her brief journey into space proved that primates could survive and function in the weightlessness and accelerations of spaceflight.

As 1985 began, the second meeting of ministers from the 11 member nations and 3 associate member nations of the European Space Agency (ESA) took place in Rome on January 30. At the meeting the members agreed to participate in the program proposed by U.S. Pres. Ronald Reagan to launch a permanent space station into Earth orbit in the 1990s. The ESA contribution would be a manned scientific module named *Columbus.* It could be detached from the space station to form a building block in an ESA space station if the need arose.

Also early in 1985 Great Britain announced that it would establish the British National Space Centre, probably at the Royal Aircraft Establishment at Farnborough. Its mission would be to foster the development of space technology

The crew of the space shuttle *Challenger*'s July–August mission: Red team (bottom row, left to right) Loren Acton, Roy Bridges, and Karl Henize; Blue team (top row) John-David Bartoe, F. Story Musgrave, and Anthony England. The crew commander (striped shirt) was C. Gordon Fullerton.
NASA

within the U.K. and coordinate a national space policy. In October ESA member nations unanimously approved the acceptance of Austria and Norway to full membership. The two countries had been associate members since 1981.

Manned Flight. In Japan the National Space Development Agency announced that three astronauts had been selected from 533 applicants. One of them would be tapped to fly aboard the U.S. space shuttle in January 1988. In April the U.S.S.R. invited Japan to provide an astronaut to fly aboard a Soviet spacecraft at some future time.

After extensive screening by the U.S. National Aeronautics and Space Administration (NASA), a schoolteacher was selected to undertake astronaut training in preparation for a space shuttle mission in early 1986. She was Sharon Christa McAuliffe of Concord, N.H. NASA also announced in June that 13 new astronauts had been selected, bringing the total to 103.

On Jan. 24, 1985, space shuttle orbiter *Discovery* lifted off from the Kennedy Space Center in Florida. The crew was all military, as was the mission. Few details about the flight were released by the U.S. Department of Defense. The mission commander was Navy Capt. Thomas K. Mattingly, and Air Force Lieut. Col. Loren J. Shriver was the pilot. Mission specialists included Air Force Maj. Ellison S. Onizuka and Marine Corps Lieut. Col. James F. Buchli. Also aboard was Air Force Maj. Gary Payton, a Department of Defense spaceflight engineer.

Informed sources in the technical and scientific media reported that the primary purpose of the mission was to place in orbit a satellite designed to track Soviet missile tests and intercept military and diplomatic communications in the U.S.S.R. and elsewhere. In addition to the secret satellite, *Discovery* also carried an Australian blood experiment that was not military. The experiment, provided by Sydney Hospital, was designed to investigate how zero gravity affects human blood. *Discovery* returned to Earth on January 27, landing at the Kennedy Space Center.

Discovery again was launched from the Kennedy Space Center on April 12. Aboard were mission commander Air Force Col. Karol J. Bobko and pilot Navy Capt. Donald Williams, accompanied by mission specialists Navy Capt. David Griggs, Jeffrey Hoffman, and Rhea Seddon. Also on the flight were Sen. Jake Garn (Rep., Utah) and Charles Walker, as payload specialists. The primary mission was to launch the Anik C-1 and Leasat 3 satellites, which

was accomplished. However, Leasat 3 failed to activate in orbit. A variety of scientific experiments were performed aboard the *Discovery* orbiter, including one involving electrophoresis that had potential commercial applications in pharmacology. Garn participated as a subject in several medical experiments. The shuttle orbiter returned to the Kennedy Space Center on April 19.

On April 29 the *Challenger* shuttle orbiter took off from Kennedy Space Center with a crew of seven, including scientists from two nations, The Netherlands and the U.S. Mission commander was Marine Col. Robert F. Overmyer, and the pilot was U.S. Air Force Col. Frederick D. Gregory. Mission specialists included Don L. Lind, Norman E. Thagard, and William A. Thornton. Payload specialists were Taylor G. Wang and Lodewijk van den Berg, the latter from The Netherlands. The flight was dedicated to materials processing and life sciences experiments in the first operational Spacelab. While the materials-processing experiments went well, a life sciences project to evaluate an animal holding cage stocked with two monkeys and 24 rats did not fare as well. It indicated the need to improve the design for such a facility. Lind also took a series of spectacular photographs of auroras within the Earth's atmosphere while looking down upon them. *Challenger* returned to Earth on May 6, landing at Edwards Air Force Base in California.

Discovery was launched from the Kennedy Space Center on June 17. It was commanded by Navy Capt. Daniel C. Brandenstein and piloted by Navy Comdr. John O. Creighton. Mission specialists included Air Force Col. John M. Fabian, Air Force Lieut. Col. Steven R. Nagel, and Shannon Lucid. In addition, there were two payload specialists: Prince Sultan Salman as-Saud, a nephew of King Fahd of Saudi Arabia and an experienced jet pilot, and Patrick Baudry of France.

It was a busy mission. The Arabsat 1-B, Morelos 1, and Telstar 3D communications satellites were launched. A small, free-flying platform, Spartan 1, was deployed from the shuttle cargo bay by the craft's remote manipulator arm. It made astronomical measurements and was later retrieved. Baudry and Prince Sultan participated in a number of medical experiments. Baudry had earlier trained in the Soviet Union for a possible mission aboard the Salyut 7 space station. On June 24 *Discovery* landed at Edwards Air Force Base.

Next in the busy schedule for the space shuttle was the launch of *Challenger* on July 29 from the Kennedy Space Center. Its crew consisted of mission commander Air Force Col. C. Gordon Fullerton and pilot Air Force Col. Roy D. Bridges, Jr. Mission specialists were F. Story Musgrave, Anthony England, and Karl Henize. John-David Bartoe and Loren Acton were payload specialists. The primary mission was to perform a series of scientific experiments on the first pallet-only flight of the Spacelab 2. *Challenger* landed at Edwards Air Force Base on August 6.

Discovery was launched on August 27 from the Kennedy Space Center. Mission commander was Air Force Col. Joe H. Engle, and the pilot was Air Force Lieut. Col. Richard O. Covey. Mission specialists were James van Hoften, John M. Lounge, and William F. Fisher.

In one of the busiest missions to date, *Discovery* launched three satellites and retrieved an inoperative one, repaired it, and redeployed it. Several scientific experiments were also on board. In addition, crew members used a 70-mm movie camera to take footage for a film to be released later as *The Dream Is Alive*.

Launched as planned were the Aussat 1 (Australia), ASC 1, and Leasat 4 communications satellites. The high point

In April the crew of the space shuttle *Discovery* jury-rigged a "fly-swatter" attachment to the shuttle's extending robot arm in a fruitless attempt to trip an activating lever on the Leasat 3 communications satellite they had just deployed.
NASA

of the mission, however, was the capture and repair of the Leasat 3, which had failed during an earlier mission. For two days astronauts van Hoften and Fisher spent hours in the cargo bay of the shuttle orbiter. With the repairs completed, van Hoften mounted supports on the end of the remote maneuvering arm and manually deployed the satellite into space after spinning it by hand to 3 rpm. The success of the repairs was not known until late in October when Earth controllers of the Leasat 3 fired the satellite's perigee kick motor to place it into the desired orbit. The highly successful mission ended with a landing at Edwards Air Force Base on September 3.

The shuttle orbiter *Atlantis* was launched for the first time on October 3. Mission commander was Air Force Col. Karol J. Bobko, and the pilot was Air Force Lieut. Col. Ronald J. Grabe. Mission specialists were Marine Corps Maj. David C. Hilmers and Army Col. Robert Stewart. Air Force Maj. William Pailes was the payload specialist. Even though the details of the flight were classified by the U.S. Department of Defense, it was believed that an objective of the mission was to launch two Defense Satellite Communications System (DSCS, phase 3) satellites. They were successfully placed in orbit. *Atlantis* landed on October 7 at Edwards Air Force Base.

Atlantis was launched into orbit again on November 26 from the Kennedy Space Center. The mission commander was Air Force Lieut. Col. Brewster Shaw, Jr., and the pilot was Marine Corps Lieut. Col. Bryan O'Connor. Also on board were Air Force Maj. Jerry Ross, Army Lieut. Col. Sherwood Spring, Mary Cleave, Charles Walker, and a Mexican, Rodolfo Neri Vela. During the mission the crew successfully launched into orbit Morelos-B, a Mexican communications satellite; Australia's Aussat-2 communications satellite; and a Satcom K-2 for RCA American Communications Inc.

On November 29 Ross and Spring stepped out of *Atlantis* into space to practice construction techniques that would be used to build future space stations. The men worked with aluminum tubes and end connectors to assemble and disassemble various structures. The 5½-hour exercise left the men fatigued. Two days later they repeated the exercise for 6 hours 42 minutes; again they were successful in their endeavours but reported being very tired when they were finished. *Atlantis* returned to Earth on December 3, landing at Edwards Air Force Base.

Also during the year the Soviet Union continued its

On August 31–September 1 another *Discovery* crew captured and repaired the errant Leasat 3 satellite and returned it to orbit, and in October it responded to ground control by firing its rocket motor and climbing to permanent orbit some 35,900 kilometres (22,300 miles) above the Earth.

NASA

program of manned spaceflight, concentrating on the further development of activities that would lead to larger and more versatile space stations. On June 6 Soyuz T-13 was launched from Tyuratam. Aboard were Vladimir Dzhanibekov and Viktor Savinykh. The former had been ferried to the Salyut 7 space station on Soyuz T-12 on July 17, 1984. Their mission was to accomplish repairs on the Salyut 7, which had been seriously disabled. Soyuz T-13 returned to the Earth on September 26 with cosmonauts Dzhanibekov and Georgiy Grechko aboard, their tasks finished in the repair work. Savinykh remained on the Salyut 7 with two cosmonauts who were already aboard.

Soyuz T-14 was launched from Tyuratam on September 17. In it were Lieut. Col. Vladimir Vasyutin, Lieut. Col. Aleksandr Volkov, and Georgiy Grechko. They took supplies and supplemented the Salyut crew.

On July 19 a new type of spacecraft was launched from Tyuratam and docked with the Salyut 7 space station. Cosmos 1669 was apparently a free-flying, unmanned module that could be used to enlarge the Salyut. The Soviets said that the new vehicle was based on the *Progress* unmanned ferry spacecraft. It was detached from Salyut 7 on August 29, after which it reentered the atmosphere and was destroyed.

Yet another extension module was added to Salyut 7 on September 27 when Cosmos 1686 was launched from Tyuratam by a Proton launch vehicle. On October 2 it docked with the space station. The new addition more than doubled the length of the space station, to 35 m (115 ft). On November 21 the three cosmonauts aboard Salyut 7 returned to the Earth because of the illness of one of them, Vladimir Vasyutin.

West Germany paid NASA $64 million to fly *Challenger* on a mission that lasted from October 30 to November 6. Mission commander was Henry W. Hartsfield, Jr., and the pilot was Air Force Lieut. Col. Steven R. Nagel. Also aboard were Marine Corps Col. James F. Buchli, Air Force Col. Guion S. Bluford, Jr., Bonnie J. Dunbar, West German physicists Ernst Messerschmid and Reinhard Furrer, and Dutch physicist Wubbo Ockels. The first manned spaceflight to be managed by a country other than the U.S. or U.S.S.R., the mission was dedicated to scientific experiments in metallurgy, crystal growth, biology, and human physiology.

Unmanned Satellites. The year 1985 was notable for demonstrating the utility of unmanned satellites in saving human life. A young Belgian race car driver owed his life to the combined efforts of the U.S. NOAA 9 and Soviet Cospos 1 satellites when they fixed his position after his race car had an accident in a remote area of Somalia, where there were no medical facilities or ground communications. Rescue teams dispatched by French authorities found the man and evacuated him to a hospital in Brussels, where he later recovered. By the end of May more than 400 lives had been saved by the network of three Soviet and two U.S. search-and-rescue satellites.

ATS 3 in 1985 performed yeoman's duty during the disastrous September earthquake in Mexico City. The 18-year-old satellite was pressed into service through its control centre in Malabar, Fla. It supported relief operations of the American Red Cross and the Pan-American World Health Organization. The satellite was also used by CBS to relay commercial communications and news to the U.S. from its reporters in Mexico.

On June 21 the U.S.S.R. provided the world with a mystery satellite. It broke into three pieces while in orbit. The largest piece reentered the Earth's atmosphere on June 24, and the other two followed on June 28. The largest piece was estimated to be approximately one metre (3.3 ft) long. Western experts were puzzled by the fact that the Soviets, for only the second time since their space program began, did not give the launch from Tyuratam a name or number. They theorized that it was an antisatellite test or possibly a new launch vehicle that exploded prematurely.

In September the ESA Ariane III launch vehicle veered off course from the launch site in French Guiana and had to be destroyed two minutes into the mission. Lost were the ECS 3 and Spacenet 3 satellites. It was the third failure in 15 attempts for Ariane, and some potential customers had second thoughts about using it as a launch vehicle.

Probes. During the year both the U.S.S.R. and the U.S. announced plans for future probes. The Soviet announcement was couched in terms that showed that considerable planning had gone into the future missions. Scheduled for a June 1988 launch were two probes to Mars and a rendezvous with and possible landing on its satellite Phobos. If the landing attempt succeeded, the second probe would go on to rendezvous with the planet's other satellite, Deimos. Other Soviet probes planned for 1989 and 1990 included a polar-orbiting Mars probe to study the geochemical makeup of the surface and ice caps in the dark polar caps.

The U.S. said that if approval was obtained it would launch in March 1991 a probe for a rendezvous with the comet Wild 2. The probe would drop a penetrator on the nucleus of the comet that would relay data.

As 1984 ended, the Soviets launched two probes, Vega 1 and Vega 2, to visit Venus and then rendezvous with Halley's Comet. Each probe consisted of a main body, a landing module, and a helium-filled balloon. The instrumented three-metre (ten-foot)-diameter balloon deployed from Vega 1 in the Venusian atmosphere was tracked for 46 hours by an international network of ground stations on Earth in June. In addition, there were 11 radio telescopes around the world receiving data from the balloon's instrumented gondola. Transmission failed when batteries in the gondola were exhausted. The balloon drifted through the atmosphere at an altitude of 54.7 km (34 mi) above the surface.

The balloon from Vega 2 was deployed on June 15 and transmitted data until June 17. Its gondola also transmitted data for 46 hours until its batteries failed. At the altitude above Venus's surface of 54.7 km (34 mi), preliminary analysis of data indicated an atmospheric temperature of 37.8° C (100° F) and a wind velocity of 239 km/h (148.5 mph).

Major Satellites and Space Probes Launched Oct. 1, 1984–Sept. 30, 1985

Name/country/ launch vehicle/ scientific designation	Launch date, lifetime*	Physical characteristics Weight in kg†	Shape	Diameter in m†	Length or height in m†	Experiments	Orbital elements Perigee in km†	Apogee in km†	Period (min)	Inclination to Equator (degrees)
ERBS/U.S./Space Shuttle/ 1984-108B	10/5/84	2,268 (5,000)	rectangular body with trapezoidal superstructure and two solar panels	4.6 (15)	3.8 (12.5)	Measure Earth radiation budget	598 (372)	608 (378)	96.8	57.0
STS 51-A/U.S/Space Shuttle/1984-113A	11/8/84 11/16/84	2,041,166 (4,500,000)	delta-shaped vehicle with two solid boosters and external tank	24 (78.7)	37 (121.4)	Launch two communications satellites and retrieve two other satellites from orbit	288 (179)	299 (186)	90.4	28.5
Anik D-2/Canada/Space Shuttle/1984-113B	11/10/84	‡	cylinder	‡	‡	Communications satellite	‡	‡	‡	‡
NOAA 9/U.S./Atlas E/ 1984-123A	12/12/84	‡	box-shaped with two solar panels	‡	‡	Weather satellite	841 (523)	862 (536)	102.0	98.9
Vega 1/U.S.S.R./SL-12/ 1984-125A	12/15/84	‡	‡	‡	‡	Venus and Halley's Comet probe	Heliocentric orbit			
Vega 2/U.S.S.R./SL-12/ 1984-128A	12/21/84	‡	‡	‡	‡	Venus and Halley's Comet probe	Heliocentric orbit			
Sakigake/Japan/ ‡ / 1985-001A	1/8/85	‡	cylinder	‡	‡	Solar wind experiments	Heliocentric orbit			
Meteor 2/U.S.S.R./ A I/1985-013A	2/6/85	2,760 (6,085)	cylinder with two solar panels	1.5 (4.92)	5 (16.4)	Weather satellite	950 (590)	975 (606)	‡	82.5
Arabsat 1A/Arab League/ Ariane 3/1985-015A	2/8/85	1,195 (2,635)	cube	‡	‡	Communications satellite	‡	‡	‡	‡
Brazilsat 1/Brazil/ Ariane 3/1985-015B	2/8/85	1,140 (2,513)	cylinder	‡	‡	Communications satellite	‡	‡	‡	‡
Geosat/U.S./ Atlas F/1985-021A	3/13/85	635 (1,400)	‡	‡	‡	Provide geodesic data for the U.S. Navy	760 (472)	817 (508)	100.67	108.05
Ekran/U.S.S.R./ D le/1985-024A	3/22/85	2,000 (4,409)	cylinder with two solar panels	2 (6.6)	5 (16.4)	Television satellite	‡	‡	‡	‡
STS 51-D/U.S/Space Shuttle/1985-028A	4/12/85 4/19/85	2,043,380 (4,504,882)	delta-shaped vehicle with two solid boosters and external tank	24 (78.7)	37 (121.4)	Launch two satellites and perform scientific experiments	315 (196)	460 (286)	92.12	28.52
Prognoz 10/U.S.S.R./ A Ile/1985-033A	4/26/85	1,000 (2,205)	cylinder with instrument package	2 (6.6)	1.5 (4.92)	Study interaction of solar wind on magnetosphere	400 (249)	200,000 (124,274)	64.81	65.0
STS 51-B/U.S/Space Shuttle/1985-034A	4/26/85 5/6/85	2,042,814 (4,503,634)	delta-shaped vehicle with two solid boosters and external tank	24 (78.7)	37 (121.4)	Material processing and life sciences experiments	346 (215)	358 (222)	91.6	57.0
Nusat/U.S./Space Shuttle/1985-034B	4/29/85	52 (115)	26-sided polyhedron	0.48 (1.57)	‡	Air traffic control radar calibration	346 (215)	355 (221)	91.5	57.0
Soyuz T-13/U.S.S.R./ A II/1985-043A	6/6/85	7,000 (15,432)	sphere and cylinder with two solar panels	2.2 (7.22)	7.3 (23.95)	Ferry crew to Salyut 7 space station	299 (186)	334 (208)	90.8	51.6
Morelos 1/Mexico/ Space Shuttle/1985-048B	6/17/85	512 (1,129)	cylinder	2.2 (7.22)	6.6 (21.65)	Communications satellite	‡	‡	‡	‡
Arabsat 1B/Arab League/ Space Shuttle/1985-048C	6/18/85	1,270 (2,800)	box-shaped with two solar panels	2.6 (8.53)	1.5 (4.92)	Communications satellite	‡	‡	‡	‡
Progress 24/U.S.S.R./ A II/1985-051A	6/21/85 7/15/85	‡	sphere	‡	‡	Ferry repair parts and supplies to Salyut 7 space station	190 (118)	240 (149)	88.7	51.6
Giotto/ESA/ Ariane 1/1985-056A	7/2/85	960 (2,116)	cylinder	1.8 (5.91)	1.6 (5.25)	Probe to study Halley's Comet	Interplanetary trajectory			
STS 51-F/U.S/Space Shuttle/1985-063A	7/29/85 8/6/85	2,041,166 (4,500,000)	delta-shaped vehicle with two solid boosters and external tank	24 (78.7)	37 (121.4)	Solar and astronomical observations using Spacelab 2 instruments; launch small satellite and retrieve it	311 (193)	319 (198)	90.8	49.5
Planet A/Japan/ Mu-35-2/1985-073A	8/18/85	139.7 (308)	cylinder	1.4 (4.59)	0.7 (2.3)	Scientific probe to Halley's Comet	Interplanetary trajectory			
Soyuz T-14/U.S.S.R./ ‡ / 1985-081A	9/17/85	7,000 (15,432)	sphere and cylinder with two solar panels	2.2 (7.22)	7.5 (24.61)	Ferry new crew to Salyut 7 space station	210 (130)	275 (171)	‡	‡

* All dates are in universal time (UT).   † English units in parentheses: weight in pounds, dimensions in feet, apogee and perigee in statute miles.   ‡ Not available.

(MITCHELL R. SHARPE)

Both Vega 1 and 2 also ejected landing modules to the surface of Venus. They were instrumented to telemetre atmospheric pressure, temperature, X-ray fluorescence, and gamma-ray radiation. Because of the extreme heat and high atmospheric pressure on the surface, the landers transmitted data for only about 20 minutes.

Meanwhile, the main bodies of the Vegas continued on their trajectories for their rendezvous with Halley's Comet in March 1986. Other probes to Halley's Comet included two by Japan and one by ESA. The contribution of the U.S. to cometary exploration took place on September 11 when ICE (International Cometary Explorer) flew through the tail of the distant Comet Giacobini-Zinner. (For additional information on the cometary probes, *see* ASTRONOMY.)

(MITCHELL R. SHARPE)

See also Astronomy; Earth Sciences; Industrial Review: *Aerospace; Telecommunications;* Military Affairs; Television and Radio.

This article updates the *Macropædia* article EXPLORATION: *Space Exploration*.

Sports and Games

AERIAL SPORTS

Brig. Gen. Charles ("Chuck") Yeager, first man to break the sound barrier and hero of the book and movie *The Right Stuff,* made 1985 a memorable year for aerial sports by setting no fewer than 17 world-class records at the age of 62. Flying a Piper Cheyenne 400LS, Yeager on April 16 set four time-to-climb records in Class C-1e, turboprop aircraft, after taking off from Portland, Ore., and reaching 12,000 m (39,372 ft) in 11 min, 8 sec. The previous record was 14 min, set in 1981. Two days later Yeager set a speed record in that class, flying from San Francisco to New York City in 6 hr 39 min 28 sec. for an average speed of 622.7 km/h (386.8 mph). Between July 26 and August 14, flying between various cities in the U.S., Yeager set 12 additional speed records in the 400LS, covering 12,161.5 km (7,553.7 mi) in a flight time of 19 hr 13 min 6 sec for an average speed of 632.9 km/h (393.1 mph).

Bob Hoover, Yeager's backup pilot in the historic Oct. 14, 1947, faster-than-sound flight, set a speed record for piston-engined airplanes of unlimited weight (Class C-1) on March 28, 1985. Hoover flew a World War II P-51 Mustang 3,532 km (2,194 mi) from Los Angeles to Daytona Beach, Fla., in 5 hr 20 min 25 sec, averaging 659.52 km/h (409.83 mph).

The pilot holding the greatest total of world flying records at the end of 1985 was Marie McMillan, 59, the "flying grandmother" of Las Vegas, Nev., who had compiled 656 U.S. national and Fédération Aéronautique Internationale certified world-class records. The FAI confirmed more than 300 of those set by McMillan on a 30,000-km (18,000-mi) multistop flight in the U.S., Central America, and the Caribbean during March 1984, in a Beechcraft Bonanza.

Dan Bookout of Texarkana, Ark., became the man with the most aviation records when he set seven new world speed marks for Class C-1d piston aircraft on an Oct. 22, 1985, flight between Texarkana and Washington, D.C., in his Piper Lance. Between May 30 and June 20 he established 29 other world records on city-to-city flights throughout the U.S.

Poland, using radical-design PZL Wilga aircraft, was the big winner in the World Precision Flight Championship for piston-engine airplanes held August 11–18 at Kissimmee, Fla. Only 248 points were deducted from Poland's score. Sweden finished second with 540 points deducted, and Finland was third with 816 deducted points. A record 67 pilots from 16 countries took part in the contest.

In the accident-plagued World Gliding Championships, July 27–August 8 at Rieti, Italy, Doug Jacobs of the U.S. finished first in the 15-m class with 10,901 points, flying an LS-6. In the standard class gliding competition Luigi Brigliadori of Italy was first with 9,697 points flying a Discus. The Open class was won by Ingo Renner of Austria with 9,933 points in a Nimbus 3.

The world speed record for single-place gliders over a 750-km (465-mi) triangular course was set by Hans Werner Grosse of West Germany on January 8. Grosse maintained 158.41 km/h (98.42 mph) in an ASW 22 at Alice Springs, Australia. A 100-km (62-mi) triangular course speed record of 128 km/h (79.54 mph) for motor gliders was established January 15 at Kenilworth, South Africa, by Willibald Collee of West Germany, flying a Janus M.

Grosse's Dec. 9, 1984, record of 162.22 km/h (100.79 mph) around a 300-km (186-mi) triangular course in an ASW 22 was confirmed by the FAI. The organization also confirmed the Nov. 11, 1984, world women's glider record for speed around a 750-km (450-mi) triangular course, set

ROBERT FRANZESE—AERIAL DIMENSIONS

At the World Freefall Convention at Freeport, Illinois, in August, 100 skydivers jumped from four DC-3 airplanes at 5,500 metres (18,000 feet) and attempted to link up into formation. One diver (lower left) failed to connect but the formation of 99 (held for 17 seconds) broke the previous record of 72.

by Pamela Hawkins of the U.K. in an ASW 17 at Waikerie, Australia.

In the World Hang Gliding Championships held May 25–June 9 at Kossen, Austria, John Pendry of the U.K. finished first with 1,392 points. The team competition was won by the U.K. with 5,191 points. A new hang-glider flexible-wing women's world record for straight distance to a goal was set by Valerie Ann Wallington of Australia at Ben Nevis, Australia, on January 4, when she attained 118.09 km (73.38 mi) in her Magic III 155. The FAI confirmed the flexible-wing triangular course hang-glider record of 18.45 km (11.46 mi) set at Bond Springs, Australia, by fellow Australian Denis Cummings in a Magic III on Nov. 26, 1984.

At the World Parachute Relative Work Championships at Mali Losing, Yugos., on September 16 the U.S. won the four-person team competition with 118 points. The eight-person team event was won by the U.S. with 120 points.

A team of 23 Americans set a world record for largest canopy formation in parachute relative work at Houston (Texas) Gulf Airport on June 16. A mark of 22 persons had been achieved by French jumpers on June 1 at La Ferte Gaucher, France. An Oct. 3, 1984, women's world record for largest canopy formation, set by a team of eight Soviet women at Televi, U.S.S.R., was confirmed by the FAI.

The world hot-air ballooning championship at Battle Creek, Mich., July 13–21, was won by David Levin of the U.S. with 9,533 points. Winners of the FAI's 1985 Montgolfier awards for balloonists were Joe Kittinger of the U.S., who set a number of records in becoming the first man to fly the Atlantic solo in a balloon in 1984, and John Petrehn of the U.S., who set a 851.3-km (529-mi) distance record and 24-hour duration record for hot-air balloons in a 1984 South Dakota-to-Illinois flight.

(MICHAEL D. KILIAN)

ARCHERY

Rick McKinney of Glendale, Ariz., won his third men's world championship in 1985, and Irina Soldatova of the Soviet Union became the women's champion. The world championships were held October 2–5 in Seoul, South Korea, at the facility scheduled to be used for the 1988 Olympic Games. There were 77 entrants in men's singles, 67 in women's singles, 16 in men's teams, and 14 in women's teams.

Each man shot two rounds for a total of 288 arrows—72 each from 30, 50, 70, and 90 m. The women shot the same total number of arrows but from 30, 50, 60, and 70 m. For men and women a perfect score would be 2,880.

McKinney had won the biennial world championship in 1977 and 1983, and in the 1984 Olympics he took the silver medal behind Darrell Pace of Hamilton, Ohio. In 1985 the 32-year-old McKinney scored 2,601 to 2,592 for second-place Koo Ja Chong of South Korea. Pace finished eighth with 2,535.

The women's leaders were Soldatova with 2,595 points and Ludmilla Arzhanikova, her Soviet teammate, with 2,589. Pauline Edwards (fourth with 2,561) was the leading Briton, while Melanie Skillman of Laureldale, Pa., was the best of the U.S. competitors (13th with 2,505).

In men's team competition South Korea won with 7,660 to 7,643 for the second-place United States. Among women's teams the Soviet Union defeated South Korea handily, 7,721 to 7,628.

McKinney dominated the major U.S. competitions during the year and won his seventh national championship. He led the men in the U.S. world trials August 12–15 in St. Louis, Mo., with 2,652; the U.S. championships

August 6–9 in Oxford, Ohio, with 2,624; and the U.S. field championships June 15–16 in Staunton, Va., with 992. He finished second behind Pace (2,592 to 2,590) in the National Sports Festival July 24–August 4 at Baton Rouge, La.

Skillman won the women's competition in the U.S. world trials with 2,507, in the National Sports Festival with 2,459, and in the U.S. field championships with 923. Terry Pesho of Tempe, Ariz., took the U.S. championship with 2,487. Skillman did not enter that tournament.

(FRANK LITSKY)

AUTOMOBILE RACING

Grand Prix Racing. In international Formula One automobile racing in 1985, the rules remained virtually unchanged, with turbocharged 1½-litre engines predominating and road-holding capabilities enhanced by the use of air foil wings. Tires were also crucial, and toward the end of the season Pirelli staged a comeback, competing against U.S. Goodyear. Michelin withdrew as a tire supplier. Engine power rose appreciably, to about 600 brake horsepower (bhp) at some 10,000 rpm from the better units. This resulted in speeds of more than 320 km/h (1 km = 0.62 mi) on the longer straightaways, as at Paul Ricard, France, and at Monza, Italy, where Nelson Piquet (Brazil) went through the speedtrap at 333.71 km/h in training for the Italian Grand Prix. Honda, in particular, was getting high power from its V6-cylinder engines.

The drivers' world championship was won for the first time by a Frenchman, Alain Prost. He clinched the title at Brands Hatch, England, in the European Grand Prix, with two more races still to be contested.

The first Grand Prix race took place at Rio de Janeiro, Brazil. Prost's McLaren-TAG-Porsche had the fastest lap at 187.292 km/h and won the race with an average time of 181.527 km/h. Michele Alboreto (Italy) placed second in a Ferrari, and Elio De Angelis (Italy) was third in a Renault-powered Lotus. The scene then moved to Portugal, at Estoril Autodrome. Ayrton Senna (Brazil) was the winner at 145.162 km/h after establishing the fastest lap at 150.404 km/h in a Lotus-Renault 97T. Alboreto's Ferrari was the only other car to complete the full distance, Patrick Tambay (France) finishing third in a Renault RE60, a lap behind. At Imola, Italy, in the San Marino Grand Prix, ten cars survived out of 25. The victor was De Angelis in his Lotus-Renault, at 191.798 km/h; Alboreto achieved the best lap speed, at 199.470 km/h. Thierry Boutsen (Belgium) finished second for Arrows, and Tambay's Renault was third.

In the tortuous Monaco street race, Prost (McLaren MP4) drove to a smooth victory, at 138.434 km/h; Alboreto finished second in his Ferrari, just ahead of De Angelis in the Lotus-Renault. A faulty track surface caused the Belgian Grand Prix at Spa to be postponed. In the Canadian Grand Prix at Montreal, Senna had the fastest lap at 181.554 km/h, and Alboreto won in his Ferrari at 174.688 km/h from teammate Stefan Johansson (Sweden); Prost's McLaren was third. The Detroit Grand Prix was won by Keke Rosberg (Finland) for the Williams-Honda team, at 131.486 km/h, ahead of the Ferraris of Johansson and Alboreto; Senna had the fastest lap, at 137.131 km/h.

In the French Grand Prix, Piquet finished just ahead of Rosberg, with Prost third—a varied trio of Brabham-BMW, Williams-Honda, McLaren-Porsche; Piquet's average speed was 201.323 km/h, and Rosberg had the fastest lap at 209.340 km/h. The British Grand Prix, at Silverstone, was notable for a remarkable 160-mph (257.6-km/h) qualifying lap and a race lap record of more than 150

At the Indianapolis 500 in May, Danny Sullivan, the eventual winner, experienced some difficulty just 21 laps from the finish. In spinning a full circle he narrowly missed the wall and fellow racer Mario Andretti.
AP/WIDE WORLD

mph (243.067 km/h) by Prost, who also won the race at 235.404 km/h over Alboreto and Jacques Lafitte (France) in a Ligier. A new, inferior, Nürburgring was the setting for the German Grand Prix, won by Alboreto, at 191.147 km/h, from Prost and Lafitte. Niki Lauda (Austria) had the fastest lap, at 197.464 km/h. Prost then won the Austrian Grand Prix at 231.132 km/h from Senna and Alboreto and had the best lap at 239.701 km/h as well; 9 finished out of 25.

The Dutch Grand Prix at Zandvoort ended in a win for Lauda (McLaren), at 193.089 km/h, from Prost, who had the fastest lap, at 199.995 km/h; Senna was third. In the Italian Grand Prix, Prost was the winner at 227.565 km/h from Piquet and Senna; Nigel Mansell (Great Britain) had the fastest lap at 236.512 km/h. Spa then had its postponed Belgian Grand Prix, with Senna (at 189.811 km/h), Mansell, and Prost in the first three places; Prost had the fastest lap at 205.241 km/h. Mansell gained a convincing win at Brands Hatch in the European Grand Prix, averaging 203.625 km/h; Senna and Rosberg placed second and third. Lafitte had the fastest lap at 211.734 km/h.

The Williams-Honda FW10s came in first and second at Kyalami, South Africa, as Mansell won from Rosberg at 206.744 km/h. Prost was third, and Rosberg had the fastest lap at 215.536 km/h. In the final Grand Prix, over the excellent new Australian circuit near Adelaide, Rosberg gained the third consecutive victory for the Canon Williams-Honda team, at 135.168 km/h, and also achieved a lap record at 153.168 km/h.

Rallies and Other Races. Porsche again dominated endurance races in 1985, at Mugello, Monza, Silverstone, Hockenheim, Mosport, Canada, Brands Hatch, and in the Le Mans, France, 24-hour competition. The winners lost no speed while using 15% less fuel and developed over 600 bhp. A Lancia-Martini won at Spa, and Nissan-March was victorious in Fiji. Rothmans-Porsche won the world endurance championship for teams. Derek Bell (Great Britain) and Hans-Joachim Stuck (West Germany) won the world endurance championship for drivers. The Daytona, Fla., 24-hour race was won by a Porsche 962.

An Audi Quattro won the Monte Carlo Rally, and in Sweden Peugeot 205 T16s sandwiched an Audi Sport. The African Safari Rally and the Ivory Coast Rally were victories for Toyota Celicas. A Renault 5 won the Tour of Corsica, while Peugeot beat Audi in the Acropolis Rally and Malcolm Wilson's Audi Quattro won the Scottish Rally. Peugeot took the first two places in New Zealand and won in Argentina. With the 1,000 Lakes Rally in Finland, Timo Salonen of Finland took the 1985 world

drivers' championship and Peugeot Sport the manufacturers' championship from Audi. Audi won the San Remo Rally from Peugeot, and in Cyprus a Lancia Rally won. The Lombard RAC Rally was won by Henri Toivonen of Finland in a four-wheel-drive Lancia Delta S4, 56 seconds ahead of teammate Markku Alen in another Lancia.

(WILLIAM C. BODDY)

U.S. Racing. The Roger Penske racing team in 1985 collected both the Indianapolis 500 and the Championship Auto Racing Teams (CART) crowns. The 1985 Indianapolis victory went to Danny Sullivan of Louisville, Ky., in a March-Cosworth by a margin of 2.47 seconds over Mario Andretti. Roberto Guerrero of Colombia finished third, and Sullivan's teammate, Al Unser, Sr., was fourth. Pancho Carter won pole position at 212.7 mph (342.4 km/h).

Al Unser, Sr., who drove at Indianapolis only because Rick Mears failed to recover sufficiently from injuries, won the CART crown on the final race of the season by finishing ahead of his son Al Unser, Jr. Andretti, best man in the Lola T-900 chassis, finished fifth in the season standings as the March-Cosworths proved dominant. Sullivan, fourth for the season, won the final race of the CART/PPG series at the new Tamiami, Fla., track before some 60,000 people. Third for the season was Bobby Rahal, who captured three races.

Bill Elliott, who drove in the Winston Cup series of the National Association for Stock Car Auto Racing (NASCAR), won the Elier driver of the year award over Sullivan and representatives from other forms of U.S. racing, but he lost the NASCAR season crown to Darrell Waltrip in the final race of the season 4,292 points to 4,191. Elliott, driving a Thunderbird, won 11 of 19 superspeedway events including the prestigious Daytona 500 and the Darlington Southern 500. His winnings for the year totaled over $2 million, more than any other driver had earned in one season. The steady Waltrip, driving a Chevrolet for Junior Johnson, won his third Winston Cup crown in five years. He also won three races plus the Winston invitational at Charlotte, N.C. But Elliott won the Winston Million, a $1 million bonus for victories at specified locales.

Porsche's 962 won 16 of the 17 International Motor Sports Association's Camel GT races, and Al Holbert, Porsche's U.S. competition director, won the season championship for Grand Touring prototypes. In the other GT classes, Jim Downing won the 750-kg prototype Camel Lights class in a Mazda-Argo; John Jones of Canada in a Ford Mustang won in the GTOver 2.8-litre class; and Jack Baldwin became the first IMSA GT repeat champion

since 1968 by winning the GTUnder 2.8-litre category in a Mazda RX-7. In the 24 Hours of Daytona and in the 12 Hours of Sebring, a Porsche 962 driven by A. J. Foyt, Bob Wollek, and Preston Henn won for Henn's Swap Shop team. The races were more notable as the swan song of Chevrolet-powered cars for the 1985 season. Porsche 962 pilots occupied seven of the top ten driver positions. Jaguar drivers finished third, fourth, and ninth. In the new Firestone Firehawk Endurance series, Porsche 944 won car of the year honours over Toyota's MR2, the touring division champion. Walt Maas and Jon Milledge piloted the winning Porsche.

In the year's closest competition, the Champion Spark Plug Challenge for small front-drive sedans, Mazda's Dennis Shaw defeated Dodge's Kal Showket in the final race of the season. Shaw won four races to Showket's seven but was more consistent.

Winning nine of a possible ten races, Tommy Riggins won the Kelly American Challenge title and his Buick Somerset took the manufacturers' crown. Irv Hoerr in a Chevrolet Camaro finished second.

The Sports Car Club of America's most successful professional series in 1985 was the Trans-Am. Two Ford-mounted drivers dominated the competition, with Wally Dallenbach, Jr., nipping Willie T. Ribbs for season honours. The new Playboy Endurance Series was totally dominated by Corvettes over Porsche 944s. The Can-Am series for prototypes was won by Lou Sell.

(ROBERT J. FENDELL)

BADMINTON

The major event in the world of badminton during 1985 was the fourth world badminton championships, held for the first time on the North American continent. Calgary, Alta., was the host city for this event, which took place during June 10–16.

In the men's singles Han Jian of China won the championship, defeating Morten Frost of Denmark in the final match 14–18, 15–10, 15–8. Han Aiping, also of China, won the women's singles with a final-round 6–11, 12–11, 11–2 victory over Wu Jianqi of China. Park Joo Bong and Kim Moon Soo of South Korea won the men's doubles, beating Li Yongbo and Tian Bingyi of China in the final match 5–15, 15–7, 15–9. In the women's doubles Han Aiping and Li Lingwei of China defeated Lin Ying and Wu

Dixi of China in the finals 15–9, 14–18, 15–9. The mixed doubles were won by the South Korean pair of Park Joo Bong and Yoo Sang Hee; they defeated Stefan Karlsson and Maria Bengtsson of Sweden in the final match 15–10, 12–15, 15–12.

Chosen as host for the next world championships was the Badminton Association of China. The tournament was scheduled to be played in Beijing (Peking) in May 1987. During the 1985 competition it was announced that badminton would be included in the summer Olympic Games in 1992. The organizing committee for the 1988 Olympics requested that badminton be an exhibition sport during those games.

(C. R. ELI)

BASEBALL

Though beset by problems such as a two-day strike and a drug investigation, major league baseball in 1985 produced an attendance record of 46,838,819 spectators. There were also several landmark achievements and yet another new champion at the end of the longest season in history.

World Series. The Kansas City Royals, decided underdogs, won the first championship in their 17-year existence. They downed the St. Louis Cardinals four games to three in an all-Missouri World Series after trailing in the best-of-seven set three games to one. By rallying for their victory, the Royals became the first team in the 82-year annals of the World Series to triumph after losing its first two games at home.

In the Series opener at Kansas City on October 19, the Cardinals defeated the Royals 3–1 behind the strong pitching of John Tudor and Todd Worrell. One evening later the Royals appeared to have victory in hand, leading 2–0 after eight innings. But Kansas City left-hander Charlie Leibrandt, who had yielded only two hits until that time, was victimized by a four-run ninth inning, and the Cardinals prevailed 4–2 to assume what appeared to be an insurmountable 2–0 lead in games as the Series moved to St. Louis. There, during the regular season, the Cardinals had posted a 55–26 record.

However, in the third game of the Series on October 22, the Royals downed the Cardinals 6–1 on a strong six-hitter by right-hander Bret Saberhagen and three runs batted in by second baseman Frank White. On October 23 Tudor, considered the ace of the St. Louis pitching staff, surrendered only five hits and beat the visiting Royals 3–

A jubilant Bret Saberhagen is mobbed by his Kansas City Royals teammates after pitching his second World Series victory in the deciding seventh game.

The year 1985 was a vintage one for three of baseball's most durable performers. In August of his 19th season, Tom Seaver (left) became just the 17th pitcher in major league history to win 300 games. In the same month, Rod Carew (centre) became the 16th major leaguer to reach the 3,000-hit mark. And in September player-manager Pete Rose (right) got his 4,192nd major league hit, passing the 57-year-old mark set by Ty Cobb.

(LEFT) RONALD C. MODRA, SPORTS ILLUSTRATED; (CENTRE) V. J. LOVERO, SPORTS ILLUSTRATED; (RIGHT) FOCUS ON SPORTS

0. Willie McGee and Tito Landrum hit home runs for the Cardinals.

Anticipating a celebration the following evening, the Cardinals instead fell 6–1 as Kansas City's Danny Jackson worked a complete game. The Series now stood 3–2 in favour of St. Louis.

The Cardinals again appeared on the verge of their second World Series crown in four years and 14th in the franchise's history when they took a 1–0 lead into the bottom of the ninth at Royals Stadium on October 26. However, the resilient Royals scored two runs for a dramatic 2–1 victory. Pinch hitter Dane Iorg singled to drive in the runs soon after the Cardinals had argued heatedly about a call made at first base by umpire Don Denkinger. The Cardinals contended that Denkinger's "safe" ruling deprived them of a much-needed out and fueled the Royals' comeback aspirations.

The low-scoring pace of the World Series changed markedly on October 27, when the Royals treated a wildly cheering home crowd to an 11–0 rout at the expense of Tudor and six successors. Tudor was knocked out of the game in the third inning, his earliest departure in an otherwise splendid season. Joaquín Andújar, one of the Cardinal relief pitchers, was ejected from the contest, as was Cardinal manager Whitey Herzog. Saberhagen pitched a complete five-hitter in the final game and was voted most valuable player for the World Series, having won half of Kansas City's games.

All the Kansas City pitching staff was commended for restricting the Cardinals to a .185 batting average, the lowest mark ever recorded for a team participating in a seven-game Series. Moreover, the Cardinals, who led the National League in batting average (.264) and runs during the regular season, managed only one multiple-run inning in the Series.

The Kansas City triumph was the third straight World Series conquest for the American League. Beyond that, the success of the Royals underscored baseball's balance of power. Since the New York Yankees achieved consecutive World Series titles in 1977 and 1978, no champion had repeated.

Championship Series. In 1985 the intraleague championship series, or play-offs, were expanded from a best-of-five format to best-of-seven. That afforded the Royals another opportunity to exhibit their special methods of survival.

The Toronto Blue Jays assumed a 3–1 advantage in games over the Royals, who then rebounded with three victories in a row to claim the American League pennant. The last two wins occurred at Toronto on October 15 and 16, by scores of 5–3 and 6–2. The Blue Jays, favoured to prevail in that play-off, also had difficulties with the young, talented Kansas City pitching staff.

In the National League the Cardinals began their championship series with the Los Angeles Dodgers by dropping the first two contests in Dodger Stadium. But after returning home to St. Louis, the Cardinals arose for three triumphs, the last being achieved on a tie-breaking home run in the ninth inning by normally light-hitting shortstop Ozzie Smith. His blow, off Tom Niedenfuer, gave the Cardinals a 3–2 decision and a 3–2 lead in games. Back at Los Angeles, on October 16, the Dodgers were clinging to a 5–4 margin when powerful Jack Clark clubbed a clutch three-run ninth-inning home run off the luckless Niedenfuer. The Cardinals won the contest 7–5 and the National League pennant in six games.

Regular Season. Undoubtedly, the most awaited event of the 1985 season took place in Cincinnati on September 11. On that evening the indefatigable Pete Rose (*see* BIOGRAPHIES), 44-year-old player-manager of the Reds, stepped up against Eric Show of the San Diego Padres and stroked his 4,192nd major league career hit. That broke a mark established more than a half century earlier by Ty Cobb. Rose, performing in his hometown, was accorded a standing ovation of several minutes.

Other veterans shared the limelight in a summer of touchstone achievements. On the same Sunday in August, Tom Seaver of the Chicago White Sox pitched his 300th career victory and Rod Carew of the California Angels garnered his 3,000th hit. On the last Sunday of the regular season 46-year-old Phil Niekro, the oldest player in the major leagues, notched his 300th victory as the New York Yankees beat the Blue Jays in Toronto.

That setback did not matter to the Blue Jays, for one day earlier they had clinched the American League East title after just nine years as a major-league team. The Blue Jays enjoyed a comfortable lead for most of the season and then fended off a late challenge by the Yankees. The defending World Series champion Detroit Tigers were never a factor in the race.

In the American League West division the Royals strug-

gled with erratic hitting and were as many as 7½ games out of first place in late July. But they overtook the California Angels during a crucial four-game series in the last week of the regular season.

The Cardinals, picked to finish in fifth or sixth place, surprised most observers by winning 101 games during the regular season, the most in the major leagues. But, paced by the 24–4 record of their spectacular young pitching sensation, Dwight Gooden (see BIOGRAPHIES), the New York Mets won 98 and were a close second throughout the year.

The Dodgers, also dismissed as also-rans before the season, had few problems claiming first place in the National League West. Rose and the Reds were runners-up.

Willie McGee of St. Louis captured the National League batting crown with a .353 average. Resurgent Dave Parker of Cincinnati led the league with 125 runs batted in, and rookie Vince Coleman of the Cardinals accumulated 110 stolen bases (the Cardinals had 314 as a team). Dale Murphy of the Atlanta Braves had 37 home runs to lead in that department. Besides Gooden, there were three other 20-game winners. Tudor and Andújar each collected 21 for St. Louis, while Tom Browning had 20 for Cincinnati.

Wade Boggs of the Boston Red Sox amassed 240 hits to win the American League batting crown with a .368 average. Darrell Evans of the Detroit Tigers clubbed 40 home runs and became the first player in history to reach that plateau in both leagues during his career. Don Mattingly of the New York Yankees easily claimed the runs-batted-in title with 145; teammate Rickey Henderson stole the most bases, 80. Ron Guidry, also of the Yankees, led American League pitchers with 22 triumphs. Saberhagen of Kansas City had 20.

St. Louis dominated the postseason awards in the National League, winning three of the four. Shortstop Willie McGee was named most valuable player; outfielder Vince Coleman was voted rookie of the year; and Whitey Herzog was manager of the year. Gooden of the New York Mets won the Cy Young award as the league's best pitcher. In the American League Kansas City's Bret Saberhagen was the Cy Young winner; first baseman Don Mattingly of the New York Yankees was the most valuable player; and shortstop Ozzie Guillen of the Chicago White Sox was voted rookie of the year. Bobby Cox of Toronto was named manager of the year.

Off-Field Problems. Baseball, which endured a 50-day player strike during 1981, was girding itself for another protracted impasse when the players again walked off the job in August. But on this occasion the two sides were quickly brought together, and the dispute lasted only two days. Much of the credit for the settlement was given to Peter V. Ueberroth, who in October completed his first year as commissioner.

Baseball's image was not so fortunate during a federal trial investigating the use of cocaine and other illegal drugs in the major leagues. Several present and past players testified under immunity. Based on their disclosures, it appeared that drugs constituted a serious problem for the sport. Ueberroth called on the major league players to submit to voluntary and random testing for drug use.

(ROBERT WILLIAM VERDI)

Latin America. The Dominican Republic's Licey Tigers for the fifth time captured the Caribbean Series, which was played in February at Mazatlán, Mexico. The Tigers thus became the most successful team in the 15-year history of the Series. They registered five victories on their way to the championship, losing only one game, to Mexico's Culiacán Tomato Growers, which finished second in the series with an even record of three wins and three losses. The San Juan Metros from Puerto Rico and the La Guaira Sharks from Venezuela were tied with two victories and four defeats each.

The Licey Tigers earned the right to represent the Dominican Republic in the Caribbean Series by defeating the Eastern Sugar Growers, from the city of La Romana, four games to one. Culiacán had a more difficult time in the final play-off of Mexico's Pacific League and had to go the entire length of a best-of-seven series to overcome the Mexicali Eagles. La Guaira blanked the heavily favoured Aragua Tigers in the championship series of the Venezuelan League, while the San Juan Metros clinched the Puerto Rican title four games to two against the Santurce Crabs.

During the summer the Mexico City Red Devils captured the pennant of the AAA Mexican Baseball League after winning the southern division. In the play-offs the Red Devils defeated the Mexico City Tigers, their traditional rivals, and the Nuevo Laredo Owls.

Cuba, a country where there was no professional baseball, overwhelmed its competition in the first Pan-American Championship of Amateur Baseball. Puerto Rico was second, and the U.S. placed third. (SERGIO SARMIENTO)

Japan. Osaka's Hanshin Tigers of the Central League defeated Tokorozawa's Seibu Lions of the Pacific League in the best-of-seven Japan Series four games to two. It was the Tigers' first championship in the 36-year-old postseason contest. First baseman Randy Bass hit a three-run home run to lead the Tigers to a 3-0 victory in the series' opener. Tiger right-hander Chikafusa Ikeda allowed only six hits. The Lions led off the second game with a home run by shortstop Hironori Ishige, but Bass's two-run round-tripper gave the Tigers a 2-1 victory.

The Lions came back to defeat the Tigers in the third game, tallying 12 hits and scoring 6 runs. Bass chalked up his third home run of the series. Called in to pinch hit with two down in the top of the ninth, outfielder Yoshihiro Nishioka stroked a two-run homer off Tiger reliever Osamu Fukuma, helping the Lions win the fourth game 4-2 and thus tying the series two games to two.

The Tigers jumped to a 4-0 lead in the first inning of the fifth game with third baseman Masayuki Kakefu's three-run home run and a base hit by shortstop Katsuo Hirata. The Osaka club eventually won 7-2 as outfielder Keiji Nagasaki hit a two-run homer, his first in the series. In the sixth game the Tigers scored 9 runs on 11 hits, including Nagasaki's grand-slam homer and Kakefu's two-run round-tripper. Starter Richard Gale went the full nine innings and gave up only three runs, giving the Tigers the game and the series.

Final Major League Standings, 1985

AMERICAN LEAGUE East Division					NATIONAL LEAGUE East Division				
Club	W.	L.	Pct.	G.B.	Club	W.	L.	Pct.	G.B.
Toronto	99	62	.615		St. Louis	101	61	.623	
New York	97	64	.602	2	New York	98	64	.605	3
Detroit	84	77	.522	15	Montreal	84	77	.522	16½
Baltimore	83	78	.516	16	Chicago	77	84	.478	23½
Boston	81	81	.500	18½	Philadelphia	75	87	.463	26
Milwaukee	71	90	.441	28	Pittsburgh	57	104	.354	43½
Cleveland	60	102	.370	39½					

West Division					West Division				
Club	W.	L.	Pct.	G.B.	Club	W.	L.	Pct.	G.B.
Kansas City	91	71	.562		Los Angeles	95	67	.586	
California	90	72	.556	1	Cincinnati	89	72	.553	5½
Chicago	85	77	.525	6	Houston	83	79	.512	12
Minnesota	77	85	.475	14	San Diego	83	79	.512	12
Oakland	77	85	.475	14	Atlanta	66	96	.407	29
Seattle	74	88	.457	17	San Francisco	62	100	.383	33
Texas	62	99	.385	28½					

Randy Bass was voted the most valuable player of the series. He was the third U.S. player to receive the honour, following Joe Stanka in 1964 and Jim Lyttle in 1980.

Bass won the Central League triple crown (.350, 54 home runs, 134 runs batted in). His tally of 54 home runs was just one short of the Japanese record, set in 1964 by Sadaharu Oh, now manager of Tokyo's Yomiuri Giants. Bass was the second U.S. player to win the triple crown, Greg ("Boomer") Wells of Nishinomiya's Hankyu Braves having done so in 1984. Bass was also voted most valuable player in the Central League.

Third baseman Hiromitsu Ochiai of Kawasaki's Lotte Orions was voted the Pacific League's most valuable player and also won the triple crown. Ochiai belted 52 home runs (tying the Pacific League record), hit .367 (an all-Japan record for a right-hander), and collected 146 runs batted in (Pacific League record). It was his second triple crown, a feat equaled only by Sadaharu Oh.

(RYUSAKU HASEGAWA)

BASKETBALL

United States. *Professional.* The 1984–85 season belonged to Kareem Abdul-Jabbar. No stranger to the winner's circle, the 2.19-m (7-ft 2-in) centre had helped the Los Angeles Lakers reach the NBA finals five times in six seasons. The 1985 triumph over the Boston Celtics, Abdul-Jabbar's third NBA championship as a member of the Lakers and the fourth of his career, was the sweetest one of all.

The superstar had turned 38 on April 16, two days before the Lakers opened their play-off schedule by crushing Phoenix 142–114 in a first-round game. For two straight years the Lakers had been humbled in the final play-off round, first by Philadelphia and then by Boston, and they hungered for revenge.

No one was more motivated than Abdul-Jabbar, who took it as a personal affront when the Celtics battered his team into submission in their seven-game 1984 showdown. He, Magic Johnson, and the rest of the Lakers endured taunts about being intimidated physically by the Celtics and mentally by boisterous crowds in Boston Garden.

So when the Celtics humiliated the Lakers 148–114 in the first game of their 1985 final round, it seemed like a replay of the previous year to elated Boston backers and depressed Los Angeles fans. This was the second-worst margin of defeat ever in a game in the final play-off round, topped only by Washington's 117–82 rout of Seattle in 1978.

Undaunted, team captain Abdul-Jabbar held a players' meeting before the second game, aware that returning to Los Angeles with a deficit of 0–2 in the best-of-seven series would probably prove too big an obstacle to overcome. Then he backed up his words with action, silencing the packed Boston Garden with a 30-point, 17-rebound barrage. The Lakers survived 109–102 in what proved to be the pivotal contest of the series. They went to the West Coast, confidence restored, to take two of the next three confrontations with the Celtics, setting up the long-awaited final match in Boston on June 9. The Lakers climaxed their comeback by triumphing 111–100 in that contest. Never before had a visiting team won the decisive play-off game in Boston Garden. Abdul-Jabbar and superior depth made the difference. The towering centre unleashed his fearsome skyhook, averaging 25.7 points per game against the Celtics while making 60.4% of his shots. He also became the leading all-time NBA play-off scorer, topping the record of 4,457 points set by the Lakers' Jerry West.

After being named most valuable player of the series, Abdul-Jabbar agreed that this had been his most satisfying

Kareem Abdul-Jabbar's patented skyhook shot led the Los Angeles Lakers past Larry Bird and the Boston Celtics in the National Basketball Association championship series in June. The Celtics had never before lost a championship series on their home court at the Boston Garden.
AP/WIDE WORLD

moment in 16 pro seasons. In 1971, then known as Lew Alcindor, he first took play-off MVP honours for leading the Milwaukee Bucks to the NBA championship.

The exciting climax capped a successful NBA season, with attendance and interest on the upswing. The sensational debut of Olympic hero Michael Jordan was a major reason. Jordan drew huge crowds throughout the league, averaging 28.2 points per game, leading the Chicago Bulls into the play-offs, and outpolling Houston's Akeem Olajuwon for rookie of the year laurels.

College. It was called the impossible dream, the classic upset, and many other things by stunned spectators, television viewers, the nation's media, and even the participants. No label could begin to convey the drama, bordering on sheer fantasy, of Villanova's incredible 66–64 triumph over Georgetown for the 1985 National Collegiate Athletic Association (NCAA) basketball championship. The Wildcats, seeded 29th in the 64-team NCAA tournament field, had no business even reaching the final, according to most experts. They were given little chance of prevailing against mighty Georgetown, led by 2.14-m (7-ft) centre Patrick Ewing.

Georgetown, top-ranked in every college basketball poll, had won 35 of 37 games, and the Hoyas were supremely confident of adding their second straight national title. With Ewing dominating the middle to block shots and

intimidate foes, they had compiled a 121–23 record during the centre's four years. And Georgetown needed just one more victory to become the first team since UCLA in 1973 to wear back-to-back NCAA crowns. Oklahoma A&M, Kentucky, San Francisco, and Cincinnati had accomplished that feat previously.

But the Hoyas' rendezvous with destiny was detoured by coach Rollie Massimino and his aptly named Wildcats. Beaten twice by the Hoyas during the regular season, Villanova also had lost eight other games before entering the NCAA tournament with an unimpressive 19–10 record. In semimiraculous fashion they then knocked off six straight favourites, becoming the first team not ranked among the nation's top ten to win the championship since City College of New York (CCNY) in 1950. Every time Massimino's disciplined team faltered, Ed Pinckney brought things under control. The 2.08-m (6-ft 10-in) centre was the leader in both word and deed. Still, conquering supposedly unbeatable Georgetown required a superb game from all the Wildcats, and they answered the challenge.

The sellout crowd of 23,124 at the University of Kentucky's Rupp Arena was only mildly surprised when Harold Pressley tipped in a basket to put Villanova on top 29–28 at halftime. Noted for strong finishes, Georgetown was accustomed to wearing down opponents in the closing minutes, cashing in on relentless defensive pressure throughout the game. The Hoyas' strategy usually forced critical turnovers at the moment of decision.

Besides, the underdogs had shot at a sizzling 72.2% in the initial 20 minutes, making 13 of 18 field goal attempts. Georgetown supporters were confident that no team could sustain that pace. But neither Hoya coach John Thompson nor anyone else expected what happened in the second half. Villanova made an unbelievable nine of ten shots, roared from behind in the closing minutes, and hung on for one of the biggest upsets in the history of college basketball. The new champions finished with 22 baskets in 28 tries, an NCAA tournament record shooting percentage of 78.6.

More than pinpoint shooting was needed. The Hoyas, expected to roll up a huge rebounding margin, were held to a 17–17 standoff on the backboards. Villanova's sticky 2–3 zone defense prevented Ewing from taking command under the basket. Most significant of all, the winners turned in a virtually flawless floor game.

The key man was Wildcat point guard Gary McLain. Despite being hounded all over the court by Georgetown's Tony Jackson, McLain brought the ball up with sure-handed grace, committing only two turnovers. That assured good shots for Pinckney, who scored 16 points; Dwayne McClain, who got a game-high 17; and the unlikely Wildcat hero, guard Harold Jensen.

Shooting a torrid 79% from the field, the Wildcats of Villanova upset the Hoyas of Georgetown University 66–64 in the National Collegiate Athletic Association championship final in April. Dwayne McClain (shooting) got 17 of Villanova's points and as time ran out fell on the ball until the final buzzer sounded.

RICHARD MACKSON/SPORTS ILLUSTRATED

Coming off the bench, Jensen snapped a shooting slump by sinking all five of his field goal attempts, plus four of five free throws. Jensen clicked with the clutch 4.9-m (16-ft) jumper that put Villanova back on top for good with 2 minutes and 36 seconds left to play. He added four more points in the frantic closing minutes, frustrating repeated Georgetown rallies.

The National Invitation Tournament (NIT) was won by UCLA, which defeated Indiana 65–62 in the final. The women's NCAA basketball championship was won by Old Dominion (31–3) in a 70–65 decision over Georgia (29–5). Medina Dixon scored 18 points and added 15 rebounds for the Lady Monarchs, who took control with an impressive 57–30 domination of rebounds.

The NCAA rules committee voted to use the 45-second shot clock in 1985. Designed to eliminate stalling, it requires the offensive team to shoot within 45 seconds of gaining possession or surrender the ball.

(ROBERT G. LOGAN)

World Amateur. The major confrontation in world basketball in 1985 took place at Kobe (Japan) University where a powerful U.S. collegiate team suffered a surprise 96–93 defeat by the Soviet Union in the men's final. Earlier in the tournament, during the preliminary games, the U.S. had beaten the Soviet Union 91–87, but the threat posed by the tournament-dominating 2.21-m (7-ft

NBA Final Standings, 1984–85

EASTERN CONFERENCE Atlantic Division			WESTERN CONFERENCE Midwest Division		
Team	Won	Lost	Team	Won	Lost
Boston	63	19	Denver	52	30
Philadelphia	58	24	Houston	48	34
New Jersey	42	40	Dallas	44	38
Washington	40	42	San Antonio	41	41
New York	24	58	Utah	41	41
			Kansas City	31	51

Central Division			Pacific Division		
Team	Won	Lost	Team	Won	Lost
Milwaukee	59	23	L.A. Lakers	62	20
Detroit	46	36	Portland	42	40
Chicago	38	44	Phoenix	36	46
Cleveland	36	46	Seattle	31	51
Atlanta	33	49	L.A. Clippers	31	51
Indiana	23	59	Golden State	22	60

3-in) Soviet centre Arvidas Sabonis kept the outcome of the final an open question. The game was tied at 80–80 when Sabonis fouled out with 4½ minutes remaining. The lead then fluctuated until the score reached 93–93, when Vladimir Khomitchus sank a three-point jump shot from the corner with just two seconds on the clock to clinch a Soviet victory. The Soviet Union also won the women's gold medal, defeating the U.S. 87–81 in the final. The first world championship for junior women took place at the Olympic Center at Colorado Springs, Colo., and completed a clean sweep for the Soviet Union, which beat Korea 80–75 in the final.

The world championship finals were scheduled to be held in Spain in 1986, and the European qualification system was based for the first time on qualifying groups playing their games on a home-and-away basis over a two-year period. Highlights of the first three rounds of matches were victories by England 69–68 over Czechoslovakia, by Greece 94–90 against France in overtime, and by The Netherlands 67–66 over Belgium.

The European men's championship finals were held in Stuttgart, West Germany. Once again the Soviet Union emerged the victors, beating surprise finalists Czechoslovakia 120–89. The women's European championship finals took place in Italy in September 1985. The title was retained by the Soviet Union, which thereby maintained an unbroken sweep of victories stretching back to 1960. In the final the Soviets defeated Bulgaria 103–69. (Bulgaria had finished second in the previous European championships, in 1983, and was the last team to beat the Soviet women in a European championship match, in 1958.) The third-place match was won by Hungary, which defeated Czechoslovakia 103–76.

The World Club Championship resulted in a win for the host club, FC Barcelona, which was victorious against Monte Libano of Brazil 93–89 in the final. The 1984–85 European Champions' Cup for men was won by KK Cibona of Zagreb, Yugos., which defeated seven-time previous winner Real Madrid 87–78 in the final at Athens. FC Barcelona took the Cup-Winners' Cup at Grenoble, France, with a 77–73 win over Zahlgiris Kaunas of the Soviet Union to gain a European cup for the first time after three times as finalists. In the final of the other European cup competition, the Korac Cup, Olimpia Milan defeated Pall Varese 91–78 in an all-Italian affair. In the women's European Champions' Cup final Fiorella Vicenza of Italy regained the title it had won in 1983 by defeating TTT Daugawa Riga of Latvia 63–55.　　(MELVIN D. WELCH)

BILLIARD GAMES

Billiards. Raymond Ceulemans of Belgium captured his 19th world three-cushion billiard title in The Netherlands in April, narrowly edging defending champion Nobuaki Kobayashi of Japan 50–49 in the final match. For these 40th world championships the governing World Billiard Union again disdained the traditional full round-robin competition of 60-point games. Instead, two separate six-player round-robins were contested, with the top two finishers from each advancing to a single elimination final phase. All matches were to 50 points.

Ceulemans won the B bracket, with Junichi Komori (41st All-Japan champion) finishing solidly in second place. In the A bracket Kobayashi was the winner, with 1985 European champion Torbjorn Blomdahl in second.

The two Japanese faced each other in the semifinal round. Kobayashi posted a 1.351 points-per-inning average to advance handily. Ceulemans was even tougher in the other semifinal as he scorched the cushions at a 2.273

scoring pace to crush the 23-year-old Swede 50–14. A Ceulemans-Kobayashi final was thus assured for the eighth time, with the typically dramatic one-point victory giving Ceulemans a 7–1 record in those meetings.

The 43rd European championships in three-cushion billiards took place in The Netherlands in March. A field of 16, led by defending champion Rini Van Bracht and Ceulemans, was divided into four flights for 50-point matches. In the semifinal round Blomdahl upset Ceulemans 50–48 in 39 innings. The loss ended any hope for a 22nd European title for Ceulemans in 1985; he and Egidio Vierat of France, a victim of a 50–25 defeat by Van Bracht, played for third place. Ceulemans beat Vierat 50–37 in 40 innings to finish third and qualify for the world tournament. Blomdahl played stiff defense on the way to a 50–30 win over Van' Bracht to win the title, needing just 39 innings.

The $20,000 third *Billiards Digest* three-cushion championships, the richest open three-cushion event in the world, drew 42 competitors, including Ceulemans and Blomdahl, to Chicago in July. As in the European tournament, Blomdahl upset the Belgian master by a 50–29 count. It earned Blomdahl third place and meant that Ceulemans had to beat Richard Bitalis of France twice to 50 points for the title, which he did in 27- and 26-inning masterpieces.

The seventh Denver Athletic Club open followed, with Ceulemans and Bitalis adding both great talent and international flavour to the 22-player field. The two popular stars repeated their 1-2 finish, with the final match won by Ceulemans 50–42 in 30 innings.

The Billiard Federation of the USA 18th annual national championship in San Jose, Calif., was won by Frank Torres over Allen Gilbert, despite the latter's setting new records for high run (14) and best 50-point game (28 innings). The *National Billiard News* open in Oak Park, Mich., attracted a field of 30, with Bob Ameen of Detroit taking first place and Adrian Viguera of Chicago placing second.

Pocket Billiards. U.S. players continued to enjoy an increasing number of tournaments offered on the professional-size 4½-ft by 9-ft tables as players, promoters, and sponsors alike sought to establish a solid, ongoing annual "tour" of tournaments. By 1985 virtually all professional competitions in the U.S. were contested in the fast short-rack rotation game of nine-ball.

The 1984 U.S. nine-ball open in Norfolk, Va., with $34,200 in prizes in two divisions, was won by the *National Billiard News* and *Billiards Digest* players of the year, Earl Strickland (men) and Jean Balukas (women).

The sixth annual Women's Professional Billiards Association Carleton Slims nationals in South Fallsburg, N.Y., a $10,000, 32-player nine-ball test, was won easily by the 25-year-old Balukas. The Brooklyn native later became the youngest member and only the second woman elected to the Billiard Congress of America (BCA) Hall of Fame.

Yet another big win for Balukas came at the $50,000 Sands Regent open in Reno, Nev., over a strong field of 32. Mike Sigel of Towson, Md., won the 66-player men's event.

Strickland capped a string of three straight tour wins at the $40,000 Clyde Childress open in Richmond, Ky., over a tough field of 57. Truman Hogue of Louisville, Ky., won an added 32-player nine-ball bank pool event.

The fourth Caesars Tahoe Billiard Classic at Lake Tahoe, Calif., with $78,000 at stake in three divisions, was won by Cecil ("Buddy") Hall (men), Robin Hansen-Bell (women), and Bob Vanover (seniors). The $75,000 Red's open in Houston, Texas, drew 108 men and 32 women for nine-ball plus 30 men for an added one-pocket event won by

Grady Mathews. Efren Reyes (alias Caesar Morales) of the Philippines took the men's title, and Lori Jon Ogonowski of New Jersey the women's.

The year's richest event, the $136,000 Resorts open in Atlantic City, N.J., was contested by 115 men, 25 women, and 32 seniors. Wade Crane, Hansen-Bell, and Larry ("Boston Shorty") Johnson were the divisional winners, respectively.

In eight-ball competition, most often held on 3½-ft by 7-ft tables, the $33,000 seventh Pabst U.S. team open drew 89 men's and 49 women's teams to Milwaukee, Wis., in March. Miller Time (Moline, Ill.) took the men's title, with the Breaking Point (West Allis, Wis.) gaining the women's crown. The $25,000 Valley National 8-Ball Association team championships took place during 1985 in Las Vegas, Nev. Kozak's of Windsor, Ont., was the men's winner, and Cannon Lanes of Cannon Falls, Minn., took the women's championship.

The BCA held its ninth national eight-ball (individual) and seventh All-American eight-ball (team) tournaments in Fort Worth, Texas, with more than $57,000 in prizes. The team winners were Starlight No. 2 (men) and Golden Nugget (women), both of Arlington, Texas. Individual titlists were Steve Matlock, Cedar Rapids, Iowa, and Linda Hoffman, Arlington. "The Place" of Baltimore, Md., won the $10,000 first prize in the $35,000 Busch Pool League national championship team tournament in St. Louis, Mo.

The $150,000 fifth Lite Beer World Series of Tavern Pool in Las Vegas attracted 1,374 men and 426 women for individual eight-ball play. John Herron of Baker, Calif., and Ellen Sellers of Chicago were the victors. Herron's victory was worth $10,000, while Sellers won $7,500.

(BRUCE H. VENZKE)

Snooker. Dennis Taylor (Northern Ireland) won the world professional snooker title for the first time when he defeated the defending champion, Steve Davis (England), by 18 frames to 17 in an epic final at Sheffield, England, in April 1985. Davis, who in February had won the English championship by beating Tony Knowles 8–2 in the final, turned the tables on Taylor in October by defeating him 10–9 in the Rothmans Grand Prix final. Cliff Thorburn (Canada) regained the Benson and Hedges Masters title and went on to win the Scottish Masters tournament and the Goya Matchroom Trophy. Silvino Francisco (South Africa) became the first Dulux British Open champion in March when he defeated Kirk Stevens (Canada) 12–9 in the final. (SYDNEY E. FRISKIN)

BOBSLEDDING

Wolfgang Hoppe, an East German driver who had won both Olympic bobsledding events in 1984, defeated his compatriot Detlef Richter in the two-man race at the world championships at Cervinia, Italy, in January 1985; Zintis Ekmanis took the bronze medal for the U.S.S.R. East Germany completed a gold and silver double when, in the four-man contest, Bernhard Lehmann finished ahead of Richter; Silvio Giobellina placed third for Switzerland.

Giobellina retained the European four-man title at St. Moritz, Switz., in February, with Hoppe runner-up and the 40-year-old veteran Hans Hiltebrand of Switzerland third. The two-man championship was gained by Ekmanis, with Hoppe and Hiltebrand second and third.

An inaugural World Cup was awarded for performances at four tournaments. The three best scores made by each contestant were added together to achieve the total. Jeffrey Jost of the United States was the winner, with Nick Phipps of Great Britain second and Anton Fischer of West Germany third.

New regulations, to be ratified by the Fédération Internationale de Bobsleigh et de Tobogganning (FIBT), were expected to restrict the future size and weight of sleds and thus challenge manufacturers' expertise with aerodynamics to produce competitive bobs of a more strictly standardized form. This would outlaw the East German, Soviet, and Swiss sleds used in 1985.

Followers of the sport were saddened by news of the impending closure of the Cervinia track, one of the world's best, because of high maintenance costs. Italy's winter sports federation decided that all that country's future competitions would be staged at Cortina d'Ampezzo.

(HOWARD BASS)

BOWLING

World Tenpins. The international tenpin season of 1985 opened with the eighth Asian Zone amateur championships of the Fédération Internationale des Quilleurs in Singapore in November 1984. Australia's John Sullivan and Thailand's Kunarksorn Luyong won the individual titles. Sullivan defeated Hiroshi Ishihara of Japan 211–196 in his final match, and Luyong defeated Bec Nautanabe of the Philippines in his final 204–170. The six-game singles was won by Ollie Reformado of the Philippines with a score of 1,390; the doubles went to Singapore with 2,532; Malaysia won the trios with a record high 3,666 series; and South Korea won the five-man event with 5,820. Paeng Nepomuceno of the Philippines won the all-events gold medal with 4,978.

In the women's division the Philippines' Bong Coo won the singles gold with 1,261; the Philippines took the doubles with 2,317, Australia the trios with 3,521, and Japan the five-game event with 5,827. The all-events gold went to Jeanette Baker of Australia, who totaled 4,689 for the 24 games.

The European amateur tenpin championships took place in Vienna in July 1985. From 12 events Finland, whose men won every team event, went home with four gold medals, four silver, and two bronze, while Sweden gained five gold medals, two silver, and two bronze. Tony Rosenqvist of Sweden was the champion above champions with victories in each men's individual event. In the women's events Finland won the trios; Italy claimed its first gold medal ever when Coletta Marcuzzo won the six-game event; the doubles competition was won by Åsa Larsson of Denmark and Lena Sulkanen of Sweden; France took the five-women team event; the 24-game all-events gold medal went to Great Britain with Meg Shaw; and in the match play final Larsson defeated Nora Haveneers of Belgium.

At the World Games II in or near London, tenpin bowlers of 24 top nations took part in singles for men and women and mixed doubles. Dominique de Nolf and Haveneers of Belgium won the mixed doubles. The men's eight-game singles was won by Raymond Jansson of Sweden with 1,699 and the women's singles by Adelene Wee of Singapore with 1,601; both winners were also representatives of a new generation, being only 19 years of age.

(YRJÖ SARAHETE)

U.S. Tenpins. Scores of the championship matches on the Professional Bowlers Association (PBA) tour in 1985 often disappointed viewers and sponsors, but Mike Aulby did not share the blame. Aulby had won five PBA titles going into the final weeks of the year, and the 25-year-old left-hander from Indianapolis, Ind., was consistently strong when first prize was at stake. In Union City, Calif., Aulby won his final match 245–190; in Toledo, Ohio, 253–211; in Garden City, N.Y., 233–220; in Denver, Colo., 210–159; and in Chicago, 245–189. In the PBA doubles cham-

pionship in Las Vegas, Nev., Aulby and his brother-in-law, Steve Cook of Roseville, Calif., teamed for a 224–209 victory.

The six championships helped Aulby accumulate $199,-800, surpassing Earl Anthony's one-year record of $164,-735. Second on the money list was Pete Weber of St. Louis, Mo., 23-year-old son of Bowling Hall of Fame member Dick Weber, who also passed Anthony's record with $173,356. Missing from the list of 25 leading money winners was the 1984 Bowler of the Year, Mark Roth of Spring Lake Heights, N.J., who averaged 211.3 in 1985 but had little success in the tournaments.

A bowler who had long puzzled followers of the sport because of his inability to win a title despite numerous opportunities, Steve Wunderlich of St. Louis, won one of the year's richest events, the American Bowling Congress (ABC) Masters Tournament in Tulsa, Okla. In the final match Wunderlich defeated Tommy Kress of Rochester, N.Y., 256–171 and won $40,600.

In the ABC tournament for nonprofessionals in Tulsa, the Regular Division winners were: team, Terry's Pro Shop, Solon, Ohio, 3,233; doubles, Howard Higby and Clyde Gibson, Lake Jackson, Texas, 1,366; singles, Glenn Harbison, Pittsburgh, Pa., 774; all-events, Barry Asher, Anaheim, Calif., 2,033.

For the second time in three years Aleta Sill of Cocoa, Fla., won the biggest prize available to women bowlers when she topped Linda Graham 279–193 in the title match of the Maxim/Women's International Bowling Congress (WIBC) Queens Tournament in Toledo. Sill, who was runner-up to Japan's Kazue Inahashi in 1984, gained $20,-700 for her victory. Graham, from Des Moines, Iowa, received $11,600.

Sill and Graham both were champions in the WIBC tournament in Toledo, with Sill taking the Open Division all-events honours with 1,900 for her nine games. Graham and Melody Philippson of Colfax, Iowa, each bowled 623 to win the doubles title with 1,246. A 2,934 total by a Toledo quintet, Don Redman Insurance, won the Open Division team crown, and Polly Schwarzel of Cheswick, Pa., rolled 694 for the singles championship.

Division I winners in the WIBC were: team, Taylor Chiropractic, Howell, Mich., 2,834; doubles, Sara Hennessey and Laura Lyons, Piqua, Ohio, 1,232; singles, Vicki Baker, St. Paris, Ohio, 656; and all-events, Barb Hansen, Marstons Mills, Mass., 1,800.   (JOHN J. ARCHIBALD)

BOXING

The biggest upset in heavyweight boxing in 1985 was the defeat of Larry Holmes (U.S.) by light heavyweight champion Michael Spinks (U.S.) on points over 15 rounds. Both fighters had been undefeated, and though Holmes had relinquished the World Boxing Council (WBC) title in 1983 to become International Boxing Federation (IBF; not internationally recognized) champion, he was still considered the world's top heavyweight. Earlier he had successfully defended his IBF crown by stopping David Bey (U.S.) in ten rounds and outpointing Carl Williams (U.S.). Holmes had won all of his 48 professional contests and was a firm favourite to beat Spinks and so equal the record of Rocky Marciano, who won every one of his 49 fights before retiring as undefeated heavyweight champion. Though Holmes failed to equal Marciano's record, Spinks established two new records. He became the first light heavyweight champion to beat a heavyweight champion and, because Leon Spinks (U.S.) had won the heavyweight title from Muhammad Ali in 1978, it was the first time that two brothers could claim they had won the heavyweight championship.

Marvelous Marvin Hagler gave away four years in age and four inches in height and reach but won the undisputed world middleweight championship in April with a third-round technical knockout of Thomas ("Hit Man") Hearns.
AP/WIDE WORLD

Pinklon Thomas (U.S.) continued as WBC champion, knocking out former WBA champion Mike Weaver (U.S.) in eight rounds. Tony Tubbs (U.S.) became new WBA champion by outpointing Greg Page (U.S.).

The WBC cruiserweight championship changed hands twice. Alfonso Ratliff (U.S.) won it from Carlos de León (P.R.) but was then beaten by Bernard Benton (U.S.). Piet Crous (South Africa) retained the WBA title by stopping Randy Stephens (U.S.) in three rounds at Sun City, South Africa, but Dwight Muhammad Qawi (U.S.) later stopped Crous in 11 rounds, also at Sun City. Qawi was banned from appearing in WBC ratings for two years because he had fought in South Africa. Michael Spinks (U.S.) retained both the WBC and WBA light heavyweight titles, halting David Sears (U.S.) in three rounds and Diamond Jim McDonald (U.S.) in eight. However, after winning the IBF heavyweight title from Holmes, Spinks was stripped of his light heavyweight crown by the WBC and WBA. J. B. Williamson (U.S.) then won the WBC crown by outpointing Prince Mama Mohammed (Ghana).

Marvin Hagler (U.S.) remained the undisputed middleweight king, knocking out Thomas Hearns (U.S.), the WBC junior middleweight champion, in three rounds. Hearns remained the junior middleweight titleholder without making a defense during the year, but Mike McCallum (U.S.) made two successful defenses of the WBA version, stopping Luigi Minchillo (Italy) in 13 rounds and David Braxton (U.S.) in 8. Milton McCrory (U.S.) kept the WBC welterweight crown with two victories in France, outpointing Pedro Vilella (U.S.) and stopping Carlos Trujillo (Panama) in three, but then lost it on a two-round knockout by Don Curry (U.S.). Curry made only one defense of his WBA welterweight title, beating Colin Jones (Wales) in four rounds.

After retaining the WBC junior welterweight championship by outpointing Leroy Haley (U.S.), Billy Costello (U.S.) lost the title to Lonnie Smith (U.S.) after being knocked out in the eighth round. It was Costello's first defeat after 30 consecutive victories. The WBA championship at this weight passed from Gene Hatcher (U.S.), who was halted in nine rounds by Ubaldo Sacco (Arg.). The WBC lightweight title changed hands; Hector Camacho (P.R.) outpointed the titleholder, José Luis Ramírez (Mexico), but Livingstone Bramble (U.S.) retained the WBA version by outpointing Ray Mancini (U.S.). Julio César Chávez

(Mexico) remained WBC junior lightweight champion in a busy year. He stopped Ruben Castillo (U.S.) in six rounds and Roger Mayweather (U.S.), the former WBA champion, in two; he then outpointed Dwight Pratchett (U.S.) to bring his record to 46 wins without a defeat. Rocky Lockridge (U.S.), having retained the WBA crown against Kamel Bou Ali (Tunisia), lost it to Wilfred Gómez (P.R.). Gómez thus joined the select number of champions who had won three titles, having previously held the WBC featherweight and junior featherweight crowns.

Azumah Nelson (Ghana) kept the WBC featherweight championship, stopping Juvenal Ordénes (Chile) in three rounds and dismissing Pat Cowdell (England) in the first. After retaining the WBA featherweight championship for the 19th time with a win on points over Jorge Lujan (Panama), Eusebio Pedroza (Panama) lost the title to Barry McGuigan (Northern Ireland) over 15 rounds. McGuigan then remained champion by stopping Bernard Taylor (U.S.), who had been undefeated in his previous 34 contests.

One of the biggest surprises of the year was the defeat of WBC junior featherweight champion Juan Meza (Mexico) by Lupe Pintor (Mexico), the former bantamweight champion. Pintor had been omitted from the world rankings for some time. The WBA junior featherweight crown remained with Víctor Callejas (P.R.), who outpointed Lee Seung Hoon (South Korea). Albert Davila (U.S.) relinquished the WBC bantamweight title, and this was later won by Daniel Zaragoza (Mexico) when Freddie Jackson (U.S.) was disqualified in the seventh round for butting. Zaragoza lost the crown in his first defense to Miguel Lora (Colombia). Richie Sandoval (U.S.) had no difficulty retaining the WBA title, stopping Cardenio Ulloa (Chile) in eight rounds.

Jiro Watanabe (Japan), who had been stripped of the superflyweight championship by the WBA, was still recognized by the WBC and successfully defended this title three times, knocking out Payao Poontaret (Thailand) in 11 rounds, outpointing Julio Soto Solane (Dominican Republic), and stopping Katsuo Katsuma (Japan) in seven. The vacant WBA championship went to Kaosai Galaxy (Thailand) with a sixth-round win against Eusebio Espina (Dominican Republic). Kaosai followed this with victories against Lee Dong Choon (South Korea) in seven rounds and Rafael Orono (Venezuela) in five. Sot Chitalada (Thailand) continued as WBC flyweight champion by stopping Charlie Magri (England) in four rounds and drawing with Gabriel Bernal (Mexico). After defending the WBA flyweight crown for the ninth time by outpointing Antoine Montero (France), Santos Laciar (Arg.) relinquished the title and Hilario Zapata (Panama) won it.

Chang Jung Koo (South Korea) retained the WBC junior

Michael Spinks (left) upset heavyweight champion Larry Holmes in a unanimous 15-round decision in September. Holmes, who had confidently expected to equal Rocky Marciano's record of 49 straight victories, had beaten Spink's older brother Leon in a 1981 bout.
MANNY MILLAN/SPORTS ILLUSTRATED

flyweight crown with wins against Germán Torres (Mexico) and Francisco Montiel (Mexico). Joey Olivio (U.S.) made boxing history in winning the WBA title from Francisco Quiroz (Dominican Republic), becoming the first American ever to win the junior flyweight championship. Later, however, he lost it to Yuh Myung Woo (South Korea).

In Europe the heavyweight championship changed hands twice. Anders Eklund (Sweden) knocked out Steffen Tangstad (Norway) in four rounds; because Sweden and Norway had banned professional boxing, the fight was held in Copenhagen. In his first defense Eklund was knocked out in four rounds by Frank Bruno (England).

Alex Blanchard (Neth.) retained the light heavyweight crown when he fought Richard Caramanolis (France) to a draw. In their previous meeting Blanchard had knocked out Caramanolis to win the championship. Tony Sibson (England) was stripped of the middleweight title by the European Boxing Union (EBU) when he was unable to meet the organization's date to defend the championship against Ayub Kalule, born in Uganda but living in Denmark. Kalule was then matched with Pierre Joly (France) for the vacant title and beat the Frenchman in eight rounds. Said Skouma (France) became the junior heavyweight champion, stopping Enrico Scacchia (Switzerland) in six rounds. Lloyd Honeyghan (England) took over the welterweight championship by knocking out Gianfranco Rosi (Italy) in three rounds. After retaining the junior welterweight championship, Patrizio Oliva (Italy), who defeated Alessandro Scapecchi (Italy), gave up the title in order to challenge for

European, Commonwealth, and British Boxing Champions
as of Dec. 31, 1985

Division	Europe	Commonwealth	Britain
Heavyweight	Frank Bruno, England	Trevor Berbick, Canada	Hughroy Currie, England
Cruiserweight	. . .	Chisanda Mutti, Zambia	Sammy Reeson, England
Light heavyweight	Alex Blanchard, Neth.	Leslie Stewart, Trinidad	Dennis Andries, England
Middleweight	Ayub Kalule, Denmark	Tony Sibson, England	Herol Graham, England
Junior middleweight	George Steinherr, West Germany	Nick Wilshire, England	Prince Rodney, England
Welterweight	Lloyd Honeyghan, England	Lloyd Honeyghan, England	Sylvester Mittee, England
Junior welterweight	Terry Marsh, England	Billy Famous, Nigeria	Terry Marsh, England
Lightweight	René Weller, West Germany	Barry Michael, Australia	Tony Willis, England
Junior lightweight	Vacant	John Sichula, Zambia	Vacant
Featherweight	Jim McDonnell, England	Vacant	Barry McGuigan, N.Ire.
Junior featherweight	. . .	. . .	. . .
Bantamweight	Ciro De Leva, Italy	Paul Ferreri, Australia	Ray Gilbody, England
Superflyweight	. . .	. . .	. . .
Flyweight	Charlie Magri, England	Vacant	Duke McKenzie, England
Junior flyweight	. . .	. . .	. . .

world honours. The vacant championship was then won by Terry Marsh (England), who halted Scapecchi in six rounds.

René Weller (West Germany) remained Europe's best lightweight, stopping Frederic Geoffroy (France) in 11 rounds. Pat Cowdell (England) did not defend the junior lightweight crown, but after he was stopped in one round in a WBC challenge against Azumah Nelson, the EBU stripped him of the title. Barry McGuigan (Northern Ireland) retained the European featherweight championship by knocking out Clyde Ruan (England) in four rounds, but he then relinquished the title in order to concentrate on his quest for the world crown. The vacant title was later won by Jim McDonnell (England) when he knocked out José Luis Vicho (Spain) in four rounds. Boxers from Britain won a total of five European championships during the year.

Ciro de Leva (Italy) remained bantamweight champion with wins over José Antunez (Spain), Walter Ciorgetti (Italy), and Alain Limarola (France). Charlie Magri (England) gained the flyweight championship for the third time, knocking out defending champion Franco Cherchi (Italy) in two rounds. Only two other British fighters had won a European title at one weight on three separate occasions—Henry Cooper and Joe Bugner, both of them at heavyweight.

There were few changes among Commonwealth champions. Trevor Berbick (Canada) and Chisanda Mutti (Zambia) remained heavyweight and cruiserweight champions, respectively. There was a change at light heavyweight when Leslie Stewart (Trinidad) beat the titleholder, Lotte Mwale (Zambia).

Tony Sibson (England) retained the middleweight crown without defending it. Nick Wilshire (England) became the new junior middleweight champion by stopping Ken Salisbury (Australia) in two rounds. Sylvester Mittee (England) retained the welterweight title with a win on points over Martin McGough (England) but then lost it to Lloyd Honeyghan (England). Billy Famous (Nigeria) carried on as junior welterweight champion, but Barry Michael (Australia) regained the lightweight title he had lost to Graeme Brooke (Australia). John Sichula (Zambia) replaced Lester Ellis (Australia) as junior lightweight champion. The featherweight championship was declared vacant, and Paul Ferreri (Australia) retained the bantamweight title.

(FRANK BUTLER)

CHESS

On Nov. 9, 1985, after a marathon encounter stretching across 14 months and 72 games, Garry Kasparov of the U.S.S.R. (*see* BIOGRAPHIES) became the chess champion of the world by defeating the titleholder, Anatoly Karpov, 13–11. At 22 Kasparov was the youngest world champion in the history of chess.

The long contest between the two Soviet grand masters began in September 1984. The first man to win six games was to be declared the champion. Karpov began strongly, winning four of the first nine games (the other five were drawn) in his effort to retain the title that he had held since 1975. But Kasparov became more cautious, and many of the subsequent contests ended in draws. Karpov eventually pulled ahead 5–0, but Kasparov then won one game and, in succession, two more, the 47th and 48th. At that time, in February 1985, the president of the International Chess Federation, Florencio Campomanes of the Philippines, halted the match on the grounds that both players were too exhausted to continue.

Both players at once protested against the decision, which was clearly against the rules as laid down by the chess federation congress. The president later said that he was acting in response to a request from the Soviet Chess Federation, which believed that Karpov's health might suffer if the match were allowed to continue. But the correct procedure under the rules would have been for the Soviet

16th game of the world championship match			
White	Black	White	Black
A. Karpov	G. Kasparov	A. Karpov	G. Kasparov
1 P–K4	P–QB4	22 BxB	QxB
2 N–KB3	P–K3	23 P–N3	N–Q2
3 P–Q4	PxP	24 B–N2	Q–KB3
4 NxP	N–QB3	25 P–QR3	P–QR4
5 N–N5	P–Q3	26 PxP	PxP
6 P–QB4	N–B3	27 Q–R2	B–N3
7 QN–B3	P–QR3	28 P–Q6	P–N5
8 N–R3	P–Q4	29 Q–Q2	K–N2
9 BPxP	PxP	30 P–B3	QxQP
10 PxP	N–QN5	31 PxB	Q–Q5 ch
11 B–K2	B–QB4	32 K–R1	N–B3
12 Q–Q	Q–Q	33 R–B4	N–K5
13 B–B3	B–B4	34 QxN	N–B7 ch
14 B–N5	R–K1	35 RxN	BxQ
15 Q–Q2	P–N4	36 R(B2)–Q2	Q–K6
16 QR–Q1	N–Q6	37 RxB	B–B8
17 KN–N1	P–R3	38 N–N2	Q–B7
18 B–R4	P–N5	39 N–Q2	RxR ch
19 N–R4	B–Q3	40 NxR	R–K8 ch
20 B–N3	R–QB1	resigns	
21 P–N3	P–N4		

Federation to submit its request to the match arbiter, who would then have advised Karpov to consult the match physician. If the physician thought that the world champion's health was endangered, he would then have advised him to resign the match. Eventually, nonetheless, both competitors said that they were prepared to abide by the president's decision.

In September 1985 the contest resumed in Moscow, with new scoring rules. The scores of the first round were canceled, and the two men ere to play a maximum of 24 games, with one point awarded for a win and ½ point given to each player for a draw. The first player to gain 12½ points would win the match.

Kasparov won the first two games and proceeded to play in brilliant style. The 16th game, a win for Kasparov, was a particularly interesting one (*see* box). In the 19th game Karpov made a desperate attempt at a counterattack, but Kasparov refuted him and again won the game.

The 24th, and last, game of the match took place on November 9. Ahead 12–11, Kasparov needed only a draw to gain the championship. Karpov began play aggressively with a king-side assault, and Kasparov responded with a firm defense. But Karpov maintained his pressure, and Kasparov changed his tactics, adopting a more risky offensive style. The strategy was successful, and Karpov resigned the game and his title after 43 moves.

In other competition during the year, Evgeny Sveshnikov of the Soviet Union won the Hastings international tournament in the U.K. Sharing second place were Stefan Djuric of Yugoslavia, Jim Plaskett of the U.K., and Joel Benjamin and John Fedorowicz of the U.S. Jan Timman of The Netherlands was successful in his native land, winning the Wijk aan Zee international tournament and solidifying his third-place ranking in the world behind Kasparov and Karpov. Tied for second were John Nunn of the U.K. and Aleksandr Beljavsky of the Soviet Union.

At the Commonwealth championships in London, Kevin Spraggett of Canada and Praveen Thipsay of India tied for first place. Spraggett had tied for first in the event in 1984. At the Reggio Emilia international tournament in Italy, Lajos Portisch of Hungary was the winner, his first victory since the Toluca interzonal tournament in 1982. Robert Hübner of West Germany and Ljubomir Ljubojevic of Yugoslavia tied for first in the Linares international tournament in Spain.

The Copenhagen international tournament in Denmark was won by Josef Pinter of Hungary, while second place was shared by two Danes, Curt Hansen and Bent Larsen, and an Icelander, Helgi Olafsson. Tied for first in the Windy City international tournament at Chicago were James Rizzitano and Vincent McCambridge, both of the U.S. Cris Ramayrat of the Philippines won the San Francisco international tournament; Jay Whitehead of the U.S. placed second. At the Baden-Baden international tournament in West Germany, Jan Smejkal of Czechoslovakia was the winner, and Efim Geller of the Soviet Union was runner-up. In one of the finest performances by a woman in the history of chess, Maya Chiburdanidze of the Soviet Union defeated an all-male opposition that included eight grand masters to win the Banja Luka international tournament in Yugoslavia.

The world junior championships, held in the United Arab Emirates, was won by Maxim Dlugy of the U.S. The world under-14 championships, which took place in Argentina, was also won by a U.S. player, Ilya Gurevich. Lev Alburt, a former Soviet grand master who moved to New York City, won his second consecutive U.S. championship.

Three interzonal tournaments were held in 1985 to determine challengers for the world championship. The top four finishers in each tournament qualified for the next round of competition, the Candidates Tournament. In the first interzonal the four qualifiers were Artur Yusupov, Beljavsky, and Aleksandr Chernin of the Soviet Union and Portisch. The top four finishers in the second interzonal were Timman, Jesús Noguieras of Cuba, Mikhail Tal of the Soviet Union, and Spraggett. Qualifying from the third interzonal tournament were Rafael Vaganian and Andrey Sokolov of the Soviet Union, Yasser Seirawan of the U.S., and Nigel Short of the U.K. (HARRY GOLOMBEK)

CONTRACT BRIDGE

Two world championships, the Bermuda Bowl for open teams and the Venice Trophy for women's teams, dominated contract bridge in 1985. The new format for both events provided for a maximum participation of ten teams in each. In recognition of their size, zones 1 and 2, Europe and North America, of the four competing zones were each entitled to double participation in both events. The leading

The Bermuda Bowl produced what was probably the best played hand of the tournament:

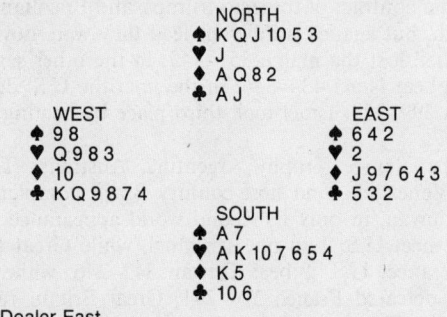

```
                    NORTH
                    ♠ K Q J 10 5 3
                    ♥ J
                    ♦ A Q 8 2
                    ♣ A J
    WEST                              EAST
    ♠ 9 8                             ♠ 6 4 2
    ♥ Q 9 8 3                         ♥ 2
    ♦ 10                              ♦ J 9 7 6 4 3
    ♣ K Q 9 8 7 4                     ♣ 5 3 2
                    SOUTH
                    ♠ A 7
                    ♥ A K 10 7 6 5 4
                    ♦ K 5
                    ♣ 10 6
```

Dealer East,
East-West game.

The same boards were played in both finals. In the Venice Trophy the U.S. was two down in seven spades, while the British women bid and made six spades. In the Bermuda Bowl Australia was two down in seven spades, but Hugh Ross of the U.S. made seven spades after the following auction:

East (Jan Fucik)	South (Peter Pender)	West (Franz Terraneo)	North (Hugh Ross)
Pass	1 ♥	1 no trump	Double
2 ♦	4 ♥	Pass	4 no trump
Pass	5 ♣	Double	5 ♦
Pass	5 ♥	Pass	5 no trump
Pass	6 ♦	Pass	7 ♠
(All Pass)			

Perhaps the normal way to play the hand is to play for a diamond split no worse than 5–2. Cash the king and ace of diamonds, ruff a diamond high, and the second top heart will provide a discard for the losing club. Ross decided that there had been too much bidding, and he drew the right conclusions. West's "comic" no trump followed by his double of four clubs was clearly based on a long club suit. East's diamond bid, lacking high cards in the suit, could be based only on considerable length. A second diamond might not stand up, but all the ingredients for a classic double squeeze were there.

Ross won the opening club lead and immediately led out his trumps. After the last trump he played the king, ace, and queen of diamonds, forcing East to reduce to three cards. East, who had to guard against declarer's fourth diamond, was obliged to keep one diamond and could not hold two hearts. Dummy's last three cards were three hearts, and West had to reduce to three cards. He took his best chance by discarding the king of clubs and relying on his partner for the jack of clubs—in vain. As a result of that hand, the U.S. drew 44 points ahead after 64 boards and was never seriously challenged thereafter.

country in each of those two zones would be exempted until the semifinal round; the remaining teams would play an eight-day round-robin for two places in each event.

In the Bermuda Bowl competition, the U.S. and Canada qualified from Zone 2 and Austria and Israel from Zone 1. The U.S. and Austria went through to the semifinals. In the Venice Trophy U.S. 1 and U.S. 2 represented North America, while Europe was represented by France and Great Britain, the defending champions; U.S. 1 and France were exempted until the semifinal. The other qualifying nations in the Bermuda Bowl were Argentina, Indonesia, New Zealand, Pakistan (which withdrew, as did India, which had taken Pakistan's place, later), Venezuela, and the host country, Brazil. The Bermuda Bowl semifinal match between Brazil and the U.S. provided the highest drama of the championships. On the next to last board, Brazil led by six points; the brothers Branco bid six clubs, were doubled, and were down one after a trump finesse failed. In the replay, however, Sergio Barbosa and Gabino Cintra of Brazil capped their opponents' bid of five clubs with a sacrifice of five hearts that cost only 50 points. Thus with one board to play, the score was tied. In the Closed Room Bob Hamman and Bob Wolff of the U.S. made ten tricks in a contract of one no trump. Barbosa and Cintra reached a contract of three no trumps, and Brazilian hopes ran high, but against a different lead they were down two and Brazil lost the match 351–342. In the other semifinal Austria beat Israel 434–346. In the final the U.S. defeated Austria 399–324. Israel took third place by beating Brazil 174–152.

In the Venice Trophy Argentina, Australia, Taiwan, India, Venezuela, and host country Brazil completed the field. Taiwan, in only its second world appearance, qualified to meet U.S. 1 in one semifinal, while Great Britain faced France. U.S. 1 beat Taiwan 342–246, while Great Britain defeated France 276–241. Great Britain retained the Venice Trophy with a victory in the final over U.S. 1 323–213. France beat Taiwan 188–149 to take third place. The U.S. Bermuda Bowl winners were Bob Hamman and Bob Wolff, Chip Martel and Lew Stansby, Hugh Ross and Peter Pender, and Alfred Sheinwold (nonplaying captain). The British Venice Trophy winners were Sally Horton and Sandra Landy, Pat Davies and Nicola Smith, Jill Scott-Jones and Michelle Brunner, and Grattan Endicott (nonplaying captain). (HAROLD FRANKLIN)

CRICKET

In test matches in 1984–85 England emerged as the outstanding success, while India and Pakistan were supreme in one-day matches. West Indies maintained its overall excellence in five-day tests but proved vulnerable in shorter competitions. Pakistan outplayed New Zealand and India in tests, and Australia had an unhappy year that ended by losing the Ashes 3–1 in England.

Pakistan and India played two tests and, predictably, batsmen dominated both matches and ensured two draws. Centuries for Pakistan were made by the captain, Zaheer Abbas (168 not out), Qasim Umar (210), Mudassar Nazar (199), and Saleem Malik (102 not out); scoring centuries for India were Mohinder Amarnath (101 not out), S. M. Patel (127), and R. J. Shastri (139). The most successful bowlers were Pakistan's fast-medium, left-arm Azeem Hafeez (11 wickets) and India's all-rounder Shastri (4 wickets in 96 overs) and Chetan Sharma (4 wickets in 61 overs). (Because of India's mourning for the death of Prime Minister Indira Gandhi, the third match of the series was not played.)

In Australia, West Indies under C. H. Lloyd overwhelmed the home team by winning the first three tests

easily. The fourth test was drawn, and the fifth was won by Australia, under A. R. Border, who had replaced K. J. Hughes as captain after the second test; the victory, by an innings, was due to splendid spin bowling by R. G. Holland and M. J. Bennett and a brilliant 173 by K. C. Wessels. Earlier the West Indies batsmen had amassed centuries by Lloyd, H. A. Gomes (2), P. J. Dujon, R. B. Richardson, and I. V. A. Richards. The West Indies fast bowlers, M. D. Marshall, Joel Garner, M. A. Holding, and C. A. Walsh, carried all before them until the final test. Holding took rise for 21 in the first test and Marshall five in each innings in the third and another five in the fourth. Wessels was the outstanding Australian batsman, passing 50 five times, and A. M. J. Hilditch was the only other centurion. Fast bowler G. F. Lawson (23 wickets) was Australia's main strike force.

A three-match series between host country Pakistan and New Zealand ended with the home side winning 2–0. Pakistan won the first two tests comfortably, but New Zealand's batsmen J. G. Wright (107) and J. F. Reid (97), supported by brothers M. D. and J. D. Crowe and the captain, J. V. Coney, helped to achieve a draw in the third. Pakistan, led by Zaheer, had in Javed Miandad the outstanding batsman in the series; he scored a century in each innings in the second test. Other centurions were Malik and Nazar, who also opened the bowling. Left-arm spinner Iqbal Qasim (Pakistan, 18 wickets) and S. L. Boock (New Zealand, 17 wickets) were the leading bowlers.

A month later the teams met again in New Zealand under different captains, G. P. Howarth and Javed. There New Zealand gained a healthy revenge, winning 2–0. Fine batting by the left-handed Reid (two centuries) and Coney, whose 111 not out ensured a two-wicket victory in the third test, and good support from all-rounder R. J. Hadlee and batsman M. D. Crowe saw New Zealand safely home. No Pakistan batsman made a century, the best being Umar. Pakistan's bowling was dominated by two young seamers, Wasim Akram and Hafeez (12 wickets each).

England, under D. I. Gower, lost the first test by eight wickets against host team India but then won the second and fourth contests and achieved a remarkable triumph for an underrated side. India, under the veteran S. M. Gavaskar, produced an 18-year-old leg-spinner, L. Sivaramakrishnan, who took 12 wickets in his first test and 7 in his second. But England finally mastered him, thanks primarily to an innings of 160 by opening batsman R. T. Robinson in the second test and to dedicated batting by M. W. Gatting and G. Fowler, who in the fourth test each made a double century. Other factors in the English victory were fine bowling by spinners P. H. Edmonds and the veteran P. I. Pocock. India also included a batting prodigy in M. Azharuddin, who made centuries in his first three tests. Other centurions were Shastri (2), S. M. H. Kirmani, and D. B. Vengsarkar.

The wealth of West Indian batting and the fast bowling of Marshall proved too much for New Zealand, which put up a brave fight in the Caribbean but after drawing the first two tests was battered and beaten in the last two by ten wickets each. The top five West Indians, who were led by I. V. A. Richards, accumulated three centuries (by R. B. Richardson, Richards, and C. G. Greenidge) and averaged over 50. For New Zealand, led by Howarth again, the Crowe brothers made centuries. Marshall took 27 wickets, including 11 in the third test, and the gifted all-rounder Hadlee (15 wickets) and fast-medium E. J. Chatfield (13) were New Zealand's best bowlers.

England at home under Gower defeated Australia 3–1. The Australians began their tour by winning two of the

Test Series Results, November 1984–September 1985

Test	Host country and its scores		Visiting country and its scores		Result
1st	Pakistan	428 for 9 wkt dec	India	155 and 371 for 6 wkt	Match drawn
2nd	Pakistan	674 for 6 wkt	India	500	Match drawn
1st	Australia	76 and 226	West Indies	416	West Indies won by an innings and 112 runs
2nd	Australia	175 and 271	West Indies	424 and 26 for 2 wkt	West Indies won by 8 wkt
3rd	Australia	284 and 173	West Indies	356 and 292 for 7 wkt dec	West Indies won by 191 runs
4th	Australia	296 and 198 for 8 wkt	West Indies	497 and 186 for 5 wkt dec	Match drawn
5th	Australia	471 for 9 wkt dec	West Indies	163 and 253	Australia won by an innings and 55 runs
1st	Pakistan	221 and 181 for 4 wkt	New Zealand	157 and 241	Pakistan won by 6 wkt
2nd	Pakistan	230 and 230 for 3 wkt	New Zealand	267 and 189	Pakistan won by 7 wkt
3rd	Pakistan	328 and 308 for 5 wkt	New Zealand	426	Match drawn
1st	India	465 for 8 wkt dec and 51 for 2 wkt	England	195 and 317	India won by 8 wkt
2nd	India	307 and 235	England	418 and 127 for 2 wkt	England won by 8 wkt
3rd	India	437 for 7 wkt and 29 for 1 wkt	England	276	Match drawn
4th	India	272 and 412	England	652 for 7 wkt and 35 for 1 wkt	England won by 9 wkt
5th	India	533 for 8 wkt dec and 97 for 1 wkt dec	England	417 and 91 for 0 wkt	Match drawn
1st	New Zealand	492 and 103 for 4 wkt	Pakistan	322	Match drawn
2nd	New Zealand	451 for 9 wkt	Pakistan	169 and 183	New Zealand won by an innings and 99 runs
3rd	New Zealand	220 and 278 for 8 wkt	Pakistan	274 and 223	New Zealand won by 2 wkt
1st	West Indies	307 and 261 for 8 wkt dec	New Zealand	262 and 187 for 6 wkt	Match drawn
2nd	West Indies	511 for 6 wkt dec and 268 for 6 wkt dec	New Zealand	440	Match drawn
3rd	West Indies	336 and 10 for 0 wkt	New Zealand	94 and 248	West Indies won by 10 wkt
4th	West Indies	363 and 59 for 0 wkt	New Zealand	138 and 283	West Indies won by 10 wkt
1st	England	533 and 123 for 5 wkt	Australia	331 and 324	England won by 5 wkt
2nd	England	290 and 261	Australia	425 and 127 for 6 wkt	Australia won by 4 wkt
3rd	England	456 and 196 for 2 wkt	Australia	539	Match drawn
4th	England	482 for 9 wkt dec	Australia	257 and 340 for 5 wkt	Match drawn
5th	England	595 for 5 wkt dec	Australia	335 and 142	England won by an innings and 118 runs
6th	England	464	Australia	241 and 129	England won by an innings and 94 runs

three one-day internationals 2–1. They then held their own early in the test series by winning at Lord's but lost the last two tests. England's top batsmen exposed the weakness of the Australian bowling by making huge scores, Gower, G. A. Gooch, Gatting, and Robinson each totaling more than 150; the only bowler to hold them in check was 20-year-old fast-medium C. J. McDermott, with 30 wickets. For England I. T. Botham took 31 wickets as well as playing some fine hitting innings; R. M. Ellison (fast-medium) took 17 wickets in the last two tests; and spinners Edmonds and J. E. Emburey shared 34 wickets. Border, the captain, was in a class of his own as a batsman, winning the Lord's test with an innings of 196.

In one-day cricket competition in Australia, West Indies beat Australia 2–1 in the Benson & Hedges World Series Cup Finals. Australia won the first match through a brilliant 127 not out by Border, but the all-round strength of West Indies gained it victories in the other two. In what was known as the World Championship of Cricket, the final was fought out between India and Pakistan. India won by eight wickets.

Middlesex and Essex were the two best sides in the English domestic season. Middlesex won the county championship, with Hampshire second and Gloucestershire third. Essex won the NatWest Trophy and the John Player Special League but lost to Leicestershire in the Benson & Hedges Cup. In Australia, New South Wales won the Sheffield Shield, and in South Africa, Transvaal won the Currie Cup. In West Indies, Trinidad and Tobago won the Shell Shield, and in New Zealand, Wellington won the Shell Trophy. In India, Bombay won the Ranji Trophy, South Zone the Duleep Trophy, and Rest of India the Irani Cup. In Pakistan, United Banks won the Paco Pentangular and Qaid-i-Azam Trophy, and Karachi Whites took the Patron's Trophy.   (REX ALSTON)

CURLING

Canada extended its record number of wins to 16 by defeating Sweden 6–2 in the final of the 27th men's world championship for the Air Canada Silver Broom at Kelvin Hall, Glasgow, Scotland, on March 24–31. The winning skip, Al Hackner from Ontario, supported by Rick Lang,

Ian Tetley, and Pat Peroud, confirmed his reputation as the world's top curler with a near-perfect performance; his crucial last two shots ended the challenge of Stefan Hasselborg, backed by his brother Michael, Hans Nordon, and Lars Wernbom. Hackner became only the third player to figure in a championship victory twice (previously in 1982). Canada had overcome the U.S. 9–4 in one semifinal, and Sweden had eliminated Denmark 4–2 in the other. The other participating nations were Norway, Scotland, West Germany, Switzerland, Italy, and England.

Canada also won the seventh women's world championship, beating Scotland 5–2 in the final at Jönköping, Sweden, March 17–24. Switzerland defeated Sweden 6–4 for third place. Canadian depth was evident in its victory over Switzerland in the final of the 11th world junior championship in Perth, Scotland, on March 10–17; Scotland and Norway placed third and fourth.

Curling schools continued to open in Switzerland on almost as large a scale as the country's well-organized ski-teaching system. In Japan curling advanced sufficiently to justify that nation's application to participate in the 1986 world championship. The sport's steady expansion had its frustrations, however. Although England was able to enter a world championship team, efforts to increase activity south of the Anglo-Scottish border were severely limited because of the great hold that recreational skating maintained at England's ice rinks. A converse situation existed at most of Scotland's rinks, where few managements could afford to take much time from curling.

Although curling was added to the program of the 1988 Winter Olympics in Calgary, Alta., the host country was disappointed that it would be contested only as a demonstration sport, as it had at three previous Olympic Games. The main stumbling block was the existence of another form of curling, known as Eisstockschiessen, played primarily in West Germany and Austria.   (HOWARD BASS)

CYCLING

Bernard Hinault of France defied a broken nose and stitches in a head wound to win the 1985 Tour de France and join Jacques Anquetil and Eddy Merckx as the only riders to have won professional cycling's most

important race on five occasions. Hinault dominated the 3½-week race (June 28–July 21) despite the injuries he received in a crash at the finish of the 14th stage in Saint-Étienne. He also won his preparatory event, the Tour of Italy, and so completed the sport's most famous double—a feat achieved only by Fausto Coppi, Anquetil, Merckx, and Hinault himself—for the second time. English-speaking competitors enjoyed unprecedented prominence in the Tour de France. Runner-up Greg LeMond, riding for the same trade team as Hinault, recorded the first stage victory by a rider from the U.S. when he won the 47.5-km time trial at Lake Vassivière. The next three positions overall were filled by Ireland's Stephen Roche and Sean Kelly and Australia's Phil Anderson. Kelly won the Super Prestige Pernod trophy for the second consecutive year.

At the 1985 world championships in the Veneto region of Italy, 38-year-old Joop Zoetemelk of The Netherlands won the professional road race title. Three other road titles were also decided there. After remeasurement of the course, the Soviet Union was credited with an Olympic-record-breaking average speed of 50.9 km/h (31.6 mph) in winning the team time trial. The amateur men's road race was won by Lech Piasecki of Poland, after a series of early crashes left 60 riders in need of medical treatment. Jeannie

The 1985 Tour de France was won by Bernard Hinault (centre) of France, who became only the third man to win the event five times. Finishing second was his teammate, Greg LeMond of the United States. Hinault, 31, expected to retire after one more year of competition.
VANDYSTADT/ALL SPORT

1985 Cycling Champions

Event	Winner	Country
WORLD AMATEUR CHAMPIONS—TRACK		
Men		
Sprint	L. Hesslich	East Germany
Tandem sprint	R. Rehounek, V. Voboril	Czechoslovakia
Individual pursuit	V. Ekimov	U.S.S.R.
Team pursuit	R. Amadio, G. Grisandi	Italy
	M. Brunelli, S. Martinello	
1,000-m time trial	J. Glücklich	East Germany
50-km points	M. Penc	Czechoslovakia
50-km motor paced	R. Dotti	Italy
Women		
Sprint	I. Nicoloso	France
Individual pursuit	R. Twigg	U.S.
WORLD PROFESSIONAL CHAMPIONS—TRACK		
Sprint	K. Nakano	Japan
Individual pursuit	H.-H. Oersted	Denmark
50-km points	U. Freuler	Switzerland
One-hour motor paced	B. Vicino	Italy
Keirin	U. Freuler	Switzerland
WORLD AMATEUR CHAMPIONS—ROAD		
Men		
Individual road race	L. Piasecki	Poland
100-km team time trial	V. Jdanov, I. Sumnikov	U.S.S.R.
	V. Klimov, A. Zinoviev	
Women		
Individual road race	J. Longo	France
WORLD PROFESSIONAL CHAMPION—ROAD		
Individual road race	J. Zoetemelk	The Netherlands
WORLD CHAMPIONS—CYCLO-CROSS		
Amateur	M. Kluge	West Germany
Professional	K.-P. Thaler	West Germany
MAJOR PROFESSIONAL ROAD-RACE WINNERS		
Tour de France	B. Hinault	France
Tour of Italy	B. Hinault	France
Tour of Spain	P. Delgado	Spain
Paris–Nice	S. Kelly	Ireland
Milan–San Remo	H. Kuiper	The Netherlands
Tour of Flanders	E. Vanderaerden	Belgium
Paris–Roubaix	M. Madiot	France
Flèche Wallonne	C. Criquelion	Belgium
Liège–Bastogne–Liège	M. Argentin	Italy
Dauphiné–Libéré	P. Anderson	Australia
Bordeaux–Paris	B. Cornillet	France
G.P. de Midi Libre	S. Contini	Italy
Tour of Switzerland	P. Anderson	Australia
Circuit Het Volk	E. Planckaert	Belgium
Amstel Gold	G. Knetemann	The Netherlands
G.P. de Frankfurt	P. Anderson	Australia
Paris–Brussels	A. van der Poel	The Netherlands
Dunkirk 4-day	J.-L. Vandenbroucke	Belgium
Tirenno Adriatico	J. Zoetemelk	The Netherlands
Ghent–Wevelgem	E. Vanderaerden	Belgium
Tour of Romandie	J. Müller	Switzerland
Tour of Lombardy	S. Kelly	Ireland
Tour de l'Avenir*	M. Ramirez	Colombia
Tour of Britain*	E. van Lancker	Belgium
Berlin–Prague–Warsaw†	L. Piasecki	Poland

*Mixed professional and amateur.
†Amateur.

Longo of France took the women's title after previously winning three silver and three bronze medals on the road and track. The track program produced a world best of 5 min 43.02 sec from Hans-Henrik Oersted of Denmark during his successful defense of the professional 5,000-m pursuit title. Oersted returned to the 400-m cement track two weeks later and broke the nonaltitude world record for one hour, covering 48.149 km (29.852 mi). Two long winning sequences were extended when Japanese millionaire Koichi Nakano won the professional sprint for the ninth year, and Urs Freuler of Switzerland collected his fifth consecutive professional points race title as well as winning the keirin for a second time. Rebecca Twigg of the U.S. scored her third victory in the women's pursuit, but compatriot Connie Paraskevin lost the sprint title to Isabelle Nicoloso of France. (JOHN R. WILKINSON)

FENCING

Mauro Numa of Italy and Philippe Boisse of France retained their individual titles in the foil and épée events, respectively, during the world fencing championships at Barcelona, Spain, in July. When the week-long competition had ended, however, it was the West Germans who emerged with the most gold medals—three. Paced by the seasoned Cornelia Hanisch, they captured first places in the women's individual and team foil and in the men's team épée. Italy won the men's team foil.

Honours in sabre were shared by Hungary and the Soviet Union. Gyoergy Nebald, the Hungarian stylist, proved best in the individual competition, defeating Bulgaria's Khristo Etropolski for the gold medal. Unable to place among the first three in individual sabre, the Soviet Union gained its only gold medal by triumphing in the team event.

Two unexpected episodes provided extra excitement. Italy's Stefano Cerioni, who had finished third in the individual foil a year earlier at the Olympic Games in Los Angeles, was ordered out of that weapon's final match for "unsportsmanlike behaviour"; it was alleged that he had used insulting language. His exclusion marked the first time in the history of the annual championships that such an action had been taken by officials.

Even more startling was an injury to the lower abdomen

suffered by France's Philippe Conscience. He was hurt when a blade wielded by Poland's Boguslav Zych pierced the former's padded jacket and tore through his iliac vein. Only the presence of a Spanish surgeon, who immediately made the correct diagnosis, and a portable operating unit in a van kept outside the sports hall's premises for emergencies averted more serious consequences.

(MICHAEL STRAUSS)

FIELD HOCKEY

At the sixth Champions Trophy tournament in Karachi, Pak., in December 1984, Australia defeated Pakistan, the world and Olympic champion, 2–0 in the deciding match of the round-robin series. Great Britain finished third, The Netherlands fourth, New Zealand fifth, and Spain sixth. West Germany and India had withdrawn.

In May 1985 West Germany defeated England 1–0 at Mülheim, West Germany, and then went on to win the four-nations tournament in June at Amsterdam, where England placed second, The Netherlands third, and India fourth. In July–August England toured Australia, which won the six-match series 5–1. At Barcelona in October Spain won the Intercontinental Cup, defeating New Zealand in the final on a penalty stroke competition after the game had ended in a 2–2 tie. Finishing behind those two teams were (3) Poland, (4) Canada, (5) Argentina, (6) Ireland, (7) Kenya, (8) Malaysia, (9) Belgium, (10) Japan, (11) South Korea, and (12) Zimbabwe. The Netherlands won the four-nations tournament in London. The Soviet Union finished second, England third, and India fourth.

Indoors, West Germany reaffirmed its superiority by winning the eight-nations tournament at Bad Neuenahr, West Germany, in December 1984, defeating England 14–3 in the final. Austria placed third, followed in order by Poland, Wales, Denmark, Italy, and France. Scotland regained the home countries championship in January 1985, defeating England 8–6 in Cardiff, Wales. Wales was third and Ireland fourth.

In women's hockey England defeated Scotland 3–0 at Wembley, London, and later won the home countries championship. The Soviet Union won the Intercontinental Cup at Buenos Aires, Arg., in March–April, defeating Argentina 3–2 in the final. South Korea won the bronze medal by defeating Japan 2–1. Other placings were (5) India, (6) Wales, (7) Zimbabwe, (8) Jamaica, (9) Switzerland, (10) Paraguay, and (11) Uruguay.

The Netherlands defeated Great Britain 1–0 at Gateshead, England, in June, and the second match ended in a 0–0 tie. In August–September England toured Australia, which won the five-match series 4–1. At home in May West Germany defeated Scotland 5–1 at Dortmund and England 3–0 at Mülheim. At Glasgow, Scotland, in June Australia defeated Great Britain 4–1 and Scotland twice, 2–0 and 4–0.

Indoors, West Germany won the European championship at Crystal Palace, London, in January, defeating The Netherlands 8–7 in the final. They were followed by (3) England, (4) Scotland, (5) Canada, (6) Austria, (7) Ireland, and (8) Italy. (SYDNEY E. FRISKIN)

FOOTBALL

Association Football (Soccer). Crowd tragedies and qualifying for the 1986 World Cup finals in Mexico were the focal points in soccer during 1985. The Brussels Heysel Stadium riot (see Sidebar), which led to the banning of English clubs from international competition for at least three years, was the most serious of the season. But the fire at the English Third Division club Bradford on May 11, during a match against Lincoln, cost 56 spectators their lives and was seen on television by millions of viewers. Fire gutted the old wooden stand and caused a stampede. There was also a riot in Birmingham, England, in May 1985 during which, mercifully, only one fan died, probably because the policing and crowd control were strong and efficient—and a little luck was granted when a group of supporters burst through a door and fell some 4.5 m (15 ft) into a parking lot, and only one was seriously hurt.

On the playing front, Canada for the first time qualified for a place in the final rounds of the World Cup. Canada thus joined host country Mexico, which was sure it could stage the event despite the massive earthquake of September 1985, and defending champion Italy. Other nations to qualify by October included Argentina, Brazil, Hungary, Poland, and Uruguay.

Unfortunately, bribery and corruption were again evident during the year, particularly in Bulgaria, where some clubs bribed opposition goalkeepers and referees. Players in Bulgaria were theoretically amateurs, but their jobs outside football involved little work. In an attempt to curb the unsavoury element in the sport, the Bulgarian government banned trades between teams, and Levski Spartak and CSKA Sofia (teams that were involved in violent scenes at the cup final in 1985) were disbanded. They were reformed as Vitosha and Sredec, respectively, but kept the bulk of the same playing staffs.

During the year several notable figures in football died, including Jock Stein (see OBITUARIES), the manager of Scotland, who collapsed with a heart attack immediately after the end of the Wales-Scotland international at Cardiff on September 10. (The match ended in a 1–1 draw.)

Table I. Association Football National Champions

Nation	League winners	Cup winners
Albania	17 Nendori	Flamurtari
Argentina	Argentinos Juniors	
Austria	FK Austria	Rapid Vienna
Belgium	Anderlecht	Cercle Bruges
Bolivia	Blooming	
Brazil	Coritiba	
Bulgaria	Trakia Plovdiv	CSKA Sofia
Chile	Universidad Católica	
Colombia	América	
Costa Rica	Liga Deportiva Alajuense	
Cyprus	Omonia	AEL Limassol
Czechoslovakia	Sparta Prague	Dukla Prague
Denmark	Vejle	Lyngby
Ecuador	Nacional	
El Salvador	F.A.S.	
England	Everton	Manchester United
Finland	Kuuysi Lahti	Haka
France	Bordeaux	Monaco
Germany, East	Dynamo Berlin	Dynamo Dresden
Germany, West	Bayern Munich	Bayern Uerdingen
Greece	PAOK Salonika	Larissa
Guatemala	Deportivo Suchitepéquez	
Honduras	Olimpia	
Hungary	Honved	Honved
Iceland	IK Akranes	IK Akranes
Ireland	Shamrock Rovers	Shamrock Rovers
Italy	Verona	Sampdoria
Luxembourg	Jeunesse d'Esch	Red Boys
Malta	Rabat Ajax	Zurrieg
Mexico	América	América
Netherlands, The	Ajax, Amsterdam	Utrecht
Northern Ireland	Linfield	Glentoran
Norway	Vålerengen	Fredrikstad
Paraguay	Guaraní	
Peru	Universitario de Deportes / Sport Boys	
Poland	Gornik Zabrze	Widzew Lodz
Portugal	Porto	Benfica
Romania	Steaua Bucharest	Steaua Bucharest
Scotland	Aberdeen	Celtic
Spain	Barcelona	Atletico Madrid
Sweden	IFK Göteborg	AIK Stockholm
Switzerland	Servette	Aarau
Turkey	Fenerbahce	Galatasaray
U.S.S.R.	Zenit Leningrad	Dynamo Kiev
U.S.		
Uruguay	Central Español	
Venezuela	Deportivo Táchira	
Wales	—	Shrewsbury
Yugoslavia	Sarajevo	Red Star, Belgrade

The Heysel Stadium Riot

The European Champions' Cup final in Brussels on May 29, 1985, produced a major soccer tragedy when 39 people died as a result of injuries received in the Heysel Stadium. In addition, more than 200 people who had gone to see the game between Liverpool of England and Italian champions Juventus of Turin were hurt after a wall and a safety fence collapsed during a riot. At the subsequent inquiry English clubs were banned indefinitely from international competition by the Union of European Football Associations (UEFA), though there was reason to think that this ban might be lifted after three years.

The rioting started an hour before the evening kickoff, with drink inflaming the usual animosity between rival fans. Ugly scenes at the stadium were witnessed by millions worldwide on television. The kickoff was delayed for 85 minutes before the understaffed police and stewards could restore order sufficiently for the game to start. Opinion was divided as to whether UEFA officials should have allowed the match to go on, and the argument would long continue.

The high number of fatalities was caused by the collapse of a wall that crushed some fans and caused others to fall and pile up on one another; ambulance men had the hard task of extricating the dead, dying, and injured. Other injuries were occasioned by fighting between the two sets of supporters, with lumps of concrete and other missiles being hurled. The riot was believed to have begun when some Italian fans threw fireworks at the Belgian police. The British supporters, who already had a disgraceful reputation in Europe for unruly behaviour, charged toward the sections reserved for the Juventus contingent. Thuggery followed as the rival factions clashed and the overworked and confused police were caught off guard. Moreover, there was no clearly defined segregation of the two sets of fans in the stadium. Yet no sociological arguments could excuse the terrible behaviour of the British invaders. The Liverpool contingent was infiltrated, as were other British traveling football parties, by a hooligan element, which, fueled by liquor, wrought the most havoc.   (TREVOR WILLIAMSON)

DAVID CANNON—ALL SPORT/TIME MAGAZINE

European Champions' Cup. Against the tragic backdrop of the events that preceded it, it was not surprising that the cup final at Brussels' Heysel Stadium lacked the sparkle that might have been expected of a match between Europe's top two clubs. It was settled by a single penalty goal scored by Michel Platini, the French midfielder and star of the Juventus effort, 12 minutes into the second half. Liverpool's Gary Gillespie had brought down Zbigniew Boniek as the Pole was dashing through, having headed in a long pass from Platini. Liverpool protested that the incident was outside the penalty box but to no avail, and Platini stepped up to do the rest. Liverpool had a penalty appeal turned down when Ronnie Whelan was brought down by Massimo Bonini, and goalkeeper Stefano Tacconi made several good saves in the last quarter of the game as Liverpool intensified its effort to score. But it was not to be; the Italians used both substitutes, thereby bringing on fresh legs, and held on for victory.

European Cup-Winners' Cup. Everton, the English entry, proved equal to the task of returning the cup to England after 14 years. The English team beat Rapid Vienna of Austria 3–1 in the final at Rotterdam on May 15. Everton built its game from a position of sound defense, and indeed all five members of that department, including goalkeeper Neville Southall, were international competitors. On its way to the final in Rotterdam's Feyenoord stadium, Everton had conceded only one goal, to Bayern Munich in the semifinals. Thus it was small wonder that the Austrians realized it would be a hard job to pierce so efficient a rear guard. Yet Rapid's manager, Otto Baric, also appreciated that Everton had plenty of goal potential and so planned a containing strategy; this worked for almost an hour, though goalkeeper Michael Konsel was kept busy by the Everton raiders.

Andy Gray of Scotland broke the deadlock after 57 minutes when Graeme Sharp collected a bad back pass from Leo Lainer and turned the ball back for Gray to shoot into an untenanted net. Then three minutes later Baric made his first substitution, sending in Hans Gross for Peter Pacult in an attempt to boost the attack; after another seven minutes Antonin Panenka joined the midfield to bolster the efforts of the lively Zlatko Kranjcar. Yet with Rapid pushing forward, Everton discovered more opportunities to attack and, after Konsel had made a fine save from Trevor Steven, the young attacking midfielder headed a second goal from a Kevin Sheedy corner. Everton's concentration lapsed momentarily in the closing minutes, and Hans Krankl, Rapid's danger man, topped off a fine pass by Gross, but within two minutes the energetic Irish winger Sheedy had restored the two-goal margin when he collected a through pass by Sharp and shot past Konsel.

UEFA Cup. This two-legged final produced a reversal of the norm in 1985 in that the trophy was won by Real Madrid on the away leg rather than the home game. The Spanish team triumphed against Videoton of Hungary 3–1 on aggregate, having laid the groundwork with their triumph in Szekesfehervar on May 8. In the first encounter Real Madrid, after the usual exploratory feints and forays, started to get the better of a Videoton team crippled by injuries and suspensions. The Spaniards translated that superiority into tangible evidence with a goal by Miguel Gonzáles Michel from Ricardo Gallego's cross. Though Videoton increased its attacks, the Real Madrid defense, with Uli Stielike of West Germany as the pivot, maintained a firm grip, and some 20 minutes into the second half the Spaniards made their presence felt with a goal by Carlos Santillana after he had wasted an earlier chance to score. The long-serving Juanito (Juan Gómez), having

entered the contest as a substitute, and Michel sprang the Hungarians' offside trap to present Jorge Valdano with a last-minute goal. In the return at Madrid two weeks later, Real could afford to squander a penalty, missed by Valdano, and two "goals" disallowed for offside. Though Real carried the major threat, the efforts of Miguel Ángel, their long-serving goalkeeper, foiled all that the Hungarians could throw at him except a rising shot from Lajos Majer four minutes before the end of the match.

United States. Suffering from declining attendance in recent years, the North American Soccer League went out of existence in March and, consequently, had no season in 1985. Competition did continue in the Major Indoor Soccer League, however. Baltimore and San Diego were winners of the Eastern and Western divisions, respectively. In the play-offs San Diego emerged as champion by defeating Baltimore four games to one in the final round. San Diego's Steve Zungul was named the most valuable player in the play-offs.   (TREVOR WILLIAMSON)

Latin America. It was a good year for soccer in Argentina. Not only did the national team qualify easily for the 1986 World Cup final rounds, but its national league champion, Argentinos Juniors, went on to win the Libertadores de América Cup, South America's club championship. This was the second year in a row that an Argentine team had captured the coveted cup.

By contrast, Brazilian soccer was in turmoil. The national team did, indeed, qualify for the World Cup final rounds—as it had done for every single competition for the cup—but it was less than its usual overwhelming self in the qualifying round, where it even tied a game with Paraguay. Telé Santana, the much-criticized coach of the national team in the 1982 World Cup, returned to the helm in May, just in time for the qualifying games. No Brazilian team, moreover, was able to enter into the final play-off series for the Libertadores de América Cup. Coritiba, of Paraná, won the national championship in 1985.

Uruguay was the first South American team to qualify for the World Cup, while Paraguay was the last one, since it had to play an additional series after placing second in Brazil's group. In the national championships, Central Español won in Uruguay for the second year in a row, while Guaraná replaced Olimpia as the national Paraguayan champion.

Mexico, as the host country, did not have to play to qualify for the World Cup, but its national team played a full 12-game schedule during the year. The Mexican championships were dominated by América of Mexico City, which won both the league and the cup titles.

América of Cali continued its dominance over Colombia's football as it won a third league championship in a row. It was also a surprise runner-up in the Libertadores de América Cup. Nacional of Quito also repeated as a national champion in Ecuador.

Blooming won the Bolivian title, while Universidad Católica became the champion in Chile. In Venezuela Deportivo Táchira won the pennant. Two separate championships took place in Peru, where the professional league faced its most serious financial crisis ever—the Regional was won by Universitario de Deportes, while the Decentralized went to Sport Boys. In Central America Liga Deportiva Alajuense became the champion in Costa Rica, F.A.S. (Futbolistas Asociados Santaneros) in El Salvador, Deportivo Suchitepéquez in Guatemala, and Olimpia in Honduras.   (SERGIO SARMIENTO)

Rugby. *Rugby Union.* The outstanding event of the 1984–85 period was the tour of the British Isles by the Wallabies of Australia in October–December 1984. They played spectacular attacking rugby and became the first Australian team to win victories over each of the four home countries on one tour. The Wallabies defeated England 19–3, Ireland 16–9, Wales 28–9, and Scotland 37–12. In those four matches they scored 12 tries and had only one scored against them. They played 18 games throughout the British Isles and won 13, drew 1, and lost 4, with points for 400, against 232. Their total number of tries was 51. The Wallabies were captained by Andy Slack, coached by Alan Jones, and managed by Chilla Wilson. Their stand-off half, Mark Ella, scored a try in each of the four international matches.

Playing against England at Twickenham on Jan. 5, 1985, Romania was beaten 22–15 by an experimental England side. The Romanians also lost their two other games in England; the North of England defeated them 17–8 and the SouthWest 15–3.

At the Five Nations Tournament, Scotland, which had won the grand slam in 1984, lost all four of its games. Conversely, Ireland, which had lost all of its 1984 matches, won the triple crown and the championship. France, which had been favoured to win, beat Wales and Scotland but tied

COLORSPORT

Donal Lenihan carries the ball for Ireland while Phil Orr fends off England's David Cooke in Ireland's victory over England in the Five Nations Tournament in March.

with England and Ireland. England, which had lost 27–10 to a multinational team in a game staged to celebrate 75 years of the Twickenham ground, held France to a score of 9–9 and beat Scotland 10–7 but then fell to both Ireland and Wales.

In May and June 1985 England made a seven-match tour of New Zealand, including two tests. In the first of the tests the All Blacks beat England 18–13, and they then also won the second 42–15, the worst defeat ever suffered by England. The All Blacks, captained by Andy Dalton, played devastatingly efficient all-round rugby.

France made a seven-match tour of Argentina, losing the first of the two tests against the Pumas 24–16 in Buenos Aires but winning the second test there 23–15. Canada played nine matches in Australia, losing the two tests 59–3 and 43–15. Fiji played three tests in Australia, being beaten 52–28, 12–9, and 32–9. New Zealand defeated Australia 10–9 at Auckland to win the Bledisloe Cup.

The International Rugby Football Board in March 1985 decided to stage rugby's first World Cup in Australia and New Zealand in 1987. For the first time the board held its annual meeting in Paris.

Rugby League. Great Britain beat France resoundingly 50–4 at Leeds, but France gained revenge with a 24–16 win at Perpignan a few weeks later. Ellery Hanley, who had scored 55 tries for Bradford Northern and Great Britain, was transferred to Wigan for a world record fee of £150,000. John Risman, son of Bev Risman, a former England Rugby Union and Great Britain Rugby League player, became the first man to play for Oxford University against Cambridge at both Union and League. Wigan beat Hull 28–24 at Wembley in what was considered the most exciting Challenge Cup Final for many years. The attempt to establish Rugby League in the south of England met with a setback when both Invicta, based at Southend, and Bridgend (formerly Cardiff) were suspended for a year for lack of proper organization.   (DAVID FROST)

U.S. Football. *College.* Oklahoma won its sixth national U.S. college football championship when it was the only one of the four contenders to win a bowl game on Jan. 1, 1986. The Sooners finished with a won-lost record of 11–1 after defeating previously top-ranked Penn State 25–10 in the Orange Bowl. Penn State (11-1) fell to third in the Associated Press (AP) and United Press International (UPI) polls. Iowa and Miami (Fla.) also went into their

final games hoping to rank first. But Iowa (10–2) lost 45–28 in the Rose Bowl to UCLA (9–2–1), and Miami (10–2) lost 35–7 in the Sugar Bowl to Tennessee (9–1–2), which thereby gained a ranking of fourth. Michigan (10–1–1) won second in the polls by beating Nebraska (9–3) in the Fiesta Bowl 27–23.

Florida (9–1–1) was ranked fifth by the AP but was ineligible for a bowl game or UPI ranking because of National Collegiate Athletic Association (NCAA) violations. The UPI's fifth-ranked team was Air Force (12–1), which tied Brigham Young for the Western Athletic Conference championship. Other top ten teams included Southwest Conference champion Texas A&M (10–2), Pacific Ten champion UCLA, Miami, Big Ten champion Iowa, and Nebraska.

Oklahoma won the Big Eight, and Tennessee took the Southeast Conference. Other conference champions were Maryland in the Atlantic Coast, Pennsylvania in the Ivy League, Bowling Green in the Mid-American, Fresno State in the Pacific Coast, and Furman in the Southern. Fresno State (11–0–1) was the only undefeated team in the NCAA's top Division I-A after its 51–7 California Bowl victory over Bowling Green (11–1) but was downgraded in the polls because it played against comparatively weak teams.

The highest individual honour, the Heisman Trophy, went to Auburn halfback Bo Jackson by three percentage points over Iowa quarterback Chuck Long, the closest margin in the award's 51 years. Jackson rushed for 1,786 yd, second in Division I-A to Michigan State's Lorenzo White with 1,908, and scored 17 touchdowns, second to Bowling Green's Bernard White with 19. A national magazine suggested that Joe Dudek of Plymouth (N.H.) State should be the first Heisman winner from Division III after he ran for 1,615 yd and 24 touchdowns. Dudek's 79 touchdowns and 474 points in his 41-game career were the most ever for a college player. Two defensive nose tackles won the awards for top linemen: Oklahoma's Tony Casillas the Lombardi Trophy and Boston College's Mike Ruth the Outland.

Navy's Napoleon McCallum was the Division I-A all-purpose running leader with 2,330 yd on rushes, pass receptions, and kick returns. He set a career record with 7,172 yd. Navy salvaged its 4–7 season with a 17–7 upset of Army, which finished 9–3.

Utah's Erroll Tucker became the first player to lead

Freshman quarterback Jamelle Holieway led the Sooners of Oklahoma to a 25-10 win over Penn State in the Orange Bowl. As the only one of the top four teams to win its New Year's Day classic, Oklahoma bagged its sixth national championship.

Chicago Bears quarterback Jim McMahon executes a pitchout during the Super Bowl game on January 26. Execution, on offense and especially on defense, was the key to the Bears' 46–10 win over the New England Patriots.

AP/WIDE WORLD

Division I-A both in average kickoff returns (29.1 yd) and in punt returns (24.3 yd). He set a record with seven returns for touchdowns, including three on interceptions. John Lee of UCLA set career records with 79 field goals and an .859 accuracy rate (79 for 92). For the season his .875 percentage (21 for 24) tied Washington's Jeff Jaeger, while Ball State's John Diettrich led in total field goals with 25 and Tennessee's Carlos Reveiz had the most points on kicks, 102.

Division I-A passing leaders were Michigan's Jim Harbaugh with a 163.7 efficiency rating, Long Beach State's Doug Gaynor with a .710 completion percentage, Brigham Young's Robbie Bosco with 30 touchdowns and 4,273 yd, and Purdue's Jim Everett with 326.3 yd per game of total offense. The top pass receivers were Purdue's Rodney Carter with 98 catches, Kansas's Richard Estell with

1,109 yd, and Brigham Young's Mark Bellini with 14 touchdowns. Tennessee's Chris White and East Carolina's Kevin Walker tied for the interception lead with nine, and Air Force's Mark Simon had the highest punting average, 47.3 yd.

In Division III Augustana (Ill.) won its third straight national championship by beating Ithaca (N.Y.) College 20–7, its 37th consecutive victory and 12th of the season. North Dakota State (11–2–1) beat North Alabama 35–7 for the Division II crown, and Georgia Southern defeated Furman 44–42 for the Division I-AA title. Coach Eddie Robinson (see BIOGRAPHIES) of 9–3 Grambling finished the year with 329 victories, exceeding Paul ("Bear") Bryant's former college record of 323 and George Halas's professional record of 326.

Professional. The Chicago Bears climaxed an 18–1 season and gained their first National Football League (NFL) championship since 1963 by defeating the New England Patriots 46–10 in the Super Bowl at New Orleans, La., on Jan. 26, 1986. The margin of victory was the largest in Super Bowl history. Dominating the game was the Bear defense, which allowed the Patriots only one first down during the first half and held them to only seven yards gained by rushing during the entire game. The Bears also tied a Super Bowl record by sacking the Patriot quarterbacks seven times. Voted the most valuable player of the game was Bear defensive end Richard Dent. Outstanding on offense for the Bears was quarterback Jim McMahon.

The Bears won the National Conference with the second 15-win season in NFL history. They captured the national fancy with an aggressive defense and William ("the Refrigerator") Perry (see BIOGRAPHIES), the 138.5-kg (305-lb) rookie defensive tackle who became the largest NFL player to score a touchdown on a planned offensive play. The Bears' only defeat, at Miami after 12 straight victories, drew the highest television ratings ever for a Monday night game. With help from four play-off teams in New York and Los Angeles, the NFL reversed its three-year decline in overall television viewership.

The Bears' defense allowed the fewest points (12.4 per game), total yards (258.4 per game), and rushing yards (82.4 per game) in the NFL. They were the first team to shut out two play-off opponents. Richard Dent led the NFL with quarterback sacks. The Bears' blitzing style be-

Table II. NFL Final Standings and Play-offs, 1985

AMERICAN CONFERENCE	W	L	T	NATIONAL CONFERENCE	W	L	T
Eastern Division				**Eastern Division**			
*Miami	12	4	0	*Dallas	10	6	0
*New York Jets	11	5	0	*New York Giants	10	6	0
*New England	11	5	0	Washington	10	6	0
Indianapolis	5	11	0	Philadelphia	7	9	0
Buffalo	2	14	0	St. Louis	5	11	0
Central Division				**Central Division**			
*Cleveland	8	8	0	*Chicago	15	1	0
Cincinnati	7	9	0	Green Bay	8	8	0
Pittsburgh	7	9	0	Minnesota	7	9	0
Houston	5	11	0	Detroit	7	9	0
				Tampa Bay	2	14	0
Western Division				**Western Division**			
*Los Angeles Raiders	12	4	0	*Los Angeles Rams	11	5	0
Denver	11	5	0	*San Francisco	10	6	0
Seattle	8	8	0	New Orleans	5	11	0
San Diego	8	8	0	Atlanta	4	12	0
Kansas City	6	10	0				

*Qualified for play-offs.

Play-offs

Wild-card round	American finals
New York Giants 17, San Francisco 3	New England 31, Miami 14
New England 26, New York Jets 14	
American semifinals	**National finals**
New England 27, Los Angeles Raiders 20	Chicago 24, Los Angeles Rams 0
Miami 24, Cleveland 21	
National semifinals	**Super Bowl**
Chicago 21, New York Giants 0	Chicago 46, New England 10
Los Angeles Rams 20, Dallas 0	

came such an example for the league that five teams had at least 61 sacks, a total that was third highest in league history before 1984.

Offensively, the Bears' 28.5 points per game ranked second in the league, and their 172.6 yd rushing per game ranked first for the third year in a row. Walter Payton had a record third straight 2,000-yd season on runs and catches. He set a record by rushing for at least 100 yd in nine consecutive games. Kicker Kevin Butler's 144 points led the league.

The Bears also led in possession time and turnover differential, taking the ball away 23 more times than they lost it. They swept the top individual awards with NFL coach of the year Mike Ditka (*see* BIOGRAPHIES), NFL defensive player of the year Mike Singletary, and NFC offensive player of the year Payton.

The Patriots were the third team to reach the Super Bowl as a "wild card," the term for two play-off teams in each conference that do not win division championships. They became the first team to win three play-off games on the road. They made 16 turnovers and lost only 2 in those victories, which included triumphs over the Los Angeles Raiders and the Miami Dolphins, regular season leaders of the American Conference with 12 victories and 4 defeats. The Patriots' stars included Andre Tippett, whose 16½ sacks led the American Conference, and Irving Fryar, who led the NFL with 14.1 yd per punt return.

The Cleveland Browns became the first NFL team to win a divisional championship without a winning record, taking the American Conference Central at 8–8. They produced the third pair of 1,000-yd rushers in league history, Kevin Mack and Earnest Byner. As division champions they went to the play-offs instead of the Denver Broncos, the first 11–5 team to miss postseason play.

The Bears and Dolphins were the only teams to repeat as division champions. The Dallas Cowboys had gone three years without a championship, the Browns four, and the Los Angeles Rams five. The Browns, Cowboys, Patriots, and New York Jets were the teams in the play-offs that had not qualified for them a year earlier. The San Francisco 49ers were the fifth defending champions in six years that failed to win their division or a play-off game.

The Raiders had the leading defense in the American Conference and their first NFL rushing leader, Marcus Allen. Allen tied Payton's record of nine straight 100-yd games in the last game of the regular season, when he finished with 1,759 rushing yards and passed National Conference leader Gerald Riggs of Atlanta by 40 yd. Allen's 2,314 yd on runs and pass receptions set a league record.

The Dolphins' Dan Marino led NFL passers with 30 touchdowns and 4,137 yd. San Diego was the best passing team, with league highs of 304.4 passing yards, 408.4 total yards, and 29.2 points per game. The leader in passing efficiency was the Jets' Ken O'Brien, with a 96.2 rating largely attributable to the fact that he was intercepted only eight times. San Francisco's Joe Montana led National Conference passers, and his .613 completion percentage led the league.

Fullback Roger Craig contributed 1,050 rushing yards and 1,016 receiving yards to the 49ers' National Conference-leading offense, becoming the first player ever to make more than 1,000 yd in both categories in one season and one of two backs ever to gain 1,000 yd receiving. The other was San Diego's Lionel ("Little Train") James, who set records during the 1985 season with 1,027 yd receiving by a back and 2,535 total yards on runs, catches, and kick returns.

Craig led the NFL with 92 catches, and James the American Conference with 86. Washington's Art Monk led wide receivers with 91, and the Raiders' Todd Christensen led tight ends with 82. Seattle had two receiving leaders, Daryl Turner with 13 touchdowns and Steve Largent with 1,287 yd. Largent became the fifth and youngest player to gain more than 10,000 yd receiving during his career. Kansas City's Stephone Paige broke a 40-year-old record with 309 yd receiving in one game.

Paige's teammate Deron Cherry tied a record with four interceptions in a game. Everson Walls's nine interceptions for Dallas led the league a record-setting third time in only his fifth season.

The Rams' success stemmed largely from their kicking teams. Dale Hatcher led NFL punters with a 38-yd net average; Henry Ellard led National Conference punt returners with a 13.5-yd average; and Ron Brown led NFL kickoff returners with a 32.8-yd average and three touchdowns. Nick Lowery's 58-yd field goal for Kansas City was the season's longest, and his .889 percentage (24 for 27) the league's highest. Minnesota's Jan Stenerud retired at 43 as the all-time field goal leader with 373.

Joe Morris led the NFL with 21 touchdowns for the Giants, all rushing. Washington allowed 171.6 passing yards per game, fewest in the league. The Jets had the best rushing defense in the American Conference, and the Pittsburgh Steelers led the conference in pass defense but had their first losing season since 1971.

The United States Football League finished its third and last spring season with the Baltimore Stars winning their second straight championship 28–24 against the Oakland Invaders at East Rutherford, N.J., on July 14. The league planned to resume play in the autumn of 1986, but in the meantime it lost several star players, a handful of franchises, and its network television contract. It hoped to regain financial footing through a $1.2 billion lawsuit against the NFL, charging it with monopolizing network professional football telecasts.

Canadian Football. The British Columbia Lions defeated the Hamilton Tiger-Cats 37–24 for the Grey Cup championship of the Canadian Football League (CFL) on November 24 at Montreal. Roy Dewalt was named the outstanding player after throwing touchdown passes of 84, 60, and 66 yd. Lui Passaglia of the Lions was the game's leading scorer with a total of 19 points, including five field goals.

The Lions, with a 13–3 record, won the Western Division for the third straight time. They had the season's most outstanding player, Mervyn Fernandez, who led CFL receivers with 1,727 yd and 15 touchdowns on 95 catches. Dewalt led league passers with 4,237 yd and 27 touchdowns. Defensive tackle Michael Gray was the most outstanding rookie.

The Tiger-Cats streaked from a 1–6 start to an 8–8 finish, still the CFL's worst division championship record ever. Tiger-Cat safety Paul Bennett was the most outstanding Canadian player and tied teammate Less Browne with 12 interceptions, the most in the league.

Winnipeg, second in the Western Division at 12–4, had the other two Schenley Award winners for top individual performances. They were linebacker Tyrone Jones for most outstanding defensive player and guard Nick Bestaja for most outstanding offensive lineman. Other leaders from Winnipeg were Willard Reaves with 1,323 yd rushing and Trevor Kennard with 43 field goals and a record-setting 198 points. Saskatchewan's Craig Ellis led the CFL with 102 catches, 17 touchdowns, and 14 rushing touchdowns.

(KEVIN M. LAMB)

GOLF

Suspicions that the U.S. was not quite the force it had been in world golfing competition were confirmed in 1985. For the first time in 28 years, the U.S. was defeated in the Ryder Cup, though the team that beat it was admittedly European and not purely British, as had been the case in 1957. The agreed-upon base of selection, embracing the continent of Europe, had been made in 1977 because U.S. domination was undermining the match's appeal. Also during the year Sandy Lyle became the first British winner of the British Open since Tony Jacklin 16 years earlier, and Bernhard Langer of West Germany became only the third overseas player to win the U.S. Masters. Never in modern times had European golf enjoyed such a year of success.

It was Europe's Ryder Cup victory at the Belfry, near Birmingham, England, that most caught the public imagination, and the ultimate margin of $16\frac{1}{2}$–$11\frac{1}{2}$ was conclusive. No one derived greater satisfaction than Jacklin, the European nonplaying captain and winner of the British and the U.S. Open in 1969 and 1970, respectively. With his inspirational leadership, he outmaneuvered his opposite number, Lee Trevino.

Before record crowds (approximately 80,000 for the three days), Europe did not make the fast start that was thought to be important. The U.S. won the opening series of foursomes by 3–1 but, inspired by Severiano Ballesteros and his fellow Spaniard Manuel Piñero, with whom he won twice on that opening day, the Europeans closed the overall gap to a single point after the afternoon four-ball matches. A crucial small putt missed on the 18th green by Craig Stadler of the U.S. just before lunch on the second day brought the teams to a tie, and by nightfall Europe was ahead 9–7. Europe increased its advantage in the singles, again being given a fine example by the diminutive Piñero, who beat Lanny Wadkins in the top match. But it was Sam Torrance who had the distinction of holing the decisive putt for a birdie three to defeat Andy North, the U.S. Open champion, on the 18th green. At that moment the Ryder Cup, first contested in 1927, passed back into European possession. Among other winners of their singles were both Lyle and Langer, who thereby completed a notable season during which both had won their first major championships.

On the first day of the British Open championship at Royal St. George's, Sandwich, Kent, Christy O'Connor (Ireland) broke Henry Cotton's course record of 65 (which had also stood as a British Open record until 1977) with a 64 that included a run of seven consecutive birdies. Bad weather on the afternoon of the first day and morning of the second made conditions difficult for some players, among them Jack Nicklaus of the U.S., who failed to qualify for the last two rounds for the first time in his career. After three rounds the destiny of the title seemed to lie between Langer and Australia's David Graham, who in 1981 had won the U.S. Open. They were tied three strokes ahead of the field but, perhaps with eyes only for one other, fell away with last rounds of 75 apiece. This left the door open for their pursuers, and it was Lyle who stepped through it with a final round of 70 for a two-over-par aggregate of 282. He won by a stroke from Payne Stewart (U.S.), with Langer, Graham, O'Connor, Mark O'Meara (U.S.), and José Rivero (Spain) all sharing third place. Lyle's birdies on the 14th and 15th holes hoisted him to the top of the leader board, though he had an anxious wait after bogeying at the 18th.

Langer did the same thing at the last hole in the

Bernhard Langer tries on the traditional green jacket after winning the Masters Tournament at Augusta, Georgia, in April. He was the first West German to win one of the four major golf tournaments, and he took home $126,000 for his effort.
JOHN IACONO/SPORTS ILLUSTRATED

U.S. Masters at Augusta, Ga., as did North in the U.S. Open. The West German had nevertheless played beautifully over the last two rounds, scoring 68 each time and beating Ballesteros, Raymond Floyd, and Curtis Strange (both U.S.) by two strokes. Langer's total of 282 was six under par, while Strange's share of second place reflected a remarkable recovery. After an opening round of 80, he had booked a flight home the following evening. Instead he came back with a 65, followed it with a 68, and went into the last round only a stroke off the lead.

North, standing 1.93 m (6 ft 4 in) tall, gained his second U.S. Open victory in eight years. He had won at Cherry Hills Country Club near Denver, Colo., in 1978 and now did so again at Oakland Hills Country Club near Detroit by a stroke from Denis Watson of South Africa. A total of 279 for the four rounds left North the only player under par. For a time there had been the distinct possibility that a player from Asia would win the championship, because at one stage in the last round, T. C. Chen of Taiwan led by four strokes. However, he foundered at the fifth hole when, in chipping to the green, he hit the ball twice and took an eight. It was also an agonizingly near miss for Watson, whose first round of 70 included a two-stroke penalty when he waited beyond the permitted ten seconds for a putt that had stopped on the edge of the hole to drop. Except for that penalty he would have finished a stroke ahead of North.

North, at 35, was hardly one of the rising generation of U.S. golfers. Nor was Hubert Green, 38, who won the U.S. Professional Golfers' Association (PGA) championship at Cherry Hills by two strokes from the defending champion, Trevino, seven years his senior. Throughout the tournament it was nearly always a two-horse race, Trevino leading through the first two days but Green overtaking him in the third round before being caught again with nine holes to play. However, it was Green, the 1977 U.S. Open champion, who had the stronger finish. He had a total of 278, six under par, on a course that drew much criticism for its severity.

The U.S. Tournament Player's Championship at the Tournament Players' Club course, Ponte Vedra, Fla., was won in fine style by Calvin Peete, the tournament having some claim to being the world's fifth "major." But the player of the year was Strange, who won three tournaments—the

Honda Classic, the Panasonic Las Vegas International, and the Canadian Open—on the way to becoming the leading money winner with a record of $542,321. But he decided not to enter the British Open, and at the year's end he had not yet won a major championship.

A remarkable feature of U.S. golf was the success of the Seniors' tour for players over 50. Peter Thomson of Australia, who had won the British Open five times during the 1950s and '60s, was so dominant that his earnings of $386,724 were exceeded only by Strange and Wadkins on the main tour.

Lyle, who won only one other tournament—the Benson and Hedges International—besides the British Open, was nevertheless the leading money winner in Europe with £162,552, well ahead of Langer. It was the third time that he had headed the money list since 1979, and in those seven seasons he had not once finished outside the top five. In third place was Ballesteros, whose five victories included yet another in the Suntory world match-play championship at Wentworth, England. He had now won this event four times in five years. The event promised an epic final when Ballesteros came face to face with Langer, as he had done 12 months earlier. But the West German was well below his best, his defeat by six and five being the most conclusive since the match-play competition was launched in 1964.

The U.S. was beaten by Australia in the new Dunhill Cup, a medal match-play event at St. Andrews, Scotland, with teams of three men on each side. Graham Marsh, David Graham, and Greg Norman defeated Raymond Floyd, Mark O'Meara, and Curtis Strange by 3–0 in the final.

It was therefore left to the U.S. amateurs to restore some pride as they defeated Great Britain and Ireland in the Walker Cup at Pine Valley, Clementon, N.J. The margin of 13–11 was, however, much closer than most people had

Kathy Baker won her first professional golf victory in convincing fashion, taking the U.S. Women's Open in July with an eight-under-par 280, three strokes ahead of runner-up Judy Clark. Baker, 24 years old, was in her second year on the professional tour.

expected and contrasted sharply with the whitewash inflicted on the British when last the Walker Cup was played at Pine Valley, in 1936. After the first day the two teams were even, and the turning point came in the second series of foursomes, which the Americans took by 3–0 with the other game halved. The British managed to close the gap in the last series of singles and, for their tenacity, made a big impression on crowds that had to be limited to 3,000 each day because of the difficulties of spectator control on a notoriously difficult but scenically beautiful course. On the victorious U.S. team was Scott Verplank, who a few weeks earlier had become the first amateur in 29 years to win a professional event when he took the Western Open at Butler National Golf Club in Oak Brook, Ill. Verplank failed, however, in his defense of the U.S. amateur championship at Montclair, N.J., the title going to Sam Randolph, another Walker Cup player, who defeated Peter Persons on the last green in the 36-hole final.

The British amateur championship broke new ground at Royal Dornoch, Scotland, and it produced in Garth McGimpsey the first Irish champion since Joe Carr in 1960. He beat Graham Homewood, a little-known Englishman, by eight and seven over 36 holes. One other amateur deserved special mention. When the young Spaniard José-Maria Olazabal took the Youths' championship at Ganton, England, he became the first golfer to have completed the hat trick of Amateur (1984), Boys' (1983), and now Youths' championships.

Nancy Lopez, whose crowd appeal and skill were among the main reasons for the expansion of the Ladies Professional Golf Association (LPGA) tour in the U.S. in the late 1970s, enjoyed her best year for some time. She won five tournaments, was leading money winner for the third time in her career with an astonishing $416,472, and was named LPGA golfer of the year. However, it was Kathy Baker who took the most treasured prize, the U.S. Women's Open at Baltusrol, N.J. With a four-round total of 280, she finished three strokes ahead of Judy Clark.

The British Women's Open championship, thrown into disarray by the withdrawal of the 1984 sponsor, Hitachi, was salvaged first by the Royal and Ancient Golf Club of St. Andrews and then by Burberry's. Between them they raised prize money of £60,000, and the title went to a visiting American, Betsy King, whose aggregate of 300 for the 72 holes beat Marta Figueras-Dotti of Spain by two strokes. Once again the British made little impact on their own championship, but Laura Davies, who hit the ball as far as most men do, was leading money winner on the Women's Professional Golf Association circuit, in her first year as a professional, with earnings of £21,736.

(MICHAEL E. J. WILLIAMS)

GYMNASTICS

Gymnasts from the Soviet Union regained their top world ranking by winning both the men's and women's team titles, the all-around titles, and more individual championships than competitors from any other country. The world championships, held November 4–10 at Montreal, climaxed the Soviet renaissance, which also included the women's European championship and the male and female all-around champions in the World University Games at Kobe, Japan.

For the first time in the history of the world championships, there was a tie for the all-around title. A pair of 16-year-old Soviet newcomers, Elena Shoushounova and Oksana Omeliantchik, finished even. Two East German gymnasts, Dagmar Kersten and Gabriele Fahnrich, trailed the Soviet duo. In winning the uneven parallel bars,

Li Ning of China won three medals, including a share of the rings title, at the world gymnastics championships in Montreal in November.
AP/WIDE WORLD

Fahnrich had the highest individual score in the apparatus finals, 19.950 out of a possible 20.000.

In the men's competition at the world championships, Valentin Moglinyi of the Soviet Union and Sylvio Kroll of East Germany shared the parallel bars title, and Moglinyi also won the pommel horse. Tong Fei of China won the floor exercise, and Li Ning of China shared the rings title with Yury Korolev of the Soviet Union. Korolev won the side horse vault outright.

In the women's events Shoushounova won the vault, and teammate Omeliantchik was the gold medalist in the floor exercise. Fahnrich was the winner on the uneven parallel bars, and Romania's Daniela Silvas defeated her more experienced teammate Ecaterina Szabo on the balance beam.

Few gymnasts were scored "ten" by the judges in comparison with the comparatively large number of perfect marks at the 1984 Olympic Games. There were two tens in the women's apparatus finals. Silvas received a perfect score on the balance beam, and Omeliantchik received a perfect mark for her routine in the floor exercise.

In the men's competition the U.S.S.R. won a total of nine medals to seven for China, and by a margin of seven to four the Soviets outscored Romania in the women's competition. Only one United States gymnast qualified for the apparatus finals; Sabrina Mar tied for sixth place in the vault.

Natalia Yurchenko of the U.S.S.R. retained her all-around honours in the World University Games, while teammate Dmitry Bilozerchev won the men's all-around title. A broken leg sidelined Bilozerchev for the world championships. (CHARLES ROBERT PAUL, JR.)

HANDBALL

Naty Alvarado of Hesperia, Calif., won his seventh United States Handball Association (USHA) national open singles title in 1985 by defeating Vern Roberts, Jr., of Tucson, Ariz., 21-18, 21-6 at the Tucson Athletic Club. Alvarado's seventh title (his fourth in a row) set a new USHA record for number of titles won and put him in a position to challenge the Amateur Athletic Union (AAU) record of nine singles titles set by Joe Platak in the 1930s and '40s.

Alvarado teamed with Roberts to win the open doubles title, defeating Jaime Paredes and Dennis Haynes of Los Angeles 21-2, 21-17. For Alvarado the singles and doubles victories, known as handball's Grand Slam, marked the fourth year in a row he had achieved that feat, also a record.

Peanut Motal of Martinez, Calif., won the women's open singles title by defeating LeaAnn Tyson of Austin, Texas, 21-7, 21-13. Tyson teamed with Susan Oakleaf of Austin to win the open doubles title, defeating Motal and Nancy Molter of Fall River, Mass., 21-10, 21-11.

In other action Neal Manning of Tucson defeated Pat Kirby, also of Tucson, 10-21, 21-7, 11-8 for the masters singles title for men aged 40 and over. Gordy Pfeifer of Tacoma, Wash., and Dave Lynch of Tucson teamed to win the masters doubles title by defeating Kirby and Fred Munsch of New York City 21-8, 21-8. Other winners included Tom Rohrback, Pasadena, Calif. (golden singles for players 50 and over); Tom Ciasulli, Scotch Plains, N.J. (super singles for players 60 and over); and Sal Espinosa, San Jose, Calif. (diamond singles for players 70 and over).

In the Canadian national championships, held at Oakville, Ont., Merv Deckert of Toronto won his eighth Canadian title by defeating Keith Gracey of Montreal 21-15, 21-8. Earlier in the year Deckert had won an international tournament at Dublin that matched players from Canada, the U.S., Mexico, and Ireland.

(TERRY CHARLES MUCK)

HORSE RACING

Thoroughbred Racing and Steeplechasing. *United States and Canada.* Winners in five of the seven Breeders' Cup races were named divisional champions in the Eclipse Award voting conducted by the Thoroughbred Racing Associations, the National Turf Writers Association, and the *Daily Racing Form.* They included: two-year-old colt, Tasso; older filly or mare, Life's Magic; male turf horse, Cozzene; female turf horse, Pebbles; and sprinter, Precisionist. Other horses earning Eclipse Award honours were: two-year-old filly, Family Style; three-year-old colt, Spend a Buck; three-year-old filly, Mom's Command; older male horse, Vanlandingham; and steeplechaser, Flatterer, which had won the previous two years. Life's Magic, champion three-year-old filly in 1984, was the only other Eclipse Award winner to repeat. Spend a Buck and Mom's Command, which had been retired because of injury, did not take part in the Breeders' Cup competition.

Other Eclipse Award winners included: owner, Mr. and Mrs. Eugene Klein; trainer, D. Wayne Lukas; breeder, Nelson Bunker Hunt; jockey, Laffit Pincay, Jr.; and apprentice jockey, Art Madrid, Jr. The Kleins, who raced Family Style, Life's Magic, and Lady's Secret, established a record for stable earnings with $5,446,401. Their horses, some of them owned jointly with others, won 30 stake races. Lukas, who trained for the Kleins and others, had a record total of 70 stakes victories for the year. He saddled horses that nearly doubled his record 1984 earnings by accumulating $11,160,111. Pincay, previously named champion jockey in 1971, 1973, 1974, and 1979, became the first individual to win five Eclipse Awards. Each time he also gained the earnings title. In 1985 his mounts earned $13,353,299 to smash the record of $12,045,813 established in 1984 by Chris McCarron.

Probably the outstanding champion of the year was the English-bred four-year-old filly Pebbles, Europe's best female Thoroughbred. Racing as the 2.20-1 favourite, the daughter of Sharpen Up defeated 13 male rivals in the Breeders' Cup Turf at 1½ mi. Because that was Pebbles's

U.S.-born jockey Steve Cauthen, who began racing in Great Britain in 1979, rode his first Epsom Derby winner in June. Slip Anchor, a 9–4 favourite, led the field of 14 from the start and finished easily with a seven-length lead.

SYNDICATION INTERNATIONAL/PHOTO TRENDS

only start in the U.S., many voters ignored her in the Eclipse Award competition.

Lady's Secret was successful in eight consecutive stakes, which included three Grade I events—the Maskette, Ruffian, and Beldame—but was outvoted by Mom's Command. The latter, owned and bred by Peter Fuller and ridden by his daughter Abby, won seven stakes in nine starts and finished second in two others. Her victories included the Triple Crown for fillies—the Acorn, Mother Goose, and Coaching Club American Oaks.

Spend a Buck, which won the Kentucky Derby and Garden State's $2 million bonus for victory in a series of races, set a single-season earnings mark of $3,552,704. The three-year-olds comprised a vintage crop. Besides Spend a Buck they included Proud Truth, winner of the Breeders' Cup Classic; Chief's Crown; Creme Fraiche, winner of the Belmont Stakes; Stephan's Odyssey; and Tank's Prospect, winner of the Preakness Stakes.

Spend a Buck and Mom's Command were among the contenders for horse of the year honours, won in 1984 by John Henry. That marked a record seventh Eclipse Award for the then nine-year-old gelding and his second prize as horse of the year. John Henry did not compete in 1985 because of physical problems and was retired with record earnings of $6,597,947.

The versatile Vanlandingham scored in four stakes, including the Suburban, Jockey Club Gold Cup, and the Washington, D.C., International. The International was his first start on turf. Family Style finished second to stablemate Twilight Ridge in the Breeders' Cup race for two-year-old fillies but won three stakes, including the Spinaway, the Arlington-Washington Lassie, and the Frizette.

Sam-Son Farm's Imperial Choice was the unanimous choice as Canada's horse of the year. The gelding also was named champion grass horse and champion three-year-old male. Imperial Choice's victories included the Prince of Wales Stakes, one of Canada's Triple Crown races for three-year-olds. In the others, the filly La Lorgnette won the Queen's Plate (she also took the Canadian Oaks), and Crowning Honors was first in the Breeders' Stakes.

Sam-Son Farm raced another champion, Grey Classic, in the two-year-old male division. Other Sovereign Award winners included: two-year-old filly, Stage Flite; three-year-old filly, La Lorgnette; older male, Ten Gold Pots; older mare, Lake Country; and sprinter, Summer Mood.

(JOSEPH C. AGRELLA)

Europe and Australia. Almost all of the quality events in European racing take place between mid-April and late October, but the proliferation of valuable international prizes at the end of the year was altering the shape of the European season in 1985. It was becoming increasingly worthwhile to concentrate on the big autumn prizes, the most important of which were provided by the Breeders' Cup program in the U.S., run in 1985 at Aqueduct Race Track in New York City. There, on November 2, Pebbles set a new course record of 2 min 27 sec for the 1½ mi in the Breeders' Cup Turf. Pebbles had started her season on April 26, when she won the newly instituted Trusthouse Forte Mile at Sandown Park, but the Aqueduct race was only her fifth of the year. She was beaten 1½ lengths by the 33–1 Bob Back in the Prince of Wales's Stakes at Royal Ascot but avenged that defeat in beating Rainbow Quest and Bob Back by 2 lengths and 1½ lengths in the Coral-Eclipse Stakes on July 6. Pebbles became ill soon afterward and did not race again until October 19, when she gained an impressive success in the Dubai Champion Stakes at Newmarket, beating the Epsom Derby winner, Slip Anchor, by three comfortable lengths.

The 1984 St. Leger winner, Commanche Run, developed into one of the stars of the season with consecutive front-running victories in the Benson & Hedges Gold Cup and Ireland's Phoenix Champion Stakes. He would have earned a $1 million bonus if he could have added the Dubai Champion, but he finished only eighth.

Commanche Run and Pebbles were members of an exceptionally strong group of older horses in Europe. The French-trained five-year-old Sagace seemed likely to prove the best of them when he won the Prix Ganay, Prix d'Ispahan, and Prix Foy. His training was directed toward a second success in the Prix de l'Arc de Triomphe and an entry in the Breeders' Cup Turf, but plans went awry. Sagace injured himself shortly before the Arc and was not at his peak. Although he passed the post a neck in front of Rainbow Quest, he had bumped his rival twice in the final furlong and the placings were reversed. Rainbow Quest thus gained the first British success in Europe's most prestigious race since Rheingold in 1973. Sagace was then retired to stud in Kentucky, and his stable fielded the ex-Australian six-year-old Strawberry Road in the Breeders' Cup Turf. Strawberry Road, which had won the Grand Prix de Saint-Cloud in July, raced strongly at Aqueduct and failed by only a neck to catch Pebbles.

Rousillon, Never So Bold, and Teleprompter were other older British stars. Rousillon won Europe's two most important races for milers, the Swettenham Stud Sussex Stakes at Goodwood and the Prix du Moulin at Longchamp. Never So Bold won the only three Group I sprints at home and, although fourth behind the Irish-trained mare Committed in the Prix de l'Abbaye de Longchamp, was indisputably Europe's champion sprinter. Teleprompter may not have

Spend a Buck, ridden by Angel Cordero, finished better than five lengths ahead of his nearest rival in the Kentucky Derby in May. The margin of victory was the largest in the Churchill Downs classic since 1946.

been in the same class as this pair, but the exclusion of geldings from Group I races in Europe prevented him from being placed where he might have challenged that assessment. He showed what he could do when winning the Budweiser-Arlington Million.

Europe's 1985 three-year-olds were much less exciting than their seniors, and the two-year-old fillies beat the colts in all four Group I races open to both sexes in France. Baiser Volé, which won two, may have been the best of them, while the William Hill Futurity winner, Bakharoff, appeared to be the best in Britain. Slip Anchor, which won the Epsom Derby by seven lengths from the subsequent Irish Derby victor, Law Society, injured himself after that race and, when he returned in the autumn, was beaten by Shernazar in the September Stakes and by Pebbles in the Dubai Championship. Oh So Sharp, which carried the same colours as Pebbles, those of Sheikh Mohammed, but hailed from a different stable, won the One Thousand Guineas, Oaks, and St. Leger, a feat last achieved by Meld in 1955. She was beaten by a neck by Petoski, with Rainbow Quest third, in the King George VI and Queen Elizabeth Diamond Stakes and by ³/₄ length by Commanche Run in the Benson and Hedges, but she was clearly the champion three-year-old filly. Petoski did not race again, but Oh So Sharp held a strong claim to be considered champion of her age group. She and Slip Anchor did most to make Henry Cecil champion trainer in Britain for the sixth time in ten years. Dermot Weld was champion in Ireland, with 126 successes, while Patrick-Louis Biancone, trainer of the winners of eight Group I races, including Sagace, led all rivals in France.

Lester Piggott, one of the greatest jockeys ever to have ridden in Britain, ended his career on his home turf at Nottingham on October 29, a week before his 50th birthday, although he continued to ride overseas after that date. He would train at Newmarket beginning in 1986. Piggott, who rode 4,349 winners at home and many more throughout the world, raised his record number of British classic victories to 29 with a hard-fought victory on Shadeed in the Two Thousand Guineas. British racing also lost another senior jockey in Joe Mercer, less celebrated than

Piggott but widely recognized as a supreme stylist. The British jockeys' championship went to Steve Cauthen (*see* BIOGRAPHIES) for the second year in a row.

In Australia What a Nuisance beat a strong field in the Fosters-Melbourne Cup, which carried a total prize, thanks to the introduction of a sponsor, of $A1 million and thus claimed the title of the richest handicap in the world.

Burrough Hill Lad was the best steeplechaser in Britain, but injury prevented him from attempting a repeat victory in the Cheltenham Gold Cup, which was won by the much inferior Forgive 'n Forget. Sir Gain, in the Grand Steeplechase de Paris, and Rhyme 'n Reason, in the Irish Grand National, were successful favourites, but the 50–1 Last Suspect caused a surprise in the Seagram Grand National at Aintree, Liverpool.   (ROBERT W. CARTER)

Harness Racing. In 1985 Nihilator, son of the record-breaking Niatross and himself holder of the two-year-old and three-year-old mile pacing track records of 1 min 52⁴/₅ sec and 1 min 49³/₅ sec, respectively, won the $350,730 Little Brown Jug. Later in the year, however, Falcon Seelster won an invitational pace in a world record 1 min 51 sec for a competitive race. The two-year-old trotting fillies' Breeders' Crown of $632,803 was won by Caressable, and the $367,850 Kentucky Pacing Derby by Sherman Almahurst; Prakas won the World Trotting Derby of $553,750 in 1 min 53²/₅ sec, a new world's three-year-old record, and then went on to win the Hambletonian. The Roosevelt International Trot of $250,000 was won by Lutin d'Isigny of France for the second time. The $1,344,000 Woodrow Wilson final for two-year-old pacers was taken by Grade One. Nihilator won the $1,018,000 Meadowlands Pace, and Chairmanoftheboard the $600,000 Cane Pace. The richest Standardbred of all time, On The Road Again, with earnings of more than $2,750,000, swept the World Cup Series of pacing with a 1-min 52²/₅-sec final at the Meadowlands. Meadow Road of Sweden made a clean sweep of the $320,000 International Statue of Liberty Trot, winning the second leg in a world record 1 min 54⁴/₅ sec from Sandy Bowl (U.S.) and Mon Tourbillon (France), and also won the Meadowlands $400,000 International Series.

In voting by the United States Trotting Association and

Major Thoroughbred Race Winners, 1985

Race	Won by	Jockey	Owner
United States			
Acorn	Mom's Command	A. Fuller	Peter Fuller
American Derby	Creme Fraiche	E. Maple	Brushwood Stable
Arkansas Derby	Tank's Prospect	G. Stevens	Mr. and Mrs. E. V. Klein
Arlington Classic	Smile	J. Vásquez	F. A. Genter Stable
Arlington-Washington Futurity	Meadowlake	J. Diaz	C. J. Robertson
Arlington-Washington Lassie	Family Style	L. Pincay, Jr.	E. V. Klein
Belmont	Creme Fraiche	E. Maple	Brushwood Stable
Blue Grass	Chief's Crown	D. MacBeth	Star Crown Stable and Three Chimneys Farm
Breeders' Cup Juvenile	Tasso	L. Pincay, Jr.	G. Robins and T. H. Sams
Breeders' Cup Juvenile	Fillies Twilight Ridge	J. Velásquez	E. V. Klein
Breeders' Cup Sprint	Precisionist	C. McCarron	F. W. Hooper
Breeders' Cup Mile	Cozzene	W. Guerra	J. S. Nerud
Breeders' Cup Distaff	Life's Magic	A. Cordero, Jr.	E. V. Klein
Breeders' Cup Turf	Pebbles	Pat Eddery	Sheikh Mohammed
Breeders' Cup Classic	Proud Truth	J. Velásquez	Darby Dan Farm
Brooklyn	Bounding Basque	A. Graell	J. D. Wimpfheimer
Budweiser-Arlington Million	Teleprompter	T. Ives	Lord Derby
Champagne	Mogambo	A. Cordero, Jr.	Peter M. Brant
Coaching Club American Oaks	Mom's Command	A. Fuller	Peter Fuller
Delaware	Basie	J. Cruguet	F. A. Genter Stable
Flamingo	Chief's Crown	D. MacBeth	Star Crown Stable and Three Chimneys Farm
Florida Derby	Proud Truth	J. Velásquez	Darby Dan Farm
Futurity	Ogygian	W. Guerra	Tartan Stable
Gulfstream Park	Dr. Carter	J. Velásquez	F. A. Genter Stable
Hialeah Turf Cup	Selous Scout	R. Platts	Double Eagle Stable
Hollywood Derby	Charming Duke	Y. Saint-Martin	Green Horn Stable
(2 divisions)	Slew the Dragon	J. Velásquez	Equusequity Stable
Hollywood Futurity	Snow Chief	A. Solis	Carl Grinstead and Ben Rochelle
Hollywood Gold Cup	Greinton	L. Pincay, Jr.	Mrs. M. J. Bradley
Jockey Club Gold Cup	Vanlandingham	P. Day	Loblolly Stable
Kentucky Derby	Spend a Buck	A. Cordero, Jr.	Hunter Farm
Kentucky Oaks	Fran's Valentine	P. Valenzuela	Green Thumb Farm Stable
Man o'War	Win	R. Migliore	S. Bailie, F. Ephraim, and P. Cornman
Marlboro Cup Invitational	Chief's Crown	D. MacBeth	Star Crown Stable and Three Chimneys Farm
Meadowlands Cup	Bounding Basque	R. Davis	J. D. Wimpfheimer
Metropolitan	Forzando II	D. MacBeth	S. C. Chillingworth
Preakness	Tank's Prospect	P. Day	Mr. and Mrs. E. V. Klein
Santa Anita Derby	Skywalker	L. Pincay, Jr.	Oak Cliff Stable
Santa Anita	Lord At War	W. Shoemaker	Peter Perkins
Suburban	Vanlandingham	D. MacBeth	Loblolly Stable
Travers	Chief's Crown	A. Cordero, Jr.	Star Crown Stable and Three Chimneys Farm
Turf Classic	Noble Fighter	A. Lequeux	Buckram Oak Farm
Washington (D.C.) International	Vanlandingham	D. MacBeth	Loblolly Stable
Widener	Pine Circle	D. MacBeth	Loblolly Stable
Wood Memorial Invitational	Eternal Prince	R. Migliore	B. J. Hurst
Woodward	Track Barron	A. Cordero, Jr.	Peter M. Brant
England			
One Thousand Guineas	Oh So Sharp	S. Cauthen	Sheikh Mohammed
Two Thousand Guineas	Shadeed	L. Piggott	Maktoum al-Maktoum
Derby	Slip Anchor	S. Cauthen	Lord Howard de Walden
Oaks	Oh So Sharp	S. Cauthen	Sheikh Mohammed
St. Leger	Oh So Sharp	S. Cauthen	Sheikh Mohammed
Coronation Cup	Rainbow Quest	Pat Eddery	K. Abdulla
Ascot Gold Cup	Gildoran	B. Thomson	R. Sangster
Coral-Eclipse Stakes	Pebbles	S. Cauthen	Sheikh Mohammed
King George VI and Queen Elizabeth Diamond Stakes	Petoski	W. Carson	Marcia, Lady Beaverbrook
Sussex Stakes	Rousillon	G. Starkey	K. Abdulla
Benson & Hedges Gold Cup	Commanche Run	L. Piggott	I. Allan
Dubai Champion Stakes	Pebbles	Pat Eddery	Sheikh Mohammed
France			
Poule d'Essai des Poulains	No Pass No Sale	Y. Saint-Martin	R. Strauss
Poule d'Essai des Pouliches	Silvermine	F. Head	Mme A. Head
Prix du Jockey-Club	Mouktar	Y. Saint-Martin	The Aga Khan
Prix de Diane Hermès	Lypharita	L. Piggott	L.-T. al Swaidi
Prix Royal-Oak	Mersey	J.-L. Kessas	D. Wildenstein
Prix Ganay	Sagace	Y. Saint-Martin	D. Wildenstein
Prix Lupin	Metal Precieux	A. Lequeux	D. Wildenstein
Grand Prix de Paris	Sumayr	Y. Saint-Martin	The Aga Khan
Grand Prix de Saint-Cloud	Strawberry Road	Y. Saint-Martin	D. Wildenstein
Prix Vermeille	Walensee	E. Legrix	D. Wildenstein
Prix de l'Arc de Triomphe	Rainbow Quest	Pat Eddery	K. Abdulla
Grand Critérium	Femme Elite	A. Lequeux	S. Fradkoff
Ireland			
Irish 2,000 Guineas	Triptych	C. Roche	A. Clore
Irish 1,000 Guineas	Al Bahathri	A. Murray	Hamdan al-Maktoum
Irish Sweeps Derby	Law Society	Pat Eddery	S. S. Niarchos
Irish Oaks	Helen Street	W. Carson	Sir M. Sobell
Irish St. Leger	Leading Counsel	Pat Eddery	R. Sangster
Phoenix Champion Stakes	Commanche Run	L. Piggott	I. Allan
Italy			
Derby Italiano	Don Orazio	M. Jerome	Lady M Stable
Grand Premio del Jockey-Club	St. Hilarion	G. Starkey	A. Christodoulou
West Germany			
Deutsches Derby	Acatenango	A. Tylicki	Gestüt Fährhof
Grosser Preis von Baden	Gold and Ivory	S. Cauthen	P. Mellon
Grosser Preis von Berlin	Ordos	P. Alafi	Gestüt Zoppenbroich
Preis von Europa	Sumayr	Y. Saint-Martin	The Aga Khan

Urged on by driver William O'Donnell, harness racer and pacer of the year Nihilator trots a record-breaking 1-minute 49.6-second mile at the Meadowlands in August.

AP/WIDE WORLD

the United States Harness Writers Association, Nihilator was selected harness horse of the year and pacer of the year. Prakas was voted trotter of the year. Divisional winners for pacers were: Barberry Spur, two-year-old colt; Follow My Star, two-year-old filly; Nihilator, three-year-old colt; Stienam, three-year-old filly; On the Road Again, aged pacer; and Green With Envy, aged mare. Divisional trotting winners included: Express Ride, two-year-old colt; Britelite Lobell, two-year-old filly; Prakas, three-year-old colt; Armbro Devona, three-year-old filly; Sandy Bowl, aged trotter; and Babe Kosmos, aged mare.

Champion trotting mare Scotch Notch took the Inter-Dominion Trotters championship in Australia. Preux Chevalier won the Inter-Dominion Pacing championship final of $A180,000 from Village Kid and Game Oro. West Australian-bred two-year-old Prince of Princes paced a world record mile rate of 1 min 59.6 sec in a 2,100-m race. Anne Frawley became the first woman to drive a Derby winner in Australia when she won the New South Wales Pacers' Derby with Vanderport. Australia's greatest money winner, Gammalite, retired with $A1,386,480 from 94 wins. In New Zealand the premier two-year-old Sapling Stakes was won by Sir Alba. New Zealand's famous pacer Roydon Glen made it 12 in succession when he broke the track record at Cambridge in 1 min 57 sec. Juvenile champion Nardinski won the $NZ120,000 Great Northern Derby. The $NZ125,000 New Zealand Pacing Cup went to Camelot, while the Trotters Free for All was won by Sir Castleton. In the $100,000 Sires Stakes final, Arveeae won from Nardinski and Master Mood; the $200,000 Max Harvey Auckland Cup went to Roydon Glen.

In Sweden Legolas won the Swedish V65 final. The Onion won the Gold Divison at Göteborg, and Meadow Road took the Elitlopp final in a world record 1 min 55.2 sec (5/8-mi track) from Rosalind's Guy and Brandy Hanover. The sponsored Matchline Cup final at Stockholm went to Glenn Kosmos. In Finland The Onion won the Vermo Cup at Helsinki, and at Seinejoki Glenn Kosmos set a track record of 1 min 59.3 sec. Meadow Road won the Finland V65 Gold Division over 2,140 m.

In Denmark Minou du Doujon won the Copenhagen Cup, and the Tuborg Open Trot went to Norway's Victoria S. In Norway the Oslo Grand Prix was won by French-owned Ogorek; Toyota Moulin captured the Gold Division final, and Jarlsberg took the Grand International.

In France the Prix D'Amérique of F 1.1 million at Vincennes, Paris, was won by Lutin d'Isigny from Mon Tourbillon and Minou du Doujon. Mon Tourbillon went on to win the Prix d'Atlantique at Enghien and the Prix de France. The Prix de Paris was taken by Malouin. Italy's Gran Premio di Europa in Milan went to Passionant with a record 2 min 1.5 sec over 2,100 m.   (NOEL SIMPSON)

ICE HOCKEY

North America. The Edmonton Oilers in 1985 once more proved their dominance over the National Hockey League (NHL) by winning their second straight Stanley Cup, this time by beating the up-and-coming Philadelphia Flyers in the final series four games to one. The speedy, high-scoring champions dropped the series' first game in Philadelphia but then reeled off four straight victories, ending with an 8–3 win at their home rink. Invincible at home, the Oilers compiled a record 16 straight play-off victories there.

The Flyers' appearance in the finals was testimony to the managerial skills of Bobby Clarke, former player and Flyer captain, in his first year as general manager. The recharged team had finished the regular season with the best overall record in the league. On the way to the Stanley Cup series the Flyers defeated two formidable foes, the New York Islanders in the quarterfinals and the Quebec Nordiques in the semifinals.

But Edmonton, with youth, depth, experience, and confidence, claimed the cup. Wayne Gretzky, the incomparable centre, once more set several scoring records, but there were other outstanding Edmonton players as well.

REUTERS/BETTMANN NEWSPHOTOS

Captain Wayne Gretzky (left) and Mike Krushelnyski hoist the Stanley Cup in celebration after their Edmonton Oilers won the National Hockey League championship for the second consecutive year, defeating the Philadelphia Flyers four games to one.

The 24-year-old Gretzky achieved a record sixth consecutive Hart Trophy as the league's most valuable player. In the National Hockey League only Bobby Orr had won any award for more than six straight years, having been named top defenseman for eight seasons beginning in 1967. Gretzky also won a fifth straight league scoring championship, surpassing the mark of four that he shared with Detroit's Gordie Howe and Boston's Phil Esposito. Gretzky had 73 goals and 135 assists in the regular season for a total of 208 points. In the play-offs Gretzky scored 47 points on 17 goals and 30 assists, the most points and assists ever achieved by one player in one play-off season. That feat earned him the Conn Smythe Trophy as the play-offs' most valuable player.

Gretzky's teammate Paul Coffey won the Norris Trophy as the league's best defenseman. Jari Kurri, another Oiler and a native of Finland, won the Lady Byng Award as the league's most gentlemanly player.

Pelle Lindbergh of the Philadelphia Flyers won the Vezina Trophy as the league's best goaltender. Lindbergh missed the final game of the Stanley Cup series with a knee injury. Tragedy struck, however, on the morning of November 10 when Lindbergh, driving home intoxicated after a team party, lost control of his sports car and crashed into a concrete wall. The 26-year-old player died of brain and spinal cord injuries.

Flyers Coach Mike Keenan, in his rookie NHL season, won the Adams Trophy for coach of the year. The William Jennings Trophy for the goaltending team with the fewest goals scored against it went to the Buffalo pair of Tom Barrasso and Bob Sauve.

Mario Lemieux, a 1.93-m (6-ft 4-in) centre for the Pittsburgh Penguins, was named rookie of the year. Lemieux had been selected first overall in the previous year's amateur draft and had signed the richest rookie contract in NHL history. He led the Penguins in regular-season scoring with 43 goals and 57 assists.

The Buffalo Sabres' Craig Ramsay won the Selke Award as the league's best defensive forward. Anders Hedberg of the New York Rangers, whose last year before retirement was cut short by an eye injury, won the Bill Masterton Trophy for sportsmanship and dedication to hockey.

In accepting his trophies, Gretzky criticized an NHL rule change set for the 1985–86 season that would virtually eliminate the four-on-four skating situations on which Gretzky has thrived. The new rule would allow teams to remain at full strength when coincidental minor penalties were assessed—as had been the case with coincidental major penalties. (In a coincidental penalty each team loses the same number of players for the same amount of time.) Gretzky said the rule change would rob the game of some excitement.

The 1984–85 season was marked by the retirement at age 33 of the great Guy Lafleur, one of the legendary "Flying Frenchmen" who propelled the Montreal Canadiens to five Stanley Cup championships during the 1970s. One of the most graceful and exciting skaters ever to play the game, Lafleur retired in November. The right wing's accomplishments included six straight seasons (beginning in 1970) with 50 or more goals.

A dizzying flurry of coaching changes took place during the 1984–85 season. In Boston Gerry Cheevers resigned during the season, and general manager Harry Sinden took over. At the season's end a newly retired player, Butch Goring, was named head coach. In Buffalo general manager Scotty Bowman, who had also been coaching the team, replaced himself with Jim Schoenfeld, a recently retired player. Bowman's 17-year coaching career had included guiding the Montreal Canadiens to five Stanley Cup championships. He went to Buffalo as coach and general manager in 1979.

Orval Tessier of Chicago, who was named coach of the year in 1983, was dismissed by general manager Bob Pulford, who then took over as coach. In Detroit coach Nick Polano was dismissed after the season and replaced by Harry Neale.

Neale had been general manager of Vancouver. During the season Neale fired Vancouver coach Bill LaForge and took over himself behind the bench. But after Vancouver's poor finish, Neale was fired as general manager. Named as Vancouver's new general manager was Jack Gordon, and the new coach was Tom Watt.

Minnesota general manager Lou Nanne fired coach Bill Mahoney early in the season and replaced him with Glen Sonmor as interim coach. After the season Lorne Henning was named head coach. In Montreal coach Jacques Lemaire resigned and was replaced by Jean Perron. Herb

Table I. NHL Final Standings, 1985

	Won	Lost	Tied	Goals	Goals against	Points
Prince of Wales Conference						
PATRICK DIVISION						
*Philadelphia	53	20	7	113	348	241
*Washington	46	25	9	101	322	240
*New York Islanders	40	34	6	86	345	312
*New York Rangers	26	44	10	62	295	345
New Jersey	22	48	10	54	264	346
Pittsburgh	24	51	5	53	276	385
ADAMS DIVISION						
*Montreal	41	27	12	94	309	262
*Quebec	41	30	9	91	323	275
*Buffalo	38	28	14	90	290	237
*Boston	36	34	10	82	303	287
Hartford	30	41	9	69	268	318
Clarence Campbell Conference						
NORRIS DIVISION						
*St. Louis	37	31	12	86	299	288
*Chicago	38	35	7	83	309	299
*Detroit	27	41	12	66	313	357
*Minnesota	25	43	12	62	268	321
Toronto	20	52	8	48	253	358
SMYTHE DIVISION						
*Edmonton	49	20	11	109	401	298
*Winnipeg	43	27	10	96	358	332
*Calgary	41	27	12	94	363	302
*Los Angeles	34	32	14	82	339	326
Vancouver	25	46	9	59	284	401

*Clinched playoff berth.

Table II. World Ice Hockey Championships, 1985

	Won	Lost	Tied	Goals	Goals against	Points
GROUP A Championship Section						
Czechoslovakia	3	0	0	18	6	6
Canada	2	1	0	9	8	4
U.S.S.R.	1	2	0	12	8	2
United States	0	0	3	7	24	0
GROUP A Relegation Section						
Finland	4	4	2	39	33	10
Sweden	4	6	0	37	40	8
West Germany	3	6	1	28	41	7
East Germany	0	8	2	16	64	2
GROUP B						
Poland	6	0	1	37	13	13
Switzerland	5	1	1	29	13	11
Italy	5	2	0	29	22	10
Austria	3	4	0	18	24	6
Japan	3	4	0	31	36	6
Netherlands, The	3	4	0	36	25	6
Norway	2	5	0	28	38	4
Hungary	0	0	7	17	54	0
GROUP C						
France	6	0	1	54	13	13
Yugoslavia	6	1	0	36	13	12
China	5	1	1	45	22	11
Romania	4	3	0	51	29	8
Denmark	3	4	0	16	23	6
Bulgaria	2	5	0	27	45	4
North Korea	1	6	0	18	56	2
Spain	0	7	0	9	55	0

Brooks was fired as coach of the New York Rangers during the season. General manager Craig Patrick took over himself. At the season's end he named a new coach, Ted Sator.

In the minor leagues the Sherbrooke Canadiens won the American Hockey League championship. The Peoria Rivermen won the International Hockey League title.

(ROBIN CATHY HERMAN)

European and International. The 50th world championships reached a climactic conclusion when the eight Group A nations contested the title in Prague, Czech., on April 17–May 3. Left-winger Jiri Sejba rose from relative obscurity to national hero by scoring a hat trick to give the host nation a 5–3 victory over Canada in the match that decided the gold and silver medalists.

Wildly supported by the majority of a 14,000-strong crowd, Sejba made the best and most decisive of his three goals in the 13th minute of the middle period, when the score was 2–2 and the Canadians held a one-man advantage. Sejba gained possession from defenseman Larry Murphy and then cleverly outmaneuvered Scott Stevens to put the puck deftly past goaltender Pat Riggin. This was the turning point of a game in which Canada had a chance to win its first world title since 1961.

This first Czechoslovak triumph since 1977 followed a preliminary round in which the Soviet title defenders had won all their seven games. When the four top teams moved to the medal round, the Soviets unexpectedly ran out of steam, losing 2–1 to the Czechoslovaks and 3–1 to Canada before salvaging the bronze medal with a 10–3 win over the fourth-place U.S. team.

Although Hannu Jarvempaa of Finland was the tournament's leading goal scorer with nine, Sergey Maharov from the U.S.S.R. collected the most points, 14 from 8 goals and 6 assists. The all-star selection afterward comprised Jiri Kralik, the Czechoslovak goaltender; Aleksey Karanotov and Vyacheslav Fetisov, the Soviet defensemen; Vladimir Ruzicka, the Czechoslovak centre; and Maharov and Vladimir Krutov, the Soviet wings.

As usual, the 24 participating nations were divided into three sections, the eight in Group B playing at Fribourg, Switz., on March 21–31. Poland, the winner after losing only one game, was promoted to Group A for the 1986 competition in Moscow, changing places with East Germany, which finished last in Group A in 1985.

Norway and Hungary, finishing at the bottom of Group B, were relegated to Group C for 1986. They were to be replaced by France and Yugoslavia, which had placed first and second, respectively, in Group C competition at Saint-Gervais, Chamonix, and Mégève, France, on March 14–23.

The ninth world junior (under 21) championship, played in Helsinki, Turku, and Myyrmäki, Fin., on Dec. 23, 1984–Jan. 1, 1985, was recaptured by Canada, the 1982 winner. Czechoslovakia placed second, and the U.S.S.R., the defending champion, finished third. The other Group A contestants included Finland, Sweden, the U.S., West Germany, and Poland. Fourteen other nations took part in tournaments for Groups B and C, held in Japan and Belgium, respectively.

It became compulsory during the year for all world junior championship players to wear face masks. The International Ice Hockey Federation (IIHF) expressed the hope that the juniors would continue wearing such masks after becoming seniors. Studies showed that the number of serious injuries had declined since the players had become better protected. The admission of Kuwait, following Brazil and Mexico, increased membership in the IIHF to 36 nations.

It was decided by the executive board of the International Olympic Committee that professionals would be eligible to participate in the 1988 Winter Olympic Games in Calgary, Alta., provided that they were younger than 23 on February 1 of that year. Former professionals would also be eligible if they held no contract after Sept. 1, 1987.

(HOWARD BASS)

ICE SKATING

A profusion of new indoor rinks throughout the world underlined a continuing upsurge of recreational and competitive participation in all branches of ice skating. A higher standard of competition was particularly evident in Japan, corresponding with that country's improved instructional facilities. The popularity of ice dancing widened, while a decline in the number of pair skaters was attributed to the increased risk of the sport brought about by the attempt to perform more ambitious lifts and jump throws. Speed skating seemed likely to benefit from a decision by the International Skating Union to introduce a World Cup series in 1986 and by the addition of an extra Olympic Games women's event, the 5,000 m, as well as through an increasing interest in short-track indoor racing.

Figure Skating. The departure from competition of several stars after the 1984 Winter Olympics sparked a fascinating new cycle of growth, with highly promising challengers to the more established performers enhancing the drama of top-level contests. The men's technical progress was especially noticeable, with an added degree of athleticism. The triple axel jump was now being seen more than once in a performance; other triples became more commonplace, and even an occasional quadruple toe loop jump was landed correctly.

There were 117 competitors in the four events of the 75th world championships in Tokyo on March 4–9. Aleksandr Fadeev captured the vacant men's crown, resisting strong late challenges from Brian Orser, the Canadian runner-up in the 1984 Winter Olympics, and Brian Boitano, who won the bronze for the U.S. Six judges gave Fadeev a score of 5.9 (out of a possible 6.0) for technical merit despite his touching down from a double salchow. Orser collected the same mark from four judges for presentation, three more than the Soviet victor. Both competitors achieved clean triple axels.

Katarina Witt, the East German Olympic gold medalist, came from behind to retain the women's title. Not for the first time, she showed a champion's cool when the chips were down, overtaking Kira Ivanova of the Soviet Union and third-place Tiffany Chin of the U.S. with a personal

Katarina Witt of East Germany glides out of third place and into first for her second consecutive victory in the world figure skating championships.

Andrea Schöne of East Germany sets a world-record pace in the 5,000-metre event at the women's speed skating world championship in Yugoslavia in February. She also won the three shorter events to dominate the meet and regain the title she had held in 1983.

AP/WIDE WORLD

best performance that inspired five judges to award her 5.9 for presentation.

In a generally improved women's competition, runner-up Ivanova came within an ace of completing an unprecedented Soviet sweep of the four titles. Chin, a U.S. resident of Chinese parentage, proved a powerful jumper and elegant spinner. Her fall from a double axel near the end surely cost her the silver medal. The host country suffered a harsh setback when Midori Ito, the outstanding jumper in the previous year's contest, had to withdraw after breaking her ankle in training.

With superior overhead lifts and well-landed triple throws, Oleg Vasiliev and Elena Valova recaptured the pairs title they had previously won in 1983. They overhauled their Soviet compatriots Oleg Makarov and Larissa Selezneva in spite of a touch down from a double axel by Vasiliev. Lloyd Eisler and Katherina Matousek, the Canadian bronze medalists, led a significant challenge to Eastern European dominance by three North American partnerships.

After three frustrating years as runners-up to Britain's invincible Christopher Dean and Jayne Torvill, who had turned professional, Andrey Bukin and Natalia Bestemianova succeeded to the ice dance title. Sergey Ponomarenko and Marina Klimova, also of the Soviet Union, finished second. Michael Seibert and Judy Blumberg of the U.S. won the bronze medal for a third time.

Speed Skating. Hein Vergeer of The Netherlands outpaced the Soviet defender, Oleg Bozhiev, to capture the men's world championship in Hamar, Norway, on February 16–17. Another Dutchman, Hilbert van der Duim, the 1982 winner, gained the bronze medal. In the individual events Vergeer won the 5,000 m and Bozhiev the 1,500 m, with Gaetan Boucher of Canada and Geir Karlstad from Norway taking the 500 m and 10,000 m, respectively.

In the women's world championship at Sarajevo, Yugos., on February 9–10, Andrea Schöne of East Germany regained the title she had held in 1983, this time dominating the competition with wins in all four distances. In the 5,000 m she set a world record time of 7 min 32.82 sec. Gabi Schönbrunn, also of East Germany, finished second

in the overall competition, with Sabine Brehm completing an East German clean sweep.

In the separate world sprint championships, at Heerenveen, Neth., on February 23–24, Igor Zhelezovsky of the U.S.S.R. gained the men's title, with Boucher, the defending champion, finishing in second place and Dan Jensen of the U.S. in third. Christa Rothenburger defeated her fellow East German Angela Stahnke to take the women's title, with Erwina Rys-Ferens of Poland third.

At the fifth world short-track (indoor) championships, in Amsterdam on March 15–17, Toshinobu Kawai won the men's title for Japan, followed by his compatriot Tatsuyoshi Ishihara, runner-up for a second successive time; Louis Grenier from Canada finished third. Japanese ascendancy was further emphasized by the victory in women's competition of Eiko Shishii, who proved too good for Bonnie Blair of the U.S. and Nathalie Lambert of Canada, second and third, respectively. With shorter laps and sharper corners than on the larger open-air circuits, indoor racing required a quite different technique and offered more opportunity for success to competitors from nations with no outdoor tracks.   (HOWARD BASS)

LACROSSE

Men. In the United States in 1985 Johns Hopkins University beat Syracuse University 11–4 to win the National Collegiate Athletic Association (NCAA) championship. In the North versus South game the South collegiate all-stars defeated the North 16–7. Hobart University defeated Washington College (Maryland) 15–8 to win the NCAA Third Division title. In club lacrosse, Long Island defeated Maryland 21–20 in a sudden-death play-off in overtime. The best player awards for the year went to Larry Quinn (Johns Hopkins, goalkeeper), John DeTommaso (Johns Hopkins, defense), Del Dressel (Johns Hopkins, midfield), and Tim Nelson (Syracuse, attack). In 1985 the U.S. Intercollegiate Lacrosse Association membership stood at an all-time high of 192 clubs.

Australia continued to develop a modified game of lacrosse known as "soft crosse," accepted there as a school recreational activity. Western Australia won the interstate championship for the fourth time in five years. State champion teams were: Victoria, Williamstown, with G. Purdie of Chadstone Club "fairest and best" player; South Australia, Stuart, with K. Humphreys of East Torrans Club fairest and best player; Western Australia, East Fremantle, with J. Gower of Wembley Club fairest and best player.

In England Cheadle was the champion club, winning an easy victory over the University of London to gain the Iroquois Cup. Cheadle also won the North of England Senior Flags by defeating Old Hulmeians 12–5. The First Division of the league in the North of England was headed by Cheadle, and Cheshire was county champion at both senior and junior levels. In the South the Flag winner, University of London, defeated Hillcroft. Hampstead won the South of England league championship.

(CHARLES DENNIS COPPOCK)

Women. Preparation for the second World Cup, scheduled for June 1986 at Swarthmore (Pa.) College, dominated the 1984–85 season. England convincingly defeated Wales 12–3 but struggled painfully to gain a fortunate 3–2 victory over ever improving Scotland. Australia's wins over Great Britain in the summer of 1985 suggested that Australia would provide the greatest threat to the World Cup holders, the U.S. On tour Great Britain defeated Victoria State 8–5, Tasmania 24–0, South Australia 10–7, and Western Australia 8–5. However, Australia won four test matches 6–3, 9–4, 6–4, and 7–5, although England retrieved some

honour with a 6–5 victory in the final test. Differences in technique were marked, with Australia displeased by close stick-checking and Great Britain objecting to the degree of physical contact on and off the ball, but the Australians deserved their victories because of their superior shooting skills and better utilization of both speed and possession.

In Britain a severe winter took its toll of the league program, and sadly, after the first games had shown the territories more evenly matched than usual, the territorial championship had to remain unresolved when snow caused the cancellation of the second territorial weekend. The Territorial Reserves Tournament did take place, though some matches were played in blizzard conditions, with the South retaining the title. The All-England Counties Tournament was won by Cheshire, which defeated defending champion Middlesex. In the All-England Clubs and Colleges Tournament, West London, with its team of internationals, defeated one of the main challengers, Bedford College of Higher Education, 2–0 only to be defeated 4–2 in overtime by the defending champions, St. Mary's College, Twickenham. (MARGARET-LOUISE O'KEEFFE)

LAWN BOWLS

Predictably, Australians dominated the women's lawn bowls world championships, held at the Reservoir Bowling Club, near Melbourne, Australia, from Feb. 11 to March 2, 1985. They captured three of the four events, together with the *Daily Mirror* (London) Trophy for winning most points spread across the individual events. Scotland's Sarah Gourlay, Elizabeth Christie, Annette Evans, and Frances Whyte won the fours competition and so stopped an Australian whitewash, but Australia's Merle Richardson was the tournament's outstanding player, winning both the singles—always the prime event—and the pairs with Fay Craig. Altogether, 19 countries competed, a new record.

The Mazda international masters championship was staged at Beaumaris, also near Melbourne. It was won by Kenny Williams of New South Wales, after Tony Allcock of England came within one-eighth of an inch of victory. David Bryant of England won the Gateway Masters tournament at Worthing, England, for the fifth time. The world indoor championships, at Coatbridge, Scotland, went to Terry Sullivan of Wales. (C. M. JONES)

MARTIAL ARTS

Judo. The 14th world judo championships in Seoul, South Korea, in late September highlighted judo activities in 1985. Japan won the unofficial team championship with four gold medals, a silver, and a bronze. Next came South Korea with two gold and two silver medals, followed by the Soviet Union with one gold and five bronze. Yoshimi Masaki of Japan won the open category and became the unofficial world judo champion, replacing Yasuhiro Yamashita, who had retired. Hitoshi Saito of Japan, who was heavily favoured to win the title, dropped out of the heavyweight final when his left elbow was dislocated in a match with Cho Yong Chul of South Korea. Earlier in the year at the Budokan in Tokyo, Yamashita had narrowly defeated Saito to win the all-Japan championships. It was the ninth straight time that Yamashita had won the only major world tournament without weight classes. In mid-June he officially retired from tournament competition.

In the 25-nation 34th European judo championships in May at Hamar, Norway, winners included heavyweight Grigory Veritchev of the Soviet Union, light heavyweight Robert van der Walle of Belgium, and light middleweight Neil Adams of Britain. Karen Briggs, Dianne Bell, and Dawn Netherwood of Great Britain won gold medals in the

second international women's championships in Fukuoka, Japan; 125 women from 19 countries competed. Japan and South Korea each won three gold medals in the University Games at Kobe, Japan, in August.

Karate. During the 13th all-Japan all-styles karate-do championships at the Budokan in December, both the men's and women's *kumite* defending champions won their respective competitions. *Nidan* (second-degree black belt) Yorihisa Uchida, a 22-year-old specialist in the *shotokan* style, defeated *sandan* (third degree) Masamichi Yokomichi 3–1 with two *jodan-tsuki* (upper punches) and a *chudan-tsuki* (centre punch). Earlier in the year Uchida had won a gold medal in the second World Games in London. In the women's contest, 21-year-old Tomoko Konishi, an Osaka Educational University student and a *sandan karateka* who fought in the *kushin-kai* style, edged *sandan* Yukari Yamakura 3–2. It was Konishi's third national title. She also won a gold medal in the world karate championships in The Netherlands in 1984.

At the World Games in London during the summer, 2,000 athletes from 60 countries competed in a variety of sports. Japan won gold medals in karate in the men's and women's *kata* (prescribed forms) and the 60-kg and 75-kg weight classes in the *kumite* (fighting) competition. Britain won three *kumite* gold medals in the open-weight, super-heavyweight, and 70-kg divisions; Italy won the 80-kg class and The Netherlands the 65-kg category.

The Japan Karate Association (JKA) held its national and world championship tournaments at the Nippon Budokan in Tokyo in late September. Masao Kagawa won both the *kata* and *kumite* all-Japan titles, while runner-up Minoru Kawawada won the JKA world *kata* and *kumite* titles. Masaaki Yokomichi was second in the world *kumite* competition. Kyokushin-kai held its national contact karate tournament in November at the Tokyo Municipal Gym, with 128 *karateka* competing. Akiyoshi Matsui, a third-degree black belt, defeated Hiroaki Kurosawa in the final match. Some 650 students from 135 high schools competed in the high school championships at the Budokan in March; Meguro High School in Tokyo won the boys' *kumite* team title. More than 800 children participated in the 39th primary and junior high school tournament in August in Hyogo Prefecture. In an important development, the International Olympic Committee (IOC) recognized the World Union of Karate-do Organizations (WUKO). Ryoichi Sasakawa, president of WUKO, expressed the hope that karate would be approved as an Olympic sport by 1992.

Kendo. In April Japan walked off with the major honours in the sixth world kendo championships in Paris, with Kunihide Koda defeating Ogawa with two *kote* (forearm) strikes in an all-Japanese final. A pair of South Koreans tied for third place. In the team competition, in which 22 countries participated, Japan blanked Brazil 3–0, with Canada and South Korea tying for third place. The seventh world championships were to be held in Seoul in 1988. A 34-year-old Osaka policeman, Yoshifumi Ishizuka, won first place in the all-Japan men's individual championships at the Budokan in November. He outlasted Wataru Kondo 1–0 in the finals, scoring the winning point with a *men* (helmet) strike. In the all-Japan women's championships in May in Osaka, Sachi Mitani used *do* (breastplate) and *kote* strikes to edge Fujita 2–1 in the finals. Miyagi Prefecture beat Saitama Prefecture 3–2 for the national team title in Osaka that same day. A Tokyo policeman, Masaaki Endo, won the men's title in the all-Japan police championships at the Budokan on May 31, while Satomi Fukunoue, also of Tokyo, took the policewomen's title for the third time

with a *men* strike against Mizue Morita. The Toray Spinning Co. team won the all-Japan industrial championships 4–1 against the Toppan Printing Co. in September.

(ANDREW M. ADAMS)

MOTORBOATING

Lee ("Chip") Hanauer of Seattle, Wash., driver of the newly sponsored Miller American unlimited hydroplane, led the assault on the American Power Boat Association (APBA) record books in 1985, winning the coveted APBA Gold Cup for the fourth consecutive year. In doing so, Hanauer became the first driver since Gar Wood some 60 years earlier to win four Gold Cups in a row, surpassing the late Bill Muncey and Ron Musson, who each took three straight. Hanauer also set the sport's first lap record of more than 150 mph (240 km/h) in 1985, pushing his turbine-powered Lucero hull to a qualifying mark of 153.061.

Other unlimited newsmakers were the aircraft-powered *Executone* and *Miss Budweiser* teams. Drivers Scott Pierce and Jim Kropfeld fought off challengers and finished second and third, respectively, behind Hanauer in the national high point competition.

George Morales of Miami, Fla., continued his trek through the APBA record books with a record-breaking Offshore run from Miami to New York City. Morales's four 700-hp MerCruiser engines pushed his 14-m (46-ft) Cougar catamaran over the 2,224-km (1,257-mi) course in 19 hr, 38 min, 35 sec, chopping more than three hours off the former record set in 1974. Even the second-place finisher, Al Copeland of New Orleans, La., broke the former mark, finishing an hour behind Morales.

Morales added another gem to his Offshore crown in 1985, winning the world championship in the Superboat class, for his third championship title in as many years. Copeland, on the other hand, swept the Superboat class on the national circuit, winning the national high point title. Other 1985 national high point winners in Offshore competition included Miami's Sal Magluta in the Open class, Chris Lavin of Westport, Conn., in Modified, John Emmons of East Hanover, N.J., in Pro-Stock, Bob Erickson of Minnetonka, Minn., in Stock A, and Bill Kaye of Chicago in Stock B.

In the two-litre outboard tunnel boat class, the British International Harmsworth Trophy—known as the "America's Cup" of powerboat racing—remained on its home turf despite a hard-fought challenge by the U.S. The British team, led by Mark Wilson of Brighton, England, and Jon Jones of Cardigan, Wales, won convincing victories in both legs of the contest, clinching the historic prize for the second year in a row.

U.S. drivers fared better in the Formula One outboard season as Ben Robertson of Charleston, S.C., finished second in the international points competition, 11 points behind leader Bob Spalding of England. Robertson's teammate, Gene Thibodaux of Winter Haven, Fla., tied for third place with Sweden's Bertil Wik.

(HILARY R. SPITTLE)

MOTORCYCLING

In 1985 Freddie Spencer of the U.S. became the first man to win both the 500-cc and 250-cc motorcycle world championships in the same road-racing season. Riding a Rothman's Honda, he defeated the 1984 500-cc champion, Eddie Lawson (U.S.; Yamaha), who finished second, and mastered the West German Anton Mang (Honda) in the 250-cc series. Spencer recorded 14 wins and 4 seconds in 21 grand prix starts. In the 250-cc competition he won six consecutive races.

Fausto Gresini (Italy; Garelli) was the 125-cc champion, with countryman Pierpaulo Bianchi (MBA) finishing second. In the sidecar class the leaders were the Dutch team of Egbert Streuer and Bernhard Schneiders, driving a Yamaha. The 80-cc class was won, for the second year, by Stefan Dörflinger (Switz.; Krauser). World Formula One champion was Joey Dunlop of Northern Ireland (Honda).

The 1985 world champion endurance team was Gerard Coudray and Patrick Igoa (France; Honda). The Le Mans, France, 24-hour event was won by the team of Guy Bertin, Bernard Millet, and Philippe Guichon (France; Suzuki).

In world motocross competition the 500-cc title went to Britain's Dave Thorpe (Honda). Heinz Kinigadner (Austria; KTM) was the 250-cc champion, and Hansi Bachtold and Fritz Fuss (Switz.; EML) took the sidecar class.

Thierry Michoud (France; Fantic), who set a record in winning 9 of the 12 rounds in the contest, was world trials champion. Eddie Lejeune (Belgium; Honda) finished in second place.

Winners of the main World Trophy in the International Six Days Enduro, held in Spain, were the Swedish team; East Germany took the subsidiary Junior Trophy contest. Runners-up, in both categories, were teams entered by Spain. Erik Gundersen (Denmark) retained his world speedway championship.

(CYRIL J. AYTON)

MOUNTAINEERING

The Union Internationale des Associations d'Alpinisme (UIAA) held its annual General Assembly for 1985 in Venice, Italy, in October. The Chinese Mountaineering Association was elected to membership, and so the national mountaineering bodies of all the major Himalayan countries had become UIAA members. The new president was Carlo Sganzini (Italy). A main topic for discussion was competition climbing. After previous unsuccessful proposals to introduce it as a sport in the Olympic Games, the Mountaineering Federation of the U.S.S.R. proposed a European cup competition in the Crimea under the existing Soviet competition rules and with UIAA patronage. This was rejected by the assembly, but individual countries were left to accept or reject Soviet invitations.

The UIAA approached the Himalayan countries with two requests: to reduce the compulsory personnel for lightweight expeditions, and to introduce a winter climbing season in India and Pakistan (previously Nepal had been the only country with such a season). The Indian government announced limited arrangements for climbing in the eastern Karakoram, to be undertaken by joint Indian-foreign expeditions. Noteworthy new routes were on Masherbrum northwest side by a Japanese party and on Gasherbrum I northwest face by Poles.

In Nepal in 1984 after the monsoon, 49 expeditions took place. Particularly noteworthy was the completion by a Spanish party of a route on the south face of Annapurna I. In 1985 before the monsoon, only 26 expeditions took place, including several on Mt. Everest (among them a successful ascent by British mountaineer Chris Bonnington); Everest was fully booked until 1997. The Nepalese government announced a 10% increase in the royalty charge after the 1985 monsoon. Reinhold Messner of Italy climbed Annapurna I and Dhaulagiri I and so had only two 8,000-m (26,200-ft) peaks still to climb.

A new development in the Alps in 1984–85 was the wholehearted application of modern rock-climbing techniques and attitudes in the higher mountains, particularly in the Chamonix Aiguilles. Also noteworthy on Mont Blanc was the climbing of several difficult routes by one party in one day, such as the north face of the Grand Pilier

d'Angle, the 1961 Freney route, the Freney-Bardill direct route, and the Innominata Arête in one day of 22 hours.

The British mountaineer Don Whillans died in August (*see* OBITUARIES). (JOHN NEILL)

POLO

The Guards Polo Club in England was the site of the 1985 International Polo Day. In the competition for the Coronation Cup, Mexico (R. Gracida [7], C. Gracida [9], G. ["Memo"] Gracida [10], and J. Baez [5]) defeated England I (W. P. Churchward [6], A. J. Kent [8], J. Hipwood [9], and H. Hipwood [9]) 8–6. In the supporting Silver Jubilee Cup, England II (the prince of Wales [4], J. Horswell [6], R. Graham [5], and Lord C. Beresford [6]) achieved a 6–5 victory over Brazil (P. de Meirelles [4], M. Junquiera [7], S. Novaes [7], and R. de Lima [3]).

The British Open championship for the Cowdray Park Gold Cup was won by the Maple Leafs (M. Glue [4], J. Hipwood [9], A. Devcich [7], and W. Galen Weston [2]) 11–10 over Les Diables Bleus (G. Wildenstein [3], J. Baez [5], G. ["Memo"] Gracida [10], and the prince of Wales [4]). The Charles Heidsieck Warwickshire Cup was won by the Centaurs (D. Yeoman [3], A. J. Kent [8], O. Rinehart [8], and D. Jamison [3]) by a score of 9–5 over Los Locos (Mrs. S. Tomlinson [4], S. Tomlinson [4], L. Macaire [7], and S. Macaire [6]).

In the United States, Retama (J. Gose [4], C. Gracida [9], G. ["Memo"] Gracida [10], and S. Gose [2]) won the U.S. Open. The German championship open was taken by the Springbok (J. Schneider, K. Winter, G. Holter, and P. Withers). (COLIN J. CROSS)

RACKETS

William Boone became the first left-hander to win the world rackets title when he unseated the defending champion, John Prenn, in December 1984. Twice postponed because of injuries to Prenn, the first leg of the final round was played in Montreal in November. Boone took it by four games to two and then won the second leg at Queen's Club, London, by three to zero. Boone repeated that win in the final of the amateur championship but lost to Prenn in the open championship by four games to one.

Prenn won the Canadian championship, beating David McLernon in Montreal, while the brothers Andrew and Randall Crawley won the doubles. Prenn won the U.S. Open in Detroit, beating James Male, the first player with a two-handed backhand to make his mark in rackets. Together they won the U.S. doubles, having earlier taken the Manchester Gold Racquet competition. Boone and Randall Crawley won the British Open doubles title but lost to Prenn and Charles Hue Williams in the final of the British amateur championship. (ROY MCKELVIE)

RACQUETBALL

Mike Yellen of Southfield, Mich., won his third consecutive U.S. national championship in 1985 by once again taking the number one ranking from former champion Marty Hogan at the last tournament of the professional season in June. Yellen's third national title left him only one short of Hogan's all-time record.

A new star, 20-year-old Gregg Peck of Austin, Texas, emerged during the men's tour. Peck, the younger brother of former national champion Dave Peck, won two tournaments, including the season-ending $40,000 DP Leach national championships in Boston, and finished the year a close third behind Yellen and Hogan.

Lynn Adams of Costa Mesa, Calif., continued her total domination of women's racquetball by losing only a single

Gregg Peck won the DP Leach national, racquetball's richest tournament, in June and took $40,000 home from Boston.

DREW STODDARD, COMMISSIONER RMA MEN'S PRO TOUR

match during the entire women's professional season. She won six tournaments and became the first woman ever to win the "triple crown"—consecutive victories at the Ektelon, WPRA, and DP national championships.

Former world squash champion Heather McKay of Canada retired from professional racquetball competition in June. In her seven-year career on the women's racquetball tour, McKay won 19 tournaments and 3 national championships, her last coming in 1984 at the age of 42.

Amateur racquetball made further strides in international competition. The U.S. team continued to dominate the field by sweeping both the North American regional championships in Ecuador and the World Games II in London. Fifteen countries fielded teams for the London competition, generally regarded as a precursor to full Olympic Games recognition. (DREW W. STODDARD)

REAL TENNIS

Christopher Ronaldson of the U.K., the professional at Hampton Court, London, again successfully defended his world title against Wayne Davies of Australia. At Queen's Club, London, in March 1985 Ronaldson won three of four well-fought sets on the first day and romped home on the second to win seven sets to one, 6–5, 6–3, 5–6, 6–3, 6–1, 6–2, 6–4, 6–1. Davies won the U.S. Open, beating fellow Australian Lachlan Deuchar three sets to zero in New York City after losing to him in the U.S. professional championship 6–5 in the final set at Newport, R.I.

Alan Lovell won the British amateur championship at Queen's Club for the third successive year, beating former titleholder Howard Angus. A newcomer, Kevin McCollum, a Briton working in New York and an expert at the boomerang service (invented by the Australians), won the U.S. amateur championship by beating two former champions, Gene Scott and Ralph Howe. In the Bathurst Cup played in Hobart, Tasmania, in April 1985, Australia again beat the U.S. and lost to Britain, repeating the 1984 result. Judy Clarke of Melbourne, Australia, beat Lesley Ronaldson, wife of Christopher, in the final of the first women's real tennis world championship 6–3, 5–6, 6–5 at the Royal Melbourne Tennis Club. (ROY MCKELVIE)

RIVER SPORTS

The world white-water championships were held June 6–16 in Garmisch and Augsburg, West Germany. In the slalom Richard Fox of the U.K. won the men's kayak class, and David Hearn and Jon Lugbill of the U.S. finished first and second in the men's canoe class. In wild-water (downriver white-water) racing Marco Previde Massara of Italy won the men's kayak class.

The U.S. national white-water canoe and kayak championships took place July 8–12 on the Nantahala River in North Carolina. In the slalom Chris Doughty won the men's kayak class, Cathy Hearn won the women's, and her brother David Hearn won the men's canoe class. In wildwater racing Jon Fishburn won his fourth consecutive title in men's kayaking; Hearn won the women's championship and Angus Morrison the men's canoe class.

The U.S. marathon championships took place August 16–18 on the Wabash River at Lafayette, Ind. In canoeing Alan Rudquist won the men's solo class and then also took the tandem class with partner Mike Fries. In kayaking Ann Hopkinson won the women's competition, Kenny Holton won the men's, and Scott Randolph and Fletcher Anderson won the men's tandem.

In the U.S. national flat-water championships, held August 21–24 in Sacramento, Calif., Greg Barton won all three men's kayak races, as he had the previous year. Leslie Klein won the women's kayaking, and Bruce Merrit won the men's canoeing. Barton became the first American ever to become a world champion in flat-water competition when he won the men's 10,000-m single kayak race at the world championships, held August 15–18 at Hazewinkel, Belgium. Hungarian and East German racers won most of the other competitive events.   (ERIC LEAPER)

RODEO

In 1985 professional rodeo captured a larger share of sports entertainment dollars than ever before. The Professional Rodeo Cowboys Association (PRCA) instituted its first full season of the $1 million Winston Tour rodeos, which included six contests at various sites around the U.S. The 18 teamlike "outfits" featured the previous season's top winners who had been "drafted." In addition, more than 600 regular PRCA-sanctioned rodeos were held in North America during the year, with more than $14 million in prize money.

The tour rodeos met with mixed responses from cowboys and fans alike. The cowboys who qualified for the competitions were quite satisfied, especially from a financial standpoint. Many of those who could not compete felt that too much prize money had been allocated to too few rodeos. A survey of fans who attended at least one of the tour rodeos indicated they appreciated the high calibre of competition, but for the most part attendance was lacking, possibly because the tour sites were new to rodeo. PRCA officials planned to continue the tour in 1986.

The entire association and the fans seemed well pleased with the 1985 National Finals Rodeo. The season's top 15 winners in each of seven events, including the Women's Professional Rodeo Association barrel racers, competed December 7–15 for a record $1,790,000. The sport's "Super Bowl" moved from Oklahoma City, Okla., where it had been held for 20 years, to Las Vegas, Nev. The city of Las Vegas had nearly doubled the 1984 prize money to book the event.

The 1985 world champions, selected on the basis of the most money won over the entire season in each event, were named at the end of the rodeo. The world all-around championship, which was awarded to the cowboy who won the most money in two or more events, went to Lewis Feild of Elk Ridge, Utah, with $130,347 in bareback riding and saddle bronc riding. Feild also took the bareback championship with $103,247.

Other world champions included Joe Beaver of Victoria, Texas, with $95,869 in calf roping; Ote Berry of Gordon, Neb., with $97,273 in steer wrestling; Jake Barnes of Bloomfield, N.M., and Clay O'Brien Cooper of Gilbert, Ariz., who earned $99,048 each in team roping; Brad Gjermundson of Marshall, N.D., with $84,652 in saddle bronc riding; Ted Nuce of Manteca, Calif., with $107,872 in bull riding; and Charmayne James of Clayton, N.M., with $93,848 in barrel racing. Two weeks earlier Jim Davis of Bandera, Texas, had won the steer roping championship with $35,631. The National Finals Steer Roping was held at Guthrie, Okla.

All-around champions named by other, smaller rodeo associations in North America included Greg Schlosser of Okotoks, Alta., in the Canadian Professional Rodeo Association, and Dan Dailey of Tulsa, Okla., in the International Professional Rodeo Association (for 1984); the 1985 champions would be named at the association's International Finals, to be held Jan. 16–19, 1986, in Tulsa.

In the National Intercollegiate Rodeo Association's Finals, held in June at Bozeman, Mont., Kent Richard of McNeese State University, Lake Charles, La., took the men's all-around, and Lisa Scheffer of the University of Montana won the women's all-around title for 1985.

(RANDALL E. WITTE)

ROWING

The 1985 world rowing championships revealed some slackening in East German and Soviet dominance. The medals in the 35 open, lightweight, and junior events were shared among 21 countries from a record high overall number of entries. East Germany won 12 world titles, while 7 went to the Soviet Union, 4 each to West Germany and Romania, and 3 to Italy. Other countries to win titles were Australia, Canada, Finland, France, and Great Britain. In the world medals table the highest scores were East Germany 23, the Soviet Union 14, Romania 13, the U.S. 11, and Italy 10.

In the world championships, at Hazewinkel, Belgium, East Germany was eclipsed in the men's events by the Soviet Union. Italy also earned distinction, and nine other nations shared the medals. East Germany won the double

In the University Boat Race on London's Thames River in April, the Oxford University eight (left) won a record tenth consecutive victory, outpacing the crew from Cambridge by nearly five lengths. Cambridge still led the annual series by 68 victories to 62.

Gary Jobson led a four-man crew representing the United States (right) to victory over teams from seven other nations in the Liberty Cup series of 14 rounds of match races in New York Harbor in July.

sculls from the Soviet Union by 3.99 sec but lost narrowly to Canada by 0.28 sec in the quadruple sculls and could secure only bronze medals in three other events.

The most dramatic finish took place in the coxless pairs when the 1981 world champions, the brothers Nikolay and Yury Pimenov of the Soviet Union, just held out to beat Great Britain by 0.08 sec. The Soviet Union defeated Italy by 1.56 sec in coxed fours but was given a tighter struggle by the Italians before winning the eights by 0.87 sec. Italy took the coxed pairs by 2.64 sec from Romania, and West Germany finished 1.06 sec ahead of the Soviet Union in coxless fours. The men's single sculls provided a classic race when the Finnish triple Olympic champion, Pertti Karppinen, sculled past the U.S. newcomer Andrew Sudduth in the last 250 m to win by a length.

The East Germans dominated the women's events, which were held over 2,000 m for the first time. They won four gold medals, one silver, and one bronze; Romania won a gold, three silvers, and a bronze; and the Soviet Union finished with a gold and a silver. The other medalists were Bulgaria, Canada, and the U.S. In the two closest finals East Germany was pressed by the Soviet Union before winning the quadruple sculls by 1.52 sec, but the Soviets then held off East Germany to win the eights by 0.89 sec.

Italy stole the limelight with two gold medals and two silver medals in the men's lightweight events, which carried "world" status for the first time. France and West Germany won the two other titles, and Austria, Spain, and the U.S. also gained medals. Eastern European countries competed for the first time and also supported the new lightweight events for women. The title winners in that competition were Australia, Great Britain, and West Germany, with France, Romania, and the U.S. also winning medals.

In the world junior championships on their home waters at Brandenburg, East Germany shared six of the gold medals in the men's events with the Soviet Union and took two silver medals and a bronze. Other medalists were Denmark, France, Great Britain, Greece, Italy, Poland, and the U.S. In the women's events only Austria and West Germany, with a bronze medal each, broke the Eastern European stranglehold.

In England the Henley Royal Regatta attracted a record 348 entries, and in an all-American final of the Grand Challenge Cup, Harvard University beat Princeton University by more than three lengths. Ridley College won the Thames Cup for Canada, and the third overseas winners were Bjørn Eltang and Lars Kruse of Denmark in the Double Sculls Cup. Oxford won the 131st University Boat Race by 4¾ lengths after a close struggle for the first 2½ mi. This was Oxford's tenth consecutive win and reduced the Cambridge lead in the series to 68–62. Oxford also made rowing history in South America in August when a group of students rowed a racing eight 1,600 km (1,000 mi) down the Amazon.   (KEITH OSBORNE)

SAILING

In February 1985 the cream of the U.S. ocean-racing yachts, along with several boats from Europe, gathered in Florida for the Southern Racing Circuit competition. Charley Scott's J41 *Smiles* one-tonner took the overall honours.

With interest in the 1987 America's Cup series gathering momentum, more and more match-race series were being organized. In the Congressional Cup, sailed off Long Beach, Calif., three top U.S. helmsmen tied at the end of the regular series, and in the sail-off Rod Davis, the Soling class Olympic gold medalist, narrowly beat defending champion Dave Perry and John Kolius. The British match-race series was held off Lymington, Hampshire, in Westerley Fulmar yachts. Nine group races were sailed to select the four semifinalists. Iain Murray from Australia won the preliminary series with eight victories, ahead of Gary Jobson of the U.S., Harold Cudmore, sailing for Ireland, and Chris Law of the U.K. Murray and Cudmore qualified for the finals, in which Murray badly lost the start and never recovered. Cudmore thus again won the Lymington Cup.

The Round Britain race took place again in 1985, and once more the big multihulled craft dominated the scene. Because of the vast difference in size and speed of the boats that were entered, the leaders finished before the smaller boats had gained the halfway mark. Most interest was naturally focused on the leading craft, with Michael Whipp and David Allen-Williams establishing a seven-hour lead in *BCA-Paragon* by the halfway stage, but soon afterward

World Class Boat Champions

Class	Winner	Class	Winner
Albacore	Graham Child (United Kingdom)	Optimist	Serge Kats (The Netherlands)
Contender	Barry Watson (Australia)	6 Metre	Phillippe Durr (Switzerland)
Dragon	Wolfgang Rappel (West Germany)	Soling	Dave Curtis (United States)
Europe	Ole Petter Pollen (Norway)	Tempest	Rolf Bahr (West Germany)
Flying Dutchman	Jørgen Schonherr (Denmark)	Tornado	Robert White (United Kingdom)
GP 14	Simon Relph (United Kingdom)	Youth Laser	Andy Beadsworth (United Kingdom)
International 14	Jamie Kidd (Canada)	Youth 420	Jens Olbrysch (West Germany)
International Moth	Roger Angell (United Kingdom)	$\frac{1}{4}$ Ton	Geoff Meek (South Africa)
Laser	Lawrence Crispen (United Kingdom)	$\frac{3}{4}$ Ton	Niels Jeffeson (Denmark)
OK	Leith Armit (New Zealand)	1 Ton	Larry Wooddell (United Kingdom)

they had to retire into Peterhead. This left Tony Bullimore and Nigel Irons in the lead in *Apricot,* and they finished some 15 hours ahead of *Moor Energy* (Jeff Houlgrave and Bob Bradford), with *Marlow Ropes* (Mark Gatehouse and Peter Rowsell) a close third.

The field for the 1987 America's Cup challenge, due to be sailed in Australian waters, was whittled down to 14 teams: six U.S., two Canadian, two French, two Italian, and one each from Great Britain and New Zealand. The elimination series to determine the one challenger to sail against the Australian defender was scheduled to start with a round-robin series off Fremantle, Australia, on Oct. 5–20, 1986. The designs of keels and underwater shapes remained cloaked in secrecy, while technical advances in equipment continued unabated at huge costs; masts were estimated to cost up to about £40,000 each.

In the Admiral's Cup series 18 teams entered. The British team was clearly a strong one, with three of the best one-tonners, including world champion *Jade* (Larry Wooddell), supported by *Panda* (Peter Whipp) and *Phoenix* (Lloyd Bankson). The West German team, holders of the cup, were in no mood to give the trophy up easily and had their boats *Rubin VIII* (Hans-Otto Schumann), *Outsider* (Tilmar Hansen), and *Diva (85)* (Diekel and Westphall Langloh) in top trim. The very windy channel conditions of late July and early August took a heavy toll of the fleet, particularly in the English Channel race. The Fastnet race was a rough one that caused many boats to retire, but the West German victory was in doubt until *Jade* suffered mast damage and had to withdraw. *Phoenix,* skippered by Cudmore, finished the series as top boat, and Great Britain took second place behind West Germany.

(ADRIAN JARDINE)

SHOOTING

The IV Championships of the Americas were held at Ft. Benning, Georgia, with 187 marksmen representing 14 nations competing. The 1985 world moving target championships took place at Montecatini Terme, Italy, while the world air gun championships were conducted at Mexico City.

Trap and Skeet. At the Championships of the Americas, the gold medal for trap was taken by the U.S. team with a score of 419 of a possible 450. The Brazilian team took the silver medal with 403, while the Canadians won the bronze with 385. The individual winner was Dayne Johnson of the U.S., who took the gold medal with a 191 of a possible 200. In the women's division Frances Strodtman of the U.S. won the gold medal with a 180 out of 200.

At the world moving target championships, the Italian men's trap team placed first with a 434. The Soviet Union was second with 428, while the tie-breaking rules awarded the Czechoslovakian team third place. The individual high score was a 197 of a possible 200 by M. Bednarik of Czechoslovakia. The Chinese team scored 383 to take first place in the women's division. The Italians were second with 377, while the Canadian women scored 366 to finish third. Li Liu of China was high individual with a 188.

In skeet the gold medal at the Championships of the Americas went to the U.S. team for its score of 433. The Cuban team scored 427 to take the silver medal, while Argentina won the bronze with 420. Matt Dryke of the U.S. won the individual gold medal with a 196, besting in a shoot-off Michael Schmidt of the U.S., who took the silver. The individual gold medal in the women's division was won by Eva Funes of the U.S. with a 190.

At the world moving target championships, the U.S. team score of 433 was awarded the gold medal in skeet under tie-breaking rules over Italy, which placed second. Czechoslovakia finished third with 432. The individual gold medal was won by B. Hochwald of East Germany with a 196 out of 200. China scored 412 to win the gold medal in the women's division. The U.S. won the silver medal with 405, and Italy the bronze with 386. T. Carlisle of the U.S. with a 190 was the individual winner.

Rifles. At the Championships of the Americas, the 300-m standard rifle event was won by the U.S. team, which fired a score of 1,676 to take the gold medal. Brazil placed second with 1,580, and Canada was third with 1,568. The individual gold medal was awarded to Robert Aylward of the U.S. for his 567 of a possible 600. The U.S. team won the gold medal for 300-m free rifle with its score of 3,413. Canada finished second with 3,227, and Brazil was third with 3,193. Aylward won the individual gold medal with 1,140.

The U.S. won the 50-m standard rifle contest with a 1,729 and the 50-m free rifle event with a 3,446. Lones Wigger of the U.S. took the individual gold medal with a 1,154. The 50-m running game matches were won by the U.S. team with 1,725. Colombia finished second with 1,714, and Guatemala third with 1,707. Mike English of the U.S. scored 581 to win the individual gold medal. In the air rifle events the Canadian team placed first with a 1,739, with the individual gold medal going to Canada's J. F. Senecal for his 587. The 10-m running game event was won by the U.S. with 1,100. The individual gold medal went to Randy Stewart of the U.S. for his 372.

France won over 21 other nations competing in the rifle events at the world air gun championships with a score of 1,752. Yugoslavia placed second with 1,746, while West Germany was third with 1,745. High individual score was 588 by Philippe Heberle of France.

Handguns. The U.S. won all team events for handguns at the Championships of the Americas. Individual gold medals were won by Donald Nygord of the U.S. in the standard pistol, free pistol, and air pistol. In the centrefire pistol Bernardo Tober of Colombia was the winner, and Mark Howkins of Canada took the individual gold medal in the rapid-fire pistol.

The Soviet Union won the air pistol event at the world air gun championships with a score of 1,726. France was second with 1,719, and the U.S. placed third with 1,710. R. Beutler of Switzerland fired a 580 for individual high score. The Soviet women's team also finished first with 1,130. Sweden was second with 1,127, and West Germany placed third with 1,114. Marlia Dobrantcheva of the Soviet Union won the individual gold medal with 384.

(ROBERT N. SEARS)

SHOW JUMPING

Great Britain, represented by Nick Skelton (on Everest St. James), John Whitaker (Hopscotch), Malcolm Pyrah (Towerlands Anglezarke), and Michael Whitaker (Warren Point) won the European show jumping team title at Dinard, France, during the first weekend in August. The team score for the gold medal was 21.56 penalty points; Switzerland won the silver with 42.08 and West Germany the bronze with 44.75. Paul Schockemöhle on Deister, his mighty Olympic Games and world champion, won his third consecutive individual European championship for West Germany with 15.06 faults. Heidi Robbiani of Switzerland, winner of the 1984 Olympic bronze medal, was second on Jessica V with 16.29, and John Whitaker took the bronze medal for Britain on Hopscotch with 17.71. At Copenhagen, West Germany's Reiner Klimke, on Ahlerich, added the European dressage championship to his Olympic gold medal, and West Germany won the dressage team championship.

The European three-day event championship took place at Burghley, England. The British team of Lucinda Green on her Australian-bred world champion Regal Realm, Virginia Holgate on Priceless, Lorna Clarke on Myross, and Ian Stark on Oxford Blue won the championship with 172.8 penalty points from France (353.8), West Germany (372.6), Ireland (685.2), and Poland (710.8). Virginia Holgate and Priceless, the only combination with no further penalties to add to their dressage score of 49, took the individual gold medal, and the silver went to Clarke on Myross, with 61.8. Hard on her heels was Stark on Oxford Blue with 62.   (PAMELA MACGREGOR-MORRIS)

SKIING

The worst weather and snow conditions for many decades early in the 1984–85 season failed to block the major contests. Spectator attendance understandably fell in December and early January but then rose to unprecedented heights in North America during March. Some 1,800 competitions were held worldwide in the Alpine and Nordic disciplines.

Alpine Racing. The 28th world championships, at Bormio, Italy, from January 31 to February 10, confirmed a distinct swing from extreme specialization to all-round ability. Thus, an outstanding technician, Pirmin Zurbriggen of Switzerland, won the 60th men's downhill and the combined downhill and slalom and finished second in the giant slalom—all within weeks of having undergone knee surgery.

Markus Wasmaier of West Germany, a noted down-

hiller, unexpectedly won the giant slalom title, foiling Zurbriggen's attempt at a hat trick of gold medals. Peter Müller, another Swiss, and Doug Lewis of the U.S. finished second and third in the downhill. Jonas Nilsson of Sweden won the slalom, followed by Austrian-born Marc Girardelli of Luxembourg and Robert Zoller of Austria. Girardelli took the bronze medal in the giant slalom, but though he was the top-seeded skier of the season, he failed to win a gold. Also denied a gold medal was one-time Swedish ace Ingemar Stenmark. Second and third to Zurbriggen in the combined event were an Austrian, Ernst Riedlsperger, and a Swiss, Thomas Bürgler.

Swiss racers won two of the four women's events. The Olympic gold medalist, Michela Figini, took the downhill with a convincing margin of 1.61 sec over her compatriot Ariane Ehrat and Katrin Gutensohn of Austria, who tied for second. The experienced Erika Hess, who had won three gold medals in 1982, took the combined event for Switzerland, ahead of Sylvia Eder of Austria and Tamara McKinney of the U.S. A Hess fall allowed Perrine Pelen and Christelle Guignard to gain the first and second slalom spots for France, followed by Paoletta Magoni of Italy. A surprise giant slalom winner was 17-year-old Diann Roffe of the U.S. Second-place Elisabeth Kirchler of Austria denied a U.S. clean sweep, with Eva Twardokens and Debbie Armstrong finishing third and fourth.

Thus, in the eight men's and women's events, Switzerland won four gold medals, and West Germany, Sweden, the U.S., and France took one apiece.

A greater test of consistency, the 19th Alpine World Cup series, concluded on March 24 at Heavenly Valley, Calif. The winners in the men's and women's divisions were Girardelli and Figini. Girardelli, helped by an injury to his rival, Zurbriggen, won the overall, slalom, and giant slalom titles, finishing first in seven slalom races during the series to equal the record set by Stenmark. Zurbriggen, the defending champion, was second in the overall standings, followed by Andreas Wenzel of Liechtenstein.

Figini took the women's overall and downhill titles and shared the giant slalom with Marina Kiehl of West Germany. Hess won the slalom and Brigitte Oertli took the combined to emphasize Swiss women's domination. Oertli was overall runner-up to Figini, with Maria Walliser finishing third to complete a Swiss clean sweep. The concurrently decided Nations Cup was retained by Switzerland, ahead of Austria and West Germany.

Nordic Events. Norway, the most successful nation in Nordic competition, took 5 of the 13 gold medals in the 35th world championships, at Seefeld, Austria, on January 18–27. Two cross-country superstars were Gunde Svan of

Two of the gold medalists at the world alpine racing championships in Bormio, Italy, were Diann Roffe (left) of the U.S., in the giant slalom, and Pirmin Zurbriggen (right) of Switzerland, in the combined, one of his two wins.

Sweden, winner of the 30 km and 50 km, and Anette Boe of Norway, the fastest woman in the 5 km and 10 km.

Kari Haerkoenen of Finland won the men's 15 km, and Norway took the team relay. Per Bergerud of Norway proved the outstanding jumper, winning the 90-m event and finishing third in the 70 m, which was won by Jens Weissflog of East Germany. The individual Nordic combination went to a West German, Hermann Weinbuch, who was also one of his country's victorious trio in the team event.

Grete Nykkelmo of Norway won a gold medal in the women's 20 km and also finished third over each of the distances won by Boe. In the team relay the U.S.S.R. outpaced the Norwegian runners-up despite the presence of Boe and Nykkelmo.

Svan retained the men's title in the sixth Nordic World Cup competition for cross-country racing, a series of events spanning four months. Tor-Haakon Holte was runner-up for Norway, with third place shared by Thomas Wassberg (Sweden) and Ove Robert Aunli (Norway). Boe captured the women's crown, with Nykkelmo and Britt Pettersen completing a Norwegian grand slam. The Nations Cup went to Norway, followed by Finland and Sweden.

The second World Cup in Nordic combination, linking cross-country and jumping, was gained by Geir Andersen of Norway. Weinbuch and Hubert Schwarz finished second and third for West Germany, and a Nations Cup for this competition went to Norway, with West Germany second and East Germany third.

In the world biathlon championships, combining cross-country skiing with rifle shooting, at Ruhpolding, West Germany, on February 14–17, Frank-Peter Rötsch of East Germany won the 10-km event from Erik Kvalfoss of Norway. Rötsch took the silver medal in the 20 km, which was won by Yury Kaschkarov of the Soviet Union. The team relay went to the U.S.S.R., with East Germany runner-up and West Germany third.   (HOWARD BASS)

SPELUNKING

During 1985 several of the world's longest caves were extended. The longest of all, the combined Mammoth Cave-Flint Ridge system in Kentucky, increased to 484.3 km (301 mi) when explorers followed up new leads. An unconfirmed rumour indicated yet another discovery there, resulting in a total length of more than 500 km (311 mi). The Optimisticheskaya gypsum cave in the U.S.S.R. had some 5 km (3 mi) added to its 153-km (95-mi) length, making it the second longest in the world. In the Swiss Hölloch there were new discoveries in the upper levels, but recomputation of the survey data for the cave as a whole reduced its overall length to 133 km (82.7 mi); this left it still in third place. Jewel Cave in South Dakota increased by a few kilometres to 114.3 km (71 mi) and so remained fourth, while Ozyornaya (U.S.S.R.) was fifth at 107.6 km (66.9 mi). Another Soviet cave, Zoluska, increased from some 60 km (37 mi) to 80 km (49.7 mi) and thus took seventh place, after Ojo Guareña in Spain (still 83 km; 50.3 mi).

Réseau Jean Bernard in France remained the world's deepest cave at 1,535 m (5,036 ft). In the U.S.S.R., Snezhnaya was said to have been explored to a new depth of 1,470 m (4,823 ft), a substantial increase but still leaving it in second place. The Franco-Spanish cave Pierre Saint-Martin (1,342 m; 4,403 ft) is joined to the Réseau d'Arphidia, giving a total depth of about 1,570 m (5,151 ft); however, because the connection is impassable by humans, the larger figure did not constitute a depth record and the cave remained only the third deepest. The deepest cave in the Southern Hemisphere, Nettlebed in New Zealand, was extended to 687 m (2,254 ft) in the course of a five-day exploration by Australians and New Zealanders.

British reconnaissance expeditions went to the Indonesian islands of Sumba and Irian Jaya. An Anglo-Australian team in Java mapped 20 km (12.4 mi) of cave passage in 20 days, including 11.3 km (7 mi) in Luweng Jaran, the longest cave yet known in Indonesia. A French expedition on the island of New Britain explored 8.5 km (5.3 mi) of new caves there. In Britain an above-water connecting passage between Peak Cavern and Speedwell in Derbyshire, sought for at least 80 years, was found. The combined length of the two caves was 10.3 km (6.4 mi). Of particular interest were some unusual caves explored by French and Icelandic spelunkers in Iceland. They had been formed beneath glaciers by streams of geothermal water, sometimes as hot as 95° F (35° C), which had cut into the rock below while leaving the cave roof of glacier ice. One of these caves was 2.9 km (1.8 mi) long.   (T. R. SHAW)

SQUASH RACKETS

In November 1985 the men's world individual and team championships were held in Cairo. Jahangir Khan of Pakistan won his fifth World Open title, and in the team event played between three men from each country, Pakistan beat England in the semifinal and then defeated New Zealand 2–1 to retain the championship. Runner-up New Zealand beat Australia 2–1 in their semifinal. During the year Khan also won the French and British Open titles.

In the 1985 British Open finals, a revolutionary new squash ball was used for the first time. The development involved drilling a large number of small holes in the ball and filling the base of the holes with a retroreflective chemical. Lights lined up close to the television cameras sent beams that were reflected to produce a glowing, highly vis-

Jahangir Khan, scion of a Pakistani family long dominant in squash competition around the world, scores a point against Steve Bowditch on his way to his second consecutive North American (softball) championship in New York City in April.

ible ball; while there was no visible effect for the spectators at the site, television viewers could now follow the games far more satisfactorily. In November the English championships became the first national tournament in the world to be played on a fully transparent Perspex squash court.

In women's competition Susan Devoy from New Zealand won her second British Open title in April following her surprising defeat by Lucy Soutter of England in the final of the Women's Masters challenge in Warrington, England. In the British Open final Devoy beat Martine Le Moignan from Guernsey 9–6, 5–9, 9–6, 9–5. Le Moignan had won the British title in December 1984.

The 1985 women's world championships were held in Dublin in August. In the junior events Soutter won the world individual championship, beating Sarah Fitzgerald of Australia; in the team event Soutter again beat Fitzgerald, but Australia won 2–1 overall. In the senior competition Devoy again triumphed, beating another Guernsey player, Lisa Opie, in the final; England beat New Zealand 2–1 for the team championship. The England women had retained their European team title in Barcelona, Spain, in April, as had England's men.　　　　(ANDREW SHELLEY)

SURFING

The 1984–85 competition for the championship of the Association of Surfing Professionals concluded with the Bells Beach Rip Curl in Australia. Tom Carroll of Australia defeated South Africa's Shaun Tomson to retain the world crown. Mark Occhilupo of Australia finished third. In the women's division Frieda Zamba of Florida finished first, followed by Kim Mearig of the U.S. and Pam Burridge of Australia.

Interest in surfing in Australia appeared to be at an all-time high, as athletes from that nation won 9 of the top 16 places in the professional competition. Of a total of 19 professional events, Australia scheduled 7 and raised almost one-third of the total prize money.

The 1985–86 season was marred by the boycott of the South African contests by Carroll, Tom Curren of the U.S., and Martin Potter of Great Britain. As a result of his lack of participation in those events, Carroll dropped from first position to seventh in the world standings.

(JACK C. FLANAGAN)

SWIMMING

Competitive swimming in the year after the 1984 Olympic Games marked time, with many of the leading athletes pointing toward the world championships in 1986 at Madrid, when all of the swimming powers would meet head-on for the first time since 1982. The expected decline in the number of new world records emphasized the general mediocrity of competition on the world scene as most of the U.S. Olympic medalists retired and many of the European world record holders took a year's break from heavy training.

The first world record of 1985 was not set at any of the three major international tournaments but was established in the annual dual meet between the Soviet Union and East Germany at Erfurt, East Germany. There on March 3 Igor Polianskiy of the Soviet Union lowered the 200-m backstroke record from 1 min 58.41 sec to 1 min 58.14 sec. At the East German national championship competition in June at Leipzig, Silke Hoerner lowered the world-record 200-m breaststroke set in 1979 from 2 min 28.36 sec to 2 min 28.33 sec. This was the only world record set by women in 1985.

West Germany's Michael Gross, winner of two gold medals in world-record time at the 1984 Olympics, shaved

0.52 sec off the world mark of 3 min 48.32 sec to 3 min 47.80 sec in the 400-m freestyle at the West German championships at Remscheid on June 27. Two days later he regained the 200-m butterfly world record, slicing 0.03 sec from the old mark for a time of 1 min 57.01 sec. On August 10 in the XVII European Championships at Sofia, Bulg., Gross again lowered the 200-m butterfly mark by 0.36 sec with a time of 1 min 56.65 sec, thereby equaling Mark Spitz's feat of holding four world records at the same time.

Matt Biondi, a junior at the University of California, in only his third year of major swimming competition, lowered the 100-m freestyle world record of 49.36 sec set by Olympic champion Rowdy Gaines in 1981. Biondi's 49.24 sec was set in a preliminary of the 1985 U.S. swimming long course championships at Mission Viejo, Calif., August 6. In the final Biondi set a new record of 48.95 sec.

With the exception of Biondi's outstanding performance, lacklustre swims were the rule in almost every male event in the U.S. championships. In the women's competition this was even more evident. Mary T. Meagher, an Olympic champion, was the only woman to have a better time than the Germans, achieving this in the butterfly. Mark Schubert coached his Mission Viejo Nadadores to the women's team and combined team championships, making him the most successful coach in U.S. swim history.

Two world records were set by the U.S. men's national team in the Pan Pacific meet, held in August at Tokyo. On August 17 the quartet of Scott McCadam, Mike Heath, Paul Wallace, and Biondi were timed at 3 min 17.08 sec for the 4 × 100-m freestyle relay, taking nearly two seconds off the previous mark set in 1984. A day later the team of Rick Carey, John Moffet, Pablo Morales, and Biondi took 1.02 seconds off the 4 × 100-m medley relay with a time of 3 min 38.28 sec.

The XVII European Championships, held at Sofia in August, was marked by the absence of Soviet champion Vladimir Salnikov, holder of three world records. East Germany dominated the women's events, winning 14 out of 15. However, it was the first time since 1977 that East Germany had lost a gold medal, as Bulgaria's Tania Bogomilova won the 200-m breaststroke. Heike Friedrich was the outstanding competitor at the meet, winning the 100-m and 200-m freestyle events and swimming on three winning relays. The East German women also won ten silver and three bronze medals.

In the men's European competition, Igor Polianskiy of the U.S.S.R. won both the 100-m and 200-m backstroke races, setting a European record of 55.24 sec for the shorter event. Michael Gross was the outstanding male competitor, winning six gold medals: the 200-m freestyle, 100-m and 200-m butterfly, and three relays. This effort contributed

Michael Gross of West Germany strokes to a victory and a new world record in the 200-metre butterfly at the West German championship meet in Remscheid in June. Earlier Gross had shaved more than half a second from the world 400-metre freestyle record.

Matt Biondi of California wins the 100-metre freestyle event in the Pan Pacific swimming championship in Tokyo in August. A few days earlier he had set two successive world marks in that event at the U.S. swimming long course meet at Mission Viejo, California.
AP/WIDE WORLD

to West Germany's medal count of six gold, two silver, and three bronze. East Germany was runner-up with two gold, six silver, and two bronze medals. For the first time since 1970 France won a gold medal as Stephan Caron took the 100-m freestyle.

At the Pan Pacific meet, out of 16 events U.S. men won 12 gold, 6 silver, and 5 bronze medals, outdistancing Australia with 2 gold, 5 silver, and 5 bronze. Matt Biondi paced the Americans with five gold medals, one silver, and one bronze, winning the 50-m and 100-m freestyle and anchoring three winning relays. The U.S. women surpassed the men, winning 13 gold, 8 silver, and 4 bronze medals. Canada was their nearest rival, with two golds, one silver, and five bronze. Olympic 100-m champion Carrie Steinseifer of the U.S. was the outstanding female, winning a gold medal in the 200-m freestyle, a silver in the 100-m freestyle, and golds in two relays. A U.S. record was set in the 4 × 200-m freestyle relay as Mary Wayte, Trina Radke, Laura Walker, and Steinseifer were timed in 8 min 6.74 sec, taking 0.57 second off the previous time.

Diving. The Federation Internationale de Natation Amateur (FINA), the world governing organization for amateur aquatics, conducted the IV World Cup diving championships, held in April at Shanghai. The event attracted 67 divers representing 14 nations, competing as teams and in individual events. The overall team trophy was captured by the host nation, China, with a total of 4,334.07 points. The Soviet Union, scoring 3,983.01, was second, and the United States finished third with 3,942.09. The women's team trophy and men's team trophy were each won by China, followed by the U.S.S.R. and the U.S. In the women's 3-m springboard the winner was Li Yihua of China, followed by teammate Li Qiaoxian. Brita Baldus of East Germany finished third. Michele Mitchell of the U.S. defeated Chen Xiaoxia of China to win the platform competition; Alla Lobankina of the U.S.S.R. was third. In the men's 3-m springboard Tan Liangde of China defeated Mark Bradshaw of the U.S., with Ron Meyer of the U.S. third. Tong Hui of China won the platform by only 0.78 points over Vyacheslav Troshin of the U.S.S.R., giving China three of the four gold medals. Third place in the platform went to Li Kongzheng of China.

At the McDonald's International Diving Invitational, at Fort Lauderdale, Fla., in May, Li Yihua again won the women's 3-m springboard event, followed by the U.S. pair of Kelly McCormick and Michele Mitchell. Mitchell won the platform, upsetting Chen Xiaoxia, with Veronica Ribot

of Argentina third. Tan Liangde won his second international men's 3-m springboard, outpointing Niki Stajkovic of Austria and Ron Meyer. Li Kongzheng defeated Tong Hui in the platform with Bruce Kimball of the U.S. placing third.

Following the McDonald's meet, the U.S. defeated China in a dual competition at Orlando, Fla., in May. McCormick and Mitchell won the women's 3-m springboard and platform, respectively. Tan Liangde and Li Kongzheng won the men's 3-m springboard and platform for China.

At Clayton, Mo., in August at the U.S. outdoor diving championships, McCormick won the 3-m springboard and Mitchell the platform. Greg Louganis, who did not compete in the international tournaments because of a shoulder injury, continued his unbeaten season by winning both the 3-m springboard and platform.

The Soviet Union dominated the European championships, winning three of the four contests. Zhanna Tsirulnikova won the women's 3-m springboard, followed by teammate Irina Sidorava, with Heidemarie Grecka of Czechoslovakia third. Anjela Stasyulevi of the U.S.S.R. outpointed Ramona Patow-Wenzel of East Germany for a Soviet victory in the women's platform. Alla Lobankina of the U.S.S.R. placed third. In men's diving Nikolay Drozhzhin of the U.S.S.R. won the 3-m springboard, with Bulgaria's Peter Georgiev and West Germany's Dieter Doerr placing second and third. Thomas Kunths of East Germany prevented a Soviet sweep by diving off the platform with enough consistency to outpoint Albin Killat of West Germany and Domenico Rinaldi of Italy.

Synchronized Swimming. At the U.S. championships, held in Fort Lauderdale, Fla., from June 30 to July 7, Sarah Josephson of Ohio State University won the solo event, scoring 145.858 points. Mary Visniski of Walnut Creek, Calif., barely outpointed Karen Josephson of Ohio State University 139.550 to 138.333 for the silver medal. The Josephson sisters won the duet title with 140.296 points, followed by Kristen Babb and Michelle Svitenko of Walnut Creek, Calif., with 134.787. Alice and Margarita Smith of the University of Arizona were third with 134.775. Walnut Creek won the team crown with 138.679 points, followed by Ohio State with 137.541 and Santa Clara, Calif., with 135.872.

The II FINA World Cup at Indianapolis, Ind., on August 23–25, attracted 90 athletes from nine countries. Canada swept all three titles; Carolyn Waldo of Montreal was almost perfect in her solo routine, receiving five scores of 9.9 out of a possible 10; after winning that title she then paired with Michelle Cameron to win the duet. Canada edged the United States for the team victory 189.900 to 187.717, with Japan third at 184.723. Winners at the European championships were Carolyn Wilson of Great Britain in solo competition, Alexandra Worisch and Eva-Marie Edinger of Austria in the duet, and France as the team champion.   (ALBERT SCHOENFIELD)

TABLE TENNIS

The biennial world championships got under way in Göteborg, Sweden, at the end of March with 66 men's and 55 women's associations participating in the competition. China retained possession of both the Swaythling and Marcel Corbillon cups, which are awarded to the men's and women's team champions. Sweden's men's team once again finished second, ahead of Poland, Japan, North Korea, Yugoslavia, Czechoslovakia, and France. In the women's team standings, North Korea was runner-up, followed by South Korea, The Netherlands, the U.S.S.R., Hungary, Japan, and Czechoslovakia.

1985 World Rankings

MEN	WOMEN
1. Jiang Jialiang (China)	1. Cao Yanhua (China)
2. Chen Longcan (China)	2. Geng Lijuan (China)
3. Xie Saike (China)	3. Dai Lili (China)
4. Wang Huiyuan (China)	4. Qi Baoxiang (China)
5. Teng Yi (China)	5. Tong Ling (China)
6. Andrzej Grubba (Poland)	6. Ni Xialian (China)
7. Lo Chuen Tsung (Hong Kong)	7. Jiao Zhimin (China)
8. Chen Xinhua (China)	8. Bettine Vriesekoop (Neth.)
9. Mikael Appelgren (Sweden)	9. Yang Young Ja (South Korea)
10. Jan-Ove Waldner (Sweden)	10. Marie Hrachova (Czechoslovakia)

Chinese athletes also won four of the five individual world titles, losing only the men's doubles. In that event the Swedish team of Mikael Appelgren and Uls Carlsson defeated Jindrich Pansky and Milan Orlowski of Czechoslovakia in two straight sets. In other individual competitions, Jiang Jialiang was crowned men's singles champion after defeating his fellow countryman Chen Longcan. The women's singles final, which also featured two Chinese, was won by Cao Yanhua, who needed four sets to defeat Geng Lijuan. In the women's doubles, Dai Lili and Geng Lijuan defeated Cao Yanhua and Ni Xialian in two sets. The mixed doubles title was taken by Cai Zhenhua and Cao Yanhua, who dropped the first set but took the next two to triumph over Pansky and Marie Hrachova of Czechoslovakia.

During the tournament the Congress of the International Table Tennis Federation admitted Guinea, Gabon, and Chinese Taipei to full membership, bringing the total number of affiliated associations to 126. Options to organize future world championships were granted to India (1987) and West Germany (1989). The Congress ruled that only red and black could be used on a racket's surfaces.

In early February the European top 12 players tournament was held in Barcelona, Spain. After the men's competition, Andrzej Grubba (Poland) was ranked number one. Next in order were Pansky, Appelgren, J. Secretin (France), J.-O. Waldner (Sweden), and D. Douglas (England). Bettine Vriesekoop (Neth.) was ranked first among the women players. Next in order were Z. Olah (Hungary), Hrachova, O. Nemes (West Germany), and F. Bulatova (U.S.S.R.).

The European League winners for 1984–85 were Sweden in the Super Division, France in Division 1, and Bulgaria in Division 2.

The sixth World Cup competition, featuring 16 of the top men players in the world, was held in Foshan, China, in late August. In the final rankings, Chen Xinhua (China) was first, Grubba second, Jiang Jialiang third, Chen Longcan fourth, and Lo Chuen Tsung (Hong Kong) fifth.

(ARTHUR KINGSLEY VINT)

TENNIS

Dominance in men's tennis in 1985 shifted from the U.S. to Europe. In the three leading championships, those of France, Wimbledon (England), and the U.S., the only men's title exclusively won by Americans was the U.S. doubles. In singles a Swede, Mats Wilander, won the French title; a West German, Boris Becker (*see* BIOGRAPHIES), won at Wimbledon; and a native of Czechoslovakia, Ivan Lendl, won the U.S. In addition, West Germany beat the U.S. in the second round of the Davis Cup. Spectator interest increased at the main events. Total paid attendance at the U.S. Open in New York City was a record 409,455.

Sponsorship was maintained at a high level, and earnings of leading players grew with the increased prize money. For the French Open total prize money was F 10,523,650, for Wimbledon £1,934,760, and for the U.S. Open $3,073,500. Sponsorship of the two world's team championships, the men's Davis Cup and the women's Federation Cup, was maintained by the Japanese corporation NEC. A U.S. corporation, Nabisco, replaced Volvo of Sweden as sponsor of the men's Grand Prix, a worldwide series for individual competition throughout the year.

Concern about possible adverse effects of intensive play at too young an age resulted in restrictions in the rules of the respective Men's and Women's International Professional Tennis councils. In Grand Prix events all boys under 14 were made ineligible; those aged 14 were restricted to 8 tournaments in a year and the 15-year-olds to 12. Girls under 15 were limited to 10 international series tournaments in a year; those aged 15 to 16 could play only 12; and all girls under 16 were limited to three successive tournaments and had to take at least two rest periods of 30 days. No minimum age limit was imposed.

The Wimbledon championships produced the youngest men's singles champion of all time. Becker was 17 years 227 days old; the previous youngest winner was Wilfred Baddeley of Great Britain, who in 1891 was 19 years 175 days old—nor was any men's singles champion of France or the U.S. younger.

Unacceptable court behaviour caused problems throughout the year. Following the defeat of the U.S. by Sweden in the Davis Cup final in Göteborg in 1984, the U.S. Tennis Association took the unprecedented step of requiring its players to sign an agreement to conform to a code of good sportsmanship. Neither John McEnroe nor Jimmy Connors signed, and they were not selected for the 1985 Davis Cup team. In September Connors was suspended from Grand Prix competition for 42 days; it was an automatic suspension when fines for violations of the code of conduct totaled $7,500. McEnroe was asked to resign his honorary membership in Queen's Club, London, after complaints about his language.

Men's Competition. McEnroe was again named as "world champion" by the International Tennis Federation (ITF). He ended 1984 as leader of the Grand Prix series and earned the top bonus of $600,000. The last major tournament of the season, the Australian championships in Melbourne in December 1984, was won by Wilander. He beat Kevin Curren (South African-born, naturalized U.S.) 6–7, 6–4, 7–6, 6–2 in the final.

McEnroe won the Grand Prix Masters' event in Madison Square Garden, New York City, in January. He defeated Wilander 6–1, 6–1 in the semifinals and Lendl 7–5, 6–0, 6–4 in the final. McEnroe's form subsequently declined. In the finals of a tournament in Dallas, Texas, in April, the

D. FINEMAN—SYGMA

Boris Becker of West Germany makes a characteristic lunge for the ball on his way to his stunning victory at Wimbledon in July. He was the first West German, the first unseeded player, and the youngest man ever to the win the title.

The usually composed Hana Mandlikova of Czechoslovakia allows herself a brief expression of satisfaction after defeating former compatriot Martina Navratilova for the U.S. Open championship at Flushing Meadow, New York, in September.

TREVOR JONES—ALL SPORT/WOODFIN CAMP & ASSOCIATES

most important of World Championship Tennis (WCT) events and, in 1985, part of the Grand Prix series, Joakim Nyström (Sweden) beat McEnroe in the opening round. In the final Lendl defeated Tim Mayotte (U.S.) 7–6, 6–4, 6–1. In another WCT event, the Tournament of Champions at Forest Hills, N.Y., in May, Lendl defeated McEnroe 6–3, 6–3 in the final. Wilander won the French championship for the second time, defeating McEnroe 6–1, 7–5, 7–5 in the semifinal and Lendl 3–6, 6–4, 6–2, 6–2 in the final.

Wimbledon had not only its youngest but, uniquely, an unseeded winner in Becker. That the West German was unseeded was due to the logic of the computer ranking list rather than the sharp form he had revealed two weeks earlier when he won the Queen's Club, London, tournament. Even so his victory at Wimbledon was unexpected. There were many other surprises at Wimbledon. Wilander lost in the first round to Slobodan Zivojinovic (Yugos.), and Henri Leconte (France) beat Lendl 3–6, 6–4, 6–3, 6–1 in the fourth round. Curren beat McEnroe 6–2, 6–2, 6–4 in the quarterfinals. Becker beat Nyström, seeded seventh, by 3–6, 7–6, 6–1, 4–6, 9–7 in round three and Mayotte by 6–3, 4–6, 6–7, 7–6, 6–2 in the fourth. He was a winner in four sets in the later rounds, 7–6, 3–6, 6–3, 6–4 in the quarterfinal against Leconte, 2–6, 7–6, 6–3, 6–3 against fifth-seeded Anders Jarryd (Sweden) in the semifinal, and 6–3, 6–7, 7–6, 6–4 in the final against Curren, the eighth seed. Becker's total loss of eight sets in the tournament was equaled only by Ted Schroeder (U.S.) in 1949.

Becker did not rise to the same heights in the U.S. Open at the National Tennis Center in Flushing Meadow, New York City, in September. Nyström beat him 6–3, 6–4, 4–6, 6–4 in the fourth round. McEnroe in turn defeated Nyström 6–1, 6–0, 7–5 and then triumphed over Wilander 3–6, 6–4, 6–3, 6–3 in the semifinals. Lendl defeated

Connors 6–2, 6–3, 7–5 in the other semifinal and won his first U.S. Open by beating McEnroe 7–6, 6–3, 6–4 in the final. No pair dominated doubles. The outstanding pair, Peter Fleming (U.S.) and McEnroe, won the Masters' tournament in January 1985 for the seventh consecutive year but later split. The Australian title for 1984 went to Mark Edmondson (Australia) and Sherwood Stewart (U.S.), and Edmondson also won the French title with Kim Warwick (Australia). Heinz Günthardt (Switz.) and Balazs Taroczy (Hung.) won the Wimbledon championship. The U.S. title was taken by Ken Flach and Robert Seguso (both U.S.).

The World Team Cup, with eight nations qualifying by the world ranking of their players, was staged for the eighth time in Düsseldorf, West Germany, in May. In the final the U.S. (McEnroe, Connors, Flach, Seguso) beat Czechoslovakia (Lendl, Miroslav Mecir, Tomas Smid) 2–1 to win for the third time.

The Davis Cup attracted an entry of 62 nations. The four zonal sections were won by Denmark, Great Britain, Mexico, and New Zealand; as a result of their victories each of those nations gained promotion to the World Group for 1986. In the World Group of 16 nations, Japan, Argentina, France, and Chile lost in the first round and the subsequent play-off and so were relegated to the zonal sections for 1986. The most notable casualty was France, which first lost to Paraguay 3–2 in Asunción and then to Yugoslavia 4–1 in Belgrade. Surprising, too, was the defeat of the U.S. in the second round. Without its best singles players the U.S. (Eliot Teltscher, Aaron Krickstein, Flach, Seguso) beat Japan 5–0. In the second round, however, West Germany (Becker, Hans Schwaier, Andreas Maurer) beat the U.S. 3–2 in Hamburg. Becker's powerful play then helped West Germany defeat Czechoslovakia, with Lendl able to play only in doubles, 5–0 in Frankfurt.

The defending champion, Sweden (Wilander, Jarryd, Stefan Edberg, Henrik Sundström), beat Chile 4–1 in Santiago, India 3–0 at Bangalore, and Australia 5–0 in Malmö to reach the final against West Germany. It marked the fourth time that Sweden had reached the final round. West Germany's only previous appearance was in 1970. In the final round Sweden successfully defended its championship by defeating West Germany 3–2. With the two nations tied 2–2, Edberg defeated West Germany's Michael Westphal in the final singles match 3–6, 7–5, 6–4, 6–3.

Women's Competition. Martina Navratilova (Czechoslovakian-born, naturalized U.S.) was again the outstanding player but by a less wide margin. She was declared "world champion" for the fourth time. After success in six straight "Grand Slam" (Wimbledon, French, U.S., and Australian championships) singles titles, she lost in the Australian semifinals in December 1984. Helena Sukova (Czech.) defeated her 1–6, 6–3, 7–5. Chris Evert Lloyd (U.S.) then beat Sukova 6–7, 6–1, 6–3 to win the title for the second time.

Navratilova won the Virginia Slims series, which ended in March, and won a bonus of $185,000 for her triumphs in singles and doubles. In the concluding tournament at Madison Square Garden, she won the final 6–3, 7–5, 6–4 against Sukova. Evert Lloyd won the West German championship in Berlin, defeating a young West German, Steffi Graf, in the final. Evert Lloyd's greatest triumph came in the French Open, where she ended a long series of losses to Navratilova by defeating her 6–3, 6–7, 7–5 in an exhilarating final. It was Evert Lloyd's sixth French title win. At Wimbledon, however, Navratilova reasserted her dominance. She defeated Evert Lloyd 4–6, 6–3, 6–2 in the final for her sixth singles championship in that tournament.

The U.S. Open at Flushing Meadow had a more surprising victor. With disciplined, brilliant strokes, Hana

Mandlikova (Czech.) beat Evert Lloyd 4–6, 6–2, 6–3 in the semifinals and Navratilova 7–6, 1–6, 7–6 in the final. As a youngster in Prague, Mandlikova had been a ball boy for Navratilova before the latter became a U.S. citizen.

Navratilova was also less dominant in doubles. She and Pam Shriver (U.S.) retained only the Australian and French titles. In winning the French doubles in June, they gained their eighth successive Grand Slam crown. At Wimbledon Kathy Jordan (U.S.) and Elizabeth Smylie (Australia) defeated them 5–7, 6–3, 6–4 in the final. In the U.S. Open final Claudia Kohde-Kilsch (West Germany) and Sukova beat them 6–7, 6–2, 6–3.

Navratilova expanded her activities by competing in mixed doubles. She won at Wimbledon with Paul Mc-Namee (Australia). Because of rain they played the last three rounds in one day. They won the semifinal 6–7, 7–5, 23–21 against Scott Davis (U.S.) and Betsy Nagelsen (U.S.), the longest mixed doubles ever staged at Wimbledon, and played a total of 117 games in the seven sets. Navratilova also won the mixed doubles in the U.S. Open with Heinz Günthardt (Switz.).

The Federation Cup, the women's world team championship, was held in Nagoya, Japan, in October with an entry of 38 countries. Czechoslovakia (Mandlikova, Sukova, Andrea Holikova, Regina Marsikova) beat the U.S. (Kathy Jordan, Elise Burgin) 2–1 in the final to win the title for the third straight year and the fourth time in all.

The U.S. beat Great Britain 7–0 at Williamsburg, Va., for the Wightman Cup. It was the 47th win in 57 contests for the U.S. (Evert Lloyd, Shriver, Kathy Rinaldi, Betsy Nagelsen, Anne White). Great Britain (Annabel Croft, Jo Durie, Ann Hobbs, Virginia Wade) last won in 1978.

(LANCE TINGAY)

TOBOGGANING

Michael Walter gained the men's title in the world luge championships at Oberhof, East Germany, on January 26–27, leading a clean sweep for the host nation. His aggregate time for the four runs was more than half a minute better than that of the runner-up, Jörg Hoffmann, who was separated by only one one-hundredth of a second from the third man, Jens Müller.

Steffi Martin retained the women's title in another East German grand slam, completed by runner-up Bettina Schmidt and third-place Ute Weiss. The three women repeated the order of their finish in the 1984 Winter Olympics.

Hoffmann won the two-seater event with Jochen Pietzsch, followed by their compatriots Rene Keller and Lutz Kühnlenz. An East German medals monopoly was prevented only by Vitali Meinik and Dmitry Alekseev, who took the bronze for the U.S.S.R.

The centenary of the Cresta Run for skeleton tobogganing at St. Moritz, Switz., was celebrated by a week of festivities that ended on February 10 with the 76th and fastest-ever Grand National, contested by specially invited riders. The championship was retained by the previous year's winner, Franco Gansser of Switzerland, whose six runs included the season's fastest descent in 52.54 sec, just 0.79 sec slower than the track record he had set in 1984. Finishing second was Urs Nater and third was Patrick Latscha, both also of Switzerland. (HOWARD BASS)

TRACK AND FIELD SPORTS

Three new worldwide competitions graced the 1985 track and field season. Added to the schedule of the worldwide governing body, the International Amateur Athletic Federation, were the first World Indoor Games, World Cup

Steve Cram of Great Britain edges Said Aouita of Morocco by just 0.04 second in the 1,500-metre race in Nice, France, on July 16 and sets a new world record in doing so. By the end of the 1985 season, each man held two world records.
THE ASSOCIATED PRESS LIMITED

marathon, and the Grand Prix invitational circuit. All were pronounced successes by the IAAF and were to be scheduled regularly, with the indoor meet becoming an official world indoor championship in 1987.

Men's International Competition. Two young but experienced middle-distance runners provided much of the excitement during the year as they competed against each other and the clock with equal vigour. They were Steve Cram of Great Britain, the 1983 world champion at 1,500 m, and Said Aouita of Morocco, the 1984 Olympic champion at 5,000 m. Born just 19 days apart in late 1960, the pair accounted for five world records in four events and for near misses at two other distances.

The stage was set early in the European season when the two clashed at 1,500 m on July 16 at Nice, France. Both smashed Steve Ovett's two-year-old world record, with Cram hanging on for the win in 3 min 29.67 sec and Aouita just 0.04 sec behind. Both claimed a world record 11 days later in separate events at Oslo. Cram took away the one-mile record of Britain's Sebastian Coe, the improvement again being more than a second as Cram clocked 3 min 46.32 sec. It was the first loss for Coe in a record-breaking race; previously he had won nine contests in world best time. The Oslo track also was kind to Aouita as he claimed his first world record. He covered 5,000 m in 13 min 00.40 sec, bettering David Moorcroft's three-year-old mark, made on the same track, by the narrowest possible margin, 0.01 sec.

Cram and Aouita then went their separate ways but remained aware of each other as each continued to seek additional triumphs. The Briton was the first to score as he added the less frequently run 2,000-m mark to his collection. At Budapest, Hung., on August 4, Cram ran the 2,000 m in 4 min 51.39 sec, surpassing John Walker's nine-year-old record by 0.01 sec. Just five days later, at Gateshead, England, Cram narrowly failed to collect his fourth world record in 24 days. He ran 1,000 m in 2 min 12.85 sec,

Valerie Brisco-Hooks crosses the finish line of the women's 400-metre race at the Dallas Times Herald Invitational track meet in February with a new U.S. indoor record of 52.99 seconds, a full 0.3 second faster than the previous mark.

AP/WIDE WORLD

missing Coe's mark of 2 min 12.18 sec while running the second fastest time ever. This, however, marked the end of fast racing for Cram in 1985, as an injury did what no opponent was able to do.

The spotlight then shifted to Aouita, who made clear his determination to hold all world records from 1,500 m to 5,000 m. He first went after Cram's new mile mark. He barely missed it on August 21 at Zurich, Switz., running 3 min 46.92 sec; this was 0.61 sec short of Cram but the second best time ever recorded. At West Berlin, two days later and reportedly suffering leg problems, Aouita earned his second world record by overtaking Cram's 1,500-m mark. Aouita covered the distance in 3 min 29.46 sec, 0.21 sec faster than Cram. Next Aouita turned his attention to the 3,000-m record of 7 min 32.1 sec. At Brussels on August 30 he missed by less than a second, and his 7-min 32.94-sec time was the third fastest ever. Hurting badly, Aouita missed Cram's new 2,000-m record by a substantial margin in September, but his 4 min 54.02 sec still was the fourth fastest ever.

As the season neared its end, Cram was left with world records in the mile and 2,000 m and the second best performances in history in the 1,000 m and 1,500 m. Aouita also had two world marks, in the 1,500 m and 5,000 m. His mile time was the second best ever, his 3,000-m mark the third best, and his 2,000-m time the fourth.

The two rivals thus accounted for 5 of the 11 male world records for 1985. In other action, three of the four jumping records were bettered, along with the marathon, 30-km walk, and shot put. Maurizio Damilano of Italy set a new mark for the 30-km walk of 2 hr 6 min 27.3 sec.

Three of the five field-event records went to Soviet athletes. In the high jump little-known Rudolf Povarnitsin improved his personal pre-1985 best by 0.19 m (7½ in) when he jumped 2.40 m (7 ft 10½ in). This surprising record was achieved August 11 at Donyetsk, U.S.S.R., but Povarnitsin was destined to hold it for just 24 days. Then on September 4 Igor Paklin of the U.S.S.R. won the World University Games at Kobe, Japan, with a leap of 2.41 m (7 ft 10¾ in). The new pole vault mark was far from surprising, as it was made by Sergey Bubka, who had scored four world records in 1984. His 1985 feat took place on July 13 in Paris and broke a major barrier. It was the first 6-m (19-ft 8¼-in) vault ever.

There was considerable surprise surrounding the triple jump record. Willie Banks of the United States had fallen to sixth in the 1984 Olympics and, as he had reached the age of 29, there was considerable speculation that his prime had passed. The first intimation that this was not true came when Banks jumped 17.67 m (57 ft 11¾ in), the second best leap in history, on June 8. Just eight days later, in the U.S. national championships in Indianapolis, Ind., Banks astounded everyone by reaching 17.97 m (58 ft 11½ in). The lone throwing record of the year was set by East Germany's Ulf Timmermann, who put the shot 22.62 m (74 ft 2½ in) on September 22. This broke the previous mark by 0.40 m (15¾ in) and brought the amateur record to within 0.24 m (9½ in) of the all-time best made by professional Brian Oldfield in 1975.

The IAAF's Grand Prix program was a major step in freeing track and field athletes from restrictions on their ability to benefit financially from their sport. While still defined as an amateur, a track and field athlete was now allowed to earn cash prizes and endorsement fees as long as the money passed through a trust fund administered by the national governing body. Under the Grand Prix formula certain major invitational meetings participated in the awarding of a total of $542,000. Points were awarded for placings in the prescribed meets, and those with the most points at the end of the season won cash prizes. The highest scorer among the men was 5,000-m runner Doug Padilla of the United States, and he won $35,000. Distance runner Mary Decker Slaney of the U.S. was the women's leading money winner, also with $35,000.

The World Cup brought together at Canberra, Australia, eight national and regional teams. The 1985 winner of this quadrennial affair was the United States, while the best individual performance belonged to Ben Johnson of Canada. His 10.00 sec for 100 m was the fastest time ever for a race into a head wind.

The World Indoor Games in Paris was scheduled too early (January 18–19) for peak performances, but the interest shown by 75 competing countries spoke well for the first World Indoor Championships, to be held in 1987. World indoor best performances during the year (there were no officially recognized indoor world records) included two in the 400 m; the first was set by Thomas Schonlebe of East Germany (45.60 sec), and it was then broken by Todd Bennett of Great Britain (45.56 sec). Greg Foster of the United States lowered the 50-m hurdle best to 6.35 sec, and Timmermann put the shot 22.15 m (72 ft 8 in). The high jump best fell twice, Patrik Sjoberg of Sweden leaping 2.38 m (7 ft 9¾ in) and Dietmar Moegenburg of West Germany, the 1984 Olympic titlist, clearing 2.39 m (7 ft 10 in).

Two of the sport's brighter stars did not dominate their events in 1985 as they usually did. Hurdler Edwin Moses, two-time Olympic champion, missed the entire season because of injuries. And Carl Lewis, winner of four Olympic

gold medals in the 1984 Games, also had injury problems. He started the year in his usual manner, leading the world in both sprinting and long jumping. But an injury in mid-season kept him out of competition for more than a month, and when he did return he could not regain his usual form.

Women's International Competition. Winning the World Cup with a record score and accounting for half of the ten world records set during the year, the women of East Germany had an outstanding season. Furthermore, they accounted for all five of the world records set at recognized Olympic distances. Leading the way was veteran champion and record breaker Marita Koch. She climaxed her season on October 6 by regaining the 400-m record, which had been regarded as somewhat untouchable after Jarmila Kratochvilova of Czechoslovakia lowered the mark to 47.99 sec in 1983. Koch, however, ran the distance in 47.60 sec. And as a fitting climax to a season during which she also had come within 0.07 sec of her own 200-m world record of 21.71 sec, she ran a fast 47.9-sec leg on the winning 4 x 400-m relay team. The World Cup also produced an international record in the 4 x 100-m relay, the East German quartet of Sabine Rieger, Silke Gladisch, Ingrid Auerswald, and Marlies Gohr running 41.37 sec.

The East Germans also produced two world records in a September 22 meeting. Moving from the 400 m to the 400-m hurdles, Sabine Busch climaxed a successful debut in that event when she ran 53.56 sec. And in the long jump Heike Drechsler (Heike Daute when she won the world championships in 1983) leaped 7.44 m (24 ft 5 in). Petra Felke achieved two world javelin marks on June 4, throwing first 75.26 m (246 ft 11 in) and then 75.40 m (247 ft 4 in).

Also earning a record under a new married name was Mary Slaney of the United States, known as Mary Decker until 1985. She lowered the record in the mile, a non-Olympic event, to 4 min 16.71 sec. Zola Budd of Great Britain, who had collided with Decker in the 1984 Olympic 3,000 m, claimed a record in the 5,000 m, which was not scheduled for the Olympics. She ran the distance in 14 min 48.07 sec. Ingrid Kristiansen of Norway ran two world bests, but the 10,000 m had not yet been run in the Olympics, and no world records were recognized for the marathon. She ran the 10,000 m in 30 min 59.42 sec. In the infrequently contested 5,000-m walk, Maryanne Torrellas of the United States earned a record with her performance of 22 min 51.10 sec.

Indoors there were three world bests of note. Drechsler long jumped 6.99 m (22 ft 11¼ in) but lost the record two weeks later when Galina Chistyakova of the Soviet Union leaped 7.25 m (23 ft 9½ in). And Koch dashed 60 m in 7.04 sec.

U.S. Competition. U.S. men produced only one world record in 1985 but did achieve 16 national records in nine events. As with the world records, the U.S. successes were almost entirely in the middle distances and jumps. Sydney Maree led the way, establishing U.S. records in the 1,500-m, 2,000-m, and 5,000-m events. A former world record holder at 1,500 m, Maree lost his U.S. mark to Steve Scott but gained it back with a time of 3 min 29.77 sec, the third best time ever. He ran the 2,000 m in 4 min 54.20 sec, the fifth fastest ever, and pushed Aouita to the latter's record in the 5,000 m. In that race Maree was timed in 13 min 1.15 sec, a mark bettered only by two others.

Banks scored two U.S. bests in the triple jump. Two others broke U.S. standards twice or more. Jud Logan upped the hammer throw best four times, finally reaching 77.24 m (253 ft 5 in). And Joe Dial twice cleared heights never before attained by U.S. vaulters, leaping 5.83 m (19 ft 1½ in) and 5.85 m (19 ft 2¼ in). Two names were recorded in the U.S. high jump record book when Dennis Lewis tied the previous best with 2.34 m (7 ft 8 in) and Jim Howard then cleared 2.35 m (7 ft 8½ in). On the track Johnny Gray improved on his own 800-m national best, running 1 min 42.60 sec, and veteran Henry Marsh recorded a time of 8 min 9.17 sec in the steeplechase, the fifth fastest in history.

A dozen national records were earned by U.S. women. Slaney led the way with her world mile best and U.S. records in the 800 m (1 min 56.90 sec), the 3,000 m (8 min 29.69 sec and then 8 min 25.83 sec), and the 5,000 m (15 min 6.53 sec). Three new marks were set in the 400-m hurdles, Latanya Sheffield and Judi Brown-King each running 54.66 sec and then Brown-King completing the season with 54.38 sec. The long jump also produced three new bests, Carol Lewis leaping 7.01 m (23 ft) and 7.04 m (23 ft 1¼ in) only to see Jackie Joyner stretch out to 7.24 m (23 ft 9 in). Ramona Pagel completed the national record activity with a shot put of 19.13 m (62 ft 9¼ in).

U.S. indoor records went to Foster with 6.35 in the 50-m hurdles, Gray with 1 min 46.9 sec for 800 m, Padilla with 7 min 44.9 sec for 3,000 m and 8 min 15.3 sec for two miles, and Howard twice in the high jump with a best of 2.35 m (7 ft 8½ in). For the women Diane Dixon and three-time Olympic gold medalist Valerie Brisco-Hooks took turns breaking the 400-m mark, each doing it twice with Dixon finally bringing the time down to 52.20 sec. Lewis long jumped 6.78 m (22 ft 3 in).

The National Collegiate Athletic Association indoor and outdoor men's championships were won by Arkansas. For the women Florida State won the indoor team title and Oregon the outdoor championship.

Marathon Running and Cross Country. The first World Cup marathon ever to be held took place in Hiroshima, Japan, and resulted in very fast times. The surprising individual and team wins came from the African country of Djibouti, which never before had produced outstanding runners. Ahmed Salah won the race in 2 hr 8 min 9 sec, the second fastest time ever, and teamed with two countrymen to win the team title by more than 4½ minutes over Japan. The women's race, held a day earlier on April 13, was won by Katrin Dörre of East Germany in 2 hr 33 min 30 sec, and Italy was the winning team.

The men's world marathon best performance (there are no official world records inasmuch as conditions vary considerably from race to race) was achieved by 1984 Olympic Games marathon champion Carlos Lopes of Portugal. Running at Rotterdam, Neth., on April 20, Lopes took 53 seconds off the previous best time with a performance of 2 hr 7 min 12 sec. The former world's best, Steve Jones of Great Britain, made a brilliant effort to regain his record but lost by one second while winning at Chicago on October 20. And at London on April 21 the women's best time was lowered to 2 hr 21 min 6 sec by Kristiansen.

The men's world cross-country championship was won by Lopes, the defending champion, and the women's title went to Budd. Ethiopia won the men's team race for the fifth year in a row, defeating Kenya and the United States, while the U.S. women's team won its third consecutive championship. In college competition Wisconsin won both the men's and women's team title and also the individual men's race, which went to Tim Hacker. Suzie Tuffey of North Carolina State became the women's winner.

(BERT NELSON)

VOLLEYBALL

The year 1985 was a quiet one for volleyball, as it always is in the year after an Olympics. Dual matches between national teams, traditional tournaments under the auspices of the host nation, and the World Cup in November were highlights of the season.

The men's national teams of the United States, the Soviet Union, Brazil, and Cuba continued to occupy the top rungs of world rankings. The home team seemed to enjoy a slight advantage, as the U.S.S.R. defeated the U.S. at home to capture the eight-team Savvin Memorial Championship and the U.S. then returned the favour by winning the four-team USA Cup.

In women's competition China and Cuba, followed closely by the U.S.S.R. and Japan, were at the top of the world rankings. China remained unchallenged as number one, a position it had successfully defended for five years. Without any of the 1984 Olympians continuing to play on its national team, the U.S. for the first time in six years could not claim a position among the top five women's teams.

The 1985 World Cup was played once again in Japan. China successfully defended the women's title that it won in 1981 but received a strong challenge from the Cuban women, who finished second. The Soviets placed third, and Japan was fourth. Brazil, South Korea, Peru, and Tunisia rounded out the eight-team competition. For the Chinese women it was the fifth straight year at the top of the world list, starting with the 1981 World Cup and including the 1982 world championships and the 1984 Olympic Games title.

The 1985 men's World Cup confirmed the previous year's Olympic title for the U.S., which went through the eight-team tournament undefeated to finish two games ahead of second-place Soviet Union. Czechoslovakia finished third and Brazil fourth, with Argentina, Japan, South Korea, and Egypt rounding out the field. It was the first World Cup medal for the U.S. (ALBERT M. MONACO, JR.)

WATER POLO

Traditionally the year following the Olympic Games is one of rebuilding and experimentation for many national teams. With new coaches and players coming onto the scene, it is difficult to determine clear-cut favourites in many international tournaments. Such was the case in 1985, when as many as four teams could be said to be outstanding.

Perhaps the best team was the Soviet Union. Because the Soviets did not participate in the 1984 Olympics, they were not eligible for the 1985 Fédération Internationale de Natation Amateur (FINA) Cup, the premier event of the year. However, the Soviet Union won the European championships because of their record after tying with West Germany and Yugoslavia. Teams from the Soviet Union also won the world junior championships and the world university games.

Another of the top four teams was from Yugoslavia. The Olympic gold medalists did not do well in the FINA Cup, finishing fourth, but they placed second in the European championships. The Yugoslavians also finished second at the world university games and third at the world junior championships.

The winners of the FINA Cup, the West Germans, also were one of the top four. They were undefeated in the FINA Cup and placed third in the European championships. The best team outside of Europe was the United States, the Olympic silver medalists. They placed second in the FINA Cup, finishing the tournament with an exciting come-from-behind tie with the West Germans. The U.S. athletes also did well in the world university games, where they finished fourth. (WILLIAM ENSIGN FRADY)

WATER SKIING

Sammy Duvall of the United States and Karen Bowkett Neville of Australia won the overall titles in the 19th world water ski championships at Toulouse, France, in September. Although Duvall finished no better than sixth in any of the individual disciplines, he edged Karen's husband, Mick Neville, 2,736 to 2,726 for his third consecutive overall triumph in the biennial world meet.

Team honours again went to the U.S. skiers, who scored a total of 8,550 points, but the Nevilles and their Australian teammates were close behind with 8,375. Skiers from Great Britain and France finished third and fourth with 7,812 and 7,790 points, respectively.

Event winners among the men, with their two-round cumulative scores, were Bob Lapoint, U.S., slalom, 118½ buoys; Patrice Martin, France, tricks, 19,300 points; and Geoff Carrington, Australia, jumping, 112.60 m (369 ft). Gold medals among the women were won by Camille Duvall, U.S., slalom, 101 buoys; Judy McClintock, Canada, tricks, 13,730 points; and Deena Brush, U.S., jumping, 79.50 m (261 ft).

In the U.S. national championships Carl Roberge of Orlando, Fla., won the men's open overall title for the fourth time in five years, while his sister, Karin, became the women's overall champion. Carl also won the slalom with 62½ buoys. Cory Pickos of Eagle Lake, Fla., continued his mastery of the tricks event with 10,300 points. The men's jumping title went to Mike Morgan of Lake Wales, Fla., with a best leap of 55.51 m (182 ft). Event winners for women were Camille Duvall, Windermere, Fla., slalom, 55½ buoys; Tawn Larsen, Madison, Wis., tricks, 8,110 points; and Deena Brush, Fruitland Park, Fla., jumping, 40.87 m (134 ft).

Sammy Duvall also successfully defended his U.S. Masters overall title, and Deena Brush was the winner among the women. Andy Mapple of Great Britain won the men's slalom in the head-to-head finals of the new Masters format; Duvall won tricks; and Mike Hazelwood of Great Britain was first among the jumpers. Brush was the women's slalom winner. Kristie Overton of Greenville, N.C., was best in tricks, and Karen Morse of Great Britain won the jumping competition. (THOMAS C. HARDMAN)

WEIGHT LIFTING

Bulgaria succeeded the Soviet Union as the top weight-lifting nation at the 1985 world championships, held August 23–31 at Sodertalje, Sweden. The Bulgarians won six gold and three silver medals. The U.S.S.R. earned four gold, including a tie in the 90-kg (198-lb) class, and four silver medals. The other gold medal was won by Hungary.

The outstanding lifter was Naum Shalamanov of Bulgaria, who competed in the 60-kg (132-lb) class. In 1985 he set two of the three world records recorded. At the world championships he had a snatch lift of 143 kg (314.6 lb) and then improved his record to 145 kg (319.66 lb) in the World Cup on November 9.

The other world record in the world championships was credited to Aleksandr Varbanov of the U.S.S.R. with a clean and jerk of 210 kg (466.27 lb) as he won the 75-kg (165-lb) class. For the sixth time Yurik Vardanyan of the Soviet Union claimed a world title, this time in the 82.5-kg (181.5 lb) class.

In the team competition Bulgaria edged the Soviet Union

for top honours 439 to 425 points. The two leaders were trailed by Hungary, China, and East Germany.

Ten nations shared in the medals awarded for total lifts. After Bulgaria and the U.S.S.R. with nine and eight medals, respectively, Hungary had one gold and one bronze; China garnered one silver and two bronze; Czechoslovakia won one silver; Romania and Poland accounted for two bronze each; and Italy and West Germany each won a single bronze medal.　　　　　　　(CHARLES ROBERT PAUL, JR.)

WRESTLING

Wrestling. There were no surprises in the 1985 wrestling world championships. After the Soviet team boycotted the 1984 Olympic Games, they again proved in 1985 that they were the best in the world in both freestyle and Greco-Roman wrestling. The world freestyle championships were held in Budapest, Hung., from October 10 to 13. The Soviet Union placed first with 89 points, followed by Bulgaria with 63 points and the U.S. with 59 points. Five Soviet wrestlers won individual championships.

The Greco-Roman championships took place August 10 at Kolboth, Norway. The U.S.S.R. was again the winner, with 48 points, and Bulgaria placed second with 34 points. Each team had three individual champions. Romania was third with 30 points. (For a table of the winners of the world championships, see *Sporting Record,* below.)

Just as the U.S.S.R. dominated the world championships, the University of Iowa continued to reign supreme in the National Collegiate Athletic Association wrestling championships, held in Oklahoma City from March 8 to 10. Iowa scored 145¼ points for its eighth consecutive NCAA championship. The University of Oklahoma finished second with 98½ points, and Iowa State was third with 70.

(MARVIN G. HESS)

Sumo. The year in Japanese sumo wrestling was highlighted by the retirement of Kitanoumi, one of the greatest *yokozuna* (grand champions) of modern times; the powerful resurgence of *yokozuna* Chiyonofuji (*see* BIOGRAPHIES); and the continued decline of the third *yokozuna,* Takanosato. Other major events in 1985 included an official visit by sumo wrestlers to the United States highlighted by a three-day tourney in New York City's Madison Square Garden, the promotion of Onokuni and Kitao to the second-highest rank of *ozeki* (champion), Kotokaze's retirement after his knee injury and subsequent demotion from *ozeki,* and the opening of Tokyo's new national arena for sumo, the Ryogoku Kokugikan, in January.

Among other developments, former *yokozuna* Tochinishiki (currently chairman of the Japan Sumo Association) celebrated his 60th birthday by performing the traditional *kanreki dohyoiri* (60th-anniversary ring-entrance ceremony); two veteran *sekiwake* (junior champions), Fujizakura and Washuyama, retired; and a 2.1-m, 200-kg (6-ft 9-in, 440-lb) Canadian named John Tenta entered sumo. *Yokozuna* Chiyonofuji won four of the six annual 15-day tournaments (including all three held in Tokyo), while *ozeki* Hokutenyu and *ozeki* Asashio each won one.

In the Hatsu *basho* (New Year's tournament) in January, Chiyonofuji chalked up a perfect 15–0 record to win his 11th tourney title and his second *zensho yusho* (perfect tourney victory). After 6½ years in Makuuchi (the highest of sumo's six divisions), *ozeki* Asashio, 186-kg (410-lb) ex-college sumo champion, finally won his first *yusho* (tourney title) in the Haru *basho* (Spring tournament) in March in Osaka with a fine 13–2 record after having lost twice previously in play-offs.

Chiyonofuji continued to dominate sumo by winning the Natsu *basho* (Summer tournament) in May with a near-

In the final match of a three-day sumo tournament staged at Madison Square Garden in New York City in June, *yokozuna* Chiyonofuji lifts his opponent, Takanosato, out of the ring to win yet another title. He finished the 1985 season with more wins than any other competitor.
UPI/BETTMANN NEWSPHOTOS

perfect 14–1 mark, while Samoan-American Konishiki—the heaviest *rikishi* (sumo wrestler) in history at 230 kg (506 lb)—finished second as a *komusubi* (subjunior champion) with a fine 12–3 record. *Ozeki* Hokutenyu achieved an outstanding 13–2 record to capture the championship of the Nagoya *basho* in July, with *sekiwake* Onokuni and top-ranked *maegashira* Kitao tying for second place with 12–3 marks. *Yokozuna* Chiyonofuji bounced back in September to grab the *yusho* of the Aki *basho* (Autumn tournament) with another perfect 15–0 record for his 13th title and his third *zensho yusho*. Newly promoted *ozeki* Onokuni was runner-up again with a 12–3 record, but *sekiwake* Konishiki was sidelined after injuring his tailbone when the small wooden stool he was sitting on collapsed while he was taking a bath. Finally, in the sixth and last tournament, the Kyushu *basho,* in November—the most exciting tournament of the year—Chiyonofuji once again asserted his dominance to win the *yusho* and tie former *yokozuna* Wajima for third place on the all-time list for most tourney titles with his 14th. He also won *rikishi* of the year honours for most wins in 1985, collecting 80 victories against only 10 losses. *Ozeki* Hokutenyu and *sekiwake* Kitao finished in a tie for second at the Kyushu *basho* with 12–3 records, resulting in a promotion for Kitao to *ozeki*.

(ANDREW M. ADAMS)

This article updates the *Macropædia* article Major Team and Individual SPORTS and *Micropædia* entries on the various sports.

SPORTING RECORD

Automobile Racing, 1985

Formula One Grand Prix Race Results:

Race	Driver	Car	Average Speed
Brazilian	A. Prost	McLaren-TAG-Porsche	181.527 km/h
Portuguese	A. Senna	Lotus-Renault 97T	145.162 km/h
San Marino	E. De Angelis	Lotus-Renault 97T	191.798 km/h
Monaco	A. Prost	McLaren-TAG-Porsche	138.434 km/h
Canadian	M. Alboreto	Ferrari	174.688 km/h
Detroit	K. Rosberg	Williams-Honda FW 10	131.486 km/h
French	N. Piquet	Brabham-BMW	201.323 km/h
British	A. Prost	McLaren-TAG-Porsche	235.404 km/h
German	A. Alboreto	Ferrari	191.147 km/h
Austrian	A. Prost	McLaren-TAG-Porsche	231.132 km/h
Dutch	N. Lauda	McLaren-TAG-Porsche	193.089 km/h
Italian	A. Prost	McLaren-TAG-Porsche	227.565 km/h
Belgian	A. Senna	Lotus-Renault 97T	189.811 km/h
European	N. Mansell	Williams-Honda FW10	203.625 km/h
South African	N. Mansell	Williams-Honda FW10	206.744 km/h
Australian	K. Rosberg	Williams-Honda FW10	135.168 km/h

World Drivers' Championship: Prost, 73 pt; Alboreto, 53 pt; K. Rosberg, 40 pt
Constructors' World Championship: McLaren; Ferrari.
World endurance championship for teams: Rothmans-Porsche
World endurance championship for drivers: D. Bell (U.K.) and H.-J. Stuck (W.Ger.)
Le Mans 24-hour endurance: Porsche
World rally drivers' championship: T. Salonen (Finland)
World rally manufacturers' championship: Peugeot Sport
Monte Carlo Rally: Audi Quattro
CART (Championship Auto Racing Team):
1985 Individual champion: A. Unser, Sr.
NASCAR (National Association for Stock Car Auto Racing):
1985 Driver champion: D. Waltrip
SCCA (Sports Car Club of America)
1985 Driver champion: W. Dallenbach, Jr.
Indianapolis 500: D. Sullivan in a March-Cosworth, aver. speed: 152.982 mph (246.301 km/h)

Baseball, 1985

Hall of Fame inductees: Lou Brock, Enos Slaughter, Arky Vaughan, Hoyt Wilhelm
New Record for Career Base Hits: P. Rose 4,204
World Series Results: Kansas City (AL) 4 games, St. Louis (NL) 3 games
Japan Series Results: Hanshin (Central League) 4 games, Seibu (Pacific League) 2 games

Basketball, 1985

National Basketball Association (NBA), professional championship 1984–85: Los Angeles 4 games, Boston 2 games
New NBA Record for Career Scoring: K. Abdul-Jabbar 33,262 points (at end of 1984–85 season)
National Collegiate Athletic Association (NCAA): *men:* Villanova, *women:* Old Dominion
National Invitational Tournament (NIT): UCLA
World Amateur Champions: *men:* U.S.S.R., *women:* U.S.S.R.

Bowling, 1985

Tenpins World Games Champions:
Singles: *men:* R. Jansson (Sweden), *women:* A. Wee (Singapore)
American Bowling Congress (ABC) tournament for amateurs:
Regular Division:
Singles: G. Harbison
Doubles: H. Higby and C. Gibson
All-events: B. Asher
Team: Terry's Pro Shop, Solon, Ohio
Maxim/Women's International Bowling Congress (WIBC):
Open Division:
Singles: P. Schwarzel
Doubles: L. Graham and M. Philippson
All-events: A. Sill
Team: D. Redman Insurance, Toledo, Ohio

Boxing

Champions as of Dec. 31, 1985:

	World Boxing Council (WBC)	World Boxing Assn. (WBA)
Heavyweight	P. Thomas (U.S.)	T. Tubbs (U.S.)
Cruiserweight	B. Benton (U.S.)	D. M. Qawi (U.S.)
Lt. heavyweight	J. B. Williamson (U.S.)	vacant
Middleweight	M. Hagler (U.S.)	M. Hagler (U.S.)
Jr. middleweight	T. Hearns (U.S.)	M. McCallum (Jamaica)
Welterweight	D. Curry (U.S.)	D. Curry (U.S.)
Jr. welterweight	L. Smith (U.S.)	U. Sacco (Argentina)
Lightweight	H. Camacho (Puerto Rico)	L. Bramble (U.S.)
Jr. Lightweight	J. C. Chávez (Mexico)	W. Gómez (Puerto Rico)
Featherweight	A. Nelson (Ghana)	B. McGuigan (N.Ireland)
Jr. featherweight	L. Pintor (Mexico)	V. Callejas (Puerto Rico)
Bantamweight	M. Lora (Colombia)	R. Sandoval (U.S.)
Super flyweight	J. Watanabe (Japan)	K. Galaxy (Thailand)
Flyweight	S. Chitalada (Thailand)	H. Zapata (Panama)
Jr. flyweight	Chang Jung Koo (S.Korea)	Yuh Myung Woo (S.Korea)

Cycling, 1985

World Amateur Champions—Track:
men: Sprint — L. Hesslich (E.Ger.)
Tandem sprint — R. Rehounek, V. Voboril (Czech.)
Individual pursuit — V. Ekimov (U.S.S.R.)
Team pursuit — R. Amadio, G. Grisandi, M. Brunelli, and S. Martinello (Italy)
1,000-m time trial — J. Glücklich (E.Ger.)
50-km points — M. Penc (Czech.)
50-km motor paced — R. Dotti (Italy)
women: Sprint — I. Nicoloso (France)
Individual pursuit — R. Twigg (U.S.)
World Professional Champions—Track:
Sprint — K. Nakano (Japan)
Individual pursuit — H.-H. Oersted (Denmark)
50-km points — U. Freuler (Switzerland)
One-hour motor paced — B. Vicino (Italy)
Keirin — U. Freuler (Switzerland)
World Amateur Champions—Road:
men: Individual road race — L. Piasecki (Poland)
100-km team time trial — V. Jdanov, I. Sumnikov, V. Klimov, and A. Zinoviev (U.S.S.R.)
women: Individual road race — J. Longo (France)
World Professional Champion—Road:
Individual road race — J. Zoetemelk (Neth.)
Tour de France: B. Hinault (France)

Fencing, 1985

World fencing champions:
men's foil: *indiv.:* M. Numa (Italy), *team:* Italy
men's épée: *indiv.:* P. Boisse (France), *team:* W.Ger.
men's sabre: *indiv.:* G. Nebald (Hungary), *team:* U.S.S.R.
women's foil: *indiv.:* C. Hanische (W.Ger.), *team:* W.Ger.

Football

Association Football Major Tournaments:
Inter-Continental Cup won by Juventus of Italy
European Champions' Cup won by Juventus of Italy
European Cup-Winners' Cup won by Everton of England
UEFA Cup won by Real Madrid of Spain
Libertadores de América Cup won by Argentinos Juniors of Argentina
World Youth Cup won by Brazil
U.S. Professional National Football League (NFL) results:
National Football Conference Championship: Chicago 24, Los Angeles 0
American Football Conference Championship: New England 31, Miami 14
Super Bowl XX: Chicago 46, New England 10
U.S. College Football:
Rose Bowl: UCLA 45, Iowa 28
Cotton Bowl: Texas A&M 36, Auburn 16
Orange Bowl: Oklahoma 25, Penn State 10
Sugar Bowl: Tennessee 35, Miami 7
Canadian Football League professional championship (Grey Cup):
British Columbia 37, Hamilton 24

Rugby Union International Matches, 1871–Dec. 31, 1985*:

	Eng.	Scot.	Ire.	Wales	Brit. Isles	S.Af.	N.Z.	Aust.	France
England	...	48/16	54/8	35/12	...	2/1	3/0	4/0	32/7
Scotland	37/16	...	47/4	37/2	...	3/0	0/2	6/0	26/2
Ireland	35/8	44/4	...	29/5	...	1/1	0/1	6/0	25/5
Wales	43/12	50/2	53/5	...	...	0/1	3/0	7/0	36/3
British Isles	...	...	...	...	...	14/6	5/3	12/0	...
South Africa	6/1	5/0	8/1	6/1	20/6	...	20/2	21/0	11/4
New Zealand	12/0	10/2	8/1	8/0	24/3	15/2	...	56/4	16/0
Australia	7/0	4/0	4/0	4/0	2/0	7/0	19/4	...	4/1
France	21/7	27/2	28/5	19/3	...	3/4	4/0	8/1	...

Rugby League Test Matches, 1908–Dec. 31, 1985*:

	Great Britain	Australia	New Zealand	France
Great Britain	...	49/4	6/3	8/2
Australia	43/4	...	35/0	22/3
New Zealand	24/3	20/0	...	13/3
France	13/2	12/3	11/3	...

*Reading across, the first figure is the all-time number of wins and the second the number of drawn matches against a given opponent.

Golf, 1985

Major Tournament Winners:

	men	women
U.S. Open	A. North (U.S.)	K. Baker (U.S.)
U.S. Amateur	S. Randolph (U.S.)	M. Hattori (Japan)
British Open	S. Lyle (U.K.)	B. King (U.S.)
British Amateur	G. McGimpsey (Ireland)	L. Beham (Ireland)
U.S. PGA	H. Green (U.S.)	N. Lopez (U.S.)
U.S. Masters	B. Langer (W.Ger.)	
U.S. Tournament Players Championship	C. Peete (U.S.)	...

Ryder Cup (pro.) — Europe 16½, U.S. 11½
Walker Cup (amat.) — U.S. 13, Great Britain and Ireland 11

PGA leading money winner: C. Strange (U.S.) $542,321
LPGA leading money winner: N. Lopez (U.S.) $416,472

Gymnastics, 1985

World championships:

	men	women
Team	U.S.S.R.	U.S.S.R.
Indiv. all-around	Y. Korolev (U.S.S.R.)	E. Shushunova (U.S.S.R.) and O. Omelyanchik (U.S.S.R.) (tie)
Parallel bars	S. Kroll (E.Ger.) and V. Mogilny (U.S.S.R.) (tie)	—
Uneven parallel bars	—	G. Fahnrich (E.Ger.)
Horizontal bar	Tong Fei (China)	—
Horse vault	Y. Korolev (U.S.S.R.)	E. Shushunova (U.S.S.R.)
Side horse	V. Mogilny (U.S.S.R.)	E. Shushunova (U.S.S.R.)
Balance beam	—	D. Silvas (Romania)
Rings	Li Ning (China) and Y. Korolev (U.S.S.R.) (tie)	—
Floor exercise	Tong Fei (China)	O. Omelyanchik (U.S.S.R.)

World amateur champion: Czechoslovakia

Ice Skating, 1985

World championships:
Figure skating:
 Individual: *men:* A. Fadeev (U.S.S.R.), *women:* K. Witt (E.Ger.)
 Pairs: O. Vasiliev and E. Valova (U.S.S.R.)
 Dancing: A. Bukin and N. Bestemianova (U.S.S.R.)

Speed skating:	men	women
Overall	H. Vergeer (Neth.)	A. Schöne (E.Ger.)
500 m	G. Boucher (Canada)	A. Schöne (E.Ger.)
1,500 m	O. Bozhiev (U.S.S.R.)	A. Schöne (E.Ger.)
5,000 m	H. Vergeer (Neth.)	A. Schöne (E.Ger.)
10,000 m	G. Karlstad (Norway)	A. Schöne (E.Ger.)
Sprint:	I. Zhelezovsky (U.S.S.R.)	C. Rothenburger (E.Ger.)

Rowing, 1985

World champions:

men:	Double sculls	E.Ger.
	Quadruple sculls	Canada
	Coxless pairs	U.S.S.R.
	Coxed fours	U.S.S.R.
	Eights	U.S.S.R.
	Coxed pairs	Italy
	Coxless fours	W.Ger.
	Single sculls	Finland
women:	Quadruple sculls	E.Ger.
	Eights	U.S.S.R.

Shooting, 1985

Championships of the Americas:

	team	individual
Team trap	U.S.	
Men's trap		D. Johnson (U.S.)
Women's trap		F. Strodtman (U.S.)
Men's skeet	U.S.	M. Dryke (U.S.)
Women's skeet		E. Funes (U.S.)
300-m standard rifle event	U.S.	R. Aylward (U.S.)
300-m free rifle	U.S.	R. Aylward (U.S.)
50-m standard rifle	U.S.	L. Wigger (U.S.)
50-m free rifle	U.S.	L. Wigger (U.S.)
50-m running game	U.S.	M. English (U.S.)
10-m running game	U.S.	R. Stewart (U.S.)
Air rifle	Canada	J. Senecal (Canada)
Standard pistol	U.S.	D. Nygord (U.S.)
Free pistol	U.S.	D. Nygord (U.S.)
Air pistol	U.S.	D. Nygord (U.S.)
Centrefire pistol	U.S.	B. Tober (Colombia)
Rapid-fire pistol	U.S.	M. Howkins (Canada)

Show Jumping, 1985

European championships:
 Jumping: *team:* U.K., *indiv.:* P. Schockemöhle (W.Ger.) on Deister
 Dressage: *team:* W.Ger., *indiv.:* R. Klimke (W.Ger.) on Ahlerick
 3-day event: *team:* U.K., *indiv.:* V. Holgate (U.K.) on Priceless

Skiing, 1985

	men	women
World championships—Alpine:		
Downhill	P. Zurbriggen (Switz.)	M. Figini (Switz.)
Combined event	P. Zurbriggen (Switz.)	E. Hess (Switz.)
Giant slalom	M. Wasmaier (W.Ger.)	D. Roffe (U.S.)
Slalom	J. Nilsson (Sweden)	P. Pelen (France)
World Cup championships—Alpine:		
Overall	M. Girardelli (Luxem.)	M. Figini (Switz.)
Slalom	M. Girardelli (Luxem.)	M. Figini (Switz.)
Giant slalom	M. Girardelli (Luxem.)	M. Figini (Switz.) and M. Kiehl (W.Ger.) (tie)
Slalom		E. Hess (Switz.)
Combined		B. Oertli (Switz.)

Nations Cup—Alpine: Switzerland

World championships—Nordic:		
5-km cross country		A. Boe (Norway)
10-km cross country		A. Boe (Norway)
15-km cross country	K. Haerhoenen (Fin.)	
20-km cross country		G. Nykelmo (Norway)
30-km cross country	G. Svan (Sweden)	
50-km cross country	G. Svan (Sweden)	
Team relay	Norway	
70-m jump	J. Weissflag (E.Ger.)	
90-m jump	P. Bergerud (Norway)	
Combination indiv.	H. Weinbach (W.Ger.)	
Combination team	W.Germany	
World Cup championships—Nordic:		
Cross country	G. Svan (Sweden)	A. Boe (Norway)
Combination	G. Anderson (Norway)	
Nations Cup—Nordic:		
Cross country	Norway	
Combination	Norway	
Biathlon:		
10-km	F.-P. Rötsch (E.Ger.)	
20-km	Y. Kaschkarov (U.S.S.R.)	
Team relay	U.S.S.R.	

Swimming, 1985

World swimming records set—men:

100-m freestyle	M. Biondi (U.S.)	49.24 sec
100-m freestyle	M. Biondi (U.S.)	48.95 sec
400-m freestyle	M. Gross (W.Ger.)	3 min 47.80 sec
200-m backstroke	I. Polianskiy (U.S.S.R.)	1 min 58.14 sec
200-m butterfly	M. Gross (W.Ger.)	1 min 57.01 sec
200-m butterfly	M. Gross (W.Ger.)	1 min 56.65 sec
4 × 100-m freestyle relay	S. McCadam, M. Heath, P. Wallace, M. Biondi (U.S.)	3 min 17.08 sec
4 × 100-m medley relay	R. Carey, J. Moffet, P. Morales, M. Biondi (U.S.)	3 min 38.28 sec

World swimming record set—women:

200-m breaststroke	S. Hoerner (E.Ger.)	2 min 28.33 sec

World diving championships:
 Team: *men:* China, *women:* China
 3-m springboard: *men:* Tan Liangde (China), *women:* Li Yihua (China)
 Platform: *men:* Tong Hui (China), *women:* M. Mitchell (U.S.)

Tennis, 1985

	men's singles	women's singles
French Open:	M. Wilander (Sweden)	C. Evert Lloyd (U.S.)
Wimbledon:	B. Becker (W.Ger.)	M. Navratilova (U.S.)
U.S. Open:	I. Lendl (Czech.)	H. Manlikova (Czech.)
Australian Open:	M. Wilander (Sweden)	C. Evert Lloyd (U.S.)

Davis Cup (men): Sweden; World Team Cup (men): U.S.; Wightman Cup (women): U.S.; Federation Cup (women): Czech.

Track and Field, 1985

World outdoor records set—men:

1 mile	S. Cram (U.K.)	3 min 46.31 sec
1,500 m	S. Cram (U.K.)	3 min 29.67 sec
	S. Aouita (Morocco)	3 min 29.45 sec
2,000 m	S. Cram (U.K.)	4 min 51.39 sec
5,000 m	S. Aouita (Morocco)	13 min 00.40 sec
Marathon	C. Lopes (Portugal)	2 hr 7 min 12 sec*
30-km walk	M. Damilano (Italy)	2 hr 6 min 27.3 sec
High jump	R. Povarnitsin (U.S.S.R.)	2.40 m (7 ft 10½ in)
	I. Paklin (U.S.S.R.)	2.41 m (7 ft 10¾ in)
Pole vault	S. Bubka (U.S.S.R.)	6.00 m (19 ft 8¼ in)
Triple jump	W. Banks (U.S.)	17.97 m (58 ft 11½ in)
Shot put	V. Timmermann (E.Ger.)	22.62 m (74 ft 2½ in)

World outdoor records set—women:

400 m	M. Koch (E.Ger.)	47.60 sec
1 mile	M. Slaney (U.S.)	4 min 16.71 sec
5,000 m	Z. Budd (U.K.)	14 min 48.07 sec
10,000 m	I. Kristiansen (Norway)	30 min 59.42 sec
Marathon	I. Kristiansen (Norway)	2 hr 21 min 06 sec*
400-m hurdles	S. Busch (E.Ger.)	53.56 sec
4 × 400-m relay	East Germany	41.37 sec
5,000-m walk	M. Torrelles (U.S.)	22 min 51.10 sec
Long jump	H. Dreschler (E.Ger.)	7.44 m (24 ft 5 in)
Javelin throw	P. Felke (E.Ger.)	75.26 m (246 ft 11 in)
	P. Felke (E.Ger.)	75.40 m (247 ft 4 in)

*World best time; there is no world record because courses vary

Wrestling, 1985

World championships:

weight	freestyle	Greco-Roman
48 kg (105.5 lb)	Kim Chol Hwan (N.Korea)	M. Allakhverdiev (U.S.S.R.)
52 kg (114.5 lb)	V. Jordanov (Bulgaria)	J. Ronningen (Norway)
57 kg (125.5 lb)	S. Beloglazov (U.S.S.R.)	S. Balov (Bulgaria)
62 kg (136.5 lb)	V. Alekseev (U.S.S.R.)	J. Vangelov (Bulgaria)
68 kg (149.5 lb)	A. Fadzaev (U.S.S.R.)	S. Negrisan (Romania)
74 kg (163 lb)	R. Cascaret (Cuba)	M. Mamiachvili (U.S.S.R.)
82 kg (180.5 lb)	M. Schultz (U.S.)	B. Daras (Poland)
90 kg (198 lb)	B. Scherr (U.S.)	M. Houck (U.S.)
100 kg (220 lb)	L. Khabelov (U.S.S.R.)	A. Dimitrov (Bulgaria)
130 kg (Hvy)	D. Gobedjisvili (U.S.S.R.)	I. Rostortsky (U.S.S.R.)

Television and Radio

Some form of radio and television service was available in all major countries in 1985. Approximately 980 million radio sets were in use throughout the world, including 554 million, 56% of the total, in the United States. There were about 475 million television sets, of which approximately 175 million, or 37%, were in the U.S. The Soviet Union, with 75 million, or 16%, ranked second, and Japan was third with 30.2 million, or 6.4%, according to estimates published in the 1985 *Broadcasting/Cablecasting Yearbook.* Other *Broadcasting* estimates of television sets by country included West Germany, 21.8 million; Brazil, 21.4 million; France, 19 million; United Kingdom, 18.6 million; Italy, 13.6 million; Canada, 12.4 million; Spain, 11.6 million; China, 9.7 million; Poland, 8.2 million; Mexico, 7.6 million; Australia, 6.5 million; The Netherlands, 6.2 million; Argentina, 5.9 million; East Germany, 5.8 million; Yugoslavia, 4.4 million; Czechoslovakia, 4.3 million; Egypt, 3.9 million; Turkey, 3.6 million; Saudi Arabia, 3.5 million; and Sweden, 3.2 million.

Television stations on the air or under construction throughout the world numbered approximately 8,300. About 2,200 were in the Far East, 2,110 in Western Europe, 1,492 in the U.S., 920 in Eastern Europe, 180 in South America, 105 in Mexico, 100 in Canada, and 50 in Africa. There were about 18,000 radio stations, most of which employed the amplitude-modulation (AM) system of transmission, but the number of frequency-modulation (FM) stations was growing. In the U.S. there were about 10,610 radio stations, of which 5,641 (53%) were FM.

Organization of Services. In the U.S. Pres. Ronald Reagan's deregulation policies continued to ease restrictions on broadcasters and cable operators, but by 1985 much had already been done and further opportunities were diminishing. The regulatory body, the Federal Communications Commission (FCC), found one major opportunity for deregulation but could not take action on it. Finishing a proceeding that it originated the year before, the FCC in August concluded that the so-called fairness doctrine—a long-established policy that required a station to present all sides of important controversial issues if it presented any side—was contrary to the public interest, inhibiting rather than encouraging the presentation of public issues, as it had been intended to do. But the doctrine had been approved by the U.S. Supreme Court in a 1969 decision, and the commission therefore would continue to enforce it.

What might prove to be the most significant deregulatory move of the year came not from the FCC but from a U.S. appeals court in Washington, D.C. To the delight of cable operators and the consternation of broadcasters, the court ruled in July that the FCC's "must-carry" rules, which for 20 years had required local cable systems to include the programming of local TV stations on their cable channels, were too broad to meet the requirements of the First Amendment to the Constitution. Many cable operators had long wanted to be free of the rules, which they said deprived them of channels they wanted to devote to other programs, while broadcasters insisted that the rules were essential to them in maintaining the availability of local broadcast service to cable subscribers as well as nonsubscribers. The court's decision left the way open for the FCC to try to redraft the rules, but many commission officials doubted that the commission could do it in a way that would meet the court's criteria. The FCC at first said that it would not appeal the court's decision, but later, under pressure from broadcasters and a number of congressmen,

The rapid proliferation of satellite-dish television antennas for private use—about 1.2 million of them had been installed in the U.S. so far—prompted some 700 exhibitors to show their wares at an industry convention in Nashville, Tennessee, in September.
STEVE HARBISON/TIME MAGAZINE

it said that it would call a hearing to see what might be done and would welcome proposals. Broadcasters, in the meantime, opened a campaign to repeal or modify the compulsory license under which cable companies gained access to broadcasting and other programs in return for a modest fee, and at the end of November the National Cable Television Association tentatively empowered its officers to talk with broadcasters about the possibility of finding a "mutually tolerable" alternative to the must-carry rules.

The financial structure of some of broadcasting's oldest, biggest, and most prestigious companies underwent basic changes in 1985, a year marked by takeovers and mergers. The American Broadcasting Cos., owner of the ABC-TV network, a variety of radio networks, television stations in five of the largest U.S. markets, and 12 important radio stations, agreed to be acquired by the much smaller but prestigious Capital Cities Communications, a major broadcaster, publisher, and cable TV operator, in a cash-and-stock transaction valued at $3.5 billion. The first transfer of a network's ownership since ABC itself was formed more than 30 years earlier, the transaction was approved by the FCC in November on condition, as expected, that the merged company dispose of enough stations and other interests to bring it into compliance with the FCC's various multiple-ownership rules.

The ABC-Capital Cities deal, impressing investors with the value of broadcasting stocks, was one of many takeovers, attempted takeovers, bidding wars, and straightforward acquisitions undertaken during the year. CBS, a broadcasting leader since its formation in the late 1920s, finally succeeded in fighting off a takeover bid by the relatively small Turner Broadcasting System, but only at the expense of more than $1 billion in debt (from buying up 21% of its own stock); this led to the sale of several of its major nonbroadcasting properties, disposal of the limited cable TV interests that it owned, a commitment to reduce 1987 expenses by 20%, extensive personnel layoffs, and an offer of early retirement that was accepted by more than 500 of its executives. Turner Broadcasting, meanwhile, turned its acquisitive attentions elsewhere and came up with a deal to buy the Metro-Goldwyn-Mayer/United Artists (MGM/

UA) film company in a cash-and-stock transaction valued at about $1.5 billion. And in December a second change in network ownership was set in motion when RCA, owner of the NBC network, agreed to be acquired by the General Electric Corp. for something over $6 billion, the most money ever paid for a non-oil company.

Cable television continued to expand. The A. C. Nielsen Co., the leading TV audience measurement service, estimated that in July the number of cable-equipped U.S. homes totaled 38,955,150, or 45.7% of all U.S. television homes, compared with 36,105,500, or 42.9%, in July 1984. Cable was still experiencing growing pains, however. Many system operators were uncertain as to whether the fundamental business should be basic cable (supported by advertising) or pay cable, or part of a new trend, "pay per view," in which cable homes could order—and pay for—only those movies or other special events they particularly wanted to see.

Cable also had another problem: program piracy. More and more homes were buying small satellite receiving antennas, or "backyard dishes," that enabled them to receive cable programs without paying for them. A number of pay cable services were beginning to "scramble" their signals to thwart these interceptions, and an industrywide movement was under way late in the year to develop a single scrambling policy applicable to all.

Videocassette recorders (VCRs), the devices that record TV programs and play them back later and also play prerecorded movies and other programs, were again television's biggest growth area. Industry estimates put the total of VCR-equipped homes in 1985 at about 28.1% of all U.S. TV homes, more than double the 13% estimated in 1984. A. C. Nielsen Co. found that in July the average VCR was used for 2 hours 14 minutes a week for recording and 4 hours 18 minutes for playback.

In the U.K. the British Broadcasting Corporation (BBC) had a traumatic year. In August Director General Alasdair Milne (*see* BIOGRAPHIES) had to contend with a serious crisis over the issue of political censorship. This arose when the BBC board of governors, under pressure from Home Secretary Leon Brittan, canceled a program about Northern Ireland.

Aside from the question of independence, the BBC's future financing arrangements were a matter of continuing concern during the year. The government used the regular license fee review to raise the question as to whether the BBC should be financed by advertising. In March it decided to hold down the license fee to the fairly low level of £58 a year for two years (instead of the expected three years) and to appoint a committee (chaired by economist Alan Peacock) to examine different ways of financing the BBC. It was widely predicted that one of the committee's preferred options would be a limited amount of BBC advertising, possibly on radio. The BBC was already showing signs of becoming more commercial and more competitive. Several cost-cutting committees were set up, and 4,000 jobs were eliminated. A management reshuffle led to the appointment of an accountant, Michael Checkland, as deputy director general, the first time the job had not been held by a program maker. BBC Enterprises, the corporation's commercial arm, was significantly expanded.

Independent Television (ITV) suffered financial losses during the early part of the year when advertising revenues fell. The reason for the decline remained inexplicable even when, in the autumn, revenues recovered. Thames TV, the largest ITV company, was one of the worst hit. Separately from their U.K. businesses, the ITV companies were actively developing a new Super Channel to be delivered by satellite throughout Europe. In November the BBC indicated that it wished to supply programs to the channel (it rejected an offer of investing in the company that would run it). The channel would present primarily ITV and BBC material already seen in the U.K., with some live news and sports, and was likely to begin operating in 1987.

A series of decisions by France's Socialist government was expected to result in the French having more than twice as many television channels as any other European country. In a speech in January, Pres. François Mitterrand gave official blessing to private, advertising-financed television. There would be two national channels and 40–50 local channels. One national channel would provide music; the other, news and general-interest programs. These new channels, which were likely to be supported by major French public and private companies as well as by Radio-Télé Luxembourg (RTL) and possibly some U.K. companies, were expected to start broadcasting in 1986.

Several other European countries moved toward starting new TV channels. The Dutch government agreed to allow a third TV channel, starting in 1987, to be financed by advertising. In June the Icelandic Atthing (parliament) stripped the state TV and radio service of its monopoly powers and set up a new body to issue licenses to private companies. Swedish Television continued to develop a new channel, which seemed likely to be financed by subscriptions instead of advertising as originally intended. There were also plans for a second channel in Denmark, where two private companies started experimental services.

There were significant changes in radio broadcasting during the year. In July the U.K. government announced a two-year trial of community radio. It invited proposals for 10-w "neighbourhood" stations and 100-w "community-of-interest" stations in London and 12 other areas. The Community Radio Association strongly criticized the government's technical guidelines and also the two-year limit. The changes in radio were not all positive. Many U.K. local stations were forced to close or merge in the face of continuing financial losses. In West Germany the country's first commercial radio services, in Munich, got off to a bad start when the Bavarian government allocated the stations only three wavelengths; each station was able to broadcast for only a few hours a day and therefore was unable to achieve sufficient revenues.

Programming. Comedies and other programs intended primarily for the young adult viewer gained new emphasis in the prime-time television schedules that the major U.S. networks offered for the 1985–86 season. The number of half-hour situation comedies, relatively small only a few years earlier, increased 10% over the previous season, reaching 24 a week; in addition, there were two new comedy series, "Stir Crazy" and "Hometown," of an hour each, an uncharacteristically long form for comedy. Action-adventure dramas, which dominated the 1984–85 schedules, increased by one, to 36. Together, the three networks introduced 20 new series totaling 16½ hours.

The 1984–85 season had produced a major turnaround in the network audience rankings. CBS again finished first, but NBC, which for years had seemed to have permanent possession of third place, continued a dramatic rise and not only ousted ABC from second place but gave CBS a close run for first. The new rankings were reflected in the amount of new programming introduced for 1985–86. ABC replaced more than one-third of its prime-time schedule, with eight new programs totaling 7½ hours; CBS, pushing hard to hold onto first place, introduced six new series, adding up to 5 hours; while NBC, confident of the momentum in its current schedule, made the fewest

changes it had undertaken in 15 years, deciding to get by with six new series totaling 4 hours, or 18% of its prime-time lineup.

In nonseries programming, made-for-television movies and miniseries continued to play a greater role, while the use of theatrical motion pictures declined. Because of the motion picture industry's practice of releasing movies so that they could be shown on pay cable six months in advance of their network release—and with pay cable's habit of showing each movie several times—most theatrical pictures had been seen by large audiences by the time the networks could broadcast them, and their ratings were far below what they would have been otherwise. For the most part, therefore, the networks found that they could attract larger audiences with made-for-TV movies.

In cable, too, the trend toward creation of special programming continued. As the supply of new theatrical movies dwindled, more and more of the large pay-cable operators, such as Home Box Office, Cinemax, Showtime, and The Movie Channel, were producing or underwriting the production of new comedy, drama, and children's series, miniseries, and specials for their own use. By 1985 some of these shows, especially situation comedies, had become so successful that their owners were considering syndicating them to broadcast TV stations after their cable runs.

The most widely seen and heard program of 1985, and perhaps of any year, was the 16-hour Live Aid concert on July 13, a multinational, multimedia event. The concert, organized by Bob Geldof (*see* BIOGRAPHIES) to raise money for famine relief in Africa, was held simultaneously in Philadelphia and London. Produced by Worldwide Sports & Entertainment and featuring some 60 contemporary rock and country music acts, it was carried in whole or in part by—among others—ABC-TV, ABC Radio, the Music Television cable network, the BBC, and more than 100 independent stations. It was beamed live via satellite to more than 110 countries and on a tape-delayed basis to

Journalists stage a one-day strike to protest the decision of the British Broadcasting Corporation to cancel a planned documentary program on the situation in Northern Ireland that included an interview with an alleged leader of the Irish Republican Army.

about 40 others. In all it reached more than 1,500,000,000 people throughout the world.

The summit conference between President Reagan and the Soviet Union's Mikhail Gorbachev in Geneva in November was among the most extensively covered events of the year, though it was far from the newsiest, thanks to a news blackout imposed by both sides until the meetings were over. The hijacking of TWA Flight 847 by terrorists in the Middle East in June and the plight of the passenger-hostages became the subject of continuous reporting, much of it live, for more than two weeks and led to a public controversy—and to introspection by the networks themselves—as to whether so much coverage, especially so much live coverage, had played into the hands of the terrorists and delayed a resolution of the crisis.

In the 37th annual Emmy awards, the Academy of Television Arts and Sciences named "Cagney & Lacey" as the outstanding drama series and "The Cosby Show" the outstanding comedy series. "Motown Returns to the Apollo" won for variety, music, or comedy programs; "The Jewel in the Crown" for limited series; "Do You Remember Love?" for drama/comedy specials; and "Garfield in the Rough" for animated programs.

Emmys for lead actor and actress in a drama series went to William Daniels of "St. Elsewhere" and Tyne Daly of "Cagney & Lacey." Robert Guillaume of "Benson" and Jane Curtin of "Kate & Allie" won for lead actor and actress in a comedy series, while lead actor and actress awards for limited series or specials went to Richard Crenna of "The Rape of Richard Beck" and Joanne Woodward of "Do You Remember Love?" Outstanding supporting actor and actress Emmys were won by Edward James Olmos of "Miami Vice" and Betty Thomas of "Hill Street Blues" in the drama series category, John Larroquette of "Night Court" and Rhea Perlman of "Cheers" for comedy series, and Karl Malden of "Fatal Vision" and Kim Stanley of "Cat on a Hot Tin Roof" for limited series or specials. In the 12th annual Emmy awards for daytime programming, top honours went to "The Young and the Restless" as the outstanding drama series, "$25,000 Pyramid" in the game show category, "Sesame Street" for children's series, "Donahue" for talk/service shows, "Jim Henson's Muppet Babies" in the animated program classification, and "All the Kids Do It" in the children's specials category.

Sports remained one of television's major audience attractions. After a 1984 Supreme Court ruling voided the National Collegiate Athletic Association's control over television coverage of its members' football games, there was a surge in the number of college teams shown on TV; this surge, along with substantially increased exposure of both college and professional football on cable TV, was blamed for an apparent waning of football audience ratings late in 1984. With the start of the new season in September 1985, however, the ratings indicated that the viewers had returned. Up to mid-November, TV audience ratings of National Football League games on the three broadcasting TV networks were running from 8 to 17% higher than in the same period in 1984.

Broadcasting estimated that TV and radio networks and stations and cable operators would pay $530 million for college and professional football TV and radio rights in 1985, about 6% more than in 1984. For similar professional baseball rights, *Broadcasting* estimated, the broadcasters' and cable operators' rights payments for 1985 games totaled $278 million, a 3.7% increase over 1984.

In radio, music and news remained the staples. Listeners could find stations that catered to an almost endless variety of tastes: jazz, classical, country, or rock music; ethnic, re-

One of the bright spots in network television programming in 1985 was the return of Mary Tyler Moore in a comedy series, called simply "Mary." The show also featured John Astin.
CBS

ligious, talk, and information combinations; and all news. Among radio stations generally, country music was first in popularity, with adult contemporary second, and middle-of-the road/nostalgia third.

The Public Broadcasting Service (PBS) reported in midyear that during the 1984–85 season its programs reached 48,050,000 homes and 95,145,000 viewers in an average week, or 75% more homes and 86% more people than in 1977–78, when PBS started regular audience measurements. In prime time the totals were 28,870,000 homes and 53.7 million people, for gains of 113 and 120%, respectively. Compiled by A. C. Nielsen Co. and published by PBS, the figures also showed that 97% of all U.S. television homes could receive at least one public television station—a statistic, PBS noted, that was unmatched by any cable TV service. PBS said the research showed that "strong prime-time programming" such as "Nova," "The Living Planet," and "National Geographic Specials" led the 1984–85 advances.

During 1985 arts programs continued at their low level of broadcasting expenditure and viewing hours (if not of production values) in Western Europe and their conspicuously higher profile in most countries of Eastern Europe. While the best programs were in a sad vein, a majority of drama productions were devoted to such familiar frothy escapist formulas as the gun-toting and fast-moving detective duo "Dempsey and Makepeace" from Britain's London Weekend Television or the soap-cum-melodrama account of prosperous suburban lives and loves in "Sons and Daughters" from Australia's Grundy Organization.

In the bleak school, "Displaced Persons," also from Australia, took the viewer back to view a stream of Poles and others in a refugee quarantine station in 1945. World War II remained one of the very strongest themes for grim drama. Long gone, however, was the image of a good-looking soldier rushing to victory with his machine gun cracking fire. Modern war drama was more likely to centre upon a harassed, middle-aged bureaucrat making meek compromises to allow an inhuman ideology greater scope, before the outbreak of war. "Charlie Grant's War" from Canada, set in Vienna in the 1930s, was of this kind; so was "A Woman's Pale Blue Handwriting," made by Austria's ÖRF network and also set there in the 1930s.

Other outstanding dramas of the year included "Silent Poison," a contemporary West German thriller about a hapless photographer who believes he has stumbled upon a shady conspiracy responsible for a factory explosion; from Japan, "Sakuma," a striking, possibly allegorical account of a convict who repeatedly escapes from prison but nevertheless wins the esteem and finally the affection of his jailer; "The Four Seasons," Polish Television's imaginative drama with metaphysical concerns about fertility and waste in nature, all bound up in a taut and witty treatment; and "The Kidnapping," a Swiss melodrama in a pastoral

WTTW, CHICAGO

Robin Bailey and Diana Rigg were Lord and Lady Dedlock in "Bleak House," another remarkable British production brought to U.S. audiences as part of the Public Broadcast Service's "Masterpiece Theatre" series.

Alpine setting that belied the fast pace and tension of its plot. Australia produced a number of stirring dramas that reached the TV screens of several other nations in 1985. Among them were "Waterfront," a love story set against the background of industrial unrest and dockland violence, "The Flying Doctor," a characteristic drama from the outback, and "The Dunera Boys," about Australian and German refugees shipped from England to remote areas of Australia during World War II. From Sweden came "Beyond Sorrow, Beyond Pain," a memorable drama telling of the director's own reactions to an appalling accident that left her boyfriend blind and brain-damaged.

For British television, often looked to by other countries for the highest standards in drama and other types of production, 1985 was no vintage year. The most imaginative new drama series was the BBC's "Edge of Darkness," about a detective pained and puzzled by the death of his daughter; he gradually learns of her involvement in an extreme left-wing and conservationist group, and a story of nuclear-weapons conspiracy and private profiteering unfolds. Anglia TV, the ITV company that produced the distinguished string of "Tales of the Unexpected," also produced a masterly detective series in "The Black Tower," adapted from P. D. James's book. "Heart of the High Country" from Central Television was set in New Zealand at the turn of the century.　　　(PAUL A. BARRETT; RUFUS W. CRATER; JOHN HOWKINS; LAWRENCE B. TAISHOFF)

Amateur Radio. The number of amateur ("ham") radio operators continued to grow. The American Radio Relay League, the leading organization of ham operators, put the U.S. total in October 1985 at 413,127, up from 410,066 in October 1984. Throughout the world licensed ham radio operators were estimated to number 1,511,000 in 1985.

Ham operators provide vital communications links in emergency or other conditions when normal communications lines are down. In the fall of 1985, for example, when an earthquake demolished buildings and killed thousands of people in Mexico, and in November, when thousands more died in mud slides triggered by a volcanic eruption in Colombia, ham operators provided communications between the devastated areas and the outside world.

　　　　　(RUFUS W. CRATER; LAWRENCE B. TAISHOFF)

See also Industrial Review: *Advertising; Telecommunications; Motion Pictures; Music.*

This article updates the *Macropædia* article BROADCASTING.

Theatre

Great Britain and Ireland. Conflicts involving the Arts Council of Great Britain (ACGB) and its clients became more acute as the arts minister, Lord Gowrie, increased the ACGB's grant for 1985–86 by 2% to £106 million, well below the inflation rate. There was criticism of the ACGB's apparent acceptance of this defeat and of the ensuing demise of several theatrical companies. Government policy was opposed by the new National Campaign for the Arts, members of Parliament, and such public figures as Sir Claus Moser, chairman of the Royal Opera House Board, and Sir Peter Hall, head of the National Theatre (NT).

Condemnation by subsidized theatres in Britain and the resignations of half of the ACGB's drama panel, its drama director, and its financial director forced a reversal of policy. The ACGB's demand for £161 million for 1986–87 was in keeping with Lord Gowrie's pledge that the arts world would not be let down after the abolition in April 1986 of the Greater London Council (GLC) and six regional metropolitan authorities. Yet the government broke its promise, increasing the grant to £135 million, far below the figure required to make up the shortfall or to enable the ACGB to help launch the new South Bank Board as successor to the GLC. Concern about the government's commitment to the arts was heightened in September when Richard Luce, replacing Lord Gowrie as arts minister, was not included in the Cabinet.

A number of official surveys upheld the case for the arts establishment, and this was strengthened when the Policy Studies Institute revealed that box-office receipts in the state-subsidized theatres had been steadily rising. Nonetheless, the first of these theatres to have their grants axed were five leading "touring date" theatres, headed by the historic Sadler's Wells in London.

Sir Peter Hall's concerns about the reduced subsidy for the NT led to his decision to close the Cottesloe Theatre, where *The Mysteries* won for NT director Bill Bryden prizes from all four award juries—the Laurence Olivier (LO), London Standard (LS), *Plays and Players* (*P&P*), and *Drama Magazine* (*DM*) awards. A special grant from the GLC reopened the Cottesloe, where the NT group led by Ian McKellen and Edward Petherbridge excelled in Mike Alfreds's unconventional production of *The Cherry*

Patti LuPone starred in Trevor Nunn's 3½-hour musical version of Victor Hugo's *Les Misérables* for the Royal Shakespeare Company.

Athol Fugard (left) and Zakes Mokae starred as South African brothers divided by skin colour in a 25th-anniversary production of Fugard's remarkable first play, *The Blood Knot*, at the Yale Repertory Theatre in New Haven, Connecticut.

ROBERT R. MCELROY/NEWSWEEK

Orchard. The NT annual report for 1984–85 showed an excellent record, with earned income rising to £7.5 million against a grant of £7.8 million.

At the Lyttelton *Mrs. Warren's Profession* featured a superb performance by Joan Plowright in the title role. The best of two award-winning productions at the Olivier was Alan Ayckbourn's comedy of backstage amateur theatricals, *A Chorus of Disapproval,* in which Michael Gambon as a much-harassed director and Imelda Staunton as his patient wife won several awards. As the Machiavellian newspaper proprietor in David Hare and Howard Brenton's award-winning satire on Fleet Street, *Pravda,* Anthony Hopkins won the new LO Ken Tynan award. Other prizes went to designer William Dudley for his innovative work on *The Mysteries,* to David Essex's *Mutiny!* at the Piccadilly Theatre, to *The Merry Wives of Windsor* at the Stratford home of the Royal Shakespeare Company (RSC), and to the uproarious NT double bill at the Olivier of *The Critic* and *The Real Inspector Hound.*

In its annual report the RSC claimed that the 1.9% increase in its grant from the ACGB was insufficient to maintain standards. The RSC's awards were fewer in 1985; the LO best comedy prize was given to Peter Barnes's religious satire *Red Noses,* and the best actress in a musical award went to Patti LuPone of the U.S. in *Les Misérables* (at the Barbican) and in Marc Blitzstein's *The Cradle Will Rock,* one of several U.S. plays at the Old Vic. The LO and LS best actor awards went to Antony Sher as Richard III and as the camp hero of *Torch Song Trilogy,* both RSC productions.

Bill Hamon, author of *Grafters,* a social drama at the Hampstead Theatre, was named most promising playwright (LS), and Gary Oldman was voted most promising actor (*DM*) in Edward Bond's *The Pope's Wedding* at the Royal Court. Two *P&P* "most promising" awards were won at the Royal Court, by Timberlake Wertenbaker for her pastiche 18th-century drama, *The Grace of Mary Traverse,*

and by Janet McTeer in its title role. *DM* selected Espen Skjønberg of Norway as best supporting actor in his role as Chebutykin in *Three Sisters* at the Royal Exchange Theatre in Manchester and gave a new general merit award to the Kick Company's *King Lear.* Another "most promising" (LO) award went to the Cheek by Jowl company in three plays at the Donmar Warehouse.

Awards in the private sector went to Vanessa Redgrave (best actress: *DM, LS,* and *P&P*) in *The Seagull;* the shared *P&P* newcomer award to her daughter Natasha Richardson in the same play; the LS best musical to Alan Bleasdale's biography of Elvis Presley (from Liverpool), *Are You Lonesome Tonight?;* and to *Me and My Girl* for best musical (LO) and best actor in a musical (LO) for its star, Robert Lindsay. There were memorable performances by Liv Ullmann (*see* BIOGRAPHIES) in *Old Times;* Charlton Heston in *The Caine Mutiny Court-Martial;* Michael Denison in *Twelfth Night* (at the Open Air Theatre); Sian Philips in *Gigi;* Maggie Smith in Ronald Harwood's *Interpreters;* and the hilarious Donald Sinden in *The Scarlet Pimpernel,* from Chichester.

Though Ted Nealon, Ireland's arts minister, admitted that Irish arts were underfunded and advocated a lottery, and Joe Dowling resigned as head of the Abbey Theatre in protest against cuts in funding, the Dublin Festival, under Michael Scott, was able to present a bumper program of new Irish works from both North and South. Also, the Abbey, with Christopher Fitz-Simmons as new head and with a £100,000 Arts Council grant, yielded a fine dramatic crop, including Siobhan McKenna in *Long Day's Journey into Night;* a revival of John B. Keane's modern classic *Sive;* Marie Keane in a Beckett double bill; Ulick O'Connor's Irish Republican Army (IRA) drama of 1922, *Execution;* Frank McGuinness's play on Ulster Protestantism, *Observe the Sons of Ulster Marching Towards the Somme* (also seen at the Belfast Festival); Tom MacIntyre's *Rise Up Lovely Sweeney;* Maureen Toal in McGuinness's monodrama *Baglady;* Thomas Murphy's saloon-bar comedy *Conversation on a Homecoming;* and Eoghan Harris's 1840 potato famine drama *Souper Sullivan.* The best Lyric Belfast Players' productions were Brian Moore's *Catholics;* Martin Lynch's *The Minstrel Boys,* about the hunger strike by IRA prisoners; and Stewart Parker's historical *Northern Star,* also seen at the Dublin Festival.

France, Italy, Spain, Low Countries, Greece. New festivals were a sign of success for the French theatre under the tutelage of Arts Minister Jack Lang. The early resignation of Jean-Pierre Vincent as head of the Comédie Française left a gap that would be hard to fill. The company's few real successes were Vincent's much-debated *Macbeth,* with Philippe Clévenot; a Feydeau threesome; and *The Balcony,* staged by Georges Lavaudant. Antoine Vitez at the Chaillot put on two Victor Hugo plays to mark the poet's centenary celebrations; *Ubu Roi,* which won Dominique Valadié the best actor Critics' Prize (CP); and Karl Michael Grüber's *King Lear,* from West Berlin, starring Bernhard Minetti. Other successes in the subsidized theatres were Guy Rétoré's *Georges Dandin* at the Théâtre de l'Est Parisien, Georges Lavaudant's staging of *Richard III* and Jean Mercure's swan-song production of *Volpone* at the Théâtre de la Ville, and, at the Théâtre de l'Europe, Giorgio Strehler's *L'Illusion comique* with Gérard Desarthe as best actor (CP), Ingmar Bergman's *John Gabriel Borkman* from Munich, West Germany, and his *King Lear* from Stockholm, and Tadeusz Kantor's *Perish the Artists!* from Krakow, Poland.

Jean-Louis Barrault's *The Birds* at the Rond-Point was followed by his *Le Cid,* with Francis Huster, and five mod-

ern No plays by Yukio Mishima, with Natasha Parry. Peter Brook's nine-hour version of the Indian epic *The Mahabharata,* adapted by Jean-Claude Carrière and first seen at the Avignon Festival, went on a European tour that ended at his own Bouffes du Nord. The new Spring Festival in Paris featured Tennessee Williams's *Paradise on Earth,* in which Christiane Cohendy won the CP for best actress. At the Avignon Festival Chekhov's *On The Highroad,* staged by Klaus Michael Grüber, shared the CP best play award with the Comédie de Caen's version of Bond's *Summer.* The City of Paris prizes went to Marianne Epin in Gildas Bourdet's *Le Saperleau* at the Théâtre de la Ville and to Loleh Bellon for her play *Such Tender Bonds.*

In the private sector Jean Bouchard won the CP for best French play with *A Strange Present* at the Mathurins. The main attractions elsewhere were Edouard Bourdet's *The Weaker Sex* with Patachou, Marcel Pagnol's *The Baker's Wife* with Michel Galabru, Robert Hossein's spectacular *Julius Caesar* at the Sports Palace, Pierre Etaix's *Monsieur Is Getting On a Bit* with François Perier, *Gigi* with Danielle Darrieux and Suzanne Flon, and Louis Calaferte's *The Battle of Waterloo.*

The Milan, Italy, Piccolo Teatro celebrated its 40th birthday with Vitez's *The Triumph of Love* from Paris and news of the opening of a new school and theatre studio in May 1986. Other notable events were Strehler's version of Eduardo de Filippo's *The Great Magic; The Genius* by Damiano Damiani and Raffaele La Capria (with Giorgio Albertazzi acting and directing); *La Venexiana* and *Much Ado About Nothing,* starring Valeria Moriconi; Luca Ronconi's youth-group staging of Schnitzler's *Comedy of Seduction;* Pirandello's *To Clothe the Naked* with Mariangela Melato; Paola Borboni in a one-woman version of *King Lear;* and the premiere of Karol Wojtyla's (Pope John Paul II's) 1940 drama of *Job.*

Highlights in Barcelona, Spain, at the International Catalan Theatre Congress included *Cyrano de Bergerac* with José-Maria Flotats, Nuria Espert in *Salome,* and the "Els Comediants" company in *Alè (Breath).* In Madrid Luis

William Petersen's performance in the Wisdom Bridge company's production of *In the Belly of the Beast* helped bring Chicago's lively and provocative local theatre scene to international attention. Wisdom Bridge also scored with its *Kabuki Medea.*

Pasqual's staging of the Marlowe/Brecht *Edward II* was the main new work at the Teatro Maria Guerrero. Spain and Spanish arts were featured at the 1985 Europalia in Belgium, with, among others, Lope de Vega's *Punishment Without Vengeance* from the Teatro Español at the Belgian National Theatre (BNT). Jacques Huisman, the retiring head of the BNT, to be succeeded by Jean-Claude Drouot, took his valedictory *Le Misanthrope* to the Edinburgh (Scotland) Festival before retiring. East German director Fritz Marquandt staged *The Imaginary Invalid* at the Amsterdam City Theatre, while West German Stephan Stroux was the director of the world premiere of Bernard-Marie Koltès's *Quai Ouest,* which dealt with the clash of alien cultures. Flemish playwright Hugo Klaus adapted Valle-Inclán's *Divine Words* at the Europalia.

At the Athens Festival the main foreign items were Brook's *Mahabharata,* the London NT's *Coriolanus,* the Milan Piccolo's *Storm,* Peter Stein's *Oresteia* from West Berlin, Vitez's *Lucrezia Borgia* from Paris, and Ingmar Bergman's *Borkman* from Munich. Greek productions ranged from the Greek national theatre's *Bacchae,* the Northern Greek national theatre's *Suppliants,* Karolos Koun's Art Theatre's *Acharnians,* and the Modern Theatre's *Thesmophoriazusae* to Mastrosimone's *Extremities,* staged by Jules Dassin, husband of the arts minister, Melina Mercouri.

Switzerland, West and East Germany, Austria. In Zürich, Switz., Gerhard Klingenberg, the new head of West Berlin's Renaissance Theatre, returned as guest director of *The Importance of Being Earnest* to the Schauspielhaus, which also put on the Swiss premiere of Thomas Hürlimann's drama of a dying farmer, *Deadline,* staged by West German (formerly East German) director Matthias Langhoff. The Gerhardt Hauptmann Prize went to 25-year-old newcomer Stefan Dähnert, and the Georg Büchner award to East German Heiner Müller. Benno Besson revived his famous East German production of *The Dragon,* in French, at the Comédie de Genève. Alessandro Manzoni's bicentenary was celebrated by the Teatro della Svizzera Italiana with Luigi Lunari's stage version of *I promessi sposi.*

Luc Bondy's first production as successor to Peter Stein at the West Berlin Schaubühne was a triumphant *The Triumph of Love* by Pierre Marivaux. No less auspicious a beginning was Peter Zadek's *Yerma,* starring former East German Jutta Hoffmann, at the Hamburg Schauspielhaus; that theatre was represented at the annual spring meeting in Berlin with Zadek's production of *Ghetto* by Joshua Sobol and with a thriller by John Hopkins. A Hebrew production of *Ghetto* and Sobol's *Soul of a Jew,* both from Haifa, Israel, were also presented. Wesker's *Shylock* received its West German premiere in Augsburg, but the Frankfurt world premiere of Fassbinder's controversial posthumous drama about a "wicked Jew" had to be abandoned in the light of massive public protests. A highlight of the East Berlin Festival was Alexander Lang's acclaimed production of *Iphigenia on Tauris,* which won for Katja Paryla both the Berliner Zeitung award and the Helene Weigel medal. The Hans-Otto medal was awarded to the 87-year-old Elisabeth Bergner, who was invited to revisit her old prewar home, the Deutsches Theater (DT), for the occasion. Other events in East Berlin were the revival of Ernst Barlach's 1926 morality play, *Blue Boll,* at the DT and *The Dance of Death,* directed at the Palace Theatre by Britain's David Leveaux.

The city of Vienna's Joseph Kainz Medal was given to Yury Lyubimov for his Burgtheater production of *Crime and Punishment.* The Burg also put on *Hamlet,* with Karl Maria Brandauer, and *Borkman,* with Romuald Pekny,

Roshan Seth, as an urbane Indian novelist in Britain, was one of the chief debaters in David Hare's *A Map of the World,* an exploration of relations between developed and third world nations that had its U.S. debut off-Broadway.

MARTHA SWOPE/TIME MAGAZINE

while Israel's Joseph Millo staged Sobol's *Ghetto* at the Volkstheater, with Andrea Jonasson.

Eastern Europe, Scandinavia, Israel. An unusual production for Moscow, at the Stanislavsky Theatre, was Arkady Stavitsky's *40 Sholom Aleichem Street,* in which Zionist Jews are favourably portrayed. The new head of the Taganka, Anatoly Efros, directed Gorky's *The Lower Depths* at his theatre, while Oleg Tabakov made his acting debut at the Moscow Arts in Rolf Hochhuth's *The Jurists,* staged by West Germany's Günther Fleckenstein. Galina Volchok, codirector of the Sovremennik, made a rare acting appearance there in *Who's Afraid of Virginia Woolf?*

At Warsaw's Polski, Kazimierz Dejmek staged T. S. Eliot's *The Elder Statesman;* at the Popular Theatre Zygmunt Hübner put on Gorky's *Enemies;* and at the Contemporary Maciej Englert produced *Three Sisters.* At the Bucharest (Rom.) national theatre, Marcela Rusu appeared in a feminist drama by Slovak writer Natasha Tanska, directed by Mihai Berechet. Also in Bucharest a rural family drama, *Olelie* by Fanus Neagu, starring George Constantin, was featured at the Nottara, and there were new works by Dumitru Solomon at the Bulandra and by Tudor Popescu at the Comedy. New plays by Nikolay Haitov, Stanislav Stratiev, and Yordan Radichkov were among some 20 staged in Sofia, Bulg., where, at the Drama Theatre, Georgy Karaslavov's *Tango,* directed by Vily Tsankov, was highly praised.

Andras Forgach's Dostoyevsky-inspired *The Gambler* at the national theatre in Budapest ranked in importance in Hungary with Akos Kertesz's drama of adultery, *A House with an Attic,* at the Castle Theatre. Also noteworthy was a revised version of Miklos Hubay's drama about Freud, *The Dreamreader's Dream,* also at the national theatre.

A tour of *Borkman* in Denmark, pending completion of the rebuilt Royal Theatre, was directed by East Germany's Peter Kupke. An important revival there was that of Henry Nathansen's *Within the Walls.* The royal opening of the £33 million new "Norwegian Theatre" in Oslo, with *Romeo and Juliet* and *Cats,* was the theatrical event of the year in Norway, closely followed by *Peer Gynt* at the national theatre with a triple cast. A new Ingmar Bergman production at Stockholm's Royal Dramatic Theatre was *Miss Julie,* while Lasse Pöysti was replaced as head of the theatre by Lars Löfgren. The completion of the new £4 million Workers' Theatre in the city of Tampere, where Czech director Jiri Menzel staged *The Taming of the Shrew* at the unique rotating open-air theatre in Pyynikki Park, was the best news in Finland. At the Helsinki national theatre, Ritva Siikala staged Strindberg's *The Father,* and Eeva-Kaarina Volanen made her debut as Arkadina in *The Seagull.*

Omri Nitzan, the new head of the Habimah national theatre in Tel Aviv, Israel, began making plans for the theatre's 70th anniversary in 1987. The Haifa Theatre staged for the Israel Festival two parallel versions of *Waiting for Godot,* in Hebrew and Arabic. The Berlin Schaubühne's two-character version of *The Dybbuk* (with Urs Bihler and Miriam Goldschmidt) closely rivaled the Jerusalem Khan Theatre's version of the play, with which the Habimah had been launched by Stanislavsky in Moscow in 1917. A rare experience in Jerusalem was the Palestinian El-Makawati company in Françoise Abu Salem's production in Arabic of *The Story of the Eye and the Tooth,* a drama inspired by the Israeli-Arab conflict.   (OSSIA TRILLING)

United States. The death of Yul Brynner (*see* OBITUARIES) late in the year symbolized the state of Broadway in 1985. For the first time in memory even the producers in New York City were forced to concede that Broadway was not in good health, and as evidence of this, for the first time in their history, the major performance categories of the annual Tony awards were reduced for want of deserving nominees. The central question was crucial: Was this crisis just the cyclical one, to be survived as usual by this "fabulous invalid," or had the commercial theatre undone itself with unrecoupable production costs and unaffordable ticket prices?

The situation was not helped by a hitless musical year. More than ever, Broadway's morale was determined by its musical stage, and New York City was offering a menu only of old hits, one of them (*A Chorus Line*) ten years old. Indeed, the most popular musical of the year was over 30 years old—the endlessly popular revival of *The King and I*—and it closed only because the star, Brynner, was mortally ill.

If there was any sunshine in Broadway's wintry year, it came from Neil Simon's delightful *Biloxi Blues.* The second in a projected autobiographical trilogy that had been inaugurated in 1983 with *Brighton Beach Memoirs,* this play took its youthful protagonist from his Brooklyn adolescence into the maturing ritual of military basic training in the 1940s. Few disagreed that here was Simon's most substantial and well-wrought play, a thoughtful and touching study of a young man's confusion and his struggle toward adulthood. Simon was rewarded with a Tony award for the best play of the year—astonishingly enough, the first ever won by this author of *Barefoot in the Park,* *The Odd Couple,* and *Plaza Suite,* among others.

Another of the few bright spots in the 1985 Broadway year was, of all things, a revival of Frederick Lonsdale's 1923 drawing-room comedy *Aren't We All?,* starring the redoubtable Claudette Colbert and Rex Harrison. Some took this success to suggest an audience hungry for sophistication and the traditional values of wit, civility, and polish. That would be reassuring were it true, but it was difficult to make out any current young Claudette Colberts, Rex Harrisons, or, for that matter, Frederick Lonsdales.

The musical show that did win the year's Tony award, if merely for want of competition, was the decidedly un-Broadway *Big River*. This adaptation of *The Adventures of Huckleberry Finn* emanated from the American Repertory Theatre at Harvard University. It was not produced by people associated with Broadway, nor was it created by them, and it did not have the brash music or the tough glitter of traditional Broadway shows. It was not so wonderful either, but if *Big River* was not a great show, it did teach a valuable lesson—that there are musical theatre languages that audiences can appreciate other than that of orthodox show business.

As for the failures in the Broadway year, they were at least more diverse than the hits. The once infallible producer-director Harold Prince continued his catastrophic downslide with the $5 million *Grind*. Other musical flops ranged from the vaudevillian *Harrigan 'n Hart* to the rock-and-rolling *Leader of the Pack*. There were also unsuccessful Broadway revivals of Peter Nichols's *Joe Egg*, Rod Serling's *Requiem for a Heavyweight*, and Eugene O'Neill's *Strange Interlude*, although in October Jason Robards propelled another marathon O'Neill play, *The Iceman Cometh*, to a successful Broadway engagement. If theatre lovers hoped that this signaled a new fall season and a fresh start, their hopes were dashed. Not that there were many failures in the fall of 1985. Worse, there were few attempts, although Lily Tomlin did make a great hit with her appropriately titled one-woman show, *The Search for Signs of Intelligent Life in the Universe*. It certainly was the year's most intelligent Broadway entertainment. A most unlikely hit turned out to be *Tango Argentino*, an evening devoted entirely to tangos played by a small

Wrestling: Raw Power on the Stage

To begin with, it's the ultimate in-the-round performance. Viewers not only are on all four sides of this stage; they are practically on top of it. Here Bertolt Brecht's platform stage is brought to perfection; here the reductio ad absurdum trappings of the likes of John Napier (the brilliant environmental designer of *Cats, The Life and Adventures of Nicholas Nickleby,* and other wonders) is at its simplest, cleanest, most bare visual elegance.

Theatrical visionaries, in stripping away lighting, elaborate scenery, and all those three-dimensional nooks and crannies of a Broadway stage, are trying to make a point about drama, and it is this: The mythic power of the art form, the elemental heroes and forces that the best dramas succeeded in illustrating, thunder forth at their loudest and most subliminal when their surroundings are unadorned and spartan. Give me a bare stage and a few great actors, and I can show you life in a handful of magic stardust.

All this is in reference to a just completed evening of drama, which, to recall now, more than an hour after its conclusion, still makes my fingers tremble at my typewriter, still makes my spine tingle in my swivel chair. It was one of those evenings—so startling, so moving, so total, and so innovative—that critics (and, naturally, press agents) live for. It is called *Wrestling*, and although I saw it at a theatre called the Rosemont Horizon near Chicago, I'm told it's available as well via any number of cable and local television outlets.

In any event the mastermind or minds behind *Wrestling* (the program credits no author—come to think of it, the usher neglected to give me a program) have stripped theatre bare and dished up its essence. Even the performers are virtually stripped, clothed in brilliantly simple bathing-trunk attire that reveals most of their rolling flesh, warts and all.

The plot is base, vile, combative. Four characters—bearing such cartoon names as Hulk Hogan and Mighty Manfred—leap onstage and attack each other. What begins as a kind of fracas of brute fisticuffs soon grows into a verbal tirade without bounds. (Hogan at one point implies an illicit tie between Manfred and his sister, an obvious allusion to Oedipus.)

But the performance doesn't stop at name-calling and assault. In the midst of the conflict—an obvious allegory of the raging forces at war in the heart and soul of mankind—these characters erupt in breathless, athletic choreographic reveries. Hogan leaps over Manfred, landing on the palms of his hands and then pushing back up in a springboard antic, as if at loose in a buoyant rubber landscape. I haven't seen ballet as spartan and deft as that since Edward Villella.

Wrestling then introduces the innovative touch of a microphoned narrator—this in a work so simple that a narrator is the last imaginable adornment. But there he is, a kind of inverse absurdist symbol of our desire to understand, even that which ought to appear so obvious. These are dramatists (when will we be given their names?) whose levels simply don't quit. Does a backyard brawl need a narrator? Does, in fact, the human condition?

Human and dramatic traditions, present in both poetic bareness and satiric sting; stage simplicity and stage expansiveness; elemental conflicts and up-to-the-minute technology; all are combined in one breathless story and performance, one as simple as a neighbourhood melee and as moving and poetically sparse as something by Samuel Beckett.

Critics, of course, are not supposed to sully their hands with discussions of commercial prospects for a work; their realm is properly aesthetic. But some theatrical endeavours demand a breaking of the rules, and I, for one, wish to go on record predicting: *Wrestling* is one drama whose run will last forever.

(SID SMITH)

WALLY MCNAMEE—WOODFIN CAMP & ASSOCIATES

Hulk Hogan and other dramatis personae: No sets, no props, no script, no dialogue, hardly any costume; just *drama*.

onstage orchestra, sung by several ardent vocalists, and, most importantly, danced by a company of middle-aged, overdressed, and gloriously sensual ballroom dancers. This was the sort of unpredictability that should characterize a healthy theatre.

Off-Broadway in New York City the year was not much more encouraging except that serious dramas, which had all but disappeared from the uptown theatres, were regularly settling down for long runs in the smaller houses. Sam Shepard, who had yet to be produced on Broadway, had three plays running in smaller theatres at various times during the year: *Fool for Love, Curse of the Starving Class,* and *A Lie of the Mind.* Herb Gardner's *I'm Not Rappaport,* thanks to a charming script and ingratiating performances by Cleavon Little and Judd Hirsch, survived unkind reviews to settle down for a run off-Broadway and then in a big house. Perhaps the season's most disturbing play was *Orphans* by Lyle Kessler. It was typical of the dramas that seemed to be appealing to audiences across the country—tense, threatening, darkly comic plays dealing with family relationships. Such works, inspired most notably by Harold Pinter via Sam Shepard, were particularly propagated by the Steppenwolf Theatre Company of Chicago, which produced both *Orphans* and a recent successful revival of Shepard's *True West.*

Indeed Chicago, once clucked over by show folk as a bad theatre town, had developed into one of the nation's most active stage centres. In addition to Steppenwolf, the city offered such professional and ambitious production companies as the Organic Theatre Company, the Body Politic, Wisdom Bridge, and, of course, the celebrated Goodman Theatre. Indeed, when New York City's repertory theatre in Lincoln Center was finally started anew after several years of shameful inactivity, it was the Goodman Theatre's artistic director, Gregory Mosher, who was called in to run the place. Lincoln Center reopened its doors at the year's end with a double bill of plays by David Mamet, *The Shawl* and *Prairie du Chien.* Mosher had originally staged them at the Goodman.

Los Angeles had long since developed into one of the nation's busiest stage centres, originating commercial productions as well as institutional ones. One of the year's most interesting stage events, in fact, occurred there with the autumn revival of Harold Pinter's *Old Times,* starring Liv Ullmann, Nicola Paget, and the playwright himself. As actor, Pinter was not equipped to communicate his lines well, and the production's projected tour was canceled following a tepid Los Angeles reception.

Canada. In Canada the Stratford Festival continued to endure endless crises while appearing prosperous. Artistic director John Hirsch, who had rescued this most prestigious of North American theatres when it was said to be on the brink of disaster five years earlier, announced his resignation at the end of the summer. The 1985 season had been acceptable for this major but tourist-oriented festival theatre. It might have been accused of a certain commercialism, presenting *The Pirates of Penzance* and a punk version of *Measure for Measure,* but a perking up was welcome after years of deadly institutionalism. The year's rising attendance and dropping deficits surely eased the threat of governmental interference that always seemed to overshadow Stratford's well-trimmed lawns.

Other production choices for the Canadian institution's 1985 season were unexceptional: *King Lear, Twelfth Night,* Oliver Goldsmith's *She Stoops to Conquer,* and, for a contemporary touch, Williams's *The Glass Menagerie.* John Neville was engaged to succeed Hirsch in 1986, and that at least ensured a smooth transition of administrations unlike several in the past.   (MARTIN GOTTFRIED)

See also Dance; Music.

This article updates the *Macropædia* article The History of Western THEATRE.

Transportation

The Economic and Social Commission for Asia and the Pacific with its 44 member states designated 1985 as the start of a Decade of Transport and Communications. Meanwhile, during the year two developments illustrated weaknesses in the world's transportation system. The African famines and the Latin-American natural disasters highlighted the costs of inadequate transport in times of distress, and the spate of airline crashes and hijackings that led to more than 1,900 passenger fatalities served as a reminder of the millions of people who are killed and injured in transportation accidents every year. Paradoxically, the long-term risks from air accidents were still of the order of one fatality in one million passenger journeys.

(DAVID BAYLISS)

In June United Airlines' parent company, UAL Inc., announced its intention to acquire Hertz, the world's oldest and largest automobile rental company. Together with UAL's Westin Hotel subsidiary, the deal would create a full-service travel operation.

AVIATION

The year was a black one for airline safety. Among the major disasters, on June 23 an Air-India 747 crashed in the Atlantic southwest of Ireland with the loss of all 329 on board. Sabotage was suspected but at year's end was unproved. On August 2 an L-1011 of Delta Air Lines crashed while on its final approach to the Dallas-Fort Worth (Texas) Airport. The death toll was 135 on board and one person on the ground. Investigation centred on the possibility that the aircraft encountered severe wind shear. On August 12 a Japan Air Lines 747 crashed in mountainous country in Japan while on a domestic flight. Of the 524 passengers on board, 4 survived. The aircraft was disabled in flight and became uncontrollable, possibly because the rear bulkhead of the pressurized fuselage failed. On August 22 a British Airtours 737 caught fire during the takeoff run at Manchester (England) International Airport. The captain brought the aircraft to a halt, but it was engulfed by the fire, which had begun when an engine combustion chamber failed. There were 55 fatalities, and 14 were seriously injured. On September 6 a DC-9 of Midwest Express crashed shortly after takeoff from Milwaukee, Wis., with the loss of 31 lives, and on December 12 a chartered DC-8 operated by Arrow Air of Miami, Fla., crashed just after taking off from Gander, Newfoundland; all 256 on board, including 248 U.S. soldiers, were killed.

In 1984, by contrast, the International Civil Aviation Organization (ICAO) had reported 224 passenger fatalities on scheduled services, with a fatality rate of 0.02 per 100 million passenger-km, both figures the lowest for many years. The 1985 fatality total surpassed that of 1974, when there were 1,299 passenger fatalities and a fatality rate of 0.24. Traffic then was at less than half the level of 1985, however, so the 1985 fatality rate was likely to be substantially lower.

Despite continued growth in traffic during 1985, there were renewed fears about financial prospects for the airlines. The International Air Transport Association (IATA) reported a growth of 8.5% in scheduled international passenger traffic during the first seven months of the year and a 6.3% increase in capacity. The strong growth in freight reported in 1984 for international traffic scheduled by IATA—14.3%—dwindled during the first seven months of 1985 to 2.8%. As a result, although total traffic was up 6.4%, it was outstripped by capacity, which rose 6.9%.

Financial results for IATA airlines in 1984 were considerably worse than anticipated. The association, in October of that year, had predicted an operating profit of $2.9 billion on international services and a profit after interest of $1.2 billion. The actual result was an operating profit of $2.2 billion, which became $500 million after interest payments. The forecasts were scaled down appropriately, and the after-interest result for 1985 might prove to be little more than one of breaking even. The situation was all the more disappointing because the 1984 forecasts, coming after the severe losses of 1979–83, had foreseen profits improving into 1986 at least.

Route 66, U.S. highway (b. 1926—d. June 27, 1985, Duluth, Minn.), was celebrated in song, in literature, and on television during its 59 years as perhaps the best-known automobile road in the United States. Although it was formally designated U.S. Route 66 in 1926, it did not actually constitute a continuous paved route until 1932, when it became a 3,540-km (2,200-mi) concrete trail running from the intersection of Jackson Boulevard and Michigan Avenue in Chicago to Santa Monica Boulevard and Ocean Avenue in Santa Monica, Calif. Across Missouri the highway paralleled the old "Wire Road," the first telegraph line to the Southwest, which in turn was originally an Osage Indian trail; the trail from Ft. Smith, Ark., to Santa Fe, N.M., was surveyed by army topographers in 1849, and the way into California was laid out as a wagon route in 1857 by an army exploring party using more than 70 imported camels to traverse the Mojave Desert. In the years of the Great Depression and the Dust Bowl, 66 became the escape route for the "Okies," impoverished Midwestern farmers and workers lured by the promise of California. In *The Grapes of Wrath,* John Steinbeck called it "the path of a people in flight. . . . 66 is the mother road." A decade later the singer Nat King Cole struck a lighter note when he crooned a suggestion to "get your kicks on Route 66." And in the early 1960s a popular television series depicted a couple of footloose young adventurers cruising Route 66 in their Corvette.

The immediate cause of death was acute decertification by the American Association of State Highway and Transportation Officials, but the victim had suffered for years from a chronic case of Interstate Highway System.

(ROBERT MCHENRY)

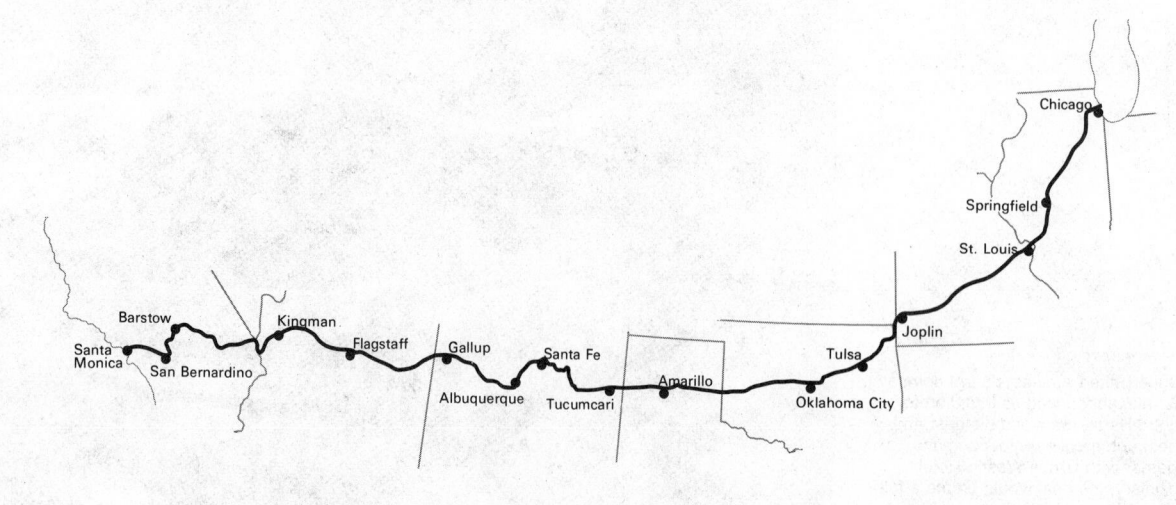

For once the deterioration could not be laid at the door of fuel prices. Fuel accounted for 25% of IATA members' operating costs, the highest single item, but prices had been stable and even decreasing slightly. Alarm expressed by U.K. airlines in particular during October about sudden and major price increases before the end of the year could not immediately be confirmed as a general trend, and some oil industry analysts argued that it was a local and temporary phenomenon.

A steady reduction in yield—the rate of revenue per unit of traffic—during 1980–84 had been matched by a fall in unit operating costs, achieved largely through improved staff productivity and the introduction of more efficient aircraft. However, this trend could not be maintained in 1985, when yield became static but costs began to rise.

In the U.S. traffic growth appeared to slow toward the end of 1985, but during the first nine months of the year there was a 14.3% increase in passenger traffic over the same period of 1984. Capacity grew only by 8.4%. International passenger traffic of the 20 Western European flag carriers in the first eight months of 1985 was 8.5% above that for the same period of 1984, while international freight traffic rose 3.6%.

In the U.S. Pan American agreed to sell its profitable Pacific division to United Air Lines. Control of TWA was won by financier Carl Icahn in a contest with Texas Air. Frontier Airlines was taken over by the fast-growing People Express.   (DAVID WOOLLEY)

SHIPPING AND PORTS

Hopes generated during the previous year that some sectors of the world shipping industry might be emerging from the recession in freight rates were dashed in 1985. As a result of inaccurate projections, wrong incentives, and doubtful national policies, the world's merchant fleet had doubled since the mid-1970s, while the growth in the amount of trade carried by sea was less than one-third of the increase in capacity. During 1985 several major shipping companies went out of business, the largest being Japan's Sanko Line. Behind all the shipowners' problems was the still massive amount of tonnage that was not being used. At midyear the number of tankers in lay-up was 343 vessels with an aggregate of 53.6 million metric tons deadweight (dw); the number of dry-cargo ships laid up numbered 969, totaling 10.5 million metric tons dw. Governments continued to make the situation worse by providing financial subsidies, and many shipyards offered vessels for sale at well below their true cost. A positive development was the rise in the volume of tonnage scrapped. This reached a record level of more than 40 million metric tons dw and included four of the world's largest tankers, all over 500,000 tons dw.

The total tonnage of the world merchant fleet fell slightly from 419 million gross registered tons (grt) to 395 million grt. Liberia's remained the largest national fleet with 58 million grt, and Panama (40.6 million grt) took second place from Japan (39.9 million grt). Greece remained in fourth place with 31 million grt. The U.K., which had once had one of the largest merchant fleets in the world, was in ninth place with 14.3 million grt.

New investment in port development continued unabated, particularly in China, despite the unstable conditions in world shipping. Access to the port of Amsterdam was improved to enable ships of 150,000 tons dw to enter via the North Sea Canal. To serve the massive coal project of El Cerrejon, Colombia, the port of Puerto Bolívar was equipped to handle up to 10,000 metric tons per hour of highly volatile bituminous coal suitable for U.S. eastern seaboard and Western European markets. Because of the

Workers pour concrete to replace a 55-metre (180-foot) section of wall that collapsed in Lock Seven of the Welland Canal near Thorold, Ontario, on October 14. By the time the canal reopened on November 7, a backlog of about 140 ships had built up.
JOE TRAVER/THE NEW YORK TIMES

high cost of providing deeper water at their berths, many ports invested in bulk loading and discharging operations offshore, using a transfer rig stationed in sheltered or even in open waters.

Following the agreement by the British and French governments in March that the two countries could be joined by a fixed link across the English Channel, opponents of such a link pointed out that it would destroy many British and French ports on the Channel coasts.   (W. D. EWART)

FREIGHT AND PIPELINES

Freight traffic was relatively buoyant during the year, with European air cargo up by more than 14% and European rail traffic up 11%. Concern about the environmental effects of heavy trucks continued to be expressed, and in London a nighttime and weekend ban on trucks was to be introduced. There were no such concerns about train size, and more countries were planning larger trains; 10,-000-metric-ton coal trains were being planned for China's Datang (Ta-t'ang) to Guangzhou (Canton) line, which was being electrified. Generally, freight packaging was being made more efficient, as illustrated by the introduction of double stacking of containers on rail freight services in the U.S.

As of the end of 1985 there were 193,000 km (1 km = 0.62 mi) of pipelines in the construction, planning, and study phases, with starts in 1985 on 32,000 km of new construction. Despite this, the capacity of the world's pipeline construction industry was not being fully utilized; pricing was, therefore, competitive, and there was sustained innovation in construction techniques in hostile environments such as deep waters, where an increasing proportion of new pipelines were being laid.

Among major projects completed in 1985 was the 3,380-km, 140-cm (56-in)-diameter oil line between Novosibirsk and Yelets in the U.S.S.R.; in the same area a 250-km coal slurry pipe was opened. In Utah a 153-km phosphate slurry line was commissioned, and a 217-km carbon dioxide pipe was brought into service in the U.S. Central Basin area. A growing proportion of new pipelines in the Middle East were for water rather than for oil or gas. An example was the 345-km pipeline to Asir in Saudi Arabia. The biggest pipeline project started in 1985 was the $1.7 billion, 1,600-km Indian oil and gas line from the western offshore fields to inland fertilizer plants to the north.

Much pipeline activity was geared to the modernization and maintenance of existing pipelines; thus a 725-km line between Texas and Oklahoma formerly used to carry crude oil was converted at a cost of $150 million to carry natural gas. The use of high-density plastics in networks of pipes of small diameter was growing.

ROADS AND TRAFFIC

The shift in policies toward deregulation and private ownership appeared to have boosted interest in toll roads. As of the end of 1985 there were more than 4,000 km of toll roads in Japan, and 900 km were planned in Malaysia. China was building a toll expressway to link Shenyan (Shenyen)-Guangzhou and Zhuhai (Chu-hai) at a cost of $900 million. The Turkish government planned a $500 million toll road to run from Bulgaria over the second Bosporus crossing to Ankara in Turkey. In the U.S. 27 km were in the planning stage in the Chicago area, and the Dallas (Texas) North Tollway was under construction. Perhaps the most impressive toll facility that was opened in 1985 was the 8.4-km Penang Bridge linking the island of Penang to the mainland of Malaysia.

Other major highway facilities opened in 1985 were the 480-m Iguaçu Bridge linking Argentina and Brazil, the Fort McHenry Tunnel under the Baltimore, Md., harbour, the cross-Denmark motorway between Vejle and the West German border, and the Ali Ayub expressway in Iraq. At $750 million for 218 km, the four-tube Fort McHenry Tunnel was one of the most expensive sections of highway ever built.

Traffic growth appeared to be greater in 1985 than in recent years. This was consistent with the increased demand for new vehicles, with the U.S. automobile industry again profitable. Concerns about oil supplies and prices persisted, and the use of alcohol-based fuels was spreading among less developed countries that had little or no indigenous oil. In Britain the innovative Sinclair electric three-wheeler came and went, showing that cleanliness and low cost were less important to consumers than was performance.

Maintaining the growing length of heavily traveled superhighways continued to be a major problem, as illustrated by the shutdown of a section of Britain's busiest motorway, the M-1, for two weeks for reconstruction. Standards were being revised upward, and new motorway pavements in the U.K. were to be built to provide an 85% chance of lasting 20 years without requiring strengthening.

INTERCITY RAIL

In a year marking the 150th anniversary of the first German railway (Nürnberg to Fürth), the West German rail system was being electrified at a rate of 280 km per year, and its intercity experimental train was unveiled. In Japan the main bore of the Seikan Tunnel was completed, and another section of the Tohoku Shinkansen (high-speed rail line) was opened. In France the Lille-to-Lyon Train à Grande Vitesse (TGV) service began operating, and work started on the 280-km TGV-Atlantique, scheduled for completion in 1990. In the U.S.S.R. the Baikal-to-Amur railway was fully operational, reducing rail hauls between European Russia and Western Siberia by 200 to 450 km. The project had necessitated the construction of 32 km of bridges and 25 km of tunnels.

As of 1985 China had one of the world's busiest railway systems. Extending over 56,000 route-km, it carried 220,000,000,000 passenger-km and 800,000,000,000 metric ton-km in 1985. Chinese passenger trains consisted of as many as 25 coaches; to help cope with the growth in demand, 420 diesel and 150 twin electric locomotives, along with double-decker passenger coaches, were ordered. In Denmark the world's first three-phase asynchronous 25-kv locomotives were in service, and in the U.K. the High Speed Train set a new world record for a diesel-hauled train by covering the 432 km between Newcastle and London at an average speed of 186 km/h and achieving a maximum speed of 232 km/h. Electrification projects were being implemented in most industrialized countries and increasingly were introduced in less developed countries. The two extremes were to be seen in China, where the Datang to Beijing (Peking) line was electrified while steam locomotives were still being built in significant numbers.

Serious train crashes occurred in Portugal, where 54 people were killed, and in Ethiopia, where 392 people died. The latter was one of the worst disasters in railway history. (*See* DISASTERS.)

SUSAN GREENWOOD/THE NEW YORK TIMES

Perhaps in keeping with Miami's growing reputation for chic, the Florida city's new elevated mass transit system was widely admired for design, cleanliness, and efficiency, but fiscal problems, notably a cut in federal subsidies, and low ridership clouded its future.

The 870-kilometre (542-mile) Transgabonais railway continued to advance through dense West African jungle. At a cost of $2.7 million per kilometre, the railway, intended to link the capital, Libreville, with the chief interior cities, was one of the world's largest active public works projects.

C. FRANCOIS—FIGARO—GAMMA/LIAISON

URBAN MASS TRANSIT

One of the most far-reaching changes in urban transit policy in industrial countries occurred with the passing of the Transport Act 1985 in the U.K. Essentially, this gave the market prime place in providing local transport services, with publicly sponsored services occupying a secondary role.

Recent innovations in bus transport included reopening of the defunct Trinidadian railways as busways and the opening of new busways in Ottawa and Pittsburgh, Pa. Bus transportation projects were being planned in five other U.S. cities. Energy conservation systems on buses, using high-speed flywheels and compressed gases, were tried successfully, and electrically steered buses were being tested in Fürth, West Germany. The strong interest in light rail (a railway system equipped to carry only light traffic) over recent years resulted in the opening of several new systems in 1985. In Vancouver, B.C., a 23-km system began operation and would serve Expo 86—the 1986 World Exposition of Transport and Communications—when it opened in May 1986. In Buffalo, N.Y., the first ten kilometres of the city's $530 million system was operating. Other light railways recently opened included the Island Line in Hong Kong, the central section of Pittsburgh's South Hills Line, the first half of Manila's 15-km system, the Scarborough, Ont., 7-km system, and a new line in Volgograd, U.S.S.R. Work was under way on new lines in Strasbourg, Grenoble, and Paris in France and in Los Angeles and Dallas, Texas, in the U.S. The Dallas system would eventually extend to 258 km.

New subways were opened in Tianjin (Tientsin), China, and Odessa, which became the 19th city in the U.S.S.R. to have a subway, the largest number in any country. Extensions to existing systems were opened in Washington, D.C., Miami, Fla., Atlanta, Ga., Asphoro, Japan, Seoul, South Korea, Paris, Leningrad, Novosibirsk, U.S.S.R., and Moscow (whose system was now 200 km in length). London's subway stations were being extensively modernized, and automatic ticketing programs were under way. In New York City one-fifth of the 6,200 subway cars were being replaced, and extensive modernization of the Paris and Madrid systems was under way. (DAVID BAYLISS)

See also Energy; Engineering Projects; Environment; Industrial Review: Aerospace; Automobiles.

This article updates the Macropædia article TRANSPORTATION.

World Affairs

Relations between the two superpowers had reached a low point in 1983, but a slow thaw set in during the following year and this continued in 1985, culminating in the Geneva summit meeting in November between U.S. Pres. Ronald Reagan and Mikhail Gorbachev, the new Soviet leader. (See BIOGRAPHIES.) Earlier, Gorbachev had made a state visit to France, and there were other high-level contacts between West and East. Given the conflicting basic interests of the superpowers, far-reaching agreements at Geneva were ruled out in advance; the significance of the summit was that it took place at all, that the leaders of the two most powerful nations were again on speaking terms. Soviet offers to accept cuts in strategic missiles if the U.S. ceased work on the Strategic Defense Initiative ("Star Wars") signified a new approach in Soviet foreign policy after years of apparent lack of interest in serious arms control negotiations.

Ronald Reagan was reelected president of the United States on Nov. 6, 1984; there were no major changes in the key positions of his administration as he entered his second term. Far more significant changes took place in the Soviet Union. Konstantin Chernenko, who had succeeded Yury Andropov in February 1984, died on March 10, 1985, aged 73. (See OBITUARIES.) He had been ill for a long time, and effective control had slipped out of his hands well before his death. Gorbachev succeeded him and strengthened his new position within a few weeks. There were many new appointments; Andrey Gromyko, who had been foreign minister for almost three decades, became head of state, and Nikolay Ryzhkov (see BIOGRAPHIES) replaced Nikolay Tikhonov as chairman of the Council of Ministers.

There was no reason to expect any significant change in the basic orientation of Soviet domestic and foreign policies. But there was certainly a greater urgency and activity in both fields. Above all, a great deal of effort went into the attempt to increase Soviet output in industry and agriculture in both quantity and quality. Only time would tell whether the attempt on the part of the new Soviet leadership to provide a new impetus to a stagnating economy would be stronger than the inbuilt inertia of the system.

In foreign policy Gorbachev and his colleagues certainly did not show themselves more "dovish" or "liberal," as some in the West had expected. There was a marked change in style from that of their predecessors; officials spent more time at their desks, and no vodka was offered at official parties. But the essential aims of Soviet foreign policy had in no way changed. There was, if anything, greater toughness in pursuing those aims, especially in regard to the U.S.S.R.'s Eastern European allies, who were given to understand that they were expected to toe the Soviet line. Though the new masters in the Kremlin had no hope of obtaining significant concessions from the Republican administration in the U.S., the two superpowers still

World Affairs: Contents

For your convenience this article groups the countries of the world by the geopolitical regions to which they belong. Certain related topics, such as United Nations, Dependent States, and various regional affairs articles (*e.g.*, Middle Eastern Affairs), are also included. An alphabetical list of these topics appears below, indicating the page where each may be found. Articles on the various countries update the *Macropædia* articles of the same name (except where otherwise noted), as do the more extensive statistical treatments in the *World Data* section.

seemed to inch toward certain arms-control agreements. The bilateral arms talks in Geneva were resumed on the day after the announcement of Chernenko's death.

The Soviet leaders also showed some greater willingness to normalize relations with China and to improve their ties with Western Europe. But since there were narrow limits to their readiness to make concessions, such improvement was by and large restricted to the climate of relations rather than to issues of substance.

No significant events took place inside Europe. As in previous years, governments were preoccupied with major domestic problems such as the high unemployment rate. The ruling parties in Britain, France, and West Germany came under growing pressure, and there were misgivings with regard to the "Star Wars" plans of the U.S. But there were no plausible alternative defense strategies—such as the strengthening of conventional forces or closer cooperation between the European countries.

The most prominent victim of a worldwide temporary upsurge of terrorism was Indira Gandhi, who was shot by Sikh nationalists on Oct. 31, 1984; she was succeeded by her son Rajiv, who worked against heavy odds during 1985 for a reconciliation between India's various nationalities. Other major manifestations of terrorism were the explosion in midair of an Air-India plane, with heavy loss of life, and the hijacking of a TWA airplane from Athens on June 14. The Shi'ah Muslim hijackers demanded the release of more than 700 coreligionists, who were imprisoned in Israel on suspicion of having performed terrorist acts. The most dramatic terrorist incident was the hijacking of the Italian luxury liner *Achille Lauro* in the Mediterranean Sea by a splinter group of the Palestine Liberation Organization (PLO) in October and the subsequent killing of an elderly U.S. passenger. The interception by U.S. aircraft of the

Egyptian plane that was to fly the perpetrators of the crime to safety led to diplomatic tension in U.S. relations with Egypt and Italy. In December Palestinian groups claimed responsibility for terrorist attacks at the Israeli airline terminals in the Rome and Vienna airports; several people were killed.

Israel unilaterally withdrew from Lebanon in three stages, leaving behind in the border area the South Lebanon Army to police the buffer zone between Israel and Lebanon. Inside Lebanon fighting between various Muslim militias continued almost without interruption. The almost forgotten war between Iran and Iraq also continued, and various attempts to arrange negotiations between the PLO and Israel, in which King Hussein of Jordan took a leading part, made no visible progress.

Africa during 1985 witnessed the overthrow of the governments of three countries, The Sudan (in April), Uganda (in July), and Nigeria (in August). While the new Sudanese military leaders took a more neutralist line in foreign affairs, the Nigerian coup was motivated chiefly by domestic affairs. More important in its implications for the rest of the world was the deepening of the famine in central Africa. Most publicity was given to starvation in Ethiopia, where more than 40% of the population were said to be affected, but international rescue efforts had also to be directed to neighbouring countries. Violence and protests against the policy of apartheid (racial separation) increased dramatically in South Africa. On July 20 Pres. P. W. Botha announced a state of emergency.

With all the misfortunes that befell mankind during the year, including such natural disasters as an earthquake in Mexico and a volcanic eruption in Colombia, 1985 was a quiet year; no new wars or civil wars were reported from any part of the world, and those that continued did not

grow in intensity. But it was also true that developments that went largely unreported cast a lengthening shadow on the years to come. These included the unresolved international debt crisis, the growing international U.S. trade deficit, and the increasing danger of protectionism in world trade. World leaders continued to postpone making hard decisions on these and other subjects. (WALTER LAQUEUR)

This article updates the *Macropædia* article 20th-Century INTERNATIONAL RELATIONS.

UNITED NATIONS

In October 1985 the UN commemorated its 40th birthday in a ten-day celebration at UN headquarters. On UN Day itself (October 24), Secretary-General Javier Pérez de Cuéllar reminded the delegates of their "single, collective constituency," the human race, that "vast, silent majority which wants peace with justice and dignity, with freedom from fear and the hope of a better tomorrow."

The anniversary Preparatory Committee had wanted the General Assembly to adopt a celebratory declaration but was unable to agree on a text. The Assembly did, however, proclaim 1986 the "International Year of Peace."

Middle East. On October 21 Shimon Peres, Israel's prime minister, called for immediate termination of the state of war between Jordan and Israel. Peres offered to go to Jordan or to any other mutually acceptable place to attend a peace conference with King Hussein, a Jordanian-Palestinian delegation, or even with the U.S.S.R. if the Soviet Union restored diplomatic relations with Israel. Hussein praised Peres as a "man of vision." These mutually conciliatory remarks were generally welcomed after a year of concern about Israeli-Arab military and terrorist clashes. On October 9, for instance, the Security Council, while welcoming Arab terrorists' release of the passengers and crew of the hijacked Italian cruise ship *Achille Lauro,* deplored the killing of a passenger, an American Jew in a wheelchair. The Council also condemned terrorism "in all its forms wherever and by whomsoever committed."

On a U.S. initiative and with the support of the U.S.S.R., the Council on December 18, for the first time in its history, unanimously and "unequivocally" condemned all acts of "hostage-taking and abduction" and called for the "immediate, safe release of all hostages. . . ." On December 6 the Assembly had adopted a similar resolution.

On October 1, the Council debated Israel's air strike on Palestine Liberation Organization (PLO) headquarters near Tunis, Tunisia. Israelis called the attack "an act of self-defense" because the PLO allegedly had used the base for planning terrorist operations against Israel and Jews everywhere. On October 4 the Security Council "vigorously" condemned (14–0–1, the U.S. abstaining) "Israel's armed aggression" and asserted Tunisia's "right to appropriate reparations." On December 16 the Assembly declared that Israel was not "peace-loving" and urged (86–23–37) members "totally to isolate" it. The Council's October 4 concern, that Israel's raid on Tunis would provoke reprisals, was borne out on December 27 when Palestinians attacked airports in Rome and Vienna, killing and wounding a number of people.

Lebanon. After Israel announced (January 14) a plan to withdraw its troops from southern Lebanon, where they had been stationed since 1982, Undersecretary-General Brian Urquhart (the longest-serving member of the Secretariat, who retired at year's end) went to the Middle East to coordinate Israel's troop movements with those of the UN Interim Force in Lebanon (UNIFIL). He also tried unsuccessfully to persuade Israel to allow UNIFIL to patrol the border, replacing the South Lebanon Army (SLA), an Israeli-backed 2,000-man Christian militia that the Shi‘ah Muslims distrusted.

On February 16 Israel completed the first phase of a three-stage withdrawal. Six days later Lebanon complained to the secretary-general about Israeli "raids, arrests, killings, and repression." Israeli officials called their "iron fist" essential to thwart Shi‘ah Muslim attacks on their troops. The Security Council met on February 28 to consider what Lebanon called Israel's "continuing acts of aggression." On March 2 UNIFIL reported that Israel was mounting a huge crackdown, and on March 6, fearing Shi‘ah reprisals if the U.S. vetoed a Council resolution criticizing Israel, UNIFIL relieved its U.S. nationals of field responsibilities. On March 12 the U.S. did veto an anti-Israeli draft resolution (Australia, Denmark, and the U.K. abstained), preferring an alternate text expressing regret for the violence in Lebanon and sympathy for its victims.

On May 31 the Council unanimously called on all concerned "to end acts of violence against the civilian population . . . particularly in and around Palestinian refugee camps," which still housed over 100,000 people. The Council also asked all parties to facilitate the humanitarian work of both the UN Relief and Works Agency for Palestine Refugees (UNWRA) and the International Com-

AP/WIDE WORLD

Harold Stassen (left) of the United States, Charles H. Malik (centre) of Lebanon, and Gen. Carlos Romulo (right) of the Philippines were among the original signers of the United Nations Charter who met to mark the 40th anniversary of the event in San Francisco in June.

mittee of the Red Cross (ICRC). Israel withdrew its last units from Lebanon on June 10 but left military advisers and plainclothes agents to watch over a "security zone" 13 to 19 km (8 to 12 mi) deep in Lebanon.

Unidentified gunmen abducted a British journalist, Alec Collett, preparing articles for UNWRA, just outside Beirut on March 25, from a clearly marked UN vehicle. He was the first known UN employee to be kidnapped in Lebanon. On May 15 Aidan Walsh, an Irish national and UNWRA's deputy director, was dragged out of his car, forced into another car, and abducted, but he was freed unharmed 36 hours later. On June 7 Finnish soldiers of UNIFIL turned over to the Shi'ah Muslim militia, Amal, 11 SLA militiamen who wanted to defect. The SLA accused UNIFIL of forcing the men to leave and took 21 UNIFIL soldiers, all Finns, hostage. The Finns were freed on June 15 after ICRC representatives convinced the SLA that the militiamen were genuine defectors. On December 16 the secretary-general reported to the Council that UNIFIL was threatened by Israel's unwillingness to allow it into the security zone, by possible cuts in U.S. contributions to the UN, and by increasing violence in the area.

Other Conflicts. *Cyprus.* On January 17 Cypriot Pres. Spyros Kyprianou and Rauf Denktash, head of the self-proclaimed Turkish Cypriot state, met for the first time in more than five years to discuss reunifying Cyprus. The two leaders greeted each other with what Denktash characterized as the "handshake of the century," but their problems remained unresolved at year's end. On September 20 the secretary-general told the Security Council that his initiative had brought the two sides closer, and the Council called on all parties in Cyprus to make a special effort to agree soon. A UN force of about 2,300 personnel from eight countries still served on the island.

Iran-Iraq War. The UN conducted its first on-site investigation of prisoner-of-war (POW) camps, and three experts concluded, in a report made public February 21, that both parties had violated the Geneva Convention, though neither side treated POWs as badly as the other side alleged. The experts asked both sides to release as many of the estimated 60,000 prisoners as possible. Iraq's foreign minister urged the Security Council on March 4 to arrange a prisoner exchange, but Iran, which claimed that the Council favoured Iraq, asked the secretary-general to work for an exchange independent of the Council. On December 12, however, Iran's UN delegate said he would join in Council deliberations if the Council condemned chemical weapons and the bombing of civilian targets.

Civilians reportedly became the targets of both sides in intensified fighting in March, despite the moratorium of June 1984 forbidding such attacks. The moratorium was not renewed. Pérez de Cuéllar proposed (March 26) that the belligerents stop attacking unarmed merchant ships, threatening international civil aviation, and using chemical weapons (mustard gas and a nerve agent known as *tabun*). He visited Teheran and Baghdad on April 7 and 8, having emerged as the only go-between both sides trusted, but the gap between the belligerents remained "as wide as ever," and in May they were again attacking population centres.

Afghanistan. Undersecretary-General Diego Cordovez conducted "proximity talks" with Pakistani and Afghan officials in Geneva in June about Afghanistan, which Soviet troops, estimated to number about 115,000, had entered in December 1979. Afterward, he expressed his growing conviction that parties to the Afghan war now agreed that a military solution was unattainable. He held further talks in June, August, and December, but the core issue, establishing a timetable for withdrawing Soviet troops, remained.

On December 11, however, the U.S. endorsed a draft treaty negotiated with UN help between Afghanistan and Pakistan that incorporated Soviet guarantees to withdraw its troops from Afghanistan in exchange for U.S. pledges to stop siding with Afghan rebels. In the December round of proximity talks, the Afghans informally showed Cordovez a timetable for Soviet troop withdrawal, to be considered at meetings in early 1986.

Vietnam. The secretary-general visited Vietnam in January, and his special representative went in July to arrange for a U.S. team to search on Vietnamese territory for unrecovered bodies. The team began working in November. On November 5 the General Assembly urged Vietnam (114–21–16) to withdraw its forces from Kampuchea.

South Africa. South Africa's policies of apartheid (racial separation), intervening militarily in neighbouring states, and refusing to grant independence to South West Africa/Namibia were condemned frequently by the Security Council, the UN Council on Namibia, and the Special Committee Against Apartheid.

On April 15 South African Foreign Minister R. P. ("Pik") Botha said that South Africa would pull its forces out of Angola, where they were fighting guerrillas of the South West Africa People's Organization (SWAPO). He hoped that the move would lead Cuban troops to withdraw from Angola. On May 22, however, Angola announced that it had killed two South Africans and taken one prisoner when they tried to sabotage oil installations in Cabinda Province. Angola then broke off negotiations on Cuban troop withdrawal.

South African troops continued operating in Angola, and on June 20, September 20, and October 7 the Security Council unanimously condemned the Pretoria government's actions. On June 21 the Council condemned South Africa for mounting an "unprovoked . . . military attack" on Botswana one week earlier. On December 6 the Council again condemned South Africa's "continued and

AP/WIDE WORLD

With United Nations Secretary-General Javier Pérez de Cuéllar looking on, Jaime de Piniés of Spain addresses the 40th UN General Assembly after being elected president of the body in September. De Piniés had nearly 30 years' experience in the Spanish mission to the UN.

unprovoked acts of aggression" against Angola, and on December 30 it demanded compensation for "killings and . . . unprovoked and premeditated violence" on December 20, when South African commandos invaded the Lesotho capital of Maseru.

On June 17 South Africa installed an interim administration in Namibia that the UN Council for Namibia characterized as a "puppet regime." Two days later the Security Council mandated the secretary-general to resume immediate contact with South Africa to implement a UN plan for Namibian independence and "strongly" warned (13–0–2, the U.K. and U.S. abstaining) that South Africa's failure to cooperate would "compel" the Council to consider sanctions. On November 15 Britain and the U.S. vetoed a draft resolution seeking to impose "mandatory selective sanctions" (France abstained). On March 12 the Council unanimously condemned South Africa for killing 18 blacks at a squatter camp in clashes with police and for detaining 16 leading opponents of the government. On July 26 it censured South Africa for imposing a national state of emergency and urged states to apply sanctions, and on August 21 it strongly condemned South Africa for continued killings and mass arrests.

International Court of Justice (ICJ). The U.S. Department of State announced on January 18 that President Reagan had decided the U.S. would no longer take part in Nicaragua's suit against it for allegedly mining its harbours and supporting paramilitary attacks on Nicaragua itself. The action marked the first time that the U.S. had walked out of an ICJ case since the court began operating in 1946. (*See* LAW: *International Law.*)

Women's Rights. The secretary-general announced on November 15 a personal commitment to correct "severe disparities in women's representation" at the professional levels of the UN Secretariat. He aimed to have women compose 30% of all recruits in two years. Mercedes Pulido de Briceno, assistant secretary-general for the improvement of the status of women, whom Pérez de Cuéllar had appointed on February 26, urged a 50% goal, as well as the vigorous affirmative action program endorsed in July by the UN Decade for Women Conference in Nairobi, Kenya.

Economic and Social Problems. The World Health Organization (WHO) convened a two-day conference in Geneva on September 25 on acquired immune deficiency syndrome (AIDS). In October the UN Office of Emergency Operations in Africa said that, although Africa's need for international food aid would decline in 1986, more than $1 billion in drought-related assistance and supplies was required to assist 19 million people still facing famine. The UN Commission on Environment and Development, meeting in São Paulo, Brazil, on October 28, received a new multibillion-dollar plan to save the world's rapidly disappearing tropical forests.

On November 9, as the Unesco General Conference ended, delegates unanimously approved a proposed work program. The $398 million budget for 1986 and 1987 was cut by 25% to make up for the loss of contributions by the U.S., which resigned at the end of 1984. Despite these reforms, the U.K. announced on December 5 that it would withdraw at the end of the year. On December 11 staff members staged a one-day work stoppage, and five began a hunger strike "to protest the arbitrariness and inconsistency in Unesco's recruitment and staff management." The hunger strike ended after four days, when the director general agreed to give a joint management-staff committee wide powers to deal with personnel adjustments.

(RICHARD N. SWIFT)

This article updates the *Macropædia* article UNITED NATIONS.

COMMONWEALTH OF NATIONS

On June 20, 1985, the Maldives and St. Vincent and the Grenadines attained full membership in the Commonwealth of Nations. Both countries had been special members of the Commonwealth, the Maldives since 1982 and St. Vincent since 1979. Of the Commonwealth's 49 members, only two—Nauru and Tuvalu—now retained special-member status, which carried the right to participate in all Commonwealth activities with the exception of the biennial Commonwealth heads of government meeting (CHOGM). In July the Commonwealth Secretariat, established at the 1965 CHOGM to provide a central organization for consultation and cooperation among member countries, celebrated its 20th anniversary.

All 47 full members of the Commonwealth were represented at the CHOGM held in Nassau, The Bahamas, on October 16–22. Since the previous CHOGM, held in 1983 at New Delhi, India, there had been changes of leadership not only in India itself but also in several other Commonwealth countries. Among leaders attending their first CHOGM in 1985 were those of Barbados, Belize, Canada, Grenada, Guyana, Malta, New Zealand, and Nigeria. During the course of 1985 Pres. Forbes Burnham of Guyana and Prime Minister J. M. G. Adams of Barbados died (*see* OBITUARIES); Pres. Julius Nyerere of Tanzania and Pres. Siaka Stevens of Sierra Leone handed over to their successors. Nigeria experienced its second coup in 20 months.

The main focus of the CHOGM was to formulate a means of applying pressure on the government of South Africa to dismantle apartheid and speed up the process of granting independence to South West Africa/Namibia. The meeting was concerned to reach a compromise that would be acceptable to the leaders of black African nations, who favoured stringent sanctions, on the one hand and to U.K. Prime Minister Margaret Thatcher, a staunch opponent of economic sanctions, on the other. On the final day the leaders agreed on a number of limited economic "measures" (the word sanctions was not used in the final communiqué) that included a ban on loans to South Africa, action to prevent the importation of Krugerrands, an embargo on the sale of petroleum, arms, ammunition, and computer equipment capable of being used by the security forces, and the discouragement of cultural and scientific contacts. The agreement also proposed that a group of "eminent Commonwealth persons" seek to facilitate a dialogue with the South African government to encourage internal political reform and that further measures be considered if adequate progress had not been made at the end of a six-month period.

The CHOGM also discussed trouble spots in India and Sri Lanka, where Sikh and Tamil populations, respectively, were seeking self-determination; expressed concern at the rising incidence of drug abuse and stressed the need for greater cooperation in fighting drug trafficking; and endorsed the report of a consultative committee established at the New Delhi CHOGM to examine the particular vulnerability, both political and economic, of small states. Pacific members of the Commonwealth criticized France for continuing to conduct nuclear tests in French Polynesia.

In 1984 the Commonwealth Development Corporation (CDC) initiated 31 new projects worth £101.4 million in 20 countries to bring total investment to £590 million in 49 countries. Most of the new projects supported by the CDC were concerned with developing renewable natural resources in African countries. The CDC made its first commitment in Sri Lanka, to develop sugarcane production, and supported a hydroelectricity project in Papua

New Guinea. The Commonwealth Fund for Technical Cooperation (CFTC) increased its funding to £27 million in 1985–86, compared with £23 million in 1984–85. The U.K. provided 30% of the CFTC's total funding, and a large proportion of the U.K.'s overseas aid budget was directed toward poorer Commonwealth countries.

(MOLLY MORTIMER)

POLITICAL PARTIES

The following table is a general world guide to political parties. All countries that were independent on Dec. 31, 1985, are included; there are a number for which no analysis of political activities can be given. Parties are included in most instances only if represented in parliaments (in the lower house in bicameral legislatures); the figures in the last column indicate the number of seats obtained in the last general election (figures in parentheses are those of the penultimate one). The date of the most recent election follows the name of the country.

The code letters in the affiliation column show the relative political positions of the parties within each country; there is, therefore, no entry in this column for single-party states. There are obvious difficulties involved in labeling parties within the political spectrum of a given country. The key chosen is as follows: F-fascist; ER-extreme right; R-right; CR-centre right; C-centre; L-non-Marxist left; SD-social democrat; S-socialist; EL-extreme left; and K-Communist.

The percentages in the column "Voting strength" indicate proportions of the valid votes cast for the respective parties, or the number of registered voters who went to the polls in single-party states.

Political Parties

Country / Name of party	Affiliation	Voting strength (%)	Parliamentary representation
Afghanistan			
Pro-Soviet government since April 27, 1978	—	—	—
Albania (November 1982)			
Albanian Labour (Communist)	—	99.9	250 (250)
Algeria (March 1982)			
National Liberation Front	—	99.9	281 (261)
Angola (August 1980)			
Movimiento Popular de Libertaçao de Angola (MPLA)	—		203
Antigua and Barbuda (April 1984)			
Antigua Labour Party	C	...	16 (13)
Progressive Labour Movement	L	...	0 (3)
Independents	—	...	1 (1)
Argentina (November 1985)			
Movimiento Justicialista Nacional (Peronist)	CR	34.5	103 (111)
Unión Cívica Radical	C	43.0	130 (129)
Others	—	22.5	21 (14)
Australia (December 1984)			
National	R	...	21 (17)
Liberal	C	...	45 (33)
Labor	L	...	82 (75)
Austria (April 1983)			
Freiheitliche Partei Österreichs	R	5.0	12 (11)
Österreichische Volkspartei	C	43.2	81 (77)
Sozialistische Partei Österreichs	SD	47.8	90 (95)
Others	—	4.0	0 (0)
Bahamas, The (June 1982)			
Progressive Liberal Party	CR	53	32 (30)
Free National Movement	L	43	8 (2)
Others	—	...	3 ...
Bahrain			
Emirate, no parties	—	—	—
Bangladesh			
On March 24, 1983, Gen. Hossain Ershad seized power from the civilian government	—	—	—
Barbados (June 1981)			
Democratic Labour	C	47.1	10 (7)
Barbados Labour	L	52.2	17 (17)
Belgium (October 1985)			
Vlaams Blok	ER	1.4	1 (1)
Volksunie	R	7.8	16 (20)
Front Démocratique des Francophones	R	1.2	3 (8)
Liberals { Flemish	CR	10.7	22 (28)
{ French	CR	10.2	24 (24)
Social Christians { Flemish	C	21.3	49 (43)
{ French	C	7.9	20 (18)
Socialists { Flemish	SD	14.5	32 (26)
{ French	SD	13.7	35 (35)
Others	—	6.2	10 (11)
Belize (December 1984)			
United Democratic Party	R	...	21 (5)
People's United Party	C	...	7 (13)
Benin (November 1979)			
People's Revolutionary Party	—	—	336
Bhutan			
A monarchy without parties	—	—	—
Bolivia (July 1985)			
Acción Democrática Nacionalista	R	37.0	52
Movimiento Nacionalista Revolucionario	C	42.0	60
Christian Democratic Party	C	2.0	3
Movimiento de la Izquierda Revolucionaria	L	11.0	16

Country / Name of party	Affiliation	Voting strength (%)	Parliamentary representation
Small left-wing parties	L	15.0	22
Botswana (September 1984)			
Botswana Democratic Party	C	...	29 (29)
Botswana People's Party	L	...	1 (1)
Botswana National Front	EL	...	4 (2)
Brazil (November 1982)			
Movimiento Democrático Brasileiro	CR	44.1	200
Partido Democrático Social	C	39.4	234
Partido Trabalhista Democrático	S	6.7	24
Partido Trabalhista Brasileiro	S	5.5	13
Partido dos Trabalhadores	EL	4.3	8
Brunei			
Legislative Council	—	...	33
Bulgaria (June 1981)			
Fatherland Front			
Bulgarian Communist Party	—	99.9 {	271
Bulgarian Agrarian Union			99 400 (400)
No party affiliation			30
Burkina Faso			
National Revolutionary Council since August 1983	—	—	—
Burma (October 1985)			
Burma Socialist Program Party	—	...	489 (475)
Burundi (October 1974)			
Tutsi ethnic minority government	—	—	—
Cameroon (May 1983)			
Cameroonian National Union	—	99.3	120 (120)
Canada (September 1984)			
Progressive Conservative	CR	50.0	211 (103)
Liberal	C	28.0	40 (147)
New Democratic	L	19.0	30 (32)
Others	—	...	1 (0)
Cape Verde (December 1980)			
African Party for the Independence of Guinea-Bissau and Cape Verde	—	93.0	—
Central African Republic			
Military Committee of National Recovery took power on Sept. 1, 1981	—	...	—
Chad			
Military government since 1975	—	—	—
Chile			
Military junta since Sept. 11, 1973	—	—	—
China, People's Republic of (February 1978)			
Communist (Kungchantang) National People's Congress	—	...	3,500
Colombia (March 1982)			
Partido Conservador	R	...	84 (86)
Partido Liberal	C	...	114 (109)
Unión Nacional de Oposición	L	...	1 (4)
Comoros (March 1982)			
Federal Assembly	—	...	38
Congo (July 1979)			
Parti Congolais du Travail	—	—	115
Costa Rica (February 1982)			
Partido de Liberación Nacional	R	55	33 (25)
Partido Cristiano Democrático	C	30	18 (27)
Three left-wing parties	L	15	6 (5)
Cuba (December 1981)			
Partido Comunista Cubano	—	99.0	499 (481)
Cyprus			
Greek Zone (December 1985)			
Democratic Rally	CR	33.56	19 (12)
Democratic Party (DIKO)	C	27.65	16 (8)

Country / Name of party	Affiliation	Voting strength (%)	Parliamentary representation
Socialist Party (EDEK)	SD	11.07	6 (3)
Communist Party (AKEL)	K	27.43	15 (12)
Turkish Zone (June 1985)			
National Turkish Party	—	...	24
Communal Liberation Party	—	...	10
Turkish Republican Party	—	...	12
New Dawn Party (Renaissance)	—	...	4
Czechoslovakia (June 1981)			
National Front	—	99.5	200 (200)
Denmark (January 1984)			
Conservative	R	23.4	42 (26)
Liberal Democratic (Venstre)	CR	12.1	22 (21)
Christian People's	CR	2.7	5 (4)
Progress	C	3.6	6 (16)
Radical Liberal (Radikale Venstre)	C	5.5	10 (9)
Centre Democrats	C	4.6	8 (15)
Social Democrats	SD	31.6	56 (59)
Socialist People's	EL	11.5	21 (20)
Left Socialists	EL	2.7	5 (5)
Faeroe Islands and Greenland	—	...	4 (4)
Djibouti (May 1982)			
One-party state: National Assembly	—	...	65
Dominica (July 1985)			
Freedom Party	C	59.0	15 (17)
Labour Party	L	...	5 (2)
Independents	—	...	1 (2)
Dominican Republic (May 1982)			
Partido Reformista	R	37.0	... (42)
Partido Revolucionario	L	48.4	... (49)
Others	—	...	...
Ecuador (January 1984)			
Popular Democracy	R	...	4
Democratic Party	CR	...	5
National Reconstruction Front			
Social Christian Party			9
Radical Liberal Party			4
Conservative Party	CR	...16 {	2
National Revolutionary Party			1
Others			0
Concentration of Popular Forces	C	...	7
Democratic Left (Izquierda Democrática)	L	...	25
Democratic Popular Movement	EL	...	3
Left Broad Front	EL	...	2
Others	—	...	9
Egypt (May 1984)			
New Wafd Party	R	15.12	57
National Democratic Party	CR	72.99	391
Socialist Labour Party	L	7.07	0
National Progressive Unionist Party	L	4.17	0
El Salvador (March 1985)			
Alianza Republicana Nacionalista	R	29	13 (19)
Partido Auténtico Institucional Salvadoreño	R	...	1 (0)
Partido de Conciliación Nacional	CR	8	12 (13)
Partido Acción Democrática	CR	...	1 (18)
Partido Cristiano Democrático	C	54	33 (40)
Equatorial Guinea (August 1983)			
National Assembly	—	...	41
Ethiopia			
Military government since 1974	—	—	—
Fiji (July 1982)			
Alliance Party (mainly Fijian)	—	...	28 (36)
National Federation (mainly Indian)	—	...	22 (15)
Others	—	...	2 (1)
Finland (March 1983)			
National Coalition Party (Conservative)	R	22.1	44 (47)
Swedish People's	R	4.6	11 (10)

Political Parties

Country Name of party	Affili-ation	Voting strength (%)	Parlia-mentary represen-tation
Centre (including former Liberal)			
Party	C	17.6	38 (40)
Christian League	C	3.0	3 (9)
Rural Party	C	9.7	17 (7)
Social Democratic	SD	26.7	57 (52)
People's Democratic League			
(Communist)	K	14.0	27 (35)
Green Party	—	1.5	2 —
Others	—	...	1 (0)
France (June 1981)			
Centre-Right:			
Gaullists (Rassemblement pour			
la République)	R	...	83 (148)
Giscardians (Union pour la			
Démocratie Française)	CR	...	64 (137)
Other	—	...	11 (6)
Union of Left:			
Parti Radical	L	...	14 (10)
Parti Socialiste	SD	...	269 (103)
Parti Communiste	K	...	44 (86)
Others	—	...	6 (1)
Gabon (February–March 1985)			
Parti Démocratique Gabonais	—	95.44	111 (84)
Gambia, The (April 1982)			
People's Progressive Party	C	61.7	27 (28)
Three other parties	—	...	8 (7)
German Democratic Republic (June 1981)			
National Front	—	99.2	500 (500)
(Sozialistische Einheitspartei and others)			
Germany, Federal Republic of (March 1983)			
Christlich-Demokratische Union	R	38.2	191 (174)
Christlich-Soziale Union		10.6	53 (52)
Freie Demokratische Partei	C	6.9	34 (53)
Sozialdemokratische Partei			
Deutschlands	SD	38.2	193 (218)
The Green (Ecology) Party	—	5.6	27 (0)
Ghana			
Military dictatorship since Dec. 31, 1981	—	—	—
Greece (June 1985)			
New Democracy Party	CR	40.8	126 (115)
Panhellenic Socialist Movement (Pasok)	SD	45.8	161 (172)
Greek Communist Party (KKE)	K	9.4	12 (13)
Eurocommunists	K	1.4	1 (0)
Grenada (December 1984)			
New National Party	C	...	14
Grenada United Labour Party	R	...	1
Guatemala (November 1985)			
Movimiento de Liberación Nacional	ER	...	...
Partido Democrático de Cooperación Nacional	CR	...	...
Unión de Centro Nacional	C	...	...
Democrácia Cristiana	C	...	...
Partido Socialista Democrático	SD	...	...
Guinea			
Military Committee for National Redress in power since April 1984	—	—	—
Guinea-Bissau			
Governed by the Council of the Revolution since Nov. 14, 1980	—	—	—
Guyana (December 1985)			
People's National Congress	R	77.0	42 (41)
People's Progressive Party	L	11.0	8 (10)
Others	...	0.5	3 (0)
Haiti (February 1984)			
Conseil National d'Action Jean-Claudiste	—	...	59
Honduras (November 1985)			
Partido Nacional	R	...	63 (34)
Partido Liberal	CR	...	66 (44)
Others	C	...	3 (4)
Hungary (June 1985)			
Patriotic People's Front	—	...	361
Independents	—	...	25
Iceland			
Independence (Conservative)	R	38.7	23 (21)
Progressive (Farmers' Party)	C	19.0	14 (17)
Social Democratic	SD	11.7	6 (10)
Social Democratic Alliance	EL	7.3	4 —
People's Alliance	K	17.3	10 (11)
Feminists		5.5	3 —
India (December 1984; figures incomplete)			
Congress (I)	C	...	395 (351)
Communist Party of India (Marxist)	K	...	22 (35)
Communist Party (pro-Soviet)	K	...	6 (10)
Other opposition parties and independents		...	121

Country Name of party	Affili-ation	Voting strength (%)	Parlia-mentary represen-tation
Indonesia (May 1982)			
Golkar (Functional Groups)	—	64.3	342
United Development Party	—	27.8	94
Indonesian Democratic Party (merger of five nationalist and Christian parties)	—	7.9	24
Iran (May 1984)			
Islamic Republican Party	R	...	251
Iraq			
Military and B'ath Party governments since 1958	—	...	...
Ireland (November 1982)			
Fianna Fail (Sons of Destiny)	C	...	75 (81)
Fine Gael (United Ireland)	C	...	70 (63)
Irish Labour Party	L	...	16 (15)
Others	—	...	5 (7)
Israel (July 1984)			
Tehiya	ER	4.0	5 (3)
Kach	ER	1.2	1 —
Likud { Herut / Liberal }	R	31.9	41 (48)
National Religious	CR	3.5	4 (6)
Agudat Israel	C	1.7	2 (4)
Yahad	C	2.2	3 —
Ometz	C	1.2	1 —
Labour Alignment { Labour / Mapam }	SD	34.9	44 (47)
Civil Rights	SD	2.4	3 (1)
Shinui	SD	2.6	3 (2)
Progressive List for Peace	EL	1.8	2 —
Hadash	K	3.4	4 (4)
Others			7 (5)
Italy (June 1983)			
Movimento Sociale Italiano	F	6.8	42 (30)
Partito Liberale Italiano	CR	2.9	16 (9)
Democrazia Cristiana	C	32.9	225 (262)
Partito Repubblicano Italiano	C	5.1	29 (16)
Partito Social-Democratico Italiano	L	4.1	23 (20)
Partito Socialista Italiano	SD	11.4	73 (62)
Partito Radicale	EL	2.2	11 (18)
Partito Comunista Italiano	K	29.2	198 (201)
Südtiroler Volkspartei	—	0.5	3 (4)
Others	—	4.2	10 (8)
Ivory Coast (October 1980)			
Parti Démocratique de la Côte d'Ivoire	—	99.9	100
Jamaica (December 1983)			
Jamaica Labour Party	L	60	60 (51)
People's National Party	SD	(Boycotted)	(9)
Japan (December 1983)			
Liberal-Democratic	R	...	250 (284)
Komeito (Clean Government)	CR	...	58 (33)
Democratic-Socialist	SD	...	38 (32)
Socialist	S	...	112 (107)
Communist	K	...	26 (29)
Others	—	...	27 (26)
Jordan			
Royal government, no parties	—	...	60
Kampuchea (May 1981)			
Kampuchean United Front for National Salvation (Vietnamese-backed)	—	99.0	117
Kenya (September 1983)			
Kenya African National Union	—	48.0	158
Kiribati (January 1983)			
House of Assembly, no formal parties	—	...	35
Korea, North (February 1982)			
Korean Workers' (Communist) Party	—	100.0	615 (579)
Korea, South (February 1985)			
Korea National Party	CR	9.2	20 (25)
Democratic Justice Party	C	35.3	148 (151)
New Korea Democratic Party	L	28.6	67 —
Democratic Korea Party	L	17.6	35 (81)
Independents and others	—		6 (19)
Kuwait (February 1985)			
Princely government with elected National Assembly, no parties	—	50	(30)
Laos, People's Democratic Republic of			
Lao People's Revolutionary Party	—	...	...
Lebanon (April 1972)			
Maronites (Roman Catholics)	—		30
Sunni Muslims	—		20
Shi'ah Muslims	—		19
Greek Orthodox	—		11
Druzes (Muslim sect)	—		6
Melchites (Greek Catholics)	—		6
Armenian Orthodox	—		4
Other Christian	—		2
Armenian Catholics	—		1
Lesotho			
Constitution suspended Jan. 30, 1970	—	—	—

Country Name of party	Affili-ation	Voting strength (%)	Parlia-mentary represen-tation
Liberia (October 1985)			
National Democratic Party of Liberia	R	...	45
Opposition	L	...	19
Libya			
Military government since Sept. 1, 1969	—	—	—
Liechtenstein (February 1982)			
Vaterländische Union	CR	53.5	8 (8)
Fortschrittliche Bürgerpartei	C	46.5	7 (7)
Luxembourg (June 1984)			
Parti Chrétien Social	CR	...	25 (24)
Parti Libéral	C	...	14 (15)
Parti Ouvrier Socialiste	SD	...	21 (14)
Parti Communiste	K	...	2 (2)
Ecologists	—	...	2 (0)
Madagascar (August 1983)			
Advance Guard of the Malagasy Revolution (Arema)	C	64.8	117 (112)
Madagascar Independence Congress	L	8.8	9 (16)
Movement for Proletarian Power	L	11.1	3 —
People's Party for National Unity	L	10.6	6 (7)
Madagascar National Independence Movement (Monima)	L	3.7	2 —
Malawi (June 1983)			
Malawi Congress Party	—	...	101 (87)
Malaysia (April 1982)			
National Front (Barisan Nasional)			
United Malays National Organization		70	
Malaysian Chinese Association		24	
Malaysian Indian Congress		4	}133 (131)
Gerakan		5	
Sabah and Sarawak		30	
Opposition Parties			
Democratic Action Party		9	
Partai Islam Malaysia		5	} 21 (23)
Independents		7	
Maldives (February 1975)			
Presidential rule since 1975			
Mali (June 1985)			
Union Démocratique du Peuple Malien	—	...	82
Malta (December 1981)			
Nationalist Party	R	...	31 (31)
Labour Party	SD	...	34 (34)
Mauritania			
Military government since April 25, 1981	—	—	—
Mauritius (August 1983)			
Independence (Labour) Party			(2)
Parti Mauricien Social-Démocrate	C	41	(2)
Mouvement Socialiste Mauricien			(2)
Mouvement Militant Mauricien	L	...	19 (42)
Parti Socialiste Mauricien	—	—	(18)
Organisation du Peuple Rodriguais	—	...	2 (2)
Mexico (July 1985)			
Partido Revolucionario Institucional	CR	64.8	289 (299)
Partido Acción Nacional	CR	16.2	9 (1)
Partido Auténtico de la Revolución	CR	3.1	2 (0)
Monaco (January 1978)			
Union Nationale et Démocratique	—	...	18 (17)
Mongolia (June 1981)			
Mongolian People's Revolutionary Party	—	99.9	354 (354)
Morocco (September 1984)			
Union Constitutionelle	CR	...	83 —
Rassemblement National des Indépendants	CR	...	61 (141)
Mouvement Populaire	CR	...	47 (44)
Istiqlal (Independence)	C	...	41 (49)
Union Socialiste des Forces Populaires	L	...	36 (16)
Others	—	...	38 (14)
Mozambique (December 1977)			
Frente da Libertação do Moçambique (Frelimo)	—	...	210
Nauru (December 1983)			
Independents	—	...	18
Nepal (May 1981)			
140-member Parliament, 122 elected and 28 appointed by the king; no parties			
Netherlands, The (September 1982)			
Christian Democratic Appeal	CR	29.3	45 (48)
Liberals (VVD)	C	23.0	36 (26)
Democrats 1966	C	4.3	6 (17)
Labour (PVDA)	SD	30.4	47 (44)
Others	—	13.0	16 (15)
New Zealand (July 1984)			
New Zealand Party	CR	12.0	0 —
National (Conservative)	CR	36.0	37 (47)

Political Parties

Country Name of party	Affili- ation	Voting strength (%)	Parlia- mentary represen- tation	
Social Credit	C	8.0	2	(2)
Labour Party	L	43.0	56	(43)
Nicaragua (November 1984)				
Democratic Conservative Party	CR	14.0	14	
Independent Liberal Party	C	9.6	9	
Popular Social Christian Party	L	5.6	6	
Sandinista National Liberation Front	L	66.8	61	
Socialist Party of Nicaragua	EL	1.4	2	
Communist Party of Nicaragua	K	1.5	2	
Marxist-Leninist Popular Action Movement	K	1.0	2	
Niger				
Military government since April 1974	—	—	—	
Nigeria				
Military government since December 1983	—	—	—	
Norway (September 1985)				
Høyre (Conservative)	R	30.1	50	(53)
Kristelig Folkeparti	CR	8.3	16	(15)
Senterpartiet (Agrarian)	C	6.7	12	(11)
Venstre (Liberal)	C	3.1	0	(2)
Progress Party	C	3.7	2	(4)
Arbeiderpartiet (Labour)	SD	41.2	71	(66)
Sosialistisk Venstreparti (Socialist Left)	S	5.4	6	(4)
Oman				
Independent sultanate, no parties	—	—	—	
Pakistan (February 1985)				
National Assembly (no parties)	—	...	237	
Panama				
Since July 1982 a civilian president under "indirect" military supervision	—	—	—	
Papua New Guinea (June 1982)				
Pangu Party	—	34.0	50	(39)
United Party	—	7.2	9	(38)
People's Progress Party	—	10.0	14	(18)
National Party	—	10.0	13	(3)
Independents	—	20.9	4	
Paraguay (February 1983)				
Partido Colorado (A. Stroessner)	R	90.0	40	
Opposition parties	—	10.0	20	
Peru (April 1985)				
Convergencia Democrática	R	...	12	
Acción Popular	CR	...	10	
Alianza Popular Revolucionaria Americana	SD	...	107	
Izquierda Unida	L	...	48	
Izquierda Nacionalista	L	...	1	
Independents	—	...	2	
Philippines				
Martial law lifted Jan. 17, 1981	—	—	—	
Poland (October 1985)				
Front of National Unity				
Polish United Workers' Party			245	(261)
United Peasants' party			106	(113)
Democratic Party	—	78.86	35	(37)
Non-party			74	(49)
Portugal (October 1985)				
Democratic and Social Centre	R	15.0	22	(30)
Democratic Renewal Party	CR	21.0	45	—
Social Democratic Party	C	29.0	88	(75)
Socialist Party	SD	20.0	57	(101)
United People's Alliance	K	15.0	38	(44)
Qatar				
Independent emirate, no parties	—	—	—	
Romania (March 1985)				
Social Democracy and Unity Front	—	99.99	389	(369)
Rwanda (December 1983)				
National Revolutionary Development Movement	—	...	70	
Saint Christopher and Nevis (June 1984)				
People's Action Movement	CR	...	6	(3)
Nevis Reformation Party	CR	...	3	(2)
Labour Party	L	...	2	(4)
Saint Lucia (May 1982)				
United Workers' Party	C	...	14	(5)
St. Lucia Labour Party	S	...	2	(12)
Progressive Labour Party	EL	...	1	(0)
Saint Vincent and the Grenadines (July 1984)				
St. Vincent Labour Party	CR	41.4	4	(11)
New Democratic Party	C	51.4	9	(2)
United People's Movement	L	3.2	0	(0)
San Marino (May 1983)				
Communist coalition				
Partito Comunista			15	(16)
Partito Social Democratico		...	9	(9)
Partito Socialista Unitario			8	(8)

Country Name of party	Affili- ation	Voting strength (%)	Parlia- mentary represen- tation	
Christian Democrats		...	26	(26)
São Tomé and Príncipe (1975)				
Movimento Libertaçao	—	—	—	
Saudi Arabia				
Royal government, no parties	—	—	—	
Senegal (February 1983)				
Parti Socialiste	CR	79.9	111	(83)
Parti Démocratique Sénégalais	L	14.0	8	(17)
Rassemblement National Démocratique	EL	2.6	1	—
Ligue Démocratique	K	1.1	0	—
Seychelles (August 1983)				
People's Progressive Front	—	59.3	23	
Sierra Leone (June 1978)				
All People's Congress	CR	...	85	(70)
Singapore (December 1984)				
People's Action Party	CR	64.38	77	(75)
Workers' Party	L	12.79	1	(0)
Democratic Party	—	3.70	1	(0)
Solomon Islands (October 1984)				
National Democratic Party	L	...	1	
United Party	—	...	13	
People's Alliance Party	—	...	12	
Solomone Ano Sagufenua	—	...	4	
Independents	—	...	7	
Somalia (December 1984)				
Somalian Revolutionary Socialist Party	—	99.86	171	(171)
South Africa (April 1981)				
Herstigte Nasionale Partij	ER	13.8	0	(0)
National Conservative Party	R		0	—
National Party	R	56.1	131	(134)
South Africa Party	CR	—		(3)
New Republic Party	C	7.7	8	(10)
Progressive Federal Party	L	19.1	26	(17)
Spain (October 1982)				
Alianza Popular	R	25.35	105	(9)
Unión Centro-Democrático	C	7.26	11	(168)
Partido Socialista Obrero Español	SD	46.07	201	(121)
Partido Comunista Español	K	3.87	5	(23)
Catalan nationalists	—	3.73	12	(8)
Basque nationalists	—	1.91	8	(7)
Herri Batasuna (Basque radicals)	—	0.97	2	(3)
Others	—		6	(14)
Sri Lanka (July 1977)				
United National Party	R	...	140	(19)
Freedom Party	C	...	8	(91)
Tamil United Liberation Front	C	...	18	(12)
Communists and others	—	...	2	(44)
Sudan, The				
Military Council in power since April 1985	—	—	—	
Suriname				
National Military Council since 1980	—	—	—	
Swaziland				
Royal government, no parties	—	—	—	
Sweden (September 1985)				
Conservative	R	21.4	76	(86)
Centre	CR	12.5	44	(56)
Liberal	C	14.3	51	(21)
Social Democrats	SD	44.9	159	(166)
Communists	K	5.4	19	(20)
Switzerland (October 1983)				
Christian Democrats (Conservative)	R	...	42	(44)
Republican Movement	R	...	0	(1)
National Campaign	R	...	5	(2)
Evangelical People's	R	...	3	(3)
Swiss People's (ex-Middle Class)	CR	...	23	(23)
Radical Democrats	C	...	54	(51)
League of Independents	C	...	8	(8)
Liberal Democrats	L	...	8	(8)
Social Democrats	SD	...	47	(51)
Progressive Organization (Socialists)	EL	...	3	(3)
Communist Party	K	...	1	(3)
Environmentalist Party	—	...	3	—
Others	—	...	3	(3)
Syria (November 1981)				
National Progressive Front	—	...	195	(159)
Others	—	...	0	(36)
Taiwan (Republic of China)				
Nationalist (Kuomintang)	—	...	773	
Tanzania (October 1985)				
Chama Cha Mapinduzi	—	...	111	
Thailand (April 1983)				
Prachakorn Thai	ER	...	36	
Chart Thai (Thai Nation)	R	...	73	
Social Action Party	C	...	92	
Democratic Party	C	...	56	
Siam Democratic Party	—	...	18	
National Democratic Party	—	...	15	
Independents	—	...	24	

Country Name of party	Affili- ation	Voting strength (%)	Parlia- mentary represen- tation	
Four other parties	—	...	10	
Togo (March 1985)				
Rassemblement du Peuple Togolais	—	96.0	77	(67)
Tonga (May 1981)				
Legislative Assembly (partially elected)	—	—	21	
Trinidad and Tobago (November 1981)				
People's National Movement	C	...	26	(24)
Organization for National Reconstruction	—	...	0	—
National Alliance:				
United Labour Front	L	...	8	(10)
Democratic Action Congress	EL	...	2	(2)
Tunisia (November 1981)				
National Front (led by the Parti Socialiste Destourien)	—	94.6	136	(121)
Turkey (November 1983)				
Nationalist Democracy Party	R	23.0	71	
Motherland Party	CR	45.0	212	
Populist Party	C	30.0	117	
Tuvalu (September 1985)				
House of Assembly, no political parties	—	—	12	
Uganda				
Military Council in power since July 1985	—	—	—	
Union of Soviet Socialist Republics (November 1984)				
Communist Party of the Soviet Union	—	99.99	1,500	(1,500)
United Arab Emirates				
Federal government of seven emirates	—	—	—	
United Kingdom (June 1983)				
Conservative	R	42.4	397	(339)
Alliance				
Liberal	C	25.4 {	17	(11)
Social Democratic	C		6	—
Labour	L	27.6	209	(268)
Communist	K	—	0	(0)
Scottish National Party	—	1.1	2	(2)
Plaid Cymru (Welsh Nationalists)	—	0.4	2	(2)
Ulster Unionists (three groups)	—	...	15	(10)
Social Democratic and Labour Party	—	...	1	(1)
Sinn Fein (Northern Ireland)	—	...	1	—
United States (November 1984)				
Republican	CR	...	183	(166)
Democratic	C	...	252	(267)
Uruguay (November 1984)				
Colorado Party (Conservative)	R	38.6	40	
Unión Civica	CR	2.3	2	
National (Blanco) Party	C	32.9	36	
Frento Amplio (Broad Front)	L	20.4		
Vanuatu (November 1983)				
Vanuaaku Pati	C	...	24	(26)
Others	—	...	15	(13)
Venezuela (December 1983)				
COPEI (Social Christians)	CR	28.31	...	(88)
Acción Democrática	L	44.25	118	(88)
Movimiento al Socialismo	SD	...	...	(11)
Partido Comunista Venezolano	K	...	...	(7)
Others	—	...	...	(7)
Vietnam, Socialist Republic of (April 1981)				
Communist Party	—	...	...	
Yemen, People's Democratic Republic of				
National Liberation Front	—	...	...	
Yemen Arab Republic				
Military government since 1974	—	—	—	
Yugoslavia (May 1982)				
Communist-controlled Federal Chamber	K	...	220	(220)
Zaire (October 1977)				
Legislative Council of the Mouvement Populaire de la Révolution	—	...	268	
Zambia (October 1983)				
United National Independence Party	—	67.0	125	
Zimbabwe (June–July 1985)				
Zimbabwe African National Union	—	77.0	63	(57)
Zimbabwe African People's Union	—	20.0	15	(20)
United African National Council	—	...	0	(3)
Zimbabwe African National Union (Sithole)	—	...	1	(0)
white roll				
Conservative Alliance of Zimbabwe	—	...	15	(20)
Independent Zimbabwe	—	...	4	—
Independent	—	...	1	(0)

(K. M. SMOGORZEWSKI)

Africa South of the Sahara

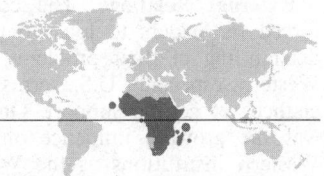

AFRICAN AFFAIRS

The African continent's economic condition slumped in 1985 to its lowest point since the rise of the modern independent nations after World War II. The combined impact of five years of drought over almost half of the land area, accelerating desertification, the world economic recession, heavy indebtedness to overseas creditors, rapid population growth, and a climate of political instability threatened many African countries with the prospect of economic collapse. Economic hardship fueled political unrest that produced a new crop of both successful and abortive political coups, while the long-standing violent conflicts in southern Africa, the Horn of Africa, Chad, and the Western Sahara were brought no closer to a settlement.

Economic and Social Affairs. The annual World Bank report warned of "the spectre of disaster" confronting Africa and the international community. Although good rainfall in 1985 broke the five-year drought in the sub-Saharan region, the area's worst in 150 years, many of the 34 affected countries were not expected to produce sufficient crops before 1986. It was estimated that by then as many as 200 million people could be desperately short of food. Unless the level of international aid was increased substantially, the immediate prospect was of a situation worse than the acute 1973–74 famine disaster.

According to the UN Food and Agriculture Organization, 1,000,000,000 tons of topsoil were lost by means of erosion every year. During the previous 20 years food production in the continent had decreased by 20%. According to the UN Economic Commission for Africa (ECA), instead of the expected modest recovery of per capita income by 3.1%, the best that might be hoped for in 1985 was 2.6%, representing a continuing drop in real per capita income.

Organization of African Unity. The summit meeting of the Organization of African Unity (OAU) held in Addis Ababa, Eth., on July 18–20 devoted itself mainly to proposals for dealing with Africa's "unprecedented economic and social crisis." In his role as chairman, Pres. Julius Nyerere of Tanzania stressed that the continent was not only underdeveloped and poor but also too fragmented to organize its resources effectively. He argued that the realities of dwindling external capital flows compelled the continent to base its development plans on its own internal resources. The OAU adopted a program for economic recovery centred on five main issues: action to rehabilitate agriculture and improve food supplies; a concerted campaign to halt the advance of the desert; the achievement of an African common market by the year 2000; negotiations with the developed nations to ease Africa's external debt, which stood at about $170 billion; and a common platform for subregional, regional, continental, and international cooperation.

Among other major decisions taken were a call for sanctions against South Africa because of its racial separation policies, criticism of South Africa and the U.S. for obstructing the liberation of South West Africa/Namibia, and a new initiative to end the fighting in both Chad and the Western Sahara. The heads of state resolved the deadlock over the appointment of a new administrative secretary-general for the OAU by agreeing on Ide Oumarou, for-

eign minister of Niger. Pres. Abdou Diouf of Senegal was elected chairman for 1985–86.

Southern Africa. Predictions that the Nkomati accord that was signed in 1984 between South Africa and Mozambique would defuse the violence and instability of the region were not fulfilled. In spite of the accord, Mozambique's security problems became more acute because of attacks by the rebel Mozambique National Resistance (MNR). Mozambique's accusations that South Africa had failed to live up to its side of the agreement brought admissions that there had been some failures, described by South Africa as technical rather than deliberate breaches.

The 1984 cease-fire agreement between Angola and South Africa also failed to live up to its promise. Although South Africa's armed forces finally withdrew from Angola in April, their military attacks and sabotage activities continued. As Jonas Savimbi's National Union for the Total Independence of Angola (UNITA), which received strong support from South Africa, stepped up military pressures, Soviet support for the Angolan Army and the Cuban combat troops stationed in Angola also increased. The U.S. Congress moved toward giving greater support to UNITA by repealing the Clark amendment, which had precluded clandestine support for such movements.

Negotiations over Namibia's independence in terms of UN Resolution 435 reached a stalemate over the issue of the withdrawal of all Cuban troops from Angola. The Angolan offer, negotiated by the U.S., to begin phasing out the Cubans failed to satisfy South Africa. Although the armed struggle for independence of the South West Africa People's Organization (SWAPO) was blunted by Angola's decision not to allow incursions across its border, its international diplomatic offensive was maintained. The new interim government installed in Namibia by South Africa was not accorded recognition by any Western power.

Meanwhile, the situation inside South Africa itself deteriorated seriously during the year with a significant rise in the level of violence. (See *South Africa:* Special Report, below.)

Horn of Africa. The violent conflicts in and around Ethiopia showed no sign of lessening. Several military offensives mounted by the government against liberation movements in Eritrea and Tigre failed to break their resistance to Ethiopia's Marxist-Leninist regime. In a bid to force The Sudan to end its support for the Eritreans, the Ethiopians increased their aid to the rebel Sudan People's Liberation Army. Efforts by the new Sudanese military regime to end the hostilities with the SPLA were unsuccessful, and relations between The Sudan and Ethiopia remained uneasy.

Coups and Inter-African Affairs. After a period of fewer coup attempts, the number again increased in 1985. In April Pres. Gaafar Nimeiry of The Sudan was toppled in a military coup, led by Gen. 'Abd ar-Rahman Siwar ad-Dahab (*see* BIOGRAPHIES). In July Pres. Milton Obote of Uganda was overthrown by the Army, which installed Lieut. Gen. Tito Okello (*see* BIOGRAPHIES) as head of state, and in August a struggle between rival factions of the Nigerian Army ended in the replacement of Maj. Gen. Mohammed Buhari by Maj. Gen. Ibrahim Babangida (*see* BIOGRAPHIES). The successful coups were comparatively bloodless, unlike abortive coup attempts in Guinea and Liberia.

The tenth anniversary of the 16-nation Economic Community of West African States (ECOWAS) became an occasion to examine why the regional grouping had failed to live up to its earlier promise. One suggested reason was that governments were still too concerned about defending

their sovereignty. The main achievements of ECOWAS were a protocol on free movement of people within the region, a major investment program to develop a regional telecommunications system, and a coordinated program to develop the trans-Sahara road network.

The 14-nation Southern African Development Coordination Conference (SADCC), in operation for five years, continued to make progress in fulfilling its major objective of lessening the dependence of its members on South Africa. Another practical example of cooperation among SADCC's members was Zimbabwe's decision to commit up to 7,000 troops to assist Mozambique in protecting its communication routes and in fighting the MNR.

Political Systems. Two African presidents voluntarily relinquished office during the year. Pres. Julius Nyerere of Tanzania was succeeded by Ali Hassan Mwinyi (*see* BIOGRAPHIES), and Pres. Siaka Stevens of Sierra Leone was succeeded by Maj. Gen. Joseph Saidu Momoh (*see* BIOGRAPHIES). The only other African leader who had previously stepped down of his own accord was Pres. Léopold Senghor of Senegal in 1980.

The first attempt in 15 years to hold multiparty elections in Lesotho was frustrated when all the opposition parties refused to participate because of objections to the new electoral system. The first elections in Liberia since the 1980 coup were conducted in an atmosphere of controversy and bitter rancour. The incumbent head of state, Gen. Samuel Doe, who secured just over half of the votes cast in the presidential election, faced and overcame an attempted military coup within weeks of his victory. After Zimbabwe's first elections since gaining independence in 1980, Prime Minister Robert Mugabe began negotiations with opposition leader Joshua Nkomo aimed at introducing a single-party system.

Population and Refugees. Africa's population continued to grow at an average of 3% a year, faster than that of any other continent. Kenya's growth rate of over 4% was the highest in the world, with Zimbabwe following close behind.

Drought and famine increased the number of refugees and substantially enlarged the number of internally displaced people. While no exact figures were available, the generally accepted estimate exceeded five million, the largest number of refugees within any continent. The situation in Ethiopia contributed by far the greatest number; about 700,000 Ethiopians had fled to Somalia and 660,-000 to The Sudan. Some 300,000 Angolans had fled to Zaire and almost 100,000 Namibians to Angola, and an estimated 130,000 Ugandans were living in exile in neighbouring countries.

External Relations. The continent's economic crisis forced its leaders to look to the West for aid and understanding of their problems and needs and to accept Western, especially U.S., terms in order to improve their chances of getting support. One immediate consequence was the growing influence on African policies of such Western institutions as the World Bank and the International Monetary Fund (IMF). A number of countries such as Guinea, The Sudan, Zambia, and Tanzania, all formerly wedded to centralized economies, undertook to expand private-sector operations, a prerequisite for IMF and U.S. aid. This situation produced strongly ambivalent attitudes toward U.S.-supported international institutions, particularly the IMF.

The U.S. strengthened its position in Mozambique, which increasingly reduced its connections with Moscow. U.S. Pres. Ronald Reagan seriously upset South Africa, which had previously regarded him as its principal Western ally, by signing an executive order for a program of selective sanctions against South Africa. Nevertheless, the OAU adopted a harshly critical resolution against the U.S. because of its failure to persuade Pretoria to implement the UN resolution on Namibia, while the possibility of the U.S. providing support for UNITA threatened to become a major point of new conflict between the majority of African countries and Washington.

Among Western European countries France continued to be the most politically active in the continent, as well as one of the largest donors of aid. Along with the Scandinavian countries, France led the Europeans in the militancy of its hostility toward South Africa. The interests of West Germany, like those of Japan, remained primarily in trade. The U.K. found itself almost isolated within the Commonwealth because of Prime Minister Margaret Thatcher's adamant opposition to economic sanctions against South Africa.

The Soviet Union, which played a relatively small part in African affairs during 1985, devoted most of its aid and attention to Ethiopia and Angola. It also contributed substantially to two liberation movements, the African National Congress of South Africa and SWAPO. The Soviet bloc suffered in the opinion of Africans because of its failure to measure up to the Western response in providing food and other aid programs to alleviate the suffering caused by the famine conditions. Cuba withdrew all its troops from Ethiopia and announced its readiness to phase out its military presence in Angola once the issue of Namibian independence had been settled.

(COLIN LEGUM)

See also *Dependent States,* below.

AP/WIDE WORLD

The 21st meeting of the Organization of African Unity, meeting in Addis Ababa, Ethiopia, in July, declared that most countries on the continent were on the brink of economic disaster and blamed a variety of causes for the situation. A resolution expressing gratitude to the international community for famine relief efforts was not approved.

ANGOLA

A people's republic, Angola is located on the Atlantic coast in southwestern Africa. The small exclave of Cabinda is separated from Angola by a strip of Congo. Area: 1,246,700 sq km (481,350 sq mi). Pop. (1985 est.): 8,754,000. Cap.: Luanda. Monetary unit: kwanza, with (Oct. 21, 1985) a free rate of 29.50 kwanzas to U.S. $1 (42.30 kwanzas = £1 sterling). President in 1985, José Eduardo dos Santos.

Addressing the national conference of the ruling Movimento Popular de Libertação de Angola (MPLA) in Luanda in January 1985, Angolan Pres. José Eduardo dos Santos reaffirmed his government's commitment to Marxism-Leninism and to strengthening its material links with the socialist world. In practice this did not prevent the development of economic relations with Western nations. Within days of making his speech, President dos Santos welcomed a number of senior representatives of Gulf Oil and the Chevron Corp. to Luanda, and at the same time attempts were made to arrange the exchange of oil for food from Brazil. Spain agreed to work toward extending trading links with Angola, while Sweden offered aid to develop the fishing industry. During 1984 oil exports rose by 30%, and there was every prospect that output would be increased still further. The MPLA elected President dos Santos to a second five-year term on December 9.

Although the military activities of the National Union for the Total Independence of Angola (UNITA) rebels continued to be limited mainly to small-scale ambushes and raids, they were widespread enough to bring virtual devastation to much of the central region of the country. Acute shortages of fuel and essential foodstuffs were exacerbated by the disruption of communications, and hundreds of thousands of displaced persons placed a heavy burden on the nation's resources. From time to time the rebels attempted a more spectacular strike intended to demonstrate to the outside world that they were a force to be reckoned with. In December 1984 UNITA forces attacked the diamond-mining town of Cafunfo in the north, claiming to have killed more than 100 government troops and to have captured a number of European technicians. The attack achieved its main objective of arousing external attention while at the same time striking a blow at the recently reorganized diamond industry, Angola's second highest export earner. However, President dos Santos refused to contemplate any coalition government that included UNITA representatives.

Some South African troops remained in southern Angola, ostensibly to guard against incursions by forces of the South West Africa People's Organization (SWAPO) into Namibia. The government believed, however, that South Africa's objective was to accomplish its overthrow and to ensure the withdrawal of Cuban troops from the country. South Africa had not been appeased by President dos Santos's offer in November 1984 to agree to withdraw Cuban troops after South Africa had withdrawn its own forces from Angola and ceased to assist UNITA, and after Namibia had achieved independence. U.S. mediation brought about a new agreement in April by which Angola agreed to send home 10,000 Cuban troops as an initial gesture and South Africa promised to withdraw its forces from Angola immediately.

It emerged that South Africa had not fully honoured the agreement when a small South African raiding party was intercepted by Angolan forces in the Cabinda enclave in May. While South Africa described the party as a reconnaissance force seeking out SWAPO and African National

At a press conference in Jamba in September, Jonas Savimbi, leader of the National Union for the Total Independence of Angola (UNITA), charged that the Soviet Union was taking a direct role in supporting the Marxist government in Luanda.
REUTERS/BETTMANN NEWSPHOTOS

Congress training areas, the Angolans believed that its aim had been to sabotage an oil refinery and accordingly announced their intention to break off negotiations with South Africa. In June President dos Santos opened the meeting of nonaligned countries in Luanda by demanding mandatory sanctions against South Africa and by calling on the U.S. to stop giving financial assistance to UNITA. There were subsequent raids into southern Angola by South African forces claiming to be in pursuit of SWAPO guerrillas in June and September. The government accused the South Africans of secretly assisting UNITA rebels, who had become increasingly hard pressed during the year. As a result of improvements in training and equipment, government forces began to achieve a notable measure of success against UNITA. The Air Force, reinforced by a number of Soviet-made aircraft, struck several damaging blows in support of ground troops.   (KENNETH INGHAM)

This article updates the *Macropædia* article SOUTHERN AFRICA: *Angola.*

BENIN

The people's republic of Benin is on the southern coast of West Africa, on the Gulf of Guinea. Area: 112,600 sq km (43,450 sq mi). Pop. (1985 est.): 4,005,000. Cap.: Porto-Novo. Monetary unit: CFA franc, with (Oct. 21, 1985) a par value of CFAF 50 to the French franc and a free rate of CFAF 402.02 to U.S. $1 (CFAF 576.50 = £1 sterling). President in 1985, Brig. Gen. Mathieu Kerekou.

During 1985 Pres. Mathieu Kerekou's government had to contend with widespread protests against its education policies among Benin's student population. Following strike action by students in April and early May, the National University of Benin and other educational establishments in Cotonou were closed until June 3. On June 11 the minister of secondary and higher education, Michel Alladaye, was removed from office and replaced by Vincent Guezodje; at the same time, a number of senior university officials were dismissed. On June 14 President Kerekou undertook a reshuffle of other ministers in the government.

Relations with France were reinforced during the year,

notably by the former colonial power's decision to increase its aid to Benin and by the visit of a French warship to Cotonou. On the other hand, efforts by Benin, together with Burkina Faso and Ghana, to improve economic and other cooperation with Libya foundered when the four countries' foreign ministers met in Ouagadougou, Burkina Faso, in January.   (PHILIPPE DECRAENE)

This article updates the *Macropædia* article WESTERN AFRICA: *Benin*.

BOTSWANA

A landlocked republic of southern Africa, Botswana is a member of the Commonwealth. Area: 581,987 sq km (224,706 sq mi). Pop. (1985 est.): 1,082,000. Cap.: Gaborone. Monetary unit: pula, with (Oct. 21, 1985) a free rate of 2.06 pula to U.S. $1 (2.96 pula = £1 sterling). President in 1985, Quett Masire.

On the night of June 14, 1985, members of the South African Defence Force attacked an alleged African National Congress (ANC) base in Botswana's capital, Gaborone. At least 15 people died in the raid. It was the culmination of several months of mounting pressure by South Africa on Botswana to deny sanctuary to ANC operatives. Earlier in the year Gaborone had been the scene of bomb attacks on refugees from South Africa.

Botswana remained extremely vulnerable to South African pressure. While only 17% of its exports went to South Africa, almost 90% of its imports came from that source, including one-fifth of its electricity and all of its petroleum. South African Pres. P. W. Botha's threat in August to expel migrant workers drew attention to the high number who were from Botswana—some 29,000, almost 19,000 of whom worked in the mines.

Nevertheless, Botswana's economy remained one of the fastest growing in Africa. Following a 15% devaluation of the pula in January, Peter Mmusi, vice-president and minister of finance and development planning, pointed out that the balance of payments position had improved and that the manufacturing sector continued to grow. Diamonds now accounted for 76% of export earnings, and the mining and livestock industries combined provided 88% of exports and 70% of government earnings. However, with inadequate rains for a fourth successive year, the grain harvest was expected to be poor.   (GUY ARNOLD)

This article updates the *Macropædia* article SOUTHERN AFRICA: *Botswana*.

BURKINA FASO

Burkina Faso (formerly Upper Volta) is a landlocked country of West Africa. Area: 274,200 sq km (105,900 sq mi). Pop. (1985 est.): 6,827,800. Cap.: Ouagadougou. Monetary unit: CFA franc, with (Oct. 21, 1985) a par value of CFAF 50 to the French franc and a free rate of CFAF 402.02 to U.S. $1 (CFAF 576.50 = £1 sterling). Head of state and chairman of the National Recovery Council in 1985, Capt. Thomas Sankara.

In the face of opposition from trade unions and students, Capt. Thomas Sankara's ruling National Revolutionary Council assumed an increasingly radical stance in 1985. The protests focused on austerity measures adopted in January and were countered by numerous arrests and the temporary closing in February of the Lycée Philippe-Zinda-Kabore, the principal educational establishment in Ouagadougou. Further arrests followed an explosion in a military camp in Ouagadougou on June 1 in which three soldiers were killed. A report released by Amnesty International on July 31 citing instances of the torture of detainees was repudiated by Sankara.

On August 4, the second anniversary of the revolution, Sankara warned opponents that they would be "judged and punished." At the same time, he suspended or reduced the sentences of several detainees, including former presidents Jean-Baptiste Ouedraogo and Saye Zerbo. A week later, on August 12, Sankara dissolved his government and appointed a new one, the third since his advent to power. On September 1, however, most of the ministers dismissed on August 12 were reinstated.

The foreign ministers of Burkina Faso, Benin, Ghana, and Libya met in Ouagadougou in January in an effort to improve relations between Libya and the other three. Negotiations were not successful, however.

On December 25 fighting broke out between troops of Burkina Faso and Mali over possession of a disputed border area known as the Agacher strip, which was believed to be rich in mineral deposits. Both sides claimed victory before a cease-fire was declared on December 29, following mediation by the Nigerian and Libyan governments.

(PHILIPPE DECRAENE)

This article updates the *Macropædia* article WESTERN AFRICA: *Burkina Faso*.

BURUNDI

Burundi is a landlocked republic of central Africa. Area: 27,834 sq km (10,747 sq mi). Pop. (1985 est.): 4,655,000. Cap.: Bujumbura. Monetary unit: Burundi franc, with (Oct. 21, 1985) a free rate of FBu 113.69 to U.S. $1 (FBu 163.03 = £1 sterling). President in 1985, Col. Jean-Baptiste Bagaza.

Relations between the Roman Catholic Church and the government of Burundi, already poor, took a turn for the worse in 1985 when the authorities threatened to arrest worshipers who attended services during working hours. In March ten Catholic missionaries were expelled from the country after they had been refused an extension of their visas. The government denied that its actions were anticlerical, claiming instead that the clergy had been "unable to adapt to the development of contemporary Burundian society."

The European Development Fund of the European Communities (EC) made a number of grants to assist with development projects. Among these was the improvement of the vital road link between Bujumbura and the market at Muzinda, an important route for the transportation of agricultural produce. Burundi remained overwhelmingly dependent on foreign aid, and its most pressing problem was to attract development advances that would keep pace with its fast-growing population.   (GUY ARNOLD)

This article updates the *Macropædia* article CENTRAL AFRICA: *Burundi*.

CAMEROON

A republic of western central Africa, Cameroon lies on the Gulf of Guinea. Area: 465,458 sq km (179,714 sq mi). Pop. (1985 est.): 9,635,000. Cap.: Yaoundé. Monetary unit: CFA franc, with (Oct. 21, 1985) a par value of CFAF 50 to the French franc and a free rate of CFAF 402.02 to U.S. $1 (CFAF 576.50 = £1 sterling). President in 1985, Paul Biya.

The year was marked by the consolidation of Pres. Paul Biya's personal authority. In March, at its first congress since his advent to power, the ruling Cameroonian National Union (UNC) was reconstituted as the Democratic Assembly of the Cameroonian People (RDPC), and Biya was reelected to the party's presidency. On August 24, in a major reshuffle of the government, the Ministry of Defense was placed under control of the presidency, while a

number of the UNC "old guard" were replaced by younger reformist RDPC members.

Cameroon's relations with France, worsened by the latter's believed complicity in the failed April 1984 mutiny, were improved by Biya's official visit to Paris in February. During the visit Biya stated that members of the Cameroonian Peoples' Union (UPC) were free to return to Cameroon, "but not with a UPC label." In August the former bishop of Nkongsamba, Msgr. Albert Ndongmo, was authorized to return from exile. The decision preceded by a few days the visit of Pope John Paul II to Cameroon on August 10–14.   (PHILIPPE DECRAENE)

This article updates the *Macropædia* article WESTERN AFRICA: *Cameroon.*

CAPE VERDE

The republic of Cape Verde occupies an island group in the Atlantic Ocean about 620 km (385 mi) off the west coast of Africa. Area: 4,033 sq km (1,557 sq mi). Pop. (1985 est.): 314,000. Cap.: Praia. Monetary unit: Cape Verde escudo, with (Oct. 21, 1985) a free rate of 89.21 escudos to U.S. $1 (127.92 escudos = £1 sterling). President in 1985, Aristide Pereira; prime minister, Pedro Pires.

During an official visit to Bulgaria in June 1985, Pres. Aristide Pereira of Cape Verde signed economic, commercial, scientific, cultural, and political accords. In 1985 Cape Verde also agreed to allow U.S. investment in the country. Closer ties were established with Morocco.

In drawing up the second five-year (1985–89) development plan, the government paid special attention to mobilizing the resources of its large overseas population. There were an estimated 600,000 Cape Verdians living overseas, about twice the population of the islands. In 1983, 2.8 billion escudos flowed into the islands in the form of repatriated earnings, enough to cover 93.9% of import costs. The government hoped to increase income from this source, but it also wished to encourage a return to the islands. The main investments under the development plan were to be in the fishing sector, the principal source of exports, and in small industries. The plan also provided favourable terms for expatriates to repatriate investment profits.

Praia's population, now approaching 50,000, was increasing at a rate of 5% a year, largely as a result of the exodus from rural areas. Ten years of drought had forced many peasants to move to the towns or to emigrate. Cape Verde remained heavily dependent upon aid.

(GUY ARNOLD)

This article updates the *Macropædia* article WESTERN AFRICA: *Cape Verde.*

CENTRAL AFRICAN REPUBLIC

The Central African Republic is a landlocked state in central Africa. Area: 622,436 sq km (240,324 sq mi). Pop. (1985 est.): 2,567,000. Cap.: Bangui. Monetary unit: CFA franc, with (Oct. 21, 1985) a par value of CFAF 50 to the French franc and a free rate of CFAF 402.02 to U.S. $1 (CFAF 576.50 = £1 sterling). Head of state in 1985 and chairman of the Military Committee of National Recovery to September 21, Gen. André Kolingba.

Opposition to Gen. André Kolingba's military regime increased during 1985. A communiqué published in Paris in January announced the formation of a government-in-exile headed by Gen. Alphonse M'Baikoua, one of the leaders of the failed coup of March 1982. François Guéret, minister of justice under former president David Dacko, was arrested on February 13 and on July 31 was sentenced

to ten years in prison for "an appeal for destabilization" of the regime. On September 21 General Kolingba dissolved the Military Committee of National Recovery and formed a new government in which six of the former military ministers were replaced by civilians. On several occasions during the year Chadian forces crossed the northern frontier to attack villages on the Central African side that were sheltering refugees from southern Chad.

Pope John Paul II arrived in Bangui on August 14 during his third African tour. In a court ruling in Paris in May, passages in *Ma Vérité* ("My Truth"), the autobiography of former emperor Jean-Bedel Bokassa, were held to defame former French president Valéry Giscard d'Estaing, and copies of the book were ordered destroyed.

(PHILIPPE DECRAENE)

This article updates the *Macropædia* article CENTRAL AFRICA: *Central African Republic.*

CHAD

Chad is a landlocked republic of central Africa. Area: 1,284,000 sq km (495,755 sq mi). Pop. (1985 est.): 5,018,000. Cap.: N'Djamena. Monetary unit: CFA franc, with (Oct. 21, 1985) a par value of CFAF 50 to the French franc and a free rate of CFAF 402.02 to U.S. $1 (CFAF 576.50 = £1 sterling). President in 1985, Hissen Habré.

Throughout 1985 the situation in Chad remained at an impasse, both politically and militarily. Pres. Hissen Habré's authority was diminished in the north by the presence of Libyan forces deployed as far as the 16th parallel and by former president Goukouni Oueddei's Libyan-backed Popular Armed Forces (FAP; the military wing of Goukouni's Transitional Government of National Union [GUNT]). The south was virtually controlled by dissident commandos ("codos") united under the command of Col. Alphonse Kotiga. Nevertheless, in March and April Habré toured the southern region, seeking to gain additional support. In June France provided supplementary budgetary aid of F 4.5 million to enable him to meet promises of financial support to dissident rebel groups that had agreed to rally to his government.

AP/WIDE WORLD

Continued drought and famine in Chad drove nomad families to seek temporary homes in refugee camps. A project developed by CARE distributed quarter-acre plots of land to nomad families and sponsored instruction in farming and shelter building.

In July Goukouni, Habré's chief rival for power, and leaders of the various other opposition factions met in Brazzaville (Congo). A further meeting was held in Cotonou (Benin) in August, but no substantive agreement on cooperation emerged from either of these meetings.

In January Chadian Minister of Foreign Affairs Gouara Lassou accused Libya of an attempt to assassinate Habré in September 1984. On a visit to Togo in March, Habré stated that Libya was reinforcing its troops and military equipment in the north. Later in the year there were reports of violent clashes in the Faya-Largeau area between the FAP and their Libyan allies. Subsequent rumours that Goukouni had been replaced by a former FAP leader, Mahamat Issa Idriss, were denied in October.

In February a spokesman of Exxon Corp. announced that petroleum prospecting, suspended since January 1979, was to be resumed in the Sarh region. Chad remained the country with the world's lowest per capita gross national product—$80.   (PHILIPPE DECRAENE)

This article updates the *Macropædia* article WESTERN AFRICA: *Chad.*

COMOROS

The republic of Comoros is an island state in the Indian Ocean off the east coast of Africa. Area: 1,862 sq km (719 sq mi), excluding the island of Mayotte, which continued to be a de facto dependency of France. Pop. (1985 est., excluding Mayotte): 403,000. Cap.: Moroni. Monetary unit: CFA franc, with (Oct. 21, 1985) a par value of CFAF 50 to the French franc and a free rate of CFAF 402.02 to U.S. $1 (CFAF 576.50 = £1 sterling). President in 1985, Ahmed Abdallah.

On March 8, 1985, while Pres. Ahmed Abdallah was on a private visit to France, an attempted coup by members of the presidential guard, three of whom were reported killed, was overcome. According to government sources, some 60 persons were arrested in connection with the attempt. At a trial held in Moroni in November, 18 persons were sentenced to life imprisonment and 47 others received lesser sentences.

During the year Abdallah twice reshuffled his government. In January former prime minister Ali Mroudjae was appointed minister of state for the interior; in September, among changes that included a reduction in the Cabinet to 9 ministers and 3 secretaries of state from a previous total of 16, he was dropped again.

In January Comoros, together with France, was admitted to membership in the Indian Ocean Commission, which previously comprised Madagascar, Mauritius, and Seychelles. In October, during a second, official, visit to France by Abdallah, the future status of the French dependency of Mayotte, over which Comoros claimed sovereignty, was discussed.   (PHILIPPE DECRAENE)

This article updates the *Macropædia* article INDIAN OCEAN ISLANDS: *Comoros.*

CONGO

A people's republic, Congo is in central Africa on the Atlantic Ocean. Area: 342,000 sq km (132,047 sq mi). Pop. (1985 est.): 1,740,000. Cap.: Brazzaville. Monetary unit: CFA franc, with (Oct. 21, 1985) a par value of CFAF 50 to the French franc and a free rate of CFAF 402.02 to U.S. $1 (CFAF 576.50 = £1 sterling). President in 1985, Col. Denis Sassou-Nguesso; prime minister, Ange-Édouard Poungui.

At a meeting of the ruling Congolese Labour Party (PCT) Central Committee in June 1985, Pres. Denis Sassou-Nguesso warned that the country's economy was heading toward catastrophe. After five years of economic expansion during which offshore oil production had more than doubled, declining demand had reduced revenue from oil exports—the main source of foreign exchange—to a "disappointing" level. Meanwhile, the country's external debt approached $1.5 billion, with debt service absorbing some 45% of state revenue. In the hope of avoiding recourse to the International Monetary Fund, President Sassou-Nguesso presented a program of austerity measures, involving heavy cuts in expenditure.

Efforts by Congo to mediate the conflict in Chad continued. In July leaders of the various Chadian opposition factions met in Brazzaville.   (PHILIPPE DECRAENE)

This article updates the *Macropædia* article CENTRAL AFRICA: *Congo.*

DJIBOUTI

The republic of Djibouti is in the Horn of northeastern Africa on the Gulf of Aden. Area: 23,200 sq km (8,950 sq mi). Pop. (1985 est.): 430,000. Cap.: Djibouti. Monetary unit: Djibouti franc, with (Oct. 21, 1985) a free rate of DF 163.88 to U.S. $1 (DF 235 = £1 sterling). President in 1985, Hassan Gouled Aptidon; prime minister, Barkat Gourad Hamadou.

During 1985 little news of Djibouti's domestic affairs filtered through to the outside world. Under Pres. Hassan Gouled Aptidon's authoritarian regime, the former French Territory of the Afars and Issas, which had received its independence in 1977, appeared to be developing increasingly into an Issa-dominated ethnocracy. In June it was officially stated that Defense Minister Habib Mohamed Loita had been dismissed from office.

The continued presence in Djibouti of a 5,000-strong French military contingent accounted for the frequent comings and goings of high-ranking French officials concerned with matters of defense. Total French aid to Djibouti was set at F 24 million for 1985–86. One of the main projects in progress was the extensive modernization of Djibouti's international port, with finance from the UN Development Program and from Arab and other Western European countries as well as France. Ambouli international airport was also being upgraded. In July, at a meeting of their joint ministerial council, Djibouti and Ethiopia signed an agreement on cooperation in agriculture, fisheries, transportation, and communications.

A new television transmitter situated at Arta, some 35 km (22 mi) from the capital, was inaugurated by President Gouled in June. It would extend reception of national programs to all parts of the country.

(PHILIPPE DECRAENE)

This article updates the *Macropædia* article EASTERN AFRICA: *Djibouti.*

EQUATORIAL GUINEA

The republic of Equatorial Guinea consists of Río Muni, on the Atlantic coast of West Africa, and the offshore islands of Bioko and Annobon. Area: 28,051 sq km (10,831 sq mi). Pop. (1985 est.): 317,000. Cap.: Malabo. Monetary unit: ekwele (plural: bipkwele), with (Oct. 21, 1985) a free rate of 402.02 bipkwele to U.S. $1 (576.50 bipkwele = £1 sterling). President of the Supreme Military Council in 1985, Lieut. Col. Teodoro Obiang Nguema Mbasogo; prime minister, Capt. Cristino Seriche Bioko.

Following Equatorial Guinea's 1983 decision to join the Central African Customs and Economic Union, formalities were completed by January 1985 for the country's entry into the Central Bank of West African States and the CFA franc zone. In December 1984 France agreed to provide

budgetary aid worth F 41.5 million to ease the transition. Pres. Teodoro Obiang Nguema's visit to France in June 1985 was further evidence of the increase in French influence at the expense of Spain, the former colonial power. However, membership in the CFA franc zone was unlikely to yield substantial benefits, given the severe economic problems facing the country.

Spain remained the principal trading partner and source of aid. In July the International Monetary Fund approved a standby arrangement for a maximum of 9.2 million Special Drawing Rights. Equatorial Guinea also had its debts rescheduled during the year.

In March Nigeria evacuated several hundred Nigerian workers who had been recruited to work in Equatorial Guinea's cocoa plantations. The move followed the fatal shooting of a Nigerian worker by security forces in February. (GUY ARNOLD)

This article updates the *Macropædia* article WESTERN AFRICA: *Equatorial Guinea.*

ETHIOPIA

The socialist state of Ethiopia is in the Horn of northeastern Africa, on the Red Sea. Area: 1,223,600 sq km (472,400 sq mi). Pop. (1985 est.): 43,551,000. Cap.: Addis Ababa. Monetary unit: birr, with (Oct. 21, 1985) a par value of 2.07 birr to U.S. $1 (free rate of 2.93 birr = £1 sterling). Head of state and chairman of the Provisional Military Administrative Council in 1985, Lieut. Col. Mengistu Haile Mariam.

A major development in Ethiopia during 1985 concerned a reassessment of the population and its distribution in light of the country's first national census, conducted with UN assistance in May 1984. The census claimed to have covered 85% of the population. Estimates were made from various sources for the remainder, largely the population of rural highland regions in Eritrea and Tigre and pastoral lowland areas in all regions. The new total was declared to be 42,020,000, compared with the previous Statistical Office estimate of 34.6 million for the same date. The annual growth rate was put at 2.9%. The evidence showed that population distribution was significantly different from the estimates. The population of the central region of Shewa,

By May 1985, in response to urgent appeals, the world community had sent more than 500,000 tons of cereal grain to famine-wracked Ethiopia. Distribution of the food, however, was hampered by the frequently obstructive policies of the Ethiopian government.

including the capital, Addis Ababa, was found to be nearly 23% of the total. The urban population of 4.7 million represented only 11.3% of the total, compared with estimates of around 15.2%.

The distribution of population had been significantly altered in the aftermath of the 1983–85 drought, which affected virtually all regions, most seriously Eritrea, Tigre, Welo (Wallo), and certain areas of northern Shewa. Drought also hit regions such as Gojam, which previously had produced an exportable surplus of grain. In some areas the major factor in the disruption of the rural economy had been the uncertainty and inadequacy of rainfall in marginal areas of cultivation. It was also clear, however, that the northern regions had reached the end of a long historical period of traditional land use during which soil fertility had declined, and vegetation degradation had reached a point where long-term environmental upgrading would be required. In these circumstances the government was concerned to resettle people in more fertile areas. As of June 1985 more than 170,000 families had been resettled in the western provinces, and more than 300,000 families were to be resettled by year's end. The majority had their origins in Tigre and Welo. To assist in building up the necessary infrastructure for new villages, the government launched a campaign that mobilized some 20,000 students and teachers during a three-month period in mid-1985. A French medical group, Médecins Sans Frontières, was ordered from the country after its chairman claimed that 100,000 people had died in the resettlement effort.

No figure had yet been put on the number of people who died during the famine. The problem had been compounded by the fact that extensive areas in the north were not under permanent government control as a result of secessionist activities. Figures released by the Relief and Rehabilitation Commission indicated that the total population requiring urgent relief supplies or supplementary feeding in various parts of the country rose to nine million in July. The response was a large, if somewhat belated, program of support from the international community, contributed mainly through nongovernmental organizations and inspired by television films transmitted by Western news media. At the same time, the airports from which airlifts of grain were organized offered the unique spectacle of transport planes from the U.S., the U.S.S.R., the U.K., East Germany, West Germany, Poland, Libya, and Italy lined up side by side on the tarmac.

The year brought rain to most regions in the country at the right time, but it remained to be seen whether the 1985 harvest would be sufficient. Grave doubts were expressed because the long period of food shortage and starvation had disorganized the agricultural economy. There was a shortage of seed grain; people were returning from feeding centres without farm implements or oxen; and the farming population in general was in a debilitated state. Further disruptions to food production occurred in the south where maize (corn) crops were attacked by an invasion of army worms, and the enset (false banana) plant, which provided the staple food for some three million people, was affected by disease. Livestock herds had been seriously reduced by shortages of water and pasture. Finally, a battle was being waged against the coffee berry disease, which was threatening the most important export crop.

Against this background of rural disaster, which would require a considerable volume of external assistance to combat, the September celebrations of the Ethiopian new year and the 11th anniversary of the revolution were somewhat subdued. The urban population, which provided the bulk of participants in the annual parades, had been very

seriously affected by food shortages, rising prices, and a general freeze on incomes that were frequently tapped for relief operations. The expected announcement of the new constitution for a republic, following the formation of the Workers' Party of Ethiopia in September 1984, did not materialize. The responsibility for drawing up the new constitution was handed to a special commission at the party congress held in September 1985.

There appeared to be no movement toward a settlement with the rebels in the north, where the fighting absorbed a significant proportion of government resources. Relations with Somalia also remained poor, and there were sporadic engagements along the lengthy border of the Ogaden. The Ethiopian regime reacted with anger when news broke in January of Israel's secret evacuation of thousands of Falashas (Ethiopian Jews) from Ethiopia to Israel.

This article updates the *Macropædia* article EASTERN AFRICA: *Ethiopia.*

GABON

Gabon is a republic of central Africa, on the Atlantic Ocean. Area: 267,667 sq km (103,347 sq mi). Pop.: in 1985 estimates varied from 564,000 to 1,682,000. Cap.: Libreville. Monetary unit: CFA franc, with (Oct. 21, 1985) a par value of CFAF 50 to the French franc and a free rate of CFAF 402.02 to U.S. $1 (CFAF 576.50 = £1 sterling). President in 1985, Omar Bongo; prime minister, Léon Mébiame.

Legislative elections held in Gabon on Feb. 17 and March 3, 1985, returned the ruling Gabonese Democratic Party (the only permitted party) to power with 99.48% of the votes cast in a 95.44% poll. In August Pres. Omar Bongo announced the release of six members of the banned Movement for National Renewal (Morena) imprisoned since 1982; he claimed that there were now no political detainees in Gabon. Some days previously (August 11), Capt. Alexandre Mandja Ngokouta, sentenced to death for plotting against the state, had been executed.

In January President Bongo initiated a campaign to track down and expel foreigners who entered the country illegally to undertake "anarchic" commercial activities. Lebanese storekeepers were singled out as the worst offenders. Franco-Gabonese cooperation was strengthened by a defense agreement signed in Paris on April 25. An irritant in the relationship was the presence in Paris of Morena, which in August announced the formation of a government-in-exile.

On May 1 Tenneco Inc. confirmed an important new oil strike 40 km (25 mi) off Port-Gentil.

(PHILIPPE DECRAENE)

This article updates the *Macropædia* article CENTRAL AFRICA: *Gabon.*

GAMBIA, THE

A republic and member of the Commonwealth, The Gambia extends from the Atlantic Ocean along the lower Gambia River in West Africa; it is surrounded by Senegal, with which it has formed an administrative union called Senegambia. Area: 10,690 sq km (4,127 sq mi). Pop. (1985 est.): 749,200. Cap.: Banjul. Monetary unit: dalasi, with (Oct. 21, 1985) a free rate of 3.49 dalasis to U.S. $1 (5 dalasis = £1 sterling). President in 1985, Sir Dawda Jawara.

Development of the Senegambian confederation, which entered its fourth year in February 1985, received a setback in March when Senegal's ambassador to The Gambia was recalled to Dakar at Banjul's request following an incident at a football match when the diplomat ordered Senegalese troops to restore calm. The presence of the Senegalese Army in The Gambia since the attempted coup of 1981 had been a source of some resentment. In February Pres. Sir Dawda Jawara lifted the state of emergency that had been in force since the coup attempt.

The poor state of the economy seriously hindered negotiations aimed at achieving economic integration with Senegal. Early in 1985 the International Monetary Fund (IMF) withdrew its standby arrangement, forcing the government to turn to the U.S. for food aid and to The Netherlands for fuel aid. Nevertheless, by July there were severe shortages of fuel and rice. Public anger was directed not against the government, which was perceived to be doing its best, but against the IMF and the Organization of Petroleum Exporting Countries, which were accused of holding the country ransom by imposing conditions that it could not meet. (GUY ARNOLD)

This article updates the *Macropædia* article WESTERN AFRICA: *The Gambia.*

GHANA

A republic of West Africa and member of the Commonwealth, Ghana lies on the Gulf of Guinea. Area: 238,533 sq km (92,098 sq mi). Pop. (1985 est.): 12,815,300. Cap.: Accra. Monetary unit: cedi, with (Oct. 21, 1985) a free rate of 60.16 cedis to U.S. $1 (86.27 cedis = £1 sterling). Chairman of the Provisional National Defense Council in 1985, Jerry John Rawlings.

During 1985 there were signs that hard effort and aid combined were enabling Ghana to tackle some of its more serious economic problems. Inflation was reduced to 19%, compared with 39% the previous year, and the government was committed to implementing the economic reform measures proposed by the International Monetary Fund and the World Bank: devaluation, reduction of the budget deficit, and reorganization of the public sector.

The economy received massive injections of aid during the year, a sign that Jerry John Rawlings's administration had won recognition and support from key Western

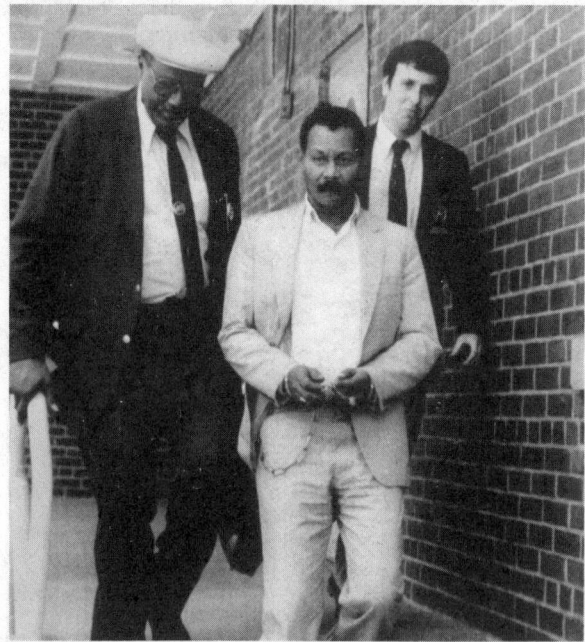

Michael Agbotui Soussoundis of Ghana was arrested by FBI agents in July and charged with receiving classified information about Central Intelligence Agency operations in Ghana from Sharon Scranage, a CIA employee who was also charged with espionage.

donors, notably Canada, The Netherlands, and the U.K. In June the International Development Association approved a $40 million credit to assist a three-year (1986–88) program to rehabilitate a section of the Accra–Kumasi road.

Relations with the U.S. remained strained, however. A widespread CIA operation in Ghana was revealed in July when the U.S. authorities arrested Sharon Scranage, a CIA agent in Accra, who admitted providing details of the agency's intelligence-gathering network to a Ghanaian national. As Scranage's trial revealed the extent of her alleged disclosures, a number of senior Ghanaian officials fled the country.

At the end of November sources in Lomé reported that almost 9,000 Ghanaians had fled to Togo following violent clashes between rival tribes.   (GUY ARNOLD)

This article updates the *Macropædia* article WESTERN AFRICA: *Ghana.*

GUINEA

The republic of Guinea is located in West Africa, on the Atlantic Ocean. Area: 245,857 sq km (94,926 sq mi). Pop. (1985 est.): 5,429,000. Cap.: Conakry. Monetary unit: syli, with (Oct. 21, 1985) a free rate of 23.26 sylis to U.S. $1 (33.35 sylis = £1 sterling). President in 1985, Brig. Gen. Lansana Conté.

An attempted coup on the night of July 4–5, 1985, led by Education Minister Col. Diara Traoré (prime minister during April–December 1984), was put down at the cost of 18 dead and 229 wounded (official figures). The attempt was made during the absence of Brig. Gen. Lansana Conté, head of the ruling Military Committee for National Redress (CMRN), at a meeting in Togo of the Economic Community of West African States.

On his return to Conakry, Conté (recently promoted by the CMRN from his previous rank of colonel) indicated that the coup leaders would face execution. A military tribunal was established on August 13 to try those implicated, who included several other members of the government besides Traoré. No reports of the trials were subsequently released. Frontiers with Guinea's neighbours, closed immediately after the coup attempt, were reopened on July 12, and a curfew was rescinded. Earlier, in May, some 30 leading figures of the regime of the late Pres. Ahmed Sékou Touré had been released from detention, charges against them having been dropped.

Encouraged by increased popular support after the failed coup, the CMRN sought ways to revive the bankrupt economy, drained by currency trafficking and a ubiquitous black market.   (PHILIPPE DECRAENE)

This article updates the *Macropædia* article WESTERN AFRICA: *Guinea.*

GUINEA-BISSAU

A republic of West Africa, Guinea-Bissau lies on the Atlantic Ocean. Area: 36,125 sq km (13,948 sq mi). Pop. (1985 est.): 873,000. Cap.: Bissau. Monetary unit: peso, with (Oct. 21, 1985) a free rate of 147.22 pesos to U.S. $1 (211.11 pesos = £1 sterling). President in 1985, João Bernardo Vieira.

In January 1985 Guinea-Bissau's attorney general, Nicandro Barreto, was dismissed from his post, accused of supporting former prime minister Victor Saúde Maria in his alleged attempt to seize power from Pres. João Bernardo Vieira in 1984. In November 1985 the government claimed that it had foiled another plot to overthrow Vieira. Vice-Pres. Paulo Correia, who was accused of masterminding the plan, was arrested.

In February the International Court of Justice at The Hague delivered its verdict in the dispute between Guinea-Bissau and Guinea over their maritime boundary. The decision awarded Guinea-Bissau almost two-thirds of the contested area. It was later confirmed that petroleum deposits had been discovered there.

Angola granted credit worth $2.5 million to Guinea-Bissau for the purchase of Angolan refined petroleum products and promised to supply petroleum by-products over a five-year period in exchange for agricultural and industrial products from Guinea-Bissau. West Germany provided a loan worth DM 8 million to finance development projects. During the year President Vieira visited Gabon, South Korea, and Pakistan, as well as neighbouring Guinea and Senegal.   (GUY ARNOLD)

This article updates the *Macropædia* article WESTERN AFRICA: *Guinea-Bissau.*

IVORY COAST

A republic of West Africa, the Ivory Coast lies on the Gulf of Guinea. Area: 320,763 sq km (123,847 sq mi). Pop. (1985 est.): 10,163,000. Cap.: Abidjan. Monetary unit: CFA franc, with (Oct. 21, 1985) a par value of CFAF 50 to the French franc and a free rate of CFAF 402.02 to U.S. $1 (CFAF 576.50 = £1 sterling). President in 1985, Félix Houphouët-Boigny.

Pres. Félix Houphouët-Boigny's reelection to a sixth five-year term on Oct. 27, 1985, by 100% of the voters in a 99.98% poll, did nothing to dispel concern at home and abroad over the still open question of his successor. This uncertainty continued to affect the recession-hit economy. Even so, stringent austerity measures and record harvests of cocoa (more than 500,000 metric tons), coffee (270,000 tons), and cotton (212,000 tons) helped to secure an International Monetary Fund standby credit of 66.2 million SDRs (Special Drawing Rights) for the year.

Relations with neighbouring Ghana and Burkina Faso were of particular concern during the year. In June, in a drive against illegal immigrants, Ivory Coast expelled some 500 of the 300,000 Ghanaians resident there. In September, following a soccer match between Ivorian and Ghanaian teams at Kumasi, Ghana, there was widespread violence directed against the Ghanaian community in Ivory Coast. Relations with Burkina Faso, already at a low ebb for ideological reasons, worsened in April when a prominent Burkinabe businessman was murdered in Abidjan. In December Ivory Coast and Israel announced that they intended to resume diplomatic relations.

On August 10, in the course of his African tour, Pope John Paul II inaugurated St. Paul's Cathedral in Abidjan. He had laid its cornerstone in May 1980.

(PHILIPPE DECRAENE)

This article updates the *Macropædia* article WESTERN AFRICA: *Ivory Coast.*

KENYA

A republic and member of the Commonwealth, Kenya is in eastern Africa, on the Indian Ocean. Area: 582,646 sq km (224,961 sq mi), including 11,230 sq km of inland water. Pop. (1985 est.): 20,312,000. Cap.: Nairobi. Monetary unit: Kenya shilling, with (Oct. 21, 1985) a free rate of K Sh 16.53 to U.S. $1 (K Sh 23.70 = £1 sterling). President in 1985, Daniel arap Moi.

The setbacks caused by three years of drought in Kenya were compounded in January 1985 when about 36,500 ha (90,000 ac) of land were devastated by army worms. By April, however, following plentiful and widely dispersed rainfall, the situation had improved greatly. In 1985 the

country as a whole was self-sufficient in food production, with food supplies from more fertile districts being diverted to areas badly hit by prolonged famine. In order to reimburse farmers who had been affected by the drought, the prices of milk, tea, sugar, rice, and beef were raised in February. Later in the year, higher production costs led to price increases of 16% for bread and more than 20% for maize (corn) meal.

Prices offered on the world market for the main export crops, tea and coffee, were low. However, a loan of more than $40 million from a consortium of British banks allowed the government to finance existing coffee stocks until a market could be found for them. As a result, in spite of the reduction in the 1984–85 coffee crop, Kenya met the export quota permitted by the International Coffee Organization in full. The government's close adherence to the stabilization program prepared by the International Monetary Fund maintained economic growth and brought a reduction in the trade deficit, along with a proportionate fall in the inflation rate.

The reopening of the rail link between Taveta, Kenya, and Kahe, Tanzania, in February provided evidence of the improving relations between the two countries. Initially, only freight trains operated across the border. However, both passengers and freight were carried on the weekly steamer service across Lake Victoria connecting Kisumu, Kenya, and Mwanza, Tanzania, which was restored at the same time. The following month, under pressure from the European Communities, ministers met with their counterparts from Tanzania and Uganda and agreed to the revival of a number of joint projects involving the three countries. Initially, they planned to work out means of cooperation in the fields of transport and communications, tourism, and scientific research. Then, in October, the three heads of government met to consider the wider implications of cooperation, though it was clear that there was no intention of reviving the East African Community, which had linked the three countries before it broke up in 1977.

June elections within the ruling Kenya African National Union introduced a number of new members into the party hierarchy. In August there was a reshuffle of the Cabinet with a view to increasing efficiency in economic planning. Of particular importance was the appointment of Robert Ouko as minister of planning and national development. Ouko had considerable experience as foreign minister and as minister of labour and was well known to a number of international financiers.

In February students at the University of Nairobi once again came into conflict with the government after three of their leaders were expelled without explanation and five others were deprived of their scholarships. In the course of the demonstrations that followed, a student was killed when riot police tried to disperse protesters. Some 2,500 students were ordered to leave the university and report to their local chiefs.

Echoes of a more serious clash were reawakened in September with the announcement of the release of Stephen Muriithi, jailed after the attempted coup against Pres. Daniel arap Moi in 1982, and reports—neither confirmed nor denied by the government—that 12 leaders of the coup attempt had been executed in July. Two men connected with the coup remained in detention: Raila Odinga, the son of former vice-president Oginga Odinga, and a journalist, Otemo Mak'onyango.

The conference ending the UN Decade for Women was held in Nairobi in July.   (KENNETH INGHAM)

This article updates the *Macropædia* article EASTERN AFRICA: *Kenya.*

LESOTHO

A constitutional monarchy of southern Africa and member of the Commonwealth, Lesotho forms a landlocked enclave within South Africa. Area: 30,355 sq km (11,720 sq mi). Pop. (1985 est.): 1,499,600. Cap.: Maseru. Monetary unit: loti (plural: maloti), at par with the South African rand, with (Oct. 21, 1985) a free rate of 2.60 maloti to U.S. $1 (3.72 maloti = £1 sterling). King, Moshoeshoe II; prime minister in 1985, Chief Leabua Jonathan.

On July 31, 1985, Lesotho's prime minister, Chief Leabua Jonathan, announced that general elections would take place in September. Two weeks later, however, the elections were canceled after the opposition parties refused to take part. Had they taken place, the elections would have been the first since 1970, when Chief Jonathan suspended the constitution before the results were announced.

South African Pres. P. W. Botha's threat to repatriate migrant workers from neighbouring countries if economic sanctions were applied to South Africa highlighted Lesotho's vulnerability to economic pressure from its neighbour. South Africa's mines provided employment for more than 100,000 people from Lesotho, whose remitted wages accounted for 50% of Lesotho's gross national product. Nevertheless, King Moshoeshoe II urged Western nations to enforce sanctions despite the possible consequences. Pretoria denied the Lesotho government's claim that South Africa was behind the killing of nine persons, allegedly South African refugees, in a raid on Maseru December 20.

(GUY ARNOLD)

This article updates the *Macropædia* article SOUTHERN AFRICA: *Lesotho.*

LIBERIA

The republic of Liberia is located in West Africa, on the Atlantic Ocean. Area: 99,067 sq km (38,250 sq mi). Pop. (1985 est.): 2,232,000. Cap.: Monrovia. Monetary unit: Liberian dollar, at par with the U.S. dollar, with a free rate (Oct. 21, 1985) of L$1.43 to £1 sterling. Head of state in 1985, Gen. Samuel K. Doe.

In a year that was deeply troubled both politically and economically, events in Liberia were dominated by presidential and legislative elections and two attempts to assassinate the country's chief of state. The elections, postponed from October 1984, took place on Oct. 15, 1985. Gen. Samuel K. Doe, military leader since the 1980 coup, won 51% of the presidential vote, while his National Democratic Party of Liberia secured more than two-thirds of the seats in both the Senate and the House of Representatives. (For tabulated results, see *Political Parties,* above.) The newly elected administration was to take office in January 1986. The elections were not without incident. Prior to polling day opposition groups suffered overt harrassment, and a number of their leaders were banned from political activity. The Liberian People's Party and the United People's Party were refused the certification required to contest the elections. Jackson Doe, leader of the Liberian Action Party and runner-up in the presidential vote, accused the government of extensive interference in the voting.

Early in the year the U.S. earmarked aid worth $93 million for Liberia in 1985–86. Subsequently, the U.S. Congress decided not to release the funds until it was satisfied that a return to civilian rule—accompanied by the release of political prisoners—had been effected.

In April Lieut. Col. Moses Flanzamaton, a member of the presidential guard, was executed for leading an attempt

to assassinate General Doe. In November rebel troops under the leadership of Brig. Gen. Thomas Quiwonkpa shelled the Executive Mansion; Quiwonkpa announced over the radio that he had overthrown Doe, but Doe later told his listening countrymen that the coup had failed. Quiwonkpa, who five years before had helped Doe to seize power, was subsequently apprehended and executed.   (GUY ARNOLD)

This article updates the *Macropædia* article WESTERN AFRICA: *Liberia*.

MADAGASCAR

The republic of Madagascar occupies the island of the same name and minor adjacent islands in the Indian Ocean off the southeast coast of Africa. Area: 587,041 sq km (226,658 sq mi). Pop. (1985 est.): 10,012,000. Cap.: Antananarivo. Monetary unit: Malagasy franc, with (Oct. 21, 1985) a free rate of FMG 537.31 to U.S. $1 (FMG 770.50 = £1 sterling). President in 1985, Didier Ratsiraka; prime minister, Lieut. Col. Désiré Rakotoarijaona.

A ministerial reshuffle announced by Pres. Didier Ratsiraka on Feb. 21, 1985, put newcomers in charge of social affairs, rural development, industry, and information. Three of the new ministers were young technocrats, while the fourth, Simon Pierre, who took over the information portfolio, was a leading ideologist of President Ratsiraka's ruling Advance Guard of the Malagasy Revolution.

Social unrest and violence continued to characterize daily life in Madagascar. In January an Italian missionary was decapitated and mutilated—the second foreign priest to be murdered within a few months. On July 31–August 1 security forces supported by tanks attacked the Antananarivo headquarters of the antigovernment kung fu sect that had been banned the previous year. Pierre Mizael Andrianarijaona, the sect's leader, was killed with 19 of his followers.

In foreign relations, Ratsiraka sought closer links with France and the U.S. In February Andriana Rahinjaka, president of the National Assembly, led a parliamentary delegation to Washington, D.C. In June, in the course of celebrations marking the tenth anniversary of Ratsiraka's accession to the presidency, Antananarivo gave a spectacular welcome to Mme Danielle Mitterrand, wife of the French president. There were also moves to normalize relations with Comoros. In May the Paris Club of creditor countries agreed to a rescheduling of Madagascar's external debt of approximately $2 billion.   (PHILIPPE DECRAENE)

This article updates the *Macropædia* article INDIAN OCEAN ISLANDS: *Madagascar*.

MALAWI

A republic and member of the Commonwealth, Malawi is a landlocked state in eastern Africa. Area: 118,484 sq km (45,747 sq mi). Pop. (1985 est.): 7,058,800. Cap.: Lilongwe. Monetary unit: kwacha, with (Oct. 21, 1985) a free rate of 1.69 kwacha to U.S. $1 (2.42 kwacha = £1 sterling). President in 1985, Hastings Kamuzu Banda.

Unlike many of its neighbours, Malawi escaped the effects of the 1984 drought, and in 1985 agricultural production again reached record levels. There remained, however, three serious problems. First, earlier heavy demand for Malawi's surplus maize (corn) crop seemed unlikely to be sustained because of the excellent rainfall throughout the region in 1985. Second, troubles in Mozambique disrupted the railway system on which Malawi depended for the export of its main cash crops (tobacco, tea, and sugar). Third, since nearly 40% of revenue in the 1985–86 budget

was earmarked for the servicing of external and internal debt, it was necessary to curtail external borrowing and to curb the budget deficit, to the detriment of a number of services. Nevertheless, though inflation remained high, the economy was buoyant. More than 30% of capital expenditure was set aside to alleviate transport problems.

Maintaining his pragmatic approach to foreign relations, Pres. Hastings Kamuzu Banda announced at the annual convention of the Malawi Congress Party in September that, while disliking the Communist system, he was prepared to have friendly relations with Soviet-bloc countries. This in no way affected Malawi's contacts with South Africa and Israel. In April President Banda paid a four-day visit to the U.K.   (KENNETH INGHAM)

This article updates the *Macropædia* article SOUTHERN AFRICA: *Malawi*.

MALI

Mali is a landlocked republic of West Africa. Area: 1,240,192 sq km (478,841 sq mi). Pop. (1985 est.): 7,904,000. Cap.: Bamako. Monetary unit: CFA franc, with (Oct. 21, 1985) a par value of CFAF 50 to the French franc and a free rate of CFAF 402.02 to U.S. $1 (CFAF 576.50 = £1 sterling). President in 1985, Gen. Moussa Traoré.

On June 9, 1985, Pres. Moussa Traoré, whose personal authority had been reinforced by changes in the government at the end of the previous year, was reelected unopposed for an additional six-year term. In parliamentary elections held on the same day, all the candidates on the list of the ruling and sole political party, the Democratic Union of the Malian People (UDPM), were duly elected to the National Assembly. Previously, at the UDPM party congress in March, President Traoré had been reappointed secretary-general of the UDPM central executive bureau.

Mali was one of the sub-Saharan countries worst hit by drought. In January Interior Minister Lieut. Col. Abderhamane Maiga stated that six of the seven economic regions and 60% of the total population were affected. In April the UN Food and Agriculture Organization estimated Mali's food grain deficit for 1984–85 at almost 500,000 metric tons; more than 100,000 tons of emergency food aid was needed.

On December 25 Mali and Burkina Faso went to war over possession of the Agacher strip, a disputed border area. A cease-fire was declared on December 29.

In February 50 people were killed when an Air Mali Antonov-24 passenger aircraft crashed at Timbuktu shortly after taking off.   (PHILIPPE DECRAENE)

This article updates the *Macropædia* article WESTERN AFRICA: *Mali*.

MAURITANIA

The republic of Mauritania is on the Atlantic coast of West Africa. Area: 1,030,700 sq km (398,000 sq mi). Pop. (1985 est.): 1,656,000. Cap.: Nouakchott. Monetary unit: ouguiya, with (Oct. 21, 1985) a free rate of 76.85 ouguiya to U.S. $1 (110.21 ouguiya = £1 sterling). President of the Military Committee for National Salvation and prime minister in 1985, Lieut. Col. Maaouya Ould Sidi Ahmed Taya.

Following Lieut. Col. Maaouya Ould Sidi Ahmed Taya's December 1984 takeover of the presidency of the Military Committee for National Salvation (CMRN), 1985 was marked by a series of ministerial reshuffles. These left Taya as head of state and of government and also in charge of defense.

During the year diplomatic relations with Libya and

Morocco were reestablished. Relations with the former had been severed in April 1984 during Lieut. Col. Mohamed Khouna Ould Haidalla's presidency of the CMRN because of subversive student activity allegedly financed from Libya. Agreement with Morocco was reached on delimitation of the two countries' common frontier.

Mauritania continued to suffer from the effects of drought, which affected some two-thirds of the population and required the nation to receive 155,000 tons of food aid during 1984–85. At a meeting of creditor and donor countries in Paris in March, the Mauritanian delegation outlined an emergency rehabilitation plan that called for 2.5 billion ouguiya (about $33.2 million) of financial aid.

(PHILIPPE DECRAENE)

This article updates the *Macropædia* article WESTERN AFRICA: *Mauritania.*

MAURITIUS

The parliamentary state of Mauritius, a member of the Commonwealth, occupies an island in the Indian Ocean about 800 km (500 mi) east of Madagascar and includes the island dependencies of Rodrigues, Agalega, and Cargados Carajos Shoals. Area: 2,040 sq km (787.5 sq mi). Pop (1985 est.): 1,024,900. Cap.: Port Louis. Monetary unit: Mauritian rupee, with (Oct. 21, 1985) a free rate of Mau Rs 14.47 to U.S. $1 (Mau Rs 20.75 = £1 sterling). Queen, Elizabeth II; governor-general in 1985, Sir Dayendranath Burrenchobay; prime minister, Aneerood Jugnauth.

The bitter political row between Prime Minister Aneerood Jugnauth and the leader of the opposition, Paul Berenger, which had dominated political affairs in Mauritius for years, showed signs of abating during 1985. Berenger offered to withdraw his accusations of government corruption after the Legislative Assembly passed a bill extending the Declaration of Assets Act. The law now required members of Parliament to make a full declaration of all possessions and debts. In his turn, Jugnauth began to refer to Berenger as "my good friend the leader of the opposition."

Faced with a rapidly increasing population, the government took as its first priority the fight against unemployment. Substantial aid from the European Communities was being used to combat rural desertification. Recent efforts to expand the tourist sector began to bring returns. Nevertheless, sugar still dominated the economy. Following the collapse of sugar prices in 1980, the government had followed International Monetary Fund guidelines in implementing economic reforms, with the result that both consumption and investment had been reduced in real terms. The measures had succeeded in reducing the budget deficit, but the price had been a marked increase in unemployment. The government launched a program designed to rehabilitate the sugar industry. Sir Seewoosagur Ramgoolam (*see* OBITUARIES), the first prime minister of Mauritius, died December 15 at age 85.   (GUY ARNOLD)

This article updates the *Macropædia* article INDIAN OCEAN ISLANDS: *Mauritius.*

MOZAMBIQUE

The people's republic of Mozambique is located in eastern Africa, on the Indian Ocean. Area: 799,380 sq km (308,642 sq mi). Pop. (1985 est.): 14,074,000. Cap.: Maputo. Monetary unit: metical, with (Oct. 21, 1985) a free rate of 42.06 meticals to U.S. $1 (60.31 meticals = £1 sterling). President in 1985, Samora Machel.

The year 1985 began with sporadic acts of violence against people and property by the Mozambique National Resistance (MNR, or Renamo). The attacks were a repetition and escalation of similar acts that, over several years, had contributed to the breakdown of the country's economy and left most rural areas in a state of insecurity and urban centres virtually under siege. The government believed that funds and matériel were being supplied to the guerrillas from Portuguese and South African sources. In January, after some hesitation due to the constitutional principles involved, Portuguese Prime Minister Mário Soares responded to complaints from Mozambique by placing restrictions on MNR activists who had previously operated freely in Lisbon.

The South African government insisted that it was attempting to act as mediator between the government of Mozambique and the MNR and was fulfilling the terms of the 1984 Nkomati accord, under which it had promised not to give assistance to the MNR. After a meeting of the joint South African-Mozambican security commission in February, however, South African Foreign Minister R. F. ("Pik") Botha admitted that his government found it difficult to prevent supplies of aid from reaching the guerrillas by way of Portuguese who had left Mozambique and taken refuge in his country. Although Mozambican Pres. Samora Machel appeared skeptical about South Africa's sincerity and declared that in his opinion the Nkomati accord had failed, both countries reaffirmed their commitment to it in March.

In a further move away from the socialist doctrine upon which Machel had formerly insisted, the People's Assembly in June approved incentives to encourage Western investment in Mozambique and, simultaneously, the government signed its first loan agreement with the World Bank. In recognition of this shift in policy, the U.S. and the U.K. made limited offers of assistance to areas affected by drought and of nonlethal military supplies, while the U.K. also promised to provide a training program for the Army. Machel visited both countries in September. In July an estimated 5,000 Zimbabwean troops joined the 2,000 already stationed in Mozambique to help protect the railway and the petroleum pipeline running from the Zimbabwean border to the Mozambican port of Beira. Toward the end of August a joint action by Mozambican and Zimbabwean troops resulted in the capture of an MNR headquarters known as Casa Banana. However, because the guerrillas did not rely upon a central organization but operated in separate bands, each pursuing its own advantage, the overall effect on the MNR's activities was small.

Accusations of complicity with the guerrillas were again leveled against South Africa by the government. In reply the South African government admitted on September 19 that it had violated the Nkomati accord but had done so only in a technical sense and with the clear aim of bringing the MNR into meaningful negotiations with the government of Mozambique. As if to signal their continuing opposition, MNR representatives in Lisbon claimed that their movement had been responsible for huge explosions in a military arsenal near Maputo.

In June celebrations of ten years of independence were muted because of the ruined state of the economy, widespread insecurity, and the scarcity of food in the markets. President Machel told Parliament that it was essential to adopt a "war economy" because of the impact of guerrilla activities. The MNR actions, together with the effects of the drought conditions suffered during the previous year, resulted, according to Finance Minister Rui Baltazar, in a 22% decline in the value of exports in 1984 and a 25% drop in industrial production.   (KENNETH INGHAM)

This article updates the *Macropædia* article SOUTHERN AFRICA: *Mozambique.*

NIGER

Niger is a landlocked republic of West Africa. Area: 1,186,408 sq km (458,075 sq mi). Pop. (1985 est.): 6,253,200. Cap.: Niamey. Monetary unit: CFA franc, with (Oct. 21, 1985) a par value of CFAF 50 to the French franc and a free rate of CFAF 402.02 to U.S. $1 (CFAF 576.50 = £1 sterling). Chief of state and president of the Supreme Military Council in 1985, Brig. Gen. Seyni Kountché; prime minister, Ahmid Algabid.

Faced with a flagging economy and foreign-backed subversive activity, Pres. Seyni Kountché sought to improve relations with the U.S. In December 1984 he visited Washington, and in March 1985 U.S. Vice-Pres. George Bush paid a return visit to Niamey.

During the night of May 29–30 a 14-man commando unit of Nigerian Tuaregs attacked the subprefecture of Tchin Tabaraden, 500 km (300 mi) northeast of Niamey; one of the commandos was killed, two escaped, and the rest were taken prisoner. On June 3 Kountché attributed the attack to the Libyan-based Popular Front for the Liberation of Niger. One of the movement's leaders, he said, was Abdoulaye Diori, son of ex-president Hamani Diori.

In a ministerial reshuffle on September 23, Mahamane Sani Bako replaced Ide Oumarou as foreign minister, following the latter's appointment as secretary-general of the Organization of African Unity.   (PHILIPPE DECRAENE)

This article updates the *Macropædia* article WESTERN AFRICA: *Niger*.

NIGERIA

A republic and member of the Commonwealth, Nigeria is located in West Africa, on the Gulf of Guinea. Area: 923,768 sq km (356,669 sq mi). Pop. (1985 est.): 96,015,000. Cap.: Lagos. Monetary unit: naira, with (Oct. 21, 1985) a free rate of 0.89 naira to U.S. $1 (1.28 naira = £1 sterling). Chairman of the Supreme Military Council to Aug. 27, 1985, Maj. Gen. Mohammed Buhari; president and chairman of the Armed Forces Ruling Council from August 30, Maj. Gen. Ibrahim Babangida.

Maj. Gen. Mohammed Buhari, Nigeria's leader since the Army seized power on the last day of 1983, was himself toppled from power on Aug. 27, 1985, in a bloodless coup. During 20 months in power the Buhari administration had clearly been unsuccessful in its efforts to solve Nigeria's pressing economic problems, while it had become deeply unpopular as a result of its repressive tactics.

The new leader was Maj. Gen. Ibrahim Babangida (*see* BIOGRAPHIES), who declared on coming to power: "We recognize that a government, be it civilian or military, needs the consent of the people to govern if it is to reach its objectives." The Supreme Military Council was replaced by the Armed Forces Ruling Council and the Federal Executive Council by a National Council of Ministers. Six of the previous ministers were retained, among them two civilians—Tam David-West, minister of petroleum and energy, and Alhaji Lukman, minister of mines, power, and steel. The majority of ministers were military officers. Two important new appointments were those of Bolaji Akinyemi as external affairs minister and Kalu Idika Kalu as finance minister. The new regime replaced 13 of the 19 state governors.

Nigerians had been prepared for sacrifices and accepted austerity measures imposed by the Buhari regime. They found, however, that individual freedom was also curtailed, in particular the right to comment upon government actions, and that the regime showed a marked unwillingness to take public opinion into account. Its most unpopular measure was Decree 4, which effectively muzzled the press. The new government at once repealed Decree 4 and released about 100 detainees, many of whom had been in prison for 20 months without charge or trial. In addition, the powers of the much-criticized and feared Nigerian Security Organization were greatly reduced.

Although the Buhari government blamed its predecessors for the state of the economy, both unemployment and prices continued to rise. When the coup took place, the inflation rate was 40%, the industrial sector was operating at 50% of capacity, and an unrealistic 44% of foreign earnings was earmarked for debt servicing. The question of whether or not to accept a loan from the International Monetary Fund (IMF), together with the conditions that would be attached to it, had been under debate for three years. Although the new regime appeared to favour such a loan as a short-term means of assisting the economy, Babangida at once invited a public debate on the issue. Public opinion was overwhelmingly hostile; opponents of the IMF loan insisted that Nigeria opt for a policy of self-reliance that would also entail rejecting external borrowing from other sources. The external debt amounted to just short of $21.4 billion at the end of 1984.

Setting out the objectives of his government, Babangida emphasized economic reconstruction, social justice, and self-reliance. It became clear to Nigerians that the military

In the second wave of mass expulsions in two years, the Nigerian government rounded up tens of thousands of illegal aliens and trucked them to border points for repatriation, along with what household goods they could carry.

would be in power for a considerable time and that all decision making would be dominated by economic factors. On October 1 Babangida declared a state of economic emergency for the next 15 months, during which time the aim would be to turn the economy around. On December 20 several high-ranking military officers were seized for plotting to overthrow the Babangida government.

U.K. Foreign Secretary Sir Geoffrey Howe paid an official visit to Nigeria in early September. Although nothing concrete was achieved during his trip, the fact that it proceeded as planned so soon after the coup emphasized the desire of both countries to improve relations, which had been strained since the attempted kidnapping of Umaru Dikko, former transport minister in the civilian government, in London in 1984. However, relations took a downturn in October 1985 when the U.K. government expressed official concern over the 14-year prison sentences passed by a Lagos court on two British engineers found guilty of stealing a light aircraft.   (GUY ARNOLD)

This article updates the *Macropædia* article WESTERN AFRICA: *Nigeria.*

RWANDA

The landlocked republic of Rwanda is situated in central Africa. Area: 26,338 sq km (10,169 sq mi). Pop. (1985 est.): 6,115,000. Cap.: Kigali. Monetary unit: Rwanda franc, with (Oct. 21, 1985) a free rate of RF 95.19 to U.S. $1 (RF 136.50 = £1 sterling). President in 1985, Maj. Gen. Juvénal Habyarimana.

Development was the most important activity in Rwanda in 1985. The Saudi Fund for Development provided $14 million toward construction of a road linking Kayonza with Kagitumba, on the border with Uganda. At a total cost estimated at $56 million, the project would provide Rwanda with a link to the Ugandan road system and thence to the port of Mombasa, Kenya.

Funding was being provided by the European Communities (EC) for a scheme to improve water supplies in the district to the south of Kigali. The EC was also helping to finance the development of a cottage industry in tin mining. During 1980–85 tin output had dropped by 85%. By supplying technical assistance, tools, and small-scale mining equipment, the project aimed to create over 300 new jobs and to improve the average daily income of another 1,000 people. The World Bank's International Development Association provided $4.8 million to fund a training program that would assist the government in budget preparation and financial planning.

In June death sentences were passed on five people, including a former army commander, found guilty of murdering political prisoners in 1975–76. On Independence Day, July 5, Pres. Juvénal Habyarimana commuted all death sentences to life imprisonment.   (GUY ARNOLD)

This article updates the *Macropædia* article CENTRAL AFRICA: *Rwanda.*

SÃO TOMÉ AND PRÍNCIPE

The republic of São Tomé and Príncipe comprises two main islands and several smaller islets that straddle the Equator in the Gulf of Guinea, off the west coast of Africa. Area: 964 sq km (372 sq mi). Pop. (1985 est.): 106,500. Cap.: São Tomé. Monetary unit: dobra, with (Oct. 21, 1985) a free rate of 42.64 dobras to U.S. $1 (61.14 dobras = £1 sterling). President in 1985, Manuel Pinto da Costa.

In his capacity as chairman of the Portuguese-speaking African countries, Pres. Manuel Pinto da Costa of São Tomé and Príncipe paid official visits to both Angola and Mozambique in April 1985. His talks were mainly concerned with the situation in southern Africa. He pledged his country's solidarity with Angola, and in Maputo he promised "concrete support in material and military terms." São Tomé was host to a summit meeting of Africa's five Portuguese-speaking countries in February.

During the year the government adopted measures to encourage the private sector, which had been almost entirely neglected since independence. The measures included providing import quotas for private businesses and urging entrepreneurs to import goods to meet some of the most pressing needs of the home market. The Angolan News Agency, Angop, was to provide assistance to São Tomé in setting up a national news agency.

In February the president dismissed the ministers of foreign affairs and of planning and took over both functions himself. On September 30 Pinto da Costa, who had been head of state since independence in 1975, was reelected for a further five-year term of office by the People's Assembly.

                (GUY ARNOLD)

This article updates the *Macropædia* article CENTRAL AFRICA: *São Tomé and Príncipe.*

SENEGAL

The republic of Senegal is located in West Africa, on the Atlantic Ocean; it surrounds the country of The Gambia, with which it has formed an administrative union called Senegambia. Area: 196,722 sq km (75,955 sq mi). Pop. (1985 est.): 6,520,000. Cap.: Dakar. Monetary unit: CFA franc, with (Oct. 21, 1985) a par value of CFAF 50 to the French franc and a free rate of CFAF 402.02 to U.S. $1 (CFAF 576.50 = £1 sterling). President in 1985, Abdou Diouf.

In his capacity as chairman of the Organization of African Unity (OAU), Pres. Abdou Diouf undertook a tour of southern Africa in October 1985, with the object of reaffirming OAU members' support for the struggle against apartheid in South Africa and for the independence of South West Africa/Namibia. In November President Diouf paid a state visit to France, where he discussed with Pres. François Mitterrand the situations in South Africa and in Chad. Also discussed was the possibility of increased French development and budgetary aid. France remained Senegal's major source of aid, with a total of F 1,358,000,-000 for 1985, but following Diouf's visit to Washington, D.C., in April, Senegal also hoped for an increase in the amount of U.S. aid. Meanwhile, Senegal's economic situation remained at a low ebb.

Multipartyism continued to flourish. The launching on February 1 of the Senegalese Democratic Union brought the total number of political parties to 16. In July five left-wing parties joined in a Senegalese Democratic Alliance (ADS), subsequently banned by the government on the grounds that such groupings were illegal. In August Abdoulaye Wade, leader of the main opposition party, the Senegalese Democratic Party, and 14 others were arrested for having taken part in an unauthorized demonstration against South Africa's apartheid policy organized by ADS; they were released after three days when charges against them were dropped.

A minor government reshuffle took place in January, when changes were also made in the Cabinet of the Senegambian Confederation. The uneasy relationship between the confederation's partners was underlined by the withdrawal in March of Senegal's ambassador to The Gambia.   (PHILIPPE DECRAENE)

This article updates the *Macropædia* article WESTERN AFRICA: *Senegal.*

SEYCHELLES

A republic and member of the Commonwealth, the Seychelles consists of about 100 islands in the Indian Ocean, 1,450 km (900 mi) from the east coast of Africa. Area: 453 sq km (175 sq mi). Pop. (1985 est.): 65,100. Cap.: Victoria. Monetary unit: Seychelles rupee, with (Oct. 21, 1985) a free rate of SR 6.71 to U.S. $1 (SR 9.62 = £1 sterling). President in 1985, France-Albert René.

During 1985 the government of Seychelles launched its five-year (1985–89) national plan. The three principal aims of the plan were to reduce unemployment, to improve the balance of payments by increasing exports and reducing imports and by maximizing the benefits from tourism, and to increase growth through investment in the productive sectors. The plan envisaged investment of SR 2.8 billion, almost all from external sources.

The tourist sector continued to improve. Following the sharp upturn in 1984, there was a further 17% increase in tourist arrivals in the first eight months of 1985. However, other sectors of the economy were sluggish.

Both the U.S.S.R. and the U.S. provided substantial amounts of aid during the year. The U.S.S.R. supplied 4,000 metric tons of marine diesel fuel for the Seychelles Navy, while the U.S. provided SR 14 million for fuel for the Seychelles Electricity Corporation. The lease agreement for U.S. use of the satellite tracking station on Mahé was renewed in November.

Gérard Hoarau, exiled leader of the opposition to Pres. France-Albert René, was shot and killed in front of his London home on November 29.   (GUY ARNOLD)

This article updates *Macropædia* article INDIAN OCEAN IS-LANDS: *Seychelles*.

SIERRA LEONE

A republic of West Africa and member of the Commonwealth, Sierra Leone lies on the Atlantic Ocean. Area: 71,740 sq km (27,699 sq mi). Pop. (1985 est.): 3,580,000. Cap.: Freetown. Monetary unit: leone, with (Oct. 21, 1985) an official rate of 5.30 leones to U.S. $1 (7.60 leones = £1 sterling). Presidents in 1985, Siaka Stevens and, from November 28, Maj. Gen. Joseph Saidu Momoh.

In presidential elections held in Sierra Leone on Oct. 1, 1985, voters endorsed Maj. Gen. Joseph Saidu Momoh (*see* BIOGRAPHIES), the sole candidate, as successor to Siaka Stevens, who had held the office since 1971. Earlier in the year Stevens's seven-year term of office, due to expire in June, was extended for six months. While the reported reason was to allow time to prepare new voters' lists, some sources suggested that Stevens needed the extra time to make arrangements for a successor. Arrangements were completed in August at the convention of the ruling All People's Congress (APC), the country's sole legal party. Momoh was endorsed as new leader of the APC, and thus its presidential candidate, after the other two contenders—Sorie Koroma and Francis Minah, first and second vice-presidents, respectively—withdrew.

Momoh, who relinquished his position as head of the armed forces when he took up the presidency, faced formidable problems, not least among them the level of corruption. He announced that he would give priority to the agricultural sector. In June Finance Minister Joe Amara-Bangali presented a budget that revealed marginal growth in 1984–85.   (GUY ARNOLD)

This article updates the *Macropædia* article WESTERN AFRICA: *Sierra Leone*.

SOMALIA

A republic in the Horn of northeastern Africa, the Somali Democratic Republic, or Somalia, lies on the Gulf of Aden and the Indian Ocean. Area: 637,000 sq km (246,000 sq mi). Pop. (1985 est.): 5,817,200. Cap.: Mogadishu. Monetary unit: Somali shilling, with (Oct. 21, 1985) a free rate of 36.58 Somali shillings to U.S. $1 (52.45 Somali shillings = £1 sterling). President in 1985, Maj. Gen. Muhammad Siyad Barrah.

Following general elections in Somalia on Dec. 31, 1984, 46 new members took their seats in the 171-member People's Assembly. The elections were the second to take place since the Somali Revolutionary Socialist Party (SRSP) was established as the country's sole legal party in 1976.

Antigovernment forces based in Ethiopia maintained their attacks during the year. The Somali Democratic Salvation Front (SDSF), one of the main rebel groups, continued its occupation of the strip of land on the Somali-Ethiopian border that it had occupied with the backing of Ethiopian troops in 1983. Government sources blamed the Ethiopians for an air attack in September on the town of Abudwaq in which 17 people were reported killed; in response the Ethiopians accused the government of blaming them for problems internal to Somalia. Meanwhile, divisions within the SDSF led to internecine violence. In October Col. Abdullahi Yusuf, leader of the SDSF, was arrested by Ethiopian authorities.

An estimated 700,000 refugees originally made homeless by the 1977–78 war with Ethiopia over the Ogaden region were housed in more than 30 camps throughout Somalia. Early in the year a fresh influx of refugees, reportedly fleeing from political and religious repression in Ethiopia, began arriving in the northeast of the country. By March the new arrivals numbered some 45,000. There followed an outbreak of cholera that spread through the refugee camps and to the general public. By mid-May, as the result of a government quarantine and immunization measures supported by the efforts of International Red Cross teams, the outbreak was reported to be under control.

In a speech to the SRSP Central Committee in February, Pres. Muhammad Siyad Barrah referred to Somali-U.S. relations as "limping," apparently because of U.S. reluctance to supply more than minimal military aid. On the same occasion, he spoke of his desire to "normalize" relations with the U.S.S.R., a former ally with whom relations had been severed in 1977 when Moscow backed Ethiopia in the Ogaden war. Nevertheless, Somalia during 1985 remained firmly within the Western camp.

Against a background of continuing economic difficulties, the effect of government policy was increasingly to move away from central control toward a free-market economy. Throughout 1984 the government was involved in negotiations with the International Monetary Fund (IMF) to establish terms for an extended credit facility. After agreement had been reached in principle, the government in January introduced a dual exchange rate for the Somali shilling and allowed exporters to retain 65% of profits, compared with 35% previously. The IMF provided a standby credit worth $54 million in February. Meanwhile, a special meeting of aid donor countries pledged an estimated $80 million over and above their previous aid commitments.

An otherwise bleak economic outlook was improved by an exceptionally good grain harvest in midyear. This ended a five-year period of drought and shortages.

(VIRGINIA R. LULING)

This article updates the *Macropædia* article EASTERN AFRICA: *Somalia*.

SOUTH AFRICA

The Republic

South Africa occupies the southern tip of Africa, with the Atlantic Ocean to the west and the Indian Ocean to the east. It partially surrounds the four former black states of Bophuthatswana, Ciskei, Transkei, and Venda (whose independence is not recognized by the international community). Area: 1,123,226 sq km (433,680 sq mi). Pop. (1985 est.): 27,424,000. (Area and population figures exclude the four former black states.) Executive cap., Pretoria; judicial cap., Bloemfontein; legislative cap., Cape Town. Monetary unit: rand, with (Oct. 21, 1985) a free rate of R 2.60 to U.S. $1 (R 3.72 = £1 sterling). Executive state president in 1985, Pieter Willem Botha.

Domestic Affairs. In January 1985, opening the first full session of the tricameral Parliament created under the controversial Constitution Act of 1983, executive State Pres. Pieter W. Botha (*see* BIOGRAPHIES) spoke of the National Party (NP) government's plans for constitutional development and racial reform. In the eyes of most South Africans and of other observers throughout the world, however, the government proposals were completely overshadowed by unrest in the black townships. Beginning in the Vaal Triangle in September 1984, the unrest continued unremittingly in one part of the country or another throughout 1985. In response, the government declared a state of emergency in 36 districts of the Transvaal and Eastern Cape on July 20. The state of emergency was lifted in six districts but on October 25–26 was extended to an additional eight in the Western Cape.

Botha's proposals included setting up an "informal, nonstatutory" negotiating forum for discussion with black leaders, removing the "negative and discriminatory" aspects of influx control, restoring South African citizenship to residents of the former homelands, and granting freehold rights to Africans in urban areas. In later speeches during the year, Botha and other government ministers stated that the government was considering including African members on the appointed President's Council and that it intended to repeal the only remaining statutory job colour bar, contained in the Mines and Works Act. At the same time, the government continued to defend residential and school apartheid (racial separation) and the separate political identity of the homelands. (*See* Special Report.)

Parliament repealed the Prohibition of Mixed Marriages Act and sections of the Immorality Act and also the Prohibition of Political Interference Act, which had prohibited multiracial political parties. Parliament also passed the Re-

gional Services Council Act, providing for the creation of multiracial metropolitan councils. The President's Council issued a report whose most publicized recommendations were that influx control, "as applied at present in terms of Act 25 of 1945, be abolished . . . in an orderly manner" and that uniform identity documents be issued to all citizens. It put forward numerous other proposals for the ordering and directing of the process of urbanization. The report was under consideration by the government.

While there were many localized causes for the unrest, it was rooted in opposition to apartheid policies and in the nation's worsening economic conditions. Protest took many forms, including mass boycotts of school classes, rent strikes, work stay-aways, and street fighting against government security forces. By November, for example, some 350,000 residents of Vaal Triangle townships had been on a rent strike for 14 months, and such strikes were also widespread in the Eastern Cape. In November it was estimated that more than 90% of the eligible students were boycotting matriculation exams.

The government claimed that the unrest was created by a small minority of "Communist-inspired agitators" of the banned African National Congress (ANC). However, the most marked feature of the situation in the townships—not only in major centres but in tiny towns throughout the country—was the spread of grass-roots organizations, in many cases embracing entire communities, and the involvement in protest actions of blacks of all ages, including boys and girls in primary school. Organization took place largely under the banner of the United Democratic Front (UDF), which had spearheaded the widespread boycott of the 1984 elections to the Coloured and Asian chambers of Parliament and was demanding political rights for all South Africans. Opinion polls conducted among blacks during the year showed the huge popularity of leaders identified with the ANC, in particular the imprisoned Nelson Mandela (*see* BIOGRAPHIES).

In dealing with the unrest the police were increasingly reinforced in the townships by units of the South African Defence Force (SADF), following the precedent established in Sebokeng and Sharpeville in October 1984. The use of troops and security-force methods and the imposition of the state of emergency were factors leading to the nationwide spread of a boycott of white businesses that was launched, and remained most effective, in the Eastern Cape. There was widespread criticism of police methods. Among the most publicized incidents were police shootings in Uitenhage on March 21, which resulted in 19 deaths

Elijah Barayi (second from left) was elected president of the Congress of South African Trade Unions at its founding convention in Durban, South Africa, in December. Claiming to represent some 500,000 predominantly black workers, the Congress was the largest labour federation in South African history.

according to official sources and 43 according to others, and the "Trojan Horse" affair in the Western Cape in October, when police hiding in containers on the back of a delivery vehicle emerged to open fire on demonstrators. The government-appointed commission inquiring into the Uitenhage incident made some criticisms of the police but concluded that they had had no option but to open fire, although the commission also pointed out that the majority of the victims had been shot in the back.

According to the Institute of Race Relations, there were 825 deaths resulting from the unrest between September 1984 and the end of October 1985. Official sources claimed, up to the same date, 504 deaths from security-force action and 232 others. Among other ominous developments were disappearances, murders, and mutilations allegedly carried out by white "death squads." By Nov. 8, 1985, the number of people who had been detained without trial under the state of emergency had reached 5,253, of whom 3,063 had been released. Thousands of other blacks had also been arrested, and there were widespread allegations of torture.

During the year a number of UDF leaders were charged with treason, which on conviction carried a maximum penalty of death. In December charges were dropped against 12 of the 16 defendants in one trial; a further 22 UDF leaders faced the same charge in a separate trial. In August the Rev. Allan Boesak (see BIOGRAPHIES), patron of the UDF, was charged with subversion. Winnie Mandela, wife of Nelson Mandela, was arrested twice in late December for defying a banning order forbidding her to enter Soweto, which she regarded as her home. She was released under bail conditions that repeated the ban.

In an attempt to curtail the worldwide publicity that the situation was receiving, the government on November 2 prohibited foreign journalists from filming, or being present at, scenes of unrest. During the same month, Anthony Heard, editor of the Cape Times, was charged under security legislation for publishing an interview with exiled ANC leader Oliver Tambo (see BIOGRAPHIES).

The government argued that much of the township violence was directed by blacks against other blacks. It appeared for the most part, however, to be directed against blacks who were regarded as "collaborators" with apartheid—those who had taken office in the unpopular local community councils, black policemen, and blacks regarded as police informers. In Natal in August there was a severe outbreak of violence between Africans and Indians. While Gatsha Buthelezi (see BIOGRAPHIES), head of the KwaZulu government and of the Inkatha movement, blamed the violence on black youths from outside Natal, UDF leaders in Natal identified its roots in the violent hostility of Inkatha vigilante groups toward the UDF. At the end of December there were violent clashes between members of the Zulu and Pondo tribes south of Durban. Over 50 people died in the fighting, which was apparently unrelated to the year's political violence.

The political strife entered a new phase in December with an increase in the number of attacks on whites. The most serious incident took place on December 23 when a bomb exploded in a crowded shopping centre at Amanzimtoti, a resort south of Durban. The government blamed the ANC for the attack, which killed five people, all white.

Throughout the year there were growing indications of dissatisfaction among influential sections of white opinion, especially the business community, with the NP government's handling of the situation. This increased during the state of emergency and also following President Botha's speech on August 15 to the Natal NP congress, in which he failed to announce anticipated new initiatives. In September

Frederick van Zyl Slabbert, leader of the opposition Progressive Federal Party (PFP), together with Chief Buthelezi, launched the National Convention Alliance. Its aims were to persuade the government to repeal all discriminatory legislation, to legalize all banned organizations, to set free unconditionally all political prisoners and detainees, and to allow free political association as the basis for calling a representative national convention to formulate a new constitution.

A surprising new development was the decision of major business leaders to fly to Lusaka, Zambia, on September 13 for informal talks with leaders of the ANC, including Tambo. Leaders of the PFP followed, but the government refused passports to Afrikaner church and student leaders who also wished to talk with the ANC. The business leaders expressed their concern that black opinion in the country was increasingly hostile to the free enterprise system, regarding it as intimately bound up with apartheid. They also rejected calls for government based on one person, one vote in a unitary South Africa, favouring instead a "federal" system reflecting the "plural" character of the population. At the same time, recognizing the popularity of the ANC, they wished to ascertain from its leaders the conditions under which they would enter negotiations. Besides enumerating preconditions for negotiations, ANC leaders stated that the only matter for negotiation was "the transfer of power to the majority." They also stated that they were not willing to abandon their strategy of armed struggle against the apartheid regime.

The Conservative Party and Herstigte Nasionale Partij (HNP), both to the right of the NP, played on white fears by blaming the unrest on the government's reform policies. By-elections in May showed only a slight swing to the right, but in by-elections held on October 30 the HNP won its first seat in Parliament.

A major development during the year was the decision by the majority of nonracial (predominantly African) trade unions to unite as the Congress of South African Trade Unions. Initial membership was estimated at more than 500,000, making the organization the largest trade-union coordinating body in the country.

Foreign Relations. The major feature of the year was the intensified international isolation of South Africa, principally as a result of the domestic unrest and the state of emergency. A number of Western countries instituted or intensified sanctions on investment, trade, and military-related transactions and withdrew their ambassadors. In partial reversal of his previous policy of "constructive engagement" with the apartheid government to encourage reform, U.S. Pres. Ronald Reagan in September restricted new bank loans and banned sales of computer systems to the security forces, sales of nuclear technology, and the importation of Krugerrands. The move came after strong pressures from the U.S. Congress, whose members were in turn affected by widespread antiapartheid campaigning in the U.S. During his tour of South Africa in January, Sen. Edward Kennedy (Dem., Mass.) publicized black grievances and promised to campaign in the U.S. for intensified sanctions. Most strongly resistant to any form of sanctions was Prime Minister Margaret Thatcher's Conservative government in Britain. However, the British government came into line with mild sanctions measures instituted by the European Communities and with similar measures agreed upon by the Commonwealth conference.

Within southern Africa the Nkomati agreement with Mozambique and negotiations with Angola in 1984 had appeared to herald a halt to the armed conflict punctuating South Africa's relations with those countries. However,

such hopes proved overoptimistic. The Mozambique National Resistance (MNR) movement continued its insurgency against the Mozambique government, and increasing evidence emerged that there was continued support for it from within the South African regime, particularly with the publication in October by the Mozambique government of diaries captured from MNR leader Alfonso Dlakhama. The South African government admitted that "technical violations" of the accord had occurred. Military officers alleged to be responsible for the violations were moved to other posts, and Gen. Constand Viljoen, chief of the SADF, retired prematurely.

SADF troops withdrew from Angola in April but were again in action in the country in subsequent months. In September–October the SADF openly admitted its support for the National Union for the Total Independence of Angola (UNITA) rebels who were fighting the Angolan government. Its troops were involved in operations to defend UNITA bases against a government offensive, in which there was evidence of intensified military assistance from the U.S.S.R.

Pressures were maintained internationally for the implementation of UN Resolution 435, calling for independence for South West Africa/Namibia from South African control and for democratic elections. After April, however, the South African government unilaterally went ahead with the establishment of a transitional government in Namibia formed from the six parties of the Multi-Party Conference on the basis of a 62-person legislature. An eight-member Cabinet was appointed and began to take steps toward drawing up a new constitution.

On June 14 in South Africa's first military offensive against Botswana, SADF commandos raided houses in Gaborone that allegedly served as bases for ANC guerrilla activity. At least 15 people were killed. The ANC and the Botswana government vigorously denied the charges, and the raid was widely condemned internationally. In response to pressure for increased international sanctions, South African government spokesmen on several occasions appeared to threaten retaliation against the country's southern African neighbours in the form of cutting economic ties and repatriating foreign migrant workers.

The Economy. At the beginning of 1985 the economy was suffering severely from the effects of anti-inflationary austerity measures, including spending cuts and raised interest rates, that were instituted in August 1984. The consequences were considerable rises in unemployment and a marked increase in the number of bankruptcies. In the year to June 1985 some 48,400 jobs, almost two-thirds belonging to blacks, were lost in manufacturing. Official statistics on unemployment among blacks were unreliable, but it was widely estimated that the total exceeded three million. In March the government provoked considerable protest among public servants by announcing a one-third cut in annual bonuses. The March budget continued the austerity policies, particularly in government spending, and raised the general sales tax to 12%.

The slowing down of economic activity, by reducing the demand for imports, created a massive turnaround in the current account of the balance of payments. An annualized deficit of more than R 2 billion in the third quarter of 1984 was replaced by an annualized surplus of R 5.4 billion in the second quarter of 1985. Important contributions came from gold exports and a revival in agriculture. (While the dollar gold price remained relatively static, rand earnings rose to record levels because of the decline in value of the rand.) At the same time, because of the lack of profitable investment opportunities and the climate of unrest, there was a steady net outflow of capital, amounting to some R 2 billion during the year.

The rand weakened against foreign currencies and then dropped sharply as a result of the state of emergency and the disappointment induced by Botha's speech of August 15. The fall in the rand increased the burden of foreign-debt repayment. When several U.S. banks refused to refinance loans, the government responded on August 27 by suspending foreign-exchange dealings and the stock exchange for five days and by announcing a freeze on debt-servicing repayments and the reestablishment of the "financial rand" as the means for investment and disinvestment; thus, the "two-tier" currency system that had been abandoned in February 1983 was revived. The freeze, initiated for four months only, seemed likely to last longer because of the reluctance of foreign banks to agree on a loan-rescheduling arrangement.

The austerity measures were markedly unsuccessful in diminishing inflation, which reached a record rate of 16.8% in October. Nevertheless, because of internal pressures, during the second half of the year the government embarked on mildly reflationary measures, including a reduction of interest rates and an injection of R 900 million into job-creation measures.

Bophuthatswana

The republic of Bophuthatswana consists of six discontinuous, landlocked geographic units, entirely surrounded by South Africa except for one unit that borders Botswana on the northwest. Area: 40,000 sq km (15,444 sq mi). Pop. (1985 est.): 1,527,000. Cap.: Mmabatho. Monetary unit: South African rand. President in 1985, Lucas Mangope.

Ciskei

Bordering the Indian Ocean in the south, Ciskei is surrounded on land by South Africa. Area: 5,386 sq km (2,080 sq mi). Pop. (1985 est.): 777,000. Cap.: Bisho. Monetary unit: South African rand. President in 1985, Lennox Sebe.

Transkei

Bordering the Indian Ocean and surrounded on land by South Africa, Transkei comprises three discontinuous geographic units, two of which are landlocked and one of which borders Lesotho. Area: 43,553 sq km (16,816 sq mi). Pop. (1985 est.): 2,681,000. Cap.: Umtata. Monetary unit: South African rand. President in 1985, Kaiser Daliwonga Matanzima; prime minister, George Matanzima.

Venda

The landlocked republic of Venda is located in extreme northeastern South Africa. Area: 6,198 sq km (2,393 sq mi). Pop. (1985 est.): 424,000. Cap.: Thohoyandou. Monetary unit: South African rand. President in 1985, Patrick Mphephu.

The four former homelands, regarded as politically independent of South Africa by the South African government alone, continued to depend overwhelmingly on revenue generated in the central South African economy, on the one hand in the form of wages paid to migrant workers and on the other in the form of direct and indirect payments from the government of the republic. In 1984 Transkei received from South Africa R 616 million, Bophuthatswana R 353 million, Ciskei R 333 million, and Venda R 160 million. It appeared that preparations were in motion for KwaNdebele to become the fifth "independent" homeland in 1986.

(continued on page 472)

South Africa's Apartheid Policy

BY COLIN LEGUM

South Africa entered the most difficult period of its modern history in 1985 when its government formally committed itself to unscrambling the policy of apartheid (racial separation) that it had pursued with vigour and ruthlessness since the National Party came to power in 1948. The core of apartheid ideology was the belief that peaceful racial coexistence could be secured only by separating the country's four communities—the 23.9 million blacks, 4.8 million whites, 3 million Coloureds (people of mixed race), and 1 million Asians (mainly Indians)—into different social and political societies that would nevertheless remain economically interdependent. The objective was to be achieved by dividing the country between whites, who were allocated more than two-thirds of the territory, and blacks. It was proposed that the blacks should achieve their separate political independence within ten ethnic homelands scattered across the remaining one-third of the nation; those blacks living in the designated white area would be treated as "temporary sojourners." Such a policy called for a major effort to reverse the influx of blacks into the economically prosperous white areas by removing all black workers surplus to the needs of the white economy, a policy that involved uprooting millions of people.

Apart from the moral questions that it raised, this policy ran up against a number of practical difficulties. For example, insufficient land was allocated to absorb the "surplus" black labour; a rapidly expanding industrial society called for many more, not fewer, black workers in the white-designated areas; and millions of urban blacks had long since lost all contact with their ethnic roots. These basic fallacies in the ideology of apartheid finally came to be acknowledged by the South African government.

In a speech in August, Pres. Pieter Botha (see BIOGRAPHIES) announced that he was "not prepared to lead white South Africans and other minority groups on a road to abdication and suicide." The U.S. and other foreign governments were dismayed; they had been led to expect an announcement of significant reforms that would lead to the end of apartheid. In September Botha made some concessions, promising to grant citizenship to blacks who lived in urban areas but were nominally citizens of "independent" homelands and to scrap the law that required blacks to carry passes designed to restrict "unauthorized" blacks from white-designated areas.

During the 37 years of apartheid rule, the political attitudes of black South Africans had been transformed. A new generation of young blacks had been radicalized by

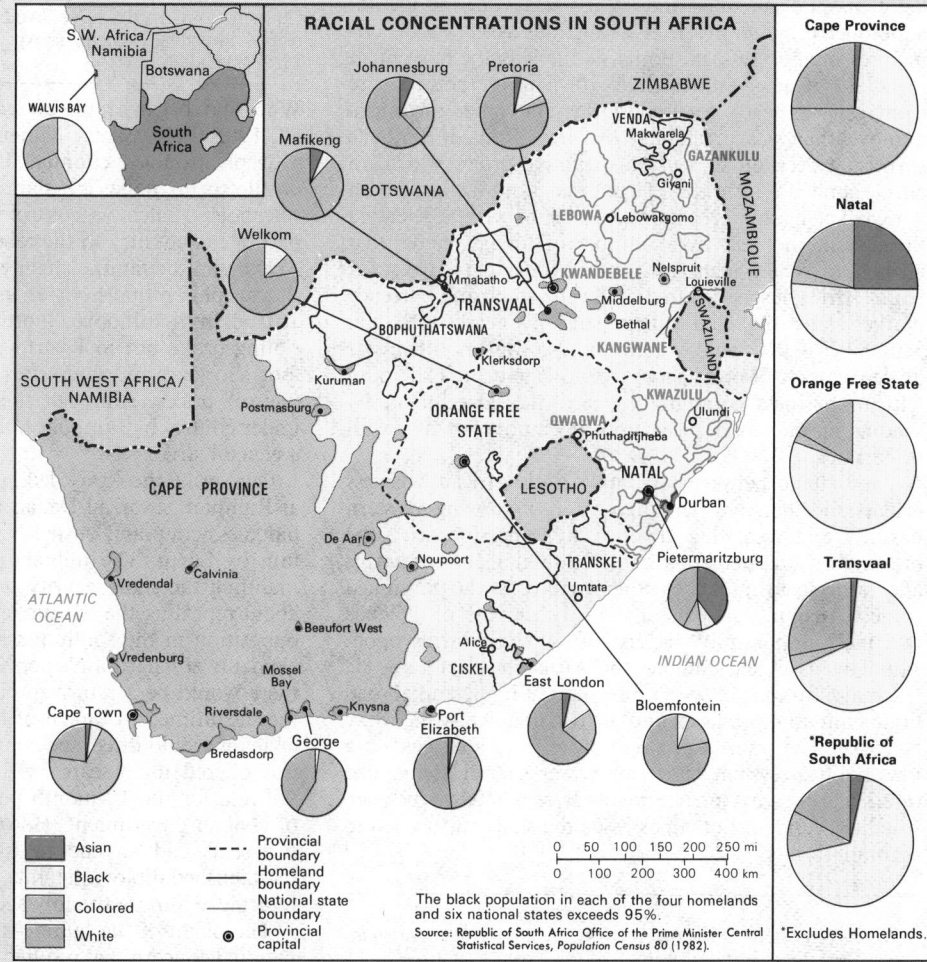

Apartheid, legally embodied in the Population Registration Act of 1950, made the separation of South Africa's four racial groups mandatory and resulted in the creation of so-called black areas: six homelands, designated for settlement by black South Africans, and four national states, not recognized as independent by the international community. Together these comprised some 14% of the total land area.

The 1980 census underenumerated the black population by excluding an estimated 4.6 million people living in the homelands. Blacks living in the six homelands and four national states made up at least 72% of the total South African population.

RACIAL CONCENTRATIONS IN SOUTH AFRICA

Asian
Black
Coloured
White

Provincial boundary
Homeland boundary
National state boundary
Provincial capital

Cape Province
Natal
Orange Free State
Transvaal
*Republic of South Africa

0 50 100 150 200 250 mi
0 100 200 300 400 km

The black population in each of the four homelands and six national states exceeds 95%.

Source: Republic of South Africa Office of the Prime Minister Central Statistical Services, *Population Census 80* (1982).

*Excludes Homelands.

their struggle against discriminatory laws and an inferior education system, and an increasing number of blacks had come to believe that their only hope for change was through violent struggle. They were inspired by the success of the armed struggles in neighbouring countries and by the example of Umkonto We Sizwe (Spear of the Nation, underground military wing of the banned African National Congress [ANC]), which had been launched by Nelson Mandela (*see* BIOGRAPHIES) in 1961. Mandela, in the 21st year of a life sentence in prison, had come to be regarded as the symbol of African resistance.

A revolt of young black militants, which had first manifested itself in Soweto in 1976, spread across South Africa in 1985. Angry young people, many still teenagers, took over the leadership of some communities. They organized school and consumer boycotts and began a campaign to make the black ghettos ungovernable by attacking police and others who collaborated with the system. This forceful black resistance called forth strong police and military reaction by the authorities. There were also other centres of black opposition led by such movements as the Zulu-dominated Inkatha, whose leader was Chief Gatsha Buthelezi (*see* BIOGRAPHIES), and the newly legalized black trade unions.

South Africa's leaders also came under greater pressure from an increasingly hostile Western community. Until 1985 foreign investors had viewed South Africa as a stable country, but with the increase in racial tensions, doubts crept in. Western governments, including those of the U.S. and Britain, showed their concern over the slow progress in ending apartheid; though they remained opposed to blanket economic sanctions, they began to favour the idea of adopting a program of selective sanctions as a way of exerting pressure on President Botha. In the U.S. the movement in favour of disinvestment had grown to the point where Congress was ready to support this and other measures, a move that was preempted by Pres. Ronald Reagan's surprising decision to sign an executive order, which, in effect, applied a series of selective sanctions against South Africa. The country's economic problems were accelerated throughout the year by a number of foreign banks that refused to renew loans to South Africa. On August 27 South Africa suspended trading on the stock and currency markets after the rand fell in value by nearly 60%. On September 1 the country announced a four-month freeze on repayments of principal on the foreign debt. The South African business community defied the government by sending an influential delegation to Zambia for talks with leaders of the ANC.

The détente between powerful South African business leaders and the ANC, coming on top of growing Western hostility and escalating violence at home, increased the pressure on President Botha to stop talking about reforms and to begin to implement them. However, he continued to delay action, partly because of the climate of violence but, more importantly, because of signs of growing opposition to his policies among the Afrikaner electorate. He felt himself trapped between pressures at home and abroad urging him to move faster and the risk of a right-wing white backlash. The transition period away from apartheid to a new political system based on power sharing demanded rare skills in crisis management. It remained to be seen whether President Botha possessed the statecraft needed to accomplish this.

Colin Legum is an authority on African affairs and a regular contributor to the Britannica Book of the Year.

(continued from page 470)

Through provision of incentives, these areas attracted a continual trickle of private investment. There were increasing complaints from trade unions in South Africa, however, that the territories were undercutting production within the republic by methods to ensure cheap labour, including severely restricting labour organizations.

The effects of the unrest throughout the republic spilled over into the former homelands, Ciskei and Transkei in particular. Many people were detained by the governments of those two territories and of Bophuthatswana; 880 people were detained in September in Transkei alone. Fort Hare University (Ciskei), the universities of Transkei, Venda, and Bophuthatswana, and other educational institutions were closed because of student unrest at various times during the year. In a characteristic incident, Bathandwa Ndondo, former vice-president of the Students Representative Council of the University of Transkei, was shot eight times and his corpse dumped at a hospital in Umtata. A police chief confirmed that police were responsible. Subsequently, Ndondo's lawyer and several other people associated with him were detained without trial.

(MARTIN LEGASSICK)

See also *Dependent States,* below.

SUDAN, THE

A republic of North Africa, The Sudan has a coastline on the Red Sea. Area: 2,503,890 sq km (966,757 sq mi). Pop. (1985 est.): 23,645,000. Cap.: Khartoum. Monetary unit: Sudanese pound, with (Oct. 21, 1985) a par value of LSd 2.50 to U.S. $1 (free rate of LSd 3.58 = £1 sterling). President to April 6, 1985, Gen. Gaafar Nimeiry; chairman of the Transitional Military Council from April 9, Gen. 'Abd ar-Rahman Siwar ad-Dahab; prime ministers, Nimeiry to April 6 and, from April 22, al-Jazuli Daf'allah.

When he began a private visit to the U.S. on March 27, 1985, Pres. Gaafar Nimeiry of The Sudan left behind a deeply troubled country. The professional classes were hostile to his policy of islamization; the government had surrendered effective control over much of the southern part of the country to the rebel Sudan People's Liberation Army; and the famine already affecting large areas reached catastrophic proportions as thousands of starving refugees arrived from Ethiopia. Shortly after Nimeiry's departure, rioting broke out in Khartoum, principally as a result of food shortages and sharp rises in sugar, bread, and gasoline (petrol) prices. Although the disturbances were brought under control by riot police, they were quickly followed by a general strike.

On April 6 the Army, led by Defense Minister Gen. 'Abd ar-Rahman Siwar ad-Dahab (*see* BIOGRAPHIES), staged a bloodless coup and ousted Nimeiry, who was granted asylum by Egypt. The military junta at once set about dismantling the state security services, but nothing was said about repealing the Islamic law that had aroused so much opposition in the south and among the more westernized elements of Khartoum's population. It was announced that there would be a return to civilian rule in 12 months. In the meantime, a Council of Ministers that included some civilians would direct the country's affairs. The rebel south was offered three seats on the Council of Ministers and self-rule for the 12-month period before the introduction of civilian government. However, the southerners wanted five seats and an end to Islamic law. The new regime reestablished diplomatic links with Ethiopia and attempted to achieve a more friendly accord with Libya.

The plight of the famine-stricken areas prompted international concern that resulted in a vast increase in food aid.

Later in the year distribution was hampered when heavy rains disrupted rail traffic to the regions where starvation was most widespread. However, the rains offered some hope that subsequent harvests might alleviate the disaster.

(KENNETH INGHAM)

SWAZILAND

Swaziland is a landlocked monarchy of southern Africa and a member of the Commonwealth. Area: 17,364 sq km (6,704 sq mi). Pop. (1985 est.): 659,200. Cap.: Mbabane. Monetary unit: lilangeni (plural: emalangeni), at par with the South African rand, with (Oct. 21, 1985) a free rate of 2.60 emalangeni to U.S. $1 (3.72 emalangeni = £1 sterling). Regent in 1985, Queen Ntombi; prime minister, Prince Bhekimpi Dlamini.

Presenting the 1985–86 budget to Parliament in February 1985, Finance Minister Barnabas Dlamini indicated that there had been no improvement in Swaziland's economy. The country was suffering from the effects of world recession, drought conditions in 1982–83, and the devastation caused by Cyclone Domoina in 1984. With the population growing by 3.4% a year, per capita income was falling and unemployment was on the increase. The budget included a number of financial incentives designed to encourage investment. Among the major development projects that were announced during the year were an international-standard hotel at Piggs Peak and a textile mill at the Matsapa industrial estate.

At the Southern African Development Coordination Conference meeting in Mbabane, Prime Minister Prince Bhekimpi Dlamini shocked the delegates by defending his country's "good neighbour" policy toward South Africa. His stance was explained in part by Swaziland's extreme vulnerability to economic pressure from the republic. As the crisis in South Africa deepened, the government of the republic threatened to expel migrant workers, including over 13,000 from Swaziland.   (GUY ARNOLD)

This article updates the *Macropædia* article SOUTHERN AFRICA: *Swaziland*.

TANZANIA

The republic of Tanzania, a member of the Commonwealth, consists of Tanganyika, on the east coast of Africa, and Zanzibar, just off the coast in the Indian Ocean, which includes Zanzibar Island, Pemba Island, and small islets. Area: 945,037 sq km (364,881 sq mi). Pop. (1985 est.): 21,730,000. Seat of government, Dar es Salaam; capital designate, Dodoma. Monetary unit: Tanzania shilling, with (Oct. 21, 1985) a free rate of T Sh 16.53 to U.S. $1 (T Sh 23.70 = £1 sterling). Presidents in 1985, Julius Nyerere and, from November 5, Ali Hassan Mwinyi; prime minister, Salim Ahmed Salim.

On Nov. 5, 1985, Julius Nyerere, who had led the country since independence, resigned as president of Tanzania and handed over the office to his elected successor. As chairman of the sole party, Chama Cha Mapinduzi (CCM), a post that he planned to retain until 1987, Nyerere would continue to exert considerable influence over Tanzanian affairs.

At a special congress of the CCM in August, Ali Hassan Mwinyi (*see* BIOGRAPHIES) was chosen ahead of Prime Minister Salim Ahmed Salim and Rashidi Kawawa, the CCM general secretary, as sole candidate to succeed Nyerere. He received the endorsement of the electorate in presidential elections on October 27. Elections to the National Assembly took place on the same day. Mwinyi, who had taken over the joint offices of Tanzanian vice-president and president of Zanzibar following the resignation of Aboud Jumbe in early 1984, had achieved considerable success in improving Zanzibar's economy and handling its potentially delicate relations with the mainland.

As president of Tanzania, Mwinyi inherited a unified country with no organized opposition but with serious economic problems that provided a possible breeding ground for discontent. Not least among them was the shortage of food. Potentially capable of supplying all its own food requirements, Tanzania was forced to use some of its meagre foreign-exchange reserves to pay for imported maize (corn). At the same time, the fall in prices offered for its main cash crops (sisal, cotton, and cashew nuts) reduced reserves still further. Nyerere had consistently refused to accept aid from the International Monetary Fund (IMF) because he rejected the conditions imposed by that organization.

Nyerere felt impelled by circumstances to permit some relaxation of his principles. He ordered the sisal industry, nationalized in 1967, returned to private ownership because state control had proved unsuccessful. Controls on imports were relaxed to a limited extent to reduce public discontent, while private enterprise was allowed to take over certain areas of business. However, Nyerere insisted that the government would continue to control the most important sectors of the economy. On taking office, President Mwinyi promised to adhere to the program of socialism and self-reliance drawn up by his predecessor in his Arusha Declaration of 1967. However, the steadily worsening balance of payments deficit, coupled with rising inflation, rendered the need for an accommodation with the IMF increasingly urgent.

Addressing the Southern African Development Coordination Conference summit in August, Nyerere attacked the U.S., the U.K., and West Germany for their failure to impose economic sanctions on South Africa. He urged African nations to mount a trade boycott against South Africa, while stressing that such action would invite retaliation.   (KENNETH INGHAM)

This article updates the *Macropædia* article EASTERN AFRICA: *Tanzania*.

TOGO

A republic of West Africa, Togo is situated on the Bight of Benin. Area: 56,785 sq km (21,925 sq mi). Pop. (1985 est.): 2,989,000. Cap.: Lomé. Monetary unit: CFA franc, with (Oct. 21, 1985) a par value of CFAF 50 to the French franc and a free rate of CFAF 402.02 to U.S. $1 (CFAF 576.50 = £1 sterling). President in 1985, Gen. Gnassingbe Eyadema.

Legislative elections on March 24, 1985, duly returned the Togolese People's Assembly (RPT—the sole permitted party) to power. For the first time, candidates were not confined to a single RPT list.

While Pres. Gnassingbe Eyadema enjoyed good standing on the international scene, exiled opponents continued their efforts to destabilize his regime. A press conference to have been held by the Paris-based Togolese Democratic Movement on June 6—four days before Eyadema's arrival on a state visit to France—was forbidden by the Paris police. A series of bomb incidents in Lomé during August was followed by numerous arrests; these in turn led to allegations by Amnesty International of torture and detention without trial of those arrested. Two further bomb attacks on December 4 killed one person and injured others.

In June the creditor nations in the Club of Paris agreed to a rescheduling of Togo's external debt (F 6,280,000,000 in 1984) over 11 years. Pope John Paul II visited Togo on August 8–10.   (PHILIPPE DECRAENE)

This article updates the *Macropædia* article WESTERN AFRICA: *Togo*.

Following July's military coup, Uganda's new leaders—Prime Minister Paulo Muwanga (left), Minister of Internal Affairs Paul Ssemogerere (right), and Gen. Tito Okello—observe the release of political prisoners.

UPI/BETTMANN NEWSPHOTOS

UGANDA

A landlocked republic and member of the Commonwealth, Uganda is located in eastern Africa. Area: 241,140 sq km (93,100 sq mi), including 44,081 sq km of inland water. Pop. (1985 est.): 14,716,100. Cap.: Kampala. Monetary unit: Uganda shilling, with (Oct. 21, 1985) a free rate for traditional exports, essential imports, and official loans of U Sh 669.46 to U.S. $1 (U Sh 960 = £1 sterling) and with (Dec. 31, 1984) a free rate for other transactions of U Sh 520 to U.S. $1 (U Sh 745.68 = £1 sterling). President until July 27, 1985, Milton Obote; chairman of the Military Council from July 29, Gen. Tito Okello; prime ministers, Erifasi Otema Allimadi to July 27, Paulo Muwanga from August 1, and Abraham Waligo from August 25.

The steady economic recovery that had taken place with the support of the World Bank and the International Monetary Fund since Pres. Milton Obote was returned to office in Uganda in 1980 was increasingly threatened in the early months of 1985 by the activities of antigovernment rebels and the heavy-handed reprisals of government troops. In response to a request from Obote, the U.K. government agreed in April to renew and increase military assistance; at the same time, the British voiced their disquiet over reports of army excesses. Hopes of a more stable future were undermined when the National Resistance Army (NRA), the main guerrilla force, opened a new front in the Western Province. In the eyes of many Ugandans, the new offensive gave credence to the rebels' claim that they were not merely conducting a tribal struggle for power in support of the interests of a section of the Baganda people who had opposed Obote ever since he drove their ruler, the kabaka, into exile 20 years earlier.

During a visit to the U.K. in June, Paul Ssemogerere, leader of the main parliamentary opposition, the Democratic Party, pleaded with the British government to intervene to protect democracy in Uganda. He claimed that half a million people, more than during the years (1971–79) of former president Idi Amin's tyrannous rule, had died since Obote took office. Shortly afterward Amnesty International published a report in which detailed charges of torture were leveled against the security forces. Obote invited Amnesty representatives to examine the situation for themselves, but before the offer could be taken up, his government was overthrown by a military coup on July 27. Obote fled first to Kenya and later to Zambia.

The origins of the coup lay in the disaffection among Acholi members of the Army who were critical of the favoured treatment that, they said, was given to soldiers from Lango, Obote's own tribal district. The northern brigade, under Brig. Bazilio Olara Okello, mutinied and advanced southward to Kampala, which they seized without much resistance but with an excess of looting.

The NRA, which claimed foreknowledge of the coup, hoped to take a share in government. They were angry, therefore, when, without consultation, the mutineers appointed a Military Council under Gen. Tito Okello (*see* BIOGRAPHIES), the army commander, to supervise the government of the country for a year. They were even more disturbed when Paulo Muwanga, vice-president under Obote, whom they distrusted as much as Obote himself, was appointed prime minister of an interim government on August 1, and when the Military Council enlisted the aid of some of Amin's former soldiers. While the NRA threatened to continue its military activities, Ssemogerere accepted office as minister of internal affairs. His first duty was to release more than 1,000 prisoners detained by the Obote regime, many of whom testified to the truth of the Amnesty report.

The dismissal of Muwanga within a month did little to reassure the NRA. However, talks between the leaders of the Military Council and the NRA began in Kenya in August, with Kenyan Pres. Daniel arap Moi as mediator, and on December 17 a peace treaty was signed in Nairobi. Under the agreement, power in the Military Council would be shared by the NRA, and the guerrillas would be absorbed into the national army. An observer force provided by Kenya, Tanzania, Britain, and Canada would monitor the accord. Earlier, on December 11, the government announced that elections would be held in July 1986.

(KENNETH INGHAM)

This article updates the *Macropædia* article EASTERN AFRICA: *Uganda*.

ZAIRE

The republic of Zaire is located in central Africa with a short coastline on the Atlantic Ocean. Area: 2,344,885 sq km (905,365 sq mi). Pop. (1985 est.): 33,052,000. Cap.: Kinshasa. Monetary unit: zaire, with (Oct. 21, 1985) a free rate of 53.13 zaires to U.S. $1 (76.18 zaires = £1 sterling). President in 1985, Mobutu Sese Seko; prime minister, Kengo wa Dondo.

Fighting in the town of Moba, Shaba Province, in mid-November 1984 was attributed by the government of Zaire to the activities of rebels based in Tanzania. However, the Tanzanian government denied that it harboured Zairian rebels, and opposition groups in Brussels said that the fighting was the result of a mutiny in the Zairian Army. It was significant, therefore, that shortly afterward Pres. Mobutu Sese Seko retired six generals and five lieutenant colonels and announced that a new army unit was to be set up with the special task of providing information for the head of state. A subsequent attack on Moba in June 1985 was blamed once again on "hostile elements" from Tanzania.

In late 1984 and early 1985 Mobutu carried out a substantial reorganization of his Cabinet. On February 1 he himself assumed the justice portfolio. The government's adherence to the austerity program laid down in the 1985 budget evoked confidence and induced the International Monetary Fund to agree to a standby credit arrangement of $160 million in April. Other sources of foreign aid also remained available. Italy offered a loan to promote agricultural development in the Bas-Zaire (Lower Zaire) and

Bandundu regions, and the U.S. Agency for International Development offered a further loan for road building and for medical and water projects in Shaba region. The UN Development Program and Food and Agriculture Organization also agreed to make a grant of $1.9 million.

Zaire was granted an increase in its coffee export quota under the International Coffee Agreement, a concession granted to only two other African countries. In February it was announced that Zaire expected to meet its domestic petroleum needs from its own resources by exchanging its light, sulfur-free crude oil for imports of heavier oils and refined products. Like neighbouring Zambia, Zaire had suffered for nearly a decade from the low price paid for copper on the world market, but there was a modicum of encouragement to be gleaned from the announcement that Western European countries intended to increase their consumption of copper by 2–3%.

In June several members of the banned Zairian Union pour la Démocratie et le Progrès Social (UDPS) who had been under house arrest since 1982, when they campaigned against the government's one-party policy, were released. They claimed that the government had agreed to release all political prisoners and to halt political arrests in return for the cessation of public activity by the UDPS. On July 18, however, a Belgian employee of the European Parliament, Ronald van den Bogaert, was arrested on his arrival in Kinshasa and charged with possessing seditious material intended for members of the UDPS. He was tried and sentenced to ten years' imprisonment, though both the trial and sentence were fiercely criticized by Belgium's Flemish Socialist Party, of which he was a member. Shortly afterward the UDPS charged the government with failing to respect the truce. On October 9 a UDPS meeting in Kinshasa in the home of the party chairman, Kibassa Maliba, was broken up by government troops; the UDPS claimed that 13 of its members had been arrested, though the government said only one person had been detained. At the end of June former prime minister Nguza Karl-I-Bond was reported to have renounced his opposition to Mobutu and returned to Zaire, ending four years of voluntary exile in Belgium.

Relations with Zambia continued to be strained because of the expulsion by each country of nationals belonging to its neighbour, a situation that was aggravated by the influx of hundreds of refugees into Zambia after the fighting in Moba in 1984. On February 9, at the end of a visit to Kinshasa by Pres. José Eduardo dos Santos of Angola, Zaire signed a number of bilateral agreements with Angola covering defense and security, trade, conservation, and health. Each country agreed to prevent the launch of attacks against the other from within its borders, and the two presidents also discussed the question of refugees.

In September Minister of Foreign Affairs Mokolo wa Mpombo paid an official visit to South Korea, where he sought that country's participation in agricultural and hydroelectricity projects and urged South Korea to import Zairian cobalt and zinc. The two countries reaffirmed their desire for bilateral cooperation in the fields of economics, technology, and culture.

In May President Mobutu paid a six-day official visit to Israel, where he reportedly secured favourable credit terms for the purchase of military hardware from Israel. In 1982 Zaire had been the first of the black African nations to break a boycott of Israel. During the course of his African tour in August, Pope John Paul II visited Zaire for the second time.   (KENNETH INGHAM)

This article updates the *Macropædia* article CENTRAL AFRICA: *Zaire*.

ZAMBIA

A landlocked republic and member of the Commonwealth, Zambia is in eastern Africa. Area: 752,614 sq km (290,586 sq mi). Pop. (1985 est.): 6,666,000. Cap.: Lusaka. Monetary unit: kwacha, with (Oct. 21, 1985) a free rate of 5.72 kwacha to U.S. $1 (8.20 kwacha = £1 sterling). President in 1985, Kenneth Kaunda; prime ministers, Nalumino Mundia and, from April 24, Kebby Musokotwane.

Austerity was the theme of all the Zambian government's pronouncements in 1985. Estimates of expenditure for the year rose by $55.5 million, all of it attributable to debt servicing. Although Pres. Kenneth Kaunda deplored the "terrifying" demands attached by the International Monetary Fund to its loans, the government found it essential to borrow. When the value of the kwacha was more than halved in October, the finance minister declared he was confident that it would stabilize at a higher level once the business sector calmed down. Speaking at the opening of the 20th national council meeting of the ruling United National Independence Party in October, Kaunda said that industry had become too capital intensive.

Over the recent years of drought, Zambia had found it necessary to use its scarce supplies of foreign currency to import maize (corn). With the drought broken, the potential benefits were threatened by low prices offered by the government to producers and by the danger that a fuel shortage might hamper harvesting. The fuel crisis was averted when a new loan was raised from a consortium of banks.   (KENNETH INGHAM)

This article updates the *Macropædia* article SOUTHERN AFRICA: *Zambia*.

ZIMBABWE

A republic and member of the Commonwealth, Zimbabwe is a landlocked state in eastern Africa. Area: 390,759 sq km (150,873 sq mi). Pop. (1985 est.): 8.1 million. Cap.: Harare. Monetary unit: Zimbabwe dollar, with (Oct. 21, 1985) a free rate of Z$1.68 to U.S. $1 (Z$2.41 = £1 sterling). President in 1985, the Rev. Canaan Banana; prime minister, Robert Mugabe.

During the opening months of 1985 Joshua Nkomo, leader of Zimbabwe's main opposition party, the Zimbabwe African People's Union (ZAPU), experienced increasing difficulty in addressing public meetings because of the violent intervention of supporters of the ruling Patriotic Front party, the Zimbabwe African National Union (ZANU [PF]). At the end of February five supporters of another party, the United African National Council (UANC), led by former prime minister Bishop Abel Muzorewa, were shot dead at Hwange railway station after a party meeting, while on the same day, supporters of ZAPU and ZANU (PF) fought pitched battles in the streets of Bulawayo. On March 2 Bulawayo was sealed off by hundreds of troops who then spent two days searching the city for antigovernment rebels in an attempt, they claimed, to prevent a recurrence of the previous week's violence. Nkomo, who had already complained of mass abductions of his supporters, described the military action as another attempt by the government to demoralize his followers. His complaint was reinforced a few days later when the Roman Catholic Church's Commission for Justice and Peace handed the government its report on violent incidents by supporters of the government and ZANU (PF) against their critics in Matabeleland.

Parliamentary elections planned for the end of March

were postponed because electoral registers had not been completed in time to allow the delimitation commission to define new constituency boundaries. The new date for voting was fixed for June, but when, after further delays, legislation was passed in May to hasten the electoral process, opposition parties were vocal in their criticism because they believed the new measures did not allow them adequate time to choose and allocate candidates. The High Court rejected an application from ZAPU to postpone the closing date for nominations, but the date was postponed by one and a half days by presidential order. Elections were fixed for June 27 for voters on the white roll and July 1–2 for voters on the common roll.

In the elections on the white roll, Ian Smith's Conservative Alliance of Zimbabwe won a surprisingly convincing victory, taking 15 of the 20 seats reserved for whites in the National Assembly; the breakaway Independent Zimbabwe Group won 4, and the final seat was taken by an independent. The result did not please Prime Minister Robert Mugabe, who was highly critical of the lack of cooperation shown to the government by Smith and his supporters. Claiming that the trust bestowed by the government upon the white minority clearly had not been deserved, the prime minister promised to abolish white representation at an early date.

When the black voters went to the polls, clumsy polling procedures caused lengthy delays with the result that the period allowed for the elections had to be extended by two days. Although there had been some harassment of opposition supporters in the days leading up to the elections, the voting went off without incident. However, the militancy of some ZANU (PF) members was demonstrated in areas near Harare and Kwekwe, where members of the opposition were threatened with eviction from their homes if they did not join the government party. As expected, Mugabe's ZANU (PF) won an overwhelming victory, polling half a million more votes than in 1980 and increasing its representation from 57 to 63 seats. ZAPU secured 15 seats, 5 fewer than in 1980. Even in Matabeleland, where support for ZAPU remained strong, there were some ZANU (PF) gains. Worst hit of all was Muzorewa's UANC, which failed to win a single seat in Parliament. (For tabulated results, see *Political Parties,* above.)

As a snub to those who voted for Smith, Mugabe dropped Denis Norman, minister of agriculture, from his Cabinet, though he appointed Chris Andersen, the only independent white member of Parliament, to a ministerial post. ZAPU leaders were angered by the appointment of Enos Nkala as minister of home affairs in charge of police. Though Ndebele himself, Nkala had always advocated harsh measures against the government's opponents in Matabeleland. Nkala responded to criticism of his appointment by threatening to ban, and later to destroy, ZAPU.

Following the elections the government began to take a more lenient line toward Conservative Alliance supporters, though a televised talk by Smith, during a November visit to the U.K., aroused strong resentment. Subsequently, a parliamentary committee was established to consider reprimanding Smith for making derogatory remarks about Zimbabwe's government and its black population. Douglas Collard ("Boss") Lilford, former chairman of the Rhodesia Front, the forerunner of the Conservative Alliance, and a major political figure during the period of Rhodesia's unilateral declaration of independence, was found murdered on November 29. Whites were more affected than blacks by a constitutional amendment that, as of early December, barred Zimbabweans from holding dual nationality.

The pressure on ZAPU was sharply increased by a number of incidents, including the arrest of Sydney Malunga, a senior ZAPU official and member of Parliament, and of Nick Mabodoko, mayor of Bulawayo; the eviction of ZAPU from its Harare headquarters; and the seizure of Nkomo's passport. Muzorewa's retirement from politics in November further weakened opposition to the government, but hopes of a more stable future were raised by talks between Mugabe and Nkomo with a view to a merger between their two parties.

At the beginning of the year the first steps were taken to implement the leadership code laid down by ZANU (PF) in August 1984 that banned party officials from receiving more than one salary, owning more than 20 ha (50 ac) of land, or engaging in any form of business activity. A month later Wiriddzayi Nguruve, commissioner of police, was suspended from office pending an inquiry into charges of serious misconduct. Mugabe was criticized by trade unionists within his party for labour legislation that outlawed strikes and gave the labour minister power over union finances and officeholders—measures seen as constituting a denial of the Socialist policies that ZANU (PF) professed to uphold.

There was better news for the government on the agricultural front when it was announced in March that the maize (corn) crop seemed likely to reach a record three million metric tons. The tobacco crop, an important source of export earnings, was also expected to reach record levels. As a gesture of goodwill, 25,000 metric tons of maize were promised to famine-stricken Ethiopia, while the government paid $1 million to the emergency assistance fund set up by the Organization of African Unity in 1984. As a further response to the improved economic outlook, and with an eye to the parliamentary elections, in April Mugabe announced a 15% increase in the wages of the lowest paid workers to take effect July 1. At the same time, allocations of foreign currency for imports were increased by 30%, and restrictions on payments to foreign shareholders living abroad were relaxed in an effort to encourage foreign investors to take a more active part in the economy.

The budget introduced by Finance Minister Bernard Chidzero on July 30 provoked a mixed response. The public was relieved that no obviously oppressive measures appeared to be contemplated, but economists feared that the proposed 28% increase in the budget deficit might adversely affect relations with the International Monetary Fund. They also forecast considerable increases in the prices of food and fuel.   (KENNETH INGHAM)

This article updates the *Macropædia* article SOUTHERN AFRICA: *Zimbabwe.*

Middle East and North Africa

MIDDLE EASTERN AND NORTH AFRICAN AFFAIRS

The Gulf war between Iran and Iraq, which entered its sixth year in September 1985, dominated Middle Eastern affairs, although the year was also marked by the opening of a new U.S. peace initiative aimed at reconciling Israel and the Arab nations on the issue of Palestine. Israeli forces withdrew from Lebanon, leaving the stage clear for Syria's Pres. Hafez al-Assad to try to negotiate a settlement between the leaders of Christian, Druze, and Muslim militias,

who signed an armistice accord on December 28. There was an increase in incidents of kidnapping and political terrorism, which during the year included the seizure of the Italian cruise ship *Achille Lauro,* the hijacking of a Trans World Airlines passenger aircraft, and an assassination attempt on Emir Sheikh Jabir of Kuwait. In North Africa Libyan leader Col. Muammar al-Qaddafi faced increased internal opposition and also angered Tunisia and Egypt by expelling thousands of guest workers who had been recruited in previous years to aid the oil boom.

The Gulf War. The year brought little hope of an end to the long conflict between Iran and Iraq. Iran maintained its insistence that its objective was to overthrow Iraq's Pres. Saddam Hussein at-Takriti. In March fighting flared to a pitch of ferocity rarely seen since the early weeks of the conflict. The move to escalate the fighting came initially from Baghdad as Iraqi bombers attacked first the Iranian petroleum-exporting terminal at Kharg Island and then Iranian cities, breaking an agreement made in June 1984 not to attack civilian targets. Iran opened an offensive on March 12 that aimed to establish a bridgehead on the west bank of the Tigris River to cut the Baghdad–Basra road, a principal communications artery. The attack was repulsed by Iraq, which also stepped up its raids on oil tankers. Despite possessing superior air power, Iraq was unable to halt loading at the Kharg Island terminal for more than short periods. Although a moratorium on air and missile strikes on civilian targets was announced on June 14, Iraq renewed the onslaught on July 1, claiming that the attacks would continue until a just and honourable peace had been reached on terms to be set by President Hussein.

Iraq's main financial support was from the Gulf Cooperation Council (GCC) member states, which continued to help their "Arab brother" with oil swaps and direct subsidies. Iran maintained its war effort through income from petroleum exports and by making use of its larger population and more plentiful natural resources. Iran was confident of being able to maintain its 2.3 million-bbl-a-day quota set by the Organization of Petroleum Exporting Countries (OPEC). In early October Iran mounted naval maneuvers in the Strait of Hormuz, through which tankers enter the Gulf. Iranian Pres. Sayyed Ali Khamenei warned Western powers against military intervention; Iran made it clear that it was determined to close the strait if its own oil supply lines were cut. Iraq immediately retaliated on November 6 with a strike on Iran's Ahwaz pipe mill.

At the GCC summit held in Muscat, Oman, in November, GCC leaders showed some signs of taking a more neutral stance on the war. However, mediation initiatives taken by the GCC after its summit were rebuffed by Iran, which declined to meet the GCC envoy, Omani Minister of State for Foreign Affairs Yusuf al-Alawi.

Gulf Cooperation Council. Defense and security were the major concerns voiced by leaders of the GCC countries—Saudi Arabia, Kuwait, Bahrain, Qatar, Oman, and the United Arab Emirates (U.A.E.)—at the 1985 summit in Oman. Their talks ended on November 6 with renewed calls for an end to the Gulf war and pledges to stop the spread of terrorism. In May Emir Sheikh Jabir of Kuwait survived unhurt when a bomb attack was made on his motor cavalcade in Kuwait's normally peaceful Corniche. Preoccupation with these subjects pushed to one side regional topics, including economic integration and industrial strategy, which had been expected to dominate the summit agenda. The final communiqué used two UN Security Council resolutions on the war—Resolution 540 of October 1983 and Resolution 552 of June 1984—as points of departure for renewed contacts between the GCC

and the warring parties. Both resolutions had been rejected by Iran.

In August the defense forces of the six GCC states held joint exercises at the King Khalid Military City in northeastern Saudi Arabia. It was also understood that progress was being made on the idea of forming a GCC rapid-deployment force that could assist in the event of a localized emergency, such as the attempted coup in Bahrain in December 1981. While contacts between GCC members remained good at the government level, private-sector interests in the richest of the GCC states—Saudi Arabia and Kuwait—still favoured a nationalist and protectionist approach to trade policies. It was decided to postpone until December 1986 the opening of the $1 billion road causeway linking Bahrain with Saudi Arabia to allow more time to study its social and economic impact.

In what could be regarded as diplomatic gains for the U.S.S.R. in its superpower rivalry with the U.S., two GCC member states announced their decision to recognize the Soviet Union during the year. Oman made the announcement on September 26, and the U.A.E. made a similar statement on November 15. Each country affirmed that its decision was a strictly bilateral one. Oman's rapprochement with the U.S.S.R. represented a major policy reversal; relations between the two countries had been poor since the 1970s, when the U.S.S.R. had supported a guerrilla insurgency movement in the Dhofar region of Oman from bases in Marxist-led South Yemen. Diplomatic sources in Muscat said that Oman's decision reflected a desire to establish credentials as a nonaligned state, an interpretation that was reinforced by the invitations to many third world leaders to attend the 15th anniversary celebrations for Sultan Qabus ibn Sa'id of Oman on November 18. The diplomatic initiatives brought to three the number of GCC states that recognized the U.S.S.R.—Kuwait had already done so—but it was considered unlikely that Qatar and Saudi Arabia would follow suit because of their distaste for the treatment of Muslims in the U.S.S.R.

GCC states remained on excellent terms with most Western countries, although relations were soured by the move by the European Communities (EC) to put tariffs on methanol and polyethylene imports from the GCC to Europe. A meeting in Luxembourg in October revealed a lack of communication between the EC and the GCC.

The Arab World and Arab-Israeli Relations. A major development during 1985 was the Jordanian-Palestinian response to U.S. moves to break the deadlock between Arab countries and Israel over the Palestine issue. In February it was announced that King Hussein of Jordan and Palestine Liberation Organization (PLO) chairman Yasir Arafat had reached agreement on a joint peace initiative based on urging Israel to hand over the occupied territories in exchange for peace. Throughout the year King Hussein was at the forefront of efforts to arrange a meeting between a joint Palestinian-Jordanian team and U.K. Secretary of State for Foreign Affairs Sir Geoffrey Howe as a first step toward a meeting between a Jordanian delegation and U.S. representatives. Although the meeting with Howe was called off at the last minute, assurances were given on November 4 that the EC would receive a joint Jordanian-Palestinian delegation. On the same day, Luxembourg's Foreign Minister Jacques Poos said that King Hussein's plan also involved recognition of Israel by the PLO and a meeting between a Palestinian-Jordanian group and U.S. negotiators that would take place within the framework of an international conference including all five permanent members of the UN Security Council.

Arafat disputed this interpretation when, in a speech in

Cairo on November 5, he described the demand for PLO recognition of Israel as amounting to a precondition to negotiations and, as such, unacceptable. He maintained that the PLO had no intention of renouncing violence outside Israel and the occupied territories and claimed that the demand for the PLO to halt military action outside Israel was "unreasonable" as long as Israel continued to attack Palestinians "all over the world."

The Arab summit conference in Casablanca, Morocco, ended on August 9 with a resolution that gave implicit backing to the joint Jordanian-PLO peace initiative with Israel. However, the significance of the meeting was diminished by the fact that it was attended by fewer than half the Arab heads of state, while five countries boycotted the meeting altogether. Later in the year a rapprochement between Syria and Jordan increased Arafat's isolation. During Jordanian Prime Minister Zaid ar-Rifai's visit to Damascus, Syria, on November 12–13, both Jordan and Syria rejected any bilateral deal with Israel and called for an international conference on the Arab-Israeli conflict. This was followed by a two-day meeting between Hussein and Assad in Damascus at the end of December.

Many Israeli officials were convinced that King Hussein was serious in his commitment to reviving peace talks. They believed that moderate Arab nations would have more success in curbing the activities of the PLO following its implication in the *Achille Lauro* affair (*see* below). Israel's Prime Minister Shimon Peres made a significant move to assist King Hussein by embracing the idea of convening some kind of international meeting to begin peace talks. As a result Peres faced, and overcame, an internal government crisis in November.

Peres insisted that the U.S.S.R. mend fences with Israel before taking part in such an international conference, and beginning in midyear there were reports suggesting that Moscow was stepping up its contacts with Israel. The Soviet Union had severed diplomatic ties with Israel following the 1967 Arab-Israeli war. Since assuming power in March 1985, Soviet leader Mikhail Gorbachev was understood to have initiated moves to bring the U.S.S.R. into a cen-

tral role in Middle Eastern diplomacy. Peres was sharply criticized, however, by Israeli Foreign Minister Yitzhak Shamir in July for sending a goodwill message to Gorbachev through Edgar Bronfman, president of the World Jewish Congress. In return for Israeli help, King Hussein was attempting to find a solution to the main problem facing Peres by seeking Palestinian negotiators who would be acceptable to the Israeli prime minister. In the fall of 1986 Peres was due to hand over power to the Likud, his partners in the government of national unity, who were regarded as being hostile to any deal with the Palestinians; this fact brought a sense of urgency to negotiations.

U.S. Policy. The U.S. resumed its role as broker in the cause of peace in the region when during May 10–13 U.S. Secretary of State George Shultz visited Israel, Egypt, and Jordan. Although the tour was regarded as having been fruitless in terms of major achievements, it provided the backdrop to the meeting between King Hussein and U.S. Pres. Ronald Reagan on May 29. With Pres. Hosni Mubarak of Egypt already supporting his stand, King Hussein was anxious to secure the involvement of the U.S., which was regarded by many moderate Arab countries, including Saudi Arabia, as being indispensable to any major peace initiative. President Reagan subsequently yielded to pressure from Republican senators to block a proposed sale of weapons, worth $1.9 billion, to Jordan unless Jordan and Israel began direct talks. Speaking at the UN General Assembly on October 21, Peres appeared to acknowledge the progress made by U.S. diplomacy when he agreed to entertain the Jordanian idea of an international peace conference while continuing to push for bilateral talks between Israel and Jordan. Israel's air strike on the PLO headquarters near Tunis, Tunisia, on October 1, carried out in revenge for the murder of three Israelis in Cyprus, was not well received in Washington. However, U.S. outrage over the *Achille Lauro* seizure just one week later did much to redress the balance.

The U.S. had insisted since 1975 that it would negotiate with the PLO only after the guerrilla organization recognized Israel and pledged support for UN resolutions

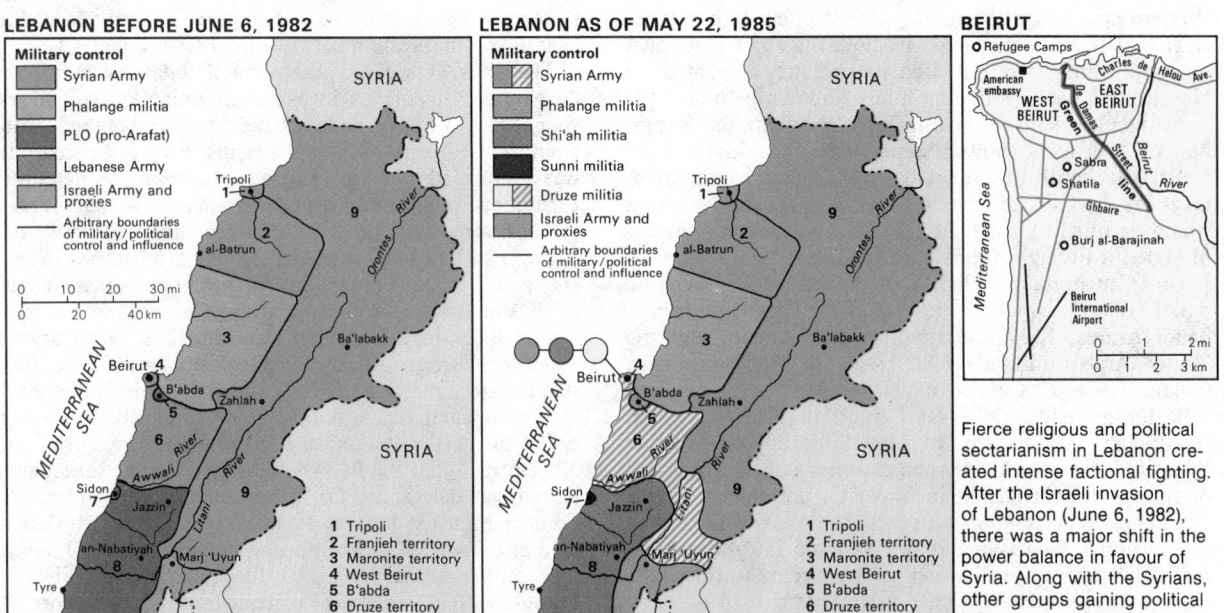

Fierce religious and political sectarianism in Lebanon created intense factional fighting. After the Israeli invasion of Lebanon (June 6, 1982), there was a major shift in the power balance in favour of Syria. Along with the Syrians, other groups gaining political influence were the Druze and the Shi'ah, while the Maronites and the Sunni were the losers.

Source: *The Economist.*

242 and 338, which were generally interpreted as implying recognition of the Jewish state. What appeared to be a softening of this stance in 1985 was interpreted by hard-line Likud politicians as merely a "flexing of commitment," which would not be followed by any real change in U.S. support for Israel.

Terrorism. The rash of terrorist attacks affecting civilians, particularly U.S. citizens, was a feature of the year's events that worried Western leaders. On June 14 a U.S. Trans World Airlines passenger aircraft flying from Athens to Rome was hijacked by Lebanese Shi'ah Muslims, who demanded the release of prisoners held by the Israelis. One U.S. passenger was killed and a number were held hostage for two weeks in Beirut before the crisis was ended following negotiations conducted by Nabih Berri (*see* BIOGRAPHIES), Lebanon's minister of justice and political leader of the Lebanese Shi'ah community. Shi'ah gunmen later kidnapped four officials of the Soviet embassy in Lebanon; they killed one diplomat before releasing the others at the end of October after holding them for a month.

The Italian cruise liner *Achille Lauro* was seized on October 7 off the coast of Egypt by four gunmen who were reported to be members of the Palestine Liberation Front, a splinter group of the PLO. The gunmen killed one U.S. passenger, 69-year-old Leon Klinghoffer, before surrendering to the Egyptian authorities on October 9. As part of the surrender pact the gunmen were to be flown to Tunisia, but their plane was intercepted by U.S. fighters and forced to land in Sicily, bringing the Palestinians to trial in Italy.

An EgyptAir airliner flying from Athens to Cairo on November 23 was hijacked to the airport at Valletta, Malta. During the hijacking and the ensuing gun battle as Egyptian troops stormed the plane, 57 of the 98 passengers and crew were killed. It was the heaviest loss of life ever suffered during an airliner hijack. Responsibility for the hijacking was claimed by the Abu Nidal group, a Palestinian faction that was opposed to Arafat's leadership of the PLO and to any rapprochement between Jordan, the PLO, and Israel. The Abu Nidal group was believed by some sources to be based in Libya. The same group was reported to have carried out attacks on Israeli El Al check-in counters at airports in Rome and Vienna on December 27. The attacks, in which 18 people died, embarrassed the Italian and Austrian authorities, both of which had expressed support for the PLO. The Israelis, who promised retaliatory action, refused to accept PLO claims that it was not involved in the incidents.

The Economy. Saudi Arabia appeared to be prepared to break ranks with OPEC by increasing its petroleum extractions toward its OPEC quota of 4.3 million bbl a day and so abandoning its pivotal role as OPEC's "swing producer." Speaking in Mecca on September 22, Saudi Arabia's King Fahd underlined his country's continued support for OPEC, but he also warned that Saudi Arabia would increase its output if other members raised their production quotas. At the December OPEC meeting in Geneva, the oil ministers agreed to cease defending the $28-a-barrel price in favour of increasing sales.

North Africa. The year was marked by the growing ostracism of Libya and by a polarization among the nations of the Maghrib—Morocco, Algeria, Tunisia, and Libya. The crisis began on August 5 when Libya, following the example of Nigeria, started sending home foreign workers in an attempt to improve its economic position. The country most affected was Tunisia, which retaliated by expelling more than 250 Libyans, including some diplomats. The Tunisian government also claimed that Libya was massing

troops on its border and subsequently called for all its nationals to return home and halted all economic cooperation with the Qaddafi regime. With Libya and Morocco allied by the Oujda accord of 1984, Algeria was moving closer to Tunisia. When Algerian Pres. Chadli Bendjedid visited Tunis on September 2, he assured Pres. Habib Bourguiba of Tunisia of Algeria's support.

On October 23 Moroccan Prime Minister Mohammad Karim Lamrani told the UN that Morocco wished the UN to organize a referendum in January 1986 about the future of the disputed Western Sahara. Morocco had declared a unilateral cease-fire in the territory, where it had been fighting guerrillas from the Popular Front for the Liberation of Saguia el Hamra and Río de Oro (Polisario Front) independence movement since 1975.   (JOHN WHELAN)

ALGERIA

Algeria is a republic of North Africa on the Mediterranean Sea. Area: 2,381,741 sq km (919,595 sq mi). Pop. (1985 est.): 21,731,000. Cap.: Algiers. Monetary unit: dinar, with (Oct. 21, 1985) a free rate of 4.87 dinars to U.S. $1 (6.99 dinars = £1 sterling). President in 1985, Col. Chadli Bendjedid; prime minister, Abdelhamid Brahimi.

During 1985 Algeria continued to concentrate on domestic affairs, particularly economic reorganization. In February Pres. Chadli Bendjedid instructed his administration to concentrate on developing the south of the country, revising the National Charter—the national development plan drawn up by his predecessor, Houari Boumédienne—and ensuring that his policies were properly understood by the population. The revision of the National Charter, which began in mid-July, was a potentially far-reaching move, since it implied the rejection of Boumédienne's legacy, and the former president was criticized in the media for the first time. In December two of modern Algeria's founders, Ahmed Ben Bella and Hocine Aït-Ahmed, announced in London the formation of a united front to oppose the National Liberation Front, Algeria's only party.

Algeria's economic problems stemmed from the fact that oil and gas revenues, while expected to maintain the 1984 level of around $12 billion, were substantially lower than they had been in the early 1980s. As a result, the 1985–89 plan was revised, and Algeria turned to international money markets for massive loans, making it one of the most heavily indebted nations in Africa. The foreign debt exceeded $16 billion by the end of the year. Algeria resisted price cuts proposed by the Organization of Petroleum Exporting Countries in December 1984 and January 1985, only reluctantly agreeing to a cut of $1 a barrel in March. Liquefied natural gas sales suffered from the decision of the U.S. company Distrigas to cancel its contracts. However, Spain agreed to pay $500 million in compensation for its failure to honour a 1975 gas purchase contract, and a revised agreement was signed.

The radical changes taking place inside Algeria were underlined in late April when serious riots broke out in Algiers to protest poor housing conditions. Riots in the southern town of Ghardaïa in June were the result of a dispute over land distribution to the private sector. Islamic fundamentalism continued to pose a serious problem, despite the leniency shown during trials in Médéa in April, when 135 fundamentalists accused of involvement in the 1982 disturbances were either given light sentences or released. Algeria's accelerated arabization campaign was opposed by the Berber population and by elements in the administration who considered French a more appropriate official language.

In foreign affairs Algeria continued to support the Popular Front for the Liberation of Saguia el Hamra and Río de Oro (Polisario Front) in its struggle against Morocco for control of the Western Sahara. A proposed meeting of North African heads of state had to be abandoned in February when Algeria refused to exclude the Western Sahara issue from the agenda. Chadli tried to wean the U.S. from its support for Morocco during his state visit there in April. The subject also figured on the agenda when the president visited Madrid on July 1. Relations with France worsened during the year, partly because of France's close relations with Morocco. (GEORGE JOFFÉ)

This article updates the *Macropædia* article NORTH AFRICA: *Algeria*.

BAHRAIN

The monarchy (emirate) of Bahrain consists of a group of islands in the Persian Gulf between the Qatar Peninsula and Saudi Arabia. Area: 678 sq km (262 sq mi). Pop. (1985 est.): 431,000. Cap.: Manama. Monetary unit: Bahrain dinar, with (Oct. 21, 1985) a free rate of 0.38 dinar to U.S. $1 (0.54 dinar = £1 sterling). Emir in 1985, Isa ibn Sulman al-Khalifah; prime minister, Khalifah ibn Sulman al-Khalifah.

The opening of the $1 billion Bahrain–Saudi Arabia causeway, rescheduled from December 1985 to December 1986 to allow for the completion of customs and immigration formalities, was expected to give a much-needed boost to the claims of Bahrain as a financial and services centre for the Persian Gulf. The attractions of Bahrain as an offshore financial haven suffered a number of setbacks during the year. Three U.S.-based banks announced cuts in their establishments because of high operating costs. A leading Bahraini-born banker was arrested on April 23 after irregularities in the accounts of an offshore banking unit were allegedly detected by the monetary authority. Officials countered by blaming the overall situation on declining bank profits worldwide and hoped soon to announce new banking licenses for institutions seeking representation in Bahrain.

Intercommunal tensions continued between the politically dominant Sunnis, from whom the ruling family was drawn, and the Bahraini Shi'ah, constituting more than half the native population. A small minority of Shi'ah sympathized with the Iranian revolution and sought radical change in Bahrain, including discrimination against women and the closing of bars and nightclubs. On June 23 six Bahrainis were deported from the U.K. after being arrested on suspicion of plotting against the Bahraini government. (JOHN WHELAN)

This article updates the *Macropædia* article ARABIA: *Bahrain*.

CYPRUS

An island republic and member of the Commonwealth, Cyprus is in the eastern Mediterranean Sea. Area: 9,251 sq km (3,572 sq mi). Pop. (1985 est.): 685,000. Area and population figures include the Turkish Cypriot state that has occupied the northern third of the island since 1974, though its existence is not internationally recognized. Official population estimates may not take into account the recent and reportedly extensive Turkish immigration and Greek emigration. Cap.: Nicosia. Monetary unit: Cyprus pound, with (Oct. 21, 1985) a free rate of £C 0.56 to U.S. $1 (£C 0.80 = £1 sterling). President in 1985, Spyros Kyprianou.

There were high hopes for the January summit meeting in New York City between Pres. Spyros Kyprianou and Turkish Cypriot leader Rauf Denktash. The meeting was the culmination of efforts by UN Secretary-General Javier

Pérez de Cuéllar to produce a draft agreement for a federal solution to end the division between the Greek and Turkish Cypriot communities. The summit collapsed, however, as it became clear that the two leaders were not of one mind. Kyprianou viewed the draft accord as nothing more than a basis for further negotiations. Denktash accepted the draft as a finished product, ready to be signed; he was willing to leave unresolved issues to be worked out later.

The talks ended amid bitter recriminations. Kyprianou returned home to severe criticism from the two powerful opposition parties, the Communist AKEL and the right-wing Rally. In an unprecedented move the executive president was censured by the House of Representatives, where his small Democratic Party, supported by three Socialists, was outvoted 23–12 in a motion calling for him to sign the draft agreement and submit to the will of the parliamentary majority or resign. Kyprianou refused to resign, as was his right, and the opposition proceeded to bring the legislature to a virtual standstill by blocking all measures sent to the House by Kyprianou's Council of Ministers.

In the north the ebullient Denktash was riding high as the Greeks squabbled. He proceeded to give the south a threefold lesson in democracy by calling a referendum on a new constitution and then presidential and parliamentary elections. The constitution received 70% backing, and even Denktash himself confessed surprise when he won a six-way presidential race with a landslide 70% of the vote. In the northern assembly elections the National Turkish Party, founded by Denktash, won 24 seats and formed an alliance with the 10-seat Communal Liberation Party (TKP). The left-wing Turkish Republican Party won 12 seats, and New Dawn (YDP), a party of settlers from the mainland, won 4 seats.

In October the southern House unanimously voted to dissolve itself, setting parliamentary elections for December 8. The House was expanded from 35 to 56 seats. The elections were a personal triumph for Kyprianou, whose party had been expected to lose heavily against the powerful opposition. At the expense of AKEL, which won only 15 seats, the Democrats won 16, the Socialist EDEK won 6, and the Rally became the major party with 19. The House deadlocked at its first and second sessions, however, and failed to elect a House leader, carrying the paralysis of governmental business into 1986.

The economy, not helped by the political crisis, faltered but remained basically sound. Estimates for the growth of gross domestic product in 1985 showed a drop of 1.5% from the 6% of 1984. However, optimism surrounded 1986 forecasts, with agriculture, tourism, and service industries expected to continue booming. Inflation was reasonably stable at about 5.5%, as was unemployment at about 3%. In December Cyprus began detailed talks with the European Communities (EC) aimed at a transition to a full customs union with the EC. (THOMAS O'DWYER)

EGYPT

A republic of North Africa, Egypt has coastlines on the Mediterranean and Red seas. Area: 997,739 sq km (385,229 sq mi). Pop. (1985 est.): 48,503,000. Cap.: Cairo. Monetary unit: Egyptian pound (LE), with a par value of LE 1 = U.S. $1.42857 and a main official rate (for most business transactions) of LE 0.82 = U.S. $1 (LE 1.18 = £1 sterling). President in 1985, Hosni Mubarak; prime ministers, Kamal Hassan Ali and, from September 4, Ali Lutfi.

Deteriorating economic circumstances and growing Islamic fundamentalism in Egypt were two factors worrying Pres. Hosni Mubarak as he began his fifth year in office in Octo-

ber 1985. They threatened to undermine the achievements of his presidency, which had been, first and foremost, his success in healing the wounds—both at home and abroad—of the turbulent years of his predecessor, Pres. Anwar as-Sadat.

Domestic Affairs. The lifting of restrictions placed on Shenuda III, the spiritual leader of the Coptic Church, on January 1 represented a major reversal of policy adopted in the Sadat years. (*See* RELIGION: *Eastern Non-Chalcedonian Churches.*) However, this gain for community understanding was offset by a worsening crisis in relations between the government and Islamic fundamentalists. In July Hafez Salama, the leader of a campaign to apply Shari'ah (Islamic law) in Egypt, was arrested along with 45 of his followers in the first crackdown on Muslim activists since Mubarak took office. In May the People's Assembly cut short a debate on the adoption of Shari'ah at the request of the ruling National Democratic Party. The government had determined to move slowly on the question of introducing Islamic law in a bid to please all parties.

Mubarak indicated his concern about internal developments with an angry speech on June 26 that was clearly directed against Islamic groups, whom—in a departure from his normally cautious style—he labeled "extremists." By promising a tough line against agitation, Mubarak put in doubt one of his earlier political goals—the creation of a wider and more active democratic franchise.

Underlying these political troubles were economic difficulties that provided the motivation for the major new appointment in a reshuffle of the Cabinet announced in September. Former finance minister Ali Lutfi was appointed prime minister in place of Kamal Hassan Ali on September 4, following the resignation of Ali and his Cabinet. Lutfi was considered to be a close confidant of Mubarak, who had appointed him to a special committee on the economy established earlier in 1985. The Cabinet announced on September 5 involved few other changes, but one significant promotion was that of Kamal Ahmad al-Ganzouri, the minister of planning and international cooperation, who became one of four deputy prime ministers. A number of other moves, including the appointment of Abdel-Rahman Labib to replace an army general as housing minister, served to diminish the influence of the military in the government.

The government was striving to fulfill an ambitious urban renewal program. Some two million new homes would be required by the end of the century if Egypt was to cope with the expected growth of its population. The visit of U.K. Prime Minister Margaret Thatcher on September 16–18 was marked by the signing of a £12.5 million grant for the development of coal mining and the unveiling of a plaque opening the Greater Cairo Wastewater Project, in which British companies were participating.

The Economy. Two of Egypt's principal sources of revenue—income from oil exports and remittances from expatriate workers—were being curtailed by recession within the Gulf region and weak world energy prices. The country was suffering from a chronic shortage of hard currency at a time when talks with the International Monetary Fund (IMF) on financial aid were delicately poised. The government had resisted the IMF's earlier calls to end food price subsidies. Finance Minister Salaheddin Hamid and Ali Negm, governor of the central bank, took part in talks with the IMF that began in Washington, D.C., on August 5. Their aim was to secure for Egypt a standby credit to support the balance of payments. It was believed the IMF acknowledged that the Mubarak administration had taken some steps toward easing public-spending burdens

Pres. Hosni Mubarak of Egypt (right) awards a medal for bravery to the pilot of the Egyptian airliner that had been forced down in Italy by U.S. Navy fighters while transporting Palestinian terrorists.
EL KOUSSY—SYGMA

but considered that efforts by midyear had fallen short of what was required.

In a further move to come to grips with economic problems, Mubarak visited Spain on September 20–21 and France on September 29–30, where he discussed ways of reducing the arrears on Egypt's military debts to both countries. Prime Minister Ali announced in August that talks about rescheduling the $1.2 billion in military debt to the U.S.S.R. had been inconclusive but were to be resumed later in the year. On July 8 a trade protocol with Moscow valued at more than $800 million was ratified.

The introduction in January of a controlled floating exchange rate for the Egyptian pound and a new tariff system to restrict imports brought stability to the currency market, but this was threatened in September by a slide in the value of the pound. On September 18 Mubarak announced the suspension of all new credits or loans, apart from those for productive, profit-yielding schemes. The statement indicated the government's concern to reduce the widening trade deficit, which was estimated at $6 billion for the year to July 1985. In a move to boost the economy, the government announced on September 30 that a 3.4% increase in tolls for ships using the Suez Canal was to be introduced with effect from Jan. 1, 1986.

Egypt's consistent calls for higher oil prices upset the consensus on the matter among other Arab nations. When the petroleum and mineral resources minister, Abdel-Hadi Muhammad Kandil, attended a meeting of the Organization of Petroleum Exporting Countries (OPEC) as an observer in January, he criticized the OPEC resolutions as "indecisive" and claimed that they would not halt the decline in prices on world markets. Overseas sales of cotton, Egypt's second biggest merchandise export, were on the increase, and the government was forecasting an 18% rise in cotton production in 1985–86.

Foreign Relations. President Mubarak continued his policy of improving relations with Arab nations, with the aim of maneuvering the country back into the Arab mainstream. The decision to grant political asylum to Gen. Gaafar Nimeiry following the coup that deposed him as president of The Sudan in April was in the tradition established when the government granted similar hospitality to

the exiled shah of Iran in 1979. Of greater concern was the move by Libya to expel hundreds of Egyptian expatriate workers, although the Cairo authorities said they could foresee no problem in integrating them.

On the wider question of bringing peace to the Middle East, in February Mubarak launched an initiative aimed at establishing a dialogue between the U.S. and a Jordanian-Palestinian delegation. The suggestion was viewed as a first step toward opening Arab-Israeli talks on the future of the West Bank and Gaza Strip. Mubarak pursued the idea when he visited the U.S. on March 9–13. Although any gains from his talks with officials there were not immediately clear, the U.S. administration subsequently gave weight to attempts to revive the stalled peace process.

Egypt came under renewed pressure from the U.S. to normalize its relationship with Israel, which had been frozen since the Israeli invasion of Lebanon in 1982 and the subsequent massacre of Palestinians by Lebanese Christian militia at the Sabra and Shatila refugee camps. However, Mubarak was seeking a more flexible attitude from Israel toward the Palestinian question, as well as the remaining bilateral territorial dispute (over Taba in the Sinai Peninsula), before he would risk losing the diplomatic gains that came from better relations with moderate Arab states. On May 28 the petroleum minister visited Israel to discuss oil sales. This apparent improvement in relations was spoiled, however, when an Israeli diplomat was assassinated in a suburb of Cairo on August 20 by a group calling itself the Egyptian Revolution.

Egypt's relations with the U.S. suffered in the aftermath of the hijacking of an Italian cruise liner, the *Achille Lauro,* by Palestinians in October. On hearing that one passenger, a U.S. citizen, had been killed during the hijack, the U.S. administration was strongly critical of Egypt's decision to grant safe passage to the hijackers, and the Egyptian airliner carrying them to Tunisia was intercepted by U.S. military planes and forced to land at a NATO base in Italy. Anti-U.S. demonstrations erupted in Cairo, and President Mubarak angrily demanded an apology to "all Egyptians." However, tensions over the incident had eased by year's end. In November the same EgyptAir plane involved in the *Achille Lauro* affair was hijacked by members of a Palestinian splinter group and flown to Malta, where Egyptian commandos stormed it with considerable loss of life. (*See* Western Europe: *Malta,* below.)   (JOHN WHELAN)

IRAN

The Islamic republic of Iran is in southwestern Asia on the Caspian and Arabian seas and the Persian Gulf. Area: 1,648,-000 sq km (636,000 sq mi). Pop. (1985 est.): 45 million. Cap.: Teheran. Monetary unit: rial, with (Oct. 21, 1985) a free rate of 85.84 rials to U.S. $1 (123.10 rials = £1 sterling). Supreme *faqih* (spiritual leader) in 1985, Ayatollah Ruhollah Khomeini; president, Sayyed Ali Khamenei; prime minister, Mir Hossein Moussavi.

Pressures arising from the continuing Gulf war between Iran and Iraq permeated all aspects of Iranian life during 1985. Iran remained firmly locked in the conflict, which entered its sixth year in September. Furthermore, the Iranian regime remained internationally isolated. The major powers were without exception aligned against the Iranian struggle to bring about the downfall of Iraqi Pres. Saddam Hussein at-Takriti and to seize part or all of Iraq. Iran was all but denied access to the arms, financial credits, and diplomatic support that were channeled to Iraq by the U.S.S.R., France, and the Arab nations. Among the few countries offering support to Iran were Syria and Libya;

on June 23 the latter concluded an agreement providing for close political and military cooperation with Iran.

In March the Iranians launched a major new land offensive in the southern marshlands of Iraq. Iranian forward troops succeeded in crossing the Tigris River. However, lacking logistical support and air cover, the attack fell victim to punishing countermoves by the Iraqis. The campaign resulted in heavy losses on the Iranian side, and any possibility that the Iranians might have regained the initiative in the war receded. The Iraqis mounted a number of air raids against Iranian cities, bombing civilian targets in Teheran, Isfahan, Tabriz, Shiraz, and many other settlements. By April the "war of the cities" had developed into a series of tit-for-tat exchanges in which the Iranians shelled Basra and Baghdad and bombed Iraqi border areas. With neither side apparently able to sustain the war against city populations, the attacks faded out in mid-April, though there were reports of further intensive air raids on Teheran in June.

As a counterstrategy to Iraqi control of the air war, Iran adopted a tactic of small-scale attacks along the 1,450-km (900-mi) frontier with a view to undermining Iraqi morale. Attacks on the northern front and, later, in the central sector were augmented by infiltration of Iraqi positions in the marsh areas of the south during late April and May. The Iraqis responded by carrying out a series of intensive air raids on the Kharg Island oil terminal beginning on July 15. For the first time, considerable damage was inflicted, and Iraq maintained an intermittent bombardment of the terminal throughout the remainder of the year. The Iraqi raids, though they did not bring Iranian oil exports to a complete halt, succeeded in making the operation extremely difficult. There were reports that Iranian troops were again massing in preparation for an offensive in the southern marshlands in late December.

Representing a marked change, there was open debate in the country about the issues involved in the war and the need for peace. Nevertheless, Iranian conditions for peace were relaxed scarcely at all. Efforts at mediation came to nothing despite a clear desire on the part of Iraq for an end to the confrontation.

Sayyed Ali Khamenei was returned for a second four-year term as president when he won over 85% of the vote in elections held on August 16. Speculation that the prime minister might be replaced ended when Mir Hossein Moussavi was reappointed to the post in October. He brought a number of new ministers into his Cabinet and promised a more radical program for the coming year. In November it was announced that the Council of Experts had designated Ayatollah Hussein Ali Montazeri to succeed Ayatollah Ruhollah Khomeini as the country's supreme spiritual leader, although there were no signs that Khomeini would step down in the near future.

Economic conditions deteriorated considerably as a result of the demands of the war budget. Foreign exchange receipts fell in response to the softening international market for crude oil and difficulties in exporting oil. The country's ability to pay for its imports declined as reserves of foreign exchange fell below $3 billion.

(KEITH S. MCLACHLAN)

IRAQ

A republic of southwestern Asia, Iraq has a short coastline on the Persian Gulf. Area: 438,317 sq km (169,235 sq mi). Pop. (1985 est.): 15,676,000. Cap.: Baghdad. Monetary unit: dinar, with (Oct. 21, 1985) a par value of 0.31 dinar to U.S. $1 (free rate of 0.44 dinar = £1 sterling). President in 1985, Saddam Hussein at-Takriti.

Iraqi soldiers guard Iranian prisoners of war following an Iranian offensive across the Tigris River intended to cut the Baghdad–Basra highway in March. Casualties numbered in the thousands.

PIERRE PERRIN—GAMMA/LIAISON

The Gulf war entered a new phase in mid-1985 when Iraq stepped up its air attacks on the Iranian oil terminal at Kharg Island. Iraqi raids on a steel complex in Ahwaz and a partially constructed nuclear power plant in Bushehr on March 4 led to an Iranian attack on the city of Basra. Using this breach of an earlier pledge to avoid civilian targets as justification, Pres. Saddam Hussein at-Takriti launched the "war of the cities" campaign and ordered attacks on 30 cities. In the same month, after intensive fighting on the ground, Iranian forces briefly held a section of the road from Baghdad to Basra before they were driven back. During five years of hostilities 70,000 Iraqis had been killed, 150,000 wounded, and 50,000 taken prisoner by Iran. Some $35 billion in foreign-currency reserves had been spent on the war, and the government had accumulated more than $40 billion in foreign debt.

In order to fuel the war effort, Iraq sought an increase in its oil-exporting quota from the Organization of Petroleum Exporting Countries in Vienna on October 4. Oil Minister Qasim Ahmad Taqi argued that new development projects had rendered its 1.2 million-bbl-a-day quota unrealistic. The first phase of a new pipeline to link Iraq's southern oil fields with the Saudi Arabian pipeline was commissioned on October 4. On June 2 Taqi announced that the latest estimate of Iraq's oil reserves was 145,000,000,000 bbl, a figure that, if confirmed, would put them second only to those of Saudi Arabia in world terms. On July 17 President Hussein claimed that he expected oil production would soon return to the levels attained before the start of the Gulf war.

The government faced difficulties in repaying in full rescheduled debts to its trading partners. While Iraq owed some $25 billion to the Arab Gulf states, principally Kuwait and Saudi Arabia, other creditors included France, West Germany, the U.K., and Japan. The surge of oil through the Saudi pipeline, estimated at 500,000 bbl a day by late 1985, was expected to help settle these accounts, but not before 1986. The extent of the problem could not be assessed accurately since the government, among the most secretive in the Middle East, had released very little economic information to the International Monetary Fund since 1977.

The five-year (1986–90) plan was described by First Deputy Prime Minister Taha Yassin Ramadan as "the beginning of a new era." Development plans concentrated on improving and extending infrastructure and social services. Investment in oil was to remain a high priority, but diversification into the agricultural and light industrial sectors was also to be encouraged. Ramadan said the government had prepared two plans, one based on the war ending within two years and the other assuming that hostilities would continue indefinitely.

President Hussein continued to command a large degree of support at home. However, a bomb attack on the Rafidain Bank headquarters on March 14 indicated the existence of local opposition in Baghdad. In the north a nighttime curfew was in force as a result of the activities of Kurdish guerrillas. In September the leader of the Democratic Party of Kurdistan, Masoud Barzani, claimed that his forces controlled much of the area around Iraq's northern border with Syria.

The government took heart from the support offered by the Gulf Cooperation Council countries and by the Arab summit that took place in Morocco in August. On June 27 an economic, cultural, and scientific agreement was signed with Egypt. On June 26 Iraq suspended diplomatic relations with Libya after the latter joined Iran in a strategic alliance with the aim of resisting any effort by Egypt, Iraq, Jordan, and the Palestine Liberation Organization to seek an accommodation with Israel. An indication of the improvement in Iraq's relations with the U.S. came in September when the two countries initialed a wide-ranging trade agreement. There was also evidence of better relations with nonaligned countries, particularly India and Yugoslavia, and with Soviet-bloc countries, from whom Iraq received military equipment.   (JOHN WHELAN)

ISRAEL

A republic of southwestern Asia, Israel is situated on the Mediterranean Sea. Area: 20,700 sq km (7,992 sq mi), not including territory occupied in the June 1967 war. Pop. (1985 est.): 4,306,000. Cap.: Jerusalem (but see Israel table in Britannica World Data). Monetary unit: shekel, with (Oct. 21, 1985) a free rate of 1,479.78 shekels to U.S. $1 (2,122 shekels = £1 sterling). President in 1985, Chaim Herzog; prime minister, Shimon Peres.

Israel embarked on an entirely new political experience in September 1984 when the government of national unity—in which neither the Labour Party on the left wing nor Likud on the right was dominant—took office. To the surprise of many, the government survived throughout 1985. In accordance with the coalition agreement, Prime Minister Shimon Peres and Deputy Prime Minister and Foreign Minister Yitzhak Shamir were to exchange portfolios at the midpoint of the government's term of office in October 1986. The prospect of the moderate, flexible Peres being replaced by the hard-line, unbending Shamir preoccupied

politicians at home and both friends and adversaries of Israel abroad. It also brought a sense of urgency to the efforts of Peres to resolve Israel's economic crisis and to search for a peace settlement in the Middle East. In the opinion of Peres, the central issue was the rehabilitation of the economy, which was a necessary prerequisite to restoring Israel's position on the international scene. In his view, once the former was achieved, the latter would take care of itself.

Domestic Affairs. The events of 1985 made sense only when interpreted against the background of the drama being acted out between the two major parties, each of which—while rarely losing sight of the national interest—sought a position of advantage. There were, moreover, domestic complications for the leaders of both the major parties. When Prime Minister Peres (Labour) had taken office, his own standing in the country had not been particularly high. Furthermore, a strong element within the Labour Party leadership believed that Labour should seek fresh elections before the time came to hand over the office of prime minister to Likud. For his part, Peres insisted that he would honour the agreement to hand over leadership to Shamir after 25 months unless in the meantime Likud decided to withdraw from the government.

Shamir was concerned with preserving conditions that would allow the fulfillment of the agreement and the rotation of portfolios. This fact clearly inhibited his opposition to government measures that were unpalatable to the Likud rank and file, especially the more extreme nationalist and religious groups who saw their views better represented by the populist Likud politicians and rivals of Shamir, deputy party leader and Housing and Construction Minister David Levy and Trade and Industry Minister Ariel Sharon. However, their radicalism was also tempered by the ultimate threat available to Peres: to dissolve the agreement and call for new elections.

During the course of 1985, the personal popularity of the prime minister soared, while that of Shamir and other Likud leaders declined. The opinion polls gave Peres an all-time-high rating for a prime minister of 67%. Shamir and his colleagues barely reached 20%. Similarly, in terms of popularity Labour was drawing away from Likud and began to appear the major party most likely to attract the necessary support from the smaller parties to form a coalition government that was not based on national unity. Likud leaders therefore decided not to risk the probable

Months after their secret airlift from Ethiopia, Falashas (Ethiopian Jews) demonstrated in Israel against the refusal of some rabbinical authorities to recognize them as Jews unless they underwent conversion rituals.

consequences for their party of an election challenge.

The government survived a threat to its unity in December 1984 when Yitzhak Peretz, leader of the Shas Party, resigned from the government in protest against not being offered the religious affairs portfolio; he withdrew his resignation, however, on being offered the interior ministry. A more serious crisis began to develop in mid-October 1985 when Sharon and Levy led Likud's criticism of Peres for speeches, made during a visit to the U.S., in which he suggested that Israel might respond to Jordan's call for an international conference to discuss the Middle East peace process. (See Middle Eastern and North African Affairs, above.) Likud ministers were completely opposed to the idea of Israel's making any territorial concessions. Later, in particularly vitriolic language, Sharon publicly accused Peres of seeking secret talks with Syria, of conducting secret negotiations with Jordan, and of being prepared to enter into negotiations with the Palestine Liberation Organization (PLO). Peres responded by demanding that Sharon either apologize or resign. On November 15 Peres accepted a letter of apology from Sharon and withdrew the threat of dismissal, thus averting the collapse of the government.

In July, 15 members of the so-called Jewish underground, among them prominent members of the orthodox settlers movement, the Gush Emunim, were found guilty of terrorist acts against Palestinians on the West Bank. The trial had become a focus of intensified controversy following the government's release on May 20 of 1,150 Palestinians held in Israel in exchange for three Israeli soldiers held by a PLO group based in Damascus, Syria. Among the freed Palestinians were many convicted terrorists and murderers. Their release may have eased security problems in Israel's overextended prison system, but it undermined the country's hitherto firm stance against terrorism both at home and abroad. In the view of some, the release of the Palestinians was an outstanding political blunder on the part of the Peres government.

The government's new austerity measures announced on May 28 made a sharp impact on the entire nation; the cost of subsidized food was increased by 25%, fuel by 25%, and gasoline (petrol) by 45%. By mid-July the government had begun to implement its fairly ruthless economic emergency plan, the main features of which were a three-month price freeze, an 18.8% depreciation of the shekel, a freeze on the new exchange rate and on salaries, and savage cuts in government budgets and public-sector staffing levels. Banks were ordered to restrict credit and to take other measures to control and encourage growth rather than inflation. A new shekel worth 1,000 old shekels was introduced on September 3. By the end of the year, there was evidence of the first signs of improvement in the economy.

Peres summarized his objectives in his speech to Israeli industrialists and foreign investors who met in Jerusalem on September 10. He told them that, despite the generous aid Israel received from the U.S. (some $3.5 billion overall in 1985) and from world Jewry, the country had to turn inward "to conquer the ruinous phenomenon of inflation, to alter the structure of our economy, to curtail government expenditure, to do without and to save—in order to reduce our dependence on foreign aid to a minimum."

Foreign Affairs. From the first day of 1985, uncharted and unforeseeable problems emerged and demanded instant attention, rather than long-term plans, from government ministers. The year had hardly dawned when premature publicity endangered the secret airlift of Ethiopian Jews carried out by Israel with some assistance from the U.S.; some 7,000 Falashas, members of an ancient community of Jews reputedly dating back to the days of the queen of

Sheba, had already been transported from Ethiopia via the Sudan to Israel, and more were to come later.

On January 14 the government announced plans for the total withdrawal of Israeli troops from Lebanon, to commence within five weeks and to be concluded in three phases. Following the commencement of the withdrawal, a small number of Shi'ah militants apparently organized from the Iranian embassy in Damascus began to launch hit-and-run attacks on Israeli troops. While they inflicted almost daily casualties, the effect of their actions was greatly magnified by the massive coverage provided by the Israeli press and television of grieving families at funerals. The theme was taken up worldwide and exploited most effectively in militant Shi'ah propaganda from Damascus. Even serious Western commentators accepted at face value claims by Shi'ah militants that they were "chasing" the Israelis from southern Lebanon. The PLO and the West Bank Palestinians were enjoined to emulate this most effective Shi'ah uprising, which was said to have forced the Israelis to flee. By early May, however, the Shi'ah "uprising" had evaporated. It emerged that barely 20 or 30 of the 200 or more Shi'ah villages in southern Lebanon had given succour to the militants. What had seemed to be a crisis turned out to be little more than a swiftly forgotten incident.

The country heaved a collective sigh of relief when the withdrawal from Lebanon was completed in early June. Few had time to give due consideration to the fate of those Lebanese who had allied themselves to the Israelis, especially the Christian community in the areas now threatened by Druze and Shi'ah militias. Prime Minister Peres announced that the Lebanese would have to look after themselves.

The proposals for peace in the Middle East revealed in February by King Hussein of Jordan and Yasir Arafat, chairman of the PLO, were presented as a dramatic initiative to bring Jordan, the Palestinians, and Israel to the negotiating table for a settlement that would exchange peace for territorial concessions by Israel. As the year unfolded, the initial euphoria was progressively tempered by unresolved ambiguities concerning the position of the PLO and the willingness of Hussein to enter into direct negotiations with Israel.

In the second half of the year, Israel appeared to be benefiting from a change in the international climate. Israel's retaliatory attack (a response to the killing of three Israelis in the Cypriot port city of Larnaca) on the PLO headquarters near Tunis on October 1 did not evoke the storm of condemnation that it would have done earlier. Peres's leadership was apparently bringing dividends for Israel and consequential benefits for Peres and his party at home. The failure of the PLO leadership to embarrass Israel also contributed to a new confidence in the Israeli government. However, a rare opportunity for dissent between Israel and its closest ally, the U.S., was afforded in November when it was revealed that a U.S. citizen, a civilian intelligence analyst with the U.S. Navy, had been accused of supplying Israel with classified military information. The prime minister immediately apologized, and the Israeli government promised a full-scale investigation of the matter.

Talks with Egypt about the disputed Taba enclave in the Sinai Peninsula, which was controlled by Israel and claimed by both countries, made only limited progress. Nevertheless, after all the gloom at the start of the year, Israel appeared set to end 1985 on an upbeat note. Southern Lebanon had been quiet for months. The Galilee was no longer threatened, and there was a dialogue of sorts with Jordan and the West Bank Palestinians. However,

developments at the end of the year curbed the mood of optimism. Israel claimed that Syria's deployment of surface-to-air missiles along its border with Lebanon posed a threat to Israel's security. Then on December 27 terrorists attacked the Israeli airline check-in desks at Rome and Vienna airports; 18 people were killed. Israel refused to accept the PLO's claim that it was not involved in the attacks, which were blamed by some sources on Abu Nidal, a Palestinian group opposed to the PLO.   (JON KIMCHE)

JORDAN

A constitutional monarchy, Jordan is located in southwestern Asia and has a short coastline on the Gulf of Aqaba. Area: 89,206 sq km (34,443 sq mi). Pop. (1985 est.): 2,590,000. Cap.: Amman. Monetary unit: dinar, with (Oct. 21, 1985) a free rate of 0.38 dinar to U.S. $1 (0.54 dinar = £1 sterling). King, Hussein I; prime ministers in 1985, Ahmad Abdel Obeidat and, from April 4, Zaid ar-Rifai.

During 1985 King Hussein of Jordan was at the centre of efforts to secure a lasting peace in the Middle East. In partnership with Palestine Liberation Organization (PLO) chairman Yasir Arafat, he proposed that Israel relinquish "in exchange for peace" the territories that it had occupied since 1967. The two leaders also declared that the future of the Israeli-occupied territories lay in the setting up of an autonomous Palestinian entity in confederation with Jordan. The agreement between Hussein and Arafat, announced in February, had the aim of bringing the U.S. into the peace process as a first step toward securing an international conference, at which direct Arab-Israeli talks could take place.

King Hussein journeyed to the U.S. at the end of September to promote his initiative in an address to the UN and talks with U.S. Pres. Ronald Reagan. Hopes were raised when, following her visits to Jordan and Egypt in mid-September, U.K. Prime Minister Margaret Thatcher invited to London a joint Palestinian-Jordanian team that was to include two members of the PLO executive. However, when the talks were called off at the last minute—amid a welter of recriminations from both British and PLO representatives—the initiative was dangerously undermined. An Israeli peace proposal, presented in October at the UN, was regarded by Hussein as "positive" in spirit but brought no forward movement in negotiations between the two countries.

Thatcher's visit to Amman culminated in the signing of a $350 million arms deal in which the U.K. agreed to supply military vehicles, radio equipment, tank ammunition, patrol boats, and battlefield command systems. The U.S. administration was eager to cement relations with Jordan by supplying military interceptor aircraft and other air defense equipment, but the U.S. Congress voted to refuse any arms sales to Jordan before March 1, 1986, unless in the interim Jordan and Israel were to begin "meaningful" peace negotiations. In January the Jordanians announced that the U.S.S.R. had agreed to supply ground and air defense systems, without specifying the value of the deal or the type of weapons involved. The deal with the Soviets followed the U.S.'s refusal in 1984 to supply Jordan with Stinger antiaircraft missiles.

On April 5 Zaid ar-Rifai, newly appointed prime minister, swore in a new Cabinet in which only five ministers were retained from the previous government. Rifai placed priority on improving relations with Syria and stimulating the private sector of the economy. On September 16–17, following mediation by Saudi Arabia, talks took place in Jidda between Rifai and his Syrian counterpart, Abdul

Rauf al-Kasm. The growing rapprochement between the two countries was underlined by the meeting between King Hussein and Syrian Pres. Hafez al-Assad in Damascus on December 30, the first time the two leaders had met since 1979.

The 1985 budget called for a 5% increase in public spending and set total expenditure at 811.2 million dinars ($2.2 billion). Foreign finance was vital to the success of the program. In 1984 Arab aid totaled $606 million, showing a decline for the fourth consecutive year, but remittances from the thousands of Jordanians working abroad increased because of the strong dollar. Economic growth of nearly 2% in 1984 was the result of higher industrial and mining output and growth in the financial sector. Two recently discovered oil wells near the border with Saudi Arabia and Iraq were producing more oil than had been expected, although it was too early to estimate the extent of reserves. In 1984 the visible trade gap narrowed by more than 14%, although the deficit still exceeded $2 billion.

Turkey agreed to buy 500,000 metric tons of phosphates from Jordan during 1985, but the industry still faced difficulties because of a temporary decline in world demand for its product. In August Jordan and India reached their first countertrade (barter) agreement, a $2 million deal to exchange phosphate rock for earth-moving machinery.

In September the Arab Fund for Economic and Social Development agreed to lend the equivalent of $27 million for an irrigation project in the Jordan River valley. The U.S. also agreed to provide a $250 million aid package, to be administered under the supervision of the U.S. Agency for International Development. In July Saudi Arabia delivered a second portion, worth $119 million, of its $358 million annual aid commitment.   (JOHN WHELAN)

KUWAIT

A constitutional monarchy (emirate), Kuwait is in the northeastern Arabian Peninsula, on the Persian Gulf. Area: 17,818 sq km (6,880 sq mi). Pop. (1985 est.): 1,911,000. Cap.: Kuwait City. Monetary unit: dinar, with (Oct. 21, 1985) a free rate of 0.29 dinar to U.S. $1 (0.42 dinar = £1 sterling). Emir, Sheikh Jabir al-Ahmad al-Jabir as-Sabah; prime minister in 1985, Crown Prince Sheikh Saad al-Abdullah as-Salim as-Sabah.

An attempt on the life of Emir Sheikh Jabir of Kuwait narrowly failed when a suicide bomber drove a vehicle into a motorcade in which the emir was traveling on May 25, 1985. Two bodyguards, a passerby, and the suicide driver, who was a member of the underground Iraqi radical group al-Dawa, were killed, and 11 others were injured. The attack was believed to be linked to demands by the terrorist group Islamic Jihad ("Islamic Holy War") for the release of 17 Shi'ah Muslims convicted of involvement in bomb attacks on Kuwait City in 1983. On July 11 two bomb explosions in seaside cafés in the capital killed 9 people and injured more than 80 others. The authorities believed that they were the work of al-Dawa, although a little-known group based in Beirut claimed responsibility. On July 17 a bill calling for the death penalty for terrorist acts was overwhelmingly passed in the National Assembly. By early September over 6,000 people had been deported.

Elections to the National Assembly, in which only Kuwaiti males could vote, took place on February 20. Among the 50 directly elected members of parliament, the veteran nationalist Ahmad al-Khatib and 11 of his supporters were returned to office. Although conservative supporters of the government retained their majority, the opposition made unexpected gains. Crown Prince Sheikh Saad formed a new government in which he remained

prime minister, but a number of his ministers came under attack, including Oil and Industry Minister Sheikh Ali al-Khalifah as-Sabah.

In 1984 Kuwait's petroleum production totaled 1,160,-000 bbl a day, slightly more than the quota set by the Organization of Petroleum Exporting Countries. Despite cutbacks attributable to lower income from oil exports, Kuwait remained the world's leading donor to the third world, giving 3.8% of its gross national product in aid during 1984.   (JOHN WHELAN)

This article updates the *Macropædia* article ARABIA: *Kuwait.*

LEBANON

A republic of southwestern Asia, Lebanon is situated on the Mediterranean Sea. Area: 10,230 sq km (3,950 sq mi). Pop. (1985 est.): 2,668,000. (The population of Lebanon, including about 500,000 Palestinian refugees, is thought to have declined since the outbreak of civil war in 1974, but reliable figures are not available.) Cap.: Beirut. Monetary unit: Lebanese pound, with (Oct. 21, 1985) a free rate of LL 17.62 to U.S. $1 (LL 25.26 = £1 sterling). President in 1985, Amin Gemayel; prime minister, Rashid Karami.

The withdrawal of the Israeli Army from Lebanon and plans for closer cooperation between Pres. Amin Gemayel and Syria's Pres. Hafez al-Assad took place against a background of continued sectarian fighting in Lebanon during 1985. Beirut airport was the scene of an international hostage drama involving a Trans World Airlines passenger airliner hijacked on June 14 by Shi'ah gunmen demanding the release of some 700 Shi'ah Lebanese and Palestinians being detained by the Israelis. One U.S. passenger, a navy diver, was shot dead by the hijackers. A solution to the crisis, resulting in the release on June 30 of the 39 remaining U.S. hostages, was brought about through the mediation of Nabih Berri (*see* BIOGRAPHIES), leader of the Amal, Lebanon's dominant Shi'ah militia. All of the detainees were released by Israel before the end of the year, but the hostage incident inevitably provoked some discomfort for U.S. Pres. Ronald Reagan and the Israeli leadership. The hijack had been masterminded by a semiautonomous wing of Amal led by Akel Hamiyeh, who was also prominent in the earlier month-long attack on Palestinian refugee camps in Beirut.

The Israeli withdrawal from Lebanon, reportedly completed on June 10, did not end Israel's involvement in Lebanon's internal affairs; Israeli military advisers were to remain behind to assist the South Lebanon Army, a 2,000-strong militia composed mainly of Maronite Christians, which the Israelis supported as a buffer against violence that would otherwise be directed at their own country. Earlier, in mid-February, Israel had pulled out of Sidon after 32 months of occupation. The Shi'ah, a minority in Sidon itself, were seen as having mounted a successful guerrilla campaign that greatly influenced Israel's decision to withdraw. On the strength of this success, the Shi'ah began to press more strongly for an end to their inferior status under the constitution.

Syria's central role in the forging of a settlement between rival Lebanese Christian and Muslim factions emerged clearly during the year. The Syrian government made its most determined effort to end the ten-year-old civil war since Damascus sent its troops into Lebanon in June 1976. The peace initiative made a promising start in July when West Beirut militia leaders agreed to keep their fighters off the streets. Syrian officers then organized a meeting of Muslim and Druze leaders in the Bekaa Valley. At the meeting it was agreed that plans would be drawn up for a conference between all of Lebanon's factions to decide on

Pro-Syrian militiamen take part in the attack on Tripoli while Sunni Muslim fundamentalists entrenched in the city fight back. The city was finally given over to the Syrian Army in October.

PATRICK CHAUVEL—SYGMA

a new power-sharing formula. These hopeful moves were thwarted by a new outbreak of violence that included a spate of murderous car bombings in Beirut and Tripoli, the first occurring on August 14 in a suburb of Christian East Beirut. The explosions were sufficient to trigger the heaviest artillery exchanges experienced in the capital for some months. In early October, following three weeks of fighting between Muslim fundamentalists and Syrian-supported leftist militias, the Syrian Army took over the Lebanese port of Tripoli. The fighting in Tripoli resulted in at least 200 dead.

The Lebanese relationship with the U.S.S.R. was another casualty of the hostilities in Tripoli. In October four officials of the Soviet embassy in Beirut were kidnapped. One was killed, the others held hostage but released unharmed on October 30. Responsibility for the incident was claimed by Sunni Muslims who were demanding Syrian intervention to end the fighting in Tripoli. The Soviets responded by evacuating nonessential embassy staff and families of diplomats stationed in Beirut.

On April 17 Prime Minister Rashid Karami announced the resignation of his nine-member Cabinet, but the collapse of his national unity government was avoided when, a week later, he agreed to remain in office. The government, which had been formed in May 1984, gave factional leaders ministerial responsibilities, but it had failed to make much impact on the political deadlock or on Lebanon's economic misery. Complicating factors were the revolt of the Christian militia against President Gemayel's Christian Phalange Party and the emergence of a semiautonomous Druze statelet in the Shuf Mountains.

On October 16 it was announced in Damascus that Christian, Druze, and Shi'ah militia representatives had agreed on draft proposals for political reforms at talks chaired by Syria's Vice-Pres. 'Abd al-Halim Khaddam. The proposals called for the gradual abolition of Lebanon's Christian-dominated system of government. An accord incorporating the proposals and providing for the disbanding of the militias was signed in Damascus on December 28 by Berri, Druze leader Walid Jumblatt, and Elie Hobeika, commander of the (Christian) Lebanese forces.

In January, following a serious slide of the Lebanese pound against the U.S. dollar, the Karami administration decided to seek assistance from the International Monetary Fund. The economy had declined markedly in 1984. The balance of payments deficit reached $1.4 billion, and foreign-exchange reserves dwindled alarmingly. Industrial

production fell by 4% to $250 million. Despite attempts by Lebanese authorities to tighten security at Beirut international airport, by late 1985 the national carrier, Middle East Airlines, was the only airline serving the airport; passenger traffic had slumped to its lowest level since 1953, with slightly more than 1,000 passengers a day using the facility.

President Gemayel made an urgent appeal to Saudi Arabia's King Fahd for economic aid, but it was noted that Saudi Arabia delayed disbursement of $460 million worth of aid promised at the 1979 Arab summit held in Tunisia. The industrial sector suffered from factors other than the direct effects of the conflict, including the increased cost of raw materials, a rise in energy prices, high interest rates, and recession in the Gulf states, the destination of many Lebanese exports.

The fate of six U.S. citizens, some missing since June 1984, remained uncertain. They were believed to be captives of the group known as Islamic Jihad ("Islamic Holy War"). The murder of one of the six, William Buckley, an officer of the U.S. embassy in Beirut, was announced in October, but the report was not confirmed. A seventh U.S. prisoner, a Presbyterian minister who had been held for 16 months, was freed in September. Other kidnapped or missing foreign nationals, some British and French, were still unaccounted for at year's end.   (JOHN WHELAN)

See also *Middle Eastern and North African Affairs*, above.

LIBYA

A socialist country of North Africa, Libya lies on the Mediterranean Sea. Area: 1,749,000 sq km (675,000 sq mi). Pop. (1985 est.): 3,630,000. Cap.: Tripoli. Monetary unit: Libyan dinar, with (Oct. 21, 1985) a free rate of 0.30 dinar to U.S. $1 (0.42 dinar = £1 sterling). Chief of state in 1985, Col. Muammar al-Qaddafi; secretary-general of the General People's Committee (premier), Muhammad az-Zaruq Rajab.

In common with all petroleum-exporting countries, during 1985 Libya suffered from the slack world demand for oil and the consequent drop in prices. The value of oil exports was further eroded from midyear by the long-anticipated fall in the value of the U.S. dollar, the currency in which oil was traded. Observers put the annual level of oil revenues as low as $8 billion, compared with the peak of $23 billion in 1980. The consequences for all aspects of the economy were severe. New investment in the development of infrastructure virtually ceased as the bills for medium-term and long-term projects in industry, agriculture, and infrastructure initiated in the boom years of the late 1970s fell due. Some major projects retained a prominent place, among them the "great man-made river" water pipeline scheme for the transportation of water from the southeast of the country to the coast at the Gulf of Sidra; but the future of this project, estimated to cost a minimum of $11 billion, was precarious.

The cost of the large immigrant work force could not be sustained, and it was reported that more than 100,000 foreign workers were expelled or laid off during the year. In August an estimated 25,000 Tunisians and a smaller number of Egyptians and African nationals were ordered to leave on very short notice. Domestic consumption was also restricted, and widespread shortages were reported in the shops as a result of the disruption of imports by overseas suppliers dissatisfied by delays in payment. Restrictions on the movement of capital out of Libya were increased, and international flights were reduced.

Libyan leader Col. Muammar al-Qaddafi attempted to improve relations with the U.K. government, which had

severed diplomatic relations after the shooting of a po- licewoman outside the Libyan People's Bureau (embassy) in April 1984. Four Britons detained in Libya since May 1984 were sent home in February 1985. The Libyans tried, unsuccessfully, to secure the release of a number of Libyans accused of involvement in a series of bombings aimed at anti-Qaddafi Libyans in London and Manchester in March 1984. Four of the accused were found guilty and given prison sentences ranging from 5 to 15 years. Very few Libyans received visas for access to the U.K. during 1985, although there was no decline in the level of com- mercial activity by British companies in Libya. The size of the British community in Libya, estimated at 8,000–9,000, remained unchanged, and the large Libyan community in the U.K. declined only a little.

A number of terrorist attacks in Rome and Bonn were directed at Libyan diplomats serving overseas and at op- ponents of the Qaddafi regime. In June a member of the Libyan mission to the UN was expelled from the U.S., charged with involvement in plots against Libyan dissi- dents there. Relations with the U.S. remained cool and deteriorated markedly at the end of the year when the U.S. accused Libya of involvement in bomb attacks at Rome and Vienna airports on December 27. While relations with the U.S.S.R. continued to be cordial, during Qaddafi's visit to Moscow in October it was clear that Libya's economic role was no longer as valued as it had been in the 1970s, when it had been a particularly useful customer because of its ability to settle in hard currency.

Relations with other North African countries were again often tense. Libyan troops remained in Chad and, although no serious hostilities were reported in Chad itself, the situ- ation was further complicated in October by rumours that former Chadian president Goukouni Oueddei—who had received Libyan backing in his efforts to regain power— had been removed as head of the Popular Armed Forces, one of 11 groups making up the self-styled opposition gov- ernment. (*See* Africa South of the Sahara: *Chad,* above.) The revolution and change of government in Sudan in April were welcomed by Qaddafi, whose offer of military training facilities in Libya was accepted by the new lead- ership. Tunisia responded swiftly to the expulsion of its nationals by expelling more than 250 Libyans on charges of spying. The union with Morocco remained an impor- tant element of policy in North Africa, a region in which Libya's initiatives were widely mistrusted.   (J. A. ALLAN)

This article updates the *Macropædia* article NORTH AFRICA: *Libya.*

MOROCCO

A constitutional monarchy of North Africa, Morocco has coast- lines on the Atlantic Ocean and the Mediterranean Sea. Area: 458,730 sq km (177,117 sq mi). Pop (1985 est.): 24,370,000. (Area and population figures refer to Morocco as constituted prior to the purported division of Western Sahara between Mo- rocco and Mauritania and the subsequent Moroccan occupation of the Mauritanian zone in 1979.) Cap.: Rabat. Monetary unit: dirham, with (Oct. 21, 1985) a free rate of 9.78 dirhams to U.S. $1 (14.02 dirhams = £1 sterling). King: Hassan II; prime minister in 1985, Mohammad Karim Lamrani.

During 1985 events in Morocco were once again domi- nated by the country's continuing struggle with the Popular Front for the Liberation of Saguia el Hamra and Río de Oro (Polisario Front) and its associated government-in- exile, the Saharan Arab Democratic Republic (SADR), for control of the Western Sahara. Morocco tightened its hold on the territory by building two new defensive walls that extended and consolidated its control eastward and south-

ward. The Polisario Front continued its attacks and shot down several aircraft, including a Belgian civilian plane in January and a West German plane in February.

Morocco's diplomatic isolation increased as the number of states recognizing the SADR rose to 64. The Orga- nization of African Unity (OAU), from which Morocco had withdrawn in protest in 1984, confirmed the member status of the SADR by electing the SADR president as OAU vice-president at its summit in July 1985. During an address to the UN on October 23, Prime Minister Moham- mad Karim Lamrani announced that his government had declared a unilateral cease-fire in the area and was willing to allow the UN to organize a referendum to decide its future. The speech made no move toward recognizing the validity of Polisario claims to represent Western Saharans.

Anxious to maintain good relations with Morocco in view of its claims on the Spanish enclaves of Ceuta and Melilla, Spain expelled Polisario Front representatives in September. Following a visit by French Prime Minister Laurent Fabius in April, France agreed to provide F 1 billion in development aid and 1.3 million metric tons of cereals by the end of the year. Relations with the U.S. con- tinued to be threatened by Morocco's treaty of union with Libya. King Hassan canceled plans to visit Washington, and a joint military commission meeting was postponed in May. The rapprochement with Libya was itself somewhat soured by King Hassan's decision to call an Arab summit in August to discuss the proposed Jordanian-Palestinian Middle East peace initiative, which Libya opposed, and by Morocco's disapproval of the closer links between Libya and Iran.

At home the majority opposition party, the National Union of Popular Forces, was critical of the administra- tion's willingness to follow requirements laid down by the International Monetary Fund (IMF) for restructuring the economy. The government's 1986–88 plan underlined this commitment by reducing the role of the public sector, while in September subsidies on essential foodstuffs were cut by up to 20%. Foreign debt stood at almost $12 billion at the start of the year. In September the IMF renewed its standby credit at 315 million Special Drawing Rights, while official creditors in the Club of Paris agreed to reschedule $1 billion of debt some days later.   (GEORGE JOFFÉ)

This article updates the *Macropædia* article NORTH AFRICA: *Morocco.*

OMAN

The sultanate of Oman occupies the southeastern part of the Arabian Peninsula, facing the Persian Gulf, the Gulf of Oman, and the Arabian Sea. A small part of the country lies to the north and is separated from the rest of Oman by the United Arab Emirates. Area: 300,000 sq km (120,000 sq mi). Pop.: in 1985 estimates ranged from 1 million to 1.5 million; no census has ever been taken. Cap.: Muscat. Monetary unit: rial Omani, with (Oct. 21, 1985) a free rate of 0.35 rial to U.S. $1 (free rate of 0.50 rial = £1 sterling). Sultan and prime minister in 1985, Qabus ibn Sa'id.

The announcement on Sept. 26, 1985, that Oman and the U.S.S.R. were to establish diplomatic relations was re- garded as a coup for Soviet diplomacy in the Middle East, given the past opposition of Sultan Qabus ibn Sa'id to Communist regimes. Until then Kuwait had been the only Gulf Cooperation Council country with an ambassador in Moscow. Minister of State for Foreign Affairs Yusuf al- Alawi said that Oman's relations with the U.S. and other Western countries would not be affected. The position of the U.S. and the U.K. as the country's principal suppliers of weapons appeared unlikely to be changed by the Soviet

move. Oman was expected to take delivery in 1986 of 300 U.S.-made Sidewinder missiles, to be deployed on Tornado fighter aircraft supplied by the U.K. under a multimillion-dollar deal signed in London on August 14.

Petroleum production reached record levels during the year as the government made preparations for a new five-year (1986–90) plan. The third plan, based on a production level of 450,000 bbl a day, involved a shift in emphasis from infrastructure to non-oil income-generating schemes as part of a long-term strategy to prepare for the time, 20 or 30 years ahead, when petroleum supplies would be exhausted.

Relations with Yemen (Aden; South Yemen), a supporter of the Dhofar rebellion against the sultan in the 1970s, continued to improve, following the resumption of diplomatic ties in 1983. In April Radio Oman reported that South Yemen had agreed to a proposal that ambassadors be exchanged. South Yemen later appointed a nonresident ambassador.   (JOHN WHELAN)

This article updates the *Macropædia* article ARABIA: *Oman*.

QATAR

A monarchy (emirate) on the Arabian Peninsula, Qatar occupies a desert peninsula on the west coast of the Persian Gulf. Area: 11,400 sq km (4,400 sq mi). Pop. (1985 est.): 301,000. Cap.: Doha. Monetary unit: riyal, with (Oct. 21, 1985) a free rate of 3.65 riyals to U.S. $1 (5.23 riyals = £1 sterling). Emir and prime minister in 1985, Sheikh Khalifah ibn Hamad ath-Thani.

During 1985 Qatar maintained petroleum production at or close to the 280,000-bbl-a-day quota set by the Organization of Petroleum Exporting Countries. Almost all of the petroleum came from the onshore Dukhan Field. Proven reserves would be sufficient to last for 40 years at current levels of extraction. Japan, the largest customer, took almost half of petroleum exports in 1984.

The most important economic project was the development of the North Field. Lying off the northeast coast of Qatar, it contained the world's largest known reserves of natural gas. The project was expected to require investment of up to $6 billion. In September it was announced that the Japanese Marubeni Corp. had taken a 7.5% stake in the company established to develop the find, a tripartite venture of the Qatar government, British Petroleum, and the Compagnie Française des Pétroles-Total. The development intensified concern about Qatar's security arrangements. The Iran-Iraq conflict had at times come close, when Iran had carried out attacks on shipping within Qatar's waters. Following the government's purchase of 14 French-built Mirage F-1C jet fighters in 1984, the construction of a military air base had become a priority.

In February 1985 Emir Sheikh Khalifah ibn Hamad ath-Thani opened an extension of the University of Qatar. When it first opened, for the 1973–74 academic year, the university had 150 students; by 1985 there were over 4,500. Accompanied by senior ministers, Sheikh Khalifah visited the U.K. on November 12–15 and then went on to tour France.   (JOHN WHELAN)

This article updates the *Macropædia* article ARABIA: *Qatar*.

SAUDI ARABIA

The kingdom of Saudi Arabia occupies four-fifths of the Arabian Peninsula, with coastlines on the Red Sea and the Persian Gulf. Area: 2,240,000 sq km (865,000 sq mi). Pop. (1985 est.): 11,240,000. Cap.: Riyadh. Monetary unit: riyal, with (Oct. 21, 1985) a free rate of 3.65 riyals to U.S. $1 (5.24 riyals = £1 sterling). King and prime minister in 1985, Fahd.

Saudi Arabia's decision in 1985 to increase oil production to close to its Organization of Petroleum Exporting Countries (OPEC) quota of 4.3 million bbl a day put strains on the unity of OPEC during a year that was increasingly dominated by Saudi Arabian moves to improve its security. In taking this fresh direction in its oil policy, Saudi Arabia triggered debate about the need for OPEC to find market-related pricing mechanisms, while also throwing down the gauntlet to non-OPEC producers who had come to depend on the kingdom's acting as a "swing producer" to avoid oversupplying the market. The agreement at the December OPEC meeting to stop defending oil prices in favour of defending the cartel's market share in essence legitimized recent practices.

The Gulf Cooperation Council (GCC) summit in Oman ended on November 8 with renewed calls to end the Gulf war and prevent terrorism. Saudi Arabia reiterated that these issues were of more importance to the GCC than the secondary goal of economic integration.

Following a visit by U.K. Prime Minister Margaret Thatcher in April, on September 26 Defense and Aviation Minister Prince Sultan ibn Abdel-Aziz and U.K. Secretary of State for Defense Michael Heseltine signed a memorandum of understanding on the purchase of military aircraft from British Aerospace. Valued at some $4.2 billion, it was described as the largest export order ever negotiated by Britain. Part of the payment was to be met through oil barter, and the deal might also be linked with an offset investment program similar to one already agreed on with the U.S. for the "Peace Shield" defense program. In February the Ministry of Defense and Civil Aviation awarded the U.S. company Boeing Aerospace Corp. three contracts valued at $1.1 billion under the offset program, which was now monitored by a Saudi government committee; 35% of the value of the contracts had to be reinvested in the kingdom in high-technology ventures in which Saudi Arabian investors would match the investment.

The government was eager to diversify its sources of weapons supplies to include countries such as Brazil in order to avoid dependence on the U.S., where the pro-Israel lobby had often blocked sales of advanced weapons to the kingdom. Nevertheless, according to a *New York Times* report on September 5, the government had made a verbal commitment to allow U.S. forces to operate from its bases in the event of Soviet aggression or if the kingdom was unable to handle a Gulf crisis on its own. While informal contacts had taken place between the government and Moscow, no progress was made on the question of establishing formal links.

The Hajj (pilgrimage to Mecca) passed off peacefully in August. Some 1.6 million people took part, including 150,000 pilgrims from Iran. On May 18 two explosions rocked the Sulaymani district of Riyadh, killing one person and injuring three. Responsibility was claimed by the externally based Islamic Jihad ("Islamic Holy War") group. The incident was the first serious terrorist attack since the 1979 siege of the Grand Mosque in Mecca. Religious sentiment in Saudi Arabia remained extremely conservative. In June prominence was given in the media to a statement by Islamic leader Sheikh Abdel-Aziz ibn Baz that allowing men and women to mix at work would open an evil door that would be hard to close. Young Saudi Arabians of both sexes were inspired by the example of Prince Sultan Salman ibn Abdel-Aziz, who in June became the first Arab astronaut when he joined the crew of the U.S. space shuttle "Discovery."

In 1984 Saudi Arabia moved up to 11th place among the world's top 20 trading nations in terms of both imports and

exports, according to a General Agreement on Tariffs and Trade assessment. After two years in which the kingdom balanced its budgets by drawing down its foreign-exchange reserves, the government determined to take tough action to keep spending under control. Both the 1985–86 budget and the fourth five-year (1985–90) plan were based on oil production of not less than 3,850,000 bbl a day. The 1985 budget included cuts in nearly every spending department. At a meeting with representatives of the private sector in Riyadh on March 27, King Fahd called for greater commitment by the private businessman in his own country. The largest project to be affected by the new mood of realism was the proposed refinery at Qassim. Development of the $1 billion project was suspended by royal decree on March 11. It was later announced that work would resume within five years. During the plan period, some subsidiaries of the state hydrocarbons agency, Petromin, were expected to be privatized, along with the national airline, Saudia.

Although King Fahd had previously championed the cause of joint ventures between home and foreign businesses, in 1985 he came under growing pressure from the business lobby to support protectionist legislation. In June he issued a royal decree urging government departments to heed earlier orders to award more contracts to local companies. Under the five-year plan, production and private initiative replaced construction and public enterprise as key themes. The plan envisaged a cut of 600,000 jobs, mainly in the unskilled categories, in the expatriate population by 1990 and the creation of 375,000 new jobs for Saudi Arabians, particularly graduates now emerging from the kingdom's universities. By 1990 the government also hoped to have introduced national military service.

The difficulties faced by Saudi Arabia in its industrialization drive were highlighted by a growing atmosphere of confrontation with the European Communities (EC). On August 3 the EC slapped 13.4–14% tariffs on imports of Saudi Arabian polyethylene. The Saudi Basic Industries Corporation claimed that the duty was based on "exaggerated data and unfounded fears regarding the purported impact of Saudi exports." The government was understood to be reviewing its options, including the possibility of imposing retaliatory tariffs on imports of manufactured goods from the EC. Industry and Electricity Minister Sheikh Abdel-Aziz az-Zamil told the *Al-Riyadh* daily newspaper in January that the kingdom should aim at 50% self-sufficiency in industrial goods. Total imports were now running at more than $40 billion a year.

The Eastern Province, home of the petroleum industry and the major industrial complex of Jubail, was expected to benefit from the road causeway link with Bahrain; the opening of the causeway, scheduled for December 1985, was postponed until December 1986. On September 30 the industrial city of Yanbu on the Red Sea coast received its first shipment of crude oil from Iraq via the new pipeline linking Iraq with Saudi Arabia's main east–west pipeline. In February Prince Muhammad ibn Fahd, second son of King Fahd, was appointed governor of the Eastern Province, replacing Prince Abdel-Mohsin ibn Jiluwi, who retired for health reasons. The Jiluwi family, which had ruled the area since 1913, was considered unsympathetic to the needs of the 300,000-strong Shi'ah minority.

On October 1 the government confirmed the appointment of Hamad Saud as-Sayyari as governor of the Saudi Arabian Monetary Agency (SAMA). The kingdom was the sixth largest contributor to the International Monetary Fund, and SAMA was one of the largest institutional investors outside the industrialized countries. Commercial banking in the kingdom remained profitable, although some foreign banks experienced difficulties in securing judicial recognition of loan defaults because of Islamic strictures against usury. During 1985 the Saudi Fund for Development, an aid agency, agreed to provide India, Senegal, Niger, Rwanda, and Mali with loans, largely to assist construction of infrastructure and improvement of social welfare. Prime Minister Turgut Ozal of Turkey, who concluded a six-day visit on March 22, claimed that he had secured an agreement to encourage joint production of sophisticated weapons and spare parts for military equipment.   (JOHN WHELAN)

This article updates the *Macropædia* article ARABIA: *Saudi Arabia.*

SYRIA

A republic of southwestern Asia, Syria is on the Mediterranean Sea. Area: 185,180 sq km (71,498 sq mi). Pop. (1985 est.): 10,267,000. Cap.: Damascus. Monetary unit: Syrian pound, with (Oct. 21, 1985) a commercial rate of LS 3.67 to U.S. $1 (LS 5.25 = £1 sterling). President in 1985, Gen. Hafez al-Assad; prime minister, Abdul Rauf al-Kasm.

On Feb. 11, 1985, Gen. Hafez al-Assad won a third seven-year term as president of Syria when he secured 99.97% of the votes cast in a national referendum in which 99.38% of eligible voters took part, according to official figures. At the ruling Ba'ath Party congress in January, the first in five years, Assad was endorsed by the party as secretary-general. Five members of the party's 21-member Regional Command were replaced at the 16-day congress; President Assad's younger brother, Rifaat al-Assad, previously thought to be in disgrace, was reappointed to both the Regional Command and the 90-member Central Committee. President Assad's position was considered to have been greatly enhanced by his show of strength at the congress, coming as it did after a period during which he had reportedly suffered from poor health. A revised government list revealed on April 8 contained few significant changes apart from a reshuffle of economic portfolios.

Syria made its most determined effort since its army intervened in Lebanon in 1976 to bring about a settlement between the warring Christian and Muslim factions in that divided country. On December 28 an agreement was signed by leaders of Christian, Shi'ah, and Druze militia following talks chaired by Syrian Vice-Pres. 'Abd al-Halim Khaddam. The agreement called for a gradual phasing out of the built-in Christian majority in Lebanon's Chamber of Deputies (parliament).

FRANK VIELJEUX—SYGMA

Some of the 39 U.S. citizens held by hijackers in Beirut hold a press conference in Damascus after their release in June. Syrian Pres. Hafez al-Assad had played a key role in obtaining their release.

In early October the Syrian Army took control of the northern Lebanese port of Tripoli following three weeks of fighting between Muslim fundamentalists and Syrian-backed leftist militia. Syria was widely believed to have been behind Shi'ah attacks on Palestinian refugee camps in Lebanon that followed the withdrawal of the Israeli Army. Syria firmly denied the charge, blaming the violence at the camps in May and June on the Palestine Liberation Organization (PLO). Damascus was opposed to the efforts of PLO chairman Yasir Arafat and King Hussein of Jordan to revive peace negotiations with Israel, though at the same time there was a marked improvement in relations between Syria and Jordan. The meeting between Hussein and Assad in Damascus on December 30 was the first for six years.

Syria's radical stance in Arab and Middle Eastern affairs continued to be reflected in support for Iran in the Gulf war, opposition to any policy of rapprochement with Israel, and close friendship with the U.S.S.R. and other Soviet-bloc countries. Assad refused to attend the emergency Arab summit called by King Hassan II of Morocco in August because, in Damascus's view, the summit was designed to justify the Jordanian-Palestinian peace moves. Assad visited Moscow on June 19–22 for talks with Soviet leader Mikhail Gorbachev. In May Syria signed an economic and technical cooperation agreement with the U.S.S.R., and in September a separate agreement covering Soviet aid for petroleum exploration was concluded.

Expectations of petroleum production from the recently discovered field in the northeastern Deir az-Zor region were revised downward to some 50,000 bbl a day. The field was scheduled to begin commercial production in 1986. Total crude petroleum production stood at around 170,000 bbl a day, while 200,000 bbl a day were imported for use in local refineries. Most of the imports were supplied by Iran at concessionary rates in return for Syria's decision to deny Iraq the right to export its crude petroleum through Syria.

Syria received assurances from Kuwait that it intended to honour its aid obligations, despite a vote to the contrary in the Kuwait National Assembly. In 1985 Syria was scheduled to receive $186 million from Kuwait. The 1985 budget, passed by the People's Council in June, reflected the government's commitment to tight control over public spending. Defense spending accounted for more than 50% of current expenditure, while the investment budget gave priority to the agricultural sector. Among the major sources of foreign finance were the Arab Fund for Economic and Social Development, the European Communities, and the World Bank. (JOHN WHELAN)

TUNISIA

A republic of North Africa, Tunisia lies on the Mediterranean Sea. Area: 154,530 sq km (59,664 sq mi). Pop. (1985 est.): 7,158,000. Cap.: Tunis. Monetary unit: dinar, with (Oct. 21, 1985) a free rate of 0.78 dinar to U.S. $1 (1.12 dinars = £1 sterling). President in 1985, Habib Bourguiba; prime minister, Mohammed Mzali.

At a meeting of the Central Committee of the ruling Parti Socialiste Destourien (PSD) on March 9, 1985, Tunisia's Pres. Habib Bourguiba gave the clearest indication yet that his successor, "when the time came," would be Prime Minister Mohammed Mzali. In a ministerial reshuffle on October 23 Zine El Abidine Ben Ali was promoted from state secretary to minister-delegate in charge of national security, and Nourredine Hached, ambassador to Algeria, was appointed minister of labour.

Meanwhile, the government faced increasing opposition. The year began with a strike by students at the University of Tunis to mark the anniversary of the previous year's "bread riots." Local elections on May 12 were boycotted by opposition parties. Tension between the government and the labour union organization, the Union Générale des Travailleurs Tunisiens (UGTT), grew throughout the year. In October the UGTT headquarters in Tunis was closed by government order, and in November UGTT Secretary-General Habib Achour was placed under house arrest. Following an agreement reached on December 4 between the UGTT and Minister of Labour Hached, Achour was replaced as secretary-general by Sadok Allouche.

The government also had to contend with two crises in Tunisia's foreign relations. The first of these arose in August when Libya began to expel Tunisian workers (of whom there were some 80,000–90,000 in Libya). In all, some 30,000 were expelled, adding to Tunisia's already severe economic problems. Relations worsened with the expulsion by Tunisia of 253 Libyans accused of espionage. Efforts at mediation were made by the Arab League, and Tunisia was supported by Algeria, whose Pres. Chadli Bendjedid visited Bourguiba at Monastir on September 2. On September 26 Tunisia severed relations with Libya.

The second crisis involved Tunisia's relations with the U.S., previously a trusted ally. Tunisia was outraged by Pres. Ronald Reagan's initial approval of the Israeli air raid on the headquarters of the Palestine Liberation Organization on the outskirts of Tunis on October 1, when many Tunisians were among those killed or injured. The visit to Tunis on October 21–23 of U.S. Deputy Secretary of State

Workers begin to sort out the rubble left after Israeli jets bombed the headquarters of the Palestine Liberation Organization near Tunis in October.

John C. Whitehead, with an offer of increased U.S. aid, helped to repair the rift.

Franco-Tunisian relations remained cordial. French Foreign Minister Roland Dumas visited Tunis twice during the year. In June, when Bourguiba visited France privately, Pres. François Mitterrand met with him at the Tunisian embassy. In August Edith Cresson, French minister of industrial redeployment and foreign trade, visited Tunis for discussions on economic cooperation. During the Tunisian-Libyan confrontation a French naval squadron patrolled off Gabès.   (PHILIPPE DECRAENE)

This article updates the *Macropædia* article NORTH AFRICA: *Tunisia.*

TURKEY

A republic of Asia Minor and southeastern Europe, Turkey has coastlines on the Aegean, Black, and Mediterranean seas. Area: 779,452 sq km (300,948 sq mi), including 23,698 sq km in Europe. Pop. (1985): 51.4 million. Cap.: Ankara. Monetary unit: Turkish lira, with (Oct. 21, 1985) a free rate of 544.01 liras to U.S. $1 (780.11 liras = £1 sterling). President in 1985, Gen. Kenan Evren; prime minister, Turgut Ozal.

During 1985 the political scene in Turkey changed as the opposition to the government of Prime Minister Turgut Ozal, leader of the right-of-centre Motherland Party, chose new leaders and regrouped. On the left the extraparliamentary Social Democratic Party merged with the main opposition party in Parliament, the Populist Party, under its new leader, Aydin Guven Gurkan. However, a further division was introduced by the formation on November 14 of the Democratic Left Party, based on the personal following of Bulent Ecevit, former prime minister, who had been banned from political activity for ten years under the 1982 constitution. In the ranks of the right-wing opposition, the Nationalist Democracy Party, under its new leader, Umit Soylemezoglu, drew closer to the extraparliamentary Right Path Party, led by Husamettin Cindoruk, a supporter of former prime minister Suleyman Demirel.

Restrictions imposed after the 1980 military takeover continued to be eased. At the end of the year only 9 of the country's 67 provinces remained under martial law, while in 16 others civil administrators still held emergency powers. The area still under martial law was in the southeast, where the outlawed Kurdish Workers Party (PKK) continued its campaign of violence. Launched in August 1984, by the end of November 1985 the campaign had caused 241 deaths, 59 of them among the security forces. Abroad, Armenian nationalists attacked the Turkish embassy in Ottawa, killing a security guard. Charges of politically motivated offenses continued to be heard. Many detainees were released, and several death sentences, mainly against Kurdish separatists, awaited confirmation. On October 23 the European Parliament accepted a report critical of the human rights situation and decided that relations with Turkey should remain suspended. In December, however, five Western European countries—France, Denmark, The Netherlands, Norway, and Sweden—agreed to drop charges of human rights violations, ending three years of litigation in the European Court of Human Rights. The Turkish government in turn agreed to submit periodic reports on the situation and to allow on-site inspections by representatives of European human rights organizations.

The government was preoccupied with the plight of ethnic Turks in neighbouring Bulgaria, who had allegedly been subjected to forcible assimilation. Several notes of protest and offers to take in the Bulgarian Turks failed to produce results. Following the temporary partial closure of the frontier, the mutual blockading of consulates, and the suspension of sporting contacts, the Turkish government voiced its complaints at international gatherings and canvassed other Muslim countries for support.

There was no improvement in relations with Greece, which accused both Turkish and U.S. aircraft of violating its airspace during periodic maneuvers. During his visit in November, Michael Armacost, U.S. assistant secretary of state for political affairs, discussed the revision of the U.S.-Turkish defense and economic cooperation agreement, which was to expire in December. A $100 million economic aid agreement between the two countries was signed at year's end. The consolidation of the self-proclaimed Turkish Republic of Northern Cyprus was supported by Turkey, the only country to recognize the state. At the same time, Turkey continued to support the efforts of the UN to solve the Cyprus dispute. (See *Cyprus,* above.) There was agreement on this point with U.K. Foreign Secretary Sir Geoffrey Howe, who visited Ankara in February. He was followed in July by West German Chancellor Helmut Kohl.

The economy continued to grow, although at a slower rate than in 1984. The trade balance improved, and Turkey was able to service its foreign debt and to obtain further external finance. Prime Minister Ozal's primary concerns during his visits to the U.S. in April and the Far East in July were to promote trade and to attract foreign investment.

(ANDREW MANGO)

This article updates the *Macropædia* article TURKEY AND ANCIENT ANATOLIA.

UNITED ARAB EMIRATES

Consisting of Abu Dhabi, Ajman, Dubai, Fujairah, Ras al-Khaimah, Sharjah, and Umm al-Qaiwain, the United Arab Emirates is a federation of seven largely autonomous emirates located on the eastern Arabian Peninsula. Area: 77,700 sq km (30,000 sq mi). Pop.: (1985 est.): 1,280,000. Cap.: Abu Dhabi. Monetary unit: dirham, with (Oct. 21, 1985) a free rate of 3.67 dirhams to U.S. $1 (5.27 dirhams = £1 sterling). President in 1985, Sheikh Zaid ibn Sultan an-Nahayan; prime minister, Sheikh Rashid ibn Said al-Maktum.

Two developments in 1985 strengthened the regional position of the United Arab Emirates (U.A.E.). A new national airline, called Emirates Airlines and based in Dubai, began operations in October with initial traffic rights to Kuwait (later withdrawn), Pakistan, and India. The new carrier was in competition to some extent with Gulf Air, in which the U.A.E. was a shareholder. The Dubai National Travel Agency began promoting "winter sunshine" package tours to the U.A.E. with a view to boosting tourism from Europe. The second development, announced on April 23, was the setting up of a free-trade zone authority at the Jebel Ali port area outside the town of Dubai. Although Abu Dhabi remained the most important member of the federation in terms of its petroleum production and influence on policy-making, Dubai moved ahead as a commercial centre.

The aim of a number of mergers among local banks during the year was to restrain the unfettered growth of the banking sector. In June the Petroleum and Mineral Resources Ministry revealed a multimillion-dollar plan to stockpile enough petroleum to meet the country's needs for at least 45 days.

In November the U.A.E. announced that it was establishing diplomatic relations with the U.S.S.R. Before 1985 only Kuwait, among the Gulf emirates, had maintained relations with the Soviets.   (JOHN WHELAN)

This article updates the *Macropædia* article ARABIA: *United Arab Emirates.*

YEMEN, PEOPLE'S DEMOCRATIC REPUBLIC OF

The People's Democratic Republic of Yemen (Yemen [Aden]: South Yemen) is located in the southern coastal region of the Arabian Peninsula, on the Gulf of Aden and the Arabian Sea. Area: 336,870 sq km (130,070 sq mi). Pop. (1985 est.): 2,124,-000. Cap.: Aden. Monetary unit: dinar, with (Oct. 21, 1985) a par value of 0.34 dinar to U.S. $1 (free rate of 0.49 dinar = £1 sterling). Chairman of the Presidium of the Supreme People's Council (president) in 1985. Ali Nasir Muhammad Husani; prime ministers, Muhammad Husani and, from February 14, Haidar Abu Bakr al-Attas.

Pres. Ali Nasir Muhammad Husani of South Yemen was reelected for another five-year term as secretary-general of the ruling Yemeni Socialist Party (YSP) at the party's third general congress in October 1985. At the same time, the new Politburo contained a number of the president's critics, among them 'Abd al-Fattah Ismail, whom Muhammad had replaced as head of state in April 1980 and who had returned from exile earlier in 1985.

In February President Muhammad relinquished the post of prime minister, which he had held for 14 years, when he appointed a new Cabinet under Haidar Abu Bakr al-Attas. The new prime minister announced that the government would continue attempts to build links with North Yemen. In his report to the YSP congress he stressed the importance of developing strong relations with socialist countries, in particular the U.S.S.R.

Since coming to power President Muhammad had sought better relations with other Arab countries, most notably Oman. According to a statement issued in November by the Omani government, South Yemen and Oman were to exchange ambassadors in early 1986.   (JOHN WHELAN)

This article updates the *Macropædia* article ARABIA: *People's Democratic Republic of Yemen.*

YEMEN ARAB REPUBLIC

The Yemen Arab Republic (Yemen [San'a']; North Yemen) is situated in the southwestern coastal region of the Arabian Peninsula, on the Red Sea. Area: 200,000 sq km (77,200 sq mi). Pop. (1985 est.): 6,547,000. Cap.: San'a'. Monetary unit: rial, with (Oct. 21, 1985) a par value of 5.86 rials to U.S. $1 (free rate of 7.02 rials = U.S. $1; 10.06 rials = £1 sterling). President in 1985, Col. Ali Abdullah Saleh; prime minister, Abdel Aziz Abdel Ghani.

In a Cabinet reshuffle announced on Nov. 14, 1985, Pres. Ali Abdullah Saleh of North Yemen promoted a number of ministers who favoured closer ties with Saudi Arabia, despite a history of interference by the latter nation in Yemeni politics. Saleh's brother, Muhammad Abdullah Saleh, was appointed deputy interior minister and security chief. It was reported in August that both North and South Yemen had indicated separately to Saudi Arabia their willingness to discuss the demarcation of the borders separating the three countries. Although generally considered pro-Western in stance, President Saleh pursued a policy of friendship toward the U.S.S.R. by entertaining a Soviet economic delegation early in 1985.

On September 25 President Saleh announced that exploration in the Marib al-Jawf basin by Yemen Hunt Oil Co., a subsidiary of the U.S. Hunt Oil Co., had revealed crude petroleum reserves of 300 million bbl and sufficient gas reserves to justify commercial exploitation. He added that a pipeline would be built to connect the oil field with the Red Sea.   (JOHN WHELAN)

This article updates the *Macropædia* article ARABIA: *Yemen Arab Republic.*

East Asia

CHINA

The People's Republic of China is situated in eastern Asia, with coastlines on the Yellow Sea and the East and South China seas. Area: 9,572,900 sq km (3,696,100 sq mi), including Tibet and excluding Taiwan. (See *Taiwan,* below.) Pop. (1985 est., excluding Taiwan): 1,043,074,000. Cap.: Beijing (Peking). Monetary unit: yuan, with (Oct. 21, 1985) a market rate of 3.05 yuan to U.S. $1 (4.37 yuan = £1 sterling). General secretary of the Chinese Communist Party in 1985, Hu Yaobang (Hu Yao-pang); president, Li Xiannian (Li Hsien-nien); premier, Zhao Ziyang (Chao Tzu-yang).

During 1985 China continued its pursuit of far-reaching reforms of the country's political and economic institutions and of expanded commercial and technical ties with the industrialized world. Under the guidance of elder statesman Deng Xiaoping (Teng Hsiao-p'ing), the Chinese Communist Party (CCP) accelerated the promotion of younger, better educated leaders into positions of political responsibility, hoping thereby to assure long-term policy continuity. In an unprecedented turnover of high-level political leadership, Deng secured the resignation of 10 out of 24 members of the CCP Central Committee's Political Bureau, replacing them with more vigorous officials in their 50s and 60s. But complications arose in China's departures from rigid central economic control, including, in particular, unchecked expenditures by individual enterprises and financial abuses by trading companies. Notwithstanding these difficulties, the leadership reiterated its support for the economic reforms and the open-door economic policy. Relations with the United States encountered some difficulties but generally experienced stability and forward movement. Relations with the Soviet Union, although subject to larger differences and uncertainties, also made headway.

Domestic Affairs. Deng Xiaoping's principal energies in 1985 were devoted to further entrenching reformist policies by placing his supporters in key leadership positions. Deng engineered a major political victory at a special party conference held in September, when 64 members of the CCP Central Committee (including a number of senior officials considered unsympathetic to the political and economic reforms) relinquished their posts. But the retirees were allowed to retain their salaries and official privileges, thereby reducing the possibility of disgruntlement or disaffection. Key backers of Deng's policies were also among those stepping down, reflecting the importance now attached to age and technical competence in leadership assignments.

However, Deng's decision not to relinquish his leadership position reversed his earlier intention to retire from political life by 1985 and indicated that his role remained vital to further development of the reforms. Despite evident good health at age 81, Deng increasingly sought to restrict his formal political activities. Principal responsibility for managing the reform program was delegated to Deng's chief lieutenants, 70-year-old party General Secretary Hu Yaobang (Hu Yao-pang) and 66-year-old Premier Zhao Ziyang (Chao Tzu-yang). But newly elected members of the Political Bureau, most notably 56-year-old Hu Qili (Hu Ch'i-li) and 57-year-old Li Peng (Li P'eng; *see* BIOGRAPHIES), were also entrusted with increased responsibility. The latter two officials (both trained as engineers)

were expected to succeed to the top party and state posts, probably in 1987.

Leadership turnover at the top was paralleled by an effort to rejuvenate the CCP at other levels. Since the institution of a mandatory retirement system in 1980, more than one million party officials had given up their posts. Despite a membership of more than 40 million, the CCP remained woefully short of personnel capable of overseeing China's ambitious plans for economic modernization. To fill this gap, the CCP actively sought to recruit intellectuals and scientists, but many educated Chinese preferred to steer clear of political involvement.

Equally far-reaching steps were under way within the military establishment, long a source of resistance to Deng's reforms. In March plans were publicized for retiring 47,-000 veteran officers from active duty by the end of 1986, approximately 10% of the officer corps. Following a series of high-level leadership meetings in the late spring, it was announced that one million men (approximately one-quarter of present troop strength) would be pared from China's military establishment over the next two years. At the same time, the regional military commands were reduced from 11 to 7. The streamlining of the armed forces was intended to increase the combat effectiveness of all three services as well as to provide additional funds for the development of more modern weapons. Perhaps most important, Deng's allies within the senior military leadership hoped that these steps would provide increased opportunities for younger, better educated officers to advance to command positions.

But some of Deng's actions met with continued skepticism and resistance. Uneasiness about the potential implications of the economic reforms topped the list. Under Deng's aegis China's economic system had departed from

Chinese construction workers climb the bamboo scaffolding around a 54-story trade centre being erected in Shenzhen (Shen-chen). In both size and purpose, the building symbolized the dominant trends in China's economy.

many of the tenets of strict central planning and moved toward a combination of market and plan. The institution of an agricultural responsibility system in 1979, whereby farmers retain excess earnings after fulfilling their production quotas, significantly reduced state intervention in the rural sector, but implementation of equivalent industrial reforms announced in October 1984 was proving more difficult. Some top leaders, including veteran economic planner Chen Yun (Ch'en Yün), expressed serious reservations about excessive tampering with the urban industrial sector, the cornerstone of China's socialist economy. Chen warned that such reforms threatened the ability of central planners to oversee the directions of the economy as a whole. He also cautioned that excessive autonomy for individual enterprises could lead to unchecked expenditures and severe imbalances among sectors of the economy.

Other critics of Deng's policies focused on the potential for ideological deviations resulting from the open-door policy. China's encouragement of increased investment from abroad and the growing presence of foreign businessmen and tourists had created a more freewheeling atmosphere in China's cities, especially in the coastal provinces. Critics voiced concern about the undesirable side effects of an enhanced foreign presence, including the attraction of Chinese youth to foreign consumer goods and Western culture.

Although Deng and other reformers did not dispute the existence of such problems, they viewed them as difficulties to be overcome rather than as the portents of a major political or ideological crisis. Deng repeatedly made clear that serious political deviations from socialism would not be tolerated and that China's increased reliance on economic incentives and market mechanisms was not the precursor of the restoration of capitalism. He stated that the leadership would not permit the emergence of major polarities between rich and poor or a shift away from state ownership of the principal means of production. But at the same time, Deng saw the encouragement of individual initiative (including the profit motive) and increased economic ties with the West as critical to enlivening the economic system and reviving public support for CCP policy.

The Economy. China was in important respects a victim of its own economic success in 1985. An extremely rapid growth rate in the first half of the year produced an overheated economy that threatened to overwhelm the country's severely burdened transportation and resource-allocation systems. A number of these problems were traceable to steps undertaken in late 1984 to free Chinese industry from the pervasive grip of central planning and to encourage increased innovation and risk taking. With many enterprises informed that they were now responsible for their own profits and losses, some factory managers aggressively pursued opportunities for increasing their market shares. But these actions produced a number of unwelcome consequences, including what Premier Zhao described as the "indiscriminate" issuing of bonuses to workers, an exponential growth in bank loans, and a rapid expansion of money supply. At the same time, the abrupt jump in industrial output—a rise of more than 23% in the first six months of 1985 alone, compared with a 14% increase for all of 1984—severely taxed China's energy resources and transportation system.

Some of the most acute problems concerned the rapid depletion of China's foreign exchange. Increased demand for consumer goods and the enhanced ability of provinces and some individual enterprises to make decisions on the spending of hard currency resulted in a ballooning inter-

(continued on page 496)

An Interview with Deng Xiaoping

On Sept. 10, 1985, Frank Gibney, vice-chairman of Encyclopædia Britannica's board of editors, interviewed Chinese leader Deng Xiaoping (Teng Hsiaop'ing) in the Great Hall of the People in Beijing (Peking). Following are excerpts from Deng's wide-ranging remarks.

On the Modernization Program. In 1981 China began the sixth five-year plan. We set out at that time to achieve a growth rate of 4%, while we hoped that it would reach 5%. But in the event we were able to register 9.5%—indeed, almost 10% for the past four years. In 1985, the growth rate even exceeded 10%. Thus, the policy of opening China to the outside world has yielded excellent results. However, the tangible changes do not explain everything. We can only say at this point that initial successes have been achieved. Better results will be achieved when we solve the problems of urban reform.

Starting from the second half of 1984, we began to modernize the urban economy, much as we had worked with the rural economy in previous years. To say we are working on the urban economy, of course, means that we are attempting now to achieve a comprehensive reform of China's economy as a whole. If we succeed, we will lay the foundation for a stable economy that will serve this country in good stead for the rest of the century—and indeed through the first 30 or 50 years of the next century. By the end of the first half of the next century, we hope that China will have caught up with the advanced countries. Nonetheless, economic reform is highly complex. It invites problems, and we inevitably must run risks. In the process of working toward our goals, we have to face the fact that many errors will be made, big and small. Errors are unavoidable, and we can only do our best to correct them when they occur. And at the same time, we must try to avoid major errors.

The past five years were only our first steps. Per capita income in 1979 was only $250. It is now more than $300. That may not seem like such a big change, but it is a sign of our progress. We are now formulating the seventh five-year plan for China's economic development. Here we are aiming at an annual growth rate of 7 to 8%. This is not so high. Nonetheless, we think we can quadruple the gross national product by the end of this century.

I say these goals are not so high advisedly, because we do not want to stress the growth rate only. The average growth rate for last year and, indeed, for the second half of this year has been entirely too fast. To grow this fast is bad for sustained growth and the stable economic foundation we seek. Now, therefore, we must begin to avoid shooting for excessively high growth rates. The people are rather optimistic about our future prospects. We do not wish to disappoint them, but in many ways we must proceed cautiously from this point on.

On Problems. Of course we had our problems. At the very beginning the rural reform did not proceed fast enough. Some provinces were halfhearted in supporting rural reforms. Indeed, they went at a very halting pace. They were reluctant. It was not until they found out that

other provinces had achieved very good results that they tried to imitate the reforms and correct their past mistakes. All regions that really followed our reforms in the rural area achieved very good results. Indeed, it is fair to say that by now 90% of our rural areas have been changed and vastly improved. The remaining 10% is the problem area. There are still areas in China where peasants have trouble feeding and clothing themselves. In this territory we must now mobilize the resources of the state to assist the people. Provinces that have succeeded early should now bend their efforts to assist those provinces that have lagged behind.

On the Market Economy. We adhere to the socialist system. Whatever we do, we must not forget that we are trying to accomplish our goals under a socialist system. What are the two most important guiding principles behind our efforts to achieve reform through a socialist system? First, there must be public ownership of production. That is to say, the public sector must predominate; enterprises owned by the state or owned by the people or collectively owned should continue to have predominant roles in our economic growth. Our second goal is to achieve common prosperity for all. We have encouraged some regions and some people to be well off first, and we are happy to find that they are achieving prosperity. Yet we do not want a polarization of incomes to occur. Therefore, regions that have prospered are urged to help those that are behind. Naturally, we are happy to have foreign enterprises come and assist in China's development, and we will get a certain amount of free enterprise ownership in China itself. But we do not intend to let this lead to capitalism. I have recently read in the American press that quite a few Americans are now saying that China will not really turn capitalist, as people had been saying before. Of course this is a sound judgment. These Americans are right. China will not take the capitalist road. China will continue its march toward socialist development in its own way.

On the Soviet Economy. The Soviets have found out that they have really very bad defects in their economy and that what they have practiced has not proved effective. Alternatives must be found. This is an obvious fact. Of course, it is also true that it is far more difficult for the Soviet Union to make constructive changes because of the political structure they have there. There is a rigidity and a lack of flexibility that we do not have. Nonetheless, I would say that the Soviets could do very well if they wanted to. The country has the capability of improving.

On the Pacific Basin. The matter of [participation in] the Pacific Basin is really not on our government's agenda yet. In the first place, we are not sure whether China is in a position to play its role in this field. In fact, none of the countries in the area, like the United States, Japan, or the Southeast Asian countries, has approached us in this regard. But there is one thing I would like to mention and to stress. China is a country on the Pacific. Indeed, it is the Pacific country with the largest population. Thus, China has a concern in any question involving the Pacific, and China is concerned in this relationship.

On Sino-U.S. Relations. The most important issue between us is technology transfer. I must say that, on the whole, the relations between the United States and China have done very well. The development of the Sino-U.S. relationship has been satisfactory, but it has not achieved what it could. And one of the big reasons is this matter of technology transfer. I know that the economic community in the United States is enthusiastic about more technology transfer to China. The real obstacles are in the United States Congress.

In front of the Gate of Heavenly Peace in Beijing (Peking), two Chinese workers display headlines announcing September's shakeup in the Communist Party leadership.
AP/WIDE WORLD

(continued from page 494)

national trade deficit and a 30% drop in China's foreign exchange reserves in the first six months of 1985 alone.

The biggest problems were associated with Japan, China's largest trading partner. An explosive demand for Japanese consumer items and industrial products and the importation of numerous production lines (especially in consumer electronics) contributed to a surge in China's imports that was not matched by comparable increases in exports. As a result China's 1985 trade imbalance with Japan was expected to exceed $5 billion, imposing a strain on relations between the two countries.

Unprecedented economic abuses also developed as a consequence of China's increased ties with the outside world. To attract foreign investment and technology, China in 1979 created a limited number of special economic zones in the country's southern coastal regions, where foreign firms were granted preferential tax treatment and related incentives for establishing factories and supplying advanced technology. Although many senior leaders (including Deng) had earlier deemed the special economic zones proof of the "correctness" of the open-door policy, mounting problems in the spring and summer produced a much more cautious view. Exposure of a major scandal on Hainan Island involving unauthorized imports of Japanese cars, motorcycles, and consumer electronics worth more than $1 billion graphically revealed the extent of such problems. The boomtown atmosphere in the zones not only created a ready climate for corruption but also raised the issue of whether the substantial costs required to develop new industrial areas had yielded a reasonable return on investment.

To cope with these problems, officials in Beijing (Peking) sought to curb much of the autonomy previously granted to the zones. A number of local officials were dismissed or reassigned, and far stricter controls on the expenditure of funds and disbursement of hard currency were imposed. In July it was announced that April 1984 plans to expand the zones to an additional 14 cities had been delayed, with near-term expansion to be limited to 4 major cities where the industrial and management infrastructure was already fairly well developed.

China also experienced complications in the introduction of price reform, long recognized as a crucial if extremely difficult step in the transition to a more mixed economy. In May government price controls on meat and vegetables were lifted, and prices were allowed to fluctuate according to supply and demand. The initial effects were an abrupt rise in food prices and local shortages of nonstaple items such as pork. Wage increases and price subsidies for city dwellers offset much of this increased cost to consumers, and the State Council also announced that no major steps in price reform would be taken in 1986. By allowing a longer period to establish such changes, government planners hoped to achieve a successful transition to the new arrangements.

This mood of continued yet more sober optimism was also evident in deliberations over the seventh five-year plan, scheduled to begin in 1986. Annual economic growth for the plan was targeted at approximately 7%, 3% lower than the average increases achieved in the sixth five-year plan. By concentrating investment in the underdeveloped transportation, communications, and energy sectors and in the technological upgrading of existing industrial enterprises, planners hoped to eliminate crucial economic bottlenecks, reduce sectoral imbalances, and lay the basis for sustained growth in the 1990s. The plan also called for the continued expansion of China's service economy, which had experienced remarkable development in recent years. More than ten million Chinese were now self-employed, and planners hoped to convert almost all retail establishments to individual or collective ownership by 1990.

Foreign Affairs. China continued to increase its international visibility in 1985, emphasizing the expansion of political and economic relations with virtually all nations and reiterating its independent foreign-policy stance toward the two superpowers. Senior Chinese officials visited numerous less developed and industrialized countries, stressing China's commitment to peaceful coexistence and its hopes for long-term amicable ties with the outside world. The maintenance of regional stability was considered especially crucial since the existence of major tensions in East Asia posed a serious risk to the requirements of domestic economic construction.

Sino-Soviet relations were more active than at any point since the early 1960s, with both sides testing the opportunities for an expanded relationship in the aftermath of Mikhail Gorbachev's succession to power in the U.S.S.R. At Konstantin Chernenko's funeral in March, Gorbachev and Li Peng, leader of the Chinese delegation, both pledged renewed efforts to improve relations. In July Vice-Premier Yao Yilin (Yao Yi-lin) traveled to the Soviet Union, re-

ciprocating the visit of Deputy Premier Ivan Arkhipov to China in December 1984. The two countries signed a long-term trade agreement for the 1986–90 period totaling $13.5 billion. Under the agreement two-way trade in 1990 was expected to reach $3.5 billion, more than double its present level. A separate agreement provided for the resumption of Soviet technical assistance to China for the first time since 1960, including the upgrading of 17 factories built by the U.S.S.R. in the 1950s and the construction of 7 new industrial plants. Official relations between the legislative bodies and the trade unions of the two countries were also restored, but China stated that it was not yet willing to consider the resumption of Communist Party ties. In December the two sides announced that the Soviet and Chinese foreign ministers would exchange visits to one another's capitals during 1986.

However, China repeatedly insisted that full political ties depended on elimination of the "three obstacles" to the normalization of relations: Moscow's occupation of Afghanistan, Soviet support for Vietnam's occupation of Kampuchea, and Soviet military deployments in East Asia, including the presence of ground forces in Mongolia and 171 SS-20 intermediate-range missiles east of the Urals. Moscow not only remained unyielding on these issues but also stepped up the level of its military activity on all three fronts. Quite possibly because of the need for regional stability, China concluded that a less hostile relationship was nevertheless possible under those circumstances.

Sino-Soviet relations remained much more modest than the burgeoning ties between the United States and China. China continued to voice complaints about three areas of U.S. policy: U.S. dealings with Taiwan (especially continued arms sales to the island), restrictions on the sale of sensitive technologies to China, and protectionist sentiment that threatened to limit Chinese textile exports to the United States. Despite these differences China made clear its desire for expanded ties, with a particular emphasis on economic, scientific, and technical collaboration. U.S.-China trade reached a record $6.1 billion in 1984, and two-way trade for 1985 seemed certain to surpass it. U.S. investment in China (much of it in offshore oil exploration) exceeded $1 billion by 1985, well in excess of that of any other nation. Perhaps most important, an estimated 15,000 Chinese students were enrolled in U.S. universities, more than had been sent to all other countries combined.

Ranking military officials of the two countries also maintained their dialogue on security issues. In January, Gen. John Vessey became the first chairman of the Joint Chiefs of Staff to visit China. Discussions continued on sales of selected defense technologies to Beijing, including diesel engines for several new Chinese destroyers and an artillery shell production line. But an impending U.S. Navy port visit to Shanghai was postponed during April when the United States, in accord with long-standing U.S. policy, refused to either confirm or deny the presence of nuclear weapons on board the ships.

High-level political visits took place and achieved important results. In July Pres. Li Xiannian (Li Hsien-nien) made the first visit ever of a Chinese chief of state to the United States, reciprocating U.S. Pres. Ronald Reagan's April 1984 visit to China. The two countries signed a long-delayed accord on peaceful nuclear cooperation, which appeared to pave the way for sales of U.S. civilian nuclear-power technology to China. However, U.S. congressional concern about reports of Chinese assistance to Pakistan's nuclear program and the insistence of numerous legislators that China provide more binding pledges of its commitment to nuclear nonproliferation delayed final approval of

the accord until December. President Li's visit to the U.S. was followed by Vice-Pres. George Bush's visit to China in October, at which time the U.S. announced new measures to expedite the flow of advanced Western technologies to China.

Sino-Japanese relations experienced some troubling moments during the year. An August visit by Prime Minister Yasuhiro Nakasone to a Tokyo shrine honouring Japan's war dead provoked a strong diplomatic reaction from China, and Nakasone later pledged not to undertake similar visits in the future. In September Chinese university students staged protests against China's growing trade dependence on Japan and the mounting influx of Japanese goods, which they described as a "second occupation." But senior officials quickly interceded and sought to prevent subsequent demonstrations from assuming an anti-Japanese coloration. Admonitions to the students and reassurances to Tokyo reiterated that China's opening to the outside world remained unchanged but that ways had to be sought to achieve more balanced economic relations in the future. (JONATHAN D. POLLACK)

JAPAN

A constitutional monarchy in the northwestern Pacific Ocean, Japan comprises an archipelago with four major islands (Hokkaido, Honshu, Kyushu, and Shikoku), the Ryukyus (including Okinawa), and minor adjacent islands. Area: 377,765 sq km (145,856 sq mi). Pop. (1985): 120,760,000. Cap.: Tokyo. Monetary unit: yen, with (Oct. 21, 1985) a free rate of 215.66 yen to U.S. $1 (309.25 yen = £1 sterling). Emperor, Hirohito; prime minister in 1985, Yasuhiro Nakasone.

Domestic Affairs. In October 1984, despite intraparty criticism, Yasuhiro Nakasone had been reelected president of Japan's ruling Liberal-Democratic Party (LDP) and was thus assured of continuing as prime minister. He appointed a new Cabinet, in which portfolios were distributed among recent rivals and LDP faction leaders. On Jan. 25, 1985, in a speech at the resumption of the 102nd session of the Diet (parliament), Nakasone promised to continue, during his second term, policies pressing for nuclear disarmament, free trade, and domestic reforms, including further deregu-

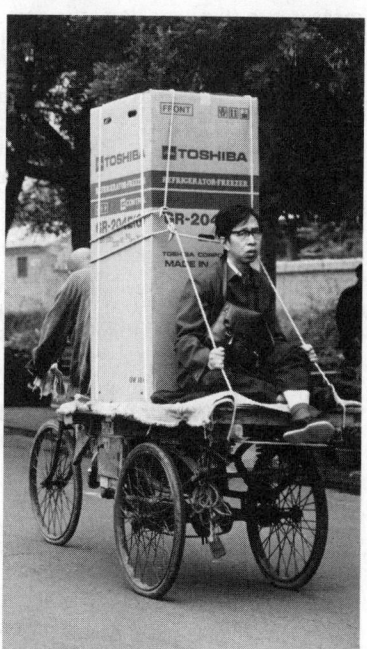

J.-P. LAFFONT—SYGMA

Japanese exports to China reached record levels in 1985 as Japan became China's chief source of imported goods, particularly consumer durables.

lation of public corporations, reduction of the deficit, and alteration of the system of education. The prime minister would not rule out the possibility that defense spending in fiscal 1985 might exceed the politically established limit of 1% of Japan's gross national product (GNP). On October 16, in the lower house, Nakasone suggested elimination of the ceiling.

Meanwhile, there were behind-the-scenes moves in the LDP toward a "post-Nakasone" era. On February 7 a member of Nakasone's Cabinet, Finance Minister Noboru Takeshita, announced the organization of a study group (the Soseikai), in effect a faction within a faction. It brought together 40 members of the Diet, one-third of the powerful 123-man Tanaka faction. Former prime minister Kakuei Tanaka, found guilty in the Lockheed aircraft procurement case, was not technically an LDP member while his case was on appeal, but he still managed the largest party faction. He denounced Takeshita's move, as did LDP Vice-Pres. Susumu Nikaido, nominal head of the Tanaka faction and a possible successor to Nakasone.

LDP Secretary-General Shin Kanemaru openly stated that the inauguration of the study group signaled Takeshita's intention to be a contender for the presidency of the LDP in the election scheduled for November 1986. The faction led by former prime minister Zenko Suzuki reaffirmed its ties with the Tanaka group. Suzuki backed a senior faction member and former chief Cabinet secretary, Kiichi Miyazawa, for future leadership. Foreign Minister Shintaro Abe was also considered a "new leader," along with Takeshita and Miyazawa.

On February 27 Tanaka suffered what at the time was called a "mild stroke," but on March 4 doctors reported that his condition was worse than announced. Masayuki Fujio, a leader of the faction attached to former prime minister Takeo Fukuda, stated openly in April that Tanaka had a slim chance for political recovery. On June 6 Tanaka was moved to a villa in Karuizawa, and his Tokyo political office was closed. At first these developments seemed to presage additional intraparty friction, since Prime Minister Nakasone had originally been raised to power by the Tanaka faction.

Indeed, LDP leaders were revealing sharp policy differences. Miyazawa, for example, called for government measures to stimulate domestic demand. So did State Minister Toshio Komoto, who argued that Japan had to alter its economic structure from one that relied heavily on imports. Ippei Kaneko, director general of the Economic Planning Agency (EPA), urged that business stimulation be incorporated in the fiscal 1986 budget. Chief Cabinet Secretary Takao Fujinami, however, stated that the government had no intention of taking drastic steps to stimulate demand. Takeshita stated that the Finance Ministry was opposed to issuing additional deficit-financing bonds. Kanemaru urged that the introduction of indirect taxation to restore fiscal balance not be ruled out. Meanwhile, Takeshita's new group and non-Soseikai members led by Nikaido groped for a compromise that would guarantee unity in the Tanaka faction. In April a Kyodo opinion survey reported that the prime minister enjoyed the highest level of support (at 58.7%) in his 28 months in office. Despite his popularity, Nakasone faced opposition within the party to any plan to amend LDP rules so that he could run for a third term.

The Nakasone administration also faced stiff opposition in the Diet. In late January and again in late February, the Japan Socialist Party (JSP) brought parliamentary debate to a halt in protest against Nakasone's apparent intention to exceed the 1%-of-GNP ceiling on defense spending. On

March 6 opposition parties accepted a compromise worked out by Kanemaru, who promised that the LDP would "earnestly" consider tax reduction and would also try to hold down defense costs.

On April 5, four days after the beginning of the new fiscal year, an austere budget bill received the approval of the Diet. General account expenditures totaled 52,499,-600,000,000 yen, an increase of 3.7% over the previous year. Debt service expense, which topped 10 trillion yen for the first time, and defense expenditure, which rose 5.1%, accounted for the increase. Otherwise, the LDP draft budget placed emphasis on research toward the construction of new bullet-train lines and technology fitted to the 21st century. According to the EPA, Japan's real GNP for calendar 1984 totaled 223,056,600,000,000 yen ($857.9 billion) at 1975 prices, an increase of 5.8% (the sharpest annual rise since 1973). Exports expanded 16.2% and accounted for much of the gain. Imports rose only 11.2%.

On June 25 the 102nd Diet closed its 207-day session, carrying over such controversial legislation as an antiespionage bill, revision of the election law, and a measure for reforming the public pension law. As of early July party strength in the (lower) House of Representatives was: LDP (including New Liberal Party allies) 262; JSP 112; Clean Government Party (Komeito) 59; Democratic Socialist Party (DSP) 38; Japan Communist Party (JCP) 27; independents 8; vacancies 5 (total 511). In the (upper) House of Councillors it was: LDP 139; JSP 42; Komeito 27; DSP 13; JCP 14; independents 13; vacancies 4 (total 252).

On May 31 the LDP had submitted to the Diet its "6–6 plan" to rectify disproportionate representation in the lower house. The bill would add one seat to each of the six most densely populated districts and decrease one in each of the six most sparsely populated areas. Opposition parties rejected the plan. In any case, on July 17 the Supreme Court ruled that the last general election was unconstitutional because of disproportionate distribution of votes. The court did not, however, set aside the results of the 1983 poll. The LDP "6–6" bill was resubmitted to an extraordinary session of the Diet that opened October 14.

The Nakasone administration was more successful with other reforms. On April 1, under a law passed in 1984, Nippon Telegraph & Telephone Public Corporation (Denden Kosha) was deregulated and became a private joint-stock firm, NTT Corp. (Shindenden), with 318,000 employees and capital of 780 billion yen (one-third of its stock was held by the government). Similarly, on April 1 the Japan Tobacco & Salt Public Corporation was changed into a private concern. On June 25 Prime Minister Nakasone replaced Iwao Nisugi as president of Japanese National Railways (JNR) with Takaya Sugiura, former vice-minister of transportation. Nisugi had opposed a plan to deregulate the deficit-ridden JNR. On July 26 a government committee recommended that the JNR be split into 24 regional, private companies. Sabotage to rail communications and signal systems that disrupted Tokyo commuter traffic during the morning rush hour on November 29 was thought to have been perpetrated by a far left group to protest the privatization scheme. The government also had plans to privatize Japan Air Lines (JAL).

In June Michio Okamoto, chairman of the Ad Hoc Advisory Council on Education Reform, presented his first set of recommendations. His report praised the present system of education for its egalitarian nature but called for deemphasis on examinations and reform of the system's uniformity and parochial outlook. Ichiro Tanaka, president of the Japan Teachers Union (Nikkyoso), attacked proposals made by the council, which, he said, was determined to

privatize and commercialize education. (*See* EDUCATION.)

On August 12 a JAL domestic flight to Osaka crashed in rugged mountains 110 km (70 mi) northwest of Tokyo. All but 4 of the 524 persons aboard perished. It was the worst single-aircraft accident in history.

Foreign Affairs. In 1985 Japan used a world's fair to advertise its own progress and to forecast a worldwide high-tech transition to the 21st century. Officially known as the International Exposition-Tsukuba, Expo '85 opened March 17 for a six-month run in the science city of Tsukuba, about 50 km (30 mi) northeast of Tokyo, already the site of 46 Japanese research institutes. Expo '85 included exhibits from 49 nations, 37 international organizations, and 28 private corporations. The total cost of the fair was $2.6 billion.

Meanwhile, back in the 20th century, in 1984 Japan produced a record annual trade surplus of $44,350,000,-000 (current account surplus of $35,020,000,000). Japan's reserves in gold, currencies, and Special Drawing Rights stood at $27,330,000,000 at the end of May 1985. This position exacerbated trade friction with the U.S., the Western industrial democracies, and the members of the Association of Southeast Asian Nations (ASEAN). However, because Japan had initiated a market-opening package in April in an effort to increase imports, the leaders attending the May 2–4 Bonn summit of major industrialized nations held back criticism of Prime Minister Nakasone.

Nevertheless, relations with the U.S. were dominated by trade considerations. In 1984 exports to the U.S. (about one-third of Japan's total) soared 40% to a record high of $60 billion. At their meeting in Los Angeles on Jan. 2, 1985, U.S. Pres. Ronald Reagan pressed Nakasone for steps that would increase Japan's imports. Nakasone agreed to take such measures in several categories: telecommunications, computers, forestry products, pharmaceuticals, and medical equipment. When Vice-Foreign Minister Nobuo Matsunaga was appointed the new ambassador to the U.S. on January 29, he stated that his biggest task was to head off protectionist sentiment in the U.S. Congress.

On March 2 the minister of international trade and industry, Keijiro Murata, called on Japanese automakers to exercise moderation in exports to the U.S., even after "voluntary restraints" expired. The government announced on March 28 that auto exports would be limited to 2,330,000 units (a rise of 24% over the 1984 quota). Also in March, the prime minister asked Murata and State Minister Komoto to coordinate all agency negotiations with the U.S. on trade. On April 9 Nakasone unveiled his "substantial" package of measures, following meetings with a special envoy, Gaston Sigur, of the U.S. National Security Council. Late in June the government announced another package featuring a uniform 20% tariff reduction on 1,790 items. On July 29 the administration adopted measures that would ease standards and certification and other procedures.

When the two leaders met in January, President Reagan asked Nakasone for an "understanding" of the U.S. Strategic Defense Initiative (SDI). Back in Japan, the prime minister was much more cautious in comments on the "Star Wars" proposal, indicating that he would abide by Japan's constitution and remember the Diet's 1969 resolution against military use of space. As to more conventional weapons, in April and in September some 26 U.S. F-16 fighter-bombers were deployed at Misawa in Aomori Prefecture. A second squadron was scheduled to arrive in 1987 to enhance—according to the Japan Defense Agency (JDA)—the "American-Japanese deterrent" against a potential Soviet threat from the north.

Relations with the Soviet Union remained tentative. On February 7 the Japanese observed "Northern Territories Day," a government-sponsored campaign designed to publicize Japan's claim to four islands northeast of Hokkaido still occupied by the U.S.S.R. 40 years after the end of World War II. Prime Minister Nakasone told an audience that Japan "is fully resolved to regain Habomai, Shikotan, Kunashiri, and Etorofu by peaceful means." When Nakasone met the new Soviet leader in Moscow on March 14, however, Mikhail Gorbachev refused to discuss the territorial issue.

On March 11 the new Soviet ambassador to Tokyo, Petr Abrasimov, proposed to Foreign Minister Abe that they address four issues: (1) promotion of bilateral trade; (2) cultural exchange (among major nations only Japan and the U.S. had no treaty on this subject with the U.S.S.R.); (3) a tax treaty to avoid double levies; and (4) a proposal to lift the Soviet embassy personnel ceiling. On June 6, more than five years after the Soviet invasion of Afghanistan prompted Japan to cut off all talks, the Foreign Ministry handed Abrasimov a revised draft for a comprehensive cultural exchange treaty.

Trade between Japan and China during 1984 set a record high, with Japanese exports totaling $7.2 billion and imports, $5.9 billion. On March 27 LDP Vice-President Nikaido began a five-day visit to China, his sixth trip since 1972 when, as Cabinet secretary, he accompanied Prime Minister Tanaka to the mainland to start negotiations toward normalization of relations.

Since 1965 Japan had had normal relations with South Korea, despite various strains in the relationship. On February 7 South Korean opposition leader Kim Dae Jung made an overnight stopover in Tokyo on his way home. He was reported as saying, "I am overwhelmed to be setting foot on Japanese soil again, almost 12 years after I was kidnapped and taken away to Korea from Japan." The Japanese press and public watched developments carefully as Kim was placed under house arrest immediately upon his arrival in Seoul. (See *Korea,* below.) As of January 1 the government lifted sanctions against North Korea, 14 months after they were imposed to protest the 1983 terrorist bombing that killed 17 South Korean officials in Rangoon, Burma. Tokyo had not, however, established official relations with Pyongyang.

A Pacific Basin Cooperation Plan was accelerated by Nakasone's eight-day trip to Oceania beginning January 13. His tour included Australia, New Zealand, Papua New Guinea, and Fiji. Prime Minister Rajiv Gandhi of India arrived in Japan for a four-day visit in late November, the first such visit by an Indian head of government in 16 years.   (ARDATH W. BURKS)

See also Feature Article: *The New Asia-Pacific Era.*

KOREA

A country of northeastern Asia, bordered by the Sea of Japan, the Korea Strait, and the Yellow Sea, Korea is divided into two parts roughly at the 38th parallel.

During 1985 there were unprecedented developments in the relationship between the two governments of Korea. In September 1984 North Korea had offered relief aid to its rival regime after floods devastated many areas in South Korea. The offer was, surprisingly, accepted. Discussions on economic cooperation begun by the two sides in 1984 continued into 1985. On the agenda were such topics as trading complementary items, reopening railway links severed decades ago, opening ports, pursuing joint ventures in mining, and setting up standing consultative committees. However, North Korea continued to protest fiercely

against the annual military exercises conducted jointly by South Korean and U.S. forces.

A significant breakthrough occurred in May when North and South Korea agreed to resume bilateral Red Cross talks, initiated in 1972 but canceled a year later when the North accused the South of anti-Communist activities. The two-day sessions, characterized by a rare lack of rancour, focused on the prospect of exchange visits among some ten million Koreans who were separated from relatives by the division of their country. Follow-up negotiations in midyear eventually produced results. In September 50 ordinary citizens from each side, accompanied by performing artists, journalists, and officials, crossed the demilitarized zone for reunions with their kinfolk. The occasion, lasting four days and three nights, marked the first time such an exchange had taken place since the nation was divided in 1945.

North and South Korea also opened dialogues on parliamentary affairs. In addition, both governments agreed to discuss a possible role for North Korea in the 1988 Olympic Games, to be held in Seoul, South Korea. The Japanese press carried a surprising report that Ho Dam, a member of the North Korean Politburo, had visited Seoul in September for secret talks with Pres. Chun Doo Hwan. Both sides, however, denied the story.

Republic of Korea (South Korea)

Area: 99,091 sq km (38,259 sq mi). Pop. (1985 est.): 41,215,-000. Cap.: Seoul. Monetary unit: won, with (Oct. 21, 1985) a free rate of 881.74 won to U.S. $1 (1,264.42 won = £1 sterling). President in 1985, Chun Doo Hwan; prime ministers, Chin Iee Chong and, from February 18, Lho Shin Yong.

In South Korea the year began with two highly significant political events: the return from exile of leading dissident Kim Dae Jung (*see* BIOGRAPHIES) and the elections for a new National Assembly. On February 8, under the glare of extensive media publicity, Kim arrived in Seoul after two years of self-exile in the U.S. "I am coming home to join my people's struggle for democracy," he declared. With 17 years left of a 20-year jail sentence on sedition charges, Kim was immediately escorted to his home and placed under house arrest. The standing ban against his participation in political activities meant that he could not become directly involved in the parliamentary elections.

On February 12 South Koreans went to the polls to elect the 276-seat unicameral legislature, which constitutionally shared power equally with the executive branch of government. President Chun's Democratic Justice Party (DJP), as expected, topped the lists by taking 35% of the popular vote. Much to the government's consternation, however, a newly formed opposition party performed unexpectedly well. Backing both Kim Dae Jung and another outspoken opposition leader, Kim Young Sam, the uncompromisingly antigovernment New Korea Democratic Party (NKDP) gained 29% of the vote. (For tabulated results, see *Political Parties,* above.) The return of Kim Dae Jung had apparently provided a significant morale boost to the opposition.

Clearly taken aback by the election results, President Chun reshuffled both his Cabinet and the top leadership of the DJP. The new prime minister was Lho Shin Yong, former head of national security, while Rho Tae Woo, head of the National Olympic Committee and a close friend of the president, took over as DJP chairman. Both Lho and Rho were considered political moderates.

A new challenge to Chun's authority arose in April when the NKDP merged with the smaller Democratic Korea Party, a moderate opposition party. Together they

Opposition leader Kim Dae Jung returned to South Korea accompanied by several U.S. supporters, including Robert White (left), former ambassador to El Salvador, and Thomas M. Foglietta (right), member of the House of Representatives from Pennsylvania.
AP/WIDE WORLD

commanded the one-third majority needed to call an extraordinary session or block constitutional changes in the National Assembly. Chun's response was to make conciliatory overtures. He also lifted the political ban from 14 opposition leaders, including both Kim Dae Jung and Kim Young Sam.

Another political storm blew up in August when Chun tried to introduce a law under which students found guilty of having engaged in "violent" demonstrations would be sent to detention centres for ideological "reorientation." According to government authorities the Campus Stabilization bill was intended to stanch the rising level of violence among student radicals before it became a threat to national security. However, opposition to the bill was so broad and so heated that the president shelved it, at least temporarily.

Although South Korea had no diplomatic ties with China, both had clearly indicated a desire in recent years for improved relations. Two incidents during the year tested South Korea's attitude toward the matter. In March a Chinese torpedo boat drifted into Korean waters following a mutiny during which a number of crew members died. Three Chinese warships that entered Korean waters in search of the vessel were "strongly invited" by Seoul to leave. China quickly obliged and even apologized. In return, South Korea sent back the boat and the survivors, among them an unknown number believed to have requested passage to Taiwan. The latter, a friend of South Korea, expressed its "profound discontent." When a comparable incident occurred in August, however, the Koreans appeased Taiwan. The defecting pilot of a Chinese air force bomber was allowed to go to Taiwan, though the damaged plane and a second crewman were returned to China.

A weakening of the exporting and industrial prowess that in recent years had powered South Korea's growth took place during the year. Though the government initially projected a 7.5% expansion in gross national product (GNP) for the year, the estimate was revised to 6.5% and then to 5–6% as overseas markets remained depressed and protectionist sentiment continued to gain ground in the developed countries. Particularly hard hit were the construction and shipbuilding industries. Concern was also mounting over the country's huge external debt of $45 billion, and targets for trimming the current account deficit were not being met. The won suffered on financial markets, falling from 830 to the U.S. dollar in January to 880

by September. The government was obliged to moderate its tight monetary policies in an effort to stimulate the domestic economy.

Democratic People's Republic of Korea (North Korea)

Area: 122,370 sq km (47,250 sq mi). Pop. (1985 est.): 20,082,-000. Cap.: Pyongyang. Monetary unit: won, with (Oct. 21, 1985) a nominal exchange rate of 0.94 won to U.S. $1 (1.35 won = £1 sterling). General secretary of the Central Committee of the Workers' (Communist) Party of Korea and president in 1985, Marshal Kim Il Sung; chairman of the Council of Ministers (premier), Kang Song San.

The political scene in Pyongyang continued to be dominated by speculation about when 73-year-old Pres. Kim Il Sung would pass power on to his son, Kim Chong Il. While the timing remained uncertain, the course itself was further confirmed during massive celebrations surrounding the president's birthday on April 15. Eulogies of the "Great Leader" (the father) invariably referred to the "Dear Leader" (the son) as well. The younger Kim, already supreme commander of the armed forces, had reportedly taken over the day-to-day management of the Workers' (Communist) Party, the government, and the military establishment. Though some resistance to his accession apparently remained among veteran generals, these opponents were expected to be retired or otherwise swept aside before long.

North Korea had long practiced a delicate balancing act in keeping roughly equidistant relations with its giant neighbours, China and the U.S.S.R. However, in 1985 there was evidence of a distinct tilt toward the Soviets. The first hint came in May when China disclosed that Chinese Communist Party General Secretary Hu Yaobang (Hu Yao-pang) had made a sudden, secret trip to meet Kim Il Sung in North Korea. The next day a squadron of Soviet MiG-23 fighter aircraft landed outside Pyongyang; later it was reliably reported that the Soviets had left behind ten of the aircraft, probably as a gift to the Kim leadership. Shortly afterward, in an unprecedented gesture of friendship, both Kims appeared separately at special functions at the Soviet embassy in Pyongyang. In September the Soviets were allowed to conduct at least one reconnaissance flight against China over North Korean air space.

The economy continued to perform indifferently. The second seven-year (1978–84) plan had aimed to achieve a 9.6% annual growth in GNP, but most independent experts estimated the attained figure to be 4–5%. The delay in announcing a third plan prompted some analysts to suggest that unforeseen problems had arisen. North Korea, which spent 20–25% of its GNP on the armed forces, had been obliged to seek foreign investment during the previous two years. However, President Kim's personal approaches to Japan and his government's traditional archenemy, the U.S., met with cool responses.

(THOMAS HON WING POLIN)

MONGOLIA

A landlocked people's republic of eastern Asia, Mongolia occupies the geographic area known as Outer Mongolia. Area: 1,565,000 sq km (604,000 sq mi). Pop. (1985 est.): 1,907,000. Cap.: Ulan Bator. Monetary unit: tugrik, with (Oct. 21, 1985) a nominal exchange rate of 3.35 tugriks to U.S. $1 (4.81 tugriks = £1 sterling). First secretary of the Mongolian People's Revolutionary (Communist) Party and chairman of the Presidium of the Great People's Hural (chief of state) in 1985, Zhambyn Batmunkh; chairman of the Council of Ministers (premier), Dumaagiyn Sodnom.

The top-level reshuffle of government posts that followed the removal of Mongolia's long-serving leader Yumzhagiyen Tsedenbal from power in August 1984 was completed during a session of the Great People's Hural in December of that year. Zhambyn Batmunkh (see BIOGRAPHIES), who had already replaced Tsedenbal as first secretary of the Mongolian People's Revolutionary (Communist) Party, was unanimously elected to the post of chairman of the Presidium of the Great People's Hural. Batmunkh was replaced as premier by Dumaagiyn Sodnom.

During 1985 Mongolia's close links with the U.S.S.R. appeared unaffected by the changes. On August 29, during a visit by Batmunkh to Moscow, Soviet leader Mikhail Gorbachev noted that cooperation between the two countries had spread to all sectors. Batmunkh pointed out that Mongolia was attempting to improve relations with China and was therefore interested in the consultations aimed at normalizing Sino-Soviet relations. The two leaders signed a 15-year agreement on political and economic cooperation.

Premier Sodnom's official visit to Poland in June 1985 was returned the following month when a delegation from the Polish Politburo spent a week in Mongolia. In September Foreign Minister Mangalyn Dugersuren traveled to Moscow to visit his new Soviet counterpart, Eduard Shevardnadze.

(K. M. SMOGORZEWSKI)

TAIWAN

Taiwan, which consists of the island of Taiwan (Formosa) and surrounding islands off the coast of China, is the seat of the Republic of China (Nationalist China). Area: 36,000 sq km (13,900 sq mi), including the island of Taiwan and its 85 outlying islands, 21 in the Taiwan group and 64 in the Pescadores group. Pop. (1985 est.): 19,135,000. (Area and population figures exclude the Quemoy and Matsu groups, which are administered as an occupied part of Fujian [Fukien] Province.) Cap.: Taipei. Monetary unit: new Taiwan dollar, with (Oct. 21, 1985) a free rate of NT$40.07 to U.S. $1 (NT$57.46 = £1 sterling). President in 1985, Chiang Ching-kuo; president of the Executive Yuan (premier), Yu Kuo-hwa.

The year 1985 proved to be a trying one for leaders on Taiwan. Economic uncertainties combined with mounting concern about the political succession to Pres. Chiang Ching-kuo, 75 years old and in questionable health. The increasing presence of China on the world scene accentuated Taiwan's growing diplomatic isolation. Officials in Taipei continued to resist pressures from the government in China to reach a political accommodation, regarding China's overtures as a subterfuge for Taiwan's eventual incorporation under Communist control. But trade tensions with the United States also clouded the island's position and long-term prospects, a fact underscored by the U.S. government's repeated denials of Taiwan's requests for new, advanced military hardware.

The behaviour of Taipei's internal security apparatus also proved highly vexing at home and abroad. A court found the former head of Taiwan's intelligence forces guilty of involvement in the late 1984 murder in California of Henry Liu, a Chinese-American writer who had written a highly critical book about Chiang Ching-kuo and his family. During a September visit to the island, a Taiwan publisher, now residing in the U.S., was arrested for allegedly distributing propaganda from the Chinese mainland, charges that she denied following her release on lesser charges. These activities prompted protests from the U.S. Department of State and the Congress and suggested erosion in U.S. political support for Taiwan, a crucial factor in maintaining the island's viability.

Major economic uncertainties were also of great con-

cern to the leadership. Protectionist sentiment and reduced external demand for Taiwan's products slowed economic growth from a robust 11% in 1984 to less than 5% in 1985. Taiwan was also under mounting pressure to open its markets much more fully to U.S. goods and services in the expectation that such steps would reduce a trade surplus with the United States that exceeded $10 billion in 1984. However, the small size of the domestic market precluded the possibility that increased internal demand could compensate fully for lost sales abroad. Business failures increased substantially, especially among firms already heavily in debt. In addition, Taiwan's largest savings and loan institution collapsed in February under the strain of mounting financial irregularities, causing the resignation of the nation's finance minister.

To counteract these trends and the continuing flight of capital, the government announced plans to spend approximately $20 billion for 14 major construction projects between 1985 and 1991. But this commitment to key projects was not expected to settle the uncertain economic outlook in the immediate future.

Despite these setbacks and the generally low morale among senior officials, the ruling Kuomintang (Nationalist Party) demonstrated continued political strength in November elections for local and provincial government offices, garnering nearly 70% of the vote. However, in more politically active Taipei the 11 opposition candidates all won handily, reflecting the growing vigour and assertiveness of nonparty politicians. Nor did the Kuomintang's electoral successes obscure the potential crisis associated with the impending succession to Chiang Ching-kuo. Although 62-year-old Vice-Pres. Lee Teng-hui (a Taiwan native and U.S.-trained agronomist) seemed a logical successor to some observers, others doubted that the former mainlanders, who had long been dominant within the Kuomintang, would permit it.

Underlying these domestic uncertainties was the challenge posed by the growing power of China. In the spring the government publicly acknowledged the existence of an increasingly robust trade (estimated as high as $1 billion) between China and Taiwan, which authorities in Taipei no longer actively curtailed. In late November Taiwan received a major setback when the Asian Development Bank announced plans to admit China to full membership.

(JONATHAN D. POLLACK)

South Asia

AFGHANISTAN

Afghanistan is a landlocked people's republic in central Asia. Area: 652,225 sq km (251,825 sq mi). Pop. (1985 est.): 18,120,-000 (though estimates vary, by 1984 the exodus to Pakistan and Iran accounted for approximately 4.5 million). Cap.: Kabul. Monetary unit: afghani, with (Oct. 21, 1985) a free rate of 69.04 afghanis to U.S. $1 (99 afghanis = £1 sterling). President of the Revolutionary Council in 1985, Babrak Karmal; prime minister, Sultan Ali Keshtmand.

Afghanistan was locked in military stalemate throughout 1985, with neither the Muslim insurgents nor the Soviet-backed government troops mounting any decisive military offensive, though there were numerous operations and

At a camp overlooking the ruins of their native village, Afghan rebels clean their weapons. The village was one of many destroyed by Soviet forces trying to cut off the flow of men, arms, and supplies from Pakistan.

ARTHUR BONNER/THE NEW YORK TIMES

clashes. The insurgents appeared better equipped than previously, with antiaircraft weapons in particular, in their efforts to counter government forces, who were aided by an estimated 115,000 Soviet soldiers. An antiguerrilla onslaught launched by the joint Soviet-Afghan military command in eastern Afghanistan in mid-August fell far short of success. However, the offensive, described by area experts as among the biggest since the Soviet intervention in 1979, brought the war closer to the Pakistani border, a fact that worried Islamabad. Afghanistan remained completely dependent on Moscow.

On the diplomatic front, the UN special representative for Afghanistan, Diego Cordovez, shuttled between Islamabad and Kabul. Three times during the year, in June, August, and December, he shuttled between separate rooms in the UN building in Geneva, meeting alternately with Afghan Foreign Minister Shah Mohammad Dost and his Pakistani counterpart, Sahabzada Yaqub Khan. The foreign ministers did not meet directly, since to do so would amount to recognition by Pakistan of Pres. Babrak Karmal's regime. Iran once again boycotted the talks but was kept informed. The last round of talks adjourned on December 19 to allow the parties to study new UN proposals. Earlier, the U.S. announced its willingness to act as guarantor of a settlement that would involve Soviet troop withdrawal and an end to U.S. aid to the guerrillas.

Reports on the ongoing war in Afghanistan were sketchy, often confusing, and contradictory. In the absence of impartial reports, the world press gained its information largely from Western diplomats and Kabul Radio. News also reached the West from visitors who toured Afghanistan clandestinely. There were several major clashes during the year. In January Soviet-Afghan troops launched an offensive in the provinces of Konarha, Nangarhar, and Paktia in eastern Afghanistan and Nimruz and Herat in the west, part of a move designed to cut off guerrilla supply routes. On March 23, according to resistance sources in Pakistan, some 400 Soviet and Afghan troops were killed when a series of chain-reaction explosions triggered by a time bomb engulfed a military convoy at Ollamd, near the Salang

tunnel. In April Western diplomats claimed that several hundred civilians had been killed in late March during Soviet-Afghan attacks in the provinces of Laghman in the east, Qonduz and Samangan in the north, and Herat. On June 12 at least 20 Afghan Air Force planes were blown up at Shindand air base in the western province of Farah. On September 4 an Afghan airliner traveling from Kabul to Farah crashed near Qandahar, killing all 52 people on board. The government blamed the guerrillas for the incident.

A UN report on human rights in Afghanistan accused Soviet forces in March of "bombarding villages, destroying food supplies, massacring civilians, and disregarding the Geneva convention." The report claimed that the government was holding 50,000 political prisoners and that tortures in jails were "commonplace." The government rejected the claims as "fabrication."

At home, President Karmal announced on January 10 that membership of the ruling Communist Party had increased from 16,000 at the time it came to power to 120,000. On the same day, Afghanistan marked the 20th anniversary of the party's founding. A three-day Loya Jirga (grand council) held on April 23–25 was attended by 1,796 delegates. This traditional national tribal assembly had not been convened since the 1979 coup.

On the international front, Kabul's relations with China and Iran deteriorated further. In August Foreign Minister Dost visited India, the only country outside the Soviet bloc with which relations improved.   (DILIP GANGULY)

BANGLADESH

A republic and member of the Commonwealth, Bangladesh is in the northeastern part of the Indian subcontinent, on the Bay of Bengal. Area: 143,998 sq km (55,598 sq mi). Pop. (1985 est.): 98.7 million. Cap.: Dhaka. Monetary unit: taka, with (Oct. 21, 1985) a free rate of 29.43 taka to U.S. $1 (42.20 taka = £1 sterling). President in 1985, Lieut. Gen. Hossain Mohammad Ershad; prime minister, Ataur Rahman Khan.

On May 24, 1985, Bangladesh suffered a devastating cyclone that drove huge tidal waves across the low-lying islands in the Ganges River delta. It was the worst natural disaster to hit the country since 1970, when a cyclone and tidal waves killed at least 200,000 people. According to unofficial estimates the death toll was as high as 40,000, but the official report, released two weeks after the disaster, numbered the dead at 4,264, with 17,000 houses destroyed and another 123,000 damaged. The government appealed for $50 million worth of foreign assistance to aid recovery. In addition to the immediate problems of providing food and shelter for survivors, there were longer-term concerns, such as buying seed for the next harvest to replace that which had been destroyed in the floods.

During the year Lieut. Gen. Hossain Mohammad Ershad ruled Bangladesh with a carrot-and-stick approach that brought some semblance of stability to his military regime and kept the fragmented opposition at bay. Following an opposition threat to boycott them, Ershad shelved plans to hold parliamentary and presidential elections in April. On March 1, announcing his decision to cancel the polls, Ershad reimposed full martial-law restrictions, including the banning of political activities. He claimed that he had conceded more to the opposition parties than was the case in any other country under martial law and berated the opposition for refusing to agree to his terms for holding elections in spite of this fact.

Ershad ordered a referendum to be held on March 21, when the people were asked to vote on the question of

Few survivors remained on Sandwip Island, one of many in the Ganges River delta, after huge cyclone-driven tidal waves swept the area in May, killing thousands and wiping out homes and crops.
AP/WIDE WORLD

whether they wished the president to remain in office. He faced severe criticism from the opposition and from the international press, who alleged that the polls were rigged and that the turnout had been minimal, perhaps as low as 10 or 15%. They dismissed the referendum as a "farce." According to the official results, however, 72% of the electorate voted, and almost 95% of those, some 33 million people, cast their votes in favour of Ershad's remaining in office. There were reports of at least one death during referendum-related violence.

On May 16 and 20 elections were held for council leaders in the *upazillas* (subdistricts), the new units of local government. The elections were held on a nonparty basis. At least 11 people died in violence connected with the polling. Two major opposition leaders, Sheikh Hasina Wajad of the Awami League and Begum Khalida Zia of the Bangladesh Nationalist Party, who had been placed under house arrest on March 2, were freed on May 25.

In July Minister of Finance Mohammad Syed ud-Zaman presented the 1985–86 budget; it totaled $1,390,000,000, an increase of $111 million over that of the previous year. The minister predicted in his budget speech that the country would face difficult times in the upcoming two years because of an "appreciable deterioration in the aid climate" and pledged to take steps to boost private-sector production and investment. In the meantime, Bangladesh continued to be deeply dependent on foreign-aid disbursements, which in 1984 accounted for 40% of the government's total resources. The World Bank's International Development Association had approved 94 interest-free loans totaling $3 billion.

On the international front, Bangladesh's relations with China continued to improve, with China pledging a loan worth 100 million yuan. During a visit by Ershad to China on July 4–9, he told a press conference that his country enjoyed a "very special relationship with China" and admitted that Bangladesh was receiving military aid from that country. Ershad also visited Japan, South Korea, Saudi Arabia, and Iraq during the year. A three-year pact on sharing the waters of the Ganges River was signed with India in November.   (DILIP GANGULY)

BHUTAN

The monarchy of Bhutan is a landlocked state situated in the eastern Himalayas between China and India. Area: 47,000 sq km (18,100 sq mi). Pop. (1985 est.): 1,423,000. Official cap., Thimphu; administrative cap., Paro. Monetary unit: ngultrum, at par with the Indian rupee (which is also in use), with (Oct. 21, 1985) a free rate of 11.92 ngultrums to U.S. $1 (17.10 ngultrums = £1 sterling). Druk gyalpo (king) in 1985, Jigme Singye Wangchuk.

The tiny kingdom of Bhutan was thrust into the international limelight in July 1985 when it was the site for talks between the Sri Lankan government and Tamil separatists campaigning for autonomy of Tamil-dominated areas in Sri Lanka. Though the talks failed to end the dispute, Bhutan received prominence as a nation in attempting to bring about a resolution.

The country's first permanent representative to the UN and its associated bodies presented credentials on April 24. In a major development, on November 5 Bhutan established its first diplomatic links with countries outside South Asia—Denmark, Sweden, and Switzerland. South Asian foreign ministers met in Thimphu on May 13–14 to discuss plans to establish the South Asian Association for Regional Cooperation, which was inaugurated in December.

Bhutan's cordial relations with India were further consolidated by King Jigme Singye Wangchuk's visit to New Delhi in February and Indian Prime Minister Rajiv Gandhi's trip to Bhutan in September. The announcement on May 15 that Bhutan had no plans to establish diplomatic relations with China allayed one of India's major fears. However, the government pursued talks with China aimed at demarcating 500 km (310 mi) of their common boundary. Bhutan claimed its boundaries were well defined in historical and geographic terms.   (DILIP GANGULY)

This article updates the *Micropædia* article BHUTAN.

INDIA

A federal republic of southern Asia and member of the Commonwealth, India is situated on a peninsula extending into the Indian Ocean with the Arabian Sea to the west and the Bay of Bengal to the east. Area: 3,064,063 sq km (1,183,041 sq mi), excluding the Indian-occupied portion of Jammu and Kashmir. Pop. (1985 est.): 768 million, including Indian-occupied Jammu and Kashmir. Cap.: New Delhi. Monetary unit: rupee, with (Oct. 21, 1985) a free rate of Rs 11.92 to U.S. $1 (Rs 17.10 = £1 sterling). President in 1985, Zail Singh; prime minister, Rajiv Gandhi.

Domestic Affairs. In India 1985 was the year of Rajiv Gandhi, of political reconciliation, and of new moves in economic policy. Succeeding his murdered mother, Indira Gandhi, on Oct. 31, 1984, the young prime minister established himself within 12 months as a resourceful, dynamic, and farsighted leader. The election he ordered in December 1984 to the Lok Sabha (lower house of the national Parliament) gave his party, the Congress (I), a record 401 seats out of the 515 for which polling took place—a higher proportion than it had secured under either Jawaharlal Nehru or Indira Gandhi. The Council of Ministers that he formed on December 31 confirmed that Rajiv Gandhi was a man with a mind of his own. He followed this up by announcing that finding solutions to the problems of Sikh separatism in the Punjab and agitation against immigrants in Assam would be his highest priority. Another early move of the new government was a bill to ban defections from parties. The bill was unanimously adopted by Parliament in January.

Elections to assemblies were held in the first week of March in 11 states and one union territory (Pondicherry). The Congress (I) won in Bihar (192 seats out of 324), Gujarat (149 out of 182), Himachal Pradesh (55 out of 68), Madhya Pradesh (250 out of 320), Maharashtra (162 out of 288), Orissa (117 out of 147), Rajasthan (113 out of 200), Uttar Pradesh (266 out of 425), and Pondicherry (15 out of 30). In Karnataka the Janata Party under Ramakrishna Hegde emerged victorious; in Andhra Pradesh the Telugu Desam of N. T. Rama Rao retained power; and in Sikkim the Sikkim Sangram Parishad under N. B. Bhandari swept the polls.

In a surprise move the Madhya Pradesh chief minister, Arjun Singh, was appointed governor of Punjab on March 12, with Motilal Vora succeeding him. A day earlier several leaders of the Akali Dal, which was agitating for an autonomous Sikh state, had been released from jail. In April a judicial inquiry was ordered into the riots that took place in New Delhi after the assassination of Indira Gandhi. Negotiations undertaken through the governor of Punjab resulted in the signing on July 24 of an agreement between Sant Harchand Singh Longowal (*see* OBITUARIES), president of the Akali Dal, and Prime Minister Gandhi. The agreement reaffirmed that the city of Chandigarh would go to Punjab and that certain Hindi-speaking areas of Punjab would be transferred to neighbouring Haryana state on the advice of a commission. It also entrusted to a Supreme Court judge the question of the sharing of river waters between Punjab and Haryana.

While the agreement was widely welcomed, it was not to the liking of extremists. Terrorists continued their attacks throughout the year, one of their victims being the head priest of the Akal Takht in the Golden Temple, Amritsar. Nearly 80 people were killed in New Delhi, Haryana, and Uttar Pradesh in simultaneous bomb explosions on May 10. The country was stunned when an Air-India jet crashed into the Atlantic Ocean off Ireland on June 23 with 329 persons aboard. There were no survivors. It was widely believed that the aircraft had been blown up by Sikh extremists, although commissions of inquiry had not given their verdict by the end of the year. The chain of killings did not stop with the signing of the accord. On July 31 Lalit Maken, a member of Parliament, was gunned down; and on August 20, three days after plans to hold elections in Punjab were announced, Sant Longowal was assassinated while addressing a meeting.

Elections in Punjab went ahead as planned on September 25. Polling proved to be peaceful and heavy, in spite of a boycott call by extremists. The Akali Dal secured 73 out of 117 seats in the state assembly as against 32 seats won by Congress (I). A Dal government, headed by Surjit Singh Barnala, was sworn in. Elections were also held to fill Punjab's 13 seats in the Lok Sabha; the Dal won 7 and the Congress (I) 6.

On August 15 a settlement of the long-drawn-out problem of foreigners (emigrants from Bangladesh) in Assam was reached. It was decided that for the purpose of detecting foreigners and deleting their names from the electoral roll in the state, Jan. 1, 1966, would be regarded as the base date. The names of foreigners who had entered the state between then and March 24, 1971, would be deleted from existing electoral rolls and would be restored on the expiration of a ten-year period. Foreigners who had arrived after March 25, 1971, would be expelled. Elections were held to the state assembly on December 16. The Assam Gana Parishad, formed by the parties and groups that had carried on the agitation, won 63 of the 125 seats, while Congress (I) won 23 and the United Minorities Front 17.

Gujarat was in the grip of violent agitation for several months after the state government announced that concessions reserved for the scheduled castes would be extended to some other backward castes. When Madhavsinh Solanki stepped down as chief minister in July, tempers finally cooled. He was succeeded by Amarsinh Chowdhury. Changes took place in the chief ministerships of Maharashtra, where Shivajirao Patil Nilangekar took over from Vasantdada Patil in June, and of Uttar Pradesh, where Bir Bahadur Singh succeeded Narayan Dutt Tiwari in September. Earlier, after the state assembly elections in March, Bindeshwari Dubey was sworn in as chief minister in Bihar and Harideo Joshi gained the post in Rajasthan. On September 25 Rajiv Gandhi carried out a major reshuffle of the Council of Ministers. Bali Ram Bhagat, Narayan Dutt Tiwari, and A. B. A. Ghani Khan Chowdhury were made ministers of external affairs, industry, and program implementation, respectively. Gandhi took over the defense portfolio from P. V. Narasimha Rao, who was appointed to the newly created Ministry of Human Resource Development. In November Arjun Singh resigned as governor of Punjab to take up the post of minister of commerce.

Among other major political moves during the year was the enactment of a bill to permit donations from companies to political parties and the introduction of a bill to appoint an ombudsman to investigate complaints against holders of high political office. A bill to prevent terrorist and disruptive activities was also enacted, and a stringent law was adopted to deal with the drug menace.

In January India was rocked by the revelation that secret papers had been stolen from the Prime Minister's Office and given to foreign governments. Many employees were arrested. In an important verdict the Supreme Court ruled that women divorced under Muslim law were entitled to maintenance. The Jawaharlal Nehru award for international understanding was conferred upon Bruno Kreisky, former chancellor of Austria, and, posthumously, on Indira Gandhi. She was also awarded the Lenin Prize by the U.S.S.R. and the José Martí Order of Cuba. India filed a suit in the U.S. against Union Carbide Corp. for compensation for the victims of the poison-gas tragedy at Bhopal in 1984. Celebrations of the centenary of the Indian National Congress took place in December.

The Economy. The union government budget, presented on March 16, contained a new approach to direct taxes. It reduced the highest income-tax level to 50% and raised the exemption limit. Total receipts during 1985–86 were set at Rs 479,460,000,000, including Rs 3,110,000,000 from new taxes and Rs 21,440,000,000 from external loans. Total disbursements were estimated at Rs 512,950,000,000, leaving a deficit of Rs 33,490,000,000. The allocation for defense was Rs 93.9 billion and that for the development plan Rs 185,090,000,000.

A meeting of the national development council in November adopted the draft of the seventh five-year (1985–90) plan. The plan envisioned an outlay of Rs 1.8 trillion by the union and state governments during the five-year period, with priority being given to agriculture, industrial modernization, and programs providing direct assistance to the poor. The plan aimed at an annual growth rate of 5% and the creation of 40 million jobs over five years.

Foreign Policy. A conference of India, Argentina, Greece, Mexico, Sweden, and Tanzania was held in New Delhi in January to pursue a six-nation disarmament initiative. It called on nuclear powers to halt all tests, refrain from adding to their stockpiles, and start a dialogue on disarmament. In March Prime Minister Gandhi attended the funeral of Soviet leader Konstantin Chernenko in Moscow. He paid an official visit to the U.S.S.R. in May and held wide-ranging talks with the new leader, Mikhail Gorbachev. A 1 billion ruble credit and an agreement on scientific and technical cooperation until the year 2000 were signed.

The following month Gandhi visited Egypt, France, Algeria, the U.S., and Switzerland. In Washington he held talks with Pres. Ronald Reagan and also addressed a joint session of the U.S. Congress. Discussions were held on closer cooperation between the two countries in several fields of advanced technology, for which a memorandum was signed. Gandhi also paid brief visits to Bangladesh and Bhutan. In October he went on a visit to the U.K., The Bahamas (to attend the Commonwealth heads of government meeting), Cuba, the UN (for its 40th anniversary celebrations), and The Netherlands. On his return trip he went to Moscow. In November he visited Vietnam and Japan. Before his trips to the U.S. and the U.K., the governments of both countries announced that they had uncovered and foiled plots to kill Gandhi.

The desire to improve relations with Pakistan appeared to be blocked by concern about Pakistan's intentions regarding the production of nuclear weapons and its alleged support of extremists. Talks were held with a Chinese delegation in November on the border question. The trouble

BALDEV—SYGMA

Four weeks after signing an agreement with Indian Prime Minister Rajiv Gandhi that was to end three years of confrontation with the government, Sant Harchand Singh Longowal, president of the Sikh political party Akali Dal, was shot dead by two Sikh extremists. Thousands of mourners joined the procession to his funeral pyre.

in Sri Lanka between Tamils, whose traditional home was India, and the government of Sri Lanka continued to cause anxiety. The two sides held several meetings under Indian auspices, and a cease-fire was arranged. An extraordinary meeting of the coordinating bureau of nonaligned countries was held in April in New Delhi. India also participated in the inauguration of the South Asian Association for Regional Cooperation in Dhaka, Bangladesh, in December.

Among notable foreign visitors to India were Presidents Raúl Alfonsín of Argentina, Miguel de la Madrid of Mexico, Julius Nyerere of Tanzania, Junius Jayawardene of Sri Lanka, Maumoon Abdul Gayoom of the Maldives, Hammer DeRoburt of Nauru, and Zia-ul-Haq of Pakistan and Prime Ministers Olof Palme of Sweden, Andreas Papandreou of Greece, Gen. Wojciech Jaruzelski of Poland, Milka Planinc of Yugoslavia, Aneerood Jugnauth of Mauritius, Margaret Thatcher of the U.K., David Lange of New Zealand, and George Chambers of Trinidad and Tobago.

(H. Y. SHARADA PRASAD)

MALDIVES

A republic and member of the Commonwealth in the Indian Ocean, the Maldives consists of about 2,000 small islands southwest of the southern tip of India. Area: 298 sq km (115 sq mi). Pop. (1985): 181,453. Cap.: Male. Monetary unit: rufiyaa, with (Oct. 21,1985) a free rate of 7.04 rufiyaa to U.S. $1 (10.10 rufiyaa = £1 sterling). President in 1985, Maumoon Abdul Gayoom.

Faced with a rate of population increase of 3% a year, and with 45% of the people under the age of 15, the government of the Maldives was granted virtually no margin for error in its economic planning. Per capita income, which had actually declined during the 1970s, stood at $470 in 1985. Tourism was rapidly establishing itself as the most important economic activity in the islands as the number of visitors increased to about 50,000 a year. Other important contributors to the economy included fishing, shipping, coconut processing, and agriculture.

As one of the smallest and geographically most diffuse island states in the world, the Maldives was well qualified to comment on the problems faced by very small nations. In this connection it regarded membership in the Commonwealth as particularly valuable because the organization regarded the matter as one worthy of concern. Indeed, the Maldives was a member of a Commonwealth study group established to investigate the issue. The group's findings were presented to the Commonwealth heads of government meeting held at Nassau, The Bahamas, in October. Pres. Maumoon Abdul Gayoom represented the Maldives at the heads of government meeting for the first time.

(GUY ARNOLD)

This article updates the *Macropædia* article INDIAN OCEAN ISLANDS: *Maldives*.

NEPAL

A constitutional monarchy, Nepal is a landlocked country in the Himalayas between India and the Tibetan Autonomous Region of China. Area: 147,181 sq km (56,812 sq mi). Pop. (1985 est.): 16,525,000. Cap.: Kathmandu. Monetary unit: Nepalese rupee, with (Oct. 21, 1985) a free rate of NRs 18.28 to U.S. $1 (NRs 26.22 = £1 sterling). King, Birendra Bir Bikram Shah Deva; prime minister in 1985, Lokendra Bahadur Chand.

In June 1985 terrorism spread to Nepal when a series of bomb attacks killed eight people, including a member of Parliament, and triggered a government crackdown. A previously unknown group called United Liberation Torch-bearers claimed responsibility. Police detained more than 1,500 people amid reports that Nepalese antimonarchists based in India were the architects of the bloodletting. The opposition continued to protest against the partyless government system, and during the year more than 4,000 opposition supporters were arrested.

Relations with China continued to improve. In June a $19 million water conservation and irrigation project built with Chinese aid was inaugurated. The two countries signed a memorandum of understanding in March to open the border between Tibet and Nepal to foreign visitors. Relations with India remained friendly and did not show any remarkable shift. King Birendra Bir Bikram Shah Deva visited India in September. The king appointed Randhir Subba to replace the ailing Padma Bahadur Khatri as foreign affairs minister in May.

On the economic front the government announced a major shift from agriculture to industry and energy in the seventh five-year (1985–90) plan, which began on July 16. The $2.8 billion program was to be financed by foreign grants and loans.

(DILIP GANGULY)

PAKISTAN

A federal republic, Pakistan is in the northwestern part of the Indian subcontinent, on the Arabian Sea. Area: 796,095 sq km (307,374 sq mi), excluding the Pakistani-controlled section of Jammu and Kashmir. Pop. (1985 est., including some 3 million Afghan refugees and 1.6 million residents of Pakistani-controlled Jammu and Kashmir): 100,356,000. Cap.: Islamabad. Monetary unit: Pakistan rupee, with (Oct. 21, 1985) a free rate of PRs 15.83 to U.S. $1 (PRs 22.70 = £1 sterling). President in 1985, Gen. Mohammad Zia-ul-Haq; prime minister from March 24, Mohammad Khan Junejo.

Official results of the referendum held in Pakistan on Dec. 19, 1984, revealed that 97.7% of voters in a turnout of 62% had approved the islamization policy of Pres. Mohammad Zia-ul-Haq and the continuation of his chosen course in transferring power to an elected assembly. Zia interpreted the vote as a mandate to remain in office as president for a further five years. However, opposition leaders accused the government of ballot rigging on a massive scale.

Undeterred by opposition criticism, on Jan. 12, 1985, Zia announced a six-point islamization plan and elections to provincial and national assemblies. The 11-party opposition grouping, the Movement for the Restoration of Democracy (MRD), boycotted the elections because the ban on political activities had not been lifted. In a government crackdown during the week before polling day, many MRD leaders were jailed or placed under house arrest. The government admitted that 369 people had been arrested, but the MRD alleged that the total was at least 1,500. At least ten people died in election-day violence. Although elections to the National Assembly, which took place on February 25, were conducted on a nonparty basis, an official analysis of the results revealed that the greatest number of seats had been won by supporters of the Pakistan People's Party (PPP)—the party of the executed former prime minister Zulfikar Ali Bhutto—and the Muslim League. Voters expressed disapproval of the government by failing to return five of the nine ministers in the Cabinet.

Before Parliament assembled on March 23, Zia restored some of the suspended 1973 constitution; he also introduced constitutional amendments that increased the power of the president at the expense of the prime minister and prevented any presidential order that Zia had made since coming to power in 1977 from being altered or repealed without the sanction of the president. On March 24 the National Assembly gave a vote of confidence to the new

A traffic accident in Karachi, Pakistan, in April turned into a six-day riot whose targets were chiefly Pashtuns, an ethnic minority with ties to Afghanistan. At least 50 people died and 250 were injured.
SANDRO TUCCI—GAMMA/LIAISON

prime minister, Mohammad Khan Junejo. Opposition leaders were again placed under house arrest in September when the Assembly debated the controversial indemnity bill, which sought to legalize all decisions made by Zia and the military courts during the years of martial law. The bill was passed on October 16 after the government offered a compromise amendment limiting the power of the military in future administrations. Zia officially declared martial law at an end on December 30.

Benazir Bhutto, daughter of the late prime minister and leader of the PPP, ended 19 months of self-imposed exile when she returned to Pakistan on August 21. She returned for the burial of her brother, Shahnawaz Bhutto, a leader of the Al Zulfikar guerrilla group, who had died under mysterious circumstances the previous month in Cannes, France. Within days of her arrival Benazir Bhutto was placed under house arrest. She was later allowed to leave the country again. The military courts handed down stiff punishments on a number of occasions during the year to people found guilty of plotting against the regime. In March life sentences (25 years under Pakistani laws) were passed on 54 people, allegedly members of Al Zulfikar.

Relations with India, increasingly uneasy during the year, were improved by Zia's visit to New Delhi in December, during which he and Prime Minister Rajiv Gandhi pledged not to attack one another's nuclear installations. In September the U.S. revealed a proposal to sell $103 million worth of arms to Pakistan. Although the conflict in Afghanistan advanced closer to Pakistan's borders during the year, this produced no discernible change in relations with the U.S.S.R. There was marked improvement in relations with China.

The economy performed well in 1985. On May 23 a balanced budget with no deficit financing was presented for 1985–86. The Aid-to-Pakistan Consortium met in Paris on May 6–7 and pledged assistance worth $2.1 billion; Pakistan had requested $1.8 billion.   (DILIP GANGULY)

SRI LANKA

A republic and member of the Commonwealth, Sri Lanka occupies an island in the Indian Ocean off the southeast coast of peninsular India. Area: 65,610 sq km (25,332 sq mi). Pop. (1985 est.): 16,109,000. Cap., Colombo; capital designate, Sri Jayawardenapura. Monetary unit: Sri Lanka rupee, with (Oct. 21, 1985) a free rate of SL Rs 27.30 to U.S. $1 (SL Rs 39.15 = £1 sterling). President in 1985, Junius Richard Jayawardene; prime minister, Ranasingne Premadasa.

Sri Lanka entered its third successive year of emergency rule during 1985 as a section of the Tamil community continued its ten-year-old campaign for an autonomous Tamil state in the north and east of the country. The first half of the year was dominated by fierce clashes between Tamil militants and the national security forces, most of whom were drawn from the country's Sinhalese majority, and the second half by negotiations aimed at resolving the ethnic conflict. In July the government claimed to have foiled a Tamil attempt to assassinate Pres. Junius Jayawardene.

On June 18 the government and a number of Tamil guerrilla groups agreed to cease hostilities until mid-September in an effort to reach a peaceful settlement. Peace talks took place in July and August at Thimphu, Bhutan, under the auspices of the Indian government. However, the second round broke down on August 17 when all six participating Tamil organizations walked out in protest after the two sides traded charges of truce violations. Although the talks failed to produce results, they at least succeeded in bringing each side to a greater understanding of the other. On September 16 the government announced a unilateral

AP/WIDE WORLD

Near Paranthan in northern Sri Lanka, a group of young Tamil recruits learn the use of automatic rifles and grenade launchers as part of a six-month training course conducted by a Tamil separatist organization opposed to the Sinhalese-dominated national government.

extension of the cessation of hostilities for an indefinite period, and later it accepted in part a Tamil proposal to enlarge the multiracial committee that was monitoring the cease-fire.

The government admitted that defense spending had increased tenfold to almost $600,000 a day since the start of the upsurge in ethnic violence. The economy was also suffering from a slump in tourism and from the disruption of road, rail, and sea transport. Economists warned of possible long-term consequences, including both a brain and a capital drain and loss of confidence among investors.

In April Margaret Thatcher became the first British prime minister to visit Sri Lanka in 25 years.

(DILIP GANGULY)

Southeast Asia

SOUTHEAST ASIAN AFFAIRS

During 1985, for the seventh successive year, the diplomatic calendar of Southeast Asia was dominated by efforts to resolve the conflict over Kampuchea, where the regime was supported by some 170,000 Vietnamese troops. This activity intensified after Hanoi mounted its fiercest ever dry-season military offensive against Khmer resistance guerrillas between November 1984 and April 1985 and knocked out all their major bases near the border with Thailand. (See *Kampuchea,* below.) A number of political initiatives issued from both major camps involved in the conflict: the Association of Southeast Asian Nations (ASEAN), which supported the Democratic Kampuchea (DK) resistance coalition, and Vietnam-led Indochina.

Sensing military victory, the foreign ministers of Vietnam, Laos, and the Phnom Penh regime met in Ho Chi Minh City, Vietnam, in mid-January to chart a diplomatic course. They put forward what they described as a new proposal to break the deadlock. Its chief elements were a withdrawal of Vietnamese forces from Kampuchea and the holding of internationally monitored elections, provided the "genocidal clique" headed by Pol Pot of the Khmer Rouge, one of the three parties in the DK resistance coalition, was eliminated. The foreign ministers also suggested an international conference on Kampuchea, to consist not only of regional and global powers but of other nations, such as Australia and Sweden, that had "contributed to peace in Southeast Asia." However, ASEAN officials were skeptical about the plan, seeing little in it that was new. "The proposal," in the words of one Thai diplomat, "was probably intended to deflect international criticism of the suffering inflicted upon masses of Kampuchean refugees by Hanoi's soldiers during their attacks on Khmer resistance camps."

Australian Foreign Minister William (Bill) Hayden tried to mediate the dispute by flying to Indochina in March and giving the proposal a sympathetic hearing. Not surprisingly, Hayden met a cool reception when he subsequently arrived in Thailand to elaborate on the Indochinese plan. That same week Thailand had complained that Vietnamese troops had entered its territory and clashed with its Army. Hanoi's leaders had denied the allegation to Hayden. After being shown videotaped evidence supporting Thailand's claim when he was in Bangkok, Hayden admitted that

he had been misled by Vietnam. The Australian initiative stalled.

In April an ASEAN effort was launched when Malaysia suggested proximity talks between representatives of the UN-recognized DK resistance coalition and the Phnom Penh regime. The proposal was designed to overcome Phnom Penh's refusal to meet the Khmer Rouge by bringing the two sides to a common venue but keeping them in different rooms, where communications would be effected through a neutral mediator. Although ASEAN governments showed interest, at the end of May Indonesian Foreign Minister Mochtar Kusumaatmadja proposed a separate peace plan, with the normalization of relations between Vietnam and the U.S. as its centrepiece. Seen at first as a competitive move on Jakarta's part, Mochtar's proposal was later presented as being complementary to the Malaysian one.

Initially the proposal to hold proximity talks envisaged discussions between the two warring Khmer sides only. By the time it had been officially endorsed at the annual meeting of ASEAN foreign ministers in July, however, it had undergone a significant change. The modified version proposed that DK representatives meet officials not only from Phnom Penh but also from Hanoi. A senior ASEAN official said the DK had rejected the original initiative on the grounds that it was not involved in a civil war, and therefore it wished to talk directly with the aggressor, Vietnam. Though Hanoi did not formally reject proximity talks, the Vietnamese media referred to the idea in derogatory terms. According to well-informed sources, the Vietnamese had been interested in the first version but found the second unacceptable.

The communiqué issued at the end of the ASEAN foreign ministers' conference included other references to Indochina. It deplored the latest Vietnamese dry-season offensive that had driven a quarter of a million Khmer refugees into Thailand and drew attention to their plight. It also noted "with serious concern" Hanoi's use of Kampuchean forced labour in war zones.

Indonesia further developed its designated role as ASEAN's interlocutor with Vietnam on the Kampuchean issue. Relations between Jakarta and Hanoi continued to improve, culminating in November in reciprocal visits by trade delegations and a decision to resume direct commerce. However, controversy broke out within ASEAN earlier in the year when Gen. Benny Murdani, chief of the Indonesian armed forces, remarked after a visit by Vietnamese Defense Minister Gen. Van Tien Dung that Jakarta would step up its military ties with Hanoi.

The U.S.S.R., already involved in the Kampuchean conflict through its ally, Vietnam, sought a higher diplomatic profile in the region to complement its broadened military presence. During a month-long tour of Southeast Asian capitals, Soviet Deputy Foreign Minister Mikhail Kapitsa said that Moscow was prepared to act as a guarantor of peace once the region's key nations had settled the Kampuchean issue. The offer, however, was not well received. ASEAN members became increasingly uncomfortable as the U.S.S.R. continued its military buildup at strategic points in the Indian Ocean, the sea-lanes of East Asia, and the former U.S. naval base at Cam Ranh, Vietnam. To meet the perceived threat to security posed by the arrival of Soviet MiG-21 and MiG-23 fighter aircraft in Ho Chi Minh City and Kampuchea, the Malaysian Air Force was to buy 40 Skyhawks over several years, while Thailand was seeking to acquire sophisticated F-16 jet fighters from the U.S. With virtually full access to the Cam Ranh and Da Nang bases on Vietnam's coast, the Soviets were able

A Thai soldier hails a Vietnamese soldier, to warn him that he is intruding on Thai territory. Thailand's border with Kampuchea remained tense through the year as a result of Vietnamese operations against Kampuchean guerrillas and refugees.

REUTERS/BETTMANN NEWSPHOTOS

to maintain medium-range Tu-16 Badger bombers, long-range patrol craft, and several submarines in the Pacific Ocean. They were also well positioned to conduct maritime surveillance and to gather intelligence on radar and air defenses throughout Southeast Asia.

The increase in Soviet activities put pressure on the U.S. to raise its own profile in the region, which had been low ever since the U.S. military withdrawal from Vietnam in 1975. In July the U.S. Congress passed a bill that would allow $5 million in aid to the two non-Communist partners of the DK resistance coalition. In a significant shift from its previous stance, the U.S. administration stated that it would no longer refuse military assistance to the resistance forces.

While busily cultivating trade and business links with non-Communist Southeast Asia, China was less active than usual on the diplomatic scene. Nonetheless, a significant milestone was passed when Chinese Foreign Minister Wu Xueqian (Wu Hsueh-ch'ien) went to Indonesia in April to meet President Suharto and Foreign Minister Mochtar. Though the meetings produced no substantive breakthrough, they marked the first time since bilateral relations were suspended in 1967 that top-level officials from the two countries had met on either's home territory. Later, Jakarta and Beijing (Peking) announced the resumption of direct trade links. The progress of Sino-Indonesian relations was watched closely by the other members of ASEAN.

Links between Japan and the region were bedeviled by growing frustration over the trade pattern that had developed between them. At a meeting in June of economics ministers from all the nations concerned, ASEAN officials characterized the pattern as "distorted" and "lopsided." Some 90% of ASEAN's exports to Japan consisted of raw materials and primary products, while a similar proportion of Japanese exports to the region was made up of manufactured goods. The conference even heard references to Tokyo's wartime attempt to colonize Southeast Asia.

Though ASEAN's economic performance in 1985 remained superior to that of the rest of the world, it slipped noticeably from the levels of the previous year. For much of 1985 growth rates for exports and gross national prod-

uct fell short of projections. Prime reasons included sluggish commodity prices and slow economic performance by ASEAN's major trading partners. The latter factor in turn fueled a high tide of protectionist sentiment in Western countries, particularly the U.S. Throughout the year ASEAN countries joined the chorus of protest from Asia against the protectionist laws being introduced by the U.S. Congress. The battle against a controversial bill that threatened to cut deeply into East and Southeast Asia's textile exports to the U.S. was especially heated. In October, just before the House of Representatives voted on the bill, Prime Minister Lee Kuan Yew of Singapore made an impassioned, lucid speech on the dangers of protectionism before the full U.S. Congress. The bill passed, but it failed to muster the two-thirds majority needed to override the veto that Pres. Ronald Reagan had promised to exercise if necessary.   (THOMAS HON WING POLIN)

BRUNEI

The sultanate of Brunei is located on the northern coast of the island of Borneo, on the South China Sea. Area: 5,765 sq km (2,226 sq mi). Pop. (1985 est.): 224,000. Cap.: Bandar Seri Begawan. Monetary unit: Brunei dollar, with (Oct. 14, 1985) a free rate of Br$2.13 to U.S. $1 (Br$3.06 = £1 sterling). Sultan and prime minister in 1985, Sir Muda Hassanal Bolkiah Mu'izzadin Waddaulah.

Potentially one of the most important developments in the public life of Brunei in 1985 was the formation of the Brunei National Democratic Party (BNDP), the sultanate's sole political party. The move was seen by some analysts as a possible harbinger of a livelier political climate in the oil-rich state, ruled by the absolute monarch Sultan Sir Muda Hassanal Bolkiah. While the BNDP supported an "Islamic monarchy," it also pledged to struggle for a more open administration (currently both the government and Parliament were dominated by the royal family). The new party, which planned to press for elections "soon," had apparently attracted a number of local Malay intellectuals into its ranks.

In general, Brunei's citizens remained content with their rulers, largely because the sultanate's oil wealth enabled the establishment of a generous, cradle-to-grave welfare program. Dominating the generation of that wealth was the Brunei Shell Petroleum Co. (BSPC), owned half by the Royal Dutch/Shell group and half by the government. In 1985 the government set in motion plans to exert greater control over the industry, which produced 99% of the country's exports. One plan was for the creation of a government energy-control board to oversee BSPC's operations.   (THOMAS HON WING POLIN)

This article updates the *Macropædia* article EAST INDIES: *Brunei.*

BURMA

Burma is a people's republic of Southeast Asia with coastlines on the Bay of Bengal and the Andaman Sea. Area: 676,577 sq km (261,228 sq mi). Pop. (1985 est.): 37,686,000. Cap.: Rangoon. Monetary unit: kyat, with (Oct. 21, 1985) a free rate of 7.67 kyats to U.S. $1 (11 kyats = £1 sterling). Chairman of the State Council in 1985, U San Yu; prime minister, U Maung Maung Kha.

Rebels opposed to the Burmese government blew up a passenger train traveling between Rangoon and Mandalay on July 24, 1985, killing 67 people and injuring at least 100 others. The blast was caused by a land mine powerful enough to derail six coaches and the engine. Area experts

believed that the explosion was the worst single act of sabotage against a civilian target during the rule of the Burma Socialist Program Party. In a similar incident, a troop train was blown up near Port Moulmein in May. Though no organization claimed responsibility for the explosions, the government believed that Karen insurgents were behind them. The Karens were one of several groups—others were the Burmese Communists, Kachin, Shan, Lahu, and Karenni (Kayah)—resisting the government, which was dominated by ethnic Burmese.

In February a security operation involving more than 3,000 troops was launched against insurgents who controlled the opium trade in eastern Burma. Though the outcome of the offensive was not made public, there were reports of clashes with rebels in several locations. Besides dealing in drugs, the smugglers exchanged Burmese gold, teak, gems, tin ore, and cattle for manufactured goods from Thailand and guns from unknown sources.

When Chinese Pres. Li Xiannian (Li Hsien-nien) visited Burma in March, the New China News Agency described the occasion as a "major event" in Sino-Burmese relations. In May Pres. Mohammad Zia-ul-Haq became the first Pakistani head of state to visit Burma in a quarter of a century. During his trip to Rangoon in July, Khurshi Alam Khan, India's junior external affairs minister, said Indo-Burmese relations were "excellent."　　(DILIP GANGULY)

INDONESIA

A republic of Southeast Asia, Indonesia consists of the major islands of Sumatra, Java, Kalimantan (Indonesian Borneo), Celebes, and Irian Jaya (West New Guinea) and approximately 3,000 smaller islands and islets. Area: 1,919,443 sq km (741,101 sq mi). Pop. (1985 est.): 167,550,000. (Area and population figures include former Portuguese Timor.) Cap.: Jakarta. Monetary unit: rupiah, with (Oct. 21, 1985) a free rate of 1,121.22 rupiah to U.S. $1 (1,607.83 rupiah = £1 sterling). President in 1985, Suharto.

The main theme of Indonesia's domestic affairs in 1985 was the government's ongoing campaign to bring all spheres of national life under its secular ideology, *pancasila* (the five principles: belief in a supreme deity, nationalism, democracy, humanitarianism, and social justice). A climax was reached in May when a controversial law was passed by Parliament requiring all civic and religious bodies to adopt *pancasila* as their sole guiding principle within two years. Groups that received funds from abroad without official clearance, aided foreigners threatening to harm the nation's interests, or professed anti-*pancasila* doctrines (Communism was the only one named outright) could be disbanded. Though the law stipulated that the state creed would not regulate the observance of religious duties, some faith-based groups and political parties remained concerned about interference, noting that the government was empowered to "guide" organizations. Such worries were widely believed to have been a key motivation behind a series of mysterious bombings and fires that began in late 1984 and continued into 1985. However, most groups apparently sympathized with the authorities' underlying goal of preserving national unity by dampening Muslim fundamentalist or secessionist ambitions.

The government's determination to act against extremist-inspired violence became apparent when the trials of more than 40 people charged with involvement in the bombing incidents began in January. The testimony indicated that the violence had been sparked by a volatile mix of emotions: frustration that the authorities were taking control of Islam and resentment that Indonesia's ethnic Chinese continued to dominate the national economy. After five

months of court hearings, nine defendants were found guilty of participation in the bomb attacks, including H. M. Sanusi, a former Cabinet minister. Meanwhile, attacks on some of the country's major buildings continued. A historic palace in central Java was burned down in January, barely a week after unexplained explosions damaged the world-renowned Buddhist temple at Borobudur. The headquarters of Radio Indonesia and a shopping complex in Jakarta were razed in separate incidents in July.

Having consolidated its position at home, President Suharto's administration clearly indicated its desire to play a more prominent role on the international stage. The highlight of the year took place in April when Indonesia was host to the commemoration of the watershed Afro-Asian Conference held in Bandung, Java, 30 years earlier. Some 240 delegates, representing more than 80 nations, 4 liberation movements, and three-quarters of the world's population, gathered in Java to draft a new Bandung declaration. Of particular interest was the presence of Chinese Foreign Minister Wu Xueqian (Wu Hsüeh-ch'ien). His talks with Suharto marked the first contact at such high levels between the two governments since bilateral relations were frozen 18 years earlier, after Jakarta accused Beijing (Peking) of fomenting an abortive coup attempt. Later the two countries agreed to reopen bilateral trade links.

The year was one of continued moderate economic growth, despite soft world oil prices and rising protectionism in the developed countries. In his budget for fiscal 1985–86, Suharto set total expenditure at 23,046,000,000,-000 rupiah, an increase of 12% over the previous year. Growth in gross domestic product recovered in 1984 to about 5%, more than twice the low of 2.2% in 1982. However, more domestic and foreign business investment was deemed necessary. The Indonesia Commodity Exchange began trading in April, and in the same month the new $600 million international airport opened at Cengkareng, some 25 km (15.5 mi) west of Jakarta.

(THOMAS HON WING POLIN)

This article updates the *Macropædia* article EAST INDIES: *Indonesia*.

KAMPUCHEA

A people's republic of Southeast Asia, Kampuchea occupies the southwestern part of the Indochinese Peninsula, on the Gulf of Thailand. Area: 181,035 sq km (69,898 sq mi). Pop. (1985 est.): 7,280,000. Cap.: Phnom Penh. Monetary unit: riel. Secretary-general of the People's Revolutionary (Communist) Party of Kampuchea and president of the Council of State in 1985, Heng Samrin; president of the Council of Ministers (prime minister) from January 14, Hun Sen.

Events in Kampuchea during 1985 were again dominated by the struggle for control of the country's political destiny. Kampuchea's Vietnamese occupiers launched unprecedentedly fierce and successful attacks against Democratic Kampuchea (DK) resistance bases on the border with Thailand. The tripartite resistance coalition—made up of the (Communist) Khmer Rouge, the (non-Communist) Khmer People's National Liberation Front (KPNLF), and the Armée Nationale Sihanoukist (ANS)—was forced to rethink its military strategy. Hanoi's forces began their annual dry-season assault on the resistance earlier than usual. Their successes of the last two months of 1984, when they gained control of four important KPNLF camps, continued in 1985. In January nearly 4,000 Vietnamese troops overran Ampil camp, the KPNLF's political, military, and social nerve centre. The following month the Vietnamese won control of the Khmer Rouge mountain redoubt of

Some 250,000 refugees fled across the border from Kampuchea to Thailand in January as Vietnamese troops overran camps of the chief resistance organizations.

ROLAND NEVEU—GAMMA/LIAISON

Phnom Malai, and in March the frontier stronghold of the ANS at Tatum fell.

The conflict sent some 250,000 Khmer civilians fleeing across the border to Thailand, greatly exacerbating that country's refugee problem. In addition, Vietnam's military strikes often penetrated into Thai territory, resulting in clashes with the Thai Army. The offensive also brought forth threats of military retaliation from China, chief backer of the Khmer Rouge. China's actions, however, were limited to skirmishes along the tense Sino-Vietnamese frontier. Analysts surmised that China's apparent restraint was motivated by a desire to encourage a thaw in relations with the U.S.S.R., Vietnam's principal ally. The Association of Southeast Asian Nations (ASEAN), main supporter of the KPNLF and the ANS, reacted with concern to the collapse of the guerrilla bases but did not waver in its pledge to continue backing the resistance.

The DK abandoned its attempts to defend stationary camps in favour of guerrilla tactics in the Kampuchean interior. The switch had little effect on the Khmer Rouge, who were used to the rigours of jungle operations, but experts predicted that the adjustment would be more difficult for their non-Communist partners. Faced with the prospect of losing credibility, DK forces launched numerous pin-prick attacks on the Vietnamese and their installations. Resistance leaders, meanwhile, traveled to sympathetic countries in search of military and political assistance.

China was quick to deliver fresh supplies of arms not only to the Khmer Rouge but to the other two factions as well. After intensive lobbying by former prime minister Son Sann, the KPNLF leader, and Prince Norodom Sihanouk, president of the DK government-in-exile, the U.S. Congress changed its policy and authorized $5 million in assistance. Factional frictions within the resistance surfaced once again, however, and Sihanouk threatened to resign as head of the DK alliance after hearing reports that the Khmer Rouge had killed 38 of his troops. Even so, the KPNLF and the ANS buried their differences and formed a joint military command.

In August a meeting of Indochinese foreign ministers pledged that Vietnamese troops would leave Kampuchea by 1990. It was the first time that Hanoi had publicly announced a specific date for withdrawal. It was believed the process might begin even sooner if the Khmer Rouge and its notorious leader, Pol Pot, were "eliminated." Barely two weeks later, Khmer Rouge radio announced that Pol Pot had retired as military chief to assume an "advisory" po-

sition. Though the statement was received with skepticism in Hanoi, ASEAN officials welcomed it.

The Vietnam-backed administration continued to make limited progress in stabilizing conditions at home. Following good rice harvests in 1982 and 1983, adverse weather conditions played havoc with the 1984 crop, and supplies from international organizations were again required. The major political change was the elevation of Foreign Minister Hun Sen to the post of prime minister on January 14 following the death of the incumbent, Chan Sy, in December 1984.   (THOMAS HON WING POLIN)

This article updates the *Macropædia* article Mainland SOUTH-EAST ASIA: *Kampuchea.*

LAOS

A landlocked people's republic, Laos is in the northern part of the Indochinese Peninsula. Area: 236,800 sq km (91,400 sq mi). Pop. (1985 est.): 4,117,000. Cap.: Vientiane. Monetary unit: new kip, with (Oct. 21, 1985) a free rate of 34.98 new kip to U.S. $1 (50.16 new kip = £1 sterling). President in 1985, Prince Souphanouvong; chairman of the Council of Ministers (prime minister), Kaysone Phomvihan.

Attracting much attention throughout 1985 were the tense and apparently deteriorating relations between Laos and its larger neighbour, Thailand. A dispute between the two governments over three strategically located border hamlets that began in 1984 simmered well into 1985. By August the issue had provoked more than 120 armed encounters between Laotian and Thai troops. Bangkok put the casualties at 2 Thai soldiers killed and 11 wounded and 8 Laotians dead and an unspecified number injured. Intermittent diplomatic attempts to resolve the dispute came to nothing. There were reports that villagers living in the vicinity had been killed, and Thailand accused the Laotians of sending "spies" trained by Vietnam into its territory in an attempt to convert its hill-tribe people to Communism.

Vietnam's involvement in Laos was the subject of two documents issued early in the year. A paper on the "Soviet-Vietnamese condominium" in Laos was the work of a former senior official of the ruling Pathet Lao who had received training in Vietnam and the U.S.S.R. The author, now based in Paris, asserted that his country was home to 8,000 Vietnamese and 1,600 Soviet advisers as well as 400,-000 Vietnamese settlers. The second document, a White Paper issued by the Thai Foreign Ministry, also decried the vietnamization of Laos and claimed that Hanoi cadres

had infiltrated every government organization. The report noted that since the Communists came to power in Laos a decade earlier, more than 280,000 Laotians had fled to Thailand. After slowing in recent years, the exodus picked up again in 1984 and 1985, with more than a thousand refugees crossing the border in some months. Laotian officials blamed the departures on "Western policies" aimed at "parasites who don't want to work, preferring to be unemployed in the United States."

Opponents of the Vientiane regime who stayed behind posed no real threat. Some 6,000 were still believed to be in two dozen "reeducation" camps. Resistance groups, spearheaded by borderland minority tribes such as the Hmong, the Yao, the Khmu, and the Muser, remained fragmented and lacked the resources to mount a serious challenge to the Laotian Army, which was strengthened by the presence of 60,000 Vietnamese troops.

The government continued to rely heavily on foreign aid for economic development. In 1984 and 1985, however, the amount declined some 15–20% from the annual average of around $100 million during 1978–82 because lack of infrastructure and expertise slowed absorption. The funds came mostly from the Soviet bloc, the UN, and a handful of Western countries. Socialization of agriculture remained slow, but the country maintained self-sufficiency in food production. More than $20 million worth of hydroelectricity, representing 90% of exports, was sold to Thailand.

(THOMAS HON WING POLIN)

This article updates the *Macropædia* article Mainland SOUTH-EAST ASIA: *Laos.*

MALAYSIA

A federal constitutional monarchy of Southeast Asia and member of the Commonwealth, Malaysia consists of the former Federation of Malaya at the southern end of the Malay Peninsula (excluding Singapore) and Sabah and Sarawak on the northern part of the island of Borneo. Area: 330,434 sq km (127,581 sq mi). Pop. (1985 est.): 15,551,000. Cap.: Kuala Lumpur. Monetary unit: ringgit, with (Oct. 21, 1985) a free rate of 2.45 ringgits to U.S. $1 (3.52 ringgits = £1 sterling). Supreme head of state in 1985, with the title of *yang di-pertuan agong,* Tuanku Mahmood Iskandar ibni al-Marhum Sultan Ismail; prime minister, Datuk Seri Mahathir bin Mohamad.

Though Malaysian Prime Minister Mahathir bin Mohamad was not required to call general elections until April 1987, he had been expected to do so before the end of 1985. The chief reason that he did not was the continuation throughout the year of a bitter leadership dispute within

the Malaysian Chinese Association (MCA), the country's largest Chinese-based political party and a key member of the ruling National Front coalition. The MCA feud was touched off in March 1984 when Neo Yee Pan was challenged for the job of party president by his deputy and rival, Tan Koon Swan. In February 1985 an accord was signed in which Neo agreed to reinstate Tan and 13 of his associates in the party and to clean up the party membership rolls, while Tan promised not to contest the MCA presidency in party elections to be held later in the year.

By April, however, the rivals were again publicly blaming each other for breaching terms of understanding over the question of the party rolls. Under the mediation of National Front leaders, they settled on a second compromise in May; Tan would withdraw a proposed motion of no confidence in Neo, a special committee would be formed to clean up membership lists, and the MCA presidential election would be open to all contestants, including Tan. When barely three months later disagreements between Neo and another party stalwart, Mak Hon Kam, again split the MCA, the National Front response was swift and dramatic. Mahathir dismissed Neo from his Cabinet post as minister of housing and local government, and the MCA was given a three-month period to put its house in order.

Prime Minister Mahathir's standing within his own United Malays National Organization (UMNO), the dominant party within the National Front, remained strong. Moderation emerged as the country's political keynote—a trend that influenced even the opposition fundamentalist Partai Islam (PAS). In a remarkable reversal PAS leader Hadi Awang wooed the Chinese community by declaring that a non-Malay could be Malaysia's prime minister as long as he was a good Muslim.

An unexpected political storm blew up in the state of Sabah. In state assembly elections held in April the ruling Berjaya Party of Chief Minister Harris Salleh was defeated by the Partai Bersatu Sabah (Sabah United Party; PBS), a new grouping led by Joseph Pairin Kitingan. The PBS took 25 seats, while Berjaya dropped from its previous tally of 44 to 6, and the United Sabah National Organization (USNO) garnered 16. The success of PBS was attributed by analysts to the growing feelings of alienation and discrimination among Christian Kadazans, Sabah's largest single ethnic community.

Stunned by the returns, Harris promised to support a government formed by USNO leader Tun Mustapha Harun, his erstwhile rival. Arguing that together their parties had won more than half the popular vote, the

A patrol of Malaysian soldiers keeps watch on the road leading to Betong, Thailand. The frontier crossing was heavily used by Communist guerrillas and by smugglers.

two leaders persuaded Adnan Roberts, the state governor, to swear in Mustapha as chief minister. However, many Malaysians viewed the move as unconstitutional, and the citizens of Sabah feared that violence would follow. Within hours, following talks with Pairin, consultations with a team of lawyers, and a message from Kuala Lumpur in support of Pairin, the governor agreed that PBS had the right to form a government. Mustapha's appointment as chief minister was withdrawn, and Pairin was sworn in.

Like many less developed countries, Malaysia felt the economic impact of sluggish commodity prices. Prices were soft during much of the year for the country's major commodity exports: palm oil, rubber, timber, tin, and petroleum. The gross domestic product was expected to achieve a 4–5% growth in 1985, compared with 7.3% a year earlier. In the first quarter government debt increased slightly, but external debt declined by a small amount for the first time. Inflation remained low at just over 4%. Prime Minister Mahathir paid an official visit to China in November.   (THOMAS HON WING POLIN)

This article updates the *Macropædia* article Mainland SOUTHEAST ASIA: *Malaysia*.

PHILIPPINES

Situated in the western Pacific Ocean off the southeast coast of Asia, the republic of the Philippines consists of an archipelago of about 7,100 islands. Area: 300,000 sq km (115,800 sq mi). Pop (1985 est.): 54,669,000. Cap.: Manila. Monetary unit: peso, with (Oct. 21, 1985) a free rate of 18.13 pesos to U.S. $1 (26 pesos = £1 sterling). President in 1985, Ferdinand E. Marcos; prime minister, Cesar Virata.

A year of increasing Communist guerrilla activity and worsening economic conditions ended in December 1985 with a presidential election campaign. Pres. Ferdinand E. Marcos, seeking reelection, was opposed by Corazon C. Aquino, who blamed him for the 1983 murder of her husband, opposition leader Benigno S. Aquino, Jr., despite a court finding that a lone Communist gunman was probably responsible.

Marcos arranged to have the election more than a year ahead of schedule. On Aug. 25, 1985, the presidential palace had said that public opinion reports showed "an overwhelming rejection" of an early election, but on December 2 Marcos signed a National Assembly bill amid mounting domestic and U.S. criticism of his regime; the bill called for elections to be held on Feb. 7, 1986. U.S. Pres. Ronald Reagan had sent a close friend, Sen. Paul Laxalt (Rep., Nev.), to Manila in October to express concern over deteriorating conditions and to urge economic, political, and military reforms.

The constitutionality of the early election was challenged because the presidency was not vacant, but Marcos said he would resign only when a winner was ready to be sworn in. A prominent critic of this arrangement was national assemblyman Arturo Tolentino, who had been fired from the post of foreign minister on March 4 for criticizing Marcos's retention of power to rule by decree after martial law ended in 1981. Nevertheless, on December 11 Marcos chose Tolentino, the ruling New Society Movement's best vote getter, as his vice-presidential candidate.

Marcos signed the election law a few hours after a special court acquitted 26 persons accused of conspiracy to murder Aquino. The government had contended that Aquino was shot by a man acting on Communist orders, who was then killed by security forces. However, a yearlong investigation led to the indictment of one civilian and 25 security men, including Gen. Fabian C. Ver, the

Corazón Aquino, widow of opposition figure Benigno Aquino, who was killed on his return to the Philippines in 1983, and Salvador Laurel, head of the United Nationalist Democratic Organization, headed a ticket opposing Pres. Ferdinand Marcos.
ALBERT GARCIA—GAMMA/LIAISON

armed forces chief of staff. The Supreme Court barred from their trial some of the evidence the investigation had used, weakening the prosecution case that a Manila policeman supposedly guarding Aquino had shot him. The U.S. State Department said it was "very difficult to reconcile" the acquittal with the investigation's results. Ver, who had been suspended during the trial, was reinstated by Marcos as chief of staff and immediately began reorganizing the armed forces. Although ostensibly done in response to U.S. pressure for reform, the changes were described by foreign observers as tightening Marcos's personal control.

The head of a 12-party opposition coalition, Salvador Laurel, announced his candidacy for president, as did Mrs. Aquino, who said she wanted a popular verdict on Marcos's possible blame for her husband's murder. The archbishop of Manila, Jaime Cardinal Sin, interceded to avoid a splitting of the anti-Marcos vote, and Laurel agreed to run for vice-president with Mrs. Aquino.

Marcos said on December 14 that 10,000 "innocent civilians" had been killed during 1985 by guerrillas of the Communist New People's Army (NPA). A government White Paper issued in May estimated NPA strength at between 10,000 and 12,000, but Communists claimed 30,-000. Most observers agreed that the guerrillas' strength was growing. The U.S. Defense Department warned that within three years the guerrillas could achieve military parity with government forces.

The Communist insurgency fed on economic distress. Falling world prices for sugar and coconuts cut farmers' incomes, and Filipino industries were in recession. The average person's income dropped 6.8% between the first half of 1984 and the same period of 1985.

(HENRY S. BRADSHER)

SINGAPORE

Singapore, a republic of Southeast Asia and member of the Commonwealth, occupies a group of islands, the largest of which is Singapore, at the southern extremity of the Malay Peninsula. Area: 618 sq km (239 sq mi). Pop. (1985 est.): 2,558,200. Monetary unit: Singapore dollar, with (Oct. 21, 1985) a free rate of S$2.13 to U.S. $1 (S$3.06 = £1 sterling). Presidents in 1985, Chengara Veetil Devan Nair to March 28, Yeoh Ghim Seng (acting) to September 3, and, from September 3, Wee Kim Wee; prime minister, Lee Kuan Yew.

The year 1985 proved to be an unusually eventful one in Singapore. Following general elections in December 1984, in which the ruling People's Action Party (PAP) won 77 of 79 parliamentary seats, the long-standing question of who would eventually succeed Lee Kuan Yew as prime minister was resolved. Defense Minister Goh Chok Tong became the heir apparent when he was named first deputy prime minister by Lee in the new Cabinet announced on December 31, 1984. Lee said that the choice of Goh had been made by his peers in the Cabinet, including several of his prospective rivals for the top post. Using an analogy drawn from soccer, Lee described his position in the leadership team as that of "goalkeeper," while his younger colleagues would play "centre forward" and "strikers."

Another political benchmark was the resignation due to alcoholism of Pres. Chengara Veetil Devan Nair, a veteran PAP stalwart, in March. Lee's revelation in Parliament of Nair's alcoholism stunned politicians and the public at large. Nair, whose four-year term would have expired in October, had not been known as a heavy drinker. He had been one of the prime minister's closest associates for decades and a key ally during the political struggles of Singapore's formative years. Though Lee seemed determined to make an example of Nair on moral and ethical grounds, many thought his public censure unnecessarily harsh. His replacement was Wee Kim Wee, a former journalist and diplomat. In October Nair announced his intention to immigrate to the U.S.

Singapore's economy, which had grown by an impressive 8.2% in 1984, slowed dramatically to register a contraction of 1.4% in the second quarter of 1985. It appeared likely to record the worst annual performance since independence. In his National Day address in August, Lee frankly admitted that the outlook was poor. Slow growth and rising protectionism in the U.S., Singapore's major trading partner, and sluggishness in important economic sectors such as shipbuilding and oil refining were key factors. Furthermore, the competitiveness of Singapore's exports had been sapped by high wage levels, which in recent years had soared above those in Hong Kong, Taiwan, and South Korea. In November Pan-Electric Industries Ltd., a major concern with 68 subsidiaries around the world, went into receivership.   (THOMAS HON WING POLIN)

This article updates the *Macropædia* article Mainland SOUTH-EAST ASIA: *Singapore*.

Wee Kim Wee (centre), flanked by Prime Minister Lee Kuan Yew (left) and Chief Justice Wee Chong Jin, was sworn in as Singapore's fourth president in September following the unexpected resignation of Pres. Chengara Veetil Devan Nair.

THAILAND

Thailand is a constitutional monarchy in Southeast Asia, on the Andaman Sea and the Gulf of Thailand. Area: 513,115 sq km (198,115 sq mi). Pop. (1985 est.): 51,301,000. Cap.: Bangkok. Monetary unit: baht, with (Oct. 21, 1985) a free rate of 26.50 baht to U.S. $1 (38 baht = £1 sterling). King, Bhumibol Adulyadej; prime minister in 1985, Gen. Prem Tinsulanond.

On Sept. 9, 1985, Thailand was shaken by the 16th attempted coup d'état since the abolition of absolute monarchy in 1932. Some 500 rebel soldiers, backed by 22 tanks, proclaimed on radio at 7:30 AM that "the Revolutionary Party, which comprises military, police, and civilian parties, has seized national sovereignty." Barely eight hours later, however, the rebellion had fizzled out, aborted by an evident lack of support both within the powerful military establishment and among the public. In the meantime, however, two bloody battles in the streets of Bangkok involving tanks and small arms killed 5 people, including 2 foreign journalists, injured approximately 60 others, and caused damage amounting to several million baht. Thailand's recent record of political stability received a sharp jolt.

The coup attempt was apparently masterminded by Manoon Roopkachorn, a charismatic former army colonel who had been cashiered after leading a similarly unsuccessful revolt in 1981, and his brother Manas, an officer in the Air Force. Among those who reportedly gave their support once the coup was under way were former prime minister Kriangsak Chamanand, Gen. Serm Na Nakhorn, a former supreme commander of the armed forces, and Gen. Yos Thephasdin, a former deputy commander in chief of the Army. It soon became clear, however, that dominant forces within the military remained loyal to Prime Minister Prem Tinsulanond. Manoon negotiated with government authorities to secure safe passage out of the country in return for a prompt, peaceful conclusion to the rebellion. Following the surrender he flew to Singapore and then to West Germany, after U.S. authorities had denied his request for asylum.

The government arrested Kriangsak, Serm, and Yos, despite their protests that they had been forced to support the coup, as well as some 100 others. Since Kriangsak was the leader of the National Democratic Party, a partner in the governing coalition, Prem was obliged to reshuffle his Cabinet. Chief motives for the coup attempt were widely believed to be economic hardship and Manoon's own ambitions.

Long-standing tensions between the military and the politicians also came to the fore in July when Parliament passed the most controversial bill of the 1985 session. The constitutional amendment, which would change the country's electoral system, had been introduced by the Social Action Party, the largest partner in the ruling coalition. It provided for provinces to be divided into constituencies in a way that many believed would improve the chances of smaller parties against bigger ones and against individual candidates backed by the military. The bill was passed by a narrow but decisive majority.

The nation's financial circles were jolted by the collapse in February of a "chit fund" run by businesswoman Chamoy Thipyaso. Chit funds, money pools that pay interest at a rate many times higher than banks, had been outlawed by the government in 1984. The collapse of Chamoy's fund left 80,000 investors angrily seeking recovery of the $350 million they had deposited with her.

The readings on Thailand's economy were mixed. There

Loyal soldiers of the Thai Army battle rebel troops, estimated to be 500 strong, supporting a coup attempt by a former army colonel and an air force officer.
SYGMA

was concern about falling exports, rising unemployment, and slow growth, but both the World Bank and the government were cautiously optimistic. Though it passed a zero-growth budget of $8 billion for 1985–86, the government set an average growth target of 5% a year in its sixth (1987–91) development plan. Some economists criticized the goal as unrealistic, noting that such major commodity exports as rice, sugar, tapioca, and maize (corn) were expected to face soft prices for some time into the future.

(THOMAS HON WING POLIN)

This article updates the *Macropædia* article Mainland SOUTH-EAST ASIA: *Thailand.*

VIETNAM

The socialist republic of Vietnam occupies the eastern part of the Indochinese Peninsula in Southeast Asia and is bounded on the south and east by the South China Sea. Area: 331,653 sq km (128,052 sq mi). Pop. (1985 est.): 59,239,000. Cap.: Hanoi. Monetary unit: dong, with (Oct. 21, 1985) an official rate of 94.22 dong to U.S. $1 (135.11 dong = £1 sterling). Secretary-general of the Communist Party in 1985, Le Duan; president of the National Assembly, Nguyen Huu Tho; president of the State Council (president), Truong Chinh; president of the Council of Ministers (prime minister), Pham Van Dong.

In 1985 Vietnam experienced a quiet year in terms of developments at the top levels of political power. Though 77 years old and ailing, Communist Party Secretary-General Le Duan remained firmly in control. Hanoi's decision to seek more normal economic links with the outside world was largely motivated by years of economic stagnation at home. An even more significant shift was under way in the diplomatic field. Spurred by a growing need for development aid as well as by a desire to lessen its dependence on the U.S.S.R., Vietnam's leaders launched initiatives to repair its long-frayed relationship with the U.S.

Throughout the year Le Duan maintained his characteristic low profile. However, suspicions that he might be losing his grip were dispelled by the reinstatement of Nguyen Van Linh, a confidant of Le Duan, in the Communist Party's 15-member Politburo. A veteran revolutionary, Linh had been expected to fade into obscurity when he was dropped from the Politburo in 1982. The importance of another centre of Vietnamese power, the Army, was underscored in December 1984 during commemorations of the 40th anniversary of its founding, when two senior officers were promoted; Le Duc Anh, in charge of military operations in Kampuchea, and Le Trong Tan, chief of general staff, became only the fifth and sixth men to attain the rank of full general.

During 1985 Hanoi marked the 40th anniversary of the August Revolution, which brought the late president Ho Chi Minh to power in the north, and the 10th anniversary of Hanoi's conquest of the south. The latter celebration was attended by a phalanx of U.S. press and television journalists compiling in-depth retrospectives on their country's fateful involvement in Vietnam.

A major current in the social and religious life of Vietnam went largely unnoticed in the outside world. The authorities stepped up the political crackdown launched the previous year against major religious groups in the south, especially Buddhists and Christians, who had long constituted an important political force in that part of the country. During 1984 some leading Buddhist figures were retired, many others were jailed, and a few died mysteriously. In 1985 the authorities extended their suppression to grassroots elements. According to Vietnamese exiles in clandestine contact with Buddhists at home, the campaign was a "systematic" part of Hanoi's policy to curb criticism of the state. Only 15,000 or so monks remained in the temples and monasteries of southern Vietnam, compared with more than 100,000 a decade earlier. The authorities withdrew the traditional exemption of clergy from service in the armed forces; placed pliant monks, often from the north, in key positions in leading Buddhist organizations; disseminated revised, party-sanctioned versions of Buddhist teachings; and required monastery schools to teach Marxism-Leninism to their pupils. Monks were also removed from monasteries to work in factories or the fields.

Christians were not spared. A number of Roman Catholic leaders were detained because of their opposition to government-controlled religious committees. Constant pressure was applied against the Evangelical Church of Vietnam, the nation's largest and oldest Protestant church. Some 100 pastors were reportedly confined to çamps. One result was that Christianity was beginning to go underground in Vietnam, with video recordings of religious programs apparently being smuggled into the country.

Meeting at the end of 1984, the seventh plenum of the Communist Party's Central Committee concentrated on economic matters. It identified the need to boost food production and the manufacture of consumer goods as major priorities. Though food output in 1984 had grown by 300,000 metric tons, the total fell short of the target of 18 million metric tons. The plenum blamed the shortfall on inclement weather, bad management, and disruptive efforts by China. The agricultural sector faced further setbacks in the third quarter of 1985 when several powerful typhoons destroyed large areas of rice paddy.

Watched by a portrait of Ho Chi Minh, troops representing Vietnam's 1.2 million-man Army march past a reviewing stand full of dignitaries. The Liberation Day parade in Ho Chi Minh City (formerly Saigon) marked the tenth anniversary of North Vietnam's victory over the south.

EDDIE ADAMS—GAMMA/LIAISON

Faced with a foreign debt estimated at more than $6 billion and meagre reserves of $16 million, Hanoi began actively to solicit closer ties with the international financial community. At a conference of Southeast Asian central bankers in Malaysia in February, Hanoi's representatives announced that they intended to seek $200 million in loans from the International Monetary Fund. Officials of the IMF were noncommittal, pointing out that the Fund had stopped lending to Vietnam three years earlier.

The plenum endorsed a policy aimed at improving diplomatic relations with Western countries, especially the U.S. The strategy involved fostering the normalization of ties with Washington by being more cooperative on bilateral matters and encouraging the U.S. to play a more active role in Southeast Asia in order to counter China's influence. Besides softening its customary anti-U.S. rhetoric, Vietnam made a significant gesture on the unresolved, emotional issue of U.S. servicemen who remained missing in action (MIA) from the Indochina wars. During talks in Hanoi in August, Vietnamese negotiators promised that their government would unconditionally complete the search for MIAs within two years. Previously, Vietnam had always demanded in return that the U.S. declare willingness to normalize relations, deliver financial aid, or stop "colluding" with China. On this occasion Hanoi announced that it would conduct investigations of crash sites and carry out necessary excavations on its own, but the U.S. offered to bear the costs of the digging and proposed that joint searches be arranged. The first such search, at the crash site of a B-52 bomber about 14 km (9 mi) north of Hanoi, was completed December 1. Human remains were found and removed for possible identification.

Spurred perhaps by an apparent thaw in Sino-Soviet relations, Vietnamese officials repeatedly stated that their government attached no preconditions to renewed amity with China, although the latter, like the U.S., continued to insist on a withdrawal of Vietnamese troops from Kampuchea. (See *Kampuchea,* above.) There was some evidence of easing in the troubled relationship, but analysts agreed that substantive improvement probably remained some way off.   (THOMAS HON WING POLIN)

This article updates the *Macropædia* article Mainland SOUTH-EAST ASIA: *Vietnam.*

Western Europe

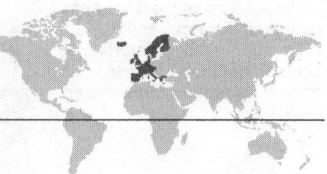

WESTERN EUROPEAN AFFAIRS

Some further tentative steps toward greater political unity among member countries of the European Communities (EC; the European Economic Community [EEC], the European Coal and Steel Community [ECSC], and Euratom), together with continued failure to solve Western Europe's underlying economic ills, were the main characteristics of 1985. The year ended as it had begun with a serious unemployment crisis and further evidence that Western Europe was losing the industrial and technological struggle with the U.S. and Japan.

Although no clear or agreed strategy to make up lost ground had emerged, there was a growing consensus that existing policies had failed. There were signs of moves away from the monetarist orthodoxy that had guided national economic thinking in almost all Western European states from the beginning of the decade. There was also more questioning of existing trade and financial links binding Western Europe with the U.S. and the rest of the industrialized world.

Throughout the year Western Europe maintained pressure on the U.S. administration to act decisively to reduce its budget and balance of payments deficits. As the year drew to a close, however, there were fears that a new economic downturn in the U.S. might further delay and obstruct Western European efforts to reverse industrial stagnation and mass unemployment. The problems experienced by the U.S. dollar also exacerbated fears in Western Europe about the impact of third world indebtedness on international monetary and banking stability. This, in turn, revived Western European desires to strengthen and expand the European monetary system (EMS) as an autonomous element in the world monetary system.

The new EC Commission that took office in January under the presidency of Jacques Delors, former French finance minister, made the removal of internal economic and trade barriers one of its major priorities. With the total number of people out of work within the EC approaching 14 million, economists were gloomy about an early improvement in job prospects. Apart from encouraging faster technological innovation and development and strengthening the EMS, the EC committed itself in January to completing the internal Common Market. However, the task of removing institutional and other barriers to form a completely integrated European market appeared likely to require several years to accomplish.

Meanwhile, despite serious internal economic problems and unresolved issues affecting its political future, the EC pressed on with enlargement. After more than five years of negotiations, the EC summit held in Brussels on March 29–30 agreed to admit Portugal and Spain as new member states from Jan. 1, 1986. The final stages were among the most difficult of the lengthy negotiations. There was a sharp dispute among the ten existing member countries about the speed with which Spain, a major fishing nation, should be integrated and given full rights in the Community's common fisheries policy. The final obstacle concerned a demand by the Greek government for a major package of financial aid to compensate for the effect Spain's entry was expected to have on its competitive position as a producer

of Mediterranean goods. In the end agreement was reached on an aid package totaling $3 billion, with Greece as the prime beneficiary. The treaties formalizing the accession of Portugal and Spain to the Community were signed at the EC summit held in Milan, Italy, on June 29.

In the same year that the decision was taken to increase substantially the geographic area and population of the Community, Greenland became the first territory to leave the EC. Greenland formally withdrew on February 1. In a referendum three years earlier, the majority of the tiny population of the self-governing Danish territory had voted to abandon membership because of dissatisfaction with the effect of EC fishing policy on its economy and the lack of development aid.

With further enlargement looming, EC member governments were greatly preoccupied with disagreements over the Community's budget and its decision-making processes. The year started with the EC budget being financed on an emergency basis because of disagreements between the member governments and the directly elected European Parliament about the proper level of expenditure. The difficulties of fixing the Community's budget were exacerbated by the unresolved issue of reform of the EC common agricultural policy and by the 1984 agreement strictly limiting the net financial contributions to be made to the EC budget by the U.K. With public concern growing about surpluses of farm products and the fact that agricultural spending accounted for some 70% of the budget, both the Commission and some member governments worked to reduce production incentives. Because of internal conflicts, the agreement setting price levels for agricultural production was delayed until May, when only very slight increases in guaranteed price levels for most products were adopted. Even then the West German government refused to implement an agreement made by the other nine member countries to impose a slight cut in the guaranteed price for cereals. The controversy over Europe's "food mountains" revived during the autumn, following a visit to the European Parliament by a delegation of voluntary workers who had organized aid for famine-stricken Ethiopia. (*See* BIOGRAPHIES: *Geldof, Bob.*)

The inadequacies of the Community's decision-making institutions also preoccupied the Milan summit. A proposal by the Italian government, at the time holding the presidency of the EC Council of Ministers, to call a special conference to review the founding treaties of the Community was accepted. However, the British, Danish, and Greek governments expressed serious reservations about the agreement and claimed that reform of the decision-making rules of the Community could be achieved without revising the founding treaties. When EC foreign ministers began a review of the treaties in September, it seemed likely that agreement on any changes in the rules—for instance, to allow a greater acceptance of majority voting, rather than unanimous voting, in the Council—would take many months.

In the event, the Luxembourg summit in December went some way toward healing the disunity evident in Milan. In Luxembourg agreement was reached on a package of reforms that, if approved by national governments, would form the basis for amendments to the treaty. The package contained the prospect of a very limited extension in the use of majority voting on proposals designed to develop the internal market, an increased consultative role for the European Parliament, and "progressive realization" of economic and monetary union. However, while the U.K. emerged content with special provisions allowing it to retain border controls in view of its island status, in the

As Italian Prime Minister Bettino Craxi observes, Felipe González, prime minister of Spain, signs the treaty that would admit his country and Portugal to membership in the European Communities in January 1986, raising EC membership to 12. The signing took place in Madrid in June.
CONTIFOTO/SYGMA

opinion of some member countries the reform package was rendered ineffective by the number of national exemptions it contained.

Concern about the extent to which European industry was falling behind its major world industrial competitors surfaced regularly throughout the year. In April Pres. François Mitterrand of France proposed, with West German government support, a major project named Eureka, designed to keep Western Europe in the high-technology race by encouraging firms to coordinate high-technology research and development, particularly in the area of information systems, lasers, and artificial intelligence.

Trade frictions with the U.S., Japan, and some of the newly industrialized nations were another recurring source of concern in Western Europe. In October the U.S. and the EC each announced plans to bring action against the other under the General Agreement on Tariffs and Trade for unfairly subsidizing exports of cereals. Open trade conflict with the U.S. over steel exports was only narrowly avoided when, in November, an uneasy agreement was reached involving "voluntary restraint" of certain types of European steel exports to the U.S. The closing months of the year saw renewed pressure on Japan to further liberalize imports from Europe and to take action through exchange-rate policy to improve its balance of trade with Europe.

In May the EC and China signed a new trade agreement that greatly expanded cooperation in industrial research and development. During the year the Council for Mutual Economic Assistance, the Soviet-bloc trading organization, opened diplomatic contacts and sought a formal bilateral agreement with the EC. However, the Europeans, while eager to conclude separate agreements with individual Eastern-bloc countries on trade and other matters and encouraged over the U.S.S.R.'s apparent readiness to recognize EC institutions, indicated their desire first to observe the results of the U.S.-Soviet summit in November.

A major event in the Western European calender was the official visit of U.S. Pres. Ronald Reagan, who took part in the celebrations in May of the 40th anniversary of

the Allied victory in Europe at the end of World War II. Controversy surrounded the president's decision to include a visit to a West German military cemetery that contained the graves of some members of the Waffen SS, which had been responsible for administering the Nazi concentration camps. (See *Germany, Federal Republic of,* below.) Despite this, his speech to the European Parliament was widely hailed as a success.

A major issue during September was the worsening unrest in South Africa and growing pressure within Western European countries for stronger action to express opposition to apartheid. The 12 EC governments (including Spain and Portugal, whose foreign ministers began attending discussions on political cooperation in midyear) agreed on largely symbolic trade and other sanctions against South Africa. Agreement came after three weeks during which the U.K. government had withheld its full support.

Much discussion took place during the year about the deterioration in relations between the nuclear superpowers. It was widely feared that President Reagan's Strategic Defense Initiative, the so-called Star Wars proposal, might jeopardize the prospects for progress at the nuclear arms reduction negotiations between the U.S. and the U.S.S.R. in Geneva. There was relief during October when it emerged that Reagan and Soviet leader Mikhail Gorbachev would be meeting to try to give new impetus to the Geneva talks. On the other hand, it was felt that, in terms of Western European public opinion, the Soviet leader had stolen a march on the U.S. by making proposals for radical cuts in nuclear arms in the late summer. While no major breakthrough was achieved at the summit, both leaders reaffirmed their commitment to arms control negotiations. In December a meeting of foreign ministers from Western European countries expressed disappointment that the summit had not made concrete progress toward arms reductions.

During the year there were several meetings of the revived Western European Union, an association of the principal European members of the NATO alliance. This was interpreted by many on both sides of the Atlantic as an indication that European members wanted to play a greater, and more independent, role within NATO and in their own defense decisions.

The European Court of Human Rights in Strasbourg was not in the headlines as often as in previous years. There were, however, significant rulings confirming the right of citizens in individual Western European countries to appeal to the court against decisions made by national governments and courts.

Further steps were taken to integrate the trading and financial systems of the European Free Trade Association, which linked non-EC countries of Western Europe, with the Community. The two organizations not only concerted their international policies on trade barriers, technical standards, and monetary cooperation but also discussed steps to tackle common problems such as environmental pollution.   (JOHN PALMER)

See also Economic Affairs; Military Affairs.

ANDORRA

A landlocked independent coprincipality of Europe, Andorra is in the Pyrenees Mountains between Spain and France. Area: 464 sq km (179 sq mi). Pop. (1985 est.): 43,000. Cap.: Andorra la Vella. Monetary units: French franc and Spanish peseta. Coprinces: the president of the French Republic and the bishop of Urgel, Spain, represented by their *veguers* (provosts) and *batlles* (prosecutors). An elected Council General of 28 members elects the first syndic, in 1985 Francesc Cerqueda Pascuet; chief executive, Josep Pintat-Solans.

During 1985 Andorra expressed a desire to negotiate directly with the authorities of the European Communities (EC) about the future of the coprincipality in light of Spain's impending membership in the EC, to be formalized in January 1986. In his new year's message, broadcast in January 1985, Josep Pintat-Solans, Andorra's chief executive, made it clear that Andorra desired from the EC some form of special status similar to that which Spain was negotiating for the Canary Islands. During the year he consulted with Bishop Juan Marti Alanis of Urgel and French Pres. François Mitterrand, the coprinces responsible for Andorra's foreign relations. Agreement was reached on sending a delegation to Brussels representing the chief executive and the coprinces. Although Andorrans apparently enjoyed a prosperous existence, Pintat-Solans's action was prompted by concern about the economic future. Andorra's income was derived almost exclusively from tourism and trading in imported goods.

In July Andorra's principal supermarket was destroyed by a serious fire caused by a gas explosion. Nine people were killed . On December 12 elections were held to renew the Council General. They were the first to take place under new legislation that lowered the voting age to 18.

(K. M. SMOGORZEWSKI)

This article updates the *Micropædia* article ANDORRA.

AUSTRIA

The republic of Austria is a landlocked state of central Europe. Area: 83,855 sq km (32,376 sq mi). Pop. (1985 est.): 7,552,000. Cap.: Vienna. Monetary unit: schilling, with (Oct. 21, 1985) a free rate of 18.53 schillings to U.S. $1 (26.58 schillings = £1 sterling). President in 1985, Rudolf Kirchschläger; chancellor, Fred Sinowatz.

World attention focused uncomfortably on Austria in 1985 with the discovery that a "wine mafia" had been lacing local wines with harmful diethylene glycol, an automobile antifreeze additive that enhanced sweetness and alcoholic content. As doctored wines began turning up all over Europe and the U.S., the government was forced virtually to halt exports, and later in the year it introduced tough new wine laws.

The year had an unpropitious start with the welcome home after more than 30 years' imprisonment in Italy given to Nazi war criminal Walter Reder by Defense Minister Friedhelm Frischenschlager of the rightist Freedom Party of Austria, coalition partner of Chancellor Fred Sinowatz's Socialist Party of Austria. Reder had been condemned for his part in the massacre of 600 hostages in the northern Italian village of Marzabotto in 1944. As he arrived, the World Jewish Congress was meeting in Vienna for the first time; the ensuing protests at home and abroad forced the minister to apologize, though he resisted pressure to resign.

Protection of employment and conservation of the environment were prime concerns of Austria's economic policymakers. The government's conservation program provided for the reduction of harmful emissions from vehicles and industrial plants, the purification of rivers, and protection of the countryside from dangerous chemicals. A priority was the provision of clean hydroelectric power. However, the strength of feeling among Austria's nature conservationists continued to hinder government plans for the Hainburg hydroelectric plant near the Czechoslovak border; opponents mounted mass demonstrations and occupied the Danube banks, and there was a public outcry led by Nobel Prize winner Konrad Lorenz. The government postponed moves to restart operations after a serious political crisis threatened to erode Austria's traditional social

A chemist at the laboratory of the U.S. Bureau of Alcohol, Tobacco and Firearms checks an array of Austrian wines being tested for contamination. Diethylene glycol, usually used as an additive in automobile antifreeze solutions, was discovered in a number of Austrian export wines.

GEORGE TAMES/THE NEW YORK TIMES

consensus. In July the frustrated shareholders in the mothballed 20 billion-schilling Zwentendorf nuclear power plant decided to dismantle it and sell off its components, arousing further fierce argument among the political parties.

Controversy also followed the government's decision in March to buy 24 Draken fighter aircraft from Sweden. Inhabitants of the areas surrounding the airfields where the aircraft were to be sited protested against atmospheric pollution and increased noise levels. In May the Steyr-Daimler-Puch works' decision to repurchase 50 Kürassier light tanks from the Army for subsequent sale to Morocco was blocked by Socialist Interior Minister Karl Blecha, a supporter of the Polisario Front guerrillas' fight for an independent Western Sahara.

An opportunity to dwell on less controversial matters came with the 30th anniversary of the State Treaty by which Austria had returned to full sovereignty after World War II. Eleven foreign ministers, including those of the signatory powers—Great Britain, France, the Soviet Union, and the U.S.—attended the celebrations in Vienna on May 15.

An Organization for Economic Cooperation and Development report in early 1985 welcomed Austria's overall economic performance, although it warned of possible longer-term dangers from increasing budget deficits, outmoded industrial structures, and distortions caused by industrial subsidies. Forecasts for 1985 estimated growth at 3%, investment up 4.5%, exports up 12.5%, inflation at 3.3–4%, and unemployment just under 5%.

In August Austria experienced the worst floods since 1954. Many lives were lost, and material damage amounted to billions of schillings. Vienna airport was the scene of one of two attacks on Israeli airline passengers on December 27.   (ELFRIEDE DIRNBACHER)

BELGIUM

A constitutional monarchy, the Benelux country of Belgium is situated on the North Sea coast of northwestern Europe. Area: 30,519 sq km (11,783 sq mi). Pop. (1985 est.): 9,859,000. Cap.: Brussels. Monetary unit: Belgian franc, with (Oct. 21, 1985) a commercial rate of BF 53.42 to U.S. $1 (BF 76.60 = £1 sterling) and a financial rate of BF 53.80 to U.S. $1 (BF 77.15 = £1 sterling). King, Baudouin I; prime minister in 1985, Wilfried Martens.

The Belgian government of Prime Minister Wilfried Martens narrowly failed to complete its full four-year term of office when, on Sept. 2, 1985, King Baudouin I dissolved Parliament and called general elections for October 13. The results gave a slightly increased majority to the outgoing coalition of Flemish and French Social Christian and Liberal parties. The loss of six seats by the Flemish Liberals was more than compensated by the extra eight seats won by the Social Christian parties. While the Flemish Socialists increased their representation by six seats, the (Flemish nationalist) Volksunie and the Front Démocratique des Francophones both lost support. (For tabulated results, see *Political Parties,* above.)

The dissolution of Parliament was prompted in the main by tensions between the Flemish and French Social Christians. The latter refused to support a proposed constitutional amendment that would devolve responsibility for educational matters to the communities. They believed the move would pose a threat to Roman Catholic schools in French-speaking Wallonia, where the Socialists, in opposition on the national level, were the major party.

Further tension resulted from the parliamentary inquiry into the riot in Heysel stadium, Brussels, that broke out before the start of the European Cup final soccer match between Liverpool (England) and Juventus of Turin (Italy) on May 29. The violence resulted in the deaths of 39 spectators. The inquiry concluded that the actions of the Belgian police had revealed serious shortcomings. When Interior Minister Charles-Ferdinand Nothomb, a French Social Christian, refused to assume responsibility, French Liberal Justice Minister Jean Gol tendered his own resignation, and a number of other French Liberal ministers followed suit. Martens offered the resignation of the entire government on July 16, but the king refused to accept it. (*See* SPORTS AND GAMES: *Football:* Sidebar.)

Following the elections, Martens maintained the same Social Christian-Liberal coalition. In the new Cabinet sworn in on November 28, both Nothomb and Gol retained their posts. The list contained a new defense minister, François-Xavier de Donéa, and a new budget minister, Guy Verhofstadt.

The regionalization laws of 1980 continued to cause controversy as regional and community executives attempted to wrest more powers from the national government. The Walloon regional council approved a decree imposing the compulsory affiliation of all communes to a public power-distribution authority. After an appeal was lodged by the national government with the newly installed Court of Arbitration, the decree was rescinded.

Earlier in the year the government gave the green light to the installation of the first 16 U.S. cruise missiles at the Florennes air force base. The missiles arrived in March. Even after the installation, Flemish Socialists insisted on their withdrawal.

A left-wing terrorist group calling itself the Cellules Communistes Combattantes (CCC) attacked more than a dozen buildings, causing considerable damage. Its targets were the political headquarters of the Liberals and Social Christians and property belonging to U.S. "imperialists." On November 9 an armed gang killed eight people during a raid on a supermarket in Aalst. The incident was the worst in a series of armed robberies on stores belonging to a single chain. Martens and Foreign Relations Minister Léo Tindemans made an official trip to the U.S. in January. Pope John Paul II visited Belgium in May during his tour of the Benelux countries.   (JAN R. ENGELS)

This article updates the *Macropædia* article THE LOW COUNTRIES: *Belgium.*

DENMARK

A constitutional monarchy of north central Europe, Denmark lies between the North and Baltic seas. Area: 43,080 sq km (16,633 sq mi), excluding the Faeroe Islands and Greenland. Pop. (1985 est.): 5,107,000. Cap.: Copenhagen. Monetary unit: krone, with (Oct. 21, 1985) a free rate of 9.56 kroner to U.S. $1 (13.71 kroner = £1 sterling). Queen, Margrethe II; prime minister in 1985, Poul Schlüter.

When Prime Minister Poul Schlüter delivered his speech at the opening of the Danish Folketing (parliament) on Oct. 1, 1985, he could claim that his four-party coalition government had fulfilled at least some of the promises made when it came to power three years earlier. During the first six months of 1985 the inflation rate was 2%—only Japan, West Germany, Switzerland, and The Netherlands, among countries belonging to the Organization of Economic Cooperation and Development, had lower inflation rates. The Danish krone was among the world's strongest currencies, despite the large foreign debt and balance of payments deficit. Unemployment, though still acknowledged to be too high, had been reduced by 90,000 during the previous year. The deficit on the internal budget had been cut, and a majority in the Folketing had reached agreement in principle on tax reform.

The Achilles' heel of the government's economic policy was the balance of payments deficit. While the government aimed to achieve balance in this area by 1988, most economists believed it would take a year or so longer. The deficit for 1985 appeared likely to exceed the 1984 figure of 17 billion kroner, as well as government forecasts. However, the government had no plans to intervene to slow the rise in the deficit, in the belief that it was an inevitable result of the recent boom in the economy and that intervention would threaten investment activity.

Paradoxically, in view of the 250,000 unemployed, certain industries were suffering from a lack of skilled workers. Official statistics, covering only a fraction of the job market, gave a strong indication of the trend; the number of unfilled jobs had risen to 2,000, compared with 200 at the end of 1982. The paradox led to debates about whether enough resources were being channeled into the education of unskilled labour and whether, perhaps, certain unemployed people felt they could live a reasonable life on the approximately 102,000 kroner a year provided by the state.

At the end of March the failure of wage negotiations between trade unions and employers' federations sparked the worst wave of industrial unrest that Denmark had witnessed in over a decade. The government introduced an emergency package of austerity measures that included the limitation of wage increases to no more than 2% until 1987, cuts in social services, reductions in some social benefits in real terms, and an increase in company tax from 40 to 50%. The immediate result was an intensification of unofficial strike action among both public- and private-sector workers. When the labour disputes had calmed down, the government won some praise for its efficiency; in the opinion of others, its policies were responsible for dividing the country into "haves" and "have-nots."

A recent liberalization of the legislation governing the admittance of refugees had resulted in a rush of refugee arrivals, notably from the Middle East. In November the Folketing began to consider changes to the legislation. The killing of a taxi driver in Copenhagen on October 19 was thought to have been perpetrated by an extreme right-wing group that had demanded that its call for the expulsion of immigrants and refugees be broadcast on television.

During the year there was a great deal of debate about the country's security policy and its attitude toward NATO, subjects on which there was dissent among the parties. There was general agreement, however, on the question of moves toward greater unity within the European Communities; Denmark was determined not to give up its right to a national veto on policy-making decisions.

(STENER AARSDAL)

FINLAND

The republic of Finland is in northern Europe, on the Gulf of Bothnia and the Gulf of Finland. Area: 338,145 sq km (130,559 sq mi). Pop. (1985 est.): 4,910,000. Cap.: Helsinki. Monetary unit: markka, with (Oct. 21, 1985) a free rate of 5.66 markkaa to U.S. $1 (8.12 markkaa = £1 sterling). President in 1985. Mauno Koivisto; prime minister, Kalevi Sorsa.

Foreign ministers of the 35 countries that endorsed the Final Act of the Conference on Security and Cooperation in Europe met in Helsinki on July 30–Aug. 1, 1985, exactly ten years after the document was signed. Attention was diverted from the plenary session to some 200 bilateral and multilateral fringe meetings. Most important of these was the first meeting between U.S. Secretary of State George Shultz and his hitherto untried Soviet counterpart, Eduard Shevardnadze, who prepared the ground for the meeting between their respective leaders in November. In July.Helsinki was host to a ministerial conference of the UN Economic Commission for Europe, at which 19 states approved a protocol binding them to reduce national emissions and transboundary fluxes of sulfur dioxides to 30% of their 1980 levels by 1993. (*See* ENVIRONMENT.)

On January 2 Finnish defense staff announced that an "unidentified flying object" had penetrated Finland's airspace five days earlier. They gave the news only after the Norwegians revealed that a Soviet missile had crossed a neck of their territory between the Arctic Ocean and Finland. Within 48 hours Moscow issued an unprecedented admission and apology to both Helsinki and Oslo, thereby defusing an incident that could have had serious consequences. Wreckage of the projectile, which the Soviets said had been "inadvertently" fired during shooting practice in the Barents Sea, was recovered from in and around Lake Inari, Finnish Lapland. Finnish experts confirmed that the weapon was an obsolescent Shaddock cruise missile used as a target.

By the time Pres. Mauno Koivisto had his first full meeting with the new Soviet leader, Mikhail Gorbachev, in Moscow on September 19, two unforeseen problems had emerged to trouble bilateral relations. First, a nagging shortfall in Soviet crude-oil shipments to Finland had developed. Since Finland could not export more than it imported on bilateral account, the reassurances that Koivisto received on the oil flow were important. Second, the Soviets had issued a warning to the Finnish Communists that a split in their party would jeopardize interstate relations. At an extraordinary congress of the Finnish Communist Party in March, the national-minded majority had increased its influence at the expense of the pro-Moscow orthodox minority when the majority-controlled Central Committee (CC) was granted the power to eject district organizations that did not obey party rules. Despite Soviet intimidation, the CC later set October as the deadline to begin expulsions.

Pressure from the Kremlin proved abortive in another context. The Soviet news agency TASS pilloried a "peace and freedom" cruise mounted by exiles from the former Baltic republics of Estonia, Latvia, and Lithuania. The

Finnish searchers inspect the wreckage of a Soviet cruise missile after it was recovered from the frozen Lake Inari. The missile went astray during exercises over the Barents Sea, and the Soviet Union subsequently apologized for the accident.
AP/WIDE WORLD

effect of the Soviet action was to increase publicity for the event. Despite its embarrassment, the government allowed the ship to dock in Finland, and an unprecedented anti-Soviet march was staged in Helsinki on July 28.

On the other hand, the authorities received some criticism for enacting an emergency law—described as "illiberal"—designed to keep security tight during the foreign ministers' meeting. There was also concern about the government's handling of information during an incident in June in which 21 Finnish soldiers from the UN Interim Force in Lebanon were held captive for eight days by the Israeli-backed South Lebanon Army (SLA). After much official evasion and a clampdown on media criticism, it was revealed that the troops had helped to stage-manage the desertion of 11 SLA militiamen.

A survey carried out by the Organization for Economic Cooperation and Development suggested that Finland was likely to achieve annual economic growth of around 3%.

(DONALD FIELDS)

FRANCE

A republic of western Europe, France includes the island of Corsica in the Mediterranean Sea and has coastlines on the English Channel, the Mediterranean, and the Atlantic Ocean. Area: 543,965 sq km (210,026 sq mi). Pop. (1985 est.): 55,191,-000. Cap.: Paris. Monetary unit: franc, with (Oct. 21, 1985) a free rate of F 8.04 to U.S. $1 (F 11.53 = £1 sterling). President in 1985, François Mitterrand; prime minister, Laurent Fabius.

The year 1985 was not a good one for France. Under the shadow of the legislative elections scheduled to take place in 1986, left and right in French politics confronted each other without noticeable benefit to the country and without advancing the debate about what would happen if, after the elections, a left-wing president had to govern with a right-wing parliamentary majority. Cantonal elections in March 1985 confirmed the advance of the right and the decline in the fortunes of the left. The strengthening of the European Communities (EC) did not progress as had been hoped; moves toward granting the new status of independence in association with France to New Caledonia might be reversed by a future right-wing administration; and the "Greenpeace affair" did nothing to enhance the image of France in the world.

Domestic Affairs. At the start of the year, Pres. François Mitterrand (*see* BIOGRAPHIES) launched a campaign to revive the failing electoral fortunes of the left, emphasizing the achievements of the Socialist Party (PS) government and appealing for unity. He was immediately countered by Georges Marchais, general secretary of the Communist Party (PC), who at the 25th PC congress in February attacked government policies over the previous three years. According to Marchais, most of the social reforms of 1981 had been gradually eroded before being abolished completely. On the grounds that "the class struggle is worldwide," Marchais refused to break with the countries of the Eastern bloc. The congress was an important one, leading to a radicalization of PC policies and confirming a state of war between it and the Socialist Party, following the breakup of the Union of the Left when the PC left the government in 1984.

In the cantonal elections, in which 2,044 seats, more than half the total, were contested, the right-wing opposition parties—the Rassemblement pour la République (RPR) and the Union pour la Démocratie Française (UDF)—won their fourth victory over the government since the start of President Mitterrand's seven-year term in 1981; previously, they had won cantonal elections in 1982, municipal elections in 1983, and elections to the European Parliament in 1984. In the first round the opposition won 58% of the vote, as against 42% for the left-wing parties, while in the second round it took 53.51%, as against 46.28% for the left, and won control of ten départements previously held by its opponents. The left gained control of Guadeloupe and French Guiana. Overall the PS took 424 seats, a loss of 155; the PC took 149 seats, a loss of 80; the Left Radicals (MRG) lost 13 seats; and various other left-wing parties gained 4 seats. Among the opposition parties, the RPR emerged with 400 seats, a gain of 155; the UDF took 525 seats, a gain of 102; various other right-wing parties increased their representation to 425 seats, a gain of 124; while the far-right National Front, lead by Jean-Marie le Pen, won a single seat. The right now controlled 69 départements, as against 26 for the left.

Meanwhile, the Cabinet made an important decision that was subsequently passed by Parliament: the 1986 legislative elections were to be held under a system of proportional representation in a single round of voting.

A plan by the Renault company to assemble cars in Spain and other low-wage countries for subsequent import into France sparked a protest demonstration in August. Workers blocked traffic on the Champs-Élysées with new automobiles, which had to be towed by Paris authorities.

ROBERT COHEN—AGIP/PICTORIAL PARADE

Under the new system, the National Assembly would have its seats distributed, in each département, among the different party lists according to the highest average obtained. One round of voting would replace the two rounds under the existing majority-vote system, and consequently there would be no possibility of candidates standing down in favour of each other. The new system allowed for one representative for each 100,000 inhabitants and not fewer than two for each département. Accordingly, the number of deputies was to be increased by 86, giving a National Assembly of 577 seats.

The legislative electoral reforms put great pressure on government solidarity. The first victim was Michel Rocard, who resigned as minister of agriculture in April on the grounds that he could not subscribe to a reform that he had always opposed. He was replaced by Henri Nallet, technical adviser at the Elysée Palace. Later, revealing that his decision to resign had another cause, Rocard announced that he would be a candidate to succeed Mitterrand as president of the republic in 1988.

Despite profound differences within the party, the PS congress in October ended with a synthesis of the motions proposed by Lionel Jospin, PS first secretary, and Rocard. In response to President Mitterrand's appeal, unity was achieved by one means or another. After four and a half years in power, the Socialists had finally broken with the Communists, their former allies, and were attempting to regroup. Rocard did not win the day, but his cause moved forward; Jospin confirmed his position as party leader; and Prime Minister Laurent Fabius brilliantly stole the limelight and appeared the most likely Socialist candidate for the presidency.

The political right, though it enjoyed a substantial lead in polls showing voting intentions, still lacked charisma. Furthermore, it, too, was suffering from internal quarrels. In June the three opposition leaders—former president Valéry Giscard d'Estaing (UDF) and his former prime ministers Raymond Barre (UDF) and Jacques Chirac (RPR)— met together for the first time at what was described as a Liberal convention. According to Giscard, presenting himself as a "federator" between Chirac and Barre, there

were two conditions for the opposition's return to power: the means (the union of the opposition parties) and a doctrine (Liberalism). In October an electoral agreement was concluded between the RPR and the UDF concerning the lists of candidates they would present at the 1986 legislative elections. The two major parties were to offer separate lists in one half of the départements and joint lists in the other half. Immediately after the agreement was reached, however, the conflict in the UDF between Giscardians and Barrists flared up again.

The television confrontation between Prime Minister Fabius and Chirac at the end of October signaled the start of the election campaign for the following year. The tone of the debate was frequently heated. Chirac painted a picture of a country that was "disappointed, weakened, and uneasy," while Fabius took advantage of the opportunity to restate the main direction of his policies. Chirac discounted the possibility that his party would take part in a government that included the National Front, while Fabius, in his turn, said that he would not govern with the support of the Communists. The majority of viewers polled after the debate considered Chirac to have been the more convincing, clear, and competent of the two.

The second half of the year saw a slowing down of inflation, justifying the government's austerity policy. The rise in retail prices was virtually nil in September (0.1%), after a period of near stability in the preceding months. Consequently, the inflation rate for 1985 was expected to be barely over 5%, compared with 6.7% in 1984. On the other hand, unemployment remained a black spot, with the number of those out of work holding steady at around 2.5 million. Government measures to reduce unemployment were hampered by the size of the national debt. There was no improvement in foreign trade, and by September the cumulative balance of payments deficit since the start of the year had reached F 2.6 billion, equivalent to the total for all of 1984.

The Confédération Générale du Travail (CGT), the main trade union federation, which received the support of the PC, continued its campaign against the government throughout the year. The image of trade unionism was tarnished, however, by the failure of strike action at the Renault automobile plant. The CGT's day of action on October 24 brought together some hundreds of thousands of workers in Paris and the main cities outside the capital. However, while the one-day strike was well supported by certain sections of the public sector, overall it attracted less support than expected and was little followed in the private sector.

The territory of New Caledonia in the South Pacific Ocean, a French possession since 1853, was the scene of violent confrontations between Kanak (indigenous Melanesian) members of the Front de Libération Nationale Kanake et Socialiste (FLNKS) under Jean-Marie Tjibaou (see BIOGRAPHIES) and the population of European (mainly French) descent, the caldoches. Faced with increased violence on the island, the government appointed Edgard Pisani first as high commissioner and then, in May, as minister for New Caledonia with a brief to speed up the process of granting self-determination. Despite a lightning visit by President Mitterrand on January 19, the state of emergency imposed a week earlier was extended and was not lifted until June. The French government decided to institute a transitional regime to allow the different population groups to express their views on the territory's progress toward independence in association with France. Four regions were set up—the Loyalty Islands, the Northern Region, the Central-Southern Region, and Nouméa

and district—while France was to strengthen its military presence in the territory.

Regional elections took place as planned in September. Although the *caldoche* parties, which were opposed to independence, received 60.84% of the vote, as against 35.18% for those favouring independence, the pro-independence faction emerged with majorities in three of the four new regions; the Rassemblement pour la Calédonie dans la République, the main *caldoche* party, won control in Nouméa. Each side could claim a victory, and New Caledonia emerged from the elections more divided than ever. In the short term the new political regime was designed to effect a change in the balance in local public life in favour of the Kanaks and, in theory, lead to a referendum before Dec. 31, 1987, on the question of the territory's achieving independence in association with France. However, in the event of an opposition victory in the 1986 elections in France, this proposed new status for the territory was likely to be challenged.

Foreign Affairs. As usual, France's concerns and aspirations were centred mainly, though not exclusively, on Western Europe. The meeting of the EC Council (the heads of state or government of EC member countries) held in Brussels in March took place in a morose atmosphere, with differences of interest getting in the way of any agreement. Nonetheless, June 12 proved to be a red-letter day with the signing in Lisbon and Madrid of the act enlarging the EC from 10 to 12 members from 1986. France believed that the enlargement of the Community would strengthen the position of Western Europe in relation to the superpowers. The EC Council meeting in Milan at the end of June was notable chiefly for an agreement on the principle of technological cooperation among Western European nations through the French-proposed Eureka project. When EC foreign ministers met to prepare for the Luxembourg summit in December, they were unable to achieve progress on the problem of the proposed revision of the Treaty of Rome, and differences emerged over the matter of imposing sanctions against South Africa. Despite the fact that the Luxembourg summit went some way toward resolving differences among EC members, Paris still questioned the future of a Europe in which intensified national interests caused confrontation and wondered when Europe would speak with a single voice.

At the Bonn summit of the seven most industrialized countries in May, there were considerable differences of opinion between President Mitterrand and U.S. Pres. Ronald Reagan, particularly over Reagan's Strategic Defense Initiative. Mitterrand remained opposed to the U.S. concept of "Star Wars" because, in his view, it would deprive Europe of its autonomy. Mitterrand went to West Berlin together with West German Chancellor Helmut Kohl to express France's continuing friendship toward the Federal Republic. He also spent four days in Brazil and Colombia. During the year he welcomed to Paris Pres. Miguel de la Madrid Hurtado of Mexico, King Juan Carlos I of Spain, Japanese Prime Minister Yasuhiro Nakasone, and Pres. Raúl Alfonsín of Argentina. However, the event that excited the most interest was undoubtedly Mikhail Gorbachev's four-day visit to Paris in October, the Soviet leader's first visit to the West after he took power in March. Several private discussions between Gorbachev and Mitterrand made up what was described as "a dialogue, with no major concessions." On December 4 Gen. Wojciech Jaruzelski of Poland visited Paris. Fabius was among the French politicians who criticized Mitterrand for becoming the first Western head of state to meet the Polish leader since martial law was imposed in Poland in 1981.

French involvement in the "Greenpeace affair" was extensively covered by the world press. Agents of the Direction Générale de Sécurité Extérieure (DGSE), the French external security service, were responsible for sabotaging the *Rainbow Warrior*, flagship of the environmental movement Greenpeace, which sank on July 10 in the port of Auckland, New Zealand. In November two French agents, Maj. Alain Mafart and Capt. Dominique Prieur, received prison sentences of ten years after pleading guilty to charges of sabotage and manslaughter, the latter charge resulting from the death of a Greenpeace photographer. The pretext for their action was the fact that the boat's mission was to spy on the firing ground for French nuclear tests at Mururoa Atoll, French Polynesia. This excuse appeared all the more ridiculous in the light of the fact that French Navy ships could easily prevent Greenpeace boats from entering Mururoa's territorial waters.

An official inquiry headed by Bernard Tricot issued a report exonerating the French government in August. The following month, however, Prime Minister Fabius admitted that Tricot had been misled during his inquiry and that the agents had indeed acted on government orders, though he did not reveal the source of the orders. Adm. Pierre Lacoste was dismissed as head of the DGSE and replaced by Gen. René Imbot, chief of staff of the Army. Minister of Defense Charles Hernu tendered his resignation and was succeeded by Paul Quilès, who moved from his post as minister for town planning, housing, and transport. Following these changes, according to the Elysée Palace, the "Greenpeace affair" was closed.

The other side of the matter emerged when President Mitterrand visited Mururoa Atoll on September 13 and presided over a meeting of representatives from French territories in the South Pacific. Twenty years after Gen. Charles de Gaulle, Mitterrand restated the need for a French presence in the Pacific and French determination to continue the subterranean nuclear tests at Mururoa for the sake of French independence. In general, France's right-wing opposition approved of the visit, thus demonstrating a degree of consensus over the country's policy of nuclear deterrence that had yet to be achieved in other fields.

(JEAN KNECHT)

See also *Dependent States,* below.

GERMANY, FEDERAL REPUBLIC OF

The Federal Republic of Germany (West Germany) is in central Europe, on the North and Baltic seas. Area: 248,706 sq km (96,026 sq mi). Pop. (1985 est., including West Berlin, which is an enclave within East Germany): 60,940,000. Provisional cap.: Bonn. Monetary unit: Deutsche Mark, with (Oct. 21, 1985) a free rate of DM 2.64 to U.S. $1 (DM 3.78 = £1 sterling). President in 1985, Richard von Weizsäcker; chancellor, Helmut Kohl.

Despite an economic upturn marred only by the high level of unemployment, the popularity of West Germany's centre-right coalition government of the Christian Democratic Union (CDU), its Bavarian wing, the Christian Social Union (CSU), and the Free Democratic Party (FDP) decreased in 1985. This was largely the result of disappointment over the leadership of federal Chancellor Helmut Kohl (*see* BIOGRAPHIES), who showed an unsteady hand in his management of both domestic and foreign policies, though his position was not seriously challenged.

Domestic Affairs. The biggest setback to the coalition parties was the outcome of the elections for the state parliament of North Rhine-Westphalia on May 12. Under the leadership of Johannes Rau, the charismatic state premier,

Personal problems, with alcohol and money, were thought to be the chief motives for the defection of Hans Joachim Tiedge, West Germany's chief of counterintelligence activity against East Germany. Other defectors were believed to be moles planted by East Germany.
SVEN SIMON—KATHERINE YOUNG

the Social Democratic Party (SPD) won 52.1% of the vote. The CDU's share fell by almost seven percentage points to 36.5%, compared with the 1980 state elections. The Social Democrats won majorities in towns previously regarded as safe for the Christian Democrats. Roman Catholic industrial workers in the Ruhr deserted the CDU, while farmers in Westphalia who might have voted for the CDU showed their anger over reduced subsidies from the European Communities (EC) by staying home. Clearly Rau, a jolly man of 54 and a churchgoing Protestant, had become the new star of the Social Democrats on a national level. It was assumed he would be the party's choice as candidate for chancellor in the federal elections due in 1987.

In March the Social Democrats scored a notable success in state elections in the Saarland, polling 49.2% of the vote, compared with 45.4% in 1980. The CDU's share fell from 44 to 37.3%. In the same month, however, the Christian Democrats held their position with only marginal losses in West Berlin. The results confirmed Eberhard Diepgen in office as governing mayor; he had held the office since February 1984 when he took over from Richard von Weizsäcker, who went on to become federal president.

The first coalition between the Social Democrats and the Green Party was formed in October in the state of Hesse. The move, which brought the Greens into government for the first time, was forced on the Social Democrats because they lacked an overall majority in the state legislature. The development took place at a time when the Greens were falling in the opinion polls, perhaps as voters grew bored with their irreverent behaviour in the Bundestag (federal parliament). In Hesse the Greens took over the state Environment Ministry set up to run waste management, water pollution control, nature conservation, and general energy policy. The SPD remained responsible for nuclear energy policy decisions.

The Christian Democrats claimed that a national coalition between the Social Democrats and the Greens could be expected if the Social Democrats emerged as the largest party, but without an overall majority, in the 1987 federal elections. Federal Minister of Finance Gerhard Stoltenberg went so far as to say that having Greens in a state gov-

ernment presented a danger to internal security. Some industrial firms made it known that they were considering moving out of Hesse, a state whose largest city is Frankfurt.

In February the FDP congress elected Martin Bangemann, the federal economics minister, as the party's leader in succession to Hans-Dietrich Genscher, the federal foreign minister. Bangemann expressed strong commitment to a continuation of the FDP's alliance with the Christian Democrats. In 1982 the FDP had withdrawn its support from the Social Democratic government of the time in order to form an alliance with the Christian Democrats.

The 11th annual economic summit of seven industrialized countries (Canada, France, West Germany, Italy, Japan, the U.K., and the U.S.) took place in Bonn in May. A shadow was cast over the event by a row concerning an act of reconciliation at a German military cemetery to mark the 40th anniversary of Victory in Europe (VE) Day at the end of World War II. U.S. Pres. Ronald Reagan, who attended the summit, had accepted Chancellor Kohl's invitation to visit the cemetery at Bitburg, not knowing that it contained the graves of soldiers of the Waffen SS, which had administered Hitler's concentration camps. Despite a storm of protest from many groups in the U.S., Kohl stuck to his plans, and Reagan felt obliged to go along with them, though in the event the visit to the cemetery was scaled down. On the same day, May 5, the two leaders visited the site of the Bergen-Belsen concentration camp. Some West Germans reacted with scorn to the fuss caused by the Bitburg affair in the U.S. In an editorial, the *Frankfurter Allgemeine Zeitung* daily newspaper blamed the U.S. media for breathing new life into the "caricature of the ugly German."

President Weizsäcker made a strong attack on German attitudes toward Jews in the Third Reich in a remarkable speech on the anniversary of VE Day, May 8. He said that at the time, Germans with their eyes and ears open could not have failed to notice that Jews were being deported; at the end of World War II too many Germans had claimed they had not known anything. President Weizsäcker said that scarcely any country had remained free from blame of war or violence. The genocide suffered by the Jews was, however, unparalleled in history. While the perpetration of the crime had been in the hands of a few people, and had been concealed from the eyes of the public, every German could have seen for himself the misery of his Jewish compatriots.

West Germans, and their allies as well, were shaken by a series of spy scandals in August and September. The most serious of these was the defection to East Germany of Hans Joachim Tiedge, third in command of West German counterintelligence. In his position as head of a department of the Verfassungsschutzmt (the federal Office for the Protection of the Constitution), Tiedge had access to the most secret information. He had worked for the service for 19 years and was also well informed about the activities of allied counterintelligence organizations. Around the time of his disappearance, no fewer than eight other alleged spies fled to East Germany. Among them were Sonja Lüneburg, for 12 years secretary to Economics Minister Bangemann, Ursula Richter, another government secretary, and Lorenz Betzing, a messenger who had once worked in an underground bunker intended as a command post in time of war.

Neighbours of Tiedge had been warning the service for years about his drinking habits, and a woman who cleaned his house said she had often seen documents marked top secret lying about. It was subsequently reported that the service had called back all its agents from the Eastern bloc because it was presumed that Tiedge had blown their

covers. In the wake of the affair, Heribert Hellenbroich was dismissed as head of the Bundesnachrichtendienst (the West German intelligence organization) after only a month in office. Hellenbroich had previously been in charge of counterintelligence. Hans-Georg Wieck, West German ambassador to NATO, took his place as chief of the intelligence service.

Court proceedings against two former federal Cabinet ministers, Count Otto Lambsdorff and Hans Friderichs, in connection with the so-called Flick affair opened in August. The prosecution alleged that the Flick industrial concern had paid out large sums of money to buy influence in Bonn and that the two men had accepted bribes. Both strongly denied the charges. Lambsdorff had resigned as economics minister in June 1984 when he was charged with corruption. Friderichs, who had been Lambsdorff's predecessor at the Economics Ministry, had resigned in 1977 to become chief executive of the Dresdner Bank. Both were members of the FDP. Charged with them was Eberhard von Brauchitsch, former chief executive of the Flick holding company. It was alleged that the two politicians had accepted money for party funds rather than for personal gain.

More than 300,000 Turks had returned home from West Germany since the federal government introduced a cash incentive scheme to encourage repatriation in 1983. The scheme was available to people of all non-EC countries but was aimed principally at reducing the large Turkish population in West Germany. Even so, there were still four million foreigners in the country, about 6% of the total population. The government said that foreigners who elected to stay in the country would be encouraged to acquire German nationality.

In late September and early October a wave of violent protests that involved widespread looting and destruction of property swept through a number of West German towns and cities. The incident that apparently sparked the violence was the death of a demonstrator during a rally against neo-Nazism in Frankfurt on September 28. The man, Günther Sare, died after being run over by a police water-cannon vehicle. Violent confrontations with the police followed. While Frankfurt was the scene of some of the worst incidents, riots erupted in several other centres, including Hamburg, West Berlin, Hanover, and Stuttgart.

West German tennis player Boris Becker (*see* BIOGRAPHIES) became a national hero by winning the men's singles championship at Wimbledon at the age of 17. Becker, who came from the town of Leimen, near Heidelberg, was the youngest player, the first German, and the first unseeded player to win the title.

The novelist Heinrich Böll, Nobel Prize winner in 1972, described as an honest rebel and the father figure of postwar German literature, died on July 16. Axel Springer, the newspaper publisher whose publications included *Bild Zeitung* and *Die Welt,* died on September 22. (*See* OBITUARIES.)

The government's economic policies could have been regarded as reasonably successful had it not been for the level of unemployment, which remained stubbornly unchanged at around two million. The inflation rate was about 2%; real gross national product was likely to rise by 2.5% for the year; export trade was increasing; and the health of state finances improved.

Foreign Affairs. Chancellor Kohl's pronounced pro-U.S. stance at the Bonn economic summit in May irritated the French. Kohl sided with President Reagan on two key issues: European involvement in the Strategic Defense Initiative (SDI) research program, and the need for a new round of international trade talks under the auspices of the General Agreement on Tariffs and Trade (GATT). West German observers spoke of cracks in the foundations of Europe's greatest postwar achievement, the close relationship between Bonn and Paris. The French were afraid that the U.S., in a new round of GATT talks, would succeed in removing restrictions on trade in agricultural products. Should this happen, the EC common agricultural policy, which the French saw as the cornerstone of the Community, could no longer be maintained in its existing form.

A cautious willingness for West Germany to take part in the SDI research program could be detected in the Chancellor's Office, though Foreign Minister Genscher was far from enthusiastic. Kohl had apparently been persuaded by West German industry that it stood to win lucrative contracts through collaboration with the project. Genscher feared that a bilateral agreement with the U.S. on "Star Wars" would place a further burden on West Germany's relations with its Communist neighbours. Genscher prompted Kohl to express support for West German collaboration in Eureka, the French-inspired project for a community of European technologies. Kohl made it clear, however, that participation in Eureka would not be linked with a rejection of Reagan's SDI plans. This suggested that Eureka would not become a rival project to SDI, something the French would, perhaps, have liked.

France continued to stress the importance of its relationship with West Germany. In October French Pres. François Mitterrand flew to West Berlin with Kohl to reaffirm France's commitment, as one of its guarantor powers, to the city's security. "You should interpret my presence here as a sign of solid, durable, and vigilant friendship," said Mitterrand at a welcoming ceremony. His visit, only the second by a French head of state, followed a meeting with Kohl in Bonn at which they discussed the implications of the forthcoming Geneva summit meeting between Reagan and Soviet leader Mikhail Gorbachev.

In October President Weizsäcker paid a visit to Israel, the first by a German head of state. Within the limits imposed by history, it was a success, and at the end of

DEUTSCHE PRESSE–AGENTUR/PHOTOREPORTERS

As party chairman Willy Brandt looks on, Johannes Rau, the rising star of West Germany's Social Democratic Party, announces his willingness to be the party's candidate for federal chancellor in the 1987 election.

it Israeli Pres. Chaim Herzog was able to say: "We used merely to respect you. We have now found a place for you in our hearts." Weizsäcker skirted sensitive questions about West German arms shipments to Saudi Arabia, saying policy-making was not part of his responsibility. It was a sensitive issue. Just before President Weizsäcker left Bonn, preliminary approval had been given to plans for a West German group to supply $2.5 billion worth of munitions plant to Saudi Arabia. Both the Social Democrats and the Greens denounced the possible contract, and Genscher was believed to have strong reservations about such a deal.

Minister of the Interior Friedrich Zimmermann (CSU) paid a visit to Paraguay in October, during which his civilities toward Gen. Alfredo Stroessner, the president of Paraguay, were considered by many people in West Germany to have been above and beyond the call of duty. Stroessner had ancestral links with Bavaria. At a press conference in Paraguay Zimmermann regretted what he called the campaign against Stroessner in the West German media in May, when the president was planning to visit West Germany. At the time, Paraguay was widely believed to be harbouring Josef Mengele, the Nazi doctor notorious for his experiments on inmates of the Auschwitz concentration camp during World War II. Later in the year the body of a man who died six years earlier in Brazil was identified as almost certainly that of Mengele.

Genscher visited China in November for the fourth time as foreign minister. He called for closer cooperation between the two countries and especially for more trade. When the Chinese expressed interest in Eureka, he told them the project would remain a European undertaking, though he softened the blow by saying that the world should have no technological divide.

(NORMAN CROSSLAND)

This article updates the *Macropædia* article GERMANY: *Federal Republic of Germany.*

GREECE

The republic of Greece occupies the southern part of the Balkan Peninsula and several adjoining island groups in southeastern Europe, in and between the Ionian and Aegean seas. Area: 131,957 sq km (50,949 sq mi). Pop. (1985 est.): 9,967,000. Cap.: Athens. Monetary unit: drachma, with (Oct. 21, 1985) a free rate of 154.31 drachmas to U.S. $1 (221.28 drachmas = £1 sterling). Presidents in 1985, Konstantinos Karamanlis until March 10 and, from March 30, Christos Sartzetakis; prime minister, Andreas Papandreou.

Political developments in Greece in 1985 were dominated by two events: the sudden resignation of Pres. Konstantinos Karamanlis on March 10, and the decisive victory of the ruling Panhellenic Socialist Movement (Pasok) in the general elections on June 2. Economic difficulties forced the government to introduce a program of rigorous economies. Frequent incidents of international terrorism on Greek territory induced the government to tighten security and coordinate counterterrorist action with other Western law-enforcement services.

Prime Minister Andreas Papandreou's sudden decision to withdraw his promised support for President Karamanlis, former New Democracy Party (conservative) prime minister, who was seeking reelection by Parliament for a second five-year term, forced Karamanlis to resign. Taking his own Pasok parliamentary group by surprise, Papandreou nominated instead Christos Sartzetakis (*see* BIOGRAPHIES), a Supreme Court judge, as the next chief of state. At the same time, he put forward proposals for a revision of the constitution in order to curtail presidential prerogatives. Employing methods whose legitimacy was questioned by

the opposition as well as by constitutional experts, Papandreou succeeded in securing the required three-fifths majority to elect Sartzetakis as president in the third round of voting. When the New Democracy Party challenged the legality of the new president and called for general elections, Papandreou obliged, but not before Parliament approved the constitutional reforms. The reforms would go into effect only if the next Parliament endorsed them.

The results of the elections of June 2 proved that Papandreou was right to discount the theory that, by withdrawing support from Karamanlis, he would lose the moderate vote. The Greek countryside, once the stronghold of conservatism, went solidly behind Pasok for the second time, despite Pasok's opposition to Greece's membership in the European Communities (EC), which had brought increased prosperity to the agricultural sector. Pasok took nearly 46% of the vote and 161 seats, and New Democracy nearly 41% and 126 seats, while the pro-Moscow Greek Communist Party (KKE) won 12 seats and the Eurocommunists one seat. (For tabulated results, see *Political Parties,* above.)

Still suffering from the shock of its second successive electoral defeat, New Democracy faced a new crisis when its leader, Konstantinos Mitsotakis, resigned abruptly in the belief that his leadership was being put in question by his parliamentary deputy, Kostis Stefanopoulos. The party's parliamentary group promptly reelected Mitsotakis. Stefanopoulos, who did not turn up to challenge him, left the party and, along with nine other dissident deputies, formed the Democratic Renewal Party, whose conservative platform was spiced with populism.

There was speculation about whether Pasok, in its second four-year term, would reach out for its more radical strategic objectives. However, it soon became clear that the constraints that had tempered Papandreou's aims during his first term remained in place and were, if anything, stronger. An abrupt deterioration in the state of the economy was evidenced by rising unemployment, two-digit inflation, and soaring foreign and domestic debts. After some hesitation, Papandreou shuffled his Cabinet to bring in a new economic team under former agriculture minister Kostas Simitis, who became minister of national economy, and on October 11 he launched a rigid austerity program. The government resisted the wave of strikes and protests that followed and disciplined its own party's recalcitrant trade union leaders by summary dismissals. The austerity budget for 1986 introduced in November included proposals to increase tax revenues and cut government spending.

At the same time, Papandreou turned to both the EC and the U.S. for support in the form of loans and investments that would inject some life into the stagnant economy. Rapprochement with the U.S. was a difficult objective, however. Incensed by years of anti-U.S. rhetoric from Papandreou, Washington was not eager to help. Indeed, following the hijacking on June 14 of a Trans World Airlines passenger aircraft that had taken off from Athens airport, U.S. Pres. Ronald Reagan admonished Papandreou for showing laxity toward terrorists and declared Athens airport unsafe. A dramatic decline in arrivals of U.S. tourists was estimated to have cost Greece about $300 million in lost revenue. Furthermore, the U.S. Defense Department withheld approval of the sale of 40 F-16 fighter aircraft to the Greek Air Force on the grounds that Greece was suspected of leaking Western high-technology secrets to the U.S.S.R. The revelations of Sergey Bokhan, a Soviet diplomat who defected to the U.S. from Athens in May, seemed to corroborate the existence of such leaks.

In both instances, the government acted promptly. It stepped up its counterterrorist activities and warned its

Arab friends that illicit activity conducted through Greece would no longer be tolerated. At the same time, a naval officer and two civilian electronics experts named by Bokhan were arrested and charged with selling defense secrets to the Soviets. However, Washington's main concern focused on whether Papandreou could be induced to drop his threat to expel the U.S. from its military bases in Greece when the current agreement expired in 1988.

While mending fences with the U.S., Papandreou also tried to improve relations with the U.S.S.R. He paid an official visit to Moscow in February. Papandreou joined the leaders of Argentina, India, Mexico, Sweden, and Tanzania in a joint appeal to the superpowers for a nuclear freeze. Although Greece's relations with its Balkan neighbours, including Albania, continued to improve, the plan for a nuclear-free Balkan zone was shelved because of Turkish objections. No effort was made to improve bilateral relations with Turkey.   (MARIO MODIANO)

ICELAND

Iceland is an island republic in the North Atlantic Ocean, near the Arctic Circle. Area: 103,000 sq km (39,769 sq mi). Pop. (1985 est.): 243,000. Cap.: Reykjavík. Monetary unit: króna, with (Oct. 21, 1985) a free rate of 41.65 krónur to U.S. $1 (59.72 krónur = £1 sterling). President in 1985, Vigdís Finnbogadóttir; prime minister, Steingrímur Hermannsson.

Throughout 1985 the Icelandic economy experienced moderate growth, largely under the influence of a limited fish catch, while other industries performed only passably well. Real gross national product (GNP) rose by an estimated 1.5% in volume, following a 2.5% rise in the previous year and a 5.7% decline in 1983. Despite the slow rate of growth in 1985, the economy was under considerable demand pressure, which found an outlet in substantial wage and price increases and a sizable current account deficit. Inflation averaged 31%, and the current account deficit was estimated at some 5% of GNP.

Iceland's relations with the U.S., which over the years had been excellent, were soured in 1985 by the fact that the U.S. base in Iceland ceased using Icelandic vessels for its freight import needs and resorted instead to using ships of U.S. registry, thus depriving two local shipping companies of important revenue. The matter was taken up directly by Foreign Minister Geir Hallgrímsson with U.S. Secretary of State George Shultz. The latter did his utmost to smooth over the issue by visiting Iceland twice during the year, in March and again in November. Soviet Foreign Minister Eduard Shevardnadze also paid a goodwill visit to the country in November.

The long-running dispute between the Icelandic government and Alusuisse, the Swiss corporation that owned an aluminum smelter in Iceland, was finally resolved in July when the Icelandic government signed an agreement settling all outstanding issues. The agreement increased the price of electric power supplied to the smelter and at the same time settled a dispute over the amount of tax that the smelter was to pay. The company had been accused of tax evasion.

The Althing (parliament) dealt with two unusual bills early in 1985. The first, which called for abolition of the state monopoly of radio and television, was passed; the second called for an end to the ban on alcoholic beer and was rejected. Both issues were hotly contested. The temperance movement, an influential force in Icelandic life, threw its considerable weight behind the campaign against the beer bill and lobbied successfully for its defeat. Later in the year, the government introduced a ban on artificial alcoholic beer, a homemade blend of grain spirits and alcohol-free beer.

The right-of-centre coalition government of the Progressive Party and the Independence Party, led by Prime Minister Steingrímur Hermannsson of the Progressive Party, continued in office throughout the year. In October the Independence Party, which held six of the ten posts in the Cabinet, reshuffled its ministers. The major objective of the reshuffle was to facilitate the entry into the Cabinet of Thorsteinn Pálsson as finance minister. Pálsson had succeeded Hallgrímsson as chairman of the party in November 1983. Sverrir Hermannsson moved from the Energy and Industry Ministry to Education, replacing Ragnhildur Helgadóttir, who moved to the Health and Social Security Ministry. The moves followed Hallgrímsson's announcement that he intended to resign his post of foreign minister on Jan. 1, 1986.

On October 24 the women of Iceland staged a one-day strike as they had done ten years earlier on the same date. The strike was intended to emphasize the role and importance of women in the economy and everyday life. Factories and offices were largely shut down and, since housewives also participated in the strike, most husbands had to take over the duties of cooking and child care.

Pres. Vigdís Finnbogadóttir contributed to the strike by refusing to sign an important emergency bill that had been passed during an all-night session of the Althing the night before. After delaying her signature for several hours, Finnbogadóttir eventually relented and affixed her signature to the bill, thus making it law. The law ordered an end to a strike by flight attendants that had virtually halted air transportation between Iceland and the rest of the world.

(BJÖRN MATTHÍASSON)

IRELAND

The republic of Ireland, separated from Great Britain by the North Channel, the Irish Sea, and St. George's Channel, shares its island with Northern Ireland to the northeast. Area: 70,285 sq km (27,137 sq mi). Pop. (1985 est.): 3,614,000. Cap.: Dublin. Monetary unit: Irish pound (punt), with (Oct. 21, 1985) a free rate of Ir£0.85 to U.S. $1 (Ir£1.22 = £1 sterling). President in 1985, Patrick J. Hillery; prime minister, Garret FitzGerald.

The Irish government, midway through its term of office, faced economic difficulties that showed little sign of improvement during 1985. The foreign debt, at 70% of gross national product, reached Ir£2,000 million. Unemployment continued to rise and in mid-1985 stood at 17.7% of the work force. With one million people totally or partially dependent on social-welfare payments, and one-half of the population below the age of 25, the burden of taxation continued to be borne by the middle-income groups. There was considerable discontent over the policies being pursued by the government, and demands were made throughout the year for a change in the taxation system, under which the average wage earner paid tax at around 40%. Discontent reached acute levels in October when the public-service unions confronted the government by staging the country's first comprehensive strike in the public sector, while individual unions went on strike in support of teachers' wage claims.

Though inflation, down to 5.2% and falling, was below the average for the European Communities (EC), improved industrial performance did little to help the economic situation. Government strategy, which hoped to combine modest cuts in taxation with curtailment of public expenditure, failed to reach the targets set in the January budget.

Prime Ministers Garret FitzGerald of Ireland (left) and Margaret Thatcher of Great Britain sign a treaty whereby the government of the Irish Republic would have a formal consultative role on issues relating to the status of and policy toward Northern Ireland.
AP/WIDE WORLD

More significantly, performance was well short of the targets set by the government for the three-year period 1985–87 in the overall economic strategy document, "Building on Reality," published in October 1984. Agriculture was adversely affected by the worst summer in 30 years as widespread flooding destroyed grain and hay harvests. Despite government and EC measures to aid the worst-affected areas, the general mood of discontent spread to rural areas.

The ruling coalition of Fine Gael and the Labour Party lost some parliamentary support early in the year over its measure designed to liberalize the availability of contraceptives. The new law allowed the sale of nonmedical contraceptives to persons over the age of 18, whereas previously contraceptives had been available only to married people on prescription. The bill passed the Dail (lower house of parliament) in February, despite the fact that some members of both government parties refused to support it, and became law in March.

The introduction of the new legislation was followed by a severe political setback for the coalition in local elections held in June. The main opposition party, Fianna Fail, made substantial gains throughout the country and took control of a number of local authorities, councils, and corporations. The reverse was heralded by the declining fortunes of the administration in the opinion polls, in which Fianna Fail was seen to lead the combined coalition partners by as much as 18 percentage points. Riding on this tide of public popularity, Fianna Fail leader Charles J. Haughey forced the expulsion of his main rival, Desmond O'Malley, from the party.

The trend in political affairs toward divergence and confrontation hindered progress in the talks between the British and Irish governments on a new initiative aimed at solving the problem of Northern Ireland. While Prime Minister Garret FitzGerald, together with Deputy Prime Minister Dick Spring and Foreign Affairs Minister Peter Barry, worked throughout the year to ensure that the Republic of Ireland would have a say in Northern Ireland's future, the opposition leader declared himself to be increasingly opposed to any approach that was not structured toward eventual achievement of a united Ireland. His stance placed considerable strain on negotiations and led to delays in the planning of a summit meeting between FitzGerald and U.K. Prime Minister Margaret Thatcher.

When the summit took place at Hillsborough Castle, County Down, Northern Ireland, on November 15 the two leaders signed an agreement setting up an Anglo-Irish Conference for Northern Ireland that would bring together, as joint chairmen, the U.K. secretary of state for Northern Ireland and the Irish Republic's foreign minister. The principle behind the plan was that the Republic of Ireland representative, accompanied by additional aides, would act as guarantor for the minority nationalist community in Northern Ireland. The concept received widespread support in both the U.K. and the Republic, although it was accompanied by considerable risks and earned growing opposition among the unionists in Northern Ireland as the details emerged. The Hillsborough agreement was approved by both the U.K. and Irish parliaments by the end of the year.

Another area that continued to provoke political confrontation was law and order. An increase in vandalism, robbery with violence, and drug abuse brought divided reactions, not just between the government and the opposition but within political parties. In general, the controversy was well handled by Justice Minister Michael Noonan. However, his plan to open a prison for young offenders on Spike Island, in the estuary of the River Lee at Cork, received a setback when rioting destroyed the building. In February, following the discovery of a large bank deposit believed to belong to the Irish Republican Army, an emergency law was passed allowing the government to seize money thought to be owned by illegal organizations.

In a year of political and economic gloom and despondency, a ray of optimism came from an unlikely source. Bob Geldof (see BIOGRAPHIES), a pop musician from Dublin, organized the Live Aid concert, staged on July 13 in London and Philadelphia and broadcast round the world, which raised over £50 million ($71.5 million) for the relief of famine in Africa. The Irish contribution reached £6 million ($8.6 million), outstripping that of any other country on a per capita basis.

On October 25 the first flights arrived at the newly completed international airport at the tiny village of Knock, County Mayo. The airport was built largely at the instigation of Msgr. James Horan, parish priest of Knock, and had been funded in the main by public money in a time of acute stringency. Since Knock was fogbound for much of the year and would have difficulty producing sufficient traffic to justify the expenditure, the airport's future was uncertain.　(MAVIS ARNOLD)

See also United Kingdom, below.

ITALY

A republic of southern Europe, Italy occupies the Apennine Peninsula, Sicily, Sardinia, and a number of smaller islands in the Mediterranean Sea. Area: 301,277 sq km (116,324 sq mi). Pop. (1985 est.): 57,079,000. Cap.: Rome. Monetary unit: lira, with (Oct. 21, 1985) a free rate of 1,778.94 lire to U.S. $1 (2,551 lire = £1 sterling). Presidents in 1985, Alessandro Pertini and, from July 9, Francesco Cossiga; prime minister, Bettino Craxi.

Italy's coalition government of Christian Democrats, Socialists, Republicans, Social Democrats, and Liberals, in office since Aug. 4, 1983, faced a severe crisis that forced Socialist Prime Minister Bettino Craxi to offer his own

An EgyptAir jetliner is guarded by Italian and U.S. troops at a military base in Sigonella, Sicily, after having been forced to divert from its intended destination in Tunisia by U.S. Navy fighters. Four hijackers of the *Achille Lauro* were taken into custody from the plane.

G. GIANSANTI—SYGMA

and his government's resignation on Oct. 17, 1985. The first link in a chain of events that precipitated the crisis was the hijacking of the Italian cruise ship *Achille Lauro,* with over 400 people aboard, by four Palestinians claiming to be members of the Palestine Liberation Front (PLF), a splinter group of the Palestine Liberation Organization (PLO). The hijacking took place on October 7 as the ship was sailing in the Mediterranean Sea between Alexandria and Port Said, Egypt. Craxi, who had held several friendly meetings with PLO chairman Yasir Arafat, turned to him to use his good offices. Fifty-two hours later the four hijackers surrendered to the Egyptians, and Rome celebrated Craxi's triumph.

As the four Palestinians were being flown in an Egyptian aircraft to Tunisia as part of the surrender pact, however, their plane was intercepted by U.S. Tomcat fighters operating from an aircraft carrier. U.S. Pres. Ronald Reagan telephoned Craxi for permission to force the Egyptian plane to land at the NATO base at Sigonella, Sicily. With Craxi's consent, the plane landed, bringing the four hijackers physically under Italian jurisdiction. Italy already had legal jurisdiction over them for the crimes they had committed aboard the Italian ship, including the murder of one U.S. passenger. Also aboard the aircraft, as it turned out, were Arafat's negotiator, Abul Abbas, and another aide. The U.S. claimed that Abbas, a PLF leader, had been responsible for planning the original objective of the mission, which apparently had been to attack the Israeli port of Ashdod. Already frustrated by Craxi's refusal to turn over the four hijackers, Reagan again telephoned Craxi and demanded the arrest and extradition of Abbas. Craxi, instead, allowed him and the other Arafat aide to leave the country, arguing that they were under Egypt's protection and that Abbas also carried an Iraqi diplomatic passport.

As far as was known, Craxi was the first Italian prime minister to say no to a U.S. president, but no other prime minister had ever faced a similar situation. It was possible that his refusal to agree to Reagan's demands increased his popularity among those Italians with latent antipathy toward the Western superpower. If Craxi could be accused of being pro-Arab, it was a policy that all previous Italian governments had followed more or less implicitly, and without ever being seen as anti-Israeli. However, some members of the government did not agree with Craxi's actions. Defense Minister Giovanni Spadolini, claiming he had not been consulted on the decision to allow Abbas to depart, led his fellow Republicans out of the Cabinet, forcing Craxi to offer his resignation. The makeup of Parliament was such that Craxi's five-party coalition commanded only a 55% majority, which without the support of the Republicans would be reduced to a highly vulnerable 51%.

However, Pres. Francesco Cossiga (*see* BIOGRAPHIES), only four months into his term of office, neither refused nor accepted the proffered resignation. By the end of October, following talks with the various party leaders, Craxi was in a position to assure Cossiga that he could continue with the same coalition. On November 6 Craxi won a vote of confidence in the Chamber of Deputies by a secure margin.

Domestic Affairs. Regional and municipal elections took place in most of the nation in May. The results brought a return to the status quo of the previous decade. The Communists, who had shown a fractional lead over the Christian Democrats in the 1984 elections to the European Parliament, received only 30% of the national vote while the Christian Democrats' share increased to 35%. The Christian Democrats also regained control of Rome's city administration after nine years of Communist domination. In other cities with more than 500,000 population, the Communists held onto their vote, dropping a fraction here and there. However, a fractional loss was never taken lightly, and Alessandro Natta, Communist leader since 1984, was advised to call an early party conference for the spring of 1986.

Pres. Alessandro Pertini's seven-year term of office ended in July. In the preceding months, every opinion poll had shown that the majority of Italians wished to see him reelected as head of state. However, with Pertini soon to turn 89, Parliament perhaps felt him too old for another term, and the Christian Democrats did not disguise their desire to have one of their own in the office, after seven years of occupancy by a Socialist. On June 16 Pertini announced that he would not seek reelection. On June 24 Parliament elected Cossiga, a Christian Democrat who was chairman of the Senate at the time. Although he was, at 56, the youngest Italian president of the post-World War II era, at times the Quirinale Palace's new occupant seemed to be an older man than his buoyant and peppery predecessor. During the year two of the smaller political parties, the Social Democrats and the Liberals, quietly chose new leaders in Franco Nicolazzi and Alfredo Biondi, respectively.

In March Michele Sindona, already convicted in the U.S. of bank fraud offenses, received a 12-year prison sentence in his native Italy for similar offenses in connection with the collapse of his Banca Privata Finanziara in 1974. In June he was charged with having hired an Italian-American to fly to Milan and kill Giorgio Ambrosoli, who had been assigned the task of investigating Sindona's bank failure and other shady dealings in Italy.

Two other trials that took place during the year attracted more public attention. The first, which began in February, was of 251 defendants accused of crimes related to the activities of the Camorra, the Neapolitan-based organization

of criminal gangs. It was the first trial resulting from the massive crackdown on Camorra activities in June 1983. The motive for the public's interest was the fact that one of the defendants, Enzo Tortora, was one of Italy's most popular television personalities. His fans, and the Italian press in general, were unable to accept the sentence of ten years passed on Tortora, who was accused of being a drug peddler for the Camorra. Tortora lodged an appeal.

The second trial was that of four Turks and three Bulgarians whom Mehmet Ali Agca, the Turk who was serving a life sentence for his 1981 attempt to kill Pope John Paul II, accused of being his accomplices and paymasters. Ably presided over by Judge Severino Santiapichi (*see* BIOGRAPHIES), the trial nevertheless rapidly turned into black farce. Agca, the sole accuser, was found out in at least one lie on each day that he testified. He retracted much that he had said in pretrial sworn statements, and on several occasions he announced that he was Jesus Christ incarnate. As he named additional Turks as his accomplices, evidence of the existence of a Bulgarian connection in the plot diminished.

Terrorism did not cease, but some of the acts perpetrated on Italian soil were "imported" and apparently related in different ways to the Palestinian conflict. Two Jordanians were killed in an ambush in Rome; hand grenades thrown among the tables of an outdoor café injured approximately 40 people; and in September a 16-year-old Arab was apprehended after a bomb exploded in the British Airways ticket office in Rome, injuring 13 people and killing an Italian woman clerk. On December 27 Palestinian gunmen using grenades and machine guns attacked passengers at the Israeli airline check-in desk at Rome's Leonardo da Vinci Airport.

On July 19 an earthen dam gave way in the Fiemme Valley, near Trento in the Dolomite Alps, releasing a flood of mud and water that killed some 250 people. However, the tragedy that left an indelible impression upon Italians because it was transmitted live on television was the death of 31 Italian football fans, who were among those who died in Heysel soccer stadium, Brussels, on May 29. The fans had gone there to support Juventus of Turin in the European Cup final match against the English club Liverpool. The deaths, most of them caused by crushing and suffocation, were blamed primarily on the hooliganism of the English fans and secondarily on the seating arrangements and inadequate policing in the stadium. (*See* SPORTS AND GAMES: *Football:* Sidebar.)

Mafia attempts, some successful, on the lives of policemen and public figures in Sicily suggested that the law was indeed beginning to interfere with the Mafia's drug trafficking, which was now apparently its main business. Formerly, the Mafia had attacked rival gangland criminals but had left public servants alone. In the space of eight days in August, two Mafia experts with the Palermo police force were gunned down.

Venice and the surrounding lagoon area received 600 billion lire from the government to spend on flood protection and housing before the end of 1986. Permission was granted to start excavation work in Rome on the Forum of Nerva and the two-thirds of Julius Caesar's Forum that remained below street level. The biggest archaeological dig ever undertaken in a modern urban centre, it was not expected to be completed before the end of the century.

The Economy. Though the government's goal was to bring inflation down from its 1984 level of 10% to 7%, Italy seemed certain to close the year with double-digit inflation again. The 1984 record budget deficit of 93.9 trillion lire, representing 16.7% of the gross domestic product, seemed sure to be overtaken by the 1985 fiscal deficit. During the

year imports grew faster (by 5%) than exports (down by 7.3%), reflecting the facts that the percentage of dollar-determined prices was higher for imports than for exports and that Italy had to import most of its prime materials and 80% of its energy supplies. The government sought to curb inflation with austere fiscal clampdowns and to entrap tax evaders. Without the tourism boom, expected to bring in $8.8 billion, the picture would have been bleak indeed.

(GEORGE ARMSTRONG)

LIECHTENSTEIN

A landlocked constitutional monarchy of central Europe, Liechtenstein is united with Switzerland by a customs and monetary union. Area: 160 sq km (62 sq mi). Pop. (1985 est.): 26,800. Cap.: Vaduz. Monetary unit: Swiss franc, with (Oct. 21, 1985) a free rate of Sw F 2.17 to U.S. $1 (Sw F 3.11 = £1 sterling). Sovereign prince, Francis Joseph II; deputy head of state in 1985, Prince Hans Adam; chief of government, Hans Brunhart.

On July 1, 1985, Sovereign Prince Francis Joseph II of Liechtenstein, who a year earlier had transferred much of his executive power to his son, Prince Hans Adam, was admitted to a hospital in Switzerland. He was thought to be suffering from a heart complaint. Within a week his condition was described as very much improved.

On September 8 Pope John Paul II paid the first official visit by a Roman Catholic pope to the principality. He traveled by helicopter from Zürich, Switz., to the north of the country, between Eschen and Mauren, where he was greeted by Prince Francis Joseph, his wife, Princess Georgine, and Prince Hans Adam. The mass at the nearby stadium was attended by a congregation of 30,000, greater than the total population of Liechtenstein. The pope then flew on to Vaduz. The political result of his ten-hour visit was that Liechtenstein and the Vatican agreed to establish diplomatic relations.   (K. M. SMOGORZEWSKI)

This article updates the *Micropædia* article LIECHTENSTEIN.

LUXEMBOURG

The Benelux country of Luxembourg is a landlocked constitutional monarchy in western Europe. Area: 2,586 sq km (999 sq mi). Pop. (1985 est.): 366,200. Cap.: Luxembourg. Monetary unit: Luxembourg franc, at par with the Belgian franc, with (Oct. 21, 1985) a free rate of Lux F 53.42 to U.S. $1 (Lux F 76.60 = £1 sterling). Grand duke, Jean; prime minister in 1985, Jacques Santer.

During his pilgrimage to the Benelux countries in 1985, Pope John Paul II paid a two-day visit to Luxembourg on May 15–16. In contrast to his turbulent reception in The Netherlands, he received a warm welcome from the people of Luxembourg, over 90% of whom are Roman Catholic. After celebrating mass at the cathedral of Luxembourg, John Paul visited Grand Duke Jean and his family, met with Prime Minister Jacques Santer and members of his government, and was shown around the complex of buildings belonging to the European Communities (EC) in the capital.

The Grand Duchy began its six-month presidency of the EC Council on July 1. In June Luxembourg was one of five EC member countries—the others were Belgium, France, West Germany, and The Netherlands—who agreed that citizens of the EC should be free to cross their common frontiers without undergoing police checks. At their meeting in Brussels on March 27, EC industry ministers agreed that the government of Luxembourg, along with those of Belgium, France, and Italy, should be permitted to grant

extra subsidies to its steel industry during 1985, on condition that serious consideration be given to reducing the industry's output capacity in the future.

Grand Duchess Charlotte (*see* OBITUARIES) died on July 9. Mother of Grand Duke Jean, she was the ruler of the Grand Duchy during the period 1919–64, at the end of which she abdicated in favour of her son.

(K. M. SMOGORZEWSKI)

This article updates the *Macropædia* article The Low COUNTRIES: *Luxembourg.*

MALTA

The republic of Malta, a member of the Commonwealth, comprises the islands of Malta, Gozo, and Comino in the Mediterranean Sea between Sicily and Tunisia. Area: 316 sq km (122 sq mi). Pop. (1985 est.): 333,000. Cap.: Valletta. Monetary unit: Maltese lira (formerly Maltese pound), with (Oct. 21, 1985) a free rate of 0.43 lira to U.S. $1 (0.62 lira = £1 sterling). President in 1985, Agatha Barbara; prime minister, Carmelo Mifsud Bonnici.

Under the leadership of Prime Minister Carmelo Mifsud Bonnici (*see* BIOGRAPHIES), who succeeded Dom Mintoff in December 1984, the Maltese government sought to repair links with Western Europe during 1985. In September a three-year agreement was signed with the European Communities under which Malta was to receive aid. Restrictions on travel to and trade with Italy, imposed in late 1984, were lifted in September 1985.

Following mediation by the Vatican, the government and the Roman Catholic Church signed an agreement in April providing for the gradual phasing out of fees in Malta's church schools and setting up a joint commission to handle any further church-state disputes. The accord settled a long disagreement over the issue of free education.

On November 23 a hijacked EgyptAir passenger airliner landed at Valletta airport. Mifsud Bonnici authorized the storming of the plane by a group of Egyptian commandos after the hijackers had killed two passengers. A further 57 persons died in the ensuing gun battle and fire on the plane. One of the hijackers, reportedly Palestinian, survived and was taken into custody.

On June 3 the International Court of Justice at The Hague delivered its judgment in the dispute between Malta and Libya over their maritime boundary. Malta, which had pressed for the boundary to be drawn at an equal distance from either country, was awarded a substantially smaller area of the continental shelf than Libya because of the latter's longer coastline.   (ALBERT GANADO)

MONACO

A sovereign principality on the northern Mediterranean coast, Monaco is bounded on land by the French département of Alpes-Maritimes. Area: 1.90 sq km (0.73 sq mi). Pop. (1985 est.): 28,000. Monetary unit: French franc, with (Oct. 21, 1985) a free rate of F 8.04 to U.S. $1 (F 11.53 = £1 sterling). Chief of state, Prince Rainier III; minister of state in 1985, Jean Herly.

The principality of Monaco, perhaps best known for its gambling casinos, welcomed the establishment of two very different institutions during 1985. An impressive new sports complex was officially inaugurated on January 25. While the centrepiece of the complex was a soccer and athletics stadium that could seat 20,000 spectators, facilities for many other sports were also included. Costing F 600 million, the new complex was built on some 20 ha (50 ac) of land that had been reclaimed from the Mediterranean Sea.

A source of even greater pride in the palace of Monaco, according to some reports, was the Princess Grace Irish Library, newly housed in two rooms of an old residence on the Rock of Monaco. During the 1960s the late Princess Grace, of Irish-American background, had built up a collection of books about Ireland. This collection formed the core of the new library.   (K. M. SMOGORZEWSKI)

This article updates the *Micropædia* article MONACO.

NETHERLANDS, THE

A constitutional monarchy of northwestern Europe, The Netherlands, a Benelux country, is on the North Sea. Area: 41,-508 sq km (16,026 sq mi). Pop. (1985 est.): 14,472,000. Cap., Amsterdam; seat of government, The Hague. Monetary unit: guilder, with (Oct. 21, 1985) a free rate of 2.98 guilders to U.S. $1 (4.27 guilders = £1 sterling). Queen, Beatrix; prime minister in 1985, Ruud Lubbers.

During 1985 three issues dominated public life in The Netherlands: the visit of Pope John Paul II; the decision regarding the deployment of U.S. medium-range cruise missiles; and the "Elfstedentocht," a traditional ice-skating race around 11 cities in Friesland Province. A cold spell allowed the race to take place on February 21 for the first time in 22 years. Attracting 16,000 competitors, the event caused skating fever to grip the country. The race was won by Evert van Benthem, a 26-year-old farmer, in a time of 6 hr 46 min 46 sec. He received a wreath of honour from Queen Beatrix and became a national hero, at least for a time.

Pope John Paul received rather less attention when he

SYGMA

Egyptian commandos surround the sole surviving hijacker of an EgyptAir plane at Valletta airport in Malta. The other hijackers, believed to be Palestinians, were killed in the storming of the plane, along with 57 passengers and crew.

paid a four-day official visit in May. The majority of Dutch people had mixed feelings about his visit; on the one hand, they appreciated his disarming nature and his efforts to deliver his speeches in Dutch; on the other, they disapproved of the Roman Catholic Church's views on divorce, abortion, contraception, and the role of women in the church. In the face of protests that began a week before his arrival and continued throughout his visit, the pope remained firm. Among several groups who declined to meet him were the Dutch Jews, who refused because he chose not to apologize for the fact that the church did not speak out against Nazi persecution of Jews during World War II. The pope's reception revealed the independent nature of Dutch culture more clearly than Catholic officials could express it to the Vatican.

On November 1 Prime Minister Ruud Lubbers announced that the government had agreed to sign a treaty with the U.S. allowing NATO to deploy 48 cruise missiles in The Netherlands by 1988 and guaranteeing its permission for five years. The agreement, expected to come into force in 1986, marked the end of more than six years of emotional political discussion and followed an attempt in June 1984 to link the decision with the progress of East-West arms-control negotiations. Days earlier Lubbers had been handed a petition signed by some 3,750,000 people opposed to deployment. In October the U.S.S.R. launched an intensive political offensive aimed at influencing the government. At the last minute the government was invited to discuss disarmament proposals with the Soviets if it would abandon its intention to accept the missiles.

The government decision was strongly opposed by the Socialist Party (PVDA) and the smaller left-wing parties, which claimed that it was unconstitutional and that the government had not tried to negotiate with the U.S.S.R. The two major government parties favoured the decision, though for different reasons. The Liberals (VVD) were satisfied that the move showed The Netherlands to be a reliable member of NATO, while the Christian Democratic Appeal accepted it as the inevitable consequence of the failure of its attempt to influence arms-control negotiations.

Queen Beatrix's speech to Parliament on September 17 underlined the government's priorities: to encourage a recovery of trade and industry and to reduce the budget deficit. While the budget, presented by Finance Minister Onno Ruding, revealed a slight reduction in the deficit, the government intended to accelerate the process by cutting spending by 8 billion guilders.

Queen Beatrix and Prince Claus paid an official visit to Spain on October 8–10, returning the visit by King Juan Carlos to The Netherlands in 1980. The occasion was seen as a final gesture of reconciliation. After more than three centuries, the war in which The Netherlands won independence from Spain was banished to the history books.

(DICK BOONSTRA)

See also *Dependent States,* below.

This article updates the *Macropædia* article The Low COUNTRIES: *The Netherlands.*

NORWAY

A constitutional monarchy of northern Europe, Norway occupies the western part of the Scandinavian Peninsula, with coastlines on the Skagerrak, the North Sea, the Norwegian Sea, and the Arctic Ocean. Area: 323,895 sq km (125,057 sq mi), excluding the Svalbard Archipelago and Jan Mayen Island. Pop. (1985 est.): 4,157,000. Cap.: Oslo. Monetary unit: krone, with (Oct. 21, 1985) a free rate of 7.89 kroner to U.S. $1 (11.32 kroner = £1 sterling). King, Olav V; prime minister in 1985, Kåre Isaachsen Willoch.

Parliamentary elections held on Sept. 9, 1985, returned to power the three-party, right-of-centre coalition led by Kåre Willoch, who thus became the first Conservative in the 20th century to win a second term as Norway's prime minister. Willoch's government, in which the Christian Democrat (Christian People's) and Centre (agrarian) parties were junior partners, lost ground, however, in terms of both parliamentary strength and share of the total vote. It emerged with a lead of only one seat over the Socialist opposition, comprising the Labour and Socialist Left parties. The balance of power in the Storting (parliament), expanded from 155 members to 157, was held by the right-wing Progress Party, although its representation shrank from four seats to two. (For tabulated results, see *Political Parties,* above.) The new Storting contained the highest proportion (35%) of women of any national assembly in the world.

Increased support for the Labour and Socialist Left parties reflected widespread discontent with government spending curbs, aimed at slowing inflation, which had adversely affected health and social services in particular. The budget for 1986, introduced on October 14, sought to repair the damage by sharply increasing expenditure in these sectors. The minority coalition was expected to face a difficult four years. On a number of issues, including defense, foreign affairs, and regional development, many Christian Democrat and Centre Party members leaned more toward the views of Labour than those of their own government. The Progress Party, piqued at Willoch's refusal to grant it any influence over coalition policy, would not promise unconditional support.

The Cabinet was reshuffled at the end of September to reflect the increased parliamentary strength of the Christian Democrat and Centre parties. Eivind Reiten, a Centre Party representative, replaced a Conservative as minister of fisheries, while Religious Affairs and Education Minister Kjell Magne Bondevik, a Christian Democrat, became deputy prime minister.

In February the U.K. government vetoed a provisional £20,000 million deal between Statoil, the state petroleum company, and the British Gas Corporation for the supply of gas from the Sleipner field to Britain in the 1990s. As a result, the development of Sleipner was shelved temporarily. Later in the year gas exports to the U.K. and other countries in Europe from the Anglo-Norwegian Statfjord field began. The mainland economy prospered. Gross national product was expected to show 3.75% growth over the previous year, with industrial output up 3%. Unemployment dropped from an average of 3% in 1984 to 2.25%, and industrial wages rose by over 9%. Expansionist fiscal policies, adopted with an eye to the elections, partly accounted for the boom. Another factor was the strong U.S. dollar in the first part of the year, which boosted krone revenues from petroleum and gas, as well as from more traditional exports.

The weakening of petroleum prices, and the fall in the value of the dollar in the latter half of the year, seemed likely to continue into 1986 and were expected to reduce state revenues from petroleum to 35.8 billion kroner in 1986, down from an estimated 46 billion kroner in 1985. The 1986 budget foresaw a deficit of almost 1 billion kroner, compared with an expected 1985 surplus of 19.3 billion kroner. The deficit was due mainly to the drop in petroleum revenues but also to the fact that revenue from other sources was not expected to match the rise in state expenditure and transfers. Modest personal income tax concessions were aimed at encouraging moderation in 1986 wage demands.

A news event of international interest during the year

was the trial on spying charges of former diplomat and government minister Arne Treholt. In June a tribunal found Treholt guilty of spying for both the U.S.S.R. and Iraq. He was sentenced to 20 years' imprisonment and ordered to pay costs of 100,000 kroner, as well as the 1 million kroner he allegedly received from the Soviet and Iraqi secret services. Treholt appealed to the Supreme Court. In October his account of his imprisonment, interrogation, and trial was published.   (FAY GJESTER)

See also *Dependent States,* below.

PORTUGAL

A republic of southwestern Europe, metropolitan Portugal is on the Atlantic coast of the Iberian Peninsula, which it shares with Spain. Area: 91,985 sq km (35,516 sq mi), including the Azores and Madeira island groups/archipelagoes in the Atlantic. Pop. (1985 est.): 10,151,300. Cap.: Lisbon. Monetary unit: escudo, with (Oct. 21, 1985) a free rate of 162.48 escudos to U.S. $1 (233 escudos = £1 sterling). President in 1985, Gen. António dos Santos Ramalho Eanes; prime ministers, Mário Soares and, from November 6, Aníbal Cavaço Silva.

Factional squabbling within the Social Democratic Party (PSD), which, together with the Socialist Party (PSP), formed Portugal's coalition government, led the PSD leader, Deputy Prime Minister and Defense Minister Carlos Mota Pinto (*see* OBITUARIES), to resign both his party and government posts in February 1985. Mota Pinto, who died three months later, was replaced in both capacities by Rui Machete. Machete's following in the PSD was weak, however, and on May 19 he himself was replaced as head of the party by Aníbal Cavaço Silva, leader of the party's right wing. A professor of economics, Cavaço Silva had been a close associate of the late prime minister Francisco Sá Carneiro and had been finance minister in his 1980 government. Socialist prime minister Mário Soares was angered by the PSD's choice of leader. Speaking at a political rally on June 2, Cavaço Silva called into question the future of the coalition between the PSP and PSD. He went on to call for the formation of a rejuvenated PSD, which, in his view, would be unable to agree to remain in the government. The PSD faction headed by Cavaço Silva was strongly opposed to PSP policies, especially on the subjects of labour and agrarian reform.

On June 3 the political committee of the PSD met and decided to pull the party out of the coalition on June 13, the day after the country signed its accession treaty with the European Communities (EC). Meanwhile, the Communist-led unions staged nationwide strikes in the industrial and transport sectors and organized demonstrations calling for an end to the coalition government. They were joined in this demand by the right-wing Democratic and Social Centre (CSD), whose leader, Francisco Lucas Pires, called for snap elections. Pres. António dos Santos Ramalho Eanes brooded for six days on the breakup of the coalition before asking the Assembly if it could muster a new Cabinet without elections. Two days later he called a meeting of the 16-member Council of State to consider a date for elections. Prime Minister Soares offered his resignation on June 25; the Assembly was dissolved on July 12; and general elections were set for October 6. The PSP agreed to remain in office in the meantime as a minority caretaker government.

In mid-July António Almeida Santos was chosen by the PSP as its candidate for the premiership. Santos, who had served in the Cabinet eight times since the 1974 revolution, was a lawyer and a close friend of Soares. On July 18 Soares formally announced his intention to run in the presidential elections due in January 1986. The following day a new party, the Democratic Renewal Party (DRP), was formally recognized. The party was set up by supporters of President Eanes to provide him with a vehicle for reentering the political arena once his term of office expired. Eanes, completing his second term of office, was constitutionally barred from running again. Shortly after the parliamentary elections the PSD, with the strong support of Cavaço Silva, formally adopted Diogo Freitas Amaral, a former leader of the CSD, as its presidential candidate.

In the general elections the PSD overtook the PSP to become the largest single party in the 250-seat Assembly. While the PSD increased its representation from 75 to 88 seats, the PSP, whose representation dropped from 101 to 57 seats, lost support largely to the DRP, which emerged with 45 seats. Both the (Communist) United People's Alliance and the CSD lost seats. (For tabulated results, see *Political Parties,* above.) A constitutional crisis threatened when, immediately after the polling, Prime Minister Soares announced that he was handing over his official duties to PSD Deputy Prime Minister Machete. President Eanes stepped in and secured a promise from Soares that he would continue as caretaker prime minister until a new government had been formed.

After receiving the endorsement of his party on October 20, Cavaço Silva was appointed prime minister of a minority PSD government on October 28. The CSD offered working support, and the DRP declared that it was "not opposed." Cavaço Silva's Cabinet, sworn in on November 6, retained three ministers from the previous coalition administration and included two independent ministers, Foreign Affairs Minister Pedro Pires de Miranda and Labour and Social Security Minister Luis Mira Amaral. Referring to the size of his Cabinet, the smallest of any government since the revolution, Cavaço Silva announced that it was his first contribution toward eliminating wasteful spending of public funds. The PSD had campaigned on a platform that envisaged a free-market economy in which job-security laws would be liberalized and state control of industry reduced.

Despite a security crackdown in 1984 against suspected members of the Popular Forces of April 25 (FP-25) urban guerrilla group, acts of terrorism continued. The FP-25 had claimed responsibility for a series of bomb attacks on banks, property, and NATO installations and the killing of 14 people since 1980. In February 1985 the FP-25 carried out a bomb attack on the West German air base at Beja in southeastern Portugal. Among those detained in 1984 was Lieut. Col. Otelo Saraiva de Carvalho, a major figure of the revolution. During his trial, which began in July 1985, he admitted that FP-25 forces had infiltrated his organization and that some of his own men had carried out acts of violence, but he denied that terrorism was part of his plan. Carvalho revealed that since 1978 he had been preparing the ground for a resistance movement opposed to the return of fascism. To that end, he had set up a four-tier organization that comprised the Forces of Popular Unity, a grouping of seven radical left-wing parties; Carvalho himself; the Civilian Armed Structure, which was to recruit workers for armed struggle; and a fourth structure known by the code name Barracks, which was to recruit military personnel. According to the prosecution, the third-named part of the organization was, in fact, the FP-25.

U.S. Pres. Ronald Reagan visited Portugal during his European tour in May. As he prepared to deliver an address to the Assembly, Communist deputies walked out to protest U.S. policy toward Nicaragua.

(MICHAEL WOOLLER)

See also *Dependent States,* below.

SAN MARINO

The republic of San Marino is a landlocked enclave in north-eastern Italy. Area: 61 sq km (24 sq mi). Pop. (1985 est.): 22,-300. Cap.: San Marino. Monetary unit: Italian lira, with (Oct. 21, 1985) a free rate of 1,778.94 lire to U.S. $1 (2,551 lire = £1 sterling). The republic is governed by two *capitani reggenti,* or coregents, appointed every six months by a popularly elected Grand and General Council. Executive power rests with the Congress of State, composed of the coregents, three secretaries of state (for foreign and political affairs, internal affairs, and economic affairs), and seven ministers.

San Marino's left-wing coalition government of Communists, Socialists, and United Socialists entered its eighth year in power during 1985. The coregents Marino Bellini and Giuseppe Amici, appointed by the Grand and General Council on Oct. 1, 1984, completed their six-month term of office and were succeeded on April 1, 1985, by Enzo Colombini and Severiano Tura. They were replaced in their turn by Pier Paolo Gasperoni and Ubaldo Biordi on October 1.

In December 1984 legislation was passed allowing foreigners who had lived in San Marino for 30 years or more to attain citizenship of the republic. It was estimated that some 1,400 people would immediately become eligible for citizenship as a result.

International PEN (*P*oets and playwrights, *E*ssayists and editors, and *N*ovelists) held a five-day conference in San Marino at the end of May 1985 on the theme of "Literature for Youth—the Youth of Literature." In the same month, the republic was host to the Small States Games for the first time.   (K. M. SMOGORZEWSKI)

This article updates the *Micropædia* article SAN MARINO.

SPAIN

A constitutional monarchy of southwestern Europe with coastlines on the Bay of Biscay, the Atlantic Ocean, and the Mediterranean Sea, Spain shares the Iberian Peninsula with Portugal; it includes the Balearic and Canary island groups, in the Mediterranean and the Atlantic, respectively. Area: 504,750 sq km (194,885 sq mi). Pop. (1985 est.): 38,765,000. Cap.: Madrid. Monetary unit: peseta, with (Oct. 21, 1985) a free rate of 160.83 pesetas to U.S. $1 (230.63 pesetas = £1 sterling). King, Juan Carlos I; prime minister in 1985, Felipe González Márquez.

The Cabinet reshuffle announced by Prime Minister Felipe González Márquez of Spain in July 1985 included the surprise resignation of Miguel Boyer, minister of economy and finance, who reportedly quit after failing in his attempt to persuade González to appoint him as his deputy. Instead the prime minister closed ranks with Deputy Prime Minister Alfonso Guerra González, arguing that Guerra commanded support from various parts of the ruling Partido Socialista Obrero Español (PSOE; Spanish Socialist Workers Party) machine. Foreign Minister Fernando Morán was also dismissed, mainly because of his anti-NATO attitude. Morán was replaced by Francisco Fernández Ordóñez, while Boyer was succeeded by Carlos Solchaga, former minister of industry and energy. The fact that four other posts were filled by technocrats, rather than by mainstream PSOE politicians, was taken by the press as an indication that early elections were likely in the event of a defeat for the government in a referendum planned for early 1986 on the question of Spain's membership in NATO. The González government, now in favour of NATO membership, had suspended it upon coming to power in December 1982.

The efforts of Gerardo Iglesias, secretary-general of the Partido Comunista Español (PCE), to set up a new broadly based left-wing front, Convergencia de Izquierda, were publicly opposed by his predecessor, Santiago Carrillo. In order to reduce Carrillo's considerable support among party members, Iglesias resolved to have his supporters elected to regional power centres. Carrillo and several of his supporters were dropped from the PCE Central Committee in April. Ramón Tamames, who left the PCE at the end of 1984, set up the Federación Progresista, which defined itself as federalist and progressive.

A general strike supported by both the Communist-led Comisiones Obreras and the Socialist Unión General de Trabajadores took place in mid-June. The strike and demonstration signaled the growing impatience of the unions with official economic policy and with the government's impotence in the face of a 22% unemployment rate. Pressure from union members to abandon the national wages accord grew more intense, especially after the employers' federation threatened to withdraw from the accord when it became evident that the government would not concede further tax cuts or incentives to increase jobs. The general strike was the first since the death of Gen. Francisco Franco ten years earlier. In November the anniversary of Franco's death was commemorated by a demonstration in Madrid, attended by at least 50,000 right-wing Spaniards and led by one of Franco's daughters.

The government was also unpopular with environmentalists, who teamed up with anti-NATO demonstrators to hold a weekend of street parties and protests in November. While reiterating his own and his party's commitment to NATO, González announced that he would seek a reduction in the number of U.S. troops stationed in Spain. At the same time, Spain was reportedly upgrading the naval base at Rota to prepare for its use in conjunction with NATO partners and bringing the armed services up to NATO standards.

As a result of a series of agreements signed between the Basque and Catalan regional governments on the one hand and the central government and local Socialist parties on the other, relations between the central and autonomous governments improved markedly. In the Basque Country the Basque Nationalist Party (PNV) began the year with-

Carrying signs reading "No to NATO" and "No to military expenses," demonstrators in Madrid held protest marches before the visit of U.S. Pres. Ronald Reagan in May.

King Juan Carlos confers with U.S. Pres. Ronald Reagan during their walk through the garden of El Pardo near Madrid on the second day of Reagan's visit.

AP/WIDE WORLD

out a working majority in the regional parliament. The endorsement by the parliament of José Antonio Ardanza, a moderate PNV member, as premier of the regional government led to the Basque Socialist Party's agreeing to support the PNV and paved the way for a formal statement, issued by the PNV in March, urging Basques to assist efforts to end violence in the region. The PNV, however, avoided entanglement in negotiations between Madrid and the military wing of the Euzkadi ta Azkatasuna (ETA; Basque Homeland and Liberty) aimed at facilitating the return of former ETA members to the region after standing trial and formally abjuring violence.

In Catalonia promises that further powers would be transferred to the region at first proved sufficient to calm tensions. Catalans felt that their lack of autonomy in raising taxes to fund regional activities placed the region in an inferior position compared with that of the Basque region and Navarra. Jordi Pujol, president of the Catalan government, sponsored a new centre party, the Democratic Reform Party. In elections to the regional parliament in Galicia on November 24, Manuel Fraga Iribarne's Popular Coalition (PC) failed to win an absolute majority. The results gave 34 seats to the PC, 11 to the Galician Coalition, an offshoot of the newly formed Democratic Reform Party, and 22 to the Socialists.

Early in the year there were major demonstrations against a proposed law to reform the education system; the changes would have the effect of making the state more responsible for education at the expense of the Roman Catholic Church. Demonstrations against a law allowing abortion in strictly limited circumstances were backed by certain members of the medical profession who refused to implement the provisions for reasons of conscience.

At the end of March the European Communities (EC) Council of Ministers released a statement noting that key issues such as fisheries, agriculture, and social affairs (emigration) had been resolved and that enlargement of the EC to include Spain and Portugal could take place as planned on Jan. 1, 1986. At the end of April an agreement was reached regulating bilateral Spanish-Portuguese trade relations within the EC context during the next ten years. Spanish import duties and restrictions on most Portuguese goods were to be abolished from the date of entry into the EC. Despite a last-minute rush to complete negotiations, there were unresolved issues—and therefore blank pages in the treaty—when it was formally signed in Madrid in June.   (MICHAEL WOOLLER)

SWEDEN

A constitutional monarchy of northern Europe, Sweden occupies the eastern side of the Scandinavian Peninsula, with coastlines on the North and Baltic seas and the Gulf of Bothnia. Area: 449,964 sq km (173,732 sq mi). Pop. (1985 est.): 8,345,-000. Cap.: Stockholm. Monetary unit: krona, with (Oct. 21, 1985) a free rate of 7.93 kronor to U.S. $1 (11.37 kronor = £1 sterling). King, Carl XVI Gustaf; prime minister in 1985, Olof Palme.

General elections held in Sweden on Sept. 15, 1985, resulted in the widely predicted return to power of Prime Minister Olof Palme's Social Democratic Party government for another three-year term. Less predictable were the narrow margin of the Socialist victory and the sudden reemergence of the Liberals as a force to be reckoned with. The Social Democrats won 159 seats in the Riksdag (parliament). However, in losing seven seats they no longer commanded a majority over the combined forces of the three non-Socialist parties (the Conservative, Centre, and Liberal parties) and were forced to rely on the Communists, who won 19 seats, for support.

Every party lost support except the Liberals, who, under their new leader, Bengt Westerberg, won 51 seats, a gain of 30. Westerberg's rapidly rising star eclipsed the two other non-Socialist leaders. The Conservatives, under Ulf Adelsohn, won 76 seats, a loss of 10, while the Centre Party, led by former prime minister Thorbjörn Fälldin, won 44, a loss of 12. (For tabulated results, see *Political Parties, above.*)

Palme had also suffered a partial eclipse and was clearly irked. He described the election as "an enormous victory," declared that reliance on Communist support was nothing new for his party, and derided the Westerberg phenomenon. Communist leader Lars Werner was in the Eurocommunist mold, having denounced the Soviets for alleged incursions by their submarines into Swedish territorial waters and for their involvement in Afghanistan. However, he declared that his party would seek to move the Social Democratic Party's policies further to the left. The election result was a bitter blow for Adelsohn, who would have been the most likely candidate for prime minister in the event of a non-Socialist victory. Fälldin came under pressure to resign the Centre Party leadership to make way for a younger leader.

A month after the elections, Palme revealed a limited reshuffle of his Cabinet in which the most important change was the demotion of Lennart Bodström from foreign affairs minister to education and cultural affairs minister. Earlier in the year, Bodström had been at the centre of a political row when he expressed skepticism about the findings of an official inquiry that blamed the U.S.S.R. for the alleged incursions into Swedish waters. Bodström was replaced by Sten Andersson, previously health and social affairs minister.

The election indicated that, while the average Swede feared the erosion of the welfare state, the Social Democrats were unlikely to see a return to the days before 1976 when for 44 years their election victories had been virtually automatic. An echo of those days was sounded earlier in the year when more than 50,000 people paraded through the streets of Stockholm to pay tribute to the memory of Tage Erlander (*see* OBITUARIES), prime minister during 1946–69, who died on June 21.

At the beginning of May some 20,000 public-sector employees, including air-traffic controllers, customs officials, and postal workers, began one of the most disruptive labour disputes in Sweden's post-World War II history. Air traffic

Bengt Westerberg, leader of Sweden's Liberal Party, is elated by his party's showing in the September elections. The Liberals more than doubled their representation in the Riksdag.

AP/WIDE WORLD

came to a halt, and the land borders were virtually closed to imports. A compromise agreement on wage increases was reached on May 20 following secret meetings between Palme and trade-union leaders.

A speech to Sweden's Young Socialists during which Palme criticized U.S. policies in Central America brought a strong reaction from the U.S. State Department, which labeled the speech "one-sided and provocative." Palme was more cautious in his conduct of domestic affairs. He allowed Finance Minister Kjell-Olof Feldt to pursue a fiscal policy aimed at holding down inflation and reducing the budget deficit. The economy experienced moderate expansion, while unemployment remained steady at around 3%.

(CHRIS MOSEY)

SWITZERLAND

A landlocked federal republic in west central Europe, Switzerland consists of a confederation of 26 cantons (six of which are demicantons). Area: 41,293 sq km (15,943 sq mi). Pop. (1985 est.): 6,473,000. Cap.: Bern. Monetary unit: Swiss franc, with (Oct. 21, 1985) a free rate of Sw F 2.17 to U.S. $1 (Sw F 3.11 = £1 sterling). President in 1985, Kurt Furgler.

Switzerland experienced another year of political, economic, and social stability in 1985. Political affairs were dominated by a proposal to revise the constitution. The existing constitution, dating from 1848 and revised for

the first time in 1974, was a bewildering mixture of basic principles and detailed amendments on a wide range of matters that in other countries were left to legislative procedure. A draft revision submitted in 1977 had met with considerable opposition from those who favoured increased powers at the cantonal level and supporters of free enterprise. Toward the end of 1985 Elisabeth Kopp, minister at the Department of Justice and Police, submitted for parliamentary discussion a report incorporating a revised version of the earlier draft and two other proposed models for revision. The left-wing parties expressed indifference toward the matter, while the centre and right-wing parties advanced other ideas of their own. Public reaction reflected the view that the existing constitution worked, despite its drawbacks, and that there were far more urgent problems to be tackled. In December Parliament elected Minister of the Interior Alphons Egli, a Christian Democrat, to serve as president for 1986.

A number of plebiscites were conducted during the course of the year. A proposal to update the existing marital and family law in order to increase the rights of women in terms of authority and property ownership was accepted. On the other hand, a proposal to ban scientific experiments involving live animals suffered a massive defeat; the motion was strongly opposed by pharmaceutical companies and many university research laboratories. Also rejected was a constitutional amendment that would have severely limited abortions.

Kopp's department was at the centre of controversy surrounding refugees from third world countries. The granting of asylum to persons whose lives were endangered by political persecution in their own countries, on condition that they did not threaten Switzerland's security or public order, was a sacrosanct principle of Swiss tradition and constitutional practice. At first Kopp allowed a liberal interpretation of these laws. However, she changed her approach rapidly and without hesitation when it was discovered that numerous refugees had sought asylum on the basis of insufficient or fraudulent information and documents. Some Tamil refugees from Sri Lanka were reportedly found to be actively engaged in a worldwide heroin-trafficking network. Kopp ordered some drastic expulsions in an effort to counter hostile public reaction to the foreigners and a corresponding emergence of right-wing anti-immigration groups, which began to make a showing in a few municipal elections. On December 11 Jean-Pierre Hocké accepted appointment as the UN high commissioner for refugees, to take office in January 1986.

GAMMA/LIAISON

As preparations for the summit meeting between U.S. Pres. Ronald Reagan and Soviet leader Mikhail Gorbachev were completed, some 10,000 advocates of peace and other causes marched quietly through the streets of Geneva.

Gross domestic product appeared set to maintain a modest growth rate of about 2%, while the inflation rate remained unchanged at about 3%. Unemployment did not exceed the comparatively moderate proportions of the previous few years, although the watch and precision-instrument manufacturing industries were still experiencing serious difficulties in adapting to pressure from foreign competition.

A subtle but significant change appeared to be under way in the conception and application of Switzerland's time-honoured principle of neutrality. This conclusion could be drawn from the unprecedented appearance at the UN of a highly placed Swiss diplomat, Edouard Brunner, who accepted an invitation to address the UN during its 40th anniversary celebrations in October. His speech contained a lucid statement of Switzerland's combination of neutrality and increasingly intense participation in the international scene, a practice that was proving useful to the international community as a whole. A plebiscite on Switzerland's proposed accession to full membership in the UN was to take place in 1986. Meanwhile, Switzerland remained a member of Unesco, a specialized agency of the UN, and the Swiss government committed itself to working within the agency to effect the internal reform. In late November world attention was focused on Geneva, the setting for the summit meeting between U.S. Pres. Ronald Reagan and Soviet leader Mikhail Gorbachev. (*See* Eastern Europe and the U.S.S.R.: *Union of Soviet Socialist Republics,* below.)

(MELANIE STAERK)

UNITED KINGDOM

A constitutional monarchy in northwestern Europe and member of the Commonwealth, the United Kingdom comprises the island of Great Britain (England, Scotland, and Wales) and Northern Ireland, together with many small islands. Area: 244,100 sq km (94,248 sq mi), including 3,218 sq km of inland water but excluding the crown dependencies of the Channel Islands and Isle of Man. Pop. (1985 est.): 56,518,000. Cap.: London. Monetary unit: pound sterling, with (Oct. 21, 1985) a free rate of £0.70 to U.S. $1 (U.S. $1.43 = £1 sterling). Queen, Elizabeth II; prime minister in 1985, Margaret Thatcher.

Domestic Affairs. On March 5, 1985, with bands playing and heads held high, the striking miners marched back to their pits. For the defeated strikers it was a day of bitterness and humiliation. For the government of Prime Minister Margaret Thatcher (*see* BIOGRAPHIES), it was the moment of victory. The strike ended a year almost to the day after it had begun with the announcement by the National Coal Board (NCB) of a plan to close 20 uneconomic pits and thereby make redundant some 20,000 of the industry's 186,000 workers. Throughout the bitter and often violent dispute, Arthur Scargill, president of the National Union of Mineworkers (NUM), had insisted that there was no such thing as an uneconomic pit. But the strike was about more than the economic future of the British coal industry. It was about the constitutional and political authority of the government; it was about the rule of law over disorder; and it was about the cohesion of the Labour movement—the Trades Union Congress (TUC) and the Labour Party—and the power of the trade unions.

For Scargill the strike was a single battle in a revolutionary class struggle. This viewpoint had given the strike a political character from the outset and had increased the government's determination to win and to be seen to win decisively. Not least this was because folk memories of the events of 1974—when the Conservative Party government of Edward Heath had been destroyed at the hands of the miners, or had perhaps destroyed itself with their aid—

Terry Waite (upper left), special envoy of the archbishop of Canterbury and frequently described as a "gentle giant," conducted private and at times hazardous diplomacy on behalf of hostages in Lebanon.
ARAL—SIPA/SPECIAL FEATURES

were still strong. For Thatcher the strike was also a trial of will.

By the beginning of the year the outcome of the dispute was no longer in doubt. The miners were effectively beaten. Coal stocks were more than sufficient to see the winter through; not an electric light bulb had been extinguished, in contrast to the blackouts of 1974, when industry had been reduced to a three-day working week. Moreover, once the New Year arrived the drift back to work of defeated or disaffected miners gathered pace until, toward the end of February, the NCB could claim that more than 50% of the miners were at work, including the 26%, mainly in Nottinghamshire, who had refused to join the strike in the first place. Scargill remained recalcitrant to the very last. In the end, at a delegate conference of the NUM, the miners voted by the narrowest margin for a return to work without any terms at all. In effect, it was unconditional surrender. Nevertheless, Scargill claimed victory. "All our future struggles will be stronger as a result," he declared. Few other leaders of the Labour movement agreed with him.

The financial cost of the 12-month dispute was not easy to assess, although one global estimate put it at above £3 billion. There were other costs, too. Relationships between management and workers, between strikers and "scabs" (strikebreakers), and between communities and the police had been damaged in ways that might take a generation to repair. Moreover, the NUM was effectively split, a state of affairs that was formalized later in the year with the formation of the breakaway Democratic Union of Mineworkers, centred in Nottinghamshire. Another consequence of the dispute was that policing in Britain was unlikely ever to be the same again. Britain had moved a step closer to possessing a national police force and had come to rely upon paramilitary riot squads for the quelling of civil disorders, as had long been the practice in most of continental Europe.

From the government's point of view, the government was seen to govern, as Thatcher had resolved would be the case, and the ghosts of 1974 were laid at last. Furthermore, victory over the miners confirmed and dramatized the tilt in the balance of power against the trade union movement in general that had been evident since the Conservatives came to office in 1979. The defeat of the miners left the unions in disarray.

After the strike, normality returned to British political life, although there were some surprising, and unforeseen, consequences. One was a sharp decline in the government's

popularity. Any hope that the "Scargill factor" would do for the prime minister's popularity what the "Falklands factor" had in 1982 was soon dispelled. The acquittal of Clive Ponting (*see* BIOGRAPHIES) in February on charges of breaching the Official Secrets Act might also have adversely affected the government's standing. The opposition sought, with some success, to capitalize on suggestions, vigorously denied by Thatcher, that the prime minister herself had been involved in the decision to prosecute.

In January the government's average standing in the three major opinion polls was 41% to Labour's 33% and the Liberal-Social Democratic Party Alliance's 24%. By May, in which month the Conservatives experienced severe setbacks in local elections to fill the nonmetropolitan county councils, the government's standing had fallen to 36%. On July 4 the Alliance narrowly won a parliamentary by-election in the constituency of Brecon and Radnor, Wales, in which the Conservative candidate was relegated to a humiliating third place.

Was this merely a case of "midterm blues" or something more serious? Thatcher was not bound to fight another general election until May 1988, but with unemployment still well above the three million mark and showing little sign of improvement, an increasing number of Conservative members of Parliament began to wonder whether the party could win again on its existing economic policies. Following the local elections, doubts were openly expressed as to whether the prime minister remained an electoral asset to her party. A standard of rebellion was raised by Francis Pym, former foreign secretary whom Thatcher had sacked from her Cabinet after the 1983 election victory. Pym placed himself at the head of a new grouping, launched in May, of traditional and progressive Conservative backbenchers that called itself Centre Forward.

Apart from a brief spurt in its popularity ratings in March, coinciding with the ending of the miners' strike, the Labour Party was not the chief beneficiary of the government's sagging popularity. Its weighted average standing in the polls remained around the 36% mark. In contrast, the Alliance began the year at 25% and by September was leading the field with 35%. Opinion-poll projections suggested that a "hung" or minority Parliament was likely after the next elections, and at the time of the party conferences in the autumn, there was much talk of coalitions.

Yet even while the opposition parties were benefiting from the media exposure during their annual conferences, a quiet recovery was taking place in the government's standing. Compared with the low point in August, by the end of November it had recovered by some four percentage points to run neck and neck with Labour, while support for the Alliance quickly subsided to little more than it had been at the beginning of the year. Conservative spirits brightened, Thatcher's popularity ratings rose again, and any suggestion that she might not lead her party into the next elections was dispelled along with the autumn mists.

During the first half of September, Thatcher announced a number of new government appointments and a major reshuffle of her Cabinet. Within the Cabinet, Douglas Hurd moved to the Home Office from the Northern Ireland Office, where he was replaced by Tom King. Hurd succeeded Leon Brittan, who took over as trade and industry secretary from Norman Tebbit (*see* BIOGRAPHIES). Tebbit remained in the Cabinet as chancellor of the duchy of Lancaster and also took over from John Selwyn Gummer as chairman of the Conservative Party. Lord Young of Graffham (*see* BIOGRAPHIES) replaced King as employment secretary. Kenneth Baker entered the Cabinet as environment secretary in place of Patrick Jenkin, who left the government.

In what was to prove a controversial party appointment, Jeffrey Archer (*see* BIOGRAPHIES) was chosen to be deputy chairman of the Conservative Party.

Whatever the cause of the recovery in the government's popularity, it was clear that the "Scargill factor" continued to haunt the Labour movement. Both the TUC and the Labour Party were split down the middle on the question of whether to support retrospective reimbursement of legal fines and penalties incurred by the NUM during the strike. At the Labour Party conference in October, Labour leader Neil Kinnock was defeated on this electorally embarrassing issue, but he was resolved to leave no doubt as to where he, and a future Labour government, would stand. He denounced both Scargill and, in a stirring piece of oratory, the leaders of the Liverpool city council, members of the Trotskyist Militant Tendency faction of the Labour Party, who, in protest against the government's policy of limiting the local rates (property taxes) that local councils could levy, were following a course that would bankrupt the city. (A compromise was later reached that allowed the city's immediate financial crisis to be resolved.) Kinnock's speech won him personal kudos but could not dispel the spectacle of a Labour Party divided and preoccupied with internal issues, plagued by extremists, and ambivalent in its attitudes toward the rule of law.

According to the pollsters, more than 80% of the population believed that unemployment was the chief issue facing the country, but all the while the average real living standards of those who did have jobs was increasing. It had been rising by about 2% a year since the end of the recession in 1981, and in 1985 the increase may have been a little greater. The budget introduced in March was a cautious one in which the overriding priority remained the further reduction of inflation. Chancellor of the Exchequer Nigel Lawson was widely regarded as having laid the ground for substantial tax cuts in the years leading up to general elections in 1987 or 1988. In the meantime, the chancellor was clearly taking no chances. In his 1985 budget, tax thresholds were lowered by £730 million—less than half the sum that had been talked about a few months earlier—and some £2,000 million was set against future government spending to allow for a fall in the value of the U.S. dollar and declining oil revenues.

In general the British financial community applauded the budget, while Conservative backbenchers were content that their lobbying endeavours had headed off further radical reforms of the kind that might upset the Conservative middle classes, notably the taxation of private pensions. There was talk of "Thatcherism" being dead. Financial pundits concluded that monetarism in the technical sense was dead when it became clear that the government's interest-rate policy was geared to controlling the exchange rate of sterling rather than the money supply. However, there was more to "Thatcherism" than monetarism. In early June the government published its long-awaited review of the social security system, billed as the most important exercise of its kind since the original Beveridge report of 1942. This was expected to show whether political caution had taken over from radical reforming zeal—and so it did, although not immediately.

The most radical and most controversial feature of the review announced by Secretary of State for Health and Social Services Norman Fowler was the proposed abolition of the State Earnings-Related Pension Scheme (SERPS), established in 1978. Thatcher herself was reported to be an enthusiastic abolitionist. However, the proposal soon ran into deep trouble. From the outset the Treasury had been alarmed by the more immediate shorter-term costs of phas-

ing out SERPS; industry was not eager to contribute to the private pension arrangements of its employees; and there was political opposition to abandoning a scheme that had been set up with bipartisan support only a few years earlier. Opposition to abolition proved overwhelming. Before the end of the year, the Cabinet had reversed its decision and settled for a reform of SERPS that would reduce its future costs somewhat. In some other respects, too, the Fowler review failed to live up to its radical intents.

Meanwhile, another important shift in government policy had occurred. At the end of the autumn annual review of public expenditure, it became plain that the government had held to its expenditure target of £139,000 million only by the device of raiding its contingency fund and stepping up the sale of state assets. Within the conventions of Britain's accounting of governmental spending, asset sales counted as negative spending. In economic terms the planned increase in actual spending programs would be reflationary to the tune of some £4,000 million, and the government's Keynesian critics, the "wets," were quick to congratulate the government on its "L-turn," if not a complete "U-turn."

Concern about the emphases of economic policy was matched by concern about its social consequences. These reached a new pitch in the autumn when a series of unconnected disturbances brought violence to the inner cities once more. In Handsworth, an inner-city area of Birmingham, a whole street was destroyed in an orgy of gasoline (petrol) bombing on September 9. Brixton, in south London, scene of some of the worst riots in 1981, exploded a few weeks later after a black woman was shot and injured by police during a dawn raid on her home. On October 6 there was a similar but even more violent outburst in Tottenham, in north London, following the accidental death of another black woman, who suffered a heart attack during a police raid. During the Tottenham riots a police officer was stabbed to death. Although in Handsworth, for example, 50% of black youths were out of work, government ministers were quick to assert that unemployment was not the cause of the violence; they attributed it rather to criminal behaviour. These disturbances prompted renewed concern about inner-city conditions. In December a commission set up by the archbishop of Canterbury published a report called "Faith in the Cities" that listed familiar but costly measures for dealing with the physical decay and human despair in economically declining inner-city areas.

The riots increased concern not only about the social condition of the poor and unemployed but also about the general tide of violence in British society. The government's political recovery after September owed at least something to its firm handling of the disturbances. The year had already been marred by an appalling outbreak of hooliganism on May 29 when Liverpool soccer fans ran amok before the start of a match against the Italian club Juventus in Heysel Stadium, Brussels. The violence resulted in 39 deaths. (*See* SPORTS AND GAMES: *Football: Sidebar.*) These images of violence, later reinforced by the riots and reminiscent of the picket-line clashes of the previous year, were linked in people's minds with what appeared to be a contagion of violent crime, gratuitous violence to individuals, child abuse, and rape. There were gruesome cases in all these categories during the course of the year, leading to calls for sterner penal measures. There was also new concern, voiced by the prime minister herself, about violence on television, which she refused to believe was unconnected with the enactment of violence in real life.

The horror of the Heysel Stadium riot was compounded by the fact that it took place just over two weeks after another soccer ground had provided the setting for what was on this occasion a tragic accident. On May 11 fire engulfed a spectators' stand during a match at Bradford City soccer club. The blaze killed 56 people and injured more than 200 others.

Foreign Affairs. Thatcher was more active than usual in foreign affairs. In April she toured Malaysia, Singapore, Brunei, Indonesia, Sri Lanka, India, and Saudi Arabia. During her trip to the Middle East in September, when she visited Jordan and Egypt, she agreed that her government would meet representatives of the Palestine Liberation Organization, but the meeting was later canceled. The government gave conditional support to U.S. Pres. Ronald Reagan's Strategic Defense Initiative (known as "Star Wars") and toward the end of the year reached an agreement for British industry to participate in the research program.

Thatcher suffered a setback at the Milan summit of the European Communities (EC) in June when her pragmatic approach to reforming the EC's decision-making machinery was overruled by those who wanted more ambitious revisions to the Treaty of Rome. By the time EC leaders met again in Luxembourg in December, however, realism and national interests had prevailed over European idealism and, although the British made some concessions, the resulting compromise was closer to Thatcher's view than

Pallbearers including Sinn Fein leader Martin McGuinness (left) and Martin Galvin (right), a leader of U.S. supporters of the Irish Republican Army, head the mourners at the funeral of an IRA terrorist in August.

to the declarations made in Milan. Commonwealth affairs were dominated chiefly by concern about developments in South Africa. At the biennial Commonwealth heads of government conference in Nassau, The Bahamas, in October, Thatcher was forced to give some ground—although not much—in agreeing to economic measures against Pres. P. W. Botha's regime.

Northern Ireland. The most potentially important development of the year in foreign affairs was the accord signed in November with the Republic of Ireland giving the latter a consultative role in the governing of Northern Ireland. The Hillsborough agreement was reached after long and painstaking secret diplomacy between Dublin and London. In effect, it exchanged a role for the Republic on behalf of the nationalist minority in the north for a de facto recognition by Dublin of Northern Ireland's union with Britain. It was hoped that the agreement would result in a more coordinated and effective drive against the Irish Republican Army (IRA) while at the same time preventing the alienation of the Roman Catholic population from the political process and keeping them from the electoral arms of Sinn Fein, political wing of the IRA. At the end of December 18 prominent members of Sinn Fein were arrested and charged with possession of explosive substances.

Although London insisted that the Hillsborough agreement did nothing to alter the status of Northern Ireland as a province of the U.K., the Ulster loyalists exploded in predictable wrath, crying treason and threatening to overthrow the agreement by whatever means. The government had prepared itself on this occasion to face down or defeat a Protestant backlash of the kind that had wrecked the Sunningdale agreement in 1974, but as 1985 ended, that confrontation was still to come.   (PETER JENKINS)

See also *Commonwealth of Nations,* above; *Dependent States,* below.

VATICAN CITY STATE

The independent sovereignty of Vatican City State is surrounded by but is not part of Rome. As a state with territorial limits, it is properly distinguished from the Holy See, which constitutes the worldwide administrative and legislative body for the Roman Catholic Church. Area: 44 ha (108.8 ac). Pop. (1985 est.): 1,000. As sovereign pontiff, John Paul II is the chief of state. Vatican City is administered by a pontifical commission of five cardinals headed by the secretary of state, in 1985 Agostino Cardinal Casaroli.

The 28 new cardinals created by Pope John Paul II at a consistory held in St. Peter's Square on May 25, 1985, included five from Italy, three from the U.S., two each from Canada, France, Poland, and West Germany, and one each from Austria, Belgium, Chile, Czechoslovakia, Ethiopia, India, Nicaragua, Nigeria, the Philippines, Spain, The Netherlands, and Venezuela. Among them were Archbishops Bernard Law of Boston, John O'Connor of New York, and Myroslav Ivan Lubachivsky of Philadelphia. The last-named succeeded Josyf Cardinal Slipyj (d. 1984) as head of the Ukrainian Catholic Uniate Church, based in Rome. The pope's compatriots elevated to the now 152-strong Sacred College were Andrzej Maria Deskur, president emeritus of the Commission for Social Communications, and Archbishop Henryk Roman Gulbinowicz of Wroclaw.

Notable visitors to the Vatican during the year included the prince and princess of Wales, U.S. Vice-Pres. George Bush, Soviet Foreign Minister (later President) Andrey Gromyko, the queen and prince consort of The Netherlands, Pres. Erich Honecker of East Germany, Japanese Prime Minister Yasuhiro Nakasone, and Israeli Prime Minister Shimon Peres.

In March a commission of 14 cardinals met to discuss organizational and financial reform within the Vatican, in particular the future operations of the Institute for Religious Works (the Vatican bank). The pope called a plenary session of the Sacred College in November to discuss draft proposals for reform.   (MAX BERGERRE)

See also Religion: *Roman Catholic Church.*

This article updates the *Micropædia* article VATICAN CITY STATE.

Eastern Europe and the U.S.S.R

EASTERN EUROPEAN AFFAIRS

The central event of 1985 in Eastern European politics took place, as so often before, in the U.S.S.R. with the accession of Mikhail Gorbachev (*see* BIOGRAPHIES) to the

Pope John Paul II listens intently to one of the 161 delegates to the Extraordinary Synod of Bishops of the Roman Catholic Church held at the Vatican in November–December.

leadership of the Communist Party of the Soviet Union (CPSU) on March 11. Though Eastern Europe had become far more independent of Soviet desires than it had been under Stalin, it remained dependent on the Kremlin and on Soviet preferences. In this context the Gorbachev succession was important. Under his two short-lived predecessors, Yury Andropov and Konstantin Chernenko (*see* OBITUARIES), the Soviet preference for the direction of Eastern European policies remained unclear. Gorbachev, it was expected, would change this. In particular, the new leader enjoyed something of a reputation as a reformer, a term that was undefined and open to interpretation.

By the end of 1985 there was little hard evidence of Gorbachev's true wishes for the future of Eastern Europe. Indeed, the picture was muddy and confused. Considerable alarm was occasioned in some Eastern European countries by an article published in *Pravda,* the CPSU daily newspaper, in June. The article was harshly critical of national deviations in Eastern European countries and asserted that the Soviet road to communism was the only true road. These were code words for centralization and reassertion of the supremacy of Soviet methods, something that several Eastern European countries were plainly reluctant to contemplate. Reactions to the article varied between those in Hungary, where it met with apprehension because it was felt that the entire Hungarian reform course was threatened by its implications, and those in Poland, where the article elicited barely a whisper.

Subsequent statements in the Soviet press—none of them, it should be noted, coming from politicians—served only to balance the picture. An article in *Kommunist,* the CPSU's theoretical monthly and, therefore, of high ideological persuasiveness, appeared to go in the other direction from the one in *Pravda* toward the acceptance of national differences in the "construction of socialism." There was no public statement from Gorbachev himself to clarify matters by the end of the year.

As against this, those Eastern European countries favouring relatively relaxed relations with the West, notably East Germany, Hungary, Romania, and, to a lesser extent, Bulgaria, took heart from the relatively optimistic note on which the Geneva summit between Gorbachev and U.S. Pres. Ronald Reagan in November ended. In terms of atmosphere, if not in content, the summit appeared to offer encouragement to those who favoured easier contacts between East and West.

Yet, at the same time, the Budapest Cultural Forum, one of the meetings designed to maintain the process established by the 1975 Helsinki Accords by discussing, in this instance, East-West cultural relations and the political obstacles to them, ended in virtual failure when the delegates were unable to agree on any final document. With Western delegations stressing the unacceptability of Soviet and Eastern European restrictions on cultural contacts, there had been no doubt from the outset that the fairly tough Western line would make it difficult to reach agreement. Nevertheless, to end the forum without any kind of final document whatsoever reflected poorly on the six weeks of discussions. There was little doubt that the intransigent attitude of the Soviet and Czechoslovak delegations contributed materially toward the outcome, although at the end it was the Romanian delegation that vetoed the innocuous final communiqué drafted by the Hungarian hosts, mainly because Romania had been repeatedly pilloried during the forum for its discriminatory policies against its two million-strong ethnic Hungarian minority.

Celebration of the 30th anniversary of the signing of the Warsaw Treaty, which included a ceremonial renewal of the treaty at a Warsaw Pact summit in Poland in April, turned out to be a rather low-key affair. Despite the presence of all party leaders and heads of state and government from the seven Warsaw Pact countries, little more was done than to sign the text of the treaty, without amendments. The treaty itself was renewed for an additional 20 years with an automatic prolongation of another 10 years.

A clear new line was emerging in economic relations between the U.S.S.R. and Eastern Europe. Evidently the Soviet Union was no longer prepared to accept the relatively low-quality goods that many Eastern European nations had grown used to delivering to Soviet purchasers. For decades the Soviet market had been regarded as "soft," that is, prepared to absorb goods of a quality that was well below the world level. The Soviet delegation to the Council for Mutual Economic Assistance meeting in June served notice that this would no longer be the case and that, as the U.S.S.R. delivered raw materials that were up to the standard expected in world markets, it would in the future expect the equivalent in manufactured goods. In several Eastern European countries the press carried reports warning that Soviet buyers were actually returning shoddy goods.

The implications of this move, which was clearly in line with Gorbachev's attempt to improve discipline within the U.S.S.R. itself, were disturbing for Eastern Europeans. In the medium term the change also had repercussions for investment, as it would evidently require the Eastern Europeans to retool and to introduce costly quality-control measures in order to upgrade the quality of their output.

Overall, 1985 could be regarded as a transitional year, though with potentially major changes on the horizon. As ever, there was underlying tension between the desire among Eastern Europeans for greater room for maneuver in international politics and economics, as well as in the running of their domestic affairs, and pressure from the U.S.S.R. for stricter conformity to Soviet ideological requirements. This, in effect, was the perennial dilemma of Soviet-Eastern European relations. Despite the inauguration of what was clearly to be an entirely new era in the U.S.S.R. with the accession to power of Gorbachev, coupled with the likelihood that he could well remain in office long enough to see a change of leadership in all the Eastern European countries, there were as yet few signs as to what shape the Gorbachev era would actually assume. Those signs that could be read pointed in the direction of tighter rather than looser Soviet control.

(GEORGE SCHÖPFLIN)

See also Economic Affairs; Military Affairs.

ALBANIA

A people's republic in the western Balkan Peninsula of southeastern Europe, Albania is situated on the Adriatic Sea. Area: 28,748 sq km (11,100 sq mi). Pop. (1985 est.): 3 million. Cap.: Tirane. Monetary unit: lek, with (Oct. 21, 1985) a free rate of 7.15 leks to U.S. $1 (10.25 leks = £1 sterling). First secretaries of the Albanian (Communist) Party of Labour in 1985, Enver Hoxha to April 11 and, from April 13, Ramiz Alia; chairman of the Presidium of the People's Assembly (president), Alia; chairman of the Council of Ministers (premier), Adil Carcani.

On April 11, 1985, Enver Hoxha (*see* OBITUARIES), leader of Albania for over 40 years and the longest-serving head of a Communist country, died after suffering a heart attack. Two days later he was succeeded as first secretary of the Albanian Party of Labour by Ramiz Alia (*see* BIOGRAPHIES), chairman of the Presidium of the People's Assembly since 1982. In his speech at Hoxha's funeral in Tirane on April 15, Alia made it clear that no changes in

Albanian domestic or foreign policy should be expected. Departing from international diplomatic practice, he did not allow representatives of foreign governments to attend the funeral, and the Soviet telegram of condolence was returned as "unacceptable." In August Alia said that moves to broaden ties with the outside world would not include the opening of diplomatic relations with either superpower. On the occasion of Albania's national day at the end of November, an article in the Soviet daily *Pravda* again signaled the U.S.S.R.'s willingness to seek friendlier relations, but the overture met no response.

In August U.K. Prime Minister Margaret Thatcher revealed that Britain was holding secret talks with Albania in an attempt to settle a 40-year-old diplomatic rift between the two countries. Britain was claiming nearly £850,000 in compensation for two destroyers mined off the Albanian coast, with the loss of more than 40 British lives, in 1946. Albania refused to pay until Britain handed over Albanian gold looted by the Germans during World War II. The gold, held jointly by Britain, France, and the U.S., was worth around £44 million at current prices.

(K. M. SMOGORZEWSKI)

BULGARIA

The people's republic of Bulgaria is on the eastern Balkan Peninsula of southeastern Europe, along the Black Sea. Area: 110,912 sq km (42,823 sq mi). Pop. (1985 est.): 8,979,000. Cap.: Sofia. Monetary unit: lev, with (Oct. 21, 1985) a free rate of 0.99 lev to U.S. $1 (1.43 leva = £1 sterling). General secretary of the Bulgarian Communist Party and chairman of the State Council (president) in 1985, Todor Zhivkov; chairman of the Council of Ministers (premier), Grisha Filipov.

The marked deterioration in relations between Bulgaria and Turkey that occurred during 1985 was deeply rooted in the past. An estimated one-tenth of Bulgaria's total population of almost nine million people consisted of ethnic Turks, a consequence of five centuries of Ottoman domination. Before the Communist government came to power in 1944, the Turks had lived in relative harmony with

TASS/SOVFOTO

General Secretary Mikhail Gorbachev (left) of the U.S.S.R. joins Pres. Todor Zhivkov of Bulgaria in laying flowers on the Lenin monument in Sofia during the biennial Warsaw Pact summit meeting in October.

the Bulgar population. In 1951, however, the Bulgarian Communist Party (BCP) began a campaign to bulgarianize the minority. At first the Turks successfully resisted these pressures, but in 1974 the government struck two major blows by prohibiting Turkish language teaching and closing down over 1,300 mosques.

In December 1984, according to the Turkish government, Bulgarians launched a campaign aimed at forcing the Turks to change their names to the Bulgarian equivalents—for example, from Ismail to Ivan or from Mehmet to Mikhail—in preparation for the census due to take place at the end of 1985. Family names were to be chosen from a list of 2,000 with Slavonic roots, all ending with "-ov," "-ev," or "-ski." The Bulgarian authorities, who maintained that the Turks had adopted the new names voluntarily, claimed that the charge had been fabricated with the aim of damaging relations between the two countries. Turkish Pres. Kenan Evren addressed a sharply worded letter of protest to BCP General Secretary Todor Zhivkov, and on Feb. 14, 1985, Turkey withdrew its ambassador to Sofia.

Turkey later applied economic pressure on Bulgaria by concluding an agreement to establish ferry services with Romania. Bulgaria responded in kind; during an official visit to Athens in July, Zhivkov and Greek Prime Minister Andreas Papandreou agreed to set up a train and ferry service that would provide both countries with access to Syria without passing through Turkey.

On February 10–11 Sir Geoffrey Howe became the first U.K. foreign secretary to pay an official visit to Bulgaria during the 100 years of diplomatic relations between the two countries. Zhivkov was the official guest of Gen. Wojciech Jaruzelski in Poland on April 2–3, and on October 21 Soviet leader Mikhail Gorbachev visited Zhivkov in Sofia.

(K. M. SMOGORZEWSKI)

CZECHOSLOVAKIA

The federal socialist republic of Czechoslovakia is a landlocked state of central Europe. Area: 127,896 sq km (49,381 sq mi). Pop. (1985 est.): 15,508,500. Cap.: Prague. Monetary unit: koruna, with (Oct. 21, 1985) a commercial rate of 6.45 koruny to U.S. $1 (9.25 koruny = £1 sterling). General secretary of the Communist Party of Czechoslovakia and president in 1985, Gustav Husak; federal premier, Lubomir Strougal.

Throughout 1985 the economy continued to occupy most attention in Czechoslovakia. It became evident to economists at home and abroad that no remedy had been found for the ills that had plagued the economy for years and that the outlook was bleak. Failure to modernize and to increase investment had left the country's once-modern industry resembling a 19th-century industrial scrap heap. Observers were particularly alarmed because Czechoslovak products were no longer always competitive within the Communist world. The diagnosis—overcentralization, excessive bureaucracy, insufficient market discipline, too much political interference in the running of the economy, high levels of waste—was widely accepted. The fact that one-fifth of all enterprises failed to fulfill plan targets indicated the extent of the problem.

The Central Committee (CC) of the Communist Party of Czechoslovakia (CPC) projected a growth rate of 3.2% in net material product for 1985. Labour productivity was expected to rise by 4.7%. The 1984 growth figure of 2.8% barely prevented serious economic problems. Although the figure was on the positive side of the balance, it concealed deficits in a number of crucial economic areas. The gap between supply and demand in domestic trade remained unbridged. The severe winter of 1984–85, when tempera-

tures dropped to −25° C (−13° F), left several areas of the economy exposed. Shortages of energy resulted in shortened work time in several sectors.

In October 1984 the CC had discussed another problem area—agriculture. It found that this sector too was riddled with "weaknesses and shortcomings," notably in the quality of produce and in the relatively low rates of growth in output. The result was that Czechoslovakia was slipping badly in terms of productivity compared with other countries. For example, since the end of World War II Czechoslovakia had fallen from 15th to 21st place in Europe in sugar-beet production, as measured by hectare yield. Excessive use of chemical fertilizers was blamed for lower yields and the diminishing fertility of land, while persistent shortages of agricultural machinery were blamed on the failure of industry to meet demand.

Calls for changes in the economic system surfaced from time to time. The arguments of the reformers were restrained, however. They called for expansion of the service sector and attempts to curb the wastefulness of heavy industry by subjecting it to competition for resources. Valtr Komarek, one of the more prominent figures among the reformers, argued in a series of articles that the need for intensive, as opposed to extensive, methods was urgent, and that this need required a radical transformation of the approach to economics as a whole. However, Komarek came up against a political constraint—the refusal of the CPC leadership to contemplate economic reform for fear it would undermine the party's political position.

At a CC meeting in June 1985, CPC General Secretary Gustav Husak indicated once again that no market-oriented, decentralizing reform of the system was contemplated. The statement was taken to be the Czechoslovak leadership's response to the slight optimism generated by the succession of Mikhail Gorbachev to the leadership of the Communist Party of the Soviet Union in March. A major anticorruption drive that led to a purge of CPC members was not expected to alter the balance of forces significantly, even though it claimed a number of relatively senior officials as victims. In October there were reports that Finance Minister Leopold Ler and two of his deputy ministers had been placed under house arrest for alleged involvement in smuggling activities.

The Charter 77 opposition group maintained its activities at, if anything, a somewhat higher level than in previous years. In November 1984 it issued a joint appeal with East German peace groups for "a missile-free Europe," the first time that such a joint appeal had been made. Charter later protested against the intensifying level of "disinformation" in the official press. The number of those who adhered to the Charter was growing slowly and had reached almost 2,000 by mid-1985. In October Charter sent an open letter to the Budapest Cultural Forum, one of the meetings held as part of the official follow-up to the 1975 Helsinki Accords. The letter contained accusations concerning the damaging effects of the Czechoslovak regime's repressive practices.

Vaclav Havel, the opposition dramatist, was increasingly emerging as a political thinker of considerable stature. His essay pointing out the difficulty that Eastern Europeans had in accepting the activities of Western European peace movements as untainted by pro-Soviet sentiment was widely regarded as an influential document. The awarding of the 1984 Nobel Prize for Literature to the poet Jaroslav Seifert proved embarrassing to the authorities in view of Seifert's refusal to compromise with the government, and their response to the event was grudging. The popular response was much more positive.

The year 1985 marked the 1,100th anniversary of the death of St. Methodius, regarded as the founding father of Christianity in the Czech and Slovak lands. Both the Roman Catholic Church and the state were determined to celebrate the event in their own ways. The authorities insisted that the significance of St. Methodius had been political, involving the founding of the proto-Czech and Slovak state of the Great Moravian Empire. The church emphasized the religious content of the saint's message. The July 7 anniversary attracted around 150,000 pilgrims to Velehrad, site of the saint's tomb. This sizable public demonstration in the teeth of official disapproval indicated the depth of religious feeling. In April Pope John Paul II appointed Msgr. Jozef Tomko as the first Slovak cardinal.

(GEORGE SCHÖPFLIN)

GERMAN DEMOCRATIC REPUBLIC

A socialist republic, the German Democratic Republic (East Germany) is in central Europe on the Baltic Sea. Area: 108,333 sq km (41,827 sq mi). Pop. (1985 est.): 16,703,000. Cap.: East Berlin. Monetary unit: Mark of Deutsche Demokratische Republik, with (Oct. 21, 1985) a free rate of M 2.64 to U.S. $1 (M 3.78 = £1 sterling). General secretary of the Socialist Unity (Communist) Party and chairman of the Council of State (president) in 1985, Erich Honecker; chairman of the Council of Ministers (premier), Willi Stoph.

The visit to East Berlin in June 1985 of French Prime Minister Laurent Fabius was an important milestone in East Germany's policy of improving relations with Western nations. Fabius was the first head of government of one of the three Western allied powers (the U.K., the U.S., and France, which, together with the U.S.S.R., had taken administrative control of Berlin at the end of World War II) to have political talks there. However, the French made it clear that, while they recognized East Berlin as East Germany's de facto seat of government, they did not acknowledge it to be the East German capital city. Nor could they grant it such a status, since they, the French, shared responsibility for Berlin as a whole.

One of the main purposes of the visit was to improve economic links between France and East Germany, the Eastern bloc's most powerful industrial country after the U.S.S.R. French interest in increasing trade was reflected in the unusually large French representation at the Leipzig trade fair in September. There the East German leader Erich Honecker was told by the French ambassador that a new stage had been reached in relations between the two countries, made possible in part by East Germany's reliability as a trading and financial partner.

Honecker paid a state visit to Greece in October, reciprocating a visit by Prime Minister Andreas Papandreou to East Germany in 1984. In Athens they signed an agreement on industrial and technological cooperation, and both expressed concern at the prospect of the "arms race being extended to outer space." East German opposition to the U.S. Strategic Defense Initiative was a theme of the speech by Foreign Minister Oskar Fischer at the opening of the UN General Assembly in September. Following the Soviet example, Fischer called for a pledge by all nuclear states to forgo the first use of nuclear weapons, declare a freeze on nuclear arsenals, and prohibit nuclear tests.

In a speech on October 7, the 36th anniversary of the founding of the East German state, Honecker claimed that East Germany was making impressive economic progress. He said national income was up by 4.4%, productivity by nearly 8%, and retail trade turnover by 4.4%. Many thousands of apartments had been built or modernized, and the harvest of 11.6 million metric tons of grain was the

Willy Brandt (left), former chancellor of West Germany, continued his policy of *Ostpolitik* on an unofficial basis in meeting East German leader Erich Honecker in East Berlin in September.
REGIS BOSSU—SYGMA

biggest on record. Honecker went on to say that citizens of East Germany appreciated the fact that they were living in the first German state to guarantee freedom, democracy, full employment, and material security. Honecker declared that the 11th congress of the Socialist Unity (Communist) Party, scheduled to take place in early 1986, would adopt measures to strengthen and develop socialist society.

However, the Communist Party was evidently not certain of receiving total commitment from all of its 2.2 million members. It gave orders that each member be questioned "in a comradely atmosphere" about his or her political views, style of life, and attitude to work. A screening in 1980 had resulted in the expulsion of some 4,000 members; the biggest purge had been in 1951, when 150,000 members had been forced to leave the party. This time workers were being asked to pledge support for the country's economic plan. The party was also using the research to determine the extent of its members' contacts with Western countries. From the beginning of 1984 until September 1985, some 40,000 East German citizens had been allowed to move to West Germany; it was estimated that another 500,000 applications were in the pipeline.

Willy Brandt, former Social Democratic federal chancellor of West Germany, met Honecker on a semiofficial visit to East Berlin in September. According to West German sources, Honecker promised to make further "easements" in travel between East and West Germany. Brandt also received the impression that Honecker would like to visit Bonn. In 1984 Honecker had decided that the time was not ripe for such a visit, since it was obvious that East German expectations would not be met.

The spy scandal that broke in West Germany in August demonstrated the effectiveness of the East German intelligence service. After the sensational defection of Hans Joachim Tiedge, a senior officer in the West German counterintelligence organization, it was disclosed that Tiedge had been an East German spy for years. The importance of the Tiedge case was comparable to that of Werner Stiller of the East German Ministry of State Security, who had fled to the West in 1979 and enabled 40 East German spies to be identified.

On March 24 Maj. Arthur Nicholson, a member of the U.S. Army's military liaison mission in East Germany, was shot dead by a Soviet soldier near the town of Ludwigslust, close to the border with West Germany. The incident provoked a serious row between the U.S.S.R. and the U.S.;

the former claimed that Nicholson had been spying on a Soviet military installation in a restricted zone, while the latter denied that the incident had taken place in an area that was restricted.

Cultural relations between East and West Germany flourished during the year, though a formal cultural agreement between Bonn and East Berlin still had not been signed. A West German publisher, Suhrkamp Verlag of Frankfurt, and the state publishing house in East Berlin decided to publish the first uniform edition of the writings of Bertolt Brecht.   (NORMAN CROSSLAND)

This article updates the *Macropædia* article GERMANY: *German Democratic Republic.*

HUNGARY

A people's republic, Hungary is a landlocked state in central Europe. Area: 93,036 sq km (35,921 sq mi). Pop. (1985 est.): 10,645,000. Cap.: Budapest. Monetary unit: forint, with (Oct. 21, 1985) a free rate of 48.06 forints to U.S. $1 (68.92 forints = £1 sterling). General secretary of the Hungarian Socialist Workers' (Communist) Party in 1985, Janos Kadar; chairman of the Presidential Council (chief of state), Pal Losonczi; chairman of the Council of Ministers (premier), Gyorgy Lazar.

The 13th national congress of the Hungarian Socialist Workers' (Communist) Party took place in Budapest on March 25–28, 1985. The congress, the first to be held since 1980, was attended by 935 delegates representing the 871,000 party members, as well as by delegates from 50 other Communist parties around the world. In his opening address, General Secretary Janos Kadar made a passionate defense of his government's program of reform aimed at decentralizing and liberalizing the economy, promised an improvement in living standards, and pledged to continue contracts with Western nations. His speech included dismissive references to dissident Hungarian intellectuals. Kadar said that the Warsaw Treaty members had decided to renew their alliance—they did so the following month at a summit meeting held in Warsaw—because NATO powers had rejected the idea that both the military blocs might be dissolved and had turned down a Soviet-bloc offer of a European nonaggression pact.

The Soviet representative at the congress was Grigory Romanov, at the time still a senior Soviet Politburo member. His speech indicated that the Kremlin extended cautious approval to Hungary's economic reforms. He noted that the U.S.S.R. approved of closer links with capitalist nations in order to prevent a situation in which "imperialist forces" could apply economic pressure as a means of interfering in internal affairs.

Kadar's concern to reassure the people of Hungary that the reforms had a long-term future led the Communist Party to become the first in Eastern Europe to create the post of deputy party leader. The appointment went to Karoly Nemeth, a loyal supporter of Kadar on the Politburo and an opponent of both right-wing and left-wing deviation. The congress reelected Kadar as general secretary and approved a Politburo in which 3 of the 13 members were replaced; Valeria Benke, Mihaly Korom, and Lajos Mehes were replaced by Karoly Grosz, head of the Budapest party organization, Csaba Hamori, secretary of the Communist Youth League, and Istvan Szabo, head of the collective farm movement.

Elections to the 387-seat National Assembly took place on June 8. A second round of voting on June 22 was necessary in those constituencies where no candidate won an outright majority. Each voter had two ballot papers, one for 35 unopposed deputies on a list of national candidates,

Janos Kadar, general secretary of the Hungarian Socialist Workers' Party, opens the party's 13th national congress in Budapest in March with a ringing defense of his reform policies.
INTERFOTO MTI/EASTFOTO

the other to select a single deputy to represent the constituency, of which there were 352 in all. A new electoral law stipulated that at least two candidates must contest each constituency. Before the elections, each candidate was obliged to sign a declaration of support for the program of the Patriotic People's Front. Dissident groups were unsuccessful in their efforts to have candidates nominated. The results showed that independent opposition candidates secured 25 seats. The new Assembly returned Pal Losonczi for a further five-year term as chairman of the Presidential Council on June 28.

During Kadar's working trip to Moscow on September 25, he and Soviet leader Mikhail Gorbachev issued a joint communiqué stating that Hungary and the U.S.S.R. intended to continue their collaboration according to the principles of "Marxism-Leninism, democratic centralism, and socialist internationalism." On January 21 Minister of Foreign Affairs Peter Varkonyi held talks with his Romanian counterpart, Stefan Andrey, in Bucharest. They discussed the problem of Romania's Hungarian minority, which numbered between 1.7 million and 2 million.

On April 18 Princess Margaret, sister of Queen Elizabeth II, arrived in Budapest on a five-day visit that, although styled unofficial, was regarded by some diplomats as having political significance. Returning Prime Minister Margaret Thatcher's trip to Hungary in February 1984, Kadar paid a three-day official visit to the U.K. beginning on Oct. 31, 1985. During his tour of European countries in December, U.S. Secretary of State George Shultz visited Hungary, where he met Kadar and discussed trade issues with government ministers.   (K. M. SMOGORZEWSKI)

POLAND

A socialist republic of eastern Europe, Poland is on the Baltic Sea. Area: 312,683 sq km (120,727 sq mi). Pop. (1985 est.): 37,160,000. Cap.: Warsaw. Monetary unit: zloty, with (Oct. 21, 1985) a free rate of 148.38 zlotys to U.S. $1 (212.78 zlotys = £1 sterling). First secretary of the Polish United Workers' (Communist) Party in 1985, Gen. Wojciech Jaruzelski; chairmen of the Council of State (chiefs of state), Henryk Jablonski and, from November 6, Jaruzelski; chairmen of the Council of Ministers (premiers), Jaruzelski and, from November 6, Zbigniew Messner.

General elections took place in Poland on Oct. 13, 1985. In previous elections all candidates had been approved by a special committee of the Front of National Unity, composed of delegates from the three existing political parties: the Polish United Workers' (Communist) Party (PUWP), the United Peasants' Party, and the Democratic Party. The 1985 elections were the first to be held under a new electoral law. Each eligible citizen had two votes: one for 50 unopposed candidates on a national list, and the other for one of two candidates in local constituencies, of which there were 410 in total. The national list of candidates was prepared by the Patriotic Movement for National Renaissance (PRON), a government-appointed body set up in 1983 under the chairmanship of Jan Dobraczynski, a nonparty man of letters. The list comprised 22 candidates from the PUWP, 8 from the Peasants' Party, 4 from the Democratic Party, and 16 independents, with the notable lack of an independent sponsored by the Roman Catholic Church. All candidates in the elections pledged loyalty to the existing political system.

Official results of the elections published on October 16 revealed a turnout of 78.64%. The final distribution of seats among the three parties was close to that in the previous Sejm (parliament), with a slight increase in the number of independents. (For tabulated results, see *Political Parties,* above.) The government, pointing to the fact that more than three-quarters of the electorate had voted, claimed that it had triumphed over the boycott called by Solidarnosc (Solidarity), the banned trade union movement, and urged Western nations to drop remaining economic sanctions in view of the approval that it had won from voters. Solidarity in turn expressed skepticism about the results; Solidarity leader Lech Walesa claimed that in his hometown of Gdansk 50% of voters had boycotted polling, while the government claimed a 66% turnout. Walesa was later accused of slander by the Polish authorities.

Significant shifts in the mechanism of power were announced on November 6, the date that the new Sejm was inaugurated. Gen. Wojciech Jaruzelski stepped down as premier and handed over the reins of government to Zbigniew Messner, an economist, who was a member of the PUWP Politburo and had been one of Jaruzelski's deputy premiers. The Sejm elected a new Council of State in which Jaruzelski succeeded Henryk Jablonski as chairman (head of state). Since Jaruzelski also retained the post of first secretary of the PUWP, he remained, incontestably, Poland's leader. At its second sitting on November 12 the Sejm approved a new Council of Ministers, reduced from 27 to 26 members. Messner dismissed nine ministers, principal among them being Janus Obodowski, who had been deputy premier in charge of planning, and Stefan Olszowski, foreign minister, who had resigned from the Politburo the previous day. The latter was replaced by Marian Orzechowski, a professor of history and deputy member of the Politburo.

On his first visit to the West since he became premier in February 1981, General Jaruzelski flew to New York City on September 24 to attend the UN General Assembly. The visit did not fulfill any expectations he might have entertained that it would end the period of diplomatic isolation imposed by the U.S. and its European allies when martial law was declared in December 1981. On August 31 the U.S. administration announced that Pres. Ronald Reagan would refuse to meet Jaruzelski during the visit. The snub was in protest against the continuing arrests of supporters of Solidarity.

In his address to the UN General Assembly on September 27, Jaruzelski deprecated the "correctors of history" who were trying to undermine the existing frontiers enacted at the Teheran, Yalta, and Potsdam conferences during and at the end of World War II. During his five-day stay in

New York he met many foreign statesmen. Talking to U.S. journalists, Jaruzelski admitted that Poland's relations with the U.S. were as bad as they had ever been but maintained that Poland was not to blame. "We are prepared for full normalization in our bilateral relations. . . . But this has to be paralleled by a return to elementary political realism," he stated.

There were signs that some Western European nations were prepared to seek an improvement in relations. In April U.K. Foreign Secretary Sir Geoffrey Howe visited Poland, and on December 4 Jaruzelski arrived in Paris for a meeting with French Pres. François Mitterrand. Mitterrand's decision, announced only days before the visit, to become the first Western head of state to agree to meet the Polish leader since December 1981 provoked deeply hostile reactions at home.

Although officially banned, Solidarity remained active. May Day demonstrations in support of Solidarity took place in Warsaw and several other Polish cities. While Walesa himself was prevented from joining the march in Gdansk, two leading dissidents, Jacek Kuron and Seweryn Jaworski, received prison sentences of three months for or-

---

The Popieluszko Trial

The trial that followed the murder in October 1984 of the pro-Solidarity Polish priest Father Jerzy Popieluszko was seen in the West as an unprecedented event in a Communist country within the Soviet orbit. The four accused were members of the state security police—generally considered to be above the law—and the trial was open to the public and to Western reporters, with the proceedings broadcast live by Polish Radio. Nevertheless, the conduct of the trial clearly had been carefully planned by the Interior Ministry and the Politburo. Nothing emerged to implicate high-ranking officials, while both the presiding judge and counsel for the defense took every opportunity to mention the hostility of some Roman Catholic priests toward the socialist state.

The events leading to the trial began on October 19, when Father Popieluszko and his driver, Waldemar Chrostowski, were intercepted late at night en route from Bydgoszcz to Warsaw by three of the accused, Capt. Grzegorz Piotrowski and Lieutenants Waldemar Chmielewski and Leszek Pekala. Popieluszko was savagely beaten and, bound and weighted with rocks, thrown into a reservoir. But Chrostowski managed to escape, with the result that, by the following morning, both the ecclesiastical and state authorities were aware of the crime. Threatened with a possible public outcry, the latter were forced to take action.

Interior Minister Gen. Czeslaw Kiszczak, appointed by Premier Gen. Wojciech Jaruzelski to investigate the circumstances of Popieluszko's disappearance, announced on October 27 that Piotrowski, Chmielewski, and Pekala had been arrested and reduced to the ranks. On December 27 they and their immediate superior, Col. Adam Pietruszka, were brought to trial in Torun, charged with the murder of Popieluszko, whose body had been found on October 30. State Prosecutor Leszek Pietrasinski, demanding the death penalty for Piotrowski, called him "a cold, calculating, merciless murderer." For the other three defendants he demanded 25-year prison terms—the maximum under Polish law. Dismissing the death penalty as a "sign of vengeance," Presiding Judge Artur Kujawa, on Feb. 7, 1985, sentenced Piotrowski to 25 years' imprisonment. Pietruszka also received 25 years, but Pekala and Chmielewski—"victims of their superiors' action"—were given sentences of 15 and 14 years, respectively. The sentences were upheld by the Supreme Court on April 22.

Who authorized the action that resulted in Father Popieluszko's murder? No clear answer emerged. The most senior official to give evidence at the trial was Gen. Zenon Platek, head of the Interior Ministry department concerned with monitoring church affairs. Platek's questioning by the prosecution was perfunctory, but his probable complicity was indicated by his suspension from duty before the trial opened and his subsequent dismissal from his post. More importantly, Gen. Miroslaw Milewski, a Politburo member and Central Committee secretary, resigned from all state and party positions on May 14.

Soviet reaction to the affair could be gauged by *Pravda*'s reference, in a report of the trial, to the Polish church's support for "hostile activities against the socialist state." Some weeks before the crime, on Sept. 11, 1984, *Izvestiya* had rebuked the Polish government for weakness in its dealings with "anti-Soviet provocateurs such as Jerzy Popieluszko."

(K. M. SMOGORZEWSKI)

LASKI—BLACK STAR

ganizing the Warsaw demonstration. However, arguing that he had been attempting to negotiate a peaceful end to the rally, Kuron appealed successfully against his sentence. In June three Solidarity activists, Adam Michnik, Bogdan Lis, and Wladyslaw Frasyniuk, arrested in Gdansk in February, were found guilty of attempting to incite public unrest and received jail sentences ranging from 2½ to 3½ years. The number of political prisoners in Poland rose from 25 at the end of 1984 to some 370 by mid-November 1985. In that month, following the elections, the authorities granted a limited amnesty to political prisoners; because it excluded those freed under earlier amnesties and subsequently re-arrested, it did not extend to most imprisoned Solidarity activists.

After the Sejm passed a controversial law in July granting the government greater power of control over the universities, the minister of education in November dismissed the rectors of a number of academic institutions, including the universities of Poznan, Gdansk, and Wroclaw. According to Solidarity sources, those dismissed were Solidarity sympathizers. The trial of four state security police charged with the murder of pro-Solidarity priest Jerzy Popieluszko in October 1984 attracted intense interest both at home and abroad. (*See* Sidebar.)　　　　(K. M. SMOGORZEWSKI)

ROMANIA

A socialist republic on the Balkan Peninsula in southeastern Europe, Romania has a coastline on the Black Sea. Area: 237,500 sq km (91,700 sq mi). Pop. (1985 est.): 22,715,000. Cap.: Bucharest. Monetary unit: leu, with (Oct. 21, 1985) a commercial rate of 4.06 lei to U.S. $1 (5.82 lei = £1 sterling). General secretary of the Romanian Communist Party, president of the republic, and president of the State Council in 1985, Nicolae Ceausescu; chairman of the Council of Ministers (prime minister), Constantin Dascalescu.

Official results revealed a turnout of 99.9% in general elections held on March 17, 1985, to fill Romania's 369-seat Grand National Assembly (parliament). All candidates were nominated by the Socialist Democracy and Unity Front, which included the Romanian Communist Party (RCP) and various other Communist organizations. While 97.7% of votes were cast in favour of candidates, the percentage voting against was 2.3%, compared with 1.5% in the previous elections in 1980. The new National Assembly convened on March 29 and reelected Nicolae Ceausescu for another five-year term as president of the republic and thus, automatically, as president of the State Council.

Ceausescu, reelected general secretary of the RCP in November 1984, celebrated 20 years in that office in 1985. Members of the Politburo paid tribute to his achievements at a meeting on July 23. In his own speech Ceausescu outlined the developments that had transformed Romania into an "industrial-agricultural country with a modern developed industry and an advanced socialist agriculture." During the two decades that he had been in power, he pointed out, industrial output had increased sixfold, while agricultural production had increased by 250%. The standard of living had risen steadily, and wages were almost three times higher than they had been in 1965. Ceausescu admitted that he had encountered difficulties during his years in power; he had faced distrust from those at home who doubted the party's ability to implement the necessary measures to solve the country's problems and accusations from abroad that he was guilty of deviation from the true path of socialism.

During the year a number of changes were made to the Council of Ministers. In December Gen. Constantin Olteanu was replaced as defense minister by his former

deputy, Gen. Vasile Milea. On October 17 Ioan Avram, deputy prime minister responsible for supervision of the energy sector, Nicolae Busui, minister of electric power, and Marin Stefanache, minister of mines, were dismissed, and at about the same time, high army officers were placed in command of coal-burning power stations. The moves were occasioned by a crisis in the energy sector to which weather conditions during the previous year had contributed. The winter of 1984–85 had been the most severe in four decades, and long periods of dry weather in both 1984 and 1985 had depleted water supplies in rivers and reservoirs, resulting in an unprecedented slump in hydroelectric power production. At the same time, production in the coal-mining industry failed to reach targets, and the country's petroleum extraction was on the decline.

During the early months of 1985, the authorities took drastic action to save fuel. Romanians were barred from using many electrical appliances; private cars were banished from the streets; and only minimal street lighting was permitted. Icy conditions in the Danube River ports affected exports. Later in the year some of those measures were reintroduced as the country took steps to guard against the effects of another hard winter. Addressing a plenary session of the RCP Central Committee on November 14, Ceausescu called for firm action to develop "responsibility, honesty, discipline, and order."

The shortages of fuel and food were aggravated by Ceausescu's drive to reduce the foreign debt. In this endeavour he claimed success; from a peak in 1982, when some estimates put the total at $14 billion, the foreign debt had been reduced to $4 billion by late 1985 according to the government.

Despite reports that Romania might raise objections to the renewal of the Warsaw Pact treaty, the extension of the treaty was signed by Ceausescu along with leaders of the six other Warsaw Pact countries at a summit meeting in Warsaw on April 26. The only Warsaw Pact leader to maintain friendly links with China, Ceausescu paid his fourth official visit to that country in October. In December he visited Yugoslavia. During U.K. Foreign Secretary Sir Geoffrey Howe's visit to Bucharest in February, he and Ceausescu discussed trade. On December 15 U.S. Secretary of State George Shultz made the first stop of his European tour in Romania. Shultz was reported to have warned Ceausescu that unless his government improved its human rights record, the U.S. would withdraw from Romania its "most-favoured-nation" status, a trade privilege enjoyed only by Romania and Hungary among Eastern-bloc nations.

(K. M. SMOGORZEWSKI)

UNION OF SOVIET SOCIALIST REPUBLICS

The Union of Soviet Socialist Republics is a federal state covering parts of eastern Europe and northern Asia. Area: 22,402,200 sq km (8,649,500 sq mi). Pop (1985 est.): 277.5 million. Cap.: Moscow. Monetary unit: ruble, with (Oct. 21, 1985) a free rate of 0.77 ruble to U.S. $1 (1.11 rubles = £1 sterling). General secretaries of the Communist Party of the Soviet Union in 1985, Konstantin U. Chernenko to March 10 and, from March 11, Mikhail S. Gorbachev; chairman of the Presidium of the Supreme Soviet (presidents), Chernenko until March 10 and, from July 27, Andrey A. Gromyko; chairmen of the Council of Ministers (premiers), Nikolay A. Tikhonov and, from September 27, Nikolay I. Ryzhkov.

Domestic Affairs. The death of Konstantin Chernenko (*see* OBITUARIES) on March 10, 1985, was a watershed in Soviet politics, representing the final passing from the scene of a generation of leaders who had come to power under Leonid Brezhnev. The new general secretary of the Communist

In a Moscow parade marking the 68th anniversary of the Bolshevik Revolution, workers carry a sign calling on the "peoples of the world" to unite in opposition to "the militarization of space."
WALLY MCNAMEE/NEWSWEEK

Party of the Soviet Union (CPSU), Mikhail Gorbachev (*see* BIOGRAPHIES), was at 54 the youngest man to become leader since Joseph Stalin. In nominating Gorbachev as the new general secretary at a meeting of the CPSU Central Committee (CC) on March 11, Foreign Minister Andrey Gromyko stated that Gorbachev had taken the chair at CC Politburo meetings when Chernenko had been too ill to attend. Of Gorbachev's chairmanship he said: "Without exaggeration, he conducted himself brilliantly"; he also praised the flexibility and lack of dogma in his approach to problems.

There was little doubt that Gromyko's praise was genuine, and it underlined the fact that Gorbachev was the most able man in the Politburo. The succession battle had been between him and Grigory Romanov, the only other CC secretary who was a full member of the Politburo. Since Gorbachev had been running the CC Secretariat in Chernenko's absence, he was ideally placed to take over. At the last moment he had to fight off a challenge from Viktor Grishin, a Politburo member and survivor from the Brezhnev era. However, Grishin was not in the Secretariat, and his bid for supreme office was doomed to failure. In December he was removed from his post as head of the Moscow party organization.

Events moved so rapidly that Chernenko's death and Gorbachev's election were announced on the same day, posing a problem for the Soviet daily newspaper *Pravda,* which decided to place Gorbachev's photograph on page one and that of Chernenko on page two. In contrast to his three aged predecessors, Gorbachev presented a picture of health, vitality, dynamism, and, despite his limited experience of life among Moscow's political elite, remarkable self-confidence.

Because the CPSU had changed only its leader and not its policies, Gorbachev could not make sweeping changes in the Politburo, but he was in a stronger position to bring new people into the Secretariat. In order to build up his own authority, he needed to bring in those who shared his own vision of the future. Egor Ligachev became a full member of the Politburo and was responsible in the Secretariat for personnel appointments. As such, he emerged as Gorbachev's deputy. Others who became full members of the Politburo were Nikolay I. Ryzhkov (*see* BIOGRAPHIES), CC secretary for economics; Gen. Viktor Chebrikov, head of the KGB state security force; and Eduard Shevardnadze (*see* BIOGRAPHIES), first secretary of the party in Georgia.

Lev Zaikov, CC secretary for the defense industries, and Boris Eltsin, CC secretary for construction, were elected candidate (nonvoting) members of the Politburo. The most startling demotion was that of Grigory Romanov, who was removed from both the Politburo and the Secretariat.

Since 1977 the general secretary of the CPSU had always been chairman of the Presidium of the Supreme Soviet (president) as well, but in July this vacant post was filled by Gromyko, who thus ended 28 years as foreign minister. If this was a surprise—most foreign observers had expected Gorbachev to become head of state—the appointment of Shevardnadze to replace Gromyko as foreign minister astonished many. The Georgian had little experience of the outside world and was a beginner in foreign affairs. The effect of these two appointments was to increase Gorbachev's authority and allow him greater flexibility in external policy. Gromyko appeared to be a stopgap president, and it seemed likely that in the near future Gorbachev would add the post to those he already held, those of head of the CPSU and chairman of the Defense Council. Another significant promotion was that of Anatoly Dobrynin, longtime Soviet ambassador in Washington, who became first deputy foreign minister. Dobrynin's considerable ability and expertise made him a key adviser to Gorbachev on U.S. policy.

As expected, Premier Nikolay Tikhonov (80) gave way to a younger man in September. Some observers had expected either Geidar Aliyev, first deputy premier, or Vitaly Vorotnikov, premier of the Russian S.F.S.R., to get the job, but it went instead to Ryzhkov (56), an able technocrat. He immediately left his post in the CC Secretariat. Soon afterward Nikolay Baibakov was replaced as head of the state planning commission, Gosplan, by Nikolay Talyzin, an electronics specialist. In December Boris Gostev was appointed to fill the post of finance minister left vacant by the death of Vasily Garbuzov, and Boris Bratchenko was replaced as minister of the coal industry by his former deputy, Mikhail Shchadov.

While there were many changes at the top of the party in 1985, there were even more lower down. Over 40% of the first secretaries of oblasts or *krai*s (provinces) changed between March and December. Directed by Ligachev, the aim was to sweep away the old guard and install able, technically competent functionaries capable of increasing the effectiveness of Soviet economic life. Another reason for removals was the pervasiveness of corruption, which had

spread rapidly during the final years of the Brezhnev era.

Marshal Nikolay Ogarkov, dismissed as chief of general staff in September 1984, appeared to make a comeback as commander in chief of the Western theatre of military operations. The post probably also included command over the Northwestern theatre and Warsaw Pact forces. In the event of a conflict with NATO forces, Ogarkov would be the key field commander. His thinking on military strategy, operational art, and tactics was systematically implemented in the Soviet armed forces throughout the year. It appeared certain that the reason for Ogarkov's dismissal in 1984 concerned disagreements over resource allocations and not over military doctrine. Ogarkov wanted more high-technology weapons immediately, whereas the CPSU leadership judged that such a demand would impose too great a burden on the civilian economy. The leaders were willing to produce the weapons but only in limited quantities.

A new generation of military and naval commanders took over, although not all of them could be connected with Ogarkov. There were new commanders in charge of almost all 16 Soviet military districts, all four groups of Soviet forces (in East Germany, Poland, Czechoslovakia, and Hungary), all theatres of military operation, and the Baltic, Northern, and Black Sea fleets. Gen. Aleksey Lizichev became the new head of the main political administration of the Soviet armed forces, and Adm. Vladimir Chernavin was appointed commander in chief of the Navy in place of Adm. Sergey Gorshkov, who had held the post for 29 years. All these changes represented the most rapid turnover at the top of the Soviet military since 1945. Marshal Sergey Sokolov, appointed minister of defense in December 1984, became a candidate member of the Politburo, continuing the tradition, begun in 1973, that the defense minister become ex officio a member of that body. However, the appointment of Sokolov (73) had the appearance of being an interim measure, and Gorbachev might soon wish to pick his own defense minister.

Gorbachev began to develop a distinctive style of leadership. On walkabouts in Leningrad, Tselinograd, and other cities, he sought to communicate directly to the citizens his views about how the U.S.S.R. should develop. When editors and journalists from the press and television were invited to see him, he greeted them not with the long speeches they had come to expect but with requests for their own opinions, telling them that he had come to listen. He was critical of poor discipline in all its guises, be it overconsumption of alcohol, poor timekeeping, or failure to meet one's obligations. As a nondrinker as well as a nonsmoker, Gorbachev led the campaign against alcoholism. The general secretary castigated those who were quite capable of making long-winded speeches but were quite incapable of fulfilling their plans. The unity of word and deed became one of his slogans. In his official speeches Gorbachev displayed a refreshing ability to express himself in clear, forthright language and to avoid dogma and cliché.

The number of Jews and Germans permitted to emigrate declined to a trickle during the year. It was thought, however, that Gorbachev's desire to improve relations with Israel, the U.S., and West Germany might result in an increase in 1986. Yelena Bonner, wife of the dissident Soviet physicist Andrey Sakharov, was granted permission to journey to the West to seek medical treatment.

The draft version of a new program and statute of the CPSU, due to be presented to the 27th congress in February–March 1986, was published for discussion in October. A new party program had been promised for years and was certainly necessary in the light of promises made in the previous program, published in 1961, which had looked forward to the Soviet public living under communism in the 1980s. The new program was intended to guide the population through to the year 2000. It forecast that over the 15-year period economic output would double and living standards would rise substantially. There was sharp criticism of the Brezhnev leadership, which was accused of failure to assess "in due time and proper manner alterations in the economic situation and the need for profound change in all spheres of life." The optimistic objective was an annual growth of 4.7% over the 15-year period. The key to the future was declared to be scientific and technical progress. However, the program contained few tangible suggestions as to how the country's economic problems were to be solved. Generalizations were the rule. Since Soviet industry was incapable of supplying all the new equipment necessary to achieve such progress, an increase in East-West cooperation appeared probable.

The Economy. The increase in industrial production between January and September was 3.7% over the same period in 1984, while labour productivity grew by 3.3%. In the third quarter of 1985 the daily rate of output rose by 5%; in the energy and electrification sector production was up by 4%, and in chemicals and the oil machinery industry it rose 5% over the same quarter of 1984. The oil industry achieved 96% of its plan target and mineral fertilizers 97%, but the coal industry recorded a 1% growth to achieve 100.2%—quite an achievement given the great problems of the industry. However, coal output was well below the original goals set in the five-year (1981–85) plan. Light industry also failed to meet its target. The transportation sector continued to experience difficulties, with only air transport and the merchant marine fulfilling plan objectives. The railroad network was overburdened and would require considerable investment.

In October the government newspaper *Izvestiya* stated that those ministries, associations, and enterprises selected to participate in the "economic experiment" had done especially well. This factor was increasingly significant in assessing economic performance, as some 2,300 enterprises, accounting for over 12% of Soviet output, now worked under "new conditions." However, the performance of some ministries failed to live up to expectations. While the Belorussian Ministry of Light Industry and the Ukrainian Ministry of the Food Industry were praised, the Ukrainian Ministry of Local Industry did not fulfill its goals. A decree issued in August stated that selected enterprises were to be permitted to use their own profits to renew equipment during the 12th five-year (1986–90) plan, and enterprise funds were to be channeled into the construction of homes and recreational buildings for workers.

The harvest attained an estimated 180 million metric tons, greater than that achieved in 1984 but nevertheless disappointing because it fell short of expectations. Output and economic efficiency in the agricultural sector remained generally unsatisfactory despite some trends for the better. Besides problems in grain production, the output of sugar beets, sunflowers, and cotton remained inadequate. Animal products improved, thanks mainly to imported fodder, but productivity remained low. In 1984 grain imports reached 45 million metric tons, including 26.4 million metric tons of wheat; the importation of 5.5 million metric tons of sugar made the Soviet Union the leading importer of sugar on the world market. Imports of agricultural products over the years 1982–84 cost an estimated $16.1 billion. A new agreement on agricultural cooperation concluded with the U.S. included a new five-year pact on grain sales that foresaw Moscow purchasing at least nine million metric tons of grain a year from the U.S.

For the world's media, at least, one of the high points of Mikhail Gorbachev's visit to Paris in October was the meeting of his wife, Raisa, and couturier Yves St.-Laurent.

P. PERRIN—GAMMA/LIAISON

While Gorbachev hinted that fewer resources might be devoted to the rural sector, he did not articulate any solutions to the perennial problems facing agriculture. Waste was still evident on a massive scale. In July *Pravda* revealed that since 1981 in Chimkent Oblast, Kazakhstan, almost one billion rubles had been invested in agriculture, and yet the output of grain, potatoes, vegetables, and milk yield per cow had declined. Not surprisingly, overall agricultural output in the oblast had also dropped. In November it was announced that a superministry of agriculture was to be formed by merging the Ministries of Agriculture, Agricultural Procurement, the Meat and Dairy Industry, and the Food Industry, as well as the State Committee for the Production and Technical Supervision of Agriculture.

Foreign Affairs. The year was dominated by the summit meeting between Gorbachev and U.S. Pres. Ronald Reagan in Geneva on November 19–20. It was the first meeting between the superpower leaders since 1979. Given the poor state of Soviet-U.S. relations, such a meeting had appeared improbable earlier in the year. It appeared that the Soviets agreed to the conference mainly because of their apprehension about the U.S. Strategic Defense Initiative (SDI), popularly known as the "Star Wars" defense system.

The shooting of Maj. Arthur Nicholson, a U.S. military liaison officer, by a Soviet guard in East Germany in March angered the U.S. administration. It was the first U.S. fatality in 40 years of liaison work with the Soviet Army. Later the U.S. accused the Soviet Union of using "spydust" to keep track of U.S. diplomats in the U.S.S.R. Then the U.S.S.R. accused the U.S. of "kidnapping and terrorism" when Vitaly Yurchenko (*see* BIOGRAPHIES), a KGB officer, appeared in the Soviet embassy in Washington in November claiming that he had been held in the U.S. against his will. At a press conference in Moscow on his return, Yurchenko stated that he had been seized in Rome on August 1 and taken to the U.S., where he had been put under pressure to betray his country. The U.S. Central Intelligence Agency claimed that Yurchenko had been a genuine defector but had changed his mind; another possible interpretation of events was that Yurchenko had been sent on a reconnaissance mission by the KGB in order to learn about CIA debriefing techniques and also to permit the U.S.S.R. to attack the U.S. on human rights, widely held to be the Soviets' and Gorbachev's weakest card.

In the weeks preceding the summit the Soviet Union conducted a fierce campaign against SDI, skillfully utilizing opposition to the program in the West to bolster its position. Gorbachev's visit to France in October revealed the Soviet leader to be highly persuasive. His wife, Raisa, charmed Western viewers even more. President Reagan was considered to be at a disadvantage; an old U.S. leader pitted against a young Soviet leader provided quite a contrast to the recent past.

At Geneva long discussions between the two leaders established a basis for mutual trust that augured well for the future. Although Gorbachev had stated beforehand that only an agreement to halt SDI would represent success, and Reagan refused to make any concessions on this point, the summit was a success. In a joint statement both sides agreed that a nuclear war could not be won and must not be fought. Neither side would seek to achieve military superiority. They called for early progress in arms control negotiations and supported the idea of an interim agreement on intermediate nuclear forces. Further steps would be taken to reduce nuclear risk. Both underlined their commitment to the nuclear non-proliferation treaty. Bilateral discussions involving technical experts would aim to achieve a ban on chemical weapons, including the questions of verification that would ensue. Both sides favoured positive results from the NATO-Warsaw Pact talks on mutual and balanced force reductions in Vienna. The U.S. and the U.S.S.R. intended to facilitate an early and successful conclusion to the Stockholm Conference on Confidence and Security-Building Measures and Disarmament in Europe. Dialogue between the superpowers was to be intensified at both foreign minister and other levels. Safety on air routes in the northern Pacific was to increase. Air services between the two countries were to resume. A Soviet consulate general was to open in New York City and a U.S. one in Kiev. There was to be cooperation on environmental protection, while educational and cultural exchanges were to be expanded. Both countries favoured the expansion of international cooperation in utilizing controlled thermonuclear fusion for peaceful purposes. The two leaders agreed to meet again in Washington in 1986 and in Moscow in 1987.

Anglo-Soviet relations reached a new low in September when 31 Soviet diplomats and media people were expelled from the U.K. and the same number of Britons were ordered out of Moscow. The Soviets expelled by Britain were accused of spying on the evidence of Oleg Gordiyevsky, KGB head in Britain, who had defected in August. British intelligence claimed that Gordiyevsky had been a double agent for 19 years, during which time he had provided much valuable information. He was the highest ranking KGB officer ever to defect to Britain. However, relations between the two countries recovered rapidly, and by the end of the year Soviet visas had been granted for some replacement British diplomats.

Sino-Soviet relations improved slightly during the year. Yao Yilin (Yao Yi-lin), Chinese vice premier, visited Moscow and signed a new five-year trade agreement; he was the highest ranking Chinese official to visit the U.S.S.R. in more than 20 years. However, while relations at the state level improved, contacts at party level made little progress.

The war in Afghanistan continued into its sixth year with no military or political victory in sight. The Soviet Union suffered a humiliating defeat at the UN in November when a record 122 nations censured its occupation of Afghanistan, with only 19 countries supporting Moscow and 12 abstaining. The subject caused sharp disagreements at the Geneva summit, and Gorbachev was apparently well aware that the issue had become a liability.

In the Middle East Oman established diplomatic relations with Moscow in September, and the United Arab Emirates did so in November. Kuwait, which had already

recognized the Soviet Union, deployed the first of its Soviet missiles, bought in 1984 for $325 million. Saudi Arabia and its allies were considering establishing diplomatic relations with the U.S.S.R. The Soviet Union continued its policy of cultivating better relations with Israel in an effort to increase its influence in the area. When Col. Muammar al-Qaddafi of Libya visited Moscow in October, attempts were made to persuade him to moderate his anti-Israeli stance.

The U.S.S.R.'s charmed existence in Lebanon ended when three diplomats and an embassy physician were kidnapped in September by left-wing guerrillas. One diplomat was murdered before the release of the others was negotiated. (MARTIN MCCAULEY)

See also Feature Article: *The Soviet Union under Gorbachev.*

YUGOSLAVIA

A federal socialist republic, Yugoslavia is in southern Europe on the Adriatic Sea. Area: 255,804 sq km (98,766 sq mi). Pop. (1985 est.): 23,235,000. Cap.: Belgrade. Monetary unit: Yugoslav dinar, with (Oct. 21, 1985) a free rate of 285.33 dinars to U.S. $1 (409.17 dinars = £1 sterling). Presidents of the Presidium of the League of Communists in 1985, Ali Sukrija and, from June 25, Vidoje Zarkovic; presidents of the Collective Presidency, Veselin Djuranovic and, from May 15, Radovan Vlajkovic; president of the Federal Executive Council (premier), Milka Planinc.

In 1985 Yugoslavia grappled with serious economic and financial problems against a background of growing political ferment at home, while in foreign policy the country maintained its nonaligned stance. Premier Milka Planinc visited the U.S. in May for talks that chiefly concerned the country's financial position. In July she visited Moscow, and in the same month Gen. Wojciech Jaruzelski, Poland's premier, visited Yugoslavia. In November Bulgarian Premier Grisha Filipov journeyed to Belgrade to return Planinc's visit to Bulgaria in 1984. He was followed in December by Romanian Pres. Nicolae Ceausescu and by U.S. Secretary of State George Shultz.

Relations with Albania improved slightly after the death of Enver Hoxha, the Albanian Communist Party leader, in April. In November the two countries signed an agreement to open the railway linking Shkoder with Titograd, Albania's first direct rail link with the outside world, in early 1986. Trade between the two countries doubled in 1985. However, polemics continued about the situation in Yugoslavia's Kosovo Province, with its predominantly Albanian population. Albania complained of the oppression of Albanians in Kosovo, while Yugoslavia accused Albania of interfering in its internal affairs.

The situation in Kosovo remained Yugoslavia's main internal security problem. Throughout the year there were trials of Kosovo Albanians who were agitating for the province to be granted the status of a full federal republic. Emigration of Serbs and Montenegrins from Kosovo continued against a background of complaints that they were leaving under pressure. In Serbia there was growing demand for revision of the 1974 constitution, which had granted considerable autonomy not only to the six federal republics but also to the two provinces of Kosovo and Vojvodina, both part of Serbia.

Three of six accused dissidents were sentenced in February to prison sentences ranging from one to two years; one was released for lack of evidence, and the trial of the other two was postponed. The six had been arrested in Belgrade in April 1984. Others arrested at the same time, including Milovan Djilas, Yugoslavia's best-known dissident, had already been released. In spite of the continuing crackdown against the Roman Catholic Church in Croatia and Bosnia, some 15,000 young Croatian Catholics attended a rally in Zagreb Cathedral at the end of October. Pope John Paul II was refused permission to attend the ceremonies in July marking the 1,100th anniversary of the death of St. Methodius, the Greek-born missionary who for a time had been bishop of what is today a part of Yugoslavia. A large crowd attended the rededication in Belgrade on May 12 of the foundations of the Serbian Orthodox Church of St. Sava, patron saint of Serbia.

In July two draft laws on the redistribution of hard currency failed to receive the required two-thirds majority in the federal Parliament, largely because of opposition from Croatia and Slovenia. They objected to a larger share of hard-currency earnings being handed over to the National Bank for general needs, including debt repayment, on the grounds that the move would discourage exports. Negotiations begun in 1984 with Western banks about Yugoslavia's $19.5 billion debt resulted in agreement in September 1985 to reschedule $3.5 billion worth of repayments falling due in the period 1985–88. The agreement cleared the way for payment of a further installment of an International Monetary Fund credit. In the first six months of 1985, exports to the hard-currency area increased by only 2%, instead of the planned 15%, while those to member countries of the Council for Mutual Economic Assistance rose 15%. In the same period, imports from both East and West went up 7% and industrial output rose 2.9% as compared with the first half of 1984. The inflation rate reached 80% in the second half of 1985, while unemployment exceeded one million and the number of strikes was double the 1984 level.

(K. F. CVIIC)

Premier Milka Planinc (far right) of Yugoslavia meets with Mikhail Gorbachev (far left), general secretary of the Communist Party of the Soviet Union, during her visit to Moscow in July.

North America

CANADA

Canada is a federal parliamentary state and member of the Commonwealth covering North America north of conterminous United States and east of Alaska. Area: 9,970,610 sq km (3,849,675 sq mi). Pop (1985 est.): 25,427,000. Cap.: Ottawa. Monetary unit: Canadian dollar, with (Oct. 21, 1985) a free rate of Can$1.36 to U.S. $1 (Can$1.96 = £1 sterling). Queen, Elizabeth II; governor-general in 1985, Jeanne Sauvé; prime minister, Brian Mulroney.

Domestic Affairs. The new Progressive Conservative administration headed by Brian Mulroney marked its first year in office in 1985. On Sept. 4, 1984, the Conservatives had triumphed in one of the most decisive electoral victories in Canadian history, winning 211 of the 282 seats in the House of Commons. Given this decisive mandate, Canadians had expected forceful leadership and sweeping change from the new government, but Mulroney, even though he concentrated executive power in the prime minister's office, proved a cautious leader. His legislative accomplishments during his first year were few, and he showed a tendency to retreat from policies when they proved to be controversial. The result was a first year in office for the Conservatives that many Canadians characterized as disappointing. Mulroney's personal standing declined in the polls, and the popularity of his party fell to 40% during the summer, as compared with the 50% rating the Conservatives had enjoyed on coming to power.

Mulroney, faced by an embarrassingly large group of followers in the Commons, chose 40 for his Cabinet, the largest number in Canadian history. He put real power in the hands of a veteran member from Yukon who was a shrewd parliamentary tactician, Erik Nielsen. Holding the honorific title of deputy prime minister, Nielsen was placed in charge of a task force to review government operations and propose reductions in personnel and expenditures. On February 27, after Robert Coates resigned as minister of national defense following a visit to a seedy West German bar (an episode the prime minister characterized as an error in judgment), Nielsen was named to that post as well, and he retained it in a minor Cabinet shuffle on August 20. Nielsen was also a member of the Priorities and Planning Committee, whose 16 members made the important decisions of the administration and reviewed the work of other Cabinet committees. In late September two senior ministers resigned: John Fraser from British Columbia, minister of fisheries, who admitted overruling fisheries inspectors in releasing a consignment of rancid canned tuna meat for public consumption, and Marcel Masse, minister of communications, who asked to be relieved of Cabinet duties while a complaint regarding the reporting of his election expenses was being investigated. Masse, a powerful figure on the Quebec political scene, was returned to the Cabinet on November 30 when the charges against him were determined to be unfounded. A new fisheries minister was appointed from British Columbia.

Parliament sat from Nov. 5, 1984, to June 28, 1985, when it adjourned for the summer recess. A total of 49 bills were approved, most of them housekeeping measures introduced by the previous Liberal administration. The Mulroney government moved swiftly to demolish one of the pillars of its predecessor's economic policy: the Foreign Investment Review Agency (FIRA), a body set up in 1973, during a period of heightened concern over the effects of foreign investment in Canada. Its role was to screen investments from abroad and takeovers of Canadian businesses. The agency had been a source of contention with the U.S. during the early 1980s and was not popular with Canadian business. It was now replaced by Investment Canada, whose task was to encourage new investment, whether from foreign or domestic sources. The Conservatives also backed away from the Liberals' controversial metric policy, deciding that although metric measurement would continue to be mandatory in Canada, retailers could also use the imperial system.

The equality rights section of Canada's Charter of Rights and Freedoms came into effect on April 17, three years after the Charter had been formally proclaimed. The delay had been intended to give Parliament and the provincial legislatures time to bring their laws into conformity with the Charter. Seven of the ten provinces had taken the necessary steps or announced their intention of doing so. Quebec, which did not recognize the 1982 Charter, had its own comprehensive charter of rights. It was, however, an ordinary statute that could be repealed at any time, whereas the federal Charter was entrenched in the constitution.

Two important agreements were reached with the provinces during 1985. On February 11 Prime Minister Mulroney signed a 68-clause memorandum of understanding with Premier Brian Peckford of Newfoundland governing the management of oil and gas resources lying off the island-province's coast. Newfoundland was given the authority to tax these resources as if they were on land. The agreement was more generous to the province than one signed by the Liberal government in 1982 with Nova Scotia. That accord left ultimate power to manage offshore resources with the federal majority on the control board and with the federal energy minister. The Newfoundland document provided for the province and Ottawa each to appoint three members to the management board, which would have an independent chairman. Mulroney described the Atlantic Accord as the most important agreement Newfoundland had entered into with Ottawa since it joined the Canadian confederation in 1949. Peckford called an election for April 2, which his Conservative Party won, but with a reduced majority of 36 of the 52 seats.

An agreement relating to oil prices was signed with the western producing provinces of Alberta, Saskatchewan, and British Columbia on March 28. It provided for Canadian oil prices to be decided by the market rather than by government decree. Under the plan, Canadian oil prices were to be permitted to compete at world levels by June 1. The federal government agreed to eliminate five of its taxes and special charges on petroleum as soon as possible and to phase out its royalties on oil and natural gas. The oil industry stood to gain a possible $1.3 billion in additional revenue during the first year of the pact. The agreement effectively demolished most of the Liberal government's 1980 National Energy Program. (*See* Special Report.)

The Economy. The Canadian economy showed encouraging growth during 1985, with employment and incomes higher than the year before. Consumer demand, especially for automobiles, was the strongest component in the increase, although spending on plant and equipment (capital goods) was also strong. Exports to all major markets—the U.S., Europe, and Japan—were down. This condition contrasted with Canada's flourishing export performance in recent years. The gross national product, seasonally adjusted, was expected to reach $449 billion, representing an

U.S. Pres. Ronald Reagan and Canadian Prime Minister Brian Mulroney stroll past the cannons of the Citadel overlooking the St. Lawrence River at Quebec during their "shamrock summit," as it was dubbed by the press, in March.

DIANA WALKER—GAMMA/LIAISON

annual growth rate of about 4% in real terms in the first six months of the year. During the third quarter the rate increased to 6%. The Canadian dollar continued to feel the impact of high interest rates in the U.S. as it hovered between 71 and 73 U.S. cents during the year. Unemployment showed the usual regional and seasonal variations; in October it was running at 10.3%, compared with 11.2% in January. The jobless rate was still significantly higher in the 15–24-year age group, in Quebec, and in the outlying provinces of Canada. Inflation continued to be under control, with an annual rate of 4.2% recorded for October. Interest rates were also lower than they had been in previous years, the trend-setting Bank of Canada rate standing at 8.7% in mid-October.

Several major corporate takeovers occurred in Canada in 1985. On May 9 it was announced that British Telecom of London had acquired a controlling interest in Mitel Corp., a leading Ottawa-based telecommunications firm. On August 2 a Toronto financial group, Olympia & York Developments Ltd., purchased control of Gulf Canada, an oil company owned by Chevron Corp. of San Francisco, for $2.8 billion. Ten days later it was announced that Petro-Canada would buy Gulf Canada's petroleum refining and marketing assets west of Quebec. This would make Petro-Canada the largest gasoline retailer in the country.

An understanding was reached with Japan on July 3 by which Japanese car imports into Canada would be limited to 18% of the anticipated Canadian car market for 1985. The undertaking differed from those reached in previous years in that it did not specify the number of vehicles to be admitted into Canada. The new formula would allow Japanese manufacturers to increase the number of vehicles shipped to Canada in a year of strong consumer demand. A large Korean auto manufacturer, Hyundai, announced it would build an assembly plant at an undisclosed location in Canada, its first overseas facility. Korean cars had enjoyed booming sales in Canada since they were first introduced in 1984.

The Canadian banking system, long a symbol of stability, suffered a pair of shocks in September when two smaller banks failed. The Canadian Commercial Bank and the Northland Bank, both based in Alberta, dealt largely with business and institutional clients. The fall in value of real estate in western Canada and the recession in the oil industry in the early 1980s had left them holding nonperforming or troubled loans. The federal government promised to pay $900 million to the uninsured depositors in the two banks. At the same time, it set up a judicial inquiry to look into the factors that contributed to their collapse, the first in Canada since 1923.

A long-standing link between Canada and the U.S. was dissolved on March 30 when the Canadian branch of the United Automobile Workers (UAW) formally split from its international parent union. The Canadian union had unsuccessfully sought full autonomy for Canadian workers in 1984. The new Canadian union received $36 million as its share of UAW assets, thus providing a strike fund of $30 million, the largest of any union in Canada.

In his first budget, produced on May 23, Finance Minister Michael Wilson cut net spending by $1.8 billion and increased revenues by $200 million in the 1985–86 fiscal year. These measures were expected to reduce the deficit to $33.8 billion. Income and consumer taxes were raised, most notably through a 10% surtax on basic federal income tax on salaries of over $30,000, to last for 18 months from July 1. Large corporations were also to pay an income surtax of 5%, while the gasoline tax, excise taxes, and sales taxes were all increased or extended to formerly exempt items. A lifetime capital gains tax exemption of $500,000 was provided in an effort to instill investment incentives and create jobs. Most controversial was a plan to partially deindex old-age pensions and family allowances. Wilson proposed, beginning in 1986, to reduce indexing on these payments to the amount of the annual increase in the consumer price index that exceeded 3%. The proposal roused a storm of protest from citizens over 65, and on June 27 the finance minister announced that he would continue to index old-age pensions fully, offsetting the loss of savings through increases in corporate and gasoline taxes.

Foreign Affairs. Two issues dominated the agenda of Canada's relations with the U.S.: the possibility of free trade and cooperation in the Strategic Defense Initiative ("Star Wars") research project. The trade issue gained public attention in Canada as protectionist proposals in the U.S. Congress were seen as threatening to jeopardize Canada's entry into the valuable U.S. market. (About 75% of Canada's trade is with the U.S.) When Pres. Ronald Reagan met Mulroney at the "shamrock summit" in Quebec City on March 17–18, the reduction of trade barriers was a major item of discussion. The two leaders agreed to work toward freer trade, the president reportedly telling Mulroney in a private session that he would "go to bat" for Canada in opposing protectionist measures.

In Canada a royal commission on the country's economic prospects appointed by former prime minister Pierre

(continued on page 556)

A Mood for Change

BY PETER WARD

The overwhelming victory of the federal Progressive Conservative Party in the Canadian election of Sept. 4, 1984, seemed to open the floodgates, because the most constant thing about Canadian politics in 1985 was change. In some areas regional strongmen—allies or foes of former prime minister Pierre Trudeau—chose to leave public life, perhaps because the political wars had lost some of their zest. In other areas provincial governments were threatened by the same mood of discontent that had led voters to decimate the federal Liberals in 1984. Major upheavals took place or were threatened in Quebec, Ontario, New Brunswick, Manitoba, Saskatchewan, Alberta, British Columbia, and the Yukon Territory.

A Shift from Separatism. Perhaps the most significant change came in Quebec. Nine years earlier, in 1976, Quebecers had elected a provincial government dedicated to independence, headed by René Lévesque and his Parti Québécois (PQ). But in the 1984 federal election they did an about-face, giving a resounding victory to the federal Progressive Conservative Party and, by implication, support to continued adherence to the Canadian confederation. The fact that Prime Minister Brian Mulroney himself was from Quebec was a major factor in helping to solidify public opinion behind federalism. By early 1985 former premier Robert Bourassa and his rejuvenated Liberal Party—traditionally the party of federalism in Quebec—were far ahead in the public opinion polls.

With the next provincial election looming, Lévesque realized his party could not win on an independence platform and sought a more moderate party stance, in line with the polls. The result was a high-level revolt within his government. Several senior Cabinet ministers, men who had been in the vanguard of the independence movement, resigned. Defections and resignations reduced the PQ majority in the Quebec National Assembly to the point where it was dangerously close to defeat. Discouraged by political developments and suffering from ill health, Lévesque resigned on June 20.

In the subsequent contest for leadership of the PQ, the choice of the moderates, Justice Minister Pierre-Marc Johnson (see BIOGRAPHIES), won handily, but the December 2 Quebec election proved to be a disaster for him and his party. Liberals won 99 seats in the 122-seat Quebec Assembly, while the PQ won only 23 seats. Liberal leader Bourassa failed to win his personal seat, but he was expected to win a by-election early in 1986 in a safe Liberal Montreal district. Quebec ended 1985 with Bourassa as premier, already forming an alliance with Ontario's new Liberal government to oppose free trade between Canada and the U.S.

Fall of a Machine. The most surprising change of the year came in Canada's largest province, Ontario, ruled by a succession of Conservative governments since 1943. In late 1984 William Davis, premier since 1971, resigned

and called a leadership convention for early 1985. Cabinet veteran Frank Miller emerged victorious, but his tenure as premier was brief. From his accession to office on February 8 to the election on May 2, his fortunes went steadily downhill. Some blamed him for shunning the advice of the old provincial Conservative machine, which had been instrumental in Mulroney's victory. Others gave credit to the energetic and effective campaigning of the Ontario Liberal leader, David Peterson (see BIOGRAPHIES). In any case, election day resulted in a near stalemate, with the Conservatives capturing 52 of the legislature's 125 seats, the Liberals 48, and the New Democratic Party (NDP) 25.

After several weeks of negotiation, the NDP decided to support the Liberals, assuring the end of the Conservative monopoly of power in Ontario. The legislature met, and on June 18 Liberals, supported by the New Democrats, defeated the Miller government on a nonconfidence vote. Miller resigned as required, and after 42 years of Conservative rule, Liberal David Peterson became premier of Ontario. Citizens of Ontario seemed to like the change. By the end of the summer Peterson was leading in the polls with 47% support, compared with 29% for the Conservatives and 23% for the NDP. Conservatives ended the year with a convention to choose a new leader. On the second ballot, Larry Grossman of Toronto, a former provincial treasurer, won by the narrow margin of 848 votes to 829 for Dennis Timbrell, formerly municipal affairs minister in the provincial government.

From Maritimes to Prairies. New Brunswick, ruled by Conservative Premier Richard Hatfield since 1970, also appeared to be heading for a change of governing parties, although a provincial election was not legally required until October 1987. In New Brunswick it was the alleged adventures of the premier that brought Conservative for-

AP/WIDE WORLD

Pierre-Marc Johnson (left) succeeded to the leadership of the Parti Québécois after René Lévesque (right), who founded the party in 1968, resigned in June. The party's troubles were not over, however; it lost an election in December to the Liberals under Robert Bourassa.

Peter Ward operates Ward News Services Canada in the Parliamentary Press Gallery, Ottawa.

tunes to a 15-year low. In September 1984 Hatfield, who had acquired a nationwide reputation for unconventional behaviour, was accompanying Queen Elizabeth II on a tour of the province. Before their plane took off, police dogs, sniffing the baggage for explosives, discovered a political explosive in the form of marijuana in an outer pocket of Hatfield's suitcase. After a great deal of discussion and investigation, Hatfield was charged with possession.

He was acquitted in a sensational trial in January 1985, but within days of the verdict, newspaper stories appeared claiming Hatfield had picked up two young students and taken them to his home for a marijuana and cocaine party in 1981. Hatfield denied the allegations and claimed the Royal Canadian Mounted Police were out to get him. Nonetheless, the damage to his image was severe, and in August he had to face down demands from some fellow Conservatives that he resign. He was determined to lead his party in at least one more provincial election, and his political skills were such that observers hesitated to bet on the outcome.

In Manitoba, which since November 1981 had had Canada's only left-wing NDP government, Premier Howard Pawley was considering an election call, although polls showed his popularity about even with that of Conservative leader Gary Filmon. One of the biggest issues in Manitoba was bilingualism. The courts had ruled that a late 19th-century government acted illegally when it made Manitoba English-speaking, and it ordered all provincial legislation translated so it would be available in both English and French. Pawley favoured seeking accommodation on the language issue and increasing the availability of French services in the province. This stand gave him political trouble in some rural areas, but the coming election appeared to be a toss-up.

Conservatives were the party with problems in Saskatchewan. Premier Grant Devine, who overwhelmed the NDP in an April 1982 election, had until April 1987 to call another one, but tradition favoured a new election after four years. A summer sampling of public opinion in Regina, the provincial capital, showed the NDP ahead of the Conservatives—25% of the voters, compared with 16%—but 53% were undecided. The province led the country in economic growth, but a severe drought in traditionally Conservative southern Saskatchewan spelled economic disaster for farmers. Any massive provincial aid program for the farmers could signal an early election. At best, Devine was expected to lose some of the 56 Conservative seats in the 64-seat legislature.

No such troubles threatened the Conservative Party in Alberta, but there was a major change as Peter Lougheed, premier since September 1971, decided to retire. His departure marked the end of an era that had seen Alberta emerge as a major energy supplier. His successor, businessman Donald Getty, inherited a 65–4 majority in the provincial legislature. Once energy minister under Lougheed and a former teammate of the ex-premier on the Edmonton Eskimos professional football team, Getty was slightly to the right of Lougheed politically and could be expected to champion provincial rights in dealings with Ottawa. The new premier was expected to call an election sometime in 1986, though one was not due until November 1987.

Far West, Far North. British Columbia's Social Credit dynasty might be coming to a close. Premier William Bennett did not have to call an election until May 1988, but only two years after being returned to power by a healthy majority, his Social Credit Party (Socreds), out of power for only three years since 1952, was in trouble. A summer public opinion survey of the province's heavily populated

One of many Canadian political leaders to benefit from a national mood of impatience with incumbents and eagerness for change, David Peterson became premier of Ontario in June, ending 42 years of Conservative government in the province.
CANAPRESS

lower mainland showed 25.7% of voters favouring the NDP to only 22.6% for the Socreds (9.6% supported the Liberals, 3% the Conservatives, and the rest were undecided).

Bennett's problems were economic. The world recession had devastated British Columbia's two chief industries, lumber and mining, and unemployment throughout 1985 hovered around 15%, compared with 10.5% for Canada as a whole. The NDP, gaining ground under its new leader, Robert Skelly, blamed Bennett for making things worse with his efforts to balance the provincial budget by raising taxes and cutting government services. In two years 12,686 civil servants and teachers had been dropped from the public payroll. Nor had Bennett achieved much success in recruiting federal aid to attract major industries to the province. His best hope, observers felt, might be to make capital from the public enthusiasm expected to accompany the Expo 86 world's fair in Vancouver.

Discontent with the political establishment extended far into the Canadian north in 1985. In a May election in the Yukon Territory the Conservatives, led by lawyer Willard Phelps, were defeated by the NDP under actor-playwright Tony Penikett. The Conservatives had been in power in the Yukon since 1978, the year party politics arrived in the territory, and they had been expected to win again. Phelps and his party captured only 6 of the 16 seats in the Legislative Council, to 8 seats for the NDP and 2 for the Liberals. The result was a setback for Erik Nielsen, the federal deputy prime minister and defense minister, who had been Conservative MP for the Yukon since 1957.

Meanwhile, the Mulroney government was not immune from the prevailing mood. A year after the 1984 election, an extensive public opinion poll showed that 60% of those surveyed thought Mulroney had not kept his election promises. At the same time, 46% still said they would vote for him, compared with 29% for the Liberals and 21% for the NDP.

The U.S. Coast Guard icebreaker *Polar Sea* is shadowed by the Canadian cutter *Sir John A. MacDonald* in Lancaster Sound. The *Polar Sea*'s voyage through the Northwest Passage, claimed as territorial waters by Canada, roused sharp protests from Canadian nationalists.
CANAPRESS

(continued from page 553)

Trudeau recommended strongly in favour of a free trade agreement with the U.S. that would eliminate all tariffs over ten years. A joint committee of the Senate and the House of Commons, representing all three political parties, also reported in favour of "broad discussions with the United States to determine their receptivity to liberalizing bilateral trade." On September 26 Mulroney told the House of Commons that he had called President Reagan to inform him that he wished to begin negotiations on a broad package of tariff reductions. The 1965 pact allowing free trade in auto vehicles and parts was not to enter into the negotiations.

Arrangements for strengthening North America's air defense were a more controversial topic in Canada. Although Canada permitted tests of free-flying cruise missiles over 2,500 km (1,550 mi) of its northern territory in late February, the government made it clear that U.S. nuclear arms could not be based in Canada without its consent. Air defense figured in the "shamrock summit" when the two leaders signed an agreement for a U.S. $1.5 billion upgrade to the northern radar defense system. It was made clear that there was no connection between the land-based radar system in the north, now 30 years old, and weapons in space that were aimed at antiballistic missiles. The matter was likely to be raised in parliamentary hearings dealing with renewal of the North American Aerospace Defense Command (formerly NORAD), due to expire in March 1986. In common with some of the U.S.'s European allies, Canada took a cautious stand on the $26 billion Star Wars research program. The government supported research but stopped short of endorsing development and deployment of the system. In September Mulroney stated that the Canadian government would not participate in the research phase of Star Wars but would not bar private interests in Canada from doing so.

The March meeting between the two leaders referred the controversial acid rain issue to two high-profile former public officials, who were to study and report on the question before the next Mulroney-Reagan meeting in 1986: William Davis, Ontario's premier until February, and Drew Lewis, Reagan's transport secretary during his first term. The status of the historic Northwest Passage through Canada's Arctic islands was back in the news. Fifteen years earlier, Canada had asserted pollution-control regulations over the Arctic waters. The U.S. challenged this jurisdiction, claiming the waters were part of the international sea, and the issue of sovereignty remained uncertain. During

early August the U.S. Coast Guard icebreaker *Polar Sea* made a successful transit of the occasionally ice-blocked passage. At first the Mulroney government reacted mildly, but Inuit groups living along the route protested, and many Canadians felt the government had not presented its objections forcefully enough to Washington.

On September 10, claiming that Soviet submarines had been operating in Arctic waters and citing the *Polar Sea* voyage, the Canadian government spelled out new measures to enforce its control in the Arctic. Straight baselines, authorized in international law, would be drawn around the islands, giving Canada ownership of the internal waters they enclosed. Military surveillance flights over the Arctic would be increased, and the government would build a Class 8 icebreaker capable of crushing through ice 2½ m (8 ft) thick. More naval operations would also take place in the eastern Arctic in 1986. There would be an effort to cooperate more closely with the U.S. in the face of common security concerns, but this would have to be based on a recognition of Canada's sovereignty in the area.

Measures to persuade South Africa to move away from its repressive racial policies were under intense consideration by the government during the year. On July 6 External Affairs Minister Joe Clark announced sanctions to discourage trade. The export of sensitive electronic equipment to South African government agencies would be banned, a double taxation agreement would be abrogated, Canadian banks would be encouraged not to sell South African gold coins, and Canada would terminate all contracts for the processing of uranium from South West Africa/Namibia when current agreements ended in 1988. Additional funds were to be provided to help in the training of black South African students in Canada and in their home country. On September 13 Clark announced that he was meeting bankers and businessmen to discuss further measures to influence the South African government. Canadian banks were also to be asked to ban new loans to the South African government or its agencies. In a strongly worded address September 25, Clark told the UN General Assembly that "measures to make all South Africans equal within their state must be pursued to the end." Prime Minister Mulroney carried the same message to the Commonwealth heads of government conference at Nassau in The Bahamas in the week of October 14. Mulroney helped to mediate between Britain and most other Commonwealth members in an effort to work out a single Commonwealth position on the vexed question of economic sanctions against South Africa.   (D. M. L. FARR)

UNITED STATES

The United States of America is a federal republic composed of 50 states, 49 of which are in North America and one of which consists of the Hawaiian Islands. Area: 9,372,571 sq km (3,618,770 sq mi), including 205,856 sq km of inland water but excluding the 156,492 sq km of the Great Lakes that lie within U.S. boundaries. Pop. (1985 est.): 236.9 million. Cap.: Washington, D.C. Monetary unit: U.S. dollar, with (Oct. 21, 1985) a free rate of U.S. $1.43 to £1 sterling. President in 1985, Ronald Reagan.

Foreign Affairs. Thinking perhaps about how his administration would be judged by historians of a future day, U.S. Pres. Ronald Reagan (*see* BIOGRAPHIES) indicated a yearning for lasting global peace in his second inaugural address, Jan. 21, 1985. He accused the Soviet Union of mounting "the greatest military buildup in the history of man" but pledged to "meet with the Soviets hoping that we can agree on a way to rid the world of the threat of nuclear destruction."

This offer led eventually to a summit conference in Geneva on November 19–20 between Reagan and Soviet leader Mikhail Gorbachev (*see* BIOGRAPHIES). In a televised address five days before the meeting, the president said: "My mission, stated simply, is a mission for peace. It is to engage the new Soviet leader in what I hope will be a dialogue for peace that endures beyond my presidency. It is to sit down across from Mr. Gorbachev and try to map out, together, a basis for peaceful discourse even though our disagreements on fundamentals will not change."

The actual encounter went much as Reagan evidently had envisioned it. Appearing together in the Swiss city on November 21, the two leaders voiced their determination to restrain the arms race and to "improve U.S.-Soviet relations and the international situation as a whole." But they made no mention of any specific steps to limit or reduce their nuclear arsenals. Instead, they acclaimed agreements on cultural exchanges and stressed their concurrence on the need for a fresh start in East-West relations.

On his return to the United States, Reagan delivered a generally optimistic report to a November 21 joint session of Congress. "It was a constructive meeting," he said. "So constructive, in fact, that I look forward to welcoming Mr. Gorbachev to the United States next year. And I have accepted his invitation to go to Moscow the following year."

The tenth anniversary of the end of the Vietnam war was marked in New York City in May with a ticker-tape parade of veterans on Broadway and the dedication of a Vietnam Veterans Memorial by Mayor Edward Koch.
ANDERSON—GAMMA/LIAISON

Much of the potential drama of the Geneva summit had been undercut by previous developments. In a September 9 *Time* magazine interview that caused consternation in official Washington, Gorbachev took the Reagan administration to task for playing down the Geneva meeting as a "get-acquainted" session. And in a speech to the United Nations General Assembly on October 24, Reagan urged

GENE BASSET/ATLANTA JOURNAL, UNITED FEATURE SYNDICATE

More than 60 homes were destroyed or severely damaged and some 240 persons left homeless by a fire that raged through a Philadelphia neighbourhood after police bombed the fortified headquarters of the sect known as Move.
STEVEN FALK--GAMMA/LIAISON

the Soviet Union to join the U.S. in finding peaceful solutions to five regional conflicts—in Afghanistan, Angola, Cambodia (Kampuchea), Ethiopia, and Nicaragua—that involved regimes supported by Moscow.

However, the main breakthrough in U.S.-Soviet relations in 1985 was not the Reagan-Gorbachev meeting but the resumption of talks, also in Geneva, between lower-level representatives of the two superpowers on reduction of nuclear arms. Renewal of the negotiations was agreed upon in early January by U.S. Secretary of State George P. Shultz and Soviet Foreign Minister Andrey A. Gromyko. The Soviets had withdrawn from the Intermediate Nuclear Forces talks in November 1983 and from the Strategic Arms Reduction Talks the following month. The resumption of negotiations was made possible when the Soviets agreed to drop their earlier insistence that they would not return to the bargaining table unless the U.S. halted its deployment of medium-range cruise and Pershing II missiles in Western Europe.

The renewed bilateral arms discussions got under way at the insistence of the U.S.S.R. on March 12 despite the death two days earlier of Soviet Pres. Konstantin U. Chernenko (see OBITUARIES). The two sides agreed on March 14 to divide their negotiating teams into subgroups on strategic nuclear weapons, intermediate-range nuclear arms, and space-based weapons. The talks were adjourned for a month on April 24 amid reports that no progress had been made because of a continuing dispute over how the talks should be conducted.

Resumption of the Geneva arms talks on May 30 brought no improvement in atmosphere. It soon became obvious that the main sticking point was the Strategic Defense Initiative (the so-called Star Wars plan). The Soviets continued to insist that the United States make "necessary adjustments" in this program, while the U.S. made it clear that Star Wars was a nonnegotiable issue.

Given these inflexible positions, the second round of arms talks ended July 16 with no apparent progress. White House spokesman Larry Speakes asserted that Soviet negotiators preferred to explore "concepts" rather than "deal in concrete terms and with hard numbers."

The third round opened September 19 amid a mood of pessimism. At the end of the month Soviet negotiators proposed a 50% reduction in the strategic nuclear arsenals of both countries. Viktor P. Karpov, head of the Soviet team, called the proposal a "well-balanced package of drastic new arms-control measures." U.S. negotiators responded

by offering on November 1 a disarmament package that included a new limit on the maximum number of nuclear warheads in the arsenals of the United States and the Soviet Union. The U.S. offer contained no Star Wars concessions, and U.S. officials privately acknowledged that the proposals amounted to a "repackaging" of previous offers.

The generally favourable media coverage of Reagan's meeting with Gorbachev contrasted sharply with the negative commentary that accompanied the president's trip to Western Europe in May in connection with observances commemorating the 40th anniversary of the end of World War II in Europe. Reagan came under fire when it was disclosed that he intended to lay a wreath at a military cemetery in Bitburg, West Germany, where the graves included those of some members of the Waffen SS, Hitler's elite troops, who had administered the concentration camps.

Announcement of the president's plans, which the White House refused to alter, elicited sharp complaints from Jewish and veterans' groups. Far from disavowing his plans, however, Reagan said on April 18 that German soldiers had been "victims" of the Nazis "just as surely as the victims in the concentration camps." But he blunted criticism of his visit to Bitburg by stopping earlier the same day at the nearby Bergen-Belsen Nazi prison camp.

The controversy over Bitburg overshadowed what was supposed to have been the highlight of the president's trip to Europe—his participation in the 11th annual summit meeting of the seven major industrial democracies, held May 2–4 at Bonn, West Germany. The communiqué issued on May 4 asserted that "world economic conditions are better than they have been for a considerable time," that inflation had been reduced, and that the "recovery in the industrial countries has begun to spread to the developing world." The leaders agreed to work to strengthen their individual economies, halt protectionism, improve world monetary stability, increase job opportunities, and reduce social inequities.

Another focus of concern for U.S. foreign-policy makers in 1985 was South Africa. Early in the year it seemed that the troubles in that country could possibly be turned to the Republican administration's advantage. This was because of the unexpected hostility that greeted the visit to South Africa on January 5–13 of Sen. Edward M. Kennedy (Dem., Mass.). Kennedy had been invited to the country by Bishop Desmond Tutu, winner of the 1984 Nobel Peace Prize, and the Rev. Allan Boesak (see BIOGRAPHIES), president of the World Alliance of Reformed Churches.

Kennedy's reception was chillier than expected. Both black and white South Africans accused him of making the trip to stage a "media event" that would help his chances of gaining the Democratic Party's presidential nomination in 1988. The Kennedy trip soon faded into insignificance, however, as a nationwide movement aimed at pressuring South Africa to dismantle its apartheid system of racial separation gathered momentum. Protest demonstrations held almost daily outside the South African embassy in Washington, D.C., were augmented by similar activities on college campuses across the country.

In Congress, meanwhile, more than 20 bills were introduced with the aim of persuading South Africa to abandon apartheid. Reagan, succumbing to the pressure, reversed his previous position and on September 9 ordered limited trade and financial sanctions against the country. Among other measures, he ordered a ban on trade in nuclear technology, on computer sales to South African government security agencies, and on bank loans to Pretoria, except for those that financed projects that clearly benefited all racial groups.

Reagan, however, remained firm in his opposition to the leftist Sandinista government of Nicaragua. The Department of State announced on January 18 that the United States would not participate in proceedings in the International Court of Justice (World Court) concerning Nicaragua's suit against U.S. aggression. Administration officials said the same day that the U.S. had suspended talks with the Sandinista government, begun in June 1984, on easing tensions between the two countries. And on October 7 the United States announced that it would no longer automatically comply with World Court rulings, stating that the tribunal had been "abused for political ends" by nations such as Nicaragua.

Reagan ordered an embargo on trade with Nicaragua on May 1 and banned Nicaraguan aircraft and ships from the United States. The measures followed a decisive defeat in Congress during the previous week of Reagan's request for $14 million in aid to the Nicaraguan *contra* rebel forces. Congress subsequently had a change of heart. In a major victory for the White House, the House of Representatives voted June 12 to provide $27 million in humanitarian aid to the Nicaraguan *contras.* The Senate had voted June 6 to approve $38 million in nonmilitary aid to the *contras* and also voted to bar the use of U.S. funds for operations against Nicaragua that would flout international law or the charter of the Organization of American States.

U.S.-Canadian relations took a turn for the better with Reagan's meeting in Quebec City March 17–18 with Prime Minister Brian Mulroney. The meeting was named the "shamrock summit" since it began on St. Patrick's Day and both participants were of Irish descent. The two leaders signed an agreement to upgrade the North American radar defense system, known as the Distant Early Warning (DEW) Line, and also agreed to appoint "special envoys" to search for solutions to the problem of acid rain. In addition, Reagan and Mulroney signed agreements on trade, fishing, space projects, and coordination of law-enforcement efforts in cross-border criminal investigations.

Domestic Affairs. Economic policy dominated the Reagan administration's domestic program in 1985 as the White House pursued the twin goals of tax reform and a program to achieve a balanced federal budget. The president referred indirectly to those objectives in his second inaugural address when he declared: "We must act now to protect future generations from government's desire to spend its citizens' money and tax them into servitude when the bills come due. Let us make it unconstitutional

for the federal government to spend more than the federal government takes in."

Reagan outlined his tax reform proposals in detail during a nationally televised address on May 28. He called the current tax system "unwise, unwanted, and unfair" and said that his own plan would "reduce tax burdens on the working people of this country, close loopholes that benefit a privileged few," and simplify the U.S. tax code.

The plan, based on a set of Treasury Department recommendations made public in November 1984, proposed to merge the existing 14 personal income-tax brackets into just three, with a substantial lowering of the maximum tax rate. It would, the administration said, mean a tax reduction for virtually all of the two-thirds of U.S. taxpayers who did not itemize deductions. It would cut overall personal income taxes by 7% while collecting 9% more revenue from business. And it would eliminate a variety of credits, deductions, incentives, and preferences.

As expected, the president's tax proposals came under attack from special interest groups and members of Congress. The battle was joined in earnest on September 26, when Rep. Dan Rostenkowski (Dem., Ill.; *see* BIOGRAPHIES), chairman of the tax-writing House Ways and Means Committee, unveiled his plan for overhauling the federal tax code. Rostenkowski's proposals followed the general outline of Reagan's but modified them in a number of respects. The Rostenkowski plan allowed less generous personal exemptions for taxpayers who itemized deductions than did the president's plan, and it proposed

AP/WIDE WORLD

Most of the 39 U.S. citizens who had been held hostage in Beirut, Lebanon, by radical Shi'ah Muslims arrive at Andrews Air Force Base, Maryland, after their release in June. Pres. Ronald Reagan and his wife, Nancy, were there to greet them.

Protesters approach the Soviet freighter *Marshal Koniev* near Reserve, Louisiana, in November. They were demonstrating against the U.S. Immigration Service's actions in returning to Soviet authorities a Ukrainian sailor who had twice jumped ship but then apparently changed his mind about seeking asylum in the U.S.

AP/WIDE WORLD

to continue to allow individuals to deduct a portion of their state and local income taxes from federal taxable income. It also called for a higher maximum tax rate on capital gains. On December 18 the House passed a bill that incorporated most of Rostenkowski's proposals and sent the legislation to the Senate.

In the meantime, Congress was wrestling with its annual round of appropriations legislation, including a measure requiring a balanced federal budget by fiscal year 1991. The balanced-budget proposal, a program of forced deficit reductions, took the form of an amendment to legislation raising the ceiling on the federal debt from $1,824,000,-000,000 to $2,079,000,000,000. Congress approved the bill on December 11, just in time to forestall a possible default by the federal government on its debt obligations.

Approval came shortly after Reagan said that he would sign the measure despite provisions that could lead to substantial reductions in defense spending. Department of Defense officials calculated that the potential cuts could amount to as much as $18 billion.

In another major economic development the U.S. took part in international efforts to check the long rise in the value of the U.S. dollar against other major currencies. On February 27 the U.S. Federal Reserve Board and the central banks of six European countries—Austria, Belgium, the U.K., France, Italy, and West Germany—intervened in world currency markets in a successful attempt to force the dollar down.

A new campaign to lower the dollar's value began on September 22 in New York City at a meeting of central bankers and finance ministers of the five leading non-Communist industrial nations—the U.S., West Germany, Japan, France, and Britain. On the next day, intervention in the international currency markets by some or all of the so-called Group of Five nations helped to cause a record one-day decline in the value of the dollar. By the end of the week the dollar had fallen 5.2% in value against major currencies, according to the Federal Reserve Board.

The decline of the dollar from what many economists regarded as an unrealistically high value was seen as one factor in the stock market surge that occurred at the end of the year. Also contributing to the steep rise in share values were continued low inflation and declining interest rates. In November alone the closely watched Dow Jones average of 30 industrial stocks exceeded the 1300 and then the 1400 level for the first time in Wall Street history. Then, on December 11, the Dow broke the 1500 barrier.

The year was a busy one for corporate merger activity, much of it involving well-known print or broadcast media properties. For example, the magazine publishing world was surprised on March 8 by the news that directors of *The New Yorker* had agreed to sell the periodical for $142 million to Samuel I. Newhouse, Jr. It was the first time that the magazine had changed hands in its 60-year history. In a takeover attempt that many did not take seriously at first, Atlanta broadcaster Ted Turner announced in April that he would ask CBS Inc. shareholders to sell him a controlling interest in the television network. The proposed deal eventually fell through after CBS announced plans to buy back nearly $1 billion worth of its own stock from shareholders, a defensive maneuver that left the company with a heavy burden of debt and forced it to introduce a series of painful cost-cutting measures.

The two other major national commercial TV networks did change ownership during the year, however. The sale of American Broadcasting Cos. for at least $3.5 billion to Capital Cities Communications Inc. was announced March 18. Then, on December 11, it was disclosed that General Electric Co. had agreed to purchase RCA Corp.—parent company of the NBC television network—for $6,280,-000,000. The merger was expected to produce a defense, communications, and consumer products powerhouse with few equals anywhere. In yet another takeover involving a group of television stations, the owners of Twentieth Century-Fox Film Corp. agreed in May to buy the seven independent television stations owned by Metromedia Inc. for $2 billion.

The Reagan administration experienced substantial personnel changes. One of the more unusual shifts involved the exchange of jobs, announced on January 8, between White House Chief of Staff James Baker and Secretary of the Treasury Donald Regan (*see* BIOGRAPHIES). Baker was designated to head the Treasury, a Cabinet post that required Senate confirmation, which was forthcoming Jan-

uary 29. No such action was needed for Regan to take over as the top White House aide in Reagan's second term.

A week after clearing Baker's appointment, the Senate confirmed three other new Cabinet appointees: William J. Bennett as secretary of education, Donald P. Hodel as secretary of the interior, and John S. Herrington as secretary of energy. Seeking speedy action on the Bennett nomination, Reagan had assured Congress that he had dropped plans to abolish the Education Department "at this time." Secretary of Labor Raymond J. Donovan resigned March 15 after a New York State judge refused to dismiss fraud and larceny charges pending against him. Donovan was the first Cabinet member ever to be indicted while in office. He was succeeded as labour secretary by U.S. Trade Representative Bill Brock.

By far the most controversial Cabinet confirmation of the year was that of Edwin Meese III as attorney general on February 23. The Senate vote was 63 to 31, with Democrats casting all the nays. The confirmation came more than a year after Meese, a former White House counselor, had been nominated by Reagan to succeed William French Smith in the post. Opponents of the nomination argued that Meese was insensitive to civil rights and the concerns of minority groups generally.

Meese subsequently made headlines by attacking certain opinions of the U.S. Supreme Court. In a speech before the American Bar Association July 9, he admonished the court for what he called "policy choices" instead of decisions based on "constitutional principle." He specifically condemned recent rulings concerning school prayer, government aid to religious schools, and a state law giving employees the right to a day off to observe their Sabbath. The attorney general later described as "wrong" the court's decision in *Miranda* v. *Arizona,* a celebrated 1960s case that established the right of a criminal defendant to have a lawyer present before questioning by police. In turn, Meese's views on constitutional law were publicly assailed by Supreme Court Justices John Paul Stevens and William Brennan, Jr.

President Reagan announced on October 1 that Health and Human Services Secretary Margaret Heckler had agreed to leave her Cabinet post and become ambassador to Ireland. Though the White House took pains to portray the move as a "promotion," it followed weeks of rumours that Regan was seeking her ouster. Regan also was reported to have engineered the departure from the White House of Robert McFarlane, Reagan's national security adviser.

In a move that was not unexpected, UN Ambassador Jeane Kirkpatrick told the president on January 30 that

President Reagan and Mrs. Reagan welcome Li Xiannian (Li Hsiennien), president of China, and his wife to a state dinner at the White House in July. During Li's visit to the U.S. an agreement on the sale of nuclear technology to China was signed.
UPI/BETTMANN NEWSPHOTOS

she was leaving government to "speak out clearly" on U.S. foreign policy. She was succeeded in the post by Lieut. Gen. Vernon Walters (*see* BIOGRAPHIES), who had been deputy director of the Central Intelligence Agency under presidents Richard Nixon and Gerald Ford.

Budget Director David Stockman, one of the leading architects of the administration's campaign to reduce federal spending, quit his post effective August 1 to join the New York investment banking firm of Salomon Brothers Inc. Succeeding him as head of the Office of Management and Budget was James C. Miller III, who was chairman of the Federal Trade Commission at the time of his appointment.

One of the year's most disconcerting developments was the large number of espionage cases that came to light. Of particular interest was a spy ring including three members of the same family: John Walker, Jr. (*see* BIOGRAPHIES), a retired navy warrant officer, charged in May with spying for the Soviet Union for nearly 20 years; Michael Walker, John Walker's son and a navy yeoman aboard the aircraft carrier USS *Nimitz,* charged with providing classified documents to his father; and Arthur Walker, John Walker's brother and a retired navy lieutenant commander, also charged with delivering classified documents to his brother. The fourth principal figure in the case—described by federal officials as the largest and most damaging in recent U.S. history—was Jerry Whitworth, a former navy enlisted man charged with passing classified materials to John Walker.

The U.S. citizens implicated in other spy cases in 1985 included: Sharon Scranage, a clerk in the CIA's Ghana station, charged with passing classified intelligence information to her Ghanaian lover; Edward Howard, a former CIA officer charged with passing intelligence information to the Soviet Union; Jonathan Jay Pollard, a civilian employee of the Naval Investigative Service, charged with spying for Israel; Larry Wu-tai Chin, a retired CIA analyst accused of spying for China for 30 years; and Ronald Pelton, a former communications specialist for the National Security Agency, charged with spying for the Soviet Union from 1965 to 1979. Commenting on this in a nationwide radio address on November 30, Reagan said: "Some of you may be wondering if the large number of spy arrests

STEVE KELLEY/SAN DIEGO UNION

in recent weeks means that we are looking harder or that there are more spies to find. Well, I think the answer to both questions is yes."

At least as worrisome to the public as revelations of espionage were incidents and threats of terrorism. One such drama began to unfold on October 7 when Palestinian terrorists hijacked an Italian cruise ship with more than 400 passengers and crew off Egypt and demanded that Israel free Palestinian prisoners. After a two-day ordeal during which a wheelchair-bound U.S. tourist was slain by the hijackers, they surrendered in Egypt in exchange for a pledge of safe conduct out of the country. When an Egyptian jet tried to fly the terrorists to a safe haven on October 10, U.S. Navy F-14 fighters intercepted the craft and forced it to land in Sicily. The incident strained relations between the United States and both Egypt and Italy. (*See* Western Europe: *Italy,* above.)

In an earlier hijacking episode that lasted far longer, two Lebanese Shi'ah gunmen on June 14 commandeered a Trans World Airlines passenger jet carrying 153 passengers and crew, 104 of them American, shortly after takeoff from Athens airport. Over the next two days, as the plane was forced to shuttle back and forth across the Mediterranean between Beirut and Algiers, one U.S. passenger was killed and more than 100 others were freed by the hijackers. The remaining 39 U.S. hostages were freed on June 30. On July 8 Reagan accused five nations—Cuba, Iran, Libya, Nicaragua, and North Korea—of making up a "confederation of terrorist states" that was guilty of "outright acts of war" against the United States.

A potentially more serious assault on the country, in the opinion of many health professionals, was the growing incidence of acquired immune deficiency syndrome (AIDS), an almost invariably fatal condition caused by a virus that attacks and destroys the body's defenses against disease, leaving it vulnerable to a host of common and exotic infections. Concern about AIDS, mounting in some urban areas for the past several years, gained a national focus in July with the disclosure that film and television actor Rock Hudson (*see* Obituaries) was suffering from the ailment. In the United States most AIDS patients had been either male homosexuals or intravenous drug users. According to the federal Centers for Disease Control in Atlanta, Ga., nearly 16,000 AIDS cases had been diagnosed by December, and more than 8,000 persons had died of complications arising from the condition. Hudson died October 2, some 15 months after his case had been diagnosed. (*See* Health and Disease.)

The Coca-Cola Co. announced in April that it was changing the formula for its flagship soft drink, Coca-Cola, or Coke. The move came as the 99-year-old product, a symbol of the U.S. throughout the world, was facing a heated challenge in the domestic market from PepsiCo's Pepsi-Cola. Only three months later, however, Coca-Cola Co. announced that it would soon begin to sell again a cola drink made with the original formula. The turnaround came in response to consumer unhappiness with the reformulated beverage, which many long-time Coke fans pronounced too sweet. (RICHARD L. WORSNOP)

See also *Dependent States,* below.

Church Membership in the United States

Religious body	Total clergy	Inclusive membership	Religious body	Total clergy	Inclusive membership
Baptist bodies			Jehovah's Witnesses	None	697,660
American Baptist Association	...	225,000	Jews	6,500	5,817,000
American Baptist Churches in the U.S.A.	7,350	1,620,153	Latter Day Saints (Mormons)		
Baptist Bible Fellowship, International	4,500	1,400,900	Church of Jesus Christ of Latter-day Saints	27,745	3,602,000
Baptist General Conference	1,526	130,193	Reorganized Church of Jesus Christ of L.D.S.	16,545	192,445
Baptist Missionary Association of America	2,800	228,868	Lutherans		
Conservative Baptist Association of America	...	225,000	American Lutheran Church	7,443	2,339,946
Free Will Baptists	2,895	212,527	Evangelical Lutheran Churches, The Assn. of	665	110,934
General Baptists (General Association of)	1,476	75,028	Lutheran Church in America	8,407	2,910,281
Liberty Baptist Fellowship	374	130,000	Lutheran Church—Missouri Synod	7,823	2,628,133
National Baptist Convention of America	28,574	2,668,799	Wisconsin Evangelical Lutheran Synod	1,437	415,630
National Baptist Convention, U.S.A., Inc.	27,500	5,500,000	Mennonite Church	2,328	90,347
National Primitive Baptist Convention	636	250,000	Methodists		
Primitive Baptists	...	72,000	African Methodist Episcopal Church	6,550	2,210,000
Progressive National Baptist Convention	863	521,692	African Methodist Episcopal Zion Church	6,275	1,202,229
Regular Baptist Churches, General Association of	2,045	300,839	Christian Methodist Episcopal Church	2,650	718,922
Southern Baptist Convention	62,600	14,341,822	Free Methodist Church of North America	1,755	72,072
Buddhist Churches of America	115	100,000	United Methodist Church	37,228	9,291,936
Christian and Missionary Alliance	2,106	223,141	Wesleyan Church	2,636	109,140
Christian Congregation	1,446	102,813	North American Old Roman Catholic Church	148	62,380
Church of God (Anderson, Ind.)	3,192	185,404	Pentecostals		
Church of the Brethren	2,108	161,824	Apostolic Overcoming Holy Church of God	350	75,000
Church of the Nazarene	8,438	514,937	Assemblies of God	25,986	2,036,453
Churches of Christ—Christian Churches			Church of God	2,737	75,890
Christian Church (Disciples of Christ)	6,771	1,132,510	Church of God (Cleveland, Tenn.)	9,638	505,775
Christian Churches and Churches of Christ	...	1,043,642	Church of God in Christ	10,425	3,709,661
Churches of Christ	...	1,600,500	Church of God in Christ, International	1,600	200,000
Community Churches, International Council of	300	185,000	Church of God of Prophecy	8,051	74,430
Congregational Christian Churches, Natl. Assn. of	826	108,115	Full Gospel Fellowship of Churches and Ministers, Intl.	850	65,000
Eastern Churches			International Church of the Foursquare Gospel	3,242	171,928
American Carpatho-Russian Orthodox Greek Catholic Ch.	68	100,000	Pentecostal Church of God	1,593	93,338
Antiochian Orthodox Christian Archdiocese of N. Am.	180	280,000	Pentecostal Holiness Church, International	3,422	113,000
Apostolic Catholic Assyrian Ch. of the East, N. Am. Dioc.	57	80,000	United Pentecostal Church, International	6,775	475,000
Armenian Apostolic Church of America	23	225,000	Plymouth Brethren	500	98,000
Armenian Church of America, Diocese of the	61	450,000	Polish National Catholic Church of America	141	282,411
Bulgarian Eastern Orthodox Church	11	86,000	Presbyterians		
Coptic Orthodox Church	27	100,000	Cumberland Presbyterian Church	761	98,829
Greek Orthodox Archdiocese of N. and S. America	655	1,950,000	Presbyterian Church in America	1,562	168,239
Orthodox Church in America	531	1,000,000	Presbyterian Church (U.S.A.)	19,116	3,092,151
Romanian Orthodox Episcopate of America	67	60,000	Reformed bodies		
Russian Orth. Ch. in the U.S.A., Patriarchal Parishes	60	51,500	Christian Reformed Church in North America	1,020	224,764
Russian Orthodox Church Outside of Russia	168	55,000	Reformed Church in America	1,576	341,866
Serbian Eastern Orth. Ch. in the U.S.A. and Canada	73	97,123	Roman Catholic Church	57,317	52,286,043
Ukrainian Orthodox Church in the U.S.A.	131	87,745	Salvation Army	5,194	420,971
Episcopal Church	13,548	2,775,424	Seventh-day Adventist Church	5,070	638,929
Evangelical Covenant Church of America	900	84,185	Triumph the Church and Kingdom of God in Christ	1,375	54,307
Evangelical Free Church of America	...	90,000	Unitarian Universalist Association	1,018	170,510
Friends United Meeting	590	57,432	United Church of Christ	10,157	1,696,107
Independent Fundamental Churches of America	1,366	120,446			

Table includes churches reporting a membership of 50,000 or more and represents the latest information available.
Source: National Council of the Churches of Christ in the U.S.A.

(CONSTANT H. JACQUET)

Developments in the States in 1985

Severe deficit problems restricted the federal government's ability to develop innovative solutions to national problems during 1985, allowing state governments to share the spotlight in a variety of areas. The states moved forward on such concerns as education reform and child abuse and accelerated attempts to find common solutions to environmental and taxation problems.

It was a particularly troubling year in the ethical arena, with record numbers of state officials facing conflict of interest or criminal charges. But the withdrawal of the federal government from some areas of activity, despite a U.S. Supreme Court decision constricting states' rights, left many commentators predicting at the year's end that state government was entering a "golden age" of influence in national affairs.

All states except Kentucky held regular legislative sessions during 1985. Fourteen (including Kentucky) staged special sessions, often on problems concerning education.

Party Strengths. Voters made few significant changes in political party lineups during limited state elections in 1985, leaving Democrats in control of both chambers of 26 state legislatures and Republicans enjoying a two-house majority in only 11. Democrats dominated legislatures in all states except Arizona, Colorado, Connecticut, Idaho, Indiana, Kansas, New Hampshire, North Dakota, South Dakota, Utah, and Wyoming (where Republicans had control in both houses); Alaska, Michigan, New Mexico, New York, Ohio, and Pennsylvania (where Republicans organized the upper house and Democrats the lower chamber); Delaware, Minnesota, Nevada, New Jersey, and Vermont (where Democrats controlled the upper body and Republicans the lower house); Montana (Democratic Senate and evenly divided House); and Nebraska (a nonpartisan, one-house legislature). The breakdown exaggerated Democratic strength, since GOP candidates made modest gains in 1985 elections and came close to achieving majority status in many legislative bodies.

Voters reelected a Republican governor in New Jersey and retained a Democratic gubernatorial regime in Virginia, leaving the lineup of governors for 1986 at 34 Democrats and 16 Republicans. Democrats controlled the governorship and both legislative chambers in 18 states, while the Republicans had total control in only 4 states.

Government Structures, Powers. Preoccupation with problems of federalism and education typically made 1985 a quiet year for structural changes in state governments. Arizona and Idaho established new departments of commerce. Mississippi moved to review and update its 1890 state constitution. Under terms of a new mandate, Alabama legislators were required to approve education and general fund appropriations before taking up any other spending legislation.

The North Dakota Supreme Court ruled on January 5 that Democratic Governor-elect George Sinner had the right to office as of January 1. Republican Gov. Allen I. Olson wanted to hold his term over until at least January 6, apparently to name two replacements to the state Supreme Court. Arizona state Sen. Tony Gabaldon, a former teacher displeased by perceived legislative hostility toward professionals, especially teachers, introduced a bill requiring an IQ test for legislative candidates, with the result to be printed on the ballot beside their names. The bill died in committee.

Government Relations. The year was a tumultuous and historic one in regard to state relationships with other levels in the federal system. In an unexpected development the U.S. Supreme Court reversed a precedent of only nine years and ruled that states must be held subject to certain federal laws, such as wage and hour strictures. The 5 to 4 vote in *Garcia* v. *San Antonio Metropolitan Transit Authority* occurred because a single justice, Harry Blackmun, changed his position on the issue. Late in the year the U.S. Congress approved a bill exempting state and local governments from most federal wage laws, thus saving state governments from $1 billion to $3 billion annually in higher labour costs, but the judgment diminishing state powers remained.

State officials were badly split over a federal tax-reform plan, initially proposed by the administration of Pres. Ronald Reagan, that would have eliminated the deduction for state property and income taxes. A survey of 38 governors found 24 opposing the Reagan proposal and only 9 favouring it; leaders of high-tax Northeastern and Midwestern states were vigorous in their opposition to it, saying that the measure amounted to "double taxation." Supporters of the Reagan plan argued that it would broaden the federal tax base (to which many state income tax schemes are tied) and increase state tax receipts. State and local tax deductibility was restored in the reform plan reported out by the Democratic-controlled House Ways and Means Committee.

A proposed amendment to the U.S. Constitution that would give congressional voting rights to the District of Columbia failed during the year, passing its seven-year deadline for ratification with only 16 of the required 38 states having signed it. A previously obscure constitutional amendment that would delay the effective date of any congressional pay raise until after a subsequent election picked up steam during the year, with South Dakota, New Hampshire, Arizona, Tennessee, and Oklahoma ratifying it. The amendment had been originally proposed in 1789 without any deadline for state ratification; confused records over the years indicated that from 6 to 10 states (of the 38 required) had endorsed it prior to the 1985 flurry. A proposed state call for a constitutional convention to write a balanced-budget amendment remained stalled during the year, with no states joining the 32 demanding the convention; convention resolutions failed during the year in Michigan, Hawaii, Illinois, Maine, Minnesota, Montana, and Washington.

All but 2 of the 105-member South Dakota legislature visited Washington, D.C., during the winter to lobby for relief from severe agricultural economic conditions. Oregon revoked a 1983 law that had forced most commuters from the state of Washington into a higher tax bracket in Oregon's income tax.

Despite adverse court decisions and reduced federal assistance, state leaders expressed confidence during the year that state governmental powers and prestige were enjoying a substantial resurgence as deficit problems forced the federal government to reduce its activism on domestic issues. The U.S. government has "no choice but to unload substantial responsibilities" onto the states, Virginia Gov. Charles Robb declared. It thus appeared that the Reagan administration's "New Federalism" program, widely scorned after its 1982 publication, might become national policy by default as a result of fiscal and deficit pressures.

Finances. As the nation's economic recovery completed its third year, pressures on state treasuries eased, making the year an unremarkable one for tax legislation. Overall, tax rates in the 50 states were modestly lowered during 1985, with only inflation and economic growth pushing

In August the New York state lottery offered its biggest prize ever, a $41 million jackpot. One of the three winning tickets had been purchased by a pool of 21 workers, many of them immigrants, from a manufacturing plant in Mount Vernon, New York.

revenues higher. A survey by the Tax Foundation found that eight states (Michigan, Minnesota, New Jersey, New York, North Carolina, Ohio, Oregon, and Pennsylvania) had cut taxes by $100 million or more, while only five (Florida, Illinois, Indiana, Oklahoma, and Tennessee) had raised taxes by a similar amount. Several states found it necessary to cut spending during the year, often by the use of hiring freezes; Arkansas, Colorado, Illinois, Idaho, Iowa, Nebraska, and Louisiana were among states trimming budgets in order to balance year-end books.

Oregon voters for the seventh time rejected a proposed state sales tax, leaving the number of states without such a levy at five. New Hampshire, New Jersey, and Vermont abandoned the federal surplus food program as U.S. funds for food distribution ran out. Six farm states—Minnesota, Illinois, Wisconsin, Indiana, Ohio, and North Dakota—initiated interest-rate subsidy programs to assist hard-pressed farmers.

Figures compiled in 1985 revealed that state revenue from all sources totaled $397.1 billion during the 1984 fiscal year, an increase of 11% over the preceding 12 months. General revenue (excluding state liquor and state insurance trust revenue) was $330.7 billion, up 13.9%. Total state expenditures rose only 5.2% to $351.4 billion, the smallest percentage increase in 23 years and one creating a technical surplus of $45.7 billion for the year. General expenditures, not including outlays of the liquor stores and insurance-trust systems, amounted to $309.7 billion, up 8.6% over fiscal 1983. Of general revenue, 59.6% came from state taxes and licenses, 15.8% from charges and miscellaneous revenue, including educational tuition, and 24.6% from intergovernmental revenue (mostly from the federal government).

The largest state outlay was $116.1 billion for education, of which $40 billion went to state colleges and universities and $67.5 billion to local public schools. Other major outlays included $62.7 billion for public welfare, $28.9 billion for highways, and $24.9 billion for health and public hospitals.

Ethics. An extraordinary outbreak of criminal and ethical accusations against current and past state officials took place in 1985. The most sensational involved Louisiana Gov. Edwin W. Edwards, indicted February 28 on 50 fraud and racketeering counts centring on state approval for hospital and nursing-home construction. A mistrial was declared in December after a federal jury was unable to agree on a verdict.

Retired Hawaii Supreme Court Justice Kazuhisa Abe was indicted on theft and conspiracy charges in connection with alleged fraudulent sales of commodities. Minnesota Supreme Court Justice John Todd resigned after being accused of cheating on a Florida bar examination. A grand jury investigated, but absolved, West Virginia Chief Justice Richard Neely, who admitted firing his secretary because she refused to baby-sit for his son. Rhode Island's chief justice, Joseph A. Bevilacqua, was suspended for four months and publicly censured for bringing his office "into serious disrepute" by his friendships with reputed mobsters. A New York jury con-

Chicago's controversial State of Illinois Center opened in 1985. The structure, designed by Helmut Jahn, includes offices, shops, restaurants, and a 16-story atrium that emerges from the roof as a cylinder. In front is "Monument with Standing Beast," sculptured by Jean Dubuffet.

AP/WIDE WORLD

victed state Supreme Court Justice William C. Brennan of taking bribes in return for fixing four criminal cases.

Nebraska's attorney general, Paul Douglas, resigned in December 1984 after being convicted of perjury before a state legislative committee; in March 1985 he was ordered to perform 1,500 hours of volunteer work and to pay a $25,000 fine. Mississippi state Sen. Thomas N. Brooks was indicted and convicted of attempted extortion in soliciting $50,000 in return for helping to pass a horse-racing bill.

Kansas Attorney General Robert T. Stephan dropped his gubernatorial election bid after it was revealed that his supporters had paid more than $20,000 to settle a sexual harassment suit against him brought by a former employee. Two ranking New Mexico treasury officials, Kenneth Johnson and Philip Troutman, were convicted in federal court of attempting to extort payoffs from a New York bank. Later in the year the New Mexico state treasurer, Earl Hartley, pleaded guilty to neglect of duty and resigned from office; he was accused of spending funds from a state treasurers' group for personal purposes.

Louisiana's education superintendent, Tom Clausen, was indicted on payroll fraud and obstruction-of-justice charges. Former Rhode Island House speaker Edward Manning and onetime state housing director Ralph A. Pari were indicted on embezzlement and conspiracy charges related to fraudulent low-interest mortgage loans. Maryland state Sen. Jerome F. Connell was suspended from office after his conviction for tax evasion; he was sentenced to a year in prison and fined $5,000. Alabama state docks supervisor John E. Brittain was indicted for theft and bid-rigging on contracts.

Education. Numerous educational reform measures, including upgrading of teacher pay and of teacher examinations, were proposed in most state capitols during 1985. One survey found that all but five states were in the process of testing teacher competency despite vigorous objections from some teacher groups. Results of the first serious teacher literacy and competency exams, in Arkansas, revealed that more than 95% passed. Georgia, South Dakota, Illinois, and Kentucky were among states taking major educational reform steps during the year.

New Hampshire moved to equalize spending among school districts of varying economic resources. A federal appeals court ruled unconstitutional Louisiana's "creationism" law; it had required that the biblical theory of creation be taught alongside evolution. Similar creationism bills were considered by 31 states during 1985, but none was approved.

Health, Welfare. Thirteen additional states approved "living will" laws during 1985, bringing to 35 the number of jurisdictions where individuals could forbid heroic lifesaving measures in the event of terminal illness. New Mexico and West Virginia regulated smoking in public, bringing the number of states with such laws to 38; New Jersey and Washington toughened existing smoking regulations. California became the first state to attack problems associated with Alzheimer's disease, appropriating $5 million for treatment and research.

Seeking to combat problems associated with the growing numbers of the homeless ill, Georgia joined North Carolina and Hawaii in allowing courts to require mandatory outpatient services for the mentally afflicted. Texas and Washington required school postural screening for spinal curvatures, bringing to 19 the states with such laws. Virginia, Louisiana, and South Carolina experimented with helping pregnant teenagers by hiring unemployed mothers to counsel them.

Oregon and New York became the first states to require hospitals to ask survivors of terminally ill patients for organ donations. Massachusetts became the first state to require labels on snuff cans warning of possible addiction, oral cancer, and other diseases associated with smokeless tobacco.

Illinois experienced a virulent outbreak of food poisoning, with several thousand cases of salmonella and 3 deaths attributed to a couple of faulty valves at a dairy. Although the office of state health director Thomas Kirkpatrick published releases

indicating that he was holding daily meetings on the problem, Kirkpatrick was fired by Gov. James Thompson after it was revealed that he had left the state on vacation in mid-crisis.

Law, Justice. Reacting to national outrage over abuse and victimization of children, many states stiffened their laws governing day-care, exploitation of minors, and courtroom requirements for children during the year. A dozen states provided for videotaped testimony by underage witnesses in child-abuse cases, and Florida, Nevada, Washington, Tennessee, Alabama, Utah, New Mexico, and Alaska were among states that expanded and toughened their child-abuse statutes. Several states innovated in publicizing missing children; Georgia helped place photographs of such children in monthly gas bills, and New York printed their pictures on state tollway tickets.

New Mexico became the first state to declare as a felony an injury to a pregnant woman that causes the loss of her child. Texas repealed its Sunday-closing "blue law," and South Carolina softened its version. Montana and South Dakota joined 23 states in outlawing the rape of an estranged spouse. New York's governor vetoed a bill that would have severely restricted hostile corporate takeovers.

Rhode Island legislators, overriding a gubernatorial veto, ordered the dismissal of charges for any minor driving violations (such as speeding) for drivers who had maintained a good safety record over the previous three years. Explained Sen. James Donelan, "Under the law, even a dog is entitled to one bite in most cases."

Drugs. Under the threat of a cutoff of federal highway funds, 13 more states—New York, Connecticut, Alabama, Florida, Georgia, Kansas, Mississippi, New Hampshire, Maine, North Carolina, South Carolina, Texas, and Virginia—raised their minimum drinking age to 21 during the year, undoing a move in the 1970s toward lower age minimums for alcoholic consumption. A total of 33 states had returned to 21 years by the end of 1985; the deadline for doing so in order to avoid congressionally mandated cuts in highway funding was Oct. 1, 1986. After several years of nationwide grass-roots campaigning against drunk driving, Oregon emerged as the toughest enforcement state; inebriation was classified there as a blood alcohol content of only 0.08%, and first-time offenders would have their licenses suspended for a year.

California outlawed synthetic cocaine. Georgia toughened its penalties for cocaine trafficking. Nevada allowed the death penalty for drug dealers whose customers die of a drug overdose.

Arizona, Indiana, Kansas, and Oklahoma moved to curb "happy hour" drink promotions, but there were signs that the antidrinking campaign was meeting opposition. Illinois, Rhode Island, and South Dakota moved to set limits on their "dram shop" acts, which hold bar owners liable if they serve patrons too much liquor.

Prisons. The population of state prisons rose to another record level during 1985, forcing more than $200 million worth of new construction. A midyear census by the Bureau of Justice Statistics found 452,372 inmates in state prisons, up from 419,968

a year earlier. Officials attributed the continued increase, which was occurring at a period of generally declining crime rates, to tougher state laws, hardened judicial attitudes, and a cutback in early-release programs for prisoners.

The South Carolina Supreme Court ruled that surgical castration is a cruel and unusual punishment and thus is an unconstitutional alternative to a 30-year term for rape. The U.S. Supreme Court gave its approval to lethal injections, authorized by 13 states as a means of capital punishment.

A federal judge, citing delay and official indifference to overcrowding, ordered a closing of Tennessee prisons to new convicts, throwing them entirely on city and county jails. State officials rushed new funds into prison construction and considered the possibility of having a private, profit-making corporation take over the operation of state prisons. (*See* CRIME, LAW ENFORCEMENT, AND PENOLOGY: *Sidebar*.)

Gambling. State-run games of chance continued to gain public acceptance, with Iowa becoming the 22nd state to authorize a state lottery. Three New England states started the first multistate lottery as a means of boosting prizes to compete with neighbouring games in Massachusetts and New York; Maine furnished the computer for the "megabucks" game, New Hampshire conducted the drawing, and Vermont handled the administration.

Environment. States continued to band together to combat perceived environmental threats, either bypassing or combating the federal government in pursuing polluters vigorously. Connecticut, Massachusetts, Maine, New Hampshire, New York, New Jersey, and Vermont sued the U.S. Environmental Protection Agency over its failure to impose emission controls on acid rain suspects in the Midwest. Six Northeastern states signed an agreement with five Canadian provinces to reduce sulfur dioxide emissions. The governors of Illinois, Indiana, Michigan, Minnesota, New York, Ohio, Pennsylvania, and Wisconsin initialed a pact with Canadian officials to register and monitor major freshwater withdrawals from the Great Lakes.

Following a major leak at a Union Carbide Corp. facility at Institute, W.Va., officials approved a law requiring that stores of hazardous substances be reported to local health and fire officials. Vermont approved major legislation protecting groundwater and providing for the cleanup of toxic-waste sites. Maine voters insisted on approving any future low-level radioactive-waste storage plan.

Connecticut state Rep. Mae Schmidle, claiming that uncooked rice can kill birds that ingest it, proposed a law banning the throwing of rice at weddings. A prominent biology professor said, however, that the rice would be harmful to birds "only if they're hit in the face with it," and the bill died.

Equal Rights. Comparable worth, a concept that calls for equal pay for jobs requiring similar training and responsibility, received a major judicial blow during the year when a federal appeals panel threw out a major Washington State claim. California state workers had earlier filed the largest gender discrimination wage claim in history on behalf of 38,000 female workers in 400 job categories, but the court decision

cast doubt on its legal merit. After several years of examination five states (Iowa, Massachusetts, Minnesota, Washington, and Wisconsin) were providing some funding for equalizing female state workers' pay, and ten more were studying compensation issues without comparable worth legislation. But governors in Ohio and Oregon vetoed similar expenditures, and experts doubted whether additional states would agree to the expensive proposition.

Vermont's legislature approved a state equal rights amendment for submission to state voters in 1986. Montana became the first state to prohibit gender distinctions in all insurance premiums and payments. Idaho lawmakers, overriding a gubernatorial veto, made that state the nation's 21st right-to-work state and the first new one since 1970.

Although Oregon's governor vetoed a bill ordering divestment of state pension funds from South Africa, divestment mandates were approved in Iowa, New Jersey, and Rhode Island. Among the other states 26 considered anti-South Africa action during 1985, and by the end of the year nine had divestment laws on their books.

Consumer Protection. Following the lead of New York and New Jersey, 14 additional states made the use of seat belts mandatory for adult automobile passengers during 1985. Transportation Secretary Elizabeth Dole had asserted that unless 67% of the population was covered by strict seat-belt laws by 1989, she would require that 1990 automobiles throughout the nation have automatic seat belts or air bags. Many of the state laws did not provide for the $25 fine specified in the Dole order, however, and it appeared that air bags would be required eventually.

There was much additional action on auto safety. Massachusetts became the first state to require use of the seat belts in both front and rear passenger areas, and 21 states required their employees to wear belts at all times when driving or riding in a car. North Carolina and Wyoming became the 49th and 50th states to require seat belts for minors, and several states raised the age limit for those covered.

Kansas and Mississippi approved new "lemon laws" protecting automobile buyers from chronic defects. Rhode Island extended the concept to used cars and New Hampshire to motorcycles. Maine sued Sears, Roebuck and Co. over its sale of service contracts, which state investigators said often duplicated warranty coverage. Iowa declared a state of economic emergency, allowing farmers to obtain a one-year reprieve from foreclosure on their homesteads. Georgia placed the E. F. Hutton brokerage firm on suspension for a year following the disclosure by federal authorities that it had been involved in an account overdrafting scheme.

Ohio and Maryland, two of five states furnishing extensive state insurance to savings and loan associations, experienced a serious loss of investor and saver confidence during the spring, leading to a shutdown of all privately insured thrift institutions in both states. Ohio Gov. Richard Celeste managed to reopen most of the institutions after 11 days, but depositors were still barred from full access to their funds at a half dozen Maryland thrifts at the year's end.   (DAVID C. BECKWITH)

Latin America
and
the Caribbean

LATIN-AMERICAN
AFFAIRS

In 1985 Latin America's economic difficulties showed few signs of abating, and its external indebtedness gave grounds for concern. Elections in several countries continued a trend toward civilian rule that had begun in 1980. (*See* Special Report.) Following presidential and general elections held in Peru and Bolivia in April and July, the new presidents, Alan García Pérez and Víctor Paz Estenssoro, respectively (*see* BIOGRAPHIES), took office in July and August. Presidential and general elections also took place in Guatemala and Honduras in November and December. The victor in the second round between the two leading presidential contenders in Guatemala was Vinicio Cerezo, who was to take office in January 1986. In Honduras, after legal wrangles delayed the announcement of official results, José Azcona Hoyo was declared the winner at year's end. Legislative and state gubernatorial elections held in Mexico in July were won by the government party, the Partido Revolucionario Institucional. In November Pres. Raúl Alfonsín's Radical Civic Union in Argentina increased its majority by one seat in midterm elections for the Chamber of Deputies. Also in November, in elections for mayors of state capitals in Brazil, the Brazilian Democratic Movement Party, chief party in the governing coalition, won an overall victory but lost in São Paulo, Rio de Janeiro, and several smaller cities.

No solution to the Falkland Islands/Islas Malvinas dispute between Argentina and the U.K. was in sight, although during President Alfonsín's official visits to France and Spain in September and October, he held meetings with U.K. opposition party leaders. On November 25 the UN General Assembly adopted an Argentine-backed resolution calling for talks between the two countries.

Central America remained subject to political and social disorders, with guerrilla activity continuing in El Salvador, Guatemala, and Nicaragua. Peace initiatives were in progress throughout the year. The Contadora Group, formed in January 1983 by Colombia, Mexico, Panama, and Venezuela, presented the second draft of a peace and cooperation treaty for the region to the governments of Costa Rica, El Salvador, Honduras, Guatemala, and Nicaragua and to the UN in October. It proposed that military activity of all kinds be monitored by an international corps of inspectors. The Contadora Group announced that it would not persist with negotiation efforts if the treaty was not accepted. The previous proposed treaty, prepared in 1984, had been accepted by Nicaragua but was rejected by El Salvador, Honduras, Costa Rica, and the U.S.

In November the European Communities (EC) formalized links with Central America by signing a five-year cooperation agreement. It granted most-favoured-nation status to Costa Rica, El Salvador, Guatemala, Honduras, Nicaragua, and Panama and committed the EC to increasing substantially its aid to the region, which stood at about $30 million a year. The agreement was also signed by Spain and Portugal, due to join the EC in 1986.

On October 1 the Central American Common Market (CACM) countries—Costa Rica, El Salvador, Guatemala, Honduras, and Nicaragua—began implementing a new set of customs nomenclature and import tariffs, based on the EC nomenclature. Negotiations were completed in July on 85% of the new tariffs, which were to range between 5 and 80%. The lowest were to be for capital goods, raw materials, and inputs for the productive sectors. The agreement was one of the most important initiatives designed to revive the moribund CACM since the late 1970s.

Neither the Latin American Integration Association (LAIA), which consisted of Argentina, Bolivia, Brazil, Chile, Colombia, Ecuador, Mexico, Paraguay, Peru, Uruguay, and Venezuela, nor the Andean Group of Bolivia, Colombia, Ecuador, Peru, and Venezuela made much headway during the year. The LAIA was to begin using a new customs nomenclature from Jan. 1, 1986, for negotiations on tariff reductions, for designating products under LAIA mechanisms, and for the presentation of trade statistics. Representatives of industrial sectors continued efforts to negotiate tariff reductions with modest success. Within the Andean Group, Colombia and Venezuela introduced liberal foreign investment regulations that departed significantly from the strict rules laid down by the group.

In February the state-owned banks in Argentina, Brazil, and Mexico established Latinequip, a trinational company, to try to increase Latin America's share in the market for capital goods and engineering services. Latin-American industrial concerns were to draw on lines of credit from the founder banks, while the World Bank and the Inter-American Development Bank (I-ADB) were to be approached for funding.

When heads of government of the 13-nation Caribbean Community (Caricom) met in Bridgetown, Barbados, in July, trade was the main item on the agenda. They agreed to raise the common external tariff by 15% as of the end of August on imports of cement, steel products, automotive parts, and a range of other goods from outside the Caricom area. The U.S. Caribbean Basin Initiative (CBI) functioned fitfully throughout the year. The CBI, which had become law in January 1984, was an integrated program of tax and trade measures that included an agreement offering duty-free access to the U.S. market for 12 years for a wide range of Caribbean and Central American products, mainly manufactured goods. In 1984 only 7.5% of exports from Caribbean Basin countries to the U.S. carried the CBI's duty-free status, and all exports from those countries in the period January–June 1985 were down, compared with the same period in 1984. In November Canada announced a plan, designed to help make up for the CBI's shortcomings, that would allow duty-free entry into Canada for a wide variety of Caribbean and Central American goods.

An upturn in the world economy in 1984 helped Latin America to reverse somewhat the declines registered during the period 1980–83. A growth in gross domestic product of 3.1% in 1984 resulted in an increase in per capita product of 0.6%, compared with a decline in the latter of 10% in 1982–83. Exports from Latin America reached $99 billion, as against $89 billion in 1983, while tight controls contributed to imports of $61 billion, compared with $59 billion in 1983. The increase in the external debt slowed to 5.6% during the year, compared with 6% in 1983. The region's total external debt reached $360 billion by the end of 1984 and was estimated at $370 billion in mid-1985. Interest payments on the debts amounted to $38 billion in 1984, as against $35 billion in 1983 and $36 billion in 1982. Inflation remained a major problem as the average regional rate reached 175.4% in 1984, up from 130.8% in 1983. Preliminary estimates indicated that in 1985 the growth rate would be lower than that of 1984 and that exports would be reduced significantly because of

(continued on page 569)

The Swing Toward Democracy

BY GEORGE PHILIP

Between 1980 and 1985 military government went into retreat across Latin America. Although Maj. Gen. Augusto Pinochet Ugarte in Chile and Gen. Alfredo Stroessner in Paraguay remained obdurate, the list of countries that experienced transitions toward civilian and democratic rule included Argentina, Bolivia, Uruguay, Brazil, Peru, Panama, and Honduras. In Ecuador an elected civilian president replaced a military junta in 1979, and in Guatemala elections took place in late 1985. Although civilian rule remained precarious in a number of the countries where it had been instituted, the cumulative effect of this transformation was considerable. In most of these

countries, moreover, the military showed no particular wish to force its way back into power.

There was no single or simple explanation for this trend. Some cases of democratization owed much to particular historic experiences. These included the military defeat of the Argentine junta in the South Atlantic in 1982, the cocaine connection in Bolivian politics, and the near defeat of the Salvadoran military by Marxist insurgents in 1981–82. It should also be remembered that almost every South American country had enjoyed periods of democratic rule in the past. There had been many swings between civilian and military rule, although recent military governments had tended to be more technocratic, more durable, and often more repressive than their predecessors. The return to the barracks, therefore, was by no means definitive, but in many cases it seemed to have been established more firmly than in prior years. Nevertheless, some recently democratized countries might well fall back under military rule one day.

Forces for Change. Circumstances differed in each country, but there were two general factors behind the recent democratizing trend. One was that, in South America, recession and economic setbacks were, perhaps surprisingly, democratizing forces. The other was that the U.S. had been pressing for democratization in Central America as part of

DEMOCRACY IN LATIN AMERICA, 1985

Status:
- Democratic
- Partially democratic
- Not democratic
- Dependent state

Source: *The Economist.*

In the past decade Latin America experienced a notable democratizing trend, with more and more governments changing through an electoral process in which opposing parties vied for votes. It continued to be true, however, that most of the countries in the region moved toward only partial democracy, with opposition parties having political impact but not being allowed to win elections and thereby to come to power.

Liberation Theology

"Liberation theology" was born in Latin America in the late 1960s. Its advocates insist that it is not a theology "about" liberation but a theology "for" liberation. It is politically committed. It is deliberately partisan. It has made what it calls the "option for the poorest," by which is meant that one has a better chance of understanding the Christian gospel if one is on the side of the oppressed. While the traditional Christian God is seen by liberationists as the prop of an unjust social system, with a message of resignation in this world and hope only in the next, the God of liberation theology brings hope into the here and the now.

At Medellín, Colombia, in 1968, the Latin-American bishops denounced "social sin" and "structural injustice." This paved the way for the Peruvian Indian Gustavo Gutiérrez to write *Teología de la liberación* (1971; Eng. trans. *A Theology of Liberation*, 1973).

Countless other works in the same genre followed. The best-known authors were the Jesuits Juan Segundo (Uruguay) and Jon Sobrino (El Salvador) and the Brazilian Franciscan Leonardo Boff (*see* BIOGRAPHIES), together with his brother Clodovis. Many of the issues raised by liberation theology were considered by the third Conference of Latin American Bishops held in Puebla, Mexico, in 1979. The bishops strongly endorsed the church's involvement in social problems but warned of "the risk of ideologization of theological thought when Marxist analysis is used as its starting point." In 1974 Karol Cardinal Wojtyla (later Pope John Paul II) criticized liberation theology as too thisworldly, and he subsequently criticized liberationists' substitution of the concept of class struggle for the traditional Christian idea of charity.

(PETER HEBBLETHWAITE)

---

its response toward the Sandinista revolution in Nicaragua.

The impact of recession on South American politics was affected by the fact that recent military regimes generally projected a technocratic image and pretended that they were superior to civilians at economic management. When international conditions were favourable, this pretense could be sustained; when export prices fell and international interest rates rose, the bluff was called. Faced with the need to impose unpopular austerity measures, military authorities often sought (with some success) to limit popular unrest by easing political conditions and promising an eventual return to democracy.

The original supporters of military rule, seeing that political conditions were changing, sought to find a basis for compromise with the opposition. Where this was achieved, as in the case of Brazil, the transition to democracy was relatively smooth. Where it was not, as in Chile, the dictatorship was able to continue. In most cases, however, the military failed to control its own succession and eventually was forced to return power to moderate opposition figures: Fernando Belaúnde Terry in Peru (whom the military had overthrown in 1968), Tancredo Neves in Brazil (before his unexpected death; *see* OBITUARIES), and Raúl Alfonsín in Argentina. Civilian politicians who had maintained too close an association with the military regime suffered some notable setbacks when democracy returned.

In Central America, the early 1980s were dominated by the various responses to the Nicaraguan revolution. Some countries in the region, notably El Salvador, became heavily dependent on U.S. support to combat Marxist insurgents. Although the U.S. had not always been an unqualified supporter of Latin-American democracy, Washington was anxious to ease out the hard-line military dictatorships that had provided rebel movements with recruits and grist for propaganda. U.S. pressure, therefore, played a major part in democratizing El Salvador and in persuading the Guatemalan government to agree to hold elections. Interestingly enough, the U.S. government proved unable fully to control the outcome of these democratic openings; Washington was unenthusiastic about José Napoleón Duarte until he was elected president of El Salvador in 1984 and won an outright congressional majority in 1985. The situation in Central America remained unstable, however, and continuing U.S. support for democratic reform was crucial if the military was to be kept out of the presidential palaces.

The Road Ahead. Although welcome, democratization was taking place at a particularly difficult time for Latin America. The very factors that precipitated military withdrawal from office—high inflation, domestic recession, a severe foreign debt problem—were burdens on incoming civilian regimes. In addition, these civilian governments often had to face insurgencies originally directed against the military rulers, and they had to decide how far to pursue cases of human rights abuses committed by the military. Prolonged recession, in particular, might intensify the cynicism and disillusionment already common enough in Latin America with regard to democratic institutions.

Despite these difficulties, some civilian presidents were surprisingly successful in maintaining domestic confidence while, at the same time, tackling their countries' most severe outstanding problems. They were helped by the fact that the political atmosphere had quieted down since the 1960s. Hopes and fears that Cuban-style revolution was imminent in South America had largely evaporated. Crushed beyond redemption in many South American countries, the armed left remained active only in Chile, Colombia, and Peru. Even in Central America, the armed left had little prospect of short-term success outside its existing bastions in Cuba and Nicaragua. There remained a long-term possibility of further revolutions.

Similarly, in the larger South American countries, right-wing hopes of a military-technocratic miracle had been effectively dashed by the world recession. In some countries (notably Argentina), relations between the military and the business sector broke up amid some acrimony as a result. There was now a more realistic appreciation of the limits of what was politically possible in Latin America. This, however, did not necessarily entail political quiescence. The more successful democratic leaders were those able to maintain a degree of presence and to exercise leadership. Argentina's Alfonsín and El Salvador's Duarte were good examples. Now that the nonsolution of military rule had been largely discredited, political leaders would have a better chance of coming to grips with the many problems confronting them.

George Philip is lecturer in Latin-American politics at the London School of Economics and Political Science and at the Institute of Latin-American Studies, University of London. He is author of Oil and Politics in Latin America: Nationalist Movements and State Companies.

(continued from page 566)

a fall in demand from advanced industrialized countries and because of depressed commodity prices. Inflation was expected to remain at a high level.

Although Latin-American governments expressed increased anxiety about the foreign debt, no coordinated approach to tackling the problem emerged. On taking office in Peru in July, President García stated that his country's debt repayments during the upcoming 12 months would be limited to 10% of export earnings, although in fact the policy was not strictly adhered to later. Several Latin-American leaders, including Pres. José Sarney (*see* BIOGRAPHIES), new leader of Brazil, pointed out that concessions on repayments were necessary to help foster internal development and growth. Representatives of the Cartagena Group, comprising the 11 principal debtor countries in the region, held talks on the debt problem with the EC in April. A call by Pres. Fidel Castro of Cuba in July for a regionwide default was rebuffed by other governments in the area.

The region's two largest borrowers were in disagreement with the International Monetary Fund (IMF). In September the IMF declared Mexico out of compliance with austerity objectives and suspended payment of $900 million in pending loans; however, a rapprochement was likely in view of the large expenditures involved in repairing damage caused by the Mexico City earthquake during the same month. (See *Mexico:* Sidebar, below.) The Brazilian government, the IMF, and creditor banks failed to agree on economic policy and the rescheduling of $45.3 billion of debts due in 1985–89, despite the fact that concurrence in principle on the latter point had been reached with creditor banks in February. On the other hand, after Argentina began implementing an austerity program that was even more severe than that previously agreed upon with the IMF, Argentina and creditor banks signed a contract in August that provided for the rescheduling of debts and provision of $4.2 billion in new credits.

U.S. Secretary of the Treasury James Baker presented a "Program for Sustained Growth" to the IMF/World Bank meetings at Seoul, South Korea, in October. The program aimed to encourage less developed countries with recent debt-servicing problems (reportedly including Argentina, Bolivia, Brazil, Chile, Colombia, Ecuador, Mexico, Peru, Uruguay, and Venezuela) to follow market-oriented economic policies promoting growth, as well as IMF fiscal, monetary, and exchange-rate policies. In return they would be eligible for enhanced assistance from international financial institutions. The World Bank and the I-ADB were requested to increase disbursements by 50% in 1986–88, and commercial banks were asked to increase their lending by some 2¹⁄₂% a year during the same period.

(ROBIN CHAPMAN)

ANTIGUA AND BARBUDA

A parliamentary state and member of the Commonwealth, Antigua and Barbuda comprises the islands of Antigua, Barbuda, and Redonda in the eastern Caribbean Sea. Area: 442 sq km (171 sq mi). Pop. (1985 est.): 80,500. Cap.: Saint John's. Monetary unit: East Caribbean dollar, with (Oct. 21, 1985) a par value of EC$2.70 to U.S. $1 (free rate of EC$3.87 = £1 sterling). Queen, Elizabeth II; governor-general in 1985, Sir Wilfred E. Jacobs; prime minister, Vere Cornwall Bird.

An improved growth rate of 5% was forecast for 1985 in Antigua and Barbuda as tourist arrivals and earnings continued to increase. However, the government announced in April that it was preparing a structural adjustment

plan aimed at dealing with the external debt and current account deficit. In January the government imposed an indefinite wage freeze for public employees, and in March it closed the country's only sugar factory, which had incurred substantial losses. Efforts to attract foreign investment continued during the year. In February a U.S. company opened an electronics assembly plant, the first project to be established under the U.S. Caribbean Basin Initiative. Discussions were held with an Israeli company with a view to starting vegetable production for export. A visit by Deputy Prime Minister Lester Bird to China in June produced an aid package worth EC$5 million.

In July Tim Hector, leader of the left-wing Antigua Caribbean Liberation Movement and a persistent critic of the government, was sentenced to six months in prison on a charge of undermining confidence in a public official. In March the National Democratic Party was formed, under the leadership of Ivor Heath, a surgeon.   (ROD PRINCE)

This article updates the *Macropædia* article The WEST INDIES: *Antigua and Barbuda.*

ARGENTINA

The federal republic of Argentina occupies the eastern section of the Southern Cone of South America, along the Atlantic Ocean. Area: 2,780,092 sq km (1,073,399 sq mi). Pop. (1985 est.): 30,563,800. Cap.: Buenos Aires. Monetary unit: austral, with (Oct. 21, 1985) a free rate of 0.80 australes to U.S. $1 (1.15 australes = £1 sterling). President in 1985, Raúl Alfonsín.

Domestic Affairs. During 1985 public attention in Argentina was once again concentrated on the role that the armed forces had played in the "dirty war" against subversives in the 1970s. Worldwide attention was drawn to the trials on charges of murder and human rights abuses of nine former junta members who had governed Argentina during 1976–82. Public hearings began on April 22, 1985. The prosecution case lasted for five months, during which nearly 1,000 witnesses appeared before the tribunal to provide evidence of hundreds of cases of kidnapping, murder, and torture allegedly perpetrated by the security forces. The prosecution called for life imprisonment for five of the nine accused men and sentences of between 10 and 15 years for the other four. The case for the defense, which opened at the end of September, was based on the argument that the hearings were unconstitutional and politically orchestrated. The military remained unrepentant, claiming that its actions had been morally justified by the need to save Argentina from subversion. The verdict, issued December 9, resulted in the conviction of five of the defendants. Ex-president Jorge Videla and former navy commander Adm. Emilio Massera both received life sentences, while ex-president Gen. Roberto Eduardo Viola and two other former officers were given lesser prison terms. Four of the defendants, including ex-president Leopoldo Galtieri, were acquitted, although three of them (including Galtieri) remained in detention on charges connected with the 1982 Falklands war with Great Britain. A decision in that case was expected early in 1986.

Sharp cuts were made during the year in defense expenditure. The Navy put several ships up for sale; the Army claimed to be running out of ammunition; and military living standards plummeted. Discontent led to the appearance of right-wing subversion. A wave of bomb attacks, often on military targets, and of bomb threats against schools was blamed on rightist plotters aiming to destabilize the administration of Pres. Raúl Alfonsín and provoke a military coup. In mid-October six military officers and six civilians were ordered arrested for alleged involvement

in the campaign. The officers included Col. Pascual Guer-
rieri, deputy head of J-2, the army intelligence service,
and Gen. Guillermo Soarez Mason, former commander
of the 1st Army Corps. Among the civilians named were
two journalists who were alleged to have collaborated with
hard-line military officers and to have published a series of
provocative articles claiming that the country was on the
brink of social and political chaos.

While relations between Alfonsín and the military remained strained, the possibility of a coup was ruled out.
The tactics of the alleged conspirators did not command
wide support from the armed forces, and Alfonsín was seen
to be popular and to have political and economic matters
largely under control. The decree under which the 12 suspects were arrested was found to be unconstitutional by the
judiciary, who ruled that they could be detained without
trial only when a state of siege was in force. Principally
in response to this ruling, the government declared a 60-
day state of siege at the end of October. The courts then
upheld the arrest order, and several of the suspects were
detained again after having been freed.

Alfonsín's Radical Civic Union (UCR) fared well in the
November 3 elections, filling more than half of the 254-
seat Chamber of Deputies (the first midterm congressional
elections to be held for 20 years) and half of the seats
in the provincial legislatures. Campaigning concentrated
on economic issues such as inflation, the decline in real
wages, and the rise in unemployment, calculated to have
increased from 4.4% in May 1984 to 6.3%, the highest
level in 11 years, by May 1985. The Peronists, the major opposition, were beset by divisions so deep that they
presented two separate slates of candidates in the key electoral districts of Buenos Aires and its province. Both the
Peronists and the UCR saw their share of the vote decline
in comparison with the 1983 general elections. However,
while the Peronists lost eight seats to emerge with a total
of 103 in the Chamber of Deputies, the UCR increased its
representation by one to 130.

The labour unions achieved little success in their resistance to the government's economic policies, and various
strike calls during the year received only meagre response.
Union strength was expected to increase and to pose more
of a problem to the Labour Ministry, however, following

CARLOS CARRION—SYGMA

The trial of nine former
military commanders in
Argentina was the focus
of continuing public
demonstrations. The
nine were charged with
responsibility for the
deaths or disappearance
of thousands of citizens
during the 1970s.

the appointment on September 19 of Saúl Ubaldini as
secretary-general of the Peronist-dominated Confederación
General de Trabajo, replacing the four-member secretariat
of which he had been a member. Ubaldini had the reputation of being a hard-liner and a straight-talking popular
militant. He stressed that he would put pressure on the
government through mass rallies rather than through strike
action that would result in workers' losing income.

Foreign Relations. Relations with the U.K. remained
cool, and there was little progress on the Falkland Islands/
Islas Malvinas dispute. In July the U.K. government lifted
trade sanctions imposed on Argentina during the 1982
conflict over the islands, but the move was not reciprocated. Argentina refused to declare a formal cessation of
hostilities unless the question of sovereignty of the islands
was discussed, and at the United Nations there was a renewed campaign to persuade the U.K. to include the issue
in negotiations.

Alfonsín met British politicians Neil Kinnock, leader of
the Labour Party, and David Steel, leader of the Liberal
Party, in September and October. As a result of these meetings, Argentine Foreign Minister Dante Caputo declared
that there was "clear proof that we are not in conflict
with a nation, but a government." Both British politicians
agreed that there should be a formal cessation of hostilities,
that the protection zone should be lifted, that full commercial and diplomatic links should be restored, and, more
importantly, that the issue of sovereignty over the islands
could be included in future talks. During a European tour
in September to promote exports and attract investment,
Alfonsín tried to gather support for Argentina's territorial claim, but he was unable to drive a wedge between
the U.K. and other member countries of the European
Communities.

The Economy. Radical economic policy changes announced on June 14 marked an abrupt departure from the
gradualist approach to economic decision making previously adopted by the Alfonsín administration. The Austral
Plan introduced a new currency, the austral, pegged at
U.S. $0.80. Other measures included an indefinite price
and wage freeze, a severely restrictive monetary policy, and
a move to stabilize public finance through spending cuts,
higher public utility tariffs, and tax reforms. Automatic financing of the public-sector deficit by the central bank was
suspended. The key objectives of the plan were to control
inflation, which reached 1,129% in the year to June 1985,
and to reduce the public-sector deficit from 12% of gross
domestic product (GDP) in 1984 to 4.1% in 1985. The
measures were in some instances even more stringent than
those agreed upon with the International Monetary Fund
(IMF).

The price freeze brought an immediate reduction in the
inflation rate; the monthly rate declined in September to
2%—the lowest monthly increase for ten years—while the
annual rate fell to 640% by the end of September and was
officially forecast to drop to 150% by March 1986. The
public-sector deficit was reduced from 13.1% of GDP in the
second quarter of the year to 2% in the third. The spread
between the official and the parallel rates of exchange was
reduced, with the latter quoted at U.S. $0.90 in October.

Progress was also made on the foreign debt issue. Following the government's failure to reach IMF economic
targets, in February the IMF suspended the credit facility
agreed upon in December 1984. A bridging loan of $483
million, over one-third of which was provided by the U.S.,
was arranged in June to help meet interest payments and to
keep repayment arrears within the sensitive 90-day period.
After the implementation of the Austral Plan, the IMF

allowed Argentina to resume drawing on its credit facility. The move unlocked the door for agreement with commercial bank creditors on a major rescheduling of debt. At the end of August a pact was signed that included a $4.2 billion new-money facility, a $9.9 billion restructuring of public-sector debt and public-guaranteed private-sector debt, and a restructuring of $3.5 billion in private-sector debt maturing in 1984–85. Argentina eliminated interest arrears with a payment of $900 million to creditor banks in September.　　　　　　　　　　　(SARAH CAMERON)

BAHAMAS, THE

A parliamentary state and member of the Commonwealth, The Bahamas comprise an archipelago of about 700 islands in the North Atlantic Ocean just southeast of the United States. Area: 13,939 sq km (5,382 sq mi). Pop. (1985 est.): 230,000. Cap.: Nassau. Monetary unit: Bahamian dollar, with (Oct. 21, 1985) a par value of B$1 to U.S. $1 (free rate of B$1.43 = £1 sterling). Queen, Elizabeth II; governor-general in 1985, Sir Gerald Cash; prime minister, Sir Lynden O. Pindling.

Prime Minister Sir Lynden Pindling of The Bahamas remained securely in office throughout 1985 after defeating a parliamentary motion of no confidence in May. The motion was brought in the wake of the royal commission report on drug-related corruption, issued in December 1984, which recommended legal action against several people including a former Cabinet minister, George Smith. Following the commission's report, the government hired a U.S. lobbying firm to improve its image with the U.S. administration. The government cooperated with U.S. agents in a major operation against the drug trade in April.

Tourism, the mainstay of the economy, continued its upturn, with a 12% rise in stopover arrivals reported for the January–April period. Earnings for 1985 were projected at U.S. $900 million, against U.S. $820 million in 1984, and substantial investments were being made in the hotel industry by U.S. companies. In March The Bahamas was designated as qualifying for benefits under the U.S. Caribbean Basin Initiative.

In October the 1985 Commonwealth heads of government conference was held in Nassau, the first to be held in the Caribbean since the 1975 conference in Kingston, Jamaica. (See *Commonwealth of Nations*, above.)
　　　　　　　　　　　(ROD PRINCE)

This article updates the *Macropædia* article The WEST INDIES: *The Bahamas*.

BARBADOS

The parliamentary state of Barbados, a member of the Commonwealth, occupies the most easterly island in the southern Caribbean Sea. Area: 430 sq km (166 sq mi). Pop. (1985 est.): 252,700. Cap.: Bridgetown. Monetary unit: Barbados dollar, with (Oct. 21, 1985) a free rate of BDS$2 to U.S. $1 (BDS$2.88 = £1 sterling). Queen, Elizabeth II; governor-general in 1985, Sir Hugh Springer; prime ministers, J. M. G. Adams and, from March 11, Bernard St. John.

The sudden death of Prime Minister J. M. G. ("Tom") Adams (*see* OBITUARIES) on March 11, 1985, cast a shadow over the prospects of the governing Barbados Labour Party (BLP), which faced general elections in 1986. Under the new prime minister, Bernard St. John (*see* BIOGRAPHIES), there were reports that various groups within the BLP were maneuvering for position. In a reorganization of the Cabinet in June, St. John separated the posts of attorney general and foreign minister. The latter post went to former information minister Nigel Barrow, while the new attorney

general was David Simmons, winner of a by-election held in May in the constituency left vacant by Adams's death.

With tourist arrivals declining and a continued slump in manufacturing, the government halved its 1985 economic growth target from 2 to 1% in June. Unemployment rose from 17.4 to 19.3% between March and June, following a number of factory closures. A major cause was the continuing trade impasse between Trinidad and Tobago and other members of the Caribbean Community (Caricom), including Barbados. The Caricom summit held in Barbados in July set a deadline of August 31 for implementation of a common external tariff and other measures. When Trinidad and Tobago failed to meet this deadline, St. John threatened to impose retaliatory trade restrictions.
　　　　　　　　　　　(ROD PRINCE)

This article updates the *Macropædia* article The WEST INDIES: *Barbados*.

BELIZE

A parliamentary state and member of the Commonwealth, Belize is on the Caribbean coast of Central America. Area: 22,965 sq km (8,867 sq mi). Pop. (1985 est.): 162,000. Cap.: Belmopan. Monetary unit: Belize dollar, with (Oct. 21, 1985) a free rate of BZ$2 to U.S. $1 (BZ$2.87 = £1 sterling). Queen, Elizabeth II; governor-general in 1985, Dame Minita Gordon; prime minister, Manuel Esquivel.

At the start of 1985, the political climate in Belize was one of uncertainty because the United Democratic Party (UDP), which had won 21 of the 28 seats in the House of Representatives in the national elections on Dec. 14, 1984, was expected to chart a new course for the nation. Prime Minister Manuel Esquivel noted in his 1985 budget address that the government faced a giant task in reviving the country's economy. During the months that followed, Belize found itself being drawn closer to the U.S. because U.S. markets accounted for about half of Belize's imports and exports. During the year Belize reportedly became the world's fourth largest exporter of marijuana. The U.S. agreed to spray the illegal crop in an effort to control illicit trafficking in the drug.

The UDP was also committed to reaching an honourable settlement with neighbouring Guatemala over the border

Elijio Briceno, a former government minister of Belize, was arrested in Miami in April and charged with complicity in a scheme to smuggle marijuana into the United States by way of airstrips in his home country. Three others were also arrested.

dispute between the two countries. Hopes for an amicable agreement appeared to increase when the Guatemalan Assembly drew up a draft for a new constitution that contained no mention of the disputed territory. On October 9 Britain's Queen Elizabeth II began a three-day visit to Belize on her way to the Commonwealth heads of government meeting in The Bahamas. This was the first visit ever made to Belize by the queen.   (INEZ T. BAPTIST)

This article updates the *Macropædia* article CENTRAL AMERICA: *Belize*.

BOLIVIA

Bolivia is a landlocked republic in central South America. Area: 1,098,581 sq km (424,164 sq mi). Pop. (1985 est.): 6,429,000. Judicial cap., Sucre; administrative cap., La Paz. Monetary unit: peso, with (Oct. 21, 1985) an official rate of 74,948 pesos to U.S. $1 (107,475 pesos = £1 sterling). Presidents in 1985, Hernán Siles Zuazo and, from August 6, Víctor Paz Estenssoro.

Pressure from within Congress and widespread discontent with the government's economic record forced Pres. Hernán Siles Zuazo of Bolivia to cut short his term of office by a year and call general elections for June 1985. The preelection period was marked by growing political unrest and rumours of a coup d'état, and these factors, combined with the slow registration of voters, served to delay the elections by a month. Foreign Minister Edgar Camacho Omiste resigned the day before polling to protest against the strengthening of relations with China and the consequent breaking of ties with Taiwan.

When polling took place on July 14, the right-wing Acción Democrática Nacionalista party, led by Gen. Hugo

AP/WIDE WORLD

Víctor Paz Estenssoro (wearing sash) congratulates his vice-president, Julio Garret Ayllón, after being inaugurated president of Bolivia in August. Paz Estenssoro had won a congressional ballot required by the absence of a majority winner in the popular vote.

Banzer Suarez, Bolivia's military ruler during 1971–78, received 29% of the vote, as against 26% for the Movimiento Nacionalista Revolucionaria (MNR). Since no party gained an outright majority, the new president was chosen by congressional ballot. Víctor Paz Estenssoro (*see* BIOGRAPHIES), the MNR's centrist candidate, defeated Banzer by 94 votes to 51 and was inaugurated as president for the fourth time on August 6. Although he could count on the support of the left-wing parties, who were eager to keep the right out of power, his position in Congress was fairly weak, since he did not command a majority.

The year was one of continuing economic crisis, with inflation reaching an estimated 14,000% by midyear. Minimal growth of 1% in 1984 was mainly accounted for by the recovery in agriculture, as mining output fell to the lowest level since the 1930s. There was little evidence of improvement in 1985. The official exchange rate of 75,000 pesos to U.S. $1 was grossly overvalued when compared with the black-market rate of 1.4 million pesos to U.S. $1 (August figures). As a result, more and more business transactions were carried out on the black market, and Bolivians reverted to a barter economy. Bank deposits dwindled because of highly negative real interest rates, and traditional business ventures were being replaced by speculative activities.

At the end of August the new government announced a series of economic measures that included lifting exchange controls and introducing a "controlled float" to unify the free and official exchange rates. A new unit of currency, equivalent to 1 million pesos, was also promised. The government eliminated many price subsidies, raised domestic fuel prices, and imposed a four-month freeze on wages of workers in the public sector. A complete reorganization of public-sector companies, aimed at decentralizing control, was planned.

The package was greeted with protests from the workers. The Bolivian Workers' Central Labour Federation called a general strike in early September, and the government declared a state of siege. However, the business sector and foreign creditors welcomed the new government's stance, and debt negotiations resumed with optimism on both sides. Foreign governments also pledged aid to help with the implementation of the measures. The strike ended in early October with an agreement that included the release of detained labour leaders.   (INGRID IVERSEN)

BRAZIL

Brazil is a federal republic in eastern South America on the Atlantic Ocean. Area: 8,512,000 sq km (3,286,500 sq mi). Pop. (1985 est.): 135,564,000. Cap.: Brasília. Monetary unit: cruzeiro, with (Oct. 21, 1985) a free rate of 8,267.43 cruzeiros to U.S. $1 (11,855.50 cruzeiros = £1 sterling). Presidents in 1985, Gen. João Baptista de Oliveira Figueiredo to March 15, acting president from March 15 and president from April 22, José Sarney.

Domestic Affairs. The political year in Brazil was dominated by the transition to civilian rule and the unusual circumstances surrounding the presidential succession. On Jan. 15, 1985, the 686-member electoral college, made up of members of Congress together with representatives of the state assemblies, voted in the first presidential contest involving civilian candidates since the military came to power in 1964. The successful candidate was Tancredo de Almeida Neves (*see* OBITUARIES), supported by the main opposition grouping, the Brazilian Democratic Movement Party (PMDB), who received 480 votes to 180 for the only other candidate, Paulo Salim Maluf of the ruling Social

Democratic Party (PDS). Neves was due to take office on March 15 but was prevented from doing so by an illness that required repeated surgery and eventually led to his death on April 21. José Sarney (*see* BIOGRAPHIES), who had been chosen as Neves's vice-president, was sworn in as acting president on March 15 and as president the day after Neves's death. Sarney was a leader of the Liberal Front Party, a breakaway faction of the PDS that had joined with the PMDB to sponsor Neves's candidacy.

In May Congress passed legislation that paved the way for direct presidential elections, legalized all political parties, and gave votes to illiterates, adding some 20 million people to the electoral roll. A new constitution was expected to be ready by the end of 1987. Direct elections took place in November 1985 for mayors in the state capitals, in those towns previously considered national security areas, and in other towns that had not held local elections since 1964. The PMDB suffered some unexpected defeats in the elections, losing a number of important towns to candidates of the extreme right and left.

Although not enjoying the same degree of popular support as Neves, Sarney steadily improved his position as the year progressed. He persevered with the government team chosen by Neves until the end of August, when he accepted the resignations of Finance Minister Francisco Dornelles and Antônio Carlos Lemgruber, governor of the central bank, who favoured a continuation of recessionary economic policies advocated by the International Monetary Fund (IMF). They were replaced by Dilson Funaro and Fernão Bracher, respectively.

After four months of deliberation Sarney announced the main lines of his economic strategy in a speech on July 22. Growth of 5–6% a year was to be fostered principally by the private sector, and the role of the state sector in the economy was to be progressively reduced. Inflation was to be tackled by price controls and measures to reduce prices of basic foodstuffs. Public spending would be redirected to social and small-scale projects and was expected to fall in real terms in the long run. Programs to reduce poverty, particularly in the northeast, would take priority. The government would not adopt policies that would depress living standards and would honour all financial commitments at home and abroad.

The Sarney administration tried, though with little success, to persuade employers and labour to conclude a social pact leading to restraint in price and pay increases. Throughout the year there were crippling strikes in major industries, the most serious by metalworkers in the Greater São Paulo area in April–June. Sarney implemented a number of social measures in an effort to bolster his administration's standing. The most important of these was a decree, signed in October, providing for the distribution of land to 7.1 million peasant families by the year 2000.

On June 21 a group of forensic scientists announced that they had reached a "reasonable scientific certainty" that a body exhumed earlier in the month from a cemetery at Embu, Brazil, was that of Nazi war criminal Josef Mengele, the so-called Angel of Death of the Auschwitz-Birkenau concentration camp. The body was that of a man who had died in a drowning accident in 1979.

The Economy. Gross domestic product was expected to rise by 5–6% during 1985, compared with an increase of 4.5% in 1984. Agricultural output grew by 7–8% as a result of an increase of 11% in production of principal crops. Overall industrial production was expected to expand by some 7%. Considerable growth in the service sectors followed upon greater consumer demand arising from pay increases in excess of the inflation rate and from increased

Daniel Muñoz, a Brazilian forensic anthropologist, exhibits the skull from the remains that were identified by an international team of experts as those of Josef Mengele, the long-sought Nazi physician responsible for as many as 400,000 deaths at the Auschwitz-Birkenau concentration camp.
BOB NICKELSBERG—GAMMA/LIAISON

public expenditure on socially oriented projects. The inflation rate remained a considerable problem. The general price index rose by 222.9% in the year ended in September 1985, compared with the annual rate of 223.8% in 1984. The major causes of inflation were the high prices of foodstuffs, indexation of wages and government securities, and depreciation of the cruzeiro.

Brazil's external accounts remained sound. Based on January–September figures, the $12 billion trade surplus target for the year was expected to be attained easily. Exports reached $18.4 billion, 7.6% less than in the same period of 1984, while imports were reduced by 10.3% to $9.2 billion. The balance of payments deficit in the first half of the year was $779 million, compared with $185 million in the first half of 1984. Gross international reserves stood at $11.6 billion in mid-1985.

Negotiations on rescheduling servicing of $45.3 billion of external debt due in 1985–90 remained stalled. Although the government reached an agreement in principle with creditor banks in January, negotiations were cut short after the suspension of IMF credits in February. In October the U.S., creditor banks, and the IMF informed Brazil that a multiannual rescheduling could not be concluded without the IMF's stamp of approval. In November the government announced that it no longer intended to seek agreement with the IMF.   (ROBIN CHAPMAN)

CHILE

The republic of Chile extends along the Pacific coast of the Southern Cone of South America. Area: 736,905 sq km (284,520 sq mi), not including Chile's Antarctic claim. Pop. (1985 est.): 12,074,000. Cap.: Santiago. Monetary unit: peso, with (Oct. 21, 1985) a free rate of 179.57 pesos to U.S. $1 (257.50 pesos = £1 sterling). President in 1985, Maj. Gen. Augusto Pinochet Ugarte.

The sacking of Interior Minister Sergio Onofre Jarpa Reyes and of Finance Minister Luis Escobar Cerda in February 1985 marked the end of an attempt by the Chilean regime of Pres. Augusto Pinochet Ugarte to negotiate with the political parties. Jarpa, who was replaced by Ricardo García Rodríguez, had been responsible for an initiative that was aimed at attracting and consolidating middle-class

Mothers and other relatives of *desaparecidos*, "the disappeared ones" (persons believed to have been abducted by police and other government forces), organized a public protest demonstration in Santiago, Chile, on August 9. They were dispersed by police.

and right-wing support by promising an earlier return to democracy than was possible under the ruling constitution. However, after various interviews given by President Pinochet, the political parties involved in the dialogue with the government decided that the president had withdrawn his support from the initiative. On the financial front, Escobar Cerda was replaced by Hernán Buchi Buc, a former superintendent of banks, who had also served as an undersecretary in the Economic Affairs and Health ministries. The new minister's appointment was a cause of alarm among the domestic business community because Buchi was seen as a chief promoter of the Chicago-style monetarism that Escobar had been specifically appointed to change. The replacement of Modesto Collados Núñez by Juan Carlos Delano as minister of economy, development, and reconstruction in a later Cabinet reshuffle in August confirmed the policy of strict austerity based on monetary control.

Membership in the Communist Party was once again declared illegal because of the party's endorsement of violent means to overthrow the regime. Repression of party members was on the increase. In March two Communist leaders and a left-wing dissident were found murdered after they had been kidnapped. Five months later, as a result of information made available by the state intelligence agency (the Central Nacional de Informaciones; CNI), 14 members of the police force were charged with the murders, while five police officials were accused of arranging the abduction of five teachers' union personnel in March. The accused belonged to the police force's intelligence division, the Dirección de Comunicaciones y Informaciones de Carabineros (Dicomcar). Gen. César Mendoza Durán,

commander of the police force and member of the military junta, where he was President Pinochet's closest ally, resigned and was replaced in both positions by his assistant, Gen. Rodolfo Stange Delckers, who earlier had offered his own resignation. One of Stange's first acts was to announce that Dicomcar was to be dissolved.

Attacks by unidentified persons on human-rights and trade-union organizers intensified just before the year's first organized day of protest, which took place on August 9. A three-day protest organized by the trade unions on September 4–6 was significant in that it drew support from middle-class shop owners, truck drivers, and taxi owners, previously strong supporters of the regime, who had been hit by debts caused by higher taxes and inflation, as well as increased gasoline (petrol) prices. Ten people were killed and 120 injured during September's demonstrations. As a result, the state of emergency, which had been partially modified in June, was reimposed for a further six months. The Roman Catholic Church described the situation as an "escalating spiral of madness." Although President Pinochet had rejected the idea of dialogue with the opposition at the end of August, 11 political parties, claiming to represent 80% of the electorate, joined the church in sponsoring a petition calling for a rapid return to civilian rule. The document called for a return to democracy based on direct congressional and presidential elections in 1989. At the end of September the courts ordered the arrest of Rodolfo Seguel and Manuel Bartos, leaders of the miners' union and the textile workers' union, respectively, on charges relating to September's demonstrations.

The earthquake that hit Chile in the early evening on March 3 registered more than 8 on the Richter scale and caused at least 177 deaths and more than $1.8 billion worth of damage. With the epicentre located offshore from Valparaíso, near the village of Algarrobo, the earthquake tremors, lasting over a minute, caused extensive damage to ports and infrastructure. Emergency relief was channeled by the government, while donations by friendly governments and loans from the World Bank were used to repair the damage.

On May 2 the Beagle Channel treaty between Chile and Argentina was formally ratified, ending six years of mediation by the Vatican. The agreement, which awarded Chile practically all it had been seeking, helped bring about a reduction of tension between the two countries. Chile's relations with the U.S. were more mixed. On the one hand, concern over the human-rights situation caused the U.S. to abstain in a vote to grant Chile an Inter-American Development Bank loan in February and to welcome the church-supported petition for a rapid return to democracy as "a positive step." On the other hand, the U.S. supported a much larger World Bank cofinancing loan that allowed Chile to close its 1985 external financing program. In May it was disclosed that the U.S. had approached the government for permission to develop Easter Island as an emergency landing strip for the space shuttle program. Opponents of the government condemned the proposal on the grounds that it would ruin the island's environment, violate the island's sovereignty, and create a permanent U.S. military base that would make the area a possible target in the event of a war between the superpowers.

An external financing agreement and an arrangement with the International Monetary Fund (IMF) were reached in late June. The government agreed to guarantee private-sector debt if creditors so wished. Following the accord, the peso was devalued by 8.4% and import duties were reduced from an average of 30% to 20% in order to encourage exports without adding to inflation. Record low

copper prices as well as disappointing export performance had made the negotiations difficult and slow. Nevertheless, Chile was unusual among debtor nations in that during 1984 it had managed to meet the targets agreed on with the IMF. A $1 billion financing plan was signed with creditor banks in November. (MICHAEL WOOLLER)

COLOMBIA

A republic in northwestern South America, Colombia has coastlines on the Caribbean Sea and the Pacific Ocean. Area: 1,141,748 sq km (440,831 sq mi). Pop. (1985 est.): 28,842,000. Cap.: Bogotá. Monetary unit: peso, with (Oct. 21, 1985) a free rate of 159.14 pesos to U.S. $1 (228.21 pesos = £1 sterling). President in 1985, Belisario Betancur Cuartas.

During 1985 events in Colombia were dominated by a resurgence of violence and increased social tensions arising from higher unemployment. Of the four main guerrilla movements, only one, the Colombian Revolutionary Armed Forces (FARC), upheld its cease-fire agreement made with the government in 1984. Some of its members later organized themselves into the Patriotic Union Party to participate in parliamentary and presidential elections scheduled to take place in 1986. The other guerrilla groups, notably the April 19 Movement (M-19), took advantage of the truce agreement to regroup, following the amnesty granted to their leaders. Claiming persistent attacks by the armed forces, M-19 intensified its guerrilla activity in southwestern Colombia, gained control of some of the slum areas of the main urban centres, and finally broke its cease-fire in June. The National Liberation Army resorted to new tactics of kidnapping and extorting money, and the Popular Army of Liberation continued its indiscriminate killings in the ranching districts of the northwest. On November 6, M-19 guerrillas seized the Palace of Justice in Bogotá and took most of the occupants hostage. Pres. Belisario Betancur Cuartas refused to negotiate, and the following day government forces stormed the building. About 100 persons were killed in the fighting, including the Supreme Court president, Alfonso Reyes Echandía, and ten other Supreme Court judges. It was believed that all the guerrillas also died.

Violence also arose from the government's crusade against drug trafficking. As the U.S. began acting on its newly ratified extradition treaty with Colombia, some drug dealers fled the country, while others went into hiding and in some cases entered into a marriage of convenience with guerrilla factions. That they continued to wield power was demonstrated by the killing in July of Tulio Manuel Castro Gil, the judge in charge of investigations into the murder of Minister of Justice Rodrigo Lara Bonilla in April 1984.

Security problems had a significant effect on the economy. Apart from the direct cost of protecting personnel and installations, many peasant farmers migrated to the large cities. To overcome some of these problems, President Betancur promoted the idea of regional devolution, starting with the direct election of mayors who were currently appointed by the executive. However, land reform remained a more intractable issue.

In a reshuffle of his Cabinet in August, President Betancur replaced the ministers of agriculture, education, and labour and social security. Pressure mounted later in the year for the replacement of Gen. Miguel Vega Uribe, appointed defense minister in January, because of his connection with the administration of former president Julio César Turbay (1978–82); at midyear the State Council, the highest court in the country, accused the Turbay regime of widespread human rights violations. Because ministerial posts were shared between the two main political parties, the Liberals and the Conservatives, further changes were expected to follow the New Liberal faction's break from the Liberal Party in August.

Despite economic growth in 1984, urban unemployment rose to 14.3% in June 1985. The rise was largely accounted for by the increase in the number of young people entering the labour force. The rising trend of unemployment was accelerated by the implementation of a tight austerity program in late 1984. The first coal shipments from the El Cerrejón mine arrived early in 1985.

Disaster struck central Colombia on November 13 when the long-dormant Nevado del Ruiz volcano erupted, sending torrents of mud down the mountainside. The town of Armero was buried; the official death count was over 25,000, and some 60,000 persons were left homeless. (ALEXANDER JOHNS CAMPBELL)

COSTA RICA

The Central American republic of Costa Rica has coastlines on the Caribbean Sea and the Pacific Ocean. Area: 51,100 sq km (19,730 sq mi). Pop. (1985 est.): 2,543,000. Cap.: San José. Monetary unit: colón, with (Oct. 21, 1985) a unified rate of 52.16 colones to U.S. $1 (74.80 colones = £1 sterling). President in 1985, Luis Alberto Monge Álvarez.

President Belisario Betancur refused adamantly to negotiate with terrorists of the group called M-19 who seized Colombia's Palace of Justice in November. Half of the 24 Supreme Court judges died; several were killed by the terrorists, others died in the storming of the building by army troops, and one died later of a heart attack.

A thin but steady stream of young men fleeing compulsory military service flowed across the San Juan River from Nicaragua to Costa Rica, where they came under the care of the Red Cross.
AP/WIDE WORLD

The reality of Costa Rica's proclaimed neutrality came under attack during 1985 as relations with Nicaragua worsened and those with the U.S. strengthened. The Nicaraguan regime pointed out that politically active Nicaraguan refugees had been allowed asylum in Costa Rica and claimed that the country was being used as a base from which to attack Nicaragua. In February Costa Rica protested the abduction of a Nicaraguan draft resister from the Costa Rican embassy in Managua, where he had sought asylum. The arrival in Costa Rica of U.S. military advisers to train the civil guard was perceived as evidence of the government's tilt toward the U.S., which supplied military assistance worth $9 million in 1985.

A marked upturn in the economy was evidenced by growth of about 5% in 1984, despite the slowing of agricultural growth following a crippling strike in the banana industry. The strike cost the Compañía Bananera de Costa Rica some $12 million in lost production and spurred the U.S.-owned parent company, United Brands, to sell all of its banana plantations in Costa Rica, causing large areas to be taken out of banana production. It would take several years before the plantations could produce another crop. Meanwhile, gross domestic product was expected to show a modest growth of 2–3% in 1985.   (INGRID IVERSEN)

This article updates the *Macropædia* article CENTRAL AMERICA: *Costa Rica.*

CUBA

The socialist republic of Cuba comprises the island of Cuba and several thousand smaller islands and cays in the Caribbean Sea. Area: 110,860 sq km (42,803 sq mi). Pop. (1985 est.):10,-058,000. Cap.: Havana. Monetary unit: Cuban peso, with (Oct. 21, 1985) a free rate of 0.93 peso to U.S. $1 (1.33 pesos = £1 sterling). President of the Councils of State and Ministers in 1985, Fidel Castro Ruz.

During 1985 there were signs of renewed life in the conduct of foreign policy as Cuba finally emerged from months of coming to terms with the shock of the U.S. intervention in Grenada in 1983. Diplomatic contacts were reestablished with a number of Latin-American nations, often for the first time since the 1959 revolution. Bolivia opened an embassy in Havana in May, Uruguay was planning to do the same, and commercial contacts were forged with several other countries, including Brazil, Argentina, and Ecuador. Pointing out that Cuba was also burdened with a large foreign debt, Pres. Fidel Castro skillfully increased

his influence among Cuba's neighbours by calling for a debtors' strike. Though governments politely disassociated themselves from Castro's views, the idea struck a chord with many sections of Latin-American society. At the same time, it diverted some attention from Cuba's failure to influence events in Central America. The country's renewed standing among South American nations was highlighted by the success of the motion to admit Cuba to the Latin-American Parliament, approved by a vote of 140–25 at that body's meeting in June.

The promise of a slight thaw in relations between Cuba and the U.S. toward the end of 1984 proved false. The launching of the U.S.-sponsored anti-Castro Radio Martí took place on May 20. If the reference to the Cuban revolutionary hero José Martí was designed to infuriate Castro, it succeeded. He suspended the immigration agreement reached with the U.S. in December 1984 and banned home visits by Cuban exiles. In fact, the output of the Florida-based station was noticeably short on political rhetoric, offering instead a safer diet of popular music and soap opera. Bilateral relations took another turn for the worse after Pres. Ronald Reagan accused Cuba of belonging to a "confederation of terrorist states" (along with Nicaragua, Libya, Iran, and North Korea). Castro responded by calling Reagan "the worst terrorist in the history of mankind" and threatening to bolster Cuba's estimated 36,000-strong garrison in Angola and Ethiopia.

At home, a purge of pro-Moscow officials conducted in February was underlined by Castro's absence from Soviet Pres. Konstantin Chernenko's funeral in March. Many university-trained technocrats were later promoted to head key ministries. Few of Castro's old allies were sacked, however, and most of the changes appeared to reflect a general trend toward increased delegation of functions. Castro himself allowed his younger brother Raúl to run many areas of domestic policy, leaving him free to play a greater role on the international stage.

The Communist Party's third congress, originally scheduled for December, was postponed until February 1986. This would allow a settling-in period for a new economic planning team, to be set up with a mandate to implement the new economic strategy announced in January 1985. Export industries were to receive investment priority to ensure the fulfillment of supply commitments to the U.S.S.R. and other members of the Council for Mutual Economic Assistance (Comecon). Soviet leader Mikhail Gorbachev's economic reforms seemed to extend to a demand that

The debut of Radio Martí, a mainly news, music, and soap opera service sponsored by the U.S. government and beamed at Cuba from Miami, provoked a sharp response from Fidel Castro.
DENNIS BRACK—BLACK STAR

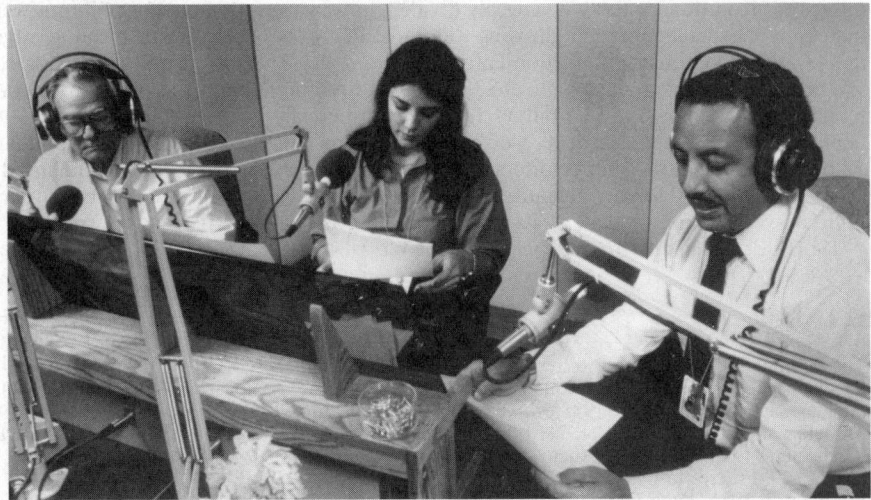

Cuba improve its delivery record in sugar, nickel, and citrus fruit. Moreover, there was increased awareness in Cuba that unrestricted Soviet assistance was unlikely to continue much longer.

The economy grew by 7.4% in 1984, surpassing the target of 5%. The most important contributions were provided by industry and construction, which registered real output increases of 7 and 16%, respectively. Sugar still dominated the economy, but its performance remained relatively disappointing. Output in both the 1983–84 and 1984–85 seasons was eight million metric tons; the former harvest was affected by too much rain, the latter by not enough. Clouding the outlook for the future, in November 1985 Hurricane Kate damaged nearly 1 million ha (2.5 million ac) of cane. Harvesting was also hindered by the perennial problems of absenteeism, labour shortages, and machinery breakdowns. In 1984 Cuba sold 3,649,996 tons of sugar, or 52% of total exports, to the U.S.S.R. The price received for these sales was about seven times the average free-market price of 5 cents a pound. Nevertheless, since Comecon sales were denominated in inconvertible rubles, Cuba valued its free-market sales as a source of hard currency. With free-market prices remaining depressed, Cuba's hard-currency trade deteriorated markedly. In 1984 the country ran a deficit in convertible currencies equivalent to 575 million pesos, compared with 45.8 million pesos in 1983.

Cuba's convertible-currency debt reached $3,430,000,-000 by the end of 1984. In March 1985 Cuba's Paris Club creditors agreed to roll over $140 million in official debt, and in July commercial bank creditors agreed to reschedule $82 million in medium-term debts and $373 million of short-term obligations maturing in 1985. Cuba's first repayment to the U.S.S.R., equivalent to $125 million and falling due in 1986, had been rescheduled to 1990. Total debt to the U.S.S.R. and other Comecon members was unknown but was believed to be in the $8.5 billion–$23 billion range.   (PAUL MILLGATE)

This article updates the *Macropædia* article The WEST INDIES: *Cuba.*

DOMINICA

An island republic within the Commonwealth, Dominica is in the eastern Caribbean Sea. Area: 750 sq km (290 sq mi). Pop. (1985 est.): 74,000. Cap.: Roseau. Monetary unit: East Caribbean dollar, with (Oct. 21, 1985) a par value of EC$2.70 to U.S. $1 (free rate of EC$3.87 = £1 sterling). President in 1985, Clarence Augustus Seignoret; prime minister, Eugenia Charles.

In general elections on July 1, 1985, the Dominica Freedom Party was returned to office with Eugenia Charles as prime minister. Her party won 15 of the 21 elected seats in Parliament, two fewer than in the previous elections, held in 1980. Among the candidates elected for the opposition Labour Party of Dominica was former prime minister Patrick John, who was facing retrial on a charge of conspiring to overthrow the government in 1981. In October John was sentenced to 12 years' imprisonment. Rosie Douglas, a left-wing independent and brother of Labour leader Michael Douglas, defeated a government-backed independent, former acting president Jenner Armour.

Presenting the 1985–86 budget in August 1985, Prime Minister Charles stated that the government had achieved a surplus of EC$400,000 on the previous year's recurrent budget, compared with a deficit of EC$17.3 million in 1980–81, its first year in office. The balance of payments deficit had been halved from EC$40.2 million in 1980 to EC$20.8 million in 1984. Inflation had declined from 30.5 to 2.2%, and unemployment had been reduced from 23 to 13%. The government indicated that during its second term it aimed to expand agricultural exports, agroprocessing, and tourism.   (ROD PRINCE)

This article updates the *Macropædia* article The WEST INDIES: *Dominica.*

DOMINICAN REPUBLIC

The Dominican Republic covers the eastern two-thirds of the Caribbean island of Hispaniola, which it shares with Haiti. Area: 48,442 sq km (18,704 sq mi). Pop. (1985 est.): 6,243,000. Cap.: Santo Domingo. Monetary unit: peso, with a free rate (Oct. 21, 1985) of 3 pesos to U.S. $1 (4.30 pesos to £1 sterling). President in 1985, Salvador Jorge Blanco.

Pres. Salvador Jorge Blanco's government appeared likely to pay a high political price for securing a 12-month standby loan worth 78.5 million Special Drawing Rights from the International Monetary Fund (IMF) in 1985. At IMF insistence the government devalued the peso by 69% against the U.S. dollar when the official and parallel exchange rates were unified in January. There were echoes of the previous year's widespread rioting when, in February, violent protests against fuel price increases left at least four people dead. Faced with the threat of a general strike, President Jorge Blanco approved a 43% increase in the public-sector minimum wage in July.

With elections scheduled for May 1986, support for the political parties seemed finely balanced. The ruling Do-

minican Revolutionary Party was deeply divided, however, increasing the chances of the right-wing Reformist Party or the left-wing Dominican Liberation Party.

The trade deficit remained high, at $388 million, and the foreign debt had grown to $3.5 billion. In June commercial bank creditors rescheduled debts worth $787 million; the following month Paris Club creditors agreed to reschedule $127 million over 11 years plus arrears amounting to $86 million over 6 years.   (PAUL MILLGATE)

This article updates the *Macropædia* article THE WEST INDIES: *Dominican Republic.*

ECUADOR

The republic of Ecuador is in western South America, on the Pacific Ocean. Area: 269,178 sq km (103,930 sq mi), including the Galápagos Islands. Pop. (1985 est.): 8,604,000. Cap.: Quito. Monetary unit: sucre, with (Oct. 21, 1985) an official rate of 67.26 sucres to U.S. $1 (81.18 sucres = £1 sterling) and a free rate of 95.90 sucres to U.S. $1 (137.52 sucres = £1 sterling). President in 1985, León Febres Cordero Rivadeneira.

For much of the first year after it came to power in Ecuador in August 1984, the government of Pres. León Febres Cordero faced severe problems in implementing policy in a Congress in which the opposition held an absolute majority. The single largest party was the opposition centre-left Izquierda Democrática (ID), which held 25 of the 71 seats in Congress. A constitutional crisis was avoided in May 1985 when two ID members shifted their allegiance to the ruling right-wing coalition, the National Reconstruction Front. This shift, with that of five independents, gave the coalition 36 seats, a slim majority. The government then was able to introduce a 29% increase in the minimum wage, which failed to match either the 1984 inflation rate of 31% or the over 60% increase that had been advocated in Congress.

Following freak weather conditions in 1983, which had severely depressed output, a 3% growth in gross domestic product was achieved in 1984. The figure was higher than expected, and a further expansion of 2–3% was forecast for 1985. Ignoring output quotas and price levels set by the Organization of Petroleum Exporting Countries, Ecuador hoped to raise petroleum production to 300,000 bbl a day by the end of the year.

Young Ecuadorians are dispersed by police tear gas in Quito during a 48-hour national strike that left six dead in January.

Foreign creditors were impressed by the government's success in meeting targets set by the International Monetary Fund (IMF) for controlling the public-sector budget and the inflation rate. A rescheduling agreement covering debts falling due in 1984 was followed by a much larger restructuring agreement, under the terms of which $4.6 billion of debt falling due between 1985 and 1989 was to be repaid over 12 years with a 3-year grace period. The IMF made available a standby facility of 105.5 million Special Drawing Rights.   (INGRID IVERSEN)

EL SALVADOR

The republic of El Salvador is situated on the Pacific coast of Central America. Area: 21,041 sq km (8,124 sq mi). Pop. (1985 est.): 5,235,700. Cap.: San Salvador. Monetary unit: colón, with (Oct. 21, 1985) a free rate of 4.06 colones to U.S. $1 (5.82 colones = £1 sterling). President in 1985, José Napoleón Duarte.

In 1985 a settlement of the six-year-old civil war in El Salvador seemed no closer. According to the Roman Catholic Church, an average of 200 people a week died in the fighting. Hope that a third round of the peace talks begun in 1984 would take place in January 1985 foundered when the parties failed to agree on a location and date for the talks and when the government rejected demands by the Farabundo Martí National Liberation Front (FMLN) guerrillas and the group's political wing, the Democratic Revolutionary Front (FDR), for discussion of a new constitution and a total reorganization of the armed forces.

In the face of heavy aerial bombardment, the relocation of civilians sympathetic to the guerrillas, and government efforts to encourage splits among the five groups that made up the FMLN, the rebels took steps in August toward unifying both the political wing and the revolutionary armies. The guerrillas concentrated on urban warfare, although in October the FMLN attacked the military base near the town of La Unión; 42 soldiers were killed and 68 were wounded.

The increase in the number of kidnappings strengthened the charge that the FMLN was merely a terrorist organization. The guerrillas demanded the release of 34 colleagues, a ban on house-to-house searches and arrests, and an end to government military operations in return for the release of Pres. José Napoleón Duarte's daughter, kidnapped along with her companion on September 10. Government claims that nine of the guerrillas were not in their hands aroused suspicions that they had died in captivity. The president's daughter was released in a complex exchange after being held for six weeks. The final arrangement involved the release of Inés Guadalupe Duarte Durán, her friend, and 23 mayors who had been abducted in previous months in exchange for the release of 22 guerrillas and the safe conduct out of El Salvador of 96 rebels disabled in the war. An urban guerrilla group affiliated with the FMLN claimed responsibility for the killing in San Salvador of 13 people, among them 4 U.S. marines, in June. The Army took retaliatory action in which 21 people were killed, and in late August 3 suspects were arrested. Reports that the U.S. had actively supported the army reprisals were later denied. The new tactics adopted by the guerrillas and the improved training and better equipment available to the armed forces—in 1985 the U.S. supplied assistance worth $460 million plus $250 million in supplementary aid—suggested that the war of attrition would continue.

Congressional elections took place on March 31. (For tabulated results, see *Political Parties,* above.) The unexpected victory of President Duarte's Christian Democratic

President José Napoleón Duarte of El Salvador embraces his daughter, Inés Guadalupe Duarte Durán (to his left), and her friend Ana Cecilia Villeda after they were released from 44 days of captivity at the hands of left-wing guerrillas.

CLAUDE URRACA—SYGMA

Party and a split within the main opposition party, the right-wing Nationalist Republican Alliance (Arena), led to the formation in early May of a new party, Patria Libre (Free Fatherland). Maj. Roberto D'Aubuisson was replaced as president of Arena in September by Alfredo Cristiani.

(BEN BOX)

See also Population and Population Movements: *Sidebar.*

This article updates the *Macropædia* article CENTRAL AMER-ICA: *El Salvador.*

GRENADA

A parliamentary state within the Commonwealth, Grenada (with its dependency, the Southern Grenadines) is in the eastern Caribbean Sea. Area: 345 sq km (133 sq mi). Pop. (1985 est.): 90,000. Cap.: Saint George's. Monetary unit: East Caribbean dollar, with (Oct. 21, 1985) a par value of EC$2.70 to U.S. $1 (free rate of EC$3.87 = £1 sterling). Queen, Elizabeth II; governor-general in 1985, Sir Paul Scoon; prime minister, Herbert A. Blaize.

During 1985 the New National Party government, which came to power in Grenada's general elections of December 1984, faced major economic problems. Despite substantial aid from the U.S. and other countries, Grenada remained heavily in debt, with arrears amounting to EC$8 million in July 1985. The main thrust of economic policy was to develop tourism. In September it was announced that a new airline, Grenada Airways, would be launched in December in conjunction with a French company, which also planned to build a 750-room hotel.

With the exception of a team of security specialists, the last U.S. forces left Grenada on June 11. Some Jamaican troops remained to carry out duties at Richmond Hill prison. The trial of 19 former ministers and other officials of the People's Revolutionary Government, charged with the murder of former prime minister Maurice Bishop and others in October 1983, underwent a number of adjournments, with the result that little progress was made during the year.

AP/WIDE WORLD

With the departure of the last U.S. forces imminent, 20 months after the invasion that ended the People's Revolutionary Government established by Maurice Bishop, this wall in St. George's, Grenada, bore an anxious sentiment.

Disagreements among different factions within the government were reported in midyear, but Prime Minister Herbert Blaize (*see* BIOGRAPHIES) survived challenges to his leadership and criticism of his manner as authoritarian. During her visit in October, Queen Elizabeth II praised the return to democracy in Grenada.   (ROD PRINCE)

This article updates the *Macropædia* article The WEST INDIES: *Grenada.*

GUATEMALA

A republic of Central America, Guatemala has coastlines on the Caribbean Sea and the Pacific Ocean. Area: 108,889 sq km (42,042 sq mi). Pop. (1985 est.): 7,675,000. Cap.: Guatemala City. Monetary unit: quetzal, at par with the U.S. dollar, with (Oct. 21, 1985) a free rate of 1.43 quetzales to £1 sterling. Chief of state in 1985, Gen. Oscar Humberto Mejía Victores.

Following congressional and presidential elections on Nov. 3, 1985, Guatemala was to return to civilian rule with the inauguration of an elected administration in January 1986. No candidate gained the 50% majority necessary to secure the presidency in the first round of voting, but in a second round on December 8, Marco Vinicio Cerezo Arévalo of the Christian Democrats (DCG) easily defeated Jorge Carpio Nicolle of the Union of the National Centre (UCN).

The final months of military rule were characterized by growing protests from all sections of society. Political instability was exacerbated by the worsening economic crisis. While gross domestic product showed marginal growth in 1985, led by the recovery of agriculture, other sectors of the economy remained depressed. At the centre of the crisis was the formerly healthy energy sector. Petroleum output plummeted from 10,000 bbl a day to 3,000 bbl a day, and construction problems delayed the completion of the Chixoy and Aguacapa hydroelectricity schemes. The resulting power shortages led to electricity rationing, which, in turn, further depressed output.

Foreign-exchange reserves fell to perilously low levels as a result of high debt servicing, estimated at over 35% of exports, and increased oil imports. In July Guatemala sold one-fifth of its gold reserves in order to finance imports, and the government increased gasoline (petrol) prices in an effort to ease the cash shortage. However, when bus fares were raised to cover the increase, Guatemalans took to the streets in protest, forcing the government to rescind the fare increase and freeze the prices of basic goods. Earlier in the year the government had faced protests from business when it tried to raise revenue through the implementation of fiscal reforms designed by the International Monetary Fund.   (INGRID IVERSEN)

See also Population and Population Movements: *Sidebar.*

This article updates the *Macropædia* article CENTRAL AMERICA: *Guatemala.*

GUYANA

A republic and member of the Commonwealth, Guyana is situated in northeastern South America, on the Atlantic Ocean. Area: 215,000 sq km (83,000 sq mi). Pop. (1985 est.): 953,000. Cap.: Georgetown. Monetary unit: Guyana dollar, with (Oct. 21, 1985) a free rate of G$4.21 to U.S. $1 (G$6.03 = £1 sterling). Presidents in 1985, Forbes Burnham and, from August 6, Desmond Hoyte; prime ministers, Hoyte and, from August 6, Hamilton Green.

Pres. Forbes Burnham (*see* OBITUARIES), who had dominated Guyanese political life since independence in 1966, died on Aug. 6, 1985, after undergoing a throat operation.

He was succeeded by Desmond Hoyte (*see* BIOGRAPHIES), first vice-president and prime minister, while Burnham's cousin Hamilton Green replaced Hoyte as prime minister. Burnham's widow, Viola, who was head of the women's section of the ruling People's National Congress, became one of the country's four vice-presidents.

Although Hoyte pledged to continue Burnham's policies, which in the months before his death had shown a strong leaning toward the U.S.S.R. and the socialist bloc, early reports indicated that the new administration was taking steps to improve the country's frayed relations with the U.S. Elections were held on December 9, four months ahead of schedule. In claiming an overwhelming victory, Hoyte denied charges of fraud leveled by the major opposition parties. The economy remained in the grip of a severe debt burden, although the government reported a 2% growth rate for 1984.   (ROD PRINCE)

This article updates the *Macropædia* article The GUIANAS: *Guyana.*

HAITI

The republic of Haiti occupies the western one-third of the Caribbean island of Hispaniola, which it shares with the Dominican Republic. Area: 27,400 sq km (10,579 sq mi). Pop. (1985 est.): 5,251,200. Cap.: Port-au-Prince. Monetary unit: gourde, with (Oct. 21, 1985) a par value of 5 gourdes to U.S. $1 (free rate of 7.17 gourdes = £1 sterling). President in 1985, Jean-Claude Duvalier.

A national referendum held on July 22, 1985, endorsed constitutional changes that set guidelines for the formation of political parties, restored the office of prime minister—to be filled in 1987—and confirmed Jean-Claude Duvalier as president for life, with the power to appoint his successor. The authorities stated that over 99.9% of the electorate had voted in favour of the changes, but reports from authoritative sources suggested that widespread voting malpractices had occurred. The new constitution incorporating the amendments had already become law following its approval by the National Assembly on June 6. The Parti Nationale Progressiste was formed in late August.

In September President Duvalier forced the resignation of Roger Lafontant, the hard-line minister for the interior and national defense, in a move to improve relations with more moderate elements in the country in general and the Roman Catholic Church in particular. In a Cabinet reshuffle December 31, 14 new ministers were appointed and 4 were given diplomatic appointments abroad. Lafontant was replaced by François Guillaume.

The economy showed a slight improvement in 1985, primarily as a consequence of a recovery in manufacturing and coffee exports. However, government finances remained unstable.   (ROBIN CHAPMAN)

This article updates the *Macropædia* article The WEST INDIES: *Haiti.*

HONDURAS

A republic of Central America, Honduras has coastlines on the Caribbean Sea and the Pacific Ocean. Area: 112,088 sq km (43,277 sq mi). Pop (1985 est.) 4,372,000. Cap.: Tegucigalpa. Monetary unit: lempira, with (Oct. 21, 1985) a par value of 2.02 lempiras to U.S. $1 (free rate of 2.89 lempiras = £1 sterling). President in 1985, Roberto Suazo Córdova.

Political wrangling in Honduras during the months preceding the November 1985 general elections provoked a constitutional crisis. The central issue was opposition in the National Assembly to Pres. Roberto Suazo Córdova's

attempts to manipulate his own Liberal Party and the rival National Party to ensure that only presidential candidates who met with his approval were nominated. A related issue was the fight for control of the Supreme Court; when the Assembly dismissed several pro-Suazo Supreme Court justices for alleged corruption, the president imprisoned the replacement Supreme Court president and charged him with treason. Pressure from the Assembly, the Roman Catholic Church, the trade unions, and the U.S. administration eventually forced Suazo to accept a compromise on May 21. The agreement included reform of the Supreme Court and of the electoral system, to allow candidates chosen by factions within a party to run for office. The Supreme Court president was released the following day.

The Liberal and National parties fielded four candidates each, and the Christian Democratic and the National Innovation and Unity parties one each. In the November 24 balloting Rafael Leonardo Callejas of the National Party was the leading candidate, with about 41% of the vote. However, under the new electoral system victory went to the leading candidate of the party gaining the most votes for all its candidates as a group, making José Azcona Hoyo of the Liberal Party the winner.

The presence in Honduras of Nicaraguan Democratic Force guerrillas (*contras*) heightened tension between Honduras and Nicaragua. The Honduran government would not admit officially that the guerrillas operated from its territory, but calls for the expulsion of the *contras* were unlikely to be heeded for fear of the effect such action would have on U.S. support. (BEN BOX)

This article updates the *Macropædia* article CENTRAL AMERICA: *Honduras.*

JAMAICA

A parliamentary state within the Commonwealth, Jamaica occupies an island in the Caribbean Sea. Area: 10,991 sq km (4,244 sq mi). Pop. (1985 est.): 2,367,000. Cap.: Kingston. Monetary unit: Jamaica dollar, with (Oct. 21, 1985) a free rate of J$6.19 to U.S. $1 (J$8.88 = £1 sterling). Queen, Elizabeth II; governor-general in 1985, Sir Florizel Glasspole; prime minister, Edward Seaga.

Street demonstrations in January 1985, in which seven people died and considerable property damage was caused, ushered in a turbulent year for the Jamaica Labour Party government of Prime Minister Edward Seaga. The demon-

Recruits of the Nicaraguan Democratic Force undergo commando training at a base in Honduras. The presence in Honduras of the FDN, one of several anti-Sandinista *contra* groups, was the source of growing tension with Nicaragua.
CLAUDIO URRACA—SYGMA

strations were in protest against a rise in gasoline (petrol) prices. At the end of June the major trade unions organized a short-lived general strike to demand wage increases, an end to public-sector layoffs, and a change in government policy to moderate the rate of price increases. During the year the opposition People's National Party rallied strongly in the opinion polls.

In July the International Monetary Fund agreed to a new $115 million standby arrangement for the period up to March 31, 1987, and a debt rescheduling agreement with foreign governments and commercial banks followed. The government nevertheless faced a worsening trade deficit, caused mainly by a slump in the bauxite industry. Gross

REUTERS/THE BETTMANN ARCHIVE

The burned-out hulk of an automobile marks the aftermath of serious rioting in Kingston, Jamaica, that was sparked by a January increase in the price of gasoline (petrol).

domestic product was expected to decline by at least 4% in 1985, while inflation was running at about 31%. The exchange rate slid from J$5 to almost J$6 to the U.S. dollar between January and October.　　(ROD PRINCE)

This article updates the *Macropædia* article The WEST INDIES: *Jamaica*.

MEXICO

A federal republic of North America, Mexico has coastlines on the Pacific Ocean, the Gulf of Mexico, and the Caribbean Sea. Area: 1,958,201 sq km (756,066 sq mi). Pop. (1985 est.): 78,027,400. Cap.: Mexico City. Monetary unit: peso, with (Oct. 21, 1985) a free rate of 399.62 pesos to U.S. $1 (573.05 pesos = £1 sterling). President in 1985, Miguel de la Madrid Hurtado.

In Mexico 1985 was ushered in with reports of violent protests in the northern states against alleged electoral fraud, a topic that dominated the political scene throughout the year. Municipal elections held on Dec. 2, 1984, gave widespread victory to the ruling Partido Revolucionario Institucional (PRI), although the opposition Partido de Acción Nacional (PAN) claimed to have won several mayoral races. The refusal to recognize PAN's claim to victory in Piedras Negras, on the border with Texas, resulted in violence that left two people dead. The Army was brought in to restore order.

These incidents heightened worries about the fair and peaceful conduct of elections due in July to fill the Chamber of Deputies (lower house of Congress) and 7 of the 31 state governorships. Many commentators saw the elections as the most important in the PRI's 56-year rule, as they were the first major elections since the economic crisis of 1982. The PRI was vulnerable, since the previous two to three years had witnessed falling real wages, rising unemployment, and high inflation rates. The PAN, which received most of its support in the prosperous americanized north, benefited from a growing dissatisfaction with the government despite lacking a coherent program of its own. However, its voters were predominantly urban, whereas PRI support continued to be strong among rural and southern voters. Although the opposition did not constitute a serious threat to the PRI's overall support, there was some evidence that the PRI went to great lengths to hinder the PAN's performance in the elections.

Polling took place on July 7. The official results, announced a week later, revealed a landslide victory for the PRI, despite indications that its support was at an all-time low. The PRI won all seven state governorships and 289 of the 300 directly elected seats in the Chamber of Deputies. (The remaining 100 were allocated by a system of proportional representation.) In a turnout of 50%, some 65% of voters supported the PRI and 16% the PAN. (For tabulated results, see *Political Parties,* above.) Allegations of fraud were strengthened by the fact that in some areas the PRI candidate announced victory before the polls closed. There were isolated incidents of clashes with the police and protests by the PAN, but the aftermath was marked by a lack of protest. During his state of the nation address in September, Pres. Miguel de la Madrid Hurtado admitted that there had been "deficiencies and electoral irregularities in some electoral districts."

Relations with the U.S. were strained at times but remained generally stable. The kidnapping and murder of a U.S. Drug Enforcement Agency official early in the year resulted in the U.S. bringing pressure to bear on Mexico to control the growing trade in drugs to the U.S. As a measure

---

The Mexican Earthquake

The earthquakes that shook Mexico City in the early morning of Sept. 19, 1985, and during the evening of the following day left thousands dead or dying in collapsed buildings. The worst damage was relatively localized in the central part of the city, which housed hotels, apartment buildings for middle-income workers, some government offices, and historic buildings. It was suggested that Spanish colonial buildings withstood the quakes far better than modern structures. While the imagination of the world was captured by dramatic rescues of newborn babies who survived for almost two weeks before being retrieved from hospital ruins, the personal, economic, and political ramifications would continue to affect the Mexican people for years to come.

The government soon came under pressure for its alleged mishandling of the rescue operation. The military, who were called in to help, received no instructions on how to proceed, and during the first few days foreign assistance was turned down. Civilians who formed their own rescue teams lacked technical expertise in dealing with a crumbling city and might in fact have caused more lives to be lost. Civilians continued to play a major role in the rescue even after international economic and technical aid was accepted.

The disaster brought to light several cases of corruption, in the construction industry in particular. A commission was set up to study construction codes for the city and examine cases of noncompliance with existing building regulations. The government's failure to act on its policy of decentralization was also highlighted. The uncontrolled growth of Mexico City had been allowed to continue, and the resulting overcrowding no doubt added to the number of deaths.

The economic cost, in terms of both reconstruction and lost revenue, was considerable. Estimates of the cost of rebuilding ranged from $2 billion upward. The International Monetary Fund (IMF) was on the verge of demanding new, stricter economic measures from the government when the earthquake struck. Although the IMF then tempered its demands, there nevertheless remained uncertainty about Mexico's relationship with its creditors. In the weeks that followed, Mexico received special aid and loans from multilateral agencies, including a $300 million loan from the World Bank and emergency assistance from the IMF. There were calls for a debt moratorium, but the government itself appeared to be trying to honour its commitments, at least in principle.

A major problem was the need to ensure that foreign aid and other inflows would not leave the country again in the shape of capital flight. Financial crisis loomed as the value of the peso plummeted, and the hoped-for boom in construction was overshadowed by external payment difficulties. Mexico's economy could recover only through careful control of foreign aid and concessions in the reconstruction period.

(INGRID IVERSEN)

of its concern over Mexico's failure to apprehend those responsible for the killing, the U.S. imposed stricter border controls. Shortly afterward, in early April, several suspected drug runners, including Ernesto Fonseca Carrillo, the alleged "godfather" of the Mexican drug trade, were arrested. Relations subsequently became more harmonious.

In the Central American region, Mexico continued to provide economic support to Nicaragua, which it supplied with petroleum, while at the same time maintaining its support for regional groupings such as the Contadora Group and the Cartagena Agreement. The government was careful not to antagonize its creditors by making radical statements on debt. President de la Madrid's 18-day visit to Europe in June was aimed at increasing trade and investment.

A spurt of growth during the latter part of 1984, resulting in part from the relaxing of austerity but also fueled by export growth, contributed to a 3.5% growth in gross domestic product (GDP) for the year as a whole; this followed a contraction of over 5% in 1983. The growth was accompanied by an acceleration of the inflation rate to 65% and a public-sector deficit of 7% of GDP, well beyond the target of 5.5% set by the International Monetary Fund (IMF). In 1985 the government restored its austerity policy with the implementation of large spending cuts. An austerity program announced in January included a freeze on public-sector employment. The government wanted to assure its creditors that fiscal discipline would continue even after IMF involvement ceased in 1985. The theme dominated the president's state of the nation address, when he warned that there was no prospect of an early end to the country's problems. While speaking out against confrontation and ultimatums over debt repayments, he stated that better terms and larger inflows of capital were required if Mexico was to maintain its debt servicing.

With the decline in oil prices on world markets seriously affecting the balance of payments, the 1984 current-account surplus was expected to be replaced by a deficit in 1985. The growth of nontraditional exports, mainly to the U.S., slowed down. Although the daily slippage of the peso was increased in February, the currency remained overvalued. In June, as pressure mounted, the government recognized the existence of a "superfree" rate by allowing banks to use it for certain transactions. Finally the "superfree" rate was fully integrated, and the "official-free" rate was abolished. On July 25 the controlled rate was devalued

Rescue workers search painstakingly through the wreckage of a building for survivors of the earthquake that battered Mexico City in September. Shortages of emergency equipment and of trained personnel greatly complicated rescue efforts.
T. CAMPION—SYGMA

by 17%, and on August 5 a regulated float replaced the daily slippage. These changes were expected to keep inflation high in 1985.

Mexico's economic and political problems were overshadowed to a great extent by the disastrous earthquake that struck Mexico City and the surrounding area on September 19 and left many thousands of people dead, injured, or homeless. (*See* Sidebar; EARTH SCIENCES: *Geophysics.*)　　　　　　　　　　　　(INGRID IVERSEN)

BILL NATION—SYGMA

As part of a campaign to pressure Mexican authorities in the case of a kidnapped U.S. narcotics agent, customs officials slowed down the processing of vehicles crossing the border from Mexico. At this crossing, from Tijuana, Mexico, to San Ysidro, California, the usual delay of 20 minutes stretched to seven hours.

NICARAGUA

A republic of Central America, Nicaragua has coastlines on the Caribbean Sea and the Pacific Ocean. Area: 127,662 sq km (49,291 sq mi). Pop. (1985 est.): 3,039,000. Cap.: Managua. Monetary unit: córdoba, with (Oct. 21, 1985) an official rate of 28.02 córdobas to U.S. $1 (40.18 córdobas = £1 sterling). Coordinator of the three-member Junta of the Government of National Reconstruction to Jan. 10, 1985, and president from January 10, Daniel Ortega Saavedra.

The Sandinista National Liberation Front government of Nicaragua decided in May 1985 to step up military action against its opponents by launching punitive strikes against the Honduran bases of the largest *contra* grouping, the Nicaraguan Democratic Force (FDN). Tens of thousands of people were moved out of areas in northern Nicaragua in order to deprive the *contras* of local support and to create "free-fire zones" that would enable the Army to operate freely. The morale of the *contras* was boosted by the U.S. administration's total embargo on trade with Nicaragua, imposed as of May 7, and by the vote in the U.S. Congress on June 12 that approved the release of $27 million in "nonlethal" aid to the rebels. Although apparently unable to retain control of captured areas, *contra* forces, particularly those based in Honduras, remained a potent threat. The effectiveness of the Democratic Revolutionary Alliance (ARDE) rebels, based in Costa Rica, was reduced by Costa Rica's stated neutrality, by their own internal divisions, and by successful Sandinista raids. Opposition groups attempted to present a united front by forming the United Nicaraguan Opposition, but the presence within the FDN of former national guardsmen who had been supporters of the late president Anastasio Somoza was deeply resented by other anti-Sandinista groups.

Following the November 1984 elections, the swearing in of the new National Assembly and the inauguration of Daniel Ortega Saavedra as president took place in January 1985. On October 15 the government reimposed the state of emergency that had been lifted shortly before the elections.

Nicaragua's economic difficulties posed a more direct threat to the government than did the actions of the *contras,* although problems were compounded by the fact

TASS/SOVFOTO

Nicaraguan Pres. Daniel Ortega Saavedra's (left) visit in May to the Soviet Union, where he met with Soviet leader Mikhail Gorbachev, prompted the U.S. Congress to reverse an earlier ban on aid to anti-Sandinista rebels.

that 40% of government spending was devoted to counterinsurgency operations. On February 8 the government announced a package of austerity measures that included production incentives for agriculture, a freeze on nonmilitary public-sector hiring, salary increases of 47–60%, the termination of most subsidies, and the devaluation of the córdoba with the introduction of a four-tier exchange rate (of 20, 28, 40, and 50 córdobas to the U.S. dollar). The value of coffee exports fell by 20.5% to $119.2 million in 1984, while sales of cotton rose by 27.5% to $133.8 million, making it the most important export. In anticipation of a U.S. trade embargo, Nicaragua had been diversifying its trading partners. In 1984 the U.S. supplied 14.6% of the country's imports and took 14.8% of its exports, compared with 1980 figures of 30 and 47.5%, respectively.

Pressure from the U.S. forced the government to abandon its application for a $58 million loan from the Inter-American Development Bank in March 1985. In its search for multilateral credits, the government was showing greater willingness to pay its debts; for example, in April the $7.5 million outstanding to the International Monetary Fund under a loan granted to the Somoza regime was repaid. President Ortega's trip to Europe in April–May apparently raised credits worth $402 million. The U.S.S.R. promised to supply from 80 to 90% of the country's petroleum needs.   (PAUL MILLGATE)

This article updates the *Macropædia* article CENTRAL AMERICA: *Nicaragua.*

PANAMA

A republic of Central America, Panama lies between the Caribbean Sea and the Pacific Ocean on the Isthmus of Panama. Area: 77,082 sq km (29,762 sq mi). Pop. (1985 est.): 2,180,000. Cap.: Panama City. Monetary unit: balboa, at par with the U.S. dollar, with a free rate (Oct. 21, 1985) of 1.43 balboas to £1 sterling. Presidents in 1985, Nicolás Ardito Barletta Vallarina and, from September 28, Eric Arturo Delvalle.

When Nicolás Ardito Barletta assumed the duties of the presidency of Panama in October 1984, he was confronted by a formidable group of obstacles. His margin of victory at the polls, counted in the hundreds, revealed a lack of strong party support, and many believed that the elections had been tainted by fraud. The immediate problem, however, was the critical state of the economy. This prompted the quick passage of austerity laws, but the pressure of discontent was so great that the president agreed to repeal them.

The austerity measures had helped to improve temporarily the fragile state of the economy. But the bankers worried about a national debt that reached well over $3 billion and also about increased competition from banking centres in Florida. The Treasury officials could not even look at the Panama Canal business without misgivings, for ship transits were decreasing in number. For various reasons the amounts of petroleum, coal, grain, and other commodities shipped through the canal were declining. Inflation was inflicting a cruel burden on everyone. The situation impelled the commander of the defense forces, Gen. Manuel Antonio Noriega, to strengthen his control over the government in May by requiring the president to remove six Cabinet members and to fill those places with figures more to his liking.

New austerity measures accompanying a $60 million loan to Panama in June produced a general strike of labourers on July 1 and 2. Their chief demand was for a freeze on payments of the national debt, but they eventually were forced to retreat.

Gen. Manuel Antonio Noriega, commander of Panama's defense forces, demonstrated his control of the civilian government in September by forcing Pres. Nicolás Ardito Barletta to resign.

CLAUDE URRACA—SYGMA

Measures of austerity were not a popular course of action with General Noriega and his forces. When he openly criticized the president, the signal for Ardito Barletta's resignation was clear. Called back to Panama from his travels, the president stepped down on September 28. The first vice-president, Eric Arturo Delvalle (*see* BIOGRAPHIES), was sworn in at a late-night meeting of the Legislative Assembly. His initial address was a plea for democracy and an end to divisiveness.   (ALMON R. WRIGHT)

This article updates the *Macropædia* article CENTRAL AMERICA: *Panama.*

PARAGUAY

Paraguay is a landlocked republic of central South America. Area: 406,752 sq km (157,048 sq mi). Pop. (1985 est.): 3,404,000. Cap.: Asunción. Monetary unit: guaraní, with (Oct. 21, 1985) an official rate of 240.17 guaraníes to U.S. $1 (344.40 guaraníes = £1 sterling). President in 1985, Gen. Alfredo Stroessner.

The political opening that Pres. Alfredo Stroessner of Paraguay appeared to have initiated in early 1984 was somewhat reversed in 1985, by a new wave of repression against unofficial opposition party leaders and by increased censorship. Opposition calls for a national dialogue were rejected by the government in July, and Radio Nandutí was accused of subversion and closed down for ten days in mid-August. The Roman Catholic Church became more outspoken in denouncing human rights violations and growing socioeconomic inequalities.

However, other factors were proving more worrisome to Stroessner. Unrest among young army officers was triggered by corruption in the higher ranks. The ruling Colorado Party was split over the question of what should happen in the post-Stroessner era. The *tradicionalistas,* who still controlled the party executive, were reported to favour a military-civilian government for a transition period to democracy. On the other hand, the *oficialistas* took advantage of the August celebrations of Stroessner's 31 years in office to proclaim his son, Gustavo Stroessner, an air force officer, as his eventual successor.

The country's involvement in the narcotics trade prompted the U.S. administration to adopt a less sympathetic stance toward the Stroessner regime. Harsh criticism by the West German public about the harbouring of Nazi war criminal Josef Mengele forced Stroessner to postpone a visit to West Germany scheduled for July.

(ALEXANDER JOHNS CAMPBELL)

PERU

The republic of Peru is located in western South America, on the Pacific Ocean. Area: 1,285,216 sq km (496,225 sq mi). Pop. (1985 est.): 19,701,000. Cap.: Lima. Monetary unit: sol, with (Oct. 21, 1985) a free rate of 13,963.74 soles to U.S. $1 (20,024 soles = £1 sterling). Presidents in 1985, Fernando Belaúnde Terry and, from July 28, Alan García Pérez; prime ministers, Luis Pércovich Roca and, from July 28, Luis Alva Castro.

On July 28, 1985, Pres. Fernando Belaúnde Terry became Peru's first freely elected ruler since 1945 to hand over power to a democratically chosen successor. General elections held on April 14 gave the centre-left Alianza Popular Revolucionaria Americana (APRA) absolute majorities in both houses of Congress. (For tabulated results, see *Political Parties,* above.) However, there was no outright winner in the presidential contest, although APRA candidate Alan García Pérez (*see* BIOGRAPHIES) fell just short of the target with 48% of the vote. In second place with 23% was Alfonso Barrantes Lingán, candidate of the Marxist coalition Izquierda Unida (IU) and mayor of Lima, while the ruling right-wing Acción Popular (AP) party was pushed into fourth place by the Convergencia Democrática, a coalition of right-wing parties. The need for a second round was obviated by Barrantes's withdrawal on April 25 and the National Election Board's announcement on June 1 that a runoff was no longer necessary.

APRA now held undisputed power for the first time in its long history. García possessed youth and dynamism, and this factor was apparently of greater importance to the electorate then his lack of experience. The swing to the left was also the result of the Belaúnde government's failure to deal with the country's ever worsening political and economic situation. The last year of Belaúnde's five-year term was marked by an increase in protests by workers and in violent acts perpetrated by the Maoist guerrilla group Sendero Luminoso (Shining Path). Its main targets were power installations, factories, and foreign businesses, and during the election campaign party offices, candidates, and polling stations were also hit. The president of the National Election Board was shot and critically wounded shortly after the election.

An Amnesty International report published in January, estimating that over 1,000 people were missing after being detained by the security forces, elicited official denials. In September President García showed his determination to act on his election pledge to establish control over the military's conduct in the antiterrorist campaign. He dismissed three top army generals held responsible for the massacre of some 40 peasants by counterinsurgency forces.

The government also faced an economic crisis. Growth in gross domestic product of 3.5% in 1984 had to be judged in the light of a contraction of almost 12% the year before. The modest recovery was led by the fishing and agricultural sectors, which had plummeted in 1983 following freak weather. Construction remained depressed by cutbacks in public projects, and although mining output showed signs of recovery—a 10% improvement in 1984—low world commodity prices kept export earnings down. The new government announced an economic package aimed at "austerity without misery." The main elements were the freezing of the exchange rate, a reduction in interest rates, a price freeze, and a wage rise of 18%.

Alan García Pérez was inaugurated president of Peru in July and quickly moved to justify the expectations of those who had voted for his youth and energy. A social democrat and something of a populist, he began his term of office with enormous popularity.

ALON REININGER—CONTACT PRESS IMAGES

The measures were announced on the heels of a radical pronouncement by García on the subject of the external debt: Peru was to restrict repayments on its $13.6 billion foreign debt to 10% of export earnings, and commercial banks were asked to grant a six-month freeze on repayments. The government was already heavily in arrears. García repeated his strong views in his address to the UN General Assembly in September when, claiming that the choice was between "debt or democracy," he pointed out that austerity measures could threaten the stability of a country. On December 17 President García announced that his government was seizing the assets of the U.S.-based Belco Petroleum Corp. because Belco had not met his demand that money from tax exemptions be invested in exploring new areas.   (INGRID IVERSEN)

SAINT CHRISTOPHER AND NEVIS

A federal parliamentary state and member of the Commonwealth, St. Christopher and Nevis is comprised of the islands of St. Christopher and Nevis in the eastern Caribbean Sea. Area: 261 sq km (101 sq mi). Pop (1985 est.): 44,000. Cap.: Basseterre. Monetary unit: East Caribbean dollar, with (Oct. 21, 1985) a par value of EC$2.70 to U.S.$1 (free rate of EC$3.87 = £1 sterling). Queen, Elizabeth II; governor-general in 1985, Sir Clement Arrindell; prime minister, Kennedy A. Simmonds.

Despite a positive economic performance in 1984, with real growth of 4% in the gross national product, the government of St. Christopher and Nevis (St. Kitts-Nevis) warned early in 1985 that the continued world recession made it increasingly difficult to maintain public services. Stamp duty and taxes on travel, vehicles, alcoholic drinks, and other items were increased in the 1985 budget to raise an extra EC$1.3 million. The weak international sugar market continued to give cause for concern.

Strong sectors included tourism, which in 1985 main-tained the momentum of the previous year, when arrivals increased by 16.3% to almost 40,000. Trade in manufactured goods, principally electronic components, also increased. New direct air links with Canada were opened in September.

The opposition Labour Party, which had suffered a crushing defeat in the 1984 general elections, retained its leader, Lee Moore, at the 1985 party convention but indicated a desire to rejuvenate its image by electing a young lawyer, Henry Browne, as deputy leader.   (ROD PRINCE)

This article updates the *Macropædia* article The WEST INDIES: *Saint Christopher and Nevis.*

SAINT LUCIA

A parliamentary state and member of the Commonwealth, St. Lucia is the second largest of the Windward Islands in the eastern Caribbean Sea. Area: 617 sq km (238 sq mi). Pop. (1985 est.): 137,600. Cap.: Castries. Monetary unit: East Caribbean dollar, with (Oct. 21, 1985) a par value of EC$2.70 to U.S. $1 (free rate of EC$3.87 = £1 sterling). Queen, Elizabeth II; governor-general in 1985, Sir Allen Lewis; prime minister, John Compton.

Increased investment in St. Lucia's industrial and tourist sectors, much of it from the U.S., held out the prospect of an economic upturn in 1985, despite continuing difficulties in the country's trading relations with fellow members of the Caribbean Community.

Tourist arrivals, which rose 13% in 1984, appeared set to continue increasing. Nevertheless, Prime Minister John Compton, presenting the 1985–86 budget, warned that difficult times lay ahead. Staffing levels in the public services were to be frozen for the coming year and reduced over the next three years; wages in this sector accounted for 55% of total current government spending. In 1984 the budget was in deficit by EC$13.1 million, while the trade deficit of EC$191.7 million reflected the fall in exports to Guyana, Jamaica, and Trinidad and Tobago. The garment industry in particular was affected by new import restrictions introduced by Trinidad.

At its party convention in August 1985, the opposition St. Lucia Labour Party (SLP) rejected a proposal from the Progressive Labour Party (PLP), led by George Odlum, to form an electoral pact. The PLP had been formed in 1981 by a breakaway faction of the SLP.   (ROD PRINCE)

This article updates the *Macropædia* article The WEST INDIES: *Saint Lucia.*

SAINT VINCENT AND THE GRENADINES

A parliamentary state within the Commonwealth, St. Vincent and the Grenadines comprises the islands of St. Vincent and the northern Grenadines in the eastern Caribbean Sea. Area: 389 sq km (150 sq mi). Pop. (1985 est.): 105,000. Cap.: Kingstown. Monetary unit: East Caribbean dollar, with (Oct. 21, 1985) a par value of EC$2.70 to U.S. $1 (EC$3.87 = £1 sterling). Queen, Elizabeth II; governors-general in 1985, Sir Sydney Gun-Munro and, from February 28, Joseph Lambert Eustace; prime minister, James Fitz-Allen Mitchell.

The New Democratic Party (NDP), which gained office in St. Vincent and the Grenadines in the July 1984 general elections, consolidated its position in February 1985 when it won a by-election in the East St. George constituency. The seat, made vacant by the retirement of former prime minister Milton Cato of the St. Vincent Labour Party, went to the NDP with a majority of 700 and brought its strength to 10 of the 13 seats in the National Assembly. Labour elected Hudson Tannis as its national leader to replace Cato.

During 1985 the government concentrated on reorganizing public enterprises and finances. The sugar industry, which had debts of EC$42 million, was closed down at the end of the 1985 season. In May the government bought the Commonwealth Development Corporation's majority holding in the country's electric power company. The 1985 budget offered tax incentives aimed at stimulating investment in the productive sector and the construction industry. Prime Minister James Mitchell pointed to reduction of the 40–50% unemployment rate as his government's highest priority. (ROD PRINCE)

This article updates the *Macropædia* article The WEST INDIES: *Saint Vincent and the Grenadines.*

SURINAME

The republic of Suriname is in northeastern South America, on the Atlantic Ocean. Area: 163,820 sq km (63,251 sq mi), not including a 17,635-km area disputed with Guyana. Pop. (1985 est.): 395,000. Cap.: Paramaribo. Monetary unit: Suriname guilder, with (Oct. 21, 1985) a par value of 1.79 Suriname guilders to U.S. $1 (free rate of 2.56 Suriname guilders = £1 sterling). Chairman of the National Military Council in 1985, Dési Bouterse; prime minister, Wim Udenhout.

A report published by the UN Human Rights Committee in February 1985 accused Suriname's National Military Council (NMC) of having murdered 15 members of the opposition in 1982. As a result, the chances of reconciliation with the government of The Netherlands remained remote. During the year Suriname thus sought financial support from other sources. In February Suriname and Colombia signed an agreement that provided for increased bilateral trade and extended a $15 million line of credit for Suriname to finance imports from Colombia. Later Dési Bouterse, chairman of the NMC, and Prime Minister Wim Udenhout visited Libya, where they secured promises of oil supplies and financial and military aid.

Five years after the military coup that brought the NMC to power, Bouterse and the leaders of the three main political parties signed an agreement in November under which the Hindustani, Creole, and Javanese populations were to be represented on a council that was to prepare for a peaceful return to democratic rule. A written constitution and a democratically elected representative body were to be introduced before April 1987. The agreement was met with skepticism in The Netherlands. (DICK BOONSTRA)

This article updates the *Macropædia* article The GUIANAS: *Suriname.*

TRINIDAD AND TOBAGO

A republic and member of the Commonwealth, Trinidad and Tobago consists of two islands in the Caribbean Sea off the coast of Venezuela. Area: 5,128 sq km (1,980 sq mi). Pop. (1985 est.): 1,189,000. Cap.: Port-of-Spain. Monetary unit: Trinidad and Tobago dollar, with (Oct. 21, 1985) a par value of TT$2.41 to U.S. $1 (free rate of TT$3.45 = £1 sterling). President in 1985, Sir Ellis Clarke; prime minister, George Chambers.

The National Alliance for Reconstruction (NAR), formed a year earlier by four of Trinidad and Tobago's opposition parties, was officially launched in September 1985. The NAR comprised the Democratic Action Congress, the United Labour Front, the Organization for National Reconstruction, and the Tapia House Movement. It was expected to present a strong challenge to the governing People's National Movement in general elections due to take place before February 1987.

The government's economic austerity measures showed some success in increasing the trade surplus and slowing the decline in international reserves. A trade surplus of TT$708 million was achieved in the first six months of 1985, compared with TT$467 million for all of 1984. Petroleum production averaged 177,639 bbl a day in the first half of the year, a 9.4% increase over the corresponding period in 1984. Despite a rise in sugar production from 64,800 metric tons in 1984 to 81,200 metric tons, the state-owned Caroni company announced a package of economy measures in October to deal with immediate cash-flow problems arising from reduced domestic demand and low world sugar prices. There were a number of labour disputes over pay and job security issues.

In July and August Prime Minister George Chambers toured the U.K., Japan, China, India, Hong Kong, South Korea, and Austria to promote trade and investment.

(ROD PRINCE)

This article updates the *Macropædia* article The WEST INDIES: *Trinidad and Tobago.*

URUGUAY

A republic of eastern South America, Uruguay lies on the Atlantic Ocean. Area: 176,215 sq km (68,037 sq mi). Pop. (1985 est.): 3,012,100. Cap.: Montevideo. Monetary unit: new peso, with (Oct. 21, 1985) a free rate of 115.30 new pesos to U.S. $1 (165.34 new pesos = £1 sterling). Presidents in 1985, Gen. Gregorio Conrado Álvarez Armelino and, from March 1, Julio María Sanguinetti Cairolo.

Following 12 years of military government, Uruguay returned to civilian rule on March 1, 1985, when Julio María Sanguinetti (*see* BIOGRAPHIES) was sworn in as president. Soon after his victory in the November 1984 elections, Sanguinetti began attempts to establish political consensus. His aim to form a government that would include all the major parties as well as his own Colorado Party was limited to the extent that members of the opposition generally declined Cabinet positions. However, the defeated presidential candidate of the Unión Cívica, Juan Vicente Chiarino, and two National (Blanco) Party sympathizers, Enrique Iglesias and Raúl Ugarte, accepted Cabinet appointments. Representatives of the parties, trade unions,

Julio María Sanguinetti (right) is congratulated by U.S. Secretary of State George Shultz upon his inauguration as president of Uruguay.

Pope John Paul II accepts gifts from representatives of the Amazon Indians of Venezuela during his January visit to that nation. During the visit the pope spoke out strongly in support of traditional church teachings.
AP/WIDE WORLD

and employers met early in the year and reached broad agreement on most political and economic issues, except for labour relations and amnesty for political prisoners.

The new government immediately lifted bans on several organizations, relaxed laws restricting freedom of the press, and allowed political exiles to return to the country. However, frustrated expectations of immediate increases in wages led to a series of damaging strikes. The militancy of labour demands ended the national dialogue and resulted in a one-day general strike in September. At the same time, efforts continued to bring army officers accused of human rights violations to justice.

(ALEXANDER JOHNS CAMPBELL)

VENEZUELA

A republic of northern South America. Venezuela lies on the Caribbean Sea. Area: 912,050 sq km (352,144 sq mi). Pop. (1985 est.): 17,317,000. Cap.: Caracas. Monetary unit: bolívar, with (Oct. 21, 1985) a main official rate of 14.57 bolívares to U.S. $1 (20.90 bolívares = £1 sterling). President in 1985, Jaime Lusinchi.

In January 1985 Luis Matos Azócar resigned as minister in charge of Venezuela's state coordination and planning office (Cordiplán) after he had been outspokenly critical of the economic austerity measures imposed by Pres. Jaime Lusinchi's government. The result of this move and a Cabinet reshuffle announced in March was to strengthen the economic hand of Minister of Development Héctor Hurtado Navarro. Leopoldo Carnevalli was transferred from the Central Budget Office to become the minister in charge of Cordiplán. A new appointment to the Cabinet was that of Carmelo Lauría Lesseur, former governor of Caracas, as secretary to the presidency. The new foreign minister was Simón Alberto Consalvi, who had held the same position under former president Carlos Andrés Pérez in the 1970s.

In August President Lusinchi vetoed a series of reforms that would have established a primary-style system for choosing presidential candidates in place of a system controlled by the parties at the national level. The change was advocated by supporters of Pérez, who had begun an informal campaign for the presidency. Lusinchi's reaction was to speak out against the reelection of any former president. He feared that the Pérez campaign would create added potential for divisions within his administration.

The debate had the effect of diverting the attention of the ruling Acción Democrática (AD) party from the opposition Social Christian Party (COPEI). In September COPEI proposed a new labour law that was more favourable to workers than was the existing AD-sponsored legislation. The labour vote had been instrumental in sweeping the AD to power in the 1983 elections. The ruling party could not therefore reject the proposed legislation without the risk of alienating the unions. A congressional committee was set up to study the proposed legislation.

In March Hemmy Croes, a leading trade unionist and member of the Central Committee of the Venezuelan Communist Party, was shot dead outside his home in Caracas. This followed the murder during the previous month of Juan Luis Ibarra Riverol, the lawyer representing Lieut. Col. Luis Alfonso Godoy, who had brought charges of corruption against three former defense ministers in the government of Lusinchi's predecessor, Luis Herrera Campíns. Godoy attributed "intellectual responsibility" for the death to the three men. It later emerged that the murder had been carried out by military personnel, apparently in revenge for the fact that they had not been paid for information supplied in support of the charges. Godoy was compulsorily retired from the Army for upsetting military discipline and promoting scandal.

In mid-May the government and its committee of advisory banks reached agreement for restructuring national debts of $21.1 billion. The agreement sanctioned the rescheduling of the debt over 12½ years at 1.125% above the London interbank rates or above the basic interest rate of the national bank of the country concerned. Venezuela was to pay $750 million to the banks once the rescheduling agreement came into effect.

At the end of June new rules amending the country's restrictive foreign-investment laws were issued. They allowed the transfer of any money arising from the sale of equity and the registration of new foreign investment in the home currency of the foreign investor as well as its equivalent in bolívares at the free-market rate of exchange. Special incentives were introduced for foreign-owned firms that exported more than 80% of their production outside the Andean Group of countries; their obligation to sell shares to domestic investors was lifted, as was the limit placed on profits they could remit from their exports.

(MICHAEL WOOLLER)

Oceania

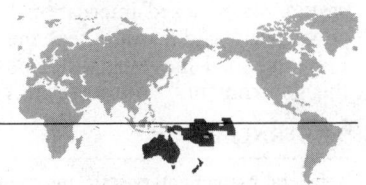

OCEANIAN AFFAIRS

During 1985 defense and nuclear issues provided an important theme in South Pacific affairs, as well as dominating relations with countries outside the region.

The South Pacific Forum. The 13 members of the South Pacific Forum—Australia, the Cook Islands, Fiji, Kiribati, Nauru, New Zealand, Niue, Papua New Guinea, the Solomon Islands, Tonga, Tuvalu, Vanuatu, and Western Samoa—held their annual meeting at Rarotonga, capital of the Cook Islands, in August 1985. A year earlier, meeting in Tuvalu, the members had agreed to work toward establishing a nuclear-free zone in the South Pacific. To that end, a working party consisting of representatives from all the member states was set up. The result was a treaty prohibiting the manufacture, testing, and stockpiling of nuclear arms in the region. The treaty also embodied a clause that guaranteed the passage of nuclear-armed or nuclear-powered vessels through the region; each country was left free to decide whether or not it would allow such ships to enter its ports.

The concept of establishing a nuclear-free zone was endorsed by all members, and eight countries—Australia, the Cook Islands, Fiji, Kiribati, New Zealand, Niue, Tuvalu, and Western Samoa—signed the treaty immediately. The remainder had to refer the document to their governments before signature. The treaty would come into effect once it had been ratified by eight member governments.

At the Forum meeting, New Zealand's Prime Minister David Lange proposed that members consider establishing a regional security pact, which would include a centre for coordinating maritime surveillance and the introduction of military training in the islands where at present there was none. Of the member countries, only Australia, New Zealand, Fiji, and Papua New Guinea possessed armies, while the other members relied on small police forces for security. Australia and New Zealand had been critical of Kiribati's proposal to grant fishing rights to the U.S.S.R.

Nevertheless, the deal was signed in August, and Tuvalu was considering entering into a similar arrangement with the Soviets. Kiribati's decision was apparently prompted mainly by frustration over extensive poaching by U.S. fishing vessels.

ANZUS Under Threat. U.S. influence within the region came under much greater threat from the disarray within the ANZUS alliance, which grouped Australia, New Zealand, and the U.S. Prime Minister Lange's Labour Party government had been elected to power in July 1984 on a manifesto that included a commitment to deny port facilities to nuclear-armed or nuclear-powered vessels. In effect, the policy would mean a total ban on U.S. naval vessels, since it was established practice within the U.S. Navy to neither confirm nor deny that any of its ships was carrying nuclear weapons.

The U.S. administration sought an immediate confrontation over the issue by requesting port facilities for one of its ships at the end of the ANZUS Sea Eagle exercises planned for March 1985. In February Lange turned down the request. The row escalated quickly, and by mid-February the U.S. government had announced retaliatory action: it would reduce significantly its intelligence-sharing cooperation with New Zealand, and it threatened to withdraw trade preferences enjoyed by New Zealand's products in U.S. markets.

In September the New Zealand government offered a compromise whereby its Cabinet would decide whether to grant port entry to a vessel according to its own evaluation of the likelihood of its carrying nuclear weapons. In reaching its decision, the Cabinet would seek no clarification from the U.S. The formula had been used successfully during ANZUS exercises in 1984, when U.S. aircraft that were nuclear capable but judged not to be carrying nuclear weapons entered the country. However, when Deputy Prime Minister Geoffrey Palmer took the proposal to the U.S. in September, it was rejected. The rift seemed no closer to being healed, and a bill that would make the ban on nuclear ships into law was introduced in Parliament in December.

The New Zealand government argued that the ANZUS alliance had been set up under a conventional treaty and that none of its articles established nuclear obligations. The U.S. administration, however, interpreted the move as a

At the August 1985 meeting of the South Pacific Forum, representatives of the 13 member states considered New Zealand's proposal to create a regional security pact.

clear threat to the alliance. The position of the third party in the alliance was an extremely difficult one. On the one hand, Australia and the U.S. already shared a substantial bilateral nuclear-arms commitment through their joint military bases in Australia, and since the end of World War II the U.S. had steadily replaced the U.K. as Australia's protector in the event of external military threat. On the other hand, New Zealand was Australia's closest partner in the old Commonwealth, and New Zealanders were among the country's oldest comrades-in-arms. Moreover, the two left-wing governments might have been expected to join forces in ideological opposition to the conservative U.S. administration. Indeed, there were sections of the Australian Labor Party who wished that Prime Minister Robert Hawke would be as resolute as Lange. Hawke's pragmatic response to the standoff within ANZUS was to blame both the parties while at the same time maintaining Australia's links with each country. However, Australia's concern over the nuclear issues was evidenced by the report of a royal commission investigation into the nuclear tests carried out in Australia by the U.K. in the 1950s and early 1960s. (See *Australia:* Sidebar, below.)

New Zealand received support from a number of other South Pacific nations, among them Papua New Guinea, which described the U.S. as "a reckless bully." The U.S.S.R. took the opportunity, when praising Lange's action, to suggest that it signaled deep dissent within the Western alliance. Lange retorted that he was not anti-American and warned the Soviets not to interfere in New Zealand's affairs. U.K. Prime Minister Margaret Thatcher, mindful of the strong antinuclear lobbies in many NATO countries, threw her weight behind the U.S. attempts to bring New Zealand to heel.

The Greenpeace Affair. New Zealand was the site of the year's single most dramatic incident in the region, and once again nuclear issues were at the heart of the matter. On July 10 the *Rainbow Warrior,* flagship of the environmental pressure group Greenpeace, sank in Auckland Harbour after explosives had torn a hole in the hull of the vessel. A Greenpeace photographer was killed. The *Rainbow Warrior* was to have led a flotilla of small boats to Mururoa Atoll, in French Polynesia, to protest against France's program of nuclear testing there. The South Pacific Forum had repeatedly expressed its opposition to the nuclear testing.

The affair sparked a serious diplomatic row between New Zealand and France. New Zealand's inquiries into the sabotage quickly uncovered a trail leading to France, and two French agents, Alain Mafart and Dominique Prieur, were arrested and charged with murder, arson, and conspiracy. French Pres. François Mitterrand's flying visit to Mururoa on September 13, while perhaps motivated by a desire to bolster his support at home in the face of mounting accusations, was viewed by South Pacific nations as inflammatory. On September 22, almost 11 weeks after the sinking of the *Rainbow Warrior,* the French government publicly admitted its responsibility when it confirmed that its external security agents had acted under orders in carrying out the attack. The two agents went on trial in November, but in a surprise move they pleaded guilty to the lesser crimes of manslaughter and sabotage, and the original charges were dropped. Both were sentenced to ten years in prison. The affair had far-reaching consequences for the French government at home (*see* Western Europe: *France,* above), but no less so in the South Pacific region, where France's standing had already suffered as a result of events in New Caledonia (see *Dependent States,* below). Lange described the *Rainbow Warrior* incident as "a sordid

case of state-backed international terrorism." The French government said it would seek the agents' early return, but Lange insisted they would not be deported "in the life of this government." (A. R. G. GRIFFITHS; LOUISE WATSON)

AUSTRALIA

A federal parliamentary state and member of the Commonwealth, Australia occupies the smallest continent and includes the island state of Tasmania. Area: 7,682,300 sq km (2,966,200 sq mi). Pop. (1985 est.): 15,749,000. Cap.: Canberra. Monetary unit: Australian dollar, with (Oct. 21, 1985) a free rate of $A1.42 to U.S. $1 ($A2.04 = £1 sterling). Queen, Elizabeth II; governor-general in 1985, Sir Ninian Martin Stephen; prime minister, Robert J. Hawke.

Domestic Affairs. Support for the government of Prime Minister Robert (Bob) Hawke, which began 1985 in a strong position, steadily deteriorated as the year progressed. After his Australian Labor Party (ALP) won a clear victory over the Liberal and National parties in the December 1984 general elections, Hawke strengthened his second ministry with some judicious appointments. Two senators who had made heavy weather of their Cabinet responsibilities were demoted; Gareth Evans was moved from the high-profile post of attorney general to become resources and energy minister, while Gordon Scholes, who was replaced as defense minister by Kim Beazley, left the Cabinet to become territories minister. By midyear, however, it was clear that the Cabinet reshuffle was not enough. Such serious defects had become evident in the Hawke government that public opinion polls suggested that the ALP would lose office to the Liberal Party should an election be held.

A series of disasters and policy turnabouts, especially in economic matters and foreign policy, led to a downward revision of popular support for the prime minister himself. Hawke accepted some of the blame but warned his ministers to think before they acted. Throughout 1985 Hawke and his Cabinet were clearly out of touch with public opinion. One of the first signs of this was the failure of the ALP to estimate correctly the strength of the antinuclear lobby. The Nuclear Disarmament Party (NDP), formed by a breakaway faction of the ALP and taking part in elections for the first time in December 1984, won a seat in the Senate. Nationwide, the NDP polled 6.8% of the Senate vote. However, at its inaugural national conference in April the NDP lost the support of several key figures, including the newly elected senator, Jo Vallentine, because of fears that the party was being taken over by the Socialist Workers Party, a far-left group with an estimated national membership of only 300. Hawke's greatest failure during the year, however, was his ill-advised attempt to call a meeting of persons interested in tax reform (*see* below).

The integrity of the government was damaged by two sensational court cases with political overtones. Norman Gallagher, general secretary of the Builders' Laborers Federation (BLF), was found guilty of accepting bribes and sent to prison. At the centre of the case were two beach houses constructed for Gallagher by major building companies as insurance against disruptions at their work sites. Directors of the companies concerned were also found guilty and fined. The ALP tried desperately and, to some extent, effectively to distance itself from the problems of the BLF. Because of the sustained record of industrial lawlessness by the BLF, and despite warnings by the Australian Council of Trade Unions (ACTU) that it was hostile to the move, Minister for Industrial Relations Ralph Willis and Prime Minister Hawke decided to introduce a special law to deregister the union.

Antinuclear demonstrations drew an estimated 170,000 persons in Sydney and some 300,000 nationwide on Palm Sunday, March 31.
AP/WIDE WORLD

Far more serious for the government was the trial of Lionel Murphy, a former ALP federal attorney general and the first Australian High Court judge to face a criminal charge, who in September was found guilty of attempting to pervert the course of justice. He was sentenced to 18 months in prison for seeking to influence committal proceedings against Morgan Ryan, a solicitor charged with forging immigration documents. While Murphy appealed his sentence, Hawke appeared to vacillate when he failed to act in reply to a call from the Liberal Party that Murphy be sacked if he refused to step down from the bench. In November an appeal court granted Murphy the right to a retrial, to take place in 1986.

In September the leadership of the Liberal Party changed hands unexpectedly. In a stormy meeting of the parliamentary party, Andrew Peacock was unsuccessful in his attempt to obtain an undertaking from his deputy, John Howard (*see* BIOGRAPHIES), that he would not challenge him for the leadership. Peacock resigned, and Howard was elected to replace him by a convincing majority. A former treasurer under Malcolm Fraser, Howard was expected, by leading the party further to the right, to present a clearer alternative to the policies of the ALP government.

In 1983 the Hawke government had established an inquiry into industrial relations to be undertaken by Keith Hancock, an economics professor, together with represen-

Fallout from the British Nuclear Tests

In July 1984 the Australian government appointed a royal commission to inquire into nuclear tests carried out by the U.K. government on the Monte Bello islands, off the coast of Western Australia, and at two sites, Emu and Maralinga, in South Australia during the period 1952–63. The impetus for the inquiry came from press reports, which reached a crescendo in the early 1980s, suggesting that servicemen and Aboriginals had died as a result of exposure to radiation.

After hearing evidence in the U.K. and Australia, the commission presented its report in November 1985. In a detailed study of 12 major bomb detonations, the report found that on several occasions tests were undertaken when weather conditions were unsuitable; the Monte Bello islands were judged inappropriate as a test site because prevailing winds carried fallout across a wide area of the mainland. On the

question of health risks to the Australian population in general, the report maintained that, although it found no positive evidence that the tests had caused deaths, "it is probable that cancers which would not otherwise have occurred have been caused."

In the first of two major recommendations, the commission held the U.K. government responsible for decontaminating test areas. Earlier efforts to clean up the sites undertaken in 1967 and 1979 were judged inadequate and misguided, and two treaties absolving the U.K. of further responsibility for decontamination were dismissed in the light of evidence that large amounts of plutonium remained scattered and buried at Maralinga, in particular. In its second recommendation the commission found the Australian government responsible for compensating Aboriginals for the loss of access to traditional lands.   (LOUISE WATSON)

Lionel Murphy, the first judge of the Australian High Court ever to face criminal indictment, speaks to reporters as he emerges from the courtroom. Murphy was convicted in September.
THE BULLETIN/AUSTRALIAN CONSOLIDATED PRESS, LTD.

tatives of capital and labour. The Hancock inquiry, which reported its findings in 1985, recommended the amalgamation of some small trade unions and the removal of penal industrial sanctions. The first major review of the arbitration system for 80 years, it contained no arguments for radical change and supported the existing established system of conciliation and arbitration. Also in 1985 Justice Robert Marsden Hope published the report of his investigation into Australia's security and intelligence organizations. While observing that these organizations were functioning well, Hope pointed out that criticism weakened morale and gave away useful information on the methods used by the security forces, thus adversely affecting their performance. The report also recommended that a new post be created—an inspector general on intelligence and security—to act as an independent overseer of the various security agencies.

Considerable controversy was generated by the organization of a cricket tour of South Africa in which major figures in Australian cricket agreed to take part—at the cost of their future careers in Australia and in defiance of government policy. Hawke made personal attacks on some members of the rebel team but at length realized that in doing so he was out of tune with elements of public opinion and withdrew his more extreme remarks.

Sir Brian Murray resigned as state governor of Victoria on October 3 after admitting that he had accepted free airline tickets from Continental Airlines. The resignation came after a period of strained relations between Murray and John Cain, ALP state premier of Victoria, who had expressed concern at the office of governor becoming the subject of gossip. The opposition charged that the state government had set out to force the resignation of Murray, who had been appointed by the previous Liberal administration.

Foreign Affairs. The year 1985 was a bad one for Australia's policymakers. Apart from the disastrous foundering of the ANZUS defense treaty between Australia, New Zealand, and the U.S. (see *Oceanian Affairs,* above), foreign relations were seriously damaged when both Hawke and Foreign Minister William (Bill) Hayden made spectacular gaffes that contributed to a loss of confidence among foreign investors.

In February Hawke left for overseas talks planned to cement relations with the European Communities (EC) and the U.S. No sooner had he arrived in Brussels than word reached him that a storm had broken at home over the government's decision to help the U.S. test its MX intercontinental ballistic missile. In Hawke's absence, Minister of Defense Beazley had revealed that deep-sea acoustic sensors necessary for the missile tests had already been laid in international waters about 320 km (200 mi) off the Tasmanian coast. Critics within the ALP were quick to point out that the government's efforts to assist the U.S. in developing the missile were inconsistent with its policy on the need for international disarmament.

Faced with the fury of his party and the condemnation of public opinion, Hawke backed down, changed the policy, and was fortunate that the U.S. administration, more concerned with the actions of New Zealand and their effects on ANZUS, tried to help Hawke out of his embarrassing loss of face. However, investors in the U.S. were not as forgiving. By selling off Australian dollars they showed that they regarded Hawke's backdown as a signal that he was still a pawn of the extreme left wing in the ALP. In explaining how he, along with Hayden and former minister of defense Scholes, had come to make the original decision on MX testing, Hawke said: "We have a security committee management which must obviously operate in certain sensitive areas. It is quite clear that not all decisions in this sort of area are capable of being taken through the full committee and Cabinet process." Hawke paid a heavy price for the committee system by being publicly attacked and humiliated by his caucus colleagues, many of whom were frustrated and concerned that such a sensitive matter had not been brought before them. Opposition leader Howard summed up feeling in the U.S., where he found surprise and disappointment that Australia had rescinded its agreement.

Relations between Australia and the U.S. had more than their usual number of ups and downs in 1985. Another potentially serious dispute arose when the *National Times* published an article alleging that the U.S. government had repositioned a spy satellite controlled from its military base at Pine Gap, Northern Territory, so that it could spy on Greece and other Mediterranean countries. Australia's large Greek community was outraged, and Greek ethnic members of Parliament demanded that Hawke prevent the U.S. from spying on what was, after all, a friendly Western government. A third difficulty arose when Australia declined to assist the U.S. with the development of its

Strategic Defense Initiative, or "Star Wars" program. The government's opposition was based on the fear that the current nuclear balance between the superpowers provided a reasonably stable deterrent, whereas the "Star Wars" program, if successful, would upset the balance.

Foreign Minister Hayden's problems concerned Australia's relations with the Association of Southeast Asian Nations (ASEAN). Hayden's situation was particularly unfortunate because he had made a point of stressing the need for Australia to have harmonious contact with ASEAN's member countries—the Philippines, Thailand, Singapore, Malaysia, Indonesia, and Brunei. The worst crisis in Australia-ASEAN relations developed when Hayden became involved in diplomatic quarrels between Thailand and Vietnam. Hayden believed Vietnamese leaders when they denied—falsely—that Vietnamese forces based in Kampuchea had made incursions into Thai territory to attack the forces of the Democratic Kampuchea government-in-exile. During his visit to Vietnam, Hayden also met with Kampuchean Prime Minister Hun Sen, thereby angering the leaders of ASEAN countries, who did not recognize the Hun Sen government. Ian McPhee, opposition spokesman for foreign affairs, described Hayden as an "amateur" and said that his poorly timed visit had undermined ASEAN's position at the United Nations and reduced Australia's credibility in the region. The Chinese government described Hayden as a "cat's-paw," and Hayden himself, with some chagrin, sent a stiff protest note to his Vietnamese counterpart, Nguyen Co Thach, regarding the misleading information he had received on Vietnamese troop movements.

The general secretary of the Chinese Communist Party, Hu Yaobang (Hu Yao-pang), was one of Australia's most important foreign visitors in 1985. Hu addressed the National Press Club as well as meeting public figures and ordinary citizens on a tour that emphasized the strengthening of bilateral ties between Australia and China.

The Economy. High unemployment and exchange-rate fluctuations proved difficult factors for the government to manage. Although the number of people out of work fell by 4,400 in May 1985, there were still more than 600,000 people registered as unemployed. The seasonally adjusted unemployment rate at that time was 8.4%, and it hovered around that figure throughout the year.

The Australian dollar suffered a major fall in value during the year. After beginning the year at U.S. $0.82, it reached its lowest value of U.S. $0.63 in late April before recovering slightly to around U.S. $0.70. It fell even further against the pound sterling and other currencies, losing about 20% of its value against the currency value of Australia's major trading partners. The dramatic and largely unpredicted decline was blamed on the country's poor international image, which, in turn, was blamed on various factors, including the Treasury's abandonment of money-supply targets, the crisis within ANZUS, the administration's strained relations with the U.S., and the triumph of the left-wing of the ALP, who prevented Hawke from reintroducing fees for university students. While in theory the depreciation of the currency might have offered unexpected relief from the widening trade deficit, in fact import businesses showed strong growth.

The dollar failed to rally and indeed might have been further harmed by Hawke's ill-advised conduct at a general meeting held in June to discuss tax reform. As part of his election policy, Hawke had pledged to gather together representatives of all sections of society—business people, trade unionists, economists, farmers, women, Aborigines, exporters, importers, and tax accountants—who together were expected, within the dignified confines of Parliament

House in Canberra, to submerge their differences and agree on a consensus policy to achieve tax reform. By the time the so-called tax summit was held, seven months after the election, the economic climate had worsened to such an extent that it appeared extremely unlikely that any consensus could be reached. Matters were made worse when Treasurer Paul Keating signaled in advance his determination to introduce a broadly based consumption tax of 12.5% in return for income tax concessions.

When the tax summit began on July 1, Parliament House was guarded by baton-carrying police. Between 20,000 and 40,000 farmers gathered on the lawns outside, encouraged in their hostility to the Hawke-Keating package by Sir Johannes Bjelke-Petersen, state premier of Queensland. Even before the summit began, public opinion polls showed that for the first time the leader of the opposition—at the time, Andrew Peacock—was more popular with the electorate than Hawke, who had hitherto been considered invincible. As the conference proceeded, the government abandoned its prepared position and fell in with the wishes of the ACTU. The views of all other participants at the meeting were ignored as Hawke retreated before the hostility of public opinion and dropped the idea of a consumption tax. Keating, who had staked his reputation on the acceptance of his consumption tax plans, quipped that the end of the conference was "like Ben Hur. We crossed the line with one wheel off the chariot." By the end of the summit, most interest groups and most members of the general public agreed that the summit had been largely a waste of time, while for both Hawke and Keating it was a political disaster.

Simon Crean, senior vice-president of the ACTU, proved to have far more influence than the Treasury expected when he said that the ACTU gave no support to Keating's package. Crean argued that the proposed consumption tax and offsetting reductions in income tax were unacceptable because they benefited those earning high incomes more than those with low and middle incomes. Any optimism among high-income earners was dashed when the government wiped out the concessional rebate system for life insurance premiums, old age pensions, tuition, and local taxes. Under the old system, about 6% of high-income earners made claims for outlays in excess of $A2,000 on such expenses. More importantly, Keating closed the tax loophole known as "negative gearing" that had allowed earners borrowing large amounts of money to buy unprofitable rental properties and claim interest payments as tax deductions. Critics of Keating's move claimed that the government would have to invest $A6 billion to make up the shortfall in rental accommodations that would be caused by the exodus of private investors discouraged by the new laws.

The agricultural sector was troubled by the U.S. administration's moves to boost its own farm exports. The Australian Wheat Board warned that up to one-third of wheat export income could be under threat. Minister for Primary Industry John Kerin personally informed the U.S. administration of Australia's concern and its fears that a trade war between the EC and the U.S. would devastate Australia's primary producers.

The year saw strong increases in retail and motor vehicle sales, while private consumption and private business investment exceeded government targets of 2.5 and 5%, respectively. The budget, presented on August 20, contained little of significance apart from a promise to establish training schemes to fight unemployment among young people and a plan to provide rebates to farmers on diesel fuel excise.   (A. R. G. GRIFFITHS)

FIJI

A parliamentary state and member of the Commonwealth, Fiji occupies an island group in the South Pacific Ocean. Area: 18,274 sq km (7,056 sq mi). Pop. (1985 est.): 692,000. Cap.: Suva. Monetary unit: Fiji dollar, with (Oct. 21, 1985) a free rate of F$1.10 to U.S. $1 (F$1.58 = £1 sterling). Queen, Elizabeth II; governor-general in 1985, Ratu Sir Penaia Ganilau; prime minister, Ratu Sir Kamisese Mara.

During 1985 the appointment of a second deputy prime minister, Minister of Finance Mosese Qionibaravi, who joined Minister of Fijian Affairs Ratu David Toganivalu, caused renewed speculation about Prime Minister Ratu Sir Kamisese Mara's eventual successor. The opposition National Federation Party remained divided. Both it and the ruling Alliance Party were threatened by the formation of the Fiji Labour Party.

A balance of payments surplus in 1984, the first in four years, was caused largely by record earnings from tourism, which surpassed those from sugar. However, cyclones in January 1985 that left 30 dead and 6,000 homeless caused a sharp downturn in tourist arrivals.

In January Japanese Prime Minister Yasuhiro Nakasone visited Fiji and promised increased aid, as well as a lower tariff for Fijian exports. When Hu Yaobang (Hu Yao-pang), the general secretary of the Chinese Communist Party, visited in April, he arranged sugar purchases from Fiji and promised $800,000 in development aid. Critical of New Zealand's antinuclear policy, Fiji took steps to strengthen ties with the U.S.   (BARRIE MACDONALD)

This article updates the *Macropædia* article PACIFIC ISLANDS: *Fiji*.

KIRIBATI

A republic in the western Pacific Ocean and member of the Commonwealth, Kiribati comprises the former Gilbert Islands, Banaba (Ocean Island), the Line Islands, and the Phoenix Islands. Area: 849 sq km (328 sq mi). Pop. (1985 est.): 65,000. Cap.: Bairiki. Monetary unit: Australian dollar, with (Oct. 21, 1985) a free rate of $A1.42 to U.S. $1 ($A2.04 = £1 sterling). President (*berititenti*) in 1985, Ieremia Tabai.

Kiribati attracted international attention and criticism in August 1985 when the government signed a fisheries agreement with the U.S.S.R. Although several Pacific Island states were approached by the Soviets, only Kiribati responded positively. The agreement allowed 16 Soviet vessels to operate in its exclusive economic zone for an annual payment of $1.5 million, but it did not include port access or victualing facilities. At home, the move drew criticism from both the Roman Catholic and Protestant churches and a motion of no confidence, defeated 19–15, from the parliamentary opposition.

Earlier in the year Kiribati protested to the U.S. against unauthorized incursions by its fishing vessels. A fishing agreement with South Korea that had lapsed in 1982 was renewed. Kiribati used more than $A10 million in aid funds provided by the European Communities, the U.K., and Japan to purchase a purse seiner and a number of smaller vessels and to construct a fisheries wharf facility. It was announced that New Zealand intended to double its aid to Kiribati over the next year, while new aid funds were to be made available by the U.S. and China. Pres. Ieremia Tabai paid a five-day visit to China in June.

(BARRIE MACDONALD)

This article updates the *Macropædia* article PACIFIC ISLANDS: *Kiribati*.

NAURU

An island republic within the Commonwealth, Nauru lies in the Pacific Ocean about 1,900 km (1,200 mi) east of New Guinea. Area: 21 sq km (8 sq mi). Pop. (1985 est.): 8,000. Cap.: Yaren. Monetary unit: Australian dollar, with (Oct. 21, 1985) a free rate of $A1.42 to U.S. $1 ($A2.04 = £1 sterling). President in 1985, Hammer DeRoburt.

The long-projected libel action by Pres. Hammer DeRoburt against the U.S. publishers of the Guam-based *Pacific Daily News* moved into the courts in 1985. A federal jury in Honolulu found that articles alleging DeRoburt had made a secret loan to separatist groups in the Marshall Islands were false and defamatory. However, it failed to find "actual malice" and so denied his $40 million claim for damages.

The Nauru Phosphate Royalties Trust continued its policy of offshore investment on a grand scale when it began planning for a residential-commercial-industrial project in Hawaii. The project involved the construction of 1,700 residential town houses in a parklike development that also included a high-rise office building and light industrial and retail space. Architects Hawaii Ltd. and other local firms were to prepare plans for the multimillion-dollar development, spread over seven hectares (17 ac) and called 404 Piikoi Street after its location.   (A. R. G. GRIFFITHS)

This article updates the *Micropædia* article NAURU.

NEW ZEALAND

New Zealand, a parliamentary state and member of the Commonwealth in the South Pacific Ocean, consists of North and South islands and Stewart, Chatham, and other minor islands. Area: 268,046 sq km (103,493 sq mi). Pop. (1985 est.): 3,291,300. Cap.: Wellington. Monetary unit: New Zealand dollar, with (Oct. 21, 1985) a free rate of $NZ1.72 to U.S. $1 ($NZ2.46 = £1 sterling). Queen, Elizabeth II; governors-general in 1985, Sir David Stuart Beattie and, from November 22, Sir Paul Reeves; prime minister, David Russell Lange.

In 1985 New Zealand's Labour Party government, brought to power in the July 1984 general elections, introduced measures to cut income tax and impose a 10% goods and

REUTERS/POPPERFOTO

The Most Reverend Sir Paul Reeves (left), the first person of Maori descent to be named governor-general of New Zealand, is offered a traditional Maori greeting by Prime Minister David Lange on his arrival at Parliament for his installation.

ED GAMBLE © 1985 THE FLORIDA TIMES-UNION

service tax (GST). The move followed years of complaint over the stifling effect of higher levels of the income-tax system and of speculation as to when politicians would act on the findings of a formal inquiry recommending that taxation be based on spending. Finance Minister Roger Douglas presented the budget proposals in two parts, on June 13 and August 20. They provided for a $NZ1.5 billion reduction in the budget deficit to $NZ1.3 billion, which, at 2.8% of gross domestic product, would make it the lowest for 12 years. Corporate taxes were increased slightly, and companies were to be taxed on the value of perks such as cars and loans given to staff.

The introduction of GST, originally planned for April 1986, was postponed until October 1986. Low-income families were to receive support to deal with the expected 5% rise in prices that GST would bring. Labour faced criticism from its own industrial wing, which feared that low earners would suffer from the changes and fought to exclude essential foods from the tax, despite the government's determination to tax all goods. The government urged restraint in wage demands as the wage freeze imposed by the previous administration came to an end. In September 1985 independent economists from the Institute of Economic Research predicted that the annual average wage increase would be 13%. The inflation rate dropped from a record 5.1% in the quarter ended in June to 2.8% in the following quarter. The annual rate was expected to reach 17%.

By the end of its first 12 months in office, the Labour Party government had, among other things, floated the New Zealand dollar, introduced a bill of rights, provided schools with more teachers, set up new ministries for women and the environment, reopened a mission in New Delhi, India, with Sir Edmund Hillary as ambassador, and cut overseas borrowing. It attracted criticism for imposing a special tax on old-age pensions, despite an earlier resolve not to do so; for identifying itself closely with a controversial campaign to decriminalize homosexuality; and for failing to control soaring interest rates. The government's 17-seat majority was reduced when it lost a by-election in what was previously considered a safe Labour seat.

From an international perspective, the most newsworthy event of 1985 in New Zealand was the bombing and subsequent sinking of the *Rainbow Warrior,* flagship of the Greenpeace organization, in Auckland Harbour in July. Prime Minister David Lange led the government's outraged response to the act, the responsibility for which was subsequently attributed to two French secret service agents. Lange continued to promote his government's decision to ban nuclear-powered and nuclear-armed vessels from the country's ports in a significant show of independence and challenge to the U.S., the country that in practice would be most affected by the ruling. (See *Oceanian Affairs,* above.) The prime minister was criticized at home for a tour of African countries that was considered by some New Zealanders as pointless. Nonetheless, Lange maintained a high profile, even as the opposition National Party lamented the failure of its new leader, former justice minister Jim McLay, to match the impact of former party leader and prime minister Sir Robert Muldoon.

Sir Basil Arthur, speaker of the House of Representatives, died in office in May and was succeeded by Gerald Wall. Paul Reeves (*see* BIOGRAPHIES), Anglican archbishop of New Zealand, resigned his church office to take up appointment as governor-general, becoming the first person of Maori descent to fill the post. (JOHN A. KELLEHER)

See also *Dependent States,* below.

PAPUA NEW GUINEA

A parliamentary state and member of the Commonwealth, Papua New Guinea is situated in the southwestern Pacific Ocean and comprises the eastern part of the island of New Guinea, the islands of the Bismarck, Trobriand, Woodlark, Louisiade, and D'Entrecasteaux groups, and parts of the Solomon Islands, including Bougainville. Area: 462,840 sq km (178,704 sq mi). Pop. (1985 est.): 3,328,000. Cap.: Port Moresby. Monetary unit: kina, with (Oct. 21, 1985) a free rate of 0.95 kina to U.S. $1 (1.37 kinas = £1 sterling). Queen, Elizabeth II; governor-general in 1985, Sir Kingsford Dibela; prime ministers, Michael Somare and, from November 21, Paias Wingti.

Papua New Guinea's Prime Minister Michael Somare had a difficult year in 1985. While relations with Indonesia reached a stable equilibrium, domestic unrest rose to sen-

sational heights. Widespread lawlessness and a shortage of law enforcement resources led to a crime wave of dangerous proportions, and in June Somare was forced to declare a state of emergency and a curfew in Port Moresby. Housebreaking, robbery, and rape were attributed by him to an unwelcome drift into the capital of unemployed from the depressed countryside. In Parliament Somare commented that public order had deteriorated to a point where the lives and safety of all law-abiding citizens were at risk. On June 4 the Cabinet endorsed a bill to provide for the castration of rapists and hanging for gang rape or rape and murder. Somare commented that the measure was a response to calls from potential investors, businessmen, and women's groups, all of whom were willing to meet force with force.

On November 21 Somare left office after losing a no-confidence vote resulting from opposition to his economic policies. Paias Wingti, former deputy prime minister under Somare who formed his own party in March, was appointed to head a caretaker government until the next general election.

In April Somare visited the U.K., where he had talks with Prime Minister Margaret Thatcher and addressed the Royal Commonwealth Society. Visitors to Papua New Guinea during the year included Japanese Prime Minister Yasuhiro Nakasone and Chinese Communist Party General Secretary Hu Yaobang (Hu Yao-pang).

The tenth anniversary of Papua New Guinea's independence was celebrated on September 16.

(A. R. G. GRIFFITHS)

This article updates the *Macropædia* article EAST INDIES: *Papua New Guinea*.

SOLOMON ISLANDS

A parliamentary state and member of the Commonwealth, the Solomon Islands comprises a 1,450-km (900-mi) chain of islands and atolls in the western Pacific Ocean. Area: 27,556 sq km (10,640 sq mi). Pop. (1985 est.): 267,270. Cap.: Honiara. Monetary unit: Solomon Islands dollar, with (Oct. 21, 1985) a free rate of SI$1.56 to U.S. $1 (SI$2.23 = £1 sterling). Queen, Elizabeth II; governor-general in 1985, Baddeley Devesi; prime minister, Sir Peter Kenilorea.

Following general elections in October 1984, Solomon Mamaloni had been replaced as prime minister of the Solomon Islands by his predecessor, Sir Peter Kenilorea. One of Kenilorea's first priorities was to break the impasse in relations between the Solomon Islands and the U.S. that had followed the seizure of a U.S. fishing vessel in mid-1984 and the imposition of a retaliatory ban on Solomon Islands imports into the U.S. The owners later repurchased the vessel, while the American Tunaboat Association opened negotiations on a fishing agreement with the Solomon Islands.

In September 1985 the government faced a vote of no confidence moved by Mamaloni, who attempted to capitalize on discontent among public servants over the government's housing policy. The motion was defeated by 20–15. Kenilorea paid official visits to Taiwan and the U.K. In October he addressed the UN while en route to the Commonwealth heads of government meeting in The Bahamas.

Strong commodity prices on world markets, for copra in particular, had resulted in a trade surplus in 1984. The government was therefore able to use some of its own funds, as well as foreign aid, for development projects.

(BARRIE MACDONALD)

This article updates the *Macropædia* article PACIFIC ISLANDS: *Solomon Islands.*

TONGA

A monarchy and member of the Commonwealth, Tonga is an island group in the Pacific Ocean east of Fiji. Area: 747 sq km (288 sq mi). Pop. (1985 est.): 97,050. Cap.: Nuku'alofa. Monetary unit: pa'anga, with (Oct. 21, 1985) a free rate of 1.42 pa'anga to U.S. $1 (2.04 pa'anga = £1 sterling). King, Taufa'ahau Tupou IV; prime minister in 1985, Prince Fatafehi Tu'ipelehake.

The year 1985 began inauspiciously when Cyclones Eric and Nigel struck Tonga in January. Although no lives were lost, there was heavy damage to crops and buildings. Despite this setback, the economy showed greater strength than for several years. Boosted by tourism, rising commodity prices (especially for copra), and remittances from Tongans working overseas, reserves reached record levels. The 1985–86 budget increased duties on fuel, tobacco, and alcohol and imposed a new tax on accommodations and entertainment. Development funds, mostly from foreign aid, totaled 50% more than in 1984–85.

After South Pacific Island Airways was grounded by the U.S. Civil Aviation Board, talks aimed at establishing an alternative international service were initiated with the U.S. company Continental Airlines. Funds provided by the European Communities were used to begin work on an extension of the harbour at Nuku'alofa. The tourist industry received a boost when passengers were permitted to disembark from cruise liners on Sundays; however, Tonga's strict laws still prevented any trading on the Sabbath.

Acting on its declared policy of offering port facilities to friendly ships, in May Tonga welcomed the nuclear-powered cruiser USS *Texas*. (BARRIE MACDONALD)

This article updates the *Macropædia* article PACIFIC ISLANDS: *Tonga.*

TUVALU

A constitutional monarchy within the Commonwealth, Tuvalu comprises nine main islands and their associated islets and reefs in the western Pacific Ocean. Area: 24 sq km (9 sq mi). Pop. (1985): 8,229. Cap.: Funafuti. Monetary unit: Australian dollar, with (Oct. 21, 1985) a free rate of $A1.42 to U.S. $1 ($A2.04 = £1 sterling). Queen, Elizabeth II; governor-general in 1985, Fiatau Penitala Teo; prime minister, Tomasi Puapua.

Following elections in September 1985, Tomasi Puapua was returned to office as prime minister of Tuvalu. In July the government rejected a request from the U.S.S.R. for a license to fish in the islands' exclusive economic zone. At the annual conference of the South Pacific Forum in Rarotonga, Cook Islands, in August, Tuvalu signed the treaty establishing a nuclear-free zone in the South Pacific.

In recognition of Tuvalu's continuing difficulty in raising development funds, New Zealand announced an increase in its annual aid grant from $NZ800,000 to $NZ1.4 million. A Japanese survey of fisheries resources was extended into 1986, and funds provided by the European Communities were used to improve electricity services on Funafuti, the capital island. West Germany agreed to offer employment in its merchant marine to up to 50 graduates of the country's Maritime Training School.

Barclay's Bank, which owned 25% of Tuvalu's National Bank, discontinued management of its operations as part of its withdrawal from most island activities. It was replaced in Tuvalu by Westpac Bank of Australia.

(BARRIE MACDONALD)

This article updates the *Macropædia* article PACIFIC ISLANDS: *Tuvalu.*

VANUATU

The republic of Vanuatu, a member of the Commonwealth, comprises 12 main islands and some 60 smaller ones in the southwestern Pacific Ocean. Area: 12,190 sq km (4,707 sq mi). Pop. (1985 est.): 140,000. Cap.: Vila. Monetary unit: vatu, with (Oct. 21, 1985) a free rate of 102.93 vatu to U.S. $1 (147.60 vatu = £1 sterling). President in 1985, George Sokomanu; prime minister, the Rev. Walter Lini.

Cyclones Eric and Nigel struck Vanuatu in January 1985, causing serious crop damage on several islands and a shipping accident in which six people died. The disaster marked the start of a year of economic difficulty. Despite high prices for copra and other commodities, the value of exports fell short of imports by $A20 million. The vatu was devalued by 9.3%. Legislation fixing the minimum wage at 15,000 vatu (U.S. $150) a month, representing a 50% increase in some unskilled wage rates, was expected to cause a rise in unemployment in some areas.

There was continuing tension in relations with France. Vanuatu sought increased aid from the former colonial power despite disagreements over the sovereignty of Matthew and Flinders islands, located between Vanuatu and New Caledonia. Matthew Island was occupied by French marines in April. The government was also severely critical of French nuclear testing in French Polynesia. At the South Pacific Forum meeting in August, Vanuatu refused to sign the Australian-backed treaty setting up a nuclear-free zone in the region on the grounds that it did not go far enough.   (BARRIE MACDONALD)

This article updates the *Macropædia* article PACIFIC ISLANDS: *Vanuatu.*

WESTERN SAMOA

A constitutional monarchy and member of the Commonwealth, Western Samoa occupies an island group in the South Pacific Ocean. Area: 2,831 sq km (1,093 sq mi). Pop. (1985 est.): 160,000. Cap.: Apia. Monetary unit: tala, with (Nov. 20, 1985) a free rate of 2.17 tala to U.S. $1 (3.11 tala = £1 sterling). Head of state (*O le Ao o le Malo*) in 1985, Malietoa Tanumafili II; prime minister, Tofilau Eti Alesana.

Following general elections on Feb. 22, 1985, in which the Human Rights Protection Party retained power by winning 31 of 47 seats, Tofilau Eti Alesana was reelected unopposed as Western Samoa's prime minister by the members of the legislature. Shortly afterward, the resignation of the party's founder, Va'ai Kolone, threatened the government's majority, but it survived until December 27, when Tofilau resigned after the legislature rejected his budget. It was expected that Kolone would be appointed to succeed him early in 1986.

The fifth development plan, unveiled in January, placed emphasis on expanding export-oriented commercial agriculture. The Sauniatu hydroelectric power station, which was opened during the year, was expected to cut fuel imports to one-quarter of previous levels. In February the tala was floated, following the lead of New Zealand. Inflation was reduced to 12%, and the arrears on overseas loans were cleared.

During his visit in April, the general secretary of the Chinese Communist Party, Hu Yaobang (Hu Yao-pang), announced a $240,000 aid grant and an increased loan for the completion of a national sports stadium.

(BARRIE MACDONALD)

This article updates the *Macropædia* article PACIFIC ISLANDS: *Samoa.*

Dependent States

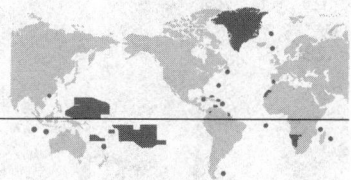

While attention was focused throughout 1985 on developments in New Caledonia, separatist movements were active in several other French overseas territories and départements. Meeting in Guadeloupe on April 5–7 for the first time, groups from Guadeloupe, Martinique, French Guiana, Réunion, Mayotte, and New Caledonia agreed to coordinate their independence strategies.

Europe and the Atlantic. At midnight on Feb. 4–5, 1985, the Spanish authorities reopened the gates at the frontier with Gibraltar, thus ending the 16-year blockade of the British colony. The move followed the signing of the Brussels agreement in November 1984 by the Spanish and U.K. governments, who had thereby agreed to implement the 1980 Lisbon Declaration, under which Spain was to lift border controls on condition that the U.K. agree to discuss the future of Gibraltar. With the implementation of the Lisbon Declaration, which removed a serious obstacle to Spain's accession to the European Communities (EC), certain rights were extended to Spaniards, including the right to work in the territory, in advance of Spain's membership coming into effect at the beginning of 1986.

The Spanish and U.K. foreign ministers opened talks on the future of Gibraltar in Geneva on February 5. The U.K. delegation included Sir Joshua Hassan, Gibraltar's chief minister. While U.K. Prime Minister Margaret Thatcher reiterated her commitment not to transfer sovereignty against the expressed wishes of Gibraltarians, the Spanish pointed out that discussion of the issue of sovereignty had not been excluded from the agenda. The Spanish were seeking to "reintegrate" Gibraltar with Spain while preserving the Gibraltarian way of life. Joe Bossano, leader of the opposition Gibraltar Socialist Labour Party and an advocate of self-determination, pledged to campaign against any Anglo-Spanish agreement.

There was little movement toward resolution of the dispute between the U.K. and Argentina over the Falkland Islands/Islas Malvinas. On November 27 the UN General Assembly overwhelmingly approved a resolution that, without mentioning sovereignty, called for talks to resolve the dispute. The vote was interpreted as a severe blow to the U.K. in its approach to the issue, since two U.K. amendments designed to include references to the islanders' right to self-determination were also heavily defeated. The new airport at Mount Pleasant, capable of taking long-range jet aircraft, was officially opened in a ceremony on May 12 attended by Prince Andrew.

On February 1 Greenland became the first country or territory to withdraw from the EC. Formalities were completed a month later than the due date of January 1 because the government of Ireland did not ratify the agreement until mid-January. Under the withdrawal terms, Greenland acquired "overseas countries and territories" status from the EC. A ten-year fisheries agreement granting EC fishing fleets access to Greenland's territorial waters was expected to bridge the gap created by the loss of EC funds.

Caribbean. Hubert Hughes was dismissed as Anguilla's minister of finance and lands in February after a dispute about a plan to introduce casino gambling. Chief Minister Emile Gumbs took over the finance portfolio. In Montser-

At a barricade erected by partisans of the Kanak Socialist National Liberation Front (FLNKS) in New Caledonia, a sign warns of their determination to win independence.
JEAN-CLAUDE FRANCOLON—GAMMA/LIAISON

rat the tourist industry continued its upturn. Overseas aid funds enabled plans to improve road and electric power systems to be initiated during the year.

Norman Saunders, chief minister of the Turks and Caicos Islands, and Stafford Missick, minister of commerce and development, were arrested on drug charges in Miami, Fla., on March 5. They resigned on March 22, and in September they were jailed for eight and ten years, respectively, and fined $50,000 each. Both were convicted of traveling to the U.S. to promote drug deals, and Missick was also found guilty of conspiring to import cocaine. Saunders was succeeded as chief minister by Nathaniel ("Bops") Francis, 72, who asked for U.S. assistance in fighting the drug trade.

In September the Cayman Islands government and Chamber of Commerce set up a joint study of ways to diversify the economy away from tourism and offshore finance. In the British Virgin Islands the chairman of the tourist board, Elihu Rhymer, who was also president of the privately owned airline company Air BVI, resigned in July over differences with Chief Minister Cyril Romney.

In general elections held in Bermuda on October 29, the governing United Bermuda Party led by Premier John Swan gained 5 seats to win 31 out of the 40 seats in the House of Assembly. The Progressive Labour Party (PLP) won seven seats, half the number it had secured in the February 1983 elections, while the National Liberal Party, newly formed by defectors from the PLP, won two. Lois Browne-Evans resigned as PLP leader in the wake of the defeat.

In the French overseas départements of French Guiana, Guadeloupe, and Martinique, elections to the *conseils généraux* in March produced gains for the left, which won control in the first two départements and increased its strength in Martinique. Early in the year a new bombing campaign by pro-independence militants in Guadeloupe killed three people, including a visitor from a U.S. cruise ship. Luc Reinette, leader of the island's banned Caribbean Revolutionary Alliance, who had been jailed in February for causing explosions, escaped from prison in June. At the end of July Guadeloupe was the scene of a week-long general strike and violent street demonstrations organized

by pro-independence groups. The demonstrations ended when a pro-independence activist, Georges Faisans, imprisoned in France, was released pending an appeal. Pres. François Mitterrand of France called for greater economic development of the départements during a three-day visit, amid tight security, to Guadeloupe and Martinique in early December.

The government of Maria Liberia-Peters in the Netherlands Antilles introduced a package of austerity measures in July to offset the effects of the closing on March 31 of the Exxon oil refinery on the island of Aruba. The government of Aruba, which depended on the refinery for one-third of its revenue, had already imposed similar measures. Aruba was due to pull out of the federation in January 1986. Closure of the Shell refinery in Curaçao, scheduled to take place at the end of September, was averted when the refinery was bought by the federal government, which then leased it to the Venezuelan state oil company, Petróleos de Venezuela.

The Puerto Rican administration of Gov. Rafael Hernández Colón, which took office in January, immediately set about improving economic relations with other Caribbean countries, notably by proposing to use $700 million of government money to promote "twin-plant" industrial projects in neighbouring islands. In October heavy rains from Tropical Storm Isabel triggered a mud-and-rock slide that buried a hillside shantytown in Ponce, killing some 150 people.

Africa. On April 18 the South African government announced that it intended to appoint a "transitional" government in South West Africa/Namibia, bringing an end to the period of direct rule from Pretoria that had begun in January 1983 when the Namibian administration resigned. The new administration, consisting of a 62-seat National Assembly and an 8-member Cabinet, was appointed in May and sworn in the following month at a ceremony in Windhoek attended by South African Pres. Pieter W. Botha. All 62 assembly members were drawn from the six-party Multi-Party Conference, a multiracial coalition; its largest member, the Democratic Turnhalle Alliance (DTA), filled 22 seats, while the remaining five parties each filled

8 seats. The South African move was directly counter to UN Resolution 435, which included a provision for direct elections in the territory in its schedule for achieving Namibian independence. In June the UN Security Council approved (by 13 votes to none, with 2 abstentions) a resolution calling for voluntary sanctions against South Africa in protest against its continued occupation of Namibia. The U.S. and the U.K. abstained; earlier they had made known their intention to veto a more strongly worded resolution calling for mandatory sanctions.

The Moroccan government announced plans to increase its military presence in Western Sahara, where it faced armed opposition from the forces of the independence movement, the Popular Front for the Liberation of Saguia el Hamra and Río de Oro (Polisario Front). Early in the year the Polisario Front shot down two light aircraft, one Belgian and the other West German, in the area. In September, claiming that it had "opened fire in legitimate self-defense," Polisario admitted responsibility for an attack on a Spanish trawler and naval patrol vessel off the coast. Two Spaniards were killed and six others held prisoner for more than a week. In response, the Spanish government closed down three Polisario Front information offices in Spain. In January the new military regime in Mauritania reaffirmed its policy of "strict neutrality" with regard to the dispute between Morocco and the Polisario Front. At the same time, it maintained its support for the Saharan Arab Democratic Republic, Western Sahara's government-in-exile established by Polisario. Since Mauritania had withdrawn its claim to part of the Western Sahara in 1979, the Moroccan government had accused Mauritania of involvement in Polisario activities.

Pacific. New Caledonia was at the centre of attention in 1985 as its constitutional status and development assumed unprecedented prominence in French politics. (*See* Western Europe: *France,* above.) Kanak demands for independence became more unified after the formation of the Kanak Socialist National Liberation Front (FLNKS), under the leadership of Jean-Marie Tjibaou (*see* BIOGRAPHIES), in September 1984. The strength of the movement was evidenced by the response to a call for a boycott of

elections to the Territorial Assembly the following month. The boycott, together with escalating violence, brought recognition in France that the proposed five-year delay before granting self-determination was not sustainable. Furthermore, progress could be made only on some basis that recognized that Kanaks were a minority in their own country and that a majority of voters in the territory would be opposed to severing links with France. A state of emergency was in force for the first six months of 1985. In January Edgard Pisani, the high commissioner, announced a revised plan that provided for a poll on the political future of New Caledonia by July and, if a majority so voted, the emergence of a "sovereign state" tied to France by a treaty of association; France would handle defense, security, economic development, and education. Also in January, President Mitterrand visited the territory and announced that France intended to establish a major naval facility, including a base for a nuclear-powered submarine, a decision that was taken as a sign of France's intention to remain in firm control of the territory.

Pisani's proposal was rejected as unworkable. He returned to Paris to take up the newly established post of minister for New Caledonian affairs and was replaced as high commissioner by Fernand Wibaux. In April French Prime Minister Laurent Fabius announced the "Fabius plan," which divided New Caledonia into four regions, each of which would have its own assembly, and established a new Territorial Assembly. Elections for these bodies were held on September 29. While the FLNKS won majorities in three of the four regions, the alliance of conservative anti-independence parties, with just over 60% of the overall vote, won control of the fourth and of the Territorial Assembly. In the worst of a series of bomb attacks apparently carried out by an anti-independence group, the Palace of Justice in Nouméa was destroyed on December 3.

French Polynesia also achieved prominence during the year when the French nuclear-testing program at Mururoa Atoll, the target of protests by the Greenpeace environmentalist pressure group, was marked by the bombing of that organization's ship *Rainbow Warrior* on July 10 by French secret service agents. (*See* Oceania: *Oceanian Af-*

GARY WILLIAMS—GAMMA/LIAISON

As much as 380 millimetres (15 inches) of rain in three days in October caused disastrous mudslides that destroyed whole communities in Puerto Rico and killed some 180 people.

fairs, above.) Despite embarrassment caused by the "Greenpeace affair" and continued protests from Pacific leaders, France carried on its tests. Visits by President Mitterrand and other leading politicians to the region during the year underlined France's commitment to the program. Under new constitutional arrangements that came into effect from September 1984, French Polynesia's leader, Gaston Flosse, was now designated as president. He obtained the agreement of both the Territorial Assembly and France to increase the number of assembly seats from 30 to 40 and to bring forward the next elections, due in 1987. He was also seeking increased powers for the Territorial Assembly once the elections were held.

In the U.S.-administered Trust Territory of the Pacific Islands, there was some slight progress toward decolonization. The conflict between the antinuclear constitution of the Republic of Palau (Belau) and the compact between three of the four island groups—the Federated States of Micronesia, Belau, and the Marshall Islands—and the U.S. governing future political, military, and economic relations remained unresolved. Nevertheless, the compact was approved by the Micronesians and was submitted to the U.S. Congress, which approved it, with amendments, in December. The compact, which provided for the retention of U.S. defense interests in the area, would require review by the island governments and endorsement of the UN before taking effect. Because of the delay in the dramatic increase in aid grants expected when final approval was forthcoming, some of the Micronesian governments were experiencing difficulties in meeting loan commitments entered into in anticipation of the new arrangements.

The U.S. announced a $3.8 million medical program for Marshall Islanders affected by nuclear testing in the 1940s and 1950s and a $42 million program to clean up Bikini Atoll. Meanwhile, some 250 Rongelap Islanders, concerned that their environment was still polluted from tests on neighbouring Eniwetok in 1954, moved to a small island in Kwajalein lagoon. Haruo Remeliik, reelected president of Belau in November 1984, was assassinated in June 1985. Political motives were assumed. Vice-Pres. Alfonso Oiterong served as acting president until Lazarus Salii was sworn in as Belau's second president in October. Salii had led Micronesia during its first political status negotiations with the U.S. in the 1960s.

In American Samoa, Peter Tali Coleman failed in his attempt to gain a third term as governor in defiance of the constitution. He was succeeded by A. P. Lutali, who sought greater involvement with Pacific neighbours rather than the U.S. The UN Special Committee on Decolonization moved to place the territory on the list of countries where it wished to see more rapid progress toward independence.

The Cook Islands was the venue for the annual meeting of the South Pacific Forum in August. The most important business was discussion of the Australian-backed treaty banning the manufacture, testing, storage, dumping, or use of nuclear weapons and materials in the South Pacific region. The treaty was signed by 8 of the 13 member states. The Forum also called for the early decolonization of New Caledonia but declined to admit a Kanak observer to its deliberations. (*See* Oceania: *Oceanian Affairs,* above.) In domestic politics, Premier Sir Thomas Davis survived in office despite an abortive motion of no confidence supported by Geoffrey Henry, who was later replaced as deputy premier by Terepai Maoate, and the collapse of the government coalition. The premier's Democratic Party retained office with the support of defectors from Henry's Cook Islands Party.

New Zealand invited a visiting mission from the UN Special Committee on Decolonization to visit Tokelau in 1986 to observe the changing situation and to hear the views of Tokelauans on their political status.

East Asia. The agreement reached between the U.K. and China in 1984 regarding the future status of Hong Kong was ratified by both the U.K. Parliament and the Chinese People's National Congress by the middle of April 1985. The agreement provided for the ending of U.K. sovereignty on July 1, 1997, when Hong Kong was to become a special administrative region of China. In 1984, addressing the question of political reform within the colony itself, Sir Edward Youde, governor of Hong Kong, had ruled out the possibility of direct elections in the immediate future to either the Executive Council or the Legislative Council, both made up of ex officio members and others appointed by the governor. However, on September 26 the first indirect elections were held to fill 24 seats on the Legislative Council, newly enlarged to 56 members. In June David Akers-Jones became chief secretary in succession to Sir Philip Haddon-Cave.

During a visit to Macão on May 27, Pres. António dos Santos Ramalho Eanes of Portugal revealed that talks between China and Portugal concerning the future of the territory were to begin in 1986. In the view of the Portuguese, the transfer of sovereignty to China was apparently inevitable. Adm. Vasco Almeida e Costa announced his intention to resign as governor of Macão at the end of the year. Eanes announced that he would leave the appointment of the next governor to his own successor as president, due to be elected in January 1986.

(BARRIE MACDONALD; ROD PRINCE; LOUISE WATSON)

This article updates the *Macropædia* articles HONG KONG; INDIAN OCEAN ISLANDS; PACIFIC ISLANDS; SOUTHERN AFRICA: *South West Africa/Namibia;* The WEST INDIES.

Polar Regions

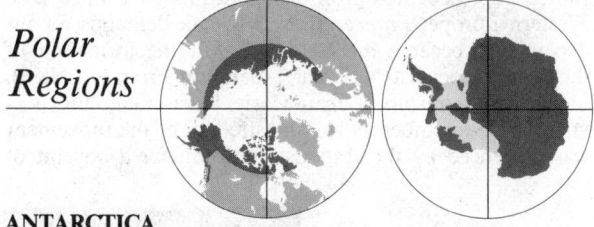

ANTARCTICA

Major events during the 1984–85 Antarctic summer field season included an international workshop on the Antarctic Treaty System held in Antarctica, the entrance of additional nations into Antarctic work, and the entrapment of a Soviet supply ship by late summer ice in the Amundsen Sea.

Fifty-seven persons from 24 nations met in early January at the Beardmore Glacier Camp only 640 km (400 mi) from the South Pole to examine the Treaty System and Antarctica's potential contributions to the nations of the world. The workshop, following the third world's challenge to the system in the UN, allowed treaty and nontreaty nations to better understand each other's views.

The Soviet vessel *Mikhail Somov* was trapped in the Amundsen Sea in March while conducting the annual resupply of Russkaya Station. The icebreaker *Vladivostok* from the Soviet Northern Sea Route fleet was sent to free the *Somov,* and by mid-July it had begun to break its way through some 640 km of ice. On July 26 the *Vladivostok* took the *Somov* in tow, and by August 3, after a lengthy struggle against ice 3.7 m (12 ft) thick in places, the *Somov* had been freed.

Other nations displayed their interest in Antarctica by establishing bases. China established the Great Wall sta-

Japanese researchers secure water samples from Don Quixote Pond in the Wright Valley of Antarctica. The pond consists of a layer of fresh water over a body of salt water.

LYNN JOHNSON—BLACK STAR

tion on Fildes Peninsula on King George Island in the South Shetlands, only 2 km (1.2 mi) from Bellingshausen (U.S.S.R.) and Rodolfo Marsh (Chile). Two ships, carrying construction workers and a scientific staff, arrived on Dec. 30, 1984, and by mid-February 1985 the station had been completed. Brazil and Uruguay also established stations on King George Island. Commandante Ferray (Brazil) supported research programs in marine biology, geology, and geophysics during the summer. Artigas (Uruguay), in Collins Harbour near the Chinese station, was the seventh station on the island.

The international conservation organization Greenpeace announced plans to establish a small four-man station in Antarctica during the 1985–86 summer season. Cuba became the 32nd nation to accede to the Antarctic Treaty; 16 of the 32 had consultative status.

National Programs. *Argentina.* Scientific work was conducted at six permanent and three temporary bases. A small party returned to burned-out Almirante Brown station in Paradise Bay and worked out of an emergency camp.

Australia. Marine biology and terrestrial geology dominated the program. Some 45 days were devoted to krill research in Prydz Bay from the *Nella Dan.* Geologic investigations concentrated on the Framnes Mountains of MacRobertson Land and on the detailed geologic mapping of the Stillwell Hills in Enderby Land.

Chile. The British Base T on Adelaide Island, unused since 1977, was transferred to Chile and renamed Teniente Carvajal. Three other bases were maintained, including Rodolfo Marsh on King George Island, where several families were living.

India. Mineral resource evaluation was emphasized in research conducted from India's permanent station, Dakshin Gangotri, on the Princess Astrid Coast. Geophysical surveys were conducted on the ice shelf and ocean bottom, and some seismic prospecting was also conducted. Fifteen men spent the 1985 winter at the base.

Japan. Marine geophysical surveys by the Japanese Agency for National Resources and Energy and the National Oil Corporation continued—in the current season, off Enderby Land. Two permanent stations were maintained, and a summer camp was established near the Sør Rondane Mountains.

New Zealand. Work began on the three-year CIROS (Cenozoic Investigations in the Ross Sea) offshore drilling project. A core was recovered through 168.9 m (554 ft) of glacial sediment down to bedrock before a major storm destroyed the drilling camp. While fieldwork was suspended until repairs could be made, the core was not damaged. Preliminary analysis suggested the scientifically rich samples are up to four million years old and contain evidence of a number of glacial events in the Ross Sea.

Norway. The largest Norwegian expedition in 25 years spent two summer months conducting geophysical, glaciological, geologic, and oceanographic research in the Weddell Sea and on the continent near longitudes 5° E and 10° W. In addition to resource-oriented research, studies were made of iceberg activity at sea and terrestrial ecology ashore.

U.S.S.R. The 30th Soviet Antarctic Expedition continued wide-ranging exploration of Antarctica. Plans were announced for the establishment of an eighth permanent station, on Berkner Island in the Weddell Sea. A new summer-only station, Soyuz, was established at Beaver Lake in the Prince Charles Mountains. Station maintenance included the construction of a packed-snow airstrip at Novolazarevskaya, similar to the one in operation at Molodezhnaya. Vostok station, deep in the interior of Antarctica, was again supplied by a tractor train from Mirnyy.

United Kingdom. The British Antarctic Survey introduced helicopters to fieldwork but continued to prohibit women scientists from working in Antarctica. Field surveys were conducted to determine the feasibility of constructing a hard runway at Rothera, where the summer snow

runway was used to support aircraft from British, Chilean, West German, and U.S. expeditions.

United States. Three permanent stations—Palmer, McMurdo, and Amundsen-Scott at the South Pole—were maintained, but Siple Station remained closed until late 1985. Major glaciologic work was concentrated at the Siple Coast on the eastern Ross Ice Shelf, where large ice streams drain the ice from Marie Byrd Land. The South Pole was the location for a major solar seismology project by U.S. and French scientists. The most significant geologic expeditions worked on Seymour Island searching for additional fossil deposits, in the Jones Mountains of Ellsworth Land, where detailed geologic mapping was emphasized, and near Mt. Takahe in Marie Byrd Land, where the volcanic geology of the area was investigated. Marine and oceanographic work was conducted from the Coast Guard icebreakers *Glacier* and *Polar Star* from the Antarctic Peninsula to Wilkes Land. The Seymour Island party also searched for Cretaceous-Tertiary boundary deposits to further study the theory that an asteroid hitting the Earth some 65 million years ago caused the extinction of the dinosaurs and other plant and animal life.

West Germany. Research continued at the permanent station, and the cooperative geologic and geophysical expedition Ganovex IV conducted research in North Victoria Land supported by two Dornier aircraft. While en route back to Germany one of the aircraft was shot down by guerrillas near Dakhla in the Western Sahara. Two pilots and the flight engineer were killed.

Other Nations. Both Sweden and The Netherlands indicated they would return to Antarctic work in the near future. Sweden had last had a major presence during the first international cooperative scientific expedition in 1949–52. Dutch scientists last worked in Antarctica in 1964–66. Italy announced plans for an Antarctic expedition and a permanent base near Terra Nova Bay, where meteorologic research would be emphasized.

International Activities. The third meeting of the Convention on the Conservation of Antarctic Marine Living Resources (CCAMLR) was held in Hobart, Tasmania. The conferees agreed to set limits on fin fishing in Antarctic waters and strongly encouraged governments to begin intensive research programs to determine how best to assist the recovery of fish stocks. Krill fishing was not affected by these limits. Krill harvesting data indicated that recent catches had decreased in quantity. It was assumed that this reflected difficulty in marketing rather than declining availability. The 13th consultative meeting of the Antarctic Treaty System was held in Brussels in October 1985. Discussions continued throughout the year on the development of a legal regime to govern possible mineral resource development in Antarctica. On December 16 the UN General Assembly voted 92–0 for a resolution affirming that all nations should share equitably in the management of Antarctic resources and in the benefits resulting from their exploitation, but the parties to the Antarctic Treaty, including the U.S. and the Soviet Union, abstained.

(PETER J. ANDERSON)

This article updates the *Macropædia* article ANTARCTICA.

ARCTIC REGIONS

Alaska. Despite falling oil prices, the development of Alaska's North Slope continued. Production of 250,000 bbl of oil daily was expected to begin in 1986 from new developments, such as the Kuparuk and Lisburne fields, just when the giant Prudhoe Bay field would start to decline. Thus North Slope oil output, critical to Alaska's economy, should be stable at least through 1988–89. In February it

was reported that the Sohio company estimated that up to 1,800,000,000 more barrels of oil should be recoverable from Prudhoe Bay than had originally been calculated, using new technology expected to be available within five years. Initial estimates of recoverable oil from the Prudhoe field were 9,600,000,000 bbl, of which just over 3,000,-000,000 bbl had been extracted by the end of 1984. In March ARCO Alaska announced that an $85 million pilot project had been undertaken to determine whether it was economically feasible to develop the oil-bearing sand 1,065 m (3,500 ft) beneath the Earth's surface at West Sak, on the North Slope.

In May two giant Korean and Japanese companies announced they were considering the feasibility of building an oil refinery at Valdez, the terminus of the trans-Alaska pipeline, to process products for the Far East. Processing the oil in Alaska would sidestep the U.S. ban on the export of crude oil from the North Slope. A potential roadblock was the fact that the state, which owned one-eighth of Prudhoe Bay's production, had already committed most of its oil in long-term contracts. Late in October Alaska Gov. William Sheffield announced an agreement between U.S. Pres. Ronald Reagan and Prime Minister Yasuhiro Nakasone of Japan to ship Alaskan crude oil to Japan starting early in 1986. The agreement, expected to earn the U.S. an estimated $461 million, involved oil from Cook Inlet and not from Prudhoe Bay.

The October issue of the journal *Alaska* reported that oil exploration in the Arctic National Wildlife Refuge had been completed in April. The program of oil and gas exploration had been mandated by the Alaska National Interests Lands Conservation Act of 1980. More than 1,930 km (1,200 mi) of seismic testing was done to determine how much oil and gas lie under the 5.6 million-ha (1.4 million-ac) coastal plain. Late in the year a federal appeals court issued a preliminary injunction prohibiting exploration for oil and gas on federally owned land on Alaska's outer continental shelf. The lawsuit had been brought by two native communities who argued that energy exploration would interfere with their aboriginal hunting and fishing rights.

The 85 million-ton-reserve Red Dog zinc-lead deposit, one of the richest zinc deposits ever discovered in the Western world, moved to the threshold of commercial development with the state government's agreement to advance $175 million in transport development costs. The funds would be used by Cominco Alaska to bring the concentrates to market from their remote location, 145 km (90 mi) north of Kotzebue in northwestern Alaska, along a 9-m (30-ft)-wide highway to a port on the Chukchi Sea coast. At full production of 700,000 tons of concentrate per year in 1989, the $250 million mine would be the world's most important zinc producer. Cominco's partner in the project was NANA, a corporation of Alaskan native people, which owned the land and mineral deposit.

After almost two years of study, the Alaska Native Review Commission, sponsored by the Inuit Circumpolar Conference and headed by Justice Thomas R. Burger, issued its review of the Alaska Native Claims Settlement Act (ANCSA) of 1971. In making his recommendations, Justice Burger listed the three main concerns of Alaska natives as land, self-government, and subsistence. The report, entitled *Village Journey: The Report of the Alaska Native Review Commission,* recommended that lands under the control of native corporations be transferred to tribal governments to keep the land in native ownership; that tribal governments established in all of Alaska's villages assert their native sovereignty; and that tribal governments have exclusive jurisdiction over fish and wildlife on native lands.

Crewmen from the Soviet ice-breaker *Moskva* work to free some of the thousands of beluga whales that were discovered in February trapped by ice in the narrow Senyavin Strait off the Chukchi Peninsula.
APN/TASS/GAMMA/LIAISON

Canada. The $530 million Norman Wells oil field expansion and pipeline project, Canada's first major northern hydrocarbon development, reached production in May. While not big by world standards, its 25,000 bbl a day made up 2% of Canada's crude oil requirements and would save Canada $250 million a year in imported oil.

Early in the year the new Progressive Conservative government of Canada began to undo the regulatory regimes established by previous governments. The new regime was intended to reward drilling results, not drilling per se, and what this would mean for frontier exploration was not yet clear. In June the minister of energy told a gathering of businessmen in New York that Canada would continue to be a reliable, long-term energy supplier for the U.S. and that foreign investment in the energy sector would be encouraged by elimination of the government's right to take a 25% share of frontier discoveries without compensation. The minister said the best incentive for oil and gas development in the Mackenzie River-Beaufort Sea area would be a natural-gas pipeline from the Mackenzie to southern Canada or the extension of the Norman Wells oil pipeline into the Beaufort.

A three-year study and public review by the Beaufort Sea Environmental Assessment Panel concluded that the earliest commercial shipments of oil and gas from the Beaufort could come by 1988. In August the Canadian Petroleum Association forecast in its annual review that there would be no dramatic increase in frontier drilling, but at least two wells would be drilled in the central region of Hudson Bay. Several major developers announced plans for increased spending in 1985. Imperial Oil announced a $1 billion spending plan, while B. P. Canada declared a target of nearly $200 million. Important oil discoveries were being reported by other operators, including Panarctic Oils Ltd. at Cape Allison in the High Arctic and Esso Resources Canada Ltd. in the Beaufort Sea north-

west of Tuktoyaktuk. The two-week voyage of the U.S. Coast Guard icebreaker *Polar Sea* in August through the Northwest Passage and the Canadian Arctic Islands led to a reaffirmation of Canada's claims to sovereignty over the passage. (*See* North America: *Canada,* above.)

In July the minister of Indian affairs and northern development announced that a task force would conduct a fundamental review of federal policy on native claims. The existing policy predated such developments as the 1982 and 1983 constitutional amendments on aboriginal rights, the report of a special committee on Indian self-government, and numerous court cases related to claims issues. In early January the Constitutional Alliance of the Northwest Territories (NWT) reached a tentative agreement on a boundary for division of the NWT into two separate northern territories. The federal government had already agreed in principle to the creation of a new territory in the eastern Arctic as a homeland for a majority of Canada's Inuit.

The Soviet North. As reported in the August *Arctic News-Record,* Gregory Argranat of the Academy of Sciences of the U.S.S.R. stated that economic development of the Soviet Union's northern regions was not simply a matter of learning how to exploit the raw materials. Commenting on future resource development planning, Argranat said experience showed that development without a sound social and economic infrastructure is expensive, complicated, and generally unsatisfactory. He stated that it was a goal of Soviet northern policy not only to exploit the resources but to populate the region, and in this connection it was pointed out that the value of the northern regions is the vast space they can provide for population expansion. Argranat emphasized also the vital role of the Soviet North in maintaining the biochemical balance of the Northern Hemisphere and as a potential source of fresh water.

(KENNETH DE LA BARRE)

This article updates the *Macropædia* article The ARCTIC.

CONTRIBUTORS

Aarsdal, Stener. Journalist, *Børsen* (Denmark's Business Daily), Copenhagen.
WORLD AFFAIRS: *Denmark*
Adams, Andrew M. Free-lance Foreign Correspondent; Editor and Publisher, *Sumo World* magazine.
SPORTS AND GAMES: *Martial Arts; Wrestling (in part)*
Agrella, Joseph C. Correspondent, *Blood-Horse* magazine; former Turf Editor, *Chicago Sun-Times.*
SPORTS AND GAMES: *Horse Racing (in part)*
Allaby, Michael. Free-lance Writer and Lecturer. Author of *Who Will Eat?*
ENVIRONMENT *(in part)*; LIFE SCIENCES: Special Report *(in part)*
Allan, J. A. Reader in Geography, School of Oriental and African Studies, University of London.
WORLD AFFAIRS: *Libya*
Alston, Rex. Broadcaster and Journalist. Author of *Watching Cricket.*
SPORTS AND GAMES: *Cricket*
Amedeo, Michael. Writer, Encyclopædia Britannica Educational Corp.
BIOGRAPHIES *(in part)*
Anderson, Peter J. Assistant Director, Institute of Polar Studies, Ohio State University.
WORLD AFFAIRS: *Antarctica*
Archibald, John J. Feature Writer, *St. Louis Post-Dispatch;* Adjunct Professor, Washington University, St. Louis, Mo.
SPORTS AND GAMES: *Bowling (in part)*
Armstrong, George. Rome Correspondent, *The Guardian.*
BIOGRAPHIES *(in part)*; WORLD AFFAIRS: *Italy*
Arnold, Guy. Free-lance Writer. Author of *Modern Nigeria; Aid in Africa.*
BIOGRAPHIES *(in part)*; WORLD AFFAIRS: *Botswana; Burundi; Cape Verde; Equatorial Guinea; Gambia, The; Ghana; Guinea-Bissau; Lesotho; Liberia; Maldives; Mauritius; Nigeria; Rwanda; São Tomé and Príncipe; Seychelles; Sierra Leone; Swaziland*
Arnold, Mavis. Free-lance Journalist, Dublin.
WORLD AFFAIRS: *Ireland*
Arrington, Leonard J. Formerly Church Historian, Church of Jesus Christ of Latter-day Saints.
RELIGION: *Church of Jesus Christ of Latter-day Saints*
Ashenhurst, Robert Lovett. Professor, Graduate School of Business, University of Chicago.
INFORMATION PROCESSING AND INFORMATION SYSTEMS: Special Report
Auerbach, Alan J. Professor of Economics, University of Pennsylvania.
INDUSTRIAL REVIEW: Special Report
Ayton, Cyril J. Editor, *Motorcycle Sport,* London.
SPORTS AND GAMES: *Motorcycling*
Baptist, Ines T. Free-lance Writer.
WORLD AFFAIRS: *Belize*
Barford, Michael F. Editor and Director, *Tabacosmos,* London.
INDUSTRIAL REVIEW: *Tobacco*
Bargad, Warren. Associate Professor of Hebrew Literature and Director, Center for Jewish Studies, University of Florida.
LITERATURE: *Hebrew*
Barrett, Paul A. Contributing Editor, *Financial Times' New Media Markets* newsletter and *TV World* magazine, London.
TELEVISION AND RADIO *(in part)*
Bass, Howard. Journalist and Broadcaster. Editor, *Winter Sports,* 1948–69.
SPORTS AND GAMES: *Bobsledding; Curling; Ice Hockey (in part); Ice Skating; Skiing; Tobogganing*
Bayliss, David. Director of Planning, London

Regional Transport. Coauthor of *Developing Patterns of Urbanization.*
TRANSPORTATION *(in part)*
Beattie, Roger A. Secretariat Member, International Social Security Association, Geneva.
SOCIAL SECURITY AND WELFARE SERVICES *(in part)*
Beckwith, David C. National Correspondent, *Time* magazine, Washington, D.C.
WORLD AFFAIRS: *United States:* Developments in the States in 1985
Bergerre, Max. Vatican Affairs Correspondent, *La Vie Catholique,* Paris.
WORLD AFFAIRS: *Vatican City State*
Berkovitch, Israel. Writer and Consultant. Author of *Coal on the Switchback;* Editor of *World Energy: Looking Ahead to 2020.*
ENERGY: *Coal*
Beyer, Reginald Ian. Deputy Curator, Royal Botanic Gardens, Kew, England.
BOTANICAL GARDENS AND ZOOS *(in part)*
Bickelhaupt, David L. Professor of Insurance and Finance, College of Administrative Science, Ohio State University, Columbus.
INDUSTRIAL REVIEW: *Insurance*
Bilefield, Lionel. Technical Journalist.
INDUSTRIAL REVIEW: *Paints and Varnishes*
Bird, Thomas E. Director, Council for the Study of Ethics and Public Policy, Queens College, City University of New York.
LITERATURE: *Yiddish (in part)*
Blooston, George. Writer; Contributor to *Publishers Weekly* magazine.
PUBLISHING: *Books (in part)*
Boddy, William C. Editor, *Motor Sport.* Full Member, Guild of Motoring Writers.
SPORTS AND GAMES: *Automobile Racing (in part)*
Boden, Edward. Editor, *Veterinary Record.*
HEALTH AND DISEASE: *Veterinary Medicine*
Bolt, Peter H. Secretary, British Committee, World Methodist Council.
RELIGION: *Methodist Churches*
Boltz, C. L. Science Writer; formerly Science Editor, *Financial Times.*
ENERGY: *Electricity*
Boonstra, Dick. Assistant Professor, Department of Political Science, Free University, Amsterdam.
WORLD AFFAIRS: *Netherlands, The; Suriname*
Booth, John Nicholls. Lecturer and Writer. Author of *The Quest for Preaching Power.*
RELIGION: *Unitarian (Universalist) Churches*
Boswall, Jeffery. Producer of Sound and Television Programs, BBC Natural History Unit, Bristol, England.
LIFE SCIENCES: *Ornithology*
Box, Ben. Free-lance Writer and Researcher on Latin America and Iberia.
WORLD AFFAIRS: *El Salvador; Honduras*
Boye, Roger. Coin columnist, *Chicago Tribune.*
PHILATELY AND NUMISMATICS: *Coins and Paper Money*
Bradsher, Henry S. Foreign Affairs Writer.
WORLD AFFAIRS: *Philippines*
Braidwood, Robert J. Professor Emeritus of Old World Prehistory, Oriental Institute and Department of Anthropology, University of Chicago. Author of *Prehistoric Men.*
ARCHAEOLOGY: *Eastern Hemisphere*
Brazee, Rutlage J. Geophysical Consultant.
EARTH SCIENCES: *Geophysics*
Brecher, Kenneth. Professor of Astronomy and Physics, Boston University. Coauthor and coeditor of *Astronomy of the Ancients.*
ASTRONOMY; ASTRONOMY: Sidebar
Brobyn, Allen F. Assistant Director (Marketing), Glass Manufacturers Federation, London.

INDUSTRIAL REVIEW: *Glass*
Brogan, Hugh. Lecturer in History, University of Essex, Colchester, England.
Macropædia: THE FORMS OF GOVERNMENT
Burdin, Joel L. Professor of Educational Administration, City College of the City University of New York.
EDUCATION *(in part)*
Burke, Donald P. Executive Editor, *Chemical Week,* New York City.
INDUSTRIAL REVIEW: *Chemicals*
Burks, Ardath W. Emeritus Professor of Asian Studies, Rutgers University, New Brunswick, N.J.
WORLD AFFAIRS: *Japan*
Buss, Robin. Lecturer in French, Woolwich College of Further Education, London. Author of *Vigny's Chatterton.*
LITERATURE: *French (in part)*
Butler, Frank. Former Sports Editor, *News of the World,* London. Author of *A History of Boxing in Britain.*
SPORTS AND GAMES: *Boxing*
Cameron, Sarah. Economist, Group Economics Department, Lloyds Bank PLC, London.
WORLD AFFAIRS: *Argentina*
Campbell, Alexander Johns. Latin-American Economist, Lloyds Bank Group Economics Department.
BIOGRAPHIES *(in part)*; WORLD AFFAIRS: *Colombia; Paraguay; Uruguay*
Carter, Robert W. Journalist, London.
BIOGRAPHIES *(in part)*; SPORTS AND GAMES: *Horse Racing (in part)*
Cassidy, Richard J. Senior Public Relations Officer, British Gas Corporation.
ENERGY: *Natural Gas*
Chapman, Christine Patton. Writer, *International Herald Tribune;* English Lecturer, Tsuda College, Tokyo.
BIOGRAPHIES *(in part)*
Chapman, Kenneth F. Former Editor, *Stamp Collecting* and *Philatelic Magazine.*
PHILATELY AND NUMISMATICS: *Stamps*
Chapman, Robin. Senior Economist, Group Economics Department, Lloyds Bank PLC, London.
BIOGRAPHIES *(in part)*; WORLD AFFAIRS: *Brazil; Haiti; Latin-American Affairs*
Chappell, Duncan. Professor, Department of Criminology, Simon Fraser University, Vancouver, B.C.
CRIME, LAW ENFORCEMENT, AND PENOLOGY: *Crime; Law Enforcement*
Chuprinin, Sergey. Journalist, Novosti Press Agency, Moscow.
LITERATURE: *Russian (in part)*
Clarke, R. O. Writer, Paris.
LABOUR–MANAGEMENT RELATIONS
Cleveland, William A. Editor, Britannica World Data and *Britannica Atlas.*
MINING AND METALLURGY: *Mining*
Cogle, T. C. J. Editor, *Electrical Review,* London.
INDUSTRIAL REVIEW: *Electrical*
Coppock, Charles Dennis. Honorary Member, English Lacrosse Union.
SPORTS AND GAMES: *Lacrosse (in part)*
Costin, Stanley H. British Correspondent, *Herrenjournal International,* and others.
FASHION AND DRESS *(in part)*
Crater, Rufus W. Senior Editorial Consultant, *Broadcasting,* New York City.
TELEVISION AND RADIO *(in part)*
Cross, Colin J. Editor, *The Polo Times;* U.K. Chairman, European Polo Academy.
SPORTS AND GAMES: *Polo*
Crossland, Norman. Former Bonn Correspondent, *The Economist,* London.

BIOGRAPHIES *(in part)*; WORLD AFFAIRS: *German Democratic Republic; Germany, Federal Republic of*
Curley, Robert. Editorial Researcher, Encyclopædia Britannica, Inc.
BIOGRAPHIES *(in part)*
Cviic, K. F. East European Specialist, *The Economist,* London.
WORLD AFFAIRS: *Yugoslavia*
David, Tudor. Managing Editor, *Education,* London.
EDUCATION *(in part)*; EDUCATION: Sidebar
Davies, C. R. M. Research Lecturer in Criminology and Penology, University of Liverpool, England.
CRIME, LAW ENFORCEMENT, AND PENOLOGY: *Prisons and Penology*
Davis, Donald A. Editor, *Drug & Cosmetic Industry* and *Cosmetic Insider's Report,* New York City.
INDUSTRIAL REVIEW: *Pharmaceuticals*
Deam, John B. Technical Director, National Machine Tool Builders Association, McLean, Va.
INDUSTRIAL REVIEW: *Machinery and Machine Tools*
Decraene, Philippe. Head, Center for Advanced Studies on Modern Africa and Asia, Paris.
WORLD AFFAIRS: *Benin; Burkina Faso; Cameroon; Central African Republic; Chad; Comoros; Congo; Djibouti; Gabon; Guinea; Ivory Coast; Madagascar; Mali; Mauritania; Niger; Senegal; Togo; Tunisia*
de la Barre, Kenneth. Director, Katimavik, Montreal.
WORLD AFFAIRS: *Arctic Regions*
Denselow, Robin. Rock Music Critic, *The Guardian,* London; Current Affairs Reporter, BBC Television.
MUSIC: *Popular*
De Puy, Norman R. Minister, First Baptist Church, Newton Centre, Mass.; Columnist, *American Baptist* magazine.
RELIGION: *Baptist Churches*
Deshayes-Creuilly, Marie-Jose. Head of Documentation Service, International Vine and Wine Office, Paris.
INDUSTRIAL REVIEW: *Beverages (in part)*
Dirnbacher, Elfriede. Austrian Civil Servant.
WORLD AFFAIRS: *Austria*
Dixon, Bernard. Science Writer and Consultant. Editor (1969–79), *New Scientist* magazine. Author of *Magnificent Microbes; Medicine and Care.*
HEALTH AND DISEASE: *Mental Health; Overview (in part)*
Dorris, Thomas Hartley. Editor, Ecumenical Press Service, Geneva.
RELIGION: *Lutheran Communion*
Eli, C. R. Former Executive Director, U.S. Badminton Association.
SPORTS AND GAMES: *Badminton*
Engels, Jan R. Director, Centre Paul Hymans; Editor, *Vooruitgang-Progrès* magazine.
WORLD AFFAIRS: *Belgium*
Evans, Harold Matthew. Editorial Director, *U.S. News & World Report.* Former Editor, *The Sunday Times* and *The Times.*
PUBLISHING: Special Report
Ewart, W. D. Marine Consultant, London. Author of *Bunkers; Bulk Carriers.*
INDUSTRIAL REVIEW: *Shipbuilding;* TRANSPORTATION *(in part)*
Farr, D. M. L. Professor of History, Carleton University, Ottawa.
WORLD AFFAIRS: *Canada*
Faust, Joan Lee. Garden Editor, *New York Times.*
GARDENING *(in part)*
Felknor, Bruce L. Editorial Consultant, Encyclopædia Britannica, Inc.
BRITANNICA AWARDS; Feature Sidebar: SHEVCHENKO
Fendell, Robert J. Auto Editor, *Science &*

Mechanics. Author of *The New Era Car Book and Auto Survival Guide.*
SPORTS AND GAMES: *Automobile Racing (in part)*
Ferrier, R. W. Group Historian, The British Petroleum Company PLC, London.
ENERGY: *Petroleum*
Fiddick, Peter. Media Editor, *The Guardian,* London.
BIOGRAPHIES *(in part)*; PUBLISHING: *Newspapers (in part); Magazines (in part)*
Fields, Donald. Helsinki Correspondent, BBC, *The Guardian,* and *The Sunday Times,* London.
WORLD AFFAIRS: *Finland*
Firth, David. Editor, *The Friend,* London; formerly Editor, *Quaker Monthly,* London.
RELIGION: *Religious Society of Friends*
Fisher, David. Civil Engineer, Freeman Fox & Partners, London.
ENGINEERING PROJECTS: *Bridges*
Flanagan, Jack C. Travel Counselor.
SPORTS AND GAMES: *Surfing*
Frady, William Ensign, III. Editor, *Water Polo Scoreboard,* Newport Beach, Calif.
SPORTS AND GAMES: *Water Polo*
Franklin, Harold. Editor, *English Bridge Quarterly.* Bridge Correspondent, *Yorkshire Post.*
SPORTS AND GAMES: *Contract Bridge*
Franz, Frederick W. President, Watch Tower Bible and Tract Society of Pennsylvania.
RELIGION: *Jehovah's Witnesses*
Fridovich, Irwin. James B. Duke Professor of Biochemistry, Duke University Medical Center, Durham, N.C.
LIFE SCIENCES: *Molecular Biology (in part)*
Fridovich-Keil, Judith L. Graduate Student and Ph.D. Candidate, Biology Department, Massachusetts Institute of Technology.
LIFE SCIENCES: *Molecular Biology (in part)*
Friedly, Robert Louis. Vice President for Communication, Christian Church (Disciples of Christ), Indianapolis, Ind.
RELIGION: *Christian Church (Disciples of Christ)*
Friskin, Sydney E. Hockey Correspondent, *The Times,* London.
SPORTS AND GAMES: *Billiard Games (in part); Field Hockey*
Frost, David. Rugby Union Correspondent, *The Guardian,* London.
SPORTS AND GAMES: *Football (in part)*
Gaddum, Anthony H. Chairman, H. T. Gaddum and Company Ltd., Silk Merchants, Macclesfield, Cheshire, England.
INDUSTRIAL REVIEW: *Textiles (in part)*
Ganado, Albert. Lawyer, Malta.
BIOGRAPHIES *(in part)*; WORLD AFFAIRS: *Malta*
Ganguly, Dilip. Special Correspondent, Agence France Presse, New Delhi, India.
WORLD AFFAIRS: *Afghanistan; Bangladesh; Bhutan; Burma; Nepal; Pakistan; Sri Lanka*
Garrad, Rob. Director of Information Services, International Headquarters, Salvation Army.
RELIGION: *Salvation Army*
Gastil, Raymond Duncan. Director, Comparative Survey of Freedom, Freedom House, New York City.
HUMAN RIGHTS
Gibbons, J. Whitfield. Research Ecologist, Savannah River Ecology Laboratory, Aiken, S.C.
LIFE SCIENCES: *Zoology*
Gibney, Frank. Vice-Chairman, Board of Editors, Encyclopædia Britannica, Inc. Author of *Japan: The Fragile Superpower.*
Feature Sidebar: JAPAN'S PRESIDENTIAL PRIME MINISTER; WORLD AFFAIRS: *China:* Special Report
Gillespie, Hugh M. Director of Communications, International Road Federation, Washington, D.C.
ENGINEERING PROJECTS: *Roads*

Gjester, Fay. Oslo Correspondent, *Financial Times,* London.
WORLD AFFAIRS: *Norway*
Goldsmith, Arthur. Editorial Director, *Popular Photography,* New York City.
PHOTOGRAPHY
Golombek, Harry. Chess Correspondent, *The Times,* London.
BIOGRAPHIES *(in part)*; SPORTS AND GAMES: *Chess*
Goodwin, Noël. London Correspondent, *Ballet News;* Free-lance Writer and Broadcaster. Associate Editor (to 1983) and Contributor, *Dance & Dancers.*
BIOGRAPHIES *(in part)*; DANCE *(in part)*
Gottfried, Martin. Drama Critic, New York City. Author of *A Theater Divided; Opening Nights; Broadway Musicals.*
THEATRE *(in part)*
Griffiths, A. R. G. Senior Lecturer in History, Flinders University of South Australia. Author of *Contemporary Australia.*
BIOGRAPHIES *(in part)*; WORLD AFFAIRS: *Australia; Nauru; Oceanian Affairs (in part); Papua New Guinea*
Grossman, Joel W. Archaeologist.
ARCHAEOLOGY: *Western Hemisphere*
Grudin, Robert. Associate Professor of English, University of Oregon, Eugene. Author of *Time and the Art of Living* and others. Revised *Macropædia* article: HUMANISM
Grumet, Robert S. Research Associate, Museum of the American Indian, Heye Foundation, New York City.
ANTHROPOLOGY
Hall, Peter Geoffrey. Professor of Geography, University of Reading, England; Professor of City and Regional Planning, University of California at Berkeley.
SOCIAL SECURITY AND WELFARE SERVICES: Special Report
Hallgren, Richard E. Assistant Administrator for Weather Services, National Oceanic and Atmospheric Administration.
EARTH SCIENCES: *Meteorology*
Hardman, Thomas C. Consulting Editor, *The Water Skier,* American Water Ski Assoc.
SPORTS AND GAMES: *Water Skiing*
Harper, Nicholas. Music Writer; Deputy Editor, *Classical CD,* England.
MUSIC: *Classical;* MUSIC: Sidebar
Hasegawa, Ryusaku. Editor, TBS-Britannica Co., Ltd., Tokyo.
SPORTS AND GAMES: *Baseball (in part)*
Havard-Williams, P. Professor and Head, Department of Library and Information Studies, Loughborough University, Leicestershire, England.
LIBRARIES *(in part)*
Hawkland, William D. Chancellor and Professor of Law, Louisiana State University.
LAW: *Court Decisions*
Hebblethwaite, Peter. Vatican Affairs Writer, *National Catholic Reporter,* Kansas City, Mo.
BIOGRAPHIES *(in part)*; RELIGION: *Roman Catholic Church;* WORLD AFFAIRS: *Latin-American Affairs:* Special Report: Sidebar
Hendershott, Myrl C. Professor of Oceanography, Scripps Institution of Oceanography, La Jolla, Calif.
EARTH SCIENCES: *Oceanography*
Herman, Robin Cathy. Free-lance Journalist.
SPORTS AND GAMES: *Ice Hockey (in part)*
Hess, Marvin G. Executive Vice-President, National Wrestling Coaches Association, Salt Lake City, Utah.
SPORTS AND GAMES: *Wrestling (in part)*
Higgins, Fitzgerald. Editor and Reviewer.
LITERATURE: *United States*
Hindin, Harvey J. Vice-President, Hi-Tech Editorial, Inc., Dix Hills, N.Y.
INDUSTRIAL REVIEW: *Telecommunications*
Hope, Thomas W. President, Hope Reports, Inc., Rochester, N.Y.
MOTION PICTURES *(in part)*

Howkins, John. Director, International Institute of Communications, London. Author of *Understanding Television.*
TELEVISION AND RADIO *(in part)*

Hunnings, Neville March. Editorial Director, European Law Centre, London. Editor, *Common Market Law Reports.*
LAW: *International Law*

Ingham, Kenneth. Professor of History, University of Bristol, England. Author of *Reformers in India.*
WORLD AFFAIRS: *Angola; Kenya; Malawi; Mozambique; Sudan, The; Tanzania; Uganda; Zaire; Zambia; Zimbabwe*

IEIS. International Economic Information Services, London.
ECONOMIC AFFAIRS: *World Economy*

Iversen, Ingrid. Economist, Group Economics Department, Lloyds Bank PLC, London.
BIOGRAPHIES *(in part)*; WORLD AFFAIRS: *Bolivia; Costa Rica; Ecuador; Guatemala; Mexico; Mexico:* Sidebar; *Peru*

Jacquet, Constant H. Staff Associate, National Council of Churches. Editor of *Yearbook of American and Canadian Churches.*
WORLD AFFAIRS: *United States (table)*

Jardine, Adrian. Company Director. Member, Guild of Yachting Writers.
SPORTS AND GAMES: *Sailing*

Jaspert, W. Pincus. Technical and Editorial Consultant. Author of *State of the Art.* Editor, *Encyclopaedia of Type Faces.*
INDUSTRIAL REVIEW: *Printing*

Jenkins, Peter. Political Columnist, *The Sunday Times,* London.
BIOGRAPHIES *(in part)*; WORLD AFFAIRS: *United Kingdom*

Joffé, George. Journalist and Writer on North African Affairs.
WORLD AFFAIRS: *Algeria; Morocco*

Jones, C. M. Consultant, *World Bowls* and *Tennis.* Author of *Winning Bowls.*
SPORTS AND GAMES: *Lawn Bowls*

Jones, D. A. N. Novelist and Critic. Author of *Parade in Pairs; Never Had It So Good.*
BIOGRAPHIES *(in part)*; LITERATURE: *Introduction; United Kingdom*

Jones, W. Glyn. Professor of Scandinavian Studies, University of Newcastle upon Tyne, England.
LITERATURE: *Danish*

Joseph, Lou. Senior Science Writer, Hill and Knowlton, Chicago.
HEALTH AND DISEASE: *Dentistry*

Katz, William A. Professor, School of Library Science, State University of New York, Albany.
PUBLISHING: *Magazines (in part)*

Kelleher, John A. Group Relations Editor, INL (newspapers), Wellington, N.Z.
BIOGRAPHIES *(in part)*; WORLD AFFAIRS: *New Zealand*

Kennedy, Richard M. Agricultural Economist, International Economics Division of the Economic Research Service, U.S. Department of Agriculture.
AGRICULTURE AND FOOD SUPPLIES *(in part)*

Khindaria, Brij. Financial Journalist, Geneva. Specialist in relationships among multinational companies, consumer activists, and international regulatory bodies.
CONSUMER AFFAIRS: Special Report

Kilian, Michael D. Washington Columnist, *Chicago Tribune.* Author of *Flying Can Be Fun.*
SPORTS AND GAMES: *Aerial Sports*

Killheffer, John V. Associate Editor, *Encyclopædia Britannica.*
BIOGRAPHIES *(in part)*

Kimche, Jon. Formerly Editor, *New Middle East; Afro-Asian Affairs,* London. Author of *Second Arab Awakening; Palestine or Israel.*
WORLD AFFAIRS: *Israel*

Kind, Joshua B. Professor of Art History, Northern Illinois University, De Kalb. Au-

thor of *Rouault; Geometry as Abstract Art.*
MUSEUMS *(in part)*

Kitagawa, Joseph M. Emeritus Professor of History of Religions, Divinity School, University of Chicago. Author of *Religions of the East.*
RELIGION: *Buddhism*

Kloos, Jean Clark Cameron. Markets Editor, *Timber Trades Journal.*
INDUSTRIAL REVIEW: *Wood Products*

Knecht, Jean. Formerly Assistant Foreign Editor, *Le Monde,* Paris.
BIOGRAPHIES *(in part)*; WORLD AFFAIRS: *France*

Knox, Richard A. Technical Author; formerly Editor, *Nuclear Engineering International,* London.
INDUSTRIAL REVIEW: *Nuclear Industry*

Kolata, Gina. Writer, *Science* magazine, Washington, D.C. Coauthor of *The High Blood Pressure Book.*
HEALTH AND DISEASE: *Overview (in part)*

Kriegsman, Sali Ann. Dance Writer and Consultant. Washington, D.C.; Correspondent, *Ballet News; Washington DanceView.*
DANCE *(in part)*

Kushnick, Louis. Lecturer, Department of American Studies, University of Manchester, England.
POPULATIONS AND POPULATION MOVEMENTS: *International Migration;* RACE RELATIONS

Laberis, William E. Managing Editor, *Computerworld.*
INFORMATION PROCESSING AND INFORMATION SYSTEMS

Lamb, Kevin M. Sportswriter, *Chicago Sun-Times.* Author of *Quarterbacks, Nickelbacks & Other Loose Change.*
BIOGRAPHIES *(in part)*; SPORTS AND GAMES: *Football (in part)*

Laqueur, Walter. Director, Institute of Contemporary History and Wiener Library, London. Author of *Europe Since Hitler.*
WORLD AFFAIRS: *Introduction*

Larson, Roy. Editor and Publisher, *The Chicago Reporter.*
RELIGION: *Introduction*

Larsson, Gerd. Tokyo Correspondent, *Dagens Industri.*
BIOGRAPHIES *(in part)*

Leaper, Eric. Executive Director, National Organization for River Sports, Colorado Springs, Colo.
SPORTS AND GAMES: *River Sports*

Leerburger, Benedict A. Editorial Consultant and Science Writer. Author of *The Complete Consumers Guide to the Latest Telephones; Josiah Willard Gibbs.*
LIFE SCIENCES: Special Report *(in part)*

Legassick, Martin. Coordinator (honorary), Southern Africa Labour Education Project; formerly Senior Lecturer in Sociology, University of Warwick, Coventry, England.
WORLD AFFAIRS: *South Africa*

Legum, Colin. Associate Editor (1947–81), *The Observer;* Editor, *Africa Contemporary Record,* London; and others.
BIOGRAPHIES *(in part)*; WORLD AFFAIRS: *African Affairs; South Africa:* Special Report

Lennox-Kerr, Peter. Editor, *High Performance Textiles;* European Editor, *Textile World.* Author of *The World Fibres Book.*
INDUSTRIAL REVIEW: *Textiles (in part)*

Litsky, Frank. Sportswriter, *New York Times.*
SPORTS AND GAMES: *Archery*

Littell, Franklin H. Professor of Religion, Temple University, Philadelphia. Author of *Macmillan Atlas History of Christianity.*
RELIGION: *World Church Membership*

Logan, Robert G. Sportswriter, *Chicago Tribune.* Author of *The Bulls and Chicago—A Stormy Affair; Miracle on 35th Street.*
SPORTS AND GAMES: *Basketball (in part)*

Luling, Virginia R. Social Anthropologist.
WORLD AFFAIRS: *Somalia*

McCauley, Martin. Senior Lecturer in Soviet and East European Studies, School of Slavonic and East European Studies, University of London.
WORLD AFFAIRS: *Union of Soviet Socialist Republics*

Macdonald, Barrie. Reader in History, Massey University, Palmerston North, N.Z.
WORLD AFFAIRS: *Dependent States (in part); Fiji; Kiribati; Solomon Islands; Tonga; Tuvalu; Vanuatu; Western Samoa*

MacDonald, Trevor J. Manager, International Affairs, British Steel Corporation.
INDUSTRIAL REVIEW: *Iron and Steel*

MacGregor-Morris, Pamela. Equestrian Correspondent, *Horse and Hound,* London.
SPORTS AND GAMES: *Show Jumping*

McKelvie, Roy. Former Rackets and Real Tennis Correspondent, *The Times,* London.
SPORTS AND GAMES: *Rackets; Real Tennis*

McLachlan, Keith S. Senior Lecturer, School of Oriental and African Studies, University of London.
WORLD AFFAIRS: *Iran*

Mallett, H. M. F. Editor, *Wool Record Weekly Market Report,* Bradford, England.
INDUSTRIAL REVIEW: *Textiles (in part)*

Mango, Andrew. Orientalist and Broadcaster.
WORLD AFFAIRS: *Turkey*

Marty, Martin E. Fairfax M. Cone Distinguished Service Professor of the History of Modern Christianity, University of Chicago.
RELIGION: Special Report

Mateja, James L. Auto Editor and Financial Reporter, *Chicago Tribune.*
INDUSTRIAL REVIEW: *Automobiles*

Mathias, Charles McC., Jr. Retired U.S. Senator from Maryland (1969–86) and former Representative in Congress (1961–69).
ECONOMIC AFFAIRS: Special Report

Matthíasson, Björn. Economist, Central Bank of Iceland.
WORLD AFFAIRS: *Iceland*

Mazie, David M. Associate of Carl T. Rowan, syndicated columnist. Free-lance Writer.
SOCIAL SECURITY AND WELFARE SERVICES *(in part)*

Mazze, Edward Mark. Dean and Professor of Marketing, School of Business Administration, Temple University, Philadelphia.
CONSUMER AFFAIRS *(in part)*; INDUSTRIAL REVIEW: *Advertising*

Menkes, Suzy. Fashion Editor, *The Times,* London.
FASHION AND DRESS: Special Report

Mermel, T. W. Consultant; formerly Chairman, Committee on World Register of Dams.
ENGINEERING PROJECTS: *Dams; Dams table*

Meyendorff, John. Professor, Dean of St. Vladimir's Orthodox Theological Seminary; Professor of History, Fordham University, New York City.
RELIGION: *The Orthodox Church; Eastern Non-Chalcedonian Churches*

Miles, Peter W. University of Adelaide, Australia.
LIFE SCIENCES: *Entomology*

Millgate, Paul. Economist, Group Economics Department, Lloyds Bank PLC, London.
WORLD AFFAIRS: *Cuba; Dominican Republic; Nicaragua*

Millikin, Sandra. Architectural Historian.
ARCHITECTURE; ART EXHIBITIONS AND ART SALES: *Art Exhibitions;* BIOGRAPHIES *(in part)*; MUSEUMS *(in part)*

Modiano, Mario. Athens Correspondent, *The Times,* London.
BIOGRAPHIES *(in part)*; WORLD AFFAIRS: *Greece*

Monaco, Albert M., Jr. Executive Director, United States Volleyball Association, Colorado Springs, Colo.
SPORTS AND GAMES: *Volleyball*

Moore, John E. Hydrologist, Reston, Va.
EARTH SCIENCES: *Hydrology*

Morgenstern, Dan M. Director, Institute of

Jazz Studies, Rutgers, The State University of New Jersey. Author of *Jazz People.*
MUSIC: *Jazz*

Morris, Jacqui M. Editor, *Oryx* magazine.
ENVIRONMENT *(in part)*

Morrison, Donald. Senior Editor, *Time.*
PUBLISHING: *Newspapers (in part)*

Mortimer, Molly. Commonwealth Correspondent, *The Spectator,* London. Author of *Trusteeship in Practice; Kenya.*
WORLD AFFAIRS: *Commonwealth of Nations*

Mosey, Chris. Associate Editor, *Sweden Now,* Stockholm; Nordic Correspondent, *The Observer* and *Worldwatch;* Swedish Correspondent, *Daily Mail* and *The Times.*
WORLD AFFAIRS: *Sweden*

Muck, Terry Charles. Editor, *Leadership* magazine, Carol Stream, Ill.
SPORTS AND GAMES: *Handball*

Mullen, Joan. Vice-President, Manager of the Law and Justice Area of Abt Associates Inc.
CRIME, LAW ENFORCEMENT, AND PENOLOGY: Sidebar

Nakasone, Yasuhiro. Prime Minister of Japan (since November 1982). Author of *Ideal of Youth; Frontier in Japan.*
Feature Article: THE NEW ASIA-PACIFIC ERA

Napier, Elspeth. Editor of publications of the Royal Horticultural Society.
GARDENING *(in part)*

Naylor, Ernest. Lloyd Roberts Professor of Zoology, University College of North Wales.
LIFE SCIENCES: *Marine Biology*

Neill, John. Consultant, Submerged Combustion Ltd.; President, British Mountaineering Council. Author of Climbers' Club Guides.
SPORTS AND GAMES: *Mountaineering*

Nelson, Bert. Editor, *Track and Field News.* Author of *Olympic Track and Field.*
SPORTS AND GAMES: *Track and Field Sports*

Netschert, Bruce C. Vice-President, National Economic Research Associates, Inc., Washington, D.C.
ENERGY: *World Summary*

Neusner, Jacob. University Professor, Brown University, Providence, R.I. Author of *Judaism, The Evidence of the Mishnah.*
RELIGION: *Judaism*

Noblett, Geoffrey J. Tunneling Division Manager, Tarmac Construction International, Wolverhampton, England.
ENGINEERING PROJECTS: *Tunnels*

Noel, H. S. Editor, *World Fishing,* England.
AGRICULTURE AND FOOD SUPPLIES: *Fisheries*

Norman, Geraldine. Saleroom Correspondent, *The Times,* London. Author of *The Sale of Works of Art; Nineteenth Century Painters and Painting;* Coauthor of *The Fake's Progress.*
ART EXHIBITIONS AND ART SALES: *Art Sales*

Oberman, Bonnie. Writer and Editor.
BIOGRAPHIES *(in part)*

O'Donoghue, Michael. Curator, Science Reference Library, London; Lecturer in Gemmology, City of London Polytechnic.
INDUSTRIAL REVIEW: *Gemstones*

O'Dwyer, Thomas. Director, Levant Bureau; Writer on East Mediterranean Affairs, Nicosia, Cyprus.
WORLD AFFAIRS: *Cyprus*

O'Keeffe, Margaret-Louise. Retired Press Officer, All England Women's Lacrosse Association.
SPORTS AND GAMES: *Lacrosse (in part)*

Olney, P. J. Curator of Birds and Reptiles, Zoological Society of London. Editor, *International Zoo Yearbook.*
BOTANICAL GARDENS AND ZOOS: *Zoos*

Osborne, Keith. Editor, *British Rowing Almanack.* Author of *Boat Racing in Britain, 1715–1975.*
SPORTS AND GAMES: *Rowing*

Osterbind, Carter C. Associate, Gerontology Center, and Professor Emeritus of Economics, University of Florida.

INDUSTRIAL REVIEW: *Building and Construction*

Palmer, John. Former European Editor, *The Guardian,* London.
WORLD AFFAIRS: *Western European Affairs*

Palmer, S. B. Reader, Department of Applied Physics, University of Hull, England.
PHYSICS

Parker, Sandy. Publisher of weekly international newsletter on fur industry; Copublisher, *Fur World.*
INDUSTRIAL REVIEW: *Furs*

Patterson, Robert P., Jr. Partner, Patterson, Belknap, Webb & Tyler, New York City.
CRIME, LAW ENFORCEMENT, AND PENOLOGY: Sidebar *(in part)*

Paul, Charles Robert, Jr. Special Assistant to the Secretary General, U.S. Olympic Committee, Colorado Springs.
SPORTS AND GAMES: *Gymnastics; Weight Lifting*

Penfold, Robin C. Free-lance Writer in industrial topics. Editor, *Shell Polymers.* Author of *A Journalist's Guide to Plastics.*
INDUSTRIAL REVIEW: *Plastics*

Pertile, Lino. Reader in Italian, University of Sussex, England.
LITERATURE: *Italian*

Petherick, Karin. Reader in Swedish, University of London.
LITERATURE: Swedish

Pfeffer, Irving. Attorney. Author of *The Financing of Small Business.*
ECONOMIC AFFAIRS: *Stock Exchanges (in part)*

Philip, George. Lecturer in Latin-American Politics, London School of Economics and Political Science and Institute of Latin-American Studies, University of London. Author of *Oil and Politics in Latin America.*
WORLD AFFAIRS: *Latin-American Affairs:* Special Report

Pinfold, Geoffrey M. Director, NCL Consulting Engineers, London. Author of *Reinforced Concrete Chimneys and Towers.*
ENGINEERING PROJECTS: *Buildings*

Plotkin, Arthur. Editor, *American Libraries* magazine, American Library Association.
LIBRARIES *(in part)*

Polin, Thomas Hon Wing. Assistant Managing Editor, *Asiaweek,* Hong Kong.
BIOGRAPHIES *(in part);* WORLD AFFAIRS: *Brunei; Indonesia; Kampuchea; Korea; Laos; Malaysia; Singapore; Southeast Asian Affairs; Thailand; Vietnam*

Pollack, Jonathan D. Senior Staff Member, Political Science Department, Rand Corp., Santa Monica, Calif.
WORLD AFFAIRS: *China; Taiwan*

Poppeliers, John. Chief, Section for Technical Cooperation and Training, Cultural Heritage Division, Unesco, Paris.
HISTORIC PRESERVATION

Post, Avery D. President, United Church of Christ, New York City.
RELIGION: *United Church of Christ*

Prasad, H. Y. Sharada. Information Adviser to the Prime Minister, New Delhi, India.
WORLD AFFAIRS: *India*

Prince, Rod. Journalist specializing in Caribbean matters.
BIOGRAPHIES *(in part);* WORLD AFFAIRS: *Antigua and Barbuda; Bahamas, The; Barbados; Dependent States (in part); Dominica; Grenada; Guyana; Jamaica; Saint Christopher and Nevis; Saint Lucia; Saint Vincent and the Grenadines; Trinidad and Tobago*

Ranger, Robin. Associate Professor, Defense and Strategic Studies, School of International Relations, University of Southern California.
MILITARY AFFAIRS; MILITARY AFFAIRS: Special Report

Ray, G. F. Senior Research Fellow, National Institute of Economic and Social Research, London.
INDUSTRIAL REVIEW: *Introduction*

Read, Anthony A. Director, Book Development Council, London.
PUBLISHING: *Books (in part)*

Rebelo, L. S. Reader, Department of Portuguese Studies, King's College, University of London.
LITERATURE: *Portuguese (in part)*

Redlich, Edward. Associate, Patterson, Belknap, Webb & Tyler, New York City.
CRIME, LAW ENFORCEMENT, AND PENOLOGY: Sidebar *(in part)*

Reid, J. H. Reader in German, University of Nottingham, England. Author of *Heinrich Böll: Withdrawal and Re-emergence.*
LITERATURE: *German*

Reid, Philip D. Professor of Biological Sciences, Smith College, Northampton, Mass.
LIFE SCIENCES: *Botany*

Ripley, Michael D. Senior Public Relations Officer, Brewers' Society, U.K.; formerly Editor, *Brewing Review.*
INDUSTRIAL REVIEW: *Beverages (in part)*

Robinson, David. Film Critic, *The Times,* London. Author of *A History of World Cinema; Chaplin: His Life and Art.*
MOTION PICTURES *(in part)*

Saeki, Shoichi. Professor of Literature, Chuo University, Tokyo. Author of *In Search of Japanese Ego.*
LITERATURE: *Japanese*

Saint-Amour, Robert. Professor, Department of Literary Studies, University of Quebec at Montreal.
LITERATURE: *French (in part)*

Sanders, Thomas H. B., Jr. Professor of Metallurgy, Purdue University, West Lafayette, Ind.
MINING AND METALLURGY: *Metallurgy*

Sarahete, Yrjö. General Secretary, Fédération Internationale des Quilleurs, Helsinki.
SPORTS AND GAMES: *Bowling (in part)*

Sarmiento, Sergio. Editor in Chief, Spanish-language publications, Encyclopædia Britannica Publishers, Inc.
BIOGRAPHIES *(in part);* SPORTS AND GAMES: *Baseball (in part); Football (in part)*

Schoenfield, Albert. Formerly Publisher, *Swimming World;* Vice-Chairman, U.S. Olympic Swimming Committee; Honoree, International Swimming Hall of Fame.
SPORTS AND GAMES: *Swimming*

Schöpflin, George. Lecturer in East European Political Institutions, London School of Economics and School of Slavonic and East European Studies, University of London.
WORLD AFFAIRS: *Czechoslovakia; Eastern European Affairs*

Schulman, Elias. Adjunct Professor, Queens College, City University of New York. Author of *Soviet-Yiddish Literature.*
LITERATURE: *Yiddish (in part)*

Sears, Robert N. Editor, National Rifle Association, Washington, D.C.
SPORTS AND GAMES: *Shooting*

Sell, Alan P. F. Theological Secretary, World Alliance of Reformed Churches, Geneva.
RELIGION: *Reformed, Presbyterian, and Congregational Churches*

Shackleford, Peter. Chief of Studies, World Tourism Organization, Madrid.
INDUSTRIAL REVIEW: *Tourism*

Sharpe, Mitchell R. Science Writer; Historian, Alabama Space and Rocket Center, Huntsville. Author of *The Rocket Team.*
SPACE EXPLORATION

Shaw, T. R. Advisory Editor, *International Journal of Speleology.* Author of *History of Cave Science.*
SPORTS AND GAMES: *Spelunking*

Shelley, Andrew. Competitions Manager, Squash Rackets Association, England.
SPORTS AND GAMES: *Squash Rackets*

Shepherd, Melinda. Copy Editor, Encyclopædia Britannica, Inc.
BIOGRAPHIES *(in part)*

Sherwood, Martin A. Employed in the pharmaceutical industry. Author of *New Worlds in Chemistry.*
CHEMISTRY

Shevchenko, Arkady N. Former UN Under Secretary-General for Political and Security Council Affairs; former Ambassador to the UN from the U.S.S.R. Author of *Breaking with Moscow.*
Feature Article: THE SOVIET UNION UNDER GORBACHEV

Simpson, Noel. Managing Director, Sydney Bloodstock Proprietary Ltd., Sydney.
SPORTS AND GAMES: *Horse Racing (in part)*

Singer, Peter. Professor of Philosophy; Director, Centre for Human Bioethics, Monash University, Victoria, Australia. Author of *Practical Ethics.*
Macropædia: ETHICS

Smith, Donald. Editor, *Rubber World* magazine, Akron, Ohio.
INDUSTRIAL REVIEW: *Rubber*

Smith, Reuben W. Dean, Graduate School, and Professor of History, University of the Pacific, Stockton, Calif.
RELIGION: *Islam*

Smith, Sid. Entertainment Writer, *Chicago Tribune.*
THEATRE: Sidebar

Smogorzewski, K. M. Writer on contemporary history. Founder and Editor, *Free Europe,* London.
BIOGRAPHIES *(in part);* WORLD AFFAIRS: *Albania; Andorra; Bulgaria; Hungary; Liechtenstein; Luxembourg; Monaco; Mongolia; Poland; Poland: Sidebar; Political Parties; Romania; San Marino*

Spelman, Robert A. President, Home Furnishings Services, Washington, D.C.
INDUSTRIAL REVIEW: *Furniture*

Spittle, Hilary R. Publications Editor, American Power Boat Association.
SPORTS AND GAMES: *Motorboating*

Staerk, Melanie. Former Executive Editor, *Swiss Review of World Affairs* (Zurich) and *Unescopresse* (Berne).
WORLD AFFAIRS: *Switzerland*

Steen, Lynn Arthur. Professor of Mathematics, St. Olaf College, Northfield, Minn. Author of *Mathematics Today.*
MATHEMATICS

Stern, Irwin. Assistant Professor of Portuguese, Columbia University, New York City.
LITERATURE: *Portuguese (in part)*

Sternberg, Charles. Executive Director Emeritus, International Rescue Committee.
POPULATIONS AND POPULATION MOVEMENTS: Sidebar

Stoddard, Drew W. Commissioner, Men's Professional Racquetball; Editor, *National Racquetball Magazine.*
SPORTS AND GAMES: *Racquetball*

Støverud, Torbjørn. Honorary Research Fellow, University College, London.
LITERATURE: *Norwegian*

Strauss, Michael. Ski, Sports, and Feature Writer, *New York Times* (retired); Sports Editor, *Palm Beach Daily News.*
SPORTS AND GAMES: *Fencing*

Sullivan, H. Patrick. Dean of the College and Professor of Religion, Vassar College, Poughkeepsie, N.Y.
RELIGION: *Hinduism*

Sweetinburgh, Thelma. Fashion Writer, Paris.
FASHION AND DRESS *(in part)*

Swift, Richard N. Professor Emeritus of Politics, New York University, New York City.
WORLD AFFAIRS: *United Nations*

Synan, Vinson. Assistant General Superintendent, Pentecostal Holiness Church. Author of *The Old Time Power.*
RELIGION: *Pentecostal Churches*

Taggart, Charles Johnson. Free-lance Writer.
BIOGRAPHIES *(in part)*

Taishoff, Lawrence B. President, Broadcasting Publications, Inc., and Publisher, *Broadcasting* magazine and others.
TELEVISION AND RADIO *(in part)*

Tak, Jean van der. Senior Editor, Population Reference Bureau, Inc.
POPULATIONS AND POPULATION MOVEMENTS: *Demography*

Talbot, Nathan A. Manager, Committees on Publication, The First Church of Christ, Scientist, Boston.
RELIGION: *Church of Christ, Scientist*

Talbott, John A. Professor of Psychiatry, Cornell University Medical College, Ithaca, N.Y. Author of *Death of the Asylum.*
HEALTH AND DISEASE: Special Report *(in part)*

Tallan, Norman M. Chief, Metals and Ceramics Division, Materials Laboratory, Wright-Patterson Air Force Base, Dayton, Ohio.
INDUSTRIAL REVIEW: *Ceramics*

Theiner, George. Editor, *Index on Censorship,* London. Coauthor of *The Kill Dog;* editor of *New Writing in Czechoslovakia.*
LITERATURE: *Eastern European; Russian (in part)*

Thomas, Theodore V. Free-lance Journalist and Press Consultant. Editor (1961–79), *British Toys and Hobbies.*
INDUSTRIAL REVIEW: *Games and Toys*

Tingay, Lance. Former Tennis Correspondent, *Daily Telegraph,* London. Author of *100 Years of Wimbledon; Tennis Facts and Feats.*
SPORTS AND GAMES: *Tennis*

Trigg, Robert H. Assistant Vice-President, Economic Research, New York Stock Exchange.
ECONOMIC AFFAIRS: *Stock Exchanges (in part)*

Trilling, Ossia. Coeditor and Contributor, *International Theatre.* Contributor, BBC and *The Times,* London.
BIOGRAPHIES *(in part);* THEATRE *(in part)*

UNHCR. The Office of the United Nations High Commissioner for Refugees.
POPULATIONS AND POPULATION MOVEMENTS: *Refugees*

Utt, Roger L. Assistant Professor of Spanish, Department of Romance Languages and Literatures, University of Chicago.
LITERATURE: *Spanish (in part)*

Vale, Norman K. Retired Director of News Services, The United Church of Canada.
RELIGION: *The United Church of Canada*

Venzke, Bruce H. Chief Correspondent, *National Billiard News;* Member, Rules Committee, Billiard Congress of America.
SPORTS AND GAMES: *Billiard Games (in part)*

Verdi, Robert William. Sportswriter, *Chicago Tribune.*
SPORTS AND GAMES: *Baseball (in part)*

Vermeer, Ruth. Development Officer, International Organization of Consumer Unions, The Hague, Neth.
CONSUMER AFFAIRS *(in part)*

Vint, Arthur Kingsley. Counselor, International Table Tennis Federation, Hastings, East Sussex, England.
SPORTS AND GAMES: *Table Tennis*

Ward, Peter. Owner and Operator, Ward News Services Canada, Parliamentary Press Gallery, Ottawa.
WORLD AFFAIRS: *Canada:* Special Report

Warner, Antony C. Editor, *Drinks Marketing,* London.
INDUSTRIAL REVIEW: *Beverages (in part)*

Watson, Louise. Staff Editor, Encyclopædia Britannica, London.
BIOGRAPHIES *(in part);* WORLD AFFAIRS: *Australia:* Sidebar; *Dependent States (in part); Oceanian Affairs (in part)*

Way, Diane Lois. Historical Researcher.
BIOGRAPHIES *(in part)*

Webber, Frederick L. President, National Soft Drink Association, Washington, D.C.
INDUSTRIAL REVIEW: *Beverages (in part)*

Weinthal, John R. Automotive Writer.
INDUSTRIAL REVIEW: *Automobiles (in part)*

Welch, Melvin D. Secretary, English Basket Ball Association; Editor (1971–78), *Basketball Magazine.*
SPORTS AND GAMES: *Basketball (in part)*

Whelan, John. Publisher, *Middle East Economic Digest* and *Africa Economic Digest,* London.
BIOGRAPHIES *(in part);* WORLD AFFAIRS: *Bahrain; Egypt; Iraq; Jordan; Kuwait; Lebanon; Middle Eastern and North African Affairs; Oman; Qatar; Saudi Arabia; Syria; United Arab Emirates; Yemen, People's Democratic Republic of; Yemen Arab Republic*

Whitney, Barbara. Senior Copy Editor, Encyclopædia Britannica, Inc.
BIOGRAPHIES *(in part)*

Wilkinson, John R. Sportswriter, East Midland Provincial Newspapers Ltd., U.K.
SPORTS AND GAMES: *Cycling*

Williams, Michael E. J. Golf Correspondent, *Daily Telegraph,* London.
SPORTS AND GAMES: *Golf*

Williams, Raymond L. Associate Professor of Spanish, Washington University, St. Louis, Mo.
LITERATURE: *Spanish (in part)*

Williamson, Trevor. Chief Sports Subeditor, *Daily Telegraph,* London.
SPORTS AND GAMES: *Football (in part);* Football: Sidebar

Wilson, Michael. Editor, *Avionics,* Jane's Publishing Co. Ltd.
INDUSTRIAL REVIEW: *Aerospace*

Witte, Randall E. Editor, *The Western Horseman* magazine, Colorado Springs, Colo.
SPORTS AND GAMES: *Rodeo*

Wood, Kenneth H. Retired Editor, *Adventist Review;* President, and Chairman of Trustees, Ellen G. White Estate, Inc.
RELIGION: *Seventh-day Adventist Church*

Woods, Elizabeth. Writer. Author of *The Yellow Volkswagen; Gone; Men; The Amateur.*
LITERATURE: *English (in part)*

Woollen, Anthony. Editor (1959–79), *Food Manufacture,* London. Editor, *Food Industries Manual* (20th ed.).
AGRICULTURE AND FOOD SUPPLIES: *Food Processing*

Wooller, Michael. Economist, Group Economics Dept., Lloyds Bank PLC, London.
WORLD AFFAIRS: *Chile; Portugal; Spain; Venezuela*

Woolley, David. Air Transport Editor, *Interavia,* London.
TRANSPORTATION *(in part)*

Worsnop, Richard L. Associate Editor, Editorial Research Reports, Washington, D.C.
WORLD AFFAIRS: *United States*

Wright, Almon R. Retired Senior Historian, U.S. Department of State.
WORLD AFFAIRS: *Panama*

Wyllie, Peter John. Chairman, Division of Geological and Planetary Sciences, California Institute of Technology.
EARTH SCIENCES: *Geology and Geochemistry*

Yang, Winston L. Y. Professor of Chinese Studies, Department of Asian Studies, Seton Hall University, South Orange, N.J.
BIOGRAPHIES *(in part);* LITERATURE: *Chinese*

Young, M. Norvel. Chancellor Emeritus, Pepperdine University, Malibu, Calif. Author of *Preachers of Today.*
RELIGION: *Churches of Christ*

Young, Susan. News Editor, *Church Times,* London.
RELIGION: *Anglican Communion*

Yuge, Yasushi. Staff writer; *The Japan Economic Journal,* Tokyo.
INFORMATION PROCESSING AND INFORMATION SYSTEMS *(in part)*

Zollo, Stephen M. New Products Editor, *Electronics* magazine, McGraw-Hill Inc.
INDUSTRIAL REVIEW: *Microelectronics*

Plate 1

Flags of the Nations

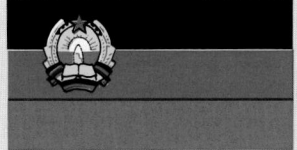

Afghanistan

Albania

Algeria

Andorra*

Angola

Antigua and Barbuda

Argentina*

Australia

Austria*

*State flag shown; national flag does not carry coat of arms.

Plate 2   Flags of the Nations

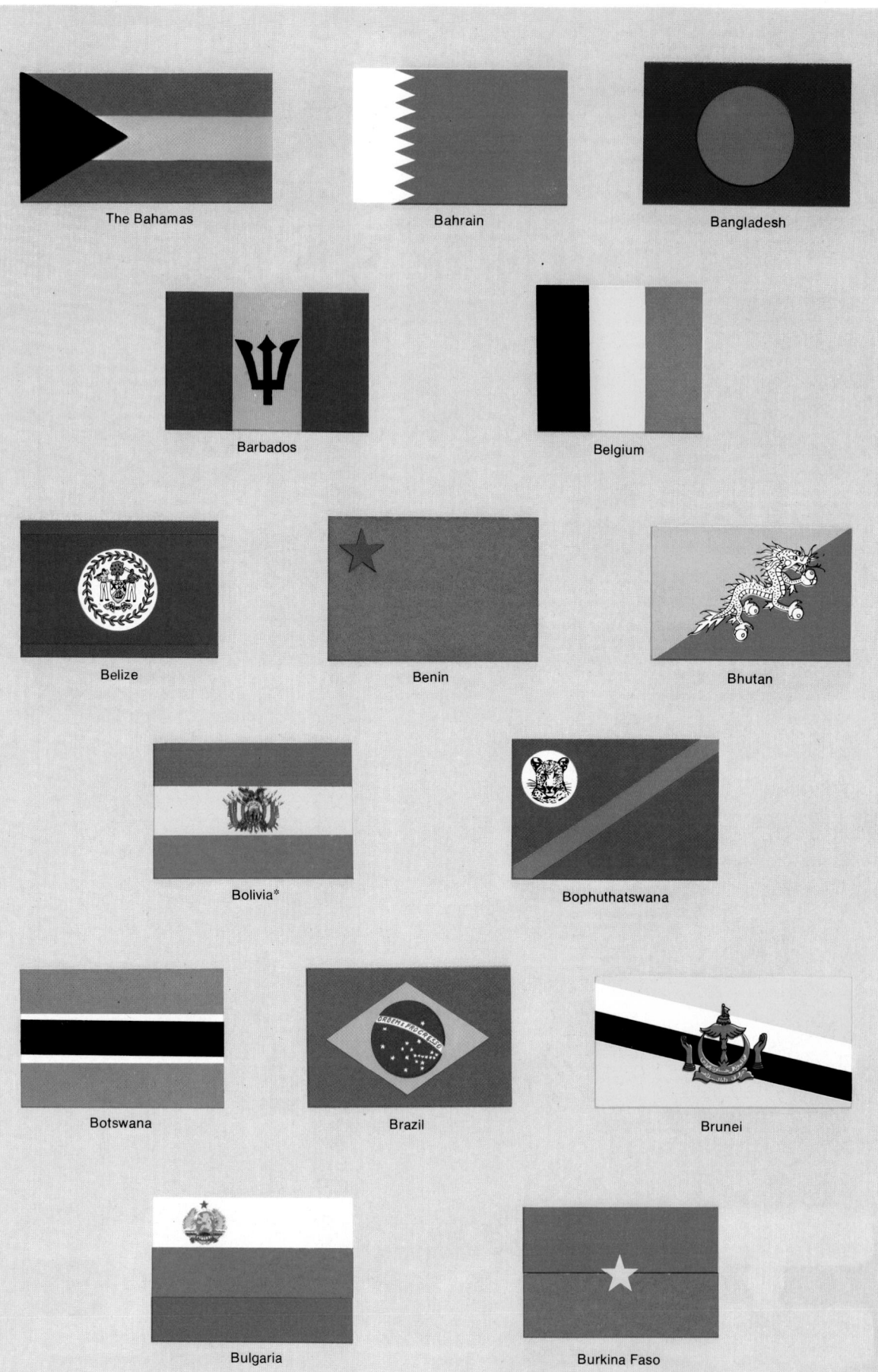

The Bahamas

Bahrain

Bangladesh

Barbados

Belgium

Belize

Benin

Bhutan

Bolivia*

Bophuthatswana

Botswana

Brazil

Brunei

Bulgaria

Burkina Faso

*State flag shown; national flag does not carry coat of arms.

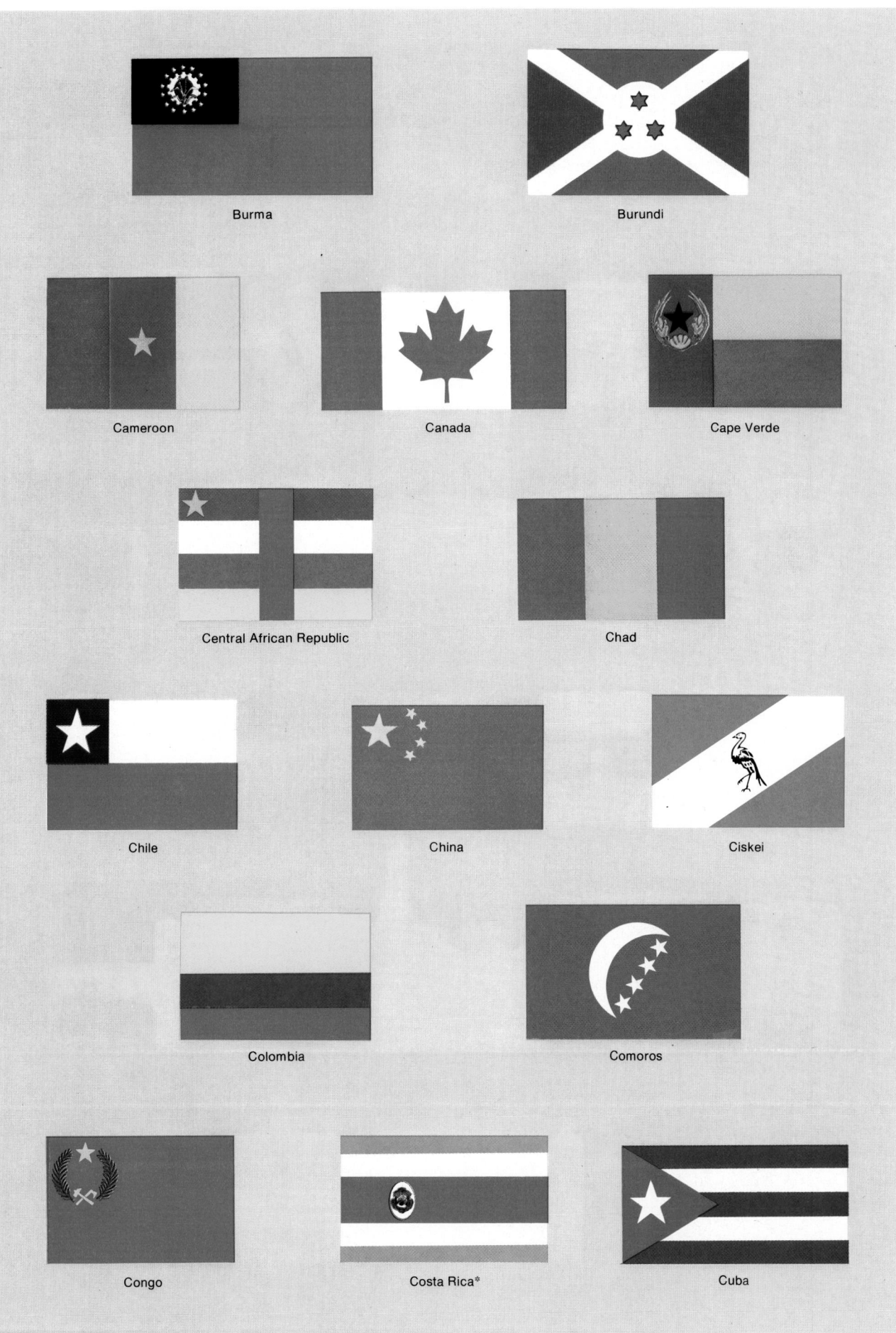

Burma

Burundi

Cameroon

Canada

Cape Verde

Central African Republic

Chad

Chile

China

Ciskei

Colombia

Comoros

Congo

Costa Rica*

Cuba

*State flag shown; national flag does not carry coat of arms.

Plate 4   Flags of the Nations

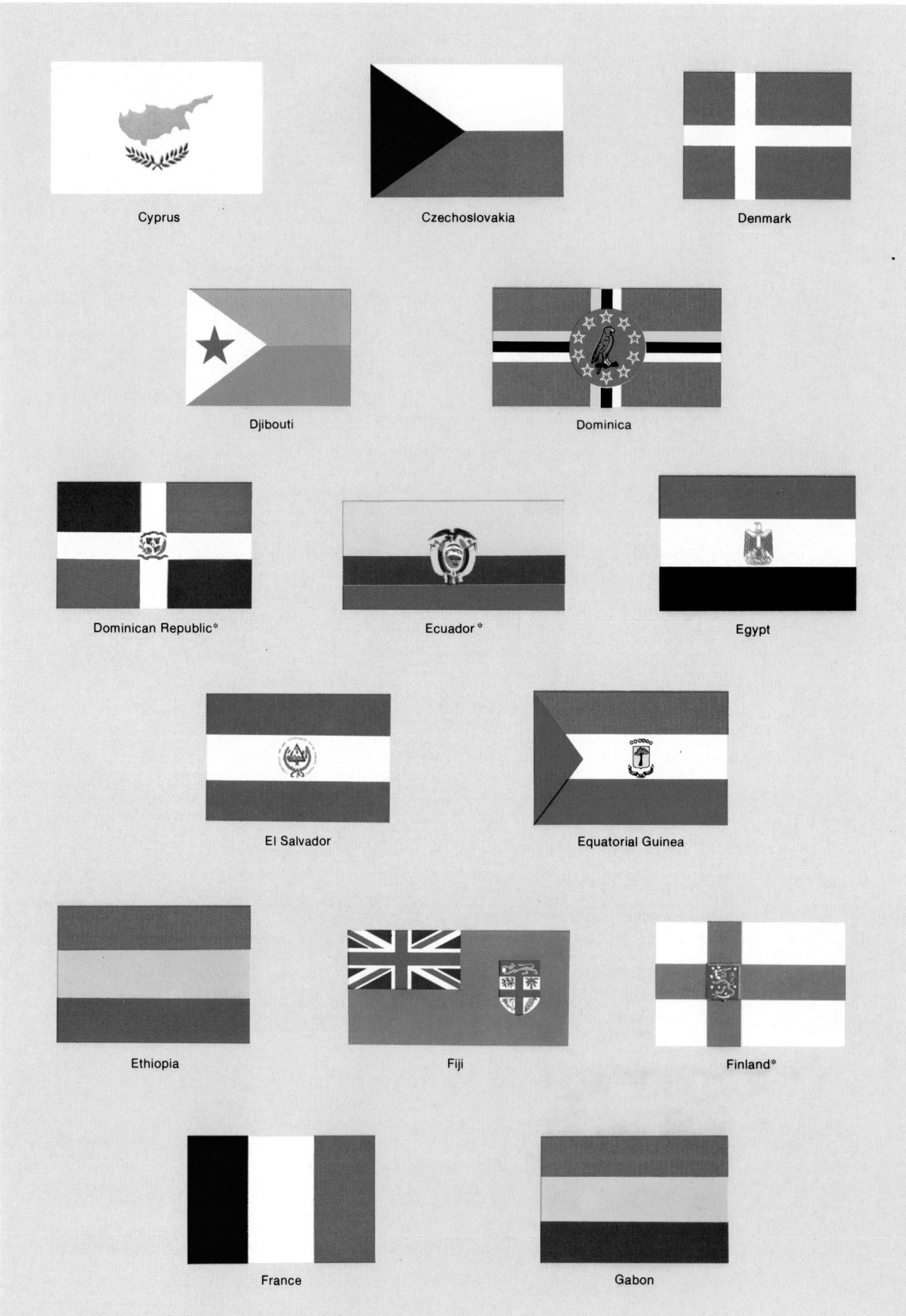

Cyprus

Czechoslovakia

Denmark

Djibouti

Dominica

Dominican Republic*

Ecuador*

Egypt

El Salvador

Equatorial Guinea

Ethiopia

Fiji

Finland*

France

Gabon

*State flag shown; national flag does not carry coat of arms.

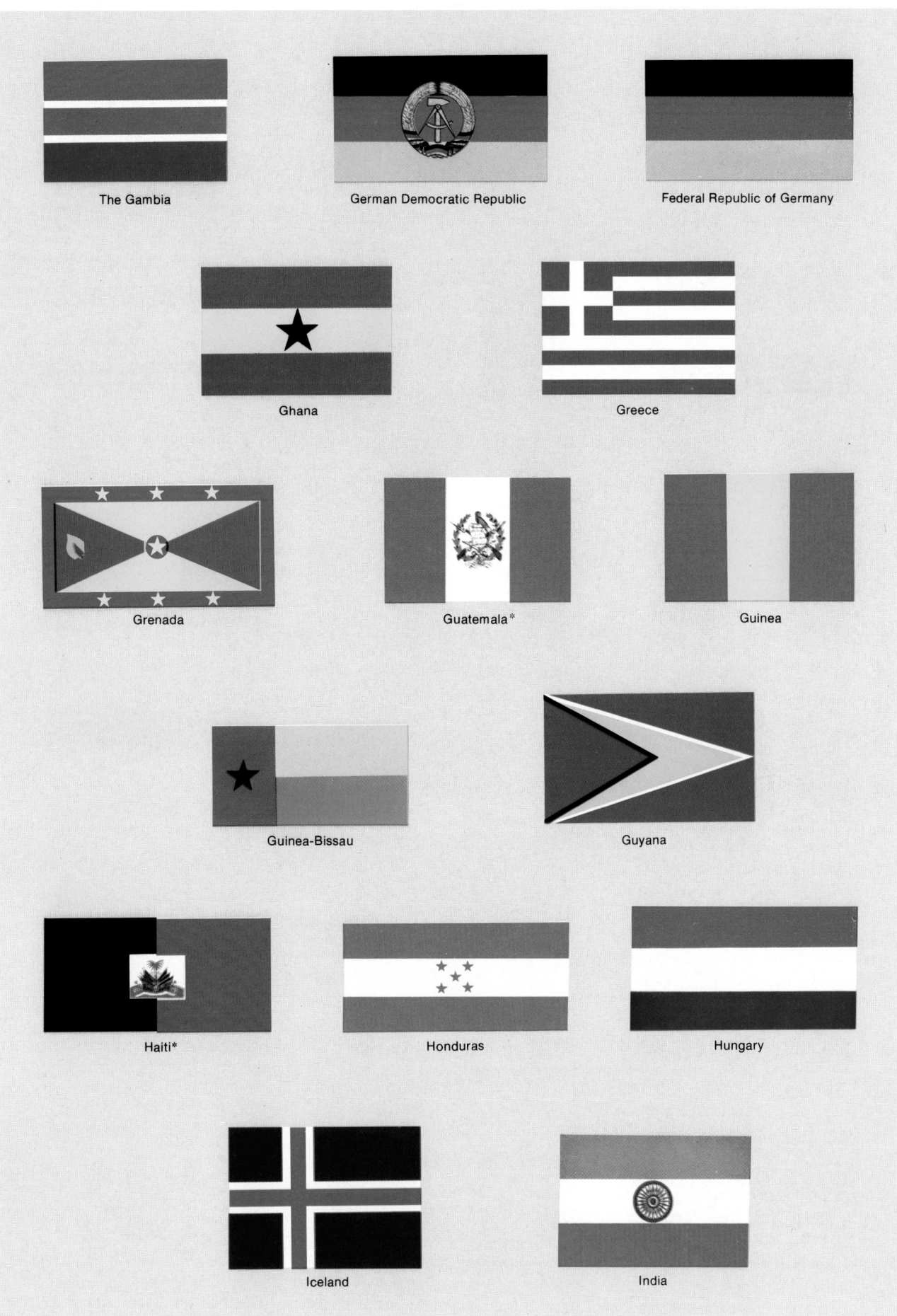

The Gambia

German Democratic Republic

Federal Republic of Germany

Ghana

Greece

Grenada

Guatemala*

Guinea

Guinea-Bissau

Guyana

Haiti*

Honduras

Hungary

Iceland

India

*State flag shown; national flag does not carry coat of arms.

Plate 6　Flags of the Nations

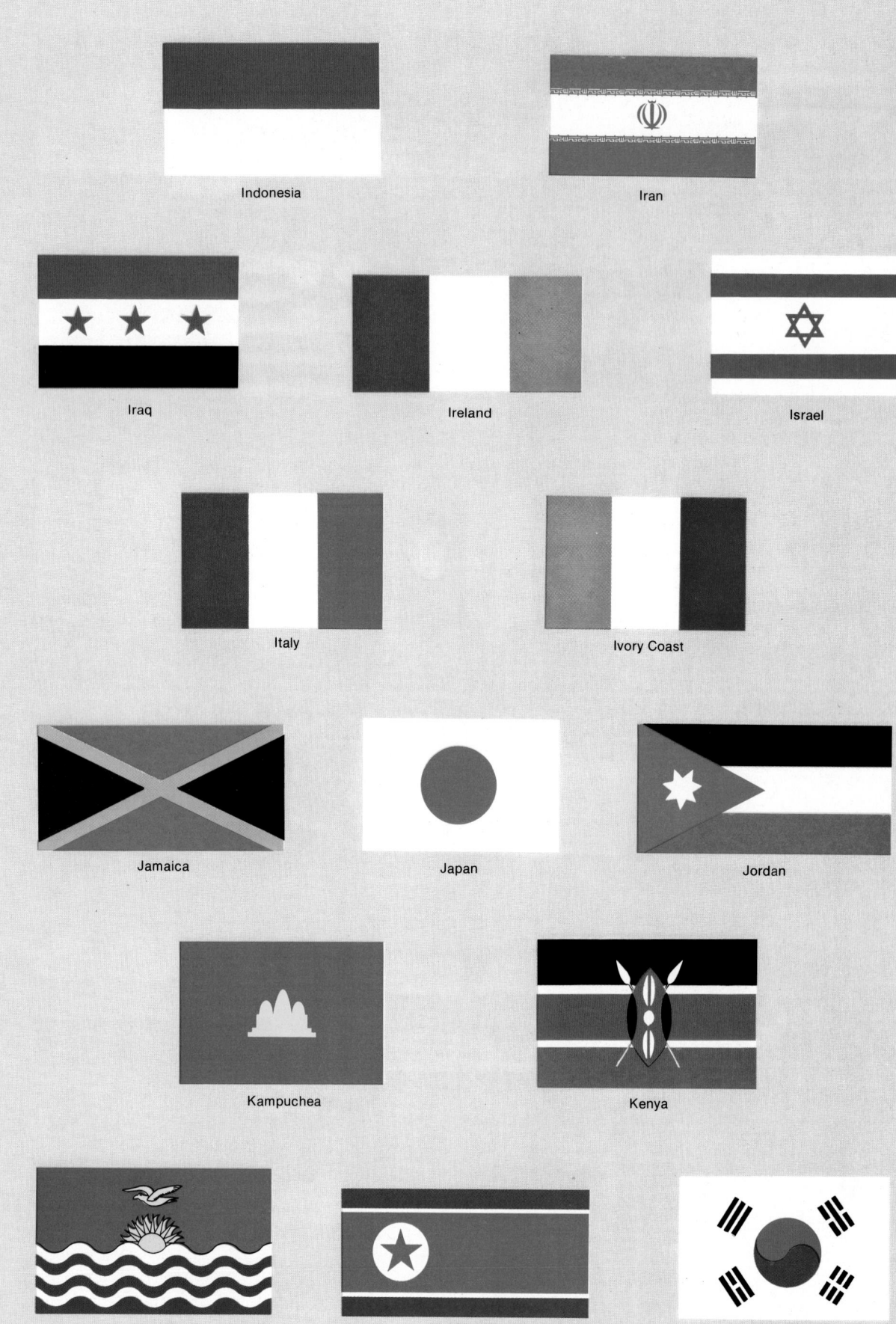

Indonesia

Iran

Iraq

Ireland

Israel

Italy

Ivory Coast

Jamaica

Japan

Jordan

Kampuchea

Kenya

Kiribati

North Korea

South Korea

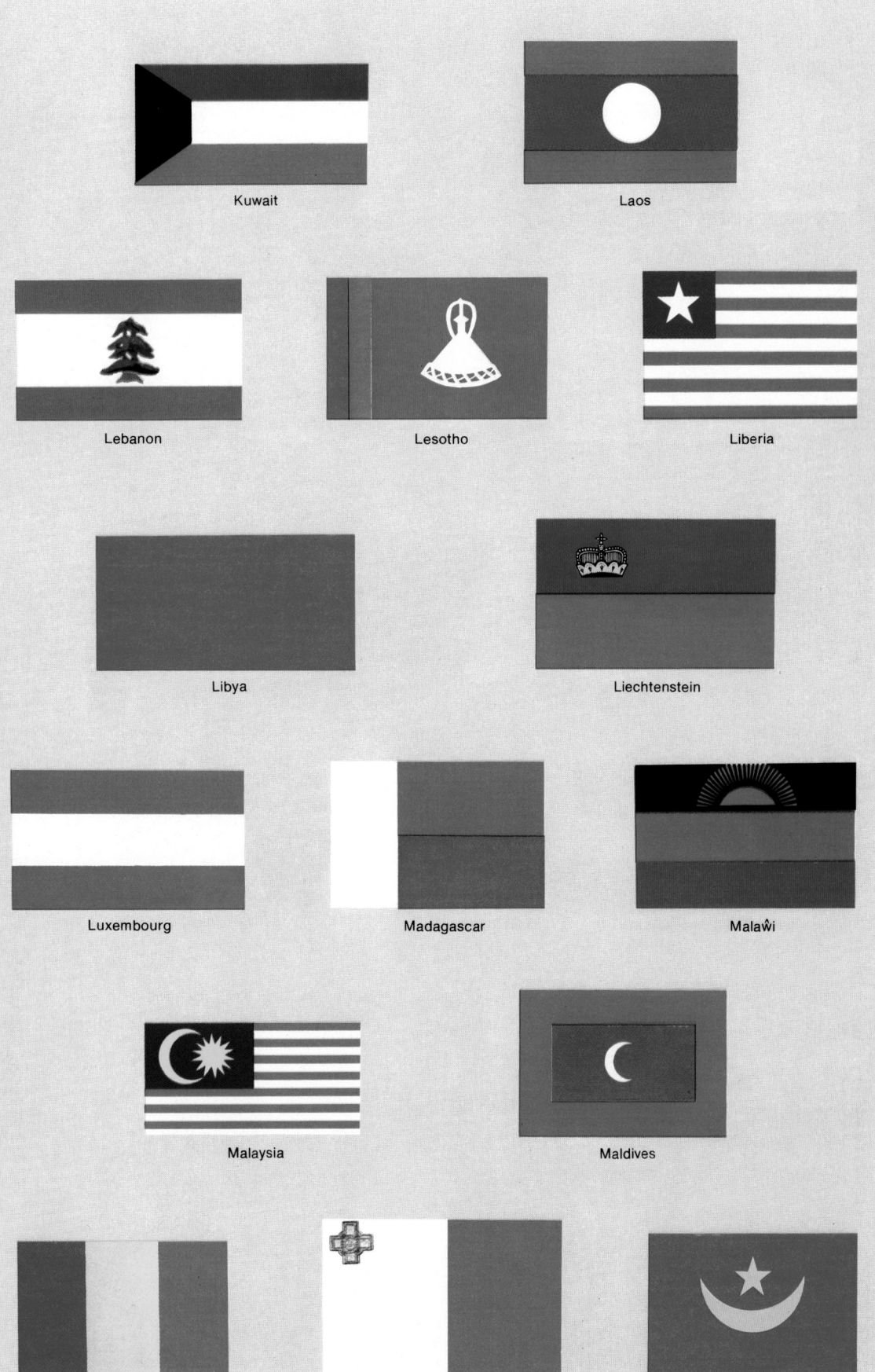

Kuwait

Laos

Lebanon

Lesotho

Liberia

Libya

Liechtenstein

Luxembourg

Madagascar

Malaŵi

Malaysia

Maldives

Mali

Malta

Mauritania

Plate 8 Flags of the Nations

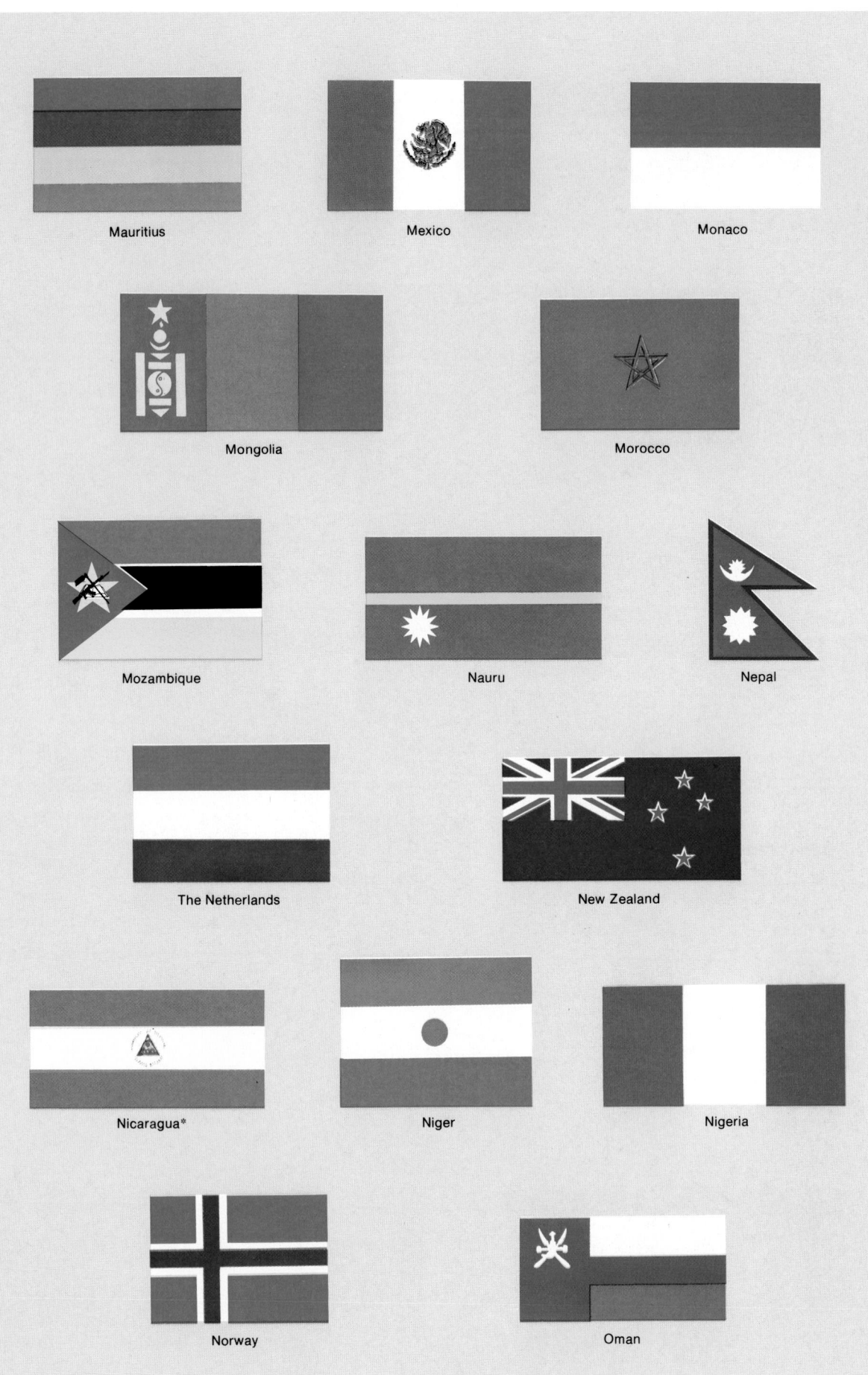

Mauritius

Mexico

Monaco

Mongolia

Morocco

Mozambique

Nauru

Nepal

The Netherlands

New Zealand

Nicaragua*

Niger

Nigeria

Norway

Oman

*State flag shown; national flag does not carry coat of arms.

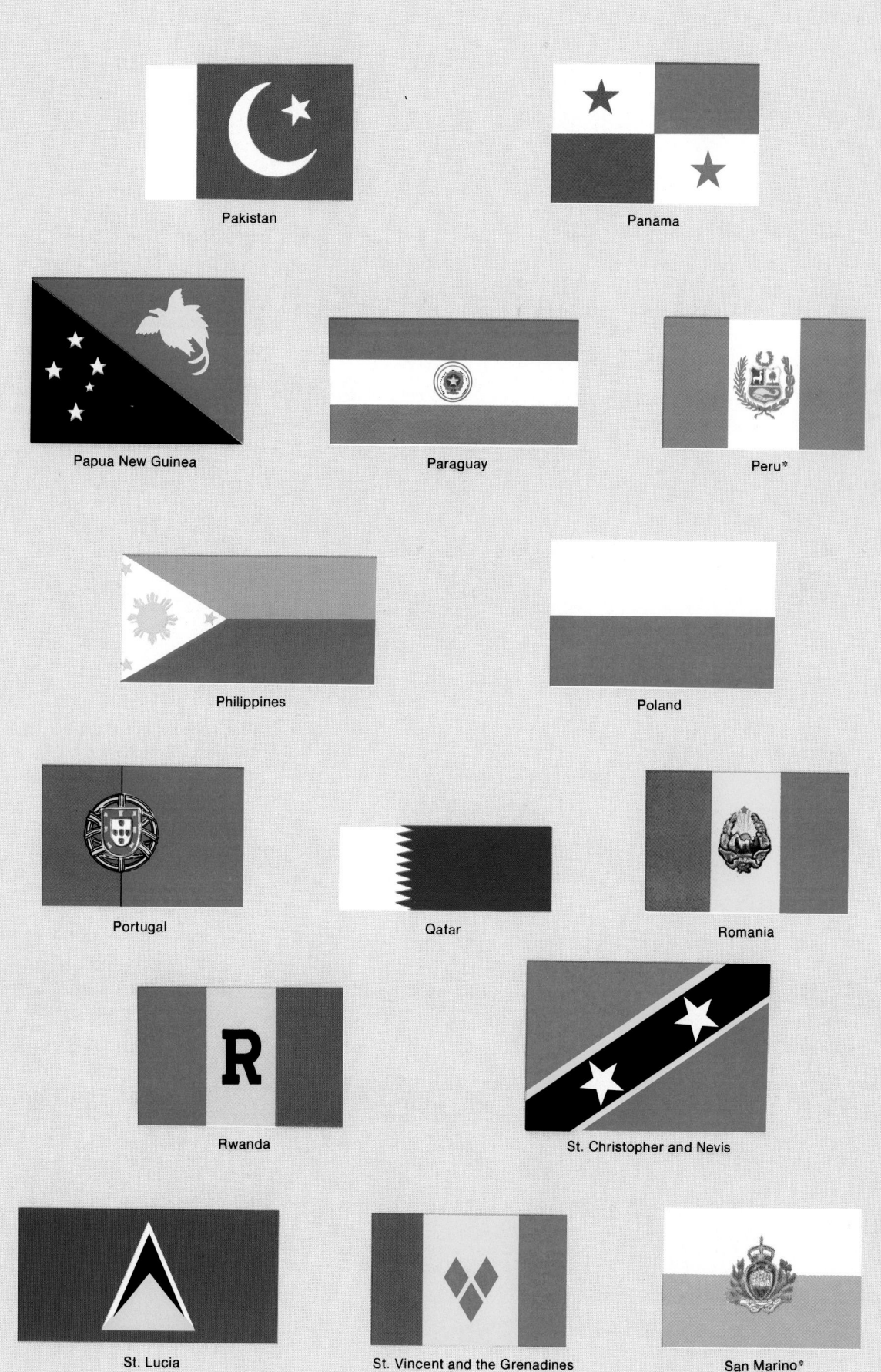

Pakistan

Panama

Papua New Guinea

Paraguay

Peru*

Philippines

Poland

Portugal

Qatar

Romania

Rwanda

St. Christopher and Nevis

St. Lucia

St. Vincent and the Grenadines

San Marino*

*State flag shown; national flag does not carry coat of arms.

Plate 10   Flags of the Nations

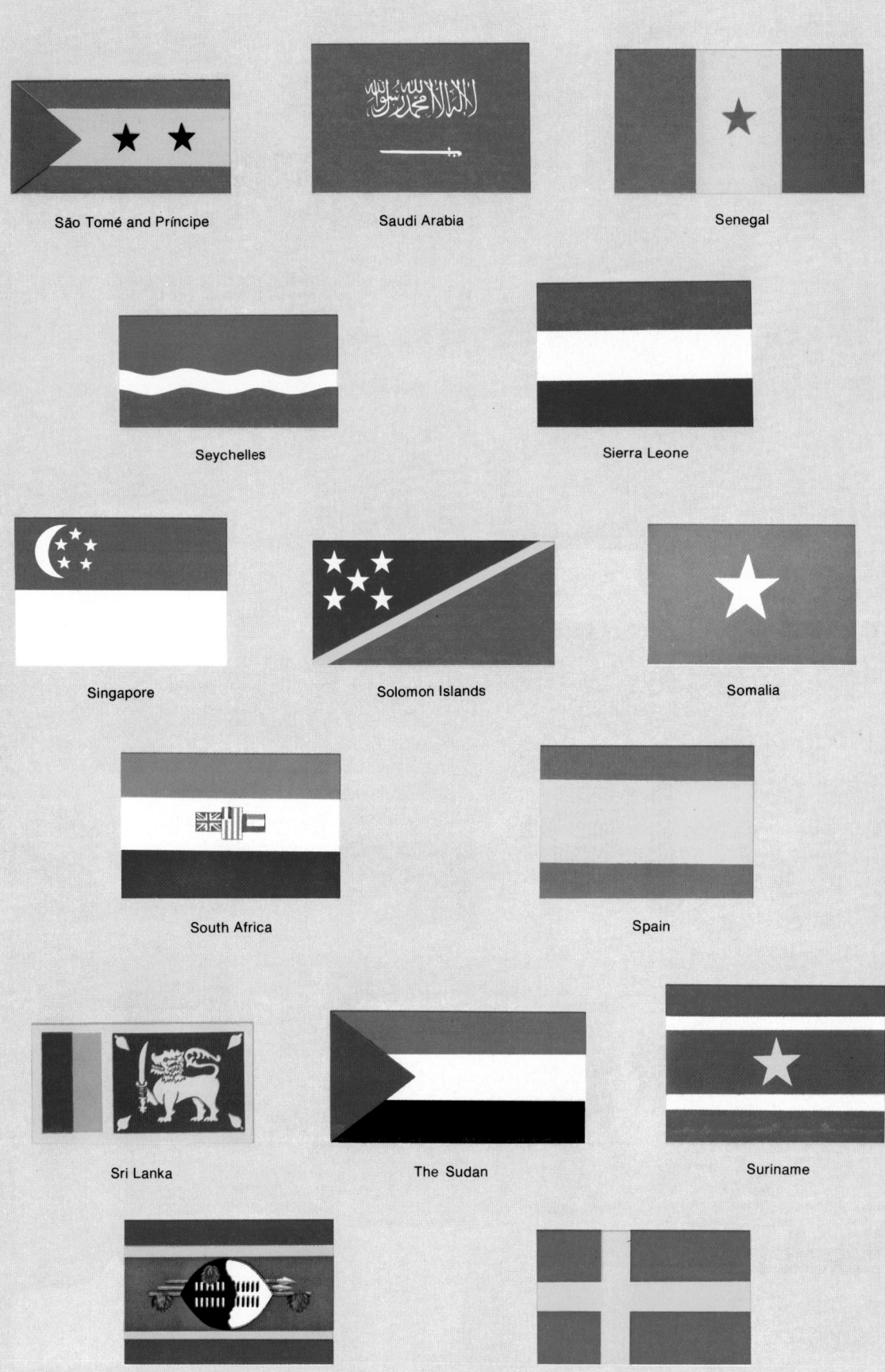

São Tomé and Príncipe

Saudi Arabia

Senegal

Seychelles

Sierra Leone

Singapore

Solomon Islands

Somalia

South Africa

Spain

Sri Lanka

The Sudan

Suriname

Swaziland

Sweden

Switzerland

Syria

Taiwan

Tanzania

Thailand

Togo

Tonga

Transkei

Trinidad and Tobago

Tunisia

Turkey

Tuvalu

Uganda

Union of Soviet Socialist Republics

United Arab Emirates

Plate 12 Flags of the Nations

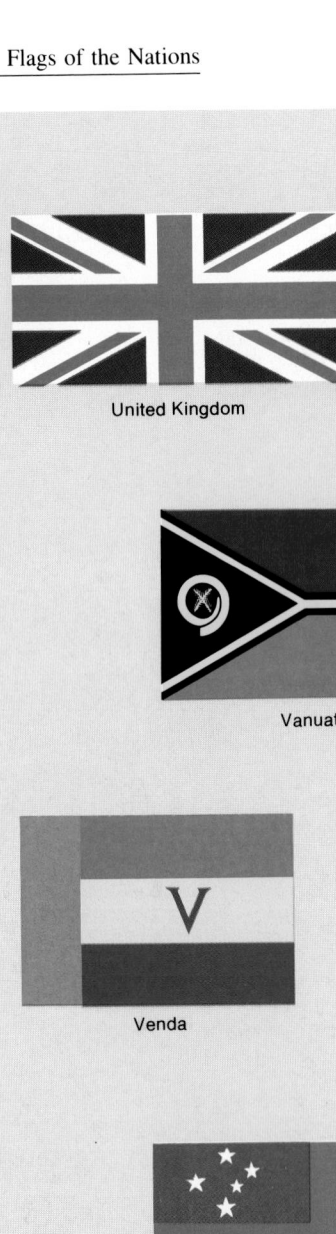

United Kingdom

United States

Uruguay

Vanuatu

Vatican City

Venda

Venezuela*

Vietnam

Western Samoa

People's Democratic Republic of Yemen

Yemen Arab Republic

Yugoslavia

Zaire

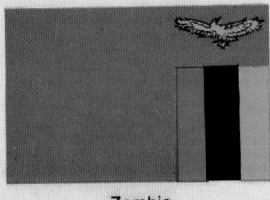

Zambia

Zimbabwe

*State flag shown; national flag does not carry coat of arms.

1986
Britannica
World Data

Encyclopædia Britannica, Inc.
Chicago
Auckland/Geneva/London/Manila/Paris/Rome
Seoul/Sydney/Tokyo/Toronto

CONTENTS

INTRODUCTION

Britannica World Data provides a statistical portrait of each of some 215 countries and dependencies of the world, at a level appropriate to the size and importance of each. It contains 186 country statements, ranging in length from one to four pages, for the largest and most significant of these, and permits, in the development of more than a score of major thematic subject areas (employment, agriculture, trade), simultaneous comparison among all of these larger countries and 29 additional smaller dependent states.

Updated annually, *Britannica World Data* can be consulted as a separate work of reference developing a particular body of subject matter, but it is particularly intended as direct, structured support for many of Britannica's other reference works—encyclopedias, yearbooks, atlases—at a level of detail that their editorial style or space requirements do not permit.

Like the textual, graphic, or cartographic modes of expression of these other products, statistics possess their own inherent editorial virtues and weaknesses. Two principal goals in the creation of *Britannica World Data* were up-to-dateness and comparability, each possible separately, but not always possible to combine. If, for example, research on some subject (say, registered motor vehicles) is completed during a particular year (x), figures may be available for 100 countries for the preceding year ($x-1$), for 140 countries for the year before that ($x-2$), and for 180 countries for the year before that ($x-3$).

Which year should be the basis of a thematic compilation for 215 countries so as to give the best combination of up-to-dateness and comparability? And, should $x-1$ be adopted for the thematic table, ought up-to-dateness in the country table (for which year x is already available) be sacrificed for agreement with the thematic table? In general, the editors have opted for maximum up-to-dateness in the country statistical boxes and maximum comparability in the thematic tables, so as to take the best advantage of late information, published and unpublished.

Comparability, however, also resides in the meaning of the numbers compiled, which may differ greatly from country to country. The headnotes to the thematic tables explain many of these definitional problems; the Glossary serves the same purpose for the country statistical pages. Since the researcher or editor does not always find a neat, unambiguous choice between a datum compiled on two different bases (say, railroad track length, or route length), one of which is wanted and the other not, a choice must be made between the latest official national data (which may be incomplete, published only after a delay of several years, politically suspect, compiled on the wrong basis [for international comparability], or may refer to some time period other than a standard Gregorian calendar year) and some external figure, often only an estimate, compiled by an international organization (such as the UN, FAO, or IMF), on the desired basis, but often at a considerable remove from the country's own most recent data, both in time and distance. Every effort has been made to obtain the best combination of comparability and up-to-dateness from available sources, and, when the completeness of a country's published data permitted, to analyze it further for better agreement in coverage, scope, and datedness, For certain subjects, especially population, the editors have prepared their own estimates.

The published basis of the information compiled is the statistical collections of Encyclopædia Britannica, Inc., some of the principal elements of which are enumerated in the Bibliography. All of these sources are held, and updated continuously for editorial use, in Britannica's editorial offices. The publications themselves are issued in some 75 languages in common use among the countries of the world; the information contained in them is supplemented by unpublished data received in correspondence from the countries concerned. Usual holdings for a country with a well-developed statistical and publishing program may include any of the following kinds of documents: the national statistical abstract; the most recent censuses of population; periodic or occasional reports on vital statistics, social indicators, agriculture, mining, labour, manufacturing, wholesale and retail trade, finance and banking, development planning, foreign trade, transportation, and communication. These primarily statistical sources are supplemented by other kinds of national reference works, such as gazetteers (of place names), national atlases, constitutions, and monographs by domestic or external analysts.

No reference work on the countries of the world can, or should, be used in isolation. To say that the population density of The Netherlands is 1,100 per square mile will not be misleading, because the population is rather evenly distributed across the landscape outside the cities. To give a density for Greenland calculated on the same basis (total population ÷ total area) *would* be misleading (and would amount to only 0.06 persons per square mile) because much of Greenland is uninhabitable ice cap. Similarly, the great majority of the social, economic, and financial data contained in this work should not be interpreted in isolation. Interpretive text of long perspective, such as that of the *Encyclopædia Britannica* itself; political, geographic, and topical maps; and recent analysis of political events and economic trends, such as that contained in the articles of the *Book of the Year*, will all help to supply balance, physical framework, and analytical focus that numbers alone cannot provide. By the same token, study of those sources will be amplified and made more concrete by use of the *Britannica World Data* to supply up-to-date geographic, demographic, economic, and financial data to illuminate the generalized and more impressionistic methodology of those works.

GLOSSARY

A number of terms that are used to classify and report data in the "Nations of the World" section require some explanation.

Those italicized terms that are used regularly in the country compilations to introduce specific categories of information (*e.g.*, "birth rate," "budget") appear in this glossary in italic boldface type, followed by a description of the precise kind of information being offered and how it has been edited and presented. In some instances, additional discussion is provided on aspects of data collection and classification.

All other terms are printed here in roman boldface type. Many terms have rather specific meanings in statistical reporting, and they are so defined here. Other terms have less specific application as they are used in different countries or by different reporting organizations. Any ambiguities in the application of terms used in the country compilations and any departures from the definitions given in this glossary are usually annotated or footnoted at the appropriate places.

Terms that appear in small capitals in certain definitions are themselves defined at their proper alphabetical locations.

Terms whose definitions are marked by an asterisk (*) refer to data that are supplied only in the larger two- to four-page country compilations.

access to services, a group of measures indicating level of access to public services for the general population, including electrical power, treated public water, sewage removal, and fire protection.*

age breakdown, the distribution of a given population by age, usually reported here as percentages (of total population) based on the number of persons in each 15-year age bracket. For some censuses there are substantial numbers of persons for whom age is unknown or from whom there is no response, which imparts a degree of uncertainty to the distribution.

area and population, usually the first-order administrative subdivisions of the country (such as the states of the United States), with capital or administrative seat, area, and population. Occasionally, when these subdivisions are either especially numerous, or, occasionally, nonexistent, a regional, political, electoral, census, or other scheme has been substituted.

associated state, *see* state.

autonomous, *see* self-governing.

balance of payments, a statistical statement for a given period showing the balance among: (1) transactions in goods, services, and income between a country and the rest of the world; (2) changes in ownership or valuation of that country's monetary gold, SPECIAL DRAWING RIGHTS, and claims on and liabilities to the rest of the world; and (3) unrequited transfers and counterpart entries needed (in an accounting sense) to balance transactions and changes among any of the foregoing types of exchange that are not mutually offsetting. The United Nations *System of National Accounts* (SNA) provides a framework for international comparability in classifying such transactions, but detail of local law as to what constitutes a

transaction, valuation and reporting periods, and the size of a holding or transaction visible to national authorities all result in differences in the meaning of a particular national statement.

balance of trade, the net value of all international goods trade of a country, usually excluding reexports (goods received only for transshipment), and the percentage that this net represents of total trade.

More generally, the balance of trade, also known as merchandise account, is the difference between the value of a country's imports and the value of its exports of goods as usually recorded by customs authorities. Balance of trade refers only to the visible international trade of goods and is thus a segment of a country's BALANCE OF PAYMENTS, which takes all visible and invisible trade with other countries into account. (Invisible trade refers to imports and exports of services such as transport, tourism, and insurance.) A country has a favourable balance of trade when the value of exports exceeds that of imports.

barrel (bbl), a unit of liquid measure. The barrel conventionally used for reporting crude petroleum and petroleum products is equal to 42 U.S. gallons or 159 litres. The number of barrels of crude petroleum per metric ton ranging typically from 6.65 to 8.09, depends upon the specific gravity of the petroleum. The world average is roughly 7.33 barrels per ton.

birth rate, the number of live births annually per 1,000 population.

See also crude birth rate.

budget, the annual receipts and expenditures of the central government for its activities only; does not include the revenues and expenditures of state, provincial, and other local governments unless otherwise specified. Figures for budgets are limited to ordinary receipts and matching expenditures and wherever possible exclude capital expenditures, *i.e.*, funds for development and other special projects and foreign-aid grants (which nonetheless often appear as receipts on the budgets of recipient countries).

When both a recurrent and a capital budget exist for a single country, the former is the budget funded entirely from national resources (taxes, duties, excises, etc.) that would recur (be generated by economic activity) every year. It funds the most basic governmental services, those least able to stand interruption. The capital budget is usually funded, particularly in less developed countries, by external aid and may change its size very considerably from year to year. Sometimes a capital budget may be funded by transfers from a recurrent budget.

capital, usually the actual seat of administration and government of a political entity. When more than one capital exists, each is identified by kind; when interim arrangements

exist during the creation of a new national capital, the de facto situation is described.

Anomalous cases where the de jure designation under the country's laws differs from actual local practice, as when Yemen (Aden) or Libya formerly possessed two cocapitals in constitutional law, but only one in practice; or where international recognition does not support a country's claim, as with the proclamation by Israel of a capital on territory not fully recognized as part of Israel; or the proclamation of both a state and a capital on territory recognized as part of another state, as with the Turkish Republic of Northern Cyprus, are footnoted.

capital budget, *see* budget.

causes of death, as defined by the World Health Organization, "the disease or injury which initiated the train of morbid events leading directly to death, or the circumstances of accident or violence which produced the fatal injury." This principle, the "underlying cause of death," is the basis of the medical judgment as to cause; the statistical classification system according to which these causes are grouped and named is the *International List of Causes of Death,* the latest revision of which is the Ninth, although a number of countries continue to report according to the Eighth, or even earlier, versions. Reporting is usually in terms of events per 100,000 population (sometimes 10,000 for smaller countries).

chief of state / head of government, as prescribed or practiced, although divergences in form and practice are considerable.

In general usage, the chief of state is the formal head of a national state. The primary responsibilities of the chief of state are usually ceremonial—convening legislatures, greeting foreign officials, hosting state dinners, and bestowing honours. The head of government of a national state is the chief executive officer who effectively exercises the majority of actual executive powers. The head of government of a dependent political unit is the chief executive officer, either appointive or elective, who wields the most local executive powers, regardless of administrative prerogatives reserved elsewhere. In some countries the two positions may be merged.

In communist countries the official given as the chief of state is the chairman of the policy-making organ, and the official given as the head of government is the chairman of the nominal administrative/executive organ.

c.i.f. (trade valuation): *see* imports.

colony, an area annexed to, or controlled by, an independent state but not an integral part of it; a non-self-governing territory. A colony has a charter and may have a degree of self-government. A crown colony is a colony originally chartered by the British government.

commonwealth (U.S.), a self-governing political entity associated with the United States; examples are the Philippines from 1935 to 1946 and Puerto Rico since 1952.

Commonwealth, formerly called the Commonwealth of Nations, a loose voluntary association of states, including the United Kingdom and a number of its former dominions, colonies, and dependencies, established under the Statute of Westminster in 1931.

communications, collectively, the means available for the public transmission of information within a country. Data are provided for daily newspapers, their number and total circulation, and the per capita rate of circulation implied by that total; for radio, television, and telephone receivers, total numbers and rates of availability are supplied.

constitutional monarchy, *see* monarchy.

consumer price index, also known as the retail price index or the cost-of-living index, a series of index numbers assigned to the price of a selected "basket," or assortment, of basic

consumer goods and services in a country or region to measure changes over time in prices paid by a typical household for those goods and services. Items included in the consumer price index are ordinarily determined by governmental surveys of typical household expenditures, and are assigned weights relative to their proportion of those expenditures.

coprincipality, *see* monarchy.

crude birth rate, the number of live births annually per 1,000 of midyear population. Birth rates for individual countries may be compared with the world annual average of 29 births per 1,000 population between 1980 and 1985.

crude death rate, the number of deaths annually per 1,000 of midyear population. Death rates for individual countries may be compared with the world annual average of 11 deaths per 1,000 population between 1980 and 1985.

daily per capita caloric intake (supply), the calories equivalent to the known average daily supply of foodstuffs for human consumption in a given country divided by the population of the country. This estimated measure may differ from actual daily per capita consumption of food as a result of waste, inefficient distribution, and exploitation of sources of food not included in the known supply of foodstuffs. The daily per capita caloric intake of a country may be compared with the corresponding daily per capita caloric requirement. The latter is calculated by the Food and Agriculture Organization (FAO) of the United Nations from the age and sex distributions, average body weights, and environmental temperatures in a given country to determine the calories needed to sustain a person there at normal levels of activity and health. The daily per capita caloric requirement ranges from 2,200 to 2,400 in most Asian, African, and Latin-American countries to 2,500 and more in North America and most European and Oceanian countries. The world daily per capita caloric requirement approaches 2,400.

See also food.

de facto population, for a given area, the population enumerated on the basis of those present at a particular time, including temporary visitors and excluding legal residents temporarily absent.

de jure population, for a given area, the population enumerated on the basis of legal residence, excluding temporary visitors and including legal residents temporarily absent.

deadweight tonnage, the maximum weight of cargo, fuel, fresh water, stores, and persons that may safely be carried by a ship. It is customarily measured in long tons of 2,240 pounds each, equivalent to 1.016 metric tons. Deadweight tonnage is the difference between the tonnage of a fully loaded ship and the fully unloaded tonnage of that ship.

death rate, the number of registered deaths or, where registration is incomplete, the estimated number of deaths annually per 1,000 population.

See also crude death rate.

density (of population), usually the total area of the country divided into its DE FACTO POPULATION. Special adjustment is made for inland water or other uninhabitable areas, *e.g.,* excluding the lake area of Finland, the ice area of Greenland, or the desert area of Egypt.

The crude density of population of a particular country can be compared with the world average of 93 persons per square mile (36 persons per square kilometre) in 1985.

department, a first-order civil administrative subdivision. *Overseas department* (France), an overseas subdivision of the French Republic, almost equivalent to a department of metropolitan France, with elected representation in the French Parliament.

dependency, any area outside of and under the jurisdiction of an independent state but not formally annexed to it.

direct taxes, taxes levied directly on firms and individuals, such as taxes on income, profits, and capital gains. The immediate incidence, or burden, of direct taxes is on the firms and individuals thus taxed; the incidence of direct taxes on firms may, however, be passed on to consumers and other economic units in the form of higher prices for goods and services, with the result that the distinction between direct and indirect taxes is not always clear. Figures given for individual countries are limited to direct taxes levied by their respective central governments unless otherwise specified.

distribution of income/wealth, the portion of national household income or wealth accruing to households or individuals comprising each respective decile (tenth) or quintile (fifth) of the total number of households or individuals.*

See also household income and expenditures.

divorce rate, the number of legal, civilly recognized divorces annually per 1,000 population.

doubling time, the number of complete years required for a country to double its population at its current rate of natural increase; it does not take into account expected demographic change during the period, such as changes in birth rate, death rate, or population migration.

earnings index, a series of index numbers comparing average wages in selected industries in a country or region with the same industry at a previous period to measure changes over time in those wages. It is most commonly collected for wages paid on a daily, weekly, or monthly basis. The scope of the earnings index varies from country to country; the index is often limited to earnings in manufacturing industries. The index for each country applies to all wage earners in a designated group and ordinarily takes into account basic wages (overtime is normally distinguished), bonuses, cost-of-living allowances, and contributions toward social security by the wage earners in question. Some countries include payments in kind. Contributions toward social security by employers are usually excluded, as are social security benefits received by wage earners.

See also price and earnings indexes.

economically active population, *see* population economically active.

education, tabulation of the principal elements of the country's educational establishment, classified as far as possible according to the country's own system of primary, secondary, and higher levels (the usual age limits for these levels being identified in parentheses), with total number of schools (physical facilities) and of teachers and students (whether full- or part-time). The student–teacher ratio is calculated whenever available data permit.

educational attainment, the distribution of the adult population by the highest level of formal education attained or completed.

emirate, *see* monarchy.

empire, *see* monarchy.

enclave, a portion of a state separated geographically from its main part and having boundaries only with some other state or states. The surrounded area is said to be an enclave with respect to the area that borders on it and an *exclave* with respect to the state of which it is a part.

ethnic/linguistic composition, ethnic, racial, or linguistic composition of a national population, reported here according to the most reliable breakdown published in official sources (when available) or external analysis (when the subject is not addressed in national sources [usually because of social or political sensitivity about the consequences of publishing such

data]). For a discussion of some of the classificational problems, *see* the "Language" table at page 838.

exchange rate, the value of one currency compared to another, or to a standardized value such as the SPECIAL DRAWING RIGHT, or as mandated by local statute when one currency is "tied" by a par value to another. Rates given usually refer to market values when the currency itself is traded, or to the value of trade transactions either averaged over the period of a year, or as of a single date during the year.

exclave, *see* enclave.

exports, material goods legally leaving a country (or customs area) and subject to customs regulations. The total value and distribution by percentage of the major items (in preference to groups of goods) exported are given, together with the distribution of trade among major trading partners (usually single countries or trading blocs). Figures given for goods exported are free on board (f.o.b.) unless otherwise specified. The value of goods exported and imported free on board (f.o.b.) is calculated from the cost of production and excludes the cost of transport, which is passed on to the consumer.

external debt, public debt with an original or extended maturity of more than one year that is owed to nonnationals of a country, and is repayable in foreign currency, goods, or services. The debt may be an obligation of a national or subnational governmental body (or an agency of either), or of an autonomous public body. The debt is usually classed as either outstanding (the proportion valued on concessional terms, indicating dependency on official lenders) or disbursed (the proportion carrying variable interest rates, indicating dependence on capital markets).

external territory (Australia), *see* territory.

fabricated metal, refined metal that has been converted through processing into finer or more finished forms, such as rolled shapes, from ingots.

farm, economic unit comprising an operator and the land on which agricultural operations are conducted. The legal tenure of the farm may be under the control of a person, partnership, or corporation. In the United States, a farm is such a place with annual gross sales of farm products of $1,000 or more.

federal, consisting of first-order political subdivisions that are prior to and independent of the central government in certain functions.

federal republic, *see* republic.

federation, a union of coequal political entities that retain some degree of autonomy within the union.

fertility rate, *see* general fertility rate; total fertility rate.

financial aggregates, tabulation of seven-year time series, providing principal measures of the financial condition of a country: the exchange rate of the national currency against the U.S. dollar, the pound sterling, and the International Monetary Fund's SPECIAL DRAWING RIGHT (SDR); the amount and kind of international reserves (holdings of SDRs, gold, and foreign currencies) and reserve position of the country in the International Monetary Fund; principal economic rates and prices (central bank discount rate, government bond yields, and industrial stock [share] prices). For BALANCE OF PAYMENTS, the origin in terms of component balance of trade items and balance of invisibles (net) is given.*

fish catch, the live-weight equivalent of the aquatic animals (including fish, crustaceans, mollusks, etc., but excluding whales, seals, and other aquatic mammals) caught in freshwater or marine areas by national fleets and landed in domestic or foreign harbours for commercial, industrial, or subsistence purposes.

f.o.b. (trade valuation): *see* exports.

food, total per capita supply of food (assumed to equal actual consumption since detailed data on waste, or actual consumption logs, are seldom available), summarized in calories and distributed as percentages by vegetable and animal origin.

See also daily per capita caloric intake.

form of government/political status, the structure of a country's administration provided for in normal constitutional operation, whether or not suspended by extralegal military or civil action, although such de facto administrations are identified; together with the number of members (as prescribed by the constitution) for each legislative house, named according to its English rendering. Dependencies are classified according to the status of their political association with the administering country.

general fertility rate, the number of live births per 1,000 females of childbearing age, generally considered to be between the ages of 15 and 49. Stillborn births are generally excluded from the general fertility rate.

See also total fertility rate.

gross domestic product (GDP), the total value of the final goods and services produced by residents and nonresidents within a given country during a given year. The GDP excludes the value of net income earned abroad, which is included in the GROSS NATIONAL PRODUCT (GNP).

gross national product (GNP), the total per capita value of final goods and services produced both from within a given country *and* from external (foreign) transactions in a given year. GNP is equal to GROSS DOMESTIC PRODUCT plus net factor income from abroad (the latter including balance-of-goods trade and international financial transactions).

gross output in factor values, the total market value of goods and services produced in a given period in a given country, less all INDIRECT TAXES on production but including all current subsidies received in support of production activity.

gross output value in producers' prices, the total market value of goods and services produced in a given period in a given country, including all INDIRECT TAXES on production but excluding subsidies.

gross (register) ton, unit of measure of the permanently enclosed volume of a ship, less certain exempted spaces such as those devoted to machinery, bunkers, crew accommodations, and so on; the gross register tonnage of a ship is thus a rough estimation of its volumetric cargo capacity. The gross register ton is equivalent to 100 cubic feet or 2.83 cubic metres.

head of government, *see* chief of state/head of government.

health, total number of accredited physicians (according to Western criteria) by specialization and their ratio to the total population; similarly for hospital beds, except that psychiatric and other specialized institutional beds are excluded.

household income and expenditure, data for average household size (by number of individuals) and for average household income (often reported alternatively as consumption expenditure). Sources of income and expenditures for major items of consumption (but not for savings, investment, or insurance) are reported as percentages.

In general, household income is the amount of funds, usually measured in monetary units, received by the members (generally those 14 years old and over) of a HOUSEHOLD in a given time period. The income can be derived from wages or salaries, nonfarm or farm SELF-EMPLOYMENT, pensions, investments, rental property, public assistance, unemployment benefits, etc. The income of a household is expressed as a gross amount before deductions

for taxes. Data on expenditure refer to consumption of personal or household goods and services; they normally exclude savings, taxes, and insurance. National practice with regard to inclusion of credit purchases differs markedly.

households, groups of related or unrelated individuals living in the same HOUSING UNIT, distributed by size of household. A family household is one composed principally of individuals related by blood or marriage.*

housing unit, a single room or a group of rooms occupied exclusively as separate living quarters, whose occupants do not live or eat with other occupants (if any) in the same structure. A housing unit has direct access from the outside of its building and also has exclusive kitchen facilities.

immigration, usually the number and origin of those immigrants admitted to a nation in a legal status that would eventually permit the granting of the right to settle permanently or to acquire citizenship.*

imports, material goods legally entering a country (or customs area) and subject to customs regulations; excludes financial movements. The total value and distribution by percentage of the major items (in preference to groups of goods) imported are given, together with the direction of trade among major trading partners (usually single countries), trading blocs (such as the European Economic Community), or customs areas (such as Belgium–Luxembourg). The value of goods imported is given free on board (f.o.b.) unless otherwise specified; f.o.b. is defined above under EXPORTS.

The principal alternate basis for reporting valuation of goods in international trade is that of cost, insurance, and freight (c.i.f.); its use is restricted to imports, as it comprises the principal charges needed to bring the goods to the customs house in the country of destination. Because it inflates the value of imports relative to exports, more countries have, latterly, been providing estimates of imports on an f.o.b. basis as well.

incorporated territory (U.S.), *see* territory.

independent, of a state, autonomous and controlling both its internal and external affairs.

indirect taxes, taxes levied on sales or transfers of selected intermediate goods and services, including excises, value-added taxes, and tariffs, that are ordinarily passed on to the ultimate consumers of the goods and services. Figures given for individual countries are limited to indirect taxes levied by their respective central governments unless otherwise specified.

infant mortality rate, the number of children born live who die before their first birthday per 1,000 live births. Total infant mortality includes neonatal mortality, which is deaths of children within one month of birth.

kingdom, *see* monarchy.

land use, distribution by classes of vegetational cover or economic use of the land area only (excluding inland water, for example, but not marshland), reported as percentages.

leisure, the principal uses or reported preferences in the use of the individual's free time for personal recreation, rest, or self-improvement.*

life expectancy, the number of years a person born within a particular population group would be expected to live, based on actuarial calculations.

Life expectancy at birth is usually lower than after the first year of life because of INFANT MORTALITY. Life expectancy is often used to compare the general health of populations of different countries. Life expectancy in the early 1980s ranges from lows of 40 years or less at birth for men in some of the least developed countries to highs of more than 80 years for women in the most developed countries.

literacy, the ability to read and write a language with some degree of competence; the precise

degree constituting the basis of a particular national statement is usually defined by the national census and is often tested by the census enumerator. Elsewhere, particularly where much adult literacy may be the result of literacy campaigns, rather than the consequence of passage through a formal educational system, definition and testing of literacy may be better standardized, albeit of a lower overall standard.

machinery, for purposes of trade or industrial classification, goods having moving parts, except toys and instruments.

major cities, usually the five largest cities proper whose population is at least one-tenth that of the primate (largest) city; fewer will be listed if the size disparity is very great. For multipage tables, ten or more* will be listed without regard for the size of the primate city. All populations will refer to the most specific administrative or demographically defined city proper, unless a municipality or METROPOLITAN AREA is specified.

manufacturing, mining, and construction enterprises, a detailed tabulation of the principal industries in these three sectors, showing for each industry the number of enterprises and employees, wages in that industry as a percentage of the general average wage, and the value of that industry's output in terms of value added or turnover.*

marriage rate, the number of legal, civilly recognized marriages annually per 1,000 population.

material (or social) product, in the national accounting systems of the socialist countries, the aggregate value of all "productive" services, generally omitting personal (nonpublic) services, financial activities, and the like that in conventional Western national accounts would contribute to the GROSS DOMESTIC PRODUCT, a more comprehensive measure that not only includes material output but also every identifiable service element of a national economy. Socialist countries that are members of the International Monetary Fund have begun, however, to report gross domestic, and national, product according to the *System of National Accounts* that forms the basis of international reporting of national accounts.

material well-being, a group of measures indicating the percentage of households or dwellings possessing certain goods or appliances, including automobiles, telephones, television receivers, refrigerators, air conditioners, and washing machines.*

merchant marine, the privately or publicly owned ships of a nation (limited to those in Lloyd's of London statistical reporting of 100 or more GROSS REGISTER TONS) that are employed in commerce. It usually consists of oil and chemical tankers; liquefied gas, ore, and bulk carriers; and general cargo and container ships.

metropolitan area, region of dense, predominantly urban, settlement around a city; the population so designated is usually economically dependent upon the central city to some degree, either for employment, shopping, transportation services, or the like. Such areas are usually compact and contiguous, containing no physically discontinuous elements, except islands or other elements separated from the central city by geography rather than by economic or commuting patterns.

military expenditure, the apparent value of all identifiable military expenditure by the central government on hardware, personnel, pensions, research and development, etc., reported here as a percentage of the GNP, with a comparison to the world average.

military personnel, *see* total active duty personnel.

mobility, a measure of the rate at which individuals or households change dwellings (or

remain in them), usually measured between censuses and including international as well as domestic migration.*

monarchy, a government in which the CHIEF OF STATE holds office, usually hereditarily, but sometimes electively, and for life (sometimes electively for a term). The state may be a coprincipality, emirate, empire, kingdom, principality, shaykhdom, or sultanate. The powers of the monarch may range from absolute, *i.e.,* he or she both reigns and rules, through various degrees of limitation of authority, to merely nominal, as in a constitutional monarchy, in which the titular monarch reigns but others, as elected officials, rule or participate in the ruling.

monetary unit, currency in official use in a given country; name, spelling, and abbreviation in English according to International Monetary Fund recommendations or local practice; valuation usually according to market or commercial rates.

See also exchange rate.

natural increase, also called natural growth or the balance of births and deaths, the excess of births over deaths in a population; the rate of natural increase is the difference between the CRUDE BIRTH RATE and the CRUDE DEATH RATE of a given population. Natural increase rates for individual countries may be compared with the world annual average increase of 18 persons per 1,000 population (1.8%) annually between 1980 and 1985. Natural increase is added to the balance of migration to calculate the total growth of that population.

nonferrous metal, metal that does not contain significant quantities of iron and its alloys; usually this term is reserved for base metals such as copper or lead.

official language(s), that (or those) prescribed for actual day-to-day conduct and publication of a country's official business. Other languages may have local protection, may be permitted in legal action (such as a trial), or may be "national languages," for the protection of which special provisions have been made, but these are not deemed official.

official name, the local official form(s) short or long, of a country's legal name(s) taken from the country's constitution or from other official documents. The English-language form is usually the protocol form in use by the country, the U.S. Department of State, and the United Nations.

official religion, generally, any religion prescribed or given special protection by the constitution or legal system of the country.

organized territory (U.S.), *see* territory.

overseas department (France), *see* department.

overseas territory (France), *see* territory.

parliamentary state, *see* state.

part of a realm, a dependent political entity with some degree of self-government and having a special status above that of a colony (*e.g.,* the prerogative of rejecting for local application any law enacted by the motherland).

participation rate, a measure of the extent to which any adult population is engaged in economically productive activities. It is usually calculated as the percentage of those employed or economically active as compared to the larger population from whom they are drawn—those over age 15, or between the ages of 15 and 64, or some other nationally or demographically standardized group.

passenger-miles or **passenger-kilometres,** carriage by public or commercial means of a single passenger a distance of one mile (or kilometre); in aggregate the total miles or kilometres traveled by all passengers in a given country via specified means of transportation. Figures given for countries are calculated from ticket sales and ordinarily exclude passengers carried free of charge.

people's republic, *see* republic.

place of birth/national origin, if the former, numbers of native- and foreign-born population of a country by actual place of birth; if the latter, any of several classifications, including those based on origin of passport at original admission to country, on cultural heritage of family name, on self-designated (often multiple) origin of (some) ancestors, and on other systems for assigning national origin.*

population economically active, the total number of persons (above a set age for economic labour, usually 10–15 years) in all employment statuses—self-employed, wage- or salary-earning, part-time, seasonal, unemployed, etc.

The United Nations' *Yearbook of Labour Statistics* defines the economically active population as "all persons of either sex who furnish the supply of labour for the production of economic goods and services." National practices vary between countries as regards the treatment of such groups as armed forces, inmates of institutions, persons living on reservations, persons seeking their first job, seasonal workers and persons engaged in part-time economic activities. In some countries, all or part of these groups may be included among the economically active while in other countries the same groups may be treated as inactive. However, in general, the data on economically active population do not include students, women occupied solely in domestic duties, retired persons, persons living entirely on their own means, and persons wholly dependent upon others.

population projection, the expected population in 1990 and 2000, embodying the country's own projections wherever possible. Estimates of the future size of a population are usually based on assumed future levels of fertility, mortality, and migration. Assumptions about these future levels are commonly made from cohort analysis, which describes a group of persons who experience a particular life event, such as birth or marriage, within the same period of time. Projections in the tables, whether based on external estimates by the United Nations, World Bank, U.S. Department of Commerce, or on those of the country itself, unless otherwise specified, are medium (*i.e.,* most likely) variants wherever possible.

price and earnings indexes, tabulation comparing the change in the CONSUMER PRICE INDEX over a period of seven years with the change in the general labour force's EARNINGS INDEX for the same period. No adjustment is possible, however, for other measures of disposable income.

principality, *see* monarchy.

processed mineral, mineral that is not in its original raw form but that has undergone any of a number of physical, chemical, or metallurgical processes such as crushing, sorting, sizing, or concentrating by chemical, magnetic, electrostatic, or other treatment.

production, the physical quantity or monetary value of the output of an industry, usually tabulated here as the most important items or groups of items (depending on the available detail) of primary (extractive) and secondary (manufactured) production. When a single consistent measure of value, such as "value added," can be obtained, this is given, ranked by value; otherwise, quantity of production is given for the major groups and items.

public debt, the current outstanding debt of all periods of maturity for which the central government and its organs are obligated. For many developing countries, only figures for external public debt are available.

quality of working life, a group of measures including weekly hours of work (including overtime); rates per 100,000 for job-connected injury, illness, and mortality; coverage of labour force by insurance for injury, permanent dis-

ability, and death; work days lost to labour strikes and stoppages; and commuting patterns (length of journey to work in minutes and usual method of transportation).*

railroads, mode of transportation by self-driven or locomotive-drawn cars over fixed rails. Length of track figures given for individual countries ordinarily include the total length of all mainline and spurline running track and exclude switching sidings and yard track. Route length, when given, does not compound multiple running tracks laid on the same trackbed. Auxiliary lines traversed by ferries and motor vehicles are excluded unless otherwise specified.

recurrent budget, *see* budget.

religious affiliation, distribution of practicing or nominal religionists, by percentage of total population. This usually assigns to children the religion of their parents, since few sources conform to any other practice. For a discussion of some of the classificational problems of religious membership and practice, *see* the "Religion" table at p. 842.

republic, a state with elected leaders and a centralized presidential form of government, local subdivisions being subordinate to the national government. *Federal republic* (as distinguished from a unitary republic), a republic in which power is divided between the central government and local subdivisions (*e.g.,* states, provinces, or cantons) in whom it is held to originate, the division of power being defined in a written constitution and jurisdictional disputes usually being settled in a court; sovereignty usually rests with the authority that has the power to amend the constitution. *People's republic,* in the dialectics of Communism, the first stage of development toward a communist state, the second stage being a *socialist republic. Soviet republic,* a republic governed by an elected soviet (council). *Unitary republic* (as distinguished from a federal republic), a republic in which power is held by a central authority and not derived from constituent subdivisions.

retail price index, *see* consumer price index.

roundwood, wood obtained from removals from forests, felled or harvested (with or without bark), in various forms such as round, split, roots, stumps, etc. It can be broadly divided into two classes: softwoods, from coniferous trees, and hardwoods, from nonconiferous trees.

rural, see urban–rural.

self-employment, work in which income derives from direct employment in one's own business, trade, or profession, as opposed to work in which salary or wages are earned from an employer.

self-governing, of a state, in control of its internal affairs in degrees ranging from control of most internal affairs (though perhaps not of public order or of internal security) to complete control of all internal affairs (*i.e.,* the state is autonomous) but having no control of external affairs or defense. In this list the term self-governing refers to the final state in the successive stages of increasing self-government, generally followed by independence.

service/trade enterprises, a detailed tabulation for the largest sectors of the domestic economy—services and wholesale and retail trade—as defined, surveyed, and reported by individual countries, providing: number of enterprises and employees, wages as a percentage of the general average wage, and the value of that industry's output in terms of value added or turnover.*

sex distribution, ratios, calculated as percentages, of male and female population to total population.

shaykhdom, *see* monarchy.

social deviance, a group of measures, usually reported as rates per 100,000, for principal categories of socially deviant behaviour, including crime, alcoholism, drug abuse, and suicide.*

social participation, a group of measures indicative of the degree of social engagement possessed by a particular population, including rates of participation or membership in public activities such as elections, voluntary work (or non-job-connected organizational memberships), trade unions, and religious organizations.*

social security, public programs designed to protect individuals and families from loss of income owing to unemployment, old age, sickness or disability, or death and to provide other assistance, such as medical care or other services. Such programs may include social insurance, health and welfare programs, income maintenance programs, or other modes of public aid.

socialist republic, *see* republic.

soviet republic, *see* republic.

Special Drawing Right (SDR), a unit of account utilized by the International Monetary Fund (IMF) to denominate monetary reserves available under a quota system to IMF members to maintain the value of their national currency unit in international transactions.

state, an autonomous political entity; also, a first-order civil administrative subdivision, especially of a federated union. *Associated state,* an autonomous state in free association with another that conducts its external affairs and defense. *Parliamentary state,* an independent state in the COMMONWEALTH that is governed by a parliament and that recognizes the British monarch as its titular head.

structure of gross domestic product and labour force, tabulation of the principal elements of the national economy, according to standard industrial categories, together with the distribution of the labour force (when possible POPULATION ECONOMICALLY ACTIVE) that generates the GROSS DOMESTIC PRODUCT.

subsidy, financial aid or grant given by a government to a private or public enterprise deemed to be in the public interest. Subsidies may be employed for a wide range of purposes, such as to support a vital industry (*e.g.,* agriculture, steelmaking) or to keep prices of certain goods low or stable.

sultanate, *see* monarchy.

tenure, the legal or customary forms and methods by which real property is held, such as lease, fee, title, loan, communal grant, and the like. Tenure of housing is the legal form of occupancy (owned, rented, or subrented) by a HOUSEHOLD of its living quarters.

territory, a noncategorized political dependency; a first-order administrative subdivision; a dependent political entity with some degree of self-government, but with fewer rights and less autonomy than a colony since there is no charter. *External territory* (Australia), a territory situated outside the area of the country. *Incorporated territory* (U.S.), a part of the United States with nonvoting representation in the Congress, but with most constitutional provisions extended to its inhabitants (*e.g.,* Alaska until 1959). *Organized territory* (U.S.), a territory for which a system of laws and a settled government have been provided by an act of the United States Congress. *Overseas territory* (France), an overseas subdivision of the French Republic with elected representation in the French Parliament, having individual statutes, laws, and internal organization adapted to local conditions. *Trust territory,* a non-self-governing former mandate of the League of Nations, administered by an independent state under trust arrangements with the United Nations, with the goal of eventual self-government. *Unincorporated territory* (U.S.), a dependency of the United States with limited self-government, whose inhabitants can claim the fundamental but not all of the procedural rights (*e.g.,* trial by jury) guaranteed by the United States Constitution.

theocracy, a state governed by hierarchs, *i.e.,* by religious leaders.

ton-miles or **ton-kilometres,** aggregate measure of freight hauled in a specified period of time, equal to tons of freight multiplied by the miles (or kilometres) each ton is transported. Figures given for individual countries indicate the aggregate ton-miles (or ton-kilometres) traveled by freight via the means of transportation indicated. Figures are compiled from way-bills (nationally) and ordinarily exclude mail, specie, passengers' baggage, the fuel and stores of the conveyance in question, and goods carried free of charge.

total active duty personnel, full-time active duty military personnel (excluding militias and part-time, informal, or other paramilitary elements), with their distribution by percentages among the major services.

See also military expenditure.

total fertility rate, the average number of children each woman in a particular age group would have during her lifetime if she were to live to the end of her childbearing years.

See also general fertility rate.

tourism, service industry comprising activities connected with domestic and international travel for pleasure or recreation; confined here to international travel and reported as number of border crossings, or estimated expenditures by tourists of all nationalities visiting a particular country and, conversely, the estimated expenditures of that country's nationals in all countries of destination.

transport, all mechanical methods of moving persons or goods. Data reported for national establishments include: for railroads, length of track and volume of traffic for passengers and cargo (but excluding mail, etc.); for roads, length of network and numbers of passengers cars and of commercial vehicles, *i.e.,* trucks and buses (no data on traffic); for merchant marine, the number of vessels of more than 100 gross tons and their total deadweight tonnage (no data on traffic); for air transport, traffic data for passengers and cargo, and the number of airports with scheduled flights.

trust territory, *see* territory.

unincorporated territory (U.S.), *see* territory.

unitary republic, *see* republic.

urban–rural, social characteristic of local or national populations, defined by predominant economic activities, "urban" referring to a group of predominantly nonagricultural pursuits, "rural" to agricultural pursuits. The distinction is usually based on the country's own definition of urban, which may depend only upon the size (population) or a place, or upon factors like employment, density of housing, public services, etc.

value added, also called value added by manufacture, the GROSS OUTPUT VALUE of a firm or industry minus the cost of inputs—raw materials, supplies, and other inputs for which other firms are paid—required to produce it. Value added is the portion of the sales value of gross output value that is actually created by the firm or industry. Value added generally includes labour costs, administrative costs, and operating profits. The terms net output and value added are sometimes used synonymously.

The Nations of the World

Afghanistan

Official name: Da Afghānestān
Dimukratik Jamhuriyat (Pashto);
Dowlat-e Jumhūrī-ye Dimukrātik-e
Afghānestān (Dari) (Democratic
Republic of Afghanistan).
Form of government: unitary single-
party people's republic with
one transitional legislative body
(Revolutionary Council [57])*.
Chief of state: President of the
Revolutionary Council.
Head of government: Prime Minister.
Capital: Kābul.
Official languages: Pashto; Dari
Persian.
Official religion: Islām.
Monetary unit: 1 afghani (AF) = 100
puls (puli); valuation (Oct. 21, 1985)
1 U.S.$ = AF69.04; 1 £ = AF99.00.

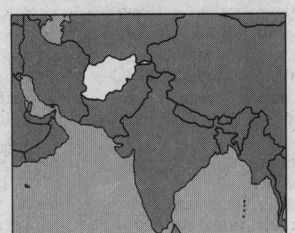

Area and population	area		population
Regions	sq mi	sq km	1982 estimate
Eastern	28,664	74,240	1,853,000
North-central	20,461	52,994	1,983,000
North-east	29,910	77,468	1,651,000
North-west	50,581	131,005	2,278,000
South-central	32,963	85,375	1,099,000
South-east	12,546	32,494	3,390,000
Western	76,698	198,649	1,493,000
TOTAL	251,824	652,225	16,363,000†

Demography

Density‡ (1985): persons per sq mi 71.9, persons per sq km 28.2.
Urban–rural§ (1985): urban 18.5%; rural 81.5%.
Sex distribution§ (1982): male 51.42%; female 48.58%.
Age breakdown§ (1982): under 15, 44.6%; 15–29, 26.8%; 30–44, 15.8%; 45–
59, 8.5%; 60–74, 3.7%; 75 and over, 0.6%.
Population projection: (1990) 19,349,000; (2000) 24,180,000.
Doubling time§: 27 years.
Ethnic composition (1984): Pashtun 50%; Tadzhik 25%; Uzbek 9%; other
16%.
Religious affiliation (1983): Sunnī Muslim 87%; Shī'ah Muslim 12%;
other 1%.
Major cities (1981–82): Kābul 1,036,407; Qandahār 191,345; Herāt 150,497.

Vital statistics

Birth rate per 1,000 population (1980–85): 49.6 (world avg. 29.0).
Death rate per 1,000 population (1980–85): 27.3 (world avg. 11.0).
Natural increase rate per 1,000 population (1980–85): 22.3 (world avg. 18.0).
Total fertility rate (avg. births per childbearing woman; 1980–85): 6.9.
Life expectancy at birth (1984): male 37.2 years; female 37.9 years.
Major reported illness (1981–82): tuberculosis 17,499.

National economy

Budget (1981–82). Revenue: AF40,464,100,000 (internal revenue sources
74.1%, of which natural gas revenues 43.9%; loans and grants-in-aid 25.9%).
Expenditures: AF40,464,100,000 (governmental ministries 50.0%; developmental budget 31.9%; foreign debt service 13.9%; surplus 1.6%).
Public debt (external, outstanding; 1982): U.S.$1,324,000,000.
Production (metric tons except as noted). Agriculture, forestry, fishing (1984):
wheat 2,850,000, corn (maize) 800,000, rice 466,000, grapes 430,000, barley
365,000; livestock (number of live animals) 20,000,000 sheep, 3,750,000
cattle, 3,000,000 goats, 1,250,000 asses, 410,000 horses, 270,000 camels;
roundwood 6,538,000 cu m ‖ ; fish catch 1,500 ‖ . Mining and quarrying
(1983): cement 150,000; salt 8,000; gypsum 5,000; barite 2,000. Manufacturing (by production value in afghanis; 1981–82): food products 3,762,-
000,000; textiles (all forms) 2,770,000,000; industrial chemicals (including
fertilizers) 751,000,000; printing and publishing 539,000,000. Construction
(1981–82): nonresidential 113,176 cu m, of which educational buildings
29,779, industrial buildings 21,171. Energy production (consumption): electricity (kW-hr; 1984) 1,300,000,000 (1,300,000,000); coal (metric tons; 1983)
165,000 (165,000); petroleum products (metric tons; 1983) 1,000 (313,000);
natural gas (cu m; 1983) 2,550,000,000 (179,000,000).
Land use (1983): forested 2.9%; meadows and pastures 46.3%; agricultural
and under permanent cultivation 12.4%; other 38.4%.
Gross national product (1982): U.S.$3,500,000,000 (U.S.$214 per capita).

Structure of net material product and labour force				
	1982–83		1981–82	
	in value AF'000,000¶	% of total value	labour force	% of labour force
Agriculture	64,700	68.8	2,194,770	57.3
Manufacturing, mining, and public utilities	13,000	13.8	466,860	12.2
Construction	3,000	3.2	48,880	1.3
Transp., commun.	3,300	3.5	65,650	1.7
Education, public health	...	...	70,520	1.8
Trade	8,600	9.1	126,100	3.3
Public administration	...	...	79,260	2.1
Public services	...	...	134,420	3.5
Other	1,500	1.6	642,360	16.8
TOTAL	94,000	100.0	3,828,820§	100.0

Population economically active (1979–80): total 3,634,600; participation rate
of total population 27.9% (female 8.2%, unemployed 5.5%).

Price indexes (1980 = 100)							
	1977	1978	1979	1980	1981	1982	1983
Consumer price index	72.8	78.8	99.1	100.0	104.9	...	...

Household size. Average household size§ (1979): 6.2.

Foreign trade

Balance of trade (current prices)♀							
	1976	1977	1978	1979	1980	1981	1982
AF'000,000	+2,899	+943	−1,019	+4,551	+8,404	+7,573	+5,217
% of total	12.4%	3.5%	3.4%	12.3%	16.6%	12.4%	7.9%

Imports (1981–82): AF30,797,800,000 (vehicles 22.7%, petroleum products
18.0%, sugar 8.1%, woven fabrics of flax or ramie 7.9%, processed animal
and vegetable oils 4.2%, tea 4.0%). *Major import sources:* U.S.S.R. 58.6%;
Japan 12.6%; Hong Kong 4.4%; India 2.7%; West Germany 2.7%.
Exports (1981–82): AF34,354,300,000 (natural gas 39.2%, dried fruit 25.2%,
carpets and rugs 10.5%, fresh fruit 7.3%, wool and hides 3.4%). *Major
export destinations:* U.S.S.R. 59.4%; Pakistan 8.8%; India 6.2%.

Transport and communications

Transport. Railroads (1984): length 6 mi, 10 km. Roads (1981–82): total
length 11,789 mi, 18,974 km (paved 42%). Vehicles (1981–82): passenger
cars 31,754; trucks and buses 30,997. Merchant marine: none. Air transport (1981–82): passenger-mi 117,750,000, passenger-km 189,500,000; short
ton-mi cargo 14,500,000, metric ton-km cargo 21,169,000; airports (1985) 3.
Communications. Daily newspapers (1984): total number 4; total circulation 92,200; circulation per 1,000 population 5.2. Radio (1984): receivers
135,000 (1 per 131 persons). Television (1984): receivers 12,600 (1 per 1,402
persons). Telephones (1984): 31,200 (1 per 566 persons).

Education and health

Education (1981–82)	schools	teachers	students	student/ teacher ratio
Primary	3,820	35,364	1,115,993	31.6
Secondary	447	6,170	124,488	20.2
Vocational□	45	1,314	14,431	11.0
Higher	19	1,569	17,542	11.2

Educational attainment (1980). Percent of population over age 25 having: no
formal schooling 88.5%; some primary education 6.8%; complete primary
0.3%; some secondary 1.2%; postsecondary 3.2%. *Literacy* (1980): total population over age 15 literate 1,436,000 (20.0%); males 33.2%; females 5.8%.
Health (1981–82): physicians 1,215 (1 per 13,467 persons); hospital beds
6,875 (1 per 2,380 persons); infant mortality rate per 1,000 live births
(1981) 204.8.
Food (1979–81): daily per capita caloric intake 2,055 (vegetable products
90%, animal products 10%); 84% of FAO recommended minimum.

Military

Total active duty personnel (1984): 46,000 (army 87.0%, air force 13.0%).
Military expenditure as percent of GNP (1981): 3.0% (world 5.7%); per
capita expenditure U.S.$6.

*The provisional Basic Principles of the Democratic Republic of Afghanistan, adopted
in 1980, provides for the eventual election of a Grand National Assembly. †Total
includes 2,615,000 nomads not distributed by province. Afghan refugees in Pakistan
number almost 3,000,000 and in Iran 1,850,000. ‡Includes both settled and nomadic
population. §Based on settled population only. ‖ 1982. ¶At 1978 prices. ♀Excluding
imports and special transactions. □Includes technical institutes.

Albania

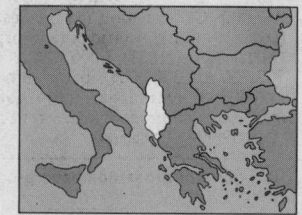

Official name: Republika Popullore Socialiste e Shqipërisë (People's Socialist Republic of Albania).
Form of government: unitary single-party people's republic with one legislative house (People's Assembly [250]).
Chief of state: President (Chairman of the Presidium of the People's Assembly).
Head of government: Premier (Chairman of the Council of Ministers).
Capital: Tiranë.
Official language: Albanian.
Official religion: none.
Monetary unit: 1 lek (plural leks) = 100 qindars; valuation (Oct. 21, 1985) 1 U.S.$ = 7.15 leks; 1 £ = 10.25 lekë.

Area and population

Provinces	Capitals	area sq mi	area sq km	population 1982 census
Berat	Berat	396	1,026	154,000
Dibër	Peshkopi	605	1,568	134,800
Durrës	Durrës	327	848	217,000
Elbasan	Elbasan	572	1,481	208,000
Fier	Fier	454	1,175	212,000
Gjirokastër	Gjirokastër	439	1,137	60,300
Gramsh	Gramsh	268	695	38,000
Kolonjë	Erseka	311	805	22,300
Korçë	Korçë	842	2,181	199,000
Krujë	Krujë	234	607	93,000
Kukës	Kukës	514	1,331	86,000
Lezhë	Lezhë	185	479	53,000
Librazhd	Librazhd	391	1,013	63,000
Lushnjë	Lushnjë	275	712	115,400
Mat	Burrel	397	1,028	67,000
Mirditë	Rrëshen	335	867	45,000
Përmet	Përmet	359	930	36,400
Pogradec	Pogradec	280	725	62,000
Pukë	Pukë	399	1,033	45,000
Sarandë	Sarandë	424	1,097	76,700
Shkodër	Shkodër	976	2,528	206,200
Skrapar	Çorovoda	299	775	42,000
Tepelenë	Tepelenë	315	817	45,200
Tiranë	Tiranë	478	1,238	310,000
Tropojë	Bajram	403	1,043	39,800
Vlorë	Vlorë	621	1,609	155,000
TOTAL		11,100*	28,748	2,786,100

Demography

Population (1985 est.): 3,000,000.
Density (1985): persons per sq mi 274.8, persons per sq km 106.1.
Urban-rural (1983): urban 33.8%; rural 66.2%.
Sex distribution (1982): male 51.60%; female 48.40%.
Age breakdown (1980): under 15, 37.3%; 15–29, 28.9%; 30–44, 16.5%; 45–59, 10.2%; 60–74, 5.5%; 75 and over, 1.6%.
Population projection: (1990) 3,400,000; (2000) 4,000,000.
Doubling time: 28 years.
Ethnic composition (1980): Albanian 93.1%; Gypsy 2.5%; Greek 2.4%; other 2.0%.
Religious affiliation (1980): Muslim 20.5%; Christian 5.4%; atheist 18.7%; nonreligious 55.4%.
Major cities (1982): Tiranë 202,000; Durrës 72,600; Shkodër 70,000; Elbasan 68,000; Vlorë 60,000.

Vital statistics

Birth rate per 1,000 population (1984): 26.0 (world avg. 29.0).
Death rate per 1,000 population (1984): 6.0 (world avg. 11.0).
Natural increase rate per 1,000 population (1984): 20.0 (world avg. 18.0).
Total fertility rate (avg. births per childbearing woman; 1980): 3.6.
Marriage rate per 1,000 population (1984): 9.0.
Divorce rate per 1,000 population (1982): 0.8.
Life expectancy at birth (1983): male 66.9 years; female 71.6 years.
Major causes of death per 100,000 population: n.a.

National economy

Budget (1984). Revenue: 9,200,000,000 leks (surplus from state enterprises 93.0%, other 7.0%). Expenditures: 9,150,000,000 leks (national economy 55.3%, social and cultural services 26.2%, defense 11.0%, administration 1.6%).
Public debt: n.a.
Tourism (1982): number of tourists 6,000; receipts from visitors, n.a.; expenditures by nationals abroad, n.a.
Production (metric tons except as noted). Agriculture, forestry, fishing (1984): wheat 600,000, corn (maize) 400,000, vegetables and fruit except grapes 353,000, sugar beets 320,000, potatoes 136,000, grapes 83,000, sunflower seeds 53,000, barley 34,000, oats 30,000, olives 25,000, tobacco 18,000; livestock (number of live animals) 1,200,000 sheep, 700,000 goats, 600,000 cattle, 200,000 pigs, 74,000 mules and asses, 43,000 horses; roundwood 2,330,000 (1983) cu m; fish catch (1983) 4,000. Mining and quarrying

(1983): chromite ore 1,200,000; iron ore 650,000; salt 70,000; copper 16,500; nickel 5,600. Manufacturing (1983): bitumen (asphalt) 1,800,000; cement 1,100,000; distillate fuel oils 272,000; nitrogenous and phosphate fertilizers 102,000; raw sugar 40,000; paper and paperboard 17,000†; olive oil 7,000; wine 230,000 hectolitres‡; beer 160,000 hectolitres†; cigarettes 6,200,-000,000 units‡; cotton and woolen fabrics 60,900,000 m‡. Construction (1980): 1,821,000,000 leks. Energy production (consumption): electricity (kW-hr; 1983) 2,885,000,000 (2,885,000,000); coal (metric tons; 1983) 1,700,-000 (1,900,000); crude petroleum (barrels; 1983) 10,995,000 (10,995,000); petroleum products (metric tons; 1983) 1,280,500 (1,280,500); natural gas (cu m; 1983) 397,435,500 (397,435,000).
Gross national product (at current market prices; 1981): U.S.$2,380,000,000 (U.S.$850 per capita).

Structure of net material product and labour force

	1978 value	% of total value	labour force	% of labour force
Agriculture	...	37.9	557,800	50.0
Manufacturing, mining, public utilities	...	45.4	221,400	19.8
Construction	...	7.2	49,700	4.5
Transportation and communication			33,000	3.0
Trade	...	9.5	38,600	3.5
Pub. admin., defense			80,300	7.2
Other			134,000	12.0
TOTAL	...	100.0	1,115,000	100.0

Population economically active (1978): total 1,115,000; participation rate of total population over age 15, 66.6% (female 46.0%, unemployed, n.a.).
Price and earnings indexes: n.a.
Household income and expenditure. Average household size (1980) 4.5; average annual income per household: n.a.; source of income: n.a.; expenditure: n.a.
Land use (1983): forested 45.3%; meadows and pastures 19.7%; agricultural and under permanent cultivation 25.9%; other 9.1%.

Foreign trade

Balance of trade (current prices)

	1978	1979	1980	1981	1982	1983
'000,000 leks	...	100	...	...	...	...
% of total	...	5.3	...	...	...	...

Imports§ (1979): 900,000,000 leks (chromite ore and concentrates, electricity, iron ore, nickel, petroleum products, copper, pyrite ore, bauxite, dolomite, chemicals, building materials [cement, marble facings], textile and leather goods, fruit and vegetables, and wine). *Major import sources:* Czechoslovakia 12.0%; Yugoslavia 12.0%; China 10.0%; Italy 8.0%; Poland 8.0%; West Germany 7.0%.
Exports§ (1979): 1,000,000,000 leks (machinery and equipment, iron and steel, and consumer goods). *Major export destinations:* Czechoslovakia 11.0%; Yugoslavia 10.0%; Italy 10.0%; China 9.0%; Poland 7.0%; West Germany 7.0%.

Transport and communications

Transport. Railroads (1984): length 253 mi, 408 km; passenger-mi 181,000,-000‡, passenger-km 291,000,000‡; short ton-mi cargo 87,000,000‡, metric ton-km cargo 127,000,000‡. Roads (1981): total length 13,049 mi, 21,000 km (paved 14%). Vehicles (1970): passenger cars 3,500; trucks and buses 11,200. Merchant marine (1984): vessels (100 gross tons and over) 20; total deadweight tonnage 79,940. Air transport: passengers, n.a.; cargo, n.a.; airports (1985) with scheduled flights 1.
Communications. Daily newspapers (1981): total number 2; total circulation 145,000; circulation per 1,000 population 54.2. Radio (1984): total number of receivers 210,000 (1 per 13.3 persons). Television (1984): total number of receivers 185,740 (1 per 15 persons). Telephones, n.a.

Education and health

Education (1982–83)

	schools	teachers	students	student/ teacher ratio
Primary (age 6–13)	1,617	26,440	532,300	20.1
Secondary (age 14–17)	23‖	1,250	21,900¶	10.2¶
Voc., teacher tr.	242‖	3,750	64,800¶	17.3¶
Higher	17‖	1,240	17,500¶	14.1

Educational attainment, n.a. *Literacy* (1970): total population over age 15 literate 1,234,376 (75.0%).
Health (1982): physicians 3,861 (1 per 720 persons); hospital beds (1978) 17,000 (1 per 151 persons); infant mortality rate per 1,000 live births 44.0.
Food (1980–82): daily per capita caloric intake 3,060 (vegetable products 87%, animal products 13%); 127% of FAO recommended minimum requirement.

Military

Total active duty personnel (1984): 40,400 (army 74.3%, navy 7.9%, air force 17.8%). *Military expenditure as percent of GNP* (1981): 8.1% (world 5.8%); per capita expenditure U.S.$69.

*Detail does not add to total given because of rounding. †1980. ‡1981. §No figures are available for commodity breakdown since 1964. ‖1979–80. ¶Excludes students enrolled in evening courses.

Algeria

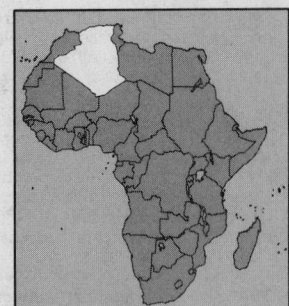

Official name: al-Jumhūrīyah
al-Jazā'irīyah ad-Dīmuqrāṭīyah
ash-Sha'bīyah (Arabic) (Democratic
and Popular Republic of Algeria).
Form of government: single-party
republic with one legislative house
(The National People's Assembly
[281]).
Head of state and government:
President.
Capital: Algiers.
Official language: Arabic.
Official religion: Islām.
Monetary unit: 1 Algerian dinar
(DA) = 100 centimes; valuation (Oct.
21, 1985) 1 U.S.$ = DA4.87:
1 £ = DA6.99.

Area and population

Wilāyat*	Capitals	area sq mi	area sq km	population 1984 estimate
Adrar	Adrar	163,127	422,498	161,936
Alger	Algiers	303	786	2,442,303
Annaba	Annaba	1,347	3,489	650,096
Batna	Batna	5,746	14,882	691,079
Béchar	Béchar	118,147	306,000	184,069
Bejaïa	Bejaïa	1,329	3,442	659,040
Biskra	Biskra	42,366	109,728	662,778
Blida	Blida	1,430	3,704	1,126,303
Bouira	Bouira	1,744	4,517	454,805
ech-Cheliff	ech-Cheliff	3,350	8,677	1,040,563
Constantine	Constantine	1,375	3,562	809,245
Djelfa	Djelfa	8,844	22,905	403,500
Guelma	Guelma	3,330	8,624	633,733
Jijel	Jijel	1,431	3,705	604,319
Laghouat	Laghouat	43,263	112,052	391,817
Mascara	Mascara	2,257	5,846	526,644
Médéa	Médéa	3,360	8,704	575,305
Mostaganem	Mostaganem	2,712	7,024	896,767
M'Sila	M'Sila	7,654	19,825	540,013
Oran	Oran	703	1,820	889,800
Ouargla	Ouargla	215,921	559,234	261,760
Oum el-Bouaghi	Oum el-Bouaghi	3,136	8,123	464,806
Saïda	Saïda	41,227	106,777	450,594
Sétif	Sétif	3,996	10,350	1,176,673
Sidi bel Abbès	Sidi bel Abbès	4,497	11,648	604,773
Skikda	Skikda	1,833	4,748	597,530
Tamanrasset	Tamanrasset	214,673	556,000	62,680
Tébessa	Tébessa	6,400	16,575	439,638
Tiaret	Tiaret	9,056	23,456	731,542
Tizi Ouzou	Tizi Ouzou	1,450	3,756	1,028,864
Tlemcen	Tlemcen	3,585	9,284	678,025
TOTAL		919,594†	2,381,741	20,841,000

Demography

Population (1985): 21,731,492.
Density (1985): persons per sq mi 23.6, persons per sq km 9.1.
Urban–rural (1984): urban 66.6%; rural 33.4%.
Sex distribution (1984): male 49.94%; female 50.06%.
Age breakdown (1982): under 15, 46.1%; 15–29, 27.1%; 30–44, 12.8%; 45–59, 8.3%; 60–74, 4.3%; 75 and over, 1.4%.
Population projection: (1990) 25,300,000; (2000) 36,000,000.
Doubling time: 21 years.
Ethnic composition (1980): Arab 83.5%; Berber 16.1%; French 0.4%.
Religious affiliation (1980): Sunnī Muslim 99.1%; Roman Catholic 0.5%; other 0.4%.
Major cities (1984): Algiers 2,442,303.

Vital statistics

Birth rate per 1,000 population (1982): 42.9‡ (world avg. 29.0); legitimate, n.a.; illegitimate, n.a.
Death rate per 1,000 population (1982): 10.5‡ (world avg. 11.0).
Natural increase rate per 1,000 population (1982): 32.4‡ (world avg. 18.0).
Total fertility rate (avg. births per childbearing woman; 1979): 7.2.
Marriage rate per 1,000 population (1982): 6.3‡.
Divorce rate per 1,000 population: n.a.
Life expectancy at birth (1980–85): male 56.7 years; female 58.9 years.
Major causes of death per 100,000 population (1982): scarlet fever 696.5; chicken pox 151.4; dysentery 63.4.

National economy

Budget (1983). Revenue: DA98,667,000,000 (petroleum and gas revenues 60.8%). Expenditures: DA98,667,000,000 (education 13.8%; housing 14.0%).
Public debt (external, outstanding; 1982): U.S.$12,915,600,000.
Tourism (1982): receipts from visitors, n.a.; expenditures by nationals abroad U.S.$452,000,000.
Production (metric tons except as noted). Agriculture, forestry, fishing (1984): wheat 1,200,000, potatoes 600,000, barley 588,000, grapes 360,000, tomatoes 298,000, oranges 228,000; livestock (number of live animals) 14,-700,000 sheep, 3,000,000 goats, 1,450,000 cattle, 164,000 camels; roundwood 1,685,000 cu m§; fish catch 64,500§. Mining and quarrying (1983): iron ore 4,200,000; barite 110,000; clay 57,000; zinc 52,700; sulfur 15,000; lead 6,000; copper 730; silver 120,000 troy oz. Manufacturing (1982): cement 5,000,000; pig iron and ferroalloys 1,097,000; crude steel 550,000; wine

262,000. Construction (1981): residential 28,000 units. Energy production (consumption): electricity (kW-hr; 1983) 8,926,000,000 (8,926,000,000); coal (metric tons; 1983) 7,000 (907,000); crude petroleum (barrels; 1984) 233,-300,000 (31,300,000§); petroleum products (metric tons; 1983) 28,770,000 (4,689,000); natural gas (cu m; 1983) 13,034,000,000 (3,556,000,000).
Gross national product (at current market prices; 1983): U.S.$49,450,000,000 (U.S.$2,400 per capita).

Structure of gross domestic product and labour force

	1981 in value DA'000,000	1981 % of total value	1982 labour force ‖	1982 % of labour force
Agriculture	11,240	6.2	960,000	28.1
Mining	56,681	31.4 }		
Manufacturing	20,101	11.1	468,000	13.7
Construction	21,113	11.7	552,000	16.1
Public utilities	1,867	1.0 }		
Transportation and communication			148,000	4.3
Trade	41,268	22.9 }	541,000	15.8
Finance				
Services				
Pub. admin., defense	19,864	11.0	705,000	20.6
Other	8,400¶	4.7	47,000	1.4
TOTAL	180,534⁹	100.0	3,421,000	100.0

Population economically active (1982): total 4,163,643; participation rate of population over age 10, 21.1% (female 6.8%, unemployed, n.a.).

Price and earnings indexes (1980 = 100)

	1978	1979	1980	1981	1982	1983	1984
Consumer price index	81.9	91.3	100.0	114.6	122.3	127.9	136.3
Earnings index							

Household income and expenditure. Average household size (1980) 4.9; average annual income per household: n.a.; expenditure: n.a.
Land use (1983): forested 1.8%; meadows and pastures 13.2%; agricultural and under permanent cultivation 3.2%; built-up, wasteland, and other 81.8%.

Foreign trade

Balance of trade (current prices)

	1979	1980	1981	1982	1983	1984
DA'000,000	+6,939	+19,493	+19,836	+11,151	+14,686	+18,672
% of total	10.4%	19.4%	19.0%	10.1%	13.9%	17.2%

Imports (1982): DA49,384,000,000 (machines and transport equipment 39.1%, of which transport equipment 14.8%; food and food preparations 17.7%; consumer products 7.6%). *Major import sources:* France 20.9%; West Germany 13.9%; Italy 8.8%; Spain 7.6%; Japan 7.3%; United States 7.0%.
Exports (1982): DA60,535,000,000 (mineral fuels and lubricants 98.2%, of which petroleum 84.2%). *Major export destinations:* European Economic Community 66.2%; United States 17.1%; Japan 3.8%; U.S.S.R. 0.7%.

Transport and communications

Transport. Railroads (1983): route length 2,576 mi, 4,146 km; passenger-mi, n.a., passenger-km, n.a.; short ton-mi cargo, n.a., metric ton-km cargo, n.a. Roads (1981): total length 44,795 mi, 72,091 km (paved 54%). Vehicles (1981): passenger cars 573,573; trucks and buses 265,577. Merchant marine (1984): vessels (100 gross tons and over) 147; total deadweight tonnage 1,984,586. Air transportð (1984): passenger-mi 1,560,772,000, passenger-km 2,511,824,000; short ton-mi cargo 9,073,000, metric ton-km cargo 13,246,-000; airports (1985) with scheduled flights 26.
Communications. Daily newspapers (1985): total number 4; total circulation 480,000; circulation per 1,000 population 22.1. Radio (1985): total number of receivers 3,500,000 (1 per 6 persons). Television (1985): total number of receivers 1,440,000 (1 per 15 persons). Telephones (1982): 606,869 (1 per 33 persons).

Education and health

Education (1981–82)

	schools	teachers	students	student/ teacher ratio
Primary (age 6–11)	9,263	104,500	4,250,000	40.7
Secondary (age 12–18)	1,178	38,845□	1,350,000	...
Voc., teacher tr.□	71	2,292	26,218	11.4
Higher	15	8,573	100,000	11.7

Educational attainment, n.a. *Literacy* (1980): total population over age 15 literate 4,342,300 (41.8%); males literate 2,771,400 (55.6%); females literate 1,570,900 (29.1%).
Health (1982): physicians 6,508 (1 per 3,002 persons); hospital beds 45,830 (1 per 426 persons); infant mortality rate per 1,000 live births (1982) 92.2.
Food (1980–82): daily per capita caloric intake 2,644 (vegetable products 89%, animal products 11%); 108% of FAO recommended minimum.

Military

Total active duty personnel (1984): 130,000 (army 84.6%, navy 6.2%, air force 9.2%). *Military expenditure as percent of GNP* (1983): 2.7% (world 6.1%); per capita expenditure U.S.$61.

*Separate area and population figures are not available for the 16 new wilāyāt created in February 1984. †Detail does not add to total given because of rounding. ‡For Algerian population only. §1983. ‖ Employed persons only. ¶Net indirect taxes only. ⁹At current prices. ðAir Algérie international flights only. □1980–81.

Andorra

Official name: Principat (Co-Principat) or Senyoriu (Co-Senyoriu) d'Andorra; les Valls d'Andorra (Principality [or Co-Principality] of Andorra; the Valleys of Andorra).
Form of government: co-principality with one nonpartisan legislative house (General Council of the Valleys [28]).
Chiefs of state: President of France; Bishop of Urgel, Spain.
Head of government: Syndic (Chairman) of the General Council of the Valleys.
Capital: Andorra la Vella.
Official language: Catalan.
Official religion: Roman Catholicism.
Monetary unit: There is no local currency of issue; the French franc and Spanish peseta are both in circulation. 1 franc (F) = 100 centimes; 1 peseta (Pta) = 100 céntimos.
Valuation (Oct. 21, 1985)
1 U.S.$ = F8.04, 1 £ = F11.53;
1 U.S.$ = Ptas 160.83,
1 £ = Ptas 230.63.

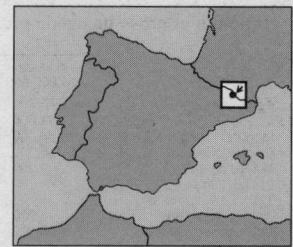

Area and population		area*		population
Parishes	Capitals	sq mi	sq km	1983 estimate
Andorra la Vella	Andorra la Vella	23†	59†	15,698
Canillo	Canillo	47	121	794
Encamp	Encamp	29	74	4,558
La Massana	La Massana	24	61	2,705
Les Escaldes–Engordany	...	†	†	10,758
Ordino	Ordino	34	89	780
Sant Julià de Lòria	Sant Julià de Lòria	23	60	4,647
TOTAL		179‡	464	39,940

Demography

Population (1985): 43,000.
Density (1985): persons per sq mi 238.2, persons per sq km 91.9.
Urban–rural (1983): urban 66.2%; rural 33.8%.
Sex distribution (1982): male 53.74%; female 46.26%.
Age breakdown§ (1973): under 18, 31.0%; 19–50, 51.6%; 51 and over, 17.4%.
Population projection: (1990) 53,000; (2000) 80,000.
Doubling time: 17 years.
Ethnic composition (1983): Spanish 58.6%; Andorran 27.1%; French 6.2%; Portuguese 3.5%; British 1.1%; other 3.5%.
Religious affiliation (1980): Roman Catholic 94.2%; Jewish 0.4%; Jehovah's Witnesses 0.3%; Protestant 0.2%; other 4.9%.
Major city (1983): Andorra la Vella 15,698.

Vital statistics

Birth rate per 1,000 population (1983): 14.4 (world avg. 29.0); legitimate, n.a.; illegitimate, n.a.
Death rate per 1,000 population (1983): 4.4 (world avg. 11.0).
Natural increase rate per 1,000 population (1983): 10.0 (world avg. 18.0).
Total fertility rate (avg. births per childbearing woman): n.a.
Marriage rate per 1,000 population (1981): 4.1.
Divorce rate per 1,000 population: n.a.
Life expectancy at birth: (1980; both sexes) 70 years.
Major causes of death per 100,000 population: n.a.; however, health problems are those of a developed country—cardiovascular disease, hypertension, malignant neoplasms (cancers).

National economy

Budget (1983). Revenue: Ptas3,719,700,000 (excise taxes on imported consumer goods and gasoline *c.* 90.0%; additional revenue is derived from a 3% tax on alcoholic beverages). Expenditures: Ptas3,683,400,000 (primarily administrative services and education; Andorra has virtually no military or social welfare expenditures).
Production. Agriculture, forestry, fishing (1981): potatoes 472 metric tons, tobacco 264 metric tons, and unknown amounts of hay, rye, buckwheat, olives, and grapes; livestock (number of live animals; 1982) 9,000 sheep, 1,115 cattle, 217 horses. Mining and quarrying (1983): building stone and sometimes worked, small deposits of lead and iron ore. Manufacturing (1982): ceramics, cigars and cigarettes, alcoholic beverages (including anisette and brandy), clothing, jewelry, textiles, and wooden furniture. Construction (1973): 10.3% residential; 89.7% nonresidential. Energy production (consumption): electricity (kW-hr; 1984) 140,000,000 (n.a. ‖); coal, none (n.a.); crude petroleum, none (n.a.); petroleum products, none (n.a.); natural gas, none (n.a.).
Population economically active (1982): total 17,184; participation rate of total population 45.2% (female, n.a.; unemployed, n.a.)

Price and earnings indexes (1980 = 100)♀							
	1978	1979	1980	1981	1982	1983	1984
Consumer price index	74.8	86.5	100.0	114.6	131.0	147.0	163.6
Earnings index	...	...	...	...	...	...	...

Public debt: n.a.
Gross national product (at current market prices; 1983): U.S.$360,000,000 (U.S.$9,000 per capita)¶.

Structure of labour force		
	1982	
	labour force	% of labour force
Agriculture and forestry	87	0.5
Mining	386	2.2
Manufacturing	2,244	13.1
Construction	2,295	13.4
Transportation and communication	275	1.6
Trade	4,337	25.2
Finance	1,049	6.1
Pub. admin., defense	1,101	6.4
Services and hotel	4,603	26.8
Other	807	4.7
TOTAL	17,184	100.0

Household income and expenditure. Average household size: n.a.; income per household: n.a.; source of income: n.a.; expenditure: n.a.
Land use (1983): forested 23.7%; meadows and pastures 44.2%; agricultural and under permanent cultivation 4.0%; other 28.1%.
Tourism (1983): receipts from tourist arrivals, n.a.; expenditures by nationals abroad, n.a.; number of tourist arrivals, approximately 10,000,000 annually, most of whom do not stay overnight; number of hotels 235; number of hotel rooms 9,085.

Foreign trade

Balance of trade (current prices)♂				
	1976	1977	1978	1979
U.S.$'000,000	−150	−204	−208	−338
% of total	92.4%	94.6%	94.9%	94.8%

Imports (1979): U.S.$347,300,000, of which from France U.S.$219,600,000, from Spain U.S.$127,700,000 (includes fuels, food, perfumes, clothing, and radio and television sets)□.
Exports (1979): U.S.$9,200,000, of which to France U.S.$5,200,000, to Spain U.S.$4,000,000 (includes wooden furniture, handicrafts, cigarettes, cigars, leather goods, and electricity).

Transport and communications

Transport. Railroads: none; however, both French and Spanish railways stop near the border. Roads (1981): total length 138 mi, 220 km (paved 55%). Vehicles (1982): passenger cars 26,000; trucks and buses, n.a. Merchant marine (1984): vessels (100 gross tons and over) none. Airports with scheduled flights (1985): none; the airport at nearby Seo de Urgel, Spain, has scheduled daily flights to Barcelona and Palma (on Majorca).
Communications. Daily newspapers (1983): total number 1; circulation (2 principal weeklies) 6,000; circulation per 1,000 population 144.5 Radio (1983): total number of receivers 7,000 (1 per 5.7 persons). Television (1983): total number of receivers 4,000 (1 per 10.0 persons). Telephones (1982): 17,719 (1 per 2.1 persons).

Education and health

Education (1979–80)	schools	teachers	students	student/ teacher ratio
Primary (age 6–12)	12	305	4,711	15.4
Secondary (age 12–18)	1	120◊	2,134	17.8
Voc., teacher tr.	8	...	...	...
Higher	...	...	...	...

Educational attainment, n.a.; education is compulsory to age 16, however.
Literacy (1981): total population literate (virtually 100%).
Health (1981): physicians 42 (1 per 852 persons); hospital beds 110 (1 per 325 persons); infant mortality rate per 1,000 live births (1980) 16.0.
Food (1980–82)△: daily per capita caloric intake 3,420 (vegetable products 68%, animal products 32%); 137% of FAO recommended minimum requirement.

Military

Total active duty personnel (1982): none. France and Spain provide for Andorra's defense. The city of Barcelona police and French *gendarmerie* alternate year-by-year in assisting the 32-member Andorran police force.
Military expenditure as a percent of central government expenditure (1981): 0.0001% (world 19.0%).

Total area of Andorra per survey of 1978 is 181 sq mi (468 sq km). †Andorra la Vella includes Les Escaldes-Engordany. ‡Detail does not add to total given because of rounding. §Andorra la Vella only. ‖40% of consumption is produced within Andorra; the remainder is imported from Spain. ¶Trade, tourism (including winter-season sports, fairs, and festivals), and the banking system (of some importance as a tax haven for foreign financial investment and transactions) are the primary sources of GNP. ♀Spanish peseta. ♂The trade value of French francs and Spanish pesetas are converted into U.S. dollars for purposes of standardization. □Imported manufactured items are less expensive in Andorra than in neighbouring countries because they are duty free. As a result, smuggling remains a profitable sideline for some. ◊1974–75. △Composite values derived from Spanish and French food data.

Angola

Official name: República Popular de
Angola (People's Republic of Angola).
Form of government: people's republic
with one legislative house (People's
Assembly [207]).
Head of state and government:
President.
Capital: Luanda.
Official language: Portuguese.
Official religion: none.
Monetary unit: 1 kwanza (Kw) = 100
lwei; valuation (Oct. 21, 1985)
1 U.S.$ = Kw29.50; 1 £ = Kw42.30.

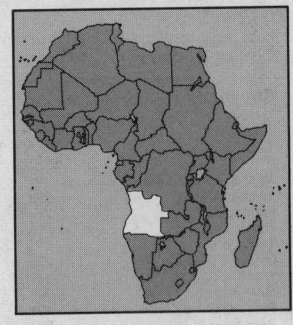

Area and population

Provinces	Capitals	area* sq mi	area* sq km	population 1985 estimate
Bengo	Caxito	14,173	36,708	133,000
Benguela	Benguela	15,116	39,151	664,000
Bié	Kuito	27,149	70,317	891,000
Cabinda	Cabinda	2,744	7,107	108,000
Huambo	Huambo	12,796	33,141	1,204,000
Huíla	Lubango	30,499	78,992	774,000
Kuando Kubango	Menongue	76,671	198,577	161,000
Kuanza Norte	N'Dalatando	7,717	19,988	440,000
Kuanza Sul	Sumbe	21,281	55,117	658,000
Kunene	N'Giva	29,327	75,956	233,000
Luanda	Luanda	570	1,477	1,030,000
Lunda Norte	Lucapa	39,685	102,784	288,000
Lunda Sul	Saurimo	29,860	77,336	138,000
Malanje	Malanje	33,686	87,247	788,000
Moxico	Lwena	77,870	201,683	263,000
Namibe	Namibe	22,043	57,090	74,000
Uíge	Uíge	23,728	61,455	560,000
Zaire	M'Banza Kongo	14,281	36,989	166,000
TOTAL		481,350†‡	1,246,700†‡	8,573,000§

Demography

Population (1985): 8,573,000.
Density (1985): persons per sq mi 17.8, persons per sq km 6.9.
Urban–rural (1985): urban 30%; rural 70%.
Sex distribution (1985): male 51.11%; female 48.89%.
Age breakdown (1985): under 15, 42.2%; 15–29, 27.5%; 30–44, 16.4%; 45–59, 9.5%; 60 and over, 4.4%.
Population projection: (1990) 9,978,000; (2000) 12,257,000.
Doubling time: 22 years.
Ethnic composition (1978): Ovimbundu 35.7%; Mbundu 22.3%; Kongo 12.6%; Luimbe 8.6%; Chokwe 8.2%; Nyaneka 4.2%; Humbe 2.5%; Ambo 2.4%; Lunda 0.9%; other 2.6%.
Religious affiliation (1980): affiliated Christian 65.7%, of which Roman Catholic 55.1%, Protestant 9.2%; nominal Christian 24.3%; tribal religionist 9.5%; other 0.5%.
Major cities (mid-1980s): Luanda 960,000; Lubango 105,000; Namibe 100,000 ‖.

Vital statistics

Birth rate per 1,000 population (1983): 49.0 (world avg. 29.0).
Death rate per 1,000 population (1983): 22.0 (world avg. 11.0).
Natural increase rate per 1,000 population (1983): 27.0 (world avg. 18.0).
Total fertility rate (avg. births per childbearing woman; 1983): 6.5.
Marriage rate per 1,000 population: n.a.
Divorce rate per 1,000 population: n.a.
Life expectancy at birth (1983): male 42.0 years; female 44.0 years.
Major causes of death: n.a.; however, major diseases are malaria, tuberculosis, and tetanus.

National economy

Budget¶ (1981). Revenue: Kw93,478,000,000 (taxes 57.0%; loans 21.1%; state returns from mixed enterprises 12.6%; other 9.3%). Expenditures: Kw91,640,000,000 (economic and social development 37.5%; defense 20.2%♀; education, health, and other social services 15.1%; administration 12.9%; other 14.3%).
Public debt (external, outstanding; 1982): U.S.$553,000,000.
Tourism: n.a.
Production (metric tons except as noted). Agriculture, forestry, fishing (1984): cassava 1,950,000, sugarcane 360,000, bananas 280,000, corn (maize) 260,000, sweet potatoes 180,000, palm oil 40,000, coffee 27,000, peanuts (groundnuts) 20,000; livestock (number of live animals) 3,350,000 cattle, 955,000 goats, 460,000 pigs, 245,000 sheep; roundwood 9,003,000 cu mö; fish catch 112,414ö. Mining and quarrying (1983): diamonds, of which gem quality 775,000 carats, industrial quality 259,000 carats; cement 220,000; salt 55,000. Manufacturing (1981): raw sugar 65,000; crude steel 10,000; soaps 6,000; paints 5,000; beer 1,350,000 hectolitres□; matches 55,000 boxes; cigarettes 2,400,000,000 units; shirts 2,300,000 units; skirts 967,000 units; leather shoes 306,000 pairs. Construction: n.a. Energy production (consumption): electricity (kW-hr; 1984) 1,650,000,000 (1,650,000,000); coal (metric tons; 1983) none (minuscule); crude petroleum (metric tons; 1983) 6,800,000 (1,504,000); petroleum products (metric tons; 1983) 1,030,000 (515,000); natural gas (cu m; 1983) 102,500,000,000 (102,500,000,000).
Gross national product (at current market prices; 1982): U.S.$7,634,000,000 (U.S. $1,032 per capita).

Structure of gross domestic product and labour force

	1981 in value Kw'000,000	% of total value	labour force	% of labour force
Agriculture	68,400	34.3	1,123,360	59.0
Mining	41,000	20.6		
Manufacturing	4,200	2.1		
Construction	3,300	1.7		
Trade, finance	9,500	4.8	304,640	16.0
Public utilities	700	0.3		
Transportation and communication	8,300	4.2		
Pub. admin., defense	20,400	10.2		
Services	...	...	476,000	25.0
Other	43,700	21.9		
TOTAL◊	199,500	100.0‡	1,904,000	100.0

Population economically active (1983): total 1,986,000; participation rate of total population 23.8% (female 9.5%, unemployed, n.a.).
Price and earnings indexes: n.a.
Household income and expenditure. Average household size (1980) 4.8; average annual income per household: n.a.; source of income: n.a.; expenditure: n.a.
Land use (1983): forested 42.9%; meadows and pastures 23.3%; agricultural and under permanent cultivation 2.8%; other 31.0%.

Foreign trade

Balance of trade (current prices)

	1978	1979	1980	1981	1982	1983
Kw'000,000	+8,600	+11,400	+4,100	+3,200	+22,024	+32,959
% of total	18.3%	16.9%	3.8%	3.1%	26.6%	41.5%

Imports (1981): Kw49,500,000,000 (mostly purchases of military hardware, food [particularly grains], and other machinery and transport equipment). *Major import sources:* Portugal 15%; France 11%; U.S.S.R. 9%; South Africa 9%; Brazil 8%; United Kingdom 7%.
Exports (1981): Kw52,700,000,000 (crude petroleum 74%, petroleum products 10%, diamonds 10%, coffee 5%). *Major export destinations:* United States 49%; The Bahamas 15%; Spain 7%; Brazil 7%.

Transport and communications

Transport. Railroads (1981): route length 1,834 mi, 2,952 kmö; passenger journeys 7,622,000; cargo transported 725,000 metric tons. Roads (1975): total length 44,900 mi, 72,300 km (paved 12%). Vehicles (1982): passenger cars 75,000; trucks and buses 25,000. Merchant marine (1984): vessels (100 gross tons and over) 87; total deadweight tonnage 138,555. Air transport△ (1984): passenger-mi 570,025,000, passenger-km 917,368,000; short ton-mi cargo 17,158,500, metric ton-km cargo 25,051,000; airports (1985) with scheduled flights 19.
Communications. Daily newspapers (1984): total number 4; total circulation 111,500; circulation per 1,000 population 13.5. Radio (1984): total number of receivers 130,000 (1 per 66 persons). Television (1984): total number of receivers 23,000 (1 per 371 persons). Telephones (1981): 65,900 (1 per 120 persons).

Education and health

Education (1981–82)

	schools	teachers	students	student/ teacher ratio
Primary (age 7–10)	7,026	40,027	1,258,858	31.5
Secondary (age 11–16)	...	3,870	132,205	34.2
Voc., teacher tr.	...	410	5,206	12.7
Higher	1	300	3,150	10.5

Educational attainment, n.a. *Literacy* (1980): total population literate (over age 15) 1,196,000 (about 28%); males literate 771,000 (36.2%); females literate 425,000 (19.3%).
Health (1980): physicians 436 (1 per 17,500 persons); hospital beds 20,700 (1 per 373 persons); *infant mortality rate* per 1,000 live births (1983) 148.0.
Food (1979–81): daily per capita caloric intake 2,353 (vegetable products 92%, animal products 8%); 100% of FAO recommended minimum requirement.

Military

Total active duty personnel (1984): 43,000† (army 93.0%, navy 3.5%, air force 3.5%). *Military expenditure as percent of GNP* (1981): 11.4% (world 5.7%); per capita expenditure U.S.$101.

*Provincial detail and totals independently reported and converted. †Total contains adjustments of unspecified nature amounting to 2,156 sq mi (5,585 sq km). ‡Detail does not add to total given because of rounding. §Unified national estimates and projections based on sample surveys, partial censuses, and analysis of provincial vital statistics. ‖1981 estimate; population (1970 census) of other important towns was: Huambo 61,885; Lobito 59,258; and Benguela 40,996. ¶Budget for 1983 was: Revenue Kw83,900,000,000; Expenditure Kw83,900,000,000. ♀According to unofficial estimates, defense consumed more than 50% of the budget in 1981. ö1983. □1979. ◊In current prices. △TAAG airline only. †In 1984, about 19,000 Cuban troops and several hundred other Soviet-bloc advisers and technicians were assisting government forces.

Antigua and Barbuda

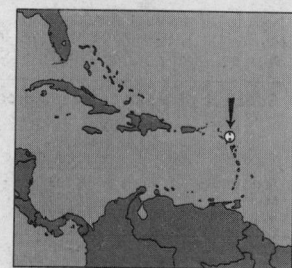

Official name: Antigua and Barbuda.
Form of government: parliamentary
state with appointed Senate (17) and
elected House of Representatives (17).
Chief of state: British Monarch
represented by governor-general.
Head of government: Prime Minister.
Capital: Saint John's.
Official language: English.
Official religion: none.
Monetary unit: 1 East Caribbean dollar
(EC$) = 100 cents; valuation (Oct. 21,
1985) 1 U.S.$ = EC$2.70;
1 £ = EC$3.87.

Area and population	area		population
Parishes*	sq mi	sq km	1984 estimate
Saint George	10.2	26.4	
Saint John's	26.2	67.9	
Saint Mary	25.1	65.0	78,000
Saint Paul	17.7	45.8	
Saint Peter	12.8	33.2	
Saint Phillip	16.0	41.4	
Islands*			
Barbuda	62.0	160.6	1,500
Redonda	0.5	1.3	†
TOTAL	170.5	441.6	79,500

Demography

Population (1985): 80,500.
Density (1985): persons per sq mi 472.1, persons per sq km 182.3.
Urban–rural (1985): urban 31.0%; rural 69.0%.
Sex distribution (1982): male 48.00%; female 52.00%.
Age breakdown (1970): under 15, 44.0%; 15–29, 24.2%; 30–44, 12.0%; 45–59
11.7%; 60 and over, 8.1%.
Population projection: (1990) 86,000; (2000) 99,000.
Doubling time: 52 years.
Ethnic composition (1980): black 94.4%; European 1.3%; other 4.3%.
Religious affiliation (1980): Anglican 44.5%; other Protestant (largely Mora-
vian and Methodist) 41.6%; Roman Catholic 10.2%; other 3.7%.
Major cities (1982): Saint John's 30,000; Codrington 1,200.

Vital statistics

Birth rate per 1,000 population (1983): 15.1 (world avg. 29.0); legitimate
18.7%; illegitimate 81.3%.
Death rate per 1,000 population (1983): 4.6 (world avg. 11.0).
Natural increase rate per 1,000 population (1983): 10.5 (world avg. 18.0).
Total fertility rate (avg. births per childbearing woman; 1980): 2.6.
Marriage rate per 1,000 population (1983): 2.3.
Divorce rate per 1,000 population (1983): 0.4.
Life expectancy at birth (1982): 72.0 years.
Major causes of death per 100,000 population (1983): malignant neoplasms
(cancers) 62.6; hypertensive heart diseases 42.2; cerebrovascular disease
28.1; pneumonia 25.6; diabetes mellitus 20.4.

National economy

Budget (1983). Revenue: EC$88,812,000 (indirect taxes 76.5%, of which con-
sumer taxes 39.7%, import duties 27.9%; transfer payments from abroad
4.6%). Expenditure: EC$94,595,000 (salaries 55.8%; goods and services
32.1%; interest on public debt 6.9%; pensions and gratuities 6.6%)‡.
Public debt (external, outstanding; 1983): U.S.$80,000,000.
Tourism (1983): receipts from visitors U.S.$51,200,000; expenditures by na-
tionals abroad, n.a.
Production (metric tons except as noted). Agriculture, forestry, fishing (1983):
sugarcane 4,600, sweet potatoes 353, tomatoes 285, yams 273, pineapples
181, cabbage 166, carrots 148, cucumbers 140, pumpkins 116; livestock
(number of live animals; 1984): 16,000 cattle, 12,000 sheep, 12,000 goats,
70,000 poultry§; fish catch (1983) marine fishes 1,013, lobsters 50. Mining
and quarrying (1983): gravel 49,212. Manufacturing (value of sales of local
manufactures in EC$; 1981): clothing 84,410,000; mattresses 23,429,000;
household appliances 6,350,000; paint and paint products 2,937,000; plastic
products 1,758,000. Construction (1983): total building applications 557;
gross value EC$60,402,960. Energy production (consumption): electricity
(kW-hr; 1983) 63,000,000 (63,000,000); coal, none (n.a.); crude petroleum,
none (negligible); petroleum products (metric tons; 1983) negligible (48,-
000); natural gas, none (n.a.).
Labour force (1983): total 30,843; participation rate of population over age
16, 39.4% (female 39.6%, unemployed 24.1%).

Price and earnings indexes (1980 = 100)							
	1978	1979	1980	1981	1982	1983	1984
Consumer price index	72.2	84.0	100.0	111.5	116.3	118.5	123.5
Weekly earnings index	76.5	85.8	100.0	...	...	...	...

Household income and expenditure. Average household size (1970) 4.2;
average annual income per household: n.a.; source of income: n.a.; expenditure: n.a.
Gross national product (at current market prices; 1983): U.S.$140,000,000
(U.S.$1,730 per capita).

Structure of gross domestic product and labour force				
	1984		1980	
	in value EC$'000,000	% of total value	labour force	% of labour force
Agriculture, fishing	20.1	5.4	2,092	9.5
Quarrying	2.8	0.8	75	0.3
Manufacturing	18.2	4.9	1,539	7.0
Construction	22.8	6.2	2,476	11.2
Public utilities	10.0	2.7	319	1.4
Transp. and commun.	62.1	16.8	2,596	11.8
Trade, restaurants, and hotels	101.8	27.6	4,867	22.1
Finance	70.3	19.0	742	3.4
Pub. admin., defense	58.5	15.8	}	
Services	20.2	5.5	} 7,322	33.3
Other	−17.5 ‖	−4.7 ‖		
TOTAL	369.30	100.0	22,028	100.0

Land use (1983): forested 15.9%; meadows and pastures 6.8%; agricultural
and under permanent cultivation 18.2%; other 59.1%.

Foreign trade

Balance of trade (current prices)						
	1978	1979	1980	1981	1982	1983
EC$'000,000	−77	−169	−158	−207	−189	−178
% of total	53.2%	72.1%	51.2%	52.9%	63.6%	64.2%

Imports (1983): EC$25,719,100 (food and live animals 34.0%; chemicals
21.1%; beverages and tobacco 15.1%; machinery 3.4%). *Major import
sources:* United States 49.6%; United Kingdom 13.2%; Canada 5.5%..
Exports (1983): EC$49,688,000 (reexports 40.0%, of which miscellaneous
manufactured articles 44.3%; machinery 38.9%; domestic exports 60.0%, of
which miscellaneous manufactured goods 54.9%, machinery 13.2%, chemicals 7.9%, beverages and tobacco 7.5%). *Major export destinations:* United
States 32.0%; United Kingdom 17.2%; Canada 11.2%.

Transport and communications

Transport. Railroads¶ (1982): 48 mi (78 km). Roads (1982): total length 237
mi, 380 km (paved 63%). Vehicles (1983): passenger cars 7,120; trucks and
buses 1,209♀. Merchant marine (1984): vessels (100 gross tons and over) 3;
total deadweight tonnage 443. Air transport (1981): passenger-mi 67,691,-
000ŏ; passenger-km 108,938,000ŏ; short ton-mi cargo 14,812,000◻, metric
ton-km cargo 21,625,000◻; airports (1985) with scheduled flights 1.
Communications. Daily newspapers (1983): total number 2; total circulation
5,500; circulation per 1,000 population 71. Radio (1984): total receivers
20,000 (1 per 4.0 persons). Television (1984): total receivers 16,600 (1 per
4.8 persons). Telephones (1983): 10,470 (1 per 7.5 persons).

Education and health

Education (1983)	schools	teachers	students	student/ teacher ratio
Primary (age 5–10)	48	426	9,933	23.3
Secondary (age 11–16)	16	331	4,197	12.7
Voc., teacher tr.	1	...	...	...
Higher	...	...	...	...

Educational attainment, n.a. *Literacy* (1980): total adult population literate
88%.
Health (1983): physicians 29 (1 per 2,698 persons); hospital beds 226 (1 per
346 persons); infant mortality rate per 1,000 live births (1982) 32.0.
Food (1980–82): daily per capita caloric intake 2,039 (vegetable products 72%,
animal products 28%); 82%◊ of FAO recommended minimum requirement.

Military

Total active duty personnel (1983): c. 700. *Military expenditure as percent of
GNP:* n.a.

*Community councils are the actual organs of local governments. †Uninhabited.
‡Excludes adjustment for receipts on government goods and services (−6.0%). §1982.
‖ Less imputed bank service charges. ¶Serving sugarcane plantations only. ♀1981.
ŏLeeward Island Air Transport Company. ◻1982 Seagreen airlines. ◊1979–81.

ANTIGUA DEPARTMENT OF TOURISM

Nelson's Dockyard, commissioned 1755, today a museum, Antigua.

Argentina

Official name: República Argentina
(Argentine Republic).
Form of government: federal republic,
with two legislative houses (Senate
[46]; Chamber of Deputies [254]).
Head of state and government:
President.
Capital: Buenos Aires.
Official language: Spanish.
Official religion: Roman Catholicism.
Monetary unit: 1 austral (pl. australes)*
($a) = 1,000 pesos; valuation (Oct. 21,
1985) 1 U.S.$ = $a0.80; 1 £ = $a1.15.

Area and population

Provinces	Capitals	area sq mi	area sq km	population 1984 estimate
Buenos Aires	La Plata	118,754	307,571	11,829,000
Catamarca	San Fernando del Valle de Catamarca	38,984	100,967	223,000
Chaco	Resistencia	38,469	99,633	762,000
Chubut	Rawson	86,752	224,686	297,000
Córdoba	Córdoba	65,161	168,766	2,567,000
Corrientes	Corrientes	34,054	88,199	706,000
Entre Ríos	Paraná	30,418	78,781	953,000
Formosa	Formosa	27,825	72,066	327,000
Jujuy	San Salvador de Jujuy	20,548	53,219	462,000
La Pampa	Santa Rosa	55,382	143,440	226,000
La Rioja	La Rioja	34,626	89,680	175,000
Mendoza	Mendoza	57,462	148,827	1,299,000
Misiones	Posadas	11,506	29,801	658,000
Neuquén	Neuquén	36,324	94,078	288,000
Río Negro	Viedma	78,384	203,013	442,000
Salta	Salta	59,759	154,775	733,000
San Juan	San Juan	34,614	89,651	504,000
San Luis	San Luis	29,633	76,748	229,000
Santa Cruz	Río Gallegos	94,187	243,943	132,000
Santa Fe	Santa Fe	51,354	133,007	2,616,000
Santiago del Estero	Santiago del Estero	52,222	135,254	639,000
Tucumán	San Miguel de Tucumán	8,697	22,524	1,071,000
Other federal entities				
Distrito Federal	Buenos Aires	77	200	2,924,000
Tierra del Fuego	Ushuaia	8,210	21,263	35,000
TOTAL		1,073,399†	2,780,092	30,097,000

Demography

Population (1985): 30,563,800.
Density (1985): persons per sq mi 28.5, persons per sq km 11.0.
Urban–rural (1983): urban 83.0%; rural 17.0%.
Sex distribution (1980): male 49.22%; female 50.78%.
Age breakdown (1980): under 15, 30.4%; 15–29, 23.9%; 30–44, 18.8%; 45–59, 15.1%; 60–74, 9.0%; 75 and over, 2.8%.
Population projection: (1990) 33,094,000; (2000) 38,788,000.
Doubling time: 47 years.
Ethnic composition (1983): European 98%; mestizo 2%.
Religious affiliation (1981): Roman Catholic 92.8%; other 7.2%.
Major cities (1980): Buenos Aires 2,923,000 (Greater Buenos Aires 9,766,-000); Córdoba 969,000; Rosario 876,000; La Plata 455,000.

Vital statistics

Birth rate per 1,000 population (1983): 24.6 (world avg. 29.0); (1979) legitimate 70.2%; illegitimate 27.4%; unknown 2.4%.
Death rate per 1,000 population (1983): 8.7 (world avg. 11.0).
Natural increase rate per 1,000 population (1983): 15.9 (world avg. 18.0).
Total fertility rate (avg. births per childbearing woman; 1981): 2.8.
Marriage rate per 1,000 population (1979): 6.2.
Divorce rate per 1,000 population: ‡.
Life expectancy at birth (1981): male 68.6 years; female 73.3 years.
Major causes of death per 100,000 population (1979): circulatory diseases 388.7; malignant neoplasms (cancers) 151.2; respiratory diseases 47.3.

National economy

Budget (1982). Revenue: $12,173,150,000§ (taxes on goods and services 46.0%, customs and excise tax 18.7%, income tax 4.6%, wealth tax 2.3%). Expenditures: $a14,055,420,000§ (economic development 35.1%, defense 18.6%, social welfare 16.3%, culture and education 10.4%, general administration 9.4%, security 5.7%, science and technology 2.9%, health 2.2%).
Public debt (external, outstanding; 1983): U.S.$24,592,500,000.
Tourism (1982): receipts from visitors U.S.$516,000,000; expenditures by nationals abroad U.S.$559,000,000.
Production (metric tons except as noted). Agriculture, forestry, fishing (1984): sugarcane 15,468,000, wheat 12,300,000, corn (maize) 9,200,000, sorghum 7,740,000, soybeans 6,000,000, grapes 2,759,000, potatoes 2,097,-000, alfalfa 1,522,000, flax 660,000, raw cotton 561,400; livestock (number of live animals) 53,500,000 cattle, 30,000,000 sheep; roundwood 10,520,000 cu m ‖; fish catch 416,300 ‖. Mining and quarrying (1983): gold 20,898 troy oz; silver 2,636,000 troy oz; uranium 504. Manufacturing (by value in $a'000,000; 1983): motor vehicles 18,933; cigars and cigarettes 8,410; cast iron, steel, and ferroalloys 6,857; vegetable oil (edible and nonedible) 6,702; sugar 6,469; paper and paper products 6,322. Construction (authorized; 1983) 780,000 sq m¶. Energy production (consumption): electricity (kW-hr; 1984) 40,848,000,000 (42,992,000,000 ‖); coal (metric tons; 1983) 486,000 (978,000); crude petroleum (barrels; 1984) 180,670,000 (183,073,000 ‖);

petroleum products (metric tons; 1983) 21,926,000 (20,094,000); natural gas (cu m; 1983) 13,138,000,000 (15,365,000,000).
Gross national product (1983): U.S.$58,560,000,000 (U.S.$2,030 per capita).

Structure of gross domestic product and labour force

	1983 in value U.S.$'000,000	1983 % of total value	1980 labour force	1980 % of labour force
Agriculture	8,796.7	15.4	1,200,992	12.0
Mining	1,553.0	2.7	47,171	0.5
Manufacturing	13,552.8	23.7	1,985,995	19.9
Construction	3,052.3	5.3	1,003,175	10.1
Public utilities	2,314.3	4.1	103,256	1.0
Transp. and commun.	6,379.6	11.2	460,476	4.6
Trade	7,266.5	12.7	1,702,080	17.0
Finance	4,869.6	8.5	395,704	4.0
Pub. admin., defense	6,167.1	10.8 }	2,399,039	24.0
Services	3,162.1	5.5 }		
Other	...	...	691,302	6.9
TOTAL	57,114.0❡	100.0†	9,989,190	100.0

Population economically active (1983): total 10,815,000; participation rate of total population 38.3% (female 26.4%, unemployed 5.7%).

Price and earnings indexes (1980 = 100)

	1980	1981	1982	1983	1984	1985δ
Consumer price index	100.0	204.0	541.0	2,403	17,462	74,204
Monthly earnings index□	100.0	183.3	434.3	1,742	15,407	58,541

Land use (1983): forested 21.9%; meadows and pastures 52.2%; agricultural and under permanent cultivation 13.0%; other 12.9%.

Foreign trade◇

Balance of trade (current prices)

	1979	1980	1981	1982	1983	1984△
U.S.$'000,000	+1,769	−1,360	+713	+2,768	+3,710	+756
% of total	12.8%	7.8%	4.1%	22.2%	31.0%	22.2%

Imports (1983): U.S.$4,504,306,000 (chemicals 20.9%; nonelectrical machinery 15.4%; petroleum and petroleum products 9.8%; electrical machinery 7.8%; cast-iron and steel products 7.4%; road vehicles and transport equipment 4.1%; plastics, cellulose, and artificial resins 3.8%). *Major import sources:* United States 21.6%; Brazil 14.8%; West Germany 10.5%.
Exports (1983): U.S.$7,836,146,000 (cereals 36.9%; feeding stuff for animals 8.2%; vegetables, fruits, and nuts 7.4%; vegetable oils, fats, and waxes 6.9%; meat and meat preparations 5.5%; petroleum and petroleum products 4.5%; hides and skins 3.4%; cast-iron and steel products 2.6%). *Major export destinations:* U.S.S.R. 20.8%; United States 9.6%; The Netherlands 9.4%; China 6.4%; Japan 4.8%; Brazil 4.6%; Italy 4.3%.

Transport and communications

Transport. Railroads (1984): length 22,484 mi, 36,185 km; passenger-km 10,524,000,000; metric ton-km cargo 11,244,000,000. Roads (1983): total length 131,920 mi, 212,305 km (paved 26%). Vehicles (1984): passenger cars 3,685,000; commercial vehicles and buses 1,388,000. Merchant marine (1984): vessels (100 gross tons and over) 530; total deadweight tonnage 3,498,236. Air transport (1983): passenger-km 6,058,924,000; metric ton-km cargo 191,309,000; airports (1985) 65.
Communications. Daily newspapers (1982): total number 159; total circulation 2,485,000†; circulation per 1,000 population 85❍. Radio (1984): receivers 10,500,000 (1 per 3.0 persons). Television (1984): receivers 5,915,-000 (1 per 5.1 persons). Telephones (1983): 2,717,061 (1 per 11 persons).

Education and health

Education (1984)

	schools	teachers	students	student/teacher ratio
Primary (age 6–12)	20,619	218,520	4,430,513	20.3
Secondary (age 13–17)❍	1,987	86,874	656,521	7.6
Vocational	3,117	119,309	905,755	7.6
Higher	1,251	64,230	677,535	10.5

Educational attainment (1980). Percent of adult population over age 25 having: no formal schooling 6.0%; less than primary education 32.0%; primary 34.6%; secondary 20.5%; higher 6.9%. *Literacy* (1980): total population over age 15 literate 94.9%; males literate 95.5%; females literate 94.4%.
Health: physicians (1979) 79,216 (1 per 351 persons); hospital beds (1980) 150,010 (1 per 182 persons); infant mortality rate per 1,000 live births (1983) 35.3.
Food (1980–82): daily per capita caloric intake 3,368 (vegetable products 67%; animal products 33%); 128% of FAO recommended minimum requirement.

Military

Total active duty personnel (1984): 153,000 (army 65.4%, navy 23.5%, air force 11.1%). *Military expenditure as percent of GNP* (1983): 2.7% (world 6.1%); per capita expenditure: U.S.$51.

*Introduced June 14, 1985, at the rate of 1 austral = 1,000 pesos. †Detail does not add to total given because of rounding. ‡Argentina has no legal provision for divorce. §In new pesos, which prior to June 14, 1985, had a rate of 1 new peso = 10,000 old pesos. ‖ 1983. ¶Distrito Federal only. ❡At 1982 prices. δMarch. □Skilled workers in manufacturing only. ◇Import figures are f.o.b. (free on board) in balance of trade and c.i.f. (cost, insurance, and freight) for commodities and trading partners. △Second quarter. †Partial circulation only. ❍Teacher training included with secondary.

Australia

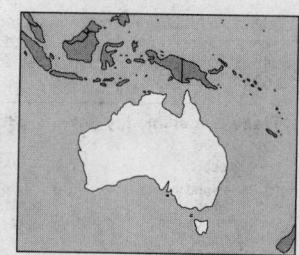

Official name: Commonwealth of Australia.
Form of government: federal parliamentary state with two legislative houses (Senate [76]; House of Representatives [148]).
Chief of state: British Monarch represented by governor-general.
Head of government: Prime Minister.
Capital: Canberra.
Official language: English.
Official religion: none.
Monetary unit: 1 Australian dollar ($A) = 100 cents; valuation (Oct. 21, 1985) 1 U.S.$ = $A1.42; 1 £ = $A2.04.

Area and population

| | | area | | population |
| | | | | 1984 |
States	Capitals	sq mi	sq km	estimate
New South Wales	Sydney	309,500	801,600	5,405,100
Queensland	Brisbane	666,900	1,727,200	2,505,100
South Australia	Adelaide	379,900	984,000	1,353,000
Tasmania	Hobart	26,200	67,800	437,300
Victoria	Melbourne	87,900	227,600	4,075,900
Western Australia	Perth	975,100	2,525,500	1,382,600
Territories				
Australian Capital Territory	Canberra	900	2,400	245,600
Northern Territory	Darwin	519,800	1,346,200	138,900
TOTAL		2,966,200	7,682,300	15,543,600*

Demography

Population (1985 est.): 15,749,000.
Density (1985): persons per sq mi 5.3, persons per sq km 2.1.
Urban–rural (1981): urban 85.7%; rural 14.3%.
Sex distribution (1985): male 49.88%; female 50.12%.
Age breakdown (1985): under 15, 23.7%; 15–29, 25.1%; 30–44, 21.9%; 45–59, 14.6%; 60–74, 10.8%; 75 and over, 3.9%.
Population projection: (1990) 16,724,000; (2000) 18,580,000.
Doubling time: 58 years.
Ethnic composition (1980): Anglo-Australian 81.8%; British 5.7%; Italian 2.0%; Scottish 1.5%; Greek 1.2%; aboriginal 1.0%; German 0.8%; Dutch 0.7%; other 5.3%.
Religious affiliation (1981): Christian 76.4%, of which Anglican Church of Australia 26.1%, Roman Catholic 26.0%, other Protestant 20.8% (Uniting Church 4.9%, Presbyterian 4.4%, Methodist 3.4%), Orthodox 2.9%; Muslim 0.5%; Jewish 0.4%; Buddhist 0.2%; no religion 10.8%; other 11.7%.
Major cities (1983): Sydney 3,334,950; Melbourne 2,864,600; Brisbane 1,138,370; Adelaide 969,160; Perth 948,800†; Newcastle 410,300†; Canberra 255,900; Wollongong 233,700†; Gold Coast 178,800†‡; Hobart 172,500†.
Place of birth (1981): 78.2% native-born; 20.6% foreign-born, of which United Kingdom 7.8%§, Italy 1.9%, New Zealand 1.2%, Greece 1.0%, Yugoslavia 1.0%, East and West Germany 0.8%, The Netherlands 0.7%, Poland 0.4%, Malta 0.4%, Lebanon 0.3%; not stated 1.2%.
Mobility (1982). Population living in the same residence as in 1981: 84.0%; different residence, same state 9.4%; different states and territories 6.6%.
Households (1981). Total number of households (1982) 5,213,900. Average household size 3.1; 1 person 18.0%, 2 persons 29.2%, 3 persons 16.9%, 4 persons 19.1%, 5 persons 10.5%, 6 persons 4.1%, 7 or more persons 2.2%. Family households (1982): 4,001,800 (76.8%), nonfamily 1,212,100 (23.2%).
Immigration (1983): permanent immigrants admitted 78,391, from United Kingdom and Ireland 25.0%, New Zealand 7.9%, Malaysia and Singapore 7.2%, East and West Germany 4.9%, Philippines 4.8%, South Africa 3.4%, Indonesia 3.3%, South Asia (Bangladesh, India, Pakistan, Sri Lanka) 2.6%, United States 2.5%, Yugoslavia 1.9%, Austria 1.8%. Refugee arrivals (1985) 14,000.

Vital statistics

Birth rate per 1,000 population (1985): 15.8 (world avg. 29.0); (1982) legitimate 86.3%; illegitimate 13.7%.
Death rate per 1,000 population (1985): 7.1 (world avg. 11.0).
Natural increase rate per 1,000 population (1985): 8.7 (world avg. 18.0).
Total fertility rate (avg. births per childbearing woman; 1983): 1.9.
Marriage rate per 1,000 population (1983): 7.5.
Divorce rate per 1,000 population (1983): 2.8.
Life expectancy at birth (1983): male 72.1 years; female 78.7 years.
Major causes of death per 100,000 population (1983): diseases of the circulatory system 355; malignant neoplasms (cancers) 168; diseases of the respiratory system 51; accidents, poisonings, and violence 49; diseases of the digestive system 24; endocrine, nutritional, and metabolic diseases and immunity disorders 14.

Social indicators

Educational attainment (1982). Percent of adult population over age 20 having: primary and secondary education 57.6%; vocational 16.9%; certificate/ diploma 17.1%; university 6.8%.
Quality of working life (1985 ‖). Average workweek: 33.4 hours (3.7% overtime). Annual rate per 100,000 workers for: injury or accident, n.a.; industrial illness, n.a.; death, n.a.. Proportion of employed persons insured for damages or income loss resulting from: injury 100%; permanent disability 100%; death 100%. Average days lost to labour stoppages per 1,000 workdays (1984): 0.7. Means of transportation to work (1981): 62.2% private automobile; 13.9% public transportation; 1.3% bicycle; 5.4% foot; 17.2% other. Proportion of unemployed workers discouraged (considered by employers to be too young or too old and no vacancies in line of work; 1982): 31.6%.

Distribution of family income (1982)

income group	$A0–5,000	$A6,000–13,000	$A14,000–18,700	more than $A18,700
% of population	11.2%	28.4%	32.4%	28.0%

Access to services (1976). Proportion of dwellings having access to: electricity 99.5%; bathroom 96.0%; flush toilet 92.2%; kitchen 97.9%; public sewer 73.4%.
Social participation. Eligible voters participating in last national election: 86.8%. Population participating in voluntary work: n.a. Trade union membership in total work force (1983): 55%. Practicing religious population in total affiliated population: n.a.
Social deviance (1982). Offense rate per 100,000 population for: murder 3.2, rape 17.2; serious assault 44.8; auto theft 533.9; burglary and housebreaking 1,438.8; fraud and forgery 438.4. Incidence per 100,000 in general population of (1981): alcoholism, n.a.; drug and substance abuse (charges) 214.1, of which marijuana 177.6, narcotics 25.1, amphetamines 4.2, barbiturates and hypnotics 2.3, tranquilizers 1.8, hallucinogens 1.8; suicide 11.5.
Leisure, n.a.
Material well-being (1983). Households possessing: automobile 86%; telephone 85%; refrigerator 99.6%; air conditioner 32.3%; washing machine 91.7%; hot water 98.7%; central heating 3.9%; swimming pool 10.1%.

National economy

Gross national product (at current market prices; 1984): U.S.$170,000,000,000 (U.S.$10,940 per capita).

Structure of gross domestic product and labour force

| | 1982–83 | | 1984 | |
	in value $A'000,000	% of total value	labour force¶	% of labour force
Agriculture	5,839	4.0	400,100	6.2
Mining	6,542	4.5	93,200	1.4
Manufacturing	26,775	18.4	1,141,400	17.7
Construction	9,022	6.2	423,200	6.5
Public utilities	5,433	3.7	147,900	2.3
Transportation and communication	12,344	8.5	485,700	7.5
Trade	19,276	13.2	1,271,400	19.7
Finance	31,990	22.0	619,300	9.6
Pub. admin., defense	6,930	4.8	321,700	5.0
Services	25,573	17.6	1,558,400	24.1
Other	−4,278⁹	−2.9⁹	...	...
TOTAL	145,446⁵	100.0	6,462,300	100.0

Budget (1985–86). Revenue: $A64,100,000,000 (income tax 61.9%, of which individual 51.0%, corporate 10.0%; excise duties 14.0%; sales tax 9.4%). Expenditures: $A69,100,000,000 (social security and welfare 27.6%; transfers to state governments 19.6%; health 9.7%; interest on public debt 9.7%; defense 9.5%; education 7.2%; general public services 6.9%; economic services 6.3%; housing 2.0%; culture and recreation 1.2%).
External debt (1984–85): $A33,100,000,000.
Tourism (1983): receipts from visitors U.S.$1,008,000,000; expenditures by nationals abroad U.S.$1,713,000,000.

Manufacturing, mining, and construction enterprises (1983–84)

	no. of establishments	no. of employees	weekly wages as a % of avg. of all wages□	annual value added ($A'000,000)
Manufacturing				
Food, beverages, and tobacco	3,423	168,889	100.8	6,364
Paper, printing, and publishing	2,921	99,722	104.8	3,397
Basic metal products	533	77,240	115.5	3,363
Transport equipment	1,290	116,550	93.2	3,319
Chemical, petroleum, and coal products	917	56,430	102.4	3,099
Fabricated metal products	4,179	95,587	98.5	2,829
Wood, wood products, and furniture	3,991	69,833	...	1,925
Nonmetallic mineral products	1,718	38,187	...	1,709
Clothing and footwear	1,947	71,132	...	1,540
Textiles	625	31,862	74.8	907
Mining				
Coal	136	33,115 }	153.3	2,769
Metallic minerals	308	31,071 }		2,762
Construction⋄	51,351	246,510	104.0	3,925

Production (gross value in $A'000 except as noted). Agriculture, forestry, fishing (1983–84): livestock slaughtered—cattle 2,064,000, sheep and lambs 568,400, pigs 374,700; wool 2,030,500; wheat 3,625,900, vegetables 739,500, barley 730,500, sugarcane 516,700, potatoes 282,700, cotton 263,700, sorghum 244,900, grapes 206,800, oats 200,000, apples 133,900, bananas 83,900, sunflower seeds 54,600, peanuts (groundnuts) 40,300, pears 36,800, pineapples 30,600, peaches 25,400; livestock (number of live animals; 1984) 139,242,000 sheep, 22,161,000 cattle, 2,527,000 pigs, 48,000,000 poultry; roundwood 16,015,000 cu m△; fish catch 168,580 metric tons△. Mining and quarrying (metric tons; 1983–84): iron ore 79,879,000; bauxite 21,662,400; refined metals—aluminum 617,921, zinc 299,738, lead 190,121, copper 166,429, tin 2,937, gold 30,661 kilograms. Manufacturing (metric

tons; 1983–84): raw steel 6,161,000; cement 5,130,000; iron and steel slabs 3,889,000; super phosphate 2,663,000; sulfuric acid 1,726,000; beef and veal 1,338,100; wheat flour 1,137,600; refined sugar 682,100; newsprint 378,100; lamb 292,500; mutton 164,000; pork 253,300; plaster sheets 60,401,000 sq m; textile floor coverings 38,861,000 sq m; woven cotton cloth 35,452,000 sq m; concrete roofing tiles 15,658,000 cu m; woven woolen cloth 10,-039,000 sq m; automotive gasoline 149,680,000 hectolitres□; furnace fuel 30,380,000 hectolitres□; beer 18,520,000 hectolitres; finished and partly finished motor vehicles 368,267 units. Construction (building starts by value in $A'000; 1983–84): new dwellings 6,441,400; alterations and additions to dwellings 753,800; other buildings in private sector 3,031,400.

Retail sales and service enterprises (1979–80)

	no. of establishments	no. of employees	total wages and salaries ($A'000,000)	annual turnover ($A'000,000)
Motor vehicle dealers, gasoline and tire dealers	26,516	175,995	1,319	18,203
Food stores	39,416	260,266	1,131	12,747
Department and general stores	857	99,569	717	4,254
Clothing, fabrics, and furniture stores	17,908	81,797	519	4,143
Household appliances and hardware stores	8,196	43,542	320	2,966
Restaurants, hotels and accommodations	17,702	183,310	1,022	4,670
Licensed clubs	3,243	52,297	697	1,515
Laundries and dry cleaners	1,365	12,106	91	224
Motion picture theatres	577	6,777	45	178
Hairdressers and beauty salons	2,265	12,282	78	173

Energy production (consumption): electricity (kW-hr; 1983–84) 111,658,000,-000 (106,287,000,000); coal (metric tons; 1982–83) 142,292,000 (49,271,000); crude petroleum (barrels; 1984) 169,700,000 (201,768,500△); petroleum products (metric tons; 1983–84) 26,308,000 (23,642,000); natural gas (cu m; 1983) 12,433,575,000 (12,433,575,000).

Population economically active (April 1985): total 7,179,000; participation rate of population over age 15, 60.3% (female 38.4%, unemployed 8.6%).

Price and earnings indexes (1980 = 100)

	1979	1980	1981	1982	1983	1984	1985 ‖
Consumer price index	90.8	100.0	109.7	121.9	134.2	139.6	147.4
Weekly earnings index	89.3	100.0	111.4	124.5	133.3	146.0	151.9

Household income and expenditure. Average household size (1982) 3.3; average annual income per household (1983–84) $A10,444 (U.S.$9,190); sources of income (1983–84): wages and salaries 60.8%, income from property and entrepreneurship 23.2%, current transfers from government 12.8%; expenditure (1983–84): rent 19.9%, food 16.3%, transport and communications 15.3%, household equipment and operation 9.7%, clothing and footwear 6.4%.

Land use (1983): forested 13.9%; meadows and pastures 58.4%; agricultural and under permanent cultivation 6.1%; other 21.6%.

Financial aggregates

	1979	1980	1981	1982	1983	1984	1985 (8 mos.)
Exchange Rate, $A1.00 per:							
U.S. Dollar	1.12	1.14	1.15	1.02	0.90	0.88	0.71
£	0.53	0.49	0.57	0.50	0.59	0.64	0.51
SDR	0.84	0.93	0.97	0.89	0.85	0.84	0.68
International reserves (U.S.$)							
Total (excl. gold; '000,000)	1,424	1,690	1,671	6,371	8,869	7,441	6,366
SDRs ('000,000)	42	---	52	86	81	209	273
Reserve pos. in IMF ('000,000)	206	325	294	---	114	183	199
Foreign exchange ('000,000)	1,176	1,365	1,325	6,285	8,675	7,049	5,893
Gold ('000,000 fine troy oz)	7.93	7.93	7.93	7.93	7.93	7.93	7.93
% world reserves	0.8	0.8	0.8	0.8	0.8	0.8	0.8
Interest and prices							
Central bank discount (%)	...	...	...	...	...	...	...
Gov't. Bond yield (%)†	9.8	11.6	14.0	15.4	14.3	13.8	13.4⊙
Industrial share prices (1980 = 100)	66.9	100.0	104.2	79.5	100.4	117.0	145.6⊙
Balance of payments (U.S.$'000,000)							
Balance of visible trade	2,511	1,378	−2,329	−2,612	18	−1,040	...
Imports, f.o.b.	16,066	20,181	23,545	23,407	19,474	23,644	...
Exports, f.o.b.	18,577	21,559	21,216	20,795	19,492	22,604	...
Balance of invisibles	−4,641	−5,161	−5,517	−5,047	−5,335	−6,741	...
Balance of payments, current account	−2,646	−4,136	−8,244	−8,126	−5,787	−8,251	...

Foreign trade

Balance of trade (current prices)

	1978–79	1979–80	1980–81	1981–82	1982–83	1983–84
$A'000,000	+1,194	+1,515	−1,755	−2,099	+1,331	+742
% of total	6.1%	7.0%	4.4%	4.6%	3.0%	1.5%

Imports (1983–84): $A24,062,896,000 (machinery 26.0%, of which office machines and automatic data-processing equipment 4.7%; transport equipment 12.9%, of which road motor vehicles 9.6%; mineral fuels and lubricants 9.2%; chemicals and related products 8.9%; food and live animals 4.2%; crude materials (inedible) excluding fuels 3.2%; paper and paperboard 2.6%; beverages and tobacco 0.8%). *Major import sources:* Japan 22.3%; United States 21.6%; United Kingdom 7.2%; New Zealand 3.8%; Italy 3.1%; Saudi Arabia 2.8%; Hong Kong 2.3%; France 2.1%; Singapore 2.0%.

Exports (1983–84): $A24,805,243,000 (metalliferous ores and metal scrap 16.6%; coal, coke, and briquettes 13.4%; cereals 10.9%; textile fibres and their waste 8.3%; petroleum, petroleum gases, and petroleum products 7.6%; nonferrous metals 6.2%; meat 5.6%; sugar and honey 2.6; iron and

steel 1.7%). *Major export destinations:* Japan 26.5%; United States 10.9%; New Zealand 5.6%; United Kingdom 4.6%; Singapore 3.8%; West Germany 2.9%; Hong Kong 2.5%; China 2.4%; U.S.S.R. 2.3%; Papua New Guinea 2.0%.

Trade by commodity group (1983–84)

SITC Group	imports $A'000,000	imports %	exports $A'000,000	exports %
00 Food and live animals	1,015.3	4.2	6,155.5	24.8
01 Beverages and tobacco	196.1	0.8	73.4	0.3
02 Crude materials, excluding fuels	762.1	3.2	6,855.2	27.6
03 Mineral fuels, lubricants, and related materials	2,204.1	9.2	5,224.0	21.1
04 Animal and vegetable oils, fat and over	111.1	0.5	105.4	0.4
05 Chemicals and related products, n.e.s.	2,151.1	8.9	500.8	2.0
06 Basic manufactures	3,984.8	16.6	2,582.2	10.4
07 Machinery and transport equipment	9,315.4	38.7	1,340.1	5.4
08 Miscellaneous manufactured articles	3,119.6	13.0	510.6	2.1
09 Goods not classified by kind	691.9	2.9	711.2	2.9
Nonmerchandise trade	511.4	2.1	746.8	3.0
TOTAL	24,062.9	100.0*	24,805.2	100.0

Direction of trade (1983–84)

	imports $A'000,000	imports %	exports $A'000,000	exports %
Africa	154.8	0.6	721.7	2.9
Asia	10,521.7	43.7	13,535.3	54.6
Japan	5,366.2	22.3	6,570.0	26.5
South America	194.7	0.8	110.2	0.4
North and Central America	5,679.1	23.6	3,036.3	12.2
United States	5,188.4	21.6	2,704.7	10.9
Europe	6,130.3	25.5	4,487.1	18.1
EEC	5,106.3	21.2	3,363.8	13.6
U.S.S.R.	12.1	0.1	581.8	2.3
Other Europe	1,011.9	4.2	541.5	2.2
Oceania	1,000.6	4.2	1,927.5	7.8
New Zealand	921.7	3.8	1,400.8	5.6
Other countries, including destinations unknown	381.7	1.6	987.1	3.4
TOTAL	24,062.9	100.0*	24,805.2	100.0*

Transport and communications

Transport. Railroads** (1983): route length 24,200 mi, 38,900 km; passenger-mi 1,359,051,000◊, passenger-km 2,187,120,000◊; short ton-mi cargo 23,622,000,000, metric ton-km cargo 34,488,000,000. Roads (1984): total length 507,700 mi, 817,000 km (paved 47%). Vehicles (1983): passenger cars 7,322,500; trucks and buses 789,000. Merchant marine (1984): vessels (100 gross tons and over) 622; total deadweight tonnage 3,227,001. Air transport (1984): passenger-mi 16,233,000,000, passenger-km 26,124,000,000; short ton-mi cargo 543,930,000, metric ton-km cargo 794,124,000; airports (1984) with scheduled flights 441.

Communications. Daily newspapers (1979): total number 63; total circulation 4,851,000; circulation per 1,000 population 337. Radio (1983): total number of receivers 20,000,000 (1 per 0.8 person). Television (1983): total number of receivers 6,500,000 (1 per 2.4 persons). Telephones (1984): 8,328,714 (1 per 1.9 persons).

Education and health

Education (1983)

	schools	teachers	students	student/teacher ratio
Primary (age 6–12)	8,336	94,233	1,809,035	19.2
Secondary (age 13–17)	1,572	93,273	1,206,771	12.9
Voc., teacher tr.	373	44,776	729,291	16.3
Higher	64	21,866	349,243	16.0

Literacy (1980): total population over age 15 literate 99.5%.

Health: physicians (1982) 27,500 (1 per 552 persons); hospital beds (1984) 91,654 (1 per 170 persons); infant mortality rate per 1,000 live births (1983) 10.4.

Food (1980–82): daily per capita caloric intake 3,113 (vegetable products 66%, animal products 34%); 115% of FAO recommended minimum requirement.

Military

Total active duty personnel (1984): 72,345 (army 45.2%, navy 23.5%, air force 31.3%). *Military expenditure as percent of GNP* (1983): 2.8% (world 6.1%); per capita expenditure U.S.$303.

*Detail does not add to total given because of rounding. †1982 estimate. ‡Includes Tweed Heads. §Includes both Northern Ireland and Republic of Ireland. ‖ Second quarter. ¶Employed persons only. ⁹Less imputed bank service charges. ᵟAt current prices. □1982–83. ◊1978–79. △1983. †Long term only. ⊙July. **Government railways only.

Austria

Official name: Republik Österreich
(Republic of Austria).
Form of government: federal multi-party republic with two legislative houses (Federal Council [63]; National Council [183]).
Chief of state: President.
Head of government: Chancellor.
Capital: Vienna.
Official language: German.
Official religion: none.
Monetary unit: 1 schilling (S) = 100 groschen; valuation (Oct. 21, 1985)
1 U.S.$ = S18.53; 1 £ = S26.58.

Area and population

States	Capitals	area sq mi	area sq km	population 1984 estimate
Burgenland	Eisenstadt	1,531	3,965	268,300
Kärnten	Klagenfurt	3,681	9,534	538,700
Niederösterreich	Vienna	7,402	19,172	1,423,200
Oberösterreich	Linz	4,626	11,980	1,278,000
Salzburg	Salzburg	2,762	7,154	451,200
Steiermark	Graz	6,327	16,387	1,183,800
Tirol	Innsbruck	4,883	12,647	594,400
Vorarlberg	Bregenz	1,004	2,601	307,600
Wien	—	160	415	1,505,800
TOTAL		32,376	83,855	7,551,000

Demography

Population (1985): 7,552,000.
Density (1985): persons per sq mi 233.2, persons per sq km 90.4.
Urban–rural (1981): urban 55.1%; rural 44.9%.
Sex distribution (1984): male 47.53%; female 52.47%.
Age breakdown (1981): under 15, 19.1%; 15–29, 24.3%; 30–44, 20.5%; 45–59, 16.5%; 60–74, 13.3%; 75 and over, 6.3%.
Population projection: (1990) 7,579,000; (2000) 7,625,000.
Ethnic composition (national origin; 1981): Austrian 96.1%; Yugoslavian 1.7%; Turkish 0.8%; German 0.5%; other 0.9%.
Religious affiliation (1981): Roman Catholic 84.3%; Protestant 5.6%; non-religious and atheist 6.0%; other 4.1%.
Major cities (1981): Vienna 1,505,800*; Graz 243,166; Linz 199,910; Salzburg 139,426; Innsbruck 117,287.

Vital statistics

Birth rate per 1,000 population (1984): 11.7 (world avg. 29.0); (1982) legitimate 77.6%; illegitimate 22.4%.
Death rate per 1,000 population (1984): 11.6 (world avg. 11.0).
Natural increase rate per 1,000 population (1984): 0.1 (world avg. 18.0).
Total fertility rate (avg. births per childbearing woman; 1980–85): 1.6.
Marriage rate per 1,000 population (1983): 7.4.
Divorce rate per 1,000 population (1983): 1.9.
Life expectancy at birth (1981): male 71.2 years; female 75.9 years.
Major causes of death per 100,000 population (1983): heart and circulatory disease 663.0, of which ischemic heart disease 188.2; malignant neoplasms (cancers) 249.3; accidents 63.7; diseases of the respiratory system 67.3.

National economy

Budget (1984). Revenue: S302,900,000,000 (taxes 85.4%, of which direct income 28.3%, indirect 52.2%, corporate 4.9%). Expenditures: S324,500,000,000 (goods and services 27.0%; transfers 42.7%; interest on public debt 10.0%).
Tourism (1983): receipts from visitors U.S.$5,142,000,000; expenditures by nationals abroad U.S.$2,830,000,000.
Production (metric tons except as noted). Agriculture, forestry, fishing (1984): sugar beets 2,605,000, corn (maize) 1,542,000, barley 1,517,000, wheat 1,501,000, potatoes 1,138,000, grapes 360,000, rye 381,000, milk 3,650,000; livestock (number of live animals) 3,881,000 pigs, 2,633,325 cattle, 15,215,121 chickens; roundwood (1983) 13,647,000. Mining and quarrying (1983): iron ore 3,540,000†; magnesite 1,090,000; zinc 22,688†; lead 5,750†. Manufacturing (value in S'000,000; 1981) machinery 54,584, of which electrical 21,509, transport 11,382; metal products (including steel) 18,681; beverages and tobacco 17,469; textiles and apparel 16,068; chemical products 15,107; food products 12,587. Construction (dwellings completed; 1981): residential 4,500,000 sq m; nonresidential 100,000 sq m. Energy production (consumption): electricity (kW-hr; 1983) 42,609,000,000 (39,114,000,000); coal (metric tons; 1983) 3,041,000 (6,289,000); crude petroleum (barrels; 1983) 9,984,000 (47,332,000); petroleum products (metric tons; 1983) 6,866,700 (9,086,500); natural gas (cu m; 1983) 1,213,400,000 (4,413,950,000).
Population economically active (1983): total 3,420,976; participation rate of total population 45.3% (female 38.8%, unemployed 3.7%).

Price and earnings indexes (1980 = 100)

	1978	1979	1980	1981	1982	1983	1984
Consumer price index	90.7	94.0	100.0	106.8	112.6	116.3	122.9
Monthly earnings index	87.6	92.7	100.0	106.1	123.7	117.8	123.7

Gross national product (at current market prices; 1983): U.S.$66,800,000,000 (U.S.$8,450 per capita).

Structure of gross domestic product and labour force

	1983 in value S'000,000	% of total value	labour force	% of labour force
Agriculture	44,250	3.7	315,900	9.6
Mining	} 326,960	27.1	15,600	0.5
Manufacturing			935,000	28.4
Construction	88,3070	7.3	298,800	9.1
Public utilities	38,790	3.2	41,700	1.3
Transportation and communication	67,410	5.6	209,700	6.4
Trade	202,400	16.8	434,100	13.2
Finance	169,460	14.1	177,800	5.4
Pub. admin., defense	174,510	14.5	718,200	21.8
Services	40,370	3.4	140,500	4.3
Other	53,360	4.4	6,300	0.2
TOTAL	1,205,810	100.0‡	3,293,600	100.0‡

Household income and expenditure. Average household size (1983) 2.7; income per household§ (1983) S171,000 (U.S.$9,520); sources of income (1980): wages and salaries 60.0%, social security benefits and social assistance grants 16.9%, self-employment 15.7%; expenditure (1983): food 26.7%, housing and utilities 23.8%, clothing and footwear 8.0%.
Land use (1983): forested 38.7%; meadows and pastures 24.4%; agricultural and under permanent cultivation 18.3%; other 18.6%.

Foreign trade

Balance of trade (current prices)

	1979	1980	1981	1982	1983	1984
S'000,000	−63,609	−89,677	−82,741	−65,690	−71,200	−77,590
% of total	13.4%	16.5%	14.1%	11.0%	11.4%	11.0%

Imports (1983): S348,339,135,000 (machinery and transport equipment 29.8%, of which road vehicles 9.8%; manufactured goods 14.8%, of which textile yarn 4.7%, iron and steel 2.7%; petroleum and related materials 9.9%; chemicals and related products 10.1%). *Major import sources:* West Germany 41.5%; Italy 8.9%; Switzerland 4.8%; U.S.S.R. 4.3%; France 4.1%; Japan 3.5%.
Exports (1983): S277,139,438,000 (manufactured goods 34.1%, of which iron and steel 8.7%; textile yarn 5.8%; machinery and transport equipment 30.2%, of which road vehicles 4.3%; chemicals 9.4%). *Major export destinations:* West Germany 30.8%; Italy 8.9%; Switzerland 6.8%; United Kingdom 4.1%; U.S.S.R. 3.9%; France 3.7%.

Transport and communications

Transport. Railroads (1983): length 4,174 mi, 6,718 km; passenger-mi 4,365,000,000, passenger-km 7,025,000,000; short ton-mi cargo 7,003,000,000, metric ton-km cargo 10,224,000,000. Roads (1984): total length 66,736 mi, 107,402 km (paved 100%). Vehicles (1984): passenger cars 2,468,452; trucks and buses 232,528. Merchant marine (1984): vessels (100 gross tons and over) 26; total deadweight tonnage 215,385. Air transport (1984): passenger-mi 872,400,000, passenger-km 1,404,000,000; short ton-mi cargo 16,093,000, metric ton-km cargo 23,496,000; airports (1985) with scheduled flights 6.
Communications. Daily newspapers (1983): total number 30; total circulation, n.a.; circulation per 1,000 population, n.a. Radio (1983): total number of receivers 5,520,000 (1 per 1.4 persons). Television (1983): total number of receivers 3,180,000 (1 per 2.4 persons). Telephones (1983): 3,330,171 (1 per 2.3 persons).

Education and health

Education (1983–84)

	schools	teachers	students	student/ teacher ratio
Primary (age 6–9)	3,421	27,942	364,548	13.0
Secondary (age 10–18)	298	16,636	171,806	10.3
Voc., teacher tr.	1,228	22,850	385,571	16.9
Higher	44	10,897	143,459	13.2

Educational attainment (1981). Percent of adult population over age 25 having: secondary 47.5%; postsecondary 3.3%. *Literacy* (1983): virtually 100%.
Health (1984): physicians 20,390 (1 per 370 persons); hospital beds 83,716 (1 per 90 persons); infant mortality rate per 1,000 live births (1983) 11.9.
Food (1980–82): daily per capita caloric intake 3,595 (vegetable products 64%, animal products 36%); 130% of FAO recommended minimum requirement.

Military

Total active duty personnel (1983): 50,000 (army 90.6%; navy, none; air force 9.4%). *Military expenditure as percent of GNP* (1983): 1.3% (world 6.1%); per capita expenditure U.S.$119.

*1984. †Metal content only. ‡Detail does not add to total given because of rounding. §Represents net household or disposable income.

Bahamas, The

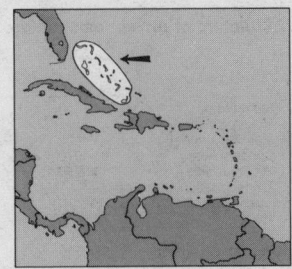

Official name: The Commonwealth of The Bahamas.
Form of government: parliamentary state with two legislative houses (Senate [16]; House of Assembly [43]).
Chief of state: British Monarch represented by governor-general.
Head of government: Prime Minister.
Capital: Nassau.
Official language: English.
Official religion: none.
Monetary unit: 1 Bahamian dollar (B$) = 100 cents; valuation (Oct. 21, 1985) 1 Bahamian dollar = U.S.$1.00 = £0.70.

Area and population

Islands and Island Groups†	Residence of Commissioner†	area* sq mi	area* sq km	population 1980 census
Abaco, Great and Little, and Mores Island and cays	Marsh Harbour	649	1,681	7,324
Acklins Island	Pompey Bay	192	497	616
Andros Island	Kemps Bay	2,300	5,957	8,397
Berry Islands	Nicolls Town	12	31	509
Biminis, North and South, Cay Lobos, and Cay Sal	Alice Town	11	28	1,432
Cat Island	Arthur's Town	150	388	2,143
Crooked Island	Colonel Hill	84	218	517
Eleuthera, Harbour Island, and Spanish Wells	Rock Sound	200	518	10,600
Exuma, Great and Little, and cays	George Town	112	290	3,672
Grand Bahama	Freeport	530	1,373	33,102
Inagua, Great and Little	Matthew Town	599	1,551	939
Long Cay	...	9	23	33
Long Island	Clarence Town	230	596	3,358
Mayaguana	Abraham's Bay	110	285	476
New Providence	Nassau	80	207	135,437
Ragged Island and cays	Duncan Town	14	36	146
San Salvador and Rum Cay	Cockburn Town	90	233	804
TOTAL		5,382‡	13,939‡	209,505§

Demography

Population (1985): 230,000.
Density (1985): persons per sq mi 42.7, persons per sq km 16.5.
Urban–rural (1985): urban 57.3%; rural 42.7%.
Sex distribution (1980): male 48.77%; female 51.23%.
Age breakdown (1980): under 15, 38.1%; 15–29, 27.8%; 30–44, 17.9%; 45–59, 9.8%; 60–74, 5.1%; 75 and over, 1.3%.
Population projection: (1990) 247,000; (2000) 282,000.
Doubling time: 36 years.
Ethnic composition (1980): black 72.3%; mixed 14.2%; white 12.9%; other 0.6%.
Religious affiliation (1980): non-Anglican Protestant (Baptist and Church of God [Anderson Ind.]) 46.6%; Roman Catholic 25.5%; Anglican 20.7%; other 7.2%.
Major cities (1980): Nassau 135,437 ‖ ; Freeport 25,423.

Vital statistics

Birth rate per 1,000 population (1982): 24.3 (world avg. 29.0); legitimate 39.7%, illegitimate 60.3%.
Death rate per 1,000 population (1982): 5.4 (world avg. 11.0).
Natural increase rate per 1,000 population (1982): 18.9 (world avg. 18.0).
Total fertility rate (avg. births per childbearing woman; 1980): 3.3.
Marriage rate per 1,000 population (1982): 7.0.
Divorce rate per 1,000 population (1982): 0.7.
Life expectancy at birth (1980): male 64.0 years; female 69.0 years.
Major causes of death per 100,000 population (1982): malignant neoplasms (cancers) 107.8; heart diseases 80.7; accidents 39.0; chronic bronchitis, emphysema, and asthma 38.5; cerebrovascular disease 31.2.

National economy

Budget (1984). Revenue: B$325,745,000 (customs receipts 56.7%, nontax revenue 19.6%, stamp taxes 6.1%, service taxes 5.6%, business and professional licenses 3.9%, departure tax 3.5%). Expenditures: B$338,013,000 (education 23.0%, health 16.4%, interest on the public debt 12.5%, general administration 10.8%, police 9.6%, tourism 7.9%).
Public debt (external, outstanding; 1984): U.S.$199,271,000.
Tourism (1983): receipts from visitors U.S.$770,000,000; expenditures by nationals abroad U.S.$96,000,000.
Production (value in U.S.$000 except as noted). Agriculture, forestry, fishing (1983): poultry products 17,200, fruits and vegetables 8,300¶, beef and mutton 800, dairy products, none♀; livestock (number of live animals; 1984) 38,000 sheep, 19,000 pigs, 18,000 goats, 4,000 cattle, 1,000,000 chickens; roundwood 115,000 cu m♂; crawfish 4,965, marine fishes 3,526, conchs 1,332. Mining and quarrying (metric tons; 1983): aragonite 3,000,000; salt (unrefined) 862,000. Manufacturing (metric tons; 1982): residual fuel oil 4,000,000; gas-diesel oil 1,650,000; cement 71,000□; dressed poultry 6,000; rum 100,000 hectolitres. Construction (1984): residential 57,582; nonresidential 16,913. Energy production (consumption): electricity (kW-hr; 1983)

920,000,000 (920,000,000); coal, none (n.a.); crude petroleum (barrels; 1983) none (62,305,000); petroleum products (metric tons; 1983) 6,750,000 (717,-000); natural gas, none (n.a.).
Gross national product (at current market prices; 1983): U.S.$900,000,000 (U.S.$4,050 per capita).

Structure of gross domestic product and labour force

	1983◊ in value B$'000,000	1983◊ % of total value	1979 labour force	1979 % of labour force
Agriculture	71.3	4.4	1,415	1.9
Mining△	...	...	74	0.1
Manufacturing, pub. util.	177.7	10.9	5,137	6.9
Construction	46.8	2.9	5,361	7.2
Transp. and commun.	174.9	10.8	7,523	10.1
Trade	432.7	26.6	22,334	30.0
Finance	191.2	11.8	4,247	5.7
Pub. admin., defense	283.7	17.4	23,820	32.0
Other services	247.8	15.2	4,542	6.1
TOTAL	1,626.1†	100.0	74,453	100.0

Population economically active (1979): total 77,056; participation rate of total population 36.8% (female 45.8%, unemployed [1983 est.] 25.0%).

Price and earnings indexes (1980 = 100)

	1979	1980	1981	1982	1983	1984	1985
Consumer price index	89.2	100.0	111.1	117.8	122.6	127.4	133.1⊙
Annual earnings index**	77.7	100.0	112.5	115.7	...	...	...

Household income and expenditure. Average household size (1980) 4.3; income per household (1979) B$13,537 (U.S.$13,537); sources of income: n.a.; expenditure (1982): food and beverages 20.5%, housing and fuel 17.7%, transport and communication 15.1%, recreation and education 6.6%, household furnishings and operation 6.0%, clothing and footwear 4.0%.
Land use (1983): forested 32.2%; meadows and pastures 0.2%; agricultural and under permanent cultivation 0.9%; other†† 66.7%.

Foreign trade

Balance of trade (current prices)

	1978	1979	1980	1981	1982	1983	1984
B$'000,000	−215	+39	−269	−436	−408	−454	−460
% of total	4.8%	0.5%	2.7%	5.8%	7.7%	8.1%	8.8%

Imports (1983): B$3,230,000,000 (crude petroleum 75.2%; manufactured goods, chemicals, machinery and transport equipment, food, live animals, beverages, tobacco 24.8%). *Major import sources*‡‡: United States 74%; United Kingdom 13%; Canada 3%.
Exports (1983): B$2,581,000,000 (petroleum products 90.5%; salt, aragonite, timber, beverages, chemicals 9.5%). *Major export destinations*: United States 41%; United Kingdom 7%; Canada 4%.

Transport and communications

Transport. Railroads: none. Roads (1983): total length 2,548 mi, 4,100 km (paved 43%). Vehicles (1983): passenger cars 52,341; trucks and buses 8,678. Merchant marine (1984): vessels (100 gross tons and over) 163; total deadweight tonnage 5,681,862. Air transport (1981): passenger-mi 72,313,000, passenger-km 116,377,000; short ton-mi cargo 6,343,000, metric ton-km cargo 9,261,000; airports (1985) with scheduled flights 21.
Communications. Daily newspapers (1984): total number 4; total circulation 30,000; circulation per 1,000 population 133. Radio (1984): total receivers 115,000 (1 per 2.0 persons). Television (1984): total receivers 50,500 (1 per 4.5 persons). Telephones (1983): 67,544 (1 per 3.3 persons).

Education and health

Education (1983)

	schools	teachers	students	student/ teacher ratio
Primary (age 5–11)	187	1,972	37,097	18.8
Secondary (age 11–16)	38	1,334	23,202	17.4
Higher§§	1	127	4,093	32.2

Educational attainment (1970). Percent of adult population over age 25 having: no formal schooling 6.7%; primary education only 15.4%; secondary 63.0%; postsecondary or higher 14.9%. *Literacy* (1984): total population over age 15 literate 201,000 (89.0%).
Health (1983): physicians 218 (1 per 1,018 persons); hospital beds 948 (1 per 234 persons); infant mortality rate per 1,000 live births (1982) 25.3.
Food (1980–82): daily per capita caloric intake 2,490 (vegetable products 65%, animal products 35%); 90% of FAO recommended minimum requirement.

Military

Defense is divided between the Royal Bahamas Police Force (1,500 in 1984) and the Royal Bahamas Defense Force. In 1982 $28.7 million, about 7.7% of the total budget, was spent on defense.

*Land area only of individual islands or island groups. †Out Islands (all islands and island groups excluding New Providence) are governed by commissioners assigned by the central government. ‡10 sq mi (27 sq km) are unaccounted for in breakdown. §Census total includes Bahamian residents abroad, but excludes 14,010 nonresident visitors. ‖ Figure refers to whole island of New Providence, which is considered as the metropolitan area of Nassau. ¶Primarily bananas, cabbages, cucumbers, pineapples, sugarcane, and tomatoes. ♀Local dairy ceased production in 1982. δ1983. □1981. ◊Preliminary estimate. △Included in the manufacturing and public utilities portion of the gross domestic product. †At current prices. ⊙July. **Based on government salaries. ††Mostly swamps and mangroves. ‡‡Does not include sources of crude petroleum. §§1980–81.

Bahrain

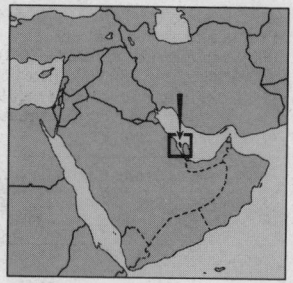

Official name: Dawlat al-Baḥrayn (State of Bahrain).
Form of government: monarchy (emirate) with a cabinet appointed by the Emir.
Chief of state: Emir.
Head of government: Prime Minister.
Capital: Manama.
Official language: Arabic.
Official religion: Islām.
Monetary unit: 1 Bahrain dinar (BD) = 1,000 fils; valuation (Oct. 21, 1985) 1 BD = U.S.$2.63 = £1.85.

Area and population

Regions	area		population
	sq mi	sq km	1981 census
Towns/villages			
Central	...	...	16,776
Central villages	...	...	16,776
Judd Ḥafṣ	...	...	33,693
Judd Ḥafṣ	...	...	7,232
Judd Ḥafṣ villages	...	...	26,461
al-Manāmah	...	...	121,986
Manama	...	...	108,684
al-Manāmah villages	...	...	13,302
al-Muḥarraq	...	...	61,853
al-Muḥarraq	...	...	46,061
al-Muḥarraq villages	...	...	15,792
Northern	...	...	22,117
Northern villages	...	...	22,117
Rifā'	...	...	28,150
ar-Rifā'	...	...	22,408
Rifā' villages	...	...	5,742
Sitrah	...	...	22,993
Sitrah villages	...	...	22,993
Western	...	...	14,503
Western villages	...	...	14,503
Towns with special status			
al-Ḥadd	...	...	7,111
Madīnat 'Īsā	...	...	21,275
Islands			
Ḥawār and other	...	...	341
TOTAL	261.7*	677.9*	350,798

Demography

Population (1985): 431,000.
Density (1985): persons per sq mi 1,647, persons per sq km 635.8.
Urban–rural (1981): urban 80.7%; rural 19.3%.
Sex distribution (1981): male 58.38%; female 41.62%.
Age breakdown (1981): under 15, 32.9%; 15–29, 34.5%; 30–44, 20.0%; 45–59, 8.8%; 60–74, 3.1%; 75 and over, 0.7%.
Population projection: (1990) 518,000; (2000) 688,000.
Doubling time: 16 years.
Ethnic composition (1981): Bahraini 70.0%; non-Bahraini 30.0%.
Religious affiliation (1981): Muslim 85.0%; Christian 7.3%; other 7.7%.
Major cities (1981): Manama 108,684; al-Muḥarraq 46,061; ar-Rifā' 22,408.

Vital statistics

Birth rate per 1,000 population (1981): 32.9 (world avg. 29.0).
Death rate per 1,000 population (1981): 5.5 (world avg. 12.0).
Natural increase rate per 1,000 population (1981): 27.4 (world avg. 17.0).
Total fertility rate (avg. births per childbearing woman; 1981): 4.8.
Marriage rate per 1,000 population (1982): 6.4.
Divorce rate per 1,000 population (1981): 2.1.
Life expectancy at birth (1980–85): male 65.7 years; female 69.9 years.
Major causes of death per 100,000 population (1981): diseases of the circulatory system 89.8; ill-defined diseases 43.0; accidents and acts of violence 33.1; malignant neoplasms (cancers) 23.1; respiratory diseases 18.8.

National economy

Budget (1982). Revenue: BD497,800,000 (energy taxes 74.8%; taxes on international trade 6.6%; social security contributions 3.8%). Expenditures: BD473,700,000 (defense 22.3%; public utilities 15.9%; education 10.7%).
Population economically active (1982): total 141,110; participation rate of total population 37.1% (female [1981] 11.4%, unemployed [1981] 3.2%).

Price and earnings indexes (1980 = 100)

	1978	1979	1980	1981	1982	1983	1984
Consumer price index	94.2	96.3	100	111.3	121.2	124.8	125.2
Monthly earnings index	...	...	...	...	...	...	...

Production (metric tons except as noted). Agriculture, forestry, fishing (1984): dates 40,000, tomatoes 12,000, cow's milk 6,000; livestock (number of live animals) 15,000 goats, 7,000 sheep, 6,000 cattle. Manufacturing (1982): petroleum products 9,280,000, asphalt 232,000. Construction (permits issued; 1981): residential 4,611; nonresidential 1,665. Energy production (consumption): electricity (kW-hr; 1983) 2,026,000,000 (2,026,000,000); coal, none (n.a.); crude petroleum (barrels; 1983) 15,019,000 (63,954,000); petroleum products (metric tons; 1983) 7,352,000 (343,000); natural gas (cu m; 1983) 5,487,796,000 (2,816,151,000†).
Gross national product (1983): U.S.$4,120,000,000 (U.S.$10,360 per capita).

Structure of gross domestic product and labour force

	1981		1982	
	value in BD'000,000	% of total value	labour force	% of labour force
Agriculture	16.5	1.1	3,510	2.5
Mining			410	0.3
Manufacturing	} 292.7	18.9	16,340	11.6
Construction			28,250	20.0
Public utilities			2,900	2.1
Transp. and commun.			11,060	7.8
Trade			18,600	13.2
Finance	} 1,233.8	80.0	4,080	2.9
Pub. admin., defense			45,740	32.4
Services	}			
Other			10,220	7.2
TOTAL	1,543.0‡	100.0	141,110	100.0

Households. Average household size (1981) 6.0.
Land use (1983): meadows and pastures 6.5%; agricultural and under permanent cultivation 3.2%; other§ 90.3%.
Public debt (external, outstanding; 1983): BD91,200,000.
Tourism (1982): receipts from visitors U.S.$129,000,000; expenditures by nationals abroad U.S.$202,000,000.

Foreign trade‖

Balance of trade (current prices)

	1979	1980	1981	1982	1983	1984
BD'000,000	+96	+173	+238	+201	+71	−16
% of total	5.4%	6.8%	7.9%	7.6%	3.0%	0.7%

Imports (1984): BD1,324,900,000 (crude petroleum 47.5%, machinery 21.8%, manufactured goods 17.1%, food 6.3%). *Major import sources¶*: Japan 18.6%; United States 14.0%; United Kingdom 13.6%; Italy 11.8%.
Exports (1984): BD1,179,000,000 (petroleum products 86.5%, aluminum 9.7%). *Major export destinations¶*: Saudi Arabia 20.8%; Japan 19.4%; United Arab Emirates 11.0%; India 7.7%; United States 7.7%.

Transport and communications

Transport. Railroads: none. Roads (1984): total length 155 km (paved 100.0%). Vehicles (1982): passenger cars 67,240; trucks and buses 21,288. Merchant marine (1984): vessels (100 gross tons and over) 72; total deadweight tonnage 59,167. Air transport⁹ (1983): passenger-km 890,400,000; metric ton-km cargo 23,817,000; airports (1985) with scheduled flights 1.
Communications. Daily newspapers (1984): total number 3; total circulation 25,500; circulation per 1,000 population 59.2 Radio (1984): total receivers 140,000 (1 per 2.5 persons). Television (1983): total receivers 122,000 (1 per 2.9 persons). Telephones (1983): 87,607 (1 per 4.0 persons).

Education and health

Education (1980–81)

	schools	teachers	students	student/teacher ratio
Primary (age 6–11)	114	2,963	48,406	16.3
Secondary (age 12–17)	21	951	23,727	24.9
Voc., teacher tr.	5	233	2,846	12.2
Higher	2	159	3,650	22.9

Educational attainment: n.a. *Literacy* (1981): total population literate 164,-176 (69.8%); males literate 112,116 (76.5%); females literate 52,060 (58.6%).
Health (1980): physicians 363 (1 per 964 persons); hospital beds 1,107 (1 per 316 persons); infant mortality rate per 1,000 live births (1981) 51.8.

Military

Total active duty personnel (1984): 2,800 (army 82.1%, navy 10.7%, air force 7.2%). *Military expenditure as percent of GNP* (1983): 4.0% (world 6.1%); per capita expenditure U.S.$403.

*Total area includes numerous small uninhabited islands and dependencies of Bahrain. †1983. ‡At current prices. §Mostly sandy plains and salt marshes. ‖Import figures are f.o.b. (free on board) in balance of trade and c.i.f. (cost, insurance, and freight) for commodities and trading partners. ¶Percentage shares for trading partners derived from nonoil portion of foreign trade only. ⁹Gulf Air is based in Bahrain.

STATE OF BAHRAIN/MINISTRY OF INFORMATION

King Faisal Road and Diplomatic Area, Manama, Bahrain.

Bangladesh

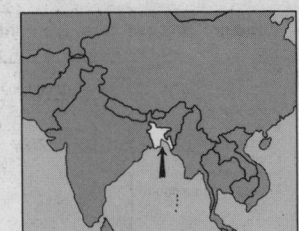

Official name: Gana Prajātantrī Bangladesh (People's Republic of Bangladesh).
Form of government: currently under martial law; constitution suspended and unicameral parliament dissolved in 1982.
Head of state and government: President (Chief Martial Law Administrator).
Capital: Dhākā (formerly Dacca).
Official language: Bengali.
Official religion: Islām.
Monetary unit: 1 Bangladesh Taka (Tk) = 100 paisa; valuation (Oct. 21, 1985) 1 U.S.$ = Tk29.43; 1 £ = Tk42.20.

Area and population

Divisions Districts	Administrative centres	area sq mi	area sq km	population 1984 estimate
Chittagong	Chittagong	17,535	45,415	25,415,000
Bāndarban	Bāndarban	1,738	4,501	193,000
Chittagong	Chittagong	2,879	7,457	6,176,000
Chittagong Hill Tracts	Rangamati	3,351	8,679	653,000
Comilla	Comilla	2,548	6,599	7,739,000
Noākhāli	Maijdi Court	2,108	5,460	4,292,000
Sylhet	Sylhet	4,911	12,719	6,362,000
Dhākā	Dhākā	11,881	30,772	29,512,000
Dhākā	Dhākā	2,884	7,470	11,260,000
Farīdpur	Farīdpur	2,657	6,882	5,359,000
Jamālpur	Jamālpur	1,293	3,349	2,759,000
Mymensingh	Mymensingh	3,733	9,668	7,387,000
Tangail	Tangail	1,314	3,403	2,747,000
Khulna	Khulna	12,963	33,574	19,291,000
Barisāl (Bakerganj)	Barisāl	2,818	7,299	5,249,000
Jessore	Jessore	2,538	6,573	4,521,000
Khulna	Khulna	4,698	12,168	4,870,000
Kushtia	Kushtia	1,328	3,439	2,578,000
Patuākhāli	Patuākhāli	1,581	4,095	2,073,000
Rājshāhi	Rājshāhi	13,219	34,237	23,768,000
Bogra	Bogra	1,501	3,888	3,068,000
Dinājpur	Dinājpur	2,535	6,566	3,599,000
Pābna	Pābna	1,827	4,732	3,852,000
Rājshāhi	Rājshāhi	3,651	9,456	5,927,000
Rangpur	Rangpur	3,705	9,596	7,322,000
TOTAL				97,986,000

Demography

Population (1985): 98,699,000.
Density (1985): persons per sq mi 1,775, persons per sq km 685.
Urban–rural (1985): urban 11.9%; rural 88.1%.
Sex distribution (1985): male 51.55%; female 48.45%.
Age breakdown (1985): under 15, 45.7%; 15–29, 27.3%; 30–44, 13.9%; 45–59, 8.3%; 60 and over, 4.8%.
Population projection: (1990) 115,244,000; (2000) 145,800,000.
Doubling time: 27 years.
Ethnic composition (1980): Bengali 97.8%; Bihārī 1.5%; tribal (Chakmā, Gāro, Khāsi, Santāl, etc.) 0.7%.
Religious affiliation (1984): Muslim 86.6%; Hindu 12.1%; Buddhist 0.6%; Christian 0.3%; other 0.4%.
Major cities (1981): Dhākā 3,430,312; Chittagong 1,391,877; Khulna 646,359; Rājshāhi 253,740.

Vital statistics

Birth rate per 1,000 population (1980–85): 44.8 (world avg. 29.0).
Death rate per 1,000 population (1980–85): 17.5 (world avg. 11.0).
Natural increase rate per 1,000 population (1980–85): 27.3 (world avg. 18.0).
Total fertility rate (avg. births per childbearing woman; 1980–85): 6.2.
Marriage rate per 1,000 population (1982): 9.0.
Life expectancy at birth (1980–85): male 48.3 years; female 47.3 years.
Major causes of death per 100 deaths (1976): diseases of the respiratory system 20.9; malignant neoplasms (cancers) 19.8; infectious intestinal diseases 15.5; diseases of the liver and kidney 11.4.

National economy

Budget (1983–84). Revenue: Tk33,968,000,000 (customs duties 39.2%, excise duties 16.1%, sales tax 12.8%, income taxes 9.1%, railways 5.2%, interest receipts 2.7%). Expenditures: Tk24,135,000,000 (defense 17.3%, education 13.2%, debt service 10.4%, administration 10.2%, health and food subsidy 10.0%, justice and police 9.7%, transport and communications 8.9%).
Public debt (external, outstanding; 1983): U.S.$4,184,500,000.
Tourism (1983): receipts from visitors U.S.$17,000,000; expenditures by nationals abroad U.S.$18,000,000†.
Production (metric tons except as noted). Agriculture, forestry, fishing (1984): paddy rice 21,500,000, sugarcane 7,350,000, wheat 1,200,000, jute and jute-like fibres 733,000, sweet potatoes 780,000, bananas 680,000, mangoes 185,000, pineapples 165,000, tobacco leaves 52,000, tea 46,000, peanuts (groundnuts) 27,000, sesame seed 20,000; livestock (number of live animals) 36,300,000 cattle, 12,050,000 goats, 1,750,000 buffalo, 2,000,000 sheep, 76,000,000 chickens; roundwood 32,051,000 cu m‡; fish catch 728,500‡. Mining and quarrying (1983): sea salt 250,000; limestone 32,000. Manufacturing (1983–84): chemical fertilizers 732,000; jute textiles 536,000; cement 274,000; iron and steel 174,000; paper and newsprint 58,000; cot-

ton yarn 46,000; cigarettes 14,860,000,000 units. Construction: n.a. Energy production (consumption): electricity (kW-hr; 1983) 3,758,000,000 (3,758,-000,000); coal (metric tons; 1983) none (163,000); crude petroleum (barrels; 1983) 80,630 (7,530,000); petroleum products (metric tons; 1983) 729,000 (1,142,000); natural gas (cu m; 1983) 2,020,700,000 (2,020,700,000).
Gross national product (at current market prices; 1983): U.S.$12,530,000,000 (U.S.$130 per capita).

Structure of gross domestic product and labour force

	1983–84 in value Tk'000,000	1983–84 % of total value	1983–84 labour force	1983–84 % of labour force
Agriculture	144,557	45.7	14,000,000	53.6
Mining	4	0.0	...	...
Manufacturing	30,314	9.6	1,800,000	6.9
Construction	14,558	4.6	700,000	2.7
Public utilities	1,257	0.4	25,000	0.1
Transportation and communication	26,994	8.5	561,000	2.1
Trade	27,344	8.6	1,067,000	4.1
Finance	28,142	8.9	354,000	1.4
Public admin., defense	11,843	3.7	1,158,000	4.4
Services and other	31,130	9.8	6,448,000	24.7
TOTAL	316,143§	100.0*	26,113,000	100.0

Population economically active (1981): total 30,855,961; participation rate of population over age 15, 66.3% (female 11.4%, unemployed and underemployed [1983] 37.4%).

Price and earnings indexes (1980 = 100)

	1978	1979	1980	1981	1982	1983	1984
Consumer price index	78.4	88.3	100.0	113.2	123.7	133.7	149.8
Hourly earnings index‖	59.3	64.5	100.0	105.4	106.3	106.4	...

Household income. Average household size (1981) 5.8; median annual income per household (1976–77) Tk8,166 (U.S.$531); sources of income: agriculture 44.7%, wages and salaries 26.9%, finance and trade 11.8%, real estate 6.0%, other 10.6%; expenditure (1976–77): food and drinks 74.5%, fuel and lighting 9.1%, rent 5.8%, clothing and footwear 5.3%, other 5.2%.
Land use (1983): forested 16.0; meadows and pastures 4.5%; agricultural and under permanent cultivation 68.2%; other 11.3%.

Foreign trade

Balance of trade (current prices)

	1979	1980	1981	1982	1983	1984
Tk'000,000	−16,541	−24,380	−29,692	−28,528	−30,055	−40,882
% of total	44.7%	51.0%	51.2%	45.6%	45.7%	46.4%

Imports (1983–84): Tk43,311,800,000 (machinery 15.4%; chemicals 14.7%; petroleum and petroleum products 8.8%; wheat 8.8%). *Major import sources:* Japan 16.0%; Singapore 10.4%; United States 10.3%; China 6.9%.
Exports (1983–84): Tk19,456,200,000 (jute manufactures 42.3%; raw jute and jute mesta 13.8%; leather 10.6%; tea 8.7%). *Major export destinations* (1981): United States 11.6%; Mozambique 10.5%; Pakistan 6.7%; Iran 6.2%.

Transport and communications

Transport. Railroads (1982–83): route length¶ 1,791 mi, 2,883 km; passenger-mi 3,994,000,000, passenger-km 6,428,000,000; short ton-mi cargo 498,000,000, metric ton-km cargo 727,000,000. Roads (1982): total length 98,522 mi, 21,401 km (paved 12%). Vehicles (1981–82): passenger cars 35,-488; trucks and buses 21,401. Merchant marine (1984): vessels (100 gross tons and over) 248; total deadweight tonnage 496,935. Air transport (1982): passenger-mi 813,000,000, passenger-km 1,308,000,000; short ton-mi cargo 15,600,000, metric ton-km cargo 22,800,000; airports (1985) 8.
Communications. Daily newspapers (1984): total number 32; total circulation 569,000; circulation per 1,000 population 5.9. Radio (1984): total receivers 800,000 (1 per 121 persons). Television (1984): total receivers 255,000 (1 per 379 persons). Telephones (1982): 122,190 (1 per 758 persons).

Education and health

Education (1983–84)

	schools	teachers	students	student/ teacher ratio
Primary (age 5–9)	43,865	183,793	9,643,000	52.5
Secondary (age 10–14)	8,551	95,275	2,608,000	27.4
Voc., teacher tr.	797	16,713	450,911	27.0
Higher	45	3,842	59,775	15.6

Educational attainment (1974). Percent of adult population over age 25 having: no formal schooling, or less than one full year, 78.0%; primary education 10.0%; some secondary 6.9%; postsecondary 0.9%. *Literacy* (1981): total population over age 14 literate 13,600,000 (29.2%); males literate 9,560,000 (39.7%); females literate 4,036,000 (18.0%).
Health (1982): physicians 12,306 (1 per 7,526 persons); hospital beds 24,233 (1 per 3,822 persons); infant mortality rate per 1,000 live births (1980–85) 133.0.
Food (1980–82): daily per capita caloric intake 1,869 (vegetable products 96%, animal products 4%); 85% of FAO recommended minimum.

Military

Total active duty personnel (1984): 81,300 (army 89.8%, navy 6.5%, air force 3.7%). *Military expenditure as percent of GNP* (1983): 1.4% (world 6.1%); per capita expenditure U.S.$2.

*Detail does not add to total given because of rounding. †1982. ‡1983. §At current prices. ‖Skilled wage earnings in manufacturing. ¶1981–82.

Barbados

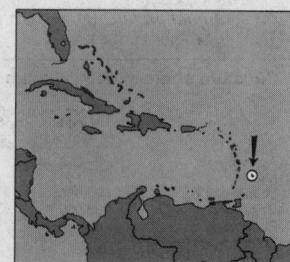

Official name: Barbados.
Form of government: parliamentary state with two legislative houses (Senate [21]; House of Assembly [27]).
Chief of state: British Monarch represented by governor-general.
Head of government: Prime Minister.
Capital: Bridgetown.
Official language: English.
Official religion: none.
Monetary unit: 1 Barbados dollar (BDS$) = 100 cents; valuation (Oct. 21, 1985) 1 U.S.$ = BDS$2.00; 1 £ = BDS$2.88.

Area and population

Parishes*	area		population
	sq mi	sq km	1980 census
Christ Church	22	57	40,790
St. Andrew	14	36	6,731
St. George	17	44	17,361
St. James	12	31	17,255
St. John	13	34	10,330
St. Joseph	10	26	7,211
St. Lucy	14	36	9,264
St. Michael†	15	39	99,953
St. Peter	13	34	10,717
St. Philip	23	60	18,662
St. Thomas	13	34	10,709
TOTAL	166	430‡	248,983§

Demography

Population (1985): 252,700.
Density (1985): persons per sq mi 1,522, persons per sq km 586.
Urban–rural (1985): urban 42.2%; rural 57.8%.
Sex distribution (1983): male 47.70%; female 52.30%.
Age breakdown (1980): under 15, 29.6%; 15–29, 30.1%; 30–44, 15.0%; 45–59, 11.1%; 60–74, 10.3%; 75 and over, 3.9%.
Population projection: (1990) 257,000; (2000) 264,000.
Doubling time: not applicable; population growth is negligible.
Ethnic composition (1980): black 91.9%; white 3.3%; mulatto 2.6%; East Indian 0.5%; other 1.7%.
Religious affiliation (1980): Anglican 49.7%; other Protestant 38.3% (mainly Methodist, Pentecostal, and Seventh-day Adventist); Roman Catholic 5.9%; nonreligious 5.2%.
Major cities (1980): Bridgetown 7,552 (metropolitan area 99,953); other cities cannot be identified because no other bounded localities exist.

Vital statistics

Birth rate per 1,000 population (1984): 16.7 (world avg. 29.0); (1975) legitimate 23.9%; illegitimate 76.1%.
Death rate per 1,000 population (1984): 7.7 (world avg. 11.0).
Natural increase rate per 1,000 population (1984): 9.0 (world avg. 18.0).
Total fertility rate (avg. births per childbearing woman; 1980–85): 2.2.
Marriage rate per 1,000 population (1980): 4.2.
Divorce rate per 1,000 population (1979): 0.6.
Life expectancy at birth (1980–85): male 68.9 years; female 74.5 years.
Major causes of death per 100,000 (1980): diseases of the circulatory system 257.7; malignant neoplasms (cancers) 130.5; heart diseases 99.6; diabetes mellitus 49.0.

National economy

Budget (1984–85). Revenue: BDS$571,974,000 (tax revenue 88.5%, of which individual income tax 21.9%, consumption tax 16.8%, import duties 14.7%, corporate tax 8.9%; nontax revenue 11.5%). Expenditures: BDS$559,810,000 (health 16.6%; general public services 15.7%; economic services 14.1%, of which road and other transportation 9.5%; social security and welfare 9.2%; defense 3.6%; agriculture 2.9%; education 2.4%).
Public debt (external, outstanding; 1983): U.S.$172,700,000.
Production (metric tons except as noted). Agriculture, forestry, fishing (1984): sugarcane 900,000, vegetables (mainly carrots, cucumbers, and cabbages) 10,000, yams and sweet potatoes 10,000, eggs 1,050; livestock (number of live animals) 50,000 pigs, 54,000 sheep, 18,000 cattle, 4,000 mules and asses, 1,000,000 chickens; roundwood, n.a.; marine fish catch 6,422‖. Manufacturing (1982): electronic assembly for reexport (including microprocessors and computer chips), n.a.; clothing, n.a.; sugar 100,000; animal feed 50,000; cigarettes 271; beer 88,000 hectolitres; rum 46,000 hectolitres; fuel oil 95,000; gasoline 45,000. Construction, n.a. Energy production (consumption): electricity (kW-hr; 1984) 361,600,000 (382,000,000); coal, none (negligible); crude petroleum (barrels; 1984) 634,000 (1,457,000‖); petroleum products (metric tons; 1983) 195,000 (211,000); natural gas (cu m; 1984) 25,300,000 (10,330,000).
Population economically active (1984): total 111,600; participation rate of total population 44.2% (female 45.5%, unemployed 18.3%).

Price and earnings indexes (1980 = 100)

	1980	1981	1982	1983	1984	1985
Consumer price index	100.0	114.6	126.4	133.0	139.2	145.3¶
Monthly earnings index	100.0	109.8	121.6	128.3	...	...

Household income and expenditure. Average household size (1980) 3.6; income per household: n.a.; sources of income: n.a.; expenditure (1980): food 43.2%, housing 13.1%, household operations 9.6%, alcohol and tobacco 8.4%, fuel and light 6.2%, medical and personal care 6.0%, clothing and footwear 5.1%, transportation 4.6%, education and recreation 3.8%.
Tourism (1983): receipts from visitors U.S.$252,000,000; expenditures by nationals abroad U.S.$26,000,000♀.
Gross national product (at current market prices; 1984): U.S.$1,035,000,000 (U.S.$4,109 per capita).

Structure of gross domestic product and labour force

	1984		1983	
	in value BDS$'000	% of total value	labour force	% of labour force
Agriculture, fishing	141,382	6.1	8,400	7.5
Mining	29,392	1.3 }		
Manufacturing	264,056	11.5 }	15,400	13.7
Construction	129,996	5.6	9,200	8.2
Public utilities	68,004	3.0	2,100	1.9
Transportation and communication	171,019	7.4	5,900	5.2
Trade	619,035	26.9	25,200	22.4
Finance	270,890	11.8	3,700	3.3
Pub. admin., defense, and services	381,223	16.5	38,800	34.4
Other	228,195ō	9.9ō	3,900	3.5
TOTAL	2,303,192□	100.0	112,600	100.0‡

Land use (1983): meadows and pastures 9.0%; agricultural and under permanent cultivation 77.0%; other 14.0%.

Foreign trade◊

Balance of trade (current prices)

	1979	1980	1981	1982	1983	1984
BDS$'000,000	−478.8	−507.1	−665.1	−498.6	−499.0	−427.7
% of total	44.0%	35.8%	46.0%	32.5%	27.9%	21.4%

Imports (1984): BDS$1,324,662,000 (electrical components 18.1%, machinery 13.3%, food and beverages 12.1%, fuels 5.1%; construction materials 4.4%, chemicals 3.3%). *Major import sources:* United States 47.8%; United Kingdom 7.5%; Trinidad and Tobago 8.5%; other European Economic Community 4.5%; Canada 5.7%.
Exports (1984): BDS$583,668,000 (electrical components 57.6%, clothing 11.1%, sugar 9.8%, chemicals 4.4%, molasses and rum 2.6%). *Major export destinations:* United States 27.6%; Trinidad and Tobago 9.5%; EEC 8.2%, of which United Kingdom 6.9%; Guyana 6.7%.

Transport and communications

Transport. Railroads: none. Roads (1983): total length 994 mi, 1,600 km (paved 95%). Vehicles (1984): passenger cars 30,984; trucks and buses 5,454. Merchant marine (1984): vessels (100 gross tons and over) 35; total deadweight tonnage 9,466. Air transport (1980): passenger-mi 205,000,000, passenger-km 330,000,000; short ton-mi cargo 342,000, metric ton-km cargo 500,000; airports (1985) with scheduled flights 1.
Communications. Daily newspapers (1984): total number 2; total circulation 40,000; circulation per 1,000 population 159. Radio (1984): total number of receivers 192,000 (1 per 1.3 persons). Television (1983): total number of receivers 55,000 (1 per 4.6 persons). Telephones (1983): 72,850 (1 per 3.4 persons).

Education and health

Education (1982–83)

	schools	teachers	students	student/ teacher ratio
Primary (age 4–11)	139	1,492△	34,848	...
Secondary (age 12–16)	36	1,281△	26,552	...
Vocational†	6		2,343	...
Higher⊕	2	216	2,954	13.7

Educational attainment (1980). Percent of population over age 15 having: no formal schooling 0.6%; primary education 50.0%; secondary 41.0%; higher 3.8%. *Literacy* (1980): total population over age 15 literate** 169,894 (98.0%); males literate 78,022 (98.3%); females literate 91,872 (97.7%).
Health: physicians (1979) 208 (1 per 1,195 persons); hospital beds (1980) 2,126 (1 per 117 persons); infant mortality rate per 1,000 live births (1984) 10.9.
Food (1980–82): daily per capita caloric intake 3,067 (vegetable products 74%, animal products 26%); 125% of FAO recommended minimum requirement.

Military

Total active duty personnel (1983): 154 (paramilitary marine and coast guard components only). *Military expenditure as percent of GNP* (1983): 0.7% (world 6.1%); per capita expenditure U.S.$26.

*Parishes have no local administrative function. †Includes Bridgetown. ‡Detail does not add to total given because of rounding. §Excludes nonresident visitors. ‖1983. ¶July. ♀1982. ōIncludes net indirect taxes. □At current prices. ◊Import figures are f.o.b. (freight on board) in balance of trade and c.i.f. (cost, insurance, and freight) for commodities and trading partners; export figures include reexports in balance of trade and trading partners and are excluded from commodities. △Public schools only. †1981–82. ⊕1983–84. **National literacy standard based solely on school attendance. Functional literacy may be appreciably lower.

Belgium

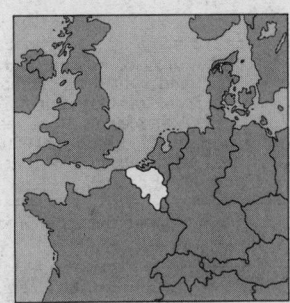

Official name: Koninkrijk België
(Dutch); Royaume de Belgique
(French) (Kingdom of Belgium).
Form of government: constitutional
monarchy with two legislative
houses (Senate [182]; House of
Representatives [212]).
Chief of state: Monarch.
Head of government: Prime Minister.
Capital: Brussels.
Official languages: Dutch; French;
German.
Official religion: none.
Monetary unit: 1 Belgian franc
(BF) = 100 centimes; valuation (Oct.
21, 1985) 1 U.S.$ = BF53.42;
1 £ = BF76.60.

Area and population		area		population
				1983
Provinces	Capitals	sq mi	sq km	estimate
Antwerp	Antwerp	1,107	2,867	1,577,000
Brabant	Brussels	1,297	3,358	2,221,000
East Flanders	Ghent	1,151	2,982	1,332,000
Hainaut	Mons	1,462	3,787	1,292,000
Liège	Liège	1,491	3,862	996,000
Limburg	Hasselt	935	2,422	724,000
Luxembourg	Arlon	1,715	4,441	223,000
Namur	Namur	1,415	3,665	409,000
West Flanders	Brugge	1,210	3,134	1,084,000
TOTAL		11,783	30,519*	9,858,000

Demography

Population (1985): 9,859,000.
Density (1985): persons per sq mi 836.7, persons per sq km 323.1.
Urban–rural (1980): urban 72.4%; rural 27.6%.
Sex distribution (1981): male 48.84%; female 51.16%.
Age breakdown (1982): under 15, 20.0%; 15–29, 23.7%; 30–44, 19.1%; 45–59,
18.6%; 60–74, 12.8%; 75 and over, 5.8%.
Population projection: (1990) 9,890,000; (2000) 9,925,000.
Doubling time: not applicable; population growth is negligible.
Nationality (1981): Belgian 91.1%; Italian 2.8%; Moroccan 1.1%; French
1.1%; Dutch 0.7%; Turkish 0.6%; other 2.6%.
Religious affiliation (1983): Roman Catholic 96.0%; other 4.0%.
Major cities (1983): Antwerp 490,524; Ghent 236,540; Charleroi 216,144;
Liège 207,496; Brussels 137,738 (metropolitan area; 1982, 994,774).

Vital statistics

Birth rate per 1,000 population (1984): 11.7 (world avg. 29.0); (1981) legiti-
mate 95.5%; illegitimate 4.5%.
Death rate per 1,000 population (1984): 11.1 (world avg. 11.0).
Natural increase rate per 1,000 population (1984): 0.6 (world avg. 18.0).
Total fertility rate (avg. births per childbearing woman; 1982): 1.1.
Marriage rate per 1,000 population (1984): 6.4.
Divorce rate per 1,000 population (1982): 1.6.
Life expectancy at birth (1985): male 70.1 years; female 76.7 years.
Major causes of death per 100,000 population (1978): heart disease 287.9;
malignant neoplasms (cancers) 268.3; cerebrovascular disease 146.6.

National economy

Budget (1984). Revenue: BF1,318,200,000,000 (direct taxes 60.3%; value-
added, stamp, and similar duties 26.8%; customs and excise duties 7.4%).
Expenditures: BF1,636,200,000,000 (government departments 44.2%; public
debt 17.8%; educational and cultural services 15.5%; pension 9.8%; defense
5.4%).
Public debt (1984): U.S.$56,276,800,000.
Tourism (1983): receipts from visitors U.S.$1,653,000,000; expenditures by
nationals abroad U.S.$2,015,000,000.
Production (metric tons except as noted). Agriculture, forestry, fishing (1984):
sugar beets 5,723,000, potatoes 1,650,000, wheat 1,330,000, barley 935,000,
apples 260,000, tomatoes 130,000, oats 118,000, corn (maize) 39,000, milk
4,150,000; livestock (number of live animals) 3,115,000 cattle, 5,300,000
pigs, 120,000 sheep, 35,000 horses; roundwood 3,041,000 cu m†; fish catch
48,580†, of which European plaice (flounder) 10,591, Atlantic cod 7,715,
Atlantic herring 5,970. Mining and quarrying (1983): copper 431,000; zinc
275,800; lead 134,200. Manufacturing (value added in BF'000,000; 1982):
metal products and machinery 264,600; food and beverages 160,200; chemicals and chemical products 89,800, of which drugs and medicines 14,400;
textiles 47,200; glass and glass products 38,200,000; furniture and fixtures
36,300; iron and steel 32,400; printing and publishing 28,500; paper and
paper products 21,600; wearing apparel 20,800. Construction (1984): residential 14,976,000 cu m; nonresidential 18,168,000 cu m. Energy production
(consumption): electricity (kW-hr; 1984) 54,657,000,000 (52,388,000,000†);
coal (metric tons; 1984) 6,301,000 (15,540,000‡); petroleum (barrels; 1984)
none (155,125,000‡); natural gas (cu m; 1984) 32,500,000 (9,332,400,000‡).
Household income and expenditure. Average household size (1981) 2.7;
sources of income (1983): wages and salaries 53.0%, self-employment 24.2%,
transfer payments 21.5%; expenditure (1983): housing 25.0%, food 21.1%,
personal care and health 9.4%, clothing and footwear 6.1%, other 38.4%.
Land use‡ (1983): forested 21.4%; meadows and pastures 20.7%; agricultural
and under permanent cultivation 25.4%; other 32.5%.

Gross national product (at current market prices; 1983): U.S.$81,162,481,000
(U.S.$8,240 per capita).

Structure of gross domestic product and labour force				
	1983			
	in value BF'000,000	% of total value	labour force	% of labour force
Agriculture	99,800	2.4	139,000	3.3
Mining	20,100	0.5	29,500	0.7
Manufacturing	1,020,900	24.4	969,000	23.0
Construction	238,000	5.7	265,400	6.3
Public utilities	148,700	3.5	37,900	0.9
Transportation and communication	321,900	7.7	307,500	7.3
Trade	818,000	19.5	838,400	19.9
Finance	234,900	5.6	286,500	6.8
Pub. admin., defense	349,700	8.3 }	1,238,600	29.4
Services	847,300	20.2 }		
Other	90,700	2.2	101,200§	2.4
TOTAL	4,190,000	100.0	4,213,000	100.0

Population economically active (1983): total 4,213,000; participation rate of
total population 42.7% (female 37.4%, unemployed 13.8%).

Price and earnings indexes (1980 = 100)						
	1979	1980	1981	1982	1983	1984	1985 ‖
Consumer price index	92.8	100.0	107.6	117.0	126.0	134.0	140.5
Hourly earnings index	91.5	100.0	110.1	116.9	122.0	128.0	130.8

Foreign trade

Balance of trade (current prices)					
	1979	1980	1981	1982	1983	1984
BF'000,000	−123,129	−210,448	−236,884	−247,817	−166,257	−205,100
% of total	3.6%	5.3%	5.4%	4.9%	3.0%	3.3%

Imports (1983): BF2,817,019,000,000 (machinery and transport equipment
22.0%, of which road vehicles and parts 10.3%; mineral fuels and lubricants 19.0%, of which petroleum and petroleum products 14.7%; natural
gas 2.4%; chemicals and chemical products 9.4%; food and live animals
9.2%; nonindustrial diamonds 5.1%). *Major import sources:* West Germany
21.0%; The Netherlands 18.4%; France 14.3%; United Kingdom 8.7%;
United States 6.5%.
Exports (1983): BF2,650,762,000,000 (machinery and transport equipment
22.4%, of which passenger cars 9.5%; chemicals and chemical products
11.9%, of which plastics 4.0%; food and live animals 8.8%; iron and steel
8.0%; petroleum and petroleum products 7.9%; nonindustrial diamonds
6.0%; textile yarns and fabrics 5.5%). *Major export destinations:* West
Germany 21.1%; France 18.2%; The Netherlands 14.2%; United Kingdom
9.8%; United States 5.1%.

Transport and communications

Transport. Railroads (1984): length 2,442 mi, 3,930 km; passenger-mi 4,007,-
000,000, passenger-km 6,448,000,000; short ton-mi cargo 5,391,000,000,
metric ton-km cargo 7,871,000,000. Roads (1984): total length 79,341 mi,
127,688 km (paved 95%). Vehicles (1984): passenger cars 3,300,248; trucks
and buses 310,685. Merchant marine (1984): vessels (100 gross tons and
over) 338; total deadweight tonnage 3,890,428. Air transport (1984): passenger-mi 3,512,000,000, passenger-km 5,652,000,000; short ton-mi cargo
371,004,000; metric ton-km cargo 541,656,000; airports (1985) with scheduled flights 4.
Communications. Daily newspapers (1983): total number 30; total circulation 2,222,600§; circulation per 1,000 population 226¶. Radio (1983): total
number of receivers 4,607,000 (1 per 2.1 persons). Television (1983): total number of receivers 2,981,497 (1 per 3.3 persons). Telephones (1983):
3,984,295 (1 per 2.5 persons).

Education and health

Education (1982–83)				
	schools	teachers	students	student/ teacher ratio
Primary (age 6–12)	2,261	24,106	814,089	33.8
Secondary (age 12–18)	759	56,719	848,590	15.0
Voc., teacher tr.	209	6,864	218,717	31.9
Higher	...	...	108,689	...

Educational attainment (1977). Percent of population over age 13 having:
less than secondary education 61.3%; lower secondary 17.8%; upper secondary 11.4%; vocational 3.6%; teacher's college 2.3%; university 3.6%.
Literacy (1984): virtually 100% literate.
Health (1981): physicians 25,629 (1 per 384 persons); hospital beds 92,436
(1 per 106 persons); infant mortality rate per 1,000 live births (1984) 10.7.
Food‡ (1980–82): daily per capita caloric intake 3,668 (vegetable products 59%, animal products 41%); 130% of FAO recommended minimum
requirement.

Military

Total active duty personnel (1984): 93,607 (army 69.5%, navy 4.9%, air force
22.4%). *Military expenditure as percent of GNP* (1983): 3.3% (world 6.1%);
per capita expenditure U.S.$272.

*Detail does not add to total given because of rounding. †1983. ‡Includes Luxem-
bourg. §Includes unemployed and persons in the armed forces. ‖ June. ¶For 27
newspapers only.

Belize

Official name: Belize.
Form of government: constitutional
  monarchy with two legislative houses
  (Senate [8]; House of Representatives
  [28]).
Chief of state: British Monarch
  represented by governor-general.
Head of government: Prime Minister.
Capital: Belmopan.
Official language: English.
Official religion: none.
Monetary unit: 1 Belize dollar
  (BZ$) = 100 cents; valuation (Oct. 21,
  1985) 1 U.S.$ = BZ$2.00*;
  1 £ = BZ$2.87.

Area and population

Districts	Capitals	area		population
		sq mi	sq km	1985 estimate
Belize	Belize City	1,624	4,206	54,500
Cayo	San Ignacio	2,061	5,338	27,400
Corozal	Corozal	718	1,860	28,000
Orange Walk	Orange Walk	1,829	4,737	26,660
Stann Creek	Dangriga	840	2,176	16,500
Toledo	Punta Gorda	1,795	4,649	13,400
TOTAL		8,867	22,965†	166,400

Demography

Population (1985): 166,400.
Density (1985): persons per sq mi 18.8, persons per sq km 7.2.
Urban–rural (1980): urban 51.7%; rural 48.3%.
Sex distribution (1984): male 50.63%; female 49.37%.
Age breakdown (1984): under 15, 45.3%; 15–29, 27.9%; 30–44, 11.8%; 45–59,
  7.9%; 60–74, 5.0%; 75 and over, 2.1%.
Population projection: (1990) 181,000; (2000) 226,000.
Doubling time: 32 years.
Ethnic composition (1980): Creole 39.7%; mestizo 33.1%; Garifuna (black
  Carib) 7.6%; Maya 6.8%; white 4.2%; other 8.6%.
Religious affiliation (1980): Roman Catholic 61.7%; Anglican 11.8%;
  Methodist 6.0%; Mennonite 3.9%; Seventh-day Adventist 3.0%; Baha'i
  2.5%; Pentecostal 2.2%; Nazarene 1.1%; Jehovah's Witnesses 1.0%; Baptist
  0.9%; other 5.9%.
Major cities (1980): Belize City 39,770; Orange Walk 8,440; Corozal 6,900;
  Dangriga 6,660; Belmopan 2,940.

Vital statistics

Birth rate per 1,000 population (1984): 38.0 (world avg. 29.0); legitimate
  46.1%; illegitimate 53.9%.
Death rate per 1,000 population (1984): 4.9 (world avg. 11.0).
Natural increase rate per 1,000 population (1984): 34.9 (world avg. 18.0).
Total fertility rate (avg. births per childbearing woman; 1980): 3.7.
Marriage rate per 1,000 population (1984): 5.3.
Divorce rate per 1,000 population (1984): 0.5.
Life expectancy at birth (1979–81): male and female 71.2 years.
Major causes of death per 100,000 population (1984): heart disease 43.8;
  bronchitis, emphysema, and asthma 42.6; malignant neoplasms (cancers)
  34.5; pneumonia 32.0; perinatal mortality 24.7; cerebrovascular diseases
  23.4.

National economy

Budget (1983–84 est.). Revenue: BZ$194,600,000 (current revenue BZ$101,-
  600,000, of which import duties 35.1%, income tax 18.8%, stamp duties
  8.1%, excise taxes 7.0%). Expenditures: BZ$194,600,000 (energy and com-
  munications 18.3%, natural resources 17.4%, public works 13.6%, health,
  housing, and coops 11.7%, education and legal affairs 11.1%).
Public debt (external, outstanding; 1983): U.S.$55,700,000.
Tourism (1983): receipts from visitors U.S.$7,200,000; expenditures by na-
  tionals abroad, n.a.
Production (metric tons except as noted). Agriculture, forestry, fishing
  (1984): sugarcane 1,038,000, oranges 46,000, grapefruits 28,000, bananas
  19,000, corn (maize) 16,000, rice 4,000, coconuts 3,000, vegetables and
  melons 3,000, dry beans 3,000; livestock (number of live animals) 51,000
  cattle, 20,000 pigs, 350,000 chickens; roundwood 113,000 cu m‡; fish catch
  2,824‡. Mining and quarrying (1984): sand and gravel 554,370; limestone
  608,860. Manufacturing (1983): sugar 103,100; molasses 33,500; fertilizer
  4,641; wheat flour 1,264; beer 28,640 hectolitres; cigarettes 64,600,000
  units; garments 1,966,000 units; batteries 5,555 units. Construction (1977):
  residential 7,150 sq m, nonresidential 2,018 sq m. Energy production (consumption): electricity (kW-hr; 1983) 58,000,000 (58,000,000); coal, none
  (n.a.); crude petroleum, none (n.a.); petroleum products (metric tons; 1983)
  none (56,000); natural gas, none (n.a.).
Population economically active (1984): total 47,325; participation rate of
  working-age population 29.2% (female 32.5%, unemployed 14.0%).

Price and earnings indexes (Feb. 1980 = 100)

	July 1980	July 1981	July 1982	Feb. 1983
Consumer price index	104.4	116.7	127.9	134.4
Earnings index	...	...	...	...

Gross national product (at current market prices; 1983): U.S.$170,000,000
  (U.S.$1,140 per capita).

Structure of gross domestic product and labour force

	1984		1981	
	in value BZ$'000	% of total value	labour force	% of labour force
Agriculture	65,500	20.8	14,000	28.6
Mining	800	0.2	...	...
Manufacturing	46,000	14.6	6,900	14.1
Construction	18,000	5.7 }	5,900	12.0
Transportation and communication	34,800	11.0 }		
Trade	55,000	17.5	3,900	8.0
Finance	33,400	10.6	...	...
Public utilities	6,100	1.9 }		
Pub. admin., defense	32,800	10.4 }	9,800	20.0
Services	33,000	10.5	...	...
Other	11,000	3.5	8,500	17.3
TOTAL	314,800†	100.0†	49,000	100.0

Household income and expenditure. Average household size (1984) 5.2; income per household: n.a.; source of income: n.a.; expenditure: n.a.
Land use (1983): forested 44.4%; meadows and pastures 1.9%; agricultural
  and under permanent cultivation 2.3%; other 51.4%.

Foreign trade¶

Balance of trade (current prices)

	1980	1981	1982	1983	1984	April 1985
BZ$'000,000	11.7	+24.0	16.0	−24.9	−4.0	+1.3
% of total	0.4%	5.3%	1.7%	7.4%	1.1%	4.8%

Imports (1984): BZ$260,273,000 (manufactured goods 29.8%, food 21.5%,
  machinery and transport 19.9%, fuels 16.7%, chemicals 8.3%, beverages
  2.4%). Major import sources: United States 43.6%; United Kingdom 8.3%;
  Canada 2.3%.
Exports (1984): BZ$145,719,000 (food 75.2%, manufactured goods 21.5%,
  crude materials except fuels 2.2%, chemicals 0.6%). Major export destinations: United States 57.8%; United Kingdom 20.5%; Canada 2.6%.

Transport and communications

Transport. Railroads: none. Roads (1983): total length 1,620 mi, 2,607 km
  (paved 15%). Vehicles (1983): passenger cars 3,098; trucks and buses 4,916.
  Merchant marine (1984): vessels (100 gross tons and over) 3; total deadweight tonnage 805. Scheduled international air transport (1984): passenger
  arrivals 40,064, passenger departures 43,157; cargo loaded 899 metric tons,
  cargo unloaded 1,301 metric tons; airports (1985) with scheduled flights 7.
Communications. Daily newspapers: none. Radio (1984): total number of
  receivers 72,000 (1 per 2.2 persons). Television: total number of receivers,
  n.a. Telephones (1984): 9,350 (1 per 17 persons).

Education and health

Education (1984)

	schools	teachers	students	student/ teacher ratio
Primary (age 5–14)	225	1,515	37,753	24.9
Secondary (age, n.a.)	24	491	6,532	13.3
Voc., teacher tr. } Higher	5	58	737	12.7

Educational attainment (1980). Percent of population over age 15 having:
  no formal schooling 7.3%; primary education 73.5%; secondary 14.2%;
  higher 1.6%; other 3.4%. Literacy (1982 est.): total population over age 15
  literate 95,400 (90%).
Health (1984): physicians 78 (1 per 2,078 persons); hospital beds 584 (1 per
  278 persons); infant mortality rate per 1,000 live births 23.4.
Food (1980–82): daily per capita caloric intake 2,692 (vegetable products 74%,
  animal products 26%); 118% of FAO recommended minimum requirement.

Military

Total active duty personnel (1984): about 500; a British garrison of 1,800
  troops remains in the country.

*The Belize dollar is officially pegged to the U.S. dollar. †Detail does not add to
total given because of rounding. ‡1983. §Public utilities are included with public
administration and defense. ‖Transportation and communication is included with
construction. ¶Import value in balance of trade is f.o.b. (free on board) and in the
major import categories section is c.i.f. (cost, insurance, and freight).

Benin

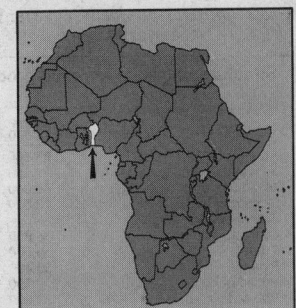

Official name: République Populaire du
Bénin (People's Republic of Benin).
Form of government: unitary
single-party people's republic with
one legislative house (National
Revolutionary Assembly [196]).
Head of state and government:
President.
Capitals: Porto-Novo (official);
Cotonou (de facto).
Official language: French.
Official religion: none.
Monetary unit: 1 CFA franc
(CFAF) = 100 centimes; valuation
(Oct. 21, 1985) 1 U.S.$ = CFAF402.02;
1 £ = CFAF576.50.

Area and population

Provinces	Capitals	area sq mi	area sq km	population 1982 estimate
Atacora	Natitingou	12,050	31,200	522,000
Atlantique	Cotonou	1,250	3,200	752,000
Borgou	Parakou	19,700	51,000	532,000
Mono	Lokossa	1,450	3,800	517,000
Ouémé	Porto-Novo	1,800	4,700	680,000
Zou	Abomey	7,200	18,700	618,000
TOTAL		43,450	112,600	3,621,000

Demography

Population (1985): 4,005,000.
Density (1985): persons per sq mi 92.2, persons per sq.km 35.6.
Urban–rural (1983): urban 16.0%; rural 84.0%.
Sex distribution (1980): male 49.26%; female 50.74%.
Age breakdown (1980): under 15, 43.6%; 15–29, 25.8%; 30–44, 15.8%; 45–59, 9.2%; 60 and over, 5.6%.
Population projection: (1990) 4,861,000; (2000) 6,756,000.
Doubling time: 22 years.
Ethnic composition (1980): Fon 58.9%; Somba 10.4%; Yoruba 10.4%; Bariba 8.9%; Fulani 5.6%; other 5.8%.
Religious affiliation (1980): traditional beliefs 61.4%; Christian 21.6%, of which Roman Catholic 17.4%, Protestant 2.2%; Muslim 15.2%; other 1.8%.
Major cities (1982): Cotonou 487,000; Porto-Novo 208,000; Parakou 66,000; Abomey 54,000; Kandi 53,000.

Vital statistics

Birth rate per 1,000 population (1983): 49.0 (world avg. 29.0).
Death rate per 1,000 population (1983): 18.0 (world avg. 11.0).
Natural increase rate per 1,000 population (1983): 31.0 (world avg. 18.0).
Total fertility rate (avg. births per childbearing woman; 1983): 6.5.
Marriage rate per 1,000 population (1980–85): 12.8.
Divorce rate per 1,000 population (1980–85): 0.8.
Life expectancy at birth (1983): male 46.0 years; female 50.0 years.
Major causes of death per 100,000 population (1977): malaria 227.7; diseases of the respiratory system 206.5; diseases of the digestive system 200.7.

National economy

Budget (1984). Revenue: CFAF55,900,000,000 (indirect taxes 65.1%, direct taxes 25.8%, other 9.1%). Expenditures: CFAF55,900,000,000 (administration and services 70.5%, economic development 10.7%).
Public debt (external, outstanding; 1983): U.S.$614,800,000.
Production (metric tons except as noted). Agriculture, forestry, fishing (1984): cassava 639,000, corn (maize) 379,000, sorghum 82,000, palm kernels 75,000, seed cotton 73,000, peanuts (groundnuts) 58,000, dry beans 37,000; livestock (number of live animals) 1,050,000 sheep, 1,000,000 goats, 875,000 cattle, 520,000 pigs, 5,000,000 chickens; roundwood 4,006,000 cu m*; fish catch 21,050*. Mining and quarrying (1983): cement 315,000. Manufacturing (1981): sugar 47,000; cotton fibre 15,438; palm oil 14,849. Construction: n.a. Energy production (consumption): electricity (kW-hr; 1984) 87,594,000 (182,487,000); coal, none (n.a.); crude petroleum (barrels; 1984) 3,285,000† (n.a.); petroleum products (metric tons; 1983) none (115,000).
Gross national product (1983): U.S.$1,102,000,000 (U.S.$290 per capita).

Structure of gross domestic product and labour force

	1981 in value CFAF'000,000	1981 % of total value	1980 labour force	1980 % of labour force
Agriculture	100,500‡	38.6‡	726,000	46.0
Mining, manufacturing, and public utilities	16,100§	6.2§	253,000	16.0
Construction	13,200	5.1		
Trade and finance	58,200	22.4		
Transp. and commun.	15,700	6.0	600,000	38.00
Pub. admin., defense	26,000	10.0		
Other				
Net indirect taxes	30,400	11.7	—	—
TOTAL	260,100	100.0	1,579,000	100.0

Tourism: receipts from visitors (1982) U.S.$10,000,000; expenditures by nationals abroad (1981) U.S.$4,000,000.
Population economically active (1980): total 1,579,000; participation rate of total population 45.4% (female 45.3%; unemployed, n.a.).

Price and earnings indexes (1977 = 100)

	1978	1979	1980	1981	1982	1983	1984
Consumer price index	106.9	117.8	130.7	147.8	...	...	...
Hourly earnings index	100.0	100.0	115.0	115.0	115.0	180.4	180.4 ‖

Household income and expenditure. Average household size (1979) 5.4; income per household: n.a.; sources of income: n.a.; expenditure: n.a.
Land use (1983): forested 34.5%; meadows and pastures 4.0%; agricultural and under permanent cultivation 16.3%; other 45.2%.

Foreign trade¶

Balance of trade (current prices)

	1975	1976	1977	1978	1979	1980
CFAF'000,000	−35,109	−41,474	−55,674	−64,057	−58,327	−56,697
% of total	71.6%	65.1%	69.2%	82.5%	74.9%	68.1%

Imports (1980): CFAF69,969,000,000 (manufactured goods 40.1%; machinery and transport equipment 20.3%, of which electrical equipment 7.7%; tobacco 14.0%; food products 9.8%, of which cereals 4.9%). *Major import sources* (1984): France 22.8%; Austria 8.8%; Brazil 7.7%; India 6.3%; The Netherlands 5.9%; Italy 5.2%; China 4.2%; Japan 4.1%; United States 3.8%; West Germany 2.2%.
Exports (1980): CFAF13,272,000,000 (food products 30.2%, of which cocoa beans 22.1%; palm kernel oil 29.8%; cotton 22.2%; energy 3.3%; cement 0.4%). *Major export destinations* (1984): Spain 31.9%; West Germany 20.6%; France 15.7%.

Transport and communications

Transport. Railroads (1981): length 359 mi, 578 km; passenger-mi 116,600,000, passenger-km 187,600,000; short ton-mi cargo 120,900,000, metric ton-km cargo 176,500,000. Roads (1983): total length 5,219 mi, 8,400 km (paved? 10%). Vehicles (1980): passenger cars 9,592; trucks and buses 7,025. Merchant marine (1984): vessels (100 gross tons and over) 13; total deadweight tonnage 4,880. Air transport◊ (1982): passenger-mi 137,840,000, passenger-km 221,830,000; short ton-mi cargo 15,432,000, metric ton-km cargo 22,531,000; airports (1985) with scheduled flights 5.
Communications. Daily newspapers (1984): total number 3; total circulation 12,000□; circulation per 1,000 population 3.5□. Radio (1984): total receivers 68,000 (1 per 51 persons). Television (1984): total receivers 17,250 (1 per 203 persons). Telephones (1981): 18,000 (1 per 200 persons).

Education and health

Education (1981–82)

	schools	teachers	students	student/ teacher ratio
Primary	2,480	10,381	404,297	38.9
Secondary	...	1,215◊	83,207△	...
Vocational	...	...	4,441△	...
Higher	1	304	4,730	15.6

Educational attainment, n.a. *Literacy* (1980): total population over age 15 literate 530,000 (27.9%); males 39.8%; females 16.6%.
Health: physicians (1980) 204 (1 per 17,485 persons); hospital beds (1981) 4,025 (1 per 905 persons); infant mortality rate per 1,000 live births (1983) 148.0.
Food (1980–82): daily per capita caloric intake 2,142 (vegetable products 96%, animal products 4%); 95%† of FAO recommended minimum requirement.

Military

Total active duty personnel (1982): 3,300 (army 90.9%, navy 6.1%, air force 3.0%). *Military expenditure as percent of GNP* (1983): 2.6% (world 6.1%); per capita expenditure U.S.$5.

*1983. †Production of offshore petroleum began in 1982, reaching a daily flow rate of 9,000 barrels in 1984. A surplus is expected for export. ‡Includes hunting, forestry, and fishing. §Includes public utilities. ‖ January 1984. ¶Figures do not include unaccountable reexports of black market goods, which originate mainly in Nigeria and amounted to an estimated 90% of Benin's actual exports in 1981. ◊1981. ◊Cotonou airport only. □Circulation for government daily only. ◊1978. △1980–81. †1979–81.

Traditional Bermudian domestic
architecture, with lapped roofs
and walls of native limestone.

Bermuda

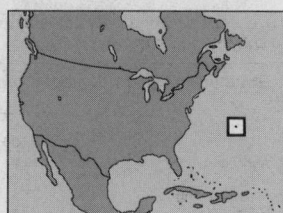

Official name: Colony of Bermuda.
Political status: colony (United
  Kingdom) with two legislative houses
  (Senate [11]; House of Assembly [40]).
Chief of state: British Monarch,
  represented by Governor.
Head of government: Premier.
Capital: Hamilton.
Official language: English.
Official religion: none.
Monetary unit: 1 Bermuda dollar
  (Ber$) = 100 cents; valuation (Oct. 21,
  1985) 1 U.S.$ = Ber$1.00*;
  1 £ = Ber$1.43.

Area and population	area		population
			1980
Municipalities	sq mi	sq km	census
Hamilton	0.3	0.8	1,617
St. George	0.5	1.3	1,647
Parishes			
Devonshire	1.9	4.9	6,843
Hamilton	2.0	5.2	3,784
Paget	2.0	5.2	4,497
Pembroke†	1.8	4.7	10,443
St. Georges‡	1.7	4.4	2,940
Sandys	1.9	4.9	6,255
Smiths	1.9	4.9	4,463
Southampton	2.2	5.7	4,613
Warwick	2.2	5.7	6,948
TOTAL	21.0§ ‖	54.0§ ‖	54,050¶

Demography

Population (1985)¶: 56,700.
Density (1985)¶: persons per sq mi 3,060, persons per sq km 1,180.
Urban–rural (1985): urban 100.0%; rural, none.
Sex distribution (1985): male 48.81%; female 51.19%.
Age breakdown (1985): under 15, 21.3%; 15–29, 24.6%; 30–44, 25.0%; 45–59, 16.1%; 60–74, 9.7%; 75 and over, 3.3%.
Population projection: (1990) 59,000; (2000) 63,000.
Doubling time: 100 years.
Ethnic composition (1980): black 61.3%; white 37.3%; other 1.4%.
Religious affiliation (1980): Anglican 42.1%; other Protestant (principally African Methodist Episcopal and Methodist) 37.0%; Roman Catholic 18.6%.
Major cities (1985): St. George 1,707; Hamilton 1,676.

Vital statistics

Birth rate per 1,000 population (1983): 16.4 (world avg. 29.0); legitimate 70.3%; illegitimate 29.7%.
Death rate per 1,000 population (1983): 7.0 (world avg. 11.0).
Natural increase rate per 1,000 population (1983): 9.4 (world avg. 18.0).
Total fertility rate (avg. births per childbearing woman; 1975–80): 1.9.
Marriage rate per 1,000 population (1983): 12.1.
Divorce rate per 1,000 population (1983): 4.8.
Life expectancy at birth (1980): male 68.8 years; female 76.3 years.
Major causes of death per 100,000 population (1978): diseases of the circulatory system 333.0; malignant neoplasms (cancers) 140.0; endocrine and metabolic disorders 50.0; diseases of the respiratory system 43.0.

National economy

Budget (1984). Revenue: Ber$178,400,000 (customs duty 43.3%, employment tax 9.3%, hospital levy 9.2%, international companies tax 4.8%, land tax 4.7%, hotel occupancy tax 4.0%). Expenditures: Ber$195,300,000 (health and social services 21.9%, education 16.4%, public works and agriculture 15.1%, police 8.0%, tourism 7.1%).
Public debt (external, outstanding; 1982): U.S.$279,000,000.
Tourism (1984): receipts from visitors U.S.$336,800,000; expenditures by nationals abroad, n.a.
Production (value in Ber$ except as noted). Agriculture, forestry, fishing (1983): vegetables 4,300,000, milk 901,000, fruits 808,000, eggs 720,000, meat 420,000, honey 140,000, flowers 55,000؟; livestock (number of live animals) 2,000 pigs, 1,000 cattle, 1,000 horses, 47,000 chickens; fish catch 500. Mining and quarrying: limestone quarried for construction material. Manufacturing: major industries are pharmaceuticals, electronics wares, fish processing, handicrafts, woodworking, small boat building, and textiles. Construction (value in Ber$; 1984): residential 59,000,000; nonresidential 36,700,000. Energy production (consumption): electricity (kW-hr; 1983) 368,000,000 (368,000,000); coal, none (negligible); crude petroleum, none (n.a.); petroleum products (metric tons; 1983) none (144,000); natural gas, none (n.a.).
Population economically active (1984): total employed 32,033; participation rate of population over age 15, 71.8% (female [1983] 45.3%, unemployed 0.7%).

Price and earnings indexes (1975 = 100)							
	1979	1980	1981	1982	1983	1984	1985δ
Consumer price index	113.7	130.7	146.2	157.6	170.2	175.0	173.7
Monthly earnings index	107.2	113.5	129.2	180.7	...	...	...

Gross national product (at current market prices; 1983): U.S.$840,000,000 (U.S.$15,000 per capita).

Structure of gross domestic product and labour force				
	1982–83		1984	
	in value Ber$'000	% of total value	labour force	% of labour force
Agriculture	...	...	326	1.0
Mining	...	...⎫		
Manufacturing	...	...⎬	1,150	3.6
Construction	...	...	2,205	6.9
Public utilities	...	...	410	1.3
Transportation and communication	...	...	2,142	6.7
Trade	...	...	11,393	35.5
Finance	...	...	4,292	13.4
Pub. admin., defense	...	...⎫		
Services	...	...⎬	7,774	24.3
Other	...	...	2,341	7.3
TOTAL	787,300	100.0	32,033	100.0

Household income and expenditure. Average household size (1982) 2.7; income per household Ber$23,700 (U.S.$23,700); sources of income (1982): wages and salaries 72.2%, imputed income from owner occupancy 9.7%, investments including rents 8.0%, self-employment 6.7%; expenditure (1982): housing 22.6%, food, alcohol, and tobacco 19.5%, household goods and services 15.2%, transportation 9.4%, recreation and education 9.0%, foreign travel 6.9%, other 17.4%.
Land use (1983): forested 14.7%; meadows and pastures, 0.6%; agricultural and under permanent cultivation, 4.7%; built-on, wasteland, and other 80.0%.

Foreign trade

Balance of trade (current prices)					
	1980	1981	1982	1983	1984
Ber$'000,000	−274.7	−293.4	−333.8	−355.0	−363.4
% of total	78.9%	83.3%	90.6%	88.6%	81.7%

Imports (1984): Ber$403,931,000 (food, beverages, and tobacco 20.3%, of which meat and meat preparations 5.6%, fruit and vegetables 3.9%; petroleum and petroleum products 12.5%; electrical machinery, including apparatus and appliances 10.2%; clothing 7.8%; chemicals 7.3%; transport equipment 7.1%; nonelectrical machinery 5.2%). *Major import sources:* United States 57.3%; United Kingdom 8.0%; Canada 6.5%; Japan 4.8%.
Exports (1984): Ber$40,544,500 (drugs and medicine 55.9%; electrical supplies 15.3%; electronic supplies 4.5%; scientific supplies 1.3%; books and papers 1.3%; aircraft supplies 0.7%; liquor 0.2%). *Major export destinations* (1983): Italy 30.7%; United States 24.9%; United Kingdom 7.5%; Canada 7.1%; The Netherlands 6.7%; Brazil 5.3%.

Transport and communications

Transport. Railroads: none. Roads (1982): total length 249 mi, 400 km (paved 100%). Vehicles (1983): passenger cars 15,840; trucks and buses 3,690. Merchant marine (1984): vessels (100 gross tons and over) 76; total deadweight tonnage 1,307,260. Air transport (passengers; 1983): arrivals 530,537, departures 527,482; short ton cargo handled 9,567, metric ton cargo handled 8,679; airports (1985) with scheduled flights 1.
Communications. Daily newspapers (1984): total number 1; total circulation 15,021; circulation per 1,000 population 267. Radio (1984): total number of receivers 100,000 (1 per 0.6 person). Television (1983): total number of receivers 66,000 (1 per 0.8 person). Telephones (1983): 51,374 (1 per 1.1 persons).

Education and health

Education (1984–85)	schools	teachers	students	student/ teacher ratio
Primary (age 5–11)	22	312	5,413	17.3
Secondary (age 11–16)	13	350	4,134	11.8
Vocational	1	52	502	9.7
Higher	1	13	105	8.1

Educational attainment (1980). Percent of total population over age 5 having: no formal schooling 1.6%; primary education 32.4%; secondary 45.2%; some higher 16.0%; other 4.8%. *Literacy* (1980): total population over age 15 literate 39,577 (96.9%); males literate 19,026 (96.7%); females literate 20,551 (97.0%).
Health: physicians (1982) 108 (1 per 513 persons); hospital beds (1978) 477 (1 per 114 persons); infant mortality rate per 1,000 live births (1983) 8.7.
Food (1980–82): daily per capita caloric intake 2,521 (vegetable products 59%, animal products 41%); 106% of FAO recommended minimum requirement.

Military

Total active duty personnel (1982): 1,550□.

---

*The Bermuda dollar is at par with the U.S. dollar. †Excludes the area and population of the city of Hamilton. ‡Excludes the area and population of the town of St. George. §Grand total includes 2.3 sq mi (5.4 sq km) leased to the United States for military bases. ‖ Detail does not add to total given (less area for the military bases) because of rounding. ¶Excludes on-base military personnel, Bermudians residing abroad, and institutionalized persons. ؟1982. δSecond quarter. □Includes troops of both the United Kingdom and the United States.

Bhutan

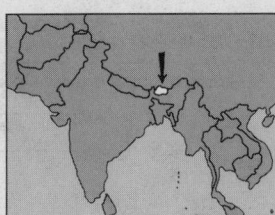

Official name: Druk-Yul (Kingdom of Bhutan).
Form of government: monarchy with one legislative house (National Assembly [150]).
Head of state and government: Monarch.
Capital: Thimphu (official); Paro (administrative and summer).
Official language: Dzongkha (a Tibetan dialect).
Official religion: Mahāyāna Buddhism.
Monetary unit: 1 Ngultrum* (Nu) = 100 chetrum; valuation (Oct. 21, 1985) 1 U.S.$ = Nu11.92; 1 £ = Nu17.10.

Area and population

Districts	Capitals	area sq mi	area sq km	population 1982 estimate
Bumthang	Jakar	1,150	2,990	23,200
Chirang	Damphu	310	800	116,200
Dagana	Dagana	540	1,400	34,900
Gasa	Gasa	2,000	5,180	11,600
Gaylegphug	Gaylegphug	1,020	2,640	116,200
Ha	Paro	830	2,140	11,600
Lhuntsi	Lhuntshi	1,120	2,910	46,500
Mongar	Mongar	710	1,830	81,300
Paro	Paro	580	1,500	46,500
Pema Gatsel	Pema Gatsel	150	380	34,900
Samchi	Samchi	830	2,140	185,900
Samdrup Jongkhar	Samdrup Jongkhar	900	2,340	69,700
Shemgang	Shemgang	980	2,540	46,500
Tashigang	Tashigang	1,640	4,260	185,900
Thimphu	Thimphu	960	2,480	81,300
Tongsa	Tongsa	570	1,470	23,200
Wangdi Phodrang	Wangdi Phodrang	1,160	3,000	46,500
TOTAL		18,150†	47,000†	1,162,000‡

Demography

Population (1985 est.): 1,423,000.
Density (1985): persons per sq mi 78.6, persons per sq km 30.3.
Urban–rural (1985): urban 4.5%; rural 95.5%.
Sex distribution (1985): male 51.59%; female 48.41%.
Age breakdown (1985): under 15, 40.0%; 15–29, 26.9%; 30–44, 17.4%; 45–59, 10.4%; 60–69, 3.7%; 70 and over, 1.8%.
Population projection: (1990) 1,569,000; (2000) 1,893,000.
Doubling time: 34 years.
Ethnic composition (1980): Bhutia 60.9%; Gurung 15.4%; Assamese 13.1%; other 10.6%.
Religious affiliation (1985): Buddhist 69.6%; Hindu 24.6%; Muslim 5.0%; other 0.8%.
Major cities (1982 est.): Thimphu 12,000; Phuntsholing 10,000.

Vital statistics

Birth rate per 1,000 population (1980–85): 38.4 (world avg. 29.0); legitimate, n.a.; illegitimate, n.a.
Death rate per 1,000 population (1980–85): 18.1 (world avg. 11.0).
Natural increase rate per 1,000 population (1980–85): 20.3 (world avg. 18.0).
Total fertility rate (avg. births per childbearing woman; 1980–85): 5.5.
Marital status of population 15 years and over (1985): married 71.3%; single 19.7%; widowed 7.5%; divorced 1.6%.
Divorce rate per 1,000 population: n.a.
Life expectancy at birth (1980–85): male 46.6 years; female 45.1 years.
Major causes of death: n.a.; however, malaria, tuberculosis, gastrointestinal infectious diseases, influenza, and pneumonia are major health problems.

National economy

Budget (1983–84). Revenue: Nu628,107,000 (grants from government of India 40.6%, internal sources 30.1%, grants from UN and other international agencies 21.9%, loans 7.4%). Expenditures: Nu628,107,000 (agriculture 27.2%§, secretariat 23.0%, public works 20.1%, education 10.9%, health 6.2%, communications 2.0%).
Public debt (external, outstanding): n.a.
Tourism (1981–82): receipts from visitors U.S.$1,411,400; expenditures by nationals abroad, n.a.
Production (metric tons except as noted). Agriculture, forestry, fishing (1984): corn (maize) 85,000, rice 61,000, fruit 48,000, potatoes 27,000, wheat 10,000, vegetables and melons 10,000, millet 7,000, barley 5,000, jute 4,000, tobacco 1,000; livestock (number of live animals) 315,000 cattle, 74,000 pigs, 45,000 goats, 43,000 sheep, 28,000 buffalo, 26,000 yaks ‖, 16,000 horses; roundwood 3,224,000 cu m¶; fish catch 1,000¶. Mining and quarrying: n.a.; however, some slate is quarried, and gypsum and graphite are mined. Manufacturing (value in Nu; 1980–81): distillery products 47,000,000; cement 36,000,000; chemical products 19,000,000; processed food 14,000,000; forest products 3,000,000. Construction (number of buildings completed; 1977–78): residential 10; nonresidential (guest house) 1. Energy production (consumption): electricity (kW-hr; 1983) 26,000,000 (26,000,000); coal, none (n.a.); crude petroleum, none (n.a.); petroleum products (metric tons; 1983) none (1,000); natural gas, none (n.a.).

Gross national product (at current market prices; 1981): U.S.$124,402,400 (U.S.$95 per capita).

Structure of gross domestic product and labour force

	1981–82 in value Nu'000,000	1981–82 % of total value	labour force	% of labour force
Agriculture	478.9	40.1	613,000	94.3
Mining	9.6	0.8	}	
Manufacturing	27.5	2.3 }	6,000	0.9
Construction	21.5	1.8 }		
Trade	34.6	2.9	9,000	1.4
Public utilities	3.6	0.3 }		
Transportation and communication	39.4	3.3 }		
Finance	16.7	1.4	22,000	3.4
Pub. admin., defense	124.2	10.4		
Other	438.2⁹	36.7⁹		
TOTAL	1,194.2⁵	100.0⁵	650,000	100.0

Population economically active (1984): total 664,000; participation rate of population over age 15, 79.7% (female, n.a.; unemployed, n.a.).

Price and earnings indexes (1980–81 = 100)

	1977–78	1978–79	1979–80	1980–81	1981–82
Consumer price index	71.8	80.4	91.3	100.0	110.3
Earnings index	...	...	...	...	...

Household income and expenditure. Average household size (1980): 5.4; income per household: n.a.; source of income: n.a.; expenditure: n.a.
Land use (1983): forested 69.8%; meadows and pastures 4.6%; agricultural and under permanent cultivation 2.1%; other 23.5%.

Foreign trade□

Balance of trade (current prices)

	1978	1979	1980	1981	1982	1983
Nu'000,000	...	...	...	...	...	−226.5
% of total	...	...	...	...	...	38.9%

Imports (1981–82): Nu404,521,000 (machinery and equipment 22.1%, petroleum products 14.2%, iron and steel products 8.1%, motor vehicles 7.3%, rice 3.9%, fabrics 3.0%, stationery and books 2.2%, wheat and wheat flour 1.6%). *Major import source:* India.
Exports (1981–82): Nu177,981,000◇ (cement 26.6%, oranges 9.6%, sawn timber 9.0%, potatoes 8.7%, talcum powder 6.1%, cardamom 6.1%, rosin 4.0%, menthol products 2.7%). *Major export destination:* India 96.5%.

Transport and communications

Transport. Railroads: none. Roads (1984): total length 1,270 mi, 2,050 km (paved about 50%). Vehicles (1982): passenger cars 1,363; trucks and buses 706. Merchant marine: none. Air transport: n.a.; airports (1984) with scheduled flights 1.
Communications. Daily newspapers: none△. Radio (1984): total number of receivers 12,500 (1 per 112 persons). Television (1983): total number of receivers 200 (1 per 6,800 persons). Telephones (1982): 1,866 (1 per 714 persons).

Education and health

Education (1983)

	schools	teachers	students	student/ teacher ratio
Primary (age 7–11)	136	1,167	41,372	35.5
Secondary (age 12–16)	32	251	3,109	12.4
Voc., teacher tr.	4	143	2,189	15.3
Higher	2	16	204	12.8

Educational attainment, n.a. *Literacy* (1977): total population over age 15 literate 124,000 (18.0%); males literate 98,000 (31.0%); females literate 26,000 (9.0%).
Health (1982): physicians 64 (1 per 18,100 persons); hospital beds 600 (1 per 2,000 persons); infant mortality rate per 1,000 live births (1980–85) 144.
Food (1975–77): daily per capita caloric intake 2,058 (vegetable products 98%, animal products 2%); 89% of FAO recommended minimum requirement.

Military

Total active duty personnel: about 4,000 (army 100%).

*Indian currency is also accepted legal tender; the Ngultrum is at par with the Indian rupee. †2,700 sq mi (7,000 sq km) are not included in the district area totals. ‡Detail does not add to total given because of rounding. §Includes irrigation, animal husbandry, and forestry. ‖1982. ¶1983. ⁹Includes tourism. ⁵At current prices. □Only with India. ◇An additional Nu6,432,000 in commodities was exported to countries other than India. △A government weekly is published from Thimphu in Dzongkha, Nepalese, and English, circulation 5,000.

Bolivia

Official name: República de Bolivia (Republic of Bolivia).
Form of government: unitary, multiparty republic with two legislative houses (Chamber of Senators [27]; Chamber of Deputies [130]).
Head of state and government: President.
Capital: La Paz (administrative); Sucre (judicial).
Official languages: Spanish, Aymara, Quechua.
Official religion: Roman Catholicism.
Monetary unit: 1 Bolivian peso ($b) = 100 centavos; valuation (Oct. 21, 1985) 1 U.S.$ = $b74,948; 1 £ = $b107,475.

Area and population

Departments	Capitals	area sq mi	area sq km	population 1984 estimate
Beni	Trinidad	82,458	213,564	232,000
Chuquisaca	Sucre	19,893	51,524	454,600
Cochabamba	Cochabamba	21,479	55,631	954,800
La Paz	La Paz	51,732	133,985	2,029,000
Oruro	Oruro	20,690	53,588	403,300
Pando	Cobija	24,644	63,827	45,600
Potosí	Potosí	45,644	118,218	859,700
Santa Cruz	Santa Cruz	143,098	370,621	1,011,700
Tarija	Tarija	14,526	37,623	262,000
TOTAL		424,164	1,098,581	6,252,700

Demography

Population (1985 est.): 6,429,000.
Density (1985): persons per sq mi 15.2, persons per sq km 5.9.
Urban–rural (1985): urban 47.7%; rural 52.3%.
Sex distribution (1984): male 49.38%; female 50.62%.
Age breakdown (1984): under 15, 43.0%; 15–29, 26.6%; 30–44, 15.9%; 45–59, 9.3%; 60–74, 4.4%; 75 and over, 0.8%.
Population projection: (1990) 7,314,000; (2000) 9,724,000.
Doubling time: 25 years.
Ethnic composition (1982): mestizo 31.2%; Quechua 25.4%; Aymara 16.9%; white 14.5%; other 12.0%.
Religious affiliation (1981): Roman Catholic 94.0%; Bahā'ī 2.6%; other 3.4%.
Major cities (1984): La Paz 953,634; Santa Cruz 419,042; Cochabamba 304,960; Oruro 172,814; Sucre 84,505.

Vital statistics

Birth rate per 1,000 population (1982): 44.0 (world avg. 29.0).
Death rate per 1,000 population (1982): 16.8 (world avg. 11.0).
Natural increase rate per 1,000 population (1982): 27.2 (world avg. 18.0).
Total fertility rate (avg. births per childbearing woman; 1980–85): 6.2.
Marriage rate per 1,000 population (1980): 4.8.
Divorce rate per 1,000 population: n.a.
Life expectancy at birth (1980–85): male 48.6 years; female 53.0 years.
Major causes of death per 100,000 population: n.a.

National economy

Budget (1983). Revenue: $b45,641,100,000 (internal taxes 43.9%, customs taxes 12.7%, royalties on petroleum 7.7%). Expenditures: $b249,241,200,000 (services 32.4%, transfers and contributions 10.7%, public debt 4.6%, materials and equipment 3.6%).
Public debt (external, outstanding; 1983): U.S.$2,968,900,000.
Tourism (1982): receipts from visitors U.S.$36,000,000*; expenditures by nationals abroad U.S.$40,000,000.
Production (metric tons except as noted). Agriculture, forestry, fishing (1984): sugarcane 2,195,000, corn (maize) 489,000, potatoes 650,000, bananas 160,000, oranges 95,000, rice 194,000, wheat 69,000; livestock (number of live animals): 9,200,000 sheep, 4,300,000 cattle, 3,200,000 goats, 1,700,000 pigs, 800,000 asses, 420,000 horses; roundwood 1,272,000 cu m†; fish catch 5,617†. Mining and quarrying (metric tons of pure metal; 1984): zinc 38,280; tin 17,875; antimony 9,675; lead 8,023; tungsten 2,590; copper 1,981†; gold 1,100 kilograms. Manufacturing (gross value in $b; 1981): food and beverages 16,080,982,808, of which food 12,254,780,842; nonferrous metals 7,606,061,069; nonmetallic mineral products 1,328,121,249; metal products 1,194,120,108; wood and wood products 999,542,335; machinery and equipment 516,844,375. Construction‡ (1983): residential dwellings 323. Energy production (consumption): electricity (kW-hr; 1983) 1,680,000,000 (1,228,200,000); coal (metric tons; 1983) none (1,000); crude petroleum (barrels; 1984) 7,027,000 (7,393,000†); petroleum products (metric tons; 1983) 1,065,900 (1,061,900); natural gas (cu m; 1983) 3,296,400,000 (412,464,000).
Population economically active (1982): total 1,871,600; participation rate of population over age 15, 31.6% (female 23.2%, unemployed, n.a.).

Price and earnings indexes (1980 = 100)

	1979	1980	1981	1982	1983	1984	1985
Consumer price index	67.9	100.0	132.1	295.4	1,109	15,325	538,145§
Monthly earnings index	...	...	...	...	...	...	...

Gross national product (at current market prices; 1983): U.S.$3,070,000,000 (U.S.$510 per capita).

Structure of gross domestic product and labour force

	1983 in value $b'000,000	1983 % of total value	1982 labour force ‖	1982 % of labour force
Agriculture	341,435	22.5	792,600	46.4
Mining	100,504	6.6	76,200	4.5
Manufacturing	246,005	16.2	155,500	9.1
Construction	28,002	1.8	56,500	3.3
Public utilities	15,594	1.0	7,200	0.4
Transportation and communication	130,526	8.6	94,700	5.5
Trade	362,454	23.9	128,800	7.5
Finance	93,057	6.1	13,300	0.8
Pub. admin., defense	106,253	7.0		
Services	110,939	7.3	382,600	22.4
Other	−18,984¶	−1.2¶		
TOTAL	1,515,785⌀	100.0⌀	1,707,400	100.0⌀

Land use (1983): forested 51.7%; meadows and pastures 24.9%; agricultural and under permanent cultivation 3.1%; other 20.3%.

Foreign trade□

Balance of trade (current prices)

	1978	1979	1980	1981	1982	1984
U.S.$'000,000	−96.6	−53.2	+261.8	+229.0	+399.0	+275.0
% of total	7.1%	3.4%	16.1%	14.4%	31.8%	22.8%

Imports (1983): U.S.$768,669,000 (capital goods 45.4%, of which capital goods for industry 28.2%, transport equipment 14.5%; raw materials 33.5%, of which raw materials for industry 25.9%; consumer goods 20.6%, of which nondurable consumer goods 12.5%, durable consumer goods 8.1%). *Major import sources:* United States 28.1%; Argentina 14.2%; Brazil 13.9%; Japan 7.3%; Mexico 6.1%; West Germany 5.5%; France 4.0%; United Kingdom 3.9%; Chile 3.0%.
Exports (1983): U.S.$788,608,600 (natural gas 44.6%; tin 25.4%; coffee 1.7%; sugar 1.6%; wood 0.9%). *Major export destinations:* Argentina 47.6%; United States 20.1%; The Netherlands 6.0%; Belgium 3.1%; West Germany 2.9%; United Kingdom 2.3%; Switzerland 2.0%; Japan 1.9%; France 1.9%; Peru 1.8%.

Transport and communications

Transport. Railroads: length (1983) 2,320 mi, 3,733 km; passenger-mi 345,000,000◇, passenger-km 555,000,000◇; short ton-mi cargo 1,160,000,000, metric ton-km cargo 1,693,000,000. Roads (1983): total length 25,461 mi, 40,975 km (paved 4%). Vehicles (1983): passenger cars 40,638; trucks and buses 36,951. Merchant marine (1984): vessels (100 gross tons and over) 2; total deadweight tonnage 18,934. Air transport (1984): passenger-mi 544,000,000, passenger-km 876,000,000; short ton-mi cargo 27,300,000, metric ton-km cargo 39,900,000; airports (1985) with scheduled flights 16.
Communications. Daily newspapers (1984): total number 14; total circulation 253,000; circulation per 1,000 population 40. Radio (1984): total number of receivers 482,000 (1 per 13 persons). Television (1984): total number of receivers 387,000 (1 per 16 persons). Telephones (1983): 204,747 (1 per 30 persons).

Education and health

Education (1983)

	schools	teachers	students	student/ teacher ratio
Primary (age 6–13)	8,514	50,703	1,154,819	22.8
Secondary (age 14–17)	845	8,091	174,982	21.6
Higher	25	1,487	13,388	9.0

Educational attainment (1976). Percent of adult population over age 25 having: no formal schooling 48.6%; primary education 28.5%; secondary 17.9%; higher 5.0%. *Literacy* (1976): total population over age 15 literate 1,706,718 (63.2%); males literate 990,408 (75.8%); females literate 716,310 (51.4%).
Health (1978): physicians 3,410 (1 per 1,433 persons); hospital beds 9,353 (1 per 523 persons); infant mortality rate per 1,000 live births (1984) 213.0.
Food (1980–82): daily per capita caloric intake 2,116 (vegetable products 83%, animal products 17%); 89% of FAO recommended minimum requirement.

Military

Total active duty personnel (1984): 27,600 (army 72.5%, navy 13.0%, air force 14.5%). *Military expenditure as percent of GNP* (1982): 1.9% (world 6.1%); per capita expenditure U.S.$17.

*1981. †1983. ‡National government sponsored only. §July. ‖ Employed persons only. ¶Less imputed bank service charges. ⌀At current prices. ◇Detail does not add to total given because of rounding. □Import figures are f.o.b. (free on board) in balance of trade and c.i.f. (cost, insurance, and freight) for commodities and trading partners. ◇1982.

Botswana

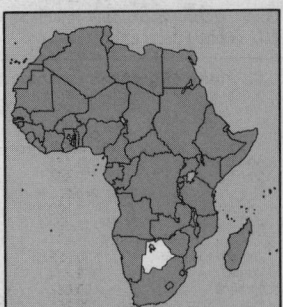

Official name: Republic of Botswana.
Form of government: multiparty republic with one legislative body (National Assembly [39]).
Head of state and government: President.
Capital: Gaborone.
Official language: English.
Official religion: none.
Monetary unit: 1 pula (P) = 100 thebe; valuation (Oct. 21, 1985) 1 U.S.$ = P2.06; 1 £ = P2.96.

Area and population

Districts	Capitals	area sq mi	area sq km	population 1984 estimate
Central	Serowe	57,039	147,730	355,000
Ghanzi	Ghanzi	45,525	117,910	21,000
Kgalagadi	Tshabong	41,290	106,940	26,000
Kgatleng	Mochudi	3,073	7,960	49,000
Kweneng	Molepolole	13,857	35,890	128,000
North East	Masunga	1,977	5,120	40,000
North West				
Chobe	Kasane	8,031	20,800	9,000
Ngamiland	Maun	42,135	109,130	75,000
Southern	Kanye	10,992	28,470	138,000
South East	Ramotswa	687	1,780	34,000
Towns				
Francistown	—	27	70	36,000
Gaborone	—	27	71*	79,000
Lobatse	—	25	64	22,000
Orapa	—	*	*	5,800
Selebi-Pikwe	—	20	52	33,000
TOTAL		224,706†	581,987	1,051,000†

Demography

Population (1985): 1,082,000.
Density (1985): persons per sq mi 4.8, persons per sq km 1.9.
Urban–rural (1981): urban 16.1%; rural 83.9%.
Sex distribution (1981): male 47.09%; female 52.91%.
Age breakdown (1981): under 15, 46.8%; 15–29, 24.7%; 30–44, 12.5%; 45–59, 8.0%; 60–74, 5.5%; 75 and over, 2.5%.
Population projection: (1990) 1,292,000; (2000) 1,865,000.
Doubling time: 19.2 years.
Ethnic composition (1980): Bantu 93.6%; Bushman 4.8%; European 0.7%; other 0.9%.
Religious affiliation (1980): folk religionist 49.2%; Protestant 26.6%; indigenous Christian 11.8%; Roman Catholic 9.4%; other 3.0%.
Major cities (1984): Gaborone 79,000; Francistown 36,000; Selebi-Pikwe 33,000; Serowe 29,000; Mahalapye 25,000; Molepolole 24,000.

Vital statistics

Birth rate per 1,000 population (1980–85): 50.0 (world avg. 29.0); legitimate, n.a.; illegitimate, n.a.
Death rate per 1,000 population (1980–85): 13.0 (world avg. 11.0).
Natural increase rate per 1,000 population (1980–85): 37.3 (world avg. 18.0).
Total fertility rate (avg. births per childbearing woman; 1981): 6.2.
Marriage rate per 1,000 population: n.a.
Divorce rate per 1,000 population: n.a.
Life expectancy at birth (1981): male 52.7 years; female 59.3 years.
Major causes of death (as percent of total deaths; 1977): measles 16.3%; heart disease 8.4%; influenza and pneumonia 7.6%; diarrheal diseases 7.5%; malignant neoplasms (cancers) 6.0%.

National economy

Budget (1983–84). Revenue: P511,372,000 (property income 33.2%, import duties 30.7%, income tax 27.5%). Expenditures: P453,946,000 (government services 15.0%, education 12.1%, public works 8.6%, local government and lands 8.2%, agriculture 5.2%, health 4.0%).
Production (metric tons except as noted). Agriculture, forestry, fishing (1984): cereals 10,000 (of which sorghum 6,000, corn [maize] 2,000, millet 1,000, wheat 1,000), vegetables and melons 16,000, pulses 15,000, fruit 11,-000, roots and tubers 7,000, seed cotton 3,000, cotton seed 2,000, peanuts (groundnuts) 1,000; livestock (number of live animals) 2,900,000 cattle, 800,000 goats, 165,000 sheep, 144,000 mules and asses, 25,000 horses; roundwood 788,000 cu m‡; fish catch 1,250‡. Mining and quarrying (1983): diamonds 10,731,165 carats (P538,300,000); nickel–copper matte 48,083, of which copper 20,260, nickel 18,210, cobalt 220. Manufacturing (1984): beer 155,000 hectolitres. Construction (1982): residential 75,200 sq m; nonresidential 103,300 sq m. Energy production (consumption): electricity (kW-hr; 1983) 622,000,000 (604,408,000§); coal (metric tons; 1982) 414,778 (n.a.); crude petroleum, none (n.a.); petroleum products, n.a. (n.a.); natural gas, none (n.a.).
Population economically active (1981): total 315,475; participation rate of total population 33.6% (female 40.3%, unemployed [1982] 166,000).

Price and earnings indexes (1980 = 100)

	1978	1979	1980	1981	1982	1983	1984
Consumer price index	78.7	87.8	100.0	116.2	129.6	142.9	153.4
Earnings index	...	...	...	...	...	...	...

Public debt (external, outstanding; 1983): U.S.$230,200,000.
Tourism (1983): receipts from visitors U.S.$47,000,000; expenditures by nationals abroad U.S.$16,000,000.
Gross national product (at current market prices; 1983): U.S.$920,000,000 (U.S.$920 per capita).

Structure of gross domestic product and labour force

	1982–83 in value P'000,000	1982–83 % of total value	1983 labour force	1983 % of labour force
Agriculture	73.5	7.4	4,500	4.5
Mining	286.3	28.7	7,200	7.2
Manufacturing	81.7	8.2	9,900	9.9
Construction	43.2	4.3	9,500	9.5
Public utilities	29.5	3.0	1,900	1.9
Transportation and communication	29.8	3.0	3,900	3.9
Trade	223.5	22.4	15,300	15.2
Finance	95.9	9.6	6,000	6.0
Pub. admin., defense	147.4	14.8 }	42,200	42.0
Services	38.3	3.8 }		
Other	−52.0 ‖	−5.2 ‖		
TOTAL	997.1¶	100.0	100,400	100.0†

Household income and expenditure. Average household size (1981) 5.7; average annual income per household, n.a.; sources of income (1980): wages and salaries 71.1%, self-employment 23.3%, transfers 5.5%; expenditure (1980): food, beverages, and tobacco 48.2%, rent and services 12.6%.
Land use (1983): forested 1.6%; meadows and pastures 75.2%; agricultural and under permanent cultivation 2.3%; other 20.9%.

Foreign trade♀

Balance of trade (current prices)

	1979	1980	1981	1982	1983	1984
P'000,000	−48.5	−120.6	−318.4	−232.5	−70.9	+34.5
% of total	6.4%	13.4%	33.6%	19.9%	4.8%	2.0%

Imports (1983): P835,735,000 (food, beverages, and tobacco 19.6%; machinery and electrical goods 12.7%; mineral fuels 12.6%; vehicles and transport equipment 11.5%; metal and metal products 9.8%; textiles and footwear 9.2%; chemicals and rubber 8.3%; wood and paper 3.4%). *Major import sources:* CUSA (Customs Union of Southern Africa, which includes Botswana, Lesotho, South West Africa/Namibia, South Africa, and Swaziland) 82.4%; United Kingdom 1.2%; United States 1.0%.
Exports (1983): P717,702,000 (diamonds 66.6%; meat and meat products 11.3%; copper–nickel matte 9.4%; textiles 4.7%; animal hides and skins 0.7%). *Major export destinations:* CUSA 8.3%; United States 7.4%; United Kingdom 4.4%.

Transport and communications

Transport. Railroads (1982–83): length 444 mi, 714 km; number of passengers 566,372; short ton-mi cargo 944,353, metric ton-km cargo 1,378,732. Roads (1983): total length 4,987 mi, 8,026 km (paved 22%). Vehicles (1983): passenger cars 11,039; trucks and buses 20,739. Merchant marine: none. Air transport (1980): passenger-mi 355,000,000, passenger-km 570,000,000; short ton-mi cargo 24,180,000, metric ton-km cargo 35,300,000; airports (1985) with scheduled flights 4.
Communications. Daily newspapers (1984): total number 1; total circulation 18,000; circulation per 1,000 population 17.1. Radio (1984): total number of receivers 75,800 (1 per 14 persons). Television (1983): none. Telephones (1984): 11,700 (1 per 90 persons).

Education and health

Education (1984)

	schools	teachers	students	student/ teacher ratio
Primary (age 7–13)	518	6,753	209,345	31.0
Secondary (age 14–19)	56	1,065	27,326	25.7
Voc., teacher tr.	17	...	2,321	...
Higher	1	137‡	1,232	...

Educational attainment (1981). Percent of population over age 12 having: no formal schooling 42.9%; some primary education 34.9%; complete primary 14.5%; complete secondary 6.2%; higher 0.9%. *Literacy* (1981): total population over age 15 literate 262,000 (52.4%); males literate 106,841 (47.7%); females literate 155,159 (56.2%).
Health (1981): physicians 113 (1 per 8,319 persons); hospital beds 2,067 (1 per 463 persons); infant mortality rate per 1,000 live births (1981) 68.4.
Food (1980–82): daily per capita caloric intake 2,468 (vegetable products 84%, animal products 16%); 106% of FAO recommended minimum requirement.

Military

Total active duty personnel (1985): 2,850 (army 94.7%; navy, none; air force 5.3%). *Military expenditure as percent of GNP* (1983): 3.0% (world 6.1%); per capita expenditure U.S.$25.

*Area included with Central District. †Detail does not add to total given because of rounding. ‡1983. §1982. ‖ Less imputed bank service charge. ¶At current prices. ♀Import figures are f.o.b. (free on board) in balance of trade and c.i.f. (cost, insurance, and freight) for commodities and trading partners.

Brazil

Official name: República Federativa do Brasil (Federative Republic of Brazil).
Form of government: multiparty federal republic with 2 legislative houses (Federal Senate [69]; Chamber of Deputies [479]).
Chief of state and government: President.
Capital: Brasília.
Official language: Portuguese.
Official religion: none.
Monetary unit: 1 Cruzeiro (Cr$) = 100 centavos; valuation (Oct. 21, 1985)
1 U.S.$ = 8,267 cruzeiros;
1 £ = 11,856 cruzeiros.

Area and population		area*		population
				1985
States	Capitals	sq mi	sq km	estimate
Acre	Rio Branco	58,915	152,589	358,000
Alagoas	Maceió	10,707	27,731	2,245,000
Amazonas	Manaus	604,035	1,564,445	1,728,000
Bahia	Salvador	216,613	561,026	10,731,000
Ceará	Fortaleza	58,159	150,630	5,893,000
Espírito Santo†	Vitória	17,605	45,597	2,287,000
Goiás	Goiânia	247,913	642,092	4,453,000
Maranhão	São Luís	126,897	328,663	4,641,000
Mato Grosso	Cuiabá	340,156	881,001	1,480,000
Mato Grosso do Sul	Campo Grande	135,347	350,548	1,604,000
Minas Gerais	Belo Horizonte	226,708	587,172	14,600,000
Pará	Belém	482,906	1,250,722	4,201,000
Paraíba	João Pessoa	21,765	56,372	3,016,000
Paraná	Curitiba	77,048	199,554	8,074,000
Pernambuco	Recife	37,946	98,281	6,775,000
Piauí	Teresina	96,886	250,934	2,430,000
Rio Grande do Norte	Natal	20,469	53,015	2,126,000
Rio Grande do Sul	Pôrto Alegre	108,952	282,184	8,486,000
Rio de Janeiro	Rio de Janeiro	17,092	44,268	12,767,000
Rondônia	Pôrto Velho	93,840	243,044	731,000
Santa Catarina	Florianópolis	37,060	95,985	4,096,000
São Paulo	São Paulo	95,714	247,898	29,657,000
Sergipe	Aracaju	8,492	21,994	1,287,000
Other federal entities				
Distrito Federal	Brasília	2,245	5,814	1,579,000
Amapá	Macapá	54,161	140,276	214,000
Fernando de Noronha‡	Fernando de Noronha	10	26	1,000
Roraima	Boa Vista	88,844	230,104	104,000
TOTAL		3,286,487§	8,511,965	135,564,000

Demography

Population (1985): 135,564,000.
Density (1985): persons per sq mi 41.2, persons per sq km 15.9.
Urban-rural (1980): urban 67.6%; rural 32.4%.
Sex distribution (1985): male 49.92%; female 50.08%.
Age breakdown (1985): under 15, 36.4%; 15–29, 28.9%; 30–44, 17.8%; 45–59, 10.3%; 60–74, 5.2%; 75 and over, 1.4%.
Population projection: (1990) 150,368,000; (2000) 179,487,000.
Doubling time: 31 years.
Ethnic composition (1980): Brazilian white 53.0%, of which Portuguese 15.0%, Italian 11.0%, Spanish 10.0%, German 3.0%; mulatto 22.0%; mestizo 12.0%; black 11.0%; Japanese 0.8%; indigenous Indian 0.1%; other 1.1%.
Religious affiliation (1980): Roman Catholic 87.8%, of which Spiritist Catholic 15.7% ‖, Evangelical Catholic 9.0%¶; Protestant (mostly Assemblies of God, other Pentecostal, and Baptist) 6.1%.¶; Afro-American Spiritist 2.0%♀; Spiritist 1.7%♂; nonreligious 1.0%; atheist 0.4%; Buddhist 0.3%; Jewish 0.2%; other 0.5%.
Major cities (1980): São Paulo 7,033,000 (metropolitan area 12,589,000); Rio de Janeiro 5,091,000 (metropolitan area 9,014,000); Salvador 1,492,000 (metropolitan area 1,767,000); Belo Horizonte 1,442,000 (metropolitan area 2,540,000); Recife 1,184,000; Pôrto Alegre 1,109,000; Curitiba 844,000; Belém 758,000; Goiânia 703,000; Fortaleza 649,000; Brasília 411,000.
Total number of immigrants entering Brazil (1884–1973): 5,072,000; *place of national origin:* Portugal 31.1%; Italy 30.2%; Spain 13.8%; Japan 4.9%; Germany 4.0%; Russia (U.S.S.R.) 2.2%; other 13.8%.
Mobility (1980). Households living in same residence as in 1970: 25.0%.
Families (1983). Average family size 4.3; 1–2 persons 23.7%, 3 persons 19.7%, 4 persons 19.6%, 5–6 persons 23.1%, 7 or more persons 13.9%. Family households: n.a.
Immigration (1981): permanent immigrants admitted 4,303, from United Kingdom 29.2%, Japan 15.4%, Uruguay 10.1%.

Vital statistics

Birth rate per 1,000 population (1980–85): 30.6 (world avg. 29.0).
Death rate per 1,000 population (1980–85): 8.4 (world avg. 11.0).
Natural increase rate per 1,000 population (1980–85): 22.2 (world avg. 18.0).
Total fertility rate (avg. births per childbearing woman; 1980–85): 3.8.
Marriage rate per 1,000 population (1981): 7.5.
Divorce rate per 1,000 population (1981): 0.2.
Life expectancy at birth (1980–85): male 60.9 years; female 66.0 years.
Major causes of death per 100,000 population (1980): diseases of the circulatory system 156.2, of which cerebrovascular disease 51.5, diseases of pulmonary circulation 40.5, acute myocardial infarction 30.7; accidents 58.0; infectious and parasitic diseases 57.4; diseases of the respiratory system 49.3, of which pneumonia 29.3; malignant neoplasms (cancers) 49.3;

perinatal conditions 42.5; other, ill-defined conditions 131.8; homicide and other violence 22.6.

Social indicators

Educational attainment (1983). Percent of population over age 5 having: no formal schooling 6.0%; primary 79.9%; secondary 9.6%; higher 4.5%.

Distribution of income (1980)									
percent of national income by decile									
1	2	3	4	5	6	7	8	9	10 (highest)
1.2	2.0	3.0	3.6	4.4	5.6	7.2	9.9	15.4	47.9

Quality of working life. Average workweek (1980): 80.6% of the labour force works 40 or more hours per week. Annual estimated rate per 100,000 insured urban workers (1982) for: injury or accident 5,500; industrial illness, n.a.; death 21. Proportion of labour force participating in national social insurance system: 51.8%. Average days lost to labour stoppages per 1,000 workdays: n.a. Average duration of journey and method of transport to work: n.a. Rate per 1,000 workers of discouraged (unemployed no longer seeking work): n.a.
Access to services (1980). Proportion of households having access to: electricity 67.4%, of which urban households having access 88.5%, rural households having access 20.5%; safe public (piped) water supply 53.2%, of which urban households having access 75.8%, rural households having access 3.2%; public sewage collection or septic tank 41.5%, of which urban households having access 57.4%, rural households having access 6.2%; public fire protection, n.a.
Social participation. Eligible voters participating in last national election: 82.7%□. Population participating in voluntary work: n.a. Trade union membership in total work force (1980 est.): 10–15%. Practicing religious population in total affiliated population: Most men, and in particular Portuguese-Brazilian men, attend Mass only on special occasions. They believe religion is the domain and duty of women.
Social deviance: The incidence of crime is not accurately reported. Felonies per official statistics (1978): 64,915, of which murder and bodily assault 42.0%, robbery, extortion, and fraud 39.0%, rape and pandering 4.5%, trafficking or using illegal narcotics 10.5%. Suicide (1983): 5,368; additional potential suicides (1981) 9,698.
Leisure. Favourite leisure activities: n.a.
Material well-being (1980). Households possessing: automobile 22.4% (urban 28.3%, rural 9.5%); telephone 12.4% (urban 17.5%, rural 0.9%); television receiver 54.9% (urban 73.1%, rural 14.7%); refrigerator 49.5% (urban 66.2%, rural 12.6%); air conditioner, n.a.; washing machine, n.a.

National economy

Gross national product (at current market prices; 1983): U.S.$245,590,000,-000 (U.S.$1,890 per capita).

Structure of gross domestic product and labour force				
	1983			
	in value U.S.$'000,000◇	% of total value	labour force△	% of labour force
Agriculture	18,445	8.4	13,115,200	27.1
Mining	1,824	0.8		
Manufacturing	53,083	24.1 }	7,664,600	15.8
Construction	13,136	6.0	4,627,700	9.5
Public utilities	8,462	3.8	...	...
Transportation and communication	16,608	7.5	1,777,700	3.7
Trade	31,691	14.4	5,112,200	10.5
Finance	40,733	18.5	†	†
Pub. admin., defense	18,185	8.2	2,010,500	4.1
Services	18,328	8.3	12,721,300†	26.2†
Other	...	...	1,437,300	3.0
TOTAL	220,495	100.0	48,466,500	100.0§

Budget (1985). Revenue: Cr$88,872,115,000,000 (tax revenue 64.6%, of which property taxes 33.7%, taxes on goods and services 20.9%, customs duties 5.3%; economic services 10.8%; social security contributions 9.7%). Expenditures: Cr$88,872,115,000,000 (transportation 19.0%; regional development 18.5%; administration 11.8%; education and culture 9.3%; manpower 8.4%; defense 5.7%; energy and mineral resources 4.3%; agriculture 3.8%; health 10.9%).
Public debt (external, outstanding; 1983): U.S.$71,985,000,000.
Tourism (1983): receipts from visitors U.S.$1,533,000,000; expenditures by nationals abroad U.S.$839,000,000.

Manufacturing enterprises (1981)				
	no. of enterprises	number of labourers	wages of labourers as a % of avg. of all wages	value added in producer's prices (Cr$'000,000)
Chemicals	2,813	122,739	157.5	1,161,916
Metallurgy	9,032	391,670	113.9	799,797
Mechanical products	7,835	405,690	162.7	784,716
Food products	22,942	419,215	61.3	768,480
Textiles	5,295	380,828	73.8	458,510
Transportation equipment	2,634	196,632	153.6	531,123
Electric and communications equipment	2,752	186,490	120.2	500,213
Combustible fuels (not metals)	15,043	257,892	75.2	402,914
Clothing and footwear	8,966	354,625	55.3	314,594
Paper and paper products	1,377	80,498	102.4	183,214
Publishing and printing	5,004	103,074	117.5	207,294
Lumber	9,085	165,420	58.8	158,575
Plastics	2,145	104,301	89.6	158,452
Pharmaceutical products	443	22,688	113.7	145,835
Furniture	5,812	122,015	64.9	116,353

Production (metric tons except as noted). Agriculture, forestry, fishing (1984): sugarcane 241,518,000, cassava 21,275,000, corn (maize) 21,174,000, soybeans 15,537,000, oranges 13,372,000, rice 9,023,000, bananas 6,968,-000, haricots and other dry beans 2,621,000, potatoes 2,210,000, unginned cotton 1,872,000, wheat 1,830,000, tomatoes 1,791,000, coffee 1,353,000, pineapples 956,000, papayas 470,000, tobacco 415,000, cocoa beans 346,-000, castor beans 225,000, sisal 225,000; livestock (number of live animals) 132,801,000 cattle, 33,000,000 pigs, 17,500,000 sheep, 8,500,000 goats, 5,200,000 horses; roundwood (1983) 220,248,000 cu m; fish catch (1983) 844,500, of which sardines 240,000. Mining and quarrying (value of production in U.S.$'000,000; 1982): petroleum 4,930⊕; iron ore 790⊕; gold 763⊕; natural gas 388; granite 372; limestone 345; coal 273; tin 223⊕; clay 173; bauxite 158; phosphates 144; manganese 131; sand 105; asbestos 57; magnesium 49; diamonds and other precious stones 41. Manufacturing (value of production for export in U.S.$'000,000; 1979): automobiles and trucks including engines 936; steel 331; wood pulp 190; pig iron 163; electronic parts and equipment 153; ships 146; tubes and pipes 144; auto radios 139; vehicle parts and components 126; computers 92; paper and cardboard 82; airplanes 72; earthmovers 58; tires 53; optical instruments 50; tractors including parts 49; microelectronic parts 49; military vehicles 47. Construction (new buildings completed; 1982) residential 20,404,000 sq m; nonresidential 3,513,000 sq m.

Retail trade enterprises (1980)

	no. of enterprises	total no. of employees	annual wage as a % of all wages	annual value of sales (Cr$'000,000)
Food, beverages, and tobacco stores	538,638	963,106	16.5	586,249
Automobile dealers and auto parts stores	25,284	157,285	205.4	581,354
General merchandise stores (including food products)	16,186	274,379	145.5	658,096
Gasoline stations	21,588	140,865	127.6	594,063
Stores selling clothing, fabrics, and textiles	117,595	452,641	102.3	434,793
Hardware stores	37,396	208,783	134.5	407,266
Stores selling radios, televisions, and related electronic goods	26,114	168,431	180.1	353,169
Drugstores	33,631	142,030	118.0	217,781
Agricultural machinery and heavy equipment dealers	6,565	59,244	329.5	204,332
General merchandise stores (excluding food products)	3,367	58,729	239.9	124,359
Book, magazine, and office supply stores	20,192	63,529	123.1	60,327

Energy production (consumption): electricity (kW-hr; 1983) 161,970,000,000 (161,728,000,000); hard coal (metric tons; 1983) 6,737,000 (11,485,000); crude petroleum (barrels; 1984) 172,000,000 (347,000,000); petroleum products (metric tons; 1983) 43,200,000 (37,646,000); natural gas (cu m; 1983) 1,660,383,000 (1,660,383,000); alcohol** (hectolitres; 1984) 93,000,000 (n.a.).
Population economically active (1983): total 50,940,700; participation rate of population over age 10, 54.8% (female 33.0%, unemployed 6.0%).

Price and earnings indexes (1980 = 100)

	1979	1980	1981	1982	1983	1984	1985
Consumer price index	54.7	100.0	205.6	407.0	984.9	2,922.5	6,759.3††
Earnings index‡‡	52.0	100.0	223.1	494.8	1,109.8	2,212.3††	...

Household income and expenditure. Average family size (1983) 4.3; average annual income per household of families having income (1981) Cr$488,-124 (U.S.$5,241); source of income: n.a.; expenditure (1974)§§: housing and household furnishings 33.5%, food 27.1%, clothing and footwear 7.0%, transportation 6.7%, health and hygiene 6.4%, education 2.7%, tobacco 2.0%, recreation 1.9%, other 12.7%.
Land use (1983): forested 67.1%; meadows and pastures 19.4%; agricultural and under permanent cultivation 8.8%; other 4.7%.

Financial aggregates‖ ‖

	1980	1981	1982	1983	1984	1985 (7 mo.)
Exchange rate, Cr$ per:						
U.S. dollar	65.5	127.8	252.7	984.0	3,184.0	6,440.0
£	156.2	243.8	407.9	1,427.4	3,682.2	9,200.8
SDR	83.5	148.8	278.7	1,030.2	3,121.0	6,680.7
International reserves (U.S.$)						
Total (excl. gold; '000,000)	5,769	6,604	3,928	4,355	11,508	10,588¶¶
SDRs ('000,000)	384	452	99	99	1	2
Reserve pos. in IMF ('000,000)	344	264	287	99	99	99
Foreign exchange ('000,000)	5,042	5,888	3,641	4,355	11,507	10,581¶¶
Gold ('000,000 fine troy oz)	1.88	2.20	0.15	0.54	1.47	2.87
% world reserves	0.20	0.23	0.02	0.06	0.16	0.30öö
Interest and prices						
Central bank discount (%)	38.0	49.0	49.0	156.6	187.3öö	...
Gov't. bond yield (%)	...	...	...	...	...	...
Industrial share prices	...	...	...	...	...	...
Balance of payments (U.S.$'000,000)						
Balance of visible trade	−2,823	1,202	780	6,470	13,089	4,293◻◻
Imports, f.o.b.	22,955	22,091	19,395	15,429	13,916	5,146◻◻
Exports, f.o.b.	20,132	23,293	20,175	21,899	27,005	9,439◻◻
Balance of invisibles	−10,152	−13,135	−17,082	−13,414	...	...
Balance of payments, current account	−12,806	−11,751	−16,312	−6,837	...	...

Foreign trade

Balance of trade (current prices)◇◇

	1979	1980	1981	1982	1983	1984
U.S.$'000,000	−4,560	−4,828	−786	−894	+5,098	+11,795
% of total	13.0%	10.7%	1.7%	2.2%	13.2%	27.9%

Imports (1983): U.S.$16,801,000,000 (mineral fuels 57.2%, of which crude petroleum 55.9%, chemicals 8.7%, of which organic chemicals 4.2%, fertilizers 1.0%; food products 7.5%, of which cereals 6.0%, fruits and melons 0.5%; nonelectric machinery 6.9%; transport equipment 3.8%, of which aircraft 1.5%, boats etc. 1.1%, automobiles and other road vehicles 0.9%; basic manufactures 2.4%, of which iron and steel 1.1%; synthetic rubber and plastic materials 2.0%; surgical and photographic instruments 1.4%; paper and paper products 1.2%; animal products 0.7%, of which fish products 0.2%; textiles 0.5%). *Major import sources* (1983): United States 15.4%; Saudi Arabia 14.4%; Iraq 13.4%; West Germany 4.6%; Venezuela 4.3%; Japan 3.6%; China 3.5%; Canada 3.2%; France 3.0%; Iran 2.5%; Argentina 2.2%; Qatar 1.6%; Angola 1.4%.
Exports (1983): U.S.$21,899,000,000 (food and live animals 38.1%, of which coffee 9.9%, feedstuffs for animals 9.0%, legumes and beans 3.0%, cocoa 2.8%, sugar 2.6%, oilseeds and fruits 1.5%, fish 0.6%; mineral products 13.3%, of which mineral fuels 5.3%; basic manufactures 10.0%, of which iron and steel 7.8%; nonelectrical machinery 5.1%; transport equipment 6.6%, of which automobiles and other road vehicles 4.7%; textile yarns and fabrics 4.9%, of which cotton fabric 2.5%; chemicals 4.1%, of which organic chemicals 2.3%; leather footwear 3.3%; plastic and related products 1.9%; timber 1.5%). *Major export destinations* (1983): United States 22.8%; Japan 6.5%; The Netherlands 5.7%; West Germany 5.2%; Italy 4.5%; France 4.1%; United Kingdom 3.3%; U.S.S.R. 3.1%; Spain 2.4%; Belgium–Luxembourg 2.3%; Iraq 1.9%; Saudi Arabia 1.8%; Iran 1.6%; India 1.3%; China 1.2%.

Transport and communications

Transport. Railroads (1983): route length 18,148 mi, 29,207 km; passenger-mi 8,573,000,000, passenger-km 13,797,000,000; short ton-mi cargo 51,200,-000,000, metric ton-km cargo 74,751,000,000. Roads (1983): total length 709,359 mi, 1,141,605 km (paved 7%). Vehicles (1983): passenger cars 10,-077,000; trucks and buses 1,118,000. Merchant marine (1984): vessels (100 gross tons and over) 706; total deadweight tonnage 9,420,000. Air transport (1984)△△: passenger-mi 10,484,254,000, passenger-km 16,872,803,000; short ton-mi cargo 568,216,000, metric ton-km cargo 829,580,000; airports (1984) with scheduled flights 126.
Communications. Daily newspapers (1983): total number 265; total circulation 5,722,000; circulation per 1,000 population 44. Radio (1984): total number of receivers 25,000,000 (1 per 5.3 persons). Television (1984): total number of receivers 23,000,000 (1 per 5.8 persons). Telephones (1983): 9,309,000 (1 per 14 persons).

Education and health

Education (1983)

	schools	teachers	students	student/ teacher ratio
Primary (age 7–14)	190,917	967,975	24,555,789	25.4
Secondary (age 15–17)	8,853	180,354	2,944,097	16.3
Higher	868	122,697	1,438,992	11.7

Literacy (1983): total population over age 14 literate 61,297,000 (78.1%); males literate 30,474,000 (79.6%); females literate 30,823,000 (76.6%).
Health: physicians (1980) 97,100 (1 per 1,246 persons); hospital beds (1982) 530,501 (1 per 239 persons); infant mortality rate per 1,000 live births (1980–85) 71.0.
Food (1980–82): daily per capita caloric intake 2,574 (vegetable products 86%, animal products 14%); 108% of FAO recommended minimum requirement.

Military

Total active duty personnel (1984): 274,000 (army 66.8%, navy 16.8%, air force 16.4%). *Military expenditure as percent of GNP* (1983): 0.7% (world 6.1%); per capita expenditure U.S.$14.

*Total area, including 1,035 sq mi (2,680 sq km) in dispute between the states of Amazonas and Pará and 1,009 sq mi (2,614 sq km) in dispute between Ceará and Piauí. Land area excluding inland water is 3,265,075 sq mi (8,456,508 sq km). †Includes the islands of Trinidade and Martin Vaz. ‡Includes Rocas atoll and the rocks of São Pedro and São Paulo. §Detail does not add to total given because of rounding. ‖ Spiritist Catholics are actively and regularly involved in the practice of medium religions; about 60,000,000 Roman Catholics defer to spiritist dogma and participate in organized spiritism occasionally. ¶Evangelical Catholics are persons who are officially regarded as Roman Catholic, but who are affiliated to Protestant churches. ♀Non-Christian followers of Afro-Brazilian syncretistic religions ("low spiritism"). ♂Non-Christian followers of Kardecism ("high spiritism"). ◻1982 election for state governors, federal senators, and federal deputies. Detail cited here is based on the electoral returns for federal deputies. ◇1982 prices. △Age 10 and over. †Services include finance. ⊕1984. **Fuel produced from sugarcane used in the operation of locally produced automobiles as either hydrous alcohol or gasohol. ††Average of first two quarters. ‡‡Manufacturing sector only. §§State of Rio de Janeiro only. ‖ ‖ Exchange rates, international reserves, and interest and prices are all based on end of year figures. ¶¶End of April. ♀♀Less than 0.5. ööEnd of June. ◻◻First five months only. ◇◇Imports c.i.f. (cost, insurance, and freight); exports f.o.b. (free on board). △△Cruzeiro do Sul, TransBrasil, Varig, and Vasp airlines only.

Brunei

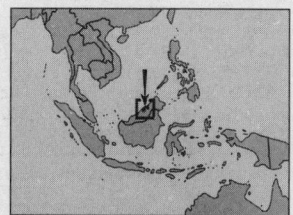

Official name: Negara Brunei Darussalam (State of Brunei, Abode of Peace).
Form of government: monarchy.
Chief of state: Sultan.
Head of government: Prime Minister.
Capital: Bandar Seri Begawan.
Official language: Malay.
Official religion: Islām.
Monetary unit: 1 Brunei dollar (Br$) = 100 cents; valuation (Oct. 14, 1985) 1 U.S.$ = Br$2.13; 1 £ = Br$3.06.

Area and population

Districts	Capitals	area sq mi	area sq km	population 1982 estimate
Belait	Kuala Belait	1,053	2,727	52,763
Brunei and Muara	Bandar Seri Begawan	220	570	119,139
Temburong	Bangar	503	1,303	6,443
Tutong	Tutong	450	1,165	22,045
TOTAL		2,226	5,765	200,390

Demography

Population (1985): 224,000.
Density (1985): persons per sq mi 100.6, persons per sq km 38.9.
Urban–rural (1981): urban 80.8%; rural 19.2%.
Sex distribution (1982): male 53.39%; female 46.61%.
Age breakdown (1982): under 15, 38.1%; 15–29, 32.1%; 30–44, 17.3%; 45–59, 8.1%; 60–69, 2.6%; 70 and over, 1.8%.
Population projection: (1990) 258,000; (2000) 341,000.
Doubling time: 20 years.
Ethnic composition (1983): Malay 65.2%; Chinese 20.0%; other indigenous 8.1%; other 6.7%.
Religious affiliation (1982): Muslim 63.4%; Buddhist 14.0%; Christian 9.7%; other 12.9%.
Major cities (1981): Bandar Seri Begawan 63,868; Seria 23,511; Kuala Belait 19,281.

Vital statistics

Birth rate per 1,000 population (1983): 27.9 (world avg. 29.0); (1978) legitimate 99.3%; illegitimate 0.7%.
Death rate per 1,000 population (1983): 3.3 (world avg. 11.0).
Natural increase rate per 1,000 population (1983): 24.6 (world avg. 18.0).
Total fertility rate (avg. births per childbearing woman): n.a.
Marriage rate per 1,000 population (1982): 6.7.
Divorce rate per 1,000 population (1982): 0.9*.
Life expectancy at birth (1981): male 70.1 years; female 72.7 years.
Major causes of death per 100,000 population (1981): diseases of the circulatory system 41; accidents, poisoning, and violence 36; malignant neoplasms (cancers) 25; diseases of the respiratory system 16; infectious and parasitic diseases 5.

National economy

Budget (1984). Revenue: Br$6,500,000,000 (largely from petroleum profits). Expenditures: Br$2,650,000,000 (development fund 35.8%, defense 12.8%, public works 8.7%, education 8.2%).
Public debt (external, outstanding; 1983): U.S.$10,000,000.
Tourism (1983): number of visitors 5,347.
Production (metric tons except as noted). Agriculture, forestry, fishing (1984): rice 6,000, roots and tubers 5,000, vegetables and melons 4,000, bananas 4,000, pineapples 4,000, cassava 4,000, oranges 1,000, eggs 2,320; livestock (number of live animals) 15,000 pigs, 15,000 buffaloes, 4,000 cattle, 2,000 goats, 1,000,000 chickens; roundwood (1983) 296,000 cu m; fish catch (1983) 3,105. Mining and quarrying (1983): other than petroleum and natural gas (see below), none except sand and gravel for construction. Manufacturing (1983): gasoline 80,600; distillate fuel oils 47,600; liquefied natural gas 29,400, naphtha 6,800. Construction (number of buildings completed; 1981): residential 12, nonresidential, 60. Energy production (consumption): electricity (kW-hr; 1983) 728,000,000 (728,000,000); coal, none (none); crude petroleum (barrels; 1983) 59,234,000 (n.a.); petroleum products (metric tons; 1983) 644,000 (699,000); natural gas (cu m; 1983) 7,508,000,000 (1,045,000,000).
Population economically active (1981): total 70,690; participation rate of total population 36.4% (female 23.8%, unemployed 3.6%).

Price and earnings indexes (1977 = 100)♀

	1976	1977	1978	1979	1980	1981	1982
Consumer price index	...	100.0	...	...	118.2	129.0	137.2
Monthly earnings index	92.2	100.0	113.3	114.8	133.0	143.0	...

Household income and expenditure. Average household size (1971) 5.8.; income per household: n.a.; source of income: n.a.; expenditure (1981): food 45.1%; transportation and communication 17.2%; recreation, education, and cultural services 8.9%; household furnishings 8.3%; clothing and footwear 6.1%; rent and utilities 5.0%.
Gross national product (at current market prices; 1983): U.S.$4,420,000,000 (U.S.$21,140 per capita).

Structure of gross domestic product and labour force

	1982 in value Br$'000,000	1982 % of total value	1981 labour force	1981 % of labour force
Agriculture	75.0	0.9	3,440	4.9
Mining	5,963.1	67.2	3,860	5.5
Manufacturing	879.8	9.9	2,780	3.9
Construction	268.5	3.0	12,650	17.9
Public utilities	13.1	0.2	1,960	2.8
Transportation and communication	63.9	0.7	4,530	6.4
Trade	868.3	9.8	7,360	10.4
Finance	282.2	3.2	2,010	2.8
Services	546.0	6.2	29,280	41.4
Other	−91.4†	−1.0	2,820‡	4.0‡
TOTAL	8,868.5§	100.0 ‖	70,690	100.0

Land use (1983): forested 78.7%; meadows and pastures 1.1%; agricultural and under permanent cultivation 1.3%; other 18.9%.

Foreign trade

Balance of trade (current prices)

	1978	1979	1980	1981	1982	1983
Br$'000,000	+3,556	+4,934	+8,622	+7,327	+6,582	+5,629
% of total	73.6%	74.1%	77.8%	74.3%	67.7%	64.6%

Imports (1983): Br$1,542,200,000 (machinery and transport equipment 38.1%, basic manufactures 21.0%, food and live animals 12.3%, miscellaneous manufactured articles 9.3%, chemicals 7.6%, beverages and tobacco 4.2%, mineral fuels and lubricants 1.4%, animal and vegetable oils and fats 0.5%). *Major import sources:* Singapore 22.8%; United States 19.5%; Japan 19.2%; United Kingdom 7.9%; Malaysia 3.8%¶; Australia 2.7%; West Germany 2.3%; Thailand 2.3%.
Exports (1983): Br$7,170,000,000 (crude petroleum 55.7%, natural gas 40.3%, petroleum products 2.8%, all other products 1.2%). *Major export destinations:* Japan 67.7%; United States 8.1%; South Korea 7.5%; Singapore 6.2%; Thailand 4.6%; Taiwan 2.8%.

Transport and communications

Transport. Railroads♀ (1983): length 12 mi, 19 km. Roads (1984): total length 766 mi, 1,233 km (paved 35%). Vehicles (1983): passenger cars 63,177; trucks and buses 9,603. Merchant marine (1984): vessels (100 gross tons and over) 2; total deadweight tonnage 961. Air transport (1982): passenger arrivals 171,390, passenger departures 159,075; cargo loaded 543 metric tons, cargo unloaded 6,228 metric tons; airport (1985) with scheduled flights 1. Marine transport (1983): cargo loaded 19,157,700 metric tons, cargo unloaded 697,400 metric tons.
Communications. Daily newspapers (1984): none. Radio (1984): total number of receivers 52,000 (1 per 4 persons). Television (1984): total number of receivers 31,000 (1 per 7 persons). Telephones (1982): 21,928 (1 per 9 persons).

Education and health

Education (1982–83)

	schools	teachers	students	student/ teacher ratio
Primary (age 5–11)	177	1,922	31,682	16.5
Secondary (age 12–20)	27	1,396	17,698	12.7
Voc., teacher tr.	6	252	1,324	5.3
Higherδ	1	57	143	2.5

Educational attainment (1981). Percent of adult population over age 25 having: no formal schooling 32.2%; primary education 28.3%; secondary 30.1%; postsecondary and higher 9.4%. *Literacy* (1981): total population over age 15 literate 92,253 (77.8%); males literate 55,179 (85.2%); females literate 37,074 (69.0%).
Health (1981): physicians 97 (1 per 2,000 persons); hospital beds 615 (1 per 315 persons); infant mortality rate per 1,000 live births (1983) 11.5.
Food (1980–82): daily per capita caloric intake 2,558 (vegetable products 82%, animal products 18%); 116% of FAO recommended minimum requirement.

Military

Total active duty personnel (1984): 3,950□ (army 88.6%, navy 8.9%, air force 2.5%). *Military expenditure as percent of GNP* (1982): 4.7% (world 6.0%); per capita expenditure U.S.$810.

*For Muslim population only. †Imputed bank service charge. ‡Includes unemployed. §At current prices. ‖ Detail does not add to total because of rounding. ¶Peninsular Malaysia only. ♀For industrial purposes only. δ1980–81. □All services form part of the army.

Bulgaria

Official name: Narodna Republika Bŭlgaria (People's Republic of Bulgaria).
Form of government: unitary single-party people's republic with one legislative house (National Assembly [400]).
Chief of state: Chairman of the State Council (president).
Head of government: Chairman of the Council of Ministers (premier).
Capital: Sofia.
Official language: Bulgarian.
Official religion: none.
Monetary unit: 1 lev (leva) = 100 stotinki; valuation (Oct. 21, 1985) 1 lev = U.S.$1.01; 1 £ = 1.43 leva.

Area and population		area		population
				1982
Provinces	**Capitals**	sq mi	sq km	estimate
Blagoevgrad	Blagoevgrad	2,496	6,464	337,615
Burgas	Burgas	2,936	7,605	435,274
Gabrovo	Gabrovo	798	2,068	177,512
Khaskovo	Khaskovo	1,547	4,008	295,996
Kŭrdzhali	Kŭrdzhali	1,552	4,020	285,538
Kyustendil	Kyustendil	1,159	3,002	198,571
Lovech	Lovech	1,594	4,128	211,398
Mikhaylovgrad	Mikhaylovgrad	1,401	3,629	233,521
Pazardzhik	Pazardzhik	1,691	4,379	322,206
Pernik	Pernik	909	2,355	175,042
Pleven	Pleven	1,685	4,364	373,358
Plovdiv	Plovdiv	2,167	5,612	753,093
Razgrad	Razgrad	1,022	2,646	193,240
Ruse	Ruse	1,002	2,595	297,466
Shumen	Shumen	1,303	3,374	251,626
Silistra	Silistra	1,104	2,859	173,943
Sliven	Sliven	1,397	3,618	235,635
Smolyan	Smolyan	1,358	3,518	174,438
Sofiya	Sofia	2,822	7,310	308,883
Stara Zagora	Stara Zagora	1,935	5,012	411,165
Tolbukhin	Tolbukhin	1,821	4,716	251,993
Tŭrgovishte	Tŭrgovishte	1,063	2,754	172,424
Varna	Varna	1,471	3,810	467,265
Veliko Tŭrnovo	Veliko Tŭrnovo	1,822	4,719	346,857
Vidin	Vidin	1,184	3,066	169,293
Vratsa	Vratsa	1,547	4,006	291,303
Yambol	Yambol	1,607	4,162	205,324
City Commune				
Sofia		430	1,113	1,155,602
TOTAL		42,823	110,912	8,905,581

Demography

Population (1985): 8,979,000.
Density (1985): persons per sq mi 209.7, persons per sq km 81.0.
Urban–rural (1984): urban 65.0%; rural 35.0%.
Sex distribution (1983): male 49.73%; female 50.27%.
Age breakdown (1982): under 15, 22.1%; 15–29, 21.1%; 30–44, 20.3%; 45–59, 20.3%; 60–74, 12.1%; 75 and over, 4.1%.
Population projection: (1990) 9,413,000; (2000) 9,698,000.
Doubling time: not applicable; population stable.
Ethnic composition (1980): Bulgarian 88.2%; Turkish 8.5%; other 3.3%.
Religious affiliation (1982): Eastern Orthodox 26.7%; Muslim 7.5%; Protestant 0.7%; Roman Catholic 0.5%; other 0.1%; atheist 64.5%.
Major cities (1983): Sofia 1,094,000*; Plovdiv 367,195; Varna 295,038; Ruse 178,920; Burgas 178,239.

Vital statistics

Birth rate per 1,000 population (1984): 13.6 (world avg. 29.0); (1980) legitimate 89.1%; illegitimate 10.9%.
Death rate per 1,000 population (1984): 11.4 (world avg. 11.0).
Natural increase rate per 1,000 population (1984): 2.2 (world avg. 18.0).
Total fertility rate (avg. births per childbearing woman; 1980): 2.2.
Marriage rate per 1,000 population (1984): 7.5.
Divorce rate per 1,000 population (1984): 1.6.
Life expectancy at birth (1984): male 68.0 years; female 74.0 years.
Major causes of death per 100,000 population (1981): diseases of the circulatory system 615.6; malignant neoplasms (cancers) 152.3.

National economy

Budget (1983). Revenue: 16,800,000,000 leva (turnover tax, taxes from state enterprises, and income tax 64.8%). Expenditures: 16,700,000,000 leva (economy 51.2%, education and health 18.1%, social security 17.4%).
Public debt (external, outstanding; 1981): U.S.$2,975,000,000.
Tourism (1983): number of tourists 5,771,163; receipts from visitors U.S.$269,000,000†; expenditures by nationals abroad, n.a.
Production (metric tons except as noted). Agriculture, forestry, fishing (1984): wheat 3,600,000, corn (maize) 3,000,000, vegetables 1,963,000, barley 1,800,000, sugar beets 1,300,000; livestock (number of live animals) 1,814,000 cattle, 10,978,000 sheep, 3,769,000 pigs; roundwood 3,800,000 cu m‡; fish catch 151,000‡. Mining and quarrying (1983): iron ore 1,803,000; lead 96,000; copper 70,000; zinc 65,000; manganese 43,000. Manufacturing (1983): cement 5,600,000; pig iron and crude steel 4,480,000; fertilizers 687,000; wood pulp and paper 516,000; cotton fabrics 371,000,000 m; mo-

tor vehicles 17,707 units; wine 3,769,000 hectolitres. Construction (1984): residential 4,483,000 sq m. Energy production (consumption): electricity (kW-hr; 1983) 42,642,000,000 (47,955,000,000); coal (metric tons; 1983) 32,545,000 (39,632,000); crude petroleum (barrels; 1983) 9,675,000 (93,-824,000); petroleum products (metric tons; 1983) 11,390,000 (13,310,000); natural gas (cu m; 1983) 112,820,000 (2,164,000,000).
Gross national product (1982): U.S.$26,000,000,000 (U.S.$2,920 per capita).

Structure of net material product and labour force				
	1983			
	in value '000,000 leva	% of total value	labour force	% of labour force
Agriculture	3,945.0	16.8	895,000	22.3
Mining				
Manufacturing	13,265.0	56.5	1,377,170	34.3
Public utilities			50,400	1.3
Construction	2,270.0	9.7	350,000	8.7
Transportation and communication	1,845.0	7.8	259,000	6.4
Trade	1,529.0	6.5	354,000	8.8
Finance	—	—		
Pub. admin., defense	—	—	731,000	18.2
Services	—	—		
Other	625.0§	2.7		
TOTAL	23,479.0 ‖	100.0	4,017,000	100.0

Population economically active (1984): total 4,142,000; participation rate of population over age 15, 59.5% (female 49.3%, unemployed, n.a.).

Price and earnings indexes (1970 = 100)							
	1977	1978	1979	1980	1981	1982	1983
Consumer price index	101.6	103.2	107.8	122.9	123.5	123.7	125.3
Monthly earnings index	121.8	126.6	133.1	155.6	163.7	167.7	170.1

Household income and expenditure. Average household size (1982) 3.3; income per household 5,092 leva (U.S.$5,249); sources of income: wages and salaries 62.9%, social welfare 20.0%, other 17.1%; expenditure (1981): food 36.5%, clothing and footwear 8.6%, housing 6.7%, transportation 5.4%.
Land use (1983): forested 34.9%; meadows and pastures 18.4%; agricultural and under permanent cultivation 37.5%; other 9.2%.

Foreign trade

Balance of trade (current prices)					
	1978	1979	1980	1981	1982	1983
'000,000 leva	−151.3	+303.4	+618.6	−97.6	−121.3	−148.5
% of total	1.1%	2.0%	3.5%	0.5%	0.6%	0.6%

Imports (1983): 11,966,000,000 leva (fuels, mineral raw materials, and metals 46.3%; machinery and equipment 34.2%; of which transport equipment 14.5%; power and electrical machinery 3.0%, tractors and agricultural machinery 2.4%; chemical fertilizers and rubber 5.2%; crop and livestock crude material 4.7%). *Major import sources:* U.S.S.R. 58.1%; East Germany 5.7%; Poland 4.3%; Czechoslovakia 4.1%; West Germany 3.9%.
Exports (1983): 11,817,500,000 leva (machinery and equipment 48.4%, of which transport equipment 12.0%; fuels, mineral raw materials, and metals 11.4%; food, beverages, and tobacco 16.4%). *Major export destinations:* U.S.S.R. 56.0%; East Germany 5.5%; Libya 4.0%; Czechoslovakia 4.0%.

Transport and communications

Transport. Railroads (1984): length 4,379 mi, 7,626 km; passenger-km 8,233,000,000; metric ton-km cargo 18,060,000,000. Roads (1984): total length 23,384 mi, 37,633 km (paved 91%). Vehicles (1983): passenger cars 937,579; trucks and buses 519,200. Merchant marine (1984): vessels (100 gross tons and over) 197; total deadweight tonnage 1,840,794. Air transport (1984): passenger-km 2,870,000,000; metric ton-km cargo 51,800,000; airports (1985) 13.
Communications. Daily newspapers (1984): total number 14; total circulation 2,221,000‡; circulation per 1,000 population 249.4. Radio (1984): receivers 2,056,000 (1 per 4.3 persons). Television (1984): receivers 1,691,-000 (1 per 5.3 persons). Telephones (1984): 1,655,000 (1 per 5.4 persons).

Education and health

Education (1983-84)				
	schools	teachers	students	student/ teacher ratio
Primary and secondary (age 7–17)	3,535	71,300	1,206,000	16.9
Voc., teacher tr.	511	18,320	212,900	11.6
Higher	33	13,400	68,500	5.1

Educational attainment¶ (1983): Percent of adult population having: 2-year college degree 15.6%; 4-year college degree 7.5%. *Literacy* (1980): total population over age 15 literate 95.5%.
Health (1984): physicians 24,000 (1 per 373 persons); hospital beds 81,500 (1 per 110 persons); infant mortality rate per 1,000 live births 16.8.
Food (1980–82): daily per capita caloric intake 3,663 (vegetable products 78%, animal products 22%); 146% of FAO recommended minimum.

Military

Total active duty personnel (1984): 147,300 (army 71.3%, navy 5.8%, air force 22.9%). *Military expenditure as percent of GNP* (1983): 8.1% (world 6.1%); per capita expenditure U.S.$461.

*1984. †1980. ‡1983. §Includes other material activities and cost of nonmaterial services. ‖At current prices. ¶In labour force.

Burkina Faso*

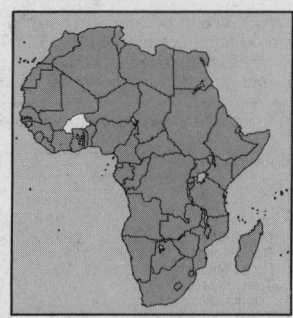

Official name: Burkina Faso
(Burkina Faso).
Form of government: military
government†.
Head of state and government:
Chairman of the National
Revolutionary Council.
Capital: Ouagadougou.
Official language: French.
Official religion: none.
Monetary unit: 1 CFA franc
(CFAF) = 100 centimes; valuation
(Oct. 21, 1985) 1 U.S.$ = CFAF402.02;
1 £ = CFAF576.50.

Area and population

Provinces	Capitals	area‡ sq mi	area‡ sq km	population 1985 estimate§
Bam	Kongoussi	1,551	4,017	175,100
Bougouriba	Diébougou	2,736	7,087	213,000
Boulgou	Tenkodogo	3,722	9,639	358,600
Burkina	Koudougou	3,592	9,303	582,000
Comoé	Banfora	7,102	18,393	210,800
Ganzourgou	Zorgho	1,578	4,087	149,800
Gnagna	Bogandé	2,528	6,548	147,600
Gourma	Fada Ngourma	11,067	28,664	231,100
Houet	Bobo Dioulasso	6,360	16,472	370,800
Kénédougou	Orodara	3,207	8,307	118,600
Kossi	Nouna	5,088	13,177	244,300
Nahouri	Pô	1,484	3,843	88,300
Namentenga	Boulsa	3,545	9,182	329,800
Nouhoun	Dédougou	4,032	10,442	240,300
Oubritenga	Ouagadougou	4,315	11,175	787,000
Passoré	Yako	1,575	4,078	262,500
Poni	Gaoua	4,000	10,361	216,600
Sahel	Dori	9,081	23,519	265,400
Sanmatenga	Kaya	3,557	9,213	340,900
Sissili	Léo	5,303	13,736	144,600
Soum	Djibo	5,154	13,350	160,000
Sourou	Tougan	3,663	9,487	279,200
Tapoa	Diapaga	5,707	14,780	110,600
Yatenga	Ouahigouya	4,746	12,293	637,000
Zoundwéogo	Manga	1,099	2,847	110,000
TOTAL		105,869	274,200	6,773,900

Demography

Population (1985): 6,827,800.
Density (1985): persons per sq mi 64.5, persons per sq km 24.9.
Urban–rural (1980): urban 8.5%; rural 91.5%.
Sex distribution (1985): male 49.46%; female 50.54%.
Age breakdown (1980): under 15, 44.5%; 15–29, 26.0%; 30–44, 15.6%; 45–59, 9.1%; 60–74, 4.1%; 75 and over, 0.7%.
Population projection: (1990) 7,400,000; (2000) 8,600,000.
Doubling time: 45 years.
Ethnic composition (1980): Mossi 53.6%; Lobi 6.9%; Bobo 6.9%; Fulani 5.6%; Gurunsi 5.1%; Tuareg 4.1%; Gurma 4.0%; other 13.8%.
Religious affiliation (1980): tribal religionist 44.8%; Muslim 43.0%; Christian 12.2%, of which Roman Catholic 9.8%, Protestant 2.4%.
Major cities (1985): Ouagadougou 359,801; Bobo Dioulasso 202,807; Koudougou 59,644; Ouahigouya 41,595.

Vital statistics

Birth rate per 1,000 population (1981): 47.8 (world avg. 29.0); legitimate, n.a.; illegitimate, n.a.
Death rate per 1,000 population (1981): 21.5 (world avg. 11.0).
Natural increase rate per 1,000 population (1981): 26.3 (world avg. 18.0).
Total fertility rate (avg. births per childbearing woman; 1981): 6.5.
Marriage rate per 1,000 population (1975): 9.4.
Divorce rate per 1,000 population (1975): 1.3.
Life expectancy at birth (1981): male 43.2 years; female 45.0 years.
Major diseases (1980): bilharziasis, kwashiorkor, malaria, measles, and onchocerciasis ("river blindness").

National economy

Budget (1984). Revenue: CFAF57,600,000,000 (indirect taxes 66.1%, of which customs duties 40.4%; direct taxes 19.6%; other 14.3%). *Expenditures:* CFAF62,700,000,000 (general public services 26.7% ‖; defense 17.5% ‖; education 16.8% ‖; debt payment 14.2% ‖; investment 7.2% ‖).
Public debt (external, outstanding; 1983): U.S.$398,400,000.
Tourism (1983): receipts from visitors U.S.$4,000,000; expenditures by nationals abroad, n.a.
Production (metric tons except as noted). Agriculture, forestry, fishing (1984): sorghum and millet 1,019,618, sugarcane 320,000, pulses 155,600, roots and tubers 119,000, seed cotton 79,287, peanuts (groundnuts) 78,000, corn (maize) 77,599, karite 66,675, sweet potatoes 43,000, rice 40,996, sesame 3,717; livestock (number of live animals; 1983) 2,950,000 cattle, 2,500,000 goats, 2,000,000 sheep, 14,000,000 chickens; roundwood 7,149,000 cu m ‖; fish catch 7,000 ‖. Mining and quarrying (1983): phosphates 3,000. Manufacturing (1983): flour 21,009; soap 10,006; cotton yarn 373; motorcycles and scooters 4,700 units; footwear 1,313,000 pairs; beer 701,447 hectolitres; soft drinks 139,558 hectolitres. Construction: n.a. Energy production (consumption): electricity (kW-hr; 1984) 121,217,000 (107,136,000); coal, none (n.a.); crude petroleum, none (n.a.); petroleum products (metric tons; 1983) 140,000 (140,000); natural gas, none (n.a.).

Gross national product (at current market prices; 1983): U.S.$1,210,000,000 (U.S.$210 per capita).

Structure of gross domestic product and labour force

	1982 in value CFAF'000,000	% of total value	labour force	% of labour force
Agriculture	143,030.2	41.2	2,763,000	82.0
Mining	27.5	¶		
Manufacturing‡	43,010.7	12.4		
Construction	13,985.1	4.0	438,000	13.0
Public utilities	4,876.4	1.4		
Transportation and communication	24,460.6	7.0		
Trade	40,599.8	11.7		
Pub. admin., defense	⌀	⌀	168,000	5.0
Services	56,516.9⌀	16.3⌀		
Other	20,481.5ō	5.9ō	...	...
TOTAL	346,988.7□	100.0◇	3,369,000	100.0

Population economically active: total (1982) 3,369,000; participation rate of total population 49.7% (female 46.1%, unemployed, n.a.).

Price and earnings indexes (1980 = 100)

	1978	1979	1980	1981	1982	1983	1984
Consumer price index	77.5	89.1	100.0	107.6	120.5	130.6	133.4
Hourly earnings index	80.0	100.0	100.0	126.7	126.7	126.7	126.7

Household income and expenditure. Average household size (1984) 4.9; average annual income per household CFAF303,000 (U.S.$640); source of income: n.a.; expenditure: (1984): food 34.6%; transportation and communication 18.6%; electricity (light) and fuel 13.7%; alcohol and beverages 9.0%; health 5.2%; housing 5.1%.
Land use (1983): forested 25.6%; meadows and pastures 36.5%; agricultural and under permanent cultivation 9.6%; other 28.3%.

Foreign trade

Balance of trade (current prices)

	1978	1979	1980	1981	1982	1983
CFAF'000,000	−41,475	−47,678	−56,548	−71,524	−95,599	−87,864
% of total	68.4%	67.9%	59.7%	64.2%	72.5%	66.9%

Imports (1983): CFAF109,576,100,000 (machines and transport equipment 23.4%, of which transport equipment 10.9%; electrical machinery 4.8%; manufactured goods 20.5%; petroleum products 17.5%; chemicals 10.3%; cereals 7.3%; preserved dairy products 3.7%; tobacco 3.3%; cement 2.7%). *Major import sources:* France 27.9%; Ivory Coast 23.6%; United States 9.4%; The Netherlands 5.1%; Japan 4.3%; West Germany 3.4%; China 2.2%.
Exports (1983): CFAF21,712,000,000 (raw cotton 54.7%; karite nuts 11.8%; manufactured goods 6.3%; live animals 5.9%; vegetables 2.6%). *Major export destinations:* Taiwan 27.0%; France 11.9%; China 11.4%; Ivory Coast 8.9%; United Kingdom 7.5%; Mali 5.2%; Japan 4.3%; Togo 2.6%.

Transport and communications

Transport. Railroads (1982)△: length 321 mi, 517 km; passenger-mi 532,000,000, passenger-km 856,000,000; short ton-mi cargo 457,000,000, metric ton-km cargo 668,000,000. Roads (1984): total length 5,395 mi, 8,684 km (paved 23%). Vehicles (1983): passenger cars 21,182; trucks and buses 6,647. Merchant marine: none. Air transport (1980): passenger-mi 112,000,000, passenger-km 180,000,000; short ton-mi cargo 12,300,000, metric ton-mi cargo 18,000,000; airports (1985) 9.
Communications. Daily newspapers (1984): total number 6; total circulation, n.a. Radio (1984): total number of receivers 116,000 (1 per 59 persons). Television (1984): total number of receivers 20,000 (1 per 341 persons). Telephones (1981): 10,625 (1 per 588 persons).

Education and health

Education (1984)

	schools	teachers	students	student/ teacher ratio
Primary	1,037	4,796	276,732	57.7
Secondary	79	1,553	43,001	27.7
Vocational	27	484	4,492	9.3
Higher	1	216	3,870	17.9

Educational attainment, n.a. *Literacy* (1975): total population literate 267,500 (9.1%); males literate 217,000 (15.1%); females literate 50,500 (3.2%).
Health: physicians (1981) 127 (1 per 49,220 persons); hospital beds (1979) 3,444 (1 per 1,755 persons); infant mortality rate per 1,000 live births (1984) 149.0.
Food (1980–82): daily per capita caloric intake 1,922 (vegetable products 95%, animal products 5%); 82% of FAO recommended minimum requirement.

Military

Total active duty personnel (1984): 3,775 (army 98.0%; navy, none; air force 2.0%). *Military expenditure as percent of GNP* (1983): 2.8% (world 6.1%); per capita expenditure U.S.$4.

*Known as Upper Volta before Aug. 4, 1984. †The functions of the legislative house (National Assembly; [57]) and all political parties have been suspended since 1980. ‡Total land area is 105,792 sq mi (274,000 sq km) and is shown for the provinces; the total area (both land and water) is shown in the grand total. §Beginning of the year. ‖1983. ¶Less than 0.1%. ⌀Public administration and defense are included with services. ōImport duties. ◇At current prices. □Detail does not add to total given because of rounding. △Passenger-mi and short ton-mi cargo figures are based on traffic between Abidjan (Ivory Coast) and Ouagadougou.

Burma

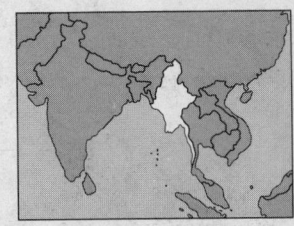

Official name: Pyeidaungzu Socialist Thammada Myanma Naingngandaw (Socialist Republic of the Union of Burma).
Form of government: single-party people's republic with one legislative house (People's Assembly [475]).
Chief of state: President (Chairman).
Head of government: Prime Minister.
Capital: Rangoon.
Official language: Burmese.
Official religion: none.
Monetary unit: 1 Burmese kyat (K) = 100 pyas; valuation (Oct. 21, 1985) 1 U.S.$ = K7.67; 1 £ = K11.00.

Area and population

| | | area | | population |
| | | sq mi | sq km | 1983 census |
Divisions	Capitals			
Irrawaddy	Bassein	13,567	35,138	4,991,057
Magwe	Magwe	17,305	44,820	3,241,103
Mandalay	Mandalay	14,295	37,024	4,580,923
Pegu	Pegu	15,214	39,404	3,800,240
Rangoon	Rangoon	3,927	10,171	3,973,782
Sagaing	Sagaing	36,535	94,625	3,855,991
Tenasserim	Tavoy	16,735	43,343	917,628
States				
Chin	Falam	13,907	36,019	368,985
Kachin	Myitkyinā	34,379	89,041	903,982
Karen	Pa-an	11,731	30,383	1,057,505
Kayah	Loi-kaw	4,530	11,733	168,355
Mon	Moulmein	4,748	12,297	1,682,041
Rakhine (Arakan)	Sittwe (Akyab)	14,200	25,778	2,045,891
Shan	Taunggyi	60,155	155,801	3,718,706
TOTAL		261,228	676,577	35,306,189

Demography

Population (1985): 37,686,000.
Density (1985): persons per sq mi 144.3, persons per sq km 55.7.
Urban-rural (1983): urban 24.0%; rural 76.0%.
Sex distribution (1983): male 49.59%; female 50.41%.
Age breakdown (1985): under 15, 41.2%; 15–29, 27.2%; 30–44, 15.3%; 45–59, 10.3%; 60–74, 5.0%; 75 and over, 1.0%.
Population projection: (1990) 44,548,000; (2000) 49,749,000.
Doubling time: 35 years.
Ethnic composition (1983): Burman 68.0%; Shan 6.9%; Karen 6.6%; Rakhine 4.4%; other 14.1%..
Religious affiliation (1980): Buddhist 87.2%; Christian 5.6%; Muslim 3.6%; tribal religions 1.9%; other 1.7%.
Major cities (1983): Rangoon 2,458,712; Mandalay 532,895; Moulmein 219,991; Pegu 150,447; Bassein 144,092.

Vital statistics

Birth rate per 1,000 population (1980–85): 37.9 (world avg. 29.0).
Death rate per 1,000 population (1980–85): 12.7 (world avg. 11.0).
Natural increase rate per 1,000 population (1980–85): 25.2 (world avg. 18.0).
Total fertility rate (avg. births per childbearing woman; 1980–85): 5.3.
Marriage rate per 1,000 population, n.a.
Divorce rate per 1,000 population, n.a.
Life expectancy at birth (1980–85): male 53.4 years; female 56.7 years.
Major causes of death per 100,000 population (1978): pneumonia 16.1; heart diseases 10.5; enteritis and other diarrheal diseases 10.0; tuberculosis 9.4; malignant neoplasms (cancers) 6.5; cerebrovascular disease 4.1; malaria 3.5.

National economy

Budget (1981–82). Revenue: K7,572,000,000 (taxes on goods and services 37.6%; property income 29.3%; import duties 16.1%; sales and excise taxes 10.9%; grants 3.6%; corporate and individual income taxes 2.6%). Expenditures: K7,046,000,000 (agriculture, forestry, and fishing 26.1%; defense 21.7%; general public services 14.2%; education 10.1%; health 6.1%; social security and welfare 5.8%).
Public debt (external, outstanding; 1983): U.S.$2,226,100,000.
Tourism (1982): receipts from visitors U.S.$13,000,000; expenditures by nationals abroad U.S.$3,000,000.
Production (metric tons except as noted). Agriculture, forestry, fishing (1984): rice 14,500,000, sugarcane 3,842,000, vegetables and melons 2,022,000, fruits 1,083,000, peanuts (groundnuts) 601,000, pulses 573,000 (of which dry beans 329,000, chick peas 183,000), plantains 438,000, corn (maize) 360,000, roots and tubers 242,000 (of which potatoes 155,000), sesame seed 216,000, wheat 191,000, seed cotton 108,000, millet 88,000, tobacco leaves 62,000, sunflower seed 60,000, jute 55,000, natural rubber 16,000; livestock (number of live animals) 9,550,000 cattle, 2,750,000 pigs, 2,100,000 water buffalo, 1,000,000 goats, 32,000,000 chickens; roundwood 19,254,000 cu m*, of which teak 168,500; fish catch 585,800*, of which marine fishing areas 442,930. Mining and quarrying (by metal content except as noted; 1983): lead 17,000; zinc 4,537; copper 4,200; tin 1,642; tungsten 930; jadeite 29,109 kg; silver 558,000 troy oz. Manufacturing (1983–84): cement 370,000; fertilizer 150,000; sugar 44,500; soap 34,200; cotton yarn 12,700; cigarettes 2,740,000,000 units. Construction† (units; 1976): residential 73; nonresidential 50. Energy production (consumption): electricity (kW-hr; 1983) 1,872,000,000 (1,872,000,000); coal (metric tons; 1983) 54,000 (234,-

000); crude petroleum (barrels; 1983) 11,144,000 (10,771,000); petroleum products (metric tons; 1983) 1,025,000 (1,026,000); natural gas (cu m; 1983) 475,970,000 (475,970,000).
Gross national product (1983): U.S.$6,500,000,000 (U.S.$180 per capita).

Structure of gross domestic product and labour force

| | 1983–84 | | | |
	in value K'000,000	% of total value	labour force	% of labour force
Agriculture	24,045	48.4	9,590,000	66.2
Mining	602	1.2	85,000	0.6
Manufacturing	4,687	9.4	1,198,000	8.3
Construction	916	1.8	225,000	1.6
Public utilities	230‡	0.5‡	16,000	0.1
Transportation and communication	1,917	3.9	480,000	3.3
Trade	11,861	23.9	1,413,000	9.7
Finance, Pub. admin., Services	} 5,472‡	11.0‡	872,000	6.0
Other			618,000	4.3
TOTAL	49,730§	100.0§	14,497,000	100.0‖

Population economically active (1981–82): total 14,462,000; participation rate of total population 41.6% (female 28.2%, unemployed 4.6%).

Price and earnings indexes (1980 = 100)

	1979	1980	1981	1982	1983	1984	1985
Consumer price index	99.4	100.0	100.3	105.6	116.6	117.0	121.0¶
Monthly earnings index⁹	95.7	100.0	101.9	105.1	...	...	...

Household income and expenditure. Average household size (1980) 5.1; average annual income per household: n.a.; source of income: n.a.; expenditure (1976)ᵟ: food and beverages 75.5%, fuel and power 7.5%, clothing 3.7%, household rent and utilities 3.4%, charities and ceremonials 1.9%, medical care 1.0%, education 1.0%, travel 0.8%.
Land use (1983): forested 48.9%; meadows and pastures 0.5%; agricultural and under permanent cultivation 15.3%; other 35.3%.

Foreign trade□

Balance of trade (current prices)

	1978	1979	1980	1981	1982	1983	1984
K'000,000	−428.3	+625.2	+997.8	+1,006.2	+172.9	+1,084.1	+630.5
% of total	11.8%	14.0%	19.0%	17.0%	2.9%	21.7%	14.7%

Imports (1982–83): K6,566,800,000 (nonelectrical machinery and transport equipment 54.3%; base metals and manufactures 9.0%; chemicals, fertilizers, and pharmaceuticals 6.7%; electrical machinery 6.5%). *Major import sources* (1983): Japan 30.8%; West Germany 24.4%; Singapore 9.3%; United Kingdom 5.7%; United States 2.6%.
Exports (1982–83): K3,036,300,000 (rice and rice products 37.7%; teak 24.1%; base metals and ores 6.9%; prawns 2.9%). *Major export destinations* (1983): Singapore 20.3%; Indonesia 15.5%; Japan 14.8%.

Transport and communications

Transport. Railroads (1984): route length 1,949 mi, 3,137 km; passenger-mi 1,802,000,000, passenger-km 2,900,000,000; short ton-mi cargo 304,800,000, metric ton-km cargo 445,000,000. Roads (1983–84): total length 14,207 mi, 22,863 km (paved 17%). Vehicles (1980): passenger cars 43,300; trucks and buses 44,700. Merchant marine (1984): vessels (100 gross tons and over) 105; total deadweight tonnage 128,316. Air transport (1983–84): passenger-mi 139,194,000, passenger-km 224,005,000; short ton-mi cargo 1,739,000, metric ton-km cargo 2,539,000; airports (1985) with scheduled flights 32.
Communications. Daily newspapers (1984): total number 6; total circulation 565,000; circulation per 1,000 population 15. Radio (1984): total receivers 800,000 (1 per 46 persons). Television (1984): total receivers 32,000 (1 per 1,030 persons). Telephones (1983–84): 53,988 (1 per 678 persons).

Education and health

Education (1983–84)

	schools	teachers	students	student/ teacher ratio
Primary (age 5–9)	27,499	104,754	4,696,289	44.8
Secondary (age 10–15)	2,338	41,668	1,210,329	29.0
Voc., teacher tr.	53	1,314	15,554	11.8
Higher	35	5,622	171,245	30.5

Educational attainment, n.a. *Literacy* (1980): total population over age 15 literate 13,673,800 (65.9%); males literate 7,709,800 (75.9%); females literate 5,964,000 (56.3%).
Health (1983–84): physicians 8,931 (1 per 4,099 persons); hospital beds 25,919 (1 per 1,412 persons); infant mortality rate per 1,000 live births (1980–85) 94.
Food (1980–82): daily per capita caloric intake 2,360 (vegetable products 96%, animal products 4%); 109% of FAO recommended minimum.

Military

Total active duty personnel (1984): 180,500 (army 90.3%, navy 5.5%, air force 4.2%). *Military expenditure as percent of GNP* (1983–84): 3.4% (world 6.1%); per capita expenditure U.S.$6.

---

*1983. †Government building activity only. ‡Gas and water are included with finance, pub. admin., services, and other. §At current prices. ‖ Detail does not add to total given because of rounding. ¶April. ⁹Males in manufacturing only. ᵟBased on five rural townships. □Import figures are f.o.b. (free on board) in balance of trade and c.i.f. (cost, insurance, and freight) for commodities and trading partners.

Burundi

Official name: République du Burundi (French); Republika y'Uburundi (Rundi) (Republic of Burundi).
Form of government: unitary single-party republic with one legislative house (National Assembly [65]).
Chief of state and government: President.
Capital: Bujumbura.
Official languages: French; Rundi.
Official religion: none.
Monetary unit: 1 Burundi franc (FBu) = 100 centimes; valuation (Oct. 21, 1985) 1 U.S.$ = FBu113.69; 1 £ = FBu163.04.

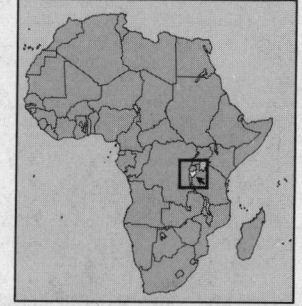

Area and population		area*		population
Provinces	Capitals	sq mi	sq km	1984 estimate
Bubanza	Bubanza	422	1,093	186,200
Bujumbura	Bujumbura	510	1,321	547,600
Bururi	Bururi	966	2,503	355,400
Cankuzo	Cankuzo	749	1,939	122,300
Cibitoke	Cibitoke	633	1,640	218,200
Gitega	Gitega	774	2,004	534,900
Karuzi	Karuzi	563	1,458	244,300
Kayanza	Kayanza	413	1,070	426,900
Kirundo	Kirundo	661	1,711	338,000
Makamba	Makamba	767	1,986	144,600
Muramvya	Muramvya	626	1,622	419,700
Muyinga	Muyinga	721	1,867	297,600
Ngozi	Ngozi	571	1,479	451,200
Rutana	Rutana	709	1,837	167,600
Ruyigi	Ruyigi	932	2,414	194,900
TOTAL		10,747	27,834	4,649,500†

Demography

Population (1985 est.): 4,784,300.
Density‡ (1985): persons per sq mi 477.6, persons per sq km 184.4.
Urban–rural (1985): urban 2.5%; rural 97.5%.
Sex distribution (1985): male 48.79%; female 51.21%.
Age breakdown (1985): under 15, 44.3%; 15–29, 25.1%; 30–44, 15.7%; 45–59, 9.6%; 60–74, 4.5%; 75 and over, 0.8%.
Population projection: (1990) 5,305,000; (2000) 6,951,000.
Doubling time: 26 years.
Ethnic composition (1980): Hutu 83.3%; Tutsi 12.8%; Tutsi from Rwanda 1.6%; Zairian 1.2%; Twa Pygmy 1.0%; other 0.1%.
Religious affiliation (1980): affiliated Christian 79.5%, of which Roman Catholic 73.3%, Protestant 4.4%; tribal religionist 13.5%; nominal Christian 6.0%; Muslim 0.9%; other 0.1%.
Populated places (1982): Bujumbura 235,400§; Gitega 35,000; Ngozi 20,000.

Vital statistics

Birth rate per 1,000 population (1980–85): 47.6 (world avg. 29.0).
Death rate per 1,000 population (1980–85): 20.9 (world avg. 11.0).
Natural increase rate per 1,000 population (1980–85): 26.7 (world avg. 18.0).
Total fertility rate (avg. births per childbearing woman; 1980–85): 6.4.
Marriage rate per 1,000 population: n.a.
Divorce rate per 1,000 population: n.a.
Life expectancy at birth (1980–85): male 42.4 years; female 45.6 years.
Major causes of death per 100,000 population (1983) ‖: measles 18.5; bacillary dysentery 10.8; other diarrheal diseases 3.2; malaria 3.0; pulmonary tuberculosis 1.1.

National economy

Budget (1983)¶. Revenue: FBu11,167,900,000 (income tax 31.6%, customs duties 23.5%, excise duties 19.3%, other indirect taxes 18.6%, administrative receipts 6.1%, property tax 1.0%). Expenditures: FBu13,706,500,000 (goods and services 60.5%, subsidies and transfers 15.6%, loans 0.2%, other 23.8%).
Public debt (external, outstanding; 1983): U.S.$284,000,000.
Tourism (1981): receipts from visitors U.S.$22,000,000; expenditures by nationals abroad U.S.$18,000,000.
Production (metric tons except as noted). Agriculture, forestry, fishing (1984): bananas 980,000, sweet potatoes 450,000, cassava 430,000, pulses 292,000, sorghum 150,000, yams and taros 107,000, corn (maize) 103,000, millet 35,000, coffee 32,000, peanuts (groundnuts) 12,000, cotton seed 4,000, tea 2,000; livestock (number of live animals) 770,000 goats, 565,000 cattle, 315,000 sheep, 3,000,000 chickens; roundwood 3,522,000 cu m?; fish catch 12,000?. Mining and quarrying (1983): peat 13,293; kaolin clay 4,053; lime 300; gold 272 troy oz. Manufacturing (1983): beer 89,486,600 bottles; carbonated beverages 1,952,400 cases; cigarettes 293,950,000 units; blankets 358,800 units; footwear 300,900 pairs. Construction: n.a. Energy production (consumption): electricity (kW-hr; 1983) 2,000,000 (142,000,-000); coal, none (n.a.); crude petroleum, none (n.a.); petroleum products (metric tons; 1983) none (36,000); natural gas, none (n.a.); peatõ (metric tons; 1983) 8,000 (8,000).
Land use (1983): forested 2.4%; meadows and pastures 35.5%; agricultural and under permanent cultivation 50.9%; other 11.2%.
Gross national product (at current market prices; 1983): U.S.$1,050,000,000 (U.S.$240 per capita).

Structure of gross domestic product and labour force				
	1983		1979	
	in value FBu'000,000	% of total value	labour force	% of labour force
Agriculture	55,202	55.6	2,246,200	93.1
Mining	◇	◇	1,400	0.1
Manufacturing	4,806	4.8	36,700	1.5
Construction	5,742	5.8	14,700	0.6
Public utilities	593◇	0.6◇	1,700	0.1
Transportation and communication	2,835	2.9	6,400	0.3
Trade	7,991	8.1	20,900	0.9
Finance	1,591	1.6	1,300	0.1
Pub. admin., defense	7,112	7.2	80,700	3.3
Services	5,254	5.3		
Other	8,114△	8.2△	3,100	0.1
TOTAL	99,240†	100.0†	2,413,100	100.0†

Population economically active (1983): total 2,480,841; participation rate of total population 56.1% (female, n.a.; unemployed, n.a.).

Price and earnings indexes (1980 = 100)							
	1979	1980	1981	1982	1983	1984	1985□
Consumer price index	91.4	100.0	112.0	118.4	128.3	146.7	158.5
Monthly earnings index	76.5	100.0	162.1	147.5	134.9	...	...

Household income and expenditure. Average household size (1980) 4.9; average annual income per household: n.a.; source of income: n.a.; expenditure: n.a.

Foreign trade⊕

Balance of trade (current prices)					
	1979	1980	1981	1982	1983	1984
FBu'000,000	−2,570	−7,259	−5,873	−8,866	−7,352	−7,635
% of total	12.1%	38.2%	30.3%	35.9%	32.9%	24.4%

Imports (1983): FBu17,074,900,000 (intermediate goods 41.4%, capital goods 30.5%, consumer goods 28.1%). *Major import sources:* Belgium–Luxembourg 15.4%; France 10.3%; West Germany 8.7%; Japan 6.4%; Italy 3.9%; The Netherlands 3.8%.
Exports (1983): FBu7,505,700,000 (coffee 87.1%; raw cotton 3.5%; tea 3.0%; animal hides and skins 0.9%; minerals 0.1%). *Major export destinations:* West Germany 49.5%; Belgium–Luxembourg 4.6%; Italy 3.4%; United States 2.1%; United Kingdom 2.1%.

Transport and communications

Transport. Railroads: none. Roads (1981): total length 3,196 mi, 5,144 km (paved 7%). Vehicles (1983): passenger cars 7,016, trucks and other vehicles 5,700. Merchant marine (1979): vessels (100 gross tons and over) 1; total gross tonnage 385. Air transport (1983)**: passenger arrivals 21,754, departures 21,834; cargo loaded 3,278 short tons (2,974 metric tons), unloaded 5,010 short tons (4,545 metric tons); airports (1985) with scheduled flights 2.
Communications. Daily newspapers (1984): total number 1; total circulation 20,000; circulation per 1,000 population 4.3. Radio (1984): total number of receivers 160,000 (1 per 29 persons). Television: total number of receivers, n.a. Telephones (1982): 5,601 (1 per 769 persons).

Education and health

Education (1983–84)				
	schools	teachers	students	student/ teacher ratio
Primary (age 6–11)	874	6,164	302,611	49.1
Secondary (age 12–18)	25	475	7,854	16.5
Voc., teacher tr.	36	594	6,033	10.2
Higher	6	372	2,479	6.7

Educational attainment, n.a. *Literacy* (1980): total population over age 14 literate 544,200 (22.6%); males literate 455,800 (38.7%); females literate 88,400 (7.2%).
Health (1983): physicians 216 (1 per 20,942 persons); hospital beds 2,893 (1 per 1,564 persons); infant mortality rate per 1,000 live births (1980–85) 137.
Food (1980–82): daily per capita caloric intake 2,244 (vegetable products 97%, animal products 3%); 96% of FAO recommended minimum requirement.

Military

Total active duty personnel (1984): 5,200 (army 96.2%, navy 0.9%, air force 2.9%). *Military expenditure as percent of GNP* (1983): 3.2% (world 6.1%); per capita expenditure U.S.$9.

*Total land area is 10,017 sq mi (25,944 sq km) and is shown for the provinces; the total area (both land and water) is shown in the grand total. †Detail does not add to total given because of rounding. ‡Based on land area. §1984 estimate. ‖ Data shown is for four provinces only. ¶1984: revenue FBu15,192,300,000; expenditure FBu17,394,900,000. 1985: revenue FBu17,152,000,000; expenditure FBu18,¶57,000,-000. ?1983. õPeat is not yet popularly accepted as a fuel. It is mostly used by industries, schools, and the military. □March. ◇Mining included with public utilities. △Indirect taxes, less subsidies. ↑At current prices. ⊕Import figures are f.o.b. (free on board) in balance of trade and c.i.f. (cost, insurance, and freight) for commodities and trading partners. **Bujumbura Airport only.

Cameroon

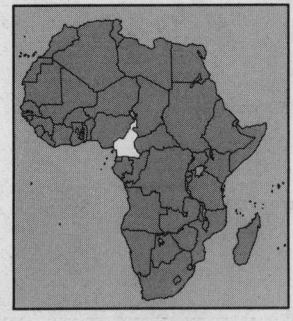

Official name: République du Cameroun (French); Republic of Cameroon (English).
Form of government: republic with one legislative house (National Assembly [120]).
Head of state and government: President.
Capital: Yaoundé.
Official languages: French; English.
Official religion: none.
Monetary unit: 1 CFA franc (CFAF) = 100 centimes; valuation (Oct. 21, 1985) 1 U.S.$ = CFAF402.02; 1 £ = CFAF576.50.

Area and population

Provinces	Capitals	area sq mi	area sq km	population 1983 estimate
Adamaoua	Ngaoundéré	24,680	63,910	350,000
Centre	Yaoundé	25,580	66,240	1,497,000
Est	Bertoua	42,080	109,000	433,000
Extrême-Nord	Maroua	13,250	34,320	1,549,000
Littoral	Douala	7,810	20,220	1,286,000
Nord	Garoua	25,410	65,820	549,000
Nord-Ouest	Bamenda	6,720	17,410	1,110,000
Ouest	Bafoussam	5,360	13,880	1,252,000
Sud	Ebolowa	19,190	49,700	372,000
Sud-Ouest	Buea	9,540	24,710	709,000
TOTAL		179,720*	465,460*	9,107,000

Demography

Population (1985): 9,635,000.
Density (1985): persons per sq mi 53.6, persons per sq km 20.7.
Urban–rural (1982–83): urban 33.8%; rural 66.2%.
Sex distribution (1982–83): male 49.89%; female 50.11%.
Age breakdown (1983): under 15, 42.9%; 15–29, 26.3%; 30–44, 16.3%; 45–59, 9.5%; 60 and over, 5.0%.
Population projection: (1990) 10,885,000; (2000) 13,893,000.
Doubling time: 29 years.
Ethnic composition (1982): Cameroon Highland Bantu 27%; Equatorial Bantu 25%; Kirdi 15%; Fulani 9.5%; Northwestern Bantu 8%; Hausa 8%; Baya and Bamum (Mbum) 6%; other 1.5%.
Religious affiliation (1980): Roman Catholic 35%; Protestant 18%; animist 25%; Muslim 22%.
Major cities (1983): Douala 708,000; Yaoundé 485,000; Nkongsamba 86,900†; Maroua 81,900†; Garoua 77,900†.

Vital statistics

Birth rate per 1,000 population (1982–83): 45.0 (world avg. 29.0).
Death rate per 1,000 population (1982–83): 20.3 (world avg. 11.0).
Natural increase rate per 1,000 population (1982–83): 24.7 (world avg. 18.0).
Total fertility rate (avg. births per childbearing woman; 1982–83): 6.2.
Life expectancy at birth (1982–83): male 43.2 years; female 45.6 years.
Major causes of death per 100,000 population: n.a.; however, major health problems include malaria, tuberculosis, parasitic infestations, and nutritional deficiency diseases.

National economy

Budget‡ (1985–86). Revenue: CFAF740,000,000,000 (direct and assimilated taxes 49.5%; customs duties and taxes 26.9%; receipts for services 8.6%; indirect taxes 8.1%). Expenditures: CFAF740,000,000,000 (investment 41.9%, of which development operations 31.1%; education 9.3%; armed forces 6.6%; health 3.6%; agriculture 2.3%).
Gross national product (1983): U.S.$7,640,000,000 (U.S.$834 per capita).

Structure of gross domestic product and labour force

	1981 in value CFAF'000,000,000	1981 % of total value	1982 labour force	1982 % of labour force
Agriculture	455.6	26.8	2,594,800	73.2
Mining	91.8	5.4	1,580	0.1
Manufacturing	140.0	8.2	159,560	4.5
Construction	78.3	4.6	62,860	1.8
Trade and finance	251.2	14.7	149,200	4.2
Public utilities	19.6	1.2	3,230	0.1
Transp. and commun.	96.8	5.7	47,400	1.3
Pub. admin., defense, services, and other	569.7	33.4	524,370	14.8
TOTAL	1703.0¶	100.0	3,543,000	100.0

Households. Average household size (1976) 5.2.
Population economically active (1983): total 4,112,000; participation rate of total population 45.5%, (female [1982] 37.5%, unemployed [1982] 4.6%).

Price index (1980 = 100)

	1979	1980	1981	1982	1983	1984	1985 ‖
Consumer price index	91.3	100.0	110.7	125.4	146.3	162.9	170.4

Production (metric tons except as noted). Agriculture (1984): sugarcane 1,100,000, cassava 620,000, corn (maize) 400,000, millet 400,000, coffee 127,000, cocoa 115,000, palm oil 81,000, peanuts (groundnuts) 80,000; livestock—3,730,000 cattle, 2,180,000 sheep, 2,000,000 goats, 1,000,000 pigs; roundwood 9,904 cu m§; fish catch 84,277§. Mining and quarrying (1983): aluminum 77,600, limestone 50,700, gold 8 kilograms. Manufacturing (CFAF, gross value; 1981): beverages and tobacco 52,185,000,000; textiles and clothing 22,070,000,000; metal products 20,622,000,000; foods, prepared 20,000,000,000; chemical products 17,106,000,000. Construction (CFAF, gross value; 1981): 12,522,000,000. Energy production (consumption): electricity (kW-hr; 1983) 1,804,000,000 (1,804,000,000); coal, n.a. (none); petroleum (barrels; 1983) 41,633,800 (23,756,800); petroleum products (metric tons; 1983) 2,655,000 (2,671,000); natural gas, none (n.a.).
Land use (1983): forested 53.9%; meadows and pastures 17.7%; agricultural and under permanent cultivation 14.8%; other 13.6%.
Tourism (1983): receipts from visitors U.S.$29,000,000; expenditures by nationals abroad (1982) U.S.$70,000,000.
Public debt (external, outstanding; 1983): U.S.$1,883,000,000.

Foreign trade

Balance of trade (current prices)

	1979	1980	1981	1982	1983	1984
CFAF'000,000,000	−30.6	−47.0	−89.3	−65.7	−94.8	−103.1
% of total	6.0%	7.5%	13.0%	9.2%	11.3%	11.9%

Imports (1982): CFAF392,575,000,000 (machines and transport equipment 34.8%, chemical products 13.2%, textile yarn 6.6%, iron and steel 5.0%, petroleum and products 3.6%). *Major import sources:* France 44.7%; United States 7.6%; West Germany 6.9%; Japan 6.1%; Italy 4.2%.
Exports (1982): CFAF326,891,000,000 (crude petroleum 46.8%, coffee 15.6%, cacao 14.2%, cork and wood 5.9%). *Major export destinations:* United States 40.1%; The Netherlands 19.5%; France 15.8%; West Germany 5.0%.

Transport and communications

Transport. Railroads (1982–83): length 729 mi, 1,173 km; passenger-mi 242,000,000, passenger-km 389,000,000; short ton-mi cargo 566,000,000, metric ton-km cargo 827,000,000. Roads (1984): total length 38,836 mi, 64,905 km (paved 5%). Vehicles (1983): passenger cars 62,500; trucks and buses 17,000. Merchant marine (1984): vessels (100 gross tons and over) 48; total deadweight tonnage 87,752. Air transport (1983): passenger-mi 345,511,000, passenger-km 547,999,000; short ton-mi cargo 34,291,000, metric ton-km cargo 50,064,000; airports (1985) with scheduled flights 10.
Communications. Daily newspapers (1984): 1; circulation 35,000; circulation per 1,000 population 3.7. Radio (1984): 785,000 receivers (1 per 12.0 persons). Television: n.a. Telephones (1981): 26,000 (1 per 333 persons).

Education and health

Education (1983–84)

	schools	teachers	students	student/ teacher ratio
Primary (age 6–14)	5,582	31,030	1,563,852	50.4
Secondary (age 15–24)	365	6,795	218,057	32.1
Voc., teacher tr.	199	2,974	70,671	23.8
Higher²	13	557	11,407	20.5

Educational attainment (1976). Percent of population over age 15 having: no schooling 51.1%; primary education 41.7%; some postprimary 0.2%; secondary 5.7%; some postsecondary 0.3%; higher 0.2%; other 0.8%. *Literacy* (1980): total population literate (over age 15) 2,344,100 (55.2%); males literate 1,453,200 (70.2%); females literate 890,900 (41.0%).
Health: physicians (1981) 640 (1 per 13,527 persons); hospital beds (1980) 24,541 (1 per 353 persons); infant mortality rate per 1,000 births (1983) 116.
Food (1980–82): daily per capita caloric intake 2,148 (vegetable products 94%, animal products 6%); 93% of FAO recommended minimum requirement.

Military

Total active duty personnel (1984): 7,300 (army 90.4%, navy 4.8%, air force 4.8%). *Military expenditure as percent of GNP* (1983): 1.2% (world 6.0%); per capita expenditure U.S.$10.

*Total includes 100 sq mi (248 sq km) of water area. †1981. ‡Revenue breakdown is for 1982–83. §1983. ‖ First quarter. ¶In current prices. ²1981–82.

SALGADO—MAGNUM

Lumber being loaded for export, port of Douala, Cameroon.

Canada

Official name: Canada.
Form of government: federal multiparty parliamentary state with two legislative houses (Senate [104]; House of Commons [282]).
Chief of state: British Monarch represented by governor-general.
Head of government: Prime Minister.
Capital: Ottawa.
Official languages: English; French.
Official religion: none.
Monetary unit: 1 Canadian dollar (Can $) = 100 cents; valuation (Oct. 21, 1985) 1 U.S.$ = Can$1.36; 1 £ = Can$1.96.

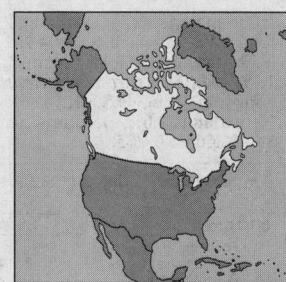

Area and population

		area		population
Provinces	**Capitals**	sq mi	sq km	1985* estimate
Alberta	Edmonton	248,800	644,390	2,344,600
British Columbia	Victoria	358,971	929,730	2,888,700
Manitoba	Winnipeg	211,723	548,360	1,067,900
New Brunswick	Fredericton	27,834	72,090	718,400
Newfoundland	Saint John's	143,510	371,690	579,700
Nova Scotia	Halifax	20,402	52,840	879,600
Ontario	Toronto	344,090	891,190	9,047,900
Prince Edward Island	Charlottetown	2,185	5,660	127,000
Quebec	Quebec	523,859	1,356,790	6,572,300
Saskatchewan	Regina	220,348	570,700	1,018,200
Territories				
Northwest Territories	Yellowknife	1,271,442	3,293,020	50,900
Yukon Territory	Whitehorse	184,931	478,970	22,800
TOTAL		3,849,675†	9,970,610†	25,318,000

Demography

Population (1985): 25,427,000.
Density (1985): persons per sq mi 7.1, persons per sq km 2.8.
Urban–rural (1981): urban 75.7%; rural 24.3%.
Sex distribution (1981): male 49.80%; female 50.20%.
Age breakdown (1981): under 15, 23.4%; 15–29, 28.9%; 30–44, 20.0%; 45–59, 15.0%; 60–74, 9.6%; 75 and over, 3.1%.
Population projection: (1990) 26,826,000; (2000) 29,028,000.
Doubling time: 58 years.
Ethnic composition (by language; 1981): English 61.2%; French 25.6%; Italian 2.2%; German 2.1%; Ukrainian 1.2%; other European 4.6%; Asiatic 2.3%; Amerindian and Inuktitut (Eskimo) 0.8%.
Religious affiliation (1981): Roman Catholic 46.5%; Protestant 41.2%; Eastern Orthodox 1.5%; Jewish 1.2%; Muslim 0.4%; Hindu 0.3%; nonreligious 7.4%; other 1.5%.
Major metropolitan areas (1984): Toronto 3,140,500; Montreal 2,865,900; Vancouver 1,331,000; Ottawa–Hull 756,600; Edmonton 687,500; Calgary 619,700; Winnipeg 603,500; Quebec 589,100; Hamilton 554,400; Saint Catharines–Niagara 307,500.

Other metropolitan areas (1984)

	population		population		population
Chcoutimi– Jonquière	138,700	Oshawa	166,900	Sudbury	148,800
Halifax	285,900	Regina	173,400	Thunder Bay	121,700
Kitchener	298,400	Saint John's	160,100	Trois Rivières	114,000
London	290,100	Saint John	115,500	Victoria	242,000
		Saskatoon	165,100	Windsor	247,900

Place of birth (1971): 84.7% native-born; 15.3% foreign-born, of which United Kingdom 4.3%, other European 3.5%, other 7.5%.
Mobility (1981). Population living in the same residence as in 1976: 52.4%; different residence, same province 24.9%; different province 22.7%.
Households (1981). Total number of households 8,281,531‡. Average household size 2.9; 1 person 20.3%, 2 persons 28.9%, 3 persons 17.5%, 4 persons 18.6%, 5 persons 9.1%, 6 persons 3.5%, 7 or more persons 2.1%. Family households: 6,324,976 (76.4%), nonfamily 1,956,555 (23.6%, of which 1 person 20.3%).
Immigration (1984): permanent immigrants admitted 88,199, from Asia 47.5%, Europe 24.4%, United States 7.8%, West Indies 6.3%, other 14.0%.

Vital statistics

Birth rate per 1,000 population (1984): 15.0 (world avg. 29.0); (1983) legitimate 91.0%; illegitimate 9.0%.
Death rate per 1,000 population (1984): 7.1 (world avg. 11.0).
Natural increase rate per 1,000 population (1984): 7.9 (world avg. 18.0).
Total fertility rate (avg. births per childbearing woman; 1983): 1.7.
Marriage rate per 1,000 population (1984): 7.4.
Divorce rate per 1,000 population (1982): 2.9.
Life expectancy at birth (1983): male 73.0 years; female 79.0 years.
Major causes of death per 100,000 population (1982): diseases of the circulatory system 329.7; malignant neoplasms (cancers) 172.3; accidents 59.8; diseases of the respiratory system 36.7.

Social indicators

Educational attainment (1976). Percent of adult population over age 25 having: no formal schooling 1.8%; less than full primary education 18.5%;

primary 12.2%; secondary 36.6%; postsecondary 30.9%, of which (graduates by level; 1985): 4-year higher degree 100,760, master's 14,890, doctorate 1,940.

Distribution of income (1981)

percent of national income by quintile

1	2	3	4	5 (highest)
5.3%	11.8%	18.9%	24.0%	40.0%.

Quality of working life (1984). Average workweek: 38.5 hours (6.7% overtime). Annual rate per 100,000 workers for (1978): injury, accident, or industrial illness 4,924; death 8.3. Proportion of labour force insured for damages or income loss resulting from (1983): injury 99%; permanent disability 99%; death 99%. Average days lost to labour stoppages per 1,000 employee-workdays (1984): 1.5. Average duration of journey to work (1977)§: 23 minutes (26.0% public transportation, 74.0% other). Rate per 1,000 workers of discouraged (unemployed no longer seeking work; 1983): 10.5.
Access to services (1978). Proportion of households having access to: electricity 87.2%; public water supply (1976) 98.5%; public sewage collection 98.5%; public fire protection 90.4%.
Social participation. Eligible voters participating in last national election: 69.7%. Population over 18 years of age participating in voluntary work: n.a. Trade union membership in total work force: 39.0%. Practicing religious population in total affiliated population: 92.7%.
Social deviance (1980). Offense rate per 100,000 population for: murder 6.0; rape 14.1; grand and auto theft 436.7; burglary and housebreaking 1,497.1. Incidence per 100,000 in general population of: alcoholism (1976) 27; drug and substance abuse 322.4; suicide (1982) 14.0.
Leisure (1982). Favourite leisure activities: watching television 23.7 hrs/week; listening to radio 18.5 hrs/week.
Material well-being (1978). Households possessing: automobile 78.5%; telephone 96.5%; television receiver 97.3%; refrigerator 99.4%; central air conditioner 4.5%; automatic washing machine 59.1%.

National economy

Gross national product (at current market prices; 1984): U.S.$317,326,000,-000 (U.S.$12,650 per capita).

Structure of gross domestic product and labour force

	1983			
	in value Can$'000,000	% of total value	labour force	% of labour force
Agriculture	12,987	3.2	587,000	4.8
Mining	22,443	5.6	170,000	1.4
Manufacturing	63,403	15.9	1,886,000	15.5
Construction	18,411	4.6	566,000	4.6
Public utilities	14,578	3.6	120,000	1.0
Transportation and communication	29,004	7.3	750,000	6.2
Trade	36,982	9.3	1,850,000	15.2
Finance			602,000	4.9
Pub. admin., defense			782,000	6.4
Services	201,493	50.5	3,421,000	28.1
Other			1,448,000 ‖	11.9 ‖
TOTAL	393,301¶	100.0	12,182,000	100.0

Budget (1984–85). Revenue: Can$67,326,000,000 (personal income tax 48.7%; corporation income tax 14.6%; sales tax 10.9%; excise taxes and import duties 9.8%). Expenditures: Can$98,200,000,000 (education, health, and welfare 40.4%; public debt interest 20.7%; economic development 11.5%; defense 8.9%).
National debt (1984): Can$163,419,000,000.
Tourism (1983): receipts from visitors U.S.$2,613,000,000; expenditures by nationals abroad U.S.$3,887,000,000.

Manufacturing, mining, and construction enterprises (1981)

	no. of enter- prises	no. of employees	hourly wages as a % of avg. of all wages	annual value added (Can$'000,000)
Manufacturing				
Food and beverages	4,492	234,077	86.6	10,354.5
Transport equipment	1,270	178,612	110.7	8,041.1
Paper and related products	758	131,024	96.9	6,965.5
Metal fabricating	5,072	158,832	101.4	6,137.7
Chemicals and chemical products	1,232	90,186	102.6	6,099.5
Primary metals	439	125,168	93.8	5,836.6
Electrical products	1,121	127,924	99.0	5,163.4
Machinery	1,620	108,531	85.0	4,690.5
Printing, publishing, and related products	4,508	107,488	91.7	4,082.5
Wood	3,394	112,570	103.5	3,442.3
Petroleum and coal products	111	26,638	133.3	2,722.9
Building materials	1,574	55,269	104.0	2,510.5
Textile	952	67,673	73.3	2,283.9
Clothing	2,125	95,850	59.8	2,148.4
Rubber and plastic	1,030	61,504	97.0	2,280.4
Furniture and fixtures	2,464	53,361	92.0	1,456.1
Tobacco products industries	25	8,744	117.9	642.7
Leather industries	415	26,207	60.8	617.9
Knitting mills	262	20,495	73.3	463.4
Mining	...	178,200	147.9	17,288.7
Construction	...	475,100	144.7	18,239.6

Production (farm cash receipts in Can$'000 except as noted). Agriculture, forestry, fishing (1984): wheat 3,745,200, rapeseed 941,600, barley 663,300, corn (maize) 564,900, vegetables 514,700, tobacco 365,700, floriculture 349,-600, potatoes 308,400, fruits 270,900, soybeans 205,200; livestock (number of live animals) 12,308,000 cattle, 10,655,000 pigs, 790,000 sheep, 96,300,000

poultry; roundwood 141,502,000 cu m; pelts 4,423,395 metric tons?; fish catch 1,337,300 metric tons. Mining and quarrying (metric tons; 1984): iron ore 40,264,000; zinc 1,022,200; copper 706,200; lead 249,200; nickel 161,680; molybdenum 10,500; uranium 9,244; silver 1,305; gold 77. Manufacturing (metric tons; 1984): wood pulp 20,410,700; crude steel 14,699,000; pig iron 9,643,000; newsprint 9,007,000; cement 7,856,000; sulfuric acid 4,054,000; caustic soda 1,574,000; synthetic rubber 97,500; road motor vehicles 1,854,-570, of which passenger cars 1,032,789 units, truck and buses 808,232 units; refrigerators 692,810 units; washing machines and dryers 656,870 units; footwear 45,431,000 pairs; beer 235,580,000 hectolitres. Construction (1984): residential Can$8,513,200,000; nonresidential Can$6,988,400,000.

Service enterprises (1984)

	no. of enter- prises	no. of employees	weekly wages as a % of all wages	annual sales (Can$'000,000)
Retail trade				
Food stores	...	213,400	...	28,044.5
Motor vehicle dealers	...	79,800	...	20,846.5
Department stores	...	ᵟ	...	11,384.9
Service stations	...	63,700	...	11,313.4
Clothing stores	...	50,200	...	5,295.3
Pharmacies	...	52,400	...	4,727.2
Furniture and appliance stores	...	62,100	...	2,983.2
Automotive stores	...	31,500	...	2,606.2
General merchandise	...	231,700ᵟ	...	2,395.1
General stores	...	ᵟ	...	1,890.9
Variety stores	...	45,100	...	1,207.0
Shoe stores	...	18,400	...	1,171.1
Hardware stores	...	17,300	...	1,046.5
Jewelry stores	...	14,000	...	867.1

Energy production (consumption): electricity (kW-hr; 1984) 424,853,000,000 (383,417,000,000); coal (metric tons; 1984) 57,401,000 (50,616,000); crude petroleum (barrels; 1984) 540,200,000 (494,800,000); petroleum products (metric tons; 1984) 87,616,000 (78,323,000); natural gas (cu m; 1984) 101,-578,500,000 (47,558,400,000).

Population economically active (1985): total 13,103,000; participation rate of population over age 15, 67.6% (female 37.6%, unemployed 9.7%).

Price and earnings indexes (1981 = 100)

	1979	1980	1981	1982	1983	1984	1985◻
Consumer price index	80.7	88.9	100.0	110.8	117.2	122.3	127.6
Monthly earnings index	81.7	89.3	100.0	111.8	118.1	123.3	...

Household income and expenditure. Average household size (1984) 2.8; average annual income per household Can$36,800 (U.S.$27,900); sources of income: wages and salaries 64.1%, social welfare 14.9%, interest, dividends, and other investment income 13.1%, other 7.9%; expenditure (1982): food 18.0%, housing 17.1%, transportation 14.4%, clothing 6.3%, health 3.4%, education 2.8%.
Land use (1983): forested 35.4%; meadows and pastures 2.6%; agricultural and under permanent cultivation 5.0%; built-on, wasteland, and other 57.0%.

Financial aggregates

	1979	1980	1981	1982	1983	1984	1985 (7 mo.)
Exchange rate, Can$ per:							
U.S. dollar	1.17	1.17	1.20	1.23	1.23	1.29	1.35
£	2.60	2.84	2.42	2.15	1.88	1.50	1.86
SDR	1.54	1.52	1.38	1.36	1.30	1.30	1.40
International reserves (U.S.$)							
Total (excl. gold; '000,000)	2,856	3,041	3,492	3,000	3,465	2,491	2,799
SDRs ('000,000)	586	453	174	71	21	72	63
Reserve pos. in IMF ('000,000)	391	579	402	365	703	678	697
Foreign exchange ('000,000)	1,879	2,009	2,916	2,564	2,741	1,741	2,039
Gold ('000,000 fine troy oz)	22.18	20.98	20.46	20.26	20.17	20.16	20.14
% world reserves	2.35	2.20	2.00	2.14	2.13	2.13	2.13
Interest and prices							
Central bank discount (%)	14.00	17.26	14.66	10.26	10.04	10.16	10.91
Gov't. bond yield (%)	10.21	12.48	15.22	14.26	11.79	12.75	10.88
Industrial share prices							
(1980 = 100)	73.3	100.0	97.4	76.8	111.4	110.6◇	...
Balance of payments (U.S.$'000,000)							
Balance of visible trade,	4,180	8,002	6,609	14,959	14,877	16,585	...
of which:							
Imports, f.o.b.	53,471	59,475	65,940	55,470	60,829	72,369	...
Exports, f.o.b.	57,650	67,477	72,552	70,429	75,706	88,954	...
Balance of invisibles	−8,877	−9,981	−12,925	−13,961	−14,147	−15,414	...
Balance of payments, current account	−4,120	−953	−5,055	2,110	1,365	1,893	...

Foreign trade

Balance of trade (current prices)

	1978	1979	1980	1981	1982	1983	1984
Can$'000,000,000	3.0	2.8	6.9	4.5	15.8	19.4	16.6
% of total	2.9%	2.2%	4.7%	2.8%	9.9%	11.8%	8.0%

Imports (1984): Can$95,842,400,000 (machinery and transport equipment 65.9%, of which motor vehicle parts 13.5%, road motor vehicles 11.0%, machinery 8.7%; food, feed, beverages, and tobacco 6.1%; crude petroleum 3.5%; nonferrous metals 2.5%; chemicals 2.0%; plastics and synthetic rubber 1.7%; textiles 1.7%). *Major import sources:* United States 71.5%; Japan 6.0%; United Kingdom 2.4%; West Germany 2.3%; Mexico 1.5%; Taiwan 1.3%; France 1.3%; Hong Kong 1.1%.
Exports (1984): Can$112,495,400,000 (road motor vehicles and parts 26.1%;

crude materials 15.4%, of which crude petroleum 3.9%, natural gas 3.5%; food 9.1%, of which wheat 4.2%; newsprint 4.3%; lumber 3.8%; wood pulp 3.5%; machinery 3.1%; chemicals 2.3%; iron and steel 2.0%; aluminum 1.7%). *Major export destinations:* United States 75.6%; Japan 5.0%; United Kingdom 2.3%; U.S.S.R. 1.9%; China 1.1%; West Germany 1.1%; The Netherlands 1.0%; Belgium–Luxembourg 0.7%; France 0.7%; Brazil 0.7%; South Korea 0.6%.

Trade by commodities (1982)

SITC Group	imports U.S.$'000	imports %	exports U.S.$'000	exports %
00 Food and live animals	3,594,208	6.6	7,787,449	11.4
01 Beverages and tobacco	349,560	0.6	503,421	0.7
02 Crude materials, excluding fuels	2,644,367	4.8	10,144,651	14.8
03 Mineral fuels, lubricants, and related materials	5,492,446	10.0	10,100,847	14.8
04 Animal and vegetable oils, fat, and waxes	80,436	0.2	170,537	0.3
05 Chemicals and related products, n.e.s.	3,310,637	6.0	3,405,584	5.0
06 Basic manufactures	6,038,278	11.0	10,973,403	16.0
07 Machinery and transport equipment	26,300,264	48.0	21,820,796	31.9
08 Miscellaneous manufactured articles	5,471,088	10.0	1,809,417	2.6
09 Goods not classified by kind	1,542,730	2.8	1,676,663	2.5
TOTAL	54,824,014	100.0	68,392,768	100.0

Direction of trade (1984)

	imports U.S.$'000,000	imports %	exports U.S.$'000,000	exports %
Africa	886.5	1.2	1,135.0	1.3
Asia	13,881.9	18.8	12,941.3	14.9
Americas	51,578.1	69.7	62,987.4	72.5
United States	48,253.1	65.2	60,725.8	69.9
South America	1,718.4	2.3	1,189.8	1.4
Other America	1,606.6	2.2	1,071.8	1.2
Europe	7,296.3△	9.9	9,183.6△	10.6
EEC	5,778.2	7.8	5,074.0	5.8
Eastern Europe	215.4	0.3	1,778.2	2.0
Other Europe	1,302.8	1.8	2,331.5	2.7
Oceania	361.1	0.5	615.0	0.7
TOTAL	74,003.9	100.0△	86,862.3	100.0

Transport and communications

Transport. Railroads (1984): length 74,564 mi, 120,000 km; passenger-mi 1,299,000,000, passenger-km 2,090,000,000; short ton-mi cargo 167,574,-000,000, metric ton-km cargo 244,669,000,000. Roads (1984): total length 549,462 mi, 884,249 km (paved 81%). Vehicles (1983): passenger cars 10,731,000; trucks and buses 3,362,000. Merchant marine (1984): vessels (100 gross tons and over) 1,310; total deadweight tonnage 4,209,824. Air transport† (1984): passenger-mi 19,402,000,000, passenger-km 31,224,000,-000; short ton-mi cargo 713,877,000, metric ton-km cargo 1,042,300,000; airports (1985) with scheduled flights 60.
Communications. Daily newspapers⊕ (1984): total number 114; total circulation 5,500,000; circulation per 1,000 population 217. Radio (1983): total number of receivers 28,000,000 (1 per 0.9 person). Television (1983): total number of receivers 12,400,000 (1 per 2 persons). Telephones (1983): 16,-802,000 (1 per 1.5 persons).

Education and health

Education (1985–86)

	schools	teachers	students	student/ teacher ratio
Primary and secondary (age 6–18)	15,459	269,775	4,948,110	18.3
Higher	266	59,250	781,270	10.7

Literacy (1975): total population over age 14 literate 16,185,000 (95.6%); males literate 8,003,000 (95.6%); females literate 8,182,000 (95.7%).
Health (1979): physicians 43,192 (1 per 546 persons); hospital beds 270,118 (1 per 110 persons); infant mortality rate per 1,000 live births (1984) 9.3.
Food (1980–82): daily per capita caloric intake 3,438 (vegetable products 62%, animal products 38%); 129% of FAO recommended minimum requirement.

Military

Total active duty personnel (1984): 82,858 (army 15.7%, navy 6.7%, air force 18.5%, not identified by service 59.2%). *Military expenditure as percent of GNP* (1983): 2.2% (world 6.1%); per capita expenditure U.S.$265.

*April. †Total land area is 3,558,096 sq mi (9,215,430 sq km) and is shown for the provinces and territories; the total area (both land and inland water) is shown in the grand total. ‡In 1984 the total number of households was 8,857,000. §Urban areas. ‖ Unemployed. ¶At current prices. ⁹1982. ᵟDepartment and general stores included with general merchandise. ◻July. ◇November 1984. △Detail does not add to total given because of rounding. †Air Canada and CP Air only. ⊕English and French only.

Cape Verde

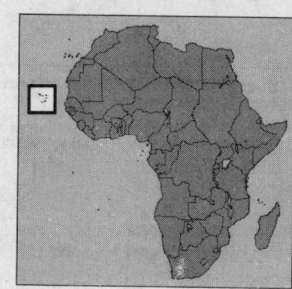

Official name: República de Cabo Verde (Republic of Cape Verde).
Form of government: unitary single-party republic with one legislative house (People's National Assembly [63]).
Chief of state: President.
Head of government: Premier.
Capital: Praia.
Official language: Portuguese.
Official religion: none.
Monetary unit: 1 escudo (CV Esc) = 100 centavos; valuation (Oct. 21, 1985) 1 U.S.$ = CV Esc89.21; 1 £ = CV Esc127.92.

Area and population

Islands Counties	Capitals	area sq mi	area sq km	population 1980 census*
Boa Vista		239	620	3,245
Boa Vista	Sal Rei			
Brava		26	67	6,896
Brava	Nova Sintra			
Fogo		184	476	30,233
Fogo	São Filipe			
Maio		104	269	3,888
Maio	Porto Inglês			
Sal		83	216	5,851
Sal	Santa Maria			
Santiago		383	991	141,843
Praia	Praia			55,318
Santa Catarina	Assomada			39,614
Santa Cruz	Pedra Badejo			22,743
Tarrafal	Tarrafal			24,168
Santo Antão		301	779	42,613
Paúl	Pombas			7,931
Porto Novo	Porto Novo			12,998
Ribeira Grande	Ponta Sol			21,684
São Nicolau		150	388	13,314
São Nicolau	Ribeira Brava			
São Vicente		88	227	40,962
São Vicente	Mindelo			
TOTAL		1,557†	4,033	288,845

Demography

Population (1985): 314,000.
Density (1985): persons per sq mi 201.7, persons per sq km 77.9.
Urban–rural (1980): urban 35.1%; rural 64.9%.
Sex distribution (1980): male 46.32%; female 53.68%.
Age breakdown (1980): under 15, 46.0%; 15–29, 27.6%; 30–44, 9.1%; 45–59, 9.0%; 60–74, 6.3%; 75 and over, 2.0%.
Population projection: (1990) 343,000; (2000) 382,000.
Doubling time: 36 years.
Ethnic composition (1980): mixed 70%; black 28%; white 2%.
Religious affiliation (1982): Roman Catholic 98.0%; Protestant 2.0%.
Major cities (1980): Praia 37,676; Mindelo 36,746; São Filipe 4,370.

Vital statistics

Birth rate per 1,000 population (1983): 38.2 (world avg. 29.0); (1975) legitimate 55.2%; illegitimate 44.8%.
Death rate per 1,000 population (1983): 9.4 (world avg. 11.0).
Natural increase rate per 1,000 population (1983): 28.8 (world avg. 18.0).
Total fertility rate (avg. births per childbearing woman; 1980–85): 2.6.
Marriage rate per 1,000 population (1975): 5.4.
Divorce rate per 1,000 population: n.a.
Life expectancy at birth (1980–85): male 60.3 years; female 64.0 years.
Major causes of death per 100,000 population (1980): enteritis and other diarrheal diseases 85.5; heart disease 51.9; cerebrovascular disease 45.7; malignant neoplasms (cancers) 34.6; measles and other infectious and parasitic diseases 34.6; pneumonia 27.2; bronchitis, emphysema, and asthma 20.4; avitaminoses and other nutritional deficiencies 14.5.

National economy

Budget (1981)‡. Revenue: CV Esc1,076,475 (indirect taxes 52.1%, of which import duties 42.8%; direct taxes 28.7%, of which taxes from industry 8.6%; receipts from petroleum 8.2%). Expenditures: CV Esc4,896,320 (investment expenditure CV Esc3,814,320 [77.9%], of which industry and energy 28%, transportation 25%, agriculture 17%).
Public debt (external, outstanding; 1984): U.S.$67,100,000.
Tourism: n.a.
Production (metric tons except as noted). Agriculture, forestry, fishing (1984): coconuts 10,000, sugarcane 9,000, bananas 3,000, corn (maize) 3,000, potatoes 3,000, sweet potatoes 2,000, cassava 2,000; livestock (number of live animals) 77,000 goats, 23,000 pigs, 13,000 cattle; roundwood, n.a.; fish catch (1983) 13,205, of which tuna 6,068 (46.0%), other marine fishes 5,838 (44.2%). Mining and quarrying (1982): salt CV Esc3,485,000. Manufacturing (1983): flour 9,996, bread 2,331; frozen fish 1,120; biscuits 429; cigars 37; alcoholic beverages 195,036 litres; soft drinks 132,954 litres. Construction (1982): residential CV Esc280,800,000; nonresidential CV Esc1,900,000. Energy production (consumption): electricity (kW-hr; 1983) 12,000,000 (12,000,000); coal, none (none); crude petroleum, n.a. (n.a.); petroleum products (metric tons; 1982) n.a. (32,000); natural gas, n.a. (n.a.).

Gross national product (at current market prices; 1983): U.S.$110,000,000 (U.S.$363 per capita).

Structure of gross domestic product and labour force

	1981 in value CV Esc'000,000	% of total value	labour force	% of labour force
Agriculture, forestry, and fishing	560.0	17.6	58,000	55.8
Manufacturing and public utilities	125.0	3.9	1,700	1.6
Mining	9.0	0.3		
Construction	645.0	20.3		
Pub. admin., defense	550.0	17.3	44,300	42.6
Trade, finance, and other	1,290	40.6		
TOTAL	3,179	100.0	104,000	100.0

Population economically active (1983): total 109,000; participation rate of total population 36.0% (female [1981] 9.5%, unemployed [1980] 21.0%).

Price and earnings indexes (1975 = 100)

	1976	1977	1978	1979	1980	1981
Consumer price index	101.2	108.3	122.7	131.2	150.4	167.7
Monthly earnings index	...	...	...	...	...	...

Household income and expenditure. Average household size (1980) 4.3; average annual income per household: n.a.; source of income: n.a.; expenditure: n.a.
Land use (1983): forested 0.2%; meadows and pastures 6.2%; agricultural and under permanent cultivation 9.9%; other 83.7%.

Foreign trade

Balance of trade (current prices)

	1978	1979	1980	1981	1982	1983
CV Esc'000,000	−1,833	−1,895	−2,743	−3,300	−3,978	−5,482
% of total	92.4%	91.1%	99.9%	91.5%	89.8%	92.0%

Imports (1983): CV Esc5,720,241,000 (machinery and electrical equipment 16.6%, mineral products 13.6%, foodstuffs and beverages 13.3%, vegetable products 13.1%, transport equipment 7.8%, chemical products 4.2%, textiles and textile products 3.3%, plastics and resins 2.5%). *Major import sources* (1981): Portugal 31.7%; The Netherlands 12.9%; Iceland 6.5%; West Germany 6.3%.
Exports (1983): CV Esc238,039,000 (animals and animal products 49.2%, vegetable products 20.3%, foodstuffs and beverages 20.2%, mineral products 6.5%). *Major export destinations* (1981): Algeria 25.5%; The Netherlands 17.0%; Portugal 8.5%; Central African Republic 2.1%; Zaire 2.1%; Spain 2.1%.

Transport and communications

Transport. Railroads: none. Roads (1982): total length 1,398 mi, 2,250 km (paved 29%). Vehicles (1981): passenger cars 4,000; trucks and buses 1,343. Merchant marine (1984): vessels (100 gross tons and over) 24; total deadweight tonnage 21,728. Air transport (1982)§: passenger arrivals 21,200, passenger departures 23,106; metric tons of cargo loaded 104.7, metric tons of cargo unloaded 615.3; airports (1985) with scheduled flights 9.
Communications. Daily newspapers: none. Radio (1984): total number of receivers 47,000 (1 per 6.6 persons). Television: none. Telephones (1981): 1,739 (1 per 168 persons).

Education and health

Education (1982–83)

	schools	teachers	students	student/ teacher ratio
Primary (age 7–10)	436	1,459	50,000	34.3
Secondary (age 10–17)	16	603	10,454	17.3
Voc., teacher tr.	4	76	923	12.1
Higher	...	...	...	...

Educational attainment, n.a. *Literacy* (1981): total population over age 15 literate 78,839 (49.3%); males literate 43,814 (55.3%); females literate 35,025 (43.4%).
Health (1980): physicians 51 (1 per 5,664 persons); hospital beds 632 (1 per 457 persons); infant mortality rate per 1,000 live births (1983) 30.0.
Food (1980–82): daily per capita caloric intake 2,716 (vegetable products 91%, animal products 9%); 116% of FAO recommended minimum requirement.

Military

Total active duty personnel (1985): 1,100 (army 90.9%, navy 6.8%, air force 2.3%). *Military expenditure as percent of GNP* (1982): 2.2% (world 6.0%); per capita expenditure U.S.$7.

*Preliminary. †Detail does not add to total given because of rounding. ‡Budget for 1984 was: Revenue Cv Esc1,630,000,000; Expenditure CV Esc2,134,500,000. §Data for Amílcar Cabral airport only.

Central African Republic

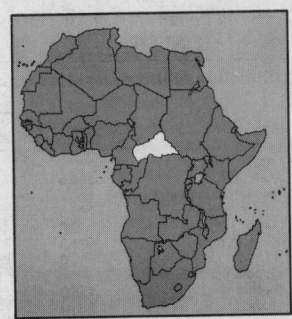

Official name: République Centrafricaine (Central African Republic).
Form of government: military dictatorship with one ruling body (Military Committee for National Recovery [23]).
Head of state and government: Chairman.
Capital: Bangui.
Official language: French.
Official religion: none.
Monetary unit: 1 CFA franc (CFAF) = 100 centimes; valuation (Oct. 21, 1985) 1 U.S.$ = CFAF402.0; 1 £ = CFAF576.5.

Area and population

Prefectures	Capitals	area sq mi	area sq km	population 1985* estimate
Bamingui-Bangoran	Ndélé	22,471	58,200	29,400
Bangui	Bangui	26	67	473,800
Basse-Kotto	Mobaye	6,797	17,604	187,200
Gribingui-Économique	Kaga-Bandoro	7,720	19,996	85,700
Haut-Mbomou	Obo	21,440	55,530	52,200
Haute-Kotto	Bria	33,456	86,650	233,100
Haute-Sangha	Berbérati	11,661	30,203	37,400
Kemo-Gribingui	Sibut	6,642	17,204	78,300
Lobaye	Mbaïki	7,427	19,235	160,700
Mbomou	Bangassou	23,610	61,150	132,900
Nana-Mambere	Bouar	10,270	26,600	197,600
Ombella-Mpoko	Bimbo	12,292	31,835	127,900
Ouaka	Bambari	19,266	49,900	216,200
Ouham	Bossangoa	19,402	50,250	269,300
Ouham-Pendé	Bozoum	12,394	32,100	242,100
Sangha-Économique	Nola	7,495	19,412	59,600
Vakaga	Birao	17,954	46,500	24,200
TOTAL		240,324†	622,436	2,607,600

Demography

Population (1985): 2,658,000.
Density (1985): persons per sq mi 11.0, persons per sq km 4.3.
Urban–rural (1983): urban 44.0%; rural 56.0%.
Sex distribution (1980): male 47.86%; female 52.14%.
Age breakdown (1981): under 15, 42.4%; 15–59, 54.1%; 60 and over, 3.5%.
Population projection: (1990) 2,965,000; (2000) 3,736,000.
Doubling time: 28 years.
Ethnic composition (1978): Banda 44.6%; Baya 14.3%; Ngbandi 10.7%; Azande 9.6%; Mbaka 4.3%; Sara 3.9%; Kare 2.5%; other 10.1%.
Religious affiliation (1980): Protestant 50.0%; Roman Catholic 33.1%; tribal 12.0%; Muslim 3.2%; Baha'i 0.3%; other 1.4%.
Major cities (1984): Bangui 473,800; Bambari 44,500; Bouar 42,000; Berbérati 38,000; Bossangoa 35,800.

Vital statistics

Birth rate per 1,000 population (1983): 41.0 (world avg. 29.0); legitimate, n.a.; illegitimate, n.a.
Death rate per 1,000 population (1983): 17.0 (world avg. 11.0).
Natural increase rate per 1,000 population (1983): 24.0 (world avg. 18.0).
Total fertility rate (avg. births per childbearing woman; 1983): 5.5.
Marriage rate per 1,000 population: n.a.
Divorce rate per 1,000 population: n.a.
Life expectancy at birth (1983): male 46.0 years; female 49.0 years.
Major causes of death per 100,000 population (1978): infectious and parasitic diseases 59.0.

National economy

Budget (1982). Revenue: CFAF29,995,000,000 (indirect taxes 52.4%, nonfiscal receipts 21.1%, direct taxes 20.3%). Expenditures: CFAF38,203,000,000 (education and culture 13.9%, defense 8.3%, repayment of public debt 8.1%).
Public debt (external, outstanding; 1983): U.S.$315,000,000.
Tourism (1981): receipts from visitors U.S.$3,000,000; expenditures by nationals abroad, n.a.
Production (metric tons except as noted). Agriculture, forestry, fishing (1984): roots and tubers 1,154,000, cassava 900,000, peanuts (groundnuts) in shell 130,000, bananas 82,000, plantains 65,000, millet 59,000, corn (maize) 43,000, seed cotton 20,000, coffee 15,000, rice 13,000; livestock (number of live animals) 1,500,000 cattle, 960,000 goats, 140,000 pigs, 82,000 sheep, 1,637,000 chickens; roundwood 3,049,000 cu m‡; fish catch 13,000‡. Mining and quarrying (1983): diamonds 295,300 carats; gold 134 kg. Manufacturing (1981): footwear 380,000 pairs; motorcycles 7,000 units; bicycles 5,000 units; beer 208,000 hectolitres; soft drinks 34,000 hectolitres; woven cotton fabrics 5,000,000 sq m. Construction: n.a. Energy production (consumption): electricity (kW-hr; 1983) 69,000,000 (69,000,000); coal, none (n.a.); crude petroleum, none (n.a.); petroleum products (metric tons; 1983) none (69,000); natural gas, none (n.a.).
Land use (1983): forested 63.7%; meadows and pastures 4.8%; agricultural and under permanent cultivation 3.1%; other 28.4%.

Gross national product (at current market prices; 1983): U.S.$690,000,000 (U.S.$280 per capita).

Structure of gross domestic product and labour force

1983	in value U.S.$'000,000	% of total value	labour force	% of labour force
Agriculture	177	35.5	1,114,000	85.8
Mining	16	3.2		
Manufacturing	39	7.8	55,000	4.2
Construction	22	4.4		
Public utilities	8	1.6		
Transportation and communication				
Trade	236	47.4	130,000	10.0
Finance				
Pub. admin., defense				
Services				
TOTAL	498§	100.0†	1,299,000	100.0

Population economically active (1983): total 1,322,000; participation rate of total population 50.7% (female [1981] 47.7%, unemployed, n.a.).

Price and earnings indexes (1980 = 100)

	1979	1980	1981	1982	1983	1984	1985 ‖
Consumer price index	85.4	100.0	112.6	127.5	144.5	151.1	161.2
Earnings index	...	...	...	...	...	...	...

Household income and expenditure. Average household size (1980) 4.3; average annual income per household CFAF91,985 (U.S.$435); source of income: n.a.; expenditure: n.a.

Foreign trade

Balance of trade (current prices)

	1977	1978	1979	1980	1981	1982
CFAF'000,000	+8,260	+6,738	+5,713	+11,300	+1,595	+3,679
% of total	26.0%	26.3%	20.3%	30.2%	3.9%	5.5%

Imports (1980): CFAF13,084,000,000 (machinery and equipment 33.9%, food 20.9%, chemicals and plastics 12.2%, textiles 8.4%, fuels and lubricants 1.8%). *Major import sources:* France 61%; Japan 7%.
Exports (1980): CFAF24,384,000,000 (diamonds 36.3%, wood 28.8%, coffee 27.4%, cotton 7.5%). *Major export destinations:* France 52%; Belgium–Luxembourg 14%; Israel 8%; United States 5%.

Transport and communications

Transport. Railroads: none. Roads (1982): total length 14,018 mi, 22,560 km (paved 1%). Vehicles (1984): passenger cars 43,121; trucks and buses 3,861. Merchant marine: vessels (100 gross tons and over) none. Air transport (1982): passenger-mi 105,804,000, passenger-km 170,276,000; short ton-mi cargo 20,677,000, metric ton-km cargo 30,188,000; airports (1985) with scheduled flights 1.
Communications. Daily newspapers: none. Radio (1982): total number of receivers 135,000 (1 per 18 persons). Television (1982): total number of receivers 1,200 (1 per 2,000 persons). Telephones (1983): 2,737 (1 per 1,117 persons).

Education and health

Education (1983–84)

	schools¶	teachers	students	student/ teacher ratio
Primary (age 6–11)	853	4,263	291,444	68.4
Secondary (age 12–18)	...	616	52,417	85.1
Voc., teacher tr.	...	90	1,712	19.0
Higher¶	7	297	4,571	15.4

Educational attainment, n.a. *Literacy* (1980): total population over age 15 literate 447,800 (38.5%); males literate 322,800 (58.8%); females literate 125,000 (20.4%).
Health (1980): physicians 108 (1 per 21,204 persons); hospital beds 3,605 (1 per 616 persons); infant mortality rate per 1,000 live births (1983) 142.0.
Food (1980–82): daily per capita caloric intake 2,151 (vegetable products 93%, animal products 7%); 94% of FAO recommended minimum requirement.

Military

Total active duty personnel (1984): 2,300 (army 87.0%; navy, none; air force 13.0%). *Military expenditure as percent of GNP* (1983): 2.0% (world 6.1%); per capita expenditure U.S.$5.

---

*Beginning of year. †Detail does not add to total given because of rounding. ‡1983. §At current factor cost. ‖ May. ¶1981–82.

Chad

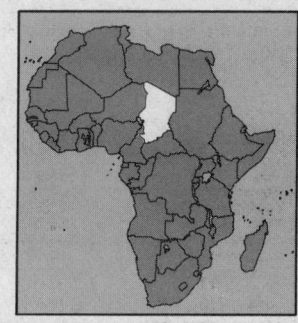

Official name: République du Tchad (Republic of Chad).
Form of government: military regime with no political parties or legislative bodies.
Head of state and government: President.
Capital: N'Djamena.
Official language: French.
Official religion: none.
Monetary unit: 1 CFA franc (CFAF) = 100 centimes; valuation (Oct. 21, 1985) 1 U.S.$ = CFAF402.00; 1 £ = CFAF576.5.

Area and population		area		population
Préfectures	Capitals	sq mi	sq km	1980 estimate
Batha	Ati	34,285	88,800	358,000
Biltine	Biltine	18,090	46,850	179,000
Borkou-Ennedi-Tibesti	Faya	231,795	600,350	90,000
Chari-Baguirmi	N'Djamena	32,010	82,910	700,000
Guéra	Mongo	22,760	58,950	211,000
Kanem	Mao	44,215	114,520	203,000
Lac	Bol	8,620	22,320	137,000
Logone Occidental	Moundou	3,355	8,695	303,000
Logone Oriental	Doba	10,825	28,035	313,000
Mayo-Kebbi	Bongor	11,625	30,105	707,000
Moyen-Chari	Sarh	17,445	45,180	536,000
Ouaddaï	Abéché	29,435	76,240	350,000
Salamat	Am Timan	24,325	63,000	109,000
Tandjilé	Laï	6,965	18,045	308,000
TOTAL		495,755*	1,284,000	4,504,000

Demography

Population (1985): 5,018,000.
Density (1985): persons per sq mi 10.1, persons per sq km 3.9.
Urban–rural (1983): urban 20.0%; rural 80.0%.
Sex distribution (1980): male 47.90%; female 52.10%.
Age breakdown (1980): under 15, 41.8%; 15–29, 26.1%; 30–44, 16.0%; 45–59, 10.3%; 60–74, 4.9%; 75 and over, 0.9%.
Population projection: (1990) 5,558,000; (2000) 7,063,000.
Doubling time: 33 years.
Ethnic composition (1980): Sudanic Arab 30.3%; Bagirmi, Sara, and Kreish 25.8%; Teda 7.7%; Mbum 6.7%; Masalit 6.5%; Tama 6.3%; Mubu 4.2%; Kanuri 2.3%; Hausa 2.2%; other 8.0%.
Religious affiliation (1980): Muslim 44.0%; Christian 33.0%, of which nominal only 15.5%, Protestant 8.8%, Roman Catholic 8.3%; traditional beliefs 22.8%; other 0.2%.
Major cities (1979): N'Djamena 225,000†; Moundou 66,000; Sarh 65,000; Abéché 54,000; Kélo 27,000.

Vital statistics

Birth rate per 1,000 population (1983): 42.0 (world avg. 29.0); legitimate, n.a.; illegitimate, n.a.
Death rate per 1,000 population (1983): 21.0 (world avg. 11.0).
Natural increase rate per 1,000 population (1983): 21.0 (world avg. 18.0).
Total fertility rate (avg. births per childbearing woman; 1983): 5.0.
Marriage rate per 1,000 population: n.a.
Divorce rate per 1,000 population: n.a.
Life expectancy at birth (1983): male 42.0 years; female 45.0 years.
Major causes of death: n.a.

National economy

Budget (1984). Revenue: CFAF11,200,000,000 (indirect taxes 73.2%, of which customs receipts 60.1%; direct taxes 21.7%). Expenditures: CFAF37,635,000,000 (defense 46.5%; education 10.9%; community projects 9.1%; health 3.8%).
Public debt (external, outstanding; 1983): U.S.$233,300,000.
Tourism (1981): receipts from visitors U.S.$2,000,000; expenditures by nationals abroad, n.a.
Production (metric tons except as noted). Agriculture, forestry, fishing (1984): roots and tubers 436,000, millet 320,000, sugarcane 250,000, cassavas 210,000, seed cotton 115,000, peanuts (groundnuts) 80,000, cotton seed 72,000, rice 51,000, lint cotton 43,000, dry beans 35,000, sweet potatoes 35,000, mangoes 30,000, dates 30,000, raw sugar 22,000; livestock (number of live animals) 3,400,000 cattle, 2,200,000 sheep, 2,000,000 goats, 3,000,000 chickens; roundwood 8,112,000 cu m†; fish catch 110,000†. Mining and quarrying: clay and natron. Manufacturing (1984): beef and veal 24,000; mutton and lamb 8,000; goat meat 7,000; salted, dried, or smoked fish 20,000‡; refined sugar 4,000; wheat flour 4,000‡; woven cotton fabrics 15,600,000 metres‡; beer 163,000 hectolitres‡; cigarettes 349,000,000 units‡. Construction: n.a. Energy production (consumption): electricity (kW-hr; 1983) 65,000,000 (65,000,000); coal, none (n.a.); crude petroleum, none (n.a.); petroleum products (metric tons; 1983) none (90,000); natural gas, none (n.a.).
Household income and expenditure. Average household size (1980) 3.9; average annual income per household CFAF96,806 (U.S.$458); source of income: n.a.; expenditure: n.a.
Land use (1983): forested 16.3%; meadows and pastures 35.7%; agricultural and under permanent cultivation 2.5%; other 45.5%.

Gross national product (at current market prices; 1983): U.S.$282,000,000 (U.S.$59 per capita).

Structure of gross domestic product and labour force				
	1983			
	in value U.S.$'000,000	% of total value	labour force	% of labour force
Agriculture	316.0	51.6	1,476,000	81.0
Mining	3.0	0.5		
Manufacturing	44.0	7.2	151,000	8.3
Construction	8.0	1.3		
Public utilities	3.0	0.5		
Transportation and communication				
Trade	238.0	38.9	196,000	10.7
Finance				
Pub. admin., defense				
Services				
TOTAL	612.0§	100.0	1,823,000	100.0

Population economically active (1984): total 1,862,000 (participation rate of total population 38.0% (female [1977] 23.2%, unemployed, n.a.).

Price and earnings indexes (1975 = 100)							
	1972	1973	1974	1975	1976	1977	1978¶
Consumer price index	73.7	77.7	86.5	100.0	103.3	112.0	128.6

Foreign trade ‖

Balance of trade (current prices)						
	1978	1979	1980	1981	1982	1983
CFAF'000,000	−26,705	+644	−534	−6,684	−16,733	−9,420
% of total	37.4%	1.7%	1.7%	12.9%	30.6%	53.3%

Imports (1983): CFAF13,539,600,000 (petroleum products 16.8%; cereal products 16.8%; pharmaceutical products and chemicals 11.5%; machinery and transport equipment 8.5%, of which transport equipment 7.3%; electrical equipment 5.7%; textiles 2.9%; raw and refined sugar 2.3%). *Major import sources* (1975): France 40.7%; Nigeria 10.7%; The Netherlands 7.1%; United States 5.8%; Cameroon 5.7%.
Exports (1983): CFAF4,120,000,000 (raw cotton 91.1%; live cattle and frozen bovine meat 1.8%). *Major export destinations* (1975): Nigeria 19.6%; France 6.8%; Congo 5.5%; Niger 4.1%; Cameroon 2.9%; Central African Republic 1.9%; Zaire 1.7%.

Transport and communications

Transport. Railroads: none. Roads (1983): total length 24,855 mi, 40,000 km (paved 1%). Vehicles (1982): passenger cars 7,000; trucks and buses 5,000. Merchant marine vessels (100 gross tons and over) none. Air transport¶ (1983): passenger-mi 129,311,000, passenger-km 208,106,000; short ton-mi cargo 26,217,000, metric ton-km cargo 38,278,000; airports (1985) with scheduled flights 2.
Communications. Daily newspapers (1983): total number 3; total circulation 1,500♀; circulation per 1,000 population 3,300♀. Radio (1984): total number of receivers 75,000 (1 per 65 persons). Television: none. Telephones (1981): 900 (1 per 5,085 persons).

Education and health

Education (1976–77)				
	schools	teachers	students	student/ teacher ratio
Primary (age 6–12)	783	2,610	210,882δ	77.0
Secondary (age 13–19)	...	590	18,382	31.2
Voc., teacher tr.	...	...	1,198	...
Higher□	1	85	550	6.5

Educational attainment, n.a. *Literacy* (1980): total population over age 15 literate 466,500 (17.8%); males literate 459,700 (35.6%); females literate 6,800 (0.5%).
Health: physicians (1980) 94 (1 per 47,640 persons); hospital beds (1977) 3,553 (1 per 1,182 persons); infant mortality rate per 1,000 live births (1983) 142.0.
Food (1980–82): daily per capita caloric intake 1,821 (vegetable products 92%, animal products 8%); 77% of FAO recommended minimum requirement.

Military

Total active duty personnel (1984): 4,200 (army 95.2%; navy, none; air force 4.8%). *Military expenditure as percent of GNP* (1983): 2.4% (world 6.1%); per capita expenditure U.S.$1.

*Detail does not add to total given because of rounding. †1983. ‡1980. §At current factor cost. ‖ Imports c.i.f. (cost, insurance, and freight); exports f.o.b. (free on board). ¶The airport at N'Djamena is underutilized because of the political and military unrest in Chad. ♀Partial circulation only. δExcluding Islámic private education (9,453 students in 1975). □1981–82.

Chile

Official name: República de Chile (Republic of Chile).
Form of government: military regime.
Head of state and government: President (general) assisted by a four-member junta.
Capital: Santiago.
Official language: Spanish.
Official religion: none.
Monetary unit: 1 peso (Ch$) = 100 centavos; valuation (Oct. 21, 1985) 1 U.S.$ = Ch$179.57; 1 £ = Ch$257.50.

Area and population

Regions	Capitals	area sq mi	area sq km	population 1985 estimate*
Tarapacá	Iquique	22,422	58,073	266,400
Antofagasta	Antofagasta	48,381	125,306	336,200
Atacama	Copiapó	30,219	78,268	214,700
Coquimbo	La Serena	15,308	39,647	439,900
Valparaíso	Valparaíso	6,220	16,109	1,326,800
Libertador General Bernardo O'Higgins	Rancagua	7,024	18,193	589,300
Maule	Talca	11,783	30,518	739,300
Bío-Bío	Concepción	14,218	36,824	1,569,400
Araucanía	Temuco	12,263	31,760	678,000
Los Lagos	Puerto Montt	25,904	67,090	904,600
Aisén del General Carlos Ibáñez del Campo	Coihaique	42,085	108,999	71,400
Magallanes y de la Antártica Chilena	Punta Arenas	43,363†	112,310†	117,400
Región Metropolitana de Santiago	Santiago	5,331	13,808	4,722,500
TOTAL		284,520†‡	736,905†	11,976,000‡

Demography

Population (1985): 12,074,000.
Density (1985): persons per sq mi 42.4, persons per sq km 16.4.
Urban–rural (1984): urban 83.1%; rural 16.9%.
Sex distribution (1984): male 49.52%; female 50.48%.
Age breakdown (1984): under 15, 31.4%; 15–29, 29.0%; 30–44, 19.4%; 45–59, 11.9%; 60–74, 6.3%; 75 and over, 1.9%‡.
Population projection: (1990) 13,061,000; (2000) 14,017,000.
Doubling time: 42 years.
Ethnic composition (1980): mestizo 92%; Indian (mostly Mapuche) 6%; others (mainly European) 2%.
Religious affiliation (1982): Roman Catholic 79.2%; Protestant 6.0%; atheist and nonreligious 2.0%; other 12.8%.
Major cities (1985*): Greater Santiago 4,271,500; Viña del Mar 311,600; Valparaíso 266,900; Talcahuano 218,900; Concepción 215,800; Antofagasta 174,100; Temuco 170,200; Rancagua 149,700; Talca 143,000; Chillán 127,600; Arica, 126,700; Valdivia 118,900; Iquique 118,700.

Vital statistics

Birth rate per 1,000 population (1984): 21.2 (world avg. 29.0); (1980) legitimate 72.4%; illegitimate 27.6%.
Death rate per 1,000 population (1984): 6.3 (world avg. 11.0).
Natural increase rate per 1,000 population (1984): 14.9 (world avg. 18.0).
Total fertility rate (avg. births per childbearing woman; 1981): 3.0.
Marriage rate per 1,000 population (1982): 7.0.
Divorce rate per 1,000 population (1982): 0.3.
Life expectancy at birth (1981): male 65.4 years; female 70.1 years.
Major causes of death per 100,000 population (1982): circulatory diseases 168.2; malignant neoplasms (cancers) 102.5; accidents and poisonings 74.6.

National economy

Budget (1983). Revenue: Ch$941,879,000,000 (nontax revenue 67.9%, income tax 32.1%). Expenditures: Ch$645,585,000,000 (current transfers 61.4%, salaries 18.6%, goods and services 7.8%, interest on public debt 2.8%).
Public debt (external, outstanding; 1983): U.S.$6,827,500,000.
Tourism: receipts from visitors (1983) U.S.$85,000,000; expenditures by nationals abroad (1981): U.S.$260,000,000.
Production (metric tons except as noted). Agriculture, forestry, fishing (1984): sugar beets 2,194,000, grapes 1,050,000, potatoes 988,000, wheat 988,000, corn (maize) 721,000, apples 235,000, tomatoes 162,000, oats 163,000; livestock (number of live animals) 6,300,000 sheep, 3,870,000 cattle, 1,150,000 pigs; roundwood 12,849,000 cu m§; fish catch 3,978,078§. Mining and quarrying (1984): iron ore 7,116,000,000; copper 1,308,000; nitrates 622,500§; molybdenum 15,300; iodine 2,793§; silver 465,159 kilograms; gold 17,716 kilograms. Manufacturing (1984): cement 1,296,000; crude steel ingots 684,000; pig iron and ferroalloys 600,000; newsprint 172,800; beer 1,760,000 hectolitres§; cigarettes 7,680,000,000 units§; tires 595,000 units§; motor vehicles (assembled) 6,744 units. Construction ‖ (value in '000,000 of Ch$; 1983) residential 16,174; nonresidential 4,643. Energy production (consumption): electricity (kW-hr; 1984) 13,356,000,000 (11,871,000,000¶); coal (metric tons; 1984) 1,236,000 (1,193,000¶); crude petroleum (barrels; 1983) 13,301,000 (27,457,000); petroleum products (metric tons; 1983) 4,009,000 (4,670,000); natural gas (cu m; 1983) 939,511,000 (939,511,000).
Gross national product (at current market prices; 1983): U.S.$21,890,000,000 (U.S.$1,870 per capita).

Structure of gross domestic product and labour force

	1983 in value Ch$'000,000	% of total value	labour force♀	% of labour force
Agriculture	138,400	9.4	509,400	15.8
Mining	131,800	8.9	59,400	1.8
Manufacturing	293,300	19.9	405,900	12.6
Construction	75,600	5.1	93,500	2.9
Public utilities	37,000	2.5	23,700	0.7
Transportation and communication	80,500	5.5	195,800	6.1
Trade	255,200	17.3	550,400	17.1
Finance	239,200	16.2	110,100	3.4
Pub. admin., defense	74,400	5.0		
Services	150,200	10.2	1,267,900	39.4
Other				
TOTAL	1,475,600δ	100.0	3,216,100	100.0‡

Population economically active (1982): total 3,659,100; participation rate of population over age 15, 45.7% (female 29.9%, unemployed 16.7%).

Price and earnings indexes (1980 = 100)

	1979	1980	1981	1982	1983	1984	1985
Consumer price index	74.0	100.0	119.7	131.6	167.5	200.7	274.1□
Monthly earnings index	68.1	100.0	130.3	142.9	162.5	192.3	...

Household income and expenditure. Average household size (1982) 4.5; income per household, n.a.; expenditure (1978): food 41.9%, housing 13.3%, transportation and communication 11.8%, recreation and education 8.2%, household goods 7.8%, clothing and footwear 7.6%.
Land use (1983): forested 20.7%; meadows and pastures 15.9%; agricultural and under permanent cultivation 7.4%; other 56.0%.

Foreign trade◊

Balance of trade (current prices)

	1979	1980	1981	1982	1983	1984
U.S.$'000,000	+320	+329	−1,487	+720	+1,320	+953
% of total	4.3%	3.6%	16.0%	10.7%	20.8%	15.0%

Imports (1984): U.S.$3,481,000,000 (intermediate goods 62.0%; consumer goods 14.9%; capital goods 14.6%). *Major import sources* (1983): United States 25.5%; Venezuela 8.2%; Argentina 7.3%; Brazil 6.9%; West Germany 6.7%; Japan 5.9%.
Exports (1984): U.S.$3,657,600,000 (mining 54.2%, of which copper 43.4%; fruits and vegetables 8.0%; fish meal 7.5%; paper and paper products 7.1%; chemical and petroleum products 3.4%). *Major export destinations:* United States 26.0%; Japan 11.1%; West Germany 10.0%; Brazil 6.2%; United Kingdom 5.4%; France 4.5%; Italy 4.4%.

Transport and communications

Transport. Railroads (1984): length 5,300 mi, 8,500 km; passenger-mi 887,300,000, passenger-km 1,428,000,000; short ton-mi cargo 1,578,100,000, metric ton-km cargo 2,304,000,000. Roads (1983): total length 54,761 mi, 88,129 km (paved 11%). Vehicles (1983) passenger cars 620,000; trucks and buses 257,000. Merchant marine (1984): vessels (100 gross tons and over) 219; total deadweight tonnage 731,511. Air transport (1984): passenger-mi 969,337,000, passenger-km 1,560,000,000; short ton-mi cargo 77,393,000, metric ton-km cargo 112,992,000; airports (1985) with scheduled flights 13.
Communications. Daily newspapers (1983): total number 66; total circulation 1,407,300; circulation per 1,000 population 120. Radio (1984): 17,000,000 receivers (1 per 0.7 person). Television (1984): 2,645,000 receivers (1 per 4.5 persons). Telephones (1983): 608,200 (1 per 19 persons).

Education and health

Education (1983)

	schools	teachers¶	students	student/ teacher ratio
Primary (age 6–13)	8,858	62,746	2,139,155	...
Secondary (age 14–17)	1,282	...	541,739	...
Vocational	347	...	143,689	...
Higher	24	10,372	125,363	...

Educational attainment (1970). Percent of adult population over age 25 having: no formal schooling 12.4%; primary education 57.2%; secondary 26.6%; higher 3.8%. *Literacy* (1983): total population over age 12 literate 8,301,000 (95.6%); males literate 4,100,000 (95.0%)△; females literate 4,201,000 (93.8%)△.
Health: physicians (1981) 10,877 (1 per 1,038 persons); hospital beds (1982) 38,254 (1 per 300 persons); infant mortality rate per 1,000 live births (1984) 20.1.
Food (1980–82): daily per capita caloric intake 2,706 (vegetable products 84%, animal products 16%); 113% of FAO recommended minimum requirement.

Military

Total active duty personnel (1984): 96,000 (army 55.2%, navy 29.2%, air force 15.6%). *Military expenditure as percent of GNP* (1982): 4.8% (world 6.0%); per capita expenditure: U.S.$121.

---

*1984 year-end estimate. †Excludes 490,243 sq mi (1,269,723 sq km) of Antártica Chilena, portions of which are disputed with the United Kingdom and Argentina. ‡Detail does not add to total given because of rounding. §1983. ‖ Includes both private and public authorized construction. ¶1982. ♀Employed persons only. δAt current prices. □September. ◊Import figures are f.o.b. (free on board) in balance of trade and c.i.f. (cost, insurance, and freight) for commodities and trading partners. △Calculated from the 1981 literacy rate of 94.4%.

China

Official name: Chung-hua Jen-min Kung-ho-kuo (People's Republic of China).
Form of government: single-party people's republic with one legislative house (National People's Congress [2,978]).
Chief of state: President.
Head of government: Premier.
Capital: Peking (Beijing).
Official language: Mandarin Chinese.
Official religion: none.
Monetary unit: 1 Renminbi (yuan) (Y) = 10 jiao = 100 fen; valuation (Oct. 21, 1985) 1 U.S.$ = Y3.05; 1 £ = Y4.37.

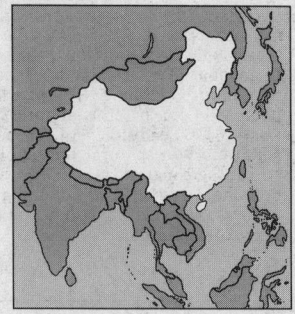

Area and population*†		area		population
		sq mi	sq km	1983 estimate
Provinces	**Capitals**			
Anhwei (Anhui)	Ho-fei (Hefei)	54,000	139,900	50,560,000
Chekiang (Zhejiang)	Hangchow (Hangzhou)	39,300	101,800	39,630,000
Fukien (Fujian)	Foochow (Fuzhou)	47,500	123,100	26,400,000
Heilungkiang (Heilongjiang)	Harbin (Harbin)	179,000	463,600	33,060,000
Honan (Henan)	Cheng-chou (Zhengzhou)	64,500	167,000	75,910,000
Hopeh (Hebei)	Shih-chia-chung (Shijiazhuang)	78,200	202,700	54,200,000
Hunan (Hunan)	Ch'ang-sha (Changsha)	81,300	210,500	55,090,000
Hupeh (Hubei)	Wu-han (Wuhan)	72,400	187,500	48,350,000
Kansu (Gansu)	Lan-chou (Lanzhou)	141,500	366,500	19,880,000
Kiangsi (Jiangxi)	Nan-ch'ang (Nanchang)	63,600	164,800	33,840,000
Kiangsu (Jiangsu)	Nanking (Nanjing)	39,600	102,600	61,350,000
Kirin (Jilin)	Ch'ang-ch'un (Changchun)	72,200	187,000	22,690,000
Kwangtung (Guangdong)	Canton (Guangzhou)	89,300	231,400	60,750,000
Kweichow (Guizhou)	Kuei-yang (Guiyang)	67,200	174,000	29,020,000
Liaoning (Liaoning)	Shen-yang (Shenyang)	58,300	151,000	36,290,000
Shansi (Shanxi)	T'ai-yüan (Taiyuan)	60,700	157,100	25,720,000
Shantung (Shandong)	Tsinan (Jinan)	59,200	153,300	75,640,000
Shensi (Shaanxi)	Sian (Xi'an)	75,600	195,800	29,310,000
Szechwan (Sichuan)	Ch'eng-tu (Chengdu)	219,700	569,000	100,760,000
Tsinghai (Qinghai)	Hsi-ning (Xining)	278,400	721,000	3,930,000
Yunnan (Yunnan)	K'un-ming (Kunming)	168,400	436,200	33,190,000
Autonomous regions				
Inner Mongolia (Nei Monggol)	Hu-ho-hao-t'e (Hohhot)	454,600	1,177,500	19,560,000
Kwangsi Chuang (Guangxi Zhuang)	Nan-ning (Nanning)	85,100	220,400	37,330,000
Ningsia Hui (Ningxia Hui)	Yin-ch'uan (Yinchuan)	25,600	66,400	3,980,000
Sinkiang Uighur (Xinjiang Uygur)	Urumchi (Urumqi)	635,900	1,646,900	13,330,000
Tibet (Xizang)	Lhasa (Lhasa)	471,700	1,221,600	1,930,000
Municipalities				
Peking (Beijing)	—	6,500	16,800	9,540,000
Shanghai (Shanghai)	—	2,400	6,200	11,940,000
Tientsin (Tianjin)	—	4,400	11,300	7,880,000
TOTAL		3,696,100‡	9,572,900‡	1,021,060,000§

Demography

Population (1985): 1,043,100,000.
Density (1985): persons per sq mi 282.3, persons per sq km 109.0.
Urban-rural (1982): urban 20.6%; rural 79.4%.
Sex distribution (1982): male 51.53%; female 48.47%.
Age breakdown (1982): under 15, 33.6%; 15–29, 29.1%; 30–44, 17.5%; 45–59, 12.2%; 60–74, 6.3%; 75 and over 1.3%.
Population projection: (1990) 1,098,000,000; (2000) 1,269,000,000.
Doubling time: 60 years.
Ethnic composition (1982): Han (Chinese) 93.30%; Chuang 1.33%; Hui 0.72%; Uighur 0.59%; Yi 0.54%; Miao 0.50%; Manchu 0.43%; Tibetan 0.39%; Mongolian 0.34%; Tuchia 0.28%; Puyi 0.21%; Korean 0.18%; Tung 0.14%; Yao 0.14%; Pai 0.11%; Hani 0.11%; Kazakh 0.09%; Tai 0.08%; Li 0.08%; other 0.44%.
Religious affiliation (1980): nonreligious 59.2%; Chinese folk-religionist 20.1%; atheist 12.0%; Buddhist 6.0%; Muslim 2.4%; Christian 0.2%.
Major cities (1982): Shanghai 6,270,000; Peking 5,550,000; Tientsin 5,130,000; Shen-yang 4,020,000; Wu-han 3,230,000; Canton 3,120,000; Chungking (Chongqing) 2,650,000; Harbin 2,550,000; Ch'eng-tu 2,470,000; Sian 2,180,000; Nanking 2,130,000; T'ai-yüan 1,750,000; Ch'ang-ch'un 1,740,000; Ta-lien (Dalian) 1,480,000; Lan-chou 1,430,000; K'un-ming 1,430,000; Tsinan 1,320,000; An-shan (Anshan) 1,210,000; Fu-shun (Fushun) 1,190,000; Ch'ing-fao (Qingdao) 1,180,000.
Households (1982). Average rural household size 5.5; urban household size 4.1. Family households: 220,100,755 (99.5%); collective 1,073,010 (0.5%).

Vital statistics

Birth rate per 1,000 population (1984): 17.5 (world avg. 29.0); legitimate, n.a.; illegitimate, n.a.
Death rate per 1,000 population (1984): 6.7 (world avg. 11.0).
Natural increase rate per 1,000 population (1984): 10.8 (world avg. 18.0).
Total fertility rate (avg. births per childbearing woman; 1980–85): 2.3.
Marriage rate per 1,000 population (1982): 16.7.
Divorce rate per 1,000 population: n.a.
Life expectancy at birth (1980–85): male 65.5 years; female 69.4 years.
Major causes of death per 100,000 population (1981) ‖ : diseases of the heart 139.9; malignant neoplasms (cancers) 113.0; diseases of the circulatory

system 111.2; diseases of the respiratory system 43.0; accidents (including suicide) 31.3; gastrointestinal diseases 25.9; infectious diseases 23.7.

Social indicators

Educational attainment (1982). Percent of population over age 5 having: no schooling or some primary 31.9%; completed primary 39.9%; completed junior secondary 20.0%; completed senior secondary 7.5%; some higher 0.2%; completed higher 0.5%.

Distribution of rural income (1980)				
percent of household income by quintile				
1	2	3	4	5 (highest)
8.5%	12.9%	17.4%	23.5%	37.7%

Quality of working life (1982). Average workweek: 48 hours. Annual rate per 100,000 workers for: injury or accident, n.a.; industrial illness, n.a.; death, n.a. Money spent on labour insurance and collective amenities (including pensions for the retired): Y20,940,000,000¶. Average days lost to labour stoppages per 1,000 workdays: n.a. Average duration of journey to work: n.a. Method of transport: n.a. Rate per 1,000 workers of discouraged (unemployed no longer seeking work): n.a.
Access to services (1979). Proportion of communes having access to: electricity 87.1%; safe public water supply, n.a.; public sewage collection, n.a.; public fire protection, n.a.
Social participation. Eligible voters participating in last national election: n.a. Population participating in voluntary work: n.a. Trade union membership in total work force: 62.5%. Practicing religious population in total affiliated population: n.a.
Social deviance. Annual reported offense rate per 100,000 population (1979–81) for: theft 60.0; violent crime (including murder, rape, and robbery) 4.5; other 10.59.
Leisure. Favourite leisure activities: n.a.
Material well-being (1983). Urban families possessing (number per family): wristwatches 2.7; bicycles 1.6; sewing machines 0.8; radios 1.0; televisions 0.8. Rural families possessing (number per family): wristwatches 0.9; bicycles 0.6; sewing machines 0.4; radios 0.6; televisions 0.04.

National economy

Gross national product (at current market prices; 1983): U.S.$301,840,000,000 (U.S.$296 per capita).

Structure of national income and labour force				
	1983		1982	
	in value Y'000,000,000	% of total value	labour force ('000)	% of labour force
Agriculture	180.1	28.2	320,130	71.6
Mining	...	...	δ	δ
Manufacturing	352.1	55.1	59,300δ	13.3δ
Construction	60.1	9.4	13,400	3.0
Public utilities	...	...	...	...
Transp. and commun.	17.9	2.8	8,500	1.9
Trade	28.8	4.5	18,200	4.1
Finance	...	...	...	...
Pub. admin., defense	...	...	6,110	1.4
Services	...	...	16,460	3.7
Other	...	...	4,960	1.1
TOTAL	639.0	100.0	447,060	100.0□

Budget (1983). Revenue: Y124,900,000,000 (taxes 62.1%; receipts from state enterprises 19.3%). Expenditures: Y129,300,000,000 (capital construction 29.6%; culture, education, public health 17.3%; defense 13.7%).
Tourism (1983): receipts from visitors U.S.$941,000,000; expenditures by nationals abroad, n.a.

Retail and service enterprises (1982)				
	no. of enterprises	no. of employees	annual wage as a % of all wages	annual gross output value○ (Y'000,000)
Retail trade	2,607,000	8,709,000	...	...
Grocery stores	150,000	1,160,000	...	...
Department stores	122,000	1,217,000	...	...
Other food shops	91,000	669,000	...	...
Agricultural supplies stores	55,000	254,000	...	...
Household supplies stores	51,000	269,000	...	...
Grain and oil shops	35,000	378,000	...	...
Textile stores	21,000	143,000	...	...
Electrical appliances stores	20,000	202,000	...	...
Drug stores	20,000	150,000	...	...
Book stores	14,000	66,000	...	...
Coal stores	12,000	135,000	...	...
Service trade	597,000	1,824,000	...	...
Repair shops	217,000	414,000	...	...
Barber shops	83,000	264,000	...	...
Hotels	49,000	393,000	...	...
Photo studios	41,000	139,000	...	...

Production (metric tons except as noted). Agriculture, forestry, fishing (1984): grains—rice 181,400,000, wheat 87,700,000, corn (maize) 72,600,000, sorghum 8,510,000, millet 6,600,000, barley 3,000,000; oilseeds—peanuts 4,130,000, rapeseed 3,960,000, sunflower 1,400,000, sesame 420,000; fruits and nuts—apples 3,810,000, pears 2,020,000, oranges 1,495,000, bananas 436,000, chestnuts 240,000, walnuts 120,000¶; others—roots and tubers 158,500,000, sugarcane 38,400,000, soybeans 10,000,000, sugar beets 7,520,000, pulses 6,100,000, cotton 5,700,000, tobacco 1,530,000, jute and hemp 1,020,000, tea 440,000, silk 35,000; livestock (number of live animals) 298,500,000 pigs, 98,900,000 sheep, 68,000,000 goats, 58,600,000 cattle, 18,700,000 water buffalo, 10,800,000 horses, 9,400,000 asses, 564,000

camels; roundwood (1983) 231,650,000 cu m; fish catch (1983) 5,213,000, of which 2,660,000 freshwater fish, 1,446,000 marine fish, 367,000 clams, 308,000 marine crabs. Mining and quarrying (1983): metals (metal content of ores)—copper 350,000, zinc 170,000, lead 170,000, tin 16,000, tungsten 15,000, molybdenum 2,000; other metals—iron ore 75,000,000, bauxite 1,950,000, nickel 15,000, gold 2,000,000 troy oz; nonmetals—salt 16,130,-000, gypsum 5,400,000, barite 1,000,000, talc 1,000,000, fluorspar 650,000, graphite 185,000, asbestos 160,000. Manufacturing (1983)⊕: cement 108,-250,000; steel 40,020,000; chemical fertilizer 13,789,000; sugar 3,770,000; cloth 14,880,000,000 metres; wristwatches 34,690,000 units; bicycles 27,-580,000 units; sewing machines 10,870,000 units; television sets 6,840,000 units. Construction (value in Y; 1982): residential 12,177,000,000; nonresidential 8,888,000,000. Distribution of industrial production (percent of total value of output by sector; 1978 [1984]): state-operated enterprises 80.6% (73.8%); collectives 19.2% (25.0%); privately operated enterprises 0.2% (1.2%). Retail sales (percent of total sales by sector; 1978 [1984]): state-operated enterprises 90.5% (45.8%); collectives 7.4% (39.6%); privately operated enterprises 2.1% (14.6%).

Manufacturing and mining enterprises (1981)◇

	no. of enterprises	no. of employees	annual wages as a % of avg. of all wages△	annual gross output value† (Y'000,000)
Manufacturing				
Machinery, transport equipment, and basic manufactures,	104,100	10,151,000	96.7	107,995
of which,				
Industrial equipment	7,600	...	...	19,001
Transport equipment	2,700	...	...	12,420
Electronic goods	4,100	1,015,000	...	11,888
Metalware for daily use	11,200	...	...	9,617
Textiles,	17,100	3,890,000	95.5	85,602
of which,				
Cotton	5,100	...	...	51,791
Foodstuffs,	55,600	2,561,000	87.5	69,012
of which,				
Grains and edible oils	24,800	...	...	20,398
Processed meat	2,500	...	...	11,797
Tobacco manufactures	300	...	...	10,051
Chemicals,	23,800	3,071,000	92.1	59,143
of which,				
Organic chemicals	2,700	...	...	11,956
Fertilizers	3,600	1,133,000	...	10,286
Building materials,	48,500	1,921,000	93.0	19,507
of which,				
Brick, tile, other	32,000	...	...	8,442
Cement (all forms)	11,600	...	...	7,235
Secondary forest products (including paper and stationery)	20,000	1,081,000	96.1	19,116
Primary forest products	17,500	1,318,000	114.3	10,490
Mining				
Nonferrous and ferrous metals	4,600	3,192,000	107.6	45,669
Petroleum,	300	569,000	114.0	28,213
of which,				
Crude petroleum	190	...	...	13,049
Coal	8,200	3,959,000	119.8	14,626

Energy production (consumption): electricity (kW-hr; 1983) 351,440,000,000 (351,690,000,000); coal (metric tons; 1983) 714,530,000 (710,114,000); crude petroleum (barrels; 1983) 774,296,000 (666,081,000); petroleum products (metric tons; 1983) 64,451,000 (60,601,000); natural gas (cu m; 1983) 12,-177,000,000 (12,177,000,000).

Population economically active (1982): total 474,384,000; participation rate of total population 47.3% (female 32.0%**; unemployed, n.a.). Urban work force by sector of employment, 1978 (1984): state-run enterprises 74,500,-000 (86,700,000); collectives 20,000,000 (32,500,000); self-employment or privately run enterprises 150,000 (3,400,000).

Price and earnings indexes (1980 = 100)

	1977	1978	1979	1980	1981	1982	1983
Consumer price index	90.5	91.3	93.1	100.0	102.6	104.5	106.7
Earnings index	...	...	...	...	...	...	...

Land use (1983): forested 14.0%; meadows and pastures 30.7%; agricultural and under permanent cultivation 10.8%; other 44.5%.

Financial aggregates††

	1979	1980	1981	1982	1983	1984	1985 (6 mo.)
Exchange rate, Y per:							
U.S. dollar	1.50	1.53	1.75	1.92	1.98	2.80	2.88
£	3.33	3.65	3.33	3.10	2.87	3.23	3.73
SDR	1.97	1.95	2.03	2.12	2.07	2.74	2.87
International reserves (U.S.$)							
Total (excl. gold; '000,000)	2,154	2,545	5,048	11,339	14,853	15,081	12,221‡‡
SDRs ('000,000)	—	92	275	214	335	406	426
Reserve pos. in IMF ('000,000)	—	191	—	176	223	308	
Foreign exchange	2,154	2,262	4,773	11,125	14,342	14,420	11,505‡‡
Gold ('000,000 fine troy oz)	12.8	12.8	12.7	12.7	12.7	12.7	12.7‡‡
% world reserves	1.4	1.5	1.3	1.3	1.3	1.3	1.3‡‡
Interest and prices							
Central bank discount (%)	...	...	...	...	...	...	...
Gov't bond yield (%)	...	...	...	...	...	...	...
Industrial share prices	...	...	...	...	...	...	...
Balance of payments (Y'000,000)							
Balance of visible trade,	−1,110	−290	3,030	8,610	5,130	1,590	−6,020§§
of which:							
Imports, f.o.b.	22,280	27,410	33,730	32,820	38,700	56,370	21,690§§
Exports, f.o.b.	21,170	27,120	36,760	41,430	43,830	57,960	15,670§§
Balance of invisibles	...	...	...	...	...	...	...
Balance of payments, current account	...	...	...	...	...	...	...

Household income and expenditure. Average household size (1982), n.a.; rural household 5.5, urban household 4.1. Average annual income per household, n.a.; rural household Y1,475, urban household Y2,216. Sources of income (1982): rural household—income from the collective 51.9%, sideline production 38.1%, of which selling privately tended livestock or poultry 13.3%, or crop or forest produce 12.2%; urban household—time wages 64.4%, subsidies 14.1%, bonuses 10.9%, piece-rate wages 7.6%. Expenditure (1982): rural household—food 60.5%, clothing 11.3%, housing 10.2%, personal effects 10.2%, fuel 5.6%, cultural activities 2.2%; urban household—food 58.7%, clothing 14.4%, personal effects 9.2%, cultural activities 6.6%, fuel 2.9%, housing 1.5%, transportation and communication 1.5%, other 5.2%.

Foreign trade ‖ ‖

Balance of trade (current prices)

	1979	1980	1981	1982	1983	1984
Y'000,000	−3,120	−2,760	−10	+5,660	+1,650	−3,480
% of total	6.9%	4.8%	0.0%	7.3%	1.9%	2.9%

Imports (1982): Y35,769,000,000 (wheat 15.2%, rolled steel 9.1%, manufactured fertilizers 6.5%, synthetic fibres 4.7%, uncombed cotton 3.7%, sugar 3.4%, synthetic polymers 2.9%, logs 2.6%, aluminum, copper, zinc [all forms] 2.4%, wool 1.5%). *Major import sources:* United States 22.7%; Japan 20.6%; Hong Kong 6.9%; Canada 6.6%; West Germany 5.1%; Australia 4.8%; Romania 2.2%; Thailand 1.8%.
Exports (1982): Y41,433,000,000 (crude petroleum 14.8%, garments 7.2%, petroleum products 6.4%, cotton cloth 3.2%, coal 1.6%, canned food 1.6%, aquatic products 1.4%, raw silk 1.3%, cotton and polyester cloth 1.3%, cereals 1.3%, live pigs 1.1%). *Major export destinations:* Hong Kong 23.7%; Japan 22.0%; United States 8.0%; Jordan 6.0%; West Germany 3.5%; Singapore 2.9%; Brazil 1.7%; Yemen (Ṣan'a') 1.5%.

Transport and communications

Transport. Railroads (1983): length 32,600 mi, 52,500 km; passenger-mi 110,191,300,000, passenger-km 177,336,000,000; short ton-mi cargo 454,-421,000,000, metric ton-km cargo 663,444,000,000. Roads (1982): total length 563,600 mi, 907,000 km (paved, n.a.). Vehicles (1982): passenger cars 265,000; trucks 1,768,000. Merchant marine (1984): vessels (100 gross tons and over) 1,262; total deadweight tonnage 20,301,848¶¶. Air transport (1982): passenger-mi 3,700,000,000, passenger-km 6,000,000,000; short ton-mi cargo 126,200,000, metric ton-km cargo 184,200,000; airports (1985) with scheduled flights 73.
Communications. Daily newspapers (1984): total number 27; total circulation 24,826,000; circulation per 1,000 population 24. Radio (1984): total number of receivers 15,000,000 (1 per 69 persons). Television (1984): total number of receivers 9,900,000 (1 per 104 persons). Telephones (1982): 2,342,500 (1 per 430 persons).

Education and health

Education 1982

	schools	teachers	students	student/ teacher ratio
Primary (age 7–13)	880,516	5,505,000	139,720,000	25.4
Secondary (age 13–17)	101,649	2,871,000	45,285,000	15.8
Secondary specialized	3,076	...	1,039,000	...
Higher	715	287,000	1,154,000	4.0

Literacy (1982): total population over age 11 literate 511,000,000 (68.0%)♀♀; males literate, n.a.; females literate, n.a.
Health (1982): physicians 857,000♂♂ (1 per 1,176 persons); hospital beds 2,054,000 (1 per 491 persons); infant mortality rate per 1,000 live births (1980–85) 38.0.
Food (1980–82): daily per capita caloric intake 2,490 (vegetable products 93%, animal products 7%); 106% of FAO recommended minimum requirement.

Military

Total active duty personnel (1984): 4,000,000 (army 79.0%, navy 8.8%, air force 12.2%). *Military expenditure as percent of GNP* (1982): 7.1% (world 6.0%); per capita expenditure U.S.$49.

*Names of the provinces, autonomous regions, and municipalities are stated in conventional form followed by Pinyin transliteration; names of capitals are stated in conventional form or Wade–Giles transliteration followed by Pinyin transliteration. †Data for Taiwan, Quemoy, and Matsu are excluded. ‡Includes 4,600 sq mi (11,900 sq km) not shown separately. §1982 census population is 1,008,175,288. ‖ Based on rural sample population of 3,800,000. ¶1983. ♀Excludes arrests for anti-Communist activities. ♂Mining is included in manufacturing. □Detail does not add to total given because of rounding. ◇State-owned industries only. △1979. †In 1980 constant prices. ⊕Most important manufactured products. **Estimate. ††Exchange rates and international reserves are based on end of year figures. ‡‡4 months. §§3 months. ‖‖Imports, c.i.f. (cost, insurance, and freight); exports, f.o.b. (free on board). ¶¶Deadweight tonnage includes 543 vessels of Taiwan (100 gross tons and over). ♀♀Estimate of literacy excludes semiliterates. ♂♂Includes doctors of traditional Chinese medicine, but excludes practitioners of traditional Chinese medicine.

Colombia

Official name: República de Colombia (Republic of Colombia).
Form of government: unitary, multiparty republic with two legislative houses (Senate [114]; House of Representatives [199]).
Head of state and government: President.
Capital: Bogotá.
Official language: Spanish.
Official religion: Roman Catholicism.
Monetary unit: 1 peso (Col$) = 100 centavos; valuation (Oct. 21, 1985) 1 U.S.$ = Col$159.14; 1 £ = Col$228.21.

Area and population		area		population
				1983
Commissariats	**Capitals**	sq mi	sq km	estimate
Amazonas	Leticia	42,342	109,665	18,000
Guainía	San Felipe (Obando)	27,891	72,238	11,000
Guaviare	Guaviare	16,342	42,327 ⎫	
Vaupés	Mitú	25,200	65,268 ⎬	37,000
Vichada	Puerto Carreño	38,703	100,242	14,000
Departments				
Antioquia	Medellín	24,561	63,612	4,081,700
Atlántico	Barranquilla	1,308	3,388	1,379,100
Bolívar	Cartagena	10,030	25,978	1,076,800
Boyacá	Tunja	8,953	23,189	1,100,400
Caldas	Manizales	3,046	7,888	870,600
Caquetá	Florencia	34,349	88,965	302,300
Cauca	Popayán	11,316	29,308	821,700
Cesar	Valledupar	8,844	22,905	542,600
Chocó	Quibdó	17,965	46,530	253,500
Córdoba	Montería	9,660	25,020	861,900
Cundinamarca	Bogotá	8,735	22,623	1,288,000*
Huila	Neiva	7,680	19,890	272,900
La Guajira	Riohacha	8,049	20,848	510,200
Magdalena	Santa Marta	8,953	23,188	610,100
Meta	Villavicencio	33,064	85,635	384,800
Nariño	Pasto	12,845	33,268	947,000
Norte de Santander	Cúcuta	8,362	21,658	878,300
Quindío	Armenia	712	1,845	352,700
Risaralda	Pereira	1,598	4,140	630,800
Santander	Bucaramanga	11,790	30,537	1,367,600
Sucre	Sincelejo	4,215	10,917	398,400
Tolima	Ibagué	9,097	23,562	1,128,900
Valle	Cali	8,548	22,140	2,848,600
Intendancies				
Arauca	Arauca	9,196	23,818 ⎫	
Casanare	Yopal	17,236	44,640 ⎬	82,000
Putumayo	Mocoa	9,608	24,885	79,000
San Andrés and Providencia	San Andrés	17	44	30,000
Special District				
Bogotá		613	1,587	4,483,300
TOTAL		440,831†	1,141,748	27,663,200

Demography

Population (1985): 28,842,000.
Density (1985): persons per sq mi 65.4, persons per sq km 25.3.
Urban–rural (1983): urban 65.4%; rural 34.6%.
Sex distribution (1980): male 50.11%; female 49.89%.
Age breakdown (1980): under 15, 39.4%; 15–29, 30.2%; 30–44, 15.7%; 45–59, 9.2%; 60–74, 4.6%; 75 and over, 0.9%.
Population projection: (1990) 31,900,000; (2000) 38,000,000.
Doubling time: 32 years.
Ethnic composition (1980): mestizo 47.8%; mulatto 23.0%; white 20.0%; black 6.0%; Amerindian 1.6%; other 1.6%.
Religious affiliation (1983): Roman Catholic 97%; other 3%.
Major cities (1982): Bogotá 4,483,300‡; Medellín 1,664,000; Cali 1,450,000; Barranquilla 924,000; Cartagena 470,000.

Vital statistics

Birth rate per 1,000 population (1982): 30.6 (world avg. 29.0); legitimate 75.2%; illegitimate 24.8%.
Death rate per 1,000 population (1982): 5.8 (world avg. 11.0).
Natural increase rate per 1,000 population (1982): 24.8 (world avg. 18.0).
Total fertility rate (avg. births per childbearing woman; 1980–85): 3.9.
Marriage rate per 1,000 population (1977): 3.5.
Life expectancy at birth (1980–85): male 61.4 years; female 66.0 years.
Major causes of death per 100,000 population (1977): diseases of the circulatory system 129.2; infectious and parasitic diseases 86.6.

National economy

Budget (1983). Revenue: Col$357,958,000,000 (indirect taxes 54.3%, direct taxes 22.2%, credit resources 17.0%). Expenditures: Col$401,799,000,000 (education 21.5%, public debt 11.3%, defense 9.9%, public works 8.6%).
Public debt (external, outstanding; 1983): U.S.$6,898,300,000.
Tourism (1983): receipts from visitors U.S.$235,000,000; expenditures by nationals abroad U.S.$445,000,000.
Production (metric tons except as noted). Agriculture (1984): sugarcane 13,992,000, potatoes 2,016,900, rice 1,780,300, cassava 1,716,800, bananas 1,220,500, corn (maize) 889,600, coffee (green) 816,000, sorghum 610,900, tobacco 51,900; roundwood 16,553,000 cu m‡; fish catch 57,537‡; livestock (number of live animals) 24,251,000 cattle, 2,311,000 pigs, 2,255,000

sheep. Mining and quarrying (1984): iron ore 444,000; gold 501,552 troy oz; silver 96,452 troy oz. Manufacturing (value added in Col$'000,000; 1982): processed food 70,903; beverages 67,685; chemicals 62,112; textiles 41,854; nonmetal products 19,924; transport equipment 19,255. Construction (1983)§: residential 7,296,000 sq m; nonresidential 1,284,000 sq m. Energy production (consumption): electricity (kW-hr; 1983) 27,096,000,-000 (27,070,000,000); coal (metric tons; 1983) 6,000,000 (5,400,000); crude petroleum (barrels; 1983) 55,644,000 (65,917,000); petroleum products (metric tons; 1983) 8,522,000 (7,492,000); natural gas (cu m; 1983) 4,635,925,000 (4,635,925,000).
Gross national product (at current market prices; 1983): U.S.$38,830,000,000 (U.S.$1,410 per capita).

Structure of gross domestic product and labour force				
	1983		**1980**	
	in value Col$'000,000	% of total value	labour force	% of labour force
Agriculture	568,572	18.7	2,412,413	28.5
Mining	88,328	2.9	49,740	0.6
Manufacturing	630,819	20.8	1,136,735	13.4
Construction	153,824	5.1	242,191	2.9
Public utilities	66,606	2.2	44,233	0.5
Transp. and commun.	246,001	8.1	352,623	4.2
Trade	405,881	13.4 ⎱	1,539,843	18.1
Finance		⎰		
Pub. admin., defense	876,630	28.9	1,998,460	23.6
Services				
Other			690,762	8.2
TOTAL	3,036,661‖	100.0†	8,467,000	100.0

Population economically active (1980): total 8,467,000; participation rate of population over age 15, 52.3% (female, 26.2%, unemployed 3.8%).

Price and earnings indexes (1980 = 100)							
	1979	1980	1981	1982	1983	1984	1985
Consumer price index	79.0	100.0	127.5	158.8	190.2	220.8	280.1¶
Monthly earnings index	78.0	100.0	129.8	167.1	...	...	...

Average household size (1981) 5.4.
Land use (1983): forested 49.7%; meadows and pastures 28.9%; agricultural and under permanent cultivation 5.4%; other 16.0%.

Foreign trade

Balance of trade (current prices)						
	1979	1980	1981	1982	1983	1984
U.S.$'000,000	+387.6	−255.5	−1,729.0	−1,841.8	−1,390.7	−590.4
% of total	6.2%	3.1%	22.6%	22.9%	18.4%	7.9%

Imports (1984): U.S.$4,051,948,000 (machinery and equipment 34.2%, chemicals 17.1%, crude petroleum and petroleum products 11.7%, base metals and metal manufactures 9.8%, paper and paper products 5.0%). *Major import sources* (1983): United States 34.7%; EEC countries 14.4%; Venezuela, Ecuador, and Peru 13.6%; Japan 7.9%.
Exports (1984): U.S.$3,461,583,000 (coffee 51.1%, crude petroleum and petroleum products 12.8%, bananas 5.8%, fresh-cut flowers 3.9%, chemicals 2.9%, cotton 2.8%). *Major export destinations* (1983): EEC countries 37.8%; United States 28.6%; Venezuela, Ecuador, and Peru 5.9%.

Transport and communications

Transport. Railroads (1984): length 2,115 mi, 3,403 km; passenger-mi 119,-000,000, passenger-km 192,000,000; short ton-mi cargo 493,000,000, metric ton-km cargo 720,000,000. Roads (1983): total length 65,369 mi, 105,201 km (paved 28%). Vehicles (1981): cars 672,385; trucks and buses 168,096. Merchant marine (1984): vessels (100 gross tons and over) 82; total deadweight tonnage 480,556. Air transport (1983): passenger-km 4,116,000,000; metric ton-km cargo 226,728,000; airports (1985) 79.
Communications. Daily newspapers (1984): 31; circulation 1,323,800; circulation per 1,000 population 47. Radio (1984): 3,025,000 receivers (1 per 9.3 persons). Television (1984): 1,801,000 receivers (1 per 16 persons). Telephones (1983): 2,547,222 (1 per 11 persons).

Education and health

Education (1983)				
	schools	teachers	students	student/ teacher ratio
Primary	33,974	132,210	4,065,546	30.8
Secondary♀	4,369	91,646	1,846,458	20.1
Higher	216	39,238	365,772	9.3

Educational attainment (1973). Percent of population over age 20 having: no schooling 22.4%; primary education 55.9%; secondary 18.4%; higher 3.3%. *Literacy* (1981): population over age 15 literate 11,923,900 (74.2%).
Health: physicians (1977) 12,720 (1 per 1,969 persons); hospital beds (1980) 44,495 (1 per 586 persons); infant mortality rate per 1,000 live births (1980–85) 39.5.
Food (1980–82): daily per capita caloric intake 2,536 (vegetable products 85%, animal products 15%); 111% of FAO recommended minimum requirement.

Military

Total active duty personnel (1984): 69,700 (army 81.8%, navy 12.2%, air force 6.0%). *Military expenditure as percent of GNP* (1982): 0.8% (world 6.1%); per capita expenditure U.S.$12.

*Population for the city of Bogotá is included with the special district. †Detail does not add to total given because of rounding. ‡1983. §Includes 56 urban centres. ‖At current prices. ¶Aug. ♀Secondary excludes vocational and teacher training.

Comoros*

Official name: Jumhurīyat al-Qumur al-Ittihādīyah al-Islāmīyah (Arabic); République Fédéral Islamique des Comores (French) (Federal Islāmic Republic of the Comoros).
Form of government: federal Islāmic republic with one legislative house (Federal Assembly [38]).
Head of state and government: President.
Capital: Moroni.
Official languages: Arabic; French.
Official religion: Islām.
Monetary unit: 1 Comorian franc (CF) = 100 centimes; valuation (Oct. 21, 1985) 1 U.S.$ = CF402.0; 1 £ = CF576.5.

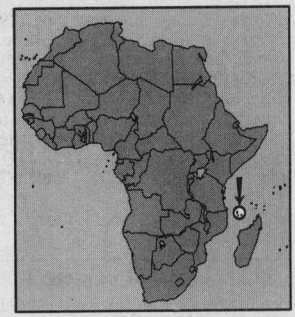

Area and population		area		population
		sq mi	sq km	1980 census
Islands†	Capitals			
Moili (Mohéli)	Fomboni	112	290	17,194
Ngazidja (Grande Comore)	Moroni	443	1,148	192,177
Ndzouani (Anjouan)	Mutsamudu	164	424	137,621
TOTAL		719	1,862	346,992

Demography

Population (1985): 403,000.
Density (1985): persons per sq mi 560.5, persons per sq km 216.4.
Urban–rural (1980)‡: urban 33.4%; rural 66.6%.
Sex distribution (1985): male 49.75%; female 50.25%.
Age breakdown (1985): under 15, 45.7%; 15–29, 26.2%; 30–44, 14.8%; 45–59, 8.7%; 60–74, 3.8%; 75 and over, 0.8%.
Population projection: (1990) 466,000; (2000) 637,000.
Doubling time: 23 years.
Ethnic composition (1980): Comorian (a mixture of Bantu, Arab, and Malagasy peoples) 96.9%; Makua (a Bantu people from East Africa) 1.6%; French 0.4%; other 1.1%.
Religious affiliation (1980): Sunnī Muslim 99.7%; Christian 0.2%; Bahā'ī 0.1%.
Major cities (1980): Moroni 20,112; Mutsamudu 12,518; Domoni 7,658; Quani 7,051; Iconi 5,770; Fomboni 5,663.

Vital statistics

Birth rate per 1,000 population (1980–85): 45.7 (world avg. 29.0).
Death rate per 1,000 population (1980–85): 17.2 (world avg. 11.0).
Natural increase rate per 1,000 population (1980–85): 28.5 (world avg. 18.0).
Total fertility rate (avg. births per childbearing woman; 1980–85): 6.3.
Marriage rate per 1,000 population: n.a.
Divorce rate per 1,000 population: n.a.
Life expectancy at birth (1980): male 44.0 years; female 47.0 years.
Major causes of death per 100,000 population: n.a.; however, major diseases (1980) are malaria (afflicts 80% of the adult population), tuberculosis, leprosy, and kwashiorkor (a nutritional deficiency disease).

National economy

Budget (1984). Revenue: CF6,659,000,000 (current revenues CF6,066,000,-000, of which indirect taxes on foreign trade 81.9%, turnover tax 7.2%, income from state enterprises 3.2%, registry and stamps 2.2%). Expenditures: CF8,008,000,000 (current expenditure CF7,008,000,000, of which defense 19.0%, education, youth, and recreation 18.7%, general administration 11.3%, foreign affairs 6.8%, community expenses 6.6%, public debt payments 6.5%, public works 4.1%, infrastructure and environment 3.9%, transport and tourism 3.4%, health 2.4%).
Public debt (external, outstanding; 1983): U.S.$83,300,000.
Tourism (1984): visitor arrivals 14,000.
Production (metric tons except as noted). Agriculture, forestry, fishing§ (1984): cassava 90,000, coconuts 43,000, bananas 34,000, sweet potatoes 17,000, rice 15,000, corn (maize) 6,000, copra 3,000, pulses 2,000, cloves 1,134 ‖, vanilla 177 ‖; livestock (number of live animals) 92,000 goats, 83,000 cattle, 9,000 sheep, 4,000 asses, 300,000 chickens; roundwood, n.a.; fish catch (1983) 4,000. Mining and quarrying: sand and gravel for local construction. Manufacturing (1983): copra 684; ylang-ylang essence 49; other important products are cement, handicrafts, soaps, and soft drinks. Construction: n.a. Energy production (consumption): electricity (kW-hr; 1984) 10,450,000 (10,450,000); coal, none (n.a.); crude petroleum, none (n.a.); petroleum products (metric tons; 1983) none (12,000); natural gas, none (n.a.).
Population economically active§ (1984): total 158,000; participation rate of total population 40.4% (female 35.1%, unemployed, n.a.).

Price and earnings indexes (1979 = 100)						
	1976	1977	1978	1979	1980	1981
Consumer price index	70.1	75.5	87.9	100.0	111.2	...
Monthly earnings index	...	...	...	...	...	...

Household income and expenditure. Average household size (1980) 5.3; average annual income per household: n.a.; source of income: n.a.; expenditure: n.a.

Gross national product (at current market prices; 1982): U.S.$120,000,000 (U.S.$326 per capita).

Structure of gross domestic product and labour force				
	1982		1980	
	in value U.S.$'000,000	% of total value	labour force¶	,% of labour force
Agriculture	41.4	44.8	1,349	10.6
Mining	—	—	—	—
Manufacturing	4.5	4.9	685	5.4
Construction	9.7	10.5	3,579	28.1
Public utilities	0.7	0.8	206	1.6
Transportation and communication			975	7.6
Trade, restaurants, hotels	36.0	39.0	1,210	9.5
Finance, insurance			146	1.1
Public administration, services			4,597	36.1
TOTAL	92.4⁹	100.0	12,747	100.0

Land use§ (1983): forested 16.0%; meadows and pastures 7.0%; agricultural and under permanent cultivation 42.0%; other 35.0%.

Foreign tradeᵟ

Balance of trade (current prices)						
	1979	1980	1981	1982	1983	1984
CF'000,000	−2,406	−4,185	−4,330	−4,291	−5,680	−15,700
% of total	24.4%	51.6%	32.5%	25.0%	27.7%	71.7%

Imports (1984): CF18,878,800,000 (foodstuffs 30.5%, of which rice 14.4%, meat 3.8%; petroleum products 11.1%; construction equipment and materials 10.9%, of which cement 4.4%; medicinal products 1.6%; iron and steel tubes and pipes 1.0%). *Major import sources* (1981): France 51.1%; Pakistan 13.5%; Kenya–Tanzania 7.3%; Madagascar 6.2% China 2.0%; United Kingdom 0.7%.
Exports (1984): CF3,079,100,000 (cloves 56.0%; vanilla 19.1%; ylang-ylang 13.8%; motor fuels 7.0%; basil and other essences 2.5%; copra 1.0%; coffee and cocoa 0.2%). *Major export destinations:* France 43.0%; West Germany 10.0%; Singapore 9.0%; The Netherlands 7.0%; United States 6.0%; United Kingdom 5.9%; Mauritius 5.0%.

Transport and communications

Transport. Railroads: none. Roads (1982): total length of paved roads 278 mi, 448 km. Vehicles (1983): passenger cars, 3,600; trucks and buses, 2,000. Merchant marine (1984): vessels (100 gross tons and over) 2; total deadweight tonnage 1,793. Air transport (1983)▢: passenger arrivals and departures 30,537; cargo loaded and unloaded 172 metric tons; airports (1985) with scheduled flights 3.
Communications. Daily newspapers: none. Radio (1984): total number of receivers 40,000 (1 per 9.8 persons). Television: total number of receivers, none. Telephones (1977): 1,035 (1 per 307 persons).

Education and health

Education (1980–81)				
	schools	teachers	students	student/ teacher ratio
Primary (age 7–13)	236	1,292	59,709	46.2
Secondary	32	434	13,528	31.2
Voc., teacher tr.	4	27	327	12.1

Educational attainment (1981). Percent of total population over age 15 having: no formal schooling 60%; some formal education 40%. *Literacy* (1984)§: total population over age 5 literate 15%.
Health: physicians (1978) 20 (1 per 16,900 persons); hospital beds (1978) 686 (1 per 497 persons); infant mortality rate per 1,000 live births (1980) 200.0.
Food (1980–82)§: daily per capita caloric intake 2,291 (vegetable products 95%, animal products 5%); 98% of FAO recommended minimum requirement.

Military◇

Total active duty personnel (1983): 700–800 (army 100%). *Military expenditure as percent of GNP* (1983): 1.9% (world 6.1%); per capita expenditure U.S.$6.

*Excludes Mayotte, a *collectivité territoriale* (territorial collectivity) of France, unless otherwise indicated. †Island names in Comorian Swahili and French. ‡Urban defined as being all settlements of more than 3,000 inhabitants. §Includes Mayotte. ‖ Excludes Mayotte. ¶Salaried employees only. ⁹Detail does not add to total given because of rounding. ᵟImport figures c.i.f. (cost, insurance, and freight), export figures f.o.b. (free on board). ▢Air Comores only. ◇In 1983 France assumed sole responsibility for the defense of the Comoros.

Congo (Brazzaville)

Official name: République Populaire de Congo (People's Republic of the Congo).
Form of government: people's republic with one legislative body (People's National Assembly [151]).
Head of state and government: President (Chairman of the Central Committee).
Capital: Brazzaville.
Official language: French.
Official religion: none.
Monetary unit: 1 CFA franc (CFAF) = 100 centimes; valuation (Oct. 21, 1985) 1 U.S.$ = CFAF402.02; 1 £ = CFAF576.50.

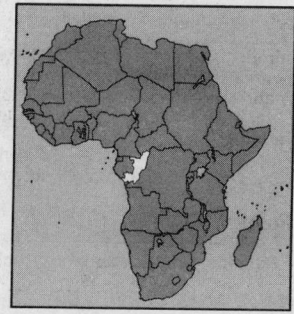

Area and population

		area		population
Regions	Capitals	sq mi	sq km	1980 estimate
Bouenza	Nkayi	4,736	12,265	129,000
Cuvette	Owando	28,900	74,850	121,000
Kouilou	Pointe-Noire	5,287*	13,694*	76,000
Lékoumou	Sibiti	8,089	20,950	63,000
Likouala	Impfondo	25,500	66,044	32,000
Niari	Loubomo	10,016†	25,942†	106,000
Plateaux	Djambala	14,826	38,400	103,000
Pool	Kinkala	13,127	34,000	208,000
Sangha	Ouesso	21,544	55,800	41,000
Communes				
Brazzaville		21	55	422,000
Loubomo		†	†	31,000
Nkayi		†	†	33,000
Pointe-Noire		*	*	185,000
TOTAL		132,047	342,000	1,550,000

Demography

Population (1985): 1,740,000.
Density (1985): persons per sq mi 13.2, persons per sq km 5.1.
Urban–rural (1985): urban 39.5%; rural 60.5%.
Sex distribution (1985): male 49.31%; female 50.69%.
Age breakdown (1985): under 15, 43.6%; 15–29, 25.8%; 30–44, 15.6%; 45–59, 9.5%; 60–74, 4.6%; 75 and over, 0.9%.
Population projection: (1990) 1,995,000; (2000) 2,646,000.
Doubling time: 27 years.
Ethnic composition (1978): Kongo 52.3%; Teke 24.0%; Bubangui 5.2%; Kota 4.5%; Mboshi 3.4%; other 10.6%.
Religious affiliation (1980): Roman Catholic 53.9%; Protestant 24.4%; animist 19.0%; other 2.7%.
Major cities (1980): Brazzaville 422,400; Pointe-Noire 185,110; Nkayi 32,520; Loubomo 30,830.

Vital statistics

Birth rate per 1,000 population (1980–85): 44.5 (world avg. 29.0); legitimate, n.a.; illegitimate, n.a.
Death rate per 1,000 population (1980–85): 17.1 (world avg. 11.0).
Natural increase rate per 1,000 population (1980–85): 27.4 (world avg. 18.0).
Total fertility rate (avg. births per childbearing woman; 1980–85): 6.0.
Marriage rate per 1,000 population: n.a.
Divorce rate per 1,000 population: n.a.
Life expectancy at birth (1980–85): male 45.0 years; female 48.1 years.
Major causes of death per 100,000 population: n.a.; however, the major diseases are malaria, diseases of the respiratory system, tuberculosis, and parasitic diseases.

National economy

Budget (1985). Revenue: CFAF311,000,000,000 (petroleum revenue 58.0%, domestic taxes 19.3%, customs duties 15.0%). Expenditures: CFAF311,000,000,000 (public works, construction, and housing 29.6%, hydraulic energy 18.1%, civil aviation and transport 9.5%, industries and crafts 6.5%, agriculture and livestock 6.1%, health 6.0%, defense 3.8%).
Public debt (external, outstanding; 1983): U.S.$1,487,000,000.
Tourism (1982): receipts from visitors U.S.$13,000,000§; expenditures by nationals abroad U.S.$54,000,000.
Production (metric tons except as noted). Agriculture, forestry, fishing (1984): cassava 600,000, sugarcane 250,000, bananas 32,000, palm oil 15,300, peanuts (groundnuts) 15,000, yams 14,000, sweet potatoes 13,000, corn (maize) 7,000, coffee 3,000, cacao beans 2,000, rice 2,000; livestock (number of live animals) 182,000 goats, 68,000 cattle, 60,000 sheep; roundwood (1983) 2,238,000 cu m; fish catch (1983) 31,926. Mining and quarrying (1983): cement 15,034; lead 4,000‡; copper 35‡; gold 8.3 kilograms‡. Manufacturing (1983): cement 39,242; raw sugar 21,000; wheat flour 8,000; soap 5,100; peanut oil 1,000; cigarettes 895; beer 788,000 hectolitres; soft drinks 246,000 hectolitres; veneer sheets 63,000 cu m; footwear 928,000 pairs. Construction: n.a. Energy production (consumption): electricity (kW-hr; 1983) 185,000,000 (212,000,000); coal, none (n.a.); crude petroleum (barrels; 1983) 37,925,000 (36,500); petroleum products (metric tons; 1983) none (96,000); natural gas, none (n.a.).
Land use (1983): forested 62.4%; meadows and pastures 29.3%; agricultural and under permanent cultivation 2.0%; other 6.3%.

Gross national product (at current market prices; 1983): U.S.$2,180,000,000 (U.S.$1,320 per capita).

Structure of gross domestic product and labour force

	1981			
	in value CFAF'000,000,000	% of total value	labour force	% of labour force
Agriculture	42.7	7.9	180,200	34.0
Mining	212.8	39.3		
Manufacturing	34.3	6.3		
Construction	25.1	4.6		
Public utilities	3.5	0.6	137,800	26.0
Transportation and communication	43.9	8.1		
Trade, finance	60.1	11.1		
Pub. admin., defense	56.3	10.4		
Services	63.0	11.7	212,000	40.0
Other	...	...		
TOTAL	541.7	100.0	530,000	100.0

Population economically active (1983): total 563,000; participation rate of total population 34.1% (female 44.6% ‖, unemployed, n.a.).

Price and earnings indexes (1980 = 100)

	1978	1979	1980	1981	1982	1983	1984
Consumer price index	86.2	93.2	100.0	117.0	132.0	142.3	160.0
Earnings index	...	...	...	...	...	...	...

Household income and expenditure. Average household size (1980) 4.7; average annual income per household CFAF1,016,000¶ (U.S.$ 4,500); source of income: n.a.; expenditure: n.a.

Foreign trade

Balance of trade (current prices)

	1977	1978	1979	1980	1981	1982
CFAF'000,000,000	−0.7	5.0	46.5	73.0	66.5	55.7
% of total	0.8%	4.4%	27.3%	23.7%	12.9%	9.5%

Imports (1982): CFAF244,600,000,000♀ (machinery 17.7%; finished steel products 11.4%; electrical machinery 10.4%; petroleum products 8.3%; automobiles 7.0%; minerals, including cement 3.9%; library materials 3.2%; meat 3.2%; cotton textiles 2.6%; pharmaceutical products 2.1%). *Major import sources:* France 63.5%; Brazil 7.0%; Belgium–Luxembourg 3.1%; Japan 3.1%; The Netherlands 3.1%; United States 3.0%; Italy 2.0%.
Exports (1982): CFAF326,100,000,000 (crude petroleum 89.6%; wood and wood products 4.7%; pearls and precious stones 2.7%; petroleum products 0.8%; coffee, cocoa, and tobacco 0.7%). *Major export destinations:* United States 50.8%; Italy 21.0%; Spain 10.4%; France 10.0%; Belgium–Luxembourg 2.7%.

Transport and communications

Transport. Railroads (1982): length 498 mi, 802 km; passenger-mi 242,000,000, passenger-km 390,000,000; short ton-mi cargo 350,000,000, metric ton-km cargo 511,000,000. Roads (1982): total length 5,124 mi, 8,246 km (paved 10.3%). Vehicles (1982): passenger cars 30,500; trucks and buses 78,600. Merchant marine (1984): vessels (100 gross tons and over) 21; total deadweight tonnage 10,840. Air transportô (1983): passenger-mi 129,311,000, passenger-km 208,106,000; short ton-mi cargo 26,218,000, metric ton-km cargo 38,278,000; airports (1985) with scheduled flights 17.
Communications. Daily newspapers (1984): total number 4; total circulation 24,000; circulation per 1,000 population 14.2. Radio (1984): total number of receivers 97,000 (1 per 17 persons). Television (1984): total number of receivers 4,800 (1 per 353 persons). Telephones (1982): 8,899 (1 per 180 persons).

Education and health

Education (1980–81)

	schools	teachers	students	student/ teacher ratio
Primary (age 6–13)	1,310	7,186	390,676	54.4
Secondary (age 14–18)	122	3,649	168,718	46.2
Voc., teacher tr.	36	1,468	18,867	12.9
Higher□	1	681	6,848	10.1

Educational attainment◊ (1974). Percent of population over age 15 having: secondary education 30%, of which males 37%, females 23%. *Literacy* (1980): total population over age 15 literate 375,060 (56.4%); males literate 230,740 (69.5%); females literate 144,320 (44.0%).
Health: physicians (1980) 278 (1 per 5,500 persons); hospital beds (1978) 6,876 (1 per 211 persons); infant mortality rate per 1,000 live births (1980–85) 124.
Food (1980–82): daily per capita caloric intake 2,466 (vegetable products 95%, animal products 5%); 111% of FAO recommended minimum requirement.

Military

Total active duty personnel (1984): 8,700 (army 92.0%, navy 2.3%, air force 5.7%). *Military expenditure as percent of GNP* (1982): 4.7% (world 6.0%); per capita expenditure U.S.$58.

*Area of Pointe-Noire commune is included with Kouilou. †Areas of Loubomo and Nkayi communes are included with Niari. ‡Metal content of ores. §1981. ‖1974. ¶Derived from GNP. ♀Import figures are c.i.f. (cost, insurance, and freight). ôAir Afrique only. □1979–80. ◊For the Commune of Brazzaville only.

Costa Rica

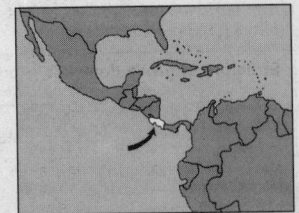

Official name: República de Costa Rica
(Republic of Costa Rica).
Form of government: unitary multiparty
republic with one legislative house
(Legislative Assembly [57]).
Head of state and government:
President.
Capital: San José.
Official language: Spanish.
Official religion: Roman Catholicism.
Monetary unit: 1 Costa Rican colón
₡ = 100 céntimos; valuation (Oct. 21,
1985) 1 U.S.$ = ₡52.16; 1 £ = ₡74.80.

Area and population

Provinces	Capitals	area		population
		sq mi	sq km	1984 census
Alajuela	Alajuela	3,766	9,753	427,962
Cartago	Cartago	1,206	3,125	271,671
Guanacaste	Liberia	3,915	10,141	195,208
Heredia	Heredia	1,026	2,656	197,575
Limón	Limón	3,548	9,188	168,076
Puntarenas	Puntarenas	4,354	11,277	265,883
San José	San José	1,915	4,960	890,434
TOTAL		19,730	51,100	2,416,809

Demography

Population (1985): 2,543,000.
Density (1985): persons per sq mi 128.9, persons per sq km 49.8.
Urban–rural (1982): urban 47.3%; rural 52.7%.
Sex distribution (1984): male 50.04%; female 49.96%.
Age breakdown (1982): under 15, 36.4%; 15–29, 31.3%; 30–49, 19.7%; 50–69, 9.4%; 70 and over and unknown 3.2%.
Population projection: (1990) 2,937,000; (2000) 3,596,000.
Doubling time: 26 years.
Ethnic composition (1981): European 86.8%; mestizo 7.0%; other 6.2%.
Religious affiliation (1982): Roman Catholic 91.7%; other 8.3%.
Major cities (1984): San José 241,464; Limón 52,602; Alajuela 34,556; Puntarenas 29,224; Cartago 23,928.

Vital statistics

Birth rate per 1,000 population (1983): 30.0 (world avg. 29.0).
Death rate per 1,000 population (1983): 3.9 (world avg. 11.0).
Natural increase rate per 1,000 population (1983): 26.1 (world avg. 18.0).
Total fertility rate (avg. births per childbearing woman; 1981): 3.5.
Marriage rate per 1,000 population (1982): 7.7.
Life expectancy at birth (1981): male 70.5 years; female 74.7 years.
Major causes of death per 100,000 population (1980): diseases of the circulatory system 105.2; malignant neoplasms (cancers) 67.3; accidents 42.9.

National economy

Budget (1982). Revenue: ₡12,708,000,000 (taxes on foreign trade 38.1%, income tax 22.8%, property tax 0.9%). Expenditures: ₡12,187,000,000 (goods and services 49.4%, transfers and subsidies 35.5%, interest payments 15.1%).
Public debt (external, outstanding; 1983): U.S.$3,314,600,000.
Population economically active (1984): total 835,314; participation rate of population over age 16, 34.0% (female [1981] 30.3%, unemployed [1983] 9.8%).

Price index (1980 = 100)

	1979	1980	1981	1982	1983	1984	1985
Consumer price index	84.7	100.0	137.1	260.6	345.6	386.9	447.6¶

Gross national product (1983): U.S.$2,420,000,000 (U.S.$1,020 per capita).

Structure of gross domestic product and labour force

	1983		1984	
	in value ₡'000,000	% of total value	labour force‡	% of labour force
Agriculture	30,040.9	21.0	224,064	26.8
Mining	29,227.3	20.4	131,954	15.8
Manufacturing				
Construction	4,959.6	3.5	46,479	5.5
Public utilities	5,008.9	3.5	48,267	5.8
Transp. and commun.	11,003.9	7.7	155,875	18.7
Trade	21,260.0	14.8		
Finance	19,632.8	13.7		
Public admin., defense, services	15,914.2	11.1	228,675	27.4
Other	6,221.0	4.3		
TOTAL	143,268.5§‖	100.0	835,314	100.0

Production (metric tons except as noted). Agriculture, forestry, fishing (1984): sugarcane 2,850,000, bananas 950,000, rice 127,000, coffee 124,000, corn (maize) 104,000; livestock (number of live animals): 2,550,000 cattle, 223,000 pigs, 6,000,000 chickens; roundwood 2,631,000 cu m†; fish catch 10,902†. Mining and quarrying (1983): gold 30,000,000 troy oz, silver 2,000 troy oz. Manufacturing (production value in ₡; 1980): cigarettes and beer 3,449,000,000; chemical and rubber products 1,133,000,000; textiles and leather goods 731,000,000; machinery and fabricated metal products 716,000,000; lumber and wooden products 526,000,000. Construction (1981): residential 805,000 sq m; nonresidential 1,049,000 sq m. Energy production

(consumption): electricity (kW-hr; 1983) 2,700,000,000 (2,700,000,000); coal, none (n.a.); crude petroleum (barrels; 1983) none (3,660,000); petroleum products (metric tons; 1983) 440,000 (693,000); natural gas, none (n.a.).
Tourism (1983): receipts from visitors U.S.$130,000,000; expenditures by nationals abroad U.S.$36,000,000*.
Family income and expenditure: average family size (1977) 5.0; income per family ₡29,318 (U.S.$3,421).
Land use (1983): forested 31.5%; meadows and pastures 42.8%; agricultural and under permanent cultivation 12.5%; other 13.2%.

Foreign trade

Balance of trade (current prices)

	1978	1979	1980	1981	1982	1983	1984
₡'000,000	−1,572	−2,796	−3,308	−1,755	+2,261	+3,557	−1,755
% of total	9.6%	14.9%	16.2%	3.9%	3.9%	5.2%	2.0%

Imports (1981): ₡26,301,000,000♀ (machinery 23.4%, of which telecommunications equipment 4.0%; manufactured goods 22.4%, of which paper and paper products 5.2%, iron and steel [all forms] 4.3%; chemicals 19.6%; petroleum 10.5%). *Major import sources:* United States 32.9%; Japan 9.5%; Mexico 9.1%; Venezuela 7.0%; Guatemala 5.3%; El Salvador 3.0%.
Exports (1981): ₡22,006,000,000♀ (coffee 23.7%; bananas 22.8%; basic manufactures 11.4%; chemical products, including pharmaceuticals 8.0%; beef 7.3%; sugar 4.2%). *Major export destinations:* United States 28.7%; West Germany 11.6%; Nicaragua 8.7%; Guatemala 7.9%; El Salvador 4.5%.

Transport and communications

Transport. Railroads (1983): route length 700 km; passenger-km, n.a.; metric ton-km cargo, n.a. Roads (1983): total length 29,586 km (paved 8%). Vehicles (1983): passenger cars 101,251; trucks and buses 76,485. Merchant marine (1984): vessels (100 gross tons and over) 27; total deadweight tonnage 19,262. Air transport (international; 1984): passenger-km 540,000,000; metric ton-km cargo 24,300,000; airports (1985) 8.
Communications. Daily newspapers (1983): total number 5; total circulation 182,152; circulation per 1,000 population 76. Radio (1984): total 190,000 receivers (1 per 12.5 persons). Television (1984): total 450,000 receivers (1 per 5.3 persons). Telephones (1983): 281,040 (1 per 8.5 persons).

Education and health

Education (1983)

	schools	teachers†	students	student/ teacher ratio
Primary (age 5–11)	3,511	11,615	343,800	...
Secondary (age 12–17)	242	8,213	153,971	...
Vocational	...	...	...	...
Higher	14	...	58,942	...

Educational attainment (1973). Percent of adult population over age 25 having: no formal schooling 16.1%; less than primary education 49.1%; primary 17.8%; secondary 11.2%; postsecondary and higher 5.8%. *Literacy* (1980): total population literate 93.0%; males 93.2%; females 92.8%.
Health: physicians (1979) 1,506 (1 per 1,477 persons); hospital beds (1980) 7,570 (1 per 295 persons); infant mortality per 1,000 live births (1982) 18.9.
Food (1980–82): daily per capita caloric intake 2,638 (vegetable products 82%, animal products 18%); 118% of FAO recommended minimum requirement.

Military

Military expenditure as percent of GNP (1983): 0.7% (world 6.1%); per capita expenditure U.S.$6. Army officially abolished in 1948. About 3,000 long-term volunteers conduct both police and paramilitary activities.

*1982. †1983. ‡Employees only. §At current prices. ‖Detail does not add to total given because of rounding. ¶August. ♀Based on conversion of U.S.$ (used in official government sources) into ₡ using the average exchange rate of 1981.

Hand-painted oxcart, a national symbol of Costa Rica, at Sarchi, near San José, the national capital.

Cuba

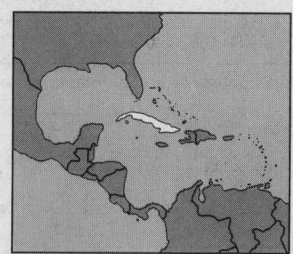

Official name: República de Cuba (Republic of Cuba).
Form of government: unitary socialist republic with one legislative house (National Assembly [499]).
Head of state and government: President.
Capital: Havana.
Official language: Spanish.
Official religion: none.
Monetary unit: 1 peso = 100 centavos; valuation (Oct. 21, 1985)
1 peso = U.S.$0.93 = £1.33.

Area and population		area		population
Provinces	**Capitals**	sq mi	sq km	1983 estimate
Camagüey	Camagüey	5,466	14,158	685,400
Ciego de Avila	Ciego de Avila	2,441	6,321	331,400
Cienfuegos	Cienfuegos	1,613	4,177	333,900
Ciudad de la Habana*	—	281	727	1,961,100
Granma	Bayamo	3,229	8,362	749,300
Guantánamo	Guantánamo	2,388	6,184	470,500
Holguín	Holguín	3,589	9,295	926,100
La Habana†	Havana	2,197	5,691	598,000
Las Tunas	Las Tunas	2,542	6,584	447,400
Matanzas	Matanzas	4,532	11,739	568,200
Pinar del Río	Pinar del Río	4,194	10,861	652,700
Sancti Spiritus	Sancti Spiritus	2,599	6,732	405,800
Santiago de Cuba	Santiago de Cuba	2,382	6,170	924,000
Villa Clara	Santa Clara	3,067	7,944	775,200
Special political entity				
Isla de la Juventud	Nueva Gerona	849	2,200	61,900
TOTAL		42,803‡	110,860‡	9,890,900

Demography

Population (1985): 10,058,000.
Density (1985): persons per sq mi 235.0, persons per sq km 90.7.
Urban–rural (1984): urban 70.3%; rural 29.7%.
Sex distribution (1984): male 50.45%; female 49.55%.
Age breakdown (1983): under 15, 28.7%; 15–29, 28.4%; 30–44, 19.5%; 45–59, 12.4%; 60 and over, 11.0%.
Population projection: (1990) 10,540,000; (2000) 11,718,000.
Doubling time: 78 years.
Ethnic composition (1980): white 72%; mulatto 15%; black 12%; other 1%.
Religious affiliation (1980): nonreligious 48.7%; Roman Catholic 39.6%; atheist 6.4%; Afro-American Spiritist 1.6%; Protestant 1.4%; other 2.3%.
Major cities (1983): Havana 1,972,000§; Santiago de Cuba 348,900; Camagüey 251,000; Holguín 189,600; Santa Clara 173,700.

Vital statistics

Birth rate per 1,000 population (1983): 16.7 (world avg. 29.0).
Death rate per 1,000 population (1983): 5.9 (world avg. 11.0).
Natural increase rate per 1,000 population (1983): 10.8 (world avg. 18.0).
Total fertility rate (avg. births per childbearing woman; 1980–85): 2.0.
Marriage rate per 1,000 population (1983): 7.7.
Divorce rate per 1,000 population (1983): 3.0.
Life expectancy at birth (1980–81): male 71.9 years; female 75.4 years.
Major causes of death per 100,000 population (1978): heart disease 141.2; cancers 99.8; accidents 63.9; cerebrovascular disease 53.9; pneumonia 44.2.

National economy

Budget (1983). Revenue: 12,128,200,000 pesos (government sector 98.6%; taxes 1.4%). Expenditures: 11,393,600,000 pesos (production capital 40.3%; education and public health 19.4%; social, cultural, and scientific activities 14.8%; defense, internal security 9.9%; housing, community services 5.5%).
Public debt (external, outstanding; 1982): U.S.$12,000,000,000 ‖ .
Production (metric tons except as noted). Agriculture, forestry, fishing (1984): sugarcane 75,000,000, rice 555,000, oranges 410,000, sweet potatoes 335,000, potatoes 259,000, bananas 185,000, corn (maize) 97,000, tobacco 45,000, coffee 26,000; livestock (number of live animals): 6,400,000 cattle, 2,300,000 pigs, 759,000 horses; roundwood (1983) 3,193,000 cu m; fish catch (1983) 198,000, of which mackerel 72,000. Mining and quarrying (1983): nickel 39,200; chromite 30,000. Manufacturing (value of production in '000 of pesos; 1983): processed food (excluding sugar and fish) 1,846,300; sugar (all forms) 1,397,600; nonelectrical machinery 742,300; fuels 538,200; beverages and tobacco 412,900. Construction (value added in '000 of pesos; 1982): residential 79,100; nonresidential 277,000. Energy production (consumption): electricity (kW-hr; 1984) 12,300,000,000 (12,300,000,000); coal (metric tons; 1983) none (90,000); crude petroleum (barrels; 1983) 5,438,000 (50,577,000); petroleum products (metric tons; 1983) 6,030,000 (9,419,000); natural gas (cu m; 1983) 8,256,000 (8,256,000).
Population economically active (1984): total 3,118,000; participation rate of population over age 15, 44.6% (female [1983] 36.1%, unemployed [1981] 3.4%).

Price and earnings indexes (1980 = 100)							
	1976	1977	1978	1979	1980	1981	1982
Consumer price index	...	...	...	...	...	...	...
Monthly earnings index	87.6	93.3	94.7	97.0	100.0	114.7	119.1

Tourism (1984): receipts from visitors, about U.S.$100,000,000; expenditures by nationals abroad, n.a.
Gross material product (1982): U.S.$21,971,000,000 (U.S.$2,241 per capita).

Structure of net material product and labour force				
	1984		1983	
	in value '000,000 pesos	% of total value	labour force¶	% of labour force¶
Agriculture	3,654	14.1	595,000	21.7
Mining and manufacturing	11,598	44.7	631,000	23.0
Public utilities			96,900	3.5
Construction	2,311	8.9	284,000	10.4
Transportation and communication	1,981	7.6	185,000	6.8
Trade	6,254	24.1	348,000	12.7
Public admin., defense	—		600,500	21.9
Services	—			
Other	145⁹	0.6⁹	...	...
TOTAL	25,943⁵	100.0	2,740,400	100.0

Household income and expenditure. Number of households (1980) 2,331,000; average household size (1980) 4.2; income, n.a.; expenditure, n.a.
Land use (1983): forested 17.4%; meadows and pastures 22.5%; agricultural and under permanent cultivation 29.0%; other 31.1%.

Foreign trade

Balance of trade (current prices)						
	1979	1980	1981	1982	1983	1984
'000,000 pesos	−186.6	−578.0	−948.0	−881.4	−1,024.0	−1,921
% of total	2.6%	6.8%	10.1%	5.7%	5.9%	14.6%

Imports (1983): 6,217,700,000 pesos (machinery and transport equipment 30.5%, mineral fuels and lubricants 30.0%, foodstuffs and beverages 12.7%, basic manufactures 12.3%). *Major import sources* (1984): U.S.S.R. 66.3%; East Germany 3.7%; China 3.4%; Japan 3.0%; Bulgaria 2.6%; Czechoslovakia 2.4%; Romania 2.0%.
Exports (1983): 5,522,700,000 pesos (sugar and sugar products 74.0%, minerals and concentrates 5.2%, fish and fish preparations 1.9%, tobacco and tobacco products 1.9%). *Major export destinations* (1984): U.S.S.R. 72.1%; East Germany 4.0%; China 3.7%; Bulgaria 3.4%; Czechoslovakia 3.0%; Spain 1.2%.

Transport and communications

Transport. Railroads□ (1984): length 3,058 mi, 4,922 km; passenger-mi 1,332,000,000, passenger-km 2,144,000,000; short ton-mi cargo 1,792,000,000, metric ton-km cargo 2,617,000,000. Roads (1984): total length 21,000 mi, 34,000 km (paved 30%). Vehicles (1981): passenger cars 18,657; trucks and buses 28,098. Merchant marine (1984): vessels (100 gross tons and over) 418; total deadweight tonnage 1,230,077. Air transport (1983): passenger-mi 1,337,000,000, passenger-km 2,151,000,000; short ton-mi cargo 22,900,000, metric ton-km cargo 33,400,000; airports with scheduled flights, n.a.
Communications. Daily newspapers (1984): total number 16; total circulation 1,281,000; circulation per 1,000 population 129. Radio (1984): receivers 2,135,000 (1 per 4.7 persons). Television (1984): receivers 1,500,000 (1 per 6.6 persons). Telephones (1982): 406,355 (1 per 24 persons).

Education and health

Education (1982–83)				
	schools	teachers	students	student/ teacher ratio
Primary (age 6–11)	11,213	83,358	1,363,078	16.4
Secondary (age 12–17)	1,319	65,101	774,410	11.9
Voc., teacher tr.	431	23,098	243,146	10.5
Higher	32	12,222	173,403	14.2

Educational attainment (1981). Percent of adult population over age 24 having: no formal schooling and some primary education 39.6%; completed primary 26.6%; some secondary 13.8%; completed secondary 15.8%; some higher 1.6%; completed higher 2.6%. *Literacy* (1980): total population over age 15 literate 6,087,000 (91.1%); males literate 3,101,000 (91.1%); females literate 2,986,000 (91.1%).
Health (1984): physicians 19,200 (1 per 518 persons); hospital beds 49,000 (1 per 203 persons); infant mortality rate per 1,000 live births (1983) 15.0.
Food (1980–82): daily per capita caloric intake 2,917 (vegetable products 77%, animal products 23%); 123% of FAO recommended minimum requirement.

Military

Total active duty personnel (1984)◊: 153,000 (army 81.7%, navy 7.8%, air force 10.5%). *Military expenditure as percent of GNP* (1983): 8.0% (world 6.1%); per capita expenditure: U.S.$126.

*Province contiguous with the city of Havana. †Province bordering the city of Havana on the east, south, and west. ‡Includes 1,434 sq mi (3,715 sq km) of unpopulated cays not distributed by province. §1984. ‖ Debt to U.S.S.R. and Western countries only. ¶State sector. ⁹Other material activities. ⁵At current prices. □Figures exclude 4,888 mi (7,867 km) of railway serving sugar plantations or sugar factories. ◊U.S. forces at Guantánamo: 2,500.

Cyprus

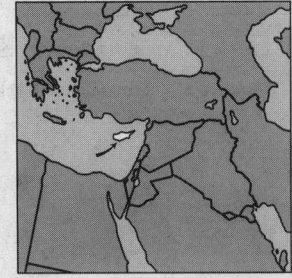

Official name*: Kipriakí Demokratía (Kípros) (Greek)/Kıbrıs Cumhuriyeti (Turkish) (Republic of Cyprus).
Form of government: unitary multiparty republic with a unicameral legislature (House of Representatives [50]).
Chief of state: President.
Head of government: Minister to the President.
Capital: Nicosia.
Official languages: Greek; Turkish.
Official religion: none.
Monetary unit†: 1 Cyprus pound (£C) = 1,000 mils; valuation (Oct. 21, 1985) 1£C = U.S.$1.79 = £1.25.

Area and population

Districts	Capitals	area sq mi	area sq km	population‡ 1982 census
Famagusta	Famagusta	766	1,984	24,187
Kyrenia	Kyrenia	247	640	...
Larnaca	Larnaca	433	1,121	83,151
Limassol	Limassol	538	1,393	143,847
Nicosia	Nicosia	1,049	2,717	207,290
Paphos	Paphos	539	1,396	45,023
TOTAL		3,572	9,251	503,498

Demography

Population (1985): 685,000.
Density (1985): persons per sq mi 191.8, persons per sq km 74.0.
Urban–rural§ (1982): urban 63.6%; rural 36.4%.
Sex distribution§ (1983): male 49.76%; female 50.23%.
Age breakdown§ (1983): under 15, 25.0%; 15–29, 26.5%; 30–44, 20.3%; 45–59, 13.9%; 60–69, 7.2%; 70 and over, 7.1%.
Population projection: (1990) 708,000; (2000) 793,000.
Doubling time: 53 years.
Ethnic composition (1983): Greek 80.7%; Turk 18.7%; other 1.3%.
Religious affiliation (1980): Greek Orthodox 76.2%; Muslim 18.7%; other Christian 2.7%; other 2.4%.
Major cities (1982): Nicosia§ 123,298; Limassol 100,254; Larnaca 35,823.

Vital statistics§

Birth rate per 1,000 population (1983): 22.3 (world avg. 29.0); (1983) legitimate 99.7%; illegitimate 0.3%.
Death rate per 1,000 population (1983): 8.5 (world avg. 11.0).
Natural increase rate per 1,000 population (1983): 13.8 (world avg. 18.0).
Total fertility rate (avg. births per childbearing woman; 1983): 2.5.
Marriage rate per 1,000 population (1983): 11.2.
Divorce rate per 1,000 population (1983): 0.5.
Life expectancy at birth (1979–81): male 72.3 years; female 76.0 years.
Major causes of death per 100,000 population: n.a.; however major infectious diseases in 1983 included measles, leprosy, and tuberculosis.

National economy§

Budget ‖ (1984). £C257,768,900 (indirect taxes 45.9%; direct taxes 27.7%; interest, dividends, rents, and royalties 6.1%; sales of goods and services 5.8%). Expenditures: £C301,384,200 (payments on public debt 20.6%; subsidies and contributions 18.4%; education 14.2%; police 7.6%; medical 7.4%).
Public debt (external, outstanding; 1983): U.S.$649,700,000.
Tourism¶ (1983): receipts from visitors U.S.$332,000,000; expenditures by nationals abroad U.S.$68,000,000.
Production (metric tons except as noted). Agriculture, forestry, fishing (1984): grapes 205,000, potatoes 180,000, oranges 147,000, grapefruit 89,000, barley 90,000, lemons 49,000, wheat 18,000; livestock (number of live animals) 500,000 sheep, 360,000 goats, 250,000 pigs, 43,000 cattle; roundwood (1983) 65,000 cu m; fish catch (1983) 2,058. Mining and quarrying (1984): iron pyrites 31,039; asbestos 8,215; terra umbra (brown earth) 7,362. Manufacturing (1984): cement 852,700; mosaic tiles 1,634,000 sq m; wine 442,100 hectolitres; beer 233,000 hectolitres; footwear 7,296,000 pairs; cigarettes 2,586,000,000 units. Construction (value added in £C; 1983) 130,500,000. Energy production (consumption): electricity (kW-hr; 1983) 1,222,000,000 (1,073,000,000); coal, none (none); crude petroleum (barrels; 1983) none (4,090,000); petroleum products (metric tons; 1983) 532,000 (856,000); natural gas, n.a. (n.a.).
Population economically active (1983): total 209,089; participation rate of total population 32.2% (female 39.2%, unemployed 3.7%).

Price and earnings indexes (1980 = 100)§

	1979	1980	1981	1982	1983	1984	1985
Consumer price index	88.1	100.0	110.6	117.7	123.6	131.1	137.6⁹
Monthly earnings index	90.2	100.0	106.7	117.8	122.7	...	...

Household income and expenditure. Average household size§ (1982) 3.5; average annual income per household: n.a.; source of income: n.a.; expenditure (1981): food, beverages, and tobacco 28.1%; transport and communication 23.2%; household furnishings and operation 11.8%; clothing and footwear 10.8%; housing 8.4%; restaurants and hotels 8.4%; recreation 7.5%.
Land use (1983): forested 18.5%; meadows and pastures 10.1%; agricultural and under permanent cultivation 46.8%; other 24.6%.

Gross national product§δ (at current market prices; 1983): U.S.$2,430,000,-000 (U.S.$3,720 per capita).

Structure of gross domestic product and labour force§

	1983 in value £C'000,000	% of total value	labour force	% of labour force
Agriculture	97.3	8.9	43,400	20.7
Mining	8.1	0.7	1,194	0.6
Manufacturing	178.9	16.4	41,742	20.0
Construction	126.1	11.5	20,359	9.7
Public utilities	21.9	2.0	1,470	0.7
Transportation and communication	90.9	8.3	10,670	5.1
Trade	154.9	14.2	38,372	18.3
Finance	80.4	7.4	8,179	3.9
Pub. admin., defense	130.6	12.0	13,527	6.4
Services	159.2	14.6	26,369	12.6
Other	43.5	4.0	4,046	2.0
TOTAL	1,091.8	100.0	209,328	100.0

Foreign trade§□

Balance of trade (current prices)

	1979	1980	1981	1982	1983	1984
£C'000,000	−196.9	−236.6	−251.9	−322.8	−376.6	−381.4
% of total	37.9%	38.7%	34.7%	38.4%	41.5%	36.1%

Imports (1984): £C796,520,000 (machinery and transport equipment 26.3%, petroleum and petroleum products 17.5%, cereals and cereal preparations 4.9%, iron and steel 3.2%). *Major import sources:* United Kingdom 12.1%; Italy 10.5%; Japan 8.3%; West Germany 7.0%; U.S. 5.2%; Iraq 5.2%.
Exports (1984): £C336,826,000 (clothing and accessories excluding footwear 20.2%, vegetables and fruit 19.4%, machinery and transport equipment 8.6%, beverages 4.5%, tobacco 3.4%). *Major export destinations:* United Kingdom 17.0%; Lebanon 14.1%; Libya 11.4%; Saudi Arabia 7.5%; U.S.S.R. 3.0%; United Arab Emirates 2.4%; Iraq 1.8%; Syria 1.5%.

Transport and communications

Transport. Railroads: none. Roads (1984): total length 7,156 mi, 11,517 km (paved 48%). Vehicles (1984): passenger cars 113,078; trucks and buses 43,-095. Merchant marine (1984): vessels (100 gross tons and over) 737; total deadweight tonnage 11,801,233. Air transport (1983): passenger-mi 577,-362,000, passenger-km 929,176,000; short ton-mi cargo 70,331,000, metric ton-km cargo 102,681,000; airports (1985) with scheduled flights 2.
Communications. Daily newspapers (1984): total number 17; total circulation 74,886; circulation per 1,000 population 116.5. Radio (1984): total number of receivers 300,000 (1 per 2.2 persons). Television (1984): total number of receivers 167,000 (1 per 3.9 persons). Telephones (1983): 164,000 (1 per 4.0 persons).

Education and health§

Education (1984–85)

	schools	teachers	students	student/ teacher ratio
Primary (age 5–12)	396	2,193	47,381	21.6
Secondary (age 12–18)	93	2,644	43,511	16.5
Vocational	16	492	5,375	10.9
Higher	15	250	2,580	5.2

Educational attainment (1976). Percent of population over age 20 having: primary education 54.9%; secondary 36.7%; higher 7.7%. *Literacy* (1980): total population over age 10 literate 416,000 (89.0%); males literate 216,000 (93.5%); females literate 200,000 (84.5%).
Health (1983): physicians 635 (1 per 1,024 persons); hospital beds 5,375 (1 per 121 persons); infant mortality rate per 1,000 live births (1984) 21.0.
Food (1979–81): daily per capita caloric intake 3,378 (vegetable products 74%, animal products 26%); 136% of FAO recommended minimum requirement.

Military

Total active duty Greek-Cypriot personnel (1984): 10,000 (army 100.0%). *Military expenditure* (1982): U.S.$45,311,000; per capita expenditure U.S.$91. *Total active duty Turkish-Cypriot personnel* (1984): 4,500. *Military expenditure* (1982): U.S.$4,980,000; per capita expenditure U.S.$33.

*In July 1974 Turkey invaded Cyprus, and an autonomous Turkish-Cypriot administration was established in the northern part of the island. On Feb. 13, 1975, the occupied territory was declared the "Turkish Federated State of Cyprus." Following a unilateral declaration of independence in November 1983, the autonomous sector was renamed the "Turkish Republic of Northern Cyprus." The state is not recognized internationally. †Monetary unit of the Turkish sector is the Turkish lira (LT); valuation (Oct. 29, 1984) 1 U.S.$ = LT416.51; 1 £ = LT502.73. ‡Population for government-controlled areas (the Greek south) was officially 503,498. The 1982 estimated population for the Turkish sector was given as 153,239; the total population of the island therefore amounted to about 657,000 in that year. Its size distribution and makeup have been extensively altered since the Turkish invasion, now embodying internal refugees no longer resident in their home districts, recent Turkish immigrants, and international immigrants. §Data refer to government-controlled area only. ‖ Budget for the Turkish sector (1984). Revenue: LT17,760,000,000 (local taxes 36.9%, local loans 30.8%, foreign aid 32.3%). Expenditures: LT17,760,000,000 (personnel 39.8%, investment 25.5%, defense 6.0%). ¶The Turkish sector contains the two most popular resorts, Famagusta and Kyrenia. ⁹August. δGDP for Turkish sector (1981) U.S.$237,000,000 (U.S.$1,558 per capita). □Foreign trade for the Turkish sector (1982). Imports: LT19,402,900,000. Major import sources: Turkey 30.4%; United Kingdom 16.3%; West Germany 5.2%; Italy 3.9%. Exports: LT6,371,300,000 (citrus fruit, potatoes, carob, tobacco). Major export destinations: United Kingdom 45.3%; Turkey 16.1%.

Czechoslovakia

Official name: Československá Socialistická Republika (Czechoslovak Socialist Republic).
Form of government: federal socialist republic with two legislative houses (House of the People [200]; House of Nations [150]).
Chief of state: President.
Head of government: Premier.
Capital: Prague.
Official languages: Czech; Slovak.
Official religion: none.
Monetary unit: 1 koruna (Kčs) = 100 halura; valuation (Oct. 21, 1985) 1 U.S.$ = Kčs6.45; 1 £ = Kčs9.25.

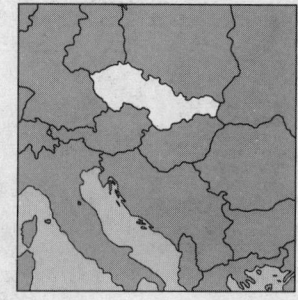

Structure of net material product and labour force

	1983			
	in value Kčs'000,000	% of total value	labour force	% of labour force
Agriculture	45,176	8.9	1,019,000	13.6
Mining and manufacturing	309,468†	61.0†	2,837,000†	37.9†
Construction	52,644	10.3	714,000	9.5
Public utilities	†	†	†	†
Transportation and communication	25,762	5.1	495,000	6.6
Trade	70,814	14.0	669,000	8.9
Finance	—	—	‡	‡
Pub. admin., defense	—	—	120,000	1.6
Services	—	—	1,078,000	14.4
Other	3,461§	0.7§	561,000‡	7.5‡
TOTAL	507,325	100.0	7,493,000	100.0

Population economically active (1983): total 7,736,000; participation rate of population over age 15, 66.3% (female 45.8%, unemployed, n.a.).

Price and earnings indexes (1970 = 100)

	1977	1978	1979	1980	1981	1982	1983
Consumer price index	103.0	104.6	108.6	111.8	112.7	118.4	119.5
Monthly earnings index	127.9	132.2	136.1	139.2	142.8	114.6	117.3

Public debt (external, outstanding, to the West; 1981): U.S.$4,620,000,000.
Household income and expenditure. Average household size (1983) 3.0; income per household Kčs76,670 (U.S.$11,887); sources of income: wages and salaries 62.6%, welfare 19.8%, other 17.6%; expenditure (1983): food 26.3%, clothing and footwear 26.6%, services 12.6%.

Area and population

		area		population
Republics Regions	Capitals	sq mi	sq km	1984 estimate
Czech Socialist Republic	Prague			
Jihočeský	České Budějovice	4,380	11,345	694,100
Jihomoravský	Brno	5,802	15,028	2,053,500
Severočeský	Ústí nad Labem	3,015	7,810	1,177,400
Severomoravský	Ostrava	4,273	11,067	1,949,000
Středočeský	Prague	4,248	11,003	1,144,400
Východočeský	Hradec Králové	4,340	11,240	1,247,100
Západočeský	Plzeň	4,199	10,876	876,500
Slovak Socialist Republic	Bratislava			
Středoslovenský	Banská Bystrica	6,944	17,985	1,559,400
Východoslovenský	Košice	6,250	16,188	1,440,500
Západoslovenský	Bratislava	5,595	14,491	1,707,500
Capital Cities				
Prague	—	191	495	1,186,200
Bratislava	—	142	368	401,400
TOTAL		49,381*	127,896	15,437,000

Demography

Population (1985): 15,508,000.
Density (1985): persons per sq mi 314.1, persons per sq km 121.3.
Urban–rural (1984): urban 74.1%; rural 25.9%.
Sex distribution (1984): male 48.70%; female 51.30%.
Age breakdown (1984): under 15, 24.4%; 15–29, 21.7%; 30–44, 21.5%; 45–59, 16.2%; 60–74, 11.7%; 75 and over, 4.5%.
Population projection: (1990) 15,758,000; (2000) 16,278,000.
Doubling time: not applicable; population growth is negligible.
Ethnic composition (1984): Czech 63.8%; Slovak 31.0%; Hungarian 3.8%; Polish 0.4%; German 0.4%; Ukrainian 0.3%; other 0.3%.
Religious affiliation (1980): Roman Catholic 65.6%; atheist 20.1%; Czechoslovak Church 4.4%; Evangelist Church of Czech Brethren 1.4%; other 8.5%.
Major cities (1984): Prague 1,186,200; Bratislava 401,400; Brno 380,900; Ostrava 323,700; Košice 214,300.

Vital statistics

Birth rate per 1,000 population (1984): 14.7 (world avg. 29.0); (1982) legitimate 94.2%; illegitimate 5.8%.
Death rate per 1,000 population (1984): 11.8 (world avg. 11.0).
Natural increase rate per 1,000 population (1984): 2.9 (world avg. 18.0).
Total fertility rate (avg. births per childbearing woman; 1982): 2.3.
Marriage rate per 1,000 population (1984): 6.6.
Divorce rate per 1,000 population (1984): 2.3.
Life expectancy at birth (1982): male 67.1 years; female 74.4 years.
Major causes of death per 100,000 population (1984): cerebrovascular disease 340.6; ischemic heart disease 325.1; malignant neoplasms (cancers) 232.8; bronchitis, emphysema, and asthma 86.3; accidents and poisoning 74.3; diseases of the digestive system 47.1.

National economy

Budget (1983). Revenue: Kčs324,127,000,000 (receipts from enterprises 71.4%; taxes 13.7%). Expenditures: Kčs323,890,000,000 (education, health, social welfare, and culture 41.6%; national economy 38.6%; defense 11.8%).
Tourism (1983): receipts from visitors U.S.$299,000,000; expenditures by nationals abroad U.S.$229,000,000.
Production (metric tons except as noted). Agriculture, forestry, fishing (1984): sugar beets 7,600,000, wheat 5,317,000, potatoes 3,700,000, barley 3,276,000, corn (maize) 722,000; livestock (number of live animals) 7,070,000 pigs, 5,190,000 cattle, 51,000,000 chickens; roundwood 18,800,000 cu m; fish catch 19,600. Mining and quarrying (1983): iron ore 1,903,000; copper 25,-746; zinc 14,199. Manufacturing (1984): crude steel 14,831,000; rolled steel 10,910,000; cement 10,530,000; wood pulp and paper 1,605,000; sulfuric acid 1,246,000; plastic and resins 1,039,000; chemical fertilizers 1,021,000; cotton fabrics 597,932,000 m; beer 23,768,000 hectolitres; wine 1,265,000 hectolitres; road motor vehicles 227,022 units. Construction (1983): 7,216,-000 sq m. Energy production (consumption): electricity (kW-hr; 1984) 78,349,000,000 (81,804,000,000); coal (metric tons; 1984) 127,105,000 (132,-133,000); crude petroleum (barrels; 1983) 682,000 (126,025,000); petroleum products (metric tons; 1982) 13,452,000 (13,083,000); natural gas (cu m; 1983) 613,000,000 (9,883,000,000).
Land use (1984): agricultural 40.4%; forested 35.9%; meadows and pastures 13.0%; other 10.7%.
Gross national product (at current market prices; 1983): U.S.$87,601,000,000 (U.S.$5,690 per capita).

Foreign trade

Balance of trade (current prices)

	1979	1980	1981	1982	1983	1984
Kčs'000,000	−5,604	−1,377	+1,413	+1,345	+826	+761
% of total	3.8%	0.9%	0.8%	0.8%	0.4%	0.3%

Imports (1983): Kčs103,012,000,000 (machinery and transport equipment 33.2%, of which industrial machinery 9.3%, agricultural and construction machinery 8.9%, transport equipment 6.3%; crude petroleum and petroleum products 21.2%; chemicals 7.8%; food 7.1%; nonferrous metals 3.5%; iron and steel 3.2%). *Major import sources:* U.S.S.R. 46.2%; East Germany 10.3%; Poland 6.2%; Hungary 5.0%; West Germany 4.5%.
Exports (1983): Kčs103,838,000,000 (machinery and transport equipment 54.8%, of which industrial machinery 11.2%, road vehicles and parts 9.0%, textile and leather machinery 4.6%; iron and steel 7.1%; mineral fuels and lubricants 6.2%; footwear 3.5%). *Major export destinations:* U.S.S.R. 41.8%; East Germany 9.0%; Poland 7.1%; Hungary 5.3%; West Germany 4.7%; Yugoslavia 4.3%; Austria 2.8%; Bulgaria 2.8%; Romania 1.8%.

Transport and communications

Transport. Railroads (1984): length 8,165 mi, 13,141 km; passenger-mi 11,-734,000,000, passenger-km 18,884,000,000; short ton-mi cargo 46,785,000,-000, metric ton-km cargo 68,309,000,000. Roads (1983): total length 46,043 mi, 74,100 km (paved 100%). Vehicles (1983): passenger cars 2,221,379; trucks and buses 358,736. Merchant marine (1984): vessels (100 gross tons and over) 19; total deadweight tonnage 276,647. Air transport (1983): passenger-mi 1,198,000,000, passenger-km 1,928,000,000; short ton-mi cargo 35,204,000, metric ton-km cargo 51,400,000; airports (1985) 14.
Communications. Daily newspapers (1984): total number 30; total circulation 4,353,000 ‖; circulation per 1,000 population 284. Radio (1984): total number of receivers 4,165,000 (1 per 3.7 persons). Television (1984): total number of receivers 4,323,000 (1 per 3.6 persons). Telephones (1984): 3,401,775 (1 per 4.5 persons).

Education and health

Education (1984–85)

	schools	teachers	students	student/ teacher ratio
Primary (age 6–14)	6,398	94,404	2,037,121	21.6
Secondary (age 15–18)	342	9,302	138,436	14.9
Voc., teacher tr.	565	16,748	271,234	16.2
Higher	36	19,135	174,304	9.1

Educational attainment (1980). Percent of adult population having: less than full primary education 1.7%; primary and secondary 47.6%, of which secondary 45.9%; higher 6.0%. *Literacy* (1980): total population over age 15 literate 11,524,716 (99.6%); males literate 5,525,860 (99.6%); females literate 5,998,856 (99.5%).
Health (1984): physicians 45,600 (1 per 339 persons); hospital beds 155,000 (1 per 99 persons); infant mortality rate per 1,000 live births (1984) 15.6.
Food (1980–82): daily per capita caloric intake 3,508 (vegetable products 67%, animal products 33%); 140% of FAO recommended minimum requirement.

Military

Total active duty personnel (1984): 218,250 (army 72.9%; navy, none; air force 27.1%). *Military expenditure as percent of GNP* (1983): 5.9% (world 6.1%); per capita expenditure U.S.$445.

---

*Detail does not add to total given because of rounding. † Public utilities are included with manufacturing. ‡Finance is included with other. §Includes other activities of the material sphere. ‖ 27 newspapers only.

Denmark

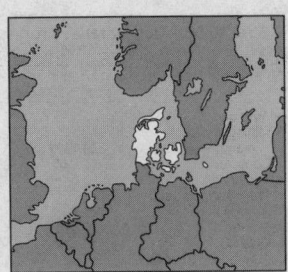

Official name: Kongeriget Danmark (Kingdom of Denmark).
Form of government: parliamentary state and constitutional monarchy with one legislative house (Folketing [179]).
Chief of state: Danish Monarch.
Head of government: Prime Minister.
Capital: Copenhagen.
Official language: Danish.
Official religion: Evangelical Lutheran.
Monetary unit: 1 krone (Dkr; plural kroner) = 100 øre; valuation (Oct 21, 1985) 1 U.S.$ = Dkr9.56; 1 £ = Dkr13.71.

Area and population*		area		population
		sq mi	sq km	1985 estimate†
Counties	**Capitals**			
Århus	Århus	1,761	4,561	582,200
Bornholm	Rønne	227	588	47,200
Frederiksborg	Hillerød	520	1,347	335,000
Fyn	Odense	1,346	3,486	454,300
København	—	202	522	612,200
Nordjylland	Ålborg	2,383	6,173	482,000
Ribe	Ribe	1,209	3,132	215,400
Ringkøbing	Ringkøbing	1,874	4,853	264,500
Roskilde	Roskilde	344	891	209,000
Sønderjylland	Åbenrå	1,517	3,930	249,700
Storstrøm	Nykøbing	1,312	3,398	257,100
Vejle	Vejle	1,157	2,997	326,800
Vestsjælland	Sorø	1,152	2,984	278,800
Viborg	Viborg	1,592	4,122	230,400
Cities				
Copenhagen (København)	—	34	88	478,600
Frederiksberg	—	3	9	88,000
TOTAL		16,633	43,080‡	5,111,100‡

Demography

Population (1985): 5,109,000.
Density (1985): persons per sq mi 307.2, persons per sq km 118.6.
Urban–rural (1982): urban 84.0%; rural 16.0%.
Sex distribution (1985): male 49.25%; female 50.75%.
Age breakdown (1985): under 15, 18.6%; 15–29, 22.7%; 30–44, 22.4%; 45–59, 16.0%; 60–74, 14.0%; 75 and over, 6.3%..
Population projection: (1990) 5,068,400; (2000) 4,951,300.
Growth rate: During the early 1980s Denmark's population has been decreasing.
Ethnic composition (1985): Danish 98.8%; other Scandinavian 0.4%; Turkish 0.4%; other 0.4%.
Religious affiliation (1980): Evangelical Lutheran 95.6%; Roman Catholic 0.6%; Muslim 0.2%; Jewish 0.1%; atheist 1.2%; other 2.3%.
Major cities (1984): Greater Copenhagen 1,365,760; Århus 250,404; Odense 170,961; Ålborg 154,840.

Vital statistics

Birth rate per 1,000 population (1984): 10.1 (world avg. 29.0); (1983) legitimate 59.4%; illegitimate 40.6%.
Death rate per 1,000 population (1984): 11.2 (world avg. 11.0).
Natural increase rate per 1,000 population (1984): −1.1 (world avg. 18.0).
Total fertility rate (avg. births per childbearing woman; 1983): 1.4.
Marriage rate per 1,000 population (1984): 5.6.
Divorce rate per 1,000 population (1982): 2.9.
Life expectancy at birth (1982–83): male 71.5 years; female 77.5 years.
Major causes of death per 100,000 population (1983): ischemic heart disease 323.3; malignant neoplasms (cancers) 288.1; cerebrovascular disease 101.6.

National economy

Budget (1984). Revenue: Dkr177,789,000,000 (customs and excise taxes 46.3%, income and property taxes 40.0%, other 13.7%). Expenditures: Dkr231,950,000,000 (social services 24.0%, education 6.9%, defense 4.9%, other 64.2%).
Public debt (1984): U.S.$41,650,000,000.
Tourism (1983): receipts from visitors U.S.$1,306,000,000; expenditures by nationals abroad U.S.$1,210,000,000.
Production (metric tons except as noted). Agriculture, forestry, fishing (1984): barley 6,072,000, sugar beets 2,616,000, wheat 2,446,000, milk 5,387,000§; livestock (number of live animals) 2,749,900 cattle, 8,717,000 pigs; roundwood 2,953,000 cu m§; fish catch 1,862,130§. Manufacturing (value added in kroner; 1983): fabricated metal products and machinery 31,599,000,000; food, beverages, and tobacco 20,376,000,000, chemicals and petroleum products 11,521,000,000; paper and printed products 9,265,000,000. Construction (1983 ‖): residential 2,264,000 sq m; nonresidential 3,774,000 sq m. Energy production (consumption): electricity (kW-hr; 1983) 22,186,000,000 (26,393,000,000); coal (metric tons; 1983) none (8,666,000); crude petroleum (barrels; 1983) 15,785,000 (36,887,000); petroleum products (metric tons; 1983) 6,466,000 (9,052,000); natural gas (1983) none (n.a.).
Land use (1983): forested 11.6%; meadows and pastures 5.7%; agricultural and under permanent cultivation 62.3%; other 20.4%.
Gross national product (at current market prices; 1983): U.S.$54,600,000,000 (U.S.$10,680 per capita).

Structure of gross domestic product and labour force				
	1984		1983	
	in value Dkr'000,000	% of total value	labour force	% of labour force
Agriculture	29,816	6.2	177,000	7.3
Mining	3,963	0.8	3,000	0.1
Manufacturing	98,988	20.5	503,000	20.8
Construction	30,568	6.3	157,000	6.5
Public utilities	5,982	1.2	14,000	0.6
Transportation and communication	39,862	8.2	177,000	7.3
Trade	71,055	14.7	320,000	13.2
Finance	11,830	2.4	156,000	6.4
Pub. admin., defense	109,270	22.6	739,000	30.6
Services	93,461	19.4	147,000	6.1
Other	−11,957♀	−2.5	25,000	1.0
TOTAL	482,658	100.0†	2,418,000	100.0†

Population economically active (1983): total 2,732,000; participation rate of working age (15–64) population 79.4% (female 45.4%, unemployed 11.5%).

Price and earnings indexes (1980 = 100)							
	1978	1979	1980	1981	1982	1983	1984
Consumer price index	81.2	89.0	100.0	111.7	123.0	131.5	139.8
Monthly earnings index	80.5	89.8	100.0	108.9	120.5	128.4	135.3♀

Household income and expenditure. Average household size (1982) 2.4; income per household (1981) Dkr105,218 (U.S.$14,772); principal sources of income (1981): wages and salaries 59.1%, self-employment 14.3%, pensions and other 26.6%; expenditure (1983): housing 33.7%, food and beverages 22.0%, transportation and communication 15.8%, education, recreation, and culture 9.4%, clothing and footwear 5.7%.

Foreign trade

Balance of trade (current prices)					
	1979	1980	1981	1982	1983	1984
'000,000 kroner	−19,478	−13,717	−10,373	−10,692	−3,325	−6,972
% of total	11.2%	6.7%	4.3%	4.0%	1.1%	2.1%

Imports (1984): Dkr171,782,500,000 (machinery and transportation equipment 25.9%, of which road vehicles 6.1%; mineral fuels 17.7%, of which crude petroleum and petroleum products 15.0%; manufactured goods 13.5%, of which iron and steel 4.5%; chemicals and related products 11.4%; food and live animals 8.1%). *Major import sources:* West Germany 20.4%; Sweden 13.9%; United Kingdom 9.0%; The Netherlands 5.4%; United States 5.2%.
Exports (1984): Dkr164,810,660,000 (food and live animals 27.3%, of which meat and meat preparations 12.0%, dairy products 4.6%, fish and shellfish 4.8%; machinery and transport equipment 24.5%; chemicals and related products 9.0%). *Major export destinations:* West Germany 16.1%; United Kingdom 12.9%; Sweden 11.4%; United States 9.6%; Norway 6.4%.

Transport and communications

Transport. Railroads (1982): length 1,529 mi, 2,461 km; passenger-mi 2,747,300,000, passenger-km 4,421,400,000; short ton-mi cargo 1,036,200,000, metric ton-km cargo 1,667,600,000. Roads (1984): total length 43,388 mi, 69,827 km (paved 100%). Vehicles (1983): passenger cars 1,390,339; trucks and buses 242,883. Merchant marine (1984): vessels (100 gross tons and over) 1,101; total deadweight tonnage 7,973,433. Air transport (1984): passenger-mi 1,909,000,000, passenger-km 3,072,000,000; short ton-mi cargo 87,289,000, metric ton-km cargo 127,440,000; airports (1985) with scheduled flights 12.
Communications. Daily newspapers (1983): total number 47; total circulation 1,805,000; circulation per 1,000 population 353. Radio (1984): total number of receivers 2,018,000 (1 per 2.5 persons). Television (1984): total number of receivers 1,900,000 (1 per 2.7 persons). Telephones (1983): 3,634,000 (1 per 1.4 persons).

Education and health

Education (1983–84)				
	schools	teachers	students	student/ teacher ratio
Primary and lower secondary (age 7–12)	2,892	66,008	735,188	11.5
Upper secondary (age 13–18)	165	7,897	82,583	10.5
Vocational	271δ	...	140,621	...
Higher	96δ	10,411δ	122,535	...

Educational attainment (1983). Percent of population over age 14 having: primary and secondary education 84.5%; some postsecondary 6.7%; graduated from university 8.8%. *Literacy* (1983): 99.5%.
Health (1983): physicians 8,016 (1 per 422 persons); hospital beds 37,900 (1 per 130 persons); infant mortality rate per 1,000 live births 7.7.
Food (1979–81): daily per capita caloric intake 3,548 (vegetable products 55%, animal products 45%); 127% of FAO recommended minimum requirement.

Military

Total active duty personnel (1984): 31,400 (army 57.6%, navy 18.8%, air force 23.6%). *Military expenditure as percent of GNP* (1983): 2.1% (world 6.1%); per capita expenditure U.S.$223.

*Excluding Greenland and the Faeroe Islands (*qq.v.*). † January 1. ‡Detail does not add to total given because of rounding. §1983. ‖ Completed during year. ¶Includes imputed bank service charges. ♀Sept., 1984. δ1982–83.

Djibouti

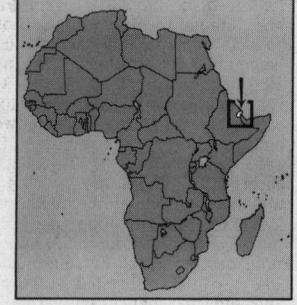

Official name: Jumhūrīyah Jībūtī (Arabic); République de Djibouti (French) (Republic of Djibouti).
Form of government: unitary single-party republic with one legislative house (National Assembly [65]).
Chief of state: President.
Head of government: Prime Minister.
Capital: Djibouti.
Official languages: Arabic; French.
Official religion: none.
Monetary unit: 1 Djibouti Franc (DF) = 100 centimes; valuation (Oct. 21, 1985) 1 U.S.$ = DF163.88; 1 £ = DF235.00.

Area and population

Districts	Capitals	area* sq mi	sq km	population 1982 estimate
Ali-Sabieh	Ali-Sabieh	925	2,400	15,000
Dikhil	Dikhil	2,775	7,200	30,000
Djibouti	Djibouti	225	600	200,000
Obock	Obock	2,200	5,700	15,000
Tadjourah	Tadjourah	2,825	7,300	30,000
TOTAL		8,950	23,200	335,000†

Demography

Population (1985 est.): 430,000‡.
Density (1985): persons per sq mi 48.0, persons per sq km 18.5.
Urban-rural (1985): urban 77.7%; rural 22.3%.
Sex distribution (1980): male 49.24%; female 50.76%.
Age breakdown (1980): under 15, 42.3%; 15–24, 18.1%; 25–64, 36.2%; 65 and over, 3.4%.
Population projection: (1990) 498,000; (2000) 670,000.
Doubling time: 23 years.
Ethnic composition (1984): Issa 47%; Afar 37%; European (mostly French) 8%; Arabic (mostly Yemeni) 6%; other 2%.
Religious affiliation (1983): Sunnī Muslim 94%; Christian 6%, of which Roman Catholic 4%, Protestant 1%, Orthodox 1%.
Major city and towns (1982): Djibouti 200,000§; Ali-Sabieh 4,000; Tadjourah 3,500; Dikhil 3,000.

Vital statistics

Birth rate per 1,000 population (1980–85): 49.2 (world avg. 29.0).
Death rate per 1,000 population (1980–85): 18.3 (world avg. 11.0).
Natural increase rate per 1,000 population (1980–85): 30.9 (world avg. 18.0).
Total fertility rate (avg. births per childbearing woman; 1980–85): 6.8.
Marriage rate per 1,000 population (1982): 6.7.
Divorce rate per 1,000 population (1982): 1.9.
Life expectancy at birth (1982): 50 years.
Major causes of death‖ (1984): percentage of total deaths from diarrhea and acute dehydration 16.0%; malnutrition 16.0%; intoxication 11.0%; tuberculosis 6.0%; acute respiratory disease 6.0%; malaria 6.0%; anemia 6.0%; heart disease 2.0%; kidney disease 1.0%; other ailments 19.0%; no diagnosis 11.0%.
Major reported diseases per 100,000 population (1984): diarrhea 2,219.0; gonorrhea 542.2, of which men 437.5, women 104.7; tuberculosis 380.0; malaria 296.8; syphilis 181.2, of which men 84.2, women 97.0; measles 64.0; viral hepatitis 59.3; whooping cough 21.5; leprosy 8.1; acute poliomyelitis 7.4; tetanus 2.5.

National economy

Budget (1984). Revenue: DF21,854,600,000 (indirect taxes 53.1%, direct taxes 24.1%, customs duties 5.9%, excises 3.1%). Expenditures: DF21,854,600,-000 (defense 21.7%, general administration 16.2%, economic development and services 9.0%, social welfare and health 7.6%, education 6.7%, debt payment 3.1%).
Public debt (external, outstanding; 1983): U.S.$32,900,000.
Tourism: n.a.
Production (metric tons except as noted). Agriculture¶, forestry, fishing (1984): vegetables and melons 12,000; livestock (number of live animals) 543,000 goats, 400,000 sheep, 54,000 camels, 44,000 cattle, 7,000 asses; fish catch 426♀. Mining and quarrying (1983): mineral production limited to locally used construction material and evaporated salt. Manufacturing (1983): n.a.; main items produced are furniture, nonalcoholic beverages, light electromechanical goods, and mineral water. Construction (1984): residential 27,738 sq m; nonresidential 52,225 sq m. Energy production (consumption): electricity (kW-hr; 1983) 126,000,000 (126,000,000); coal, none (n.a.); crude petroleum, none (n.a.); petroleum products (metric tons; 1983) none (154,000); natural gas, none (n.a.).
Population economically active: n.a.

Price and earnings indexes (1975 = 100)

	1977	1978	1979	1980	1981	1982	1983
Consumer price index	136.6	163.4	187.6	210.5	222.2	217.0	...
Monthly earnings index	...	...	...	...	...	...	...

Gross national product (at current market prices; 1984): U.S.$307,980,000 (U.S.$760 per capita).

Structure of gross domestic product and labour force

	1984 in value DF'000,000	1984 % of total value	1982 labour force▫	1982 % of labour force
Agriculture	2,690	4.5	63	0.4
Mining	—	—	—	—
Manufacturing	4,920	8.2	726	4.5
Construction	4,490	7.5	2,309	14.3
Public utilities	1,942	3.2	456	2.8
Transportation and communication	6,010	10.0	2,711	17.0
Trade	9,400	15.6	3,148	19.5
Finance	6,530	10.8	1,296	8.0
Pub. admin., defense	16,170	26.8	3,347	20.7
Services	950	1.6	915	5.6
Other	7,132◊	11.8◊	1,168	7.2
TOTAL	60,234△	100.0	16,139	100.0

Household income and expenditure. Average household sizeŏ (1982) 5.6; income per household: n.a.; source of income: n.a.; expenditure: n.a.
Land use (1983): forested 0.3%; meadows and pastures 9.1%; agricultural and under permanent cultivation¶; other 90.6%.

Foreign trade†

Balance of trade (current prices)

	1977	1978	1979	1980	1981	1982	1983
DF'000,000	−15,585	−25,963	−31,431	−35,699	−28,311	−37,965	−12,599
% of total	69.8%	80.4%	88.7%	88.9%	90.1%	89.5%	24.7%

Imports (1982): DF40,197,000,000 (food and live animals 20.5%; machinery and transport equipment 20.1%, of which electrical machinery and appliances 9.0%; textiles and clothing 15.2%; petroleum products 9.6%; kat [a narcotic leaf] 8.0%; special transactions, including importation of gold coins, personal effects, and military goods, 4.5%; tobacco and tobacco products 3.6%). *Major import sources* (1980): France 50.3%; Ethiopia 6.5%; North America 5.6%; Benelux 5.2%; Japan 5.0%; United Kingdom 4.2%.
Exports (1982): DF2,232,000,000 (unspecified special transactions 51.7%; live animals [including camels] 12.2%; food and food products 14.2%). *Major export destinations* (1980): France 65.7%; Italy 5.7%; Somalia 5.0%; Benelux 2.4%; United Kingdom 0.4%.

Transport and communications

Transport. Railroads (1982): length 66 mi, 106 km; short tons cargo 169,980,-000, metric tons cargo 154,200,000⊙. Roads (1983): total length 1,806 mi, 2,906 km (paved 11%). Vehicles (1982): passenger cars 9,000; trucks and buses 1,500. Merchant marine (1984): vessels (100 gross tons and over) 7; total deadweight tonnage 2,853. Air transport** (1983): passenger arrivals 63,662, passenger departures 58,479; cargo loaded 1,575 metric tons, cargo unloaded 6,542 metric tons; airports (1985) with scheduled flights 3.
Communications. Daily newspapers: none. Radio (1984): total number of receivers 17,500 (1 per 23 persons). Television (1984): total number of receivers 11,200 (1 per 36 persons). Telephone subscribers (1983): 3,624 (1 per 106 persons).

Education and health

Education (1983–84)

	schools	teachers	students	student/ teacher ratio
Primary (age 6–14)	52	496	21,847	44.0
Secondary (age 12–20)	9	211	4,791	22.7
Voc., teacher tr.	10	123	1,540	12.5
Higher	—	—	161	

Educational attainment, n.a. *Literacy* (c. 1980): population over age 14 literate 11.9%; 8.8% if discounting the expatriate population.
Health (1984): physicians 46 (1 per 8,804 persons); hospital beds 1,182 (1 per 343 persons); infant mortality rate per 1,000 live births 150–200.
Food: n.a.

Military

Total active duty personnel (1984): 2,700 (army 96.3%, navy 0.7%, air force 3.0%)††. *Military expenditure as percent of GNP* (1982): 13.1% (world 6.0%); per capita expenditure U.S.$74.

*Approximate figures given in sq km; sq mi equivalent rounded to appropriate level of generality. †Including 45,000 unaccounted, not shown separately. ‡Nearly 31,000 refugees from Ethiopia were repatriated by year's end 1984; over 14,000 were still residing in Djibouti in January 1985. §District population. ‖ Infants and children to age 10, district of Djibouti only. ¶In 1982 only 450 ac (200 ha) of land were cultivated. ♀1983. ŏCity of Djibouti only. ▫Salaried employees only. ◊Import duties, less imputed bank service charge. △At current prices. †The value of imports includes merchandise destined for Ethiopia and northern Somalia; that of exports excludes reexports coming from those areas. In 1980 the value of reexports from Ethiopia and northern Somalia was approximately five times greater than the value of domestic exports. ⊙Total weight of Ethiopian exports and imports transported to and from the port of Djibouti. **Djibouti International Airport only. ††In 1984, 3,250 French military personnel were also stationed in Djibouti.

Dominica

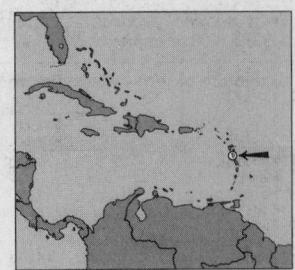

Official name: Commonwealth of Dominica.
Form of government: multiparty republic with one legislative house (House of Assembly [31]).
Chief of state: President.
Head of government: Prime Minister.
Capital: Roseau.
Official language: English.
Official religion: none.
Monetary unit: 1 East Caribbean dollar (EC$) = 100 cents; valuation (Oct. 21, 1985) 1 U.S.$ = EC$2.70*; 1 £ = EC$3.87.

Area and population	area		population
Parishes	sq mi	sq km	1970 census
St. Andrew	69	179	11,998
St. David	49	127	6,709
St. George	21	54	20,114
St. John	23	60	5,283
St. Joseph	46	119	6,393
St. Luke	4	10	1,622
St. Mark	4	10	1,943
St. Patrick	32	83	10,085
St. Paul	26	67	4,459
St. Peter	11	29	1,696
TOTAL	290†‡	750†	70,302§

Demography

Population (1985): 77,400.
Density (1985): persons per sq mi 256.0, persons per sq km 99.0.
Urban-rural (1970): urban 46.2%; rural 53.8%.
Sex distribution (1981): male 49.85%; female 50.15%.
Age breakdown (1981): under 15, 39.8%; 15–29, 28.6%; 30–44, 11.9%; 45–59, 9.2%; 60–74, 7.4%; 75 and over, 3.1%.
Population projection: n.a.
Doubling time: 122 years.
Ethnic composition (1980): black 89.0%; mulatto 7.3%; Amerindian 1.7%.
Religious affiliation (1981): Roman Catholic 91.8%; Protestant 8.0%.
Major towns (1981): Roseau 8,346; Portsmouth 2,220.

Vital statistics

Birth rate per 1,000 population (1983): 24.3 (world avg. 29.0); (1980) legitimate 35.0%; illegitimate 65.0%.
Death rate per 1,000 population (1983): 5.1 (world avg. 11.0).
Natural increase rate per 1,000 population (1983): 19.2 (world avg. 18.0).
Total fertility rate (avg. births per childbearing woman; 1980–85): 3.0.
Marriage rate per 1,000 population: n.a.
Divorce rate per 1,000 population: n.a.
Life expectancy at birth (1980–85): male 66.5 years; female 72.8 years.
Major causes of death per 100,000 population (1981): diseases of the circulatory system 180.4; malignant neoplasms (cancers) 68.1; infectious and parasitic diseases 52.1; accidents, poisoning, and violence 36.1.

National economy

Budget (1983–84) ‖. Revenue: EC$69,700,000 (consumption tax 32.3%, income tax 26.8%, import duties 14.6%, licenses 2.2%, stamp duty 1.9%). Expenditures: EC$69,500,000 (general administration 14.4%; education 19.4%; health 13.7%; social security and welfare 7.6%; roads 6.6%; agriculture and forestry 6.2%; communication 2.6%).
Tourism (1983): receipts from visitors U.S.$5,130,000; expenditures by nationals abroad, n.a.
Gross national product (1983): U.S.$79,400,000 (U.S.$1,073 per capita).

Structure of gross domestic product and labour force	1983			
	in value EC$'000,000	% of total value	labour force	% of labour force
Agriculture	52.5	29.8	3,255	13.1
Mining	1.3	0.7	...	...
Manufacturing	14.1	8.0	1,359	5.5
Construction	12.6	7.2	3,061	12.3
Public utilities	5.2	3.0	264	1.1
Transp. and commun.	19.7	11.2	2,127	8.6
Trade, hotels, restaurants	16.1	9.2	2,852	11.5
Finance, real estate, insurance	11.5	6.5	498	2.0
Pub. admin., defense, services	40.6	23.1	11,440	46.0
Other	2.3	1.3	...	...
TOTAL	175.8δ	100.0	24,856	100.0‡

Population economically active (1981); participation rate of total population 34.4% (female 35.0%, unemployed 18.6%).

Price and earnings indexes (1975 = 100)							
	1978	1979	1980	1981	1982	1983	1984
Consumer price index	63.9	76.6	100.0	113.3	118.4	123.2	125.8
Earnings index	...	...	...	...	...	...	...

Household income and expenditure. Average household size (1970) 4.7; average annual income per household: n.a.; expenditure: n.a.
Production (metric tons except as noted). Agriculture, forestry, fishing (1984): bananas 37,000, root crops (mostly dasheens and tanias) 25,000, coconuts 15,000, grapefruits 8,000, limes 6,000, cucumbers 2,498¶, oranges 2,000, cocoa 450¶; livestock (number of live animals) 9,000 pigs, 6,000 goats, 4,000 cattle, 115,000 chickens9; roundwood, n.a.; fish catch (1983) 1,500. Mining and quarrying (1983): pumice 110,000. Manufacturing (value in '000 EC$; 1983): laundry soap 10,594; toilet soap 8,839; coconut oil 7,220; galvanized sheets 5,528; copra 3,622; soft drinks 1,985; garments 527. Construction: n.a. Energy production (consumption): electricity (kW-hr; 1984) 20,200,000 (16,300,000); coal, none (n.a.); crude petroleum, none (n.a.); petroleum products (metric tons; 1983) none (12,000); natural gas, none (n.a.).
Public debt (external, outstanding; 1984): U.S.$42,688,000.
Land use (1983): forested 41.0%; meadows and pastures 3.0%; agricultural and under permanent cultivation 23.0%; other 33.0%.

Foreign trade

Balance of trade (current prices)□						
	1979	1980	1981	1982	1983	1984
EC$'000,000	−34.6	−102.4	−82.3	−62.2	−49.5	−78.8
% of total	40.5%	66.1%	44.3%	32.0%	25.5%	35.9%

Imports (1984): EC$149,310,000 (food, beverages, and tobacco 25.1%, manufactured goods 22.8%, oils and fats 3.8%; machinery and transport equipment 26.0%; fuels and lubricants 10.3%; chemicals 9.2%). *Major import sources:* United States 26.6%; United Kingdom 12.8%; Canada 7.7%.
Exports (1984◊): EC$70,470,000 (bananas 40.3%, soap 27.0%, galvanized sheets 7.2%, coconut oil 5.8%, vegetables 2.2%, grapefruit 2.2%). *Major export destinations:* United Kingdom 46.9%; United States 1.6%.

Transport and communications

Transport. Railroads: none. Roads (1984): total length 463 mi, 745 km (paved 50%). Vehicles (1980): passenger cars 3,044; trucks and buses 1,240. Merchant marine (1984): vessels (100 gross tons and over) 3; total deadweight tonnage 1,243. Air transport (1979): passengers, n.a.; cargo loaded 194 metric tons, cargo unloaded 228 metric tons; airports (1985) with scheduled flights 2.
Communications. Daily newspapers: none. Radio (1984): total number of receivers 20,000 (1 per 3.7 persons). Television: total number of receivers, n.a. Telephones (1983): 4,505 (1 per 16.4 persons).

Education and health

Education (1982–83)	schools	teachers	students	student/ teacher ratio
Primary	58	635	18,370	28.9
Secondary	8	145	3,234	22.3
Voc., teacher tr.	1	13	121	9.3
Higher†	...	59	284	4.8

Educational attainment (1981). Percent of literate adult population having: no formal schooling 5.1%; primary education 78.5%; secondary 13.5%; higher 1.3%; other 0.5%. *Literacy* (1971): total population over age 15 literate 41,903 (94.4%).
Health (1983): physicians 26 (1 per 2,846 persons); hospital beds 237 (1 per 312 persons); infant mortality rate per 1,000 live births 13.9.
Food (1980–82): daily per capita caloric intake 2,155 (vegetable products 82%, animal products 18%); 89% of FAO recommended minimum requirement.

Military

Total active duty personnel (1983): 250 police.

*Since July 1976 the par value has been U.S.$1.00 = EC$2.70. †Includes inland water area. ‡Detail does not add to total given because of rounding. §1981 census total was 74,785; breakdown by parish is not available. ‖ Estimated recurrent budget for 1984–85 was: revenue EC$76,200,000; expenditures EC$74,300,000. ¶1983. 91982. δAt current factor cost. □Imports c.i.f. (cost, insurance, and freight); exports f.o.b. (free on board). ◊Breakdown for exports is for 1983. †1980–81.

MARIO C. TOULON

Deepwater harbour, Roseau, Dominica

Dominican Republic

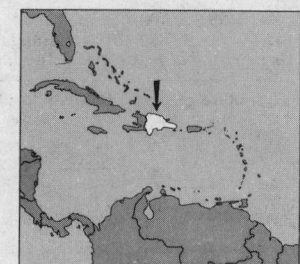

Official name: República Dominicana (Dominican Republic).
Form of government: multiparty republic with two legislative houses (Senate [27]; Chamber of Deputies [91]).
Head of state and government: President.
Capital: Santo Domingo.
Official language: Spanish.
Official religion: none.
Monetary unit: 1 Dominican peso (RD$) = 100 centavos; valuation (Oct. 21, 1985) 1 U.S.$ = RD$1.00*; 1 £ = RD$1.43.

Area and population

Provinces	Capitals	area sq mi	area sq km	population 1981 census
Azua	Azua	938	2,430	142,770
Bahoruco (Baoruco)	Neiba	531	1,376	78,636
Barahona	Barahona	976	2,528	137,160
Dajabón	Dajabón	344	890	57,709
Duarte	San Francisco de Macorís	499	1,292	235,544
El Seibo	El Seibo	1,154	2,989	157,866
Espaillat	Moca	386	1,000	164,017
Independencia	Jimaní	719	1,861	38,768
La Altagracia	Higüey	1,191	3,084	100,112
La Estrelleta	Elías Piña	690	1,788	65,384
La Romana	La Romana	209	541	109,769
La Vega	La Vega	1,304	3,377	385,043
María Trinidad Sánchez	Nagua	506	1,310	112,629
Montecristi	Montecristi	768	1,989	83,407
Pedernales	Pedernales	373	967	17,006
Peravia	Baní	626	1,622	168,123
Puerto Plata	Puerto Plata	726	1,881	206,757
Salcedo	Salcedo	206	533	99,191
Samaná	Samaná	382	989	65,699
Sánchez Ramírez	Cotuí	453	1,174	126,567
San Cristóbal	San Cristóbal	1,445	3,743	446,132
San Juan	San Juan	1,375	3,561	239,957
San Pedro de Macorís	San Pedro de Macorís	450	1,166	152,890
Santiago	Santiago de los Caballeros	1,205	3,122	550,372
Santiago Rodríguez	Sabaneta	394	1,020	55,411
Valverde	Mao	220	570	100,319
National district				
Santo Domingo	—	570	1,477	1,550,739
TOTAL		18,704†	48,442†	5,647,977

Demography

Population (1985): 6,243,000.
Density (1985): persons per sq mi 333.8, persons per sq km 128.9.
Urban–rural (1985): urban 55.7%; rural 44.3%.
Sex distribution (1981): male 50.15%; female 49.85%.
Age breakdown (1985): under 15, 40.7%; 15–29, 30.7%; 30–44, 15.4%; 45–59, 8.5%; 60–74, 3.7%; 75 and over, 1.0%.
Population projection: (1990) 6,971,000; (2000) 8,407,000.
Doubling time: 30 years.
Ethnic composition (1982): mulatto 75%; white 15%; black 10%.
Religious affiliation (1983): Roman Catholic 98%; other 2%.
Major cities (1981): Santo Domingo 1,313,170; Santiago 278,640; La Romana 91,570; San Pedro de Macorís 78,560.

Vital statistics

Birth rate per 1,000 population (1983): 38.6 (world avg. 29.0); (1976) legitimate 32.8%; illegitimate 67.2%.
Death rate per 1,000 population (1983): 8.5 (world avg. 11.0).
Natural increase rate per 1,000 population (1983): 30.1 (world avg. 18.0).
Total fertility rate (avg. births per childbearing woman; 1980–85): 4.2.
Marriage rate per 1,000 population (1981): 4.9.
Divorce rate per 1,000 population: (1981): 1.7.
Life expectancy at birth (1980–85): male 60.7 years; female 64.6 years.
Major causes of death per 100,000 population (1978): diseases of the circulatory system 63.3; infectious and parasitic diseases 60.3; accidents, poisoning, and violence 31.8; diseases of the respiratory system 29.7.

National economy

Budget (1983). Revenue: RD$1,172,600,000 (excise taxes 25.8%, import duties 22.1%, taxes on corporate profits 14.2%, nontax revenue 9.2%). Expenditures: RD$1,199,200,000 (presidency 15.6%; education 12.6%, army 11.2%, health 8.1%, police 6.4%).
Public debt (external, outstanding; 1983): U.S.$2,403,000,000.
Tourism (1981): receipts from visitors U.S.$223,000,000; expenditures by nationals abroad U.S.$133,000,000.
Production (metric tons except as noted). Agriculture (1984): sugarcane 11,750,000, plantains 605,000, rice 344,000, bananas 320,000, mangoes 184,000, tomatoes 181,000, cassava 118,000, coffee 49,000, cacao 44,000, tobacco 35,000; livestock (number of live animals) 1,994,000 cattle, 832,000 pigs, 465,000 goats, 204,000 horses; roundwood (1983) 579,000 cu m; fish catch (1983) 13,169. Mining (value of production in U.S.$'000; 1984): gold 121,850; nickel 99,620; silver 9,700. Manufacturing (value added in DR$'000; 1981): food products (excluding sugar) 173,600; beverages 70,400; chemicals 30,900; tobacco products 27,700. Construction (value in DR$'000; 1982)‡: residential 356,600; nonresidential 52,200. Energy production (consumption): electricity (kW-hr; 1983) 3,400,000,000 (3,400,000,000); coal (metric

tons; 1983) none (1,000); crude petroleum (barrels; 1983) none (10,800,000); petroleum products (metric tons; 1983) 1,464,000 (2,055,000).
Gross national product (at current market prices; 1983): U.S.$8,170,000,000 (U.S.$1,371 per capita).

Structure of gross domestic product and labour force

	1983 in value RD$'000,000	1983 % of total value	1980 labour force	1980 % of labour force
Agriculture	1,413	17.4	661,600	41.3
Mining	292	3.6	1,600	0.1
Manufacturing	1,523	18.8	325,200	20.3
Construction	522	6.4	56,100	3.5
Public utilities	125	1.5		
Transportation and communication	661	8.1		
Trade	1,336	16.5	557,500	34.8
Finance	208	2.6		
Pub. admin., defense	820	10.1		
Other	1,221	15.0		
TOTAL	8,121	100.0	1,602,000	100.0

Population economically active (1983): total 1,681,000; participation rate of population over age 15, 45.4% (female, n.a.; unemployed 25.0%).

Price and earnings indexes (1980 = 100)

	1979	1980	1981	1982	1983	1984	1985
Consumer price index	85.7	100.0	107.5	115.8	121.3	154.0	204.1§
Earnings index	...	...	...	...	...	...	...

Household income and expenditure. Average household size (1981) 5.1; average annual income per family (1975) urban family RD$2,299, rural family RD$654; source of income: n.a.; expenditure: n.a.
Land use (1983): forested 13.0%; meadows and pastures 43.2%; agricultural and under permanent cultivation 30.2%; other 13.6%.

Foreign trade ‖

Balance of trade (current prices)

	1979	1980	1981	1982	1983	1984
RD$'000,000	−186.0	−463.8	−262.8	−488.1	−489.5	−384.0
% of total	9.7%	19.4%	9.9%	24.1%	23.8%	16.8%

Imports (1983): RD$1,271,200,000 (crude petroleum and petroleum products 36.1%; machinery 8.2%; foodstuffs 8.1%; chemicals [including pharmaceuticals] 5.5%; iron and steel 4.5%). *Major import sources:* United States 34.5%; Venezuela 21.2%; Mexico 11.0%; Japan 4.3%.
Exports (1983): RD$781,700,000 (raw sugar 35.4%; gold alloy 19.8%; ferronickel 10.3%; coffee 9.8%; cacao 7.8%; furfural 2.9%). *Major export destinations:* United States 64.4%; Switzerland 5.5%; Canada 4.4%; Puerto Rico 4.1%; The Netherlands 4.0%.

Transport and communications

Transport. Railroads (1984)¶: route length 88 mi, 142 km. Roads (1982): total length 10,788 mi, 17,362 km (paved 29%). Vehicles (1983): passenger cars 94,601; trucks and buses 55,346. Merchant marine (1984): vessels (100 gross tons and over) 37; total deadweight tonnage 57,971. Air transport (1983)⊊: passenger departures 684,000, arrivals 668,000; cargo loaded 22,400 metric tons, cargo unloaded 16,700 metric tons; airports (1985) 3.
Communications. Daily newspapers (1984): total number 7; total circulation 176,900; circulation per 1,000 population 29. Radio (1984): receivers 226,000 (1 per 27 persons). Television (1984): receivers 390,000 (1 per 16 persons). Telephones (1983): 175,054 (1 per 35 persons).

Education and health

Education (1982–83)

	schools	teachers	students	student/ teacher ratio
Primary (age 7–12)	6,009	23,578	1,092,838	46.3
Secondary (age 13–18)δ	1,963	11,716	353,729	30.2
Voc., teacher tr.δ	...	...	25,648	...
Higher□	5	...	91,115	...

Educational attainment (1970). Percent of adult population over age 14 having: no formal schooling 28.8%; primary education 42.8%; junior secondary 8.3%; senior secondary 6.1%; higher 1.7%; other 12.3%. *Literacy* (1980): total population literate (over age 15) 2,329,000 (73.6%); males literate 1,161,600 (73.4%); females literate 1,167,400 (73.8%).
Health (1980)◊: physicians 2,142 (1 per 2,595 persons); hospital beds 8,953 (1 per 621 persons); infant mortality rate per 1,000 live births (1983) 28.3△.
Food (1980–82): daily per capita caloric intake 2,147 (vegetable products 87%, animal products 13%); 95% of FAO recommended minimum.

Military

Total active duty personnel (1984): 23,000 (army 60.8%, navy 19.6%, air force 19.6%). *Military expenditure as percent of GNP* (1983): 1.5% (world 6.1%); per capita expenditure U.S.$19.

*In January 1985 the value of the DR$ became free floating in relation to the U.S.$; it had been at par with the U.S.$ since 1947. †Total includes 63 sq mi (163 sq km) of offshore islands not shown separately. ‡New building construction authorized. §April. ‖ Imports and exports f.o.b. (free on board). ¶Excludes privately owned railways serving the sugar industry, totaling 1,000 mi. ⊊Santo Domingo and Puerto Plata airports only. δ1981–82. □1983–84; universities only. ◊Physicians and hospital beds under the auspices of the Institute of Social Security only. △Registered events only: the 1980–85 UN estimate is 64.0.

Ecuador

Official name: República del Ecuador (Republic of Ecuador).
Form of government: unitary multiparty republic with one legislative house (National Congress [71]).
Head of state and government: President.
Capital: Quito.
Official language: Spanish.
Official religion: none.
Monetary unit: 1 Sucre (S/.) = 100 centavos; valuation (Oct. 21, 1985) 1 U.S.$ = S/.95.90; 1 £ = S/.137.52.

Area and population

Regions Provinces	Capitals	area sq mi	area sq km	population 1982 census
Coastal				
El Oro	Machala	2,281	5,908	334,872
Esmeraldas	Esmeraldas	5,854	15,162	249,008
Guayas	Guayaquil	8,256	21,382	2,038,454
Los Ríos	Babahoyo	2,459	6,370	455,869
Manabí	Portoviejo	6,990	18,105	868,598
Eastern				
Morona-Santiago	Macas	10,200	26,418	70,217
Napo	Tena	20,200	52,318	115,110
Pastaza	Puyo	11,687	30,269	31,779
Zamora-Chinchipe	Zamora	7,102	18,394	46,691
Sierra				
Azuay	Cuenca	3,124	8,092	442,019
Bolívar	Guaranda	1,599	4,142	145,949
Cañar	Azogues	1,344	3,481	174,510
Carchi	Tulcán	1,446	3,744	127,779
Chimborazo	Riobamba	2,338	6,056	316,948
Cotopaxi	Latacunga	2,007	5,198	277,678
Imbabura	Ibarra	1,921	4,976	247,287
Loja	Loja	4,429	11,472	360,767
Pichincha	Quito	6,404	16,587	1,382,125
Tungurahua	Ambato	1,201	3,110	326,777
Island territory				
Galápagos Islands	Puerto Baquerizo Moreno	3,086	7,994	6,119
TOTAL		103,930*	269,178	8,060,712†

Demography

Population (1985): 8,604,000.
Density (1985): persons per sq mi 82.8, persons per sq km 32.0.
Urban-rural (1982): urban 49.2%; rural 50.8%.
Sex distribution (1982): male 49.88%; female 50.12%.
Age breakdown (1982): under 15, 41.9%; 15–29, 28.1%; 30–44, 15.4%; 45–59, 8.6%; 60–74, 4.5%; 75 and over, 1.5%.
Population projection: (1990) 10,949,000; (2000) 14,596,000.
Doubling time: 22 years.
Ethnic composition (1980): Quechua 49.9%; mestizo 40.0%; white 8.5%; Amerindian 1.6%.
Religious affiliation (1981): Roman Catholic 91%; other 9%.
Major cities (1982): Guayaquil 1,175,300; Quito 858,700; Cuenca 150,900; Machala 105,300; Portoviejo 101,200.

Vital statistics

Birth rate per 1,000 population: (1982) 37.0 (world avg. 29.0); legitimate 67.9%; illegitimate 32.1%.
Death rate per 1,000 population (1982): 8.0 (world avg. 11.0).
Natural increase rate per 1,000 population (1982): 29.0 (world avg. 18.0).
Total fertility rate (avg. births per childbearing woman; 1980–85): 6.0.
Marriage rate per 1,000 population (1982): 6.2.
Divorce rate per 1,000 population (1982): 0.4.
Life expectancy at birth (1981): male 59.8 years; female 63.6 years.
Major causes of death per 100,000 population (1979)‡: respiratory diseases 127.1; intestinal diseases 105.3; circulatory diseases 97.0; accidents 61.9.

National economy

Budget (1984). Revenue: S/.115,371,000,000 (income from petroleum 44.4%, import duties 14.4%, production and sales tax 13.9%, capital income [domestic and foreign aid] 11.9%, income tax 8.1%). Expenditures: S/.116,374,000,000 (no breakdown available).
Public debt (external, outstanding; 1983): U.S.$6,238,700,000.
Tourism (1983): receipts from visitors U.S.$120,000,000; expenditures by nationals abroad U.S.$152,000,000.
Production (metric tons except as noted). Agriculture, forestry, fishing (1984): bananas 1,924,000, rice 470,000, potatoes 363,000, oranges 350,000, raw sugar 328,000, corn (maize) 300,000, cassava 243,000, pineapples 92,000, coffee (green) 90,000, cacao 60,000, palm oil 43,000; livestock (number of live animals) 4,278,000 pigs, 2,311,000 sheep, 3,300,000 cattle, 42,000,000 chickens; roundwood 7,795,000 cu m§; fish catch 307,288§. Mining and quarrying (1983): limestone 1,500,000; silver 322 troy oz, gold 643 troy oz. Manufacturing (value in S/.'000,000; 1983): food products 19,432; petroleum products 16,446; textiles and clothing 6,495; beverages (including liquors) 2,706. Construction (in S/. ‖; 1981): residential 6,645,100,000; nonresidential 2,506,700,000. Energy production (consumption): electricity (kW-hr; 1983) 4,289,000,000 (4,304,000,000); crude petroleum (barrels;

1984) 93,868,400 (35,253,000§); petroleum products (metric tons; 1984) 4,254,000 (3,788,000§); natural gas (cu m; 1984) 410,300,900 (410,300,900).
Gross national product (1983): U.S.$11,690,000,000 (U.S.$1,430 per capita).

Structure of gross domestic product and labour force

	1983 in value S/.'000,000	1983 % of total value	1982 labour force	1982 % of labour force
Agriculture	76,513	13.5	786,530	33.0
Mining	81,717	14.4	7,050	0.3
Manufacturing	101,582	18.0	284,780	11.9
Construction	41,489	7.3	158,530	6.6
Public utilities	3,666	0.6	14,560	0.6
Trans. and commun.	47,903	8.5	103,850	4.4
Trade	79,510	14.1	266,640	11.2
Finance	16,902	3.0	38,420	1.6
Pub. admin., defense	42,879	7.6	614,240	25.7
Services	}			
Other	73,641	13.0	112,650	4.7
TOTAL	565,802¶	100.0	2,387,250	100.0

Population economically active (1982): total 2,387,250; participation rate of population over age 15, 51.0% (female [1981] 26.7%, unemployed [1981] 1.9%).

Price and earnings indexes (1980 = 100)

	1979	1980	1981	1982	1983	1984	1985
Consumer price index	88.5	100.0	113.0	131.3	195.0	255.8	334.4‡
Annual earnings index□	75.0	100.0	111.6	...	...	...	...

Household income and expenditure. Average household size (1982) 5.1; average annual income per household (1982) S/.28,747 (U.S.$956); sources of income (1982): self-employment 53.6%, wages and salaries 38.0%, interest, dividends, and rent 2.9%, social security 2.9%; expenditure (1982): food, beverages, and tobacco 33.8%, transportation and communication 13.0%, clothing 10.7%, housing and utilities 10.7%.
Land use (1983): forested 51.5%; meadows and pastures 16.6%; agricultural and under permanent cultivation 9.0%; other 22.9%.

Foreign trade◇

Balance of trade (current prices)

	1979	1980	1981	1982	1983	1984
U.S.$'000,000	+376.4	+532.1	+646.4	+425.8	+971.6	+1,124.3
% of total	9.8%	12.0%	14.6%	11.0%	28.0%	27.8%

Imports (1983): U.S.$1,464,954,000 (chemical products 18.5%, mineral products 15.8%, industrial machinery 12.5%, food products 9.4%, transportation equipment 8.3%). *Major import sources:* United States 34.0%; Japan 9.3%; West Germany 8.7%; Brazil 5.0%; Italy 5.0%.
Exports (1983): U.S.$2,193,614,000 (crude petroleum 67.1%, fish products 8.2%, coffee 6.8%, bananas 6.7%, petroleum products 4.8%). *Major export destinations:* United States 56.8%; Panama 9.9%; Colombia 6.1%.

Transport and communications

Transport. Railroads: (1984) route length 600 mi, 965 km; (1979) passenger-mi 42,900,000, passenger-km 69,000,000; (1979) short ton-mi cargo 19,900,000, metric ton-km cargo 29,000,000. Roads (1984): total length 22,194 mi, 35,718 km (paved 16%). Vehicles (1984): passenger cars 248,575; trucks and buses 32,624. Merchant marine (1984): vessels (100 gross tons and over) 135; total deadweight tonnage 578,805. Air transport (1982): passenger-mi 455,000,000, passenger-km 732,000,000; short ton-mi cargo 20,800,000, metric ton-km cargo 30,400,000; airports (1985) 13.
Communications. Daily newspapers (1984): total number 9; total circulation 555,000; circulation per 1,000 population 66. Radio (1984): receivers 1,875,000 (1 per 4.5 persons). Television (1984): receivers 450,000 (1 per 19 persons). Telephones (1982): 290,200 (1 per 28 persons).

Education and health

Education (1983–84)

	schools	teachers	students	student/teacher ratio
Primary (age 4–12)	13,011	50,347	1,677,364	33.3
Secondary (age 12–18)△	1,315	29,319	459,647	15.7
Vocational	466	10,590	190,631	18.0
Higher	17	11,186	267,900	23.9

Educational attainment (1974). Percent of adult population over age 25 having: no formal schooling 31.9%; primary education 53.7%; secondary 11.2%; higher 3.2%. *Literacy* (1982): total population over age 10 literate 4,875,974 (85.2%); males literate 2,492,827 (87.9%); females literate 2,383,147 (82.6%).
Health (1982): physicians (1981) 10,257 (1 per 760 persons); hospital beds 15,980 (1 per 500 persons); infant mortality rate per 1,000 live births 78.0.
Food (1980–82): daily per capita caloric intake 2,081 (vegetable products 82%, animal products 18%); 92% of FAO recommended minimum requirement.

Military

Total active duty personnel (1984): 39,300 (army 76.3%, navy 11.5%, air force 12.2%). *Military expenditure as percent of GNP* (1983): 1.6% (world 6.1%); per capita expenditure U.S.$21.

---

*Detail does not add to total given because of rounding. †Total includes 42,156 persons not shown separately. ‡Excludes nomadic Indian tribes. §1983. ‖ Authorized construction only. ¶At current prices. ⊕1981. ⬦July. □For salaried industrial workers only. ◇Import figures are f.o.b. in balance of trade and c.i.f. for commodities and trading partners. △Includes teacher training.

Egypt

Official name: Jumhūrīyah Miṣr al-'Arabīyah (Arab Republic of Egypt).
Form of government: republic with one legislative house (People's Assembly [458]).
Chief of state: President.
Head of government: Prime Minister.
Capital: Cairo.
Official language: Arabic.
Official religion: Islām.
Monetary unit: 1 Egyptian pound (LE) = 100 piastres = 1,000 millièmes; valuation (Oct. 21, 1985)
1 LE = U.S.$0.82 = £1.18.

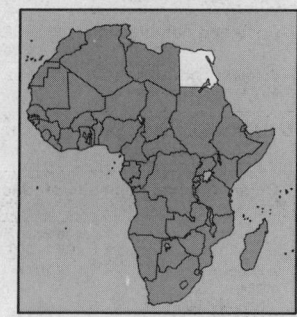

Area and population		area		population
Regions				1983
Governorates	Capitals	sq mi	sq km	estimate
Desert				
al-Baḥr al-Aḥmar	al-Ghurdaqah	78,643	203,685	68,000
Maṭrūḥ	Marsā Maṭrūḥ	81,897	212,112	156,000
Sīnā' al-Janūbīyah	aṭ-Ṭūr	...*	...*	23,000
Sīnā' ash-Shamālīyah	al-'Arīsh	23,442*	60,714*	141,000
al-Wādī al-Jadīd	al-Khārijah	145,369	376,505	106,000
Lower Egypt				
al-Buḥayrah	Damanhūr	3,911	10,130	2,976,000
ad-Daqahlīyah	al-Manṣūrah	1,340	3,471	3,281,000
Dumyāṭ (Damietta)	Dumyāṭ	227	589	690,000
al-Gharbīyah	Ṭanṭā	750	1,942	2,715,000
Kafr ash-Shaykh	Kafr ash-Shaykh	1,327	3,437	1,696,000
al-Minūfīyah	Shibīn al-Kawm	592	1,532	2,049,000
al-Qalyūbīyah	Banhā	387	1,001	2,074,000
ash-Sharqīyah	az-Zaqāzīq	1,614	4,180	3,167,000
Upper Egypt				
Aswān	Aswān	262	679	744,000
Asyūṭ	Asyūṭ	600	1,553	2,059,000
Banī Suwayf	Banī Suwayf	510	1,322	1,342,000
al-Fayyūm	al-Fayyūm	705	1,827	1,410,000
al-Jīzah	al-Jīzah	32,878	85,153	2,965,000
al-Minyā	al-Minyā	873	2,262	2,517,000
Qinā	Qinā	715	1,851	2,066,000
Sawhāj	Sawhāj	597	1,547	2,316,000
Urban				
al-Iskandarīyah (Alexandria)	—	1,034	2,679	2,708,000
al-Ismā'īlīyah (Ismailia)	—	557	1,442	447,000
al-Qāhirah (Cairo)	—	83	214	5,881,000
as-Suways (Suez)	—	6,888	17,840	241,000
Būr Sa'īd (Port Said)	—	28	72	364,000
TOTAL		385,229	997,739	44,202,000

Demography

Population (1985): 48,503,000.
Density (1985): persons per sq mi 125.9, persons per sq km 48.6.
Urban–rural (1985): urban 48.8%; rural 51.2%.
Sex distribution (1985): male 50.90%; female 49.10%.
Age breakdown (1980): under 15, 39.7%; 15–29, 27.5%; 30–44, 17.0%; 45–59, 10.1%; 60–74, 4.8%; 75 and over 0.9%.
Population projection: (1990) 53,481,000; (2000) 65,200,000.
Doubling time: 28 years.
Ethnic composition (1980): Egyptian 99.7%; other 0.3%.
Religious affiliation (1980): Sunnī Muslim 81.8%; Christian 17.8%; other 0.4%.
Major cities (1983): Cairo 5,881,000; Alexandria 2,708,000; al-Jīzah 1,509,600; Shubrā al-Khaymah 486,400; al-Maḥallah al-Kubrā 345,800.

Vital statistics

Birth rate per 1,000 population (1982): 37.3 (world avg. 29.0); legitimate, n.a.; illegitimate, n.a.
Death rate per 1,000 population (1982): 10.4 (world avg. 11.0).
Natural increase rate per 1,000 population (1982): 26.9 (world avg. 18.0).
Total fertility rate (avg. births per childbearing woman; 1980–85): 4.7.
Marriage rate per 1,000 population (1979): 9.4.
Divorce rate per 1,000 population (1979): 1.8.
Life expectancy at birth (1980–85): male 55.9 years; female 58.4 years.
Major causes of death per 100,000 population (1979): symptoms and ill-defined conditions 221.4; bronchitis, emphysema and asthma 53.4; pneumonia 47.3; ischemic heart disease 15.8.

National economy

Budget (1984–85). Revenue: LE12,877,000,000 (sovereign tax 59.4%, domestic savings and foreign credit 32.6%). Expenditures: LE18,277,000,000 (public-sector wages 18.0%, subsidies 11.3%, health and education 11.1%).
Public debt (external, outstanding; 1983): U.S.$15,530,800,000.
Tourism (1981): receipts from visitors U.S.$375,400,000; expenditures by nationals abroad U.S.$630,000,000.
Production (metric tons except as noted). Agriculture, forestry, fishing (1984): corn (maize) 3,600,000, tomatoes 2,600,000, rice 2,230,000, wheat 1,815,000, watermelons 1,250,000, potatoes 1,200,000, millet 625,000, dates 450,000, dry onions 400,000, cotton (lint) 390,000; livestock (number of live animals) 2,410,000 buffalo, 1,825,000 cattle, 1,780,000 asses, 1,500,000 goats, 1,450,000 sheep, 82,000 camels, 28,000,000 chickens; roundwood (1983) 1,935,000 cu m; fish catch (1983) 140,000. Mining and quarrying (1983): iron ore 2,223,000; crude gypsum and anhydrite 721,340; fire clay 205,000. Manufacturing (1983): cement 3,794,000; sugar 600,000†; cotton yarn 229,200; jute textile 29,640; steel castings 3,758†; cotton textiles 7,716.

Construction (value added in LE; 1980): 761,000,000. Energy production (consumption): electricity (kW-hr; 1983) 23,520,000,000 (23,520,000,000); coal (metric tons; 1982) none (1,460,000); crude petroleum (barrels; 1983) 260,221,000 (135,477,000); petroleum products (metric tons; 1983) 16,926,000 (14,650,000); natural gas (cu m; 1983) 1,520,210,000 (1,520,210,000).
Gross national product (at current market prices; 1983): U.S.$32,894,290,000 (U.S.$730 per capita).

Structure of gross domestic product and labour force				
	1981–82			
	in value LE'000,000	% of total value	labour force	% of labour force
Agriculture	3,891.5	19.8	4,247,500	36.2
Mining	} 5,610.4	28.6	24,500	0.2
Manufacturing			1,462,700	12.5
Construction	930.2	4.7	664,100	5.7
Public utilities	155.0	0.8	130,400	1.1
Transportation and communication	1,551.4	7.9	452,100	3.9
Trade and finance	3,597.0	18.3	1,175,700	10.0
Services	3,546.7	18.1	3,396,600	29.0
Other	356.6	1.8	171,300	1.5
TOTAL	19,638.8	100.0	11,724,900	100.0‡

Population economically active (1981): total 11,507,200; participation rate of total population 27.8% (female 10.6%, unemployed 5.4%).

Price and earnings indexes (1980 = 100)							
	1978	1979	1980	1981	1982	1983	1984
Consumer price index	75.4	82.9	100.0	110.4	126.8	147.2	172.3
Earnings index	...	...	...	...	...	...	...

Household income and expenditure. Average household size (1980) 4.9; average annual income per household: n.a.; source of income: n.a.; expenditure§ (1974–75): food 49.7%, clothing and footwear 14.2%, housing 12.4%, transportation 5.2%, tobacco 4.9%, recreation 1.3%.
Land use (1983): meadows and pastures 0.1%; agricultural and under permanent cultivation 2.5%; built-on, wasteland, and other 97.4%.

Foreign trade

Balance of trade (current prices)						
	1979	1980	1981	1982	1983	1984
LE'000,000	−1,398.4	−1,269.8	−3,924.5	−4,170.4	−4,982.0	−5,338.1
% of total	35.2%	22.9%	46.4%	48.8%	52.3%	54.8%

Imports (1982): LE6,354,517,000 (cereals and preparations 14.1%, transport equipment 10.6%, chemicals 7.8%, electrical machinery 6.8%). *Major import sources:* United States 19.0%; West Germany 10.1%; Italy 7.6%; France 7.5%.
Exports (1982): LE2,184,122,000 (petroleum and petroleum products 66.2%; textile fibres 13.8%). *Major export destinations:* Italy 22.1%; Israel 14.2%; France 6.9%; Romania 5.9%; The Netherlands 5.4%.

Transport and communications

Transport. Railroads (1982): length 2,725 mi, 4,385 km; passenger-mi 11,660,000,000, passenger-km 18,765,000,000; short ton-mi cargo 1,577,000,000, metric ton-km cargo 2,302,000,000. Roads (1983): total length 18,684 mi, 30,069 km (paved 47%). Vehicles (1983): passenger cars 597,869; trucks and buses 227,224. Merchant marine (1984): vessels (100 gross tons and over) 390; total deadweight tonnage 1,032,144. Air transport (1984): passenger-mi 2,725,019,000, passenger-km 4,385,501,000; short ton-mi cargo 60,441,000, metric ton-km cargo 88,243,000; airports (1985) with scheduled flights 10.
Communications. Daily newspapers (1984): total number 11; total circulation 2,824,350; circulation per 1,000 population 58.2. Radio (1984): total number of receivers 12,000,000 (1 per 3.8 persons). Television (1984): total number of receivers 3,860,000 (1 per 11.6 persons). Telephones (1982): 521,625 (1 per 82.4 persons).

Education and health

Education (1981–82)				
	schools	teachers ‖	students	student/teacher ratio
Primary (age 6–11)	11,761	140,146	4,748,414	...
Secondary (age 12–17) ‖	2,715	78,086	2,060,100	26.4
Voc., teacher tr. ‖	519	38,635	672,362	17.4
Higher	12	11,910	594,597	...

Educational attainment (1976). Percent of population over age 10 having: basic literacy or complete primary education 9.9%; secondary 5.0%; higher 2.1%; postgraduate 0.1%. *Literacy* (1980): total population over age 10 literate 10,608,000 (41.9%); males literate 7,140,000 (56.3%); females literate 3,468,000 (27.5%).
Health (1982): physicians 92,000 (1 per 467 persons); hospital beds 86,600 (1 per 497 persons); infant mortality rate per 1,000 live births (1978–80) 76.4.
Food (1980–82): daily per capita caloric intake 3,157 (vegetable products 93%, animal products 7%); 127% of FAO recommended minimum.

Military

Total active duty personnel (1984): 460,000 (army 68.5%, navy 7.2%, air force 24.3%). *Military expenditure as percent of GNP* (1983): 8.3% (world 6.1%); per capita expenditure U.S.$56.0.

*Sīnā'ash-Shamālīyah includes area of Sīnā' al-Janūbīyah governorate. †1982. ‡Detail does not add to total given because of rounding. §Urban only. ‖ 1980–81.

El Salvador

Official name: República de El Salvador (Republic of El Salvador).
Form of government: republic with one legislative house (Legislative Assembly [60]).
Chief of state and government: President.
Capital: San Salvador.
Official language: Spanish.
Official religion: none.
Monetary unit: 1 colón (₡) = 100 centavos; valuation (Oct. 21, 1985) 1 U.S.$ = ₡2.51; 1 £ = ₡3.59.

Area and population		area		population
				1983
Departments	Capitals	sq mi	sq km	estimate
Ahuachapán	Ahuachapán	479	1,240	258,500
Cabañas	Sensuntepeque	426	1,104	191,000
Chalatenango	Chalatenango	779	2,017	248,100
Cuscatlán	Cojutepeque	292	756	215,000
La Libertad	Nueva San Salvador	638	1,653	417,200
La Paz	Zacatecoluca	473	1,224	266,100
La Unión	La Unión	801	2,074	331,900
Morazán	San Francisco (Gotera)	559	1,447	227,200
San Miguel	San Miguel	802	2,077	462,000
San Salvador	San Salvador	342	886	1,043,800
Santa Ana	Santa Ana	781	2,023	471,700
San Vicente	San Vicente	457	1,184	215,000
Sonsonate	Sonsonate	473	1,226	346,000
Usulután	Usulután	822	2,130	422,200
TOTAL		8,124	21,041	5,115,800*

Demography

Population (1985): 5,235,700.
Density (1985): persons per sq mi 644.5, persons per sq km 248.8.
Urban–rural (1982): urban 39.2%; rural 60.8%.
Sex distribution (1985): male 50.01%; female 49.99%.
Age breakdown (1985): under 15, 45.3%; 15–29, 27.8%; 30–44, 14.4%; 45–59, 7.8%; 60–74, 3.7%; 75 and over, 1.0%.
Population projection: (1990) 5,997,000; (2000) 7,730,400.
Doubling time: 28 years.
Ethnic composition (1980): mestizo (white and Indian) 93.7%; Indian 5.3%; white 1.0%.
Religious affiliation (1980): Roman Catholic 96.2%; Protestant 2.4%; other 1.4%.
Major cities (1983): San Salvador 445,100; Santa Ana 132,200; Mejicanos 86,500; San Miguel 86,500; Delgado 64,600.

Vital statistics

Birth rate per 1,000 population (1983): 27.6 (world avg. 29.0); (1980) legitimate 31.1%; illegitimate 68.9%.
Death rate per 1,000 population (1983): 6.3 (world avg. 11.0).
Natural increase rate per 1,000 population (1983): 21.3 (world avg. 18.0).
Total fertility rate (avg. births per childbearing woman; 1980): 5.8.
Marriage rate per 1,000 population (1982): 4.1.
Divorce rate per 1,000 population (1982): 0.4.
Life expectancy at birth (1981): male 61.7 years; female 65.3 years.
Major causes of death per 100,000 population (1982): signs, symptoms, and ill-defined conditions 143.6; homicide and injury and other violence 112.1; tuberculosis 50.5; cerebrovascular diseases 18.1; bronchitis, emphysema, and asthma 17.1.

National economy

Budget (1983). Revenue: ₡1,723,333,000 (current revenue ₡1,228,976,000, of which direct taxes 24.9%, sales tax 18.7%, export duties 15.4%, import duties 7.3%). Expenditures: ₡1,847,065,000 (current expenditure ₡1,419,730,000, of which remunerations 55.6%, government transfers 14.5%, interest on internal and external debt 10.1%).
Public debt (1983): U.S.$1,065,000,000.
Tourism (1982): receipts from visitors U.S.$6,000,000; expenditures by nationals abroad, n.a.
Production (metric tons except as noted). Agriculture, forestry, fishing (1984): sugarcane 3,140,000, corn (maize) 509,000, coffee 166,000, sorghum 141,000, seed cotton 77,000, rice 60,000, bananas 55,000, dry beans 49,000, cassava 23,000, tobacco 5,000; livestock (number of live animals) 937,000 cattle, 379,000 pigs, 14,000 goats, 4,000,000 chickens; roundwood 4,494,000 cu m†; fish catch 7,603†. Manufacturing (value in ₡'000; 1983): processed food 509,361; beverages 222,977; refined petroleum products 145,639; clothing and footwear 94,743; chemical products 85,353; nonmetallic products 83,558; textiles 81,731; tobacco 80,126. Construction (value in ₡'000; 1983): private residential 129,500, public and private nonresidential 213,900. Energy production (consumption): electricity (kW-hr; 1983) 1,610,000,000 (1,610,000,000); coal, none (n.a.); petroleum, none (n.a.); petroleum products (metric tons; 1983) 567,000 (538,000); natural gas, none (n.a.).
Household income and expenditure. Average household size (1978) 5.1; income per household ₡8,650 (U.S.$3,460); source of income: n.a.; expenditure (1978): food 39.3%, housing 20.4%, transportation and communication 10.8%, clothing and footwear 9.4%, recreation 4.4%.
Population economically active (1980): total 1,593,353; participation rate of total population 35.5% (female 34.8%, unemployed [1982] 30%).

Price and earnings indexes (1980 = 100)						
	1978	1979	1980	1981	1982	1983	1984
Consumer price index	73.5	85.2	100.0	114.8	128.3	145.3	162.1
Monthly earnings index	...	...	...	...	...	...	...

Gross national product (at current market prices; 1983): U.S.$3,690,000,000 (U.S.$710 per capita).

Origin of gross domestic product (current prices)				
	1983		1980	
	in value ₡'000,000	% of total value	labour force	% of labour force
Agriculture	2,109.6	21.6	636,617	40.0
Mining	15.2	0.2	4,394	0.3
Manufacturing	1,524.9	15.6	247,621	15.5
Construction	343.4	3.5	80,089	5.0
Public utilities	232.7	2.4	9,681	0.6
Transportation and communication	411.5	4.2	65,593	4.1
Trade	2,331.7	23.9	256,086	16.1
Finance	912.0	9.4	15,863	1.0
Public admin., defense	1,083.9	11.1 }	250,158	15.7
Services	789.2	8.1 }		
Other	—	—	27,251‡	1.7‡
TOTAL	9,754.1§	100.0	1,593,353	100.0

Land use (1983): forested 5.9%; meadows and pastures 29.4%; agricultural and under permanent cultivation 35.0%; other 29.7%.

Foreign trade

Balance of trade (current prices)						
	1979	1980	1981	1982	1983	1984
₡'000,000	+423.0	+457.8	−287.3	−234.6	−225.3	−448.1
% of total	8.1%	9.3%	6.7%	6.3%	5.8%	19.8%

Imports (1983): ₡2,228,700,000 (chemical products 22.4%, of which medicinal and pharmaceutical products 5.7%, cosmetics and perfume 1.6%; crude petroleum 14.2%; food products 16.0%, of which dairy products 2.6%, wheat and wheat products 2.4%; electrical machinery and appliances 5.9%). *Major import sources:* United States 32.4%; Guatemala 19.3%; Mexico 9.2%; Venezuela 7.8%; Costa Rica 4.8%; West Germany 4.1%; Japan 3.5%.
Exports (1983): ₡1,838,300,000 (food products 65.6%, of which coffee 55.4%, refined sugar 5.5%, shrimp 2.0%; cotton and cotton products 9.8%; chemical products 5.5%). *Major export destinations:* United States 38.7%; West Germany 19.0%; Guatemala 16.7%; Japan 5.0%; Costa Rica 3.0%; Spain 2.3%; Panama 2.2%.

Transport and communications

Transport. Railroads (1981): length 374 mi, 602 km; passenger-mi 7,500,000, passenger-km 12,000,000; short ton-mi cargo 24,700,000, metric ton-km cargo 36,000,000. Roads (1982): total length 7,624 mi, 12,269 km (paved 14%). Vehicles (1982): passenger cars 72,547; trucks and buses 69,755. Merchant marine (1984): vessels (100 gross tons and over) 11; total deadweight tonnage 3,318. Air transport (1982): passenger-mi 208,200,000, passenger-km 335,000,000; short ton-mi cargo 7,100,000, metric ton-km cargo 10,400,000; airports (1985) with scheduled flights 1.
Communications. Daily newspapers (1981): total number 6; total circulation 240,000; circulation per 1,000 population 50. Radio (1981): total number of receivers 1,600,000 (1 per 2.8 persons). Television (1981): total number of receivers 310,000 (1 per 13 persons). Telephones (1982): 86,316 (1 per 56 persons).

Education and health

Education (1981–82)				
	schools	teachers	students	student/ teacher ratio
Primary	2,390	18,182	810,827	44.6
Secondary	233	5,123	74,258	14.6
Voc.	23	...	8,684	...
Higher	18	1,414	23,418	16.6

Educational attainment (1971). Percent of adult population over age 25 having: less than full primary education 31.9%; primary and secondary 37.9%, of which secondary 6.0%; higher 1.9%. *Literacy* (1978): total population over age 15 literate 1,514,845 (64.2%); males literate 764,815 (68.8%); females literate 750,030 (60.1%).
Health: physicians (1980) 1,491 (1 per 3,024 persons); hospital beds (1978) 7,668 (1 per 568 persons); infant mortality rate per 1,000 live births (1982) 42.2.
Food (1979–81): daily per capita caloric intake 2,155 (vegetable products 88%, animal products 12%); 94% of FAO recommended minimum requirement.

Military

Total active duty personnel (1984): 41,650 (army 93.7%, navy 0.7%, air force 5.6%). *Military expenditure as percent of GNP* (1983): 4.3% (world 6.1%); per capita expenditure U.S.$32.

*Detail does not add to total given because of rounding. †1983. ‡Includes unemployed. §At current prices.

Equatorial Guinea

Official name: República de Guinea
Ecuatorial (Republic of Equatorial
Guinea).
Form of government: unitary
single-party republic with one
legislative house (National Assembly
[41]).
Head of state and government:
President.
Capital: Malabo.
Official language: Spanish.
Official religion: none.
Monetary unit: 1 ekwele (EK, plural
bikwele) = 100 céntimos; valuation
(Oct. 21, 1985) 1 U.S.$ = EK402.09;
1 £ = EK576.50.

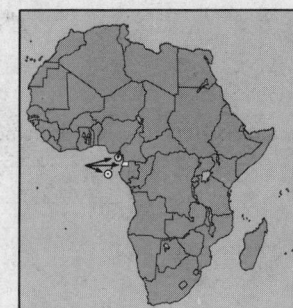

Area and population

	area		population
Islands	sq mi	sq km	1983 census*
Annobon	7	17	3,000
Bioko	779	2,017	70,000
Corisco	6	15	1,000†
Great Elobey	1	2	†
Little Elobey	0.1	0.2	†
Continent			
Rio Muni	10,038	26,000	230,000
TOTAL	10,831	28,051	304,000

Demography

Population (1985): 317,000.
Density (1985): persons per sq mi 29.3, persons per sq km 11.3.
Urban–rural (1985): urban 40.3%; rural 59.7%.
Sex distribution (1980): male 49.04%; female 50.96%.
Age breakdown (1980): under 15, 41.5%; 15–29, 25.8%; 30–44, 15.6%; 45–59,
10.6%; 60–74, 5.4%; 75 and over, 1.1%.
Population projection: (1990) 359,000; (2000) 438,000.
Doubling time: 27 years.
Ethnic composition (1978): Fang 71.5%; Bubi 14.3%; Duala 2.9%; Ibibio
1.4%; other 9.9%.
Religious affiliation (1980): Christian 88.8%; tribal 4.6%; atheist 1.4%; Muslim 0.5%; other 0.2%; none 4.5%.
Major city (1983): Malabo 37,500.

Vital statistics

Birth rate per 1,000 population (1980–85): 42.2 (world avg. 29.0); legitimate,
n.a.; illegitimate, n.a.
Death rate per 1,000 population (1980–85): 17.6 (world avg. 11.0).
Natural increase rate per 1,000 population (1980–85): 24.6 (world avg. 18.0).
Total fertility rate (avg. births per childbearing woman; 1980–85): 5.7.
Marriage rate per 1,000 population: n.a.
Divorce rate per 1,000 population: n.a.
Life expectancy at birth (1980–85): male 46.9 years; female 50.1 years.
Major causes of death per 100,000 population: n.a.; however, major diseases
are cholera, leprosy, trypanosomiasis, and malaria.

National economy

Budget (1981). Revenue: EK2,731,000,000 (import duties 45.8%, export
duties 25.6%, nontax revenue 15.7%, income tax 6.3%). Expenditures: EK2,-
887,000,000 (wages and salaries 65.9%, goods and services 20.4%, capital
expenditure 10.6%).
Public debt (external, outstanding; 1983): U.S.$109,000,000.
Tourism: n.a.
Gross national product (at current market prices; 1983): U.S.$60,000,000
(U.S.$197 per capita).

Structure of gross domestic product and labour force

	1983			
	in value EK'000,000	% of total value	labour force	% of labour force
Agriculture	2,490	41.3	80,000	73.4
Manufacturing			...	...
Construction			...	...
Public utilities	710	11.8	...	...
Transportation and communication			...	...
Trade			...	...
Finance			...	...
Pub. admin., defense	2,830	46.9	...	...
Services			...	...
Other			29,000	26.6
TOTAL	6,030	100.0	109,000	100.0

Production (metric tons except as noted). Agriculture, forestry, fishing (1984):
cassava 54,000, sweet potatoes 35,000, bananas 18,000, cacao beans 10,000,
coconuts 8,000, coffee 7,000, palm oil 5,200, palm kernels 3,000; livestock
(number of live animals) 34,000 sheep, 7,000 goats, 5,000 pigs, 4,000 cattle,
160,000 chickens; roundwood 465,000 cu m‡; fish catch 2,500‡. Mining
and quarrying: n.a.; however, iron ore, lead, zinc, and molybdenum are
present in the sedimentary rocks; traces of gold, diamonds, and radioactive ores have also been located. Manufacturing (1979): sawn wood 16,000

cu m. Construction: n.a. Energy production (consumption): electricity
(kW-hr; 1983) 15,000,000 (15,000,000); coal, none (n.a.); crude petroleum,
none (n.a.); petroleum products (metric tons; 1983) none (26,000); natural
gas, none (n.a.).
Population economically active (1984): total 111,000; participation rate of
total population 36.5% (female, n.a.; unemployed, n.a.)
Price and earnings indexes: n.a.
Household income and expenditure. Average household size (1980) 4.5;
average annual income per household: n.a.; source of income: n.a.; expenditure: n.a.
Land use (1983): forested 60.6%; meadows and pastures 3.7%; agricultural
and under permanent cultivation 8.2%; other 27.5%.

Foreign trade

Balance of trade (current prices)

	1978	1979	1980	1981	1982§	1983§
EK'000,000	+547.6	+351.9	−4,704.0	−5,400.0	−6,657.0	−9,326.0
% of total	18.6%	9.8%	54.8%	51.1%	27.5%	29.3%

Imports (1981): EK7,982,000,000 (food, beverages, and tobacco 24.9%;
petroleum and petroleum products 22.4%; motor vehicles and machinery
17.4%; iron and steel products 12.4%; clothing 6.0%). *Major import sources*
(1984): France 29.6%; Spain 26.9%; China 8.8%; Hong Kong 6.8%; Italy
6.5%.
Exports (1981): EK2,582,000,000 (cacao 71.5%; timber 24.4%; coffee 2.8%).
Major export destinations (1984): Spain 23.7%; The Netherlands 18.8%;
West Germany 16.2%; Italy 9.9%; France 8.8%.

Transport and communications

Transport. Railroads: none. Roads (1982): total length 1,715 mi, 2,760
km (paved 12%). Vehicles (1979): passenger cars 4,000; trucks and buses
3,000. Merchant marine (1984): vessels (100 gross tons and over) 2; total
deadweight tonnage 6,700. Air transport (1980): passenger-mi 4,000,000,
passenger-km 7,000,000; short ton-mi cargo 700,000, metric ton-km cargo
1,000,000; airports (1985) with scheduled flights 2.
Communications. Daily newspapers (1984): total number 2; total circulation
1,000; circulation per 1,000 population 3. Radio (1984): total number of
receivers 90,000 (1 per 3.5 persons). Television (1984): total number of
receivers 2,100 (1 per 148 persons). Telephones (1982): 1,366 (1 per 220
persons).

Education and health

Education (1980–81)

	schools	teachers	students	student/ teacher ratio
Primary (age 6–11)	511	647	40,110	62.0
Secondary (age 12–17), voc., teacher tr.	14	288	3,013	10.5

Educational attainment, n.a. *Literacy* (1980): total population literate, about
55%.
Health: physicians (1977) 5 (1 per 64,000 persons); hospital beds (1982) 3,200
(1 per 95 persons); infant mortality rate per 1,000 live births (1983) 137.
Food (1980–82): daily per capita caloric intake, n.a.; FAO recommended
minimum requirement for the region is 2,300 calories.

Military

Total active duty personnel (1984): 1,550 (army 90.3%, navy 6.5%, air force
3.2%). *Military expenditure as percent of GNP* (1981): 1.8% (world 5.8%);
per capita expenditure U.S.$9.

*Preliminary; population figures for the islands are estimated. †Corisco includes
population of Great and Little Elobey. ‡1983. §Estimated.

©TOM PIX 1976 FROM PETER ARNOLD

Santa Isabel Cathedral, Malabo (formerly Santa Isabel), Bioko (formerly
Fernando Po) Island, Equatorial Guinea

Ethiopia

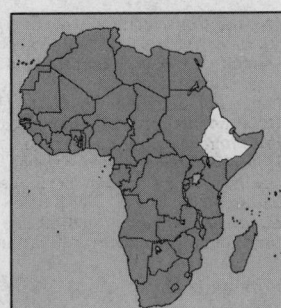

Official name: Hebretasebawit Etiyop'iya (Socialist Ethiopia).
Form of government: socialist state ruled by a Provisional Military Administrative Council (PMAC).
Head of state and government: Chairman of the PMAC and of the Council of Ministers.
Capital: Addis Ababa.
Official language: Amharic.
Official religion: none.
Monetary unit: 1 Ethiopian Birr (Br) = 100 cents; valuation (Oct. 21, 1985) 1 U.S.$ = Br2.07; 1 £ = Br2.98.

Area and population

		area		population
Regions	Capitals	sq mi	sq km	1984 census
Arsi	Asela	9,500	24,600	1,662,233
Bale	Goba	49,500	128,300	1,006,491
Eritrea*	Asmera	45,300	117,400	2,704,000
Gemu Gofa	Arba Minch	15,400	40,100	1,248,034
Gojam	Debre Markos	24,900	64,500	3,244,882
Gonder	Gonder	28,300	73,400	2,905,362
Hararge	Harer	98,400	254,800	4,151,706
Ilubabor	Metu	19,600	50,800	963,327
Kefa	Jima	20,500	53,000	2,450,369
Shewa*	Addis Ababa	33,000	85,500	9,503,140
Sidamo	Awasa	45,100	116,700	3,790,579
Tigray	Mekele	25,400	65,700	2,409,700
Welega	Nekemte	27,000	69,800	2,369,677
Wello	Dese	30,500	79,000	3,609,918
TOTAL		472,400	1,223,600	42,019,418

Demography

Population (1985): 43,551,000.
Density (1985): persons per sq mi 92.2, persons per sq km 35.6.
Urban–rural (1984): urban 11.3%; rural 88.7%.
Sex distribution (1984): male 49.85%; female 50.15%.
Age breakdown (1982): under 15, 44.9%; 15–29, 25.4%; 30–44, 16.8%; 45–59, 8.2%; 60–64, 1.5%; 65 and over, 3.2%.
Population projection: (1990) 50,243,000; (2000) 66,870,000.
Doubling time: 24 years.
Ethnolinguistic composition (1982): Amhara 30.0%; Galla 26.0%; Tigrinya 9.0%; Tigre 5.0%; Kafa 4.0%; Somali 3.0%; Gurage 3.0%; Nilotes 3.0%, of which Nuer 1.3%; Arabic 1.3%; Afar 1.0%; other 14.7%.
Religious affiliation (1980): Ethiopian Orthodox 48.9%; Muslim 31.4%; tribal religionist 11.4%; Protestant 3.5%; Evangelical 3.1%; Roman Catholic 0.7%; other 1.0%.
Major cities (1984): Addis Ababa 1,412,575; Asmera 275,385; Dire Dawa 98,104; Gonder 68,958; Dese 68,848.

Vital statistics

Birth rate per 1,000 population (1980–85): 49.2 (world avg. 29.0).
Death rate per 1,000 population (1980–85): 21.5 (world avg. 11.0).
Natural increase rate per 1,000 population (1980–85): 47.7 (world avg. 18.0).
Total fertility rate (avg. births per childbearing woman; 1980–85): 6.7.
Marriage rate per 1,000 population: n.a.
Divorce rate per 1,000 population: n.a.
Life expectancy at birth (1980–85): male 41.3 years; female 44.5 years.
Major causes of death per 1,000 population (hospital inpatients only; 1977–78): infectious and parasitic diseases 524; digestive system diseases 384; allergy, endocrine, metabolic, nutritional, and circulatory diseases 326; respiratory diseases 216.

National economy

Budget (1983–84). Revenue: Br2,202,500,000 (income and profit taxes 26.5%; excises 13.3%; export customs duties 11.4%; import customs duties 7.9%). Expenditures (recurrent and capital): Br3,427,200,000 (general government 33.0%; capital expenditure on economic development 31.5%, of which mining, industry, and tourism 9.1%, agriculture 8.4%, water resources 4.5%; education and culture 7.9%; public health 2.9%).
Public debt (external, outstanding; 1983): U.S.$1,223,000,000.
Tourism (1983): receipts from visitors U.S.$8,000,000; expenditures by nationals abroad U.S.$4,000,000†.
Production (metric tons except as noted). Agriculture, forestry, fishing (1984): sugarcane 1,650,000, corn (maize) 1,275,000, barley 848,000, wheat 675,000, vegetables and melons 513,000, coffee 240,000, fruits 210,000, millet 145,000, seed cotton 73,000, treenuts 59,000, cotton seed 48,000, sesame seed 36,000, lentils 32,000, linseed 30,000, peanuts (groundnuts) 28,000; livestock (number of live animals) 26,000,000 cattle, 23,450,000 sheep, 17,250,000 goats, 6,945,000 horses, mules, and asses, 1,020,000 camels; roundwood 29,784,000 cu m‡; fish catch 3,900‡. Mining and quarrying (1983): cement 150,000; salt 125,000; kaolin 9,000; limestone 5,000; gold 435 kilograms; platinum 3 kilograms. Manufacturing (gross value in Br'000§; 1983–84): food products 374,047; textiles 344,315; beverages 206,611; leather and shoes 138,094; metals 110,263; chemicals 99,669; paper and printing 79,555; wood 27,310. Construction (authorized; 1979): residential 122,800 sq m; nonresidential 20,800 sq m, of which commercial 11,200 sq m. Energy production (consumption): electricity (kW-hr; 1983)

753,000,000 (753,000,000); coal, n.a. (none); crude petroleum (barrels; 1983) n.a. (5,427,000); petroleum products (metric tons; 1983) 684,000 (526,000); natural gas, n.a. (n.a.).
Gross national product (at current market prices; 1984): U.S.$4,877,000,000 (U.S.$115 per capita ‖).

Structure of gross domestic product and labour force

	1984–85		1984	
	in value Br'000,000	% of total value	labour force	% of labour force
Agriculture	4,711.6	48.5	10,956,000	76.8
Mining	16.3	0.2		
Manufacturing	997.7	10.3		
Construction	353.8	3.6		
Public utilities	69.8	0.7		
Transportation and communication	606.7	6.2	3,308,000	23.2
Trade	1,002.9	10.3		
Finance	320.2	3.3		
Pub. admin., defense	775.0	8.0		
Services	662.0	6.8		
Other	199.1	2.0		
TOTAL	9,715.1¶	100.0⍷	14,264,000	100.0

Population economically active (1984): total 14,264,000; participation rate of total population 33.7% (female [1981] 33.3%, unemployed, n.a.).

Price and earnings indexes (1980 = 100)

	1979	1980	1981	1982	1983	1984	1985
Consumer price index	95.7	100.0	106.1	112.4	111.6	121.0	132.5§
Monthly earnings index	...	...	...	...	...	...	...

Household income and expenditure. Average household size (1984) 4.5; income per household: n.a.; source of income: n.a.; expenditure: n.a.
Land use (1983): forested 24.0%; meadows and pastures 41.1%; agricultural and under permanent cultivation 12.7%; other 22.2%.

Foreign trade

Balance of trade (current prices)

	1978	1979	1980	1981	1982	1983
Br'000,000	−439.9	−300.6	−614.2	−723.8	−775.6	−980.4
% of total	25.6%	14.7%	25.9%	31.0%	31.7%	37.0%

Imports (1983): Br1,813,325,000 (petroleum and petroleum products 19.3%, machinery 14.7%, food and live animals 11.9%, road motor vehicles 10.4%, electrical materials 7.8%). *Major import sources:* U.S.S.R. 20.9%; Italy 13.4%; West Germany 9.9%; Japan 9.3%; United Kingdom 7.6%.
Exports (1983): Br832,974,000,000 (coffee 62.4%, hides and skins 10.1%, kat [a narcotic leaf] 3.4%, pulses 2.9%, oilseeds 2.8%). *Major export destinations:* United States 20.4%; West Germany 16.8%; France 7.6%; Japan 7.6%; Italy 7.4%; Djibouti 6.3%.

Transport and communications

Transport. Railroads□ (1984): length 485 mi, 781 km; passenger-mi 193,000,000, passenger-km 310,000,000; short ton-mi cargo 88,000,000, metric ton-km cargo 131,000,000. Roads (1982): total length 22,612 mi, 36,391 km (paved 34%). Vehicles (1984): passenger cars 41,300; trucks and buses 11,841. Merchant marine (1984): vessels (100 gross tons and over) 21; total deadweight tonnage 46,797. Air transport (1983): passenger-mi 473,697,000, passenger-km 762,343,000; short ton-mi cargo 18,587,000, metric ton-km cargo 27,136,000; airports (1985) with scheduled flights 37.
Communications. Daily newspapers (1984): total number 3; total circulation 44,000; circulation per 1,000 population 1.0. Radio (1984): 2,000,000 receivers (1 per 21.2 persons). Television (1984): 45,000 receivers (1 per 941 persons). Telephones (1983): 100,783 (1 per 408 persons).

Education and health

Education (1980–81)

	schools	teachers	students	student/ teacher ratio
Primary (age 7–12)	6,208	37,844	2,374,362	62.7
Secondary (age 13–18)	...	11,184	487,179	43.6
Voc., teacher tr.	...	...	...	...
Higher	...	1,137	11,822	10.4

Educational attainment, n.a. *Literacy* (1980): total population over age 15 literate 1,000,000 (4.8%); males (9.3%); females (0.5%).
Health (1982): physicians 504 (1 per 79,310 persons); hospital beds 10,993 (1 per 3,636 persons); infant mortality rate per 1,000 live births (1980–85) 143.0.
Food (1979–81): daily per capita caloric intake 2,149 (vegetable products 93%, animal products 7%); 92% of FAO recommended minimum requirement.

Military

Total active duty personnel (1984): 306,000◊ (army 98.1%, navy 0.8%, air force 1.1%). *Military expenditure as percent of GNP* (1982): 9.8% (world 6.0%); per capita expenditure (1982) U.S.$11.

*Eritrea includes Aseb Administration, and Shewa includes Addis Ababa region. †1982. ‡1983. §At constant prices of 1978–79. ‖ Per capita figures are based on population calculated from 1984 census; the census population was about 16% higher than previous estimates. ¶At current prices. ⍷Detail does not add to total given because of rounding. ⬧February only. □Includes 62 mi (100 km) of the Chemin de Fer Djibouti-Ethiopien (CDE) in Djibouti; excludes 190 mi (306 km) of Northern Ethiopia Railway, not in use since 1978. ◊In 1984 about 3,000 Cuban troops and several hundred other Soviet-bloc advisers and technicians were assisting government forces.

Faeroe Islands

Official name: Faerøerne (Danish);
Føroyar (Faeroese) (Faeroe Islands).
Political status: self-governing region
of the Danish realm with a single
legislative body (Lagting [32]).
Chief of state: Danish Monarch.
Head of Government: Governor.
Capital: Tórshavn (Thorshavn).
Official languages: Danish; Faeroese.
Official religion: Evangelical Lutheran.
Monetary unit: 1 Faeroese krone
(FKr) = 100 øre; valuation (Oct. 21,
1985) 1 U.S.$ = FKr9.56;
1 £ = FKr13.71.

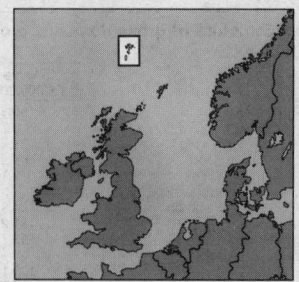

Area and population

Districts	Capitals	area		population
		sq mi	sq km	1983 estimate
Eysturoyar (Østerø)	—	110	286	9,800
Nordhoya (Norderøernes)	—	93	241	5,900
Sandoyar (Sandø)	—	48	125	1,800
Streymoyar (Strømø)	—	151	392	18,300
Sudhuroyar Nordhara (Suderø Nordre)	—	38	97	5,800
Sudhuroyar Sunnara (Suderø Søndre)	—	27	70	
Vága (Vágø)	—	73	188	2,900
TOTAL		540	1,399	44,500

Demography

Population (1985): 45,000.
Density (1985): persons per sq mi 32.3, persons per sq km 83.7.
Urban-rural (1983): urban (Tórshavn only) 29.4%; rural 70.6%.
Sex distribution (1984): male 52.26%; female 47.74%.
Age breakdown (1984): under 15, 25.9%; 15–29, 24.9%; 30–44, 19.8%; 45–59, 13.8%; 60–74, 11.5%; 75 and over, 4.0%.
Population projection: (1990) 46,900; (2000) 50,400.
Doubling time: 94 years.
Ethnic composition (by place of birth; 1970): born in Faeroe Islands 95.3%; born elsewhere 4.7%.
Religious affiliation (1980): Evangelical Lutheran Church of Denmark 74.4%; Plymouth Brethren 19.8%; Roman Catholic 0.1%; other 5.2%.
Major cities (1983): Tórshavn 13,175.

Vital statistics

Birth rate per 1,000 population (1984): 14.4 (world avg. 29.0); (1983) legitimate 67.1%; illegitimate 32.9%.
Death rate per 1,000 population (1984): 7.8 (world avg. 11.0).
Natural increase rate per 1,000 population (1984): 6.6 (world avg. 18.0).
Total fertility rate (avg. births per childbearing woman; 1983): 2.2.
Marriage rate per 1,000 population (1983): 4.6.
Divorce rate per 1,000 population (1983): 0.5.
Life expectancy at birth (1976–80): male 73.4 years; female 78.7 years.
Major causes of death per 100,000 population (1983): diseases of the circulatory system 397.1, of which ischemic heart disease 258.0, cerebrovascular disease 105.4, malignant neoplasms (cancers) 168.3; diseases of the respiratory system 47.1, of which pneumonia 29.2, bronchitis, emphysema, and asthma 17.9; automobile accidents 11.2; suicides 9.0.

National economy

Budget (1983–84). Revenue: FKr1,143,615,000 (taxes 50.2%; customs and excise duties 46.7%; interest, dividends, and other 3.1%). Expenditures: FKr1,142,889,000 (social welfare 17.0%; roads and bridges 15.0%; culture and education 11.7%; medical services 7.4%; administration 7.0%).
Public debt: n.a.
Gross national product (at current market prices; 1983): U.S.$440,000,000 (U.S.$9,850 per capita).

Structure of gross domestic product and labour force

	1980		1977	
	in value FKr'000,000	% of total value	labour force	% of labour force
Agriculture	640	24.3	282	1.6
Fishing			3,032	17.2
Manufacturing and mining	411	15.6	3,854	21.9
Construction	268	10.2	1,952	11.1
Public utilities	40	1.5	*	*
Transportation and communication	229	8.7	1,944	11.1
Trade	308	11.7	2,237*	12.7*
Finance	305	11.6	*	*
Pub. admin.			2,927	16.6
Services	429	16.3	796	4.5
Other			561	3.2
TOTAL	2,630	100.0†	17,585	100.0†

Production (metric tons except as noted). Agriculture, forestry, fishing (1982): potatoes 817, vegetables and grass are also produced; livestock (number of live animals) 47,314 sheep, 1,494 cattle; fish catch (1983) 329,879, of which cod 106,003, blue whiting 72,639, coalfish 42,446, prawn, shrimp,

and other crustaceans 10,345. Mining and quarrying: coal. Manufacturing (1983): fresh, chilled, and frozen fish 63,236; dried, salted, and smoked fish 20,759; fresh, frozen, salted, and dried crustaceans and mollusks 7,786; mutton and lamb 484; other important products include handicrafts and woolen textiles and clothing. Construction: n.a. Energy production (consumption): electricity (kW-hr; 1983) 195,000,000 (195,000,000); coal, n.a. (n.a.); crude petroleum, none (n.a.); petroleum products (metric tons; 1977) none (129,000); natural gas, none (none).
Tourism: n.a.
Population economically active (1977): total 17,585; participation rate of total population 41.9% (female 27.2%, unemployed, n.a.).

Price and earnings indexes (1980 = 100)

	1979	1980	1981	1982	1983	1984	1985
Consumer price index	85.6	100.0	116.2	132.0	145.9	153.8	158.7
Earnings index	...	...	...	...	...	...	...

Household income and expenditure. Average household size (1977) 3.7; average annual income per household: n.a.; sources of income: self-employment‡ 11.7%, wages and salaries‡ 88.3%; expenditure (1980): food and beverages 40.9%, fuel and power 18.9%, housing 17.5%, clothing and footwear 11.3%, other 11.4%.
Land use (1983): agricultural and under permanent cultivation 2.1%; other 97.9%.

Foreign trade

Balance of trade (current prices)

	1978	1979	1980	1981	1982	1983
FKr'000,000	−211.7	−325.3	−244.6	−340.0	−440.2	−626.5
% of total	12.0%	17.7%	10.8%	12.5%	15.0%	16.7%

Imports (1983): FKr2,190,400,000 (machinery and transport equipment 38.1%, of which transport equipment 24.1% [including road vehicles 4.6%], electrical machinery 5.7%; petroleum products 19.1%; food and live animals 9.5%; clothing and wearing apparel 2.5%; paper and paper products 2.5%; furniture 1.8%). *Major import sources:* Denmark 58.9%; Norway 15.1%; West Germany 14.4%; Sweden 3.0%; Italy 2.8%; United Kingdom 1.6%; Japan 1.0%.
Exports (1983): FKr1,563,900,000 (fishery products 95.3%, of which fresh and frozen 58.0%, salted, dried, and smoked 17.0%, crustaceans and mollusks 10.4%, fish products for animal feed 9.9%). *Major export destinations:* United States 27.8%; Denmark 16.2%; Italy 2.8%; United Kingdom 14.4%; West Germany 11.5%; France 6.6%; Italy 4.5%; Spain 3.8%; Sweden 2.6%.

Transport and communications

Transport. Railroads: none. Roads (1984): total length 124 mi, 200 km. Vehicles (1983): passenger cars 10,942; trucks and buses 2,360. Merchant marine (1984): vessels (100 gross tons and over) 182; total deadweight tonnage 67,497. Air transport (1985): airports with scheduled flights 1.
Communications. Daily newspapers: none. Radio (1984): total number of receivers 16,800 (1 per 2.7 persons). Television (1984): total number of receivers 9,000 (1 per 5.0 persons). Telephones (1984): 20,400 (1 per 2.2 persons).

Education and health

Education (1984–85)

	schools	teachers	students
Primary (first 7 grades)	76	...	5,583
Secondary (8th through 10th grades)		...	2,994
Vocational, teacher training§	3		607
Higher§	6		949

Educational attainment (1977). Percent of population ages 14 through 49 having: primary education 45.2%; secondary 34.2%. *Literacy* (1984): 99%.
Health: physicians (1984) 69 (1 per 648 persons); hospital beds (1982) 357 (1 per 124 persons); infant mortality rate per 1,000 live births (1983) 14.9.
Food (1979–81): daily per capita caloric intake 3,195 (vegetable products 68%, animal products 32%); 120% of FAO recommended minimum requirement.

Military

Defense responsibility lies with Denmark.

---

*Public utilities and finance included with trade. †Detail does not add to total given because of rounding. ‡Percentages are of economically active population. §1982–83.

Fiji

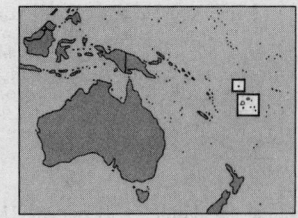

Official name: Dominion of Fiji.
Form of government: parliamentary state with two legislative houses (Senate [22]; House of Representatives [52]).
Chief of state: British Monarch represented by governor-general.
Head of government: Prime Minister.
Capital: Suva.
Official language: English.
Official religion: none.
Monetary unit: 1 Fiji dollar (F$) = 100 cents; valuation (Oct. 21, 1985) 1 U.S.$ = F$1.10; 1£ = 1.58.

Area and population

Divisions Provinces*	Capitals	area sq mi	area sq km	population 1984 estimate
Central	Suva			
Naitasiri		643	1,666	86,000
Rewa		105	272	103,600
Serua-Namosi		540	1,400	18,100
Tailevu		369	955	44,800
Eastern	Levuka			
Kandavu		185	478	8,800
Lau		188	487	13,800
Lomaiviti		159	411	13,700
Rotuma		18	46	2,600
Northern	Labasa			
Mathuata		774	2,004	69,300
Mbua		532	1,379	12,800
Thakaundrove		1,087	2,816	39,100
Western	Lautoka			
Mba		1,017	2,634	192,200
Nandronga-Navosa		921	2,385	53,200
Ra		518	1,341	28,100
TOTAL		7,056	18,274	686,000†

Demography

Population (1985): 692,000.
Density (1985): persons per sq mi 98.1, persons per sq km 37.9.
Urban–rural (1983): urban 38.4%; rural 61.6%.
Sex distribution (1983): male 50.48%; female 49.52%.
Age breakdown (1983): under 15, 37.2%; 15–29, 30.4%; 30–44, 17.7%; 45–59, 9.4%; 60–74, 4.1%; 75 and over, 1.2%.
Population projection: (1990) 758,000; (2000) 907,000.
Doubling time: 38 years.
Ethnic composition (1983): Indian 50.1%; Fijian 44.9%; part-European 1.7%; Rotuman 1.2%; Chinese 0.7%; European 0.5%; other 0.9%.
Religious affiliation (1980): Christian 49.7%; Hindu 40.9%; Muslim 7.8%; other 1.6%.
Major cities (1982 est.): Suva 71,000; Lautoka 26,000; Nadi 9,000; Ba 7,000; Nausori 6,000.

Vital statistics

Birth rate per 1,000 population (1983): 29.5 (world avg. 29.0); (1978) legitimate 82.7%; illegitimate 17.3%.
Death rate per 1,000 population (1983): 5.1 (world avg. 11.0).
Natural increase rate per 1,000 population (1983): 24.4 (world avg. 18.0).
Total fertility rate (avg. births per childbearing woman; 1983): 3.3.
Marriage rate per 1,000 population (1983): 10.1.
Divorce rate per 1,000 population (1979): 0.7.
Life expectancy at birth (1980–85): male 70.2 years; female 74.1 years.
Major causes of death per 100,000 population (1983): heart disease 133.1; ill-defined conditions 59.5; hypertensive and cerebrovascular diseases 48.1; malignant neoplasms (cancers) 44.1; pneumonia 32.6; accidents 15.0.

National economy

Budget (1984). Revenue: F$337,658,000 (income tax and gift duties 45.5%, customs and port duties 33.5%). Expenditures: F$344,407,000 (education 18.7%, economic services 15.2%, health 8.1%, general public services 12.4%, defense 3.9%).
Public debt (external, outstanding; 1984): U.S.$264,738,000.
Tourism (1983): receipts from visitors U.S.$135,000,000; expenditures by nationals abroad (1981) U.S.$19,000,000.
Production (metric tons except as noted). Agriculture, forestry, fishing (1984): sugarcane 4,290,000, coconuts 234,000, copra 23,644, paddy rice 22,171; livestock (number of live animals) 158,000 cattle, 56,000 goats, 29,000 pigs; roundwood 188,369 cu m; fish catch 11,587. Mining and quarrying (1983): gold 1,248 kilograms; silver 405 kilograms. Manufacturing (1984): refined sugar 480,000; cement 97,900; coconut oil 16,400; soap 7,252; beer 185,000 hectolitres; paint 18,000 hectolitres. Construction (1983): residential 74,016 sq m; nonresidential 26,229 sq m. Energy production (consumption): electricity (kW-hr; 1984) 369,000,000 (369,000,000); coal (metric tons; 1983) none (18,000); crude petroleum, none (n.a.); natural gas, none (n.a.).
Household income and expenditure. Average household size (1980) 4.1; income per household F$2,837 (U.S.$3,546); sources of income: wages and salaries 81.5%, self-employment 9.1%, other 9.4%; expenditure (1981): food 25.9%, transportation 13.6%, housing 12.7%, household furnishings and operation 9.2%, clothing and footwear 5.7%.
Gross national product (at current market prices; 1983): U.S.$1,190,000,000 (U.S.$1,771 per capita).

Structure of gross domestic product and labour force

	1984 in value F$'000,000	1984 % of total value	1983 labour force	1983 % of labour force
Agriculture	180.9	24.3	85,059	40.6
Mining	0.7	0.1	1,171	0.6
Manufacturing	91.4	12.3	14,348	6.8
Construction	44.6	6.0	7,450	3.6
Public utilities	9.1	1.2	2,449	1.2
Transportation and communication	84.9	11.4	7,450	3.6
Trade	127.2	17.1	15,792	7.5
Finance	98.7	13.2	5,148	2.4
Pub. admin., defense, services	129.1	17.3	25,600	12.2
Other	−21.6‡	−2.9‡	45,703§	21.8§
TOTAL	745.0 ‖	100.0 ‖	209,703	100.0

Population economically active (1984): total 234,000; participation rate of total population 34.4% (female [1983] 17.3%, unemployed [1983] 7.0%).

Price and earnings indexes (1979 = 100)

	1980	1981	1982	1983	1984	1985
Consumer price index	114.5	127.3	136.2	145.4	153.1	160.6
Annual earnings index	107.8	118.2	131.3	139.5	...	...

Land use (1983): forested 64.9%; agricultural and under permanent cultivation 12.9%; meadows and pastures 3.3%; other 18.9%.

Foreign trade

Balance of trade (current prices)

	1979	1980	1981	1982	1983	1984
F$'000,000	−177.8	−153.2	−270.9	−208.0	−248.2	−210.6
% of total	29.3%	20.0%	33.5%	28.0%	33.6%	27.6%

Imports (1984): F$487,105,000 (mineral fuels and related materials 22.0%; manufactured goods 18.7%; machinery and transport equipment 17.8%; food, beverages, and tobacco 16.1%; chemicals 9.1%). *Major import sources:* Australia 34.6%; Japan 16.2%; New Zealand 16.1%; Singapore 5.6%; United Kingdom 5.0%; United States 4.0%; China 2.5%; Taiwan 2.2%; Hong Kong 1.8%.
Exports (1984): F$279,418,000 (sugar 39.4%; gold 7.4%; coconut oil 6.6%; fish 5.1%; molasses 2.4%; manufactured goods 2.1%; wood and by-products 1.6%). *Major export destinations:* United Kingdom 28.7%; Australia 13.7%; United States 10.1%; Malaysia 8.5%; New Zealand 4.4%.

Transport and communications

Transport. Railroads (1983): length 660 mi, 1,062 km. Roads (1983): total length 2,792 mi, 4,494 km (paved 13%). Vehicles (1984): passenger cars 31,038; trucks and buses 21,467. Merchant marine (1983): vessels (100 gross tons and over) 56; total deadweight tonnage 27,754. Air transport (1983): passenger-mi 254,634,000, passenger-km 409,795,000; short ton-mi cargo 4,512,000, metric ton-km cargo 6,588,000; airports (1985) with scheduled flights 16.
Communications. Daily newspapers (1983): total number 2; total circulation 70,278; circulation per 1,000 population 106. Radio (1984): total number of receivers 300,000 (1 per 2.3 persons). Television: none. Telephones (1983): 49,542 (1 per 13.6 persons).

Education and health

Education (1983)

	schools	teachers♀	students	student/ teacher ratio
Primary (age 5–15)	660	4,256	120,244	...
Secondary (age 16–19)	140	2,467	44,415	...
Voc., teacher tr.	40	314	2,629	0.0
Higher	5	...	3,947	...

Educational attainment (1976). Percent of population 5 years old and over having: no schooling 18.8%, primary 60.8%, secondary 16.8%, postsecondary 2.8%, other 0.8%ᵟ. *Literacy* (1976): total population over age 15 literate 273,680 (79.0%); males literate 146,282 (84.0%); females literate 127,398 (74.0%).
Health (1983): physicians 325♀ (1 per 2,000 persons); hospital beds 1,736 (1 per 377.9 persons); infant mortality rate per 1,000 live births 21.0.
Food (1980–82): daily per capita caloric intake 3,046 (vegetable products 86%, animal products 14%); 115% of FAO recommended minimum requirement.

Military

Total active duty personnel (1984): 2,660 (army 94%, navy 6%, air force none). *Military expenditure as percent of GNP* (1982): 1.0% (world 6.0%); per capita expenditure: U.S.$15.

---

*The provinces are autonomous only with respect to local affairs. †Detail does not add to total given because of rounding. ‡Less imputed service charges. §Self-employed and unemployed. ‖At constant prices of 1977. ¶April. ♀1982. ᵟIncludes persons having no specific level of education.

Finland

Official name: Suomen Tasavalta (Finnish); Republiken Finland (Swedish) (Republic of Finland).
Form of government: multiparty parliamentary republic with one legislative house (Eduskunta [200]).
Chief of state: President.
Head of government: Prime Minister.
Capital: Helsinki.
Official languages: Finnish; Swedish.
Official religion: none.
Monetary unit: 1 markka (Fmk) = 100 penni; valuation (Oct. 21, 1985) 1 U.S.$ = Fmk5.66; 1 £ = Fmk8.12.

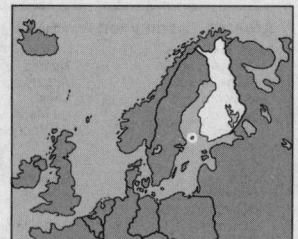

Area and population

Provinces	Capitals	land area sq mi	land area sq km	population 1984 estimate
Åland (Ahvenanmaa)	Mariehamn (Maarianhamina)	590	1,527	23,400
Häme	Hämeenlinna	6,568	17,010	672,700
Keski-Suomi	Jyväskylä	6,266	16,230	246,400
Kuopio	Kuopio	6,375	16,511	255,100
Kymi	Kouvola	4,163	10,783	342,300
Lappi	Rovaniemi	35,929	93,057	200,200
Mikkeli	Mikkeli	6,310	16,342	209,100
Oulu	Oulu	21,956	56,866	430,200
Pohjois-Karjala	Joensuu	6,866	17,782	177,700
Turku ja Pori	Turku	8,559	22,170	710,700
Uusimaa	Helsinki	3,822	9,898	1,165,400
Vaasa	Vaasa	10,211	26,447	442,600
TOTAL LAND AREA		117,615	304,623	4,875,800
INLAND WATER		12,943	33,522	
TOTAL AREA		130,558	338,145	

Demography

Population (1985): 4,910,000.
Density* (1985): persons per sq mi 41.7, persons per sq km 16.1.
Urban–rural (1983): urban 59.8%; rural 40.2%.
Sex distribution (1983): male 48.40%; female 51.60%.
Age breakdown (1983): under 15, 19.6%; 15–29, 23.5%; 30–44, 23.2%; 45–59, 16.7%; 60–74, 12.4%; 75 and over, 4.6%.
Population projection: (1990) 4,955,000; (2000) 4,964,000.
Growth rate: negligible.
Ethnolinguistic composition (1983): Finnish 93.6%; Swedish 6.2%; other 0.2%†.
Religious affiliation (1983): Lutheran 89.7%; Greek Orthodox 1.1%; nonaffiliated 8.3%; other 0.9%.
Major cities (1984): Helsinki 484,471; Tampere 167,344; Turku 163,002; Espoo 149,057; Vantaa 139,202.

Vital statistics

Birth rate per 1,000 population (1985): 12.7 (world avg. 29.0); (1983) legitimate 86.0%; illegitimate 14.0%.
Death rate per 1,000 population (1985): 9.5 (world avg. 11.0).
Natural increase rate per 1,000 population (1985): 3.2 (world avg. 18.0).
Total fertility rate (avg. births per childbearing woman; 1983): 1.7.
Marriage rate per 1,000 population (1982): 6.1.
Divorce rate per 1,000 population (1983): 2.0.
Life expectancy at birth (1982): male 70.1 years; female 78.1 years.
Major causes of death per 100,000 population (1982): ischemic heart disease 274.9; malignant neoplasms (cancers) 187.6; cerebrovascular diseases 108.5; accidents 49.2; pneumonia 29.7; suicide and self-inflicted injuries 22.7.

National economy

Budget (1985). Revenue: Fmk92,928,000,000 (tax revenue 78.4%, of which income and property taxes 27.0%, sales tax 26.8%, excise duties 13.5%, vehicle taxes 3.1%, stamp duties 2.7%). Expenditures: Fmk92,927,000,-000 (social security 17.3%; education 15.6%; health 8.8%; agriculture and forestry 8.8%; transportation 8.2%; administration 5.6%; defense 5.4%).
Public debt (1985): U.S.$7,105,000,000.
Tourism (1983): receipts from visitors U.S.$496,000,000; expenditures by nationals abroad U.S.$620,000,000.
Production (metric tons except as noted). Agriculture, forestry, fishing (1984): barley 1,715,300, oats 1,320,900, sugar beets 823,400, potatoes 745,-100, milk 3,173,000‡, pork 166,000, beef 121,000; livestock (number of live animals) 1,591,600 cattle, 1,255,800 pigs, 201,600 reindeer; roundwood 41,700,000 cu m; fish catch 119,496‡. Mining and quarrying (1983): iron ore 728,600§; chromite 446,000; copper 36,700§. Manufacturing (value added in Fmk; 1983): machinery 24,208,000,000, of which transport equipment 4,596,000,000, electrical equipment 3,909,000,000; paper and paper products 9,033,000,000; processed food 8,805,000,000; chemical products 8,292,000,000. Construction (1984): residential 17,350,000,000 cu m; nonresidential 25,900,000,000 cu m. Energy production (consumption): electricity (kW-hr; 1983) 40,336,000,000 (42,550,000,000); coal (metric tons; 1983) none (1,158,000); crude petroleum (barrels; 1983) none (74,900,000); petroleum products (metric tons; 1983) 9,306,000 (7,266,000); natural gas‖ (cu m; 1983) 4,483,000,000 (5,033,000,000).
Household income and expenditure. Average household size (1983) 2.5; income per household Fmk87,668 (U.S.$15,740); sources of income (1984): wages and salaries 76.0%, self-employment 20.6%, income from property 3.4%; expenditure (1982): housing 28.5%, food 25.2%, transportation and communications 15.7%, recreation and education 15.7%, clothing 4.9%.

Gross national product (at current market prices; 1984): U.S.$50,600,000,000 (U.S.$10,360 per capita).

Structure of gross domestic product and labour force

	1984 in value Fmk'000,000	1984 % of total value	1984 labour force	1984 % of labour force
Agriculture	16,523	7.7	294,000	12.2
Mining	843	0.4		
Manufacturing	53,757	25.2	600,000	24.9
Public utilities	5,633	2.6		
Construction	14,378	6.7	183,000	7.6
Transportation and communication	15,403	7.2	180,000	7.5
Trade	21,947	10.3	342,000	14.2
Finance	29,306	13.7	147,000	6.1
Pub. admin., defense	29,185	13.7	664,000	27.5
Services	10,871	5.1		
Other	15,750	7.4	4,000	0.2
TOTAL	213,596¶	100.0	2,413,000Ω	100.0Ω

Population economically active (1984): total 2,572,000; participation rate of working-age population ages 15–74, 69.5% (female 47.7%, unemployed 6.2%).

Price and earnings indexes (1980 = 100)

	1979	1980	1981	1982	1983	1984	1985
Consumer price index	89.6	100.0	112.0	122.4	132.7	142.4	151.5δ
Hourly earnings index	89.0	100.0	113.0	124.8	137.8	150.7	157.4□

Land use (1983): forested 76.3%; meadows and pastures 0.5%; agricultural and under permanent cultivation 7.8%; other 15.4%.

Foreign trade

Balance of trade (current prices)

	1980	1981	1982	1983	1984	1985□
Fmk'000,000	−1,410.0	+3,107.0	+1,725.0	+1,242.1	+6,222.0	+1,311.0
% of total	1.3%	2.6%	1.4%	0.9%	4.0%	3.4%

Imports (1984): Fmk74,682,000,000 (raw materials and producer goods 62.9%, of which crude petroleum 15.9%; machinery and transport equipment 16.4%, of which transport vehicles 5.8%; fuels and lubricants 6.7%). *Major import sources:* U.S.S.R. 23.1%; West Germany 13.9%; Sweden 12.3%; United Kingdom 7.7%; Japan 5.6%.
Exports (1984): Fmk80,904,000,000 (forestry products 38.0%, of which paper and paper products 29.1%, wood products 8.9%; metal and engineering products 35.5%, of which metal products and machines 28.5%, basic metals 7.0%; chemical products 12.6%; textiles and clothing 6.2%; food and beverages 2.6%). *Major export destinations:* U.S.S.R. 19.0%; Sweden 12.3%; United Kingdom 12.0%; West Germany 9.6%; United States 8.2%; Norway 4.5%.

Transport and communications

Transport. Railroads (1984): length 5,644 mi, 9,115 km†; passenger-mi 2,035,608,000, passenger-km 3,276,000,000; short ton-mi cargo 5,466,000,-000, metric ton-km cargo 7,980,000,000. Roads (1984): total length 47,015 mi, 75,663 km (paved 52%). Vehicles (1983): passenger cars 1,410,458; trucks and buses 190,200. Merchant marine (1984): vessels (100 gross tons and over) 332; total deadweight tonnage 3,209,200. Air transport (1984): passenger-mi 1,662,786,000, passenger-km 2,676,000,000; short ton-mi cargo 54,371,000, metric ton-km cargo 79,380,000; airports (1985) 21.
Communications. Daily newspapers (1983): total number 66; total circulation 2,578,000; circulation per 1,000 population 531. Radio (1983): total number of receivers 2,515,000 (1 per 1.9 persons). Television (1984): total number of receivers 1,738,432 (1 per 2.8 persons). Telephones (1983): 2,643,574 (1 per 1.8 persons).

Education and health

Education (1982–83)

	schools	teachers	students	student/ teacher ratio
Primary (age 7–12)	4,238	24,752	365,965	14.8
Secondary (age 13–19)	1,078	22,279	325,763	14.6
Voc., teacher tr.	535	14,819	106,998	7.2
Higher◊	21	5,087	127,657	25.1

Educational attainment (1982). Percent of population over age 14 having: lower secondary education 51.5%; higher secondary 28.4%; some postsecondary 8.8%; undergraduate 4.3%; graduate 6.1%; postgraduate 0.6%; other 0.3%. *Literacy* (1985): virtually 100% literate.
Health (1983): physicians 9,793 (1 per 496 persons); hospital beds 63,780 (1 per 76 persons); infant mortality rate per 1,000 live births 6.2.
Food (1980–82): daily per capita caloric intake 3,080 (vegetable products 57%, animal products 43%); 114% of FAO recommended minimum.

Military

Total active duty personnel (1984): 36,500 (army 84.6%, navy 7.4%, air force 7.9%). *Military expenditure as percent of GNP* (1983): 1.6% (world 6.1%); per capita expenditure U.S.$148.

---

*Based on land area only. †Includes English 0.04%; German 0.04%; Russian 0.04%; Lappish 0.03%; and other 0.1%. ‡1983. §Metal content of ores. ‖Manufactured gas only. ¶At 1980 prices. ΩDetail does not add to total given because of rounding. δAugust only. □First quarter only. ◊Universities only.

France

Official name: République Française (French Republic).
Form of government: republic with two legislative houses (Parliament; National Assembly [491], Senate [317]).
Chief of state: President.
Head of government: Prime Minister.
Capital: Paris.
Official language: French.
Official religion: none.
Monetary unit: 1 Franc (F) = 100 centimes; valuation (Oct. 21, 1985) 1 U.S.$ = F8.04; 1 £ = F11.53.

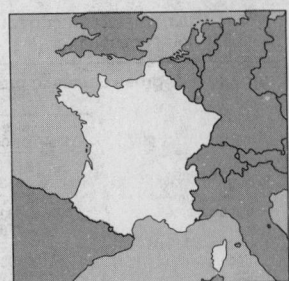

Area and population		area		population
Regions Departments	Capitals	sq mi	sq km	1984 estimate
Alsace				
Bas-Rhin	Strasbourg	1,836	4,755	926,800
Haut-Rhin	Colmar	1,361	3,525	656,200
Aquitaine				
Dordogne	Périgueux	3,498	9,060	379,100
Gironde	Bordeaux	3,861	10,000	1,147,200
Landes	Mont-de-Marsan	3,569	9,243	300,200
Lot-et-Garonne	Agen	2,070	5,361	300,600
Pyrénées-Atlantiques	Pau	2,952	7,645	561,200
Auvergne				
Allier	Moulins	2,834	7,340	367,800
Cantal	Aurillac	2,211	5,726	162,000
Haute-Loire	Le Puy	1,922	4,977	206,900
Puy-de-Dôme	Clermont-Ferrand	3,077	7,970	598,500
Basse Normandie				
Calvados	Caen	2,142	5,548	596,200
Manche	Saint-Lô	2,293	5,938	469,300
Orne	Alen	2,356	6,103	295,700
Bretagne				
Côtes-du-Nord	Saint-Brieuc	2,656	6,878	539,100
Finistère	Quimper	2,600	6,733	836,200
Ille-et-Vilaine	Rennes	2,616	6,775	762,400
Morbihan	Vannes	2,634	6,823	600,200
Bourgogne				
Côte-d'Or	Dijon	3,383	8,763	477,900
Nièvre	Nevers	2,632	6,817	238,000
Saône-et-Loire	Mâcon	3,311	8,775	571,700
Yonne	Auxerre	2,866	7,424	313,800
Centre				
Cher	Bourges	2,793	7,235	321,400
Eure-et-Loire	Chartres	2,270	5,880	370,400
Indre	Châteauroux	2,622	6,791	241,300
Indre-et-Loire	Tours	2,366	6,127	513,400
Loiret	Orléans	2,616	6,775	548,300
Loir-et-Cher	Blois	2,449	6,343	299,000
Champagne-Ardenne				
Ardennes	Charleville-Mézières	2,019	5,229	300,800
Aube	Troyes	2,370	6,139	290,500
Haute-Marne	Chaumont	2,398	6,211	210,600
Marne	Châlons-sur-Marne	3,151	8,162	547,000
Corse				
Corse-du-Sud	Ajaccio	1,550	4,014	110,900
Haute-Corse	Bastia	1,802	4,666	133,700
Franche-Comté				
Doubs	Besançon	2,021	5,234	477,700
Haute-Saône	Vesoul	2,070	5,360	234,900
Jura	Lons-le-Saunier	1,930	4,999	244,500
Territoire de Belfort	Belfort	235	609	133,300
Haute-Normandie				
Eure	Évreux	2,332	6,040	473,700
Seine-Maritime	Rouen	2,424	6,278	1,198,200
Île-de-France				
Essonne	Évry	696	1,804	1,006,300
Hauts-de-Seine	Nanterre	68	176	1,373,800
Paris	Paris	41	105	2,149,900
Seine-et-Marne	Melun	2,284	5,915	929,000
Seine-Saint-Denis	Bobigny	91	236	1,326,800
Val-de-Marne	Créteil	95	245	1,186,600
Val-d'Oise	Pontoise	481	1,246	945,000
Yvelines	Versailles	882	2,284	1,230,000
Languedoc-Roussillon				
Aude	Carcassonne	2,318	6,004	283,200
Gard	Nîmes	2,260	5,853	540,200
Hérault	Montpellier	2,356	6,101	721,900
Lozère	Mende	1,995	5,167	74,100
Pyrénées-Orientales	Perpignan	1,589	4,116	343,800
Limousin				
Corrèze	Tulle	2,261	5,857	242,100
Creuse	Guéret	2,149	5,565	138,600
Haute-Vienne	Limoges	2,131	5,520	357,000
Lorraine				
Meurthe-et-Moselle	Nancy	2,024	5,241	715,300
Meuse	Bar-le-Duc	2,400	6,216	199,700
Moselle	Metz	2,400	6,216	1,008,100
Vosges	Épinal	2,268	5,874	395,400
Midi-Pyrénées				
Ariège	Foix	1,888	4,890	135,300
Aveyron	Rodez	3,373	8,736	278,300
Gers	Auch	2,416	6,257	173,700
Haute-Garonne	Toulouse	2,436	6,309	837,500
Hautes-Pyrénées	Tarbes	1,724	4,464	228,200
Lot	Cahors	2,014	5,712	155,600
Tarn	Albi	2,223	5,758	339,400
Tarn-et-Garonne	Montauban	1,435	3,718	192,200
Nord				
Nord	Lille	2,217	5,743	2,522,200
Pas-de-Calais	Arras	2,576	6,671	1,419,100

Area and population (Continued)				
Pays de la Loire				
Loire-Atlantique	Nantes	2,631	6,815	1,012,300
Maine-et Loire	Angers	2,767	7,166	687,900
Mayenne	Laval	1,998	5,175	274,200
Sarthe	Le Mans	2,396	6,206	508,100
Vendée	La Roche-sur-Yon	2,595	6,721	490,300
Picardie				
Aisne	Laon	2,845	7,369	533,800
Oise	Beauvais	2,263	5,860	678,800
Somme	Amiens	2,382	6,170	546,300
Poitou-Charentes				
Charente	Angoulême	2,300	5,956	339,400
Charente-Maritime	La Rochelle	2,650	6,684	518,000
Deux-Sèvres	Niort	2,316	5,999	343,700
Vienne	Poitiers	2,699	6,990	374,600
Provence-Côte d'Azur				
Alpes-Maritimes	Nice	1,660	4,299	893,500
Alpes-de-Haute-Provence	Digne	2,674	6,925	121,100
Bouches-du-Rhône	Marseille	1,964	5,087	1,739,600
Hautes-Alpes	Gap	2,142	5,549	106,700
Var	Toulon	2,307	5,974	732,500
Vaucluse	Avignon	1,377	3,567	435,500
Rhône-Alpes				
Ain	Bourg-en-Bresse	2,225	5,762	431,800
Ardèche	Privas	2,135	5,529	271,300
Drôme	Valence	2,521	6,530	398,800
Haute-Savoie	Annecy	1,694	4,388	509,100
Isère	Grenoble	2,869	7,431	960,300
Loire	Saint-Étienne	1,846	4,781	739,400
Rhône	Lyon	1,254	3,249	1,450,500
Savoie	Chambéry	2,327	6,028	329,600
TOTAL		210,026	543,965	54,832,000

Demography

Population (1985): 55,163,000.
Density (1985): persons per sq mi 262.6, persons per sq km 101.4.
Urban–rural (1985): urban 77.2%; rural 22.8%.
Sex distribution (1985): male 49.16%; female 50.84%.
Age breakdown (1985): under 15, 20.0%; 15–29, 23.2%; 30–44, 21.0%; 45–59, 17.1%; 60–74, 11.9%; 75 and over, 5.8%.
Population projection: (1990) 55,600,000; (2000) 57,000,000.
Growth rate: during 1981–1984, the average growth rate was 0.3%.
Ethnic composition (1980): French 82.9%; Alsatian 2.6%; Italian 2.2%; Breton 2.0%; Algerian 1.7%; Portuguese 1.4%; Spanish 1.0%; Jewish 1.0%.
Religious affiliation (1980): Roman Catholic 76.4%; other Christian 3.7%; atheist 3.4%; Muslim 3.0%; other 13.5%.
Major cities (1982): Paris 2,165,892 (metropolitan area 10,210,059); Marseille 868,435 (1,227,901); Lyon 410,455 (1,533,305); Toulouse 344,917 (648,267); Nice 331,165 (865,492); Strasbourg 247,068 (613,380); Nantes 237,789 (558,-814); Bordeaux 201,965 (843,411); Saint-Étienne 193,938 (547,729).
Place of national origin (1982): French 90.6%; Algerians 1.5%, Portuguese 1.4%, Moroccans 0.8%, Spanish 0.6%, Italian 0.6%, other 4.5%.
Mobility (1975). Population living in same residence as in 1968: 49.5%; different residence, same region 32.6%; different region 8.7%; different country 3.2%.
Households (1982). Average household size 2.7; 1 person 24.6%, 2 persons 28.5%, 3 persons 18.8%, 4 persons 16.1%, 5 persons 7.4%, 6 persons or more 4.6%. Family households: 14,118,940 (72.1%), nonfamily 5,471,460 (27.9%, of which 1-person 24.6%).
Immigration (1984): permanent immigrants admitted 40,185, from Portugal 39.9%, Morocco 17.0%, Spain 10.3%, Tunisia 6.5%, Turkey 5.6%.

Vital statistics

Birth rate per 1,000 population (1984): 13.8 (world avg. 29.0); (1982) legitimate, 85.8%; illegitimate, 14.2%.
Death rate per 1,000 population (1984): 9.8 (world avg. 11.0).
Natural increase rate per 1,000 population (1984): 4.0 (world avg. 18.0).
Total fertility rate (avg. births per childbearing woman; 1983): 1.5.
Marriage rate per 1,000 population (1984): 5.1.
Divorce rate per 1,000 population (1984): 2.0.
Life expectancy at birth (1982): male 70.2 years; female 78.5 years.
Major causes of death per 100,000 population (1984): malignant neoplasms (cancers) 228.0; ischemic heart disease 201.8; cerebrovascular disease 118.0.

Social indicators

Educational attainment (1974). Percent of adult employed population having: less than full primary education 36.2%, primary 30.4%, secondary 21.0%, some postsecondary 7.0%, 4-year degree 2.4%, postgraduate 2.8%.

Distribution of income (1975)				
percent of household income by quintile				
1	2	3	4	5 (highest)
5.3%	11.1%	16.0%	21.8%	45.8%.

Quality of working life. Average workweek (1984): 37.5 hours (overtime, n.a.). Annual rate per 100,000 workers (1982) for: injury or accident 27.7; industrial illness 0.5; death 0.003. Proportion of labour force insured for damages or income loss resulting from: injury, n.a.; permanent disability, n.a.; death, n.a. Average days lost to labour stoppages per 1,000 workers (1982): 0.4. Average duration of journey to work (1974): 53 minutes.
Access to services (1982). Proportion of dwellings having: central heating 67.5%; piped water 99.3%; indoor plumbing 85.0%; natural gas 48.9%.
Social participation. Eligible voters participating in last national election: 65.9%. Population over 15 years of age participating in voluntary associations: 28%. Trade union membership in total workforce: n.a.

Social deviance. Offense rate per 100,000 population (1980) for: murder 3.9; rape 34.4; other assault 61.4; theft, including burglary and housebreaking 3,008.2. Incidence per 100,000 in general population of: alcoholism* (late 1970s) 3,500–4,000; drug and substance abuse, n.a.; suicide (1983) 21.8.
Leisure (1981). Favourite leisure activities: television 34%; lectures 14%; knitting 10%; conversations 10%; games 8%; walking 4%; radio 4%.
Material well-being (1982). Households possessing: automobile 72.1%; telephone 100%; television receiver 91.0%; refrigerator 96.1%; washing machine 81.7%.

National economy

Gross national product (at current market prices; 1983): U.S.$568,690,000,-000 (U.S.$10,400 per capita).

Structure of gross domestic product and labour force

| | 1983 | | | |
	in value F'000,000	% of total value	labour force	% of labour force
Agriculture	159,700	4.3	1,692,100	8.0
Mining	76,600	2.0	133,900	0.6
Manufacturing	958,700	25.5	5,065,500	23.9
Construction	240,000	6.4	1,672,600	7.9
Public utilities	98,000	2.6	201,900	1.0
Transp. and commun.	197,500	5.3	1,378,900	6.5
Trade	370,100	9.9	3,453,300	16.3
Finance	533,300	14.2	1,555,700	7.3
Other (incl. pub. admin., defense, and services)	1,118,500	29.8	6,027,600	28.4
TOTAL	3,752,400	100.0	21,181,500	100.0†

Budget (1984). Revenue: F896,100,000,000 (value-added taxes 46.5%, income tax 24.8%, corporate taxes 10.0%). Expenditure: F939,701,000,000 (education 23.7%, health and social services 21.2%, defense 16.0%, administration 11.6%).
Public debt (internal; 1984): F883,100,000,000.
Tourism (1983): receipts from visitors U.S.$7,226,000,000; expenditures by nationals abroad U.S.$4,281,000,000.

Manufacturing and mining enterprises (1982)

	no. of enter-prises‡	no. of employees	hourly wages as a % of avg. of all wages‡	annual value added (F'000,000)
Food products	...	513,000	100	117,900
Transport equipment	707	653,000	109	110,700
Electrical machinery	692	482,000	101	65,700
Petroleum refineries	47	31,000	120	44,400
Industrial chemicals	316	146,000	115	44,100
Metal products,	3,514	264,000	110	43,100
iron and steel	202	237,000	105	42,200
Textiles	1,970	260,000	84	32,600
Printing, publishing	1,736	204,000	120	25,200
Beverages	...	51,000	100	22,200
Paper and products	658	115,000	108	22,000
Wearing apparel	2,216	236,000	78	19,100
Rubber products	199	101,000	99	13,400
Tobacco	...	9,000	100	10,400
Glass products	5	65,000	120	10,300

Production (metric tons except as noted). Agriculture, forestry, fishing (1984): wheat 32,884,000, sugar beets 27,790,000, barley 11,543,000, corn (maize) 10,321,000, grapes 9,400,000, potatoes 6,200,000, apples 2,935,000, oats 1,875,000, rapeseed 1,345,000, sunflower seeds 1,000,000, tomatoes 790,000, carrots 551,000, pears 485,000, peas 480,000, peaches 454,000, rye 349,000, sorghum 256,000; livestock (number of live animals) 23,570,000 cattle, 12,260,000 sheep, 11,400,000 pigs, 1,200,000 goats; roundwood 39,-839,000 cu m§; fish catch 784,000§. Mining and quarrying (1984): iron ore 1,955,000 ‖, potash salts 1,739,000, bauxite 1,528,000, zinc 35,040 ‖, lead 1,560 ‖, gold 37,000 troy oz§. Manufacturing (1984): cement 22,716,000; crude steel 19,020,000; pig iron 15,420,000; sulfuric acid 4,520,000; rubber products 555,360, of which tires 44,316,000 units; aluminum 505,200; automobiles 2,910,000 units. Construction (dwelling units; 1983) 332,916.

Retail trade enterprises (1980)

	no. of enter-prises	no. of employees	weekly wages as a % of all wages	annual purchases (F'000,000)
Large food stores	1,844	264,639	...	144,452
Small food stores	134,083	387,537	...	100,946
butcher shops	51,994	158,019	...	34,658
Clothing stores	74,643	203,055	...	31,446
Pharmacies	19,329	95,048	...	22,191
Gas, coal, and other energy products	5,947	23,802	...	22,072
Department stores	1,464	75,374	...	20,328
Furniture stores	7,087	55,413	...	15,919
Electrical and elec-tronics stores	11,584	53,734	...	12,871
Publishing and paper	20,546	59,771	...	9,060

Energy production (consumption): electricity (kW-hr; 1984) 333,000,000,000 (299,000,000,000); coal (metric tons; 1984) 19,100,000 (42,200,000); crude petroleum (barrels; 1984) 19,400,000 (629,300,000); petroleum products (metric tons; 1983¶) 68,217,000 (74,370,000); natural gas (cu m; 1984) 5,888,300,000 (26,108,500,000).
Household income and expenditure. Average household size (1983) 2.7; average annual income per household (1983) F139,700 (U.S.$16,640). Sources of income (1984): salaries 52.8%, social security 25.4%, self-employment 21.5%; expenditure (1982): housing 26.2%, food and beverages 20.0%, transportation 13.9%, health 13.1%, clothing and footwear 6.5%, recreation 6.5%.

Population economically active (1983): total 23,045,000; participation rate of population ages 15–74, 57.2% (female 40.1%, unemployed 8.1%).

Price and earnings indexes (1980 = 100)

	1978	1979	1980	1981	1982	1983	1984
Consumer price index	79.4	87.9	100.0	113.4	126.8	139.0	149.3
Hourly earnings index	74.8	86.2	100.0	114.4	137.5	155.1	168.2

Land use (1984): forested 26.7%; meadows and pastures 23.0%; agricultural and under permanent cultivation 34.4%; other 15.9%.

Financial aggregates

	1980	1981	1982	1983	1984	1985 (7 mo.)
Exchange rate, F per:						
U.S. dollar	4.52	5.75	6.73	8.35	9.59	8.50
£	10.78	10.97	10.87	12.11	11.09	12.14
SDR	5.76	6.69	7.42	8.74	9.40	8.82
International reserves (U.S.$)						
Total (excl. gold; '000,000)	27,340	22,262	16,531	19,851	20,940	23,526
SDRs ('000,000)	935	1,257	979	442	572	686
Reserve pos. in IMF ('000,000)	1,067	1,029	958	1,352	1,265	1,293
Foreign exchange	25,338	19,976	14,594	18,057	19,102	21,547
Gold ('000,000 fine troy oz)	81.85	81.85	81.85	81.85	81.85	81.85
% world reserves	8.6	8.6	8.6	8.7	8.6	8.6
Interest and prices						
Central bank discount (%)	9.50	9.50	9.50	9.50	9.50	9.50
Gov't. bond yield (%)	12.99	15.66	15.56	13.61	12.41	10.67
Industrial share prices (1980 = 100)	100.0	88.1	74.8	101.0	136.4	159.0
Balance of payments (U.S.$'000,000)						
Balance of visible trade	−13,419	−9,970	−15,785	−8,754	−4,089	...
Imports, f.o.b.	120,934	110,843	107,289	98,460	96,392	...
Exports, f.o.b.	107,515	100,873	91,504	89,706	92,303	...
Balance of invisibles	13,360	9,393	8,326	7,664	6,965	...
Balance of payments, current account	−4,208	−4,809	−12,082	−4,904	−14	...

Foreign trade

Balance of trade (current prices)

	1979	1980	1981	1982	1983	1984
F'000,000,000	−2.8	−55.4	−54.6	−100.5	−48.3	−53.2
% of total	0.3%	4.6%	3.8%	6.1%	2.7%	3.0%

Imports (1984): F904,120,000,000 (fuels 23.4%, of which crude petroleum 15.1%; machinery 17.6%; chemicals and chemical products 13.6%; agricultural products 12.8%; transport equipment 6.7%, of which automobiles 3.4%). *Major import sources:* West Germany 16.3%; Italy 9.9%; Belgium–Luxembourg 8.2%; U.K. 8.1%; U.S. 7.7%; The Netherlands 6.1%.
Exports (1984): F850,950,000,000 (machinery 17.8%; agricultural products 16.8%; chemicals and chemical products 15.1%; transportation equipment 10.9%, of which automobiles 4.7%). *Major export destinations:* West Germany 14.7%; Italy 10.9%; Belgium–Luxembourg 8.6%; U.S. 8.1%; U.K. 7.9%; The Netherlands 4.8%.

Transport and communications

Transport. Railroads: (1983) route length 21,493 mi, 34,590 km; (1984) passenger-mi 37,530,000,000, passenger-km 60,400,000,000; short ton-mi cargo 41,180,000,000, metric ton-km cargo 60,120,000,000. Roads (1984): total length 499,945 mi, 804,585 km (paved 92%). Vehicles (1984): passenger cars 20,800,000; trucks and buses 3,310,000. Merchant marine (1984): vessels (100 gross tons and over) 1,174; total deadweight tonnage 16,093,205. Air transport (1984): passenger-mi 23,905,000,000, passenger-km 38,472,000,-000; short ton-mi cargo 1,982,185,000, metric ton-km cargo 2,893,940,000; airports (1985) with scheduled flights 60.
Communications. Daily newspapers (1984): total number 101; total circulation 13,030,000; circulation per 1,000 population 237. Radio (1983): total number of receivers 20,000,000 (1 per 2.7 persons). Television (1983): total number of receivers 17,290,000 (1 per 3.2 persons). Telephones (1983): 29,373,663 (1 per 1.9 persons).

Education and health

Education (1981–82)

	schools	teachers♀	students	student/ teacher ratio
Primary (age 2–10)	67,291	290,933	6,909,559	...
Secondary (age 11–18) } Voc., teacher tr.	11,209	256,284	5,052,452	...
Higher♀	1,094	40,585	1,017,775	25.1

Literacy (1980): total population literate 41,112,000 (98.8%); males literate 19,933,000 (98.9%); females literate 21,179,000 (98.7%).
Health (1982): physicians 113,000 (1 per 480.2 persons); hospital beds 496,784 (1 per 109.2 persons); infant mortality rate per 1,000 live births (1984) 8.2.
Food (1980–82): daily per capita caloric intake 3,525 (vegetable products 62%, animal products 38%); 140% of FAO recommended minimum requirement.

Military

Total active duty personnel (1984): 471,350 (army 64.0%, navy 13.4%, air force 18.8%, strategic nuclear forces 3.8%). *Military expenditure as percent of GNP* (1983): 3.8% (world 6.1%); per capita expenditure U.S.$392.

*Estimated as per a narrowly defined meaning of alcoholism. †Detail does not add to total given because of rounding. ‡1981. §1983. ‖ Metal content only. ¶Includes Monaco. ♀1980–81.

French Guiana

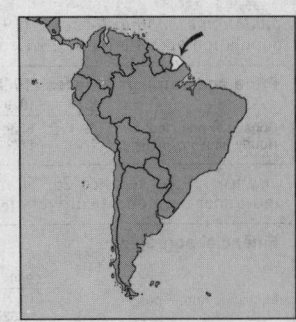

Official name: Département de la Guyane Française (Department of French Guiana).
Political status: overseas department of France with two legislative houses (General Council [16]; Regional Council [31]).
Chief of state: President of France.
Heads of government: Commissioner (for France); President of the General Council (for French Guiana); President of the Regional Council (for French Guiana).
Capital: Cayenne.
Official language: French.
Official religion: none.
Monetary unit: 1 franc (F) = 100 centimes; valuation (Oct. 21, 1985) 1 U.S.$ = F8.04; 1 £ = F11.53.

Area and population		area		population
				1982
Arrondissements	**Capitals**	sq mi	sq km	census
Cayenne	Cayenne	20,100	52,000	61,587
Saint-Laurent-du-Maroni	Saint-Laurent-du-Maroni	15,800	41,000	11,435
TOTAL		35,900	93,000*	73,022

Demography

Population (1985): 82,700.
Density (1984): persons per sq mi 2.3, persons per sq km 0.9.
Urban–rural (1982): urban 73.4%; rural 26.6%.
Sex distribution (1982): male 52.66%; female 47.34%.
Age breakdown (1982): under 15, 32.6%; 15–29, 29.2%; 30–44, 20.8%; 45–59, 10.1%; 60–74, 5.4%; 75 and over, 1.9%.
Population projection: (1990) 93,000; (2000) 125,800.
Doubling time: 19 years.
Ethnic composition (1982): Guianese (mixed) Creole 42.6%; Guiana Chinese 14.0%; French (metropolitan) 10.7%; Haitian 7.5%; French West Indian 6.6%; Bush Negro 4.7%; Brazilian 4.6%; Amerindian 4.1%; other (other West Indian, Surinamese, Hmong, and other Southeast Asian) 5.2%.
Religious affiliation (1980): Roman Catholic 87.1%; Protestant 3.9%; nonreligious 2.5%; Afro-American spiritist 2.0%; animist 1.5%; Chinese folk-religionist 1.3%; Muslim 1.0%; Bahā'ī 0.7%.
Major cities (1982): Cayenne 37,097; Kourou 6,465; Rémire-Montjoly 5,921; Saint-Laurent-du-Maroni 5,042.

Vital statistics

Birth rate per 1,000 population (1984): 28.8 (world avg. 29.0); (1984) legitimate 23%; illegitimate 77%.
Death rate per 1,000 population (1984): 5.9 (world avg. 11.0).
Natural increase rate per 1,000 population (1984): 22.9 (world avg. 18.0).
Total fertility rate (avg. births per childbearing woman; 1975–79): 3.1.
Marriage rate per 1,000 population (1984): 3.6.
Divorce rate per 1,000 population (1984): 0.3.
Life expectancy at birth (1975–79): male 63.4 years; female 69.7 years.
Major causes of death per 100,000 population (1981): cardiovascular disease 119; accidents and murders 90; malignant neoplasms (cancers) 49; illnesses of the digestive system 48; infectious diseases 43.

National economy

Budget (1983). Revenue: F449,647,000 (ordinary revenue 84.1%, of which indirect taxes 17.9%, operating receipts of government 7.7%, direct taxes 3.4%; investment income 15.9%). Expenditures: F382,415,000 (recurrent ordinary expenses 82.0%, of which nonpersonnel transfers to governmental organizations 30.1%, personnel expenses 23.3%; capital investment 18.8%, of which buildings under construction 8.2%).
Public debt (external, outstanding; 1982): U.S.$18,000,000.
Tourism (1983): visitors arriving 66,100.
Production (metric tons except as noted). Agriculture, forestry, fishing (1984): sugarcane 12,000, cassava 8,000, dasheens 3,400†, rice 3,000, plantains 1,000, corn (maize) 1,000, bananas 500, citrus fruits 400; livestock (number of live animals) 14,000 cattle, 10,000 pigs, 100,000 chickens; roundwood 69,200 cu m; fish catch 2,264. Mining and quarrying (1983): gold 249 kg; stone, sand, and gravel 400,000. Manufacturing (1984): frozen shrimp 2,874‡; frozen fish 239‡; sawnwood and veneer sheets 34,679 cu m; finished wood products 729 cu m; rum 2,159 hectolitres; other important products include wood essences, wooden boats, cement, leather goods, textiles and clothing, handicrafts, beer, and soft drinks. Construction (1983): residential 16,856 sq m; nonresidential, n.a. Energy production (consumption): electricity (kW-hr; 1983) 163,700,000 (138,100,000); coal, none (n.a.); crude petroleum, none (n.a.); petroleum products (metric tons; 1983) none (132,000); natural gas, none (n.a.); fuelwood and charcoal (cubic metres; 1981) 68,000 (68,000).
Household income and expenditure. Average household size (1982) 3.3; income per household (1980) F75,762 (U.S.$16,776); sources of income (1980): salaries 76.4%, industrial and commercial profits 12.3%, pensions and rents 3.8%, noncommercial profits 2.5%, income from stocks and bonds 1.6%, other 3.4%; expenditure (1984): food and beverages 50.0%, clothing 8.4%, housing 7.3%, household goods 5.6%, utilities 5.5%.

Land use (1983): forested 81.9%; meadows and pastures 0.1%; agricultural and under permanent cultivation 0.0%§; other 18.0%.
Gross national product (at current market prices; 1982): U.S.$210,000,000 (U.S.$3,230 per capita).

Structure of gross domestic product and labour force				
		1982		
	in value	% of total value	labour force	% of labour force
Agriculture	...	...	4,350	13.9
Mining	...	...}	3,715	11.9
Manufacturing	...			
Construction	...	...	‖	‖
Public utilities	...	...	380	1.2
Transportation and communication	...	...	1,347	4.3
Trade	...	...	2,025	6.5
Finance	...	...	444	1.4
Pub. admin.	...	...	3,218	10.3
Services	...	...	8,927	28.6
Other	...	...	6,777 ‖	21.7 ‖
TOTAL	...	...	31,163	100.0¶

Population economically active (1982): total 31,183; participation rate of population over age 15, 64.7% (female 36.7%, unemployed 15.6%).

Price and earnings indexes (1980 = 100)							
	1979	1980	1981	1982	1983	1984	1985
Consumer price index	88.9	100.0	116.5	130.3	142.4	159.0	164.6◊
Monthly earnings index	87.4	100.0	120.1	139.9	151.0	164.2	...

Foreign trade

Balance of trade (current prices)						
	1979	1980	1981	1982	1983	1984
F'000,000	−997	−973	−1,163	−1,431	−1,843	−1,831
% of total	87.7%	82.2%	75.2%	77.1%	75.8%	73.7%

Imports (1984): F2,158,110,000 (basic manufactures 23.3%, processed food products 15.5%, agricultural products 9.7%, metals and metal products 6.7%, chemicals and chemical products 6.0%, transport vehicles and parts 4.5%). *Major import sources:* France 54.7%; Trinidad and Tobago 13.0%; Japan 4.7%; United States 2.9%.
Exports (1984): F326,664,000 (agricultural products 63.9%, metals and metal products 10.9%, basic equipment 9.9%, consumer goods 8.5%). *Major export destinations:* United States 41.4%; European Economic Community 25.5%; Japan 18.1%; France 9.1%; Martinique 7.0%; Guadeloupe 6.1%.

Transport and communications

Transport. Railroads (1982): none. Roads (1982): total length 422 mi, 680 km (paved 75%). Vehicles (1981): passenger cars 16,789; trucks and buses 2,013. Fishing fleet (1982): vessels 9; total deadweight tonnage, n.a. Air transport (1984)ŏ: passenger arrivals and departures 181,266; cargo loaded and unloaded 3,914 metric tons; airports (1985) with scheduled flights 5.
Communications. Daily newspapers (1984): total number 2; total circulation 16,000□; circulation per 1,000 population 200□. Radio (1983): total number of receivers 73,000 (1 per 1 person). Television (1983): total number of receivers 40,000 (1 per 1.8 persons). Telephones (1983): 22,143 (1 per 3.7 persons).

Education and health

Education (1981–82)	schools	teachers◊	students	student/ teacher ratio
Primary (age 6–11)	66	598	13,675	...
Secondary (age 12–18)	14	365	6,339	...
Voc., teacher tr.	5	149	1,802	...
Higher	1	...	236	—

Educational attainment (1982). Percent of population over 16 having: no formal schooling 31.0%; primary education 53.8%; secondary 14.7%. *Literacy* (1982): total population over age 16 literate 38,964 (82.0%); males literate 21,021 (82.5%); females literate 17,943 (81.3%).
Health (1981): physicians 80 (1 per 885 persons); hospital beds 907 (1 per 78 persons); infant mortality rate per 1,000 live births (1984) 22.6.
Food (1980–82): daily per capita caloric intake 2,818 (vegetable products 71%; animal products 29%); 105% of FAO recommended minimum requirement.

Military

Total active duty personnel (1983)△: 4,350 (army 92.0%, navy 3.5%, air force 4.5%).

*In the mid-1980s the area south of the confluence of the Maroni and Litany rivers remained disputed by French Guiana and Suriname. †1981. ‡Export figure. §Less than 0.01%. ‖ Construction included with other. ¶Detail does not add to total given because of rounding. ◊January. ŏCommercial traffic from Rochambeau international airport (Cayenne) only. □Circulation for one daily. ◊1980–81. △Most military personnel stationed in French Guiana are from Europe; most Guianese males fulfill their military obligations elsewhere.

French Polynesia

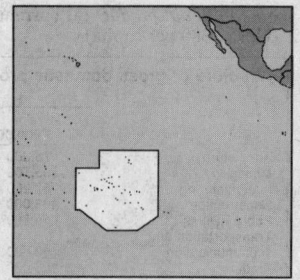

Official name: Territoire de la Polynésie Française (French) (Territory of French Polynesia).
Political status: overseas territory (France) with one legislative house (Territorial Assembly [30]), two representatives in the French National Assembly, and one senator in the French Senate.
Chief of state: President of France.
Head of government: High Commissioner.
Capital: Papeete.
Official languages: French; Tahitian.
Official religion: none.
Monetary unit: 1 Franc de la Comptoirs française du pacifique (CFP fr) = 100 centimes; valuation (Oct. 21, 1985) 1 U.S.$ = CFP fr139.47; 1 £ = CFP fr200.00.

Area and population

Circumscriptions	Capitals	area sq mi	area sq km	population 1983 census
Îles Australes	Mataura	57	148	6,283
Îles Marquises	Taiohae	405	1,049	6,548
Îles sous le Vent	Uturoa	156	404	19,060
Îles Tuamotu et Gambier	Papeete	280	726	11,793
Îles du Vent	Papeete	461	1,194	123,069
TOTAL		1,550*	4,000*	166,753

Demography

Population (1985): 175,500.
Density (1985)†: persons per sq mi 129.1, persons per sq km 49.8.
Urban–rural (1977): urban 39.7%; rural 60.3%.
Sex distribution (1983): male 52.12%; female 47.88%.
Age breakdown (1985): under 15, 37.9%; 15–29, 30.0%; 30–44, 16.5%; 45–59, 10.5%; 60–74, 4.3%; 75 and over, 0.8%.
Population projection: (1990) 204,000; (2000) 275,000.
Doubling time: 23 years.
Ethnic composition (1983): Polynesian 68.5%; mixed 14.5%, of which Polynesian-European 9.5%, Polynesian-Chinese 3.8%, European-Chinese 0.3%; European (mostly French) 11.6%; Chinese 4.5%; other 0.9%.
Religious affiliation (1980): Protestant 46.6%, of which Evangelical Church of French Polynesia 32.8%; Roman Catholic 39.4%; other Christian 8.2%, of which Mormon 3.5%; nonreligious 5.0%; other 0.8%.
Major cities (1983): Papeete 23,496; Faaa 21,927; Punaauia 12,414; Pirae 12,023; Mahina 8,954.

Vital statistics

Birth rate per 1,000 population (1984): 29.5 (world avg. 29.0); (1980) legitimate 45.1%; illegitimate 54.9%.
Death rate per 1,000 population (1984): 4.8 (world avg. 11.0).
Natural increase rate per 1,000 population (1984): 24.7 (world avg. 18.0).
Total fertility rate (avg. births per childbearing woman; 1985): 3.5.
Marriage rate per 1,000 population (1980): 6.5.
Divorce rate per 1,000 population (1980): 1.2.
Life expectancy at birth (1980–85): male 63.5 years; female 67.8 years.
Major causes of death per 100,000 population: n.a.; however, major diseases are influenza, dengue fever, and tuberculosis.

National economy

Budget (1984) Revenue: CFP fr37,591,000,000 (custom duties and taxes 73.4%, of which indirect taxes 56.9%; loans 7.5%; miscellaneous taxes 5.1%; visa and postal registrations 3.7%; property taxes 3.1%). Expenditures: CFP fr29,205,000,000 (grants and subsidies 39.2%; operating and service expenses 34.5%; public debt service 10.3%; infrastructure expenses and maintenance 7.4%; special funds 3.1%; construction 2.8%; building purchases 1.0%).
Public debt (external, outstanding; 1982): U.S.$114,000,000.
Tourism (1983): receipts from visitors U.S.$80,000,000; expenditures by nationals abroad, n.a.
Production (metric tons except as noted). Agriculture, forestry, fishing‡ (1984): coconuts 65,000, copra 7,388, cassava 5,000, vegetables (including carrots, cabbages, and cucumbers) 3,930, potatoes 3,000, watermelons 2,000, pineapples 1,277, mangoes 253, bananas 163, coffee 63, vanilla 20, flowers CFP fr190,000,000§; livestock (number of live animals) 32,000 pigs, 10,000 cattle, 3,000 goats; roundwood, n.a.; fish catch 2,378 (of which tuna 623), black cultured pearls 112 kilograms. Mining and quarrying: none. Manufacturing (1984): copra 7,358; coconut oil 5,285; *monoï* oil (a base used in cosmetics and suntan lotions) 81 ∥; beer 100,000 hectolitres¶; printed cloth 200,000 metres♀; sandals 600,000 pairs♀. Construction (value added in CFP fr'000,000; 1983): residential 2,637; nonresidential 1,150; other 2,292δ.
Energy production (consumption): electricity (kW-hr; 1984) 193,700,000 (176,700,000); coal, none (n.a.); crude petroleum, none (n.a.); petroleum products (metric tons; 1983) none (131,000); natural gas, none (n.a.).
Gross national product (at current market prices; 1983): U.S.$1,260,000,000 (U.S.$7,620 per capita).

Structure of gross domestic product and labour force

	1982 in value CFP fr'000,000	1982 % of total value	1984 labour force	1984 % of labour force
Agriculture	6,514	4.8	863□	1.7□
Manufacturing	12,421	9.1	2,548	4.9
Construction	} 12,843	9.4	8,940	17.3
Public utilities			577	1.1
Transportation and communication	8,790	6.4	3,334	6.5
Trade	} 33,029	24.1	10,441	20.3
Finance			2,247	4.4
Pub. admin., defense	32,520	23.7	18,068	35.0
Services	30,836	22.5	4,530	8.8
TOTAL	136,953◊	100.0	51,548	100.0

Population economically active (1984): total 51,548; participation rate of total population 30.3% (female 34.5%, unemployed 1.7%).

Price and earnings indexes (1980 = 100)

	1979	1980	1981	1982	1983	1984	1985△
Consumer price index	89.8	100.0	116.7	133.6	151.9	168.1	174.6
Monthly earnings index	86.8	100.0	119.8	149.4	177.2	199.2	207.1

Household income and expenditure. Average household size (1983) 5.0; average annual income per household (1977) CFP fr2,118,161 (U.S.$23,624); sources of income (1980): salaries 50.7%, self-employment 38.5%, transfer payments 9.1%, other 1.7%; expenditure (1980): food 24.2%, manufactured products 51.0%, services 12.5%, other 12.3%.
Land use (1983): forested 31.4%; meadows and pastures 5.5%; agricultural and under permanent cultivation 20.5%; other 42.6%.

Foreign trade

Balance of trade (current prices)

	1979	1980	1981	1982	1983	1984
CFP fr'000,000	−34,490	−39,690	−51,982	−58,957	−69,421	−85,622
% of total	88.6%	89.5%	90.0%	90.0%	87.8%	88.8%

Imports (1984): CFP fr85,622,000,000 (food products 20.0%, electrical machinery and appliances 17.2%, petroleum products 13.2%, transport equipment 12.0%, metal manufactures 7.9%, chemical products 5.1%, textiles 4.3%. *Major import sources* (1983): France 45.8%; United States 15.8%; New Zealand 6.0%; Singapore 4.6%; Japan 4.3%.
Exports (1984): CFP fr5,084,000,000 (reexports [primarily aeronautical parts, beer, and corned beef] 77.6%, coconut oil 9.2%, black cultured pearls 8.7%, vanilla 0.5%, *monoï* oil 0.4%, mother-of-pearl 0.4%). *Major export destinations* (1983): France 68.0%; Italy 14.5%; United States 7.0%; Japan 6.5%.

Transport and communications

Transport. Railroads: none. Roads (1982): total length 460 mi, 741 km (paved 33%). Vehicles (1975): passenger cars 16,500; trucks and buses 8,500. Merchant marine: vessels (100 gross tons and over), n.a. Air transport (1984): passenger arrivals 316,400, passenger departures 304,000; cargo unloaded 4,662 metric tons†, cargo loaded 760 metric tons†; airports (1985) with scheduled flights 32.
Communications. Daily newspapers (1984): total number 2; total circulation 21,700; circulation per 1,000 population 127. Radio (1984): total number of receivers 80,000 (1 per 2.1 persons). Television (1983): total number of receivers 25,600 (1 per 6.7 persons). Telephones (1983): 27,612 (1 per 6.2 persons).

Education and health

Education (1982–83)

	schools	teachers	students	student/ teacher ratio
Primary (age 6–10)	240	1,361	29,384	21.6
Secondary (age 11–17)	24⊙	789	12,049	15.3
Voc., teacher tr.**	17⊙	197	3,443	17.5
Higher	—	—	—	—

Educational attainment (1983): Percent of population over age 20 having: less than full primary education 61.1%; primary 20.1%; secondary 11.4%; higher 7.4%. *Literacy* (1983): total population over age 14 literate 98,314 (95.0%); males literate 51,910 (94.9%); females literate 46,404 (95.0%).
Health (1980): physicians 143 (1 per 1,034 persons); hospital beds 982 (1 per 151 persons); infant mortality rate per 1,000 live births (1984) 19.5.
Food (1980–82): daily per capita caloric intake 2,874 (vegetable products 79%, animal products 21%); 108% of FAO recommended minimum requirement.

Military

Total active duty personnel (1984): 5,000 (almost all French Army). *Military expenditure as percent of GNP:* n.a.

---

*Approximate total area including inland water; total land area is 1,359 sq mi (3,521 sq km). †Based on land area. ‡Includes marine-produced commodities, *e.g.*, pearls. §1983. ∥ 1982. ¶1980. ♀1979. δReconstruction after 1982 cyclone. □Excludes about 6,000 self-employed farmers and fishermen. ◊At current prices. △March. †Excludes 575 metric tons of nondifferentiated domestic cargo. ⊙1983–84. **Excludes one teacher-training school enrolling 120 students in 1983–84.

Gabon

Official name: République Gabonaise (Gabonese Republic).
Form of government: unitary single-party republic with one legislative house (National Assembly [120]).
Chief of state: President.
Head of government: Prime Minister.
Capital: Libreville.
Official language: French.
Official religion: none.
Monetary unit: 1 CFA franc (CFAF) = 100 centimes; valuation (Oct. 21, 1985) 1 U.S.$ = CFAF402.02; 1 £ = CFAF576.50.

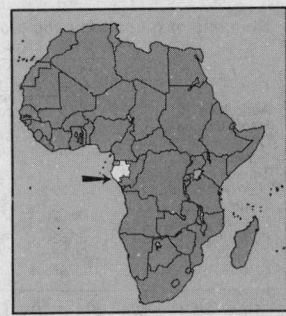

Area and population

Provinces	Capitals	area sq mi	area sq km	population 1978 estimate
Estuaire	Libreville	8,008	20,740	359,000
Haut-Ogooué	Franceville	14,111	36,547	213,000
Moyen-Ogooué	Lambaréné	7,156	18,535	49,000
Ngounié	Mouila	14,575	37,750	118,000
Nyanga	Tchibanga	8,218	21,285	98,000
Ogooué-Ivindo	Makokou	17,790	46,075	53,000
Ogooué-Lolo	Koulamoutou	9,799	25,380	49,000
Ogooué-Maritime	Port-Gentil	8,838	22,890	194,000
Woleu-Ntem	Oyem	14,851	38,465	166,000
TOTAL		103,347*	267,667	1,300,000*

Demography

Population (1985): 1,166,000.
Density (1985): persons per sq mi 11.3, persons per sq km 4.4.
Urban–rural (1980): urban 35.8%; rural 64.2%.
Sex distribution (1980): male 49.09%; female 50.91%.
Age breakdown (1970): under 15, 35.4%; 15–29, 19.3%; 30–44, 22.2%; 45–59, 16.3%; 60–74, 6.3%; 75 and over, 0.5%.
Population projection: (1990) 1,282,000; (2000) 1,611,000.
Doubling time: 42 years.
Ethnic composition (1980): Fang 34.5%; Mpongwe 14.5%; Mbete 13.6%; Punu 10.9%; French 6.0%; other 20.5%.
Religious affiliation (1980): Christian 94.5%, of which Roman Catholic 63.8%, Protestant 18.4%, African indigenous 12.1%; tribal religionist 2.9%; Muslim 0.8%; other 1.8%.
Major cities (1983): Libreville 257,000; Port-Gentil 123,000; Franceville 38,030.

Vital statistics

Birth rate per 1,000 population (1980–85): 33.7 (world avg. 29.0).
Death rate per 1,000 population (1980–85): 19.9 (world avg. 11.0).
Natural increase rate per 1,000 population (1980–85): 13.8 (world avg. 18.0).
Total fertility rate (avg. births per childbearing woman; 1980–85): 4.7.
Marriage rate per 1,000 population: n.a.
Divorce rate per 1,000 population: n.a.
Life expectancy at birth: n.a.
Major causes of death per 100,000 population: n.a.; however, major diseases are malaria, trypanosomiasis, and tuberculosis.

National economy

Budget (1983). Revenue: CFAF466,000,000,000 (taxes on petroleum organizations 35.4%; petroleum fees 24.1%; customs duties 17.8%; tax on organizations 5.2%; income tax 4.2%; business tax 3.9%). Expenditures: CFAF563,200,000,000 (development expenditure 42.8%, of which infrastructure 22.5%, social services 6.5%, defense 5.0%, administration and tourism 4.3%; current expenditure 31.9%; public debt 24.9%).
Public debt (external, outstanding; 1983): U.S.$1,282,400,000.
Tourism: receipts from visitors (1981) U.S.$15,000,000; expenditures by nationals abroad (1980) U.S.$95,000,000.
Production (metric tons except as noted) Agriculture, forestry, fishing (1984): roots and tubers 416,000, cassava 265,000, plantains 170,000, sugarcane 155,600, corn (maize) 10,000, peanuts (groundnuts) 10,000, bananas 8,000, palm oil 3,200, cacao beans 2,500, coffee 1,400; livestock (number of live animals) 150,000 pigs, 80,000 sheep, 2,000,000 chickens; roundwood 1,390,-000 cu m†; fish catch 52,638†. Mining and quarrying (1984): manganese 2,173,000; uranium 1,179; gold 550 troy oz‡. Manufacturing (1984): cement 183,000†; flour 21,600; raw sugar 15,000; beer 500,000 hectolitres; soft drinks 198,172 hectolitres; cigarettes 17,800,000 packs; textiles CFAF2,420,-000,000§. Construction: n.a. Energy production (consumption): electricity (kW-hr; 1984) 792,300,000 (677,400,000); crude petroleum (barrels; 1984) 63,865,000 (10,628,500‡); petroleum products (metric tons; 1983) 1,013,500 (387,500); natural gas (cu m; 1983) 148,500,000 (148,500,000); fuelwood and bagasse (cu m; 1983) 1,222,000 (1,222,000).
Population economically active (1984): total 533,000; participation rate of total population 46.5% (female, n.a.; unemployed, n.a.).

Price and earnings indexes (1980 = 100)

	1978	1979	1980	1981	1982	1983	1984‖
Consumer price index	82.5	89.0	100.0	108.7	126.8	137.0	151.3
Earnings index	...	...	100.0	101.1	126.6	156.3	...

Gross national product (at current market prices; 1983): U.S.$3,071,540,000 (U.S.$2,380 per capita).

Structure of gross domestic product and labour force

	1983 in value CFAF'000,000	% of total value	labour force	% of labour force
Agriculture	75,800	5.9	14,118¶	10.2¶
Mining	605,700	47.2	3,919	2.9
Manufacturing	57,200	4.5	4,123	3.0
Construction	93,000	7.3	13,154	9.5
Public utilities	19,500	1.5	⚲	⚲
Transportation and communication	50,600	4.0	⚲	⚲
Trade	105,000	8.2	3,732	2.7
Finance	10,000	0.8	⚲	⚲
Pub. admin., defense	102,600	8.0	42,678	31.0
Services	85,100	6.6	⚲	⚲
Other, including taxes on imports	77,500	6.0	56,143⚲	40.7⚲
TOTAL	1,282,000§	100.0	137,867¶	100.0

Household income and expenditure. Average household size (1980) 4.0; average annual income per household: n.a.; sources of income¶ (1983): private sector 73.4%, public sector 26.6%; expenditure: n.a.
Land use (1983): forested 77.6%; meadows and pastures 18.2%; agricultural and under permanent cultivation 1.8%; other 2.4%.

Foreign trade

Balance of trade (current prices)

	1979	1980	1981	1982	1983	1984
CFAF'000,000	+269,200	+351,000	+371,100	+252,100	+421,700	+492,600
% of total	54.3%	48.8%	45.0%	32.4%	39.4%	40.8%

Imports (1983): CFAF324,900,000,000 (machinery and mechanical equipment 23.8%; transport equipment and parts 15.1%; food, beverages, and tobacco products 12.3%; metal and metal products 10.7%; household and consumer products 5.3%; clothing and textiles 4.6%). *Major import sources* (1982): France 51.5%; United States 15.3%; Japan 6.9%; West Germany 6.1%.
Exports (1983): CFAF746,600,000,000 (crude petroleum and petroleum products 83.5%; wood 7.4%, of which okoumé and ozigo 5.5%; manganese ore and concentrate 4.2%; uranium ore and concentrate 3.3%). *Major export destinations* (1982): France 26.0%; United States 25.0%; Brazil 13.8%; United Kingdom 4.7%; Spain 4.3%; The Netherlands 4.2%.

Transport and communications

Transport. Railroads (1984): length 210 mi, 338 km; (1983) passengers carried 106,500; short ton cargo carried 609,776, metric ton cargo carried 553,180. Roads (1983): total length 4,668 mi, 7,513 km (paved 8%). Vehicles (1982): passenger cars 16,043; trucks and buses 10,695. Merchant marine (1984): vessels (100 gross tons and over) 20; total deadweight tonnage 169,212. Air transport (1983): passengers carried 850,000; cargo carried 36,376 short tons (33,000 metric tons); airports (1985) with scheduled flights 25.
Communications. Daily newspapers (1984): total number 2; total circulation 33,000; circulation per 1,000 population 35. Radio (1984): total number of receivers 100,000 (1 per 11 persons). Television (1984): total number of receivers 20,000 (1 per 57 persons). Telephones (1984): 11,600 (1 per 99 persons).

Education and health

Education (1982–83)

	schools	teachers	students	student/ teacher ratio
Primary	901	3,781	165,559	43.8
Secondary	47	1,161	22,350	19.3
Voc., teacher tr.	29	582	10,545	18.1
Higher	1	297	2,651	8.9

Educational attainment, n.a. *Literacy* (1978 est.): total population over age 15 literate 800,000 (77%); males literate, n.a.; females literate, n.a.
Health (1980): physicians 265 (1 per 4,053 persons); hospital beds 4,617 (1 per 253 persons); infant mortality rate per 1,000 live births (1980–85) 121.6.
Food (1980–82): daily per capita caloric intake 2,808 (vegetable products 88%, animal products 12%); 120% of FAO recommended minimum requirement.

Military

Total active duty personnel (1984): 3,900 (army 74.9%, navy 4.6%, air force 20.5%), not including 600 French troops. *Military expenditure as percent of GNP* (1983): 2.7% (world 6.1%); per capita expenditure U.S.$84.

*Detail does not add to total given because of rounding. †1983. ‡1982. §Value added. ‖ December. ¶Official government figures for salaried workers only, not including traditional agricultural workers; agricultural workers (FAO estimate, 1983) totaled 394,000 (74.6% of the labour force). ⚲Public utilities, transportation and communication, finance, and service employees included with other. δAt current prices.

Gambia, The

Official name: Republic of The Gambia.
Form of government: multiparty republic with one legislative house (House of Representatives [49]).
Head of state and government: President.
Capital: Banjul.
Official language: English.
Official religion: none.
Monetary unit: 1 dalasi (D) = 100 butut; valuation (Oct. 21, 1985) 1 U.S.$ = D3.49; 1 £ = D5.00.

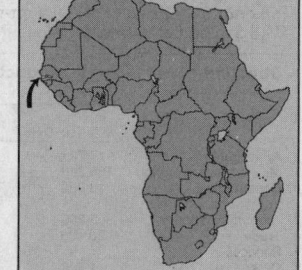

Area and population

Divisions	Capitals	area sq mi	area sq km	population 1983* census
Kombo Saint Mary	Kanifing	29	76	102,858
Lower River	Mansakonko	625	1,618	55,620
MacCarthy Island	Kuntaur/Georgetown	1,117	2,894	130,041
North Bank	Kerewan	871	2,256	111,411
Upper River	Basse	799	2,070	112,916
Western	Brikama	681	1,764	138,504
City				
Banjul		5	12	44,536
TOTAL		4,127	10,690	695,886

Demography

Population (1985): 749,200.
Density (1985): persons per sq mi 181.5, persons per sq km 70.1.
Urban–rural (1983): urban 21.2%; rural 78.8%.
Sex distribution (1980): male 49.42%; female 50.58%.
Age breakdown (1980): under 15, 44.3%; 15–29, 26.4%; 30–44, 15.4%; 45–59, 9.1%; 60–74, 4.0%; 75 and over, 0.7%.†
Population projection: (1990) 887,000; (2000) 1,244,000.
Doubling time: 20 years.
Ethnic composition (1980): Malinke 43.3%; Fulani 18.3%; Wolof 12.5%; Dyola 7.0%; Soninke 7.0%; other 11.9%.
Religious affiliation (1980): Muslim 84.8%; traditional beliefs 11.0%; Roman Catholic 1.9%; Bahā'ī 0.9%; other 1.4%.
Major cities (1983): Banjul 44,536; Brikama 20,208; Basse 5,612; Kau-Ur 5,338; Bansang 4,137.

Vital statistics

Birth rate per 1,000 population (1980–85): 47.5 (world avg. 29.0); legitimate, n.a.; illegitimate, n.a.
Death rate per 1,000 population (1980–85): 21.7 (world avg. 11.0).
Natural increase rate per 1,000 population (1980–85): 25.8 (world avg. 18.0).
Total fertility rate (avg. births per childbearing woman; 1980–85): 6.4.
Life expectancy at birth (1980–85): male 40.9 years; female 44.1 years.
Major causes of death: n.a.; however, major infectious diseases are malaria, gonococcal infections and syphilis, leprosy, chicken pox, schistosomiasis, tetanus, tuberculosis, and trypanosomiasis.

National economy

Budget (1984–85‡). Revenue: D172,642,000 (import and excise duties 52.3%; income tax 14.8%; export duties 5.5%). Expenditures: D335,801,000 (current expenditure D180,912,000, of which education, sports, and culture 13.0%; health, labour, and social welfare 8.0%; public works, transport, and communications 7.2%; agriculture and natural resources 7.0%).
Public debt (external, outstanding; 1983): U.S.$161,700,000.
Land use (1983): forested 19.8%; meadows and pastures 9.0%; agricultural and under permanent cultivation 16.0%; built-on area, wasteland, and other 55.2%.
Production (metric tons except as noted). Agriculture, forestry, fishing (1984): peanuts (groundnuts) in shell 114,000, millet 33,000, rice 22,000, corn (maize) 11,000, cassava 6,000, palm oil 2,500, palm kernels 2,000; livestock (number of live animals) 280,000 cattle, 185,000 goats, 175,000 sheep, 12,000 pigs, 320,000 chickens§; roundwood 783,000 cu m§; fish catch 9,598§. Mining and quarrying: n.a.; however, deposits of kaolin, tin, ilmenite, zircon, and rutile are important. Manufacturing: n.a.; however, major agriculture-based industries are peanut and palm kernel processing for oil and cake, fish preservation (salting, drying, and smoking), and brewing of alcoholic beverages; other industries include plastics, confectionery, furniture, and toiletries. Construction: n.a. Energy production (consumption): electricity (kW-hr; 1983) 40,000,000 (40,000,000); coal, none (n.a.); crude petroleum, none (n.a.); petroleum products (metric tons; 1983) none (51,000); natural gas, none (n.a.).
Population economically active (1983): total 312,000; participation rate of total population 44.6% (female, n.a.; unemployed, n.a.).

Price and earnings indexes (1980 = 100)

	1979	1980	1981	1982	1983	1984	1985
Consumer price index	93.7	100.0	106.1	117.6	130.1	158.9	174.3 ‖
Earnings index	...	...	...	...	...	...	...

Household income and expenditure. Average household size (1980) 4.9; average annual income per household: n.a., source of income: n.a., expenditure: n.a.
Gross national product (1983): U.S.$200,000,000 (U.S.$290 per capita).

Structure of gross domestic product and labour force

	1982–83 in value D'000,000	1982–83 % of total value	1983 labour force	1983 % of labour force
Agriculture	154.1	27.2	239,000	76.6
Mining	0.5	0.1		
Manufacturing	41.1	7.2		
Construction	45.7	8.1		
Public utilities	2.6	0.5		
Transportation and communication	47.8	8.4	73,000	23.4
Trade	134.4	23.7		
Finance	60.8	10.7		
Public administration	79.6	14.0		
Services	14.2	2.5		
Other	−13.6¶	−2.4¶		
TOTAL	567.2⁹	100.0	312,000	100.0

Tourism (1981): receipts from visitors U.S.$20,000,000; expenditures by nationals abroad U.S.$2,000,000.

Foreign tradeᵟ

Balance of trade (current prices)

	1979	1980	1981	1982	1983	1984
D'000,000	−117.6	−189.1	−156.8	−90.6	−133.4	−140.1
% of total	34.9%	63.3%	60.4%	31.5%	34.5%	30.1%

Imports (1984): D354,160,000 (food 37.3%, machinery and transport equipment 17.1%, manufactured goods 16.1%, minerals and fuel 12.3%, beverages and tobacco 5.0%; chemicals 4.4%). *Major import sources* (1982): European Economic Community countries (excluding United Kingdom) 31.2%; United Kingdom 21.5%; China 11.4%; Japan 4.4%; Senegal 3.8%.
Exports (1984): D162,568,000 (peanut oil 27.4%, shelled peanuts 24.2%, peanut meal 2.4%, fish and fish preparations 2.2%). *Major export destinations* (1982): EEC (excluding United Kingdom) 40.7%; West Africa 22.1%; United Kingdom 6.2%.

Transport and communications

Transport. Railroads: none. Roads (1983): total length 1,916 mi, 3,083 km (paved 15%). Vehicles (1983): passenger cars 6,100; trucks and buses 1,030. Merchant marine (1984): vessels (100 gross tons and over) 7; total deadweight tonnage 4,223. Air transport: passengers, n.a.; cargo, n.a.; airports (1985) with scheduled flights 1.
Communications. Daily newspapers: none. Radio (1983): total number of receivers 100,000 (1 per 7.0 persons). Television: none. Telephones (1980): 3,476 (1 per 182 persons).

Education and health

Education (1983–84)

	schools	teachers	students	student/ teacher ratio
Primary (age 6–12)	180	2,445	60,630	24.8
Secondary and post-secondary (age 13–20)	16	605	9,981	16.5
Voc., teacher tr.	16	457	8,923	19.5

Educational attainment (1973). Percent of adult population over age 20 having: no formal schooling 90.8%; primary education 6.2%; secondary 2.6%; higher 0.4%. *Literacy* (1980): total population over age 15 literate 67,700 (20.1%); males literate 47,700 (29.1%); females literate 20,000 (11.6%).
Health (1978): physicians 49 (1 per 12,069 persons); hospital beds 699 (1 per 846 persons); infant mortality rate per 1,000 live births (1975–80) 203.5.
Food (1980–82): daily per capita caloric intake 2,223 (vegetable products 93%, animal products 7%); 95% of FAO recommended minimum requirement.

Military

Total active duty personnel (1984): 475 (army 84.2%, navy 10.5%, air force 5.3%). *Military expenditure as percent of GNP* (1982): 0.0% (world 6.0%).

*Preliminary. †Detail does not add to 100.0% because of rounding. ‡Estimate. §1983. ‖May. ¶Less imputed bank charges. ⁹At current prices. ᵟImport figures are f.o.b. (free on board) in balance of trade and c.i.f. (cost, insurance, and freight) for commodities and trading partners.

E. STREICHAN—SHOSTAL

Fishing craft and market, on the Gambia River, near Banjul, The Gambia.

German Democratic Republic

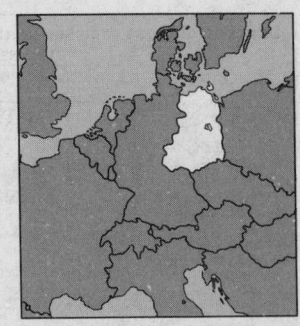

Official name: Deutsche Demokratische Republik (German Democratic Republic).
Form of government: unitary single-party republic with one legislative house (People's Chamber [500]).
Chief of state: Chairman, Council of State.
Head of government: Premier.
Capital: Berlin.
Official language: German.
Official religion: none.
Monetary unit: 1 Mark of Deutsche Demokratische Republik (M) = 100 Pfennige; valuation (Oct. 21, 1985) 1 U.S.$ = M2.64; 1 £ = M3.78.

Area and population		area		population
		sq mi	sq km	1983 estimate
Districts	**Capitals**			
Berlin, capital city	—	156	403	1,179,442
Cottbus	Cottbus	3,190	8,262	883,711
Dresden	Dresden	2,602	6,738	1,797,043
Erfurt	Erfurt	2,837	7,349	1,238,242
Frankfurt	Frankfurt	2,775	7,186	708,348
Gera	Gera	1,546	4,004	742,380
Halle	Halle	3,386	8,771	1,812,895
Karl-Marx-Stadt	Karl-Marx-Stadt	2,320	6,009	1,907,094
Leipzig	Leipzig	1,917	4,966	1,392,785
Magdeburg	Magdeburg	4,450	11,526	1,258,881
Neubrandenburg	Neubrandenburg	4,227	10,948	620,435
Potsdam	Potsdam	4,853	12,568	1,121,464
Rostock	Rostock	2,731	7,074	895,071
Schwerin	Schwerin	3,348	8,672	591,352
Suhl	Suhl	1,489	3,856	549,412
TOTAL		41,827	108,333*	16,698,555

Demography

Population (1985): 16,703,000.
Density (1985): persons per sq mi 399.3; persons per sq km 154.2.
Urban–rural (1984): urban 76.6%; rural 23.4%.
Sex distribution (1984): male 47.16%; female 52.84%.
Age breakdown (1983): under 15, 17.8%; 15–30, 25.6%; 31–45, 20.1%; 46–60, 17.7%; 61–75, 12.4%; 76 and over, 6.4%.
Population projection: (1990) 16,604,000; (2000) 16,483,000.
Doubling time: not applicable; population is declining.
Ethnic composition (1984): German 99%; other 1%.
Religious affiliation (1983): Protestant 80%; Roman Catholic 10%; atheist 10%.
Major cities (1984): Berlin (East) 1,185,500; Leipzig 559,000; Dresden 522,500; Karl-Marx-Stadt 318,900; Magdeburg 289,000; Rostock 239,400.

Vital statistics

Birth rate per 1,000 population (1984): 14.0 (world avg. 29.0); (1983) legitimate 74%; illegitimate 26%.
Death rate per 1,000 population (1984): 13.3 (world avg. 11.0).
Natural increase rate per 1,000 population (1984): 0.7 (world avg. 18.0).
Total fertility rate (avg. births per childbearing woman; 1980–85): 1.8.
Marriage rate per 1,000 population (1984): 8.0.
Divorce rate per 1,000 population: (1984): 3.0.
Life expectancy at birth (1983): male 69.1 years; female 75.1 years.
Major causes of death per 100,000 population (1983): circulatory diseases 825.0; malignant neoplasms (cancers) 212.0; pneumonia 23.0; stomach and intestinal diseases 9.0; tuberculosis 4.0.

National economy

Budget (1983). Revenue: M192,409,500,000 (revenue from nonagricultural state-owned enterprises 70.0%, social security contributions 8.6%, banking revenue 3.9%, health care contributions 3.8%). Expenditures: M191,689,100,000 (economic development 22.9%, social welfare 15.9%, economic subsidies and price supports 11.4%, health care 6.0%, education 6.0%, defense 6.0%, general administration 4.9%, cultural activities 1.8%).
Public debt (external, outstanding; 1982): U.S.$13,000,000,000.
Tourism (1983): total tourist arrivals 933,889.
Production (metric tons except as noted). Agriculture, forestry, fishing (1984): potatoes 7,753,000, sugar beets 6,500,000, barley 4,400,000, wheat 4,100,000, rye 2,300,000, oats 700,000; livestock (number of live animals; 1984) 13,058,000 pigs, 5,768,000 cattle, 2,359,000 sheep, 53,000,000 chickens; commercial timber 9,430,000 cu m, firewood 880,000 cu m†; fish catch 265,000†. Mining and quarrying (metal content except as noted; 1983): bauxite (gross amount) 60,000; iron ore 18,000; copper ore 12,000; nickel 2,200; tin 1,700; silver 1,450,000 troy oz. Manufacturing (1983): cement 11,782,000; steel 7,219,000; fertilizer 4,714,000; pig iron 2,207,000; plastics and synthetic resins 1,045,000; sulfuric acid 926,000; paper 860,000; sugar 846,000; lumber 2,246,000 cu m; 1,206,000 vacuum cleaners; 976,000 radios; 763,000 refrigerators; 667,000 television receivers; 504,000 washing machines. Construction (M; 1983): residential 6,170,300,000; nonresidential 17,688,600,000. Energy production (consumption): electricity (kW-hr; 1983) 104,928,000,000 (106,282,000,000); coal (metric tons; 1983) 277,968,000 (282,166,000); crude petroleum (barrels; 1983) 430,000 (166,076,000);

petroleum products (metric tons; 1982) 18,134,000 (15,284,000); natural gas (cu m; 1983) 7,230,000,000 (7,241,000,000).
Gross national product (at current market prices; 1983): U.S.$89,249,000,000 (U.S.$5,300 per capita).

Structure of net material product and labour force				
	1983			
	in value M'000,000	% of total value	labour force‡	% of labour force
Agriculture	17,200	7.6	895,900	10.6
Mining, manufacturing	156,600	68.8	3,539,200	41.9
Construction	13,000	5.7	563,500	6.7
Transportation and communication	9,200	4.0	643,700	7.6
Trade	20,400	9.0	850,900	10.1
Services	—	—	1,951,800§	23.1§
Other	11,200 ‖	4.9 ‖	—	—
TOTAL	227,600¶	100.0	8,445,000	100.0

Population economically active (1983): total 8,871,300; participation rate of population over age 15, 63.9% (female 48.0, unemployed, n.a.).

Price and earnings indexes (1970 = 100)							
	1977	1978	1979	1980	1981	1982	1983
Consumer price index	97.9	97.8	98.6	98.8	98.9	98.9	98.9
Monthly earnings index	124.0	128.8	132.8	135.2	138.5	142.2	144.1

Household income and expenditure. Average household size (1983) 3.1; average annual income per household M31,300 (U.S.$9,200); sources of income: wages and salaries 68.9%, social welfare 31.1%; expenditure (1983): consumer goods 28.9%, food 20.8%, education 15.4%, rent and utilities 11.0%, health and social services 6.3%.
Land use (1983): forested 27.3%; meadows and pastures 11.8%; agricultural and under permanent cultivation 47.3%; other 13.6%.

Foreign trade

Balance of trade (current prices)						
	1978	1979	1980	1981	1982	1983
M'000,000	−4,544	−4,005	−5,840	+1,073	+5,353	+8,031
% of total	4.7%	3.7%	4.9%	0.8%	3.7%	5.0%

Imports (1983): M76,196,700,000 (combustibles, minerals, and unfabricated metals 39.6%; machinery, equipment, and transportation equipment 29.9%; fabricated and partially fabricated industrial materials 17.8%; chemical products and other goods 8.3%; consumer goods 4.4%).
Exports (1983): M84,227,000,000 (machinery, equipment, and transportation equipment 47.8%; combustibles, minerals and unfabricated metals 17.7%; consumer goods 14.1%; chemical products 12.5%; fabricated industrial materials 7.9%). *Direction of total trade?:* U.S.S.R. 37.9%; Czechoslovakia 7.4%; West Germany 6.4%; Hungary 5.1%; Poland 4.9%; Bulgaria 3.0%.

Transport and communications

Transport. Railroads (1983): length 8,840 mi, 14,226 km; passenger-mi 14,046,000,000, passenger-km 22,605,000,000; short ton-mi cargo 37,590,000,000, metric ton-km cargo 54,884,000,000. Roads (1983): total length 29,440 mi, 47,380 km (paved 100%). Vehicles (1983): passenger cars 3,019,875; trucks and buses 276,364. Merchant marine (1984): vessels (100 gross tons and over) 409; total deadweight tonnage 1,791,006. Air transport (1983): passenger-mi 1,433,600,000, passenger-km 2,307,100,000; short ton-mi cargo 49,381,000, metric ton-km cargo 72,100,000; airports (1985) with scheduled flights 4.
Communications. Daily newspapers (1983): total number 39; total circulation 8,844,700; circulation per 1,000 population 530. Radio (1984): total number of receivers 6,490,000 (1 per 2.6 persons). Television (1984): total number of receivers 5,928,000 (1 per 2.9 persons). Telephones (1984): 3,441,000 (1 per 4.8 persons).

Education and health

Education (1983–84)				
	schools	teachers	students	student/ teacher ratio
Primary (age 6–10)	5,666	54,971	766,745	13.9
Secondary (age 10–18)	5,711	112,172	1,265,349	11.3
Vocational	4,500	56,577	414,044	7.3
Higher	54	29,700	434,326	14.6

Educational attainment (1983). Percent of adult population over age 20 having: primary education, virtually 100%; academic secondary 15.5%; vocational 75.9%; higher 8.6%. *Literacy* (1984): total population over age 15 literate, virtually 100%.
Health (1984): physicians 36,200 (1 per 461 persons); hospital beds 171,280 (1 per 98 persons); infant mortality rate per 1,000 live births (1983) 11.4.
Food (1980–82): daily per capita caloric intake 3,720 (vegetable products 65%, animal products 35%); 142% of FAO recommended minimum requirement.

Military

Total active duty personnel (1984): 172,000 (army 69.8%, navy 8.1%, air force 22.1%). *Military expenditure as percent of GNP* (1983): 6.4% (world 6.1%); per capita expenditure U.S.$563.

*Detail does not add to total given because of rounding. †1983. ‡Employed. §Includes finance, public administration, and defense. ‖ Other material activities. ¶At current prices. ?Separate figures are not available for import sources and export destinations.

Germany, Federal Republic of

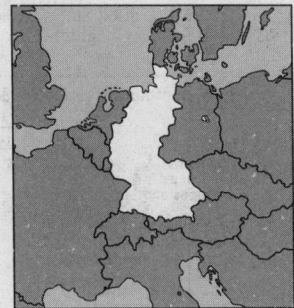

Official name: Bundesrepublik Deutschland (Federal Republic of Germany).
Form of government: federal multiparty republic with two legislative houses (Federal Council [45]; Federal Diet [520]).
Chief of state: President.
Head of government: Chancellor.
Capital: Bonn (provisional).
Official language: German.
Official religion: none.
Monetary unit: 1 Deutsche Mark (DM) = 100 Pfennige; valuation (Oct. 21, 1985) 1 U.S.$ = DM2.64; 1 £ = DM3.78.

Area and population		area		population
		sq mi	sq km	1985 estimate*
States	**Capitals**			
Baden–Württemberg	Stuttgart	13,804	35,751	9,241,000
Bayern	Munich	27,241	70,553	10,958,000
Bremen	Bremen	156	404	666,000
Hamburg	Hamburg	292	755	1,592,000
Hessen	Wiesbaden	8,152	21,115	5,535,000
Niedersachsen	Hannover	18,319	47,447	7,216,000
Nordrhein–Westfalen	Düsseldorf	13,151	34,062	16,704,000
Rheinland–Pfalz	Mainz	7,663	19,848	3,624,000
Saarland	Saarbrücken	993	2,571	1,051,000
Schleswig–Holstein	Kiel	6,069	15,721	2,614,000
Berlin (West)†	Berlin (West)	185	480	1,849,000
TOTAL		96,026‡	248,706‡	61,049,000‡

Demography

Population (1985): 60,940,000.
Density (1985): persons per sq mi 638.5, persons per sq km 246.5.
Urban–rural (1980): urban 84.7%; rural 15.3%.
Sex distribution (1984): male 47.80%; female 52.20%.
Age breakdown (1984): under 15, 15.9%; 15–29, 24.2%; 30–44, 20.8%; 45–59, 19.1%; 60–74, 13.5%; 75 and over 6.5%.
Population projection: (1990) 59,600,000; (2000) 58,800,000.
Doubling time: not applicable; population is declining.
Ethnic composition (1983): German 92.5%; Turk 2.5%; Yugoslav 1.0%; Italian 0.9%; Greek 0.5%; Austrian 0.3%; Spanish 0.3%; Dutch 0.2%; other 1.8%.
Religious affiliation (1980): Christian 92.8%, of which Protestant 46.7% (including Lutheran-Reformed tradition 23.5%, Lutheran tradition 21.7%, Reformed tradition 0.7%, other 0.8%), Roman Catholic 43.8%, New Apostolic (non-Roman) Catholic 0.8%, Greek Orthodox 0.6%, other 0.9%; nonreligious 3.7%; Muslim 2.4%; atheist 0.9%; Jewish 0.1%; other 0.1%.
Major cities (1984 est.): Berlin (West) 1,851,800; Hamburg 1,600,300; Munich 1,277,000; Cologne 932,400; Essen 628,800; Frankfurt am Main 604,600; Dortmund 584,800; Düsseldorf 570,700; Stuttgart 563,200; Bonn 291,700.
Place of birth: n.a.
Mobility: n.a.
Households (1982). Number of households 25,336,000; average household size 2.4; 1 person 31.3%, 2 persons 28.7%, 3 persons 17.6%, 4 persons 14.4%, 5 or more persons 8.0%. Family households: 17,410,000 (68.7%); nonfamily 7,926,000.
Immigration (1983): immigrants admitted 372,027, from Poland 14.9%, Italy 10.3%, Turkey 7.6%, United States 5.9%, Yugoslavia 4.8%, Austria 4.2%, United Kingdom 3.6%, German Democratic Republic 3.6%.

Vital statistics

Birth rate per 1,000 population (1984): 9.5 (world avg. 29.0); legitimate, 91.2%; illegitimate, 8.8%.
Death rate per 1,000 population (1984): 11.3 (world avg. 11.0).
Natural increase rate per 1,000 population (1984): −1.8 (world avg. 18.0).
Total fertility rate (avg. births per childbearing woman; 1983): 1.3.
Marriage rate per 1,000 population (1984): 6.0.
Divorce rate per 1,000 population (1983): 2.0.
Life expectancy at birth (1981–83): male 70.5 years; female 77.1 years.
Major causes of death per 100,000 population (1983): diseases of the circulatory system 585.0, of which cerebrovascular disease 160.1, acute myocardial infarction 134.6; malignant neoplasms (cancers) 262.3, of which stomach, colon, and rectum 64.4, bronchial, lung, and tracheal 41.9, breast 21.9; pulmonary diseases 66.4, of which pneumonia 28.0, chronic bronchitis 22.4; chronic liver disease and cirrhosis 25.1; suicide 21.3.

Social indicators

Educational attainment (1982). Percent of adult population over age 14 having: less than full primary education, virtually zero; primary and secondary 34.9%, of which primary with general secondary 15.9%; some post secondary in preparation for higher education 10.0%; completion of more advanced education 55.1%, of which trade school graduates with apprenticeship 44.7%, skilled technicians or craftsmen 4.6%, engineers 1.9%, university graduates (all levels) 3.9%.
Quality of working life (1983). Average workweek: 40.8 hours. Annual rate per 100,000 workers for: injury or accident at work 5,363; injury or accident on way to work 578; industrial illness 124; death 13.4§. Proportion of labour force insured for damages or income loss resulting from: injury, virtually 100%; permanent disability, virtually 100%; death, virtually 100%. Average days lost to labour stoppages per 1,000 workers (1983): 2. Principal means of journey to work: private automobile 32.4%; public transportation 19.2%; bicycle 6.2%; foot 37.5%; other 4.7%. Percentage of unemployed workers not eligible for unemployment benefits (1984): 28.9%.

Distribution of income (1978)				
percent of household income by quintile				
1	2	3	4	5 (highest)
6.9	11.0	15.9	21.9	44.8

Access to services. Proportion of dwellings having: electricity 99.7%; piped water supply 99.2%; flush sewage disposal 94.2%; public fire protection, n.a.
Social participation. Eligible voters participating in last national election 89.1%. Population participating in voluntary work: n.a. Trade union membership in total work force (1984): 26.6%. Practicing religious population in total affiliated population: n.a.
Social deviance (1983). Offense rate per 100,000 population for: murder 4.4; sexual abuse 69.4, of which child molestation 17.8, rape 17.6; assault and battery 107.5; larceny 4,302.5, of which burglary 367.2, auto theft 130.6. Incidence per 100,000 in general population (late 1970s) of: alcoholism 2,500 to 3,000; drug and substance abuse 650; suicide 21 ‖.
Leisure (late 1970s). Favourite leisure activities: watching television 56%; reading 30%.
Material well-being (1983). Households possessing: automobile 65%; telephone 88%; colour television receiver 73%; refrigerator 79%; air conditioner 56%¶; electric washing machine 83%.

National economy

Gross national product (at current market prices; 1983): U.S.$655,500,000,-000 (U.S.$10,672 per capita).

Structure of gross domestic product and labour force	1984		1983	
	in value DM'000,000	% of total value	labour force	% of labour force
Agriculture	35,290	2.0	1,397,000	5.1
Mining	63,930?	3.7?	336,000	1.2
Manufacturing	559,080	32.0	8,563,000	31.3
Construction	101,240	5.8	1,952,000	7.1
Public utilities	?	?	247,000	0.9
Transportation and communication	264,610	15.2	1,573,000	5.8
Trade			4,055,000	14.8
Finance	487,280	27.9	1,642,000	6.0
Services			7,005,000	25.6
Pub. admin., defense	199,540	11.4		
Other	34,000	2.0	551,000	2.0
TOTAL	1,744,990‡	100.0	27,321,000	100.0‡

Budget (1982). Revenue: DM480,730,000,000 (tax revenue 93.4%, of which social security contributions from employers 25.3%, from employees 21.2%, taxes on individual wages 13.6%, value added tax on goods and services 12.1%, taxes paid by self-employed or nonemployed 8.5%, mineral oil tax 4.7%, tobacco tax 2.5%; nontax revenue 6.0%, of which income from property 4.7%). Expenditures: DM506,030,000,000 (social security and welfare 49.7%; health 19.3%; defense 9.1%; economic services 7.4%, of which transportation and communication 5.7%; education 0.8%).
Total national debt (1984) DM367,300,000,000.
Tourism (1983): receipts from visitors U.S.$5,460,000,000; expenditures by nationals abroad U.S.$15,022,000,000.

Manufacturing, mining, and construction enterprises (1983)				
	no. of enter-prises	no. of tradesmen and professionals	wages as a % of avg. of all wages	annual gross production value§ (DM'000,000)
Road motor vehicle	1,846	789,000	112.2	147,906
Food and beverage	3,878	458,000	89.3	145,078
Chemical	1,161	568,000	121.5	144,004
Machinery (nonelectric)	4,555	952,000	104.3	137,454
Machinery and appliances (electric)	2,292	920,000	103.8	127,543
Petroleum and natural gas	54	38,000	157.4	114,466
Iron and steel	96	252,000	98.6	49,542
Mining	86	232,000	108.8	36,588
Calculator, computer	2,055	261,000	91.2	35,295
Textile	1,456	243,000	76.5	32,006
Cement, sand, and gravel	2,128	162,000	101.4	29,004
Plastics	1,639	181,000	89.5	26,461
Wood and wood products	2,248	200,000	88.6	25,100
Metalware	1,287	152,000	104.5	24,843
Construction	16,913	1,063,000	89.2	...

Production (metric tons except as noted). Agriculture, forestry, fishing (1984): sugar beets 20,018,000, barley 10,284,000, wheat 10,223,000, potatoes 7,753,000, oats 2,083,000, rye 1,930,000; livestock (number of live animals) 23,449,000 pigs, 15,552,000 cattle; 1,218,000 sheep; roundwood 29,485,000 cu m ‖; fish catch 305,620 ‖, of which Atlantic cod 68,832, Atlantic redfish 45,942, blue mussel 31,634. Mining and quarrying (1984): iron ore 312,600ŏ, zinc 95,500ŏ, lead 21,000ŏ, copper 1,000ŏ. Manufacturing (value added at factor cost in DM; 1982): machinery and transport equipment 149,247,000,000, of which electrical equipment 50,671,000,000, transport equipment 46,196,000,000; chemicals (including medicinal products) 37,630,000,000; food and beverages 23,884,000,000; calculators and computers 13,143,000,000; semiprocessed iron and steel 12,851,000,000; textiles 9,853,000,000; metalware 9,342,000,000; furniture and other wood products 9,004,000,000; plastics and other synthetic products 8,317,000,000; printed

matter 7,525,000,000; clocks and other precision products 6,936,000,000; clothing 6,294,000,000; office machines 5,795,000,000; cast metals 4,474,-000,000. Construction (1982): residential 184,821,000 cu m; nonresidential 160,532,000 cu m; restoration and conversion 2,804,000 cu m.

Service enterprises (1983)

	no. of enter-prises	no. of employees	weekly wage as a % of all wages	annual turnover (DM'000,000)
Gas	114	24,000	...	32,175
Water	157	17,000	...	3,557
Electrical power	452	229,000	...	100,704
Transport				
air	157	35,000	...	9,911
buses, trains	5,733	144,000	...	10,660
shipping	1,963	11,000	...	...
Communication				
press	2,100	204,000	...	25,155
film□	2,111	23,000	...	2,099
Mail	18,099	501,000	...	44,233
Hotels and restaurants□	119,020	653,000	...	39,895
Wholesale trade◇	132,000	1,239,000	...	...
Retail trade◇	507,000	2,282,000	...	...
Health services◇	88,000	318,000	...	...
Financial services	36,000	427,000	...	...

Energy production (consumption): electricity (kW-hr; 1984) 394,283,000,000 (373,669,000,000§); hard coal (metric tons; 1984) 84,866,000 (91,951,000§); lignite-brown coal (metric tons; 1984) 126,740,000 (130,126,000§); crude petroleum (barrels; 1984) 29,600,000 (609,570,000); petroleum products (metric tons; 1984) 84,938,000 (101,401,000); natural gas (cu m; 1984) 15,-950,000,000 (48,910,000,000§).

Population economically active (1983): total 28,542,000; participation rate of population ages 15–64, 67.3% (female 38.9%, unemployed 8.2%).

Price and earnings indexes (1980 = 100)

	1979	1980	1981	1982	1983	1984	1985
Consumer price index	94.9	100.0	106.3	111.9	115.6	118.4	120.9△
Hourly earnings index	93.8	100.0	105.5	110.5	114.1	116.8	121.6†

Household income and expenditure. Average household size (1984) 2.4; average annual net income per household (1984) DM41,693 (U.S.$14,650); sources of take home income (1984): wages 84.1%, self-employment 7.1%, investments 8.8%; expenditure (1984): food 26.0%, rent 18.4%, transportation 16.3%, household expenses 8.4%, entertainment and education 8.3%, clothing and footwear 8.1%, electricity and gas 6.6%, other 7.9%.

Land use (1983): forested 30.0%; meadows and pastures 19.0%; agricultural and under permanent cultivation 30.5%; other 20.5%.

Financial aggregates

	1978	1979	1980	1981	1982	1983	1984
Exchange rate, DM per:							
U.S. dollar	1.8280	1.7315	1.9590	2.2548	2.3765	2.7238	3.1480
£	3.7191	3.8509	4.6722	4.3022	3.8369	3.9511	3.6407
SDR	2.3815	2.2810	2.4985	2.6245	2.6215	2.8517	3.0857
International reserves (U.S.$)							
Total (excl. gold; '000,000)	48,474	52,549	48,592	43,719	44,762	42,674	40,141
SDRs ('000,000)	1,796	2,076	1,840	1,609	2,054	1,613	1,362
Reserve pos. in IMF ('000,000)	4,302	3,125	2,291	2,465	3,088	3,748	3,750
Foreign exchange	42,376	47,348	44,461	39,645	39,620	37,313	35,028
Gold ('000,000 fine troy oz)	118.64	95.25	95.18	95.18	95.18	95.18	95.18
% world reserves	11.44	10.09	9.99	10.00	10.05	10.06	10.06
Interest and prices							
Central bank discount (%)	3.0	6.0	7.5	7.5	5.0	4.0	4.5
Gov't. bond yield (%)	6.4	7.7	8.7	10.6	9.1	8.0	7.8
Industrial share prices							
(1980 = 100)	112.3	106.8	100.0	100.4	99.0	133.5	150.4
Balance of payments (U.S.$ '000,000)							
Balance of visible trade	24.73	16.85	8.99	16.58	25.26	22.25	22.24
Imports, f.o.b.	112.97	148.89	176.50	154.49	143.67	140.40	141.18
Exports, f.o.b.	137.70	165.75	185.48	171.07	168.93	162.65	163.42
Balance of invisibles	−6.62	−11.40	−11.40	−9.57	−10.05	−7.14	−4.63
Balance of payments, current account	9.27	−6.19	−16.00	−4.77	3.59	4.57	6.56

Foreign trade

Balance of trade (current prices)

	1979	1980	1981	1982	1983	1984
DM'000,000	+22,429	+8,947	+27,720	+51,277	+42,089	+53,967
% of total	3.7%	1.5%	3.6%	6.4%	5.1%	5.8%

Imports (1984): DM434,257,000,000 (machinery and transport equipment 21.9%, of which transport equipment 4.7%, electrical machinery 4.0%, office equipment 3.1%; mineral fuels 20.4%, of which crude petroleum and petroleum products 16.0%, natural gas 3.8%; food and beverages 10.2%, of which fruits and vegetables 3.1%, coffee, tea, and spices 1.7%, meat and meat products 1.3%; chemicals and chemical products 8.5%, of which plastics and synthetics 2.2%, medicinal products 0.8%; clothing and wearing apparel 4.6%; iron and steel 3.3%; textiles and yarn 3.2%; metallic ores and scrap metal 2.0%; paper and paper products 1.9%). *Major import sources:* The Netherlands 12.2%; France 10.6%; Italy 7.8%; United Kingdom 7.7%; United States 7.2%; Belgium–Luxembourg 6.6%.

Exports (1984): DM448,223,000,000 (machinery and transport equipment 44.8%, of which transport equipment 15.3%, specialized equipment for specific industries 5.8%, electrical machinery 5.5%; chemicals and chemical products 13.6%, of which plastics and synthetics 3.3%, medicinal products 1.3%, dyes and dye products 1.2%; iron and steel 4.9%; food and beverages 4.7%, of which dairy products 1.1%, meat and meat products 0.6%; textiles and yarn 3.3%; paper and paper products 1.9%). *Major export destinations:*

France 12.6%; United States 9.6%; The Netherlands 8.6%; United Kingdom 8.3%; Italy 7.7%; Belgium–Luxembourg 7.0%; Switzerland 5.3%; Austria 5.0%.

Trade by commodity group (1984)

		imports		exports	
SITC Group		U.S.$'000,000	%	U.S.$'000,000	%
00	Food and live animals	14,740	9.7	7,354	4.3
01	Beverages and tobacco	1,445	0.9	1,089	0.6
02	Crude materials, excluding fuels	10,891	7.1	3,446	2.0
03	Mineral fuels, lubricants, and related materials	31,104	20.4	5,660	3.3
04	Animal and vegetable oils, fat, and waxes	1,038	0.7	903	0.5
05	Chemicals and related products, n.e.s.	13,008	8.5	23,285	13.6
06	Basic manufactures	25,045	16.4	32,039	18.7
07	Machinery and transport equipment	33,431	21.9	76,848	44.8
08	Miscellaneous manufactured articles	17,413	11.4	16,299	9.5
09	Goods not classified by kind	4,461	2.9	4,621	2.7
TOTAL		152,576	100.0‡	171,546‡	100.0

Direction of trade (1984)⊕

	imports		exports	
	U.S.$'000,000	%	U.S.$'000,000	%
Africa	6,689	4.4	5,430	3.2
Asia	19,563	12.9‡	19,163	11.2
Middle East	6,285	4.1	10,285	6.0
Japan	6,440	4.2	2,432	1.4
other Asia	6,838	4.5	6,446	3.8
South America	4,894	3.2	3,077	1.8
North and Central America	13,203	8.7	19,082	11.2
United States	10,959	7.2	16,421	9.6
other North and Central Am.	2,244	1.5	2,661	1.6
Europe	106,595	70.2‡	122,264	71.7‡
EEC	73,097	48.1	81,827	48.0
U.S.S.R.	7,169	4.7	4,703	2.8
other Europe	26,329	17.3	35,734	21.0
Oceania	927	0.6	1,543	0.9
TOTAL	152,576	100.0	171,546	100.0

Transport and communications

Transport. Railroads (1984): length 42,992 mi ∥, 69,190 km ∥; passenger-mi 23,997,000,000, passenger-km 38,619,000,000; short ton-mi cargo 40,986,-000,000, metric ton-km cargo 59,839,000,000. Roads (1983): total length 302,764 mi, 487,251 km (paved 99%). Vehicles (1984): passenger cars 25,217,800; trucks and buses 1,348,200. Merchant marine (1984): vessels (100 gross tons and over) 1,813; total deadweight tonnage 9,519,256. Air transport (1984): passenger-mi 15,083,000,000, passenger-km 24,274,000,-000; short ton-mi cargo 1,606,368,000, metric ton-km cargo 2,345,258,000; airports (1985) with scheduled flights 26.

Communications. Daily newspapers (1981): total number 380; total circulation 20,410,000; circulation per 1,000 population 330.9. Radio (1984): total number of receivers 24,600,000 (1 per 2.5 persons). Television (1984): total number of receivers 22,127,000 (1 per 2.8 persons). Telephones (1983): 31,370,022 (1 per 2.0 persons).

Education and health

Education (1983–84)

	schools	teachers	students	student/teacher ratio
Primary (age 6–10)	21,453	307,851	4,773,336	15.5
Secondary (age 10–19)	5,374	191,730	3,216,542	16.8
Voc., teacher tr.	7,816	87,975	2,718,404	30.9
Higher	...	311,460	1,267,263	4.1

Literacy (1983): virtually 100%.
Health (1984): physicians 147,467 (1 per 415 persons); hospital beds (1983) 682,747 (1 per 90 persons); infant mortality rate per 1,000 live births 9.6.
Food (1980–82): daily per capita caloric intake 3,448 (vegetable products 62%, animal products 38%); 129% of FAO recommended minimum requirement.

Military

Total active duty personnel (1984): 495,000 (army 67.8%, navy 7.3%, air force 21.4%, other 3.5%). *Military expenditure as percent of GNP* (1983): 3.4% (world 6.1%); per capita expenditure U.S.$367.

*January 1. †Berlin (West) is under tripartite (France, United Kingdom, United States) jurisdiction and is only administratively a part of West Germany. ‡Detail does not add to total given because of rounding. §1982. ∥1983. ¶1979. ⊙Public utilities included with mining. □1981. ◇1970. △September. †Second quarter. ⊕ Totals include $705 million in imports and $987 million in exports (0.5% of all foreign trade; mostly special transactions) not distributable by region.

Ghana

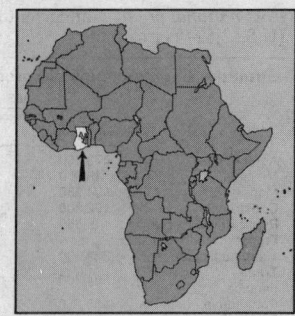

Official name: Republic of Ghana.
Form of government: republic with
  one ruling body (Provisional
  National Defense Council [6]).
Head of state and government:
  Chairman of the Provisional
  National Defense Council.
Capital: Accra.
Official language: English.
Official religion: none.
Monetary unit: 1 cedi (₵) = 100
  pesewas; valuation (Oct. 21, 1985)
  1 U.S.$ = ₵60.16; 1 £ = ₵86.27.

Area and population

		area		population
Regions	Capitals	sq mi	sq km	1984 census
Ashanti	Kumasi	9,417	24,389	2,089,683
Brong-Ahafo	Sunyani	15,273	39,557	1,179,407
Central	Cape Coast	3,794	9,826	1,145,520
Eastern	Koforidua	7,461	19,323	1,679,483
Greater Accra	Accra	1,253	3,245	1,420,066
Northern	Tamale	27,175	70,384	1,162,645
Upper East	Bolgatanga	3,414	8,842	771,584
Upper West	Wa	7,134	18,476	439,161
Volta	Ho	7,942	20,570	1,201,095
Western	Sekondi-Takoradi	9,236	23,921	1,116,930
TOTAL		92,098*	238,533	12,205,574

Demography

Population (1985 est.): 12,815,300.
Density (1985): persons per sq mi 139.1, persons per sq km 53.7.
Urban–rural (1984): urban 31.3%; rural 68.7%.
Sex distribution (1984): male 49.11%; female 50.89%.
Age breakdown (1985): under 15, 46.6%; 15–29, 26.1%; 30–44, 14.5%; 45–59, 8.3%; 60–74, 3.8%; 75 and over, 0.7%.
Population projection: (1990) 15,886,000; (2000) 21,923,000.
Doubling time: 21.2 years.
Ethno-linguistic composition (1983): Akan 44.1%; Mossi-Dagomba 15.9%; Ewe 13.0%; Ga-Adangme 8.3%; Gurma 3.5%; Yoruba 1.6%; other 13.6%.
Religious affiliation (1980): Christian 62.6%, of which Protestant 27.9%, Roman Catholic 18.7%, African indigenous 16.0%; traditional beliefs 21.4%; Muslim 15.7%, of which Ahmadīyah 7.9%; other 0.3%.
Major cities (1984): Accra 859,600; Kumasi 348,900; Tamale 136,800; Tema 99,600; Sekondi-Takoradi 93,900.

Vital statistics

Birth rate per 1,000 population (1980–85): 47.0 (world avg. 29.0); legitimate, n.a.; illegitimate, n.a.
Death rate per 1,000 population (1980–85): 14.6 (world avg. 11.0).
Natural increase rate per 1,000 population (1980–85): 32.4 (world avg. 18.0).
Total fertility rate (avg. births per childbearing woman; 1980–85): 6.5.
Marriage rate per 1,000 population: n.a.
Divorce rate per 1,000 population: n.a.
Life expectancy at birth (1980–85): male 50.3 years; female 53.7 years.
Major causes of death per 100,000 population: n.a.; however, among the major infectious diseases are malaria, tuberculosis, leprosy, trypanosomiasis (sleeping sickness), and onchocerciasis (river blindness).

National economy

Budget (1984)†. Revenue: ₵22,583,800,000 (customs and excise taxes 75.1%, of which excise duties 28.6%, import duties 19.6%, sales tax 8.7%; income and property tax estimate 24.0%). Expenditures: ₵26,871,500,000 (recurrent expenditures 83.0%; development 17.0%).
Public debt (external, outstanding; 1983): U.S.$1,095,100,000.
Tourism: receipts from visitors (1981) U.S.$1,000,000; expenditures by nationals abroad (1982) U.S.$25,000,000.
Production (metric tons except as noted). Agriculture, forestry, fishing (1984): roots and tubers 3,510,000 (of which cassava 1,900,000, yams 880,000, cocoyams 750,000, taro 730,000), cereals 872,000 (of which corn [maize] 534,000, sorghum 140,000, millet 132,000, rice 66,000), plantains 650,000, cocoa 188,000, coconuts 160,000, sugarcane 110,000, peanuts (groundnuts) 90,000, oranges 35,000, lemons 30,000, palm kernels 30,000, pulses 11,000; livestock (number of live animals) 2,000,000 goats, 2,000,000 sheep, 800,000 cattle, 375,000 pigs, 13,000,000 chickens; roundwood 9,380,000 cu m‡; fish catch 228,000‡ (of which anchovies 30,700‡). Mining and quarrying (1983): manganese ore 173,100; bauxite 70,400; gold 8,601 kg; diamonds 339,300 carats. Manufacturing (1983): kerosine, gasoline, and diesel 394,000; cement 278,000; cocoa cake, cocoa butter, and cocoa liquor 21,697; wheat flour 17,981; soap 3,147; iron rods 1,535; toothpaste 27; cloth 7,100,000 metres; beer 310,000 hectolitres; evaporated milk 100,000 hectolitres‡; ice cream 4,440 hectolitres; cigarettes 1,074,000,000 units. Construction (value added in ₵'000; 1981): 1,480,400. Energy production (consumption): electricity (kW-hr; 1983) 2,589,000,000 (2,189,000,000); coal (metric tons; 1983) none (2,000); crude petroleum (barrels; 1983) 515,000 (8,022,000); petroleum products (metric tons; 1983) 904,000 (641,000); natural gas, none (n.a.).
Household income and expenditure. Average household size (1980) 5.1; average annual income per household (1978) ₵9,600 (U.S.$ §); source of income: n.a.; expenditure (1978): food and beverages 36.9%, housing

14.8%, clothing and footwear 14.7%, transport and communication 6.1%, health care 2.3%.
Gross national product (at current market prices; 1983): U.S.$3,980,000,000 (U.S.$320 per capita).

Structure of gross domestic product and labour force

	1982			
	in value ₵'000,000	% of total value	labour force	% of labour force
Agriculture	52,798	58.2	2,292,000	50.0
Mining	360.4	0.4	91,700	2.0
Manufacturing	3,116.8	3.4	366,700	8.0
Construction	2,421.9	2.7	}	
Public utilities	513.4	0.6		
Transportation and communication	2,567.8	2.8		
Trade	22,950.5	25.3		
Finance	1,843.7	2.0	1,833,600	40.0
Pub. admin., defense	4,052.4	4.5		
Services	548.7	0.6		
Other	−435.3 ‖	−0.5 ‖		
TOTAL	90,738.3¶	100.0	4,584,000	100.0

Population economically active: total (1983) 4,719,000; participation rate of population over age 15, 50% (female [1981] 41.1%, unemployed [1982] 23.2%).

Price and earnings indexes (1980 = 100)

	1978	1979	1980	1981	1982	1983	1984
Consumer price index	43.2	66.6	100.0	216.5	264.8	590.1	824.3
Earnings index	49.0	62.0	100.0	...	139.9	...	...

Land use (1983): forested 37.2%; meadows and pastures 15.0%; agricultural and under permanent cultivation 12.0%; other 35.8%.

Foreign trade♀

Balance of trade (current prices)

	1978	1979	1980	1981	1982	1983
₵'000,000	+51.7	+605.8	+816.2	+159.5	+639.3	−946.5
% of total	1.7%	12.4%	13.4%	2.8%	15.4%	6.3%

Imports (1980): ₵3,103,600,000 (machinery and transport equipment 29.7%; petroleum products 22.8%; chemicals 15.6%; basic manufactures 12.3%; food and live animals 7.8%, of which rice 1.5%, wheat and flour 0.6%). *Major import sources:* United Kingdom 21.8%; Nigeria 20.3%; United States 12.1%; West Germany 9.4%; Japan 3.8%.
Exports (1982): ₵2,402,000,000 (cocoa beans 43.8%; gold 13.3%; cocoa products 5.6%; logs and timber 1.8%; industrial diamonds 0.6%). *Major export destinations:* United States 16.0%; United Kingdom 11.3%; Japan 8.3%; West Germany 7.9%; U.S.S.R. 6.8%; Sweden 4.6%; Romania 1.4%.

Transport and communications

Transport. Railroads (1983): length 592 mi, 953 km; passenger-mi 236,000,000, passenger-km 380,000,000; short ton-mi cargo 41,000,000, metric ton-km cargo 61,000,000. Roads (1983): total length 13,535 mi, 21,783 km (paved 3%). Vehicles (1983): passenger cars 52,864; trucks and buses 24,312. Merchant marine (1984): vessels (100 gross tons and over) 124; total deadweight tonnage 208,896. Air transport (1982): passenger-mi 181,000,000, passenger-km 291,000,000; short ton-mi cargo 21,200,000, metric ton-km cargo 31,000,000; airports (1985) with scheduled flights 4.
Communications. Daily newspapers (1984): total number 4; total circulation 460,000; circulation per 1,000 population 37. Radio (1984): 2,020,000 receivers (1 per 6.2 persons). Television (1984): 62,000 receivers (1 per 202 persons). Telephones (1982): 70,653 (1 per 168 persons).

Education and health

Education (1983–84)

	schools	teachers	students	student/ teacher ratio
Primary (6–11)	8,214δ	51,631□	1,643,455	31.8
Secondary (12–18)	4,758◇	32,795□	811,865	24.8
Voc., teacher tr.◇	62	1,727	32,288	19.3
Higher	3△	1,041◇	7,971†	...

Educational attainment (1970). Percent of adult population over age 25 having: no formal schooling 77.7%; primary education 5.8%; some secondary 12.8%; complete secondary 3.3%; higher 0.4%. *Literacy* (1980): total population over age 15 literate 44.8%; males literate 53.7%; females literate 36.2%.
Health (1981): physicians 1,665 (1 per 6,956 persons); hospital beds 20,582 (1 per 563 persons); infant mortality rate per 1,000 live births (1980–85) 98.
Food (1980–82): daily per capita caloric intake 1,657 (vegetable products 94%, animal products 6%); 82% of FAO minimum recommended requirement.

Military

Total active duty personnel (1984): 12,600 (army 79.4%, navy 9.5%, air force 11.1%). *Military expenditure as percent of GNP* (1982): 0.7% (world 6.1%); per capita expenditure U.S.$16.

*Detail does not add to total given because of rounding. †Budget (1985): revenue ₵39,900,000,000; expenditure ₵48,510,000,000; no breakdown available. ‡1983. §Unofficial exchange rate (7.5 to 9.9 times the official rate) does not allow direct conversion into other currencies. ‖ Import duties, less imputed bank service charge. ¶At current prices. ♀Import figures are f.o.b. (free on board) in balance of trade and c.i.f. (cost, insurance, and freight) for commodities and trading partners. δ1982. □Includes untrained teachers. ◇1980–81. △1984. †1982–83.

Greece

Official name: Ellinikí Dimokratía (Hellenic Republic).
Form of government: unitary multiparty republic with one legislative house (Greek Chamber of Deputies [300]).
Chief of state: President.
Head of government: Prime Minister.
Capital: Athens.
Official language: Greek.
Official religion: Eastern Orthodox.
Monetary unit: 1 drachma (Dr) = 100 leptae; valuation (Oct. 21, 1985) 1 U.S.$ = Dr154.31; 1 £ = Dr221.28.

Area and population*

Regions	area sq mi	area sq km	population 1981 census
Aegean Islands	3,522	9,122	428,533
Central Greece and Évvoia	9,417	24,391	1,099,841
Crete	3,219	8,336	502,165
Greater Athens	165	427	3,027,331
Ionian Islands	891	2,307	182,651
Ípiros	3,553	9,203	324,541
Macedonia	13,066	33,841	2,120,481
Pelopónnisos	8,254	21,379	1,012,528
Thessalía	5,420	14,037	695,654
Thráki	3,312	8,578	345,220
Autonomous administration			
Ayion Oros (Mt. Athos)	130	336	1,472
TOTAL	50,949	131,957	9,740,417

Demography

Population (1985): 9,967,000.
Density (1985): persons per sq mi 195.6, persons per sq km 75.5.
Urban–rural (1981): urban 58.1%; rural 41.9%.
Sex distribution (1982): male 49.16%; female 50.84%.
Age breakdown (1982): under 15, 22.0%; 15–29, 21.8%; 30–44, 19.2%; 45–59, 19.4%; 60–74, 12.4%; 75 and over, 5.2%.
Population projection: (1990) 10,200,000; (2000) 10,700,000.
Doubling time: 115 years.
Ethnic composition (1982): Greek 94.9%; Macedonian 1.8%; Turkish 0.6%; Albanian 0.6%; other 2.1%.
Religious affiliation (1982): Christian 98.1%, of which Greek Orthodox 97.6%, Roman Catholic 0.4%, Protestant 0.1%; Muslim 1.5%; other 0.4%.
Major cities (1981): Athens 885,737; Thessaloníki 406,413; Piraiévs 196,389; Pátrai 142,163; Iráklion 102,398.

Vital statistics

Birth rate per 1,000 population (1984): 12.7 (world avg. 29.0); legitimate 98.3%; illegitimate 1.7%.
Death rate per 1,000 population (1984): 8.9 (world avg. 11.0).
Natural increase rate per 1,000 population (1984): 3.8 (world avg. 18.0).
Total fertility rate (avg. births per childbearing woman; 1984): 2.3.
Marriage rate per 1,000 population (1984): 5.8.
Divorce rate per 1,000 population (1982): 0.7.
Life expectancy at birth (1980): male 72.2 years; female 76.4 years.
Major causes of death per 100,000 population (1984): malignant neoplasms (cancers) 177.7; cerebrovascular disease 172.2; diseases of pulmonary circulation and other forms of heart disease 112.5; ischemic heart disease 96.9.

National economy

Budget (1984)†. Revenue: Dr833,237,000,000 (indirect taxes 65.5%; direct taxes 27.5%; government entrepreneurship 3.2%). Expenditures: Dr949,-608,000,000 (personnel outlays 37.9%, of which salaries 28.7%, pensions 9.2%; servicing of public debt 16.2%; grants 10.1%; subsidies 7.8%).
Public debt (1982): U.S.$4,955,000,000.
Tourism (1983): receipts from visitors U.S.$1,176,000,000; expenditures by nationals abroad U.S.$225,000,000.
Production (metric tons except as noted). Agriculture, forestry, fishing (1984): wheat 2,646,000, tomatoes 2,250,000, corn (maize) 1,992,000, grapes 1,565,000, olives 1,400,000, potatoes 980,000, barley 831,000, apples 350,-000, tobacco 137,000, rice 91,000, oats 72,000; livestock (number of live animals) 8,500,000 sheep, 4,650,000 goats, 800,000 cattle, 230,000 asses, 100,000 horses, 37,000,000 chickens; roundwood 2,824,000 cu m‡; fish catch 100,000‡. Mining and quarrying (1983): bauxite 2,421,800; iron ore 1,332,000; zinc ore 21,300; lead ore 20,300. Manufacturing (value added in Dr; 1983): food, beverages, and tobacco 95,100,000,000; textiles 74,-270,000,000; chemicals 62,660,000,000; clothing 44,380,000,000; transport equipment 33,919,000,000. Construction (cu m; 1984): residential 28,004,-000; nonresidential 12,364,000. Energy production (consumption): electricity (kW-hr; 1983) 22,048,000,000 (21,653,000,000); coal (metric tons; 1982) 27,399,000 (27,717,000); crude petroleum (barrels; 1983) 8,647,000 (103,-096,000); petroleum products (metric tons; 1983) 12,818,000 (9,494,000); manufactured gas (cu m; 1983) 8,403,000 (8,403,000).
Household income and expenditure. Average household size (1982) 3.3; income per household (1982) Dr252,300 (U.S.$3,777); sources of income (1982): property and entrepreneurship 42.4%, wages and salaries 41.9%, social security 12.8%, other 5.2%; expenditure (1982): food, beverages, and tobacco 37.7%, housing 24.9%, transportation and communication 13.5%, clothing and footwear 8.8%, health 3.3%.

Gross national product (at current market prices; 1983): U.S.$35,700,000,000 (U.S.$3,624 per capita).

Structure of gross domestic product and labour force

	1983 in value Dr'000,000	1983 % of total value	1982 labour force	1982 % of labour force
Agriculture	473,400	17.5	1,009,800	28.1
Mining	49,950	1.8	18,800	0.5
Manufacturing	494,250	18.2	702,000	19.5
Construction	192,200	7.1	322,400	9.0
Public utilities	56,650	2.1	35,600	1.0
Transportation and communication	229,900	8.5	292,500	8.1
Trade	564,700	20.8	538,000	14.9
Finance			132,300	3.7
Pub. admin., defense	450,250	16.6	545,200	15.1
Services	200,000	7.4		
Other	...	...	2,400	0.1
TOTAL	2,709,300§	100.0	3,599,000	100.0

Population economically active (1982): total 3,706,600; participation rate of population over age 10 [1981], 44.0% (female 37.9%, unemployed 5.7%).

Price and earnings indexes (1980 = 100)

	1979	1980	1981	1982	1983	1984	1985
Consumer price index	80.1	100.0	124.5	150.6	181.1	214.5	251.6 ‖
Hourly earnings index	78.6	100.0	127.2	169.8	202.7	256.0	...

Land use (1983): forested 20.0%; meadows and pastures 40.2%; agricultural and under permanent cultivation 30.1%; other 9.7%.

Foreign trade

Balance of trade (current prices)

	1979	1980	1981	1982	1983	1984
Dr'000,000	−212.6	−231.8	−255.8	−379.6	−456.6	−541.3
% of total	42.4%	34.4%	35.0%	40.6%	36.8%	33.3%

Imports (1984): Dr1,083,940,500,000 (machinery and transport equipment 25.6%, of which passenger cars 2.3%; crude petroleum 23.3%; food, beverages, and tobacco 12.2%, of which milk and cream 1.4%, coffee 0.8%; chemical products 8.9%, of which plastics and resins 2.2%, medicinal and pharmaceutical products 1.3%). *Major import sources:* West Germany 16.6%; Italy 9.6%; Japan 7.6%; France 6.9%; Saudi Arabia 6.8%; The Netherlands 6.1%.
Exports (1984): Dr542,665,700,000 (food, beverages, and tobacco 26.6%, of which tobacco 3.8%, olive oil 3.1%, concentrated tomato puree 2.4%; clothing 12.6%; petroleum products 8.4%; textile yarn 6.3%). *Major export destinations:* West Germany 19.6%; Italy 13.5%; France 8.6%; United States 8.3%; United Kingdom 6.3%.

Transport and communications

Transport. Railroads (1984): route length 1,540 mi, 2,479 km; passenger-mi 957,500,000, passenger-km 1,541,000,000; short ton-mi cargo 526,700,000, metric ton-km cargo 769,000,000. Roads (1983): total length 66,047 mi, 106,292 km (paved 83%). Vehicles (1984): passenger cars 1,151,037; trucks and buses 589,256. Merchant marine (1984): vessels (100 gross tons and over) 2,904; total deadweight tonnage 62,236,552. Air transport (1984): passenger-mi 3,794,100,000, passenger-km 6,106,000,000; short ton-mi cargo 53,551,000, metric ton-km cargo 78,183,000; airports (1985) with scheduled flights 29.
Communications. Daily newspapers (1982): total number 131; total circulation 1,184,000¶; circulation per 1,000 population, n.a. Radio (1984): total number of receivers 4,000,000 (1 per 2.5 persons). Television (1984): total number of receivers 1,710,000 (1 per 5.8 persons). Telephones (1983): 3,113,000 (1 per 3.2 persons).

Education and health

Education (1981–82)

	schools	teachers	students	student/teacher ratio
Primary (age 6–12)	9,400	37,947	891,488	23.5
Secondary (age 13–17)	2,291	33,613	669,812	19.9
Voc., teacher tr.	766	5,828	108,212	18.6
Higher	166	11,310	124,694	11.0

Educational attainment (1981). Percent of population over age 14 having: primary education 42.3%; lower secondary 10.3%; higher secondary 15.0%; some post-secondary 4.2%; a degree from higher education school 4.4%.
Literacy (1983): total population over age 14 literate 6,914,000 (92.6%); males literate 3,429,000 (96.2%); females literate 3,465,000 (88.4%).
Health (1983): physicians 27,607 (1 per 357 persons); hospital beds 57,496 (1 per 168 persons); infant mortality rate per 1,000 live births 14.9.
Food (1980–82): daily per capita caloric intake 3,564 (vegetable products 78%, animal products 22%); 143% of FAO recommended minimum requirement.

Military

Total active duty personnel (1984): 178,000 (army 75.8%, navy 11.0%, air force 13.2%). *Military expenditure as percent of GNP* (1983): 6.8% (world 6.1%); per capita expenditure U.S.$245.

*For reasons of fit, political subdivisions or departments (*nomoi*) are not included in the table. Regions cited are geographic entities except for Ayion Oros (Mt. Athos), which is a self-governing monastic community. †Eleven months only. ‡1983. §At current prices. ‖ September. ¶For 104 dailies only.

Greenland

Official name: Grønland (Danish); Kalaallit Nunaat (Greenlandic) (Greenland).
Political status: integral part of the Danish realm with a local legislative house (Landsting [26]).
Chief of state: Danish Monarch.
Heads of government: High Commissioner (for Denmark); Prime Minister (for Greenland).
Capital: Nuuk (Godthåb).
Official languages: Greenlandic; Danish.
Official religion: Lutheran Church of Greenland (Evangelical Lutheran).
Monetary unit: 1 Danish krone (DKr) = 100 øre; valuation (Oct. 21, 1985) 1 U.S.$ = DKr 9.56; 1 £ = DKr 13.71.

Area and population

Counties		area sq mi	area sq km	population 1985 estimate
Avanersuaq (Nordgrønland)		41,200	106,700	789
Kitaa (Vestgrønland)	ice-free area	46,000	119,100	47,575
Tunu (Østgrønland)		44,800	115,900	3,278
TOTAL (ICE-FREE)		131,900	341,700	52,940†
Permanent ice*		708,100	1,833,300	
TOTAL		840,000	2,175,000	

Demography

Population (1985): 53,000.
*Density** (1985): persons per sq mi 0.40, persons per sq km 0.15.
Urban–rural (1985): urban (town) 78.2%; rural (settlement) 21.8%.
Sex distribution (1985): male 54.35%; female 45.65%.
Age breakdown (1985): under 15, 24.8%; 15–29, 34.4%; 30–44, 22.9%; 45–59, 12.4%; 60–74, 4.4%; 75 and over, 1.1%.
Population projection: (1990) 56,000; (2000) 61,000.
Doubling time: 82 years.
Ethnic composition (by place of birth; 1985): born in Greenland 82.3%; born elsewhere 17.7%.
Religious affiliation (1980): Protestant 97.8%; other 2.2%.
Major towns (1985): Nuuk (Godthåb) 10,559; Sisimiut (Holsteinsborg) 4,524; Ilulissat (Jakobshavn) 3,929; Aasiaat (Egedesminde) 3,245; Maniitsoq (Sukkertoppen) 3,122.

Vital statistics

Birth rate per 1,000 population (1983): 18.9 (world avg. 29.0); legitimate 33.2%; illegitimate 66.8%.
Death rate per 1,000 population (1983): 8.3 (world avg. 11.0).
Natural increase rate per 1,000 population (1983): 10.6 (world avg. 18.0).
Total fertility rate (avg. births per childbearing woman; 1983): 2.0.
Marriage rate per 1,000 population (1983): 5.3.
Divorce rate per 1,000 population (1983): 2.1.
Life expectancy at birth (1976–80): male 57.2 years; female 66.6 years.
Major causes of death per 100,000 population (1983): accidents 112.2; heart disease 108.4; malignant neoplasms (cancers) 100.8; suicide 78.0.

National economy

Budget (1983). Revenue: DKr1,087,500,000 (contributions from Danish government 52.6%, duties and taxes 33.3%). Expenditures: DKr1,087,500,000 (education 40.9%, social welfare 27.8%, construction 12.6%).
Public debt (external, outstanding): n.a.
Tourism: receipts from visitors, n.a.; expenditures by nationals abroad, n.a.
Gross national product (at current market prices; 1983): U.S.$550,000,000 (U.S.$10,550 per capita).

Structure of labour force

	labour force 1976	% of labour force
Agriculture, fishing, hunting, and sheep breeding	3,222	15.1
Mining, manufacturing	3,205	15.0
Construction	3,112	14.6
Public utilities	293	1.4
Transp. and commun.	1,842	8.6
Trade	2,153	10.1
Pub. admin., education	3,233	15.1
Social and health services	2,141	10.0
Other	2,177	10.2
TOTAL	21,378	100.0 ‖

Production (metric tons except as noted). Agriculture, forestry, hunting, fishing (1983): fish catch 107,725; livestock (number of live animals) 21,129 sheep, 3,000 reindeer; hunting (number of animals killed) 92,794 seals, 2,308 whales, of which 601 white whales, 492 narwhals; hunting products (number) 47,842 seal skins, 1,527 fox skins, 37 polar bear skins. Mining and quarrying (1983): zinc concentrates 75,477, cryolite 46,500, lead con-

centrates 28,000. Manufacturing (1983): principally handicrafts and food processing. Housing (1983): gross floor space of all dwellings 39,499 sq m. Energy production (consumption): electricity (kW-hr 1984) 181,700,000 (181,700,000); coal (1983) none (1,000); crude petroleum, none (n.a.); petroleum products (1984) none (155,000); natural gas, none (n.a.).
Population economically active (1976): total 21,378; participation rate of total population 43.0% (female 35.9%; unemployed, n.a.).

Price and earnings indexes (January 1980 = 100)

	1979	1980	1981	1982	1983	1984	1985
Consumer price index§	88.9	100.0	113.3	129.9	145.7	157.4	172.2
Monthly earnings index§	89.3	100.0	110.9	128.4	141.2	155.8	169.7

Household income and expenditure. Average household size (1976) 3.9; taxable income per taxpayer (1980) DKr84,160♀ (U.S.$9,200); source of income: n.a.; expenditure (1984–85): food 33.6%, housing 13.8%, clothing 9.2%, fuel and light 7.8%, transportation and communications 7.8%.
Land use (1983): forested 0.1%; meadows and pastures 0.7%; agricultural and under permanent cultivation, none; other (principally ice cap) 99.3%.

Foreign trade

Balance of trade (current prices)

	1978	1979	1980	1981	1982	1983
DK'000,000	−421	−581	−802	−772	875	−779
% of total	27.3%	25.1%	27.7%	22.4%	23.4%	19.2%

Imports (1983): DKr2,421,025,000 (machinery 21.5%, of which electrical 4.5%, road vehicles 2.4%; petroleum products 19.8%; food 20.6%, of which beverages 8.7%; metal products 6.4%). *Major import sources:* Denmark 81.2%; United States 5.1%; The Netherlands 3.2%; Norway 3.1%.
Exports (1983): DKr1,644,662,000 (shrimp and prawns 38.7%; fish 25.6%; zinc 22.0%; lead 4.8%). *Major export destinations:* Denmark 55.7%; United States 12.7%; France 10.2%; Finland 5.9%; West Germany 5.4%.

Transport and communications

Transport. Railroads: none. Roads: n.a. Vehicles (1984): passenger cars 1,346; trucks and buses 897. Merchant marine (1984): vessels (100 gross tons and over) 45; total deadweight tonnage, n.a. Air transport (1983): passenger-mi 8,664,000, passenger-km 13,944,000; short ton-mi cargo 162,000, metric ton-km cargo 236,000. Passenger conveyance within Greenland (1982): by ship 57,322; by aircraft 90,443.
Communications. Daily newspapers (1984): none. Radio (1984): 13,500 receivers (1 per 3.9 persons). Television (1984): 10,000 receivers (1 per 5.2 persons). Telephone subscribers (1984): 11,554 (1 per 4.6 persons).

Education and health

Education (1984–85)

	schools¶	teachers	students	student/ teacher ratio
Primary (age 6–15)	97		7,202	...
Secondary (age 15–19)	37	1,031	2,403♀	...
Voc., teacher tr.	5		1,537δ	...

Educational attainment (1970). Percent of adult population ages 14 through 39 having: primary education 61.7%; secondary 25.9%. *Literacy* (1979): virtually 100%.
Health (1983): physicians 58 (1 per 897 persons); hospital beds 580 (1 per 90 persons); infant mortality rate per 1,000 live births 39.6.
Food: daily per capita caloric intake, n.a.

Military

Total active duty personnel□ (1980): 320.

*Area of permanent ice not distributable by county; population density calculated with reference to ice-free area only. †Includes 1,298 people not distributed by county. §Based on January only. ‖ Detail does not add to total given because of rounding. ¶1979–80. ♀Does not include 73 students studying in Denmark. δ1983–84. □Foreign troops only. Mostly air force personnel from the United States.

Sarqaq, on the west coast of Greenland.

Grenada

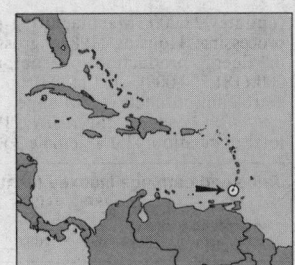

Official name: State of Grenada.
Form of government: parliamentary
  state with two legislative houses
  (Senate [13]; House of Representatives
  [15])*.
Chief of state: British Monarch,
  represented by a governor-general.
Head of government: Prime Minister.
Capital: St. George's.
Official language: English.
Official religion: none.
Monetary unit: 1 East Caribbean dollar
  (EC$) = 100 cents; valuation (Oct. 21,
  1985) 1 U.S.$ = EC$2.70;
  1 £ = EC$3.87.

Area and population†

Parishes	Capitals	area sq mi	area sq km	population 1985 estimate
Carriacou	—	13	34	...
St. Andrew	—	35	91	...
St. David	—	18	47	...
St. George's	—	26	67	...
St. John	—	15	39	...
St. Mark	—	9	23	...
St. Patrick	—	17	44	...
TOTAL		133	345	96,000

Demography

Population (1985): 96,000.
Density (1985): persons per sq mi 725.2, persons per sq km 279.9.
Urban–rural: n.a.
Sex distribution (1981): male 48.58%; female 51.42%.
Age breakdown (1980): under 15, 39.4%; 15–29, 31.2%; 30–44, 10.1%; 45–59,
  9.2; 60–74, 7.3%; 75 and over, 2.8%.
Population projection: (1990) 106,000; (2000) 131,000.
Doubling time: 34 years.
Ethnic composition (1983): black 84%; mixed 12%; East Indian 3%; white 1%.
Religious affiliation (1980): Roman Catholic 64.4%; Protestant 34.5%, of
  which Anglican 20.7%, Seventh-day Adventist 3.1%; other 1.1%.
Major cities (1980): St. George's 7,500; Gouyave 2,980.

Vital statistics

Birth rate per 1,000 population (1983): 31.2 (world avg. 29.0); (1979) legiti-
  mate 22.5%; illegitimate 77.5%.
Death rate per 1,000 population (1983): 8.6 (world avg. 11.0).
Natural increase rate per 1,000 population (1983): 22.6 (world avg. 18.0).
Total fertility rate (avg. births per childbearing woman; 1980–85): 2.9.
Marriage rate per 1,000 population (1979): 3.0.
Divorce rate per 1,000 population (1979): 0.2.
Life expectancy at birth (1980–85): male 68.5 years; female 72.5 years.
Major causes of death per 100,000 population (1981): diseases of the cir-
  culatory system 182.7; ill-defined conditions 155.2; malignant neoplasms
  (cancers) 89.1; endocrine, nutritional, and metabolic diseases 47.3.

National economy

Budget (1984)‡. Revenue: EC$87,400,000 (import duties 46.9%; income taxes
  25.4%; property taxes 5.4%; export duties 3.7%; post office 3.7%). Expenditures: EC$86,700,000 (wages and salaries 50.9%; purchases of goods and
  services 18.4%; charges on public debt 18.4%; transfer payments 14.9%).
Public debt (external, outstanding; 1984): U.S.$48,175,000.
Tourism (1984): receipts from visitors U.S.$17,000,000; expenditures by na-
  tionals abroad, n.a.
Gross national product (1983): U.S.$110,000,000 (U.S.$1,220 per capita).

Structure of gross domestic product and labour force

	1984 in value E.C.$'000,000	1984 % of total value	1981 labour force	1981 % of labour force
Agriculture	37.9	21.2	7,987	28.7
Quarrying	1.8	1.0	75	0.3
Manufacturing	4.7	2.6	1,566	5.6
Construction	13.6	7.6	2,863	10.3
Public utilities	3.7	2.1	371	1.3
Transp. and commun.	13.1	7.3	1,689	6.1
Trade	39.4	22.1	3,902	14.0
Finance	11.9	6.7	367	1.3
Pub. admin., defense	37.7	21.1		
Services	10.5	5.9	9,027	32.4
Other	4.0	2.2		
TOTAL	178.3	100.0§	27,847	100.0

Production (metric tons except as noted). Agriculture, forestry, fishing
  (1984): bananas 14,000, sugarcane 6,000, coconuts 8,000, nutmeg 2,250 ‖,
  grapefruit 2,000, cacao 2,000, mangoes 2,000, avocados 1,500, roots and
  tubers 4,000, mace 113 ‖; livestock (number of live animals) 16,000 sheep,
  13,000 goats, 11,000 pigs, 6,000 cattle, 260,000 chickens ‖; roundwood,
  n.a.; fish catch (1983) 1,801. Mining and quarrying: excavation of gravel for
  local use. Manufacturing (1983): clothing EC$6,650,000 in export sales ‖;
  beer 9,225 hectolitres; malt 4,789 hectolitres; rum 2,715 hectolitres; edible
  oil 2,126 hectolitres; coconut meal 105.6; laundry soap 25.9. Construction:
  n.a. Energy production (consumption): electricity (kW-hr; 1983) 25,000,000

(25,000,000); coal, none (n.a.); crude petroleum, none (n.a.); petroleum
  products (metric tons; 1983) none (19,000); natural gas, none (n.a.).
Household income and expenditure. Average household size (1970) 4.7; average annual income per household: n.a.; source of income: n.a.; expenditure
  (1984): food 59.0%; housing 19.0% (of which fuel and light 6.0%), clothing
  8.0%, transportation 4.0%, alcohol and tobacco 2.5%, other 7.5%.
Population economically active (1985): total 46,000; participation rate of
  total population 51.0% (female, n.a.; unemployed, 35–40%).

Price and earnings indexes (1980 = 100)

	1979	1980	1981	1982	1983	1984
Consumer price index	84.0	100.0	121.6	131.0	...	...
Monthly earnings index	...	...	...	...	...	...

Land use (1982): forested 9.0%; meadows and pastures 6.0%; agricultural
  and under permanent cultivation 41.0%; other 44.0%.

Foreign trade¶

Balance of trade (current prices)

	1979	1980	1981	1982	1983	1984
U.S.$'000,000	−25.9	−36.7	−41.7	−46.5	−45.7	−40.0
% of total	37.7%	51.3%	52.3%	55.6%	54.7%	53.9%

Imports (1983): U.S.$64,600,000 (food 21.1%, machinery 19.5%, manufac-
  tured goods 13.2%, mineral fuels 9.6%, chemicals 7.3%). *Major import
  sources:* U.K. 19.5%; U.S. 17.4%; Trinidad 17.0%; E. Germany 10.2%.
Exports (1983): U.S.$18,920,000♀ (cocoa beans 21.4%, nutmeg 17.2%, bananas
  17.1%, clothing 9.4%, mace 4.0%). *Major export destinations♂:* Trinidad
  34.3%; U.K. 25.7%; W. Germany 11.1%; Belgium–Luxembourg 11.1%.

Transport and communications

Transport. Railroads: none. Roads (1981): total length 534 mi, 860 km
  (paved 60%). Vehicles (1981): passenger cars 4,784; trucks and buses 981.
  Merchant marine (1984): vessels (100 gross tons and over) 3; total deadweight tonnage 577. Air transport (1981): passenger arrivals and departures,
  n.a.; cargo loaded 52 metric tons□, cargo unloaded 93 metric tons□; airports
  (1985) with scheduled flights 2.
Communications. Daily newspapers: none. Radio (1984): total number of
  receivers 50,000 (1 per 1.8 persons). Television: total number of receivers,
  n.a. Telephones (1983): 5,544 (1 per 16 persons).

Education and health

Education (1981–82)

	schools	teachers	students	student/ teacher ratio
Primary (age 5–11)	67	781	22,066	28.3
Secondary (age 12–18)	20	293	6,249	21.3
Vocational	1	21	213	10.1
Higher	...	71	926	13.0

Educational attainment (1970). Percent of adult population over age 14 having: no schooling 2.2%; primary 85.9%; secondary 10.1%; higher 0.7%; other
  1.1%. *Literacy* (1981): total population over age 14 literate 46,000 (85.0%).
Health: physicians (1981) 38 (1 per 2,391 persons); hospital beds (1982) 320
  (1 per 281 persons); infant mortality rate per 1,000 live births (1983) 21.2.
Food (1980–82): daily per capita caloric intake 2,162 (vegetable products 78%,
  animal products 22%); 90% of FAO recommended minimum requirement.

Military

Total active duty personnel (1985): ◇. *Military expenditure as percent of GNP*
  (1982): 4.2% (world 6.0%); per capita expenditure U.S.$60.

*Reconstituted by a general election held on Dec. 3, 1984. †Grenada is divided
  into seven parishes for administrative purposes only. There are no local government authorities. ‡Abbreviated budget (1985): revenue EC$95,000,000; expenditures
  EC$123,200,000 (international airport 33.89%, roads 12.7%); the shortfall of EC$28,-
  200,000 is funded by external sources. §Detail does not add to total given because
  of rounding. ‖ 1982. ¶Imports c.i.f. (cost, insurance, and freight); exports f.o.b. (free
  on board). ♀Of which domestic exports US$18,430,000; reexports U.S.$490,000. ♂Do-
  mestic exports only. □Excludes March. ◇A 560-member police force.

FRANK J. YURCO

Harbour, St. George's, Grenada.

Guadeloupe

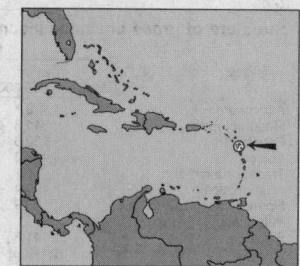

Official name: Département de
la Guadeloupe (Department of
Guadeloupe).
Political status: overseas department
(France), with two legislative houses
(General Council [36]; Regional
Council [41]).
Chief of state: President of France.
Heads of government: Commissioner
(for France); President of the
General Council (for Guadeloupe);
President of the Regional Council (for
Guadeloupe).
Capital: Basse-Terre.
Official language: French.
Official religion: none.
Monetary unit: 1 Franc (F) = 100
centimes; valuation (Oct. 21, 1985)
1 U.S.$ = F8.04; 1 £ = F11.53.

Area and population

		area		population
		sq mi	sq km	1982 census
Arrondissements	**Capitals**			
Basse-Terre*	Basse-Terre	369	957	138,242
Pointe-à-Pitre†	Pointe-à-Pitre	288	746	179,027
Saint-Martin–Saint-Barthélemy‡	Marigot	30	77	11,131
TOTAL		687	1,780	328,400

Demography

Population (1985): 330,100.
Density (1985): persons per sq mi 480.5, persons per sq km 185.4.
Urban–rural (1985): urban 45.6%; rural 54.4%.
Sex distribution (1982): male 49.10%; female 50.90%.
Age breakdown (1982): under 15, 31.1%; 15–29, 29.2%; 30–44, 16.6%; 45–59, 12.0%; 60–74, 7.8%; 75 and over, 2.8%; not specified 0.5%.
Population projection: (1990) 333,000; (2000) 348,000.
Doubling time: not applicable; population remained virtually unchanged during 1980–85.
Ethnic composition (1980): Creole (mulatto) 77.0%; black 10.0%; Guadeloupe mestizo (French–Amerindian) 10.0%; white 2.0%; East Indian and Syrian 1.0%.
Religious affiliation (1980): Roman Catholic 90.2%; Protestant (mostly Seventh-day Adventist and Reformed Church of France) 3.9%; Jehovah's Witness 1.9%; Hindu–Catholic spiritist 0.9%; Muslim 0.9%; other 2.2%.
Major cities (1982): Les Abymes 56,165; Pointe-à-Pitre 25,310; Capesterre-Belle-Eau 17,472; Basse-Terre 13,656.

Vital statistics

Birth rate per 1,000 population (1983): 20.4 (world avg. 29.0); (1980) legitimate 47.9%; illegitimate 52.1%.
Death rate per 1,000 population (1983): 6.7 (world avg. 11.0).
Natural increase rate per 1,000 population (1983): 13.7 (world avg. 18.0).
Total fertility rate (avg. births per childbearing woman; 1980–85): 2.5.
Marriage rate per 1,000 population (1982): 4.8.
Divorce rate per 1,000 population (1982): 1.3.
Life expectancy at birth (1980–85): male 67.8 years; female 73.2 years.
Major causes of death per 100,000 population (1977–80): cardiovascular diseases 220.7, of which cerebrovascular diseases 72.8; malignant neoplasms (cancers) 74.7; accidents and violent deaths 62.7; diseases of the digestive system 46.8.

National economy

Budget (1983). Revenue: F1,626,000,000 (receipts from French central government 39.4%, carried over and supplementary receipts 26.4%, taxes on motor fuels 19.9%, new loans 6.9%). Expenditures: F1,633,000,000 (health and social services 37.4%, carried over and supplementary expenses 26.7%, capital investments and works 20.4%, socioeconomic assistance 4.8%).
Public debt (external, outstanding; 1982): U.S. $68,000,000.
Tourism (1981): receipts from visitors U.S.$63,000,000; expenditures by nationals abroad, n.a.
Production (metric tons except as noted). Agriculture, forestry, fishing (1984): sugarcane 490,000, bananas 150,000, roots and tubers 27,000, eggplant 5,000, coconuts 3,000, cucumbers 3,000, pineapples 2,000; livestock (number of live animals) 93,000 cattle, 40,000 pigs, 40,000 goats, 310,000 chickens§; roundwood (1983) 17,000 cu m; fish catch (1983) 8,800. Mining and quarrying (1980): pumice, sand, and gravel for local use. Manufacturing (1983): cement 210,700; raw sugar 41,200 ‖; flour 32,600; meat products 17,500; rum 65,453 hectolitres; other products include molasses, clothing, wooden furniture and posts, metalware, glassware, and plastic goods. Construction (value in F; 1982): residential 54,000,000; commercial, industrial, and other 39,500,000. Energy production (consumption): electricity (kW-hr; 1984) 445,900,000 (386,000,000); coal, none (n.a.); crude petroleum, none (n.a.); petroleum products (metric tons; 1983) none (205,000); natural gas (cu m; 1982) none (9,359,000).
Land use (1983): forested 40.0%; meadows and pastures 12.0%; agricultural and under permanent cultivation 22.0%; other 26.0%.
Household income and expenditure. Average household size (1982) 3.7; income per household F72,898 (U.S.$16,142); sources of income: salaries 76.8%, industrial and commercial benefits 9.3%, pensions and rents 4.0%, noncommercial benefits 3.9%, income from stocks and bonds 2.6%, other 3.4%; expenditure (1972): food 44.5%, housing 17.2%, transport and communication 11.8%, clothing and footwear 8.9%, health care 6.7%, recreation 5.0%, other 5.9%.
Gross national product (at current market prices; 1982): U.S.$1,370,000,000 (U.S.$4,170 per capita).

Structure of gross domestic product and labour force

	1980		1982	
	in value F'000,000	% of total value	labour force	% of labour force
Agriculture	650	11.1	12,997	11.1
Manufacturing	539	9.2	6,643	5.7
Construction	375	6.4	9,997	8.5
Public utilities	18	0.3	703	0.6
Transportation and communication	387	6.6	4,819	4.1
Trade, restaurants, hotels	1,553	26.5	23,224	19.9
Finance, insurance, real estate	557	9.5	1,947	1.7
Pub. admin., services, other	1,781	30.4	56,512¶	48.4¶
TOTAL	5,860	100.0	116,842	100.0

Population economically active (1982): total 116,842; participation rate of total population over age 15, 53.9% (female 42.9%, unemployed 20.9%).

Price and earnings indexes (1978 = 100)♀♂

	1979	1980	1981	1982	1983	1984	1985
Consumer price index	112.5	129.3	147.4	162.5	178.6	192.5	195.7□
Monthly earnings index	114.3	130.9	157.1	183.1	201.5	215.1◇	...

Foreign trade

Balance of trade (current prices)

	1979	1980	1981	1982	1983	1984
F'000,000	−2,058	−2,628	−3,025	−3,569	−4,412	−4,480
% of total	68.1%	85.9%	74.8%	76.5%	77.9%	74.9%

Imports (1983): F5,039,000,000 (consumer goods 15.8%, food 15.6%, petroleum products 14.7%, construction materials 7.6%, tourist vehicles 6.6%, textiles and clothing 6.3%, other vehicles 2.7%). *Major import sources* (1982): France 62.4%; Martinique 9.2%; United States 5.5%; Italy 3.0%.
Exports (1983): F627,000,000 (bananas 51.7%, sugar 14.7%, rum 7.8%, and wheat flour, eggplant, fruits, and fresh-cut flowers of unknown value). *Major export destinations* (1982): France 67.8%; Martinique 18.6%; China 3.0%; Portugal 2.8%.

Transport and communications

Transport. Railroads (1983): only private, narrow-gauge railways serving sugar plantations. Roads (1983): total length 1,279 mi, 2,059 km (paved 70%). Vehicles (1983): passenger cars 82,652; trucks and buses 24,590. Merchant marine: vessels (100 gross tons and over) n.a.; total deadweight tonnage, n.a. Air transport (1983)△: passenger arrivals 528,768, passenger departures 525,203; cargo loaded 3,521 metric tons, cargo unloaded 6,944 metric tons; airports (1984) with scheduled flights 6.
Communications. Daily newspapers (1984): total number 1; total circulation 32,000; circulation per 1,000 population 97. Radio (1984): total number of receivers 55,000 (1 per 6.0 persons). Television (1983): total number of receivers 46,000 (1 per 7.2 persons). Telephones (1983): 68,518 (1 per 4.8 persons).

Education and health

Education (1981–82)

	schools	teachers	students	student/ teacher ratio
Primary (age 6–10)	284	2,744†	55,751	...
Secondary (age 11–17)	59	2,602⊙	49,606	...
Vocational	22⊕	...	10,059†	...
Higher	1	80	1,719**	...

Educational attainment (1982). Percent of population over age 14 having: no schooling 9.0%; primary education 46.7%; secondary 38.9%; higher 4.6%; other 0.8%. *Literacy* (1980): total population literate 217,900 (91.5%); males literate 106,500 (92.7%); females literate 111,400 (90.3%).
Health (1983): physicians 418 (1 per 787 persons); hospital beds 4,235 (1 per 78 persons); infant mortality rate per 1,000 live births (1980–85) 23.0.
Food (1980–82): daily per capita caloric intake 2,512 (vegetable products 76%, animal products 24%); 104% of FAO recommended minimum requirement.

Military

Total active duty personnel (1982): 2,100 (almost all army). *Military expenditure as percent of GNP:* n.a.

---

*Comprises Basse-Terre 364 sq mi (943 sq km) and Îles des Saintes 5 sq mi (14 sq km), pop. 2,901. †Comprises Grand-Terre 219 sq mi (566 sq km); Marie-Galante 58 sq mi (150 sq km), pop. 13,757; La Désirade 10 sq mi (27 sq km), pop. 1,602; and the uninhabited Îles de la Petite-Terre and Tintamarre 1 sq mi (3 sq km). ‡Comprises the French part of Saint-Martin 20 sq mi (52 sq km), pop. 8,072, and Saint-Barthélemy 10 sq mi (25 sq km), pop. 3,059. §1981. ‖ 1984. ¶Includes 24,443 unemployed. ♀Actual base year is average of April 1, 1978, through March 31, 1979. ♂All figures are end of year unless otherwise indicated. □End of March. ◇End of September. △Raizet international airport only. †1979–80. ⊙1978–79. **1982–83.

Guam

Official name: Guam.
Political Status: self-governing organized unincorporated territory of the United States with one legislative house (21).
Chief of state: President of the United States.
Head of government: Governor.
Capital: Agana.
Official language: English.
Official religion: none.
Monetary unit: 1 United States dollar (U.S.$) = 100 cents; valuation (Oct. 21, 1985) 1 U.S.$ = £0.70.

Area and population

Election Districts	area*		population†
	sq mi	sq km	1980 census
Agana	1	3	1,000
Agana Heights	1	3	3,700
Agat	10	26	4,500
Asan	6	16	2,300
Barrigada	9	23	8,700
Chalan Pago-Ordot	6	16	3,500
Dededo	30	78	26,400
Inarajan	19	49	2,300
Mangilao	10	26	7,600
Merizo	6	16	1,900
Mongmong-Toto-Maite	2	5	5,900
Piti	7	18	3,200
Santa Rita	17	44	10,300
Sinajana	1	3	2,800
Talofofo	17	44	2,200
Tamuning	6	16	15,200
Umatac	6	16	800
Yigo	35	91	11,600
Yona	20	52	4,700
TOTAL	209	541‡	118,300‡

Demography

Population (1985): 119,540.
Density (1985): persons per sq mi 572, persons per sq km 221.
Urban–rural (1980): urban 39.5%; rural 60.5%.
Sex distribution (1980): male 52.20%; female 47.80%.
Age breakdown (1980): under 15, 34.9%; 15–29, 30.6%; 30–44, 19.4%; 45–59, 10.5%; 60–74, 3.9%; 75 and over, 0.7%.
Population projection: (1990) 132,100; (2000) 146,000.
Doubling time: 52 years.
Ethnic composition (1980): Chamorro 41.8%; Filipino 21.2%; German 2.1%; Korean 1.8%; Japanese 1.8%; other 31.3%.
Religious affiliation (1980): Roman Catholic 79.5%; Protestant 15.7%; other 4.8%.
Major populated places (1980): Tamuning 8,862; Apra Harbor 5,633; Andersen Air Force Base 4,892; Mangilao 4,029.

Vital statistics

Birth rate per 1,000 population (1983): 28.7 (world avg. 29.0); (1980) legitimate 80.3%; illegitimate 19.7%.
Death rate per 1,000 population (1983): 4.2 (world avg. 11.0).
Natural increase rate per 1,000 population (1983): 24.5 (world avg. 18.0).
Total fertility rate (avg. births per childbearing woman; 1980): 1.7.
Marriage rate per 1,000 population (1983): 15.0.
Divorce rate per 1,000 population (1983): 5.6.
Life expectancy at birth (1980–82): male 69.6 years; female 74.5 years.
Major causes of death per 100,000 population (1982): heart disease 104.7; malignant neoplasms (cancers) 57.8; cerebrovascular diseases 22.6; other diseases of the central nervous system 21.7; diabetes mellitus 15.3; chronic liver diseases and cirrhosis 13.5; motor vehicle accidents 9.9.

National economy

Budget (1983). Revenue: U.S.$161,012,908 (local income taxes 50.1%, gross business receipts taxes 23.7%, revenues from United States agencies§ 13.7%, federal grants-in-aid 2.9%). Expenditures: U.S.$178,124,944 (public education 39.3%, general government operations 26.8%, continuing projects 31.7%, law and public safety 16.9%, general government 11.1%).
Public debt (external, outstanding): n.a.
Tourism (1980): receipts from visitors U.S.$117,900,000; expenditures by nationals abroad, n.a.
Production (metric tons except as noted). Agriculture, forestry, fishing (1984): coconuts 33,000, copra 2,000, roots and tubers 1,000, eggs 1,300; livestock (number of live animals) 2,000 cattle; 14,000 pigs, cattle and buffalo hides 10,000; fish catch 248¶. Mining and quarrying (1983): sand and gravel. Manufacturing (value of gross business receipts in U.S.$; 1980): petroleum refining and related products 322,083,000; food processing 11,742,000; printing and publishing 6,039,000; industrial and medical goods and materials 412,000. Construction (value of gross business receipts in U.S.$; 1980): private sector 80,609,000; military 43,331,000. Energy production (consumption): electricity (kW-hr; 1983) 1,150,000,000 (1,150,000,000); coal, none (n.a.); crude petroleum (barrels; 1983) none (11,728,000); petroleum products (metric tons; 1983) 1,454,000 (839,000); natural gas, none (n.a.).
Gross national product (at current market prices; 1983): U.S.$690,000,000 (U.S.$6,070 per capita).

Structure of gross business income and labour force

	1980		1983	
	in value U.S.$'000,000	% of total value	labour force	% of labour force
Agriculture	3.7	0.3	140	0.4
Manufacturing	340.3	30.6	1,280	4.0
Construction	80.6	7.2	1,450	4.6
Tradeǫ	445.2	40.0	5,600	17.7
Transportation and communication	26.4	2.4	1,580	5.0
Finance	75.9	6.8	1,410	4.5
Pub. admin., defense	...	...	16,000	50.5
Services	141.8	12.7	4,220	13.3
TOTAL	1,113.8‡δ	100.0	31,680	100.0

Population economically active (1983): total 34,310□; participation rate of population over age 16, 60.0% (female 15.8%, unemployed 9.6%).

Price and earnings indexes (1978 = 100)

	1979	1980	1981	1982	1983	1984	1985◇
Consumer price index	112.1	134.0	161.4	169.6	179.3	195.6	197.6
Hourly earnings index	122.1	132.2	...	...	...	...	...

Household income and expenditure. Average household size (1980) 4.1; median annual income per household (1979) U.S.$16,203; source of income: n.a.; expenditure (1978): housing 28.6%, food 24.1%, transportation 18.0%, clothing 10.6%, health and recreation 9.8%, entertainment 5.1%, medical care 4.8%, other goods and services 8.9%.
Land use (1983): forested 18.2%; meadows and pastures 14.5%; agricultural and under permanent cultivation 21.8%; other 45.5%.

Foreign trade

Balance of trade (current prices)

	1978	1979	1980	1981	1982	1983
U.S.$'000	−236,227	−403,144	−483,141	...	...	−571,519
% of total	76.7%	82.5%	79.8%	...	...	87.9%

Imports (1983): U.S.$610,743,985 (mineral fuels 46.9%, of which crude petroleum 28.8%; machinery and transport equipment 19.1%, of which passenger cars 12.4%; food and live animals 12.0%, of which beef and veal 1.5%; beverages and tobacco 4.5%, of which cigarettes 1.3%; manufactured goods 4.4%; chemicals 2.3%). *Major import sources:* United States 23.4%; Japan 19.2%; Taiwan 4.6%; Hong Kong 3.1%; Philippines 1.3%; Australia 0.6%; New Zealand 0.4%.
Exports (1983): U.S.$39,224,728 (clothing 16.9%; beverages and tobacco 12.0%, of which alcoholic beverages 4.4%, cigarettes 3.5%, nonalcoholic beverages 1.9%; machinery and transport equipment 11.4%; travel goods 3.0%; lubricating oils and greases 2.7%; fish and fish products 2.6%; cosmetics 2.6%; watches and watch cases 1.5%; cement 1.5%). *Major export destinations:* United States 24.9%; Japan 4.8%; Hong Kong 2.0%; Philippines 0.7%; Taiwan 0.5%.

Transport and communications

Transport. Railroads: none. Roads (1983): total length 419 mi, 674 km (paved 100%). Vehicles△ (1983): passenger cars 44,312; trucks and buses 15,796. Merchant marine (1980): vessels (100 gross tons and over), n.a.; surface cargo loaded, unloaded, or transshipped (1980) 623,900 metric tons. Air transport (1980): passenger arrivals 291,133; passenger departures, n.a.; cargo loaded 3,645 metric tons; cargo unloaded 5,856 metric tons; airports (1985) with scheduled flights 1.
Communications. Daily newspapers (1984): total number 1; total circulation 18,050; circulation per 1,000 population 162.5. Radio (1984): total number of receivers 300,000 (1 per 0.4 person). Television (1984): total number of receivers 78,500 (1 per 1.4 persons). Telephones (1982): 14,379 (1 per 7.7 persons).

Education and Health

Education (1981–82)

	schools	teachers	students	student/ teacher ratio
Primary (age 5–12)	37	772	17,784	23.0
Secondary (age 13–18)	19	512	11,997	23.4
Voc., teacher tr.	1	75	1,186	15.8
Higher	2†	162	3,499	21.6

Educational attainment (1980). Percent of population 25 years old and over having: primary education 21.3%; some secondary 13.1%; secondary 31.2%; college 34.4%. *Literacy:* n.a.
Health: physicians (1980) 70 (1 per 1,514 persons); hospital beds (1979) 361 (1 per 287 persons); infant mortality rate per 1,000 live births (1983) 7.5.
Food: daily per capita caloric intake, n.a.

Military

Total active duty U.S. personnel (1982): 10,800 (navy 58.4%, air force 37.0%, other 4.6%).

---

*The entire area of Guam is considered equivalent to a U.S. county for census purposes. †Includes about 23,000 active duty personnel, Department of Defense employees, and dependents. ‡Detail does not add to total given because of rounding. §Consists largely of federal income tax. ‖ 1983. ¶Employed persons only. ǫMost important industry in the private sector. δAt current prices. □Excludes nonimmigrant aliens and civilians living on military reservations. ◇Three quarters only. △Excluding military vehicles. †1982–83.

Guatemala

Official name: República de Guatemala (Republic of Guatemala).
Form of government: military regime.
Head of state and government: General, pending runoff election of a civilian president scheduled for Dec. 1985.
Capital: Guatemala City.
Official language: Spanish.
Official religion: none.
Monetary unit: 1 Guatemalan quetzal (Q) = 100 centavos; valuation (Oct. 21, 1985) 1 U.S.$ = Q1.00*; 1 £ = Q1.43.

Area and population

Departments	Capitals	area sq mi	sq km	population 1984 estimate
Alta Verapaz	Cobán	3,354	8,686	436,700
Baja Verapaz	Salamá	1,206	3,124	157,000
Chimaltenango	Chimaltenango	764	1,979	276,200
Chiquimula	Chiquimula	917	2,376	229,300
El Progreso	Progreso	742	1,922	98,500
Escuintla	Escuintla	1,693	4,384	394,000
Guatemala	Guatemala City	821	2,126	1,510,500
Huehuetenango	Huehuetenango	2,857	7,400	580,900
Izabal	Puerto Barrios	3,490	9,038	254,400
Jalapa	Jalapa	797	2,063	174,400
Jutiapa	Jutiapa	1,243	3,219	353,000
Petén	Ciudad Flores	13,843	35,854	186,300
Quezaltenango	Quezaltenango	753	1,951	461,400
Quiché	Santa Cruz	3,235	8,378	443,400
Retalhuleu	Retalhuleu	717	1,856	187,600
Sacatepéquez	Antigua Guatemala	180	465	141,400
San Marcos	San Marcos	1,464	3,791	590,100
Santa Rosa	Cuilapa	1,141	2,955	250,400
Sololá	Sololá	410	1,061	186,500
Suchitepéquez	Mazatenango	969	2,510	297,300
Totonicapán	Totonicapán	410	1,061	239,500
Zacapa	Zacapa	1,039	2,690	151,500
TOTAL		42,042†	108,889	7,599,300† ‡

Demography

Population (1985 est.): 7,675,000.
Density (1985)‡: persons per sq mi 182.5, persons per sq km 70.5.
Urban–rural (1981)§: urban 34.3%; rural 65.7%.
Sex distribution (1985): male 50.56%; female 49.44%.
Age breakdown (1985): under 15, 45.9%; 15–29, 26.5%; 30–44, 14.3%; 45–59, 8.6%; 60–74, 3.8%; 75 and over, 0.9%.
Population projection: (1990) 9,197,000; (2000) 12,222,000.
Doubling time: 30 years.
Ethnic composition (1983): Maya 55%; mestizo 42%; white or black 3%.
Religious affiliation (1983): Roman Catholic *c.* 80%; Protestant *c.* 20%.
Major cities (1981)§: Guatemala City 754,200; Quezaltenango 62,700; Escuintla 36,900; Izabal 24,200.

Vital statistics

Birth rate per 1,000 population (1983): 42.7 (world avg. 29.0).
Death rate per 1,000 population (1983): 10.5 (world avg. 11.0).
Natural increase rate per 1,000 population (1983): 32.2 (world avg. 18.0).
Total fertility rate (avg. births per childbearing woman; 1980–85): 6.1.
Marriage rate per 1,000 population (1982): 4.1.
Divorce rate per 1,000 population (1981): 0.2.
Life expectancy at birth (1981): male 57.3 years; female 60.5 years.
Major causes of death per 100,000 population (1980): typhoid and other intestinal infectious diseases 194.2; respiratory diseases 151.3; birth trauma and other conditions originating in the perinatal period 125.5; homicide 63.0; diseases of the circulatory system 49.8.

National economy

Budget (1983). Revenue: Q742,700,000 (tax revenue 78.3%, of which domestic taxes on goods and services 35.8%, corporate and capital gains tax 17.6%, taxes on international trade transactions 15.0%). Expenditures: Q1,080,200,000 (current expenditure 66.0%, of which expenditure on goods and services 48.0%, subsidies and other current transfers 10.8%).
Public debt (external, outstanding; 1983): U.S.$1,405,300,000.
Tourism (1983): receipts from visitors U.S.$61,000,000; expenditures by nationals abroad U.S.$89,348,500.
Production (metric tons except as noted). Agriculture, forestry, fishing (1984): sugarcane 6,410,000, corn (maize) 1,038,000, bananas 680,000, coffee 140,000, tomatoes 93,000, dry beans 90,000, sorghum 82,000, cottonseed 78,000; livestock (number of live animals) 2,605,000 cattle, 810,000 pigs, 660,000 sheep, 15,000,000 chickens; roundwood 6,806,000 cu m ‖ ; fish catch 4,284 ‖. Mining and quarrying (1983): feldspar 10,000; zinc 1,000¶; iron ore 860; copper concentrate 700; silver 8,000 troy oz. Manufacturing (1983): raw sugar 525,000; cheese 15,000♀; butter 5,000♀; beer 700,000 hectolitres♂; cigarettes 2,136,000,000 units; cement 466,000. Construction (1982)□: residential 147,200 sq m; nonresidential 73,600 sq m. Energy production (consumption): electricity (kW-hr; 1983) 1,700,000,000 (1,700,000,000); coal, none (n.a.); crude petroleum (barrels; 1983) 4,412,000 (6,500,000); petroleum products (metric tons; 1983) 785,000 (1,007,000); natural gas, none (n.a.).
Gross national product (at current market prices; 1983): U.S.$8,890,000,000 (U.S.$1,120 per capita).

Structure of gross domestic product and labour force

	1982 in value Q'000	1982 % of total value	1983 labour force	1983 % of labour force
Agriculture	2,406,800	25.4	1,347,381	58.1
Mining	30,800	0.3	2,319	0.1
Manufacturing	1,493,900	15.7	315,394	13.6
Construction	323,600	3.4	95,082	4.1
Public utilities	163,200	1.7	6,957	0.3
Transportation and communication	626,700	6.6	57,977	2.5
Trade	2,493,600	26.3	169,292	7.3
Finance	801,800	8.5		
Pub. admin., defense	555,600	5.9	278,289	12.0
Services	591,500	6.2		
Other			46,381	2.0
TOTAL	9,487,500◇	100.0	2,319,072	100.0

Population economically active (1984): total 1,678,000; participation rate of total population 22.1% (female [1981] 14.6%, unemployed 16.1%).

Price and earnings indexes (1980 = 100)

	1977	1978	1979	1980	1981	1982	1983
Consumer price index	75.0	81.0	90.3	100.0	111.4	111.6	115.0
Annual earnings index△	74.2	78.7	90.2	100.0	131.2	139.3	135.3

Household income and expenditure. Average household size (1980) 4.5; income per household: n.a.; source of income: n.a.; expenditure† (1975): food 40%, housing 19%, clothing and footwear 11%.
Land use (1983): forested 39.7%; meadows and pastures 12.3%; agricultural and under permanent cultivation 16.7%; other 31.3%.

Foreign trade⊕

Balance of trade (current prices)

	1978	1979	1980	1981	1982	1983
Q'000,000	−65.5	−125.1	+84.5	−286.3	−116.7	+134.7
% of total	2.9%	4.7%	2.8%	10.2%	4.8%	6.0%

Imports (1983): Q1,134,995,000 (chemical products 22.7%, mineral fuels and lubricants 22.6%, manufactured goods 20.5%; machinery and transport equipment 14.7%). *Major import sources:* United States 31.6%; El Salvador 9.1%; Mexico 7.8%; Costa Rica 7.2%; Netherlands Antilles 6.0%.
Exports (1983): Q1,158,805,600 (coffee 29.7%, sugar 10.7%, petroleum 5.2%, cotton 4.0%, bananas 3.5%, cardamom 2.7%, beans and legumes 2.3%). *Major export destinations:* United States 34.5%; El Salvador 14.1%; West Germany 5.4%; Honduras 4.6%; Costa Rica 4.5%; Nicaragua 4.4%.

Transport and communications

Transport. Railroads (1983): route length 467 mi, 751 km. Roads (1985): total length 11,200 mi, 18,000 km (paved 15.8%). Vehicles (1980): passenger cars 166,900; trucks and buses 81,500. Merchant marine (1984): vessels (100 gross tons and over) 8; total deadweight tonnage 24,138. Air transport (1984): passenger-mi 104,400,000, passenger-km 168,000,000; short ton-mi cargo 5,500,000, metric ton-km cargo 8,088,000; airports (1985) with scheduled flights 2.
Communications. Daily newspapers (1983): total number 8; total circulation 224,500; circulation per 1,000 population 30. Radio (1983): total number 500,000 (1 per 15 persons). Television (1984): total number 205,000 (1 per 37 persons). Telephones (1983 est.): 161,520 (1 per 47 persons).

Education and health

Education (1980)

	schools	teachers	students	student/ teacher ratio
Primary (age 7–12)	6,959	23,770	803,404	33.8
Secondary (age 13–18)**	...	9,613	156,612	16.3
Voc., teacher tr.**	...	...	...	...
Higher ‖	5	4,490	51,556	11.4

Educational attainment (1981). Percent of adult population over age 25 having: no formal schooling 52.9%; some primary education 26.2%; complete primary 8.3%; some secondary 5.4%; complete secondary 3.4%. *Literacy* (1980): total population over age 15 literate 2,076,500 (51.1%); males literate 1,203,000 (58.6%); females literate 873,500 (43.5%); Maya literate 450,000 (20.0%).
Health: physicians (early 1980s) 1,250 (1 per 5,700 persons); hospital beds (1981) 10,099 (1 per 728 persons); infant mortality rate per 1,000 live births (1983) 64.1.
Food (1980–82): daily per capita caloric intake 2,111 (vegetable products 91%, animal products 9%); 96% of FAO recommended minimum requirement.

Military

Total active duty personnel (1984): 40,000 (army 95.0%, navy 2.5%, air force 2.5%). *Military expenditure as percent of GNP* (1983): 2.4% (world 6.1%); per capita expenditure U.S.$25.

*The value of the quetzal is fixed at par with that of the U.S.$. †Detail does not add to total given because of rounding. ‡Based on estimated de facto population. §Based on final de jure census figure of 6,054,227. ‖ 1983. ¶1982. ♀1981. ♂1979. □Authorized private construction in Guatemala City. ◇At current prices. △Includes real annual wages and salaries paid to workers affiliated with the Guatemalan Institute of Social Security. ⊕Import figures are f.o.b. (free on board) in balance of trade and c.i.f. (cost, insurance, and freight) for commodities and trading partners. **Secondary includes vocational and teacher training.

Guinea

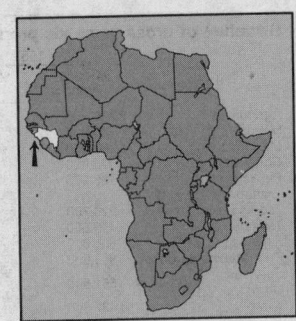

Official name: République de Guinée (Republic of Guinea).
Form of government: interim military regime ruling through the Military Committee for National Recovery (CMRN [20]) with an appointed government (41).
Head of state and government: President.
Capital: Conakry.
Official language: French.
Official religion: none.
Monetary unit: 1 Guinean syli (GS) = 100 cauris; valuation (Oct. 21, 1985) 1 U.S.$ = GS23.26; 1 £ = GS33.35.

Area and population

		area*		population
Regions	Capitals	sq mi	sq km	1977 census
Beyla	Beyla	6,738	17,452	140,000
Boffa	Boffa	2,318	6,003	121,000
Boké	Boké	4,268	11,053	149,000
Conakry	Conakry	119	308	581,000
Coyah (Dubréka)	Coyah	2,192	5,676	122,000
Dabola	Dabola	2,317	6,000	75,000
Dalaba	Dalaba	2,220	5,750	110,000
Dinguiraye	Dinguiraye	4,247	11,000	109,000
Faranah	Faranah	4,786	12,397	135,000
Forécariah	Forécariah	1,647	4,265	132,000
Fria	Fria	...	...	45,000
Gaoual	Gaoual	4,441	11,503	98,000
Guéckédou	Guéckédou	1,605	4,157	173,000
Kankan	Kankan	10,613	27,488	175,000
Kérouané	Kérouané	...	...	60,000
Kindia	Kindia	3,408	8,828	186,000
Kissidougou	Kissidougou	3,425	8,872	160,000
Koubia	Koubia	...	...	70,000
Koundara	Koundara	2,123	5,500	65,000
Kouroussa	Kouroussa	6,334	16,405	102,000
Labé	Labé	2,941	7,616	170,000
Lélouma	Lélouma	...	...	105,000
Lola	Lola	...	...	100,000
Macenta	Macenta	3,363	8,710	142,000
Mali	Mali	3,398	8,800	145,000
Mamou	Mamou	2,378	6,159	133,000
Mandiana	Mandiana	...	...	90,000
Nzérékoré	Nzérékoré	3,932	10,183	187,000
Pita	Pita	1,544	4,000	175,000
Siguiri	Siguiri	9,026	23,377	140,000
Télimélé	Télimélé	3,149	8,155	170,000
Touqué	Touqué	2,394	6,200	90,000
Yomou	Yomou	...	...	72,000
TOTAL		94,926	245,857	4,527,000

Demography

Population (1985 est.): 5,429,000.
Density (1985): persons per sq mi 57.2, persons per sq km 22.1.
Urban-rural (1985): urban 22.2%; rural 77.8%.
Sex distribution (1985): male 49.41%; female 50.59%.
Age breakdown (1985): under 15, 43.1%; 15–29, 26.2%; 30–44, 16.2%; 45–59, 9.6%; 60–74, 4.2%; 75 and over 0.7%.
Population projection: (1990) 6,145,000; (2000) 7,935,000.
Doubling time: 30 years.
Ethnic composition (1980): Fulani 40.9%; Malinke 25.9%; Susu 11.4%; Kissi 8.4%; Kpelle 4.8%; other 8.6%.
Religious affiliation (1980): Muslim 69.0%; tribal religionist 29.5%; Roman Catholic 1.1%; other 0.4%.
Major cities (1983): Conakry 656,000; Kankan 278,000; Labé 273,000; Nzérékoré 250,000.

Vital statistics

Birth rate per 1,000 population (1980–85): 46.8 (world avg. 29.0).
Death rate per 1,000 population (1980–85): 23.5 (world avg. 11.0).
Natural increase rate per 1,000 population (1980–85): 23.3 (world avg. 18.0).
Total fertility rate (avg. births per childbearing woman; 1980–85): 6.2.
Marriage rate per 1,000 population: n.a.
Divorce rate per 1,000 population: n.a.
Life expectancy at birth (1980–85): male 38.7 years; female 41.8 years.
Major causes of death per 100,000 population: n.a.; however, major diseases are malaria, venereal disease, tuberculosis, intestinal infections, measles, and schistosomiasis.

National economy

Budget (1979). Revenue: GS11,250,000,000 (no breakdown available). Expenditures: GS11,250,000,000 (current budget 60.4%; capital budget 39.6%).
Public debt (external, outstanding; 1984): U.S.$1,600,000,000.
Tourism: receipts from visitors, n.a.; expenditures by nationals abroad, n.a.
Production (metric tons except as noted). Agriculture, forestry, fishing (1984): roots and tubers 848,000 (of which cassava 650,000, sweet potatoes 83,000, yams 79,000), fruits 566,000 (of which plantains 235,000, bananas 115,000, pineapples 20,000), cereals 530,000 (of which rice 400,000, corn [maize] 56,000), vegetables and melons 389,000, sugarcane 225,000, peanuts (groundnuts) 75,000, milk 43,000, palm kernels 35,000, pulses 28,000, coffee 15,000, eggs 10,710; livestock (number of live animals) 1,850,000 cattle,

455,000 sheep, 450,000 goats, 45,000 pigs, 10,000,000 chickens; roundwood 3,644,000 cu m†; fish catch 18,453†. Mining and quarrying (1983): bauxite‡ 12,380,000; alumina 578,000; gem diamonds 23,000 carats; industrial diamonds 17,000 carats. Manufacturing (1983): palm oil 45,000; raw sugar 20,000; plywood 2,000 cu m. Construction: n.a. Energy production (consumption): electricity (kW-hr; 1983) 499,000,000 (499,000,000); coal, none (n.a.); crude petroleum, none (n.a.); petroleum products (metric tons; 1983) none (291,000); natural gas, none (n.a.).
Gross national product (at current market prices; 1983): U.S.$1,740,000,000 (U.S.$300 per capita).

Structure of gross domestic product and labour force

	1980		1983	
	in value GS'000,000	% of total value	labour force	% of labour force
Agriculture	11,600	36.6	1,968,000	82.0
Mining	7,900	24.9		
Manufacturing	1,200	3.8		
Construction	1,200	3.8		
Public utilities	300	1.0	264,000	11.0
Transportation and communication	700	2.2		
Trade	5,200	16.4		
Finance }			38,400	1.6
Pub. admin., defense			129,600	5.4
Services }	3,600	11.4		
Other			...	...
TOTAL	31,700§	100.0‖	2,400,000	100.0

Population economically active (1984): total 2,306,000; participation rate of population over age 15, 76.5% (female [1981], 34.8%, unemployed, n.a.).
Price and earnings indexes: n.a.
Household income and expenditure. Average household size (1980) 4.7; average annual income per capita (1981) GS4,815 (U.S.$230).
Land use (1983): forested 42.1%; meadows and pastures 12.2%; agricultural and under permanent cultivation 6.4%; other 39.3%.

Foreign trade¶

Balance of trade (current prices)

	1978	1979	1980	1981	1982	1983
GS'000,000	−400	−400	+1,000	+1,611	+2,511	+2,617
% of total	3.0%	2.7%	4.8%	9.9%	16.3%	16.6%

Imports (1981): GS7,349,000,000 (food, machinery and transport equipment, petroleum products, building materials, textiles). *Major import sources:* European Economic Community 60.0%, of which France 30.2%, United Kingdom 6.7%, West Germany 6.5%; United States 16.6%.
Exports (1981): GS8,960,000,000 (bauxite 10,833,030 metric tons, alumina 230,169 metric tons, coffee, pineapples, bananas, palm kernels). *Major export destinations:* EEC 32.4%, of which West Germany 16.4%, France 10.2%; United States 27.8%.

Transport and communications

Transport. Railroads (1984): route length 573 mi, 922 km. Roads (1983): total length 17,600 mi, 28,400 km (paved 5%). Vehicles (1982): passenger cars 9,948; trucks and buses 9,992. Merchant marine (1984): vessels (100 gross tons and over) 18; total deadweight tonnage 2,927. Air transport (1982): passenger-mi 89,500,000, passenger-km 144,000,000; short ton-mi cargo 9,600,000, metric ton-km cargo 14,000,000; airports (1985): with scheduled flights 1.
Communications. Daily newspapers (1979): total number 1; total circulation 20,000; circulation per 1,000 population 4. Radio (1984): total number of receivers 125,000 (1 per 42 persons). Television (1984): total number of receivers 7,600 (1 per 698 persons). Telephones (1981): 10,000 (1 per 494 persons).

Education and health

Education (1980–81)

	schools	teachers	students	student/teacher ratio
Primary (age 7–12)	2,555	7,165	257,547	35.9
Secondary (age 13–18)	...	3,520	89,900	25.5
Voc., teacher tr.♀	...	425	3,491	8.2
Higherδ	...	1,373	13,182	9.6

Educational attainment, n.a. *Literacy* (1980): total population over age 15 literate 527,900 (18.7%); males literate 464,900 (33.5%); females literate 63,000 (4.4%).
Health: physicians (1980) 301 (1 per 16,053 persons); hospital beds□ (1976) 7,650 (1 per 579 persons); infant mortality rate per 1,000 live births (1980–85) 159.
Food (1979–81): daily per capita caloric intake 1,880 (vegetable products 96%, animal products 4%); 82% of FAO recommended minimum requirement.

Military

Total active duty personnel (1985): 9,900 (army 85.8%, navy 6.1%, air force 8.1%). *Military expenditure as percent of GNP* (1981): 4.9% (world 5.8%); per capita expenditure U.S.$10.

---

*Separate area figures are not available for the newly created regions of Fria, Kérouané, Koubia, Lélouma, Lola, Mandiana, and Yomou. †1983. ‡Dry basis. §At current prices. ‖Detail does not add to total given because of rounding. ¶Trade with the Socialist bloc is not included in major import sources and major export destinations; the U.S.S.R., however, is a major trading partner. ♀1970. δ1982. □Government hospitals only.

Guinea-Bissau

Official name: República da Guiné-Bissau (Republic of Guinea-Bissau).
Form of government: single-party republic with one legislative house (National People's Assembly [150]).
Head of state and government: President.
Capital: Bissau.
Official language: Portuguese.
Official religion: none.
Monetary unit: 1 peso (PG) = 100 centavos; valuation (Oct. 21, 1985) 1 U.S.$ = PG147.22; 1 £ = PG211.11.

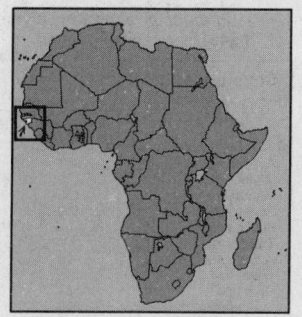

Area and population

Regions	Capitals	area sq mi	area sq km	population 1979 census*
Bafatá	Bafatá	2,309	5,981	115,656
Bissau	Bissau	324	840	51,796
Bolama	Bolama	1,013	2,624	25,449
Cacheu	Cacheu	1,998	5,175	127,514
Gabú	Gabú	3,533	9,150	103,683
Oio	Farim	2,086	5,403	131,271
Quinara	Fulacunda	1,212	3,138	35,567
Tombali	Catió	1,443	3,736	55,088
Autonomous Sector				
Bissau	—	30	78	107,281
TOTAL		13,948	36,125	753,305

Demography

Population (1985): 873,000.
Density (1985): persons per sq mi 62.6, persons per sq km 24.2.
Urban–rural (1979): urban 14.0%; rural 86.0%.
Sex distribution (1979): male 48.22%; female 51.78%.
Age breakdown (1979): under 15, 44.3%; 15–29, 25.5%; 30–44, 15.1%; 45–59, 8.2%; 60–74, 4.7%; 75 and over, 2.2%.
Population projection: (1990) 987,000; (2000) 1,241,000.
Doubling time: 33 years.
Ethnic composition (1980): Balante 41.5%; Fulani 16.3%; Malinke 12.6%; Mandyako 12.6%; other 17.0%.
Religious affiliation (1983): traditional beliefs 66%; Muslim 30%; Christian 4%.
Major cities (1979): Bissau 105,273; Bafatá 13,429; Gabú 7,803; Mansôa 5,390; Catió 5,179.

Vital statistics

Birth rate per 1,000 population (1981): 40.9 (world avg. 29.0); legitimate, n.a.; illegitimate, n.a.
Death rate per 1,000 population (1981): 21.9 (world avg. 11.0).
Natural increase rate per 1,000 population (1981): 19.0 (world avg. 18.0).
Total fertility rate (avg. births per childbearing woman; 1982): 5.4.
Marriage rate per 1,000 population: n.a.
Divorce rate per 1,000 population: n.a.
Life expectancy at birth (1975–80): male 39.4 years; female 42.6 years.
Major causes of death: n.a.; however, major diseases are tuberculosis, malaria, and pneumonia.

National economy

Budget (1981). Revenue: PG1,137,000,000 (indirect taxes 49.6%; direct taxes 25.8%; duties, fines, and other penalties 3.0%). Expenditures: PG1,944,-000,000.
Public debt (external, outstanding; 1983): U.S.$138,200,000.
Tourism: n.a.
Production (metric tons except as noted). Agriculture, forestry, fishing (1984): roots and tubers (sweet potatoes and cassava) 40,000, rice 105,000, peanuts (groundnuts) 30,000, coconuts 25,000, plantains 25,000, millet 16,000, sorghum 13,000, corn (maize) 10,000, palm kernels 10,000, cashews 10,000, copra 5,000, pulses 2,000; livestock (number of live animals) 225,000 cattle, 150,000 goats, 133,000 pigs, 420,000 chickens†; roundwood 528,000 cu m‡; fish catch 2,617. Manufacturing (in PG'000,000; 1982): beverages 143.7, of which beer 122.3, orange- and lemonade 16.5; clothing 14.0§; peanut oil 7.0; palm oil 2.4. Construction (in PG'000,000; 1982): total buildings 2.5. Energy production (consumption): electricity (kW-hr; 1983) 13,000,-000 (13,000,000); coal, none (n.a.); crude petroleum (barrels; 1981) none (210,000); petroleum products (metric tons; 1983) none (29,000); natural gas, none (n.a.).
Population economically active (1979): total 198,575; participation rate of population over age 15, 47.3% (female, n.a.; unemployed 0.5%).

Price and earnings indexes (1975 = 100)

	1975	1976	1977	1978	1979	1980	1981
Consumer price index	100.0	101.5	104.5	114.1	136.6	147.4	147.4
Earnings index	...	...	...	...	...	...	...

Household income and expenditure. Average household size (1981) 4.1; average annual income per household: n.a.; source of income: n.a.; expenditure: n.a.
Land use (1983): forested 38.2%; meadows and pastures 45.7%; agricultural and under permanent cultivation 10.3%; other 5.8%.
Gross national product (1983): U.S.$150,000,000 (U.S.$180 per capita).

Structure of gross domestic product and labour force

	1983 in value U.S.$'000,000	1983 % of total value	1979 labour force	1979 % of labour force
Agriculture	37	48.7	157,320	79.2
Mining	1	1.3	...	...
Manufacturing	1	1.3	3,006	1.5
Construction	2	2.6	1,727	0.9
Public utilities			270	0.1
Transportation and communication			2,438	1.2
Trade	35	46.1	5,250	2.6
Finance			207	0.1
Pub. admin., defense				
Services			27,417	13.8
Other	...	...	940	0.5
TOTAL	76 ‖	100.0	198,575	100.0¶

Foreign trade

Balance of trade (current prices)

	1978	1979	1980	1981	1982	1983
PG'000,000	−1,308.8	−1,588.0	−1,477.6	−1,334.1	−1,500.8	−1,227.5
% of total	60.0%	62.3%	65.9%	56.0%	61.1%	63.2%

Imports (1983): PG1,585,600,000 (food and beverages 33.7%, of which cereals 22.7%; textiles and clothing 15.8%; transport equipment 12.8%; machinery and apparatus, including electrical 8.2%). *Major import sources:* Portugal 32.7%; Italy 11.0%; The Netherlands 9.9%; France 6.9%; Senegal 5.7%.
Exports (1983): PG358,100,000 (vegetables and fruits, including peanuts and cashew nuts 66.1%; fish including shrimp 23.7%; cork and wood 4.5%). *Major export destinations:* Portugal 65.9%; Senegal 11.1%; Guinea 10.9%.

Transport and communications

Transport. Railroads: none. Roads (1982): total length 3,143 mi, 5,058 km (paved, n.a.). Vehicles (1982): private motor vehicles 4,100. Merchant marine (1984): vessels (100 gross tons and over) 15; total deadweight tonnage 2,523. Air transport (1980): passenger-mi 5,000,000, passenger-km 8,000,-000; short ton-mi cargo 700,000, metric ton-km cargo 1,000,000; airports (1985) with scheduled flights 1.
Communications. Daily newspapers (1984): total number 1; total circulation 6,000; circulation per 1,000 population 7.0. Radio (1984): total number of receivers 26,000 (1 per 33 persons). Television (1984): none. Telephones (1981): 5,000 (1 per 161 persons).

Education and health

Education (1982–83)

	schools	teachers	students	student/ teacher ratio
Primary (age 7–13)	719	3,363	74,359	22.1
Secondary (age 13–18)	8♀	543	7,667	14.1
Voc., teacher tr.	4♀	96♀	765	...

Educational attainment (1979). Percent of population over age 7 having: primary education 7.9%; secondary 0.8%; technical and higher 0.2%. *Literacy* (1979): total population over age 7 literate 26.8%.
Health: physicians (1980) 108 (1 per 7,287 persons); hospital beds (1981) 1,532 (1 per 514 persons); infant mortality rate per 1,000 live births (1980–85) 143.0.
Food (1980–82): daily per capita caloric intake 2,230 (vegetable products 93%, animal products 7%); 96% of FAO recommended minimum requirement.

Military

Total active duty personnel (1984): 6,050 (army 94.2%, navy 4.5%, air force 1.3%). *Military expenditure as percent of GNP* (1983): 8.4% (world 6.1%); per capita expenditure U.S.$11.

*Preliminary. †1982. ‡1983. §Production figure for first three quarters only. ‖ At current factor cost. ¶Detail does not add to total given because of rounding. ♀1981–82.

Shark dancer, Bubaque Island, Bijagós archipelago, Guinea-Bissau.

SUSAN PIERRES—PETER ARNOLD, INC.

Guyana

Official name: Co-operative Republic of Guyana.
Form of government: unitary single-party republic with one legislative house (National Assembly [65]).
Chief of state: President.
Head of government: Prime Minister.
Capital: Georgetown.
Official language: English.
Official religion: none.
Monetary unit: 1 Guyana dollar (G$) = 100 cents; valuation (Oct. 21, 1985) 1 U.S.$ = G$4.21; 1 £ = G$6.03.

Area and population

Regions	Capitals	area sq mi	area sq km	population 1985 estimate
East Berbice	New Amsterdam	...	...	...
East Demerara	Enmore	...	...	...
Essequibo	Suddie	...	...	...
Essequibo Islands	Enterprise	...	...	...
Georgetown*	Georgetown	...	...	200,000
Mazaruni-Potaro	Bartica	...	...	...
North West	Mabaruma	...	...	...
Rupununi	Lethem	...	...	...
West Berbice	Fort Wellington	...	...	...
West Demerara	Vreed en Hoop	...	...	...
TOTAL		83,000†	215,000†	953,000

Demography

Population (1985): 953,000.
Density (1985): persons per sq mi 11.5, persons per sq km 4.4.
Urban–rural (1983): urban 28.0%; rural 72.0%.
Sex distribution (1982): male 50.05%; female 49.95%.
Age breakdown (1982): under 15, 40.2%; 15–29, 31.3%; 30–44, 13.8%; 45–59, 8.8%; 60–74, 4.8%; 75 and over, 1.1%.
Population projection: (1990) 1,040,000; (2000) 1,196,000.
Doubling time: 38 years.
Ethnic composition (1980): East Indian 50.8%; Black African 30.4%; other 18.8%.
Religious affiliation (1980): Hindu 34.4%; Protestant 18.0%; Roman Catholic 18.0%; Anglican 16.0%; Muslim 9.0%; other 4.6%.
Major cities (1970): Greater Georgetown 200,000‡; Linden 30,000; New Amsterdam 18,000; Corriverton 17,000.

Vital statistics

Birth rate per 1,000 population (1983): 29.0 (world avg. 29.0); legitimate, n.a.; illegitimate, n.a.
Death rate per 1,000 population (1983): 7.0 (world avg. 11.0).
Natural increase rate per 1,000 population (1983): 22.0 (world avg. 18.0).
Total fertility rate (avg. births per childbearing woman; 1980–85): 3.2.
Marriage rate per 1,000 population: n.a.
Divorce rate per 1,000 population: n.a.
Life expectancy at birth (1980–85): male 67.7 years; female 73.3 years.
Major causes of death per 100,000 population (1977): circulatory disease 223.6; symptoms and ill-defined conditions 90.8; infectious and parasitic diseases 83.4; respiratory diseases 65.6.

National economy

Budget (1983). Revenue: G$610,400,000 (income tax 35.0%, excise duties 34.5%, post office and miscellaneous revenue 10.5%). Expenditures: G$1,-368,200,000 (debt charges 33.3%, education 5.3%, defense 5.3%, law and order 3.4%, health 2.9%).
Public debt (external, outstanding; 1983): U.S.$662,800,000.
Tourism (1983): receipts from visitors U.S.$4,200,000; expenditures by nationals abroad, n.a.
Production (metric tons except as noted). Agriculture, forestry, fishing (G$'000): sugarcane 3,750,000, rice 184,100, bananas and plantains 20,000, coconuts 22,000, oranges 12,000, hen eggs 4,150; livestock (number of live animals) 312,000 cattle, 142,000 pigs, 117,000 sheep, 15,000,000 chickens; roundwood 201,000 cu m§; fish catch 27,630§. Mining and quarrying (1984): bauxite 1,556,000, alumina 73,157 ‖ , gold 10,000 troy oz, diamonds 6,000 metric carats. Manufacturing (1981): rum 151,300 hectolitres¶, cigarettes 600,000,000 units, refined sugar 241,900§, stock feeds 55,000¶, flour 36,000, margarine 3,000¶. Construction: n.a. Energy production (consumption): electricity (kW-hr; 1983) 435,000,000 (435,000,000); coal, none (n.a); crude petroleum, n.a. (n.a.); petroleum products (metric tons; 1984) none (519,-000); natural gas, n.a. (n.a.).
Population economically active (1984): total 320,000; participation rate of total population 34.2% (female [1977] 25.7%, unemployed 27,039 ‖).

Price and earnings indexes (1980 = 100)

	1977	1978	1979	1980	1981	1982	1983
Consumer price index	64.6	74.4	87.7	100.0	124.7	147.8	169.9
Weekly earnings index	60.8	90.0	95.2	100.0	110.0	...	...

Household income and expenditure. Average household size (1980) 5.0; average annual income per household: n.a.; sources of income (1974): wages and salaries 73.0%, transfer payments 6.3%, other 20.7%; expenditure: n.a.

Gross national product (at current market prices; 1983): U.S.$410,000,000 (U.S.$465 per capita).

Structure of gross domestic product and labour force

	1981 in value G$'000,000	1981 % of total value	1980 labour force	1980 % of labour force
Agriculture	351	26.0	48,603	25.0
Mining	101	7.5	9,389	4.8
Manufacturing	150	11.1	27,939	14.4
Construction	110	8.1	6,574	3.4
Public utilities	...	...	2,772	1.4
Transportation and communication	90	6.7	9,160	4.7
Trade	145	10.7	14,690	7.7
Finance	64	4.7	2,878	1.5
Pub. admin., defense	276	20.4	57,416	29.5
Services	40	3.0		
Other	23	1.8	15,260	7.8
TOTAL	1,350⁹	100.0	194,681	100.0δ

Land use (1983): forested 83.2%; meadows and pastures 6.2%; agricultural and under permanent cultivation 2.5%; other 8.1%.

Foreign trade

Balance of trade (current prices)

	1978	1979	1980	1981	1982	1983
G$'000,000	+107.0	+9.4	+74.1	−155.6	−20.7	−34.7
% of total	7.6%	0.6%	3.9%	7.4%	1.4%	3.0%

Imports (1982): G$744,900,000 (fuels and lubricants 38.8%; machinery and transport equipment 16.4%; food, beverages, and tobacco 7.1%; chemicals 5.4%; clothing and footwear 3.0%). *Major import sources* (1984): Trinidad and Tobago 34.1%; United States 24.2%; United Kingdom 9.5%; Barbados 7.5%.
Exports (1982): G$724,000,000 (sugar 36.4%; calcined bauxite 25.8%; rice 8.4%; dried bauxite 8.0%; alumina 5.0%; timber 2.0%). *Major export destinations* (1984): United States 23.5%; United Kingdom 22.3%; Venezuela 16.7%; Canada 6.4%; Trinidad and Tobago 6.3%; West Germany 4.6%; France 3.3%; Jamaica 1.9%.

Transport and communications

Transport. Railroads: length (1980) 80 mi, 130 km□. Roads (1983): total length 3,426 mi, 5,513 km (paved 9%). Vehicles (1983): passenger cars 20,000; trucks and buses 4,610. Merchant marine (1984): vessels (100 gross tons and over) 104; total deadweight tonnage 22,377. Air transport (1982): total passengers 155,000; total cargo 3,100 metric tons; airports (1985) with scheduled flights 18.
Communications. Daily newspapers (1984): total number 1; total circulation 60,000; circulation per 1,000 population 64. Radio (1983): total number of receivers 350,000 (1 per 2.6 persons). Television: none. Telephones (1982): 28,500 (1 per 32 persons).

Education and health

Education (1979–80)

	schools	teachers	students	student/ teacher ratio
Primary (age 6–11)	424	6,021	164,830	27.4
Secondary (age 12–17)	87	2,513	46,595	18.5
Voc., teacher tr.	15	348	4,647	13.4
Higher	1		1,889	...

Educational attainment (1970). Percent of adult population over age 25 having: no formal schooling 12.2%; primary education 77.6%; secondary 9.2%; higher 1.0%. *Literacy* (1980): total population over age 15 literate 505,300 (95.5%); males literate 255,200 (97.1%); females literate 250,100 (94.0%).
Health: physicians (1980) 100◇ (1 per 8,820 persons); hospital beds (1979) 4,002 (1 per 212 persons); infant mortality rate per 1,000 live births (1983) 45.0.
Food (1980–82): daily per capita caloric intake 2,329 (vegetable products 88%, animal products 12%); 102% of FAO recommended minimum requirement.

Military

Total active duty personnel (1984): 6,500△ (army 92.3%, navy 4.6%, air force 3.1%). *Military expenditure as percent of GNP* (1982): 4.5% (world 6.1%); per capita expenditure U.S.$26.

*Greater Georgetown. †Estimated; no dated survey available. ‡1985 estimate. §1983. ‖ 1982. ¶1980. ⁹At current prices. δDetail does not add to total given because of rounding. □The two railways are used solely for mining and not for passenger transport. ◇Government physicians only. △All services form part of the army.

Haiti

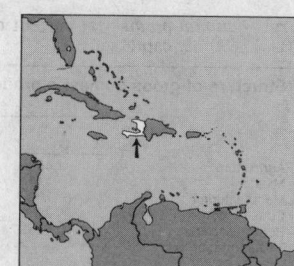

Official name: République d'Haïti (Republic of Haiti).
Form of government: republic with one legislative house (National Assembly [59]).
Head of state and government: President.
Capital: Port-au-Prince.
Official language: French.
Official religion: Roman Catholicism.
Monetary unit: 1 gourde (G) = 100 centimes; valuation (Oct. 21, 1985) 1 U.S.$ = G5.00; 1 £ = G7.17.

Area and population

Departements	Capitals	area sq mi	area sq km	population 1982 census*
Centre	Hinche	1,389	3,597	361,470
Grande Anse	Jérémie	1,917	3,100	489,957
L'Artibonite	Gonaïves	1,890	4,895	732,932
Nord	Cap-Haïtien	840	2,175	564,002
Nord-Est	Fort-Liberté	656	1,698	189,573
Nord-Ouest	Port-de-Paix	808	2,094	293,531
Ouest	Port-au-Prince	1,774	4,595	1,551,792
Sud	Les Cayes	1,005	2,602	502,624
Sud-Est	Jacmel	802	2,077	367,911
TOTAL		10,360†	26,833	5,053,792

Demography

Population (1985): 5,251,200.
Density (1985): persons per sq mi 507.0, persons per sq km 195.8.
Urban–rural (1982): urban 20.6%; rural 79.4%.
Sex distribution (1982): male 48.48%; female 51.52%.
Age breakdown (1982): under 15, 39.2%; 15–29, 26.9%; 30–44, 15.6%; 45–59, 10.0%; 60–74, 5.4%; 75 and over, 2.9%.
Population projection: (1990) 5,580,200; (2000) 6,978,000.
Doubling time: 31 years.
Ethnic composition (1980): black 95%; mulatto 5%.
Religious affiliation (1982): Roman Catholic 80.3%‡; Baptist 9.7%; Pentecostal 3.6%; other (mostly Protestant) 6.4%.
Major cities (1982)*: Port-au-Prince 449,831; Cap-Haïtien 64,406; Pétionville 35,333; Gonaïves 34,209; Les Cayes 34,090.

Vital statistics

Birth rate per 1,000 population (1980–85): 35.6 (world avg. 29.0).
Death rate per 1,000 population (1980–85): 13.0 (world avg. 11.0).
Natural increase rate per 1,000 population (1980–85): 22.6 (world avg. 18.0).
Total fertility rate (avg. births per childbearing woman; 1980–85): 5.7.
Marriage rate per 1,000 population (1980): 0.7§.
Divorce rate per 1,000 population (1980): 0.1§.
Life expectancy at birth (1980–85): male 51.2 years; female 54.4 years.
Major causes of death (1982): diarrhea, malaria, tuberculosis.

National economy

Budget (1982). Revenue: G1,113,000,000 (tax revenue 83.3%, of which import duties 19.1%, excise taxes 13.3%, taxes on corporate income 11.3%, individual income taxes 4.8; grants 8.5%; nontax revenue 7.9%). Expenditures: G1,349,600,000 (goods and services 59.4%; interest 4.3%).
Production (metric tons except as noted). Agriculture, forestry, fishing (1984): sugarcane 3,000,000, bananas and plantains 550,000, sweet potatoes 350,000, mangoes 340,000, cassava 265,000, corn (maize) 186,000, rice 124,000, sorghum 123,000, dry beans 52,000; livestock—1,350,000 cattle, 1,100,000 goats, 500,000 pigs, 425,000 horses; roundwood 5,624,000 cu m‖; fish catch 4,000‖. Mining and quarrying (1984): construction materials for local use. Manufacturing (value of production in G'000,000; 1981): refined flour 218; cement 128; baseballs and softballs 92; electronic equipment 73; livestock feed 12; edible oils 23,883 metric tons; beer and malt 1,539,000 bottles; cotton clothing 2,575,000 pieces. Construction: n.a. Energy production (consumption): electricity (kW-hr; 1983) 373,000,000 (373,000,000); coal, none (n.a.); crude petroleum, none (n.a.); petroleum products (metric tons; 1983) none (208,000); natural gas, none (n.a.).
Tourism (1981): receipts U.S.$85,000,000; expenditures U.S.$26,000,000.
Gross national product (1983): U.S.$1,700,000,000 (U.S.$333 per capita).

Structure of gross domestic product and labour force

	1983 in value U.S.$'000	1983 % of total value	1982 labour force	1982 % of labour force
Agriculture	525,800	32.2	1,222,859	57.4
Mining	1,600	0.1	19,260	0.9
Manufacturing	281,100	17.2	121,208	5.7
Construction	89,200	5.5	22,192	1.0
Public utilities	12,800	0.8	2,057	0.1
Transp. and commun.	32,900	2.0	16,386	0.8
Trade	294,800	18.1	285,728	13.4
Finance	87,300	5.3	4,030	0.2
Pub. admin., defense	173,400	10.6	...	...
Services	134,000	8.2	124,475	5.8
Other	...	...	311,463	14.6
TOTAL	1,632,900	100.0	2,129,658	100.0†

Household income and expenditure. Average household size (1980) 5.1; source of income: n.a.; expenditure (1970): food and drink 48.9%, health

8.6%, housing 7.9%, fuel and power 7.0%, household equipment and operation 4.9%, education 4.9%, clothing 3.5%, other 14.3%.
Population economically active (1982): total 2,129,658; participation rate of total population 42.1% (female 41.0%, unemployed 12.2%).

Price and earnings indexes (1980 = 100)

	1979	1980	1981	1982	1983	1984	1985
Consumer price index	84.9	100.0	110.9	119.0	131.2	140.4	151.8º
Monthly earnings index¶	72.7	100.0	120.0	120.0	...	...	...

Public debt (external, outstanding; 1983): U.S.$433,500,000.
Land use (1983): forested 3.6%; meadows and pastures 18.2%; agricultural and under permanent cultivation 32.6%; other 45.6%.

Foreign tradeठ

Balance of trade (current prices)

	1978	1979	1980	1981	1982	1983
G'000,000	−223.3	−254.0	−659.4	−1,230.8	−493.0	−620.5
% of total	12.6%	12.1%	25.3%	44.4%	23.1%	24.7%

Imports (1982–83): G1,890,000,000 (basic manufactures 19.5%, machinery and transport equipment 19.4%, food and live animals 18.7%, petroleum products 12.8%, chemicals 9.0%). *Major import sources* (1982): United States 57.2%; Japan 5.2%; Taiwan 4.5%; Canada 3.8%; France 2.8%
Exports (1982–83): G951,800,000 (light industrial products [including baseballs, clothing, electronic equipment] 50.4%, coffee 26.9%, perfume resinoids 3.7%, cordage 2.6%, cocoa 2.1%). *Major export destinations* (1982): United States 78.5%; France 4.9%; West Germany 3.3%; Italy 3.1%.

Transport and communications

Transport. Railroads (1984): ▫. Roads (1983): total length 2,292 mi, 3,688 km (paved 18%). Vehicles (1983): passenger cars 34,025; trucks and buses 4,257. Merchant marine (1984): vessels (100 gross tons and over) 6; total deadweight tonnage 851. Air transport (1983): passenger arrivals 226,000◊, passenger departures 242,000◊; short ton-mi cargo 1,301,000△, metric ton-km cargo 1,900,000△; airports (1985) with scheduled flights 2.
Communications. Daily newspapers (1983): total number 4; total circulation 20,000; circulation per 1,000 population 3.9. Radio (1984): total receivers 120,000 (1 per 43 persons). Television (1984): total receivers 65,000 (1 per 80 persons). Telephones (1983): 38,400 (1 per 133 persons).

Education and health

Education (1982–83)

	schools	teachers	students	student/ teacher ratio
Primary (age 6–12)	3,241	16,986	723,041	42.6
Secondary (age 13–18)	290	5,367	117,081	21.8
Higher	1	582	3,464	6.0

Educational attainment (1971). Percent of adult population over age 25 having: no formal schooling 83.5%; primary education 12.4%; secondary 3.8%; higher 0.3%. *Literacy* (1982): total population over age 14 literate 1,066,966 (34.7%); males literate 547,318 (37.1%); females literate 519,648 (32.5%).
Health: physicians† (1979) 600 (1 per 8,050 persons); hospital beds (1980) 3,964 (1 per 1,236 persons); infant mortality rate per 1,000 live births (1980–85) 124.0.
Food (1980–82): daily per capita caloric intake 1,906 (vegetable products 95%, animal products 5%); 84% of FAO recommended minimum requirement.

Military

Total active duty personnel (1984): 6,800 (army 92.6%, navy 4.4%, air force 3.0%). *Military expenditure as percent of GNP* (1983): 1.4% (world 6.1%); per capita expenditure U.S.$4.

*Preliminary figures. †Detail does not add to total given because of rounding. ‡About 90% of all Roman Catholics also practice Voodoo. §Registered only. ‖1983. ¶Minimum wages paid in industrial enterprises. ºJune. ठImport figures are f.o.b. (free on board) in balance of trade and c.i.f. (cost, insurance, and freight) for commodities and trading partners. ▫The only railway is privately owned and used to transport sugarcane. ◊Port-au-Prince airport only. △1980. †Physicians employed by the Ministry of Health only.

KAUFMAN & MARAFFI, INC.

National palace and statue of the "Marron Inconnu" ("Unknown Maroon" [escaped slave of the Colonial era who first took up the fight for independence]), by Albert Mangonès, Port-au-Prince, Haiti.

Honduras

Official name: República de Honduras (Republic of Honduras).
Form of government: multiparty republic with one legislative house (National Congress [82]).
Head of state and government: President.
Capital: Tegucigalpa.
Official language: Spanish.
Official religion: none.
Monetary unit: 1 Honduran lempira (L) = 100 centavos; valuation* (Oct. 21, 1985) 1 U.S.$ = L2.02; 1 £ = L2.89.

Area and population		area		population
		sq mi	sq km	1983 estimate
Departments	**Administrative centres**			
Atlántida	La Ceiba	1,641	4,251	242,200
Choluteca	Choluteca	1,626	4,211	289,600
Colón	Trujillo	3,427	8,875	128,400
Comayagua	Comayagua	2,006	5,196	211,500
Copán	Santa Rosa de Copán	1,237	3,203	217,300
Cortés	San Pedro Sula	1,527	3,954	624,100
El Paraíso	Yuscarán	2,787	7,218	206,600
Francisco Morazán	Tegucigalpa	3,068	7,946	736,300
Gracias a Dios	Puerto Lempira	6,421	16,630	35,500
Intibucá	La Esperanza	1,186	3,072	111,400
Islas de la Bahía	Roatán	100	261	18,700
La Paz	La Paz	900	2,331	86,600
Lempira	Gracias	1,656	4,290	174,900
Ocotepeque	Nueva Ocotepeque	649	1,680	64,100
Olancho	Juticalpa	9,402	24,351	228,100
Santa Bárbara	Santa Bárbara	1,975	5,115	286,800
Valle	Nacaome	604	1,565	125,600
Yoro	Yoro	3,065	7,939	304,300
TOTAL		43,277	112,088	4,092,200†

Demography

Population (1985): 4,372,000.
Density (1985): persons per sq mi 101.0, persons per sq km 39.0.
Urban–rural (1983): urban 37.0%; rural 63.0%.
Sex distribution (1982): male 50.14%; female 49.86%.
Age breakdown (1982): under 15, 47.6%; 15–29, 26.3%; 30–44, 13.6%; 45–59, 8.0%; 60–74, 3.7%; 75 and over 0.8%.
Population projection: (1990) 5,105,000; (2000) 6,978,000.
Doubling time: 24 years.
Ethnic composition (1982): mestizo 90.0%; black (including Black Caribs) 5.0%; Indian 4.0%; white 1.0%.
Religious affiliation (1980): Roman Catholic 93.6%; Protestant 3.0%; Afro-American spiritist 0.5%; Muslim 0.3%; other 2.6%.
Major cities (1983): Tegucigalpa 509,000; San Pedro Sula 323,500; La Ceiba 57,900; Choluteca 50,700; El Progreso 50,000.

Vital statistics

Birth rate per 1,000 population (1982): 43.9 (world avg. 29.0); legitimate, n.a.; illegitimate, n.a.
Death rate per 1,000 population (1982): 10.1 (world avg. 11.0).
Natural increase rate per 1,000 population (1982): 33.8 (world avg. 18.0).
Total fertility rate (avg. births per childbearing woman; 1981): 6.6.
Marriage rate per 1,000 population (1979): 4.0.
Divorce rate per 1,000 population (1979): 0.2.
Life expectancy at birth (1980–85): male 58.2 years; female 61.7 years.
Major causes of death: n.a.; however, principal causes include diseases of early infancy, gastritis and other enteric diseases (particularly typhoid fever), pneumonia and influenza, accidents, and cardiovascular diseases.

National economy

Budget (1983). Revenue: L1,543,700,000 (current revenue 50.5%, of which tax revenue 46.1%; import and export duties 18.1%; tax on production and internal trade 15.1%; individual income tax 12.3%). Expenditures: L1,543,-700,000 (current expenditure 61.5%, of which wages and salaries 31.1%; payment on public debt 12.9%; net allowance on loans 8.5%).
Public debt (external, outstanding; 1983): U.S.$1,570,300,000.
Tourism (1981): receipts from visitors U.S.$31,000,000; expenditures by nationals abroad U.S.$128,000,000.
Production (metric tons except as noted). Agriculture, forestry, fishing (1984): sugarcane 3,000,000, bananas and plantains 1,384,000, corn (maize) 552,000, milk 280,000, coffee 73,000, dry beans 52,000, seed cotton 15,000, tobacco 12,000, cotton seed 10,000; livestock (number of live animals) 2,434,000 cattle, 400,000 pigs; roundwood 5,211,000 cu m‡; fish catch 8,432‡. Mining and quarrying (1983): limestone 500,000; marble 40,000; zinc ore and concentrate 37,980; salt 30,000; lead 19,290; gold 2,151 troy oz. Manufacturing (1984): cement 583,000; iron and steel semimanufactures 20,000§; raw sugar 568,500; beef and veal 69,000‡; palm oil 7,500‡; soft drinks 1,710,600 hectolitres; beer 452,500 hectolitres; matches 5,132,000 units; cigarettes 2,024,400 units‡. Construction (value added in lempiras; 1984)‖: residential 60,596,000; commercial 13,047,000; industrial 2,612,-000. Energy production (consumption): electricity (kW-hr; 1984) 1,150,-000,000‡ (964,000,000); coal, none (n.a.); crude petroleum (barrels; 1983) none (1,985,000); petroleum products (metric tons; 1983) 245,000 (248,000); natural gas, none (n.a.).

Gross national product (at current market prices; 1983): U.S.$2,740,000,000 (U.S.$670 per capita).

Structure of gross domestic product and labour force				
	1983			
	in value L'000,000	% of total value	labour force	% of labour force
Agriculture	1,450	24.6	698,706	57.7
Mining	114	1.9	3,676	0.3
Manufacturing	785	13.3	158,940	13.2
Construction	320	5.4	41,642	3.4
Public utilities	128	2.2	4,842	0.4
Transportation and communication	403	6.8	35,952	2.9
Trade	692	11.7	102,530	8.5
Finance	629	10.7	11,742	1.0
Public admin., defense	276	4.7	}	
Services	476	8.1	152,480	12.6
Other	618¶	10.5		
TOTAL	5,891º	100.0†	1,210,510	100.0

Population economically active (1983): total 1,210,510; participation rate of population over age 15, 29.6% (female 16.5%, unemployed 21.0%).

Price and earnings indexes (1980 = 100)						
	1979	1980	1981	1982	1983	1984	1985
Consumer price index	86.5	100.0	110.2	121.2	132.7	138.8	141.2ŏ
Monthly earnings index	...	...	...	...	...	...	...

Household income and expenditure: n.a.
Land use (1983): forested 34.1%; meadows and pastures 30.4%; agricultural and under permanent cultivation 15.8%; other 19.7%.

Foreign trade□

Balance of trade (current prices)						
	1978	1979	1980	1981	1982	1983
L'000,000	−28.4	−26.9	−103.8	−114.8	−101.7	−133.0
% of total	2.2%	1.7%	5.7%	6.8%	3.7%	4.6%

Imports (1983): L1,608,616,000 (manufactured goods 23.6%, chemical products 20.9%, mineral fuels and lubricants 20.6%, machinery and transport equipment 18.4%, food products 9.1%). Major import sources: United States 37.8%; Venezuela 9.5%; Guatemala 8.4%; Costa Rica 4.5%; Trinidad and Tobago 4.3%.
Exports (1983): L1,334,701,000 (bananas 30.4%, coffee 22.7%, wood 6.1%, shrimp and lobsters 5.4%, refrigerated meat 4.7%, refined sugar 4.2%, lead and zinc 3.1%, silver 2.6%). Major export destinations: United States 51.7%; Japan 6.0%; West Germany 5.2%; Guatemala 4.4%; Belgium 4.1%.

Transport and communications

Transport. Railroads (1983): route length 624 mi, 1,004 km; passengers, n.a.; cargo, n.a. Roads (1983): total length 5,618 mi, 9,042 km (paved 22%). Vehicles (1983): passenger cars 58,920; trucks and buses 24,385. Merchant marine (1984): vessels (100 gross tons and over) 238; total deadweight tonnage 390,304. Air transport (1983): passenger-mi 216,200,000, passenger-km 348,000,000; short ton-mi cargo 1,619,000, metric ton-km cargo 2,364,000; airports (1985) with scheduled flights 3.
Communications. Daily newspapers (1984): total number 6; total circulation 236,300◊; circulation per 1,000 population 58. Radio (1983): total number of receivers 1,534,620 (1 per 2.7 persons). Television (1984): total number of receivers 136,000 (1 per 31 persons). Telephones (1983): 37,278 (1 per 110 persons).

Education and health

Education (1983)	schools	teachers	students	student/ teacher ratio
Primary (age 7–13)	6,422	19,300	802,915	41.6
Secondary (age 14–19)	356	5,853△	540,406	...
Voc., teacher tr.	11	...	56,277	...
Higher	2	2,153	30,096	14.0

Educational attainment (1974). Percentage of adult population over age 25 having: no formal schooling 52.8%; less than primary education 34.4%; primary 6.0%; some secondary 3.5%; secondary 1.8%; postsecondary 1.0%.
Literacy (1980): total population over age 15 literate 1,309,500 (68.6%); males literate 676,700 (71.1%); females literate 632,800 (66.2%).
Health (1982): physicians 1,440 (1 per 2,746 persons); hospital beds 5,506 (1 per 718 persons); infant mortality rate per 1,000 live births (1982) 87.0.
Food (1980–82): daily per capita caloric intake 2,170 (vegetable products 88%, animal products 12%); 96% of FAO recommended minimum requirement.

Military

Total active duty personnel (1984): 17,200 (army 90.1%, navy 2.9%, air force 7.0%). Military expenditure as percent of GNP (1982): 2.3% (world 6.0%); per capita expenditure U.S.$15.

*The Honduran lempira is officially pegged to the U.S. dollar; the official buying and selling rates are L2.00 and L2.02, respectively, per U.S.$1. †Detail does not add to total given because of rounding. ‡1983. §1982. ‖Tegucigalpa, San Pedro Sula, and La Ceiba only. ¶Includes net indirect taxes. ºAt current prices. ŏMarch only. □Import figures are f.o.b. (free on board) in balance of trade and c.i.f. (cost, insurance, and freight) for commodities and trading partners. ◊Circulation for 5 dailies only. △Includes vocational and teacher training.

Hong Kong

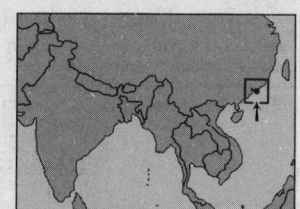

Official name: Hsiang Kang (Chinese); Hong Kong (English).
Political status: colony (United Kingdom) with three nominated advisory councils (Executive Council [16], Legislative Council [47], Urban Council [30]).
Chief of state: British Monarch.
Head of government: Governor.
Capital: Victoria.
Official languages: Chinese; English.
Official religion: none.
Monetary unit: 1 HK dollar (HK$) = 100 cents; valuation (Oct. 21, 1985) 1 U.S.$ = HK$7.80; 1 £ = HK$11.18.

Area and population

Districts	area* sq mi	area* sq km	population† 1981 census
Hong Kong Island	29.9	77.4	1,203,342
Kowloon	17.0	44.1	2,458,279
New Territories	353.6	915.7	1,324,939
TOTAL	400.5	1,037.2	4,986,560

Demography

Population (1985): 5,415,000.
Density‡ (1985): persons per sq mi 13,149.6, persons per sq km 5,077.4.
Urban–rural (1985): urban 90.8%; rural 9.2%.
Sex distribution (1984): male 51.77%; female 48.23%.
Age breakdown (1984): under 15, 23.5%; 15–29, 31.1%; 30–44, 19.9%; 45–59, 14.5%; 60–74, 8.6%; 75 and over, 2.4%.
Population projection: (1990) 6,135,000; (2000) 7,161,000.
Doubling time: 72 years.
Ethnic composition (1984): Chinese 98.6%; British 0.9%; other 0.5%.
Religious affiliation (1983): predominantly Buddhist; some Confucianist and Taoist; approximately 500,000 Christian.
Major cities (1981): New Kowloon 1,649,950; Kowloon 799,123; Victoria 590,771.

Vital statistics

Birth rate per 1,000 population (1984): 14.4 (world avg. 29.0).
Death rate per 1,000 population (1984): 4.8 (world avg. 11.0).
Natural increase rate per 1,000 population (1984): 9.6 (world avg. 18.0).
Total fertility rate (avg. births per childbearing woman; 1980–85): 2.1.
Marriage rate per 1,000 population (1984): 10.0.
Divorce rate per 1,000 population (1984): 0.9.
Life expectancy at birth (1984): male 72.7 years; female 78.3 years.
Major causes of death per 100,000 population (1984): diseases of circulatory system 137.9; malignant neoplasms (cancers) 136.3; diseases of respiratory system 79.5; diseases of the digestive system 20.8.

National economy

Budget (1984–85 est.). Revenue: HK$36,194,000,000 (earnings and profit taxes 36.9%, income from properties and investments 18.3%, excise duties 7.7%, fees and charges 7.2%). Expenditures: HK$37,332,600,000 (education 16.9%, medical 8.1%, law and order 7.9%, social welfare 5.8%, housing 4.2%, defense 4.2%).
Public debt (external, outstanding; 1983): U.S.$223,700,000.
Gross national product (at current market prices; 1983): U.S.$31,900,000,000 (U.S.$6,000 per capita).

Structure of gross domestic product and labour force

	1983 in value HK$'000,000	1983 % of total value	1984 labour force	1984 % of labour force
Agriculture	1,242	0.6	29,800	1.1
Mining	328	0.2 }		
Manufacturing	44,231	21.9	959,400	36.1
Construction	12,002	5.9	201,700	7.6
Public utilities	4,142	2.1	12,100	0.5
Transportation and communication	16,049	7.9	203,000	7.6
Trade	42,535	21.1	549,600	20.7
Finance	61,339	30.4	130,600	4.9
Pub. admin., defense, and services	31,696	15.7	455,200	17.1
Other	−11,738¶	−5.8¶	114,000	4.3
TOTAL	201,826⊘	100.0	2,655,500	100.0δ

Production (metric tons except as noted). Agriculture, forestry, fishing (1984): vegetables 159,000, fruits and nuts 2,490, rice 20, milk 3,100; livestock (number of live animals) 560,000 pigs§, 540 cattle; roundwood 180,000 cu m ‖; fish catch 200,000, of which marine 192,000. Mining and quarrying (1984): feldspar sand 92,293; feldspar 23,101; kaolin 70; quartz 34. Manufacturing (value added in HK$; 1981): wearing apparel 9,658,000,000; electrical machinery 6,773,000,000; textiles 5,202,000,000; plastic products 3,341,000,000; publishing and printed material 1,982,000,000; food, beverages, and tobacco 1,904,000,000. Construction (1984): residential 625,000 sq m; nonresidential 1,304,000 sq m. Energy production (consumption): electricity (kW-hr; 1983) 16,482,000,000 (16,114,000,000); coal (metric tons;

1983) none (3,218,000); petroleum products (metric tons; 1983) none (4,864,000); natural gas (cu m; 1983) none (151,897,000).
Population economically active (1984): total 2,707,200; participation rate of total population 50.2% (female 36.8%, unemployed 3.9%).

Price and earnings indexes (1979–80 = 100)

	1978	1979	1980	1981	1982	1983	1984
Consumer price index	80.1	89.5	103.3	117.9	130.3	143.2	154.9
Daily earnings index	80.2	92.5	107.5	125.4	136.2	...	...

Household income and expenditure. Average household size (1981) 3.9; income per household HK$45,199 (U.S.$8,081); source of income: n.a.; expenditure (1979–80): food 38.3%, housing 20.1%, personal services and entertainment 11.1%, clothing and footwear 7.8%, transportation and vehicles 6.4%, durable goods 4.6%, fuel and light 2.8%.
Tourism (1983): receipts from visitors U.S.$1,387,000,000; expenditures by nationals abroad, n.a.
Land use (1984): forested 13.0%; meadows and pastures 1.0%; agricultural and under permanent cultivation 8.0%; built-on, scrub lands, and other 78.0%.

Foreign trade

Balance of trade (current prices)

	1979	1980	1981	1982	1983	1984
HK$'000,000	−9,903	−13,408	−16,212	−15,508	−14,743	−1,929
% of total	6.1%	6.4%	6.2%	5.7%	4.4%	0.4%

Imports (1984): HK$223,370,200,000 (machinery and transport equipment 25.8%, of which electrical machinery 10.1%; textile yarn and fabrics 14.7%; food and live animals 9.0%, of which vegetables and fruits 2.2%; chemicals and related products 6.9%; photographic apparatus, watches, and clocks 5.3%; petroleum and petroleum products 4.6%). *Major import sources:* China 25.6%; Japan 23.6%; United States 10.9%; Taiwan 7.8%; Singapore 5.5%.
Exports (1984): HK$221,440,820,000□ (machinery and transport equipment 25.6%, of which electrical machinery 8.9%; clothing accessories and wearing apparel 23.7%; textile yarn and fabrics 9.3%; travel goods 1.6%). *Major export destinations:* United States 33.2%; China 17.8%; United Kingdom 4.7%; Japan 4.4%; West Germany 4.3%.

Transport and communications

Transport. Railroads (1983): length 21 mi, 34 km; passenger-mi 524,000,000, passenger-km 843,000,000; short ton-mi cargo 52,449,000; metric ton-km cargo 76,574,000. Roads (1984): total length 769 mi, 1,238 km (paved 100%). Vehicles (1984): passenger cars 198,969; trucks and buses 84,678. Merchant marine (1984): vessels (100 gross tons and over) 340; total deadweight tonnage 9,586,082. Air transport (1984): passenger arrivals 4,069,000, passenger departures 4,188,000; airports (1984) with scheduled flights 1.
Communications. Daily newspapers (1984): total number 62; total circulation 3,189,000◊; circulation per 1,000 population 602◊ Radio (1984): total number of receivers 2,700,000 (1 per 2.0 persons). Television (1984): total number of receivers 1,278,000 (1 per 4.2 persons). Telephones (1984): 2,144,000 (1 per 2.6 persons).

Education and health

Education (1984–85)

	schools	teachers	students	student/ teacher ratio
Primary (age 6–11)	757	19,824	537,345	27.1
Secondary (age 12–18)	412	...	426,553	...
Vocational	18	...	17,827	...
Higher	21	3,169	36,316	11.5

Educational attainment (1981). Percent of population over age 5 having: no schooling 15.5%; primary education 39.8%; secondary 39.2%; higher 5.5%.
Literacy (1981): total population literate 3,885,281 (77.9%); males literate 2,195,720 (84.3%); females literate 1,689,561 (70.9%).
Health (1984): physicians 4,609 (1 per 1,164 persons); hospital beds 24,073 (1 per 223 persons); infant mortality rate per 1,000 live births (1984) 9.9.
Food (1979–81): daily per capita caloric intake 2,771 (vegetable products 70%, animal products 30%); 121% of FAO recommended minimum requirement.

Military

Total active duty personnel (1984)△: 8,496 (army 92.3%, navy 7.7%, air force, n.a.). *Military expenditure as percent of GNP* (1983): 0.6% (world 6.1%); per capita expenditure U.S.$39.

---

*Excludes the surface areas of reservoirs. †Excludes 13,906 transients and 20,600 Vietnamese refugees but includes 49,747 marine population. ‡Density based on land area. §Excludes local pigs not slaughtered in abattoirs. ‖ 1983. ¶Less imputed bank service charges. ⊘At current prices. δDetail does not add to total given because of rounding. □Includes reexports. ◊Thirty-five newspapers only. △British forces with a few locally enlisted personnel in the navy.

Hungary

Official name: Magyar Népköztársaság (Hungarian People's Republic).
Form of government: unitary single-party republic with one legislative house (National Assembly [352]).
Chief of State: President.
Head of government: Premier.
Capital: Budapest.
Official language: Hungarian.
Official religion: none.
Monetary unit: 1 forint (Ft) = 100 filler; valuation (Oct. 21, 1985) 1 U.S.$ = Ft48.06; 1 £ = Ft68.92.

Area and population

Counties	Capitals	area sq mi	area sq km	population 1984 estimate
Baranya	Pécs	1,732	4,487	434,000
Bács-Kiskun	Kecskemét	3,229	8,363	564,000
Békés	Békéscsaba	2,175	5,632	429,000
Borsod-Abaúj-Zemplén	Miskolc	2,798	7,248	801,000
Csongrád	Szeged	1,646	4,263	453,000
Fejér	Székesfehérvár	1,689	4,374	423,000
Győr-Sopron	Győr	1,549	4,012	430,000
Hajdú-Bihar	Debrecen	2,398	6,212	552,000
Heves	Eger	1,404	3,637	346,000
Komárom	Tatabánya	869	2,250	323,000
Nógrád	Salgótarján	982	2,544	237,000
Pest	Budapest*	2,469	6,394	983,000
Somogy	Kaposvár	2,331	6,035	357,000
Szabolcs-Szatmár	Nyíregyháza	2,293	5,938	586,000
Szolnok	Szolnok	2,165	5,608	441,000
Tolna	Szekszárd	1,429	3,702	268,000
Vas	Szombathely	1,288	3,337	283,000
Veszprém	Veszprém	1,810	4,689	389,000
Zala	Zalaegerszeg	1,462	3,786	316,000
Capital City				
Budapest*		203	525	2,064,000
TOTAL		35,921	93,036	10,679,000

Demography

Population (1985): 10,645,000.
Density (1985): persons per sq mi 296.3, persons per sq km 114.4.
Urban-rural (1984): urban 56.0%; rural 44.0%.
Sex distribution (1984): male 48.35%; female 51.65%.
Age breakdown (1984): under 15, 21.8%; 15–29, 20.7%; 30–49, 27.3%; 50–59, 12.3%; 60 and over, 17.9%.
Population projection: (1990) 10,920,000; (2000) 10,964,000.
During the intercensal period 1970–80, the average growth rate was 0.2%; since 1980, however, the population has been decreasing.
Ethnic composition (1980): Magyar 98.8%; German 0.3%; other 0.9%.
Religious affiliation (1980): Christian 83.2%, of which Roman Catholic 53.9%, Protestant 21.6%; Jewish 0.9%; nonreligious 8.7%; atheist 7.2%.
Major cities (1985): Budapest 2,071,500; Miskolc 211,600; Debrecen 208,900; Szeged 178,600; Pécs 175,500; Győr 130,000.

Vital statistics

Birth rate per 1,000 population (1984): 11.7 (world avg. 29.0); (1982) legitimate 92.9%; illegitimate 7.1%.
Death rate per 1,000 population (1984): 13.7 (world avg. 11.0).
Natural increase rate per 1,000 population (1984): −2.0 (world avg. 18.0).
Total fertility rate (avg. births per childbearing woman; 1980–85): 2.1.
Marriage rate per 1,000 population (1984): 7.0.
Divorce rate per 1,000 population (1984): 2.5.
Life expectancy at birth (1983): male 65.6 years; female 73.5 years.
Major causes of death per 100,000 population (1983): diseases of the circulatory system 743.1; malignant neoplasms (cancers) 269.3.

National economy

Budget (1984). Revenue: Ft563,200,000,000 (payments by enterprises 82.6%, personal income tax 7.2%). Expenditures: Ft566,700,000,000 (social welfare and health 26.1%, economic tasks 23.9%, interest on public debt 9.5%, education 9.2%, defense 6.0%).
Public debt (external, outstanding; 1982): U.S.$10,030,000,000.
Tourism (1983): receipts from visitors U.S.$434,000,000; expenditures by nationals abroad U.S.$152,000,000.
Production (metric tons except as noted). Agriculture, forestry, fishing (1984): corn (maize) 6,700,000, wheat 7,300,000, sugar beets 4,200,000, potatoes 1,300,000, barley 896,000, sunflower seeds 578,110; livestock (number of live animals) 9,844,000 pigs, 2,977,000 sheep, 1,907,000 cattle, 59,155,000 poultry; roundwood 6,432,000 cu m; fish catch 43,857,000†. Mining and quarrying (1984): bauxite 2,994,000; dolomite 1,324,000†; iron ore 383,000. Manufacturing (1984): cement 4,145,000; crude steel 3,750,000; rolled steel 2,955,000; pig iron 2,096,000; chemical fertilizers 1,108,643; aluminum 74,200; cotton fabrics 303,182,000 sq m; leather footwear 44,564,000 pairs; buses and trucks 12,736,000 units. Construction (1984): residential 1,720,800; nonresidential (units) 796. Energy production (consumption): electricity (kW-hr; 1984) 26,229,000,000 (34,230,000,000); coal (metric tons; 1984) 25,047,000 (27,066,000†); crude petroleum (barrels; 1984) 14,711,300 (66,468,000†); petroleum products (metric tons; 1984) 8,881,000 (10,172,000); natural gas (cu m; 1984) 6,898,000,000 (10,716,000,000).

Land use (1983): forested 17.5%; meadows and pastures 13.8%; agricultural and under permanent cultivation 57.0%; other 11.7%.
Gross national product (1983): U.S.$18,631,000,000 (U.S.$1,750 per capita).

Structure of net material product and labour force

	1983 in value Ft'000,000,000	% of total value	labour force	% of labour force
Agriculture	97.8	13.3	1,082,800	21.8
Mining and manufacturing	276.9	37.5	1,577,500	31.7
Construction	79.1	10.7	373,000	7.5
Public utilities	3.9	0.5	77,000	1.6
Transportation and communication	57.9	7.8	393,000	7.9
Trade	81.5	11.0	497,000	10.0
Services	...	...	969,200	19.5
Other	140.7‡	19.1‡	...	...
TOTAL	737.8§	100.0 ‖	4,970,100	100.0

Population economically active (1984): total 4,940,000; participation rate of total population 46.3% (female 43.3%, unemployed, n.a.).

Price and earnings indexes (1980 = 100)

	1979	1980	1981	1982	1983	1984	1985¶
Consumer price index	91.7	100.0	104.6	111.8	120.0	129.9	138.0
Monthly earnings index	94.1	100.0	107.2	114.0	119.7	127.5	142.1

Household income and expenditure. Average household size (1983) 3.0; income per household Ft163,100 (U.S.$3,800); sources of income: wages 65.7%, social income 33.1%, other 1.2%; expenditure (1983): food 31.4%, education and culture 13.4%, alcoholic drinks 9.6%, clothing and footwear 8.8%, housing 8.1%, transportation 7.2%, health 6.4%.

Foreign trade

Balance of trade (current prices)

	1978	1979	1980	1981	1982	1983	1984
Fts'000,000,000	−60.2	−26.8	−18.9	−14.9	−0.3	9.1	23.4
% of total	11.1%	4.5%	3.2%	2.4%	0.1%	1.2%	2.9%

Imports (1983): Ft364,963,100,000 (machinery and transport equipment 28.9%; crude petroleum and petroleum products 14.0%; chemicals and related products 13.6%; food 5.6%; textile yarn and fabrics 4.7%; iron and steel 3.0%; nonferrous metals 2.9%; paper and paperboard 1.8%). *Major import sources:* U.S.S.R. 29.5%; West Germany 11.1%; East Germany 6.8%; Czechoslovakia 5.3%; Austria 5.0%; Poland 3.9%; Yugoslavia 3.1%.
Exports (1983): Ft374,107,900,000 (machinery and transport equipment 31.5%, of which electrical machinery and telecommunication equipment 15.0%; food 20.4%, of which meat 7.3%; chemicals 10.2%; petroleum products 6.1%; iron and steel 3.3%). *Major export destinations:* U.S.S.R. 33.5%; West Germany 7.2%; East Germany 6.1%; Czechoslovakia 5.6%; Austria 3.8%; Poland 3.7%; Italy 3.4%; Yugoslavia 3.3%.

Transport and communications

Transport. Railroads (1984): length 8,106 mi, 13,045 km; passenger-mi 7,005,600,000, passenger-km 11,274,400,000; short ton-mi cargo 15,646,000,000, metric ton-km cargo 22,845,000,000. Roads (1984): total length 18,445 mi, 29,684 km (paved 87.3%). Vehicles (1984): passenger cars 1,258,498; trucks and buses 153,992. Merchant marine (1984): vessels (100 gross tons and over) 21; total deadweight tonnage 112,468. Air transport (1984): passenger-mi 769,753,000, passenger-km 1,238,800,000; short ton-mi cargo 15,684,000, metric ton-km cargo 22,900,000; airports (1985) 4.
Communications. Daily newspapers (1983): total number 29; total circulation 2,842,000; circulation per 1,000 population 265.6. Radio (1980): 2,700,000 (1 per 4.0 persons). Television (1984): 2,845,000 (1 per 3.7 persons). Telephones (1984): 1,383,200 (1 per 8.0 persons).

Education and health

Education (1984–85)

	schools	teachers	students	student/ teacher ratio
Primary (age 6–13)	3,539	86,367	1,286,648	14.9
Secondary (age 14–18)	175	7,709	104,534	13.6
Vocational	729	21,801	315,570	14.5
Higher	58	14,545	99,986	6.9

Educational attainment (1983). Percent of adult population over age 25 having: higher education 7.9%. *Literacy* (1980): total population over age 15 literate 8,272,748 (98.9%); males literate 3,955,561 (99.3%); females literate 4,317,187 (98.5%).
Health (1984): physicians 33,035 (1 per 323.3 persons); hospital beds 99,098 (1 per 107.7 persons); infant mortality rate per 1,000 live births (1984) 20.0.
Food (1982): daily per capita caloric intake 3,226 (vegetable products 67%; animal products 33%); 134% of FAO recommended minimum.

Military

Total active duty personnel (1984): 105,000 (army 80.0%, air force 20.0%).
Military expenditure as percent of GNP (1983): 4.3% (world 6.1%); per capita expenditure U.S.$281.

*Budget has separate county status. The area and population of the city are excluded from the larger county (Pest), which it administers. †1983. ‡Includes other material activities, balance of taxes on products and value differences, and cost of nonmaterial services. §At current prices. ‖ Detail does not add to total given because of rounding. ¶April.

Iceland

Official name: Lýdhveldidh Ísland (Republic of Iceland).
Form of government: unitary multiparty republic with two legislative houses (Upper House [20]; Lower House [40]).
Head of state and government: President.
Capital: Reykjavík.
Official language: Icelandic.
Official religion: Evangelical Lutheran.
Monetary unit: 1 króna (ISK) = 100 aurar; valuation (Oct. 21, 1985) 1 U.S.$ = ISK41.65; 1 £ = ISK59.72.

Area and population

Regions Counties*	Administrative centres	area sq mi	area sq km	population 1984 estimate
Austurland		8,683	22,490	13,100
Austur-Skaftafellssýsla	Höfn	2,347	6,080	2,300
Nordhur-Múlasýsla	Seydhisfjördhur	4,799	12,430	3,300
Sudhur-Múlasýsla	Eskifjördhur	1,537	3,980	7,500
Nordhurland eystra		8,370	21,680	26,200†
Eyjafjardharsýsla	Akureyri	1,602	4,150	19,000
Nordhur-Thingeyjarsýsla	Húsavík	2,077	5,380	1,700
Sudhur-Thingeyjarsýsla	Húsavík	4,691	12,150	5,400
Nordhurland vestra		4,973	12,880	10,700†
Austur-Húnavatnssýsla	Blönduós	1,900	4,920	2,600
Skagafjardharsýsla	Saudhárkrókur	2,077	5,380	6,500
Vestur-Húnavatnssýsla	Blönduós	996	2,580	1,500
Rekjavíkursvaedhi og Reykjanessvaedhi		741	1,920	142,600
Gullbringusýsla	Keflavík	405	1,050	32,600
Kjósarsýsla	Hafnarfjördhur	336	870	110,000
Sudhurland		9,649	24,990	20,100†
Árnessýsla	Selfoss	3,401	8,810	10,400
Rangárvallasýsla	Hvolsvöllur	3,197	8,280	8,300
Vestur-Skaftafellssýsla	Vík	3,050	7,900	1,300
Vestfirdhir		3,676	9,520	10,400
Austur-Bardhastrandarsýsla	Patreksfjördhur	444	1,150	400
Nordhur-Ísafjardharsýsla	Ísafjördhur	1,181	3,060	5,200
Strandasýsla	Hólmavík	1,015	2,630	1,100
Vestur-Bardhastrandarsýsla	Patreksfjördhur	598	1,550	2,000
Vestur-Ísafjardharsýsla	Ísafjördhur	436	1,130	1,700
Vesturland		3,676	9,520	15,100
Borgarfjardharsýsla	Borgarnes	753	1,950	6,800
Dalasýsla	Budhardalur	815	2,110	1,100
Mýrasýsla	Borgarnes	1,262	3,270	2,600
Snaefellsnessýsla	Stykkishólmur	846	2,190	4,600
TOTAL		39,768	103,000	238,200†

Demography

Population (1985): 243,000.
Density (1985): persons per sq mi 6.1, persons per sq km 2.4.
Urban–rural (1983): urban 88.8%; rural 11.2%.
Sex distribution (1983): male 50.39%; female 49.61%.
Age breakdown (1983): under 15, 26.7%; 15–29, 27.4%; 30–44, 18.6%; 45–59, 13.6%; 60–74, 9.5%; 75 and over, 4.3%.
Population projection: (1990) 252,000; (2000) 270,000.
Doubling time: 55 years.
Ethnic composition (1983): native Icelander 97.2%; other European 2.2%; other 0.6%.
Religious affiliation (1983): Lutheran 96.9%; Roman Catholic 0.7%; other 2.4%.
Major cities (1983): Reykjavík 87,309; Kópavogur 14,433; Akureyri 13,745; Hafnarfjördhur 12,683; Keflavík 6,886.

Vital statistics

Birth rate per 1,000 population (1983): 18.4 (world avg. 29.0); legitimate 56.2%; illegitimate 43.8%.
Death rate per 1,000 population (1983): 7.0 (world avg. 11.0).
Natural increase rate per 1,000 population (1983): 11.4 (world avg. 18.0).
Total fertility rate (avg. births per childbearing woman; 1983): 2.2.
Marriage rate per 1,000 population (1983): 5.9.
Divorce rate per 1,000 population (1983): 2.1.
Life expectancy at birth (1984): male 73.5 years; female 79.5 years.
Major causes of death per 100,000 population (1981): heart and circulatory diseases 311.1; malignant neoplasms (cancers) 167.1; accidents, suicide, etc. 54.3.

National economy

Budget (1984). Revenue: ISK20,747,000,000 (indirect taxes 79.9%, of which sales tax 35.7%, import duties 14.3%; income taxes 15.6%). Expenditures: ISK19,964,000,000 (social services 55.9%, of which education 15.7%; industrial services 21.4%; government operations and subsidies 16.9%; other 5.8%).
Public debt (outstanding; 1983): U.S.$731,600,000.
Tourism (1984): receipts from visitors U.S.$64,050,000; expenditures by nationals abroad U.S.$68,400,000.
Production (metric tons except as noted). Agriculture, forestry, fishing (1984): fodder crops 3,249,000‡, potatoes 13,000, milk 130,000; livestock (number of live animals) 770,000 sheep, 64,000 cattle, 53,000 horses; fish catch, capelin 865,100, cod 274,500, herring 50,300, lobster, shrimp, and shellfish 23,600. Mining and quarrying (1983): diatomite 25,501. Manufac-

turing (1983): marine products 586,518, of which frozen fish 145,572, salted fish 83,683; cement 120,000; aluminum, refined 77,011; ferrosilicon 49,100. Construction (1982): residential 917,000 cu m, nonresidential 1,276,700 cu m. Energy production (consumption): electricity (kW-hr; 1983) 3,766,000,-000 (3,766,000,000); coal (1983) none (38,000); petroleum, none (none); petroleum products (1983) none (466,000); natural gas, none (none).
Gross national product (at current market prices; 1984): U.S.$2,169,800,000 (U.S.$9,153 per capita).

Structure of gross domestic product and labour force

	1982 in value ISK'000,000	1982 % of total value	1982 labour force	1982 % of labour force
Agriculture	1,954	6.0	8,095	7.1
Fishing and processing	5,567	17.1	15,845	13.9
Manufacturing	4,200	12.9	18,810	16.5
Construction	2,832	8.7	11,740	10.3
Transportation and communication	2,735	8.4	7,980	7.0
Trade	3,386§	10.4§	17,330§	15.2§
Pub. admin., defense, services, and other	11,884	36.5	34,200	30.0
TOTAL	32,558	100.0	114,000	100.0

Population economically active (1983): total 115,000; participation rate of total population 48.7% (female 31.5%, unemployed 1.0%).

Price and earnings indexes (1980 = 100)

	1978	1979	1980	1981	1982	1983	1984
Consumer price index	43.4	63.1	100.0	150.6	224.7	418.2	547.0
Hourly wages index	46.2	65.9	100.0	152.7	228.5	339.0	403.2

Household income and expenditure. Average household size: n.a.; disposable income per person (1982) ISK82,240 (U.S.$6,660); sources of income (1982): wages, salaries, and self-employment 80.0%, transfer payments and other 20.0%; expenditure (1984): food 25.3%, housing 25.3%, transportation and communication 18.8%, education and recreation 10.1%, clothing and footwear 8.8%, health 1.7%, other 9.4%.
Land use (1983): forested 1.2%; meadows and pastures 22.7%; agricultural and under permanent cultivation 0.1%; other 76.0% ‖.

Foreign trade

Balance of trade (current prices)

	1979	1980	1981	1982	1983	1984
ISK'000,000	+93	+153	−196	−1,885	−1,973	−2,620
% of total	1.7%	1.8%	1.5%	10.0%	5.0%	5.2%

Imports (1984): ISK26,744,000,000 (machinery and transport equipment 19.8%, of which cars and motor vehicles 3.3%; fuels and lubricants 14.3%, of which petroleum 2.9%; construction materials 5.9%). *Major import sources:* West Germany 12.6%; Denmark 9.2%; U.S.S.R. 9.1%; The Netherlands 8.8%; Sweden 8.5%; United Kingdom 8.3%.
Exports (1984): ISK23,557,000,000 (fish and fish products 67.2%, of which frozen fish fillets 30.5%, dried, salted, and smoked fish 20.6%; aluminum, refined 14.5%; agricultural products 1.7%). *Major export destinations:* United States 28.4%; United Kingdom 13.4%; West Germany 10.9%; U.S.S.R. 7.8%; Spain 4.6%.

Transport and communications

Transport. Railroads (1983): none. Roads (1983): total length 7,867 mi, 12,-661 km (paved 11.5%). Vehicles (1983): passenger cars 97,307; trucks and buses 12,272. Merchant marine (1984): vessels (100 gross tons and over) 395; total deadweight tonnage 165,927. Air transport (1984): passenger-mi 1,240,000, passenger-km 1,996,000; short ton-mi cargo 19,472,000, metric ton-km cargo 28,428,000; airports (1985) with scheduled flights 23.
Communications. Daily newspapers (1984): total number 5; total circulation 119,000; circulation per 1,000 population 507. Radio (1984): 73,088 (1 per 3.2 persons). Television (1984): 62,623 (1 per 3.8 persons). Telephones (1983): 116,856 (1 per 2.0 persons).

Education and health

Education (1982–83)

	schools	teachers	students	student/teacher ratio
Primary (age 7–12)	187	2,600	25,000	9.6
Secondary (age 12–19)	157	...	21,800	...
Voc., teacher tr.	44	...	4,280	...
Higher	4	280	4,780	17.1

Educational attainment, n.a. *Literacy* (1984): total population over age 14 literate 175,029 (100.0%).
Health (1982): physicians 532 (1 per 440 persons); hospital beds 2,595 (1 per 90 persons); infant mortality rate per 1,000 live births (1983) 6.2.
Food (1980–82): daily per capita caloric intake 3,129 (vegetable products 54%, animal products 46%); 123%¶ of FAO recommended minimum.

Military

Iceland maintains no domestic military forces; external security is guaranteed by the NATO-sponsored U.S.-manned Iceland Defense Force, numbering about 2,700 (mostly air force). A domestic coast guard of about 120 is maintained.

*Counties include county cities and towns, which are within, but administratively independent of, the counties. †Detail does not add to total given because of rounding. ‡1983. §Trade includes finance and public utilities. ‖ Glaciated, covered with peat bogs, or lava desert. ¶1979–81.

India

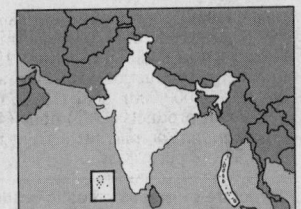

Official name: Bharat (Hindī); Republic of India (English).
Form of government: multiparty federal republic with two legislative houses (Council of States [244], House of the People [544]).
Chief of state: President.
Head of government: Prime Minister.
Capital: New Delhi.
Official languages: Hindī; English.
Official religion: none.
Monetary unit: 1 Indian rupee (Rs) = 100 paisa; valuation (Oct. 21, 1985) 1 U.S.$ = Rs11.92; 1 £ = Rs17.10.

Area and population		area		population
				1981
States	Capitals	sq mi	sq km	census
Andhra Pradesh	Hyderābād	106,200	275,100	53,549,673
Assam	Prāgjyotiṣapura	30,300*	78,500*	19,896,843†
Bihār	Patna	67,100	173,900	69,914,734
Gujarāt	Gāndhīnagar	75,700	196,000	34,085,799
Haryāna	Chandīgarh	17,100	44,200	12,922,618
Himāchal Pradesh	Simla	21,400	55,500	4,280,818
Jammu and Kashmir‡	Srinagar	86,100*	222,900*	5,987,389
Karnātaka	Bangalore	74,100	191,800	37,135,714
Kerala	Trivandrum	15,000	38,900	25,453,680
Madhya Pradesh	Bhopāl	171,200	443,400	52,178,844
Mahārāshtra	Bombay	118,800	307,700	62,784,171
Manipur	Imphāl	8,600	22,300	1,420,953
Meghālaya	Shillong	8,600	22,400	1,335,819
Nāgāland	Kohīma	6,400	16,600	774,930
Orissa	Bhubaneswar	60,100	155,700	26,370,271
Punjab	Chandīgarh	19,500	50,400	16,788,915
Rājasthān	Jaipur	132,100	342,200	34,261,862
Sikkim	Gangtok	2,700	7,100	316,385
Tamil Nādu	Madras	50,200	130,100	48,408,077
Tripura	Agartala	4,100	10,500	2,053,058
Uttar Pradesh	Lucknow	113,700	294,400	110,862,013
West Bengal	Calcutta	34,200	88,700	54,580,647
Union Territories				
Andaman and Nicobar Islands	Port Blair	3,200	8,200	188,741
Arunāchal Pradesh	Itanagar	32,300	83,700	631,839
Chandīgarh	Chandīgarh	40	100	451,610
Dādra and Nagar Haveli	Silvassa	200	500	103,676
Delhi	Delhi	600	1,500	6,220,406
Goa, Daman, and Diu	Panaji	1,500	3,800	1,086,730
Lakshadweep	Kavaratti	40	100	40,249
Mizorām	Aizawl	8,100	21,100	493,757
Pondicherry	Pondicherry	200	500	604,471
TOTAL		1,269,400*	3,287,800*	685,184,692

Demography

Population (1985): 768,000,000.
Density (1985): persons per sq mi 605.0, persons per sq km 233.6.
Urban–rural (1981): urban 23.3%; rural 76.7%.
Sex distribution (1981): male 51.72%; female 48.28%.
Age breakdown§ (1981): under 15, 39.5%; 15–29, 25.9%; 30–44, 17.4%; 45–59, 10.7%; 60 and over, 6.5%.
Population projection: (1990) 851,000,000; (2000) 1,028,000,000.
Doubling time: 31 years.
Linguistic composition (1971): Hindī 28.0%; Telugu 8.2%; Bengali 8.1%; Marāṭhī 7.6%; Tamil 6.9%; Urdu 5.2%; Gujarāti 4.7%; Malayālam 4.0%; Kannaḍa 3.9%; Oriya 3.6%; Bhojpurī 2.6%; Punjābī 2.5%; Assamese 1.6%; Chhattisgarhī 1.2%; Magadhī 1.2%; Maithilī 1.1%; other 9.6%.
Religious affiliation (1971): Hindu 82.7%; Muslim 11.2%; Christian 2.6%; Sikh 1.9%; Buddhist 0.7%; Jain 0.5%; other 0.4% ‖.
Major cities¶ (1981): Calcutta 9,194,018; Bombay 8,243,405; Delhi 5,729,283; Madras 4,289,347; Bangalore 2,921,751; Ahmadābād 2,548,057; Hyderābād 2,545,836; Pune 1,686,109; Kānpur 1,639,064; Nāgpur 1,302,066; Jaipur 1,015,160; Lucknow 1,007,604; Coimbatore 920,355; Patna 918,903; Surat 913,806.
Place of birth (foreign born; 1981): other Asia 7,875,399, of which Bangladesh 4,170,524, Pakistan 2,736,038, Nepal 501,292, Sri Lanka 211,514, Burma 134,783; Africa 42,726; Europe 13,046; United States and Canada 5,923.
Mobility (1981). Population living in same district but at different residence as in 1971: 47,604,000; different district, same state 22,557,000; different state 10,860,000; moved outside the country 1,179,000.
Households (1971). Average household size 5.6; number of rooms per household: 1 room 47.8%, 2 rooms 28.2%, 3 rooms 12.0%, 4 rooms 6.0%, 5 or more rooms 5.9%, unspecified number of rooms 0.1%. Average number of persons per room 2.8. Population in households 542,061,000 (99.1%), houseless population 1,986,000 (0.4%), institutional population 2,693,000 (0.5%).
Emigration (1980): persons living abroad 10,951,000 (accepting foreign citizenship, 6,751,000), of which in Nepal 3,800,000 (2,388,000); Sri Lanka 1,350,000 (433,000); Malaysia 1,218,000 (1,010,000); Mauritius 623,000 (612,000); Middle East 616,000 (115,000); United Kingdom 500,000 (250,000); Guyana 424,000 (424,000); Trinidad and Tobago 421,000 (420,000); Burma 350,000 (7,200); Fiji 301,000 (301,000); United States 300,000 (35,000).

Vital statistics

Birth rate per 1,000 population (1983): 33.6 (world avg. 29.0); legitimate, n.a.; illegitimate, n.a.
Death rate per 1,000 population (1983): 11.9 (world avg. 11.0).
Natural increase rate per 1,000 population (1983): 21.7 (world avg. 18.0).
Total fertility rate (avg. births per childbearing woman; 1981): 4.7.
Marriage rate per 1,000 population: n.a.
Divorce rate per 1,000 population: n.a.
Life expectancy at birth (1981): male 53.9 years; female 52.9 years.
Major causes of death (urban areas only; 1978): infectious and parasitic diseases 24.0%; diseases of the circulatory and nervous systems 19.7%; diseases of the respiratory system 8.1%; accidents, poisonings, and violence 8.3%; diseases of the digestive system 5.3%; allergic disorders and endocrine, metabolic, and blood diseases 4.9%; other, including ill-defined conditions and diseases of early infancy 29.7%.

Social indicators

Educational attainment (1981). Percent of adult population over age 25 having: no formal schooling (illiterate) 65.7%ŏ; some primary education only 11.2%; some secondary only 6.2%; completed secondary 7.1%; higher 2.5%; other 7.3%.

Distribution of income (1975–76)				
percent of household income by quintile:				
1	2	3	4	5 (highest)
7.0%	9.2%	13.9%	20.5%	49.4%

Quality of working life (1981). Average workweek: 45 hours. Rate of fatal (nonfatal) injuries per 100,000 workers: industrial workers 2.7 (1,324); miners 20.1 (220); railway workers (1981–82) 20 (1,531). Employees covered under Employee's State Insurance Scheme (1983) 7,200,000, number of beneficiaries 27,900,000. Average days lost to labour stoppages per 1,000 workdays (1982): 1.4. Average duration of journey to work: n.a. Rate per 1,000 workers of discouraged (unemployed no longer seeking work): n.a.
Access to services. Proportion of villages having: access to electricity (1982–83) 55.7%; adequate water supply (1977) 68.7%. Urban population with adequate water supply (1977) 98.0%.
Social participation. Eligible voters participating in last national election: 61.5%. Trade union membership in total workforce (1979): 4,683,000□. Practicing religious population in total affiliated population: n.a.
Social deviance (1978). Offense rate◊ per 100,000 population for: murder 2.9; dacoity (gang robbery) 2.0; other robbery 3.5; theft and housebreaking 94.7; collective criminal acts associated with riots 14.7. Incidence in general population of: alcoholism, n.a.; drug and substance abuse, n.a.△. Rate per 100,000 population of suicide (1979): 5.7.
Leisure (1983). Favourite leisure activities in urban areas: listening to the radio and attending the cinema.
Material well-being (1980). Households possessing: automobile 0.7%; telephone 2.3%; television receiver 1.6%; radio receiver 16.7%; air conditioner, n.a.; washing machine, n.a.

National economy

Gross national product (at current market prices; 1983): U.S.$190,710,000,000 (U.S.$260 per capita).

Structure of gross domestic product and labour force				
	1983–84		1981	
	in value Rs'000,000,000	% of total value	labour force	% of labour force
Agriculture	626.6	36.1	153,015,000	62.5
Mining	56.5	3.3	1,264,000	0.5
Manufacturing	258.5	14.9	25,143,000	10.3
Construction	98.4	5.7	3,565,000	1.5
Public utilities	31.3	1.8	974,000	0.4
Transportation and communication	106.4	6.1	6,069,000	2.5
Trade	247.8	14.3	12,165,000	5.0
Finance	125.3	7.2	1,764,000	0.7
Pub. admin., defense	87.4	5.1	...	...
Services	...	...	18,557,000	7.6
Other	96.0	5.5	22,089,000	9.0
TOTAL	1,734.2	100.0	244,605,000	100.0

Budget (1984–85). Revenue: Rs405,005,000,000 (tax revenue 57.2%, of which excise taxes 27.1%, customs duties 17.5%, taxes on corporations 6.3%; nontax revenue 16.0%, of which interest receipts 9.1%). Expenditures: Rs425,355,000,000 (defense 16.4%; interest payments 13.2%; industry and minerals 4.5%; social and community services 3.9%; agriculture 3.6%).
Public debt (external, outstanding; 1983): U.S.$21,429,200,000.
Production (metric tons except as noted). Agriculture, forestry, fishing (1983–84): cereals—rice 59,769,000, wheat 45,148,000, millet 12,328,000, sorghum 11,934,000, corn (maize) 7,924,000, barley 1,787,000; oilseeds—peanuts (groundnuts) 7,284,000, rapeseed and mustard 2,566,000, sesame 618,000, linseed 440,000, castor beans 407,000; spices†—chillies 525,000, turmeric 173,000, black pepper 26,000, cardamom 5,400; other⊕—sugarcane 189,129,000, pulses 11,791,000, potatoes 10,108,000, mangoes 8,700,000, cotton (all forms) 7,600,000, bananas 4,500,000, coconuts 3,900,000, jute 1,590,000, tea 595,000, tobacco 594,000, cashews 200,000, natural rubber 170,000, mulberry silk 5,500; livestock (number of live animals; 1983) 182,000,000 cattle, 78,000,000 goats, 63,000,000 water buffalo, 41,700,000 sheep, 1,050,000 camels; roundwood (1983) 232,537,000 cu m; fish catch (1983) 2,520,000, of which freshwater fishes 961,700. Mining and quarrying (value of production in Rs'000,000; 1982): crude petroleum 23,299; hard coal 20,202; iron ore 1,401; limestone 924; lignite 638; copper ore 332; man-

ganese ore 300; gold 247; phosphorite 233; zinc concentrates 155; chromite 149; dolomite 98. Manufacturing (1982–83): cement 23,200,000; steel ingots 11,000,000; sugar 8,200,000; fertilizer 4,404,000; jute textiles 1,300,000; aluminum 208,000; bicycles 4,900,000 units; electric fans 4,100,000 units, radio receivers 1,400,000 units; motorcycles and scooters 399,800 units; refrigerators 379,000 units; sewing machines 309,000 units; railway cars 15,400 units; cotton cloth 9,200,000,000 metres; man-made fibre 1,368,000,-000 metres; machinery Rs3,906,000,000, of which cotton textile machinery Rs3,151,000,000. Construction (value in Rs; 1982) residential 55,747,000,-000; nonresidential 43,408,000,000.

Manufacturing enterprises (1978–79)

	no. of factories	no. of employees	annual wages as a % of all wages	annual value added (Rs'000,000)
Chemicals and chem. products	4,881	426,000	154.5	12,990
Cotton textiles	7,601	1,118,000	96.8	11,550
Basic metals and alloys	5,250	549,000	141.2	9,570
Iron and steel	4,502	500,000	...	8,380
Cement	62	90,000	...	7,556
Machinery except electrical	6,387	384,000	132.1	6,640
Food products	16,310	1,132,000	42.5	6,300
Electrical machinery	2,882	285,000	150.8	5,750
Rubber, plastic, petroleum, and coal products	2,350	144,000	135.0	3,790
Paper products, printing, publishing, etc.	4,901	259,000	107.3	3,190
Nonmetallic mineral products	5,639	337,000	72.4	2,970
Wool, silk, and synthetic textiles	3,216	193,000	100.1	2,950
Beverages and tobacco prod.	8,240	392,000	37.5	2,460
Metal products	5,818	184,000	96.1	2,300
Jute, hemp, and mesta (kenaf) textiles	247	264,000	88.0	1,710

Energy production (consumption): electricity (kW-hr; 1983) 147,952,000,000 (147,837,000,000); coal (metric tons; 1983) 140,696,000 (144,054,000); crude petroleum (barrels; 1983) 187,126,000 (255,552,000); petroleum products (metric tons; 1983) 26,737,000 (29,824,000); natural gas (cu m; 1983) 2,732,-700,000 (2,732,700,000).

Service enterprises (1978–79)

	no. of enterprises	no. of employees	annual wage as a % of all wages	annual value added (Rs'000,000)
Public utilities (waterworks, gas)	229	13,000	122.0	160
Electrical power	216	645,000	118.0	12,190
Transport equipment (including shipbuilding and motor vehicles)	2,528	392,000	148.0	5,920
Railways**	7,072††	1,800,000	...	29,661‡‡
Communication§§				
Post and telegraph	178,246 ‖‖	852,000	...	...
Film	10,782¶¶	200,000	...	5,500‡‡
Radio and television	106ठ	...	...	172ठठ
Finance (banks)**	40,828▢▢	...	...	461,280◊◊
Wholesale trade△△	116,000	...	...	264
Retail trade△△	3,760,000	4,925,000	...	24,524
Tourism**	1,288,160††	...	...	7,500⊙⊙
Health services	29,300***	419,100†††	...	...
Cold storage services	413	7,000	46.6	60
Other: repair services	2,908	216,000	124.9	1,980

Population economically active (1981): total 244,605,000; participation rate of total population 35.7% (female 26.0%, unemployed 7.3%).

Price and earnings indexes (1980 = 100)

	1979	1980	1981	1982	1983	1984	1985‡‡‡
Consumer price index	89.7	100.0	113.0	121.9	136.3	147.7	155.4
Earnings index§§§	82.4	100.0	102.4	113.5	...	...	...

Household income and expenditure. Number of households (1981) 119,-772,545. Average household size (1981) 5.7; average annual income per household: n.a.; sources of income (1980–81): self-employment 44.9%, salaries and wages 38.7%, interest 7.6%, profits and dividends 4.8%, rent 4.0%; expenditure (1982–83): food 53.2%, transportation and communication 10.3%, clothing and footwear 9.2%, housing 5.5%, fuel and energy 5.0%, tobacco and intoxicants 3.4%, education 2.8%, medical care and health expenses 2.1%.

Financial aggregates‖ ‖ ‖

	1979	1980	1981	1982	1983	1984	1985
Exchange rate, Rs per:							
U.S. dollar	7.91	7.93	9.10	9.63	10.49	12.45	12.43‡‡‡
£	17.59	18.91	17.36	15.55	15.22	14.40	16.10‡‡‡
SDR	10.42	10.11	10.59	10.63	10.99	12.20	12.41‡‡‡
International reserves (U.S.$)							
Total (excl. gold; '000,000)	7,432	6,944	4,693	4,315	4,937	5,842	5,362¶¶¶
SDRs ('000,000)	489	480	545	374	110	331	303‡‡‡
Reserve pos. in IMF ('000,000)	213	420	384	402	510	477	486‡‡‡
Foreign exchange ('000,000)	6,731	6,043	3,764	3,539	4,318	5,034	4,754¶¶¶
Gold ('000,000 fine troy oz)	8.560	8.594	8.594	8.594	8.594	8.737	8.737¶¶¶
% world reserves	0.9	0.9	0.9	0.9	0.9	0.9	0.9¶¶¶
Interest and prices							
Central bank discount (%)	9.0	9.0	10.0	10.0	10.0	10.0	10.0ठठठ
Gov't. bond yield (%)	6.5	6.7	7.2	7.6	8.0	8.7	8.9ठठठ
Industrial share prices (1980 = 100)	92.7	100.0	122.7	120.1	126.2	134.8	173.6ठठठ
Balance of payments (U.S.$'000,000)							
Balance of visible trade	−2,222	−5,644	−5,712	−4,820	...	...	...
Imports, f.o.b.	9,819	13,947	14,149	14,046	...	...	...
Exports, f.o.b.	7,597	8,303	8,437	9,226	...	...	...
Balance of invisibles	+226	+525	+7	−621	...	...	...
Balance of payments, current account	48	−1,785	−2,698	−2,524	...	...	...

Tourism: receipts from visitors (1983) U.S.$820,000,000; expenditures by nationals abroad (1981) U.S.$220,000,000.
Land use (1983): forested 22.7%; meadows and pastures 4.0%; agricultural and under permanent cultivation 56.6%; other 16.7%.

Foreign trade

Balance of trade (current prices)ठठठ

	1979	1980	1981	1982	1983	1984▢▢▢
Rs'000,000	−16,375	−49,254	−61,599	−51,275	−50,214	−36,289
% of total	11.4%	26.7%	30.0%	22.5%	22.3%	27.3%

Imports (1982–83): Rs143,557,600,000 (crude petroleum and petroleum products 39.0%; nonelectrical machinery 9.6%; iron and steel 8.0%; precious stones [almost all gem diamonds] 4.7%; transport equipment 4.2%; wheat 2.0%; nonferrous metals 1.9%). *Major import sources:* U.S.S.R. 10.5%; Saudi Arabia 10.4%; United States 9.5%; Japan 7.5%; United Kingdom 6.2%; Iraq 6.2%; West Germany 5.6%; Iran 5.5%; Belgium 4.3%.
Exports (1982–83): Rs88,298,000,000 (precious stones [almost all gem diamonds] 9.3%; machinery and transport equipment 6.6%; ready-made garments 6.0%; iron ore 4.2%; tea and maté 4.2%; fish, crustaceans, and mollusks 4.0%; leather and leather manufactures 3.9%; chemicals 3.4%; cotton fabrics 3.0%). *Major export destinations:* U.S.S.R. 17.6%; United States 10.8%; Japan 9.0%; United Kingdom 5.2%; West Germany 3.9%; Saudi Arabia 2.6%; United Arab Emirates 2.5%; Belgium 2.4%.

Transport and communications

Transport. Railroads (1983): route length 37,861 mi, 60,933 km; passenger-mi 129,592,000,000, passenger-km 208,558,000,000; short ton-mi cargo 119,-000,000,000◊◊◊, metric ton-km cargo 173,700,000,000◊◊◊. Roads (1982): total length 1,077,000 mi, 1,734,000 km (paved 42%). Vehicles (1983): passenger cars 1,171,900; trucks and buses 807,500. Merchant marine (1984): vessels (100 gross tons and over) 710; total deadweight tonnage 10,368,343. Air transport (1984): passenger-mi 14,488,000,000, passenger-km 23,316,000,000; short ton-mi cargo 717,400,000, metric ton-km cargo 1,047,400,000; airports (1985) with scheduled flights 70.
Communications. Daily newspapers (1984): total number 212; total circulation 18,561,000; circulation per 1,000 population 25. Radio (1984): total number of receivers 22,500,000 (1 per 33 persons). Television (1984): total number of receivers 2,100,000 (1 per 358 persons). Telephones (1983): 3,215,379 (1 per 228 persons).

Education and health

Education (1982–83)

	schools	teachers	students	student/teacher ratio
Primary (age 5–10)	503,741	1,389,356	55,220,443	39.7
Secondary (age 10–17)	175,702	1,849,504	57,398,203	31.0
Voc., Teacher tr.	4,878	...	468,993	...
Higher△△△	9,056	259,745	4,924,794	19.0

Literacy (1981): total population over age 14 literate 168,900,000 (40.8%); males literate 117,600,000 (54.8%); females literate 51,300,000 (25.7%).
Health (1981): physicians 268,712††† (1 per 2,615 persons); hospital beds (1982) 476,226 (1 per 1,509 persons); infant mortality rate per 1,000 live births (1981) 117.
Food (1980–82): daily per capita caloric intake 2,030 (vegetable products 95%, animal products 5%); 92% of FAO recommended minimum requirement.

Military

Total active duty personnel (1984): 1,120,000 (army 85.7%, navy 4.2%, air force 10.1%). *Military expenditure as percent of GNP* (1983): 3.5% (world 6.1%); per capita expenditure U.S.$8.

*Area data for Assam and Jammu and Kashmir are from 1971. †Estimated figure. ‡Area data include 32,400 sq mi (83,800 sq km) of Pakistani-occupied Jammu and Kashmir; population figure pertains to the Indian-occupied portion only. §Excludes Assam. ‖ Includes 91,000 Zoroastrians. ¶Populations cited are for urban agglomerations. ठIncludes New Delhi (population 273,036). ठIncludes 0.9% literate population having no formal schooling. ▢Total of reporting unions only (about 20%). ◊Reported criminal acts. △India's codeine consumption in 1983 was fourth highest in the world. †All data for spices, 1981–82. ⊙All data included under other, 1983, except mulberry silk, 1982–83. **1982. ††Number of railway stations. ‡‡Gross revenue. §§1981. ‖‖Number of post and telegraph offices. ¶¶Number of cinemas. ठठNumber of radio and television stations. ठठEarnings from commercials. ◊◊Total deposits. △△1970. ††Number of tourists. ⊙⊙Foreign exchange earned. ***Number of hospitals, dispensaries, and primary health centres. †††Number of physicians and nurses. ‡‡‡End of June. §§§Average daily wage rate of male agricultural workers. ‖‖‖Excepting 1985, exchange rates and international reserves are end of year figures, and other categories are yearly averages. ¶¶¶End of February. ठठठApril average. ठठठImports c.i.f. (cost, insurance, and freight); exports f.o.b. (free on board). ▢▢▢First two quarters. ◊◊◊1984. △△△1979–80. †††Registered persons. Not all are resident in the country.*

Indonesia

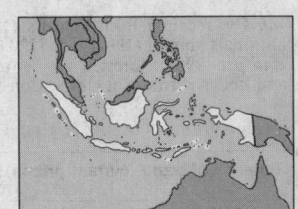

Official name: Republik Indonesia
(Republic of Indonesia).
Form of government: unitary multiparty
republic with two legislative
houses (People's Consultative
Assembly [920]; House of People's
Representatives [460]).
Head of state and government:
President.
Capital: Jakarta.
Official language: Bahasa Indonesia.
Official religion: none.
Monetary unit: 1 Indonesian rupiah
(Rp) = 100 sen; valuation (Oct. 21,
1985) 1 U.S.$ = Rp1,121.22;
1 £ = Rp1,607.83.

Area and population		area		population
		sq mi	sq km	1984 estimate
Metropolitan district	**Capitals**			
Jakarta Raya	Jakarta	228	590	7,585,449
Provinces				
Bali	Denpasar	2,147	5,561	2,632,900
Bengkulu	Bengkulu	8,173	21,168	909,000
Irian Jaya	Jayapura	162,928	421,981	1,299,900
Jambi	Jambi	17,345	44,924	1,690,200
Jawa Barat	Bandung	17,877	46,300	30,395,425
Jawa Tengah	Semarang	13,207	34,206	26,997,500
Jawa Timur	Surabaya	18,503	47,922	30,868,700
Kalimantan Barat	Pontianak	56,664	146,760	2,714,500
Kalimantan Selatan	Banjarmasin	14,541	37,660	2,241,600
Kalimantan Tengah	Palangkaraya	58,919	152,600	1,088,700
Kalimantan Timur	Samarinda	78,162	202,440	1,518,800
Lampung	Tanjung Karang	12,860	33,307	5,769,000
Maluku	Ambon	28,767	74,505	1,575,500
Nusa Tenggara Barat	Mataram	7,790	20,177	2,980,900
Nusa Tenggara Timur	Kupang	18,485	47,876	2,947,900
Riau	Pakanbaru	36,511	94,562	2,442,800
Sulawesi Selatan	Ujung Pandang	28,101	72,781	6,475,000
Sulawesi Tengah	Palu	26,921	69,726	1,495,400
Sulawesi Tenggara	Kendari	10,690	27,686	1,061,200
Sulawesi Utara	Menado	7,345	19,023	2,309,400
Sumatera Barat	Padang	19,219	49,778	3,705,500
Sumatera Selatan	Palembang	40,034	103,688	5,259,200
Sumatera Utara	Medan	27,331	70,787	9,231,700
Timor Timur	Dili	5,743	14,874	598,100
Special autonomous districts				
Aceh	Banda Aceh	21,387	55,392	2,920,500
Yogyakarta	Yogyakarta	1,224	3,169	2,865,200
TOTAL		741,101*	1,919,443	161,579,500

Demography

Population (1985): 167,550,000.
Density (1985): persons per sq mi 226.1, persons per sq km 87.3.
Urban–rural (1980): urban 22.3%; rural 77.7%.
Sex distribution (1980): male 49.72%; female 50.28%.
Age breakdown (1980): under 15, 40.8%; 15–29, 27.0%; 30–44, 16.4%; 45–59, 10.2%; 60–74, 4.5%; 75 and over, 1.1%.
Population projection: (1990) 178,370,000; (2000) 204,486,000.
Doubling time: 33 years.
Ethnolinguistic composition (1980): Javanese 40.1%; Sundanese 15.3%; Indonesian 12.0%; Madurese 4.8%; other 27.8%.
Religious affiliation (1980): Muslim 83.6%; Christian 7.5%; other 8.9%.
Major cities (1983): Jakarta 7,636,000; Surabaya 2,289,000; Medan 1,966,000; Bandung 1,602,000; Semarang 1,269,000.

Vital statistics

Birth rate per 1,000 population (1980–85): 30.7 (world avg. 29.0).
Death rate per 1,000 population (1980–85): 13.0 (world avg. 11.0).
Natural increase rate per 1,000 population (1980–85): 17.7 (world avg. 18.0).
Total fertility rate (avg. births per childbearing woman; 1980–85): 3.9.
Marriage rate per 1,000 population (1980): 8.1.
Divorce rate per 1,000 population (1980): 1.4.
Life expectancy at birth (1980–85): male 51.2 years; female 53.9 years.
Major causes of death: n.a.; however, major diseases are tuberculosis, malaria, dysentery, cholera, and plague.

National economy

Budget (1985–86 est.). Revenue: Rp23,046,000,000 (taxes from energy production 48.4%, foreign aid receipts 19.0%, income tax 13.3%, import and excise taxes 7.3%, sales tax 7.2%). Expenditures: Rp23,046,000,000 (development 46.2%, debt service 15.4%, salaries and pensions 13.5%).
Public debt (external, outstanding; 1983): U.S.$21,685,300,000.
Tourism: receipts from visitors (1983): U.S.$440,000,000; expenditures by nationals abroad (1982) U.S.$557,000,000.
Production (metric tons except as noted). Agriculture, forestry, fishing (1984): paddy rice 37,500,000, sugarcane 23,726,000, cassava 14,000,000, rubber 1,150,000, coffee 329,000, nutmeg 7,751†; livestock (number of live animals) 7,910,000 goats, 6,800,000 cattle, 4,790,000 sheep, 3,620,000 pigs, 2,391,000 water buffalo; roundwood 122,249,000 cu m‡; fish catch 2,112,230‡. Mining and quarrying (1984): nickel ore 1,066,776; bauxite 1,033,233; copper ore§ 190,349; iron ore§ 82,967; tin ore§ 23,225; silver 1,999,662 kg. Manufacturing (1984): cement 6,607,400; paper 84,578; cotton yarn 129,903 bales; beer 474,040 hectolitres; transportation vehicles 155,400 units‡.

Energy production (consumption): electricity (kW-hr; 1983) 15,294,000,000 (15,294,000,000); coal (metric tons; 1984) 1,084,652 (325,000)‡; crude petroleum (barrels; 1983) 490,491,000 (183,649,000); petroleum products (metric tons; 1983) 20,769,000 (22,526,000); natural gas (cu m; 1983) 17,682,000,000 (3,774,000,000).
Gross national product (at current market prices; 1983): U.S.$87,120,000,000 (U.S.$560 per capita).

Structure of gross domestic product and labour force				
	1983		**1980**	
	in value Rp'000,000	% of total value	labour force	% of labour force
Agriculture	18,772	26.4	28,040,462	54.8
Mining	13,824	19.4	369,282	0.7
Manufacturing	8,918	12.5	4,360,657	8.5
Construction	4,434	6.2	1,573,142	3.1
Public utilities	503	0.7	84,684	0.2
Transp. and commun.	3,325	4.7	1,467,771	2.9
Trade	10,875	15.3	6,611,397	12.9
Finance			231,935	0.5
Pub. admin., defense	} 10,564	} 14.8	} 8,452,182	} 16.5
Services and other				
TOTAL	71,215‖	100.0	51,191,512	100.0*

Population economically active (1980): total 52,153,345; participation rate of total population 35.6% (female 33.0%, unemployed 1.7%).

Price and earnings indexes (1980 = 100)							
	1978	1979	1980	1981	1982	1983	1984
Consumer price index	70.0	84.4	100.0	112.2	122.9	137.4	151.7
Monthly earnings index¶	74.4	87.2	100.0	108.5	122.6	...	...

Household income and expenditure. Average household size (1980) 4.9; income per household: n.a.; source of income: n.a.; expenditure (1980): food 69.3%, housing, fuel, light, and water 12.2%, clothing, footwear, and headwear 5.1%, durable goods 3.8%.
Land use (1983): forested 67.2%; meadows and pastures 6.6%; agricultural and under permanent cultivation 11.2%; other 15.0%.

Foreign trade♀

Balance of trade (current prices)					
	1979	1980	1981	1982	1983	1984
U.S.$'000,000	+9,165	+12,235	+10,410	+7,240	+6,545	+9,508
% of total	41.6%	38.7%	30.5%	19.4%	18.3%	27.7%

Imports (1984): U.S.$13,882,075,000 (machinery and transport equipment 36.1%; mineral fuels 20.6%; chemicals 11.9%; base metals 10.5%; food and live animals 1.9%). *Major import sources:* Japan 23.8%; United States 18.4%; Singapore 12.9%.
Exports (1984): U.S.$21,887,765,000 (petroleum and petroleum products 57.0%; natural gas 16.2%; wood products 4.5%; rubber 4.2%; coffee 2.6%). *Major export destinations:* Japan 47.3%; U.S. 20.6%; Singapore 9.7%.

Transport and communications

Transport. Railroads: (1984) length 4,317 mi, 6,947 km; (1983) passenger-km 5,573,000,000; (1983) metric ton-km cargo 553,000,000. Roads (1983): total length 83,300 mi, 134,000 km (paved 41%). Vehicles (1984): passenger cars 912,997; trucks and buses 962,026. Merchant marine (1984): vessels (100 gross tons and over) 1,484; total deadweight tonnage 2,627,275. Air transport (1983): passenger-km 7,860,000,000; metric ton-km cargo 199,572,000; airports (1985) 94.
Communications. Daily newspapers (1982): total number 89; total circulation 2,603,190; circulation per 1,000 population 16.8. Radio (1984): 6,800,000 receivers (1 per 24 persons). Television (1984): 3,005,000 receivers (1 per 55 persons). Telephones (1983): 669,301 (1 per 238 persons).

Education and health

Education (1982–83)	schools	teachers	students	student/ teacher ratio
Primary (age 7–12)	120,162	841,833	24,700,075	29.3
Secondary (age 13–18)	16,028	336,336	5,697,231	16.9
Voc., teacher tr.	2,752δ	65,528δ	853,000	...
Higher	50δ	56,322δ	692,700	...

Educational attainment (1980). Percent of population over age 10 having: no formal education 27.3%; less than primary 40.6%; primary 21.2%; less than secondary 6.0%; secondary 4.3%; postsecondary 0.3%; higher 0.2%.
Literacy (1980): total population literate 72.0%; males literate 80.5%; females literate 63.8%.
Health: physicians (1983) 10,262 (1 per 15,542 persons); hospital beds (1984) 103,500 (1 per 1,586 persons); infant mortality rate per 1,000 live births (1980–85) 90.3.
Food (1980–82): daily per capita caloric intake 2,363 (vegetable products 98%, animal products 2%); 109% of FAO recommended minimum.

Military

Total active duty personnel (1984): 281,000 (army 74.7%, navy 14.9%, air force 10.4%). *Military expenditure as percent of GNP* (1983): 2.8%; (world 6.1%); per capita expenditure U.S.$15.

*Detail does not add to total given because of rounding. †1983 export figure only. ‡1983. §Concentrates. ‖ At current prices. ¶Based on prices received by farmers for sale of produce. ♀Import figures are f.o.b. (free on board) in balance of trade and c.i.f. (cost, insurance, and freight) for commodities and trading partners. δ1981–82.

Iran

Official name: Jomhūrīyeh Islāmīyeh
Īrān (Islāmic Republic of Iran).
Form of government: unitary Islāmic
republic with a single legislative house
(Islāmic Consultative Assembly [270]).
Chief of state: Velayat Faghih
(religious leader).
Head of state: President.
Head of government: Prime Minister.
Capital: Tehrān.
Official language: Farsī (Persian).
Official religion: Islām.
Monetary unit: 1 rial (Rls) = 100 dinars;
valuation (Oct. 21, 1985)
1 U.S.$ = Rls85.84; 1£ = Rls123.10.

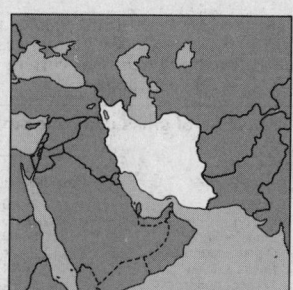

Area and population

Provinces	Capitals	area sq mi	area sq km	population 1984 estimate
Āzārbāijān-e Gharbī	Orūmīyeh	15,000	38,850	1,915,000
Āzārbāijān-e Sharqī	Tabrīz	25,908	67,102	4,097,000
Bākhtarān	Bākhtarān	9,137	23,667	1,177,000
Boyer Aḥmad-e Kohkilūyeh	Yāsūj	5,506	14,261	390,000
Būshehr	Būshehr	10,676	27,653	519,000
Chahār Mahāl-e Bakhtiārī	Shahr Kord	5,741	14,870	601,000
Eṣfahān	Eṣfahān	40,405	104,650	3,012,000
Fārs	Shīrāz	51,466	133,298	2,806,000
Gīlān	Rasht	5,679	14,709	2,069,000
Hamadān	Hamadān	7,638	19,784	1,407,000
Hormozgān	Bandar ʿAbbās	25,818	66,870	694,000
Īlām	Īlām	7,352	19,044	308,000
Kermān	Kermān	71,997	186,472	1,535,000
Khorāsān	Mashhad	120,980	313,337	4,441,000
Khūzestān	Ahvāz	24,981	64,702	2,284,000
Kordestān	Sanandaj	9,651	24,998	906,000
Lorestān	Khorramābād	12,117	31,383	1,306,000
Markazī	Arāk	15,403	39,895	1,430,000
Māzandarān	Sārī	18,291	47,375	2,880,000
Semnān	Semnān	34,764	90,039	370,000
Sīstān-e Balūchestān	Zāhedān	70,107	181,578	997,000
Tehrān	Tehrān	7,381	19,118	7,243,000
Yazd	Yazd	24,673	63,905	569,000
Zanjān	Zanjān	14,053	36,398	1,488,000
TOTAL		634,724	1,643,958	44,444,000

Demography

Population (1985): 45,000,000.
Density (1985): persons per sq mi 70.9, persons per sq km 27.4.
Urban–rural (1980): urban 49.9%; rural 50.1%.
Sex distribution (1980): male 50.72%; female 49.28%.
Age breakdown (1981–82): under 15, 43.5%; 15–29, 28.7%; 30–44, 14.7%; 45–59, 8.7%; 60–64, 1.6%; 65 and over, 2.8%.
Population projection: (1990) 51,033,000; (2000) 64,916,000.
Doubling time: 26 years.
Ethnic composition (1980): Persian 45.0%; Azerbaijani 16.0%; Kurdish 8.2%; Luri 2.2%; Bakhtiari 1.9%; Baluchi 1.9%; Arab 1.6%; other 23.2%.
Religious affiliation (1985): Muslim 98% (Shīʿī 93.0%, Sunnī 5%); other 2%.
Major cities (1982): Tehrān 5,734,199; Mashhad 1,119,748; Eṣfahān 926,601; Shīrāz 800,416; Ahvaz 470,927.

Vital statistics

Birth rate per 1,000 population (1983): 51.1 (world avg. 29.0).
Death rate per 1,000 population (1983): 4.8 (world avg. 11.0).
Natural increase rate per 1,000 population (1983): 46.3 (world avg. 18.0).
Total fertility rate (avg. births per childbearing woman; 1981): 6.0.
Marriage rate per 1,000 population (1983): 9.7.
Divorce rate per 1,000 population (1983): 0.9.
Life expectancy at birth (1981): male 57.1 years; female 59.0 years.
Major causes of death per 100,000 population: n.a.; however, major infectious diseases are influenza, strep throat, dermatomycosis, typhoid and paratyphoid fevers, measles, malaria, brucellosis, and chicken pox.

National economy

Budget (1982–83). Revenue: Rls3,104,627,000,000 (oil and gas 47.9%, taxes 21.5%, investment 7.5%, trade and services 2.6%, other 20.5%). Expenditures: Rls2,980,000,000,000 (development 26.2%, Iran–Iraq war 13.4%, other 60.4%).
Tourism (1983): receipts from visitors U.S.$31,000,000; expenditures by nationals abroad, n.a.
Production (metric tons except as noted). Agriculture, forestry, fishing (1984): wheat 5,500,000, potatoes 1,550,000, barley 1,550,000, grapes 1,300,000, rice (paddy) 1,230,000, watermelons 950,000; livestock (number of live animals) 34,000,000 sheep, 13,600,000 goats, 8,200,000 cattle, 1,800,000 asses, 350,000 horses, 74,000,000 chickens; roundwood 6,721,000 cu m*; fish catch 34,500*. Mining and quarrying (1983): kaolin 100,000; barite 85,000; chromium ore (oxide content) 50,000; copper ore 48,500; zinc ore 39,000; lead 26,000. Manufacturing (value in Rls; 1981): textiles 131,500,000,000; processed food 67,410,000,000; transport equipment 47,000,000,000; electrical machinery 35,660,000,000; chemicals 31,833,000,000; iron and steel 21,100,000,000. Construction (1982): new buildings completed 18,809,000 sq m, of which residential 16,654,000 sq m. Energy production (consumption): electricity (kW-hr; 1983) 29,900,000,000 (29,900,000,000); coal (metric

tons; 1983) 800,000 (860,000); petroleum (barrels; 1984) 791,200,000 (193,-000,000*); petroleum products (metric tons; 1983) 25,520,000 (25,445,000); natural gas (cu m; 1983) 6,707,999,000 (6,707,999,000).
Gross national product (at current market prices; 1977): U.S.$75,257,512,857 (U.S.$2,123 per capita).

Structure of gross domestic product and labour force

	1982 in value Rls'000,000	1982 % of total value	1976 labour force	1976 % of labour force
Agriculture	1,912.1	17.8	3,615,314	36.9
Mining	1,927.8	17.9	90,230	0.9
Manufacturing	894.4	8.3	1,682,188	17.2
Construction	685.6	6.4	1,202,061	12.3
Public utilities	98.6	0.9	61,761	0.6
Transp. and commun.	709.8	6.6	433,364	4.4
Trade	1,702.8	15.8	671,735	6.9
Finance	...	...	100,653	1.0
Pub. admin., defense	...	...	...	...
Services	...	...	1,523,688	15.6
Other	2,825.2	26.3	415,061	4.2
TOTAL	10,756.3	100.0	9,796,055	100.0

Population economically active (1976): total 9,796,055; participation rate of total population 28.5% (female 20.3%, unemployed, n.a.).

Price and earnings indexes (1980 = 100)

	1978	1979	1980	1981	1982	1983
Consumer price index†	75.0	82.9	100.0	124.2	147.4	176.5
Monthly earnings index‡	49.9	73.8	100.0	108.9	119.7	138.1

Household income and expenditure. Average household size (1982) 4.3; income per household (1975) Rls298,761 (U.S.$4,235); sources of income: wages 40.8%, self-employment 28.2%, assistance 4.5%; expenditure† (1975): food and tobacco 43.8%, housing and energy 22.3%, clothing and footwear 9.4%, furniture and household equipment 7.7%, transportation 6.8%.
Land use (1983): forested 11.0%; meadows and pastures 26.9%; agricultural and under permanent cultivation 8.4%; other 53.7%.

Foreign trade

Balance of trade (current prices)§

	1978	1979	1980	1981	1982	1983
Rls'000,000	+330,600	+878,500	+228,200	+119,200	+587,500	+275,800
% of total	11.9%	20.6%	12.9%	6.5%	27.0%	8.9%

Imports (1981): Rls861,600,000,000 (machinery and transport equipment 28.0%, chemicals 14.5%, food and live animals 13.9%). *Major import sources:* West Germany 15.2%; Japan 9.8%; U.S.S.R. 7.6%; United Kingdom 7.3%; Switzerland 4.2%; Austria 3.3%.
Exports (1981): Rls980,800,000,000 (petroleum and petroleum products 96.3%). *Major export destinations:* West Germany 45.2%; U.S.S.R. 12.4%; Italy 8.1%; Saudi Arabia 3.6%; France 3.1%.

Transport and communications

Transport. Railroads (1983): route length 2,837 mi, 4,567 km. Roads (1983): total length 67,710 mi, 108,970 km (paved 31%). Vehicles (1981): passenger cars 1,532,269; trucks and buses 313,006. Merchant marine (1984): vessels (100 gross tons and over) 306; total deadweight tonnage 3,410,649. Air transport (1984): passenger-mi 2,407,412,000, passenger-km 3,874,362,000; short ton-mi cargo 61,829,000, metric ton-km cargo 90,269,000; airports (1985) with scheduled flights 14.
Communications. Daily newspapers (1984): 14; circulation 962,000 ‖ ; circulation per 1,000 population 22.2 ‖ . Radio (1984): receivers 8,000,000 (1 per 5.4 persons). Television (1984): receivers 2,000,000 (1 per 21.7 persons). Telephones (1983): 2,118,080 (1 per 19.1 persons).

Education and health

Education (1982–83)

	schools	teachers	students	student/ teacher ratio
Primary (age 7–11)	44,900	250,167	5,592,808	22.4
Secondary (age 12–18)	9,312	63,611	1,717,097	26.9
Voc., teacher tr.	3,707	66,010	1,002,569	15.2
Higher	114	9,042	117,148	12.9

Educational attainment (1971). Percent of population over age 7 having: no formal schooling 9.2%; primary education 67.2%; secondary 21.2%; higher 1.9%; certificate not reported 0.5%. *Literacy* (1980): total population over age 15 literate 10,980,000 (42.8%); males literate 7,163,000 (55.4%); females literate 3,817,000 (30.1%).
Health (1981): physicians 15,182 (1 per 2,604 persons); hospital beds 61,443 (1 per 644 persons); infant mortality rate per 1,000 live births (1980–85) 101.0.
Food (1978–80): daily per capita caloric intake 2,912 (vegetable products 90%, animal products 10%); 121% of FAO recommended minimum requirement.

Military

Total active duty personnel (1984): 555,000 (revolutionary guard corps 45.1%, army 45.0%, navy 3.6%, air force 6.3%). *Military expenditure as percent of GNP* (1983): 5.0% (world 6.1%); per capita expenditure U.S.$124.

*1983. †For urban areas only. ‡Compensation paid to employees in large manufacturing establishments. §Imports derived from the Direction of Trade Statistics (DOTS). ‖ Circulation based on 10 dailies only.

Iraq

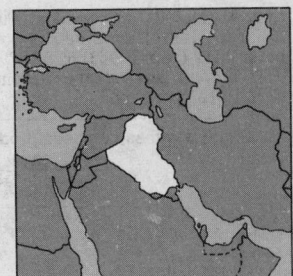

Official name: al-Jumhūrīyah
al-ʻIrāqīyah (Republic of Iraq).
Form of government: unitary
single-party republic with one
legislative house (National Assembly
[250]).
Head of state and government:
President.
Capital: Baghdād.
Official language: Arabic.
Official religion: Islām.
Monetary unit: 1 Iraqi dinar (ID) = 20
dirhams = 1,000 fils; valuation (Oct.
21, 1985) 1 ID = U.S.$3.23;
1 ID = £2.27.

Area and population

Governorates	Capitals	area* sq mi	area* sq km	population 1982 estimate
al-Anbār	ar-Ramādī	53,175	137,723	535,627
Bābil	al-Ḥillah	2,030	5,258	680,700
Baghdād	Baghdād	1,992	5,159	4,038,430
al-Baṣrah	al-Baṣrah	7,363	19,070	1,184,500
Dhī Qār	an-Nāṣirīyah	5,261	13,626	683,537
Diyālā	Baʻqūbah	7,449	19,292	650,211
Karbalāʼ	Karbalāʼ	1,944	5,034	305,627
Maysān	al-ʻAmārah	5,445	14,103	395,666
al-Muthannā	as-Samāwah	19,702	51,029	239,044
an-Najaf	an-Najaf	10,751	27,844	438,971
Ninawā	Mosul	14,838	38,430	1,258,001
al-Qādisiyah	ad-Dīwāniyah	3,285	8,507	475,676
Ṣalāḥ ad-Din	Sāmarrāʼ	11,198	29,004	411,734
at-Taʼmīm	Kirkūk	3,729	9,659	587,079
Wasiṭ	al-Kūt	6,683	17,308	455,583
Kurdish Autonomous Region				
Dahūk	Dahūk	2,363	6,120	296,339
Irbīl	Irbīl	5,587	14,471	657,294
as-Sulaymānīyah	as-Sulaymānīyah	6,083	15,756	816,406
LAND AREA		168,878	437,393	14,110,425
INLAND WATER		357	924	
TOTAL AREA		169,235	438,317	

Demography

Population (1985): 15,676,000.
Density (1985): persons per sq mi 92.6, persons per sq km 35.8.
Urban–rural (1982): urban 68.0%; rural 32.0%.
Sex distribution (1982): male 51.46%; female 48.54%.
Age breakdown (1982): under 15, 46.4%; 15–29, 27.0%; 30–44, 13.6%; 45–59, 7.7%; 60–74, 3.9%; 75 and over 1.4%.
Population projection: (1990) 18,136,000; (2000) 24,198,000.
Doubling time: 26 years.
Ethnic composition (1978): Arab 76.9%; Kurd 18.6%; Turkmen 1.5%; Persian 1.3%; Assyrian 0.8%; other 0.9%.
Religious affiliation (1980): Muslim 95.8% (of which Shīʻī 53.5%, Sunnī 42.3%); Christian 3.5%; other 0.7%.
Major cities (1979): Baghdād 3,400,000†; Mosul 900,000; Kirkūk 500,000.

Vital statistics

Birth rate per 1,000 population (1980–85): 45.1 (world avg. 29.0).
Death rate per 1,000 population (1980–85): 11.5 (world avg. 11.0).
Natural increase rate per 1,000 population (1980–85): 33.6 (world avg. 18.0).
Total fertility rate (avg. births per childbearing woman; 1980–85): 6.7.
Marriage rate per 1,000 population (1982): 4.0.
Divorce rate per 1,000 population (1981): 0.1.
Life expectancy at birth (1980–85): male 55.9 years; female 59.1 years.
Major causes of death per 100,000 population (1975): heart disease (except ischemic) 69.9; accidents (all types) 27.6; pneumonia 27.2; malignant neoplasms (cancers) 19.6; during the early 1980s, however, there were high war casualities and high incidence of trachoma, influenza, measles, whooping cough, and tuberculosis.

National economy

Budget (1981). Revenue: ID5,025,000,000 (revenue from oil and public enterprises 88.5%, sales tax 7.7%, income tax 1.3%). Expenditures: ID5,025,-000,000 (economic services 44.9%, defense 24.0%, local government 8.3%, internal security 5.2%, health 4.6%, education 2.9%).
Public debt (external, outstanding; 1980): U.S.$481,000,000.
Tourism (1981): receipts from visitors U.S.$170,000,000; expenditures by nationals abroad, n.a.
Production (metric tons except as noted). Agriculture, forestry, fishing (1984): wheat 300,000, barley 300,000, sugarcane 200,000‡, potatoes 110,000‡, rice 95,000, corn (maize) 90,000, eggs 22,000,000, milk 1,125,000; livestock (number of live animals) 8,300,000 sheep, 2,300,000 goats, 3,000,000 cattle, 250,000 camels, 250,000‡ buffalo, 45,000,000 poultry; roundwood 131,000‡ cu m; fish catch 26,219‡. Mining and quarrying (1983): elemental sulfur 340,000; gypsum 170,000; salt 80,000. Manufacturing (1983): cement 5,600,-000; paper and paperboard 12,186†; beer 669,390 hectolitres†. Construction (1982): authorized residential 15,516,000 sq m; authorized nonresidential 1,173,000 sq m. Energy production (consumption): electricity (kW-hr; 1983) 13,700,000,000 (13,700,000,000); coal, n.a. (n.a.); crude petroleum (barrels;

1984) 437,800,000 (61,499,000‡); petroleum products (metric tons; 1983) 7,650,000 (5,900,000); natural gas (cu m; 1983) 435,663,000 (435,663,000).
Gross national product (at current market prices; 1981): U.S.$31,300,000,000 (U.S.$2,300 per capita).

Structure of gross domestic product and labour force

	1981 in value ID'000,000	1981 % of total value	1981 labour force	1981 % of labour force
Agriculture	977.0	10.3	1,313,000	39.6
Mining	2,265.5	23.9	3,350	0.1
Manufacturing	594.9	6.3	325,804	9.8
Construction	1,645.4	17.3	364,397	10.9
Public utilities	68.4	0.7	38,342	1.2
Transportation and communication	726.6	7.6	13,250	0.4
Trade	851.2	8.9	...	...
Finance	290.7	3.1	...	...
Pub. admin., defense	...	...	...	...
Services	2,075.6	21.9	...	...
Other	...	...	1,257,857	38.0
TOTAL	9,495.3	100.0	3,316,000	100.0

Population economically active (1977): total 3,133,939; participation rate of total population 26.1% (female 17.0%, unemployed 2.4%).

Price and earnings indexes (1973 = 100)

	1981	1982	1983
Consumer price index	129.4	157.9	177.1
Earnings index			

Household income and expenditure. Average household size (1980) 5.8; average annual income per household: n.a.; source of income: n.a.; expenditure (1971–72): food and beverages 55.4%, housing 18.2%, clothing and footwear 10.3%, transport and communications 5.3%, medical care and health 2.4%, recreation 1.2%.
Land use (1982): forested 3.4%; meadows and pastures 9.2%; agricultural and under permanent cultivation 12.6%; built-on, wasteland, and other 74.8%.

Foreign trade§

Balance of trade (current prices)

	1977	1978	1979	1980	1981
ID'000,000	+1,668	+2,155	+4,776	+5,789	+1,026
% of total	41.4%	49.2%	60.6%	59.5%	19.8%

Imports (1981): ID2,333,845,000 (machines electrical and nonelectrical, airplanes, and other 63.2%; consumer goods 20.7%; chemical and pharmaceutical products 3.4%). *Major import sources:* Japan 30.4%; West Germany 15.9%; France 5.4%; United States 3.5%.
Exports (1981): ID16,859,000 (foodstuffs 55.9%; rubber, paper, and fertilizers 23.0%). *Major export destinations:* Pakistan 14.1%; United Kingdom 6.2%; India 5.3%; Italy 3.2%; France 2.7%; Brazil 2.4%.

Transport and communications

Transport. Railroads (1982): length 1,265 mi, 2,035 km; passenger-mi 543,-300,000 ‖, passenger-km 874,300,000 ‖; short ton-mi cargo 1,977,000,000 ‖, metric ton-km cargo 2,887,000,000 ‖. Roads (1981): total length 15,699 mi, 25,265 km (paved 65%). Vehicles (1981): passenger cars 229,530; trucks and buses 152,768. Merchant marine (1984): vessels (100 gross tons and over) 153; total deadweight tonnage 1,790,466. Air transport (1982): passenger-mi 917,000,000, passenger-km 1,476,000,000; short ton-mi cargo 37,463,000, metric ton-km cargo 54,696,000; airports (1985) with scheduled flights 1.
Communications. Daily newspapers (1984): total number 6; total circulation 324,000; circulation per 1,000 population 23. Radio (1984): total number of receivers 2,200,000 (1 per 6 persons). Television (1984): total number of receivers 635,000 (1 per 22 persons). Telephones (1983): 624,685 (1 per 23 persons).

Education and health

Education (1982–83)

	schools	teachers	students	student/ teacher ratio
Primary (age 6–11)	10,223	107,364	2,614,927	24.4
Secondary (age 12–17)	1,977	32,556	971,827	29.8
Voc., teacher tr.	200	5,974	94,057	15.7
Higher	25	6,674	116,260	17.4

Educational attainment, n.a. *Literacy* (1980): total population over age 15 literate 3,044,500 (43.4%); males literate 2,233,100 (62.9%); females literate 811,400 (23.3%).
Health (1982): physicians 7,634 (1 per 1,773 persons); hospital beds 24,772 (1 per 570 persons); infant mortality rate per 1,000 live births (1981) 31.
Food (1979–81): daily per capita caloric intake 2,789 (vegetable products 88%, animal products 12%); 116% of FAO recommended minimum requirement.

Military

Total active duty personnel (1984): 642,500 (army 93.4%, navy 0.7%, air force 5.9%). *Military expenditure as percent of GNP* (1983): 47.2% (world 6.1%); per capita expenditure U.S.$787.

*Excluding Iraq–Saudi Arabia Neutral Zone. †1981. ‡1983. §Balance of trade is based on f.o.b. (free on board) valuation of imports and exports; however, commodities traded and trade partners information are based on c.i.f. (cost, insurance, and freight) valuation. ‖ 1980.

Ireland

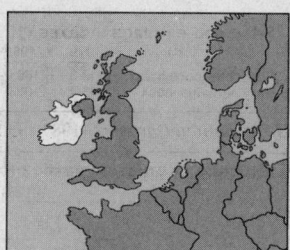

Official name: Éire (Irish); Ireland*
(English).
Form of government: unitary multiparty
republic with two legislative houses
(Senate [60]; House of Representa-
tives [166]).
Chief of state: President.
Head of government: Prime Minister.
Capital: Dublin.
Official languages: Irish; English.
Official religion: Roman Catholic.
Monetary unit: 1 Irish pound (IR£) =
100 new pence; valuation (Oct. 21,
1985) 1 IR£ = U.S.$1.22 = £0.85.

Area and population	area		population
Provinces Counties	sq mi	sq km	1981 census
Connacht	6,611	17,122	424,410
Galway	2,293	5,940	172,018
Leitrim	581	1,525	27,609
Mayo	2,084	5,398	114,766
Roscommon	951	2,463	54,543
Sligo	693	1,796	55,474
Leinster	7,580	19,633	1,790,521
Carlow	346	896	39,820
Dublin	356	922	1,003,164
Kildare	654	1,694	104,122
Kilkenny	796	2,062	70,806
Laoighis	664	1,719	51,171
Longford	403	1,044	31,140
Louth	318	823	88,514
Meath	902	2,336	95,419
Offaly	771	1,998	58,312
Westmeath	681	1,763	61,523
Wexford	908	2,351	99,081
Wicklow	782	2,025	87,449
Munster	9,315	24,127	998,315
Clare	1,231	3,188	87,567
Cork	2,880	7,460	402,465
Kerry	1,815	4,701	122,770
Limerick	1,037	2,686	161,661
Tipperary North Riding	771	1,996	58,984
Tipperary South Riding	872	2,258	76,277
Waterford	710	1,838	88,591
Ulster	3,093	8,012	230,159
Cavan	730	1,891	53,855
Donegal	1,865	4,830	125,112
Monaghan	498	1,291	51,192
TOTAL LAND AREA	26,600	68,895†	3,443,405
INLAND WATER	537	1,390	
TOTAL AREA	27,137	70,285	

Demography
Population (1985): 3,614,0000.
Density (1985): persons per sq mi 135.9, persons per sq km 52.4.
Urban–rural (1985): urban 57.0%; rural 43.0%.
Sex distribution (1985): male 50.06%; female 49.94%.
Age breakdown (1985): under 15, 30.5%; 15–29, 24.4%; 30–44, 17.4%; 45–59,
12.7%; 60–74, 10.8%; 75 and over, 4.2%.
Population projection: (1990) 3,800,000; (2000) 4,200,000.
Doubling time: 70 years.
Ethnic composition (1981): more than 94% Irish nationality.
Religious affiliation (1983): Catholic 94.0%; Anglican 4.0%; other 2.0%.
Major cities (1981): Dublin 525,882; Cork 136,344; Limerick 60,736.

Vital statistics
Birth rate per 1,000 population (1984): 18.2 (world avg. 29.0); (1980) legiti-
mate 95.0%; illegitimate 5.0%.
Death rate per 1,000 population (1984): 9.1 (world avg. 11.0).
Natural increase rate per 1,000 population (1984): 9.1 (world avg. 18.0).
Total fertility rate (avg. births per childbearing woman; 1980–85): 3.2.
Marriage rate per 1,000 population (1984): 5.2.
Life expectancy at birth (1980–85): male 70.4 years; female 75.7 years.
Major causes of death per 100,000 population (1981): heart and circulatory
diseases 477.4, malignant neoplasms (cancers) 178.6; pneumonia 61.3.

National economy
Budget (1984). Revenue: IR£5,952,000,000 (income taxes 32.7%, value-added
tax 23.1%; excise taxes 21.1%). Expenditures: IR£6,991,000,000 (debt service 24.2%; social welfare 18.9%; health 12.9%; education 12.1%).
Public debt (1984): U.S.$18,205,400,000.
Tourism: receipts from visitors (1983) U.S.$457,000,000; expenditures by
nationals abroad (1981) U.S.$511,000,000.
Production (metric tons except as noted). Agriculture, forestry, fishing
(1984): sugar beets 1,650,000, barley 1,600,000, potatoes 1,000,000, wheat
660,000, oats 140,000, milk 5,880,000; livestock (number of live animals)
6,759,000 cattle, 3,754,000 sheep, 1,117,000 pigs; roundwood (1983) 1,026,-
000 cu m; fish catch (1983) 203,400. Mining and quarrying (1984): iron
ore 385,000‡; gypsum 325,000; barite 222,000; zinc ore 206,000‡; lead ore
37,200‡. Manufacturing (value added in IR£; 1979): food and beverages
678,200,000; machinery and transport equipment 428,900,000; chemical
products 337,300,000; nonmetallic mineral products 192,000,000; textiles
124,400,000; printing and publishing 114,200,000; clothing and footwear
109,700,000. Construction (1982): 2,690,000 sq m. Energy production (consumption): electricity (kW-hr; 1984) 11,568,000 (11,568,000); coal (metric

tons; 1983) 74,800 (1,500,000); crude petroleum (barrels; 1983) none (8,590,-
000); petroleum products (metric tons; 1983) 480,000 (4,700,000); natural
gas (cu m; 1983) 2,076,900,000 (2,077,000,000).
Gross national product (1983): U.S.$16,960,000,000 (U.S.$4,810 per capita).

Structure of gross domestic product and labour force	1982		1983	
	in value IR£'000,000	% of total value	labour force	% of labour force
Agriculture	1,296	11.3	189,400	16.8
Mining			9,500	0.8
Manufacturing	1,180	36.6	217,900	19.4
Construction			87,700	7.8
Public utilities			15,100	1.3
Transp. and commun.	2,221	19.4	69,900	6.2
Trade			186,000	16.5
Pub. admin., defense	830	7.3	267,000	23.7
Services				
Finance	2,910	25.4	78,200	7.0
Other			4,500	0.4
TOTAL	11,437	100.0	1,125,200	100.0†

Population economically active (1982): total 1,283,000; participation rate of
total population 36.8% (female 28.8%, unemployed 10.7%).

Price and earnings indexes (1980 = 100)	1978	1979	1980	1981	1982	1983	1984
Consumer price index	74.7	84.6	100.0	120.4	141.0	155.8	169.2
Weekly earnings index	73.5	84.6	100.0	116.7	131.7	147.1	165.1

Household income and expenditure. Average household size (1983) 3.9;
income per household: n.a.; sources of income (1982): wages and salaries
58.4%, self-employment 15.1%, interest and dividends 4.8%; expenditure
(1982): food 30.9%, transportation 13.0%, rent and household goods 10.1%.
Land use (1983): forest 4.9%; pasture 70.5%; agricultural 14.1%; other 10.5%.

Foreign trade

Balance of trade (current prices)	1979	1980	1981	1982	1983	1984
IR£'000,000	−1,365	−1,342	−1,698	−1,120	−420	−15.3
% of total	16.7%	14.3%	15.1%	9.1%	2.9%	0.1%

Imports (1983): IR£7,355,400,000 (machinery and transport equipment
28.8%, petroleum and petroleum products 11.7%, chemical products 11.4%,
food products 4.2%, textiles 3.8%, paper and paper products 2.9%, iron and
steel 1.9%). *Major import sources:* United Kingdom 45.4%; United States
14.7%; West Germany 8.0%; France 4.7%; The Netherlands 3.7%; Japan
3.3%.
Exports (1983): IR£6,935,900,000 (machinery and transport equipment
26.2%, of which office machinery and data-processing equipment 13.8%,
electrical machinery 5.7%; food and beverages 23.9%, of which meat and
meat products 8.0%; dairy products 5.7%; beverages 2.2%; chemical products 13.9%; clothing and footwear 2.0%). *Major export destinations:* United
Kingdom 36.9%; West Germany 9.9%; France 8.2%; United States 8.1%.

Transport and communications
Transport. Railroads (1983): route length 1,236 mi, 1,989 km; passenger-km
819,000,000; metric ton-km cargo 540,000,000. Roads (1982): total length
57,349 mi, 92,294 km (paved 94%). Vehicles (1983): passenger cars 718,555;
trucks and buses 73,832. Merchant marine (1984): vessels (100 gross tons
and over) 154; total deadweight tonnage 270,450. Air transport (1984):
passenger-km 2,190,000,000; metric ton-km cargo 104,900,000; airports
(1985) 3.
Communications. Daily newspapers (1983): 10; circulation 939,000; circulation per 1,000 population 266. Radio (1983): receivers 2,036,100 (1 per
1.7 persons). Television (1983): receivers 721,100 (1 per 4.9 persons). Telephones (1983): 779,600 (1 per 4.5 persons).

Education and health

Education (1982–83)	schools	teachers	students	student/ teacher ratio
Primary (age 6–14)	3,391	20,424	560,874	27.5
Secondary (age 12–18)	572	14,086	238,620	16.9
Voc., teacher tr.	252	5,090	77,347	15.2
Higher	27	3,713	43,521	11.7

Educational attainment (1981). Percent of population over age 14 having:
primary education 45.6%; secondary 27.3%; some postsecondary 19.4%;
university or like institution 7.6%. *Literacy* (1985): virtually 100% literate.
Health: physicians (1981) 4,443 (1 per 775 persons); hospital beds (1980)
33,028 (1 per 103 persons); infant mortality rate per 1,000 live births (1983)
9.8.
Food (1980–82): daily per capita caloric intake 3,970 (vegetable products 62%,
animal products 38%); 143% of FAO recommended minimum requirement.

Military
Total active duty personnel (1984): 13,943 (army 87.5%, navy 6.4%, air force
6.0%). *Military expenditure as percent of GNP* (1983): 1.9% (world 6.1%);
per capita expenditure U.S.$92.

*As provided by the constitution; the 1948 Republic of Ireland Act provides prece-
dent for this longer formulation of the official name but, per official sources, "has not
changed the usage *Ireland* as the name of the state in the English language." †Detail
does not add to total given because of rounding. ‡Metal content only.

Israel

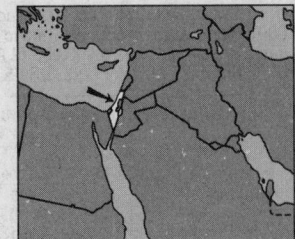

Official name: Medinat Yisra'el
(Hebrew); Isrā'īl (Arabic) (State
of Israel).
Form of government: multiparty
republic with one legislative house
(Knesset [120]).
Chief of state: President.
Head of government: Prime Minister.
Capital: Jerusalem is the proclaimed
capital of Israel (from Jan. 23, 1950)
and the actual seat of government,
but recognition of its status as capital
by the international community has
largely been withheld pending final
settlement of territorial and other
issues through peace talks between
Israel and the Arab parties concerned.
Official languages: Hebrew; Arabic.
Official religion: none.
Monetary unit: 1 Israeli shekel
(IS) = 100 new agorot; valuation (Oct.
21, 1985) 1 U.S.$ = IS1,480;
1 £ = IS2,122.

Area and population

Districts	Capitals	area* sq mi	area* sq km	population 1983 census†
Central (Ha Merkaz)	Ramla	479	1,242	830,700
Haifa (Ḥefa)	Haifa	330	854	575,300
Jerusalem (Yerushalayim)	Jerusalem	215	557	472,900
Northern (Ha Ẕafon)	Tiberias	1,347	3,490	656,000
Southern (Ha Darom)	Beersheba	5,555	14,387	478,800
Tel Aviv	Tel Aviv-Yafo	66	170	1,000,200
TOTAL		7,992	20,700	4,037,600

Demography†

Population (1985): 4,306,000.
*Density** (1985): persons per sq mi 538.8, persons per sq km 208.0.
Urban–rural (1983): urban 86.9%; rural 13.1%.
Sex distribution (1983): male 49.82%; female 50.18%.
Age breakdown (1983): under 15, 32.1%; 15–29, 24.3%; 30–44, 18.0%; 45–59, 12.6%; 60–74, 9.7%; 75 and over, 3.3%.
Population projection‡: (1990) 4,638,800; (2000) 5,339,600.
Doubling time: 41 years.
Ethnic composition (1980): Jewish 83.1%; Arab 16.7%; other 0.2%.
Religious affiliation (1983): Jewish 83.0%; Muslim (mostly Sunnī) 13.1%; Christian 2.3%; Druze and other 1.6%.
Major cities (1983): Jerusalem 431,800; Tel Aviv–Yafo 330,400; Haifa 227,-900; Ḥolon 133,900; Bat Yam 129,700.

Vital statistics†

Birth rate per 1,000 population (1984): 23.6 (world avg. 29.0); (1980) legitimate 97.5%; illegitimate 2.5%.
Death rate per 1,000 population (1984): 6.6 (world avg. 11.0).
Natural increase rate per 1,000 population (1984): 17.0 (world avg. 18.0).
Total fertility rate (avg. births per childbearing woman; 1983): 2.8.
Marriage rate per 1,000 population (1984): 7.0.
Divorce rate per 1,000 population (1984): 1.1.
Life expectancy at birth (1982): male 72.8 years; female 76.2 years.
Major causes of death per 100,000 population (1982): heart disease 256.7; malignant neoplasms (cancers) 133.9; cerebrovascular disease 82.0.

National economy

Budget (1983). Revenue: IS466,495,000,000 (indirect taxes 67.9%; direct taxes 20.1%). Expenditures: IS787,505,000,000 (consumption expenditure 57.3%; subsidies 16.9%, of which on domestic production 7.2%, on exports 5.9%, to the business sector 3.8%).
Tourism (1984): receipts from visitors U.S.$1,268,000,000; expenditures by nationals abroad U.S.$860,000,000.
Production (metric tons except as noted). Agriculture, forestry, fishing (1984): oranges 921,000, tomatoes 359,000, potatoes 207,000, wheat 130,000, apples 118,000, watermelons 82,000, lemons and limes 62,000, cucumbers 59,000, onions 57,000, grapes 43,000; livestock (number of live animals) 330,-000 cattle, 240,000 sheep, 115,000 goats, 26,000,000 chickens; roundwood 118,000 cu m§; fish catch 22,402§. Mining and quarrying (1984–85): phosphate rock 2,250,000; potash 1,825,000; phosphoric acid 150,000; bromine and bromine compounds 136,000; periclase 47,000. Manufacturing (1984): wheat flour 516,000; polyethylene 73,953; cardboard 47,695; ammonium sulfate 42,155; tires 32,029; writing and printing paper 772. Construction (1984): residential 6,439,000 sq m; nonresidential 331,000 sq m. Energy production (consumption): electricity (kW-hr; 1984) 14,908,800,000 (13,-074,100,000); coal (metric tons; 1984) none (2,678,300); crude petroleum (barrels; 1984) 13,140 (51,700,000); petroleum products (metric tons; 1983) 6,953,000 (5,841,000); natural gas (cu m; 1984) 53,300,000 (53,300,000).
Land use (1983): forested 5.7%; meadows and pastures 40.2%; agricultural and under permanent cultivation 21.5%, other 32.6%.
Population economically active (1985) ‖ : total 1,456,000; participation rate of population over age 14, 49.7% (female 34.7%, unemployed 5.9%).

Price and earnings indexes (1980 = 100)

	1979	1980	1981	1982	1983	1984	1985¶
Consumer price index	43.3	100.0	216.8	477.8	1,173.5	5,560.4	21,100
Daily earnings index	43.4	100.0	245.4	553.8	1,414.8	7,028.0	...

Gross national product (1983): U.S.$21,990,000,000 (U.S.$5,360 per capita).

Structure of gross domestic product and labour force

	1983 in value IS'000,000	1983 % of total value	1985 labour force	1985 % of labour force
Agriculture	60,470	5.3	76,700	5.6
Manufacturing, mining	226,892	20.0	309,800	22.6
Construction	75,631	6.6	72,300	5.3
Public utilities	25,393	2.2	13,000	0.9
Transp. and commun.	81,717	7.2	83,800	6.1
Trade	146,093	12.9	164,100	12.0
Finance	...	...	133,400	9.7
Public and community services	...	...	411,200	30.0
Services, other	520,121	45.8	105,400	7.8
TOTAL	1,136,317	100.0	1,369,700	100.0

Public debt (external, outstanding; 1983): U.S.$15,148,800,000.
Household income and expenditure. Average urban household size (1983) 3.5; monthly income per household IS42,825 (U.S.$762); sources of income (1983): salaries and wages 90.5%, property, interest and dividends, pensions, allowances and assistance 8.6%, self-employment 0.9%; expenditure (1984): food, beverages, and tobacco 26.2%, housing and furnishings 26.0%, clothing, footwear, and personal effects 4.5%, fuel and light 4.0%, transportation 2.9%, other goods and services 36.4%.

Foreign trade

Balance of trade (current prices)

	1979	1980	1981	1982	1983	1984
IS'000,000	−8,049	−16,310	−40,089	−68,787	−212,187	−1,198
% of total	24.9%	21.5%	22.9%	21.2%	26.2%	26.0%

Imports (1984): US$8,411,400,000 (raw materials, including precious metals and chemical products 42.8%; fuel and lubricants 18.9%; machinery and industrial equipment 18.7%; diamonds 11.6%). *Major import sources:* United States 21.1%; West Germany 11.2%; Belgium–Luxembourg 9.2%; United Kingdom 8.3%; Switzerland 5.4%.
Exports (1984): US$5,803,700,000 (electrical and nonelectrical machinery 30.2%; diamonds 20.9%; chemicals 12.9%; textiles, clothing, and leather 6.4%; food, beverages, and tobacco 6.4%). *Major export destinations:* United States 28.2%; United Kingdom 8.3%; West Germany 6.2%; France 4.1%; Belgium–Luxembourg 4.0%; Italy 3.7%.

Transport and communications

Transport. Railroads (1983): length 333 mi, 536 km; passenger-mi 129,-000,000, passenger-km 207,000,000; short ton-mi cargo 594,000,000, metric ton-km cargo 867,000,000. Roads (1983): total length 7,756 mi, 12,482 km (paved 100%). Vehicles (1983): passenger cars 571,515; trucks and buses 124,253. Merchant marine (1984): vessels (100 gross tons and over) 64; total deadweight tonnage 677,450. Air transport (1984): passenger-mi 3,792,139,-000, passenger-km 6,102,868,000; short ton-mi cargo 362,616,000, metric ton-km cargo 529,411,000; airports (1985) with scheduled flights 6.
Communications. Daily newspapers (1984): total number 25; total circulation 1,240,200; circulation per 1,000 population 294. Radio (1984): total receivers 1,055,000 (1 per 4.0 persons). Television (1984): total receivers 605,000 (1 per 6.9 persons). Telephones (1983): 1,410,000 (1 per 2.9 persons).

Education and health

Education (1983–84)

	schools	teachers	students	student/ teacher ratio
Primary (age 6–13)	1,831	45,607	616,852	13.5
Secondary (age 14–17)♀	888	35,508	310,242	8.7
Voc., teacher tr.	341	...	96,547	...
Higher	7	...	64,605	...

Educational attainment (1983). Percent of population over age 14 having: no formal schooling 7.0%; primary education 25.1%; secondary 47.0%; higher 20.9%. *Literacy* (1979): total population over age 15 literate 2,412,200 (91.6%); males literate 1,241,900 (95.6%); females literate 1,170,300 (87.7%).
Health: physicians (1981) 10,200 (1 per 387 persons); hospital beds (1983) 26,402 (1 per 155 persons); infant mortality rate per 1,000 live births (1984) 6.6.
Food (1980–82): daily per capita caloric intake 2,989 (vegetable products 78%, animal products 22%); 119%♂ of FAO recommended minimum.

Military

Total active duty personnel (1984): 141,000 (army 73.8%, navy 6.4%, air force 19.8%). *Military expenditure as percent of GNP* (1983): 29.0% (world 6.1%); per capita expenditure U.S.$1,494.

*Excluding West Bank, Gaza Strip, Golan Heights, and East Jerusalem. †De jure; includes population of East Jerusalem and about 23,700 Israeli residents living in occupied territories. ‡Based on migration balance of +5,000 per year in the 1980s and nil in the 1990s. §1983. ‖ Excludes armed forces; includes Israelis in occupied territories. ¶End June. ♀Includes intermediate education age 12–14. ♂1979–81.

Italy

Official name: Repubblica Italiana (Italian Republic).
Form of government: republic with two legislative houses (Senate [315]; Chamber of Deputies [630]).
Chief of state: President.
Head of government: Prime Minister.
Capital: Rome.
Official language: Italian.
Official religion: none; Roman Catholicism disestablished 1985.
Monetary unit: 1 lira (Lit, plural lire) = 100 centesimi; valuation (Oct. 21, 1985) 1 U.S.$ = Lit1,779; 1 £ = Lit2,551.

Area and population		area		population
Regions				1984
Provinces	Capitals	sq mi	sq km	estimate
Abruzzi	L'Aquila	4,168	10,794	1,236,060
Chieti	Chieti	999	2,587	376,667
L'Aquila	L'Aquila	1,944	5,034	295,288
Pescara	Pescara	473	1,225	290,366
Teramo	Teramo	752	1,948	273,739
Basilicata	Potenza	3,858	9,992	614,522
Matera	Matera	1,331	3,447	205,551
Potenza	Potenza	2,527	6,545	408,971
Calabria	Catanzaro	5,823	15,080	2,098,137
Catanzaro	Catanzaro	2,026	5,247	758,035
Cosenza	Cosenza	2,568	6,650	759,463
Reggio di Calabria	Reggio di Calabria	1,229	3,183	580,639
Campania	Naples	5,249	13,595	5,563,230
Avellino	Avellino	1,078	2,792	440,377
Benevento	Benevento	800	2,071	293,140
Caserta	Caserta	1,019	2,639	777,674
Napoli	Naples	452	1,171	3,020,816
Salerno	Salerno	1,900	4,922	1,031,223
Emilia-Romagna	Bologna	8,542	22,123	3,952,304
Bologna	Bologna	1,429	3,702	925,113
Ferrara	Ferrara	1,016	2,632	378,391
Forlì	Forlì	1,123	2,910	604,936
Modena	Modena	1,039	2,690	596,782
Parma	Parma	1,332	3,449	398,723
Piacenza	Piacenza	1,000	2,589	276,799
Ravenna	Ravenna	718	1,859	356,485
Reggio nell'Emilia	Reggio nell'Emilia	885	2,292	415,075
Friuli-Venezia Giulia	Trieste	3,030	7,847	1,228,280
Gorizia	Gorizia	180	467	143,858
Pordenone	Pordenone	878	2,273	276,631
Trieste	Trieste	82	212	277,475
Udine	Udine	1,890	4,895	530,316
Lazio	Rome	6,642	17,203	5,056,119
Frosinone	Frosinone	1,251	3,239	470,085
Latina	Latina	869	2,251	447,771
Rieti	Rieti	1,061	2,749	144,060
Roma	Rome	2,066	5,352	3,722,053
Viterbo	Viterbo	1,395	3,612	272,150
Liguria	Genoa	2,091	5,416	1,789,225
Genova	Genoa	2,091	1,834	1,028,348
Imperia	Imperia	446	1,155	223,943
La Spezia	La Spezia	341	882	239,818
Savona	Savona	596	1,545	297,116
Lombardia	Milan	9,211	23,857	8,891,318
Bergamo	Bergamo	1,066	2,760	902,932
Brescia	Brescia	1,846	4,782	1,024,631
Como	Como	798	2,067	780,734
Cremona	Cremona	684	1,771	331,083
Mantova	Mantova	903	2,339	375,566
Milano	Milan	1,066	2,762	4,001,423
Pavia	Pavia	1,145	2,965	508,865
Sondrio	Sondrio	1,240	3,212	175,327
Varese	Varese	463	1,199	790,757
Marche	Ancona	3,743	9,694	1,420,829
Ancona	Ancona	749	1,940	436,391
Ascoli Piceno	Ascoli Piceno	806	2,087	355,231
Macerata	Macerata	1,071	2,774	293,928
Pesaro e Urbino	Pesaro	1,117	2,893	335,279
Molise	Campobasso	1,713	4,438	331,670
Campobasso	Campobasso	1,123	2,909	238,645
Isernia	Isernia	590	1,529	93,025
Piemonte	Turin	9,807	25,399	4,431,064
Alessandria	Alessandria	1,375	3,560	460,373
Asti	Asti	583	1,511	213,277
Cuneo	Cuneo	2,665	6,903	548,763
Novara	Novara	1,388	3,594	505,785
Torino	Turin	2,637	6,830	2,311,649
Vercelli	Vercelli	1,159	3,001	391,217
Puglia	Bari	7,470	19,348	3,946,871
Bari	Bari	1,980	5,129	1,488,158
Brindisi	Brindisi	710	1,838	399,573
Foggia	Foggia	2,774	7,185	691,597
Lecce	Lecce	1,065	2,759	785,528
Taranto	Taranto	941	2,437	582,015
Sardegna	Cagliari	9,301	24,090	1,617,265
Cagliari	Cagliari	2,662	6,895	744,032
Nuoro	Nuoro	2,720	7,044	276,123
Oristano	Oristano	1,016	2,631	157,145
Sassari	Sassari	2,903	7,520	439,965
Sicilia (Sicily)	Palermo	9,926	25,708	5,006,684
Agrigento	Agrigento	1,175	3,042	479,809
Caltanissetta	Caltanissetta	822	2,128	290,904
Catania	Catania	1,371	3,552	1,029,515
Enna	Enna	989	2,562	193,536
Messina	Messina	1,254	3,247	677,634
Palermo	Palermo	1,927	4,992	1,223,892
Ragusa	Ragusa	623	1,614	281,235
Siracusa	Siracusa	814	2,109	401,123
Trapani	Trapani	951	2,462	429,036

Area and population	(continued)			
Toscana	Florence	8,877	22,992	3,581,291
Arezzo	Arezzo	1,248	3,232	313,409
Firenze	Florence	1,498	3,879	1,201,263
Grosseto	Grosseto	1,739	4,504	220,683
Livorno	Livorno	468	1,213	347,478
Lucca	Lucca	684	1,773	385,059
Massa-Carrara	Massa-Carrara	447	1,157	203,851
Pisa	Pisa	945	2,448	389,010
Pistoia	Pistoia	373	965	265,552
Siena	Siena	1,475	3,821	254,986
Trentino-Alto Adige	Bolzano	5,259	13,620	875,780
Bolzano-Bozen	Bolzano	2,857	7,400	432,231
Trento	Trento	2,402	6,220	443,549
Umbria	Perugia	3,265	8,456	813,507
Perugia	Perugia	2,446	6,334	586,400
Terni	Terni	819	2,122	227,107
Valle d'Aosta	Aosta	1,259	3,262	113,418
Veneto	Venice	7,090	18,363	4,361,527
Belluno	Belluno	1,420	3,678	219,295
Padova	Padova	827	2,142	813,061
Rovigo	Rovigo	691	1,789	252,644
Treviso	Treviso	956	2,477	726,271
Venezia	Venice	950	2,460	839,978
Verona	Verona	1,195	3,096	778,898
Vicenza	Vicenza	1,051	2,721	731,380
TOTAL		116,324	301,277	56,929,101

Demography

Population (1985): 57,079,000.
Density (1985): persons per sq mi 490.7, persons per sq km 189.4.
Urban–rural (1985): urban 71.7%; rural 28.3%.
Sex distribution (1985): male 48.96%; female 51.04%.
Age breakdown (1985): under 15, 19.9%; 15–29, 22.8%; 30–44, 19.8%; 45–59, 18.7%; 60–74, 13.2%; 75 and over 5.6%.
Population projection: (1990) 57,400,000; (2000) 58,100,000.
Doubling time: greater than 100 years.
Ethnic composition (1980): Italian 98.1%; other 1.9%.
Religious affiliation (1980): Roman Catholic 83.2%; nonreligious 13.6%; atheist 2.6%; other 0.2%.
Major cities (1984): Rome 2,830,650; Milan 1,561,438; Naples 1,208,545; Turin 1,069,013; Genoa 746,785; Palermo 712,342; Bologna 447,971.
National origin (1980): 98.1% Italian; 1.9% foreign, of which Austrian 0.2%, French 0.2%, Slovene 0.2%, Albanian 0.1%, other 1.2%.
Mobility (1977). Population living in the same residence as in 1967: 52.0%.
Households. Average household size (1982) 3.0; composition of households (1980) 1 person 13.9%, 2 persons 23.4%, 3 persons 22.6%, 4 persons 21.6%, 5 persons 11.1%, 6 or more persons 7.4%. Family households: 13,088,040 (74.3%); nonfamily 4,527,088 (25.7%), of which 1-person 13.9%.
Immigration (1982): immigrants admitted 92,423, from Europe 76.9%, of which West Germany 34.3%, Switzerland 25.7%, France 6.0%; Africa 6.0%; Latin America 5.7%; United States 5.2%; Asia 2.6%.

Vital statistics

Birth rate per 1,000 population (1984): 10.5 (world avg. 29.0); legitimate 95.2%; illegitimate 4.8%.
Death rate per 1,000 population (1984): 9.4 (world avg. 11.0).
Natural increase rate per 1,000 population (1984): 1.1 (world avg. 18.0).
Total fertility rate (avg. births per childbearing woman; 1983): 1.5.
Marriage rate per 1,000 population (1984): 5.2.
Divorce rate per 1,000 population: (1984): 0.3.
Life expectancy at birth (1983): male 73.0 years; female 79.0 years.
Major causes of death per 100,000 population (1983): diseases of the circulatory system 459.0, of which myocardial infarction 72.4, ischemic heart disease 66.5; malignant neoplasms (cancers) 225.4; diseases of the respiratory system 69.0; diseases of the digestive system 55.3.

Social indicators

Educational attainment (1980). Percent of adult population having: less than full primary education 14.4%; primary 42.8%; junior secondary 27.5%; upper secondary 12.5%; 4-year higher degree 2.8%.

Distribution of income (1977)				
percent of household income by quintile				
1	2	3	4	5 (highest)
6.2	11.3	15.9	22.7	43.9

Quality of working life. Average workweek (1983): 38.5 hours. Annual rate per 100,000 workers (1978) for: injury or accident 5,928; industrial illness 405; death 66. Proportion of labour force insured for damages or income loss (1982) resulting from: injury 100%; permanent disability 100%; death 100%. Average days lost to labour stoppages per 1,000 workdays (1984): 0.8. Average duration of journey to work: n.a. Rate per 1,000 workers of discouraged (unemployed no longer seeking work; 1982): 0.9.
Access to services (1978). Proportion of dwellings having access to: electricity 99.9%; safe water supply 99.7%; toilet facilities 96.1%; bath facilities 87.0%.
Social participation. Eligible voters participating in last national election: 89.0%. Population participating in voluntary work: n.a. Trade union membership in total workforce (1982): 62.4%. Practicing religious population in total affiliated population (1980): 65.7%, of which weekly 28.0%.
Social deviance (1984). Offense rate per 100,000 population for: murder 1.8; rape 1.5; other assault 29.1; theft, including burglary and housebreaking 1,616. Incidence per 100,000 in general population of: alcoholism (1978) 2.0; drug and substance abuse (1978) 25.1; suicide (1984) 5.6.
Leisure (1982). Favourite leisure activities (as percent of public spending on culture): cinema 35.6%; sporting events 16.3%; theatre 10.6%.

Material well-being. Rate per 1,000 of population possessing (1983): automobile 345; telephone 380. Households possessing (1979): television 72%; refrigerator 91%; air conditioner 9%; washing machine 88%.

National economy

Gross national product (at current market prices; 1983): U.S.$350,038,850,-000 (U.S.$6,170 per capita).

Structure of gross domestic product and labour force

	1983			
	in value 000,000,000 lire	% of total value	labour force	% of labour force
Agriculture	31,146	5.8	2,504,000	10.9
Mining	17,509	3.2	657,900	2.8
Manufacturing	127,768	23.8	4,643,100	20.2
Construction	41,730	7.8	1,726,000	7.5
Public utilities	26,320	4.9	195,000	0.8
Transportation and communication	35,357	6.5	1,242,900	5.4
Trade	83,084	15.5	4,189,800	18.2
Finance	63,373	11.8	373,300	1.6
Pub. admin., defense	75,283	14.1	3,098,000	13.4
Services	43,210	8.1	2,130,000	9.2
Other	—8,876*	—1.6*	2,278,000†	9.9†
TOTAL	535,904	100.0‡	23,038,000	100.0‡

Budget (1983). Revenue: 176,944,000,000,000 lire (property and income taxes 45.9%, business taxes 22.2%, transfer payments 15.3%, sales taxes 9.9%). Expenditures: 259,890,000,000,000 lire (social services 21.7%, regional and local subsidies 13.4%, education and culture 10.6%, transportation and communication 8.2%, national defense 4.0%).
Public debt (1984): U.S.$293,000,000,000.
Tourism (1983): receipts from visitors U.S.$9,034,000,000; expenditures by nationals abroad U.S.$1,822,000,000.

Manufacturing, mining, and construction enterprises (1981)

	no. of enterprises	no. of employees	hourly wages as a % of avg. of all wages	annual value added (000,000,000 lire)
Transport equipment	730	402,000	117.7	10,388
Industrial chemicals	1,037	244,000	119.7	10,128
Machinery, nonelectrical	2,484	299,000	98.0	9,777
Electrical machinery	1,145	310,000	112.1	8,249
Pottery, ceramics, and glass	2,427	207,000	83.4	6,767
Iron and steel	872	236,000	122.6	6,702
Food products	1,607	172,000	92.2	6,429
Textiles	2,935	275,000	84.4	6,348
Metal products	2,379	197,000	86.7	5,734
Wearing apparel	1,729	165,000	75.8	3,157
Printing, publishing	776	85,000	103.2	3,075
Petroleum and gas	7	7,000	138.6	2,460
Plastic products	916	71,000	84.4	2,090
Paper and paper products	607	64,000	102.1	2,030
Nonmetal mining and quarrying	301	18,000	82.9	536
Construction	326,000	1,199,000	...	31,920

Production (metric tons except as noted). Agriculture, forestry, fishing (1984): sugar beets 11,591,400, grapes 11,300,000, wheat 10,136,700, corn (maize) 6,816,000, tomatoes 6,719,400, potatoes 2,519,300, olives 2,130,000, apples 2,036,600, oranges 1,945,800, barley 1,634,000, peaches 1,360,000, pears 1,069,000, rice 998,000; livestock (number of live animals) 9,113,000 cattle, 9,228,000 sheep, 9,187,000 pigs, 110,000,000 chickens; roundwood 80,444,-000 cu m; fish catch 428,674. Mining and quarrying (1984): rock salt 3,255,-400; potash 1,481,400; feldspar 985,600; asbestos 147,300; barite 107,100; zinc 41,100; lead 21,500; magnesium 9,300. Manufacturing (1984): cement 38,304,000; crude steel 23,072,000; pig iron 11,891,000; olive oil 3,900,000; sulfuric acid 2,650,000; pasta 2,485,000; plastics and resins 2,436,000§; chemical fertilizers 1,830,000§; caustic soda 1,072,000; soaps and detergents 1,058,600; textiles and cloth 253,400§; wine 71,200,000 hectolitres ‖; beer 9,333,000 hectolitres ‖; 2,437,300 motorized road vehicles, of which 1,395,500 automobiles, 853,900 motorcycles, scooters, and mopeds, 187,800 trucks and buses; 331,500,000 pairs of shoes; 50,000,000 women's dresses. Construction (buildings completed 1983): residential 185,323; commercial, industrial, and other 25,101.

Service enterprises (1981)

	no. of enterprises	no. of employees	hourly wage as a % of all wages	annual value added (000,000,000 lire)
Public utilities	61	11,000	...	5,082
Electrical power	49	125,000	...	4,017
Transportation	195,828	1,135,950	...	24,760
Communication }			...	5,842
Finance	234,334	938,904	...	46,343
Wholesale and retail trade	1,589,785	3,694,238	...	61,884
Pub. admin., services	494,153	3,553,304	...	57,333

Energy production (consumption): electricity (kW-hr; 1984) 188,000,000 (193,962,000,000); coal (metric tons; 1984) 1,805,845 (2,550,000); crude petroleum (barrels; 1984) 14,600,000 (634,370,000); petroleum products (metric tons; 1983) 69,932,000 (77,988,000); natural gas (cu m; 1984) 13,-853,910,000 (31,378,500,000).
Population economically active (1985): total 22,893,000; participation rate of population over age 15, 50.3% (female 34.8%, unemployed 10.8%).

Price and earnings indexes (1980 = 100)

	1979	1980	1981	1982	1983	1984	1985¶
Consumer price index	82.5	100.0	117.8	137.2	157.3	160.8	172.8
Monthly earnings index	68.8	82.0	100.0	123.9	145.7	186.7	...

Household income and expenditure. Average household size (1982) 3.0; average annual income per household 16,969,000 lire (U.S.$12,467); sources of income: salaries and wages 49.2%, self-employment 31.1%, social security 11.8%; expenditure (1983): food and beverages 28.3%, housing 25.2%, transport and communications 13.8%, recreation and education 5.6%.
Land use (1983): forested 21.6%; meadows and pastures 17.4%; agricultural and under permanent cultivation 42.2%; other 18.8%.

Financial aggregates

	1979	1980	1981	1982	1983	1984
Exchange rate, Lit per:						
U.S. dollar	830.9	856.4	1,136.8	1,352.5	1,518.8	1,757.0
£	1,762.8	1,992.2	2,305.3	2,367.6	2,304.0	2,347.9
SDR	1,059.0	1,186.8	1,396.8	1,511.3	1,737.4	1,897.6
International reserves (U.S.$)						
Total (excl. gold; '000,000)	18,197	23,140	20,134	14,090	19,840	20,796
SDRs ('000,000)	592	665	783	785	591	633
Reserve pos. in IMF ('000,000)	312	823	734	696	990	1,074
Foreign exchange ('000,000)	17,294	21,652	18,617	12,610	18,259	19,089
Gold ('000,000 fine troy oz)	66.71	66.67	66.67	66.67	66.67	66.67
% world reserves	7.1	7.0	7.0	7.0	7.1	7.1
Interest and prices						
Central bank discount (%)	15.00	16.50	19.00	18.00	17.00	16.50
Gov't. bond yield (%)	14.05	16.11	20.58	20.90	18.02	14.95
Industrial share prices (1980 = 100)	78.7	100.0	151.7	123.1	153.1	171.9
Balance of payments (U.S.$'000,000)						
Balance of visible trade	—990	—16,417	—10,901	—8,130	—4,390	—5,994
Imports, f.o.b.	—72,379	—93,236	—85,803	—80,678	—75,215	—78,976
Exports, f.o.b.	71,389	76,819	74,902	72,548	70,827	72,982
Balance of invisibles	6,614	5,402	1,537	1,701	2,555	2,026
Balance of payments, current account	5,414	—9,801	—8,604	—5,684	555	—2,871

Foreign trade

Balance of trade (current prices)

	1979	1980	1981	1982	1983	1984
'000,000,000 lire	—1,905	—15,716	—14,056	—16,966	—11,465	—19,163
% of total	1.4%	9.2%	6.7%	7.9%	4.9%	6.9%

Imports (1983): 122,001,933,000,000 lire (crude petroleum 19.8%; machinery and transport equipment 19.4%, of which transport equipment 7.4%, precision machinery 3.8%; chemicals and chemical products 9.7%; food and live animals 8.4%; metal and semiprocessed metal 7.6%; refined petroleum products 7.1%). *Major import sources:* West Germany 15.9%; France 12.6%; United States 5.9%; U.S.S.R. 4.5%; Switzerland 3.9%; Saudi Arabia 3.7%.
Exports (1983): 110,537,203,000,000 lire (nontransport machinery 26.3%; transport equipment 10.9%, of which automobiles 3.6%, tractors and construction equipment 0.9%; clothing and wearing apparel 8.6%, of which shoes 4.2%; textiles 8.4%; metal and processed metal 8.3%; chemicals and chemical products 7.2%; refined petroleum products 5.6%). *Major export destinations:* West Germany 16.6%; France 14.7%; United States 7.7%; United Kingdom 6.3%; Switzerland 4.1%; Saudi Arabia 4.1%.

Transport and communications

Transport. Railroads (1984): route length 12,292 mi, 19,782 km; passenger-mi 23,070,000,000, passenger-km 37,128,000,000; short ton-mi cargo 12,-181,000,000, metric ton-km cargo 17,785,000,000. Roads (1983): total length 184,981 mi, 297,698 km (paved 100%). Vehicles (1983): passenger cars 20,450,000; trucks and buses 1,720,000. Merchant marine (1984): vessels (100 gross tons and over) 1,590; total deadweight tonnage 14,938,899. Air transport (1984): passenger-mi 8,474,000,000, passenger-km 13,638,000,000; short ton-mi cargo 486,289,000, metric ton-km cargo 709,970,000; airports (1985) 36.
Communications. Daily newspapers (1982): total number 79; total circulation 4,632,000; circulation per 1,000 population 81.8. Radio (1984): total number of receivers 14,007,892 (1 per 4.1 persons). Television (1984): total number of receivers 13,831,260 (1 per 4.1 persons). Telephones (1983): 21,670,001 (1 per 2.6 persons).

Education and health

Education (1983–84)

	schools	teachers♀	students♂	student/ teacher ratio
Primary (age 6–10)	28,786	276,716	3,909,365	...
Secondary (age 11–13)	13,135	333,062	3,301,625	...
Voc., teacher tr.	4,430	199,268	2,042,913	...
Higher	74	47,844	1,096,454	...

Literacy (1971): total population literate 38,421,342 (93.9%); males literate 18,767,897 (95.3%); females literate 19,653,445 (96.6%).
Health: physicians (1981) 97,003 (1 per 583.9 persons); hospital beds (1982) 515,152 (1 per 109.8 persons); infant mortality rate per 1,000 live births (1984) 11.6.
Food (1980–82): daily per capita caloric intake 3,589 (vegetable products 76%, animal products 24%); 143% of FAO recommended minimum requirement.

Military

Total active duty personnel (1984): 375,100 (army 69.3%, navy 11.9%, air force 18.8%). *Military expenditure as percent of GNP* (1983): 2.9% (world 6.1%); per capita expenditure U.S.$181.

*Imputed bank charges less indirect duties on import. †Unemployed. ‡Detail does not add to total given because of rounding. §1983. ‖ 1982. ¶April. ♀1982–83. ♂1984–85.

Ivory Coast

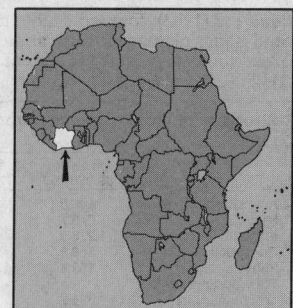

Official name: République de Côte
d'Ivoire (Republic of Ivory Coast).
Form of government: republic with
one legislative house (National
Assembly [147]).
Head of state and government:
President.
Capital: Abidjan
(Capital designate: Yamoussoukro).
Official language: French.
Official religion: none.
Monetary unit: 1 CFA franc
(CFAF) = 100 centimes; valuation
(Oct. 21, 1985) 1 U.S.$ = CFAF402.02;
1 £ = CFAF576.50.

Area and population		area		population
Departments	Capitals	sq mi	sq km	1975 census*
Abengourou	Abengourou	2,664	6,900	177,692
Abidjan	Abidjan	5,483	14,200	1,389,141
Aboisso	Aboisso	2,413	6,250	148,823
Adzopé	Adzopé	2,019	5,230	162,837
Agboville	Agboville	1,486	3,850	141,970
Biankouma	Biankouma	1,911	4,950	75,711
Bondoukou	Bondoukou	6,382	16,530	296,551
Bongouanou	Bongouanou	2,151	5,570	216,907
Bouaflé	Bouaflé	2,189	5,670	164,817
Bouaké	Bouaké	9,189	23,800	808,048
Bouna	Bouna	8,290	21,470	84,290
Boundiali	Boundiali	3,048	7,895	96,449
Dabakala	Dabakala	3,734	9,670	56,230
Daloa	Daloa	4,483	11,610	265,529
Danané	Danané	1,776	4,600	170,249
Dimbokro	Dimbokro	3,293	8,530	258,116
Divo	Divo	3,058	7,920	202,511
Ferkessedougou	Ferkessedougou	6,845	17,728	90,423
Gagnoa	Gagnoa	1,737	4,500	174,018
Guiglo	Guiglo	5,463	14,150	137,672
Issia	Issia	1,386	3,590	104,081
Katiola	Katiola	3,637	9,420	77,875
Korhogo	Korhogo	4,826	12,500	276,816
Lakota	Lakota	1,054	2,730	76,105
Man	Man	2,722	7,050	278,659
Mankono	Mankono	4,116	10,660	82,358
Odienné	Odienné	7,954	20,600	124,010
Oumé	Oumé	927	2,400	85,486
Sassandra	Sassandra	6,768	17,530	116,644
Séguéla	Séguéla	4,340	11,240	75,181
Soubré	Soubré	3,193	8,270	75,350
Tingréla	Tingréla	849	2,200	35,829
Touba	Touba	3,367	8,720	77,786
Zuénoula	Zuénoula	1,093	2,830	98,792
TOTAL		123,847†	320,763	6,702,866

Demography

Population (1985): 10,163,000.
Density (1985): persons per sq mi 82.1, persons per sq km 31.7.
Urban–rural (1985): urban 42.0%; rural 58.0%.
Sex distribution (1985): male 51.09%; female 48.91%.
Age breakdown (1985): under 15, 45.1%; 15–29, 25.4%; 30–44, 15.6%; 45–59,
9.2%; 60–74, 4.0%; 75 and over 0.7%.
Population projection: (1990) 12,568,000; (2000) 19,088,000.
Doubling time: 16 years.
Ethnic composition (1978): Bete 19.7%; Senufo 14.4%; Baule 11.8%; Anui
10.5%; Malinke 6.6%; Dan 5.6%; Lobi 5.3%; other 26.1%.
Religious affiliation (1980): folk religionist 43.8%; Christian 32.0%; Muslim
24.0%; other 0.2%.
Major cities (1975): Abidjan 1,800,000‡; Bouaké 175,264; Daloa 60,837; Man
50,288; Korhogo 45,250.

Vital statistics

Birth rate per 1,000 population (1983): 46.0 (world avg. 29.0); legitimate,
n.a.; illegitimate, n.a.
Death rate per 1,000 population (1983): 14.0 (world avg. 11.0).
Natural increase rate per 1,000 population (1983): 32.0 (world avg. 18.0).
Total fertility rate (avg. births per childbearing woman; 1983): 6.6.
Marriage rate per 1,000 population: n.a.
Divorce rate per 1,000 population: n.a.
Life expectancy at birth (1983): male 50.0 years; female 53.0 years.
Major causes of death: n.a.; however, the major infectious diseases are
malaria, dysentery, yaws, pneumonia, leprosy, and syphilis and gonorrhea.

National economy

Budget (1985). Revenue: CFAF418,130,000,000. Expenditures: CFAF418,-
130,000,000.
Public debt (external, outstanding; 1983): U.S.$4,824,200,000.
Tourism (1981): receipts from visitors U.S.$74,000,000; expenditures by na-
tionals abroad U.S.$239,000,000.
Production (metric tons except as noted). Agriculture (1984): sugarcane
1,800,000, plantains 850,000, cassava 800,000, rice 490,000, corn (maize)
468,000, cacao beans 411,000, pineapples 220,000, cotton 212,000, coconuts
170,000, palm oil 145,000, coffee 85,000; livestock (number of live animals) 1,400,000 goats, 1,400,000 sheep, 760,000 cattle; roundwood (1983)
11,839,000 cu m; fish catch (1983) 93,960. Mining and quarrying (1982):
diamonds 37,000 carats. Manufacturing (1982): cement 1,000,000‡; motor

gasoline 240,000; raw sugar 170,000; wheat flour 145,000; cocoa powder
75,000; cigarettes 3,500; sawn wood 748,000 cu m; veneer sheets 38,000
cu m. Construction (in CFAF; 1982): 229,000,000,000. Energy production (consumption): electricity (kW-hr; 1983) 1,965,000,000 (933,510,000);
coal, none (n.a.); crude petroleum (barrels; 1983) 7,513,250 (12,534,000);
petroleum products (metric tons; 1983) 1,541,000 (1,089,000).
Gross national product (at current market prices; 1983): U.S.$6,730,000,000
(U.S.$720 per capita).

Structure of gross domestic product and labour force				
	1981			
	in value CFAF'000,000,000	% of total value	labour force	% of labour force
Agriculture	639.4	27.1	3,255,590	79.0
Mining	15.8	0.7		
Manufacturing	289.5	12.3		
Construction	188.8	8.1		
Public utilities	41.2	1.7	164,840	4.0
Transportation and communication	189.0	8.0		
Pub. admin., defense	272.5	11.6		
Trade, finance Services	718.7	30.5	700,570	17.0
Other				
TOTAL	2,354.9§	100.0	4,121,000	100.0

Population economically active (1983): total 4,338,000; participation rate of
population ages 15–64, 53.0% (female, n.a.; unemployed, n.a.).

Price and earnings indexes (1980 = 100)							
	1979	1980	1981	1982	1983	1984	1985
Consumer price index	87.2	100.0	108.8	116.8	123.7	129.0	127.1 ‖
Annual wage index	...	100.0	107.0	117.4	...	...	...

Household income and expenditure. Average household size (1980) 4.5;
average annual income per household CFAF500,000; sources of income:
wages 44.9%, self-employment 49.9%, transfers and other resources 5.2%;
expenditure (1979): food 51.1%, housing 11.6%, clothing 8.4%.
Land use (1983): forested 26.3%; meadows and pastures 9.4%; agricultural
and under permanent cultivation 12.5%; other 51.8%.

Foreign trade

Balance of trade (current prices)							
	1977	1978	1979	1980	1981	1982	1983
CFAF'000,000,000	+99.6	−1.8	+6.0	+49.5	+7.8	+36.8	+92.5
% of total	10.4%	0.1%	0.6%	3.9%	0.6%	2.0%	6.2%

Imports (1983): CFAF704,249,000,000 (machinery and transport equipment
24.5%, of which nonelectrical machinery 7.9%; crude petroleum 13.3%;
chemicals 10.8%; cereals 7.3%; dairy products 2.8%). *Major import sources:*
France 35.2%; West Germany 5.4%; Nigeria 5.3%; Japan 4.5%.
Exports (1983): CFAF796,774,000,000 (coffee 21.8%; cacao beans 20.4%;
wood 12.5%; energy products 11.5%; cacao butter 4.9%; cotton 4.0%; canned
fish 2.5%; chemicals 2.2%). *Major export destinations:* France 19.0%; United
States 12.4%; The Netherlands 11.6%; Italy 8.1%; United Kingdom 4.5%.

Transport and communications

Transport. Railroads (1983): length 761 mi, 1,225 km; passenger-mi 620,-
382,000, passenger-km 998,410,000; short ton-mi cargo 360,759,000, metric
ton-km cargo 526,700,000. Roads (1984): total length 33,390 mi, 53,736
km (paved 6%). Vehicles (1982): passenger cars 182,956; trucks and buses
52,491. Merchant marine (1984): vessels (100 gross tons and over) 64; total
deadweight tonnage 173,679. Air transport¶ (1983): passenger-mi 178,682,-
000, passenger-km 287,561,000; short ton-mi cargo 37,582,000, metric ton-
km cargo 54,869,000; airports (1985) with scheduled flights 15.
Communications. Daily newspapers (1984): total number 1; total circulation 80,000; circulation per 1,000 population 8.2. Radio (1984): 900,000
receivers (1 per 10.8 persons). Television (1984): 340,000 receivers (1 per
28.7 persons). Telephones (1980): 88,000 (1 per 94 persons).

Education and health

Education (1979–80)				
	schools	teachers	students	student/ teacher ratio
Primary (age 6–11)	4,419	24,441	963,246	39.4
Secondary (age 12–18)	113⁹	4,569	172,409	37.7
Voc., teacher tr.	38	650⁵	44,481	...
Higher	1	475□	10,772	...

Educational attainment (1975). Percent of population over age 6 having: no
formal schooling 75.3%; primary education 17.3%; secondary 5.1%; higher
0.5%. *Literacy* (1980): total population literate 1,560,000 (35.0%).
Health (1978): physicians 429 (1 per 16,795 persons); hospital beds 9,962 (1
per 723 persons); infant mortality rate per 1,000 live births (1983) 121.
Food (1980–82): daily per capita caloric intake 2,658 (vegetable products
93%, animal products 7%); 115% of FAO recommended minimum.

Military

Total active duty personnel (1984): 6,000 (army 75.0%, navy 11.7%, air force
13.3%). *Military expenditure as percent of GNP* (1983): 1.3% (world 6.1%);
per capita expenditure U.S.$8.

*Preliminary. †Detail does not add to total given because of rounding. ‡1983. §At
current factor cost. ‖ April. ¶Air Afrique only. ⁹Public schools only. δ1976–77.
□1978–79.

Jamaica

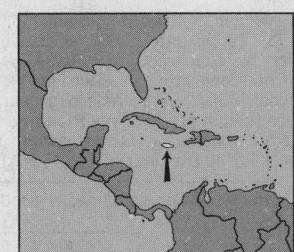

Official name: Jamaica.
Form of government:
parliamentary state with two
legislative houses (Senate [21]; House
of Representatives [60]).
Chief of state: British Monarch
represented by governor-general.
Head of government: Prime Minister.
Capital: Kingston.
Official language: English.
Official religion: none.
Monetary unit: 1 dollar (J$) = 100
cents; valuation (Oct. 21, 1985)
1 U.S.$ = J$6.19; 1 £ = J$8.88.

Area and population

		area		population
Counties Parishes	Capitals	sq mi	sq km	1985 estimate
Cornwall				
Hanover	Lucea	174	450	64,000
Saint Elizabeth	Black River	468	1,212	142,400
Saint James	Montego Bay	230	595	145,300
Trelawny	Falmouth	338	875	72,200
Westmorland	Savanna-la-Mar	312	807	125,600
Middlesex				
Clarendon	May Pen	462	1,196	212,100
Manchester	Mandeville	321	830	153,800
Saint Ann	Saint Ann's Bay	468	1,213	144,600
Saint Catherine	Spanish Town	460	1,192	388,000
Saint Mary	Port Maria	236	611	109,900
Surrey				
Kingston	Kingston	8	22	*
Portland	Port Antonio	314	814	76,200
Saint Andrew	—	166	431	625,800*
Saint Thomas	Morant Bay	287	743	83,800
TOTAL		4,244	10,991	2,343,700

Demography

Population (1985): 2,343,700.
Density (1985): persons per sq mi 552.2, persons per sq km 213.2.
Urban–rural (1982): urban 46.3%; rural 53.7%.
Sex distribution (1982): male 48.95%; female 51.05%.
Age breakdown (1982): under 15, 40.6%; 15–29, 29.0%; 30–44, 11.6%; 45–59, 10.0%; 60–64, 6.8%; 65 and over, 2.0%.
Population projection: (1990) 2,535,000; (2000) 2,872,000.
Doubling time: 40 years.
Ethnic composition (1983): black 76.3%; Afro-European 15.1%; East Indian and Afro-East Indian 3.4%; white 3.2%; other 2.0%.
Religious affiliation (1980): Protestant (mostly Anglican, Baptist, Seventh-day Adventist) 70.7%; Roman Catholic 9.6%; indigenous Christian 8.6%; spiritist (mostly Rastafarian) 7.1%; other 4.0%.
Major cities (1982): Kingston 104,041; Spanish Town 89,097; Portmore 66,-976; Montego Bay 59,614.

Vital statistics

Birth rate per 1,000 population (1984): 23.5 (world avg. 29.0).
Death rate per 1,000 population (1984): 5.4 (world avg. 11.0).
Natural increase rate per 1,000 population (1984): 18.1 (world avg. 18.0).
Total fertility rate (avg. births per childbearing woman; 1981): 3.4.
Marriage rate per 1,000 population (1983): 3.7.
Divorce rate per 1,000 population (1983): 0.3.
Life expectancy at birth (1981): male 69.2 years; female 73.3 years.
Major causes of death per 100,000 population (1978): cerebrovascular disease 81.7; malignant neoplasms (cancers) 74.8; heart disease 72.4; diseases of the respiratory system 41.7%; infectious and parasitic diseases 39.3.

National economy

Budget (1982–83). Revenue: J$1,749,660,000 (tax revenue 76.4%, of which income taxes 37.0%; consumption taxes 21.7%; customs duties 6.9%; special bauxite transaction 6.4%). Expenditures: J$1,818,500,000 (public debt 26.8%; education 19.9%; general administration 17.3%; public order and defense 13.0%; health 10.0%).
Public debt (external, outstanding; 1983): U.S.$1,949,000,000.
Tourism (1983): receipts from visitors U.S.$399,000,000; expenditures by nationals abroad U.S.$11,000,000.
Production (metric tons except as noted). Agriculture, forestry, fishing (1984): sugarcane 2,655,000, roots and tubers 186,000, bananas 160,000, coconuts 120,000, vegetables (including pumpkins, tomatoes, and carrots) 91,000, citrus fruits 87,000, cocoa beans 3,000, spices (1983) 2,666, coffee 2,000, tobacco 2,000; livestock (number of live animals) 420,000 goats, 318,000 cattle, 270,000 pigs; roundwood (1983) 39,000 cu m; fish catch (1983) 8,653. Mining and quarrying (1984): bauxite 8,570,000, gypsum 111,000. Manufacturing (purchasers' values in J$000,000; 1981): food (excluding sugar-based products) 124; tobacco products 115; alcoholic beverages (excluding rum) 106; fabricated metals, machinery, and equipment 104; chemicals 85; refined petroleum 80. Construction (new buildings authorized; 1983): residential J$184,000,000; nonresidential J$165,000,000. Energy production (consumption): electricity (kW-hr; 1983) 2,350,000,000 (2,350,000,000); coal, none (negligible); crude petroleum (barrels; 1983) none (7,100,000); petroleum products (metric tons; 1983) 886,000 (2,084,000); natural gas, none (none).

Land use (1983): forested 27.9%; meadows and pastures 18.5%; agricultural and under permanent cultivation 24.8%; other 28.8%.
Gross national product (at current market prices; 1983): U.S.$2,940,000,000 (U.S.$1,285 per capita).

Structure of gross domestic product and labour force

	1983			
	in value J$'000,000	% of total value	labour force	% of labour force
Agriculture	446.8	6.6	248,600	33.4
Mining	278.7	4.1	6,600	0.9
Manufacturing	1,273.8	18.9	94,400	12.7
Construction	566.8	8.4	35,000	4.7
Public utilities	163.5	2.4	} 32,400	4.3
Transportation and communication	386.7	5.7		
Trade	1,370.7	20.3	106,800	14.3
Pub. admin., defense	1,001.4	14.9	101,000	13.6
Finance	1,132.6	16.8	} 120,300	16.1
Other	129.4	1.9		
TOTAL	6,750.4	100.0	745,100	100.0

Population economically active (1983): total 1,019,900; participation rate of total population 44.6% (female 45.5%, unemployed 26.9%).

Price and earnings indexes (1980 = 100)

	1979	1980	1981	1982	1983	1984	1985
Consumer price index	78.6	100.0	112.7	120.1	134.0	171.3	209.8†
Monthly earnings index	...	...	...	...	...	...	...

Household income and expenditure. Average household size (1982) 4.2; income per household, n.a.; sources of income (1982): wages and salaries 70.9%, self-employment 27.3%, transfers 1.8%; expenditure (1983): food 32.3%, transportation 13.7%, alcohol and tobacco 8.1%, rent 7.7%, household furnishings 5.6%, energy 4.8%, recreation 3.2%, clothing and footwear 2.6%, medical care 2.3%, education 0.2%, other 19.5%.

Foreign trade ‡

Balance of trade (current prices)

	1980	1981	1982	1983	1984	1985§
J$'000,000	−107.4	−556.1	−841.2	−1,071.2	−1,130.8	−1,008.8
% of total	3.0%	13.8%	24.5%	27.8%	16.5%	26.8%

Imports (1983): J$2,841,000,000 (crude petroleum and petroleum products 29.7%, chemical products 10.3%, cereals and cereal preparations 6.2%, road vehicles 5.7%, industrial machinery and parts 4.5%, textile yarn and fabrics 3.7%). *Major import sources:* United States 39.1%; Venezuela 11.0%; Netherlands Antilles 10.8%; United Kingdom 6.7%; Mexico 4.9%.
Exports (1983): J$1,364,000,000 (alumina 44.7%, bauxite 15.9%, raw sugar 7.5%, petroleum products 4.0%, clothing 2.2%, cigars and cigarillos 1.9%, coffee 1.4%, rum 1.3%). *Major export destinations:* United States 33.4%; United Kingdom 20.0%; Canada 12.2%; Trinidad and Tobago 9.3%.

Transport and communications

Transport. Railroads (1984): route length 205 mi, 330 km; passenger-mi 79,308,357, passenger-km 49,279,833; short ton-mi cargo (‖) 88,514,000, metric ton-km cargo 129,228,000. Roads (1984): total length 7,442 mi, 11,977 km (paved 40%). Vehicles (1983): passenger cars 40,271; trucks and buses 20,167. Merchant marine (1984): vessels (100 gross tons and over) 13; total deadweight tonnage 12,878. Air transport (1983)¶: passenger arrivals 492,088, passenger departures 461,595; cargo unloaded 3,933 metric tons, cargo loaded 5,186 metric tons; airports (1985) with scheduled flights 2.
Communications. Daily newspapers (1984): total number 3; total circulation 104,300; circulation per 1,000 population 45. Radio (1984): 858,000 (1 per 2.7 persons). Television (1984): 200,500 (1 per 12 persons). Telephones (1983): 132,517 (1 per 17 persons).

Education and health

Education (1983–84)

	schools	teachers	students	student/ teacher ratio
Primary (age 6–11)	819	10,630	455,486	42.8
Secondary (age 12–16)	142	8,139	166,815	20.4
Voc., teacher tr.	12	...	4,651	...
Higher	16	415º§	1,913º§	...

Educational attainment (1970). Percent of population over age 14 having: no formal schooling 3.9%; primary education 82.6%; secondary 10.5%; higher 1.0%; other 2.0%. *Literacy* (1980): total population over age 14 literate 1,100,600 (88.6%); males literate 542,600 (88.2%); females literate 558,000 (89.1%).
Health (1983): physicians (1982) 319 (1 per 7,033 persons); hospital beds 6,346 (1 per 360 persons); infant mortality rate per 1,000 live births 9.2.
Food (1980–82): daily per capita caloric intake 2,531 (vegetable products 85%, animal products 15%); 113% of FAO recommended minimum requirement.

Military

Total active duty personnel (1984): 3,720 (army 94.1%; navy 3.8%; air force 2.1%). *Military expenditure as percent of GNP* (1983): 1.3% (world 6.1%); per capita expenditure U.S.$16.

*Kingston included with Saint Andrew. †May. ‡Exports figures are f.o.b. (free on board); import figures are f.o.b. in balance of trade and c.i.f. (cost, insurance, and freight) for commodities. §Through May. ‖ 1981. ¶Airports at Kingston and Montego Bay. ºUniversity of the West Indies. ♂1982.

Japan

Official name: Nihon (Japan).
Form of government: constitutional monarchy with a National Diet consisting of two legislative houses (House of Councillors [252]; House of Representatives [511]).
Chief of state: Emperor.
Head of government: Prime Minister.
Capital: Tōkyō.
Official language: Japanese.
Official religion: none.
Monetary unit: 1 Yen (¥) = 100 sen; valuation (Oct. 21, 1985) 1 U.S.$ = ¥215.65; 1 £ = ¥309.25.

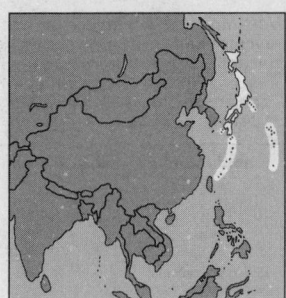

Area and population

Regions Prefectures	Capitals	area sq mi	area sq km	population 1984 estimate
Chūbu				
Aichi	Nagoya	1,983	5,136	6,405,000
Fukui	Fukui	1,618	4,191	809,000
Gifu	Gifu	4,091	10,596	2,014,000
Ishikawa	Kanazawa	1,620	4,197	1,142,000
Nagano	Nagano	5,245	13,585	2,121,000
Niigata	Niigata	4,856	12,578	2,472,000
Shizuoka	Shizuoka	3,001	7,773	3,537,000
Toyama	Toyama	1,642	4,252	1,115,000
Yamanashi	Kōfu	1,723	4,463	820,000
Chūgoku				
Hiroshima	Hiroshima	3,269	8,466	2,806,000
Okayama	Okayama	2,737	7,089	1,902,000
Shimane	Matsue	2,559*	6,628*	789,000
Tottori	Tottori	1,349*	3,493*	613,000
Yamaguchi	Yamaguchi	2,357	6,105	1,601,000
Hokkaidō				
Hokkaidō (Territory)	Sapporo	32,247	83,519	5,667,000
Kantō				
Chiba	Chiba	1,987	5,146	5,071,000
Gumma	Maebashi	2,454	6,356	1,903,000
Ibaraki	Mito	2,353	6,094	2,690,000
Kanagawa	Yokohoma	927	2,402	7,305,000
Saitama	Urawa	1,467	3,799	5,776,000
Tochigi	Utsunomiya	2,476	6,414	1,844,000
Kinki				
Hyōgo	Kōbe	3,234	8,377	5,256,000
Mie	Tsu	2,231	5,777	1,732,000
Nara	Nara	1,425	3,692	1,292,000
Shiga	Ōtsu	1,551	4,016	1,139,000
Wakayama	Wakayama	1,824	4,724	1,090,000
Kyūshū				
Fukuoka	Fukuoka	1,914	4,958	4,702,000
Kagoshima	Kagoshima	3,538	9,164	1,810,000
Kumamoto	Kumamoto	2,860	7,407	1,828,000
Miyazaki	Miyazaki	2,986	7,735	1,174,000
Nagasaki	Nagasaki	1,587	4,111	1,596,000
Ōita	Ōita	2,447	6,337	1,244,000
Saga	Saga	939	2,433	876,000
Ryukyu				
Okinawa	Naha	870	2,254	1,161,000
Shikoku				
Ehime	Matsuyama	2,190	5,671	1,522,000
Kagawa	Takamatsu	727	1,882	1,018,000
Kōchi	Kōchi	2,744	7,107	835,000
Tokushima	Tokushima	1,600	4,145	831,000
Tohoku				
Akita	Akita	4,483†	11,611†	1,253,000
Aomori	Aomori	3,713†	9,617†	1,530,000
Fukushima	Fukushima	5,322	13,784	2,068,000
Iwate	Morioka	5,899	15,279	1,431,000
Miyagi	Sendai	2,815	7,292	2,160,000
Yamagata	Yamagata	3,601	9,327	1,257,000
Metropolis				
Tōkyō‡	Tōkyō	835	2,162	11,797,000
Urban prefectures				
Kyōto§	Kyōto	1,781	4,613	2,584,000
Ōsaka§	Ōsaka	721	1,867	8,640,000
TOTAL		145,862 ‖ ¶	377,781 ‖ ¶	120,235,000¶

Demography

Population (1985): 120,760,000.
Density (1985): persons per sq mi 127.9, persons per sq km 319.7.
Urban–rural (1980): urban 76.2%; rural 23.8%.
Sex distribution (1985): male 49.20%; female 50.80%.
Age breakdown (1985): under 15, 21.6%; 15–29, 20.6%; 30–44, 24.0%; 45–59, 19.1%; 60–69, 7.9%; 70 and over, 6.8%.
Population projection: (1990) 122,834,000; (2000) 128,119,000.
Doubling time: During the intercensal period 1975–80, the annual growth rate was 0.9%; since 1981, however, the population growth rate has been decreasing.
Ethnic composition (1984): Japanese 99.4%; other (mainly Korean) 0.6%.
Religious affiliation: most Japanese consider themselves to be adherents of both Shintō (87%), a body of indigenous beliefs and practices, and Buddhism (73.1%). A small proportion of the population is Christian (1.3%). Most of the others are members of "new religions," which incorporate to varying degrees Shintō, Buddhist, Taoist, and Christian beliefs.
Major cities (1985): Tōkyō 8,425,000; Yokohama 2,984,000; Ōsaka 2,634,000; Nagoya 2,118,200; Sapporo 1,543,000; Kyōto 1,480,000; Kōbe 1,413,000; Fukuoka 1,162,000; Kawasaki 1,079,000♀; Kitakyūshū 1,054,000♀.

Other principal cities (1984)

	population		population		population
Akashi	263,825	Kashiwa	267,994	Sagamihara	474,440
Akita	295,369	Kawagoe	280,194	Sakai	818,050
Amagasaki	511,930	Kawaguchi	399,510	Sasebo	250,092
Aomori	293,811	Kōchi	306,830	Sendai	666,593
Asahigawa	361,701	Koriyama	299,126	Shimonoseki	268,345
Chiba	782,277	Kumamoto	551,795	Shizuoka	464,662
Fujisawa	322,412	Kurashiki	410,062	Suita	348,630
Fukushima	269,105	Machida	314,573	Takamatsu	325,901
Fukuyama	356,422	Maebashi	274,496	Takatsuki	345,285
Funabashi	504,864	Matsudo	422,355	Tokorozawa	266,200
Gifu	409,812	Matsuyama	422,313	Tokushima	255,624
Hachiōji	418,838	Miyazaki	277,840	Toyama	311,792
Hakodate	320,529	Nagano	333,523	Toyohashi	318,278
Hamamatsu	508,856	Nagasaki	450,346	Toyonaka	412,449
Higashiosaka	526,024	Naha	302,507	Toyota	302,092
Himeji	452,099	Nara	322,807	Urawa	374,152
Hirakata	378,036	Neyagawa	259,390	Utsunomiya	399,744
Hiroshima	936,227	Niigata	471,813	Wakayama	402,271
Ichikawa	393,748	Nishinomiya	420,197	Yao	278,084
Ichinomiya	256,463	Ōita	384,708	Yokkaichi	260,942
Iwaki	347,875	Okayama	565,559	Yokosuka	427,351
Kagoshima	526,905	Okazaki	280,469		
Kanazawa	427,379	Ōmiya	369,677		

Place of birth (1984): 99.4% native-born; 0.6% foreign-born (mainly Korean).
Mobility (1980). Population living in same residence as in October 1975: 68.0%; different residence, same prefecture 24.2%; different prefecture 7.7%.
Households (1984). Total households 37,338,000; average household size 3.1; composition of households (1980) 1 person 15.8%, 2 persons 17.6%, 3 persons 19.0%, 4 persons 26.6%, 5 persons 11.7%, 6 persons 6.0%, 7 or more persons 3.3%. Family households (1984) 28,166,000 (75.4%); nonfamily 9,172,000 (24.6%), of which 1-person 1,779,000 (19.4%).

Type of households (1983)
Total number of dwelling units: 34,745,000

	number of dwellings	percent of total
by kind of dwelling		
exclusive entry (do not share bathroom or kitchen)	31,929,000	91.9
combined with nondwelling	2,487,000	7.2
detached house	22,372,000	64.3
apartment building	9,324,000	26.8
tenement (substandard or overcrowded building)	2,890,000	8.3
by legal tenure of householder		
owned	21,641,000	62.3
rented	12,900,000	37.1
by government	2,602,000	7.5
by private owner	8,454,000	24.3
other	204,000	0.6
by kind of amenities		
running water	32,570,000	93.7
flush toilet♂	20,107,000	57.9
bathroom	30,602,000	88.1
by year of construction		
prior to 1945	3,693,000	10.6
1945–60	4,702,000	13.5
1961–70	8,799,000	25.3
1971–75	7,499,000	21.6
1976–83	9,693,000	27.9

Immigration (1984): permanent immigrants/registered aliens 833,265, from South Korea 81.4%, Taiwan 8.1%, United States 3.3%, Philippines 1.2%, United Kingdom 0.8%, Vietnam 0.5%, West Germany 0.4%.

Vital statistics

Birth rate per 1,000 population (1984): 12.5 (world avg. 29.0); (1980) legitimate 99.2%; illegitimate 0.8%.
Death rate per 1,000 population (1984): 6.2 (world avg. 11.0).
Natural increase rate per 1,000 population (1983): 6.3 (world avg. 18.0).
Total fertility rate (avg. births per childbearing woman; 1983): 1.8.
Marriage rate per 1,000 population□ (1985): 5.2.
Divorce rate per 1,000 population□ (1985): 1.4.
Life expectancy at birth (1983): male 74.2 years; female 79.8 years.
Major causes of death per 100,000 population (1984): malignant neoplasms (cancers) 151.6; cerebrovascular diseases 116.5; heart diseases 113.2; pneumonia and bronchitis 37.4; accidents and adverse effects 24.2; senility without mention of psychosis 24.0; suicide 20.2; cirrhosis of the liver 14.1; hypertensive diseases 10.9; nephritis, nephrotic syndrome, and nephrosis 10.5.

Social indicators

Educational attainment (1980). Percent of population 15 years old and over having: no schooling 0.3%; primary and lower secondary education 38.5%; higher secondary 38.0%; junior college and technical college 5.7%; university and postgraduate 8.0%; still in school 9.5%.

Distribution of income (1980)

percent of average household income by decile

1	2	3	4	5	6	7	8	9	10 (highest)
35.8	53.6	64.6	73.5	82.9	93.2	105.2	120.4	145.4	224.8.

Quality of working life. Average workweek (1984): 46.7 hours (10.7% overtime). Annual rate of industrial deaths per 100,000 workers (1983): 3.7. Proportion of labour force insured for damages or income loss resulting

from injury, permanent disability, and death (1984): 45.8%. Average mandays lost to labour stoppages per 1,000 workdays (1984): 0.09. Average duration of journey to work (1983): 32 minutes (26.7%◊ private automobile, 67.4%◊ public transportation, 5.5%◊ taxi, 0.4%◊ other). Rate per 1,000 workers of discouraged (unemployed no longer seeking work; 1982): 64.7.
Access to services (1980). Proportion of households having access to: gas supply 63.0%; safe public water supply 91.4%; public sewage collection 89.4%.
Social participation. Eligible voters participating in last national election (December 1983): 67.9%. Population over 15 years of age participating in social service activities on a voluntary basis (1981): 26.0%. Trade union membership in total work force (1984): 21.0%. Practicing religious population in total affiliated population: n.a.
Social deviance (1983). Offense rate per 100,000 population for: murder 1.5; rape 1.7; larceny and theft 1,119.6; robbery 1.9. Incidence in general population of: alcoholism, n.a.; drug and substance abuse, n.a. Rate of suicide per 100,000 population (1984) 20.3.

Leisure/use of personal time
Daily activities (1981)
(both sexes)

Social activities	daily average hrs./min.	% of day
Work	4.35	19.1
Meals	1.50	7.6
Housekeeping and childcare	1.49	7.6
Commuting to work/school	.36	2.5
Schoolwork	.32	2.2
Shopping	.22	1.5
Personal activities		
Sleep	7.57	33.1
Rest and relaxation	1.19	5.5
Personal care and grooming	.57	4.0
Transportation (excluding commuting)	.12	.8

Recreational activities (1981)

	weekday hrs./min.	% of total leisure time	weekend hrs./min.	% of total leisure time
Males				
Personal associations and friendships	2.30	18.7	3.20	18.2
Television, radio, newspapers, and magazines	2.27	18.4	2.59	16.3
Study and research (excluding schoolwork)	2.23	17.9	2.45	15.0
Hobbies and amusements	2.12	16.5	3.18	18.1
Voluntary social activities	2.11	16.3	3.04	16.8
Sports	1.38	12.2	2.51	15.6
Females				
Television, radio, newspapers, and magazines	2.29	19.1	2.37	16.3
Study and research (excluding schoolwork)	2.24	18.4	2.34	16.0
Voluntary social activities	2.21	18.1	2.32	15.7
Hobbies and amusements	2.07	16.3	2.48	17.4
Personal associations and friendships	2.06	16.1	2.51	17.7
Sports	1.34	12.0	2.43	16.9

Material well-being (1984). Households possessing: automobile 64.8%; telephone, virtually 100%; colour television receiver, virtually 100%; refrigerator, 99.2%; air conditioner 49.3%; washing machine, virtually 100%; videocassette recorder 18.7%.

National economy
Gross national product (at current market prices; 1984): U.S.$1,215,189,000,000 (U.S.$10,120 per capita).

Structure of gross domestic product and labour force

	1983		1984	
	in value ¥'000,000,000	% of total value	labour force	% of labour force
Agriculture	9,098.8	3.3	5,120,000	8.6
Mining	1,164.0	0.4	80,000	0.1
Manufacturing	83,832.1	30.5	14,380,000	24.3
Construction	21,674.1	7.9	5,270,000	8.9
Public utilities	9,833.8	3.6	350,000	0.6
Transportation and communication	19,081.9	6.9	3,410,000	5.8
Trade	33,519.3	12.2	13,190,000	23.3
Finance	46,394.4	16.9	2,160,000	3.6
Pub. admin., defense	13,132.7	4.8	1,950,000	3.3
Services	49,284.6	17.9	11,540,000	19.5
Other	−12,096.6△	−4.4	1,820,000†	3.1
TOTAL	274,919.0	100.0	59,270,000	100.0¶

Budget (1985)⊕. Revenue: ¥52,500,000,000,000 (income tax 29.5%, corporation tax 23.9%, public bonds 22.2%, liquor tax 3.7%, stamp duties 2.6%, custom duties 1.3%). Expenditures: ¥52,500,000,000,000 (national debt 19.5%, local finance 18.5%, social security 18.2%, public works 12.1%, education and science 9.2%, national defense 6.0%).
Public debt (1984): U.S.$496,439,471,000.
Population economically active (1985)**: total 60,390,000; participation rate of population over age 15, 63.8% (female 40.1%, unemployed 2.5%).

Price and earnings indexes (1980 = 100)

	1979	1980	1981	1982	1983	1984	1985**
Consumer price index	92.6	100.0	104.9	107.7	109.7	112.1	114.6
Monthly earnings index	94.1	100.0	105.3	110.0	113.8	118.9	123.8

Household income and expenditure†† (1984). Average household size 3.8; average annual income per household ¥5,088,300 (U.S.$20,225); sources of income: wages and salaries 76.3%, other 23.7%; expenditure: food 21.2%, housing 8.8%, transportation 7.8%, reading and recreation 7.1%, clothing 5.5%, education 3.4%, furniture and household utensils 3.4%, medical care 2.0%; net savings 11.9%.

Manufacturing, mining, and construction enterprises (1982)

	no. of enter-prises‡‡	avg. no. of employees§§	monthly contract wages as a % of avg. of all contract wages§§	annual value added (¥'000,000,000)
Electrical machinery	40,982	847,000	102.0	10,612
Nonelectrical machinery	71,042	705,000	102.0	8,446
Transport equipment	25,801	690,000	104.3	7,660
Food products	84,894	425,000	92.5	7,339
Chemical products	8,666	369,000	111.8	6,505
Iron and steel	9,051	353,000	111.0	4,729
Fabricated metal products	111,003	410,000	93.7	4,704
Printing and publishing	61,993	293,000	110.6	4,126
Ceramic, stone, and clay	37,662	303,000	92.9	3,653
Ordnance and miscellaneous	...	262,000	94.1	3,491
Textiles	118.183	194,000	91.3	2,958
Paper and paper products	19,879	167,000	97.2	1,967
Nonferrous metal products	6,635	133,000	106.7	1,631
Apparel products	63,366	86,000	83.5	1,478
Precision instruments	15,841	162,000	97.2	1,465
Petroleum and coal products	1,338	40,000	120.9	1,443
Lumber and wood products	44,012	130,000	79.1	1,405
Furniture and fixtures	48,451	114,000	84.3	1,219
Rubber products	10,287	95,000	100.0	994
Leather products	15,527	22,000	87.8	357
Mining	6,993	63,000	100.4	406
Construction	550,798	1,622,000	94.9	22,649‡‡

Tourism (1983): receipts from visitors U.S.$825,000,000; expenditures by nationals abroad U.S.$4,428,000,000.

Financial aggregates

	1979	1980	1981	1982	1983	1984	1985 (6 mo.)
Exchange rate, ¥ per:							
U.S. dollar	219.14	226.74	220.54	249.08	237.52	237.52	248.99
£	464.93	527.47	447.23	435.96	360.32	317.40	318.93
SDR	315.76	258.91	255.95	259.23	243.10	246.13	248.52
International reserves (U.S.$)							
Total (excl. gold; '000,000)	19,522	24,636	28,208	23,334	24,602	26,429	27,631
SDRs ('000,000)	1,688	1,738	1,934	2,091	1,935	1,927	2,081
Reserve pos. in IMF ('000,000)	1,477	1,331	1,558	2,071	2,303	2,219	2,171
Foreign exchange ('000,000)	16,357	21,567	24,716	19,172	20,364	22,283	23,379
Gold ('000,000 fine troy oz)	24.23	24.23	24.23	24.23	24.23	24.23	24.23
% world reserves	2.6	2.5	2.5	2.6	2.6	2.6	2.6 ‖
Interest and prices							
Central bank discount (%)	6.25	7.25	5.50	5.50	5.00	5.00	5.00 ‖
Gov't. bond yield (%)	7.69	9.22	8.66	8.06	7.42	6.81	6.37 ‖
Industrial share prices (1980 = 100)	94.9	100.0	116.3	115.8	136.5	172.1	207.5 ‖
Balance of payments (U.S.$'000,000,000)							
Balance of visible trade	1.9	2.1	20.0	18.1	31.5	44.4	...
Imports, f.o.b.	99.4	124.6	129.6	119.6	114.0	123.9	...
Exports, f.o.b.	101.2	126.7	149.5	137.7	145.5	168.3	...
Balance of invisibles	−9.5	−11.4	−13.6	−9.9	−9.1	−7.8	...
Balance of payments, current account	−8.8	−10.8	4.8	6.9	20.8	35.0	...

Production (metric tons except as noted). Agriculture, forestry, fishing (1984): rice 14,848,000, potatoes 3,707,400, mandarin oranges 2,008,000, radishes 2,617,000, cabbages 1,614,000, Chinese cabbages 1,548,000, sweet potatoes 1,400,000; onions 1,096,000, cucumbers 1,070,000, apples 811,000, tomatoes 801,600, wheat 741,000, carrots 640,500; livestock (number of live animals) 10,423,000 pigs, 4,682,000 cattle, 176,581,000 hens, 143,024,000 broiler chickens; roundwood (1983) 65,729,000 cu m; fish catch 12,793,000, of which sardines 4,176,200, mackerel 802,900, tuna 373,100. Mining and quarrying (1984): limestone 169,824,000; quicklime 7,583,000; gypsum 5,761,000; dolomite 4,386,000; pyrophyllite 1,064,000; fire clay 1,308,145; iron ore 297,817; zinc 255,712. Manufacturing (1984): crude steel 105,586,000; semifinished steel 96,753,000; hot-rolled steel products 82,765,000; pig iron 80,403,000; cement 78,851,000; asbestos slate 73,840,000; cold-rolled steel strips 20,226,000; number of units—315,553,000 fluorescent lamps; 147,164,000 watches; 143,311,000 motor vehicle tires; 83,714,000 electronic desk calculators; 39,277,000 motor vehicle tubes; 27,124,000 videotape recorders; 14,557,000 35mm cameras; 14,478,000 colour television receivers; 7,073,200 passenger cars; 4,380,600 trucks and buses; 1,578,300 electronic computer processors. Construction (floor area started; 1984): residential 92,788,000 sq m; nonresidential 84,268,000 sq m; combined residential and business 19,082,000 sq m.

Service enterprises (1982)

	no. of enter-prises ‡‡	avg. no. of em-ployees§§	monthly contract wages as a % of all contract wages §§	gross output at producers' value (¥'000,000,000)
Eating and drinking services	794,758	155,000	82.3	...
Real estate	238,358	88,000	105.5	36,156
Transport and communication	160,643	2,313,000	100.0	29,505
Road passenger transport	45,499	538,000	96.9	...
Road freight transport	48,267	664,000	101.6	...
Finance and insurance	84,136	680,000	127.6	20,210
Public utilities	10,914	237,000	116.5	14,869
Retail trade	1,781,075	926,000	89.4	} 49,920
Wholesale trade	445,447	1,965,000	100.8	
Medical services	157,879	174,000	134.6	...
Educational services	82,059	214,000	117.3	...

Energy production (consumption): electricity (kW-hr; 1984) 580,410,000,000 (524,530,000,000); coal (metric tons; 1984) 16,645,000 (104,839,000); crude petroleum (barrels; 1984) 3,095,000 (1,227,000,000); petroleum products (metric tons; 1984) 152,664,000, of which heavy fuel oil 42.5%, gasoline 20.2%, kerosene and jet fuel 17.0% (161,035,000, of which heavy fuel oil 40.4%, kerosine and jet fuel 15.0%, gasoline 19.0%, diesel 13.0%, naphtha 12.6%); natural gas (cu m; 1984) 2,133,000,000 (27,847,000,000).
Land use (1983): forested 67.9%; meadows and pastures 1.6%; agricultural and under permanent cultivation 13.0%; other 17.5%.

Foreign trade¶¶

Balance of trade (current prices)

¥'000,000,000	1979	1980	1981	1982	1983	1984
¥'000,000,000	+591	+55	+4,603	+4,473	+7,373	+10,674
% of total	1.3%	0.1%	7.4%	6.9%	11.8%	20.9%

Imports (1984): ¥32,321,100,000,000 (crude petroleum 28.8%; machinery and equipment 8.9%; chemicals 6.1%; metal ores and scrap 4.8%, of which iron ore 2.3%; petroleum products 4.5%; coal 3.9%; nonferrous metals 3.4%; fish and shellfish 3.0%; wood 2.9%; textiles 2.8%). *Major import sources*: United States 19.7%; Saudi Arabia 10.8%; Indonesia 8.2%; United Arab Emirates 5.7%; Australia 5.3%; China 4.4%; Canada 3.6%; Malaysia 3.2%.
Exports (1984): ¥40,325,300,000,000 (motor vehicles 17.5%; iron and steel 8.1%; tape recorders 4.9%; chemicals 4.5%; office machinery 4.4%; vessels 4.3%; textiles and allied products 4.0%; scientific and optical equipment 3.6%; electron tubes, etc. 3.4%; power-generating machinery 2.3%). *Major export destinations*: United States 35.3%; China 4.3%; South Korea 4.2%; West Germany 3.9%; Hong Kong 3.9%; Saudi Arabia 3.3%; Australia 3.0%; United Kingdom 2.7%; Singapore 2.7%; Canada 2.5%; Panama 2.0%.

Trade by commodity group (1984)

SITC group	imports U.S.$'000,000	%	exports U.S.$'000,000	%
00 Food and live animals	15,191	11.1	1,290	0.8
01 Beverages and tobacco	836	0.6	150	0.1
02 Crude materials, excluding fuels	19,153	14.0	1,250	0.7
03 Mineral fuels, lubricants, and related materials	60,337	44.2	505	0.3
04 Animal and vegetable oils, fats, and waxes	372	0.3	148	0.1
05 Chemicals and related products, n.e.s.	8,346	6.1	7,626	4.5
06 Basic manufactures	11,932	8.7	30,137	17.7
07 Machinery and transport equipment	10,809	7.9	102,680	60.4
08 Miscellaneous manufactured articles	6,088	4.5	24,654	14.5
09 Goods not classified by kind	3,439	2.5	1,674	1.0
TOTAL	136,503	100.0¶	170,114	100.0¶

Direction of trade (1984)

	imports U.S.$'000,000	%	exports U.S.$'000,000	%
Africa	3,112	2.3	6,358	3.7
Asia	70,778	51.9	56,912	33.5
South America	4,247	3.1	2,466	1.4
North America and Central America	34,804	25.5	70,319	41.3
United States	26,862	19.7	59,937	35.2
other North and Central Am.	7,942	5.8	10,382	6.1
Europe	14,909	10.9	27,170	16.0
EEC	9,336	6.8	19,404	11.4
USSR	1,394	1.0	2,518	1.5
other Europe	4,179	3.1	5,248	3.1
Oceania	8,650	6.3	6,890	4.1
TOTAL	136,500	100.0	170,114	100.0

Transport and communications

Transport. Railroads: length (1983) 16,720 mi, 26,908 km; rolling stock (1983) locomotives 4,000, passenger cars 47,022, freight cars 65,142; passengers carried (1984) 18,769,000,000; passenger-mi (1984) 201,954,000,000, passenger-km 325,014,000,000; short ton-mi cargo (1984) 16,045,000,000, metric ton-km cargo 23,425,000,000. Roads (1983): total length 697,985 mi, 1,123,300 km (paved 53%). Vehicles (1985): passenger cars 25,075,000; trucks 8,444,000; buses 230,000. Merchant marine (1984): vessels (100 gross tons and over) 10,495; total deadweight tonnage 64,624,307. Air transport (1984): passengers carried 50,074,000; passenger-mi 39,318,000,000, passenger-km 63,267,000,000; short ton-mi cargo 1,834,400,000, metric ton-km cargo 2,678,200,000; airports (1985) with scheduled flights 72. Shares of domestic passenger traffic by mode of transportation (1983): automobiles 44%; railway 39%; buses 13%; ships and airplanes 4%.

Distribution of traffic (1983)

	cargo carried ('000,000 tons)	% of nat'l total	passengers carried ('000,000)	% of nat'l total
Road	5,123.0	90.2	33,809	47.9
Rail (intercity)	122.0	2.1	18,538	26.3
Urban transport	—	—	17,985	25.5
road	—	—	14,356	20.4
rail	—	—	3,629	5.1
Inland water	438.0	7.7	153	0.2
Air	0.4	0.0	41	0.1
Pipeline	...	...		
TOTAL	5,682.0	100.0	70,526	100.0

Communications. Daily newspapers (1984): total number 125; total circulation 67,380,000; circulation per 1,000 population 565. Radio (1984): total number of receivers 94,000,000 (1 per 1.3 persons). Television (1984): total number of receivers 30,799,000 (1 per 3.9 persons). Telephones (1983): 63,976,000 (1 per 1.9 persons).

Other communication media (1983)

Print	titles	Electronic	traffic ('000)
Books (new titles)	31,297	Telegrams♀	43,526
of which		Domestic	41,684
Social sciences	7,100	International	1,842
Fiction	6,505	Telex (in minutes)♀♀	165,822
Business	1,173	Domestic	111,103
Children's	2,222	International	54,719
Natural sciences	2,735		
History	1,974	Post♀	
Arts	3,233	Mail	16,579,443
Magazines/journals	3,565	Domestic	16,344,000
Weekly	95	International	235,443
Monthly	2,349	Parcels	144,528
		Domestic	140,636
Cinema		International	3,892
Feature films (greater than 1,600 m)	317		

Education and health

Education (1985)

	schools	teachers	students	student/ teacher ratio
Primary (age 6–11)	25,040	461,249	11,095,711	24.1
Secondary (age 12–17)	16,584	551,962	11,168,212	20.2
Higher	1,066	133,867	2,445,206	18.3

Literacy (1984): total population over age 15 literate 93,210,000 (100%); males literate 45,300,000 (100%); females literate 47,910,000 (100%).
Health (1982): physicians 167,952 (1 per 707 persons); dentists 58,362 (1 per 2,034 persons); nurses 546,597 (1 per 217 persons); pharmacists 124,390 (1 per 954 persons); midwives 25,416 (1 per 4,670 persons); hospital beds (1983) 1,440,381 (1 per 82.4 persons), of which general 71.0%, mental 22.7%, tuberculosis 4.4%, other 1.9%; infant mortality per rate 1,000 live births (1984) 6.0.
Food (1983): daily per capita caloric intake 2,593 (vegetable products 75%, animal products 25%); 111% of FAO recommended minimum requirement.

Military

Total active duty personnel (1984): 245,000 (army 63.3%, navy 18.0%, air force 18.7%). *Military expenditure as percent of GNP* (1984): 1.0% (world 6.1%); per capita expenditure U.S.$99.

*Excludes Lake Naka (38 sq mi [98 sq km]), which is part of both Tottori and Shimane prefectures. †Excludes Lake Towada (23 sq mi [60 sq km]), which is part of both Akita and Aomori prefectures. ‡Part of Kanto geographical region. §Part of Kinki geographical region. ‖ 1984 survey; also includes Lake Naka and Lake Towada. ¶Detail does not add to total given because of rounding. ♀1984. ♂Includes septic tank. □Figures relate only to Japanese nationals in Japan. ◇Applies to passengers carried within the metropolitan areas of Tōkyō, Ōsaka, and Nagoya only. △Import duties and statistical discrepancy less imputed bank service charge. ⊺Includes unemployed. ⊙Initial budget. **June. ††Worker's household. ‡‡1981. §§1983. ‖ ‖ May. ¶¶Import figures are f.o.b. (free on board) in balance of trade and c.i.f. (cost, insurance, and freight) for commodities and trading partners. ♀♀1982.

JEANNE HOLLE

Shintō ceremony of *hatsu-miya-mairi* ("first shrine visit," at which the month-old infant formally becomes a communicant), at the Meiji Shrine, Tokyo.

Jordan

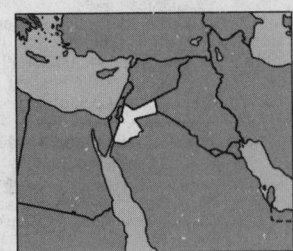

Official name: al-Mamlakah al-Urdunnīyah al-Hāshimīyah (al-Urdun) (Hashemite Kingdom of Jordan).
Form of government: constitutional monarchy with two legislative houses (Senate [30 appointed by king]; House of Deputies [60 elected]).
Chief of state: Monarch.
Head of government: Prime Minister.
Capital: Amman.
Official language: Arabic.
Official religion: Islām.
Monetary unit: 1 Jordan Dinar (JD) = 1,000 fils; valuation (Oct. 21, 1985) JD1.00 = U.S.$2.65 = £1.85.

Area and population

Governorates	Capitals	area sq mi	area sq km	population 1985 estimate*
al-ʿĀṣimah	Amman	6,904	17,882	1,427,300
al-Balqāʾ	as-Salt	413	1,069	179,100
al-Karak	al-Karak	1,777	4,601	153,100
Irbid	Irbid	8,747	22,654	744,800
Maʿān	Maʿān	16,602	43,000	90,800
TOTAL		34,443	89,206	2,595,000

Demography

Population (1985): 2,647,000.
Density (1985): persons per sq mi 76.9, persons per sq km 29.7.
Urban-rural (1981): urban 59.5%; rural 40.5%.
Sex distribution (1985): male 52.31%; female 47.69%.
Age breakdown (1979): under 15, 51.8%; 15–29, 23.3%; 30–44, 13.4%; 45–59, 4.2%; 60 and over, 4.2%.
Population projection: (1990) 3,055,000; (2000) 4,249,000.
Doubling time: 21 years.
Ethnic composition (1982): Arab 98.0%; Circassian 1.0%; Armenian 1.0%.
Religious affiliation (1980): Sunnī Muslim 93.0%; Christian 4.9%; other 2.1%.
Major cities (1984): Amman 777,500; az-Zarqā 265,700; Irbid 136,200; ar-Raṣayfah 61,300.

Vital statistics

Birth rate per 1,000 population (1980–85): 45.3 (world avg. 29.0).
Death rate per 1,000 population (1980–85): 9.1 (world avg. 11.0).
Natural increase rate per 1,000 population (1980–85): 36.2 (world avg. 18.0).
Total fertility rate (avg. births per childbearing woman; 1980–85): 7.1.
Marriage rate per 1,000 population (1984): 7.1.
Divorce rate per 1,000 population (1984): 1.0.
Life expectancy at birth (1980–85): male 60.3 years; female 64.2 years.
Major causes of death per 100,000 population: n.a.; however, major diseases are tuberculosis, typhoid, paratyphoid, salmonella, hepatitis, and dysentery; nonvenereal syphilis is widespread in the southern desert region.

National economy

Budget (1983). Revenue: JD762,000,000 (foreign grants and loans 44.4%, indirect taxes 21.6%, fees 8.0%, direct taxes 10.4%). Expenditures: JD775,-370,000 (development expenditure 39.2%, defense 21.7%, education 7.6%, police 3.3%, health and social welfare 2.8%).
Public debt (external, outstanding; 1983): U.S.$1,940,100,000.
Tourism (1983): receipts from visitors U.S.$512,000,000; expenditures by nationals abroad U.S.$370,000,000.
Production (metric tons except as noted). Agriculture, forestry, fishing (1984): tomatoes 208,700, eggplant 51,100, olives 50,000, wheat 49,700, citrus fruit (mostly oranges and lemons) 48,300, squash 42,700, hot and sweet peppers 16,200, bananas 14,300, watermelons 14,000, cauliflower 12,-400, barley 11,900, grapes 8,600, tobacco 2,400; livestock (number of live animals; 1983) 980,000 sheep, 442,000 goats, 34,000 cattle, 17,000 camels; roundwood (1983) 4,000 cu m; fish catch (1983) 17. Mining and quarrying (1984): phosphate ore 6,120,000; potash 486,000; gypsum 41,000. Manufacturing (1984): cement 1,994,000; phosphate fertilizer 365,000†; steel 112,000; cigarettes 460; beer 50,200 hectolitres; arrack 8,500 hectolitres; wine 4,200 hectolitres. Construction (1983): residential 2,378,100 sq m; nonresidential 632,300 sq m. Energy production (consumption): electricity (kW-hr; 1984) 2,265,000,000 (1,925,000,000); coal, none (n.a.); crude petroleum (barrels; 1983) none (18,900,000); petroleum products (metric tons; 1983) 2,325,000 (2,078,000); natural gas none (n.a.).
Population economically active (1979): total 446,316; participation rate of total population over age 14, 44.1% (female 7.5%, unemployed 9.0%).

Price and earnings indexes (1975 = 100)

	1978	1979	1980	1981	1982	1983	1984
Consumer price index	136.6	156.0	173.3	194.2	200.5	210.6	218.7
Daily earnings index†	152.7	164.7	200.0	213.3	...	...	...

Household income and expenditure. Average household size (1979) 6.4; income per household (1979) JD1,820‡ (U.S.$6,055); source of income: n.a.; expenditure (1980): food and beverages 42.3%, household supplies 20.4%, rent 14.6%, education 7.2%, clothing and footwear 6.6%, health care 2.4%, transportation 1.5%, tobacco 0.9%, recreation 0.3%, other 3.8%.

Gross national product (at current market prices; 1983): U.S.$4,400,000,000 (U.S.$1,710 per capita).

Structure of gross domestic product and labour force

	1981 in value JD'000,000	1981 % of total value	1979 labour force	1979 % of labour force
Agriculture	69.4	5.8	46,051	10.3
Mining	46.8	3.9	6,066	1.4
Manufacturing	145.5	12.1	32,196	7.2
Construction	104.3	8.7	63,861	14.3
Public utilities	22.8	1.9	2,387	0.5
Transportation and communication	114.7	9.6	26,827	6.0
Trade	212.8	17.7	41,404	9.3
Finance	145.8	12.2	8,243	1.9
Pub. admin., defense	191.2	15.9	179,034	40.1
Services	35.3	2.9		
Other	110.5	9.3	40,247	9.0§
TOTAL	1,199.1	100.0	446,316	100.0

Land use (1983): forested 0.4%; meadows and pastures 1.0%; agricultural and under permanent cultivation 4.3%; other 94.3% ‖.

Foreign trade

Balance of trade (current prices)¶

	1979	1980	1981	1982	1983	1984
JD'000,000	−465	−545	−805	−878	−893	−781
% of total	58.7%	51.3%	52.9%	52.9%	61.0%	45.7%

Imports (1984): JD1,071,300,000 (mineral fuels [mostly crude petroleum] 19.9%; nonelectrical machinery and equipment 6.1%; cereals [including wheat, wheat flour, rice, and corn] 6.1%; iron and steel 5.7%; motor vehicles 5.4%; electrical machinery and equipment 4.8%; metal manufactures [mostly structures and parts] 4.4%). *Major import sources:* Saudi Arabia 19.5%; United States 11.1%; Japan 7.4%; United Kingdom 6.8%; West Germany 6.3%; Italy 5.8%.
Exports (1984)♀: JD261,100,000 (worked building stone and asbestos cement 28.1%; natural phosphate fertilizer 22.6%; food and live animals [mostly assorted vegetables, tomatoes, olives, citrus fruit, and spices] 14.0%; wearing apparel, textiles, and yarn 4.9%; pharmaceuticals 4.3%; wood and wooden products 3.2%). *Major export destinations:* Iraq 26.0%; Saudi Arabia 14.8%; India 13.1%; Romania 4.9%; Pakistan 4.3%; Kuwait 4.0%.

Transport and communications

Transport. Railroads (1983): route length 384 mi, 618 km; passenger-mi 3,700,000, passenger-km 6,000,000□; short ton-mi cargo, n.a. Roads (1984): total length 3,934 mi, 6,332 km (paved 74.4%). Vehicles (1982): passenger cars 118,852; trucks and buses 48,884. Merchant marine (1984): vessels (100 gross tons and over) 8; total deadweight tonnage 75,525. Air transport (1984): passenger-mi 2,243,264,000, passenger-km 3,610,191,000; short ton-mi cargo 95,815,000, metric ton-km cargo 139,888,000; airports (1985) with scheduled flights 2.
Communications. Daily newspapers (1984): total number 5; total circulation 176,000; circulation per 1,000 population 68. Radio (1984): total number of receivers 550,000 (1 per 4.1 persons). Television (1984): total number of receivers 280,000 (1 per 8.0 persons). Telephones (1981): 70,781 (1 per 31 persons).

Education and health

Education (1983–84)

	schools	teachers	students	student/ teacher ratio
Primary (age 5–11)	1,148	15,179	487,890	32.1
Secondary (age 12–17)	1,515	13,153	286,092	21.8
Vocational	19	1,290	25,310	19.6
Higher	47	2,465§	55,575	...

Educational attainment (1979). Percent of population over age 14 having: no formal schooling 47.9%; primary education 19.8%; secondary 26.4%; higher 5.9%. *Literacy* (1980): total population over age 15 literate 357,400 (31.2%); males literate 253,670 (42.1%); females literate 103,730 (19.1%).
Health (1984): physicians 2,310 (1 per 1,102 persons); hospital beds 3,578 (1 per 711 persons); infant mortality rate per 1,000 live births (1981) 67.0.
Food (1979–81): daily per capita caloric intake 2,498 (vegetable products 89%, animal products 11%); 102% of FAO recommended minimum requirement.

Military

Total active duty personnel (1984): 76,300 (army 89.1%, navy 0.4%, air force 10.5%). *Military expenditure as percent of GNP* (1982): 21.3% (world 6.0%); per capita expenditure U.S.$298.

*January 1. †1983. ‡Households involved in nonagricultural activities only. §Unemployed. ‖ Mostly desert. ¶Includes reexports. ♀Domestic exports only. ♂1982–83. □1980.

Kampuchea

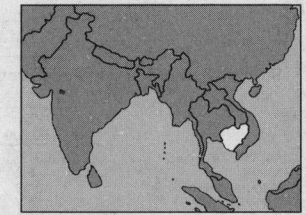

Official name: Sathearanakrath Pracheachon Kampuchea (People's Republic of Kampuchea)*.
Form of government: single-party people's republic with one legislative house (National Assembly [117]).
Chief of state: President, Council of State.
Head of government: Prime Minister.
Capital: Phnom Penh.
Official language: Khmer.
Official religion: none.
Monetary unit: 1 riel = 100 sen; valuation (Dec. 31, 1983) 1 U.S.$ = 4.00 riels; 1 £ = 5.81 riels.

Area and population

Provinces	Capitals	area sq mi	area sq km	population 1981 census
Bătdâmbâng	Bătdâmbâng	7,407	19,184	719,000
Kâmpóng Cham	Kâmpóng Cham	3,783	9,799	1,070,000
Kâmpóng Chhnăng	Kâmpóng Chhnăng	2,132	5,521	221,000
Kâmpóng Saôm	Kâmpóng Saôm	26	68	53,000
Kâmpóng Spœ	Kâmpóng Spœ	2,709	7,017	340,000
Kâmpóng Thum	Kâmpóng Thum	10,657†	27,602†	379,000
Kâmpôt	Kâmpôt	2,320	6,008	354,000
Kândal	...	1,472	3,812	720,000
Kaôh Kŏng	Krŏng Kaôh Kŏng	4,309	11,161	25,000
Krâchéh	Krâchéh	4,283	11,094	157,000
Môndôl Kiri	Senmonorom	5,517	14,288	16,000
Phnom Penh	Phnom Penh	18	46	329,000
Poŭthisăt	Poŭthisăt	4,900	12,692	175,000
Preăh Vihéar	Phnum Tbéng Meanchey	†	†	70,000
Prey Vêng	Prey Vêng	1,885	4,883	672,000
Rôtânôkiri	Lumphăt	4,163	10,782	45,000
Siĕmréab	Siĕmréab	6,354	16,457	477,000
Stœng Trêng	Stœng Trêng	4,283	11,092	39,000
Svay Riĕng	Svay Riĕng	1,145	2,966	292,000
Takêv	Takêv	1,376	3,563	531,000
TOTAL		69,898‡	181,035‡	6,684,000

Demography

Population (1985): 7,280,000.
Density (1985): persons per sq mi 104.1, persons per sq km 40.2.
Urban–rural (1980): urban 13.9%; rural 86.1%.
Sex distribution (1980): male 49.96%; female 50.04%.
Age breakdown (1984): under 15, 32.6%; 15–64, 64.8%; 65 and over, 2.6%.
Population projection: (1990) 8,572,000; (2000) 9,772,000.
Doubling time: 27 years.
Ethnic composition (1982): Khmer 93%; Chinese 3%; Vietnamese 4% (although recent Vietnamese immigration may have raised their proportion to as much as 8%).
Religious affiliation (1980): Buddhist 88.4%; Muslim 2.4%; other 9.2%.
Major cities (1971): Phnom Penh 600,000§; Kâmpóng Cham 34,706; Kâmpóng Chhnăng 15,813; Kratié 14,765; Pursat 14,736; Svay Riĕng 13,766.

Vital statistics

Birth rate per 1,000 population (1984): 44.3 (world avg. 29.0); legitimate, n.a.; illegitimate, n.a.
Death rate per 1,000 population (1984): 18.7 (world avg. 11.0).
Natural increase rate per 1,000 population (1984): 25.6 (world avg. 18.0).
Total fertility rate (avg. births per childbearing woman; 1984): 5.0.
Marriage rate per 1,000 population: n.a.
Divorce rate per 1,000 population: n.a.
Life expectancy at birth (1984): male 43.5 years; female 46.4 years.
Major causes of death per 100,000 population (registered deaths only; 1966): tuberculosis of the respiratory system 154; all accidents other than vehicle accidents 111; malaria 55; pneumonia 51.

National economy

Budget. The lack, since the mid-1970s, of a taxable domestic economic base or of any income-earning export markets has left Kampuchea without a central governmental budget other than the dispersal of foreign aid and the management of development investments.
Public debt: n.a.
Tourism: none.
Production (metric tons except as noted). Agriculture, forestry, fishing (1984): rice 1,300,000, roots and tubers 130,000, cassava 95,000, corn (maize) 75,000, beans 30,000, sweet potatoes 26,000, tobacco 5,000, rubber 1,000§; livestock (number of live animals) 1,466,000 cattle, 1,008,000 pigs, 600,000 buffalo, 6,000,000 chickens; roundwood 5,239,000 cu m§; fish catch 63,800§. Mining and quarrying (1980): salt 30,000. Manufacturing (1983): cement 50,000‖; pork 20,000; beef and veal 14,000; sawn wood 43,000 cu m; plywood 2,000 cu m; cigarettes 4,100,000,000 units‖. Construction: n.a. Energy production (consumption): electricity (kW-hr; 1983) 140,000,-000 (140,000,000); coal, n.a. (n.a.); crude petroleum, n.a. (n.a.); petroleum products (metric tons; 1983), n.a. (11,000); natural gas, n.a. (n.a.).
Household income and expenditure. Average household size (1980) 5.6; average annual income per household: n.a.; source of income: n.a.; expenditure: n.a.
Land use (1983): forested 75.8%; meadows and pastures 3.3%; agricultural and under permanent cultivation 17.2%; other 3.7%.
Origin of gross domestic product: n.a.

Gross national product (at current market prices; 1975): U.S.$1,132,000,000 (U.S.$159 per capita).

Structure of gross domestic product and labour force

	1966 in value '000,000 riels	% of total value	labour force	% of labour force
Agriculture	13,100	40.9	2,543,000	80.0
Mining and manufacturing	3,300	10.3		
Construction	1,700	5.3		
Public utilities	400	1.3	246,000	4.0
Transportation and communication	700	2.2		
Trade	7,300	22.8		
Public admin., defense	3,900	12.2	3,353,000	16.0
Services	1,600	5.0		
TOTAL	32,000	100.0	6,142,000	100.0

Population economically active (1984): total 2,696,000; participation rate of population ages 15–64, 59.0% (female, n.a.; unemployed, n.a.).

Price and earnings indexes (1970 = 100)

	1967	1968	1969	1970	1971	1972	1973
Consumer price index¶	79.5	84.1	89.4	100.0	172.0	215.2	556.1
Earnings index	...	...	...	...	...	...	...

Foreign trade♀

Balance of trade (current prices)

	1978	1979	1980	1981	1982	1983
U.S.$'000,000	...	...	...	−60	...	−20
% of total				41.1%	...	67.0%

Imports (1973): 14,200,100,000 old riels (agricultural and food products 54.4%, textiles 12.4%, mineral products 11.7%, pharmaceuticals 9.8%, metals and metal products 9.0%, chemicals 2.3%). *Major import sources* (1972): Japan 17.8%; Thailand 16.5%; Hong Kong 14.9%; France 14.4%; United States 10.1%; Singapore 5.3%.
Exports (1973): 2,732,500,000 old riels (rubber 93.1%, haricot beans 4.4%, sesame seeds 2.0%, rice 0.5%). *Major export destinations* (1972): South Vietnam 54.8%; Hong Kong 18.3%; Singapore 10.2%; Japan 4.1%; France 4.1%; United States 3.0%.

Transport and communications

Transport. Railroads (1981): length 403 mi, 649 km; passenger-mi 33,554,-000, passenger-km 54,000,000; short ton-mi cargo 6,850,000, metric ton-km cargo 10,000,000. Roads (1981): total length 8,296 mi, 13,351 km (paved 20%). Vehicles (1981): passenger cars 700; trucks 1,800. Merchant marine (1984): vessels (100 gross tons and over) 3; total deadweight tonnage 3,839. Air transport (1977): passenger-mi 26,098,800, passenger-km 42,000,000; short ton-mi cargo 274,000, metric ton-km cargo 400,000; airports (1985) with scheduled flights 1.
Communications. Daily newspapers (1984): total number 16; total circulation, n.a. Radio (1983): total number of receivers 200,000 (1 per 35 persons). Television (1983): total number of receivers 51,000 (1 per 139 persons). Telephones (1981): 7,315 (1 per 790 persons).

Education and health

Education (1981–82)

	schools	teachers	students	student/ teacher ratio
Primary (age 6–11)	3,629	38,600	1,548,419	40.1
Secondary	5	78	1,521	19.5
Voc., teacher tr.	6	...	2,754	...
Higher	...	...	...	...

Educational attainment, n.a. *Literacy* (1980): total population over age 15 literate 48.0%.
Health: physicians (1971) 438 (1 per 15,297 persons); hospital beds (1980) 6,300 (1 per 951 persons); infant mortality rate per 1,000 live births (1984) 151.0.
Food (1980–82): daily per capita caloric intake 1,930 (vegetable products 95%, animal products 5%); 87% of FAO recommended minimum requirement.

Military

Total active duty personnel (1983): 30,000δ. *Military expenditure as percent of GNP:* n.a.; per capita expenditure, n.a.

---

*The UN continues to seat Democratic Kampuchea (DK), whose present leadership calls itself the Coalition Government of Democratic Kampuchea and is composed of Khmer People's National Liberation Front, the DK, and the organization of Norodom Sihanouk. †Area of Preăh Vihéar included with Kâmpóng Thum. ‡Total land area is 68,721 sq mi (177,987 sq km) and is shown for provinces; the total area (both land and water) is shown in the grand total. §1983. ‖1982. ¶Phnom Penh only. ♀In 1981 imports were estimated to be U.S.$103,000,000; exports were estimated to be U.S.$43,000,000. Major trading partners are the U.S.S.R., Vietnam, Czechoslovakia, Bulgaria, East Germany, Hungary, Cuba, Poland, Mongolia, and Laos. δExcludes about 175,000 Vietnamese troops and about 45,000 opposition forces of Democratic Kampuchea.

Kenya

Official name: Jamhuri ya Kenya (Swahili); Republic of Kenya (English).
Form of government: unitary single-party republic with one legislative house (National Assembly [172]).
Head of state and government: President.
Capital: Nairobi.
Official languages: Swahili; English.
Official religion: none.
Monetary unit: 1 Kenyan shilling (K Sh) = 100 cents; valuation (Oct. 21, 1985) 1 U.S.$ = K Sh16.53; 1 £ = K Sh23.70.

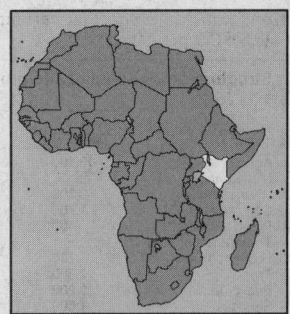

Area and population

		area		population
Provinces	Provincial headquarters	sq mi	sq km	1984 estimate
Central	Nyeri	5,087	13,176	2,926,200
Coast	Mombasa	32,279	83,603	1,688,000
Eastern	Embu	61,734	159,891	3,423,500
Nairobi	Nairobi	264	684	1,103,600
North Eastern	Garissa	48,997	126,902	484,700
Nyanza	Kisumu	6,240	16,162	3,508,500
Rift Valley	Nakuru	67,131	173,868	4,132,400
Western	Kakamega	3,228	8,360	2,269,400
TOTAL		224,961*	582,646*	19,536,300

Demography

Population (1985): 20,312,000.
Density† (1985): persons per sq mi 92.1, persons per sq km 35.5.
Urban–rural (1985): urban 16.7%; rural 83.3%.
Sex distribution (1985): male 49.77%; female 50.23%.
Age breakdown (1983): under 15, 51.4%; 15–29, 25.2%; 30–44, 13.0%; 45–59, 6.9%; 60–74, 3.0%; 75 and over, 0.5%.
Population projection: (1990) 24,911,000; (2000) 38,499,000.
Doubling time: 17 years.
Ethnic composition (1979): African 98.5% (Kikuyu 20.9%, Luhya 13.8%, Luo 12.8%, Kamba 11.3%, Kalenjin 10.8%); Asian 0.5%; Arab 0.3%; European 0.3%; other 0.4%.
Religious affiliation (1980): Roman Catholic 26.4%; Protestant 19.3%; other Christian 27.3%; tribal religionist 18.9%; Muslim 6.0%; other non-Christian 2.1%.
Major cities (1983): Nairobi 1,162,200‡; Mombasa 425,600§; Kisumu 167,100; Nakuru 101,700; Machakos 92,300.

Vital statistics

Birth rate per 1,000 population (1980–85): 55.1 (world avg. 29.0).
Death rate per 1,000 population (1980–85): 14.0 (world avg. 11.0).
Natural increase rate per 1,000 population (1980–85): 41.1 (world avg. 18.0).
Total fertility rate (avg. births per childbearing woman; 1980–85): 8.1.
Life expectancy at birth (1980–85): male 51.2 years; female 54.7 years.
Major causes of death per 100,000 population: n.a.; however, major health problems include malaria, gastroenteritis, venereal diseases, diarrhea and dysentery, trachoma, and schistosomiasis.

National economy

Budget ‖ (1983–84). Revenue: K Sh19,337,640,000 (sales tax 31.5%, income tax 20.1%, import duties 19.1%, excise duties 8.4%). Expenditures: K Sh25,156,020,000 (economic services 24.1%, education 16.3%, public administration 15.3%, defense 11.2%).
Public debt (external, outstanding; 1983): U.S.$2,384,000,000.
Production (metric tons except as noted). Agriculture, forestry, fishing (1984): sugarcane 3,910,000, corn (maize) 1,275,000, cassava 680,000, potatoes 416,000, sweet potatoes 350,000, plantains 255,000, pulses 250,000, pineapples 165,000, sorghum 150,000, bananas 142,000, tea 115,000, coconuts 110,000, wheat 100,000, coffee 95,000, barley 85,000, millet 75,000, tomatoes 57,000, sisal 50,000, seed cotton 27,000, sunflower seeds 17,000, cottonseed 17,000, cashew nuts 15,000, copra 10,000, peanuts (groundnuts) 9,000, tobacco 5,000; livestock (number of live animals) 12,000,000 cattle, 8,000,000 goats, 6,700,000 sheep; roundwood 29,330,000 cu m¶; total fish catch 78,442, of which freshwater fish 93.6%. Mining and quarrying (metric tons; 1983): soda ash 193,960, salt 83,427; fluorspar 59,084; lime and limestone 26,166; corundum (ruby) 98 kilograms. Manufacturing (metric tons except as noted; 1983): wheat flour 271,669; corn meal 227,545; animal feeds 154,006; refined salt 54,470; cotton woven fabrics 61,733,000 sq m; bedsheets 513,000 sq m; shirts 3,074,000 units; blankets 2,303,000 units. Construction (1982): residential 252,000 sq m; nonresidential 91,000 sq m. Energy production (consumption): electricity (kW-hr; 1983) 1,814,430,-000 (2,000,700,000); coal (metric tons; 1983) none (32,000); crude petroleum (barrels; 1983) none (16,684,000); petroleum products (metric tons; 1983) 1,918,100 (1,103,000).
Population economically active (1983): total 6,903,000; participation rate of population over age 15, 75.6% (female, n.a.; unemployed, n.a.).

Price and earnings indexes (1980 = 100)

	1978	1979	1980	1981	1982	1983	1984
Consumer price index	81.4	87.9	100.0	111.8	134.7	150.2	165.4
Monthly earnings index	82.1	89.5	100.0	117.1	123.8	131.4	...

Gross national product (at current market prices; 1983): U.S.$6,450,000,000 (U.S.$344 per capita).

Structure of gross domestic product and labour force

	1983			
	in value K £'000,000	% of total value	labour force§	% of labour force
Agriculture	1,091.6	33.2	155,162	17.3
Mining	6.2	0.2	1,221	0.1
Manufacturing	408.3	12.4	125,697	14.0
Construction	180.3	5.5	37,551	4.2
Public utilities	76.8	2.3	8,066	0.9
Transportation and communication	195.3	5.9	48,866	5.4
Trade	346.3	10.5	67,535	7.5
Finance	489.4	14.6	41,633	4.6
Pub. admin., defense	481.4	14.6 ⎫		
Services	112.7	3.4 ⎬	413,032	46.0
Other	–97.1□	–2.9□	...	...
TOTAL	3,291.2◊	100.0	898,763	100.0

Tourism: receipts from visitors (1983) U.S.$135,216,000; expenditures by nationals abroad (1980) U.S.$33,000,000.
Household income and expenditure. Average household size (1980) 6.3; average annual income per household: n.a.; source of income: n.a.; expenditure (1975)♀: food 40.0%, transportation 7.9%, recreation 4.5%, clothing and footwear 11.9%, housing 16.0%, miscellaneous 19.7%.
Land use (1983): forested 4.2%; meadows and pastures 6.6%; agricultural and under permanent cultivation 4.2%; other 85.0%.

Foreign trade

Balance of trade (current prices)

	1979	1980	1981	1982	1983	1984
K Sh'000,000	–4,117	–8,867	–8,001	–6,746	–4,811	–6,720
% of total	20.7%	30.1%	29.3%	22.9%	15.3%	17.7%

Imports (1983): K Sh18,112,000,000 (crude petroleum 31.3%; machinery and transport equipment 22.5%, of which transport equipment 11.4%, electrical machinery 4.7%; chemicals 14.1%, of which fertilizers 2.7%, pharmaceuticals 2.1%; iron and steel 5.3%). *Major import sources:* United Kingdom 13.5%; United Arab Emirates 12.0%; Saudi Arabia 9.5%; Japan 9.3%; West Germany 7.6%; United States 6.1%.
Exports (1983): K Sh11,372,000,000 (coffee, not roasted 25.4%; tea 19.6%; petroleum products 18.7%; vegetables and fruit 8.7%, of which canned pineapple 3.2%, beans, peas, and lentils 2.2%; cement 3.9%; corn (maize) 1.9%; sisal fibre and tow 1.9%). *Major export destinations:* United Kingdom 14.8%; West Germany 12.6%; Uganda 10.6%; United States 6.0%; The Netherlands 5.0%.

Transport and communications

Transport. Railroads (1983): length 1,650 mi, 2,650 km; passenger-mi 452,-109,000, passenger-km 727,600,000; short ton-mi cargo 1,432,000, metric ton-km cargo 2,091,000. Roads (1983): total length 33,900 mi, 54,500 km (paved 12%). Vehicles (1983): passenger cars 115,348; trucks and buses 90,034. Merchant marine (1984): vessels (100 gross tons and over) 25; total deadweight tonnage 3,672. Air transport△ (1984): passenger-mi 634,291,000, passenger-km 1,020,794,000; short ton-mi cargo 21,547,000, metric ton-km cargo 31,458,000; airports (1985) with scheduled flights 9.
Communications. Daily newspapers: total number (1984) 4; total circulation (1980) 258,859; circulation per 1,000 population (1980) 16. Radio (1984): total number of receivers 600,000 (1 per 33 persons). Television (1984): total number of receivers 76,000 (1 per 257 persons). Telephones (1983): 216,674 (1 per 87 persons).

Education and health

Education (1983)

	schools	teachers	students	student/ teacher ratio
Primary (age 5–11)	11,966	117,475	4,323,822	36.8
Secondary (age 12–17)	2,230	18,960	493,710	26.0
Voc., teacher tr.	40	1,925	20,554	10.8
Higher	3	...	10,133	...

Educational attainment (1979). Percent of population over age 15 having: no formal schooling 44.1%; primary education 40.1%; secondary 13.7%; postsecondary 1.3%; other 0.8%. *Literacy* (1980): total population over age 15 literate 3,814,900 (47.1%); males literate 2,377,200 (60%); females literate 1,437,700 (34.8%).
Health (1983): physicians 2,366 (1 per 7,935 persons); hospital beds 29,294 (1 per 641 persons); infant mortality rate per 1,000 live births 81.
Food (1980–82): daily per capita caloric intake 2,036 (vegetable products 89%, animal products 11%); 87% of FAO recommended minimum requirement.

Military

Total active duty personnel (1984): 13,650 (army 95.2%; navy 4.8%; air force reorganized as part of army since 1982, air force personnel about 2,400 in 1982). *Military expenditure as percent of GNP* (1983): 2.1% (world 6.1%); per capita expenditure U.S.$7.

*Total includes 4,336 sq mi (11,230 sq km) of inland water area. †Land area only. ‡1985. §1984. ‖ Budget for 1985–86: Revenue K Sh 31,622,000,000; Expenditure K Sh 31,704,000,000. ¶1983. ♀Nairobi only. δEmployees only. □Imputed bank service charge. ◊At current prices. △Kenya Airways only.

Kiribati

Official name: Republic of Kiribati.
Form of government: unitary republic
with one legislature (House of
Assembly [36]).
Head of state and government:
President.
Capital: Bairiki, on Tarawa Atoll.
Official language: English.
Official religion: none.
Monetary unit: 1 Australian Dollar
($A) = 100 cents; valuation (Oct. 21,
1985) 1 U.S.$ = $A1.42; 1 £ = $A2.04.

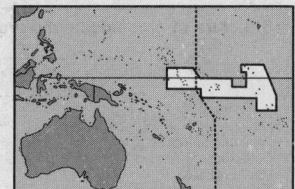

Area and population		area*		population
Island Groups				1983
Islands	**Capitals**	**sq mi**	**sq km**	**estimate**
Gilberts Group	Bairiki Islet	110	285	58,100
Abaiang		7	17	3,800
Abemama		10	27	2,700
Aranuka		5	12	1,000
Arorae		3	9	1,700
Banaba			6	100
Beru		7	1	2,500
Butaritari		5	13	3,500
Kuria		6	15	900
Maiana		7	17	1,900
Makin		3	8	1,600
Marakei		5	14	2,600
Nikunau		7	19	2,100
Nonouti		8	20	2,700
Onotoa		6	16	2,300
Tabiteuea		15	38	4,600
Tamana		2	5	1,600
Tarawa		12	31	22,500
Line Group	Kiritimati	207	535	2,300
Northern		167	432	2,300
Kiritimati (Christmas)		150	388	1,400
Tabuaeran (Fanning)		13	34	400
Teraina (Washington)		4	10	500
Southern		40	103	—
(Caroline, Flint, Malden,				
Starbuck, Vostok)				
Phoenix Group	Kanton	11	29	—
(Birnie, Enderbury,				
Kanton [Canton], McKean,				
Manra [Sydney], Nikumaroro				
[Gardner], Orona [Hull],				
Rawaki [Phoenix])				
TOTAL		328	849	60,300†

Demography

Population (1985): 65,000.
Density‡ (1985): persons per sq mi 234.7, persons per sq km 90.7.
Urban–rural (1983): urban 33.2%; rural 66.8%.
Sex distribution (1978): male 49.32%; female 50.68%.
Age breakdown (1978): under 15, 41.1%; 15–29, 28.1%; 30–44, 15.0%; 45–59, 10.0%; 60–74, 4.8%; 75 and over, 1.0%.
Population projection: (1990) 72,000; (2000) 89,000.
Doubling time: 39 years.
Ethnic composition (1978): Micronesian 97.9%; Polynesian 1.5%; European, Chinese, and other 0.6%.
Religious affiliation (1978): Roman Catholic 50.4%; Kiribati Protestant (Congregational) 44.0%; Bahā'ī 2.1%; Seventh-day Adventist 1.6%; other 1.9%.
Major cities (1983 est.): Urban Tarawa 20,050 .

Vital statistics

Birth rate per 1,000 population (1978): 34.9 (world avg. 30.5); legitimate, n.a.; illegitimate, n.a.
Death rate per 1,000 population (1978): 14.0 (world avg. 12.0).
Natural increase rate per 1,000 population (1978): 20.9 (world avg. 18.5).
Total fertility rate (avg. births per childbearing woman; 1980–85): 4.5.
Marriage rate per 1,000 population (1973): 4.5.
Divorce rate per 1,000 population: n.a.
Life expectancy at birth (1978): male 50.3 years; female 53.8 years.
Major causes of death (1979)§: tuberculosis, diarrheal and respiratory diseases, and nutritional disorders.

National economy

Budget (1982). Revenue: $A15,871,000 (external aid and income 53.3%, indirect taxes 23.8%, direct taxes 6.3%). Expenditures: $A16,956,000 (education 18.3%, communications 18.1%, home affairs 10.5%, health 10.0%, works and energy 8.3%, police 6.6%).
Public debt: n.a.
Tourism (1977): visitors 796.
Production (metric tons except as noted). Agriculture, forestry, fishing (1984): coconuts 85,000, roots and tubers 13,000 (of which taro 3,000), copra 12,000, fruit 5,000, vegetables and melons 4,000, bananas 4,000, eggs 113; livestock (number of live animals) 10,000 pigs, 191,000 chickens ‖ ; fish catch 24,212¶, of which snapper 3,000, emperor 2,500, yellowfin tuna 2,100, skipjack tuna 2,000. Mining and quarrying: none♀. Manufacturing (1981): copra $A2,930,000; other important products are processed fish, baked goods, clothing, boats, and handicrafts. Energy production (consumption): electricity (kW-hr; 1983) 6,000,000 (6,000,000) coal: none (n.a.); crude petroleum: none (n.a.); petroleum products (metric tons; 1983) none (9,000); natural gas: none (n.a.).

Gross national product (at current market prices; 1983): U.S.$30,000,000 (U.S.$492 per capita).

Structure of gross domestic product and labour force				
	1978			
	in value $A'000	% of total value	labour force	% of labour force
Agriculture	7,300	18.5	495	7.0
Mining	16,800	42.5	317	4.5
Manufacturing	700	1.8	183	2.6
Construction	3,100	7.9	972	13.8
Public utilities	600	1.5	193	2.8
Transportation and communication	1,000	2.5	691	9.8
Trade	2,400	6.1	913	13.0
Finance	600	1.5	32	0.5
Pub. admin., defense	4,700	11.9	1,016	14.4
Services			1,805	25.6
Other, including unemployed	2,300	5.8	424	6.0
TOTAL	39,500δ	100.0	7,041	100.0

Population economically active (1978): total 7,041; participation rate of total population 12.5% (female 20.2%, unemployed 5.9%).

Price and earnings indexes (1980 = 100)							
	1978	1979	1980	1981	1982	1983	1984
Consumer price index	80.3	86.1	100.0	107.7	113.7	120.8	128.1
Monthly earnings index	...	...	...	...	...	...	...

Household income and expenditure. Average household size (1978) 6.2; income per household: n.a.; source of income: agriculture 35.9%, wages only 27.5%, wages and other 19.3%, agriculture and other 12.6%, other 4.7%; expenditure (1982): food 50.0%, tobacco and alcohol 14.0%, clothing 8.0%, transportation 8.0%, housing and household operation 7.5%.
Land use (1983): forested 2.8%; agricultural and under permanent cultivation 50.7%; other 46.5%.

Foreign trade

Balance of trade (current prices)						
	1978	1979	1980	1981	1982	1983	1984
$A'000	+7,281	+5,664	−14,422	−16,312	−15,681	−15,900	−10,800
% of total	20.5%	15.4%	74.8%	−71.2%	77.2%	65.4%	38.0%

Imports (1981): $A19,912,000 (machines and transport equipment 32.8%, food and live animals 24.9%, basic manufactured goods 12.5%, petroleum products 12.0%, miscellaneous manufactured articles 8.0%, beverages and tobacco 5.6%). *Major import sources:* Australia 42.2%; Japan 13.2%; New Zealand 7.4%; Italy 2.5%; United Kingdom 2.0%.
Exports (1981): $A3,534,000 (copra 74.6%, fish and fish preparations 25.4%). *Major export destinations:* South Korea 40.0%; The Netherlands 36.0%; Australia 8.0%.

Transport and communications

Transport. Roads (1984): total length 398 mi, 640 km (paved, n.a.). Vehicles (1978): passenger cars and trucks 163; motorcycles 2,822. Merchant marine (1984): vessels (100 gross tons and over) 4; total deadweight tonnage 1,832. Air transport (1978): passengers carried 14,593; airports (1985) with scheduled flights 17.
Communications. Daily newspapers: none. Radio (1984): total number of receivers 10,000 (1 per 6.4 persons). Television: n.a. Telephones (1984): 1,400 (1 per 45.7 persons).

Education and health

Education (1982–83)	schools	teachers	students	student/ teacher ratio
Primary (age 6–13)	106	450	13,836	30.7
Secondary (age 14–18)	5	65	950	14.6
Voc., teacher tr.	2	14	122	8.7
Higher□	1	17	113	6.6

Educational attainment (1978): Percent of population over age 15 having: no schooling 5.3%, less than full primary education 44.1%, primary 39.8%, some secondary 4.6%, secondary 5.9%, diploma and university 0.3%. *Literacy* (1982): Total population over age 15 literate 31,806 (90.0%).
Health: (1981) physicians 16 (1 per 3,690 persons); hospital beds 283 (1 per 208 persons); infant mortality rate per 1,000 live births (1978) 8.7.
Food (1980–82): daily per capita caloric intake 3,120 (vegetable products 76%, animal products 24%); 117% of FAO recommended minimum requirement.

*Includes uninhabited islands. †Detail does not add to total given because of rounding. ‡Density based on inhabited island areas (277 sq mi [717 sq km]). §Leading causes of death at Tungaru Central Hospital. ‖ 1982. ¶1983. ♀Mining of phosphates on Banaba (Ocean Island) ceased in 1979. δAt current prices. □Teachers college.

Korea, North

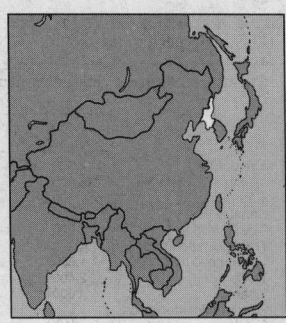

Official name: Chosŏn Minjujuŭi
In'min Konghwaguk (Democratic
People's Republic of Korea).
Form of government: unitary
single-party republic with one
legislative house (Supreme People's
Assembly [615]).
Chief of state: President.
Head of government: Premier.
Capital: P'yŏngyang.
Official language: Korean.
Official religion: none.
Monetary unit: 1 won = 100
chon; valuation (Oct. 21, 1985)
1 U.S.$ = 0.94 won; 1 £ = 1.35 won.

Area and population

Provinces	Capitals	area* sq mi	area* sq km	population 1968 estimate
Chagang-do	Kanggye	6,300	16,200	780,000
Hamgyŏng-namdo	Hamhŭng	7,400	19,200	1,315,000
Hamgyŏng-pukto	Ch'ŏngjin	6,100	15,900	1,110,000
Hwanghae-namdo	Haeju	2,900	7,600	1,340,000
Hwanghae-pukto	Sariwŏn	3,300	8,600	1,060,000
Kangwŏn-do	Wŏnsan	4,100	10,700	1,030,000
P'yŏngan-namdo	P'yŏngsan	4,700	12,300	2,250,000
P'yŏngan-pukto	Sinŭiju	4,600	12,000	1,760,000
Yanggang-do	Hyesan	5,400	14,100	435,000
Special cities				
Ch'ŏngjin-si	—	700	1,900	385,000
Hamhŭng-si	—	300	800	530,000
P'yŏngyang-si	P'yŏngyang	700	1,800	1,275,000
Special district				
Kaesŏng-chigu	Kaesŏng	500	1,200	289,000
TOTAL		47,300†	122,400†	13,559,000

Demography

Population (1985): 20,082,000.
Density (1985): persons per sq mi 426.6, persons per sq km 164.7.
Urban–rural (1985): urban 62.0%; rural 38.0%.
Sex distribution (1985): male 49.58%; female 50.42%.
Age breakdown (1980): under 15, 40.0%; 15–29, 28.7%; 30–44, 15.9%; 45–59, 9.6%; 60–74, 4.7%; 75 and over, 1.1%.
Population projection: (1990) 22,443,000; (2000) 27,256,000.
Doubling time: 30 years.
Ethnic composition (1980): Korean 99.3%; other 0.7%.
Religious affiliation (1980): atheist or nonreligious 67.9%; traditional beliefs 15.6%; Ch'ŏndogyo 13.9%; Buddhist 1.7%; Christian 0.9%.
Major cities (1981): P'yŏngyang 1,283,000; Hamhŭng-Hŭngnam 775,000; Ch'ŏngjin 490,000; Kaesŏng 240,000; Wŏnsan 240,000.

Vital statistics

Birth rate per 1,000 population (1983): 31.0 (world avg. 29.0).
Death rate per 1,000 population (1983): 7.5 (world avg. 11.0).
Natural increase rate per 1,000 population (1983): 23.5 (world avg. 18.0).
Total fertility rate (avg. births per childbearing woman; 1983): 4.0.
Marriage rate per 1,000 population: n.a.
Divorce rate per 1,000 population: n.a.
Life expectancy at birth (1983): male 63 years; female 67 years.
Major causes of death: n.a.; however, major diseases are malignant neoplasms (cancers), hypertensive and heart diseases, and intestinal infections.

National economy

Budget (1984). Revenue: 26,237,000,000 won (detail, n.a.). Expenditures: 26,237,000,000 (national economy 59.0%‡, social and cultural affairs 23.0%‡, defense 15.1%‡, other 2.9%‡).
Public debt (external, outstanding; 1983): U.S.$3,000,000,000.
Production (metric tons except as noted). Agriculture, forestry, fishing (1984): rice 5,400,000, corn (maize) 2,580,000, potatoes 1,700,000, apples 560,000, millet 500,000, barley 500,000, soybeans 400,000; livestock (number of live animals) 2,700,000 pigs, 1,025,000 cattle, 340,000 sheep, 260,000 goats, 18,100,000 chickens; roundwood 6,200,000 cu m§; fish catch 1,600,000§. Mining and quarrying (1983): iron ore 8,000,000; crude magnesite 1,900,000; calcined magnesite 800,000; pyrites 620,000; salt 570,000; zinc 120,000‡; barite 110,000; lead 95,000 ‖; silver 1,300,000 troy oz ‖; gold 160,000 troy oz ‖. Manufacturing (1983): cement 7,300,000; crude steel 3,600,000; steel semimanufactures 3,400,000; pig iron 3,100,000; chemical fertilizers 3,900,000; machine tools 29,000 units; tractors 25,000; textile fabrics 490,000,000 m. Construction: n.a. Energy production (consumption): electricity (kW-hr; 1983) 41,000,000,000 (41,000,000,000); coal (metric tons; 1983) 48,500,000 (48,500,000); crude petroleum (barrels; 1983) none (14,700,000); petroleum products (metric tons; 1983) 2,170,000 (2,650,000); natural gas, none (n.a.).
Population economically active (1983): total 8,695,000; participation rate of population over age 15, 75.5% (female, n.a.; unemployed, n.a.).
Price and earnings indexes: n.a.
Household income and expenditure. Average household size (1980) 5.7; average annual income per household 3,677 won (U.S.$4,275); source of income: n.a.; expenditure: n.a.
Gross national product (1982): U.S.$16,200,000,000 (U.S.$790 per capita).

Structure of gross domestic product and labour force

	1982 in value '000,000 won	% of total value	labour force	% of labour force
Agriculture	...	...	3,276,000	44.1
Mining and manufacturing	...	...	} 2,790,000	33.0
Construction	...	...		
Public utilities	...	...		
Transp. and commun.	...	...	418,000	4.9
Trade	...	...	} 1,521,000	18.0
Finance	...	...		
Pub. admin., defense	...	...		
Services	...	...		
Other	...	...		
TOTAL	11,800	100.0	8,455,000	100.0

Land use (1983): forested 74.4%; meadows and pastures 0.4%; agricultural and under permanent cultivation 18.7%; other 6.5%.
Tourism: n.a.

Foreign trade

Balance of trade (current prices)

	1974	1976	1978	1979	1980	1981
'000,000 won	−601	−176	−53	+165	−256	−285
% of total	31.6%	11.5%	3.3%	6.3%	9.4%	10.3%

Imports (1981): 1,520,000,000 won (crude petroleum, machinery and equipment [including trucks], industrial chemicals, coking coal, and grain are among the major imports). *Major import sources:* U.S.S.R. 22.0%; Japan 18.0%; China 17.0%.
Exports (1981): 1,235,000,000 won (minerals [including lead, magnesite, and zinc], metallurgical products, agricultural products, and manufactured goods are among the major exports). *Major export destinations:* U.S.S.R. 26.0%; China 17.0%; Japan 9.0%; Saudi Arabia 9.0%; India 5.0%.

Transport and communications

Transport. Railroads (1984): length 2,720 mi, 4,380 km; passengers, n.a.; cargo, n.a. Roads (1981): total length 12,600 mi, 20,280 km (paved 2%). Vehicles: n.a. Merchant marine (1984): vessels (100 gross tons and over) 61; total deadweight tonnage 739,885. Air transport (1979): passenger-mi 52,200,000, passenger-km 84,000,000; short ton-mi cargo 1,370,000, metric ton-km cargo 2,000,000; airports (1985) with scheduled flights 1.
Communications. Daily newspapers (1984): total number 10; total circulation, n.a. Radio (1984): total number of receivers 4,100,000 (1 per 5 persons). Television (1984): total number of receivers 1,050,000 (1 per 19 persons). Telephones: n.a.

Education and health

Education (1982)

	schools	teachers	students	student/ teacher ratio
Primary (age 5–9)	4,700¶	} c. 100,000	c. 2,500,000	...
Secondary (age 10–15)			c. 2,500,000º	...
Voc., teacher tr.	...		...	...
Higher	175	9,244	200,000	21.6

Educational attainment, n.a. *Literacy* (1979): 90%.
Health (1982): physicians 45,000 (1 per 417 persons); hospital beds 244,000 (1 per 77 persons); infant mortality rate per 1,000 live births (1983) 32.
Food (1980–82): daily per capita caloric intake 3,065 (vegetable products 94%, animal products 6%); 130% of FAO recommended minimum requirement.

Military

Total active duty personnel (1984): 784,500 (army 89.2%, navy 4.3%, air force 6.5%). *Military expenditure as percent of GNP* (1983): 16.7% (world 6.1%); per capita expenditure U.S.$179.

*Areas approximate. †Detail does not add to total given because of rounding. ‡1979. §1983. ‖ By metal content. ¶1976. ºIncludes vocational students.

TASS FROM SOVFOTO

Palace of Sports, P'yŏngyang, North Korea.

Korea, South

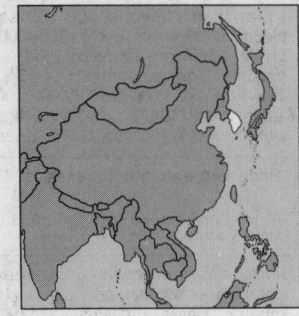

Official name: Taehan Min'guk
(Republic of Korea).
Form of government: unitary republic
with a National Assembly (276
members).
Chief of state: President.
Head of government: Prime Minister.
Capital: Seoul.
Official language: Korean.
Official religion: none.
Monetary unit: 1 won (W) = 100 chon;
valuation (Oct. 21, 1985)
1 U.S.$ = W881.74; 1 £ = W1,264.42.

Area and population

| | | area | | population |
| | | sq mi | sq km | 1984 estimate* |
Provinces	Capitals			
Cheju-do	Cheju	705	1,825	482,000
Chŏlla-namdo	Kwangju	4,720	12,225	3,824,300
Chŏlla-pukto	Chŏnju	3,108	8,050	2,288,700
Ch'ungch'ŏng-namdo	Taejŏn	3,410	8,833	3,056,200
Ch'ungch'ŏng-pukto	Ch'ŏngju	2,869	7,431	1,419,900
Kangwŏn-do	Ch'unch'ŏn'	6,523	16,894	1,816,400
Kyŏnggi-do	Inch'ŏn†	4,191	10,856	4,581,000
Kyŏngsang-namdo	Masan	4,576	11,851	3,083,700
Kyŏngsang-pukto	Taegu†	7,501	19,428	3,574,000
Special cities				
Inch'ŏn-si	Inch'ŏn	78	202	1,295,100
Pusan-si	Pusan	168	434	3,495,300
Sŏul-t'ŭkpyŏlsi	Seoul	234	605	9,501,400
Taegu-si	Taegu	176	455	2,012,000
TOTAL		38,259	99,091	40,430,000‡

Demography

Population (1985): 41,215,000.
Density (1985): persons per sq mi 1,077.3, persons per sq km 415.9.
Urban–rural (1984): urban 64.0%; rural 36.0%.
Sex distribution (1984): male 50.15%; female 49.85%.
Age breakdown (1981): under 15, 34.0%; 15–29, 30.0%; 30–44, 18.4%; 45–59, 11.4%; 60–74, 5.1%; 75 and over, 1.1%.
Population projection: (1990) 44,475,000; (2000) 52,849,000.
Doubling time: 44 years.
Ethnic composition (1982): Korean 99.9%; other 0.1%.
Religious affiliation (1981): Buddhist 37.4%; Protestant 25.7%; Confucian 17.5%; Roman Catholic 4.8%; Ch'ondogyo 3.6%; Wonbulgyo 3.2%; other 7.8%.
Major cities (1983): Seoul 9,204,300; Pusan 3,395,200; Taegu 1,958,800; Inch'ŏn 1,220,300; Kwangju 843,500.

Vital statistics

Birth rate per 1,000 population (1984): 23.0 (world avg. 29.0).
Death rate per 1,000 population (1984): 6.2 (world avg. 11.0).
Natural increase rate per 1,000 population (1984): 16.8 (world avg. 18.0).
Total fertility rate (avg. births per childbearing woman; 1980–85): 2.6.
Marriage rate per 1,000 population (1981): 3.1.
Divorce rate per 1,000 population (1981): 0.4.
Life expectancy at birth (1985): male 64.9 years; female 76.3 years.
Major causes of death per 100,000 population: n.a.

National economy

Budget (1985). Revenue: W12,275,000,000,000 (income and excise taxes 60.0%, customs duties 13.7%, defense surtax 12.3%, monopoly profits 6.8%). Expenditures: W11,396,015,000,000,000 (defense 33.6%, education 21.9%, economic development 16.1%, subsidies and transfer payments 8.8%, social programs 6.8%).
Tourism (1983): receipts from visitors U.S.$596,245,000; expenditures by nationals abroad U.S.$555,000,000.
Production (metric tons except as noted). Agriculture, forestry, fishing (1984): fruits and vegetables 10,351,000 (of which cabbages 3,457,000, apples 528,-000, oranges 261,000, garlic 200,000), rice 7,970,000, barley 804,000, potatoes 436,000, soybeans 226,000, corn (maize) 133,000; livestock (number of live animals) 2,215,000 cattle, 3,649,000 pigs, 350,000 goats; roundwood (1983) 10,189 cu m; fish catch (1983) 2,400,387. Mining and quarrying (1984): iron ore 552,000; zinc ore 108,500; lead ore 20,118; tungsten ore 4,465; refined silver 51,872 kilograms. Manufacturing (1984): cement 23,500,000; pig iron 8,904,000; crude steel 5,016,000; urea fertilizer 737,000§; man-made fibres 394,011§; cotton yarn 274,800; cotton fabrics 394,000,000 sq m; passenger cars 128,490 units§. Construction (1984): residential 20,556,000 sq m; non-residential 19,008,000 sq m. Energy production (consumption): electricity (kW-hr; 1984) 53,628,000,000 (62,338,000,000); coal (metric tons; 1984) 20,-640,000 (36,820,000); crude petroleum (barrels; 1983) none (191,300,000); petroleum products (metric tons; 1983) 22,694,000 (23,222,000).
Household income and expenditure. Average household size (1983) 4.5; income per household W3,258,000 (U.S.$4,100); sources of income: wages and salaries 60.3%, other 39.7%; expenditure (1984): food 37.6%, housing including utilities 11.8%, education 9.9%, clothing and footwear 9.8%, health 7.5%, transportation 6.2%.
Land use (1983): forested 66.5%; meadows and pastureland 0.7%; agricultural and under permanent cultivation 22.0%; other 10.8%.

Public debt (external, outstanding; 1983): U.S.$23,071,700,000.
Gross national product (at current market prices; 1984): U.S.$78,976,000,000 (U.S.$1,950 per capita).

Structure of gross domestic product and labour force

| | 1983 | | | |
	in value W'000,000,000	% of total value	labour force	% of labour force
Agriculture	8,260.4	16.0	4,314,000	28.5
Mining	850.4	1.6	108,000	0.7
Manufacturing	12,534.1	24.3	3,275,000	21.7
Construction	4,703.7	9.1	816,000	5.4
Public utilities	1,204.8	2.3	31,000	0.2
Transportation and communication	4,564.8	8.9	626,000	4.1
Trade	7,671.5	14.9	3,237,000	21.4
Finance	3,942.9	7.7	445,000	2.9
Pub. admin., defense	2,676.8	5.2	} 1,663,000	11.0
Services	5,168.4	10.0		
Other	...	...	613,000 ‖	4.1 ‖
TOTAL	51,577.8	100.0	15,128,000	100.0

Population economically active (1983): total 15,128,000; participation rate of working age population over age 15, 55.8% (female 37.7%, unemployed 4.0%).

Price and earnings indexes (1980 = 100)

	1978	1979	1980	1981	1982	1983	1984
Consumer price index	65.6	77.7	100.0	121.3	130.1	134.5	137.6
Monthly earnings index	63.1	81.3	100.0	120.0	137.7	154.6	167.1

Foreign trade

Balance of trade (current prices)

	1979	1980	1981	1982	1983	1984
US$'000,000	−4,396	−4,384	−3,628	−2,400	−1,970	−1,386
% of total	13.0%	11.3%	8.1%	5.4%	3.9%	2.3%

Imports (1984): U.S.$30,631,400,000 (machinery and transport equipment 32.0%, mineral fuels and related products 23.7%, crude materials except fuels 12.9%, chemicals and chemical products 9.0%). *Major import sources* (1983): United States 25.9%; Japan 25.8%; Saudi Arabia 8.3%; Australia 4.0%; Malaysia 3.2%; Kuwait 2.9%; West Germany 2.7%; United Kingdom 1.9%.
Exports (1984): U.S.$29,244,900,000 (manufactured goods 52.2%, machinery and transport equipment 35.3%, food and live animals 3.9%, chemicals and chemical products 3.1%). *Major export destinations* (1983): United States 31.0%; Japan 12.8%; Saudi Arabia 5.4%; Hong Kong 3.1%; West Germany 3.0%; Canada 2.4%; Kuwait 2.3%.

Transport and communications

Transport. Railroads (1984): length 4,278 mi, 6,884 km; passenger-mi 13,-477,000,000, passenger-km 21,689,000,000; short ton-mi cargo 7,965,000,-000, metric ton-km cargo 11,630,000,000. Roads (1984): total length 33,926 mi, 54,599 km (paved 39%). Vehicles (1984): passenger cars 465,119; trucks and buses 483,170. Merchant marine (1984): vessels (100 gross tons and over) 1,799; total deadweight tonnage 11,211,472. Air transport (1983): passenger-mi 7,494,000,000, passenger-km 12,060,000,000; short ton-mi cargo 813,570,793,000, metric ton-km cargo 1,187,868,000; airports (1985) with scheduled flights 3.
Communications. Daily newspapers (1984): total number 25; total circulation 6,748,100§; circulation per 1,000 population 171§. Radio (1984): total number of receivers 10,250,000 (1 per 4.0 persons). Television (1984): total number of receivers 8,113,483 (1 per 5.0 persons). Telephones (1984): 5,947,536 (1 per 6.8 persons).

Education and health

Education (1985)

	schools	teachers	students	student/ teacher ratio
Primary (age 6–13)	6,528	126,233	5,040,958	39.9
Secondary (age 14–19)	3,230	103,385	3,936,073	38.1
Vocational	644	29,265	891,953	30.5
Higher	486	33,157	1,190,219	35.9

Educational attainment (1980). Percent of adult population over age 25 having: no formal schooling 21.1%; primary education 36.1%; secondary 16.7%; postsecondary 7.2%. *Literacy* (1981): total population literate 13,191,432 (92.7%); males literate 6,937,242 (97.5%); females literate 6,254,190 (87.9%).
Health (1983): physicians 26,473 (1 per 1,509 persons); hospital beds 59,099 (1 per 676 persons); infant mortality rate per 1,000 live births (1983): 37.0.
Food (1980–82): daily per capita caloric intake 2,938 (vegetable products 91%, animal products 9%); 125% of FAO recommended minimum requirement.

Military

Total active duty personnel (1984): 622,000 (army 86.8%, navy 7.9%, air force 5.3%). *Military expenditure as percent of GNP* (1984): 5.3% (world *c.* 6.0%); per capita expenditure: U.S.$106.

*October 1. †During 1981–82 Inch'ŏn and Taegu also became special cities. ‡Detail does not add to total given because of rounding. §1983. ‖ Unemployed.

Kuwait

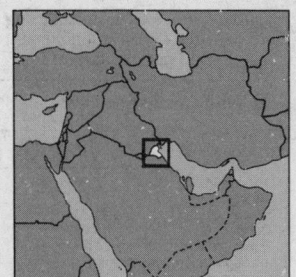

Official name: Dawlat al-Kuwayt (State of Kuwait).
Form of government: Constitutional monarchy with a single parliamentary house (National Assembly [50]).
Chief of state: Emir.
Head of government: Prime Minister.
Capital: Kuwait City.
Official language: Arabic.
Official religion: Islām.
Monetary unit: 1 Kuwaiti dinar (KD) = 1,000 fils; valuation (Oct. 21, 1985) 1 KD = U.S.$3.39 = £2.36.

Area and population

Governorates	Capitals	area		population
		sq mi	sq km	1985 census†
al-Aḥmadī	al-Aḥmadī	1,984	5,138	304,662
al-Jahrah	al-Jahrah	4,372	11,324	279,466
Capital	Kuwait City	38	98	167,750
Ḥawallī	Ḥawallī	138	358	943,250
Islands*	—	348	900	...
TOTAL		6,880	17,818	1,695,128

Demography

Population (1985): 1,695,128.
Density (1985): persons per sq mi 259.5, persons per sq km 100.2.
Urban–rural (1985): urban 93.7%; rural 6.3%.
Sex distribution (1985): male 58.10%; female 41.90%.
Age breakdown (1980): under 15, 40.2%; 15–29, 28.2%; 30–44, 21.7%; 45–59, 7.7%; 60 and over, 2.2%.
Population projection: (1990) 2,101,000; (2000) 2,936,000.
Doubling time: 14.4 years.
Ethnic composition (1980): Kuwaiti 41.7%; other Arab 42.3%; Asian 15.0%; other 1.0%.
Religious affiliation (1980): Muslim 91.5% (Sunnī about 80%, Shī'ah about 20%); Christian 6.4%; other 2.1%.
Major cities (1980): Ḥawallī 152,402; as-Sālimīyah 145,991; al-Jahrah 67,311; Kuwait City 60,525; al-Farwānīyah 57,841.

Vital statistics

Birth rate per 1,000 population (1980–85): 40.9 (world avg. 29.0); legitimate, n.a.; illegitimate, n.a.
Death rate per 1,000 population (1980–85): 4.1 (world avg. 11.0).
Natural increase rate per 1,000 population (1980–85): 36.9 (world avg. 18.0).
Total fertility rate (avg. births per childbearing woman; 1980–85): 6.2.
Marriage rate per 1,000 population (1984): 3.0.
Divorce rate per 1,000 population (1984): 1.5.
Life expectancy at birth (1980–85): male 68.0 years; female 72.9 years.
Major causes of death per 100,000 population (1981): circulatory diseases 94.7; accidents, poisonings, and violence 49.4; malignant neoplasms (cancers) 28.1; respiratory diseases 26.3.

National economy

Budget (1983–84). Revenue: KD4,439,100,000 (oil revenue 63.0%, investment income 29.0%, tax income 4.5%, customs duties 1.5%). Expenditures: KD3,012,900,000 (development 19.2%, defense 12.4%, education 8.1%, social services 1.5%, capital expenditure 0.8%).
Public debt: none.
Tourism (1982): receipts from visitors U.S.$198,000,000; expenditures by nationals abroad U.S.$1,306,000,000.
Gross national product (at current market prices; 1983): U.S.$30,290,000,000 (U.S.$18,180 per capita).

Structure of gross domestic product and labour force

	1983			
	in value KD'000,000	% of total value	labour force	% of labour force
Agriculture	34	0.5	3,182	0.7
Mining (oil sector)	3,094	49.8	6,475	1.3
Manufacturing	401	6.4	39,664	8.1
Construction	289	4.6	81,363	16.5
Public utilities	34	0.5	5,365	1.1
Transportation and communication	191	3.1	31,561	6.4
Trade	508	8.2	54,797	11.1
Finance	319	5.1	17,575	3.6
Pub. admin., defense, services, and other	1,349	21.8	251,896	51.2
TOTAL	6,219	100.0	491,878	100.0

Production (metric tons except as noted). Agriculture, forestry, fishing (1984): milk 31,000, poultry meat 20,000, tomatoes 14,000, melons 3,000, onions 2,000; livestock (number of live animals) 600,000 sheep, 8,000,000 chickens; fish catch 4,566. Mining and quarrying (1983): cement 1,560,000; nitrogen (N content of ammonia) 234,000; sulfur 145,000; lime 14,000. Manufacturing (1984): flour 176,500,000; urea 611,000; asbestos pipes 30,-204; salt 22,239; liquefied caustic soda 8,656; chlorine gas 8,128; hydrogen gas 2,522,000 cu m; concrete 93,288 cu m; hydrochloric acid 451,100 gallons; concrete pipes 29,900 units. Construction (1984): residential 3,131,000

sq m; nonresidential 755,000 sq m. Energy production (consumption): electricity (kW-hr; 1984) 13,894,000,000 (11,827,000,000); coal, none (none); crude petroleum (barrels: 1984) 424,400,000,000 (181,125,000‡); petroleum products (metric tons; 1984) 24,362,000 (3,678,000‡); natural gas (cu m; 1984) 5,816,000,000 (5,199,000,000).
Labour force (1983): total 491,878; participation rate of total population over age 15, 31.5% (female 18.8%, unemployed [1980] 0.3%).

Price and earnings indexes (1980 = 100)

	1978	1979	1980	1981	1982	1983	1984
Consumer price index	87.4	93.5	100.0	107.4	115.7	121.2	122.6
Monthly earnings index	...	...	...	...	...	...	...

Household income and expenditure. Average household size (1980) 6.9; annual income per household (1973)§ KD4,246 (U.S.$12,907); sources of income: wages and salaries 53.8%, self-employment 20.8%, other 25.4%; expenditure (1983): food 35.7%, housing and maintenance 18.7%, transportation 15.3%, household appliances 11.0%, clothing and footwear 10.0%, other 9.3%.
Land use (1983): forested 0.1%; meadows and pastures 7.5%; agricultural and under permanent cultivation 0.1%; other, built-up, and wasteland 92.3%.

Foreign trade

Balance of trade (current prices)

	1979	1980	1981	1982	1983	1984
KD'000,000	+3,652	+3,604	+2,585	+885	+1,204	+1,239
% of total	56.6%	50.5%	39.9%	16.8%	23.1%	21.4%

Imports (1984): KD1,039,000,000 (machinery and transport equipment 43.6%, manufactured goods 22.1%, miscellaneous manufactured articles 15.3%, food and live animals 12.3%, chemicals 3.6%, crude materials except fuels 1.6% ‖). *Major import sources:* Japan 20.6%; France 10.3%; United States 9.1%; United Kingdom 5.8%.
Exports (1984): KD2,277,800,000 (crude petroleum 49.7%, refined petroleum 37.1%). *Major export destinations:* Japan 13.6%; Italy 9.9%; Singapore 7.6%; The Netherlands 7.5%; Iraq 6.8%.

Transport and communications

Transport. Railroads: none. Roads (1983): total length 1,066 mi, 1,715 km (paved 100%). Vehicles (1984): passenger cars 383,460; trucks and buses 115,730. Merchant marine (1984): vessels (100 gross tons and over) 250; total deadweight tonnage 3,879,889. Air transport (1983): passenger-mi 2,354,045,000, passenger-km 3,788,476,000; short ton-mi cargo 338,751,000, metric ton-km cargo 494,568,000; airports (1985) with scheduled flights 1.
Communications. Daily newspapers (1985): total number 7; total circulation 453,000; circulation per 1,000 population 267. Radio (1984): total number of receivers 710,000 (1 per 2 persons). Television (1984): total number of receivers 575,000 (1 per 2.4 persons). Telephones (1983): 258,325 (1 per 6.5 persons).

Education and health

Education (1983–84)

	schools	teachers	students	student/teacher ratio
Primary (age 6–9)	252	8,968	165,696	18.5
Secondary (age 10–17)¶	337	16,871	219,758	13.0
Higher	9	763	13,233	17.3

Educational attainment (1980). Percent of adult population over age 25 having: no formal schooling 60.1%; primary education 7.9%; secondary education 21.0%; higher education 11.0%. *Literacy* (1980): total population over age 10 literate 829,000 (86.2%); males literate 535,000 (92.9%); females literate 295,000 (76.2%).
Health (1983): physicians 2,596 (1 per 602 persons); hospital beds 5,479♀ (1 per 285 persons); infant mortality rate per 1,000 live births (1982) 22.8.
Food (1980–82): daily per capita caloric intake 3,404 (vegetable products 74%, animal products 26%); 147% of FAO recommended minimum requirement.

Military

Total active duty personnel (1984): 12,500 (army 80%, navy 4.0%, air force 16.0%). *Military expenditure as percent of GNP* (1983): 4.0% (world 6.1%); per capita expenditure U.S.$662.

*Bubian Island and Warba Island. †Provisional. ‡1983. §Kuwaiti households only. ‖ 1982. ¶Includes vocational and teacher-training schools. ♀Government hospitals only.

Laos

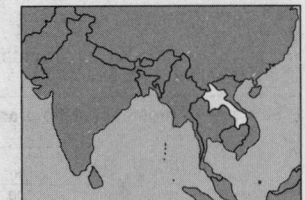

Official name: Sathalanalat Paxathipatai Paxaxôn Lao (Lao People's Democratic Republic).
Form of government: unitary single-party people's republic with one legislative house (National Congress of People's Representatives [264]).
Chief of state: President.
Head of government: Prime Minister.
Capital: Vientiane.
Official language: Lao.
Official religion: none.
Monetary unit: 1 kip (KN) = 100 at; valuation (preferential rate; Oct. 21, 1985) 1 U.S.$ = KN34.98; 1 £ = KN50.16.

Area and population

Provinces	Capitals	area sq mi	area sq km	population 1984 estimate
Attapu	Attapu	4,595	11,900	81,000
Champasak	Champasak	5,600	14,500	437,000
Houaphan	Xam Nua	6,290	16,300	234,000
Khammouan	Khammouan	10,195	26,400	327,000
Louang Namtha	...	4,980	12,900	166,000
Louangphrabang	Louangphrabang	7,300	18,900	336,000
Oudomxay	...	7,070	18,300	267,000
Phôngsali	Phôngsali	6,100	15,800	139,000
Saravan	Saravan	8,340	21,600	265,000
Savannakhét	Savannakhét	8,380	21,700	536,000
Vientiane	Vientiane	7,950	20,600	721,000
Xaignabouri	Xaignabouri	7,105	18,400	348,000
Xiangkhoang	Xiangkhoang	7,530	19,500	176,000
TOTAL		91,430*	236,800	4,033,000

Demography

Population (1985): 4,117,000.
Density (1985): persons per sq mi 45.0, persons per sq km 17.4.
Urban–rural (1985): urban 15.9%; rural 84.1%.
Sex distribution (1985): male 50.37%; female 49.63%.
Age breakdown (1985): under 15, 42.8%; 15–29, 26.5%; 30–44, 16.1%; 45–59, 9.6%; 60–74, 4.3%; 75 and over, 0.7%.
Population projection: (1990) 4,989,000; (2000) 6,213,000.
Doubling time: 29 years.
Ethnic composition (1983 est.): Lao 48%; Mon-Khmer tribes 25%; tribal Thai 14%; Sino-Tibetan tribes, including the Hmong (Meo) and Yao 13%.
Religious affiliation (1980 est.): Buddhist 57.8%; tribal religionist 33.6%; Christian 1.8%, of which Roman Catholic 0.8%, Protestant 0.2%; Muslim 1.0%; atheist 1.0%; Chinese folk-religionist 0.9%; none 3.8%; other 0.1%.
Major cities (1975): Vientiane 210,000†; Savannakhét 53,000; Pakxé 47,000; Louangphrabang 46,000.

Vital statistics

Birth rate per 1,000 population (1980–85): 30.7 (world avg. 29.0).
Death rate per 1,000 population (1980–85): 13.0 (world avg. 11.0).
Natural increase rate per 1,000 population (1980–85): 17.7 (world avg. 18.0).
Total fertility rate (avg. births per childbearing woman; 1980–85): 3.9.
Marriage rate per 1,000 population: n.a.
Divorce rate per 1,000 population: n.a.
Life expectancy at birth (1980–85): male 48.3 years; female 51.2 years.
Major causes of death: n.a; however, during the 1970s malaria, influenza, dysentery, and pneumonia were among the country's major health problems.

National economy

Budget (1981). Revenue: KN930,000,000 (private sector taxes 15.1%, state enterprises 75.3%). Expenditures: KN2,160,000,000 (current expenditure 56.0%, capital expenditure 44.0%).
Public debt (external, outstanding; 1982): U.S.$60,000,000.
Tourism (1982): total number of tourists 29,000.
Population economically active (1984): total 2,002,000; participation rate of population over age 15, 86.8% (female 44.9%; unemployed, n.a.).

Price and earnings indexes (1976 = 100)

	1980
Consumer price index	793
Monthly earnings index	...

Production (metric tons except as noted). Agriculture, forestry, fishing (1983): rice 1,322,000, cassava 76,000, potatoes 46,000, corn (maize) 40,000, pineapples 38,000, sweet potatoes 38,000, onions 35,000, melons 30,000, sugarcane 30,000, oranges 26,000; livestock (number of live animals) 1,350,000 pigs, 910,000 water buffalo, 490,000 cattle, 60,000 goats, 6,000,000 chickens; roundwood 3,920,000 cu m; fish catch 20,000. Mining and quarrying (1983): gypsum 13,000‡; rock salt 11,000; tin 3,500. Manufacturing (1983): domestic animal feed 3,000; washing powder 970; plastic products 185; textiles 1,451,400 metres; clothing 474,900 pieces; cigarettes 12,000,000 packets; bricks 10,900,000 units; rubber tires and tubes 1,000,000 units; beer 13,000 hectolitres; soft drinks 12,370 hectolitres. Construction: n.a. Energy production (consumption): electricity (kW-hr; 1983) 1,250,000,000

(502,000,000); coal (metric tons; 1981) 1,000 (1,000); crude petroleum, n.a. (n.a.); petroleum products (metric tons; 1983) none (162,000); natural gas, n.a. (n.a.).
Gross national product (at current market prices; 1983): U.S.$601,570,000 (U.S.$152 per capita).

Structure of gross domestic product and labour force

	1983 value in '000,000 KN	1983 % of total value	1981 labour force	1981 % of labour force
Agriculture	12,994	72.0	...	75.0
Manufacturing	1,263	7.0	...	6.0
Mining				
Construction				
Public utilities				
Transportation and communication	3,790	21.0		19.0
Trade				
Finance				
Pub. admin., defense				
Services				
TOTAL	18,047	100.0		100.0

Household income and expenditure. Average household size (1980) 5.3; average annual income per household KN3,710 (U.S.$371); source of income: n.a.; expenditure: n.a.
Land use (1983): forested 55.0%; meadows and pastures 3.5%; agricultural and under permanent cultivation 3.9%; other 37.6%.

Foreign trade

Balance of trade (current prices)

	1979	1980	1981	1982	1983	1984
U.S.$'000,000	−67.0	−100.0	−68.1	−61.9	−66.8	−36.7
% of total	65.9%	68.2%	66.8%	54.7%	56.7%	61.9%

Imports (1984): U.S.$47,994,000 (important imports are cereals, other food products, petroleum products, and agricultural and general machinery). *Major import sources:* Thailand 39.6%; unspecified countries 20.7%; Singapore 14.3%; Japan 11.8%; United Kingdom 2.2%; Vietnam 1.6%.
Exports (1984): U.S.$11,287,000 (important exports are wood [76.5% of all exports in 1980], coffee, electricity transferred to Thailand, and tin). *Major export destinations:* China 43.1%; United States 17.7%; Thailand 7.9%; Belgium 5.9%; Iran 5.7%; unspecified countries 5.2%.

Transport and communications

Transport. Railroads: none. Roads (1981): total length 6,340 mi, 10,200 km (paved 13%). Vehicles (1982): passenger cars 15,000; trucks and buses 3,000. Merchant marine: none. Air transport (1982): passenger-mi 5,000,000, passenger-km 8,000,000; short ton-mi cargo 70,000, metric ton-km cargo 100,000; airports (1985): with scheduled flights 7.
Communications. Daily newspapers (1983): total number 2; total circulation 12,500; circulation per 1,000 population 3.0. Radio (1984): total number of receivers 225,000 (1 per 18 persons). Television (1984): total number of receivers 30,000 (1 per 134 persons). Telephones (1983): 4,300 (1 per 921 persons).

Education and health

Education (1980–81)

	schools	teachers	students	student/ teacher ratio
Primary (age 6–10)§	6,525	16,454	480,871	29.2
Secondary (age 11–16)	...	3,666	78,925	21.5
Voc. teacher tr.	...	939	11,510	12.3
Higher	1	140	1,408	10.1

Educational attainment, n.a. *Literacy* (1980): total population over age 15 literate 997,600 (45.2%); males literate 586,600 (52.8%); females literate 412,500 (37.6%).
Health (1983): physicians 1,654 (1 per 2,394 persons); hospital beds 9,495 (1 per 417.1 persons); infant mortality rate per 1,000 live births 121.
Food (1980–82): daily per capita caloric intake 1,927 (vegetable products 90%, animal products 10%); 87% of FAO recommended minimum requirement.

Military

Total active duty personnel (1984): 53,700 (army 93.1%, navy 3.2%, air force 3.7%). *Military expenditure as percent of GNP* (1981): 9.0% (world 5.7%); per capita expenditure U.S.$7.

*Detail does not add to total given because of rounding. †1981 estimate. ‡Province of Savannakhét only. §1982–83.

Lebanon

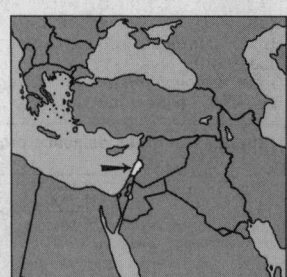

Official name: al-Jumūrīyah al-Lubnānīyah (Republic of Lebanon).
Form of government: multiparty republic with one legislative house (National Assembly [99]).
Chief of state: President.
Head of government: Prime Minister.
Capital: Beirut.
Official language: Arabic.
Official religion: none.
Monetary unit: 1 Lebanese pound (LL) = 100 piastres; valuation (Oct. 21, 1985) 1 U.S.$ = LL17.62; 1 £ = LL25.26.

Area and population

Governorates	Capitals	area sq mi	area sq km	population 1970 estimate
Bayrūt	Beirut (Bayrūt)	7	18	474,870
al-Biqā'	Zaḥlah	1,653	4,280	203,520
Jabal Lubnān	B'abdā	753	1,950	833,055
al-Janūb	Şaydā	364	943	249,945
an-Nabaṭīyah*	...	408	1,058	...
ash-Shamāl	Tripoli (Ṭarābulus)	765	1,981	364,935
TOTAL		3,950	10,230	2,126,325

Demography

Population (1985): 2,668,000.
Density (1985): persons per sq mi 784.8, persons per sq km 303.0.
Urban–rural (1985): urban 83.7%; rural 16.3%.
Sex distribution (1985): male 48.53%; female 51.47%.
Age breakdown (1984): under 15, 35.6%; 15–29, 30.4%; 30–44, 15.0%; 45–59, 11.0%; 60–74, 6.0%; 75 and over, 2.0%.
Population projection: (1990) 3,301,000; (2000) 3,992,000.
Doubling time: in the period 1970–75 the average growth rate was 2.6%; however, since 1976 the population is decreasing from the massive emigration resulting from the civil war.
Ethnic composition (1983): Lebanese 82.6%; Palestinian 9.6%; Armenian 4.9%; Syrian, Kurd, and other 2.9%.
Religious affiliation: no official data exist subsequent to the 1932 census, when Christians (predominantly Maronite Roman Catholic) were a slight majority; it is thought that Muslims today constitute the majority but by what margin is impossible to ascertain. An unofficial estimate (1983) indicated that the main religious groups were distributed as follows: Shī'ī Muslim 35%; Maronite Christian 25%; Sunnī Muslim 25%; Greek Orthodox 7.5%; Druze 7.5%.
Major cities (1982): Beirut 509,000; Tripoli 198,000; Şaydā 105,000; Zaḥlah 45,000.

Vital statistics

Birth rate per 1,000 population (1982): 29.9 (world avg. 29.0); legitimate, n.a.; illegitimate, n.a.
Death rate per 1,000 population (1982): 8.3 (world avg. 11.0).
Natural increase rate per 1,000 population (1982): 21.6 (world avg. 18.0).
Total fertility rate (avg. births per childbearing woman; 1982): 2.0.
Marriage rate per 1,000 population (1981): 7.0.
Divorce rate per 1,000 population (1973): 0.6.
Life expectancy at birth (1980–85): male 65.0 years; female 68.9 years.
Major causes of death (mid-1970s): heart ailments and gastrointestinal diseases, including typhoid and dysentery; violence and acts of war have been principal causes of mortality for the last decade.

National economy

Budget (1985). Revenue: LL8,217,000,000 (customs duties *c.* 35%). Expenditure: LL10,892,000,000 (defense 21.6%, education 15.0%, public works 6.7%, housing 0.1%).
Production (metric tons except as noted). Agriculture, forestry, fishing (1984): oranges 200,000, grapes 160,000, tomatoes 125,000, potatoes 120,-000, apples 128,000, lemons and limes 50,000, olives 50,000, sugar beets 50,000, apricots 25,000, peaches and nectarines 22,000, wheat 18,000, bananas 13,000, olive oil 10,000, centrifugal sugar (raw value) 6,000, almonds 5,500, tobacco 4,000; livestock (number of live animals) 440,000 goats, 130,000 sheep, 45,000 cattle, 9,000,000 chickens; roundwood (1983) 252,000 cu m; fish catch (1983) 1,400. Mining and quarrying (1982): gypsum 5,000. Manufacturing (1982): cement 1,980,000. Construction (1981): 5,863,000 sq m. Energy production (consumption): electricity (kW-hr; 1983) 1,220,000,-000 (1,260,000,000); coal, n.a. (none); crude petroleum (barrels; 1983) n.a. (3,665,000); petroleum products (metric tons; 1983) 490,000 (1,301,000); natural gas, none (n.a.).
Labour force (1982): 1,149,000; participation rate of total population 44.9% (female 19.9%, unemployed 5.8%).

Price and earnings indexes (1970 = 100)

	1970	1971	1972	1973	1974
Consumer price index	100.0	101.6	106.6	113.0	125.5
Earnings index	...	...	...	...	...

Household income and expenditure. Average household size (1980) 5.3; average annual income per household: n.a.; source of income: n.a.; expenditure: n.a.

Public debt (external, outstanding; 1983): U.S.$181,600,000.
Tourism: n.a.
Gross national product (at current market prices; 1983): U.S.$4,600,000,000–$5,500,000,000 (U.S.$1,636–$1,956 per capita).

Structure of gross domestic product and labour force

	1977 in value LL'000,000	1977 % of total value	1982 labour force	1982 % of labour force
Agriculture	700	8.5	238,188	20.7
Mining	...	...	223,136	19.4
Manufacturing	1,070	13.1		
Construction	280	3.4	71,698	6.2
Public utilities	445	5.4	8,503	0.7
Transportation and communication	630	7.7	62,161	5.4
Finance	...	...		
Trade	2,320	28.3	203,258	17.7
Pub. admin., defense	835	10.2		
Services	1,920	23.4	342,057	29.8
Other	...	...		
TOTAL	8,200	100.0	1,149,001	100.0†

Land use (1983): forested 6.8%; meadows and pastures 0.9%; agricultural and under permanent cultivation 29.1%, wasteland, built-up, and other areas 63.2%.

Foreign trade

Balance of trade (current prices)

	1978	1979	1980	1981	1982	1983
LL'000,000	–3,031	–5,601	–8,631	–8,906	–9,890	–12,461
% of total	40.5%	52.8%	59.1%	45.0%	48.5%	69.0%

Imports (1982): LL15,146,000,000 (consumer goods 40.0%; machinery and transport equipment 35.0%; petroleum products 20.0%). *Major import sources:* Italy 15.2%; France 10.3%; United States 9.1%; West Germany 7.6%; Saudi Arabia 5.7%.
Exports (1982): LL5,256,000,000 (agricultural products 21.3%, of which vegetables 15.9%; textile products 11.3%; metal products 8.5%; precious metals, jewelry, and coins 5.0%). *Major export destinations:* Saudi Arabia 29.7%; Iraq 22.1%; Jordan 10.8%; Syria 7.4%; Kuwait 5.5%.

Transport and communications

Transport. Railroads (1982): length 258 mi, 415 km; passenger-mi 5,325,-000, passenger-km 8,570,000; short ton-mi cargo 28,770,000, metric ton-km cargo 42,010,000. Roads (1982): total length 4,300 mi, 7,000 km (paved 80%). Vehicles (1982): passenger cars 460,400; trucks and buses 35,000. Merchant marine (1984): vessels (100 gross tons and over) 251; total deadweight tonnage 696,676. Air transport‡ (1984): passenger-mi 516,117,000, passenger-km 830,612,000; short ton-mi cargo 13,544,000, metric ton-km cargo 19,774,000; airports (1985) with scheduled flights 1.
Communications. Daily newspapers (1984): total number 39; total circulation 603,458; circulation per 1,000 population 228.2. Radio (1984): total number of receivers 1,500,000 (1 per 1.8 persons). Television (1984): total number of receivers 450,000 (1 per 5.9 persons). Telephones (1973): 227,000 (1 per 12 persons).

Education and health

Education (1981–82)

	schools	teachers	students	student/ teacher ratio
Primary (age 5–9)	1,116		398,977	...
Secondary (age 10–16)	1,405	53,450	250,028	...
Voc., teacher tr.	181	3,563	39,045	11.0
Higher	18	...	70,314	...

Educational attainment, n.a. *Literacy* (1980): total population over age 10 literate 1,183,000 (73.4%); males literate 643,000 (82.6%); females literate 540,000 (64.2%).
Health (1982): physicians 3,000 (1 per 1,000 persons); hospital beds 11,400 (1 per 263 persons); infant mortality rate per 1,000 live births (1981) 40.2.
Food (1979–81): daily per capita caloric intake 2,995 (vegetable products 84%, animal products 16%); 121% of FAO recommended minimum requirement.

Military

Total active duty personnel (1984): 20,300 (army 93.6%, navy 1.5%, air force 4.9%); factional armies (1984) Lebanese forces (Maronite) 6,000; Progressive Socialist Party/Druze forces 5,000, Amal (Shī'ī) 3,500; Murā biṭun (Sunnī) 1,500. *Military expenditure as percent of GNP* (1983): 8.2% (world 6.1%); per capita expenditure: U.S.$161.

*Created in 1975; includes the districts of Nabaṭīyah, Bint Jubayl, Marj 'Uyūn, and Ḥāşbayya, which were formerly part of al-Janūb. †Detail does not add to total given because of rounding. ‡International flights only.

Lesotho

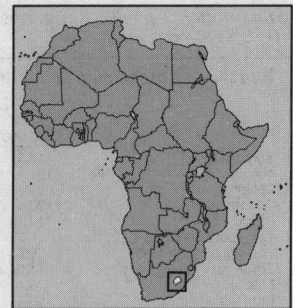

Official name: Lesotho (Sesotho); Kingdom of Lesotho (English).
Form of government: constitutional monarchy with two legislative houses (National Assembly [93]; Senate [33]).
Chief of state: King.
Head of government: Prime Minister.
Capital: Maseru.
Official languages: Sesotho; English.
Official religion: Christianity.
Monetary unit: 1 loti (plural maloti [M]) = 100 lisente; valuation (Oct. 21, 1985) 1 U.S.$ = M2.60; 1 £ = M3.72.

Area and population

Districts	Capitals	area sq mi	area sq km	population 1982 estimate
Berea	Teyateyaneng	858	2,222	166,100
Butha-Buthe	Butha-Buthe	682	1,767	86,700
Leribe	Leribe	1,092	2,828	240,000
Mafeteng	Mafeteng	818	2,119	180,300
Maseru	Maseru	1,652	4,279	299,400
Mohale's Hoek	Mohale's Hoek	1,363	3,530	155,800
Mokhotlong	Mokhotlong	1,573	4,075	82,700
Qacha's Nek	Qacha's Nek	907	2,349	86,500
Quthing	Quthing	1,126	2,916	100,500
Thaba-Tseka	Thaba-Tseka	1,649	4,270	...
TOTAL		11,720	30,355	1,398,200

Demography

Population (1985 est.): 1,499,600.
Density (1985): persons per sq mi 127.9, persons per sq km 49.4.
Urban-rural (1985): urban 5.8%; rural 94.2%.
Sex distribution (1985): male 48.45%; female 51.55%.
Age breakdown (1985): under 15, 42.3%; 15–29, 25.9%; 30–44, 16.2%; 45–59, 9.9%; 60–74, 4.7%; 75 and over, 1.0%.
Population projection: (1990) 1,731,000; (2000) 2,251,000.
Doubling time: 27 years.
Ethnic composition (1984): Sotho 99.7%; other 0.3%.
Religious affiliation (1980): Roman Catholic 43.5%; Protestant (mostly Lesotho Evangelical) 29.8%; Anglican 11.5%; other Christian 8.0%; tribal 6.2%; other 1.0%.
Major urban centres (1976): Maseru 55,031 (Maseru-Roma-Morija metropolitan area; 1982, 82,099); Maputsoe 15,823; Teyateyaneng 8,589.

Vital statistics

Birth rate per 1,000 population (1980–85): 41.7 (world avg. 29.0); legitimate, n.a.; illegitimate, n.a.
Death rate per 1,000 population (1980–85): 16.4 (world avg. 11.0).
Natural increase rate per 1,000 population (1980–85): 25.3 (world avg. 18.0).
Total fertility rate (avg. births per childbearing woman; 1980–85): 5.8.
Marriage rate per 1,000 population: n.a.
Divorce rate per 1,000 population: n.a.
Life expectancy at birth (1980–85): male 47.7 years; female 51.0 years.
Major causes of death: n.a.

National economy

Budget (1984–85). Revenue: M314,000,000 (current revenue 73.6%, of which customs and excise taxes 48.1%; development grants 15.0%; loans and borrowing 11.9%; personal income tax 6.4%). Expenditures: M315,000,000 (current expenditures 39.4%; development 37.7%, of which international airport 8.6%, food program 3.5%; debt service 19.0%; administration 3.5%).
Production (metric tons except as noted). Agriculture, forestry, fishing (1984): corn (maize) 90,000, sorghum 26,000, vegetables and melons 25,000, fruit 15,000, pulses 15,000, roots and tubers 6,000, wheat 5,000; livestock (number of live animals) 1,350,000 sheep, 1,020,000 goats, 560,000 cattle, 105,000 horses, 105,000 asses, 72,000 pigs, 1,000,000 chickens; roundwood 293,000 cu m†; fish catch 20†. Mining and quarrying (1982)*: diamonds 42,000 carats. Manufacturing (1983): n.a.; however, food processing, cottage industry weaving, and handicrafts were the main manufacturing activities. Construction: n.a. Energy production (consumption): electricity (kW-hr; 1984) 1,000,000 (n.a.); coal, none (n.a.); petroleum, none (n.a.); natural gas, none (n.a.).
Gross national product (at current market prices; 1983): U.S.$670,000,000 (U.S.$470 per capita).

Structure of gross domestic product and labour force

	1981–82‡ in value M'000	1981–82‡ % of total value	1981 labour force	1981 % of labour force
Agriculture	67,144	19.3	430,000	60.0
Mining	16,036	4.6		
Manufacturing	17,928	5.1	107,000	15.0
Construction	31,787	9.1		
Public utilities	1,725	0.5		
Transp. and commun.	4,550	1.3		
Trade	38,694	11.1		
Finance	36,045	10.3	179,000	25.0
Pub. admin., defense	48,467	13.9		
Services	3,475	1.0		
Other	82,607§	23.7§		
TOTAL	348,458 ‖	100.0¶	716,000⌀	100.0

Public debt (external, outstanding; 1983): U.S.$145,200,000.
Tourism (1981): number of tourists entered 153,528.
Population economically active (1984): total 757,000; participation rate of total population 51.7% (female [1978–79] 46.1%, unemployed [1978–79] 2.2%).

Price and earnings indexes (1980 = 100)

	1979	1980	1981	1982	1983	1984	1985
Consumer price index	86.4	100.0	114.9	125.9	147.1	164.0	183.6§
Monthly earnings index	...	...	...	...	...	...	...

Household income and expenditure. Average household size (1980) 4.4; average annual income per household (1979–80) M1,550 (U.S.$1,150); sources of income (1978–79): agriculture 49.2%, wages and salaries 42.0% (of which migrant workers' remittances 32.4%), home industry 2.4%, other 6.4%; expenditure (1973): food 34.0%, clothing 19.3%, housing 9.7%, transportation 9.5%, education 4.1%, health 1.8%.
Land use (1983): meadows and pastures 65.9%; agricultural and under permanent cultivation 9.8%; other 24.3%.

Foreign trade◻

Balance of trade (current prices)

	1978	1979	1980	1981	1982	1983
M'000,000	−198.0	−251.2	−298.3	−384.6	−504.8	−596.1
% of total	78.1%	76.8%	76.7%	81.7%	86.6%	92.0%

Imports (1981): M439,375,000 (manufactured goods [excluding chemicals, machinery, and transport equipment] 37.4%, of which clothing 8.4%, blankets and traveling rugs 3.6%, footwear 3.3%; food and live animals 18.9%, of which cereals [all forms] 5.9%, sugar [all forms] 2.6%; machinery and transport equipment 17.0%, of which trucks and vans 3.5%; petroleum products 8.6%). *Major import sources:* Customs Union of Southern Africa 97.1%; European Economic Community 1.5%.
Exports (1981): M43,124,000 (diamonds 42.1%; food and live animals 10.3%; umbrellas, brooms, brushes, and basketwork 8.1%; mohair 8.0%; road vehicles 3.1%; footwear 3.0%). *Major export destinations:* Customs Union of Southern Africa 46.7%; Switzerland 41.8%; West Germany 7.0%.

Transport and communications

Transport. Railroads (1984): length 1 mi, 2 km. Roads (1983): total length 2,363 mi, 3,803 km (paved 11%). Vehicles (1982): passenger cars 5,129; trucks and buses 11,962. Merchant marine (1984): vessels (100 gross tons and over) none. Air transport (1981): passenger-mi 8,000,000, passenger-km 13,000,000; short ton-mi cargo 70,000, metric ton-km cargo 100,000; airports (1985) with scheduled flights 15.
Communications. Daily newspapers (1984): total number 3; total circulation 44,000; circulation per 1,000 population 30. Radio (1984): total number of receivers 42,000 (1 per 35 persons). Television (1984): none. Telephones (1981): 7,910 (1 per 173 persons).

Education and health

Education (1982)

	schools	teachers	students	student/teacher ratio
Primary (age 6–12)	1,103	5,295	277,945	52.5
Secondary (age 13–17)	108	1,368	27,799	20.3
Voc., teacher tr.	12	196◇	2,054	...
Higher◇	1	149	1,091	7.3

Educational attainment (1976). Percent of population over age 10 having: no formal education 28.8%; primary 64.6%; secondary 2.3%; higher 0.6%.
Literacy (1980): total population over age 15 literate 534,700 (69.9%); males literate 217,500 (57.5%); females literate 317,200 (80.0%).
Health (1982): physicians 114 (1 per 12,265 persons); hospital beds 2,300 (1 per 608 persons); infant mortality rate per 1,000 live births (1980–85) 110.
Food (1980–82): daily per capita caloric intake 2,355 (vegetable products 93%, animal products 7%); 103% of FAO recommended minimum requirement.

Military

Total active duty personnel (1980): 1,500△. *Military expenditure as percent of GNP* (1981): 1.8% (world 5.7%); per capita expenditure U.S.$9.

*Mining activities ended in late 1982 with the closure of Lesotho's one commercial mine. Plans to reopen the mine were being considered in 1984. †1983. ‡April 1 to March 30. §Includes other producers and other adjustments, less imputed bank service charge. ‖ At current prices. ¶Detail does not add to total given because of rounding. ⌀In 1981 about 23% of the total labour force were employed in South Africa; about 140,000 men, representing about 50% of the adult male labour force, were employed in South African mines in 1984. ◊April. ◻Import figures are f.o.b. (free on board) in balance of trade and c.i.f. (cost, insurance, and freight) for commodities and trading partners. ◇1981. △Lesotho Paramilitary Force.

Liberia

Official name: Republic of Liberia.
Form of government: multiparty
republic with one legislative house
(Interim National Assembly [58]).
Head of state and government:
President.
Capital: Monrovia.
Official language: English.
Official religion: none.
Monetary unit: 1 Liberian dollar
(L$) = 100 cents; valuation (Oct. 21,
1985) 1 U.S.$ = L$1.00; 1 £ = L$1.43.

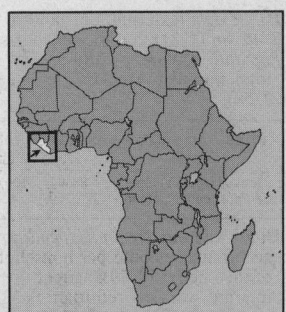

Area and population

Counties	Capitals	area sq mi	area sq km	population 1981 estimate
Bong	Gbarnga	3,650	9,454	230,700
Grand Bassa	Buchanan	5,075	13,144	163,400
Grand Cape Mount	Robertsport	2,250	5,827	78,600
Grand Gedeh	Zwedru	6,575	17,029	91,700
Lofa	Voinjama	7,475	19,360	219,800
Maryland	Harper	1,675	4,338	100,900
Montserrado*	Monrovia	2,550	6,605	625,300
Nimba	Sanniquellie	4,650	12,044	324,100
Sinoe	Greenville	4,350	11,266	76,600
TOTAL		38,250	99,067	1,911,100

Demography

Population (1985): 2,232,000.
Density (1985): persons per sq mi 58.3, persons per sq km 22.5.
Urban–rural (1985): urban 39.5%; rural 60.5%.
Sex distribution (1985): male 49.57%; female 50.43%.
Age breakdown (1985): under 15, 46.8%; 15–29, 24.9%; 30–44, 14.7%; 45–59, 8.7%; 60–74, 4.1%; 75 and over, 0.8%.
Population projection: (1990) 2,571,000; (2000) 3,564,000.
Doubling time: 21 years.
Ethnic composition (1980): Bakwe 26.7%; Kpelle 20.8%; Gere and Basse 14.4%; Loma 8.0%; Mano 6.9%; Gola 6.9%; Liberians 1.3%; other 15.0%.
Religious affiliation (1983): traditional beliefs 75%; Muslim 15%; Christian 10%.
Major cities (1980): Monrovia 243,243; Yekepa 14,189†; Tubmanburg 14,089†; Gbarnga 10,860.

Vital statistics

Birth rate per 1,000 population (1980–85): 48.7 (world avg. 29.0).
Death rate per 1,000 population (1980–85): 17.2 (world avg. 11.0).
Natural increase rate per 1,000 population (1980–85): 31.5 (world avg. 18.0).
Total fertility rate (avg. births per childbearing woman; 1980–85): 6.9.
Marriage rate per 1,000 population: n.a.
Divorce rate per 1,000 population: n.a.
Life expectancy at birth (1980–85): male 47.4 years; female 50.7 years.
Major causes of death per 100,000 population‡ (1981): complications during pregnancy 613.8; diarrheal dysentery 257.7; malaria 174.6; pneumonia 168.4; anemia 73.7; measles 49.4.

National economy

Budget (1983–84). Revenue: L$306,000,000 (income and wealth taxes 32.8%; development grants 19.3%; import duties 18.6%; excise tax 11.8%; tax on foreign vessels 9.2%). Expenditures: L$348,400,000 (current expenditure 68.3%, of which wages and salaries 34.8%, interest on public debt 15.8%, goods and services 10.6%, subsidies and grants 7.2%; development expenditure 31.7%).
Public debt (external, outstanding; 1983): U.S.$699,100,000.
Tourism: n.a.
Production (metric tons except as noted). Agriculture, forestry, fishing (1984): cassava 300,000, rice 230,000, sugarcane 155,000, bananas 79,000, natural rubber 78,000, plantains 33,000, sweet potatoes 17,000, green coffee 12,000, oranges 7,000, pineapples 7,000, cocoa beans 6,000; livestock (number of live animals) 235,000 sheep, 234,000 goats, 120,000 pigs, 42,000 cattle, 3,000,000 chickens; roundwood 4,580,000 cu m§; fish catch 13,553§. Mining and quarrying (1983): iron ore 14,937,000; diamonds 400,000 carats; gold 25,000 troy oz. Manufacturing (1982): cement 79,000; palm oil 20,000; cigarettes 20,000,000 units; beer 161,000 hectolitres ‖ . Construction: n.a. Energy production (consumption): electricity (kW-hr; 1983) 1,100,000,000 (1,100,000,000); coal, none (n.a.); crude petroleum (barrels; 1983) none (4,670,000); petroleum products (metric tons; 1983) 622,000 (503,000); natural gas, none (n.a.).
Population economically active (1981): total 1,232,387; participation rate of total population 62.5% (female 31.4%, unemployed 7.6%).

Price and earnings indexes (1980 = 100)

	1979	1980	1981	1982	1983	1984	1985
Consumer price index	87.2	100.0	107.6	114.0	117.2	118.6	118.7¶
Monthly earnings index	...	...	...	...	...	...	...

Household income and expenditure. Average household size (1980) 4.9; income per household: n.a.; source of income: n.a.; expenditure (1979): food 34.3%, rent 14.9%, clothing and footwear 13.8%, household goods and services 6.1%, beverages and tobacco 5.7%, fuel and light 5.0%.

Gross national product (at current market prices; 1983): U.S.$990,000,000 (U.S.$470 per capita).

Structure of gross domestic product and labour force

	1981 in value L$'000,000	% of total value	labour force♀	% of labour force
Agriculture	118.3	13.6	515,000	79.3
Mining	131.4	15.1	20,000	3.1
Manufacturing	68.3	7.8	11,000	1.7
Construction	30.1	3.5	7,500	1.2
Public utilities	19.1	2.2	1,500	0.2
Transportation and communication	56.8	6.5	12,000	1.8
Trade	74.2	8.5	32,000	4.9
Finance	79.4	9.1	} 32,000	4.9
Pub. admin., defense	155.8	17.9		
Services	28.4	3.3		
Other	109.1	12.5	18,500	2.9
TOTAL	870.9§	100.0	649,500	100.0

Land use (1983): forested 39.0%; meadows and pastures 2.5%; agricultural and under permanent cultivation 3.9%; other 54.6%□.

Foreign trade

Balance of trade (current prices)

	1978	1979	1980	1981	1982	1983
L$'000,000	+66.9	+76.1	+114.4	+120.8	+105.5	+54.6
% of total	7.1%	7.6%	10.5%	12.9%	12.4%	6.8%

Imports (1983): L$411,622,000 (machinery and transportation equipment 26.5%, food and live animals 22.6%, petroleum and petroleum products 21.6%, basic manufactures 17.0%, miscellaneous manufactured articles 5.9%, chemicals 4.9%, beverages and tobacco 2.2%, animal and vegetable oils 1.3%). *Major import sources* (1982): United States 27.8%; West Germany 10.0%; The Netherlands 7.3%; Japan 6.2%; United Kingdom 4.2%; France 2.6%; China 2.2%; Norway 2.0%; Sweden 1.3%.
Exports (1983): L$427,600,000 (iron ore 62.5%, rubber 17.1%, logs and timber 5.5%, coffee 4.3%, diamonds 4.0%, cocoa 2.7%). *Major export destinations* (1982): West Germany 31.5%; United States 17.5%; Italy 14.4%; France 8.9%; Belgium–Luxembourg 5.8%; Spain 4.4%; The Netherlands 4.2%; United Kingdom 4.1%; Denmark 1.2%.

Transport and communications

Transport. Railroads◇ (1982–83): route length 304 mi, 490 km; short ton-mi cargo 1,421,700,000△, metric ton-km cargo 2,075,700,000△. Roads (1981): total length 6,268 mi, 10,087 km (paved 7%). Vehicles (1980): passenger cars 13,070; buses and other commercial vehicles 12,415. Merchant marine (1984): vessels (100 gross tons and over) 1,934; total deadweight tonnage 121,394,635. Air transport (1980): passenger-mi 10,600,000, passenger-km 17,000,000; short ton-mi cargo 68,000, metric ton-km cargo 100,000; airports (1985) with scheduled flights 8.
Communications. Daily newspapers (1984): total number 3; total circulation 25,000; circulation per 1,000 population 12. Radio (1984): total number of receivers 330,000 (1 per 6.5 persons). Television (1984): total number of receivers 35,000 (1 per 62 persons). Telephones (1983): 8,510 (1 per 246 persons).

Education and health

Education (1980)

	schools	teachers	students	student/ teacher ratio
Primary (age 6–12)	1,151	9,099	227,431	25.0
Secondary (age 13–18)	275	1,146	52,301	45.6
Voc., teacher tr.	6	63	2,322	36.9
Higher	3	190	3,789	19.9

Educational attainment, n.a. *Literacy* (1980): total population ages 15–19 literate 84,800 (45.6%); males literate 61,400 (66.3%); females literate 23,400 (25.1%).
Health (1981): physicians 236 (1 per 8,305 persons); hospital beds 3,000 (1 per 653 persons); infant mortality rate per 1,000 live births 151.5.
Food (1980–82): daily per capita caloric intake 2,261 (vegetable products 95%, animal products 5%); 99% of FAO recommended minimum requirement.

Military

Total active duty personnel (1984): 5,600 (army 87.5%, navy 8.0%, air force 4.5%). Liberia also had a domestic militia numbering 1,750 in 1982. *Military expenditure as percent of GNP* (1983): 2.8% (world 6.1%); per capita expenditure U.S.$13.

*Area and population of the commonwealth district of Monrovia are included with Montserrado county. †1974 census. ‡Hospital inpatient morbidity rates. §1983. ‖ 1980. ¶March. ♀Employed persons only. ♂At current prices. □Primarily swampy lowland. ◇For iron ore transport only. △Refers to Liberian American-Swedish Minerals Company railroad only.

Libya

Official name: al-Jamāhīrīyah al-ʿArabīyah al-Lībīyah ash-Shaʿbīyah al-Ishtirākīyah (Socialist People's Libyan Arab Jamahiriya).
Form of government: socialist state with one policy-making body (General People's Congress [approx. 1,000]).
Chief of state*: Muammar al-Qaddafi.
Head of government: Secretary-general of the General People's Committee (premier).
Capital: Tripoli.
Official language: Arabic.
Official religion: Islām.
Monetary unit: 1 Libyan dinar (LD) = 1,000 dirhams; valuation (Oct. 21, 1985) 1 Libyan dinar = U.S.$3.38 = £2.36.

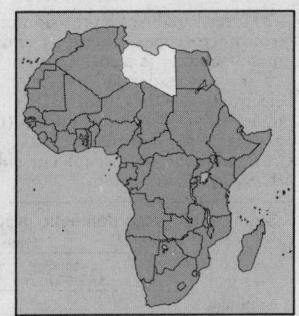

Area and population		area		population
		sq mi	sq km	1984 census
Baladīyāt	**Capitals**			
Ajdābiyā	Ajdābiyā	...	...	100,547
Awbāri	Awbāri	...	...	48,701
al-ʿAzīzīyah	al-ʿAzīzīyah	...	...	85,068
Banghāzi	Banghāzi	...	...	485,386
Darnah	Darnah	...	...	105,031
al-Fatah	al-Marj	...	...	102,763
Ghadamis	Ghadamis	...	...	52,247
Gharyān	Gharyān	...	...	117,073
al-Jabal al-Akhḍar	al-Bayḍā'	...	...	120,662
al-Khums	al-Khums	...	...	149,642
al-Kufrah	al-Kufrah	...	...	25,139
Marzuq	Marzuq	...	...	42,294
Miṣrātah	Miṣrātah	...	...	178,295
Niqāt al-Khums	Zuwārah	...	...	181,584
Sabhā	Sabhā	...	...	76,171
Sawfajjin	Bani Walīd	...	...	45,195
ash-Shāṭi	Birāk	...	...	46,749
Surt	Surt	...	...	110,996
Ṭarābulus	Tripoli (Ṭarābulus)	...	...	990,697
Tarhunah	Tarhunah	...	...	84,640
Ṭubruq	Ṭubruq	...	...	94,006
Yafran	Yafran	...	...	73,420
az-Zāwiyah	az-Zāwiyah	...	...	220,075
Zlīṭan	Zlīṭan	...	...	101,107
TOTAL		685,524	1,775,500	3,637,488

Demography

Population (1985): 3,786,000.
Density (1985): persons per sq mi 5.5, persons per sq km 2.1.
Urban–rural (1985): urban 64.5%; rural 35.5%.
Sex distribution (1985): male 52.72%; female 47.28%.
Age breakdown (1980): under 15, 46.6%; 15–29, 25.1%; 30–44, 16.2%; 45–59, 8.3%; 60–74, 3.2%; 75 and over, 0.6%.
Population projection: (1990) 4,416,700; (2000) 6,538,800.
Doubling time: 17 years.
Ethnic composition (1982): Libyan (Berber and Arab with some Negro stock) 82.4%; foreign nationals 17.6%.
Religious affiliation (1982): Sunnī Muslim 97.0%; other 3.0%.
Major cities (1979): Tripoli 587,400; Banghāzi 267,700; Miṣrātah 52,200.

Vital statistics

Birth rate per 1,000 population (1980–85): 46.0 (world avg. 29.0).
Death rate per 1,000 population (1980–85): 11.2 (world avg. 11.0).
Natural increase rate per 1,000 population (1980–85): 34.8 (world avg. 18.0).
Total fertility rate (avg. births per childbearing woman; 1980–85): 7.2.
Marriage rate per 1,000 population (1979): 6.0.
Divorce rate per 1,000 population (1979): 1.5.
Life expectancy at birth (1980–85): male 56.1 years; female 59.4 years.
Major causes of death: n.a.; however, major diseases are trachoma, tuberculosis, malaria, and dysentery.

National economy

Budget (1982). Revenue and expenditure: LD3,855,000,000 (development 67.4%, administrative 32.6%).
Public debt (external, outstanding; 1982): U.S.$844,000,000.
Tourism (1981): receipts from visitors U.S.$14,000,000; expenditures by nationals abroad U.S.$645,000,000.
Production (metric tons except as noted). Agriculture, forestry, fishing (1984): tomatoes 245,000, wheat 150,000, potatoes 120,000, olives 110,000, dates 98,000, barley 70,000, oranges 45,000, grapes 23,000, peanuts (groundnuts) in shells 14,000; livestock (number of live animals) 4,800,000 sheep, 1,500,000 goats, 200,000 cattle, 135,000 camels, 60,000 asses; roundwood 631,000 cu m†; fish catch 7,500†. Mining and quarrying (1983): gypsum 180,000; salt 12,000. Manufacturing (1985): lime 270,000,000; cement 4,600,000; urea 668,300; ammonia 495,000; methanol 495,000; ethylene 247,500; asphalt 150,000; crude steel 10,000. Construction (gross value in LD; 1981): residential 61,671,000; nonresidential 256,904,000. Energy production (consumption): electricity (kW-hr; 1983) 7,150,000,000 (7,150,000,000); coal (metric tons; 1983) none (1,000); crude petroleum (barrels; 1984) 391,250,000 (43,587,000†); petroleum products (metric tons; 1983) 4,975,000 (5,527,000); natural gas (cu m; 1983) 9,853,669,000 (8,315,962,000).

Gross national product (at current market prices; 1983): U.S.$25,100,000,000 (U.S.$7,500 per capita).

Structure of gross domestic product and labour force				
	1982		1985	
	in value LD'000,000	% of total value	labour force	% of labour force
Agriculture	217	2.5	178,000	16.8
Mining	4,265	48.2	24,500	2.3
Manufacturing	305	3.4	112,000	10.5
Construction	1,054	11.9	256,500	24.2
Public utilities	69	0.8	25,500	2.4
Transportation and communication	387	4.4	93,000	8.7
Trade	523	5.9	41,000	3.9
Finance	...	...	13,000	1.2
Pub. admin., defense	...	...	69,000	6.5
Services	...	...	183,500	17.3
Other	2,026	22.9	66,000	6.2
TOTAL	8,846	100.0	1,062,000	100.0

Population economically active (1985): total 1,062,000; participation rate of total population 29.3% (female 9.4%; unemployed, n.a.).

Price and earnings indexes (1975 = 100)							
	1973	1974	1975	1976	1977	1978	1979
Consumer price index	85.3	91.6	100.0	105.4	112.1	145.0	137.1
Monthly earnings index	...	...	...	...	...	...	...

Household income and expenditure. Average household size (1980) 5.1; average annual income per household: n.a.; source of income: n.a.; expenditure (1977): food 37.2%, housing 32.2%, transportation 9.4%, education and recreation 8.5%, clothing 6.9%, medical care 3.3%.
Land use (1983): forested 0.4%; meadows and pastures 7.6%; agricultural and under permanent cultivation 1.2%; desert and built-up areas 90.8%.

Foreign trade

Balance of trade (current prices)						
	1978	1979	1980	1981	1982	1983
LD'000,000	+1,794	+3,345	+4,674	+2,238	+1,894	+1,348
% of total	42.2%	54.1%	56.3%	32.0%	29.8%	25.9%

Imports (1981): LD2,481,422,000 (food and live animals 16.3%, transport equipment and parts 14.9%, nonelectrical machinery 13.1%, electrical machinery 10.2%, metal manufactured products 9.7%, textiles and clothing 6.2%, iron and steel 5.1%, chemicals 4.5%). *Major import sources:* Italy 30.2%; West Germany 10.5%; Japan 7.6%; United Kingdom 6.9%; France 6.3%; United States 6.3%; Spain 3.0%; Turkey 2.3%.
Exports (1981): LD4,609,851,000 (crude petroleum 99.6%, chemicals 0.4%). *Major export destinations:* United States 27.4%; Italy 23.8%; West Germany 10.3%; Spain 6.7%; Turkey 5.1%; Greece 5.0%.

Transport and communications

Transport. Railroads: none. Roads (1982): total length 12,000 mi, 19,300 km (paved 56%). Vehicles (1982): passenger cars 415.509; trucks and buses 334,405. Merchant marine (1984): vessels (100 gross tons and over) 105; total deadweight tonnage 1,514,077. Air transport‡ (1981): passenger-mi 831,027,000, passenger-km 1,337,411,000; short ton-mi cargo 9,004,000, metric ton-km cargo 13,146,000; airports (1985) with scheduled flights 8.
Communications. Daily newspapers (1984): total number 1; circulation 40,000; circulation per 1,000 population 11.5. Radio (1984): total number of receivers 166,000 (1 per 21.1 persons). Television (1984): total number of receivers 171,000 (1 per 20.5 persons). Telephones (1976): 59,000 (1 per 42.0 persons).

Education and health

Education (1982–83)	schools	teachers	students	student/ teacher ratio
Primary (age 6–12)	2,744	42,202	741,502	17.6
Secondary (age 13–18)	1,555	25,044	301,415	12.0
Voc., teacher tr.	195	3,883	50,363	12.9
Higher§	8	1,340‖	25,700§	...

Educational attainment (1973). Percent of population over age 10 having: no formal schooling (illiterate) 43.1%; ability to read only 8.7%; ability to read and write 32.1%; primary education 9.8%; secondary 5.8%; higher 0.5%.
Literacy (1985): total population over age 10 literate 2,701,446 (74.4%); males literate 1,666,170 (85.0%); females literate 1,035,276 (62.0%).
Health (1981): physicians 4,690¶ (1 per 660 persons); hospital beds 15,375 (1 per 201 persons); infant mortality rate per 1,000 live births (1981) 97.5.
Food (1980–82): daily per capita caloric intake 3,667 (vegetable products 84%, animal products 16%); 156%⸿ of FAO recommended minimum requirement.

Military

Total active duty personnel (1984): 73,000 (army 79.5%, navy 8.9%, air force 11.6%). *Military expenditure as percent of GNP* (1983): 17.5% (world 6.1%); per capita expenditure U.S.$6,608.

---

*No formal titled office exists. †1983. ‡International scheduled flights only. §1981–82. ‖1979–80. ¶Personnel in government services only. ⸿1979–81.

Liechtenstein

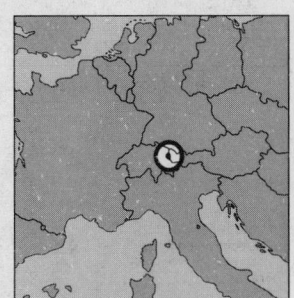

Official name: Fürstentum Liechtenstein (Principality of Liechtenstein).
Form of government: constitutional monarchy with one legislative house (Diet [15]).
Chief of state: Prince.
Head of government: Prime Minister.
Capital: Vaduz.
Official language: German.
Official religion: none.
Monetary unit: 1 Swiss franc (SFr) = 100 centimes; valuation (Oct. 21, 1985) 1 U.S.$ = SwF2.16; 1 £ = SwF3.11.

Area and population

Communes	area sq mi	area sq km	population 1985 estimate*
Balzers	7.6	19.6	3,500
Eschen	4.0	10.3	2,700
Gamprin	2.4	6.1	900
Mauren	2.9	7.5	2,700
Planken	2.0	5.3	300
Ruggell	2.9	7.4	1,300
Schaan	10.4	26.8	4,600
Schellenberg	1.4	3.5	600
Triesen	10.2	26.4	3,000
Triesenberg	11.5	29.8	2,200
Vaduz	6.7	17.3	4,900
TOTAL	61.8†	160.0	26,700

Demography

Population (1985): 26,800.
Density (1985): persons per sq mi 432.3, persons per sq km 167.5.
Urban–rural: n.a.
Sex distribution (1985): male 49.02%; female 50.98%.
Age breakdown (1985): under 15, 19.2%; 15–29, 27.2%; 30–44, 25.3%; 45–59, 14.1%; 60–74, 10.1%; 75 and over, 4.1%.
Population projection: (1990) 27,700; (2000) 29,600.
Doubling time: not applicable; population growth is negligible.
Ethnic composition (1985): Liechtensteiner 64.1%; Swiss 16.0%; Austrian 6.0%; German 4.0%; other 9.9%.
Religious affiliation (1985): Roman Catholic 85.9%; Protestant 8.5%; other 5.6%.
Major cities (1985): Vaduz 4,872; Schaan 4,653.

Vital statistics

Birth rate per 1,000 population (1984): 15.2 (world avg. 29.0); legitimate 93.6%; illegitimate 6.4%.
Death rate per 1,000 population (1984): 6.6 (world avg. 11.0).
Natural increase rate per 1,000 population (1984): 8.6 (world avg. 18.0).
Total fertility rate: n.a.
Marriage rate per 1,000 population (1984): 14.2.
Divorce rate per 1,000 population (1984): 7.3.
Life expectancy at birth (1980–84): male 71.1 years; female 77.8 years.
Major causes of death per 100,000 population (1984): diseases of the circulatory system 213.6, of which heart disease 161.2 (including ischemic heart disease 71.2); malignant neoplasms (cancers) 157.4; diseases of the digestive system 52.5; accidents, poisonings, and acts of violence 52.5; diseases of the respiratory system 26.2.

National economy

Budget (1983). Revenue: SwF260,378,000 (taxes and interest 67.3%; post, telephone, and telegraph 20.0%; other revenue sources include real estate capital-gains taxes and death and estate taxes). Expenditures: SwF252,896,-000 (financial affairs 45.8%; education 13.7%; post, telephone, and telegraph 12.9%; social affairs 9.5%).
Public debt: none.
Tourism (1984): 83,589 tourist arrivals; receipts from visitors, n.a.; expenditures by nationals abroad, n.a.
Population economically active (1985): total 12,456; participation rate of total population 46.5% (female 34.4%, unemployed 0.2%).

Price and earnings indexes (1980 = 100)

	1978	1979	1980	1981	1982	1983	1984
Consumer price index‡	92.8	96.1	100.0	106.5	112.5	115.9	119.3
Monthly earnings index	...	...	...	...	...	...	...

Household income and expenditure. Average household size (1980) 3.0; average annual income per household: n.a.; sources of earned income: wages and salaries 91.2%, self-employment 8.8%; expenditure (1983): insurance 14.9%, rent 12.7%, education and self-improvement 12.7%, food 12.5%, taxes 10.3%, transportation 10.1%, health 5.5%, clothing 4.7%.
Production (metric tons except as noted). Agriculture, forestry, fishing (1983): silo corn (maize) 25,000, milk 10,558, potatoes 400, barley 210, wheat 160; livestock (number of live animals; 1984) 6,260 cattle, 3,575 pigs, 2,265 sheep; commercial timber (1983) 11,291 cu m. Mining and quarrying: n.a. Manufacturing (1983): whipped cream 1,494; yogurt 55; cheese 9; wine 80,-

120 litres; small-scale precision manufacturing includes optical lenses, electron microscopes, electronic equipment, and high-vacuum pumps; metal manufacturing is also important. Construction (1983): residential 187,821 cu m; nonresidential 194,906 cu m. Energy production (consumption): electricity (kW-hr; 1983) 52,280,000 (155,928,000); coal (metric tons; 1983) none (90); petroleum products (metric tons; 1983) none (39,600); natural gas (kg; 1983) none (2,297,762).
Gross national product (at current market prices; 1980): U.S.$523,960,000 (U.S.$20,960 per capita).

Structure of gross domestic product and labour force

	1980 in value SwF'000	1980 % of total value	1985 labour force	1985 % of labour force
Agriculture	...	...	372	3.0
Mining	...	...	53	0.4
Manufacturing	...	...	4,319	34.7
Construction	...	...	1,040	8.4
Public utilities	...	...	121	1.0
Transportation and communication	...	...	365	2.9
Trade	...	...	1,628	13.1
Finance	...	...	745	6.0
Pub. admin., defense	...	...	598	4.8
Services	...	...	2,960	23.8
Other	...	...	255	2.0
TOTAL	876,000	100.0	12,456	100.0†

Land use (1983): forested 18.7%; meadows and pastures 37.5%; agricultural and under permanent cultivation 25.0%; other 18.8%.

Foreign trade

Balance of trade (current prices)

	1978	1979	1980	1981	1982	1983
SwF'000,000	+235.6	+398.0	+454.6	+531.9	+523.5	+560.7
% of total	28.3%	35.3%	34.1%	38.6%	39.3%	41.6%

Imports (1983): SwF393,106,000 (machinery and transport equipment 28.3%; hardware 12.6%; chemical products 6.8%; unrefined and semi-fabricated metal 4.8%; limestone, cement, and other building materials 3.4%; food, beverages, and tobacco 2.1%, of which fruits and vegetables 0.7%; wood and cork 1.3%). *Major import sources:* n.a.
Exports (1983): SwF953,802,000 (machinery and transport equipment 47.1%; hardware 23.2%; other finished goods 20.1%; chemical products 6.7%; limestone, cement, and other building materials 1.6%). *Major export destinations:* European Economic Community countries 37.9%; Switzerland 22.9%; other European Free Trade Association countries 7.7%.

Transport and communications

Transport. Railroads (1984): length 11.5 mi, 18.5 km; passenger and cargo traffic, n.a. Roads (1979): total length 205 mi, 330 km. Vehicles (1985): passenger cars 14,804; trucks and buses 1,631. Merchant marine: none. Air transport: none.
Communications. Daily newspapers (1984): total number 2; total circulation 14,500; circulation per 1,000 population 545. Radio (1983): total number of receivers 8,234 (1 per 3.2 persons). Television (1983): total number of receivers 7,743 (1 per 3.4 persons). Telephones (1983): 23,261 (1 per 1.1 persons).

Education and health

Education (1985–86)

	schools	teachers	students	student/ teacher ratio
Primary (age 7–12)	14	100	1,732	17.3
Secondary (age 13–19)	9	108	1,774	16.4
Vocational§	1	35	75	...

Educational attainment, n.a.; 9 years of formal education are compulsory, however. *Literacy:* virtually 100%.
Health (1983): physicians 20 (1 per 1,325 persons); hospital beds, n.a; infant mortality rate per 1,000 live births (1984) 7.4.
Food: daily per capita caloric intake 3,530 (vegetable products 62%, animal products 38%); 130% of FAO recommended minimum requirement ‖ .

Military

Total active duty personnel: none. *Military expenditure as percent of GNP:* none.

*January 1, 1985. †Detail does not add to total given because of rounding. ‡The index is for Switzerland, which is united with Liechtenstein in a customs and monetary union. §One evening school with part-time teachers. ‖ Figures are derived from statistics for Switzerland and Austria.

Luxembourg

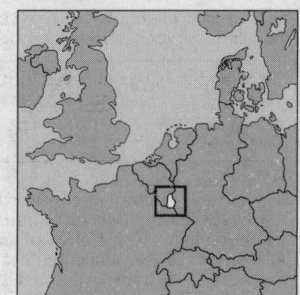

Official name: Grand-Duché de Luxembourg (French); Grossherzogtum Luxemburg (German) (Grand Duchy of Luxembourg).
Form of government: constitutional monarchy with one legislative house (Chamber of Deputies [64]).
Chief of state: Grand Duke.
Head of government: Prime Minister.
Capital: Luxembourg.
Official languages: French; German.
Official religion: none.
Monetary unit: 1 Luxembourg franc (LFr., plural LFr.) = 100 centimes; valuation (Oct. 21, 1985) 1 U.S.$ = LFr.53.42; 1 £ = LFr.76.60.

Area and population

	area		population
Districts Cantons	sq mi	sq km	1981 census
Diekirch	447	1,157	53,363
Clervaux	128	332	9,580
Diekirch	92	239	21,873
Redange	103	267	10,271
Vianden	21	54	2,642
Wiltz	102	265	8,997
Grevenmacher	203	525	38,836
Echternach	72	186	10,653
Grevenmacher	82	211	16,393
Remich	49	128	11,790
Luxembourg	349	904	272,407
Capellen	77	199	27,159
Esch	94	243	114,474
Luxembourg (Ville et Campagne)	92	238	114,228
Mersch	86	224	16,546
TOTAL	999	2,586	364,606

Demography

Population (1985): 366,200.
Density (1985): persons per sq mi 366.6, persons per sq km 141.6.
Urban–rural (1980): urban 78.4%; rural 21.6%.
Sex distribution (1984): male 48.67%; female 51.33%.
Age breakdown (1981): under 15, 18.5%; 15–29, 23.7%; 30–44, 21.2%; 45–59, 18.8%; 60–74, 12.8%; 75 and over, 5.0%.
Population projection: (1990) 375,000; (2000) 400,000.
Doubling time: 110 years.
Ethnic composition (1981): Luxemburger 73.7%; Portuguese 8.0%; Italian 6.1%; French 3.3%; German 2.4%; other 6.5%.
Religious affiliation (1980): Roman Catholic 93.0%; Protestant 1.2%; other 5.8%.
Major cities (1981): Luxembourg 78,924; Esch-sur-Alzette 25,142; Dudelange 14,074; Differdange 8,588.

Vital statistics

Birth rate per 1,000 population (1984): 11.5 (world avg. 29.0); (1982) legitimate 91.9%; illegitimate 8.1%.
Death rate per 1,000 population (1984): 11.1 (world avg. 11.0).
Natural increase rate per 1,000 population (1984): 0.4 (world avg. 18.0).
Total fertility rate (avg. births per childbearing woman; 1984): 1.4.
Marriage rate per 1,000 population (1984): 5.4.
Divorce rate per 1,000 population (1984): 1.7.
Life expectancy at birth (1983): male 68.3 years; female 74.8 years.
Major causes of death per 100,000 population (1984): circulatory diseases 554.8, of which cerebrovascular disease 198.4, ischemic heart disease 149.3; malignant neoplasms (cancers) 261.3; accidents and suicides 39.0.

National economy

Budget (1984). Revenue: LFr.68,484,300,000 (income tax 45.7%; indirect taxes 33.6%, of which value added taxes 16.2%, customs taxes 9.2%). Expenditures: LFr.67,656,400,000 (social security 25.7%; transport and power 21.8%; education and arts 14.0%; debt service 12.6%; administration 7.8%; defense 3.0%).
Public debt (1985): U.S.$760,400,000.
Tourism: receipts from visitors, n.a.; expenditures by nationals abroad, n.a.
Production (metric tons except as noted). Agriculture, forestry, fishing (1983): barley 35,100, wheat 21,800, potatoes 17,200, oats 9,600; livestock (number of live animals) 224,645 cattle, 48,205 pigs; roundwood 336,050 cu m*. Mining and quarrying (1983): metal ores, none; nonmetals 9,600,000, of which stone 4,400,000, sand and gravel 4,000,000, gypsum 400,000. Manufacturing (1984): steel ingots and castings 3,987,000; finished rolled products 3,068,000; pig iron 2,768,000; meat products 20,500; butter 8,100; cheese 2,900; wine 152,300 hectolitres. Construction (1982): residential and semiresidential 417,732 sq m; nonresidential 105,521 sq m. Energy production (consumption): electricity (kW-hr; 1984) 905,000,000 (3,252,000,000); coal (metric tons; 1984) none (297,000); crude petroleum, none (n.a.); petroleum products (metric tons; 1984) none (971,000); natural gas (cu m; 1984) none (261,096,000).
Gross national product (at current market prices; 1981): U.S.$4,470,000,000 (U.S.$12,190 per capita).

Structure of gross domestic product and labour force

	1983		1982	
	in value LFr.'000,000,000	% of total value	labour force	% of labour force
Agriculture	5.6	2.7	7,700	4.8
Mining	0.2	0.1	40,800	25.7
Manufacturing	52.9	25.7 }		
Construction	12.1	5.9	16,000	10.1
Public utilities	5.4	2.6	1,400	0.9
Transportation and communication	11.1	5.4	14,700	9.2
Trade	30.5	14.8	48,800	30.7
Finance	32.9	16.0	9,200	5.8
Pub. admin., defense	23.9	11.6	17,400	11.0
Services	31.3	15.2 }	2,900	1.8
Other	...	... }		
TOTAL	205.9†	100.0	158,900	100.0

Population economically active (1984): total 161,000; participation rate of population over age 15, 53.7% (female [1982]) 33.0%, unemployed 1.7%).

Price and earnings indexes (1980 = 100)

	1978	1979	1980	1981	1982	1983	1984
Consumer price index	88.9	93.8	100.0	109.3	118.2	128.4	138.2
Hourly earnings index‡	87.4	92.4	100.0	104.6	116.9	127.6	137.6

Household income and expenditure. Average household size (1982) 2.8; income per household LFr.751,800 (U.S.$16,455); source of income: n.a.; expenditure (1982): housing 29.2%, food 18.6%, transportation 18.5%, health care 7.3%, clothing and footwear 7.0%, recreation 3.6%.
Land use (1983): forested 31.7%; meadows and pastures 27.3%; agricultural and under permanent cultivation 21.3%; other 19.7%.

Foreign trade

Balance of trade (current prices)

	1978	1979	1980	1981	1982	1983
LFr.'000,000	−8,652	−6,062	−12,704	−17,192	−15,868	−16,492
% of total	5.7%	3.4%	6.7%	8.8%	7.2%	6.9%

Imports (1983): LFr.127,913,000,000 (metal products, machinery, and transport equipment 36.6%, of which electrical machinery 12.8%, transport equipment 9.3%; mineral products 18.4%; chemical products 7.8%; food, beverages, and tobacco 7.6%). *Major import sources:* Belgium 38.1%; West Germany 33.1%; France 12.0%; The Netherlands 3.4%; United States 2.7%; Italy 2.4%.
Exports (1983): LFr.111,421,000,000 (metal products, machinery, and transport equipment 58.5%, of which electrical machinery 8.9%; plastic materials and rubber manufactures 14.2%; textile yarn, fabrics, and related products 6.4%; chemical products 3.3%; food, beverages, and tobacco 3.0%). *Major export destinations:* West Germany 29.8%; Belgium 16.7%; France 15.4%; The Netherlands 6.1%; United States 4.0%; Italy 3.5%.

Transport and communications

Transport. Railroads (1984): length 168 mi, 270 km; passenger-mi 177,000,000, passenger-km 285,000,000; short ton-mi cargo 400,000,000, metric ton-km cargo 584,000,000. Roads (1984): total length 3,204 mi, 5,157 km (paved 99%). Vehicles (1985): passenger cars 151,640; trucks and buses 13,691. Merchant marine: vessels (100 gross tons and over) n.a.; total deadweight tonnage, n.a. Air transport (1984): passenger arrivals 377,000, departures 405,000; cargo loaded and unloaded 74,648 metric tons; airports (1985) with scheduled flights 1.
Communications. Daily newspapers (1983): total number 6; total circulation 130,000; circulation per 1,000 population 365. Radio (1984): total number of receivers 227,000 (1 per 1.6 persons). Television (1984): total number of receivers 91,200 (1 per 4.0 persons). Telephones (1984): 147,074 (1 per 2.5 persons).

Education and health

Education (1984–85)

	schools	teachers§	students	student/ teacher ratio
Primary (age 6–15)	...	1,685	21,979	...
Secondary (age 12–18)	...		8,705	...
Voc., teacher tr.	...	3,482 ‖	16,571	...
Higher	...		785	...

Educational attainment, n.a. *Literacy* (1983): virtually 100% literate.
Health (1983): physicians 627 (1 per 604 persons); hospital beds 4,740 (1 per 76 persons); infant mortality rate per 1,000 live births (1983) 11.2.
Food (1980–82): daily per capita caloric intake¶ 3,668; (vegetable products 59%, animal products 41%); 142% of FAO recommended minimum requirement.

Military

Total active duty personnel (1983): 720 (army 100.0%). *Military expenditure as percent of GNP* (1983): 0.7% (world 6.1%); per capita expenditure U.S.$85.

*1984. †At factor cost and current prices. ‡Manufacturing only. §1982–83. ‖ Includes part-time teachers. ¶Figures for Belgium–Luxembourg.

Macau

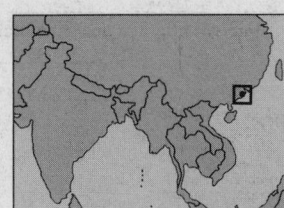

Official name: Macau.
Political status: overseas territory
(Portugal).
Head of state and government:
Governor (appointed).
Capital: Macau.
Official language: Portuguese.
Official religion: Roman Catholicism.
Monetary unit: 1 pataca* = 100 avos;
valuation (Oct. 21, 1985)
1 U.S.$ = 8.10 patacas; 1 £ = 11.62
patacas.

Area and population		area		population
		sq mi	sq km	1981 census
Districts Parishes	Capital			
Marine Area	—	—	—	13,011
Islands		3.9	10.1	9,478
São Francisco Xavier (Coloane)	—	1.4	3.5	4,082
Nossa Senhora Carmo (Taipa)		2.5	6.6	5,396
Macau	Macau	2.1	5.4†	225,337
Santo António	—	0.3	0.9	78,325
São Lázaro	—	0.3	0.8	20,787
São Lourenço	—	0.3	0.8	38,941
Sé	—	0.4	1.0	28,495
Nossa Senhora Fátima	—	0.8	2.0	58,789
TOTAL		6.0	15.5	247,826

Demography

Population (1985 est.): 314,000.
Density (1985): persons per sq mi 52,333, persons per sq km 20,258.
Urban–rural (1981): urban 94.9%‡.
Sex distribution (1981): male 51.88%; female 48.12%.
Age breakdown (1981): under 15, 22.9%; 15–29, 36.2%; 30–44, 16.7%; 45–59, 12.7%; 60 and over, 11.5%.
Population projection: (1990) 341,000; (2000) 388,000.
Doubling time: 36 years.
Nationalities (1981): Chinese 73.5%; Portuguese 20.3%; English 0.9%; other 5.3%.
Religious affiliation (1984): Buddhist and Taoist 69.9%; Roman Catholic 6.2%; nonreligious 14.1%; other 9.8%.
Major city (1981): Macau 223,581.

Vital statistics

Birth rate per 1,000 population (1984): 19.4 (world avg. 29.0).
Death rate per 1,000 population (1984): 4.6 (world avg. 11.0).
Natural increase rate per 1,000 population (1984): 14.8 (world avg. 18.0).
Total fertility rate (avg. births per childbearing woman; 1980–85): 3.4.
Marriage rate per 1,000 population (1984): 8.6.
Divorce rate per 1,000 population (1982): 0.1.
Life expectancy at birth (1979): male 68.0 years; female 73.0 years.
Major causes of death per 100,000 population (1982): diseases of the circulatory system 124.9; malignant neoplasms (cancers) 83.4; infectious and parasitic diseases 33.1.

National economy

Budget (1984). Revenue: 1,442,800,000 patacas (1983; direct taxes 25.3%, indirect taxes 14.0%, transitory accounts 9.6%). Expenditures: 1,153,900,000 patacas (1983; security forces 14.1%, health and social welfare 4.6%, education 4.0%).
Production (metric tons except as noted). Agriculture, forestry, and fishing (1984): grapes 4,000, eggs 615; livestock (number of live animals) 5,000 pigs; fish catch 7,014§. Mining and quarrying (1982): granite 656,920. Manufacturing (1983): clothing 27,184; knitwear 13,230; meat 9,021; furniture 2,335; wine 796; explosive and pyrotechnic products 586; footwear 376; optical materials 312. Construction (1984): residential 207,472 sq m; commercial 217,177 sq m. Energy production (consumption): electricity (kW-hr; 1984) 425,000,000 (425,000,000); coal (metric tons; 1983) none (1,000); petroleum (barrels; 1981) none (2,559); petroleum products (metric tons; 1983) none (167,000); natural gas, none (n.a.).
Gross national product (at current market prices; 1983): U.S.$780,000,000 (U.S.$2,560 per capita).

Structure of labour force		
	1981	
	labour force	% of labour force
Agriculture	7,551	6.0
Mining	71	0.1
Manufacturing	56,304	45.0
Construction	9,937	7.9
Public utilities	876	0.7
Transportation and communication	5,776	4.6
Trade	14,134	11.3
Finance	2,191	1.8
Public administration	4,056	3.2
Services	8,714	7.0
Other	15,450	12.4
TOTAL	125,060	100.0

Population economically active (1981): total 127,359; participation rate of population over age 10, 61.5% (female 37.1%, unemployed 2.4%).

Price and earnings indexes (Oct. 1982–Sept. 1983 = 100)			
	1983 ‖	1984 ‖	1985 ‖
Consumer price index	100	112.2	115.9
Earnings index	...	...	...

Public debt: none.
Tourism (1984): number of tourists 4,155,343.
Household income and expenditure. Average household size: n.a.; income per household: n.a.; source of income: n.a.; expenditure (1982–83): food 42.0%, rent 21.2%, education, health, and other services 8.1%, clothing and footwear 7.3%, transportation 4.9%.
Land use (1979): forested 50.0%; agricultural and under permanent cultivation 4.0%; built-on area, wasteland, and other 46.0%.

Foreign trade

Balance of trade (current prices)						
	1979	1980	1981	1982	1983	1984
'000,000 patacas	+196.4	−38.0	−112.2	+38.5	+250.3	+919.4
% of total	5.1%	−0.7%	−1.4%	0.4%	2.3%	6.7%

Imports (1984): 6,385,600,000 patacas (industrial raw materials 51.6%, food and beverages 10.3%, machinery and electrical equipment 7.9%, building materials 6.8%, mineral fuels 6.0%, transport equipment 1.9%). *Major import sources:* Hong Kong 39.5%; China 28.0%; Japan 10.0%; United States 7.0%; United Kingdom 1.6%; Australia 1.3%; West Germany 1.3%; France 0.6%.
Exports (1984): 7,305,000,000 patacas (textiles and garments 70.0%, toys 10.0%, artificial flowers 3.8%, electronics 3.2%, leather articles 2.1%, ceramics 0.7%, fish and seafood 0.8%, furniture 0.8%, optical products 0.7%). *Major export destinations:* United States 30.4%; Hong Kong 20.1%; West Germany 10.6%; France 10.5%; United Kingdom 6.7%; China 5.2%; Italy 3.6%; Australia 1.9%; Japan 1.5%.

Transport and communications

Transport. Railroads: none. Roads (1982): total length 56 mi, 90 km (paved 100%). Vehicles (1984): passenger cars 17,543; trucks and buses 2,153. Merchant marine (1982): vessels 311¶; total gross tonnage 15,288. Air transport: none.
Communications. Daily newspapers (1984): total number 10; circulation, n.a. Radio (1984): total number of receivers 80,000 (1 per 3.9 persons). Television (1979): total number of receivers 59,000 (1 per 4.8 persons). Telephones (1985): 27,716 (1 per 11 persons).

Education and health

Education (1983–84)	schools	teachers	students	student/ teacher ratio
Primary (age 6–11)	77	1,043	31,481	30.2
Secondary (age 12–18)	28	664	11,594	17.5
Voc., teacher tr.	1	25	480	19.2
Higher	4	56	3,968	70.8

Educational attainment (1981). Percent of economically active population over age 10 having: no formal schooling 13.8%; primary education 22.6%; some secondary 27.2%; secondary 20.5%; some postsecondary 13.0%; higher 2.9%. *Literacy* (1981): total population over age 10 literate 127,359 (61.3%); males literate 80,102 (76.4%); females literate 47,257 (46.2%).
Health (1984): physicians (1982) 386 (1 per 772 persons); hospital beds 1,360 (1 per 227 persons); infant mortality rate per 1,000 live births 12.0.
Food (1980–82): daily per capita caloric intake 2,467 (vegetable products 73%, animal products 27%); 107% of FAO recommended minimum requirement.

Military

Total active duty personnel (1982): 1,800 (army 100%).

*The pataca free floats with the Hong Kong dollar and has a parity of 1 pataca = HK$0.96. †Detail does not add to total given because of rounding. ‡5.1% of Macau's population lives on sampans and other vessels. §1983. ‖ March. ¶All registered vessels including barges, tugboats, floating casinos, sampans, dredgers, but excluding barges used for restaurants and recreation.

Madagascar

Official name: Repoblika Demokratika Malagasy (Malagasy); République Démocratique de Madagascar (French) (Democratic Republic of Madagascar).
Form of government: multiparty republic with one legislative house (National People's Assembly [137]).
Chief of state: President.
Head of government: Prime Minister.
Capital: Antananarivo.
Official languages: Malagasy; French.
Official religion: none.
Monetary unit: 1 franc (FMG) = 100 centimes; valuation (Oct. 21, 1985) 1 U.S.$ = FMG537.31; 1 £ = FMG770.56.

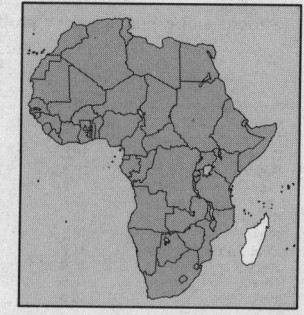

Area and population

Provinces	Capitals	area sq mi	area sq km	population 1985 estimate
Antananarivo	Antananarivo	22,503	58,283	3,195,800
Antsiranana	Antsiranana	16,624	43,046	689,800
Fianarantsoa	Fianarantsoa	39,526	102,373	2,209,700
Mahajanga	Mahajanga	57,924	150,023	1,075,300
Toamasina	Toamasina	27,765	71,911	1,444,700
Toliary	Toliary	62,319	161,405	1,396,700
TOTAL		226,662*	587,041	10,012,000

Demography

Population (1985 est.): 10,012,000.
Density (1985): persons per sq mi 42.3, persons per sq km 16.3.
Urban–rural (1985): urban 21.8%; rural 78.2%.
Sex distribution (1985): male 49.61%; female 50.39%.
Age breakdown (1985): under 15, 44.0%; 15–29, 25.4%; 30–44, 15.5%; 45–59, 9.6%; 60–74, 4.6%; 75 and over, 0.9%.
Population projection: (1990) 11,575,000; (2000) 15,552,000.
Doubling time: 25 years.
Ethnic composition (1978): Malagasy 98.8%, of which Merina 25.9%, Betsimisaraka 14.6%, Betsileo 12.0%, Tsimihety 7.3%, Sakalava 6.1%; Antandroy 54.4%; Comorian 0.3%; Indian and Pakistani 0.2%; French 0.2%; other 0.5%.
Religious affiliation (1980): Christian 51.0%, of which Roman Catholic 26.0%, Protestant 22.8%; traditional beliefs 47.0%; Muslim 1.7%; other 0.3%.
Major cities (1980): Antananarivo 547,139; Toamasina 95,505; Fianarantsoa 83,250; Mahajanga 80,881.

Vital statistics

Birth rate per 1,000 population (1980–85): 44.4 (world avg. 29.0); legitimate, n.a.; illegitimate, n.a.
Death rate per 1,000 population (1980–85): 16.5 (world avg. 11.0).
Natural increase rate per 1,000 population (1980–85): 27.9 (world avg. 18.0).
Total fertility rate (avg. births per childbearing woman; 1980–85): 6.1.
Marriage rate per 1,000 population: n.a.
Divorce rate per 1,000 population: n.a.
Life expectancy at birth (1980–85): male 48.9 years; female 50.4 years.
Major causes of death per 100,000 population: n.a.; however, major diseases are malaria, leprosy, and tuberculosis.

National economy

Budget (1985): Revenue: FMG241,000,000,000 (no breakdown available). Expenditures: FMG436,200,000,000 (current expenditure 71.8%, of which education 15.5%, defense 10.7%, health 5.9%, agriculture 1.9%, public works 0.9%).
Public debt (external, outstanding; 1983): U.S.$1,489,800,000.
Tourism (1981): receipts from visitors U.S.$5,000,000; expenditures by nationals abroad U.S.$38,000,000.
Production (metric tons except as noted). Agriculture, forestry, fishing (1984): roots and tubers 2,866,000 (of which cassava 2,047,000, sweet potatoes 463,000, potatoes 264,000, taro 93,000), rice 2,132,000, sugarcane 1,660,000, fruit 741,000, bananas 224,000, vegetables and melons 302,000, corn (maize) 141,000, coffee 81,000, pulses 57,000, peanuts (groundnuts) 32,000, sisal 20,000, cloves 2,800*, black pepper 2,600*, cacao 2,000, vanilla 500*; livestock (number of live animals) 10,400,000 cattle, 1,800,000 goats, 1,350,000 pigs, 700,000 sheep; roundwood 6,262,000 cu m†; fish catch 54,500†. Mining and quarrying (1983): chromite concentrate 41,598; graphite 13,548; industrial calcite 2,000; mica 1,085; beryl 65,000 kg; celestine 30,000 kg; agate 20,000 kg; jasper 17,000 kg; tourmaline 1,750 kg. Manufacturing (1983): raw sugar 95,822; gasoline 38,536; cement 36,237; soap 10,978; cigarettes 1,780; chewing tobacco 1,442; beer 236,268 hectolitres. Construction (1982): residential 21,400 sq m; nonresidential 7,800 sq m. Energy production (consumption): electricity (kW-hr; 1983) 450,000,000 (450,000,000); coal (metric tons; 1983) none (13,000); crude petroleum (barrels; 1983) none (2,269,200); petroleum products (metric tons; 1983) 199,000 (341,000); natural gas, none (n.a.).
Population economically active: total (1983) 4,544,000; participation rate of population over age 15, 48.0% (female [1981] 44.5%, unemployed [1982] 0.6%).

Price and earnings indexes (1980 = 100)

	1979	1980	1981	1982	1983	1984	1985
Consumer price index	84.6	100.0	130.5	172.0	205.3	225.5	244.9‡
Earnings index	...	...	...	...	...	...	...

Gross national product (at current market prices; 1983): U.S.$2,730,000,000 (U.S.$290 per capita).

Structure of gross domestic product and labour force

	1981 in value FMG'000,000	1981 % of total value	1982 labour force	1982 % of labour force
Agriculture	276,400	35.3	3,335,000	75.0
Mining			89,000	2.0
Manufacturing	113,000	14.4	445,000	10.0
Construction				
Public utilities				
Transportation and communication	304,600	38.8	578,000	13.0
Trade				
Finance				
Services				
Pub. admin., defense	90,000	11.5		
TOTAL	784,000§	100.0	4,447,000 ‖	100.0

Household income and expenditure. Average household size (1980) 4.7; average annual income per household (1981) FMG4,485 (U.S.$1,650); source of income: n.a.; expenditure: n.a.
Land use (1983): forested 22.3%; meadows and pastures 58.5%; agricultural and under permanent cultivation 5.2%; other 14.0%.

Foreign trade¶

Balance of trade

	1976	1977	1978	1979	1980	1981	1982
FMG'000,000,000	+11.3	+14.6	+6.5	−25.7	−17.9	−34.1	−12.7
% of total	9.3%	9.6%	3.8%	13.3%	9.5%	16.6%	5.6%

Imports (1982): FMG148,601,000,000♀ (mineral products 26.5%, of which crude petroleum 19.8%; chemical products 13.0%; machinery 11.9%; vehicles and parts 10.3%; metal products 6.2%; electrical equipment 6.1%; textiles 2.7%). *Major import sources:* France 34.1%; West Germany 6.1%; Japan 5.7%; United States 5.6%; Italy 3.6%; Belgium–Luxembourg 1.6%.
Exports (1982): FMG108,347,000,000 (coffee 30.1%; cloves and clove oil 24.2%; vanilla 15.4%; petroleum products 3.5%; sugar 1.1%). *Major export destinations:* France 24.5%; United States 15.5%; West Germany 9.8%; Japan 6.7%; Italy 2.3%; Réunion 2.2%.

Transport and communications

Transport. Railroads (1983): route length 644 mi, 1,036 km; passenger-mi 173,861,000, passenger-km 279,802,000; short ton-mi cargo 152,507,000, metric ton-km cargo 222,657,000. Roads (1982): total length 9,703 mi, 15,615 km (paved 30%). Vehicles (1981): passenger cars 26,300; trucks and buses 14,245. Merchant marine (1984): vessels (100 gross tons and over) 60; total deadweight tonnage 106,782. Air transport (1983): passenger-mi 239,000,000, passenger-km 384,000,000; short ton-mi cargo 14,400,000, metric ton-km cargo 21,100,000; airports (1985) with scheduled flights 35.
Communications. Daily newspapers (1984): total number 7; total circulation, n.a. Radio (1984): total number of receivers 1,100,000 (1 per 8.8 persons). Television (1984): total number of receivers 15,000 (1 per 649 persons). Telephones (1983): 37,100 (1 per 255 persons).

Education and health

Education (1978)

	schools	teachers	students	student/ teacher ratio
Primary (age 6–11)	8,002	23,937	1,311,000	54.8
Secondary (12–18)	104δ	5,088□	131,836□	25.9□
Voc., teacher tr.δ	126	759	9,213	12.1
Higher	3◇	557	32,599△	...

Educational attainment, n.a. *Literacy* (1980): total population over age 15 literate 2,826,000 (53.0%); males literate, n.a.; females literate, n.a.
Health (1981): physicians 901 (1 per 9,943 persons); hospital beds 21,300 (1 per 420 persons); infant mortality rate per 1,000 live births (1980–85) 67.
Food (1980–82): daily per capita caloric intake 2,522 (vegetable products 93%, animal products 7%); 110% of FAO recommended minimum requirement.

Military

Total active duty personnel (1984): 21,100 (army 94.8%, navy 2.8%, air force 2.4%). *Military expenditure as percent of GNP* (1983): 2.1% (world 6.1%); per capita expenditure U.S.$6.

*Quantity exported, 1983–84. †1983. ‡April. §At current prices. ‖ Includes unemployed. ¶Import figures are f.o.b. (free on board) in balance of trade and c.i.f. (cost, insurance, and freight) for commodities and trading partners. ♀Excludes gold and military equipment. δ1971–72. □1975. ◇1984; two colleges and one university with six regional centres. △1982.

Malaŵi

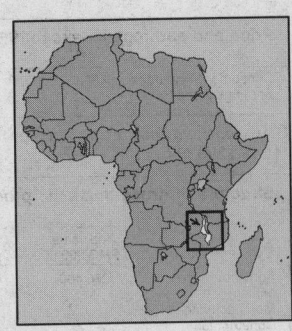

Official name: Malaŵi (Chewa);
Republic of Malaŵi (English).
Form of government: single-party
republic with one legislative house
(National Assembly [101]).
Head of state and government:
President.
Capital: Lilongwe.
Official languages: Chewa; English.
Official religion: none.
Monetary unit: 1 Malaŵi kwacha
(MK) = 100 Tambala; valuation (Oct.
21, 1985) 1 U.S.$ = MK1.69;
1 £ = MK2.42.

Area and population		area*		population
Regions **Districts**	**Capitals**	sq mi	sq km	1985 estimate
Central	Lilongwe	13,742	35,592	2,835,900
Dedza	Dedza	1,399	3,624	395,000
Dowa	Dowa	1,174	3,041	327,300
Kasungu	Kasungu	3,042	7,878	257,500
Lilongwe	Lilongwe	2,378	6,159	931,300
Mchinji	Mchinji	1,296	3,356	209,800
Nkhotakota	Nkhotakota	1,644	4,259	124,800
Ntcheu	Ntcheu	1,322	3,424	299,500
Ntchisi	Ntchisi	639	1,655	116,000
Salima	Salima	848	2,196	174,700
Northern	Mzuzu	10,398	26,931	794,300
Chitipa	Chitipa	1,353	3,504	88,300
Karonga	Karonga	1,141	2,955	131,100
Mzimba	Mzimba	4,027	10,430	368,600
Nkhata Bay	Nkhata Bay	1,579	4,090	129,600
Rumphi	Rumphi	2,298	5,952	76,700
Southern	Blantyre	12,260	31,753	3,428,600
Blantyre	Blantyre	777	2,012	508,100
Chikwawa	Chikwawa	1,836	4,755	241,700
Chiradzulu	Chiradzulu	296	767	219,400
Machinga	Machinga	2,303	5,965	425,200
Mangochi	Mangochi	2,422	6,272	376,100
Mulanje	Mulanje	1,332	3,450	594,500
Mwanza	Mwanza	886	2,295	89,200
Nsanje	Nsanje	750	1,942	135,400
Thyolo	Thyolo	662	1,715	400,500
Zomba	Zomba	996	2,580	438,500
TOTAL		45,747	118,484	7,058,800

Demography

Population (1985): 7,058,800.
Density (1985): persons per sq mi 187.9, persons per sq km 72.5.
Urban-rural (1985): urban 12.3%; rural 87.7%.
Sex distribution (1985): male 48.54%; female 51.46%.
Age breakdown (1985): under 15, 47.6%; 15–29, 25.5%; 30–44, 14.5%; 45–59,
8.1%; 60–74, 3.6%; 75 and over, 0.6%.†
Population projection: (1990) 8,288,900; (2000) 11,630,500.
Doubling time: 23 years.
Ethnic composition (1980): Maravi (including Nyanja, Chewa, Tonga, and
Tumbuka) 58.6%; Lomwe 18.4%; Yao 13.4%; Ngoni 6.7%; other 2.9%.
Religious affiliation (1980): Christian 57.2%, of which Protestant 25.7%, Ro-
man Catholic 25.0%; traditional beliefs 19.0%; Muslim 16.2%; other 7.6%.
Major cities (1984 est.): Blantyre 333,800; Lilongwe 172,100; Mzuzu 70,200.

Vital statistics

Birth rate per 1,000 population (1983): 54.0 (world avg. 29.0).
Death rate per 1,000 population (1983): 23.0 (world avg. 11.0).
Natural increase rate per 1,000 population (1983): 31.0 (world avg. 18.0).
Total fertility rate (avg. births per childbearing woman; 1985): 7.6.
Marriage rate per 1,000 population (1977): 7.8.
Divorce rate per 1,000 population (1977): 1.4.
Life expectancy at birth (1981): male 42.7 years; female 45.4 years.
Major causes of death per 100,000 population‡ (1981): pneumonia 14.7;
measles 11.1; malnutrition 10.4; anemia 8.9; diarrheal diseases 7.9.

National economy

Budget (1984–85). Revenue: MK329,500,000 (surtax 25.8%, import duties
20.4%, corporate taxes 17.3%, income tax 12.4%). Expenditures: MK363,-
000,000 (debt charges 36.2%, goods and services 27.3%, wages 24.7%).
Public debt (external, outstanding; 1983): U.S.$718,600,000.
Tourism (1983): receipts from visitors U.S.$6,800,000; expenditures by na-
tionals abroad, n.a.
Production (metric tons except as noted). Agriculture (1984): sugarcane
1,670,000, corn (maize) 1,400,000, peanuts (groundnuts) 180,000, sorghum
140,000, potatoes 122,000, tobacco 70,000, tea 34,000; livestock (number
of live animals) 910,000 cattle, 770,000 goats, 220,000 pigs, 89,000 sheep;
roundwood 6,468,000 cu m§; fish catch 58,416§. Mining and quarrying
(1983): limestone 109,000; cement 70,000. Manufacturing (1982): beer 657,-
000,000 hectolitres; cigarettes 743,000,000 units. Construction (value in MK;
1982) ‖ : residential 3,120,000; nonresidential 6,467,000. Energy production
(consumption): electricity (kW-hr; 1984) 467,460,000 (406,040,000); coal
(metric tons; 1983) none (45,000); crude petroleum, none (none); petroleum
products (metric tons; 1983) none (134,000); natural gas, none (n.a.).
Gross national product (at current market prices; 1983): U.S.$1,390,000,000
(U.S.$210 per capita).

Structure of gross domestic product and labour force				
	1983		**1982**	
	in value MK'000,000	% of total value	labour force¶	% of labour force
Agriculture⁹	330.1	39.5	179,215	52.1
Mining	...	...	609	0.2
Manufacturing	103.3	12.4	31,397	9.1
Construction	36.8	4.4	24,725	7.2
Public utilities	16.8	2.0	4,272	1.2
Transportation and communication	45.7	5.5	16,729	4.9
Trade	148.1	17.7	21,812	6.3
Finance	40.9	4.9	10,036	2.9
Public administration	91.9	11.0	} 55,257	16.1
Services	30.9	3.7		
Other	−8.9δ	−1.1δ		
TOTAL	835.6□	100.0	344,052	100.0

Population economically active (1984): total 2,967,000◊; participation rate of
population over age 15, 80.2% (female [1977] 46.2%, unemployed [1977]
1.9%).

Price and earnings indexes (1980 = 100)						
	1978	1979	1980	1981	1982	1983	1984
Consumer price index	75.7	84.0	100.0	111.8	122.8	139.4	167.3
Monthly earnings index	81.5	85.7	100.0	112.9	126.3	...	...

Household income and expenditure (1979–80). Average household size△ 4.5;
income per household MK1,934 (U.S.$2,419†); sources of income: wages
83.3%, household enterprise 6.0%; expenditure: food 23.7%, transportation and communication 13.7%, household equipment 9.9%, clothing and
footwear 8.0%, housing 7.6%.
Land use (1983): forested 44.0%; meadows and pastures 19.6%; agricultural
and under permanent cultivation 24.9%; other 11.5%.

Foreign trade⊕

Balance of trade (current prices)						
	1979	1980	1981	1982	1983	1984
MK'000,000	−103.7	−82.9	−31.7	−26.5	−54.0	+72.0
% of total	22.2%	15.2%	6.1%	4.9%	9.2%	9.4%

Imports (1983): MK363,752,000 (gasoline 12.2%, fertilizers 8.9%, road vehi-
cles 4.7%, medicinal products 2.0%, dairy products 0.9%). *Major import
sources:* South Africa 38.8%; United Kingdom 13.4%; West Germany 7.9%;
Japan 6.8%; Zimbabwe 5.5%.
Exports (1983): MK265,167,000 (tobacco 51.6%, tea 21.1%, sugar 10.2%, corn
4.2%, beans and peas 3.6%, unbleached cotton fabric 2.0%, peanuts 1.1%).
Major export destinations: United Kingdom 27.6%; South Africa 8.3%;
West Germany 6.5%; Zimbabwe 6.3%; United States 6.0%.

Transport and communications

Transport. Railroads (1984): route length 490 mi, 789 km; passenger-mi
44,700,000, passenger-km 72,000,000; short ton-mi cargo 82,200,000, metric ton-km cargo 120,000,000. Roads (1983): total length 7,172 mi, 11,542
km (paved 19%). Vehicles (1981): passenger cars 14,102; trucks and buses
17,247. Merchant marine (1984): vessels (100 gross tons and over) 2; total
deadweight tonnage 400. Air transport (1984): passenger-mi 44,700,000,
passenger-km 72,000,000; short ton-mi cargo 822,000, metric ton-km cargo
1,200,000; airports (1985) with scheduled flights 4.
Communications. Daily newspapers (1984): total number 2; total circulation
32,000; circulation per 1,000 population 5. Radio (1984): total number of
receivers 550,000 (1 per 12 persons). Television (1983): total number of
receivers, n.a. Telephones (1981): 15,130 (1 per 412 persons).

Education and health

Education (1982–83)				
	schools	teachers	students	student/ teacher ratio
Primary (age 6–13)	2,411	13,714	868,849	63.4
Secondary (age 14–18)	60	825	17,232	20.9
Teacher tr., voc.**	10	155	2,322	15.0
Higher	4	305	1,849	6.1

Educational attainment (1977). Percent of adult population over age 25
having: primary education 4.7%; secondary 2.5%; higher 0.2%. *Literacy*
(1983): total population over age 15 literate 1,121,934 (31.3%).
Health†† (1982): physicians 121 (1 per 51,461 persons); hospital beds 6,596
(1 per 840 persons); infant mortality rate per 1,000 live births 164.0§.
Food (1980–82): daily per capita caloric intake 2,220 (vegetable products
96%, animal products 4%); 95% of FAO recommended minimum.

Military

Total active duty personnel (1984): 4,650 (army 96.8%, navy 2.1%, air force
1.1%). *Military expenditure as percent of GNP* (1983): 1.7% (world 6.1%);
per capita expenditure U.S.$3.

*Total land area is 36,400 sq mi (94,276 sq km) and is shown for regions and
districts; the total area (both land and water) is shown in the grand total. †Detail does
not add to total given because of rounding. ‡Reported inpatient deaths in hospitals.
§1983. ‖ New construction in the cities of Blantyre and Lilongwe only. ¶Employed
persons only. ⁹Both estate and smallholder agriculture. δLess imputed bank service
charges. □At 1978 prices. ◊Includes 2,402,000 people working in agriculture. △Based
on a sample survey of the city of Blantyre. †Based on end of 1979 conversion
factor. ⊕Import figures are f.o.b. (free on board) in balance of trade and c.i.f. (cost,
insurance, and freight) for commodities and trading partners. **Public only. ††1981.

Malaysia

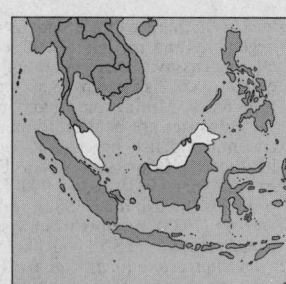

Official name: Malaysia.
Form of government: federal constitutional monarchy with two legislative houses (Senate [68]; House of Representatives [176]).
Chief of state: Yang di-Pertuan Agong.
Head of government: Prime Minister.
Capital: Kuala Lumpur.
Official language: Malay.
Official religion: Islām.
Monetary unit: 1 ringgit, or Malaysian dollar (M$) = 100 cents; valuation (Oct. 21, 1985) 1 U.S.$ = M$2.45; 1 £ = M$3.52.

Area and population

Regions States	Capitals	area sq mi	area sq km	population 1984 estimate
East Malaysia				
Sabah*	Kota Kinabalu	28,460	73,711	1,176,400
Sarawak	Kuching	48,050	124,449	1,442,100
West Malaysia				
Johor	Johor Baharu	7,330	18,985	1,818,900
Kedah	Alor Setar	3,639	9,425	1,233,000
Kelantan	Kota Baharu	5,765	14,931	1,016,200
Melaka	Melaka	640	1,658	511,500
Negeri Sembilan	Seremban	2,565	6,646	631,500
Pahang	Kuantan	13,884	35,960	895,000
Pinang	Pinang	398	1,031	1,029,300
Perak	Ipoh	8,110	21,005	1,976,900
Perlis	Kangar	307	795	162,900
Selangor	Shah Alam	3,072	7,956	1,682,800
Terengganu	Kuala Terengganu	5,002	12,955	617,000
Federal Territory				
Kuala Lumpur	—	94	243	1,076,100
TOTAL LAND AREA		127,317	329,750	15,269,600
INLAND WATER		264	684	
TOTAL AREA		127,581	330,434	

Demography

Population (1985): 15,676,700.
Density (1985): persons per sq mi 122.8, persons per sq km 47.4.
Urban–rural (1980): urban 34.2%; rural 65.8%.
Sex distribution (1980): male 50.16%; female 49.84%.
Age breakdown (1980): under 15, 39.5%; 15–29, 29.1%; 30–44, 16.5%; 45–59, 9.2%; 60–74, 4.6%; 75 and over, 1.1%.
Population projection: (1990) 17,338,000; (2000) 20,615,000.
Doubling time: 30 years.
Ethnic composition (1983): Malay 55.8%; Chinese 33.3%; other 10.9%.
Religious affiliation (1980): Muslim 52.9%; Buddhist 17.3%; Chinese folk-religionist 11.6%; Hindu 7.0%; Christian 6.4%; other 4.8%.
Major cities (1980): Kuala Lumpur 919,610; Ipoh 293,849; Pinang 248,241; Johor Baharu 246,395; Petaling Jaya 207,805.

Vital statistics

Birth rate per 1,000 population (1984): 29.6 (world avg. 29.0).
Death rate per 1,000 population (1984): 5.2 (world avg. 11.0).
Natural increase rate per 1,000 population (1984): 24.4 (world avg. 18.0).
Total fertility rate (avg. births per childbearing woman; 1983): 3.5.
Marriage rate per 1,000 population (1979): 1.7.
Divorce rate per 1,000 population (1979): 0.02.
Life expectancy at birth (1983): male 68.2 years; female 72.9 years.
Major causes of death per 100,000 population (1981)†: heart disease 29.1; infectious and parasitic diseases 19.2; malignant neoplasms (cancers) 18.6; cerebrovascular diseases 14.4; pneumonia 10.6.

National economy

Budget (1985). Revenue: M$21,877,000,000 (income tax 38.7%, import and export duties 23.6%, nontax revenue 10.6%). Expenditures: M$28,591,000,000 (economic development 22.7%, debt service 19.2%, education 16.3%, defense 9.4%, administration 8.7%, internal security 5.9%, health 4.5%).
Public debt (external, outstanding; 1983): U.S.$10,665,200,000.
Tourism (1982): receipts from visitors U.S.$436,000,000; expenditures by nationals abroad U.S.$480,000,000‡.
Production (metric tons except as noted). Agriculture (1984): palm oil 3,717,000, rice 1,755,000, rubber 1,530,000, palm kernels 1,046,000, pineapples 181,000, cacao 93,000, peppers 23,800; livestock (number of live animals) 2,100,000 pigs, 575,000 cattle, 335,000 goats, 255,000 buffalo, 69,000 sheep, 78,000,000 chickens; roundwood (1983) 41,877,000 cu m; fish catch (1983) 741,089. Mining and quarrying (1983): bauxite 501,800; copper 123,400; iron ore 113,700; tin concentrates 41,400; gold 75,912 troy oz. Manufacturing (1983)§: cement 3,231,000; iron and steel products 287,900; bars and rods for reinforced concrete 241,000; sweetened condensed milk 113,800; tin 53,300; soap 46,400; biscuits 45,500; canned pineapple 39,300; cigars, cigarettes, and other manufactured tobacco products 14,500; rubber compounds 12,000; footwear 26,105,000 pairs; rubber tires and tubes 10,280,000 units. Construction: n.a. Energy production (consumption): electricity (kW-hr; 1983) 12,200,000,000 (9,700,000,000); coal (metric tons; 1983) none (136,000); petroleum (barrels; 1984) 181,784,000 (46,220,000 ‖); petroleum products (metric tons; 1983) 5,253,000 (8,658,000); natural gas (cu m; 1983) 1,380,000,000 (2,256,000,000).

Gross national product (at current market prices; 1983): U.S.$27,760,000,000 (U.S.$1,870 per capita).

Structure of gross domestic product and labour force

	1984 in value M$'000,000	1984 % of total value	1985 labour force	1985 % of labour force
Agriculture	7,157	21.3	1,980,900	35.5
Mining	1,638	4.9	63,400	1.1
Manufacturing	6,185	18.4	876,300	15.7
Construction	1,825	5.4	386,800	6.9
Public utilities	876	2.6	¶	¶
Transportation and communication	2,758	8.2	272,300	4.9
Trade	4,597	13.7	773,500	13.9
Finance	2,704	8.0		
Pub. admin., defense	4,410	13.1	895,500	16.1
Services	852	2.5		
Other	625♀	1.9♀	327,000¶⌀	5.9¶⌀
TOTAL	33,627□	100.0	5,575,900	100.0

Population economically active (1985): total 5,575,900; participation rate of population over age 15, 58.8% (female [1980] 33.6%, unemployed [1983] 5.4%).

Price and earnings indexes (1980 = 100)

	1979	1980	1981	1982	1983	1984	1985
Consumer price index	93.7	100.0	109.7	116.1	120.4	125.1	125.6◇
Earnings index							

Household income and expenditure. Average household size (1980) 5.2; average annual income per household: n.a.; source of income: n.a.; expenditure (1980): food 36.2%, housing 24.1%, transportation 16.6%, recreation and education 6.7%, clothing and footwear 4.7%, health 1.3%.
Land use (1983): forested 66.0%; meadows and pastures 0.1%; agricultural and under permanent cultivation 13.2%; other 20.7%.

Foreign trade△

Balance of trade (current prices)

	1980	1981	1982	1983	1984	1985†
M$'000,000	+7,045	+3,141	+1,961	+5,028	+8,954	+367
% of total	14.3%	6.1%	3.6%	8.3%	13.1%	5.6%

Imports (1983): M$30,721,100,000 (petroleum products 7.8%; crude petroleum 5.3%; cereals 2.7%, of which corn [maize] 1.1%, wheat 0.8%, rice 0.8%; passenger cars 2.7%). *Major import sources:* Japan 25.3%; United States 16.1%; Singapore 13.9%; West Germany 5.2%; Saudi Arabia 4.3%.
Exports (1983): M$32,823,300,000 (crude petroleum 24.0%; sawlogs and sawn lumber 12.2%; rubber 11.2%; palm oil and palm kernel oil 10.6%; tin and concentrates 5.2%) *Major export destinations:* Singapore 22.5%; Japan 19.7%; United States 13.2%; The Netherlands 5.4%; South Korea 4.7%.

Transport and communications

Transport. Railroads (1983): length 1,666 mi, 2,681 km; passenger-mi 932,000,000§, passenger-km 1,500,000,000§; short ton-mi cargo 723,000,000§, metric ton-km cargo 1,056,000,000§. Roads (1982): total length 24,084 mi, 38,759 km (paved 65%). Vehicles (1983): passenger cars 974,170; trucks and buses 288,362. Merchant marine (1984): vessels (100 gross tons and over) 429; total deadweight tonnage 2,409,607. Air transport (1984): passenger-mi 3,705,800,000, passenger-km 5,964,000,000; short ton-mi cargo 137,000,000, metric ton-km cargo 200,000,000; airports (1985) with scheduled flights 39.
Communications. Daily newspapers (1984): total number 42; circulation, n.a. Radio (1983): total number of receivers 282,893⊕ (1 per 52.5 persons). Television (1983): total number of receivers 1,672,845⊕ (1 per 8.9 persons). Telephones (1983): 976,500 (1 per 15 persons).

Education and health

Education (1984)

	schools	teachers	students	student/ teacher ratio
Primary (age 7–12)	6,557	83,760	2,148,832	25.7
Secondary (age 13–19)	1,102	54,134	1,245,159	23.0
Voc., teacher tr.	44	1,653	19,701	11.9
Higher	38	6,854	86,368	12.6

Educational attainment (1980). Percent of population over age 5 having: no formal education 25%; primary 44%; some secondary 18%; secondary and higher 13%. *Literacy* (1980): total population over age 10 literate 7,133,775 (75.0%); males literate 3,913,865 (83.0%); females literate 3,219,910 (67.1%).
Health (1981): physicians (1983) 4,234 (1 per 3,510 persons); hospital beds 34,538 (1 per 411 persons); infant mortality rate per 1,000 live births 21.1.
Food (1980–82): daily per capita caloric intake 2,636 (vegetable products 87%, animal products 13%); 113% of FAO recommended minimum requirement.

Military

Total active duty personnel (1984): 124,500 (army 80.7%, navy 8.8%, air force 10.5%). *Military expenditure as percent of GNP* (1983): 8.1% (world 6.1%); per capita expenditure U.S.$160.

*Includes Labuan federal territory. †Medically certified deaths only. ‡1981. §Peninsular Malaysia and Singapore. ‖ 1983. ¶Public utilities included with other. ⌀Includes import duties and bank service charges. ◇Includes unemployed. □At constant 1970 prices. ◇June. △Import figures are f.o.b. (free on board) in balance of trade and c.i.f. (cost, insurance, and freight) for commodities and trading partners. †March. ⊕Licenses issued and renewed.

Maldives

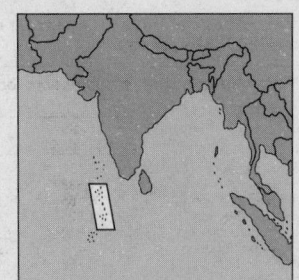

Official name: Divehi Jumhuriyya (Republic of Maldives).
Form of government: republic with one legislative house (People's Council [48]).
Head of state and government: President.
Capital: Male.
Official language: Divehi.
Official religion: Islām.
Monetary unit: 1 Maldivian Rufiyaa (Rf) = 100 laaris; valuation (Oct. 21, 1985) 1 U.S.$ = Rf7.04; 1 £ = Rf10.10.

Area and population*

Administrative atolls	Capitals	area sq mi	area sq km	population 1985 census†
Haa-Alifu	Dhidhdhoo	...	...	9,891
Haa-Dhaalu	Nolhivaranfaru	...	...	10,848
Shaviyani	Farukolhu Funadhoo	...	...	7,529
Noonu	Manadhoo	...	...	6,874
Raa	Ugoofaaru	...	...	9,516
Baa	Eydhafusni	...	...	6,945
Lhaviyani	Naifaru	...	...	6,402
Kaafu	Male	...	...	54,908
Alifu	Mahibadhoo	...	...	7,695
Vaavu	Felidhoo	...	...	1,423
Meemu	Muli	...	...	3,493
Faafu	Magoodhoo	...	...	2,148
Dhaalu	Kudahuvadhoo	...	...	3,576
Thaa	Veymandhoo	...	...	6,942
Laamu	Hithadhoo	...	...	7,158
Gaafu-Alifu	Viligili	...	...	6,081
Gaafu-Dhaalu	Thinadhoo	...	...	8,870
Gnyaviyani	Foah Mulah	...	...	6,189
Seenu	Hithadhoo	...	...	14,965
TOTAL		115	298	181,453

Demography

Population (1985): 182,000.
Density (1985): persons per sq mi 1,577.8†, persons per sq km 608.9†.
Urban–rural (1985): urban 25.5%; rural 74.5%.
Sex distribution (1977): male 51.84%; female 48.16%.
Age breakdown (1977): under 15, 44.6%; 15–29, 24.8%; 30–44, 16.4%; 45–59, 9.6%; 60 and over, 4.6%.
Population projection: (1990) 202,000; (2000) 254,000.
Doubling time: 25 years.
Ethnic composition: Sinhalese; Dravidian; Arab; African.
Religious affiliation: virtually 100% Muslim.
Major cities (1985): Male 46,334.

Vital statistics

Birth rate per 1,000 population (1983): 43.1 (world avg. 29.0).
Death rate per 1,000 population (1983): 10.4 (world avg. 11.0).
Natural increase rate per 1,000 population (1983): 32.7 (world avg. 18.0).
Total fertility rate: n.a.
Marriage rate per 1,000 population (1981): 34.6.
Divorce rate per 1,000 population (1981): 25.5.
Life expectancy at birth (1977): male 52 years; female 49 years.
Major causes of death per 100,000 population: n.a.; however, epidemics of waterborne diseases (including gastroenteritis, cholera, and typhoid fever) occurred in the 1960s and 1970s, and the incidence of leprosy and tuberculosis remains high. Cases of malaria are also still reported.

National economy

Budget (1983). Revenue: Rf137,400,000 (import duties 22.0%; revenue from tourism 17.4%; foreign aid 16.7%, of which nonbudgetary-fund receipts 7.7%, cash receipts 6.3%, food aid 0.8%; charges associated with the airlines industry 11.1%; charges associated with all aspects of fishing 7.3%). Expenditures Rf165,500,000 (president's office and residence 14.7%; main airport 11.5%; Islāmic centre 11.5%; education 9.0%; defense 8.5%; health 7.6%; administration 6.0%; social services 5.7%; reclamation 4.9%).
Public debt (external, outstanding; 1983) U.S.$46,500,000.
Gross national product (at current market prices; 1983): U.S.$56,028,000 (U.S.$334 per capita).

Structure of gross domestic product and labour force

	1983 in value Rf'000	1983 % of total value	1980 labour force‡	1980 % of labour force
Agriculture§	143,760	29.6	35,900	54.9
Mining	6,200	1.3		
Manufacturing	} 22,960	4.7	13,600	20.8
Public utilities			200	0.3
Construction	34,220	7.1	3,100	4.7
Transportation and communication	42,050	8.7	3,300	5.0
Trade	52,370	10.8	2,000	3.1
Pub. admin., defense	75,780	15.6	...	...
Finance	}		...	...
Services	} 108,010	22.2	5,300	8.1
Other			2,000	3.1
TOTAL	485,420 ‖	100.0	65,400	100.0

Production (metric tons except as noted). Agriculture, forestry, fishing (1984): vegetables and melons 17,000, coconuts 9,000, roots and tubers 8,000 (including cassava, sweet potatoes, and yams), fruits excluding melons 8,000, copra 1,000; fish catch 38,500, of which skipjack tuna 19,700, yellow-fin tuna 6,200. Mining and quarrying: n.a. Manufacturing: n.a.; however, major industries are boat building and repairing, coir yarn and mat weaving, coconut and fish processing, lacquer work, garment manufacturing, and handicrafts. Construction: n.a. Energy production (consumption): electricity (kW-hr; 1983) 10,000,000 (10,000,000); coal, none (n.a.); petroleum products (metric tons; 1982) none (7,000); natural gas, none (n.a.).
Tourism (1983): receipts from visitors U.S.$11,000,000; expenditures by nationals abroad, U.S.$3,000,000.
Population economically active (1980): total 65,410; participation rate of working-age (15–59) population 79.8% (female 38.8%, unemployed, n.a.).
Household income and expenditure. Average household size (1977) 6.1; income per household: n.a.; source of income: n.a.; expenditure: n.a.
Land use (1983): forested 3.3%; meadows and pastures 3.3%; agricultural and under permanent cultivation 10.0%; built-on, wasteland, and other 83.4%.

Foreign trade¶

Balance of trade (current prices)

	1978	1979	1980	1981	1982	1983
Rf'000,000	−63.9	−98.6	−119.9	−35.6	−91.2	−269.9
% of total	46.5%	58.9%	50.5%	21.4%	39.4%	58.7%

Imports (1983): Rf 364,600,000 (food, beverages, and tobacco 28.7%, of which rice 6.9%, alcoholic and nonalcoholic beverages 3.6%, tobacco 3.2%; sugar and sugar products 2.5%; machinery and transport equipment 19.4%; petroleum products 18.9%; chemicals 7.4%; wood and wood products 3.6%; steel 2.7%; cement 2.0%). *Major import sources:* Singapore 62.1%; Japan 11.4%; Sri Lanka 7.9%; India 4.5%; Hong Kong 3.1%; United Kingdom 1.9%.
Exports (1983): RF 94,800,000 (clothing and wearing apparel 46.7%; fresh skipjack tuna 28.9%; dried skipjack 5.5%; salted reef fish [including grouper, perch, and snapper] 4.9%; other fresh fish 4.6%; ambergris 2.8%). *Major export destinations:* United States 41.5%; Japan 18.8%; Sri Lanka 15.7%; Thailand 7.9%; Singapore 5.2%; Saudi Arabia 2.8%.

Transport and communications

Transport. Railroads: none. Roads: total length, n.a. Vehicles (1984): passenger cars 310; trucks 107. Merchant marine (1984): vessels (100 gross tons and over) 32; total deadweight tonnage 204,124. Air transport (1983): passenger arrivals 78,819, passenger departures 79,860; cargo loaded 104 metric tons, cargo unloaded 1,599 metric tons; airports (1985) with scheduled flights 1.
Communications. Daily newspapers (1984): total number 2; circulation, n.a. Radio (1983): total number of receivers 15,083 (1 per 11 persons). Television (1983): total number of receivers 2,270 (1 per 74 persons). Telephones (1982): 1,540 (1 per 103 persons).

Education and health

Education (1983–84)

	schools	teachers	students	student/ teacher ratio
Primary (age 6–11)	65	590	42,598	72.2
Secondary (age 11–18)	4	93	841	9.0
Voc., teacher tr.	3	27	206	7.6
Higher	—	—	—	—

Educational attainment (1977). Percent of adult population over age 25 having: no formal schooling 80.2%; primary education 15.1%; secondary 3.9%; postsecondary 0.1%; higher 0.1%; not stated 0.6%. *Literacy* (1982): total population over age 15 literate 62,365 (81.1%); males literate 31,896 (80.2%); females literate 30,469 (82.0%).
Health (1983): physicians 17 (1 per 9,882 persons); hospital beds (1977)♀ 40 (1 per 3,863 persons); infant mortality rate per 1,000 live births 77.0.
Food (1979–81): daily per capita caloric intake 1,983 (vegetable products 91%, animal products 9%); 90% of FAO recommended minimum requirement.

Military

Total active duty personnel: Maldives maintains one security force numbering about 700–1,000; it performs both army and police functions.

---

*Maldives is divided into 19 administrative districts corresponding to atoll groups; arrangement shown here is from north to south; total area excludes 34,634 sq mi (89,702 sq km) of water. †March 25–28. ‡Employed persons only. §Primarily fishing. ‖ Detail does not add to total given because of rounding. ¶Import figures are f.o.b. (free on board) in balance of trade and c.i.f. (cost, insurance, and freight) for commodities and trading partners. ♀In government establishments only.

Mali

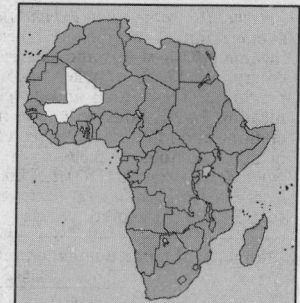

Official name: République du Mali (Republic of Mali).
Form of government: unitary single-party republic with one legislative house (National Assembly [82]).
Head of state and government: President.
Capital: Bamako.
Official language: French.
Official religion: none.
Monetary unit: 1 CFA franc (CFAF)* = 100 centimes; valuation (Oct. 21, 1985) 1 U.S.$ = CFAF402.02; 1 £ = CFAF576.50.

Area and population

		area		population
Regions	Capitals	sq mi	sq km	1985 estimate
Gao	Gao	124,323	321,996	451,800
Kayes	Kayes	76,356	197,760	1,071,300
Koulikoro	Koulikoro	34,685	89,833	1,144,200
Mopti	Mopti	34,257	88,752	1,384,600
Ségou	Ségou	21,671	56,127	1,297,200
Sikasso	Sikasso	29,529	76,480	1,348,200
Tombouctou†	Tombouctou	157,907	408,977	590,300
District				
Bamako	Bamako	103	267	801,500
TOTAL		478,841	1,240,192	8,089,500

Demography

Population (1985): 8,089,500.
Density (1985): persons per sq mi 16.9, persons per sq km 6.5.
Urban–rural (1985): urban 20.8%; rural 79.2%.
Sex distribution (1985): male 48.39%; female 51.61%.
Age breakdown (1985): under 15, 46.0%; 15–29, 25.8%; 30–44, 14.9%; 45–59, 8.7%; 60–74, 3.9%; 75 and over, 0.7%.
Population projection: (1990) 8,825,000; (2000) 11,306,000.
Doubling time: 28 years.
Ethnic composition (1980): Bambara 32.9%; Fulani 12.2%; Senufo 11.5%; Malinke 9.0%; Soninke 8.6%; Dogon 7.4%; Songai 6.0%; Tuareg 5.4%; Dyula 3.2%; Bobo 2.5%; other 1.3%.
Religious affiliation (1983): Muslim 90%; traditional beliefs 9%; Christian 1%.
Major cities (1976): Bamako 801,500‡; Ségou 64,890; Mopti 53,885; Sikasso 47,030; Kayes 44,736.

Vital statistics

Birth rate per 1,000 population (1980–85): 50.2 (world avg. 29.0); legitimate, n.a.; illegitimate, n.a.
Death rate per 1,000 population (1980–85): 22.4 (world avg. 11.0).
Natural increase rate per 1,000 population (1980–85): 27.8 (world avg. 18.0).
Total fertility rate (avg. births per childbearing woman; 1980–85): 6.7.
Marriage rate per 1,000 population: n.a.
Divorce rate per 1,000 population: n.a.
Life expectancy at birth (1980–85): male 40.4 years; female 43.6 years.
Major causes of death per 100,000 population: n.a.; however, major infectious diseases are malaria, syphilis and gonococcal infections, influenza, measles, amebiasis, and strep throat.

National economy

Budget (1983). Revenue: MF190,233,000,000 (current revenue 57.4%, of which capital gains and corporate taxes 14.2%, general sales and value-added tax 11.8%, import duties 10.8%, excise tax 7.5%, sales tax on imports 7.1%, sales tax on domestic goods 4.8%). Expenditures: MF259,069,000,000 (loans and grants 47.6%, education 10.1%, defense 7.9%, economic services 7.1%, social security and welfare 4.6%, agriculture including forestry and fishing 4.2%, health 2.5%).
Public debt (external, outstanding; 1983): U.S.$880,800,000.
Tourism (1983): receipts from visitors U.S.$13,000,000; expenditures by nationals abroad U.S.$18,000,000.
Population economically active (1982): total 3,906,000; participation rate of population ages 15–64, 52.3% (female 17.0%♀, unemployed 1.3%♂).

Price and earnings indexes (1970 = 100)

	1977	1978	1979	1980	1981	1982	1983
Consumer price index□	245.0	327.0	313.0	382.7	429.5	439.4	482.6
Earnings index	...	...	...	...	...	...	...

Production (metric tons except as noted). Agriculture, forestry, fishing (1984): millet 800,000, seed cotton 152,000, rice 125,000, sugarcane 107,000, peanuts (groundnuts) in shell 100,000, cottonseed 96,000, cassava 75,000, sweet potatoes 54,000, cotton lint 54,000, corn (maize) 50,000, wheat 2,000, tobacco 1,100; livestock (number of live animals) 6,000,000 goats, 6,300,000 sheep, 6,000,000 cattle, 800,000 asses, 400,000 camels, 75,000 horses, 14,000,000 chickens; roundwood 4,583,000 cu m§; fish catch 33,000§. Mining and quarrying (1983): gold 13,000 troy oz, salt 4,500. Manufacturing (1985): cotton fibre 67,900; goat, mutton, and lamb 47,000 ‖ ; soft drinks 43,700; beef and veal 39,000 ‖ ; cement 26,000¶; sugar 24,000; molasses 8,400; butter 4,355 ‖ ; beer 17,000 hectolitres ‖ . Construction: n.a. Energy production (consumption): electricity (kW-hr; 1983) 110,000,000 (110,000,-000); coal, none (n.a.); crude petroleum, none (n.a.); petroleum products (metric tons; 1983) none (137,000); natural gas, none (n.a.).
Gross national product (at current market prices; 1983): U.S.$1,110,000,000 (U.S.$150 per capita).

Structure of gross domestic product and labour force

	1982			
	in value MF'000,000,000	% of total value	labour force	% of labour force
Agriculture	388.7	53.1	3,355,300	85.9
Mining	} 53.8	7.3	195,300	5.0
Manufacturing				
Construction	42.1	5.7	}	
Public utilities	4.7	0.6		
Transportation and communication	25.2	3.4		
Trade	120.9	16.5	} 355,400	9.1
Finance				
Pub. admin., defense	} 97.5	13.3		
Services				
Other				
TOTAL	732.9◇	100.0△	3,906,000	100.0

Household income and expenditure. Average household size (1980) 5; average annual income per household: n.a.; source of income: n.a.; expenditure: n.a.
Land use (1983): forested 7.1%; meadows and pastures 24.6%; agricultural and under permanent cultivation 1.7%; other 66.6%.

Foreign trade

Balance of trade (current prices)

	1978	1979	1980	1981	1982	1983
CFAF'000,000,000	−21.2	−25.3	−25.6	−35.7	−33.0	−33.6
% of total	35.2%	28.7%	22.8%	29.8%	25.6%	20.9%

Imports (1983): U.S.$254,900,000 (machinery, appliances, and transportation equipment 35.5%; petroleum products 19.1%; construction materials 11.8%; food products 10.5%; chemicals and pharmaceutical products 10.5%). *Major import sources:* Ivory Coast 25.6%; France 22.6%; West Germany 10.0%; United Kingdom 7.0%; Senegal 4.2%; Japan 2.9%; United States 2.9%; Italy 2.6%; Spain 2.6%; The Netherlands 2.2%; Belgium–Luxembourg 1.9%; Hong Kong 1.2%; China 1.2%; Switzerland 1.0%.
Exports (1983): U.S.$166,800,000 (raw cotton and cotton products 40.9%; live animals 30.4%; salted, dried, or smoked fish 1.2%; peanuts 1.0%). *Major export destinations:* Belgium–Luxembourg 24.6%; France 15.6%; West Germany 10.1%; Japan 7.0%; United Kingdom 5.4%; China 4.4%; The Netherlands 4.0%; Niger 3.7%; Italy 3.6%; Ivory Coast 2.6%.

Transport and communications

Transport. Railroads (1981): length 401 mi, 646 km; passenger-mi 195,000,000, passenger-km 314,000,000; short ton-mi cargo 93,500,000, metric ton-km cargo 136,500,000. Roads (1981): total length 8,080 mi, 13,004 km (paved 14%). Vehicles (1982): passenger cars 20,000; trucks and buses 5,000. Merchant marine: vessels (100 gross tons and over) none. Air transport (1982): passenger-mi 59,000,000, passenger-km 95,000,000; short ton-mi cargo 411,000, metric ton-km cargo 600,000; airports (1985) with scheduled flights 9.
Communications. Daily newspapers (1984): total number 1; total circulation 40,000; circulation per 1,000 population 5.2. Radio (1984): total number of receivers 110,000 (1 per 70 persons). Television: total number of receivers, n.a. Telephones (1983): 9,537 (1 per 789 persons).

Education and health

Education (1982–83)

	schools	teachers	students	student/ teacher ratio
Primary (age 6–14)	1,558	10,912	364,382	33.4
Secondary (age 15–17)	20	...	13,227	...
Voc., teacher tr.	11	890	12,612	14.2
Higher†	7	...	5,792	...

Educational attainment (1976). Percent of adult population over age 25 having: no formal schooling 95.4%; primary education 3.8%; secondary 0.6%; postsecondary and higher 0.2%. *Literacy* (1980): total population over age 15 literate 361,800 (10.1%); males literate 329,200 (18.6%); females literate 32,600 (1.8%).
Health (1980): physicians 319 (1 per 21,890 persons); hospital beds 4,056 (1 per 1,722 persons); infant mortality rate per 1,000 live births (1980–85) 149.0.
Food (1980–82): daily per capita caloric intake 1,749 (vegetable products 91%, animal products 9%); 81% of FAO recommended minimum requirement.

Military

Total active duty personnel (1984): 4,950 (army 92.9%, navy 1.0%, air force 6.1%). *Military expenditure as percent of GNP* (1983): 2.7% (world 6.1%); per capita expenditure U.S.$4.

*In June 1984, the Mali franc (MF) was replaced by the CFA franc at the rate of 1 CFA franc = 2 Mali francs; older data may be reported in Mali francs. †Area for Tombouctou region is estimated as a residue between total reported area and the remainder of the regions. ‡1985 estimate. §1983. ‖ 1982. ¶1980. ♀1976. ♂Urban areas; estimated. □Includes food index for Bamako only. ◇At current prices. △Detail does not add to total given because of rounding. †1978–79.

Malta

Official name: Repubblika ta' Malta
(Maltese); Republic of Malta (English).
Form of government: unitary multiparty
republic with one legislative house
(House of Representatives [65]).
Chief of state: President.
Head of government: Prime Minister.
Capital: Valletta.
Official languages: Maltese; English.
Official religion: Roman Catholicism.
Monetary unit: 1 Maltese lira
(Lm) = 100 cents = 1,000 mils;
valuation* (Oct. 21, 1985)
1 Lm = U.S.$2.32 = £1.62.

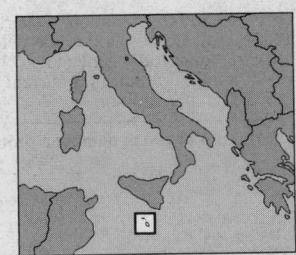

Area and population	area		population
			1984
Census regions†	sq mi	sq km	estimate
Gozo and Comino	27	70	23,800
Inner Harbour	6	15	119,700
Northern	30	78	25,900
Outer Harbour	12	32	86,200
South Eastern	20	53	38,100
Western	27	69	38,300
TOTAL	122	316‡	332,000

Demography

Population (1985): 333,000.
Density (1985): persons per sq mi 2,730.0, persons per sq km 1,050.0.
Urban–rural (1985): urban 85.4%; rural 14.6%.
Sex distribution (1985): male 48.65%; female 51.35%.
Age breakdown (1984): under 15, 24.5%; 15–29, 23.7%; 30–44, 23.5%; 45–59, 15.3%; 60–74, 9.4%; 75 and over, 3.6%.
Population projection: (1990) 345,000; (2000) 360,000.
Doubling time: more than 100 years.
Ethnic composition (1980): Maltese 95.7%; British 2.1%; other 2.2%.
Religious affiliation (1980): Roman Catholic 97.3%; Anglican 1.2%; other 1.5%.
Major cities (1984): Sliema 20,100; Birkirkara 18,000; Qormi 16,900§; Valletta 14,000§; Hamrun 14,100.

Vital statistics

Birth rate per 1,000 population (1984): 14.8 (world avg. 29.0); legitimate 99.3%, illegitimate 0.7%.
Death rate per 1,000 population (1984): 7.9 (world avg. 11.0).
Natural increase rate per 1,000 population (1983): 6.9 (world avg. 18.0).
Total fertility rate (avg. births per childbearing woman; 1980–85): 2.0.
Marriage rate per 1,000 population (1984): 8.0.
Divorce rate per 1,000 population: n.a.
Life expectancy at birth (1983): male 70.4 years; female 73.8 years.
Major causes of death per 100,000 population (1984): diseases of the circulatory system 485.7; malignant neoplasms (cancers) 159.9; endocrine, nutritional, and metabolic diseases of the blood and blood-forming organs 93.9; diseases of the respiratory system 27.6; diseases of the digestive system 27.6; accidents, poisoning, and violence 25.1.

National economy

Budget (1984). Revenue: Lm212,840,000 (national insurance 23.6%, income tax 20.3%, customs and excise taxes 20.3%, property income 9.7%). Expenditures: Lm183,074,000 (national insurance benefits 28.8%, health 10.9%, education 8.5%).
Tourism (1983): receipts from visitors U.S.$148,000,000; expenditures by nationals abroad U.S.$53,000,000.
Production (value added in Lm except where noted). Agriculture, forestry, fishing (1983): vegetables 7,912,000 (of which tomatoes 2,751,000, melons 387,000, onions 223,000), cereals 2,417,000 (of which wheat 929,000, barley 333,000), fruits 1,900,000 (of which citrus fruits 731,000, strawberries 553,000), potatoes 1,617,000; livestock (number of live animals) 53,366 pigs, 12,794 cattle, 3,395 sheep, 1,062,900 chickens; fish catch 1,032,000. Mining and quarrying (1983): quarrying 971,100, of which building stone 968,300. Manufacturing (1983): textiles and wearing apparel 35,193,100, of which clothing 26,684,000, textiles, 4,144,000, footwear 4,020,000; machinery and transport equipment 26,211,800, of which electrical equipment 11,566,200, transport equipment 2,140,800; food and beverages 18,426,000, of which wine, beer, and malt products 4,678,800, nonalcoholic beverages 4,291,500, bakery products 3,076,000; chemicals 7,406,700, of which rubber tires and rubber products 2,826,100, plastics 1,585,000; wood, cork, and furniture 5,738,800; tobacco and tobacco products 3,005,000. Construction (1983): 20,584,800. Energy production (consumption): electricity (kW-hr; 1984) 722,600,000 (722,600,000); coal (metric tons; 1983) none (52,000); crude petroleum, none (n.a.); petroleum products (metric tons; 1983) none (275,000); natural gas, none (n.a.).
Population economically active (1983): total 120,922; participation rate of total population 36.9% (female 24.5%, unemployed 8.5%).

Price and earnings indexes (1980 = 100)							
	1978	1979	1980	1981	1982	1983	1984
Consumer price index	80.6	86.4	100.0	111.5	118.0	117.0	116.5
Annual earnings index	....	....	100.0	108.7	120.2	....	....

Household income and expenditure. Average household size (1982) 3.6; average annual income per household Lm4,736 (U.S.$11,399); sources of income (1984): wages and salaries 48.9%, professional and unincorporated enterprises 17.0%, transfer payments 14.6%, property income 12.1%; expenditure (1984): food and beverages 33.2%, transportation and communication 14.2%, housing 11.6%, furniture and household operations 9.9%, clothing and footwear 7.6%, recreation, entertainment, and education 6.3%, health 3.7%, tobacco 3.6%.
Public debt (1983): U.S.$31,127,000.
Gross national product (at current market prices; 1983): U.S.$1,310,000,000 (U.S.$4,000 per capita).

Structure of gross domestic product and labour force				
	1984		1983	
	in value Lm'000	% of total value	labour force	% of labour force
Agriculture	19,346	4.6	5,478	5.0
Manufacturing	124,706	29.6	34,111	30.8
Mining }	19,660	4.7	1,183	1.1
Construction }			5,809	5.2
Public utilities	24,985	5.9	1,280	1.2
Transportation and communication	23,391	5.5	7,841	7.1
Trade	66,077	15.7	11,234	10.1
Finance	18,631	4.4	3,173	2.9
Pub. admin., defense	56,090	13.3 }		
Services	33,605	8.0	40,530	36.6
Other	34,886	8.3 }		
TOTAL	421,377	100.0	110,639	100.0

Land use (1983): agricultural and under permanent cultivation 43.8%; other (infertile clay soil with underlying limestone) 56.2%.

Foreign trade

Balance of trade (current prices)						
	1979	1980	1981	1982	1983	1984
Lm'000,000	−92.8	−124.9	−125.6	−123.8	−128.1	−149.1
% of total	23.4%	27.3%	26.6%	26.8%	28.9%	29.1%

Imports (1984): Lm330,489,000 (semimanufactures 28.0%, of which textile fabrics and yarn 11.8%, metal and metal manufactures 6.5%; machinery and transport equipment 22.1%, of which electrical equipment 8.3%, power-generating machinery 3.5%; food and beverages 14.3%, of which cereals 2.7%, meats 1.3%, fruits and nuts 1.0%; fuels 12.8%; chemicals 7.0%; tobacco 1.9%). *Major import sources:* Italy 30.7%; United Kingdom 18.0%; West Germany 17.2%; United States 6.0%; France 3.6%; The Netherlands 2.8%; Spain 1.8%.
Exports (1984): Lm181,364,000 (clothing and footwear 35.1%; machinery and transport equipment 22.2%, of which electrical equipment 13.2%; semimanufactures 10.5%, of which rubber 3.1%; printed material 5.4%; food and beverages 5.4%; chemicals 1.0%). *Major export destinations:* West Germany 31.2%; United Kingdom 15.0%; Italy 10.4%; The Netherlands 5.3%; United States 5.1%; Belgium 3.2%.

Transport and communications

Transport. Railroads: none. Roads (1984): total length 823 mi, 1,324 km (paved 92%). Vehicles (1984): passenger cars 77,419; trucks and buses 17,368. Merchant marine (1984): vessels (100 gross tons and over) 195; total deadweight tonnage 2,102,016. Air transport (1984): passenger-mi 351,700,000, passenger-km 566,000,000; short ton-mi cargo 2,648,500, metric ton-km cargo 3,867,000; airports (1985) with scheduled flights 1.
Communications. Daily newspapers (1981): total number 4; total circulation 81,000; circulation per 1,000 population 250. Radio (1983): total number of receivers 150,000 (1 per 2.2 persons). Television (1983): total number of receivers 90,000 (1 per 3.6 persons). Telephones (1983): 98,125 (1 per 3.3 persons).

Education and health

Education (1984–85)	schools	teachers	students	student/ teacher ratio
Primary (age 5–13)	122	1,648	33,987	20.6
Secondary (age 11–20)	66	1,589	22,664	14.3
Voc., teacher tr.	21	443	5,237	11.8
Higher	1	156	1,337	8.6

Educational attainment, n.a. *Literacy* (1980): total population over age 14 literate 261,900 (81.4%); males literate 129,500 (83.4%); females literate 132,400 (79.7%).
Health: physicians (1975) 382 (1 per 794 persons); hospital beds (1980) 3,431 (1 per 93 persons); infant mortality rate per 1,000 live births (1984) 11.6.
Food (1980–82): daily per capita caloric intake 2,918 (vegetable products 72%, animal products 28%); 118% of FAO recommended minimum requirement.

Military

Total active duty personnel (1984): 800 (paramilitary forces). *Military expenditure as percent of GNP* (1983): 1.2% (world 6.1%); per capita expenditure U.S.$35.

*The Maltese lira is tied to the currencies of several principal trading partners. †Malta has no first-order administrative subdivisions; data are reported according to census regions. ‡Detail does not add to total given because of rounding. §1983.

Martinique

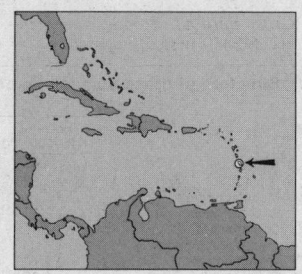

Official name: Département de la Martinique (Department of Martinique).
Political status: overseas department (France) with two legislative houses (General Council [36]; Regional Council [41]).
Chief of state: President of France.
Heads of government: Commissioner (for France); President of the General Council (for Martinique); President of the Regional Council (for Martinique).
Capital: Fort-de-France.
Official language: French.
Official religion: none.
Monetary unit: 1 Franc (F) = 100 centimes; valuation (Oct. 21, 1985) 1 U.S.$ = F8.04; 1 £ = F11.53.

Area and population

		area		population
				1982
Arrondissements	Capitals	sq mi	sq km	census
Fort-de-France	Fort-de-France	141	365	176,749
Le Marin	Le Marin	154	399	78,329
La Trinité	La Trinité	126	327	73,488
TOTAL		421	1,091	328,566

Demography

Population (1985): 330,000.
Density (1985): persons per sq mi 783.8, persons per sq km 302.5.
Urban–rural (1982): urban 57.1%; rural 42.9%.
Sex distribution (1982): male 48.49%; female 51.51%.
Age breakdown (1982): under 15, 28.3%; 15–29, 30.3%; 30–44, 16.2%; 45–59, 13.2%; 60–74, 8.5%; 75 and over, 3.3%; not specified, 0.2%.
Population projection: (1990) 334,000; (2000) 357,000.
Doubling time: not applicable; population growth was negligible during 1980–85.
Ethnic composition (1980): mulatto 94.7%; French (metropolitan) 2.3%; East Indian 1.9%; Creole (Martinique white) 0.7%; other 0.4%.
Religious affiliation (1980): Roman Catholic 91.4%; Protestant (mostly Seventh-day Adventist) 4.7%; syncretist 1.6%; nonreligious 1.2%; other 1.1%.
Major cities (1982): Fort-de-France 96,649; Schœlcher 16,412; Le Lamentin 6,872; Saint-Pierre 4,923.

Vital statistics

Birth rate per 1,000 population (1984): 17.3 (world avg. 29.0); (1983) legitimate 65.1%; illegitimate 34.9%.
Death rate per 1,000 population (1984): 6.3 (world avg. 11.0).
Natural increase rate per 1,000 population (1984): 11.0 (world avg. 18.0).
Total fertility rate (avg. births per childbearing woman; 1980–85): 2.4.
Marriage rate per 1,000 population (1984): 3.9.
Divorce rate per 1,000 population (1984): 1.0.
Life expectancy at birth (1980–85): male 68.4 years; female 73.5 years.
Major causes of death per 100,000 population (1981): cardiovascular diseases 215.7; malignant neoplasms (cancers) 94.4; accidents and murders 46.3; illnesses of the nervous system (including industrial alcohol poisoning) 45.4.

National economy

Budget (1983). Revenue: F1,493,000,000 (receipts from French central government 43.2%, carried over and supplementary receipts 20.2%, taxes on motor fuels 14.9%, new loans 5.8%, receipts from public health and social welfare clinics 3.1%). Expenditures: F1,493,000,000 (health and social assistance 35.6%, infrastructure and public works 24.2%, deferred and supplementary expenses 20.2%).
Production (metric tons except as noted). Agriculture, forestry, fishing (1984): sugarcane 255,000, bananas 185,000, pineapples 23,000, yams 9,000, sweet potatoes 7,000, avocados 6,500, carrots 5,000, tomatoes 4,000, cucumbers 3,000, limes 2,300, anthuriums 55*, other flowering and nonflowering plants 37*; livestock (number of live animals) 72,000 sheep, 55,000 cattle, 40,000 pigs, 26,000 goats; roundwood (1983) 11,000 cu m; fish catch 5,174. Mining and quarrying (1983): pumice 150,000; sand and gravel for local construction. Manufacturing (1984): petroleum products 700,000; cement 189,000; pineapple preserves 7,149, pineapple juice 1,046†, rum 104,000 hectolitres; other products include leather goods, clothing, fabricated metals, and yawls and sails. Construction: n.a. Energy production (consumption): electricity (kW-hr; 1984) 409,000,000 (362,000,000); coal, none (n.a.); crude petroleum (barrels; 1983) none (3,299,000); petroleum products (metric tons; 1984) 700,000 (361,000); natural gas, none (n.a.).
Population economically active (1982): total 125,987; participation rate of total population over age 14, 55.9% (female 45.4%, unemployed 26.9%).

Price and earnings indexes (1979 = 100)‡

	1978	1979	1980	1981	1982	1983	1984
Consumer price index	90.7	100.0	118.5	136.8	150.4	166.6	179.7
Monthly earnings index	87.5	100.0	114.5	137.4	160.1	176.3	192.3

Tourism (1982): receipts from visitors U.S.$89,000,000; expenditures by nationals abroad, n.a.

Public debt (external, outstanding; 1982) U.S.$48,000,000.
Gross national product (at current market prices; 1983): U.S.$1,330,000,000 (U.S.$4,040 per capita).

Structure of gross domestic product and labour force

	1979		1982	
	in value F'000	% of total value	labour force	% of labour force
Agriculture	424,470	7.7	9,844	7.8
Manufacturing	304,994	5.5	5,862	4.7
Construction	168,476	3.0	7,832	6.2
Public utilities	108,159	2.0	1,006	0.8
Transportation and communication	201,102	3.6	5,197	4.1
Trade	791,826	14.3	9,864	7.8
Finance	262,191	4.7	2,063	1.6
Pub. admin., defense	1,739,565	31.4	29,370	23.3
Services	1,009,806	18.3	15,815	12.6
Other, including unemployed	527,475	9.5	39,134	31.1
TOTAL	5,538,064	100.0	125,987	100.0

Household income and expenditure. Average household size (1982) 3.8; income per household (1979) F70,009 (U.S.$17,415); sources of income (1979): salaries 74.2%, industrial and commercial profits 10.0%, pensions and rents 4.8%, income from stocks and bonds 3.9%, noncommercial profits 3.4%, other 3.7%; expenditure (1977): services 36.2%, food 30.7%, goods for current consumption 19.8%, energy and utilities 5.7%, durable goods 4.7%, intermediate goods 2.9%.
Land use (1983): forested 26.0%; meadows and pastures 30.0%; agricultural and under permanent cultivation 18.0%; other 26.0%.

Foreign trade

Balance of trade (current prices)

	1979	1980	1981	1982	1983	1984
F'000,000	−2,303	−3,011	−3,211	−3,819	−4,359	−4,632
% of total	67.0%	73.1%	62.2%	65.3%	62.4%	63.2%

Imports (1984): F5,983,000,000 (crude petroleum and petroleum products 24.6%, food products 20.2%, electrical machinery and equipment 11.7%, chemical products 8.2%, metal manufactures [including iron and steel] 5.6%, textiles and clothing 4.5%). *Major import sources:* France 54.0%; Venezuela 11.0%; Saudi Arabia 5.0%; United Arab Emirates 5.0%; Italy 3.0%; United States 3.0%.
Exports (1984): F1,351,000,000 (bananas 37.6%, petroleum products 29.4%, rum 6.6%, pineapples and pineapple preserves 5.8%, fertilizer 3.8%). *Major export destinations:* France 54.2%; Guadeloupe 35.8%; West Germany 5.6%; French Guiana 1.9%.

Transport and communications

Transport. Railroads: none. Roads (1983): total length 1,130 mi, 1,819 km (paved 82%). Vehicles (1983): passenger cars 134,923; trucks and buses 3,726. Fishing fleet (1984): vessels (100 gross tons and over) 2. Air transport (1984): passenger arrivals 385,900, passenger departures 389,600; cargo unloaded 5,235 metric tons, cargo loaded 4,831 metric tons; airports (1985) with scheduled flights 1.
Communications. Daily newspapers (1984): total number 1; total circulation 30,000; circulation per 1,000 population 91. Radio (1984): total number of receivers 46,000 (1 per 7 persons). Television (1984): total number of receivers 42,500 (1 per 8 persons). Telephones (1983): 83,600 (1 per 4 persons).

Education and health

Education (1982–83)

	schools	teachers	students	student/ teacher ratio
Primary (age 6–11)	297	3,222§	57,532	...
Secondary (age 12–18)	...	...	38,778‖	...
Vocational	...	...	9,854¶	...
Higher	1	40	1,220	30

Educational attainment (1982). Percent of population over age 15 having: no formal schooling 6.1%; primary education 46.2%; secondary 41.8%; higher 4.8%; other 1.1%. *Literacy* (1982): total population over age 15 literate 206,807 (92.5%); males literate 97,538 (91.8%); females literate 109,269 (93.2%).
Health: physicians (1981) 376 (1 per 873 persons); hospital beds (1982) 3,973 (1 per 83 persons); infant mortality rate per 1,000 live births (1984) 8.7.
Food (1980–82): daily per capita caloric intake 2,671 (vegetable products 81%, animal products 19%); 110% of FAO recommended minimum requirement.

Military

Total active duty personnel: n.a.; France is responsible for defense.

---

*Quantity of production for export only. †1983. ‡All figures are end of year. §Public school teachers only. ‖1980–81. ¶1979–80.

Mauritania

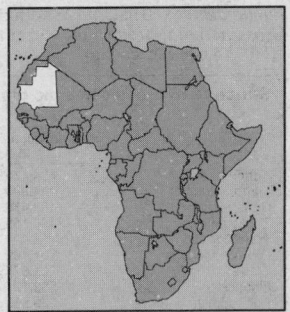

Official name: al-Jumhūrīyah
  al-Islāmīyah al-Mūrītānīyah (Arabic),
  République Islamique de Mauritanie
  (French) (Islāmic Republic of
  Mauritania).
Form of government: military regime.
Head of state and government:
  President assisted by Military
  Committee for National Salvation
  (24).
Capital: Nouakchott.
Official languages: Arabic; French.
Official religion: Islām.
Monetary unit: 1 Mauritanian Ouguiya
  (UM) = 5 khoums; valuation (Oct. 21,
  1985) 1 U.S.$ = UM76.85;
  1 £ = UM110.21.

Area and population

Regions	Capitals	area sq mi	area sq km	population 1982 estimate
el-'Açâba	Kiffa	14,100	36,600	149,000
Adrar	Atar	83,100	215,300	59,000
Brakna	Aleg	12,700	33,000	165,000
Dakhlet Nouadhibou	Nouadhibou	8,600	22,300	30,000
Gorgol	Kaédi	5,200	13,600	163,000
Guidimaka	Sélibaby	4,000	10,300	100,000
Hodh ech-Chargui	Néma	70,500	182,700	230,000
Hodh el-Gharbi	'Ayoûn el-'Atroûs	20,600	53,400	150,000
Inchiri	Akjoujt	18,100	46,800	20,000
Tagant	Tidjikdja	36,800	95,200	80,000
Tiris Zemmour	Fdérik	97,600	252,900	25,000
Trarza	Rosso	26,200	67,800	240,000
District				
Nouakchott	Nouakchott	46	120	150,000
TOTAL		397,700*	1,030,020	1,561,000

Demography

Population (1985): 1,656,000.
Density (1985): persons per sq mi 4.2, persons per sq km 1.6.
Urban–rural (1983): urban 25.0%; rural 75.0%†.
Sex distribution (1985): male 49.48%; female 50.52%.
Age breakdown (1980): under 15, 45.9%; 15–29, 26.2%; 30–44, 14.7%; 45–59, 8.7%; 60–74, 3.9%; 75 and over, 0.6%.
Population projection: (1990) 1,828,000; (2000) 2,229,000.
Doubling time: 35 years.
Ethnic composition (1980): Moor 79.6%; Tukulor 12.2%; Fulani 5.0%; Soninke 3.0%; other 0.2%.
Religious affiliation (1980): Muslim 99.4%; Christian 0.4%; other 0.2%.
Major cities (1981): Nouakchott 150,000‡; Nouadhibou 22,000; Kaédi 21,000; Zouérate (Zouîrât) 17,500§.

Vital statistics

Birth rate per 1,000 population (1983): 43.0 (world avg. 29.0); legitimate, n.a.; illegitimate, n.a.
Death rate per 1,000 population (1983): 19.0 (world avg. 11.0).
Natural increase rate per 1,000 population (1983): 24.0 (world avg. 18.0).
Total fertility rate (avg. births per childbearing woman; 1983): 6.0.
Marriage rate per 1,000 population: n.a.
Divorce rate per 1,000 population: n.a.
Life expectancy at birth (1983): male 44.0 years; female 47.0 years.
Major causes of death per 100,000 population: n.a.; however, major diseases are malaria, typhoid fever, and cholera.

National economy

Budget (1982). Revenue: UM11,466,000,000 (tax revenue 69.5%, of which taxes on international trade 42.8%, taxes on income and profits 16.6%; capital receipts 10.1%; loans 8.7%; subsidies and grants 7.4%). Expenditures: UM11,326,000,000 (administration 56.6%, of which defense 18.1%, education 12.4%; health and social affairs 3.6%; public debt service 12.6%; investments 4.9%).
Public debt (external, outstanding; 1983): U.S.$1,171,000,000.
Tourism (1981): receipts from visitors U.S.$6,000,000; expenditures by nationals abroad U.S.$15,000,000.
Land use (1983): forested 14.7%; meadows and pastures 38.1%; agricultural and under permanent cultivation 0.2%; desert 47.0%.
Production (metric tons except as noted). Agriculture, forestry, fishing (1984): pulses 19,000, millet 15,000, rice 14,000, dates 10,000, vegetables 8,000, roots and tubers 5,000, corn (maize) 3,000, sweet potatoes 2,000, peanuts (groundnuts) 2,000; livestock (number of live animals) 5,000,000 sheep, 3,200,000 goats, 1,300,000 cattle, 780,000 camels, 3,000,000 chickens; roundwood (1983) 53,000 cu m; fish catch (1983) 53,849. Mining and quarrying (1983): iron ore (gross weight) 7,400,000; hydraulic cement 60,000; gypsum 4,000. Manufacturing (1984): meat 43,000, of which fresh beef and veal 16,000, fresh mutton and lamb 7,000, goat meat 5,000; crude steel 7,000; hides and skins 4,900; cheese 1,700. Construction (value added in U.S.$; 1982): 60,000,000. Energy production (consumption): electricity (kW-hr; 1983) 103,000,000 (103,000,000); coal (metric tons; 1983) none (7,000); crude petroleum, none (n.a.); petroleum products (metric tons; 1983) none (198,000); natural gas, none (n.a.).

Gross national product (at current market prices; 1983): U.S.$720,000,000 (U.S.$450 per capita).

Structure of gross domestic product and labour force

	1981 in value UM'000,000	% of total value	labour force	% of labour force
Agriculture	8,545	25.2	353,000	69.0
Mining	2,898	8.5		
Manufacturing	2,249	6.6	40,000	8.0
Public utilities				
Construction	2,141	6.3		
Transportation and communication	2,700	8.0		
Trade and finance	6,024	17.7	118,000	23.0
Pub. admin., defense	5,910	17.4		
Services	...	...		
Other	3,477	10.2		
TOTAL	33,944‖	100.0*	511,000	100.0

Population economically active (1984): total 552,000; participation rate of population over age 15, 62.4% (female 4.3%¶; unemployed, n.a.).

Price and earnings indexes (1980 = 100)

	1978	1979	1980	1981	1982	1983	1984
Consumer price index	82.8	90.3	100.0	119.1	134.1	135.3	144.9
Earnings index	...	...	...	...	...	...	...

Household income and expenditure. Average household size (1980) 5.0; average annual income per household: n.a.; source of income: n.a.; expenditure: n.a.

Foreign trade

Balance of trade (current prices)

	1979	1980	1981	1982	1983	1984
UM'000,000	−3,771	−2,694	+1,178	−530	+4,969	+7,877
% of total	21.9%	13.1%	4.9%	2.1%	18.4%	27.0%

Imports (1983): UM11,013,000,000 (machinery and transport equipment 40.0%, food 25.0%, crude petroleum and petroleum products 18.6%). *Major import sources* (1984): France 21.9%; Spain 19.8%; West Germany 9.6%; United States 7.6%; Senegal 6.9%; Algeria 6.0%; Thailand 5.7%; China 3.0%; Egypt 3.0%; Italy 2.7%; Belgium–Luxembourg 2.6%; The Netherlands 2.5%; Japan 1.4%; Denmark 1.3%; United Kingdom 1.1%; Canada 0.9%; Ivory Coast 0.8%; India 0.8%; South Korea 0.4%.
Exports (1983): UM15,982,000,000 (fish 54.9%, iron ore 45.1%). *Major export destinations* (1984): Italy 24.5%; Japan 22.1%; Belgium 17.9%; France 15.1%; Spain 7.3%; United Kingdom 5.0%; West Germany 3.2%; Algeria 1.5%; Portugal 1.0%; Senegal 0.9%; Greece 0.9%; Turkey 0.6%; United States 0.4%.

Transport and communications

Transport. Railroads (1983): route length 428 mi, 689 km; passenger-mi 7,705,000, passenger-km 12,400,000; short ton-mi cargo 2,967,000,000, metric ton-km cargo 4,332,000,000. Roads (1981): total length 4,685 mi, 7,540 km (paved 18%). Vehicles (1981): passenger cars 11,262; trucks and buses 8,437. Merchant marine (1984): vessels (100 gross tons and over) 40; total deadweight tonnage 7,094. Air transport (1980): passenger-mi 135,000,000, passenger-km 218,000,000; short ton-mi cargo 12,739,000, metric ton-km cargo 18,600,000; airports (1985) with scheduled flights 8.
Communications. Daily newspapers (1984): total number 1; total circulation, n.a. Radio (1984): total number of receivers 95,000 (1 per 17 persons). Television: total number of receivers, n.a. Telephones (1982): 3,161 (1 per 493 persons).

Education and health

Education (1980–81)

	schools	teachers	students	student/ teacher ratio
Primary (age 6–11)	599	2,183	90,530	41.5
Secondary (age 12–17)	...	646	20,248	31.3
Voc., teacher tr.	...	...	1,854	...
Higher	3º	25	1,374º	...

Educational attainment, n.a. *Literacy* (1978): total adult population literate 17.0%.
Health: physicians (1980) 103 (1 per 14,500 persons); hospital beds (1979) 561 (1 per 2,653 persons); infant mortality rate per 1,000 live births (1983) 136.0.
Food (1980–82): daily per capita caloric intake 2,228 (vegetable products 76%, animal products 24%); 97% of FAO recommended minimum requirement.

Military

Total active duty personnel (1984): 8,470 (army 94.4%, navy 3.8%, air force 1.8%). *Military expenditure as percent of GNP* (1983): 5.8% (world 6.1%); per capita expenditure U.S.$25.

*Detail does not add to total given because of rounding. †The percentage of nomads in Mauritania declined from about 80% of the total population in 1970 to about 25% of the total population in 1983. ‡1982. §1977. ‖At current prices. ¶1981. º1983.

Mauritius

Official name: Mauritius.
Form of government: unitary multiparty state with one legislative house (Legislative Assembly [70]).
Chief of state: British Monarch represented by governor-general.
Head of government: Prime Minister.
Capital: Port Louis.
Official language: English.
Official religion: none.
Monetary unit: 1 Mauritian Rupee (Mau Re; plural Mau Rs) = 100 cents; valuation (Oct. 21, 1985) 1 U.S.$ = Mau Rs14.47; 1 £ = Mau Rs20.75.

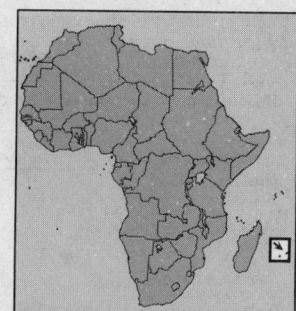

Area and population

Islands Districts	area sq mi	area sq km	population 1983 census*
Mauritius	720	1,865	960,200
Black River	100	259	36,700
Flacq	115	298	107,400
Grand Port	101	262	92,300
Moka	89	230	61,300
Pamplemousses	69	179	90,200
Plaines Wilhems	78	202	301,300
Port Louis	17	44	132,200
Rivière du Rampart	57	148	80,500
Savanne	94	243	58,300
Rodrigues	40	104	33,000
Agelega	27	70	350
Saint Brandon	1	3	150
TOTAL	788	2,041†	993,700

Demography

Population (1985 est.): 1,024,900.
Density (1985): persons per sq mi 1,300.6, persons per sq km 502.2.
Urban–rural‡ (1984): urban 41.7%; rural 58.3%.
Sex distribution (1984): male 50.22%; female 49.78%.
Age breakdown‡ (1983): under 15, 32.4%; 15–29, 32.0%; 30–44, 17.7%; 45–59, 11.0%; 60–74, 5.7%; 75 and over, 1.2%.
Population projection: (1990) 1,117,000; (2000) 1,248,000.
Doubling time: 43 years.
Ethnic composition (1982): Indian 68.0%; Creole 27.0%; Chinese 3.0%; English and French 2.0%.
Religious affiliation (1980): Hindu 46.1%; Roman Catholic 31.2%; Muslim 16.4%; Protestant 1.5%; Baha'i 1.0%; Buddhist 0.6%; other 3.2%.
Major cities (1983): Port Louis 148,040; Beau Bassin–Rose Hill 87,520; Quatre Bornes 56,676; Vacoas–Phoenix 56,011; Curepipe 57,613.

Vital statistics

Birth rate per 1,000 population (1984)‡: 21.1 (world avg. 29.0).
Death rate per 1,000 population (1984)‡: 6.6 (world avg. 11.0).
Natural increase rate per 1,000 population (1984)‡: 14.5 (world avg. 18.0).
Total fertility rate (avg. births per childbearing woman; 1982)‡: 2.4.
Marriage rate per 1,000 population (1984)‡: 10.8.
Divorce rate per 1,000 population (1982)‡: 0.4.
Life expectancy at birth (1980–85)‡: male 63.3 years; female 68.4 years.
Major causes of death per 100,000 population (1983): heart diseases 293.0; respiratory diseases, including pneumonia, bronchitis, emphysema, and asthma 80.2; injury and poisoning 48.2; malignant neoplasms (cancers) 46.9.

National economy

Budget (1984–85 est.). Revenue: Mau Rs3,575,000,000, (import duties 24.9%, stamp duties 11.9%, income tax 11.9%, export duties 11.5%, excise duties 7.6%). Expenditures: Mau Rs4,230,000,000 (debt servicing 38.2%, education and cultural affairs 12.7%, general administration 10.9%, social security 7.9%, health 6.7%, transfers to local government 5.8%).
Public debt (external, outstanding; 1983): U.S.$332,500,000.
Tourism (1983): receipts from visitors U.S.$42,000,000; expenditures by nationals abroad U.S.$13,000,000.
Gross national product (at current market prices; 1983): U.S.$1,250,000,000 (U.S.$1,000 per capita).

Structure of gross domestic product and labour force

	1984 in value Mau Rs'000,000	% of total value	labour force§	% of labour force
Agriculture	1,695	14.4	49,777	26.2
Mining	19	0.2	164	0.1
Manufacturing	1,988	16.8	41,716	21.9
Construction	700	5.9	3,959	2.1
Public utilities	285	2.4	4,084	2.2
Transportation and communication	1,320	11.2	8,191	4.3
Trade	1,660	14.1	8,723	4.6
Finance	2,038	17.3	4,784	2.5
Pub. admin., defense	1,385	11.7	62,796	33.0
Services	710	6.0		
Other	...	...	5,864	3.1
TOTAL	11,800 ‖	100.0	190,058	100.0

Production (metric tons except as noted). Agriculture, forestry, fishing (1984): sugarcane 5,250,000, tea (green) 6,000, potatoes 14,000, tomatoes 12,000, bananas 7,000, peanuts (groundnuts) 2,000, tobacco 1,000, corn (maize) 1,000; livestock (number of live animals) 70,000 goats, 59,000 cattle, 10,000 pigs, 4,000 sheep; roundwood 30,000 cu m¶; fish catch 9,536¶. Manufacturing (1984): sugar, refined 575,600; molasses 150,000; fertilizers 51,796¶; processed tea 8,000; soft drinks 273,000 hectolitres; beer and stout 166,200 hectolitres; rum 50,800 hectolitres; matches 192,200 boxes. Construction (1983): residential 4,196,000 sq m; nonresidential 785,000 sq m. Energy production (consumption): electricity (kW-hr; 1984) 378,800,000 (427,000,000¶); coal (metric tons; 1983) none (1,000); crude petroleum, none (n.a.); petroleum products (metric tons; 1983) none (185,000); natural gas, none (n.a.).
Population economically active (1981): total 332,000; participation rate of population over age 15, 34.2% (female 22.8%, unemployed 18.1%).

Price and earnings indexes (1980 = 100)

	1979	1980	1981	1982	1983	1984	1985
Consumer price index	70.4	100.0	114.5	127.5	134.7	144.6	153.0♀
Monthly earnings index	82.8	100.0	114.3	130.5	143.8	153.6	...

Household income and expenditure. Average household size (1980) 4.6; income per household (1979) Mau Rs15,540 (U.S.$2,430); source of income: n.a.; expenditure (1982): food and nonalcoholic beverages 43.9%, clothing, footwear, and furnishings 10.5%, housing 10.4%, transportation 10.0%, alcohol and tobacco 6.5%.
Land use (1983): forested 31.4%; meadows and pastures 3.8%; agricultural and under permanent cultivation 57.8%; other 7.0%.

Foreign trade♂

Balance of trade (current prices)

	1979	1980	1981	1982	1983	1984
Mau Rs'000,000	−570.9	−560.7	−1,113.9	−183.4	+53.0	−479.8
% of total	10.5%	7.7%	15.7%	2.2%	0.6%	4.4%

Imports (1984): Mau Rs6,485,700,000 (manufactured goods classified chiefly by material 30.0%, food 19.7%, mineral fuels and lubricants 16.6%, machinery and transport equipment 11.6%, chemicals 7.0%, inedible crude materials excluding fuels 4.6%, animal and vegetable oils and fats 3.5%). *Major import sources:* France 11.6%; Bahrain 10.5%; South Africa 8.0%; United Kingdom 7.9%; Japan 6.2%; China 5.9%; New Zealand 3.0%.
Exports (1984): Mau Rs5,180,300,000 (sugar 48.7%, clothing 30.9%, tea 4.8%, fish and fish preparations 2.1%, textile yarn and fabric 1.9%, pearls and precious and semiprecious stones 1.7%, watches and clocks 1.6%). *Major export destinations:* United Kingdom 50.5%; France 17.3%; United States 12.3%; West Germany 5.2%; Italy 2.6%; Canada 1.9%; Réunion 1.7%.

Transport and communications

Transport. Railroads: none. Roads (1983): total length 1,110 mi, 1,787 km (paved 92%). Vehicles (1983): passenger cars 26,082; trucks and buses 17,929. Merchant marine (1984): vessels (100 gross tons and over) 18; total deadweight tonnage 57,455. Air transport (1984): passenger-mi 276,000,000, passenger-km 444,000,000; short ton-mi cargo 5,712,400, metric ton-km cargo 8,340,000; airports (1985) with scheduled flights 2.
Communications. Daily newspapers (1984): total number 8; total circulation 76,000; circulation per 1,000 population 75. Radio (1984): total number of receivers 129,414 (1 per 7.8 persons). Television (1984): total number of receivers 98,130 (1 per 10 persons). Telephones (1983): 47,155 (1 per 21 persons).

Education and health

Education (1984)

	schools	teachers	students	student/ teacher ratio
Primary (age 5–12)	281	6,460	135,391	21.0
Secondary (age 12–20)	128	3,563	73,961	20.8
Voc., teacher tr.¶	7	69□	444	...
Higher¶	2	184□	610	...

Educational attainment (1972). Percent of adult population over age 25 having: no formal education 36.0%, less than primary 32.6%, primary 18.3%, secondary 11.9%, higher 1.2%. *Literacy* (1980): total population over age 15 literate 557,100 (84.6%); males literate 297,700 (90.5%); females literate 259,400 (78.8%).
Health (1984): physicians (1983) 690 (1 per 1,439 persons); hospital beds‡◊ 2,811 (1 per 359 persons); infant mortality rate per 1,000 live births‡ 24.7.
Food (1980–82): daily per capita caloric intake 2,811 (vegetable products 90%, animal products 10%); 119% of FAO recommended minimum requirement.

Military

Total active duty personnel: none; however, a special police mobile unit ensures internal security. *Military expenditure as percent of GNP* (1983): 0.2% (world 6.1%); per capita expenditure U.S.$2.

---

*Preliminary. †Detail does not add to total given because of rounding. ‡Island of Mauritius only. §Employed persons as of March 1984. ‖ At current prices. ¶1983. ♀May. ♂Import figures are f.o.b. (free on board) in balance of trade and c.i.f. (cost, insurance, and freight) for commodities and trading partners. □1982. ◊Government hospitals only.

Mayotte

Official name: Collectivité Territoriale de Mayotte (Territorial Collectivity of Mayotte).
Political status: overseas dependency of France with one legislative house (General Council [17]), one representative in the French National Assembly, and one senator in the French Senate*.
Chief of state: President of France.
Head of government: Commissioner.
Capital: Dzaoudzi (Capital designate, Mamoudzou).
Official language: French.
Official religion: none.
Monetary unit: 1 French (metropolitan) franc (F) = 100 centimes; valuation (Oct. 21, 1985) 1 U.S.$ = F8.04; 1 £ = F11.53.

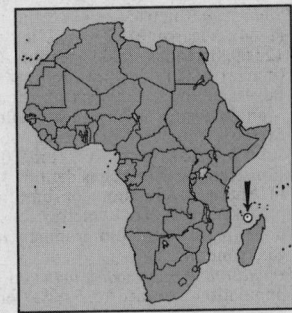

Area and population

Islands Communes	Capitals	area sq mi	area sq km	population 1985 census†
Grande Terre				
Acoua	—	4.9	12.6	2,714
Bandraboua	—	12.5	32.4	3,510
Bandrele	—	14.1	36.5	2,989
Boueni	—	5.4	14.1	3,000
Chiconi	—	3.2	8.3	4,035
Chirongui	—	10.9	28.3	3,380
Dembeni	—	15.0	38.8	2,369
Kani-Keli	—	7.9	20.5	2,785
Koungou	—	11.0	28.4	3,458
Mamoudzou	—	16.2	41.9	12,119
Mtsamboro	—	5.3	13.7	3,978
M'tsangamouji	—	8.4	21.8	3,248
Ouangani	—	7.3	19.0	2,586
Sada	—	4.3	11.2	4,163
Tsingoni	—	13.4	34.8	3,029
Petite Terre				
Dzaoudzi	—	2.6	6.7	5,675
Pamandzi	—	1.7	4.3	4,100
TOTAL		144.1	373.2‡	67,138

Demography

Population (1985): 67,138†.
Density (1985): persons per sq mi 465.9, persons per sq km 179.9.
Urban–rural: n.a.§.
Sex distribution (1978): male 49.94%; female 50.06%.
Age breakdown (1978): under 15, 50.2%; 15–29, 23.4%; 30–44, 13.9%; 45–59, 7.0%; 60–74, 3.8%; 75 and over, 1.7%.
Population projection: (1990) 86,300; (2000) 142,600.
Doubling time: 14 years.
Ethnic composition (1985): Comorian (a mixture of Bantu, Arab, and Malagasy peoples) 96.9%; Europeans 2.5%; Indian Méti 0.4%; other 0.1%.
Religious affiliation (1985): Sunnī Muslim 96.9%; Christian, principally Roman Catholic, 3.0%; other 0.1%.
Major towns (1985) ‖ : Mamoudzou 12,119; Dzaoudzi 5,675.

Vital statistics

Birth rate per 1,000 population (1978): 49.8 (world avg. 30.0); legitimate (monogamous marriage) 70.8%; legitimate (polygamous marriage) 18.4%; illegitimate 10.8%.
Death rate per 1,000 population: n.a.
Natural increase rate per 1,000 population: n.a.
Total fertility rate (avg. births per childbearing woman): n.a.
Marital status of adult population (1978): monogamous marriage 51.8%; unmarried 27.3%; polygamous marriage 11.0%; divorced 6.6%; widowed 3.3%.
Life expectancy at birth: n.a.
Major causes of death per 100,000 population: n.a.; however, malaria is a significant contagion; filariasis, formerly widespread, and leprosy are now practically nonexistent.

National economy

Budget (1984). Revenue: F137,089,000 (subsidies 44.0%, indirect taxes 22.9%, receipts from public property 17.7%, direct taxes 6.8%). Expenditures: F148,393,000 (roads 14.1%, health 11.5%, debt service 9.9%, education 9.9%, construction 6.9%).
Public debt: n.a.
Tourism: n.a.
Production (metric tons except as noted). Agriculture, forestry, fishing (1983): rice 1,500–2,000¶, mangoes 1,500, bananas 1,300, breadfruit 700, citrus fruit 600, cassava 500, taro 200, pineapples 200, coffee 18♀, cinnamon 12,500 kilograms¶, ylang-ylang 12,240 kilograms¶, vanilla 2,700 kilograms, cloves 400 kilograms; coconut palm trees (number of producing trees) 350,000; livestock (number of live animals; 1984) 10,000–15,000 goats, 3,000–4,000 cattle, 1,500–2,000 sheep; fish catch 700¶. Mining and quarrying: minuscule. Manufacturing (1983): mostly involves processing of agricultural products for export. Construction (gross value in F'000; 1983): residential 11,050; commercial and other 32,185. Energy production (consumption): electricity (kW-hr; 1982) 5,000,000 (5,000,000); coal, none

(n.a.); crude petroleum, none (n.a.); petroleum products, none (n.a.); natural gas, none (n.a.).
Gross national product (at current market prices): n.a.

Structure of gross domestic product and labour force

	1978 in value	% of total value	labour force	% of labour force
Agriculture, forestry, and fishing	...	...	9,298	65.4
Mining	...	...	19	0.1
Manufacturing	...	...	833	5.9
Construction	...	...	1,361	9.6
Public utilities	...	...	133	0.9
Transportation and communication	...	...	287	2.0
Trade	...	...	672	4.7
Finance	...	...	220	1.5
Pub. admin., defense	...	...	218	1.5
Education, health	...	...	348	2.4
Other	...	...	825	5.8
TOTAL	...	...	14,214	100.0‡

Population economically active (1978): total 14,214; participation rate of total population over age 15, 30.0% (female 37.5%, unemployed, n.a.).

Price and earnings indexes (1982 = 100)

	1978	1979	1980	1981	1982	1983	1984
Consumer price indexδ	...	...	...	...	100.0	113.3	139.1
Hourly earnings index□	54.5	72.8	72.8	81.7	100.0	111.4	117.2

Household income and expenditure. Average household size (1978) 4.7; average annual income per household: n.a.; source of income: n.a.; expenditure: n.a.
Land use (1984): agricultural 64.3%, of which 21.4% is under permanent cultivation; other 35.7%.

Foreign trade◊

Balance of trade (current prices)

	1979	1980	1981	1982	1983	1984
F'000,000	−56	−69	−96	−110	−140	−173
% of total	76.9%	83.8%	83.9%	91.1%	90.1%	89.6%

Imports (1984): F182,836,000 (food products 23.7%, mineral fuels 22.6%, machinery 14.9%, transport equipment 6.7%, metal and metal products 8.2%, chemical products 5.2%, wood and wood products 5.2%, textiles and clothing 4.2%). *Major import sources:* France 52.9%; Bahrain 11.3%; Kenya 7.7%; Thailand 7.0%; South Africa 5.9%; Réunion 2.8%.
Exports (1984): F3,581,000 (ylang-ylang 47.7%, vanilla 33.4%, coffee 11.9%, copra 5.3%). *Major export destinations:* France 81%; Réunion 6%; United States 6%.

Transport and communications

Transport. Railroads: none. Roads (1983): total length 139 mi, 224 km (paved 46%). Vehicles (1983): 1,528. Merchant marine: vessels (100 gross tons and over) n.a. Air transport (1984): passenger arrivals and departures 15,570; cargo loaded and unloaded (metric tons) 162; airports (1985) with scheduled flights 1.
Communications. Daily or weekly newspapers (1984): none. Radio (1984): total number of receivers 6,000 (1 per 9.4 persons). Television: total number of receivers, n.a. Telephone subscribers (1981): 400 (1 per 130 persons).

Education and health

Education (1984–85)

	schools△	teachers	students	student/ teacher ratio
Primary (age 6–11)	72	407	14,992	36.8
Secondary (age 12–18)	1	66△	1,374	20.0
Voc., teacher tr.	2	△	475	...
Higher†	—		31⊕	

Educational attainment (1978). Percent of population 15 years and over having: no formal education 82.0%; some primary 10.6%; early secondary 5.4%; late secondary 1.5%; postsecondary and higher 0.5%. *Literacy* (1978): total population over age 15 literate 4,279 (18.0%); males literate 3,230 (27.5%); females literate 1,049 (8.7%).
Health: physicians (1979) 9 (1 per 5,400 persons); hospital beds (1981) 86 (1 per 599 persons); infant mortality rate per 1,000 live births, n.a.
Food: daily per capita caloric intake, n.a.

Military

Total active duty personnel: Mayotte maintains no domestic military force; however, French military personnel of about 300 are in residence.

---

*Final status of Mayotte is not yet determined; it is claimed by the Comoros as an integral part of that country. †August. ‡Detail does not add to total given because of rounding. §In the late 1970s, 87% of all residents of Mayotte lived in villages of less than 1,000 inhabitants. ‖Populations cited are for villages with adjoining communes. ¶1984. ♀1984 export figure. δBased on January prices except for 1984, which is a mid-year average. □Based on pay increases for salaried employees occurring in January 1978, February 1979, January 1981, January 1982, April 1983, and January 1984. ◊Reexports are included in balance of trade; reexports are not included with commodities and trading partners. △General secondary includes vocational and teacher training. †1983–84. ⊕Students are enrolled in either France or Réunion.

Mexico

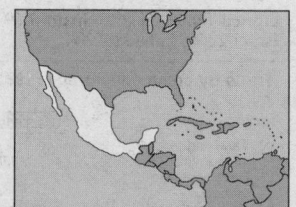

Official name: Estados Unidos Mexicanos (United Mexican States).
Form of government: federal republic with two legislative houses (Senate [64] and Chamber of Deputies [400]).
Chief of state and head of government: President.
Capital: Mexico City.
Official language: Spanish.
Official religion: None.
Monetary unit: 1 peso (Mex$) = 100 centavos; valuation (Oct. 21, 1985)
1 U.S.$ = Mex$312.28;
1 £ = Mex$447.81.

Area and population

States	Capitals	area* sq mi	sq km	population 1984 estimate
Aguascalientes	Aguascalientes	2,112	5,471	615,000
Baja California Norte	Mexicali	26,997	69,921	1,327,000
Baja California Sur	La Paz	28,369	73,475	263,000
Campeche	Campeche	19,619	50,812	514,000
Coahuila	Saltillo	57,908	149,982	1,776,000
Colima	Colima	2,004	5,191	399,000
Chiapas	Tuxtla Gutiérrez	28,653	74,211	2,332,000
Chihuahua	Chihuahua	94,571	244,938	2,186,000
Durango	Durango	47,560	123,181	1,295,000
Guanajuato	Guanajuato	11,773	30,491	3,358,000
Guerrero	Chilpancingo	24,819	64,281	2,354,000
Hidalgo	Pachuca	8,036	20,813	1,714,000
Jalisco	Guadalajara	31,211	80,836	4,887,000
México	Toluca	8,245	21,355	9,840,000
Michoacán	Morelia	23,138	59,928	3,118,000
Morelos	Cuernavaca	1,911	4,950	1,121,000
Nayarit	Tepic	10,417	26,979	814,000
Nuevo León	Monterrey	25,067	64,924	2,933,000
Oaxaca	Oaxaca	36,275	93,952	2,526,000
Puebla	Puebla	13,090	33,902	3,751,000
Querétaro	Querétaro	4,420	11,449	872,000
Quintana Roo	Chetumal	19,387	50,212	324,000
San Luis Potosí	San Luis Potosí	24,351	63,068	1,860,000
Sinaloa	Culiacán	22,521	58,328	2,147,000
Sonora	Hermosillo	70,291	182,052	1,717,000
Tabasco	Villahermosa	9,756	25,267	1,208,000
Tamaulipas	Ciudad Victoria	30,650	79,384	2,148,000
Tlaxcala	Tlaxcala	1,551	4,016	622,000
Veracruz	Jalapa	27,683	71,699	6,171,000
Yucatán	Mérida	14,827	38,402	1,215,000
Zacatecas	Zacatecas	28,283	73,252	1,220,000
Federal District				
Distrito Federal	—	571	1,479	9,750,000
TOTAL		756,066	1,958,201	76,377,000

Demography

Population (1985): 78,027,400.
Density† (1985): persons per sq mi 103.5, persons per sq km 39.9.
Urban–rural (1980): urban 66.3%; rural 33.7%.
Sex distribution (1984): male 50.07%; female 49.93%.
Age breakdown (1980): under 15, 43.0%; 15–29, 27.8%; 30–44, 14.9%; 45–59, 8.5%; 60–74, 4.0%; 75 and over, 1.8%.
Population projection: (1990) 89,012,000; (2000) 109,180,000.
Doubling time: 43 years.
Ethnic composition (1981): mestizo 55.0%; Amerindian 29.0%; Caucasian 15.0%; black 0.5%; other 0.5%.
Religious affiliation (1980): Roman Catholic 92.6%; Protestant (including Evangelical) 3.3%; Jewish 0.1%; other 0.9%; none 3.1%.
Major cities (1980): Mexico City 8,831,079; Guadalajara 1,626,152; Ciudad Netzahualcóyotl 1,341,230; Monterrey 1,090,009; Puebla 835,759; León 593,002; Juárez 544,496; Tijuana 429,500; Mérida 400,142; Chihuahua 385,603.
Place of birth (1980): 98.4% native-born; 1.6% foreign-born and unknown.
Mobility (1970). Population living in the same state as in 1960: 87.2%; different state 12.8%.
Households (1980). Total households 12,074,609; average household size 5.5; 1 person 5.4%, 2 persons 10.2%, 3 persons 12.4%, 4 persons 14.3%, 5 persons 13.5%, 6 persons 11.7%, 7 or more persons 32.5%. Family households: 11,421,286 (94.6%); nonfamily 653,323 (5.4%).
Immigration (1980): permanent immigrants admitted 73,260.
Emigration (1981): legal immigrants to the United States 101,268.

Vital statistics

Birth rate per 1,000 population (1983): 32.7 (world avg. 29.0); (1978) legitimate 91.0%, illegitimate 7.9%, unspecified 1.1%.
Death rate per 1,000 population (1983): 7.0 (world avg. 11.0).
Natural increase rate per 1,000 population (1983): 25.7 (world avg. 18.0).
Total fertility rate (avg. births per childbearing woman; 1980–85): 4.9.
Marriage rate per 1,000 population (1981): 7.1.
Divorce rate per 1,000 population (1981): 0.3.
Life expectancy at birth (1980–85): male 63.9 years; female 68.2 years.
Major causes of death per 100,000 population (1981): diseases of the circulatory system 100.2; accidents, including alcohol-related deaths 97.6; diseases of the respiratory system 77.2; infectious and parasitic diseases 73.0; diseases of the digestive system 43.8; malignant neoplasms (cancers) and nonmalignant tumours 41.7; signs, symptoms, and ill-defined conditions 37.9; conditions originating in the perinatal period 36.9.

Social indicators

Educational attainment (1980). Percent of population 15 years and over having: no primary education 13.7%; up to 3 years of primary 19.0%; 4 to 6 years of primary 28.0%; some post-primary 26.7%; unspecified 12.6%.

Distribution of income (1977)

percent of household income by quintile

1	2	3	4	5 (highest)
2.9	7.0	12.0	20.4	57.7

Quality of working life. Average workweek (1980): 46.0 hours. Annual rate (1979) per 100,000 workers for: temporary disability 2,789; indemnification 41; death 7. Labour conflicts (1982): 51,420, involving 146,419 workers. Labour stoppages (1982): 1,925, involving 25,173 workers. Average duration of journey to work: n.a. Method of transport: n.a. Rate per 1,000 workers of discouraged (unemployed no longer seeking work): n.a.
Access to services (1980). Proportion of dwellings having access to: electricity 74.6%; safe public water supply 71.2%; public sewage collection 49.2%.
Social participation. Eligible voters participating in last national election: 74.9%. Population participating in voluntary work: n.a. Trade union membership in total work force: n.a. Practicing religious population in total affiliated population (1970): weekly 10% of urban dwellers, 25% of rural dwellers; yearly 55% of urban dwellers, 73% of rural dwellers.
Social deviance (1975). Criminal cases tried by local authorities per 100,000 population for: murder 10.4; rape 3.0; other assault 31.4; theft 21.0. Incidence per 100,000 in general population of: alcoholism, n.a.; drug and substance abuse, n.a.‡; suicide 0.86§.
Leisure (1982). Favourite leisure activities (average daily attendance): cinema 430,486; museums and archaeological sites 29,220; live theatre 7,676; sporting events 5,056; bullfights 330.
Material well-being (1970). Households possessing: radio 46.3%; television 1.8%; radio and television 29.4% .

National economy

Gross national product (at current market prices; 1983): U.S.$168,070,000,-000 (U.S.$2,240 per capita).

Structure of gross domestic product and labour force

	1984 in value Mex$'000,000	% of total value	1980 labour force	% of labour force
Agriculture	2,509,923.5	8.5	5,699,971	25.8
Mining	3,533,824.9	12.0	477,017	2.2
Manufacturing	7,021,263.1	23.9	2,575,124	11.7
Construction	1,431,551.7	4.9	1,296,337	5.9
Public utilities	293,471.1	1.0	115,932	0.5
Transportation and communication	1,934,563.4	6.6	672,011	3.0
Trade	6,489,352.0	22.0	1,729,296	7.8
Finance	} 1,838,928.9	6.2	405,754	1.8
Pub. admin., defense			‖	‖
Services	4,635,693.8	15.7	2,418,114	11.0
Other	−249,714.6	−0.8	6,676,428 ‖	30.3 ‖
TOTAL	29,438,857.8¶	100.0	22,065,984	100.0

Budget (1984 est.). Revenue: Mex$4,943,000,000,000 (revenue from state petroleum company 36.4%, property taxes 23.6%, value added taxes 16.6%, taxes on gasoline and diesel 9.4%, excise taxes 3.9%, import duties 3.4%). Expenditures: Mex$7,110,000,000,000 (transfer payments and interest on public debt 56.1%, government services 35.1%).
Public debt (external, outstanding; June 1985): U.S.$94,407,000,000.
Tourism (1983): receipts from visitors U.S.$1,625,000,000; expenditures by nationals abroad U.S.$441,000,000.

Manufacturing, mining, and construction enterprises (1983)

industry	no. of large enterprises	no. of employees (000)	yearly wages as a % of avg. of all wages	annual value added (Mex$'000,000)
Manufacturing	1,209	526.5⁹	100.0	2,167,421⁹
Food, beverages, and tobacco	476	150.5	78.1	586,032
Metal products	149	92.5	109.8	472,463
Chemicals	141	59.4	120.2	333,228
Nonelectrical machinery and transport equipment	47	53.8	132.2	224,053
Paper and printing	96	29.0	107.0	145,781
Nonmetallic mineral products	54	25.7	103.9	130,516
Textiles and apparel	153	58.8	78.6	107,828
Electrical machinery	66	31.4	87.8	84,239
Wood and wood products	6	5.0	100.7	19,129
Other manufactures	21	20.3	110.6	64,154
Mining (petroleum and coal products)	14	5.1	97.5	35,358
Construction	...	...	...	...

Production (metric tons except as noted). Agriculture, forestry, fishing (1981): sugarcane 36,500,000, corn (maize) 14,050,000, sorghum 6,729,000, wheat 4,262,000, bananas 1,500,000, oranges 1,600,000, dry beans 1,270,000, tomatoes 1,320,000, potatoes 830,000, soybeans 789,000, rice 635,000, lemons and limes 600,000, barley 635,000, grapes 585,000, cottonseed 395,000, coffee 262,000, cotton lint 257,000, tobacco 62,000; livestock (number of live animals) 37,500,000 cattle, 18,370,000 pigs, 10,000,000 goats, 6,400,000 sheep, 2,820,000 asses, 3,619,000 mules, 197,000,000 chickens; roundwood (1983) 19,805,000 cu m; fish catch (1983) 1,070,045, of which sardines 316,-000, anchovies 236,600. Mining and quarrying (metals by metal content; 1984): iron ore 5,489,300; zinc 290,200; copper 189,100; lead 183,300; manganese 180,900; silver 63,873,500 troy oz; gold 226,900 troy oz; (nonmetals; 1984) sulfur 1,825,700; fluorite 627,400; phosphate rock 518,300; barite 426,100; graphite 41,500. Manufacturing (value added Mex$'000,000,000;

1983): iron and steel products 358.2; transport vehicles 202.4; printing and paper products 145.8; animal and vegetable oil and margarine 105.4; beer 98.5; plastic and other artificial fibres 88.6; beverages 83.8; cereals and cereal preparations 82.4; cement 81.3; soaps, detergents, and other products 80.7; rubber tires and tubes 77.3; electrical machinery and appliances 71.1; meat and dairy products 58.0; cotton, linen, and other finished products 47.1. Construction (gross value of new construction in Mex$'000,000,000; 1982): residential 453.9; nonresidential 107.0.

Service enterprises (1970)

	no. of establishments	no. of employees	weekly wage as a % of all wages	annual value added (Mex$'000,000)
Food and beverage preparation	71,524	177,399	...	3,236
Recreation and resorts	20,850	78,149	...	3,189
Food and beverage service	51,884	141,105	...	2,539
Lodging	6,708	54,509	...	2,515
Exhibitions and shows	3,550	33,323	...	2,143
Repair, excluding industries requiring parts	41,572	95,553	...	1,908
Professional services	9,522	32,058	...	1,772
Medical and social assistance	16,244	43,731	...	1,449
Educational services	5,016	43,781	...	1,355
Personal grooming and cleaning	29,708	65,060	...	1,212
Automobile repair	18,848	51,588	...	1,105
Alcoholic beverages	19,640	36,294	...	697
Mechanical repair	8,195	17,562	...	404
Shoe repair	4,532	6,737	...	73

Energy production (consumption): electricity (kW-hr; 1983) 82,343,000,000 (82,271,000,000); coal (metric tons; 1983) 7,800,000 (8,350,000); crude petroleum (barrels; 1984) 1,050,800,000 (412,000,000§); petroleum products (metric tons; 1983) 63,802,000 (60,187,000); natural gas (cu m; 1984) 28,077,000,000 (24,334,000,000).

Population economically active (1980): total 22,066,084; participation rate of total population 33.0% (female 27.8%, unemployed, n.a.)

Price and earnings indexes (1980 = 100)

	1979	1980	1981	1982	1983	1984	1985
Consumer price index	79.1	100.0	127.9	203.3	410.2	679.0	1,001.3ŏ
Monthly earnings index	83.0	100.0	133.0	222.0▭	...	...	...

Household income and expenditure. Average household size (1980) 5.5; average annual income per household: n.a. Source of income: n.a.; expenditure (1980): food and beverages 36.8%, housing 23.2%, clothing and footwear 11.1%, transportation and communication 10.0%, recreation and entertainment 5.5%, health and medical services 4.4%.

Land use (1983): forested 24.4%; meadows and pastures 38.7%; agricultural and under permanent cultivation 12.3%; other 24.6%.

Financial aggregates◇

	1980	1981	1982	1983	1984	1985△
Exchange Rate, Mex$ per:						
U.S. Dollar	22.95	24.51	56.40	120.09	167.83	209.57
£	53.39	49.70	98.73	182.18	224.89	248.63
SDR	29.87	28.90	62.27	128.38	171.80	205.67
International reserves (U.S.$)						
Total (excl. gold; '000,000)	2,960	4,074	834	3,913	7,272	6,119
SDRs ('000,000)	144	178	6	23	3	—
Reserve pos. in IMF ('000,000)	128	187	—	95	—	—
Foreign exchange	2,688	3,709	828	3,795	7,269	6,119
Gold ('000,000 fine troy oz)	2.06	2.26	2.07	2.31	2.42	2.30
% world reserves	0.22	0.24	0.22	0.24	0.26	0.24
Interest and prices						
Treasury bill rate	27.73	33.23	57.44	53.78	49.18	...
Balance of payments (U.S.$'000,000)						
Balance of visible trade, of which:	−2,830	−4,099	+7,646	+14,507	...	...
Imports, f.o.b.	18,896	24,037	14,435	7,721	...	...
Exports, f.o.b.	16,066	19,938	22,081	22,228	...	...
Balance of invisibles	−5,607	−10,089	−13,660	−9,654	...	...
Balance of payments, current account	−8,162	−13,899	−5,753	+5,208	...	...

Foreign trade†

Balance of trade (current prices)

	1979	1980	1981	1982	1983	1984
U.S.$'000,000	−3,103	−4,667	−5,642	+6,173	+13,340	+12,943
% of total	14.7%	13.4%	12.7%	17.0%	45.3%	36.2%

Imports (1983): U.S.$8,058,000,000 (unprocessed agricultural products [excluding livestock] 21.0%, of which corn [maize] 8.2%, sorghum 5.6%, soybean seed 2.8%; industrial machinery 18.0%, of which metalworking equipment 3.3%; chemicals 10.6%; transportation and communication equipment 8.8%, of which maritime vessels, parts, and equipment 3.1%; manufactured food products 6.8%; electrical machinery and apparatus 5.9%; petrochemicals 4.8%; iron and steel 4.7%). *Major import sources:* United States 60.5%; West Germany 4.5%; Japan 4.4%; Canada 2.8%; United Kingdom 2.1%; Italy 2.1%; Spain 2.1%.

Exports (1983): U.S.$21,399,000,000 (crude petroleum 66.6%; petroleum products 3.3%; transportation and communication equipment 3.3%, of which automobile motors 1.8%; chemicals 2.2%; coffee 2.2%; silver bars 1.8%; frozen shrimp 1.7%; natural gas 1.6%). *Major export destinations:*

United States 58.2%; Spain 7.6%; Japan 7.1%; France 3.9%; Brazil 3.0%; Israel 2.5%; Canada 2.2%.

Trade by commodity group (1983)

SITC group	imports U.S.$'000,000	imports %	exports U.S.$'000,000	exports %
00 Food and live animals	1,622	20.1	1,543	7.2
01 Beverages and tobacco	—	—	90	0.4
02 Crude materials, excluding fuels	580	7.2	587	2.7
03 Mineral fuels, lubricants, and related materials	599	7.4	15,979	74.7
04 Animal and vegetable oils, fats, and waxes	101	1.2	—	—
05 Chemicals and related products, n.e.s.	644	8.0	895	4.2
06 Basic manufactures	1,039	12.9	1,189	5.6
07 Machinery and transport equipment	3,351	41.6	1,044	4.9
08 Miscellaneous manufactured articles	119	1.5	67	0.3
09 Good not classified by kind	4	0.1	5	—
TOTAL	8,059	100.0	21,399	100.0

Direction of trade (1983)

SITC group	imports U.S.$'000,000	imports %	exports U.S.$'000,000	exports %
Africa	21	0.3	58	0.3
Asia	453	5.6	2,380	11.1
South America	193	2.4	886	4.1
North and Central America	5,219	64.8	13,775	64.4
United States	4,873	60.5	12,495	58.4
other North and Central Am.	346	4.3	1,280	6.0
Europe	1,554	19.3	4,286	20.0
EEC	1,190	14.8	2,273	10.6
U.S.S.R.	3	—	6	—
other Europe	361	4.5	2,007	9.4
Oceania	23	0.3	9	0.1
unknown	172	2.1	5	—
freight and insurance charges	423	5.2	—	—
TOTAL	8,059	100.0	21,399	100.0

Transport and communications

Transport. Railroads (1983): route length 16,031 mi, 25,799 km; passenger-mi 3,654,000,000, passenger-km 5,880,000,000; short ton-mi cargo 28,957,000,000, metric ton-km cargo 42,276,000,000. Roads (1983): total length 133,265 mi, 214,470 km (paved 50%). Vehicles (1982): passenger cars 5,221,159; trucks and buses 1,978,327. Merchant marine (1984): vessels (100 gross tons and over) 624; total deadweight tonnage 2,146,277. Air transport⊕ (1984): passenger-mi 10,633,000,000, passenger-km 17,112,000,000; short ton-mi cargo 102,183,000, metric ton-km cargo 149,200,000; airports (1985) 72.

Communications. Daily newspapers (1983): total number, more than 350; total circulation, n.a.; circulation per 1,000 population, n.a. Radio (1983): total number of receivers 22,000,000 (1 per 3.4 persons). Television (1983): total number of receivers 7,550,000 (1 per 9.9 persons). Telephones (1983): 5,845,400 (1 per 12.8 persons).

Education and health

Education (1983–84)

	schools	teachers	students	student/teacher ratio
Primary (age 6–12)	79,202	428,029	15,376,153	35.9
Secondary (age 12–18)	16,411	225,141	4,277,606	19.0
Voc., teacher tr.**	3,738	104,804	1,725,601	16.5
Higher	1,092	92,338	1,121,252	12.1

Literacy (1980): total population literate 31,475,670 (83.0%); males literate 15,955,272 (86.2%); females literate 15,520,398 (79.9%).

Health: physicians (1980) 53,053 (1 per 1,260 persons); hospital beds (1978) 66,093 (1 per 1,011 persons); infant mortality rate per 1,000 live births (1983) 53.0.

Food (1980–82): daily per capita caloric intake 2,930 (vegetable products 86%, animal products 14%); 124% of FAO recommended minimum requirement.

Military

Total active duty personnel (1984): 120,000 (army 78.8%, navy 16.6%, air force 4.6%). *Military expenditure as percent of GNP* (1983): 0.6% (world 6.1%); per capita expenditure U.S.$11.

*Total land area is 754,107 sq mi (1,953,128 sq km); the area shown for the states, federal district, and the grand total includes both land and water area. †Based on land area. ‡Through 1982, cannabis remained the most abused drug. §1983. ‖ Public administration and defense included with other. ¶At current prices. ♀Detail does not add to total given because of rounding. ŏMay. ▭Third quarter. ◇Exchange rates and treasury bill rates are expressed in period averages; international reserves are expressed in end of period rates. △First six months only. †All exports f.o.b. (free on board), imports c.i.f. (cost, insurance, and freight). ⊕All scheduled traffic of Mexicana and AeroMexico airlines. **1982–83.

Mongolia

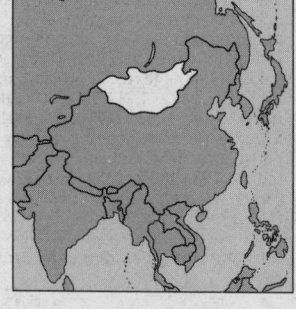

Official name: Büged Nayramdah Mongol Arad Ulas (Mongolian People's Republic).
Form of government: unitary single-party republic with one legislative house (People's Great Hural [370]).
Chief of state: Chairman of the Presidium of the People's Great Hural.
Head of government: Premier.
Capital: Ulaanbaatar.
Official language: Khalkha Mongolian.
Official religion: none.
Monetary unit: 1 tugrik = 100 möngös; valuation (Oct 21, 1985) 1 U.S.$ = 3.35 tugriks; 1 £ = 4.81 tugriks.

Area and population		area		population
		sq mi	sq km	1984 estimate
Provinces	**Capitals**			
Arhangay	Tsetserleg	21,000	55,000	83,800
Bayanhongor	Bayanhongor	45,000	116,000	69,500
Bayan-Ölgiy	Ölgiy	18,000	46,000	84,000
Bulgan	Bulgan	19,000	49,000	46,000
Dornod	Choybalsan	47,000	122,000	67,800
Dornogovi	Saynshand	43,000	111,000	47,400
Dundgovi	Mandalgov	30,000	78,000	44,100
Dzavhan	Uliastay	32,000	82,000	88,100
Govi-Altay	Altay	55,000	142,000	62,500
Hentiy	Öndörhaan	32,000	82,000	60,500
Hovd	Hovd	29,000	76,000	71,600
Hövsgöl	Mörön	39,000	101,000	96,600
Ömnögovi	Dalandzadgad	64,000	165,000	35,500
Övörhangay	Arvayheer	24,000	63,000	93,200
Selenge	Sühbaatar	16,000	42,000	76,400
Sühbaatar	Baruun-urt	32,000	82,000	47,200
Töv	Dzuunmod	31,000	81,000	90,200
Uvs	Ulaangom	27,000	69,000	81,400
Autonomous municipalities				
Darhan	—	100	200	63,600
Erdenet	—	300	800	40,500
Ulaanbaatar	—	800	2,000	470,500
TOTAL		604,000*	1,565,000	1,820,400

Demography

Population (1985): 1,907,000.
Density (1985): persons per sq mi 3.2, persons per sq km 1.2.
Urban–rural (1984): urban 51.5%; rural 48.5%.
Sex distribution (1983): male 50.05%; female 49.95%.
Age breakdown (1980): under 15, 43.1%; 15–29, 26.1%; 30–44, 16.2%; 45–59, 9.5%; 60–74, 4.1%; 75 and over, 1.0%.
Population projection: (1990) 2,170,000; (2000) 2,686,000.
Doubling time: 26 years.
Ethnic composition (1980): Khalkha Mongol 83.9%; Kazakh 4.8%; Dörbed Mongol 2.8%; Buryat Mongol 2.2%; Dariganga Mongol 1.9%; other 4.4%.
Religious affiliation: n.a.
Major cities (1984): Ulaanbaatar 470,500; Darhan 63,600; Erdenet 40,500.

Vital statistics

Birth rate per 1,000 population (1983): 36.2 (world avg. 29.0); legitimate, n.a.; illegitimate, n.a.
Death rate per 1,000 population (1983): 9.8 (world avg. 11.0).
Natural increase rate per 1,000 population (1983): 26.4 (world avg. 18.0).
Total fertility rate (avg. births per childbearing woman; 1982): 4.8.
Marriage rate per 1,000 population (1983): 5.7.
Divorce rate per 1,000 population (1983): 0.3.
Life expectancy at birth (1980–85): male 62.9 years; female 66.8 years.
Major causes of death: n.a.

National economy

Budget (1984). Revenue: 5,410,000,000 tugriks (turnover tax 65.1%, deductions from profits 21.3%, social insurance contributions 3.3%). Expenditures: 5,400,000,000 tugriks (social and cultural services 39.9%, national economy 39.8%, defense 14.1%, administration and other 6.2%).
Public debt: heavily dependent on U.S.S.R.
Tourism (1983): number of tourists 170,000; receipts from visitors, n.a.; expenditures by nationals abroad, n.a.
Production (metric tons except as noted). Agriculture, forestry, fishing (1983): wheat 648,000, potatoes 97,500, barley 88,800, oats 57,200; livestock (number of live animals; 1984) 14,110,000 sheep, 4,548,000 goats, 2,374,000 cattle, 1,960,000 horses, 45,100 pigs; roundwood 2,210,000 cu m; fish catch 300. Mining and quarrying (1983): fluorspar 700,000; copper 104,000. Manufacturing (1983): cement 165,000; flour 165,000; lime 89,300; meat 64,400; woolen cloth 1,020,500 m; leather shoes 2,200,000 pairs; sheep skins 3,510,400† units; goat skins 1,186,900† units; beer 91,100,000 hectolitres. Construction (1980): residential 183,400 sq m; nonresidential 113,300 sq m. Energy production (consumption): electricity (kW-hr; 1984) 1,885,000,000 (2,375,000,000); coal (metric tons; 1983) 4,974,000 (4,974,000); crude petroleum, none (n.a.); petroleum products (metric tons; 1983) none (677,000); natural gas, none (n.a.).

Gross national product (at current market prices; 1983): U.S.$1,803,000,000 (U.S.$1,000 per capita).

Structure of net material product and labour force		1983		
	value	% of total value	labour force	% of labour force
Agriculture	...	17.3	345,200	51.1
Mining and manufacturing	...		82,200	12.2
Construction	...}	33.3	26,700	3.9
Public utilities	...		16,400	2.4
Transportation and communication	...	10.5	34,600	5.1
Trade	...	37.2	38,900	5.8
Services	...	...	97,700‡	14.4‡
Other§	...	1.7	34,300	5.1
TOTAL	...	100.0	676,000	100.0

Population economically active (1984): total 691,000; participation rate of total population 38.0% (female [1983] 46.0%, unemployed, n.a.
Price and earnings indexes: n.a.
Household income and expenditure. Average household size (1980) 5.0; average annual income per household: n.a.; source of income: n.a.; expenditure: n.a.
Land use (1983): forested 9.7%; meadows and pastures 78.8%; agricultural and under permanent cultivation 0.8%; other 10.7%.

Foreign trade

Balance of trade (current prices)						
	1978	1979	1980	1981	1982	1983
U.S.$'000,000	−133.7	−207.5	−138.7	−225.7	−220.0	−305.0
% of total	19.6%	18.5%	15.2%	20.1%	17.0%	20.7%

Imports (1983): U.S.$889,000,000 (machinery and equipment 35.5%; fuels, minerals, and metals 29.6%; consumer goods 18.9%; food products 8.3%; chemical products, fertilizers, and rubber 5.7%; raw materials except food 2.0%). *Major import sources:* U.S.S.R. and socialist countries 98.5%; capitalist countries 1.5%.
Exports (1983): U.S.$584,000,000 (minerals and metals 39.2%; raw materials and food products 46.2%; consumer goods 13.5%). *Major export destinations:* U.S.S.R. and socialist countries 99.4%; capitalist countries 0.6%.

Transport and communications

Transport. Railroads (1983): length 1,062 mi, 1,710 km; passenger-mi 240,000,000, passenger-km 386,000,000; short ton-mi cargo 3,081,000,000, metric ton-km cargo 4,498,000,000. Roads (1983): total length 29,000 mi, 46,700 km (paved 2%). Vehicles: n.a. Merchant marine: vessels (100 gross tons and over) none. Air transport (1983): passenger-mi 162,000,000, passenger-km 261,000,000; short ton-mi cargo 3,425,000, metric ton-km cargo 5,000,000; airports (1985) with scheduled flights 1.
Communications. Daily newspapers (1984): total number 2; total circulation 177,000 ‖; circulation per 1,000 population 99.7 ‖. Radio (1984): total number of receivers 187,000 (1 per 9.7 persons). Television (1984): total number of receivers 70,700 (1 per 25.7 persons). Telephones (1984): 44,600 (1 per 40.8 persons).

Education and health

Education (1983–84)	schools	teachers	students	student/ teacher ratio
Primary and secondary (age 8–18)	674	15,900	410,000	25.8
Voc., teacher tr.	37	1,100	23,600	21.4
Higher	8	1,400	26,000	18.6

Educational attainment (1983). Percent of employed population having: vocational education 9.1%; some postsecondary and higher 7.1%. *Literacy* (1980): total population over age 15 literate 849,000 (89.5%); males literate 443,000 (93.4%); females literate 406,000 (85.5%).
Health (1984): physicians 4,234 (1 per 430.0 persons); hospital beds 19,900 (1 per 91.3 persons); infant mortality rate per 1,000 live births (1982) 49.0.
Food (1980–82): daily per capita caloric intake 2,757 (vegetable products 64%, animal products 36%); 114% of FAO recommended minimum requirement.

Military

Total active duty personnel (1984): 36,500 (army 90.4%; navy, none; air force 9.6%). *Military expenditure* (1983): 935,100,000 tugriks ($247,394,000); estimated foreign military assistance $600,000; per capita expenditure U.S.$136.

*Detail does not add to total given because of rounding. †1982. ‡Includes finance, public administration, and defense. §Other material activities. ‖ 1983.

Morocco

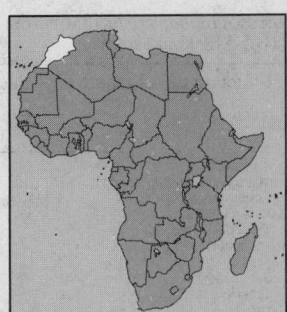

Official name: al-Mamlakah al-Maghribīyah (Kingdom of Morocco).
Form of government: constitutional monarchy with one legislative house (House of Representatives [306]).
Chief of state: King.
Head of government: Prime Minister.
Capital: Rabat.
Official language: Arabic.
Official religion: Islām.
Monetary unit: 1 Moroccan dirham (DH) = 100 Moroccan francs; valuation (Oct. 21, 1985) 1 U.S.$ = DH9.78; 1 £ = DH14.02.

Area and population

Provinces	Capitals	area sq mi	area sq km	population 1982 census
Agadir	Agadir	6,741	17,460	579,741
Azilal	Azilal	3,880	10,050	387,115
Beni Mellal	Beni Mellal	2,732	7,075	668,703
Ben Slimane	Ben Slimane	1,066	2,760	174,464
Boulemane	Boulemane	5,558	14,395	131,470
Chaouen (Chefchaouen)	Chaouen	1,680	4,350	309,024
Essaouira	Essaouira	2,446	6,335	393,683
Fès	Fès	2,085	5,400	805,464
Figuig	Figuig	21,618	55,990	101,359
Guelmim*	Guelmim	11,100	28,750	116,138
el-Hoceima	el-Hoceima	1,371	3,550	311,298
Ifrane	Ifrane	†	†	100,255
el-Jadida	el-Jadida	2,317	6,000	763,351
el-Kelaa Sraghna	el-Kelaa Sraghna	3,888	10,070	577,595
Kenitra	Kenitra	3,400	8,805	715,967
Khémisset	Khémisset	3,207	8,305	405,836
Khenifra	Khenifra	4,292	11,115	363,716
Khouribga	Khouribga	1,641	4,250	437,002
Laayoune*	El Aaiún	...	...	9,044
Marrakech	Marrakech	5,697	14,755	1,266,695
Meknès	Meknès	3,286†	8,510†	626,868
Nador	Nador	2,367	6,130	593,255
Ouarzazate	Ouarzazate	17,938	46,460	533,892
Oujda	Oujda	7,992	20,700	780,762
er-Rachidia	er-Rachidia	23,006	59,585	421,207
Safi	Safi	2,813	7,285	706,618
Settat	Settat	3,764	9,750	692,359
Sidi Kacem	Sidi Kacem	...	...	514,127
Tangier	Tangier	461	1,195	436,227
Tan-Tan	Tan-Tan	6,678	17,295	47,040
Taounate	Taounate	2,156	5,585	535,972
Taroudannt	Taroudannt	...	...	558,501
Tata	Tata	10,010	25,925	99,950
Taza	Taza	5,799	15,020	613,485
Tétouan	Tétouan	2,326	6,025	704,205
Tiznit	Tiznit	2,687	6,960	313,140
Prefectures				
Ain Chok–Hay Hassani		...	...	298,376
Ain Sebaa–Hay Mohammadi		...	...	421,272
Ben Msik–Sidi Othmane		...	...	639,558
Casablanca–Anfa		623	1,615	923,630
Mohammedia–Znata		...	...	153,828
Rabat–Salé		492	1,275	1,020,001
TOTAL		177,117	458,730	20,252,193

Demography

Population (1985): 24,370,000.
Density (1985): persons per sq mi 137.6, persons per sq km 53.1.
Urban–rural (1985): urban 43.9%; rural 56.1%.
Sex distribution (1985): male 50.05%; female 49.95%.
Age breakdown (1981): under 15, 45.6%; 15–29, 26.8%; 30–44, 14.8%; 45–59, 8.4%; 60–74, 3.7%; 75 and over, 0.7%.
Population projection: (1990) 27,840,000; (2000) 36,509,000.
Doubling time: 24 years.
Ethnic composition (1982): Arab–Berber 99.1%; other 0.9%.
Religious affiliation (1982): Muslim (mostly Sunnī) 98.7%; Christian 1.1%.
Major cities (1982): Casablanca 2,139,204; Rabat 518,616; Fès 448,823.

Vital statistics

Birth rate per 1,000 population (1980–85): 44.1 (world avg. 29.0).
Death rate per 1,000 population (1980–85): 11.7 (world avg. 11.0).
Natural increase rate per 1,000 population (1980–85): 32.4 (world avg. 18.0).
Total fertility rate (avg. births per childbearing woman; 1980–85): 6.4.
Marriage rate per 1,000 population: n.a.
Divorce rate per 1,000 population: n.a.
Life expectancy at birth (1980–85): male 56.1 years; female 59.4 years.
Major causes of death per 100,000 population (1981)‡: conjunctivitis of the newborn 819.0; measles 508.0; trachoma 108.5; bilharzia 37.8.

National economy

Budget (1986). Revenue: DH55,420,000,000 (loans 38.7%). Expenditures: DH68,310,000,000 (current 32.5%, investment 30.0%).
Public debt (external, outstanding; 1983): U.S.$9,445,300,000.
Tourism (1983): receipts from visitors U.S.$417,000,000; expenditures by nationals abroad 83,000,000§.
Production (metric tons except as noted). Agriculture, forestry, fishing (1984): wheat 1,989,000, barley 1,405,000, oranges 746,000, potatoes 550,-000; livestock (number of live animals) 12,000,000 sheep, 4,500,000 goats, 3,300,000 cattle; roundwood 1,697,000 cu m‖; fish catch 439,895‖. Mining and quarrying (1984): phosphate rock 21,233,000; lead 100,100; zinc 88,700. Manufacturing (value in DH; 1985): foodstuffs 16,662,000,000; chemicals 9,450,000,000; textiles and leather 6,146,000,000. Construction (value added in DH; 1982): 4,211,300,000. Energy production (consumption): electricity (kW-hr; 1983) 6,010,000,000 (6,010,000,000); coal (metric tons; 1983) 817,000 (745,000); crude petroleum (barrels; 1983) 121,600 (33,364,000); petroleum products (metric tons; 1983) 4,023,000 (3,943,000); natural gas (cu m; 1983) 80,213,000 (80,213,000).
Gross national product (at current market prices; 1983): U.S.$15,620,000,000 (U.S.$750 per capita).

Structure of gross domestic product and labour force

	1981 in value DH'000,000	1981 % of total value	1983 labour force	1983 % of labour force
Agriculture	10,887	14.2	2,934,000	49.4
Mining	4,283	5.6		
Manufacturing	13,416	17.6		
Construction	5,364	7.0		
Public utilities	2,935	3.8	3,004,000	50.6
Trade and finance	14,965	19.6		
Pub. admin., defense	9,958	13.0		
Other	14,637	19.2		
TOTAL	76,445	100.0	5,938,000	100.0

Population economically active (1981): total 5,451,000; participation rate of total population 26.4% (female 15.9%, unemployed, n.a.).

Price and earnings indexes (1980 = 100)

	1978	1979	1980	1981	1982	1983	1984
Consumer price index	84.4	91.4	100.0	112.5	124.4	132.1	148.5
Monthly earnings index	...	...	...	...	...	...	...

Household income and expenditure. Average household size (1982) 5.9; income per household: n.a.; source of income: n.a.; expenditure (1981): food 54.0%, transportation 18.5%, housing 13.5%, clothing 8.5%.
Land use (1983): forested 11.6%; meadows and pastures 28.0%; agricultural and under permanent cultivation 18.8%; other 41.6%.

Foreign trade

Balance of trade (current prices)

	1979	1980	1981	1982	1983	1984
DH'000,000	−4,987	−5,136	−7,406	−10,405	−8,173	−15,287
% of total	24.6%	21.0%	23.1%	29.5%	22.2%	28.6%

Imports (1982): DH25,990,248,000 (petroleum 25.4%; machinery 20.7%; food 13.4%, iron and steel 4.8%). *Major import sources:* France 24.7%; Saudi Arabia 13.5%; U.S. 6.0%; U.S.S.R. 5.2%; West Germany 4.8%.
Exports (1982): DH12,439,745,000 (nonmetallic minerals, metals, and ores 33.1%; food, beverages, and tobacco 24.3%; chemicals and chemical products 16.5%; textile products and wearing apparel 8.3%). *Major export destinations:* France 24.0%; West Germany 7.9%; Spain 6.7%; Italy 6.7%.

Transport and communications

Transport. Railroads (1984): route length 1,105 mi, 1,779 km; passenger-km 1,404,000,000♀; metric ton-km cargo 4,188,000,000♀. Roads (1983): total length 35,778 mi, 57,577 km (paved 45%). Vehicles (1983): passenger cars 470,239; trucks and buses 232,857. Merchant marine (1984): vessels (100 gross tons and over) 261; total deadweight tonnage 641,229. Air transport (1984): passenger-km 1,739,466,000; metric ton-km cargo 38,068,000; airports (1985) 14.
Communications. Daily newspapers (1984): total number 8; total circulation 282,000; circulation per 1,000 population 12.3. Radio (1984): receivers 2,500,000 (1 per 8.4 persons). Television (1984): receivers 1,032,955 (1 per 20.3 persons). Telephones (1983): 265,672 (1 per 86.9 persons).

Education and health

Education (1982)

	schools	teachers	students	student/ teacher ratio
Primary (age 7–12)	2,498	63,157	2,418,385	38.3
Secondary (age 14–21)	644	39,035	900,694	23.1
Voc., teacher tr.	...	...	10,300	...
Higher	19	2,558	98,513	38.5

Educational attainment, n.a. *Literacy* (1980): total population over age 15 literate 7,655,000 (70.7%); males literate 4,459,000 (82.4%); females literate 3,196,000 (58.7%).
Health (1981): physicians 1,153 (1 per 17,906 persons); hospital beds 24,342 (1 per 848 persons); infant mortality rate per 1,000 live births (1975–80) 114.4.
Food (1980–82): daily per capita caloric intake 2,635 (vegetable products 93%, animal products 7%); 109% of FAO recommended minimum requirement.

Military

Total active duty personnel (1984): 144,000 (army 86.8%, navy 4.2%, air force 9.0%). *Military expenditure as percent of GNP* (1983): 8.2% (world 6.1%); per capita expenditure U.S.$55.

---

*Excludes area and population of the portion of the provincial territory in Moroccan-occupied Western Sahara. †Area of Meknès includes Ifrane. ‡Reported cases only. §1982. ‖1983.

Mozambique

Official name: República Popular de
Moçambique (People's Republic of
Mozambique).
Form of government: people's republic
with a single legislative house
(People's Assembly [226]).
Chief of state and head of government:
President.
Capital: Maputo.
Official language: Portuguese.
Official religion: none.
Monetary unit: 1 metical (MT, plural
meticais) = 100 centavos; valuation
(Oct. 21, 1985) 1 U.S.\$ = MT42.06;
1 £ = MT60.31.

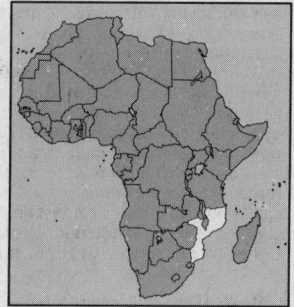

Area and population

Provinces	Capitals	area* sq mi	area* sq km	population 1982 estimate
Cabo Delgado	Pemba	31,902	82,625	977,600
Gaza	Xai-Xai	29,231	75,709	1,030,500
Inhambane	Inhambane	26,492	68,615	1,037,500
Manica	Chimoio	23,807	61,661	666,800
Maputo	Maputo	9,944	25,756	511,500
Nampula	Nampula	31,508	81,606	2,498,800
Niassa	Lichinga	49,829	129,056	534,700
Sofala	Beira	26,262	68,018	1,107,800
Tete	Tete	38,890	100,724	864,200
Zambézia	Quelimane	40,544	105,008	2,600,200
City				
Maputo	—	232	602	785,500
TOTAL		308,642†	799,380	12,615,200†

Demography

Population (1985 est.): 14,074,000.
Density‡ (1985): persons per sq mi 46.3, persons per sq km 17.9.
Urban–rural (1980): urban 8.7%; rural 91.3%.
Sex distribution (1980): male 48.71%; female 51.29%.
Age breakdown (1980): under 15, 43.7%; 15–29, 25.2%; 30–44, 16.0%; 45–59,
9.7%; 60–74, 4.6%; 75 and over, 0.8%.
Population projection: (1990) 16,132,000; (2000) 21,713,000.
Doubling time: 25 years.
Ethnic composition (1980): Makua 52.3%; Tsonga 23.6%; Malawi 12.0%;
Shona 5.8%; Yao 3.2%; Swahili 0.7%; Makonde 0.5%; Portuguese 0.2%;
other 1.7%.
Religious affiliation (1980): tribal religionist 47.8%; Muslim 16.5%; Christian
16.5%, of which Roman Catholic 14.3%; other 19.2%.
Major cities (1982): Maputo 785,500; Nampula 126,126§; Beira 113,770§.

Vital statistics

Birth rate per 1,000 population (1980–85): 44.6 (world avg. 29.0); (1974)
legitimate 73.1%; illegitimate 26.9%.
Death rate per 1,000 population (1980–85): 17.2 (world avg. 11.0).
Natural increase rate per 1,000 population (1980–85): 27.4 (world avg. 18.0).
Total fertility rate (avg. births per childbearing woman; 1980–85): 6.1.
Marriage rate per 1,000 population (1974): 0.7.
Divorce rate per 1,000 population (1973): 0.01.
Life expectancy at birth (1980–85): male 47.8 years; female 51.1 years.
Major infectious diseases per 100,000 population (1980): measles 227.4;
pulmonary tuberculosis 55.9; viral hepatitis 19.2; leprosy 13.8; cholera
4.6; tetanus 4.5.

National economy

Budget (1982). Revenue: MT20,962,600,000 (indirect taxes 43.9%, direct
taxes 30.1%). Expenditures: MT19,167,800,000 (economic sector 75.8%, social and administrative sector 7.4%).
Public debt (external, outstanding; 1982): U.S.\$583,000,000.
Tourism: n.a.
Production (metric tons except as noted). Agriculture, forestry, fishing (1984):
cassava 3,150,000, sugarcane 1,000,000, corn (maize) 330,000, sorghum 180,-
000, bananas 70,000, copra 65,000, peanuts (groundnuts) 70,000; livestock
(number of live animals) 1,320,000 cattle, 19,000,000 chickens; roundwood
14,685,000 cu m ‖; fish catch 42,440 ‖. Mining and quarrying (1983): marine salt 28,000; hydraulic lime 10,000; copper 1,000; bentonite 500; garnet
12,000 kg. Manufacturing (1982): cement 270,000; sugar 126,000; feed 66,-
000¶; coconut oil 23,000¶; soap 22,000; hoes 808,000 units; tires 132,000
units; inner tubes 135,000 units¶; beer 450,000 hectolitres. Construction
(1974): residential 247,000 sq m; nonresidential 121,000. Energy production
(consumption): electricity (kW-hr; 1983) 6,426,000,000 (1,500,000,000); coal
(metric tons; 1983) 380,000 (420,000); crude petroleum (barrels; 1983) none
(4,245,600); petroleum products (metric tons; 1983) 528,000 (495,000); natural gas, none (none).
Population economically active (1980): total 5,671,290; participation rate of
population over age 15, 46.7% (female 52.4%, unemployed 1.7%).

Price and earnings indexes (1970 = 100)

	1971	1973	1975	1977
Consumer price index	115.7	130.6	164.2	195.5
Monthly earnings index	...	...	...	...

Household income and expenditure. Average household size (1980) 4.2;
average annual income per household: n.a.; source of income: n.a.; expenditure: n.a.
Gross national product (at current market prices; 1981): U.S.\$4,466,000,000
(U.S.\$360 per capita).

Structure of gross domestic product and labour force

	1981 in value MT'000,000	1981 % of total value	1980 labour force	1980 % of labour force
Agriculture	64,374	40.0	4,754,831	83.8
Mining	684	0.4	346,794	6.1
Manufacturing	13,276	8.3		
Construction	8,925	5.6	42,121	0.7
Public utilities	2,168	1.3	♀	♀
Transportation and communication	6,032	3.8	77,025	1.4
Trade and finance	38,482	23.9	112,244	2.0
Pub. admin., defense	12,816	8.0	243,449♀	4.3♀
Services	...	...		
Other	14,002	8.7	94,826	1.7
TOTAL	160,759♂	100.0	5,671,290	100.0

Land use (1983): forested 19.3%; meadows and pastures 56.1%; agricultural
and under permanent cultivation 3.9%; other 20.7%.

Foreign trade

Balance of trade (current prices)

	1979	1980	1981	1982	1983	1984□
MT'000,000	−10,264	−16,897	−18,392	−22,918	−20,286	−22,000
% of total	38.2%	48.2%	48.1%	57.0%	65.7%	64.7%

Imports (1983): MT25,572,200,000 (capital goods 22.4%, foodstuffs 22.3%,
machinery and spare parts 15.4%, crude petroleum 14.4%, chemicals 5.6%,
metals 4.9%). *Major import sources* (1980): South Africa 19.8%; West Germany 14.9%; Portugal 9.6%; Iraq 9.1%; United Kingdom 7.2%.
Exports (1983): MT5,286,600,000 (shrimps 23.7%, petroleum products 16.6%,
raw cotton 12.9%, cashews 12.2%, tea 11.2%, sugar 6.6%). *Major export
destinations* (1980): United States 26.9%; Portugal 16.1%; South Africa
7.0%; United Kingdom 6.9%; The Netherlands 5.7%.

Transport and communications

Transport. Railroads: length (1984) 2,388 mi, 3,843 km; passenger-mi (1981)
377,000,000, passenger-km 606,000,000; short ton-mi cargo (1981) 3,532,-
000,000, metric ton-km cargo 5,156,000,000. Roads (1982): total length
16,200 mi, 26,000 km (paved, n.a.). Vehicles (1981): passenger cars 49,-
500; trucks and buses, n.a. Merchant marine (1984): vessels (100 gross
tons and over) 98; total deadweight tonnage 45,822. Air transport (1982):
passenger-mi 417,649,000, passenger-km 672,142,000; short ton-mi cargo
9,122,000, metric ton-km cargo 13,318,000; airports (1985) with scheduled
flights 7.
Communications. Daily newspapers (1984): total number 2; total circulation
54,000; circulation per 1,000 population 3.9. Radio (1983): total number
of receivers 275,000 (1 per 48 persons). Television (1983): total number
of receivers 1,000 (1 per 13,310 persons). Telephones (1982): 56,000 (1
per 231 persons).

Education and health

Education (1983)

	schools	teachers	students	student/teacher ratio
Primary (age 5–9)◇	8,528	29,634	1,402,541	47.3
Secondary (age 10–16)	136	2,523	106,975	42.4
Voc., teacher tr.	62	1,228	19,627	16.0
Higher	1	352	1,106△	...

Educational attainment (1970). Percent of population over age 5 having: no
schooling 87.0%; primary education 11.7%; secondary 1.2%; higher 0.1%.
Literacy (1980): total population over age 15 literate 1,959,000 (33.2%);
males literate 1,272,000 (44.4%); females literate 687,000 (22.7%).
Health (1981): physicians 365 (1 per 34,329 persons); hospital beds 12,927
(1 per 969 persons); infant mortality rate per 1,000 live births (1982) 105.0.
Food (1980–82): daily per capita caloric intake 1,864 (vegetable products 97%,
animal products 3%); 80% of FAO recommended minimum requirement.

Military

Total active duty personnel (1984): 15,650 (army 89.5%, navy 4.2%, air force
6.3%). *Military expenditure as percent of GNP* (1982): 3.4% (world 6.0%);
per capita expenditure U.S.\$13.

*Total land area is 303,623 sq mi (786,380 sq km); total area is shown for the
provinces and also in the grand total. †Detail does not add to total given because of
rounding. ‡Density is based on land area. §1970. ‖ 1983. ¶1981. ♀Public utilities are
included with services. ♂At current prices. □At 1983 prices. ◇Includes initiation classes
in which pupils learn Portuguese. △Includes some teacher training from second level.

Nauru

Official name: Naoero (Republic of Nauru).
Form of government: republic with one legislative house (Parliament [18]).
Head of state and government: President.
Capital: Yaren*.
Official language: Nauruan.
Official religion: none.
Monetary unit: 1 Australian dollar ($A) = 100 cents; valuation (Oct. 21, 1985) 1 U.S.$ = $A1.42; 1 £ = $A2.04.

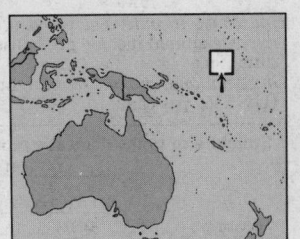

Area and population

Districts	area sq mi	area sq km	population 1977 census
Aiwo	0.4	1.1	439
Anabar	0.6	1.5	102
Anetan	0.4	1.0	149
Anibare	1.2	3.1	55
Baiti	0.5	1.2	254
Boe	0.2	0.5	448
Buada	1.0	2.6	334
Denigomodu	0.3	0.9	151
Ewa	0.5	1.2	235
Ijuw	0.4	1.1	52
Meneng	1.2	3.1	637
Nibok	0.6	1.6	278
Uaboe	0.3	0.8	231
Yaren	0.6	1.5	413
TOTAL	8.2	21.2	7,254†

Demography

Population (1985): 8,000.
Density (1985): persons per sq mi 975.6, persons per sq km 377.4.
Urban–rural (1984): urban 100%; rural 0%.
Sex distribution‡ (1981): male 51.30%; female 48.70%.
Age breakdown‡ (1981): under 15, 43.8%; 15–24, 23.0%; 25–34, 13.7%; 35–44, 8.2%; 45–55, 6.1%; 55–64, 3.1%, 65 and over 2.1%.
Population projection: (1990) 8,000; (2000) 9,000.
Doubling time: 45 years.
Ethnic composition (1977): Nauruan 57.5%, of whom Eamwit 30.2%, Irvwa 25.2%, Eamwidamwit 17.7%; other Pacific islander 26.1%, of whom Gilbertese 67.9%, Tuvaluan 32.1%; Chinese 8.6%; European and other 7.8%.
Religious affiliation (1980): Nauruan Protestant Church (Congregational) 57.6%; Roman Catholic 24.0%; Confucian and Taoist 8.4%; Buddhist 1.7%; Baha'i 1.7%; nonreligious 6.6%.
Major cities: none.

Vital statistics

Birth rate per 1,000 population (1982): 34.0 (world avg. 29.0); legitimate, n.a.; illegitimate, n.a.
Death rate per 1,000 population (1982): 9.2 (world avg. 11.0).
Natural increase rate per 1,000 population (1982): 24.8 (world avg. 18.0).
Total fertility rate (avg. births per childbearing woman): n.a.
Marriage rate per 1,000 population‡ (1977): 6.3.
Divorce rate per 1,000 population‡ (1977): 0.3.
Life expectancy at birth‡ (1976–81): male 48.9 years; female 62.1 years.
Major causes of death per 100,000 population (1976–81)§ ‖ : accidents, suicide, and violence 116.0; diseases of the circulatory system 89.0; diseases of the digestive system 53.0; malignant neoplasms (cancers) 38.0; infectious and parasitic diseases 33.0.

National economy

Budget (1984–85). Revenue: $A88,273,000¶ (no breakdown available). Expenditures: $A88,130,600 (no breakdown available).
Public debt (external, outstanding): none.
Tourism: receipts from visitors, n.a; expenditures by nationals abroad, n.a.
Gross national product (at current market prices; 1981): U.S.$155,400,000 (U.S.$21,400 per capita).

Distribution of gross domestic product and labour force

	1982 value in A$'000,000	1982 % of total value	1966 labour force	1966 % of labour force
Agriculture	...	...	2	0.1
Mining	...	...	1,725	68.9
Manufacturing	...	...	2	0.1
Construction	...	...	173	6.9
Public utilities	...	...	1	—
Transport and communications	...	...	22	0.9
Trade	...	...	87	3.5
Finance	...	...	1	—
Services	...	...	308	12.3
Pub. admin., defense	...	...	148	5.9
Other	...	...	35	1.4
TOTAL	100	100.0	2,504⁹	100.0

Production (metric tons except as noted). Agriculture, forestry, fishing (1984): coconuts 2,000, and noncommercial quantities of bananas, pineapples, and vegetables are produced, but most foodstuffs and beverages are imported; livestock (number of live animals) 2,000 pigs; roundwood, none;

fish catch, n.a. (fish caught are for local consumption only). Mining and quarrying (1983): phosphate rock 1,684,000. Manufacturing: none. Construction (1977): 65 units. Energy production (consumption): electricity (kW-hr; 1983) 27,000,000 (27,000,000); coal, none (n.a.); crude petroleum, none (n.a.); petroleum products (metric tons; 1983) none (41,000); natural gas, none (n.a.).
Population economically active (1977): total 2,211; participation rate of total population 30.5% (female, n.a.; unemployed, n.a.).
Price and earnings indexes: n.a.
Household income and expenditure. Average household size (1977) 8.0; average annual income per household: δ; source of income: □; expenditure: n.a.
Land use (1983): forested 40%; meadows and pastures, nil; agricultural and under permanent cultivation, nil; built-on, wasteland, and other *c.* 60%◊.

Foreign trade

Balance of trade (current prices)

	1978	1979	1980	1981	1982	1983
$A'000,000	+42.9	+66.8	+81.6	+61.9	...	+98.6
% of total	65.4%	75.9%	59.2%	67.5%	...	57.4%

Imports (1979): $A10,600,000 (food, fuel, water, machinery for phosphate industry, and building materials). *Major import sources:* Australia 58.0%; United Kingdom, New Zealand, and Japan.
Exports (1979): $A77,400,000 (phosphate 100%). *Major export destinations:* Australia 51.0%; New Zealand 41.0%; Japan 4.0%; South Korea 3.0%.

Transport and communications

Transport. Railroads (1984): length 3 mi, 5 km; (1983–84) passenger traffic, n.a.; short ton-mi cargo 4,670,000, metric ton-km cargo 6,820,000. Roads (1984): total length 12 mi, 19 km (paved 100%). Vehicles (1977): passenger cars, trucks, and buses 1,761. Merchant marine (1984): vessels 8; total deadweight tonnage, 93,391. Air transport (1982): passenger-mi 147,886,-000, passenger-km 238,000,000; short ton-mi cargo 1,096,000, metric ton-km cargo 1,600,000; airports (1985) with scheduled flights 1.
Communications. Daily newspapers: none; 1 bimonthly, total circulation 750; circulation per 1,000 population, about 95. Radio (1984): total number of receivers 4,000 (1 per 2.1 persons). Television: no broadcast TV; videotaped television is commonplace, however. Telephones (1979): 1,500 (1 per 5.3 persons).

Education and health

Education (1980)

	schools	teachers	students	student/teacher ratio
Primary (age 5–11)△	9	102	1,704	16.7
Secondary (age 12–16)	2	36	339	9.4
Vocational	1	4	70	17.5
Teacher training (at second level)	1	1	10	10.0
Higher	—	—	—	—

Educational attainment. n.a. *Literacy* (1979): total population over age 15 literate 99.0%.
Health (1980): physicians, 11 (1 per 700 persons); hospital beds 200 (1 per 40.0 persons); infant mortality rate per 1,000 live births (1981) 31.2.
Food (1978–80): daily per capita caloric intake 3,202 (vegetable products 64%, animal products 36%); 120% of FAO recommended minimum requirement.

Military

Total active duty personnel (1984): Nauru does not have any military establishment; there is a police force of about 60 Nauruans.

*Seat of government. †Total includes 396 Nauruans unable to complete census forms; also included are 564 Europeans, 626 Chinese, and 1,890 other Pacific islanders not distributable by district. ‡Nauruan population only. §Annual average. ‖ Of the 191 deaths during the six years, the leading specific causes by actual number were: motor vehicle accidents 31; viral hepatitis 17; acute cerebrovascular disease 16; diabetes mellitus 11; drownings 9; cirrhosis 8. ¶Largely from phosphate exports. ⁹The Nauruan economy is heavily dependent on contract immigrant labour, largely engaged in phosphate production. In 1981 Nauruans constituted only 36.9% of the employment structure (most of whom worked in the administrative–governmental sector); foreign contract labour as a percent of labour force included I-Kiribati 26.7%, Tuvaluans 17.0%, Chinese 8.0%, Filipinos 3.6%, and others 7.8%. δIndividual landownership, distribution of phosphate royalties according to landownership, and sequential working of phosphate deposits have combined to produce considerable inequities in income distribution among Nauruans. Similar inequities exist between the Nauruans and the alien work force, especially the phosphate workers from Kiribati and Tuvalu. □Nearly complete dependence on phosphate revenues. ◊About 80% of Nauru's land area is classified as phosphate-bearing, of which about 60% had been mined out by the early 1980s. △Includes pre-primary.

Nepal

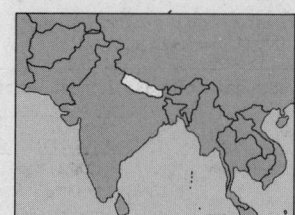

Official name: Nepāl Adhirājya (Kingdom of Nepal).
Form of government: constitutional monarchy with one legislative house (National Panchayat [140]).
Chief of state: King.
Head of government: Prime Minister.
Capital: Kāthmāndu.
Official language: Nepālī.
Official religion: none.
Monetary unit: 1 Nepalese rupee (NRs) = 100 paisa (pice); valuation (Oct. 21, 1985) 1 U.S.$ = NRs18.28; 1 £ = NRs26.22.

Area and population

Development regions Geographic regions	Capitals	area sq mi	area sq km	population 1981 census
Eastern	Dhankūtā	10,987	28,456	3,708,923
Mountain				338,439
Hill				1,257,042
Tarai				2,113,442
Central	Kāthmāndu	10,583	27,410	4,909,357
Mountain				413,143
Hill				2,108,433
Tarai				2,387,781
Western	Pokharā	11,351	29,398	3,128,859
Mountain				19,951
Hill				2,150,939
Tarai				957,969
Mid-western	Surkhet	16,362	42,378	1,955,611
Mountain				242,486
Hill				1,042,365
Tarai				670,760
Far-western	Dipāyal	7,544	19,539	1,320,089
Mountain				288,877
Hill				604,336
Tarai				426,876
TOTAL		56,827	147,181	15,022,839

Demography

Population (1985 est.): 16,525,000.
Density (1985): persons per sq mi 290.8, persons per sq km 112.3.
Urban–rural (1981): urban 6.4%; rural 93.6%.
Sex distribution (1981): male 51.22%; female 48.78%.
Age breakdown (1981): under 15, 41.4%; 15–29, 25.5%; 30–44, 17.4%; 45–59, 10.0%; 60–74, 4.7%; 75 and over, 1.0%.
Population projection: (1990) 18,500,000; (2000) 23,048,000.
Doubling time: 26 years.
Ethnic composition (1980): Nepalese 54.4%; Bihārī (including Maithilī and Bhojpurī) 18.7%; Tamang 6.1%; Newār 4.4%; Thārū 4.1%; other 12.3%.
Religious affiliation (1981): Hindu 89.5%; Buddhist 5.3%; Muslim 2.7%; Jain 0.1%; other 2.4%.
Major cities (1981): Kāthmāndu 235,160; Birātnagar 93,544; Lalitpūr 79,875; Bhaktapūr 48,472; Pokharā 46,642.

Vital statistics

Birth rate per 1,000 population (1984): 41.7 (world avg. 29.0).
Death rate per 1,000 population (1984): 18.0 (world avg. 11.0).
Natural increase rate per 1,000 population (1984): 23.7 (world avg. 18.0).
Total fertility rate (avg. births per childbearing woman; 1984): 6.2.
Marriage rate per 1,000 population: n.a.
Divorce rate per 1,000 population: n.a.
Life expectancy at birth (1984): male 47.2 years; female 45.7 years.
Major causes of death per 100,000 population: n.a.; however, major diseases are cholera, malaria, tuberculosis, and typhoid.

National economy

Budget (1984–85 est.). Revenue: NRs4,190,100,000 (taxes on goods and services 39.4%, customs duties 20.7%, income tax 10.7%, interest on loans 9.5%, registration taxes 6.9%, land revenue 6.3%, government services 5.5%). Expenditures: NRs3,079,200,000 (loan repayment 22.5%, defense 17.2%, general administration 13.6%, social services 8.5%, economic services 6.9%, education 5.4%, revenue and economic administration 3.2%).
Public debt (external, outstanding; 1983): U.S.$346,400,000.
Tourism (1983): receipts from visitors U.S.$35,000,000; expenditures by nationals abroad U.S.$20,000,000.
Production (metric tons except as noted). Agriculture, forestry, fishing (1984): rice 2,760,000, corn (maize) 751,000, wheat 634,000, sugarcane 509,000, potatoes 383,000, millet 114,000, jute 25,000, tobacco 7,000, milk (cow, buffalo, goat) 823,000, eggs 17,500; livestock (number of live animals) 7,000,000 cattle, 4,400,000 buffalo, 2,600,000 goats, 2,480,000 sheep, 395,000 pigs; roundwood 14,684,000 cu m*; fish catch 2,112*. Mining and quarrying (1983): limestone 50,422; talc 15,263; magnesite 15,016; garnet 23,000 kilograms. Manufacturing (1983–84): jute 20,528; sugar 18,464; cement 10,355; cotton textiles 11,973,000 metres; synthetic textiles 3,639,000 metres; beer 27,840 hectolitres; cigarettes 3,709,000,000 units; shoes 68,-000 pairs. Construction: n.a. Energy production (consumption): electricity (kW-hr; 1983) 257,000,000 (336,000,000); coal (metric tons; 1983) none (70,000); petroleum products (metric tons; 1983) none (90,000); natural gas, none (none).

Gross national product (at current market prices; 1983): U.S.$2,660,000,000 (U.S.$170 per capita).

Structure of gross domestic product and labour force

	1981–82 in value NRs'000,000	1981–82 % of total value	1981 labour force	1981 % of labour force
Agriculture	16,792	55.5	6,244,289	91.1
Mining	68	0.2	971	†
Manufacturing	1,189	3.9	33,029	0.5
Construction	2,537	8.4	2,022	†
Public utilities	90	0.3	3,013	†
Transportation and communication	1,992	6.6	7,424	0.1
Trade	1,070	3.5	109,446	1.6
Finance	2,351	7.8	9,850	0.1
Services	2,174	7.2	313,570	4.6
Other	2,002‡	6.6	127,272§	1.9§
TOTAL	30,265 ‖	100.0	6,850,886	100.0¶

Population economically active (1981): total 6,850,886; participation rate of population ages 15–60, 85.1% (female 34.6%, unemployed, n.a).

Price and earnings indexes (1980 = 100)

	1978	1979	1980	1981	1982	1983	1984
Consumer price index	84.2	87.2	100.0	111.1	124.1	139.5	138.9°
Monthly earnings index	...	...	...	...	...	...	...

Household income and expenditure. Average household size (1980) 5.3; income per household (1973–74) NRs791 (U.S.$75); sources of income (1973–74)ŏ: wages and salaries 39.2%, self-employment 33.6%, owner-occupied dwellings 17.5%; expenditure (1973–75)ŏ: food and beverages 48.0%, housing 20.0%, clothing and footwear 8.8%, fuel and power 4.2%, recreation 3.4%, education 3.2%.
Land use (1983): forested 32.5%; meadows and pastures 13.1%; agricultural and under permanent cultivation 17.0%; other 37.4%.

Foreign trade□

Balance of trade (current prices)

	1979	1980	1981	1982	1983	1984◇
NRs'000,000	−1,602.3	−2,947.5	−2,601.2	−3,827.2	−5,054.2	−1,080.3
% of total	38.0%	60.4%	42.9%	62.2%	65.0%	51.9%

Imports (1983–84): NRs6,514,300,000 (basic manufactured goods 27.7%; machinery and transport equipment 25.3%; mineral fuels 11.5%; food and live animals, chiefly for food 11.2%; chemicals 10.7%; miscellaneous manufactured articles 7.2%; crude materials except fuels 4.1%). *Major import sources:* India 46.9%; Japan 24.8%; South Korea 7.5%; Singapore 4.7%; United States 4.2%; Hong Kong 2.3%.
Exports (1983–84): NRs1,703,900,000 (food and live animals, chiefly for food 34.3%; basic manufactures 32.6%; crude materials except fuels 21.8%; machinery, transport equipment, and other manufactured articles 4.9%; animal and vegetable oils 4.0%). *Major export destinations:* India 68.1%; United Kingdom 12.9%; United States 8.5%; Singapore 3.8%; Japan 3.0%.

Transport and communications

Transport. Railroads (1982–83): length 32 mi, 52 km; passengers carried 114,-500; freight handled 19,800 tons. Roads (1983–84): total length 3,485 mi, 5,608 km (paved 46%). Vehicles (1978): passenger cars 14,201; trucks and buses 9,988. Merchant marine: none. Air transport (1982): passenger-mi 155,000,000, passenger-km 250,000,000; short ton-mi cargo 2,100,000, metric ton-km cargo 3,100,000; airports (1985) with scheduled flights 6.
Communications. Daily newspapers (1983): total number 51; total circulation, n.a.; circulation per 1,000 population, n.a. Radio (1984): total number of receivers 310,000 (1 per 50 persons). Television: total number of receivers, n.a. Telephones (1984): 23,500.

Education and health

Education (1982–83)

	schools△	teachers	students	student/ teacher ratio
Primary (age 6–11)	10,340	38,016	1,727,000	45.4
Secondary (age 12–17)	4,253	15,903	418,000	26.3
Higher	10	2,918△	52,070	...

Educational attainment, n.a. *Literacy* (1981): total population over age 6 literate 2,833,440 (23.3%); males literate 2,117,030 (34.0%); females literate 716,410 (12.0%).
Health (1983–84): physicians 571 (1 per 28,270 persons); hospital beds 3,048 (1 per 5,296 persons); infant mortality rate per 1,000 live births (1984) 140.0.
Food (1980–82): daily per capita caloric intake 2,005 (vegetable products 93%, animal products 7%); 91% of FAO recommended minimum requirement.

Military

Total active duty personnel (1984): 25,000 (army 100.0%). *Military expenditure as percent of GNP* (1983): 1.1% (world 6.1%); per capita expenditure U.S.$1.

*1983. †Less than 0.1%. ‡Indirect taxes less subsidies. §Includes activities not adequately defined. ‖At current prices. ¶Detail does not add to total given because of rounding. °Second quarter. ŏFor Kāthmāndu only. □Import figures are f.o.b. (free on board) in balance of trade and c.i.f. (cost, insurance, and freight) for commodities and trading partners. ◇First quarter. △1981–82.

Netherlands, The

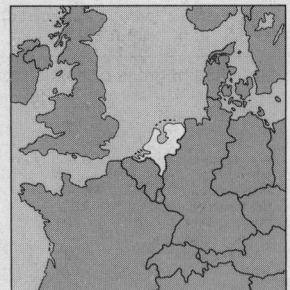

Official name: Koninkrijk der Nederlanden (Kingdom of The Netherlands).
Form of government: constitutional monarchy with two legislative houses (First Chamber [75]; Second Chamber [150]).
Chief of state: Monarch.
Head of government: Prime Minister.
Seat of government: The Hague.
Capital: Amsterdam.
Official language: Dutch.
Official religion: none.
Monetary unit: 1 Netherlands guilder (f.) = 100 cents; valuation (Oct. 21, 1985) 1 U.S.$ = f.2.98; 1 £ = f.4.27.

Area and population

Provinces	Capitals	area		population
		sq mi	sq km	1985 estimate*
Drenthe	Assen	1,025	2,654	429,500
Friesland	Leeuwarden	1,295	3,355	597,600
Gelderland	Arnhem	1,937	5,016	1,745,300
Groningen	Groningen	902	2,335	561,100
Limburg	Maastricht	838	2,170	1,085,700
Noord-Brabant	Eindhoven	1,914	4,957	2,113,000
Noord-Holland	Haarlem	1,030	2,668	2,311,500
Overijssel	Zwolle	1,471	3,811	1,044,900
Utrecht	Utrecht	514	1,332	936,100
Zeeland	Middelburg	689	1,785	355,400
Zuid-Holland	's-Gravenhage	1,122	2,905	3,151,300
Municipalities†				
Almere	—	57	148	40,300
Dronten	—	129	333	22,400
Lelystad	—	105	271	56,600
Zeewolde	—	86	223	1,900
TOTAL LAND AREA		13,113‡	33,963	14,453,800
INLAND WATER		2,913	7,545	
TOTAL AREA		16,026	41,508	

Demography

Population (1985): 14,472,000.
Density (1983): persons per sq mi 1,094.0, persons per sq km 422.4.
Urban–rural (1984): urban 88.5%; rural 11.5%.
Sex distribution (1984): male 49.49%; female 50.51%.
Age breakdown (1984): under 15, 20.4%; 15–29, 25.6%; 30–44, 22.0%; 45–59, 15.5%; 60–74, 11.6%; 75 and over, 4.9%.
Population projection: (1990) 14,783,000; (2000) 15,380,000.
Doubling time: n.a.; vital rates and net migration in near balance.
Ethnic composition (by nationality; 1984): Netherlander 96.2%; Turkish 1.1%; Moroccan 0.7%; German 0.3%; other 1.7%.
Religious affiliation (1983): Roman Catholic 36.1%; Dutch Reformed Church 19.3%; Reformed Churches 7.9%; other 4.4%; no religion 32.3%.
Major cities (1985): Amsterdam 675,600; Rotterdam 571,100; 's-Gravenhage 443,500; Utrecht 230,000; Eindhoven 191,700.

Vital statistics

Birth rate per 1,000 population (1984): 12.1 (world avg. 29.0); legitimate 92.4%; illegitimate 7.6%.
Death rate per 1,000 population (1984): 8.3 (world avg. 11.0).
Natural increase rate per 1,000 population (1984): 3.8 (world avg. 18.0).
Total fertility rate (avg. births per childbearing woman; 1983): 1.5.
Marriage rate per 1,000 population (1984): 5.7.
Divorce rate per 1,000 population (1983): 2.3.
Life expectancy at birth (1983): male 72.8 years; female 79.5 years.
Major causes of death per 100,000 population (1984): malignant neoplasms (cancers) 225.3, of which lung cancer 56.0; ischemic heart diseases 172.6; cerebrovascular diseases 83.9; accidents, poisoning, and violence 40.7.

National economy

Budget (1984). Revenue: f.131,187,000,000 (income and corporate taxes 36.3%, natural gas royalties 11.8%, excise and import taxes 7.6%). Expenditures: f.166,549,000,000 (social security and public health 20.4%, education and culture 17.6%, defense 7.8%).
Public debt (1984): U.S.$63,297,000,000.
Tourism (1983): receipts from visitors U.S.$1,421,000,000; expenditures by nationals abroad U.S.$3,223,000,000.
Production (metric tons except as noted). Agriculture (1984): sugar beets 6,955,000, potatoes 6,673,000, vegetables and melons 2,855,000, wheat 1,131,000; livestock (number of live animals) 5,516,000 cattle, 11,146,000 pigs, 760,000 sheep; roundwood 906,000 cu m; fish catch 503,275. Manufacturing (value of sales in f.'000,000; 1983): synthetic fibres 27,200; foodstuffs 22,800; petroleum products 16,900; electrical machinery 12,800; transport equipment 6,300. Construction (1982): residential 58,947,000 sq m; nonresidential 51,620,000 sq m. Energy production (consumption): electricity (kW-hr; 1984) 62,778,000,000 (61,782,000,000 ‖); coal (metric tons; 1982) none (7,443,000); crude petroleum (barrels; 1984) 21,140,000 (282,400,000¶); petroleum products (metric tons; 1984) 62,059,000 (24,186,000¶); natural gas (cu m; 1984) 77,251,000,000 (38,905,000,000 ‖).
Land use (1983): forested 8.7%; meadows and pastures 33.7%; agricultural and under permanent cultivation 25.5%; other 32.1%.

Gross national product (at current market prices; 1984): U.S.$122,448,000,-000 (U.S.$8,492 per capita).

Structure of gross domestic product and labour force

	1983			
	in value f.'000,000	% of total value	labour force	% of labour force
Agriculture	13,470	4.4	64,500	1.1
Mining }	77,140	25.4	8,500	0.1
Manufacturing			704,600	12.1
Construction	20,860	6.9	278,700	4.8
Public utilities	5,650	1.9	301,200	5.2
Transp. and commun.	20,660	6.8	282,800	4.9
Trade	45,360	15.0	645,000	11.1
Pub. admin., defense	46,980	15.5	762,000	13.1
Finance }	89,080	29.4	407,200	7.0
Services			1,284,200	22.1
Other	−15,940⁹	−5.3⁹	1,075,300⁵	18.5⁵
TOTAL	303,260□	100.0	5,814,000	100.0

Population economically active (1984): total 5,884,000; participation rate of total population 40.8% (female 34.9%; unemployed 14.0%).

Price and earnings indexes (1980 = 100)

	1979	1980	1981	1982	1983	1984	1985◊
Consumer price index	93.9	100.0	106.7	113.0	116.2	120.0	121.6
Hourly earnings index	96.0	100.0	103.0	110.0	113.0	115.0	118.0

Household income and expenditure. Average household size (1984) 2.7; income per household (1983) f.74,200 (U.S.$26,000); sources of income: wages 40.9%, transfer payments 28.7%, self-employment 17.8%, other 12.6%; expenditure (1983): housing 31.8%, food 11.2%, clothing 4.7%.

Foreign trade△

Balance of trade (current prices)

	1979	1980	1981	1982	1983	1984
f.'000,000	−1,341	+499	+12,834	+15,984	+18,191	+22,421
% of total	0.5%	0.2%	3.9%	4.7%	5.2%	5.6%

Imports (1984): f.198,922,000,000 (manufactured goods 26.0%; petroleum and petroleum products 23.9%; machinery and transport equipment 19.1%; foodstuffs, beverages, and tobacco 12.4%; chemicals 9.3%). *Major import sources:* West Germany 22.0%; Belgium–Luxembourg 11.1%; United States 8.9%; United Kingdom 8.7%; France 5.9%.
Exports (1984): f.210,691,000,000 (mineral fuels and natural gas 23.0%; manufactured goods 19.8%, of which metal products 6.1%; food and beverages 18.7%; chemical products 16.7%; machinery and transport equipment 14.0%). *Major export destinations:* West Germany 29.7%; Belgium–Luxembourg 13.9%; France 10.4%; United Kingdom 9.5%; Italy 5.6%.

Transport and communications

Transport. Railroads (1984): length 2,852 km; passenger-km 8,938,000,000; metric ton-km cargo 2,782,000,000 ‖ . Roads (1983): total length 110,140 km (paved 86.5%). Vehicles (1983): passenger cars 4,728,000; trucks and buses 357,000. Merchant marine (1984): vessels (100 gross tons and over) 1,337; total deadweight tonnage 6,653,523. Air transport† (1983–84): passenger-km 16,814,000,000; metric ton-km cargo 1,275,000,000; airports (1985) 9.
Communications. Daily newspapers (1984): total number 79; total circulation 4,500,000; circulation per 1,000 population 312. Radio (1984): total receivers 4,750,000 (1 per 3.0 persons). Television (1984): total receivers 4,454,000 (1 per 3.2 persons). Telephones (1983): 8,023,000 (1 per 1.8 persons).

Education and health

Education (1983–84)

	schools	teachers	students	student/ teacher ratio
Primary (age 6–12)	9,606	63,058	1,237,422	19.6
Secondary (age 12–18)	1,471	53,770	832,990	15.5
Voc., teacher tr.	1,892	56,963	633,966	11.1
Higher	402	29,952	306,416	10.2

Educational attainment (1981). Percent of population ages 15–64 having: primary education 19.3%; secondary 62.8%; higher 14.0%. *Literacy* (1985): virtually 100% literate.
Health (1984): physicians 29,951 (1 per 481 persons); hospital beds 68,943 (1 per 209 persons); infant mortality rate per 1,000 live births 8.3.
Food (1980–82): daily per capita caloric intake 3,553 (vegetable products 57%, animal products 43%); 132% of FAO recommended minimum requirement.

Military

Total active duty personnel (1984): 103,267 (army 67.4%, navy 16.3%; air force 16.3%). *Military expenditure as percent of GNP* (1983): 3.2% (world 6.1%); per capita expenditure U.S.$325.

---

*January 1st estimate; includes about 1,200 persons having no fixed municipality of residence. †Former parts of IJsselmeerpolders not yet included in any province. ‡Detail does not add to total given because of rounding. §Delivered at factories only; about 97% of all milk produced. ‖ 1983. ¶1982. ⁹Imputed bank service charge. ⁵Primarily unemployed and self-employed. □At current prices. ◊First quarter. △Import figures are f.o.b. (free on board) in balance of trade and c.i.f. (cost, insurance, and freight) for commodities and trading partners. †KLM (Royal Dutch Airlines) only.

Netherlands Antilles

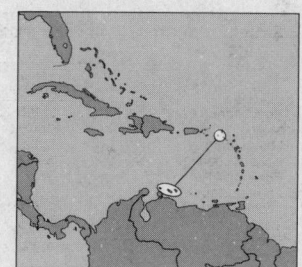

Official name: Nederlandse Antillen (Netherlands Antilles).
Political status: nonmetropolitan territory of The Netherlands with one legislative house (Parliament [22])*.
Chief of state: Dutch Monarch represented by the governor.
Head of government: Prime Minister.
Capital: Willemstad.
Official language: Dutch.
Official religion: none.
Monetary unit: 1 Netherlands Antillean guilder (NA f.) = 100 cents; valuation (Oct. 21, 1985) 1 U.S.$ = NA f.1.80; 1 £ = NA f.2.58.

Area and population

Island authorities	Capitals	area sq mi	area sq km	population 1981 census
Aruba	Oranjestad	75	193	60,312
Bonaire	Kralendijk	111	288	8,753
Curaçao	Willemstad	171	444	147,388
Windward Islands	—	26	68	15,479
Saba	The Bottom	5	13	965
Sint Eustatius or Statia	Oranjestad	8	21	1,358
Sint Maarten (Dutch part only)	Philipsburg	13	34	13,156
TOTAL		383	993	231,932

Demography

Population (1985): 244,000.
Density (1985): persons per sq mi 637.1, persons per sq km 245.7.
Urban–rural (1985): urban 92.4%; rural 7.6%.
Sex distribution (1981): male 48.80%; female 51.20%.
Age breakdown (1972): under 15, 38.1%; 15–29, 26.7%; 30–44, 16.6%; 45–59, 10.3%; 60–74, 6.5%; 75 and over, 1.8%.
Population projection: (1990) 262,000; (2000) 300,000.
Doubling time: population growth is negligible.
Ethnic composition (1980): Netherlands Antillean (Dutch/black) creole 84.0%; white 6.1%; other West Indian 4.9%; Suriname creole 2.9%; other 2.1%.
Religious affiliation (1980): Roman Catholic 87.2%; Protestant (mostly Lutheran–Reformed tradition and Methodist) 9.7%; nonreligious 1.9%; Jewish 0.4%; other 0.8%.
Major cities (1980 est.): Willemstad (urban area) 100,000; Oranjestad 20,000; Philipsburg 10,000.

Vital statistics

Birth rate per 1,000 population (1980)†: 18.8 (world avg. 29.0); legitimate 60.4%; illegitimate 39.6%.
Death rate per 1,000 population (1980)†: 5.3 (world avg. 11.0).
Natural increase rate per 1,000 population (1980)†: 13.5 (world avg. 18.0).
Total fertility rate (avg. births per childbearing woman): n.a.
Marriage rate per 1,000 population (1980)†: 6.3.
Divorce rate per 1,000 population (1980)†: 2.3.
Life expectancy at birth (1974–79)‡: male 69.8 years; female 75.7 years.
Major causes of death per 100,000 population (1973): malignant neoplasms (cancers) 94.8; diseases of the circulatory system 89.9; accidents, poisoning, and violence 44.7.

National economy

Budget (1983)§. Revenue: NA f.290,000,000 (import duties 34.1%, tax sharing from Aruba and Curaçao 33.4%, excise taxes 14.1%, foreign exchange tax 5.9%, Dutch development aid 4.5%, other taxes 3.1%). Expenditures: NA f.313,000,000 (social service expenditures 62.3%, pensions 9.6%, interest on domestic debt 7.7%, transfers to Aruba and Curaçao governments 6.8%, national airline subsidy 6.7%).
Public debt (external, outstanding; 1982): U.S.$623,000,000.
Tourism: receipts from visitors (1984) U.S.$314,000,000, of which Windward Islands 41%, Aruba 36%, Curaçao 22%, Bonaire 1%; expenditures by nationals abroad (1981) U.S.$63,000,000.
Production (metric tons except as noted). Agriculture, forestry, fishing (value of production in NA f.'000; 1982): eggs 3,863, fruits and vegetables 2,850, pork 1,250, goat meat 555; livestock (number of live animals; 1984) 23,000 goats, 9,000 cattle, 8,000 pigs, 8,000 sheep; roundwood, n.a.; fish 11,000. Mining and quarrying (1983): unrefined salt 399,000; calcium phosphate 15,000 ‖. Manufacturing (1982)¶: heavy fuel oils 19,400,000; motor gasoline 2,600,000; lubricating oils 500,000; beer 134,000 hectolitres♀; other manufactures include cigarettes, textiles, rum. Construction (value of new buildings in NA f.'000; 1982) 74,059. Energy production (consumption): electricity (kW-hr; 1983) 2,350,000,000 (2,350,000,000); coal, none (n.a.); crude petroleum (barrels; 1983) none (175,700,000); petroleum products (metric tons; 1983) 22,155,000 (2,116,000); natural gas, none (n.a.).
Household income and expenditure. Average household size (1980) 4.5; average annual income per household: n.a.; source of income: n.a.; expenditure (1984)♂: food 22.1%, transportation and communication 19.4%, housing 18.8%, household supplies 10.0%, clothing and footwear 8.7%, recreation and education 5.9%, health 2.2%, other 12.9%.
Gross national product (at current market prices; 1982): U.S.$1,370,000,000 (U.S.$5,730 per capita).

Structure of gross domestic product and labour force

	in value	% of total value	1983 labour force	% of labour force
Agriculture	...	...	320	0.3
Mining	...	...	177	0.2
Manufacturing	...	...	8,428	8.8
Construction	...	...	7,029	7.3
Public utilities	...	...	1,697	1.7
Transportation and communication	...	...	5,876	6.1
Trade	...	...	21,865	22.8
Finance	...	...	4,941	5.1
Services	...	...	30,232	31.5
Other	...	...	15,628	16.2
TOTAL	...	...	96,193	100.0

Population economically active (1983): total 96,193; participation rate of total population 39.9% (female 39.6%, unemployed 16.1%).

Price and earnings indexes (1980 = 100)

	1978	1979	1980	1981	1982	1983	1984
Consumer price index	78.3	87.2	100.0	112.2	119.0	122.4	125.0
Monthly earnings index◇	...	88.9	100.0	114.7	127.9	...	...

Land use (1983): forested, negligible; meadows and pastures, negligible; agricultural and under permanent cultivation 8.0%; other (dry savanna) 92.0%.

Foreign trade△

Balance of trade (current prices)

	1977	1978	1979	1980	1981	1982	1983
NA f.'000,000	−805.4	−925.0	−772.0	−924.0	−1,335.4	−1,088.0	−209.0
% of total	6.9%	8.0%	5.1%	4.7%	5.9%	5.6%	1.3%

Imports (1979)‡: NA f.7,911,000,000 (crude petroleum 73.3%; petroleum products 10.6%, of which heavy fuel oils 9.5%; machines and transport equipment 3.2%; food and live animals 3.1%; basic manufactures 2.6%; chemicals 1.6%). *Major import sources:* Venezuela 70.6%; United States 6.9%; Nigeria 5.9%; Qatar 2.9%; The Netherlands 2.5%.
Exports (1979)‡: NA f.7,139,000,000 (petroleum and petroleum products 98.4%, of which heavy fuel oils 59.2%, gasoline 15.9%, kerosine 12.4%, crude petroleum 4.0%, lubricating oils 3.6%; chemicals 0.7%). *Major export destinations:* United States 51.3%; United Kingdom 3.1%; Colombia 3.0%; Jamaica 2.8%.

Transport and communications

Transport. Railroads: none. Roads (1984): total length 590 mi, 950 km (paved 32%). Vehicles (1982): passenger cars 55,000; trucks and buses 8,000. Merchant marine vessels (100 gross tons and over) n.a. Air transport (1983)†: passenger-mi 110,570,000, passenger-km 177,950,000; short ton-mi cargo 732,000, metric ton-km cargo 1,069,000; airports (1985) with scheduled flights 6.
Communications. Daily newspapers (1984): total number 6; total circulation 53,500; circulation per 1,000 population 221. Radio (1984): receivers 160,000 (1 per 1.5 persons). Television (1984): receivers 57,000 (1 per 4.3 persons). Telephones (1983): 65,163 (1 per 3.7 persons).

Education and health

Education (1981)

	schools	teachers	students	student/ teacher ratio
Primary (age 6–12)	125	1,543	32,832	21.3
Secondary (age 12–17)	...	669	10,931	16.3
Voc., teacher tr.	...	734	10,318	14.1
Higher⊕	1	20	500	25.0

Educational attainment (1971). Percent of adult population over age 25 having: no formal schooling 52.2%; primary education 25.0%; secondary 18.4%; higher 4.4%. *Literacy* (1980): total population over age 15 literate 95.0%.
Health: physicians (1975) 164 (1 per 1,393 persons); hospital beds (1983) 2,410 (1 per 100 persons); infant mortality rate per 1,000 live births (1980) 13.4†.
Food (1980–82): daily per capita caloric intake 2,735 (vegetable products 69%, animal products 31%); 113% of FAO recommended minimum requirement.

Military

Total active duty personnel (1984): A small Dutch naval contingent is stationed permanently in the Netherlands Antilles.

*The governments of Aruba and Curaçao are partially autonomous from the central government of the Netherlands Antilles. Aruba is to withdraw from the Netherlands Antilles as of Jan. 1, 1986, and become an autonomous member of the Kingdom of The Netherlands, the same status as the whole of the Netherlands Antilles. †Excludes Sint Eustatius. ‡Aruba and Curaçao only. §Central government only. Data represent only about 18% of the combined revenue and expenditure of the Netherlands Antilles. The local government of Curaçao accounts for about 53%, Aruba 24%, the Windward Islands 4%, and Bonaire 1%. ‖ 1979. ¶The dominance of the oil-refining industry collapsed in March 1985 with the closure of Aruba's refinery. The continued operation of the Curaçao refinery also was in doubt as of late 1985. ♀1981. ♂Curaçao and Bonaire only. □In 1979 oil refining accounted for 18% of the GDP, tourism 16%, other manufacturing 9%, construction 5%, mining and agriculture 1%, and other (including offshore banking activities, crude oil transshipments, and other transportation and trade) 51%. ◇Finance and trade sectors only. △Imports c.i.f. (cost, insurance, and freight); exports f.o.b. (free on board). †ALM airlines only. ⊕1982.

New Caledonia

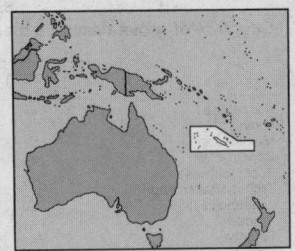

Official name: Territoire de la Nouvelle-Calédonie et Dépendances (Territory of New Caledonia and Dependencies).
Political status: overseas territory (France) with one legislative house (Territorial Assembly [43]).
Chief of state: President of France.
Head of government: High Commissioner.
Capital: Nouméa.
Official language: French.
Official religion: none.
Monetary unit: 1 franc of the Comptoirs français du Pacifique (CFP fr) = 100 centimes; valuation (Oct. 21, 1985) 1 U.S.$ = CFP fr139.46; 1 £ = CFP fr200.00.

Area and population*

Regions	Capitals	area sq mi	area sq km	population 1983 census
Loyauté	...	765	1,981	15,510
Nord	...	2,837	7,348	21,512
Nouméa	Nouméa	637	1,650	85,098
Sud	...	2,995	7,757	23,248
TOTAL		7,233†	18,734†	145,368

Demography

Population (1985): 149,400.
Density (1985): persons per sq mi 20.7, persons per sq km 8.0.
Urban–rural (1983): urban 58.5%; rural 41.5%.
Sex distribution (1983): male 51.10%; female 48.90%.
Age breakdown (1983): under 15, 36.2%; 15–29, 26.9%; 30–44, 19.5%; 45–59, 11.2%; 60–74, 5.1%; 75 and over, 1.1%.
Population projection: (1990) 159,000; (2000) 180,000.
Doubling time: 55 years.
Ethnic composition (1983): Melanesian 42.6%; European 37.1%; Polynesian 12.2%, of which Wallisian 8.4%, Tahitian 3.8%; Indonesian 3.7%; Vietnamese 1.6%; other 2.8%.
Religious affiliation (1980): Roman Catholic 71.6%; Protestant 19.0%; nonreligious 4.5%; Sunnī Muslim 4.0%, other 0.9%
Major cities (1983)‡: Nouméa 60,112; Mont-Doré 14,614; Dumbéa 5,538.

Vital statistics

Birth rate per 1,000 population (1983): 25.2 (world avg. 29.0); (1980) legitimate 57.5%; illegitimate 42.5%.
Death rate per 1,000 population (1983): 5.6 (world avg. 11.0).
Natural increase rate per 1,000 population (1983): 19.6 (world avg. 18.0).
Total fertility rate (avg. births per childbearing woman; 1980): 4.0.
Marriage rate per 1,000 population (1983): 6.9.
Divorce rate per 1,000 population (1983): 1.1.
Life expectancy at birth (1982): 68.6 years.
Major causes of death per 100,000 population (1978): malignant neoplasms (cancers) 35.1; perinatal mortality 24.9; cerebrovascular diseases 24.1; heart diseases 13.9; cranial fractures 13.9.

National economy

Budget (1983). Revenue: CFP fr29,950,000,000 (import and export taxes 31.9%, French aid 29.6%, income tax 5.9%). Expenditures: CFP fr25,950,000,000 (personnel expenditures 41.0%, education 19.0%, debt payments 10.5%).
Public debt (external, outstanding; 1982): U.S.$184,000,000.
Production (metric tons except as noted). Agriculture, forestry, fishing (1984): coconuts 11,000, sweet potatoes 4,000, vegetables 3,800, cassava 3,000, taro 3,000, bananas 2,000, potatoes 1,560, corn (maize) 731, coffee 260§, sorghum 249, wheat 244; livestock (number of live animals) 100,000 cattle, 20,000 pigs, 10,000 horses; roundwood (1983) 12,000 cu m; fish catch (1983) 2,400, of which trochus shells 501. Mining and quarrying (1984): nickel ore ‖ 2,850,000; chromite ore 140,094. Manufacturing (1984): cement 46,900¶; ferronickel (metal content) 29,158; nickel matte (metal content) 5,642; corrugated iron sheets 3,147♀; beef 2,410¶, cobalt 2,105◊, soap 362, coconut oil 263, beer 42,406 hectolitres♀. Construction: n.a. Energy production (consumption): electricity (kW-hr; 1984) 911,000,000 (907,000,000); coal (metric tons; 1983) none (97,000); crude petroleum, none (n.a.); petroleum products (metric tons; 1983) none (281,000); natural gas, none (n.a.).
Population economically active (1983): total 44,842; participation rate of total population 30.8%, (female 37.6%, unemployed 7.8%).

Price and earnings indexes (1980 = 100)□

	1978	1979	1980	1981	1982	1983	1984
Consumer price index	81.2	89.3	100.0	115.9	131.3	145.8	156.2
Hourly earnings index	81.5	89.6	100.0	115.9	138.3	153.2	164.2

Land use (1983): forested 51.2%; meadows and pastures 13.3%; agricultural and under permanent cultivation 0.5%; other 35.0%.
Gross national product (at current market prices; 1983): U.S.$1,140,000,000 (U.S.$7,820 per capita).

Structure of gross domestic product and labour force

	1982 in value CFP fr'000,000	1982 % of total value	1983 labour force	1983 % of labour force
Agriculture	1,820	1.7	9,888	22.0
Mining	13,476	12.5		
Manufacturing	4,985	4.6	7,244	16.3
Construction	6,782	6.3		
Public utilities	2,091	1.9	593	1.3
Transportation and communication	4,761	4.4	2,659	5.9
Trade	28,395	26.3	10,391	23.2
Finance	16,900	15.6	1,025	2.3
Services			12,901	28.7
Pub. admin., defense	27,791	25.7		
Other	1,092	1.0	141	0.3
TOTAL	108,093	100.0	44,842	100.0

Household income and expenditure. Average household size (1983) 4.1; average annual income per household (1980) CFP fr1,670,000 (U.S.$20,600); sources of income (1980): salaries 71.6%, other 28.4%; expenditure (1980): food 28.4%, transportation and communication 15.1%, housing 13.3%, energy 8.3%, recreation 6.4%, clothing and footwear 5.6%, household supplies 3.7%, health 2.6%, education 1.3%, other 15.3%.
Tourism: receipts from visitors, n.a.; expenditures by nationals abroad, n.a.

Foreign trade

Balance of trade (current prices)

	1979	1980	1981	1982	1983	1984
CFP fr'000,000	+10	−4,236	−7,734	−16,323	−18,971	−15,852
% of total	0.02%	6.4%	10.6%	22.9%	28.4%	19.0%

Imports (1983): CFP fr42,909,000,000 (food [including an equal distribution by value of meat products, cereals, and fruits and vegetables] 24.4%, petroleum products 23.2%, machinery and electrical goods 10.5%, transportation equipment 9.0%, chemical products 6.0%). *Major import sources* (1982): France 33.9%; United States 14.1%; Australia 14.0%; European Economic Community countries (excluding France) 9.3%; Japan 6.1%.
Exports (1983): CFP fr23,938,000,000 (ferronickel and nickel matte 62.9%, nickel ore 13.8%, chromite 4.2%). *Major export destinations* (1982): France 46.2%; United States 25.7%; Japan 19.0%; Canada 1.8%.

Transport and communications

Transport. Railroads: none. Roads (1982): total length 3,382 mi, 5,443 km (paved 14%). Vehicles (1983): passenger cars 34,100; trucks and buses 1,730. Merchant marine: vessels (100 gross tons and over) n.a. Air transport (1984)□: passengers arriving and departing 238,081; cargo unloaded 3,811 metric tons, cargo loaded 1,670 metric tons; airports (1985) with scheduled flights 1△.
Communications. Daily newspapers (1984): total number 1; total circulation 13,000; circulation per 1,000 population 88. Radio (1984): total number of receivers 80,000 (1 per 1.8 persons). Television (1984): total number of receivers 31,000 (1 per 4.7 persons). Telephones (1983): 32,578 (1 per 4.5 persons).

Education and health

Education (1984)

	schools	teachers	students	student/ teacher ratio
Primary (age 6–10)	278	1,589	33,884	21.3
Secondary (age 11–17)	41	976	12,683	13.0
Vocational	32	309	5,264	17.0
Higher	5	59	660	11.2

Educational attainment (1983). Percent of adult population over age 19 having: no formal schooling 10.0%; primary education 57.0%; secondary 27.8%; higher 5.2%. *Literacy* (1976): total population over age 13 literate 75,819 (89.4%); males literate 40,296 (90.1%); females literate 35,523 (88.7%).
Health (1981): physicians 168 (1 per 846 persons); hospital beds 1,536 (1 per 93 persons); infant mortality rate per 1,000 live births (1983) 11.2.
Food (1980–82): daily per capita caloric intake 2,821 (vegetable products 80%, animal products 20%); 106% of FAO recommended minimum requirement.

Military

Total active duty personnel (1985): 3,000 inter-service troops†. *Military expenditure as percent of GNP:* n.a.

*Internal reorganization occurred in July 1985. †Detail does not add to total given because of rounding. ‡Populations cited are for communes. §May 1, 1984, to March 15, 1985. ‖New Caledonia has nearly a third of the world's known reserves of nickel. ¶1983. ♀1981. ◊Figure reflects recovery from both ores and intermediate metallurgical products. □All figures are end of year. ◊Tontouta international airport only. △International airports only. †Excludes 600 military police, 480 riot police, and 2,280 gendarmes.

New Zealand

Official name: Dominion of New Zealand.
Form of government: multiparty parliamentary state with one legislative house (House of Representatives [95]).
Chief of state: British Monarch, represented by governor-general.
Head of government: Prime Minister.
Capital: Wellington.
Official language: English.
Official religion: none.
Monetary unit: 1 New Zealand dollar ($NZ) = 100 cents; valuation (Oct. 21, 1985) 1 U.S.$ = $NZ1.72; 1£ = $NZ2.46.

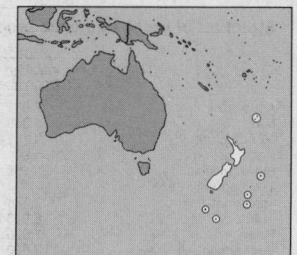

Area and population	area		population
	sq mi	sq km	1984 estimate
Statistical areas*			
North Island			
Central Auckland	2,155	5,581	882,000
East Coast	4,203	10,885	49,300
Hawke's Bay	4,359	11,289	151,700
Northland	4,885	12,653	121,600
South Auckland-			
Bay of Plenty	14,240	36,882	515,600
Taranaki	3,756	9,729	107,400
Wellington	10,720	27,766	586,800
South Island			
Canterbury†	16,736	43,346	422,000
Marlborough	3,942	10,210	36,900
Nelson	7,316	18,948	78,800
Otago	14,237	36,873	182,000
Southland‡	10,990	28,464	108,200
Westland	5,976	15,477	23,200
TOTAL	103,493	268,046	3,265,500

Demography

Population (1985): 3,291,300.
Density (1985): persons per sq mi 31.8, persons per sq km 12.3.
Urban–rural (1981): urban 83.6%; rural 16.4%.
Sex distribution (1985): male 49.63%; female 50.37%.
Age breakdown (1985): under 15, 24.7%; 15–29, 26.3%; 30–44, 20.5%; 45–59, 13.9%; 60–74, 10.7%; 75 and over, 3.9%.
Population projection: (1991) 3,506,000; (2001) 3,772,000.
Doubling time: 63 years.
Ethnic composition (1981): European 85.8%; Maori 8.9%; Pacific Island Polynesian 2.8%; other and not specified 2.5%.
Religious affiliation (1981): Anglican 25.7%; Presbyterian 16.5%; Roman Catholic 14.4%; Methodist 4.7%; other 38.7%.
Major cities (1984): Manukau 179,000; Christchurch 162,100; Auckland 143,800; Wellington 133,700; Waitemata 97,000.

Vital statistics§

Birth rate per 1,000 population (1985): 16.2 (world avg. 29.0); legitimate 76.2%; illegitimate 23.8%.
Death rate per 1,000 population (1985): 7.6 (world avg. 11.0).
Natural increase rate per 1,000 population (1985): 8.6 (world avg. 18.0).
Total fertility rate (avg. births per childbearing woman; 1985): 2.0.
Marriage rate per 1,000 population (1984): 7.8.
Divorce rate per 1,000 population (1982): 0.8 ‖ .
Life expectancy at birth (1984): male 71.2 years; female 77.7 years.
Major causes of death per 100,000 population (1981): heart disease 269.9; malignant neoplasms (cancers) 177.0; cerebrovascular disease 92.4; accidents 45.5; pneumonia 29.0.

National economy

Budget (1984–85). Revenue: $NZ12,539,100,000 (income tax 66.6%; customs, sales tax, and beer duty 20.5%; interest and profits 5.0%; highways tax 2.7%). Expenditures: $NZ15,322,600,000 (social services 29.1%; debt services and investment 17.7%; health 12.5%; education 11.3%; development of industry 11.2%).
Public debt (external, outstanding; 1984): U.S.$12,409,000,000.
Tourism (1983): receipts from visitors U.S.$237,000,000; expenditures by nationals abroad U.S.$452,000,000.
Production (metric tons except as noted). Agriculture, forestry, fishing (1984): barley 589,000, fruits 387,000, wheat 294,000, potatoes 250,000, corn (maize) 172,000, oats 55,000; livestock (number of live animals) 70,344,000 sheep, 7,910,000 cattle, 420,000 pigs, 136,000 goats; roundwood 10,021,000 cu m¶; fish catch 141,485¶. Mining and quarrying (1983): limestone 3,438,000; aluminum 227,000; serpentine 64,055; lead 6,500; gold 9,667 troy oz. Manufacturing (value added, $NZ'000; 1981–82): food, beverages, and tobacco 1,540,430, of which meat 743,343, dairy products 242,801, wine 28,535; fabricated metal products, machinery, and equipment 1,444,158; paper and paper products 684,629; textiles, wearing apparel, and leather 612,657; chemicals and chemical, petroleum, coal, rubber, and plastic products 605,934; wood and wood products 395,378. Construction (1984): residential 225,000 sq m; nonresidential 233,000 sq m. Energy production (consumption): electricity (kW-hr; 1984) 25,855,000,000 (23,027,200); coal (metric tons; 1984) 2,526,600 (2,426,300); petroleum (barrels; 1984) 16,500,000 (25,039,300); natural gas◊ (cu m; 1984) 2,888,074,000 (2,880,920,000).

Gross national product (1983): U.S.$24,000,000,000 (U.S.$7,410 per capita).

Structure of gross domestic product and labour force				
	1984			
	in value $NZ'000,000	% of total value	labour force	% of labour force
Agriculture	3,177	9.1	143,000	10.4
Mining	354	1.0	5,000	0.4
Manufacturing	7,889	22.6	302,000	22.0
Construction	1,814	5.2	88,000	6.4
Public utilities	1,013	2.9	16,000	1.2
Transp. and commun.	3,013	8.6	103,000	7.5
Trade	7,308	20.9	221,000	16.1
Finance	5,194	14.9	99,000	7.2
Pub. admin., defense	4,178	12.0 ⎫	302,000	22.0
Services	1,473	4.2 ⎭		
Other	−478ঠ	−1.4ঠ	92,000	6.7
TOTAL	34,935▢	100.0	1,371,000	100.0◊

Population economically active (1984): total 1,371,000; participation rate of population over age 15, 56.1% (female 35.2%, unemployed 5.7%).

Price and earnings indexes (1980 = 100)							
	1979	1980	1981	1982	1983	1984	1985△
Consumer price index	85.3	100.0	115.3	134.0	143.8	152.7	174.9
Weekly earnings index	84.0	100.0	119.0	133.0	134.0	137.0	148.0

Household income and expenditure. Average household size (1981) 3.2; income per household $NZ15,810 (U.S.$13,755); source of income: n.a.; expenditure (1982): housing 22.2%, food 18.7%, transportation 17.7%, household operation 15.6%, apparel 7.0%, tobacco and alcohol 4.7%.
Land use (1983): forested 38.3%; meadows and pastures 52.5%; agricultural and under permanent cultivation 1.7%; other 7.5%.

Foreign trade

Balance of trade (current prices)						
	1979	1980	1981	1982	1983	1984
$NZ'000,000	+444.4	+392.6	+383.6	+351.1	+811.5	+425.9
% of total	5.1%	3.7%	3.1%	2.4%	5.3%	2.5%

Imports (1984): $NZ8,197,900,000 (machinery and electrical equipment 23.0%; mineral fuels 14.8%, of which petroleum 7.6%; chemicals 11.7%; transport equipment 10.3%; iron, steel, and nonferrous metals 7.0%; textiles, clothing, and footwear 6.8%). *Major import sources:* Japan 20.8%; Australia 20.4%; United States 15.0%; West Germany 4.2%; United Kingdom 8.8%.
Exports (1984): $NZ8,623,800,000 (food and live animals 46.9%, of which meat and meat preparations 20.2%, dairy products and eggs 14.1%; wool 12.9%; forest products 6.2%; chemicals 4.0%). *Major export destinations:* Japan 15.2%; Australia 15.0%; United States 12.9%; United Kingdom 10.3%; Iran 4.7%; U.S.S.R. 2.9%.

Transport and communications

Transport. Railroads (1984): length 2,692 mi, 4,332 km; passenger-mi 284,687,000, passenger-km 458,160,000; short ton-mi cargo 2,168,000,000, metric ton-km cargo 3,165,000,000. Roads (1983): total length 57,731 mi, 92,909 km (paved 53%). Vehicles (1984): passenger cars 1,479,117; trucks and buses 308,270. Merchant marine (1984): vessels (100 gross tons and over) 118; total deadweight tonnage 305,898. Air transport (1984): passenger-mi 4,422,000,000, passenger-km 7,116,000,000; short ton-mi cargo 204,900,000, metric ton-km cargo 299,100,000; airports (1985) with scheduled flights 36.
Communications. Daily newspapers (1983): total number 37; total circulation 1,046,552; circulation per 1,000 population 327. Radio (1984): 2,785,000 receivers (1 per 1.2 persons). Television (1984): 943,500 receivers (1 per 3.4 persons). Telephones (1983): 1,939,488 (1 per 1.7 persons).

Education and health

Education (1983)	schools	teachers	students	student/ teacher ratio
Primary (age 5–12)	2,585	18,504	469,735	25.4
Secondary (age 13–17)	331	12,101	227,831†	18.8
Voc., teacher tr.	27	2,920	148,488†	50.8
Higher⊕	7	3,079	56,513†	18.3

Educational attainment (1981). Percent of population over age 15 having: no formal schooling 1.0%; primary education 14.9%; secondary 57.7%; vocational, postsecondary, and higher 26.4%. *Literacy* (1983): total population over age 15 literate 825,470 (100.0%).
Health (1983): physicians 7,597 (1 per 422 persons); hospital beds 31,923 (1 per 100 persons); infant mortality rate per 1,000 live births (1985) 9.5.
Food (1980–82): daily per capita caloric intake 3,492 (vegetable products 54%, animal products 46%); 136% of FAO recommended minimum requirement.

Military

Total active duty personnel (1984): 12,692 (army 43.7%, navy 22.3%, air force 34.0%). *Military expenditure as percent of GNP* (1983): 2.2% (world 6.1%); per capita expenditure U.S.$162.

*The statistical areas listed have no administrative significance; individual area figures include and total excludes 22 sq mi (57 sq km) that was not distributable by statistical area. †Includes Chatham Island county. ‡Includes Stewart Island county. §Vital statistics figures are for March 1985. ‖ Absolute decrees only. ¶1983. ◊Since 1979, data include manufactured gas. ঠIncludes import duties less imputed bank service charges. ▢At current prices. ◊Detail does not add to total given because of rounding. △Second quarter. †Includes part-time students. ⊕Universities only.

Nicaragua

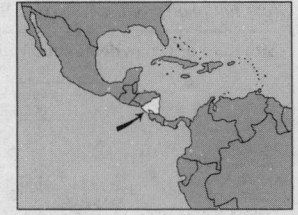

Official name: República de Nicaragua (Republic of Nicaragua).
Form of government: unitary multiparty republic with one legislative house (National Assembly [96]).
Head of state and government: President (coordinator of the junta).
Capital: Managua.
Official language: Spanish.
Official religion: none.
Monetary unit: 1 Nicaraguan córdoba (C$) = 100 centavos; valuation (Oct. 21, 1985) 1 U.S.$ = C$28.02; 1 £ = C$40.18.

Area and population

Zones Departments	Capitals	area* sq mi	sq km	population 1981 estimate
Atlantic				
Río San Juan	San Carlos	2,876	7,448	29,000
Zelaya	Bluefields	22,816	59,094	202,000
North Central				
Boaco	Boaco	1,924	4,982	89,000
Chontales	Juigalpa	1,910	4,947	98,000
Estelí	Estelí	849	2,199	110,000
Jinotega	Jinotega	3,697	9,576	127,000
Madriz	Somoto	679	1,758	72,000
Matagalpa	Matagalpa	2,623	6,794	221,000
Nueva Segovia	Ocotal	1,290	3,341	98,000
Pacific				
Carazo	Jinotepe	398	1,032	109,000
Chinandega	Chinandega	1,800	4,662	229,000
Granada	Granada	372	964	113,000
León	León	2,021	5,234	249,000
Managua	Managua	1,389†	3,597†	820,000†
Masaya	Masaya	224	581	149,000
Rivas	Rivas	830	2,149	109,000
National District				
Distrito Nacional		†	†	†
TOTAL		49,291	127,662	2,824,000

Demography

Population (1985): 3,039,000.
Density (1985)‡: persons per sq mi 66.5, persons per sq km 25.7.
Urban–rural (1983): urban 55.3%; rural 44.7%.
Sex distribution (1980): male 48.97%; female 51.03%.
Age breakdown (1980): under 15, 47.9%; 15–29, 25.7%; 30–44, 14.2%; 45–59, 7.5%; 60–74, 3.6%; 75 and over, 1.1%.
Population projection: (1990) 3,778,000; (2000) 5,261,000.
Doubling time: 25 years.
Ethnic composition (1980): mestizo (Spanish/Indian) 68.8%; white 14.0%; black 8.0%; Zambo (black/Indian) 5.0%; Amerindian 4.0%; other 0.2%.
Religious affiliation (1983): Roman Catholic 90.9%; Protestant 5.3%; other 3.8%.
Major cities (1982): Managua 750,000; León 180,000; Granada 80,000.

Vital statistics

Birth rate per 1,000 population (1983): 44.2 (world avg. 29.0).
Death rate per 1,000 population (1983): 9.5 (world avg. 11.0).
Natural increase rate per 1,000 population (1983): 34.7 (world avg. 18.0).
Total fertility rate (avg. births per childbearing woman; 1980–85): 5.9.
Marriage rate per 1,000 population (1975–80): 6.3.
Divorce rate per 1,000 population (1975–80): 0.3.
Life expectancy at birth (1982): male 56 years; female 60 years.
Major causes of death per 100,000 population (1978): heart disease 56.7; diarrheal diseases 37.3; accidents, poisoning, and violence 29.8; malignant neoplasms (cancers) 12.8.

National economy

Budget (1984). Revenue: C$11,459,800,000 (sales tax 41.2%, import duties 16.2%, social security 10.2%, property tax 7.8%). Expenditures: C$14,311,000,000 (goods and services 47.4%§, current transfers and subsidies 12.0%§, interest payments 4.6%§).
Public debt (external, outstanding; 1984): U.S.$4,259,000,000.
Tourism (1981): receipts from visitors U.S.$18,000,000; expenditures by nationals abroad U.S.$48,000,000 ‖ .
Production (metric tons except as noted). Agriculture, forestry, fishing (1984): sugarcane 3,072,000, corn (maize) 219,000, bananas and plantains 213,000, seed cotton 222,000, rice 162,000, milk 125,000, sorghum 112,000, lint cotton 85,000, coffee 46,000, dry beans 60,000, cassava 28,000; livestock (number of live animals) 2,000,000 cattle, 540,000 pigs, 5,000,000 chickens; roundwood 3,370,000 cu m§; fish catch 4,548§. Mining and quarrying (1983): gold 42,000 troy oz; salt 20,000. Manufacturing (gross value in C$'000,000; 1982): processed foods 1,624; beverages 1,293; chemical products 750; petroleum products 562; textiles 442; footwear and clothing 285; metal products 270. Construction (1981): residential 45,400 sq m; nonresidential 9,200 sq m. Energy production (consumption): electricity (kW-hr; 1983) 1,080,000,000 (1,084,000,000); coal, none (n.a.); crude petroleum (barrels; 1983) none (4,172,400); petroleum products (metric tons; 1983) 489,000 (550,000); natural gas, none (n.a.).
Gross national product (at current market prices; 1983): U.S.$2,690,000,000 (U.S.$900 per capita).

Structure of gross domestic product and labour force

	1983 in value C$'000,000	1983 % of total value	1980 labour force	1980 % of labour force
Agriculture	7,831	22.0	391,963	45.4
Mining	368	1.0	6,568	0.7
Manufacturing	9,106	25.4	91,403	10.6
Construction	941	2.6	37,322	4.3
Public utilities	758	2.1	6,652	0.8
Transportation and communication	2,335	6.5	30,064	3.4
Trade	6,973	19.5	105,053	12.2
Finance	2,676	7.5	16,761	2.0
Pub. admin., defense	3,060	8.6 }	158,789	18.4
Services	1,735	4.8 }		
Other	...		19,352	2.2
TOTAL	35,783¶	100.0	863,925	100.0

Population economically active (1982): total 868,000; participation rate of population over age 15, 31.5% (female [1981] 22.6%, unemployed [1981] 13.4%.

Price and earnings indexes (1980 = 100)

	1978	1979	1980	1981	1982	1983	1984
Consumer price index	49.9	73.9	100.0	123.9	154.6	202.6	275.0
Hourly earnings index♀	62.0	77.7	100.0	125.1	...	...	...

Household income and expenditure. Average household size (1980) 6.9; average annual income per household: n.a.; sources of income (1978): wages and salaries 70.8%, property and entrepreneurial income 27.6%, other 1.6%; expenditure (1981): food 34.0%, housing 24.2%, clothing and footwear 24.0%.
Land use (1983): forested 34.9%; meadows and pastures 42.5%; agricultural and under permanent cultivation 10.7%; other 11.9%.

Foreign trade

Balance of trade (current prices)

	1979	1980	1981	1982	1983	1984
C$'000,000	+2,198.9	−3,735.4	−4,263.7	−3,196.6	−3,158.4	−3,626.5
% of total	26.5%	29.2%	29.4%	28.2%	27.9%	34.1%

Imports (1982): C$7,272,400,000 (machinery and transport equipment 23.2%; crude petroleum 19.3%; chemicals and chemical products 15.8%; food 9.4%). *Major import sources:* Mexico 20.0%; United States 19.0%; U.S.S.R. 5.0%; France 4.2%; Cuba 3.9%; West Germany 3.7%.
Exports (1982): C$4,075,800,000 (food 62.9%, of which coffee 34.8%, beef 8.5%, sugar 8.2%; chemicals and chemical products 5.2%). *Major export destinations:* United States 22.2%; West Germany 14.2%; Japan 11.5%; Costa Rica 6.7%; China 5.3%; France 5.2%.

Transport and communications

Transport. Railroads (1984): 232 mi, 373 km; (1981) passenger-mi 12,603,000, passenger-km 20,283,000; short ton-mi cargo 9,504,000, metric ton-km cargo 13,876,000. Roads (1984): total length 15,500 mi, 25,000 km (paved 16%). Vehicles (1982): passenger cars 24,887; trucks and buses 9,789. Merchant marine (1984): vessels (100 gross tons and over) 21; total deadweight tonnage 27,304. Air transport (1980): passenger-mi 47,000,000, passenger-km 76,000,000; short ton-mi cargo 3,800,000, metric ton-km cargo 5,500,000; airports (1985) with scheduled flights 1.
Communications. Daily newspapers (1984): total number 3; total circulation 110,000; circulation per 1,000 population 37. Radio (1984): total number of receivers 200,000 (1 per 15 persons). Television (1984): total number of receivers 127,000 (1 per 23 persons). Telephones (1984): 51,237 (1 per 57 persons).

Education and health

Education (1983)

	schools	teachersδ	students	student/ teacher ratio
Primary (age 7–12)	4,976	14,105	534,996	...
Secondary (age 13–18)	323	...	151,012	...
Voc., teacher tr.	62	...	21,761δ	...
Higher	4	1,369	36,000□	...

Educational attainment (1971). Percent of adult population over age 25 having: no formal schooling 53.9%; primary and secondary education 37.4%; some postsecondary 4.4%. *Literacy* (1983): total population over age 15 literate 88.0%.
Health: physicians (1981) 1,570 (1 per 1,800 persons); hospital beds (1980) 5,115 (1 per 517 persons); infant mortality rate per 1,000 live births (1983) 75.2.
Food (1979–81): daily per capita caloric intake 2,188 (vegetable products 84%, animal products 16%); 97% of FAO recommended minimum requirement.

Military

Total active duty personnel (1984): 61,800 (army 97.1%, navy 0.5%, air force 2.4%). *Military expenditure as percent of GNP* (1983): 10.2% (world 6.1%); per capita expenditure U.S.$97.

*Total land area is 45,698 sq mi (118,358 sq km) and is shown for the departments and the national district; the total area (both land and water) is shown in the grand total. †Distrito Nacional is included with Managua. ‡Based on land area. §1983. ‖1979. ¶At current prices. ♀Nonagricultural activities. δ1982. □1984.

Niger

Official name: République du Niger (Republic of Niger).
Form of government: military government with one advisory body (National Development Council* [150]).
Head of state and government: President in conjunction with the Supreme Military Council.
Capital: Niamey.
Official language: French.
Official religion: none.
Monetary unit: 1 CFA franc (CFAF) = 100 centimes; valuation (Oct. 21, 1985) 1 U.S.\$ = CFAF402.02; 1 £ = CFAF576.50.

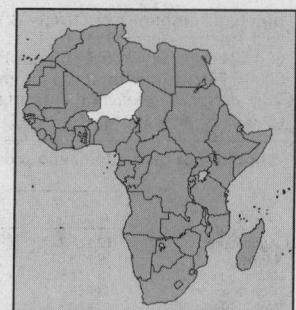

Area and population

Departments	Capitals	area† sq mi	area† sq km	population 1984 estimate
Agadez	Agadez	244,869	634,209	176,900
Diffa	Diffa	54,138	140,216	186,000
Dosso	Dosso	11,970	31,002	798,700
Maradi	Maradi	14,896	38,581	1,117,700
Niamey	Niamey	34,862	90,293	1,423,000
Tahoua	Tahoua	41,188	106,677	1,126,600
Zinder	Zinder	56,151	145,430	1,177,700
TOTAL		458,075†	1,186,408	6,006,600

Demography

Population (1985): 6,253,200.
Density (1985): persons per sq mi 12.6, persons per sq km 4.9.
Urban-rural (1985): urban 16.2%; rural 83.8%.
Sex distribution (1985): male 49.53%; female 50.47%.
Age breakdown (1985): under 15, 46.7%; 15–29, 25.6%; 30–44, 14.9%; 45–59, 8.0%; 60–74, 3.9%; 75 and over, 0.9%.
Population projection: (1990) 7,150,500; (2000) 9,350,000.
Doubling time: 26 years.
Ethnic composition (1980): Hausa 52.4%; Zerma 15.0%; Fulani 10.2%; Kanuri 9.0%; Songhai 8.0%; Tuareg 3.0%; Moors 1.9%; other 0.5%.
Religious affiliation (1983): Sunnī Muslim 97.5%; other 2.5%.
Major cities (1983): Niamey 399,100; Zinder 82,800; Maradi 65,100.

Vital statistics

Birth rate per 1,000 population (1980–85): 51.0 (world avg. 29.0).
Death rate per 1,000 population (1980–85): 22.9 (world avg. 11.0).
Natural increase rate per 1,000 population (1980–85): 28.1 (world avg. 18.0).
Total fertility rate (avg. births per childbearing woman; 1980–85): 7.1.
Life expectancy at birth (1980–85): male 40.9 years; female 44.1 years.
Major causes of death per 100,000 population (1976): malaria 317; measles 229; meningitis 145.

National economy

Budget (1983). Revenue: CFAF81,268,000,000 (customs duties 39.5%, indirect taxes 21.6%, direct taxes 16.6%). Expenditures: CFAF81,268,000,000 (operating expenses 49.8%, state expenses 25.6%, national debt 24.5%).
Public debt (external, outstanding; 1983): U.S.\$629,200,000.
Tourism (1981): receipts from visitors U.S.\$3,000,000; expenditures, n.a.
Population economically active (1982): total 1,745,000; participation rate of population ages 15–64, 51.0% (female, n.a.; unemployed, n.a.).

Price index (1980 = 100)

	1979	1980	1981	1982	1983	1984	1985
Consumer price index	90.7	100.0	122.9	137.2	133.8	145.0	151.5§

Gross national product (1983): U.S.\$1,460,000,000 (U.S.\$240 per capita).

Structure of gross domestic product and labour force

	1984 in value CFAF'000,000	1984 % of total value	1981 labour force	1981 % of labour force
Agriculture	268,200	43.6	1,481,000	87.2
Mining	53,600	8.7		
Manufacturing	25,400	4.1		
Construction	19,200	3.1		
Public utilities	10,300	1.7		
Transp. and commun.	26,900	4.4	217,000	12.8
Trade and finance	83,000	13.5		
Pub. admin., defense	52,800	8.6		
Services	52,000	8.4		
Other	24,000	3.9		
TOTAL	615,400	100.0	1,698,000	100.0

Production (value of production in CFAF except as noted). Agriculture, forestry, fishing (1983–84): millet 2,712,000,000, beans 1,177,000,000, cotton 390,000,000, sorghum 288,000,000, peanuts (groundnuts) 200,000,000; livestock (number of live animals; 1983) 7,500,000 goats, 3,500,000 cattle, 3,500,000 sheep, 503,000 asses, 412,000 camels, 285,000 horses; roundwood 3,731,000 cu m‡; fish catch 6,840 metric tons‡. Mining and quarrying (1984): uranium 97,712,000,000. Manufacturing (1980): food products 29,035,000,000; textiles and leather goods 15,298,000,000; metal products 6,420,000,000; nonmetallic mineral products (mostly cement) 4,280,000,000; chemical products (mostly plastic products) 4,280,000,000; beverages 2,791,000,000. Construction (1980): CFAF75,937,000,000. Energy production (consumption): electricity (kW-hr; 1983) 252,000,000 (380,000,000); coal (metric tons; 1983) 43,000 (43,000); crude petroleum, none (n.a.); petroleum products (metric tons; 1983) none (190,000); natural gas, none (n.a.); uranium (metric tons; 1983) 4,041 (n.a.).
Household income and expenditure. Average household size (1980) 5.2; average annual income per household: n.a.; sources of income (1977): self-employment 59.5%, family 30.1%, salary or wages 4.8%, employer 0.7%; (1983): food and beverages 50.5%, household expenses 19.1%, clothing 7.3%.
Land use (1983): forested 2.1%; meadows and pastures 7.3%; agricultural and under permanent cultivation 2.8%; other 87.8%.

Foreign trade

Balance of trade (current prices)

	1977	1978	1979	1980	1981	1982
CFAF'000,000	−8,900	−5,200	−2,800	−5,900	−14,900	−55,500
% of total	10.1%	3.9%	1.5%	2.4%	5.7%	19.8%

Imports (1982): CFAF168,041,000,000 (food products 27.8% of which cereals 13.9%, sugar and sugar products 5.5%; nonelectrical machinery 9.5%; petroleum products 9.3%; road vehicles 9.3%; chemical products 9.0%; cotton thread and fabrics 6.6%). *Major import sources* (1981): France 35.9%; Nigeria 13.3%; Algeria 7.2%; Ivory Coast 4.7%; Pakistan 4.4%.
Exports (1982): CFAF112,497,000,000 (uranium 80.6%, live animals 9.8%, cotton thread and fabrics 1.7%). *Major export destinations* (1981): France 35.7%; Japan 17.7%; Nigeria 17.2%; Libya 14.9%.

Transport and communications

Transport. Railroads (1984): none. Roads (1983): total length 11,886 mi, 19,129 km (paved 17%). Vehicles (1983): passenger cars 34,240; trucks and buses 8,761. Air transport (1983)‖: passenger arrivals 52,500, passenger departures 52,771; cargo unloaded 5,253 metric tons, cargo loaded 1,029 metric tons; airports (1985) with scheduled flights 6.
Communications. Daily newspapers (1984): total number 1; total circulation 5,000; circulation per 1,000 population 0.8. Radio (1984): 160,000 receivers (1 per 38 persons). Television (1984): 11,000 receivers (1 per 553 persons). Telephones (1981): 9,320 (1 per 603 persons).

Education and health

Education (1980–81)

	schools	teachers	students	student/ teacher ratio
Primary (age 7–12)	1,664	5,518	228,855	41.5
Secondary (age 13–19)	64	1,371	32,892	24.0
Voc., teacher tr.	8	120	2,351	19.6
Higher¶	1	189	1,825	9.7

Educational attainment (1977). Percent of population over age 9 having: no formal schooling 88.6%; primary education 10.3%; secondary 0.9%; higher 0.2%. *Literacy* (1980): total population over age 15 literate 278,000 (9.8%); males literate 195,000 (14.0%); females literate 83,000 (5.8%).
Health: physicians (1980) 136 (1 per 40,209 persons); hospital beds (1979) 3,261 (1 per 1,633 persons); infant mortality rate per 1,000 live births (1980–85) 140.0.
Food (1980–82): daily per capita caloric intake 2,462 (vegetable products 93%, animal products 7%); 99% of FAO recommended minimum requirement.

Military

Total active duty personnel (1984): 2,220 (army 96.8%, air force 3.2%). *Military expenditure as percent of GNP* (1983): 0.9% (world 6.1%); per capita expenditure U.S.\$2.

*The legislature (National Assembly) was suspended in 1974. In 1983 the National Development Council assumed the role of a constituent assembly. †Detail does not add to total given because of rounding. ‡1983. §June. ‖Niamey airport only. ¶Université de Niamey.

Ruins of the fortified Arab city of Djado, now a seasonally inhabited village (at the time of the date harvest), at the Djado oasis, in the Ténéré desert, northern Niger.

Nigeria

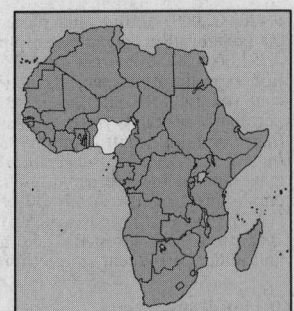

Official name: Federal Republic of
Nigeria.
Form of government: federal republic
(constitution suspended in part Dec.
31, 1983); temporarily governed under
emergency powers by Armed Forces
Ruling Council (AFRC).
Head of state and government:
President, Commander-in-Chief,
Chairman AFRC.
Capital: Lagos
(Capital designate: Abuja).
Official language: English.
Official religion: none.
Monetary unit: 1 Nigerian naira
(₦) = 100 kobo; valuation (Oct. 21,
1985) 1 ₦ = U.S.$1.12 = £0.89.

Area and population

States	Capitals	area sq mi	area sq km	population 1983 estimate
Anambra	Enugu	6,824	17,675	5,880,600
Bauchi	Bauchi	24,944	64,605	3,975,200
Bendel	Benin City	13,707	35,500	4,023,700
Benue	Makurdi	17,442	45,174	3,968,200
Borno	Maiduguri	44,942	116,400	4,901,000
Cross River	Calabar	10,516	27,237	5,696,800
Gongola	Yola	35,286	91,390	4,259,700
Imo	Owerri	4,575	11,850	6,004,900
Kaduna	Kaduna	27,122	70,245	6,700,800
Kano	Kano	16,712	43,285	9,442,000
Kwara	Ilorin	25,818	66,869	2,808,200
Lagos	Lagos	1,292	3,345	2,733,500
Niger	Minna	25,111	65,037	1,933,100
Ogun	Abeokuta	6,472	16,762	2,533,900
Ondo	Akure	8,092	20,959	4,483,100
Oyo	Ibadan	14,558	37,705	8,516,700
Plateau	Jos	22,405	58,030	3,313,600
Rivers	Port-Harcourt	8,436	21,850	2,812,100
Sokoto	Sokoto	39,589	102,535	7,421,000
Federal Capital Territory		2,824	7,315	...
TOTAL		356,669*	923,768	91,408,100

Demography

Population (1985): 96,015,000.
Density (1985): persons per sq mi 269.2, persons per sq km 103.9.
Urban–rural (1985): urban 23.0%; rural 77.0%.
Sex distribution (1985): male 49.50%; female 50.50%.
Age breakdown (1985): under 15, 48.3%; 15–29, 25.8%; 30–44, 14.1%; 45–59,
7.8%; 60–74, 3.4%; 75 and over, 0.6%.
Population projection: (1990) 108,613,000; (2000) 138,983,000.
Doubling time: 28 years.
Ethno-linguistic composition (1978): Hausa 21.5%; Yoruba 21.0%; Ibo 18.4%;
Fulani 11.1%; other 28.0%.
Religious affiliation (1980): Muslim 45.0%; Protestant 26.3%; Roman Catholic
12.1%; African indigenous 10.6%; tribal religionist 5.6%; other 0.4%.
Major cities (1983): Lagos 1,097,000; Ibadan 1,060,000; Ogbomosho 527,400;
Kano 487,100; Oshogbo 344,500.

Vital statistics

Birth rate per 1,000 population (1980–85): 50.4 (world avg. 29.0); legitimate,
n.a.; illegitimate, n.a.
Death rate per 1,000 population (1980–85): 17.1 (world avg. 11.0).
Natural increase rate per 1,000 population (1980–85): 33.3 (world avg. 18.0).
Total fertility rate (avg. births per childbearing woman; 1980–85): 7.1.
Marriage rate per 1,000 population: n.a.
Divorce rate per 1,000 population: n.a.
Life expectancy at birth (1980–85): male 46.9 years; female 50.2 years.
Major causes of death per 100,000 population: n.a.; major diseases include
malaria, tuberculosis, trypanosomiasis, onchocerciasis, and leprosy.

National economy

Budget (1985). Revenue ₦11,237,000,000 (more than 60% of the revenue is
derived from petroleum profits). Expenditures: ₦11,270,000,000 (recurrent
expenditure 48.6%; capital expenditure 51.4%, of which manufacturing
3.5%, water resources 3.5%, crops 3.2%, defense 2.8%, posts and telecommunications 2.6%, energy 2.4%, rural development 2.3%, education 1.6%).
Public debt (1983): U.S.$11,757,000,000.
Tourism (1983): receipts from visitors U.S.$102,000,000; expenditures by
nationals abroad U.S.$454,000,000.
Production (metric tons except as noted). Agriculture, forestry, fishing
(1984): cassava 11,800,000, millet 3,000,000, sorghum 3,000,000, corn
(maize) 1,600,000, sugarcane 1,200,000, pulses 800,000, rice 800,000, palm
oil 750,000, peanuts (groundnuts) 550,000, cacao 160,000, cotton lint 55,-
000; livestock (number of live animals) 11,800,000 cattle, 26,000,000 goats,
12,800,000 sheep; roundwood 85,760,000 cu m; fish catch 515,250. Mining
and quarrying (1984): limestone 867,133; cassiterite 1,768; tin metal 1,422.
Manufacturing (value added in producers' prices ₦'000,000; 1980): beverages and tobacco 737.9; transport equipment 717.5, of which motor vehicles
688.7; chemical products 417.1, of which drugs and medicines 116.2; textiles 334.9; food products 315.7; rubber products 43.3. Construction (1978):
residential ₦884,830,000; nonresidential ₦1,769,640,000. Energy produc-

tion (consumption): electricity (kW-hr; 1983) 8,785,730,000 (6,372,440,000);
coal (metric tons; 1984) 83,460 (40,000†); crude petroleum (barrels; 1984)
500,404,000 (54,975,000†); petroleum products (metric tons; 1983) 6,930,-
000 (6,236,000); natural gas (cu m; 1983) 5,640,917,400 (5,641,020,000†).
Gross national product (at current market prices; 1983): U.S.$71,030,000,000
(U.S.$777 per capita).

Structure of gross domestic product and labour force

	1983 in value ₦'000,000	% of total value	labour force	% of labour force
Agriculture	12,165.7	25.0	15,873,000	50.5
Mining	9,923.0	20.4		
Manufacturing	2,372.5	4.9		
Construction	3,268.3	6.7		
Public utilities	460.3	0.9		
Transportation and communication	2,187.7	4.5	15,563,000‡	49.5
Trade	10,490.3	21.6		
Other (including finance, pub. admin., defense, and services)	7,783.8	16.0		
TOTAL	48,651.7*§	100.0	31,436,000	100.0

Population economically active (1983): total 31,436,000 (34.4%; participation
rate of working-age population ages 15–64, 50.0% (female 39.8%, unemployed [registered] 0.6%).

Price and earnings indexes (1980 = 100)

	1979	1980	1981	1982	1983	1984	1985
Consumer price index	90.9	100.0	120.8	130.1	160.3	223.8	241.0¶
Earnings index♀	98.1	100.0	...	...	...	...	...

Household income and expenditure. Average household size (1982) 5.0; average annual income per household ₦2,600 (U.S.$3,875); source of income:
n.a.; expenditure: n.a.
Land use (1983): forested 15.4%; meadows and pastures 23.0%; agricultural
and under permanent cultivation 33.4%; other 28.2%.

Foreign trade

Balance of trade (current prices)

	1979	1980	1981	1982	1983	1984
₦'000,000	+4,507	+5,091	−2,043	−3,861	−2,111	−1,500
% of total	26.8%	21.9%	8.6%	18.2%	12.2%	9.4%

Imports (1983): ₦9,723,000,000 (machinery and transport equipment 41.3%;
manufactured goods 21.8% [important sectors include iron and steel products, textiles, paper products, and rubber products]; food and live animals
15.2%; chemicals 10.3%; mineral fuels 1.5%). *Major import sources:* United
Kingdom 21.0%; United States 14.2%; West Germany 13.3%; France 12.5%;
Japan 9.3%; The Netherlands 4.7%; Italy 4.4%.
Exports (1983): ₦7,612,300,000 (crude petroleum 96.4%; other important exports include cocoa, rubber, and palm kernels). *Major export destinations*
(1982): United States 46.2%; The Netherlands 12.1%; France 10.1%; West
Germany 6.6%; United Kingdom 2.3%; Ghana 1.2%.

Transport and communications

Transport. Railroads (1983): length 2,189 mi, 3,523 km; passenger-mi 1,275,-
000,000 ‖, passenger-km 2,053,000,000 ‖; short ton cargo handled 1,819,-
000, metric ton cargo handled 1,650,000. Roads (1981): total length 67,102
mi, 107,990 km (paved 78%). Vehicles (1981): passenger cars 262,550;
trucks 90,731. Merchant marine (1984): vessels (100 gross tons and over)
178; total deadweight tonnage 609,740. Air transportठ (1983): passenger-mi
1,505,000,000, passenger-km 2,422,000,000; short ton-mi cargo 20,448,000,
metric ton-km cargo 29,854,000; airports (1985) with scheduled flights 15.
Communications. Daily newspapers (1984): total number 15; total circulation 1,295,000▫; circulation per 1,000 population 15.2▫. Radio (1984):
5,800,000 receivers (1 per 16 persons). Television (1984): 460,000 receivers
(1 per 204 persons). Telephones (1983): 708,365 (1 per 129 persons).

Education and health

Education (1980–81)

	schools	teachers	students	student/ teacher ratio
Primary (age 6–12)	36,683	384,201	14,022,164	36.5
Secondary (age 12–17)	4,495	69,005	2,024,024	29.3
Voc., teacher tr.	470	12,156	359,817	29.6
Higher	77	...	153,306	...

Educational attainment, n.a. *Literacy* (1980): total population over age 15
literate 11,788,700 (30.0%); males 46.5%; females 14.0%.
Health (1980): physicians 8,037 (1 per 10,800 persons); hospital beds 74,901
(1 per 1,160 persons); infant mortality rate per 1,000 live births (1983) 113.
Food (1980–82): daily per capita caloric intake 2,444 (vegetable products 95%,
animal products 5%); 104% of FAO recommended minimum requirement.

Military

Total active duty personnel (1984): 133,000 (army 90.2%, navy 3.0%, air force
6.8%). *Military expenditure as percent of GNP* (1983): 2.0% (world 6.1%);
per capita expenditure U.S.$16.

*Detail does not add to total given because of rounding. †1983. ‡Nonagricultural
labour force. §At current prices. ‖ 1982. ¶April only. ♀For wages earned in nonagricultural activities only. ठNigeria Airways only. ▫1980.

Norway

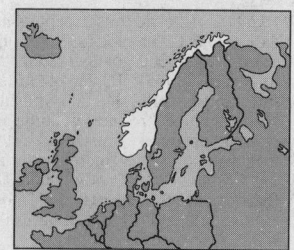

Official name: Kongeriket Norge (Kingdom of Norway).
Form of government: constitutional monarchy with one legislative house (Parliament [157]).
Chief of state: King.
Head of government: Prime Minister.
Capital: Oslo.
Official language: Norwegian.
Official religion: Evangelical Lutheran.
Monetary unit: 1 Norwegian krone (NKr) = 100 øre; valuation (Oct. 21, 1985) 1 U.S.$ = NKr7.89; 1 £ = NKr11.32.

Area and population

Counties	Capitals	area* sq mi	area* sq km	population 1985† estimate
Akershus	—	1,898	4,917	386,359
Aust-Agder	Arendal	3,557	9,212	94,244
Buskerud	Drammen	5,763	14,927	219,286
Finnmark	Vardø	18,779	48,637	76,676
Hedmark	Hamar	10,575	27,388	187,028
Hordaland	Bergen	6,036	15,634	397,480
Møre og Romsdal	Molde	5,832	15,104	237,396
Nordland	Bodø	14,798	38,327	243,569
Nord-Trøndelag	Steinkjer	8,673	22,463	126,937
Oppland	Lillehammer	9,753	25,260	182,115
Oslo	Oslo	175	454	447,109
Østfold	Moss	1,615	4,183	235,031
Rogaland	Stavanger	3,529	9,141	320,205
Sogn og Fjordane	Leikanger	7,195	18,634	106,203
Sør-Trøndelag	Trondheim	7,271	18,831	246,428
Telemark	Skien	5,913	15,315	162,255
Troms	Tromsø	10,021	25,954	147,147
Vest-Agder	Kristiansand	2,811	7,281	139,837
Vestfold	Tønsberg	856	2,216	190,481
TOTAL		125,050	323,878	4,145,786‡

Demography

Population (1985): 4,157,000.
Density (1985): persons per sq mi 33.2, persons per sq km 12.8.
Urban–rural (1985): urban 80.3%; rural 19.7%.
Sex distribution (1984): male 49.48%; female 50.52%.
Age breakdown (1984): under 15, 20.7%; 15–29, 23.1%; 30–44, 20.5%; 45–59, 14.7%; 60–74, 15.0%; 75 and over, 6.0%.
Population projection: (1990) 4,225,000; (2000) 4,325,000.
Doubling time: population growth is negligible.
Ethnic composition (by country of citizenship; 1983): Norway 98.5%; Denmark 0.4%; Sweden 0.2%; Finland 0.1%; other 0.8%.
Religious affiliation (1980): Lutheran 87.9%; other 3.8%; nonreligious 3.2%.
Major cities (1984): Oslo 447,400; Bergen 207,400; Trondheim 134,100; Stavanger 94,200; Baerum 83,000; Kristiansand 62,200; Drammen 50,700.

Vital statistics

Birth rate per 1,000 population (1984): 12.1 (world avg. 29.0); (1983) legitimate 80.7%; illegitimate 19.3%.
Death rate per 1,000 population (1984): 10.2 (world avg. 11.0).
Natural increase rate per 1,000 population (1984): 1.9 (world avg. 18.0).
Total fertility rate (avg. births per childbearing woman; 1983): 1.7.
Marriage rate per 1,000 population (1984): 5.1.
Divorce rate per 1,000 population (1983): 1.9.
Life expectancy at birth (1983): male 72.7 years; female 79.5 years.
Major causes of death per 100,000 population (1983): ischemic heart disease 265.3; malignant neoplasms (cancers) 222.3; cerebrovascular disease 129.3.

National economy

Budget (1984). Revenue: NKr139,352,000,000 (indirect taxes 52.4%, of which value added taxes 29.5%, tax on petroleum extraction 7.0%; direct taxes 30.2%, of which taxes on petroleum income 21.1%, ordinary income 8.3%; interest and dividends 12.6%). Expenditures: NKr111,308,000,000 (social security 22.5%; general subsidies 18.4%; public services 18.4%; defense 12.3%).
Tourism (1984): receipts from visitors U.S.$649,000,000; expenditures by nationals abroad U.S.$1,474,000,000.
Public debt (1983): U.S.$10,794,000,000.
Production (metric tons except as noted). Agriculture, forestry, fishing (1984): barley 700,000, potatoes 470,000, oats 527,000; livestock (number of live animals) 2,351,000 sheep, 976,100 cattle, 719,500 pigs; roundwood 9,553,000 cu m; fish catch (1984) 2,419,500, of which capelin 944,000, Atlantic cod 174,900, prawn and shrimp 85,600. Mining and quarrying (1984): iron ore 2,419,000§, titanium 650,000, zinc 29,000§, copper 22,300§. Manufacturing (gross value in NKr'000,000; 1983): machinery and equipment 49,755, of which transport equipment 13,690, electrical equipment 8,767; food products 39,466; petroleum products 13,319; wood and wood products 12,614; paper and paper products 10,300. Construction (1982): residential 3,739,000 sq m; nonresidential 2,776,000 sq m. Energy production (consumption): electricity (kW-hr; 1984) 106,625,000,000 (81,655,000,000 ‖); coal (metric tons; 1984) 470,000 (592,000 ‖); crude petroleum (barrels; 1984) 272,890,000 (51,260,000 ‖); petroleum products (metric tons; 1983) 7,680,000 (5,707,-000); natural gas¶ (cu m; 1984) 27,483,600,000 (877,000,000 ‖).
Gross national product (at current market prices; 1983): U.S.$53,400,000,000 (U.S.$12,930 per capita).

Structure of gross domestic product and labour force

	1984 in value NKr'000,000	% of total value	labour force	% of labour force
Agriculture	16,792	3.8	139,000	7.1
Mining	88,488	19.8	22,000	1.1
Manufacturing	60,773	13.6	363,000	18.5
Construction	22,069	4.9	150,000	7.6
Public utilities	18,662	4.2	22,000	1.1
Transportation and communication	41,055	9.2	176,000	9.0
Trade	58,860	13.2	325,000	16.5
Finance	37,073	8.3	119,000	6.1
Pub. admin., defense	61,427	13.8	} 650,000	33.1
Services	36,099	8.1		
Other	5,320	1.2		
TOTAL	446,618	100.0♀	1,970,000¶	100.0♀

Population economically active (1984): total 2,031,000; participation rate of population ages 16–74, 67.9% (female 58.4%, unemployed 3.0%).

Price and earnings indexes (1980 = 100)

	1978	1979	1980	1981	1982	1983	1984
Consumer price index	83.9	89.1	100.0	113.6	126.2	141.1	149.9
Hourly earnings index	89.0	91.0	100.0	110.0	121.0	132.0	145.0δ

Household income and expenditure. Average household size (1982) 2.7; consumption expenditure per household NKr88,000 (U.S.$13,600); sources of income: wages and salaries 63.0%, social security 18.8%, self-employment and property income 17.0%, other 1.2%; expenditure (1982): food 20.6%, housing 16.2%, transportation 15.1%, recreation 8.2%, clothing 7.8%.
Land use (1984): forested 27.1%; meadows and pastures 0.3%; agricultural and under permanent cultivation 2.8%; built-up and other 69.8%.

Foreign trade

Balance of trade (current prices)

	1979	1980	1981	1982	1983	1984
NKr'000,000	−811.7	8,070	14,578	13,489	32,989	40,933
% of total	−0.6%	4.6%	7.5%	6.3%	14.4%	15.3%

Imports (1984): NKr113,102,000,000 (machinery and transport equipment 28.8%, of which road vehicles 6.3%; raw materials 18.4%, of which fuels 10.3%; metals and metal products 9.3%, of which iron and steel 3.9%; food products 5.7%, of which fruits and vegetables 1.5%). *Major import sources:* Sweden 17.2%; West Germany 14.5%; United Kingdom 10.3%; United States 9.0%.
Exports (1984): NKr154,035,000,000 (fuels and fuel products 54.6%, of which crude petroleum 33.4%, natural gas 17.3%; metals and metal products 15.6%, of which aluminum 5.7%, iron and steel 2.8%; machinery and transport equipment 10.4%, of which ships and boats 3.8%; food products 5.5%, of which fish and fish products 4.1%). *Major export destinations:* United Kingdom 36.4%; West Germany 17.4%; Sweden 9.8%; The Netherlands 6.4%.

Transport and communications

Transport. Railroads (1984): length 2,636 mi, 4,242 km; passenger-mi 1,357,-000,000, passenger-km 2,184,000,000; short ton-mi cargo 1,816,000,000, metric ton-km cargo 2,652,000,000. Roads (1984): total length 52,216 mi, 84,033 km (paved 62%). Vehicles (1984): passenger cars 1,429,710; trucks and buses 214,051. Merchant marine (1984): vessels (100 gross tons and over) 2,271; total deadweight tonnage 30,604,843. Air transport (1984): passenger-mi 2,331,000,000, passenger-km 3,752,000,000; short ton-mi cargo 91,149,000, metric ton-km cargo 133,075,000; airports (1985) 41.
Communications. Daily newspapers (1984): total number 64; total circulation 1,882,000; circulation per 1,000 population 454. Radio (1984): total number of receivers 1,500,000 (1 per 2.8 persons). Television (1983): total number of receivers 1,325,964 (1 per 3.1 persons). Telephones (1985): 2,578,812 (1 per 1.6 persons).

Education and health

Education (1983–84)

	schools	teachers	students	student/ teacher ratio
Primary (age 7–13)	3,539	29,992	565,497	18.9
Secondary (age 14–18) and vocational	918	16,292	188,040□	...
Higher	225	6,883	88,008□	...

Educational attainment (1980). Percent of population over age 15 having: lower secondary education 56.8%; higher secondary 32.1%; graduated university or technical school 11.1%. *Literacy* (1984): virtually 100% literate.
Health (1983): physicians 9,722 (1 per 425 persons); hospital beds 18,729 (1 per 220 persons); infant mortality rate per 1,000 live births 7.8.
Food (1980–82): daily per capita caloric intake 3,319 (vegetable products 62%, animal products 38%); 124% of FAO recommended minimum.

Military

Total active duty personnel (1984): 36,785. *Military expenditure as percent of GNP* (1983): 3.2% (world avg. 6.1%); per capita expenditure U.S.$420.

*Excludes Svalbard and Jan Mayen (24,360 sq mi [63,080 sq km]). †Beginning of year. ‡Includes the Norwegian population of Svalbard and Jan Mayen registered as residents in municipalities on the mainland. §Metal content of ore. ‖ 1983. ¶Includes manufactured gas. ♀Detail does not add to total given because of rounding. δThird quarter. □1982–83.

Oman

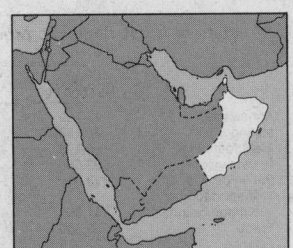

Official name: Salṭanat 'Umān
(Sultanate of Oman).
Form of government: monarchy with a
consultative council (55) appointed by
the Sultan.
Chief of state: Sultan.
Head of government: Prime Minister.
Capital: Muscat.
Official language: Arabic.
Official religion: Islām.
Monetary unit: 1 rial Omani
(RO) = 1,000 baizas; valuation (Oct.
21, 1985) 1 RO = U.S.$2.88 = £2.01.

Area and population

Region	area*		population†
Area	sq mi	sq km	1985 estimate
Dhofar	40,000	100,000	...
Southern	...	...	
Musandam (R'ūs al-Jibāl)	800	2,000	13,000
Musandam	...	...	
Other	79,200	198,000	...
al-Baṭinah	...	...	
al-Jaww and al-Buraymī	...	...	
Dhahirah (az-Ẓāhirah)	...	...	
Capital	...	...	
Eastern al-Ḥajar	...	...	
Ja'lān and Sur (Ja'lān)	...	...	
Sharqiyah	...	...	
'Uman Interior	...	...	
Western al-Ḥajar	...	...	
TOTAL	120,000	300,000	1,041,000

Demography

Population (1985): 1,041,000.
Density (1985): persons per sq mi 8.7, persons per sq km 3.5.
Urban–rural (1985): urban 8.8%; rural 91.2%.
Sex distribution (1985): male 52.85%; female 47.15%.
Age breakdown (1980): under 15, 45.2%; 15–29, 25.8%; 30–44, 15.6%; 45–59, 8.8%; 60–74, 3.9%; 75 and over, 0.7%.
Population projection: (1990) 1,218,000; (2000) 1,651,000.
Doubling time: 22.3 years.
Ethnic composition (1980): Arabic 87.0%; Baluchi 4.0%; other 9.0%.
Religious affiliation (1980): Muslim 98.9%; Hindu 0.3%; other 0.8%.
Major city (1981): Muscat 50,000.

Vital statistics

Birth rate per 1,000 population (1980–85): 47.7 (world avg. 29.0).
Death rate per 1,000 population (1980–85): 16.7 (world avg. 11.0).
Natural increase rate per 1,000 population (1980–85): 31.0 (world avg. 18.0).
Total fertility rate (avg. births per childbearing woman; 1980–85): 7.1.
Marriage rate per 1,000 population: n.a.
Divorce rate per 1,000 population: n.a.
Life expectancy at birth (1980–85): male 48.7 years; female 50.9 years.
Major causes of death per 100,000 population: n.a; however, principal health problems formerly included malaria and trachoma.

National economy

Budget (1984). Revenue: RO1,485,700,000 (oil revenue 85.9%, gas revenue 2.3%, interest from investments 1.4%). Expenditures: RO1,700,100,000 (defense 42.8%, financing of civil ministries 46.1%).
Gross national product (1983): U.S.$7,070,000,000 (U.S.$6,240 per capita).

Structure of gross domestic product and labour force

	1984		1982	
	in value RO'000,000	% of total value	labour force§	% of labour force§
Agriculture	89.0	2.9	6,583	2.9
Mining	1,449.5	47.6	3,426	1.5
Manufacturing	92.3	3.0	8,034	3.5
Construction	226.0	7.4	46,279	20.0
Public utilities	32.7	1.1	423	0.2
Transp. and commun.	84.6	2.8	2,483	1.1
Trade	369.7	12.1	33,740	14.6
Finance	275.1	9.0	3,272	1.4
Pub. admin., defense	455.6	15.0	44,087	19.1
Services	31.6	1.0	8,139	3.5
Other	−59.2 ‖	−1.9 ‖	74,442	32.2
TOTAL	3,046.9	100.0	230,908	100.0

Population economically active (1982): total 230,908; participation rate of population over age 15, 40.5% (female, n.a.; unemployed, n.a.).

Price and earnings indexes (1978 = 100)

	1978	1979	1980	1981	1982	1983	1984
Consumer price index¶	100.0	108.5	119.3	122.7	124.0	118.6	108.8
Monthly earnings index	...	...	...	...	...	...	...

Household income and expenditure. Average household size (1980) 5.5; average annual income per household: n.a.; source of income: n.a.; food expenditure (1983): meat and eggs 20.6%, cereals 15.2%, fruits and nuts 12.4%, vegetables 11.9%, dairy products 10.3%, other foods 29.6%.

Production (metric tons except as noted). Agriculture, forestry, fishing (1984): dates 75,000, bananas 35,000, limes 10,000; livestock (number of live animals) 700,000 goats, 125,000 cattle, 300,000 sheep, 1,000,000 chickens; fish catch (1983) 108,766. Mining and quarrying (1982): stone 6,220,000; sand and gravel 1,343,000; marble 50,000; copper 12,000‡. Manufacturing (1985): major products include cement blocks and floors, furniture, aluminum products, household utensils, fertilizers, and fibreglass products. Construction: n.a. Energy production (consumption): electricity (kW-hr; 1983) 1,402,000,000 (1,402,000,000); coal, none (none); crude petroleum (barrels; 1984) 152,620,000 (13,300,000§); petroleum products (metric tons; 1984) 2,400,000 (510,000); natural gas (cu m; 1983) 2,455,070,000 (n.a.).
Public debt (external, outstanding; 1982): U.S.$677,100,000.
Land use (1983): meadows and pastures 4.7%; agricultural and under permanent cultivation 0.2%; other (mostly desert and developed area) 95.1%.

Foreign trade

Balance of trade (current prices)

	1978	1979	1980	1981	1982	1983
RO'000,000	+224.8	+356.9	+696.3	+831.6	+600.4	+634.9
% of total	25.6%	29.3%	36.8%	34.5%	24.5%	29.2%

Imports (1984): RO949,200,000 (transport equipment 18.6%, manufactured goods 15.5%, food 12.9%, petroleum products 1.3%). *Major import sources:* Japan 21.3%; United Arab Emirates 17.8%; United Kingdom 16.6%.
Exports (1984): RO1,527,000,000 (crude petroleum 98.9%, fish 0.4%, copper 0.4%, fruits and vegetables 0.2%). *Major export destinations:* Japan 58.8%; Singapore 7.6%; United States 4.1%; United Kingdom 2.7%.

Transport and communications

Transport. Railroads: none. Roads (1982): total length 13,050 mi, 21,000 km (paved 14%). Vehicles (1982): private vehicles 14,930; commercial vehicles 11,822. Merchant marine (1984): vessels (100 gross tons and over) 26; total deadweight tonnage 12,129. Air transport (1983)º: passenger-mi 553,268,000, passenger-km 890,400,000; short ton-mi cargo 16,313,000, metric ton-km cargo 23,817,000; airports (1985) with scheduled flights 2.
Communications. Daily newspapers (1984): total number 2; total circulation 16,000; circulation per 1,000 population 17. Radio (1984): total receivers 800,000 (1 per 1.9 persons). Television (1984): total receivers 46,000 (1 per 32.6 persons). Telephones (1982): 19,600 (1 per 48.4 persons).

Education and health

Education (1982–83)

	schools	teachers	students	student/ teacher ratio
Primary (age 6–11)ŏ	204	6,575□	116,467	...
Secondary (age 12–17)◇	251	...	24,115	...
Voc., teacher tr.	...	...	1,994	...
Higher	none	none	1,399△	---

Educational attainment, n.a. *Literacy* (1979): total population over age 6 literate 38%; males literate 55%; females literate 20%.
Health (1985): physicians 581 (1 per 1,792 persons); hospital beds 2,565 (1 per 406 persons); infant mortality rate per 1,000 live births (1978) 200.

Military

Total active duty personnel (1984): 21,500 (army 76.7%, navy 9.3%, air force 14.0%); foreign troops 3,700. *Military expenditure as percent of GNP* (1983): 27.9% (world 6.1%); per capita expenditure U.S.$1,695.

*Cadastral areas have not been calculated. †No census has ever been taken in Oman; the total given is an unofficial estimate. For planning purposes the Omani government continues to use its own 1975 estimate of 1,500,000. ‡1984. §Civilian employees and non-Omani workers only. ‖ Less imputed bank service charges. ¶Applies to food and beverages in the capital area only. ºInternational flights only. ŏGovernment schools only; Omani statistics for private schools do not distinguish between primary and secondary levels. In 1982–83 there were 39 private schools with 6,284 students and 372 teachers; the student/teacher ratio was 16.0. □Includes teachers in preparatory and secondary schools. ◇Includes preparatory school for students 12–14 years old. △Omani students studying abroad.

CHRISTINE OSBORNE—©MEPhA

Corniche (coastal road) and harbourfront, Maṭraḥ, Oman.

Pacific Islands, Trust Territory of the

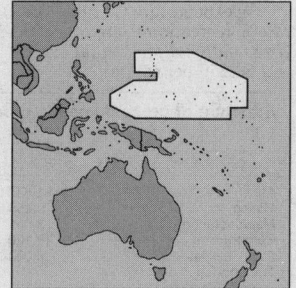

Official name: Trust Territory of the Pacific Islands.
Political status: Trust Territory (of the United Nations) under United States administration*.
Chief of state: President of the United States through the High Commissioner.
Heads of government: Marshall Islands, Federated States of Micronesia, and Palau, President; Northern Mariana Islands, Governor.
Administrative centre: Saipan.
Official language: English.
Official religion: none.
Monetary unit: 1 U.S. dollar (U.S.$) = 100 cents; valuation (Oct. 21, 1985) 1£ = U.S.$1.43.

Area and population

Island Groups Districts	Capitals	area† sq mi	area† sq km	population 1980 census
Marshall Islands	Majuro	70	181	30,873
Federated States of Micronesia	Kolonia	271	702	73,160
Kosrae	Lelu	42	109	5,491
Pohnpei	Kolonia	134	347	22,081
Truk	Moen	49	127	37,488
Yap	Colonia	46	119	8,100
Northern Mariana Is.	Saipan	184	477	16,780
Palau (Belau)	Koror	192	497	12,116
TOTAL		717	1,857	132,929

Demography

Population (1985): 149,200.
Density (1985): persons per sq mi 208.1, persons per sq km 80.3.
Urban–rural (1980): urban 28.5%; rural 71.5%.
Sex distribution (1980): male 51.41%; female 48.59%.
Age breakdown (1980): under 15, 46.0%; 15–29, 26.7%; 30–44, 13.3%; 45–59, 8.4%; 60–74, 4.5%; 75 and over, 1.1%.
Population projection: (1990) 170,000; (2000) 199,000.
Doubling time: 31 years.
Ethnic composition (1980): Trukese 22.8%; Marshallese 22.6%; Ponapean 14.4%; Palauan 9.4%; Chamorro 7.2%; Mortlockese 4.6%; Kosraean 4.2%; Yapese 3.4%; Ulithian or Woleaian 2.2%; Filipino 1.5%; other 7.7%.
Religious affiliation (1980): Christian 97.5%, of which Protestant 49.2%, Roman Catholic 45.6%, Micronesian indigenous 2.7%; Bahā'ī 1.2%; other 1.3%.
Major cities (1980): Saipan 14,549; Majuro 11,791; Moen 10,351; Koror 7,585; Tol 6,705.

Vital statistics

Birth rate per 1,000 population (1982): 26.7 (world avg. 29.0); legitimate, n.a.; illegitimate, n.a.
Death rate per 1,000 population (1982): 4.2 (world avg. 11.0).
Natural increase rate per 1,000 population (1982): 22.5 (world avg. 18.0).
Total fertility rate (avg. births per childbearing woman; 1980–85): 5.0‡.
Marriage rate per 1,000 population: n.a.
Divorce rate per 1,000 population: n.a.
Life expectancy at birth (1980–85): male 60.9 years; female 64.5 years.
Major causes of death per 100,000 population (1982): heart disease 46.8; cerebrovascular diseases 31.7; benign and malignant neoplasms (cancers) 31.7; pneumonia and influenza 24.5; diarrheal and intestinal diseases 23.8.

National economy

Budget (1983). Revenue: U.S.$208,935,000 (U.S. Department of Interior grants 45.9%, local revenue and internal resources 22.2%, covenant funds [N. Mariana Is.] 13.1%, other U.S. government grants and federal program funds 18.8%). Expenditure: n.a.; however, the total U.S. government funds of U.S.$162,527,000 were allocated as follows: Commonwealth of the Northern Mariana Islands 31.1%; Federated States of Micronesia 29.3%; Republic of the Marshall Islands 8.7%; Republic of Palau 7.6%; Trust Territory operations 11.5%; capital improvements and construction 11.3%.
Tourism (1979): receipts from visitors U.S.$2,400,000§; expenditures by nationals abroad, n.a.
Production (metric tons except as noted). Agriculture, forestry, fishing (1984): coconuts 190,000 (from which copra 26,000), cassava 10,000, sweet potatoes 3,000, vegetables and melons 3,000, fruit 3,000 (of which bananas 2,000); livestock (number of live animals) 27,000 pigs, 10,000 cattle, 4,000 goats; fish catch 5,462 ‖, of which tuna 5,388. Mining and quarrying: phosphates. Manufacturing: n.a.; however, copra is the most important product. Two processing plants (one in Palau and one in the Marshall Islands) have a combined input capacity of 60,000 metric tons of copra per year. Manufacture of handicrafts and personal items (clothing, mats, boats, etc.) by individuals is also important. Construction (1978): 103 housing units. Energy production (consumption): electricity (kW-hr; 1983) 148,000,000 (148,000,000); coal, none (n.a.); crude petroleum, none (n.a.); petroleum products (metric tons; 1983) none (50,000); natural gas, none (n.a.).

Gross national product (at current market prices; 1983): U.S.$140,000,000 (U.S.$1,000 per capita).

Structure of gross domestic product and labour force

	1978–79 in value U.S.$'000,000	1978–79 % of total value	1980 labour force	1980 % of labour force
Agriculture	...	...}	505	2.2
Mining	...			
Manufacturing	...	...	476	2.0
Construction	...	...	2,892	12.5
Public utilities	...	...		
Transportation and communication	...	...}	1,578	6.8
Trade	...	...	2,738	11.8
Finance	...	...	365	1.6
Public admin.	...	...	4,221	18.2
Services	...	...	7,703	33.2
Other	...	...	2,723¶	11.7¶
TOTAL	107.3º	100.0	23,201	100.0

Public debt: n.a.
Population economically active (1980): total 23,201; participation rate of population over age 16, 33.7% (female 21.1%, unemployed 11.5%)
Price and earnings indexes: n.a.
Household income and expenditure. Average household size (1980) 6.7; average annual income per household (1979) U.S.$2,741; source of income: n.a.; expenditure: n.a.
Land use (1983): forested 22.5%; meadows and pastures 13.5%; agricultural and under permanent cultivation 33.1%; other 30.9%.

Foreign trade

Balance of trade (current prices)

U.S.$'000,000	1973	1974	1975	1976	1977	1978
U.S.$'000,000	−28.1	−16.6	−31.5	−33.9	−28.1	−19.5
% of total	88.2%	39.7%	69.8%	62.1%	53.7%	33.5%

Imports (1978): U.S.$38,856,000 (food and live animals, chiefly for food 33.9%; miscellaneous manufactured goods 23.5%; petroluem products 12.9%; machinery and transport equipment 12.5%; beverages and tobacco 10.9%; chemicals 4.8%). *Major import sources* (1984): United States, Japan.
Exports (1978): U.S.$19,340,000 (copra and vegetable oils 62.0%; food and live animals, chiefly for food 18.0%; inedible crude materials 16.5%; miscellaneous manufactured articles 2.0%). *Major export destinations* (1984): United States, Japan, Guam.

Transport and communications

Transport. Railroads: none. Roads (1980): total length 1,000 mi, 1,600 km (paved 25%). Vehicles (1980): 6,200. Merchant marine: n.a. Air transport (1979): passenger-mi 159,300,000, passenger-km 256,300,000; short ton-mi cargo 2,220,000, metric ton-km cargo 3,241,000; airports (1985) with scheduled flights 24.
Communications. Daily newspapers (1983): total number 1; total circulation, n.a. Radio (1980): total number of receivers 12,816 (1 per 10.4 persons). Television (1980): total number of receivers 3,970 (1 per 33.5 persons). Telephones (1980): 1,350 (1 per 98.4 persons).

Education and health

Education (1981)

	schools	teachers	students	student/ teacher ratio
Primary (age 6–13)	245	1,374	31,099	22.6
Secondary (age 14–17)	32ŏ	445	6,872	15.4
Voc., teacher tr.□	2	39º	456	...
Higher△	1	158	2,129	13.5

Educational attainment (1980). Percent of population over age 15 having: no formal schooling 13.2%; some primary education 30.4%; primary 15.0%; some secondary 18.3%; secondary 14.2%; some college 6.2%; college 1.8%; post-college 0.9%. *Literacy* (1980): total population over age 15 literate 66,188 (92.2%); males literate 34,206 (93.6%); females literate 31,982 (90.8%).
Health: physicians (1983) 46† (1 per 2,100 persons†); hospital beds (1978) 462 (1 per 275 persons); infant mortality rate per 1,000 live births (1982) 22.1.
Food: daily per capita caloric intake, n.a.

Military

External security is provided by the United States.

---

*Separate administrative actions within the Trust Territory have, since 1978, created four new administrative entities that are to form the framework for local government upon termination of the UN trusteeship: the Commonwealth of the Northern Mariana Islands (1978); the Federated States of Micronesia (1979); the Republic of the Marshall Islands (1979); and the Republic of Palau (1981). The government of the Trust Territory has become progressively more vestigial as its functions are assumed by the governments of these four entities. Combined data are, thus, often no longer available. †Land area only. ‡Includes other islands in geographic Micronesia. §Excludes Northern Mariana Islands. ‖1983. ¶Includes people primarily in subsistence activity, the registered unemployed, and members of the armed forces. ºAt current prices. ŏ1976–77. □1982–83. ◊1978–79. △1980. †Excludes Marshall Islands and Palau.

Pakistan

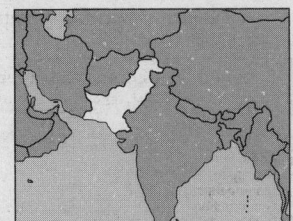

Official name: Islām-ī Jamhūrīya–e Pākistān (Islāmic Republic of Pakistan).
Form of government: federal republic with two legislative houses (Senate [87]; National Assembly [237]).
Head of state and government*: President (Chief Martial Law Administrator).
Capital: Islāmābād.
Official language: Urdū.
Official religion: Islām.
Monetary unit: 1 Pakistan Rupee (PRs) = 100 paisa; valuation (Oct. 21, 1985) 1 U.S.$ = PRs15.83; 1 £ = PRs22.70.

Area and population

Provinces	Capitals	area sq mi	area sq km	population 1983 estimate†
Baluchistān	Quetta	134,050	347,188	4,611,000
North–West Frontier	Peshāwar	28,773	74,522	11,658,000
Punjab	Lahore	79,284	205,345	50,460,000
Sind	Karāchi	54,407	140,913	20,312,000
Federally Administered Tribal Areas	...	10,510	27,221	2,329,000
Federal Capital Area				
Islāmābād	...	350	906	359,000
TOTAL		307,374	796,095	89,729,000

Demography

Population (1985): 100,356,000†.
Density (1985): persons per sq mi 326.5, persons per sq km 126.1.
Urban–rural (1981): urban 28.3%; rural 71.7%.
Sex distribution (1981): male 52.47%; female 47.53%.
Age breakdown (1981): under 15, 45.2%; 15–29, 23.9%; 30–44, 15.0%; 45–59, 9.2%; 60–74, 5.1%; 75 and over, 1.6%.
Population projection: (1990) 112,040,000; (2000) 152,050,000.
Doubling time: 23 years.
Linguistic composition (1981): Punjābī 48.2%; Pashto 13.1%; Sindhī 11.8%; Saraikī 9.8%; Urdū 7.6%; other 9.5%.
Religious affiliation (1980): Muslim 96.8%; Christian 1.8%; Hindu 1.3%; other 0.1%.
Major cities (1981): Karāchi 5,208,100; Lahore 2,952,700; Faisalābād 1,104,-200; Rāwalpindi 806,000; Hyderābād 795,000.

Vital statistics

Birth rate per 1,000 population (1984): 42.2 (world avg. 29.0).
Death rate per 1,000 population (1984): 14.9 (world avg. 11.0).
Natural increase rate per 1,000 population (1984): 27.3 (world avg. 18.0).
Total fertility rate (avg. births per childbearing woman; 1984): 5.7.
Marriage rate per 1,000 population (1975–80): 10.7.
Divorce rate per 1,000 population (1975–80): 0.3.
Life expectancy at birth (1984): male 51.6 years; female 49.7 years.
Major causes of death per 100,000 population: n.a.; however, the major diseases are tuberculosis, cancer, poliomyelitis, typhoid, dysentery, pertussis, trachoma, and malaria.

National economy

Budget (1984–85). Revenue: PRs79,416,900,000 (customs duties 29.8%, federal excise 21.4%, income from property and enterprise 12.8%, income tax and corporation tax 12.8%, sales tax 6.3%). Expenditures: PRs76,227,-100,000 (defense 38.2%, debt payment 33.7%, economic development and services 9.2%, subsidies 5.1%, general administration 4.9%, social services 3.4%).
Public debt (external, outstanding; 1984): U.S.$13,242,900,000.
Tourism (1983): receipts from visitors U.S.$201,600,000; expenditures by nationals abroad U.S.$165,000,000.
Production (metric tons except as noted). Agriculture, forestry, fishing (1983–84): sugarcane 34,287,300, wheat 11,531,000, rice 3,339,500, cottonseed 1,144,000, corn (maize) 1,013,500, cotton 572,000, tobacco 79,600; livestock (number of live animals) 28,700,000 goats, 24,200,000 sheep, 16,300,000 cattle, 12,800,000 buffalo, 890,000 camels, 79,000,000 poultry; roundwood 19,095,000 cu m; fish catch 343,402. Mining and quarrying (1983–84): limestone 4,696,443; dolomite 98,891; fire clay 83,676; barite 35,965; feldspar 5,992; chromite 4,180; bauxite 4,173; magnesite 3,338. Manufacturing (1983–84): cement 4,502,000; chemical fertilizers 2,675,689, of which urea 1,797,553; steel products 654,205; chemicals 235,497; jute textiles 79,733; tea 55,273; paper and paperboard 43,652; cotton textiles 296,596,000 sq m; beverages 961,203,000 bottles; cigarettes 40,296,000,000 units; bicycles 448,218 units; road motor vehicles 71,242 units. Construction (value in PRs; 1980): residential 5,284,000,000; nonresidential 7,816,000,000. Energy production (consumption): electricity (kW-hr; 1984) 20,721,000,000 (20,721,000,000); coal (metric tons; 1984) 2,260,000 (2,260,-000); crude petroleum (barrels; 1984) 4,803,600 (35,931,000‡); petroleum products (metric tons; 1983) 4,144,000 (5,311,000); natural gas (cu m; 1984) 9,974,000,000 (9,974,000,000).
Household income and expenditure. Average household size (1981) 6.7; income per household PRs20,530 (U.S.$2,075); sources of income (1979): wages and salaries 30.7%, self-employment 53.1%, property 11.2%, other

5.0%; expenditure (1979): food 50.8%, housing 17.5%, clothing and footwear 9.6%, recreation 0.4%, other 21.7%.
Gross national product (at current market prices; 1983): U.S.$35,000,000,000 (U.S.$370 per capita).

Structure of gross domestic product and labour force

	1983–84 in value PRs'000,000	% of total value	labour force	% of labour force
Agriculture	91,837	24.4	14,053,000	50.7
Mining	5,458	1.5	29,000	0.1
Manufacturing	75,061	20.0	3,582,000	12.9
Construction	19,120	5.1	1,279,000	4.6
Public utilities	8,053	2.1	301,000	1.1
Transportation and communication	29,108	7.7	1,224,000	4.4
Trade	61,036	16.2	3,183,000	11.5
Finance	10,651	2.8	219,000	0.8
Pub. admin., defense	32,750	8.7	2,715,000	9.8
Services	31,172	8.3		
Other	11,447	3.0	1,155,000§	4.2
TOTAL	375,693‖	100.0¶	27,740,000	100.0¶

Population economically active (1983–84): total 27,740,000; participation rate of population over age 10, 46.1% (female 11.6%, unemployed 3.9%).

Price and earnings indexes (1980 = 100)

	1979	1980	1981	1982	1983	1984	1985
Consumer price index	89.3	100.0	111.9	118.5	127.3	136.4	142.6♀
Monthly earnings index	107.0	100.0	...	...	...	...	...

Land use (1983): forested 3.8%; meadows and pastures 6.4%; agricultural and under-permanent cultivation 26.3%; built-on, wasteland, and other 63.5%.

Foreign trade

Balance of trade (current prices)

	1979	1980	1981	1982	1983	1984
PRs'000,000	−16,352	−22,450	−22,374	−30,823	−23,475	−38,927
% of total	28.7%	30.2%	28.2%	35.3%	22.5%	35.1%

Imports (1983–84): PRs76,706,700,000 (mineral fuels and lubricants 25.0%, nonelectrical machinery 13.2%, transport equipment 8.2%, iron and steel 4.4%, electrical goods 3.9%, tea 3.3%, synthetic and art silk yarn 2.1%, chemical fertilizers 2.0%). *Major import sources:* Japan 14.3%; United States 11.4%; Saudi Arabia 9.9%; Kuwait 8.1%; United Kingdom 6.7%; West Germany 6.4%; Malaysia 4.2%.
Exports (1983–84): PRs37,037,100,000 (rice 15.2%, cotton fabric 13.0%, cotton yarn 7.9%, carpets and rugs 6.2%, leather 5.3%, synthetic textiles 4.4%, fish and fish products 2.7%, sports goods 1.8%). *Major export destinations:* West Germany 12.8%; United States 9.0%; Japan 8.6%; Saudi Arabia 7.8%; United Kingdom 4.4%; France 2.1%; Kuwait 2.0%; China 1.7%.

Transport and communications

Transport. Railroads (1984): length 5,452 mi, 8,775 km; passenger-mi 11,397,-000,000, passenger-km 18,342,000,000; short ton-mi cargo 5,212,000,000, metric ton-km cargo 7,610,000,000. Roads (1983): total length 62,427 mi, 100,467 km (paved 62%). Vehicles (1983): passenger cars 197,633; trucks and buses 82,709. Merchant marine (1984): vessels (100 gross tons and over) 82; total deadweight tonnage 733,519. Air transport (1984): passenger-mi 3,298,800,000, passenger-km 5,308,914,000; short ton-mi cargo 171,370,000, metric ton-km cargo 250,211,000; airports (1985) with scheduled flights 18.
Communications. Daily newspapers (1983): total number 116; total circulation 1,991,000; circulation per 1,000 population 22. Radio (1984): 5,200,000 receivers (1 per 18 persons). Television (1984): 850,000 receivers (1 per 115 persons). Telephones (1984): 489,411 (1 per 200 persons).

Education and health

Education (1983–84)

	schools	teachers	students	student/ teacher ratio
Primary (age 5–9)	72,053	206,000	6,412,000	31.1
Secondary (age 10–14)	10,433	142,000	2,287,000	16.1
Voc., teacher tr.	266	3,798	52,000	13.7
Higher	122	9,371	137,216	14.6

Educational attainment (1981). Percent of population over age 10 having: no formal schooling 73.8%; primary education 10.2%; secondary 9.6%; some postsecondary 1.5%; higher degree 1.3%. *Literacy* (1981): total population over age 15 literate 11,938,790 (25.6%); males literate 8,709,162 (36.0%); females literate 3,229,628 (15.2%).
Health (1983): physicians 33,584 (1 per 2,654 persons); hospital beds 52,161 (1 per 1,709 persons); infant mortality rate per 1,000 live births (1984) 116.0.
Food (1980–82): daily per capita caloric intake 2,232 (vegetable products 89%, animal products 11%); 103% of FAO recommended minimum requirement.

Military

Total active duty personnel (1984): 478,600 (army 94.0%, navy 2.3%, air force 3.7%). *Military expenditure as percent of GNP* (1983): 5.4% (world 6.1%); per capita expenditure U.S.$20.

---

*Provincial estimates exclude and 1985 estimate includes Afghan refugees and residents of Pakistani-occupied Jammu and Kashmir, numbering together about 4,150,-000. †1982. ‡1983. §Includes unemployed. ‖At current prices. ¶Detail does not add to total given because of rounding. ♀May.

Panama

Official name: República de Panamá (Republic of Panama).
Form of government: multiparty republic with two legislative houses (Legislative Assembly [67]; National Assembly [505]).
Head of state and government: President.
Capital: Panama City.
Official language: Spanish.
Official religion: none.
Monetary unit: 1 balboa (B) = 100 cents; valuation (Oct. 21, 1985) 1 U.S.$ = B1.00; 1 £ = B1.43.

Area and population

Provinces	Capitals	area* sq mi	area* sq km	population 1985 estimate
Bocas del Toro	Bocas del Toro	3,443	8,917	73,500
Chiriquí	David	3,381	8,758	346,000
Coclé	Penonomé	1,944	5,035	158,700
Colón	Colón	1,915	4,961	157,600
Darién	La Palma	6,488	16,803	36,000
Herrera	Chitré	937	2,427	98,300
Los Santos	Las Tablas	1,493	3,867	80,100
Panamá	Panama City	4,642	12,022	987,700
Veraguas	Santiago	4,280	11,086	204,100
Special territory				
Comarca de San Blas	El Porvenir	1,238	3,206	38,500
TOTAL		29,762†	77,082	2,180,500

Demography

Population (1985): 2,180,500.
Density (1985): persons per sq mi 73.3, persons per sq km 28.3.
Urban-rural (1980): urban 49.3%; rural 50.7%.
Sex distribution (1983): male 51.02%; female 48.98%.
Age breakdown (1983): under 15, 38.7%; 15–29, 28.9%; 30–44, 16.5%; 45–59, 9.4%; 60–74, 5.1%; 75 and over, 1.4%.
Population projection: (1990) 2,418,000; (2000) 2,893,000.
Doubling time: 32 years.
Ethnic composition (1982): mestizo (and mulatto) 70%; white 12%; black 12%; Indian and other 6%.
Religious affiliation (1980): Roman Catholic 89.0%; Protestant 5.0%; Muslim 4.5%; Bahā'ī 1.0%; Hindu 0.3%; other 0.2%.
Major cities (1980): Panama City 389,172; San Miguelito 156,611; Colón 59,840; David 49,472.

Vital statistics

Birth rate per 1,000 population (1983): 26.2 (world avg. 29.0); (1980) legitimate 28.6%; illegitimate 71.4%.
Death rate per 1,000 population (1983): 4.1 (world avg. 11.0).
Natural increase rate per 1,000 population (1983): 22.1 (world avg. 18.0).
Total fertility rate (avg. births per childbearing woman; 1980–85): 3.6.
Marriage rate per 1,000 population (1983): 4.3.
Divorce rate per 1,000 population (1983): 0.5.
Life expectancy at birth (1980–85): male 69.2 years; female 72.9 years.
Major causes of death per 100,000 population (1983): heart disease 68.3, of which acute myocardial infarction 26.5; malignant neoplasms (cancers) 48.8; accident, suicide, homicide, and other violence 44.9, of which motor vehicle traffic accidents 14.1; cerebrovascular disease and atherosclerosis 38.9; signs, symptoms, and ill-defined conditions 34.3; congenital anomalies including birth injury, difficult labour, and other complications of pregnancy 32.2; pneumonia, influenza, and bronchitis 21.4; diabetes mellitus 9.0.

National economy

Budget (1984). Revenue: B1,372,064,000 (current revenue 65.2%, of which direct taxes 24.3%; indirect taxes 21.8%; administrative fees, charges, and sales 7.4%; income from state enterprises 4.8%). Expenditures: B1,372,064,-000 (current expenditure 87.0%, of which payment on public debt 39.3%, education 15.9%, home affairs and justice 9.2%, health 5.8%, public works 2.9%, agriculture and livestock 1.8%).
Public debt (external, outstanding; 1983): U.S.$2,986,200,000.
Tourism (1982): receipts from visitors U.S.$169,000,000; expenditures by nationals abroad U.S.$71,000,000‡.
Production (metric tons except as noted). Agriculture, forestry, fishing (1984): sugarcane 2,134,000, bananas and plantains 1,183,000, rice 175,000, corn (maize) 80,000, coffee 9,000, cacao 1,000; livestock (number of live animals) 1,470,000 cattle, 200,000 pigs; roundwood 2,047,000 cu m‡; fish catch 166,075‡. Manufacturing (value added in B; 1982): processed food 676,800,000, of which prepared meat 130,800,000, refined sugar 91,600,-000; chemical products 82,800,000; textile products 67,400,000; wood pulp and paper products 56,500,000. Construction (value added in B; 1983§): residential 51,972,400; nonresidential 32,941,000. Energy production (consumption): electricity (kW-hr; 1983) 2,238,200,000 (2,238,200,000); coal, none (n.a.); crude petroleum (barrels; 1983) none (13,200,000); petroleum products (metric tons; 1983) 1,741,000 (946,000).
Land use (1983): forested 53.7%; meadows and pastures 15.3%; agricultural and under permanent cultivation 7.7%; other 23.3%.

Gross national product (at current market prices; 1983): U.S.$4,070,000,000 (U.S.$2,070 per capita).

Structure of gross domestic product and labour force

	1983 in value B'000,000	% of total value	labour force ‖	% of labour force
Agriculture	441.3	10.0	169,900	28.3
Mining	10.0	0.2	800	0.1
Manufacturing	399.3	9.1	61,900	10.3
Construction	260.3	5.9	35,700	6.0
Public utilities	147.6	3.4	9,100	1.5
Transportation and communication	698.0	15.9	37,300	6.2
Trade	533.3	12.1	86,700	14.5
Finance	433.3	9.9	27,700	4.6
Pub. admin., defense	549.4	12.5	158,600	26.5
Services	886.6	20.2		
Other	32.7	0.7	11,600¶	1.9
TOTAL	4,391.8⁹	100.0†	599,300	100.0†

Population economically active (1983): total 663,000; participation rate of population over age 15, 51.8% (unemployed 9.6%).

Price and earnings indexes (1980 = 100)

	1979	1980	1981	1982	1983	1984	1985
Consumer price index	87.9	100.0	107.3	111.9	114.2	116.0	117.3⁵
Monthly earnings index	...	...	...	...	...	...	...

Household income and expenditure. Average household size (1980) 4.6; median income per household (1980) B2,950 (U.S.$2,950); sources of income (1979): wages and salaries 85.3%, transfers 9.2%, other 5.5%; expenditure (1978): food 47.3%, housing 12.7%, transportation 6.8%, health care 4.9%, clothing 4.8%.

Foreign trade

Balance of trade (current prices)

	1979	1980	1981	1982	1983	1984
B'000,000	−760.03	−928.41	−1,064.86	−1,032.59	−943.67	−993.77
% of total	55.6%	56.3%	61.9%	57.9%	59.4%	64.3%

Imports (1983): B1,266,173,600 (crude petroleum 25.6%, machinery and transport equipment 22.1%, manufactured products 16.2%, chemical products 11.7%, food products 8.5%). *Major import sources:* United States 31.0%; Mexico 9.6%; Venezuela 9.4%; Ecuador 8.4%; Japan 7.2%; West Germany 2.2%; Italy 1.6%.
Exports (1983): B322,498,700 (bananas 24.7%, shrimp 16.9%, sugar 13.6%, petroleum products 11.8%, coffee and cocoa 5.3%, clothing and leather products 2.5%). *Major export destinations:* United States 52.6%; West Germany 5.6%; Belgium–Luxembourg 5.1%; Costa Rica 5.0%; Italy 2.7%; Sweden 1.7%; El Salvador 1.6%.

Transport and communications

Transport. Railroads (1984): length 171 mi, 275 km; passengers carried 62,-623‡. Roads (1983): total length 5,864 mi, 9,437 km (paved 31%). Vehicles (1983): passenger cars 113,960; trucks and buses 37,051. Merchant marine (1984): vessels (100 gross tons and over) 5,499; total deadweight tonnage 62,068,888. Panama Canal traffic (1984): oceangoing transits 11,384; cargo 143,060,500 metric tons. Air transport (1982): passenger-mi 248,500,000, passenger-km 400,000,000; short ton-mi cargo 9,900,000, metric ton-km cargo 14,400,000; airports (1985) with scheduled flights 6.
Communications. Daily newspapers (1984): total number 7; total circulation 132,300; circulation per 1,000 population 62. Radio (1984): receivers 295,000 (1 per 7.2 persons). Television (1984): receivers 240,000 (1 per 8.9 persons). Telephones (1983): 202,627 (1 per 10.3 persons).

Education and health

Education (1983)

	schools	teachers	students	student/ teacher ratio
Primary (age 6–11)	2,376	12,613	335,950	26.6
Secondary (age 12–17) }	321	9,249	128,972	...
Voc., teacher tr.			49,015	...
Higher□	3	2,578	45,824	17.8

Educational attainment (1980). Percent of adult population over age 25 having: no formal schooling 17.5%; primary education 50.0%; secondary 23.1%; higher 8.2%; other 1.2%. *Literacy* (1980): total population over age 10 literate 1,193,800 (88.9%); males literate 604,800 (88.7%); females literate 589,000 (89.1%).
Health (1983): physicians 2,149 (1 per 972 persons); hospital beds 7,448 (1 per 280 persons); infant mortality rate per 1,000 live births 20.5.
Food (1980–82): daily per capita caloric intake 2,388 (vegetable products 81%, animal products 19%); 103% of FAO recommended minimum requirement.

Military

Total active duty personnel (1984): 9,500◇ (army 94.7%, navy 3.2%, air force 2.1%). *Military expenditure as percent of GNP* (1982): 0.8% (world 6.0%); per capita expenditure U.S.$16.

*Total land area is 29,341 sq mi (75,992 sq km); the area shown for provinces, special territory, and the grand total includes both land and water area. †Detail does not add to total given because of rounding. ‡1983. §Private only. ‖ Employed persons only. ¶Includes persons employed in the Canal Zone. ⁹At current prices. ⁵June. □Universities only. ◇Includes 7,500 paramilitary forces; all services form part of the army.

Papua New Guinea

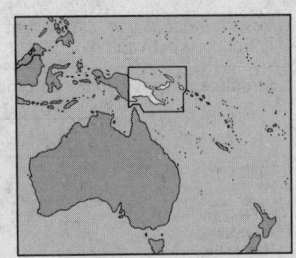

Official name: Papua New Guinea.
Form of government: unitary multiparty parliamentary state with one legislative house (National Parliament [109]).
Chief of state: British Monarch represented by governor-general.
Head of government: Prime Minister.
Capital: Port Moresby.
Official language: English.
Official religion: none.
Monetary unit: 1 Papua New Guinea kina (K) = 100 toea; valuation (Oct. 21, 1985) 1 K = U.S.$0.95 = £0.66.

Area and population

Provinces	Administrative centres	area sq mi	area sq km	population 1984 estimate*
Central	Port Moresby	11,400	29,500	122,700
Chimbu	Kundiawa	2,350	6,100	183,600
Eastern Highlands	Goroka	4,300	11,200	296,000
East New Britain	Rabaul	6,000	15,500	138,400
East Sepik	Wewak	16,550	42,800	240,800
Enga	Wabag	4,950	12,800	174,900
Gulf	Kerema	13,300	34,500	67,600
Madang	Madang	11,200	29,000	228,700
Manus	Lorengau	800	2,100	27,500
Milne Bay	Alotau	5,400	14,000	137,900
Morobe	Lae	13,300	34,500	340,600
National Capital District	Port Moresby	100	240	133,300†
New Ireland	Kavieng	3,700	9,600	70,800
Northern	Popondetta	8,800	22,800	83,800
North Solomons	Kieta	3,600	9,300	137,600
Southern Highlands	Mendi	9,200	23,800	250,900
Western	Daru	38,350	99,300	86,200
Western Highlands	Mount Hagen	3,300	8,500	287,800
West New Britain	Kimbe	8,100	21,000	98,700
West Sepik	Vanimo	14,000	36,300	120,200
TOTAL		178,703‡	462,840	3,228,000†

Demography

Population (1985): 3,345,000.
Density (1985): persons per sq mi 18.7, persons per sq km 7.2.
Urban-rural (1980): urban 13.1%; rural 86.9%.
Sex distribution (1980): male 52.35%; female 47.65%.
Age breakdown (1980): under 15, 43.0%; 15–29, 25.9%; 30–44, 17.0%; 45–59, 10.4%; 60–74, 3.5%; 75 and over, 0.2%.
Population projection: (1990) 4,125,000; (2000) 5,049,000.
Doubling time: 26 years.
Ethnic composition (1980): New Guinea Papuan 83.1%; New Guinea Melanesian 15.5%; other 1.4%.
Religious affiliation (1980): Protestant 58.4%; Roman Catholic 32.8%; Anglican 5.4%; traditional beliefs 2.5%; Baha'i 0.6%; other 0.3%.
Major cities (1984): Port Moresby 144,300; Lae 73,400; Madang 23,700; Wewak 22,100; Goroka 20,900.

Vital statistics

Birth rate per 1,000 population (1984): 35.0 (world avg. 29.0); legitimate, n.a.; illegitimate, n.a.
Death rate per 1,000 population (1984): 14.0 (world avg. 11.0).
Natural increase rate per 1,000 population (1984): 21.0 (world avg. 18.0).
Total fertility rate (avg. births per childbearing woman; 1983): 5.9.
Marriage rate per 1,000 population: n.a.
Divorce rate per 1,000 population: n.a.
Life expectancy at birth (1980–85): male 53.5 years; female 53.0 years.
Major causes of death per 100,000 population: n.a.; however, major infectious diseases are malaria, intestinal infections, and tuberculosis.

National economy

Budget (1984). Revenue: K770,056,000 (foreign government grants 30.1%, customs and excise taxes 22.2%, personal income tax 16.8%, loans 8.3%). Expenditures: K747,113,000 (no breakdown available).
Public debt (external, outstanding; 1983): U.S.$911,200,000.
Tourism: receipts from visitors (1981) U.S.$25,800,000; expenditures by nationals abroad (1983) U.S.$19,000,000.
Production (metric tons except as noted). Agriculture, forestry, fishing (1984): bananas 920,000, coconuts 782,000, sweet potatoes 464,000, sugarcane 382,000, copra 140,000, palm oil 108,000, cassava 101,000, coffee 57,000, palm kernels 44,700, cocoa 28,000, pineapples 10,000, tea 9,000, pulses 2,000, peanuts (groundnuts) 1,000; livestock (number of live animals) 1,460,000 pigs, 123,000 cattle, 16,000 goats, 1,000,000 chickens; roundwood 6,910,000 cu m ‖; fish catch 1,395 ‖. Mining and quarrying (1983): copper 183,200; silver 47,400 kg; gold 18,000 kg. Manufacturing (value added in K; 1983): food, beverages, and tobacco 126,670,000; wood and wood products 36,695,000; metals, metal products, machinery, and equipment 35,428,000. Construction (value§; 1985): residential K28,279,000; nonresidential K11,018,000. Energy production (consumption): electricity (kW-hr; 1984) 1,491,100,000 (1,491,100,000); coal, none (n.a.); crude petroleum (barrels; 1981) none (4,266,060); petroleum products (metric tons; 1983) none (626,000); natural gas, none (n.a.).
Gross national product (at current market prices; 1983): U.S.$2,510,000,000 (U.S.$790 per capita).

Structure of gross domestic product and labour force

	1980 in value K'000,000	1980 % of total value	1980 labour force	1980 % of labour force
Agriculture	575.0	33.7	564,500	77.0
Mining	225.4	13.2	4,300	0.6
Manufacturing	161.7	9.5	14,000	1.9
Construction	60.9	3.6	21,600	2.9
Public utilities	10.8	0.6	2,800	0.4
Transportation and communication	84.8	5.0	17,400	2.4
Trade	143.1	8.4	25,100	3.4
Finance	99.3	5.8	4,500	0.6
Pub. admin., defense	122.1	7.1 }	77,100	10.5
Services	202.1	11.8 }		
Other	22.9	1.3	1,500	0.2
TOTAL	1,708.1¶	100.0	732,800	100.0‡

Population economically active (1980): total 1,148,000; participation rate of population over age 15, 67.1% (female 37.5%, unemployed 12.8%♀).

Price and earnings indexes (1980 = 100)

	1979	1980	1981	1982	1983	1984	1985
consumer price index	89.2	100.0	108.1	114.0	123.0	132.2	135.6ð
Monthly earnings index	...	...	...	...	...	...	...

Household income and expenditure. Average household size (1980) 4.6; income per household (1975–76) K2,771 (U.S.$3,483); source of income: n.a.; expenditure: n.a.
Land use (1983): forested 71.2%; agricultural and under permanent cultivation 0.8%; meadows and pastures 0.2%; other 27.8%.

Foreign trade

Balance of trade (current prices)

	1978	1979	1980	1981	1982	1983	1984
K'000,000	+72.1	+125.3	+7.5	−173.7	−180.8	−138.0	−64.7
% of total	7.0%	10.0%	0.5%	13.3%	13.7%	9.2%	3.9%

Imports (1984): K866,831,000 (machinery and transport equipment 28.1%; mineral fuels, lubricants, and related materials 18.0%; food and live animals 17.8%; manufactured goods 16.2%). *Major import sources* (1983): Australia 34.9%; Japan 13.2%; Singapore 11.9%; United States 8.9%; United Kingdom 3.5%; West Germany 1.8%; Hong Kong 1.7%.
Exports (1984): K802,155,000 (copper ore and concentrates 37.2%; coffee 14.1%; cocoa beans 8.4%; timber 8.0%; palm oil 7.9%; copra 6.2%; copra oil 5.0%). *Major export destinations* (1983): Japan 29.4%; West Germany 21.4%; Australia 7.7%; United Kingdom 5.0%; Spain 3.5%; United States 1.9%.

Transport and communications

Transport. Railroads (1983): none. Roads (1982): total length 11,523 mi, 18,545 km (paved 6%). Vehicles (1982): passenger cars 18,877; trucks and buses 28,128. Merchant marine (1984): vessels (100 gross tons and over) 82; total deadweight tonnage 29,906. Air transport (1984): passenger-mi 358,000,000, passenger-km 576,000,000; short ton-mi cargo 8,500,000, metric ton-km cargo 12,500,000; airports (1985) with scheduled flights 41.
Communications. Daily newspapers (1984): total number 2; total circulation 45,000; circulation per 1,000 population 13. Radio (1984): total number of receivers 215,000 (1 per 15 persons). Television: n.a. Telephones (1984): 51,483 (1 per 63 persons).

Education and health

Education (1983)

	schools	teachers	students	student/teacher ratio
Primary (age 7–12)	2,224	10,130	322,254	31.8
Secondary (age 13–16)	111	1,629	41,702	25.6
Voc., teacher tr.	92	548	7,392	13.5
Higher ‖	3	644	3,954	6.1

Educational attainment (1980). Percent of population over age 5 having: no formal schooling 78.0%; some primary education 7.8%; completed primary 9.6%; some secondary, secondary, and higher 4.6%. *Literacy* (1980): total population over age 15 literate 757,500 (42.3%); males literate 490,100 (52.4%); females literate 267,400 (31.3%).
Health (1984): physicians 280 (1 per 11,635 persons); hospital beds 14,661 (1 per 222 persons); infant mortality rate per 1,000 live births 103.0.
Food (1980–82): daily per capita caloric intake 2,074 (vegetable products 90%, animal products 10%); 78% of FAO recommended minimum requirement.

Military

Total active duty personnel (1983): 3,232□ (army 88.0%, navy 9.3%, air force 2.7%). *Military expenditure as percent of GNP* (1983): 1.2% (world 6.1%); per capita expenditure U.S.$9.

---

*De jure. †National capital district includes noncitizens; 30,000 other noncitizens in the country bring the de facto population total to 3,258,000. ‡Detail does not add to total given because of rounding. §Private only. ‖1983. ¶At current prices. ♀1977; in six urban centres. ðFirst quarter. □All services form part of the army.

Paraguay

Official name: República del Paraguay (Republic of Paraguay).
Form of government: republic with two legislative houses (Congress [30]; Chamber of Deputies [60]).
Head of state and government: President.
Capital: Asunción.
Official language: Spanish.
Official religion: Roman Catholicism.
Monetary unit: 1 Paraguayan Guaraní (₲) = 100 céntimos; valuation* (Oct. 21, 1985) 1 U.S.$ = ₲240.15; 1£ = ₲344.41.

Area and population

Regions Departments	Capitals	area sq mi	area sq km	population 1982 census
Occidental		95,338	246,925	54,480
Alto Paraguay	Fuerte Olimpio	17,754	45,982	8,960
Boquerón	Dr. Pedro P. Peña	18,034	46,708	13,860
Chaco	Mayor Pablo Lagerenza	14,041	36,367	260
Nueva Asunción	General Eugenio A. Garay	17,359	44,961	220
Presidente Hayes	Pozo Colorado	28,150	72,907	31,180
Oriental		61,710	159,827	2,980,880
Alto Paraná	Puerto Presidente Stroessner	5,751	14,895	198,500
Amambay	Pedro Juan Caballero	4,994	12,933	68,730
Asunción	Asunción	45	117	457,210
Caaguazú	Coronel Oviedo	4,430	11,474	299,970
Caazapá	Caazapá	3,666	9,496	110,050
Canendiyú	Salto del Guairá	5,663	14,667	66,670
Central	Asunción	952	2,465	493,500
Concepción	Concepción	6,970	18,051	135,200
Cordillera	Caacupé	1,910	4,948	194,450
Guairá	Villarrica	1,485	3,846	143,430
Itapúa	Encarnación	6,380	16,525	264,020
Misiones	San Juan Bautista	3,690	9,556	78,270
Ñeembucú	Pilar	4,690	12,147	72,380
Paraguarí	Paraguarí	3,361	8,705	203,330
San Pedro	San Pedro	7,723	20,002	195,170
TOTAL		157,048	406,752	3,035,360

Demography

Population (1985): 3,404,000.
Density (1985): persons per sq mi 21.7, persons per sq km 8.4.
Urban–rural (1982): urban 42.8%; rural 57.2%.
Sex distribution (1982): male 50.07%; female 49.93%.
Age breakdown (1982): under 15, 41.1%; 15–29, 28.1%; 30–44, 15.4%; 45–59, 9.1%; 60–74, 4.8%; 75 and over, 1.5%.
Population projection: (1990) 4,231,000; (2000) 5,405,000.
Doubling time: 23 years.
Ethnic composition (1980): mestizo (Spanish–Guaraní) 90.8%; Amerindian 3.0%; German 1.7%; other 4.5%.
Religious affiliation (1980): Roman Catholic 96.0%; Protestant 1.8%; other 2.2%.
Major cities (1982): Asunción 457,210; San Lorenzo 74,240; Lambaré 67,180; Fernando de la Mora 66,450.

Vital statistics

Birth rate per 1,000 population (1980–85): 36.0 (world avg. 29.0); (1981)† legitimate 67.4%; illegitimate 32.6%.
Death rate per 1,000 population (1980–85): 7.2 (world avg. 11.0).
Natural increase rate per 1,000 population (1980–85): 28.8 (world avg. 18.0).
Total fertility rate (avg. births per childbearing woman; 1980–85): 4.9.
Marriage rate per 1,000 population (1981): 5.0.
Divorce rate per 1,000 population: n.a.
Life expectancy at birth (1980–85): male 62.8 years; female 67.5 years.
Major causes of death per 100,000 population (1980): diseases of the circulatory system 93.2; ill-defined conditions 79.7; enteritis and other diarrheal diseases 35.1.

National economy

Budget (1983). Revenue: ₲60,220,500,000 (domestic taxes on goods and services 31.5%, income tax 15.9%, customs duties 10.2%, pension funds 7.6%, real estate taxes 5.6%, sales tax 4.8%, alcohol tax 3.5%). Expenditures: ₲81,120,800,000 (defense 14.4%, education 14.1%, ministry of interior 9.4%, public debt 7.5%, public works 4.6%, public health 3.5%).
Public debt (external, outstanding; 1983): U.S.$1,161,200,000.
Tourism: receipts from visitors (1983) U.S.$49,000,000; expenditures by nationals abroad (1981) U.S.$45,000,000.
Production (metric tons except as noted). Agriculture, forestry, fishing (1984): cassava 2,200,000, sugarcane 1,700,000, soybeans 660,000, corn (maize) 500,000, bananas 325,000, seed cotton 282,000, oranges 230,000, palm kernels 150,000, sweet potatoes 120,000, wheat 100,000, lint cotton 90,000; livestock (number of live animals) 5,100,000 cattle, 1,350,000 pigs; roundwood 6,822,000 cu m‡; fish catch 3,500‡. Mining and quarrying (1983): limestone 280,000; kaolin 50,000; gypsum 6,500. Manufacturing (1983): cement 153,000; sugar 92,200; beef and veal 85,000§; tung oil 17,-000; hides 11,000; edible coconut oil 4,500; coconut pulp 3,400; woven cotton fabrics 5,842,000 metres; beer 455,930 hectolitres; alcohol 42,200 hectolitres; matches 2,979,000 boxes. Construction (1982): residential 116,-800 sq m; nonresidential 210,600 sq m. Energy production (consumption): electricity (kW-hr; 1983) 848,000,000 (846,000,000); coal, none (none); crude petroleum (barrels; 1983) none (1,410,000); petroleum products (metric tons; 1983) 186,000 (403,000); natural gas, none (none).
Gross national product (at current market prices; 1983): U.S.$4,540,000,000 (U.S.$1,410 per capita).

Structure of gross domestic product and labour force

	1983 in value ₲'000,000	1983 % of total value	1982 labour force	1982 % of labour force
Agriculture	211,615	25.9	445,720	43.3
Mining	3,487	0.4	1,130	0.1
Manufacturing	134,273	16.4	124,840	12.1
Construction	54,994	6.7	67,170	6.5
Public utilities	20,638	2.5	2,540	0.3
Transportation and communication	34,529	4.2	26,230	2.6
Trade	217,210	26.6	78,650	7.6
Finance			29,140	2.8
Pub. admin., defense	141,368 ‖	17.3 ‖ }	168,980	16.4
Services				
Other			85,110	8.3
TOTAL	818,114¶	100.0	1,029,510	100.0

Population economically active (1982): total 1,029,510; participation rate of population over age 10, 47.4% (female 20.3%, unemployed 29.0%).

Price and earnings indexes (1980 = 100)

	1979	1980	1981	1982	1983	1984	1985
Consumer price index	81.7	100.0	114.0	121.7	138.0	166.1	192.3♀
Monthly earnings index	...	...	...	...	...	...	...

Household income and expenditure: average household size (1982) 5.2.
Land use (1983): forested 51.5%; meadows and pastures 39.1%; agricultural and under permanent cultivation 4.9%; other 4.5%.

Foreign trade

Balance of trade (current prices)

	1979	1980	1981	1982	1983	1984
₲'000,000	−17,411	−26,071	−26,532	−32,301	−26,519	−42,316
% of total	18.8%	25.0%	26.3%	25.5%	23.5%	21.7%

Imports (1983): ₲69,680,000,000 (fuels and lubricants 25.1%, of which crude petroleum 12.1%, gasoline 9.0%; machines, apparatus, and engines 22.5%; iron and iron manufactures 8.3%; food, beverages, and tobacco 9.8%; transport equipment 6.2%). *Major import sources:* Brazil 28.1%; Argentina 18.7%; Algeria 13.5%; West Germany 6.9%.
Exports (1983): ₲43,161,000,000 (cotton fibres 32.9%; soybeans 31.2%; timber 6.8%; animal fodder 5.1%; tung oil 4.7%; tobacco 3.6%; cowhide 2.5%; processed meat 2.1%; sugar 1.9%). *Major export destinations:* Brazil 20.5%; The Netherlands 14.0%; West Germany 11.7%; Argentina 11.5%; United States 8.9%.

Transport and communications

Transport. Railroads (1980): length 274 mi, 441 km; passenger-mi 13,900,-000, passenger-km 22,400,000; short ton-mi cargo 23,600,000, metric ton-km cargo 34,400,000. Roads (1983): total length 7,034 mi, 11,320 km (paved 19%). Vehicles (1982): passenger cars 35,000; trucks and buses 26,000. Merchant marine (1984): vessels (100 gross tons and over) 39; total deadweight tonnage 44,298. Air transport (1982): passenger-mi 290,000,000, passenger-km 466,000,000; short ton-mi cargo 1,400,000, metric ton-km cargo 2,000,-000; airports (1985) with scheduled flights 1.
Communications. Daily newspapers (1984): total number 5; total circulation 198,000; circulation per 1,000 population 60. Radio (1984): total number of receivers 200,000 (1 per 16 persons). Television (1984): total number of receivers 82,000 (1 per 40 persons). Telephones (1983): 77,983 (1 per 60 persons).

Education and health

Education (1983)

	schools	teachers	students	student/ teacher ratio
Primary (age 7–12)	3,690	21,524	549,637	25.5
Secondary (age 13–18)δ	658	8,356	142,436	17.0
Higher	2	2,448	31,317	12.8

Educational attainment (1982). Percent of population over age 12 having: no formal schooling 9.6%; less than full primary education 47.4%; primary 17.9%; less than full secondary 15.4%; secondary 4.2%; higher 2.9%. *Literacy* (1980): total population over age 15 literate 1,459,100 (85.7%); males literate 753,000 (89.6%); females literate 706,100 (81.9%).
Health: physicians (1979) 1,795 (1 per 1,710 persons); hospital beds (1981) 3,305 (1 per 989 persons); infant mortality rate per 1,000 live births (1982) 51.2.
Food (1980–82): daily per capita caloric intake 2,824 (vegetable products 80%, animal products 20%); 123% of FAO recommended minimum requirement.

Military

Total active duty personnel (1984): 16,900 (army 74.0%, navy 14.8%, air force 11.2%). *Military expenditure as percent of GNP* (1983): 1.9% (world 6.1%); per capita expenditure U.S.$25.

*Currency pegged to U.S.$; 1 U.S.$ = ₲160.00 for luxury goods. †Among births registered on time. ‡1983. §1984. ‖ Includes hotels and restaurants. ¶At current prices. ♀April. δIncludes vocational education and teacher training.

Peru

Official name: República del Perú
(Spanish) (Republic of Peru).
Form of government: unitary multiparty
republic with two legislative
houses (Senate [60]; Chamber of
Deputies [180]).
Head of state and government:
President.
Capital: Lima.
Official languages: Spanish; Quechua.
Official religion: Roman Catholicism.
Monetary unit: 1 Peruvian sol (S/.)
= 100 centavos; valuation (Oct. 21,
1985) 1 U.S.$ = S/.13,963;
1 £ = S/.20,024.

Area and population		area		population
				1984
Departments	Capitals	sq mi	sq km	estimate
Amazonas	Chachapoyas	15,945	41,297	289,800
Ancash	Huaraz	14,158	36,669	922,900
Apurimac	Abancay	7,934	20,550	370,700
Arequipa	Arequipa	24,528	63,528	798,200
Ayacucho	Ayacucho	17,058	44,181	566,200
Cajamarca	Cajamarca	13,486	34,930	1,170,800
Cuzco	Cuzco	29,471	76,329	945,200
Huancavelica	Huancavelica	8,139	21,079	390,800
Huánuco	Huánuco	13,088	33,897	546,500
Ica	Ica	8,205	21,251	483,000
Junin	Huancayo	15,944	41,296	969,500
La Libertad	Trujillo	8,973	23,241	1,072,100
Lambayeque	Chiclayo	5,304	13,737	766,100
Lima	Lima	13,058	33,821	5,396,600
Loreto	Iquitos	146,342	379,025	513,300
Madre de Dios	Puerto Maldonado	30,271	78,403	38,700
Moquegua	Moquegua	6,065	15,709	111,600
Pasco	Cerro de Pasco	9,356	24,233	249,700
Piura	Piura	14,055	36,403	1,249,000
Puno	Puno	27,947	72,382	984,000
San Martín	Moyobamba	20,197	52,309	358,500
Tacna	Tacna	5,881	15,232	159,600
Tumbes	Tumbes	1,827	4,732	116,800
Ucayali	Pucallpa	38,931	100,831	237,300
Constitutional Province				
Callao	Callao	57	148	491,000
TOTAL		496,225*	1,285,216*	19,197,900

Demography

Population (1985): 19,701,000.
Density (1985): persons per sq mi 39.7, persons per sq km 15.3.
Urban–rural (1985): urban 70.2%; rural 29.8%.
Sex distribution (1985): male 50.38%; female 49.62%.
Age breakdown (1985): under 15, 40.5%; 15–29, 28.2%; 30–44, 16.3%; 45–59,
9.5%; 60–74, 4.5%; 75 and over, 1.0%.
Population projection: (1990) 22,332,000; (2000) 27,952,000.
Doubling time: 26 years.
Ethnic composition (1981): Quechua 47.1%; mestizo 32.0%; white 12.0%;
Aymara 5.4%; jungle Amerindian 1.7%; other 1.8%.
Religious affiliation (1981): Roman Catholic 92.4%; other 7.6%.
Major cities (1981): Lima 4,164,600; Arequipa 447,400; Callao 440,400; Tru-
jillo 354,600; Chiclayo 280,200.

Vital statistics

Birth rate per 1,000 population (1983): 35.4 (world avg. 29.0); (1977) legiti-
mate 57.8%; illegitimate 42.2%.
Death rate per 1,000 population (1983): 10.6 (world avg. 11.0).
Natural increase rate per 1,000 population (1983): 24.8 (world avg. 18.0).
Total fertility rate (avg. births per childbearing woman; 1983): 5.3.
Marriage rate per 1,000 population (1977): 2.3†.
Divorce rate per 1,000 population: n.a.
Life expectancy at birth (1980–85): male 57.6 years; female 60.7 years.
Major causes of death per 100,000 population (1978)†: influenza and pneu-
monia 76.8; enteritis and other diarrheal diseases 55.5; malignant neo-
plasms (cancers) 34.0; heart diseases 31.7.

National economy

Budget (1984). Revenue: S/.9,215,000,000,000 (tax on fuel 25.2%; tax on
external trade 23.1%; tax on goods and services 19.7%; property tax 15.4%).
Expenditures: S/.17,013,000,000,000 (current expenditure 59.6%, of which
defense and interior 19.8%, interest payments 17.3%, wages and salaries
13.0%, transfers 7.7%).
Public debt (external, outstanding; 1984): U.S.$9,775,000,000.
Tourism (1984): receipts from visitors U.S.$292,000,000; expenditures by
nationals abroad U.S.$269,000,000.
Production (metric tons except as noted). Agriculture, forestry, fishing (1984): sugarcane 7,206,000, potatoes 1,515,000, rice 1,134,000, corn
(maize) 576,000, seed cotton 255,000, coffee 92,000, wheat 88,000; livestock (number of live animals) 14,500,000 sheep, 2,825,000 cattle, 2,400,-
000 alpacas‡, 1,775,000 pigs; roundwood 7,775,000 cu m‡; fish catch
2,962,000. Mining and quarrying (1984): iron ore 4,008,000; zinc 558,000;
copper 375,000; lead 205,000; silver 1,760. Manufacturing (value added in
S/.'000,000; 1980): food, beverages, and tobacco 370.7; nonferrous metals
183.7; chemicals and plastics 159.0; textiles 151.6; transport equipment
80.0. Construction (value in S/.'000,000; 1982): buildings 1,147,369§. En-

ergy production (consumption): electricity (kW-hr; 1983) 9,328,000,000
(9,328,000,000); coal (metric tons; 1983) 80,000 (110,000); crude petroleum
(barrels; 1984) 60,800,000 (55,203,000 ‖); petroleum products (metric
tons; 1983) 7,212,000 (6,432,000); natural gas (cu m; 1983) 1,012,217,000
(1,012,217,000).
Gross national product (at current market prices; 1983): U.S.$18,650,000,000
(U.S.$1,040 per capita).

Structure of gross domestic product and labour force				
	1984		1982	
	in value S/.'000,000	% of total value	labour force	% of labour force
Agriculture	43,321	14.0	2,296,100	35.9
Mining	29,910	9.7	68,100	1.1
Manufacturing	66,611	21.5	745,800	11.7
Construction	15,368	5.0	246,300	3.8
Public utilities			12,900	0.2
Transportation and communication	127,060	41.1	282,000	4.4
Trade			976,000	15.3
Finance			104,900	1.6
Services¶	27,066	8.7	1,245,500	19.5
Other	...	...	417,100	6.5
TOTAL	309,336⁹	100.0	6,394,700	100.0

Population economically active (1982): total 6,394,700; participation rate of
population 35.1% (female 29.3%, unemployed 6.5%).

Price and earnings indexes (1980 = 100)							
	1979	1980	1981	1982	1983	1984	1985
Consumer price index	62.8	100.0	175.4	288.4	609.0	1,280.2	2,653.1ö
Monthly earnings index							

Household income and expenditure. Average household size (1981) 4.8; income per household (1971–72) S/.51,170 (U.S.$1,322); source of income:
n.a.; expenditure (1983)□: food, drink, and tobacco 38.1%, rent and utilities
15.6%, transportation 9.8%, recreation and education 7.4%.
Land use (1983): forested 54.8%; meadows and pastures 21.2%; agricultural
and under permanent cultivation 2.7%; other 21.3%.

Foreign trade

Balance of trade (current prices)						
	1979	1980	1981	1982	1983	1984
S/.'000,000,000	+429	+473	+59	+343	+1,651	+4,833
% of total	36.9%	26.7%	2.2%	8.0%	19.9%	28.3%

Imports (1984): S/.6,118,800,000,000 (capital goods 36.0%, of which public
sector 18.7%, private sector 17.3%; food items 13.5%, of which wheat 6.6%).
Major import sources: United States 33.1%; Japan 8.8%; Argentina 8.1%;
West Germany 7.4%; Brazil 5.8%.
Exports (1984): S/.10,951,500,000,000 (petroleum [all forms] 19.6%; copper
14.0%; zinc 10.8%; lead 7.4%; silver 7.2%). *Major destinations:* United
States 34.5%; Japan 9.8%; Belgium–Luxembourg 5.9%; United Kingdom
5.0%; West Germany 3.8%; Taiwan 3.3%; Italy 3.1%.

Transport and communications

Transport. Railroads (1983): route length 1,832 mi, 2,948 km; passenger-
km 563,024,000; metric ton-km cargo 839,718,000. Roads (1984): total
length 40,400 mi, 65,000 km (paved 11%). Vehicles (1982): passenger cars
359,700; trucks and buses 196,013. Merchant marine (1984): vessels (100
gross tons and over) 670; total deadweight tonnage 1,045,912. Air transport (1983): passenger-km 1,704,000,000; metric ton-km cargo 42,828,000;
airports (1985) 21.
Communications. Daily newspapers (1983): total number 59; total circulation 2,237,600◇; circulation per 1,000 population 120◇. Radio (1984): total
receivers 2,225,000 (1 per 8.6 persons). Television (1984): total receivers
875,000 (1 per 22 persons). Telephones (1983): 519,703 (1 per 36 persons).

Education and health

Education (1981–82)				
	schools	teachers	students	student/ teacher ratio
Primary (age 6–11)	25,748	116,550	3,692,273	31.7
Secondary (age 12–16)	3,289	66,874	1,429,219	21.4
Voc., teacher tr.	768	8,744	142,154	16.3
Higher	35	23,435	277,304	11.8

Educational attainment (1972). Percent of adult population over age 25
having: no formal schooling 35.0%; less than primary education 31.0%;
primary 16.1%; secondary 13.4%; higher 4.5%. *Literacy* (1981): total population literate 11,458,810 (78.7%); males literate 6,092,490 (84.3%); females
literate 5,366,320 (73.1%).
Health (1982): physicians 14,751 (1 per 1,236 persons); hospital beds 29,991
(1 per 608 persons); infant mortality rate per 1,000 live births (1983) 96.9.
Food (1980–82): daily per capita caloric intake 2,141 (vegetable products 87%,
animal products 13%); 93% of FAO recommended minimum requirement.

Military

Total active duty personnel (1984): 135,500 (army 55.4%, navy 15.1%, air
force 29.5%). *Military expenditure as percent of GNP* (1983): 5.6% (world
6.1%); per capita expenditure U.S.$57.

*Detail does not add to total given because of rounding. †Excludes Indian jungle
population; based on incomplete information. ‡1983. §Includes new construction and
capital repairs. ‖ 1983. ¶Services include public administration and defense. ⁹At current prices. öApril. □Estimate for Lima metropolitan area only. ◇Partial circulation.

Philippines

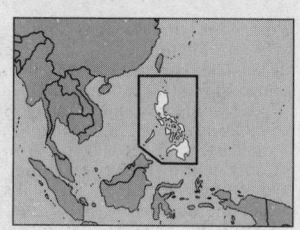

Official name: Republika ñg Pilipinas (Pilipino); Republic of the Philippines (English).
Form of government: federal parliamentary state with one legislative house (National Assembly [183]).
Chief of state: President.
Head of government: Prime Minister.
Capital: Manila.
Official languages: Pilipino; English.
Official religion: none.
Monetary unit: 1 Philippine peso (₱) = 100 centavos; valuation (Oct. 21, 1985) 1 U.S.$ = ₱18.13; 1 £ = ₱26.00.

Area and population

Regions	area sq mi	area sq km	population 1984 estimate
Bicol	6,808	17,633	3,766,000
Cagayan Valley	14,055	36,403	2,451,000
Central Luzon	7,039	18,231	5,308,000
Central Mindanao	8,994	23,293	2,451,000
Central Visayas	5,773	14,951	4,124,000
Eastern Visayas	8,275	21,432	3,031,000
Ilocos	8,328	21,568	3,783,000
National Capital Region	246	636	6,720,000
Northern Mindanao	10,937	28,328	3,117,000
Southern Mindanao	12,237	31,693	3,815,000
Southern Tagalog	18,117	46,924	6,901,000
Western Mindanao	7,214	18,685	2,770,000
Western Visayas	7,808	20,223	4,933,000
TOTAL	115,800*	300,000	53,170,000

Demography

Population (1985): 54,669,000.
Density (1985): persons per sq mi 472.0, persons per sq km 182.2.
Urban–rural (1980): urban 36.2%; rural 63.8%.
Sex distribution (1985): male 50.49%; female 49.51%.
Age breakdown (1980): under 15, 41.9%; 15–29, 29.4%; 30–44, 15.4%; 45–59, 8.8%; 60–74, 3.8%; 75 and over, 0.7%.
Population projection: (1990) 60,185,000; (2000) 78,770,000.
Doubling time: 28 years.
Ethnic composition (by mother tongue; 1975): Cebuano 24.4%; Tagalog 23.8%; Ilocano 11.1%; Hiligaynon Ilongo 10.0%; Bicol 7.0%; Samar-Leyte 4.6%; Pampango 3.4%; Pangasinan 2.3%; other 13.4%.
Religious affiliation (1980): Roman Catholic 84.1%; Aglipayan (Philippine Independent Church) 6.2%; Muslim 4.3%; Protestant 3.5%; other 1.9%.
Major cities (1980): Manila 1,630,485; Quezon City 1,165,865; Davao 610,375; Cebu 490,281; Caloocan 467,816.

Vital statistics

Birth rate per 1,000 population (1983): 32.0 (world avg. 29.0); (1980) legitimate 96.3%; illegitimate 3.7%.
Death rate per 1,000 population (1983): 6.8 (world avg. 11.0).
Natural increase rate per 1,000 population (1983): 25.2 (world avg. 18.0).
Total fertility rate (avg. births per childbearing woman; 1983): 4.2.
Marriage rate per 1,000 population (1979): 7.7.
Divorce rate per 1,000 population: n.a.
Life expectancy at birth (1983): male 63.0 years; female 66.5 years.
Major causes of death per 100,000 population (partial data; 1981): pneumonia 85.6; tuberculosis 41.7; heart diseases 33.5; enteritis and other diarrheal disease 23.6; malignant neoplasms (cancers) 16.9; accidents 16.7.

National economy

Budget (1984). Revenue: ₱47,500,000,000 (tax revenue 84.3%, of which income tax 20.0%, tax on domestic goods and services 31.4%, tax on foreign trade 30.5%; nontax revenue 15.7%). Expenditures: ₱58,830,000,000 (interest on debt 13.1%; education and culture 8.4%; general public service 6.2%; transport and communications 5.8%; defense 5.3%; agriculture 2.7%).
Public debt (external, outstanding; 1983): U.S.$10,385,000,000.
Tourism (1983): receipts from visitors U.S.$465,000,000; expenditures by nationals abroad U.S.$148,000,000†.
Production (metric tons except as noted). Agriculture, forestry, fishing (1984): rice 8,280,000, bananas 4,100,000, corn (maize) 3,743,000, sugarcane 2,380,000, cotton (lint) 73,000, peanuts (groundnuts) 45,000, copra 34,000; livestock (number of live animals) 2,900,000 buffalo, 1,920,000 cattle, 1,850,000 goats, 30,000 sheep; roundwood 35,787,000 cu m‡; fish catch 1,836,877‡. Mining and quarrying (1983): limestone 10,911,000; copper 309,000; chromite 284,400; silver 62,000; gold 25,000 kilograms. Manufacturing (gross value added in constant prices of 1972 in ₱'000,000; 1983): food items 9,246; chemicals and chemical products 2,315; electrical machinery 1,717; coal and petroleum products 1,351; footwear and wearing apparel 1,247; tobacco manufactures 1,117. Construction§ (authorized; 1983): residential 3,576,000 sq m; nonresidential 3,276,000 sq m. Energy production (consumption): electricity (kW-hr; 1983) 20,761,000,000 (20,761,000,000); coal (metric tons; 1983) 1,020,000 (1,514,000); petroleum (barrels; 1983) 5,350,900 (63,684,000); petroleum products (metric tons; 1983) 7,798,000 (9,689,000); natural gas, n.a. (n.a.).
Gross national product (at 1980 prices; 1984): U.S.$16,026,109,000 (U.S.$300 per capita).

Structure of gross domestic product and labour force

	1983 in value ₱'000,000	% of total value	labour force	% of labour force
Agriculture	84,546	22.0	10,250,000	49.9
Mining	7,021	1.8	188,000	1.0
Manufacturing	95,369	24.8	1,795,000	8.7
Construction	30,730	8.0	626,000	3.1
Public utilities	5,068	1.3	88,000	0.4
Transportation and communication	24,378	6.3	901,000	4.4
Trade } Finance }	71,085	18.5	2,257,000 313,000	11.0 1.5
Services } Other }	66,699	17.3	3,246,000 857,000	15.8 4.2
TOTAL	384,896 ‖	100.0	20,521,000	100.0

Population economically active (1983): total 20,521,000; participation rate of total population 39.4% (female 39.4%, unemployed 5.7%).

Price and earnings indexes (1980 = 100)

	1979	1980	1981	1982	1983	1984	1985
Consumer price index	84.6	100.0	113.1	124.6	137.1	206.2	257.0¶
Daily earnings index	96.2	100.0	...	...	...	...	...

Household income and expenditure. Average household size (1980) 5.6; income per family (1975) ₱5,840 (U.S.$777.5); sources of income (1971): wages and salaries 44.8%, self-employment 40.3%, owner-occupied dwellings 7.1%, pensions, social security, and related benefits 2.1%, other 5.7%; expenditure (1982): food, beverages, and tobacco 54.6%, housing 12.0%, household furnishings and operations 7.0%, clothing 6.2%, transport and communication 3.4%, education 2.7%.
Land use (1983): forested 40.4%; meadows and pastures 3.8%; agricultural and under permanent cultivation 37.7%; other 18.1%.

Foreign trade

Balance of trade (current prices)

	1979	1980	1981	1982	1983	1984
₱'000,000	−11,615	−14,898	−18,153	−22,674	−28,566	−10,907
% of total	14.7%	14.7%	16.9%	20.9%	20.7%	5.8%

Imports (1983): ₱82,270,600,000 (mineral fuels and lubricants 28.5%; nonelectrical machinery 12.0%; base metals 6.0%; electrical machinery 5.4%; transport equipment 4.6%; chemicals 3.6%). *Major import sources:* United States 23.2%; Japan 16.9%; Kuwait 11.8%; Saudi Arabia 10.9%; West Germany 4.7%; Singapore 3.9%.
Exports (1983): ₱55,003,100,000 (electrical and electronic equipment and components 21.1%; coconut products 13.6%, of which coconut oil 10.3%; garments 10.8%; mineral products 8.8%, of which copper concentrates 5.0%; forest products 6.6%; fruits and vegetables 6.5%; sugar and sugar products 6.4%). *Major export destinations:* United States 35.9%; Japan 20.4%; United Kingdom 4.7%; The Netherlands 4.5%; West Germany 4.0%; Hong Kong 3.4%; Malaysia 3.3%.

Transport and communications

Transport. Railroads (1984): length† 711 mi, 1,144 km; passenger-mi 142,000,000, passenger-km 228,000,000; short ton-mi cargo 8,000,000, metric ton-km cargo 12,000,000. Roads (1984): total length 97,641 mi, 157,139 km (paved 14%). Vehicles (1984): passenger cars 894,927; trucks and buses 128,083. Merchant marine (1984): vessels (100 gross tons and over) 946; total deadweight tonnage 5,525,609. Air transport⁹ (1984): passenger-mi 5,199,482,000, passenger-km 8,367,771,000; short ton-mi cargo 167,446,000, metric ton-km cargo 244,467,000; airports (1985) with scheduled flights 41.
Communications. Daily newspapers (1984): total number 22; total circulation 2,021,486ō; circulation per 1,000 population 38ō. Radio (1984): 2,190,000 receivers (1 per 24 persons). Television (1984): 1,000,000 receivers (1 per 53 persons). Telephones (1983): 658,415 (1 per 79 persons).

Education and health

Education (1982–83)

	schools	teachers	students	student/ teacher ratio
Primary (age 7–12)	32,114	264,653□	8,591,267	...
Secondary (age 13–16)	5,323	85,465□	2,956,576	...
Voc., teacher tr. } Higher }	1,189	261,860	150,585 1,261,096	... ...

Educational attainment (1970). Percent of adult population over age 25 having: less than elementary education 20.3%; elementary 56.1%; secondary 14.1%; college 9.5%. *Literacy* (1980): total population over age 15 literate 25,139,700 (88.7%); males literate 12,772,200 (89.9%); females literate 12,367,500 (87.5%).
Health (1983): physicians (1982) 46,579 (1 per 1,090 persons); hospital beds 76,653 (1 per 679 persons); infant mortality rate per 1,000 live births 49.
Food (1980–82): daily per capita caloric intake 2,405 (vegetable products 90%, animal products 10%); 106% of FAO recommended minimum requirement.

Military

Total active duty personnel (1984): 104,800 (army 57.3%, navy 26.7%, air force 16.0%). *Military expenditure as percent of GNP* (1983): 1.9% (world 6.1%); per capita expenditure U.S.$14.

---

*Detail does not add to total given because of rounding. †1982. ‡1983. §Private only. ‖ At current prices. ¶August. ⁹Philippines Airlines only. ōPartial circulation. □1981–82.

Poland

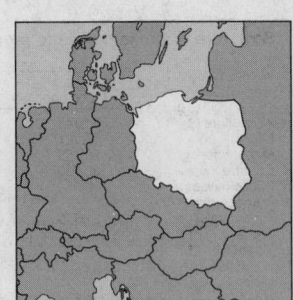

Official name: Polska Rzeczpospolita
Ludowa (Polish People's Republic).
Form of government: unitary
single-party socialist republic with one
legislative house (Sejm [460]).
Chief of state: President (Chairman).
Head of government: Prime Minister.
Capital: Warsaw.
Official language: Polish.
Official religion: none.
Monetary unit: 1 złoty = 100 groszy;
valuation (Oct. 21, 1985)
1 U.S.$ = 148.38 złotys;
1 £ = 212.78 złotys.

Area and population

Provinces	Capitals	area sq mi	area sq km	population 1984 estimate
Biała Podlaska	Biała Podlaska	2,065	5,348	293,700
Białystok	Białystok	3,882	10,055	660,000
Bielsko	Bielsko Biala	1,430	3,704	857,500
Bydgoszcz	Bydgoszcz	3,996	10,349	1,064,500
Chełm	Chełm	1,493	3,866	237,300
Ciechanów	Ciechanów	2,456	6,362	413,300
Częstochowa	Częstochowa	2,387	6,182	759,300
Elbląg	Elbląg	2,356	6,103	457,800
Gdańsk	Gdańsk	2,855	7,394	1,372,800
Gorzów	Gorzów Wielkopolski	3,276	8,484	473,800
Jelenia Góra	Jelenia Góra	1,690	4,378	503,600
Kalisz	Kalisz	2,514	6,512	686,000
Katowice	Katowice	2,568	6,650	3,854,300
Kielce	Kielce	3,556	9,211	1,093,600
Konin	Konin	1,984	5,139	452,100
Koszalin	Koszalin	3,270	8,470	477,800
Kraków	Kraków	1,256	3,254	1,197,200
Krosno	Krosno	2,202	5,702	465,000
Legnica	Legnica	1,559	4,037	478,300
Leszno	Leszno	1,604	4,154	368,800
Łódź	Łódź	588	1,523	1,146,500
Łomża	Łomża	2,581	6,684	334,000
Lublin	Lublin	2,622	6,792	967,500
Nowy Sącz	Nowy Sącz	2,153	5,576	651,800
Olsztyn	Olsztyn	4,759	12,327	707,200
Opole	Opole	3,295	8,535	996,300
Ostrołęka	Ostrołęka	2,509	6,498	378,700
Piła	Piła	3,168	8,205	454,900
Piotrków	Piotrków Trybunalski	2,419	6,266	623,500
Płock	Płock	1,976	5,117	504,000
Poznań	Poznań	3,147	8,151	1,277,700
Przemyśl	Przemyśl	1,713	4,437	389,400
Radom	Radom	2,816	7,294	719,000
Rzeszów	Rzeszów	1,698	4,397	675,000
Siedlce	Siedlce	3,281	8,499	628,700
Sieradz	Sieradz	1,880	4,869	397,400
Skierniewice	Skierniewice	1,529	3,960	404,800
Słupsk	Słupsk	2,878	7,453	385,700
Suwałki	Suwałki	4,050	10,490	437,600
Szczecin	Szczecin	3,854	9,981	924,100
Tarnobrzeg	Tarnobrzeg	2,426	6,283	572,400
Tarnów	Tarnów	1,603	4,151	627,600
Toruń	Toruń	2,065	5,348	627,100
Wałbrzych	Wałbrzych	1,609	4,168	728,300
Warszawa	Warszawa	1,463	3,788	2,381,900
Włocławek	Włocławek	1,700	4,402	421,800
Wrocław	Wrocław	2,427	6,287	1,100,400
Zamość	Zamość	2,695	6,980	483,200
Zielona Góra	Zielona Góra	3,424	8,868	631,800
TOTAL		120,727	312,683	36,745,000

Demography

Population (1985): 37,160,000.
Density (1985): persons per sq mi 307.8, persons per sq km 118.8.
Urban–rural (1984): urban 59.6%; rural 40.4%.
Sex distribution (1984): male 48.75%; female 51.25%.
Age breakdown (1984): under 15, 25.2%; 15–29, 24.0%; 30–44, 20.4%; 45–59, 16.8%; 60–74, 9.8%; 75 and over, 3.8%.
Population projection: (1990) 38,967,000; (2000) 41,217,000.
Doubling time: 78 years.
Ethnic composition (1981): Polish 98.7%; Ukrainian 0.6%; other 0.7%.
Religious affiliation (1980): Roman Catholic 81%; other 19%.
Major cities (1984): Warsaw 1,641,400; Łódź 848,600; Kraków 735,200.

Vital statistics

Birth rate per 1,000 population (1984): 19.7 (world avg. 29.0).
Death rate per 1,000 population (1984): 9.5 (world avg. 11.0).
Natural increase rate per 1,000 population (1984): 10.2 (world avg. 18.0).
Total fertility rate (avg. births per childbearing woman; 1982): 2.3.
Marriage rate per 1,000 population (1984): 8.4.
Divorce rate per 1,000 population (1984): 1.3.
Life expectancy at birth (1982): male 67.2 years; female 75.2 years.
Major causes of death per 100,000 population (1983): diseases of the circulatory system 386.9; malignant neoplasms (cancers) 175.1.

National economy

Budget (1983). Revenue: 2,575,700,000,000 złotys (tax on state enterprises 78.8%). Expenditures: 2,650,700,000,000 złotys (social insurance 12.4%, health and welfare 11.6%, education 11.2%, defense 8.3%).
Public debt (external, outstanding; 1983): U.S.$26,400,000,000.
Tourism (1983): receipts U.S.$85,000,000; expenditures U.S.$195,000,000.

Production (metric tons except as noted). Agriculture, forestry, fishing (1984): potatoes 37,400,000, sugar beets 16,000,000, rye 9,500,000, wheat 6,000,000, barley 3,600,000; livestock (number of live animals) 17,187,000 pigs, 10,903,000 cattle; (1983) roundwood 23,022,000 cu m; fish catch 671,700. Mining and quarrying (1983): copper ore 387,000; zinc 149,000; lead 59,200; silver 21,798 troy oz. Manufacturing (1984): crude steel 16,500,000; rolled steel 13,121,000; pig iron 9,369,000; cotton fabrics 808,900,000 m. Construction (1983): residential 13,188,000 sq m. Energy production (consumption): electricity ('000,000 kW-hr; 1984) 134,800 (127,166 [1983]); coal ('000 metric tons; 1984) 242,000 (199,700); crude petroleum (barrels; 1983) 1,539,300 (1,643,000); natural gas ('000,000 cu m; 1984) 6,072 (12,090).
Gross national product (1983): U.S.$140,400,000,000 (U.S.$3,860 per capita).

Structure of net material product and labour force

	1983 in value '000,000 złotys	% of total value	labour force	% of labour force
Agriculture	1,088.5	18.4	5,305,300	31.1
Mining and manufacturing	2,967.9	50.1	4,970,200	29.2
Public utilities			203,900	1.2
Construction	644.3	10.9	1,218,900	7.2
Transp., commun.	318.3	5.4	1,058,000	6.2
Trade	802.2	13.5	1,325,400	7.8
Finance	—	—	155,000	0.9
Public admin., defense	—	—	228,700	1.3
Services	—	—	2,261,200	13.3
Other	102.8	1.7	307,200	1.8
TOTAL	5,924.0	100.0	17,033,800	100.0

Population economically active (1984): total 17,731,000; participation rate of population over age 15, 64.5% (female 45.9%, unemployed, na.).

Price and earnings indexes (1980 = 100)

	1978	1979	1980	1981	1982	1983	1984
Consumer price index	85.4	91.4	100.0	121.2	243.4	294.5	341.8
Monthly earnings index	81.8	86.2	100.0	139.3	215.9	237.8	...

Household income and expenditure. Average household size (1983) 3.4; average annual income 1,453,000 złotys (U.S.$11,900); sources of income: wages 82.9%, social welfare 17.1%; expenditure (1983): food 46.8%, clothing 12.5%, housing 12.3%.
Land use (1983): forested 27.9%; meadows 13.0%; agricultural and under permanent cultivation 47.3%; other 11.8%.

Foreign trade

Balance of trade (current prices)

	1978	1979	1980	1981	1982	1983	1984
'000,000,000 złotys	−6.2	−4.1	−6.4	−7.5	+82.2	+95.3	+123.1
% of total	6.5%	3.9%	5.8%	7.7%	4.5%	4.7%	4.8%

Imports (1983): 961,185,000,000 złotys (machinery and transport equipment 27.8%, fuel and power 26.2%, chemicals 13.6%, iron and steel products 9.7%, food 5.5%). *Major import sources:* U.S.S.R. 37.1%; West Germany 6.9%; East Germany 6.8%; Czechoslovakia 6.4%.
Exports (1983): 1,057,091,000,000 złotys (machinery and transport equipment 42.7%; hard coal 12.0%, chemicals and related products 9.5%, textiles and leather articles 8.6%). *Major export destinations:* U.S.S.R. 31.2%; West Germany 8.3%; Czechoslovakia 5.2%; East Germany 4.8%; United Kingdom 3.1%.

Transport and communications

Transport. Railroads (1983): length 27,176 km; passenger-km 56,016,000,000; metric ton-km cargo 118,034,000,000. Roads (1984): total length 254,000 km (paved 62%). Vehicles (1983): passenger cars 3,181,300; trucks and buses 733,314. Merchant marine (1984): vessels (100 gross tons and over) 783; total deadweight tonnage 4,304,116. Air transport (1983): passenger-km 1,754,779,000; metric ton-km cargo 160,807,000; airports (1985) 12.
Communications (1983). Daily newspapers: total number (1984): 44; total circulation 7,902,000; circulation per 1,000 population 217. Radio: 9,050,000 receivers (1 per 4.0 persons). Television: 8,543,000 receivers (1 per 4.3 persons). Telephones: 3,846,000 (1 per 9.5 persons).

Education and health

Education (1983–84)

	schools	teachers	students	student/ teacher ratio
Primary (age 7–15)	15,020	260,000	4,530,000	17.4
Secondary (age 15–19)	879	22,000	326,000	14.8
Voc., teacher tr.	7,479	88,000	1,313,000	14.9
Higher	91	55,769	274,200	4.9

Educational attainment (1983). Percent of population over age 15 having: less than full primary education 8.0%; primary and secondary 85.9%, of which secondary 22.2%; higher 5.3%. *Literacy* (1983): total population over age 15 literate 27,352,000 (99.2%).
Health (1984): physicians 69,295 (1 per 530.0 persons); hospital beds 258,000 (1 per 142.4 persons); infant mortality rate per 1,000 live births (1983) 19.3.
Food (1980–82): daily per capita caloric intake 3,356 (vegetable products 68%, animal products 32%); 133% of FAO recommended minimum.

Military

Total active duty personnel (1984): 323,250 (army 65.0%, navy 6.8%, air force 28.2%). *Military expenditure as percent of GNP* (1983): 5.8% (world 6.1%); per capita expenditure U.S.$321.

Portugal

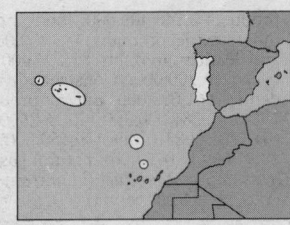

Official name: República Portuguesa (Republic of Portugal).
Form of government: parliamentary state with one legislative house (Assembly of the Republic [250]).
Chief of state: President.
Head of government: Prime Minister.
Capital: Lisbon.
Official language: Portuguese.
Official religion: none.
Monetary unit: 1 Escudo (Esc) = 100 centavos; valuation (Oct. 21, 1985) 1 U.S.$ = Esc162.48; 1 £ = Esc233.00.

Area and population		area		population
Continental Portugal				1984
Districts	Capitals	sq mi	sq km	estimate*
Aveiro	Aveiro	1,084	2,808	648,796
Beja	Beja	3,948	10,225	183,994
Braga	Braga	1,032	2,673	747,701
Bragança	Bragança	2,551	6,608	186,905
Castelo Branco	Castelo Branco	2,577	6,675	230,306
Coimbra	Coimbra	1,524	3,947	444,699
Évora	Évora	2,854	7,393	178,248
Faro	Faro	1,915	4,960	334,598
Guarda	Guarda	2,131	5,518	202,393
Leiria	Leiria	1,357	3,515	432,509
Lisboa	Lisbon (Lisboa)	1,066	2,761	2,113,400
Portalegre	Portalegre	2,342	6,065	140,493
Porto	Porto	925	2,395	1,629,399
Santarém	Santarém	2,605	6,747	459,999
Setúbal	Setúbal	1,955	5,064	723,000
Viana do Castelo	Viana do Castelo	871	2,255	263,506
Vila Real	Vila Real	1,671	4,328	266,010
Viseu	Viseu	1,933	5,007	427,397
Azores (Açores)				
Autonomous Region	Ponta Delgada	868	2,247	250,699
Madeira Autonomous				
Region	Funchal	306	794	264,787
TOTAL		35,672†	92,389†	10,128,839

Demography

Population (1985): 10,151,300.
Density (1985): persons per sq mi 284.6, persons per sq km 109.9.
Urban–rural (1981): urban 29.6%; rural 70.4%.
Sex distribution (1982): male 48.19%; female 51.81%.
Age breakdown (1981): under 15, 25.5%; 15–29, 23.5%; 30–44, 18.0%; 45–59, 17.2%; 60–74, 11.9%; 75 and over, 3.9%.
Population projection: (1990) 10,382,000; (2000) 10,732,000.
Doubling time: more than 100 years.
Nationality (1981): Portuguese 98.9%; Angolan 0.2%; Cape Verdean 0.2%; French 0.1%; Brazilian 0.1%; Spanish 0.1%; other 0.4%.
Religious affiliation (1981): Christian 96.0%, of which Roman Catholic 94.5%, Protestant 0.6%, other Christian (mostly Apostolic Catholic and Jehovah's Witness) 0.9%; nonreligious 3.8%; Jewish 0.1%; Muslim 0.1%.
Major cities (1981): Lisbon 807,167; Porto 327,368; Amadora 95,518.

Vital statistics

Birth rate per 1,000 population (1983): 14.4 (world avg. 29.0); (1975) legitimate 92.8%; illegitimate 7.2%.
Death rate per 1,000 population (1983): 9.6 (world avg. 11.0).
Natural increase rate per 1,000 population (1983): 4.8 (world avg. 18.0).
Total fertility rate (avg. births per childbearing woman; 1980–85): 2.3.
Marriage rate per 1,000 population (1983): 6.7.
Divorce rate per 1,000 population (1983): 0.8.
Life expectancy at birth (1980–85): male 67.6 years; female 74.1 years.
Major causes of death per 100,000 population (1983): cerebrovascular diseases 241.3; malignant neoplasms (cancers) 147.9; heart diseases 82.5; accidents 55.7; chronic liver disease 31.8; pneumonia 23.5.

National economy

Budget (1983). Revenue: Esc772,520,000,000 (current receipts 61.9%, of which indirect taxes 35.5%, direct taxes 21.1%; capital receipts 30.2%). Expenditures: Esc772,520,000,000 (public debt 27.1%; education 11.1%; social affairs 8.8%; defense 7.8%; public works 6.3%).
Public debt (external, outstanding; 1983): U.S.$9,950,600,000.
Tourism (1983): receipts from visitors U.S.$811,000,000; expenditures by nationals abroad U.S.$228,000,000.
Production (metric tons except as noted). Agriculture, forestry, fishing (1984): potatoes 1,080,000, grapes 1,020,000, tomatoes 881,000, corn (maize) 530,000, wheat 344,000, olives 300,000, oats 195,000, cork 99,200‡; livestock (number of live animals) 5,000,000 sheep, 3,450,000 pigs, 1,020,000 cattle; roundwood (1983) 8,278,000 cu m; fish catch (1983) 246,470. Mining and quarrying (1984): copper pyrites 334,300; anthracite 194,900; kaolin 72,700; tungsten 2,531. Manufacturing (value of production in Esc'000,000; 1983): refined petroleum 181,289; cotton and synthetic fibres 102,893; animal feedstuffs 65,649; clothing 44,231; radios, televisions, and telecommunications equipment 40,395; iron and steel 38,858; netting 36,240; motor vehicles 29,600; cement 29,487; wine 730,000 metric tons. Construction (value in Esc'000,000; 1981): residential 49,916; nonresidential 13,185. Energy production (consumption): electricity (kW-hr; 1983) 18,161,000,000 (19,477,000,000); coal (metric tons; 1983) 184,000 (524,000); crude petroleum

(barrels: 1983) none (58,985,000); petroleum products (metric tons: 1983) 7,200,000 (7,993,000); natural gas, none (n.a.).
Gross national product (at current market prices; 1983): U.S.$22,490,000,000 (U.S.$2,247 per capita).

Structure of gross domestic product and labour force				
	1981		1982	
	in value Esc'000,000	% of total value	labour force	% of labour force
Agriculture	124,443	8.5	1,018,000	23.3
Mining			27,000	0.6
Manufacturing }	440,256	30.0	1,071,000	24.6
Construction	111,011	7.6	426,000	9.8
Public utilities	23,377	1.6	21,000	0.5
Transportation and communication	85,829	5.9	165,000	3.8
Trade	322,945	22.0	511,000	11.7
Finance	113,314	7.7	107,000	2.4
Pub. admin., defense	169,617	11.6 }	864,000	19.8
Services	122,533	8.4 }		
Other	−47,882§	−3.3§	152,000	3.5
TOTAL	1,465,443	100.0	4,362,000	100.0

Population economically active (1983): total 4,362,000; participation rate of population over age 10, 54.9% (female 41.4%, unemployed 7.2%).

Price and earnings indexes (1980 = 100)							
	1978	1979	1980	1981	1982	1983	1984
Consumer price index	69.4	85.7	100.0	120.0	147.3	184.3	237.6
Daily earnings index	71.9	82.6	100.0	121.6	148.0	172.7	203.6

Household income and expenditure. Average household size (1981) 2.9; income per household: n.a.; sources of income (1981): wages and salaries 44.8%, self-employment 21.6%, transfer payments 21.1%, property and entrepreneurial income 12.5%; expenditure (1981): food 34.8%, transportation and communication 14.6%, housing 13.2%, clothing and footwear 11.2%, cafes and hotels 8.8%, health 4.3%, recreation 3.9%, other 9.2%.
Land use (1983): forested 39.7%; meadows and pastures 5.8%; agricultural and under permanent cultivation 38.7%; other 15.8%.

Foreign trade

Balance of trade (current prices)					
	1979	1980	1981	1982	1983	1984
Esc'000,000	−155,880	−243,870	−352,100	−422,240	−390,740	−377,210
% of total	30.7%	34.5%	40.7%	38.9%	27.8%	19.9%

Imports (1983): Esc899,340,000,000 (crude petroleum 20.7%, chemicals 10.0%, road vehicles 6.7%, cereals 5.9%, special industrial machinery 4.4%, petroleum products 4.3%). *Major import sources:* United States 14.1%; West Germany 11.4%; France 8.2%; United Kingdom 7.6%; Italy 5.2%.
Exports (1983): Esc508,600,000,000 (clothing 14.9%, chemicals 7.5%, finished textiles 5.4%, crude petroleum 5.0%, pulp and waste paper 4.3%, alcoholic beverages 3.9%, cork manufactures 3.8%, footwear 3.6%). *Major export destinations:* United Kingdom 14.8%; France 13.5%; West Germany 13.3%; The Netherlands 6.3%; United States 6.1%.

Transport and communications

Transport. Railroads (1983): route length 2,245 mi, 3,613 km; passenger-mi 3,228,150,000, passenger-km 5,195,214,000; short ton-mi cargo 714,842,000, metric ton-km cargo 1,043,651,000. Roads (1980): total length 32,188 mi, 51,802 km (paved 86%). Vehicles (1982): passenger cars 1,428,820; trucks and buses 96,250. Merchant marine (1984): vessels (100 gross tons and over) 359; total deadweight tonnage 2,684,923. Air transport (1984)‖ : passenger-mi 2,655,706,000, passenger-km 4,273,953,000; short ton-mi cargo 79,742,000, metric ton-km cargo 116,421,000; airports (1985) 20.
Communications. Daily newspapers (1984): total number 27; total circulation 679,700; circulation per 1,000 population 67. Radio (1984): 2,155,000 receivers (1 per 4.7 persons). Television (1984): 1,523,000 receivers (1 per 6.6 persons). Telephones (1983): 1,567,000 (1 per 6.4 persons).

Education and health

Education (1982–83)				
	schools	teachers	students	student/ teacher ratio
Primary (age 5–11)	13,069	76,141	1,305,724	17.1
Secondary (age 12–19)	629	38,809	582,495	15.0
Voc., teacher tr.	368	...	26,003	...
Higher	21	10,578	89,964	8.5

Educational attainment (1981). Percent of population over age 14 having: no formal schooling 21.8%; primary education 58.5%; secondary 15.9%; higher 3.8%. *Literacy* (1981): total population over age 14 literate 5,729,000 (78.2%); males literate 2,967,000 (84.0%); females literate 2,762,000 (72.7%).
Health (1983): physicians 22,078 (1 per 453 persons); hospital beds 51,274 (1 per 195 persons); infant mortality rate per 1,000 live births 19.3.
Food (1980–82): daily per capita caloric intake 3,106 (vegetable products 80%, animal products 20%); 127% of FAO recommended minimum requirement.

Military

Total active duty personnel (1984): 63,500 (army 61.4%, navy 23.6%, air force 15.0%). *Military expenditure as percent of GNP* (1983): 3.5% (world 6.1%); per capita expenditure U.S.$81.

*Year end, de jure. †Includes 156 sq mi (404 sq km) of inland water. ‡1983; continental Portugal only. §Less imputed bank charges. ‖ TAP (Air Portugal) only.

Puerto Rico

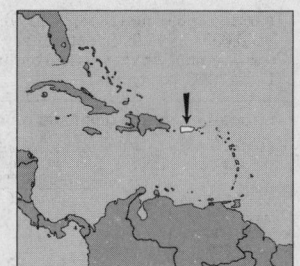

Official name: Estado Libre
Asociado de Puerto Rico (Spanish);
Commonwealth of Puerto Rico
(English).
Political status: self-governing
commonwealth associated with the
United States, having two legislative
houses (Senate [27]; House of
Representatives [51]).
Chief of state: President of the
United States.
Head of government: Governor.
Capital: San Juan.
Official languages: Spanish; English.
Official religion: none.
Monetary unit: 1 U.S. dollar
(U.S.$) = 100 cents; valuation (Oct.
21, 1985) 1 U.S.$ = 1.43 £.

Population 1984 estimate

Municipio*	population	Municipio*	population	Municipio*	population
Adjuntas	18,900	Fajardo	33,200	Naguabo	21,300
Aguada	32,400	Florida	7,600	Naranjito	25,100
Aguadilla	55,000	Guánica	18,800	Orocovis	20,900
Agunas Buenas	23,000	Guayama	40,300	Patillas	17,900
Aibonito	22,500	Guayanilla	21,000	Peñuelas	20,200
Añasco	24,400	Guaynabo	85,100	Ponce	190,900
Arecibo	87,000	Gurabo	25,000	Quebradillas	19,700
Arroyo	18,200	Hatillo	30,400	Rincón	12,400
Barceloneta	19,600	Hormigueros	15,200	Río Grande	37,700
Barranquitas	22,800	Humacao	52,400	Sabana Grande	21,100
Bayamón	202,500	Isabela	38,200	Salinas	26,600
Cabo Rojo	35,000	Jayuya	15,000	San Germán	34,200
Caguas	121,100	Juana Díaz	43,600	San Juan	428,900
Camuy	26,200	Juncos	27,000	San Lorenzo	33,300
Canóvanas	32,400	Lajas	21,300	San Sebastián	36,100
Carolina	165,700	Lares	28,000	Santa Isabel	19,500
Cataño	25,900	Las Marías	8,600	Toa Alta	33,400
Cayey	43,300	Las Piedras	23,100	Toa Baja	77,700
Ceiba	15,100	Loíza	24,600	Trujillo Alto	50,800
Ciales	17,200	Luquillo	15,400	Utuado	34,600
Cidra	29,600	Manatí	38,000	Vega Alta	30,000
Coamo	32,200	Maricao	6,700	Vega Baja	48,800
Comerio	18,400	Maunabo	11,800	Vieques	7,800
Corozal	29,600	Mayagüez	101,000	Villalba	22,500
Culebra	1,300	Moca	29,900	Yabucoa	31,400
Dorado	26,700	Morovis	21,900	Yauco	39,200
				TOTAL	3,270,000

Demography

Area: 3,515 sq mi, 9,104 sq km.
Population (1985): 3,311,100.
Density (1985): persons per sq mi 942.0, persons per sq km 363.7.
Urban–rural (1980): urban 66.8%; rural 33.2%.
Sex distribution (1980): male 48.7%; female 51.3%.
Age breakdown (1980): under 15, 31.6%; 15–29, 26.5%; 30–44, 18.4%; 45–59, 12.3%; 60–74, 8.3%; 75 and over, 2.9%.
Population projection: (1990) 3,424,100; (2000) 3,661,800.
Doubling time: not applicable.
Ethnic composition (1980): white 80.0%; black 20.0%.
Religious affiliation (1984): Roman Catholic 85.3%; Protestant 4.7%; other 10.0%.
Major cities (1984): San Juan 428,900; Bayamón 202,500; Ponce 190,900; Carolina 165,700; Caguas 121,100.

Vital statistics

Birth rate per 1,000 population (1983): 21.5 (world avg. 29.0); (1980) legitimate 79.0%; illegitimate 21.0%.
Death rate per 1,000 population (1983): 6.8 (world avg. 11.0).
Natural increase rate per 1,000 population (1983): 14.7 (world avg. 18.0).
Total fertility rate (avg. births per childbearing woman; 1980–85): 2.0.
Marriage rate per 1,000 population (1980): 10.4.
Divorce rate per 1,000 population (1980): 4.8.
Life expectancy at birth (1980–85): male 70.8 years; female 76.9 years.
Major causes of death per 100,000 population (1982): heart disease 168.9; malignant neoplasms (cancers) 83.4; cerebrovascular disease 32.8; pneumonia 24.4; diabetes mellitus 22.9; accidents and violence 22.1; conditions originating in the perinatal period 18.6; chronic liver disease and cirrhosis 18.3; atherosclerosis 14.4.

National economy

Budget (1983–84). Revenue: U.S.$3,771,000,000 (income tax 33.1%, indirect business tax 27.8%, federal government grants 18.2%, excise taxes 15.9%). Expenditures: U.S.$3,688,000,000 (health and welfare 32.2%, education 28.1%, public safety 9.2%, debt payment 7.4%, general government 6.9%).
Public debt (outstanding; 1984): U.S.$8,690,900,000.
Tourism (1984): receipts from visitors U.S.$681,227,000; (1982) expenditures by nationals abroad U.S.$473,000,000.
Production (gross value in U.S.$ except as marked). Agriculture, forestry, fishing (1984): milk 164,000,000, coffee 48,000,000, starchy vegetables 57,000,000, fruit 33,000,000, sugarcane 29,000,000, eggs 24,000,000; livestock (number of live animals; 1984) 591,972 cattle, 202,764 pigs, 6,351,259 chickens; fish catch 1,256 metric tons. Manufacturing (net income in U.S.$; 1984): chemicals and allied products 2,153,900,000; machinery and metal

products 2,146,400,000; food and food products 584,400,000; apparel and other textile products 452,200,000; building materials 84,900,000; leather and leather products 81,200,000; printing and publishing 72,800,000; tobacco 54,500,000. Construction (1984): residential 331,000,000; nonresidential 661,000,000. Energy production (consumption): electricity (kW-hr; 1984) 12,281,000,300 (10,154,600,000); coal, none (n.a.); crude petroleum (barrels; 1983) none (39,150,000); petroleum products (metric tons; 1983) 6,097,000 (7,015,000); natural gas, none (n.a.).
Gross national product (at current market prices; 1984): U.S.$14,031,000,000 (U.S.$4,294 per capita).

Structure of gross domestic product and labour force

	1984			
	in value US$'000,000	% of total value	labour force	% of labour force
Agriculture	396.7	2.1	38,000	4.0
Manufacturing	7,274.6	38.0	143,000	15.0
Mining	361.6 }	1.9	2,000	0.2
Construction			34,000	3.6
Public utilities	1,675.6 }	9.0	11,000	1.2
Transp. and commun.			30,000	3.2
Trade	2,645.5	14.2	145,000	15.2
Finance	2,409.2	12.9	22,000	2.3
Pub. admin., defense	2,153.1	11.5	177,000	18.6
Services	1,742.8	9.3	140,000	14.7
Other	11.9	0.1	210,000†	22.0†
TOTAL	18,671.0‡	100.0	952,000	100.0

Population economically active (1984): total 952,000; participation rate of population over age 16, 42.1% (female 35.1%, unemployed 22.0%).

Price and earnings indexes (1975 = 100)

	1977	1978	1979	1980	1981	1982	1983
Consumer price index	106.5	111.6	118.9	131.1	144.0	149.3	150.2
Monthly earnings index	118.6	131.7	144.8	157.2	172.4	...	...

Household income and expenditure. Average family size (1984) 4.1; income per family U.S.$16,794; source of income: n.a.; expenditure: food, beverages, and tobacco 22.8%, housing and household operations 27.6%, transportation 12.9%, clothing 12.1%, recreation 9.4%, health 5.5%.
Land use (1981): forested 20.3%; meadows and pastures 38.1%; agricultural and under permanent cultivation 15.7%; other 25.9%.

Foreign trade

Balance of trade (current prices)

	1977	1978	1979	1980	1981	1982	1983
U.S.$'000,000	−1,628	−1,788	−1,381	−1,684	−1,146	+721	+14
% of total	15.4%	15.8%	10.3%	10.8%	6.6%	4.2%	0.1%

Imports (1983): U.S.$8,506,753,000 (petroleum and petroleum products 24.6%; animal and vegetable products 20.9%; metals and metal products 19.1%; chemicals and chemical products 11.1%; textile yarn, fabrics, and related products 6.2%; wood and paper 5.5%). *Major import sources:* United States 61.2%; Japan 5.0%; Netherlands Antilles 4.9%; Venezuela 4.7%.
Exports (1983): U.S.$8,521,242,000 (chemicals and chemical products 34.0%; metal and metal products 16.3%; fish and fish preparations 11.4%; textile products 7.9%; tobacco and tobacco products 4.0%). *Major export destinations:* United States 83.5%; Virgin Islands (U.S.) 2.4%; Dominican Republic 2.1%; Trinidad and Tobago 1.3%.

Transport and communications

Transport. Railroads (1982): length 57 mi, 92 km. Roads (1982): total length 5,802 mi, 9,337 km (paved 86%). Vehicles (1984): passenger cars 973,762; trucks and buses 170,253. Merchant marine: n.a. Air transport (1984): passenger arrivals 2,533,352, passenger departures 2,571,012; cargo loaded and unloaded 165,258 metric tons; airports (1985) with scheduled flights 11.
Communications. Daily newspapers (1984): total number 5; total circulation 580,000; circulation per 1,000 population 176. Radio (1984): 2,000,000 receivers (1 per 1.6 persons). Television (1984): 810,000 receivers (1 per 4.0 persons). Telephones (1984): 808,736 (1 per 4.0 persons).

Education and health

Education (1980–81)

	schools	teachers	students	student/ teacher ratio
Primary (age 5–12)	1,618	23,154	470,089	20.3
Secondary (age 13–18)	619	13,297	337,153	25.4
Voc., teacher tr.	68	2,600	60,045	23.1
Higher	34	3,300	159,972§	...

Educational attainment (1980). Percent of adult population over age 25 having: less than full primary education 26.2%; primary 22.2%; less than full secondary 12.7%; secondary 21.2%; some postsecondary 8.5%; 4-year higher degree 6.0%; postgraduate 3.2%. *Literacy (1980):* total population over age 15 literate 1,924,100 (90.8%); males literate 934,400 (91.8%); females literate 989,700 (89.8%).
Health (1983): physicians 7,146 (1 per 457 persons); hospital beds 12,493 (1 per 262 persons); infant mortality rate per 1,000 live births 16.0.

Military

Total active duty personnel: No domestic military force is maintained; the United States is responsible for defense.

*Names of administrative seats are the same as the corresponding municipio except Isabela, whose seat is Vieques. †Unemployed. ‡At current prices. §1984.

Qatar

Official name: Dawlat Qaṭar (State
of Qatar).
Form of government: constitutional
monarchy; Islāmic law is the basis of
legislation in the state.
Head of state and government: Emir.
Capital: Doha.
Official language: Arabic.
Official religion: Islām.
Monetary unit: 1 riyal (QR) = 100
dirhams; valuation (Oct. 21, 1985)
1 U.S.$ = QR3.65; 1 £ = QR5.23.

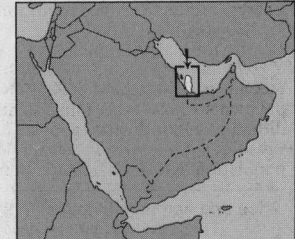

Area and population

Municipalities*	area		population
	sq mi	sq km	1970 estimate
Doha	...	...	68,400
al-Khawr	...	...	1,900
ar-Rayyān	...	...	5,800
ash-Shamāl†	...	...	2,300
Umm aṣ-Ṣilāl	...	...	2,000
al-Wakrah	...	...	1,800
nonmunicipal area			
Dukhān	...	...	700
other‡	...	...	28,200
TOTAL	4,400	11,400	111,100

Demography

Population (1985): 301,000.
Density (1985): persons per sq mi 68.4, persons per sq km 26.4.
Urban–rural (1985)§: urban 88.0%; rural 12.0%.
Sex distribution (1985): male 66.11%; female 33.89%.
Age breakdown (1981): under 15, 32.3%; 15–29, 31.8%; 30–44, 25.8%; 45–59, 7.8%; 60 and over, 2.3%.
Population projection: (1990) 354,000; (2000) 469,000.
Doubling time: 19 years.
Ethnic composition (1983): South Asian 34%; Qatari 20%; other Arab 25%; Iranian 16%; other 5%.
Religious affiliation (1980): Muslim 92.4% ‖; Christian 5.9%; Hindu 1.1%; Bahā'ī 0.2%; other 0.4%.
Major cities (1983): Doha 190,000; Musay'īd 40,000.

Vital statistics

Birth rate per 1,000 population (1983): 29.4 (world avg. 29.0); legitimate, n.a.; illegitimate, n.a.
Death rate per 1,000 population (1983): 2.9 (world avg. 11.0).
Natural increase rate per 1,000 population (1983): 26.5 (world avg. 18.0).
Total fertility rate (avg. births per childbearing woman; 1980–85): 6.8.
Marriage rate per 1,000 population (1983): 3.7.
Divorce rate per 1,000 population (1981): 5.3.
Life expectancy at birth (1980–85): male 68.2 years; female 73.2 years.
Major causes of death (1982): diseases of the circulatory system, motor vehicle accidents, and malignant neoplasms (cancers).

National economy

Budget (1985–86). Revenue: QR9,737,000,000 (crude oil 85.0%). Expenditures: QR17,048,000,000 (state capital development projects 22.3%, of which industry and agriculture 4.9%, housing and public buildings 4.1%, electricity and water 1.0%, education 0.1%; foreign commitments 8.5%; other capital development projects 7.9%).
Public debt: none.
Population economically active¶ (1981): total 111,264; participation rate of total population over age 14, 63.5% (female 8.0%, unemployed 1.4%).

Price and earnings indexes (1980 = 100)

	1979	1980	1981	1982	1983	1984
Consumer price index	93.6	100.0	...	113.9	119.5	117.3
Earnings index	...	...	...	...	...	...

Gross national product (at current market prices; 1983): U.S.$5,960,000,000 (U.S.$21,170 per capita).

Structure of gross domestic product and labour force

	1983		1970	
	in value QR'000,000	% of total value	labour force	% of labour force
Agriculture, fishing	200	0.9	3,000	3.0
Mining (petroleum)	10,714	45.9	5,000	5.0
Manufacturing	1,389	5.9	14,000	14.0
Construction	1,666	7.1	16,000	15.9
Public utilities	108	0.5		
Transportation and communication	499	2.1		
Trade	1,559	6.7	62,300	62.1
Finance, insurance, real estate	2,111	9.0		
Pub. admin., defense Services Other	5,119	21.9		
TOTAL	23,365	100.0	100,300	100.0

Tourism (1982): total number of tourists staying in hotels 126,000.
Production (metric tons except as noted). Agriculture, forestry, fishing (1983): clover 42,800, dates 6,200, tomatoes 3,700, squash 1,028, sweet melons (including honeydew) 1,023, kanari (Java almonds) 953, citrus fruit 809, barley 713, lettuce 689, watermelon 598, radishes 527, eggplant 411, livestock (number of live animals; 1984) 60,000 goats, 55,000 sheep, 6,000 camels, 5,000 cattle; roundwood, n.a.; fish catch 2,124. Mining and quarrying (1983): limestone 1,600,000; clay, sand, and gypsum are also mined for local use. Manufacturing (1984): urea 717,150; ammonia 631,760; steel bars 470,000; cement 313,330; ethylene 204,400. Construction (1983): residential 421,100 sq m; nonresidential 241,700 sq m. Energy production (consumption): electricity (kW-hr; 1983) 3,105,000,000 (3,105,000,000); coal, none (n.a.); crude petroleum (barrels; 1983) 109,780,000 (3,300,000); petroleum products (metric tons; 1983) 1,014,000 (464,000); natural gas (cu m; 1984) 5,930,000,000 (5,930,000,000).
Land use (1983): meadows and pastures 4.5%; agricultural and under permanent cultivation 0.3%; built-up, desert, and other 95.2%.

Foreign trade♀

Balance of trade (current prices)

	1979	1980	1981	1982	1983	1984
QR'000,000	+9,282	+16,040	+15,757	+9,138	+7,419	+12,698
% of total	44.1%	63.0%	61.4%	41.9%	43.9%	63.0%

Imports (1983): QR5,299,000,000 (machinery and transport equipment 43.9%, manufactured goods 32.4%, foodstuffs and live animals 12.7%, chemicals and chemical products 4.9%, beverages and tobacco 2.0%). *Major import sources* (1984): Japan 19.1%; United Kingdom 15.4%; United States 9.6%; West Germany 7.6%; France 6.3%; Italy 4.8%.
Exports (1983): QR12,150,000,000 (crude petroleum 85.3%, liquefied gas 5.5%, other, nonpetroleum exports 9.2%). *Major export destinations* (1984): Japan 51.4%; France 10.0%; Spain 6.6%; Italy 3.5%; The Netherlands 3.4%; West Germany 2.4%.

Transport and communications

Transport. Railroads: none. Roads (1983): total length 671 mi, 1,080 km (paved, n.a.). Vehicles: n.a. Merchant marine (1984): vessels (100 gross tons and over) 61; total deadweight tonnage 482,172. Air transport (1983): passenger arrivals 402,400, passenger departures 399,100; cargo unloaded 17,062 metric tons, cargo loaded 4,193 metric tons; airports (1985) with scheduled flights 1.
Communications. Daily newspapers (1984): total number 6; total circulation 43,500; circulation per 1,000 population 149.5. Radio (1984): total number of receivers 75,000 (1 per 3.8 persons). Television (1984): total number of receivers 111,000 (1 per 2.6 persons). Telephones (1984): 105,666 (1 per 2.8 persons).

Education and health

Education (1982–83)

	schools	teachers	students	student/ teacher ratio
Primary (age 6–11)	106	2,508	34,805	13.9
Secondary (age 12–17)	56 ‖	2,053	18,346	8.9
Vocational	3 ‖	86	518	6.0
Higher	1 ‖	215	4,015	18.7

Educational attainment (1981). Percent of population over age 10 having: no formal education (including illiterates) 48.9%; primary 15.0%; preparatory (lower secondary) 11.7%; secondary 12.8%; postsecondary 11.6%. *Literacy* (1981): total population over age 10 literate 96,565 (51.1%); males literate 65,151 (51.2%); females literate 31,414 (50.1%).
Health: physicians (1983) 419 (1 per 671 persons); hospital beds (1983) 891 (1 per 315 persons); infant mortality rate per 1,000 live births (1980–85) 45.0.
Food: daily per capita caloric intake, n.a.

Military

Total active duty personnel (1984): 6,000 (army 83.3%, navy 11.7%, air force 5.0%). *Military expenditure as percent of GNP* (1981): 13.1% (world 5.7%); per capita expenditure U.S.$3,896.

*Towns under the supervision of the Ministry of Minicipal Affairs. All such locales are subject to urban plan and construction projects. †Includes ar-Ruways. ‡Includes other towns, islands, and nomads. Qatar's main industrial centre, Musay 'id (Umm Sa'īd), grew substantially after the construction of an oil refinery in 1974. It is not yet a municipality. §Sex distribution (1970): Qatari (male 50.33%, female 49.67%); non-Qatari (male 74.21%, female 25.79%); total (male 64.53%, female 35.47%). ‖ Qatari nationals are almost all Sunnī Muslims of the Wahhābīyah sect. ¶Includes foreign workers. ♀Import figures are f.o.b. (free on board) in balance of trade and c.i.f. (cost, insurance, and freight) for commodities and trading partners.

Réunion

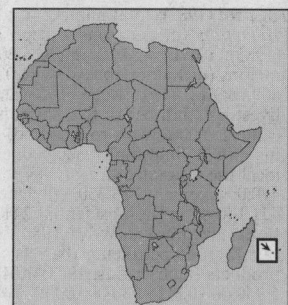

Official name: Département de la Réunion (Department of Reunion).
Political status: overseas department (France) with two legislative houses (General Council [36]; Regional Council [45]).
Chief of state: President of France.
Heads of government: Commissioner (for France); President of General Council (for Réunion); President of Regional Council (for Réunion).
Capital: Saint-Denis.
Official language: French.
Official religion: none.
Monetary unit: 1 Franc (F) = 100 centimes; valuation (Oct. 21, 1985) 1 U.S.$ = F8.04; 1 £ = F11.53.

Area and population

		area*		population
Arrondissements	Capitals	sq mi	sq km	1982 census
Saint-Benoît	Saint-Benoît	284	736	74,312
Saint-Denis	Saint-Denis	163	423	180,647
Saint-Paul	Saint-Paul	180	467	94,378
Saint-Pierre	Saint-Pierre	339	878	166,461
TOTAL		982†	2,544†	515,798

Demography

Population (1985): 546,500.
Density (1985): persons per sq mi 566.7‡, persons per sq km 218.8‡.
Urban-rural (1982): urban 52.8%; rural 47.2%.
Sex distribution (1982): male 49.05%; female 50.95%.
Age breakdown (1985): under 15, 33.1%; 15–29, 31.1%; 30–39, 11.6%; 40–49, 9.5%; 50–59, 6.9%; 60–64, 2.6%; 65 and over, 4.7%.
Population projection: (1990) 604,000; (2000) 720,000.
Doubling time: 49 years.
Ethnic composition (1980): mixed and mulatto 42.8%; East Indian 27.2%; creole (various white European) 25.7%; Chinese 4.3%.
Religious affiliation (1980): Roman Catholic 96.3%; Muslim 2.2%; Protestant 0.6%; Baha'i 0.3%; Hindu 0.2%; other 0.4%.
Major cities (1982): Saint-Denis 126,323; Saint-Pierre 90,627; Saint-Joseph 31,141; Le Port 25,377.

Vital statistics

Birth rate per 1,000 population (1984): 24.4 (world avg. 29.0); legitimate 53.9%; illegitimate 46.1%.
Death rate per 1,000 population (1984): 5.7 (world avg. 11.0).
Natural increase rate per 1,000 population (1984): 18.7 (world avg. 18.0).
Total fertility rate (avg. births per childbearing woman; 1983): 2.9.
Marriage rate per 1,000 population (1984): 6.6.
Divorce rate per 1,000 population (1984): 1.0.
Life expectancy at birth (1980–85): male 64.6 years; female 68.2 years.
Major causes of death per 100,000 population (1983): diseases of the circulatory system 175.5; accidents 71.8; malignant neoplasms (cancers) 46.8; diseases of the respiratory system 39.1; diseases of the digestive system 36.8.

National economy

Budget (1983). Revenue: F3,830,000,000 (grants from the French government 56.0%; deferred and supplementary receipts 21.9%; financial and miscellaneous revenue 18.7%; new borrowing 7.8%). Expenditures: F3,830,000,000 (current expenditures 81.1%, of which public health and social services 38.5%; investment expenditures 17.1%, of which public works 12.0%).
Tourism (1984): tourist arrivals 78,952.
Gross national product (1983): U.S.$2,060,000,000 (U.S.$3,710 per capita).

Structure of gross domestic product and labour force

	1980		1982	
	in value F'000,000	% of total value	labour force ‖	% of labour force
Agriculture	498.5	5.9	17,390	14.7
Mining }	802.0	9.5	7,369	6.2
Manufacturing }				
Construction	401.0	4.7	11,176	9.4
Public utilities	130.0	1.5	697	0.6
Transp. and commun.	346.8	4.1	5,871	5.0
Trade	1,360.1	16.1	14,328	12.1
Finance	883.2	10.5	16,297	13.8
Pub. admin., defense	2,569.1	30.4 }	44,576	37.6
Services	997.1	11.8 }		
Other	456.8‖	5.4	786	0.7
TOTAL	8,444.6	100.0†	118,490	100.0†

Production (metric tons except as noted). Agriculture, forestry, fishing (1984): sugarcane 2,340,000, corn (maize) 11,312, milk 6,000, bananas 5,100, pineapples 4,000, potatoes 3,500, tomatoes 3,154, eggs 2,450, sweet potatoes 2,000, lemons and limes 1,000; livestock (number of live animals) 72,000 pigs, 43,000 goats, 20,000 cattle; roundwood 33,000 cu m§; fish catch 2,144. Mining and quarrying (1983): gravel and sand. Manufacturing (1984): sugar 246,404; molasses 69,400; vanilla 168; rum 98,037 hectolitres; molasses alcohol 3,006 hectolitres. Construction (buildings completed; 1984): 3,041.

Energy production (consumption): electricity (kW-hr; 1984) 521,000,000 (513,300,000); fuelwood (cu m; 1983) 33,000 (33,000); petroleum products (metric tons; 1984) none (301,000).
Household income and expenditure. Average household size (1982) 4.2; income per household F24,697 (U.S.$3,672); sources of income: transfer payments 63.6%, wages and salaries 27.9%, self-employment 8.5%; expenditure (1983): industrial goods 37.8%, services 32.0%, food 29.3%.
Population economically active (1984): total 180,000; participation rate of population ages 15–64, 54.4% (female [1982] 36.0%, unemployed 30.5%).

Price and earnings indexes¶ (1980 = 100)

	1979	1980	1981	1982	1983	1984	1985⁹
Consumer price index	88.8	100.0	113.9	124.3	134.4	144.0	190.4
Hourly earnings indexᵟ	85.6	100.0	122.2	142.4	156.8	171.0	174.8

Land use (1983): forested 35.2%; meadows and pastures 4.0%; agricultural and under permanent cultivation 21.6%; other 39.2%.

Foreign trade

Balance of trade (current prices)

	1979	1980	1981	1982	1983	1984
F'000,000	−2,711	−3,368	−3,740	−4,616	−5,738	−6,077
% of total	69.5%	75.3%	76.6%	77.0%	81.1%	78.8%

Imports (1984): F6,894,600,000 (basic manufactures 25.1%, food and agricultural products 24.9%, consumer goods 23.1%, intermediate goods 16.1%, energy products 10.7%). *Major import sources:* France 64.9%; Bahrain 6.2%; South Africa 3.4%; Italy 3.4%; Japan 2.5%; West Germany 2.2%.
Exports (1984): F816,600,000 (sugar 75.0%, rum 4.2%, langouste 2.9%, vanilla 1.2%, molasses 0.3%). *Major export destinations:* France 55.0%; Portugal 7.9%; China 7.1%; Morocco 6.4%; Italy 4.5%.

Transport and communications

Transport. Railroads, none. Roads (1982): total length 2,919 km (paved 81%). Vehicles (1984): passenger cars, trucks, and buses 92,900. Fishing fleet (1982): vessels (10 gross tons and over) 4. Air transport (1984): passenger arrivals 208,698, passenger departures 210,072; cargo loaded 3,938 metric tons, cargo unloaded 6,181 metric tons; airports (1985) 1.
Communications. Daily newspapers (1984): total number 3; total circulation 61,500; circulation per 1,000 population 114. Radio (1984): total receivers 120,000 (1 per 4.5 persons). Television (1984): total receivers 87,000 (1 per 6.2 persons). Telephones (1984): 75,104 (1 per 7.1 persons).

Education and health

Education (1984–85)

	schools	teachers	students	student/ teacher ratio
Primary (age 6–11)	508	5,087	113,330	22.3
Secondary (age 12–18) }	85	3,947	69,417	17.6
Voc., teacher tr. }				
Higher	1	82	3,000	36.6

Educational attainment (1974). Percent of population over age 15 having: no formal education 21.6%; some primary 17.6%; complete primary 11.8%; some secondary 14.7%; complete secondary 5.9%; some higher 27.8%. *Literacy* (1982): total population over age 15 literate 270,200 (78.7%).
Health (1984): physicians (1985) 704 (1 per 770 persons); hospital beds 3,879 (1 per 139 persons); infant mortality rate per 1,000 live births 11.6.
Food (1980–82): daily per capita caloric intake 2,694 (vegetable products 83%, animal products 17%); 119% of FAO recommended minimum requirement.

Military

France is totally responsible for Réunion's defense☐.

*Includes 12 sq mi (32 sq km) of uninhabited islands administered as part of the département and 3 sq mi (8 sq km) of area not included in the arrondissements. †Detail does not add to total given because of rounding. ‡Based on Réunion Island area only. §1983. ‖Also includes import duties and value added tax, less imputed bank service charge. ¶End of year values. ⁹April. ᵟIn manufacturing. ☐In 1983 there were 2,700 French troops stationed on the island.

JOY SPURR—BRUCE COLEMAN INC.

Catholic church in the town of Cilaos, Réunion.

Romania

Official name: Republika Socialistă România (Socialist Republic of Romania).
Form of government: single-party socialist republic with one legislative house (Grand National Assembly [369]).
Head of state and government: President.
Capital: Bucharest.
Official language: Romanian.
Official religion: none.
Monetary unit: 1 Romanian leu (plural lei) = 100 bani; valuation (Oct. 21, 1985) 1 U.S.$ = 11.30 lei; 1 £ = 16.20 lei.

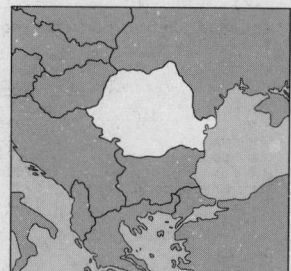

Area and population

Districts	Capitals	area sq mi	area sq km	population 1982 estimate
Alba	Alba Iulia	2,406	6,231	419,000
Arad	Arad	2,954	7,652	509,200
Arges	Piteşti	2,626	6,801	659,300
Bacău	Bacău	2,551	6,606	695,700
Bihor	Oradea	2,909	7,535	649,000
Bistriţa-Năsăud	Bistriţa	2,048	5,305	307,000
Botoşani	Botoşani	1,917	4,965	459,800
Brăila	Brăila	1,824	4,724	668,400
Braşov	Braşov	2,066	5,351	393,500
Buzău	Buzău	2,344	6,072	517,400
Caraş-Severin	Resita	3,283	8,503	400,800
Calaraşi	Calaraşi	1,915	4,959	339,900
Cluj	Cluj-Napoca	2,568	6,650	741,600
Constanţa	Constanţa	2,724	7,055	680,500
Covasna	Sfintu Gheorghe	1,431	3,705	221,900
Dimboviţa	Tirgovişte	1,558	4,035	548,900
Dolj	Craiova	2,862	7,413	767,100
Galaţi	Galaţi	1,708	4,425	619,600
Giurgiu	Giurgiu	1,471	3,810	375,800
Gorj	Tirgu Tiu	2,178	5,641	363,700
Harghita	Miercurea-Ciuc	2,552	6,610	349,400
Hunedoara	Deva	2,709	7,016	543,600
Ialomiţa	Slobozia	1,763	4,565	299,700
Iaşi	Iaşi	2,112	5,469	765,800
Maramureş	Baia Mare	2,400	6,215	526,600
Mehedinţi	Drobeta-Turnu-Severin	1,892	4,900	327,500
Mureş	Tirgu Mureş	2,585	6,696	612,600
Neamţ	Piatra Neamţ	2,274	5,890	555,000
Olt	Slatina	2,126	5,507	528,700
Prahova	Ploieşti	1,812	4,694	852,800
Sălaj	Zalău	1,486	3,850	405,700
Satu Mare	Satu Mare	1,701	4,405	265,800
Sibiu	Sibiu	2,093	5,422	502,900
Suceava	Suceava	3,303	8,555	660,500
Teleorman	Alexandria	2,224	5,760	510,500
Timiş	Timişoara	3,356	8,692	711,000
Tulcea	Tulcea	3,255	8,430	263,000
Vaslui	Vaslui	2,045	5,297	448,400
Vilcea	Rimnicu Vilcea	2,203	5,705	419,400
Vrancea	Focşani	1,878	4,863	379,200
Muncipality				
Bucharest	Bucharest	587	1,521	2,211,500
TOTAL		91,699	237,500	22,477,700

Demography

Population (1985): 22,715,000.
Density (1985): persons per sq mi 247.7, persons per sq km 95.6.
Urban–rural (1983): urban 51.6%; rural 48.4%.
Sex distribution (1983): male 49.34%; female 50.66%.
Age breakdown (1982): under 15, 27.0%; 15–29, 21.4%; 30–44, 19.3%; 45–59, 18.7%; 60–74, 10.2%; 75 and over, 3.4%.
Population projection: (1990) 23,994,000; (2000) 25,728,000.
Doubling time: not applicable; population growth is negligible.
Ethnic composition (1980): Romanian 88.5%; Hungarian 7.8%; German 1.6%; Gypsy 1.0%; other 1.1%.
Religious affiliation (1980): Romanian Orthodox 70.0%; Greek Orthodox 10.0%; Muslim 1.0%; atheist 7.0%; other 3.0%; none 9.0%.
Major cities (1983): Bucharest 1,995,000*; Braşov 331,200; Constanţa 315,700; Cluj-Napoca 301,200; Timişoara 303,500; Iaşi 305,600.

Vital statistics

Birth rate per 1,000 population (1983): 14.3 (world avg. 29.0).
Death rate per 1,000 population (1983): 9.9 (world avg. 11.0).
Natural increase rate per 1,000 population (1983): 4.4 (world avg. 18.0).
Total fertility rate (avg. births per childbearing woman; 1982): 2.4.
Marriage rate per 1,000 population (1982): 7.8.
Divorce rate per 1,000 population (1982): 1.5.
Life expectancy at birth (1980): male 67.5 years; female 72.3 years.
Major causes of death per 100,000 population (1982): diseases of the circulatory system 562.2; diseases of the respiratory system 127.9.

National economy

Budget (1982). Revenue: 277,407,600,000 lei (benefit quotas from state economic enterprises 45.2%, turnover tax 23.5%, income tax 16.1%, state social insurance 13.6%). Expenditures: 257,456,300,000 lei (national economy 61.0%, social services 32.1%, defense 4.4%).
Public debt (external, outstanding; 1984): U.S.$8,000,000,000.

Tourism (1983): receipts from visitors U.S.$202,000,000; expenditures by nationals abroad U.S.$92,000,000.
Production (metric tons except as noted). Agriculture (1984): corn (maize) 13,000,000, wheat 7,900,000, sugar beets 7,000,000, potatoes 6,500,000; livestock (number of live animals) 18,451,000 sheep, 14,347,000 pigs, 6,752,000 cattle; roundwood 22,275,000 cu m†; fish catch 251,000†. Mining and quarrying (1983): iron ore 2,146,000; bauxite 420,000; lead and zinc 73,500. Manufacturing (1984): crude steel 14,436,700; cement 14,016,000; rolled steel 10,329,400; fertilizers 3,072,700; plastics and synthetic rubber 633,000. Construction (1982): 12,689,000 sq m. Energy production (consumption): electricity (kW-hr; 1984) 71,600,000,000 (71,600,000,000); coal (metric tons; 1984) 44,279,600 (44,279,600); crude petroleum (barrels, 1984) 83,943,000 (175,832,000†); petroleum products (metric tons; 1983) 60,000 (42,100); natural gas (cu m; 1984) 33,300,000,000 (41,065,000,000†).
Gross national product (at current market prices; 1984): U.S.$45,536,300,000 (U.S.$2,019 per capita).

Structure of net material product and labour force

	1982 in value '000,000 lei	% of total value	labour force	% of labour force
Agriculture	132,000	21.0	2,986,100	28.6
Mining, manufacturing, and public utilities	352,800	56.1	3,810,900	36.5
Construction	48,400	7.7	803,300	7.7
Transportation and communication	41,500	6.6	733,000	7.0
Trade	39,000	6.2	615,300	5.9
Pub. admin., defense	...	...	62,300	0.6
Services	...	...	1,277,900	12.3
Other	15,100‡	2.4‡	139,300	1.4
TOTAL	628,800§	100.0	10,428,100§	100.0

Population economically active (1984): total 10,500,000; participation rate of population over age 15, 63.2% (female 45.9%, unemployed, n.a.).

Price and earnings indexes (1970 = 100)

	1976	1977	1978	1979	1980	1981	1982
Consumer price index	119.6	119.4	125.9	127.0	131.0	133.9	146.6
Monthly earnings index	148.5	154.7	159.0	165.1	170.0	173.2	176.9

Household income and expenditure. Average household size (1982) 3.1; income per household (1981) 73,470 lei (U.S.$4,900); sources of income: wages 62.6%, other 37.4%; expenditure (1980): food 62.7%, clothing 13.8%.
Land use (1983): forested 27.5%; meadows and pastures 19.2%; agricultural and under permanent cultivation 45.8%; other 7.5%.

Foreign trade

Balance of trade (current prices)

	1979	1980	1981	1982	1983	1984
'000,000 lei	−5,325	−8,043	+3,031	+26,987	+34,379	+67,300
% of total	5.8%	7.3%	0.9%	9.8%	12.4%	17.3%

Imports (1982): 124,850,000,000 lei (mineral fuels 53.0%, machinery 22.9%). *Major import sources:* U.S.S.R. 18.4%; Iran 8.9%; East Germany 6.1%; West Germany 4.9%; Syria 4.9%; Poland 4.2%.
Exports (1982): 151,837,000,000 lei (machinery and transport equipment 30.7%, petroleum products 26.0%, chemicals 10.2%). *Major export destinations:* U.S.S.R. 17.0%; Iraq 8.1%; West Germany 7.9%; East Germany 4.6%.

Transport and communications

Transport. Railroads (1983): length 6,913 mi, 11,125 m; passenger-km 25,578,000,000; metric ton-km cargo 62,822,000,000. Roads (1983): length 45,586 mi, 73,364 km (paved 63%). Vehicles (1980): cars 250,000; trucks and buses 130,000. Merchant marine (1984): vessels (100 gross tons and over) 393; total deadweight tonnage 3,931,543. Air transport (1983): passenger-km 2,174,000,000; metric ton-km cargo 68,000,000; airports (1985) 15.
Communications. Daily newspapers (1984): total number 36; total circulation 4,228,000; circulation per 1,000 population 187. Radio (1984): 3,350,000 (1 per 6.7 persons). Television (1984): 3,912,000 (1 per 5.8 persons). Telephones (1981): 2,027,000 (1 per 11 persons).

Education and health

Education (1983–84)

	schools	teachers	students	student/teacher ratio
Primary (age 6–13)	14,213	150,539	3,067,446	20.4
Secondary (age 14–17)	1,882	51,431	1,453,769	28.3
Higher	44	13,344	174,042	13.0

Educational attainment (1977). Percent of adult population over age 25 having: primary education 55.6%; secondary 39.8%; postsecondary 4.6%.
Literacy (1983) 95.8%.
Health (1984): physicians 46,300 (1 per 489 persons); hospital beds 211,800 (1 per 106 persons); infant mortality rate per 1,000 live births (1983) 23.9.
Food (1980–82): daily per capita caloric intake 3,343 (vegetable products 76%, animal products 24%); 126% of FAO recommended minimum.

Military

Total active duty personnel (1984): 189,500 (army 79.2%, navy 3.9%, air force 16.9%). *Military expenditure as percent of GNP* (1983): 4.7% (world 6.1%); per capita expenditure U.S.$219.

*1984. †1983. ‡Other material activities. §At current prices.

Rwanda

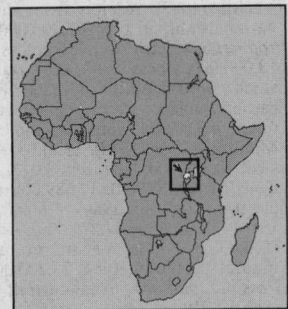

Official name: Republika y'u Rwanda (Rwanda); République Rwandaise (French) (Republic of Rwanda).
Form of government: republic with one legislative house (National Development Council [70]).
Head of state and government: President.
Capital: Kigali.
Official languages: Rwanda; French.
Official religion: none.
Monetary unit: 1 Rwanda franc (RF);
valuation (Oct. 21, 1985)
1 U.S.$ = RF95.19; 1 £ = RF136.50.

Area and population

Prefectures	Capitals	area sq mi	area sq km	population 1978 census
Butare	Butare	707	1,830	602,550
Byumba	Byumba	1,925	4,987	521,351
Cyangugu	Cyangugu	859	2,226	333,187
Gikongoro	Gikongoro	846	2,192	370,596
Gisenyi	Gisenyi	925	2,395	468,882
Gitarama	Gitarama	865	2,241	606,212
Kibungo	Kibungo	1,596	4,134	361,249
Kibuye	Kibuye	510	1,320	336,588
Kigali	Kigali	1,255	3,251	698,442
Ruhengeri	Ruhengeri	680	1,762	531,927
TOTAL		10,169*	26,338	4,830,984

Demography

Population (1985): 6,115,000.
Density (1985): persons per sq mi 601.3, persons per sq km 233.1.
Urban–rural (1985): urban 5.1%; rural 94.9%.
Sex distribution (1985): male 49.37%; female 50.63%.
Age breakdown (1980): under 15, 46.6%; 15–29, 26.0%; 30–44, 14.4%; 45–59, 8.5%; 60–74, 3.8%; 75 and over, 0.7%.
Population projection: (1990) 7,105,000; (2000) 9,845,000.
Doubling time: 22 years.
Ethnic composition (1983): Hutu 90%; Tutsi 9%; Twa 1%.
Religious affiliation (1983): Roman Catholic 56%; Protestant 12%; Muslim 9%; traditional belief systems 23%.
Major cities (1978): Kigali 117,749; Butare 21,691; Ruhengeri 16,025; Gisenyi 12,436.

Vital statistics

Birth rate per 1,000 population (1983): 52.0 (world avg. 29.0).
Death rate per 1,000 population (1983): 19.0 (world avg. 11.0).
Natural increase rate per 1,000 population (1983): 33.0 (world avg. 18.0).
Total fertility rate (avg. births per childbearing woman; 1983): 8.0.
Marriage rate per 1,000 population (1983): 2.2†.
Life expectancy at birth (1983): male 45.0 years; female 48.0 years.
Major causes of death per 100,000 population: n.a.; however, the major diseases are malaria, trypanosomiasis (sleeping sickness), pneumonia, tuberculosis, and dysentery.

National economy

Budget (1983). Revenue: RF14,682,500,000 (import and export duties 36.2%, taxes on goods and services 30.8%, income tax 20.4%, property taxes 1.6%). Expenditures: RF16,368,300,000 (education 27.4%, defense 16.4%, general administration 14.1%, economy and finance 12.3%, health 5.3%).
Public debt (external, outstanding; 1983): U.S.$219,700,000.
Tourism (1981): receipts from visitors U.S.$4,200,000; expenditures by nationals abroad U.S.$12,000,000.
Production (metric tons except as noted). Agriculture, forestry, fishing (1984): plantains 2,200,000, roots and tubers 1,878,000 (of which sweet potatoes 950,000, cassava 950,000, potatoes 330,000), cereals 291,000 (of which sorghum 200,000, corn [maize] 80,000), coffee 26,000, tea 8,000, tobacco 3,000; livestock (number of live animals) 644,000 cattle, 1,200,000 goats, 323,000 sheep, 147,000 pigs; roundwood (1983) 5,157,000 cu m; fish catch (1983) 1,210. Mining and quarrying (1983): cassiterite (tin ore) 1,526; wolframite (tungsten ore) 429; gold 623 troy oz. Manufacturing (value added at producers' prices in RF'000,000; 1982): food, beverages, and tobacco products 17,295; industrial chemicals 1,476; metal products 1,056; textiles 415; printing and published materials 119. Construction (1981): residential 59,600 sq m; nonresidential 34,400 sq m. Energy production (consumption): electricity (kW-hr; 1983) 157,000,000 (188,000,000); coal, none (n.a.); petroleum products (metric tons; 1983) none (56,000); natural gas (cu m; 1983) 1,076,000 (1,076,000).
Labour force (1983): total 2,718,000; participation rate of total population 47.7% (female [1982] 48.3%, unemployed, n.a.).

Price and earnings indexes (1980 = 100)

	1979	1980	1981	1982	1983	1984	1985
Consumer price index	93.3	100.0	106.6	119.9	127.7	134.6	137.4§
Earnings index	...	...	...	...	...	...	...

Land use (1983): forested 10.4%; meadows and pastures 17.6%; agricultural and under permanent cultivation 40.5%; other 31.5%.
Gross national product (1983): U.S.$1,540,000,000 (U.S.$270 per capita).

Structure of gross domestic product and labour force

	1983 in value RF'000,000	% of total value	labour force	% of labour force
Agriculture	56,600	39.9	2,394,000	88.1
Mining	700	0.5		
Manufacturing	26,000	18.3		
Construction	6,500	4.6		
Public utilities	200	0.1		
Transp. and commun.	4,700	3.3	324,000	11.9
Trade	20,300	14.3		
Finance				
Pub. admin., defense	26,900	19.0		
Services				
Other				
TOTAL	141,900‡	100.0	2,718,000	100.0

Household income and expenditure: Average household size (1983) 5.2; average annual income per household RF122,870 (U.S.$1,300); sources of income (1977): salaries and wages 16.5%, self-employment (profits, interest, etc.) 71.0%, transfers 9.5%; expenditure: n.a.

Foreign trade

Balance of trade (current prices)

	1979	1980	1981	1982	1983	1984
RF'000,000	−3,324	−11,093	−13,390	−12,861	−17,840	−13,858
% of total	13.2%	44.3%	46.8%	43.4%	54.6%	45.2%

Imports (1983): RF25,267,300,000 (machinery and transport equipment 24.0%, of which transport equipment 12.3%, electrical equipment 6.3%; mineral fuels and lubricants 16.5%; textiles, clothing, and footwear 10.9%; construction materials 8.5%; food 7.6%). *Major import sources:* Kenya 21.3%; Belgium–Luxembourg 17.3%; Japan 12.4%; West Germany 7.4%; China 7.0%; France 5.2%; U.S. 4.8%; Italy 3.5%; The Netherlands 3.0%.
Exports (1983): RF7,427,000,000 (coffee 69.9%; tea 12.0%; tin ores and concentrates 11.3%). *Major export destinations:* Belgium–Luxembourg 16.8%; Uganda 12.1%; West Germany 1.9%; France 1.1%; U.K. 1.1%; U.S. 0.4%.

Transport and communications

Transport. Railroads: none. Roads (1983): total length 4,910 mi, 7,900 km (paved, n.a.). Vehicles (1982): passenger cars 6,188; trucks and buses 7,168. Merchant marine: none. Air transport (1983): passenger arrivals 36,272, passenger departures 40,837; metric ton cargo loaded 16,742; metric ton cargo unloaded 12,176; airports (1985) with scheduled flights 2.
Communications. Daily newspapers: none. Radio (1984): total number of receivers 175,000 (1 per 34 persons). Television: none. Telephones (1984): 6,598 (1 per 894 persons).

Education and health

Education (1983–84)

	schools	teachers	students	student/ teacher ratio
Primary (age 7–12)	1,572	14,005	761,955	54.4
Secondary (age 13–19)	...	1,082	14,761	13.6
Voc., teacher tr.‖	...	36	640	17.8
Higher‖	...	184	1,213	6.6

Educational attainment, n.a. *Literacy* (1980): total population literate 1,295,900 (49.4%); males literate 798,800 (62.2%); females literate 497,100 (37.2%).
Health (1983): physicians 258 (1 per 22,093 persons); hospital beds 9,015 (1 per 632 persons); infant mortality rate per 1,000 live births 125.0.
Food (1980–82): daily per capita caloric intake 2,115 (vegetable products 97%, animal products 3%); 91% of FAO recommended minimum requirement.

Military

Total active duty personnel (1984): 5,150 (army 97.1%; navy, none; air force 2.9%). *Military expenditure as percent of GNP* (1983): 1.4% (world 6.1%); per capita expenditure U.S.$3.

*Detail does not add to total given because of rounding. †Excludes marriages not registered in court. ‡At current prices. §March. ‖1981–82.

CHARLES HENNEGHIEN—BRUCE COLEMAN INC.

Kabyayi School of Nursing, Gitarama Prefecture, Rwanda.

Saint Christopher and Nevis

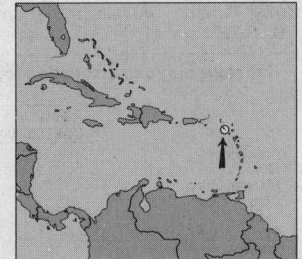

Official name: Federation of Saint Christopher and Nevis.
Form of government: federal parliamentary state with one legislative house (National Assembly [15]).
Chief of state: British Monarch represented by governor-general.
Head of government: Prime Minister.
Capital: Basseterre.
Official language: English.
Official religion: none.
Monetary unit: 1 East Caribbean dollar (ECar$) = 100 cents; valuation (Oct. 21, 1985) 1 U.S.$ = ECar$2.70; 1 £ = ECar$3.87.

Area and population		area		population
Islands				**1980**
Parishes	**Capitals**	**sq mi**	**sq km**	**census**
Saint Christopher		67.2	174.1	33,881
Christ Church Nichola Town		7.2	18.6	1,989
Saint Anne Sandy Point		4.9	12.8	3,145
Saint George Basseterre	Basseterre	11.1	28.7	14,283
Saint John Capisterre		9.6	24.8	3,163
Saint Mary Cayon		5.8	15.1	3,308
Saint Paul Capisterre		5.3	13.8	2,080
Saint Peter Basseterre		8.0	20.7	2,497
Saint Thomas Middle Island		9.4	24.3	2,255
Trinity Palmetto Point		6.0	15.4	1,161
Nevis		35.7	92.5	9,428
Saint George Gingerland		7.1	18.5	2,295
Saint James Windward		12.0	31.1	1,691
Saint John Figtree		8.2	21.3	2,224
Saint Paul Charlestown	Charlestown	1.4	3.5	1,243
Saint Thomas Lowland		7.0	18.1	1,975
TOTAL		102.9	266.6	43,309

Demography

Population (1985): 47,000.
Density (1985): persons per sq mi 455.9, persons per sq km 176.0.
Urban–rural (1980): urban 35.8%; rural 64.2%.
Sex distribution (1980): male 48.12%; female 51.88%.
Age breakdown (1980): under 15, 37.2%; 15–29, 30.4%; 30–44, 9.5%; 45–59, 9.4%; 60–74, 10.0%; 75 and over, 3.5%.
Population projection: (1990) 50,000; (2000) 53,000.
Doubling time: 40 years.
Ethnic composition (1980): black 94.3%; mixed 3.3%; white 0.9%; other 1.3%.
Religious affiliation (1980): Anglican 32.6%; Methodist 28.8%; Moravian 8.7%; Roman Catholic 7.2%; Church of God 3.5%; other 19.2%.
Major towns (1980): Basseterre 14,283; Charlestown 1,243.

Vital statistics

Birth rate per 1,000 population (1982): 29.0 (world avg. 29.0); (1980) legitimate 18.6%; illegitimate 81.4%.
Death rate per 1,000 population (1982): 11.2 (world avg. 11.0).
Natural increase rate per 1,000 population (1982): 17.8 (world avg. 18.0).
Total fertility rate (avg. births per childbearing woman): n.a.
Marriage rate per 1,000 population (1977)*: 2.6.
Divorce rate per 1,000 population (1977)*: 0.1.
Life expectancy at birth (1982): male 64.7 years; female 69.8 years.
Major causes of death per 100,000 population (1982): heart diseases 168.5; cerebrovascular diseases 168.5; malignant neoplasms (cancers) 122.0; diseases of the respiratory system 71.0.

National economy

Budget (1982). Revenue: ECar$51,098,000 (inland revenue 41.4%, import duties and excise taxes 22.3%, consumer taxes 16.3%, stamps 7.3%, charges on electricity, ice, and cold storage 6.9%). Expenditures: ECar$62,606,000 (general administration 27.6%, economic services 18.6%, education 18.6%, health 9.7%, debt payment 3.1%).
Public debt (external, outstanding; end of 1984): U.S.$15,800,000.
Tourism (1981): receipts from visitors U.S.$9,000,000; expenditures by nationals abroad, n.a.
Production (metric tons except as noted). Agriculture, forestry, fishing (1984): sugarcane 310,000, coconuts 2,000, fruits 2,000, vegetables 1,000, sweet potatoes 600, peanuts (groundnuts) 300, tanias 122†, cotton lint 7‡; livestock (number of live animals) 14,000 sheep, 10,000 pigs, 10,000 goats, 6,000 cattle; roundwood, n.a.; fish catch 1,100§. Mining and quarrying: excavation of sand for local use. Manufacturing (value of production in ECar$'000; 1982): sugar 29,291 ∥; clothing 4,597† ∥; assembly of electrical appliances 3,781 ∥; footwear 1,851† ∥; molasses 1,429 ∥; aerated water 26,500 hectolitres; beer 10,460 hectolitres. Construction: n.a. Energy production (consumption): electricity (kW-hr; 1984) 34,000,000 (26,300,000); coal, none (n.a.); crude petroleum, none (n.a.); petroleum products (metric tons; 1983) none (22,000); natural gas, none (n.a.).
Household income and expenditure. Average household size (1980) 3.7; average annual income per household: n.a.; source of income: n.a.; expenditure (1982): food and beverages 55.6%, household supplies 9.4%, housing 7.6%,

clothing and footwear 7.5%, fuel and light 6.6%, transportation 4.3%, other 9.0%.
Gross national product (at current market prices; 1983): U.S.$40,000,000 (U.S.$889 per capita).

Structure of gross domestic product and labour force				
	1982			
	in value ECar'000,000	**% of total value**	**labour force**	**% of labour force**
Agriculture	27.9	20.2	11,600	50.9
Mining	0.3	0.2	100	0.4
Manufacturing	18.7	13.5	1,800	7.9
Construction	9.8	7.1	600	2.6
Public utilities	1.2	0.9	200	0.9
Transportation and communication	16.2	11.7	500	2.2
Trade	18.9	13.7	3,800	16.7
Finance	14.1	10.2	200	0.9
Pub. admin., defense	28.1	20.3	...	...
Services	7.3	5.3	4,000	17.5
Other	−4.3¶	−3.1¶	...	...
TOTAL	138.2♀	100.0	22,800	100.0

Population economically active (1980): total 17,125; participation rate of population over age 15, 63.0% (female 41.0, unemployed 11.7%).

Price and earnings indexes (January 1978 = 100)					
	1978	**1979**	**1980**	**1981**	**1982**
Consumer price index	105.7	117.0	137.9	152.3	161.3
Earnings index	...	...	...	...	...

Land use (1983): forested 17.0%; meadows and pastures 3.0%; agricultural and under permanent cultivation 39.0%; other 41.0%.

Foreign trade

Balance of trade (current prices)♂					
	1978	**1979**	**1980**	**1981**	**1982**	**1983**
ECar$'000,000	−20.2	−41.2	−55.9	−63.3	−67.2	−91.4
% of total	18.3%	31.2%	30.0%	32.6%	39.8%	50.2%

Imports (1982): ECar$118,053,170 (food 19.5%, of which meat 4.6%, cereals and cereal preparations 3.6%; machinery and transport equipment 18.9%, of which electrical machinery 6.9%, transport equipment 6.3%; manufactured goods 12.8%, of which clothing 4.6%; mineral fuels and lubricants 11.3%, of which petroleum products 10.3%; chemicals 9.3%; crude materials except fuels 2.6%). *Major import sources:* United States 29.6%; United Kingdom 17.0%; Trinidad and Tobago 13.1%; Puerto Rico 6.7%.
Exports (1982): ECar$50,856,337 (sugar 58.9%; clothing 8.6%; machinery and appliances 8.3%; molasses 2.8%). *Major export destinations:* United Kingdom 45.5%; United States 27.9%; Trinidad and Tobago 14.3%; Netherlands Antilles 1.3%.

Transport and communications

Transport. Railroads (1983): length 36 mi, 58 km□. Roads (1983): total length 190 mi, 305 km (paved 42%). Vehicles (1983): passenger cars 2,848; trucks and buses 432. Merchant marine (1984): vessels (100 gross tons and over) 2; total deadweight tonnage 459. Air transport (1982): passenger arrivals 51,796, passenger departures 52,269; cargo handled, n.a.; airports (1985) with scheduled flights 2.
Communications. Daily newspapers (1984): none. Radio (1984): total number of receivers 21,000 (1 per 2.1 persons). Television (1984): total number of receivers 4,500 (1 per 9.8 persons). Telephones (1983): 3,259 (1 per 14 persons).

Education and health

Education (1984–85)				
	schools	**teachers**	**students**	**student/ teacher ratio**
Primary (age 5–12)	32	339	7,655	22.6
Secondary (age 13–17)	7	286	4,436	15.5
Voc., teacher tr.	2	29	240	8.3
Higher	—	—	—	—

Educational attainment (1980). Percent of population over age 14 having: no formal schooling 8.5%; primary education 80.1%; secondary 8.8%; higher 1.1%; other 1.5%. *Literacy* (1980): total population over age 15 literate 24,887 (91.5%); males literate 11,533 (90.8%); females literate 13,354 (92.2%).
Health (1982): physicians (1981) 17 (1 per 2,615 persons); hospital beds 248 (1 per 182 persons); infant mortality rate per 1,000 live births 42.8.
Food (1980–82): daily per capita caloric intake 2,231 (vegetable products 74%, animal products 26%); 92% of FAO recommended minimum requirement.

Military

Total active duty personnel (1984): the country maintains a police force and a small defense force of volunteers.

*Includes Anguilla, formerly a part of Saint Christopher and Nevis. †1981. ‡1982. §1983. ∥Export figure. ¶Bank service charge. ♀At current prices. ♂Imports c.i.f. (cost, insurance, and freight); exports f.o.b. (free on board), including reexports. □Light railway serving the sugar industry on Saint Christopher.

Saint Lucia

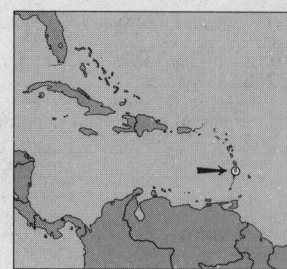

Official name: Saint Lucia.
Form of government: parliamentary
state with two legislative houses
(Senate [11]; House of Assembly [17]).
Chief of state: British Monarch
represented by governor-general.
Head of government: Prime Minister.
Capital: Castries.
Official language: English.
Official religion: none.
Monetary unit: 1 East Caribbean
Dollar (EC$) = 100 cents; valuation
(Oct. 21, 1985) 1 U.S.$ = EC$2.70;
1 £ = EC$3.87.

Area and population

		area		population
Quarters*	Capitals	sq mi	sq km	1984 estimate
Anse-la-Raye	Anse-la-Raye	11.1	28.8	5,872
Canaries	Canaries	7.4	19.2	2,467
Castries	Castries	30.7	79.5	50,798
Choiseul	Choiseul	12.1	31.3	7,682
Dennery	Dennery	27.2	70.4	11,409
Gros Islet	Gros Islet	40.0	103.6	12,012
Laborie	Laborie	14.7	38.1	8,151
Micoud	Micoud	32.3	83.7	14,104
Soufrière	Soufrière	19.5	50.5	8,620
Vieux Fort	Vieux Fort	17.3	44.8	12,951
TOTAL		238.3†	617.2†	134,066

Demography

Population (1985): 137,600.
Density (1985): persons per sq mi 577.4, persons per sq km 222.9.
Urban–rural (1982): urban 52.1%; rural 47.9%.
Sex distribution (1982): male 47.23%; female 52.77%.
Age breakdown (1981): under 15, 49.6%; 15–29, 21.3%; 30–44, 11.6%; 45–59, 9.8%; 60–74, 5.5%; 75 and over, 2.2%.
Population projection: (1990) 158,000; (2000) 208,000.
Doubling time: 25 years.
Ethnic composition (1982): black 90.3%; mixed 5.5%; East Indian 3.2%; white 0.8%; other 0.2%.
Religious affiliation (1980): Roman Catholic 86.3%; Protestant 11.3%, of which Anglican 3.0%, Seventh-day Adventist 2.5%; Rastafarian 2.2%; other 0.2%.
Major cities (1981): Castries 48,782; Soufrière 7,325; Vieux Fort 6,981.

Vital statistics

Birth rate per 1,000 population (1984): 30.1 (world avg. 29.0); (1980) legitimate 13.0%; illegitimate 87.0%.
Death rate per 1,000 population (1984): 5.5 (world avg. 11.0).
Natural increase rate per 1,000 population (1984): 24.6 (world avg. 18.0).
Total fertility rate (avg. births per childbearing woman): n.a.
Marriage rate per 1,000 population (1981): 3.4.
Divorce rate per 1,000 population (1981): 0.2.
Life expectancy at birth (1983): male 68.3 years; female 72.4 years.
Major causes of death per 100,000 population (1981): heart diseases 98.6; cerebrovascular diseases 63.9; malignant neoplasms (cancers) 57.4; influenza and pneumonia 38.0.

National economy

Budget (1982–83). Revenue: EC$137,280,000 (tax revenue 73.4%, of which income taxes 26.9%, customs duties 14.6%, consumer taxes on imports 10.6%, stamps 8.4%; grants from abroad 15.3%; nontax revenue 11.3%). Expenditures: EC$153,090,000 (current budget 76.4%; capital expenditure 23.0%; public debt repayment 0.6%).
Public debt (external, outstanding; 1983): U.S.$42,300,000.
Tourism (1982): receipts from visitors U.S.$32,000,000; expenditures by nationals abroad, n.a.
Production (metric tons except as noted). Agriculture, forestry, fishing (1984): bananas 61,000, mangoes 45,000, coconuts 30,000, yams 4,000, sweet potatoes 2,000, plantains 1,542‡, citrus fruits 784‡, vegetables (mostly tomatoes and cabbages) 710‡, ginger 115‡, cocoa beans 50‡; livestock (number of live animals) 15,000 sheep, 12,000 cattle, 12,000 pigs, 11,000 goats; roundwood, n.a.; fish catch (1983) 2,635. Mining and quarrying: excavation of sand for local construction and pumice. Manufacturing (value of production in EC$'000; 1982): cardboard boxes 22,000; copra 3,760; coconut oil 3,743; coconut meal 1,285; nonalcoholic beverages 939; clothing 556; soap 489; other manufactures include beer, batteries, electrical components, scuba-diving suits§, and wooden toys§. Construction: n.a. Energy production (consumption) (kW-hr; 1984) 65,800,000 (54,300,000); coal, none (n.a.); crude petroleum, none (n.a.); petroleum products (metric tons; 1982) none (33,000); natural gas, none (n.a.).
Population economically active (1983): 45,500; participation rate of population over age 15, 70.8% (female, n.a.; unemployed [1981] 14.5%¶).

Price and earnings indexes (1980 = 100)

	1978	1979	1980	1981	1982	1983	1984
Consumer price index	76.5	83.7	100.0	115.1	120.4	122.2	123.7
Weekly earnings index♀	65.8	81.2	100.0	...	115.0	...	...

Gross national product (at current market prices; 1983): U.S.$130,000,000 (U.S.$995 per capita).

Structure of gross domestic product and labour force

	1982		1981 ‖	
	in value EC$'000,000	% of total value	labour force	% of labour force
Agriculture	26.7	14.4	16,400	44.0
Mining	2.7	1.4		
Manufacturing	21.6	11.6	2,200	6.0
Construction	15.5	8.3	2,600	7.0
Trade	38.3	20.6	4,500	12.0
Public utilities	6.1	3.3		
Transportation and communication	21.9	11.8		
Finance	15.9	8.6	11,500	31.0
Pub. admin., defense	30.1	16.2		
Services	7.1	3.8		
TOTAL	185.9	100.0	37,200	100.0

Household income and expenditure. Average household size (1978) 4.9; average annual income per household: n.a.; source of income: n.a.; expenditure (1964): food and beverages 56.6%, housing 10.1%, clothing and footwear 8.1%, alcoholic beverages and tobacco 6.9%, fuel and light 5.6%, household supplies 5.0%, other 7.7%.
Land use (1983): forested 13.0%; meadows and pastures 5.0%; agricultural and under permanent cultivation 28.0%; other 54.0%.

Foreign trade

Balance of trade (current prices)♂

	1979	1980	1981	1982	1983	1984
EC$'000,000	−187.2	−210.0	−234.9	−206.0	−154.2	−191.7
% of total	52.1%	45.8%	51.1%	47.2%	36.5%	42.8%

Imports (1982): EC$318,300,000 (basic manufactures 25.4%, of which paper and paperboard 3.7%, iron and steel 2.2%; food and live animals 21.1%, of which meat 4.2%, wheat flour 2.2%; machinery and transport equipment 17.2%, of which motor vehicles 3.9%, electrical machinery 3.3%; chemicals 9.8%; petroleum products 9.6%). *Major import sources:* United States 36.7%; United Kingdom 12.3%; Trinidad and Tobago 10.9%; Netherlands Antilles 5.6%; Japan 4.7%.
Exports (1982)▢: EC$101,800,000 (bananas 37.6%; paper and cardboard 12.6%; clothing 9.8%; refined coconut oil 6.3%; beer and ale 5.0%). *Major export destinations:* United Kingdom 42.5%; Jamaica 12.8%; Trinidad and Tobago 11.6%; United States 7.7%; Dominica 7.5%.

Transport and communications

Transport. Railroads (1982)◇: length 13 mi, 21 km; short ton-mi cargo, n.a.; metric ton-km cargo, n.a. Roads (1983): total length 792 mi, 1,275 km (paved 90%). Vehicles (1983): passenger cars 4,479; trucks and buses 1,171. Merchant marine (1984): vessels (100 gross tons and over) 7; total deadweight tonnage 3,732. Air transport (1983)△: passenger arrivals 110,-000, passenger departures 105,500; cargo unloaded 736 metric tons, cargo loaded 624 metric tons; airports (1985) with scheduled flights 2.
Communications. Daily newspapers: none. Radio (1984): total number of receivers 90,000 (1 per 1.5 person). Television: total number of receivers, n.a. Telephones (1983): 9,587 (1 per 14 persons).

Education and health

Education (1984–85)

	schools	teachers	students	student/ teacher ratio
Primary (age 5–11)	85	1,139	33,534	29.4
Secondary (age 12–16)	11	280	5,321	19.0
Voc., teacher tr.	4	48	358	7.5
Higher	—	—	—	—

Educational attainment (1970). Percent of adult population over age 24 having: no formal schooling 28.7%; primary education 65.6%; secondary 4.7%; higher 1.0%. *Literacy* (1970): total population over age 14 literate 41,040 (81.7%); males literate 17,890 (80.8%); females literate 23,150 (82.4%).
Health (1983): physicians 36 (1 per 3,628 persons); hospital beds 363 (1 per 360 persons); infant mortality rate per 1,000 live births (1984) 17.6.
Food (1980–82): daily per capita caloric intake 2,381 (vegetable products 79%, animal products 21%); 98% of FAO recommended minimum requirement.

Military

Total active duty personnel (1984): 300†. *Military expenditure as percent of GNP:* n.a.

---

*Includes the area and population of the country's 10 town and village councils as well as rural community councils associated with particular town or village councils. †Includes the uninhabited 26.0 sq mi (67.3 sq km) Central Forest Preserve. ‡1982. §Production beginning in 1985. ‖All figures are estimates. ¶Official estimate; 1982 unofficial estimate is 27%. ♀Manufacturing and construction only. ♂Imports c.i.f. (cost, insurance, and freight); exports f.o.b. (free on board), including reexports. ▢Excludes reexports. ◇Light railways operating on banana plantations. △Data for both Castries and Vieux Fort airports. †All police.

Saint Vincent and the Grenadines

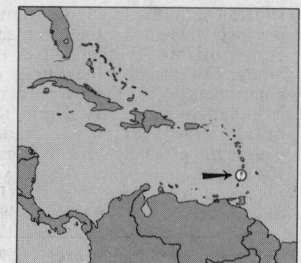

Official name: Saint Vincent and the Grenadines.
Form of government: parliamentary state with one legislative house (House of Assembly [6 senators, 13 representatives]).
Chief of state: British Monarch represented by governor-general.
Head of government: Prime Minister.
Capital: Kingstown.
Official language: English.
Official religion: none.
Monetary unit: 1 East Caribbean Dollar (EC$) = 100 cents; valuation (Oct. 21, 1985) 1 U.S.$ = EC$2.70; 1 £ = EC$3.87.

Area and population

Census divisions	area		population
	sq mi	sq km	1982 estimate
Barrouallie	14.2	36.8	6,016
Bridgetown	7.2	18.6	8,898
Calliaqua	11.8	30.6	20,666
Chateaubelair	30.9	80.1	8,476
Colonarie	13.4	34.7	9,822
Georgetown	22.2	57.5	9,072
Kingstown (city)	1.8	4.7	24,764
Kingstown (suburbs)	6.0	15.5	8,930
Layou	11.1	28.7	7,459
Marriaqua	9.4	24.3	10,956
Northern Grenadines	8.9	23.1	5,889
Sandy Bay	5.3	13.7	3,601
Southern Grenadines	7.4	19.2	3,334
TOTAL	150.3*	389.3*	127,883†

Demography

Population (1985): 105,000‡.
Density (1985)‡: persons per sq mi 698.6, persons per sq km 269.7.
Urban–rural§ (1982): urban 26.3%; rural 73.7%.
Sex distribution (1981): male 48.58%; female 51.42%.
Age breakdown (1978): under 15, 44.9%; 15–29, 29.8%; 30–44, 10.3%; 45–59, 8.2%; 60–74, 5.0%; 75 and over, 1.8%.
Population projection‡: (1990) 113,000; (2000) 130,000.
Doubling time‡: 58 years.
Ethnic composition (1980): black 65.5%; mulatto 19.9%; East Indian 5.5%; white 3.5%; other (including Amerindian, mestizo, and Arab) 5.6%.
Religious affiliation (1980): Protestant 77.3%, of which Anglican 36.0%, Methodist 20.4%, Seventh-day Adventist 4.1%, Plymouth Brethren 3.9%; Roman Catholic 19.3%; Afro-American spiritist (mostly Rastafarian) 2.0%; other 1.4%.
Major cities (1982)† ‖: Kingstown 24,764.

Vital statistics

Birth rate per 1,000 population (1982)‡: 33.2 (world avg. 29.0); legitimate, n.a.; illegitimate, n.a.
Death rate per 1,000 population (1982)‡: 7.4 (world avg. 11.0).
Natural increase rate per 1,000 population (1982)‡: 25.8 (world avg. 18.0).
Total fertility rate (avg. births per childbearing woman; 1980–85): 3.0.
Marriage rate per 1,000 population (1981)‡: 4.1.
Divorce rate per 1,000 population (1980)‡: 0.2.
Life expectancy at birth (1980–85): male 67.5 years; female 71.4 years.
Major causes of death per 100,000 population (1981)‡: diseases of the circulatory system 205.6; infectious and parasitic diseases 85.7; endocrine, nutritional, and metabolic diseases 75.6; malignant neoplasms (cancers) 50.4; diseases of the respiratory system 42.3; accidents, poisonings, and violence 40.3.

National economy

Budget (1982). Revenue: EC$68,200,000 (tax revenue 73.9%, of which import duties 34.6% [including customs duties 18.2%] and taxes on income, profits, and capital gains 24.2%; nontax revenue 18.3%). Expenditures: EC$75,300,000 (general public services 19.4%; education 16.9%; health 10.4%; defense 6.6%; roads 6.4%).
Public debt (external, outstanding; 1983): U.S.$20,900,000.
Tourism (1983): receipts from visitors U.S.$18,200,000; expenditures by nationals abroad, n.a.
Production (metric tons except as noted). Agriculture, forestry, fishing (1984): bananas 32,000, roots and tubers 25,000, coconuts 20,000, sugarcane 2,700, arrowroot 2,106¶, plantains 2,000, mangoes 2,000, peanuts (groundnuts) 400¶, carrots 350¶, ginger 286¶, nutmeg and mace 142¶, tobacco 99¶; livestock (number of live animals) 13,000 sheep, 8,000 cattle, 7,000 pigs, 4,000 goats; roundwood, n.a.; fish catch (1983) 547. Mining and quarrying (1983): salt 50,000; sand and gravel 400,000 cu m♀. Manufacturing (1984): flour 15,400♂; copra 2,000; cigarettes 20,000,000 units; rum 5,228 hectolitres♀; other products include aerated drinks, condensed milk, packing boxes for bananas, boats, concrete, and furniture. Construction, n.a. Energy production (consumption): electricity (kW-hr; 1984) 34,500,000 (24,500,000); coal, none (n.a.); crude petroleum, none (n.a.); petroleum products (metric tons; 1982) none (13,000); natural gas, none (n.a.).

Gross national product (at current market prices; 1983): U.S.$90,000,000 (U.S.$880‡ per capita).

Structure of gross domestic product and labour force

	1982		1970	
	in value EC$'000,000	% of total value	labour force	% of labour force
Agriculture	29.2	13.1	6,882	29.0
Mining	0.6	0.3	48	0.2
Manufacturing	20.7	9.3	1,851	7.8
Construction	22.4	10.0	2,871	12.1
Public utilities	5.2	2.3	214	0.9
Transportation and communication	29.8	13.3	1,068	4.5
Trade	22.7	10.1	2,871	12.1
Finance	26.7	11.9	♀	♀
Pub. admin., defense	34.0	15.2	♀	♀
Services	5.7	2.5	7,190♀	30.3♀
Other	26.8	12.0	736	3.1
TOTAL	223.8	100.0	23,731	100.0

Population economically active (1980): total 32,617□; participation rate of population over age 15, 54.6% (female 34.5%□, unemployed 25.0%◇).

Price and earnings indexes (1980 = 100)

	1978	1979	1980	1981	1982	1983	1984
Consumer price index	73.8	85.3	100.0	112.7	120.9	127.5	130.9
Earnings index	...	...	...	...	...	...	...

Household income and expenditure. Average household size (1978) 5.0; average annual income per household: n.a.; source of income: n.a.; expenditure (1982): food 55.2%, housing 11.1%, services 9.7%, clothing and footwear 6.9%, utilities 6.4%, household and miscellaneous expenses 5.4%, alcohol and tobacco 5.3%.
Land use (1983): forested 41.0%; meadows and pastures 6.0%; agricultural and under permanent cultivation 50.0%; other 3.0%.

Foreign trade

Balance of trade (current prices)

	1977	1978	1979	1980	1981	1982
EC$'000,000	−55.1	−53.4	−85.2	−111.3	−91.2	−77.1
% of total	50.1%	37.6%	51.7%	56.4%	40.9%	30.6%

Imports (1982): EC$164,500,000 (basic and miscellaneous manufactures [including paper products and clothing] 30.6%; food and live animals 29.2%, of which wheat 9.8%; machinery and transport equipment 17.2%; chemicals 10.7%; alcoholic and nonalcoholic beverages and tobacco 4.6%). *Major import sources:* United States 36.2%; United Kingdom 17.0%; Trinidad and Tobago 8.9%; Canada 6.6%; Barbados 3.7%.
Exports (1982): EC$87,400,000 (food and live animals 71.6%, of which bananas 28.6%, flour 17.8%, eddoes△ 6.6%, tanias△ 3.4%, crude coconut oil 1.5%, arrowroot starch 0.7%; basic and miscellaneous manufactures [including garments, linens, and furniture] 18.0%). *Major export destinations:* United Kingdom 31.0%; Trinidad and Tobago 30.5%; United States 9.2%; St. Lucia 6.6%; Barbados 4.9%.

Transport and communications

Transport. Railroads: none. Roads (1984): total length 450 mi, 724 km (paved 48%). Vehicles (1982): passenger cars 4,482; trucks and buses 2,400. Merchant marine (1984): vessels (100 gross tons and over) 49; total deadweight tonnage 154,762. Air transport (1981): passenger arrivals 71,097, passenger departures 70,544; airports (1985) with scheduled flights 4.
Communications. Daily newspapers: none. Radio (1984): total number of receivers 35,000 (1 per 3.0 persons). Television: total number of receivers, n.a. Telephones (1983): 6,074 (1 per 17 persons).

Education and health

Education (1982–83)

	schools	teachers	students	student/ teacher ratio
Primary (age 5–15)	62	1,251	24,551	19.6
Secondary (age 11–19)	19	292	5,170	17.7
Voc., teacher tr.	5	39	275	7.1
Higher†	1	19	105	5.5

Educational attainment (1970). Percent of adult population over age 24 having: no formal schooling 5.8%; primary education 88.2%; secondary 5.2%; higher 0.8%. *Literacy* (1983): total population over age 14 literate 54,000 (85.0%).
Health: physicians (1984) 24 (1 per 4,300 persons); hospital beds (1982) 350 (1 per 289 persons); infant mortality rate per 1,000 live births (1981) 46.8.
Food (1980–82): daily per capita caloric intake 2,353 (vegetable products 87%, animal products 13%); 97% of FAO recommended minimum requirement.

Military⊕

Total active duty personnel (1983): 489 (police 100%). *Military expenditure as percent of GNP* (1982): 6.0% (world 6.0%); per capita expenditure U.S.$18.

---

*Total area including inland water. †Country estimate. ‡Based on UN estimate. §Urban being defined as Kingstown and suburbs. ‖ Populations of other cities or locales are not available. ¶1982. ♀1981. ♂1979. □Projection based on 1970 census. ◇1984. △Particular varieties of taro rootstocks. †Teachers college. ⊕Includes local police and East Caribbean regional defense.

San Marino

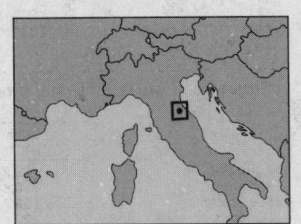

Official name: Serenissima Repubblica di San Marino (Most Serene Republic of San Marino).
Form of government: unitary multiparty republic with one legislative house (Great and General Council [60]).
Head of state and government: Captains-Regent (2).
Capital: San Marino.
Official language: Italian.
Official religion: none.
Monetary unit: 1 Italian lira (Lit; plural lire) = 100 centesimi; valuation (Oct. 21, 1985) 1 U.S.$ = Lit1,779; 1 £ = Lit2,551.

Area and population		area		population
Castles	Capitals	sq mi	sq km	1985 estimate
Acquaviva	Acquaviva	1.88	4.86	1,146
Borgo Maggiore	Borgo	3.48	9.01	4,248
Città	San Marino	2.74	7.09	4,226
Chiesanuova	Chiesanuova	2.11	5.46	700
Domagnano	Domagnano	2.56	6.62	1,828
Faetano	Faetano	2.99	7.75	746
Fiorentino	Fiorentino	2.53	6.56	1,450
Montegiardino	Montegiardino	1.28	3.31	570
Serravalle/Dogano	Serravalle	4.07	10.53	6,878
TOTAL		23.63*	61.19	21,792

Demography

Population (1985): 22,300.
Density (1985): persons per sq mi 943.9, persons per sq km 364.4.
Urban-rural (1985): urban 90.5%; rural 9.5%.
Sex distribution (1985): male 49.99%; female 50.01%.
Age breakdown (1985): under 15, 19.4%; 15–29, 25.0%; 30–44, 20.7%; 45–59, 17.6%; 60–74, 13.0%; 75 and over, 4.3%.
Population projection: (1990) 23,000; (2000) 25,000.
Doubling time: not applicable; natural population growth is negligible, averaging only 0.3% during 1980–84.
Ethnic composition (1985): Sammarinesi 88.0%; Italian 11.7%; other 0.3%.
Religious affiliation (1980): Roman Catholic 95.2%; no religion 3.0%; other 1.8%.
Major cities (1985): Serravalle/Dogano 4,672; San Marino 4,587; Murata 1,290; Domagnano 871.

Vital statistics

Birth rate per 1,000 population (1984): 10.0 (world avg. 29.0); (1981) legitimate 96.5%; illegitimate 3.5%.
Death rate per 1,000 population (1984): 7.0 (world avg. 11.0).
Natural increase rate per 1,000 population (1984): 3.0 (world avg. 18.0).
Total fertility rate (avg. births per childbearing woman): n.a.
Marriage rate per 1,000 population (1984): 8.5.
Divorce rate per 1,000 population: negligible.
Life expectancy at birth (1980–85): male 70.7 years; female 76.2 years.
Major causes of death per 100,000 population (1984): malignant neoplasms (cancers) 265.4; diseases of the circulatory system 224.9; accidents, violence, and suicide 31.5.

National economy

Budget (1983). Revenue: Lit150,638,000,000 (mainly receipts from postage stamp sales, tourism, and customs duties [collected by Italy and paid as a subsidy]). Expenditures: Lit150,638,000,000 (no breakdown available).
Public debt: n.a.
Tourism: tourist arrivals (1984) 2,787,986; receipts from visitors (1983) U.S.$56,454,000; expenditures by nationals abroad, n.a.
Gross national product (at current market prices; 1980): U.S.$176,760,000 (U.S.$8,207 per capita).

Structure of labour force (1985)		
	labour force	% of labour force
Agriculture	501	4.9
Manufacturing	3,801	37.0
Construction and public utilities	908	8.8
Transportation and communication	142	1.4
Trade	1,529	14.9
Finance and insurance	163	1.6
Services	486	4.7
Public administration and defense	2,747	26.7
TOTAL	10,275	100.0

Production (metric tons except as noted). Agriculture, forestry, fishing (1976): wheat 1,951; barley 456; grapes 1,788; livestock (number of live animals; 1975) 1,827 cattle (of which 539 dairy cattle), 1,151 pigs, 142 sheep, 81 horses, 12,045 rabbits, 50,040 quails, 19,479 chickens. Manufacturing (1984): processed meats 503,862 kilograms, of which beef 241,787 kilograms, swine 190,783 kilograms; milk 1,518,000 litres; cheese 91,657 kilograms; butter 15,849 kilograms; yogurt 10,279 kilograms; other major products include textiles, cement, paper, leather, bricks, pottery, tiles, postage stamps, gold and silver jewelry, paints, synthetic rubber, and furniture. Construction (new units completed; 1984): urban residential 155; nonresidential 55. Energy production (consumption): all electrical power is imported via electrical grid from Italy, consumption n.a.; coal (metric tons; 1983) none (n.a); crude petroleum (barrels; 1983) none (n.a.); petroleum products (metric tons; 1983) none (n.a.); natural gas (cu m; 1983) none (n.a.).
Population economically active (1985): total 11,145; participation rate of total population 50.1% (female 39.9%, unemployed 6.5%).

Price and earnings indexes (1980 = 100)					
	1981	1982	1983	1984	1985
Consumer price index	139.2	150.1	165.1	174.9	188.7
Monthly earnings index					

Household income and expenditure. Total number of households (1985): 7,653; average household size (1985) 3.0; average annual income per household: n.a.; source of income: n.a.; expenditure (1980): food, beverages, and tobacco 33.5%, transportation and communication 12.6%, clothing and footwear 10.2%, furniture, appliances, and goods and services for the home 8.0%, recreation, entertainment, education, and culture 7.9%, housing, fuel, and electrical energy 7.6%, health and sanitary services 4.0%, other goods and services 15.7%.
Land use (1983): forested 37%; agricultural and under permanent cultivation 17%; meadows and pastures 23%; built-on, wasteland, and other 23%.

Foreign trade

Balance of trade: n.a. San Marino and Italy form a single customs area; separate figures for San Marino are not available.
Imports (1982): manufactured goods of all kinds, oil, and gold. *Major import source:* Italy.
Exports (1982): wine, wheat, woolen goods, furniture, wood, ceramics, building stone, dairy products, meat, and postage stamps. *Major export destination:* Italy.

Transport and communications

Transport. Railroads: none (nearest rail terminal is at Rimini, Italy, 17 mi [27 km] northeast). Roads (1980): total length 137 mi, 220 km. Vehicles (1985): passenger cars 14,745; trucks and buses 1,699. Merchant marine: vessels (100 gross tons and over) none. Air transport: airports with scheduled flights, none; however, there is a heliport—passenger and cargo traffic, n.a.
Communications. Daily newspapers (1984): none; however, there are several journals of lesser frequency; total circulation of the oldest of these, *Il Nuovo Titano,* 1,300; circulation per 1,000 population 167. Radio (1980): total number of receivers 10,000 (1 per 2.6 persons). Television (1981): total number of receivers 6,000 (1 per 4.2 persons). Telephones (1983): 9,576 (1 per 2.9 persons).

Education and health

Education (1984–85)				
	schools	teachers	students	student/teacher ratio
Primary (age 6–10)	13	151	1,440	9.5
Secondary (age 11–18)	3	123	965	7.8
Vocational	...	...	431	...
Teacher tr.§	...	...	58	...
Higher	...	...	456 ‖	...

Educational attainment (1985). Percent of the adult labour force having: basic literacy or primary education 41.0%; secondary 28.3%; some postsecondary 15.2%; higher degree 5.6%. *Literacy* (1983): total population over age 14 literate 17,329 (97.6%); males literate 8,782 (97.7%); females literate 8,547 (97.6%).
Health: physicians (1979) 10¶ (1 per 2,030 persons); hospital beds (1980) 61 (1 per 338 persons); infant mortality rate per 1,000 live births (1984) 4.5.
Food (1978–80): daily per capita caloric intake 3,643 (vegetable products 75%, animal products 25%); 145% FAO recommended minimum requirement.

Military

Total active duty personnel (1984): none⁹. *Military expenditure as a percent of national budget* (1984): 2.0% (world *c.* 19%); per capita expenditure (1984) *c.* U.S.$2.

São Tomé and Príncipe

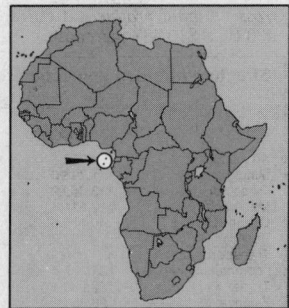

Official name: República democrática de São Tomé e Príncipe (Democratic Republic of São Tomé and Príncipe).
Form of government: republic with one legislative house (National People's Assembly [40]).
Head of state and government: President.
Capital: São Tomé.
Official language: Portuguese.
Official religion: Roman Catholicism.
Monetary unit: 1 dobra (Db) = 100 centavos; valuation (Oct. 21, 1985) 1 U.S.$ = Db42.64; 1 £ = Db61.14.

Area and population

Islands Districts	Capitals	area sq mi	area sq km	population 1984 estimate
Príncipe	São António	55	142	5,671
Paguê	Príncipe	55	142	5,671
São Tomé		332	859	98,693
Aqua Grande	São Tomé	7	17	34,997
Cantagalo	Santana	46	119	11,270
Caué	São João Angolares	103	267	4,972
Lemba	Neves	88	229	8,537
Lobata	Guadalupe	41	105	12,717
Mé-zóchi	Trinidade	47	122	26,200
TOTAL		387	1,001	104,364

Demography

Population (1985): 106,500.
Density (1985): persons per sq mi 275.2, persons per sq km 106.4.
Urban–rural (1981): urban 33.5%; rural 66.5%.
Sex distribution (1981): male 49.72%; female 50.28%.
Age breakdown (1981): under 15, 46.3%; 15–29, 25.0%; 30–44, 11.6%; 45–59, 10.0%; 60–74, 5.3%; 75 and over, 1.8%.
Population projection: (1990) 114,000; (2000) 144,000.
Doubling time: 50 years.
Ethnic composition: mestiços, angolares (descendants of Angolan slaves), forros (descendants of freed slaves), serviçais (alien contract labourers), tongas (children of serviçais), and Europeans.
Religious affiliation (1985): Roman Catholic, about 80%; remainder mostly Protestant, predominantly Seventh-day Adventist and an indigenous Evangelical Church.
Major city (1984): São Tomé 34,997.

Vital statistics

Birth rate per 1,000 population (1982): 38.7 (world avg. 29.0); legitimate, n.a.; illegitimate, n.a.
Death rate per 1,000 population (1982): 10.2 (world avg. 11.0).
Natural increase rate per 1,000 population (1982): 28.5 (world avg. 18.0).
Total fertility rate (avg. births per childbearing woman; 1980–85): 5.2.
Marriage rate per 1,000 population: n.a.
Divorce rate per 1,000 population: n.a.
Life expectancy at birth (1980–85): male 47.1 years; female 50.0 years.
Major causes of death per 100,000 population (1972): senility without mention of psychosis, and ill-defined and unknown causes 367.5; gastritis, duodenitis, enteritis, and colitis, except diarrhea of the newborn, 95.5; pneumonia 62.4; heart disease 51.7; malaria 49.1.

National economy

Budget (1977). Revenue: Db414,300,000 (indirect taxes 26.1%, direct taxes 7.5%, export duties 6.3%, import duties 13.5%, other sources 66.4%). Expenditures: Db452,600,000 (services 64.4%, wages and salaries 46.0%, interest on the public debt 0.5%).
Tourism: virtually nonexistent in the mid-1980s, although development planners expected to establish a centre at Praia das Concas (on São Tomé), with an initial capacity of 400 tourists per week.
Public debt (external, outstanding; 1983): U.S.$60,600,000.
Production (metric tons except as noted). Agriculture, forestry, fishing (1984): coconuts 42,000, cacao 7,000, copra 5,000, bananas 3,000, cassava 3,000, palmetto 3,000, vegetables and melons 3,000, cereals 1,000, palm kernels 500; livestock (number of live animals) 4,000 goats, 3,000 cattle, 3,000 pigs, 2,000 sheep, 123,000 poultry; roundwood 6,000 cu m*; fish catch 4,050*, of which marine fish 3,000, shellfish 70). Mining and quarrying: some quarrying to support local construction industry. Manufacturing (1975): bread and biscuits 1,831; palm oil 1,100†; soap 470; ice 191; limes 22; corn (maize) flour 18; sawn wood 3,000 cu m*; other products include soft drinks, beer, clothing, and bricks and clay products. Construction: (1972) buildings authorized 44 (5,561 sq m, of which residential 3,698, mixed residential–commercial 1,361, commercial 502). Energy production (consumption): electricity (kW-hr; 1983) 15,000,000 (15,000,000); coal, none (n.a.); crude petroleum, none (n.a.); petroleum products (metric tons; 1983) none (11,000); natural gas (cu m; 1983) none (n.a.).
Household income and expenditure: average household size: n.a.; income per household: n.a.; sources of income: n.a.; expenditure: n.a.
Land use (1983): meadows and pastures 1.0%; agricultural and under permanent cultivation 37.5%; forest, built-on, wasteland, and other 61.5%.

Gross national product (at current market prices; 1983): U.S.$31,700,000 (U.S.$310 per capita).

Structure of gross domestic product and labour force

	1981 in value Db'000,000	1981 % of total value	1981 labour force	1981 % of labour force
Agriculture	207.3	31.3	16,486	54.4
Mining	—	—	—	—
Manufacturing	28.7	4.3	1,629	5.4
Construction	13.3	2.0	1,805	6.0
Public utilities	3.0	0.5	287	1.0
Transportation and communication	24.7	3.7	1,036	3.4
Trade	108.0	16.3	2,040	6.7
Pub. admin., defense	112.7	17.0	5,902	19.5
Finance			187	0.6
Services	165.4†	24.9†	1,235	4.1
Other				
TOTAL	663.1	100.0	30,289	100.0

Population economically active (1981): total 30,585; participation rate of total population 31.7% (female 20.4%, unemployed, n.a.).

Price and earnings indexes (1974=100)

	1974	1975	1976	1977	1978	1979
Consumer price index	100.0	...	...	126.0	139.0	146.7
Earnings index	...	...	...	...	...	...

Foreign trade

Balance of trade (current prices)

	1974	1975	1976	1977	1978	1979
U.S.$'000,000	4.2	6.2	−5.2	−9.8	−8.7	−10.5
% of total	11.6%	11.8%	11.5%	34.2%	33.7%	36.8%

Imports (1983): Db779,864,000 (wine and beer, wheat flour, rice, petroleum products, and textiles). *Major import sources:* Portugal 27.4%; East Germany 24.0%; Belgium–Luxembourg 15.9%; Angola 11.5%; The Netherlands 4.3%; West Germany 4.0%; United Kingdom 3.3%; Soviet Union 2.5%.
Exports (1983): Db365,550,000 (cacao, copra, bananas, palm kernels, coffee, and palmetto). *Major export destinations:* East Germany 50.5%; The Netherlands, 29.9%; Portugal 13.4%; Cameroon 3.2%; West Germany 2.0%.

Transport and communications

Transport. Railroads: none. Roads (1975): total length 179 mi, 288 km (paved 69%). Vehicles (1975): passenger cars 1,774; trucks and buses 265. Merchant marine (1984): vessels (100 gross tons and over) 2; total deadweight tonnage 993. Air transport (1975): passenger arrivals 10,050, passenger departures 9,240; short ton cargo loaded 19, unloaded 112; metric ton cargo loaded 28, unloaded 164; airports (1985) with scheduled flights 1.
Communications. Daily newspapers: none; 2 government weeklies (circulation, n.a.). Radio (1984): total number of receivers 25,000 (1 per 4.2 persons). Television: none. Telephones (1983): 2,187 (1 per 46.3 persons).

Education and health

Education (1984–85)

	schools	teachers	students	student/ teacher ratio
Primary (age 6–13)	63	517	19,086	36.9
Secondary (age 14–18)	11	300	6,186	20.6
Voc., teacher tr.	2	35	370	10.6
Higher			700‡	

Educational attainment, n.a. *Literacy* (1981): total population over age 15 literate 28,114 (54.2%); males literate 17,689 (70.2%); females literate 10,425 (39.1%).
Health (1978): physicians 43 (1 per 2,000 persons); hospital beds 665 (1 per 129 persons); infant mortality rate per 1,000 live births (1983) 69.0.
Food (1980–82): daily per capita caloric intake 2,351 (vegetable products 93%, animal products 7%); 100% of FAO recommended minimum requirement.

Military

Total active duty personnel (1985): 700 Angolan and 200 Cuban troops (distribution by branch of service, n.a.). *Military expenditure as percent of GNP* (1980): 1.8% (world 5.6%).

*1983. †1982. ‡Students abroad, 1982–83.

Saudi Arabia

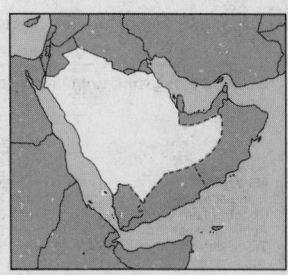

Official name: al-Mamlakah al-'Arabīyah as-Sa'ūdīyah (Kingdom of Saudi Arabia).
Form of government: monarchy.
Chief of state: King.
Head of government: Prime Minister.
Capital: Riyadh.
Official language: Arabic.
Official religion: Islām.
Monetary unit: 1 Saudi riyal (SRls) = 100 halalah; valuation (Oct. 21, 1985) 1 U.S.$ = SRls3.65; 1 £ = SRls5.24.

Area and population

Administrative Districts	Capitals	area sq mi	sq km	population 1974 census*
'Asīr	Abha	...	...	682,000
al-Bāḥah	al-Bāḥah	...	...	186,000
Ḥā'il	Ḥā'il	...	...	260,000
al-Ḥudūd ash-Shamāliyah	'Ar'ar	...	...	129,000
al-Jawf	Sakākah	...	...	65,000
Jīzān	Jīzān	...	...	403,000
al-Madīnah	Medina (al-Madīnah)	...	...	519,000
Makkah	Mecca (Makkah)	...	...	1,754,000
Najrān	Najrān	...	...	148,000
al-Qaṣim	Buraydah	...	...	316,000
al-Qurayyāt	an-Nabk	...	...	31,000
ar-Riyāḍ	Riyadh (ar-Riyāḍ)	...	...	1,272,000
ash-Sharqīyah	ad-Dammām	...	...	770,000
Tabūk	Tabūk	...	...	194,000
TOTAL		865,000	2,240,000	6,939,000†

Demography

Population (1985): 11,240,000.
Density (1985): persons per sq mi 13.0, persons per sq km 5.0.
Urban–rural (1985): urban 73.0%; rural 27.0%.
Sex distribution (1985): male 54.59%; female 45.41%.
Age breakdown (1980): under 15, 43.9%; 15–29, 26.9%; 30–44, 16.3%; 45–59, 8.4%; 60–74, 3.8%; 75 and over, 0.7%.
Population projection: (1990) 13,724,000; (2000) 20,327,000.
Doubling time: 17.3 years.
Ethnic composition (1974): Saudi 88.2%; North Yemeni 5.6%; South Yemeni 1.0%; other 5.2%.
Religious affiliation (1980): Muslim (mostly Sunnī) 98.8%; Christian 0.8%; other 0.4%.
Major cities (1974): Riyadh 1,308,000‡; Jidda (Jiddah) 1,500,000§; Mecca 366,801; aṭ-Ṭa'if 204,857.

Vital statistics

Birth rate per 1,000 population (1980–85): 43.7 (world avg. 29.0).
Death rate per 1,000 population (1980–85): 12.6 (world avg. 11.0).
Natural increase rate per 1,000 population (1980–85): 31.1 (world avg. 18.0).
Total fertility rate (avg. births per childbearing woman; 1980–85): 3.5.
Marriage rate per 1,000 population: n.a.
Divorce rate per 1,000 population: n.a.
Life expectancy at birth (1980–85): male 54.5 years; female 57.6 years.
Major causes of death per 100,000 population: n.a.; however, major diseases are cholera, cerebrospinal meningitis, yellow fever, typhoid, tuberculosis, lung infections, and asphyxia.

National economy

Budget (1985–86). Revenue: SRls200,000,000,000 (oil 77.1%). Expenditures: SRls200,000,000,000 (defense and security 32.0%, public administration and other government spending 15.0%, human resources development 11.9%, transport and communications 8.3%).
Public debt: none.
Tourism (1981): receipts from visitors U.S.$1,573,000,000; expenditures by nationals abroad U.S.$2,761,000,000.
Production (metric tons except as noted). Agriculture, forestry, fishing (1984): wheat 1,300,000, watermelons 480,000, dates 450,000, tomatoes 350,000, sorghum 87,000, grapes 75,000, onions 75,000, barley 12,000, millet 8,000, corn (maize) 4,000; livestock (number of live animals) 3,600,000 sheep, 2,350,000 goats, 550,000 cattle, 165,000 camels, 110,000 asses, 32,000,000 poultry; fish catch 26,425 ‖. Mining and quarrying (1983): hydraulic cement 8,126,000; lime 9,000; gypsum 1,000. Manufacturing (1984): methanol 956,000; urea 862,650; steel 725,000. Construction (value added in SRls; 1981): 51,689,000,000. Energy production (consumption): electricity (kW-hr; 1984) 37,000,000,000 (37,000,000,000); coal, n.a. (n.a.); crude petroleum (barrels; 1984) 1,674,900,000 (265,938,000 ‖); petroleum products (metric tons; 1983) 40,365,000 (24,699,000); natural gas (cu m; 1983) 1,281,361,000 (1,281,361,000).
Land use (1983): forested 0.7%; meadows and pastures 39.5%; agricultural and under permanent cultivation 0.5%; other, built-on, and waste 59.3%.
Population economically active (1980): total 2,330,600; participation rate of total population 27.9% (female, n.a.; unemployed, n.a.).

Price and earnings indexes (1980 = 100)

	1978	1979	1980	1981	1982	1983	1984
Consumer price index	94.6	96.4	100.0	102.7	103.8	104.8	103.7
Monthly earnings index	...	...	...	...	...	...	...

Gross national product (at current market prices; 1983): U.S.$127,080,000,-000 (U.S.$10,437 per capita).

Structure of gross domestic product and labour force

	1984–85 in value SRls'000,000	% of total value	1980 labour force	% of labour force
Agriculture	7,056.3	2.5	395,100	16.9
Mining	1,795.0	0.6	62,100	2.7
Oil sector	113,289.9	39.9		
Manufacturing	12,511.4	4.4	77,500	3.3
Construction	40,170.6	14.1	591,900	25.4
Public utilities	794.7	0.3	29,500	1.3
Transportation and communication	22,177.6	7.8	162,500	7.0
Trade	27,069.1	9.5	361,400	15.5
Finance	20,631.3	7.3		
Pub. admin., defense	30,944.2	10.9	650,600	27.9
Services and other	7,674.8	2.7		
TOTAL	284,114.9	100.0	2,330,600	100.0

Household income and expenditure. Average household size (1980) 5.5; income per household: n.a.; source of income: n.a.; expenditure (1980): food 52.2%, housing 17.2%, clothing 6.6%, furniture and utensils 5.9%, transport and communication 4.5%, health care 2.1%.

Foreign trade

Balance of trade (current prices)

	1978	1979	1980	1981	1982	1983	1984
SRls'000,000	+59.2	+110.6	+238.9	+262.9	+120.5	+49.4	+37
% of total	29.9%	40.4%	54.4%	52.2%	30.2%	17.6%	12.7%

Imports (1984): SRls127,698,000,000 (machinery and appliances 18.5%, foodstuffs 16.2%, transport equipment 13.7%, textiles and clothing 9.3%). *Major import sources:* Japan 18.5%; United States 18.3%; Italy 7.9%; France 7.6%; West Germany 7.4%; United Kingdom 6.1%; The Netherlands 2.4%; Switzerland 2.2%; Singapore 2.1%; Sweden 1.2%; Australia 1.2%; Canada 0.9%.
Exports (1984): SRls165,060,000,000 (crude petroleum 89.7%, refined petroleum 10.3%). *Major export destinations:* Japan 31.3%; United States 8.5%; Singapore 5.7%; France 4.6%; Italy 4.2%; Brazil 3.2%; Indonesia 2.9%; West Germany 2.1%; Spain 2.1%; Thailand 1.9%; United Kingdom 1.5%; Pakistan 1.2%.

Transport and communications

Transport. Railroads (1983): route length 359 mi¶, 578 km¶; passenger-mi 53,935,000, passenger-km 86,800,000; short ton-mi cargo 133,084,000, metric ton-km cargo 194,300,000. Roads (1983–84): total length 44,705 mi, 71,946 km (paved 39%). Vehicles (1983): passenger cars 1,856,398; trucks and buses 1,704,300. Merchant marine (1984): vessels (100 gross tons and over) 422; total deadweight tonnage 6,475,117. Air transport (1983): passenger-mi 9,309,256,000, passenger-km 14,981,824,000; short ton-mi cargo 1,253,634,000, metric ton-km cargo 1,830,275,000; airports (1985) with scheduled flights 18.
Communications. Daily newspapers (1985): total number 10; total circulation 638,000; circulation per 1,000 population 56.8. Radio (1984): total number of receivers 2,800,000 (1 per 3.9 persons). Television (1984): total number of receivers 2,500,000 (1 per 4.4 persons). Telephones (1983): 1,274,803 (1 per 8.2 persons).

Education and health

Education (1983–84)

	schools	teachers	students	student/ teacher ratio
Primary (age 6–12)	7,269	76,615	1,161,096	15.2
Secondary (age 13–18)	3,085	35,947	496,778	13.8
Voc., teacher tr.	26	881	2,371	2.7
Higher	73º	8,631	82,369	9.5

Educational attainment, n.a. *Literacy* (1980): total population over age 15 literate 1,234,200 (24.6%); males literate 961,500 (34.5%); females literate 272,700 (12.2%).
Health (1983): physiciansδ 6,453 (1 per 1,615 persons); hospital bedsδ 15,387 (1 per 677 persons); infant mortality rate per 1,000 live births (1975–80) 121.
Food (1980–82): daily per capita caloric intake 2,969 (vegetable products 82%, animal products 18%); 122% of FAO recommended minimum requirement.

Military

Total active duty personnel (1984): 51,500 (army 67.9%, navy 4.9%, air force 27.2%). *Military expenditure as percent of GNP* (1983): 24.3% (world 6.1%); per capita expenditure U.S.$2,508.

*Official census data are of uncertain reliability; external estimates poorly founded. Total population may number as few as 4,000,000. †Total includes 210,000 nomads not distributable by district. ‡1981 estimate. §1983 estimate. ‖ 1983. ¶1982. ºIncludes colleges, institutions, and universities. δMinistry of Health only.

Senegal

Official name: République du Sénégal (Republic of Senegal).
Form of government: republic with one legislative house (National Assembly [120]).
Head of state and government: President.
Capital: Dakar.
Official language: French.
Official religion: none.
Monetary unit: 1 CFA franc (CFAF) = 100 centimes; valuation* (Oct. 21, 1985) 1 U.S.$ = CFAF402.02; 1 £ = CFAF576.50.

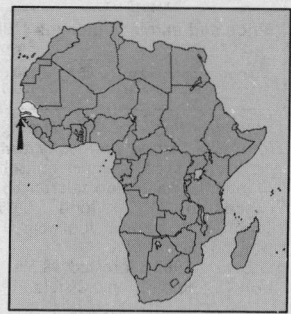

Area and population

Regions	Capitals	area sq mi	area sq km	population 1979 estimate
Cap-Vert	Dakar	212	550	1,119,000
Casamance	Ziguinchor	10,946	28,350	779,000
Diourbel	Diourbel	1,683	4,359	451,000
Fleuve	Saint-Louis	17,038	44,127	575,000
Louga	Louga	11,270	29,188	444,000
Sénégal Oriental	Tambacounda	23,012	59,602	301,000
Sine-Saloum	Kaolack	9,245	23,945	1,087,000
Thiès	Thiès	2,549	6,601	752,000
TOTAL		75,955	196,722	5,508,000

Demography

Population (1985): 6,520,000.
Density (1985): persons per sq mi 85.8, persons per sq km 33.1.
Urban–rural (1980): urban 25.4%; rural 74.6%.
Sex distribution (1985): male 49.49%; female 50.51%.
Age breakdown (1985): under 15, 45.0%; 15–29, 25.8%; 30–44, 15.4%; 45–59, 9.0%; 60–74, 4.1%; 75 and over, 0.7%.
Population projection: (1990) 7,430,000; (2000) 9,747,000.
Doubling time: 26 years.
Ethnic composition (1980): Wolof 35%; Serer 16%; Fulani (Peul) 14%; Tukulor 9%; Diola (Jola) 9%; Mandingo 7%; other 10%.
Religious affiliation (1980): Sunnī Muslim 91.0%; Roman Catholic 5.6%; tribal religionist 3.2%; other 0.2%.
Major cities (1979): Dakar 978,553; Thiès 126,886; Kaolack 115,679; Saint-Louis 96,594.

Vital statistics

Birth rate per 1,000 population (1980–85): 47.9 (world avg. 29.0).
Death rate per 1,000 population (1980–85): 21.1 (world avg. 11.0).
Natural increase rate per 1,000 population (1980–85): 26.8 (world avg. 18.0).
Total fertility rate (avg. births per childbearing woman; 1980–85): 6.5.
Marriage rate per 1,000 population: n.a.
Divorce rate per 1,000 population: n.a.
Life expectancy at birth (1980–85): male 41.8 years; female 45.0 years.
Major causes of death per 100,000 population (officially confirmed transmissible diseases only; 1978): malaria 12.7; measles 11.4, tetanus 5.5, leprosy 4.8.

National economy

Budget (1985–86). Revenue: CFAF163,856,500,000 (no breakdown available). Expenditures: CFAF153,012,100,000 (education 28.3%, defense 18.5%, public health 6.7%, economy and finance 6.6%)
Production (metric tons except as noted). Agriculture, forestry, fishing (1984): sugarcane 800,000, peanuts (groundnuts) 682,000, millet 471,000, paddy rice 136,000, corn (maize) 98,000, cotton 56,000, tomatoes 40,-000, onions 30,000; livestock (number of live animals) 2,200,000 cattle, 2,100,000 sheep, 1,000,000 goats; roundwood 3,894,000 cu m†; fish catch 212,895†. Mining and quarrying (1984): calcium phosphate 1,932,000; aluminum phosphate 279,000; salt 140,000†. Manufacturing (1981): cement 386,000; canned fish 15,200; cigarettes 2,400; nitrogenous fertilizers 6,000. Construction (authorized; 1982): residential 203,600 sq m; nonresidential 44,500 sq m. Energy production (consumption): electricity (kW-hr; 1983) 631,000,000 (631,000,000); coal, none (n.a.); crude petroleum (barrels; 1983) none (2,140,000); petroleum products (metric tons; 1983) 278,000 (682,000); natural gas, none (n.a.).
Land use (1983): forested 30.9%; meadows and pastures 29.7%; agricultural and under permanent cultivation 27.2%; other 12.2%.
Population economically active (1980): total 2,468,083; participation rate of total population 43.4% (female [1976] 39.8%; unemployed [1981] 2.9%).

Price and earnings indexes (1980 = 100)

	1978	1979	1980	1981	1982	1983	1984
Consumer price index	83.8	92.0	100.0	105.9	124.2	138.7	155.1
Hourly earnings index	80.0	80.0	100.0	105.0	105.0	113.6	113.6

Household income and expenditure§. Average household size (1975) 8.6; average annual income per household CFAF1,105,800 (U.S.$5,160); sources of income: wages and salaries 51.6%, remittances and gifts 17.5%, pensions, social security, and related benefits 12.5%, other 18.4%; expenditure (1979): food and tobacco 57.5%, housing, maintenance, and utilities 18.4%, clothing 11.9%, transport 5.4%, other 6.8%.
Gross national product (at current market prices; 1983): U.S.$2,730,000,000 (U.S.$440 per capita).

Structure of gross domestic product and labour force

	1983 in value CFAF'000,000,000	1983 % of total value	1980 labour force‡	1980 % of labour force
Agriculture	204.7	21.0	8,514	7.9
Mining			5,039	4.7
Manufacturing	249.4	25.5	23,647	22.1
Public utilities			5,726	5.3
Construction			11,723	10.9
Transportation and communication			17,003	15.9
Trade			18,599	17.4
Finance	523.6	53.5	4,208	3.9
Services			12,705	11.9
Pub. admin., defense, and other				
TOTAL	977.7	100.0	107,164	100.0

Public debt (external, outstanding; 1983): U.S.$1,504,900,000.
Tourism: receipts from visitors (1983) U.S.$63,000,000; expenditures by nationals abroad (1982) U.S.$42,225,000.

Foreign trade

Balance of trade (current prices)

	1979	1980	1981	1982	1983	1984
CFAF'000,000,000	−84.1	−121.5	−156.5	−145.9	−174.4	−229.1
% of total	27.0%	37.6%	36.5%	28.8%	27.5%	30.9%

Imports (1982): CFAF325,935,000,000 (basic manufactures 21.1%, crude petroleum 20.2%, mechanical equipment 10.3%, cereals 9.8%, chemical products 8.7%, motor vehicles 5.5%). *Major import sources* (1984): France 27.6%; United States 9.4%; Brazil 8.4%; Nigeria 6.6%; Thailand 6.0%
Exports (1982): CFAF180,037,000,000 (petroleum products 25.5%, peanut oil 17.4%, calcium phosphate 10.1%, canned fish 6.5%, fresh or frozen fish 6.1%, peanut oilcake 5.6%, fresh or frozen crustaceans 4.1%). *Major export destinations* (1984): France 30.7%; Ivory Coast 5.1%; United Kingdom 5.0%; Italy 4.0%; Mauritania 4.0%.

Transport and communications

Transport. Railroads (1983): route length 642 mi, 1,033 km; passenger-mi 82,600,000, passenger-km 133,000,000; short ton-mi cargo 212,000,000¶, metric ton-km cargo 309,000,000¶. Roads (1981): total length 9,134 mi, 14,700 km (paved 25%). Vehicles (1980): passenger cars 50,875; trucks and buses 27,767. Merchant marine (1984): vessels (100 gross tons and over) 135; total deadweight tonnage 33,583. Air transportǫ (1983): passenger-mi 23,785,000, passenger-km 208,106,000; short ton-mi cargo 26,218,000, metric ton-km cargo 38,278,000; airports (1985) with scheduled flights 3.
Communications. Daily newspapers (1984): total number 1; total circulation 31,000; circulation per 1,000 population 4.9. Radio (1984): total number of receivers 321,000 (1 per 20 persons). Television (1984): total number of receivers 51,000 (1 per 124 persons). Telephones (1979): 40,218 (1 per 137 persons).

Education and health

Education (1979–80)

	schools	teachers	students	student/ teacher ratio
Primary (age 6–11)ŏ	1,672	9,842	419,748	42.6
Secondary□ (age 12–18)	187	2,346	78,695	33.5
Voc., teacher tr.◊	32	1,475	9,632	6.5
Higher◊	9	571	10,309	18.0

Educational attainment (1970). Percent of population over age 6 having: no formal schooling 95.3%; primary education 3.9%; secondary 0.7%; higher 0.1%. *Literacy* (1980): total population over age 15 literate 1,274,000 (22.5%); males literate 1,755,000 (31.0%); females literate 804,000 (14.2%).
Health: physicians (1981) 449 (1 per 13,000 persons); hospital beds (1978) 7,092 (1 per 760 persons); infant mortality rate per 1,000 live births (1980–85) 141.0.
Food (1980–82): daily per capita caloric intake 2,364 (vegetable products 92%, animal products 8%); 99%△ of FAO recommended minimum requirement.

Military

Total active duty personnel (1984): 9,700 (army 87.6%, navy 7.2%, air force 5.2%). *Military expenditure as percent of GNP* (1983): 2.3% (world 6.1%); per capita expenditure U.S.$9.

*The value of the CFA franc is pegged to the French (metropolitan) franc. †1983. ‡Private sector only. §Among traditional African households in Dakar. ‖ In 1982 crude petroleum imports rose to 20.2%. ¶1980. ǫInternational flights only. ŏ1981. □Includes middle school. ◊1978–79.

Seychelles

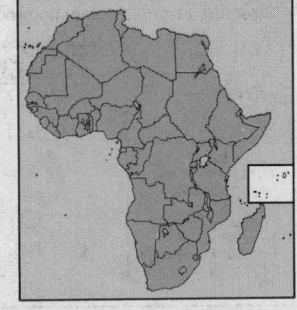

Official name: Republic of Seychelles (English); République des Seychelles (French); Repiblik Sesel (Creole).
Form of government: unitary single-party republic with one legislative house (People's Assembly [25]).
Head of state and government: President.
Capital: Victoria.
Official languages: English; French; Creole.
Official religion: none.
Monetary unit: 1 Seychelles rupee (SR) = 100 cents; valuation (Oct. 21, 1985) 1 U.S.$ = SR6.71; 1 £ = SR9.62.

Area and population

| Central (granitic) group | Capital | area | | population |
		sq mi	sq km	1984 estimate
La Digue and satellites		6	15	2,000
Mahé and satellites	Victoria	61	158	57,400
Praslin and satellites		16	42	4,650
Silhouette		8	20	200
Other islands		2	4	50
Outer (coralline) islands		83	214	400
TOTAL		175*	453	64,700

Demography

Population (1985): 65,100.
Density (1985): persons per sq mi 372.0, persons per sq km 143.7.
Urban–rural (1977): urban 37.2%; rural 62.8%.
Sex distribution (1985): male 50.26%; female 49.74%.
Age breakdown (1985): under 15, 36.3%; 15–29, 31.5%; 30–44, 12.9%; 45–64, 12.9%; 65 and over, 6.4%.
Population projection: (1990) 69,600; (2000) 82,400.
Doubling time: 36 years.
Ethnic composition (1980): Seychellois 98.0%; non-Seychellois 2.0%.
Religious affiliation (1983): Roman Catholic 96.4%; other 3.6%.
Major city (1977): Victoria 23,012.

Vital statistics

Birth rate per 1,000 population (1984): 26.9 (world avg. 29.0); legitimate 33.2%; illegitimate 66.8%.
Death rate per 1,000 population (1984): 7.5 (world avg. 11.0).
Natural increase rate per 1,000 population (1984): 19.4 (world avg. 18.0).
Total fertility rate (avg. births per childbearing woman; 1984): 3.5.
Marriage rate per 1,000 population (1984): 6.0.
Divorce rate per 1,000 population (1984): 0.8.
Life expectancy at birth (1978–81): male 66.2 years; female 73.5 years.
Major causes of death per 100,000 population (1984): circulatory diseases 146.8; malignant neoplasms (cancers) 92.7; cerebrovascular diseases 64.9; pneumonia 40.2; digestive diseases 38.6; accidents 37.1.

National economy

Budget (1984). Revenue: SR403,600,000 (import duties 33.0%; income tax 24.0%; turnover tax and excise duties 17.3%; nontax revenue 14.7%; public entities 7.6%. Expenditures: SR420,400,000 (general administration 30.4%, of which defense, police, and prisons 14.3%; debt payment 12.2%; education and information 16.7%; health 9.5%; economic services 8.4%).
Tourism (1984): receipts from visitors U.S.$39,021,000; expenditures by nationals abroad U.S.$6,400,000.
Production (metric tons except as noted). Agriculture, forestry, fishing (1984): coconuts 26,000, copra 3,722, mangoes 4,000, bananas 2,000, cinnamon bark 1,378, tea 87; livestock (number of live animals) 14,000 pigs, 4,000 goats, 1,600 cattle, 185,200 chickens; fish catch 4,021. Mining and quarrying (1983): guano 4,500. Manufacturing (1984): beer and stout 37,780 hectolitres; soft drinks 31,600 hectolitres; cigarettes 64,900,000 units. Energy production (consumption): electricity (kW-hr; 1984) 56,500,000 (56,-500,000); coal, none (n.a.); petroleum, none (n.a.); natural gas, none (n.a.).
Gross national product (1983): U.S.$141,631,000 (U.S.$2,200 per capita).

Structure of gross domestic product and labour force

| | 1983 | | 1984 | |
	in value SR'000,000	% of total value	labour force†	% of labour force
Agriculture	83.3	8.3	2,074	11.6
Manufacturing	102.9	10.3	1,767	9.9
Construction and mining	34.1	3.5	1,635	9.1
Public utilities	14.9	1.6	‡	‡
Transp. and commun.	275.7	27.7	2,143	12.0
Trade	189.6	19.1	3,185	17.8
Finance	113.5	11.4	800	4.5
Public admin., defense	177.9	17.9	2,211	12.3
Services	27.3	2.8	4,077‡	22.8‡
Other	−25.8§	−2.6§		
TOTAL	993.4	100.0	17,892	100.0

Population economically active (1984): total 25,221; participation rate of population ages 15–64, 52.1% (female, n.a.; unemployed 23.2%).

Price and earnings indexes (1980 = 100)

	1979	1980	1981	1982	1983	1984	1985
Consumer price index	88.1	100.0	110.6	109.7	116.3	120.9	121.3 ‖
Monthly earnings index	83.0	100.0	112.3	121.6	128.6	134.4	...

Public debt (external, outstanding; 1983): U.S.$41,700,000.
Household income and expenditure. Average household size (1978) 4.6; average annual income per household (1978) SR18,480 (U.S.$2,658); sources of income: wages and salaries 88.8%, agricultural sales 3.8%, pensions 1.9%; expenditure (1984): food 37.3%, beverages and tobacco 18.7%, housing 15.8%, clothing and footwear 9.0%, household and personal goods 7.5%, transportation 4.1%.
Land use (1983): forested 18.5%; agricultural and under permanent cultivation 18.5%; built-on, wasteland, and other 63.0%.

Foreign trade¶

Balance of trade (current prices)

	1979	1980	1981	1982	1983	1984
SR'000,000	−396.2	−496.2	−480.7	−541.2	−456.8	−354.8
% of total	58.8%	64.7%	68.9%	73.0%	62.5%	49.4%

Imports (1984): SR616,383,000 (petroleum, petroleum products, and related materials 30.2%; machinery and transport equipment 18.7%; food, beverages, and tobacco 18.4%; chemicals and related products 5.9%; nonmetallic mineral manufactures 4.3%; textile yarn, fabrics, and finished articles 3.2%). *Major import sources:* Bahrain 16.8%; U.K. 15.9%; South Africa 8.2%; Singapore 7.3%; Djibouti 6.6%; Japan 6.4%; France 6.2%.
Exports (1984): SR181,470,000♀ (petroleum products 78.9%ô; fish 5.6%; copra 4.5%; cinnamon bark 0.6%). *Major export destinations□:* Pakistan 38.6%; Japan 26.1%; Réunion 14.9%; U.K. 4.9%; France 2.7%.

Transport and communications

Transport. Railroads: none. Roads (1985): total length 160 mi, 257 km (paved 60%). Vehicles (1984): passenger cars 3,420; trucks and buses 1,161. Merchant marine (1984): vessels (100 gross tons and over) 3; total deadweight tonnage 321. Air transport (1984): passenger arrivals 65,000, passenger departures 65,000; metric ton cargo unloaded 1,157, metric ton cargo loaded 247; airports (1985) with scheduled flights 1.
Communications. Daily newspapers (1984): total number 2; total circulation 3,400; circulation per 1,000 population 52.5. Radio (1984): total number of receivers 16,000 (1 per 4.3 persons). Television (1984): total number of receivers 3,500 (1 per 18 persons). Telephones (1981): 7,105 (1 per 9 persons).

Education and health

Education (1985)

	schools	teachers	students	student/ teacher ratio
Primary (age 6–15)	27	664	14,444	21.8
Secondary (age 16–18)	2	193	2,435	12.6
Voc., teacher tr.	3	171	1,540	9.0

Educational attainment (1977). Percent of population over age 15 having: no formal schooling 13.7%; primary education 50.1%; some secondary 32.4%; complete secondary 1.4%; postsecondary 1.8%. *Literacy* (1971): total population literate 17,066 (57.3%); males 54.9%; females 59.6%.
Health (1984): physicians 34 (1 per 1,900 persons); hospital beds 359 (1 per 180 persons); infant mortality rate per 1,000 live births 13.8.
Food: daily per capita caloric intake, n.a.

Military

Total active duty personnel (1984): 1,200 (army 83%, navy 8.5%, air force 8.5%). *Military expenditure as percent of GNP* (1982): 5.8% (world 6.0%); per capita expenditure U.S.$129.

*Detail does not add to total given because of rounding. †Employed persons only. ‡Services include public utilities. §Net interest payments by banks. ‖ June. ¶Imports c.i.f. (cost, insurance, freight), exports f.o.b. (free on board). ♀Includes SR160 million of reexports. ôItems reexported. □Domestic export only.

WAYNE SMYTH

Fairy tern (*Sterna nereis*), on Cousin (North Cousin) Island, a private bird sanctuary, in the Seychelles.

Sierra Leone

Official name: Republic of
Sierra Leone.
Form of government: a unitary
single-party republic with one
legislative house (House of
Representatives [104]).
Head of state and government:
President.
Capital: Freetown.
Official language: English.
Official religion: none.
Monetary unit: 1 leone (Le) = 100
cents; valuation (Oct. 21, 1985)
1 U.S.$ = Le5.30; 1 £ = Le7.60.

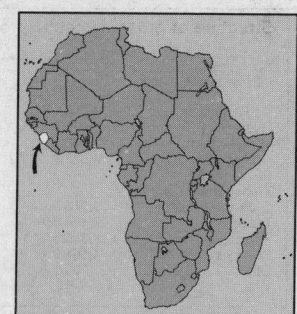

Area and population		area		population
Provinces **Districts**	**Capitals**	sq mi	sq km	1974 census
Eastern Province	Kenema	6,005	15,553	775,931
Kailahun	Kailahun	1,490	3,859	180,365
Kenema	Kenema	2,337	6,053	266,636
Kono	Sefadu	2,178	5,641	328,930
Northern Province	Makeni	13,875	35,936	1,046,158
Bombali	Makeni	3,083	7,985	233,626
Kambia	Kambia	1,200	3,108	155,341
Koinadugu	Kabala	4,680	12,121	158,626
Port Loko	Port Loko	2,208	5,719	292,244
Tonkoliii	Magburaka	2,704	7,003	206,321
Southern Province	Bo	7,604	19,694	596,758
Bo	Bo	2,015	5,219	217,711
Bonthe (incl. Sherbro)	Bonthe	1,339	3,468	87,561
Moyamba	Moyamba	2,665	6,902	188,745
Pujehun	Pujehun	1,585	4,105	102,741
Western Area	Freetown	215	557	316,312
TOTAL		27,699	71,740	2,735,159

Demography

Population (1985): 3,930,000.
Density (1985): persons per sq mi 141.9, persons per sq km 54.8.
Urban–rural (1980): urban 24.5%; rural 75.5%.
Sex distribution (1980): male 49.14%; female 50.86%.
Age breakdown (1980): under 15, 43.9%; 15–29, 26.0%; 30–44, 15.3%; 45–59, 9.5%; 60–74, 4.5%; 75 and over, 0.8%.
Population projection: (1990) 4,550,000; (2000) 6,300,000.
Doubling time: 27 years.
Ethnic composition (1978): Mende 34.4%; Temne 31.3%; Kono 5.6%; Bullom 3.7%; Fulani 3.7%; Koranko 3.7%; Limba 3.7%; Kissi 2.5%; other 11.4%.
Religious affiliation (1980): traditional beliefs 51.5%; Sunnī Muslim 39.4%; Protestant 4.7%; Roman Catholic 2.2%; Anglican 1.2%; other 1.0%.
Major cities (1984): Freetown 500,000*; Koidu-New Sembehun 136,500; Bo 56,000; Kenema 44,800; Makeni 38,100.

Vital statistics

Birth rate per 1,000 population (1980–85): 45.3 (world avg. 29.0); legitimate, n.a.; illegitimate, n.a.
Death rate per 1,000 population (1980–85): 17.4 (world avg. 11.0).
Natural increase rate per 1,000 population (1980–85): 27.9 (world avg. 18.0).
Total fertility rate (avg. births per childbearing woman; 1980–85): 6.1.
Marriage rate per 1,000 population: n.a.
Divorce rate per 1,000 population: n.a.
Life expectancy at birth (1980–85): male 46.7 years; female 50.0 years.
Major causes of death per 100,000 population: n.a.; however, the major diseases are malaria, tuberculosis, leprosy, whooping cough, measles, tetanus, and diarrhea.

National economy

Budget (1982–83). Revenue: Le170,600,000 (tax revenue 83.9%, grants 8.7%, nontax revenue 7.4%). Expenditures: Le416,100,000 (economic services 32.1%, education 14.8%, grants 6.2%).
Public debt (external, outstanding; 1983): U.S.$359,400,000.
Tourism (1981): receipts from visitors U.S.$10,000,000; expenditures by nationals abroad U.S.$10,000,000.
Production (metric tons except as noted). Agriculture, forestry, fishing (1984): rice 450,000, cassava 100,000, palm oil 37,000, palm kernels 30,000, millet 20,000, sorghum 19,000, peanuts (groundnuts) 14,000, sweet potatoes 13,000, cocoa beans 9,000, coffee 7,000; livestock (number of live animals) 330,000 cattle, 310,000 sheep, 160,000 goats, 40,000 pigs, 4,000,000 chickens; roundwood 8,142,000 cu m†; fish catch 53,038†. Mining and quarrying (1984): bauxite 1,041,200; rutile (a titanium ore) 91,289; iron ore 398,000; diamonds 107,359 carats. Manufacturing (1982): salt 52,214; nails 7,768; kerosene 159,000 hectolitres; paints 4,500 hectolitres; beer and stout 62,410 hectolitres; plastic footwear 477,000 pairs; cigarettes 1,156,000 units. Construction (value added in Le; 1981): 53,900,000. Energy production (consumption): electricity (kW-hr; 1983) 292,000,000 (292,000,000); coal, none (n.a.); crude petroleum (barrels; 1983) none (2,120,000); petroleum products (metric tons; 1983) 173,000 (159,000); natural gas, none (n.a.).
Household income and expenditure. Average household size (1980) 4.9; average annual income per household: n.a.; source of income: n.a.; expenditure (1977–78): food, beverages, and tobacco 57.5%, clothing and footwear 13.5%, transport and communication 9.5%, furniture, furnishings,

and household equipment and operation 8.4%, rent, fuel, and power 7.1%, recreation, entertainment, and education 4.0%.
Gross national product (at current market prices; 1983): U.S.$1,230,000,000 (U.S.$380 per capita).

Structure of gross domestic product and labour force				
	1980–81			
	in value Le'000,000	% of total value	labour force‡	% of labour force
Agriculture	373.5	27.9	5,994	8.5
Mining	114.5	8.6	5,774	8.2
Manufacturing	68.0	5.1	7,795	11.0
Construction	55.6	4.2	7,825	11.1
Public utilities	4.4	0.3	1,815	2.6
Transportation and communication	220.5	16.4	7,168	10.2
Trade and finance	279.6	20.9	6,934	9.8
Pub. admin., defense	84.0	6.3 }		
Services }	137.9	10.3 }	27,236	38.6
Other }				
TOTAL	1,338.0	100.0	70,541	100.0

Population economically active (1982): total 1,353,000; participation rate of total population 36.8% (female, n.a.; unemployed [registered] 0.8%).

Price and earnings indexes (1980 = 100)							
	1978	1979	1980	1981	1982	1983	1984
Consumer price index	74.2	90.0	100.0	123.3	161.8	274.2	456.3

Land use (1983): forested 28.6%; meadows and pastures 30.8%; agricultural and under permanent cultivation 24.7%; other 15.9%.

Foreign trade

Balance of trade (current prices)						
	1979	1980	1981	1982	1983	1984
Le'000,000	−129.9	−230.1	−205.9	−231.5	−85.0	−83.6
% of total	24.1%	34.6%	40.0%	45.8%	17.4%	11.1%

Imports (1983): Le286,930,000 (petroleum 30.6%; food 30.5%; minerals, fuels, and lubricants 22.4%§; machinery and transport equipment 17.5%§; manufactured goods classified by materials 15.3%§; chemicals 5.3%§). *Major import sources* (1982 est.): United Kingdom 23.0%; Japan 10.0%; United States 9.0%; West Germany 8.0%.
Exports (1983): Le201,910,000 (diamonds 32.8%; cacao 11.3%; coffee 8.3%). *Major export destinations* (1982 est.): United Kingdom 45.0%; United States 20.0%; The Netherlands 9.0%; West Germany 8.6%.

Transport and communications

Transport. Railroads (1981): length 52 mi, 84 km. Roads (1980): total length 4,635 mi, 7,459 km (paved 16%). Vehicles (1980): passenger cars 16,009; trucks and buses 4,826. Merchant marine (1984): vessels (100 gross tons and over) 23; total deadweight tonnage 1,324. Air transport ‖ (1984): passenger-mi 75,698,000, passenger-km 121,825,000; short ton-mi cargo 1,337,000, metric ton-km cargo 1,952,000; airports (1985) with scheduled flights 4.
Communications. Daily newspapers (1984): total number 1; total circulation 12,000; circulation per 1,000 population 3.4. Radio (1984): total number of receivers 100,000 (1 per 38 persons). Television (1984): total number of receivers 21,700 (1 per 175 persons). Telephones (1979): 10,350 (1 per 309 persons).

Education and health

Education (1982–83)				
	schools	teachers	students	student/ teacher ratio
Primary (age 5–11)	1,196	9,519	290,756	30.5
Secondary (age 12–18)	168	2,835	68,818	24.3
Voc., teacher tr.	6	95	969	10.2
Higher	2	303	1,917	6.3

Educational attainment (1974). Percent of population over age 5 having: no formal schooling 81.3%; primary education 12.1%; secondary 5.9%; higher 0.7%. *Literacy* (1980): total population over age 15 literate 460,300 (23.6%); males literate 294,500 (31.2%); females literate 165,800 (16.5%).
Health (1981): physicians 220 (1 per 16,232 persons); hospital beds 3,752 (1 per 952 persons); infant mortality rate per 1,000 live births (1982) 190.
Food (1980–82): daily per capita caloric intake 1,936 (vegetable products 95%, animal products 5%); 84% of FAO recommended minimum requirement.

Military

Total active duty personnel (1984): 3,100 (army 96.8%, navy 3.2%, air force, none). *Military expenditure as percent of GNP* (1983): 0.9% (world 6.1%); per capita expenditure U.S.$6.2.

*1980. †1983. ‡Includes only those employed in establishments with six or more workers. §1982. ‖ International flights only.

Singapore

Official name: Hsin-chia-p'o
 Kung-ho-kuo (Mandarin Chinese);
 Republik Singapura (Malay);
 Singapore Kudiyarasu (Tamil);
 Republic of Singapore (English).
Form of government: unitary multiparty
 republic with one legislative house
 (Parliament [79]).
Chief of state: President.
Head of government: Prime Minister.
Capital: Singapore.
Official languages: Chinese; Malay;
 Tamil; English.
Official religion: none.
Monetary unit: 1 Singapore dollar
 (S$) = 100 cents; valuation (Oct. 21,
 1985) 1 U.S.$ = S$2.13; 1 £ = S$3.06.

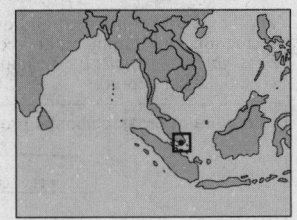

Area and population

Census areas*	area sq mi	area sq km	population 1984 estimate
Central city area	3	8	157,000
City periphery	18	46	942,800
North	7	19	228,100
Northeast	4	9	301,500
West	7	18	413,200
Suburbs	49	127	754,700
East	7	19	195,000
North	13	34	309,900
West	29	74	249,800
Outlying areas	169	437	674,600
East	46	118	301,100
North	53	137	177,500
West	70	182	196,000
TOTAL	239	618	2,529,100

Demography

Population (1985): 2,558,200.
Density (1985): persons per sq mi 10,704, persons per sq km 4,140.
Urban–rural (1985): urban 100.0%.
Sex distribution (1984): male 50.95%; female 49.05%.
Age breakdown (1984): under 15, 24.7%; 15–29, 32.8%; 30–44, 22.7%; 45–59, 12.2%; 60–74, 4.5%; 75 and over, 3.1%.
Population projection: (1990) 2,713,000; (2000) 2,967,000.
Doubling time: 60 years.
Ethnic composition (1984): Chinese 76.5%; Malay 14.8%; Indian† 6.4%; other 2.3%.
Religious affiliation (1980): Taoist 29.3%; Buddhist 26.7%; Muslim 16.3%; Christian 10.3%; Hindu 3.6%; nonreligious 13.2%; other 0.6%.

Vital statistics

Birth rate per 1,000 population (1984): 16.4 (world avg. 29.0).
Death rate per 1,000 population (1984): 5.2 (world avg. 11.0).
Natural increase rate per 1,000 population (1984): 11.2 (world avg. 18.0).
Total fertility rate (avg. births per childbearing woman; 1984): 1.6.
Marriage rate per 1,000 population (1984): 9.9.
Divorce rate per 1,000 population (1984): 6.2.
Life expectancy at birth (1983): male 70.0 years; female 75.0 years.
Major causes of death per 100,000 population (1983): diseases of the circulatory system 182.6, of which heart and hypertensive diseases 124.3; malignant neoplasms (cancers) 109.6; diseases of the respiratory system 80.2, of which pneumonia 47.5; accidents, poisoning, and violence 47.1.

National economy

Budget (1985–86). Revenue: S$10,620,653,000 (income tax 31.1%, property tax 12.1%, customs and excise duties 9.8%, taxes on motor vehicles 7.2%, interest and dividends 6.3%, regulatory charges 4.4%, premiums on land sales 4.2%). Expenditures: S$18,831,300,000 (national development 31.6%, defense 12.8%, education 10.3%, communications and information 6.2%, environment 3.1%, health 3.0%, trade and industry 2.7%).
Public debt (external, outstanding; 1983): U.S.$1,243,600,000.
Tourism (1983): receipts from visitors U.S.$1,980,000,000; expenditures by nationals abroad U.S.$531,000,000.
Production (metric tons except as noted). Agriculture, forestry, fishing (1984): vegetables 32,767, fruits 6,950, sugarcane 700, tobacco 10; livestock (number of live animals), 1,310,000 pigs, 4,000 cattle, 2,000 goats, 2,000 buffalo; fish catch 25,042. Mining and quarrying (value added in S$; 1984): granite 153,100,000. Manufacturing (value added in S$; 1984): electronic products and components 2,414,200,000; petroleum refining and petroleum products 1,387,700,000; transport equipment 968,400,000; fabricated metal products except machinery and equipment 828,900,000; nonelectrical machinery 781,800,000; paints, pharmaceuticals, and chemical products 525,300,000; printing and publishing 525,300,000. Construction (1984): residential 10,954,000 sq m; nonresidential 3,308,000 sq m. Energy production (consumption): electricity (kW-hr; 1984) 9,420,700,000 (8,325,-800,000); coal (metric tons; 1983) none (2,000); crude petroleum (barrels; 1983) none (272,676,000); petroleum products (metric tons; 1983) 29,160,-000 (9,307,000); natural gas, none (none).
Gross national product (at current market prices; 1984): U.S.$17,914,000,000 (U.S.$7,100 per capita).

Structure of gross domestic product and labour force

	1984 in value S$'000,000	% of total value	labour force	% of labour force
Agriculture	354.1	0.9	8,830	0.7
Quarrying	136.7	0.3	1,894	0.2
Manufacturing	9,728.4	25.0	322,189	26.7
Construction	4,573.9	11.8	99,787	8.3
Public utilities	792.9	2.0	9,160	0.8
Transportation and communication	5,076.0	13.1	122,408	10.1
Trade	7,454.8	19.2	264,638	21.9
Finance	8,365.7	21.6	100,940	8.4
Services	4,561.9	11.7	242,182	20.1
Other	−2,190.6‡	−5.6‡	32,573§	2.7
TOTAL	38,873.8 ‖	100.0	1,207,400	100.0¶

Population economically active (1984): total 1,207,400; participation rate of population ages 15–64, 68.0% (female 36.4%, unemployed 2.7%).

Price and earnings indexes (1980 = 100)

	1979	1980	1981	1982	1983	1984	1985
Consumer price index	92.2	100.0	108.3	112.4	113.8	116.8	117.3♀
Weekly earnings index	88.5	100.0	114.1	131.5	143.3	156.6	...

Household income and expenditure. Average household size (1984) 3.9; income per household S$20,800 (U.S.$9,700); source of income: n.a.; expenditure (1984): food and beverages 25.0%, transportation and communication 13.9%, recreation and education 11.7%, housing 9.3%, furniture and household equipment 8.8%, clothing and footwear 8.1%, health 3.0%.
Land use (1984): forested 4.6%; agricultural and under permanent cultivation 9.5%; built-up area 47.6%; other 38.3%.

Foreign trade

Balance of trade (current prices)

	1979	1980	1981	1982	1983	1984
S$'000,000	−7,394	−9,892	−13,957	−15,772	−13,349	−9,794
% of total	−10.7%	−10.7%	−13.6%	−15.1%	−12.6%	8.7%

Imports (1984): S$61,133,600,000 (crude petroleum 23.2%, petroleum products 4.5%, office machinery 3.0%, telecommunications apparatus 2.8%, crude rubber 2.4%, woven textile fabrics 2.3%, electric power machinery 2.2%). *Major import sources:* Japan 18.3%; Malaysia 15.0%; United States 14.6%; Saudi Arabia 9.3%; China 4.7%; Taiwan 3.3%; Kuwait 3.1%.
Exports (1984): S$51,340,000,000 (petroleum products 25.0%, telecommunications apparatus 5.3%, office machines 5.2%, crude rubber 4.2%, electrical circuit apparatus 2.6%, clothing 2.3%, vegetable oils 2.2%). *Major export destinations:* United States 20.0%; Malaysia 16.2%; Japan 9.4%; Hong Kong 6.2%; Thailand 4.8%; Australia 3.4%; United Kingdom 2.7%.

Transport and communications

Transport. Railroads (1984): length 16 mi, 26 km. Roads (1984): total length 1,612 mi, 2,594 km (paved 89%). Vehicles (1985): passenger cars 236,553; trucks and buses 120,051. Merchant marine (1985): vessels (100 gross tons and over) 824; total deadweight tonnage 11,038,251. Air transport (1984): passenger-mi 12,631,000,000, passenger-km 20,328,000,000; short ton-mi cargo 678,124,000, metric ton-km cargo 990,108,000; airports (1985) with scheduled flights 1.
Communications. Daily newspapers (1984): total number 12; total circulation 630,638; circulation per 1,000 population 249. Radio (1985): total number of receivers 111,009 (1 per 22.8 persons). Television (1984): total number of receivers 363,868 (1 per 7.0 persons). Telephones (1984): 972,700 (1 per 2.6 persons).

Education and health

Education (1984)

	schools	teachers	students	student/ teacher ratio
Primary (age 6–13)	210	10,657	288,623	27.1
Secondary (age 12–18)	150	8,236	187,764	22.8
Voc., teacher tr.	89	1,839	15,553	8.5
Higher	4	3,232	35,001	10.8

Educational attainment (1980). Percent of population over age 10 having: no schooling 34.9%; primary education 44.3%; secondary 12.4%; upper secondary 5.7%; higher (degree or diploma holders from universities) 2.7%.
Literacy (1984): total population over age 10 literate 1,822,800 (85.6%); males literate 998,300 (92.3%); females literate 824,500 (78.6%).
Health (1984): physicians 1,010 (1 per 2,504 persons); hospital beds 9,668 (1 per 262 persons); infant mortality rate per 1,000 live births 8.8.
Food (1980–82): daily per capita caloric intake 2,937 (vegetable products 79%, animal products 23%); 128% of FAO recommended minimum requirement.

Military

Total active duty personnel (1984): 55,500 (army 81.1%, navy 8.1%, air force 10.8%). *Military expenditure as percent of GNP* (1983): 5.8% (world 6.1%); per capita expenditure U.S.$432.

*The census areas have no administrative function. †Includes Sri Lankan. ‡Less imputed bank service charges. §Unemployed. ‖ At current prices. ¶Detail does not add to total given because of rounding. ♀May only.

Solomon Islands

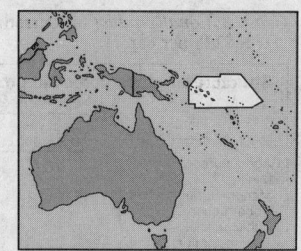

Official name: Solomon Islands.
Form of government: parliamentary state with one legislative house (National Parliament [38]).
Chief of state: British Monarch represented by governor-general.
Head of government: Prime Minister.
Capital: Honiara.
Official language: English.
Official religion: none.
Monetary unit: 1 Solomon Islands dollar (SI$) = 100 cents; valuation (Oct. 21, 1985) 1 U.S.$ = SI$1.56; 1 £ = SI$2.83.

Area and population

Provinces	Capitals	area sq mi	area sq km	population 1985 estimate
Central Islands	Tulagi	493	1,276	19,160
Guadalcanal	Honiara	2,047	5,302	41,030
Isabel	Buala	1,550	4,014	14,490
Makira	Kira Kira	1,231	3,188	19,530
Malaita	Auki	1,638	4,243	75,950
Temotu	Lata	358	926	14,360
Western	Gizo	3,310	8,573	57,770
Capital Territory				
Honiara	Honiara	13	34	24,980
TOTAL		10,640*	27,556	267,270

Demography

Population (1985): 267,270.
Density (1985): persons per sq mi 25.1, persons per sq km 9.7.
Urban–rural (1980): urban 25.2%; rural 74.8%.
Sex distribution (1976): male 52.23%; female 47.77%.
Age breakdown (1985): under 15, 49.1%; 15–29, 24.2%; 30–49, 16.4%; 50–59, 4.8%; 60 and over, 5.5%.
Population projection: (1990) 318,693; (2000) 459,061.
Doubling time: 21 years.
Ethnic composition (1976): Melanesian 93.3%; Polynesian 4.0%; Micronesian 1.4%; European 0.7%; Chinese 0.2%; other 0.4%.
Religious affiliation (1980): Christian 95.3%, of which Protestant 71.4%, Roman Catholic 19.1%; Melanesian indigenous 4.7%.
Major cities (1981): Honiara 21,334; Gizo 1,925; Tulagi 916; Auki 853.

Vital statistics

Birth rate per 1,000 population (1982): 44.6 (world avg. 29.0).
Death rate per 1,000 population (1982): 11.7 (world avg. 11.0).
Natural increase rate per 1,000 population (1982): 32.9 (world avg. 18.0).
Total fertility rate (avg. births per childbearing woman; 1982): 7.3.
Life expectancy at birth (1982): male 54 years; female 54 years.
Major causes of death per 100,000 population: n.a.; however, major diseases are malaria, tuberculosis, and leprosy.

National economy

Budget (1984). Revenue: SI$67,200,000 (recurrent revenue SI$53,300,000, of which import duties 32.1%, government earnings 22.8%, export duties 18.9%). Expenditures: SI$67,200,000 (recurrent expenditure SI$50,500,000, of which administrative infrastructure 51.1%, economic infrastructure 27.9%, education 8.5%, health 6.7%).
Public debt (external, outstanding; 1984): U.S.$14,000,000.
Tourism (1983): tourist arrivals 11,113.
Gross national product (at current market prices; 1983): U.S.$160,000,000 (U.S.$637 per capita).

Structure of gross domestic product and labour force

	1983 in value SI$'000,000	1983 % of total value	1983 labour force ‖	1983 % of labour force
Agriculture	...	...	7,061	31.7
Mining	...	...		
Manufacturing	...	...	1,798	8.1
Construction	...	...	1,381	6.2
Public utilities	...	...	301	1.4
Transportation and communication	...	...	1,933	8.7
Trade	...	...	2,115	9.5
Finance	...	...	499	2.2
Pub. admin., defense	...	...	...	...
Services	...	...	6,374	28.6
Other	...	...	800	3.6
TOTAL	180¶	100.0	22,262	100.0

Population economically active (1984): total employed 23,488; participation rate of population ages 15–64, 19.7% (female 15.7%, unemployed, n.a.).

Price and earnings indexes (1980 = 100)

	1980	1981	1982	1983	1984	1985‡
Consumer price index†	100.0	116.4	131.5	140.5	155.9	170.0
Annual earnings index§	100.0	108.0	118.8	131.4	145.9	

Household income and expenditure. Average household size (1983) 5.4; average annual income per household (1983): SI$1,010§ (U.S.$1,160); sources of income (1983): wages and salaries 74.1%, self-employment, remittances, gifts, and other assistance 25.9%; expenditure (1984): food 47.0%, housing 15.5%, drink and tobacco 9.5%, clothing 5.0%, transportation 1.1%.
Production (metric tons except as noted). Agriculture, forestry, fishing (1984): coconuts 255,000, sweet potatoes 49,000, copra 42,586, palm oil 19,700, yams 19,000, paddy rice 7,137, cocoa 1,709; livestock (number of live animals; 1983) 48,000 pigs, 23,000 cattle; roundwood 453,000 cu m; fish catch 35,927. Mining and quarrying (1983): gold 34 kilograms; silver 8 kilograms. Manufacturing: n.a.; however, major industries are palm oil, rice and saw milling, fish canning and freezing, soap and tobacco manufacturing, weaving, wood carving, boatbuilding, and leather working. Construction† (gross value in SI$; 1980): 2,551,000. Energy production (consumption): electricity (kW-hr; 1983) 25,000,000 (25,000,000); coal, none (n.a.); petroleum products (metric tons; 1982) none (37,000); natural gas, none (n.a.).
Land use (1983): forested 93.0%; meadows and pastures 1.4%; agricultural and under permanent cultivation 1.9%; other 3.7%.

Foreign trade

Balance of trade (current prices)

	1979	1980	1981	1982	1983	1984
SI$'000	+8,460	−664	−8,419	−929	+592	+34,725
% of total	7.7%	0.5%	6.8%	0.8%	0.4%	17.2%

Imports (1984): SI$83,838,000 (machinery and transport equipment 23.9%, mineral fuels and lubricants 22.7%, manufactured goods 16.2%, food 15.7%, chemicals). *Major import sources:* Australia 36.2%; Japan 15.0%; Singapore 14.5%; New Zealand 8.1%; China 4.0%; United States 3.3%.
Exports (1984): SI$118,563,000 (copra 27.2%, timber 25.5%, fish 24.3%, palm oil 14.5%, cocoa 2.8%, gold 0.6%). *Major export destinations:* Japan 33.2%; United Kingdom 12.4%; The Netherlands 11.2%; South Korea 6.4%; American Samoa 6.2%; West Germany 4.8%.

Transport and communications

Transport. Railroads (1984): none. Roads♀ (1980): total length 1,305 mi, 2,100 km (paved, n.a.). Vehicles (1982): passenger cars 1,122; trucks and buses 1,323. Merchant marine (1984): vessels (100 gross tons and over) 26; total deadweight tonnage 4,552. Air transport (1984)ठ: passenger-mi 6,852,000, passenger-km 11,027,000; short ton-mi cargo 25,000, metric ton-km cargo 37,000; airports (1983) with scheduled flights 27.
Communications. Daily newspapers (1984): none. Radio (1984): total number of receivers 25,000 (1 per 10.4 persons). Television (1984): none. Telephones (1984): 3,201 (1 per 81.2 persons).

Education and health

Education (1984)

	schools	teachers	students	student/ teacher ratio
Primary (age 7–12)	423	1,536	37,522	24.4
Secondary (age 13–18)	20	267	5,118	19.2
Voc., teacher tr.	2	63	1,142	18.1

Educational attainment, n.a. *Literacy* (1976): total population over age 15 literate 55,544 (54.1%); males 62.4%; females 44.9%.
Health (1983): physicians 38 (1 per 6,605 persons); hospital beds 1,390 (1 per 181 persons); infant mortality rate per 1,000 live births (1982) 46.
Food (1980–82): daily per capita caloric intake 2,048 (vegetable products 89%, animal products 11%); 77% of FAO recommended minimum requirement.

Military

Total active duty personnel: no military forces are maintained, but a police force of about 500 provides internal security.

*Detail does not add to total given because of rounding. †Honiara only. ‡June. §Public service earnings. ‖ Employed persons only. ¶At current prices. ♀Includes private roads. ठSolair only.

Ngusungusu, carved figureheads for canoes, inlaid with nautilus shell and representing guardian spirits; a modern cottage industry of the Solomon Islands.

Somalia

Official name: Jamhuuriyadda
  Dimuqraadiga Soomaaliya
  (Somali); Jumhūrīyah aṣ-Ṣūmāl
  ad-Dīmuqraṭīyah (Arabic) (Somali
  Democratic Republic).
Form of government:
  military-dominated, single-party
  republic with one legislative house
  (People's Assembly [177]).
Head of state and government:
  President.
Capital: Mogadishu.
Official languages: Somali; Arabic.
Official religion: Islām.
Monetary unit: 1 Somali shilling
  (So.Sh.) = 100 cents; valuation (Oct.
  21, 1985) 1 U.S.\$ = So.Sh.36.58;
  1 £ = So.Sh.52.45.

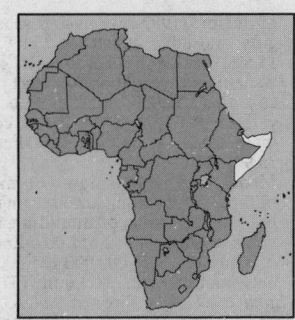

Area and population

		area		population
				1980
Regions	Capitals	sq mi	sq km	estimate
Bakool	Oddur	10,000	27,000	148,700
Bari	Bander Cassim	27,000	70,000	222,300
Banaadir	Mogadishu	400	1,000	520,100
Bay	Baidoa	15,000	39,000	451,000
Galguduud	Dusa Mareeb	17,000	43,000	255,900
Gedo	Garbahaarrey	12,000	32,000	235,000
Hiiraan	Beled Weyne	13,000	34,000	219,300
Jubbada Dhexe	Bu'aale	9,000	23,000	147,800
Jubbada Hoose	Chisimayu	24,000	61,000	272,400
Mudug	Galcaio	27,000	70,000	311,200
Nugaal	Garoe	19,000	50,000	112,200
Sanaag	Erigavo	21,000	54,000	216,500
Shabeellaha Dhexe	Giohar	8,000	22,000	352,000
Shabeellaha Hoose	Merca	10,000	25,000	570,700
Togdheer	Burao	16,000	41,000	383,900
Woqooyi Galbeed	Hargeysa	17,000	45,000	655,000
TOTAL		246,000*	637,000	5,074,000

Demography

Population (1985): 5,817,200.
Density (1985): persons per sq mi 23.6, persons per sq km 9.1.
Urban–rural (1983): urban 30.0%; rural 70.0%.
Sex distribution (1980): male 45.78%; female 54.22%.
Age breakdown (1980): under 15, 43.3%; 15–29, 24.6%; 30–44, 15.4%; 45–59, 10.5%; 60–74, 5.6%; 75 and over, 0.6%.
Population projection: (1990) 6,476,000; (2000) 7,134,000.
Doubling time: 23 years.
Ethnic composition (1981): Somali 95.0%; Bantu 2.9%; Arab 1.5%; other 0.6%.
Religious affiliation (1980): Sunnī Muslim 99.8%; Christian 0.1%; other 0.1%.
Major city (1981): Mogadishu 400,000.

Vital statistics

Birth rate per 1,000 population (1983): 50.0 (world avg. 29.0); legitimate, n.a.; illegitimate, n.a.
Death rate per 1,000 population (1983): 20.0 (world avg. 11.0).
Natural increase rate per 1,000 population (1983): 30.0 (world avg. 18.0).
Total fertility rate (avg. births per childbearing woman; 1983): 6.8.
Marriage rate per 1,000 population: n.a.
Divorce rate per 1,000 population: n.a.
Life expectancy at birth (1980–85): male 41.9 years; female 45.1 years.
Major causes of death per 100,000 population: n.a.; however, major diseases are leprosy, malaria, tetanus, and tuberculosis.

National economy

Budget (1984)†. Revenue: So.Sh.6,491,500,000 (income from government property 42.7%, import duties 18.5%, income tax 1.2%). Expenditures: So.Sh.6,491,500,000 (finance and central services 31.9%, defense 28.2%, economic services 16.8%, education 7.0%, foreign affairs 3.4%, health 2.5%, general administration 1.6%).
Public debt (external, outstanding; 1983): U.S.\$1,149,000,000.
Tourism (1982): receipts from visitors U.S.\$13,000,000; expenditures by nationals abroad U.S.\$13,000,000.
Production (metric tons except as noted). Agriculture, forestry, fishing (1984): sugarcane 500,000, sorghum 235,000, corn (maize) 120,000, bananas 98,900, vegetables 82,000, sesame seed 59,500, roots and tubers 40,000, beans 20,800, cotton 4,000, rice 3,000, wheat 1,000; livestock (number of live animals) 15,700,000 goats, 9,700,000 sheep, 5,700,000 camels, 3,600,000 cattle; roundwood (1983) 5,051,000 cu m; fish catch (1983) 15,500. Mining and quarrying (1983): salt 30,000. Manufacturing (1983): sugar 30,800; pasta and flour 10,600; boxes and bags 6,800; canned meat and fish 1,100. Construction (value added in So.Sh.; 1982): 1,687,200,000. Energy production (consumption): electricity (kW-hr; 1983) 91,900,000 (91,900,000); coal, none (n.a.); crude petroleum (barrels; 1983) n.a. (2,639,000); petroleum products (metric tons; 1983) 339,000 (362,000); natural gas, none (n.a.).
Household income and expenditure. Average household size (1980) 4.9; average annual income per household: n.a.; source of income: n.a.; expenditure: n.a.

Gross national product (at current market prices; 1983): U.S.\$1,255,000,000 (U.S.\$228 per capita).

Structure of gross domestic product and labour force

	1982			
	in value U.S.\$'000,000	% of total value	labour force	% of labour force
Agriculture	770	50.0	1,588,000	82.0
Mining				
Manufacturing				
Construction	170	11.0	155,000	8.0
Public utilities				
Transportation and communication				
Trade				
Finance	600	39.0	194,000	10.0
Pub. admin., defense				
Services				
TOTAL	1,540	100.0	1,937,000	100.0

Population economically active (1983): total 2,025,000; participation rate of total population 36.8% (female 30.0%‡, unemployed, n.a.).

Price and earnings indexes (1980 = 100)

	1977	1978	1979	1980	1981	1982	1983	1984
Consumer price index	46.1	50.7	83.0	100.0	144.4	178.5	241.4	464.1
Earnings index	...	...	...	...	...	...	...	...

Land use (1983): forested 13.9%; meadows and pastures 46.0%; agricultural and under permanent cultivation 1.8%; other 38.3%.

Foreign trade

Balance of trade (current prices)

	1978	1979	1980	1981	1982	1983
So.Sh.'000,000	−686.9	−640.3	−1,069.9	−1,841.4	−73.5	−1,421.4
% of total	34.2%	31.3%	39.0%	48.9%	1.8%	33.3%

Imports (1983): So.Sh.2,844,400,000 (petroleum 31.0%; food 16.0%; machinery and transport equipment 15.0%, of which transport equipment 7.4%; construction materials 11.8%; manufacturing raw materials 4.5%; medicinal and chemical products 4.5%; beverages and tobacco 3.9%; textiles and household goods 1.3%). *Major import sources* (1984): United States 20.3%; Italy 20.2%; Saudi Arabia 12.6%; West Germany 5.2%; United Kingdom 4.9%; France 4.8%; Bahrain 3.8%; Djibouti 3.3%; Thailand 2.9%; China 2.7%; Belgium 2.2%; The Netherlands 1.7%; Japan 1.5%; India 1.4%; Canada 1.1%; Kenya 1.0%; Denmark 1.0%; Australia 0.8%; Austria 0.7%.
Exports (1983): So.Sh.1,423,000,000 (live animals 78.8%; bananas 7.3%; myrrh 6.3%; petroleum products 3.0%; fish 2.3%; undressed hides, skins, and furs 1.5%). *Major export destinations* (1984): Saudi Arabia 59.1%; Yemen (Ṣan'ā') 11.5%; Italy 5.8%; China 5.4%; United Arab Emirates 4.7%; Iran 3.7%; Yemen (Aden) 2.6%; Hong Kong 1.5%; France 0.9%.

Transport and communications

Transport. Railroads: none. Roads (1981): total length 12,169 mi, 19,584 km (paved 13%). Vehicles (1981): passenger cars 17,754; trucks and buses 9,533. Merchant marine (1984): vessels (100 gross tons and over) 26; total deadweight tonnage 29,291. Air transport (1984): passenger-mi 176,513,000, passenger-km 284,070,000; short ton-mi cargo 3,369,000, metric ton-km cargo 4,919,000; airports (1985) with scheduled flights 9§.
Communications. Daily newspapers (1984): total number 1; total circulation, n.a. Radio (1984): total number of receivers 95,000 (1 per 60 persons). Television ‖: total number of receivers, n.a. Telephones (1981): 4,800 (1 per 782 persons).

Education and health

Education (1980–81)

	schools	teachers	students	student/ teacher ratio
Primary (age 6–14)	1,408	8,122	271,704	33.5
Secondary (age 15–18)	51	1,350	33,212	24.6
Teacher training	26	654	10,629	16.3
Higher	1	262	2,332	8.9

Educational attainment, n.a. *Literacy* (1984): total adult population literate 60%.
Health: physicians (1981) 292 (1 per 18,353 persons); hospital beds (1978) 5,232 (1 per 917 persons); infant mortality rate per 1,000 live births (1983) 142.0.
Food (1980–82): daily per capita caloric intake 2,077 (vegetable products 72%, animal products 28%); 90% of FAO recommended minimum requirement.

Military

Total active duty personnel (1984): 62,550 (army 95.9%, navy 0.9%, air force 3.2%). *Military expenditure as percent of GNP* (1983): 9.1% (world 6.1%); per capita expenditure U.S.\$21.

*Detail does not add to total given because of rounding. †Estimated. ‡1982. §Includes airfields. ‖ Since the end of 1983 television service covers Mogadishu area and Hargeysa.

South Africa

Official name: Republiek van Suid-Afrika (Afrikaans); Republic of South Africa (English).
Form of government: multiparty republic with three legislative houses (House of Assembly [166]; House of Representatives [80]; House of Delegates [40])*.
Head of state and government: State President.
Capitals: Pretoria (executive); Bloemfontein (judicial); Cape Town (legislative).
Official languages: Afrikaans; English.
Official religion: none.
Monetary unit: 1 rand (R) = 100 cents; valuation (Oct. 21, 1985) 1 U.S.$ = R2.60; 1 £ = R3.72.

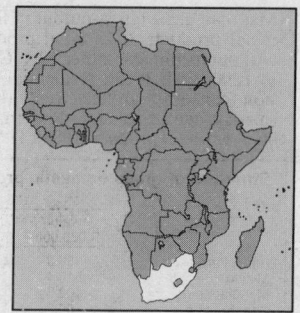

Area and population††

Provinces	Capitals	area sq mi	area sq km	population 1983 estimate
Cape	Cape Town	247,638	641,379	5,374,000
Natal	Pietermaritzburg	35,272	91,355	2,842,000
Orange Free State	Bloemfontein	49,418	127,993	2,080,000
Transvaal	Pretoria	101,352	262,499	8,950,000
National states				
Gazankulu	Giyani	2,606	6,750	585,000
KaNgwane	Nyamasane	1,436	3,720	184,000
KwaNdebele	Siyabuswa	355	920	226,000
KwaZulu	Ulundi	12,664	32,800	3,792,000
Lebowa	Lebowakgomo	8,757	22,680	1,869,000
Qwaqwa	Phuthaditjhaba	185	480	306,000
TOTAL		433,680	1,123,226	26,945,000

Demography

Population (1985): 27,424,000.
Density (1985): persons per sq mi 63.2, persons per sq km 24.4.
Urban–rural (1985)§: urban 55.9%; rural 44.1%.
Sex distribution (1985)§: male 49.58%; female 50.42%.
Age breakdown (1985)§: under 15, 41.0%; 15–29, 26.9%; 30–44, 16.1%; 45–59, 9.8%; 60–74, 5.0%; 75 and over, 1.2%.
Population projection§: (1990) 36,754,000; (2000) 46,918,000.
Doubling time: 28 years.
Ethnic composition (1983): black 67.9%, of which Zulu 23.7%, North Sotho 9.8%, Xhosa 9.7%, South Sotho 7.3%, Tswana 5.7%, other 11.7%; white 18.2%; coloured 10.6%; Asian 3.3%.
Religious affiliation (1980): tribal religionist 20.4%; Afrikaans Reformed 15.5%; Roman Catholic 9.5%; Methodist 8.5%; Anglican 6.5%; other 39.6%.
Major cities (mun., 1983): Johannesburg 1,666,000; Cape Town 1,567,000; Durban 714,000; Pretoria 712,000; Port Elizabeth 560,000.

Vital statistics

Birth rate per 1,000 population (1983): 33.6 (world avg. 29.0); (1978) legitimate 75.9% ‖ ; illegitimate 24.1% ‖ .
Death rate per 1,000 population (1983): 11.0 (world avg. 11.0).
Natural increase rate per 1,000 population (1983): 22.6 (world avg. 18.0).
Total fertility rate (avg. births per childbearing woman; 1980–85)§: 5.1.
Marriage rate per 1,000 population: n.a.
Divorce rate per 1,000 population: n.a.
Life expectancy at birth (1980–85)§: male 51.8 years; female 55.2 years.
Major causes of death per 100,000 population (1977) ‖ : heart disease 215.3; malignant neoplasms (cancers) 107.3; cerebrovascular disease 90.2; pneumonia 75.2; enteritis and other diarrheal diseases 49.1.

National economy

Budget (1984–85). Revenue: R22,518,000,000 (income tax 56.8%, sales tax 25.9%, customs duty and excise tax 13.5%). Expenditures: R25,439,000,000 (provincial administration 25.3%, defense 16.8%, interest on public debt 13.1%, education 10.7%, welfare services 8.3%).
Total debt (external; 1984): U.S.$2,629,300,000.
Tourism (1981–82): receipts from visitors U.S.$630,000,000; expenditures by nationals abroad, n.a.
Production (metric tons except as noted). Agriculture, forestry, fishing (1984): sugarcane 18,755,000, corn (maize) 4,440,000, wheat 2,150,000; livestock (number of live animals) 31,265,000 sheep, 12,895,000 cattle; forestry 20,524,000 cu m¶; fish catch 599,897¶. Mining and quarrying (1984): iron ore 24,496,000, manganese ore 3,049,000; phosphate concentrate 2,496,000, chrome 3,006,000, gold 681,300 kg, silver 217,600 kg, diamonds 10,118,910 carats. Manufacturing (value in R; 1982)♀: food 8,287,649,000; rubber products 7,116,342,000; nonelectrical machinery 4,998,518,000; chemicals 4,547,281,000; basic metal industries 3,901,157,000; electrical machinery 3,646,151,000; motor vehicles 2,446,252,000. Construction (1983): 35,832. Energy production (consumption): electricity (kW-hr; 1983)ō 109,185,000,000 (114,061,000,000); coal (metric tons; 1983) 145,838,000 (114,000,000); petroleum (barrels; 1983)ō none (88,240,000); petroleum products (metric tons; 1983)ō 14,270,000 (10,753,000); natural gas, none (none).
Land use (1983): forested 3.8%; meadows and pastures 65.4%; agricultural and under permanent cultivation 11.1%; other 19.7%.
Gross national product (1983): U.S.$76,890,000,000 (U.S.$2,450 per capita).

Structure of gross domestic product and labour force

	1983 in value R'000,000	1983 % of total value	1980 labour force	1980 % of labour force
Agriculture	3,886	4.8	1,299,840	15.0
Mining	12,451	15.3	820,300	9.5
Manufacturing	18,683	22.9	1,456,760	16.8
Construction	3,373	4.1	452,440	5.2
Public utilities	3,762	4.6	79,240	0.9
Transp. and commun.	7,195	8.8	424,040	4.9
Trade	10,883	13.3	1,008,340	11.6
Finance	11,269	13.8	285,840	3.3
Pub. admin., defense	8,749	10.7 }		
Services	1,394	1.7 }	1,986,240	22.9
Other	−21□	◊	852,660	9.9
TOTAL	81,624	100.0	8,665,700	100.0

Population economically active (1984): total 11,242,000; participation rate of total population 35.0% (female [1981] 34.4%, unemployed [1983] 6.3%).

Price and earnings indexes (1980 = 100)

	1979	1980	1981	1982	1983	1984	1985△
Consumer price index	87.9	100.0	115.2	132.1	148.4	165.7	191.9
Monthly earnings index	83.9	100.0	121.5	149.0	158.1	...	...
white (black)	(82.5)	(100.0)	(120.6)	(156.6)	(158.7)	...	...

Household income and expenditure. Average household size (1980) 5.1; average annual income per household R8,829 (U.S.$11,349); sources of income (1982): wages and salaries 82.7%, transfer payments 4.9%; expenditure (1983): food and beverages 31.8%, transportation and communication 12.4%, housing 17.8%, clothing and footwear 8.1%, energy 6.8%.

Foreign trade†

Balance of trade (current prices)

	1979	1980	1981	1982	1983	1984
R'000,000	+8,435	+5,780	−231	+914	+4,479	+3,705
% of total	35.7%	16.9%	0.6%	2.4%	12.1%	7.9%

Imports (1984): R21,666,000,000 (machinery 29.4%; transport equipment 12.3%; chemicals 8.2%; metal products 5.0%; textiles 4.8%). *Major import sources:* West Germany 15.6%; United States 15.1%; Japan 12.1%.
Exports (1984): R25,186,200,000 (gold 46.1%, of which gold coins 5.4%; minerals 12.1%; base metals 9.5%; diamonds 5.4%; food and tobacco 2.0%). *Major export destinations:* United States 14.2%; Italy 9.8%; Japan 9.3%.

Transport and communications

Transport. Railroads (1982): length⊕ 14,739 mi, 23,720 km; passenger-mi 13,049,000,000, passenger-km 21,000,000,000; short ton-mi cargo 71,156,000,000, metric ton-km cargo 103,886,000,000. Roads (1982): total length 114,830 mi, 184,802 km (paved 26%). Vehicles (1983): passenger cars 2,727,202; trucks and buses 1,153,657. Merchant marine (1984): vessels 278; total deadweight tonnage 790,707. Air transport (1983): passenger-mi 5,376,251,000, passenger-km 8,652,000,000; short ton-mi cargo 266,430,000, metric ton-km cargo 388,980,000; airports (1985) with scheduled flights 32.
Communications. Daily newspapers (1984): total number 20; total circulation 1,137,000; circulation per 1,000 population 42.5. Radio (1984): 8,300,000 receivers (1 per 3.2 persons). Television (1984): 2,100,000 receivers (1 per 12.7 persons). Telephones (1983): 3,471,519 (1 per 7.4 persons).

Education and health

Education (1985)

	schools	teachers	students	student/teacher ratio
Primary (age 6–12)	17,430**	199,949**	4,722,832	...
Secondary (age 13–17)	**	**	1,539,213	...
Vocational	132	3,733	35,394	9.5
Higher††	96	15,425	204,546	13.3

Educational attainment (1970). Percent of population over age 25 having: no formal schooling 42.1%; some primary 21.4%; complete primary 5.3%; some secondary 20.7%; postsecondary 3.7%. *Literacy*§ (1980): percent of population over age 15 literate 79.3%; males 80.6%; females 78.0%.
Health (1980): physicians (1983) 21,143 (1 per 1,219 persons); hospital beds 98,308 (1 per 246 persons); infant mortality rate per 1,000 live births 70.7.
Food (1980–82): daily per capita caloric intake 2,860 (vegetable products 85%, animal products 15%); 117% of FAO recommended minimum requirement.

Military

Total active duty personnel (1984): 83,400 (army 80.8%, navy 7.2%, air force 12.0%). *Military expenditure as percent of GNP* (1983): 4.3% (world 6.1%); per capita expenditure U.S.$97.

---

*For representation of whites, coloureds, and Indians, respectively. †Provincial figures include the national states shown separately. ‡Data exclude Bophuthatswana, Ciskei, Transkei, and Venda, which are treated as sovereign nations by the South African government. Together these entities have an area of 36,733 sq mi (95,137 sq km) and a population (1983) of 5,096,000. §Includes Bophuthatswana, Ciskei, Transkei, and Venda. ‖ Whites, Asians, and Coloureds only. ¶1983. ♀Value of sales. ōData apply to the Customs Union of Southern Africa comprising South Africa, Botswana, Lesotho, South West Africa/Namibia, and Swaziland. □Other producers less imputed bank service charge. ◊Less than 0.1%. △June. †Import figures are f.o.b. (free on board) in balance of trade and c.i.f. (cost, insurance, and freight) for commodities and trading partners. ⊕1984. **Primary includes secondary. ††Includes universities, teacher-training colleges, and technikons (advanced technical colleges), but not ordinary technical colleges and institutes.

South West Africa/ Namibia

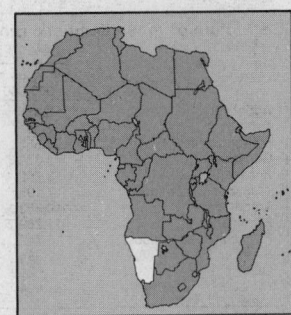

Official name: Suidwes-Afrika/Namibië (Afrikaans); South West Africa/ Namibia (English).
Political status: dependency of South Africa with one legislative house (National Assembly [62]).
Head of state and government: Administrator-General*.
Capital: Windhoek.
Official languages: Afrikaans; English.
Official religion: none.
Monetary unit: 1 South African rand (R) = 100 cents; valuation (Oct. 21, 1985) 1 U.S.$ = R2.60; 1 £ = R3.72.

Area and population†

Magisterial Districts	Capitals	area sq mi	area sq km	population 1981 census‡
Bethanien	Bethanien	6,951	18,004	2,808
Boesmanland	Tsumkwe	7,131	18,468	2,453
Caprivi Oos	Katima Mulilo	4,453	11,533	37,923
Damaraland	Khorixas	17,977	46,560	24,214
Gobabis	Gobabis	16,003	41,447	22,079
Grootfontein	Grootfontein	10,239	26,520	20,720
Hereroland-Oos	Otjinene	20,058	51,949	18,918
Hereroland-Wes	Okakarara	6,371	16,500	15,411
Kaokoland	Opuwo	22,467	58,190	16,637
Karasburg	Karasburg	14,717	38,116	9,502
Karibib	Karibib	5,108	13,230	8,953
Kavango	Rundu	19,674	50,955	105,690
Keetmanshoop	Keetmanshoop	14,788	38,302	17,608
Lüderitz	Lüderitz	20,488	53,063	14,314
Maltahöhe	Maltahöhe	9,874	25,573	4,751
Mariental	Mariental	18,413	47,689	20,578
Namaland	Gibeon	8,154	21,120	12,766
Okahandja	Okahandja	6,811	17,640	13,336
Omaruru	Omaruru	3,253	8,425	5,498
Otjiwarongo	Otjiwarongo	7,934	20,550	16,126
Outjo	Outjo	14,951	38,722	8,866
Owambo	Ondangwa	20,000	51,800	452,036
Rehoboth	Rehoboth	5,476	14,182	27,664
Swakopmund	Swakopmund	17,258	44,697	15,473
Tsumeb	Tsumeb	6,340	16,420	19,447
Windhoek	Windhoek	12,930	33,489	110,644
TOTAL		317,818	823,144	1,031,927

Demography

Population (1985): 1,097,000.
Density (1985): persons per sq mi 3.5, persons per sq km 1.3.
Urban–rural (1981): urban 26.0%; rural 74.0%.
Sex distribution (1981): male 49.21%; female 50.79%.
Age breakdown (1985): under 15, 44.3%; 15–29, 26.1%; 30–44, 15.3%; 45–59, 9.2%; 60–74, 4.3%; 75 and over, 0.8%.
Population projection: (1990) 1,360,000; (2000) 1,822,000.
Doubling time: 24.4 years.
Ethnic composition (1983): Ovambo 49.3%; Kavango 9.6%; Herero 7.3%; Damara 7.1%; white 6.8%; Nama 4.7%; other 15.2%.
Religious affiliation (1981): Lutheran 51.2%; Roman Catholic 19.8%; Dutch Reformed 6.1%; Anglican 5.0%; other 17.9%.
Major cities (1983): Windhoek 105,100; Rundu 15,000; Rehoboth 14,000; Swakopmund 13,500; Keetmanshoop 12,000.

Vital statistics

Birth rate per 1,000 population (1980–85): 45.1 (world avg. 29.0).
Death rate per 1,000 population (1980–85): 17.3 (world avg. 11.0).
Natural increase rate per 1,000 population (1980–85): 27.8 (world avg. 18.0).
Total fertility rate (avg. births per childbearing woman; 1980–85): 6.1.
Marriage rate per 1,000 population: n.a.
Life expectancy at birth (1980–85): male 47.0 years; female 49.5 years.
Major causes of death per 100,000 population: n.a.; however, major diseases are malaria, tuberculosis, and trypanosomiasis.

National economy

Budget (1984–85). Revenue: R967,000,000 (taxes 35.5%; grants from South Africa 32.9%; customs and duties 25.9%; surplus from last fiscal year [1983–84] 5.7%). Expenditures: R1,177,000,000 (current expenditure 83.7%, of which assistance to authorities 23.1%, education 8.7%, drought relief 0.6%; statutory expenditure 16.3%, of which government debt service 7.9%).
Public debt (external, outstanding; 1984): U.S.$352,000,000.
Tourism (1981): receipts from visitors U.S.$45,960,000; expenditures by nationals abroad, n.a.
Production (metric tons except as noted). Agriculture, forestry, fishing (1984): roots and tubers 140,000, corn [maize] 40,000, fruit 25,000, vegetables and melons 20,000, millet 20,000, pulses 4,000, sorghum 3,000; wool 4,470§, karakul pelts 3,000,000 units§; livestock (number of live animals) 6,000,000 sheep, 2,300,000 goats, 2,000,000 cattle; fish catch ‖ 340,981, of which anchovies 183,391, mackerel 105,273, South African pilchard 44,014. Mining and quarrying (1984): diamonds 963,000 carats, of which gem quality 915,000 carats; salt 80,719; copper 50,447; lead 38,467; zinc 33,526; uranium 4,450; limestone and marble 2,300; gold 7,460 troy oz; silver 3,535 troy oz.

Manufacturing (gross output in R'000,000; 1976): food and beverages 140.8; metal products 34.2; wood products 6.6; chemical products 3.6; printing and publishing 2.4; other 12.4. Construction (value of buildings completed in R'000,000; 1983): residential 17.0; nonresidential 10.8. Energy production (consumption): electricity (kW-hr; 1983) 910,000,000 (n.a.); coal, none (n.a.); crude petroleum, none (n.a.); natural gas, none (n.a.).
Gross national product (1983): U.S.$1,920,000,000 (U.S.$1,760 per capita).

Structure of gross domestic product and labour force

	1984 in value R'000,000	1984 % of total value	1981 labour force	1981 % of labour force
Agriculture	136.8	7.0	71,402	35.0
Mining	510.4	26.1	15,515	7.6
Manufacturing	102.6	5.3	8,017	3.9
Construction	62.2	3.2	17,654	8.7
Public utilities	74.3	3.8	1,922	0.9
Transportation and communication	131.3	6.7	9,615	4.7
Trade	272.2	13.9	22,253	10.9
Finance	150.4	7.7	3,764	1.8
Services	39.9	2.0	22,417	11.0
Public admin., defense	411.5	21.1	31,079	15.2
Other	60.9	3.1	360	0.2
TOTAL	1,952.5¶	100.0	203,998	100.0♀

Population economically active: total (1984) 471,000; participation rate of total population 43.8% (female [1977] 38.8%, unemployedδ).

Price and earnings indexes (1980 = 100)□

	1979	1980	1981	1982	1983	1984	1985◇
Consumer price index	88.9	100.0	114.8	132.7	148.5	162.1	173.9
Earnings index	...	...	...	...	...	...	...

Household income and expenditure. Average household size (1981) 4.8; average annual income per household (1980) R3,223 (U.S.$4,143); sources of income (1980): wages 80.8%, self-employment 19.2%; expenditure: n.a.
Land use (1983): forested 12.7%; meadows and pastures 64.3%; agricultural and under permanent cultivation 0.8%; other 22.2%.

Foreign trade

Balance of trade (current prices)

	1979	1980	1981	1982	1983	1984
R'000,000	374.7	243.0	−130.1	−94.3	−70.7	−11.9
% of total	23.2%	12.2%	6.7%	4.5%	3.7%	0.5%

Imports (1984): R1,094,400,000 (no breakdown available). *Major import sources:* South Africa (nearly 100%).
Exports (1984): R1,082,500,000 (minerals 80%, including diamonds, uranium, copper, zinc, lead, tin; karakul pelts; fish and fish products). *Major export destinations:* South Africa; United States; West Germany.

Transport and communications

Transport. Railroads: length (1984) 1,454 mi, 2,340 km; (1981) metric ton-km cargo 1,900,000,000. Roads (1983): total length 25,700 mi, 41,361 km (paved 10.0%). Number of registered vehicles (1981): passenger cars 27,100; trucks and buses 19,400. Merchant marine: vessels (100 gross tons and over), none. Air transport (1981–82)△: passengers handled 194,170; cargo handled 2,157 metric tons; airports (1985) with scheduled flights 10.
Communications. Daily newspapers (1982): total number 3; total circulation 20,000; circulation per 1,000 population 19.4. Radio (1984): 55,000 receivers (1 per 19.5 persons). Television (1984): 15,500 receivers (1 per 69.3 persons). Telephones (1983): 60,737 (1 per 17.3 persons).

Education and health

Education (1982–83)

	schools	teachers	students	student/ teacher ratio
Primary (age 6–12)	1,069	7,120	232,306	32.6
Secondary (age 13–19)	78	1,864	40,359	21.6
Voc., teacher tr.	6	81	1,200	14.8
Higher	4	137	537	3.9

Educational attainment, n.a. *Literacy* (c. 1980): total population, n.a.; whites literate 100%; nonwhites literate c. 28%.
Health (1983): physicians 199 (1 per 5,271 persons); hospital beds 7,300 (1 per 143 persons); infant mortality rate per 1,000 live births (1980–85) 115.
Food (1979–81): daily per capita caloric intake 2,197 (vegetable products 77%, animal products 23%); 96% of FAO recommended minimum requirement.

Military

Total active duty personnel† (1984): 14,000 (army 100%). *Military expenditure as percent of GNP* (1983): 4.2% (world 6.1%); per capita expenditure U.S.$78.

---

*Some executive powers have been delegated to a Chief Executive Officer. †Excludes area and population of Walvis Bay (part of South Africa), administered as part of South West Africa/Namibia until 1977. ‡Preliminary; total includes 7,512 transients not distributed by subdivision. §1980. ‖ 1983. ¶At current prices. ♀Detail does not add to total given because of rounding. δIn 1984 estimates of urban unemployment were in the range of 30,000–80,000, or 6–15% of the economically active population and 15–40% of those in wage employment. □Windhoek only. ◇First quarter. △South West Africa/Namibia's four largest airports only. †The South West Africa Territory Force (SWATF), largely controlled by the Republic of South Africa.

Spain

Official name*: España (Spain).
Form of government: constitutional monarchy with two legislative houses (Senate [253]; Congress of Deputies [350]).
Chief of state: King.
Head of government: Prime Minister.
Capital: Madrid.
Official language: Spanish.
Official religion: none.
Monetary unit: 1 peseta (Pta; plural Ptas) = 100 céntimos; valuation (Oct. 21, 1985) 1 U.S.$ = Ptas160.83; 1 £ = Ptas230.63.

Area and population

Autonomous communities	Capitals	area sq mi	sq km	population 1982 estimate
Andalucía	Seville (Sevilla)	33,694	87,268	6,152,600
Aragón	Zaragoza	18,398	47,650	1,161,000
Asturias	Oviedo	4,079	10,565	1,140,200
Baleares	Palma de Mallorca	1,936	5,014	669,100
Canarias	Santa Cruz de Tenerife	2,796	7,242	1,530,400
Cantabria	Santander	2,042	5,289	507,500
Castilla-La Mancha	Toledo	30,591	79,230	1,516,200
Castilla-León	Valladolid	36,368	94,193	2,381,100
Cataluña	Barcelona	12,328	31,930	6,294,700
Extremadura	Mérida	16,063	41,602	952,800
Galicia	Santiago de Compostela	11,365	29,434	2,781,200
La Rioja	Logroño	1,944	5,034	242,000
Madrid	Madrid	3,087	7,995	5,024,500
Murcia	Murcia	4,370	11,317	922,900
Navarra	Pamplona	4,023	10,421	497,200
País Vasco	Vitoria	2,803	7,261	2,299,600
Valencia	Valencia	8,998	23,305	3,760,800
TOTAL SPAIN		194,885	504,750	37,833,900†
Enclaves in Northern Morocco				
Ceuta	—	7.1	18.5	...
Melilla	—	5.4	14	...
Chafarinas	—	.24	.61	...
Vélez de la Gomera	—	.02	.04	...
Alhucemas	—	.004	.01	...
TOTAL		194,897.79†	504,783.16	...

Demography

Population (1985): 38,765,000.
Density (1985): persons per sq mi 198.9, persons per sq km 76.8.
Urban–rural (1985): urban 77.4%; rural 22.6%.
Sex distribution (1985): male 48.98%; female 51.02%.
Age breakdown (1985): under 15, 24.6%; 15–29, 24.2%; 30–44, 18,5%; 45–59, 16.8%; 60–74, 11.6%; 75 and over, 4.3%.
Population projection: (1990) 39,700,000; (2000) 41,800,000.
Doubling time: more than 100 years.
Ethnic composition (1984): Spanish 72.8%; Catalan 16.4%; Galician 8.2%; Basque 2.3%; other 0.3%.
Religious affiliation (1980): Roman Catholic 97.0%; Protestant 0.4%; other 2.6%.
Major cities (1982): Madrid 3,271,834; Barcelona 1,720,998; Valencia 770,-277; Sevilla 630,912.

Vital statistics

Birth rate per 1,000 population (1983): 12.4 (world avg. 29.0).
Death rate per 1,000 population (1983): 7.7 (world avg. 11.0).
Natural increase rate per 1,000 population (1983): 4.7 (world avg. 18.0).
Total fertility rate (avg. births per childbearing woman; 1980–85): 2.4.
Marriage rate per 1,000 population (1983): 4.8.
Life expectancy at birth (1980–85): male 71.3 years; female 77.5 years.
Major causes of death per 100,000 population (1979): circulatory diseases 391.5, of which ischemic heart disease 101.3; malignant neoplasms (cancers) 196.0; respiratory diseases 60.5.

National economy

Budget (1984). Revenue: Ptas4,068,510,000,000 (indirect taxes 40.6%, personal income taxes 36.5%, direct taxes on enterprises 7.9%). Expenditures: Ptas3,957,000,000,000 (current transfers 57.0%, wages and salaries 31.0%, goods and services 4.6%).
Public debt (1981): U.S.$36,461,000,000.
Tourism (1983): receipts from visitors U.S.$6,386,000,000; expenditures by nationals abroad U.S.$894,000,000.
Production (metric tons except as noted). Agriculture, forestry, fishing (1984): barley 10,695,000, sugar beets 9,064,000, wheat 6,044,000, potatoes 5,949,000, grapes 5,569,000, tomatoes 2,553,000, corn (maize) 2,505,000, oranges 1,310,000, onions 1,114,000, apples 1,019,000, sunflower seeds 968,000, oats 790,000; livestock (number of live animals) 5,050,000 cattle, 12,400,000 pigs, 2,400,000 goats, 1,660,000 sheep; roundwood 14,823,000 cu m‡; fish catch 1,250,000‡. Mining and quarrying (metal content in metric tons; 1984): iron ore 3,582,000, zinc 221,700, lead 95,800, copper 61,900. Manufacturing (1984): crude steel 13,260,000; pig iron 5,364,000; wine 3,554,000; sulfuric acid 3,406,000; wheat flour 2,366,000§; sugar 1,328,000; fertilizers 1,301,000‡, of which nitrogenous 852,000‡; plastic resin 1,250,-000‡. Construction (1983): residential dwellings 207,168. Energy production (consumption): electricity (kW-hr; 1983) 115,450,000,000 (112,750,000,000);

coal (metric tons; 1983) 39,600,000 (44,496,000); crude petroleum (barrels; 1983) 22,345,000 (325,760,000); petroleum products (metric tons; 1983) 39,821,000 (34,672,000); natural gas (cu m; 1983) none (2,550,143,000).
Gross national product (1983): U.S.$182,760,000,000 (U.S.$4,780 per capita).

Structure of gross domestic product and labour force

	1983 in value Ptas'000,000	% of total value	labour force	% of labour force
Agriculture	1,360,692	6.3	2,067,400	16.9
Mining			88,900	0.7
Manufacturing	6,115,903	28.4	2,978,400	24.3
Public utilities			85,200	0.7
Construction	1,556,179	7.2	1,281,200	10.4
Transportation and communication			664,600	5.4
Trade			2,416,700	19.7
Finance	12,464,987	58.0	454,100	3.7
Pub. admin., defense				
Services			2,225,100	18.1
TOTAL	21,497,761	100.0†	12,261,600	100.0†

Population economically active (1983): total 13,210,100; participation rate of population over age 15, 48.2% (female 30.3%, unemployed 7.2%).

Price and earnings indexes (1980 = 100)

	1978	1979	1980	1981	1982	1983	1984
Consumer price index	74.8	86.5	100.0	114.6	131.1	147.0	163.6
Monthly earnings index	68.5	84.4	100.0	119.9	138.1	158.8	178.7

Household income and expenditure. Average household size (1983) 2.8; income per household Ptas1,250,000 (U.S.$8,700); sources of income: wages and salaries 54.6%, profits and self-employment 26.8%, social security 17.4%; expenditure (1981): food 35.9%, housing 21.8%, transportation 11.8%, clothing and footwear 8.1%, health 6.0%, education 4.3%.
Land use (1983): forested 31.3%; meadows and pastures 21.4%; agricultural and under permanent cultivation 41.1%; other 6.2%.

Foreign trade

Balance of trade (current prices)

	1979	1980	1981	1982	1983	1984
Ptas'000,000	−482,581	−957,466	−1,086,250	−1,207,600	−1,337,900	−850,900
% of total	16.5%	24.3%	22.3%	21.1%	19.1%	10.1%

Imports (1983): Ptas4,176,500,000,000 (petroleum and petroleum products 40.0%; machinery and transport equipment 17.4%, of which cars and trucks 3.7%; food 13.0%; chemicals, plastics, and rubber 9.2%; metals and metal products 5.4%). Major import sources: Middle East 16.4%; U.S. 11.9%; West Germany 8.8%; France 8.2%; U.K. 6.1%.
Exports (1983): Ptas2,838,600,000,000 (machinery and transport equipment 26.1%, of which cars and trucks 12.3%; food 16.1%; metals and metal products 14.9%; petroleum products 8.9%). Major export destinations: France 15.8%; West Germany 9.2%; U.K. 7.7%; Middle East 7.6%; U.S. 7.3%.

Transport and communications

Transport. Railroads (1984): route length 8,433 mi, 13,572 km; passenger-km 15,576,000,000; metric ton-km cargo 11,820,000,000. Roads (1983): total length 200,170 mi, 322,143 km (paved 56%). Vehicles (1983): passenger cars 8,714,076; trucks and buses 1,604,038. Merchant marine (1984): vessels (100 gross tons and over) 2,529; total deadweight tonnage 12,122,088. Air transport (1984): passenger-km 16,332,000,000‡; metric ton-km cargo 517,152,000; airports (1985) with scheduled flights 27.
Communications. Daily newspapers (1983): total number 113; total circulation 3,400,000; circulation per 1,000 population 89. Radio (1983): 10,400,-000 receivers (1 per 3.7 persons). Television (1983): 9,912,000 receivers (1 per 3.8 persons). Telephones (1983): 12,820,190 (1 per 3.0 persons).

Education and health

Education (1983–84)

	schools	teachers	students	student/ teacher ratio
Primary (age 2–13)§	23,105	232,173	6,870,057	29.6
Secondary (age 14–17)	2,547	71,256	1,142,308	16.0
Vocational	2,397	45,339	695,180	15.3
Higher, teacher tr. ‖	33	43,037	692,152	16.1

Educational attainment (1970). Percent of population over age 13 having: less than primary education 27.1%, of which no formal schooling 11.2%; primary 65.0%; lower secondary 2.6%; upper secondary 2.2%; some postsecondary 1.8%; university degree 1.3%. Literacy (1980): total population over age 14 literate 27,571,300 (92.8%); males literate 13,276,100 (96.3%); females literate 14,294,900 (89.6%).
Health (1983): physicians 115,251 (1 per 332 persons); hospital beds 201,-035¶♀ (1 per 190 persons); infant mortality rate per 1,000 live births 7.2.
Food (1980–82): daily per capita caloric intake 3,307 (vegetable products 74%, animal products 26%); 134% of FAO recommended minimum requirement.

Military

Total active duty personnel (1984): 330,000 (army 72.7%, navy 17.3%, air force 10.0%). Military expenditure as percent of GNP (1983): 1.8% (world 6.1%); per capita expenditure U.S.$88.

*Precedent exists in official documents for both Reino de España (Kingdom of Spain) and Estado Español (Spanish State). †Detail does not add to total given because of rounding. ‡1983. §1982. ‖1982–83. ¶Includes incubators. ♀1980.

Sri Lanka (Ceylon)

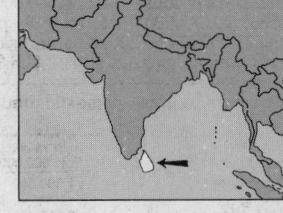

Official name: Sri Lankā Praja-thanthrika Samajavadi Janarajaya (Democratic Socialist Republic of Sri Lanka).
Form of government: unitary multiparty republic with one legislative house (Parliament [168]).
Head of state and government: President.
Capital: Colombo (Capital designate, Sri Jayawardenapura).
Official language: Sinhala.
Official religion: none.
Monetary unit: 1 Sri Lanka rupee (SL Rs) = 100 cents; valuation (Oct. 21, 1985) 1 U.S.$ = SL Rs27.30; 1 £ = SL Rs39.15.

Area and population

Districts	Capitals	area sq mi	area sq km	population 1981 census*
Amparai	Amparai	1,778	4,604	388,741
Anuradhapura	Anuradhapura	2,809	7,275	587,680
Badulla	Badulla	1,090	2,822	642,622
Batticaloa	Batticaloa	1,017	2,633	330,815
Colombo	Colombo	268	695	1,697,795
Galle	Galle	652	1,689	814,264
Gampaha	Gampaha	540	1,399	1,389,269
Hambantota	Hambantota	1,013	2,623	424,083
Jaffna	Jaffna	833	2,158	831,096
Kalutara	Kalutara	624	1,615	827,298
Kandy	Kandy	833	2,158	1,126,544
Kegalle	Kegalle	642	1,663	682,538
Kurunegala	Kurunegala	1,844	4,776	1,212,590
Mannar	Mannar	778	2,014	106,991
Matale	Matale	768	1,989	357,364
Matara	Matara	481	1,247	643,947
Moneragala	Moneragala	2,188	5,666	279,811
Mullaitivu	Mullaitivu	798	2,066	77,530
Nuwara Eliya	Nuwara Eliya	555	1,437	521,853
Polonnaruwa	Polonnaruwa	1,332	3,449	263,265
Puttalam	Puttalam	1,172	3,036	493,447
Ratnapura	Ratnapura	1,251	3,239	796,169
Trincomalee	Trincomalee	1,048	2,714	256,732
Vavuniya	Vavuniya	1,021	2,645	95,920
TOTAL		25,332†	65,610†	14,848,364

Demography

Population (1985): 16,109,000.
Density (1985): persons per sq mi 635.9, persons per sq km 245.5.
Urban–rural (1981): urban 21.5%; rural 78.5%.
Sex distribution (1981): male 50.77%; female 49.23%.
Age breakdown (1981): under 15, 35.3%; 15–29, 29.6%; 30–44, 17.9%; 45–59, 10.6%; 60–74, 5.2%; 75 and over, 1.4%.
Population projection: (1991) 18,868,000; (2001) 21,786,000.
Doubling time: 42 years.
Ethnic composition (1981): Sinhalese 74.0%; Tamil 18.2%; Sri Lankan Moor 7.1%; other 0.7%.
Religious affiliation (1981): Buddhist 69.3%; Hindu 15.5%; Muslim 7.6%; Christian 7.5%; other 0.1%.
Major cities (1982): Colombo 602,000; Dehiwala–Mount Lavinia 177,000; Moratuwa 136,000; Jaffna 121,000; Kandy 107,000.

Vital statistics

Birth rate per 1,000 population (1983): 26.2 (world avg. 29.0).
Death rate per 1,000 population (1983): 6.1 (world avg. 11.0).
Natural increase rate per 1,000 population (1982): 20.1 (world avg. 18.0).
Total fertility rate (avg. births per childbearing woman; 1983): 3.3.
Marriage rate per 1,000 population (1981): 8.1.
Divorce rate per 1,000 population (1983): 0.1.
Life expectancy at birth (1979): male 66.1 years; female 70.2 years.
Major causes of death per 100,000 population (1978): senility without mention of psychosis 122.1; heart disease 57.7; accidents other than motor vehicle 33.7; enteritis and other diarrheal diseases 31.7.

National economy

Budget‡ (1983). Revenue: SL Rs43,345,200,000 (current revenue SL Rs25,-431,900,000, of which sales and turnover taxes 40.4%, import duties 19.3%, income tax 14.2%, export duties 10.2%). Expenditures: SL Rs44,070,600,000 (current expenditures SL Rs26,222,400,000, of which interest on public debt 28.3%, administration including defense 17.0%, education, social services, and health 14.9%, pensions 7.1%, communications 5.0%).
Public debt (external, outstanding; 1983): U.S.$1,956,097,000.
Tourism (1983): receipts from visitors U.S.$127,000,000; expenditures by nationals abroad§ U.S.$79,000,000.
Production (metric tons except as noted). Agriculture, forestry, fishing (1984): rice 2,270,000, coconuts 1,460,000, cassava 650,000, tea 230,000, sweet potatoes 130,000, natural rubber 145,000, copra 100,000, mangoes 75,000; livestock (number of live animals) 1,738,000 cattle, 951,000 buffalo, 535,000 goats; roundwood 8,363,000 cu m ‖; fish catch 221,967 ‖. Mining and quarrying (1983): clays 131,890; salt 128,470; ilmenite 76,460; rutile 7,803; graphite 5,530; gemstones SL Rs936,783,600. Manufacturing (1983): cement 506,000; raw sugar 22,000; cigarettes 5,860; beer 72,000 hec-

tolitres. Construction (1982): residential 388,000 sq m. Energy production (consumption): electricity (kW-hr; 1983) 2,114,000,000 (2,114,000,000); coal (metric tons; 1983) none (28,000); crude petroleum (barrels; 1983) none (10,695,000); petroleum products (metric tons; 1983) 1,229,000 (1,335,000); natural gas (cu m; 1982) 3,063,000 (n.a.).
Gross national product (1983): U.S.$5,140,000,000 (U.S.$333 per capita).

Structure of gross domestic product and labour force

	1983 in value SL Rs'000,000	1983 % of total value	1980–81 labour force	1980–81 % of labour force
Agriculture	31,121.0	26.3	2,374,670	48.2
Mining	1,448.1	1.2	66,170	1.3
Manufacturing	17,443.0	14.7	531,065	10.8
Construction	9,710.2	8.2	223,750	4.5
Public utilities	1,633.9	1.4	18,999	0.4
Transp. and commun.	11,161.7	9.4	208,470	4.2
Trade	24,303.7	20.5	497,855	10.1
Finance	6,402.4	5.4	48,093	1.0
Pub. admin., defense, and services	10,304.0	8.7	650,981	13.2
Other	4,896.0¶	4.1¶	310,092	6.3
TOTAL	118,424.0²	100.0†	4,930,345	100.0

Population economically active: total (1983) 5,594,000; participation rate of total population 36.3% (female 27.4%ᵟ, unemployed 13.5%ᵟ).

Price and earnings indexes (1980 = 100)

	1979	1980	1981	1982	1983	1984	1985
Consumer price index	79.3	100.0	117.9	130.7	149.0	173.8	174.6□
Average wage index	80.1	100.0	100.2	118.0	129.3	162.9	...

Household income and expenditure. Average household size (1981) 5.2; income per household (1973) SL Rs3,936 (U.S.$611); sources of income (1982): wages 49.0%, property income 38.8%, government transfers 9.1%; expenditure (1983): food 50.8%, transportation 14.6%, beverages and tobacco 9.3%, housing 9.2%, clothing 5.9%, recreation 3.9%, health 1.6%.
Land use (1983): forested 36.8%; meadows and pastures 6.8%; agricultural and under permanent cultivation 33.8%; other 22.6%.

Foreign trade

Balance of trade (current prices)

	1979	1980	1981	1982	1983	1984
SL Rs'000,000	−7,278	−16,007	−14,666	−20,492	−20,370	−10,194
% of total	19.2%	31.2%	26.3%	32.3%	28.8%	11.6%

Imports (1983): SL Rs45,553,000,000 (investment goods 26.5%; consumer goods 25.6%, of which textiles 6.0%; sugar 4.4%, rice 1.7%). *Major import sources:* Japan 17.8%; Iran 10.5%; United Kingdom 6.8%; India 6.5%.
Exports (1983): SL Rs25,183,000,000 (tea 33.4%; rubber 11.5%; major coconut products 5.8%, of which desiccated coconut 3.6%; precious and semiprecious stones 3.8%). *Major export destinations:* United States 17.5%; West Germany 6.2%; United Kingdom 4.9%; Japan 4.6%; U.S.S.R. 3.8%.

Transport and communications

Transport. Railroads (1983): route length 1,453 km; passenger-km 2,421,-320,000; metric ton-km cargo 225,901,000. Roads (1981): total length 74,813 km (paved 40%). Vehicles (1983): passenger cars 136,853; trucks and buses 113,995. Merchant marine (1984): vessels (100 gross tons and over) 93; total deadweight tonnage 1,203,057. Air transport (1983): passenger-km 2,112,000,000; metric ton-km cargo 47,028,000; airports (1985) 6.
Communications. Daily newspapers (1984): total number 15; total circulation 850,000; circulation per 1,000 population 54. Radio (1982): 4,967,000 receivers (1 per 3 persons). Television (1983): 162,024 receivers (1 per 95 persons). Telephones (1982): 109,900 (1 per 135 persons).

Education and health

Education (1983)

	schools	teachers	students	student/ teacher ratio
Primary (age 5–10)	3,983	18,693	593,009	31.7
Secondary (age 11–17)	5,629	113,148	2,930,070	25.9
Voc., teacher tr.	25	466	8,382	18.0
Higher◇	8	2,168	18,073	8.3

Educational attainment (1981). Percent of adult population over age 30 having: less than primary education 30.3%; primary 37.2%; postprimary 14.7%; secondary 13.7%; higher 2.7%. *Literacy* (1981): population over age 15 literate 86.1%; males literate 90.8%; females literate 81.2%.
Health (1983): physicians△ 1,939 (1 per 7,953 persons); hospital beds 43,078 (1 per 358 persons); infant mortality rate per 1,000 live births 37.1.
Food (1980–82): daily per capita caloric intake 2,331 (vegetable products 96%, animal products 4%); 105% of FAO recommended minimum requirement.

Military

Total active duty personnel (1984): 16,560 (army 66.4%, navy 17.9%, air force 15.7%). *Military expenditure as percent of GNP* (1983): 1.5% (world 6.1%); per capita expenditure U.S.$5.

---

*Preliminary. †Detail does not add to total given because of rounding. ‡The current budget for 1984 was: revenue Sl Rs30,770,000,000; expenditures SL Rs28,950,000,-000. §1982. ‖ 1983. ¶Includes import duties. ⁰At current producers' prices. ᵟ1980–81. □August only. ◇Universities only. △Includes only those in Department of Health Services.

Sudan, The

Official name: Jumhūrīyat as-Sūdān (Republic of the Sudan)*.
Form of government: single-party republic with one legislative house (People's Assembly [153]).
Chief of state: President*.
Head of government: Prime Minister*.
Capital: Khartoum.
Official language: Arabic.
Official religion: Islām.
Monetary unit: 1 Sudanese pound (LSd) = 100 piastres; valuation (Oct. 21, 1985) 1 U.S.$ = LSd2.50; 1 £ = LSd3.58.

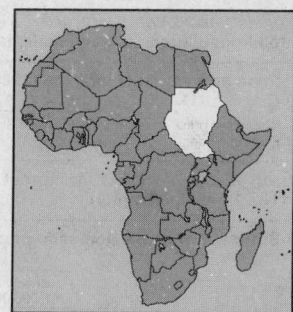

Area and population		area		population
Regions				1983
Provinces	Capitals	sq mi	sq km	census
ash-Shamālīyah (Northern)	ad-Dāmir	183,800	476,040	1,083,024
an-Nīl (Nile)	ad-Dāmir	49,167	127,343	649,633
ash-Shamālīyah (Northern)	Dunqulah	134,633	348,697	433,391
al-Wastā (Central)	Wad Madanī	53,675	139,017	4,012,543
an-Nīl al-Abyaḍ (White Nile)	ad-Duwaym	16,149	41,825	933,136
al-Jazīrah (El-Gezira)	Wad Madanī	13,536	35,057	2,023,094
an-Nīl al-Azraq (Blue Nile)	ad-Damazin	23,990	62,135	1,056,313
Kurdufān (Kordofan)	al-Ubayyiḍ	146,817	380,255	3,093,294
Kurdufān ai-Janūbīyah (Southern Kordofan)	Kāduqlī	61,141	158,355	1,287,525
Kurdufān ash-Shamālīyah (Northern Kordofan)	al-Ubayyiḍ	85,676	221,900	1,805,769
Dārfūr (Darfur)	al-Fāshir	196,404	508,684	3,093,699
Dārfūr al-Janūbīyah (Southern Darfur)	Nyala	62,753	162,529	1,765,752
Dārfūr ash-Shamālīyah (Northern Darfur)	al-Fāshir	133,651	346,155	1,327,947
ash-Sharqīyah (Eastern)	Kassalā	128,987	334,074	2,208,209
al-Baḥr al-Aḥmar (Red Sea)	Port Sudan	84,912	219,920	695,874
Kassalā (Kassala)	Kassalā	44,075	114,154	1,512,335
al-Istiwā'īyah (Equatoria)	Jūbā	76,436	197,969	1,406,181
al-Istiwā'īyah al Gharbīyah (Western Equatoria)	Yambio	30,398	78,732	359,056
al-Istiwā'īyah ash-Sharqīyah (Eastern Equatoria)	Jūbā	46,038	119,237	1,047,125
Baḥr al-Ghazāl (Bahr el-Ghazal)	Wāu	77,566	200,894	2,265,510
Baḥr al-Ghazāl al-Gharbīyah (Western Bahr el-Ghazal)	Raga	51,960	134,576	1,492,597
Baḥr al-Ghazāl ash-Sharqīyah (Eastern Bahr el-Ghazal)	Uwayl			
al-Buhayrān (El Buhayrah)	Rumbek	25,606	66,318	772,913
A'ālī an-Nīl (Upper Nile)	Malakāl	92,198	238,792	1,599,605
A'ālī an-Nīl (Upper Nile)	Nāṣir	45,231	117,148	802,354
Junqulī (Jongley)	Bor	46,781	121,164	797,251
National Capital				
Khartūm (Khartoum)	Khartoum	10,875	28,165	1,802,299
TOTAL		966,757†	2,503,890	20,564,364

Demography

Population (1985): 23,645,000.
Density (1985): persons per sq mi 24.5, persons per sq km 9.4.
Urban–rural (1983): urban 30.6%; rural 69.4%.
Sex distribution (1983): male 50.98%; female 49.02%.
Age breakdown (1985): under 15, 44.6%; 15–29, 26.0%; 30–44, 15.7%; 45–59, 8.9%; 60–74, 4.0%; 75 and over, 0.8%.
Population projection: (1990) 24,949,800; (2000) 32,885,000.
Doubling time: 25 years.
Ethnic composition (1980): Sudanese Arab 46.0%; Nilotic 25.5%; Azande 5.6%; Nuba 5.6%; Beja 5.0%; other 12.3%.
Religious affiliation (1980): Sunnī Muslim 73.0%; traditional beliefs 16.7%; Roman Catholic 5.6%; Anglican 2.3%; other 2.4%.
Major cities (1983): Omdurman 526,287; Khartoum 476,218; Khartoum North 341,146; Port Sudan 206,727.

Vital statistics

Birth rate per 1,000 population (1980–85): 45.3 (world avg. 29.0).
Death rate per 1,000 population (1980–85): 16.6 (world avg. 11.0).
Natural increase rate per 1,000 population (1980–85): 28.7 (world avg. 18.0).
Total fertility rate (avg. births per childbearing woman; 1980–85): 6.5.
Life expectancy at birth (1980–85): male 48.0 years; female 50.0 years.
Major causes of death from diseases per 100,000 population (1979)‡: pneumonia 26.4; tuberculosis 1.8; meningitis 1.3; infectious hepatitis 1.1.

National economy

Budget (1985–86). Revenue: LSd1,346,500,000 (import and export duties 55.3%; nontax revenue 19.3%; taxes on goods and services 11.7%; gross deficit LSd4,748,000,000, of which LSd3,632,500,000 financed by loans or rescheduling; net deficit LSd1,115,500,000). Expenditures: LSd6,094,500,000 (debt service 55.3%; current adminstration 33.4%, of which transfers to regions 7.4%, defense 5.5%; capital construction for development 10.5%, of which agriculture 3.8%).
Public debt (external, outstanding; 1983): U.S.$5,664,000,000.
Tourism: receipts from visitors (1981) U.S.$5,820,000§; expenditures by nationals abroad (1983) U.S.$69,000,000.
Production (metric tons except as noted). Agriculture, forestry, fishing (1984): sugarcane 4,700,000, sorghum 1,450,000, seed cotton 640,000, peanuts (groundnuts) 420,000, millet 270,000, lint cotton 219,000, sesame seeds 150,000; livestock (number of live animals) 19,600,000 cattle, 20,000,-

000 sheep, 13,000,000 goats, 2,500,000 camels; roundwood 38,157,000 cu m ‖; fish catch 29,500 ‖. Mining and quarrying (1983): hydraulic cement 200,000; salt 75,000; chromite concentrate 20,000; gypsum and anhydrite 15,000. Manufacturing (1980): crude cottonseed and peanut oils 288,000¶; wheat flour 220,000; raw sugar 195,000; cement 185,000. Construction: n.a. Energy production (consumption): electricity (kW-hr; 1983) 1,010,-000,000 (1,010,000,000); crude petroleum (barrels; 1982) none (8,210,000); petroleum products (metric tons; 1983) 1,000,000 (1,065,000).
Gross national product (1983): U.S.$8,420,000,000 (U.S.$400 per capita).

Structure of gross domestic product and labour force				
	1977–78		1979–80	
	in value LSd'000,000	% of total value	labour force	% of labour force
Agriculture	1,051.9	36.5	3,432,600	65.8
Mining	1.7	0.1	} 183,300	3.5
Manufacturing	215.1	7.5		
Construction	118.6	4.1	107,600	2.1
Public utilities	38.6	1.3	59,200	1.1
Transp. and commun.	279.1	9.6	198,800	3.8
Trade	555.8	19.3	} 220,800	4.2
Finance				
Pub. admin., defense	} 621.9	21.6	679,800	13.0
Services				
Other			340,500	6.5
TOTAL	2,882.7	100.0	5,222,600	100.0

Population economically active (1981): total 5,973,000; participation rate of total population 31.6% (female 10.9%; unemployed, n.a.).

Price indexes (1980 = 100)							
	1977	1978	1979	1980	1981	1982	1983
Consumer price index	51.0	60.8	79.8	100.0	124.6	156.6	204.5

Household income and expenditure. Average household size (1980) 5.3; average annual income per household: n.a.; source of income: n.a.; expenditure (1980)♀: food, beverages, and tobacco 66.5%, housing 12.4%, clothing 5.9%, education, health, transportation, and recreation 15.2%.
Land use (1983): forested 20.2%; meadows and pastures 23.6%; agricultural and under permanent cultivation 5.2%; desert and other 51.0%.

Foreign trade

Balance of trade (current prices)					
	1978	1979	1980	1981	1982	1983
LSd'000,000	−247.2	−244.7	−516.9	−509.7	−707.1	−761.5
% of total	37.9%	34.5%	48.8%	41.7%	44.0%	32.0%

Imports (1982): LSd1,156,404,000 (machinery 28.3%; petroleum and petroleum products 27.1%; chemicals 8.2%; sugar 5.4%). *Major import sources:* Saudi Arabia 16.2%; United Kingdom 12.0%; United States 9.6%.
Exports (1982): LSd449,338,000 (cotton 25.1%; unmilled cereals 23.3%; sheep, lambs, and goats 12.3%). *Major export destinations:* Saudi Arabia 36.6%; Italy 7.5%; Japan 6.6%.

Transport and communications

Transport. Railroads (1981–82): route length, 4,786 km; passenger-km 1,149,-000; metric ton-km cargo 1,600,000,000. Roads (1982): total length 9,018 km (paved 33%). Vehicles (1982): passenger cars 150,000; trucks and buses 22,000. Merchant marine (1984): vessels (100 gross tons and over) 23; total deadweight tonnage 128,223. Air transport (1981): passenger-km 710,-000,000; metric ton-km cargo 12,100,000; airports (1985) with scheduled flights 10.
Communications. Daily newspapers (1984): total number 2; total circulation 120,000; circulation per 1,000 population 5.3. Radio (1984): 1,450,000 receivers (1 per 15.7 persons). Television (1984): 111,000 receivers (1 per 205.2 persons). Telephones (1983): 68,838 (1 per 318.6 persons).

Education and health

Education (1981)				
	schools	teachers	students	student/ teacher ratio
Primary (age 7–12)	6,176	46,437	1,524,381	32.8
Secondary (age 13–18)	1,477δ	17,105	403,236	23.6
Voc., teacher tr.	60δ	1,584	23,696	14.9
Higher	17δ	1,934δ	33,309	...

Educational attainment, n.a. *Literacy* (1980): total population over age 15 literate 2,507,200 (21.6%); males 36.5%; females 6.5%.
Health (1981): physicians□ 2,169 (1 per 8,870 persons); hospital beds 17,328 (1 per 1,110 persons); infant mortality rate per 1,000 live births (1982) 119.
Food (1980–82): daily per capita caloric intake 2,332 (vegetable products 87%, animal products 13%); 101% of FAO recommended minimum.

Military

Total active duty personnel (1984): 58,000 (army 91.4%, navy 3.4%, air force 5.2%). *Military expenditure as percent of GNP* (1983): 1.7% (world 6.1%); per capita expenditure U.S.$8.

*On April 6, 1985, a coup replaced the existing government of The Sudan with a joint military–civilian transitional government; the chairman of the military council, however, remained the supreme authority during the transitional period. On Dec. 15 the country's name was changed from Democratic Republic to Republic of the Sudan. †Detail does not add to total given because of rounding. ‡Reported by hospitals and dispensaries. §Revenue of the departments of hotels and tourism. ‖ 1983. ¶1977. ♀Low-income households. δ1979–80. □Includes dentists.

Suriname

Official name: Republiek Suriname (Dutch); Republic of Suriname (English).
Form of government: military dictatorship with one ruling body (National Assembly [31]).
Head of state and government: Commander-in-Chief of the National Army.
Capital: Paramaribo.
Official languages: Dutch; English.
Official religion: none.
Monetary unit: 1 Suriname guilder (Sf) = 100 cents; valuation (Oct. 21, 1985) 1 U.S.$ = Sf1.78; 1 £ = Sf2.65.

Area and population

Districts	Capitals	area* sq mi	area* sq km	population 1980 census†
Brokopondo	Brokopondo	8,278	21,440	20,249
Commewijne	Nieuw Amsterdam	1,587	4,110	14,351
Coronie	Tottness	626	1,620	2,777
Marowijne	Albina	17,753	45,980	23,402
Nickerie	Nieuw Nickerie	24,946	64,610	34,480
Para	Onverwacht	378	980	14,867
Saramacca	Groningen	9,042	23,420	10,335
Suriname	...	629	1,628	166,494
Town district				
Paramaribo	Paramaribo	12	32	67,905
TOTAL		63,251	163,820	354,860

Demography

Population (1985): 395,000.
Density (1985): persons per sq mi 6.2, persons per sq km 2.4.
Urban–rural (1980): urban 44.8%; rural 55.2%.
Sex distribution (1980): male 49.49%; female 50.51%.
Age breakdown (1980): under 15, 39.3%; 15–29, 29.5%; 30–44, 13.8%; 45–59, 10.0%; 60–74, 4.5%; 75 and over, 2.8%‡.
Population projection: (1990) 405,000; (2000) 454,200.
Doubling time: 58 years.
Ethnic composition (1980): Hindustani 35%; Creole 32%; Indonesian 15%; Bush Negro 10%; Amerindian 3%; Chinese 3%; other 2%.
Religious affiliation (1980): Hindu 27.4%; Roman Catholic 22.8%; Muslim 19.6%; Protestant 18.8%; other 11.4%.
Major cities (1980): Paramaribo 67,905; Nieuw Nickerie 6,078; Meerzorg 5,355; Marienburg 3,633.

Vital statistics

Birth rate per 1,000 population (1980): 28.0 (world avg. 29.0); legitimate, n.a.; illegitimate, n.a.
Death rate per 1,000 population (1980): 7.9 (world avg. 11.0).
Natural increase rate per 1,000 population (1980): 20.1 (world avg. 18.0).
Total fertility rate (avg. births per childbearing woman; 1980): 5.7.
Marriage rate per 1,000 population (1980): 6.1§.
Divorce rate per 1,000 population: n.a.
Life expectancy at birth (1980–85): male 67.0 years; female 71.9 years.
Major causes of death per 100,000 population (1980): diseases of the circulatory system 169.4, of which cerebrovascular disease 49.4, ischemic heart disease 47.1; accidents 52.1, of which motor vehicle 18.6; malignant neoplasms (cancers) 49.6, of which stomach 5.6; infectious and parasitic diseases 38.3; diseases of the respiratory system 36.9; suicide 16.3.

National economy

Budget (1976) ‖. Revenue: Sf403,100,000¶ (import duties 23.5%; excise tax 20.6%; corporate tax 11.1%; income tax 5.8%). Expenditures: Sf424,210,000 (general public services 37.0%; education 15.9%; health 8.6%; mining, manufacturing, and construction 5.1%; social security 4.7%; roads 3.7%; housing 2.1%).
Public debt (external, outstanding; 1983): U.S.$24,000,000.
Tourism (1983): receipts from visitors U.S.$4,000,000; expenditures by nationals abroad U.S.$35,000,000.
Production (metric tons except as noted). Agriculture, forestry, fishing (1984): rice 270,000, sugarcane 150,000, fruits and vegetables 102,000 (of which bananas 41,000, oranges 7,000, other citrus fruits 2,000, cabbage 1,000, tomatoes 1,000, cucumbers 1,000), coconuts 6,000; livestock (number of live animals) 53,000 cattle, 18,000 pigs, 10,000 goats, 4,000 sheep, 1,100,000 chickens; roundwood (1983) 266,000 cu m; fish catch (1983) 3,592. Mining and quarrying (1983): bauxite 3,230,000♀; gravel and crushed stone 120,000; clay 100,000; gold 600 troy oz. Manufacturing (1983): alumina 1,240,000♀; cement 72,000; aluminum 23,000♀; sugar 11,000♂; sawn wood 61,000 cu m; wood-based panels 26,000 cu m; plywood 20,000 cu m; shoes 383,895 pairs□; soft drinks 42,328□; beer 143,000 hectolitres□; cigarettes 444,000,000 units♂. Construction: n.a. Energy production (consumption): electricity (kW-hr; 1983) 1,300,000,000 (1,300,000,000); hard coal (metric tons; 1983) none (1,000); crude petroleum (barrels; 1983) 205,000 (205,000); petroleum products (metric tons; 1983) none (537,000); fuelwood (cubic metres; 1982) 19,000 (19,000); bagasse (metric tons; 1982) 36,000 (36,000).
Land use (1983): forested 96.1%; meadows and pastures 0.1%; agricultural and under permanent cultivation 0.4%; other 3.4%.

Population economically active (1982): total 83,461; participation rate of total population 23.8% (female, n.a., unemployed [1980] 14.6%).

Price and earnings indexes (1980 = 100)

	1978	1979	1980	1981	1982	1983	1984
Consumer price index	77.5	88.3	100.0	108.7	116.6	121.8	126.2
Earnings index	...	...	...	...	...	...	...

Gross national product (at current market prices; 1983): U.S.$1,280,000,000 (U.S.$3,497 per capita).

Structure of gross domestic product and labour force

	1980 in value SF'000,000	% of total value	labour force	% of labour force
Agriculture	165	10.1	7,600	7.8
Mining	273	16.8	5,580	5.7
Manufacturing			7,260	7.4
Construction			3,940	4.1
Public utilities	302	18.6	1,260	1.3
Transportation and communication			2,930	3.0
Trade	◊	◊	11,420	11.6
Finance	◊	◊	1,970	2.1
Pub. admin., defense	318	19.6	38,040	38.9
Services	568	34.9	17,690	18.1
Other				
TOTAL	1,626△	100.0	97,690	100.0

Household income and expenditure. Average household size (1980) 3.9; average annual income per household: n.a.; source of income: n.a.; expenditure† (1968–69): food and drink 40.0%, household furniture and furnishings 12.3%, clothing and footwear 10.6%, transport and communications 9.5%, recreation 6.1%, fuel and power 5.5%.

Foreign trade

Balance of trade (current prices)

	1979	1980	1981	1982	1983	1984
Sf'000,000	+137.8	+114.4	−59.3	−49.9	−67.2	+84.1
% of total	9.5%	6.6%	3.4%	3.2%	4.9%	7.1%

Imports (1981): Sf905,000,000 (raw materials and semimanufactured goods 39.0%, machinery and equipment 28.7%, refined petroleum products 19.9%). *Major import sources:* Caribbean countries 29%; United States 28%; The Netherlands 9%.
Exports (1981): Sf845,700,000 (alumina 55.9%, bauxite 13.3%, aluminum 10.3%, shrimp 7.6%, rice 7.5%, bananas 1.4%, plywood 1.2%). *Major export destinations:* United States 35%; The Netherlands 14%; Norway 13%; United Kingdom 7%.

Transport and communications

Transport. Railroads (1983): length 104 mi, 167 km; passengers, n.a.; cargo, n.a. Roads (1983): total length 5,523 mi, 8,889 km (paved 29%). Vehicles (1983): passenger cars 31,170; trucks and buses 12,850. Merchant marine (1984): vessels (100 gross tons and over) 25; total deadweight tonnage 19,187. Air transport (1980): passenger-mi 152,240,000, passenger-km 245,000,000; short ton-mi cargo 2,466,000, metric ton-km cargo 3,600,000; airports (1985) with scheduled flights 5.
Communications. Daily newspapers (1984): total number 8; total circulation 30,000⊙; circulation per 1,000 population 80⊙. Radio (1984): total number of receivers 187,000 (1 per 2.0 persons). Television (1984): total number of receivers 43,000 (1 per 8.7 persons). Telephones (1982): 27,495 (1 per 13 persons).

Education and health

Education (1982–83)

	schools	teachers	students	student/ teacher ratio
Primary (age 6–12)	294	2,944	74,805	25.4
Secondary (age 13–17)	91	1,602	22,401	14.0
Voc., teacher tr.	19	556	9,853	17.7
Higher	2	167	734	4.4

Educational attainment, n.a. *Literacy* (1980): total population over age 15 literate 170,700 (80.7%); males literate 88,286 (85.4%); females literate 82,414 (76.3%).
Health (1980): physicians (1979) 224 (1 per 1,612 persons); hospital beds 3,169 (1 per 160.0 persons); infant mortality rate per 1,000 live births 34.9.
Food (1980–82): daily per capita caloric intake 2,470 (vegetable products 87%, animal products 13%); 110% of FAO recommended minimum requirement.

Military

Total active duty personnel (1984): 2,020** (army 89.1%, navy 7.9%, air force 3.0%). *Military expenditure as percent of GNP:* n.a.

---

*Area excludes 6,809 sq mi (17,635 sq km) of territory disputed with Guyana. †Preliminary. ‡Detail does not add to total given because of rounding. §Excludes Hindu and Muslim marriages not registered in court. ‖ Actual budget in 1983 was: revenue Sf468,780,000; expenditures Sf801,260,000. ¶Includes Sf16,870,000 in capital revenue and grants. ♀1984. ♂1982. □1981. ◊Trade and finance included with services and other. △At current prices. †For Paramaribo and environs. ⊙Partial circulation only. **All services are part of the army.

Swaziland

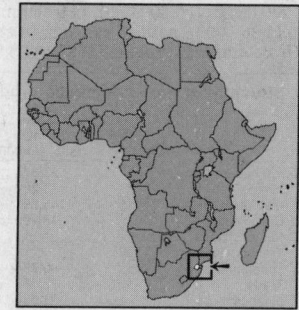

Official name: Umbuso weSwatini (Swazi); Kingdom of Swaziland (English).
Form of government: constitutional monarchy with two legislative houses (Senate [20]; House of Assembly [50]).
Chief of state: King*.
Head of government: Prime Minister.
Capitals: Mbabane (administrative); Lobamba (royal and legislative).
Official languages: Swazi; English.
Official religion: none.
Monetary unit: 1 lilangeni (plural emalangeni [E]) = 100 cents; valuation (Oct. 21, 1985) 1 U.S.$ = E2.60†; 1 £ = E3.72.

Area and population

Districts	Capitals	area sq mi	area sq km	population 1985 estimate‡
Hhohho	Mbabane	1,378	3,569	179,100
Lubombo	Siteki	2,296	5,947	133,500
Manzini	Manzini	1,571	4,068	189,700
Shiselweni	Nhlangano	1,459	3,780	145,100
TOTAL		6,704	17,364	647,400

Demography

Population (1985 est.): 647,400.
Density (1985): persons per sq mi 96.6, persons per sq km 37.3.
Urban–rural (1985): urban 26.3%; rural 73.7%.
Sex distribution (1985): male 48.84%; female 51.16%.
Age breakdown (1985): under 15, 46.1%; 15–29, 25.7%; 30–44, 14.6%; 45–59, 8.6%; 60–74, 4.2%; 75 and over, 0.8%.
Population projection: (1990) 759,000; (2000) 1,041,000.
Doubling time: 22.2 years.
Ethnic composition (1980): Swazi 87.8%; Zulu 9.2%; other 3.0%.
Religious affiliation (1980): Christian 77.0%; tribal beliefs 20.9%; other 2.1%.
Major cities (1985): Mbabane 45,000; Manzini 17,000; Havelock Mine 6,500.

Vital statistics

Birth rate per 1,000 population (1980–85): 47.5 (world avg. 29.0).
Death rate per 1,000 population (1980–85): 17.2 (world avg. 11.0).
Natural increase rate per 1,000 population (1980–85): 30.2 (world avg. 18.0).
Total fertility rate (avg. births per childbearing woman; 1980–85): 6.5.
Life expectancy at birth (1980–85): male 45.3 years; female 51.9 years.
Major causes of death per 100,000 population (1970): tuberculosis 29.5; gastroenteritis 18.3; malnutrition, unspecified 11.7; kwashiorkor 10.0.

National economy

Budget (1985–86). Revenue: E218,300,000 (no breakdown available). Expenditures: E217,300,000 (current expenditure 79.1%, of which education and training 23.8%; economic development 20.9%, of which transport and communications 9.3%, agriculture 2.8%; debt payment 16.1%).
Tourism: receipts from visitors (1983) U.S.$7,200,000; expenditures by nationals abroad (1982) U.S.$22,000,000.
Land use (1983): forested 5.9%; meadows and pastures 66.8%; agricultural and under permanent cultivation 8.0%; other 19.4%.
Production (metric tons except as noted). Agriculture, forestry, fishing (1984): sugarcane 3,500,000, fruit excluding melons 143,000, cereals 115,000 (of which corn [maize] 110,000, rice 3,000, sorghum 2,000), pineapples 35,-000, seed cotton 32,000, roots and tubers 17,000 (of which sweet potatoes 11,000, potatoes 6,000), lint cotton 12,000, pulses 3,000; livestock (number of live animals) 614,000 cattle, 298,000 goats, 40,000 sheep, 19,000 pigs, 1,000,000 chickens; roundwood (1983) 2,223,000 cu m; fish catch (1983) 44. Mining and quarrying (1984): asbestos 25,832; diamonds 16,837 carats. Manufacturing (producers' prices in E; 1981): food products and beverages 174,057,000; paper products 63,671,000; industrial chemicals 55,628,000; textiles 21,679,000; wood products, furniture, and fixtures 21,161,000. Construction (value in E; 1982): residential§ 3,798,000; nonresidential 2,822,000. Energy production (consumption): electricity (kW-hr; 1981) 310,200,000 (n.a.); coal (metric tons; 1984) 124,569 (26,350); crude petroleum, n.a. (n.a.); petroleum products, n.a. (n.a.); natural gas, n.a. (n.a.).
Public debt (external, outstanding; 1984): U.S.$118,000,000.
Gross national product (1983): U.S.$610,000,000 (U.S.$890 per capita).

Structure of gross domestic product and labour force

	1981 in value E'000,000	1981 % of total value	1982 labour force♀	1982 % of labour force
Agriculture	111.4	20.1	24,657	31.9
Mining	15.1	2.7	2,492	3.2
Manufacturing	89.1	16.1	11,708	15.1
Construction	21.4	3.9	7,426	9.6
Public utilities	7.2	1.3	1,091	1.4
Transp. and commun.	24.8	4.5	4,187	5.4
Trade	42.3	7.6	6,923	9.0
Finance			2,233	2.9
Pub. admin., defense	242.7δ	43.8	16,631	21.5
Services				
Other			—	—
TOTAL	553.9◻	100.0	77,348◊	100.0

Population economically active: total (1983) 273,000; participation rate of total population 44.2% (female [1982] 51.7%, unemployed 4.0%).

Price and earnings indexes (1980 = 100)

	1979	1980	1981	1982	1983	1984	1985 ‖
Consumer price index	84.3	100.0	120.0	133.0	148.5	167.1	198.7
Monthly earnings index¶	141.3	100.0	136.4	...	...	...	...

Household income and expenditure. Average household size (1980) 5.0; average annual income per household: n.a.; source of income: n.a.; expenditure: n.a.

Foreign trade△

Balance of trade (current prices)

	1978	1979	1980	1981	1982	1983
E'000,000	−87.3	−152.0	−159.4	−153.9	−167.9	−285.3
% of total	20.4%	27.9%	21.7%	18.4%	18.5%	30.6%

Imports (1983): E609,000,000 (machinery and transport equipment 31.2%, manufactured goods 13.9%, mineral fuels and lubricants 14.3%, chemicals and chemical products 11.6%, food and live animals 9.8%, beverages and tobacco 1.5%). *Major import sources* (1982): South Africa 94%.
Exports (1983): E323,700,000 (sugar 38.4%, wood pulp 14.0%, chemicals 13.2%, asbestos 5.8%, canned fruits 4.9%, citrus fruits 3.9%, sawn timber 3.8%). *Major export destinations* (1982): South Africa 30%; U.K 20%.

Transport and communications

Transport. Railroads (1982): route length 312 km; passengers, n.a.; metric ton-km cargo 137,800,000. Roads (1983): total length 2,719 km (paved 23%). Vehicles (1982): passenger cars 21,338; trucks and buses 8,376. Merchant marine: vessels (100 gross tons and over) n.a.; total deadweight tonnage, n.a. Air transport† (1984): passenger-km 22,494,000; metric ton-km cargo 2,201,000; airports (1985) with scheduled flights 1.
Communications. Daily newspapers (1984): total number 3; total circulation 22,000; circulation per 1,000 population 34.5. Radio (1984): 85,000 receivers (1 per 7.5 persons). Television (1984): 7,000 receivers (1 per 91.1 persons). Telephones (1983): 7,456 (1 per 83 persons).

Education and health

Education (1984)

	schools	teachers	students	student/ teacher ratio
Primary (age 6–13)	467	4,039	134,528	33.3
Secondary (age 14–18)	89	1,569	28,833	18.4
Voc., teacher tr.††	4	121	1,473	12.2
Higher‡‡	1	131	1,063	8.1

Educational attainment (1976). Percent of adult population over age 25 having: no formal schooling 53.6%; some primary education 25.4%; complete primary 9.2%; some secondary 7.9%; secondary and higher 3.9%. *Literacy* (1976): total population over age 15 literate 107,027 (41.5%); males literate 55,865 (45.5%); females literate 51,162 (37.9%).
Health (1984): physicians 80 (1 per 7,971 persons); hospital beds 1,608 (1 per 396 persons); infant mortality rate per 1,000 live births (1980–85) 129.
Food (1980–82): daily per capita caloric intake 2,526 (vegetable products 87%, animal products 13%); 109% of FAO recommended minimum requirement.

Military

Total active duty personnel (1983): 2,657. *Military expenditure as percent of GNP* (1983): 3.1% (world 6.1%); per capita expenditure U.S.$29.

*Queen acting as Regent until successor comes of age. †The lilangeni is at par with the South African rand. ‡De facto African population projection only. §Includes hotels, hostels, etc. ‖ April. ¶Based on earning of skilled workers in manufacturing. ♀Employed persons only. δIncludes imputed bank service charges. ◻At current prices. ◊In 1982 more than 12,000 Swazis were also employed in gold mines in the Republic of South Africa. △Import figures are f.o.b. (free on board) in balance of trade and c.i.f. (cost, insurance, and freight) for commodities and trading partners. †Royal Swazi National Airlines only.

T. FINCHER—FAO

Headman in traditional dress with knobstick, near Mbabane, Swaziland, overlooking a chief's cattle herd.

Sweden

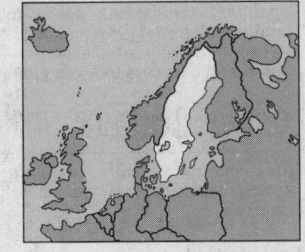

Official name: Konungariket Sverige (Kingdom of Sweden).
Form of government: constitutional monarchy and parliamentary state with one legislative house (Parliament [349]).
Chief of state: King.
Head of government: Prime Minister.
Capital: Stockholm.
Official language: Swedish.
Official religion: Church of Sweden (Lutheran).
Monetary unit: 1 Swedish krona (SKr) = 100 ore; valuation (Oct. 21, 1985) 1 U.S.$ = SKr7.93; 1 £ = SKr11.37.

Area and population		area		population
		sq mi	sq km	1984 estimate
Counties	Capitals			
Älvsborg	Vänersborg	4,400	11,395	426,300
Blekinge	Karlskrona	1,136	2,941	151,700
Gävleborg	Gävle	7,024	18,191	290,500
Göteborg och Bohus	Göteborg	1,985	5,141	712,100
Gotland	Visby	1,212	3,140	56,200
Halland	Halmstad	2,106	5,454	238,400
Jämtland	Östersund	19,090	49,443	134,700
Jönköping	Jönköping	3,839	9,944	300,900
Kalmar	Kalmar	4,313	11,170	239,400
Kopparberg	Falun	10,886	28,194	285,100
Kristianstad	Kristianstad	2,350	6,087	280,300
Kronoberg	Växjö	3,266	8,458	174,300
Malmöhus	Malmö	1,907	4,938	747,100
Norrbotten	Luleå	38,191	98,913	263,700
Örebro	Örebro	3,289	8,519	271,000
Östergötland	Linköping	4,078	10,562	392,900
Skaraborg	Mariestad	3,065	7,937	270,400
Södermanland	Nyköping	2,340	6,060	250,500
Stockholm	Stockholm	2,505	6,488	1,562,500
Uppsala	Uppsala	2,698	6,989	249,700
Värmland	Karlstad	6,789	17,584	280,500
Västerbotten	Umeå	21,390	55,401	245,200
Västernorrland	Härnösand	8,370	21,678	263,600
Västmanland	Västerås	2,433	6,302	255,700
TOTAL LAND AREA		158,661*	410,929	8,342,600*
INLAND WATER		15,071	39,035	
TOTAL		173,732*	449,964	

Demography

Population (1985): 8,345,000.
Density (1985)†: persons per sq mi 52.5, persons per sq km 20.3.
Urban–rural (1985): urban 85.5%; rural 14.5%.
Sex distribution (1984): male 49.39%; female 50.61%.
Age breakdown (1984): under 15, 18.4%; 15–29, 20.7%; 30–44, 21.9%; 45–59, 16.1%; 60–74, 15.8%; 75 and over, 7.1%.
Population projection: (1990) 8,344,500; (2000) 8,328,600.
Ethnic composition (1983): Swedish 95.2%; Finnish 1.8%; other 3.0%.
Religious affiliation (1984): Church of Sweden 90.4% (nominally; about 30% nonpracticing); Roman Catholic 1.4%; other 8.2%.
Major cities (1984): Stockholm 653,455; Göteborg 424,085; Malmö 229,107; Uppsala 152,579; Norrköping 118,451.

Vital statistics

Birth rate per 1,000 population (1984): 11.3 (world avg. 29.0); (1983) legitimate 56.4%; illegitimate 43.6%.
Death rate per 1,000 population (1984): 10.9 (world avg. 11.0).
Natural increase rate per 1,000 population (1984): 0.4 (world avg. 18.0).
Total fertility rate (avg. births per childbearing woman; 1983): 1.6.
Marriage rate per 1,000 population (1984): 4.4.
Divorce rate per 1,000 population (1984): 2.4.
Life expectancy at birth (1983): male 73.1 years; female 79.1 years.
Major causes of death per 100,000 population (1982): heart disease 439.3; malignant neoplasms (cancers) 229.4; cerebrovascular disease 113.0.

National economy

Budget (1985–86). Revenue: SKr261,952,800,000 (value-added tax 22.3%, income tax and capital gains 21.0%, social security contributions 20.9%, nontax revenue 11.3%). Expenditures: SKr323,389,000,000 (health and social affairs 24.5%, interest on national debt 23.9%, education and culture 11.8%, defense 7.8%, manpower 5.5%).
Public debt (1984): U.S.$60,908,000,000.
Tourism (1983): receipts from visitors U.S.$1,056,000,000; expenditures by nationals abroad U.S.$1,608,000,000.
Production (metric tons except as noted). Agriculture, forestry, fishing (1984): barley 2,733,000, sugar beets 2,508,000, oats 1,904,000, wheat 1,776,000, potatoes 1,307,000; livestock (number of live animals) 1,875,000 cattle, 2,670,000 pigs, 440,000 sheep; roundwood 24,800,000 cu m; fish catch 258,-800, of which Baltic herring 120,900. Mining and quarrying (1984): iron ore ‡8,123,000, zinc 383,000, copper 354,000, lead 119,000. Manufacturing (1984): crude and manufactured steel 9,176,000; paper and paperboard 6,869,000; cement 2,319,000; wood pulp 2,264,000; automobiles 314,600 vehicles. Construction (1984): 35,000 dwellings completed. Energy production (consumption): electricity (kW-hr; 1984) 119,589,000,000 (120,005,000,000); coal (metric tons; 1983) 13,000 (2,962,000); crude petroleum (barrels; 1984)

270,000‡ (100,800,000); petroleum products (metric tons; 1983) 13,106,000 (15,367,000); natural gas, n.a. (n.a.).
Gross national product (1983): U.S.$89,500,000,000 (U.S.$10,745 per capita).

Structure of gross domestic product and labour force				
	1983		1984	
	in value SKr'000,000	% of total value	labour force	% of labour force
Agriculture	21,374	3.0	218,000	5.1
Mining	3,282	0.5 }		
Manufacturing	146,891	20.8 }	1,007,000	23.7
Construction	46,708	6.6	260,000	6.1
Public utilities	...	...	...	...
Transportation and communication	40,764	5.8	294,000	6.9
Trade	75,189	10.7	586,000	13.8
Finance	81,550	11.6	316,000	7.4
Pub. admin., defense	153,438	21.8 }		
Services	27,237	3.9 }	1,574,000	37.0
Other	108,036	15.3 }		
TOTAL	704,474*§	100.0	4,255,000	100.0

Population economically active (1984): total 4,391,000; participation rate of working-age population ages 16–74, 71.9% (female 67.5%, unemployed 3.1%).

Price and earnings indexes (1980 = 100)							
	1979	1980	1981	1982	1983	1984	1985 ‖
Consumer price index	87.9	100.0	112.1	121.7	132.6	143.2	154.0
Hourly earnings index	90.5	100.0	110.2	118.2	127.4	141.2	...

Household income and expenditure. Average household size (1980) 2.4; income per household (1983) SKr98,400 (U.S.$15,165); sources of income (1982): wages and salaries 62.1%; transfer payments 21.1%, of which social security 14.8%, self-employed 17.1%, other 31.1%; expenditure (1984): housing 33.3%, food 26.1%, transportation 15.8%, recreation 9.7%.
Land use (1983): forested 64.2%; meadows and pastures 1.7%; agricultural and under permanent cultivation 7.2%; other 26.9%.

Foreign trade

Balance of trade (current prices)						
	1979	1980	1981	1982	1983	1984
SKr'000,000	−4,750	−10,700	−1,160	−5,800	10,150	24,710
% of total	2.0%	3.9%	0.4%	1.7%	2.5%	5.4%

Imports (1984): SKr218,110,000,000 (machinery and transport equipment 31.1%, of which transport equipment 8.2%, electrical machinery 8.1%; chemicals 9.4%; food and tobacco products 6.6%; clothing and footwear 4.5%). *Major import sources:* West Germany 17.5%; United Kingdom 13.6%; United States 8.1%; Norway 7.7%; Denmark 6.3%.
Exports (1984): SKr242,320,000,000 (machinery and transport equipment 40.6%, of which transport equipment 16.0%, electrical machinery 7.4%; paper products 9.4%; wood and wood pulp 8.9%; iron and steel products 6.4%; chemicals 6.2%). *Major export destinations:* West Germany 11.6%; United States 11.3%; United Kingdom 10.2%; Norway 9.2%; Denmark 5.7%.

Transport and communications

Transport. Railroads (1984): length 7,496 mi, 12,063 km; passenger-mi 4,157,000, passenger-km 6,690,000; short ton-mi cargo 12,176,000, metric ton-km cargo 17,776,000. Roads (1985): total length 108,300 mi, 174,291 km (paved 68%). Vehicles (1984): passenger cars 3,081,000; trucks and buses 223,590. Merchant marine (1984): vessels (100 gross tons and over) 679; total deadweight tonnage 5,195,995. Air transport (1984): passenger-mi 3,166,000,000, passenger-km 5,096,000,000; short ton-mi cargo 131,232,000, metric ton-km cargo 191,595,000; airports (1985) 35.
Communications. Daily newspapers (1984): total number 169; total circulation 4,782,100; circulation per 1,000 population 574. Radio (1984): 3,327,-000 receivers (1 per 2.5 persons). Television (1984): 3,251,000 receivers (1 per 2.6 persons). Telephones (1984): 7,410,000 (1 per 1.1 persons).

Education and health

Education (1984–85)	schools	teachers	students	student/ teacher ratio
Primary (age 7–12)	5,399‡¶	123,801‡¶	630,505	...
Secondary (age 13–18)	¶	¶	459,519	...
Higher	...	...	179,733	...
	...	...	216,412‡	...

Educational attainment (1979). Percent of adult population over age 24 having: lower secondary education 7.3%; higher secondary 35.7%; some post-secondary 15.4%. *Literacy* (1984): virtually 100%.
Health (1983): physicians 19,300 (1 per 432 persons); hospital beds 116,688 (1 per 71 persons); infant mortality rate per 1,000 live births (1984) 6.3.
Food (1984): daily per capita caloric intake 3,000 (vegetable products 65%, animal products 35%); 112% of FAO recommended minimum.

Military

Total active duty personnel (1984): 65,650 (army 71.6%, navy 14.7%, air force 13.7%). *Military expenditure as percent of GNP* (1983): 2.9% (world 6.1%); per capita expenditure U.S.$310.

---

*Detail does not add to total given because of rounding †Density based on land area only. ‡1983. §In current prices. ‖ For third quarter only. ¶Primary includes secondary.

Switzerland

Official name: Confédération Suisse (French); Schweizerische Eidgenossenschaft (German); Confederazione Svizzera (Italian) (Swiss Confederation).
Form of government: federal republic with two legislative houses (Council of States [46]; National Council [200]).
Head of state and government: President.
Capital: Bern.
Official languages: French; German; Italian.
Official religion: none.
Monetary unit: 1 Swiss Franc (SwF) = 100 centimes; valuation (Oct. 29, 1984) 1 U.S.$ = SwF2.52; 1 £ = SwF3.04.

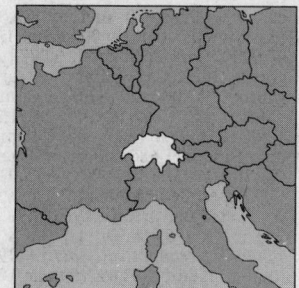

Area and population		area		population
Cantons	Capitals	sq mi	sq km	1985 estimate*
Aargau	Aarau	542	1,405	464,600
Appenzell Ausser-Rhoden†	Herisau	94	243	48,800
Appenzell Inner-Rhoden†	Appenzell	66	172	13,000
Basel-Landschaft†	Liestal	165	428	223,500
Basel-Stadt†	Basel	14	37	197,500
Bern	Bern	2,335	6,049	921,500
Fribourg	Fribourg	645	1,670	190,400
Genève	Geneva	109	282	360,500
Glarus	Glarus	264	684	36,400
Graubünden	Chur	2,744	7,106	164,800
Jura	Delémont	323	837	64,400
Luzern	Luzern	576	1,492	302,200
Neuchâtel	Neuchâtel	308	797	154,700
Nidwalden†	Stans	107	276	30,200
Obwalden†	Sarnen	189	491	27,000
Sankt Gallen	Sankt Gallen	778	2,014	398,600
Schaffhausen	Schaffhausen	115	298	69,600
Schwyz	Schwyz	351	908	100,900
Solothurn	Solothurn	305	791	218,200
Thurgau	Frauenfeld	391	1,013	189,200
Ticino	Bellinzona	1,085	2,811	273,500
Uri	Altdorf	416	1,076	33,600
Valais	Sion	2,018	5,226	227,300
Vaud	Lausanne	1,243	3,219	539,600
Zug	Zug	92	239	79,000
Zürich	Zürich	668	1,729	1,126,900
TOTAL		15,943	41,293	6,455,900‡

Demography
Population (1985): 6,473,000.
Density (1985): persons per sq mi 406.0, persons per sq km 156.8.
Urban–rural (1985): urban 60.4%; rural 39.6%.
Sex distribution (1984): male 48.71%; female 51.29%.
Age breakdown (1984): under 15, 18.1%; 15–29, 23.2%; 30–44, 22.4%; 45–59, 17.4%; 60–74, 12.8%; 75 and over, 6.1%.
Population projection: (1990) 6,600,000; (2000) 6,870,000.
Ethnolinguistic composition (1980)‡: German 65.0%; French 18.4%; Italian 9.8%; Spanish 1.6%; Romansch 0.8%; Turkish 0.6%; other 3.8%.
Religious affiliation (1980): Rom. Cath. 47.6%; Protestant 44.3%; other 8.1%.
Major cities (1985): Zürich 354,500; Basel 176,200; Geneva 159,500.

Vital statistics
Birth rate per 1,000 population (1984): 11.5 (world avg. 29.0); (1983) legitimate 94.6%; illegitimate 5.4%.
Death rate per 1,000 population (1984): 9.1 (world avg. 11.0).
Natural increase rate per 1,000 population (1984): 2.4 (world avg. 18.0).
Total fertility rate (avg. births per childbearing woman; 1983): 1.8.
Marriage rate per 1,000 population (1984): 5.9.
Divorce rate per 1,000 population (1983): 1.8.
Life expectancy at birth (1981–82): male 72.7 years; female 79.6 years.
Major causes of death per 100,000 population (1983): circulatory system diseases 388.6; malignant neoplasms (cancers) 198.2.

National economy
Budget (1982). Revenue: SwF18,868,800,000 (taxes on consumption 54.1%, of which turnover tax 29.8%, customs duties 17.3%; taxes on income and wealth 38.0%). Expenditures: SwF19,293,100,000 (defense 21.4%; social welfare 21.9%; communications and energy 15.5%; education 8.3%).
Public debt (1982): U.S.$12,298,000,000.
Tourism (1983): receipts from visitors U.S.$3,147,000,000; expenditures by nationals abroad U.S.$2,296,000,000.
Production (metric tons except as noted). Agriculture, forestry, fishing (1984): wheat 577,000, barley 311,000, potatoes 944,000, sugar beets 860,-000, apples 360,000, grapes 153,000; livestock (number of live animals) 1,943,000 cattle, 2,004,000 pigs, 361,000 sheep; roundwood 4,245,000 cu m§; fish catch 3,917§. Mining and quarrying (1983): salt 306,000; gypsum 75,000. Manufacturing (1983): cement 4,116,000; wine 3,554,000; soaps and detergents 149,000; aluminum 76,000; chocolate 61,000; woolen carpets 15,000,000 sq m; 16,500,000 watches; 1,600,000 clocks. Construction (buildings completed; 1982): residential 17,678; nonresidential 9,058. Energy production (consumption)§: electricity (kW-hr; 1983) 51,819,000,000 (42,573,000,000); coal (metric tons; 1983) none (654,000); crude petroleum

(barrels; 1983) none (31,507,000); petroleum products (metric tons; 1983) 4,150,000 (10,971,000); natural gas (cu m; 1983) none (1,294,163,000).
Gross national product (at current market prices; 1983): U.S.$105,060,000,-000 (U.S.$16,340 per capita).

Gross domestic product and structure of labour force				
	1983			
	in value SwF'000	% of total value	labour force	% of labour force
Agriculture	...	...	211,600	7.1
Mining	...	...}	914,200	30.5
Manufacturing	...			
Construction	...	...	190,200	6.4
Public utilities	...	...	29,700	1.0
Transp. and commun.	...	...	189,000	6.3
Trade	...	...	587,600	19.6
Finance	...	...	154,200	5.1
Pub. admin., defense	...	...	232,700	7.8
Services	...	...	484,500	16.2
TOTAL	203,860,000	100.0	2,993,700	100.0

Population economically active (1983): total 3,020,000; participation rate of population over age 14, 57.7% (female 35.0%, unemployed 0.9%).

Price and earnings indexes (1980 = 100)							
	1978	1979	1980	1981	1982	1983	1984
Consumer price index	92.8	96.1	100.0	106.5	112.5	115.9	119.3
Hourly earnings index	91.8	94.6	100.0	102.4	109.0	113.1	...

Household income and expenditure (1982). Average household size 2.5¶; average income per household SwF61,000 (U.S.$30,045); sources of income: wages and salaries 64.7%, self-employment 15.9%, social security 11.3%; expenditure: food and beverages 27.7%, housing 24.9%, transportation and communication 11.6%, recreation and education 9.2%, health 8.2%.
Land use (1983): forested 26.4%; meadows and pastures 40.5%; agricultural and under permanent cultivation 10.4%; other 22.7%.

Foreign trade

Balance of trade (current prices)						
	1979	1980	1981	1982	1983	1984
SwF'000,000	−4,706	−11,251	−7,272	−5,401	−7,341	−8,520
% of total	5.1%	10.2%	6.4%	4.9%	6.4%	6.6%

Imports (1983): SwF61,064,182,000 (machinery and transport equipment 26.6%, chemical products 11.5%, mineral fuels 11.3%, clothing and textiles 9.4%, precious metals and jewelry 7.9%). *Major import sources:* West Germany 28.3%; France 11.7%; Italy 10.1%; U.S. 8.2%; U.K. 5.4%; The Netherlands 4.4%.
Exports (1983): SwF53,723,465,000 (nonelectrical machinery 18.8%, electrical machinery 11.0%, pharmaceuticals 8.3%, precious-metal articles and jewelry 8.1%, watches 6.3%). *Major export destinations:* West Germany 19.9%; France 8.6%; U.S. 8.6%; Italy 7.1%; U.K. 6.5%.

Transport and communications
Transport. Railroads (1984): length♀ 3,105 mi, 4,997 km; passenger-mi 5,570,000,000, passenger-km 8,964,000,000; short ton-mi cargo 4,718,000,-000, metric ton-km cargo 6,888,000,000ð. Roads (1983): total length 42,740 mi, 68,784 km. Vehicles (1983): passenger cars 2,520,610; trucks and buses 201,175. Merchant marine (1984): vessels (100 gross tons and over) 32; total deadweight tonnage 487,358. Air transport (1984): passenger-mi 7,494,000,-000, passenger-km 12,060,000,000; short ton-mi cargo 465,920,000, metric ton-km cargo 680,232,000; airports (1985) with scheduled flights 5.
Communications. Daily newspapers (1984): total number 99; total circulation 3,112,193; circulation per 1,000 population 483. Radio (1984): 2,424,-269 receivers (1 per 2.7 persons). Television (1984): 2,199,761 receivers (1 per 3.0 persons). Telephones (1983): 4,954,828 (1 per 1.3 persons).

Education and health

Education (1984–85)				
	schools	teachers	students	student/ teacher ratio
Primary (age 6–11)	...	...	418,000	...
Secondary (age 11–18)	...	...	396,250	...
Voc., teacher tr.	...	...	251,200	...
Higher	...	...	105,900	...

Educational attainment (1970). Percent of population over age 12 having: no formal schooling 0.4%; primary education 73.5%; secondary 7.2%; some postsecondary 10.3%; university degree 2.6%. *Literacy:* virtually 100.0%.
Health (1981): physicians 7,799 (1 per 816 persons); hospital beds 35,897 (1 per 177 persons); infant mortality rate per 1,000 live births (1982) 7.7.
Food (1980–82): daily per capita caloric intake 3,465 (vegetable products 61%, animal products 39%); 129% of FAO recommended minimum.

Military
Total active duty personnel□ (1984): 625,000 (army 92.8%, air force 7.2%).
Military expenditure as percent of GNP (1983): 2.0% (world 6.1%); per capita expenditure U.S.$321.

*January 1. †Demicanton; functions as a full canton and has the same legal prerogatives as a full canton. ‡Includes resident aliens; 1983 pop. 960,200. §1983. ‖Figures include Liechtenstein. ¶1981. ♀1982. ðFederal railway only. □Mobilized personnel.

Syria

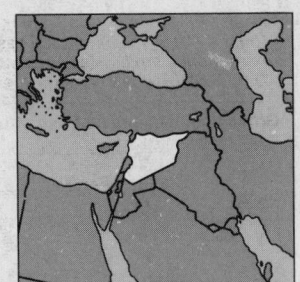

Official name: al-Jumhūrīyah al-'Arabīyah as-Sūrīyah (Syrian Arab Republic).
Form of government: unitary multiparty* republic with one legislative house (People's Council [195]).
Chief of state: President.
Head of government: Prime Minister.
Capital: Damascus.
Official language: Arabic.
Official religion: none.†
Monetary unit: 1 Syrian Pound (LS) = 100 piastres; valuation (Oct. 21, 1985) 1 U.S.$ = LS3.66; 1£ = LS5.26.

Area and population

Governorates	Capitals	area sq mi	area sq km	population 1985 estimate
Dar'ā	Dar'ā	1,440	3,730	424,000
Dayr az-Zawr	Dayr az-Zawr	12,765	33,060	458,000
Dimashq	al-Iarmouk	6,962	18,032	1,050,000
Ḥalab	Aleppo	7,143	18,500	2,126,000
Ḥamāh	Ḥamāh	3,430	8,883	834,000
al-Ḥasakah	al-Ḥasakah	9,009	23,334	759,000
Ḥimṣ	Homs	16,302	42,223	936,000
Idlib	Idlib	2,354	6,097	669,000
al-Lādhiqiyah	Latakia	887	2,297	627,000
al-Qunayṭirah	al-Qunayṭirah	719‡	1,861‡	31,000
ar-Raqqah	ar-Raqqah	7,574	19,616	395,000
as-Suwaydā'	as-Suwaydā'	2,143	5,550	225,000
Tartous	Tartous	730	1,892	506,000
Municipality				
Dimashq	Damascus	41	105	1,227,000
TOTAL		71,498‡	185,180‡	10,267,000

Demography

Population (1985): 10,267,000.
Density (1985): persons per sq mi 143.6, persons per sq km 55.4.
Urban–rural (1985): urban 48.6%; rural 51.4%.
Sex distribution (1985): male 51.08%; female 48.92%.
Age breakdown (1985): under 15, 49.3%; 15–29, 22.4%; 30–44, 14.3%; 45–59, 7.5%; 60–74, 4.8%; 75 and over, 1.7%.
Population projection: (1990) 12,774,000; (2000) 17,085,000.
Doubling time: 19 years.
Ethnic composition (1981): Arab 88.8%; Kurdish 6.3%; other 4.9%.
Religious affiliation (1980): Muslim (mostly Sunnī) 89.6%; Christian 8.9%; other 1.5%.
Major cities (1984): Damascus 1,178,000; Aleppo 1,109,100; Homs 406,300; Latakia 222,500; Ḥamāh 190,000.

Vital statistics

Birth rate per 1,000 population (1983): 43.6 (world avg. 29.0).
Death rate per 1,000 population (1983): 5.3 (world avg. 11.0).
Natural increase rate per 1,000 population (1983): 38.3 (world avg. 18.0).
Total fertility rate (avg. births per childbearing woman; 1980–85): 7.2.
Marriage rate per 1,000 population (1984): 8.2§.
Divorce rate per 1,000 population (1984): 0.6§.
Life expectancy at birth (1976–79): male 63.8 years; female 64.7 years.
Major causes of death per 100,000 population (1981): signs, symptoms, and other ill-defined conditions 207.3; diseases of the circulatory system 60.7; infectious and parasitic diseases 15.1.

National economy

Budget (1985). Revenue: LS42,984,000,000 (investment proceeds 61.1%, taxes and duties 27.4%). Expenditures: LS42,984,000,000 (defense 30.2%, education 7.9%, national security 1.2%).
Public debt (external, outstanding; 1983): U.S.$2,660,800,000.
Tourism (1983): receipts from visitors U.S.$110,000,000; expenditures by nationals abroad, n.a.
Gross national product (at current market prices; 1983): U.S.$16,510,000,000 (U.S.$1,680 per capita).

Structure of gross domestic product and labour force

	1983 in value LS'000,000	1983 % of total value	labour force	% of labour force
Agriculture	15,401	19.9	605,753	28.7
Mining	...	} 19.3	278,334	13.1
Manufacturing	14,963			
Construction	4,875	6.3	324,367	15.4
Public utilities	...	...	20,861	1.0
Transportation and communication	5,875	7.6	127,351	6.0
Trade	19,253	24.8	209,694	9.9
Finance	...	...	17,895	0.9
Pub. admin., services	...	...	478,825	22.6
Other	17,133	22.1	49,680	2.4
TOTAL	77,500	100.0	2,112,760	100.0

Production (metric tons except as noted). Agriculture, forestry, fishing (1984): wheat 1,051,000, sugar beets 900,000, watermelons 850,000, tomatoes 740,000, grapes 440,000, olives 370,000, barley 302,000, potatoes 280,000,

cucumbers 280,000, melons 280,000, cotton 160,000; livestock (number of live animals) 14,000,000 sheep, 1,000,000 goats, 770,000 cattle; roundwood 44,000 cu m‖; fish catch 3,777‖. Mining and quarrying (1983): sand and gravel 5,780,000; hydraulic cement 2,850,000; phosphate rock 1,229,000; gypsum 350,000; salt 87,000; natural asphalt 54,000. Manufacturing (market value in LS; 1984): textiles 2,011,233; cement 1,376,202; chemical products 1,208,685; sugar 1,024,485. Construction (1984): residential 3,901,000 sq m; nonresidential 686,000 sq m. Energy production (consumption): electricity (kW-hr; 1983) 6,175,000,000 (6,038,000,000); coal (metric tons; 1983) none (3,000); crude petroleum (barrels; 1983) 65,129,000 (64,684,000); petroleum products (metric tons; 1983) 7,989,000 (5,965,000); natural gas (cu m; 1983) 75,856,000 (75,856,000).
Population economically active (1983): total 2,112,760; participation rate of total population 22.4% (female 12.2%, unemployed 5.1%).

Price and earnings indexes (1980 = 100)

	1978	1979	1980	1981	1982	1983	1984
Consumer price index	80.2	84.1	100.0	118.4	135.3	143.4	157.2
Monthly earnings index	...	...	...	...	...	...	...

Average household size (1981): 6.2.
Land use (1983): steppe and pasture 45.6%; cultivable 30.5%; forested 2.7%; other 21.2%.

Foreign trade

Balance of trade (current prices)

	1978	1979	1980	1981	1982	1983
LS'000,000	−4,741	−5,590	−6,647	−9,977	−6,569	−10,281
% of total	36%	30.2%	28.7%	37.7%	29.2%	40.5%

Imports (1984): LS16,153,708 (mineral fuels and related materials 34.3%; machinery and transport equipment 19.1%; foods, beverages, and tobacco 18.1%; chemical and pharmaceutical products 7.4%; metals and metal manufactures 1.8%). *Major import sources:* Iran 22.7%; Libya 7.7%; West Germany 5.9%; France 5.1%; Italy 4.8%; Japan 4.6%.
Exports (1984): LS7,274,793 (petroleum and petroleum products 63.1%; textiles, wearing apparel, and leather 16.1%; food and live animals 5.4%). *Major export destinations:* Romania 28.2%; Italy 19.8%; France 12.1%; U.S.S.R. 11.5%; Iran 2.3%.

Transport and communications

Transport. Railroads (1984): length 1,250 mi, 2,013 km; passenger-mi 470,645,000, passenger-km 757,432,000; short ton-mi cargo 661,888,000, metric ton-km cargo 966,340,000. Roads (1983): total length 14,062 mi, 22,632 km (paved 93%). Vehicles (1984): passenger cars 114,303; trucks and buses 85,544. Merchant marine (1984): vessels (100 gross tons and over) 53; total deadweight tonnage 81,871. Air transport (1984): passenger-mi 573,628,000, passenger-km 923,167,000; short ton-mi cargo 7,759,000, metric ton-km cargo 11,328,000; airports (1985) with scheduled flights 5.
Communications. Daily newspapers (1984): total number 9; total circulation 176,400; circulation per 1,000 population 17.8. Radio (1984): total number of receivers 1,800,000 (1 per 5.5 persons). Television (1984): total number of receivers 500,000 (1 per 19.9 persons). Telephones (1983): 468,922 (1 per 20.5 persons).

Education and health

Education (1983–84)

	schools	teachers	students	student/ teacher ratio
Primary (age 6–11)	8,489	67,086	1,823,684	27.2
Secondary (age 12–18)	1,598	26,366	701,330	26.6
Voc., teacher tr.	138	5,447	64,596	11.9
Higher	41	...	123,735	...

Educational attainment (1976). Percent of population having: no schooling 40.0%; knowledge of reading and writing 27.4%; primary education 18.1%; secondary 13.1%; higher 1.4%. *Literacy* (1983): total population over age 10 literate 4,009,723 (63.3%); males literate 2,523,648 (78.4%); females literate 1,486,075 (47.7%).
Health (1984): physicians 5,543 (1 per 1,792 persons); hospital beds 11,595 (1 per 857 persons); infant mortality rate per 1,000 live births (1980–85) 57.0.
Food (1980–82): daily per capita caloric intake 3,032 (vegetable products 86%, animal products 14%); 122% of FAO recommended minimum requirement.

Military

Total active duty personnel (1984): 362,500 (army 80.0%, navy 0.7%, air force 19.3%). *Military expenditure as percent of GNP* (1983): 13.0% (world 6.1%); per capita expenditure U.S.$209.

---

*Parties other than the Communist Party form a coalition (National Progressive Front). †Islām is required to be the religion of the head of state and is the basis of the legal system. ‡Includes territory in the Golan Heights recognized internationally as part of Syria (located between the 1949 Israel–Syria Armistice line [west] and the 1974 UN Disengagement of Forces zone [east]) that has been occupied by Israel since 1967. Israel's unilateral annexation of this territory in December 1981 has received no international recognition. §Syrian Arabs only. ‖1983.

Taiwan

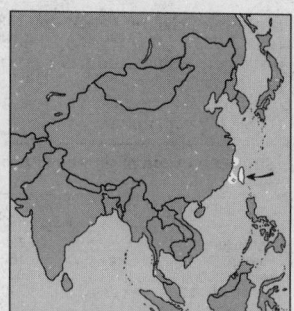

Official name: Chung-hua Min-kuo (Republic of China).
Form of government: unitary republic with a National Assembly (1,173).
Chief of state: President.
Head of government: Premier.
Capital: Taipei.
Official language: Mandarin Chinese.
Official religion: none.
Monetary unit: 1 New Taiwan dollar (NT$) = 100 cents; valuation (Oct. 21, 1985) 1 U.S.$ = NT$40.07; 1£ = NT$57.46.

Area and population

Counties	Capitals	area sq mi	area sq km	population 1985 estimate
Chang-hua	Chang-hua	415	1,074	1,218,800
Chia-i	Chia-i	706	1,829	570,100
Hsin-chu	Hsin-chu	573	1,483	365,600
Hua-lien	Hua-lien	1,787	4,629	361,500
I-lan	I-lan	825	2,137	449,000
Kao-hsiung	Feng-shan	1,078	2,793	1,071,200
Miao-li	Miao-li	703	1,820	549,600
Nan-t'ou	Nan-t'ou	1,585	4,106	534,600
P'eng-hu	Ma-kung	49	127	102,500
P'ing-tung	P'ing-tung	1,072	2,776	900,900
T'ai-chung	Feng-yuan	792	2,051	1,131,700
T'ai-nan	Hsin-ying	778	2,016	996,400
T'ai-pei	Pan-ch'iao	792	2,052	2,626,900
T'ai-tung	T'ai-tung	1,357	3,515	276,000
T'ao-yüan	T'ao-yüan	471	1,221	1,200,500
Yün-lin	Tou-liu	498	1,291	791,400
Municipalities				
Chi-lung	—	51	133	253,000
Hsin-chu	—	19	49	301,300
Kao-hsiung	—	60	156	1,296,400
Keelung	—	51	133	351,100
T'ai-chung	—	63	163	666,200
T'ai-nan	—	68	176	636,400
Taipei	—	105	272	2,483,900
TOTAL		13,900*	36,002	19,135,000

Demography

Population (1985): 19,135,000.
Density (1985): persons per sq mi 1,376.6, persons per sq km 531.5.
Urban–rural (1980): urban 70.6%; rural 29.4%.
Sex distribution (1984): male 51.94%; female 48.06%.
Age breakdown (1984): under 15, 30.2%; 15–29, 30.5%; 30–44, 18.9%; 45–59, 12.6%; 60–74, 6.5%; 75 and over, 1.3%.
Population projection: (1990) 20,791,000; (2000) 24,128,000.
Doubling time: 40 years.
Ethnic composition (1983): Taiwanese (Han Chinese) 84.0%; mainland Chinese 14.0%; other 2.0%.
Religious affiliation (1980): Chinese folk-religionist 48.5%; Buddhist 43.0%; Christian 7.4%; Muslim 0.5%; other 0.6%.
Major cities (1985): Taipei 2,483,900; Kao-hsiung 1,296,400; T'ai-chung 666,200; T'ai-nan 636,400; Keelung 351,100; Hsin-Chu 301,300.

Vital statistics

Birth rate per 1,000 population (1984): 19.6 (world avg. 29.0).
Death rate per 1,000 population (1984): 4.8 (world avg. 11.0).
Natural increase rate per 1,000 population (1984): 14.8 (world avg. 18.0).
Total fertility rate (avg. births per childbearing woman; 1984): 2.3.
Marriage rate per 1,000 population (1984): 8.2.
Divorce rate per 1,000 population (1984): 1.0.
Life expectancy at birth (1983): male 69.9 years; female 75.1 years.
Major causes of death per 100,000 population (1980): cardiovascular diseases 137.1; malignant neoplasms (cancers) 75.1; respiratory diseases 34.0.

National economy

Budget (1984). Revenue: NT$552,649,000,000 (taxes 67.3%, of which income taxes 20.0%; customs duties 18.3%). Expenditures: NT$539,053,000,000 (defense 47.9%; general administration 16.2%; economy 14.3%; social welfare and health 14.0%; education 5.7%).
Tourism (1983): receipts from visitors U.S.$990,000,000; expenditures by nationals abroad, n.a.
Production (metric tons except as noted). Agriculture, forestry, fishing (1984): sugarcane 6,545,276, vegetables 3,475,944, rice 2,244,175, sweet potatoes 424,352, citrus fruits 354,005, bananas 203,281, corn (maize) 189,-848, pineapple 123,609, peanuts 68,300, cassava 67,789, tobacco 26,441, tea 24,365; livestock (number of live animals) 129,852 cattle, 5,888,198 pigs, 196,987 goats and sheep; timber 562,637 cu m; fish catch 1,002,599. Mining and quarrying (1984): salt 79,000; copper 48; silver 10,739 kilograms; gold 1,629 kilograms. Manufacturing (1984): cement 14,234,400; crude steel 1,645,000; paper and board 1,497,800; man-made fibre 843,000; sulfuric acid 760,000; plastics and resins 635,000; fertilizers 625,000; cotton yarn 505,000; electronic calculators 43,344,114 units; audio recorders 19,632,540 units. Construction (1984): total residential and nonresidential 27,191,000 sq m. Energy production (consumption): electricity (kW-hr; 1984) 49,290,000,000 (32,725,248,000†); coal (metric tons; 1984) 2,010,775 (2,013,458); petroleum (barrels; 1983) 842,767 (n.a.); natural gas (cu m; 1984) 1,265,683,000 (n.a.).

Public debt (external, outstanding; 1983): U.S.$6,991,600,000.
Gross national product (at current market prices; 1984): U.S.$57,841,000,000 (U.S.$3,040 per capita).

Structure of gross domestic product and labour force

	1984 in value NT$'000,000	% of total value	labour force	% of labour force
Agriculture	147,946	6.5	1,286,000	17.6
Mining	14,215	0.6	41,000	0.6
Manufacturing	949,096	41.7	2,494,000	34.1
Construction	100,751	4.4	521,000	7.1
Public utilities	88,255	3.9	34,000	0.5
Transportation and communication	137,405	6.0	378,000	5.2
Trade	309,926	13.6	1,280,000	17.5
Finance	210,373	9.2	182,000	2.5
Pub. admin., defense	225,706	9.9 }	1,092,000	14.9
Services	147,609	6.5 }		
Other	−55,603§	−2.4‡	...	...
TOTAL	2,275,679§	100.0*	7,308,000	100.0

Population economically active (1985): total 7,569,000; participation rate of population over age 15, 59.0% (female 43.3%, unemployed 2.5%).

Price and earnings indexes (1981 = 100)

	1979	1980	1981	1982	1983	1984	1985‖
Consumer price index	72.2	86.0	100.0	103.4	105.3	105.5	105.9
Monthly earnings index	68.7	84.2	100.0	109.7	116.6	134.6	132.5

Household income and expenditure. Average household size (1984) 4.4; income per household NT$36,835 (U.S.$941); sources of income, n.a.; expenditure (1984): food 32.5%, housing 28.8%, recreation 10.3%, transportation 7.4%, clothing and footwear 6.3%, health 3.8%, household equipment 3.6%, other 7.3%.
Land use (1980): forested 55.0%; agricultural and under permanent cultivation 25.2%; other 19.8%.

Foreign trade

Balance of trade (current prices)

	1978	1979	1980	1981	1982	1983	1984
NT$'000,000	60,131	46,371	762	51,123	128,164	191,518	333,836
% of total	6.9%	4.2%	0.1%	3.2%	8.0%	10.5%	16.1%

Imports (1984): NT$870,861,000,000 (petroleum and petroleum products 17.1%; electronic products 11.1%; machinery, other than electrical 9.9%; chemicals and related products 9.3%; iron and steel 6.0%; nonferrous metals 3.2%). *Major import sources:* Japan 29.3%; United States 23.0%; Saudi Arabia 9.0%; Australia 3.5%; West Germany 3.5%; Kuwait 3.3%.
Exports (1984): NT$1,204,697,000,000 (electronic products and appliances 17.0%; articles of apparel and clothing 11.2%; footwear 7.6%; textile yarns and fabrics 6.1%; toys and sport goods 5.9%; metal products 5.7%; transport equipment 4.0%). *Major export destinations:* United States 48.8%; Japan 10.5%; Hong Kong 6.9%; West Germany 3.3%; Canada 3.1%.

Transport and communications

Transport. Railroads (1984): length 3,045 mi, 4,900 km; passenger-mi 5,234,-500,000, passenger-km 8,424,200,000; short ton-mi cargo 1,629,400,000, metric ton-km cargo 2,379,100,000. Roads (1984): total length 10,936 mi, 17,600 km (paved 74%). Vehicles (1985): passenger cars 844,940; trucks and buses 101,399. Merchant marine (1983): vessels (100 gross tons and over) 514; total deadweight tonnage 2,879,206. Air transport (1984): passenger-mi 6,954,420,000, passenger-km 11,192,076,000; short ton-mi cargo 1,253,-418,000, metric ton-km cargo 1,830,075,000; airports (1985) 9.
Communications. Daily newspapers (1984): total number 31; total circulation 4,917,000; circulation per 1,000 population 259. Radio (1984): 6,000,-000 receivers (1 per 3.1 persons). Television (1984): 5,235,000 receivers (1 per 3.6 persons). Telephones (1985): 4,013,517 (1 per 4.7 persons).

Education and health

Education (1984–85)

	schools	teachers	students	student/ teacher ratio
Primary (age 6–12)	2,474	71,215	2,273,390	31.9
Secondary (age 13–18)	845	60,373	1,270,092	21.0
Vocational	201	15,402	407,832	26.5
Higher	105	20,061	412,381	20.6

Educational attainment (1983). Percent of total population over age 6 having: no formal schooling 9.1%; primary education 40.2%; secondary 40.0%; higher 8.4%; other 2.3%. *Literacy* (1982): total population literate 11,294,884 (89.0%); males literate 6,297,725 (94.9%); females literate 4,997,159 (82.5%).
Health (1983): physicians 14,669 (1 per 1,268 persons); hospital beds 57,419 (1 per 324 persons); infant mortality rate per 1,000 live births 8.3.
Food (1983): daily per capita caloric intake 2,721 (vegetable products 77%, animal products 23%); 118% of FAO recommended minimum requirement.

Military

Total active duty personnel (1985): 471,000 (army 70.1%, navy 13.6%, air force 16.3%). *Military expenditure as percent of GNP* (1983): 7.5% (world 6.1%); per capita expenditure U.S.$209.

*Detail does not add to total given because of rounding. †By industry only. ‡Imputed bank service charge. §At current prices. ‖August.

Tanzania

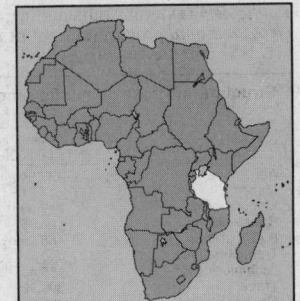

Official name: Jamhuri ya Mwungano wa Tanzania (Swahili); United Republic of Tanzania (English).
Form of government: unitary single-party republic with one legislative house (National Assembly [239]).
Chief of state: President.
Head of government: Prime Minister.
Seat of government: Dar es Salaam (Capital designate, Dodoma).
Official languages: Swahili; English.
Official religion: none.
Monetary unit: 1 Tanzanian shilling (T Sh) = 100 cents; valuation (Oct. 21, 1985) 1 U.S.$ = T Sh16.53; 1 £ = T Sh23.70.

Area and population

Regions	Capitals	area sq mi	area sq km	population 1985 estimate
Arusha	Arusha	31,698	82,098	1,183,000
Coast	Dar es Salaam	12,566	32,547	578,000
Dar es Salaam	Dar es Salaam	538	1,393	1,394,000
Dodoma	Dodoma	15,950	41,311	1,171,000
Iringa	Iringa	21,950	56,850	1,100,000
Kigoma	Kigoma	14,301	37,040	782,000
Kilimanjaro	Moshi	5,116	13,250	1,093,000
Lindi	Lindi	25,498	66,040	604,000
Mara	Musoma	8,402	21,760	862,000
Mbeya	Mbeya	23,301	60,350	1,335,000
Morogoro	Morogoro	27,268	70,624	1,134,000
Mtwara	Mtwara	6,452	16,710	878,000
Mwanza	Mwanza	7,600	19,683	1,736,000
Pemba North	Wete	380	984	*
Pemba South	Chake Chake			
Rukwa	Sumbawanga	26,500	68,635	603,000
Ruvuma	Songea	24,583	63,669	691,000
Shinyanga	Shinyanga	19,598	50,760	1,662,000
Singida	Singida	19,050	49,340	730,000
Tabora	Tabora	29,402	76,150	1,089,000
Tanga	Tanga	10,300	26,677	1,236,000
West Lake	Bukoba	10,987	28,456	1,298,000
Zanzibar North	Mkokotoni			
Zanzibar South and Central	Koani	641	1,660	571,000*
Zanzibar West	Zanzibar			
TOTAL		364,881†	945,037†	21,730,000

Demography

Population (1985): 21,730,000.
Density (1985): persons per sq mi 63.5, persons per sq km 24.5.
Urban–rural (1983): urban 14.0%; rural 86.0%.
Sex distribution (1980): male 49.49%; female 50.51%.
Age breakdown (1980): under 15, 45.9%; 15–29, 25.3%; 30–44, 14.9%; 45–59, 8.9%; 60–74, 4.2%; 75 and over, 0.8%.
Population projection: (1990) 25,635,000; (2000) 34,045,000.
Doubling time: 21 years.
Ethnic composition (1980): Nyamwezi and Sukuma 21.2%; Swahili 8.9%; Hehet and Bena 6.7%; Makonde 6.1%; Haya 5.6%; other 51.5%.
Religious affiliation (1984): Christian 40%, of which Roman Catholic 26%; Muslim 30%; traditional beliefs and other 30%.
Major cities (1978): Dar es Salaam 900,000‡; Mwanza 110,553; Tanga 103,399.

Vital statistics

Birth rate per 1,000 population (1983): 50.0 (world avg. 29.0).
Death rate per 1,000 population (1983): 16.0 (world avg. 11.0).
Natural increase rate per 1,000 population (1983): 34.0 (world avg. 18.0).
Total fertility rate (avg. births per childbearing woman; 1983): 7.0.
Marriage rate per 1,000 population (1967): 9.8.
Divorce rate per 1,000 population: n.a.
Life expectancy at birth (1983): male 49.0 years; female 52.0 years.
Major causes of death per 100,000 population: n.a.; however, the major diseases are malaria, bilharziasis, tuberculosis, and sleeping sickness.

National economy

Budget (1982–83). Revenue: T Sh9,500,000,000 (sales tax 54.9%, income tax 27.4%, customs and excise tax 6.7%). Expenditures: T Sh14,144,000,000 (general administration 44.1%, social services 34.5%).
Public debt (external, outstanding; 1983): U.S.$1,819,600,000.
Tourism (1983): receipts from visitors U.S.$13,000,000; expenditures by nationals abroad U.S.$12,000,000.
Production (metric tons except as noted). Agriculture (1984): cassava 5,600,000, corn (maize) 1,131,000, sweet potatoes 500,000, rice 400,000, coconuts 320,000, millet 285,000, seed cotton 140,000, unshelled peanuts (groundnuts) 59,000, chick peas 8,000, palm kernels 5,400; livestock (number of live animals) 14,500,000 cattle, 6,100,000 goats, 4,100,000 sheep, 26,000,000 chickens; roundwood 39,770,000 cu m‡; fish catch 272,498‡. Mining and quarrying (1983): diamonds 237,000 carats; phosphate rock 165,000. Manufacturing (1982): cement 400,000; fertilizer 13,662; wheat flour 28,000; iron sheets 16,044; rolled steel 12,104; sisal twine and ropes 11,273; aluminum 4,460; textiles 66,000,000 sq m. Construction: n.a. Energy production (con-

sumption): electricity (kW-hr; 1983) 705,000,000 (705,000,000); coal (metric tons; 1983) 1,000 (1,000); crude petroleum (barrels; 1983) none (4,118,000); petroleum products (metric tons; 1983) 515,000 (569,000); natural gas, none (n.a.).
Gross national product (at current market prices; 1983): U.S.$4,986,000,000 (U.S.$245 per capita).

Structure of gross domestic product and labour force

	1982 in value T SH'000,000	% of total value	labour force§	% of labour force
Agriculture	21,722	51.5	137,419	20.3
Mining	162	0.4	7,231	1.1
Manufacturing	3,924	9.3	118,234	17.5
Construction	1,720	4.1	51,377	7.6
Public utilities	515	1.2	21,460	3.2
Transportation and communication	2,093	5.0	60,166	8.9
Trade	3,183	7.5	38,030	5.6
Finance	5,032	11.9	16,900	2.5
Pub. admin., defense, Services }	4,793	11.4	225,170	33.3
Other	−954 ‖	−2.3 ‖	...	...
TOTAL	42,190¶	100.0	676,017	100.0

Population economically active (1984): total 8,648,000; participation rate of population ages 15–64, 50.0% (female [1978] 51.4%, unemployed, n.a.).

Price and earnings indexes (1980 = 100)

	1979	1980	1981	1982	1983	1984
Consumer price index	76.8	100.0	125.6	162.0	205.8	279.5
Monthly earnings index	94.0	100.0	...	...	...	...

Household income and expenditure. Average household size (1980) 5.1; average annual income per household: n.a.; source of income: n.a.; expenditures (1981): food 47.0%, clothing 10.8%, rent 8.6%, drinks and tobacco 7.1%, utilities 6.6%, transportation 6.4%.
Land use (1983): forested 47.2%; meadows and pastures 39.5%; agricultural and under permanent cultivation 5.9%; other 7.4%.

Foreign trade

Balance of trade (current prices)

	1978	1979	1980	1981	1982	1983
T Sh'000,000	−3,981.0	−3,794.0	−4,730.0	−4,853.0	−4,917.0	−3,384.0
% of total	35.2%	31.6%	36.1%	34.1%	36.8%	29.5%

Imports (1982): T Sh9,278,000,000 (machinery 28.1%, fuel 22.6%, consumer goods 12.5%, transport equipment 11.7%, food 11.0%). *Major import sources:* Uganda 17.0%; United Kingdom 14.4%; Japan 9.8%; India 5.2%; United States 4.9%; China 3.4%.
Exports (1982): T Sh4,295,000,000 (coffee beans 30.2%, cotton 8.8%, cloves 8.4%, sisal 4.2%, diamonds 4.2%, tobacco 3.9%, cashew nuts 2.7%, tea 2.6%). *Major export destinations:* United Kingdom 14.6%; India 6.7%; United States 3.5%; Hong Kong 3.3%; Japan 2.8%.

Transport and communications

Transport. Railroads (1982): length 2,222 mi, 3,576 km; passenger-mi 577,000,000♀, passenger-km 929,000,000♀; short ton-mi cargo 475,000,000♀, metric ton-km cargo 694,000,000♀. Roads (1984): length 50,887 mi, 81,895 km. Vehicles (1984): cars, trucks, and buses 84,190. Merchant marine (1984): vessels (100 gross tons and over) 39; deadweight tonnage 70,991. Air transport (1984): passenger-mi 163,000,000, passenger-km 262,000,000; short ton-mi cargo 18,000,000, metric ton-km 26,000,000; airports (1985) 19.
Communications. Daily newspapers (1984): total number 3; total circulation 101,000; circulation per 1,000 population 5.0. Radio (1984): 2,000,000 receivers (1 per 10 persons). Television (1984): 10,000 receivers (1 per 2,101 persons). Telephones (1983): 99,885 (1 per 204 persons).

Education and health

Education (1981–82)

	schools	teachers	students	student/ teacher ratio
Primary (age 7–13)	9,980	88,370	3,512,799	39.8
Secondary (age 14–19)	175	3,262	69,145	21.2
Voc., teacher tr.	40	744	17,914	24.1
Higher	1	893	3,780	4.2

Educational attainment (1978). Percent of population over age 10 having: no formal schooling 48.6%; some primary education 32.0%; primary 8.7%; some secondary 1.6%; completed secondary and higher 0.3%. *Literacy* (1983): 79.0%.
Health: physicians (1981) 950 (1 per 20,168 persons); hospital beds (1982) 22,350 (1 per 857 persons); infant mortality rate per 1,000 live births 97.0†.
Food (1980–82): daily per capita caloric intake 2,409 (vegetable products 94%, animal products 6%); 101% of FAO recommended minimum requirement.

Military

Total active duty personnel (1984): 43,000 (army 95.4%, navy 2.1%, air force 2.5%). *Military expenditure as percent of GNP* (1983): 2.5% (world 6.1%); per capita expenditure U.S.$6.

*Pemba North and Pemba South are included with Zanzibar. †Total land area is 342,081 sq mi (885,987 sq km) and is shown for regions; the total area (both land and water) is shown in the grand total. ‡1983. §Employed persons only. ‖ Imputed bank service charges. ¶At current prices. ♀For Tanzania Railways Corporation only.

Thailand

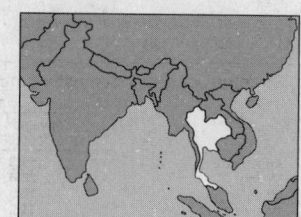

Official name: Muang Thai, or Prathet Thai (Kingdom of Thailand).
Form of government: constitutional monarchy with a multiparty National Assembly (Senate [243]; House of Representatives [324]).
Chief of state: King.
Head of government: Prime Minister.
Capital: Bangkok.
Official language: Thai.
Official religion: Buddhism.
Monetary unit: 1 Thai Baht (B) = 100 stangs; valuation (Oct. 21, 1985) 1 U.S.$ = B26.50; 1 £ = B38.00.

Area and population

Regions	area sq mi	sq km	population 1984 estimate
Bangkok Metropolis	604	1,565	5,018,300
Central*	7,236	18,742	3,393,100
Eastern	14,481	37,507	3,746,000
Northeastern	65,195	168,854	17,219,300
Northern	65,500	169,644	10,106,000
Southern	27,303	70,715	6,166,100
Western	17,795	46,088	3,866,300
TOTAL	198,115†	513,115	49,515,100

Demography

Population (1985): 51,301,000.
Density (1985): persons per sq mi 258.9, persons per sq km 100.0.
Urban–rural (1984): urban 19.5%; rural 80.5%.
Sex distribution (1985): male 50.27%; female 49.73%.
Age breakdown (1980): under 15, 40.2%; 15–29, 29.2%; 30–44, 16.2%; 45–59, 9.3%; 60–69, 3.2%; 70 and over, 1.9%.
Population projection: (1990) 55,345,000; (2000) 63,772,000.
Doubling time: 28 years.
Ethnic composition (1980): Thai 53.6%; Lao 27.6%; Chinese 10.6%; Malay 3.7%; Khmer 2.7%; other 1.8%.
Religious affiliation (1980): Buddhist 95.0%; Muslim 3.8%; Christian 0.5%; other 0.7%.
Major cities (1980): Bangkok 4,967,071; Chiang Mai 101,595; Hat Yai 93,519; Khon Kaen 85,863; Nakhon Ratchasima 78,246.

Vital statistics

Birth rate per 1,000 population (1984): 26.6 (world avg. 29.0).
Death rate per 1,000 population (1984): 7.8 (world avg. 11.0).
Natural increase rate per 1,000 population (1984): 18.8 (world avg. 18.0).
Total fertility rate (avg. births per childbearing woman; 1984): 3.3.
Marriage rate per 1,000 population (1981): 7.2.
Divorce rate per 1,000 population (1979): 0.5.
Life expectancy at birth (1984): male 61.2 years; female 65.1 years.
Major causes of death per 100,000 population (1983): accidents, poisonings, and violence 35.6; heart disease 33.8; malignant neoplasms (cancers) 27.0; tuberculosis 11.0; pneumonia 10.1; malaria 5.9.

National economy

Budget (1984–85). Revenue: B213,000,000,000 (taxes 74.9%, of which indirect taxes 56.1%; borrowing 16.4%; state enterprises 3.3%; sale of property and services 2.4%). Expenditures: B213,000,000,000 (debt services 20.8%; defense 19.4%; education 18.9%; economic services 16.4%; public utilities 6.4%; internal security 5.2%; public health 4.6%).
Public debt (external, outstanding; 1984): U.S.$8,746,565,000.
Tourism (1983): receipts from visitors U.S.$1,089,000,000; expenditures by nationals abroad (1982) U.S.$267,000,000.
Production (metric tons except as noted). Agriculture, forestry, fishing (1984): sugarcane 24,894,000, rice 19,200,000, tapioca root 18,000,000, corn (maize) 4,150,000, coconuts 1,000,000, rubber 593,000, cotton 123,000, tobacco 90,000, coffee 19,000; livestock (number of live animals) 6,150,000 buffalo, 4,620,000 cattle, 4,150,000 pigs, 30,000 goats, 65,000,000 chickens; roundwood (1983) 40,416,000 cu m; fish catch (1983) 2,259,000. Mining and quarrying (1983): limestone 8,935,900; gypsum 760,400; fluorite 237,700; barite 187,400; iron ore 40,300; tin 27,200. Manufacturing (1983): cement 7,263,400; tin plate 73,100; detergent 54,900; cigarettes 29,100; commercial vehicles 75,300 units. Construction (value in B; 1982): residential 22,717,000,000; nonresidential 41,334,000,000. Energy production (consumption): electricity (kW-hr; 1983) 18,817,000,000 (17,954,000,000); coal (metric tons; 1983) 2,252,000 (2,301,000); crude petroleum (barrels; 1983) 58,640 (56,991,000); petroleum products (metric tons; 1983) 7,785,000 (9,645,000); natural gas (cu m; 1983) 1,460,819,000 (1,460,819,000).
Population economically active (1984): total 26,580,000; participation rate of total population 53.7% (female [1982] 47.1%), unemployed 5.1%).

Price and earnings indexes (1980 = 100)

	1979	1980	1981	1982	1983	1984	1985
Consumer price index	83.5	100.0	112.7	118.6	123.0	124.1	127.7‡
Monthly earnings index	...	...	...	...	...	...	...

Household income and expenditure. Average household size (1983) 5.3; median income per household (1983) B43,476 (U.S.$1,890); sources of income

(1982): interest and profits 33.8%, wages and salaries 32.6%, agriculture 20.1%; transfer payments 8.4%, property 3.2%; expenditure (1982): food 39.1%, transportation and communication 11.7%, clothing and footwear 10.2%, miscellaneous goods and services 8.6%, alcoholic beverages and tobacco 7.1%, housing 6.3%, household utilities including furniture 5.9%, medical care and health 4.7%, recreation 4.3%, education 0.5%.
Gross national product (at current market prices; 1984): U.S.$40,628,200,000 (U.S.$812 per capita).

Structure of gross domestic product and labour force

	1983 in value B'000,000	1983 % of total value	1982 labour force§	1982 % of labour force
Agriculture	202,797	21.8	16,984,900	68.4
Mining	16,303	1.8	64,600	0.3
Manufacturing	172,532	18.6	2,006,700	8.1
Construction	46,880	5.0	520,300	2.1
Public utilities	16,390	1.8	76,300	0.3
Transportation and communication	73,043	7.9	500,900	2.0
Trade	176,577	19.0	2,298,900	9.3
Finance	71,991	7.8		
Pub. admin., defense	42,261	4.5	2,378,200	9.6
Services	98,636	10.6		
Other	11,138	1.2	500	0.0
TOTAL	928,548 ‖	100.0	24,831,300	100.0†

Land use (1983): forested 30.3%; meadows and pastures 0.6%; agricultural and under permanent cultivation 37.8%; other 31.3%.

Foreign trade¶

Balance of trade (current prices)

	1979	1980	1981	1982	1983	1984
B'000,000	−23,498	−36,790	−42,266	−17,404	−66,689	−45,587
% of total	9.8%	12.1%	12.1%	5.2%	18.5%	11.5%

Imports (1983): B236,609,000,000 (machines and transport equipment 28.9%, mineral fuels and oils 24.1%, basic manufactures 16.5%, chemicals 13.4%, crude materials excluding fuels 6.1%, miscellaneous manufactured goods 5.9%). *Major import sources:* Japan 27.4%; United States 12.6%; Saudi Arabia 10.3%; Singapore 6.2%; Malaysia 5.4%; West Germany 4.7%; China 2.5%; South Korea 2.4%; United Kingdom 2.3%; France 1.5%; Italy 1.4%.
Exports (1983): B146,472,000,000 (rice 13.8%, tapioca products 10.5%, rubber 8.0%, corn 5.8%, sugar and sugar products 5.2%, unwrought tin 3.6%, shrimps 2.2%). *Major export destinations:* Japan 15.1%; United States 14.9%; The Netherlands 10.8%; Singapore 8.1%; Hong Kong 5.0%; Malaysia 4.5%; West Germany 3.5%; Saudi Arabia 2.9%; United Kingdom 2.0%; Nigeria 2.0%; Indonesia 1.9%; France 1.9%.

Transport and communications

Transport. Railroads (1983): route length 2,321 mi, 3,735 km; passenger-mi 6,003,168,000, passenger-km 9,661,181,000; short ton-mi cargo 1,713,004,000, metric ton-km cargo 2,500,944,000. Roads (1982): total length 45,000 mi, 72,000 km (paved 35%). Vehicles (1983): passenger cars 411,982; trucks and buses 789,837. Merchant marine (1984): vessels (100 gross tons and over) 225; total deadweight tonnage 759,136. Air transport (1983): passenger-mi 5,632,978,000, passenger-km 9,065,417,400; short ton-mi cargo 225,025,000, metric ton-km cargo 328,531,400; airports (1985) with scheduled flights 10.
Communications. Daily newspapers (1984): total number 28; total circulation 2,405,000♀; circulation per 1,000 population 48△. Radio (1984): total number of receivers 7,200,000 (1 per 7 persons). Television (1984): total number of receivers 3,000,000 (1 per 17 persons). Telephones (1983): 623,368 (1 per 79 persons).

Education and health

Education (1980)

	schools	teachers	students	student/ teacher ratio
Primary (age 7–12)	33,712	346,508	8,068,252	23.3
Secondary (age 13–18)	1,437	70,201	1,309,089	18.6
Voc., teacher tr.	1,528	27,484	594,243	21.6
Higher	62	23,800	257,353	10.8

Educational attainment (1980). Percent of population over age 6 having: no formal schooling 15.8%; primary education 71.4%; secondary 9.3%; university 2.2%; other education 1.3%. *Literacy* (1980): total population over age 10 literate 29,793,848 (88.8%); males literate 15,316,986 (92.4%); females literate 14,476,862 (85.3%).
Health (1982): physicians 7,658 (1 per 6,332 persons); hospital beds 80,652 (1 per 601 persons); infant mortality rate per 1,000 live births (1984) 56.0.
Food (1980–82): daily per capita caloric intake 2,312 (vegetable products 94%, animal products 6%); 103% of FAO recommended minimum requirement.

Military

Total active duty personnel (1984): 235,300 (army 68.0%, navy 13.7%, air force 18.3%). *Military expenditure as percent of GNP* (1983): 4.1% (world 6.1%); per capita expenditure U.S.$33.

*Excluding Bangkok Metropolis. †Detail does not add to total given because of rounding. ‡August. §Employed persons only. ‖ At current prices. ¶Import figures are f.o.b. (free on board) in balance of trade and c.i.f. (cost, insurance, and freight) for commodities and trading partners. ♀Excludes circulation for two dailies.

Togo

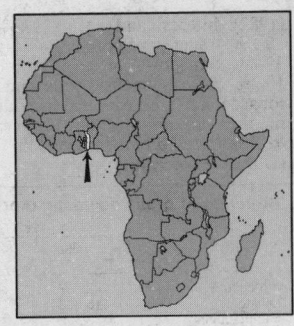

Official name: République Togolaise (Republic of Togo).
Form of government: republic with one legislative body (National Assembly [67]).
Head of state and government: President.
Capital: Lomé.
Official language: French.
Official religion: none.
Monetary unit: 1 CFA franc (CFAF) = 100 centimes; valuation (Oct. 21, 1985) 1 U.S.$ = CFAF402.02; 1 £ = CFAF576.50.

Area and population		area		population
Regions				1981
Prefectures	Capitals	sq mi	sq km	census
Centrale	Sokodé			269,174
Sotouboua	Sotouboua	2,892	7,490	128,617
Tchamba	Tchamba	*	*	44,912
Tchaoudjo	Sokodé	2,198*	5,692*	95,645
De la Kara	Kara			432,626
Assoli	Bafilo	362	938	32,444
Bassar	Bassar	2,444	6,330	118,345
Binah	Pagouda	180	465	50,077
Doufelgou	Niamtougou	432	1,120	66,120
Kéran	Kandé	653	1,692	44,762
Kozah	Kara	419	1,085	120,878
Des Plateaux	Atakpamé			561,656
Amou	Amlamé	1,692†	4,382†	72,951
Haho	Notsé	1,412	3,658	109,995
Kloto	Kpalimé	1,077	2,790	106,429
Ogou	Atakpamé	2,373	6,145	163,906
Wawa	Badou	†	†	108,375
Des Savanes	Dapaong			326,826
Oti	Sansanné-Mango	1,453	3,762	77,747
Tône	Dapaong	1,869	4,840	249,079
Maritime	Lomé			1,039,700
Golfe	Lomé	133	345	438,110
Lacs	Aného	275	712	140,006
Vo	Vogan	290	750	150,313
Yoto	Tabligbo	483	1,250	100,387
Zio	Tsévié	1,289	3,339	210,884
TOTAL		21,925‡	56,785	2,700,982§

Demography

Population (1985): 2,989,000.
Density (1985): persons per sq mi 136.3, persons per sq km 52.6.
Urban–rural (1981): urban 15.2%; rural 84.8%.
Sex distribution (1981): male 48.20%; female 51.80%.
Age breakdown (1980): under 15, 46.2%; 15–29, 25.8%; 30–44, 14.8%; 45–59, 8.6%; 60–74, 3.9%; 75 and over, 0.7%.
Population projection: (1990) 3,507,000; (2000) 4,688,000.
Doubling time: 24 years.
Ethnic composition (1978): Ewe 46.5%; Kabre 22.4%; Gurma 14.2%; Tem 4.2%; other African 11.7%; European 1.0%.
Religious affiliation (1980): animist 45.8%; Christian 37.0%; Sunnī Muslim 17.0%; other 0.2%.
Major cities (1983): Lomé 366,476; Sokodé 48,098‖; Kpalimé 27,669‖.

Vital statistics

Birth rate per 1,000 population (1980–85): 47.8 (world avg. 29.0); legitimate, n.a.; illegitimate, n.a.
Death rate per 1,000 population (1980–85): 17.1 (world avg. 11.0).
Natural increase rate per 1,000 population (1980–85): 30.7 (world avg. 18.0).
Total fertility rate (avg. births per childbearing woman; 1980–85): 6.5.
Marriage rate per 1,000 population (1979): 2.3.
Divorce rate per 1,000 population: n.a.
Life expectancy at birth (1980–85): male 46.9 years; female 50.2 years.
Major illnesses per 100,000 population (1978): infectious and parasitic diseases 26,926; diseases of the respiratory system 9,296; diseases of the digestive system 8,007; accidents, poisoning, and traumas 7,172.

National economy

Budget (1984). Revenue: CFAF76,800,000,000 (indirect tax revenue 46.7%, direct tax revenue 38.9%, stamps 3.0%). Expenditures: CFAF76,800,000,000 (administrative expenditures 40.9%, public debt 28.6%).
Public debt (external, outstanding; 1983): U.S.$805,300,000.
Tourism: receipts from visitors (1983) U.S.$12,000,000; expenditures by nationals abroad (1979) U.S.$19,000,000.
Production (metric tons except as noted). Agriculture, forestry, fishing (1984): yams 450,000, cassava 345,000, corn (maize) 163,000, millet 130,000, vegetables 70,000, fruits 44,000, dry beans 21,000, peanuts (groundnuts) 18,000, cottonseed 18,000, cacao beans 15,000, coconuts 14,000, palm oil 13,800, rice 10,000, coffee 6,000; livestock (number of live animals) 840,-000 sheep, 740,000 goats, 380,000 pigs, 250,000 cattle, 3,000,000 chickens; roundwood (1983) 745,000 cu m; fish catch (1983) 14,556. Mining and quarrying (1984): phosphate rock 2,700,000; salt 600,000¶; marble 15,087¶. Manufacturing (1980): cement 279,000¶; beer 385,000 hectolitres; woven cotton fabrics 20,000,000 m; footwear 1,155,000 pairs. Construction (1980): 4,000 sq m. Energy production (consumption): electricity (kW-hr; 1984) 84,791,000 (234,105,000); crude petroleum (barrels; 1983) none (2,336,000); petroleum products (metric tons; 1983) 485,000 (368,000).

Gross national product (at current market prices; 1983): U.S.$790,000,000 (U.S.$280 per capita).

Structure of gross domestic product and labour force				
	1981		1984	
	in value CFAF'000,000	% of total value	labour force	% of labour force
Agriculture	69.3	27.2	745,000	65.5
Mining	22.6	8.9		
Manufacturing	16.3	6.4		
Construction	11.0	4.3		
Public utilities	4.1	1.6		
Transp. and commun.	17.2	6.7	392,000	34.5
Trade	52.9	20.7		
Finance	...	...		
Pub. admin., defense	25.8	10.1		
Services	...	...		
Other	36.0	14.1		
TOTAL	255.2	100.0	1,137,000	100.0

Population economically active: total (1981) 1,104,000; participation rate of total population 40.8% (female [1980] 34.9%, unemployed [1980] 2.3%).

Price and earnings indexes (1980 = 100)							
	1978	1979	1980	1981	1982	1983	1984
Consumer price index	82.8	89.0	100.0	119.7	133.0	145.5	140.3

Household income and expenditure. Average household size (1980) 5.6; average annual income per household CFAF102,000 (U.S.$452); source of income: n.a; expenditure (1972): food 56.1%, housing 13.7%, transportation 8.6%, clothing 8.5%, health 2.2%, education 0.7%.
Land use (1983): forested 28.5%; meadows and pastures 3.7%; agricultural and under permanent cultivation 26.2%; other 41.6%.

Foreign trade

Balance of trade (current prices)						
	1978	1979	1980	1981	1982	1983
CFAF'000,000,000	−46.7	−63.8	−45.1	−60.3	−70.2	−46.2
% of total	30.1%	40.7%	24.0%	34.4%	37.6%	27.2%

Imports (1983): CFAF108,141,000,000 (food and food products 20.2%, cotton textiles 12.9%, beverages and tobacco 9.6%, transport equipment and parts 6.9%, machinery and mechanical equipment 6.0%). *Major import sources:* France 32.1%; The Netherlands 9.8%; United Kingdom 7.9%; Japan 6.1%; West Germany 5.1%; Pakistan 3.3%.
Exports (1983): CFAF61,921,000,000 (phosphates 42.0%, clinker and cement 21.4%, raw cotton 10.7%, cacao beans 8.9%, coffee 7.9%). *Major export destinations:* The Netherlands 19.9%; France 17.8%; Ivory Coast 12.3%; Yugoslavia 10.7%; Ghana 8.0%; Poland 5.5%.

Transport and communications

Transport. Railroads (1979): length 321 mi‖, 516 km‖; passenger-mi 52,-534,000, passenger-km 84,545,000; short ton-mi cargo 7,152,000, metric ton-km cargo 10,442,000. Roads (1982): total length 4,638 mi, 7,464 km (paved 20%). Vehicles (1984): passenger cars 36,372; trucks and buses 17,-963. Merchant marine (1984): vessels (100 gross tons and over) 8; total deadweight tonnage 43,199. Air transport (1983): passenger-mi 129,311,000, passenger-km 208,106,000; short ton-mi cargo 26,218,000, metric ton-km cargo 38,278,000; airports (1985) with scheduled flights 1.
Communications. Daily newspapers (1984): total number 2; total circulation 10,000♀; circulation per 1,000 population 3.4♀. Radio (1984): total number of receivers 190,000 (1 per 15.3 persons). Television (1984): total number of receivers 8,500 (1 per 342 persons). Telephones (1983): 11,105 (1 per 255 persons).

Education and health

Education (1981–82)				
	schools	teachers	students	student/ teacher ratio
Primary (age 6–11)	2,251	9,619	498,639	51.8
Secondary (age 12–18)	248	3,982	122,925	30.8
Voc., teacher tr.	22	348δ	7,306	...
Higher	1	285	4,131	14.4

Educational attainment (1970). Percent of population over age 15 having: no formal schooling 80.8%; knowledge of reading and writing 11.1%; primary education 6.4%; secondary 1.6%; higher 0.1%. *Literacy* (1980): total population over age 15 literate 490,900 (35.2%); males literate 309,800 (46.1%); females literate 181,100 (25.0%).
Health: physicians (1980) 132 (1 per 19,900 persons); hospital beds (1982) 3,655 (1 per 752 persons); infant mortality rate per 1,000 live births (1975–80) 124.0.
Food (1980–82): daily per capita caloric intake 2,160 (vegetable products 96%, animal products 4%); 92% of FAO recommended minimum requirement.

Military

Total active duty personnel (1984): 5,080□ (army□ 93.5%, navy 1.6%, air force 4.9%). *Military expenditure as percent of GNP* (1983): 2.4% (world 6.1%); per capita expenditure U.S.$6.

*Tchaoudjo includes Tchamba. †Amou includes Wawa. ‡Detail does not add to total given because of rounding. §Total includes 71,000 persons not counted separately. ‖1981. ¶1982. ♀For one daily only. δ1979–80. □Includes paramilitary personnel.

Tonga

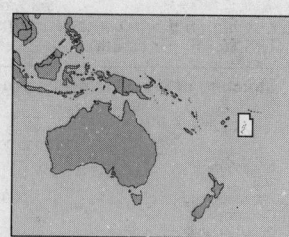

Official name: Pule'anga Tonga (Tongan); Kingdom of Tonga (English).
Form of government: constitutional monarchy with one legislative house (Legislative Assembly [28]).
Head of state and government: King.
Capital: Nukualofa.
Official languages: Tongan; English.
Official religion: none.
Monetary unit: 1 pa'anga ($T)* = 100 seniti; valuation (Oct. 21, 1985) 1 U.S.$ = $T1.42; 1 £ = $T2.04.

Area and population

Divisions		area		population
Districts	Capitals	sq mi	sq km	1984 census
Eua	Ohonua	33.7	87.4	4,017
Eua Foou		...	...	1,812
Eua Proper		...	...	2,205
Haapai	Pangai	42.2	109.3	8,561
Foa		...	...	1,299
Haano		...	...	881
Lulunga		...	...	1,461
Muomua		...	...	895
Pangai		...	...	2,665
Uiha		...	...	1,360
Niuas	Hihifo	27.7	71.7	2,517
Niuafoou		...	...	830
Niuatoputapu		...	...	1,687
Tongatapu	Nukualofa	99.8	258.6	66,420
Kolofoou		...	...	15,846
Kolomotua		...	...	13,371
Kolovai		...	...	4,356
Lapaha		...	...	7,668
Nukunuku		...	...	6,159
Tatakamotonga		...	...	7,280
Vaini		...	...	11,740
Vavau	Neiafu	46.0	119.2	15,077
Hahake		...	...	2,314
Hihifo		...	...	2,035
Leimatua		...	...	2,760
Motu		...	...	1,359
Neiafu		...	...	5,501
Pangaimotu		...	...	1,108
TOTAL LAND AREA		277.1	717.7	96,592
INLAND WATER		11.4	29.6	
TOTAL		288.5†	747.3†	

Demography

Population (1985): 97,050.
Density‡ (1985): persons per sq mi 336.4, persons per sq km 129.9.
Urban–rural (1976): urban 20.3%; rural 79.7%.
Sex distribution (1983): male 51.00%; female 49.00%.
Age breakdown (1976): under 15, 44.2%; 15–29, 26.0%; 30–44, 14.7%; 45–59, 9.5%; 60–74, 4.0%; 75 and over, 1.6%.
Population projection: (1990) 101,350; (2000) 110,540.
Doubling time: 36 years.
Ethnic composition (1976): Tongan 98.3%; other 1.7%.
Religious affiliation (1976): Free Wesleyan 47.4%; Roman Catholic 16.1%; Free Church of Tonga 13.7%; Church of Tonga 8.9%; other 13.9%.
Major city (1983): Nukualofa 20,564.

Vital statistics

Birth rate per 1,000 population (1983): 27.1 (world avg. 29.0); legitimate, n.a.; illegitimate, n.a.
Death rate per 1,000 population (1983): 3.3 (world avg. 11.0).
Natural increase rate per 1,000 population (1983): 23.8 (world avg. 18.0).
Total fertility rate (avg. births per childbearing woman; 1975): 4.9.
Marriage rate per 1,000 population (1981): 6.9.
Divorce rate per 1,000 population (1981): 0.9.
Life expectancy at birth (1976): male 58.0 years; female 60.0 years.
Major causes of death per 100,000 population: n.a.; however, major diseases are gastroenteritis, infantile diarrhea, and acute respiratory infections.

National economy

Budget (1981)§. Revenue: $T12,230,000 (import duties 31.4%; income and wealth tax 13.6%; licenses, stamp duties, registration fees 1.3%). Expenditures: $T16,275,000 (investments 37.2%; social services 22.2%; economic services 13.9%; defense 2.7%).
Public debt (external, outstanding; 1982): U.S.$16,000,000.
Production (metric tons except as noted). Agriculture, forestry, fishing (1984): roots and tubers 92,000, coconuts 56,000, sweet potatoes 17,000, cassava 11,000, fruits excluding melons 11,000, copra 7,000, bananas 3,000; livestock (number of live animals) 101,000 pigs, 17,000 goats, 12,000 horses, 11,000 cattle; roundwood 3,000 cu m ‖; fish catch 1,993 ‖. Mining and quarrying (1982): coral 150,000; sand 25,000. Manufacturing (value added in $T; 1982): food products and beverages 2,623,000; furniture fixtures and wood products 328,000; metal products 252,000; glass and china products 203,000; paper and products 26,000. Construction (value in $T; 1981): residential 2,041,400; nonresidential 5,898,600. Energy production (consumption): electricity (kW-hr; 1983) 12,000,000 (12,000,000); coal, none (n.a.); petroleum, none (n.a.); petroleum products (metric tons; 1983) n.a. (15,000); natural gas, none (n.a.).

Gross national product (1983): U.S.$80,000,000 (U.S.$777 per capita).

Structure of gross domestic product and labour force

	1983		1976	
	in value $T'000	% of total value	labour force	% of labour force
Agriculture	35,790	41.5	9,529	44.5
Mining	394	0.5	16	0.1
Manufacturing	4,271	4.9	386	1.8
Construction	3,354	3.9	1,153	5.4
Public utilities	404	0.5	114	0.5
Transportation and communication	4,950	5.7	829	3.9
Trade	12,774	14.8	825¶	3.8¶
Finance	5,189	6.0	61	0.3
Pub. admin., defense	...	...	º	º
Services	...	...	4,082º	19.0º
Other	19,149⁵	22.2º	4,440	20.7
TOTAL	86,275□	100.0	21,435	100.0

Tourism: receipts from visitors (1983) U.S.$6,000,000; expenditures by nationals abroad (1981) U.S.$1,000,000.
Population economically active (1980): total 25,100; participation rate of population over age 14, 46.5% (female, n.a.; unemployed 17.9%).

Price and earnings indexes (1976 = 100)

	1978	1979	1980	1981	1982	1983	1984
Consumer price index	135.4	151.9	187.3	207.2	223.9	238.8	240.9◊
Earnings index	...	...	...	...	...	...	...

Household income and expenditure. Average household size (1980) 6.0; average annual income per household: n.a.; source of income: n.a.; expenditure (1983): food 55.1%, household goods 12.4%, tobacco and beverages 8.5%, clothing and footwear 6.2%, transportation 6.1%, housing 3.8%.
Land use (1982): forested 11.9%; meadows and pastures 6.0%; agricultural and under permanent cultivation 80.6%; other 1.5%.

Foreign trade

Balance of trade (current prices)

	1978	1979	1980	1981	1982	1983
$T'000,000	−17.2	−19.4	−23.0	−27.3	−37.0	−35.2
% of total	62.8%	58.7%	61.7%	63.9%	81.5%	73.2%

Imports (1983): $T41,663,800 (food and live animals 23.8%, mineral fuels 15.9%, machinery and transport equipment 15.6%, chemicals 6.8%, beverages and tobacco 5.8%). Major import sources: New Zealand 36.2%; Australia 20.3%; Japan 9.0%; United Kingdom 3.2%; Hong Kong 1.2%.
Exports (1983): $T6,453,000 (coconut oil products 32.8%, vanilla beans 9.6%, desiccated coconut 7.1%, bananas 4.7%, machines and transport equipment 1.6%). Major export destinations: New Zealand 51.1%; Australia 28.6%; Japan 2.0%.

Transport and communications

Transport. Railroads: none. Roads (1984): total length 269 mi, 433 km (paved 60%). Vehicles (1983): passenger cars 443, commercial vehicles 1,343. Merchant marine (1984): vessels (100 gross tons and over) 20; total deadweight tonnage 21,168. Air transport (1980): passengers embarked and disembarked, international 44,000, domestic 14,000; cargo, n.a.; airports (1985) with scheduled flights 1.
Communications. Daily newspapers: none. Radio (1984): total number of receivers 65,000 (1 per 1.6 persons). Television: total number of receivers, n.a. Telephones (1983): 3,485 (1 per 30.0 persons).

Education and health

Education (1983)

	schools	teachers	students	student/ teacher ratio
Primary (age 6–10)	111	832	16,755	19.6
Secondary (age 13–18)	47	767	16,212	21.2
Voc., teacher tr.	12	14	554	...
Higher△	1	...	125	...

Educational attainment (1976). Percent of adult population over age 25 having: no schooling 0.4%; less than primary education 37.3%; primary 12.4%; postprimary 45.6%; secondary 0.1%; postsecondary 0.1%; higher 0.6%; special education 2.4%; other 1.1%. Literacy (1976): total population literate 46,456 (92.8%); males 92.9%; females 92.8%.
Health (1982): physicians 35 (1 per 2,881 persons); hospital beds 307 (1 per 328 persons); infant mortality rate per 1,000 live births (1983) 6.4.
Food (1980–82): daily per capita caloric intake 3,202 (vegetable products 84%, animal products 16%); 120% of FAO recommended minimum requirement.

Military

Total active duty personnel: Tonga had a national defense force of about 250 in the early 1980s.

---

*The pa'anga is at par with the Australian dollar. †Also includes 39.0 sq mi (101.1 sq km) of uninhabited islands. ‡Density is based on land area. §Estimated budget for 1983–84 was: revenue $T18,249,051; expenditures $T17,357,291. ‖ 1983. ¶Trade includes hotels and restaurants. ºPublic administration and defense are included with services. ⁵Includes indirect taxes less subsidies. □At current prices. ◊First quarter only. △1982.

Trinidad and Tobago

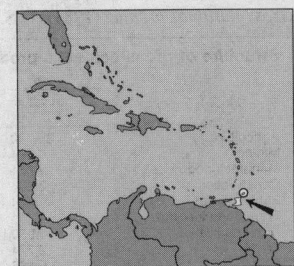

Official name: Republic of Trinidad and Tobago.
Form of government: multiparty republic with two legislative houses (Senate [31]; House of Representatives [36]).
Chief of state: President.
Head of government: Prime Minister.
Capital: Port-of-Spain.
Official language: English.
Official religion: none.
Monetary unit: 1 Trinidad and Tobago dollar (TT$) = 100 cents; valuation (Oct. 21, 1985) 1 U.S.$ = TT$2.40; 1 £ = TT$3.45.

Area and population		area		population
		sq mi	sq km	1984 estimate
Counties	**Capitals**			
Caroni	Chaguanas	213	552	156,500
Nariva/Mayaro	Rio Claro	350	906	35,000
St. Andrew/St. David	Sangre Grande	364	943	54,900
St. George	...	353	914	406,700
St. Patrick	Siparia	261	676	137,800*
Tobago	Scarborough	117	303	42,100
Victoria	Princes Town	313	811	210,300
City				
Port-of-Spain	—	4	10	60,700
Boroughs				
Arima	—	...†	...†	26,700
Point Fortin	—	...†	...†	...*
San Fernando	—	3	8	37,400
TOTAL		1,980†	5,128†	1,168,100

Demography

Population (1985): 1,189,000.
Density (1985): persons per sq mi 600.5, persons per sq km 231.9.
Urban-rural (1985): urban 22.6%; rural 77.4%.
Sex distribution (1980): male 49.98%; female 50.02%.
Age breakdown (1980): under 15, 34.2%; 15–29, 30.9%; 30–44, 16.3%; 45–59, 10.0%; 60–74, 6.2%; 75 and over, 1.7%; not stated, 0.7%.
Population projection: (1990) 1,262,000; (2000) 1,410,000.
Doubling time: 35 years.
Ethnic composition (1980): black 40.8%; East Indian 40.7%; mixed 16.3%; white 0.9%; Chinese 0.5%; Arab 0.1%; other 0.7%.
Religious affiliation (1980): Christian 61.9%, of which Roman Catholic 33.0%, Protestant 28.1% (including Anglican 14.7%, Presbyterian 3.8%, Pentecostal 3.5%, Seventh-day Adventist 2.5%); Hindu 25.0%; Muslim 6.0%; other (including Rastafarian and Yoruba syncretist) 7.1%.
Major cities (1984): Port-of-Spain 60,700; San Fernando 37,400; Arima 26,700; Point Fortin 16,710‡.

Vital statistics

Birth rate per 1,000 population (1982): 29.0 (world avg. 29.0); (1978) legitimate 56.8%; illegitimate 43.2%.
Death rate per 1,000 population (1982): 7.0 (world avg. 11.0).
Natural increase rate per 1,000 population (1982): 22.0 (world avg. 18.0).
Total fertility rate (avg. births per childbearing woman; 1980–85): 2.9.
Marriage rate per 1,000 population (1982): 8.4.
Divorce rate per 1,000 population (1979): 0.5.
Life expectancy at birth (1980–85): male 67.8 years; female 72.6 years.
Major causes of death per 100,000 population (1978): diseases of the circulatory system 244.1; malignant neoplasms 65.3; respiratory diseases 30.9.

National economy

Budget (1984). Revenue: TT$6,526,000,000 (non-oil sector 58.7%, of which tax revenue 52.5% [including individual income taxes 23.9%, taxes on goods and services 10.3%, company taxes 7.9%, import duties 7.1%], nontax revenue 6.2%; oil sector 41.3%, of which corporation taxes 33.3%, royalties 6.8%). Expenditure: TT$5,311,900,000 (education 19.2%; welfare 12.3%; health 10.6%; justice and police 7.5%; public debt 6.4%).
Tourism: receipts from visitors (1981) U.S.$152,000,000; expenditures by nationals abroad (1984) U.S.$130,000,000.
Production (metric tons except as noted). Agriculture, forestry, fishing (1984): sugarcane 893,000, coconuts 57,000, rice 18,000, taro 18,000, tomatoes 8,000, oranges 7,000, cocoa 1,717§, coffee 1,388§; livestock (number of live animals) 76,000 cattle, 62,000 pigs, 49,000 goats; roundwood (1983) 67,000 cu m; fish catch (1983) 4,461. Mining and quarrying (1984): crude petroleum 60,250,000 barrels; natural gas 2,897,100,000 cu m; natural asphalt 31,100; other quarried products include limestone, sand, and clay. Manufacturing (1984): heavy fuel oils 5,500,000‖; motor gasoline 1,560,- 000‖; nitrogenous fertilizers 1,458,000; cement 405,400; crude steel 198,- 900; methanol 180,900¶; steel rods 134,700; sugar 71,000; 20,700 motor vehicles§, 19,900 refrigerators, 21,200 television receivers§; rum (100 proof) 757,000 hectolitres; beer 240,000 hectolitres. Construction (new building authorized; 1981): residential 491,400 sq m; nonresidential 168,300 sq m. Energy production (consumption): electricity (kW-hr; 1982) 2,260,000,000 (2,260,000,000); coal, none (minuscule); crude petroleum (barrels; 1982) 62,901,000 (62,901,000); petroleum products (metric tons; 1982) 7,994,000 (1,687,000); natural gas (cu m; 1982) 3,193,000,000 (3,193,000,000).

Gross national product (at current market prices; 1983): U.S.$6,850,000,000 (U.S.$6,850 per capita).

Structure of gross domestic product and labour force				
	1984			
	in value TT$'000,000	% of total value	labour force	% of labour force
Agriculture	579	2.9	38,200	8.1
Mining	4,955	24.6 }	65,400	13.9
Manufacturing	1,323	6.6 }		
Construction	2,571	12.8 }	81,300	17.3
Public utilities	394	1.9 }		
Transportation and communication	2,289	11.4	32,300	6.8
Trade	1,805	9.0 }		
Finance	1,943	9.6 }	193,400	41.1
Pub. admin., defense	2,844	14.1 }		
Services	1,433	7.1 }		
Other	...	...	60,300♀	12.8♀
TOTAL	20,136	100.0	470,900	100.0

Public debt (external, outstanding; 1984): U.S.$1,084,800,000.
Population economically active (1984): total 470,900; participation rate of population over age 15, 62.0% (female 31.6%‖, unemployed 12.8%).

Price and earnings indexes (1980 = 100)							
	1978	1979	1980	1981	1982	1983	1984
Consumer price index	74.2	85.1	100.0	114.3	127.6	148.7	168.4
Weekly earnings index	65.9	81.4	100.0	120.6	130.8	167.4	...

Household income and expenditure. Average household size (1980) 4.2; average annual income per household: n.a.; source of income: n.a.; expenditure (1982): food 36.6%, clothing and footwear 18.9%, housing 13.8%, transportation and communications 8.6%, household supplies 8.4%, drink and tobacco 4.7%, fuel and light 2.6%, education 2.5%, health 2.5%.
Land use (1983): forested 44.2%; meadows and pastures 2.2%; agricultural and under permanent cultivation 30.8%; other 22.8%.

Foreign trade

Balance of trade (current prices)ᵟ							
	1978	1979	1980	1981	1982	1983	1984
TT$'000,000	+201	+1,214	+2,158	+1,612	−1,501	−550	+624
% of total	2.1%	10.7%	12.4%	10.3%	9.2%	4.6%	6.4%

Imports (1983): TT$6,196,700,000 (machinery and transport equipment 37.0%, basic and miscellaneous manufactures 31.0%, food and live animals 15.0%, chemicals 7.2%). *Major import sources:* U.S. 42.3%; U.K. 11.5%; Japan 9.3%; European Economic Community (excluding U.K.) 7.8%; Canada 6.5%.
Exports (1983): TT$5,646,300,000 (crude petroleum 44.3%, petroleum products 39.2%, fertilizers [anhydrous ammonia and urea] 7.2%, basic manufactures [mostly steel wire rods] 3.0%, sugar 1.0%). *Major export destinations:* U.S. 58.1%; EEC and the U.K. 12.2%; Puerto Rico and U.S. Virgin Islands 3.8%; Guyana 2.9%.

Transport and communications

Transport. Railroads: none. Roads (1984): total length 4,909 mi, 7,900 km (paved 46%). Vehicles (1983): passenger cars 200,100; trucks and buses 63,620. Merchant marine (1984): vessels (100 gross tons and over) 49; total deadweight tonnage 12,376. Air transport□ (1984): passenger-mi 1,123,177,- 000, passenger-km 1,807,582,000; short ton-mi cargo 5,799,000, metric ton-km cargo 8,465,000; airports (1985) with scheduled flights 2.
Communications (1984). Daily newspapers: total number 4; total circulation 176,000; circulation per 1,000 population 151. Radio: 375,000 receivers (1 per 3.1 persons). Television: 250,000 receivers (1 per 4.7 persons). Telephones (1983): 86,859 (1 per 13 persons).

Education and health

Education (1981–82)				
	schools	teachers	students	student/ teacher ratio
Primary (age 5–11)	464	7,272	167,452	23.0
Secondary (age 12–19)	180	2,742	90,586	33.0
Voc., teacher tr.	...	...	12,649	...
Higher◊	1	272	2,923	10.7

Educational attainment (1980). Percent of adult population over age 24 having: no formal schooling 0.3%; primary education 73.0%; secondary 23.8%; higher 2.9%. *Literacy* (1980): total population over age 14 literate 673,600 (94.8%); males literate 342,300 (96.4%); females literate 331,300 (93.3%).
Health (1982): physicians (1980) 786 (1 per 1,387 persons); hospital beds 4,321 (1 per 261 persons); infant mortality rate per 1,000 live births 26.0.
Food (1980–82): daily per capita caloric intake 3,051 (vegetable products 81%, animal products 19%); 126% of FAO recommended minimum requirement.

Military

Total active duty personnel (1984): 1,500△ (army 80.0%, navy 16.7%, air force 3.3%). *Military expenditure as percent of GNP* (1983): 3.1% (world 6.1%); per capita expenditure U.S.$202.

*St. Patrick includes the population of the borough of Point Fortin. †Areas of the boroughs of Arima and Point Fortin included with total. ‡1980. §1983. ‖1982. ¶Production began in 1984. ♀Unemployed. ᵟImports, c.i.f. (cost, insurance, and freight); exports, f.o.b. (free on board). □Trinidad and Tobago (BWIA International) Airways only. ◊1983–84; University of the West Indies, St. Augustine campus. △All services form part of the army.

Tunisia

Official name: al-Jumhūrīyah at-Tūnisīyah (Republic of Tunisia).
Form of government: multiparty republic with one legislative house (Chamber of Deputies [136]).
Head of state and government: President.
Capital: Tunis.
Official language: Arabic.
Official religion: Islām.
Monetary unit: 1 dinar (D) = 1,000 millimes; valuation (Oct. 21, 1985) D1.00 = U.S.$1.28 = £0.89.

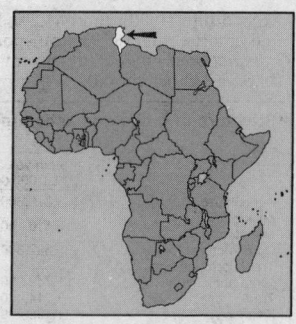

Area and population

Governorates	Capitals	area sq mi	area sq km	population 1984 census
Aryānah	Aryānah	602	1,558	374,192
Bājah	Bājah	1,374	3,558	274,706
Banzart	Banzart	1,423	3,685	394,670
Bin 'Arūs	Bin 'Arūs	294	761	246,193
Jundūbah	Jundūbah	1,198	3,102	359,429
al-Kāf	al-Kāf	1,917	4,965	247,672
Madaniyīn	Madaniyīn	3,316	8,588	295,889
al-Mahdīyah	al-Mahdīyah	1,145	2,966	270,435
al-Munastir	al-Munastir	393	1,019	278,478
Nābul	Nābul	1,076	2,788	461,405
Qābis	Qābis	2,770	7,175	240,016
Qafsah	Qafsah	3,471	8,990	235,723
al-Qaṣrayn	al-Qaṣrayn	3,114	8,066	297,959
al-Qayrawān	al-Qayrawān	2,591	6,712	421,607
Qibilī	Qibilī	8,527	22,084	95,371
Ṣafāqis	Ṣafāqis	2,913	7,545	577,992
Sidi Bū Zayd	Sidi Bū Zayd	2,700	6,994	288,528
Silyānah	Silyānah	1,788	4,631	222,038
Sūsah	Sūsah	1,012	2,621	322,491
Taṭāwin	Taṭāwin	15,015	38,889	100,329
Tawzar	Tawzar	1,822	4,719	67,943
Tūnis	Tunis (Tūnis)	134	346	774,364
Zaghwān	Zaghwān	1,069	2,768	118,743
TOTAL		59,664	154,530	6,966,173

Demography

Population (1985): 7,158,000.
Density (1985): persons per sq mi 120.4, persons per sq km 46.5.
Urban–rural (1984): urban 52.8%; rural 47.2%.
Sex distribution (1984): male 50.92%; female 49.08%.
Age breakdown (1985): under 15, 37.8%; 15–29, 30.7%; 30–44, 14.9%; 45–59, 10.5%; 60–74, 5.1%; 75 and over, 1.0%.
Population projection: (1990) 7,989,000; (2000) 9,856,000.
Doubling time: 33 years.
Ethnic composition (1980): Arab 97.9%; Berber 1.5%; French 0.2%; Italian 0.1%; other 0.3%.
Religious affiliation (1980): Sunnī Muslim 99.4%; Christian 0.3%; Jewish 0.1%; other 0.2%.
Major cities (commune; 1984): Tunis 596,654; Ṣafāqis 231,911; Aryānah 98,655.

Vital statistics

Birth rate per 1,000 population (1984): 30.9 (world avg. 29.0); (1974) legitimate 99.8%; illegitimate 0.2%.
Death rate per 1,000 population (1984): 6.6 (world avg. 11.0).
Natural increase rate per 1,000 population (1984): 24.3 (world avg. 18.0).
Total fertility rate (avg. births per childbearing woman; 1980–85): 4.9.
Marriage rate per 1,000 population (1984): 7.6.
Divorce rate per 1,000 population (1982): 0.9.
Life expectancy at birth (1980–85): male 60.1 years; female 61.1 years.
Major causes of death per 100,000 population: n.a.; however, the major illnesses are intestinal infections, trachoma, hepatitis, tuberculosis, and syphilis.

National economy

Budget (1984): Revenue: D2,613,000,000 (indirect taxes 34.1%, investment 16.7%, direct taxes 11.0%). Expenditures: D2,574,800,000 (education 11.2%, agriculture 7.9%, defense 7.5%, health 6.4%, interior affairs 4.2%, social welfare 1.1%).
Public debt (external, outstanding; 1983): U.S.$3,427,100,000.
Tourism (1983): receipts from visitors U.S.$573,000,000; expenditures by nationals abroad U.S.$102,000,000*.
Production (metric tons except as noted). Agriculture, forestry, fishing (1984): wheat 711,000, tomatoes 430,000, olives 400,000, barley 312,000, watermelons 225,000, potatoes 140,000, oranges 130,000, grapes 112,000, dates 50,000, cabbages 6,000; livestock (number of live animals) 600,000 cattle, 5,230,000 sheep, 1,030,000 goats, 177,000 camels, 16,000,000 chickens; roundwood 2,673,000 cu m†; fish catch 74,900. Mining and quarrying (1983): phosphate rock 5,924,000; iron ore 316,000; zinc 6,308; lead 4,700. Manufacturing (1984): cement 2,772,000; sulfuric acid 2,715,000; crude steel 168,000; pig iron and ferroalloys 144,000; tires 252,000 units. Construction (1982): residential building authorized 2,679,000 sq m. Energy production (consumption): electricity (kW-hr; 1983) 3,531,000,000 (3,531,300,000); coal (metric tons; 1983) none (28,000); crude petroleum (barrels; 1983) 43,001,000 (11,872,000); petroleum products (metric tons; 1983) 1,316,000 (2,489,000); natural gas (cu m; 1983) 449,740,000 (449,740,000).

Gross national product (at current market prices; 1983): U.S.$8,860,000,000 (U.S.$1,290 per capita).

Structure of gross domestic product and labour force

	1984 in value D'000,000	1984 % of total value	1981 labour force	1981 % of labour force
Agriculture	550.0	17.5	537,900	32.4
Mining	489.0	15.6	16,000	1.0
Manufacturing	571.0	18.2	359,500	21.7
Construction	247.0	7.9	179,100	10.8
Public utilities	...	...	9,500	0.6
Transportation and communication	...	...	63,200	3.8
Trade	118.0	3.7	148,500	8.9
Finance			10,900	0.7
Pub. admin., defense				
Services	1,165.0	37.1	266,500	16.1
Other	1.0	—	66,600	4.0
TOTAL	3,141.0	100.0	1,657,700	100.0

Population economically active (1980): total 1,609,300; participation rate of total population 25.3% (female 22.3%, unemployed 4.1%).

Price and earnings indexes (1980 = 100)

	1979	1980	1981	1982	1983	1984	1985‡
Consumer price index	90.9	100.0	108.9	123.8	134.9	146.2	157.8
Monthly earnings index	...	...	...	...	...	...	...

Household income and expenditure. Average household size (1984) 5.5; income per household: n.a.; source of income: n.a.; expenditure (1980): food 41.7%, housing 29.0%, clothing and footwear 8.5%, recreation 7.6%, transportation 4.9%.
Land use (1983): forested 3.6%; meadows and pastures 19.3%; agricultural and under permanent cultivation 30.2%; other 46.9%.

Foreign trade

Balance of trade (current prices)

	1979	1980	1981	1982	1983	1984
D'000,000	−430.0	−522.5	−632.9	−840.0	−845.0	−1,075.7
% of total	22.8%	22.4%	20.4%	26.4%	25.0%	27.8%

Imports (1984): D2,438,800,000 (food and live animals 7.9%, textiles 3.8%, plastic material 2.5%, yarn 2.5%, chemical products 2.5%, textile products 2.4%). *Major import sources:* France 24.9%; Italy 14.7%; West Germany 10.7%; United States 7.1%; Spain 6.2%; Japan 4.2%.
Exports (1984): D1,399,100,000 (crude petroleum 41.1%, clothing 11.9%, phosphates 10.2%, phosphoric acid 6.6%, olive oil 4.1%, dates 1.3%). *Major export destinations:* France 20.5%; United States 19.1%; Italy 17.9%; West Germany 9.5%; United Kingdom 3.9%; The Netherlands 3.3%.

Transport and communications

Transport. Railroads (1984): route length 1,251 mi§, 2,013 km§; passenger-mi 462,299,000, passenger-km 744,000,000; short ton-mi cargo 1,159,000,000 ‖, metric ton-km cargo 1,692,000,000 ‖. Roads (1982): total length 15,752 mi, 25,352 km (paved 52%). Vehicles (1982): passenger cars 141,185; trucks and buses 147,571. Merchant marine (1984): vessels (100 gross tons and over) 63; total deadweight tonnage 449,511. Air transport (1984): passenger-mi 987,376,000, passenger-km 1,589,032,000; short ton-mi cargo 12,551,000, metric ton-km cargo 18,324,000; airports (1985) with scheduled flights 3.
Communications. Daily newspapers (1984): total number 5; total circulation 250,000; circulation per 1,000 population 35.7. Radio (1984): total number of receivers 1,150,000 (1 per 6.1 persons). Television (1984): total number of receivers 400,000 (1 per 17.5 persons). Telephones (1983): 218,808 (1 per 31.4 persons).

Education and health

Education (1984–85)

	schools	teachers	students	student/ teacher ratio
Primary (age 6–11)	3,214	36,399	1,238,968	34.0
Secondary (age 12–18)	349	20,079	385,449	19.2
Voc., teacher tr.	...	...	...	...
Higher	...	5,019	38,829	7.7

Educational attainment (1975). Percent of population over age 5 having: no formal schooling 55.7%; primary education 34.4%; secondary 8.5%; higher 0.7%; no certificate 0.7%. *Literacy* (1980): total population over age 15 literate 1,855,017 (47.4%); males literate 1,190,891 (61.2%); females literate 664,126 (33.7%).
Health (1982): physicians 1,732 (1 per 3,883 persons); hospital beds 14,071 (1 per 478 persons); infant mortality rate per 1,000 live births (1984) 12.4.
Food (1980–82): daily per capita caloric intake 2,745 (vegetable products 91%, animal products 9%); 115% of FAO recommended minimum requirement.

Military

Total active duty personnel (1984): 35,100 (army 85.5%, navy 7.4%, air force 7.1%). *Military expenditure as percent of GNP* (1983): 2.9% (world 6.1%); per capita expenditure U.S.$35.

*1982. †1983. ‡August. §1981. ‖ Excluding fast service.

Turkey

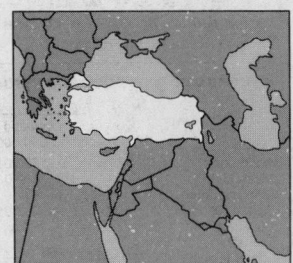

Official name: Türkiye Cumhuriyeti (Republic of Turkey).
Form of government: multiparty republic with one legislative house (Turkish Grand National Assembly [400]).
Chief of state: President.
Head of government: Prime Minister.
Capital: Ankara.
Official language: Turkish.
Official religion: none.
Monetary unit: 1 Turkish lira (LT) = 100 kurush; valuation (Oct. 21, 1985) 1 U.S.$ = LT544.01; 1 £ = LT780.11.

Area and population

Geographical regions	area sq mi	area sq km	population 1983 estimate
Akdeniz kıyısı (Mediterranean Coast)	22,933	59,395	4,280,800
Batı Anadolu (West Anatolia)	29,742	77,031	3,337,600
Doğu Anadolu (East Anatolia)	68,074	176,311	6,021,500
Güneydoğu Anadolu (Southeast Anatolia)	15,347	39,749	2,060,900
İç Anadolu (Central Anatolia)	91,254	236,347	11,435,400
Karadeniz kıyısı (Black Sea Coast)	31,388	81,295	6,483,300
Marmara ve Ege kıyıları (Marmara and Aegean coasts)	33,035	85,560	9,102,100
Trakya (Thrace)	9,175	23,764	4,734,800
TOTAL	300,948	779,452	47,456,400

Demography

Population (1985): 49,272,000.
Density (1985): persons per sq mi 157.7, persons per sq km 60.9.
Urban-rural (1980): urban 43.9%; rural 56.1%.
Sex distribution (1980): male 50.65%; female 49.35%.
Age breakdown (1980): under 15, 38.5%; 15–29, 27.7%; 30–44, 16.0%; 45–59, 11.2%; 60–64, 1.8%; 65 and over, 4.8%*.
Population projection: (1990) 54,633,000; (2000) 67,166,000.
Doubling time: 28.5 years.
Ethnic composition (1978): Turkish 87.1%; Kurdish 9.5%; Arab 1.7%; other 1.7%.
Religious affiliation (1980): Sunnī Muslim 99.2%; Eastern Orthodox 0.3%; other 0.5%.
Major cities (1980): Istanbul 2,772,708; Ankara 1,877,755; İzmir 757,854; Adana 574,515; Bursa 445,113.

Vital statistics

Birth rate per 1,000 population (1980–85): 33.6 (world avg. 29.0).
Death rate per 1,000 population (1980–85): 9.3 (world avg. 11.0).
Natural increase rate per 1,000 population (1980–85): 24.3 (world avg. 18.0).
Total fertility rate (avg. births per childbearing woman; 1980–85): 4.5.
Marriage rate per 1,000 population (1982): 3.6.
Divorce rate per 1,000 population (1982): 0.4.
Life expectancy at birth (1980–85): male 60.3 years; female 64.9 years.
Major causes of death per 100,000 population (1982): heart disease 85.2; birth injury and difficult labour 33.2; malignant neoplasms (cancers) 24.5; cerebrovascular disease 17.2.

National economy

Budget (1984). Revenue: LT3,580,530,000,000 (taxes on income 66.3%, special revenue and funds 17.7%). Expenditures: LT4,024,818,000,000 (current expenditures 35.3%, investment expenditures 18.3%).
Public debt (external, outstanding; 1983): U.S.$15,886,000,000.
Tourism (1983): receipts from visitors U.S.$408,000,000; expenditures by nationals abroad U.S.$127,000,000.
Production (metric tons except as noted). Agriculture, forestry, fishing (1984): wheat 17,200,000, sugar beets 12,600,000, barley 6,200,000, tomatoes 4,000,000, grapes 3,500,000, potatoes 3,200,000, apples 1,900,000, corn (maize) 1,500,000, cotton 1,330,000, olives 1,200,000, dry onions 1,100,000, eggplants 675,000, cotton lint 586,000, pumpkins and squash 377,000, hazelnuts 300,000, apricots 195,000, walnuts 120,000, cauliflowers 65,000, chestnuts 55,000, almonds 28,000, artichokes 8,000; livestock (number of live animals) 48,707,000 sheep, 16,732,000 goats, 17,200,000 cattle; roundwood 19,193,000 cu m†, fuelwood 15,000,000 cu m†; fish catch 567,304†. Mining and quarrying (1984): iron 3,887,097; copper 2,468,654; boron minerals 1,400,355. Manufacturing (1984): cement 13,445,000; petroleum products 11,945,000; crude iron 2,792,328; iron and steel products 2,753,388; sugar 1,500,000; cigarettes 62,000; motor vehicles 54,832 units. Construction (1984): residential 22,145,938 sq m; nonresidential 6,741,687 sq m. Energy production (consumption): electricity (kW-hr; 1983) 27,321,000,000 (29,544,000,000); coal (metric tons; 1983) 21,110,000 (21,149,000); crude petroleum (barrels; 1984) 14,839,000 (125,698,000); petroleum products (metric tons; 1984) 16,463,000 (15,150,000†); natural gas (cu m; 1983) 1,951,000 (1,951,000).
Land use (1983): forested 26.2%; meadows and pastures 11.9%; agricultural and under permanent cultivation 34.2%; other 27.7%.
Household income and expenditure‡. Average household size 5.0; income per household (1979) LT11,880 (U.S.$385); sources of income: self-employment 46.8%, wages and salaries 38.9%, transfer grant 9.4%, other 4.9%;

expenditure (1979): food 41.2%, housing 25.2%, clothing 14.8%, recreation and entertainment 6.1%, transportation 5.5%, health 3.3%, other 3.9%.
Gross national product (at current market prices; 1983): U.S.$58,260,000,000 (U.S.$1,230 per capita).

Structure of gross domestic product and labour force

	1984 in value LT'000,000	% of total value	labour force	% of labour force
Agriculture	3,373,300	18.4	9,420,000	59.9
Mining	5,116,100	28.0	110,000	0.7
Manufacturing			1,739,000	11.1
Construction	687,300	3.7	587,000	3.7
Transportation and communication	1,749,900	9.5	530,000	3.4
Trade	3,214,400	17.5	722,000	4.6
Finance	1,192,200	6.5	224,000	1.4
Public utilities	1,100,300	6.0 ‖	118,000	0.8
Pub. admin., defense				
Services	968,100	5.3	2,261,000	14.4
Other	937,800	5.1		
TOTAL	18,339,400	100.0	15,711,000	100.0

Population economically active (1982): total 19,027,000; participation rate of total population 41.1% (female 32.9%, unemployed 17.7%).

Price and earnings indexes (1980 = 100)

	1978	1979	1980	1981	1982	1983	1984
Consumer price index	30.0	47.6	100.0	136.6	178.7	230.8	350.6§
Daily earnings index ‖	48.7	68.9	100.0	127.4	161.8	221.2	306.1

Foreign trade

Balance of trade (current prices)

	1979	1980	1981	1982	1983	1984
U.S.$'000,000	−2,808	−4,999	−4,230	−3,097	−3,507	−3,624
% of total	38.3%	46.2%	31.0%	21.2%	23.4%	20.3%

Imports (1984): LT4,034,897,096,000 (liquid fuels 33.7%, machinery 20.4%, pharmaceutical products and dyes 9.5%, iron and steel 8.0%). Major import sources: Iran 14.8%; West Germany 10.8%; United States 10.1%; Libya 6.0%; Italy 5.8%; France 2.2%.
Exports (1984): LT2,608,331,529,000 (agricultural products 24.5%, clothes 9.9%, livestock and animal products 4.8%, tobacco 3.0%). Major export destinations: West Germany 17.8%; Iraq 13.4%; Iran 10.3%; Italy 6.9%; Switzerland 4.6%; United Kingdom 3.7%.

Transport and communications

Transport. Railroads (1983): route length 5,067 mi, 8,156 km; passenger-mi 3,559,000,000, passenger-km 5,728,000,000; short ton-mi cargo 9,177,000,000, metric ton-km cargo 13,398,000,000. Roads (1983): total length 188,136 mi, 302,776 km (paved, n.a.). Vehicles (1983): passenger cars 856,350; trucks and buses 488,767. Merchant marine (1984): vessels (100 gross tons and over) 776; total deadweight tonnage 5,174,046. Air transport (1984): passenger-mi 1,467,544,000, passenger-km 2,361,789,000; short ton-mi cargo 17,991,000, metric ton-km cargo 26,266,000; airports (1985) with scheduled flights 16.
Communications. Daily newspapers (1979): total number 364; total circulation 3,878,000; circulation per 1,000 population 89.1. Radio (1984): total number of receivers 4,310,000 (1 per 10.9 persons). Television (1984): total number of receivers 4,929,732 (1 per 9.5 persons). Telephones (1983): 2,664,753 (1 per 18.6 persons).

Education and health

Education (1983–84)

	schools	teachers	students	student/ teacher ratio
Primary (age 5–12)	47,324	208,393	6,495,916	31.2
Secondary (age 13–18)	5,450	90,078	1,980,523	21.9
Voc., teacher tr.	2,129	81,023	658,168	8.1
Higher	153	16,454	225,622	13.7

Educational attainment (1980). Percent of population over age 6 having: primary education 37.9%; secondary 5.1%; higher 2.2%. Literacy (1980): total population over age 6 literate 25,307,000 (67.4%); males literate 15,185,000 (79.9%); females literate 10,122,000 (54.6%).
Health (1983): physicians 32,265 (1 per 1,465 persons); hospital beds 99,396 (1 per 475 persons); infant mortality rate per 1,000 live births (1979) 131.0.
Food (1980–82): daily per capita caloric intake 3,053 (vegetable products 90%, animal products 10%); 119% of FAO recommended minimum requirement.

Military

Total active duty personnel (1984): 602,000 (army 83.1%, navy 7.6%, air force 9.3%). Military expenditure as percent of GNP (1983): 4.9% (world 6.1%); per capita expenditure U.S.$55.

*Including those of unknown age. †1983. ‡Urban areas only. §Second quarter. ‖ Insured workers only.

Tuvalu

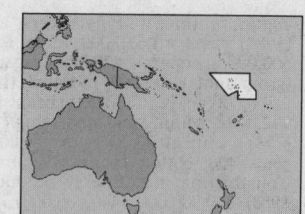

Official name: Tuvalu.
Form of government: constitutional monarchy with one legislative house (House of Assembly [13]).
Chief of state: British Monarch, represented by governor-general.
Head of government: Prime Minister.
Capital: Funafuti Atoll.
Official language: none; Tuvaluan and English widely spoken.
Official religion: none.
Monetary unit*: 1 Tuvalu Dollar = 1 Australian Dollar ($T = $A) = 100 Tuvalu and Australian cents; valuation (Oct. 21, 1985)
1 U.S.$ = $A1.42; 1 £ = $A2.04.

Area and population

Islands	Capital	area sq mi	area sq km	population 1983 estimate
Funafuti	Funafuti	0.91	2.36	2,620
Nanumaga		1.00	2.59	760
Nanumea		1.38	3.57	910
Niulakita		0.16	0.41	90
Niutao		0.82	2.12	920
Nui		1.27	3.29	650
Nukufetau		1.18	3.06	740
Nukulaelae		0.64	1.66	350
Vaitupu		1.89	4.90	1,320
TOTAL		9.25	23.96	8,360

Demography

Population (1985): 8,580.
Density (1985): persons per sq mi 927.5, persons per sq km 358.1.
Urban–rural (1983): urban 31.3%; rural 68.7%.
Sex distribution (1979): male 46.77%; female 53.23%.
Age breakdown (1979): under 15, 33.8%; 15–29, 31.0%; 30–44, 14.3%; 45–59, 13.2%; 60–74, 6.1%; 75 and over, 1.6%.
Population projection: (1990) 11,000; (2000) 15,800.
Doubling time: 19 years.
Ethnic composition (1979): Tuvaluan (Polynesian) 91.2%; mixed (part I-Kiribati or other) 6.0%; I-Kiribati 1.3%; European and other Pacific 1.5%.
Religious affiliation (1979): Church of Tuvalu (Congregational) 96.9%; Seventh-day Adventist 1.4%; Baha'i 1.0%; Roman Catholic 0.2%; other 0.5%.
Major city (1983): Funafuti (urban) 2,620.

Vital statistics

Birth rate per 1,000 population (1982): 38.7 (world avg. 29.0).
Death rate per 1,000 population (1982): 10.2 (world avg. 11.0).
Natural increase rate per 1,000 population (1982): 28.5 (world avg. 18.0).
Total fertility rate (avg. births per childbearing woman; 1979): 2.8.
Marriage rate per 1,000 population: n.a.
Divorce rate per 1,000 population: n.a.
Life expectancy at birth (1979): male 56.9 years; female 60.1 years.
Major causes of death per 100,000 population: n.a.; however, principal infectious diseases include influenza, intestinal infections, chicken pox, filarial infection and dracontiasis, and tuberculosis.

National economy

Budget (1983). Revenue: $A3,492,902 (British grant-in-aid 27.1%; philately tax 23.3%; customs duties 19.8%; personal tax 6.3%). Expenditures: $A3,-542,902 (works and communications 32.8%; social services 27.5%; office of Prime Minister 12.2%; financial services 10.8%; commerce and natural resources 5.3%; police, prisons, and immigration 4.1%; pensions and gratuities 4.0%; parliament 1.5%).
Gross national product (at current market prices; 1981): U.S.$5,000,000 (U.S.$680 per capita).

Structure of gross domestic product and labour force

	1979 in value $A	% of total value	labour force	% of labour force
Agriculture	597,100	16.0	2,955	73.7
Mining	—	—	—	—
Manufacturing	37,300	1.0	62	1.5
Construction	485,200	13.0	229	5.7
Public utilities	...	...	14	0.4
Transportation and communication	149,300	4.0	111	2.5
Trade	1,268,900	34.0	100	2.5
Finance Pub. admin., defense	1,194,200	32.0	377	9.4
Services				
Other¶	...	...	...	...
TOTAL	3,732,000⁹	100.0	4,010	100.0

Production (metric tons except as noted). Agriculture†, forestry, fishing (1984): coconuts 2,000, hens' eggs 13, honey 2, other agricultural products include breadfruit, pulaka (taro), bananas, pandanus fruit, and pawpaws; livestock (number of live animals) n.a.‡; forestry, n.a.; fish catch 793§‖. Mining and quarrying: n.a. Manufacturing (1983): copra 200 metric tons;

handicrafts; beche-de-mer; baked goods. Construction: n.a. Energy production (consumption): electricity (kW-hr; 1981) 3,000,000 (3,000,000); coal, none (n.a.); crude petroleum, none (n.a.); petroleum products, none (n.a.); natural gas, none (n.a.).
Public debt: n.a.
Tourism (1979): number of visitors 474.
Population economically active (1979): total 4,010; participation rate of total population over age 14, 83.0% (female 42.6%, employed 3.4%).

Price and earnings indexes (1978 = 100)

	1978	1979	1980	1981	1982	1983	1984
Consumer price index	100.0	104.1	117.9	129.2	141.2	150.7	...
Monthly earnings index							

Household income and expenditure. Average household size (1979) 6.8; average annual income per household: $A2,575; sources of income: agriculture and other 61.2%, cash economy only 17.9%, agriculture only 14.9%, other 6.0%; expenditure (1978): food 45.5%, housing and household operations 11.5%, transportation 10.5%, alcohol and tobacco 10.5%, clothing 7.5%, other 14.5%.
Land use (1983): agricultural and under permanent cultivation 75%ᵟ; other 25%.

Foreign trade

Balance of trade (current prices)

	1978	1979	1980	1981	1982	1983
$A'000	−1,527	−1,594	−3,061	−2,556	−2,890	...
% of total	94.3%	75.6%	94.7%	98.6%	98.7%	...

Imports (1982): $A2,890,377 (food and live animals 22.4%, of which cereals 8.9%, meat and meat preparations 4.7%, sugar and honey 2.7%, dairy products and eggs 2.0%; petroleum and petroleum products 16.5%; manufactured goods 19.1%, of which textile yarn and fabrics 2.8%, paper and paperboard 2.5%, iron and steel 1.0%; machinery and transport equipment 16.0%, of which nonelectrical machinery 7.7%, transport equipment 4.0%; chemicals 6.5%, of which dying and colouring materials 2.6%, perfume and toilet preparations 2.4%; wood, lumber and cork 2.9%; photographic goods and watches 2.7%; tobacco 2.5%; beverages 2.0%; furniture 1.0%; clothing 0.7%). *Major import sources:* Fiji 47.5%; Australia 39.7%; New Zealand 5.3%; Japan 1.4%; United Kingdom 1.0%; United States 0.1%.
Exports (1982): $A36,766▭ (copra 72.5%, reexported cinema films 27.5%).
Major export destinations: Fiji 47.5%; Australia 39.7%; New Zealand 5.3%.

Transport and communications

Transport. Railroads: none. Roads (1983): total length 5 mi, 8 km (paved, none). Vehicles: passenger cars, n.a.; trucks and buses, n.a.◇ Merchant marine (1984): vessels (100 gross tons and over) 2; total deadweight tonnage 526. Air transport (1977): passenger arrivals (Funafuti) 1,443; cargo, n.a.; airports (1985) with scheduled flights 1△.
Communications. Newspapers (1983): total number 1 (fortnightly); total circulation 250; circulation per 1,000 population 29.8. Radio (1984): total number of receivers 1,100 (1 per 7.7 persons). Television: none. Telephones (1984): 120 (1 per 71 persons).

Education and health

Education (1982–83)

	schools	teachers	students	student/teacher ratio
Primary (age 6–14)	9	41	966	23.5
Secondary (age 12–18)	1	15	250	16.7
Vocational	8	16	354	22.1
Higher	—	—	—	—

Educational attainment (1979). Percent of adult population over age 20 having: no formal schooling 0.4%; primary education 90.5%; secondary 7.7%; higher 0.5%. *Literacy* (1979): total population literate 5,509 (95.5%); males literate 2,443 (95.5%); females literate 3,066 (95.5%).
Health (1984): physicians 4 (1 per 2,118 persons); hospital beds 36 (1 per 235 persons); infant mortality rate per 1,000 live births (1979) 42.
Food: daily per capita caloric intake, n.a.

Military

Total active duty personnel: There is a police force of about 30 men.

---

*The value of the Tuvalu Dollar is pegged to the value of the Australian Dollar, which is also legal currency in Tuvalu. †Because of the poor quality of soil, agriculture is virtually nonexistent on the islands. ‡Livestock largely consists of pigs, goats, and poultry; efforts are being made to increase their number to reduce dependence on imported meat, dairy products, and eggs. §1983. ‖ Fish catch refers to marine fishes only and is largely used for local consumption, except for the export of some beche-de-mer to Fiji and Hong Kong. ¶Includes unemployed. ⁹At current prices. ᵟCapable of supporting coconut palms, pandanus, and breadfruit. ▭Sales of postage stamps to overseas philatelists was becoming an important source of foreign exchange in the mid-1980s. ◇There are several cars, tractors, trailers, and light lorries on Funafuti; a few motorcycles are in use on most islands. △Six atoll lagoons have seaplane service.

Uganda

Official name: Republic of Uganda.
Form of government: multiparty republic with one legislative house (National Assembly [156]).
Chief of state: President.
Head of government: Prime Minister.
Capital: Kampala.
Official language: English.
Official religion: none.
Monetary unit: 1 Uganda shilling (U Sh) = 100 cents; valuation (Oct. 21, 1985) 1 U.S.$ = U Sh669.46; 1 £ = U Sh960.00.

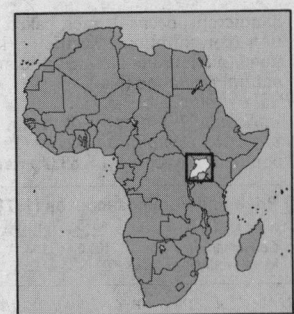

Area and population

Provinces Districts	Capitals	area sq mi	area sq km	population 1980 census
Busoga	Jinja	5,150	13,340	1,221,872
Iganga	Bulamogi	3,190	8,250	643,801
Jinja	Jinja	280	730	228,520
Kamuli	Namwendwa	1,680	4,360	349,551
Central	Kampala	2,420	6,270	1,117,648
Kampala	Kampala	70	190	478,895
Mpigi	Mpigi	2,350	6,080	638,753
Eastern	Mbale	8,600	22,260	2,015,530
Kapchorwa	Kaptanya	670	1,740	74,517
Kumi	Kumi	1,100	2,860	238,809
Mbale	Bunkoko	990	2,550	557,241
Soroti	Soroti	4,080	10,560	476,629
Tororo	Sukulu	1,760	4,550	668,334
Karamoja	Moroto	10,410	26,960	350,908
Kotido	Kotido	5,120	13,270	161,445
Moroto	Katikekile	5,290	13,690	189,463
Nile	Arua	6,070	15,730	811,755
Arua	Olaki	3,020	7,830	472,283
Moyo	Moyo	1,930	5,010	106,492
Nebbi	Nebbi	1,120	2,890	232,980
North Buganda	Bombo	10,430	27,010	1,554,371
Luwero	Luwero	3,550	9,200	412,474
Mubende	Bageza	3,980	10,310	510,260
Mukono	Kawuga Mukono	2,900	7,500	631,637
Northern	Gulu	16,030	41,520	1,261,364
Apac	Apac	2,510	6,500	313,333
Gulu	Bungatira	4,500	11,660	270,185
Kitgum	Labongo	6,210	16,090	307,594
Lira	Lira	2,810	7,270	370,252
South Buganda	Masaka	6,170	15,970	905,754
Masaka	Kaswa Bukoto	4,520	11,700	631,156
Rakai	Byakabanda	1,650	4,270	274,598
Southern	Mbarara	8,210	21,280	1,963,428
Bushenyi	Bumbaire	1,960	5,080	522,495
Kabale	Rubale	940	2,430	455,471
Mbarara	Kakika	4,320	11,200	687,803
Rukungiri	Kagunga	990	2,570	297,659
Western	Butebe	11,960	30,980	1,427,446
Bundibugyo	Busaru	720	1,880	112,126
Hoima	Hoima	3,120	8,080	294,221
Kabarole	Karambe	3,410	8,820	520,141
Kasese	Rukoki	1,200	3,120	277,708
Masindi	Nyangeya	3,510	9,080	223,250
TOTAL		93,100*	241,140*	12,630,076

Demography

Population (1985): 14,716,100.
Density (1985): persons per sq mi 158.1, persons per sq km 61.0.
Urban–rural (1980): urban 11.9%; rural 88.1%.
Sex distribution (1980): male 49.52%; female 50.48%.
Age breakdown (1980): under 15, 45.2%; 15–29, 25.9%; 30–44, 15.1%; 45–59, 8.9%; 60–74, 4.1%; 75 and over, 0.8%.
Population projection: (1990) 18,262,000; (2000) 25,396,000.
Doubling time: 22 years.
Ethnic composition (1980): Ganda 18.0%; Nyoro 14.4%; Turkana 11.0%; Gisu 10.3%; Nkole 8.2%; Soga 8.2%; Chiga 7.0%; Lango 6.5%; other 16.4%.
Religious affiliation (1980): Roman Catholic 47.5%; Protestant 31.7%; Muslim 15.8%; other 5.0%.
Major cities (1980): Kampala 458,000; Jinja 45,100; Masaka 29,120; Mbale 28,039; Mbarara 23,160.

Vital statistics

Birth rate per 1,000 population (1983): 50.0 (world avg. 29.0).
Death rate per 1,000 population (1983): 17.0 (world avg. 11.0).
Natural increase rate per 1,000 population (1983): 33.0 (world avg. 18.0).
Total fertility rate (avg. births per childbearing woman; 1983): 7.0.
Life expectancy at birth (1983): male 48.0 years; female 50.0 years.
Major causes of death per 100,000 population: n.a.; however, the major diseases are malaria, measles, venereal diseases, whooping cough, shigellosis (infection with dysentery), chicken pox, and leprosy.

National economy

Budget (1982). Revenue: U Sh21,135,000,000 (export duties 34.8%; sales tax on imported goods 22.0%; customs duties 21.0%; taxes on income and profits 9.9%; excise tax 7.4%). Expenditures: U Sh36,998,000,000 (general public services 37.9%; defense 19.6%; education 13.6%; agriculture, forestry, fishing 7.1%; health 4.0%).
Public debt (external, outstanding; 1983): U.S.$623,000,000.
Tourism (1981): receipts from visitors U.S.$5,000,000; expenditures by nationals abroad U.S.$20,000,000.

Production (metric tons except as noted). Agriculture, forestry, fishing (1984): cassava 1,650,000, millet 600,000, seed cotton 528,000, corn (maize) 500,000, sorghum 470,000, sugarcane 400,000, coffee 204,000, peanuts (groundnuts) 100,000; livestock (number of live animals) 5,200,000 cattle, 2,500,000 goats, 1,300,000 sheep; roundwood 26,255,000 cu m†; fish catch 172,000†. Mining and quarrying (1983): copper ore 1,000‡. Manufacturing (1981): cement 40,000†; tea 14,000; blister copper 1,300; soap and detergents 400; cotton fabrics 19,000,000 sq m; cigarettes 205,000,000 units. Construction: n.a. Energy production (consumption): electricity (kW-hr; 1983) 650,000,000 (440,000,000); petroleum products (metric tons; 1983) none (202,000).
Gross national product (at current market prices; 1984): U.S.$6,213,000,000 (U.S.$434 per capita).

Structure of gross domestic product and labour force

	1981 in value U Sh'000,000	1981 % of total value	1976 labour force	1976 % of labour force
Agriculture	353,347	68.1	78,200	21.4
Mining	145	0.0	4,100	1.1
Manufacturing	16,839	3.2	54,000	14.8
Construction	2,143	0.4	45,500	12.4
Transportation and communication	5,842	1.1	13,100	3.6
Trade	33,999	6.6	18,500	5.1
Pub. admin., defense	25,007	4.8	152,000	41.6
Other	81,489	15.7	...	...
TOTAL	518,811§	100.0 ‖	365,400	100.0

Population economically active (1983): total 5,860,000; participation rate of population ages 15–64, 50.0% (female [1982] 33.3%, unemployed, n.a.).

Price and earnings indexes (1981 = 100)

	1979	1980	1981	1982	1983	1984
Consumer price index	62.4	83.2	100.0	200.3	248.3	343.3
Earnings index	...	...	...	...	...	...

Household size. Average household size (1980) 5.2; average annual income per household: n.a.; source of income: n.a.; expenditure: n.a.
Land use (1983): forested 29.6%; meadows and pastures 25.0%; agricultural and under permanent cultivation 31.5%; other 13.9%.

Foreign trade

Balance of trade (current prices)

	1975	1976	1977	1978	1979	1980
U Sh'000,000	+672	+1,726	+3,124	+1,112	+2,068	+818
% of total	21.5%	40.3%	49.9%	26.1%	70.6%	19.0%

Imports (1980): USh1,740,000,000 (machinery including agricultural machinery and transport equipment 48.4%, metals and metal products excluding iron and steel 4.6%, paper and paper products 2.2%). *Major import sources:* Kenya and Tanzania 33.8%; United Kingdom 23.3%; India 13.4%.
Exports (1980): USh2,558,000,000 (unroasted coffee 96.8%, raw cotton 1.0%). *Major export destinations:* United Kingdom 17.1%; United States 14.8%; The Netherlands 13.5%; Japan 9.5%; West Germany 3.4%.

Transport and communications

Transport. Railroads (1984): route length 788 mi, 1,268 km; passengers, n.a.; cargo, n.a. Roads (1984): total length 17,289 mi, 27,824 km (paved 15%). Vehicles (1982): passenger cars 10,633; trucks and buses 11,245. Merchant marine (1984): vessels (100 gross tons and over) 1; total deadweight tonnage 2,700. Air transport? (1983): passenger-mi 88,998,000, passenger-km 143,228,000; short ton-mi cargo 26,331,000, metric ton-km cargo 38,442,000; airports (1985) with scheduled flights 7.
Communications. Daily newspapers (1984): total number 5; total circulation 23,800δ; circulation per 1,000 population 1.7δ. Radio (1985): total number of receivers 280,000 (1 per 53 persons). Television (1985): total number of receivers 76,000 (1 per 194 persons). Telephones (1980): 46,359 (1 per 276 persons).

Education and health

Education (1982)

	schools	teachers	students	student/ teacher ratio
Primary (age 6–12)	5,300	44,426	1,616,791	36.4
Secondary (age 13–18)	257	6,287	132,051	21.0
Voc., teacher tr.	23	735	13,338	18.1
Higher	4	640	7,312	11.4

Educational attainment, n.a. *Literacy* (1980): total population literate 3,484,600 (47.9%).
Health (1981): physicians 611 (1 per 21,523 persons); hospital beds 19,782 (1 per 665 persons); infant mortality rate per 1,000 live births (1983) 125.0.
Food (1980–82): daily per capita caloric intake 1,781 (vegetable products 93%, animal products 7%); 77% of FAO recommended minimum requirement.

Military

Total active duty personnel (1984): 18,000 (army 100%). *Military expenditure as percent of GNP* (1983): 1.0% (world 6.1%); per capita expenditure U.S.$4.

*Total includes 7,650 sq mi (19,820 sq km) of inland water not distributable by district. †1983. ‡Metal content. §At current prices. ‖ Detail does not add to total given because of rounding. ¶1982. ?Scheduled flights only. δPartial circulation.

Union of Soviet Socialist Republics

Official name: Soyuz Sovetskykh Sotsialisticheskikh Respublik (Sovetsky Soyuz) (Union of Soviet Socialistic Republics [Soviet Union]).
Form of government: federal socialist republic with one legislative house (Supreme Soviet [1,500]).
Chief of state: President (Chairman of the Supreme Soviet).
Head of government: Premier (Chairman of the Council of Ministers).
Capital: Moscow.
Official language: Russian.
Official religion: none.
Monetary unit: 1 ruble = 100 kopecks; valuation (Oct. 21, 1985) 1 ruble = U.S.$1.30 = £1.11.

Area and population

Soviet Federated Socialist Republic	Capitals	area* sq mi	area* sq km	population 1984 estimate
Russian S.F.S.R.	Moscow	6,592,800	17,075,400	142,108,000
Soviet Socialist Republics				
Armenian	Yerevan	11,500	29,800	3,263,000
Azerbaijan	Baku	33,400	86,600	6,498,000
Belorussian	Minsk	80,200	207,600	9,878,000
Estonian	Tallinn	17,400	45,100	1,519,000
Georgian	Tbilisi	26,900	69,700	5,171,000
Kazakh	Alma-Ata	1,049,200	2,717,300	15,654,000
Kirgiz	Frunze	76,600	198,500	3,875,000
Latvian	Riga	24,600	63,700	2,589,000
Lithuanian	Vilnius	25,200	65,200	3,539,000
Moldavian	Kishinyov	13,000	33,700	4,083,000
Tadzhik	Dushanbe	55,300	143,100	4,366,000
Turkmen	Ashkhabad	188,500	488,100	3,123,000
Ukrainian	Kiev	233,100	603,700	50,681,000
Uzbek	Tashkent	172,700	447,400	17,496,000
TOTAL		8,649,500	22,402,200	273,843,000

Demography

Population (1985): 277,500,000.
Density (1985): persons per sq mi 32.3, persons per sq km 12.5.
Urban–rural (1984): urban 64.8%; rural 35.2%.
Sex distribution (1984): male 46.90%; female 53.10%.
Age breakdown (1980): under 15, 24.3%; 15–29, 26.6%; 30–44, 19.2%; 45–59, 16.9%; 60–74, 9.6%; 75 and over, 3.4%.
Population projection: (1990) 290,155,000; (2000) 310,236,000.
Doubling time: 69 years.
Ethnic composition (1979): Russian 52.4%; Ukrainian 16.2%; Uzbek 4.8%; Belorussian 3.6%; Kazakh 2.5%; Tatar 2.4%; Azerbaijani 2.1%; Armenian 1.6%; Georgian 1.4%; Moldavian 1.1%; Tadzhik 1.1%; other 10.8%.
Religious affiliation (1980): Christian 25.5%, of which Orthodox 22.5%, Protestant 1.6%, Roman Catholic 1.4%; Muslim 11.3%; Jewish 1.2%; nonreligious 29.1%; atheist 22.1%; other 10.8%.
Major cities (1984): Moscow 8,537,000; Leningrad 4,827,000; Kiev 2,409,000; Tashkent 1,986,000; Baku 1,661,000; Kharkov 1,536,000; Minsk 1,442,000; Gorky 1,392,000; Novosibirsk 1,384,000; Sverdlovsk 1,286,000; Kuybyshev 1,251,000; Dnepropetrovsk 1,140,000; Tbilisi 1,140,000.

Other principal cities (1984)

	population		population		population
Alma-Ata	1,046,000	Krivoy Rog	680,000	Tula	529,000
Barnaul	567,000	Lvov	728,000	Ufa	1,048,000
Chelyabinsk	1,086,000	Novokuznetsk	572,000	Ulyanovsk	524,000
Donetsk	1,064,000	Odessa	1,113,000	Ustinov	603,000
Dushanbe	539,000	Omsk	1,094,000	Vilnius	535,000
Frunze	590,000	Orenburg	513,000	Vladivostok	591,000
Irkutsk	590,000	Penza	522,000	Volgograd	969,000
Karaganda	608,000	Perm	1,049,000	Voronezh	841,000
Kazan	1,039,000	Riga	875,000	Yaroslavl	623,000
Khabarovsk	569,000	Rostov-na-Donu	983,000	Yerevan	1,114,000
Kishinyov	605,000	Samarkand	515,000	Zaporozhye	844,000
Krasnodar	603,000	Saratov	894,000	Zhdanov	520,000
Krasnoyarsk	860,000	Tolyatti	576,000		

Place of birth (1983): 99.9% native-born; 0.1% foreign-born.
Mobility (1979). Population living in the same residence from birth: 52.9%; 25 years and more 10.4%; 20–24 years 3.9%; 15–19 years 5.0%; 10–14 years 5.4%; 9–6 years 6.1%; 5–2 years 8.6%; less than 2 years 7.7%.
Households† (1979). Average household size 3.5; 2 persons 29.7%, 3 persons 28.8%, 4 persons 23.0%, 5 persons 9.5%, 6 persons 4.1%, 7 or more persons 4.9%. Family households population: 232,075,245 (86.9%), nonfamily population 30,360,755 (13.1%).
Emigration: (1982) 2,700; (1979) 51,000.

Vital statistics

Birth rate per 1,000 population (1984): 19.6 (world avg. 29.0); legitimate, n.a.; illegitimate, n.a.
Death rate per 1,000 population (1984): 10.8 (world avg. 11.0).

Natural increase rate per 1,000 population (1984): 8.8 (world avg. 18.0).
Total fertility rate (avg. births per childbearing woman; 1982): 3.1.
Marriage rate per 1,000 population (1983): 10.4.
Divorce rate per 1,000 population (1983): 3.5.
Life expectancy at birth (1980): male 61.9 years; female 72.0 years.
Major causes of death per 100,000 population (1983): diseases of the circulatory system 554.3, of which cardiovascular atherosclerosis 228.2, cerebrovascular disease 121.6, hypertensive heart disease 82.7, ischemic heart disease 73.0, other diseases of the circulatory system 48.8; malignant neoplasms (cancers) 148.1.

Social indicators

Educational attainment (1984). Percent of population over age 10 having: less than full primary education 0.2%; primary and secondary 91.0%, of which secondary 60.4%; some postsecondary and higher 8.2%; postgraduate 0.6%.
Distribution of wealth: n.a.
Quality of working life (1984). Average workweek: 39.4 hours (3.0% overtime). Annual rate per 100,000 workers for: injury or accident, n.a.; industrial illness, n.a.; death, n.a. Proportion of labour force insured for damages or income loss resulting from: injury 100.0%; permanent disability 100.0%; death 100.0%. Average days lost to labour stoppages per 1,000 workdays: n.a. Average duration of journey to work: 58–68 minutes (mostly by public transportation and foot). Rate per 1,000 workers of discouraged (unemployed no longer seeking work): n.a.
Access to services‡ (1983). Proportion of dwellings having access to: electricity 100.0%; safe public water supply 91.0%; public sewage collection 88.0%; central heating 88.0%; hot water 79.0%; bathroom 81.0%.
Social participation. Eligible voters participating in last national election: 99.9%. Population participating in voluntary work (1984): 76.5%. Trade union membership in total work force: 100.0%. Practicing religious population in total affiliated population: n.a.
Social deviance. Offense rate per 100,000 population for: murder, n.a.; rape, n.a.; other assault, n.a.; grand and auto theft, n.a.; burglary and housebreaking, n.a. Incidence per 100,000 in general population of: alcoholism, n.a.; drug and substance abuse, n.a.; suicide, n.a.
Leisure (1984). Favourite leisure activities (attendance): movies 4,244,000,-000; lectures 308,700,000; museums 174,800,000; library 147,117,000; concerts 141,400,000; theatre 124,900,000.
Material well-being (1984). Households possessing: automobile, n.a.; telephone 28.5%; television receiver 95.0%; refrigerator 90.0%; air conditioner, none; washing machine 70.0%.

National economy

Gross national product (at current market prices; 1984): U.S.$734,300,000,-000 (U.S.$2,670 per capita).

Structure of net material product and labour force

	1983 in value '000,000,000 rubles	% of total value	labour force	% of labour force
Agriculture	110.1	20.1	25,334,000	19.7
Mining				
Manufacturing	254.1	46.3	37,830,000	29.4
Public utilities	§	§	4,695,000	3.6
Construction	53.2	9.7	11,315,000	8.8
Transportation and communication	33.3	6.1	12,438,000	9.7
Trade	97.4	17.8	9,899,000	7.7
Finance	...	...	681,000	0.5
Pub. admin., defense	...	...	2,626,000	2.0
Services	...	...	22,418,000	17.4
Other	...	...	1,536,000	1.2
TOTAL	548.1§	100.0	128,762,000	100.0

Budget (1983). Revenue: 357,900,000,000 rubles (share in profits of the state enterprises 29.8%, turnover tax 28.8%, income tax 7.7%). Expenditures: 354,300,000,000 rubles (national economy 57.0%, education and science 12.7%, social welfare 7.9%, defense 4.8%, health 4.7%).
Public debt: n.a.
Tourism (1982): tourist arrivals 5,000,000; tourists abroad 4,500,000.

Manufacturing, mining, and construction enterprises (1982)

	no. of enter-prises	no. of employees	monthly wages as a % of avg. of all wages	annual gross output ('000,000 rubles)
Manufacturing				
Machinery and metal products	8,180	15,011,000	111.2	182,400
Food products	7,538	2,717,000	99.2	104,100
Chemicals and chemical products	1,493	1,148,000	112.8	75,500
Textiles	1,996	2,210,000	88.4	72,700
Clothing	5,118	2,250,000	88.4	30,900
Nonmetallic products	3,200	2,088,000	103.8	24,800
Wood, furniture, and paper	2,275	1,619,000	112.8	22,300
Beverages	1,726	374,000	95.5	7,700
Iron and steel	408	1,044,000	131.1	6,200
Footwear	406	494,000	95.8	5,500
Leather and leather products	266	199,000	95.9	4,200
Tobacco	88	40,000	95.5	3,800
Glass and pottery	333	376,000	99.3	3,300
Building materials	3,938	...	107.1	2,300
Rubber and plastic	...	433,000	103.5	...
Mining				
Petroleum and gas	853	1,105,000	161.1	34,400
Coal			153.9	
Metal ores	1,070	194,000	153.9	15,900
Construction	...	11,299,000	103.3	...

Production (metric tons except as noted). Agriculture, forestry, fishing (1984): potatoes 83,000,000, sugar beets 82,000,000, wheat 76,000,000, barley 42,000,000, oats 16,000,000, corn (maize) 14,000,000, rye 13,500,000, raw cotton 2,300,000, flax fibre 9,200,000, sunflower 8,600,000, grapes 7,500,000, dry pears 5,200,000, millet and sorghum 2,400,000, tobacco 350,000; livestock (number of live animals) 145,265,000 sheep, 119,558,000 cattle, 78,722,000 pigs, 6,511,000 goats, 5,711,000 horses, 1,131,000,000 poultry; roundwood 296,000,000 cu m; fish catch 9,930,000. Mining and quarrying (1983): iron ore 245,000,000; phosphate rock 27,000,000; salt 16,200,000; potash salts 9,300,000; bauxite 4,600,000; chromium ore 3,400,000; manganese 3,100,000; asbestos 2,250,000; magnesite 2,000,000; copper 1,030,000; zinc 805,000; lead 430,000; nickel 170,000; molybdenum 11,100; tungsten 9,100; mercury 64,000 flasks; diamonds 11,000,000 carats. Manufacturing (1984): crude steel 154,000,000; cement 130,000,000; pig iron 110,500,000; rolled steel 107,000,000; mineral fertilizers 30,800,000; sulfuric acid 25,300,000; steel pipes 18,900,000; meat 16,700,000; sugar 12,500,000; paper and paperboard 9,556,000; soda ash 4,900,000; resins and plastics 4,800,000; caustic soda 2,853,000; vegetable oil 2,700,000; cotton fibre 2,586,000; cotton yarn 1,659,000; man-made fibres 1,500,000; butter 1,500,000; margarine 1,400,000; synthetic detergents 1,100,000; soap 1,098,000; insecticides 576,000; woolen yarn 447,000; woolen fibre 369,000; flax fibre 365,000; leather 126,000; cotton fabrics 7,286,000 sq m; silk fabrics 1,884,000 sq m; linen fabrics 853,000 sq m; woolen fabrics 707,000 sq m; fish products 7,000,000,000 rubles; machine tools 2,385,000,000 rubles; food-processing equipment 939,000,000 rubles; forge press machines 666,000,000 rubles; leather footwear 764,000,000 pairs; tires 62,025,000 units; radio receivers 9,298,000 units; television receivers 8,578,000 units; refrigerators 5,700,000 units; bicycles 5,060,000 units; washing machines 4,250,000 units; passenger cars 1,315,000 units; buses 85,093 units; railroad freight cars 58,433 units; railroad passenger cars 1,916 units; beer 66,081,000 hectolitres; wine 35,101,000 hectolitres. Construction (1984): residential 112,400,000 sq m, of which urban 110,800,000 sq m, rural 1,600,000 sq m.

Service enterprises (1982)

	no. of enterprises	no. of employees	monthly wage as a % of all wages
Public utilities	...	3,751,000	78.4
Electrical power	1,433	790,000	115.7
Transport: rail	...	2,231,000	111.7
Transport: road	...	2,530,000	119.7
Transport: water	...	1,920,000	140.1
Communication	90,883	5,662,000	98.1
Finance	...	676,000	95.3
Wholesale trade	...	2,047,000	80.5
Retail trade	699,900	7,816,000	80.5
Tourism	...	...	90.4
Education	275,255	2,882,000	78.5
Public services and administration	...	2,591,000	90.1
Other services	276,000	22,202,000	90.1

Energy production (consumption): electricity (kW-hr; 1984) 1,493,000,000,000 (1,354,000,000,000); coal (metric tons; 1984) 712,000,000 (608,000,000 ‖); crude petroleum (barrels; 1984) 4,493,300,000 (3,302,200,000 ‖); petroleum products (metric tons; 1982) 711,585,000 (619,585,000); natural gas (cu m; 1984) 587,000,000,000 (470,000,000,000).
Population economically active (1984): total 130,000,000; participation rate of population over age 15, 62.7% (female 46.0%, unemployed, n.a.).

Price and earnings indexes (1980 = 100)

	1978	1979	1980	1981	1982	1983
Consumer price index	94.9	96.9	100.0	101.2	104.5	105.2
Monthly earnings index	95.3	97.3	100.0	102.3	105.4	107.3

Household income and expenditure. Average household size (1983) 3.0; average annual income per household 5,472 rubles (U.S.$7,800); sources of income: wages and salaries 72.5%, social welfare 24.9%, other 2.6%; expenditure (1983): food 30.2%, alcohol 17.0%, clothing 15.4%, education and culture 15.0%, taxes 8.7%, housing 2.7%.
Land use (1983): forested 35.6%; meadows and pastures 16.7%; agricultural and under permanent cultivation 10.5%; other 37.2%.

Foreign trade

Balance of trade (current prices)

	1977	1978	1979	1980	1981	1982	1983
'000,000,000 rubles	3.2	1.1	4.6	5.2	4.5	6.7	8.3
% of total	5.0%	1.6%	5.7%	5.5%	4.1%	5.6%	6.5%

Imports (1983): 59,585,000,000 rubles (machinery and transport equipment 38.2%; cereals and food products 20.5%; consumer goods 11.5%; raw materials 8.8%; mineral fuels and lubricants 5.6%; chemicals and related products 4.6%; textile and clothing 2.1%). *Major import sources:* East Germany 10.0%; Czechoslovakia 8.6%; Bulgaria 8.1%; Poland 7.8%; Hungary 6.0%; West Germany 5.6%; Cuba 5.9%; Italy 4.4%; Yugoslavia 3.9%; Finland 3.7%; Romania 2.4%; India 1.9%; The Netherlands 1.8%; United Kingdom 1.7%; Mongolia 1.5%; Vietnam 1.3%; Japan 1.2%; Sweden 1.0%; Iran 0.8%; Switzerland 0.8%; Afghanistan 0.6%; United States 0.5%.
Exports (1983): 67,891,000,000 rubles (crude petroleum and petroleum products 41.6%; machinery and transport equipment 12.5%; mineral fuels and natural gas 9.3%; raw materials 7.6%; chemicals, fertilizers, and resins 3.1%; wood and paper products 2.8%). *Major export destinations:* East Germany 10.0%; Czechoslovakia 8.6%; Bulgaria 8.1%; Poland 7.8%; Hungary 6.0%; West Germany 5.6%; Cuba 5.0%; Italy 4.4%; Yugoslavia 3.9%; Finland 3.7%; France 3.6%; Romania 2.4%; India 1.9%; United Kingdom 1.8%; Belgium 1.5%.

Trade by commodity group (1983)

		imports		exports	
SITC Group		'000 rubles	%	'000 rubles	%
00	Food and live animals	13,406,600	22.5	1,018,400	1.5
02	Raw materials, excluding fuels	4,945,600	8.3	4,878,200	7.2
03	Mineral fuels, lubricants, and related materials	3,038,800	5.1	36,933,000	54.4
05	Chemicals and related products	2,681,300	4.5	11,881,000	17.5
65	Textile yarn, fabrics and related materials	953,000	1.6	814,700	1.2
07	Machinery and transport equipment	21,808,100	36.6	8,486,500	12.5
08	Miscellaneous manufactured articles	6,971,400	11.7	1,222,000	1.8
09	Goods not classified by kind	5,781,000	9.7	2,657,800	3.9
TOTAL		59,585,000	100.0	67,891,600	100.0

Direction of trade (1983)

	imports		exports	
	'000 rubles	%	'000 rubles	%
Communist				
Comecon	30,805,400	51.7	34,421,000	50.7
Other	2,860,000	4.8	3,326,700	4.9
Market Economy				
Industrial countries	18,709,700	31.4	19,620,700	28.9
Developing countries	7,209,900	12.1	10,523,200	15.5
TOTAL	59,585,000	100.0	67,891,600	100.0

Transport and communications

Transport. Railroads (1984): length 89,229 mi, 143,600 km; passenger-mi 225,000,000,000, passenger-km 362,000,000,000; short ton-mi cargo 2,470,000,000,000, metric ton-km cargo 3,600,000,000,000. Roads (1984): total length 605,000 mi, 973,000 km (paved 79%). Vehicles (1980): passenger cars 8,255,000; trucks and buses 7,254,000. Inland waterways (1984): length 85,687 mi, 137,941 km; passenger-mi 3,764,900,000, passenger-km 6,059,000,000; short ton-mi cargo 187,000,000,000, metric ton-km cargo 273,000,000,000. Merchant marine (1984): vessels (100 gross tons and over) 7,095; total deadweight tonnage 27,928,263. Air transport (1983): passenger-mi 110,000,000,000, passenger-km 177,000,000,000; short ton-mi cargo 2,181,000,000, metric ton-km cargo 3,185,000,000; airports (1985) with scheduled flights 52. Shares of domestic passenger traffic by mode of transportation (1983): buses 43.6%; railway 37.3%; ships and airplanes 19.1%. Pipelines (1984): length 47,364 mi, 76,225 km; short ton-mi cargo 927,000,000,000, metric ton-km cargo 1,353,000,000,000.

Distribution of traffic (1983)

	cargo carried ('000,000 tons)	% of nat'l total	passengers carried ('000,000)	% of nat'l total
Road	6,612.0	53.1	44,548.0	30.6
Rail	3,850.6	30.9	4,149.0	2.8
Urban transport	—	—	48,334.8	33.2
road	—	—	30,800.0	21.1
rail	—	—	17,534.8	12.0
Inland water	844.8	6.8	193.5	0.1
Air	3.1	0.0	109.5	0.1
Pipeline	1,146.7	9.2	—	—
TOTAL	12,457.2	100.0	145,669.6	100.0¶

Communications. Daily newspapers (1984): total number 726; total circulation 32,602,000; circulation per 1,000 population 120. Radio (1983): total number of receivers 164,885,000 (1 per 1.7 persons). Television (1984): total number of receivers 85,000,000 (1 per 3.3 persons). Telephones (1984): 27,800,000 (1 per 10 persons).

Education and health

Education (1983–84)

	schools	teachers	students	student/ teacher ratio
Primary (age 6–13)	71,200 ⎱		35,700,000	...
Secondary (age 14–17)	59,000 ⎰	2,360,000	4,714,000	...
Vocational	4,438	247,418	4,502,800	18.2
Higher	890	374,000	5,310,300	14.2

Literacy (1983): total population over age 15 literate 99.8%.
Health (1984): physicians 1,104,300 (1 per 249 persons); hospital beds 3,497,500 (1 per 79 persons); infant mortality rate per 1,000 live births (1982) 16.3.
Food (1980–82): daily per capita caloric intake 3,358 (vegetable products 74%, animal products 26%); 130% of FAO recommended minimum requirement.

Military

Total active duty personnel (1984): 5,115,000 (army 36.0%, command and general support troops 29.3%, paramilitary forces 13.2%, navy 9.6%, air force 7.8%, forces abroad 4.1%). *Military expenditure as percent of GNP* (1983): 35.0% (world 6.1%); per capita expenditure U.S.$940.

*Total land area is 8,600,400 sq mi (22,274,900 sq km) and is shown for republics; the total area (both land and water) is shown in the grand total. †Family households only. ‡Only urban dwellings. §At current prices. ‖ 1983. ¶Detail does not add to total given because of rounding.

United Arab Emirates

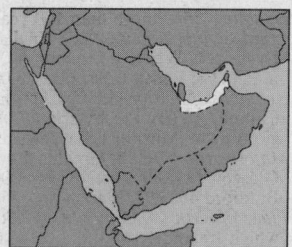

Official name: Ittiḥād al-Imārāt al-'Arabīyah (United Arab Emirates).
Form of government: monarchy; federal union of seven emirates with one legislative house (Federal National Council [40]).
Chief of state: President.
Head of government: Prime Minister.
Capital: Abu Dhabi.
Official language: Arabic.
Official religion: Islām.
Monetary unit: 1 U.A.E. Dirham (Dh) = 100 fils; valuation (Oct. 21, 1985) 1 U.S.$ = Dh3.67; 1 £ = Dh5.27.

Area and population		area		population
				1983
Emirates	Capitals	sq mi	sq km	estimate
Abu Dhabi (Abū Ẓaby)	Abu Dhabi	26,000	67,340	521,000
Ajman ('Ajmān)	Ajman	100	260	44,000
Dubai (Dubayy)	Dubai	1,500	3,890	307,000
Fujairah (Al-Fujayrah)	Fujairah	450	1,170	38,000
Ras al-Khaimah (Ra's al-Khaymah)	Ras al-Khaimah	650	1,680	86,000
Sharjah (Ash-Shāriqah)	Sharjah	1,000	2,590	185,000
Umm al-Qaiwain (Umm al-Qaywayn)	Umm al-Qaiwain	300	770	14,000
TOTAL		30,000	77,700	1,195,000

Demography

Population (1985): 1,280,000.
Density (1985): persons per sq mi 42.7, persons per sq km 16.5.
Urban-rural (1980): urban 71.8%; rural 28.2%.
Sex distribution (1980): male 68.96%; female 31.04%.
Age breakdown (1980): under 15, 30.3%; 15–29, 28.9%; 30–44, 28.3%; 45–59, 9.0%; 60–74, 2.8%; 75 and over, 0.7%.
Population projection: (1990) 1,570,000; (2000) 1,916,000.
Doubling time: 17 years.
Ethnic composition (1982): South Asian (mainly Indian, Iranian, and Pakistani) 50%; Arab 42%; other (mainly European and East Asian) 8%.
Religious affiliation (1980): Muslim 94.9%; Christian 3.8%; other 1.3%.
Major cities (1980): Dubai 266,000; Abu Dhabi 243,000; Sharjah 125,000; al-'Ayn 102,000; Ras al-Khaimah 42,000.

Vital statistics

Birth rate per 1,000 population (1980–85): 28.8 (world avg. 29.0); legitimate, n.a.; illegitimate, n.a.
Death rate per 1,000 population (1980–85): 7.1 (world avg. 11.0).
Natural increase rate per 1,000 population (1980–85): 21.7 (world avg. 18.0).
Total fertility rate (avg. births per childbearing woman; 1980–85): 6.7.
Marriage rate per 1,000 population: n.a.
Divorce rate per 1,000 population: n.a.
Life expectancy at birth (1980–85): male 61.6 years; female 65.6 years.
Major causes of accidental death per 100,000 population (1980): traffic accidents 57; fire accidents 6; electric shock 5; drowning 5.

National economy

Budget (1984). Revenue: Dh14,200,000,000 (breakdown n.a., although consists largely of oil concession receipts). Expenditures: Dh15,100,000,000 (current 90.1%, development 4.6%).
Gross national product (at current market prices; 1983): U.S.$25,770,000,000 (U.S.$21,340 per capita).

Structure of gross domestic product and labour force				
	1983		1980	
	in value Dh'000,000	% of total value	labour force	% of labour force
Agriculture	1,130	1.1	25,613	4.6
Mining	45,304	44.8	11,852	2.1
Manufacturing	9,045	9.0	34,876	6.3
Construction	11,000	10.9	154,978	27.8
Public utilities	1,976	1.9	10,952	2.0
Transportation and communication	5,110	5.1	42,038	7.5
Trade	9,936	9.8	74,332	13.3
Finance			14,946	2.7
Pub. admin., defense	17,607	17.4	90,921	16.3
Services			96,775	17.4
Other			239	...
TOTAL	101,108	100.0	557,522	100.0

Public debt (external, outstanding; 1982): U.S.$1,117,000,000.
Production (metric tons except as noted). Agriculture, forestry, fishing (1984): dates 58,000, tomatoes 37,000, watermelons 26,000, cantaloupes and other melons 18,000, pumpkins and squash 9,000, eggplants 8,000, cabbages 5,000, cucumbers and gherkins 5,000, lemons and limes 5,000, milk 5,000, cauliflower 4,000, eggs 3,800, tobacco leaves 2,000, mangoes 2,000, green peppers 2,000, wheat 1,000, barley 1,000, carrots 1,000, corn (maize) 1,000, roots and tubers 1,000, potatoes 1,000, almonds 320; livestock (number of live animals) 450,000 goats, 150,000 sheep, 70,000 camels, 30,000 cattle, 3,000,000 chickens; fish catch (1983) 73,115. Mining and quarrying (1983): limestone for hydraulic cement 4,005,000; also marble, shale for ceramic applications, and aggregate for cement. Manufacturing

(1984): cement 9,000,000; aluminum 155,355; steel 65,000; sulfur 15,000. Construction (value added in Dh; 1981): 8,850,000,000. Energy production (consumption): electricity (kW-hr; 1983) 7,900,000,000 (7,900,000,000); coal, none (n.a.); crude petroleum (barrels; 1984) 419,100,000 (10,422,000*); petroleum products (metric tons; 1983) 4,705,000 (5,374,000); natural gas (cu m; 1983) 13,895,595,000 (11,332,872,000).
Tourism: receipts from visitors, n.a.; expenditures by nationals abroad, n.a.
Population economically active (1980): total 557,521; participation rate of total population 53.5% (female [1975] 3.4%, unemployed [1975] 2.1%).
Price and earnings indexes: n.a.
Household income and expenditure: Average household size (1980) 3.8; average annual income per household: n.a.; source of income: n.a.; expenditure: n.a.
Land use (1983): forested, none; meadows and pastures 2.4%; agricultural and under permanent cultivation 0.2%; built-up, wasteland, and other 97.4%.

Foreign trade

Balance of trade (current prices)						
	1978	1979	1980	1981	1982	1983
Dh'000,000	+38,885	+29,382	+25,673	+14,668	+18,187	+24,430
% of total	35.4%	31.2%	32.6%	26.1%	31.6%	28.5%

Imports (1983): Dh30,675,000,000 (1981; nonelectrical machinery 16.7%, electrical machinery 9.5%, transport equipment 9.5%, food and live animals 9.1%, iron and steel 6.9%, textile yarn and fabric 5.8%, chemicals 5.1%). *Major import sources:* Japan 21.5%; United States 11.1%; United Kingdom 9.5%; West Germany 6.6%; Italy 4.6%; Bahrain 4.1%; France 3.5%; The Netherlands 2.8%; India 2.7%; Australia 2.0%; Switzerland 1.9%; China 1.7%; Lebanon 1.7%; Belgium–Luxembourg 1.6%; Singapore 1.6%; Pakistan 1.5%; Austria 0.9%; Syria 0.8%; Turkey 0.7%; Thailand 0.7%; Iran 0.6%.
Exports (1983): Dh55,105,000,000 (crude petroleum 86.2%, nonpetroleum exports 9.8%). *Major export destinations* (1980): Japan 34.5%; United States 13.5%; France 8.0%; Netherlands Antilles 6.7%; West Germany 6.3%; Spain 4.3%; Singapore 4.1%; United Kingdom 2.8%; Italy 2.8%; Oman 2.7%; Australia 2.1%; Pakistan 1.9%; Philippines 1.6%; Bangladesh 1.1%; The Netherlands 1.0%; Saudi Arabia 0.9%; Portugal 0.9%.

Transport and communications

Transport. Railroads: none. Roads (1981): total length 800 mi, 1,300 km (paved, n.a.). Vehicles (1981): passenger cars 130,700; trucks and buses 77,600. Merchant marine (1984): vessels (100 gross tons and over) 225; total deadweight tonnage 1,349,672. Air transport (1983): passenger-mi 2,213,000,000, passenger-km 3,562,000,000; short ton-mi cargo 65,300,000, metric ton-km cargo 95,300,000; airports (1985) with scheduled flights 2.
Communications. Daily newspapers (1984): total number 11; total circulation 272,000; circulation per 1,000 population 222.2. Radio (1984): total number of receivers 110,000 (1 per 11 persons). Television (1984): total number of receivers 110,000 (1 per 11 persons). Telephones (1983): 319,246 (1 per 4 persons).

Education and health

Education (1982–83)	schools†	teachers	students	student/ teacher ratio
Primary (age 6–11)	244	6,599	115,411	17.5
Secondary (age 12–18)	68	4,081	45,442	11.1
Vocational‡	4	154	722	4.7
Higher†	318	8,343	125,209	15.0

Educational attainment (1975). Percent of adult population over age 25 having: no formal schooling 72.2%; primary education 5.2%; secondary education 16.6%; higher education 6.0%. *Literacy* (1983): total population over age 15 literate 574,200 (68.6%); males literate 449,300 (71.0%); females literate 124,900 (60.9%).
Health (1981): physicians 1,491 (1 per 698 persons); hospital beds 3,260 (1 per 319 persons); infant mortality rate per 1,000 live births (1980–84) 49.6.
Food (1980–82): daily per capita caloric intake 3,524 (vegetable products 73%, animal products 27%); 146% of FAO recommended minimum requirement.

Military

Total active duty personnel (1984): 49,000 (army 93.0%, navy 3.5%, air force 3.5%). *Military expenditure as percent of GNP* (1983): 7.9% (world 6.1%); per capita expenditure U.S.$1,492.

*1983. †1979-80. ‡Male only.

United Kingdom

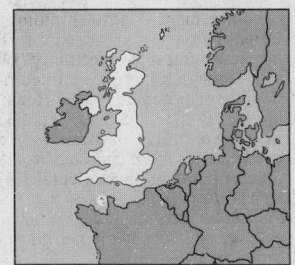

Official name: United Kingdom of Great Britain and Northern Ireland.
Form of government: constitutional monarchy with two legislative houses (House of Lords [1,178]; House of Commons [650]).
Chief of state: Sovereign.
Head of government: Prime Minister.
Capital: London.
Official language: English.
Official religion: Churches of England and Scotland "established" (protected and maintained by the state, but not "official") in their respective countries; no established church in Northern Ireland or Wales.
Monetary unit: 1 pound sterling (£) = 100 new pence; valuation (Oct. 21, 1985) 1 £ = U.S.$1.43.

Doubling time: more than 100 years.
Ethnic composition: (1980): English 78.4%; Scottish 8.9%; Irish 4.0%; Scots-Irish 1.8%; Welsh 1.3%; Indian 0.9%; Jamaican 0.7%; Pakistani 0.4%; German 0.3%; Polish 0.3%; other 3.0%.
Religious affiliation (1980): Christian 87.8%, of which Anglican 57.0%, Roman Catholic 13.0%, Presbyterian 7.0%, Methodist 4.3%, Baptist 1.4%; nonreligious 8.2%; Muslim 1.3%; Jewish 0.8%; Hindu 0.5%; Sikh 0.4%; other 1.0%.
Major cities (1983): Greater London 6,756,000§; Birmingham 1,012,900; Glasgow 751,000; Leeds 714,000; Sheffield 542,700; Liverpool 502,500; Bradford 463,900; Manchester 457,500; Edinburgh 440,900; Bristol 399,300.
Place of birth (1983): 93.1% (50,769,700) native-born; 5.9% foreign-born, of which Ireland 1.1%, India 0.9%, Caribbean 0.5%, Pakistan 0.4%.
Mobility (1981). Population living in the same residence as 1980: 90.9%; different residence, same country (of the U.K.) 8.2%; different residence, different country within U.K. 0.4%; from outside the U.K. 0.5%.
Households (1983). Average household size 2.6; 1 person 23%, 2 persons 32%, 3 persons 17%, 4 persons 18%, 5 persons 7%, 6 or more persons 3%. Family households (1982): 14,331,000 (73.5%), nonfamily 5,162,000 (26.5%, of which 1-person 21.8%).
Immigration (1984): permanent residents 201,000, from EEC ‖ 18.4%, United States 11.9%, Middle East 8.5%, Bangladesh and India 7.5%, African Commonwealth 7.0%, Australia 6.5%, Pakistan 5.0%.

Vital statistics

Birth rate per 1,000 population (1984): 12.9 (world avg. 29.0); legitimate 81.4%; illegitimate 18.6%.
Death rate per 1,000 population (1984): 11.4 (world avg. 11.0).
Natural increase rate per 1,000 population (1984): 1.5 (world avg. 18.0).
Total fertility rate (avg. births per childbearing woman; 1984): 1.8.
Marriage rate per 1,000 population (1984): 7.0.
Divorce rate per 1,000 population (1983): 2.6.
Life expectancy at birth (1980–82): male 70.8 years; female 76.9 years.
Major causes of death per 100,000 population (England, Wales, and Scotland; 1983): diseases of the circulatory system 574.9, of which ischemic heart disease 319.1, cerebrovascular disease 139.4; malignant neoplasms (cancers) 270.9; diseases of the respiratory system 171.3, of which pneumonia 108.6; injuries and poisonings 39.9. (Northern Ireland; 1982): diseases of the circulatory system 516.5, malignant neoplasms 198.0; diseases of the respiratory system 150.9, of which pneumonia 97.2.

Social indicators

Educational attainment (1981): Percent of adult population over age 18 having: primary or secondary education only, c. 90%; some postsecondary 4.5%; bachelor's or equivalent degree 4.7%; higher university degree 0.5%.

Distribution of income (1982)
percent of household income by quintile

1	2	3	4	5 (highest)
6.2	12.0	17.6	24.1	39.4

Quality of working life (1983). Average workweek (hours): male 41.4, female 37.2 (overtime male 7.7%, female 1.3%). Annual rate per 100,000 workers for: injury or accident 56.8; industrial diseases 0.5; death 2.4. Proportion of labour force (employed persons) insured for damages or income loss resulting from: injury 100%; permanent disability 100%; death 100%. Average days lost to labour stoppages per 1,000 employee workdays: 1.2. Principal means of transport to work: 55% private automobile, 20.5% public transportation, 15% foot, 2.5% bicycle, 7% other.
Access to services (1982). Proportion of households having access to: bath or shower 96%; toilet 95%; central heating 63%.
Social participation. Eligible voters participating in last national election: 75.9%. Population over 16 years of age participating in voluntary work: 23%. Trade union membership in total work force 43%.
Social deviance (1983). Offense rate per 100,000 population for: theft and handling stolen goods 3,443.2; burglary 1,673.0; fraud and forgery 263.9; violence against the person 218.5; robbery 50.0; sexual offense 46.6. Incidence per 100,000 population of: notified drug addicts 7.8; suicide 8.6.
Leisure (1983). Favourite leisure activities (attendance, except as noted): cinema 63,100,000, newspapers 33,200,000 (readership), association football matches 21,667,000¶, bingo clubs 5,700,000¶.
Material well-being (1982). Households possessing: automobile 61.3%, telephone 75.7%, television receiver 96.8%, refrigerator 96.4%, heating (full or partial) 62.8%, washing machine 81.8%.

National economy

Gross national product (at current market prices; 1983): U.S.$505,610,000,000 (U.S.$8,970 per capita).

Area and population

Countries	Capitals	area sq mi	area sq km	population 1984 estimate
England	London	50,363	130,439	46,956,400
Counties				
Avon		520	1,346	939,800
Bedfordshire		477	1,235	515,700
Berkshire		486	1,259	715,300
Buckinghamshire		727	1,883	594,600
Cambridgeshire		1,316	3,409	609,200
Cheshire		899	2,329	937,400
Cleveland		225	583	562,700
Cornwall		1,376	3,564	439,000
Cumbria		2,629	6,810	483,600
Derbyshire		1,016	2,631	911,700
Devon		2,591	6,711	978,300
Dorset		1,025	2,654	617,800
Durham		941	2,436	603,700
East Sussex		693	1,795	678,900
Essex		1,418	3,672	1,496,700
Gloucestershire		1,020	2,643	509,200
Greater London*		610	1,579	6,756,000
Greater Manchester*		497	1,287	2,588,300
Hampshire		1,458	3,777	1,509,500
Hereford & Worcester		1,516	3,927	645,300
Hertfordshire		631	1,634	980,300
Humberside		1,356	3,512	851,600
Isle of Wight		147	381	120,900
Kent		1,441	3,731	1,491,700
Lancashire		1,183	3,064	1,379,100
Leicestershire		986	2,553	866,100
Lincolnshire		2,284	5,915	556,600
Merseyside*		252	652	1,490,700
Norfolk		2,073	5,368	714,500
Northamptonshire		914	2,367	539,800
Northumberland		1,943	5,032	300,700
North Yorkshire		3,208	8,309	691,100
Nottinghamshire		836	2,164	1,000,100
Oxfordshire		1,007	2,608	555,700
Shropshire		1,347	3,490	386,600
Somerset		1,332	3,451	440,900
South Yorkshire*		602	1,560	1,305,400
Staffordshire		1,049	2,716	1,019,400
Suffolk		1,466	3,797	615,900
Surrey		648	1,679	1,014,400
Tyne and Wear*		208	540	1,142,400
Warwickshire		765	1,981	477,700
West Midlands*		347	899	2,647,000
West Sussex		768	1,989	682,700
West Yorkshire*		787	2,039	2,056,200
Wiltshire		1,344	3,480	536,200
Northern Ireland†	Belfast	5,462	14,147	1,578,500
Scotland	Edinburgh	29,794‡	77,167	5,145,700
Regions				
Borders		1,804	4,672	101,300
Central		1,016	2,631	272,800
Dumfries and Galloway		2,459	6,370	146,200
Fife		505	1,307	344,500
Grampian		3,361	8,704	497,300
Highland		9,803	25,391	197,200
Lothian		678	1,755	744,500
Strathclyde		5,227	13,537	2,373,400
Tayside		2,893	7,493	394,400
Island areas (TOTAL)		2,049	5,307	74,100
Wales	Cardiff	8,019	20,768	2,807,200
Counties				
Clwyd		937	2,427	396,300
Dyfed		2,227	5,768	335,000
Gwent		531	1,376	439,700
Gwynedd		1,494	3,869	232,700
Mid Glamorgan		393	1,018	533,900
Powys		1,960	5,077	110,600
South Glamorgan		161	416	394,400
West Glamorgan		316	817	364,600
TOTAL		94,248	244,100	56,487,800

Demography

Population (1985): 56,518,000.
Density (1985): persons per sq mi 599.7, persons per sq km 231.5.
Urban-rural (1985): urban 92.5%; rural 7.5%.
Sex distribution (1984): male 48.68%; female 51.32%.
Age breakdown (1984): under 15, 19.5%; 15–29, 23.5%; 30–44, 19.9%; 45–59, 16.5%; 60–74, 14.4%; 75 and over, 6.2%.
Population projection: (1990) 57,900,000; (2000) 59,600,000.

Structure of gross domestic product and labour force

	1984 in value £'000,000	% of total value	labour force	% of labour force
Agriculture	5,966	2.1	340,000	1.6
Mining	68,375	24.4	290,000	1.5
Manufacturing }			5,517,000	26.1
Construction	15,838	5.7	983,000	4.6
Public utilities	31,541	11.3	340,000	1.6
Transp. and commun.	19,813	7.1	1,301,000	6.2
Trade	37,048	13.2	4,324,000	20.5
Finance	53,677	19.2	1,881,000	8.9
Pub. admin., defense	18,864	6.7	1,865,000	8.8
Services	43,853	15.7	4,300,000	20.3
Other	−15,066²	−5.4²	...	...
TOTAL	279,909	100.0	21,141,000	100.0

Budget (1984). Revenue: £118,200,000,000 (customs and excise 29.8%, of which value-added tax 13.6%; income tax 28.0%; national insurance, health, and redundancy fund 18.0%). Expenditures: £131,100,000,000 (social security benefits 25.6%; debt interest 12.1%; military defense 11.9%; national health service 10.9%; education and science 9.4%).
Total national debt (1984): £143,000,000,000.

Financial aggregates

	1979	1980	1981	1982	1983	1984	1985
Exchange rate:◊							
U.S. Dollar per £	2.22	2.38	1.91	1.61	1.45	1.16	1.44□
SDRs per £	1.69	1.87	1.64	1.46	1.39	1.18	1.35□
International reserves (U.S.$)◊							
Total (excl. gold; '000,000,000)	19.74	20.65	15.24	12.40	11.34	9.44	13.19□
SDRs ('000,000,000)	1.27	0.57	0.99	1.17	0.52	0.50	0.81□
Reserve pos. in IMF ('000,000,000)	—	1.33	1.44	1.55	2.10	1.97	1.98□
Foreign exchange ('000,000,000)	18.47	18.75	12.81	9.67	8.72	6.97	10.40□
Gold ('000,000 fine troy oz)	18.25	18.84	19.03	19.01	19.01	19.03	19.03□
% world reserves	1.9	2.0	2.0	2.0	2.0	2.0	2.0□
Interest and prices◊							
Central bank discount (%)	17.00	14.00					
Gov't. Bond yield (%) long term	12.99	13.79	14.74	12.88	10.81	10.69	10.39△
Industrial share prices (1980 = 100)	93.6	100.0	112.8	130.7	164.9	196.2	243.5△
Balance of payments (U.S.$'000,000)							
Balance of visible trade,	−7,207	+3,362	+7,171	+3,423	−1,183	−5,678	...
Imports, f.o.b.	93,691	106,891	95,594	93,658	93,891	99,308	...
Exports, f.o.b.	86,484	110,253	102,765	97,081	92,708	93,630	...
Balance of invisibles	11,054	9,790	11,190	8,578	10,043	9,693	...
Balance of payments, current account	−954	8,338	14,484	8,435	4,864	736	...

Tourism (1983): receipts from visitors U.S.$5,539,000,000; expenditures by nationals abroad U.S.$6,237,000,000.

Manufacturing, mining, and construction enterprises (1982)

	no. of enterprises	no. of employees	annual wages as a % of avg. of all wages	annual gross output (£'000,000)
Manufacturing				
Food, drink, and tobacco	5,348	626,500	93.2	37,424.8
Mechanical engineering	14,007	732,500	111.1	19,667.7
Chemical engineering	2,504	303,100	118.0	18,396.7
Electrical and electronic engineering	4,751	557,100	95.3	14,565.4
Paper and paper products; printing and publishing	11,548	458,200	123.9	13,307.0
Motor vehicles	2,041	325,400	109.5	10,656.9
Metals	1,339	206,600	120.4	9,505.3
Miscellaneous machinery and equipment	5,954	244,000	106.1	6,326.4
Timber and wooden furniture	10,659	206,400	94.9	5,598.1
Aerospace equipment, manufacturing and repairing	311	187,200	119.2	5,321.6
Tobacco	19	31,100	123.6	5,138.1
Textiles	2,985	247,700	72.9	5,068.5
Mining				
Extraction of crude petroleum and natural gas	...	22,000		15,959.2
Petroleum refining	147	20,800	157.3	13,849.5
Construction	147,330†	1,158,200	...	29,263.5

Production (metric tons except as noted). Agriculture, forestry, fishing (1984): wheat 14,980,000, barley 11,030,000, sugar beets 9,015,000, potatoes 7,400,000, turnips and rutabagas 3,960,000, corn (maize) 580,000, oats 545,000; livestock (number of live animals) 12,985,000 cattle, 23,946,000 sheep, 7,793,000 pigs; roundwood 3,950,000 cu m⊙; fish catch 846,500⊙. Mining (value of production in £'000,000; 1982): sand and gravel 342; limestone and dolomite 302; clays 164; igneous rocks 91; salt 56; sandstone 39; potash 25; tin 25; fluorspar 21; iron ore 336,000 metric tons§. Manufacturing (total sales in £'000,000; 1984): motor vehicles and parts 8,900; aerospace equipment 5,039; electronic data processors 2,545; radios and televisions 2,469; boilers 1,614; packaging containers of metal 1,478; telephone and telegraph equipment 1,476; mechanical lifting and handling equipment 1,457; constructional steelwork 1,361; precision instruments 1,245. Construction (value in £; 1984): residential 4,908,000,000; nonresidential 9,285,000,000, of which public 3,833,000,000, industrial 2,342,000,000, commercial 3,110,000,000.

Retail trade enterprises (1982)

	no. of enterprises	no. of employees	weekly wage as a % of all wages	annual turnover (£'000,000)**
Food and grocery, of which	82,625	818,000	...	27,211
large grocery	113	379,000	...	16,703
other grocery	38,277	164,000	...	4,368
meats	14,954	84,000	...	2,405
Household goods, of which	39,112	269,000	...	9,358
electrical and musical goods	8,044	74,000	...	2,959
furniture	9,533	64,000	...	2,505
Drink, confectionery, and tobacco, of which	40,862	264,000	...	7,641
tobacco and confectionery	37,525	230,000	...	5,888
Clothing and footwear, of which	28,923	269,000	...	5,911
womens', girls', and infants' wear	15,105	99,000	...	2,020
footwear	3,422	77,000	...	1,467
men's and boys' wear	3,965	44,000	...	1,231
Mail order	21	44,000	...	2,421
Pharmaceuticals	7,921	66,000	...	2,074

Energy production (consumption): electricity (kW-hr; 1983) 276,227,000,000 (276,227,000,000)□; coal (metric tons; 1984) 51,252,000 (77,324,000); crude petroleum (barrels; 1984) 940,700,000 (670,000,000); natural gas (cu m; 1984) 35,000,000,000 (50,200,000,000).

Population economically active (1985††): total 27,325,000; participation rate of total population 48.4% (female 40.0%, unemployed 12.0%).

Price and earnings indexes (1980 = 100)

	1978	1979	1980	1981	1982	1983	1984
Consumer price index	74.7	84.8	100.0	111.9	121.5	127.1	133.4
Monthly earnings index	73.0	84.2	100.0	113.4	126.3	137.1	144.9

Household income and expenditure. Average household size (1983) 2.6; average annual income per household £9,550 (U.S.$14,520); sources of income: wages and salaries 65.8%, social security benefits 15.3%, rent, dividends, and interest 9.8%, income from self-employment 8.9%; expenditure (1983): food and alcohol 22.2%, housing, fuel, and power 20.2%, transport, communication, and vehicles 17.2%, recreation, entertainment, and education 9.1%, household goods and services 6.7%.
Land use (1984): forested 8.9%; meadows and pastures 46.8%; agricultural and under permanent cultivation 28.9%; other 15.4%.

Foreign trade

Balance of trade (current prices)

	1979	1980	1981	1982	1983	1984
£'000,000	−6,288	−2,409	−471	−1,420	−5,459	−8,194
% of total	7.2%	2.5%	0.5%	1.3%	4.3%	5.5%

Imports (1984): £78,705,200,000 (machinery and transport equipment 30.1%, of which road vehicles 7.6%, data-processing equipment 5.2%; petroleum and petroleum products 10.3%; food and live animals 9.9%, of which vegetables and fruits 2.4%, meat and meat preparations 1.7%; chemicals and chemical products 8.0%, of which organic chemicals 2.4%; textile yarn and fabrics 3.4%; paper and paper board 2.9%; nonferrous metals 2.5%; apparel and clothing accessories 2.6%). *Major import sources:* West Germany 14.1%; U.S. 11.9%; The Netherlands 7.8%; France 7.5%; Norway 4.9%; Japan 4.8%; Italy 4.8%; Belgium 4.7%; Ireland 3.3%.
Exports (1984): £70,511,300,000 (machinery and transport equipment 30.5%, of which road vehicles 4.7%, data-processing equipment 4.3%, power generating machinery and equipment 3.8%, machinery specialized for particular industries 3.8%; petroleum and petroleum products 21.1%; chemicals and chemical products 11.6%, of which organic chemicals 3.4%; nonmetallic mineral manufactures 3.3%; professional, scientific, and controlling instruments 2.5%; nonferrous metals 2.3%). *Major export destinations:* U.S. 14.4%; West Germany 10.6%; France 10.0%; The Netherlands 8.7%; Ireland 4.8%; Belgium 4.3%; Sweden 4.1%; Italy 4.1%.

Transport and communications

Transport. Railroads‡‡ (1984): length 25,885 mi, 41,659 km□; passenger-mi 18,693,000,000§§, passenger-km 30,084,000,000§§; short ton-mi cargo 8,532,000,000, metric ton-km cargo 12,456,000,000. Roads (1983): total length 229,080 mi, 368,670 km (paved 97%). Vehicles (1983): passenger cars 17,158,000; trucks and buses 1,856,042¶. Merchant marine (1984): vessels (100 gross tons and over) 2,468; total deadweight tonnage 24,140,368. Air transport (1983): passenger-mi 27,619,000,000, passenger-km 44,448,000,-000; short ton-mi cargo 928,388,000, metric ton-km cargo 1,355,424,000; airports (1985) with scheduled flights 40.
Communications. Daily newspapers (1981): total number 120; total circulation 25,221,000; circulation per 1,000 population 447. Radio (1984): total number of licenses 18,410,000 (1 per 3 persons). Television (1984): total number of licenses 18,632,000 (1 per 3 persons). Telephones (1984): 29,-336,000 (1 per 1.9 persons).

Education and health

Education (1982–83)

	schools	teachers	students	student/teacher ratio
Primary (age 5–10)	25,755	211,100	4,302,000	20.4
Secondary (age 11–19)	5,473	277,000	4,967,000	17.9
Voc., teacher tr.	786	...	...	...
Higher	46	31,642	801,000	25.3

Literacy (1984): total population literate, virtually 100%.
Health (1983): physicians 28,663 (1 per 1,967 persons); hospital beds 446,-378 ‖ ‖ (1 per 113 persons); infant mortality rate per 1,000 live births (1984) 9.6.
Food (1980–82): daily per capita caloric intake 3,210 (vegetable products 63%, animal products 37%); 127% of FAO recommended minimum requirement.

Military

Total active duty personnel (1984): 325,909 (army 49.6%, navy 21.8%, air force 28.6%). *Military expenditure as percent of GNP* (1983): 4.8% (world 6.1%); per capita expenditure U.S.$434.

*Metropolitan county. †Comprises 26 local government districts not shown separately. ‡Detail does not add to total given because of rounding. §1984. ‖ Excludes Republic of Ireland. ¶1982. ⍵Less imputed bank charges. ◊End of period. □October. ◊Period average. △September average. †Establishments. ⊙1983. **Includes value-added taxes. ††March. ‡‡British railways only. §§Excludes Northern Ireland. ‖ ‖ National Health Services hospitals only.

United States

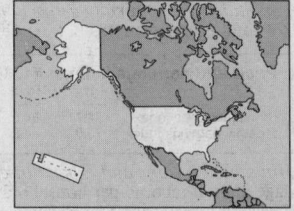

Official name: United States of America.
Form of government: federal republic with two legislative houses (Senate [100] and House of Representatives [435]).
Head of state and government: President.
Capital: Washington, D.C.
Official language: English.
Official religion: none.
Monetary unit: 1 dollar (U.S.$) = 100 cents; valuation (Oct. 21, 1985) 1 U.S.$ = £0.70; 1 £ = U.S.$1.43.

Area and population

States	Capitals	area* sq mi	area* sq km	population 1985 estimate
Alabama	Montgomery	51,705	133,915	4,021,000
Alaska	Juneau	591,004	1,530,693	521,000
Arizona	Phoenix	114,000	295,259	3,187,000
Arkansas	Little Rock	53,187	137,754	2,359,000
California	Sacramento	158,706	411,047	26,365,000
Colorado	Denver	104,091	269,594	3,231,000
Connecticut	Hartford	5,018	12,997	3,174,000
Delaware	Dover	2,044	5,294	622,000
Florida	Tallahassee	58,664	151,939	11,366,000
Georgia	Atlanta	58,910	152,576	5,976,000
Hawaii	Honolulu	6,471	16,760	1,054,000
Idaho	Boise	83,564	216,430	1,005,000
Illinois	Springfield	57,871	149,885	11,535,000
Indiana	Indianapolis	36,413	94,309	5,499,000
Iowa	Des Moines	56,275	145,752	2,884,000
Kansas	Topeka	82,277	213,096	2,450,000
Kentucky	Frankfort	40,409	104,659	3,726,000
Louisiana	Baton Rouge	47,752	123,677	4,481,000
Maine	Augusta	33,265	86,156	1,164,000
Maryland	Annapolis	10,460	27,091	4,392,000
Massachusetts	Boston	8,284	21,455	5,822,000
Michigan	Lansing	97,102	251,493	9,088,000
Minnesota	St. Paul	86,614	224,329	4,193,000
Mississippi	Jackson	47,689	123,514	2,613,000
Missouri	Jefferson City	69,697	180,514	5,029,000
Montana	Helena	147,046	380,847	826,000
Nebraska	Lincoln	77,355	200,349	1,606,000
Nevada	Carson City	110,561	286,352	936,000
New Hampshire	Concord	9,279	24,032	998,000
New Jersey	Trenton	7,787	20,168	7,562,000
New Mexico	Santa Fe	121,593	314,924	1,450,000
New York	Albany	52,735	136,583	17,783,000
North Carolina	Raleigh	52,669	136,412	6,255,000
North Dakota	Bismarck	70,702	183,117	685,000
Ohio	Columbus	44,787	115,998	10,744,000
Oklahoma	Oklahoma City	69,956	181,185	3,301,000
Oregon	Salem	97,073	251,418	2,687,000
Pennsylvania	Harrisburg	46,043	119,251	11,853,000
Rhode Island	Providence	1,212	3,139	968,000
South Carolina	Columbia	31,113	80,582	3,347,000
South Dakota	Pierre	77,116	199,730	708,000
Tennessee	Nashville	42,144	109,152	4,762,000
Texas	Austin	266,807	691,027	16,370,000
Utah	Salt Lake City	84,899	219,887	1,645,000
Vermont	Montpelier	9,614	24,900	535,000
Virginia	Richmond	40,767	105,586	5,706,000
Washington	Olympia	68,139	176,479	4,409,000
West Virginia	Charleston	24,231	62,758	1,936,000
Wisconsin	Madison	66,215	171,496	4,775,000
Wyoming	Cheyenne	97,809	253,324	509,000
District				
Dist. of Columbia	—	69	179	626,000
TOTAL		3,679,192†	9,529,063	238,740,000†

Demography

Population (1985): 238,740,000.
Density (1985): persons per sq mi 64.9, persons per sq km 25.1.
Urban–rural (1980): urban 73.7%; rural 26.3%.
Sex distribution (1984): male 48.60% female 51.40%.
Age breakdown (1984): under 15, 21.9%; 15–29, 26.0%; 30–44, 21.3%; 45–59, 14.3%; 60–74, 11.7%; 75 and over, 4.8%.
Population projection: (1990) 249,657,000; (2000) 267,955,000.
Doubling time: 78 years.
Composition by race (1984): white 85.1%; black 12.1%; other races 2.8%.
Religious affiliation (1980): Protestant 40.0%; Roman Catholic 30.0%; Jewish 3.2%; Eastern Orthodox 2.1%; Muslim 0.8%; Hindu 0.2%; nonreligious and atheist 6.9%; other 16.8%.
Place of birth (foreign-born; 1980): Mexico 2,199,221; Germany (East and West) 849,384; Canada 842,859; Italy 831,922; United Kingdom 669,149; Cuba 607,814; Philippines 501,440; Poland 418,128; U.S.S.R. 406,022; South Korea 289,885; China 286,120; Vietnam (South) 231,120; Japan 221,794; Portugal 211,614; Greece 210,998; India 206,087.
Mobility (1983). Population living in the same residence as in 1982: 83.6%; different residence, same county 10.1%; different county, same state 3.3%; different state 2.7%; moved from abroad 0.3%.
Immigration (1981): permanent immigrants admitted 596,600, from Mexico 17.0%, Caribbean countries 12.3%, Vietnam 9.3%, Philippines 7.3%, South America 6.0%, Korea 5.5%, Taiwan 4.3%, Central America 4.1%, India 3.6%, Laos 2.6%, African countries 2.5%, United Kingdom 2.5%, Kampuchea 2.1%, Canada 1.9%, Iran 1.9%, U.S.S.R. 1.5%, Portugal 1.2%, West Germany 1.1%, Pakistan 0.9%, Poland 0.8%.

Major cities (1984): New York 7,164,742; Los Angeles 3,096,721; Chicago 2,992,472; Houston 1,705,697; Philadelphia 1,646,713; Detroit 1,088,973; Dallas 974,234; San Diego 960,452; Phoenix 853,256; San Antonio 842,779.

Other principal cities (1984)

	population		population		population
Akron	226,877	Fresno	267,377	Omaha	332,237
Albuquerque	350,575	Honolulu	805,266	Pittsburgh	402,583
Anaheim	233,516	Indianapolis	710,280	Portland	365,861
Anchorage	226,663	Jackson	208,810	Richmond	219,056
Arlington	213,832	Jacksonville	577,971	Rochester	242,562
Atlanta	426,090	Jersey City	223,004	Sacramento	304,131
Austin	397,001	Kansas City	443,075	St. Louis	429,296
Baltimore	763,570	Lexington-Fayette	210,150	St. Paul	265,903
Baton Rouge	368,571	Long Beach	378,752	St. Petersburg	241,294
Birmingham	279,813	Louisville	289,843	San Francisco	712,753
Boston	570,719	Memphis	648,399	San Jose	686,178
Buffalo	338,982	Miami	372,634	Santa Ana	225,405
Charlotte	330,838	Milwaukee	620,811	Seattle	488,474
Cincinnati	370,481	Minneapolis	348,335	Shreveport	219,996
Cleveland	546,543	Mobile	204,923	Tampa	275,479
Colorado Springs	247,739	Nashville-Davidson	462,450	Toledo	343,939
Columbus	566,114	Newark	314,387	Tucson	365,422
Corpus Christi	258,067	New Orleans	559,101	Tulsa	374,535
Denver	504,588	Norfolk	279,683	Virginia Beach	308,664
El Paso	463,809	Oakland	351,898	Washington, D.C.	622,823
Fort Worth	414,562	Oklahoma City	443,172	Wichita	283,496

Households (1984). Total households 85,407,000. Average household size 2.7; 1 person 23.4%, 2 persons 31.5%, 3 persons 17.7%, 4 persons 15.9%, 5 persons 7.1%, 6 persons 2.8%, 7 or more persons 1.6%. Family households: 61,997,000 (72.6%), nonfamily 23,410,000 (27.4%, of which 1-person 23.4%).

Type of households (1983)

	number of dwellings	percent of total
by tenure of householder		
owned	54,724,000	64.7
rented	29,914,000	35.3
by kind of amenities		
with all plumbing facilities	83,016,000	98.1
lacking some or all plumbing facilities	1,621,000	1.9
by year of construction		
prior to 1940	24,641,000	29.1
1940–70	38,231,400	45.2
1970–83	21,766,800	25.7
Total in country	84,638,000	100.0

Vital statistics

Birth rate per 1,000 population (1985): 15.8 (world avg. 29.0); (1984) legitimate 80.6%; illegitimate 19.4%.
Death rate per 1,000 population (1985): 8.8 (world avg. 11.0).
Natural increase rate per 1,000 population (1985): 7.0 (world avg. 18.0).
Total fertility rate (avg. births per childbearing woman; 1984): 1.8.
Marriage rate per 1,000 population (1985): 10.3; median age at first marriage, men 25.5 years, women 23.3 years.
Divorce rate per 1,000 population (1985): 4.9.
Life expectancy at birth (1984): white male 71.8 years, black male 65.5 years; white female 78.8 years, black female 73.7 years.
Major causes of death per 100,000 population (1985): cardiovascular diseases 413.3, of which ischemic heart diseases 229.2, other forms of heart disease 80.3, cerebrovascular diseases 64.9, atherosclerosis 10.3, other cardiovascular diseases 9.1; malignant neoplasms (cancers) 192.9; diseases of the respiratory system 58.4; accidents 39.2; diabetes mellitus 15.7; suicide 11.7; chronic liver disease and cirrhosis 11.4; nephritis and nephrosis 9.1; homicide 8.2.

Social indicators

Educational attainment (1983). Percent of adult population over age 25 having: less than full primary education 8.3%; primary 6.8%; less than full secondary 12.8%; secondary 37.7%; some postsecondary 15.6%; 4-year higher degree and more 18.8%, of which postgraduate 6.7%.

Distribution of income (1983)

percent of national household income by quintile

1	2	3	4	5 (highest)
4.7	11.2	17.1	24.3	42.7

Quality of working life (1984). Average workweek: 40.7 hours (8.3% overtime). Annual rate per 100,000 workers for (1983): injury or accident 1,900; death 11.0. Proportion of labour force insured for damages or income loss resulting from: injury, permanent disability, and death (1983) 65.8%‡. Average days lost to labour stoppages per 1,000 workdays: (1983): 0.6. Average duration of journey to work (1979): 22.5 minutes (85.7% private automobile, 5.9% public transportation, 1.3% bicycle or motorcycle, 3.9% foot, 2.3% work at home, 0.9% other). Rate per 1,000 workers of discouraged (unemployed no longer seeking work; 1983): 53.5.
Access to services (1983). Proportion of dwellings having access to: electricity 100.0%; safe public water supply 98.1%; public sewage collection 73.6%§; public fire protection, n.a.
Social participation. Eligible voters participating in last national election (1984): 59.9%. Population over age 13 participating in voluntary work (1974): 22.9%. Trade union membership in total work force (1983): 13.8%. Practicing religious population in total affiliated population (weekly church

attendence; 1984): Roman Catholic 52%; Protestant 39%, of which Baptist 41%, Methodist 37%, Lutheran 35%, Episcopal 30%, Presbyterian 28%.

Social deviance (1984). Offense rate per 100,000 population for: murder 7.9; rape 35.7; robbery 205.4; other assault 290.2; motor vehicle theft 437.1; burglary and housebreaking 1,263.7; larceny-theft 2,791.3. Adult drug and substance users (1982): alcohol 56.7%; cigarettes 34.6%; marijuana 6.6%; hallucinogens 1.2%; tranquilizers 1.2%; heroin 0.6%. Rate per 100,000 population of suicide 12.3.

Crime rates per 100,000 population in metropolitan areas (1984)

	violent crime				
	total	murder	rape	robbery	assault
Atlanta	2,376.1	30.4	142.7	909.6	1,293.4
Baltimore	1,975.8	27.3	71.5	1,014.7	862.3
Boston	1,867.8	14.5	81.4	980.0	791.9
Chicago	1,990.2	24.6	75.0	947.2	943.4
Dallas	1,226.1	29.8	103.5	490.1	602.7
Detroit	2,343.4	45.3	134.0	1,618.8	545.3
Houston	839.3	26.2	70.3	507.1	235.7
Los Angeles	1,636.0	24.1	74.6	869.0	668.3
Miami	2,727.6	42.4	68.1	1,424.0	1,193.1
Minneapolis	1,047.0	7.2	105.7	469.2	464.9
New York	1,845.8	20.2	53.4	1,109.8	662.4
Philadelphia	935.5	15.8	56.2	561.6	301.9
Pittsburgh	1,098.5	11.3	53.9	773.1	260.2
St. Louis	1,746.5	28.9	78.9	703.2	935.5
San Francisco	1,302.4	10.1	68.8	725.7	497.8
Washington, D.C.	1,721.4	28.1	58.7	977.0	657.6
	property crime				
	total	burglary	larceny	auto theft	arson
Atlanta	8,662.5	2,441.1	5,443.0	718.8	59.6
Baltimore	6,385.9	1,754.6	3,871.4	686.7	73.2
Boston	9,405.3	2,025.1	4,305.3	3,046.6	28.3
Chicago	7,256.1	1,833.7	3,897.3	1,448.4	76.7
Dallas	10,342.6	3,032.9	6,388.2	838.7	82.8
Detroit	12,395.7	3,913.0	4,247.7	3,749.4	485.6
Houston	7,533.8	2,115.4	3,712.4	1,595.2	110.8
Los Angeles	7,978.3	2,184.8	4,088.0	1,542.7	162.8
Miami	10,277.6	2,666.2	6,174.5	1,384.0	52.9
Minneapolis	7,540.2	2,538.1	4,366.5	578.4	57.2
New York	6,627.6	1,795.5	3,498.7	1,234.5	98.9
Philadelphia	4,033.4	1,098.5	2,116.0	799.1	19.8
Pittsburgh	6,538.5	1,793.1	2,829.0	1,847.8	68.6
St. Louis	15,016.2	2,995.5	4,757.0	7,174.2	89.5
San Francisco	7,067.9	1,836.8	4,381.0	803.7	46.4
Washington, D.C.	6,923.5	1,758.3	4,409.5	702.1	53.6

Leisure (1977). Favourite leisure activities: watching television 30.0%; reading 15.0%; movies and theatre 6.0%; visiting friends 4.0%; listening to radio 4.0%; playing games 4.0%.

Material well-being (1982). Occupied dwellings with householder possessing: automobile 86.1%; telephone 97.0%§; television receiver 84.8%; refrigerator 63.5%; air conditioner 58.0%; washing machine 71.4%.

National economy

Gross national product (at current market prices; 1985): U.S.$3,855,100,000,000 (U.S.$16,270 per capita).

Gross national product and national income

in U.S.$000,000,000

	1980	1981	1982	1983	1984
Gross national product	2,631.7	2,957.8	3,069.3	3,304.8	3,662.8
By type of expenditure					
Personal consumption expenditures	1,668.1	1,849.1	1,984.9	2,155.9	2,341.8
Durable goods	214.7	235.4	245.1	279.8	318.8
Nondurable goods	668.8	730.7	757.5	801.7	856.9
Services	784.5	883.0	982.2	1,074.4	1,166.1
Gross private domestic investment	401.9	484.2	414.9	471.6	637.8
Fixed investment	411.7	458.1	441.0	485.1	579.6
Changes in business inventories	−9.8	26.0	−26.1	−13.5	58.2
Net exports of goods and services	23.9	30.0	19.0	−8.3	−64.2
Exports	338.8	369.9	348.4	336.2	364.3
Imports	314.8	341.9	329.4	344.4	428.5
Government purchases of goods and services	537.8	596.5	650.5	685.5	747.4
Federal	197.0	228.9	258.9	269.7	295.4
State and local	340.8	367.6	391.5	415.8	452.0
By major type of product					
Goods output	1,140.6	1,294.8	1,276.8	1,355.7	1,543.0
Durable goods	477.9	530.5	499.9	555.3	655.7
Nondurable goods	662.7	764.4	776.9	800.4	887.3
Services	1,225.2	1,373.0	1,510.8	1,639.3	1,763.3
Structures	265.9	289.9	281.7	309.8	356.5
National income	2,116.6	2,363.8	2,446.8	2,646.7	2,959.9
By type of income					
Compensation of employees	1,599.6	1,765.4	1,864.2	1,984.9	2,173.2
Proprietors' income	117.4	125.1	111.1	121.7	154.4
Rental income of persons	31.5	42.3	51.5	58.3	62.5
Corporate profits	175.4	189.9	159.1	225.2	285.7
Net interest	192.6	241.0	260.9	256.6	284.1
By industry division					
Agriculture, forestry, fishing	61.4	74.8	69.6	60.9	76.2
Mining and construction	145.7	154.2	154.3	152.3	172.3
Manufacturing	526.5	581.3	549.6	579.9	656.2
Durable	312.0	340.5	311.4	329.5	387.4
Nondurable	214.6	240.8	238.3	250.4	268.8
Transportation	80.4	84.3	83.3	87.7	99.3
Communications, pub. utilities	90.9	106.2	117.0	124.4	135.3
Wholesale and retail trade	316.7	349.4	359.0	386.4	431.6
Finance, insurance, real estate	290.9	326.0	355.1	394.0	433.9
Services	310.0	350.6	387.0	426.6	472.2
Government and government enterprise	306.3	337.0	364.1	391.7	420.4

Structure of gross domestic product and labour force

	1984			
	in value $'000,000,000	% of total value	labour force ‖	% of labour force
Agriculture	91.1	2.5	3,321,000	3.1
Mining	118.5	3.3	974,000	0.9
Manufacturing	775.7	21.4	19,412,000	18.2
Construction	148.0	4.1	4,345,000	4.1
Public utilities	109.6	3.0	960,000	0.9
Transportation and communication	232.6	6.4	4,211,000	3.9
Trade	601.8	16.6	22,134,000	20.7
Finance	598.0	16.5	5,682,000	5.3
Pub. admin., defense	421.9	11.6	15,984,000	15.0
Services	529.4	14.6	20,761,000	19.5
Other	...	...	8,918,000	8.4
TOTAL	3,626.6	100.0	106,702,000	100.0

Budget (1986). Revenue: U.S.$793,700,000,000 (individual income tax 45.2%, social insurance taxes and contributions 36.5%, corporation income tax 9.3%, excise taxes 4.4%, customs duties 1.5%). Expenditures: U.S.$973,700,000,000 (defense 29.3%, social security and medicare 27.7%, interest on debt 14.6%; income security 11.9%, health 3.6%, education 3.0%, veteran benefits and services 2.7%).

Total national debt (1985): U.S.$1,415,100,000,000.

Tourism (1983): receipts from visitors U.S.$11,187,000,000; expenditures by nationals abroad U.S.$13,944,000,000.

Land use (1983): forested 33.1%; meadows and pastures 26.2%; agricultural and under permanent cultivation 20.9%; other 19.8%.

Manufacturing, mining, and construction enterprises (1984)

	no. of enterprises	no. of employees	weekly wage as a % of all wages	annual value of shipments ($'000,000)
Manufacturing				
Food and kindred products	20,208	1,619,000	100.6	295,050
Transportation equipment	8,466	1,906,000	146.7	288,306
Chemical and allied products	11,363	1,048,000	133.0	211,833
Machinery, except electrical	48,947	2,197,000	119.6	210,168
Petroleum and coal products	2,165	189,000	161.2	200,588
Electrical and electronic machinery	15,116	2,208,000	108.5	182,534
Fabricated metal products	32,793	1,464,000	112.6	139,213
Primary metals	7,048	858,000	137.7	131,152
Paper and allied products	6,160	681,000	125.0	95,944
Textile mill products	6,192	746,000	77.6	55,078
Stone, clay, and glass products	15,591	595,000	114.9	54,993
Apparel and other related products	21,367	1,197,000	85.7	...
Instruments and related products	7,661	714,000	106.2	53,511
Rubber and plastic products	12,348	782,000	99.5	52,147
Tobacco products	117	65,000	135.3	16,918
Leather and leather products	2,558	192,000	68.4	4,850
Lumber and wood	28,293	707,000	96.4	...
Furniture and fixtures	9,160	487,000	82.2	...
Miscellaneous manufacturing indus.	14,532	1,372,000	84.5	...
Mining				
Oil and gas extraction	23,577	613,000		
Coal mining	4,133		139.6	121,100
Metal mining	985	361,000		
Nonmetallic, except fuels	5,126			
Construction				
General contractors and operative builders	112,963	1,158,000		
Heavy construction contractors	29,055	1,072,000	145.5	148,100
Special trade contractors	243,729	2,115,000		

Business activity (1982): number of businesses 9,103,688 (sole proprietorships 76.3%, active corporations 18.2%, active partnerships 5.5%), of which services 5,772,241, wholesaling and retailing 3,331,447; business receipts $2,776,933,000,000 (active corporations 83.8%, sole proprietorships 11.3%, active partnerships 4.9%), of which wholesaling and retailing $2,222,319,000,000, services $554,614,000,000; net profit $89,105,000,000 (sole proprietorships 44.3%, active corporations 40.0%, active partnerships 15.7%), of which services $51,587,000,000, wholesaling and retailing $37,518,000,000. New business concerns and business failures (1982): total number of new incorporations 567,000; total failures 24,908; failure rate per 10,000 concerns 88; current liabilities of failed concerns $15,610,800,000, average liability $626,700. Business expenditures for new plant and equipment (1983): total $269,220,000,000†, of which manufacturing businessess $111,530,000,000 (nondurable goods 53.6%, durable 46.4%), trade and services $66,680,000,000, public utilities $42,000,000,000, mining $11,830,000,000, transportation $11,200,000,000, communication and other $25,990,000,000.

Production (metric tons except as noted). Agriculture, forestry, fishing (1984): corn (maize) 194,310,000,000, wheat 70,638,000,000, soybeans 52,643,000, sugarcane 25,427,000, sorghum 21,994,000, sugar beets 20,146,000, potatoes 16,404,000, barley 12,998,000, tomatoes 8,165,000, seed cotton 7,760,000, oats 6,850,000, oranges 6,566,000, rice 6,216,000, grapes 4,644,000, apples 3,729,000, peanuts (groundnuts) 2,008,000, grapefruit 1,945,000, onions 1,885,000, sunflower seeds 1,699,000, cabbages 1,515,000, peaches and nectarines 1,365,000, green peas 1,125,000, carrots 1,025,000, dry beans 941,000, tobacco 778,000, strawberries 447,240, almonds 416,670, milk 61,436,000, cheese 2,402,000, butter 508,000, eggs 4,035,000; livestock (number of live animals) 114,000,000 cattle, 56,694,000 pigs, 11,487,000 sheep, 10,300,000 horses, 1,450,000 goats, 364,880,000 poultry; roundwood (1983) 246,238,000 cu m; fish catch 2,922,800,000. Mining and quarrying (1984): iron ore 51,274,000; phosphate rock 42,573,000; copper 1,087,000; bauxite 811,000; lead 330,700; zinc 270,000; molybdenum 46,900; uranium 5,769; silver 1,294; nickel 400; tin 100; gold 72. Manufacturing (1984): crude steel 92,528,000; cement 70,452,000; paper and paper products 68,457,000; wood pulp 55,549,000; pig iron 51,108,000; sulfuric acid 41,802,000; nitrogenous and phosphate fertilizers 17,363,000; caustic soda 9,853,000; newsprint 5,029,000; aluminum 4,099,000; man-made fibre 3,389,000; plastic and

resins 2,659,000; synthetic rubber 2,095,000; machinery and transport equipment, except electrical U.S.$220,500,000; electrical machinery U.S.$108,600,000; tires 209,375,000 units; cotton fabric 2,384,000,000 m; radio receivers 59,332,000 units; television receivers 46,420,000 units; household appliances 39,446,000 units; motor vehicles 3,075,000 units. Construction (1984): private U.S.$257,800,000,000, of which residential U.S.$145,100,000,000, commercial and industrial U.S.$61,900,000,000, other U.S.$50,900,000,000; federal, state, and local U.S.$55,200,000,000.

Retail and wholesale trade and services (1982)

	no. of enterprises	no. of employees	weekly wage as a % of all wages	annual sales (U.S.$'000,000¶)
Retail trade	1,923,228	14,467,813	...	1,293,062
Durable goods	...	...	...	465,798
Automotive dealers	91,068	1,051,174	...	278,534
Building materials, hardware, garden supply, and mobile home dealers	34,002	306,657	...	69,488
Furniture, home furnishings, equipment stores	93,734	542,635	...	61,843
Nondurable goods	...	...	...	827,264
Food stores	176,219	2,347,603	.	270,430
General merchandise group stores	34,145	1,839,158	...	152,913
Eating and drinking places	319,873	4,665,830	...	124,541
Gasoline service stations	116,188	603,886	...	99,464
Apparel and accessory stores	133,920	986,155	...	65,103
Drugstores and proprietary stores	49,527	496,217	...	43,174
Liquor stores	34,861	167,286	...	18,157
Wholesale trade	415,829	4,984,480	...	1,360,853
Durable goods	256,103	2,912,848	...	609,210
Machinery, equipment, and supplies	99,250	1,192,023	...	162,893
Motor vehicles, automotive equipment	39,460	432,982	...	121,188
Electrical goods	29,170	357,107	...	86,814
Metals and minerals, except petroleum	10,121	147,470	...	64,928
Lumber and other construction materials	17,041	184,604	...	44,561
Hardware, plumbing, heating equipment and supplies	20,815	216,596	...	37,671
Furniture and home furnishings	12,498	126,104	...	23,716
Sporting, recreational, photographic, and hobby goods	7,266	85,163	...	14,273
Miscellaneous durable goods	20,482	170,800	...	53,166
Nondurable goods	159,726	2,072,032	...	751,643
Groceries and related products	38,516	673,765	...	208,925
Farm-products raw materials	13,872	136,235	...	126,154
Apparel, piece goods, and notions	14,289	144,163	...	37,824
Beer, wine, and distilled alcholic beverages	6,378	141,286	...	37,646
Paper and paper products	13,967	186,567	...	34,473
Chemicals and allied products	10,724	124,322	...	23,585
Drugs, drug proprietaries, and druggists' sundries	3,851	105,689	...	22,143
Miscellaneous nondurable goods	39,434	372,268	...	101,373
Services°	1,261,698	11,106,144	...	426,982
Business	215,125	3,151,651	...	106,866
Health, except hospitals	346,565	2,433,061	...	95,610
Legal	115,407	569,359	...	34,325
Engineering, architectural, and surveying	45,341	581,470	...	34,315
Hotels, motels, and other lodging places	41,231	1,102,097	...	33,215
Amusement and recreation, including motion pictures	67,215	803,776	...	33,115
Automotive repair, services, garages	115,481	553,245	...	30,695
Personal	167,749	970,472	...	22,980
Accounting, auditing, and bookkeeping	51,900	330,198	...	14,596
Miscellaneous repair services	54,421	299,662	...	14,133

Energy production (consumption): electricity (kW-hr; 1984) 2,416,304,000,000 (2,279,923,000,000), of which net generation by electric utilities (by fuel type; 1983) coal 54.5%, petroleum and gas 18.1%, hydroelectric 14.4%, nuclear 12.7%, geothermal, wood, wind, and waste 0.3%; coal (metric tons; 1984) 890,143,000 (788,203,000); crude petroleum (barrels; 1984) 3,249,700,-000 (5,851,700,000); petroleum products (metric tons; 1984) 721,400,000 (783,400,000); natural gas (cu m; 1984) 488,200,000,000 (508,800,000,000).

Financial aggregates

	1979	1980	1981	1982	1983	1984	1985 (8 mo)
Exchange rate, U.S.$ per:							
£	2.12	2.33	2.03	1.75	1.52	1.34	1.38
SDR	1.29	1.30	1.18	1.10	1.07	1.02	1.03
International reserves (U.S.$)							
Total (excl. gold; '000,000,000)	7.78	15.60	18.92	22.81	22.63	23.84	26.06
SDRs ('000,000,000)	2.72	2.61	4.10	5.25	5.03	5.64	6.69
Reserve pos. in IMF ('000,000,000)	1.25	2.85	5.05	7.35	11.31	11.54	11.48
Foreign exchange ('000,000,000)	3.81	10.13	9.77	10.21	6.29	6.66	7.89
Gold ('000,000 fine troy oz)	264.60	264.32	264.11	264.03	263.39	262.79	262.66
% world reserves	28.02	27.74	27.71	27.83	27.80	27.76	...
Interest and prices							
Central bank discount (%)	12.00	13.00	12.00	8.50	8.50	8.00	7.50
Gov't. bond yield (%)δ	9.71	11.55	14.44	12.92	10.45	11.89	10.73
Industrial share prices (1980 = 100)	85.4	100.0	107.2	99.3	134.2	134.7	155.7
Balance of payments ($'000,000,000)							
Balance of visible trade	−27.56	−25.50	−27.98	−36.47	−62.02	−108.27	
Imports, f.o.b.	212.03	249.77	265.08	247.67	262.77	328.59	
Exports, f.o.b.	184.47	224.27	237.10	211.20	200.75	220.32	
Balance of invisibles	32.72	34.94	42.03	36.09	30.64	18.75	
Balance of payments, current account	−0.95	1.86	6.62	−9.23	−40.86	101.60	...

Population economically active (1985): total 117,025,000; participation rate over age 16, 65.0% (female 43.4%, unemployed 7.0%).

Average employee earnings
July figures

	average hourly earnings in U.S.$		average weekly earnings in U.S.$	
	1984	1985	1984	1985
Manufacturing				
Durable goods	9.73	10.10	397.96	410.06
Lumber and wood products	8.07	8.17	318.77	323.53
Furniture and fixtures	6.87	7.20	269.30	276.48
Stone, clay, and glass products	9.64	9.88	406.81	417.92
Primary metal industries	11.49	11.79	474.54	485.75
Fabricated metal products	9.35	9.67	381.48	394.54
Machinery, except electrical	9.96	10.32	412.34	421.06
Electrical and electronic equipment	9.00	9.47	363.60	376.91
Instruments and related products	8.88	9.21	363.19	370.24
Miscellaneous manufacturing	7.07	7.30	275.02	281.78
Nondurable goods	8.41	8.70	331.35	341.91
Food and kindred products	8.39	8.55	333.08	342.86
Tobacco manufactures	11.77	12.92	441.38	440.57
Textile mill products	6.44	6.69	253.09	258.90
Apparel and other textile products	5.53	5.69	199.08	205.98
Paper and allied products	10.52	10.89	453.41	465.00
Printing and publishing	9.38	9.66	352.69	360.32
Chemicals and allied products	11.09	11.49	462.45	479.13
Petroleum and coal products	13.25	13.99	580.35	598.77
Rubber and misc. plastics products	8.31	8.55	342.37	347.13
Leather and leather products	5.71	5.82	212.98	217.67
Nonmanufacturing				
Metal mining	13.06	13.42	522.40	556.93
Coal mining	14.91	15.30	591.07	581.39
Oil and gas extraction	10.66	10.99	472.24	484.66
Nonmetallic minerals, except fuels	9.86	10.11	449.62	463.04
Construction	12.06	12.16	464.31	469.38
Local and suburban transportation	8.01	8.06	313.19	310.31
Electric, gas, and sanitary services	12.15	12.74	503.01	529.98
Wholesale trade	8.98	9.26	348.42	359.29
Retail trade	5.86	5.94	179.90	180.58
Finance, insurance, and real estate	7.60	7.87	278.92	286.47
Hotels, motels, and tourist courts	5.33	5.72	170.03	176.18
Health services	7.78	8.11	255.18	265.20
Legal services	9.98	10.49	349.30	364.00
Miscellaneous services	11.15	11.51	432.62	447.74

Price and earnings indexes (1980 = 100)

	1979	1980	1981	1982	1983	1984	1985□
Consumer price index	88.1	100.0	110.4	117.1	120.9	126.1	131.5
Hourly earnings index	92.1	100.0	109.9	116.9	121.5	126.2	131.2

Household income and expenditure. Average household size (1985) 2.7; (1984) average annual income per household (U.S.$29,500); sources of income: wages and salaries 59.9%, personal interest income 14.4%, transfer payments 13.8%, other labour income 6.5%, proprietors' income 5.1%, other 0.3%; expenditure (1984): housing 24.0%, food 18.9%, transportation 13.6%, health 11.0%, clothing 5.9%, recreation 6.6%, education 1.8%.

Selected household characteristics (1984). Total number of households 83,-643,000, of which: (by race and Spanish origin◊) white 86.7%, black 12.8%, Spanish origin 4.8%; (by location; 1983) in metropolitan areas 68.4% (central cities 29.6%), outside metropolitan areas 31.6% (farms 1.9%); family households 60,767,000, of which married couple 80.1%, female head with children under age 18, 10.0%, other 9.9%; nonfamily households 22,876,000, of which female householder 58.9%, male 41.1%. Work disability status of householder: total number of householders (age 16–64) 66,292,000, of which having no work disability 86.9%, having work disability 13.1%; having retirement or disability income 6.3%.

Foreign trade△

Balance of trade (current prices)

	1979	1980	1981	1982	1983	1984
U.S.'000,000,000	−27.6	−25.5	−27.6	−42.6	−69.3	−123.3
% of total	7.0%	5.4%	5.6%	9.1%	14.7%	22.0%

Imports (1984): U.S.$341,177,000,000 (machinery and transport equipment 36.1%, of which passenger motor vehicles and parts 11.6%, office machines 5.8%, machinery for special purposes 4.5%, power-generating machines 4.4%, textile and knitting machines 4.3%, mining machinery 1.5%; mineral fuels and lubricants 18.6%, of which crude petroleum 11.1%, petroleum products 5.8%; manufactured goods 14.4%; miscellaneous manufactured articles 13.3%; food and live animals 5.7%; chemicals and related products 4.2%; beverages and tobacco 1.2%). Major import sources: Canada 19.6%; Japan 17.7%; Mexico 5.4%; West Germany 5.2%; Taiwan 4.7%; United Kingdom 4.4%; South Korea 2.9%; Hong Kong 2.6%; France 2.5%; Italy 2.5%; Brazil 2.4%; Venezuela 2.0%; Saudi Arabia 1.2%; Singapore 1.2%; China 1.0%.

Exports (1984): U.S.$217,888,000,000 (machinery and transport equipment 42.8%, of which nonelectrical machinery 20.3%, road motor vehicles and parts 8.1%, aircraft, spacecraft, and parts 5.8%, data-processing machines and telecommunication equipment 5.7%, scientific instruments 2.5%; food and live animals 11.4%, of which corn 3.2%, wheat 3.0%; chemicals and related products 10.4%, of which organic chemicals and products 2.3%, medicinal and pharmaceutical products 1.6%; crude materials, excluding fuels 9.4%; mineral fuels, lubricants, and related material 4.3%, of which petroleum products 1.6%; beverages and tobacco 1.3%). Major export destinations: Canada 21.2%; Japan 10.6%; United Kingdom 5.5%; Mexico 5.5%; West Germany 4.1%; The Netherlands 3.6%; France 2.8%; South Korea 2.7%; Saudi Arabia 2.3%; Australia 2.2%; Taiwan 2.2%; Italy 1.9%; Singapore 1.7%; Venezuela 1.5%; U.S.S.R. 1.5%; China 1.4%; Hong Kong 1.4%.

Trade by commodity group (1984)

SITC Group	imports (c.i.f.) U.S.$'000,000	%	exports (f.o.b.) U.S.$'000,000	%
00 Food and live animals	19,428	5.7	24,846	11.4
01 Beverages and tobacco	4,006	1.2	2,881	1.3
02 Crude materials, excluding fuels	11,882	3.5	20,404	9.4
03 Mineral fuels, lubricants, and related materials	63,297	18.5	9,481	4.3
04 Animal and vegetable oils, fat, and waxes	742	0.2	1,937	0.9
05 Chemicals and related products, n.e.s.	14,401	4.2	22,585	10.4
06 Basic manufactures	49,018	14.4	15,775	7.2
07 Machinery and transport equipment	123,104	36.1	93,161	42.8
08 Miscellaneous manufactured articles	45,361	13.3	16,515	7.6
09 Goods not classified by kind	9,938	2.9	10,301	4.7
TOTAL	341,177	100.0	217,888†	100.0

Direction of trade (1984)

	imports U.S.$'000,000	%	exports U.S.$'000,000	%
Africa	12,419	3.6	5,681	2.6
South Africa	2,577	0.7	2,265	1.0
Other	9,842	2.9	3,416	1.6
Americas	117,130	34.4	75,697	34.7
Canada	66,911	19.6	46,291	21.2
Caribbean countries and Central America	9,491	2.8	6,456	3.0
Mexico	18,267	5.4	11,978	5.5
South America	22,461	6.6	10,972	5.0
Asia	128,043	37.6	62,225	28.6
East Asia	39,135	11.5	17,355	8.0
China	3,381	1.0	3,004	1.4
Japan	60,371	17.7	23,173	10.6
Middle East	8,555	2.5	10,227	4.7
Other Asia	16,601	4.9	8,466	3.9
Europe	77,273	22.7	60,887	27.9
EEC	60,266	17.7	46,211	21.2
Other Western Europe	14,655	4.3	10,488	4.8
U.S.S.R.	600	0.2	3,284	1.5
Eastern Europe	1,752	0.5	904	0.4
Oceania	6,312	1.8	13,398	6.2
Australia	2,899	0.8	4,705	2.2
New Zealand	880	0.3	701	0.3
Other Oceania	2,533	0.7	7,992	3.7
TOTAL	341,177	100.0†	217,888	100.0

Transport and communications

Transport. Railroads (1983): length 184,235 mi, 296,489 km; passenger-mi 11,000,000,000, passenger-km 17,700,000,000; short ton-mi cargo 838,000,000,000, metric ton-km cargo 1,224,000,000,000. Roads (1985): total length 3,891,781 mi, 6,263,043 km (paved 88%). Vehicles (1985): passenger cars 130,364,000; trucks and buses 39,873,000. Merchant marine (1984): vessels (100 gross tons and over) 6,441; total deadweight tonnage 29,139,826. Air transport (1984): passenger-mi 304,458,727,000, passenger-km 489,980,000,000; short ton-mi cargo 8,168,805,000, metric ton-km cargo 11,927,000,000; airports (1984) with scheduled flights 12,653. Shares of domestic passenger traffic by mode of transportation (1983): automobiles 83.2%; airplanes 14.6%; buses 1.6%; railway 0.6%.

Distribution of commercial traffic (1982)

	cargo carried ('000,000 tons)	% of nat'l total	passengers carried ('000,000)	% of nat'l total
Rail	1.932	37.9	304	2.9
Road	493	9.6	482	4.6
Urban transport			...	...
Road	—	—	5,705	54.5
Electric railway	—	—	2,233	21.3
Heavy rail	—	—	1,433	13.7
Inland water	1,777	34.8	25	0.2
Air	4	0.1	294	2.8
Pipeline	897	17.6	—	—
TOTAL	5,103	100.0	10,476	100.0

Communications. Daily newspapers (1984): total number 1,668; total circulation 63,081,740; circulation per 1,000 population 267.1. Radio (1984): total number of receivers 485,000,000 (1 per 0.5 persons). Television (1984): total number of receivers 143,000,000 (1 per 1.6 persons). Telephones (1984): 181,091,000 (1 per 1.3 persons).

Other communication media (1983)

Print	titles (units)		titles (units)
Books (new titles)¶	41,380	Magazines/Journals	9,184
of which		of which	
Agriculture	416	Weekly	1,376
Art	1,463	Semimonthly	658
Biography	1,674	Monthly	4,096
Business	1,393	Bimonthly	1,348
Education	831	Quarterly	1,711
Fiction	4,876		
General works	2,333	**Cinema**	
History	1,791	Feature films	395
Home economics	1,022		
Juvenile	2,566		
Language	551		traffic
Law	1,125		(units, '000)
Literature	1,638	**Electronic**	
Medicine	2,502	Telegrams	39,037
Music	308	Domestic	29,857
Philosophy, psychology	1,242	International	9,200
Poetry, drama	946	Telex	69,559
Religion	1,930		
Science	2,564	**Post**	
Sociology, economics	6,257	Mail	119,381
Sports, recreation	1,072	Domestic	118,471
Technology	2,139	International	904
Travel	441		

Education and health

Education (1983–84)

	schools	teachers	students	student/ teacher ratio
Primary and preprimary (age 5–12)	...	1,359,000	30,780,000	22.6
Secondary and vocational (age 14–17)	...	1,035,000	13,495,000	13.0
Higher, including teacher-training colleges	...	870,000	12,400,000	14.2

Literacy (1980): total population over age 15 literate 166,497,565 (95.5%); males literate 79,161,126 (95.7%); females literate 87,336,439 (95.3%); other studies indicate adult "functional" literacy may not exceed 85%.

Health: physicians (1985) 527,900 (1 per 452 persons), specialties (1981) internal medicine 15.5%, general practice 12.5%, general surgery 7.1%, pediatrics 6.1%, psychiatry 5.9%, obstetrics and gynecology 5.6%, anesthesiology 3.5%, orthopedics 3.0%, pathology 2.9%, ophthalmology 2.7%, radiology 2.2%; hospital beds (1983) 1,350,000 (1 per 173 persons), of which (1982) nonfederal 91.6% (short-term general and special 74.6%, psychiatric 14.3%, long-term general and special 2.5%, tuberculosis 0.1%), federal 8.4%; infant mortality rate per 1,000 live births (1985) 10.5.

Food (1980–82): daily per capita caloric intake 3,630 (vegetable products 64%, animal products 36%); 138% of FAO recommended minimum requirement. Per capita consumption of major food groups (pounds annually; 1983): all foods 1,417.0, of which crop products 834.4, animal products 582.6; fruits and vegetables 375.9, of which vegetables 206.7 (fresh 148.4, processed 58.3), fruits 143.2 (fresh 91.8, processed 51.4), melons 26.0; dairy products 301.7; sugar and other sweeteners 136.3; potatoes and sweet potatoes 91.1; eggs 33.1; beans, peas, nuts, and soya products 20.2; coffee, tea, and cocoa 11.6.

Military

Total active duty personnel (1984): 2,135,900 (army 36.6%, navy 26.4%, air force 27.8%, marine 9.2%). *Military expenditure as percent of GNP* (1983): 6.6%† (world 6.1%); per capita expenditure U.S.$888. *Military sales and assistance* (1983)⊙: total $11,171,200,000 (Middle East and North Africa 52.7%, of which Saudi Arabia 34.8%, Egypt 9.0%, Israel 2.8%, Jordan 2.5%; Europe 25.2%, of which The Netherlands 4.7%, United Kingdom 4.2%, West Germany 2.9%, Belgium 2.5%, Norway 2.3%, Switzerland 1.9%; Asia 15.9%, of which Japan 3.9%, Taiwan 3.9%, South Korea 2.7%, Pakistan 2.3%; Thailand 1.6%; Latin America 1.5%; Oceania 1.5%, of which Australia 1.4%; Sub-Saharan Africa 0.5%; international organizations 1.0%; other 2.2%**.

*Total area excluding Great Lakes is 3,618,770 sq mi (9,372,571 sq km). †Detail does not add to total given because of rounding. ‡General health insurance. §1981. ‖ Employed persons only. ¶1984. ♀Figures for annual sales of services are for 1982. ♂Long term. □September. ◇Persons of Spanish origin may be of any race. △Import figures are c.i.f. (cost, insurance, and freight) for balance of trade, commodities, and trading partners. †1984, 6.8%. ⊙Total deliveries for year ending June 30; does not include training. ** To unidentified countries.

Pinnacles National Monument, near Trona, southern California, showing 500- to 1,200-ft (150- to 365-m) spires of tufa, formed by algal precipitation at the southern margin of Pleistocene Lake Searles.

AP/WIDE WORLD

Uruguay

Official name: República Oriental del Uruguay (Oriental Republic of Uruguay).
Form of government: republic with two legislative houses (Senate [31]; Chamber of Representatives [99]).
Head of state and government: President.
Capital: Montevideo.
Official language: Spanish.
Official religion: none.
Monetary unit: 1 Uruguayan new peso (NUr$) = 100 centésimos; valuation (Oct. 21, 1985) 1 U.S.$ = NUr$115.29; 1 £ = NUr$165.34.

Area and population		area		population
				1975
Departments	Capitals	sq mi	sq km	census
Artigas	Artigas	4,605	11,928	57,947
Canelones	Canelones	1,751	4,536	325,594
Cerro Largo	Melo	5,270	13,648	74,027
Colonia	Colonia del Sacramento	2,358	6,106	111,832
Durazno	Durazno	4,495	11,643	55,699
Flores	Trinidad	1,986	5,144	24,745
Florida	Florida	4,022	10,417	67,129
Lavalleja	Minas	3,867	10,016	65,180
Maldonado	Maldonado	1,851	4,793	76,211
Montevideo	Montevideo	205	530	1,237,227
Paysandú	Paysandú	5,375	13,922	98,508
Río Negro	Fray Bentos	3,584	9,282	50,123
Rivera	Rivera	3,618	9,370	82,043
Rocha	Rocha	4,074	10,551	60,258
Salto	Salto	5,468	14,163	103,074
San José	San José de Mayo	1,927	4,992	88,000
Soriano	Mercedes	3,478	9,008	80,614
Tacuarembó	Tacuarembó	5,961	15,438	84,535
Treinta y Tres	Trienta y Tres	3,679	9,529	45,683
TOTAL		68,037*	176,215*	2,788,429

Demography

Population (1985): 3,012,100.
Density (1985): persons per sq mi 44.3, persons per sq km 17.1.
Urban–rural (1983): urban 83.9%; rural 16.1%.
Sex distribution (1985): male 49.22%; female 50.78%.
Age breakdown (1985): under 15, 26.9%; 15–29, 23.4%; 30–44, 17.7%; 45–59, 16.6%; 60–74, 11.4%; 75 and over, 4.0%.
Population projection: (1990) 3,128,000; (2000) 3,363,900.
Doubling time: 72 years.
Ethnic composition (1980): mixed Spanish–Italian 85.9%; mestizo 3.0%; Italian 2.6%; Jewish 1.7%; mulatto 1.2%; other 5.6%.
Religious affiliation (1980): Christian 62.9%, of which Roman Catholic 59.5%; nonreligious 35.1%; Jewish 1.7%; other 0.3%.
Major city (1980): Montevideo 1,261,000; other cities (1975) Salto 72,000, Paysandú 62,000, Las Piedras 54,000.

Vital statistics

Birth rate per 1,000 population (1983): 19.0 (world avg. 29.0).
Death rate per 1,000 population (1983): 8.7 (world avg. 11.0).
Natural increase rate per 1,000 population (1983): 10.3 (world avg. 18.0).
Total fertility rate (avg. births per childbearing woman; 1982): 2.6.
Marriage rate per 1,000 population (1982): 6.9.
Divorce rate per 1,000 population (1981): 1.4.
Life expectancy at birth (1981): male 69.1 years; female 73.8 years.
Major causes of death per 100,000 population (1981): diseases of the circulatory system 375.6; malignant neoplasms (cancers) 209.6; symptoms and ill-defined conditions 67.5; accidents 54.6; infectious and parasitic diseases 24.1.

National economy

Budget (1984). Revenue: NUr$39,796,700,000 (direct taxes 70.8%, receipts from foreign trade 14.9%). Expenditures: NUr$55,473,300,000 (social security and welfare 56.6%, general public services 12.5%, interest on public debt 9.4%).
Tourism (1982): receipts from visitors U.S.$96,000,000; expenditures by nationals abroad U.S.$304,000,000.
Production (metric tons except as noted). Agriculture, forestry, fishing (1984): sugarcane 570,000, wheat 450,000, rice 340,000, sugar beets 264,000, potatoes 150,000, sorghum 140,000, corn (maize) 120,000, grapes 117,000; livestock (number of live animals) 23,337,000 sheep, 9,491,000 cattle, 540,000 horses; roundwood 2,975,000 cu m†; fish catch 144,131†. Mining and quarrying (1983): clays 300,000; glass sand 200,000. Manufacturing (value added in NUr$'000,000; 1982): food products excluding beverages 6,719; petroleum products 4,542; beverages 3,192; minerals 2,990; tobacco 2,430; clothing and footwear 1,931; transport equipment 1,805; textiles (not clothing, footwear, or leather products) 1,673; chemicals and chemical products 1,444. Construction (1982): residential 427,100 sq m; nonresidential 147,400 sq m. Energy production (consumption): electricity (kW-hr; 1983) 7,343,000,000 (3,746,000,000); coal, none (none); crude petroleum (barrels; 1983) none (9,505,000); petroleum products (metric tons; 1983) 1,194,000 (1,123,000); natural gas, none (n.a.).
Gross national product (at current market prices; 1983): U.S.$7,390,000,000 (U.S.$2,490 per capita).

Structure of gross domestic product and labour force				
	1983		1981	
	in value NUr$'000,000	% of total value	labour force	% of labour force
Agriculture	3,269	10.7	132,000	11.6
Mining	} 5,148	16.9	2,000	0.2
Manufacturing			231,000	20.3
Construction	1,012	3.3	66,000	5.8
Public utilities	446	1.5	16,000‡	1.4‡
Transportation and communication	1,726	5.6	58,000‡	5.1‡
Trade	3,689	12.1	} 171,000‡	15.0‡
Finance	} 10,666	34.9		
Pub. admin., defense			} 211,000‡	18.6‡
Services				
Other	4,576§	15.0§	250,000	22.0
TOTAL	30,532 ‖	100.0	1,137,000	100.0

Public debt (external, outstanding; 1983): U.S.$2,522,900,000.
Population economically active (1982): total 1,148,000; participation rate of total population 38.7% (female [1975] 27.7%, unemployed 9.0%).

Price and earnings indexes (1980 = 100)							
	1979	1980	1981	1982	1983	1984	1985
Consumer price index	61.2	100.0	134.0	159.5	238.0	369.6	679.9¶
Monthly earnings index♀	60.8	100.0	143.6	169.9	201.0	...	...

Household income and expenditure. Average household size (1980) 3.5; income per household: n.a.; sources of income: wages and salaries 47.5%, self-employment 21.9%, pensions, transfer payments, and other 30.6%♂; expenditure; n.a.
Land use (1983): forested 3.6%; meadows and pastures 78.5%; agricultural and under permanent cultivation 8.3%; other 9.6%.

Foreign trade□

Balance of trade (current prices)						
	1979	1980	1981	1982	1983	1984
U.S.$'000,000	−378.1	−609.7	−362.4	+218.0	+416.7	+191,4
% of total	19.3%	22.4%	12.8%	9.5%	22.0%	11.5%

Imports (1984): U.S.$735,564,000 (mineral products 38.9%; chemical products 14.0%; machinery and appliances 11.8%; synthetic plastic, resins, and rubber 6.2%; vegetable products 5.7%; textiles and textile products 4.7%; base metals and products 4.5%). *Major import sources* (1983): Nigeria 16.6%; Brazil 13.3%; Argentina 10.4%; Mexico 7.6%; United States 7.6%.
Exports (1984): U.S.$924,584,000 (textiles and textile products 30.5%; live animals and live animal products 24.7%; hides and skins 15.8%; vegetable products 14.0%; food, beverages, and tobacco 3.0%; synthetic plastics, resins, and rubber 1.1%). *Major export destinations* (1983): Brazil 14.3%; Argentina 10.7%; West Germany 9.0%; U.S.S.R. 7.7%; United States 7.4%.

Transport and communications

Transport. Railroads (1982): route length 1,867 mi, 3,004 km; passenger-mi 170,000,000, passenger-km 274,000,000; short ton-mi cargo 123,000,000, metric ton-km cargo 180,000,000. Roads (1981): total length 30,952 mi, 49,813 km (paved 10%). Vehicles (1981): passenger cars 281,275; trucks and buses 49,813. Merchant marine (1984): vessels (100 gross tons and over) 89; total deadweight tonnage 288,409. Air transport (1982): passenger-mi 173,000,000, passenger-km 278,000,000; short ton-mi cargo 685,000, metric ton-km cargo 1,000,000; airports (1985) with scheduled flights 5.
Communications. Daily newspapers (1984): total number 20; total circulation 553,100♢; circulation per 1,000 population 185♢. Radio (1984): total number of receivers 1,660,000 (1 per 1.8 persons). Television (1984): total number of receivers 440,000 (1 per 6.8 persons). Telephones (1983): 307,640 (1 per 9.6 persons).

Education and health

Education (1982)				
	schools	teachers	students	student/ teacher ratio
Primary (age 6–12)	2,291	16,821	343,957	20.4
Secondary	263	...	125,366	...
Vocational	86	...	51,697	...
Higher△†	1	4,149	36,458	8.8

Educational attainment (1975). Percent of adult population over age 25 having: no formal schooling 9.9%; less than primary education 36.7%; primary 29.6%; secondary 17.4%; higher 6.3%. *Literacy* (1983): total population over age 15 literate 96.3%; males literate (1975) 922,534 (93.5%); females literate (1975) 989,727 (94.4%).
Health (1981): physicians 5,600 (1 per 523 persons); hospital beds 23,000 (1 per 127 persons); infant mortality rate per 1,000 live births (1983) 32.0.
Food (1980–82): daily per capita caloric intake 2,809 (vegetable products 63%, animal products 37%); 107% of FAO recommended minimum requirement.

Military

Total active duty personnel (1984): 29,800 (army 74.8%, navy 15.1%, air force 10.1%). *Military expenditure as percent of GNP* (1983): 3.3% (world 6.1%); per capita expenditure U.S.$98.

*Includes 463 sq mi (1,199 sq km) of water area not shown separately. †1983. ‡Projection. §Includes indirect taxes less subsidies. ‖ At constant 1978 prices. ¶August. ♀Salaried employees only. ♂Urban only. □Import figures are f.o.b. (free on board) in balance of trade and c.i.f. (cost, insurance, and freight) for commodities and trading partners. ♢Partial circulation only. △1981. †Universidad de la República.

Vanuatu

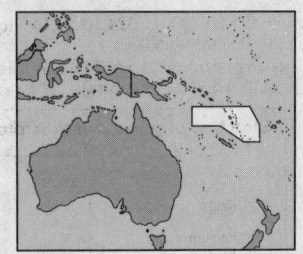

Official name: Ripablik blong Vanuatu (Bislama); République de Vanuatu (French); Republic of Vanuatu (English).
Form of government: republic with a single legislative house (Parliament [39]).
Chief of state: President.
Head of government: Prime Minister.
Capital: Vila.
Official languages: Bislama; French; English.
Official religion: none.
Monetary unit: vatu (VT); valuation (Oct. 21, 1985) 1 U.S.$ = VT102.93; 1 £ = VT147.60.

Area and population		area		population
Local Government Regions	Capitals	sq mi	sq km	1979 census
Ambrym	Eas	257	665	6,176
Aoba/Maéwo	Longana	270	700	9,576
Banks/Torres	Sola	340	880	4,958
Éfaté	Vila	357	925	19,819
Épi	Ringdove	172	445	2,597
Malekula	Lakatoro	792	2,050	15,163
Paama	Liro	23	60	2,228
Pentecost	Loltong	193	500	9,361
Santo/Malo	Luganville	1,641	4,250	19,423
Shepherd	Morua	33	85	4,444
Taféa	Isangel	629	1,630	17,506
TOTAL		4,707	12,190	111,251

Demography

Population (1985): 140,000.
Density (1985): persons per sq mi 28.4, persons per sq km 11.0.
Urban–rural (1979): urban 17.8%; rural 82.2%.
Sex distribution (1979): male 53.10%; female 46.90%.
Age breakdown (1979): under 15, 45.3%; 15–29, 27.5%; 30–44, 15.0%; 45–59, 7.7%; 60–74, 3.4%; 75 and over, 1.1%.
Population projection: (1990) 167,000; (2000) 223,000.
Doubling time: 22 years.
Ethnic composition (1979): Melanesian (Ni-Vanuatu) 93.8%; European 2.2%; part-European 0.9%; Polynesian and Micronesian 0.9%; other 2.2%.
Religious affiliation (1979): Presbyterian 35.5%; Anglican 16.2%; Roman Catholic 13.5%; animist 9.2%; Seventh-day Adventist 6.3%; Church of Christ 4.2%; nonreligious 0.7%; unknown 10.1%; other 4.3%.
Major cities (1981): Vila (Port Vila) 9,971; Santo (Luganville) 5,183*.

Vital statistics

Birth rate per 1,000 population (1984): 45 (world avg. 29.0).
Death rate per 1,000 population (1984): 12.0 (world avg. 11.0).
Natural increase rate per 1,000 population (1984): 33.0 (world avg. 18.0).
Total fertility rate (avg. births per childbearing woman; 1984): 6.5.
Life expectancy at birth (1984): male 56.2 years; female 53.7 years.
Major causes of death per 100,000 population: n.a.; however, major diseases are malaria, infantile diarrhea, influenza, hookworm, and tuberculosis.

National economy

Budget† (1981). Revenue: VT2,372,000,000 (grant aid 37.9%, import and export duties 34.8%, nontax revenue 8.6%). Expenditures: VT2,876,000,000 (education *c.* 40%).
Public debt (external, outstanding; 1983): U.S.$3,700,000.
Tourism (1983): number of visitors 32,374.
Production (metric tons except as noted). Agriculture, forestry, fishing (1984): coconuts 306,000, copra 44,000, roots and tubers 30,000, vegetables and melons 7,000, peanuts (groundnuts) 2,000, bananas 1,000, cocoa beans 1,000; livestock (number of live animals) 100,000 cattle, 71,000 pigs, 8,000 goats; roundwood 38,000 cu m‡; fish catch 2,470†, of which tuna 500. Mining and quarrying (1985): small quantities of coral reef limestone, crushed stone, sand, and gravel. Manufacturing (1980): VT326,040,000 (canned meat, frozen fish, soft drinks, furniture). Construction (approvals in Vila and Santo; 1984): residential 3,700 sq m; nonresidential 14,150 sq m. Energy production (consumption): electricity (kW-hr; 1984) 18,000,000 (21,000,000‡); coal, none (n.a.); crude petroleum (barrels; 1981) none (110,000); petroleum products (metric tons; 1983) none (16,000).
Population economically active (1981): total 61,000; participation rate of total population ages 15–55, 100%§ (female 48.3%; unemployed, n.a.).

Price and earnings indexes (1980 = 100)							
	1979	1980	1981	1982	1983	1984	1985
Consumer price index	89.9	100.0	127.5	135.3	137.6	145.2	145.7
Monthly earnings index	...	...	...	...	...	...	...

Household income and expenditure. Average household size (1980) 4.9; household income: n.a.; expenditure ‖ (1975): food 45.8%, clothing and footwear 14.1%, beverages and tobacco 10.1%, transportation and communication 9.8%, household furnishings 8.0%, housing 2.2%.
Land use (1983): forested 1.1%; meadows and pastures 1.7%; agricultural 6.4%; limestones, volcanic rock, and other 90.8%.
Gross national product (1980): U.S.$70,400,000 (U.S.$585 per capita).

Structure of gross domestic product and labour force

	1981		1979	
	in value VT'000,000	% of total value	labour force	% of labour force
Agriculture	...	...	39,296	76.8
Mining	...	...	76	0.1
Manufacturing	...	...	990	1.9
Construction	...	...	1,103	2.2
Public utilities	...	...	61	0.1
Transp. and commun.	...	...	1,323	2.6
Trade	...	...	2,178	4.3
Finance	...	...	326	0.6
Pub. admin., defense	...	...	} 5,502	10.8
Services	...	...		
Other	...	...	308	0.6
TOTAL	5,861	100.0	51,163	100.0

Foreign trade

Balance of trade (current prices)						
	1979	1980	1981	1982	1983	1984
VT'000,000	−1,780	−2,544	−2,283	−3,462	−3,320	−2,236
% of total	21.5%	34.2%	28.7%	44.0%	36.1%	20.3%

Imports (1984): VT6,631,000,000 (machines and transport equipment 20.3%, food and live animals 17.6%, basic manufactures 14.4%, mineral fuels 8.4%, chemicals 6.2%, beverages and tobacco 4.7%). *Major import sources:* Australia 35%; Japan 13%; New Zealand 10%; France 9%; Fiji 7%.
Exports (1984): VT4,395,000,000 (copra 62.2%, frozen fish 16.2%, timber 3.2%, cocoa 3.1%, beef 0.5%, cowhides 0.4%). *Major export destinations:* The Netherlands 37%; Belgium–Luxembourg 22%; Japan 13%; France 10%; Singapore 5%.

Transport and communications

Transport. Railroads: none. Roads (1981): total length 660 mi, 1,062 km; (paved 4%). Vehicles (on the islands of Espiritu Santo and Éfaté; 1984): passenger cars 3,061; trucks and buses 248. Merchant marine (1984): vessels (100 gross tons and over) 21; total deadweight tonnage 161,352. Air transport (1984): international aircraft arrivals 1,145; airports (1985) with scheduled flights 14.
Communications. Daily newspapers (1985): none. Radio (1984): total number of receivers 15,500 (1 per 9 persons). Television: none. Telephones (1983): 3,000 (1 per 44 persons).

Education and health

Education (1982)	schools	teachers	students	student/ teacher ratio
Primary (age 6–11)	286	1,063	23,595	22.2
Secondary (age 11–18)	9	126	2,067	16.4
Voc., teacher tr.	2	40	351	8.8
Higher	...	...	...	...

Educational attainment (1979). Percent of adult population over age 25 having: English qualification 45.1%, of which primary education 43.2%, postprimary 31.4%, technical and vocational 25.4%; French qualification 27.3%, of which primary 43.7%, postprimary 44.3%, technical and professional 12.0%; others 27.6%. *Literacy* (1979): total population over age 5 attended school 88,665 (73.2%); males 36,307 (76.9%); females 28,596 (69.0%).
Health: physicians (1984) 19 (1 per 7,158 persons); hospital beds (1983) 437 (1 per 300 persons); infant mortality rate per 1,000 live births (1984) 94.
Food (1980–82): daily per capita caloric intake 2,122 (vegetable products 77%, animal products 23%); 80% of FAO recommended minimum requirement.

Military

Total active duty personnel: Vanuatu has a paramilitary force of about 300 and has received military assistance from Papua New Guinea.

*1979. †Budget for 1984 was: revenue VT2,827,000,000; expenditures VT3,345,000,000. ‡1983. §Data refer to all persons in the age group of 15–55 years. ‖ For Vila and Santo only. ¶Public administration and defense are included with services.

SHOSTAL

Yasur volcano, Tanna Island, Vanuatu, which has been in virtually continuous eruption since first visited by Capt. James Cook (1774).

Venezuela

Official name: República de Venezuela (Republic of Venezuela).
Form of government: federal multiparty republic with two legislative houses (Senate [47]; Chamber of Deputies [200]).
Head of state and government: President.
Capital: Caracas.
Official language: Spanish.
Official religion: none.
Monetary unit: 1 bolívar (B., plural Bs.) = 100 céntimos; valuation (Oct. 21, 1985) 1 U.S.$ = Bs.14.57; 1 £ = Bs.20.99.

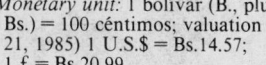

Area and population

States	Capitals	area sq mi	area sq km	population 1985 estimate
Anzoátegui	Barcelona	16,700	43,300	783,300
Apure	San Fernando de Apure	29,500	76,500	230,800
Aragua	Maracay	2,700	7,014	1,109,000
Barinas	Barinas	13,600	35,200	413,000
Bolívar	Ciudad Bolívar	91,900	238,000	824,100
Carabobo	Valencia	1,795	4,650	1,341,000
Cojedes	San Carlos	5,700	14,800	166,100
Falcón	Coro	9,600	24,800	575,800
Guárico	San Juan de Los Morros	25,091	64,986	438,500
Lara	Barquisimeto	7,600	19,800	1,096,200
Mérida	Mérida	4,400	11,300	552,300
Miranda	Los Teques	3,070	7,950	1,714,000
Monagas	Maturín	11,200	28,900	452,300
Nueva Esparta	La Asunción	440	1,150	236,200
Portuguesa	Guanare	5,900	15,200	519,400
Sucre	Cumaná	4,600	11,800	676,100
Táchira	San Cristóbal	4,300	11,100	764,700
Trujillo	Trujillo	2,900	7,400	506,800
Yaracuy	San Felipe	2,700	7,100	340,200
Zulia	Maracaibo	24,400	63,100	1,982,400
Other federal entities				
Amazonas	Puerto Ayacucho	67,900	175,750	70,800
Delta Amacuro	Tucupita	15,500	40,200	83,200
Dependencias Federales	—	50	120	...
Distrito Federal	Caracas	745	1,930	2,450,500
TOTAL		352,144*	912,050	17,316,700

Demography

Population (1985 est.): 17,317,000.
Density (1985): persons per sq mi 49.2, persons per sq km 19.0.
Urban–rural (1985): urban 85.7%; rural 14.3%.
Sex distribution (1985): male 50.00%; female 50.00%.
Age breakdown (1981): under 15, 40.5%; 15–29, 29.9%; 30–44, 15.8%; 45–59, 8.7%; 60–74, 4.0%; 75 and over, 1.1%.
Population projection: (1990) 19,700,000; (2000) 25,200,000.
Doubling time: 26 years.
Ethnic composition (1981): mestizo 69%; white 20%; black 9%; Indian 2%.
Religious affiliation (1981): Roman Catholic 92.4%; other 7.6%.
Major cities (1981): Caracas 2,661,100; Maracaibo 890,600; Valencia 616,200; Barquisimeto 497,600.

Vital statistics

Birth rate per 1,000 population (1975–80): 36.9 (world avg. 29.0); (1974) legitimate 47.0%; illegitimate 53.0%.
Death rate per 1,000 population (1975–80): 6.1 (world avg. 11.0).
Natural increase rate per 1,000 population (1975–80): 30.8 (world avg. 18.0).
Total fertility rate (avg. births per childbearing woman; 1980–85): 4.3.
Marriage rate per 1,000 population (1981): 6.4.
Divorce rate per 1,000 population (1983): 0.3.
Life expectancy at birth (1980–85): male 65.1 years; female 70.6 years.
Major causes of death per 100,000 population (1978): heart disease 82.5; malignant neoplasms (cancers) 53.4; diarrheal diseases 36.7.

National economy

Budget (1983). Revenue: Bs.76,863,000,000 (taxes on petroleum exploitation and enterprises 52.3%, excise taxes 5.6%, import duties 4.6%, social security contributions 4.1%). Expenditures: Bs.75,261,000,000 (economic services 21.1%, education 19.4%, regional and local transfers 16.8%, interest on public debt 9.1%, health 8.1%, social security and welfare 7.3%, general public services 6.5%, defense 5.3%, utilities 4.5%).
Public debt (external, outstanding; 1983): U.S.$12,911,400,000.
Tourism (1982): receipts from visitors U.S.$309,000,000; expenditures by nationals abroad U.S.$2,925,000,000.
Production (metric tons except as noted). Agriculture, forestry, fishing (1984): sugarcane 4,966,000, bananas 965,000, corn (maize) 547,000, sorghum 473,000, rice 408,000, coffee 61,000, seed cotton 46,000, sesame 38,000, cacao 12,000; livestock (number of live animals) 12,283,000 cattle; roundwood 1,300,000 cu m†; fish catch 226,869†. Mining and quarrying (1984): iron ore 13,044,000; gold 1,000 kilograms; diamonds 500,000 carats; coal 48,000; salt 350,000†. Manufacturing (1983): cement 4,151,000; steel 2,146,000; fertilizers 576,000; paper and cardboard 486,000; aluminum 385,200‡; refined sugar 348,000; automobiles 112,000 vehicles. Construction (1982§): residential 5,088,000 sq m; nonresidential 1,392,000 sq m. Energy production (consumption): electricity (kW-hr; 1983) 41,700,000,000 (41,715,000,000); coal (metric tons; 1983) 48,000‡ (79,000); petroleum (barrels; 1983)

1,695,000,000‡ (324,100,000); liquefied petroleum gas (metric tons; 1983) 1,600,000 (965,000).
Gross national product (at current market prices; 1983): U.S.$70,820,000,000 (U.S.$4,110 per capita).

Structure of gross domestic product and labour force

	1983 in value Bs.'000,000	% of total value	labour force	% of labour force
Agriculture	19,536	6.8	766,531	15.7
Mining	46,586	16.3	78,170	1.6
Manufacturing	49,261	17.3	728,113	14.9
Construction	14,269	5.0	431,341	8.8
Public utilities	5,575	2.0	63,466	1.3
Transportation and communication	31,954	11.2	343,861	7.1
Trade	27,100	9.5	921,673	18.8
Finance	22,867	8.0	235,725	4.8
Pub. admin., defense	24,568	8.6 }	1,296,368	26.5
Services	20,300	7.1 }		
Other	23,247	8.1	25,357	0.5
TOTAL	285,263 ‖	100.0*	4,890,605	100.0

Population economically active (1984): total 5,716,207; participation rate of total population 33.9% (female [1983] 27.2%, unemployed 13.3%).

Price and earnings indexes (1980 = 100)

	1979	1980	1981	1982	1983	1984	1985
Consumer price index	82.3	100.0	116.2	127.3	135.3	151.8	170.2¶
Monthly earnings index	...	...	...	...	...	...	...

Household income and expenditure: average household size (1981) 5.3; average annual income per household (1979) Bs.2,897 (U.S.$512); source of income: n.a.; expenditure (1983): food 30.7%, transportation 16.0%, recreation 10.0%, clothing and footwear 6.4%, housing 7.0%.
Land use (1983): forested 38.7%; meadows and pastures 19.7%; agricultural and under permanent cultivation 4.2%; other 37.4%.

Foreign trade

Balance of trade (current prices)

	1979	1980	1981	1982	1983	1984
Bs.'000,000	+20,134	+36,772	+35,706	+20,765	+31,427	+46,133
% of total	19.6%	28.7%	26.0%	17.2%	31.8%	32.7%

Imports (1980): Bs.45,735,000,000 (machinery other than electrical 22.1%, of which road motor vehicles 11.6%; chemicals and related products 10.5%; electrical machinery, apparatus, and equipment 9.3%; iron and steel 7.0%; cereals and cereal preparations 3.5%). *Major import sources:* United States 46.1%; Japan 8.2%; West Germany 7.0%; Canada 4.2%.
Exports (1980): Bs.82,507,000,000 (crude petroleum oils and crude oils obtained from bituminous materials 60.2%; petroleum products, refined 32.4%, of which residual fuel 22.2%). *Major export destinations:* U.S. 37.3%; Netherlands Antilles 21.7%; Canada 10.1%; U.K. 2.4%.

Transport and communications

Transport. Railroads (1982): length 273 mi, 439 km; passenger-mi 11,800,000, passenger-km 19,000,000; short ton-mi cargo 19,900,000, metric ton-km cargo 29,000,000. Roads (1981): total length 38,803 mi, 62,448 km (paved 38%). Vehicles (1981): passenger cars 1,501,382; trucks and buses 795,856. Merchant marine (1984): vessels (100 gross tons and over) 250; total deadweight tonnage 1,460,527. Air transport (1983): passenger-mi 1,737,000,000, passenger-km 2,796,000,000; short ton-mi cargo 72,338,200, metric ton-km cargo 105,612,000; airports (1985) with scheduled flights 35.
Communications. Daily newspapers (1980): total number 54; total circulation 2,476,514; circulation per 1,000 population 178. Radio (1984): total number of receivers 5,250,000 (1 per 32 persons). Television (1984): total number of receivers 2,002,000 (1 per 8.3 persons). Telephones (1983): 1,021,136 (1 per 16 persons).

Education and health

Education (1982–83)

	schools	teachers	students	student/ teacher ratio
Primary (age 7–12) } Secondary (age 13–17)♀	12,816	130,505	2,998,803	23.0
Higher	106	25,268	282,274	11.2

Educational attainment (1971). Percent of adult population over age 25 having: no formal schooling 47.1%; primary education 39.2%; secondary 11.1%; higher 2.6%. *Literacy* (1978): total population literate 6,640,816 (84.9%); males literate 3,412,181 (87.2%); females literate 3,228,635 (82.6%).
Health (1978): physicians 14,771 (1 per 888 persons); hospital beds 41,386 (1 per 317 persons); infant mortality rate per 1,000 live births (1980) 44.8.
Food (1980–82): daily per capita caloric intake 2,557 (vegetable products 79%, animal products 21%); 107% of FAO recommended minimum requirement.

Military

Total active duty personnel (1984): 44,250 (army 62.2%, navy 27.1%, air force 10.7%). *Military expenditure as percent of GNP* (1983): 1.3% (world 6.1%); per capita expenditure U.S.$55.

*Detail does not add to total given because of rounding. †1983. ‡1984. §Private only. ‖ At current prices. ¶August. ♀Includes vocational and teacher training.

Vietnam

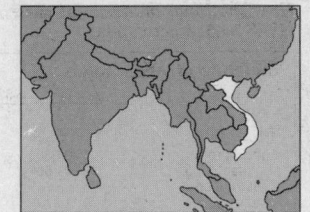

Official name: Cong Hoa Xa Hoi Chu Nghia Viet Nam (Socialist Republic of Vietnam).
Form of government: unitary single-party socialist republic with one legislative house (National Assembly [496]).
Chief of state: President.
Head of government: Premier.
Capital: Hanoi.
Official language: Vietnamese.
Official religion: none.
Monetary unit: 1 dong (D) = 10 hao = 100 xu; valuation (Oct. 21, 1985) 1 U.S.$ = D94.22; 1 £ = D135.11.

Area and population

Provinces	Capitals	area sq mi	area sq km	population 1979 census
An Giang	Long Xuyen	1,349	3,493	1,532,362
Bac Thai	Thai Nguyen	2,521	6,530	815,105
Ben Tre	Ben Tre	859	2,225	1,041,838
Binh Tri Thien	Hue	7,081	18,340	1,901,713
Cao Bang	Cao Bang	3,261	8,445	479,823
Cuu Long	Vihn Long	1,488	3,854	1,504,215
Dac Lac	Buon Me Thoat	7,645	19,800	490,198
Dong Nai	Bien Hoa	2,926	7,578	1,304,799
Dong Thap	Cao Lamh	1,309	3,391	1,182,787
Gia Lai-Cong Tum	Cong Tum	9,860	25,536	595,906
Ha Bac	Bac Giang	1,780	4,609	1,662,671
Hai Hung	Hai Duong	986	2,555	2,145,662
Ha Nam Ninh	Nam Dinh	1,453	3,763	2,781,409
Ha Son Binh	Hanoi	2,308	5,978	1,537,190
Ha Tuyen	Ha Giang	5,219	13,518	782,453
Hau Giang	Can Tho	2,365	6,126	2,232,891
Hoang Lien Son	Lao Cai	5,734	14,852	778,217
Kien Giang	Rach Gia	2,455	6,358	994,673
Lai Chau	Lai Chau	6,586	17,068	322,077
Lam Dong	Da Lat	3,835	9,933	396,657
Lang Son	Lang Son	3,161	8,187	484,657
Long An	Tan An	1,681	4,355	957,264
Minh Hai	Bac Lieu	2,972	7,697	1,219,595
Nghe Tinh	Vinh	8,688	22,502	3,111,989
Nghia Binh	Qui Nhon	4,595	11,900	2,095,354
Phu Khanh	Nha Trang	3,785	9,804	1,188,637
Quang Nam-Da Nang	Da Nang	4,629	11,989	1,529,520
Quang Ninh	Hai Duong	2,293	5,938	750,055
Song Be	Thu Dau Mo	3,807	9,859	659,093
Son La	Son La	5,586	14,468	487,793
Tay Ninh	Ho Chi Minh City	1,556	4,030	684,006
Thai Binh	Thai Binh	577	1,495	1,506,235
Thanh Hoa	Thanh Hoa	4,300	11,138	2,532,261
Thuan Hai	Phan Thiet	4,392	11,374	938,255
Tien Giang	My Tho	918	2,377	1,264,498
Vinh Phu	Viet Tri	1,786	4,626	1,488,348
Municipalities				
Haiphong	—	585	1,515	1,279,067
Hanoi	—	826	2,139	2,570,905
Ho Chi Minh City	—	787	2,029	3,419,978
Special zone				
Vung Tau-Con Dao	—	108	279	91,610
TOTAL		128,052	331,653	52,741,766

Demography

Population (1985): 60,492,400.
Density (1985): persons per sq mi 462.6, persons per sq km 178.6.
Urban–rural (1984): urban 19.1%; rural 80.9%.
Sex distribution (1985): male 48.95%; female 51.05%.
Age breakdown (1985): under 15, 40.8%; 15–29, 30.8%; 30–44, 13.5%; 45–59, 9.3%; 60–74, 4.4%; 75 and over, 1.2%.
Population projection: (1990) 68,338,000; (2000) 85,283,700.
Doubling time: 28 years.
Ethnic composition (1979): Vietnamese 88.0%; Chinese (Hoa) 1.9%; Tai 1.5%; Khmer 1.2%; Muong 1.2%; Thai 1.2%; Nung 0.9%; other 4.1%.
Religious affiliation (1980): Buddhist 55.3%; Roman Catholic 7.4%; Muslim 1.0%; other 36.3%.
Major cities (1979): Ho Chi Minh City 3,419,978; Hanoi 2,792,000*; Haiphong 1,279,067.

Vital statistics

Birth rate per 1,000 population (1985): 34.3 (world avg. 29.0); legitimate, n.a.; illegitimate, n.a.
Death rate per 1,000 population (1985): 8.8 (world avg. 11.0).
Natural increase rate per 1,000 population (1985): 25.5 (world avg. 18.0).
Total fertility rate (avg. births per childbearing woman; 1985): 4.7.
Marriage rate per 1,000 population: n.a.
Divorce rate per 1,000 population: n.a.
Life expectancy at birth (1979): male 63.6 years; female 67.8 years.
Major causes of death per 100,000 population (1979): diseases of the circulatory system 123.8; malignant neoplasms (cancers) 54.0; infectious and parasitic diseases 48.0.

National economy

Budget (1982). Revenue: U.S.$4,120,000,000. Expenditures: U.S.$5,560,000,000.
Public debt (external, outstanding; 1984): U.S.$6,000,000,000.

Production (metric tons except as noted). Agriculture, forestry, fishing (1984): rice 15,416,000, sugarcane 4,800,000, fruits 3,328,000, vegetables 2,953,000, cassava 2,900,000, sweet potatoes 1,900,000, corn (maize) 475,000, coconuts 355,000; livestock (number of live animals; 1984) 11,202,000 pigs, 4,674,000 cattle, 256,000 sheep and goats, 82,600,000 poultry; roundwood 23,676,000 cu m†; fish catch 765,000. Mining and quarrying (1981): phosphate rock 550,000; salt 500,000; chromite 15,000; zinc ore 6,000. Manufacturing (1983): cement 907,000; sugar 306,000; fertilizers 265,000; paper and paperboard 49,600; crude steel 48,000; textiles 287,000,000 sq m; beer 527,000 hectolitres; tires 15,800 units; leather footwear 200,000 pairs. Construction: n.a. Energy production (consumption): electricity (kW-hr; 1983) 4,370,000,000 (4,370,000,000); coal (metric tons; 1983) 6,000,000 (5,000,000); crude petroleum, none (n.a.); petroleum products (metric tons; 1983) none (1,345,000); natural gas, none (n.a.).
Gross national product (at current market prices; 1983): U.S.$9,818,000,000 (U.S.$170 per capita).

Structure of net material product and labour force

	1983 by value	% of total value	labour force	% of labour force
Agriculture	...	57.6	17,703,000	68.7
Mining and manufacturing	...	23.7‡	758,000	2.9
Construction	...	3.0	455,000	1.8
Public utilities	...	‡	32,300	0.1
Transportation and communication	...	1.9	180,000	0.7
Trade	...	11.7	395,000	1.5
Services	...	...	856,400	3.3
Other	...	2.1§	5,402,700 ‖	21.0
TOTAL		100.0	25,782,000	100.0

Population economically active (1983): total 25,782,000; participation rate of population ages 15–64, 55.0% (female 45.5%; unemployed, n.a.).
Price and earnings indexes: n.a.
Household income and expenditure: n.a.
Land use (1983): forested 40.4%; meadows and pastures 0.8%; agricultural and under permanent cultivation 23.3%; other 35.5%.

Foreign trade

Balance of trade (current prices)

	1978	1979	1980	1981	1982
D'000,000	−1,476	−1,899	−1,427	−1,535	−1,834
% of total	37.4%	46.4%	38.3%	49.1%	49.4%

Imports (1980): D2,577,000,000 (fuel and raw materials 44.7%, machinery 23.2%, wheat flour and food products 17.2%). *Major import sources:* U.S.S.R. 18.3%; Japan 15.8%; India 12.9%; Singapore 6.9%; Hong Kong 6.2%.
Exports (1980): D1,150,000,000 (manufactured goods 72.8%, handicrafts 18.6%, agricultural products 8.6%). *Major export destinations:* Japan 31.0%; Hong Kong 14.1%; U.S.S.R. 11.6%; Singapore 11.4%.

Transport and communications

Transport. Railroads (1983): length 1,568 mi, 2,523 km; passenger-mi 1,870,000,000, passenger-km 3,010,000,000; short ton-mi cargo 519,000,000, metric ton-km cargo 758,000,000. Roads (1983): total length 37,282 mi, 60,000 km (paved 16%¶). Vehicles (1976): passenger cars 100,000; trucks and buses 200,000. Merchant marine (1984): vessels (100 gross tons and over) 119; total deadweight tonnage 410,975. Air transport (1983): passenger-mi 180,819,000, passenger-km 291,000,000; short ton-mi cargo 2,740,000, metric ton-km cargo 4,000,000; airports (1985) with scheduled flights 3.
Communications. Daily newspapers (1984): 4; total circulation 500,000; circulation per 1,000 population 8.6. Radio (1984): total number of receivers 6,000,000 (1 per 9.7 persons). Television (1984): total number of receivers 2,250,000 (1 per 25.7 persons). Telephones (1982): 1,165,000 (1 per 48.1 persons).

Education and health

Education (1983–84)

	schools	teachers	students	student/teacher ratio
Primary and secondary (age 7–18)	11,751	427,000	11,779,000	27.6
Vocational	280	10,200	99,200	9.7
Higher	93	18,100	92,500	5.1

Educational attainment (1983). Percent of state-employed population having♀: vocational education 12.9%; higher 7.4%. *Literacy* (1979): total population over age 15 literate 28,903,500 (94.0%).
Health (1984): physicians 16,100 (1 per 3,602 persons); hospital beds 201,000 (1 per 285 persons); infant mortality rate per 1,000 live births 73.
Food (1980–82): daily per capita caloric intake 2,040 (vegetable products 92%, animal products 8%); 94% of FAO recommended minimum requirement.

Military

Total active duty personnel (1984): 1,207,000 (army 97.4%, navy 1.2%, air force 1.4%). *Military expenditure as percent of GNP:* n.a. *Foreign military aid* (1982): U.S.$1,000,000,000.

*1984 estimate. †1983. ‡Mining and manufacturing includes public · utilities. §Other material activities. ‖ Includes finance and public administration and defense. ¶1981. ♀Total state-employed 3,435,000.

Virgin Islands (U.S.)

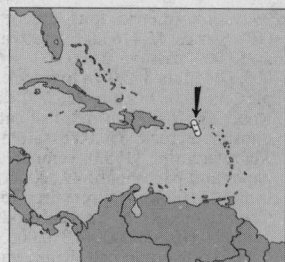

Official name: Virgin Islands of the United States.
Political status: unincorporated territory of the United States.
Chief of state: President of the United States.
Head of government: Governor.
Capital: Charlotte Amalie.
Official language: English.
Official religion: none.
Monetary unit: 1 U.S. dollar (U.S.$) = 100 cents; valuation (Oct. 21, 1985) 1 U.S.$ = £0.70.

Area and population

Islands	Capitals	area sq mi	area sq km	population 1983 estimate
St. Croix	—	84	218	52,600
St. John	—	20	52	2,500
St. Thomas	—	32	83	46,000
TOTAL		136	352*	101,200*

Demography

Population (1985 est.): 107,000.
Density (1985): persons per sq mi 772.1, persons per sq km 298.3.
Urban–rural (1980): urban 39.1%; rural 60.9%.
Sex distribution (1980): male 47.85%; female 52.15%.
Age breakdown (1980): under 15, 36.0%; 15–29, 24.2%; 30–44, 21.5%; 45–59, 11.1%; 60–74, 5.8%; 75 and over, 1.4%.
Population projection: (1990) 112,000; (2000) 128,000.
Doubling time: 49 years.
Ethnic composition (1980): black 79.7%, of which Spanish or Hispanic origin 10.3%; white 14.8%, of which Spanish or Hispanic origin 2.3%; other 5.5%, of which Spanish or Hispanic origin 3.7%.
Religious affiliation (1980): Christian 98.0%, of which Protestant 64.4% (Anglican 17.4%; Moravian 8.5%; Methodist 8.0%; Pentecostal 12.0%; Lutheran 3.2%), Baha'i 0.5%; Jewish 0.3%; nonreligious 1.2%.
Major cities (1980): Charlotte Amalie 11,842; Christiansted 2,914; Frederiksted 1,046.

Vital statistics

Birth rate per 1,000 population (1980): 21.7 (world avg. 29.0); legitimate 52.6%; illegitimate 47.4%.
Death rate per 1,000 population (1980): 4.7 (world avg. 11.0).
Natural increase rate per 1,000 population (1980): 17.0 (world avg. 18.0).
Total fertility rate (avg. births per childbearing woman; 1980–85): 3.6†.
Marriage rate per 1,000 population (1980): 9.5.
Divorce rate per 1,000 population (1980): 4.1.
Life expectancy at birth (1980–85): male 66.7 years; female 70.7 years.
Major causes of death per 100,000 population (1980): diseases of the circulatory system 215, of which heart disease 131; accidents, poisoning, and violence 88, of which homicide 25; malignant neoplasms (cancers) 68; conditions originating in the perinatal period 50; diseases of the digestive system 37, of which chronic liver disease and cirrhosis 24; diseases of the respiratory system 24; diabetes mellitus 23; congenital anomalies 11.

National economy

Budget (1983). Revenue: U.S.$252,379,000 (personal income tax 38.4%, rum excise tax 13.9%, corporate income tax 11.6%, gross receipts tax 9.7%, property tax 9.5%). Expenditures: U.S.$231,000,000 (education 25.4%, health 15.7%, executive branch 12.5%, public works 7.7%, public safety 5.7%, College of the Virgin Islands 3.8%, Territorial Court 2.7%, legislature 2.0%).
Public debt: n.a.
Tourism (1984): receipts from visitors U.S.$377,000,000; expenditures by nationals abroad, n.a.
Production (total value in U.S.$ except as noted). Agriculture, forestry, fishing (1982): milk 922,830 (3,000 metric tons), poultry and eggs 315,586, field, forage, and vegetable crops 212,155, fruits and nuts 145,796, ornamental plants and other nursery products 89,700; livestock (number of live animals; 1984) 8,000 cattle, 6,000 pigs, 6,000 goats, 5,000 sheep; roundwood, n.a.; fish catch (1983) 611 metric tons. Mining and quarrying: n.a. Manufacturing (1982): food and related products 28,771,000; watches, clocks, and watchcases 13,845,000; printing, publishing, and allied industries 5,206,000; heavy oils 10,800,000 metric tons‡, gasoline 2,400,000 metric tons‡, jet fuel 600,000 metric tons‡, kerosene 225,000 metric tons‡, liquefied petroleum gas 40,000 metric tons‡. Construction (1982): general building 64,775,000; heavy construction 52,414,000; special trade construction 24,776,000; buildings completed (1979) residential 908, nonresidential 262. Energy production (consumption): electricity (kW-hr; 1983) 775,000,000 (775,000,000); coal, none (n.a.); crude petroleum (barrels; 1983) n.a. (124,000); petroleum products (metric tons; 1983) 14,065,000 (2,599,000); natural gas, none (n.a.).
Household income and expenditure: average household size (1980) 3.4; average annual income per household (1979) U.S.$11,090; sources of income: wages and salaries 84.6%, self-employment 3.8%, interest, dividends, and rent 4.2%, transfers from government 4.1%, other 3.3%; expenditure (1982): housing 22.5%, food, beverages, and tobacco 15.7%, health care 13.3%, clothing and footwear 6.2%, personal care 2.5%, education 2.0%.

Gross national product§ (at current market prices; 1984): U.S.$898,600,000 (U.S.$8,558 per capita).

Structure of labour force

	1983 labour force	1983 % of labour force
Agriculture	3,930	9.1
Manufacturing	2,450	5.7
Construction and mining	2,370	5.5
Transportation and public utilities	2,190	5.1
Trade	7,310	16.9
Finance, insurance, real estate	1,440	3.3
Pub. admin., defense	14,020	32.4
Services	5,960	13.8
Other	3,590	8.3 ‖
TOTAL	43,260	100.0*

Population economically active (1983): total 43,260; participation rate of total population 42.8% (female [1980] 45.6%, unemployed 8.3%).

Price and earnings indexes (1980 = 100)

	1978	1979	1980	1981	1982	1983	1984
Consumer price index	79.2	88.1	100.0	110.4	117.1	120.9	126.1
Annual earnings index	76.5	88.2	100.0	108.7	109.8	110.4	...

Land use (1983): forested 5.9%; meadows and pastures 26.5%; agricultural and under permanent cultivation 20.6%; other 47.0%.

Foreign trade

Balance of trade (current prices)

	1979	1980	1981	1982	1983	1984
U.S.$'000,000	−685.4	−604.4	54.6	−300.2	−1,019.5	−786.4
% of total	10.0%	6.5%	0.5%	2.9%	12.2%	9.0%

Imports (1983): U.S.$4,668,700,000 (crude petroleum 78.8%; bauxite 0.3%). *Major import sources* (1982): United States 32.6%; Mexico 18.4%; Congo 16.2%; United Arab Emirates 15.8%; India 6.9%; Nigeria 6.7%.
Exports (1983): U.S.$3,649,200,000 (petroleum products 95.7%; alumina 3.0%¶; other major exports include rum and watch movements). *Major export destinations:* United States 96.9%; other countries 3.1%.

Transport and communications

Transport. Railroads: n.a. Roads (1984): total length 532 mi, 856 km. Registered vehicles (1983): 39,661♀. Merchant marine, n.a. Air transport km (1983): total arrivals, 478,300; airports (1984) with scheduled flights 5♂.
Communications. Daily newspapers (1982): total number 3; total circulation 17,000; circulation per 1,000 population 145. Radio (1982): total number of receivers 90,000 (1 per 1.1 persons). Television (1982): total number of receivers 54,000 (1 per 1.8 persons). Telephones (1983): 49,043 (1 per 2.1 persons).

Education and health

Education (1984–85)

	schools	teachers	students	student/ teacher ratio
Primary (age 4.5–12)	60□	981◊	18,356	...
Secondary (age 12–18)	11	799◊	14,684	...
Voc., teacher tr.△	3	27	775	28.7
Higher	1	84	765	9.1

Educational attainment (1980): Percent of adult population over age 25 having: primary education or less 35.5%; less than secondary 14.4%; secondary 25.7%; postsecondary 24.4%. *Literacy* (1982): total population over age 15 literate 90%.
Health: physicians (1974) 96 (1 per 937.5 persons); hospital beds (1983) 293 (1 per 345 persons); infant mortality rate per 1,000 live births (1980) 24.7.
Food: daily per capita caloric intake, n.a.

Military

Total active duty personnel: No domestic military force is maintained; the United States is responsible for defense and security.

---

*Detail does not add to total given because of rounding. †Represents rate for entire region, *i.e.,* the "Windward Islands." ‡1983. §Gross territorial product. ‖ Includes unemployed. ¶In 1985 the U.S.-owned alumina plant in St. Croix was in the process of closing. ♀In 1975 trucks and buses accounted for 21% of all registered vehicles. ♂Two of these are seaplane bases. □Nineteen of these are elementary/secondary schools. ◊Private school teachers not included in total. △1983–84.

Western Samoa

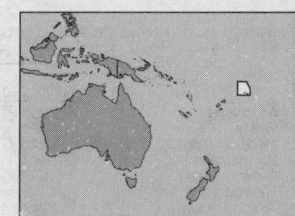

Official name: Malotuto'atasi o Samoa i Sisifo (Samoan); Independent State of Western Samoa (English).
Form of government: constitutional monarchy with one legislative house (Legislative Assembly [47]).
Chief of state: Head of State.
Head of government: Prime Minister.
Capital: Apia.
Official languages: Samoan; English.
Official religion: none.
Monetary unit: 1 tala (WS$, plural tala) = 100 sene; valuation (Nov. 20, 1985) 1 U.S.$ = WS$2.17; 1 £ = WS$3.11.

Area and population

Islands Political Districts	area sq mi	area sq km	population 1981 census*
Savaii	659	1,707	43,150
Fa'aseleleaga			11,876
Gaga'emauga			3,893
Gaga'ifomauga			5,304
Lealataua			1,934
Palauli			9,234
Satupa'itea			5,391
Vaisigano			5,518
Upolu	432	1,119	113,199
A'ana			13,149
A'ana-i-Sisifo			3,363
Aiga-i-le-Tai			3,960
Aleipata			4,236
Anoama'a			7,816
Fagaloa			1,519
Falealili			4,727
Faleata			16,821
Gaga'emauga			2,750
Lefaga			3,776
Lepa and Lotofaga			3,058
Safata			6,711
Sagaga			12,253
Vaimauga			29,060
TOTAL	1,093†	2,831†	156,349

Demography

Population (1985): 160,000.
Density (1985): persons per sq mi 146.4, persons per sq km 56.5.
Urban-rural (1981): urban 21.2%; rural 78.8%.
Sex distribution (1981): male 51.82%; female 48.18%.
Age breakdown (1981): under 15, 44.3%; 15–29, 29.1%; 30–44, 12.2%; 45–59, 9.0%; 60–74, 3.8%; 75 and over, 1.6%.
Population projection: (1990) 171,000; (2000) 182,000.
Doubling time: 83 years.
Ethnic composition (1982): Samoan (Polynesian) c. 88%; Euronesian c. 10%; European c. 2%.
Religious affiliation (1981): Congregational 47.3%; Roman Catholic 21.7%; Methodist 16.2%; Latter Day Saints 8.3%; Seventh-day Adventist 2.3%; other 4.2%.
Major cities (1981): Apia 33,170.

Vital statistics

Birth rate per 1,000 population (1984): 10.2‡ (world avg. 29.0); (1978) legitimate 43.5%; illegitimate 56.5%.
Death rate per 1,000 population (1984): 2.3‡ (world avg. 11.0).
Natural increase rate per 1,000 population (1984): 7.9 (world avg. 18.0).
Total fertility rate (avg. births per childbearing woman; 1980–85): 2.7.
Marriage rate per 1,000 population (1984): 5.0‡.
Divorce rate per 1,000 population (1984): 0.1‡.
Life expectancy at birth (1982): male 61.0 years; female 64.3 years.
Major causes of death per 100,000 population‡ (1984): diseases of the circulatory system 47.2; diseases of the respiratory system 22.6; diseases of the intestinal and digestive systems 20.7; malignant neoplasms (cancers) 17.6.

National economy

Budget (1984). Revenue: WS$58,270,720 (current revenue 96.6%, of which taxes 85.2%; loans 3.4%). Expenditures: WS$58,082,855 (current expenditure 60.3%; development expenditure 21.3%; statutory expenditure 18.4%).
Public debt (external, outstanding; 1983): U.S.$60,500,000.
Land use (1983): forested 47.0%; meadows and pastures 0.3%; agricultural and under permanent cultivation 42.8%; other 9.9%.
Production (metric tons except as noted). Agriculture, forestry, fishing (1984): coconuts 200,000, taro 37,000, bananas 22,000, papayas 11,000, mangoes 6,000, pineapples 6,000, avocados 2,000, milk 1,000, cacao 615; livestock (number of live animals) 61,000 pigs, 26,000 cattle, 1,000,000 chickens; nonconiferous roundwood 131,000 cu m§; fish catch 1,740. Mining and quarrying: n.a. Manufacturing (1984): copra 18,936, coconut oil 10,950, copra meal 4,740, sawn wood 21,000 cu m§, veneer sheets 1,061 cu m ‖; other products include coconut cream, fruit juice and fruit pulp, beer, wine, tobacco products, aluminum products, concrete blocks, handicrafts, kava (root used to brew an intoxicating beverage), and stationery. Construction (permits issued in WS$; 1984): residential 1,628,000; commercial, industrial, and other 4,135,600. Energy production (consumption): electricity (kW-hr; 1984) 33,790,000 (33,790,000).

Gross national product (at current market prices; 1980): U.S.$128,800,000 (U.S.$826 per capita).

Structure of gross domestic product and labour force

	1972 in value WS$	1972 % of total value	1981 labour force	1981 % of labour force
Agriculture	15,207,000	50.2	25,050	60.4
Mining	—	—	9	—
Manufacturing	858,900	2.8	757	1.8
Construction	1,146,800	3.8	2,279	5.5
Public utilities	...	...	447	1.1
Transportation and communication	666,600	2.2	1,353	3.3
Trade	2,861,100	9.5	1,821	4.4
Finance	1,761,800	5.8	1,305	3.1
Pub. admin., defense, government services	6,346,700	21.0	1,842	4.4
Other services	646,000	2.1	6,374	15.4
Other	769,400	2.5	269	0.6
TOTAL	30,264,300	100.0¶	41,506	100.0

Population economically active (1981): total 41,506; participation rate of total population 26.5% (female 15.0%; unemployed, n.a.).

Price and earnings indexes (1980 = 100)

	1979	1980	1981	1982	1983	1984	1985⚲
Consumer price index	75.2	100.0	120.5	142.6	166.0	185.7	202.3
Monthly earnings indexδ	91.1	100.0	112.8	...	146.6	163.0	...

Household income and expenditure. Average household size (1976) 5.9; income per household (1972) WS$1,518 (U.S.$2,200); sources of income: wages and salaries 49.4%, self-employment 22.8%, remittances, gifts, and other assistance 18.0%, land rent and royalties 8.7%, other 1.1%; expenditure: food and drink 55.1%, housing and furnishings 13.9%, clothing and footwear 11.7%, education 4.4%, tobacco 3.8%, personal care and effects 2.6%, transportation and communication 1.9%, recreation 1.8%, other 4.8%.
Tourism (1984): number of visitors 40,337; number of nationals abroad, n.a.

Foreign trade□

Balance of trade (current prices)

	1979	1980	1981	1982	1983	1984
WS$'000	−40,635	−36,902	−52,880	−39,572	−47,645	−46,953
% of total	57.9%	54.6%	72.0%	56.7%	48.3%	39.0%

Imports (1983): WS$71,242,000 (food and live animals 21.3%, machinery and transport equipment 21.0%, petroleum and petroleum products 18.4%, miscellaneous manufactured articles 7.4%, chemicals 5.9%, animals oils and fats 0.5%). *Major import sources:* New Zealand 28.8%; Australia 27.5%; United States 11.2%; Japan 11.0%; Singapore 6.0%; Fiji 4.0%.
Exports (1983): WS$27,410,000 (coconut oil 40.0%, cocoa 16.8%, taro 8.7%, beverages and tobacco 7.1%, copra 5.1%, coconut cream 4.4%, timber 2.0%, bananas 1.5%). *Major export destinations;* United States 31.3%; New Zealand 25.4%; Australia 12.7%; West Germany 10.1%; American Samoa 5.2%; Japan 3.6%.

Transport and communications

Transport. Railroads: none. Roads (1983): total length◊ 1,296 mi, 2,085 km (paved 14%). Vehicles (1984): passenger cars 1,795; trucks and buses 2,494. Merchant marine (1984): vessels (100 gross tons and over) 6; total deadweight tonnage 35,293. Air transport (1982): passengers, n.a.; cargo, n.a.; airports (1985) with scheduled flights 3.
Communications. Daily newspapers: none. Radio (1984): total number of receivers 70,000 (1 per 2.3 persons). Television (1983): total number of receivers 2,500 (1 per 64 persons). Telephones (1984): 6,037 (1 per 26 persons).

Education and health

Education (1983)

	schools ‖	teachers	students	student/ teacher ratio
Primary (age 5–11)	162	1,502△	31,447	20.9
Secondary (age 12–18)	38	520	20,404	39.2
Voc., teacher tr.	4	69	651	9.4
Higher	6	37	562	15.2

Educational attainment (1976). Percent of adult population over age 25 having: no formal schooling 60.0%; primary and secondary education 37.8%; higher 2.2%. *Literacy* (1971): total population over age 10 literate 93,360 (98.3%); males literate 48,146 (98.5%); females literate 45,214 (98.1%).
Health: physicians (1981) 63 (1 per 2,508 persons); hospital beds (1982) 735 (1 per 215 persons); infant mortality rate per 1,000 live births (1982) 42.0.
Food (1980–82): daily per capita caloric intake 2,527 (vegetable products 79%, animal products 21%); 95% of FAO recommended minimum requirement.

Military

No domestic military forces are maintained; New Zealand is responsible for defense.

---

*Preliminary. †Includes 2 sq mi (5 sq km) of small uninhabited islands. ‡Registered only. §1983. ‖1982. ¶Detail does not add to total given because of rounding. ⚲August. δGovernment employees only. □Import figures are f.o.b. (free on board) in balance of trade and c.i.f. (cost, insurance, and freight) for commodities and trading partners. ◊Total length includes 733 mi (1,180 km) of plantation roads. △Includes some secondary teachers.

Yemen (Aden)

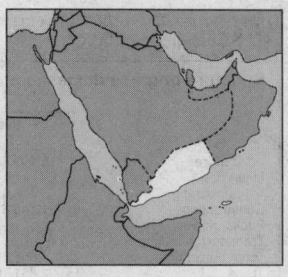

Official name: Jumhūrīyat al-Yaman ad-Dimuqrātīyah ash-Sha'bīyah (People's Democratic Republic of Yemen).
Form of government: single-party republic with one legislative house (Supreme People's Council [111]).
Head of state: Chairman of the Presidium of the Supreme People's Council.
Head of government: Prime Minister.
Capital: Aden.
Official language: Arabic.
Official religion: Islām.
Monetary unit: 1 Yemeni dinar (YD) = 1,000 fils; valuation (Oct. 21, 1985) 1 YD = U.S.$2.92 = £2.03.

Area and population

Governorates	Capitals	area sq mi	area sq km	population 1973 census
Ūlá (First)	Aden	2,690	6,980	291,376
Thāniyah (Second)	Laḥij	4,930	12,760	273,611
Thālithah (Third)	Zinjibār	8,300	21,490	311,142
Rābi'ah (Fourth)	'Atāq	28,540	73,910	161,966
Khāmisah (Fifth)	al-Mukallā	32,990	85,450	450,657
Sādisah (Sixth)	al-Ghayḍah	25,620	66,350	60,876
Directorate				
Thamūd*	Thamūd	27,000	69,930	40,647
TOTAL		130,070	336,870	1,590,275

Demography

Population (1985): 2,124,000.
Density (1985): persons per sq mi 16.3, persons per sq km 6.3.
Urban–rural (1980): urban 36.9%; rural 63.1%.
Sex distribution (1980): male 49.41%; female 50.59%.
Age breakdown (1980): under 15, 46.0%; 15–29, 25.3%; 30–44, 15.1%; 45–59, 9.0%; 60–74, 3.9%; 75 and over, 0.7%.
Population projection: (1990) 2,459,000; (2000) 3,312,000.
Doubling time: 24 years.
Ethnic composition (1980): Arab 92.9%; Indo-Pakistani 2.5%; Somali 2.2%; other 2.4%.
Religious affiliation (1984): predominantly Sunnī Muslim.
Major city (1981): Aden 365,000.

Vital statistics

Birth rate per 1,000 population (1980–85): 47.6 (world avg. 29.0); legitimate, n.a.; illegitimate, n.a.
Death rate per 1,000 population (1980–85): 18.9 (world avg. 11.0).
Natural increase rate per 1,000 population (1980–85): 28.7 (world avg. 18.0).
Total fertility rate (avg. births per childbearing woman; 1980–85): 6.9.
Life expectancy at birth (1980–85): male 45.3 years; female 47.7 years.
Major causes of death per 100,000 population: n.a.; however, major infectious diseases are shigellosis, tuberculosis, influenza, and malaria.

National economy

Budget (1980–81). Revenue: YD86,020,000 (1973–74; import duties 33.5%, excise duties 14.1%, taxes on corporate income 12.7%, taxes on personal income 8.0%). Expenditures: YD96,020,000 (1973–74; defense and security 45.9%, education 16.9%, general administration 11.8%, economic services 6.8%, health 5.1%, public works and communications 4.7%).
Public debt (external, outstanding; 1983): U.S.$1,262,800,000.
Tourism (1981): receipts from visitors U.S.$4,000,000; expenditures by nationals abroad U.S.$10,000,000.
Production (metric tons except as noted). Agriculture, forestry, fishing (1984): millet 80,000, corn (maize) 16,000, wheat 15,000, seed cotton 15,000, lint cotton 5,000, tobacco 1,000, coffee 1,000; livestock (number of live animals) 1,380,000 goats, 1,000,000 sheep, 170,000 asses, 130,000 cattle, 100,000 camels; roundwood 270,000 cu m†; fish catch 74,124†. Mining and quarrying (1981): salt 75,000. Manufacturing (1982): nails 345; aluminum cooking utensils 300; household plastic utensils 262; textiles 2,700,000 m; shirts 332,000 units; plastic sandals 1,000,000 pairs; rubber shoes 293,000 pairs; leather shoes 157,000 pairs; soft drinks 58,000,000 bottles. Construction: n.a. Energy production (consumption): electricity (kW-hr; 1983) 280,000,000 (280,000,000); coal, none (n.a.); crude petroleum (barrels; 1983) none (16,309,000); petroleum products (metric tons; 1983) 2,218,000 (1,158,000); natural gas, none (n.a.).
Population economically active (1982): total 500,000; participation rate of total population 25.5% (female 3.0%; unemployed, n.a.).

Price and earnings indexes (1980 = 100)

	1977	1978	1979	1980	1981	1982	1983
Consumer price index	77.6	79.8	90.9	100.0	103.8	113.7	126.2
Earnings index	...	...	...	...	...	...	...

Household income and expenditure. Average household size (1980) 5.5; average annual income per household: n.a.; source of income: n.a.; expenditure: n.a.
Gross national product (1983): U.S.$1,020,000,000 (U.S.$510 per capita).

Structure of gross domestic product and labour force

	1980 in value YD'000,000	1980 % of total value	1981 labour force	1981 % of labour force
Agriculture	23.4	10.1	204,600	45.2
Mining	0.3	0.1	47,800	10.5
Manufacturing	27.6	11.9		
Construction	18.3	7.9	33,800	7.5
Public utilities	2.9	1.3		
Transportation and communication	24.0	10.4	28,900	6.4
Trade	31.1	13.5	41,700	9.2
Finance	26.2	11.4		
Pub. admin., defense	52.3	22.7		
Services	1.3	0.6	95,800	21.2
Other	23.2	10.1		
TOTAL	230.6	100.0	452,600	100.0

Land use (1983): forested 7.3%; meadows and pastures 27.3%; agricultural 0.6%; built-up, wasteland, and other 64.8%.

Foreign trade

Balance of trade (current prices)

	1977	1978	1979	1980	1981	1982	1983
YD'000,000	−105.4	−110.7	−123.8	−258.4	−280.3	−277.8	−193.8
% of total	45.8%	45.4%	27.7%	32.4%	40.0%	33.6%	38.5%

Imports (1980): YD527,400,000 (1977; machinery and transport equipment 34.8%; food and live animals 23.4%, of which wheat and wheat flour 5.0%, rice 2.7%, refined sugar 2.4%; petroleum products 18.2%; chemicals 2.9%). *Major import sources* (1984): United Arab Emirates 9.3%; United States 7.5%; United Kingdom 7.4%; Japan 7.3%; Australia 6.2%.
Exports (1980): YD269,000,000 (petroleum products 95%). *Major export destinations* (1984): India 28.1%; Italy 14.1%; Japan 10.9%; The Sudan 6.4%.

Transport and communications

Transport. Railroads: none. Roads (1984): total length 1,850 km (paved, n.a.). Vehicles (1980): passenger cars 16,500; commercial vehicles 16,300. Merchant marine (1984): vessels (100 gross tons and over) 28; total deadweight tonnage 13,455. Air transport (1980): passenger-km 84,000,000; metric ton-km cargo 1,700,000; airports (1985) with scheduled flights 2.
Communications. Daily newspapers (1984): total number 4; total circulation 25,000; circulation per 1,000 population 12.1. Radio (1984): 111,000 receivers (1 per 18.6 persons). Television (1984): 38,000 receivers (1 per 54.4 persons). Telephones (1981–82): 10,054 (1 per 200 persons).

Education and health

Education (1982)

	schools	teachers	students	student/ teacher ratio
Primary (age 7–12)	890	10,915	228,893	21.0
Secondary (age 13–18)	46	1,271	27,776	21.9
Voc., teacher tr.	13	173	1,556	9.0
Higher§		246	2,517	10.2

Educational attainment, n.a. *Literacy* (1980): total population over age 15 literate 411,900 (38.9%); males literate 354,700 (66.6%); females literate 57,200 (10.9%).
Health (1980): physicians 264 (1 per 7,390 persons); hospital beds 2,900 (1 per 641 persons); infant mortality rate per 1,000 live births (1981) 142.9.
Food (1980–82): daily per capita caloric intake 2,267 (vegetable products 85%, animal products 15%); 94% of FAO recommended minimum requirement.

Military

Total active duty personnel (1984): 27,500 (army 87.3%, navy 3.6%, air force 9.1%). *Military expenditure as percent of GNP* (1983): 17.4% (world 6.1%); per capita expenditure U.S.$82.

*Thamud is administratively part of Khāmisah governorate. †1983. ‡Customs duties less production subsidies and interest. §1977–78.

Manākhah, a town of about 1,300, in the Ḥarāz massif, Yemen (San'ā'), southwest of the capital at about 7,500 feet.

Yemen (Ṣanʿāʾ)

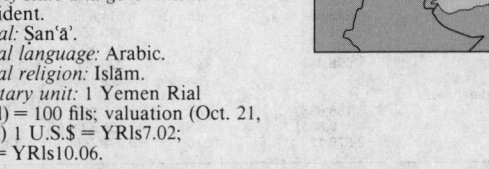

Official name: al-Jumhūrīyah al-ʿArabīyah al-Yamanīyah (Yemen Arab Republic).
Form of government: military dominated single-party republic with one legislative house (Constituent People's Assembly [159]).
Head of state and government: President.
Capital: Ṣanʿāʾ.
Official language: Arabic.
Official religion: Islām.
Monetary unit: 1 Yemen Rial (YRl) = 100 fils; valuation (Oct. 21, 1985) 1 U.S.$ = YRls7.02; 1 £ = YRls10.06.

Area and population

		area		population
Governorates	Capitals	sq mi	sq km	1980 estimate*
al-Bayḍāʾ	al-Bayḍā	4,310	11,170	182,100
al-Ḥudaydah	al-Ḥudaydah	5,240	13,580	794,300
al-Maḥwīt	al-Maḥwīt	830	2,160	195,300
Dhamār	Dhamār	3,430	8,870	506,200
Hajjah	Hajjah	3,700	9,590	450,300
Ibb	Ibb	2,480	6,430	871,700
Maʾrib	Maʾrib	15,400	39,890	76,600
Saʿdah	Saʿdah	4,950	12,810	190,300
Ṣanʿāʾ	Ṣanʿāʾ	7,840	20,310	963,900
Taʿizz	Taʿizz	4,020	10,420	981,400
TOTAL		52,210†‡	135,230‡	5,212,100

Demography

Population (1985): 6,547,000.
Density (1985): persons per sq mi 125.4, persons per sq km 48.4.
Urban–rural (1980): urban 10.2%; rural 89.8%.
Sex distribution (1980): male 47.28%; female 52.72%.
Age breakdown (1980): under 15, 45.7%; 15–29, 23.2%; 30–44, 15.1%; 45–59, 10.5%; 60–74, 4.7%; 75 and over, 0.8%.
Population projection: (1990) 7,447,000; (2000) 9,828,000.
Doubling time: 26 years.
Ethnic composition (1984): Predominantly Arabs.
Religious affiliation (1980): Shīʿah Muslim 60%; Sunnī Muslim 40%.
Major cities (1981): Ṣanʿāʾ 277,818; al-Ḥudaydah 126,386; Taʿizz 119,573.

Vital statistics

Birth rate per 1,000 population (1980–85): 48.5 (world avg. 29.0); legitimate, n.a.; illegitimate, n.a.
Death rate per 1,000 population (1980–85): 21.8 (world avg. 11.0).
Natural increase rate per 1,000 population (1980–85): 26.7 (world avg. 18.0).
Total fertility rate (avg. births per childbearing woman; 1980–85): 6.8.
Marriage rate per 1,000 population: n.a.
Divorce rate per 1,000 population: n.a.
Life expectancy at birth (1980–85): male 42.7 years; female 44.8 years.
Major causes of death per 100,000 population: n.a.; however, major infectious diseases are malaria, tuberculosis, intestinal infections, leprosy, schistosomiasis, typhoid and paratyphoid fevers, viral hepatitis, and filarial infections.

National economy

Budget (1981)§. Revenue: YRls3,282,600,000 (import duties 49.1%, income from property 13.9%, stamp tax 11.0%, excise duties 7.1%, income tax 5.2%). Expenditures: YRls6,219,900,000 (defense 32.6%, general public services 18.6%, education 14.0%, roads 6.5%, health 3.6%).
Public debt (external, outstanding; 1983): U.S.$1,573,900,000.
Production (metric tons except as noted). Agriculture, forestry, fishing (1984): sorghum 525,000, vegetables and melons 311,000, fruits 167,000, roots and tubers 160,000, potatoes 160,000, grapes 73,000, wheat 50,000, corn (maize) 50,000, barley 50,000, pulses 40,000, tobacco 7,000, dates 6,000, sesame seed 6,000, coffee 3,000, cotton lint 2,000, sugarcane 1,000, honey 300,000, milk 60,000, eggs 11,828; livestock (number of live animals) 2,227,000 goats, 1,823,000 sheep, 950,000 cattle, 520,000 asses, 60,000 camels; fish catch 12,200 ‖. Mining and quarrying (1981): salt 64,000; rock 567,000 cu m. Manufacturing (1981): cement 85,000; domestic utensils 1,600; textile fabric 3,135,000 m. Construction (value added in YRls; 1982): 1,161,000,000. Energy production (consumption): electricity (kW-hr; 1983) 285,000,000 (285,000,000); coal, none (n.a.); crude petroleum, none (n.a.); petroleum products (metric tons; 1983) none (835,000,000); natural gas, none (n.a.).
Population economically active (1982): total 1,668,000; participation rate of total population 22.7% (female 11.0%; unemployed, n.a.).

Price and earnings indexes (1980 = 100)

	1977	1978	1979	1980	1981	1982	1983
Consumer price index	67.0	75.0	95.0	100.0	105.0	108.0	114.0
Earnings index	...	...	...	...	...	...	...

Household income and expenditure. Average household size (1980) 5.8; average annual income per household: n.a.; source of income: n.a.; expenditure: n.a.

Tourism (1983): receipts from visitors U.S.$20,000,000; expenditures by nationals abroad U.S.$72,000,000.
Gross national product (at current market prices; 1983): U.S.$3,930,000,000 (U.S.$510 per capita).

Structure of gross domestic product and labour force

	1981		1975	
	in value YRls'000,000	% of total value	labour force	% of labour force
Agriculture	3,690	28.5	830,340	73.6
Mining	156	1.2	580	0.1
Manufacturing	770	5.9	33,920	3.0
Construction	1,140	8.8	52,640	4.7
Public utilities	89	0.7	1,510	0.1
Transportation and communication	483	3.7	24,710	2.2
Trade	2,263	17.5	68,980	6.1
Finance			1,980	0.2
Pub. admin., defense	4,358	33.7	...	...
Services			85,780	7.6
Other			27,330	2.4
TOTAL	12,949	100.0	1,127,770	100.0

Land use (1983): forested 8.2%; meadows and pastures 35.9%; agricultural and under permanent cultivation 14.3%; other 41.6%.

Foreign trade

Balance of trade (current prices)

	1977	1978	1979	1980	1981	1982
YRls'000,000	−4,075	−5,062	−5,857	−8,351	−6,759	−6,763
% of total	97.6%	98.8%	97.9%	−97.6%	94.0%	95.0%

Imports (1981): YRls7,340,400,000 (food and live animals 29.7%, machinery and transport equipment 25.4%, manufactured goods 22.2%, chemical products 5.6%, beverages and tobacco 1.4%). *Major import sources:* Japan 17.7%; Saudi Arabia 12.4%; France 8.8%; Italy 5.5%; West Germany 5.3%; Singapore 4.5%; Ireland 4.5%; China 4.1%; United Kingdom 3.6%; The Netherlands 3.6%; Australia 2.5%; Greece 2.1%; India 1.3%; United States 1.3%.
Exports (1981): YRls216,600,000 (machinery and transport equipment 64.5%, food and live animals 20.9%, manufactured goods 6.1%, beverages and tobacco 0.5%). *Major export destinations:* Yemen (Aden) 23.2%; Pakistan 19.3%; France 14.0%; United Arab Emirates 8.6%; Saudi Arabia 7.8%; West Germany 4.6%; United States 3.0%; The Netherlands 2.5%.

Transport and communications

Transport. Railroads: none. Roads (1984): total length 22,625 mi, 36,412 km (paved 6%). Vehicles (1984): passenger cars 105,506; trucks and buses 152,473. Merchant marine (1984): vessels (100 gross tons and over) 10; total deadweight tonnage 1,850. Air transport (1984): passenger-mi 363,087,000, passenger-km 584,333,000; short ton-mi cargo 5,373,000, metric ton-km cargo 7,844,000; airports (1985) with scheduled flights 6.
Communications. Daily newspapers (1984): total number 2; total circulation, n.a.; circulation per 1,000 population, n.a. Radio (1984): total number of receivers 110,000 (1 per 58.1 persons). Television (1984): total number of receivers 27,000 (1 per 236.5 persons). Telephones (1981): 90,350 (1 per 65.8 persons).

Education and health

Education (1980–81)

	schools	teachers	students	student/ teacher ratio
Primary (age 7–12)	2,985	9,826	412,573	39.0
Secondary (age 13–18)	314	2,023	28,852	14.3
Voc., teacher tr.	29	196	4,023	20.5
Higher	...	157	4,220	26.9

Educational attainment (1975). Percent of adult population over age 25 having: no formal schooling, c. 99%; primary education, less than 1%. *Literacy* (1980): total population over age 15 literate 350,600 (8.3%); males literate 340,100 (15.9%); females literate 10,500 (0.5%).
Health: physicians (1981) 896 (1 per 6,629 persons); hospital beds (1983) 4,000 (1 per 1,900 persons); infant mortality rate per 1,000 live births (1980–85) 154.
Food (1980–82): daily per capita caloric intake 2,328 (vegetable products 89%, animal products 11%); 94% of FAO recommended minimum requirement.

Military

Total active duty personnel (1984): 36,550 (army 95.8%, navy 1.5%, air force 2.7%). *Military expenditure as percent of GNP* (1983): 15.4% (world 6.1%); per capita expenditure U.S.$100.

*Population estimate according to the Swiss Technical Co-operation Service. †Detail does not add to total given because of rounding. ‡Area shown is according to the Swiss Technical Co-operation Service. The major part of the eastern boundary with Saudi Arabia and Yemen (Aden) is not officially defined and demarcated; however, the government of Yemen (Ṣanʿāʾ) uses a higher estimate of 77,200 sq mi (200,000 sq km). §1982–83 estimated budget was: revenue YRls5,460,000; expenditure YRls8,720,000. ‖ 1983.

Yugoslavia

Official name: Socijalistična
Federativna Republika Jugoslavija
(Slovenian); Socijalistička Federativna
Republika Jugoslavija (Macedonian,
Serbo-Croatian) (Socialist Federal
Republic of Yugoslavia).
Form of government: single-party
federal socialist republic with two
legislative houses (Chamber of
Republics and Provinces [88] and
Federal Chamber [220]).
Head of state and government: President.
Capital: Belgrade.
Official languages: Slovenian;
Macedonian; Serbo-Croatian.
Official religion: none.
Monetary unit: 1 Yugoslav dinar
(Din) = 100 paras; valuation
(Oct. 21, 1985) 1 U.S.$ = Din285.33;
1 £ = Din409.17.

Area and population

Socialist republics	Capitals	area sq mi	area sq km	population 1984 estimate
Bosnia and Hercegovina	Sarajevo	19,741	51,129	4,466,000
Croatia	Zagreb	21,829	56,538	4,648,000
Macedonia	Skopje	9,928	25,713	2,025,000
Montenegro	Titograd	5,333	13,812	623,000
Serbia	Belgrade	21,609	55,968	5,627,000
Slovenia	Ljubljana	7,819	20,251	1,866,000
Autonomous provinces*				
Kosovo	Priština	4,203	10,887	1,770,000
Vojvodina	Novi Sad	8,304	21,506	2,028,000
TOTAL		98,766	255,804	23,053,000

Demography

Population (1985): 23,235,000.
Density (1985): persons per sq mi 235.3, persons per sq km 90.8.
Urban–rural (1981): urban 46.5%; rural 53.5%.
Sex distribution (1981): male 44.43%; female 55.57%.
Age breakdown (1981): under 15, 24.5%; 15–29, 25.0%; 30–44, 19.8%; 45–59, 18.3%; 60–74, 8.9%; 75 and over, 3.1%; unknown, 0.4%.
Population projection: (1990) 24,107,000; (2000) 25,653,000.
Doubling time: 87 years.
Ethnic composition (1981): Serb 36.3%; Croat 19.7%; Bosnian Muslim 8.9%; Slovenian 7.8%; Albanian 7.7%; Macedonian 6.0%; Montenegrin 2.6%; other 11.0%.
Religious affiliation (1980): Serbian Orthodox 34.6%; Roman Catholic 26.0%; Crypto-Christian 11.3%; Muslim 10.4%; other 17.7%.
Major cities (1981): Belgrade 1,470,073; Osijek 867,646; Zagreb 768,700; Niš 643,470; Skopje 506,547.

Vital statistics

Birth rate per 1,000 population (1984): 16.4 (world avg. 29.0); (1981) legitimate 91.7%; illegitimate 8.3%.
Death rate per 1,000 population (1984): 9.3 (world avg. 11.0).
Natural increase rate per 1,000 population (1984): 7.1 (world avg. 18.0).
Total fertility rate (avg. births per childbearing woman; 1983): 2.1.
Marriage rate per 1,000 population (1984): 7.3.
Divorce rate per 1,000 population (1984): 0.9.
Life expectancy at birth (1981): male 67.7 years; female 73.1 years.
Major causes of death per 100,000 population (1981): diseases of the circulatory system 437.4; malignant neoplasms (cancers) 136.0; accidents 64.0; diseases of the respiratory system 56.3; diseases of the digestive system 38.7.

National economy

Budget (1983). Revenue: Din262,077,500,000 (share in profit of state enterprises 79.9%, import duties 17.0%, other revenue 3.1%). Expenditures: Din261,504,600,000 (education 59.1%, social welfare and health 21.0%, administration 5.8%).
Public debt (external, outstanding; 1983): U.S.$11,283,200,000.
Tourism: receipts from visitors (1983) U.S.$929,000,000; expenditures by nationals abroad (1981) U.S.$143,000,000.
Production (metric tons except as noted). Agriculture (1984): corn (maize) 11,265,000, sugar beets 6,710,000, wheat 5,596,000, potatoes 2,300,000, grapes 1,560,000, plums 991,000, barley 748,000, apples 557,000, oats 256,000, sunflower seeds 160,000, rye 81,000, tobacco 75,000, rice 36,000; livestock (number of live animals) 9,337,000 pigs, 7,458,000 sheep, 5,341,000 cattle, 74,000,000 poultry; roundwood 15,329,000 cu m†; fish catch 79,765,000†. Mining and quarrying (1984): copper ore 24,500,000; iron ore 5,316,000; lead and zinc ore 4,063,000†; bauxite 3,500,000; antimony 65,000; manganese 28,000; silver (refined) 110. Manufacturing (1984): cement 9,312,000; pig iron and crude steel 6,750,000; rolled steel 4,586,000; pulp and paper 1,768,000†; sulfuric acid 1,470,000; plastics and resins 499,000†; automobile tires 9,864,000 units; radio and television receivers 691,000 units†; leather 18,040,000 sq m†; cotton fabrics 381,000,000 sq m†. Construction (1982): residential 9,965,000 sq m; industrial 997,000 sq m; commercial 833,000 sq m. Energy production (consumption): electricity (kW-hr; 1984) 71,571,000,000 (72,626,000,000); coal (metric tons; 1984) 56,200,000 (51,900,000); crude petroleum (barrels; 1984) 29,600,000 (106,-

285,000); petroleum products (metric tons; 1983) 12,337,000 (12,906,000); natural gas (cu m; 1983) 2,090,000,000 (5,142,000,000).
Gross national product (1983): U.S.$38,979,000,000, U.S.$1,710 per capita.

Structure of gross domestic product and labour force

	1982 in value Din'000,000	1982 % of total value	1982 labour force	1982 % of labour force
Agriculture	399,203	15.5	3,638,000	36.9
Mining	57,962	2.3	197,400	2.0
Manufacturing	882,367	34.2	2,165,800	21.9
Construction	243,582	9.5	611,600	6.2
Public utilities	21,849	0.8	115,300	1.2
Transp. and commun.	167,279	6.5	415,500	4.2
Trade	606,441	23.5	822,300	8.3
Finance	...	...	209,100	2.1
Pub. admin., defense, and services	188,636	7.3	1,199,200	12.2
Other	8,805‡	0.3‡	496,500†§	5.0†§
TOTAL	2,576,124 ‖	100.0	9,870,700	100.0

Population economically active (1982): total 9,870,745; participation rate of population ages 15–64, 67.0% (female 38.0%, unemployed 12.8%).

Price and earnings indexes (1980 = 100)

	1979	1980	1981	1982	1983	1984	1985¶
Consumer price index	77.0	100.0	139.7	185.7	258.4	401.6	627.1
Monthly earnings index	82.0	100.0	137.0	175.0	223.0	324.0	499.0

Household income and expenditure. Average household size (1982) 3.6; income per household Din232,600 (U.S.$3,700); sources of income: wages and salaries 69.7%, welfare 15.4%, other 14.9%; expenditure (1982): food 39.6%, transportation 11.6%, beverages and tobacco 10.6%, clothing and footwear 10.5%, housing 9.5%, household utilities 8.8%, recreation 6.0%, health 3.4%.
Land use (1983): forested 36.6%; meadows and pastures 25.0%; agricultural and under permanent cultivation 30.6%; other 7.8%.

Foreign trade

Balance of trade (current prices)

	1979	1980	1981	1982	1983	1984
Din'000,000,000	−100.7	−117.2	−114.4	−98.5	−119.6	+116.0
% of total	29.0%	20.7%	12.9%	8.6%	6.0%	3.5%

Imports (1983): Din1,062,910,000,000 (mineral fuels and lubricants 27.2%; machinery and transport equipment 24.0%, of which nonelectric machinery 14.2%, transport equipment 4.7%; chemicals 14.5%; iron and steel 5.5%; textile yarn and fabrics 5.4%; food products 4.7%). *Major import sources:* U.S.S.R. 20.3%; West Germany 13.4%; Italy 8.1%; United States 6.4%; Czechoslovakia 5.6%; Austria 3.6%; France 3.4%; East Germany 3.4%.
Exports (1983): Din943,330,000,000 (nonelectric machinery 11.5%; clothing and footwear 10.4%; electrical machinery 10.1%; chemicals 9.7%; transport equipment 9.6%; food products 9.6%; nonferrous metals 5.1%; textile yarn and fabrics 4.1%; furniture 3.2%). *Major export destinations:* U.S.S.R. 27.2%; Italy 8.1%; West Germany 8.1%; Czechoslovakia 6.5%.

Transport and communications

Transport. Railroads (1984): length 9,389 km; passenger-km 11,500,000,000; metric ton-km cargo 28,476,000,000. Roads (1984): total length 116,460 km (paved 53%). Vehicles (1984): passenger cars 2,770,739; trucks and buses 244,770. Merchant marine (1984): vessels (100 gross tons and over) 480; total deadweight tonnage 4,130,690. Air transport (1983): passenger-km 4,901,000,000; metric ton-km cargo 85,416,000; airports (1985) 16.
Communications. Daily newspapers (1984): 27; total circulation 2,419,000; circulation per 1,000 population 104. Radio (1983): total receivers 4,689,000 (1 per 4.9 persons). Television (1983): total receivers 4,001,000 (1 per 5.7 persons). Telephones (1983): 2,796,000 (1 per 8.2 persons).

Education and health

Education (1982–83)

	schools	teachers	students	student/ teacher ratio
Primary (age 7–14)	12,413	133,661	2,807,220	21.0
Secondary (age 15–18)	28,820♀	64,783	987,481	15.2
Higher	357δ	24,905	386,356	15.5

Educational attainment (1981). Percent of total population over age 15 having: less than full primary education 44.1%; primary 24.8%; secondary 25.5%; higher 5.6%. *Literacy* (1981): total population over age 15 literate 16,945,900 (90.5%); males 95.9%; females 85.3%.
Health (1982): physicians 35,245 (1 per 642 persons); hospital beds 138,340 (1 per 164 persons); infant mortality rate per 1,000 live births (1983) 31.7.
Food (1980–82): daily per capita caloric intake 3,643 (vegetable products 78%, animal products 22%); 144% of FAO recommended minimum requirement.

Military

Total active duty personnel (1984): 239,700 (army 79.7%, navy 5.0%, air force 15.3%). *Military expenditure as percent of GNP* (1983): 3.7% (world 6.1%); per capita expenditure U.S.$97.

*The autonomous provinces are administratively part of the Socialist Republic of Serbia. †1983. ‡Includes operation of irrigation systems, water works, and supply. §Includes private sector and noneconomic activities. ‖ At current prices. ¶April. ♀Classes. δIncludes 215 university faculties.

Zaire

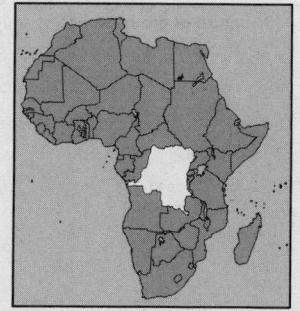

Official name: République du Zaïre (Republic of Zaire).
Form of government: single party republic with one legislative house (National Legislative Council [310]).
Head of state and government: President.
Capital: Kinshasa.
Official language: French.
Official religion: none.
Monetary unit: 1 zaire (Z) = 100 makuta (singular likuta) = 10,000 sengi; valuation (Oct. 21, 1985) 1 U.S.$ = Z53.12; 1 £ = Z76.18.

Area and population

Regions	Capitals	area sq mi	area sq km	population 1981 estimate
Bandundu	Bandundu	114,154	295,658	4,119,500
Bas-Zaire	Matadi	20,819	53,920	1,921,500
Equateur	Mbandaka	155,712	403,293	3,418,300
Haut-Zaire	Kisangani	194,302	503,239	4,541,600
Kasai Occidental	Kananga	60,605	156,967	2,935,000
Kasai Oriental	Mbuji-Mayi	64,949	168,216	2,337,000
Kivu	Bukavu	99,098	256,662	4,713,800
Shaba (Katanga)	Lubumbashi	191,879	496,965	3,823,200
Neutral City				
Kinshasa		3,848	9,965	2,338,200
TOTAL		905,365*	2,344,885	30,148,100

Demography

Population (1985): 33,052,000.
Density (1985): persons per sq mi 36.5, persons per sq km 14.1.
Urban–rural (1985): urban 44.2%; rural 55.8%.
Sex distribution (1985): male 49.30%; female 50.70%.
Age breakdown (1985): under 15, 45.2%; 15–29, 26.0%; 30–44, 15.5%; 45–59, 8.7%; 60–74, 3.9%; 75 and over, 0.7%.
Population projection: (1990) 38,445,000; (2000) 52,410,000.
Doubling time: 23 years.
Ethnic composition (1980): Luba 18.0%; Kongo 16.3%; Mongo 13.3%; Rwanda 10.0%; Azande 6.3%; Bangi and Ngale 6.1%; Mande 3.2%; Teke 3.0%; Banda 2.5%; Boa 2.5%; Chokwe 2.3%; other 16.5%.
Religious affiliation (1980): Roman Catholic 48.4%; Protestant 29.0%; indigenous Christian 17.1%; traditional beliefs 3.4%; Muslim 1.4%; other 0.7%.
Major cities (1976): Kinshasa 2,338,200†; Kananga 704,211; Lubumbashi 451,332; Mbuji-Mayi 382,632; Kisangani 339,210.

Vital statistics

Birth rate per 1,000 population (1980–85): 45.2 (world avg. 29.0); legitimate, n.a.; illegitimate, n.a.
Death rate per 1,000 population (1980–85): 15.8 (world avg. 11.0).
Natural increase rate per 1,000 population (1980–85): 29.4 (world avg. 18.0).
Total fertility rate (avg. births per childbearing woman; 1980–85): 6.1.
Marriage rate per 1,000 population (1977): 0.07‡.
Divorce rate per 1,000 population (1977): 0.02.
Life expectancy at birth (1980–85): male 48.3 years; female 51.7 years.
Major causes of death per 100,000 population§ (1977): measles 9.6; meningitis 1.1; influenza 0.4; whooping cough 0.3.

National economy

Budget ‖ (1984). Revenue: Z19,800,000,000 (direct and indirect taxes 84.3%, government investments 10.9%, administrative and judicial receipts 4.7%). Expenditures: Z21,600,000,000 (service of external debt 37.5%, government salaries 21.3%, service of internal debt 7.9%).
Public debt (external, outstanding; 1983): U.S.$4,022,000,000.
Tourism (1981): receipts from visitors U.S.$23,000,000; expenditures by nationals abroad, n.a.
Production (metric tons except as noted). Agriculture, forestry, fishing (1984): cassava 14,800,000, fruit excluding melons 2,510,000, plantains 1,480,000, vegetables and melons 803,000, sugarcane 700,000, corn (maize) 680,000, peanuts (groundnuts) 380,000, bananas 325,000, sweet potatoes 320,000, rice 260,000, potatoes 220,000, papayas 160,000, pineapples 160,000, pulses 157,000, mangoes 145,000, coffee 80,000, cotton lint 26,000, natural rubber 24,000, cocoa beans 6,000; livestock (number of live animals) 1,300,000 cattle, 760,000 pigs, 760,000 sheep, 291,000 goats, 17,000,000 chickens; roundwood 31,265,000 cu m¶; fish catch 102,000¶. Mining and quarrying (1983): copper 535,000; zinc 74,700; cobalt 11,300; manganese 4,000º; tin 3,000; silver 2,000,000 troy oz; gold 60,000 troy oz; industrial diamonds 8,266,000 carats; gem diamonds 3,172,000 carats. Manufacturing (1983): corn flour 120,360; cotton textiles 61,000,000 sq m; cigarettes 3,472,000,000 units; mattresses 2,896 units; beer 3,069,000 hectolitres; carbonated beverages 819,865 hectolitres; leather shoes 623,000 pairs. Construction (1982): residential 1,105,000 sq m; nonresidential 45,000 sq m. Energy production (consumption): electricity (kW-hr; 1983) 4,213,000,000 (4,143,000,000); coal (metric tons; 1983) 130,000 (165,000); crude petroleum (barrels; 1983) 8,273,000 (3,285,000); petroleum products (metric tons; 1983) 442,000 (894,000); natural gas, none (n.a.).
Household income and expenditure. Average household size (1982) 6.0; average annual income per household Z1,200 (U.S.$209); sources of income:

wages and salaries, small-scale trading; expenditure (1982): food 60%, other 40%.
Gross national product (at current market prices; 1983): U.S.$5,050,000,000 (U.S.$160 per capita).

Structure of gross domestic product and labour force

	1982 in value Z'000,000	% of total value	labour force	% of labour force
Agriculture	11,174.4	35.7	8,712,000	70.0
Mining	3,593.2	11.5	622,000	5.0
Manufacturing	715.4	2.3	1,244,000	10.0
Construction	1,884.3	6.0		
Public utilities	12.0	δ		
Transportation and communication	598.5	1.9		
Trade	6,644.6	21.2	1,867,000	15.0
Finance				
Pub. admin., defense	5,778.5	18.5		
Services				
Other	895.0□	2.9		
TOTAL	31,295.9◇	100.0	12,445,000	100.0

Population economically active (1984): total 13,145,000; participation rate of total population 41.0% (female [1981] 42.5%; unemployed, n.a.).

Price and earnings indexes (1980 = 100)

	1979	1980	1981	1982	1983	1984	1985△
Consumer price index	70.4	100.0	134.9	183.8	325.5	495.6	601.1
Monthly earnings index	...	...	...	...	...	...	...

Land use (1983): forested 77.9%; meadows and pastures 4.1%; agricultural and under permanent cultivation 2.8%; other 15.2%.

Foreign trade†

Balance of trade (current prices)

	1979	1980	1981	1982	1983	1984
Z'000,000	+1,569.4	+2,226	−565.6	−445.4	+7,102.7	+11,554.3
% of total	42.8%	32.3%	10.6%	9.0%	34.2%	18.9%

Imports (1982): Z2,759,775,000 (primary manufactures and semifinished products 22.0%; energy 13.0%; consumer goods 11.0%, of which food and tobacco products 5.6%, textiles and clothing 1.0%). *Major import sources:* Belgium–Luxembourg 40.2%; France 24.2%; United States and Canada 19.6%; West Germany 14.6%; Japan 9.0%.
Exports (1982): Z9,924,719,000 (copper 42.4%; industrial products 15.5%; crude petroleum 14.7%; cobalt 9.7%; coffee 6.2%; diamonds 4.4%). *Major export destinations:* United States 36.0%; Belgium–Luxembourg 31.0%; France 6.0%.

Transport and communications

Transport. Railroads (1983): length 3,263 mi, 5,252 km; passenger-mi 231,000,000⊕, passenger-km 372,000,000⊕; short ton-mi cargo 1,274,000,000⊕, metric ton-km cargo 1,860,000,000⊕. Roads (1980): total length 28,379 mi, 45,671 km (paved 18%). Vehicles (1980): passenger cars 89,471; trucks and buses 16,807. Merchant marine (1984): vessels (100 gross tons and over) 33; total deadweight tonnage 121,416. Air transport (1983): passenger-mi 365,000,000, passenger-km 588,000,000; short ton-mi cargo 20,121,000, metric ton-km cargo 29,376,000; airports (1985) with scheduled flights 33.
Communications. Daily newspapers (1983): total number 4; total circulation 45,000; circulation per 1,000 population 1.4. Radio (1984): total number of receivers 500,000 (1 per 64.2 persons). Television (1984): total number of receivers 12,500 (1 per 2,567 persons). Telephones (1983): 27,770 (1 per 1,122 persons).

Education and health

Education (1978–79)

	schools**	teachers**	students	student/ teacher ratio
Primary (age 6–11)	7,909	132,759	3,919,395	...
Secondary (age 12–17)	2,511	42,212	611,349	...
Voc., teacher tr.	20	††	192,329**	...
Higher	36	2,782	28,430	10.2

Educational attainment, n.a. *Literacy* (1980): total population over age 15 literate 8,580,000 (54.5%); males literate 5,579,000 (73.6%); females literate 2,996,000 (36.7%).
Health (1979): physicians 1,900 (1 per 14,585 persons); hospital beds 79,244 (1 per 350 persons); infant mortality rate per 1,000 live births (1980–85) 107.
Food (1980–82): daily per capita caloric intake 2,155 (vegetable products 97%, animal products 3%); 97% of FAO recommended minimum requirement.

Military

Total active duty personnel (1984): 26,000 (army 84.6%, navy 5.8%, air force 9.6%). *Military expenditure as percent of GNP* (1983): 1.5% (world 6.1%); per capita expenditure U.S.$2.

*Detail does not add to total given because of rounding. †1981 estimate. ‡Registered marriages only. §Infectious diseases only. ‖ Budget for 1985 was: revenue Z30,700,000,000 (no breakdown available); expenditures Z34,700,000,000 (no breakdown available). ¶1983. º1982. δLess than 0.1%. □Import taxes and duties less imputed bank service charge. ◇At current prices. △July. †Import figures are f.o.b. (free on board) in balance of trade and c.i.f. (cost, insurance, and freight) for commodities and trading partners. ⊕Figure is for services operated by the Zaire National Railways (SNCZ), which controls more than 90% of the country's total rail facility. **1977–78. ††Included with secondary.

Zambia

Official name: Republic of Zambia.
Form of government: republic with
one legislative house (National
Assembly [136]).
Head of state and government:
President.
Capital: Lusaka.
Official language: English.
Official religion: none.
Monetary unit: 1 Zambian kwacha
(K) = 100 ngwee; valuation (Oct. 21,
1985) 1 U.S.$ = K5.72; 1 £ = K8.20.

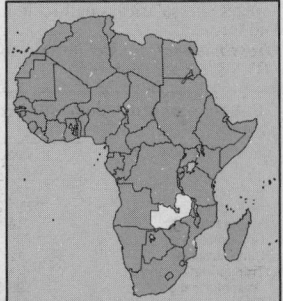

Area and population

| | | area | | population |
Provinces	Capitals	sq mi	sq km	1980 census
Central	Kabwe	36,446	94,395	513,835
Copperbelt	Ndola	12,096	31,328	1,248,888
Eastern	Chipata	26,682	69,106	656,381
Luapula	Mansa	19,524	50,567	412,798
Lusaka	Lusaka	8,454	21,896	693,878
Northern	Kasama	57,076	147,826	677,894
North-Western	Solwezi	48,582	125,827	301,677
Southern	Livingstone	32,928	85,283	686,469
Western	Mongu	48,798	126,386	487,988
TOTAL		290,586	752,614	5,679,808

Demography

Population (1985): 6,666,000.
Density (1985): persons per sq mi 22.9, persons per sq km 8.9.
Urban–rural (1980): urban 43.0%; rural 57.0%.
Sex distribution (1984): male 49.48%; female 50.52%.
Age breakdown (1984): under 15, 46.5%; 15–29, 26.5%; 30–44, 14.6%; 45–59,
8.2%; 60–74, 3.6%; 75 and over, 0.6%.
Population projection: (1990) 7,611,000; (2000) 10,276,000.
Doubling time: 23 years.
Ethnic composition (1980): Bemba 34.3%; Tonga 16.3%; Malawi 13.7%; Lozi
9.3%; Lunda 6.3%; Luena 5.0%; other 15.1%.
Religious affiliation (1980): Christian 72.0%, of whom Protestant 31.9%,
Roman Catholic 26.2%, African Christian 8.3%; traditional beliefs 27.0%;
Muslim 0.3%; other 0.7%.
Major cities (1980): Lusaka 538,469; Kitwe 314,794; Ndola 282,439; Luan-
shya 184,000; Mufulira 149,778.

Vital statistics

Birth rate per 1,000 population (1980–85): 47.4 (world avg. 29.0); legitimate,
n.a.; illegitimate, n.a.
Death rate per 1,000 population (1980–85): 15.4 (world avg. 11.0).
Natural increase rate per 1,000 population (1980–85): 32.0 (world avg. 18.0).
Total fertility rate (avg. births per childbearing woman; 1980–85): 6.9.
Marriage rate per 1,000 population: n.a.
Divorce rate per 1,000 population: n.a.
Life expectancy at birth (1980–85): male 49.1 years; female 52.5 years.
Major causes of death per 100,000 population: n.a.; however, major diseases
are avitaminosis and nutritional deficiencies and infectious and parasitic
diseases.

National economy

Budget (1983). Revenue: K1,163,200,000 (customs duties and excise taxes
55.1%, income tax 33.8%). Expenditures: K1,417,200,000 (constitutional
and statutory expenditures 27.6%, rural development 12.8%, education
10.4%, health 8.3%, police 4.5%).
Public debt (external, outstanding; 1983): U.S.$2,638,000,000.
Tourism: receipts from visitors (1983) U.S.$43,000,000; expenditures by na-
tionals abroad (1982) U.S.$43,000,000.
Production (metric tons except as noted). Agriculture, forestry, fishing
(1984): sugarcane 1,100,000, corn (maize) 857,000, fruits and vegetables
321,000 (of which tomatoes 26,000, onions 26,000, oranges 3,000), cassava
210,000, sunflower seeds 40,000, sweet potatoes 22,000, peanuts (groundnuts) 19,000, lint cotton 15,000, sorghum 14,000, millet 13,000, pulses
5,000, tobacco 3,000; livestock (number of live animals) 2,400,000 cattle,
355,000 goats, 255,000 pigs, 42,000 sheep, 19,000,000 chickens; roundwood
4,971,000*; fish catch 67,234*. Mining and quarrying (1984): copper 523,-
000; zinc 38,000; lead 15,800; cobalt 2,500; gold 10,160 oz*. Manufacturing
(1983): cement 392,000; sulfuric acid 271,000; raw sugar 132,000; nitrogen
fertilizer 86,013. Construction (value in K; 1982): residential 74,200,000;
nonresidential 79,700,000. Energy production (consumption): electricity
(kW-hr; 1983) 10,071,000,000 (6,891,000,000); coal (metric tons; 1984) 468,-
000 (468,000); crude petroleum (barrels; 1983) none (5,110,000); petroleum
products (metric tons; 1983) 700,000 (676,000); natural gas, none (none).
Population economically active (1983): total 2,263,000; participation rate of
total population 35.5% (female [1982] 17.1%, unemployed [1981] 0.9%).

Price and earnings indexes (1980 = 100)

	1979	1980	1981	1982	1983	1984	1985†
Consumer price index	89.5	100.0	114.0	128.2	153.4	184.1	240.3
Monthly earnings index	83.3	100.0	...	...	...	...	...

Gross national product (at current market prices; 1984): U.S.$2,643,000,000
(U.S.$397 per capita).

Structure of gross domestic product and labour force

| | 1983 | | | |
	in value K'000,000	% of total value	labour force	% of labour force
Agriculture	590.9	14.0	1,462,000	64.6
Mining	654.7	15.5	57,700	2.5
Manufacturing	784.4	18.6	48,800	2.2
Construction	93.6	2.2	32,100	1.4
Public utilities	81.7	1.9	7,800	0.3
Transportation and communication	237.6	5.6	23,900	1.1
Trade	510.2	12.1	30,300	1.3
Finance	306.2	7.3	22,100	1.0
Services	831.6‡	19.7‡	578,300‡	25.6‡
Other	131.2§	3.1§		
TOTAL	4,222.1 ‖	100.0	2,263,000	100.0

Household income and expenditure. Average household size (1981) 5.8; average annual income per household K1,041 (U.S.$908); sources of income:
wages and salaries 94.0%, other 6.0%; expenditure (1977): food 37.7%, housing 11.0%, clothing 8.3%, transportation 4.3%, education 2.1%, health 1.0%.
Land use (1983): forested 27.2%; meadows and pastures 47.2%; agricultural
and under permanent cultivation 7.0%; other 18.6%.

Foreign trade

Balance of trade (current prices)

	1979	1980	1981	1982	1983	1984
K'000,000	496.2	163.3	25.3	36.5	195.7	75.9
% of total	29.5%	8.3%	1.4%	1.9%	10.3%	3.3%

Imports (1981): K911,300,000 (machinery and transport equipment 34.0%;
mineral fuels, lubricants, and electricity 21.9%; basic manufactures 18.8%;
chemicals 13.7%; food 5.5%). *Major import sources:* United Kingdom
15.6%; South Africa 15.1%; United States 8.3%; West Germany 7.8%; Japan
6.0%; China 0.6%.
Exports (1982): K936,600,000 (copper 89.2%; cobalt 4.2%; zinc 2.0%; lead
0.5%). *Major export destinations:* Japan 19.4%; United Kingdom 7.5%;
United States 6.5%; West Germany 4.3%; China 1.0%; South Africa 0.6%.

Transport and communications

Transport. Railroads (1983): length 1,360 mi, 2,188 km; passengers 1,570,-
000¶; short ton cargo 5,946,000, metric ton cargo 5,394,000♀. Roads (1983):
total length 23,135 mi, 37,232 km (paved 15%). Vehicles (1982): passenger cars 105,783; trucks and buses 94,780. Merchant marine: vessels (100
gross tons and over) none. Air transport (1984): passenger-mi 343,000,000,
passenger-km 552,000,000; short ton-mi cargo 50,643,000†, metric ton-km
cargo 73,937,000†; airports (1985) with scheduled flights 14.
Communications. Daily newspapers (1984): total number 2; total circulation 109,000; circulation per 1,000 population 16.4. Radio (1983): total
number of receivers 150,000 (1 per 41 persons). Television (1984): total
number of receivers 76,000 (1 per 82 persons). Telephones (1981): 61,000
(1 per 91 persons).

Education and health

Education (1982)

	schools	teachers	students	student/ teacher ratio
Primary (age 7–13)	2,894	23,870	1,121,769	47.0
Secondary (age 14–18)	142	4,602	104,859	22.8
Voc., teacher tr.	28	406§	9,711	...
Higher	1	334§	3,648	...

Educational attainment (1969). Percent of adult population over age 14 having: no formal schooling 51.4%; primary education 39.3%; secondary 6.5%;
higher 0.5%; other 2.3%. *Literacy* (1980): total population literate 2,128,500
(68.6%); males literate 1,207,300 (79.3%); females literate 921,200 (58.3%).
Health (1982): physicians 839 (1 per 7,186 persons); hospital beds 21,257 (1
per 292 persons); infant mortality rate per 1,000 live births (1980–85) 110.6.
Food (1980–82): daily per capita caloric intake 2,124 (vegetable products
94%, animal products 6%); 92% of FAO recommended minimum daily
requirement.

Military

Total active duty personnel (1984): 14,300 (army 87.4%; navy, none; air force
12.6%). *Military expenditure as percent of GNP* (1980): 3.8% (world 5.6%);
per capita expenditure U.S.$21.

*1983. †June. ‡Public administration and defense are included with services. §In-
cludes import duties and bank service charges. ‖ At current prices. ¶1980. ♀1979.
♂1981.

Zimbabwe

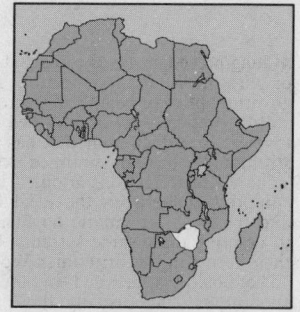

Official name: Republic of Zimbabwe.
Form of government: unitary multiparty republic with two legislative houses [Senate [40]; House of Assembly [100]).
Chief of state: President.
Head of government: Prime Minister.
Capital: Harare.
Official language: English.
Official religion: none.
Monetary unit: 1 Zimbabwe Dollar (Z$) = 100 cents; valuation (Oct. 21, 1985) 1 U.S.$ = Z$1.68; 1 £ = Z$2.41.

Area and population

Provinces	Capitals	area sq mi	area sq km	population 1982 census
Manicaland	Mutare	13,598	35,219	1,096,000
Mashonaland Central	Mount Darwin	11,383	29,482	563,000
Mashonaland East	Harare	10,353	26,813	1,491,000
Mashonaland West	Kadoma	21,520	55,737	859,000
Masvingo (Victoria)	Masvingo	21,536	55,777	1,034,000
Matabeleland North	Bulawayo	29,658	76,813	880,000
Matabeleland South	Gwanda	21,213	54,941	517,000
Midlands	Gweru	21,613	55,977	1,092,000
TOTAL		150,873*	390,759	7,532,000

Demography

Population (1985): 8,100,000.
Density (1985): persons per sq mi 53.7, persons per sq km 20.7.
Urban–rural (1983): urban 24.0%; rural 76.0%.
Sex distribution (1983): male 49.22%; female 50.78%.
Age breakdown (1983): under 15, 50.9%; 15–29, 26.3%; 30–44, 13.4%; 45–59, 6.5%; 60–74, 1.2%; 75 and over, 1.7%.
Population projection: (1990) 9,200,000; (2000) 11,300,000.
Doubling time: 25 years.
Ethnolinguistic composition (1982): Shona-speaking Bantu 70.0%; Ndebele-speaking Bantu 16.0%; white 2.3%; other 11.7%.
Religious affiliation (1980): Christian 44.8%, of which Protestant (including Anglican) 17.5%, African indigenous 13.6%, Roman Catholic 11.7%; animist 40.4%; other 14.8%.
Major cities (1982): Harare 656,000; Bulawayo 414,000; Chitungwiza 173,-000; Gweru 79,000; Mutare 70,000.

Vital statistics

Birth rate per 1,000 population (1983): 53.0 (world avg. 29.0).
Death rate per 1,000 population (1983): 13.0 (world avg. 11.0).
Natural increase rate per 1,000 population (1983): 40.0 (world avg. 18.0).
Total fertility rate (avg. births per childbearing woman; 1983): 7.0.
Marriage rate per 1,000 population (1981): n.a.
Divorce rate per 1,000 population (1981): n.a.
Life expectancy at birth (1983): male 53.0 years; female 60.0 years.
Major causes of death: n.a.; however, in 1979 measles, pneumonia, diarrhea, cardiovascular diseases, and malignant neoplasms (cancers) accounted for nearly 43% of all registered adult deaths among nonwhite residents.

National economy

Budget (1984–85). Revenue: Z$2,100,000,000 (income tax 39.1%, sales tax 18.7%, customs duties 14.9%, excise tax 12.8%, revenue from investment and property 6.0%, pension contribution 2.6%). Expenditures: Z$2,400,-000,000† (defense 20.3%, education 20.1%, health 6.6%, police 5.9%, social security and welfare 5.2%).
Tourism (1984): receipts from visitors U.S.$45,500,000; expenditures by nationals abroad, n.a.
Production (value of production in Z$ except as noted). Agriculture, forestry, fishing (1984): tobacco 254,500,000, beef 156,200,000, cotton 138,100,000, corn (maize) 130,400,000, sugar 87,100,000, milk and dairy products 65,200,-000, wheat 24,500,000, coffee 19,500,000; livestock (number of live animals) 5,550,000 cattle, 1,100,000 goats, 455,000 sheep, 195,000 pigs, 9,000,000 chickens; roundwood (1983) 6,347,000 cu m; fish catch (1983) 17,700 metric tons. Mining and quarrying (1984): gold 214,100,000; asbestos 80,800,000; nickel 59,700,000; coal 58,200,000; copper 33,700,000; chrome 29,800,000. Manufacturing (1981–82): metals and metal products 656,800,000; foodstuffs 614,700,000; chemicals and petroleum products 439,400,000; textiles, canvas, and yarns 313,800,000; clothing and footwear 203,400,000; beverages and tobacco 195,000,000; paper, printing, and publishing 148,500,000; nonmetallic mineral products 88,000,000; transport equipment 79,200,000; other manufactured goods 41,600,000. Construction (Z$; 1983): residential 29,441,000; nonresidential 72,156,000. Energy production (consumption): electricity (kW-hr; 1983) 4,116,000,000 (7,466,700,000); coal (metric tons; 1983) 3,240,000 (3,240,000); crude petroleum, none (none); petroleum products (metric tons; 1983) none (538,000); natural gas, none (none).
Population economically active (1983): total 2,628,000; participation rate of population ages 15–64, 46.0% (female [1981] 29.2%; unemployed, n.a.).

Price and earnings indexes (1980 = 100)

	1979	1980	1981	1982	1983	1984	1985‡
Consumer price index	94.9	100.0	113.1	125.2	154.1	185.2	200.2
Monthly earnings index§	81.9	100.0	123.9	149.8	...	...	...

Public debt (external, outstanding; 1984): U.S.$3,744,000,000.
Household income and expenditure. Average household size (1980) 5.8; income per household Z$1,689 (U.S.$2,628); source of income: n.a.; expenditure (1983): food 20.6%, clothing, footwear, and textiles 12.0%, alcohol and tobacco 10.8%, hotel accommodations and travel 9.4%, housing 9.0%, public utilities, coal, and petroleum products 8.2%, household equipment 7.4%, education 3.7%, medicines and drugs 2.2%, health service 1.7%, books and newspapers 1.6%.
Gross national product (at current market prices; 1983): U.S.$5,700,000,000 (U.S.$740 per capita).

Structure of gross domestic product and labour force

	1983 in value Z$'000,000	% of total value	labour force§	% of labour force
Agriculture	592	11.6	263,500	25.5
Mining	284	5.6	60,300	5.8
Manufacturing	1,385	27.3	173,400	16.8
Construction	194	3.8	49,300	4.8
Public utilities	134	2.6	6,900	0.7
Transportation and communication	364	7.2	49,600	4.8
Trade	737	14.5	80,600	7.8
Finance	333	6.6	15,800	1.5
Pub. admin., defense	375	7.4	82,500	8.0
Services	856	16.8	251,500	24.3
Other	−173 ‖	−3.4 ‖		
TOTAL	5,081¶	100.0	1,033,400	100.0

Land use (1983): forested 61.6%; meadows and pastures 12.6%; agricultural and under permanent cultivation 6.9%; other 18.9%.

Foreign trade

Balance of trade (current prices)

	1979	1980	1981	1982	1983	1984
Z$'000,000	+166.4	+99.8	−46.0	−113.4	+88.6	+213.7
% of total	13.1%	5.8%	2.3%	5.5%	4.0%	7.9%

Imports (1983): Z$1,061,600,000 (machinery and transport equipment 33.5%; petroleum products 16.9%; basic manufactures 14.5%, of which textile yarns and fabrics 3.4%, iron and steel 3.1%; chemicals 14.3%). *Major import sources:* South Africa 24.5%; United Kingdom 11.5%; United States 9.5%; West Germany 7.3%; Japan 4.7%; France 4.7%; Botswana 4.2%; Zambia 2.2%; Switzerland 1.9%; The Netherlands 1.8%.
Exports (1983): Z$1,150,200,000 (tobacco 20.5%; ferroalloys 10.3%; gold 8.7%; asbestos 6.5%; cotton 6.1%; nickel 6.0%; sugar 4.6%; corn 3.3%). *Major export destinations:* South Africa 18.2%; United Kingdom 11.5%; West Germany 7.7%; United States 6.7%; Japan 6.3%; Italy 5.2%; Botswana 4.1%; The Netherlands 3.6%; Zambia 3.4%; Zaire 2.2%; Belgium 2.1%; Spain 1.8%; France 1.7%.

Transport and communications

Transport. Railroads♀ (1984): length 2,100 mi, 3,400 km; number of passengers 2,218,000; short ton-mi cargo 3,983,000,000, metric ton-km cargo 6,411,000,000. Roads (1984): total length 105,900 mi, 170,400 km (paved 7%). Vehicles (1984): passenger cars 248,967; trucks and buses 27,914. Merchant marine: none. Air transport (1984): passenger-mi 369,816,000, passenger-km 595,163,000; short ton-mi cargo 8,126,000, metric ton-km cargo 11,864,000; airports (1985) with scheduled flights 8.
Communications. Daily newspapers (1984): total number 2; total circulation 150,000; circulation per 1,000 population 19. Radio (1984): total number of receivers 200,000 (1 per 40 persons). Television (1984): total number of receivers 99,000 (1 per 80 persons). Telephones (1983): 231,260 (1 per 33 persons).

Education and health

Education (1984)

	schoolsδ	teachersδ	students	student/teacher ratio
Primary (age 7–13)	3,880	52,502	2,147,898	...
Secondary (age 14–19)	790	10,238	422,584	...
Voc., teacher tr.	17	953	18,348	...
Higher	1□	325	4,130	...

Educational attainment (1969). Percent of adult population over age 17 having: no formal schooling 41.6%; some primary education 36.5%; primary 13.6%; secondary 3.3%; other 5.0%. *Literacy* (1980): total population literate 2,774,600 (70.8%); males literate 1,507,200 (78.0%); females literate 1,267,400 (63.8%).
Health (1980): physicians 1,148 (1 per 6,411 persons); hospital beds 21,418 (1 per 344 persons); infant mortality rate per 1,000 live births (1983) 69.0.
Food (1980–82): daily per capita caloric intake 2,164 (vegetable products 93%, animal products 7%); 90% of FAO recommended minimum requirement.

Military

Total active duty personnel (1984): 41,300 (army 96.9%, air force 3.1%). *Military expenditure as percent of GNP* (1983): 6.4% (world 6.1%); per capita expenditure U.S.$47.

*Detail does not add to total given because of rounding. †Expenditure breakdown is for 1983-84. ‡May. §Wage-earning workers only. ‖ Imputed banking service charges. ¶At current prices. ♀Includes operations in Botswana. δ1983. □1984.

Government and international organizations

This table summarizes principal facts about the governments of the countries of the world, their branches and organs, the topmost layers of local government comprising each country's chief administrative subdivisions, and the participation of their central governments in the principal intergovernmental organizations of the world.

In this table "date of independence" may refer to a variety of circumstances. In the case of the newest countries, those that attained full independence after World War II, the date given is usually just what is implied by the heading—the date when the country, within its present borders, attained full sovereignty over both its internal and external affairs. In the case of longer established countries, the choice of a single date may be somewhat more complicated: When, for example, did Switzerland become "independent"? Was it, as some authorities suggest, in 1291, the date of the formation of the Swiss Confederation?; or in 1315, with the defeat of the Habsburgs that secured independence for some of the core cantons around Luzern?; in 1499, with the acknowledgment of its status by the Holy Roman Empire through the Treaty of Basel?; or in 1638, when full recognition was granted by all the European powers through the Treaty of Westphalia? In this table 1499 has been adopted, but grounds for the other dates certainly exist. The reader interested in this subject should refer to *Macropædia* and *Micropædia* articles on national histories and relevant historical acts. In general, the date given here for any country refers either to the final act of union of a state comprised of smaller entities or to the final act of separation from a larger whole (*e.g.*, the separation of Bangladesh from Pakistan in 1971).

The date of the current, or last, constitution is in some ways a less complicated question, but governments sometimes do not, upon taking power, either adhere to existing constitutional forms or trouble to terminate the previous document and legitimize themselves by the installation of new constitutional forms. Often, however, the desire to legitimize extraconstitutional political activity by associating it with existing forms of long precedent leads to partial or incomplete modification, suspension, or abrogation of a constitution, so that the actual day-to-day conduct of government may be entirely unrelated to the provisions of a constitution still theoretically in force. When a date in this column is given in italics, it refers to a document that has been suspended, abolished by extraconstitutional action, or modified extensively.

The characterizations adopted under "kind of government" represent a compromise between the ideal forms provided for by the constitution and the more pragmatic language that a political scientist might adopt to describe these same systems. For an explanation of the application of these terms in the Britannica World Data, *see* the Glossary at p. 613.

The positions denoted by the terms "chief of state" and "head of government" are usually those identified with those functions by the constitution. Very often the position of chief of state will be a largely ceremonial one, with little or no authority over the day-to-day conduct of government, although the formal assent of the office to executive or legislative action may be required by the constitution. In other cases, such as in some of the Middle Eastern monarchies, the chief of state may also be the effective head of government. In certain countries, an official of a political party or a revolutionary figure entirely outside the constitutional structure may effectively exercise the powers of both positions.

Membership in the legislative house (-s) of each country as given here includes all elected or appointed members, as well as ex officio members (those who by virtue of some other office or title are members of the body), whether voting or nonvoting. The legislature of a country with a unicameral system is shown as the upper house in this table.

The number of administrative subdivisions for each country is listed down to the second level. A single country may, depending on its size, complexity, and historical antecedents, have as many as five levels of administrative subordination (as does the U.S.S.R.) or it may have none at all. Each level of subordination may have several kinds of subdivisions:

Government and international organizations

country	date of independence[a]	date of current or last constitution[b]	type of government	executive branch chief of state[c]	executive branch head of government[c]	legislative branch upper house[d][e] (members)	legislative branch lower house[e] (members)	admin. subdivisions first-order (number)	admin. subdivisions second-order (number)	seaward claims territorial (nautical miles)	seaward claims fishing/economic (nautical miles)
Afghanistan	Aug. 19, 1919	*Feb. 14, 1977*	people's republic	president RC	prime minister	x	x	29	185	—	—
Albania	Nov. 28, 1912	Dec. 27, 1976	people's republic	chairman PPA	chairman CM	250	—	26	200	15	1
Algeria	July 5, 1962	Nov. 19, 1976	republic	—president—		282	—	48	160	12	1
American Samoa			territory (U.S.)	U.S. president	governor	18	20	3	15	3	200
Andorra	Dec. 6, 1288	1866	coprincipality	co-princes (2)	syndic	28	—	7	—	—	—
Angola	Nov. 11, 1975	Nov. 11, 1975	people's republic	—president—		207	—	18	139	20	200
Anguilla	—	Apr. 1, 1982	territory (U.K.)	British monarch	governor	10	—	2	—	3	1
Antigua and Barbuda	Nov. 1, 1981	Nov. 1, 1981	parliamentary state	British monarch	prime minister	17	17	8	—	12	200
Argentina	July 9, 1816	July 9, 1853	federal republic	—president—		46	254	24	488	200	1
Australia	Jan 1, 1901	July 9, 1900	federal parl. state	British monarch	prime minister	76	148	8	866	3	200
Austria	c. Oct. 30, 1918	Oct. 1, 1920	federal republic	president	chancellor	63	183	9	98	—	—
Bahamas, The	July 10, 1973	July 10, 1973	parliamentary state	British monarch	prime minister	16	43	—	41	3	200
Bahrain	Aug. 15, 1971	Dec. 6, 1973	monarchy (emirate)	emir	prime minister	x	—	11	—	3	1
Bangladesh	Mar. 26, 1971	*Dec 16, 1972*	republic	—president—		(330)	—	4	21	12	200
Barbados	Nov. 30, 1966	Nov. 30, 1966	parliamentary state	British monarch	prime minister	21	27	11	—	12	200
Belgium	Oct. 4, 1830	1831	const. monarchy	monarch	prime minister	182	212	3	9	3	200[3]
Belize	Sept. 21, 1981	Sept. 21, 1981	parliamentary state	British monarch	prime minister	8	28	6	—	3	1
Benin	Aug. 1, 1960	Nov. 1979	people's republic	—president—		196	—	6	84	200	1
Bermuda	—	June 8, 1968	colony (U.K.)	British monarch	premier	11	40	11	—	3	200
Bhutan	Mar. 24, 1910		monarchy	—king—		150	—	4	17	—	—
Bolivia	Aug. 6, 1825	Feb. 1967	republic	—president—		27	130	9	99	—	—
Botswana	Sept. 30, 1966	Mar. 3, 1965	republic	—president—		15	39	14	—	—	—
Brazil	Sept. 7, 1822	Jan. 24, 1967	federal republic	—president—		69	479	27	3,963	200	4
British Virgin Islands	—	June 1, 1977	colony (U.K.)	British monarch	governor	11	—	—	—	3	200
Brunei	Jan. 1, 1984	Sept. 29, 1959	monarchy (sultanate)	sultan	prime minister	21	—	4	—	12	200
Bulgaria	Oct. 5, 1908	May 18, 1971	people's republic	chairman SC	chairman CM	400	—	28	4,823	12	1
Burkina Faso	Aug. 5, 1960	*Nov. 27, 1977*	state	—chairman CNR—		x	—	25	250	—	—
Burma	Jan. 4, 1948	Jan 4, 1974	socialist republic	president	prime minister	475	—	14	...	12	200
Burundi	July 1, 1962	Nov. 21, 1981	republic	—president—		65	—	15	114	—	—
Cameroon	Jan. 1, 1960	May 20, 1972	republic	—president—		120	—	10	40	50	1
Canada	July 1, 1867	April 17, 1982	federal parl. state	British monarch	prime minister	104	282	12	4,740	12	200
Cape Verde	July 5, 1975	Sept. 7, 1980	republic	president	premier	63	—	2	14	12[5]	200
Cayman Islands	—	Aug. 22, 1972	colony (U.K.)	British monarch	governor	15	—	3	8	3	200
Central African Republic	Aug. 13, 1960	*Feb. 6, 1981*	republic	—chairman CMRN—		(...)	—	14	47	—	—
Chad	Aug. 11, 1960	*Aug. 29, 1978*	republic	—president—		x	—	14	53	—	—
Chile	Sep. 18, 1810	March 11, 1981[6]	republic	—president—		13	41	3	200		
China	1523 BC	Dec. 4, 1982	people's republic	president	premier SC	2,978	—	29	200	12	1
Christmas Island	—		external territory (Aust.)	Australian GG	administrator	—	—	—	—	3	200
Cocos (Keeling) Islands	—		external territory (Aust.)	Australian GG	administrator	—	—	—	—	3	200
Colombia	July 20, 1810	Aug. 5, 1886	republic	—president—		114	199	32	978	12	200
Comoros	July 6, 1975	Oct. 1, 1978	federal Islamic republic	—president—		38	—	3	7	12	200
Congo	Aug. 15, 1960	July 8, 1979	people's republic	—president—		151	—	9	45	200	1
Cook Islands	—	Aug. 8, 1965	territory (N.Z.)[7]	British monarch	premier	24	—	—	—	12	200
Costa Rica	Sept. 15, 1821	Nov. 9, 1949	republic	—president—		57	—	7	80	12	200
Cuba	May 20, 1902	Feb. 24, 1976	socialist republic	—president—		499	—	14	169	12	200
Cyprus	Aug. 16, 1960	Aug. 16, 1960	republic	president	min. to pres.	50[8]	—	6[8]	604	12	1
Czechoslovakia	Oct. 28, 1918	July 11, 1960	federal socialist republic	president	premier	150	200	2	12	—	—
Denmark	c. 800	June 5, 1953	constitutional monarchy	monarch	prime minister	179	—	14	276	3	200
Djibouti	June 27, 1977	Feb. 10, 1981	republic	president	prime minister	65	—	5	11	12	200
Dominica	Nov. 3, 1978	Nov. 3, 1978	republic	president	prime minister	31	—	10	27	12	200

In the United Kingdom, for example, Greater London, 47 counties, 6 metropolitan counties (in England and Wales), and 9 regions and three island authorities (in Scotland) all coexist at a roughly comparable level of subordination to the central government. Because the regional and island authorities function less strongly as administrative entities, however, only 54 (1 + 47 + 6) subdivisions are shown at the first level for the U.K.

Finally, in the second half of the table are listed the memberships each country maintains in the principal international intergovernmental organizations of the world. This part of the table may also be utilized to provide a complete membership list for each of these organizations as of Dec. 1, 1985.

Notes for the column headings
a. As applicable, the date given may also be either that of the organization of the present form of government or the inception of the present administrative structure (federation, confederation, union, etc.).
b. Constitutions whose dates are in italic type had been wholly or substantially suspended or abolished as of late 1985.
c. For abbreviations used in this column see the list on the facing page.
d. Unicameral legislatures are also listed under this category.
e. When a legislative body has been adjourned or otherwise suspended, figures in parentheses indicate the number of members in the legislative body as provided for in the constitution. If the provision for the legislative body in the constitution has been abrogated then the space has been marked with an "X".
f. Vatican City is also a member.
g. States contributing funds to or receiving aid from UNICEF in 1981.

h. Palestine is also a member.
i. Palestine Liberation Organization is also a member.

International organizations, conventions
ACP   African, Caribbean, and Pacific (Lomé III) convention
ASEAN   Association of South East Asian Nations
COMECON   Council for Mutual Economic Assistance
EC   The European Communities
ECOWAS   Economic Community of West African States
EEC   European Economic Community
FAO   Food and Agriculture Organization
GATT   General Agreement on Tariffs and Trade
I-ADB   Inter-American Development Bank
IAEA   International Atomic Energy Agency

IBRD   International Bank for Reconstruction and Development
ICAO   International Civil Aviation Organization
ICJ   International Court of Justice
IDA   International Development Association
IDB   Islamic Development Bank
IFC   International Finance Corporation
ILO   International Labour Organisation
IMF   International Monetary Fund
IMO   International Maritime Organization
ITU   International Telecommunication Union
LAS   League of Arab States
NATO   North Atlantic Treaty Organization
OAS   Organization of American States
OAU   Organization of African Unity
OPEC   Organization of Petroleum Exporting Countries
SPC   South Pacific Commission
UNCTAD   United Nations Conference on Trade and Development
UNESCO   United Nations Educational Scientific and Cultural Organization
UNICEF   United Nations Children's Fund
UNIDO   United Nations Industrial Development Organization
UPU   Universal Postal Union
WHO   World Health Organization
WIPO   World Intellectual Property Organization

WMO   World Meteorological Organization
WTO   Warsaw Treaty of Friendship, Co-operation and Mutual Assistance (The Warsaw Pact)

Abbreviations used in the executive branch column
AFRC   Armed Forces Ruling Council
CM   Council of Ministers
CMRN   Military Committee for National Recovery
CMSN   Military Committee for National Salvation
CNR   National Council of the Revolution
CS   Council of State
GG   Governor-general
GPC   General People's Committee
MC   Military Council
PC   Presidential Council
PNDC   Provisional National Defense Council
PPA   Presidium, People's Assembly
PPGH   Presidium, People's Great Hural
PRC   People's Redemption Council
PSPC   Presidium, Supreme People's Council
PSSU   Presidium, Supreme Soviet of the U.S.S.R.
RC   Revolutionary Council
SC   State Council
SMC   Supreme Military Council
TMC   Transitional Military Council

	UN organs* and affiliated intergovernmental organizations																						Commonwealth of Nations	regional multi-purpose						economic							military		country
United Nations (date of admission)	UNCTAD*[1]	UNICEF*[g]	ICJ*	FAO	GATT	IAEA[i]	IBRD	ICAO	IDA	IFC	ILO	IMF	IMO	ITU[i]	UNESCO	UNIDO	UPU[i]	WHO	WIPO[f]	WMO		ASEAN	EC[h]	LAS[h]	OAS	OAU	SPC	ACP	COMECON	ECOWAS	EEC	I-ADB	IDB[i]	OPEC	NATO	WTO	
1946	●	●	●	●		●	●	●	●	●	●	●	●	●	●	●	●	●	●	●																	Afghanistan
1955	●	●	●	●			●	●	●	●	●	●	●	●	●	●	●	●	●	●																●	Albania
1962	●	●	●	●		●[2]	●	●	●	●	●	●	●	●	●	●	●	●	●	●				●		●								●	●		Algeria
—															●																						American Samoa
—																																					Andorra
1976	●	●	●	●		●[2]	●		●		●	●	●	●	●	●	●	●	●	●						●											Angola
1981	●	●	●	●			●	●	●	●	●	●	●	●	●	●	●	●	●	●	●							●									Anguilla
1981	●	●	●	●			●	●	●	●	●	●	●	●	●[2]	●	●	●	●	●	●				●			●									Antigua and Barbuda
1945	●	●	●	●	●	●	●	●	●	●	●	●	●	●	●	●	●	●	●	●					●							●					Argentina
1945	●	●	●	●	●	●	●	●	●	●	●	●	●	●	●	●	●	●	●	●	●						●										Australia
1955	●	●	●	●	●	●	●	●	●	●	●	●	●	●	●	●	●	●	●	●												●					Austria
1973	●	●	●	●		●[2]	●	●	●	●	●	●	●	●	●	●	●	●	●	●	●							●									Bahamas, The
1971	●	●	●	●			●	●	●	●	●	●	●	●	●	●	●	●	●	●				●									●				Bahrain
1974	●	●	●	●		●[2]	●	●	●	●	●	●	●	●	●	●	●	●	●	●	●							●					●				Bangladesh
1966	●	●	●	●	●		●	●	●	●	●	●	●	●	●	●	●	●	●	●	●				●			●				●					Barbados
1945	●	●	●	●	●	●	●	●	●	●	●	●	●	●	●	●	●	●	●	●			●								●	●			●		Belgium
1981	●	●	●	●		●[2]	●	●	●	●	●	●	●	●	●	●	●	●	●	●	●				●			●				●					Belize
1960	●	●	●	●			●	●	●	●	●	●	●	●	●	●	●	●	●	●						●		●		●							Benin
—															●																						Bermuda
1971	●			●			●	●	●	●	●	●		●	●	●	●	●		●																	Bhutan
1945	●	●	●	●	●	●	●	●	●	●	●	●	●	●	●	●	●	●	●	●					●							●					Bolivia
1966	●	●	●	●		●[2]	●	●	●	●	●	●	●	●	●	●	●	●	●	●	●					●		●									Botswana
1945	●	●	●	●	●	●	●	●	●	●	●	●	●	●	●	●	●	●	●	●				●								●					Brazil
—													●[2]		●[2]				●[2]								●										British Virgin Islands
1984	●			●									●	●			●[2]	●	●[2]		●	●															Brunei
1955	●	●	●	●		●		●			●		●	●	●	●	●	●	●	●									●							●	Bulgaria
1960	●	●	●	●			●	●	●	●	●	●	●	●	●	●	●	●	●	●						●		●		●							Burkina Faso
1948	●	●	●	●	●		●	●	●	●	●	●	●	●	●	●	●	●	●	●																	Burma
1962	●	●	●	●			●	●	●	●	●	●	●	●	●	●	●	●	●	●						●		●									Burundi
1960	●	●	●	●			●	●	●	●	●	●	●	●	●	●	●	●	●	●						●		●					●				Cameroon
1945	●	●	●	●	●	●	●	●	●	●	●	●	●	●	●	●	●	●	●	●					●							●			●		Canada
1975	●	●	●	●		●[2]	●	●	●	●	●	●	●	●	●	●	●	●	●	●						●		●									Cape Verde
—																																					Cayman Islands
1960	●	●	●	●			●	●	●	●	●	●	●	●	●	●	●	●	●	●						●		●									Central African Republic
1960	●	●	●	●			●	●	●	●	●	●	●	●	●	●	●	●	●	●						●		●									Chad
1945	●	●	●	●	●	●	●	●	●	●	●	●	●	●	●	●	●	●	●	●					●							●					Chile
1945	●	●	●	●		●	●	●	●	●	●	●	●	●	●	●	●	●	●	●																	China
—																						●															Christmas Island
—																						●															Cocos (Keeling) Islands
1945	●	●	●	●		●	●	●	●	●	●	●	●	●	●	●	●	●	●	●					●							●					Colombia
1975	●	●	●	●			●		●		●	●	●	●	●	●	●	●	●					●		●		●					●				Comoros
1960	●	●	●	●			●	●	●	●	●	●	●	●	●	●	●	●	●	●						●		●		●							Congo
—																						●					●[2]										Cook Islands
1945	●	●	●	●			●	●	●	●	●	●	●	●	●	●	●	●	●	●					●							●					Costa Rica
1945	●	●	●	●				●			●		●	●	●	●	●	●	●	●									●								Cuba
1960	●	●	●	●			●	●	●	●	●	●	●	●	●	●	●	●	●	●	●																Cyprus
1945	●	●	●	●		●		●			●		●	●	●	●	●	●	●	●									●							●	Czechoslovakia
1945	●	●	●	●	●	●	●	●	●	●	●	●	●	●	●	●	●	●	●	●			●								●	●			●		Denmark
1977	●	●	●	●			●	●	●	●	●	●		●	●	●	●	●	●	●				●		●		●					●				Djibouti
1978	●	●	●	●		●[2]	●	●	●	●	●	●		●	●	●	●	●	●	●	●				●			●									Dominica

Government and international organizations (continued)

country	date of independence[a]	date of current or last constitution[b]	type of government	executive branch chief of state[c]	head of government[c]	legislative branch upper house[de] (members)	lower house[e] (members)	admin. subdivisions first-order (number)	second-order (number)	seaward claims terri-torial (nautical miles)	fishing/economic (nautical miles)
Dominican Republic	Feb. 27, 1844	Nov. 28, 1966	republic	———president———		27	91	27	97	6	200
Ecuador	May 24, 1822	Aug. 10, 1979	republic	———president———		71	—	20	115	200	[1]
Egypt	Feb. 28, 1922	Sept. 11, 1971	republic	president	prime minister	458	—	26	...	12	200
El Salvador	Jan. 30, 1841	Dec. 20, 1983	republic	———president———		60	—	14	261	200	[1]
Equatorial Guinea	Oct. 12, 1968	Aug. 15, 1982	republic	———president———		41	—	2	6	12	[1]
Ethiopia	c. 1000 BC	July 16, 1931	socialist state	—chairman of the PMAC and CM—		x	—	15	103	12	[1]
Faeroe Islands	—	March 1948	part of Danish realm	Danish monarch	[10]	32	—	7	49	3	200
Falkland Islands	—	Nov. 21, 1977	colony (U.K.)	British monarch	civil comm.	8	—	—	—	3	200
Fiji	Oct. 10, 1970	Oct. 10, 1970	parliamentary state	British monarch	prime minister	22	52	4	14	12[5]	200
Finland	Dec. 6, 1917	July 17, 1919	republic	president	prime minister	200	—	12	461	4	12
France	Aug. 843	Oct. 4, 1958	republic	president	prime minister	317	491	22	96	12	200
French Guiana	—	—	overseas dept. (Fr.)	French president	[11]	16	31	2	20	12	200
French Polynesia	—	Aug. 2, 1984	overseas territory (Fr.)	French president	[12]	30	—	5	—	12	200
Gabon	Aug. 17, 1960	Feb. 21, 1961	republic	president	prime minister	120	—	9	37	100	150
Gambia, The	Feb. 18, 1965	April 24, 1970	republic	———president———		49	—	6	35	200	[1]
Gaza Strip	—	—	Israeli military	— area commander		—	—	3	—	—	—
Germany, East	Oct. 11, 1949	April 9, 1968	socialist republic	chairman CS	chairman CM	500	—	15	227	12	200
Germany, West	May 5, 1955	May 22–23, 1949	federal republic	president	chancellor	45	520	10	30	3	200
Ghana	March 6, 1957	Sept. 24, 1979	republic	———chairman PNDC———		(...)	—	10	58	200	[1]
Gibraltar	—	Aug. 11, 1969	colony (U.K.)	British monarch	governor	18	—	—	—	3	200
Greece	Feb. 3, 1830	June 11, 1975	republic	president	prime minister	300	—	51	147	6	[1]
Greenland	—	—	part of Danish realm	Danish monarch	prime minister	26	—	3	19	3	13
Grenada	Feb. 7, 1974	Feb. 7, 1974	parliamentary state	British monarch	prime minister	13	15	7	—	12	200
Guadeloupe	—	—	overseas dept. (Fr.)	French president	[11]	36	41	3	34	12	200
Guam	—	—	territory (U.S.)	U.S. president	governor	21	—	19	—	3	200
Guatemala	Sept. 15, 1821	Sept. 15, 1965	republic	———president———		100	—	22	326	12	200
Guernsey	—	Jan. 1949	crown dependency (U.K.)	British monarch	bailiff	60	—	3	—	3	200
Guinea	Oct. 2, 1958	May 14, 1982	republic	———president CM———		x	—	33	175	12	200
Guinea-Bissau	Sept. 24, 1973	May 16, 1984	republic	———president———		150	—	9	37	12	200
Guyana	May 26, 1966	Oct. 6, 1980	republic	president	prime minister	65	—	10	98	12	200
Haiti	Jan 1, 1804	Aug. 27, 1983	republic	———president———		59	—	9	41	12	200
Honduras	Nov. 5, 1838	Jan. 20, 1982	republic	———president———		82	—	18	282	12	200
Hong Kong	—	—	colony (U.K.)	British monarch	governor	47	—	3	18	3	[1]
Hungary	Nov. 16, 1918	Aug. 18, 1949	people's republic	president PC	premier CM	352	—	25	97	—	—
Iceland	June 17, 1944	June 17, 1944	republic	———president———		20	40	23	229	12	200
India	Aug. 15, 1947	Jan. 26, 1950	federal republic	president	prime minister	244	544	31	386	12	200
Indonesia	Aug. 17, 1945	Aug. 17, 1945	republic	———president———		920	460	27	282	12[5]	200
Iran	Oct. 7, 1906	Dec. 2–3, 1979	Islamic republic	president	prime minister	270	—	24	...	12	50
Iraq	Oct. 3, 1932	Sept. 22, 1968	republic	———president———		250	—	18	157	12	[1]
Ireland	Dec. 6, 1921	Dec. 29, 1937	republic	president	prime minister	60	166	27	49	3	200
Isle of Man	—	1961	crown dependency (U.K.)	British monarch	council pres.	11	24	10	—	3	200
Israel	May 14, 1948	June 1950[15]	republic	president	prime minister	120	—	6	14	6	[1]
Italy	March 17, 1861	Jan. 1, 1948	republic	president	prime minister	323	630	20	94	12	200
Ivory Coast	Aug. 7, 1960	Oct. 31, 1960	republic	———president———		147	—	34	162	12	200
Jamaica	Aug. 6, 1962	Aug. 6, 1962	parliamentary state	British monarch	prime minister	21	60	3	14	12	[1]
Japan	c. 660 BC	May 3, 1947	constitutional monarchy	emperor	prime minister	252	511	47	3,256	12[16]	[1]
Jersey	—	Jan. 1949	crown dependency (U.K.)	British monarch	bailiff	58	—	17	—	3	200
Jordan	March 22, 1946	Jan. 1, 1952	constitutional monarchy	king	prime minister	30	60	5	14	3	[1]
Kampuchea	Nov. 9, 1953	June 1981	people's republic	president CS	president CM	117	—	20	...	12	200
Kenya	Dec. 12, 1963	Dec. 12, 1963	republic	———president———		172	—	8	40	12	200
Kiribati	July 12, 1979	July 12, 1979	republic	———president———		37	—	23	—	12	200
Korea, North	Sept. 9, 1948	Dec. 27, 1972	people's republic	president	premier	615	—	13	152	12	200
Korea, South	Aug. 15, 1948	Oct. 27, 1980	republic	president	prime minister	276	—	13	139	12[17]	12
Kuwait	June 19, 1961	Nov. 16, 1962	const. mon. (emirate)	emir	prime minister	50	—	4	—	12	[1]
Laos	July 19, 1949	May 11, 1947	people's republic	president	chairman CM	264	—	13	...		
Lebanon	Nov. 26, 1941	May 23, 1926	republic	president	prime minister	99	—	5	26	12	[1]
Lesotho	Oct. 4, 1966	Oct. 4, 1966	constitutional monarchy	king	prime minister	33	60	10	22	—	—
Liberia	July 26, 1847	July 20, 1984	republic	———president———		26	64	14	50	200	[1]
Libya	Dec. 24, 1951	March 2, 1977	socialist state[18]	rev. leader	secretary GPC	1,112	—	25	201	12	[1]
Liechtenstein	July 12, 1806	Oct. 5, 1921	constitutional monarchy	grand duke	prime minister	15	—	11	—		
Luxembourg	May 10, 1867	Oct. 17, 1868	constitutional monarchy	grand duke	prime minister	64	—	3	12	—	—
Macau	—	—	overseas prov. (Port.)	Port. president	governor	18	—	3	5	12	[1]
Madagascar	June 26, 1960	Dec. 30, 1975	republic	president	prime minister	137	—	6	18	50	150
Malawi	July 6, 1964	July 6, 1964	republic	———president———		101	—	3	24	—	—
Malaysia	Aug. 31, 1957	Aug. 31, 1957	fed. const. monarchy	paramount ruler	prime minister	68	154	14	126	12	200
Maldives	July 26, 1965	Nov 11, 1968	republic	———president———		48	—	19	202	5, 19	19
Mali	Sept. 22, 1960	June 19, 1979	republic	———president———		82	—	8	42	—	—
Malta	Sept. 21, 1964	Sept. 21, 1964	republic	president	prime minister	65	—	—	—	12	25
Martinique	—	—	overseas dept. (Fr.)	French president	[11]	36	41	3	34	12	200
Mauritania	Nov. 28, 1960	May 20, 1961	republic	———president CMSN———		x	—	13	44	70	200
Mauritius	March 12, 1968	March 12, 1968	parliamentary state	British monarch	prime minister	70	—	12	...	12	200
Mayotte	—	—	terr. collectivity (Fr.)	French president	[21]	17	—	17	—	12	[1]
Mexico	Sept. 16, 1810	Feb. 5, 1917	federal republic	———president———		64	400	32	2,389	12	200
Monaco	Feb. 2, 1861	Dec. 17, 1962	constitutional monarchy	prince	min. of state	18	—	1	4	12	[1]
Mongolia	March 13, 1921	July 6, 1960	people's republic	chairman PPGH	premier	370	—	21	331	—	—
Montserrat	—	Jan. 1, 1960	colony (U.K.)	British monarch	governor	11	—	3	—	3	[1]
Morocco	March 2, 1956	March 10, 1972	constitutional monarchy	king	prime minister	306	—	38	131	12	200
Mozambique	June 25, 1975	June 25, 1975	people's republic	———president———		226	—	11	112	12	200
Nauru	Jan. 31, 1968	Jan. 29, 1968	republic	———president———		18	—	14	—	12	200
Nepal	Nov. 13, 1769	Dec. 16, 1962	constitutional monarchy	king	prime minister	140	—	14	75	—	—
Netherlands, The	March 30, 1814	March 29, 1814	constitutional monarchy	monarch	prime minister	75	150	11	912	3	200
Netherlands Antilles	—	—	integral part of Neth.	Dutch monarch	prime minister	22	—	4	—	3	200
New Caledonia	—	—	overseas territory (Fr.)	French president	[12]	42	48	6	32	12	200
New Zealand	Sept. 26, 1907	June 30, 1852	parliamentary state	British monarch	prime minister	95	—	239	—	12	200
Nicaragua	April 30, 1838	March 14, 1974	republic	———president———		96	—	17	136	200	[1]

membership in international organizations

United Nations (date of admission)	UN organs* and affiliated intergovernmental organizations																				Commonwealth of Nations	regional multi-purpose						economic							military		country
	UNCTAD*[1]	UNICEF*[g]	ICJ*	FAO	GATT	IAEA[i]	IBRD	ICAO	IDA	IFC	ILO	IMF	IMO	ITU[i]	UNESCO	UNIDO	UPU[i]	WHO	WIPO[i]	WMO		ASEAN	EC	LAS[h]	OAS	OAU	SPC	ACP	COMECON	ECOWAS	EEC	I-ADB	IDB[i]	OPEC	NATO	WTO	
1945	•	•	•	•	•	•	•	•	•	•	•	•	•	•	•	•	•	•	•	•					•								•				Dominican Republic
1945	•	•	•	•	•	•	•	•	•	•	•	•	•	•	•	•	•	•	•	•					•								•	•			Ecuador
1945	•	•	•	•	•	•	•	•	•	•	•	•	•	•	•	•	•	•	•	•				•[9]	•								•				Egypt
1945	•	•	•	•	•	•[2]	•	•	•	•	•	•	•	•	•	•	•	•	•	•					•								•				El Salvador
1968	•	•	•	•		•[2]	•	•	•	•	•	•	•	•	•	•	•	•	•	•						•		•									Equatorial Guinea
1945	•	•	•	•	•	•	•	•	•	•	•	•	•	•	•	•	•	•	•	•						•		•									Ethiopia
—															•			•																			Faeroe Islands
—																		•			•																Falkland Islands
1970	•	•	•	•		•[2]	•	•	•	•	•	•	•	•	•	•	•	•	•	•	•							•									Fiji
1955	•	•	•	•	•	•	•	•	•	•	•	•	•	•	•	•	•	•	•	•			•														Finland
1945	•	•	•	•	•	•	•	•	•	•	•	•	•	•	•	•	•	•	•	•			•								•				•		France
—																		•																			French Guiana
—																		•									•										French Polynesia
1960	•	•	•	•	•	•	•	•	•	•	•	•	•	•	•	•	•	•	•	•						•		•					•				Gabon
1965	•	•	•	•		•	•	•	•	•	•	•	•	•	•	•	•	•	•	•	•					•		•		•							Gambia, The
—					•										•			•						•													Gaza Strip
1973	•	•	•	•	•	•					•		•	•	•	•	•	•	•	•									•							•	Germany, East
1973	•	•	•	•	•	•	•	•	•	•	•	•	•	•	•	•	•	•	•	•			•								•		•		•		Germany, West
1957	•	•	•	•	•	•	•	•	•	•	•	•	•	•	•	•	•	•	•	•	•					•		•		•							Ghana
—																		•			•																Gibraltar
1945	•	•	•	•	•	•	•	•	•	•	•	•	•	•	•	•	•	•	•	•			•										•		•		Greece
1974	•	•	•	•		•[2]	•	•	•	•	•	•	•	•	•	•	•	•	•	•	•							•									Greenland / Grenada
—																		•																			Guadeloupe
—																		•									•										Guam
1945	•	•	•	•	•	•	•	•	•	•	•	•	•	•	•	•	•	•	•	•					•								•				Guatemala
—																		•			•																Guernsey
1958	•	•	•	•	•	•[2]	•	•	•	•	•	•	•	•	•	•	•	•	•	•						•		•		•							Guinea
1974	•	•	•	•		•	•	•	•	•	•	•	•	•	•	•	•	•	•	•						•		•		•							Guinea-Bissau
1966	•	•	•	•		•	•	•	•	•	•	•	•	•	•	•	•	•	•	•	•							•									Guyana
1945	•	•	•	•	•	•	•	•	•	•	•	•	•	•	•	•	•	•	•	•					•								•				Haiti
1945	•	•	•	•	•	•	•	•	•	•	•	•	•	•	•	•	•	•	•	•					•								•				Honduras
—					•[14]													•																			Hong Kong
1955	•	•	•	•	•	•	•	•	•	•	•	•	•	•	•	•	•	•	•	•									•							•	Hungary
1946	•	•	•	•	•	•	•	•	•	•	•	•	•	•	•	•	•	•	•	•															•		Iceland
1945	•	•	•	•	•	•	•	•	•	•	•	•	•	•	•	•	•	•	•	•	•												•				India
1950	•	•	•	•	•	•	•	•	•	•	•	•	•	•	•	•	•	•	•	•		•												•			Indonesia
1945	•	•	•	•		•	•	•	•	•	•	•	•	•	•	•	•	•	•	•				•									•	•			Iran
1945	•	•	•	•		•	•	•	•	•	•	•	•	•	•	•	•	•	•	•				•										•			Iraq
1955	•	•	•	•	•	•	•	•	•	•	•	•	•	•	•	•	•	•	•	•												•					Ireland
—																		•			•																Isle of Man
1949	•	•	•	•	•	•	•	•	•	•	•	•	•	•	•	•	•	•	•	•																	Israel
1955	•	•	•	•	•	•	•	•	•	•	•	•	•	•	•	•	•	•	•	•			•								•		•		•		Italy
1960	•	•	•	•		•	•	•	•	•	•	•	•	•	•	•	•	•	•	•						•		•		•							Ivory Coast
1962	•	•	•	•		•	•	•	•	•	•	•	•	•	•	•	•	•	•	•	•				•								•				Jamaica
1956	•	•	•	•	•	•	•	•	•	•	•	•	•	•	•	•	•	•	•	•													•				Japan
—																		•																			Jersey
1955	•	•	•	•		•[2]	•	•	•	•	•	•	•	•	•	•	•	•	•	•				•										•			Jordan
1955	•	•	•	•		•	•	•	•	•	•	•	•	•	•	•	•	•	•	•		•															Kampuchea
1963	•	•	•	•		•	•	•	•	•	•	•	•	•	•	•	•	•	•	•	•					•		•									Kenya
—		•		•[2]										•	•		•	•									•	•									Kiribati
—		•		•										•	•		•	•											•								Korea, North
—		•		•	•	•	•	•	•	•	•	•	•	•	•	•	•	•	•	•													•				Korea, South
1963	•	•	•	•		•	•	•	•	•	•	•	•	•	•	•	•	•	•	•				•										•	•		Kuwait
1955	•	•	•	•		•	•	•	•	•	•	•	•	•	•	•	•	•	•	•																	Laos
1945	•	•	•	•		•	•	•	•	•	•	•	•	•	•	•	•	•	•	•				•										•			Lebanon
1966	•	•	•	•		•[2]	•	•	•	•	•	•	•	•	•	•	•	•	•	•	•					•		•									Lesotho
1945	•	•	•	•		•	•	•	•	•	•	•	•	•	•	•	•	•	•	•						•		•									Liberia
1955	•	•	•	•		•	•	•	•	•	•	•	•	•	•	•	•	•	•	•				•		•								•			Libya
—		•		•										•	•		•	•	•																		Liechtenstein
1945	•	•	•	•	•	•	•	•	•	•	•	•	•	•	•	•	•	•	•	•			•								•				•		Luxembourg
—																		•																			Macau
1960	•	•	•	•		•	•	•	•	•	•	•	•	•	•	•	•	•	•	•						•		•									Madagascar
1964	•	•	•	•		•	•	•	•	•	•	•	•	•	•	•	•	•	•	•	•					•		•									Malawi
1957	•	•	•	•	•	•	•	•	•	•	•	•	•	•	•	•	•	•	•	•	•	•															Malaysia
1965	•	•	•	•		•	•	•	•	•	•	•	•	•	•	•	•	•	•	•	•[20]																Maldives
1960	•	•	•	•		•[2]	•	•	•	•	•	•	•	•	•	•	•	•	•	•						•		•		•							Mali
1964	•	•	•	•		•	•	•	•	•	•	•	•	•	•	•	•	•	•	•	•		•[14]					•									Malta
—																		•																			Martinique
1961	•	•	•	•		•	•	•	•	•	•	•	•	•	•	•	•	•	•	•			•[14]	•		•		•									Mauritania
1968	•	•	•	•		•	•	•	•	•	•	•	•	•	•	•	•	•	•	•	•					•		•									Mauritius
—																		•																			Mayotte
1945	•	•	•	•	•	•	•	•	•	•	•	•	•	•	•	•	•	•	•	•					•								•				Mexico
—		•		•							•			•	•		•	•																			Monaco
1961	•	•	•	•		•					•			•	•	•	•	•	•	•									•							•	Mongolia
—		•		•											•			•			•																Montserrat
1956	•	•	•	•		•	•	•	•	•	•	•	•	•	•	•	•	•	•	•				•		•		•									Morocco
1975	•	•	•	•		•[2]	•	•	•	•	•	•	•	•	•	•	•	•	•	•						•		•									Mozambique
—															•			•			•[20]						•										Nauru
1955	•	•	•	•			•	•	•	•	•	•	•	•	•	•	•	•	•	•																	Nepal
1945	•	•	•	•	•	•	•	•	•	•	•	•	•	•	•	•	•	•	•	•			•								•	•	•		•		Netherlands, The
—					•[14]													•										•					•[14]				Netherlands Antilles
—																		•									•										New Caledonia
1945	•	•	•	•	•	•	•	•	•	•	•	•	•	•	•	•	•	•	•	•	•						•										New Zealand
1945	•	•	•	•	•	•	•	•	•	•	•	•	•	•	•	•	•	•	•	•					•								•				Nicaragua

Government and international organizations (continued)

country	date of independence[a]	date of current or last constitution[b]	type of government	executive branch — chief of state[c]	executive branch — head of government[c]	legislative branch — upper house[d,e] (members)	legislative branch — lower house[e] (members)	admin. subdivisions — first-order (number)	admin. subdivisions — second-order (number)	seaward claims — territorial (nautical miles)	seaward claims — fishing/economic (nautical miles)
Niger	Aug. 3, 1960	Nov. 8, 1960	republic	president SMC		150	—	7	32	—	—
Nigeria	Oct. 1, 1960	Oct. 1, 1979	federal republic	president AFRC		x	x	20	271	30	200
Niue	—	Aug. 29, 1974	territory (N.Z.)	British monarch	premier	14	—	14	—	12	200
Norfolk Island	—	May 30, 1979	external territory (Aust.)	Australian GG	administrator	9	—	—	—	3	200
Norway	June 7, 1905	May 17, 1814	constitutional monarchy	king	prime minister	157	—	19	451	4	200
Oman	Dec. 20, 1951	—	monarchy (sultanate)	sultan	prime minister	55	—	11	41	12	200
Pacific Is., Trust Terr. of	—	—	trust territory (U.S.)	U.S. president	high comm.	—	—	4	—	3	200
Pakistan	Aug. 14, 1947	April 10, 1973	federal Islamic republic	president		87	237	6	16	12	200
Panama	Nov. 3, 1903	Oct. 11, 1972	republic	president		67	505	10	65	200	1
Papua New Guinea	Sept. 16, 1975	Sept. 16, 1975	parliamentary state	British monarch	prime minister	109	—	20	86	12[5]	200
Paraguay	May 14, 1811	Aug. 25, 1967	republic	president		30	60	20	190	200	1
Peru	July 28, 1821	July 28, 1980	republic	president		60	180	25	152	200	1
Philippines	July 4, 1946	Jan. 17, 1973	republic	president	prime minister	183	—	73	1,500	19	200
Pitcairn Island	—	Nov. 30, 1838	colony (U.K.)	British monarch	isl. magistrate	10	—	—	—	3	200
Poland	Nov. 10, 1918	July 22, 1952	socialist republic	chairman CS	prime minister	460	—	49	261	12	200
Portugal	July 25, 1139	April 2, 1976	republic	president	prime minister	250	—	22	4,123	12	200
Puerto Rico	July 25, 1952	July 25, 1952	commonwealth (U.S.)	U.S. president	governor	27	51	78	...	3	200
Qatar	Sept. 3, 1971	July 1970[22]	constitutional monarchy	emir		—	—	3	—	3	200
Réunion	—	—	overseas dept. (Fr.)	French president	[11]	36	45	4	24	12	200
Romania	May 21, 1877	Aug. 21, 1965	socialist republic	president		369	—	41	2,941	12	1
Rwanda	July 1, 1962	Dec. 20, 1978	republic	president		70	—	10	143	—	—
St. Christopher and Nevis	Sept. 19, 1983	Sept. 19, 1983	fed. parl. state	British monarch	prime minister	15	—	14	—	12	200
St. Helena and Ascension	—	Jan. 1, 1967	colony (U.K.)	British monarch	governor	15[23]	—	3	—	3	200
St. Lucia	Feb. 22, 1979	Feb. 22, 1979	parliamentary state	British monarch	prime minister	11	17	10	—	3	12
St. Pierre and Miquelon	—	—	terr. collectivity (Fr.)	French president	[21]	14	—	2	—	12	200
St. Vincent	Oct. 27, 1979	Oct. 27, 1979	parliamentary state	British monarch	prime minister	19	—	5	13	3	12
San Marino	855	1205	republic	captains-regent (2)		60	—	9	—	—	—
São Tomé and Príncipe	July 12, 1975	Dec. 12, 1975	republic	president		40	—	2	7	12[5]	200
Saudi Arabia	Sept. 23, 1932	—	monarchy	king	prime minister	—	—	14	—	12	—
Senegal	Aug. 20, 1960	March 7, 1963	republic	president		120	—	8	30	12	200
Seychelles	June 29, 1976	March 26, 1979	republic	president		25	—	—	—	12	200
Sierra Leone	April 27, 1961	June 14, 1978	republic	president		104	—	4	12	200	1
Singapore	Aug. 9, 1965	June 3, 1959	republic	president	prime minister	79	—	—	—	3	12
Solomon Islands	July 7, 1978	July 7, 1978	parliamentary state	British monarch	prime minister	38	—	8	174	12[5]	200
Somalia	July 1, 1960	Aug. 25, 1979	republic	president		177	—	16	60	200	1
South Africa	May 31, 1910	Sept. 3, 1984	republic	state president		308[24]	—	10	358	12	200
Bophuthatswana	Dec. 6, 1977[25]	Dec. 6, 1977	republic	president		105	—	12	76	—	—
Ciskei	Dec. 4, 1981[25]	Dec. 4, 1981	republic	president		87	—	7	39	—	—
Transkei	Oct. 26, 1976[25]	Dec. 1963	republic	president	prime minister	150	—	26	123	—	—
Venda	Sept. 13, 1979[25]	Sept. 13, 1979	republic	president		87	—	4	—	—	—
South West Africa/Namibia	—	—	dependency of S.Af.[26]	—	admin. general	(72)	—	26	—	6	12
Spain	1492	Dec. 29, 1978	constitutional monarchy	king	prime minister	253	350	17	50	12	200
Sri Lanka	Feb. 4, 1948	Aug. 17, 1978	republic	president	prime minister	168	—	24	682	12	200
Sudan, The	Jan. 1, 1956	Oct. 10, 1985[27]	republic	chairman TMC	prime minister	(153)	—	10	19	12	1
Suriname	Nov. 25, 1975	Nov. 25, 1975	republic	commander in chief		x	—	9	—	12	200
Swaziland	Sept. 6, 1968	Sept. 6, 1968	constitutional monarchy	king	prime minister	20	50	4	—	—	—
Sweden	before 836	Jan. 1, 1975	constitutional monarchy	king	prime minister	349	—	24	279	12	200
Switzerland	Sept. 22, 1499	May 29, 1874	federal republic	president		46	200	23	177	—	—
Syria	April 17, 1946	March 12, 1973	republic	president	prime minister	195	—	14	41	35	1
Taiwan	Oct. 25, 1945	Oct. 25, 1947	republic	president	premier	1,173	—	23	—	3	12
Tanzania	Dec. 9, 1961	April 25, 1977	republic	president	prime minister	239	—	25	105	50	1
Thailand	1350	Dec. 22, 1978	constitutional monarchy	king	prime minister	243	324	72	576	12	200
Togo	April 27, 1960	Jan. 13, 1980	republic	president		67	—	5	21	30	200
Tokelau	—	—	territory (N.Z.)	New Zealand GG	administrator	—	—	3	3	12	200
Tonga	June 4, 1970	1875	constitutional monarchy	monarch	prime minister	28	—	3	—	12	200
Trinidad and Tobago	Aug. 31, 1962	Oct. 24, 1976	republic	president	prime minister	31	36	12	30	12	200
Tunisia	March 20, 1956	June 1, 1959	republic	president	prime minister	136	—	23	199	12	1
Turkey	Oct. 29, 1923	Nov. 7, 1982	republic	president	prime minister	400	—	67	572	6[28]	200
Turks and Caicos Islands	—	Aug. 30, 1976	colony (U.K.)	British monarch	governor	19	—	3	—	3	200
Tuvalu	Oct. 1, 1978	Oct. 1, 1978	constitutional monarchy	British monarch	prime minister	13	—	2	—	12	200
Uganda	Oct. 9, 1962	Sept. 8, 1967	republic	chairman MC	prime minister	(156)	—	10	34	—	—
U.S.S.R.	c. 900	Oct. 7, 1977	fed. socialist republic	chairman PSSU	chairman CM	750	750	15	167	12	200
United Arab Emirates	Dec. 2, 1971	Dec. 2, 1971	federation of emirates	president	prime minister	40	—	7	—	3[30]	200
United Kingdom	Oct. 14, 1066	[31]	constitutional monarchy	monarch	prime minister	1,178	650	66[32]	448[32]	3	200
United States	July 4, 1776	March 4, 1789	federal republic	president		100	435	51	3,137	3	200
Uruguay	Aug. 25, 1828	Nov. 27, 1966	republic	president		31	99	19	...	200	1
Vanuatu	July 30, 1980	July 30, 1980	republic	president	prime minister	39	—	4	11	12[5]	200
Venezuela	July 5, 1811	Jan. 23, 1961	federal republic	president		47	200	23	156	12	200
Vietnam	Sept. 2, 1954	Dec. 18, 1980	socialist republic	chairman NA	chairman SC	496	—	40	391	12	200
Virgin Islands (U.S.)	—	—	territory (U.S.)	U.S. president	governor	15	—	3	—	3	200
Wallis and Futuna	—	—	overseas territory (Fr.)	French president	[34]	20	—	3	—	12	200
West Bank	—	—	Israeli military	—	area commander	—	—	7	—	—	—
Western Sahara	—	—	—			—	—	—	—	12	200
Western Samoa	Jan. 1, 1962	Oct. 28, 1960	constitutional monarchy	monarch	prime minister	47	—	21	—	12	200
Yemen (Aden)	Nov. 30, 1967	Oct. 31, 1978	people's republic	chairman, PSPC		111	—	7	27	12	200
Yemen (Ṣan'ā')	Dec. 1918	June 19, 1974	republic	president	prime minister	159	1,000	10	41	12	1
Yugoslavia	Dec. 1, 1918	Feb. 21, 1974	federal socialist republic	president		88	220	8	527	12	1
Zaire	June 30, 1960	Feb. 15, 1978	republic	president		310	—	9	37	12	200
Zambia	Oct. 24, 1964	Aug. 25, 1973	republic	president		136	—	9	53	—	—
Zimbabwe	April 18, 1980	April 18, 1980	republic	president	prime minister	40	100	8	—	—	—

[1]Territorial sea claim assumed to claim fishing/economic rights within the same zone.   [2]Full membership pending.   [3]Defined by bilateral maritime boundaries or by an equidistant line.   [4]Exclusive fishing within 100 nautical miles (nm); regulates fishing in outer 100 nm.   [5]Measured from claimed "archipelagic baselines."   [6]Not fully effective until 1989.   [7]Self-governing in free association with New Zealand.   [8]Includes the Turkish Federated State of Cyprus.   [9]Suspended in 1979.   [10]Executive responsibilities are divided between (for Denmark) the *righsombudsman* and (locally) the *løgmadur* (chairman of the Løgting [administrative council]).   [11]Executive responsibilities are divided among (for France) the Commissioner of the Republic and (locally) the President of the General Council and the President of the Regional Council.   [12]Executive responsibilities are divided between (for France) the High Commissioner and (locally) the President of the Territorial Assembly.   [13]Part 12 nm, part 200 nm, part defined by geographical coordinates.   [14]Associate member.   [15]Evolving constitution adopted by Israeli parliament.   [16]3 nm in 5 straits.   [17]3 nm in Korea Strait.   [18]The full name of Libya is The Socialist People's Libyan Arab Jamahiriya. *Jamahiriya* could be translated as "the masses of the people," "the populace," or "the multitude."   [19]Zone defined by

membership in international organizations

United Nations (date of admission)	UN organs* and affiliated intergovernmental organizations	Commonwealth of Nations	regional multi-purpose	economic	military	country

Column headers under "UN organs* and affiliated intergovernmental organizations": UNCTAD[1], UNICEF[g], ICJ[*], FAO, GATT, IAEA[i], IBRD, ICAO, IDA, IFC, ILO, IMF, IMO, ITU[j], UNESCO, UNIDO, UPU[j], WHO, WIPO[j], WMO

Column headers under "regional multi-purpose": ASEAN, EC, LAS[h], OAS, OAU, SPC

Column headers under "economic": ACP, COMECON, ECOWAS, EEC, I-ADB, IDB[j], OPEC

Column headers under "military": NATO, WTO

UN date	country
1960	Niger
1960	Nigeria
—	Niue
—	Norfolk Island
1945	Norway
1971	Oman
—	Pacific Is., Trust Terr. of
1947	Pakistan
1945	Panama
1975	Papua New Guinea
1945	Paraguay
1945	Peru
1945	Philippines
—	Pitcairn Island
1945	Poland
1955	Portugal
—	Puerto Rico
1971	Qatar
—	Réunion
1955	Romania
1962	Rwanda
1983	St. Christopher and Nevis
—	St. Helena and Ascension
1979	St. Lucia
—	St. Pierre and Miquelon
1980	St. Vincent
—	San Marino
1975	São Tomé and Príncipe
1945	Saudi Arabia
1960	Senegal
1976	Seychelles
1961	Sierra Leone
1965	Singapore
1978	Solomon Islands
1960	Somalia
1945	South Africa
—	Bophuthatswana
—	Ciskei
—	Transkei
—	Venda
—	South West Africa/Namibia
1955	Spain
1955	Sri Lanka
1956	Sudan, The
1975	Suriname
1968	Swaziland
1946	Sweden
—	Switzerland
1945	Syria
—	Taiwan
1961	Tanzania
1946	Thailand
1960	Togo
—	Tokelau
—	Tonga
1962	Trinidad and Tobago
1956	Tunisia
1945	Turkey
—	Turks and Caicos Islands
—	Tuvalu
1962	Uganda
1945[29]	U.S.S.R.
1971	United Arab Emirates
1945	United Kingdom
1945	United States
1945	Uruguay
1981	Vanuatu
1945	Venezuela
1977	Vietnam
—	Virgin Islands (U.S.)
—	Wallis and Futuna
—	West Bank
—	Western Sahara
1976	Western Samoa
1967	Yemen (Aden)
1947	Yemen (Şan'ā')
1945	Yugoslavia
1960	Zaire
1964	Zambia
1980	Zimbabwe

geographical coordinates.   20Special member participating in functional activities but not represented at meetings of Commonwealth heads of government.   21Executive responsibilities are divided between (for France) the Commissioner of the Republic and (locally) the President of the General Council.   22A 1970 basic law, though not a constitution as such, serves that purpose.   23For St. Helena only; Ascension Island and Tristan da Cunha also have local councils.   24House of Assembly—178 white members; House of Representatives—85 Coloured members; House of Delegates—45 Indian members.   25Not recognized internationally.   26The United Nations has declared itself responsible for the territory.   27Transitional constitution.   2812 nm in the Black Sea.   29Belorussian S.S.R. and Ukrainian S.S.R. are also members.   3012 nm for Sharjah.   31Unwritten constitution based on statutes and common law.   32Excludes Northern Ireland.   33Including all colonies and overseas territories.   34Executive responsibilities are divided between (for France) the Superior Administrator and (locally) the President of the Territorial Assembly.   35Membership in dispute.

Area and population

This table provides the area and population for each of the countries of the world and for all political dependencies with a permanent civilian population. Only countries such as the Vatican City State, the British Indian Ocean Territory, and similar anomalous cases are omitted. The data represent the latest published and unpublished data for both the surveyed area of the countries and their populations, the latter both as of a single year (1985) to provide the best comparability and as of the most recent census to provide the fullest comparison of certain demographic measures that are not always available in estimated form between successive national censuses. The 1985 estimates represent a combination of national, United Nations (UN) or other international organization, and *Encyclopædia Britannica* estimates so as to give the best fit to available published series, to take account of unpublished information received in correspondence, and to incorporate the results of very recent censuses for which published analyses and projections based upon them are not yet available.

One principal point to bear in mind when studying these statistics is that all of them, whatever degree of precision may be implied by the exactness of the numbers, are estimates—all of varying, and some of suspect accuracy. Even a country like the United States—which has a long tradition both of census taking and of the use of the most sophisticated analytical tools in processing the data—is unable to determine within 2.5% its total population nationally. And that is an average underenumeration. In larger cities, where enumeration of certain populations, both legal and illegal, is most difficult, the accuracy of the enumerated count may be off considerably more than 5%. When a country like Nigeria, the most populous in Africa, does not know within 20% its real population and is delayed or prevented from measuring it by political circumstances, both the amount and the margin of error are likely to increase. The editors have tried to take account of the range of variation and accuracy in published data, but it is relatively difficult to establish a value for many sources of inaccuracy unless some country or agency has made a conscientious effort to establish both the relative accuracy (precision) of its estimate and the absolute magnitude of the quantity it is trying to measure—for example, the number of people in Kampuchea (Cambodia) who died at the hands of the Khmer Rouge. Was it 1,000,000, 2,000,000, 3,000,000? If a figure of 1,000,000 is cited, what is its accuracy: ± 1%, 10%, 50%? Is the source of the figure Vietnam (potential bias on the high side to justify its invasion), China (potential bias on the low side because of its political connection with the Khmer Rouge), the United States (habitually unable to obtain or produce by analysis accurate data about Southeast Asia, complicated by political bias)?

Many similar problems exist and in endless variations: What is the extent of southern European immigration to western Europe in search of jobs? How many refugees from Uganda or Afghanistan are there in surrounding countries? How many illegal immigrants are there in the United States? How many Palestinians are there in the Middle East (they are politically inconvenient to enumerate everywhere)? How many Amerindians exist in the countries of South America (any accurate answer to that question raises the question, "Where did they go?")? How many people have died or emigrated as a result of the civil violence in Central America?

Still, much information is accurate, well founded, and updated annually. The sources of these data are censuses; national population registers

Area and population

country	area			population (latest estimate)					population (most recent census)				
	square miles	square kilometres	rank	total 1985	rank	density		% annual growth rate 1980–85	census year	total	male (%)	female (%)	urban (%)
						per sq mi	per sq km						
Afghanistan	251,825	652,225	40	18,120,000	42	72.0	27.8	2.6	1979	13,051,358[1]	51.4	48.6	15.1
Albania	11,100	28,748	126	3,000,000	109	270.3	104.4	2.3	1982	2,786,100	51.6	48.4	33.6
Algeria	919,595	2,381,741	10	21,731,000	37	23.6	9.1	2.9	1977	16,948,000	49.7	50.3	40.6
American Samoa	77	199	193	36,000	189	467.5	180.9	2.4	1980	32,297	50.7	49.3	17.5
Andorra	179	464	175	43,000	188	238.2	91.9	4.7	1982	38,051	53.7	46.3	66.8
Angola	481,350	1,246,700	21	8,573,000	68	17.8	6.9	2.5	1970	5,673,046	52.1	47.9	14.2
Anguilla	35	91	199	7,000	202	200.0	76.9	0.0	1974	6,519	47.4	52.6	—
Antigua and Barbuda	171	442	177	81,000	176	473.7	183.3	1.5	1970	65,525	48.0[2]	52.0[2]	30.7[2]
Argentina	1,073,399	2,780,092	8	30,564,000	29	28.5	11.0	1.6	1980	27,947,446	49.2	50.8	86.3
Australia	2,966,200	7,682,300	6	15,749,000	47	5.3	2.1	1.4	1981	15,053,600	50.1	49.9	89.0
Austria	32,376	83,855	109	7,552,000	73	233.3	90.1	0.1	1981	7,555,338	47.4	52.6	55.1
Bahamas, The	5,382	13,939	140	230,000	158	42.7	16.5	1.8	1980	223,545	48.8	51.2	54.4
Bahrain	262	678	169	431,000	142	1,645.0	635.7	4.3	1981	350,798	58.4	41.6	80.7
Bangladesh	55,598	143,998	89	98,699,000	9	1,775.2	685.4	2.1	1981	89,912,000	51.5	48.5	15.7
Barbados	166	430	178	253,000	155	1,524.1	588.4	0.3	1980	248,983	47.6	52.4	39.3[2]
Belgium	11,783	30,519	124	9,859,000	64	836.7	323.0	0.0	1981	9,848,647	48.7	51.3	72.4[2]
Belize	8,867	22,965	133	166,000	162	18.8	7.2	2.2	1980	144,857	50.6	49.4	52.0
Benin	43,450	112,600	96	4,005,000	99	92.1	35.6	2.9	1979	3,338,240	47.9	52.1	38.3
Bermuda	21	54	202	57,000	184	2,700.0	1,042.5	0.7	1980	54,050	48.9	51.1	100.0
Bhutan	18,150	47,000	118	1,423,000	125	78.6	30.3	2.1	1969	931,514	51.5[2]	48.5[2]	3.9
Bolivia	424,164	1,098,581	27	6,429,000	82	15.2	5.9	2.8	1976	4,613,486	49.1	50.9	41.7
Botswana	224,706	581,987	45	1,082,000	130	4.8	1.9	3.5	1981	941,027	47.1	52.9	15.9
Brazil	3,286,500	8,512,000	5	135,564,000	6	41.2	15.9	2.3	1980	119,098,992	49.7	50.3	67.6
British Virgin Islands	59	153	195	12,000	197	203.4	78.4	1.7	1980	10,985	51.1	48.9	12.0
Brunei	2,226	5,765	150	224,000	159	100.6	38.9	3.6	1981	192,832	53.4	46.6	59.4
Bulgaria	42,823	110,912	98	8,979,000	66	209.7	81.0	0.2	1975	8,727,771	49.9	50.1	58.0
Burkina Faso	105,900	274,200	68	6,828,000	77	64.5	24.9	1.9	1975	5,638,203	50.2	49.8	9.0
Burma	261,228	676,577	39	37,686,000	25	144.3	55.7	2.1	1983	35,313,905	49.6	50.4	24.0
Burundi	10,747	27,834	128	4,784,000	94	445.1	171.9	2.4	1979	4,111,310	48.3	51.7	2.3[2]
Cameroon	179,714	465,468	50	9,635,000	65	53.6	20.7	2.5	1976	7,663,246	49.0	51.0	28.5
Canada	3,849,675	9,970,610	2	25,427,000	31	6.6	2.6	1.1	1981	24,343,181	49.6	50.4	76.4
Cape Verde	1,557	4,033	152	314,000	151	201.7	77.9	1.7	1980	288,845	46.3	53.7	35.1
Cayman Islands	102	264	188	20,000	194	196.1	75.8	3.3	1979	17,340	48.8	51.2	100.0
Central African Republic	240,324	622,436	42	2,658,000	112	11.0	4.3	2.3	1975	2,054,610	48.0	52.0	34.6
Chad	495,755	1,284,000	20	5,018,000	92	10.1	3.9	2.3	1975	4,029,917	47.7	52.3	16.0
Chile	284,521	736,905	38	12,074,000	55	42.4	16.4	1.7	1982	11,275,440	49.0	51.0	81.0
China	3,696,100	9,572,900	3	1,043,100,000	1	282.3	109.0	1.2	1982	1,008,175,288	51.5	48.5	21.2
Christmas Island	52	135	196	3,000	205	57.7	22.2	0.0	1981	2,871	66.8	33.2	—
Cocos (Keeling) Islands	5.5	14	207	700	210	127.3	50.0	−7.1	1981	569	53.7	46.3	—
Colombia	440,831	1,141,748	26	28,842,000	30	65.4	25.3	2.0	1973	22,915,229	48.6	51.4	63.6
Comoros	719	1,862	158	403,000	144	560.5	216.4	3.0	1980	346,992	50.1	49.9	33.4
Congo	132,047	342,000	57	1,740,000	122	13.2	5.1	2.6	1974	1,300,120	48.5	51.5	37.8
Cook Islands	91	236	192	17,000	195	186.8	72.0	−1.1	1981	17,754	51.7	48.3	...
Costa Rica	19,730	51,100	116	2,543,000	115	128.9	49.9	2.5	1984	2,416,809	50.0	50.0	43.9
Cuba	42,803	110,860	99	10,058,000	61	235.0	90.7	0.7	1981	9,723,605	50.6	49.4	69.0
Cyprus	3,572	9,251	147	685,000	138	191.8	74.0	1.2	1976	612,851	50.0	50.0	53.0
Czechoslovakia	49,381	127,896	92	15,509,000	50	314.1	121.3	0.3	1980	15,283,095	48.7	51.3	65.5
Denmark	16,633	43,080	119	5,109,000	91	307.2	118.6	−0.1	1983[4]	5,116,464	49.3	50.7	83.9
Djibouti	8,950	23,200	132	430,000	143	48.0	18.5	3.8	1960–61	81,200	...	...	57.4
Dominica	290	750	167	74,000	178	256.0	99.0	0.0	1981	74,851	47.4[5]	52.6[5]	14.3[5]
Dominican Republic	18,704	48,442	117	6,243,000	84	333.8	128.9	2.3	1981	5,647,977	50.1	49.9	52.0
Ecuador	103,930	269,178	69	8,604,000	67	82.8	32.0	2.5	1982	8,060,712	49.9	50.1	49.2
Egypt	385,229	997,739	29	48,503,000	20	125.9	48.6	2.8	1976	36,626,204	50.9	49.1	43.8
El Salvador	8,124	21,041	134	5,236,000	90	644.5	248.8	3.0	1971	3,554,648	49.6	50.4	39.4
Equatorial Guinea	10,831	28,051	127	317,000	150	29.3	11.3	2.1	1983	304,000	49.0[2]	51.0[2]	53.6[2]

(cumulated annually); registration of migration, births and deaths, and so on; sample surveys to establish demographic conditions; and the like.

The statistics provided for area and population by country are ranked, and the population densities based on those values are also provided. The population densities, for purposes of comparison within this table, are calculated on the basis of total area of the country. Elsewhere the reader will find densities calculated on more specialized bases: land area for Finland (because of its many lakes), ice-free area for Greenland (most of which is ice cap), or inhabited area for Egypt (which has relatively enormous areas of uninhabitable desert). The data in this section conclude with the estimated growth rate for the country (including both natural growth and net migration) during 1980–85, calculated mainly from country sources. Both absolute area and population density are calculated for both square miles and square kilometres.

In the section containing census data, information supplied includes the census total (usually de facto, the population actually present, rather than de jure, the population legally resident, who might be anywhere); the male–female breakdown; the proportion that is urban (according to the country's own definition of the term "urban," which differs very much from country to country); and finally an analysis of the age structure of the population by 15-year age groups. This last analysis may be particularly useful in distinguishing the general type of population being recorded— young, fast-growing nations show a high proportion of people under 30 (some countries like Jordan or Mayotte have more than 50% of their population under 15 years), while other nations (for example Sweden, which suffered no age-group losses in World War II) exhibit quite uniform proportions among age groups.

Finally, a section is provided giving the population of each country at the end of each decade from 1930 to 2000. The data for years past represent the best available analysis of the published data by the country itself, by the demographers of the United Nations, or by the editors of Britannica. The projections for 1990 and 2000, similarly, represent the best fit of available data through the mid-1980s with projected population structure and growth rates during the next 15 years. The evidence of the last 15 years with respect to similar estimates published around 1970, however, shows how cloudy is the glass through which these numbers are read. In 1970 no respectable Western analyst would have imagined proposing that mainland China could achieve the degree of birth control that it has since then (as evidenced in the 1982 census); on the other hand, even the Chinese admit that their methods have been somewhat Draconian and that they expect some backlash in terms of higher birth-rates among those who have so far postponed larger families. How much is "some" by 2000? Compound that problem with all the social, economic, political, and biological factors that can affect 200 countries' populations, and the difficulty facing the prospective compiler of such projections may be appreciated.

Specific data about the vital rates affecting the data in this table may be found in great detail in both the country statistical boxes in "The Nations of the World" section and in the table on "Vital statistics, marriage, family," beginning at page 844.

Percentages in this table for male and female population will always total 100.0, but percentages by age group may not for reasons such as nonresponse on census forms, "don't know" responses, which are common in countries with poor birth registration systems, and the like.

age distribution (%)						population (by decade, '000s)								country
0–14	15–29	30–44	45–59	60–74	75 and older	1930	1940	1950	1960	1970	1980	1990 projection	2000 projection	
44.5	26.9	15.8	8.6	3.6	0.6	...	...	8,252	9,820	12,342	15,950	19,349	24,180	Afghanistan
37.3[2]	28.9[2]	16.5[2]	10.2[2]	5.5[2]	1.6[2]	1,003	1,088	1,215	1,607	2,136	2,670	3,350	4,000	Albania
16.1[3]	27.1[3]	12.8[3]	8.3[3]	4.3[3]	1.4[3]	6,489	7,628	8,753	10,800	14,330	18,796	25,300	36,000	Algeria
40.9	28.8	16.0	9.4	4.0	0.9	10	13	19	20	27	32	38	45	American Samoa
...	...	...	...	...	...	5	5	6	8	19	34	53	80	Andorra
41.7	23.2	17.0	7.4	3.8	1.0	3,344	3,738	4,145	4,841	5,673	7,723	9,978	12,257	Angola
43.4	22.2	10.6	10.2	10.1	3.5	...	...	...	6	6	7	7	7	Anguilla
44.0	24.2	12.0	11.7	—— 8.0 ——		30	34	45	55	66	75	86	99	Antigua and Barbuda
30.4	23.9	18.8	15.1	9.0	2.8	11,896	14,169	17,150	20,611	23,788	28,237	33,094	38,788	Argentina
25.1	25.3	20.5	15.2	10.4	3.5	6,503	7,079	8,219	10,315	12,552	14,695	16,724	18,580	Australia
19.9	23.6	20.1	17.1	13.2	6.1	6,435	6,684	6,935	7,048	7,447	7,549	7,579	7,625	Austria
38.1	27.8	17.9	9.8	5.1	1.3	61	70	79	113	169	210	247	282	Bahamas, The
32.9	34.5	20.0	8.8	3.1	0.7	...	90	127	162	215	347	518	688	Bahrain
46.6	24.6	14.9	8.2	—— 5.7 ——		35,353	41,259	45,482	54,699	68,171	88,656	115,244	145,800	Bangladesh
28.9	32.3	14.2	11.2	——13.3 ——		159	179	209	232	235	249	257	264	Barbados
20.0	23.7	19.1	18.6	12.8	5.8	8,129	8,301	8,639	9,153	9,690	9,859	9,890	9,925	Belgium
46.2	27.1	11.8	8.4	4.7	1.8	51	56	68	90	120	145	181	226	Belize
46.1[2]	25.9[2]	14.9[2]	8.6[2]	3.9[2]	0.72	1,099	1,355	1,538	1,990	2,686	3,472	4,861	6,756	Benin
22.7	27.5	22.2	15.7	9.0	2.9	28	31	37	43	53	55	59	63	Bermuda
39.2[3]	26.5[3]	16.3[3]	10.9[3]	—— 7.13 ——		440	500	726	853	1,045	1,280	1,569	1,893	Bhutan
41.5	27.0	15.4	9.8	4.6	1.7	2,153	2,508	2,765	3,405	4,265	5,600	7,314	9,724	Bolivia
56.5	19.9	10.2	6.6	3.4	3.4	212	278	387	522	650	908	1,292	1,865	Botswana
39.1	28.6	16.4	10.0	—— 5.9 ——		33,718	41,525	52,901	71,539	93,139	121,014	150,368	179,487	Brazil
34.0	29.0	18.7	9.7	6.3	2.3	5	7	7	7	10	11	17	20	British Virgin Islands
38.5	32.7	16.4	7.9	—— 4.5 ——		30	36	48	84	129	187	258	341	Brunei
21.8	22.4	20.6	18.6	13.0	3.4	5,997	6,624	7,273	7,906	8,515	8,877	9,445	9,821	Bulgaria
47.4	21.1	16.1	9.3	—— 6.1 ——		...	...	3,584	4,350	5,412	6,195	7,400	8,600	Burkina Faso
41.2[2]	25.8[2]	16.0[2]	10.9[2]	5.2[2]	0.92	14,282	16,119	18,489	22,063	26,997	33,938	44,548	49,749	Burma
42.4	29.4	13.4	8.2	4.8	1.8	...	...	2,435	2,908	3,350	4,121	5,305	6,951	Burundi
43.4	24.3	16.6	9.9	4.3	1.5	...	...	4,888	5,609	6,727	8,503	10,885	13,893	Cameroon
23.4	28.9	20.0	15.0	9.6	3.1	10,498	11,693	13,737	17,909	21,324	24,070	26,826	29,028	Canada
46.0	27.6	9.1	9.0	6.3	2.0	146	181	147	200	272	289	343	382	Cape Verde
29.1	25.8	22.1	13.1	7.3	2.6	6	7	7	8	11	17	23	27	Cayman Islands
43.5	23.5	17.1	12.4	2.7	0.8	...	...	1,311	1,500	1,793	2,290	2,965	3,736	Central African Republic
40.6	28.3	17.2	9.5	—— 4.4 ——		...	...	2,639	3,032	3,643	4,477	5,558	7,063	Chad
31.9	29.1	19.1	11.7	6.3	1.9	4,365	5,063	6,091	7,585	9,368	11,104	13,061	14,017	Chile
33.6	29.1	17.5	12.2	6.3	1.3	500,000	530,000	556,613	682,024	838,396	983,908	1,098,000	1,269,000	China
25.9	26.4	35.8	10.8	—— 1.1 ——		...	...	1	3	3	3	3	3	Christmas Island
27.4	28.3	27.2	11.2	—— 5.9 ——		...	...	1	1	1	1	1	1	Cocos (Keeling) Islands
44.1	27.3	14.9	8.5	4.1	1.0	7,280	9,097	11,268	15,321	20,884	26,056	31,900	38,000	Colombia
45.1[2]	26.9[2]	15.1[2]	8.5[2]	3.6[2]	0.82	...	...	...	177	245	347	466	637	Comoros
45.6	22.2	15.5	11.3	4.7	0.7	...	...	736	933	1,182	1,529	1,995	2,646	Congo
42.7	26.6	13.7	10.4	5.2	1.3	11	13	15	18	18	18	20	22	Cook Islands
37.9	31.5	15.8	9.2	4.4	1.2	499	619	866	1,250	1,737	2,245	2,937	3,596	Costa Rica
30.3	27.6	19.1	12.1	8.2	2.7	3,837	4,566	5,752	7,019	8,565	9,718	10,540	11,718	Cuba
25.4	29.0	17.9	13.4	10.8	3.5	357	413	494	573	615	627	708	793	Cyprus
24.3	22.9	19.9	12.7	11.5	4.3	13,964	14,713	12,389	13,654	14,334	15,265	15,758	16,278	Czechoslovakia
19.4	22.7	21.6	16.0	14.0	6.0	3,542	3,832	4,271	4,581	4,929	5,123	5,068	4,951	Denmark
42.3[2]	—— 52.1[2] ——			—— 5.6[2] ——		...	...	60	78	158	355	498	670	Djibouti
49.1[5]	21.2[5]	11.2[5]	10.0[5]	6.3[5]	2.25	41	45	51	60	70	74	77	81	Dominica
44.8[2]	29.0[2]	14.1[2]	7.8[2]	3.5[2]	0.82	1,400	1,759	2,313	3,160	4,343	5,558	6,971	8,407	Dominican Republic
41.9	28.1	15.4	8.6	4.5	1.5	2,102	2,546	3,307	4,421	5,958	7,604	10,949	14,596	Ecuador
39.9	26.7	16.6	10.6	5.2	1.0	14,822	16,942	20,461	26,085	33,329	42,126	53,481	65,200	Egypt
46.2	25.1	15.2	8.2	4.3	1.0	1,350	1,550	1,931	2,527	3,534	4,508	5,997	7,730	El Salvador
41.5[2]	25.8[2]	15.6[2]	10.6[2]	5.4[2]	1.12	...	...	211	244	291	285	359	438	Equatorial Guinea

Area and population (continued)

country	area			population (latest estimate)					population (most recent census)				
	square miles	square kilo- metres	rank	total 1985	rank	density		% annual growth rate 1980–85	census year	total	male (%)	female (%)	urban (%)
						per sq mi	per sq km						
Ethiopia	472,400	1,223,600	23	43,551,000	22	92.2	35.6	2.9	1984	42,019,418	49.9	50.1	11.3
Faeroe Islands	540	1,399	161	45,000	187	83.3	32.2	0.5	1977	41,969	52.4	47.6	87.6
Falkland Islands	4,700	12,173	142	2,000	207	0.4	0.2	0.0	1980	1,813	55.2	44.8	55.1
Fiji	7,055	18,273	137	692,000	137	98.1	37.9	1.8	1976	588,068	50.5	49.5	37.2
Finland	130,559	338,145	58	4,910,000	93	37.6	14.5	0.5	1980	4,784,710	48.3	51.7	59.9
France	210,026	543,965	46	55,191,000	16	262.8	101.5	0.5	1982	54,334,871	49.0	51.0	77.9[2]
French Guiana	35,900	93,000	106	83,000	175	2.4	0.9	4.0	1982	73,012	52.7	47.3	73.4
French Polynesia	1,359	3,521	153	175,000	161	128.8	49.7	3.4	1983	166,753	51.1	48.9	39.7
Gabon	103,347	267,667	71	1,166,000	128	11.3	4.4	1.6	1960-61	448,564	49.1	50.6[2]	35.8[2]
Gambia, The	4,127	10,690	145	749,000	136	181.5	70.1	3.4	1983	695,886	49.4[2]	50.6[2]	21.2
Gaza Strip	140	363	182	509,000	141	3,635.7	1,402.2	2.4	1983[4]	493,700	49.8	50.2	...
Germany, East	41,827	108,333	101	16,703,000	44	399.3	154.2	−0.04	1981	16,705,635	47.0	53.0	76.4
Germany, West	96,026	248,706	74	60,940,000	12	634.7	245.0	−0.2	1982[4]	61,546,101	47.8	52.2	84.7[2]
Ghana	92,098	238,533	78	12,815,000	54	139.1	53.7	2.5	1984	12,205,574	49.1	50.9	31.3
Gibraltar	2.2	5.8	209	30,000	190	13,636.4	5,172.4	0.7	1981	26,479	52.2	47.8	...
Greece	50,949	131,957	91	9,967,000	63	195.6	75.5	0.7	1981	9,740,417	49.1	50.9	58.1
Greenland	840,000	2,175,600	13	53,000	185	0.06	0.02	1.1	1984[4]	52,347	54.2	45.8	77.8
Grenada	133	345	184	96,000	174	725.2	279.2	−1.0	1980	90,821	48.8[6]	51.2[6]	25.3[5]
Guadeloupe	687	1,780	159	330,000	148	480.3	185.4	0.2	1982	327,002	49.0	51.0	...
Guam	209	541	173	120,000	169	574.2	221.8	2.3	1980	105,979	52.2	47.8	39.5
Guatemala	42,042	108,889	100	7,675,000	72	182.6	70.5	2.3	1981	6,043,559	49.8	50.2	34.3
Guernsey	30	78	200	60,000	183	2,000.0	769.2	1.0	1976	54,256	48.3	51.7	...
Guinea	94,900	245,790	75	5,429,000	87	57.2	22.1	2.3	1977	4,527,000	49.5[2]	50.5[2]	19.1[2]
Guinea-Bissau	13,948	36,125	122	873,000	134	62.6	24.2	2.1	1979	767,739	48.2	51.8	14.0
Guyana	83,000	215,000	81	953,000	133	11.5	4.4	1.9	1970	701,885	49.7	50.3	31.9
Haiti	10,579	27,400	130	5,251,000	89	496.4	191.7	1.3	1982	5,053,792	48.5	51.5	20.6
Honduras	43,277	112,088	97	4,372,000	95	101.1	39.0	3.4	1974	2,656,948	49.5	50.5	37.5
Hong Kong	400	1,037	163	5,415,000	88	13,149.6	5,077.4	1.4	1981	4,986,460	52.2	47.8	85.9
Hungary	35,921	93,036	105	10,645,000	57	296.3	114.4	−0.1	1980	10,709,463	48.4	51.6	53.2
Iceland	39,769	103,000	102	243,000	157	6.1	2.4	1.3	1983[4]	235,537	50.4	49.6	88.8
India	1,183,041	3,064,063	7	768,100,000	2	649.2	250.7	2.2	1981	685,184,692	50.3	49.7	23.7
Indonesia	741,101	1,919,443	15	167,550,000	5	226.1	87.3	2.7	1980	147,490,298	49.7	50.3	22.3
Iran	636,443	1,648,380	17	45,000,000	21	70.7	27.3	3.2	1976	33,708,744	51.5	48.5	47.0
Iraq	169,235	438,317	53	15,676,000	49	92.6	35.8	3.4	1977	12,000,497	51.5	48.5	63.7
Ireland	27,137	70,285	113	3,614,000	102	133.2	51.0	1.1	1981	3,443,405	50.2	49.8	55.6
Isle of Man	221	572	172	70,000	179	316.7	122.4	1.5	1981	66,101	47.8	52.2	...
Israel[7]	7,992	20,700	135	4,306,000	96	538.8	208.0	1.9	1983	4,037,620	49.8	50.2	86.9
Italy	116,324	301,278	65	57,079,000	14	490.7	189.5	0.4	1981	56,243,935	48.7	51.3	69.3[2]
Ivory Coast	123,847	320,763	63	10,163,000	59	82.1	31.7	4.2	1975	6,702,866	51.8	48.2	32.0
Jamaica	4,244	10,991	144	2,344,000	116	552.2	213.2	1.5	1982	2,095,878	49.0	51.0	46.3
Japan	145,862	377,781	56	120,760,000	7	827.9	319.7	0.7	1980	117,060,396	49.2	50.8	76.2
Jersey	45	116	197	78,000	177	1,733.3	672.4	1.3	1981	72,970	47.9	52.1	...
Jordan[9]	34,443	89,206	108	2,647,000	113	76.9	29.7	3.8	1979	2,123,997	52.3	47.7	59.5
Kampuchea	69,898	181,035	84	7,280,000	74	104.2	40.2	2.3	1962[10]	5,728,771	50.0	50.0	10.3
Kenya	224,961	582,646	44	20,312,000	38	90.3	34.9	4.0	1979	15,327,061	49.6	50.4	15.1
Kiribati	328	849	166	65,000	181	198.2	76.6	2.3	1985	63,045	49.5	50.5	33.9
Korea, North	47,250	122,370	94	20,082,000	39	427.2	164.7	2.3	11	—	49.4[2]	50.6[2]	59.7[2]
Korea, South	38,259	99,091	103	41,215,000	23	1,077.3	415.9	1.6	1980	37,436,315	50.1	49.9	57.3
Kuwait	6,880	17,818	138	1,911,000	120	277.8	107.3	6.6	1980	1,357,952	57.2	42.8	100.0
Laos	91,430	236,800	80	4,117,000	98	45.0	17.4	1.1	11	—	50.3[2]	49.7[2]	13.4[2]
Lebanon	3,950	10,230	146	2,668,000	111	675.4	260.8	0.01	1970	2,126,325	50.8	49.2	60.1
Lesotho	11,720	30,355	125	1,500,000	124	128.0	49.4	2.4	1976	1,216,815	48.3	51.7	17.2
Liberia	38,250	99,067	104	2,232,000	117	58.3	22.5	3.2	1974	1,503,368	50.5	49.5	29.1
Libya	685,524	1,775,500	16	3,786,000	101	5.5	2.1	4.4	1973[12]	2,249,237	53.0	47.0	59.8
Liechtenstein	62	160	194	27,000	192	435.5	168.8	1.5	1980	25,215	49.6	50.4	...
Luxembourg	999	2,586	155	366,000	146	366.4	141.5	0.1	1981	364,606	48.8	51.2	78.4[2]
Macau	6	16	206	314,000	152	52,333.3	19,625.0	1.8	1981	247,826	51.9	48.1	94.9
Madagascar	226,662	587,051	43	10,012,000	62	44.2	17.1	2.8	1975	7,603,790	50.0	50.0	16.3
Malawi	45,747	118,484	95	7,059,000	76	154.3	59.6	3.4	1977	5,547,460	48.2	51.8	8.5
Malaysia	127,581	330,434	61	15,677,000	48	122.8	47.4	2.3	1980	13,136,109	50.2	49.8	34.2
Maldives	115	298	186	182,000	160	1,582.6	611.0	3.5	1977[13]	142,832	52.7	47.3	20.7
Mali	478,841	1,240,192	22	8,090,000	71	16.9	6.4	2.5	1976	6,394,918	48.8	51.2	16.8
Malta	122	316	185	333,000	147	2,730.0	1,050.0	0.8	1967	314,216	47.9	52.1	94.3
Martinique	421	1,091	162	330,000	148	783.8	302.5	0.1	1982	328,566	48.5	51.5	57.1
Mauritania	397,700	1,030,020	28	1,656,000	123	4.2	1.6	2.0	1976–77	1,419,939	50.1	49.9	21.9
Mauritius	788	2,041	159	1,025,000	132	1,300.6	502.2	1.4	1983	993,700	49.1	50.9	42.5
Mayotte	144	373	181	67,000	180	402.8	155.5	3.0	1978[14]	47,246	49.9	50.1	53.3
Mexico	756,066	1,958,201	14	78,027,000	11	103.2	39.8	2.3	1980	67,382,581	49.4	50.6	66.3
Monaco	0.7	1.9	211	28,000	191	40,000.0	14,736.8	1.5	1975[15]	25,029	45.7	54.3	100.0
Mongolia	604,000	1,565,000	18	1,907,000	121	3.2	1.2	2.7	1979	1,594,800	50.1	49.9	51.2
Montserrat	40	102	198	12,000	197	300.0	117.6	0.0	1980	11,606	48.1	51.9	54.1
Morocco	177,117	458,730	52	24,370,000	32	137.6	53.1	3.9	1982	20,419,555	50.0[8]	50.0[8]	42.7
Mozambique	308,642	799,380	34	14,074,000	53	45.6	17.6	3.0	1980	12,130,000	48.7	51.3	8.7[2]
Nauru	8	21	205	8,000	199	1,000.0	381.0	2.7	1977	7,254	52.1[16]	47.9[16]	—
Nepal	56,827	147,181	88	16,525,000	45	290.8	112.3	2.3	1981	15,022,839	51.2	48.8	6.4
Netherlands, The	16,026	41,508	120	14,472,000	52	903.0	348.7	0.5	1984	14,394,400	49.5	50.5	88.5
Netherlands Antilles	383	993	165	244,000	156	637.1	245.7	0.7	1981	231,932	48.8	51.2	...
New Caledonia	7,233	18,734	136	149,000	165	20.6	8.0	1.2	1983	145,368	51.8	48.2	58.5
New Zealand	103,493	268,046	70	3,291,000	106	32.0	12.3	1.2	1981	3,175,737	49.7	50.3	83.6
Nicaragua	49,291	127,662	93	3,039,000	107	61.7	23.8	3.3	1971	1,877,952	48.3	51.7	48.0
Niger	458,074	1,186,408	25	6,253,000	83	13.7	5.3	2.7	1977	5,098,427	49.3	50.7	11.8
Nigeria	356,669	923,768	31	96,015,000	10	269.2	103.9	2.4	1963[17]	55,670,055	50.5	49.5	16.1
Niue	100	258	190	3,000	205	30.0	11.6	...	1981	3,281	51.0	49.0	...
Norfolk Island	14	35	203	2,000	207	142.9	57.1	...	1981	2,134	49.1	50.9	—
Norway	125,050	323,878	62	4,157,000	97	33.2	12.8	0.3	1980	4,092,340	49.5	50.5	70.3

age distribution (%)						population (by decade, '000s)								country
0–14	15–29	30–44	45–59	60–74	75 and older	1930	1940	1950	1960	1970	1980	1990 projection	2000 projection	
45.5[2]	24.4[2]	16.4[2]	8.4[2]	——5.3[2]——		...	...	16,675	20,024	24,068	37,751	50,243	66,870	Ethiopia
29.6	23.9	14.9	15.1	10.4	3.6	24	27	31	35	39	44	47	50	Faeroe Islands
26.7	22.4	——50.8——				2	2	2	2	2	2	2	2	Falkland Islands
41.1	29.8	16.2	8.8	3.3	0.8	181	218	289	394	520	634	758	907	Fiji
20.2	24.4	22.1	16.8	12.4	4.1	3,449	3,698	4,009	4,430	4,606	4,780	4,955	4,964	Finland
22.0	23.5	19.6	17.3	11.6	6.0	41,150	41,300	41,736	45,684	50,770	53,855	55,600	57,000	France
34.2	29.2	19.9	9.8	5.1	1.8	30	30	27	33	49	68	93	126	French Guiana
38.5	29.7	16.5	10.3	4.2	0.8	39	50	62	84	109	148	203	273	French Polynesia
35.4[5]	19.3[5]	22.2[5]	16.3[5]	6.3[5]	0.5[5]	...	...	...	...	950	1,074	1,282	1,611	Gabon
44.3[2]	26.4[2]	15.4[2]	9.1[2]	4.0[2]	0.7[2]	211	193	232	357	458	633	887	1,244	Gambia, The
48.7	28.0	11.0	8.2	——4.2——		...	...	...	...	370	451	589	790	Gaza Strip
19.4	24.2	20.0	17.3	12.8	6.3	15,400	16,800	18,387	17,240	17,058	16,737	16,604	16,483	Germany, East
16.5	24.0	21.0	18.6	13.6	6.3	37,500	40,600	49,986	55,433	60,714	61,566	59,600	58,800	Germany, West
46.9[5]	24.4[5]	15.8[5]	7.5[5]	3.8[5]	1.6[5]	3,110	3,636	5,297	6,958	8,789	11,293	15,886	21,923	Ghana
21.4	22.2	22.3	17.7	12.6	3.8	16	14	23	24	26	29	33	35	Gibraltar
22.3[3]	21.8[3]	19.1[3]	19.5[3]	12.4[3]	5.2[3]	6,367	7,319	7,566	8,327	8,793	9,643	10,200	10,700	Greece
25.3	34.5	22.5	12.1	4.5	1.1	16	19	23	33	41	50	56	61	Greenland
39.4	31.2	10.1	9.2	7.3	2.8	68	71	76	90	95	91	106	131	Grenada
31.1	29.2	16.6	12.0	7.8	2.8	151	180	206	265	320	327	333	348	Guadeloupe
34.9	30.6	19.4	10.5	3.9	0.5	19	22	59	67	85	107	132	146	Guam
44.9	26.8	14.8	8.5	3.9	1.1	1,771	2,201	3,024	4,005	5,263	7,262	9,197	12,222	Guatemala
21.9	22.8	17.5	17.3	14.9	5.6	40	44	44	45	51	57	63	71	Guernsey
43.8[2]	25.5[2]	16.3[2]	9.5[2]	4.2[2]	0.7[2]	...	...	2,687	3,183	3,921	4,832	6,145	7,935	Guinea
44.3	25.5	15.1	8.2	4.7	2.2	...	341	411	520	653	787	987	1,241	Guinea-Bissau
47.1	25.1	13.4	9.0	4.4	1.0	309	344	423	560	715	865	1,040	1,196	Guyana
39.2	26.9	15.6	10.0	5.4	2.9	2,422	2,827	3,097	3,723	4,234	4,922	5,580	6,978	Haiti
48.1	25.8	13.9	7.8	3.6	0.9	948	1,146	1,390	1,873	2,553	3,691	5,105	6,978	Honduras
24.8	32.7	17.7	14.6	8.2	2.0	821	1,786	1,974	3,074	3,942	5,039	6,135	7,161	Hong Kong
21.8	20.7	——57.5——				8,649	9,280	9,338	9,984	10,353	10,710	10,920	10,964	Hungary
26.7	27.4	18.6	13.6	9.5	4.3	107	121	143	176	204	228	252	270	Iceland
39.5	25.9	17.4	10.7	——6.5——		278,000	317,000	352,664	427,802	543,132	686,909	851,000	1,028,000	India
40.8	27.0	16.4	10.2	4.5	1.1	60,750	70,500	75,449	92,701	119,467	146,360	178,370	204,486	Indonesia
44.5	25.2	14.8	10.1	3.8	1.0	12,400	14,000	16,913	21,554	28,359	38,350	51,033	64,916	Iran
48.9	24.5	12.3	8.2	4.2	1.9	...	3,745	5,180	6,847	9,356	13,240	18,136	24,198	Iraq
30.1	24.9	17.2	13.1	——14.7——		2,927	2,958	2,969	2,834	2,954	3,415	3,800	4,200	Ireland
19.1	19.7	18.2	16.5	18.2	8.2	50	52	55	49	52	65	75	86	Isle of Man
32.6	26.4	18.0	12.3	9.4	3.1	...	...	...	2,114	2,958	3,906	4,639	5,440	Israel[7]
21.7[8]	22.1[8]	20.2[8]	18.6[8]	12.5[8]	4.9[8]	40,293	43,840	46,769	50,223	53,565	56,040	57,400	58,100	Italy
44.5	27.0	16.7	7.8	2.8	1.2	2,075	2,350	2,775	3,865	5,550	8,247	12,568	19,088	Ivory Coast
36.7	29.8	12.9	10.1	3.0	7.5	1,009	1,212	1,403	1,629	1,891	2,175	2,535	2,872	Jamaica
23.5	21.5	24.2	17.9	9.8	3.1	64,450	73,075	83,200	93,419	103,720	116,807	122,834	128,119	Japan
16.9	24.4	21.7	17.1	13.9	6.0	50	51	57	63	68	73	78	84	Jersey
51.8	23.3	13.4	7.3	——4.2——		...	...	1,095	1,384	1,795	2,190	3,055	4,249	Jordan[9]
43.8	24.9	16.8	9.8	4.1	0.6	2,800	3,400	4,163	5,364	7,060	6,500	8,572	9,772	Kampuchea
48.3	26.9	12.8	7.1	3.5	1.4	...	...	6,018	8,115	11,225	16,667	24,911	38,499	Kenya
38.9	29.9	16.1	9.3	4.9	0.9	27	29	33	41	49	58	72	89	Kiribati
40.0[2]	28.7[2]	15.9[2]	9.7[2]	4.7[2]	1.0[2]	...	...	9,740	10,526	13,892	17,892	22,443	27,256	Korea, North
34.0	30.0	18.4	11.5	5.1	1.0	...	...	21,147	25,142	32,976	38,124	44,475	52,849	Korea, South
40.2	28.2	21.7	7.7	1.9	0.4	...	...	145	292	748	1,375	2,101	2,936	Kuwait
42.4[2]	26.3[2]	16.7[2]	9.7[2]	4.2[2]	0.7[2]	930	1,075	1,949	2,382	2,962	3,901	4,989	6,213	Laos
42.6	23.8	16.7	9.1	——7.7——		...	965	1,364	1,786	2,470	2,669	3,301	3,992	Lebanon
39.1	25.5	15.5	10.4	3.9	5.6	537	566	766	885	1,043	1,331	1,731	2,251	Lesotho
40.9	26.7	17.7	8.8	4.6	1.3	...	...	758	1,004	1,393	1,898	2,571	3,564	Liberia
44.3	22.2	15.4	8.2	4.0	1.6	800	900	1,029	1,349	1,982	3,043	4,417	6,539	Libya
23.0	26.5	24.1	14.1	9.2	3.1	10	11	14	15	21	25	28	30	Liechtenstein
18.5	23.7	21.2	18.7	12.8	5.1	297	296	296	314	339	364	375	400	Luxembourg
22.9	36.2	16.7	12.7	——11.5——		196	375	188	169	221	287	341	388	Macau
44.4	25.7	14.2	10.0	4.6	1.1	3,722	4,034	4,330	5,370	6,720	8,714	11,575	15,552	Madagascar
44.6	25.7	14.2	9.0	1.5	4.6	1,394	1,696	3,033	3,481	4,511	5,968	8,289	11,631	Malawi
39.5	29.1	16.5	9.2	4.6	1.1	...	...	6,187	7,908	10,466	13,870	17,338	20,615	Malaysia
44.6	24.8	16.4	9.6	——4.1——		78	81	82	106	128	152	202	254	Maldives
44.0	24.9	16.1	8.7	4.8	1.5	...	...	3,426	4,224	5,690	6,983	8,825	11,306	Mali
29.8	25.9	17.6	13.8	10.2	2.7	239	270	308	329	326	320	345	360	Malta
28.4	30.3	16.2	13.2	8.6	3.3	175	200	222	252	287	328	334	357	Martinique
45.9[2]	26.2[2]	14.7[2]	8.7[2]	3.9[2]	0.6[2]	...	...	781	970	1,245	1,502	1,828	2,229	Mauritania
32.4	32.0	17.7	11.0	5.7	1.2	413	428	479	662	824	957	1,117	1,248	Mauritius
50.2	23.4	13.9	7.0	3.8	1.7	...	...	...	...	...	50	86	139	Mayotte
43.0	27.8	14.9	8.5	——5.8——		16,589	19,815	26,606	36,369	50,313	69,393	89,012	109,180	Mexico
12.7	17.8	18.6	19.9	20.7	10.0	23	20	22	23	24	26	28	30	Monaco
43.1[2]	26.1[2]	16.3[2]	9.5[2]	4.1[2]	0.9[2]	725	750	747	931	1,248	1,663	2,170	2,686	Mongolia
31.5	27.2	13.8	10.7	——16.8——		13	15	14	12	12	12	13	15	Montserrat
45.6[8]	26.8[8]	14.8[8]	8.4[8]	3.7[8]	0.7[8]	6,980	7,750	8,953	11,640	15,126	20,050	27,840	36,509	Morocco
43.7[2]	25.2[2]	16.0[2]	9.7[2]	4.6[2]	0.8[2]	3,890	5,086	5,742	7,046	9,140	12,090	16,132	21,713	Mozambique
44.1[16]	33.1[16]	11.4[16]	8.5[16]	1.9[16]	1.0[16]	3	3	4	5	7	7	8	9	Nauru
41.4	25.5	17.4	10.0	4.7	1.0	6,250	7,000	8,000	9,180	11,232	14,698	18,500	23,048	Nepal
20.4	25.6	22.0	15.5	11.6	4.9	7,936	8,834	10,027	11,417	12,958	14,150	14,783	15,380	Netherlands, The
38.0	26.7	16.7	10.3	6.4	1.8	72	107	162	192	223	236	262	300	Netherlands Antilles
36.2	26.9	19.5	11.2	5.1	1.1	54	53	59	79	110	140	159	180	New Caledonia
26.7	25.9	19.1	14.3	10.5	3.5	1,491	1,636	1,908	2,372	2,820	3,100	3,506	3,772	New Zealand
48.1	25.6	14.1	7.4	3.8	1.1	700	825	1,109	1,472	1,972	2,581	3,778	5,261	Nicaragua
46.6[2]	26.4[2]	14.4[2]	8.3[2]	3.7[2]	0.6[2]	...	...	2,291	2,913	4,016	5,468	7,151	9,350	Niger
43.0	31.9	16.5	5.1	2.5	1.0	...	...	33,320	42,366	56,346	85,039	108,613	138,983	Nigeria
40.1	27.2	14.0	9.8	5.9	3.0	4	4	4	4	4	4	4	4	Niue
22.2	21.2	21.7	19.3	——15.7——		1	1	1	1	2	2	2	2	Norfolk Island
22.1	22.7	18.9	16.0	14.4	5.9	2,807	2,973	3,265	3,581	3,877	4,086	4,225	4,325	Norway

Area and population (continued)

country	area			population (latest estimate)					population (most recent census)				
	square miles	square kilometres	rank	total 1985	rank	density		% annual growth rate 1980–85	census year	total	male (%)	female (%)	urban (%)
						per sq mi	per sq km						
Oman	120,000	300,000	66	1,041,000	131	8.7	3.5	3.1	11	—	50.6[2]	49.4[2]	7.3[2]
Pacific Is., Trust Territory of the	717	1,857	159	149,000	165	208.1	80.3	2.3	1980	132,929	51.4	48.6	28.4
Pakistan	307,374	796,095	35	100,356,000	8	326.5	126.1	3.1	1981	84,253,644	52.5	47.5	29.0
Panama	29,762	77,082	111	2,181,000	118	73.3	28.3	2.2	1980	1,831,399	50.7	49.3	49.3
Papua New Guinea	178,704	462,840	51	3,328,000	104	18.6	7.2	2.1	1980	3,010,727	52.3	47.7	13.1
Paraguay	157,048	406,752	54	3,404,000	103	21.7	8.4	3.1	1982	3,035,360	50.1	49.9	42.8
Peru	496,225	1,285,216	19	19,701,000	40	39.7	15.3	2.6	1981	17,005,210	49.7	50.3	64.9
Philippines	115,800	300,000	67	54,669,000	17	472.1	182.2	2.5	1980	48,098,460	50.2	49.8	37.2
Pitcairn Island	1.8	4.5	210	63	211	33.3	13.3	...	1981	53	54.7	45.3	—
Poland	120,727	312,683	64	37,160,000	26	307.8	118.8	0.9	1978	35,061,450	51.3	48.7	57.5
Portugal	35,672	92,389	107	10,151,000	60	284.6	109.9	0.6	1981	9,852,841	48.2	51.8	29.7
Puerto Rico	3,515	9,104	148	3,311,000	105	957.2	369.6	0.7	1980	3,196,520	48.7	51.3	66.8
Qatar	4,400	11,400	143	301,000	153	68.4	26.4	4.0	1981	244,534	63.6	36.4	86.1[2]
Réunion	982	2,544	156	547,000	140	556.4	214.8	1.6	1982	515,798	49.1	50.9	52.8
Romania	91,700	237,500	79	22,715,000	35	247.7	95.6	0.5	1977	21,559,910	49.3	50.7	48.1
Rwanda	10,169	26,338	131	6,115,000	85	601.3	232.2	3.5	1978	4,830,984	48.9	51.1	4.5
St. Christopher and Nevis	101	261	189	47,000	186	455.9	176.0	0.0	1980	43,309	48.1	51.9	37.1
St. Helena and Ascension	159	412	179	7,000	202	44.0	17.0	3.1	1976	5,147	52.0	48.0	29.6
St. Lucia	238	617	171	138,000	168	577.4	222.9	2.8	1981	120,300	47.2	52.8	52.1[3]
St. Pierre and Miquelon	93	242	191	6,000	204	64.5	24.8	0.0	1982	6,041	49.4	50.6	...
St. Vincent and the Grenadines	150	389	180	105,000	172	698.6	269.7	−3.3	1970	86,314	47.3	52.7	27.0
San Marino	24	61	201	22,000	193	943.9	364.4	0.9	1976	20,284	50.4	49.6	92.4[8]
São Tomé and Príncipe	387	1,001	164	107,000	170	275.2	106.4	2.6	1981	96,611	51.6[2]	48.4[2]	...
Saudi Arabia	865,000	2,240,000	12	11,240,000	56	13.0	5.0	3.9	1974	6,939,000	53.5[2]	46.5[2]	66.8[2]
Senegal	75,955	196,722	82	6,520,000	80	85.0	33.1	2.7	1976	4,907,507	49.5	50.5	25.4[2]
Seychelles	175	453	176	65,000	181	371.4	143.5	0.6	1977	61,898	50.4	49.6	37.1
Sierra Leone	27,699	71,740	112	3,930,000	100	141.9	54.8	4.4	1974	2,735,159	54.1	45.9	24.5[2]
Singapore	239	618	170	2,558,000	114	10,702.9	4,139.2	1.2	1980	2,413,945	51.0	49.0	100.0
Solomon Islands	10,640	27,556	129	267,000	154	25.1	9.7	3.0	1976	196,823	52.2	47.8	7.6
Somalia	246,000	637,000	41	5,817,000	86	23.6	9.1	2.7	1975	3,722,000	45.8[2]	54.2[2]	30.2[2]
South Africa	470,413	1,218,364	24	32,891,000	28	69.9	27.0	2.8	1980	27,747,359	49.6[2]	50.4[2]	49.6[2]
Bophuthatswana	15,444	40,000	—	1,527,000	—	98.9	38.2	...	1970	880,312	46.9	53.1	14.2
Ciskei	2,080	5,386	—	777,000	—	373.6	144.3	...	1970	529,635	44.3	55.7	19.6
Transkei	16,816	43,553	—	2,681,000	—	159.4	61.6	...	1970	1,745,992	41.2	58.8	3.2
Venda	2,393	6,198	—	424,000	—	177.2	68.4	...	1970	268,624	38.1	61.9	0.3
South West Africa/Namibia	317,818	823,144	33	1,097,000	129	3.5	1.3	1.7	1981	1,031,927	49.2	50.8	26.0
Spain	194,885	504,750	48	38,765,000	24	198.9	76.8	0.7	1981	37,746,260	49.1	50.9	74.3[2]
Sri Lanka	25,332	65,610	114	16,109,000	46	635.9	245.5	1.8	1981	14,848,364	50.8	49.2	21.5
Sudan, The	966,757	2,503,890	9	23,645,000	33	24.5	9.4	3.8	1983	20,564,364	51.0[18]	49.0[18]	30.6[18]
Suriname	63,251	163,820	86	395,000	145	6.2	2.4	2.1	1980	354,860	49.5	50.5	44.8[2]
Swaziland	6,704	17,364	139	647,000	139	96.6	37.3	2.9	1976	494,534	45.6	54.4	15.2
Sweden	187,901	486,661	49	8,345,000	69	44.4	17.1	0.1	1980	8,320,582	49.5	50.5	83.1
Switzerland	15,943	41,293	121	6,473,000	81	406.0	156.8	0.5	1980	6,365,960	48.9	51.1	57.1
Syria	71,498	185,180	83	10,267,000	58	143.6	55.4	3.3	1981	9,053,000	51.1	48.9	47.1
Taiwan	13,900	36,002	123	19,135,000	41	1,376.6	531.5	1.6	1980	17,968,797	52.2	47.8	70.6[2]
Tanzania	364,881	945,037	30	21,733,000	36	59.6	23.0	3.1	1978	17,512,611	49.2	50.8	13.8
Thailand	198,115	513,115	47	51,301,000	18	258.9	100.0	1.1	1980	46,961,338	50.3	49.7	17.6
Togo	21,925	56,785	115	2,989,000	110	136.3	52.6	2.8	1981	2,700,982	48.2	51.8	15.2
Tokelau	4.7	12.2	208	2,000	207	425.5	163.9	...	1981	1,572	49.4	50.6	—
Tonga	288	747	168	97,000	173	336.4	129.9	0.0	1976	90,085	51.1	48.9	20.3
Trinidad and Tobago	1,980	5,128	151	1,189,000	127	600.5	231.9	1.7	1980	1,059,825	50.0	50.0	21.5[2]
Tunisia	59,664	154,530	87	7,185,000	75	120.4	46.5	2.3	1984	6,966,173	50.9	49.1	52.8
Turkey	300,948	779,452	36	49,272,000	19	163.7	63.2	2.1	1980	44,736,957	51.6	48.4	43.9
Turks and Caicos Islands	193	500	174	8,000	199	41.5	16.0	2.7	1980	7,436	...	...	...
Tuvalu	9	24	204	8,000	199	888.0	342.9	2.4	1979	7,349	46.8	53.2	...
Uganda	93,100	241,140	77	14,716,000	51	158.1	61.0	2.8	1980	12,630,076	49.5	50.5	8.1
U.S.S.R.	8,649,500	22,402,200	1	277,500,000	3	32.1	12.4	0.9	1979	262,436,200	46.6	53.4	62.0
United Arab Emirates	30,000	77,700	110	1,280,000	126	42.7	16.5	5.3	1981	1,043,225	69.1	31.9	80.8
United Kingdom	94,248	244,100	76	56,518,000	15	599.7	231.5	0.1	1981	55,618,374	48.6	51.4	89.6
United States	3,623,461	9,384,721	4	238,816,000	4	65.5	25.3	1.0	1980	226,545,805	48.6	51.4	73.7
Uruguay	68,037	176,215	85	3,012,000	108	44.3	17.1	0.7	1975	2,788,429	49.0	51.0	83.0
Vanuatu	4,707	12,190	141	140,000	167	29.7	11.5	3.8	1979	111,251	53.1	46.9	17.8
Venezuela	352,144	912,050	32	17,317,000	43	49.2	19.0	2.5	1981	14,516,735	50.0	50.0	85.7
Vietnam	128,052	331,653	60	60,492,000	13	472.4	182.4	2.4	1979	52,741,766	48.5	51.5	19.2
Virgin Islands (U.S.)	136	352	183	107,000	170	786.8	304.0	1.8	1980	96,569	47.8	52.2	29.6
Wallis and Futuna	106	274	187	14,000	196	132.1	51.1	4.8	1983	12,408	50.5	49.5	...
West Bank	2,270	5,900	149	782,000	135	344.5	132.5	1.5	1983[4]	767,300	49.9	50.1	...
Western Sahara	103,000	266,769	72	150,000	164	1.5	0.6	2.9	1970	76,425	...	...	...
Western Samoa	1,093	2,831	153	160,000	163	146.4	56.5	0.5	1981	156,349	51.8	48.2	21.2
Yemen (Aden)	130,066	336,870	59	2,124,000	119	16.3	6.3	2.7	1973	1,590,275	49.5	50.5	33.3
Yemen (San'ā')	52,213	135,230	90	6,547,000	79	125.4	48.4	2.4	1981	7,161,851	47.3	52.7	10.2
Yugoslavia	98,766	255,804	73	23,235,000	34	235.3	90.8	0.8	1981	22,424,711	49.4	50.6	47.3
Zaire	905,365	2,344,885	11	33,052,000	27	36.5	14.1	3.1	1976	25,697,575	48.5	51.5	18.2
Zambia	290,586	752,614	37	6,666,000	78	22.9	8.9	3.3	1980	5,679,808	49.0	51.0	43.0
Zimbabwe	150,873	390,759	55	8,100,000	70	53.7	20.7	2.5	1982	7,532,000	49.3	50.7	23.0

age distribution (%)						population (by decade, '000s)								country
0–14	15–29	30–44	45–59	60–74	75 and older	1930	1940	1950	1960	1970	1980	1990 projection	2000 projection	
45.2[2]	25.8[2]	15.6[2]	8.8[2]	3.9[2]	0.7[2]	...	...	390	494	657	891	1,218	1,651	Oman
46.0	26.7	13.3	8.4	4.5	1.1	70	134	57	77	109	133	170	199	Pacific Is., Trust Territory of the
45.2	24.0	15.0	9.1	5.1	1.6	23,600	28,300	36,450	45,851	64,449	85,743	112,040	152,050	Pakistan
39.2	27.9	16.4	9.6	5.1	1.8	523	620	800	1,082	1,458	1,956	2,418	2,893	Panama
43.0	25.9	17.0	10.4	3.5	0.2	1,306	1.308	1,613	1,920	2,419	3,000	4,125	5,049	Papua New Guinea
41.1	28.1	15.4	9.1	4.8	1.5	880	1,111	1,371	1,778	2,290	2,919	4,231	5,405	Paraguay
41.3	27.7	15.6	9.3	—6.1—		5,752	6,784	7,975	9,993	13,248	17,300	22,332	27,952	Peru
41.9	29.4	15.4	8.8	3.8	0.7	13,094	16,459	20,988	27,561	36,850	48,316	60,185	78,770	Philippines
32.1	13.2	18.9	13.2	9.4	13.2	—	—	—	—	—	—	—	—	Pitcairn Island
23.9	27.4	18.5	16.9	—13.3—		29,500	31,500	24,824	29,561	32,657	35,578	38,967	41,217	Poland
25.5	23.5	18.0	17.2	11.9	3.9	6,804	7,696	8,405	8,826	9,040	9,856	10,382	10,732	Portugal
31.6	26.4	18.5	12.3	8.3	2.9	1,552	1,880	2,219	2,358	2,718	3,202	3,424	3,662	Puerto Rico
32.3	31.8	25.8	7.8	—2.3—		...	...	47	59	151	246	354	469	Qatar
38.1[8]	29.0[8]	—26.5[8]—		—6.4[8]—		198	221	244	338	447	507	604	720	Réunion
25.7	23.7	19.6	17.1	10.9	3.0	14,141	15,907	16,311	18,407	20,799	22,201	23,994	25,728	Romania
46.6[2]	26.0[2]	14.4[2]	8.5[2]	3.8[2]	0.7[2]	...	...	2,189	2,740	3,679	5,144	7,105	9,845	Rwanda
37.2	30.4	9.5	9.4	10.0	3.5	38	43	49	51	46	44	50	53	St. Christopher and Nevis
34.2	27.7	16.3	10.8	8.4	2.6	4	5	5	5	5	6	6	6	St. Helena and Ascension
49.6	21.3	11.6	9.8	5.5	2.2	60	70	79	94	100	120	158	208	St. Lucia
28.7	26.0	20.4	13.1	8.6	3.2	4	4	5	5	5	6	6	6	St. Pierre and Miquelon
51.2	21.8	11.0	8.8	5.4	1.8	53	61	67	80	86	124	113	130	St. Vincent and the Grenadines
24.4	23.0	19.9	17.4	11.4	3.9	10	10	13	15	19	21	23	25	San Marino
...	...	...	...	...	...	...	60	60	64	74	94	114	144	São Tomé and Príncipe
43.9[2]	26.9[2]	16.3[2]	8.4[2]	3.8[2]	0.7[2]	...	...	3,200	4,175	6,120	9,229	13,724	20,327	Saudi Arabia
42.5	27.3	17.2	8.6	3.7	0.1	...	...	2,600	3,076	4,267	5,687	7,430	9,747	Senegal
39.7	26.3	14.1	10.8	6.9	2.2	28	32	36	42	52	63	70	82	Seychelles
36.7	27.2	19.4	9.0	—7.6—		...	...	1,809	2,165	2,692	3,152	4,550	6,300	Sierra Leone
27.0	34.7	19.8	11.3	5.9	1.3	596	751	1,022	1,639	2,075	2,414	2,713	2,967	Singapore
47.9	24.1	14.5	8.4	3.6	1.5	94	94	104	125	163	230	319	459	Solomon Islands
43.3[2]	24.6[2]	15.4[2]	10.5[2]	5.6[2]	0.6[2]	...	...	1,826	2,226	2,790	5,074	6,476	7,134	Somalia
41.8[2]	26.2[2]	15.7[2]	9.9[2]	5.2[2]	1.2[2]	8,541	10,353	12,458	15,925	22,460	28,610	36,754	46,918	South Africa
52.6	21.3	10.4	—13.6—		2.1	...	...	...	...	880	1,335	1,741	2,273	Bophuthatswana
48.5	22.9	12.4	—14.6—		1.6	...	...	...	...	530	681	888	1,159	Ciskei
43.7	21.5	13.3	—20.3—		1.2	...	...	...	...	1,746	2,336	3,078	4,057	Transkei
43.3	20.3	12.4	—22.7—		1.3	...	...	...	...	269	317	567	1,015	Venda
44.0[2]	25.8[2]	15.6[2]	9.3[2]	4.4[2]	0.9[2]	283	336	405	522	761	1,009	1,360	1,822	South West Africa/ Namibia
25.9[2]	23.6[2]	18.0[2]	17.5[2]	11.1[2]	3.9[2]	23,445	25,757	27,868	30,303	33,779	37,430	40,541	43,362	Spain
35.3	29.6	17.9	10.6	5.2	1.4	5,253	5,972	7,678	9,889	12,514	14,740	18,066	21,076	Sri Lanka
44.1[2]	26.3[2]	15.9[2]	9.0[2]	4.0[2]	0.7[2]	7,500	8,500	9,322	11,256	14,090	19,595	24,950	32,885	Sudan, The
39.3	29.5	13.8	10.0	4.5	2.8	170	193	215	247	292	355	405	454	Suriname
47.7	25.2	13.7	7.9	4.5	2.8	139	154	253	320	409	559	759	1,041	Swaziland
19.4	20.6	21.2	16.7	15.7	6.4	6,142	6,371	7,041	7,498	8,081	8,310	8,345	8,329	Sweden
19.8	23.2	21.6	17.3	12.8	5.4	4,066	4,234	4,715	5,429	6,270	6,327	6,600	6,870	Switzerland
47.9	27.3	12.4	7.9	3.5	1.0	...	2,597	3,495	4,561	6,305	8,704	12,774	17,085	Syria
32.1	32.1	16.5	12.6	5.7	1.0	4,614	5,987	7,619	10,792	14,676	17,619	20,791	24,128	Taiwan
46.2	24.9	14.4	8.5	4.5	1.5	...	...	7,892	10,073	13,273	18,580	25,635	34,045	Tanzania
38.2	29.8	16.3	10.2	—5.5—		11,838	15,296	20,010	26,392	35,745	46,455	55,345	63,772	Thailand
45.6[2]	26.1[2]	15.0[2]	8.7[2]	3.9[2]	0.7[2]	750	834	1,201	1,465	1,954	2,601	3,507	4,688	Togo
42.9	22.5	12.7	10.2	7.2	4.5	1	1	1	2	2	2	2	2	Tokelau
44.2	26.0	14.7	9.5	4.0	1.6	28	37	50	65	80	97	101	111	Tonga
34.2	30.9	16.3	10.0	6.2	1.7	405	510	636	843	1,027	1,090	1,262	1,410	Trinidad and Tobago
41.8[3]	27.4[3]	13.6[3]	10.6[3]	5.4[3]	1.2[3]	2,381	2,887	3,530	4,221	5,137	6,392	7,989	9,856	Tunisia
38.5	27.7	16.0	11.2	—6.6—		14,448	17,723	20,809	27,509	35,232	44,438	54,663	67,166	Turkey
...	...	...	...	...	...	5	6	6	6	6	7	9	10	Turks and Caicos Islands
33.4	31.1	14.7	13.0	—7.7—		...	...	5	5	6	8	11	16	Tuvalu
45.2[2]	25.9[2]	15.1[2]	8.9[2]	4.1[2]	0.8[2]	...	...	5,969	7,551	9,806	12,792	18,262	25,396	Uganda
24.4[2]	26.6[2]	19.1[2]	16.9[2]	9.6[2]	3.4[2]	179,000	195,000	180,075	214,335	241,700	265,500	290,155	310,236	U.S.S.R.
28.6	35.1	27.8	6.6	1.7	0.2	...	...	...	...	795	980	1,570	1,916	United Arab Emirates
21.1	22.5	19.2	17.3	14.3	5.6	46,038	48,226	50,290	52,807	55,610	56,314	57,900	59,600	United Kingdom
22.6	27.4	19.1	15.2	11.3	4.4	123,616	132,594	152,271	180,671	204,879	227,236	249,657	267,955	United States
27.0	22.6	19.2	16.9	10.8	3.5	1,734	1,974	2,194	2,531	2,824	2,908	3,128	3,364	Uruguay
45.3	27.5	15.0	7.7	3.4	1.1	...	...	52	65	86	116	159	194	Vanuatu
40.5	29.9	15.8	8.7	4.0	1.1	2,980	3,740	5,145	7,635	10,559	15,256	19,700	25,200	Venezuela
41.7[2]	26.1[2]	16.0[2]	10.4[2]	4.9[2]	0.9[2]	...	...	24,600	30,200	40,064	53,740	68,338	85,284	Vietnam
36.0	24.2	21.5	11.1	5.7	1.4	22	25	27	32	75	98	110	128	Virgin Islands (U.S.)
45.8	24.8	13.8	9.0	5.7	0.9	...	...	7	8	9	11	15	18	Wallis and Futuna
-46.2	29.6	10.1	8.7	—5.5—		...	...	...	...	608	724	853	1,016	West Bank
42.9	27.2	16.3	7.4	4.4	1.8	...	...	14	32	76	130	178	229	Western Sahara
44.3	29.1	12.2	9.0	3.8	1.0	45	61	82	111	143	156	171	182	Western Samoa
47.3	20.8	15.8	8.6	—6.6—		...	...	907	1,109	1,436	1,858	2,459	3,312	Yemen (Aden)
45.7	23.2	15.1	10.5	4.7	0.8	...	...	3,622	4,429	4,840	5,817	7,447	9,828	Yemen (Şan'ā')
24.5	25.0	19.8	18.3	8.3	3.5	14,360	16,425	16,346	18,402	20,371	22,304	24,107	25,653	Yugoslavia
45.2[18]	26.0[18]	15.5[18]	8.7[18]	3.9[18]	0.7[18]	8,764	10,370	13,055	16,151	21,368	28,352	38,445	52,410	Zaire
47.1[2]	25.8[2]	14.7[2]	8.2[2]	3.6[2]	0.6[2]	1,272	1,484	2,473	3,219	4,295	5,648	7,611	10,276	Zambia
51.0	26.3	13.4	6.5	1.2	1.6	1,100	1,461	2,276	3,538	5,308	7,140	9,200	11,300	Zimbabwe

[1]Settled population only. [2]1980 estimate. [3]1982 estimate. [4]Civil register; not a census. [5]1970 census. [6]1979 estimate. [7]Excluding territory occupied after 1967. [8]1981 estimate. [9]Excluding West Bank. [10]Reported 1981 census total was 6,684,000. [11]No census ever taken. [12]Preliminary 1984 census total was 3,637,488. [13]Preliminary 1985 census total was 181,453 (males 51.8%, females 48.2%). [14]Preliminary 1985 census total was 67,138. [15]1982 census total was 27,063. [16]Indigenous inhabitants only. [17]A census was taken in 1973, but the results were repudiated. [18]1985 estimate.

Major cities and national capitals

The following table lists the principal cities and municipalities (those exceeding 100,000 in population) of the countries of the world, together with figures for each of their national capitals (indicated by a ★), regardless of size.

Most of the populations given refer to a so-called city proper, that is, a legally defined, incorporated or chartered area defined by administrative boundaries and by national or state law as a "city" (in some cases, only as a locality that is "urban" in nature, or perhaps, in the smallest countries, simply as "the settlement"). There are many variations on this basic concept, however. One that is encountered frequently is the municipality, or commune, similar to the medieval city-state in that the city is governed together with its immediately adjoining, economically dependent areas, whether urban or rural in nature. Some countries define no other demographic or legal entities within such communes or municipalities, but most identify a centre, seat, head (*cabecera*), or locality that corresponds to the most densely populated, compact, contiguous core of the municipality. Secondary centres may also be defined, and in certain countries these may be places of considerable size, depending on how long the municipality's boundaries have gone unchanged. The amount of work involved in defining these "centres" carefully may be very great, and usually the necessary manpower, employment and commuting data, and cartographic resources exist only at the time of a national census (generally five or ten years apart). Between censuses, therefore, it may be possible only to track the growth of the municipality as a whole. Thus, in order to provide the most up-to-date data for cities in this table, figures referring to municipalities or communes may be given (identified by the abbreviation "MU"), even though the country itself may define a smaller, more closely knit city proper. Specific identification of municipalities is provided in this table *only* when the country also publishes data for a more narrowly defined city proper; it is *not* provided when the sole published figure is the municipality, whether or not this is the proper local administrative term for the entity.

Since many national capitals are first-order administrative subdivisions (equivalent to a U.S. state) in their national hierarchy of local government, some care has to be taken to provide data referring to the actual urban core of the subdivision (the demographic "city proper"). Thus, data are provided for the city of Brasília, or Kuala Lumpur, but not for the national or federal capital areas that contain them. Problems also exist in the identification of cities in terms of named legal entities. There is, for example, a single municipality (*commune*) named Brussel (Brussels) at the centre of the Brussels agglomeration in Belgium; the *commune* numbers only about 140,000 population, while the agglomeration, which is understood by most people to constitute the city, numbers nearly a million. Both are shown so as to apprise the reader of the existence of a problem.

For certain countries, more than one form of the name of the city is given, usually to permit recognition of recent place name changes or of *forms* of the place name likely to be encountered in press stories if the title of the city's entry in the *Encyclopædia Britannica* is spelled according to a different romanization or spelling policy. One such case is China, for which city names are spelled first according to a long-established scholarly system called Wade–Giles, while current press references are likely to be spelled according to the more recent Chinese romanization system, Pinyin. (Peking in Wade–Giles, for example, would be spelled Peiching; in Pinyin, Beijing.) The use of the conventional Western spelling Peking in this table is supplemented by provision of the Pinyin alternative spelling, although space did not permit cross references from either alternate spellings or former names.

Sources for this data were usually the national census and statistical abstracts of the countries concerned, supplemented by correspondence with most national statistical offices to solicit data not yet issued as part of the national publishing program.

Major cities and national capitals

country / city	population	country / city	population	country / city	population	country / city	population	country / city	population
Afghanistan (1982)		Rosario	875,664	**Benin** (1982 est.)		Manaus	613,068	Sliven	100,637
Herāt	150,497	Salta	260,744	★ Cotonou (official)	487,020	Marília	103,904	Stara Zagora	141,722
★ Kābul	1,036,407	San Fernando	134,156	★ Porto-Novo (de facto)	208,258	Maringá	158,047	Varna	295,038
Mazār-e Sharīf	110,867	San Isidro	287,048	**Bermuda** (1985 est.)		Mauá	205,817	**Burkina Faso** (1985 est.)	
Qandahār	191,345	San Juan	117,731	★ Hamilton	1,676	Mogi das Cruzes	122,265	Bobo Dioulasso	202,807
Albania (1984 est.)		San Justo	946,715	**Bhutan** (1982 est.)		Montes Claros	151,881	★ Ouagadougou	359,801
★ Tiranë	220,000	San Miguel de Tucumán	392,888	★ Paro (administrative)	3,000	Mossoró	118,007	**Burma** (1983)	
Algeria (1983 est.)		San Salvador de Jujuy	124,950	★ Thimphu (official)	12,000	Natal	376,552	Bassein	144,092
★ Algiers	1,721,607	Santa Fe	287,240	**Bolivia** (1984 est.)		Nilópolis	103,033	Mandalay	523,895
Annaba	348,322	Santiago del Estero	148,758	Cochabamba	304,960	Niterói	386,185	Moulmein	219,991
Batna	122,788	Tigre	205,926	★ La Paz (administrative)	953,634	Nova Iguaçu	491,802	Pegu	150,447
Bejaia	124,122	Vicente López	289,815	Oruro	172,814	Novo Hamburgo	132,066	★ Rangoon	2,458,712
Blida (el-Boulaida)	191,314	**Australia** (1983 est.)[3]		Potosí	109,876	Olinda	266,392	**Burundi** (1984 est.)	
Boufarik	112,000[1]	Adelaide	969,200	Santa Cruz	419,042	Osasco	473,856	★ Bujumbura	235,400
ech-Cheliff	118,996	Brisbane	1,138,400	★ Sucre (judicial)	84,505	Passo Fundo	103,121	**Cameroon** (1983 est.)	
Constantine (Qacentina)	448,578	★ Canberra	255,900	**Botswana** (1984 est.)		Pelotas	197,092	Douala	708,000
Oran (Wahran)	663,504	Geelong	142,900[4]	★ Gaborone	79,000	Petrópolis	149,427	★ Yaoundé	485,000
Sétif	186,978	Gold Coast	189,100	**Brazil** (1980)		Piracicaba	179,395	**Canada** (1981)	
Sidi bel Abbes	146,653	Hobart	173,700	Americana	121,794	Ponta Grossa	171,111	Brampton	149,030
Skikda	141,159	Melbourne	2,864,600	Anápolis	160,520	Porto Alegre	1,108,883	Burlington	114,853
Tizi Ouzou	100,749	Newcastle	414,700	Aracaju	288,106	Porto Velho	101,644	Burnaby	136,494
Tlemcen (Tilimsen)	146,089	Perth	969,100	Araçatuba	113,486	Presidente Prudente	127,623	Calgary	592,743
American Samoa (1980)		Sydney	3,335,000	Barra Mansa	123,421	Recife	1,184,215	East York	101,974
★ Pago Pago	3,075	Wollongong	235,000	Bauru	178,861	Ribeirao Prêto	300,704	Edmonton	532,246
Andorra (1983)		**Austria** (1981)		Belém	758,117	Rio Claro	103,174	Etobicoke	298,713
★ Andorra la Vella	15,698	Graz	243,166	Belo Horizonte	1,442,483	Rio de Janeiro	5,090,700	Halifax	114,594
Angola (1982 est.)		Innsbruck	117,287	Blumenau	144,819	Rio Grande	124,706	Hamilton	306,434
★ Luanda	1,200,000	Linz	199,910	★ Brasília	411,305	Salvador	1,506,602	Kitchener	139,734
Lubango	105,000[2]	Salzburg	139,426	Campina Grande	222,229	Santa Maria	151,202	Laval	268,335
Namibe (Moçamedes)	100,000	★ Vienna	1,531,346	Campinas	566,517	Santarém	101,534	London	254,280
Anguilla (1974)		**Bahamas, The**		Campo Grande	282,844	Santo Andre	549,278	Longueuil	124,320
★ The Valley	760	(1982 est.)		Campos	174,218	Santos	411,023	Mississauga	315,056
Antigua and Barbuda		★ Nassau	135,000	Canoas	214,115	São Bernardo		Montreal	980,354
(1982 est.)		**Bahrain** (1981)		Carapicuiba	185,763	do Campo	381,261	North York	559,521
★ Saint John's	30,000	★ al-Manāmah	108,684	Caruaru	137,636	São Caetano do Sul	163,030	Oshawa	117,519
Argentina (1980)		**Bangladesh** (1981)[5]		Cascavel	100,351	São Carlos	109,231	★ Ottawa	295,163
Almirante Brown	332,548	Bākerganj (Barisāl)	159,298	Caxias do Sul	198,824	São Gonçalo	221,278	Quebec	166,474
Avellaneda	330,654	Chittagong	1,388,476	Contagem	111,697	São João de Meriti	210,548	Regina	162,613
Bahia Blanca	220,765	Comilla	126,130	Cuiabá	167,894	São José do Rio Prêto	171,982	Saint Catharines	124,018
Berazategui	200,926	★ Dhākā (Dacca)	3,458,602	Curitiba	843,733	São José dos		Saskatoon	154,210
★ Buenos Aires	2,922,829	Jessore	149,426	Diadema	228,594	Campos	268,073	Scarborough	443,353
Caseros	340,343	Khulna	623,184	Divinopolis	108,344	São Luis	182,466	Thunder Bay	112,486
Córdoba	968,829	Mymensingh	107,863	Duque de Caxias	306,057	São Paulo	7,033,529	Toronto	599,217
Corrientes	180,612	Pābna	101,080	Feira de Santana	225,003	São Vicente	192,770	Vancouver	414,281
Esteban Echeverria	187,969	Rājshāhi	171,600	Florianópolis	153,547	Sorocaba	254,718	Windsor	192,083
Florencio Varela	172,654	Rangpur	155,964	Fortaleza	648,815	Taubaté	155,371	Winnipeg	564,473
General San Martín	384,306	Saidpur	128,085	Franca	143,630	Teresina	339,264	York	134,617
General Sarmiento	499,648	Sirājganj	104,522	Goiânia	703,263	Uberaba	180,296	**Cape Verde** (1985 est.)	
Godoy Cruz	141,553	Sylhet	166,847	Governador Valadares	173,699	Uberlândia	230,400	★ Praia	49,500
Guaymallén	157,334	**Barbados** (1980)		Guarulhos	395,117	Vitória	144,143	**Cayman Islands** (1979)	
Lanus	465,891	★ Bridgetown	7,552	Imperatriz	111,818	Vitória da Conquista	125,717	★ George Town	7,617
La Plata	454,884	**Belgium** (1983 est.; MU)		Ipatinga	105,083	Volta Redonda	177,772	**Central African Republic**	
Lomas de Zamora	508,620	Antwerp	490,524	Itabuna	129,938	**British Virgin Islands**		(1984 est.)	
Mar del Plata	407,024	Brugge (Bruges)	118,218	Jacarei	103,652	(1980)		★ Bangui	473,817
Mendoza	118,427	★ Brussels	137,738	João Pessoa	290,424	★ Road Town	2,525	**Chad** (1983)	
Merlo	282,828	Agglomeration	989,877	Joinville	217,074	**Brunei** (1984 est.)		★ N'Djamena	225,000
Moreno	193,626	Charleroi	216,144	Juàzeiro do Norte	125,248	★ Bandar Seri Begawan	53,776	**Chile** (1985 est.)	
Morón	596,769	Ghent	236,540	Juiz de Fora	299,728	**Bulgaria** (1983 est.)		Antofagasta	174,100
Paraná	161,638	Liège (Luik)	207,496	Jundiaí	210,015	Burgas	178,239	Arica	126,700
Posadas	143,889	Namur	101,860	Lages	108,768	Pleven	135,899	Chillán	127,600
Quilmes	441,780	Schaerbeek	105,672	Limeira	137,812	Plovdiv	367,195	Concepción	215,800
Resistencia	218,438	**Belize** (1980)		Londrina	258,054	Ruse	178,920	Iquique	118,700
Rio Cuarto	110,254	★ Belmopan	2,940	Maceió	376,479	★ Sofia	1,082,815	Rancagua	149,700

country / city	population
★ Santiago	421,900
Greater Santiago	4,271,500
Talca	143,000
Talcahuano	218,900
Temuco	170,200
Valdívia	118,900
Valparaiso	266,900
Viña dal Mar	311,600
China (1982)	
An-ch'ing (Anqing)	160,000
An-shan (Anshan)	1,060,000[6]
An-shun (Anshun)	100,000
An-ta (Anda)	150,000
An-yang (Anyang)	250,000
Canton (Guangzhou)	2,420,000[6]
Chan-chiang (Zhanjiang)	300,000
Chang-chia-k'ou (Zhangjiakou)	350,000
Ch'ang-chih (Changzhi)	300,000
Ch'ang-chou (Changzhou)	425,000
Chang-chou (Zhangzhou)	160,000
Ch'ang-ch'un (Changchun)	1,390,000[6]
Ch'ang-sha (Changsha)	885,000[6]
Ch'ang-te (Changde)	175,000
Ch'ao-an (Chao'an)	130,000
Chao-ch'ing (Zhaoqing)	100,000
Ch'ao-yang (Chaoyang)	125,000
Ch'ih-feng (Chifeng)	100,000
Chen-chiang (Zhenjiang)	250,000
Cheng-chou (Zhengzhou)	921,000[6]
Ch'eng-te (Chengde)	150,000
Ch'eng-tu (Chengdu)	1,440,000[6]
Chi-an (Ji'an)	115,000
Chi-hsi (Jixi)	620,000[6]
Chi-lin (Jilin)	863,000[6]
Chi-nan (Jinan)	1,070,000[6]
Chi-ning (Jining) of Inner Mongolia	125,000
Chi-ning (Jining) of Shantung	150,000
Ch'i-t'ai-ho (Qitaihe)	125,000
Chia-hsing (Jiaxing)	175,000
Chia-mu-ssu (Jiamusi)	350,000
Chiang-men (Jiangmen)	175,000
Chiao-tso (Jiaozuo)	350,000
Ch'ih-feng (Chifeng)	100,000
Chin-chou (Jinzhou)	570,000[6]
Chin-hua (Jinhua)	125,000
Ch'in-huang-tao (Qinhuangdao)	300,000
Ch'ing-chiang (Qingjiang)	150,000
Ch'ing-tao (Qingdao)	1,110,000[6]
Ching-te-chen (Jingdezhen)	400,000
Chiu-chiang (Jiujiang)	150,000
Chou-k'ou-chen (Zhoukouzhen)	150,000
Chu-chou (Zhuzhou)	275,000
Ch'ü-hsien (Quxian)	120,000
Ch'üan-chou (Quanzhou)	175,000
Chungking (Chongqing)	1,990,000[6]
Feng-ch'eng (Fengcheng)	100,000
Fo-shan (Foshan)	200,000
Fu-chou (Fuzhou)	727,000[6]
Fu-hsin (Fuxin)	544,000[6]
Fu-shun (Fushun)	1,060,000[6]
Hai-k'ou (Haikou)	263,280
Han-chung (Hanzhong)	200,000
Han-ku (Hangu)	100,000[7]
Han-tan (Handan)	695,000[6]
Hang-chou (Hangzhou)	949,000[6]
Harbin	2,180,000[6]
Heng-yang (Hengyang)	350,000
Ho-fei (Hefei)	571,000[6]
Ho-kang (Hegang)	325,000
Ho-pi (Hebi)	200,000
Hsi-ning (Xining)	400,000
Hsia-men (Xiamen)	350,000
Hsiang-fan (Xiangfan)	175,000
Hsiang-t'an (Xiangtan)	350,000
Hsien-yang (Xianyang)	200,000
Hsin-hsiang (Xinxiang)	325,000
Hsin-yang (Xinyang)	125,000
Hsing-t'ai (Xingtai)	150,000
Hsü-ch'ang (Xuchang)	135,000
Hsü-chou (Xuzhou)	686,000[6]
Hsüan-hua (Xuanhua)	140,000[7]

country / city	population
Hu-chou (Huzhou)	135,000
Hu-ho-hao-t'e (Hohhot)	529,000
Huai-nan (Huainan)	561,000[6]
Huai-pei (Huaibei)	150,000
Huang-shih (Huangshi)	200,000
Hui-chou (Huizhou)	100,000
Hun-chiang (Hunjiang)	125,000
I-ch'ang (Yichang)	175,000
I-ch'un (Yichun)	755,000[6]
I-ning (Yining)	160,000
I-pin (Yibin)	245,240
I-yang (Yiyang)	125,000
K'ai-feng (Kaifeng)	450,000
K'ai-yüan (Kaiyuan)	100,000
Kan-chou (Ganzhou)	180,000
Kashgar (Kashi)	150,000
Ko-chiu (Gejiu)	250,000
K'o-erh-ch'in-yu-i-ch'ien-ch'i (Horqin Youyi Qianqi)	100,000
Kuei-lin (Guilin)	325,000
Kuei-yang (Guiyang)	852,000[6]
K'un-ming (Kunming)	1,050,000[6]
Lan-chou (Lanzhou)	1,120,000[6]
Le-shan (Leshan)	150,000
Leng-shui-chiang (Lengshuijiang)	150,000
Liao-yang (Liaoyang)	275,000
Liao-yüan (Liaoyuan)	300,000
Lien-yün-kang (Lianyungang)	275,000
Liu-chou (Liuzhou)	375,000
Lo-yang (Luoyang)	598,000[6]
Lu-chou (Luzhou)	250,000
Lü-ta (Lüda)	1,270,000[6]
Ma-an-shan (Ma'anshan)	275,000
Mao-ming (Maoming)	250,000
Mien-yang (Mianyang)	100,000
Mu-tan-chiang (Mudanjiang)	400,000
Nan-ch'ang (Nanchang)	853,000[6]
Nan-ch'ung (Nanchong)	228,340
Nan-ning (Nanning)	542,000[6]
Nan-p'ing (Nanping)	100,000
Nan-t'ung (Nantong)	300,000
Nan-yang (Nanyang)	100,000
Nanking (Nanjing)	1,790,000
Nei-chiang (Neijiang)	225,000
Ning-po (Ningbo)	350,000
Pai-ch'eng (Baicheng)	150,000
Pang-pu (Bengbu)	425,000
Pao-chi (Baoji)	275,000
Pao-ting (Baoding)	400,000
Pao-t'ou (Baotou)	859,000
Pei-hai (Beihai)	125,000
Pei-piao (Beipiao)	100,000[7]
★ Peking (Beijing)	5,597,972
Pen-hsi (Benxi)	669,000
P'ing-hsiang (Pingxiang)	150,000
P'ing-ting-shan (Pingdingshan)	350,000
Po-shan (Boshan)	100,000[7]
Sha-shih (Shashi)	175,000
Shan-t'ou (Shantou)	400,000
Shao-hsing (Shaoxing)	225,000
Shao-kuan (Shaoguan)	160,000
Shao-yang (Shaoyang)	250,000
Shang-ch'iu (Shangqiu)	150,000
Shanghai	6,320,872
Shen-yang (Shenyang)	3,110,000[6]
Shih-chia-chuang (Shijiazhuang)	872,000[6]
Shih-tsui-shan (Shizuishan)	135,000
Shih-yen (Shiyan)	150,000
Shuang-ya-shan (Shuangyashan)	200,000
Ssu-p'ing (Siping)	200,000
Sian (Xi'an)	1,640,000[6]
Su-chou (Suzhou)	580,000[6]
Ta-hsien (Daxian)	100,000
Ta-t'ung (Datong)	633,000[6]
T'ai-an (Tai'an)	125,000
T'ai-chou (Taizhou)	150,000
T'ai-yüan (Taiyuan)	1,320,000[6]
Tan-tung (Dandong)	400,000
T'ang-shan (Tangshan)	902,000[6]
Te-chou (Dezhou)	125,000
T'ieh-ling (Tieling)	100,000
T'ien-shui (Tianshui)	125,000
Tientsin (Tianjin)	5,142,565
Ts'ang-chou (Cangzhou)	120,000
Tsao-chuang (Zaozhuang)	150,000
Tsitsihar (Qiqihar)	936,000[6]
Tu-k'ou (Dukou)	200,000
T'ung-ch'uan (Tongchuan)	200,000

country / city	population
T'ung-hua (Tonghua)	200,000
T'ung-ling (Tongling)	100,000
Tsun-i (Zunyi)	275,000
Tzu-kung (Zigong)	450,000
Tzu-po (Zibo)	674,000[6]
Wan-hsien (Wanxian)	160,000
Wei-fang (Weifang)	275,000
Wen-chou (Wenzhou)	325,000
Wu-chou (Wuzhou)	245,250
Wu-han (Wuhan)	2,790,000[6]
Wu-hsi (Wuxi)	651,000[6]
Wu-hu (Wuhu)	360,000
Wu-lu-mu-ch'i (Ürümqi)	904,000[6]
Yang-chou (Yangzhou)	225,000
Yang-ch'üan (Yangquan)	325,000
Yen-an (Yan'an)	150,000
Yen-chi (Yanji)	100,000
Yen-t'ai (Yantai)	200,000
Yin-ch'uan (Yinchuan)	200,000
Ying-k'ou (Yingkou)	200,000
Yü-men (Yumen)	150,000
Yü-tz'u (Yuci)	120,000
Yüeh-yang (Yueyang)	125,000
Christmas Island (1980 est.)	
★ The Settlement at Flying Fish Cove	1,200
Cocos (Keeling) Islands (1981)	
★ West Island	380
Colombia (1973)	
Armenia	149,078
Barranquilla	701,945
Bello	103,039
★ Bogotá	2,845,361
Bucaramanga	317,553
Buenaventura	110,713
Cali	971,891
Cartagena	311,664
Cúcuta	234,365
Ibagué	202,850
Manizales	207,607
Medellin	1,122,099
Montería	104,129
Neiva	109,063
Palmira	140,481
Pasto	130,222
Pereira	186,776
Santa Marta	110,161
Comoros (1980)	
★ Moroni	20,112
Congo (1980)	
★ Brazzaville	422,400
Pointe-Noire	185,100
Cook Islands (1981)	
★ Rarotonga Island	9,530
Costa Rica (1984)	
★ San José	241,464
Cuba (1984 est.)	
Bayamo	103,400
Camagüey	253,800
Cienfuegos	106,500
Guantánamo	171,100
Holguín	192,200
★ Havana	1,972,400
Matanzas	103,600
Santa Clara	175,500
Santiago de Cuba	353,400
Cyprus (1982)	
Limassol	100,254
★ Nicosia	123,298
Czechoslovakia (1984 est.)	
Bratislava	401,400
Brno	380,900
Košice	214,300
Olomouc	104,300
Ostrava	323,700
Plzen	174,100
★ Prague	1,186,200
Denmark (1983)	
Ålborg	114,437
Århus	182,685
★ Copenhagen	486,593
Agglomeration	1,372,019
Odense	137,606
Djibouti (1984 est.)	
★ Djibouti	200,000
Dominica (1981)	
★ Roseau	8,346
Dominican Republic (1981)	
Santiago de los Caballeros	278,638
★ Santo Domingo	1,313,172
Ecuador (1982)	
Ambato	112,775
Cuenca	157,213
Guayaquil	1,204,532
Machala	105,283
Portoviejo	123,151
★ Quito	890,355

country / city	population
Egypt (1983 est.)	
Alexandria	2,708,000
Aswān	174,000
Asyūt	259,300
Būr Sa'īd (Port Said)	364,000
★ Cairo	5,881,000
Damanhūr	206,100
Hulwan (Helwan)	327,600
al-Ismā'īlīyah	145,478
al-Jīzah (Giza)	1,509,600
Kafr ad-Dawwar	160,554
al-Maḥallah al-Kubrā	345,800
al-Manṣūrah	310,900
al-Minya	197,000
Shubrā al-Khaymah	486,400
as-Suways (Suez)	241,000
Ṭanṭa	335,300
az-Zaqāzīq	202,637
El Salvador (1983 est.)	
★ San Salvador	445,100
Santa Ana	132,200
Equatorial Guinea (1983 est.)	
★ Malabo	37,500
Ethiopia (1984)	
★ Addis Ababa	1,412,575
Asmera	275,385
Faeroe Islands (1984 est.)	
★ Tórshavn	14,443
Falkland Islands (1980)	
★ Stanley	1,050
Fiji (1982 est.)	
★ Suva	71,000
Finland (1985 est.)	
Espoo	154,243
★ Helsinki	484,410
Tampere	168,271
Turku	161,540
Vantaa	143,188
France (1982)	
Aix-en-Provence	100,221
Amiens	130,302
Angers	135,293
Besançon	112,023
Bordeaux	201,965
Boulogne-Billancourt	102,582
Brest	154,110
Caen	112,332
Clermont-Ferrand	145,901
Dijon	139,188
Grenoble	156,437
Le Havre	198,700
Le Mans	145,976
Lille	167,791
Limoges	137,809
Lyon	410,455
Marseille	868,435
Metz	113,236
Montpellier	190,423
Mulhouse	111,742
Nantes	237,789
Nice	331,165
Nîmes	120,515
★ Paris	2,165,892
Perpignan	107,812
Reims	176,419
Rennes	190,861
Roubaix	101,488
Rouen	100,696
Saint-Étienne	193,938
Strasbourg	247,068
Toulon	177,443
Toulouse	344,917
Tours	131,265
Villeurbanne	115,378
French Guiana (1982)	
★ Cayenne	38,091
French Polynesia (1983)	
★ Papeete	23,496
Gabon (1983 est.)	
★ Libreville	257,000
Port Gentil	123,000
Gambia, The (1983)	
★ Banjul	44,536
Gaza Strip (1979 est.)	
Gaza (Ghazzah)	120,000
Germany, East (1984 est.)	
★ Berlin (East)	1,185,533
Cottbus	120,723
Dessau	103,738
Dresden	522,532
Erfurt	214,231
Gera	129,891
Halle	236,139
Jena	106,555
Karl-Marx-Stadt	318,917
Leipzig	558,994
Magdeburg	289,075
Potsdam	135,922
Rostock	241,146
Schwerin	124,975
Zwickau	120,486
Germany, West (1984 est.)	
Aachen	241,100
Augsburg	246,000

country / city	population
Bergisch Gladbach	101,000
Berlin (West)	1,851,800
Bielefeld	303,900
Bochum	387,100
★ Bonn	291,700
Bottrop	112,600
Braunschweig	255,400
Bremen	535,800
Bremerhaven	135,800
Cologne (Köln)	932,400
Darmstadt	135,600
Dortmund	584,800
Duisburg	528,000
Düsseldorf	570,700
Erlangen	101,400
Essen	628,800
Frankfurt am Main	604,600
Freiburg im Breisgau	179,400
Gelsenkirchen	290,700
Göttingen	133,000
Hagen	209,500
Hamburg	1,600,300
Hamm	167,600
Hannover	517,900
Heidelberg	133,500
Heilbronn	110,600
Herne	174,800
Hildesheim	101,600
Karlsruhe	268,700
Kassel	186,100
Kiel	246,900
Koblenz	111,500
Krefeld	219,700
Leverkusen	156,500
Lübeck	213,400
Ludwigshafen	156,000
Mainz	187,100
Mannheim	297,200
Mönchengladbach	256,300
Mülheim an der Ruhr	174,800
Munich (München)	1,277,000
Münster	273,500
Neuss	144,800
Nürnberg	471,700
Oberhausen	224,100
Offenbach	107,600
Oldenburg	138,700
Osnabrück	154,700
Paderborn	109,700
Pforzheim	104,500
Recklinghausen	118,400
Regensburg	128,100
Remscheid	123,100
Saarbrücken	189,600
Salzgitter	108,400
Siegen	108,500
Solingen	159,200
Stuttgart	563,200
Wiesbaden	268,900
Witten	102,900
Wolfsburg	122,500
Wuppertal	381,900
Würzburg	129,700
Ghana (1984 est.)	
★ Accra	859,640
Kumasi	348,880
Tamale	136,800
Gibraltar (1983 est.)	
★ Gibraltar	30,000
Greece (1981)	
★ Athens	885,737
Iráklion	102,398
Kallithéa	117,319
Larissa	102,426
Pátrai (Patras)	142,163
Peristérion	140,858
Piraiévs (Piraeus)	196,389
Thessaloníki	406,413
Greenland (1985 est.)	
★ Godthåb (Nuuk)	10,559
Grenada (1980 est.)	
★ Saint George's	7,500
Guadeloupe (1982)	
★ Basse-Terre	13,656
Guam (1980)	
★ Agana	896
Guatemala (1981)	
★ Guatemala City	754,243
Guernsey (1976)	
★ St. Peter Port	16,982
Guinea (1983 est.)	
★ Conakry	656,000
Guinea-Bissau (1979)	
★ Bissau	105,273
Guyana (1976 est.)	
★ Georgetown	72,049
Haiti (1982)	
★ Port-au-Prince	449,831
Honduras (1983 est.)	
San Pedro Sula	323,500
★ Tegucigalpa	509,000
Hong Kong (1981)	
Kowloon	799,123
New Kowloon	1,649,950
Tsun Wan	610,459
★ Victoria	590,771

Major cities and national capitals (continued)

country / city	population
Hungary (1985 est.)	
★ Budapest	2,071,500
Debrecen	208,900
Győr	130,000
Kecskemét	102,000
Miskolc	211,600
Nyíregyháza	115,000
Pécs	175,500
Szeged	178,600
Székesfehérvár	110,000
Iceland (1983 est.)	
★ Reykjavík	87,309
India (1981)	
Ādoni	108,939
Agartala	132,186
Āgra	694,191
Ahmadābād	2,059,725
Ahmadnagar	143,937
Ajmer	375,593
Akola	225,412
Alīgarh	320,861
Allahābād	616,051
Alleppey	169,940
Alwar	145,795
Ambāla	104,565
Ambattur	114,915
Amrāvati	261,404
Amritsar	594,844
Amroha	112,682
Anantapur	119,531
Arrah	125,111
Asansol	183,375
Aurangābād	284,607
Avadi	124,574
Bally	147,735
Bālurghāt	104,648
Bangalore	2,476,355
Baranagar	170,343
Bareilly	386,734
Barrackpur	115,253
Belgaum	274,430
Bellary	201,579
Bhāgalpur	225,062
Bharatpur	105,274
Bharūch	110,070
Bhatinda	124,453
Bhātpāra	260,761
Bhavnagar	307,121
Bhilai (Nagar)	290,090
Bhīlwāra	122,625
Bhīmavaram	101,894
Bhiwandi	115,298
Bhiwāni	101,277
Bhopāl	671,018
Bhubaneswar	219,211
Bhusāwal	123,133
Bihār	151,343
Bijāpur	147,313
Bīkaner	253,174
Bilāspur	147,218
Bokaro Steel City	224,099
Bombay (Greater)	8,243,405
Brahmapur	162,550
Bulandshahr	103,436
Burdwān	167,364
Burhānpur	140,986
Calcutta	3,305,006
Chandernagore	101,925
Chandīgarh	373,789
Chandrapur	115,777
Chāpra	111,564
Cochin	513,249
Coimbatore	704,514
Cuddalore	127,625
Cuddapah	103,125
Cuttack	269,950
Darbhanga	176,301
Dāvangere	196,621
Dehra Dūn	211,416
Delhi	4,884,234
Dhānbād	120,221
Dhārwār-Hubli	527,108
Dhūlia	210,759
Dindigul	164,103
Dombivli	103,222
Durg	114,637
Durgāpur	311,798
Elūru	168,154
Erode	142,252
Etāwah	212,174
Faizābād	101,873
Farīdābād	330,864
Farrukhābād-Fatehgarh	145,793
Firozābād	202,338
Gadag-Betigeri	117,368
Gangānagar	123,692
Garden Reach	191,107
Gaya	247,075
Ghāziābād	271,730
Gondia	100,423
Gorakhpur	290,814
Gulbarga	221,325
Guntūr	367,699
Gwalior	539,015
Hāpur	102,837
Hardwār	114,180
Hissār	131,309
Howrah (Haora)	744,429
Hugli Chinsurah	125,193
Hyderābād	2,150,580
Ichalkaranji	133,751
Imphāl	156,622
Indore	829,327
Jabalpur	614,162
Jadabpur	251,968
Jaipur	977,165
Jālgaon	145,335
Jālna	122,276
Jammu	206,135
Jāmnagar	277,615
Jamshedpur	438,385
Jaunpur	105,140
Jhānsi	246,172
Jodhpur	506,345
Jullundur	408,196
Junāgadh	118,646
Kākināda	226,409
Kalyān	136,052
Kāmārhāti	234,951
Kānchipuram	130,926
Kānpur	1,481,789
Karnāl	132,107
Katihār	104,781
Khandwa	114,725
Kharagpur	150,475
Kolhāpur	340,625
Kota	358,241
Kozhikode (Calicut)	394,447
Kumbakonam	132,832
Kurnool	206,362
Lātūr	111,986
Lucknow	895,721
Ludhiāna	607,052
Madras	3,276,622
Madurai	820,891
Mālegaon	245,883
Mandya	100,285
Mangalore	172,252
Masulipatam	138,530
Mathura	147,493
Meerut	417,395
Miraj	105,455
Mirzāpur-cum-Vindhyachal	127,787
Monghyr	129,260
Morādābād	330,051
Muzaffarnagar	171,816
Muzaffarpur	190,416
Mysore	441,754
Nabadwīp	109,108
Nadiād	142,689
Nāgercoil	171,648
Nāgpur	1,219,461
Naihāti	114,607
Nānded	191,269
Nāsik (Nashik)	262,428
Navsāri	106,793
Nellore	237,065
★ New Delhi	273,036
Nizāmābād	183,061
Pālghāt	111,245
Pānihāti	205,718
Pānīpat	137,927
Parbhani	109,364
Pathānkot	110,039
Patiāla	205,141
Patna	776,371
Pimpri-Chinchwad	220,966
Pondicherry	162,639
Porbandar	115,182
Proddatūr	107,070
Pune	1,203,351
Puri	100,942
Quilon	137,943
Raichūr	124,762
Raipur	338,245
Rājahmundry	203,358
Rājapālaiyam	101,640
Rājkot	445,076
Rāmpur	204,610
Rānchi	489,626
Ratlām	142,319
Raurkela Steel Township	206,821
Rewa	100,641
Rohtak	166,767
Sāgar	160,392
Sahāranpur	295,355
Salem	361,394
Sambalpur	110,282
Sambhal	108,232
Secunderābād (Cantonment)	135,994
Sāngli	152,389
Shāhjahānpur	185,396
Shillong	109,244
Shimoga	151,783
Sholāpur (Solapur)	511,103
Shrīrāmpur	127,304
Sikar	102,970
Siliguri	154,378
Sitāpur	101,210
Sonepat	109,369
South Dum-Dum	230,266
South Suburban	378,765
Srīnagar	586,038
Surat	776,583
Tamkūr	108,670
Tenāli	119,257
Thāna (Thane)	309,897
Thanjāvūr	184,015
Tiruchchirāppalli	362,045
Tirunelveli	128,850
Tirupati	115,292
Tiruppūr	165,223
Tiruvottiyūr	134,014
Titāgarh	104,534
Trivandrum	483,086
Tumkūr	108,670
Tuticorin	192,949
Udaipur	232,588
Ujjain	278,454
Ulhāsnagar	273,668
Vadodara (Baroda)	734,473
Valparai	115,452
Vārānasi (Benares)	708,647
Vellore	174,247
Vijayawāda	454,577
Vishākhapatnam	565,321
Vizianagaram	114,806
Warangal	335,150
Yamunānagar	109,304
Indonesia (1980)	
Ambon	208,898
Balikpapan	280,675
Bandung	1,462,637
Banjarmasin	381,286
Bogor	247,409
Cirebon	223,776
★ Jakarta	6,503,449
Jambi	230,373
Jember	122,712
Kediri	221,830
Madiun	150,562
Magelang	123,484
Malang	511,780
Manado	217,159
Medan	1,378,955
Padang	480,922
Pakanbaru	186,262
Palembang	787,187
Pekalongan	132,558
Pematangsiantar	150,376
Pontianak	304,778
Probolinggo	100,296
Samarinda	264,718
Semarang	1,026,671
Sukabumi	109,994
Surabaya	2,027,913
Surakarta	469,888
Tanjung Karang-Telukbetung	284,275
Tegal	131,728
Ujung Pandang	709,038
Yogyakarta	398,727
Iran (1985 est.)	
Ahvāz	508,500
Āmol	106,500
Arāk	244,300
Ardabīl	258,100
Bakhtarān	536,500
Bandar 'Abbās	212,300
Borūjerd	162,800
Dezfūl	123,000
Gorgān	113,200
Hamadan	262,200
Isfahan (Eṣfahān)	1,121,200
Karaj	431,900
Kāshān	136,000
Kermān	266,800
Khorramābād	235,600
Meshed (Mashhad)	1,103,300
Orūmīyeh	298,400
Qazvīn	205,900
Qom	637,700
Rasht	266,300
Sabzevār	129,600
Sanandaj	207,500
Shīrāz	834,800
Tabrīz	929,200
★ Tehrān	5,751,500
Yazd	223,300
Zāhedān	220,500
Zanjān	205,900
Iraq (1970 est.)	
Baghdad	2,183,800
Basra	333,700
al-Ḥillah	128,800
Irbīl	107,400
Karbalā'	107,500
Kirkūk	207,900
Mosul	293,100
an-Najaf	179,200
Ireland (1981)	
Cork	136,344
★ Dublin	525,882
Isle of Man (1981)	
★ Douglas	19,944
Israel (1983)	
Bat Yam	129,700
Beersheba (Be'er Sheva')	111,100
Haifa (Ḥefa)	227,900
Ḥolon	133,900
★ Jerusalem (Yerushalayim, Al-Quds)	431,800
Netanya	101,600
Petaḥ Tiqwa	124,600
Ramat Gan	117,600
Rishon le-Ẕiyyon	102,500
Tel Aviv–Yafo	330,400
Italy (1984 est.; MU)	
Ancona	105,657
Bari	369,576
Bergamo	121,033
Bologna	447,971
Bolzano	103,009
Brescia	204,278
Cagliari	225,009
Catania	380,370
Catanzaro	101,622
Cosenza	106,373
Ferrara	147,328
Florence (Firenze)	440,910
Foggia	157,371
Forlì	110,943
Genoa (Genova)	746,785
La Spezia	112,606
Livorno	176,298
Messina	263,924
Milan (Milano)	1,561,438
Modena	178,985
Monza	122,476
Naples (Napoli)	1,208,545
Novara	102,279
Padua (Padova)	230,744
Palermo	712,342
Parma	177,062
Perugia	144,064
Pescara	131,974
Piacenza	107,617
Pisa	103,894
Prato	161,705
Ravenna	136,786
Reggio di Calabria	175,646
Reggio nell'Emilia	131,075
Rimini	129,506
★ Rome (Roma)	2,830,650
Salerno	156,921
Sassari	119,781
Siracusa	118,690
Taranto	243,120
Terni	111,347
Torre del Greco	104,654
Turin (Torino)	1,069,013
Trieste	246,305
Udine	101,179
Venice (Venezia)	340,873
Verona	261,947
Vicenza	112,771
Ivory Coast (1983 est.)	
★ Abidjan	1,800,000
Bouaké	640,000[4]
Jamaica (1982)	
★ Kingston	104,041
Japan (1984 est.)	
Abiko	110,775
Ageo	175,949
Aizuwakamatsu	116,536
Akashi	263,825
Akita	295,369
Amagasaki	511,930
Anjō	131,138
Aomori	293,811
Asahigawa	361,701
Ashikaga	166,840
Atsugi	170,105
Beppu	134,971
Chiba	782,277
Chigasaki	182,264
Chōfu	188,624
Daitō	122,849
Fuji	211,475
Fujieda	109,929
Fujinomiya	111,378
Fujisawa	322,412
Fukui	247,983
Fukuoka	1,153,344
Fukushima	269,105
Fukuyama	356,422
Funabashi	504,864
Futyu	200,982
Gifu	409,812
Habikino	110,434
Hachinohe	241,240
Hachiōji	418,838
Hadano	138,454
Hakodate	320,529
Hamamatsu	508,856
Higashikurume	109,643
Higashimurayama	122,414
Higashiōsaka	526,024
Himeji	452,099
Hino	153,703
Hirakata	378,036
Hiratsuka	226,972
Hirosaki	176,653
Hiroshima	936,227
Hitachi	205,931
Hōfu	117,628
Ibaraki	250,198
Ichihara	232,943
Ichikawa	393,748
Ichinomiya	256,463
Ikeda	101,569
Imabari	124,809
Iruma	114,720
Ise	105,517
Isesaki	110,639
Ishinomaki	122,858
Itami	180,745
Iwaki	347,875
Iwakuni	112,409
Izumi	116,944
Izumi	134,502
Joetsu	129,966
Kadoma	140,927
Kagoshima	526,905
Kakamigahara	122,774
Kakogawa	225,290
Kamakura	175,510
Kanazawa	427,379
Kariya	110,430
Kashihara	112,369
Kashiwa	267,994
Kasugai	254,921
Kasukabe	169,287
Katsuta	100,904
Kawagoe	208,194
Kawaguchi	399,510
Kawanishi	135,491
Kawasaki	1,077,254
Kiryū	131,996
Kisarazu	119,137
Kishiwada	184,274
Kitakyūshū	1,061,092
Kitami	106,290
Kobe	1,405,978
Kodaira	158,045
Kofu	199,862
Koganei	104,189
Komaki	111,342
Komatsu	105,993
Koriyama	299,126
Koshigaya	248,093
Kumagaya	141,280
Kumamoto	551,795
Kure	229,300
Kurume	222,978
Kushiro	216,505
Kyōto	1,487,833
Machida	314,573
Maebashi	274,496
Matsubara	136,712
Matsudo	422,355
Matsue	138,569
Matsumoto	194,807
Matsusaka	115,722
Matsuyama	422,313
Minō	113,124
Misato	106,502
Mitaka	166,698
Mito	226,155
Minakoyojō	132,375
Miyazaki	277,840
Moriguchi	159,514
Morioka	234,246
Muroran	148,535
Musashino	139,060
Nagano	333,523
Nagaoka	183,484
Nagareyama	120,378
Nagasaki	450,346
Nagoya	2,109,600
Naha	302,507
Nara	322,807
Narashino	135,478
Neyagawa	259,390
Niigata	471,813
Niihama	131,109
Niiza	127,216
Nishinomiya	420,197
Nobeoka	135,854
Noda	103,997
Numazu	207,812
Obihiro	159,707
Odawara	184,097
Ōgaki	145,056
Ōita	384,708
Okayama	565,559
Okazaki	280,469
Ōme	107,737
Ōmiya	369,677
Ōmuta	159,752
Onomichi	100,811
Ōsaka	2,631,317
Ōta	131,109
Otaru	178,760
Ōtsu	231,027
Oyama	132,457
Saga	167,736
Sagamihara	474,440
Sakai	818,050

country / city	population
Sakata	102,035
Sakura	118,369
Sapporo	1,523,611
Sasebo	250,092
Sayama	140,445
Sendai	666,593
Seto	124,654
Shimizu	241,364
Shimonoseki	268,345
Shizuoka	464,662
Sōka	193,127
Suita	348,630
Suzuka	163,197
Tachikawa	144,881
Takamatsu	325,901
Takaoka	175,688
Takarazuka	192,427
Takasaki	229,364
Takatsuki	345,285
Tama	115,935
Tokorozawa	266,200
Tokushima	255,624
Tokuyama	112,010
★ Tokyo	8,390,159
Tomakomai	157,241
Tondabayashi	100,630
Tottori	135,362
Toyama	311,792
Toyohashi	318,278
Toyokawa	106,568
Toyonaka	412,449
Toyota	302,092
Tsu	149,121
Tsuchiura	118,762
Ube	173,289
Ueda	114,844
Uji	162,628
Urawa	374,152
Utsunomiya	399,744
Wakayama	402,271
Yachiyo	141,181
Yaizu	107,553
Yamagata	243,824
Yamaguchi	122,246
Yamato	175,031
Yao	278,084
Yatsushiro	108,882
Yokkaichi	260,942
Yokohama	2,943,234
Yokosuka	427,351
Yonago	131,422
Jersey (1981)	
★ St. Helier	25,698
Jordan (1984 est.)	
★ Amman	777,500
az-Zarqā'	265,700
Irbid	136,200
Kampuchea (1981 est.)	
★ Phnom Penh	400,000
Kenya (1984 est.)	
Kisumu	167,100
Mombasa	425,600
★ Nairobi	1,103,600
Nakuru	101,700
Kiribati (1983 est.)	
★ Bairiki	20,050
Korea, North (1981 est.)	
Ch'ŏngjin	490,000
Haeju	213,000[6]
Hamhŭng-Hungnam	775,000
Kaesŏng	240,000
Kimch'aek (Songjin)	490,000[6]
★ P'yŏngyang	1,283,000
Sinŭiju	200,000
Wŏnsan	240,000
Korea, South (1980)	
Andong	101,903
Anyang	253,560
Ch'angwŏn	111,676
Cheju	167,719
Chinhae	112,024
Chinju	202,717
Chi'ŏnan	120,526
Ch'ŏngju	253,192
Chŏnju	367,161
Ch'unch'ŏn	155,305
Ch'ungju	113,098
Inch'ŏn	1,083,906
Iri	145,343
Kangnŭng	116,806
Kumi	105,360
Kunsan	165,317
Kwangju	727,600
Kyŏngju	121,999
Masan	386,751
Mokp'o	221,814
P'ohang	201,174
Puch'ŏn	221,463
Pusan	3,159,766
Sŏngnam	376,840
★ Seoul (Sŏul)	8,364,379
Sunch'ŏn	114,241
Suwŏn	310,476
Taegu	1,604,934
Taejŏn	651,792
Tonghae	104,310
Uijŏngbu	133,177

country / city	population
Ulsan	418,326
Wŏnju	136,909
Yŏsu	160,988
Kuwait (1980)	
Ḥawallī	152,402
★ Kuwait (al-Kuwayt)	60,525
as-Sālimīyah	145,991
Laos (1981 est.)	
★ Vientiane	210,000
Lebanon (1982 est.)	
★ Beirut (Bayrūt)	509,000
Sidon (Ṣaydā)	105,000
Tripoli (Ṭarābulus)	198,000
Lesotho (1976)	
★ Maseru	55,031
Liberia (1980)	
★ Monrovia	243,243
Libya (1981 est.)	
Banghāzī	367,600
Miṣrātah	116,900
★ Tripoli (Ṭarābulus)	858,500
Liechtenstein (1985)	
★ Vaduz	4,872
Luxembourg (1981)	
★ Luxembourg	78,924
Macau (1981)	
★ Macau (Santo Nome de Deus)	223,581
Madagascar (1984 est.)	
★ Antananarivo	700,000
Malaŵi (1984 est.)	
Blantyre	333,800
★ Lilongwe	172,100
Malaysia (1980)	
Ipoh	293,849
Johor Baharu	246,395
Kelang	192,080
Kota Baharu	167,872
★ Kuala Lumpur	565,329
Kuala Terengganu	180,296
Kuantan	131,547
Petaling Jaya	207,805
Pinang (George Town)	248,241
Port Kelang	192,080
Seremban	132,911
Taiping	146,002
Maldives (1985)	
★ Male	46,334
Mali (1980 est.)	
★ Bamako	440,000
Malta (1983 est.)	
★ Valletta	14,000
Martinique (1982)	
★ Fort-de-France	96,649
Mauritania (1981 est.)	
★ Nouakchott	250,000
Mauritius (1985 est.)	
★ Port Louis	136,800
Mayotte (1985)	
★ Dzaoudzi	5,675
Mamoudzou (★ designate)	12,119
Mexico (1980)	
Acapulco	301,902
Aguascalientes	293,152
Atizapán de Zaragoza (Ciudad López Mateos)	188,497
Campeche	128,434
Celaya	141,675
Chihuahua	385,603
Ciudad Madero	132,444
Ciudad Obregón	165,572
Ciudad Victoria	140,161
Coatzacoalcos	127,170
Cuernavaca	192,770
Culiacán	304,826
Ensenada	120,483
Durango	257,915
Gómez Palacio	116,967
Guadalajara	1,626,152
Guadalupe	370,524
Hermosillo	297,175
Irapuato	170,138
Jalapa	204,594
Juárez	544,496
León	593,002
Los Mochis	122,531
Matamoros	188,745
Mazatlán	199,830
Mérida	400,142
Mexicali	341,559
★ Mexico City	8,831,079
Minatitlán	106,765
Monclova	115,786
Monterrey	1,090,009
Morelia	297,544
Nezahualcóyotl	1,341,230
Nuevo Laredo	201,731
Oaxaca	154,223
Orizaba	114,848
Pachuca	110,351
Poza Rica	166,799
Puebla	835,759
Querétaro	215,976
Reynosa	194,693
Saltillo	284,937
San Luis Potosí	362,371

country / city	population
San Nicolás de los Garza	280,696
Tampico	267,957
Tepic	145,741
Tijuana	429,500
Tlaquepaque	133,500
Toluca	199,778
Torreón	328,086
Tuxtla	131,096
Uruapan	122,828
Veracruz	284,822
Villahermosa	158,216
Zapopan	345,390
Monaco (1982)	
★ Monaco-Ville	1,234
Mongolia (1984 est.)	
★ Ulan Bator	470,500
Montserrat (1980)	
★ Plymouth	1,568
Morocco (1982)	
Agadir	110,479
Casablanca (Dar el-Beida)	2,139,204
Fès (Fez)	448,823
Kenitra	188,194
Khouribga	127,181
Marrakech	439,728
Meknès	319,783
Mohammedia	105,120
Oujda	260,082
★ Rabat	518,616
Safi	197,309
Salé	289,391
Tanger	266,346
Tétouan	199,615
Mozambique (1982 est.)	
Beira	110,752[7]
★ Maputo (Lourenço Marques)	785,500
Nampula	120,188[7]
Nauru (1977)	
★ Yaren	413
Nepal (1981)	
★ Kathmandu	235,160
Netherlands (1984 est.)	
★ Amsterdam (capital)	676,439
Apeldoorn	144,108
Arnhem	128,431
Breda	118,662
Dordrecht	107,475
Eindhoven	192,854
Enschede	144,938
Groningen	167,866
Haarlem	152,511
Leiden	104,261
Maastricht	113,277
Nijmegen	147,102
Rotterdam	555,349
★ The Hague (seat of government)	445,213
Tilburg	154,094
Utrecht	230,414
Zaanstad	128,413
Netherland Antilles (1980 est.)	
★ Willemstad	100,000
New Caledonia (1983)	
★ Nouméa	60,112
New Zealand (1984 est.)	
Auckland	143,800
Christchurch	162,100
Manukau	179,000
★ Wellington	133,700
Nicaragua (1982 est.)	
★ Managua	750,000
Niger (1983 est.)	
★ Niamey	399,100
Nigeria (1983 est.)	
Aba	216,000
Abeokuta	308,800
Ado-Ekiti	265,800
Akure	117,300
Benin City	165,900
Calabar	126,000
Ede	221,900
Effon-Alaiye	110,600
Enugu	228,400
Gusau	114,100
Ibadan	1,060,000
Ife	214,500
Ijebu-Ode	113,110
Ikare	101,700
Ikerre	176,800
Ilesha	273,400
Ilobu	143,800
Ilorin	343,900
Iseyin	157,000
Iwo	261,600
Jos	149,000
Kaduna	202,000
Kano	487,100
Katsina	149,300
Kumo	107,000
★ Lagos	1,097,000
Maiduguri	230,900
Mushin	240,700
Offa	142,300

country / city	population
Ogbomosho	527,400
Oka	103,500
Ondo	122,600
Onitsha	268,700
Oshogbo	344,500
Oyo	185,300
Port Harcourt	296,200
Sapele	100,600
Shaki	125,800
Shomolu	106,800
Sokoto	148,000
Zaria	274,000
Niue (1981)	
★ Alofi	986
Norfolk Island	
★ Kingston	...
Norway (1985 est.)	
Bergen	207,400
★ Oslo	447,400
Trondheim	134,100
Oman (1981 est.)	
★ Muscat	50,000
Pacific Islands, Trust Territory of the (1980)	
★ Saipan	14,549
Pakistan (1981)	
Bahāwalpur	178,000
Chiniot	106,000
Dera Ghāzi Khān	103,000
Faisalābād (Lyallpur)	1,104,209
Gujrānwāla	654,000
Gujrāt	154,000
Hyderābād	795,000
★ Islamābād	204,364
Jhelum	106,000
Jhang	195,000
Karāchi	5,208,132
Karāchi Cantonment	203,000
Kasūr	155,000
Lahore	2,952,689
Lahore Cantonment	237,000
Lārkāna	123,890
Mardān	141,842
Mirpur Khās	124,371
Multān	730,000
Nawābshāh	102,139
Okāra	154,000
Peshāwar	506,896
Quetta	285,000
Rahīm Yār Khān	119,000
Rāwalpindi	794,843
Rāwalpindi Cantonment	354,000
Sāhiwāl	152,000
Sargodha	294,000
Sheikhūpura	141,000
Siālkot	296,000
Sukkur	190,551
Wāh Cantonment	122,000
Panama (1980)	
★ Panama City	389,172
San Miguelito	156,611
Papua New Guinea (1984 est.)	
★ Port Moresby	144,300
Paraguay (1983 est.)	
★ Asunción	479,600
Peru (1981)	
Arequipa	447,431
Callao	260,581
Chiclayo	280,244
Chimbote	216,406
Cuzco	181,604
Huancayo	165,132
Ica	111,087
Iquitos	178,738
★ Lima	375,957
Metro Lima-Callao	4,605,043
Piura	186,354
Trujillo	354,557
Philippines (1980)	
Angeles	188,834
Bacolod	262,415
Baguio	119,009
Batangas	143,570
Butuan	172,489
Cabanatuan	138,298
Cadiz	129,632
Cagayan de Oro	227,312
Calbayog	106,719
Caloocan	467,816
Cebu	490,281
Davao	610,375
General Santos	149,396
Iligan	167,358
Iloilo	244,827
Lipa	121,166
Lucena	107,880
Makati	372,631
Mancaue	110,590
Mandaluyong	205,366
★ Manila	1,630,485
Metro Manila	5,925,884
Marikina	211,613
Olongapo	156,430
Ormoc	104,978
Paranaque	208,552
Pasay	287,770

country / city	population
Pasig	268,570
Quezon City	1,165,865
San Carlos	101,243
San Pablo	131,655
Silay	111,131
Tacloban	102,523
Valenzuela	212,363
Zamboanga	343,722
Pitcairn Island (1985)	
★ Adamstown	63
Poland (1983 est.)	
Białystok	240,300
Bielsko-Biała	172,000
Bydgoszcz	357,700
Bytom	238,100
Chorzów	145,100
Częstochowa	244,100
Dąbrovo Górnicza	141,600
Elbląg	115,900
Gdańsk	464,600
Gdynia	240,200
Gliwice	211,200
Gorzów Wielkopolski	113,000
Kalisz	102,900
Katowice	361,300
Kielce	197,000
Kraków	735,100
Łódź	848,500
Lublin	320,200
Olsztyn	144,400
Opole	121,900
Płock	112,400
Poznań	570,900
Radom	201,000
Ruda Śląska	162,800
Rubnik	133,000
Rzeszów	134,400
Sosnowiec	252,000
Szczecin	389,200
Tarnobrzeg	40,800
Tarnów	111,000
Toruń	182,400
Tychy	178,100
Wałbrzych	137,400
★ Warsaw (Warszawa)	1,641,300
Włocławek	113,400
Wodzislaw Śląskie	106,800
Wrocław	631,300
Zabrze	196,500
Zielona Góra	107,800
Portugal (1981)	
★ Lisbon	807,167
Porto	327,368
Puerto Rico (1984 est.)	
Bayamón	202,500
Caguas	121,100
Carolina	165,700
Ponce	190,900
★ San Juan	428,900
Qatar (1983 est.)	
★ Doha	190,000
Reunion (1982)	
★ Saint-Denis	84,400
Romania (1982 est.)	
Arrad	169,876
Bacău	151,795
Baia Mare	119,973
Brăila	212,050
Brașov	285,718
★ Bucharest	1,815,081
Buzău	116,977
Cluj-Napoca	265,824
Constanța	277,696
Craiova	235,474
Galați	247,977
Iasi	256,042
Oradea	194,189
Pitești	138,413
Ploiești	211,657
Satu Mare	117,664
Sibiu	158,025
Timișoara	256,929
Tirgu Mureș	143,128
Rwanda (1981 est.)	
★ Kigali	156,700
St. Christopher and Nevis (1980)	
★ Basseterre	14,283
St. Helena and Ascension (1978 est.)	
★ Jamestown	1,500
St. Lucia (1984 est.)	
★ Castries	50,800
St. Pierre and Miquelon (1982)	
★ Saint-Pierre	5,400
St. Vincent and The Grenadines (1982)	
★ Kingstown	24,764
San Marino (1985 est.)	
★ San Marino	4,600
São Tomé and Príncipe (1984 est.)	
★ São Tomé	35,000
Saudi Arabia (1980 est.)	
ad-Dammām	200,000[8]
Jiddah	1,308,000[9]

Major cities and national capitals (continued)

country / city	population
Mecca (Makkah)	550,000
Medina (al-Madinah)	290,000
★ Riyadh (ar-Riyad)	1,000,000[9]
aṭ-Ṭā'if	300,000
Senegal (1979 est.)	
★ Dakar	979,000
Seychelles (1977)	
★ Victoria	23,012
Sierra Leone (1980 est.)	
★ Freetown	500,000
Singapore (1985 est.)	
★ Singapore	2,558,200
Solomon Islands (1981 est.)	
★ Honiara	21,170
Somalia (1981 est.)	
★ Mogadishu	400,000
South Africa (1983 est.)	
Alberton	134,270
Benoni	227,000
★ Bloemfontein (judicial)	174,500[8]
Boksburg	246,326
★ Cape Town (legislative)	942,851
Carletonville	147,000
Durban	713,702
East London	114,929
Germiston	342,657
Johannesburg	1,666,085
Kempton Park	178,107
Kimberley	158,195
Krugersdorp	128,788
Pietermaritzburg	159,500
Port Elizabeth	560,061
★ Pretoria (executive)	711,500
Randburg	114,458
Roodepoort	148,700
Soweto	864,000[10]
Springs	147,841
Vanderbijlpark	285,974
Vereeniging	129,560
Welkom	185,500
Bophuthatswana	
★ Mmabatho	...
Ciskei (1980)	
★ Bisho	4,800[11]
Mdantsane	150,000
Transkei (1978 est.)	
★ Umtata	30,000
Venda (1982 est.)	
★ Thohoyandou	...
South West Africa/Namibia (1983 est.)	
★ Windhoek	104,100
Sri Lanka (1981)	
★ Colombo	585,776
Dehiwala-Mount Lavinia	174,385
Spain (1982 est.)	
Albacete	110,836
Alcalá de Henares	142,862
Alcorcón	140,657
Alicante	258,465
Almeria	124,925
Badajoz	102,615
Badalona	227,744
Barcelona	1,720,998
Bilbao	450,024
Burgos	150,909
Cádiz	146,048
Castellón de la Plana	129,602
Córdoba	272,309
Coruña, La	226,697
Gerona	126,030
Getafe	127,060
Gijón	255,969
Granada	244,995
Hospitalet de Llobregat	294,033
Huelva	131,073
La Laguna	112,635
Leganés	163,426
León	123,131
Lérida	115,478
Logroño	113,455
★ Madrid	3,271,834
Málaga	453,176
Móstoles	149,649
Murcia	280,237
Oviedo	165,417
Palma (de Mallorca)	319,620
Palmas de Gran Canaria, Las (Is. Canarias)	405,726
Pamplona	186,363
Sabadell	194,943
Salamanca	139,634
San Sebastián	166,980
Santa Coloma de Gramanet	140,588
Santa Cruz de Tenerife	221,660
Santander	184,094
Sevilla (Seville)	630,912
Tarragona	138,705
Terrassa	155,360
Valencia	770,277
Valladolid	358,629
Vigo	258,724
Vitoria	226,388
Zaragoza (Saragossa)	608,725
Sudan, The (1983)	
★ Khartoum	476,218
Khartoum North	341,146
Port Sudan	206,727
Omdurman	526,287
Suriname (1980)	
★ Paramaribo	67,905
Swaziland (1985 est.)	
★ Mbabane	45,000
Sweden (1985 est.; MU)	
Göteborg	424,085
Helsingborg	104,689
Jönköping	107,031
Linköping	115,600
Malmo	229,107
Norrköping	118,451
Örebro	117,569
★ Stockholm	653,455
Uppsala	152,579
Västerås	117,658
Switzerland (1985 est.)	
Basel (Bâle)	176,200
★ Bern (Berne)	140,600
Geneva (Genève)	159,500
Lausanne	126,200
Zürich	354,500
Syria (1984 est.)	
Aleppo (Halab)	1,109,100
★ Damascus (Dimashq)	1,178,000
Hamāh	190,000
Homs (Hims)	406,300
Latakia (al-Ladhiqiyah)	222,500
Taiwan (1984 est.)	
Chang-hua	193,789
Chia-i	252,906
Chi-lung (Keelung)	351,707
Chung-ho	304,430
Chung-li (80 e.)	228,567
Feng-shan (Kao-hsiung-hsien)	255,268
Fêng-yüan	134,610
Hsin-chu	292,740
Hsin-chuang	213,235
Hsin-tien	184,126
Hua-lien	103,994
Kao-hsiung	1,261,743
Pan-ch'iao (T'ai-pei-hsien)	454,948
Pa-te	106,945
Ping-chen	115,694
P'ing-tung	195,288
San-chu'ung	342,980
T'ai-chung	636,406
T'ai-nan	622,073
★ Taipei (T'ai-pei)	2,388,374
T'ai-tung	110,702
T'ao-yuan	195,895
Yüan-lin	108,126
Yung-ho	226,937
Tanzania (1978)	
★ Dar es Salaam	769,445
Mwanza	110,553
Tanga	103,399
Zanzibar	110,506
Thailand (1983 est.)	
★ Bangkok	5,018,327
Chiang Mai	150,499
Hat Yai	113,964
Khon Kaen	115,515
Nakhon Ratchasima	190,692
Ubon Ratchathani	100,255
Togo (1983)	
★ Lomé	366,476
Tokelau	
—	—
Tonga (1983 est.)	
★ Nukualofa	20,564
Trinidad and Tobago (1984 est.)	
★ Port of Spain	60,700
Tunisia (1984)	
Safāqis (Sfax)	231,911
★ Tunis	596,654
Turkey (1980)	
Adana	574,515
Adapazari	130,977
★ Ankara	1,877,755
Antalya	173,501
Balikesir	124,051
Bayrampaşa	165,723
Buca	103,105
Bursa	445,113
Denizli	135,373
Diyarbakır	235,617
Elaziğ	142,983
Erzurum	190,241
Eskişehir	309,431
Gaziantep	374,290
İskenderun	124,824
Istanbul	2,772,708
İzmir	757,854
İzmit	190,423
Kağıthane	175,540
Kahramanmaraş	178,557
Kayseri	281,320
Kirikkale	178,401
Konya	329,139
Küçükköy	100,406
Malatya	179,074
Maras	178,557
Mersin	216,308
Samsun	198,749
Sivas	172,864
Tarsus	121,074
Trabzon	108,403
Urfa	147,488
Zonguldak	109,044
Turks and Caicos Islands (1980)	
★ Cockburn Town	3,124
Tuvalu (1983 est.)	
★ Funafuti	2,620
Uganda (1980)	
★ Kampala	458,423
Union of Soviet Socialist Republics (1984 est.)	
Abakan	146,000
Achinsk	120,000
Aktyubinsk	224,000
Alma-Ata	1,046,000
Almalyk	112,000
Almetyevsk	120,000
Andizhan	267,000
Andropov	249,000
Angarsk	254,000
Angren	119,000
Anzhero-Sudzhensk	110,000
Arkhangelsk	403,000
Armavir	168,000
Arzamas	104,000
Ashkhabad	346,000
Astrakhan	487,000
Baku	1,084,000
Balakovo	176,000
Balashikha	127,000
Baranovichi	146,000
Barnaul	568,000
Batumi	130,000
Belaya Tserkov	176,000
Belgorod	274,000
Belovo	116,000
Beltsy	143,000
Bendery	118,000
Berdyansk	129,000
Berezniki	193,000
Biysk	224,000
Blagoveshchensk	192,000
Bobruysk	218,000
Borisov	128,000
Bratsk	236,000
Brest	214,000
Brezhnev	414,000
Bryansk	424,000
Bukhara	204,000
Chardzhou	155,000
Cheboksary	378,000
Chelyabinsk	1,086,000
Cherepovets	295,000
Cherkassy	267,000
Cherkessk	100,000
Chernigov	270,000
Chernovtsy	238,000
Chimkent	360,000
Chirchik	150,000
Chita	331,000
Daugavpils	123,000
Dimitrovgrad	114,000
Dneprodzerzhinsk	268,000
Dnepropetrovsk	1,140,000
Donetsk	1,064,000
Dushanbe	539,000
Dzhambul	298,000
Dzherzhinsk	272,000
Dzhezkazgan	100,000
Ekibastuz	109,000
Elektrostal	147,000
Engels	175,000
Fergana	191,000
Frunze	590,000
Gomel	452,000
Gorky	1,392,000
Grodno	239,000
Grozny	389,000
Guryev	142,000
Irkutsk	589,000
Ivano-Frankovsk	200,000
Ivanovo	476,000
Kalinin	437,000
Kaliningrad	380,000
Kaliningrad (*Moscow obl.*)	141,000
Kaluga	291,000
Kamensk-Uralsky	198,000
Kamyshin	115,000
Kanski	103,000
Karaganda	608,000
Karshi	129,000
Kaunas	400,000
Kazan	1,034,000
Kemerovo	502,000
Kerch	166,000
Khabarovsk	568,000
Kharkov	1,536,000
Kherson	340,000
Khimki	124,000
Khmelnitsky	210,000
Kiev	2,409,000
Kineshma	104,000
Kirov	407,000
Kirovabad	257,000
Kirovakan	162,000
Kirovograd	257,000
Kiselevsk	126,000
Kishinyov	605,000
Kislovodsk	107,000
Klaipėda	191,000
Kokand	163,000
Kokchetav	117,000
Kolomna	155,000
Kolpino	129,000
Komsomolsk-na-Amure	291,000
Konstantinovka	114,000
Kopeysk	134,000
Kostroma	267,000
Kovrov	151,000
Kramatorsk	189,000
Krasnodar	603,000
Krasnoyarsk	859,000
Krasny Luch	110,000
Kremenchug	222,000
Krivoy Rog	680,000
Kurgan	339,000
Kursk	413,000
Kustanay	191,000
Kutaisi	210,000
Kuybyshev	1,250,000
Kzyl-Orda	180,000
Leninabad	147,000
Leninakan	220,000
Leningrad	4,295,000
Leninsk-Kuznetsky	137,000
Liepaja	111,000
Lipetsk	440,000
Lisichansk	121,000
Lyubertsy	166,000
Lutsk	167,000
Lvov	728,000
Magadan	138,000
Magnitogorsk	421,000
Makeyevka	448,000
Makhachkala	293,000
Margilan	120,000
Maykop	138,000
Melitopol	169,000
Miass	158,000
Michurinsk	102,000
Minsk	1,442,000
Mogilyov	334,000
★ Moscow	8,275,000
Murmansk	412,000
Murom	120,000
Mytishchi	150,000
Nakhodka	148,000
Nalchik	222,000
Namangan	265,000
Nevinnomyssk	112,000
Nikolayev	480,000
Nikopol	154,000
Nizhnekamsk	163,000
Nizhnevartovsk	178,000
Nizhny Tagil	415,000
Noginsk	121,000
Norilsk	183,000
Novgorod	215,000
Novocheboksarsk	101,000
Novocherkassk	188,000
Novokuybyshevsk	110,000
Novokuznetsk	572,000
Novomoskovsk (*Tula obl.*)	147,000
Novorossiysk	174,000
Novoshakhtinsk	106,000
Novosibirsk	1,384,000
Novotroitsk	102,000
Nukus	131,000
Odessa	1,113,000
Omsk	1,094,000
Ordzhonikidze	300,000
Orekhovo-Zuyevo	136,000
Orenburg	513,000
Orsha	118,000
Orsk	263,000
Oryol	325,000
Osh	194,000
Panevėžys	114,000
Pavlodar	309,000
Pavlograd	117,000
Penza	522,000
Perm	1,048,000
Petropavlovsk	222,000
Petropavlovsk-Kamchatsky	241,000
Petrouralsk	135,000
Petrozavodsk	251,000
Pinsk	106,000
Podolsk	207,000
Poltava	296,000
Prokopyevsk	274,000
Pskov	189,000
Pyatigorsk	117,000
Riga	875,000
Rostov-na-Donu	983,000
Rovno	215,000
Rubtsovsk	163,000
Rudny	115,000
Rustavi	142,000
Ryazan	488,000
Salavat	147,000
Samarkand	515,000
Saransk	301,000
Sarapul	109,000
Saratov	893,000
Semipalatinsk	307,000
Serov	102,000
Serpukhov	142,000
Sevastopol	335,000
Severodonetsk	122,000
Severodvinsk	224,000
Shchelkovo	105,000
Shevchenko	142,000
Šiauliai	132,000
Simferopol	328,000
Slavyansk	142,000
Smolensk	326,000
Sochi	307,000
Solikamsk	104,000
Stakhanov	110,000
Stary Oskol	148,000
Stavropol	287,000
Sterlitamak	238,000
Sukhumi	124,000
Sumgait	218,000
Sumy	252,000
Surgut	188,000
Sverdlovsk (*Sverdlovsk obl.*)	1,286,000
Syktyvkar	209,000
Syzran	173,000
Taganrog	289,000
Taldy-Kurgan	103,000
Tallinn	458,000
Tambov	290,000
Tartu	110,000
Tashkent	1,986,000
Tbilisi	1,140,000
Temirtau	224,000
Ternopol	175,000
Tiraspol	158,000
Tolyatti (Togliatti)	576,000
Tomsk	467,000
Tselinograd	256,000
Tula	529,000
Tyumen	411,000
Ufa	1,048,000
Ulan-Ude	329,000
Ulyanovsk	524,000
Uralsk	188,000
Urgench	113,000
Usolye-Sibirskoye	107,000
Ussuriysk	156,000
Ust-Kamenogorsk	302,000
Ustinov	603,000
Uzhgorod	105,000
Velikiye Luki	109,000
Vilnius	535,000
Vinnitsa	360,000
Vitebsk	330,000
Vladimir	326,000
Vladivostok	590,000
Volgodonsk	160,000
Volgograd	969,000
Vologda	264,000
Volzhsky	238,000
Vorkuta	107,000
Voronezh	840,000
Voroshilovgrad	491,000
Yakutsk	175,000
Yaroslavl	623,000
Yelets	115,000
Yenakiyevo	117,000
Yerevan	1,114,000
Yevpatoriya	102,000
Yoshkar-Ola	227,000
Yuzhno-Sakhalinsk	155,000
Zagorsk	111,000
Zaporozhye	844,000
Zelenograd	141,000
Zhdanov	520,000
Zhitomir	270,000
Zlatoust	204,000
United Arab Emirates (1980)	
★ Abu Dhabi (Abū Ẓaby)	243,000
Al-'Ayn	102,000
Dubai (Dubayy)	266,000
Sharjah (ash-Shāriqah)	125,000
United Kingdom (1981)	
Aberdeen, Scot.	190,465
Belfast, N.Ire.	354,400
Birmingham	1,024,118
Blackburn	110,254
Blackpool	149,012
Bolton	143,921
Bournemouth	148,382

city	population
Bradford	295,048
Brighton	137,985
Bristol	420,234
Cardiff, Wales	266,267
Coventry	322,573
Derby	220,681
Dudley	187,367
Dundee, Scot.	174,345
Edinburgh, Scot.	420,169
Glasgow, Scot.	765,030
Gloucester	108,150
Huddersfield	148,544
Ipswich	131,131
Kingston upon Hull	325,485
Leeds	451,841
Leicester	328,835
Liverpool	544,861
★ London	6,677,928
Luton	164,743
Manchester	448,604
Middlesbrough	159,421
Newcastle upon Tyne	203,591
Newport	116,658
Northampton	155,694
Norwich	173,286
Nottingham	277,203
Oldbury/Smethwick	153,461
Oldham	107,830
Oxford	119,909
Peterborough	114,733
Plymouth	242,560
Poole	124,974
Portsmouth	177,905
Preston	168,405
Reading	198,341
Rotherham	123,312
St. Helens	114,822
Sheffield	477,257
Slough	106,822
Southampton	214,802
Southend-on-Sea	156,969
Stockport	136,792
Stoke-on-Trent	275,168
Sunderland	195,896
Sutton Coldfield	103,097
Swansea, Wales	175,172
Swindon	128,493
Walsall	178,852
West Bromwich	154,531
Wolverhampton	265,631
York	126,377
United States (1984 est.)	
Abilene (*Tex.*)	108,157
Akron (*Ohio*)	226,877
Alburquerque (*N.M.*)	350,575
Alexandria (*Va.*)	107,026
Allentown (*Pa.*)	103,899
Amarillo (*Tex.*)	162,863
Anaheim (*Calif.*)	233,516
Anchorage (*Alsk.*)	226,663
Ann Arbor (*Mich.*)	103,840
Arlington (*Tex.*)	213,832
Atlanta (*Ga.*)	426,090
Aurora (*Colo.*)	194,772
Austin (*Tex.*)	397,001
Bakersfield (*Calif.*)	130,210
Baltimore (*Md.*)	763,570
Baton Rouge (*La.*)	368,571
Beaumont (*Tex.*)	123,356
Berkeley (*Calif.*)	103,761
Birmingham (*Ala.*)	279,813
Boise City (*Idaho*)	107,188
Boston (*Mass.*)	570,719
Bridgeport (*Conn.*)	142,140
Buffalo (*N.Y.*)	338,982
Cedar Rapids (*Iowa*)	108,669
Charlotte (*N.C.*)	330,838
Chattanooga (*Tenn.*)	164,400
Chesapeake (*Va.*)	126,031
Chicago (*Ill.*)	2,992,472
Cincinnati (*Ohio*)	370,481
Cleveland (*Ohio*)	546,543
Colorado Springs (*Colo.*)	247,739
Columbus (*Ga.*)	174,500
Columbus (*Ohio*)	566,114
Concord (*Calif.*)	103,814
Corpus Christi (*Tex.*)	258,067
Dallas (*Tex.*)	974,234
Davenport (*Iowa*)	102,129
Dayton (*Ohio*)	181,159
Denver (*Colo.*)	504,558
Des Moines (*Iowa*)	190,832
Detroit (*Mich.*)	1,088,973
Durham (*N.C.*)	101,997
El Paso (*Tex.*)	463,809
Elizabeth (*N.J.*)	107,455
Erie (*Pa.*)	117,461
Eugene (*Ore.*)	101,602
Evansville (*Ind.*)	130,333
Flint (*Mich.*)	149,007
Fort Lauderdale (*Fla.*)	149,872
Fort Wayne (*Ind.*)	165,416
Fort Worth (*Tex.*)	414,562
Fremont (*Calif.*)	143,863
Fresno (*Calif.*)	267,377
Fullerton (*Calif.*)	106,901
Garden Grove (*Calif.*)	129,266
Garland (*Tex.*)	160,208
Gary (*Ind.*)	143,096
Glendale (*Ariz.*)	113,888
Glendale (*Cal.*)	147,440
Grand Rapids (*Mich.*)	183,000
Greensboro (*N.C.*)	159,314
Hampton (*Va.*)	125,992
Hartford (*Conn.*)	135,720
Hialeah (*Fla.*)	152,248
Hollywood (*Fla.*)	120,175
Honolulu (*Ha.*)	805,266
Houma (*La.*)	101,998
Houston (*Tex.*)	1,705,697
Huntington Beach (*Calif.*)	179,335
Huntsville (*Ala.*)	149,527
Independence (*Mo.*)	112,121
Indianapolis (*Ind.*)	710,280
Irving (*Tex.*)	120,057
Jackson (*Mich.*)	145,300
Jackson (*Miss.*)	208,810
Jacksonville (*Fla.*)	577,971
Jersey City (*N.J.*)	223,004
Kansas City (*Mo.*)	443,075
Knoxville (*Tenn.*)	173,972
Lakewood (*Colo.*)	121,114
Lansing (*Mich.*)	127,972
Laredo (*Tex.*)	108,676
Las Vegas (*Nev.*)	183,227
Lexington–Fayette (*Ky.*)	210,150
Lincoln (*Mich.*)	180,378
Little Rock (*Ark.*)	170,140
Livonia (*Mich.*)	100,363
Long Beach (*Calif.*)	378,752
Los Angeles (*Calif.*)	3,096,721
Louisville (*Ky.*)	289,843
Lubbock (*Tex.*)	178,529
Macon (*Ga.*)	120,226
Madison (*Wis.*)	170,747
Memphis (*Tenn.*)	648,399
Mesa (*Ariz.*)	193,931
Miami (*Fla.*)	372,634
Milwaukee (*Wis.*)	620,811
Minneapolis (*Minn.*)	358,335
Mobile (*Ala.*)	204,923
Modesto (*Calif.*)	122,234
Montgomery (*Ala.*)	184,963
Nashville–Davidson (*Tenn.*)	462,450
New Haven (*Conn.*)	124,188
New Orleans (*La.*)	559,101
New York City (*N.Y.*)	7,164,742
Newark (*N.J.*)	314,387
Newport News (*Va.*)	154,560
Norfolk (*Va.*)	279,683
Oakland (*Calif.*)	351,898
Odessa (*Tex.*)	108,690
Oklahoma City (*Okla.*)	443,172
Omaha (*Neb.*)	332,237
Ontario (*Calif.*)	106,274
Orlando (*Fla.*)	137,145
Oxnard (*Calif.*)	121,154
Pasadena (*Calif.*)	125,021
Pasadena (*Tex.*)	119,303
Paterson (*N.J.*)	138,818
Peoria (*Ill.*)	117,113
Philadelphia (*Pa.*)	1,646,713
Phoenix (*Ariz.*)	853,266
Pittsburgh (*Pa.*)	402,583
Pomona (*Calif.*)	106,979
Portland (*Ore.*)	365,861
Portsmouth (*Va.*)	107,961
Providence (*R.I.*)	154,148
Raleigh (*N.C.*)	169,331
Reno (*Nev.*)	105,615
Richmond (*Va.*)	219,056
Riverside (*Calif.*)	182,245
Roanoke (*Va.*)	100,688
Rochester (*N.Y.*)	242,562
Rockford (*Ill.*)	136,531
Sacramento (*Calif.*)	304,131
St. Louis (*Mo.*)	429,296
St. Paul (*Minn.*)	265,903
St. Petersburg (*Fla.*)	241,294
San Antonio (*Tex.*)	842,779
San Bernardino (*Calif.*)	130,391
San Diego (*Calif.*)	960,452
San Francisco (*Calif.*)	712,753
San Jose (*Calif.*)	686,178
Santa Ana (*Calif.*)	225,405
Savannah (*Ga.*)	145,014
Seattle (*Wash.*)	488,474
Shreveport (*La.*)	219,996
South Bend (*Ind.*)	107,117
Spokane (*Wash.*)	173,349
Springfield (*Mass.*)	150,454
Springfield (*Ill.*)	101,570
Springfield (*Mo.*)	136,939
Stamford (*Conn.*)	101,917
Sterling Heights (*Mich.*)	109,440
Stockton (*Calif.*)	171,659
Sunnyvale (*Calif.*)	110,600
Tacoma (*Wash.*)	159,000
Tallahassee (*Fla.*)	112,258
Tampa (*Fla.*)	275,479
Tempe (*Ariz.*)	118,336
Toledo (*Ohio*)	343,939
Topeka (*Kan.*)	118,945
Torrance (*Calif.*)	132,877
Tucson (*Ariz.*)	365,422
Tulsa (*Okla.*)	374,535
Virginia Beach (*Va.*)	308,664
Waco (*Tex.*)	104,133
Warren (*Mich.*)	152,035
★ Washington D.C.	622,823
Waterbury (*Conn.*)	102,861
Wichita (*Kan.*)	283,496
Winston-Salem (*N.C.*)	143,366
Worchester (*Mass.*)	159,843
Yonkers (*N.Y.*)	191,234
Youngstown (*Ohio*)	108,042
Uruguay (1980 est.)	
★ Montevideo	1,261,000
Vanuatu (1981)	
★ Vila	9,971
Venezuela (1981)	
Barcelona	156,461
Barinas	110,462
Barquisimeto	497,635
Cabimas	140,435
★ Caracas	2,661,088
Ciudad Bolívar	182,941
Ciudad Guayana (San Felix de Guayana)	314,497
Cumaná	179,814
Guarenas	101,742
Los Teques	112,857
Maracaibo	890,553
Maracay	387,682
Maturin	154,976
Mérida	143,209
Petare	334,800
San Cristóbal	198,793
Turmero	110,186
Valencia	616,117
Valera	102,068
Vietnam (1979)	
Bien Hoa	190,086
Can Tho	182,856
Da Nang	318,655
Haiphong	330,755
★ Hanoi	819,913
Hon Gai	115,312
Hue	165,865
Long Xuyen	112,488
My Tho	101,496
Nam Dinh	161,180
Nha Trang	172,663
Quy Nhon	130,534
Tha Nguyen	138,023
Thanh Hoa	103,981
Thanh-pho Ho Chi Minh (Saigon)	2,441,185
Vinh	154,040
Virgin Islands of the United States (1980)	
★ Charlotte Amalie	11,842
Wallis and Futuna (1983)	
★ Matautu	815
West Bank	
★ —	—
Western Sahara (1982)	
★ El Aaiún (Laayoune)	93,875
Western Samoa (1981)	
★ Apia	33,170
Yemen (Aden) (1981 est.)	
★ Aden	365,000
Yemen (Şan'ā') (1981)	
Al-Ḥudaydah	126,386
★ Şan'ā'	277,818
Ta'izz	119,573
Yugoslavia (1981; MU)	
Banja Luka	183,618
★ Belgrade (Beograd)	1,470,073
Bitola (Bitolj)	137,835
Čačak	110,676
Čakovec	116,825
Gostivar	101,188
Kragujevac	164,823
Kraljevo	121,622
Krusevac	132,972
Kumanova	126,368
Laskovac	159,001
Ljubljana	305,211
Maribor	185,699
Mostar	110,377
Niš	230,711
Novi Sad	257,685
Osijek	158,790
Pančevo	123,791
Peć	111,067
Prijedor	108,865
Priština	211,156
Prizren	134,689
Rijeka	193,044
Šabac	119,668
Sarajevo	448,500
Skopje (Skoplje)	506,547
Slavanski Brod	106,400
Smederevo	107,366
Split	235,922
Subotica	154,611
Tetova	162,414
Titograd	132,290
Titova Mitrovica	105,097
Tuzla	121,717
Uroševac	113,935
Zadar	116,174
Zagreb	768,700
Novi Zagreb	113,155
Tresnjevka	114,874
Zenica	132,733
Zrenjanin	139,300
Zaire (1976; MU)	
Bukavu	152,193
Kananga	462,621
Kikwit	172,000
★ Kinshasa	1,855,343
Kisangani	291,888
Likasi	162,000
Lubumbashi	588,307
Matadi	140,415
Mbandaka	137,484
Mbuji-Mayi	285,470
Zambia	
Chingola	145,869
Kabwe	143,635
Kitwe	314,794
Luanshya	132,164
★ Lusaka	538,469
Mufulira	149,778
Ndola	282,439
Zimbabwe (1982)	
Bulawayo	413,814
Chitungwiza	172,556
★ Harare	656,011

[1]1977.   [2]1984.   [3]All populations cited are for officially defined, widest agglomerations of metropolitan areas. Populations of city propers of larger metropolitan areas are: Sydney 51,836; Melbourne 63,388; Brisbane 689,368; Adelaide 12,656; Perth 79,398.   [4]1982.   [5]Chittagong, Dhākā, Khulna, and Rājshāni are metropolitan areas. Others are urban agglomerations (not city propers).   [6]1983 estimate.   [7]1975 estimate.   [8]1978.   [9]1981.   [10]1980.   [11]1970.

Language

This table presents data on the principal language communities of each of the countries of the world. The countries, and the principal languages used in each, are listed alphabetically; a bullet (●) indicates those languages which are designated as official by each country. The sum of the estimated populations for each language community and of the "Other" group equals the estimated de facto population of the country given in the "Area and population" table.

The estimates represent, so far as national data collection systems permit, the distribution of mother tongues (a mother tongue being the language spoken first and, usually, most fluently by an individual). Many countries do not collect data on this basis, however, and for these countries a variety of techniques have been used to approximate mother-tongue distribution. Some countries compile data on ethnic or "national" groups; for such countries ethnic distribution was often assumed to conform roughly to the distribution of language communities. This approach, however, must be used with caution, because a minority population is not always free to educate its children in its own language and because better economic opportunities often draw minority group members into the majority-language community. For some countries, a given individual may only be visible in national statistics as a passport-holder of a foreign nation, however long he may remain resident. Such persons, often guest workers, have sometimes had to be assumed to be speakers of the principal language of their home country. For example, since The Netherlands does not collect language data, holders of Moroccan passports were assumed to be speakers of Arabic (although perhaps a quarter of them might be of Berber heritage). For other countries, the language mosaic may be so complex, the language communities so minute in size, scholarly study so

inadequate, and the census base so obsolete that it was possible only to assign percentages to groups of related languages, despite their mutual unintelligibility (Papuan and Melanesian languages in Papua New Guinea, for instance). For some countries in the Americas, so few speakers of any single indigenous language remain that it was necessary to combine these groups as *Amerindian* so as to give a fair impression of their aggregate size within their respective countries.

No attempt has been made to account for populations that may legitimately be described as bilingual, unless the country itself collects data on that basis, as does Bolivia, for example. Similarly, no attempt has been made to distinguish between degrees of dialectal variance among communities *usually* classified as belonging to the same language—*e.g.,* between French and Occitan (the dialect of southern France), or between the various dialects of Chinese.

In giving the names of Bantu languages, grammatical particles specific to a language's autonym (name for itself) have been omitted (the form *Rwanda* is used here, for example, rather than *kinyaRwanda,* and *Tswana* instead of *seTswana*). Parenthetical alternatives are given for a number of languages that differ markedly from the name of the people speaking it (such as Kurukh, spoken by the Oraon tribes of India) or that may be combined with other groups distinguishable in national data but appearing here under the name of the largest member (*e.g.,* Nahuatl and others, combining data on Indian populations in El Salvador). The term *patois* as used here refers to distinguishable dialectal communities related to a national, official, or former colonial language (such as the French patois that survives in Grenada from the end of French rule in 1783).

Language

Major languages by country	Number of speakers	Major languages by country	Number of speakers	Major languages by country	Number of speakers	Major languages by country	Number of speakers	Major languages by country	Number of speakers
Afghanistan[1]		**Austria**		**Bolivia**		**Cameroon**[1]		**Chad**[1]	
● Dari (Persian), of which		Czech	10,000	● Aymara	484,000	Baloundou-Mbo	325,000	Arabic	1,515,000
Chahar Aimaq	620,000	● German	7,368,000	● Quechua	877,000	Bamileke	1,835,000	● French	...
Hazāra	1,630,000	Hungarian	19,000	● Spanish	2,340,000	Bassa	280,000	Hausa	110,000
Tadzhik	3,620,000	Serbo-Croatian	32,000	Spanish-Aymara	1,339,000	Duala	1,470,000	Kanuri	115,000
● Pashto	9,600,000	Slovak	23,000	Spanish-Quechua	1,053,000	● English	...	Masalit	326,000
Turkmen	360,000	Other	99,000	Spanish-Aymara-		Fang (Pahouin)	1,965,000	Mbum	341,000
Uzbek	1,630,000			Quechua	170,000	● French	...	Mubu	211,000
Other	660,000	**Bahamas, The**		Aymara-Quechua	81,000	Fulani	858,000	Sara, Bagirmi,	
		● English	211,000	Spanish-others	77,000	Maka	484,000	and Kreish	1,280,000
Albania[1]		English Creole	5,000	Other	10,000	Mandara	563,000	Tama	316,000
● Albanian	2,855,000	French Creole	8,000			Massa	394,000	Teda	386,000
Greek	72,000	Other	7,000	**Botswana**[1]		Tikar	730,000	Other	416,000
Macedonian	17,000			● English	...	Other	970,000		
Montenegrin	9,000	**Bahrain**		Khoisan	45,000			**Chile**	
Romanian	17,000	● Arabic	384,000	Tswana	1,000,000	**Canada**		Araucanian	676,000
Other	28,000	English	7,000	Other	38,000	Amerindian	153,000	● Spanish	11,347,000
		Persian	17,000			Arabic	52,000	Other	51,000
Algeria		Urdū	9,000	**Brazil**		Chinese	234,000		
● Arabic	17,478,000	Other	14,000	Amerindian	240,000	Croatian	33,000	**China**	
Berber	4,070,000			● Portuguese	134,200,000	Czech	28,000	Achang	21,000
French	139,000	**Bangladesh**		Other	1,160,000	Danish	27,000	Bai	1,176,000
Other	43,000	● Bengali	97,560,000			Dutch	153,000	Blang	61,000
		Urdū	250,000	**British Virgin Islands**		● English	15,510,000	Bouyei	2,203,000
American Samoa		Other	890,000	● English	11,000	Finnish	35,000	● Chinese (Han)	973,219,000
● English	...			Other	1,000	● French	6,532,000	Dai	873,000
● Samoan	36,000	**Barbados**				German	557,000	Daur	98,000
Other	...	English Creole	231,000	**Brunei**[1]		Greek	130,000	Dong	1,481,000
		● English	20,000	Chinese	46,000	Hungarian	88,000	Dongxiang	290,000
Andorra		Other	2,000	● English	...	Italian	562,000	Ewenki	20,000
● Catalan	13,000			● Malay	145,000	Japanese	21,000	Gelo	56,000
French	3,000	**Belgium**[1]		Indians	7,000	Norwegian	20,000	Hani	1,100,000
Spanish	25,000	● Dutch	5,770,000	Other	26,000	Pilipino	40,000	Hui	7,501,000
Other	2,000	● French	3,310,000			Polish	135,000	Jingpo	97,000
		● German	60,000	**Bulgaria**[1]		Portuguese	173,000	Kazakh	943,000
Angola[1]		Italian	260,000	● Bulgarian	8,082,000	Punjābi	57,000	Kirgiz	119,000
Ambo	210,000	Other	460,000	Romany	64,000	Russian	33,000	Korean	1,833,000
Chokwe	720,000			Turkish	780,000	Serbo-Croatian	46,000	Lahu	316,000
Humbe	220,000	**Belize**		Other	53,000	Slovak	21,000	Li	849,000
Kongo	1,100,000	Carib	9,000			Spanish	74,000	Lisu	500,000
Luimbe	750,000	● English	89,000	**Burkina Faso**[1,2]		Ukrainian	303,000	Manchu	4,466,000
Lunda	80,000	German	6,000	Bobo	471,000	Vietnamese	30,000	Maonan	40,000
Mbundu	1,950,000	Mayan	8,000	● French	...	Other	380,000	Miao	5,227,000
Nyaneka	370,000	Spanish	44,000	Fulani	382,000			Mongol	3,544,000
Ovimbundu	3,130,000	Other	2,000	Gurunsi	341,000	**Cape Verde**		Mulam	94,000
● Portuguese	...			Lobi	471,000	Crioulo (Cape Verdean		Naxi	254,000
Other	230,000	**Benin**[1]		Mossi	3,645,000	Creole)	314,000	Nu	24,000
		Bariba	356,000	Tuareg	279,000	● Portuguese	...	Pumi	25,000
Anguilla		Fon	2,371,000	Other	1,238,000	Other	...	Qiang	106,000
● English	7,000	● French	...					Salar	72,000
Other	...	Fulani (Peul)	236,000	**Burma**[1]		**Cayman Islands**		She	383,000
		Somba	413,000	● Burmese	25,630,000	● English	20,000	Shui	297,000
Antigua and Barbuda		Yoruba (Nago)	413,000	Karen	2,490,000	Other	...	Tadzhik	28,000
● English	77,000	Other	216,000	Rakhine (Arakanese)	1,660,000			Tibetan	4,021,000
Other	3,000			Shan	2,600,000	**Central African Republic**[1]		Tu	166,000
		Bermuda		Other	5,310,000	Banda	1,145,000	Tujia	2,944,000
Argentina		● English	53,000			Baya (Gbaya) - Mandja	367,000	Uighur	35,281,000
Guarani	280,000	Other	4,000	**Burundi**[1]		● French	...	Va	310,000
Italian	830,000			● French	...	Kare	64,000	Xibe	87,000
● Spanish	29,250,000	**Bhutan**[1]		● Rundi	4,636,000	Mbaka	110,000	Yao	1,457,000
Other	210,000	Assamese	192,000	Other[3]	19,000	Ngbandi	275,000	Yi	5,666,000
		● Dzongkha (Bhutia)	864,000			Sango	...	Zhuang	13,900,000
Australia		Gurung	225,000			Sara	100,000	Other	26,628,000
● English	15,576,000	Other	143,000			Zande (Azande)	246,000		
Other (including						Other	259,000		
Aboriginal languages)	191,000								

Major languages by country	Number of speakers
Christmas Island[1]	
Chinese	1,900
• English	...
Malay	900
Other	200
Cocos (Keeling) Islands	
• English	200
Malay	400
Other	...
Colombia	
Arawakan	182,000
Cariban	84,000
Chibchan	187,000
• Spanish	28,320,000
Other	69,000
Comoros	
• Arabic	...
Comorian (related to Swahili)	403,000
• French	...
Other	...
Congo[1,4]	
Bubangi	90,000
• French	...
Kongo	910,000
Kota	78,000
Mboshi	59,000
Teke	418,000
Other	184,000
Cook Islands	
• English	...
Maori	16,000
Other	2,000
Costa Rica	
• Spanish	2,517,000
Other	26,000
Cuba	
• Spanish	10,011,000
Other	47,000
Cyprus[1]	
• Greek	538,000
• Turkish	125,000
Other	4,000
Czechoslovakia	
• Czech	9,878,000
German	59,000
Hungarian	589,000
Polish	70,000
• Slovak	4,805,000
Ukrainian	48,000
Other	60,000
Denmark[1]	
• Danish	4,944,000
Faeroese	41,000
German	51,000
Turkish	15,000
Other	57,000
Djibouti[1]	
Afar	129,000
• Arabic	17,000
• French	...
Issa	96,000
Issachar and Gad	68,000
Other	31,000
Dominica	
• English	...
French patois	71,000
Other	3,000
Dominican Republic	
French patois	27,000
• Spanish	6,206,000
Other	11,000
Ecuador	
Quechua (and other Indian languages)	600,000
• Spanish	8,000,000
Other	...
Egypt	
• Arabic	47,920,000
Other	580,000
El Salvador	
Nahuatl (and other Indian languages)	160,000
• Spanish	5,080,000
Other	...
Equatorial Guinea[1]	
Bubi	45,000
Duala	9,000
Fang	226,000
Ibibio	4,000
• Spanish	...
Other[5]	33,000

Major languages by country	Number of speakers
Ethiopia	
• Amharic	16,420,000
Gurage	1,390,000
Oromo (Galla)	15,420,000
Tigrinya	3,660,000
Other	6,660,000
Faeroe Islands	
• Danish	...
• Faeroese	45,000
Other	...
Falkland Islands	
• English	2,000
Other	...
Fiji[1]	
• English	...
Fijian	316,000
Hindi	340,000
Other	36,000
Finland	
• Finnish	4,595,000
• Swedish	299,000
Other	16,000
France[1]	
Alsatian	1,570,000
Arabic	1,450,000
Armenian	170,000
Basque	170,000
Breton	1,220,000
Catalan	170,000
Dutch	290,000
• French	44,880,000
German	230,000
Hebrew	580,000
Polish	350,000
Other	4,000,000
French Guiana	
Creole	75,000
• French	...
Other	8,000
French Polynesia[1]	
• French	20,000
Chinese	8,000
Tahitian	130,000
Other	18,000
Gabon[1]	
Eshira	220,000
Fang	340,000
• French	70,000
Kota	130,000
Mbete	170,000
Other	230,000
Gambia, The	
Dyola	52,000
• English	...
Fulani	131,000
Malinke	330,000
Soninke	52,000
Wolof	92,000
Other	91,000
Gaza Strip	
Arabic	483,000
Hebrew	...
Other	8,000
Germany, East[1]	
• German	16,536,000
Other	167,000
Germany, West[1]	
Dutch	300,000
English	120,000
• German	57,100,000
Greek	370,000
Italian	600,000
Spanish	180,000
Turkish	1,040,000
Other	1,240,000
Ghana[1]	
Akan	6,740,000
• English	...
Ewe	1,510,000
Ga-Adangme	970,000
Mossi-Dagomba	2,040,000
Other	1,550,000
Gibraltar	
• English	10,000
Spanish	11,000
Other	9,000
Greece[1]	
Albanian	60,000
• Greek	9,460,000
Macedonian	180,000
Turkish	60,000
Other	210,000

Major languages by country	Number of speakers
Greenland	
• Danish	5,000
• Greenlandic	48,000
Other	...
Grenada	
• English	87,000
Other	3,000
Guadeloupe	
Creole and French	314,000
• French	...
Other	16,000
Guam	
Chamorro	41,000
• English	43,000
Philippine languages	20,000
Other	16,000
Guatemala	
Cakchiquel	442,000
Chorti	58,000
Ixil	77,000
Kanjobal	110,000
Kekchi	325,000
Jacaltec	50,000
Mam	650,000
Pocomcii	87,000
Quiché	932,000
• Spanish	4,316,000
Other	628,000
Guernsey	
• English	...
French	...
Other	...
Guinea[1]	
• French	...
Fulani (Peul)	2,170,000
Kissi	300,000
Mande, of which	2,730,000
Malinke	1,140,000
Susu	620,000
Other	970,000
Other	240,000
Guinea-Bissau[1]	
Balante	240,000
Fulani	200,000
Malinke	110,000
Mandyako	90,000
Pepel	90,000
• Portuguese	...
Other	150,000
Guyana	
• English	...
English Creole	...
Hindi	...
Urdū	...
Other	...
Haiti	
• French	520,000
French Creole	4,730,000
Other	...
Honduras	
• Spanish	4,280,000
Amerindian languages and other	90,000
Hong Kong	
• Chinese (Cantonese)	5,005,000
Chinese (other dialects)	333,000
• English	52,000
Other	25,000
Hungary[1]	
• Hungarian	10,540,000
Other	110,000
Iceland[1]	
• Icelandic	239,000
Other	4,000
India	
Anga (Angikā)	594,000
Assamese	12,520,000
Baghelkhandi	324,000
Bāgri	1,460,000
Banjari	662,000
Barel	323,000
Bengali	62,440,000
Bhilāli	346,000
Bhili (Bhilodi)	1,690,000
Bhojpuri	20,050,000
Bodo	714,000
Bundelkhandi	528,000
Chhattisgarhi	9,370,000
Dogri	1,770,000
• English	...
Garhwali	1,690,000
Gāro	577,000
Gojri	464,000
Gondi	2,150,000

Major languages by country	Number of speakers
Gujarāti	35,940,000
Halabi	486,000
Harauti	469,000
• Hindi	215,660,000
Ho	1,052,000
Kachchi	661,000
Kannaḍa	30,260,000
Kashmiri	3,380,000
Khāsi	539,000
Khorthā (Khottā)	707,000
Konkani	2,070,000
Korku	398,000
Koya	297,000
Kui	492,000
Kumāuni	1,690,000
Kurukh (Oraon)	1,690,000
Lamani (Banjāri)	1,610,000
Lushai (Mizo)	379,000
Maghi (Magadhi)	9,290,000
Maithili	8,520,000
Malayālam	30,720,000
Malvi	904,000
Mandeali	339,000
Marāṭhi	58,520,000
Mārwaṛi	6,600,000
Meithei (Manipuri)	1,096,000
Mewari	1,148,000
Mikir	279,000
Munda	305,000
Mundari	1,081,000
Nāgpuria	470,000
Nepāli (Gorkhali)	1,770,000
Nimadi	1,114,000
Oriyā	27,650,000
Pahāṛi	1,770,000
Punjābi	19,430,000
Rajasthani	2,920,000
Sadan (Sadri)	1,133,000
Santāli	5,150,000
Savara	311,000
Sindhi	1,690,000
Surgujia	752,000
Tamil	52,690,000
Telugu	62,670,000
Tripuri	377,000
Tulu	1,610,000
Urdū	40,090,000
Other	12,169,000
Indonesia[1]	
Achinese	3,120,000
• Bahasa Indonesia	...
Balinese	3,280,000
Batak	4,540,000
Bugi	4,370,000
Javanese	65,730,000
Madurese	10,940,000
Sundanese	21,300,000
Other	54,270,000
Iran[1]	
Arabic	710,000
Azerbaijani	7,140,000
Armenian	313,000
Bakhtiari	848,000
Baluchi	848,000
• Farsi (Persian)	20,095,000
Kurdish	3,657,000
Luri	978,000
Turkmen	665,000
Other	9,400,000
Iraq	
• Arabic	12,497,000
Assyrian	72,000
Kurdish	2,391,000
Turkish	47,000
Turkmen	257,000
Other	412,000
Ireland	
• English	2,780,000
• Irish	830,000
Other	...
Isle of Man	
• English	70,000
Other	...
Israel[1]	
• Arabic	723,000
French	51,000
German	56,000
• Hebrew	2,838,000
Romanian	82,000
Spanish	51,000
Yiddish	207,000
Other	298,000
Italy[1]	
Albanian	114,000
French	114,000
German	342,000
• Italian	55,761,000
Other	748,000

Major languages by country	Number of speakers
Ivory Coast[1]	
Akan	4,207,000
• French	...
Kru	1,686,000
Malinke	1,503,000
Southern Mande	1,036,000
Voltaic (including Senufo)	1,596,000
Other	135,000
Jamaica	
Chinese	13,000
• English	...
English and English Creole	2,069,000
Hindi and other Indian languages	36,000
Spanish	4,000
Other	83,000
Japan[1]	
• Japanese	120,110,000
Korean	570,000
Other	120,000
Jordan[1]	
• Arabic	2,550,000
Other	40,000
Jersey	
• English	...
French	...
Other	...
Kampuchea[1]	
Chinese	220,000
• Khmer	6,770,000
Vietnamese	290,000
Other[6]	...
Kenya[1]	
Arabic	82,000
Bajuni	49,000
Basua	79,000
Boran	91,000
Degodia	123,000
Embu	225,000
Gurreh	110,000
Gusii	1,115,000
Kalenjin	1,982,000
Kamba	2,287,000
Kikuyu	3,932,000
Kisi	1,251,000
Kuria	118,000
Luhya	2,604,000
Luo	2,261,000
Masai	307,000
Mbere	84,000
Meru	1,052,000
Mijikenda	886,000
Pokomo	53,000
Sambur	98,000
Somali	124,000
• Swahili	...
Taita	185,000
Teso	164,000
Turkana	213,000
Other[7]	836,000
Kiribati[1]	
• English	...
Kiribati	64,000
Other	1,000
Korea, North[1]	
• Korean	19,941,000
Other	141,000
Korea, South[1]	
• Korean	41,174,000
Other	41,000
Kuwait[1]	
• Arabic	1,497,000
Kurdish	191,000
Persian	80,000
Other	143,000
Laos[1]	
Chinese	45,000
Khmu	371,000
• Lao	2,668,000
Man	57,000
Miao	165,000
Mon-Khmer	288,000
Tai	345,000
Other[8]	178,000
Lebanon[1]	
• Arabic	2,428,000
Armenian	18,000
Kurdish	13,000
Other[6]	209,000
Lesotho	
• English	...
• Sesotho	1,495,000
Other	5,000

Language (continued)

Major languages by country	Number of speakers
Liberia[1]	
Bassa	289,000
● English	...
Gio	90,000
Gola	112,000
Grebo and Kran	357,000
Kpelle	615,000
Kru	122,000
Toma	191,000
Mano	58,000
Other	399,000
Libya	
● Arabic	3,521,000
Other[9]	109,000
Liechtenstein[1]	
● German	23,000
Other	4,000
Luxembourg[1]	
Dutch	5,000
● French	15,000
● German	10,000
Italian	23,000
Luxembourgish	279,000
Other	34,000
Macau	
Chinese	307,000
● Portuguese	...
Other	7,000
Madagascar[1]	
● French	...
Malagasy	9,892,000
Other	120,000
Malaŵi	
● Chewa	3,543,000
● English	...
Lomwe	1,024,000
Sena	246,000
Tumbuka	642,000
Yao	973,000
Other	630,000
Malaysia	
Bajau	98,000
Chinese	900,000
Chinese and others	510,000
Dusan	162,000
English	78,000
English and others	173,000
Iban	370,000
Iban and others	61,000
● Malay	6,704,000
Malay and others	2,382,000
Tamil	603,000
Tamil and others	9,000
Other	3,501,000
Maldives	
● Divehi (Maldivian)	178,000
Other	...
Mali[1]	
Bambara	2,513,000
Bobo	198,000
Dyula	253,000
Dogon	387,000
● French	...
Fulani	1,003,000
Malinke	750,000
Senufo	941,000
Songhai	466,000
Soninke	688,000
Tuareg	443,000
Other	262,000
Malta[1]	
● English	7,000
● Maltese	319,000
Other	7,000
Martinique	
Creole and French	319,000
● French	...
Other	11,000
Mauritania	
● Arabic	...
● French	1,325,000
Fulfulde (Poular)	282,000
Hassāniyah Arabic	...
Other	50,000
Mauritius	
● English	...
French	47,000
French patois	546,000
Hindi	316,000
Tamil	35,000
Urdū	28,000
Other	53,000

Major languages by country	Number of speakers
Mayotte	
Comorian (related to Swahili)	58,000
● French	...
Other	...
Mexico	
Aztec (Nahuatl)	1,869,000
Chinantec	105,000
Chol	131,000
English	...
Huastec	141,000
Huichol	70,000
Mazahua	264,000
Mazatec	169,000
Mayo	76,000
Mixtec	439,000
Mixe	101,000
Otomi	416,000
● Spanish	70,996,000
Tarahumara	85,000
Tarasco	161,000
Tlapanec	75,000
Totonac	266,000
Tzeltal	292,000
Tzotzil	181,000
Yucatec (Maya)	903,000
Zapotec	574,000
Other	713,000
Monaco[1]	
English	1,000
● French	16,000
Italian	5,000
Monegasque	4,000
Other	2,000
Mongolia[1]	
Buryat	42,000
Dariganga	36,000
Dörbed	53,000
Kazakh	84,000
● Khalkha (Mongolian)	1,535,000
Russian	25,000
Other	133,000
Montserrat	
● English	12,000
Other	...
Morocco[1]	
● Arabic	18,110,000
Berber	6,090,000
Other[6]	170,000
Mozambique[1]	
Makua	7,361,000
Malaŵi	1,689,000
● Portuguese	...
Shona	816,000
Tsonga	3,321,000
Yao	450,000
Other	437,000
Nauru	
● Nauruan	6,300
Other[7]	1,700
Nepal	
Bhojpuri	1,157,000
Hindi (Awadhi dialect)	446,000
Magar	413,000
Maithili	1,900,000
● Nepāli	8,659,000
Newāri	644,000
Rai	330,000
Tamang	793,000
Thārū	711,000
Other	1,472,000
Netherlands, The[1]	
Arabic	101,000
● Dutch	13,922,000
Turkish	159,000
Other	290,000
Netherlands Antilles[1]	
● Dutch	19,000
English	13,000
French	11,000
Papiamento	193,000
Other	7,000
New Caledonia[1]	
● French	56,000
Melanesian languages	63,000
Other	30,000
New Zealand	
● English	3,050,000
Maori	104,000
Other	111,000

Major languages by country	Number of speakers
Nicaragua[1]	
● Spanish	2,978,000
Other (including Miskito)	61,000
Niger[1]	
● French	...
Fulani	625,000
Hausa	3,258,000
Kanuri	563,000
Songhai	500,000
Tuareg	188,000
Zerma	913,000
Other	206,000
Nigeria	
Annang	1,160,000
Urhobo	1,090,000
Edo	1,640,000
● English	...
Fulani	8,250,000
Hausa	20,100,000
Ibibio	3,460,000
Ibo	15,940,000
Ijaw	1,870,000
Kanuri	3,890,000
Nupe	1,120,000
Tiv	2,400,000
Yoruba	19,500,000
Other	15,590,000
Niue	
● English	...
Niuean	3,000
Other	...
Norfolk Island	
● English	2,000
Other	...
Norway[1]	
Danish	17,000
English	21,000
Finnish	21,000
● Norwegian	4,044,000
Swedish	8,000
Other	46,000
Oman[1]	
● Arabic	904,000
Baluchi	41,000
Persian (Farsi)	35,000
Other	61,000
Pacific Islands, Trust Territory of the	
Chamorro	15,000
● English	...
Kosraean	5,000
Marshallese	33,000
Mortlockese	12,000
Palauan	15,000
Ponapean	22,000
Trukese	35,000
Woleaian	2,000
Yapese	6,000
Other	4,000
Pakistan[1]	
Baluchi	2,510,000
Brahui	900,000
Jatt	6,620,000
Pashto	8,530,000
Punjabi	60,010,000
Sindhi	12,640,000
● Urdū	7,630,000
Other[7]	1,510,000
Panama	
Cuna	47,000
Guaymí	65,000
● Spanish	2,037,000
Other	31,000
Papua New Guinea[1]	
● English	...
Papuan languages	2,773,000
Melanesian languages	515,000
Other[10]	40,000
Paraguay	
Guaraní	1,379,000
Guaraní and Spanish	1,481,000
● Spanish	132,000
Other	412,000
Peru	
Aymara	571,000
● Quechua	5,237,000
● Spanish	13,395,000
Other	498,000

Major languages by country	Number of speakers
Philippines	
Aklanon	534,000
Bicol	3,805,000
Bolinao (Zambal)	235,000
Cebuano	13,336,000
Chavacano	283,000
Chinese	136,000
Davaweno	162,000
● English	20,000
Hamtikanon	450,000
Hiligaynon/Ilongo	5,464,000
Ibanag	320,000
Ifugao	169,000
Ilocano	6,089,000
Kangkanai	200,000
Maguindanao	654,000
Manobo	172,000
Maranao	783,000
Masbate	403,000
Pampango	1,875,000
Pangasinan	1,233,000
● Pilipino (= Tagalog)	13,019,000
Romblon	225,000
Samal	317,000
Samar-Leyte (Waray-Waray)	2,527,000
Subanon	181,000
Sulu-Moro (Tau Sug)	429,000
Other	1,648,000
Pitcairn Island	
● English	60
Other	...
Poland	
Belorussian	220,000
● Polish	36,680,000
Ukrainian	220,000
Other	40,000
Portugal[1]	
● Portuguese	9,937,000
Other	101,000
Puerto Rico	
● English	16,000
● Spanish	1,878,000
Spanish and English	1,374,000
Other	43,000
Qatar[1]	
● Arabic	273,000
Other[7]	28,000
Réunion	
Creole	548,000
● French	...
Other[11]	...
Romania	
German	293,000
Hungarian	1,640,000
● Romanian	20,423,000
Other	359,000
Rwanda	
● French	...
● Rwanda	6,115,000
Other[3]	...
St. Christopher and Nevis	
● English	43,000
Other	1,000
St. Helena and Ascension	
● English	7,000
Other	...
St. Lucia	
● English	1,000
French patois	117,000
Hindi and Urdu	4,000
Other	8,000
St. Pierre and Miquelon[1]	
● French	5,900
Other	100
St. Vincent and the Grenadines	
● English	98,000
Other	7,000
San Marino[1]	
● Italian	22,000
Other	...
São Tomé and Príncipe[1]	
Fang	97,000
● Portuguese	...
Other	9,000
Saudi Arabia[1]	
● Arabic	10,903,000
Other	337,000

Major languages by country	Number of speakers
Senegal[1]	
Dyola	574,000
● French	...
Fulani	1,167,000
Mandingo	548,000
Serer	1,089,000
Tukulor	424,000
Wolof	2,399,000
Other	319,000
Seychelles	
● English	...
● French	...
Creole patois	63,000
Other	2,000
Sierra Leone[1]	
Bullom	132,000
● English	...
Fulani	132,000
Kissi	90,000
Kono	200,000
Koranko	132,000
Limba	132,000
Mende	1,232,000
Temne	1,121,000
Other[12]	408,000
Singapore[1]	
● Bahasa Malaysia	376,000
Chinese	1,961,000
● English	...
● Mandarin Chinese	...
● Tamil (and other Indian languages)	164,000
Other	57,000
Solomon Islands	
Areare	10,000
● English	...
Kwalo	9,000
Kwara'ae	18,000
Other[13]	230,000
Somalia[1]	
● Arabic	...
● Somali	5,683,000
Other	134,000
South Africa	
● Afrikaans	4,807,000
● English	1,778,000
Nguni	11,290,000
Shangana-Tsonga	835,000
Sotho	5,942,000
Venda	456,000
Other	2,374,000
Bophuthatswana	
● Afrikaans	...
● English	...
● Tswana	1,035,000
Other	492,000
Ciskei	
● English	...
● Xhosa	774,000
Other	3,000
Transkei	
● English	...
● Xhosa	2,526,000
Other	155,000
Venda	
● Afrikaans	...
● English	...
● Venda	381,000
Other	43,000
South West Africa/Namibia	
● Afrikaans	151,000
East Caprivian	39,000
● English	...
German	29,000
Herero	69,000
Khoisan	183,000
Okavango	76,000
Ovambo	505,000
Other	47,000
Spain[1]	
Basque	890,000
● Castilian Spanish	28,220,000
Catalan	6,360,000
Galician	3,180,000
Other	120,000
Sri Lanka	
English	11,000
English and Sinhalese	886,000
English and Tamil	184,000
English, Sinhalese, and Tamil	582,000
● Sinhalese	9,722,000
Sinhalese and Tamil	1,505,000
Tamil	3,165,000
Other	55,000

Major languages by country	Number of speakers	Major languages by country	Number of speakers	Major languages by country	Number of speakers	Major languages by country	Number of speakers	Major languages by country	Number of speakers
Sudan, The[1]		Nyamwezi (Sukuma)	4,586,000	**Uganda[1]**		**United Arab Emirates[1]**		**West Bank**	
● Arabic	11,630,000	Shambala	929,000	Acholi	590,000	● Arabic	1,137,000	Arabic	714,000
Beja	1,490,000	● Swahili	1,869,000	Chiga (Kiga)	1,030,000	Other	143,000	Hebrew	25,000
Dinka	2,720,000	Taita	619,000	● English	...				
Nubian	1,910,000	Other	4,186,000	Ganda (Luganda)	2,650,000	**United Kingdom**		**Western Sahara**	
Nuer	1,160,000			Gisu	1,090,000	● English	52,430,000	Arabic	150,000
Other	4,740,000	**Thailand[1]**		Lango	960,000	Scots-Gaelic	70,000	Other[15]	...
		Chinese	5,800,000	Nkole	1,210,000	Welsh	520,000		
Suriname		Khmer	720,000	Nyoro	560,000	Other	3,400,000	**Western Samoa**	
Creole	51,000	Karen	310,000	Rwanda	810,000			● English	1,000
● Dutch	138,000	Malay	1,950,000	Soga	1,210,000	**United States**		● Samoan	76,000
● English	...	● Thai	41,710,000	Turkana	1,210,000	Chinese	690,000	Samoan and English	83,000
Hindi	117,000	Other	810,000	Other[3]	3,400,000	● English	212,550,000	Other	...
Javanese	57,000					French	1,740,000		
Other	16,000	**Togo[1]**		**U.S.S.R.[1]**		German	1,740,000	**Yemen (Aden)[1]**	
		Ewe	1,390,000	Armenian	4,000,000	Greek	430,000	● Arabic	1,974,000
Swaziland		● French	...	Avar	511,000	Italian	1,770,000	Other	150,000
● English	...	Gurma	421,000	Azerbaijani	5,690,000	Japanese	360,000		
● Swazi	593,000	Kabre	669,000	Bashkir	1,452,000	Korean	290,000	**Yemen (Şan'ā')[1]**	
Other[14]	66,000	Tem	126,000	Bulgarian	382,000	Philippine languages	500,000	● Arabic	6,442,000
		Other	383,000	Buryat	374,000	Polish	880,000	Other	105,000
Sweden[1]				Byelorussian	7,440,000	Portuguese	410,000		
Finnish	292,000	**Tokelau**		Chechen	800,000	Spanish	12,730,000	**Yugoslavia[1]**	
● Swedish	7,568,000	● English	...	Dargin	304,000	Yiddish	360,000	Albanian	1,896,000
Other	485,000	Tokelauan	2,000	Estonian	1,030,000	Other	4,390,000	Hungarian	416,000
		Other	...	Gagauz	183,000			● Macedonian	1,401,000
Switzerland[1]				Georgian	3,720,000	**Uruguay**		● Serbo-Croatian	15,363,000
● French	1,208,000	**Tonga**		Greek	364,000	● Spanish	2,908,000	● Slovenian	1,789,000
● German	4,277,000	● English	...	Hungarian	181,000	Other	104,000	Other	2,370,000
● Italian	594,000	● Tongan	105,000	Ingush	197,000				
Romansh	52,000	Other	2,000	Kabardinian	341,000	**Vanuatu**		**Zaire[1]**	
Other	341,000			Kara-Kalpak	321,000	Bislama	115,000	Azande	2,016,000
		Trinidad and Tobago[1]		Kazakh	6,770,000	● English	...	● French	...
Syria[1]		● English	686,000	Kirgiz	1,970,000	● French	...	Kongo	5,354,000
● Arabic	9,117,000	Hindi (and other Indian languages)	476,000	Komi	346,000	Other	25,000	Luba	5,949,000
Armenian	288,000	Other	27,000	Komi-Permyak	160,000			Lugbara	992,000
Kurdish	647,000			Korean	412,000	**Venezuela**		Mongo	4,396,000
Other	217,000	**Tunisia**		Kumyk	241,000	● Spanish	16,870,000	Ngala	1,917,000
		● Arabic	5,371,000	Lak	106,000	Other	460,000	Rundi	1,256,000
Taiwan[1]		Arabic and French	1,704,000	Latvian	1,440,000			Rwanda	3,338,000
South Fukien Chinese	12,799,000	French	72,000	Lezgian	405,000	**Vietnam**		Teke	892,000
Hakka and Hokkien Chinese	1,911,000	Other	38,000	Lithuanian	2,940,000	Khmer	800,000	Other[16]	6,942,000
● Mandarin Chinese	3,993,000			Mari	659,000	Muong	760,000		
Other	403,000	**Turkey**		Moldavian	2,940,000	Nung	590,000	**Zambia[1]**	
		Arabic	576,000	Mordvinian	1,262,000	Tay	920,000	Bemba	2,309,000
Tanzania[1]		Kurdish	3,419,000	Ossetian	574,000	Thai	780,000	● English	...
Chagga (Chaga)	1,087,000	● Turkish	44,443,000	Polish	1,219,000	● Vietnamese	49,790,000	Lozi	633,000
● English	...	Other	833,000	● Russian	162,530,000	Other	5,590,000	Lunda	432,000
Gogo	842,000			Tadzhik	3,000,000			Luzna	339,000
Ha	693,000	**Turks and Caicos Islands**		Tatar	5,740,000	**Virgin Islands (U.S.)**		Malawi	912,000
Haya	1,282,000	● English	8,000	Turkmenian	2,110,000	● English	91,000	Ngoni	239,000
Hehet	1,478,000	Other	...	Tuvinian	176,000	Spanish	16,000	Tonga	1,091,000
Iramba	619,000			Udmurt	756,000	Other	...	Other	711,000
Luguru	1,087,000	**Tuvalu**		Uighur	223,000				
Makonde	1,282,000	English	...	Ukrainian	37,130,000	**Wallis and Futuna Islands**		**Zimbabwe[1]**	
Nyakyusa	1,174,000	Kiribati (Gilbertese)	1,000	Uzbek	12,990,000	● French	...	● English	627,000
		Tuvaluan (Ellice)	8,000	Yakut	347,000	Wallisian	14,000	Nguni	1,277,000
		Other	...	Other	3,764,000	Other	...	Nyanja	420,000
								Shona	5,738,000
								Other	38,000

[1]Figures given represent ethnolinguistic groups. [2]Majority of population speak Moré (language of the Mossi); Dyula is language of commerce. [3]Swahili also spoken. [4]Lingala and Monokutuba are patois. [5]Pidgin English and Portuguese patois also spoken. [6]French also spoken. [7]English also spoken. [8]English and French also spoken. [9]English and Italian also spoken. [10]About half the population also speaks Pisin (Pidgin English); English and Hiri (Police Motu) also spoken. [11]Gujarati and Chinese also spoken. [12]Kiro is the lingua franca. [13]Solomon Islands Pidgin (English) is the lingua franca. [14]Afrikaans and Portuguese also spoken. [15]Spanish also spoken. [16]Swahili, Tshiluba, Lingala, and Kikongo are national languages.

Religion

The following table presents statistics on religious affiliation for each of the countries of the world. An assessment was made for each country of the available data on distribution of religious communities within the total population; the best available figures, whether originating as census data, membership figures of the churches concerned, or estimated by external analysts in the absence of reliable local data, were applied as percentages to the estimated 1985 midyear population of the country to obtain the data shown below.

Several concepts govern the nature of the available data, each useful separately but none the basis of any standard of international practice in the collection of such data. The word "affiliation" was used above to describe the nature of the relationship joining the religious bodies named and the populations shown. This term implies some sort of formal, usually documentary, connection between the religion and the individual (a baptismal certificate, a child being assigned the religion of its parents, maintenance of one's name on the tax rolls of a state religion, etc.) but says nothing about the nature of the individual's personal religious practice, in that the individual may have lapsed, never been confirmed as an adult, joined another religion, or may have joined an organization that is formally atheist.

The user of these statistics should be careful to note that not only does the nature of the affiliation (with an organized religion) differ greatly from country to country, but so does the nature of individual practice. A country in which a single religion has long been predominant will often show more than 90% of its population to be *affiliated*, while in actual fact, no more than 10% may actually *practice* that religion on a regular basis. Such a situation often leads to undercounting of minority religions (where someone [head of household, communicant, child, servant] is counted at all), blurring of distinctions seen to be significant elsewhere (a Hindu country may not distinguish Protestant [or even Christian] denominations; a Christian country may not collect much data distinguishing among its Muslim or Buddhist citizens), or double-counting in countries where an individual may conscientiously practice more than one "religion" at a time.

Communist countries consciously attempt to ignore, suppress, or render invisible religious practice within their boundaries. Countries with large numbers of adherents of traditional, often animist, religions and belief systems usually have little or no formal methodology for defining the nature of local religious practice. On the other hand, countries with strong missionary traditions, or good census organizations, or few religious sensitivities may have very good, detailed, and meaningful data.

The best (indeed, at its publication, the most authoritative and exhaustive) work available is DAVID B. BARRETT (ed.), *World Christian Encyclopedia* (1982); it examines both the theoretical and practical problems of collecting and analyzing religious statistics, assembles a mine of national detail, and establishes a basis for further study.

Religion

Religious affiliation	1985 population	Religious affiliation	1985 population	Religious affiliation	1985 population	Religious affiliation	1985 population	Religious affiliation	1985 population
Afghanistan		**Benin**		**Chad**		**El Salvador**		**Grenada**	
Sunnī Muslim	15,765,000	traditional beliefs	2,459,000	Muslim	2,208,000	Roman Catholic	5,037,000	Roman Catholic	62,000
Shī'ī Muslim	2,174,000	Roman Catholic	741,000	Christian[1]	1,656,000	other	199,000	Anglican	20,000
other	181,000	Muslim	609,000	traditional beliefs	1,144,000	**Equatorial Guinea**		other	14,000
Albania		other	196,000	other	10,000	Christian[1]	281,000	**Guadeloupe**	
Muslim	615,000	**Bermuda**		**Chile**		other	36,000	Roman Catholic	298,000
Christian	162,000	Anglican	24,000	Roman Catholic	9,565,000	**Ethiopia**		Protestant	19,000
atheist	561,000	other Protestant	21,000	Protestant	725,000	Ethiopian Orthodox	22,865,000	other	13,000
nonreligious	1,662,000	Roman Catholic	11,000	other	1,784,000	Muslim	13,675,000	**Guam**	
Algeria		other	1,000	**China**		traditional beliefs	4,965,000	Roman Catholic	95,000
Muslim	21,535,000	**Bhutan**		nonreligious	617,515,000	other	2,045,000	Protestant	19,000
other	196,000	Buddhist	990,000	Chinese folk-		**Faeroe Islands**		other	6,000
American Samoa		Hindu	350,000	religionist	209,663,000	Evangelical Lutheran	34,000	**Guatemala**	
Congregational	19,000	other	83,000	atheist	125,172,000	other	11,000	Roman Catholic	6,140,000
Roman Catholic	7,000	**Bolivia**		Buddhist	62,586,000	**Falkland Islands**		Protestant	1,535,000
other	10,000	Roman Catholic	6,043,000	Muslim	25,034,000	Anglican	1,000	**Guernsey**	
Andorra		other	386,000	other	3,130,000	other	1,000	Anglican	39,000
Roman Catholic	38,000	**Botswana**		**Christmas Island**		**Fiji**		Roman Catholic	6,000
other	5,000	Christian[1]	543,000	Buddhist	1,100	Christian[1]	344,000	other	15,000
Angola		traditional beliefs	532,000	Muslim	800	Hindu	283,000	**Guinea**	
Christian[1]	7,716,000	other	7,000	Christian	500	other	65,000	Muslim	3,745,000
traditional beliefs	814,000	**Brazil**		other	600	**Finland**		traditional beliefs	1,600,000
other	43,000	Roman Catholic	119,025,000	**Cocos (Keeling) Islands**		Lutheran	4,404,000	other	80,000
Anguilla		Protestant	8,269,000	Muslim	400	other	506,000	**Guinea-Bissau**	
Anglican	3,000	other	8,270,000	Christian	200	**France**		traditional beliefs	576,000
Methodist	3,000	**British Virgin Islands**		other	100	Roman Catholic	42,166,000	Muslim	262,000
other	1,000	Methodist	5,000	**Colombia**		other Christian	2,040,000	Christian	35,000
Antigua and Barbuda		Anglican	3,000	Roman Catholic	27,977,000	atheist	1,875,000	**Guyana**	
Anglican	36,000	other	4,000	other	865,000	Muslim	1,655,000	Hindu	328,000
other Protestant	34,000	**Brunei**		**Comoros**		other	7,455,000	Roman Catholic	172,000
Roman Catholic	8,000	Muslim	142,000	Sunnī Muslim	402,000	**French Guiana**		Anglican	152,000
other	3,000	Buddhist	31,000	Christian	1,000	Roman Catholic	72,000	other Protestant	172,000
Argentina		other	51,000	**Congo**		other	11,000	Muslim	86,000
Roman Catholic	28,376,000	**Bulgaria**		Roman Catholic	938,000	**French Polynesia**		other	43,000
other	2,188,000	Eastern Orthodox	2,397,000	Protestant	433,000	Protestant	82,000	**Haiti**	
Australia		Muslim	673,000	African Christian	247,000	Roman Catholic	69,000	Roman Catholic	4,215,000
Anglican	4,110,000	atheist	5,791,000	other	122,000	other	24,000	Baptist	510,000
Uniting Church	772,000	other	118,000	**Cook Islands**		**Gabon**		other (mostly Protestant)	525,000
Presbyterian	693,000	**Burkina Faso**		Congregational	12,000	Roman Catholic	761,000	**Honduras**	
Methodist	535,000	traditional beliefs	3,059,000	Roman Catholic	3,000	Protestant	219,000	Roman Catholic	4,186,000
other Protestant	1,276,000	Muslim	2,936,000	other	2,000	African Christian	141,000	other	186,000
Roman Catholic	4,095,000	Christian[1]	833,000	**Costa Rica**		other	46,000	**Hong Kong**	
Orthodox	457,000	**Burma**		Roman Catholic	2,332,000	**Gambia, The**		Buddhist (some Confucianist	
nonreligious	1,701,000	Buddhist	32,862,000	other	211,000	Muslim	635,000	and Taoist)	4,900,000
other	2,110,000	Christian[1]	2,110,000	**Cuba**		other	114,000	Christian	515,000
Austria		Muslim	1,357,000	nonreligious	4,898,000	**Gaza Strip**		**Hungary**	
Roman Catholic	6,366,000	other	1,357,000	Roman Catholic	3,980,000	Muslim	501,000	Roman Catholic	5,738,000
Protestant	423,000	**Burundi**		atheist	644,000	other	8,000	Protestant	2,289,000
atheist and nonreligious	453,000	Christian[1]	4,093,000	other	533,000	**German Democratic Republic**		nonreligious	926,000
other	310,000	traditional beliefs	646,000	**Cyprus**		Protestant	13,363,000	atheist	766,000
Bahamas, The		other	48,000	Greek Orthodox	522,000	Roman Catholic	1,670,000	other	926,000
Anglican	48,000	**Cameroon**		Muslim	128,000	atheist	1,670,000	**Iceland**	
other Protestant	107,000	Roman Catholic	3,372,000	other	35,000	**Germany, Federal Rep. of**		Lutheran	235,000
Roman Catholic	59,000	Protestant	1,734,000	**Czechoslovakia**		Protestant	28,459,000	other	8,000
other	16,000	traditional beliefs	2,409,000	Roman Catholic	10,174,000	Roman Catholic	26,692,000	**India**	
Bahrain		Muslim	2,120,000	atheist	3,117,000	other Christian	1,401,000	Hindu	635,150,000
Shī'ī Muslim	220,000	**Canada**		other	2,218,000	nonreligious	2,803,000	Muslim	86,000,000
Sunnī Muslim	147,000	Roman Catholic	11,824,000	**Denmark**		Muslim	1,463,000	Christian	19,950,000
other	64,000	Protestant	10,476,000	Evangelical Lutheran	4,882,000	atheist	548,000	Sikh	14,600,000
Bangladesh		nonreligious	1,882,000	other	225,000	other	122,000	Buddhist	5,400,000
Muslim	85,523,000	other	1,245,000	**Djibouti**		**Ghana**		Jain	3,850,000
Hindu	11,972,000	**Cape Verde**		Sunnī Muslim	404,000	Christian[1]	8,022,000	other	3,050,000
other	1,204,000	Roman Catholic	308,000	Christian	26,000	traditional beliefs	2,742,000	**Indonesia**	
Barbados		Protestant	6,000	**Dominica**		Muslim	2,012,000	Muslim	140,070,000
Anglican	126,000	**Cayman Islands**		Roman Catholic	68,000	other	39,000	Protestant	8,040,000
other Protestant	97,000	Presbyterian	7,000	Protestant	6,000	**Gibraltar**		Roman Catholic	4,520,000
Roman Catholic	15,000	Church of God	5,000	**Dominican Republic**		Roman Catholic	22,000	other	14,920,000
other	15,000	other	8,000	Roman Catholic	6,118,000	other	8,000	**Iran**	
Belgium		**Central African Republic**		other	125,000	**Greece**		Shī'ī Muslim	41,850,000
Roman Catholic	9,465,000	Protestant	1,329,000	**Ecuador**		Greek Orthodox	9,728,000	Sunnī Muslim	2,250,000
other	394,000	Roman Catholic	880,000	Roman Catholic	7,830,000	Muslim	150,000	other	945,000
Belize		traditional beliefs	319,000	other	774,000	other	89,000	**Iraq**	
Roman Catholic	102,000	other	130,000	**Egypt**		**Greenland**		Shī'ī Muslim	8,385,000
Anglican	20,000			Sunnī Muslim	39,675,000	Protestant	52,000	Sunnī Muslim	6,630,000
Methodist	10,000			Christian	8,634,000	other	1,000	other	660,000
other	34,000			other	194,000				

Religious affiliation	1985 population
Ireland	
Roman Catholic	3,397,000
other	217,000
Isle of Man	
Anglican	43,000
Methodist	10,000
other	17,000
Israel	
Jewish	3,574,000
Muslim (mostly Sunnī)	564,000
other	168,000
Italy	
Roman Catholic	47,490,000
nonreligious	7,763,000
atheist	1,484,000
other	342,000
Ivory Coast	
traditional beliefs	4,451,000
Christian[1]	3,252,000
Muslim	2,439,000
other	20,000
Jamaica	
Protestant	1,657,000
Roman Catholic	225,000
other	462,000
Japan	
Shintoist[2]	105,060,000
Buddhist[2]	88,275,000
Christian	1,570,000
other	16,180,000
Jersey	
Anglican	48,000
Roman Catholic	18,000
other	12,000
Jordan	
Sunnī Muslim	2,462,000
other	185,000
Kampuchea	
Buddhist	6,435,000
other	845,000
Kenya	
Christian[1]	14,828,000
traditional beliefs	3,839,000
Muslim	1,219,000
other	426,000
Kiribati	
Roman Catholic	33,000
Congregational	29,000
other	3,000
Korea, North	
atheist and nonreligious	13,636,000
traditional beliefs	3,133,000
Ch'ŏndogyo	2,791,000
other	522,000
Korea, South	
Buddhist	15,415,000
Protestant	10,590,000
Confucian	7,215,000
other	7,995,000
Kuwait	
Muslim	1,749,000
other	162,000
Laos	
Buddhist	2,388,000
traditional beliefs	1,400,000
other	329,000
Lebanon	
Shīʿī Muslim	935,000
Maronite Christian	665,000
Sunnī Muslim	665,000
Greek Orthodox	200,000
Druze	200,000
Lesotho	
Roman Catholic	653,000
Protestant	620,000
other	227,000
Liberia	
traditional beliefs	1,674,000
Muslim	335,000
Christian	223,000
Libya	
Sunnī Muslim	3,672,000
other	114,000
Liechtenstein	
Roman Catholic	23,000
other	4,000
Luxembourg	
Roman Catholic	340,000
other	26,000
Macau	
Buddhist and Taoist	220,000
other	94,000
Madagascar	
Christian[1]	5,106,000
traditional beliefs	4,706,000
other	200,000
Malaŵi	
Christian[1]	4,554,000
traditional beliefs	1,340,000
Muslim	1,145,000
other	21,000
Malaysia	
Muslim	8,293,000
Buddhist	2,712,000
Chinese folk-religionist	1,819,000
other	2,853,000
Maldives	
Muslim	182,000
Mali	
Muslim	7,281,000
traditional beliefs	728,000
Christian	81,000
Malta	
Roman Catholic	324,000
other	9,000
Martinique	
Roman Catholic	315,000
other	15,000
Mauritania	
Muslim	1,646,000
other	10,000
Mauritius	
Hindu	473,000
Christian[1]	362,000
Muslim	168,000
other	22,000
Mayotte	
Sunnī Muslim	66,000
Christian	1,000
Mexico	
Roman Catholic	72,253,000
other	5,774,000
Monaco	
Roman Catholic	25,000
other	3,000
Mongolia	
atheist and nonreligious	1,027,000
traditional beliefs	484,000
other	55,000
Montserrat	
Anglican	4,000
Methodist	3,000
other	5,000
Morocco	
Muslim (mostly Sunnī)	24,050,000
other	320,000
Mozambique	
traditional beliefs	6,727,000
Muslim	2,322,000
Roman Catholic	2,013,000
other	3,012,000
Nauru	
Protestant	5,000
Roman Catholic	2,000
other	1,000
Nepal	
Hindu	14,790,000
other	1,735,000
Netherlands, The	
Roman Catholic	5,224,000
Dutch Reformed Church	2,793,000
Reformed Churches	1,143,000
nonreligious	4,674,000
other	637,000
Netherlands Antilles	
Roman Catholic	213,000
Protestant	24,000
other	7,000
New Caledonia	
Roman Catholic	107,000
Protestant	28,000
other	14,000
New Zealand	
Anglican	846,000
Presbyterian	543,000
Roman Catholic	474,000
other	1,428,000
Nicaragua	
Roman Catholic	2,974,000
other	298,000
Niger	
Muslim	6,097,000
other	156,000
Nigeria	
Muslim	43,210,000
Protestant	25,250,000
Roman Catholic	11,620,000
African Christian	10,180,000
traditional beliefs	5,380,000
other	380,000
Niue	
Congregational	2,200
other	800
Norfolk Island	
Anglican	900
other	1,100
Norway	
Lutheran	3,654,000
other	503,000
Oman	
Muslim	1,030,000
other	11,000
Pacific Islands, Trust Territory of the	
Protestant	73,000
Roman Catholic	68,000
other	8,000
Pakistan	
Muslim	97,145,000
other	3,210,000
Panama	
Roman Catholic	1,941,000
other	240,000
Papua New Guinea	
Protestant	1,944,000
Roman Catholic	1,092,000
other	292,000
Paraguay	
Roman Catholic	3,268,000
other	136,000
Peru	
Roman Catholic	18,204,000
other	1,497,000
Philippines	
Roman Catholic	45,975,000
other	8,695,000
Pitcairn Island	
Seventh-day Adventist	57
Anglican	6
Poland	
Roman Catholic	30,100,000
other	7,060,000
Portugal	
Roman Catholic	9,593,000
other	558,000
Puerto Rico	
Roman Catholic	2,824,000
other	487,000
Qatar	
Muslim	278,000
other	23,000
Réunion	
Roman Catholic	528,000
other	19,000
Romania	
Romanian Orthodox	15,900,000
Greek Orthodox	2,300,000
atheist and nonreligious	3,600,000
other	700,000
Rwanda	
Roman Catholic	3,425,000
Protestant	735,000
Muslim	550,000
traditional beliefs	1,405,000
St. Christopher and Nevis	
Anglican	15,000
Methodist	14,000
other	18,000
St. Helena and Ascension	
Anglican	6,000
other	1,000
St. Lucia	
Roman Catholic	119,000
Protestant	16,000
other	3,000
St. Pierre and Miquelon	
Roman Catholic	5,900
other	100
St. Vincent and the Grenadines	
Anglican	38,000
Methodist	21,000
Roman Catholic	20,000
other	26,000
San Marino	
Roman Catholic	21,000
other	1,000
São Tomé and Príncipe	
Roman Catholic	86,000
Protestant	21,000
Saudi Arabia	
Muslim	11,105,000
other	135,000
Senegal	
Sunnī Muslim	5,933,000
other	587,000
Seychelles	
Roman Catholic	63,000
other	2,000
Sierra Leone	
traditional beliefs	2,024,000
Muslim	1,548,000
Christian[1]	354,000
other	4,000
Singapore	
Taoist	750,000
Buddhist	685,000
Muslim	415,000
Christian	265,000
nonreligious	340,000
other	105,000
Solomon Islands	
Protestant	191,000
Roman Catholic	51,000
other	25,000
Somalia	
Sunnī Muslim	5,805,000
other	12,000
South Africa[3]	
Afrikaans Reformed (NGK)	4,256,000
Roman Catholic	2,602,000
Black independent churches	5,601,000
other Christian churches	8,605,000
Hindu	566,000
Muslim	351,000
nonreligious[4]	5,179,000
other	321,000
Bophuthatswana	
Christian	1,380,000
other	145,000
Ciskei	
Christian	600,000
other	177,000
Transkei	
Christian	1,877,000
traditional beliefs	791,000
other	13,000
Venda	
traditional beliefs	301,000
Christian	94,000
other	29,000
South West Africa/Namibia	
Lutheran	562,000
Roman Catholic	217,000
other	318,000
Spain	
Roman Catholic	37,602,000
other	1,163,000
Sri Lanka	
Buddhist	11,165,000
Hindu	2,495,000
Muslim	1,225,000
Christian	1,210,000
other	15,000
Sudan, The	
Sunnī Muslim	17,260,000
traditional beliefs	3,950,000
Christian	2,152,000
other	283,000
Suriname	
Hindu	108,000
Roman Catholic	90,000
Muslim	77,000
Protestant	74,000
other	45,000
Swaziland	
Christian[1]	498,000
traditional beliefs	135,000
other	14,000
Sweden	
Church of Sweden	7,545,000
other	800,000
Switzerland	
Roman Catholic	3,081,000
Protestant	2,868,000
other	524,000
Syria	
Sunnī Muslim	9,200,000
Christian	915,000
other	155,000
Taiwan	
Chinese folk-religionist	9,280,000
Buddhist	8,228,000
Christian[1]	1,416,000
other	211,000
Tanzania	
Christian	8,695,000
Muslim	6,520,000
traditional beliefs	6,520,000
Thailand	
Buddhist	48,735,000
Muslim	1,950,000
other	615,000
Togo	
traditional beliefs	1,370,000
Christian[1]	1,105,000
Sunnī Muslim	510,000
other	5,000
Tokelau	
Congregational	1,400
other	600
Tonga	
Free Wesleyan	46,000
Roman Catholic	16,000
other	35,000
Trinidad and Tobago	
Roman Catholic	395,000
Protestant	335,000
Hindu	300,000
other	160,000
Tunisia	
Sunnī Muslim	7,142,000
other	43,000
Turkey	
Muslim (mostly Sunnī)	48,880,000
other	390,000
Turks and Caicos Islands	
Baptist	3,300
Methodist	1,500
Anglican	1,500
other	1,700
Tuvalu	
Congregational	8,000
other	1,000
Uganda	
Roman Catholic	6,990,000
Protestant	4,665,000
Muslim	2,325,000
other	735,000
U.S.S.R.	
atheist and nonreligious	142,080,000
Eastern Orthodox	62,440,000
Muslim	31,360,000
Protestant	4,440,000
Roman Catholic	3,890,000
Jewish	3,330,000
other	29,960,000
United Arab Emirates	
Muslim	1,215,000
other	65,000
United Kingdom	
Anglican	32,102,000
other Protestant	9,099,000
Roman Catholic	7,404,000
nonreligious	4,957,000
Muslim	814,000
Jewish	458,000
other	1,684,000
United States	
Protestant	109,855,000
Roman Catholic	71,645,000
Eastern Orthodox	5,254,000
other Christian	23,045
Jewish	7,640,000
atheist and nonreligious	16,480,000
other	4,540,000
Uruguay	
Roman Catholic	1,790,000
nonreligious	1,060,000
other	165,000
Vanuatu	
Presbyterian	50,000
Anglican	23,000
Roman Catholic	19,000
other	48,000
Venezuela	
Roman Catholic	16,000,000
other	1,315,000
Vietnam	
Buddhist	33,450,000
atheist and nonreligious	11,190,000
Christian	4,475,000
other	11,375,000
Virgin Islands (U.S.)	
Protestant	60,000
Roman Catholic	45,000
other	2,000
Wallis and Futuna	
Roman Catholic	14,000
West Bank	
Muslim	734,000
other	48,000
Western Sahara	
Muslim	150,000
Western Samoa	
Congregational	76,000
Roman Catholic	35,000
Methodist	26,000
other	23,000
Yemen (Aden)	
Muslim	2,116,000
other	8,000
Yemen (Ṣanʿāʾ)	
Shīʿī Muslim	3,928,000
Sunnī Muslim	2,619,000
Yugoslavia	
Serbian Orthodox	8,039,000
Roman Catholic	6,041,000
other Christian	2,858,000
Muslim	2,416,000
atheist and nonreligious	3,880,000
Zaire	
Roman Catholic	16,000,000
Protestant	9,590,000
African Christian	5,650,000
traditional beliefs	1,120,000
other	690,000
Zambia	
Christian[1]	4,800,000
traditional beliefs	1,800,000
other	66,000
Zimbabwe	
Christian[1]	4,698,000
traditional beliefs	3,281,000
other	121,000

[1]Includes both affiliated and nominal Christians. [2]Many Japanese adhere to both Shintoism and Buddhism. [3]Excludes black independent states listed separately. [4]Includes traditional beliefs and religion not known.

Vital statistics, marriage, family

This table provides some of the basic measures that control the size, rate, and direction of population change within a country. The accuracy of these data is principally a function of the effectiveness of each respective national system for collecting information about vital and civil events (birth, death, marriage, etc.) and of the sophistication of the analysis that can be brought to bear upon the data so compiled. Calculating life expectancy, for example, requires detailed information about age structure and mortality experience, but the calculation can be made in different ways upon a single information base.

Thus data on birth rates depend not only on the completeness of registration of births in a particular country but also on the conditions under which those data are collected: Do all births take place in a hospital? Are the births reported comparably in all parts of the country? Are the records of the births tabulated in a central location with an effort to eliminate inconsistent reporting of birth events, perinatal mortality, etc.? The same difficulties apply to death rates but with the added complication of having to identify "cause of death" in a country with, say, only one physician for every 1,000 population: too few to perform autopsies to assess accurately the cause of death after the fact and also too few to provide ongoing care at a level where records would permit inference about cause of death based on prior condition or diagnosis.

Calculating natural increase, which at its most basic is simply the difference between the birth and death rates, may be complicated by the varying degrees of completeness of birth and death registrations for a given country. The total fertility rate may be understood as the average number of children that would be borne per woman if all childbearing women lived to the end of their childbearing years and bore children at each age at the average rate for that age. Calculating the fertility rate is complicated by changing age structure of the population over time, changing mortality rates among mothers, and changing medical practice at births, each improvement leading to greater numbers of live-born children and greater numbers of children who survive their first year (the basis for measurement of infant mortality, another basic control on the growth of a population).

As indicated above, data for causes of death are not only particularly difficult to obtain, since many countries are not well equipped to collect the data, but are also difficult to assess, as their accuracy may be suspect and their meaning may be subject to varying interpretation. Take the case of a citizen of a less developed country who dies of what is clearly a lung infection: Was the death complicated by chronic malnutrition, itself complicated by a parasitic infestation, these last two together so weakening the subject that he died of an infection that he might have survived had his general health been better? Similarly, in a developed country: Someone may die from what is identified in an autopsy as a cerebrovascular accident, but if that accident occurred in a vascular system that was weakened by diabetes, what was the actual cause of death? Statistics on

Vital statistics, marriage, family

country	vital rates						causes of death (rate per 100,000 population)								
	year	birth rate per 1,000 population	death rate per 1,000 population	infant mortality rate per 1,000 live births	rate of natural increase per 1,000 population	total fertility rate	year	infectious and parasitic diseases	neo-plasms (cancers)	endocrine and metabolic disorders	diseases of the nervous system	diseases of the circulatory system	diseases of the respiratory system	diseases of the digestive system	accidents, poisoning, and violence
Afghanistan	1980–85	49.6	27.3	205.0	22.3	6.9	...	...	...	...	...	...	...	...	...
Albania	1984	26.0	6.0	44.0	20.0	3.6[2]	...	...	...	...	...	...	...	...	...
Algeria	1982	42.9	10.5	92.2	32.4	7.2[3]	...	...	...	...	...	...	...	...	...
American Samoa	1983	34.4	4.2	6.8	30.2	4.9	...	...	...	...	...	...	...	...	...
Andorra	1983	14.4	4.4	16.0[4]	10.0	...	...	...	...	...	...	...	...	...	...
Angola	1983	49.0	22.0	148.0	27.0	6.5	1973	73.2	6.5	4.9	3.6	19.2	24.6	3.6	89.0
Anguilla	1982	26.2	9.5	13.6[5]	16.7	1.9[6]	...	...	...	...	...	...	...	...	...
Antigua and Barbuda	1983	15.1	4.6	32.0[2]	10.5	1.9	1978	22.7[7]	76.0	27.0	26.4[7]	183.8	40.3[7]	18.1[7]	31.1
Argentina	1983	24.6	8.7	35.3	15.9	2.8[5]	1979	35.4	151.2	21.7	13.5	388.7	47.3	40.3	205.6
Australia	1985	15.8	7.1	10.4[8]	8.7	1.9[8]	1982	3.8	168.0	14.0	9.9	355.0	51.0	4.0	49.0
Austria	1983	11.9	12.3	11.9	−0.4	0.8	1983	6.2	249.3	16.1	10.2	663.0	67.3	63.7	94.4
Bahamas, The	1982	24.3	5.4	25.3	18.9	3.3[4]	1982	8.7	107.8	18.3	18.8	130.3	71.1	37.6	39.0
Bahrain	1981	32.9	5.5	51.8	27.4	4.8	1981	11.8	23.1	6.9	1.4	89.8	18.8	6.3	32.0
Bangladesh	1980–85	44.8	17.5	133.0	27.3	6.2	1976	15.5	19.8	...	...	20.9	...	...	...
Barbados	1984	16.7	7.7	10.9	9.0	2.2[6]	1982	16.0	115.8	49.1	13.6	305.9	45.5	24.4	29.6
Belgium	1984	11.7	11.1	10.7	0.6	1.1[2]	1978	9.0	268.3	44.4	29.9	485.1	85.0	38.1	83.1
Belize	1984	38.0	4.9	23.4	33.1	3.7[4]	1984	21.0	34.5	...	...	83.9[9]	74.6[10]	...	...
Benin	1983	49.0	18.0	148.0	31.0	6.5	...	...	...	...	...	...	...	...	...
Bermuda	1983	16.4	7.0	8.7	9.4	1.9[11]	1978	4.0[7]	140.0	50.0	7.0[7]	333.0	43.0	19.6[7]	50.6[7]
Bhutan	1980–85	38.4	18.1	144.0	20.3	5.5	...	...	...	...	...	...	...	...	...
Bolivia	1982	44.0	16.8	213.0[12]	27.2	6.2	...	...	...	...	...	...	...	...	...
Botswana	1980–85	50.0	12.7	68.4[5]	37.3	6.2[5]	1977	23.9	6.0	...	...	8.4	...	...	...
Brazil	1980–85	30.6	8.4	71.0	22.2	3.8	1979	74.1	57.1	13.7	11.5	181.1	58.3	23.7	72.6
British Virgin Islands	1982	20.7	5.9	42.6	14.8	...	1982	17.6	61.8	26.5	—	158.8	79.4	26.4	52.9
Brunei	1983	27.9	3.3	11.5	24.6	...	1981	5.0	25.0	...	...	41.0	16.0	3.1	36.0
Bulgaria	1984	13.6	11.4	16.8	2.2	2.2[4]	1981	8.2	152.3	13.3	7.6	615.6	89.8	28.6	58.2
Burkina Faso	1981	47.8	21.5	149.0[12]	26.3	6.5	...	...	...	...	...	...	...	...	...
Burma	1980–85	37.9	12.7	94.0	25.2	5.3	1978	32.6	6.5	6.1	...	14.1	19.8	1.7	7.3
Burundi	1980–85	47.6	20.9	137.0	26.7	6.4	...	...	...	...	...	...	...	...	...
Cameroon	1980–85	43.2	17.8	116.0[8]	25.4	5.8	...	...	...	...	...	...	...	...	...
Canada	1984	15.0	7.1	9.3	7.9	1.7[8]	1982	3.7	172.3	15.9	8.7	329.7	36.7	29.2	56.9
Cape Verde	1981	35.7	8.2	30.0[8]	27.5	2.6[6]	1980	153.7	43.8	20.6	16.5	135.8	72.3	27.7	30.1
Cayman Islands	1984	21.4	5.9	...	15.5	...	1979	18.2	60.1	52.0	...	204.6	54.1	...	102.1
Central African Republic	1983	41.0	17.0	142.0	24.0	5.5	...	...	...	...	...	...	...	...	...
Chad	1983	42.0	21.0	142.0	21.0	5.0	...	...	...	...	...	...	...	...	...
Chile	1984	21.2	6.3	20.1	14.9	3.0[5]	1982	23.3	102.5	15.4	8.2	168.2	53.5	52.7	74.6
China	1984	17.5	6.7	38.0[6]	10.8	2.3[6]	1981[13]	23.7	113.0	6.3	9.4	251.1	43.0	25.9	31.3
Christmas Island	1982	5.6	2.0	—	3.6	...	...	...	...	...	...	...	...	...	...
Cocos (Keeling) Islands	1981	14.4	1.8	—	12.6	...	...	...	...	...	...	...	...	...	...
Colombia	1980–85	31.0	7.7	39.5	23.3	3.9	1977[15]	86.6	54.1	7.2	5.9	129.2	60.7	9.9	70.1
Comoros	1980–85	45.7	17.2	200.0[4]	28.5	6.3	...	...	...	...	...	...	...	...	...
Congo	1980–85	44.5	17.1	124.0	27.4	6.0	...	...	...	...	...	...	...	...	...
Cook Islands	1983	23.3	6.9	29.6[2]	16.4	4.1	1976–78	54.0	38.0	27.0	0.0	197.0	110.0	18.0	49.0
Costa Rica	1982	29.7	3.8	18.9	25.9	3.2	1981	29.2	75.6	13.7	9.3	106.4	36.1	18.9	44.8
Cuba	1983	16.7	5.9	15.0[12]	10.8	2.0	1980	4.1	100.7	10.0	...	55.1	47.5	...	36.9
Cyprus	1983	22.3	8.5	21.0[16]	13.8	2.5	...	...	...	...	...	...	...	...	...
Czechoslovakia	1984	14.7	11.8	15.6	2.9	2.3[8]	1984	6.8[5]	232.8	18.0[5]	...	645.7	86.3	47.1	74.3
Denmark	1984	10.1	11.2	7.7[8]	−1.1	1.4	1983	3.8	288.1	17.7	9.0[2]	470.5	76.0	21.7	74.9
Djibouti	1980–85	49.2	18.3	...	30.9	6.8	1984	...	...	...	...	...	...	...	...
Dominica	1981	22.2	4.6	11.4[2]	17.6	3.7[17]	1981	52.1	68.1	17.6	...	180.4	30.7	14.9	36.1
Dominican Republic	1983	38.6	8.5	28.3	30.1	4.2[6]	1978	60.3	21.6	5.0	9.6	63.3	29.7	18.8	31.8
Ecuador	1982	37.0	8.0	78.0	29.0	6.0[6]	1978	168.7	38.9	5.3	4.3	96.2	114.3	16.0	73.6
Egypt	1982	37.3	10.4	76.4[4]	26.9	4.7[6]	1979	29.3	19.2	8.8	0.4	194.7	187.3	288.8	47.3
El Salvador	1983	27.6	6.3	42.2[2]	21.3	5.8[4]	1980	75.0	19.1	11.5	...	54.3	37.6	2.5	305.7
Equatorial Guinea	1980–85	42.2	17.6	148.5[11]	24.6	5.7	...	...	...	...	...	...	...	...	...

causes of death seek to identify the "underlying" cause (that which sets the final train of events leading to death in motion) but often must settle for the most proximate cause or symptom. Even this kind of analysis may be misleading for those charged with interpreting the data with a view to reordering health-care priorities for a particular country.

Expectation of life is probably the most accurate single measure of the quality of life in a given society. It summarizes in a single number all of the natural and social stresses that operate upon the individuals in that society. The number may range from as few as 40 years of life in the least developed countries to as much as 80 years for women in the most developed nations. The lost potential in the years separating those two numbers is prodigious, regardless of how the loss arises—wars and civil violence, poor public health services, or poor individual health practice in matters of nutrition, exercise, stress management, and so on.

Data on marriages and marriage rates probably are less meaningful in terms of international comparisons than some of the measures mentioned above because the number, timing, and kinds of social relationships that substitute for marriage depend on many kinds of social variables—income, degree of social control, heterogeneity of the society (race, class, language communities), or level of development of civil administration (if one must travel for a day or more to obtain a legal civil ceremony, one may forgo it). Nevertheless, the data for a single country say specific things about local practice in terms of the age at which a man or woman

typically marries, and the overall rate will at least define the number of legal civil marriages, though it cannot say anything about other, less formal arrangements (here the figure for the legitimacy rate for children in the next section may identify some of the societies in which economics or social constraints may operate to limit the number of marriages that are actually confirmed on civil registers). The available data usually include both first marriages and remarriages after annulment, divorce, widowhood, or the like.

The data for families provide information about the average size of a family unit (individuals related by blood or civil register) and the average number of children under a specified age (set here at 15 to provide a consistent measure of legal minority internationally, though actual minority depends on the laws of each country). When well-defined family data are not collected as part of a country's national census or vital statistics surveys, data for households are substituted on the assumption that most households worldwide represent families in some conventional sense. In the older countries of Europe and North America increasing numbers of households are comprised of unrelated individuals (unmarried heterosexual couples, aged [or younger] groups sharing limited [often fixed] incomes for reasons of economy, or homosexual couples); such arrangements are not yet so common in the rest of the world that they represent great numbers overall. Very few census programs, even in developed countries, make adequate provision for identifying these households.

expectation of life at birth (latest year)		nuptiality, family, and family planning												country
		marriages			age at marriage (latest)						families (F), households (H) (latest)				
					groom (percent)			bride (percent)			families (households)		children		legal abortions	
male	female	year	total number	rate per 1,000 population	19 and under	20–29	30 and over	19 and under	20–29	30 and over	total ('000)	size	number under age 15	percent legitimate	number	ratio per 100 live births	
37.2	37.9	1970	6,212	0.4							H 2,110	H 6.2	H 2.8[1]	...	...	...	Afghanistan
66.9	71.6	1984	26,199	9.0	2.0	81.2	16.8	23.0	73.7	3.4		F 5.4	...	...	...	...	Albania
56.7	58.9	1982	129,200	6.3							...	H 4.9	...	...	...	...	Algeria
61.0	64.3	1980	343	10.6	5.6	65.5	28.8	24.5	60.5	15.0	H 4	H 7.1	H 2.9	86.0	...	...	American Samoa
——70.0—		1981	145	4.1											...	...	Andorra
42.0	44.0	1972	26,278	4.5	...	...	...	...	...	...		H 4.8			...	...	Angola
68.6	71.9	1982	64	9.8							H 1.6	H 4.1	H 1.8	39.4	...	...	Anguilla
——72.0—		1983	180	2.3	2.0	54.9	43.1	15.2	53.9	30.9	H 15	H 4.2	H 1.9	18.5	...	...	Antigua and Barbuda
68.6	73.3	1979	182,499[7]	6.2	4.6	70.2	25.2	24.0	60.8	15.2	H 7,104	H 3.9	H 1.2	70.2	...	...	Argentina
72.1	78.2	1983	114,860	7.5	2.2	65.9	31.9	12.3	65.9	21.8	F 4,140	F 3.1	F 0.5	86.3	...	...	Australia
71.2	75.9	1983	56,171	7.4	3.3	70.7	26.0	16.0	68.9	15.1	F 2,020	F 3.7	F 0.7	77.6	...	...	Austria
64.0	69.0	1982	1,396[4]	7.0	3.6	62.4	34.0	17.6	59.3	23.1	H 40	H 4.3	H 1.8	39.7	...	...	Bahamas, The
65.7	69.9	1982	2,356	4.4	6.2	74.4	19.4	45.9	48.5	5.6	H 34	H 6.0	H 3.0	...	...	...	Bahrain
48.3	47.3	1982	...	9.0								H 5.8			...	...	Bangladesh
68.9	74.5	1980	1,057	4.2	0.6	49.9	49.5	5.5	66.7	27.8	H 59	H 3.6	H 1.5	23.9	...	...	Barbados
70.1	76.7	1984	63,100	6.4	4.3	79.8	15.9	22.1	67.1	10.8	F 3,613	F 2.7	F 0.5	95.5	...	...	Belgium
——71.2—		1984	860	5.3	...	...	...	...	...	...	H 29	H 5.2	H 2.4	46.1	...	...	Belize
46.0	50.0	1980–85	...	12.8								H 4.9			...	...	Benin
68.8	76.3	1983	677	12.1	3.7	65.1	31.2	17.6	61.3	21.1	H 18	H 2.7	H 0.6	70.3	...	...	Bermuda
46.6	45.1	...	...	...								H 5.4			...	...	Bhutan
48.6	53.0	1980	26,990	4.8	8.3	75.1	16.6	26.1	55.4	18.5	H 1,050	H 4.4	H 1.8	80.9	...	...	Bolivia
52.7	59.3										H 125	H 5.7	H 2.0	28.0	...	...	Botswana
60.9	66.0	1981	930,000	7.5	8.1	70.7	21.2	36.5	50.5	12.9	H 27,967	H 4.7	H 1.6	...	...	...	Brazil
68.6	71.9	1981	151	11.6	0.7	49.0	50.3	7.3	57.6	35.1	H 3	H 3.3	H 1.1	44.7	...	...	British Virgin Islands
70.1	72.7	1982	1,299	6.7	4.1	76.9	19.0	19.3	71.5	9.2	H 23	H 5.8	H 2.5	99.3	...	...	Brunei
68.0	74.0	1984	67,200	7.5	6.4	75.6	18.0	37.7	51.4	10.9	F 2,627	F 3.3	F 0.7	89.1	152,370	122.5	Bulgaria
43.2	45.0	1975	...	9.4	...	...	...	...	...	...		H 4.9			...	...	Burkina Faso
53.4	56.7		...									H 5.1			...	...	Burma
42.4	45.6		...									H 4.9			...	...	Burundi
46.4	49.7		...									H 5.5			...	...	Cameroon
73.0	79.0	1984	186,000	7.4	3.1	68.1	28.8	13.3	67.3	19.4	F 6,325	F 3.9	H 1.4	91.0	66,254	17.8	Canada
60.3	64.0	1975	1,604	5.4	...	...	...	...	...	...	F 59	F 5.1		55.2	...	...	Cape Verde
68.6	71.9	1984	221	11.5	...	...	...	...	...	...	H 4	H 3.8	H 1.1	66.8	...	...	Cayman Islands
46.0	49.0		...									H 4.3			...	...	Central African Republic
42.0	45.0		...									H 3.9			...	...	Chad
65.4	70.1	1982	80,115	7.0	6.5	74.4	19.1	26.4	60.7	12.9	H 1,690	H 4.5	H 2.0	72.4	2,346	1.0	Chile
65.5	69.4	1982	8,395,000	8.3	...	...	...	...	...	...	H 221[14]	H 4.5			...	...	China
63.0	66.5	1982	25	8.3	—	90.9	9.1	45.5	36.4	18.1	—	H 5.8	H 1.5	97.1	...	...	Christmas Island
63.0	66.5	1981	6	10.8	—	100.0	—	—	100.0	—	—	H 6.3	H 2.6	93.3	2	40.0	Cocos (Keeling) Islands
61.4	66.0	1977	88,401	3.5	5.6	69.5	24.9	33.6	55.3	11.1	F 4,772	F 5.4	F 2.5	75.2	...	...	Colombia
44.0	47.0	1964	1,959	8.5	...	...	...	...	...	...		H 5.3			...	...	Comoros
45.0	48.1										H 326	H 4.7	H 2.0	...	...	...	Congo
64.0	70.0	1982	83	4.8	1.2	63.4	35.4	22.0	51.2	26.8	H 3	H 5.6	H 2.4	...	...	...	Cook Islands
70.5	74.7	1982	17,807	7.7	9.1	69.7	21.2	36.1	51.3	12.6	F 42	F 4.0	F 1.7	64.9	...	...	Costa Rica
71.9	75.4	1983	80,363[2]	7.7	12.1	54.8	33.1	36.4	41.0	22.6	F 2,002	F 4.2	H 1.6	...	...	...	Cuba
72.3	76.0	1983	7,163[5]	11.2	1.3	75.5	23.2	18.2	70.2	11.6	H 160	H 3.5	H 1.1	99.7	...	...	Cyprus
67.1	74.4	1984	117,376[5]	6.6	6.0	74.7	19.3	30.3	56.3	13.4	F 4,187	F 3.6	F 0.9	94.2	103,517	43.5	Czechoslovakia
71.5	77.5	1984	28,600	6.6	0.7	51.5	47.8	31.9	62.9	33.2	F 2,563	F 2.0	F 0.4	59.4	21,462	40.8	Denmark
——50.0—		1982	2,500	6.7								H 5.6		96.8	...	...	Djibouti
66.5	72.8	1969	234	3.3							H 12	H 4.7	H 2.2	35.0	...	...	Dominica
60.7	64.6	1981	26,862	4.9	8.0	63.0	29.0	29.7	51.0	19.3	H 753	H 5.1	H 2.5	32.8	...	...	Dominican Republic
59.8	63.6	1982[1]	49,500	6.2	13.0	65.7	21.3	39.1	47.9	13.0		H 5.1		67.9	...	...	Ecuador
55.9	58.4	1979	384,000	9.4	8.6	60.5	30.9	46.8	42.6	10.6	F 6,946	H 4.9	H 2.1	...	...	...	Egypt
61.7	65.3	1982	20,413	4.1	6.7	54.0	39.3	27.7	45.8	26.5	H 686	H 5.4	H 2.4	31.1	...	...	El Salvador
46.9	50.1	1966	209	0.8								H 4.5			...	...	Equatorial Guinea

Vital statistics, marriage, family (continued)

country	vital rates						causes of death (rate per 100,000 population)								
	year	birth rate per 1,000 population	death rate per 1,000 population	infant mortality rate per 1,000 live births	rate of natural increase per 1,000 population	total fertility rate	year	infectious and parasitic diseases	neo-plasms (cancers)	endocrine and metabolic disorders	diseases of the nervous system	diseases of the circulatory system	diseases of the respiratory system	diseases of the digestive system	accidents, poisoning, and violence
Ethiopia	1980–85	49.2	21.5	143.0	47.7	6.7	1978	39.5	3.8	24.6	2.7	5.6	16.3	28.9	15.8
Faeroe Islands	1984	14.4	7.8	14.9[8]	6.6	2.2	1983	2.2	168.3	6.7	0.0	399.4	47.1	13.5	103.2
Falkland Islands	1981	15.0	5.0	...	10.0	...									
Fiji	1983	29.5	5.1	21.0	24.4	3.3	1982	30.7	25.5	18.1	...	225.1	70.3	2.0	41.0
Finland	1983	13.8	9.3	6.2	4.5	1.7	1982	9.1	187.6	13.2	16.2[3]	444.0	72.9	7.8	76.5
France	1984	13.8	9.8	8.2	4.0	1.8[6]	1983	13.0	228.7	13.2	34.1[2]	368.4	16.8	66.4[2]	91.5
French Guiana	1984	28.8	5.9	22.6	22.9	3.1[11]	1981	31.1	49.4	16.9	21.2	149.7	21.9[7]	39.5	86.2
French Polynesia	1984	29.5	4.8	19.5	24.7	3.5[8]									
Gabon	1980–85	33.7	19.9	121.6	13.8	4.7									
Gambia, The	1980–85	47.5	21.7	203.5[11]	25.8	6.4									
Gaza Strip	1983	45.2	9.3	...	35.9	...									
Germany, East	1984	14.0	13.3	11.4[8]	0.7	1.8[6]	1981	6.1	240.0	31.3	...	825.1	70.1	10.6	40.1
Germany, West	1984	9.5	11.3	9.6	−1.8	1.3[8]	1982	7.8	270.8	21.1	13.8	585.0	68.7	58.9	68.3
Ghana	1980–85	47.0	14.6	98.0	32.4	6.5									
Gibraltar	1983	17.5	8.7	...	8.8	...									
Greece	1983	13.4	9.2	14.9	4.2	2.3	1983	8.1	178.5	36.7	12.2	424.5	60.4	34.2	51.1
Greenland	1983	18.9	8.3	39.6	10.6	2.0	1983	28.8	100.8	1.9	5.8	198.1	73.1	19.2	230.8
Grenada	1981	26.7	8.1	14.9	18.6	...	1981	26.7	89.1	47.8	...	182.7	40.7	31.1	30.0
Guadeloupe	1983	20.4	6.7	23.0[6]	13.7	2.5[6]	1979	10.0	72.5	27.6	...	220.2	13.4	3.1	96.9
Guam	1983	28.7	4.2	7.5	24.5	1.7[4]									
Guatemala	1983	42.7	10.5	64.1	32.2	5.3[5]	1980	285.1	26.0	5.0	21.2[3]	49.9	151.3	2.1	101.0
Guernsey															
Guinea	1980–85	46.8	23.5	159.0	23.3	6.2									
Guinea-Bissau	1981	40.9	21.9	143.0[6]	19.0	5.4									
Guyana	1983	29.0	7.0	45.0	22.0	3.2	1978	36.9	23.0	24.0	4.7	103.3	31.2	9.8	14.3
Haiti	1980–85	35.6	13.0	124.0	22.6	5.7									
Honduras	1982	43.9	10.1	87.0	33.8	6.6[5]	1979	88.6	18.4	4.2	21.9	48.5	36.1	22.4	50.7
Hong Kong	1984	14.4	4.8	9.9	9.6	2.1[6]	1984	13.6	136.3	4.7	3.7	137.9	79.5	20.8	30.4
Hungary	1984	11.7	13.7	20.0	−2.0	2.1[6]	1983	12.9	269.3	21.7	11.6	743.1	85.1	75.9	121.2
Iceland	1983	18.4	7.0	6.2	11.4	2.2	1982	6.0	157.3	4.7	6.2	325.0	75.1	2.6	53.0
India	1983	33.6	11.9	117.0[5]	21.7	4.3									
Indonesia	1980–85	30.7	13.0	90.3	17.7	3.9									
Iran	1983	51.1	4.8	101.0[6]	46.3	6.0[5]									
Iraq	1980–85	45.1	11.5	31.0[5]	33.6	6.7									
Ireland	1984	18.2	9.1	9.8[8]	9.1	3.2	1981	6.9	178.6	8.2	0.5	477.4	93.9	9.2	46.5
Isle of Man	1983	10.5	14.6	...	−4.1	...	1980	1.6	340.6	14.1	0.0	895.4	160.9	18.7	93.7
Israel	1984	23.6	6.6	6.6	17.0	3.1[8]	1979	10.4	147.9	10.6	...	326.6	28.2	4.7	50.1
Italy	1984	10.5	9.4	11.6	1.1	1.8	1983	6.0	225.4	35.9	13.1	459.0	69.0	55.3	66.0
Ivory Coast	1980–85	46.0	18.0	121.0[8]	28.0	6.7									
Jamaica	1984	23.5	5.4	9.2[8]	18.1	3.4[5]	1978	39.3	74.8	40.5[21]	12.0	210.9	41.7	21.4	28.0
Japan	1984	12.5	6.2	6.0	6.3	1.8[2]	1983	7.2	147.4	7.5	4.6	250.1	47.1	23.8	45.8
Jersey	1983	11.6	12.4	...	−0.8	...									
Jordan	1980–85	45.3	9.1	67.0[5]	36.2	7.1									
Kampuchea	1984	44.3	18.7	151.0	25.6	5.0									
Kenya	1980–85	55.1	14.0	81.0[8]	41.1	8.1									
Kiribati	1978	34.9	14.0	8.7	20.9	4.5[6]									
Korea, North	1983	31.0	7.5	32.0	23.5	4.0									
Korea, South	1984	23.0	6.2	37.0[8]	16.8	2.6									
Kuwait	1980–85	40.9	4.1	22.8[2]	36.8	6.2	1982	18.5	34.2	12.3	4.5	81.4	27.1	7.0	53.5
Laos	1980–85	30.7	13.0	121.0	17.7	3.9									
Lebanon	1982	29.9	8.3	40.2[5]	21.6	2.0									
Lesotho	1980–85	41.7	16.4	110.0	25.3	5.8									
Liberia	1980–85	48.7	17.2	151.5[5]	31.5	6.9									
Libya	1980–85	46.0	11.2	97.5[5]	34.8	7.2									
Liechtenstein	1984	15.2	6.6	6.1	8.6	...	1984	11.3	157.4	13.8	—	214.3	26.3	52.6	52.6
Luxembourg	1983	11.5	11.3	11.2	0.2	1.4[12]	1983	6.0	266.4	34.5	20.5	546.1	60.2	58.8	87.5
Macau	1984	19.4	4.6	12.0	14.8	3.4[6]	1982	38.9	98.0	6.4	1.0	146.7	33.9	21.1	38.3
Madagascar	1980–85	44.4	16.5	67.0	27.9	6.1									
Malaŵi	1981	56.2	22.8	169.1	33.4	7.8	1981[24]	46.4	3.4	12.5	4.8	4.7	18.3	2.9	5.4
Malaysia	1984	29.6	5.2	21.1[5]	24.4	3.5[8]	1981[16]	14.3	15.9	2.7	1.5	37.8	9.2	3.3	21.0
Maldives	1983	43.1	10.4	78.5[2]	32.7	...									
Mali	1980–85	50.2	22.4	149.0	27.8	6.7									
Malta	1984	14.8	7.9	11.6	6.9	2.0[6]	1984	0.3	159.9	93.0	2.7	485.7	27.6	27.6	25.1
Martinique	1984	17.3	6.3	8.7	11.0	2.4[6]	1981	10.4	94.4	17.1	45.4	215.7	31.4	39.6	46.3
Mauritania	1983	43.0	19.0	136.0	24.0	6.0									
Mauritius	1984	21.1	6.6	24.7	14.5	2.4[2]	1983	20.4	46.9	18.9[2]	7.4	300.4	80.2	27.1	41.7
Mayotte	1978	49.8													
Mexico	1983	32.7	7.0	53.0	25.7	4.9[6]	1981	73.0	41.7	36.0[21]	8.4	100.2	77.2	43.8	97.6
Monaco	1983	19.6	16.6	...	3.0	...									
Mongolia	1983	36.2	9.8	49.0[2]	26.4	4.8[2]									
Montserrat	1982	22.3	9.9	7.7	12.4	...	1981	17.0	95.0	103.0	...	456.0	95.0	26.0	43.0
Morocco	1980–85	44.1	11.7	114.4[11]	32.4	6.4									
Mozambique	1980–85	44.6	17.2	19.1	27.4	6.1									
Nauru	1982	34.0	9.2	31.2[5]	24.8	...	1976–81[26]	33.0	38.0	24.0	13.0	89.0	16.0	53.0	116.0
Nepal	1984	41.7	18.0	143.0	23.7	6.2									
Netherlands, The	1984	12.1	8.3	8.3	3.8	1.5[8]	1982	4.4	225.3	14.3[21]	13.7	368.7	57.4	30.4	41.7
Netherlands Antilles	1980	18.8	5.3	14.0	13.5	...	1973	8.5	94.8	19.2	0.9	89.9	22.6	8.1	44.7
New Caledonia	1983	25.2	5.6	11.2	19.6	4.0[4]	1978	17.5	35.1	1.5	9.5	43.8	...	...	13.9[28]
New Zealand	1985	16.2	7.6	9.5	8.6	2.0	1981	5.0	178.8	15.8	11.2	393.2	77.1	20.0	58.4
Nicaragua	1983	44.2	9.5	75.2	34.7	5.9[6]	1978	56.8	12.8	3.2	4.9	67.4	20.2	15.4	64.3
Niger	1980–85	51.0	22.9	140.0	28.1	7.1									
Nigeria	1980–85	50.4	17.1	113.0	33.3	7.1									
Niue	1983	29.2	7.8	—	21.4	...									
Norfolk Island	1983	9.7	9.7	...	—	...									
Norway	1984	12.1	10.2	7.8	1.9	1.7[8]	1983	6.9	222.3	10.5	0.7	481.6	81.8	15.7	75.2

male	female	year	total number	rate per 1,000 population	groom ≤19	groom 20–29	groom ≥30	bride ≤19	bride 20–29	bride ≥30	families total ('000)	size	children number under age 15	percent legitimate	abortions number	ratio per 100 live births	country
41.3	44.5	...	...	...	...	...	...	...	...	...	...	H 4.5	...	...	...	...	Ethiopia
73.4	78.7	1983	210	4.6	—	67.3	32.7	13.4	74.3	12.3	F 14	F 3.0	F 0.9	67.1	26	3.3	Faeroe Islands
		1980	11	...							H 1	H 3.3	H 0.9	75.0	...	...	Falkland Islands
70.2	74.1	1983	6,800	10.1	9.3	73.7	17.0	36.9	54.3	8.8	F 97	F 6.0	F 2.5	82.7	...	...	Fiji
70.1	78.1	1983	29,600	6.1	2.5	68.5	29.0	10.6	69.4	20.0	F 1,163	H 2.8	F 0.9	86.0	14,120	22.3	Finland
70.2	78.5	1983	300,700	5.5	1.8	75.4	22.8	14.2	70.2	15.6	H 13,177	H 2.7	H 1.0	85.8	171,218	21.4	France
63.4	69.7	1984	264	3.6							H 12	H 3.3	H 1.4	23.0			French Guiana
63.5	67.8	1984	1,100	6.5	11.3[18]	75.8[18]	12.9[18]	41.5[18]	52.5[18]	6.0[18]	H 26	H 5.0	H 2.3	45.1			French Polynesia
44.4	47.6	...	...	...							H 136	H 4.0	...	...			Gabon
40.9	44.1	...	...	...							H 123	H 4.9	H 3.4	...			Gambia, The
																	Gaza Strip
69.1	75.1	1983	128,174[5]	7.5	4.8	72.4	22.8	20.9	63.3	15.8	F 4,781	F 3.5	F 0.7	74.0	80,100	35.0	Germany, East
70.5	77.1	1984	367,000	6.0	2.7	65.3	32.0	13.5	66.9	19.6	F 22,882	F 2.7	F 0.5	91.2	91,064	14.7	Germany, West
50.3	53.7	...	...	...							H 2,272	H 5.1	H 2.2	...			Ghana
71.4	75.5	1982	406	13.5							H 7	H 3.8	H 1.0	97.1			Gibraltar
72.2	76.4	1983	66,000	6.7	2.0	65.6	32.4	29.1	57.1	13.8	H 2,990	H 3.2	H 0.7	98.4	109	0.1	Greece
57.2	66.6	1983	312[2]	5.3	—	45.7	54.3	3.4	66.2	30.4	F 25	F 2.1	F 0.4	33.2	539	51.3	Greenland
66.5	72.8	1979	330	3.0							H 20	H 2.9	H 2.2	22.5			Grenada
67.8	73.2	1982	1,577	4.8	0.9	63.1	36.0	19.2	58.7	22.1	H 70	H 3.7	H 1.9	47.9	561	8.7	Guadeloupe
69.7	78.7	1981	1,480	13.5	7.9	59.1	33.0	16.9	63.2	19.9	H 25	H 4.1	H 1.5	80.3	...	...	Guam
57.3	60.5	1980	29,519	4.1	18.3	55.7	26.0	46.2	36.2	17.6	H 1,185	H 4.5	H 2.7	34.8	...	...	Guatemala
											H 18	H 2.9					Guernsey
38.7	41.8	...	...	...							H 1,064	H 4.7	...	...			Guinea
39.4	42.6	...	...	...							H 124	H 4.4	H 2.8	11.3			Guinea-Bissau
67.7	73.3	1968	2,760	4.2							H 178	H 5.0	H 2.5	61.4			Guyana
51.2	54.4	1980	3,370[19]	0.7							H 1,131	H 5.1	H 1.8	...			Haiti
58.2	61.7	1979	14,414	4.0	9.8	62.0	28.2	38.8	46.1	15.1	H 463	H 5.7	H 2.8	...			Honduras
72.7	78.3	1984	50,756[5]	10.0	1.1	60.8	38.1	6.4	72.9	20.7	H 1,245	H 3.9	H 1.0	90.4	10,600	12.0	Hong Kong
66.1	73.7	1984	75,557[2]	7.0	6.8	70.4	22.8	30.4	52.3	17.3	F 3,028	F 3.4	F 0.8	92.9	78,682	58.9	Hungary
73.5	79.5	1982	1,303	5.9	2.4	75.8	21.8	11.1	73.4	15.5	H 49	H 3.3	H 1.3	56.2	602	13.9	Iceland
53.9	52.9	...	...	...							H 97,093	H 5.6	H 2.4	...	385,700	1.8	India
51.2	53.9	1980	...	8.1							H 30,263	H 4.9	H 2.0	...	...	...	Indonesia
57.1	59.0	1983	402,840	9.7							H 6,709	H 4.3	H 2.2	...			Iran
55.9	59.1	1982	56,440	4.0	4.0	49.1	46.9	23.9	47.2	28.9	H 1,835	H 5.5	H 3.2	...			Iraq
70.4	75.7	1984	18,590	5.2	5.2	77.1	17.7	14.9	75.2	9.9	H 726	H 3.9	H 1.3	95.0	...	...	Ireland
...	...	1981	420	6.3	4.8	58.3	36.9	16.4	60.0	23.6							Isle of Man
72.8	76.2	1984	29,480	7.0	4.3[20]	76.9[20]	18.8[20]	27.1[20]	62.9[20]	9.9[20]	H 1,026	H 3.5	H 1.3	97.5	16,829	17.4	Israel
71.1	77.8	1983	299,450	5.3	1.9	75.1	23.0	20.0	68.7	11.3	F 17,615	F 3.2	F 0.7	95.2	220,300	34.2	Italy
45.4	48.7	...	...	...							H ...	H 4.5					Ivory Coast
69.2	73.3	1983	8,465	3.7							H 420	H 4.2	H 2.0	...			Jamaica
74.2	79.8	1984	744,100	6.2	0.9[18]	65.5[18]	33.6[18]	3.2[18]	82.9[18]	13.8[18]	F 22,240	F 5.4	F 1.2	99.2	598,100	37.9	Japan
...	...										H 27	H 2.5					Jersey
60.3	64.2	1981	11,830	5.1	7.5[22]	68.5[22]	24.0[22]	54.3[22]	40.1[22]	5.6[22]	H 320	H 6.4	H 3.4	...			Jordan
43.5	46.4	...	...	...								H 5.6					Kampuchea
51.2	54.7	...	...	...							H 1,938	H 6.3	H 2.7	...			Kenya
50.3	53.8	1973	291[23]	4.5	9.9	66.7	23.5	34.7	54.5	10.8	F 12	F 5.0	F 2.0	...			Kiribati
63.0	67.0										H ...	H 5.7					Korea, North
64.9	76.3	1981	321,774	8.3	1.3	81.8	16.9	8.5	86.9	4.6	F 7,969	F 4.8	F 1.6	...			Korea, South
68.0	72.9	1982	9,338	5.9	5.2	70.4	24.4	40.5	50.6	8.9	H 143	H 6.9	H 1.6	...			Kuwait
48.3	51.2	...	...	...								H 5.3					Laos
65.0	68.9	1973	18,601	7.0							H 405	H 5.3	H 2.2	...			Lebanon
47.7	51.0	...	...	...							H 242	H 4.4	H 2.0	...			Lesotho
47.4	50.7	...	...	...								H 4.9					Liberia
56.1	59.4	1979	17,236	6.0							F 383	F 5.4	F 2.9	...			Libya
71.1	77.8	1984	377	14.2							H 8	H 3.0	H 0.7	93.4			Liechtenstein
68.3	74.8	1983	1,974	5.4	—42.3—		57.7	15.0	70.8	14.5	H 128	H 2.8	H 0.5	91.9			Luxembourg
68.0	73.0	1984	2,614	8.6	0.4	44.7	54.9	4.3	73.5	22.2	H 50	H 4.8	H 1.8	99.3			Macau
48.9	50.4	1975	19,800	2.6	14.5	60.3	25.2	49.5	36.9	13.6	H 1,709	H 4.4	H 2.0	...			Madagascar
42.7	45.4	1977	4,300	7.8							...	H 4.5[4]					Malawi
68.2	72.9	1979[25]	23,030	1.7	0.5[25]	65.3[25]	34.2[25]	7.9[25]	77.0[25]	15.1[25]	...	H 5.3					Malaysia
52.0	49.0	1982	1,404	8.9	12.3	54.1	33.6	39.5	41.4	19.1	H 23	H 6.1	H 2.7	...			Maldives
40.4	43.6	...	...	...							H 1,254	H 5.1					Mali
70.4	73.8	1982	2,788	7.7	2.3	78.5	19.2	13.2	76.3	10.5	H 76	H 3.6	H 1.2	99.3			Malta
68.4	73.5	1984	1,199[5]	3.9	0.3	60.5	39.2	12.9	60.4	26.7	H 71	H 3.8		65.1			Martinique
44.0	47.0	...	...	...							H 246	H 5.0					Mauritania
63.3	68.4	1983	10,720	10.8	1.2	55.3	43.5	20.3	62.2	17.5	F 155	F 5.3	F 2.0	55.4			Mauritius
...	...										H 10	H 4.7	H 2.3	89.2			Mayotte
63.9	68.2	1981	505,870	7.1	18.3	63.9	17.8	45.4	44.1	10.5	H 9,851	H 5.5	H 2.3	91.0			Mexico
...	...	1981	190	7.3							H 10	H 2.3	H 0.3	96.8			Monaco
62.9	66.8	1983	10,300	5.7							F 311	F 5.1					Mongolia
68.6	71.9	1982	41	4.1	2.4	39.0	58.5	7.3	58.5	34.1	H 4	H 3.1	...	23.4			Montserrat
56.1	59.4	...	...	...							H 2,819	H 5.8	H 2.5	...			Morocco
47.8	51.1	1974	6,037	0.7							F 1,860	F 4.4	F 2.0	73.1			Mozambique
48.9	62.1	1977	43[27]	6.3							H 1	H 8.0	H 2.6	...			Nauru
47.4	45.7	...	...	...							H 2,846	H 5.3	H 2.2	...			Nepal
72.8	79.5	1984	82,190	5.7	1.2	77.1	21.7	10.2	76.8	13.0	H 5,111	H 2.7	H 0.6	92.4	19,500	10.9	Netherlands, The
69.8	75.7	1980	1,488	6.3	4.0	77.0	18.9	22.2	61.1	16.7	H 41	H 4.5	H 2.1	60.4			Netherlands Antilles
—68.6—		1983	1,006	6.9	3.6	70.2	26.2	31.4	53.4	15.2	...	H 4.1		57.5			New Caledonia
71.2	77.7	1984	25,215	7.8	2.4	65.0	32.6	13.3	64.0	22.7	H 1,004	H 3.2	H 0.8	76.2	6,759	13.3	New Zealand
56.0	60.0	1980	17,174	6.3[11]	—18.1[29]—		81.9[30]	—48.2[29]—		51.8[30]	...	6.9					Nicaragua
40.9	44.1	...	...	...							H 1,029	H 5.2	H 2.4	...			Niger
46.9	50.2	...	...	...							H ...	H 5.0					Nigeria
63.0	66.5	1982	12	3.5[31]							F 1	F 4.1	F 1.9	58.2			Niue
58.0	59.9	1983	10	4.8	—	56.3	43.7	6.3	50.0	43.7				73.9			Norfolk Island
72.7	79.5	1984	21,129	5.1	2.2	71.2	26.6	12.1	71.8	16.1	F 1,684	F 2.4	F 0.6	80.7	13,496	26.3	Norway

Vital statistics, marriage, family (continued)

country	vital rates						causes of death (rate per 100,000 population)								
	year	birth rate per 1,000 population	death rate per 1,000 population	infant mortality rate per 1,000 live births	rate of natural increase per 1,000 population	total fertility rate	year	infectious and parasitic diseases	neoplasms (cancers)	endocrine and metabolic disorders	diseases of the nervous system	diseases of the circulatory system	diseases of the respiratory system	diseases of the digestive system	accidents, poisoning, and violence
Oman	1980–85	47.7	16.7	200.0[17]	31.0	7.1	...	...	...	...	...	...	...	...	...
Pacific Is., Trust Territory of the	1982	26.7	4.2	22.1	22.5	5.0[6]	1982	43.9	31.7	13.7	9.4	82.9	51.2	11.5	49.7
Pakistan	1984	42.2	14.9	116.0	27.3	5.7	...	...	...	...	...	...	...	...	...
Panama	1983	26.2	4.1	20.5	22.1	3.6[6]	1983	23.1	48.8	9.0	2.2	107.3	21.9	6.4	44.9
Papua New Guinea	1984	35.0	14.0	103.0	21.0	5.9[8]	1978	22.5	2.6	26.8	5.8	22.2	27.4	3.1	4.5
Paraguay	1980–85	36.0	7.2	51.2[2]	28.8	4.9	1980	58.0	29.9	11.1	6.5	93.2	41.5	13.7	27.7
Peru	1983	35.4	10.6	96.9	24.8	5.3	1978	113.6	33.1	3.5	5.0	44.5	93.6	14.0	27.0
Philippines	1983	32.0	6.8	49.0	25.2	4.2	1981	65.3	16.9	...	...	53.7[34]	94.6[35]	...	16.7[36]
Pitcairn Island	1982	—	—	—	—	...	...	...	...	...	...	...	...	...	...
Poland	1984	19.7	9.5	19.3[8]	10.2	2.3	1983	11.8	175.1	13.8	55.9	386.9	52.3	20.7	61.4[36]
Portugal	1983	14.4	9.6	19.3	4.8	2.3[6]	1983	10.9	147.9	12.4	1.2	425.8	53.2	36.5	67.3
Puerto Rico	1983	21.5	6.8	16.0	14.7	2.0[6]	1982	13.9	101.6	32.4	9.6	269.3	65.2	44.6	56.0
Qatar	1983	29.4	2.2	57.0[11]	27.2	6.8[6]	...	...	...	...	...	...	...	...	...
Réunion	1984	24.4	5.7	11.6	18.7	2.9[8]	1984	9.5	46.3	22.3[21]	...	173.8	38.7	36.5	71.1
Romania	1983	14.3	9.9	23.9	4.4	2.4[2]	1982	10.4	126.8	6.1	12.0	562.2	127.9	16.8	70.4
Rwanda	1983	52.0	19.0	125.0	33.0	8.0	...	...	...	...	...	...	...	...	...
St. Christopher and Nevis	1982	29.0	11.2	42.8	17.8	...	1980	105.9	101.4	49.6	6.8	398.6	60.8	47.2	24.8
St. Helena and Ascension	1982	24.6	10.0	16.3	14.6	...	...	...	...	...	...	...	...	...	...
St. Lucia	1984	30.1	5.5	17.6	24.6	...	1981	46.2	31.4	25.6	19.0	219.0	45.4	34.7	32.2
St. Pierre and Miquelon	1981	18.2	8.3	9.2	9.9	...	1977	72.9	108.3	102.1	25.0	366.7	45.8	39.6	39.6
St. Vincent and the Grenadines	1982	33.2	7.4	46.8[5]	25.8	3.0[6]	1981	85.7	50.4	75.6[21]	...	205.6	42.3	20.2	40.3
San Marino	1984	10.0	7.0	4.5	3.0	...	1984	—	267.0	14.0	—	225.0	36.0	32.0	32.0
São Tomé and Principe	1982	38.7	10.2	69.5	28.5	5.2[6]	...	...	...	...	...	...	...	...	...
Saudi Arabia	1980–85	43.7	12.6	121.1[11]	31.1	3.5	...	...	...	...	...	...	...	...	...
Senegal	1980–85	47.9	21.1	152.6[11]	26.8	6.5	...	...	...	...	...	...	...	...	...
Seychelles	1984	26.9	7.5	14.4[8]	19.4	3.4[2]	1984	40.2	92.7	27.8	15.5	233.3	83.4	38.6	37.1
Sierra Leone	1980–85	45.3	17.4	190.0[2]	27.9	6.1	...	...	...	...	...	...	...	...	...
Singapore	1984	16.4	5.2	8.8	11.2	1.6	1984	15.2	109.6	18.5	3.5	182.6	80.2	13.6	47.1
Solomon Islands	1982	44.6	11.7	46.0	32.9	7.3	...	...	...	...	...	...	...	...	...
Somalia	1983	50.0	20.0	142.0	30.0	6.8	...	...	...	...	...	...	...	...	...
South Africa	1983	33.6	11.0	70.7[4]	22.6	5.1[6]	...	...	...	...	...	...	...	...	...
Bophuthatswana	...	...	...	...	...	...	...	...	...	...	...	...	...	...	...
Ciskei	...	...	...	...	...	...	...	...	...	...	...	...	...	...	...
Transkei	...	...	...	...	...	...	...	...	...	...	...	...	...	...	...
Venda	...	...	...	...	...	...	...	...	...	...	...	...	...	...	...
South West Africa/ Namibia	1980–85	45.1	17.3	115.0	27.8	6.1	...	...	...	...	...	...	...	...	...
Spain	1983	12.4	7.7	7.2	4.7	2.4[6]	1982	14.2	153.7	20.5	11.8	361.2	67.4	42.7	43.2
Sri Lanka	1982	26.8	6.1	37.1[8]	20.7	3.3[8]	...	...	...	...	...	...	...	...	...
Sudan, The	1980–85	45.3	16.6	121.8[5]	28.7	6.5	...	...	...	...	...	...	...	...	...
Suriname	1980	28.0	7.9	34.9	20.1	5.7	1980	35.1	50.6	17.0	11.6	154.9	19.8	30.6	72.1
Swaziland	1980–85	47.5	17.2	129.0	30.3	6.5	...	...	...	...	...	...	...	...	...
Sweden	1984	11.3	10.9	7.8[8]	0.4	1.6[8]	1982	6.6	229.4	13.4	0.5	555.3	76.0	20.2	58.9
Switzerland	1984	11.5	9.1	7.7[2]	2.4	1.8[8]	1983	9.7	229.2	25.1[5]	55.5	388.6	60.1	33.8	82.3
Syria	1983	43.6	5.3	57.0[6]	38.3	7.2[6]	1981	15.1	8.4	5.0	4.0	60.7	13.2	4.5	20.0
Taiwan	1984	19.6	4.8	8.3[8]	14.8	2.3	1980	...	75.1	...	...	137.1	34.0	...	74.0
Tanzania	1983	50.0	16.0	97.0	34.0	7.0	...	...	...	...	...	...	...	...	...
Thailand	1983	21.3	5.1	12.4	16.2	3.9[8]	1983	7.8[2]	27.0	...	...	33.8	21.5[2]	17.6[2]	35.0
Togo	1980–85	47.8	17.1	114.4	30.7	6.5	...	...	...	...	...	...	...	...	...
Tokelau	1982	27.7	10.3	—	17.4	4.3	...	...	...	...	...	...	...	...	...
Tonga	1983	27.1	3.3	6.4	23.8	4.9[42]	...	...	...	...	...	...	...	...	...
Trinidad and Tobago	1982	29.0	7.0	26.0	22.0	2.9[6]	1978	22.3	65.3	6.3	5.7	244.1	30.9	3.7	59.0
Tunisia	1982	32.9	7.3	107.0[11]	25.6	4.9[6]	1980	18.2	8.9	3.9	5.2	29.3	10.0	6.2	12.4
Turkey	1980–85	33.6	9.3	131.0[3]	24.3	4.5	1982	15.0	24.5	22.6	1.7	106.7	18.1	4.0	8.4
Turks and Caicos Islands	1982	25.5	4.6	10.2	20.9	...	...	...	...	...	...	...	...	...	...
Tuvalu	1982	38.7	10.2	42.0	28.5	2.8	...	...	...	...	...	...	...	...	...
Uganda	1983	50.0	17.0	125.0	33.0	7.0	...	...	...	...	...	...	...	...	...
U.S.S.R.	1984	19.6	10.8	16.3[2]	8.8	3.1[2]	1983	...	148.1	...	...	554.3	...	...	...
United Arab Emirates	1980–85	28.8	7.1	49.6	21.7	6.7	...	...	...	...	...	...	...	...	...
United Kingdom	1984	12.9	11.7	9.6	1.2	1.8	1983	4.2	269.2	13.0[21]	15.3	573.2	171.7	32.9	40.2
United States	1985	15.8	8.8	10.5	7.0	1.8[12]	1983–84[45]	10.2	189.2	15.1	0.5	415.5	51.3	18.4	59.9
Uruguay	1983	19.0	8.7	32.0	10.3	2.6[2]	1981	24.1	209.6	...	...	375.6	32.0[31]	...	40.3[31]
Vanuatu	1984	45.0	12.0	94.0	33.0	6.5	...	...	...	...	...	...	...	...	...
Venezuela	1975–80	35.2	5.6	44.8[4]	29.6	4.3[6]	1979	48.0	54.0	10.6[17]	11.1	123.8	38.4	20.0	79.5
Vietnam	1984	31.3	10.6	73.0	20.7	4.2	1979	48.0	54.0	...	...	123.8	...	...	...
Virgin Islands (U.S.)	1980	21.7	4.7	24.7	17.0	...	1980	7.7	56.2	21.2	6.0	177.0	19.6	30.5	72.3
Wallis and Futuna	1978	41.1	10.6	40.5	30.5	...	...	...	...	...	...	...	...	...	...
West Bank	1983	39.2	9.7	...	29.5	...	...	...	...	...	...	...	...	...	...
Western Sahara	1980–85	29.0	4.5	5.3	24.5	...	...	...	...	...	...	...	...	...	...
Western Samoa	1984	10.2	2.3	42.0[2]	7.9	2.7[6]	1984	6.9	17.6	4.4	1.9	47.2	22.6	20.7	9.4
Yemen (Aden)	1980–85	47.6	18.9	142.9[5]	28.7	6.9	...	...	...	...	...	...	...	...	...
Yemen (Şan'ā')	1980–85	48.5	21.8	154.0	26.7	6.8	...	...	...	...	...	...	...	...	...
Yugoslavia	1984	16.4	9.3	31.7[8]	7.1	2.1[6]	1982	17.4	129.4	14.4	7.0	438.5	55.7	17.8	61.0
Zaire	1980–85	45.2	15.8	107.0	29.4	6.1	...	...	...	...	...	...	...	...	...
Zambia	1980–85	47.4	15.4	...	32.0	6.9	...	...	...	...	...	...	...	...	...
Zimbabwe	1981	54.4	12.7	...	41.7	8.0	1979	7.3	152.9	7.0	1.6	310.6	64.7	6.6	102.4

male	female	year	total number	rate per 1,000 population	groom 19 and under	groom 20–29	groom 30 and over	bride 19 and under	bride 20–29	bride 30 and over	families (households) total ('000)	size	children number under age 15	children percent legitimate	legal abortions number	legal abortions ratio per 100 live births	country
48.7	50.9	...	...	...	...	...	...	...	...	...	H 161	H 5.5	...	...	...	...	Oman
60.9	64.5	...	...	...	...	...	...	...	...	...	H 16	H 6.7	H 4.1	...	...	...	Pacific Is., Trust Territory of the
51.6	49.7	1971	62,900	10.7[11]	...	...	...	...	...	...		H 6.7	...	...	...	...	Pakistan
69.2	72.9	1983	8,981	4.3	5.5[32]	58.5[32]	36.0[32]	22.2[32]	52.5[32]	25.2[32]	F 347	F 4.9	...	28.6	26	—	Panama
53.5	53.0	...	...	...	...	...	...	...	...	...	F 674	H 4.6	...	...	...	...	Papua New Guinea
62.8	67.5	1981	15,550	5.0	3.2	64.5	32.3	33.0	47.0	20.0	H 345	H 5.2	...	67.4[33]	...	...	Paraguay
57.6	60.7	1977	36,777	2.3	5.5	60.4	34.1	25.9	51.4	22.6	H 2,772	H 4.8	...	57.8	...	...	Peru
63.0	66.5	1979	343,265	7.7	11.7	71.1	17.2	33.0	55.7	10.3	F 8,607	F 5.6	F 2.4	96.3	...	...	Philippines
63.0	66.5	1972	2	...	...	...	...	...	...	...			...	...	...	...	Pitcairn Island
67.2	75.2	1984	309,330	8.4	3.1	80.4	16.5	18.6	69.8	11.6	F 9,435	F 3.6	F 0.9	95.3	141,177	20.1	Poland
67.6	74.1	1983	67,060	6.7	7.7	74.5	17.8	30.2	56.7	13.1	H 3,427	H 2.9	H 0.8	92.8	...	...	Portugal
70.8	76.9	1981	31,916	9.8	12.2	57.1	30.7	29.2	48.6	22.2	F 563	H 4.1	F 1.8	79.0	...	...	Puerto Rico
54.8	58.3	1983	1,040	3.7	...	...	...	...	...	...		H 2.9	...	...	...	...	Qatar
64.6	68.2	1984	3,458	6.6	2.3	73.6	24.1	19.0	56.6	14.4	H 121	H 4.2	H 2.3	53.9	3,838	32.5	Réunion
67.5	72.3	1982	174,448	7.8	3.0	75.9	21.1	31.1	54.5	14.4	H 7,115	H 3.1	...	...	404,000	99.0	Romania
45.0	48.0	1980	13,890	2.7	...	...	...	...	...	...	H 894	H 5.2	...	...	...	...	Rwanda
63.0	68.0	1977[37]	172	2.6	...	...	...	...	...	...	H 11	H 4.3[37]	H 1.9	18.6	...	...	St. Christopher and Nevis
...	...	1982	29	5.2	8.3	58.4	33.3	38.9	44.4	16.7	H 1	H 4.4	H 1.6	56.5	...	...	St. Helena and Ascension
68.3	72.4	1981	420	3.4	0.7	46.9	52.4	8.8	53.6	37.6	H 23	H 4.9	...	13.0	...	...	St. Lucia
65.8	71.6	1981	39	6.2	...	...	...	...	...	...	H 2	H 3.3	H 0.9	83.0	...	...	St. Pierre and Miquelon
67.5	71.4	1981	508	4.1	0.7	44.2	55.1	11.1	57.2	31.7	H 20	H 5.0	...	...	...	...	St. Vincent and the Grenadines
70.7	76.2	1984	188	8.5	2.8	80.8	16.4	19.9	72.6	7.5	F 6	F 3.2	F 0.8	96.5	...	...	San Marino
47.1	50.0	1982	64	0.7	...	...	...	...	...	...			...	9.8	...	...	São Tomé and Principe
54.5	57.6	...	...	...	...	...	...	...	...	...	H 1,513	H 5.5	...	...	...	...	Saudi Arabia
41.8	45.0	...	...	...	...	...	...	...	...	...	H 1,167	H 4.8	...	...	...	...	Senegal
66.0	73.0	1981	307	4.8	2.2	69.7	28.1	31.7	50.0	18.3	H 13	H 4.6	H 1.9	33.4	...	...	Seychelles
46.7	50.0	1966	318	...	...	...	...	...	...	...	H 722	H 4.9	...	...	...	...	Sierra Leone
70.0	75.0	1984	24,467	9.9	0.8	72.2	27.0	7.8	80.1	12.1	H 510	H 3.9	H 1.3	...	15,548	36.5	Singapore
54.0	54.0	...	...	...	...	...	...	...	...	...	F 41	F 5.6	F 2.3	...	...	...	Solomon Islands
41.9	45.1	...	...	...	...	...	...	...	...	...		H 4.9	...	...	...	...	Somalia
51.8	55.2	1977	64,979[38]	...	3.5[38]	69.4[38]	27.1[38]	22.1[38]	58.6[38]	19.3[38]	F 1,403	H 5.1	...	75.9	...	...	South Africa
...	...	...	...	...	...	...	...	...	...	...			...	...	...	...	Bophuthatswana
...	...	...	...	...	...	...	...	...	...	...			...	...	...	...	Ciskei
...	...	...	...	...	...	...	...	...	...	...			...	...	...	...	Transkei
...	...	...	...	...	...	...	...	...	...	...			...	...	...	...	Venda
47.0	49.5	...	...	...	...	...	...	...	...	...		H 4.8	...	...	...	...	South West Africa/Namibia
71.3	77.5	1983	183,490	4.8	5.7	80.8	13.5	20.8	71.7	7.5	F 10,665	F 3.5	...	97.9	...	...	Spain
66.1	70.2	1981	121,668	8.1	0.4	72.4	27.2	17.8	73.4	8.8	H 2,721	H 5.2	H 1.9	92.5	...	...	Sri Lanka
48.0	50.0	...	...	...	...	...	...	...	...	...	H 3,471	H 5.3	...	...	...	...	Sudan, The
67.0	71.9	1980[39]	2,371	6.1	...	...	...	...	...	...		H 3.9	...	...	...	...	Suriname
45.3	51.9	1976	490	1.0	...	...	...	...	...	...	H 112	H 5.0	...	...	...	...	Swaziland
73.6	79.6	1984	36,685	4.4	0.5	47.4	52.1	3.0	60.0	37.0	H 3,498	H 2.4	H 0.5	56.4	32,602	35.2	Sweden
72.7	79.6	1984	38,020	5.9	0.5	62.2	37.3	5.1	72.6	22.3	H 2,500	H 2.5	...	94.6	...	...	Switzerland
63.8	64.7	1984[40]	81,460	8.2	...	...	...	...	...	...	F 1,151	F 6.2	F 2.4	...	...	...	Syria
69.9	75.1	1984	154,540	8.2	2.4	76.6	21.0	11.2	81.5	7.3	H 3,728	H 4.4	H 0.5	...	...	...	Taiwan
49.0	52.0	1967	3,475	9.8	...	...	...	...	...	...	H 3,435	H 5.1	H 2.3	...	...	...	Tanzania
59.5	65.1	1981	341,655	7.2	...	...	...	...	...	...	H 8,422	H 5.3	H 2.0	...	...	...	Thailand
46.9	50.2	1979[41]	5,753	2.3	...	...	...	...	...	...	H 479	H 5.6	...	...	...	...	Togo
63.0	66.5	1981	9	6.0	—	83.3	16.7	—	100.0	—		H 5.5	...	...	...	...	Tokelau
58.0	60.0	1981	682	6.9	...	...	...	...	...	...	F 15	F 6.1	F 2.7	...	...	...	Tonga
67.8	72.6	1982	9,483	8.4	4.5	64.0	31.5	27.2	53.6	19.2	H 193	H 4.2	H 2.1	56.8	...	...	Trinidad and Tobago
60.1	61.1	1983	52,061	7.6	1.4	72.5	26.1	35.9	54.7	9.4	H 1,313	H 5.5	...	99.8	20,500	9.5	Tunisia
60.3	64.9	1980	366,403	8.1	7.7[43]	72.4[43]	19.9[43]	35.9[43]	52.1[43]	12.0[43]	H 8,601	H 5.2	H 2.0	...	...	...	Turkey
68.6	71.9	1980	27	3.6	...	...	...	...	...	...	H 1	H 4.3	H 2.0	82.4	...	...	Turks and Caicos Islands
56.9	60.1	...	...	...	...	...	...	...	...	...	H 1	H 6.4	H 2.2	...	...	...	Tuvalu
48.0	50.0	...	...	...	...	...	...	...	...	...		H 5.2	...	...	...	...	Uganda
61.9	72.0	1983	2,834,000	10.4	4.5	76.7	18.8	25.7	59.3	15.0	F 66,307	F 3.9	...	...	10,000,000	230.0	U.S.S.R.
61.6	65.6	...	...	...	...	...	...	...	...	...		H 3.8	...	...	...	...	United Arab Emirates
70.2	76.2	1984	395,400	7.0	4.8	62.8	32.4	16.5	60.0	23.5	H 19,949	H 2.6	H 1.7	81.4	137,556[44]	17.2[44]	United Kingdom
71.8	78.8	1985	2,459,800	10.3	8.5	59.5	32.0	21.1	55.8	23.1	F 61,393	F 2.6	F 1.0	80.6	1,553,900	42.8	United States
69.1	73.8	1982	20,330	6.9	8.3	62.7	29.0	28.3	51.7	20.0	H 829	H 3.5	...	75.4	...	...	Uruguay
56.2	53.7	...	...	...	...	...	...	...	...	...		H 4.9	...	...	...	...	Vanuatu
65.1	70.6	1981[1]	91,492	6.4	10.7[1]	66.0[1]	23.3[1]	37.3[1]	49.3[1]	13.4[1]		H 5.3	...	47.0	...	...	Venezuela
57.3	61.7	...	...	...	...	...	...	...	...	...			...	...	...	...	Vietnam
68.8	71.9	1980	1,114	9.5	3.1	44.6	52.3	12.7	50.9	36.4	H 28	H 3.4	H 1.3	52.6	...	...	Virgin Islands (U.S.)
59.2	62.9	1980	60	5.6	...	...	...	...	...	...		H 6.6	H 3.0	78.3	...	...	Wallis and Futuna
...	...	...	...	...	...	...	...	...	...	...			...	...	...	...	West Bank
...	...	1972	459	4.9	...	...	...	...	...	...			...	...	...	...	Western Sahara
61.0	64.3	1984	555	5.0	0.9	58.7	40.4	7.2	68.8	24.0	F 20	F 7.8	F 3.8	43.5	...	...	Western Samoa
45.3	47.7	...	...	...	...	...	...	...	...	...		H 5.5	...	...	...	...	Yemen (Aden)
42.7	44.8	...	...	...	...	...	...	...	...	...		H 5.8	...	...	...	...	Yemen (Şan'ā')
67.7	73.1	1984	168,290	7.3	2.9	76.2	20.9	27.2	60.9	11.9	H 6,187	H 3.6	H 0.9	91.7	288,100	74.0	Yugoslavia
48.3	51.7	1975	185,300	7.5	...	...	...	...	...	...		H 6.0	...	...	...	...	Zaire
49.1	52.5	...	...	...	...	...	...	...	...	...	H 873		H 2.1	...	...	...	Zambia
53.3	56.8	1977	2,633[46]	...	2.4[46]	63.7[46]	33.9[46]	35.9[46]	54.6[46]	9.5[46]		H 5.8	...	95.8	...	...	Zimbabwe

[1]Excludes nomadic tribes. [2]1982. [3]1979. [4]1980. [5]1981. [6]1980–85. [7]1977. [8]1983. [9]Heart diseases, cerebrovascular diseases, and hypertension only. [10]Pneumonia, bronchitis, emphysema, and asthma only. [11]1975–80. [12]1984. [13]Estimates based on rural survey. [14]Millions of households. [15]Based on burial permits. [16]Medically certified deaths only. [17]1978. [18]First marriages only. [19]Port-au-Prince only. [20]Includes East Jerusalem. [21]Includes nutritional disorders. [22]Includes registered Palestinian refugees. [23]1968. [24]Reported inpatient cases only. [25]Includes Sarawak; refers to non-Muslim civil marriages and Christian ritual marriages only. [26]Annual averages. [27]1973. [28]Skull fractures only. [29]Less than 21. [30]21 and older. [31]1976. [32]Excludes tribal Indians. [33]Registered births only. [34]Heart diseases, cerebrovascular diseases, and cardiovascular diseases only. [35]Pneumonia and bronchitis only. [36]Accidents only. [37]Includes Anguilla. [38]Whites, Asians, and Coloureds only. [39]Excludes Hindu and Muslim ritual marriages. [40]Syrian Arabs only. [41]African population only. [42]1975. [43]Urban areas only. [44]Excludes Northern Ireland. [45]March 1, 1983, to February 29, 1984. [46]Non-Africans only.

National product and accounts

The national product and accounts table furnishes a breakdown of how the aggregate income (output) of a nation is produced, distributed, and spent by its population. The per capita value of a country's gross national product (GNP) provides a useful indication of the general economic well-being of its inhabitants. The several breakdowns of aggregate income or expenditure (each representing a different method of computing gross domestic product [GDP] or an element of its GNP) provide a number of specific details about each country's economy, including national patterns of consumption, investment, and foreign trade; factor costs (prices paid for the inputs of production), such as indirect taxes, capital consumption, wage compensation, and profit; industrial origin of GDP for ten principal industrial sectors; and the principal elements of a country's balance of payments (merchandise trade, invisibles, and tourism).

Measures of national output. The two most commonly used measures of national output (except for certain centrally planned economies) are GNP and GDP. Each of these measures represents an aggregate value of goods and services produced within a specific country. The GDP, the more basic of these, is a measure of the value of goods and services produced entirely within each country. It is equal to the sum of all factor costs (factor incomes) or all value added provided by the combined productive capabilities of labour and capital within each economic system. The GNP, the more comprehensive value, is composed of both domestic production and the net value added (net factor income) from transactions with other countries. When the factor income value received from other countries is greater than the value paid, a country's GNP is greater than its GDP. In theory, if all national accounts could be equilibrated, the global summation of GDP (each country's value added to the world economy) would equal the total of all GNP values.

In the first section of the table, data are provided for the nominal GNP (value in current prices for the year indicated), together with the per capita value of this product, both denominated in U.S. dollars for ease of comparison. Beside these are given figures for GDP denominated in the national currency, first as a nominal value, then as a "real" value

(adjusted, that is, to eliminate the effect of recent inflation [most often] or, occasionally, of deflation). The real values are obtained by dividing the nominal GDP by a GDP deflator (essentially a consumer price index that covers price changes in the whole economy) and are adjusted to a common base year of 1980. GNP per capita provides a rough measure of annual monetary income per person, but values should be compared cautiously, as they are subject to a number of distortions, notably of purchasing power parity (the ability of any two currencies to purchase goods in their respective domestic markets differing by more than a simple exchange rate) and in the existence of elements of national production that do not enter the monetary economy (e.g., food, clothing, or housing produced and consumed within families or in communal groups).

In a number of countries with centrally planned economies such as Afghanistan, Bulgaria, China, Cuba, Czechoslovakia, East Germany, Hungary, Laos, Mongolia, Poland, and the Soviet Union, the conventional concept for the aggregated national income/product is net material product (NMP) and includes only material goods and "productive" services. The GDP values presented in this table for free market economies are not directly comparable to the official NMP measures published by the centrally planned economies. The GDP value is more comprehensive and covers a number of sectors (especially services) excluded from the NMP value. Estimated GNPs have been supplied for most countries (including the centrally planned), based either on the country's own, or on external, analysis.

The origin, distribution, and spending of the national product. Even though GNP/GDP values allow a general comparison of relative economic development, more information is provided when these aggregates are analyzed according to their component kinds of expenditure, cost components, and industrial sectors of origin.

There are three major domestic expenditure components of GDP: private consumption (analyzed in greater detail in the "Household budgets and consumption" table), government spending, and gross domestic investment. The fourth, nondomestic, component of GDP expenditure is

National product and accounts

country	gross national product (GNP), 1983		gross domestic product (GDP), 1983		GDP by type of expenditure, 1982 (%)[a]					cost components of GDP, 1982 (%)			
					consumption		gross domestic invest-ment	foreign trade		net indirect taxes	consump-tion of fixed capital	compen-sation of employ-ees	net operating surplus
	nominal ('000,000 U.S.$)	per capita (U.S.$)	nominal ('000,000,000 national currency)	real prices of 1980 ('000,000,000 national currency)	private	govern-ment		exports	imports				
Afghanistan	3,500[1]	210[1]	94.0[2]	...	...	...	...	...	...	...	...	...	...
Albania	2,380[5]	850[5]	...	...	...	...	...	...	...	...	...	...	...
Algeria	49,450	2,400	208.7[1]	156.7[1]	46	15	37	31	-29	20[4]	8[4]	37[4]	35[4]
American Samoa	140	4,080	...	...	...	...	...	...	...	...	...	...	...
Andorra	360	9,000	...	...	...	...	...	...	...	...	...	...	...
Angola	7,634[1]	1,030[1]	199.5[5]	...	50[5]	22[5]	9[5]	——19[5]——		...	...	...	...
Anguilla	...	...	...	...	...	...	...	...	...	...	...	...	...
Antigua and Barbuda	140	1,730	0.346[1]	0.300[1]	66	23	51	72	-111	...	...	...	...
Argentina	58,560	2,030	0.150[1]	0.025[1]	69	10	18	13	-10	12	8	26	62[8]
Australia	166,230	10,810	174.0	131.5	62	18	21	15	-17	13	8	56	23
Austria	66,800	8,450	1,205.8	1,024.7	56	19	23	41	-39	13	12	54	21
Bahamas, The	900	4,050	1.449[1]	1.230[1]	59	15	27	80	-81	...	...	...	...
Bahrain	4,120	10,360	1.543[5]	...	36[5]	13[5]	37[5]	122[5]	-108[5]	...	...	...	...
Bangladesh	12,530	130	287.1	220.2	92	5	11	5	-12	...	...	...	...
Barbados	1,020	4,060	2.124	1.597	65	14	23	61	-63	14[4]	6[4]	57[4]	24[4]
Belgium	81,162	8,230	4,190.0	3,474.0	66	19	17	69	-71	10	9	58	23
Belize	170	1,140	0.352	0.332	75	26	29	53	-82	11	9	——80——	
Benin	1,102	290	385.3	...	91	9	20	22	-41	9[11]	7[11]	23[11]	61[11]
Bermuda	840	15,000	0.787	...	67[13]	14[13]	9[13]	62[13]	-54[13]	...	...	...	...
Bhutan	124[5]	95[5]	1.021[5]	...	...	...	...	...	...	...	...	...	...
Bolivia	3,070	510	1,515.8	107.4	75	11	11	26	-24	10[4]	6[4]	36[4]	47[4]
Botswana	920	920	1.022	0.985	56	26	31	62	-75	13	11	39	37
Brazil	245,590	1,890	121,055.0	12,666.0	69	10	21	8	-8	10	5	——85——	
British Virgin Islands	...	2,750[5]	...	...	...	...	...	...	...	12[11]	8	53[11]	36[8,11]
Brunei	4,420	2,140	8.868[1]	...	...	...	...	...	...	...	...	...	...
Bulgaria	26,000[1]	2,920[1]	23.479[2]	...	...	...	...	...	...	...	...	...	...
Burkina Faso	1,210	210	429.4	338.3	94	15	13	15	-36	8[13]	7[13]	24[13]	61[13]
Burma	6,500	180	49.7	45.9	——82——		25	7	-15	10	9	38	44
Burundi	1,050	240	100.4	93.5	78	20	18	9	-25	10	2	21	66
Cameroon	7,640	830	2,618.0	1,599.8	67	9	26	19	-21	13	6	29	52
Canada	300,400	12,060	402.6	303.4	57	21	18	26	-22	11	12	57	20
Cape Verde	100	360	3.179[5]	...	117[5]	11[5]	24[5]	——53[5]——		...	...	...	...
Cayman Islands	...	4,800[5]	...	...	...	...	...	...	...	...	...	...	...
Central African Republic	671	280	0.786[17]	...	9[15]	21[5]	15[5]	——26[5]——		12[18]	—	24[18]	64[18]
Chad	360[1]	80[1]	0.837[17]	...	82[4]	25[4]	9[4]	——16[4]——		6[19]	7[19]	13[19]	75[19]
Chile	21,890	1,870	1,557.7	968.0	77	15	10	22	-23	14	11	42	34
China	301,840	300	639.0[20]	...	63[2]	8[2]	29[2]	——— —— ——		...	...	...	...
Christmas Island	...	...	...	...	...	...	...	...	...	...	...	...	...
Cocos (Keeling) Islands	...	...	...	...	...	...	...	...	...	...	...	...	...
Colombia	38,830	1,410	3,036.7	1,646.1	72	11	21	12	-16	9	8	43	48[8]
Comoros	120[1]	330[1]	0.092[17]	...	65[5]	21[5]	28[5]	——14[5]——		...	...	...	...
Congo	2,180	1,320	666.0[1]	460.7[1]	41[5]	13[5]	48[5]	58[5]	-60[5]	17[5]	11[5]	29[5]	43[5]
Cook Islands	20[4]	1,110[4]	...	...	80[18]	32[18]	26[18]	32[18]	-71[18]	...	...	...	...
Costa Rica	2,420	1,020	97.0[1]	36.8[1]	58	15	23	43	-39	12	4	38	46
Cuba	14,900[1,21]	1,520[1,21]	23.079[1,2]	...	77[2]	7[2]	20[2]	——5[2]——		...	...	...	...

net foreign trade; value is given for both exports (a positive value) and imports (a negative value, representing obligations to other countries). The sum of these five percentages, excluding statistical discrepancies and rounding, should be 100% of the GDP.

The distribution of GDP by cost components usually comprises four general categories: indirect taxes (excise or value-added taxes), consumption of fixed capital (depreciation), and two income categories: (a) compensation of employees (salaries, wages, etc.) and (b) net operating surplus ("profits," interests, rent, etc.).

The distribution of GDP for ten industrial sectors is aggregated into three major industrial groups:

1. The primary sector, comprised of agriculture and mineral production (including fossil fuels).

2. The secondary sector, comprised of manufacturing, construction, and public utilities.

3. The tertiary sector, which includes all transportation and communication, trade, financial services (including real estate), personal and business services, and government.

Percentages in this section of the table may not add to 100 because the value of each industry is calculated as a percentage of the total GDP, which may contain significant monetary adjustments that are not distributable to all industries.

Average annual growth rate of real GDP. The columns show average annual growth rates of real product for the decade from 1970 to 1980, as well as for the three years from 1980 to 1983. Real GDP growth rates give an overall impression of the growth in final output achieved by various countries during the years indicated.

Balance of payments (external account transactions). The external account records the sum of all economic transactions of a current nature between one country and the rest of the world. The account shows a country's net receipts from overseas, including not only the trade of goods and services but also such invisible items as interest and dividends, short- and long-term investments, tourism, transfers to or from overseas

residents, etc. Each transaction gives rise either to a foreign claim for payment, recorded as a deficit (*e.g.*, from imports, capital outflows), or a foreign obligation to pay, recorded as a surplus (*e.g.*, from exports, capital inflows) or a domestic claim on another country. A deficit transaction in the balance of payment of one country is automatically accompanied by a surplus in that of another. By totaling the surplus and deficit transactions on the external current account for a country, a statement of its international economic relationships can be summarized. Values are given in U.S. dollars for comparability.

Tourist trade. Income from tourism is often a significant element in a country's economic balance. A tourist is defined as a visitor who stays at least 24 hours but not more than one year in the country visited and whose activities encompass business and/or pleasure. The receipts from foreign nationals reflect payments for goods and services from foreign currency resources by tourists in the given country. Expenditures by nationals abroad are also payments for goods and services, but in this case made by the residents of the given country as tourists abroad. Unless the classification is so important as to justify separate consideration, receipts and expenditures by excursionists—cruise passengers staying less than 24 hours—are included in the total tourist trade figures.

Although tourist trade is also a component of the invisible trade classification, the importance of tourism as a source of income for many countries—the Caribbean islands, for example—warrants a separate listing of this industry. The U.S. dollar is used as the common currency for comparability by the World Tourism Organization.

... Not available.

—None, less than 0.5 of last significant figure, or not applicable.

a. Detail may not add to 100 because of rounding or statistical discrepancies.

b. Detail may not add to 100 because of rounding, statistical discrepancies, or because of adjustments to the GDP such as allowances for imputed bank service charges, import duties, and value-added taxes.

origin of GDP by economic sector, 1982 (%)[b]											avg. annual growth rate of real GDP (%)		balance of payments, 1984 (current external transactions; '000,000 U.S.$)			tourist trade, 1983 ('000,000 U.S.$)		country
primary		secondary			tertiary						1970–1980	1980–1983	net transfers		current balance of payments	receipts from foreign nationals	expenditures by nationals abroad	
agriculture	mining	manufacturing	construction	public utilities	transp., communication	trade	financial svcs.	other svcs.	govt.				goods-merchandise	invisibles				
69[2]	3	14[2,3]	3[2]	3	4[2]	9[2]		2[2]			4.5	...	−200[4]	7[4]	−193[4]	1[5]	...	Afghanistan
...	...	...	...	...	...	...	...	...	...		...	...	...	...	...	...	...	Albania
6[5]	31[5]	11[5]	12[5]	1[5]			28[5]		11[5]		7.0	−1.9[6]	3,226[7]	−3,312[7]	−86[7]	167[1]	452[1]	Algeria
...	...	...	...	...	...	...	...	...	...		...	...	...	...	...	...	...	American Samoa
...	...	...	...	...	...	...	...	...	...		...	...	...	...	...	...	...	Andorra
34[5]	21[5]	2[5]	2[5]	—	4[5]		5[5]	22[5]	10[5]		−9.2	...	−34[1]	−175[1]	−209[1]	...	...	Angola
...	...	...	...	...	...	...	...	...	...		...	...	...	...	...	...	...	Anguilla
6	1	4	7	3	13	21	15	5	12		...	3.4[6]	−90[7]	75[7]	−15[7]	51	6[1]	Antigua and Barbuda
16	3	22	6	4	11	13	9	6	11		2.2	−2.7	3,982	−6,477	−2,495	516[1]	553[1]	Argentina
6[4]	6[4]	19[4]	6[4]	3[4]	7[4]	15[4]	19[4]	14[4]	4[4]		3.0	1.9	−2,144	−6,107	−8,251	1,008	1,713	Australia
4	—	27	8	4	6	17	14	3	14		3.7	1.0	−3,890	3,264	−626	5,142	2,830	Austria
4	7	3[3]	3	3	11	26	13	16	17		...	...	−678	669	−9	770	96	Bahamas, The
1[4]	32[4]	19[4]	7[4]	1[4]	8[4]	12[4]	8[4]	5[4]	7[4]		...	...	−392	381	−11	129[1]	202[1]	Bahrain
46	—	10	6	—	9	8	8	9	3		3.9	3.6	−1,434	1,007	−427	17	18[1]	Bangladesh
6	1	11	6	2	7	29	12	4	12		...	10.5[9]	−293	251	−42	252	26[1]	Barbados
2	1	24	6	4	9	10	13	10	15		3.0	0.1	−2,018[7,10]	1,256[7,10]	−762[7,10]	1,653	2,015	Belgium
19	—	11	5	2	11	15	10	9	10		...	−0.9	−678	669	−2	7.2	...	Belize
37[5]	—	6[5,12]	5[5]	12	6[5]		22[5]		10[5]		3.3	...	−159[11]	63[11]	−96[11]	10[1]	4[5]	Benin
1[11]	2[11]	4[11]	3[11]	6[11]	9[11]	32[11]	17[11]	6[11]	12[11]		...	...	−42[7]	−30[7]	−72[7]	326	...	Bermuda
63[5]	1[4]	4[5,14]	2[5]	—	3[5]	3[5]	2[5]	23[5]	...		2.0	...	−42[7]	−30[7]	−72[7]	1.4[1]	...	Bhutan
18	10	16	2	1	10	20	7	7	9		4.8	−5.7	285	−488	−203	36[5]	40[1]	Bolivia
7	29	8	4	3		10		36			...	11.8	−5	64	59	47	16	Botswana
10	1	24	5	2	5	15	17	10	6		8.4	−1.3	13,068	−12,902	166	1,533	839	Brazil
9[11]	14	6[11,14]	12[11]	2[11]	10[11]	27[11]	17[11]	1[11]	10[11]		...	...	...	...	...	82	...	British Virgin Islands
1	67	10	3	—	1	10	3	6	...		...	...	...	...	...	...	...	Brunei
20[2]	3	54[2,3]	10[2]	3	8[2]	6[2]		3[2,15]			7.1	...	...	...	...	269[5]	...	Bulgaria
41	14	12[14]	4	1	7	12		16			3.5	6.1	−233[1]	141[1]	−92[1]	4	24[5]	Burkina Faso
48	1	9	2	—	4	24	2	4	5		4.6	6.0	−353[7]	97	−344[7]	13[1]	3[1]	Burma
52	1[16]	8	5	16	2	8		25	...		2.8	2.8	...	...	...	22[5]	18[5]	Burundi
23	15	11	6	1	5	12		27	...		5.6	5.3	83[7]	−372[7]	−289[7]	29	70[1]	Cameroon
4	5	16	5	4	7	10	11	10	17		3.9	0.7	16,585	−14,692	1,893	2,613	3,887	Canada
18[5]	—	45[5,12]	20[5]	12		41[5]			17[5]		...	...	−66[13]	64[13]	−2[13]	...	...	Cape Verde
...	...	...	...	...	...	...	...	...	...		...	...	−96[7]	153[7]	57[7]	60	...	Cayman Islands
37	3	8	4	2		46			...		3.0	−0.6	−23[7]	−5[7]	−28[7]	3[5]	19[5]	Central African Republic
64[5]	—	4[5]	2[5]	1[5]	3[5]		27[5]		...		−0.2	...	−21[7]	59[7]	38[7]	2[5]	...	Chad
6	6	20	5	3	5	18	20	6	11		2.4	−3.1	293	−2,353	−2,060	85	260[5]	Chile
44[2]	3	42[2,3]	5[2]	3	4[2]	5[2]			...		5.8	6.1[6]	...	...	...	941	...	China
...	...	...	...	...	...	...	...	...	...		...	...	...	...	...	...	...	Christmas Island
...	...	...	...	...	...	...	...	...	...		...	...	...	...	...	...	...	Cocos (Keeling) Islands
19	3	20	6	2	9	14	14	6	9		5.9	1.4	330	−1,549	−1,219	235	445	Colombia
45	—	5	11	1			39				...	...	...	...	...	...	...	Comoros
8[5]	39[5]	6[5]	5[5]	1[5]	8[5]		11[5]	12[5]	10[5]		3.1	12.8[6]	417[7]	−817[7]	−400[7]	13[5]	54[1]	Congo
26[4]	—[4]	11[4]	9[4]	2[4]	7[4]	14[4]	3[4]		...		...	...	...	...	...	...	...	Cook Islands
25	1[4]	20[14]	4	3	6	20	8	3	12		5.0	−5.8[6]	−56	−287	−343	130	36[1]	Costa Rica
15[2]	3	43[2,3]	8[2]	3	8[2]	26[2]		12,15			0.4	...	...	...	...	100[22]	...	Cuba

National product and accounts (continued)

country	gross national product (GNP), 1983		gross domestic product (GDP), 1983		GDP by type of expenditure, 1982 (%)[a]					cost components of GDP, 1982 (%)			
	nominal ('000,000 U.S.$)	per capita (U.S.$)	nominal ('000,000,000 national currency)	real prices of 1980 ('000,000,000 national currency)	consumption		gross domestic invest-ment	foreign trade		net indirect taxes	consump-tion of fixed capital	compen-sation of employ-ees	net operating surplus
					private	govern-ment		exports	imports				
Cyprus	2,430	3,720	1.092	0.824	63	17	33	53	−66	7	10	——83——	
Czechoslovakia	87,601	5,690	507.3[2]	...	69[2]	8[2]	19[2]	——3[2]——		...	...	...	
Denmark	54,600	10,680	515.0	389.0	55	28	16	36	−35	15	9	55	21
Djibouti	191	570	60.3[4]	...	63[5]	34[5]	15[5]	——12[5]——		17[5]	—[5]	35[5]	48[5]
Dominica	80	1,080	0.194[1]	0.174[1]	74	26	28	40	−68	...	...	...	
Dominican Republic	8,170	1,370	7.918[1]	7.012[1]	74	10	21	14	−19	6	6	——88——	
Ecuador	11,690	1,430	565.8[1]	299.9[1]	63	13	25	21	−22	8	8	29	62[8]
Egypt	32,894	730	24.634	19.953	68	17	24	27	−36	6	8	36	59[8]
El Salvador	3,690	710	9.754	7.666	78	16	13	23	−30	6	4	——89——	
Equatorial Guinea	60	200	6.030	...	115[5]	50[5]	12[5]	——77[5]——					
Ethiopia	4,860	120	10.016	9.583	80	16	12	12	−20	...			
Faeroe Islands	440	9,850	2.630	...									
Falkland Islands	...												
Fiji	1,190	1,770	1.168	0.991	61	18	25	43	−49	8	8	47	37
Finland	50,600	10,360	274.9	207.5	55	20	24	32	−31	11	12	56	21
France	568,690	10,400	3,935.0	2,849.8	65	16	22	23	−26	13	12	56	20
French Guiana	210[1]	3,230[1]	...										
French Polynesia	1,260	7,620	87.577[4]	...	68	34	32	12	−45	6	17	46	31
Gabon	3,072	2,380	1,197.3	899.2	30[5]	16[5]	35[5]	——19[5]——		18[13]	14[13]	30[13]	37[13]
Gambia, The	200	290	0.491	...	98[5]	27[5]	45[5]	——70[5]——		...			
Gaza Strip													
Germany, East	89,249	5,300	227.6[2]	...	57[2]	20[2]	20[2]	31[2]	−28[2]	10[2]	9[2]	40[2]	41[2]
Germany, West	655,500	10,670	1,669.6	1,487.0	56	20	21	31	−29	11	13	56	20
Ghana	3,980	320	182.0	37.6	89[5]	9[5]	3[5]	3[5]	−4[5]	5[11]	3[11]	——91[11]——	
Gibraltar	130	4,330	...										
Greece	35,700	3,620	3,065.8	1,708.0	67	19	22	18	−28	10	9	40	41
Greenland	550	10,550	...										
Grenada	110	1,220	0.290[1]	0.247[1]	81	22	38	36	−76	...			
Guadeloupe	1,370	4,170	5.860[4]	...	92	33	22	7	−54	11[4]	8	70[4]	19[4,8]
Guam	690	6,070	...										
Guatemala	8,890	1,120	8.724	7,651	82	8	14	15	−19	...			
Guernsey	...												
Guinea	1,740	300	31.7[4]	...	68[5]	16[5]	16[5]	——1[5]——		...			
Guinea-Bissau	150	180	4.739[4]	...	123[5]	22[5]	17[5]	——61[5]——		...			
Guyana	410	460	1.455	1.248	61	30	26	55	−72	14	8	——78——	
Haiti	1,700	330	8.153	6.888	——97——		16	28	41	10	3	——87——	
Honduras	2,740	670	5.891	4.921	71	15	16	27	−29	10	7	——83——	
Hong Kong	31,900	6,000	201.8	...	63	8	32	85	−89	3	8	48	46[8]
Hungary	18,631	1,750	896.3	769.9	68	11	20	46	−45	...			
Iceland	2,170	9,150	56.1	12.7	64	12	29	39	−44	22	14	46	17
India	190,710	260	1,957.4	1,493.4	66	11	25	7	−10	12	7	——82——	
Indonesia	87,120	560	71,215.0	52,253.0	70	11	23	22	−26	4	7	——90——	
Iran	159,138	3,830	13,749.5	9,158.1	53	17	29	17	−12	1	7	——92——	
Iraq	31,300[5]	2,300[5]	9.495[5]	...	——51[24]——		35[24]	58[24]	−44[24]	1[24]	3[24]	21[24]	75[24]
Ireland	16,960	4,810	14.477	9.691	60	22	26	51	−59	12	9	59	19
Isle of Man	283	4,380	0.162	...									
Israel	21,990	5,340	1,430.6	114.3	60	32	22	36	−49	10	13	50	28
Italy	350,039	6,170	538,998.0	336,158.0	62	18	20	27	−28	7	10	56	26
Ivory Coast	6,730	720	2,497.7	2,045.6	63	20	22	38	−43	23[13]	8[13]	33[13]	36[13]
Jamaica	2,940	1,290	5.807[1]	4.856[1]	69	23	20	40	−52	11	10	58	22
Japan	1,204,270	10,100	274,919.0	262,073.0	59	10	30	15	−14	7	14	56	24
Jersey	910[1]	11,900[1]	0.382[1]	...									
Jordan	4,400	1,710	1.434	1.180	86	25	46	49	−106	11	5	40	44
Kampuchea	1,132[19]	160[19]	...										
Kenya	6,450	340	77.466	56.950	64	19	22	25	−30	14	8	36	51[8]
Kiribati	30	490	0.040[11]	...	93[4]	36[4]	44[4]	23[4]	−96[4]	5[4]	5[4]	30[4]	61[4]
Korea, North	16,200[1]	790[1]	11.8[1]	...									
Korea, South	73,390	1,840	59,603.0	46,734.0	63	13	25	39	−40	13	9	38	40
Kuwait	30,290	18,180	5.728[1]	6.957[1]	50	20	23	59	−53	...			
Laos	602	150	...										
Lebanon	4,600	1,750	8.2[19]	...	——110[13]——		18[13]	——28[13]——		8[25]	5[25]	——88[25]——	
Lesotho	670	470	0.384[1]	0.351[1]	182	25	37	14	−158	17[5]	3[5]	45[5]	36[5]
Liberia	990	470	0.835[1]	0.822[1]	38	18	22	57	−38	14	——86——		
Libya	25,100	7,500	8.846[1]	...	38	34	26	46	−44	4	5	30	61
Liechtenstein	524[4]	20,960[4]	...										
Luxembourg	4,470	12,190	240.6	173.6	61	18	27	——6——		12	13	64	11
Macau	780	2,560	...										
Madagascar	2,730	290	1,045.9[1]	617.8[1]	74[4]	17[4]	21[4]	16[4]	−28[4]	12[13]	11[13]	——87[13]——	
Malawi	1,390	210	1.294	0.988	71	16	20	——7——		9[13]	7[13]	27[13]	58[13]
Malaysia	27,760	1,870	67.979	62.143	54	21	35	50	−60	16[11]	8	32[11]	52[8,11]
Maldives	56	330	0.463	0.400	85	15	24	56	−80	...			
Mali	1,110	150	608.0[5]	...	79	10	29	17	−35	8	7	25	60
Malta	1,310	4,000	0.458	0.418	66	18	32	69	−85	9	3	50	38
Martinique	1,330	4,040	5.538[13]	...	86	35	19	12	−52	10[4]		66[4]	24[4]
Mauritania	720	450	31.728[4]	...	66[5]	29[5]	27[5]	——22[5]——		9[19]	6[19]	27[19]	58[19]
Mauritius	1,250	1,000	12.775	...	71	14	18	47	−50	15	8	42	43[8]
Mayotte	...												
Mexico	168,070	2,240	17,141.7	4,349.1	61	11	21	17	−11	10	6	36	49
Monaco	...												
Mongolia	1,803	1,000	...										
Montserrat		1,250[5]	0.079	...	106	21	36	14	−77	...			
Morocco	15,620	750	94.6	72.9	69	21	23	21	−34	14[4]	—	33[4]	53[4]
Mozambique	4,466[5]	360[5]	160.8[5]	...	82[5]	15[5]	9[5]	——6[5]——		...			
Nauru	...												
Nepal	2,660	170	33.621	25.906	85[5]	7[5]	18[5]	8[5]	−16[5]	...			

| origin of GDP by economic sector, 1982 (%)[b] | | | | | | | | | | avg. annual growth rate of real GDP (%) | | balance of payments, 1984 (current external transactions; '000,000 U.S.$) | | | tourist trade, 1983 ('000,000 U.S.$) | | country |
| primary | | secondary | | | tertiary | | | | | 1970–1980 | 1980–1983 | net transfers | | current balance of payments | receipts from foreign nationals | expenditures by nationals abroad | |
agri-culture	mining	manu-facturing	con-struction	public utilities	transp., communication	trade	finan-cial svcs.	other svcs.	govt.			goods-merchan-dise	invisibles				
10	1	17	12	2	8	19	12	9	8	2.2	3.5	−656[7]	471[7]	−185[7]	332	68	Cyprus
8[2]	3	62[2,3]	10[2]	3	5[2]	12[2]	—3[2,15]—			5.1	...	...	...	...	299	229	Czechoslovakia
5	1	17	5	2	7	12	14	4	21	2.5	1.4	−206	−1,431	−1,637	1,306	1,210	Denmark
4	—	8	7	3	10	16	—5[2]—			...	...	−100[1]	75[1]	−25[1]	...	...	Djibouti
31	1	8	9	2	6	13	11	—22—		...	5.6[6]	−15[7]	13[7]	−2[7]	1.5[1]	...	Dominica
18	2	18	7	1	5	17	—31—			6.6	2.8[6]	−388	162	−226	223[5]	133[5]	Dominican Republic
11	13	17	10	1	9	14	11	6	8	8.8	0.8	1,055	−1,303	−248	120	152	Ecuador
20[5]	14	29[5,14]	5[5]	1[5]	8[5]	—18[5]—		—18[5]—		7.4	9.8	−3,822[7]	3,037[7]	−785[7]	600	630[5]	Egypt
23	—	15	3	2	4	26	8	7	12	4.1	−4.9	−139	22	−117	6[1]	60[1]	El Salvador
47[13]	—	5[13]	5[13]	1[13]	2[13]	10[13]	1[13]	4[13]	16[13]	...	...	−15[5]	−3[5]	−18[5]	...	...	Equatorial Guinea
45	—	10	4	1	4	10	—27—			2.0	4.1	−433	230	−203	8	4[1]	Ethiopia
...	...	...	...	...	...	...	...	...	...	...	...	...	...	...	...	...	Faeroe Islands
...	...	...	...	...	...	...	...	...	...	...	...	...	...	...	...	...	Falkland Islands
18	—	10	7	2	8	17	—37—			4.7	0.3	−163	136	−27	135	19[5]	Fiji
8	—	24	6	3	7	10	13	3	14	3.1	2.5	1,494	−1,488	6	496	620	Finland
4	1	25	7	2	5	12	11	—33—		3.5	1.0	−4,089	4,075	−14	7,226	4,281	France
...	...	...	...	...	...	...	...	...	...	...	...	...	...	...	...	...	French Guiana
5	—	8	9	1	6	24	—46—			...	...	...	...	...	80	...	French Polynesia
6[5]	53[5]	4[5,12]	5[5]	12	—32[5]—					...	−0.2	1,275[7]	−1,200[7]	75[7]	155[5]	104[5]	Gabon
27	—	7	8	1	8	24	11	2.5	14	...	...	−84[5]	34[5]	−50[5]	20[5]	2[5]	Gambia, The
...	...	...	...	...	...	...	...	...	...	...	...	...	...	...	...	...	Gaza Strip
8[2]	14	70[2,14]	6[2]		4[2]	9[2]	—3[2,15]—			4.8	...	...	...	...	...	...	Germany, East
2	1	32	6	3	6	—28—			12	2.6	−0.0	22,340	−16,200	6,140	5,460	15,022	Germany, West
58	14	4[14]	3	1	3	25	2	1	5	−0.1	−2.8	−92[7]	−126[7]	−218[7]	15	25[1]	Ghana
...	...	...	...	...	...	...	...	...	...	...	...	...	...	...	20	...	Gibraltar
17	2	16	6	2	8	11	8	11	10	4.9	−0.1	−4,230	2,098	−2,132	1,176	225	Greece
...	...	...	...	...	...	...	...	...	...	...	...	...	...	...	...	...	Greenland
25	—	3	7	2	6	14	—41—			...	3.0[6]	−40[7]	24[7]	−16[7]	36	...	Grenada
7[4]	14	6[4,14]	4[4]	—	4[4]	17[4]	—60[4]—			...	...	...	...	...	63[5]	...	Guadeloupe
—	...	31[4]	7[4]	...	2[4]	40[4]	7[4]	—13[4]—		...	...	...	...	...	175	...	Guam
25	—	16	3	2	7	26	9	6	6	5.7	−0.9	−50	−327	−377	61	89	Guatemala
...	...	...	...	...	...	...	...	...	...	...	...	...	...	...	...	...	Guernsey
37[4]	25[4]	4[4]	4[4]	1[4]	2[4]	—16[4]—		—11[4]—		3.3	...	...	...	...	...	...	Guinea
53[4]	23	9[4,23]	23	23	1[4]	—13[4]—		—24[4]—		...	...	−46[7]	20[7]	−26[7]	...	...	Guinea-Bissau
20	6	12	7	12	6	9	7	3	16	...	−5.8	−1	−114	−113	4[5]	11[5]	Guyana
32	1	17	5	1	2	18	—24—			4.0	−1.6	−131	19	−112	85[5]	26[5]	Haiti
25	2	15	5	2	7	12	11	8	4	3.6	−0.4	−78	−174	−252	31[5]	128[5]	Honduras
1	—	21	7	1	8	18	21	14	...	9.3	...	...	...	...	1,387	...	Hong Kong
14[2]	3	37[2,3]	10[2]	3	8[2]	11[2]	—20[2,15]—			5.4	2.2	1,236	−906	330	434	152	Hungary
24[5]	—	14[5]	9[5]	4[5]	8[5]	10[5]	14[5]	—17[5]—		...	−1.8	−13	−118	−131	21	2	Iceland
29	3	14	4	2	6	15	6	5	5	3.6	5.4	−4,820[1]	2,296[1]	−2,524[6]	820	220[5]	India
26	20	13	6	1	5	15	6	2	7	7.6	4.8	5,500	−7,614	−2,114	440	557[1]	Indonesia
18	18	8	6	1	7	16	—26—			2.5	10.0	...	...	...	31	...	Iran
10[5]	24[5]	6[5]	17[5]	1[5]	8[5]	9[5]	3[5]	—22[5]—		12.1	...	...	...	...	170[5]	...	Iraq
13[13]	23	36[13,23]	23	23	—35[23]—			—17[23]—		3.5	1.8	−1,126[1]	−741[1]	−1,867[1]	457	511[5]	Ireland
...	...	...	...	...	...	...	...	...	...	...	...	...	...	...	62[7]	...	Isle of Man
6	14	19[14]	8	2	7	13	23	3	5	4.1	2.0	−2,678	1,134	−1,544	−1,029	769	Israel
6	4	25	8	4	6	16	11	8	14	3.0	−0.2	−5,995	3,124	−2,871	9,034	1,822	Italy
27[5]	15[5]	12[5]	8[5]	2[5]	8[5]	—31[5]—			12[5]	6.7	−2.6	1,277	−1,472	−195	74[5]	239[5]	Ivory Coast
7	6	16	8	2	6	24	16	3	16	−1.1	1.4[6]	−280	−32	−312	399	11	Jamaica
3	—	31	9	3	7	12	16	12	9	5.0	3.6	44,260	−9,260	35,000	825	4,428	Japan
7	—	—5—			—88—					...	...	...	...	...	223	...	Jersey
6	3	12	9	1	11	16	13	2	17	6.9	6.5	−1,721	1,502	−219	512	370	Jordan
...	...	...	...	...	...	...	...	...	...	2.4	...	...	...	...	...	...	Kampuchea
28	—	11	5	2	5	9	12	2	13	6.5	2.7	−302	164	−138	183	45[5]	Kenya
19[4]	43[4]	2[4]	8[4]	2[4]	3[4]	6[4]	2[4]	12[4]	...	...	...	...	...	...	...	...	Kiribati
...	...	...	...	...	...	...	...	...	...	...	...	...	...	...	...	...	Korea, North
16	1	28	8	2	8	15	7	8	5	9.5	7.3	−1,036	−335	−1,371	596	555	Korea, South
1	48	7	5	1	3	9	10	2	13	2.5	−3.4[6]	4,187	1,383	5,570	198[1]	1,306[1]	Kuwait
...	...	...	...	...	...	...	...	...	...	3.3	...	...	...	...	...	...	Laos
9[19]	14	13[14,19]	3[19]	5[19]	8[19]	28[19]	—23[19]—		10[19]	3.2	...	...	...	...	...	...	Lebanon
19[5]	5[5]	5[5]	9[5]	—	1[5]	11[5]	10[5]	1[5]	14[5]	7.9	...	−402	423	21	...	...	Lesotho
13	17	...	...	2	4	6	—23—		19	1.7	−5.3[6]	134	−211	−77	...	...	Liberia
3	48	3	12	1	4	6	—23—			2.2	...	1,977	−3,781	−1,804	14[5]	645[5]	Libya
...	...	...	...	...	...	...	...	...	...	...	...	...	...	...	...	...	Liechtenstein
3	14	27[14]	6	2	5	—43—			12	4.5	1.6	[10]	[10]	[10]	...	...	Luxembourg
...	...	...	...	...	...	...	...	...	...	...	...	...	...	...	...	...	Macau
35[5]	23	14[5,23]	23	23	—39[5]—				12[5]	0.3	−4.2[6]	−125[1]	−173[1]	−298[1]	5[5]	38[5]	Madagascar
38	—	10	4	2	5	12	5	15	10	6.3	0.7	28[1]	−101[1]	−73[1]	7	4[5]	Malawi
23	4	18	5	2	7	14	8	3	13	7.8	6.2	2,739	−4,435	−1,696	436[1]	480[5]	Malaysia
28	1	5[12]	8	12	6	13	—38—			...	7.7	−38	21	−17	11	3	Maldives
53	14	7[14]	6	1	3	16	—13—			4.9	...	−77	−50	−127	13	18	Mali
4	6[26]	30	26	5	5	15	5	9	14	11.8	2.2	−228	239	11	148	53	Malta
6[5]	14	5[5,14]	4[5]	2[5]	4[5]	17[5]	—63[5]—			...	...	...	...	...	89[1]	...	Martinique
25[5]	9[5]	7[5]	6[5]	—	8[5]	—18[5]—		10[5]	17[5]	1.7	...	−63[7]	−133[7]	−196[7]	6[5]	15[5]	Mauritania
13	—	14	5	2	9	11	15	5	11	...	6.8[9]	−37	−14	−51	42	13[1]	Mauritius
...	...	...	...	...	...	...	...	...	...	...	...	...	...	...	...	...	Mayotte
7	10	21	6	1	6	23	8	9	9	5.7	0.7	13,200	−9,237	3,963	1,625	441	Mexico
...	...	...	...	...	...	...	...	...	...	...	...	...	...	...	...	...	Monaco
18	3	32[23]	5	3	11	33	...	...	2	...	...	...	...	...	...	...	Mongolia
4	6	5	9	3	8	21	21	6	—	...	...	...	...	...	5[1]	...	Montserrat
14[5]	6[5]	18[5]	5[5]	4[5]	—20[5]—			19[5]	13[5]	5.6	1.3	−1,407	419	−988	417	83[1]	Morocco
40[5]	—	8[5]	6[5]	1[5]	4[5]	—24[5]—			8[5]	−29	...	−372[7]	178[7]	−194[7]	...	...	Mozambique
...	...	...	...	...	...	...	...	...	...	...	...	...	...	...	...	...	Nauru
55	—	4	8		7	14	8	1	6	2.5	3.6	−292	190	−102	35	20	Nepal

National product and accounts (continued)

country	gross national product (GNP), 1983		gross domestic product (GDP), 1983		GDP by type of expenditure, 1982 (%)[a]					cost components of GDP, 1982 (%)			
	nominal ('000,000 U.S.$)	per capita (U.S.$)	nominal ('000,000,000 national currency)	real prices of 1980 ('000,000,000 national currency)	consumption private	consumption government	gross domestic investment	foreign trade exports	foreign trade imports	net indirect taxes	consumption of fixed capital	compensation of employees	net operating surplus
Netherlands, The	142,420	9,920	376.7	329.6	60	18	18	57	-54	8	10	56	25
Netherlands Antilles	1,370[1]	5,730[1]	...	...	56[25]	21[25]	34[25]	352[25]	-364[25]	8[25]	—	66[25]	26[25]
New Caledonia	1,140	7,820	108.1	...	61	32	18	25	-40	3	11	57	29
New Zealand	24,000	7,410	39.935	...	59	17	26	28	-32	9	7	54	32
Nicaragua	2,690	900	35.783	23.939	71	22	17	15	-26	9[11]	4[11]	56[11]	31[11]
Niger	1,460	250	697.2	...	81	11	21	22	-36	...	...	...	...
Nigeria	71,030	780	44.884[1]	41.168[1]	72	11	22	19	-24	2	3	26	70
Niue	4[4]	1,160[4]	...	...	...	...	...	...	...	...	...	...	...
Norfolk Island	...	...	...	...	...	...	...	...	...	...	...	...	...
Norway	53,400	12,930	401.3	299.7	48	19	27	45	-40	10	15	50	24
Oman	7,070	6,240	2.741	...	33	27	27	59	-46	1[5]	——99[5]——		...
Pacific Is., Trust Terr. of the	140	980	...	...	...	...	...	...	...	...	...	...	...
Pakistan	35,000	370	363.8	284.2	85	10	17	11	-23	10	6	——84——	
Panama	4,070	2,070	4.379	3.927	53	23	29	39	-44	7	7	48	38
Papua New Guinea	2,510	790	1.998	1.735	67	27	30	37	-60	8	9	43	41
Paraguay	4,540	1,410	812.7	585.2	78	7	26	8	-19	7	10	33	50
Peru	18,650	1,040	26,499.1	4,556.6	71	15	17	18	-21	11	7	34	49
Philippines	39,420	760	384.5	282.6	69	9	29	16	-23	9	10	——81——	
Pitcairn Island	...	...	...	...	...	...	...	...	...	...	...	...	...
Poland	140,400	3,860	5,924.0[2]	...	62[2]	11[2]	26[2]	——1[2]——		...	...	...	...
Portugal	22,490	2,260	1,856.9[1]	1,347.2[1]	69	14	37	26	-46	9	4	54	33
Puerto Rico	12,830	3,930	16.970[1]	...	77	15	9	60	-60	6	7	46	41
Qatar	5,960	21,170	23.365	...	21	26	28	61	-35	...	...	...	...
Réunion	2,060	3,910	8.445[1]	...	85[4]	33[4]	23[4]	7[4]	-47[4]	10[4]	8	65[4]	25[4,8]
Romania	45,218	2,000	628.8[2]	...	60[2]	5[2]	32[2]	——4[2]——		...	...	...	...
Rwanda	1,540	270	132.4[1]	115.2[1]	76	19	17	9	-21	7	4	21	68
St. Christopher	40	890	0.118	...	...	...	...	...	...	...	...	...	...
St. Helena	...	...	...	...	...	...	...	...	...	...	...	...	...
St. Lucia	130	1,000	0.378	0.326	68	26	40	62	-95	...	...	...	...
St. Pierre and Miquelon	...	...	...	...	...	...	...	...	...	...	...	...	...
St. Vincent	90	880	0.248	0.185	72	23	31	63	-90	17[13]	8[13]	49[13]	26[13]
San Marino	177[4]	8,210[4]	...	...	...	...	...	...	...	...	...	...	...
São Tomé and Príncipe	32	310	0.663[5]	...	33[5]	27[5]	24[5]	——12[5]——		...	...	...	...
Saudi Arabia	127,080	10,440	415.2	377.8	33	27	31	54	-46	—	8	17[4]	83[4,8]
Senegal	2,730	440	977.7	...	78	20	16	30	-43	16[13]	7[13]	33[13]	44[13]
Seychelles	142	2,200	0.993	...	57	35	31	53	-76	19	6	42	33
Sierra Leone	1,230	360	1.939	1.277	91[5]	7[5]	19[5]	23[5]	-40[5]	9[4]	10[4]	27[4]	55[4]
Singapore	16,320	6,500	35.171	30.647	49	11	45	——5——		...	...	...	...
Solomon Islands	160	640	0.175	...	...	...	...	...	...	9[4]	12[4]	25[4]	54[4]
Somalia	1,255	230	1.540[5,17]	...	70[5]	30[5]	18[5]	——19[5]——		...	...	...	...
South Africa	76,890	2,450	89.333	62.085	56	16	27	28	-28	9	14	54	24
Bophuthatswana	...	...	0.710	...	...	...	...	...	...	...	...	...	...
Ciskei	...	...	...	...	...	...	...	...	...	...	...	...	...
Transkei	...	...	...	...	...	...	...	...	...	...	...	...	...
Venda	...	...	...	...	...	...	...	...	...	...	...	...	...
S.W. Africa/Namibia	1,920	1,760	1.720	...	...	...	...	...	...	...	...	...	...
Spain	182,760	4,780	22,778.0	15,764.0	70	12	20	18	-20	5	10	52	33
Sri Lanka	5,140	330	121.6	77.7	78	11	31	29	-48	11	6	46	36
Sudan, The	8,420	400	6.218	...	76[5]	16[5]	20[5]	——12[5]——		11[11]	7[11]	39[11]	43[11]
Suriname	1,280	3,500	2.293	...	68[4]	16[4]	20[4]	59[4]	-63[4]	14[13]	10[13]	46[13]	31[13]
Swaziland	610	890	0.651	...	73	26	29	66	-94	20[5]	6[5]	44[5]	30[5]
Sweden	103,240	12,390	704.5	541.0	54	29	18	33	-33	10	12	63	16
Switzerland	105,060	16,340	203.9	172.1	62	13	24	35	35	6	10	63	22
Syria	16,510	1,680	71.727	58.957	66	21	23	13	-23	...	...	...	...
Taiwan	49,754	2,680	1,992.6	...	52	17	24	52	-46	13[5]	8[5]	50[5]	28[5]
Tanzania	4,986	240	47.853[1]	38.718[1]	74	15	20	9	-18	12	5	27	51
Thailand	40,628	810	924.2	802.1	66	13	21	25	-25	10	8	26	57
Togo	790	280	284.7	206.6	82	15	21	33	-50	14[5]	7[5]	28[5]	51[5]
Tokelau	0.9[4]	560[4]	...	...	...	...	...	...	...	...	...	...	...
Tonga	80	780	0.086	...	96	18	27	27	-69	15	5	——81——	
Trinidad and Tobago	7,870	6,850	17.558[1]	15.403[1]	59	14	38	36	-46	...	...	...	...
Tunisia	8,860	1,290	5.520	3.888	61	16	33	37	-47	13	10	——77——	
Turkey	58,260	1,230	8,578.0	4,826.4	72	11	21	——3——		6	6	19	70
Turks and Caicos Is.	...	2,000[5]	0.028	...	...	...	...	...	...	...	...	...	...
Tuvalu	5[5]	680[5]	...	...	...	...	...	...	...	...	...	...	...
Uganda	3,090	220	518.8[5]	...	84[5]	14[5]	12[5]	——9[5]——		16[19]	8[19]	26[19]	49[19]
U.S.S.R.	706,104	2,590	548.1[2]	...	——72[2]——		26[2]	——2[2]——		...	...	...	...
United Arab Emirates	25,770	21,900	101.2	94.3	24	20	30	62	-35	-3	10	20	74
United Kingdom	505,610	8,970	300.81	238.51	61	22	16	27	-25	15	12	57	16
United States	3,292,340	14,070	3,256.5	2,738.2	66	19	17	9	-10	8	14	62	16
Uruguay	7,390	2,490	186.3	80.9	74	16	14	14	-17	12	4	——84——	
Vanuatu	67[5]	560[5]	7.742[5]	...	...	...	...	...	...	...	...	...	...
Venezuela	70,820	4,110	290.5	240.8	63	15	26	26	-29	3	7	43	47
Vietnam	9,818	170	...	...	...	...	...	...	...	...	...	...	...
Virgin Islands (U.S.)	890	8,570	...	...	...	...	...	...	...	...	...	...	...
Wallis and Futuna	10[1]	920[1]	...	...	...	...	...	...	...	...	...	...	...
West Bank	...	...	...	...	...	...	...	...	...	...	...	...	...
Western Sahara	...	...	...	...	...	...	...	...	...	...	...	...	...
Western Samoa	127[5]	810[5]	...	...	...	...	...	...	...	...	...	...	...
Yemen (Aden)	1,020	510	0.231[4]	...	106[4]	42[4]	49[4]	14[4]	-111[4]	16[4]	8[4]	58[4]	19[4]
Yemen (Ṣan'ā')	3,930	510	14.637[1]	13.285[1]	23[5]	98[5]	44[5]	9[5]	-74[5]	16[5]	3[5]	28[5]	54[5]
Yugoslavia	38,979	1,710	4,083.5[21]	1,562.12[1]	56[2]	5[2]	40[2]	20[2]	-25[2]	...	...	...	...
Zaire	5,050	160	59.134	17.350	55	19	24	32	-30	9[19]	7[19]	——84[19]——	
Zambia	3,630	580	4.181	3.099	57	31	24	31	-42	13	14	51	22
Zimbabwe	5,820	750	5.005[1]	3.735[1]	59	20	27	——6——		11	8	58	31[8]

origin of GDP by economic sector, 1982 (%)[b]										avg. annual growth rate of real GDP (%)		balance of payments, 1984 (current external transactions; '000,000 U.S.$)			tourist trade, 1983 ('000,000 U.S.$)		country
primary		secondary			tertiary							net transfers		current balance of payments	receipts from foreign nationals	expenditures by nationals abroad	
agriculture	mining	manufacturing	construction	public utilities	transp., communication	trade	financial svcs.	other svcs.	govt.	1970–1980	1980–1983	goods-merchandise	invisibles				
4	14	26[14]	7	2	7	15	—28—		16	2.9	-0.6	5,572	-576	4,996	1,421	3,223	Netherlands, The
—38[13]—			4[13]	1[13]	12[13]	24[13]	...	11[13]	11[13]	...	...	-30	223	193	314[22]	63[5]	Netherlands Antilles
2	12	5	6	2	4	26	—16—		26	...	...	...	...	...	36	...	New Caledonia
8	1	23	5	3	8	22	14	3	13	2.3	1.9	246	-1,678	-1,432	237	452	New Zealand
22	1	25	3	2	6	20	8	5	9	0.9	3.1	-319	-39	-358	18[5]	...	Nicaragua
30[5]	16[5]	8[5]	8[5]		5[5]	—9[5]—		15[5]	9[5]	2.7	-6.3[9]	-69[1]	-7[1]	-76[1]	3[5]	...	Niger
22	24	6	8	1	5	22	3	3	4	6.5	-2.4[6]	3,008	-2,478	530	102	454	Nigeria
...	...	...	...	...	...	...	...	...	...	...	...	...	...	...	...	...	Niue
...	...	...	...	...	...	...	...	...	...	...	...	...	...	...	...	...	Norfolk Island
4	16	14	6	3	9	12	11	4	14	4.8	1.7	5,115	-1,887	3,228	664	1,579	Norway
2	58	2	6	1	4	12	2	1	11	...	...	1,781	-1,633	148	...	...	Oman
...	...	...	...	...	...	...	...	...	...	...	...	...	...	...	...	...	Pacific Is., Trust. Terr. of
28	1	15	4	2	7	14	5	8	7	4.7	6.2	-2,715[7]	2,740[7]	25[7]	202	165[1]	Pakistan
9	—	9	9	4	12	16	16	8	12	4.0	3.4	-795	679	-116	168	71	Panama
34[4]	13[4]	10[4]	4[4]	1[4]	5[4]	8[4]	6[4]	12[4]	7[4]	2.3	0.8	-50	-274	-324	26[5]	19	Papua New Guinea
26	—	16	7	2	4	27	3	10	4	8.6	1.6	-200	-70	-270	49	45[5]	Paraguay
13	8	23	4	1	7	14	12	—19—		3.0	-2.6	1,007	-1,260	-253	253	162	Peru
22	2	24	9	1	6	18	8	4	5	6.3	2.6	-679	-572	-1,251	465	148[1]	Philippines
...	...	...	...	...	...	...	...	...	...	...	...	...	...	...	85	195	Pitcairn Island
19[2]	3	50[2,3]	11[2]	3	4[2]	14[2]	—2[2,15]—			...	...	...	...	...	...	...	Poland
8[5]	—	30[5]	8[5]	2[5]	6[5]	22[5]	8[5]	8[5]	12[5]	4.6	4.4[6]	-2,026	1,512	-514	811	228	Portugal
4	—	46	1	3	6	16	16	6	16	...	...	221[7]	-923[7]	-702[7]	691	473	Puerto Rico
1	53	5	7		3	9	8	1	15	...	...	1,842[7]	-1,432[7]	410[7]	...	...	Qatar
6[4]	14	9[4,14]	4[4]	2[4]	4[4]	16[4]	10[4]	12[4]	30[4]	...	...	...	...	...	...	...	Réunion
21[2]	3	56[2,3]	8[2]	3	7[2]	6[2]	—2[2,15]—			8.6	3.0	2,186	-650	1,536	202	92	Romania
45	2	15	5	—	—33—					4.1	3.3[6]	-74[7]	25[7]	-49[7]	4[5]	12[5]	Rwanda
20	—	14	7	1	12	14	10	5	20	...	...	-37[7]	23[7]	-14[7]	9[1]	...	St. Christopher
...	...	...	...	...	...	...	...	...	...	...	...	...	...	...	...	...	St. Helena
14	1	12	8	3	12	21	9	4	16	...	2.4	-57[7]	39[7]	-18[7]	32[1]	...	St. Lucia
...	...	...	...	...	...	...	...	...	...	...	...	...	...	...	...	...	St. Pierre and Miquelon
13		9	10	2	13	10	12	3	15	...	5.3	-23[7]	20[7]	-3[7]	10[1]	...	St. Vincent
...	...	...	...	...	...	...	...	...	...	...	...	...	...	...	...	...	San Marino
31[5]	...	4[5]	2[5]	1[5]	4[5]	16[5]	—25[5]—		17[5]	...	...	-6[7]	-6[7]	-12[7]	...	...	São Tomé and Príncipe
2	47	6	13	—	5	7	7	2	11	10.6	-0.4	8,829	-32,865	-24,036	1,573[5]	2,761[5]	Saudi Arabia
22	3	18.0[3]	6	3	—38—				15	2.5	2.1[9]	-544[1]	-144[1]	-400[1]	63	42[1]	Senegal
6	—	9	6	1	11	23	12	3	19	...	...	-69[7]	43[7]	-26[7]	33	7[1]	Seychelles
31[4]	9[4]	7[4]	4[4]	1[4]	15[4]	13[4]	7[4]	3[4]	6[4]	1.6	3.5	-20[7]	-5[7]	-25[7]	10[5]	10[5]	Sierra Leone
1	—	26	9	2	13	22	21	4	7	8.5	8.0	-4,389	3,388	-1,001	1,980	531	Singapore
59[27]	3	13.[3,27]	2[27]	3	2[27]	8[27]	—8[27]—		14[27]	...	...	26	-21	5	2[11]	...	Solomon Islands
60[5]	—	7[5]	3[5]	...	6[5]	6[5]	—18[5]—			3.4	...	-425	279	-146	13[1]	13[1]	Somalia
6	14	24	4	4	9	13	13	2	10	3.6	0.2	2,253	-3,063	-810	630	...	South Africa
...	...	...	...	...	...	...	...	...	...	...	...	...	...	...	...	...	Bophuthatswana
...	...	...	...	...	...	...	...	...	...	...	...	...	...	...	...	...	Ciskei
...	...	...	...	...	...	...	...	...	...	...	...	...	...	...	...	...	Transkei
...	...	...	...	...	...	...	...	...	...	...	...	...	...	...	...	...	Venda
10[5]	31[5]	5[5]	4[5]	3[5]	7[5]	15[5]	6[5]	2[5]	15[5]	...	...	...	...	...	46[5]	...	S.W. Africa/Namibia
6[5]	14	23[5,14]	7[5]		7[5]	17[5]	5[5]	15[5]	10[5]	4.0	1.3	-4,059	6,118	2,059	6,836	894	Spain
26	1	15	9	2	10	20	6	2	6	4.1	5.3	-237	244	7	127	79[5]	Sri Lanka
36[11]		8[11]	4[11]	1[11]	10[11]	19[11]	—22[11]—			4.4	...	-37	98	61	6[5]	69	Sudan, The
9	12	9	3	2	5	12	—48—			...	...	10	-53	-43	4	35	Suriname
20[5]	3[5]	16[5]	4[5]	1[5]	5[5]	8[5]	—44[5]—			...	3.8[6]	-79	68	-11	7	22[1]	Swaziland
3	—	20	7	3	6	11	12	3	22	1.7	1.0	3,601	-3,445	156	1,056	1,608	Sweden
...	...	20[3]	6	3	7	23	6	2	15	0.4	0.4	-3,042[7]	6,568[7]	3,526[7]	3,147	2,296	Switzerland
21	3	20[3]	6	3	7	23	6	2	15	10.0	5.5	-2,224[7]	1,409[7]	-815[7]	110	188[1]	Syria
7	1	40	11	4	6	13	3	—16—		8.9	...	6,107[7]	-1,498[7]	4,609[7]	1,031	1,229	Taiwan
45	—	8	4	1	4	7	11	10	—	4.9	-2.5[6]	-350[5]	71[5]	-279[5]	13	12	Tanzania
22	2	19	5	2	7	23	8	7	4	7.2	5.4	-1,930	-170	-2,100	1,089	267[1]	Thailand
27[5]	9[5]	6[5]	4[5]	2[5]	7[5]	21[5]	—14[5]—		10[5]	3.4	-4.7	16	—	16	12	19[13]	Togo
...	...	...	...	...	...	...	...	...	...	...	...	...	...	...	...	...	Tokelau
31	1	4	5	1	8	15	7	15	—	...	...	-33[5]	23[5]	-10[5]	6	5	Tonga
2	27	8	11	2	13	12	9	2	17	5.1	0.9	500	-1,287	-787	147[1]	167[5]	Trinidad and Tobago
13	12	12	6	1	5	—27—			12	7.5	3.5	-1,116	382	-734	573	102[1]	Tunisia
20	2	24	4	2	10	16	7	5	8	5.9	4.0	-2,942	1,535	-1,407	408	127	Turkey
...	...	...	...	...	...	...	...	...	...	...	...	...	...	...	...	...	Turks and Caicos Is.
...	...	...	...	...	...	...	...	...	...	...	...	...	...	...	...	...	Tuvalu
68[5]	—	3[5]			1[5]	7[5]	—16[5]—		5[5]	5.6	6.5	-49[5]	57[5]	8[5]	5[5]	20[5]	Uganda
15[2]	3	51[2,3]	10[2]	3	6[2]	18[2]	—4[2,15]—			...	...	...	...	...	...	...	U.S.S.R.
1	49	9	10	2	5	9	10	1	8	...	-3.4[6]	...	...	...	...	...	United Arab Emirates
2	7	21	5	3	6	11	16	5	13	1.9	1.2	-5,677	6,410	733	5,539	6,237	United Kingdom
3	4	21	4	3	6	17	22	9	13	3.0	1.5	-108,270	6,670	-101,600	11,187	13,944	United States
8	1	18	5	2	6	—61—				3.5	-4.2	191	-315	-124	90	304[1]	Uruguay
...	...	...	...	...	...	...	...	...	...	...	...	...	...	...	...	...	Vanuatu
6	19	16	5	2	12	9	17	4	12	5.0	-1.7	7,974	-3,002	4,972	309[1]	2,925[1]	Venezuela
58[2]	3	24[2,3]	3[2]	3	1[2]	2[2]	—2[2,15]—			8.7	...	...	...	...	...	...	Vietnam
...	...	...	...	...	...	...	...	...	...	...	...	...	...	...	315[5]	...	Virgin Islands (U.S.)
...	...	...	...	...	...	...	...	...	...	...	...	...	...	...	...	...	Wallis and Futuna
...	...	...	...	...	...	...	...	...	...	...	...	...	...	...	...	...	West Bank
...	...	...	...	...	...	...	...	...	...	...	...	...	...	...	...	...	Western Sahara
...	...	...	...	...	...	...	...	...	...	3.0	-3.2	-25	26	1	...	...	Western Samoa
10[4]	—	12[4]	8[4]	1[4]	10[4]	13[4]	11[4]	1[4]	23[4]	9.1	...	-728[7]	419[7]	-309[7]	4[5]	10[5]	Yemen (Aden)
28[5]	15	6[5]	9[5]	1[5]	4[5]	17[5]	12[5]	1[5]	15[5]	9.2	5.6[6]	-1,756[7]	1,197[7]	-559[7]	20	72	Yemen (Şan'ā')
15[2]	3	42[2,3]	9[2]	3	8[2]	22[2]	—4[2,15]—			5.8	0.2	-1,231[7]	1,506[7]	275[7]	929	143[5]	Yugoslavia
36	12	2	6	—	2	—21—		—19—		0.1	0.4	752[4]	-422[4]	330[4]	23[5]	...	Zaire
15	6	18	4	2	7	13	11	1	16	0.7	0.5	304	-419	-115	43	43[1]	Zambia
13	5	22	3	2	7	13	6	16	7	1.6	4.5[6]	184	-284	-100	35	35	Zimbabwe

[1] 1982. [2] Net material product. [3] Manufacturing includes mining and public utilities. [4] 1980. [5] 1981. [6] 1980–82. [7] 1983. [8] Net operating surplus includes consumption of fixed capital. [9] 1980–81. [10] Belgium includes Luxembourg. [11] 1978. [12] Manufacturing includes public utilities. [13] 1979. [14] Manufacturing includes mining. [15] Activities in the material sphere not elsewhere specified. [16] Mining includes public utilities. [17] U.S.$. [18] 1970. [19] 1977. [20] National income. [21] Gross material product. [22] 1984. [23] Manufacturing includes mining, construction, and public utilities. [24] 1975. [25] 1973. [26] Mining includes construction. [27] 1972.

Employment and labour

This table provides international comparisons of the world's national labour forces—giving their size, composition by demographic component, and overall growth rates.

The first part of the table focuses on the concept of "economically active population," which the International Labour Organisation (ILO) defines as persons of all ages who are either employed or looking for work. In general, "economically active population" does not include students, persons occupied solely in domestic duties, retired persons, persons living entirely on their own means, and persons wholly dependent on others. Persons engaged in illegal economic activities—smugglers, prostitutes, drug dealers, bootleggers, black marketeers, and others—also fall outside the purview of the ILO definition. Countries differ markedly in their treatment, as part of the labour force, of such groups as members of the armed forces, inmates of institutions, persons seeking their first job, seasonal workers, and persons engaged in part-time economic activities. Some countries include some or all of these groups among the economically active population, while other countries treat them as inactive.

Three principal breakdowns of the economically active total are given: (1) participation rate, or the proportion of the economically active who possess some particular characteristic, is given for women and for those of working age (ages 15 to 64); (2) activity rate, the proportion of the total population who are economically active, is given for both sexes and as a total; and (3) employment status, usually (and here) grouped as employers, self-employed, employees, family workers (usually unpaid), and others.

Each of these measures indicates certain characteristics or tendencies in a given national labour market; none should be interpreted in isolation, however, as each is influenced by a variety of incentives and constraints—demographic structure and change, social or religious customs, educational opportunity, sexual differentiation in employment patterns, degree of technological development, and the like. Participation and activity rates, for example, may be high in a particular country because it possesses an older population with few children, hence a higher proportion of working age, or because, despite a very young population with many below working age, the economy attracts eligible immigrant workers, themselves almost exclusively of working age. At the same time, low activity and participation rates might be characteristic of a country having a young population with poor employment possibilities or of a country with a good job market distorted by the presence of large numbers of "guest" or contract workers who are not part of the domestic labour force. An illiterate woman in a strongly sex-differentiated labour force is likely to begin and end as a family or traditional agricultural worker. Loss of working-age men to war, civil violence, or emigration for job opportunities may also affect the structure of a particular labour market.

The proportional distribution of the economically active population by employment status reveals that a large percentage of economically active persons in some less developed countries falls under the heading "em-

Employment and labour

country	year	economically active population										employed population by economic sector			
		total ('000)	participation rate (%)		activity rate (%)			employment status (%)				agriculture, forestry, fishing		mining, quarrying	
			female	ages 15–64	total	male	female	employers, self-employed	employees	unpaid family workers	other	number ('000)	% of labour force	number ('000)	% of labour force
Afghanistan	1982	3,829	...	43.8	27.9	...	...	...	...	...	...	2,195	60.6	...	...
Albania	1978	584	42.4	41.8	22.8	26.0	19.8	...	...	...	...	128	22.0	...	...
Algeria	1977	3,371	8.9	38.0	20.0	36.8	3.5	16.6	47.4	2.1	33.9	683	20.3	69	2.0
American Samoa	1980	11	...	58.8	32.9	...	...	2.4	97.3	0.2	0.1	0.1	1.4	—	—
Andorra	1982	...	...	...	...	...	...	...	...	...	...	0.1	0.5	0.4	2.2
Angola	1982	...	...	...	26.1	...	...	...	...	...	...	...	...	...	...
Anguilla	1974	1.2	...	42.1	18.1	...	...	...	...	...	...	0.1	8.5	...	...
Antigua and Barbuda	1980	28	39.2	56.0	37.7	47.8	28.5	12.3[1]	69.9[1]	0.6[1]	17.2[1]	2[2]	9.5[2]	0.1[2]	0.3[2]
Argentina	1983	10,815	26.4	59.1	38.3	56.6	20.1	25.2[3]	71.5[3]	—[3]	3.3[3]	1,200	12.0[3]	473[3]	0.5[3]
Australia	1984	7,128	38.0	75.1	45.9[4]	57.4[4]	34.5[4]	13.6	77.1	0.4	8.9	418	5.9	103	1.5
Austria	1983	3,294	38.7	65.2	43.6	56.3	32.2	11.2	84.6	4.2	...	316	9.6	16	0.5
Bahamas, The	1979	77	45.8	...	36.8	41.0	32.8	13.0[5]	86.7[5]	0.3[5]	...	4	5.2	0.7	0.9
Bahrain	1982	142[5]	11.4[5]	61.7[5]	40.6[5]	61.6[5]	11.1[5]	9.8[4]	88.7[4]	0.1[4]	1.4[4]	4	2.6	0.8	0.6
Bangladesh	1981	30,856	17.2	41.1	35.4	56.9	12.6	45.6	28.9	22.9	2.6	23,789	77.1	3	—
Barbados	1983	113	45.8	73.7	45.6	52.2	39.7	8.8[6]	76.4[6]	0.2[6]	14.6[6]	8	7.7	15[7]	14.2[7]
Belgium	1982	4,313	39.4	...	43.8	54.3	33.7	11.3	73.9	...	11.7	107	2.6	28	0.7
Belize	1970	33	18.7	58.6	27.6	44.8	10.3	25.1	66.3	3.6	5.0	11.1	34.0	—	0.1
Benin	1979	1,114	36.4	58.9	33.4	44.3	23.3	...	...	...	...	5	0.4	0.4	—
Bermuda	1982	31	45.2	85.1	58.2	65.4	51.3	7.7[3]	88.6[3]	0.5[3]	3.2[3]	0.2	0.7	0.1	0.3
Bhutan	1982	...	...	...	...	...	...	...	...	...	...	613	94.3	...	...
Bolivia	1982	1,872	23.2	53.3	31.6	49.2	14.5	48.9[9]	38.2[9]	9.1[9]	3.8[9]	793	46.4	76	4.5
Botswana	1981	315	40.3	63.1	33.5	42.5	25.5	3.0	39.1	45.6	12.3	10	7.3	11	8.4
Brazil	1980	43,797	27.5	57.9	36.8	53.7	20.1	27.0	65.3	5.2	2.5	13.109	30.6	7,524[10]	17.5[10]
British Virgin Islands	1980	5	38.5	72.8	45.4	54.6	35.8	18.5	79.7	0.8	1.0	0.2	5.3	—	—
Brunei	1982	71[4]	23.8[5]	61.1[4]	36.7[4]	52.3[4]	18.7[4]	7.4[4]	88.4[4]	0.6[4]	3.6[4]	3	5.0	4	5.7
Bulgaria	1982	4,448[5]	46.8[5]	75.3[5]	51.0[5]	54.3[5]	47.6[5]	...	...	...	...	929	22.8	...	...
Burkina Faso	1975	1,408	3.4	...	25.0	48.1	1.7	...	...	...	...	...	...	...	...
Burma	1982	14,462	...	...	...	...	...	...	...	...	...	9,205	66.8	71	0.5
Burundi	1982	2,368[2]	53.1[2]	94.4[2]	58.8[2]	57.0[2]	60.4[2]	35.7[2]	5.6[2]	58.5[2]	0.2[2]	17	40.7	0.8	1.9
Cameroon	1982	3,543	37.5	65.6	39.9	50.0	29.8	60.2	14.6	18.0	7.1	2,595	76.7	2	0.1
Canada	1984	12,678	41.9	79.1	49.5[4]	59.3[4]	39.9[4]	8.6	89.5	1.0	0.9	644	5.7	183	1.6
Cape Verde	1982	107	...	...	35.0	...	...	...	...	...	...	...	...	...	...
Cayman Islands	1979	8	42.0	...	48.7	58.1	39.8	10.6	80.7	—	8.7	0.1	1.7	—	—
Central African Republic	1975	649	46.7	54.0	31.6	35.2	28.3	...	...	...	...	543	83.7	7	1.0
Chad	1976	13[12]	...	...	33.5	54.3	14.7	...	...	...	...	0.9[12]	7.3[12]	0.3[12]	2.3[12]
Chile	1982	3,661	29.9	51.5	32.1	46.0	18.8	22.1	48.4	9.9	19.6	527	15.0	65	1.9
China	1982	447,060	...	...	44.0	...	...	0.3	25.2	——74.4——		320,130	71.6	[13]	[13]
Christmas Island	1981	1.6	9.8	76.4	56.3	76.0	16.6	...	...	...	...	...	0.1	1.1	68.2
Cocos (Keeling) Islands	1981	0.3	29.6	69.4	50.5	63.8	31.1	...	...	...	...	0.1	21.8	—	—
Colombia	1980	8,467	26.2	48.7	31.6	50.0	15.5	...	...	...	...	1,880[14]	34.3[14]	43[14]	0.8[14]
Comoros	1976	...	...	...	...	...	...	...	...	...	...	3[12]	35.6[12]	...	...
Congo	1982	550	...	...	...	...	...	...	...	...	...	...	...	...	...
Cook Islands	1981	6	30.3	63.1	33.7	45.6	21.1	11.0	65.7	3.7	19.6	2	29.2	—	0.3
Costa Rica	1983	844	25.5	55.6	35.5	53.1	18.0	19.6	73.9	4.5	2.0	234	28.3	138[7]	16.7[7]
Cuba	1981	3,618	31.4	58.5	30.7[1]	49.0[1]	11.5[1]	9.9[1]	88.2[1]	1.3[1]	0.6[1]	628[17]	24.1[17]	...	...
Cyprus	1983	232	36.5	...	32.7[6]	42.4[6]	22.9[6]	21.1[6]	56.0[6]	10.8[6]	12.1[6]	43	18.8	1.1	0.5
Czechoslovakia	1982	7,849[3]	46.7[3]	78.9[3]	51.4[3]	56.2[3]	46.7[3]	0.1[3]	91.2[3]	8.5[3]	0.2[3]	1,039	14.0	186	2.5
Denmark	1983	2,674	44.4	78.5	52.1	58.7	45.7	10.9	84.7	2.5	2.0	208[2]	7.8[2]	1.7[2]	0.1[2]
Djibouti	1982	...	...	...	...	...	...	...	...	...	...	...	...	0.1	4.9
Dominica	1970	19	37.2	66.2	30.4	40.1	21.8	24.8	73.0	2.2	—	7.7	36.4	—	—
Dominican Republic	1979	1,592	26.0	52.7	30.2	44.7	15.7	29.4[1]	38.2[1]	5.9[1]	26.5[1]	549[1]	44.3[1]	0.8[1]	0.1[1]
Ecuador	1982	2,387	20.8	50.1	29.7	47.0	12.3	...	...	...	...	1,337[4]	47.6[4]	9[4]	0.3[4]
Egypt	1981	11,507	10.6	...	27.8	49.0	5.9	29.0	53.3	12.3	5.4	4,006	40.3	21	0.2
El Salvador	1980	1,593	34.8	62.4	35.4	47.5	24.0	28.2	59.2	10.9	1.7	637	40.6	4	0.3
Equatorial Guinea	1982	112	...	...	...	...	...	...	...	...	...	...	...	...	...

ployers, self-employed." This occurs because the countries involved have poor, largely agrarian economies in which the average worker is a farmer who tills his own small plot of land. In countries with well-developed economies, "employees" will usually constitute the largest portion of the economically active.

Caution should be exercised when using the economically active data to make intercountry comparisons, as countries often differ in their choices of classification schemes, definitions, and coverage of groups and in their methods of collection and tabulation of data. Data on female labour-force activity, in particular, often lacks comparability. In many less developed countries, particularly those dominated by the Islāmic faith, a cultural bias favouring traditional roles for women results in the undercounting of economically active females.

The next major section of the table provides data on the distribution by economic sector of the "employed population," which consists of all persons above a specific age who, during a specified period, were either at work or formally attached to a job. Whenever possible the "employed population" has been taken to be the actively working fraction of the labour force, i.e., excluding those who are unemployed or under- and fractionally (or seasonally) employed. The data usually include such groups as unpaid family workers and members of the armed forces and usually exclude such groups as the unemployed and the severely underemployed. When comparing national labour-force data, careful regard should be given to differences in definition, sources, scope, and coverage from country to country.

The table's categorization of industrial sectors is based largely on the divisions listed in the International Standard Industrial Classification of All Economic Activities. The category "services, other" includes such activities as public administration and defense, educational services, medical and dental services, motion-picture and other entertainment services, domestic services, and activities not adequately defined.

Finally, regarding the section on labour-force growth, it should be recognized that for many economies changes in age and sex structure, in patterns and volume of unemployment and underemployment, in international and internal migration, or in technological development may significantly alter the projections.

A large part of the data presented in this table is summarized from various issues of the ILO's *Yearbook of Labour Statistics*. The ILO compiles its statistics both from official publications and from information submitted directly by national authorities. The editors have supplemented and updated ILO data with statistical information from Britannica's statistical holdings of official publications and from direct correspondence with relevant authorities. The *World Development Report*, published by the World Bank, furnishes the data for the table's last section, "Average Annual Growth of Labour Force."

manufacturing, construction		electricity, gas, water		transportation, communications		trade, hotels, restaurants		finance, real estate		services, other		average annual growth of labour force			country
number ('000)	% of labour force	number ('000)	% of labour force	number ('000)	% of labour force	number ('000)	% of labour force	number ('000)	% of labour force	number ('000)	% of labour force	1960–1970 (%)	1970–1982 (%)	1980–2000 (%)	
516	14.2	46.5	...	66	1.8	126	3.5	...	...	717	19.8	1.9	2.1	2.6	Afghanistan
271	46.5	...	...	33	5.7	39	6.6	...	...	112.7	19.3	2.3	2.7	2.4	Albania
607	18.0	30	0.9	132	3.9	214	6.4	18	0.5	1,618	48.0	0.5	3.5	4.8	Algeria
2.5	31.1	—		0.7	8.7	0.9	11.5	0.1	1.3	3.7	46.0	...	...	...	American Samoa
4.5	26.4	—	—	0.3	1.6	4.3	25.2	1.0	6.1	6.5	37.8	...	...	...	Andorra
												1.6	2.0	2.9	Angola
0.4	35.2	...	...	0.2	13.4	0.1	9.8	—	—	0.4	33.1	...	...	...	Anguilla
4.0[2]	18.2[2]	0.3[2]	1.4[2]	2.6[2]	11.8[2]	4.9[2]	22.1[2]	0.7[2]	3.4[2]	7.3[2]	33.2[2]	...	...	...	Antigua and Barbuda
2,989[3]	30.0[3]	103[3]	1.0[3]	460[3]	4.6[3]	1,702[3]	17.0[3]	395[3]	4.0[3]	3,090[3]	30.9[3]	1.3	1.3	1.3	Argentina
1,716	24.4	152	2.2	525	7.5	1,360	19.4	632	9.0	2,115	30.1	2.6	1.8	1.1	Australia
1,234	37.5	42	1.3	210	6.4	575	17.4	178	5.4	724	21.9	−0.7	0.9	0.3	Austria
8	10.4	1.2	1.6	8	10.4	22	28.6	7	9.1	26	33.8	...	...	...	Bahamas, The
45	32.1	2	1.6	15	10.3	20	14.0	7	5.0	48	33.7	...	...	...	Bahrain
1,472	4.8	11	—	481	1.5	1,159	3.8	84	0.3	3,856	12.5	2.1	2.9	3.0	Bangladesh
9[8]	8.5[8]	2	1.9	6	5.4	25	23.2	4	3.4	39	37.7	...	...	...	Barbados
1,110	26.6	33	0.8	275	6.6	694	16.6	254	6.1	1,115	26.7	0.3	0.7	0.2	Belgium
7.4	22.5	0.3	0.9	1.5	4.4	2.7	8.1	...	...	9.8	29.9	...	...	...	Belize
14	1.2	0.7	0.1	13	1.2	8	0.7	3	0.3	1,071	96.1	2.1	2.1	2.8	Benin
3	9.9	0.4	1.2	2	6.9	11	36.0	4	12.5	10	32.4	...	...	...	Bermuda
6	0.9	...	...	...	...	9	1.4	...	...	22	3.4	0.3	2.1	2.3	Bhutan
212	12.4	7	0.4	95	5.5	129	7.5	13	0.8	383	22.4	1.7	2.3	2.9	Bolivia
21	16.0	2	1.8	3	2.3	12	9.0	1	1.1	72.0	54.1	...	...	...	Botswana
3,151[8]	7.3[8]	10	10	1,816	4.1	4,111	9.6	7,090	16.5	6,113	14.3	2.7	2.3	2.6	Brazil
0.3	6.2	0.6	12.0	0.1	2.8	0.4	8.1	0.3	5.8	1.1	22.7	...	...	...	British Virgin Islands
15	22.6	2	2.9	4	6.6	7	10.8	2	3.0	29	43.4	...	...	...	Brunei
1,755	43.0	...	...	304	7.5	342	8.4	...	...	746	18.3	0.7	0.2	0.2	Bulgaria
...	...	...	...	...	...	...	...	...	...	...	...	1.6	1.6	2.5	Burkina Faso
1,312	9.5	16	0.1	458	3.2	1,310	9.5	818[11]	6.0[11]	600[11]	4.4[11]	1.1	1.5	2.3	Burma
9	20.4	0.5	1.2	1.4	3.4	1.8	4.2	1.4	3.3	10	24.9	0.9	1.6	2.8	Burundi
222	6.6	3	0.1	47	1.4	141	4.2	8	0.2	363	10.7	1.5	2.2	3.2	Cameroon
2,658	23.5	130	1.1	757	6.7	1,942	17.2	1,074	9.5	3,928	34.7	2.5	2.0	1.1	Canada
												...	...	...	Cape Verde
2	23.4	0.1	1.8	0.2	3.1	0.7	9.6	0.5	7.2	4	53.2	...	...	...	Cayman Islands
18	2.8	1	0.2	5	0.8	27	4.1	0.6	0.1	47	7.3	1.1	1.5	2.4	Central African Republic
5[12]	36.1[12]	0.4[12]	3.3[12]	0.6[12]	5.2[12]	2[12]	13.2[12]	0.6[12]	4.8[12]	3[12]	27.8[12]	1.5	1.8	2.6	Chad
680	19.4	28	0.8	225	6.4	592	16.9	133	3.8	1,255	35.8	1.4	2.1	2.1	Chile
72,700[13]	16.3[13]	...	...	8,500	1.9	18,200	4.1	...	...	27,530	6.2	1.7	1.8	1.6	China
0.1	3.4	—	0.6	0.1	4.5	0.1	4.1	...	1.5	0.3	17.1	...	...	...	Christmas Island
0.1	25.7	—	2.1	—	5.3	—	4.6	—	0.2	0.2	40.3	...	...	...	Cocos (Keeling) Islands
981[14]	17.9[14]	25[14]	0.5[14]	213[14]	3.9[14]	652[14]	11.9[14]	105[14]	1.9[14]	1,587[14]	28.9[14]	3.0	3.3	2.4	Colombia
1.3[12]	14.4[12]	...	...	0.5[12]	5.6[12]	1[12, 15]	11.1[12, 15]	15	15	3[12]	33.3[12]	...	...	...	Comoros
												1.8	2.2	3.9	Congo
0.7	12.1	0.1	2.4	0.7	12.3	0.5	9.2	0.1	2.3	2	31.4	...	...	...	Cook Islands
46[8]	5.5[8]	...	...	47[16]	5.6[16]	148	17.9	15	15	215	26.0	3.3	3.8	2.8	Costa Rica
860[17]	33.0[17]	...	...	176[17]	6.8[17]	281[17]	10.8[17]	...	...	663[17]	25.4[17]	0.8	1.8	1.8	Cuba
62	27.0	1.4	0.6	11	4.6	38	16.7	8	3.6	65	28.2	...	...	...	Cyprus
3,185	42.8	66	0.9	500	6.8	814	10.9	266	3.6	1,385	18.6	0.8	0.7	0.6	Czechoslovakia
736[2]	27.6[2]	18[2]	0.7[2]	175[2]	6.6[2]	334[2]	12.5[2]	177[2]	6.6[2]	852[2]	32.0[2]	1.1	0.6	0.4	Denmark
0.5	28.3	—	2.9	—	4.2	0.2	12.3	0.5	28.4	0.3	19.0	...	...	...	Djibouti
3.4	16.2	0.2	0.9	0.7	3.3	2.7	12.9	...	...	6.4	30.3	...	...	...	Dominica
129[1]	10.4[1]	1.7[1]	0.1[1]	43[1]	3.5[1]	77[1]	6.2[1]	20[1]	1.6[1]	419[1]	33.8[1]	2.2	3.6	3.0	Dominican Republic
431[4]	15.3[4]	15[4]	0.6[4]	68[4]	2.4[4]	297[4]	10.7[4]	32[4]	1.1[4]	567[4]	20.2[4]	2.7	2.8	3.4	Ecuador
2,092	21.0	70	0.7	552	5.6	848	8.5	131	1.3	2,224	22.4	2.2	2.5	2.4	Egypt
328	21.0	10	0.6	66	4.2	256	16.3	16	1.0	250	16.0	3.0	2.8	3.5	El Salvador
...	...									...	...				Equatorial Guinea

Employment and labour (continued)

country	year	economically active population										employed population by economic sector			
		total ('000)	participation rate (%)		activity rate (%)			employment status (%)				agriculture, forestry, fishing		mining, quarrying	
			female	ages 15–64	total	male	female	employers, self-employed	employees	unpaid family workers	other	number ('000)	% of labour force	number ('000)	% of labour force
Ethiopia	1980	14,006	38.8	75.5	45.1	54.6	35.3	...	...	...	...	...	...	...	...
Faeroe Islands	1977	18	27.2	...	41.9	58.2	23.9	11.1	86.3	...	2.6	3	18.8	0.1	0.6
Falkland Islands		...	...	...	...	...	...	...	...	...	...	...	...	...	...
Fiji	1983	163	16.8[9]	...	29.9[9]	49.3[9]	10.1[9]	33.4[9]	51.5[9]	7.8[9]	7.3[9]	85	52.1	1	0.7
Finland	1982	2,463	47.1	74.6	51.0	55.8	46.5	9.6[3]	83.6[3]	4.7[3]	2.1[3]	254	10.5	10	0.4
France	1983	23,777	40.6	65.8	43.7	53.3	34.5	15.0	76.9	...	8.1	1,758[6]	7.7[6]	137[6]	0.6[6]
French Guiana	1982	32	35.8	...	44.3	54.1	33.5	22.8[18]	70.2[18]	2.5[18]	4.4[18]	0.6[2]	4.2[2]	0.1[2]	0.8[2]
French Polynesia	1977	43	28.6	...	31.3	42.6	18.9	19.7	76.3	3.4	0.6	7	16.4	0.1	0.3
Gabon	1977	...	...	...	...	...	...	...	...	...	...	19[19]	13.6[19]	7[19]	4.8[19]
Gambia, The	1979	...	...	...	...	...	...	...	...	...	...	2	6.8	...	...
Gaza Strip	1981	82.5	34.0	32.5	33.4	...	...	...	...	...	...	...	...	...	...
Germany, East	1982	8,214	46.3	81.3	48.1	56.1	41.3	...	...	...	...	339	4.3	...	...
Germany, West	1983	28,542	38.9	66.2	46.5	59.4	34.6	8.6	88.2	3.2	—	1,493	5.6	309	1.2
Ghana	1979	3,332[1]	44.2[1]	...	38.3[1]	42.4[1]	34.1[1]	...	...	...	...	74	15.3	24	4.9
Gibraltar	1982	13[4]	27.9[4]	67.4[4]	46.2[4]	66.2[4]	26.0[4]	5.9[4]	93.8[4]	...	0.3[4]	—	—	—	—
Greece	1982	3,706	31.5	55.5	37.9	52.8	23.4	36.8	46.2	11.2	5.8	1,008	28.9	17	0.5
Greenland	1976	21	33.4	...	43.1	53.0	31.4	12.6	82.5	0.4	4.5	3	15.1	0.3	1.5
Grenada	1970	26	37.9	58.6	30.9	40.8	22.8	17.0	80.8	2.2	—	8.6	30.1	—	—
Guadeloupe	1982	124	42.5	63.7	37.9	44.5	31.6	...	...	...	...	13	14.1	7[7]	7.2[7]
Guam	1981	34[21]	38.4[21]	...	60.1[21]	75.5[21]	45.3[21]	...	...	...	...	0.1	0.3	...	...
Guatemala	1981	1,684	14.6	48.8	27.8	47.7	8.1	42.5	47.2	6.8	3.5	909	53.9	2	0.1
Guernsey	1976	26	36.8	47.1	47.1	29.8	17.4	17.9	82.1	—	—	5	17.7	0.2	0.8
Guinea		...	...	...	...	...	...	...	...	...	...	...	...	...	...
Guinea-Bissau	1979	213	3.6	42.0	38.7	78.4	2.6	...	...	...	...	153	71.9	0.1	...
Guyana	1980	239	24.7	57.3	31.5	47.9	15.5	19.8[1]	77.6[1]	2.1[1]	0.5[1]	49	25.0	9	4.8
Haiti	1982	2,130	41.0	66.2	42.1	51.3	33.5	59.4	16.6	10.4	13.6	1,223	65.4	19	1.0
Honduras	1983	1,211	16.5	53.5	29.6	49.3	9.8	...	...	...	...	699	57.7	4	0.3
Hong Kong	1983	2,568	36.3	70.2	49.6	61.6	37.0	9.6	84.5	1.8	4.1	30	1.2	2	0.1
Hungary	1982	5,069[3]	43.4[3]	72.5[3]	47.3[3]	55.3[3]	39.9[3]	2.0[3]	83.8[3]	2.0[3]	12.3[3]	1,144	22.9	...	...
Iceland	1982	124[22]	42.0[22]	79.1[22]	52.6[22]	60.6[22]	44.5[22]	...	...	...	...	14	12.4	0.1	0.1
India	1981	244,605	25.0	36.8	36.8	52.7	19.8	10.0[23]	17.1[23]	3.3[23]	69.6[23]	153,015	62.6	1,264	0.5
Indonesia	1980	52,153	33.0	59.2	35.5	47.9	23.3	39.4[22]	37.3[22]	20.8[22]	2.5[22]	28,834	56.2	387	0.8
Iran	1976	9,796	14.8	50.2	29.1	48.1	8.9	30.5	48.4	10.4	10.6	3,615	38.1	90	0.9
Iraq	1977	3,134	17.4	26.0	26.1	41.9	9.4	...	...	...	...	944	30.1	37	1.2
Ireland	1983	1,309	29.7	58.4	37.3	52.2	22.3	18.3	73.4	3.0	5.3	190	16.4	11	0.9
Isle of Man	1981	26	38.2	67.7	42.6	55.1	31.2	14.0	79.8	—	6.2	1	6.0	—	—
Israel	1983	1,403	37.3	54.8	34.2	42.9	25.4	19.0	75.1	1.4	4.5	75	5.4	31.0[7]	23[7]
Italy	1983	22,982	34.4	58.4	40.6	54.6	27.3	...	...	...	...	2,545[6]	11.3[6]	218[6]	1.0[6]
Ivory Coast	1975	2,832	32.6	...	42.2	54.9	28.5	...	...	...	...	72	21.7	1.7	0.5
Jamaica	1982	1,048	46.5	80.1	46.8	50.3	43.3	31.2[1]	67.1[1]	1.7[1]	—	261	34.5	7	1.0
Japan	1983	58,890	39.5	69.3	49.4	60.7	38.3	15.9	71.5	9.7	2.9	5,480[6]	9.5[6]	100[6]	0.2[6]
Jersey	1981	37	40.7	...	51.2	30.4	20.8	13.4	86.6	...	...	2	5.9	0.2	0.6
Jordan	1979	446	7.5	21.9	21.3	38.0	3.3	22.8	67.2	0.8	9.2	46	11.3	6	1.5
Kampuchea	1962	2,500	42.0	74.4	43.6	50.6	36.7	36.4	12.2	50.0	1.4	2,008	80.2	2	0.1
Kenya	1982	...	...	...	...	...	...	...	...	...	...	224	21.6	3	0.3
Kiribati	1978[25]	8	19.2	23.4	13.5	21.7	5.2	3.1	86.3	...	10.6	0.5	9.2	0.3	5.8
Korea, North		...	...	...	...	...	...	...	...	...	...	...	...	...	...
Korea, South	1983	15,128	38.5	58.0	37.9	46.1	29.5	32.3	47.5	16.1	4.1	4,623[6]	30.7[6]	111[6]	0.7[6]
Kuwait	1980	492	12.8	61.5	36.2	55.1	10.9	10.0	88.4	0.1	1.5	9	1.9	7	1.4
Laos	1975	1,726	...	...	52.5	...	...	...	...	...	...	1,351	78.3	...	...
Lebanon	1975	748	18.4	...	26.1	42.2	9.7	...	...	...	...	127	17.0	1	0.1
Lesotho	1976	424	32.3	56.1	34.8	48.9	21.7	7.5	50.0	36.8	5.7	99	23.3	129	30.5
Liberia	1979	433[18]	26.8[18]	47.4[18]	28.8[18]	41.7[18]	15.6[18]	...	...	...	5.4[18]	33	26.4	10	8.2
Libya	1980	814	7.3	50.9	24.1[14]	42.3[14]	3.5[14]	23.7[14]	69.6[14]	4.2[14]	2.6[14]	153	18.8	22	2.6
Liechtenstein	1980	13	35.5	73.8	51.6	66.9	36.4	9.0	87.2	3.8	...	525	4.1	44	0.3
Luxembourg	1981	154	33.3	61.3	42.2	57.7	27.4	13.9[1]	82.1[1]	3.2[1]	0.8[1]	7	5.0	0.5	0.3
Macau		...	...	...	...	...	...	...	...	...	...	...	...	...	...
Madagascar	1982	...	...	...	...	...	...	...	...	...	...	...	...	...	...
Malawi	1981	2,288[17]	46.2[17]	71.5[17]	41.3[17]	46.1[17]	36.8[17]	79.9[17]	17.8[17]	0.3[17]	2.0[17]	153	47.5	0.6	0.2
Malaysia[26]	1979	4,375	36.0	66.4	38.4	48.7	27.9	23.1	58.9	12.3	5.7	1,505	34.4	45	1.0
Maldives	1977	67	37.2	78.6	47.3	56.5	37.1	...	...	...	...	...	...	...	...
Mali	1976	2,266	17.0	52.3	35.4	60.2	11.8	45.8	4.1	42.5	7.5	1,862	84.9	8	0.4
Malta	1983	121	24.5	...	36.7	57.1	17.5	14.1	77.4	...	8.5	7[4]	5.7[4]	1.3[4]	1.1[4]
Martinique	1982	131	44.7	62.6	39.9	45.6	34.5	...	...	...	...	10	10.7	—	—
Mauritania	1982	524	...	...	...	...	...	...	...	...	...	...	...	...	...
Mauritius	1982	261	19.8	54.1	31.6	50.5	12.5	10.3	73.7	0.9	15.1	57	29.3	0.2	—
Mayotte	1978	15.1	34.3	63.3	32.1	42.0	22.1	51.0	27.9	21.0	—	9.3	65.4	—	0.1
Mexico	1980	23,988	...	60.2	35.6	...	...	...	...	...	...	7,886[2]	40.1[2]	289[2]	1.5[2]
Monaco	1975	...	...	...	...	...	...	...	...	...	...	—	—	—	0.1
Mongolia	1980	...	...	...	...	...	...	...	...	...	...	38	11.9	...	...
Montserrat	1982	3.8[1]	34.9[1]	56.1[1]	32.8[1]	45.5[1]	21.6[1]	20.4[1]	78.0[1]	1.6[1]	—	0.5	10.0	...	0.2
Morocco	1978	5,034	15.9	48.1	26.3[23]	44.5[23]	8.0[23]	28.9	66.5	4.5	0.1	1,988[23]	50.0[23]	45[23]	1.1[23]
Mozambique	1980	5,671	52.4	...	35.8[1]	53.4[1]	18.7[1]	44.4[1]	40.0[1]	14.5[1]	1.1[1]	4,755	85.3	347[7]	6.2[7]
Nauru	1977	2.2	...	...	30.5	...	...	...	...	...	...	...	...	...	...
Nepal	1981	6,851	34.6	67.5	42.0[9]	59.0[9]	24.7[9]	70.2[9]	12.3[9]	17.5[9]	...	6,244	90.9	0.5	...
Netherlands, The	1983	5,814	34.0	59.9	39.9[6]	53.6[6]	26.4[6]	9.6[4]	80.7[4]	2.0[4]	7.7[4]	248[6]	5.0[6]	8[6]	0.2[6]
Netherlands Antilles	1982	96	39.6	57.4	37.7	47.1	28.9	...	...	...	...	0.3	0.4	0.2	0.2
New Caledonia	1976	50	34.0	63.6	37.9	48.0	26.9	20.5	58.8	12.8	8.0	14	26.8	2	4.2
New Zealand	1981	1,332	34.2	65.4	42.0	55.5	28.5	12.9	81.7	0.5	4.9	142	10.8	5	0.4
Nicaragua	1980	864	21.2	...	32.0	51.4	13.3	...	...	...	...	4	2.7	2	1.6
Niger	1981	...	...	...	...	...	...	...	...	...	...	3	7.3	5	14.7
Nigeria	1982	...	...	...	...	...	...	...	...	...	...	...	...	...	...
Niue	1976	0.8	29.9	44.5	23.5	33.1	13.9	5.6	89.0	0.2	5.1	0.1	9.9	—	—
Norfolk Island	1981	1.0	43.3	80.8	46.1	53.3	39.2	...	...	...	...	—	3.0	—	0.3
Norway	1983	2,023	42.8	75.2	49.9[3]	69.1[3]	40.9[3]	9.7	84.2	2.3	3.8	146	7.5	19	1.0

manufacturing, construction		electricity, gas, water		transportation, communications		trade, hotels, restaurants		finance, real estate		services, other		average annual growth of labour force			country
number ('000)	% of labour force	number ('000)	% of labour force	number ('000)	% of labour force	number ('000)	% of labour force	number ('000)	% of labour force	number ('000)	% of labour force	1960–1970 (%)	1970–1982 (%)	1980–2000 (%)	
...	...	...	...	...	...	...	...	...	...	...	...	2.0	1.7	3.0	Ethiopia
6	31.7	0.1	0.8	1.9	11.0	2	11.9	0.3	1.9	4	23.3	...	...	...	Faeroe Islands
...	...	...	...	...	...	...	...	...	...	...	...	...	...	...	Falkland Islands
22	13.6	2	1.4	8	4.7	15	9.1	5	3.1	25	15.3	...	...	...	Fiji
723	29.8	26	1.1	169	7.0	316	13.0	139	5.7	643	26.5	0.4	0.9	0.3	Finland
6,911[6]	30.1[6]	194[6]	0.8[6]	1,360[6]	5.9[6]	3,421[6]	14.9[6]	1,567[6]	6.8[6]	5,598[6]	24.4[6]	0.7	1.0	0.6	France
2[2]	13.7[2]	0.3[2]	2.2[2]	0.6[2]	4.3[2]	1.2[2]	7.9[2]	0.9[2]	6.1[2]	8[2]	55.0[2]	...	...	...	French Guiana
8	16.9	0.3	0.7	2	5.6	8[15]	17.6[15]	[15]	[15]	19	42.5	...	...	...	French Polynesia
58[19]	41.7[19]	5[19]	3.4[19]	16[19]	11.4[19]	13[19]	9.1[19]	...	...	22[19]	16.0[19]	...	...	...	Gabon
8	25.5	2	7.6	4	13.8	5	16.1	0.5	1.7	8	28.5	...	...	...	Gambia, The
...	...	...	...	...	...	...	...	...	...	...	...	...	...	...	Gaza Strip
4,094	52.2	...	...	641	8.2	851	10.9	...	...	1,917	24.4	−0.2	0.5	0.3	Germany, East
10,723	40.5	215	0.8	1,451	5.5	3,154	11.9	898[20]	3.4[20]	8,235	31.1	0.2	0.8	0.0	Germany, West
108	22.5	16	3.3	19	3.9	32	6.6	13	2.6	197	40.9	1.6	2.3	3.9	Ghana
5	43.0	0.2	1.6	0.7	6.0	2	18.8	0.5	3.9	3	23.2	...	...	...	Gibraltar
966	27.7	35	1.0	274	7.8	523	15.3	129	3.7	539	15.4	0.0	0.8	0.5	Greece
6	27.2	0.2	1.2	1.8	8.7	3	12.5	0.3	1.6	7	32.2	...	...	...	Greenland
6.3	22.0	0.2	0.8	1.3	5.0	2.5	9.0	...	...	9.5	33.0	...	...	...	Grenada
10[8]	10.8[8]	0.7	0.7	5	5.2	10	10.9	1.5	16.4	32	34.7	...	...	...	Guadeloupe
3	8.8	...	...	3	7.4	6	17.6	1.2	3.3	20	54.0	...	...	...	Guam
264	15.7	8	0.5	43	2.6	147	8.7	21	1.3	290	17.2	2.8	3.2	2.9	Guatemala
4	14.5	0.5	2.0	2	8.5	6	24.6	1	4.2	7	27.7	...	...	...	Guernsey
...	...	...	...	...	...	...	...	...	...	...	...	1.1	1.3	2.3	Guinea
5	2.2	0.1	0.1	2	1.2	5	2.3	0.1	—	47	22.3	...	...	...	Guinea-Bissau
35	17.7	2	1.5	9	4.7	15	7.5	3	1.5	73	37.3	...	...	...	Guyana
143	7.7	2	0.1	16	0.9	286	15.3	4	0.2	176	9.4	0.6	1.3	2.0	Haiti
201	16.6	5	0.4	36	3.0	103	8.5	12	0.9	152	12.6	2.5	3.2	3.5	Honduras
1,151	45.2	14	0.5	203	7.9	545	21.3	137	5.4	469	18.4	3.3	3.5	1.4	Hong Kong
1,980	39.6	...	...	393	7.9	492	9.8	...	...	989	19.8	0.5	0.3	0.1	Hungary
40	35.7	1.2	1.1	8	7.0	12	11.3	4	4.1	32	28.3	...	...	...	Iceland
28,708	11.7	974	0.4	6,069	2.5	12,165	5.0	1,764	0.7	40,645	16.6	1.7	2.1	2.1	India
6,337	12.4	66	0.1	1,468	2.9	6,679	13.0	302	0.6	7,182	14.0	1.7	2.5	1.9	Indonesia
2,884	30.3	61	0.7	433	4.6	672	7.0	101	1.1	1,640	17.3	3.1	2.9	3.8	Iran
606	20.0	23	1.0	178	6.0	224	7.5	31	1.0	1,016	33.2	2.9	3.1	3.9	Iraq
336	28.9	14	1.2	68	5.8	162	13.9	43	3.7	338	29.2	0.0	1.3	1.5	Ireland
6	22.6	0.5	2.0	2	9.1	6	22.1	2	6.1	8	32.1	...	...	...	Isle of Man
91[8]	6.6[8]	13	0.1	89	6.5	175	13.0	129	9.4	487	36.0	3.6	2.4	2.1	Israel
7,379[6]	32.6[6]	...	...	1,144[6]	5.1[6]	4,026[6]	17.8[6]	603[6]	2.7[6]	4,627[6]	20.5[6]	−0.1	0.6	0.3	Italy
101	30.4	13	3.9	39	11.9	27	8.3	7	2.0	70	21.3	3.6	4.1	3.3	Ivory Coast
120	15.9	[24]	[24]	34[24]	4.4[24]	106	14.1	...	...	228	30.2	0.4	2.3	2.8	Jamaica
19,210[6]	33.3[6]	340[6]	0.6[6]	3,490[6]	6.0[6]	12,960[6]	22.4[6]	3,490[6]	6.0[6]	11,320[6]	19.6[6]	1.9	1.3	0.7	Japan
6	17.2	0.6	1.6	3	6.9	6	15.8	3	9.2	16	42.8	...	...	...	Jersey
96	23.7	2	0.6	27	6.6	41	10.2	8	2.0	179	44.1	2.8	2.5	4.4	Jordan
91	3.6	2	0.1	29	1.2	144[15]	5.8[15]	[15]	[15]	224	9.0	2.0	...	...	Kampuchea
207	20.0	14	1.3	53	5.1	75	7.2	44	4.2	419	40.3	2.7	3.3	4.2	Kenya
1.1	20.5	0.2	3.6	0.6	11.8	0.6	11.8	—	0.5	1.9	36.8	...	...	...	Kiribati
...	...	...	...	...	...	...	...	...	...	...	...	2.3	2.9	2.8	Korea, North
3,878[6]	25.7[6]	31[6]	0.2[6]	608[6]	4.0[6]	3,180[6]	21.1[6]	382[6]	2.5[6]	1,611[6]	10.7[6]	3.1	2.6	2.1	Korea, South
138	28.6	8	1.7	30	6.2	58	12.1	13	2.6	220	45.5	7.0	4.8	3.4	Kuwait
...	...	...	...	...	...	...	...	...	...	...	...	1.1	0.8	2.7	Laos
185	24.8	8	1.1	54	7.2	130	17.4	26	3.5	216	28.9	2.1	1.1	2.2	Lebanon
23	5.5	1	0.2	4	1.1	8	2.0	—	0.1	159	37.4	1.6	1.9	2.7	Lesotho
15	12.2	1	0.8	6	4.4	29	22.6	1.7	1.4	30	24.0	2.4	3.0	3.5	Liberia
231	28.4	20	2.4	72	8.9	43	5.3	10	1.2	264	32.4	3.6	3.6	4.4	Libya
6,465	50.1	132	1.0	432	3.3	1,726	13.4	1,647	12.8	1,934	15.0	...	...	...	Liechtenstein
49	32.3	1.1	0.7	11	7.0	23	15.4	12	7.9	47	31.4	...	...	...	Luxembourg
...	...	...	...	...	...	...	...	...	...	...	...	...	...	...	Macau
...	...	...	...	...	...	...	...	...	...	...	...	1.7	2.1	3.0	Madagascar
60	18.7	4	1.3	17	5.4	21	6.6	11	3.3	55	17.1	2.4	2.5	3.2	Malawi
964	22.0	65	1.5	185	4.2	594	13.6	...	...	1,017	23.3	2.7	2.9	3.0	Malaysia[26]
...	...	...	...	...	...	...	...	...	...	...	...	...	...	...	Maldives
26	1.2	1.2	0.1	12	0.5	45	2.0	0.2	—	239	10.9	2.1	2.1	2.9	Mali
43[4]	36.7[4]	1.2[4]	1.0[4]	8[4]	6.8[4]	15[4]	12.6[4]	...	...	42[4]	36.1[4]	...	...	...	Malta
8	8.5	1.0	1.1	5	5.6	10	10.7	4	4.5	54	58.9	...	...	...	Martinique
...	...	...	...	...	...	...	...	...	...	...	...	1.9	2.0	2.4	Mauritania
42	21.5	4	2.3	8	4.0	9	4.6	5	2.4	70	35.8	...	...	...	Mauritius
2.3	15.9	0.1	0.4	0.2	1.4	0.2	1.5	0.2	1.5	1.6	11.5	...	...	...	Mayotte
4,484[2]	22.8[2]	83[2]	0.4[2]	582[2]	2.9[2]	1,975[2]	10.1[2]	...	...	4,353[2]	22.2[2]	2.8	3.2	3.3	Mexico
1	11.8	—	0.8	0.6	6.0	3	26.1	0.9	9.4	4	45.6	...	...	...	Monaco
89	28.2	...	...	34	10.7	34	10.8	...	...	121	38.4	2.1	2.5	3.1	Mongolia
1.2	25.7	0.1	1.9	0.3	5.6	0.6	13.5	0.2	3.6	1.9	39.5	...	...	...	Montserrat
541[23]	13.6[23]	11[23]	0.3[23]	100[23]	2.5[23]	289[23]	7.3[23]	6[23]	0.1[23]	1,001[23]	25.1[23]	1.5	2.8	3.5	Morocco
42[8]	0.8[8]	...	...	77	1.3	112	2.0	...	...	243	4.4	1.8	3.4	3.1	Mozambique
...	...	...	...	...	...	...	...	...	...	...	...	...	...	...	Nauru
35	0.5	3.0	—	7	0.7	109	...	10	0.1	459	6.9	1.3	2.4	2.7	Nepal
1,380[6]	27.7[6]	45[6]	0.9[6]	315[6]	6.3[6]	871[6]	17.5[6]	463[6]	9.3[6]	1,654[6]	33.2[6]	1.6	1.3	0.5	Netherlands, The
15	19.1	1.7	2.1	6	7.3	22	27.1	5	6.1	30	37.7	...	...	...	Netherlands Antilles
10	19.7	0.5	1.1	3	5.2	5	10.6	1.1	2.2	15	30.2	...	...	...	New Caledonia
391	29.8	17	1.3	110	8.4	230	17.5	90	6.9	281	21.4	2.2	1.7	1.0	New Zealand
33	25.0	3	1.9	6	4.6	16	11.9	7	5.2	63	47.1	2.3	3.8	3.9	Nicaragua
15	42.7	2	6.8	2	6.5	3	8.8	3	8.4	1.7	4.8	3.0	3.0	3.4	Niger
...	...	...	...	...	...	...	...	...	...	...	...	1.8	1.8	3.5	Nigeria
0.1	6.9	—	3.3	0.1	13.1	0.1	6.0	—	0.2	0.5	60.5	...	...	...	Niue
0.1	14.8	—	0.7	0.1	7.6	0.3	27.8	—	4.8	0.4	41.1	...	...	...	Norfolk Island
509	26.1	21	1.1	179	9.2	337	17.2	116	5.9	626	32.0	0.5	0.7	0.6	Norway

Employment and labour (continued)

country	year	economically active population										employed population by economic sector			
		total ('000)	participation rate (%)		activity rate (%)			employment status (%)				agriculture, forestry, fishing		mining, quarrying	
			female	ages 15–64	total	male	female	employers, self-employed	employees	unpaid family workers	other	number ('000)	% of labour force	number ('000)	% of labour force
Oman	1982	229	...	...	...	...	...	...	...	...	...	9	3.9	4	1.6
Pacific Is., Trust Territory of the	1970	14	23.6	...	15.9	23.8	7.7	...	...	...	...	...	...	...	...
Pakistan	1984	27,407	12.2	52.4	31.0[21]	52.3[21]	7.9[21]	43.3[21]	25.9[21]	27.3[21]	3.5[21]	13,526[6]	52.4[6]	36[6]	0.1[6]
Panama	1982	548	27.7	52.2[3]	30.5[3]	43.5[3]	17.2[3]	27.0	64.2	5.2	3.6	155	26.8	0.7	0.1
Papua New Guinea	1980[27]	...	...	...	...	...	...	...	...	...	...	5	5.2	3	3.1
Paraguay	1982	1,030	20.3	57.1	33.9	54.0	13.8	41.2	36.7	11.6	10.5	600	44.9	12	0.9
Peru	1982	5,978	28.6	...	31.8	45.4	18.2	49.1	45.1	5.8	...	2,296	38.4	68	1.2
Philippines	1983	20,521	39.4	65.8	36.9[22]	46.3[22]	27.5[22]	36.0	38.3	21.5	4.2	8,702[22]	50.1[22]	67[22]	0.4[22]
Pitcairn Island	1981	.035	...	...	66.0	...	...	...	...	...	...	.003	8.6	—	—
Poland	1982	17,962[22]	45.4[22]	73.7[22]	51.2[22]	57.4[22]	45.4[22]	13.2[22]	74.0[22]	12.1[22]	0.7[22]	5,357	31.4	532	3.1
Portugal	1982	4,358	41.4	68.6	45.6	56.3	35.9	15.6	64.9	12.0	7.4	1,028[4]	23.9[4]	21[4]	0.5[4]
Puerto Rico	1982	935[21]	33.9[21]	47.1[21]	41.6[21]	58.0[21]	26.8[21]	12.3[21]	64.3[21]	1.1[21]	22.4[21]	35	3.8	...	...
Qatar	1976	87	2.2	...	47.2	65.5	3.5	...	...	...	...	...	...	...	...
Réunion	1982	176	35.3	...	33.5	43.8	23.6	10.4	56.3	1.1	32.2	17	14.7	7[7]	6.2[7]
Romania	1982	10,794[17]	45.6[17]	75.6[17]	50.1[17]	55.2[17]	45.1[17]	...	...	...	...	3,025	29.0	...	...
Rwanda	1978	2,661	51.5	94.3	55.1	54.6	55.6	38.8	7.2	53.8	0.2	2,472	92.9	12	0.4
St. Christopher and Nevis	1982	13	38.2	...	29.1	38.3	20.9	12.4[1]	86.6[1]	1.1[1]	—	12	50.7	0.1	0.4
St. Helena and Ascension	1976	2.6	...	...	50.7	...	...	...	...	...	...	0.1	6.3	[28]	[28]
St. Lucia	1980	49	55.2	54.4[1]	41.1	39.0	43.0	27.3[1]	70.8[1]	2.0[1]	—	10.4	35.9	—	0.1
St. Pierre and Miquelon	1982	2	31.8	60.6	39.4	54.5	24.7	12.5	76.8	...	10.7	0.1[18]	5.9[18]	[18]	[18]
St. Vincent and the Grenadines	1970	21	35.2	52.9	27.5	37.6	18.7	16.0	82.5	1.5	—	6.1	25.6	—	0.2
San Marino	1976	9	34.2	67.1	48.6	63.4	34.4	...	...	...	...	0.5	5.9	—	—
São Tomé and Príncipe	1981	31	32.4	58.5	31.7	43.0	20.4	15.9	79.9	0.1	4.1	16	56.2	2[7]	5.5[7]
Saudi Arabia	1983	2,561	...	...	...	...	...	...	...	...	...	395[3]	16.9[3]	62[3]	2.7[3]
Senegal	1983	2,893	41.5	76.6	46.3	54.6	38.1	...	...	...	...	10[17]	9.3[17]	6[17]	5.6[17]
Seychelles	1981	24	37.9	62.3	37.4	49.2	30.1	10.7	76.6	0.3	12.4	5	19.5	...	...
Sierra Leone	1981	...	...	...	...	...	...	...	...	...	...	6	8.3	6	7.9
Singapore	1983	1,208	35.5	67.0	48.3	16.3	34.0	13.5	84.3	2.2	—	12	1.0	2.4	0.2
Solomon Islands	1981	...	...	...	...	...	...	...	...	...	...	7	32.9	—	—
Somalia		...	...	...	...	...	...	...	...	...	...	...	...	...	...
South Africa	1970	7,986	32.7	68.3	37.3	50.9	24.1	...	...	...	...	2,239	28.0	676	8.5
Bophuthatswana	1979	405	...	...	31.5	...	...	0.7	...	...	...	36	8.9	12	33.8
Ciskei	1979	5	...	...	...	...	...	12.1	77.0	10.9	—	...	...	...	...
Transkei	1978	121	...	...	...	...	...	...	...	...	...	5	3.8	4	3.0
Venda	1978	19	...	...	...	...	...	...	...	...	...	0.6	3.2	5	25.5
South West Africa/Namibia	...	...	...	...	...	...	...	...	...	...	...	...	...	...	...
Spain	1983	13,210	30.3	...	35.7	52.0	20.0	18.5	67.6	6.4	7.5	1,985[4]	15.5[4]	91[4]	0.7[4]
Sri Lanka	1981	5,696	27.4	...	37.3	53.1	21.2	23.7	54.4	8.4	13.5	537	49.8	5	0.5
Sudan, The	1977	5,015	20.3	...	29.7[14]	46.7[14]	12.5[14]	59.2[14]	25.3[14]	9.9[14]	5.6[14]	3,435	68.5	185[7]	4.5[7]
Suriname	1980	98	...	38.7	27.5	...	...	...	...	...	...	8	9.1	6	6.7
Swaziland	1981	...	...	...	...	...	...	...	...	...	...	27	33.5	3	3.2
Sweden	1983	4,375	46.6	81.8	52.3[6]	56.9[6]	47.9[6]	7.2	88.9	0.4	3.5	236[6]	5.4[6]	14[6]	0.3[6]
Switzerland	1980	3,092	36.2	70.7	48.6	63.4	34.4	9.6	90.3	...	...	218	7.2	6	0.2
Syria	1983	2,113	12.2	43.3	22.4	38.5	5.6	34.0	56.2	7.4	2.4	606	29.4	278[7]	13.5[7]
Taiwan	1983	8,553[6]	34.5[6]	67.4[6]	46.3[6]	58.3[6]	33.4[6]	22.5[6]	64.2[6]	13.3[6]	...	1,291	18.0	71	1.0
Tanzania	1980	7,845[22]	51.4[22]	83.3[22]	44.8[22]	44.5[22]	45.2[22]	...	...	...	...	135	22.3	6	1.0
Thailand	1980	22,728	47.2	...	48.1	50.4	45.7	31.1	21.6	46.4	0.9	15,943	70.1	37	0.2
Togo	1980	1,019	44.0	69.3	41.1	47.9	34.9	...	...	...	...	...	...	...	...
Tokelau	1972	0.4	15.9	...	22.5	41.0	6.6	...	...	...	...	...	...	...	...
Tonga	1976	21	15.7	43.7	23.8	39.3	7.6	32.7	33.3	13.1	20.9	9.5	51.1	—	—
Trinidad and Tobago	1982	447	31.6	65.2	59.4	81.6	37.4	14.0	82.1	2.8	1.1	35	7.8	77[7]	17.4[7]
Tunisia	1982	1,810[3]	20.1[3]	51.4[3]	28.4[3]	45.1[3]	11.5[3]	24.7[3]	50.1[3]	10.5[3]	14.7[3]	539	30.2	16	0.9
Turkey	1980	19,027	33.7	67.0	42.5	54.7	29.6	23.0	33.5	38.4	5.1	10,483	57.6	179	1.1
Turks and Caicos Islands	1970	1.6	32.9	60.9	28.5	40.3	17.8	...	...	...	...	0.2	14.9	—	2.7
Tuvalu	1979	4.0	51.3	54.6	56.3	58.4	54.5	...	...	...	...	—	4.2	—	0.1
Uganda	1978	372	...	...	...	...	...	...	...	...	...	81	21.8	4	1.0
U.S.S.R.	1978	135,424[2]	49.8[2]	...	51.7[2]	55.7[2]	48.1[2]	...	82.8[5]	...	17.2[5,30]	25,646	20.9	...	...
United Arab Emirates	1980	558	3.4[5]	76.3[5]	53.1[5]	74.2[5]	5.8[6]	9.0[5]	89.3[5]	0.2[5]	1.5[5]	26	4.6	12	2.1
United Kingdom	1983	26,776	39.6	73.5[3]	47.0[3]	58.8[3]	35.9[3]	7.0[3]	85.4[3]	...	7.5[3]	349	1.6	821	3.9
United States	1983	113,226	43.0	71.3[6]	48.5[6]	57.3[6]	40.3[6]	8.3	90.1	0.6	1.2	3,884	3.4	1,103	1.0
Uruguay	1981	...	...	...	...	...	...	...	...	...	...	4	0.7	0.5	...
Vanuatu	1979	51	43.4	88.8	46.0	49.0	42.5	...	...	...	...	39	76.8	0.1	0.1
Venezuela	1983	4,891	27.2	55.7	32.0	46.4	17.4	20.5	68.2	3.2	8.1	628[4]	13.6[4]	61[4]	1.3[4]
Vietnam	1973[31]	7,031	42.6	...	35.3	41.6	29.3	...	...	...	...	...	...	...	...
Virgin Islands (U.S.)	1980	38	45.5	72.8	39.3	44.8	34.4	9.5	90.2	0.3	—	0.5	1.3	—	0.1
Wallis and Futuna	1976	3.3	35.8	65.2	36.5	46.9	26.1	42.2	18.3	39.5	—	2.7	79.2	—	—
West Bank	1981	135.3	42.2	34.2	33.6	...	...	...	...	...	...	...	...	...	...
Western Sahara	...	...	...	...	...	...	...	...	...	...	...	...	...	...	...
Western Samoa	1981	42	15.0	48.6	26.5	43.5	8.3	21.1	43.5	35.0	0.4	25	60.4	—	—
Yemen (Aden)	1973	410	18.5	...	25.8	42.4	9.4	29.8	34.2	15.1	20.9	166	49.1	2	0.6
Yemen (Ṣan'ā')	1975	1,128	11.7	...	24.8	46.0	5.6	45.2	34.0	19.1	1.7	830	73.6	0.6	0.1
Yugoslavia	1982	9,359[4]	38.4[4]	60.6[22]	43.4[4]	54.3[4]	32.9[4]	18.3[4]	70.0[4]	11.2[4]	0.5[4]	302[32]	5.1[32]	134[32]	2.2[32]
Zaire	1970	9,719	42.8	...	...	...	...	...	...	...	...	7,707	79.3	[28]	[28]
Zambia	1981	1,824	28.2	...	31.1	45.2	17.3	...	...	...	...	34	8.7	62	15.7
Zimbabwe	1982	1,033	...	...	...	...	...	...	...	...	...	263	25.5	59	5.7

manufacturing, construction number ('000)	% of labour force	electricity, gas, water number ('000)	% of labour force	transportation, communications number ('000)	% of labour force	trade, hotels, restaurants number ('000)	% of labour force	finance, real estate number ('000)	% of labour force	services, other number ('000)	% of labour force	average annual growth of labour force 1960–1970 (%)	1970–1982 (%)	1980–2000 (%)	country
54	23.7	2	0.9	6	2.6	101	43.9	4	1.6	50	21.8	...	...	...	Oman
...	...	...	...	...	...	...	...	...	...	...	...	...	...	...	Pacific Is., Trust Territory of the
4,997[6]	19.3[6]	190[6]	0.7[6]	1,215[6]	4.7[6]	2,846[6]	11.0[6]	218[6]	0.8[6]	2,663[6]	10.3[6]	1.9	2.7	3.1	Pakistan
84	14.6	6	1.1	29	5.0	71	12.3	20	3.4	162	28.0	3.4	2.4	2.5	Panama
20	19.1	2	2.0	12	11.1	16	15.3	4	3.6	42	40.6	1.7	1.7	2.0	Papua New Guinea
267	20.0	4	0.3	31	2.3	121	9.0	...	...	302	22.6	2.3	2.9	3.0	Paraguay
992	16.6	13	0.2	282	4.7	976	16.3	105	1.8	1,245	20.8	2.1	2.8	2.9	Peru
2,396[22]	13.8[22]	55[22]	0.3[22]	681[22]	3.9[22]	1,745[22]	10.1[22]	308[22]	1.8[22]	2,714[22]	15.6[22]	2.1	2.5	2.7	Philippines
—	—	.002	5.7	.005	14.3	.002	5.7	.016	45.7	.007	20.0	...	...	...	Pitcairn Island
5,559	32.6	148	0.9	1,295	7.6	1,361	8.0	350	2.1	2,440	14.3	1.7	1.4	0.8	Poland
1,407[4]	32.7[4]	22[4]	0.5[4]	152[4]	3.5[4]	489[4]	11.4[4]	90[4]	2.1[4]	733[4]	17.1[4]	0.4	0.6	0.8	Portugal
164	18.0	13	1.4	33	3.6	137	15.0	20	2.2	301	33.0	...	...	...	Puerto Rico
...	...	...	...	...	...	...	...	...	...	...	...	...	...	...	Qatar
11[8]	9.4[8]	0.7	0.6	6	4.9	14	12.1	16	13.8	45	38.3	...	...	...	Réunion
4,616	44.3	...	...	732	7.0	616	5.9	...	...	1,439	13.8	0.9	0.6	0.7	Romania
61	2.3	1	—	7	0.3	26	1.0	1	—	81	3.1	2.2	3.2	3.5	Rwanda
2	10.2	0.2	1.1	0.5	2.1	4	16.4	0.2	0.9	4	17.5	...	...	...	St. Christopher and Nevis
0.3[28]	12.0[28]	28	28	0.1	4.5	0.1	4.1	0.7	29.0	1.0	44.2	...	...	...	St. Helena and Ascension
5.2	17.8	0.5	1.7	1.1	3.7	3.1	10.6	...	...	8.7	30.0	...	...	...	St. Lucia
0.5[18]	24.7[18]	—[18]	0.8[18]	0.2[18]	11.1[18]	0.4[18]	18.8[18]	—[18]	1.2[18]	0.8[18]	37.5[18]	...	...	...	St. Pierre and Miquelon
4.2	17.6	0.2	0.8	0.9	4.0	2.5	10.7	...	...	9.8	41.1	...	...	...	St. Vincent and the Grenadines
4	...	0.0	...	0.1	...	1.3	...	0.1	...	2.7	...	...	...	...	San Marino
2[8]	6.1[8]	0.3	1.0	1	3.5	2	6.9	0.2	0.6	6	20.1	...	...	...	São Tomé and Príncipe
669[3]	28.7[3]	29[3]	1.3[3]	162[3]	7.0[3]	361[3]	15.5[3]	...	...	650[3]	27.9[3]	3.3	4.7	3.7	Saudi Arabia
36[17]	33.2[17]	5[17]	5.0[17]	18[17]	16.7[17]	21[17]	19.4[17]	4[17]	3.3[17]	8[17]	7.5[17]	1.7	2.0	2.7	Senegal
6	23.2	0.2	0.8	2	8.4	4	15.6	0.5	1.8	8	30.5	...	...	...	Seychelles
17	23.3	1.8	2.5	7	9.8	6	8.1	2	2.8	27	37.4	1.0	1.6	2.4	Sierra Leone
409	35.0	8	0.7	132	11.3	266	22.7	95	8.1	245	20.9	2.7	2.6	1.2	Singapore
4	17.2	0.3	1.3	1.4	6.4	2	9.6	0.3	1.5	7	31.1	...	...	...	Solomon Islands
...	...	...	...	...	...	...	...	...	...	...	...	2.1	2.9	2.0	Somalia
1,470	18.4	50	0.6	338	4.2	716	9.0	190	2.4	2,306	28.9	3.0	2.9	3.3	South Africa
...	...	...	...	...	...	...	...	...	...	...	...	...	...	...	Bophuthatswana
...	...	...	...	...	...	...	...	...	...	...	...	...	...	...	Ciskei
19	16.0	...	...	3	2.6	8	6.5	1	0.9	81	67.2	...	...	...	Transkei
4	22.6	...	...	...	...	0.9	5.0	...	...	8	43.7	...	...	...	Venda
...	...	...	...	...	...	...	...	...	...	...	...	...	...	...	South West Africa/Namibia
3,659[4]	28.6[4]	83[4]	0.7[4]	645[4]	5.0[4]	2,175[4]	17.0[4]	407[4]	3.2[4]	1,773[4]	13.8[4]	0.2	1.2	0.8	Spain
278	25.8	5	0.5	92	8.5	98	9.1	37	3.4	26	2.4	2.1	2.1	2.1	Sri Lanka
92[8]	1.8[8]	45	0.9	169	3.4	246	4.9	...	...	842	16.0	2.1	2.8	3.0	Sudan, The
11	13.4	1	1.5	3	3.5	11	13.7	2	2.4	41	49.7	...	...	...	Suriname
21	25.9	1.5	1.8	4	5.5	6	7.4	3	3.1	16	19.5	...	...	...	Swaziland
1,223[6]	28.1[6]	40[6]	0.9[6]	300[6]	6.9[6]	582[6]	13.4[6]	288[6]	6.6[6]	1,536[6]	35.3[6]	1.0	0.3	0.4	Sweden
1,162	38.5	22	0.7	180	6.0	586	19.4	246	8.2	592	19.6	2.0	0.4	0.2	Switzerland
324[8]	15.7[8]	21	1.0	127	6.2	210	10.2	18	0.8	479	23.2	2.1	3.3	4.4	Syria
2,758	38.4	33	0.5	377	5.2	1,236	17.2	164	2.3	1,078	15.0	...	...	...	Taiwan
154	25.4	20	3.2	58	9.6	38	6.3	14	2.3	182	29.9	2.1	2.6	3.4	Tanzania
2,225	9.8	60	0.3	456	2.0	1,916	8.4	...	...	1,887	8.3	2.1	2.8	2.2	Thailand
...	...	...	...	...	...	...	...	...	...	...	...	2.5	1.8	3.2	Togo
...	...	...	...	...	...	...	...	...	...	...	...	...	...	...	Tokelau
1.5	8.3	0.1	0.6	0.8	4.5	0.8	4.4	0.1	0.3	5.7	30.7	...	...	...	Tonga
106[8]	24.0[8]	...	...	30	6.8	93	21.0	...	...	102	22.9	2.5	1.8	2.2	Trinidad and Tobago
561	31.5	10	0.6	65	3.6	155	8.7	11	0.6	346	19.4	0.7	3.1	3.1	Tunisia
2,851	15.7	42	0.2	546	3.0	1,108	6.1	299	1.6	2,679	14.7	1.4	2.0	2.3	Turkey
0.4	23.3	—	1.0	0.1	5.9	0.1	9.1	...	...	0.7	42.7	...	...	...	Turks and Caicos Islands
0.3	31.7	—	1.6	0.1	11.9	0.1	10.9	—	1.2	0.3	38.5	...	...	...	Tuvalu
101[29]	27.1[29]	29	29	10	2.7	18	4.9	...	...	158	42.5	2.6	2.1	3.5	Uganda
47,048	38.4	...	...	11,462	9.4	9,361	7.6	604	0.5	29,033	23.7	0.7	1.2	0.6	U.S.S.R.
190	34.1	11	2.0	42	7.5	74	13.3	15	2.7	97	17.4	...	...	...	United Arab Emirates
5,836	27.5	662	3.1	1,332	6.3	4,208	19.8	1,837	8.7	6,164	29.1	0.6	0.4	0.2	United Kingdom
29,666	26.2	1,531	1.4	5,948	5.2	23,321	20.6	10,366	9.2	37,403	33.0	1.8	1.7	0.9	United States
171	31.4	7	1.3	37	6.7	83	15.2	31	5.8	175	32.1	0.8	0.3	0.9	Uruguay
2	4.1	0.1	0.1	1	2.6	2	4.3	0.3	0.6	6	11.3	...	...	...	Vanuatu
1,086[4]	23.5[4]	51[4]	1.1[4]	316[4]	6.8[4]	829[4]	18.0[4]	197[4]	4.3[4]	1,161[4]	25.2[4]	3.1	4.1	3.3	Venezuela
...	...	...	...	...	...	...	...	...	...	...	...	...	...	2.7	Vietnam
6.8	19.1	0.6	1.8	2.8	7.9	9.0	25.3	1.9	5.3	14.0	39.2	...	...	...	Virgin Islands (U.S.)
0.2	5.5	—	0.1	—	1.2	0.1	1.5	—	—	0.4	12.5	...	...	...	Wallis and Futuna
...	...	...	...	...	...	...	...	...	...	...	...	...	...	...	West Bank
...	...	...	...	...	...	...	...	...	...	...	...	...	...	...	Western Sahara
3	7.3	0.5	1.1	1	3.2	2	4.4	1	3.1	8	20.4	...	...	...	Western Samoa
30	8.8	3	0.9	13	4.0	26	7.5	0.5	0.1	98	29.0	1.7	1.7	3.6	Yemen (Aden)
86	7.7	1.5	0.1	25	2.2	69	6.1	2	0.2	113	10.0	1.6	2.0	3.4	Yemen (Şan'ā')
2,833[32]	47.4[32]	116[32]	1.9[32]	459[32]	7.7[32]	824[32]	13.8[32]	179[32]	3.0[32]	1,133[32]	18.9[32]	0.6	0.6	0.6	Yugoslavia
1,052[28]	10.8[28]	28	28	...	...	...	...	...	...	959	9.9	1.4	2.3	3.2	Zaire
94	24.0	8	2.0	22	5.7	46	11.8	22	5.6	104	26.5	2.1	2.3	3.2	Zambia
220	21.3	...	...	50	4.8	80	7.8	16	1.6	337	32.6	3.1	2.3	4.5	Zimbabwe

[1]1970. [2]1979. [3]1980. [4]1981. [5]1975. [6]1982. [7]Mining, quarrying includes manufacturing. [8]Construction only. [9]1976. [10]Mining, quarrying includes manufacturing and electricity, gas, water. [11]Finance, real estate includes services. [12]Salaried employees only. [13]Manufacturing, construction includes mining, quarrying. [14]1973. [15]Trade includes finance, real estate. [16]Transportation, communication includes finance, real estate. [17]1977. [18]1974. [19]Insured workers only. [20]Finance and insurance only. [21]1983. [22]1978. [23]1971. [24]Transportation, communications includes electricity, gas, water. [25]Active in cash economy only. [26]Peninsula only. [27]Urban areas only. [28]Manufacturing, construction includes mining, quarrying and electricity, gas, water. [29]Manufacturing, construction includes electricity, gas, water. [30]Includes communal workers and their families. [31]Former Republic of South Vietnam only. [32]All persons engaged.

Agriculture and land use

This table provides data on the structure of the agricultural sectors of the various countries of the world from the perspective of farms and farmland use. The data are taken mainly from national agricultural censuses and surveys, supplemented by reports of the United Nations Food and Agriculture Organization's (FAO's) *World Census of Agriculture*. Many of these national censuses, of course, were taken under guidelines established by the FAO for the *World Census of Agriculture* programs (the 1980 census was the fourth, and it included national censuses taken during the decade 1976–85). It represents a cooperative effort by FAO member countries to collect agricultural data within a general framework that permits international harmonization of concepts and definitions; transfer of technical expertise; and increased effectiveness in the collection, analysis, publication, and policy-related use of such statistics. More than 100 countries eventually participated in the 1970 round of censuses.

Although many nations have organized their data along FAO guidelines, differing levels of national economic and technological development, land tenure systems, as well as scope and standards of statistical coverage necessitate care in making country-to-country comparisons. All agricultural statistics, whether or not gathered under FAO guidelines, are subject to quality-control problems. Frequently scope, classificational schemes, and definitions vary from the FAO guidelines from country to country (economic planners need different information about a commercial, high-technology, multicrop agricultural sector than they do for a family-subsistence, low-technology, one-crop sector). In countries that lack sufficient manpower, financing, or transport and communications infrastructure to permit a complete census of agriculture, a sample survey may be taken. This is a limited census of a predetermined number of carefully screened holdings. From these results, nationwide projections may be prepared, but these are often of uncertain reliability. Problems of quality control include errors or biases arising from such factors as incomplete or inaccurate lists of holdings, ambiguous or misleading questions, respondents who inadvertently or willfully do not give accurate information, failure to record data for all parts of scattered or fragmented holdings, respondents' misunderstandings of the definitions of land use and cropping methods, or a failure to report livestock temporarily absent from the holding on public or common pasture land or in transit. While sample surveys can provide a check against such discrepancies, many statistical uncertainties remain.

With respect to the first section of the table, number and size of farms, for example, the Soviet bloc nations, Czechoslovakia excepted, usually publish statistics only on state collective or cooperative farms and exclude privately held plots of land, even though in some instances these provide a significant fraction of agricultural output. Many other countries impose a minimum size limit for holdings that may be covered in their census reports, and this cutoff, if not sufficiently low, can result in a substantial undercount of smaller holdings.

The land tenure statistics show a breakdown of all farms according to the rights under which the farmer holds the land. Owner-operated includes two types of ownership: outright ownership in which the holder has title and has the right to determine use and transfer of the land; and ownerlike possession in which the holder lacks the legal title to the land but uses it under terms of perpetual lease, hereditary tenure, or long-term leases

Agriculture and land use

country	year	number of farms ('000)	size of holding average (ha)	under 1 ha	1–5 ha	5–10 ha	10–20 ha	20–50 ha	50–200 ha	over 200 ha	owner-operated individual/family	corporate/state	socialized/collective	rented (including sharecroppers)	tribal/communal	other
Afghanistan	1981	126[1]	3.5[1]	44.8[1]	35.2[1]	—————20.0[1]—————					55.1[1]	—	—	25.1[1]	—	19.8[1]
Albania	...	...	...	...	...	...	...	...	...	...	...	...	...	...	...	...
Algeria	1973	899	6.2	1.1	12.7	15.8	21.7	25.6	18.0	5.1	...	...	...	...	...	...
American Samoa	1980	1.3	1.8	49.2[6]	46.4[7]	2.9	1.1	——0.4——			95.0	—	—	5.0	—	—
Andorra	...	...	...	...	...	...	...	...	...	...	...	...	...	...	...	...
Angola	1970	1,067	3.9	3.3	13.5	9.3	11.3	13.7	19.2	29.7	80.5	1.1	—	—	18.2	0.2
Anguilla	...	...	...	...	...	...	...	...	...	...	...	...	...	...	...	...
Antigua and Barbuda	1981	2.1	0.8	53.5	——46.5——		...	...	...	...	...	...	...	...	...	...
Argentina	1969	538	347	——18.6——		5.8	11.7	14.4	29.0	20.4	71.9[8]	—	—	12.7[8]	—	15.4[8]
Australia	1981	345	1,436	0.7[9]	7.2[9]	5.2[9]	6.3[9]	11.9[9]	26.2[9]	42.6[9]	95.7[9]	3.7[9]	—	—	—	0.6[9]
Austria	1980	303	24.2	2.7	31.2	17.4	20.8	21.5	5.7	0.7	59.0	—	—	2.3	—	38.7
Bahamas, The	1978	4.2	8.5	48.9	39.5	6.5	2.8	1.2	——1.2——		99.2	0.6	—	—	—	0.1
Bahrain	1974	0.9	4.3	19.6	54.5	16.4	7.4	1.9	0.2	—	37.9	0.1	—	62.0	—	—
Bangladesh	1980	6,853	1.3	54.1	——45.9——		—	—	—	—	53.2	...	...	0.5	—	46.3
Barbados	1969	0.2	95.8	...	...	...	...	...	...	...	...	...	...	...	...	...
Belgium	1970	184	8.7	29.2	24.0	17.9	18.2	9.3	——1.4——		27.3	—	1.1	71.6	—	—
Belize	1974	8.9	26.7	————69.4————			16.7	8.6	4.4	0.9	43.6	56.4	—	—	—	—
Benin	...	...	...	...	...	...	...	...	...	...	...	...	...	...	...	...
Bermuda	1981	...	...	...	...	...	...	...	...	...	...	...	...	...	...	...
Bhutan	1982	...	1.6	51.3[6]	42.9[13]	——5.8[14]——			...	...	...	...	...	...	...	...
Bolivia	1980	700	25.0[15]	...	...	...	...	...	...	...	80.0[15]	...	...	...	...	20.0
Botswana	1980	80.4	4.3	10.9	59.6	22.7	——6.8——		—	—	...	...	...	...	...	...
Brazil	1980	5,168	71.5	9.2	27.5	13.7	14.9	16.5	12.7	5.3	64.4	—	—	11.7	...	23.9
British Virgin Islands	1980	0.3	...	...	...	...	...	...	...	...	...	...	...	...	...	...
Brunei	1964	6.3	2.6	44.1[6]	40.4[13]	——15.5[14]——			52.3	1.0	—	22.0	—	24.7		
Bulgaria	1973	0.170[16]	25,700[16]	...	...	...	...	...	...	...	...	...	...	...	...	...
Burkina Faso	...	...	...	...	...	...	...	...	...	...	...	...	...	...	...	...
Burma	1981	4,300	2.3[15]	61.0[15,17]	————39.0[18]————						...	...	...	...	...	...
Burundi	1969	...	...	...	...	...	...	...	...	...	...	...	...	...	...	...
Cameroon	1973	926	1.6	42.7	53.8	3.2	0.3	—	—	—	2.4	—	—	5.2	59.5	32.9
Canada	1981	318	207	1.5[6]	——6.8[21]——		5.3	14.0	40.5	31.9	63.3	—	—	6.2	—	30.4
Cape Verde	1979	...	...	...	...	...	...	...	...	...	...	...	...	...	...	...
Cayman Islands	...	...	...	...	...	...	...	...	...	...	...	...	...	...	...	...
Central African Republic	1974	283	1.7	32.2	65.2	2.5	—	—	—	—	0.3[8]	—	—	0.1[8]	98.6[8]	1.2[8]
Chad	1973	366	2.6	19.7	69.5	10.0	——0.8——		...	...	...	...	...	...	...	...
Chile	1976	306	94.1	...	...	...	...	...	...	...	...	...	...	...	...	...
China	1982	54.4[24]	...	...	...	...	...	...	...	...	—	10.0[9]	90.0[9]	—	—	—
Christmas Island	...	...	...	...	...	...	...	...	...	...	...	...	...	...	...	...
Cocos (Keeling) Islands	...	...	...	...	...	...	...	...	...	...	...	...	...	...	...	...
Colombia	1971	1,177	26.3	22.8	——50.2——		——18.5——		6.3	2.2	68.7	—	—	5.8	4.1	21.4
Comoros	1965	25	...	...	...	...	...	...	...	...	...	42.1	—	57.9	...	...
Congo	1973	143	1.4	37.3	62.2	0.5	...	...	...	...	...	...	...	...	...	...
Cook Islands	1975	...	...	...	...	...	...	...	...	...	...	...	...	...	...	...
Costa Rica	1973	82	38.3	23.3	25.5	11.2	10.8	15.2	10.7	3.3	97.9	1.7	—	0.1	—	0.3
Cuba	1970	...	...	...	...	...	...	...	...	...	...	...	...	...	...	...
Cyprus	1977	44.5	4.6	23.4	44.6	21.7	7.3	3.0	—	—	99.3	0.1	—	—	—	0.7
Czechoslovakia	1970	1,472	8.1	91.2	6.5	1.5	——0.3——			0.5	99.4	0.1	—	—	0.6	—
Denmark	1983	99	28.8	——3.5——		17.6	27.3	38.4	——13.3——		...	...	...	...	...	...
Djibouti	...	...	...	...	...	...	...	...	...	...	...	...	...	...	...	...
Dominica	...	...	...	...	...	...	...	...	...	...	...	...	...	...	...	...
Dominican Republic	1971	305	9.0	23.0	54.0	11.1	2.4	7.1	1.9	0.4	54.7	—	—	10.1	20.0	15.1
Ecuador	1974	517	15.4	27.8	38.8	10.6	8.0	8.2	5.6	0.9	70.3	0.3	—	7.7	7.4	14.3
Egypt	1983	...	...	...	...	...	...	...	...	...	...	...	...	...	...	...
El Salvador	1971	271	5.4	48.9	37.9	5.8	3.4	2.6	1.2	0.2	41.5	—	—	28.2	6.3	24.1
Equatorial Guinea	...	...	...	...	...	...	...	...	...	...	...	...	...	...	...	...

of 30 years or more with nominal, or no, rent payment. Farms classed as owner-operated under this definition are divided into individual and family, corporate or state, and socialized or collective proprietorships. Rented includes sharecropping and related arrangements; communal/tribal includes types of customary or traditional arrangements in which title or goods do not change hands.

Statistics on types of farms by commodities produced refer as far as possible to the categories outlined by the FAO. The terms "mainly crops" and "mainly livestock" indicate that more than half of the for-sale production was either crops or livestock, and farms not clearly fitting either category were defined as mixed.

The section on technology provides some principal measures of the extent to which modern technology plays a role in the farm activities of each country (although, of course, irrigation works may employ technology and, indeed, may have been maintained in their present form from ancient times).

The classification of farmland by economic use is also subject to differing interpretations. Some countries classify land under permanent crops (those not needing to be replanted each year) as cropland or arable land; that is, land rotated between different crops. Land under temporary crops includes land requiring replanting after each harvest, but some crops—such as asparagus, strawberries, pineapples, bananas, and sugarcane—have biennial or longer growing cycles and so are sometimes arbitrarily placed under temporary and sometimes under permanent cropland. Permanently cropped land may include trees, such as cocoa, nuts, or coffee, but other trees may be grown to shade these; temporarily cropped land is some-

times simultaneously planted with permanent crops, causing confusion in classification. Many countries do not distinguish consistently between temporary and permanent meadow or pasture (land used permanently for livestock forage), and some include grassland and meadows under cropland. Land left temporarily fallow, land subject to changing use, particularly under the shifting cultivation patterns of tropical countries, may be inconsistently classified. There is also uncertainty in classifying forest and woodlands that may have commercial potential but that are also used for grazing livestock or for recreation.

Much additional information on the problems of collecting and comparing agricultural data may be found in the FAO's *World Census of Agriculture 1970: Analysis and International Comparison of the Results* and *Programme for the 1980 World Census of Agriculture,* and in the United States Department of Agriculture's *Scope and Methods of the Statistical Reporting Service.*

Measurements of area are given in hectares (1 hectare is equal to 2.4711 acres). The following notes further define the column headings:
a. All properties used wholly or partly for agricultural production. A property need not have agricultural land to be considered a farm; piggeries, hatcheries, and poultry batteries are farms because they engage in agricultural production, *i.e.,* raise livestock and produce livestock products.
b. All forms not included in the preceding categories. Includes land operated by schools, religious bodies, squatters, seasonally by nomads, and built-on, waste, and similar types of alienation.
... Not available, or no agricultural census or survey ever taken.
—None, less than half the smallest unit shown, or not applicable.

activity (% of farms)			technology (% of farms using)				farm land use										country
							land in farms		land use (%)								
									cropland				mead-ows and pastures	wood-land and forest	other[b]		
mainly crops	mainly live-stock	mixed/other	tractor	electri-city	irriga-tion works	artificial fertilizer (kg/ha)	total ('000 ha)	% of total land area	perma-nent crops	tempo-rary crops	fallow	total					
...	...	...	...	...	33[2]	2.2	14,003[3]	21.0[3]	1.8	46.3	51.9	19.9	75.4	4.8	—	Afghanistan
			15[4]	...	...	110[5]									...	Albania
5.6	1.0	93.4	4.4	39.7	13.6	26[5]	5,544	2.3	4.1	65.1	30.8	93.9	2.3	3.9		Algeria
			0.5	39.7	...	...	2.4	12.2	...	...	...	79.2	4.2	—	16.7	American Samoa
																Andorra
...	...	...	3[4]	...	89.3	3[5]	4,180	3.4	36.8	63.2	—	1.7	82.0	—	16.2	Angola
																Anguilla
...	...	...	29[4]	...	...	...	1.5	3.4	...	...	...	...	...	...	...	Antigua and Barbuda
...	...	...	5[4]	...	5[2]	3[5]	210,856	75.8	34.5	65.5	—	16.9	43.5	28.2	14.4	Argentina
29.4	70.6	—	74.9[9]	...	0.2	126.2[10]	495,442	64.5	0.4[9]	85.9[9]	13.7[9]	8.8[9]	67.5[9]	—	23.7[9]	Australia
...	...	...	196[4]	...	...	240[5]	7,324	88.5	5.6[3]	94.4[3]	—	21.3	26.6	41.5	10.6	Austria
...	...	...	8[4]	...	...	133[5]	36.2	2.6	21.5	62.9	15.6	25.1	5.0	25.7	44.2	Bahamas, The
...	...	...	...	21.3	50[2]	77.3	3.7	6.0	64.5	35.5	—	43.2	—	—	56.8	Bahrain
91.3[11]	8.7[11]	—	0.5	...	27.7	51.0	8,887	61.7	2.1	96.3	1.5	88.7	—	—11.3—		Bangladesh
...	...	...	17[4]	...	...	182[5]	19.8	45.9	...	...	...	13.7	—86.3—			Barbados
...	...	...	52.7	...	...	515[5, 12]	1,603	52.5	7.4	92.6	—	50.7	45.4	0.9	3.0	Belgium
...	...	...	25[4]	...	4[2]	27[5]	233	10.0	13.1	81.1	5.8	36.5	15.9	36.1	11.6	Belize
					1[2]	2[5]										Benin
...	...	...	...	...	...	...	0.3	6.6	24.2	63.0	12.7	83.8	10.8	5.4	—	Bermuda
						1[5]	150	3.0	...	...	...	...	...	...	...	Bhutan
...	...	...	...	...	4[2]	2[5]	84,060	76.3	19.3	80.7	...	1.4	49.4	49.2	...	Bolivia
...	...	...	2.7[3]	...	...	7.3[3]	343	5.9	—	100.0	...	83.5	...	...	...	Botswana
80.0[3]	16.2[3]	3.8[3]	2.4[3]	4.1[3]	2.1[3]	38[5]	369,588	43.7	21.3	78.7	—	11.6[3]	52.4[3]	19.7[3]	16.4[3]	Brazil
...	...	...	1[4]	...	...	...										British Virgin Islands
...	...	...	3[4]	...	...	...	16.4	2.8	78.0	22.0	—	54.8	0.1	16.4	28.7	Brunei
...	...	...	15[4]	...	28[2]	251[5]	6,071	53.0	...	...	...	70.0	24.0	—	6.0	Bulgaria
						2[5]										Burkina Faso
...	...	...	1[4]	...	10.7	21.1	10,300	15.2	—80.2[19]—		19.8[19]	14.8[19]	...	14.0[19]	71.2[19]	Burma
...	...	...	...	...	...	1[5]	1,026	40.0	...	...	...	35.5	60.0	4.5	...	Burundi
...	...	...	...	...	...	60.0[20]	1,490	3.3	...	...	...	100.0	—	—	—	Cameroon
35.3[3]	61.4[3]	3.3[3]	89.1	...	4.7[3]	42[5]	65,889	7.1	—76.1—		23.9	70.0	—	5.4	24.6	Canada
...	...	...	1[4]	...	5[2]	—	25[22]	6.2[22]	20.8[22]	79.1[22]	...	100.0[22]	...	...	...	Cape Verde
																Cayman Islands
...	...	...	...	...	...	1[5]	491	0.8	11.8	88.2	—	100.0	—	—	...	Central African Republic
...	...	...	...	...	...	1[5]	23,877[23]	45.8[23]	50.0[23]	—50.0[23]—		23.7[23]	76.3[23]	...	...	Chad
...	...	...	6[4]	...	23[2]	20[5]	28,800	39.1	6.1	65.5	28.4	11.5	42.3	20.7	25.4	Chile
...	...	...	8[4]	...	45[2]	147[5]										China
																Christmas Island
																Cocos (Keeling) Islands
...	...	...	5[4]	...	6[2]	50[5]	30,993	27.0	30.8	27.5	41.7	24.7	56.4	—	18.9	Colombia
...	...	...	...	...	...	...	115	50.0	...	...	...	34.8	9.4	10.9	44.9	Comoros
...	...	...	...	...	...	1[5]	197	0.6	49.5	50.5	—	100.0	—	—	—	Congo
...	...	...	...	...	...	...			55.9	—44.1—		100.0	—	—	—	Cook Islands
...	...	...	4.6	...	5[2]	151[5]	3,122	60.0	42.2	57.8	—	15.7	49.9	22.9	11.4	Costa Rica
...	...	...	...	...	...	...	8,100	66.0	...	...	...	...	...	...	...	Cuba
...	...	...	25[4]	...	55.1	37[5]	201	21.7	34.8	44.9	20.3	72.4	1.6	1.9	24.1	Cyprus
34.3	24.4	41.3	1.9	100.0	0.5	333[5]	11,874	92.8	2.1	97.9	—	44.3	14.4	37.3	4.1	Czechoslovakia
...	...	...	98.6	...	15.2	233[5]	2,846	66.1	0.4[3]	99.6[3]	0.1[3]	100.0[3]	—	—	—	Denmark
																Djibouti
...	...	...	5[4]	...	...	182[5]										Dominica
...	...	...	3[4]	...	12[2]	47[5]	2,736	56.5	27.8	54.3	18.0	41.8	45.8	11.6	0.8	Dominican Republic
67.8	12.4	19.8	0.1	...	20.3	26[5]	7,955	29.6	32.8	51.5	15.7	32.8	32.2	29.0	6.0	Ecuador
...	...	...	9[4]	...	100[2]	248[5]	2,731	3.0	3.5	96.5	...	100.0	...	...	...	Egypt
95.3	4.7	—	0.5	...	0.9	122[5]	1,452	69.0	25.1	58.6	16.4	44.9	38.2	11.6	5.3	El Salvador
																Equatorial Guinea

Agriculture and land use (continued)

country	farms (latest census of agriculture)[a]															
	year	number of farms ('000)	size of holding									tenure (% of farms)				
			average (ha)	size class (%)							owner-operated			rented (including share-croppers)	tribal/ communal	other
				under 1 ha	1–5 ha	5–10 ha	10–20 ha	20–50 ha	50–200 ha	over 200 ha	individual/ family	corporate/ state	socialized/ collective			
Ethiopia	1977	4,893	1.4	49.9	46.5	3.4	0.2	—	—	—	94.8	5.2	—	—	—	—
Faeroe Islands	...	...	...	...	...	...	...	...	...	...	...	...	...	...	...	...
Falkland Islands	1982	0,041	32,586[25]	...	...	...	...	...	—	100.0	—	75.0[25]	—	—	—	25.0[25]
Fiji	1969	34	7.3	25.4	33.6	23.9	11.7	—5.5—			...	...	...	...	...	...
Finland	1982	213	58.3	—	30.1	29.7	25.8	12.9	—1.5—		...	...	...	...	...	...
France	1979	1,263	22.1[9]	9.5	18.8	13.2	19.3	27.5	—11.7—		65.2[9]	—	—	33.5[9]	—	1.2[9]
French Guiana	1980	2.2	4.6	50.4	41.2	4.4	0.7	2.2	1.1	—	...	...	...	...	...	...
French Polynesia	...	...	...	...	...	...	...	...	...	...	...	...	...	...	...	...
Gabon	1975	71	1.0	68.0	—32.0—	—	—	—	—		81.8			0.3	5.3	12.5
Gambia, The	...	...	...	...	...	...	...	...	...	...	...	...	...	...	...	...
Gaza Strip	1980	...	...	...	...	...	...	...	...	...	...	...	...	...	...	...
Germany, East	1980	6.6[27]	...	...	...	...	...	...	...		...	7.4	92.6	...	—	...
Germany, West	1976	1,021	15.3[28]	12.9	29.9	17.0	20.2	17.3	2.7	—	39.5	—	—	6.7	—	53.8
Ghana	1970	805	3.2	36.6	48.7	9.0	3.9	1.8	...		...	...	...	...	...	...
Gibraltar	...	...	...	...	...	...	...	...	...	...	...	...	...	...	...	...
Greece	1978	950	3.4	25.4	54.2	14.8	4.5	1.1	0.1		...	...	...	...	...	...
Greenland	...	...	...	...	...	...	...	...	...	...	...	...	...	...	...	...
Grenada	...	...	...	...	...	...	...	...	...	...	...	...	...	...	...	...
Guadeloupe	1981	19	9.0	43.0[29]	51.6[29]	4.1[29]	0.8[29]	0.3[29]	0.2[29]	—[29]	46.6[29]	—	—	19.1[29]	—	34.3[29]
Guam	1978	2	5.8	76.1	19.2	2.4	1.0	0.7	0.6	—	80.5	—	—	5.8	5.8	7.9
Guatemala	1970	41[30]	8.4[30]	45.1	40.4	5.3	2.6	4.0	0.6	2.0	57.9	—	—	11.3	4.9	25.9
Guernsey	1985	0.125	16.0	6.7[27]	24.0[27]	23.1[27]	—46.1[27]—		—	—	32.3	—	—	23.1	—	44.6
Guinea	...	...	...	...	...	...	...	...	...	...	...	...	...	...	...	...
Guinea-Bissau	1961	87	3.0	13.4	73.3	10.0	3.0	0.3			...	...	...	...	...	...
Guyana	1964	...	...	...	...	...	...	...	...	...	...	90.0	...	...		10.0
Haiti	1971	617	1.4	58.7	37.5	—3.8—		—	—	—	...	...	...	...	...	...
Honduras	1974	195	13.5	17.3	46.6	14.5	9.8	7.8	3.3	0.8	99.7	0.1	—	—	0.2	—
Hong Kong	1978	...	...	...	...	...	...	...	...	...	...	...	...	...	...	...
Hungary	1983	1.5	5,602	...	...	...	...	...	...		1.1	26.3	72.6	—	—	—
Iceland	1981	7.0	...	15.7	9.3	11.7	23.7	35.8	—3.7—		...	...	...	...	...	...
India	1971	70,493	2.3	50.6	38.0	7.5	3.0	0.8	—0.1—		91.5	—	—	4.1	—	4.4
Indonesia[31]	1973	14,374	1.0	70.4	27.4	1.6	0.6	—	—		74.8	—	—	3.2	—	22.1
Iran	1973	...	...	...	...	...	...	...	...	...	...	...	...	...	...	...
Iraq	1971	591	9.7	20.2	29.3	21.4	18.5	9.0	1.3	0.3	52.5	—	—	40.9	—	6.6
Ireland	1980	279[3]	25.0	2.7[3]	—37.8[3]—		—52.4[3]—		7.1[3]		...	...	...	...	...	...
Isle of Man	1981	0.8	59.1	3.3	13.1	12.2	11.8	23.8	35.9	—	60.0	...	...	...		40.0
Israel	1971	40	13.4	25.9[31]	62.5[31]	8.1[31]	—3.5[31]—		—	—	77.5	—	1.8	—	—	20.7
Italy	1982	3,283	7.2	18.0[25]	30.2[25]	37.7[25]	3.1[25]	9.2[25]	1.8[25]	—	81.5[3]	—	—	6.7[3]	—	11.8[3]
Ivory Coast	1975	550	5.0	9.5	54.4	24.9	9.4	1.7	0.1	—	...	...	...	...	...	...
Jamaica	1969	193	3.1	48.1	44.4	5.3	1.2	0.5	0.3	0.1	99.5	0.2	—	—	—	0.3
Japan	1983	4,522	1.1	68.5	29.8	—1.7—			—	—	79.4[3]	...	...	...		20.6[3]
Jersey	1983	0.8	8.5	—46.2—		22.1	21.4	10.4	—	—	31.4[32]	—	—	68.6[32]	—	—
Jordan	1975	56	6.8	...	...	...	...	...	...		70.9	0.5	—	19.9	0.1	8.6
Kampuchea	...	...	...	...	...	...	...	...	...	...	...	...	...	...	...	...
Kenya	1975	1,487	4.1	31.8	58.1	9.9	—	—	0.1	0.1	...	...	...	...	...	...
Kiribati	...	...	...	...	...	...	...	...	...	...	...	...	...	...	...	...
Korea, North	...	...	...	...	...	...	...	...	...	...	...	...	...	...	...	...
Korea, South	1983	2,000	0.9	66.2	—33.8—		—	—	—	—	82.5[3]	—	—	17.4[3]	—	0.1[3]
Kuwait	1970	0.4	6.1	48.6	25.4	10.2	8.7	4.0	3.1	—	72.6	0.5	—	26.7	0.2	—
Laos	...	...	...	...	...	...	...	...	...	...	...	...	...	...	...	...
Lebanon	1970	143	4.3	47.7	—44.5—		—6.5—		1.2	0.1	...	...	...	...	...	...
Lesotho	1970	187	2.0	27.0	67.5	—5.5—		—3.7—	—0.5—		...	...	...	...	...	...
Liberia[38]	1971	122	3.0	52.8	31.0	12.0	—3.7—		—0.5—		40.0[8]	—	—	—	43.3[8]	16.7[8]
Libya	1977	170	11.0	5.0[39]	—40.0[39]—		—42.0[39, 40]—		—13.0[39, 41]—		...	...	...	...	...	...
Liechtenstein	1980	0.5	8.0	27.5	30.4	16.2	14.2	10.5	1.2	—	86.2	—	—	13.6	—	0.2
Luxembourg	1983	4.6	29	—24.7—		9.0	13.3	33.0	—20.0—		...	...	...	...	...	...
Macau	...	...	...	...	...	...	...	...	...	...	...	...	...	...	...	...
Madagascar	1971	940	1.0	65.0	35.0	—	—	—	—		...	...	...	...	...	...
Malawi	1981	1,136	1.2	54.9	45.1	—	—	—	—		...	...	...	...	...	...
Malaysia[42]	1980	920[43]	2.2[43, 44]	...	...	...	...	...	...		53.2[3, 43]	18.2[3, 45]	—	19.6[3, 43]	—	9.0[3, 43]
Maldives	...	...	...	...	...	...	...	...	...	...	...	...	...	...	...	...
Mali	1980	481	4.0	19.2	55.2	18.2	—7.5—		—		94.2[8, 47]	1.7[8]	—	—	4.1[8]	—
Malta	1983	4.4[48]	3.0[48]	38.7[48]	53.3[48]	6.9[48]	1.1	—	—		29.6	—	—	70.4	—	—
Martinique	1981	19.6	3.1	67.5	26.4	3.4	—2.1—		—0.6—		...	...	...	...	...	...
Mauritania	...	...	...	...	...	...	...	...	...	...	...	...	...	...	...	...
Mauritius	1980	32.5	1.1	61.3	36.2	1.9	0.3	0.2	—0.1—		95.8	—	—	4.2	—	—
Mayotte	1978	4.8	1.7	...	...	...	...	...	...		...	...	...	...	...	...
Mexico	1970	1,020	137	33.5	26.2	10.0	6.7	9.2	8.1	6.3	97.6[49]	0.2	—	—	2.2[49]	—
Monaco	...	...	...	...	...	...	...	...	...	...	...	...	...	...	...	...
Mongolia	1983	0.3	...	...	...	...	...	...	...		—	19.6[28, 50]	80.4[28, 50]	—	—	—
Montserrat	1972	1.2	1.9	—96.7—		2.1	0.5	0.2	0.4	0.2	14.6[10]	—	—	84.4[10]	—	1.0[10]
Morocco	1978	1,900	3.9	—75.0—		—25.0—		...	...		...	...	...	...	...	...
Mozambique	1973	1,605	3.1	—89.7[51]—		—10.0[32]—		—0.3—			0.2	0.1	—	—	99.7	—
Nauru	...	...	...	...	...	...	...	...	...	...	...	...	...	...	...	...
Nepal	1971	1,721	1.1	77.6	—21.7—		—0.7—				...	...	...	...	...	...
Netherlands, The	1983	139	14.5	10.8	21.3	17.5	24.7	22.6	3.1		44.7[10]	—	—	15.1[10]	—	40.2[10]
Netherlands Antilles	...	...	...	...	...	...	...	...	...	...	...	...	...	...	...	...
New Caledonia[31]	1976	2.3	145	2.3	9.0	11.3	22.6	25.4	17.8	11.7	45.7	...	...	...	...	...
New Zealand	1983	76	281	2.3	9.2	9.5	8.1	15.2	32.7	23.0	86.1	10.5	—	—		3.4
Nicaragua	...	...	...	...	...	...	...	...	...	...	...	...	...	...	...	...
Niger	1972	...	...	...	...	...	...	...	...	...	...	...	...	...	...	...
Nigeria	1971	...	...	92	7.8	0.2	—				...	...	...	...	...	...
Niue	...	...	...	...	...	...	...	...	...	...	...	...	...	...	...	...
Norfolk Island	...	...	...	...	...	...	...	...	...	...	...	...	...	...	...	...
Norway	1983	110	8.6	4.9	37.6	27.4	21.5	7.9	0.6		97.4[8, 10]	1.8[8, 10]	—	—	—	0.8[8, 10]

farm land use

mainly crops	mainly live-stock	mixed/other	tractor	electri-city	irriga-tion works	artificial fertilizer (kg/ha)	total ('000 ha)	% of total land area	perma-nent crops	tempo-rary crops	fallow	total	mead-ows and pastures	wood-land and forest	other[b]	country
...	...	...	...	...	...	3[5]	6,971	6.3	7.4	76.8	15.8	86.9	9.1	—	4.0	Ethiopia
...	...	...	...	...	...	...	...	...	...	...	...	...	...	...	...	Faeroe Islands
...	...	...	...	...	...	...	1,173[25]	96.4[25]	...	...	...	...	...	...	...	Falkland Islands
...	...	...	7[4]	...	...	...	245	13.4	43.8	56.2	—	59.7	15.1	—	25.2	Fiji
...	...	...	92[4]	100.0[3]	3[2]	193[5]	12,395	36.8	0.3[3]	97.6[3]	2.1[3]	19.6	1.1	58.1	21.2	Finland
...	...	...	60.8[9]	...	8.4[9]	298[5]	35,039[9]	64.4[9]	8.5[9]	89.4[9]	2.1[9]	50.2[9]	35.2[9]	8.9[9]	5.8[9]	France
...	...	...	35[4]	...	...	201[5]	10.1	0.1	8.6	41.6	49.9	63.0	35.5	—	1.5	French Guiana
...	...	...	2[4]	...	...	13[5]	...	...	...	...	...	...	...	...	...	French Polynesia
...	...	...	3[4]	...	...	3[5]	73.0	0.3	...	...	...	...	...	...	...	Gabon
...	...	...	...	...	12[2]	5[5]	...	...	...	...	...	...	...	...	...	Gambia, The
...	...	...	...	...	52.8[26]	...	26.0	52.0	74.6	25.4	...	100.0	...	...	...	Gaza Strip
33.1	66.9	—	29[4]	...	3[2]	344[5]	6,280	...	...	...	...	74.1[27]	22.3[27]	...	3.6[27]	Germany, East
...	...	...	94.1[9]	...	4[2]	418[5]	12,200[28]	49.0[28]	61.4[9]	38.6[9]	—	59.8[28]	39.3[28]	—[28]	0.9[28]	Germany, West
...	...	...	1[4]	...	1[2]	11[5]	2,574	10.8	61.4	38.6	—	100.0	...	...	...	Ghana
...	...	...	...	...	...	...	...	...	...	...	...	...	...	...	...	Gibraltar
...	...	...	19.1	...	25[2]	148[5]	3,227	24.5	23.9[9]	63.7[9]	12.1[9]	93.4	5.7	0.3	0.5	Greece
...	...	...	...	...	...	...	...	...	...	...	...	...	...	...	...	Greenland
...	...	...	2[4]	...	...	...	...	...	...	...	...	...	...	...	...	Grenada
...	...	...	3.2	...	5[2]	255	170	95.8	0.8	64.6	34.7	33.8	—	41.1	25.1	Guadeloupe
60.6	18.1	21.3	6.3	88.4	...	...	11.6	20.5	10.0	84.7	5.2	54.5	45.5	—	—	Guam
...	...	...	2[4]	...	4[2]	56[5]	3,400[30]	31.2[30]	26.6[30]	46.7[30]	26.7[30]	43.0[30]	29.0[30]	—	28.0[30]	Guatemala
...	100.0	—	...	...	...	...	2	40.0	—	100.0	...	10.6	89.4	—	—	Guernsey
...	...	...	...	...	1[2]	2[5]	...	...	...	...	...	...	...	...	...	Guinea
...	...	...	...	...	...	5[5]	169	4.7	...	...	...	...	...	...	...	Guinea-Bissau
...	...	...	7[4]	...	25[2]	36[5]	10,652	26.2	...	...	...	8.4	91.6	...	...	Guyana
...	...	...	1[4]	...	8[2]	6[5]	1,579	57.0	...	...	...	54.4	33.3	12.3	—	Haiti
...	...	...	2[4]	...	5[2]	18[5]	2,630	23.5	15.4[10]	34.6[10]	50.0[10]	52.0[10]	48.0[10]	...	—	Honduras
...	...	...	1[4]	...	38[2]	...	11	10.4	...	...	...	63.8	...	...	36.2	Hong Kong
...	...	...	104[4]	...	3[2]	279[5]	8,269	71.0	11.6	88.4	...	64.0	15.5	19.7	0.8	Hungary
...	...	...	1,688[4]	87.0[23]	...	3,764[5]	...	...	...	...	...	...	...	...	...	Iceland
...	...	...	3[4]	...	41.7	34[5]	162,124	49.3	0.6	93.2	6.2	89.5	1.9	2.8	5.8	India
86.8	—	13.2	1[4]	...	28[2]	74[5]	14,168	7.4	21.6	71.1	7.3	89.5	0.6	1.4	8.5	Indonesia[31]
...	...	...	5[4]	...	33[2]	49[5]	20,235	12.3	...	...	...	...	...	...	...	Iran
87.9	11.2	0.8	4[4]	...	32[2]	14[5]	5,732	13.1	3.0	62.4	34.6	87.2	0.7	0.2	11.9	Iraq
...	...	...	147[4]	...	...	609[5]	5,790	84.0	0.5	99.5	...	8.0	60.1	—31.8—		Ireland
...	...	...	...	...	...	...	48	85.0	2.8	97.2	...	14.1	85.8	...	...	Isle of Man
43.1[31]	30.2[31]	26.7[31]	68[4]	...	49[2]	180[5]	540	26.1	20.8	79.2	...	70.4	—	—	29.6	Israel
...	...	...	89[4]	...	23[2]	158[5]	23,579	78.3	26.3[25]	73.7[25]	...	52.4[25]	21.2[25]	17.1[25]	9.3[25]	Italy
...	...	...	1[4]	...	1[2]	13[5]	2,753	8.6	65.9	34.1	...	100.0	...	...	...	Ivory Coast
...	...	...	11[4]	...	12[2]	72[5]	603	54.8	22.2	72.2	5.6	41.3	21.6	13.5	23.6	Jamaica
80.8[14]	—19.2[14]—		54.4[3]	...	2.7[3]	38.7[5]	4,706[28]	12.7[28]	10.3[28]	87.8[28]	1.9[28]	90.4[28]	9.1[28]	0.5[28]	—[28]	Japan
85.1[33]	14.9[33]	...	...	...	...	...	6.7[33]	5.8[33]	—	100.0[33]	...	64.6[33]	34.7[33]	...	0.7[33]	Jersey
58.2[34]	14.9[34]	26.9[34]	3[4]	...	0.8	5[5]	390	4.0	8.8	64.9	26.3	80.6	0.8	0.3	18.3	Jordan
...	...	...	...	...	3[2]	6[5]	...	...	...	...	...	...	...	...	...	Kampuchea
47.0[35]	53.0[35]	—	3[4]	...	0.3	34[5]	6,132	10.8	29.4[35]	56.0[35]	14.6[35]	20.2[35]	70.7[35]	4.7[35]	4.4[35]	Kenya
...	...	...	...	...	...	...	...	...	...	...	...	...	...	...	...	Kiribati
...	...	...	14[4]	...	47[2]	349[5]	...	...	...	...	...	...	...	...	...	Korea, North
94.0[36]	0.4[36]	5.6[36]	0.4	10.3[37]	59.4[3]	351[5]	2,132[3]	21.7[3]	5.0[3]	95.0[3]	—	99.1[3]	0.7[3]	0.2[3]	—	Korea, South
56.3	20.7	23.0	1.6	...	81.3	500[5]	2.7	0.2	7.5	92.5	—	23.6	...	1.4	75.0	Kuwait
...	...	...	1[4]	...	13[2]	5[5]	...	...	...	...	...	...	...	...	...	Laos
77.0[34]	8.1[34]	14.9[34]	9[4]	...	24[2]	101[5]	275[28]	27.0[28]	36.7[28]	39.7[28]	23.6[28]	100.0[28]	—	—	—	Lebanon
5.3[34]	93.3[34]	1.4[34]	0.2	...	...	15[5]	372	12.3	—	89.6	10.4	98.8	—	—	1.2	Lesotho
...	...	...	1[4]	...	1[2]	9[5]	370	3.8	66.2[20]	33.8[20]	—	98.3[20]	—	1.7[20]	—	Liberia[38]
...	...	...	7[4]	...	11[2]	38[5]	8,800[20]	5.1[20]	—33.3[20]—		66.7[20]	20.5[20]	79.5[20]	—	—	Libya
20.9	68.8	10.3	113[4]	...	...	...	3.9	24.3	1.8	—98.2—		26.1	58.3	14.1	1.5	Liechtenstein
...	...	...	...	...	...	...[12]	127	49.3	2.5	86.0	11.5	44.4	55.6	—	—	Luxembourg
...	...	...	...	...	...	...	...	...	...	...	...	...	...	...	...	Macau
...	...	...	1[4]	...	16[2]	2[5]	2,200[19]	3.8[19]	19.0[19]	81.0[19]	—	100.0[19]	...	...	...	Madagascar
22.1	...	77.9	1[4]	...	0.2[26]	15.0	1,332	14.2	0.2	99.8	—	94.8	...	5.2	—	Malawi
...	...	...	2[4,46]	...	9[2,46]	92[5,46]	4,100[32]	31.2[32]	84.8[32]	15.2[32]	...	100.0[32]	...	...	...	Malaysia[42]
...	...	...	...	...	...	...	...	...	...	...	...	...	...	...	...	Maldives
...	...	...	...	...	6[2]	6[5]	41,500	34.0	—	18.0	82.0	28.0	72.0	—	—	Mali
...	...	...	29[4]	...	7[2]	24[5]	10.9	34.1	4.2	85.0	10.8	100.0	—	—	—	Malta
...	...	...	43[4]	...	25[2]	698[5]	75.4	71.1	39.6	60.0	0.4	36.9	33.6	10.0	19.5	Martinique
...	...	...	1[4]	...	4[2]	...	167[19]	0.2[19]	—	—	—	100.0[19]	—	...	...	Mauritania
...	...	...	3[4]	...	15[2]	209[5]	97.8[33]	52.5[33]	3.3[10]	96.7[10]	—	100.0[10]	—	—	—	Mauritius
...	...	...	...	...	...	...	8.0	21.0	...	...	...	...	...	...	...	Mayotte
66.4[34]	25.0[34]	8.6[34]	9.0	...	14.7	67[5]	139,868	72.7	6.3	58.1	35.6	16.5	53.3	14.2	16.0	Mexico
...	...	...	...	...	...	...	...	...	...	...	...	...	...	...	...	Monaco
...	...	...	8[4]	...	3[2]	11[5]	124,977	79.9	—	53.0	47.0	2.0	98.0	—	—	Mongolia
...	...	...	13[4]	...	...	...	5.9	55.1	8.2	44.3	47.5	20.1	39.0	37.6	3.3	Montserrat
...	...	...	3[4]	...	6[2]	24[5]	8,149[20]	18.3[20]	5.9[20]	63.4[20]	30.7[20]	100.0[20]	—	—	—	Morocco
...	...	...	2[4]	...	2[2]	12[5]	13,626	17.8	—44.9—		55.1	55.0	45.0	...	...	Mozambique
...	...	...	...	...	...	...	...	...	...	...	...	...	...	...	...	Nauru
...	...	...	...	...	10[2]	9[5]	1,980	14.1	...	...	...	...	...	...	...	Nepal
33.7	62.4	4.0	212[4]	...	32[2]	773[5]	2,009	59.2	14.0	85.3	0.7	41.2	58.8	—	—	Netherlands, The
...	...	...	15[4]	...	...	...	...	...	...	...	...	...	...	...	...	Netherlands Antilles
...	...	...	105[4]	...	...	555[5]	333	17.8	...	...	...	...	...	...	...	New Caledonia[31]
16.0	72.1	11.9	204[4]	...	7.2[29]	1,015[5]	21,266	79.3	...	...	...	47.7[32]	21.3[32]	4.5[32]	26.5[32]	New Zealand
...	...	...	2[4]	...	6[2]	48[5]	...	...	...	...	...	...	...	...	...	Nicaragua
...	...	...	...	...	1[2]	2[5]	15,000	12.4	—21.4—		78.6	85.2	...	4.0	10.8	Niger
...	...	...	...	...	...	7[5]	34,290	37	—20.0—		80.0	31.4	27.5	41.1	—	Nigeria
...	...	...	1[4]	...	...	...	...	...	...	...	...	...	...	...	...	Niue
...	...	...	...	...	...	...	...	...	...	...	...	...	...	...	...	Norfolk Island
...	...	...	88.3[36]	...	3.9[36]	303[5]	949	2.9	...	...	...	42.5[10]	—57.5[10]—			Norway

Agriculture and land use (continued)

country	year	number of farms ('000)	size of holding average (ha)	size class (%) under 1 ha	1–5 ha	5–10 ha	10–20 ha	20–50 ha	50–200 ha	over 200 ha	tenure (% of farms) owner-operated individual/ family	corporate/ state	socialized/ collective	rented (including share-croppers)	tribal/ communal	other
Oman	1979	65	1.3	...	...	...	...	...	...	...	...	...	...	...	...	...
Pacific Is., Trust Terr. of	1970	4.0	10.3	7.4	53.4	22.4	7.8	5.5	3.6	—	90.8	—	—	1.4	—	7.8
Pakistan	1972	3,762	5.3	13.9	54.2	21.1	7.7	2.0	1.1	—	41.7	—	—	34.5	—	23.8
Panama	1980	153	14.7	41.0	25.0	9.3	9.0	9.0	5.6	1.0	23.2	—	—	2.0	—	74.8[53]
Papua New Guinea	1981	0.9	442			—25.7—			29.6	44.7	26.5[8]	70.6[8]	—	2.9[8]	—	
Paraguay	1961	161	109	7.0	28.0	35.0	16.4	8.5	2.4	2.8	42.5	—	—	12.3	—	45.2
Peru	1972	1,391	16.9	34.7	43.3	11.0	5.7	3.3	1.4	0.6	62.2	—	—	8.6	4.8	24.4
Philippines	1980	3,439	2.6	13.6[9]	71.2[9]	10.4[9]	2.9[9]	1.8[9]	0.2[9]	—	58.0[9]	—	—	26.3[9]	—	15.8[9]
Pitcairn Island	...	...	...	...	...	...	...	...	...	...	...	...	...	...	...	...
Poland	1970	3,399	4.8	19.5	42.3	26.1	11.0	1.1	—	—	79.1	—	—	5.8	—	15.0
Portugal	1968	812	6.1	39.0	39.9	5.9	11.8	2.2	0.9	0.4	64.4	—	—	17.0	—	18.5
Puerto Rico	1978	32	13.4	5.3[6]	28.0[7]	20.4	20.3	12.8	10.8	2.5	83.0	—	—	5.0	—	11.9
Qatar	1983	0.8	42.5		—79.1[28, 54]—			—20.9[28, 55]—			...	...	...	...	...	...
Réunion	1973	39	2.0	73.9	22.6	2.5	—0.8—		—0.2—		46.1	—	—	22.5	—	31.4
Romania	1982	5.0[24]	2,814[24]	...	...	...	...	...	...	...	9.4[8]	30.0[8]	60.6[8]	—	—	—
Rwanda	1979	104	9.5	...	...	...	...	...	...	...	...	...	...	...	...	...
St. Christopher	1981	...	...	...	...	...	...	...	...	...	46.8[8]	48.0[8]	—	5.2[8]	—	—
St. Helena	1983	...	...	...	...	...	...	...	...	...	—	—	—	100.0	—	—
St. Lucia	1974	11	2.7	47.8[56]	44.9[57]	4.3[58]	1.8	0.5[59]	0.2[60]	0.8[61]	69.1	—	—	18.3	—	12.6
St. Pierre and Miquelon	...	...	...	...	...	...	...	...	...	...	...	...	...	...	...	...
St. Vincent	1983	...	...	...	...	...	...	...	...	...	...	...	...	...	...	...
San Marino	1975	0.7	7.0	21.3	47.8	—24.7—		5.1	—1.1—		39.9[8]	15.5[8]	—	29.9[8]	—	14.7[8]
São Tomé and Príncipe	1964	11.1	8.7	88.5	9.8	0.7	0.2	0.2	0.2	0.4	77.2	—	—	20.5	—	2.3
Saudi Arabia	1974	181	6.7	38.4	39.4	9.8	6.8	3.6	—2.0—		92.3	—	—	4.2	0.1	3.4
Senegal	1976	362	7.0		—99.4—				—0.6—		...	...	0.6	...	...	99.4
Seychelles	1977	4.9	1.5	...	...	...	...	...	...	...	...	...	...	...	...	...
Sierra Leone	1971	286	1.8	38.8	55.0	—6.1—			—0.1—		93.6	—	—	6.4	—	—
Singapore	1973	16	0.8	77.4	22.2	0.3		—0.1—			7.4	—	—	88.8	—	3.8
Solomon Islands	1975[43]	92	1.0	...	...	...	...	...	...	...	—	—	—	—	100.0	—
Somalia	...	...	...	...	...	...	...	...	...	...	...	...	...	...	...	...
South Africa	1978	72	1,193	...	...	...	...	...	...	...	...	...	...	...	...	...
Bophuthatswana	1976	...	...	...	...	...	...	...	...	...	...	...	...	...	...	...
Ciskei	1978	...	...	...	...	...	...	...	...	...	...	...	...	...	...	...
Transkei	1976	...	...	...	...	...	...	...	...	...	...	...	...	...	...	...
Venda	1976	53.3	9.3	...	...	...	...	...	...	...	...	...	...	...	...	...
S.W. Africa/ Namibia	1983	...	...	...	...	...	...	...	...	...	...	...	...	...	...	...
Spain	1972	2,571	17.8	24.6	38.1	15.1	10.5	7.1	3.4	1.2	80.4	1.1	0.2	18.1	—	0.2
Sri Lanka	1973	1,647	1.5	63.4	33.5	2.3	0.4	—0.4—			77.1	6.4	0.1	14.4	—	2.0
Sudan, The	1982	...	...	...	...	...	...	...	...	...	22.3	2.2	—	28.0	42.0	5.5
Suriname	1969	16	5.8	21.9	61.2	11.1	3.6	1.6	0.3	0.3	20.2	0.9	—	49.5	—	29.4
Swaziland	1972	39	19.5	26.2	60.4		—12.0—			1.4	86.1	—	—	3.4	—	10.5
Sweden	1983	114	25.8	—	17.0	20.7	23.0	27.0	—12.3—		48.1	—	—	16.1	—	35.8
Switzerland	1980	125	8.7	21.6	20.4	16.1	27.6	13.4	—0.9—		36.2	—	0.8	58.5	—	4.5
Syria	1981	485	11.5		—51.0[54]—			—42.0[62]—		6.2[63]	0.8[64]	99.2[47]	—	0.8	...[47]	—	—
Taiwan	1983	808	1.1		—98.0[51]—			—2.0[66]—			93.5	—	—	6.5	—	—
Tanzania	1972	2,489	3.0	59.7	37.7	2.1	0.4	—0.1—		0.2	87.3	—	—	3.6	—	9.1
Thailand	1982	4,585	4.3	15.9[33]	56.4[33]	21.4[33]	5.8[33]	—0.5[33]—			84.1	—	—	11.4	—	4.5
Togo	1970	233	1.4	54.0	42.4		—3.6—				...	...	...	...	...	...
Tokelau	...	...	...	...	...	...	...	...	...	...	...	...	...	...	...	...
Tonga	1976	9.1	7.6	0.7	37.7		—1.6—				8.4	8.4	—	83.2	—	—
Trinidad and Tobago	1963	35.8	6.0	46.5[17]	25.7[67]	21.1[58]	3.9	1.4[59]	0.7[60]	0.7[61]	50.2	—	—	29.6	—	20.2
Tunisia	1983	...	...	...	...	...	...	...	...	...	...	...	...	...	...	...
Turkey	1980	3,651	6.2	15.8	46.3	20.2	11.6	5.3	0.8	—	90.6	—	—	8.4	—	1.0
Turks and Caicos Is.	...	...	...	...	...	...	...	...	...	...	...	...	...	...	...	...
Tuvalu	1976	1.5	1.7	...	...	...	...	...	...	...	99.9	...	...	...	0.1	—
Uganda	1964	1,171	3.9	20.7	59.8	11.2		—8.3—			97.4	—	—	—	—	2.6
U.S.S.R.	1984	48.2[24]	11,558[24]	—	—	—	—	—	—	100.0[24]	—	46.1	53.9	—	—	...[70]
United Arab Emirates	1980	3.1[71]	5.1[71]	...	...	...	...	...	...	...	...	...	...	...	...	...
United Kingdom	1983	262	71.5	5.6[17]	8.1[72]	12.8	16.7	25.6	25.6	5.6	—68.6—			31.4	—	—
United States	1982	2,241	180.0	—8.4[57]—			—20.0[73]—		31.8[74]	23.5[75]	16.3[76]	—88.4—			11.6	—	—
Uruguay	1980	63	214.1[3]	—	14.4[3]	15.4[3]	16.0[3]	16.9[3]	18.9[3]	18.4[3]	71.2	—	—	16.3	—	12.1
Vanuatu	1980	...	...	...	...	...	...	...	...	...	65.3	34.7	—	—	—	—
Venezuela	1971	288	91.9	5.8	37.7	17.2	14.4	11.3	7.9	5.7	61.5	...	...	6.1	...	31.3[53]
Vietnam	1983	...	...	...	...	...	...	...	...	...	...	...	...	...	...	...
Virgin Islands (U.S.)	1978	0.4	26.1	24.1[6]	41.8[7]	15.1	5.3	5.6	6.0	2.1	84.7	—	—	7.4	—	7.9
Wallis and Futuna Is.	1983	...	...	...	...	...	...	...	...	...	...	...	...	...	...	...
West Bank	...	...	...	...	...	...	...	...	...	...	...	...	...	...	...	...
Western Sahara	1983	...	...	...	...	...	...	...	...	...	...	...	...	...	...	...
Western Samoa	1975	...	...	...	...	...	...	...	...	...	...	...	...	...	86.0	14.0
Yemen (Aden)	1977	0.08[24]	604[24]	...	...	...	...	...	...	...	...	44.3[24]	55.7[24]	...	...	...
Yemen (San'ā')	1976	...	...	...	...	...	...	...	...	...	...	...	...	...	...	...
Yugoslavia	1969	2,600	4.8	21.4	52.8	19.9	4.9	0.9	—0.1—		99.9	—	0.1	...	...	...
Zaire	1970	2,538	2.3	42.7[77]	55.8[77]	0.7[77]	0.2[77]	0.1[77]	0.3[77]	0.3[77]	4.2	0.1	—	...	95.6	0.1
Zambia	1971	768	3.1	50.5	45.2	—3.8—			—0.5—		...	...	—	...	...	...
Zimbabwe	1974	765	38.7	—16.7[78]—			52.8[79]	29.8[80]	—0.7[41]—		—2.0—			—	98.0	—

activity (% of farms)			technology (% of farms using)				farm land use — land in farms		land use (%)							country
mainly crops	mainly live-stock	mixed/ other	tractor	electri-city	irriga-tion works	artificial fertilizer (kg/ha)	total ('000 ha)	% of total land area	cropland — perma-nent crops	tempo-rary crops	fallow	total	mead-ows and pastures	wood-land and forest	other[b]	
...	...	...	34	...	93[2]	40[5]	83	0.3	68.6	31.4	—	49.2	—50.8—			Oman
...	...	...	14	...	...	...	40	21.1	54.2	9.8	36.0	68.7	17.5	—	13.7	Pacific Is., Trust Terr. of
...	...	...	24	...	79.5	53[5]	19,913	25.9	—92.9—		7.1	92.7	—	0.2	7.1	Pakistan
...	...	...	3.9[9]	0.5[9]	...	52[5]	2,259	29.3	21.6	43.3	35.0	24.6	57.4	15.6	2.4	Panama
...	...	...	44	...	...	33[5]	395	0.9	96.6	3.4	...	33.5	25.6	—	40.9	Papua New Guinea
98.5	0.6	0.9	24	...	3[2]	5[5]	17,473	43.0	...	...	...	...	...	...	...	Paraguay
...	...	...	5.4	0.2	34[2]	37[5]	23,545	18.3	8.5	70.3	21.2	14.6	65.5	13.1	6.7	Peru
86.7[9]	1.6[9]	11.7[9]	4.0[9]	...	21.2[9]	32[5]	9,034	30.1	35.3[9]	54.2[9]	10.5[9]	86.3	6.8	—6.9—		Philippines
...	...	...	...	...	...	...										Pitcairn Island
...	...	...	43[4]	...	1[2]	225[5]	16,419	52.5	1.5	—98.5—		69.7	17.5	7.4	5.4	Poland
...	...	...	21[4]	...	18[2]	77[5]	4,974	54.1	19.4	59.0	21.6	61.8	2.9	34.8	0.5	Portugal
...	...	...	26[4]	...	28[2]	...	426	48.1	...	...	...	55.6	25.5	13.5	5.4	Puerto Rico
99.7	0.3	—	...	...	100.0	280[5]	34	3.0	33.0	67.0	—	100.0	—	—	—	Qatar
...	...	...	23[4]	...	15.6[26]	270[5]	77	30.7	2.0	95.6	2.4	58.0	2.0	19.4	20.6	Réunion
...	...	...	15[4]	...	13.1[26]	154[5]	14,964	63.0	6.2	92.5	1.3	70.3	29.7	—	—	Romania
...	...	...	...	...	0.2[26]	...	1,460	57.1	30.7	—69.3—		67.7	32.3	—	—	Rwanda
...	...	...	15[4]	...	...	171[5]	12	45.3	31.5	—68.5—		58.1	—41.9—			St. Christopher
...	...	...	34	...	—	...	4.0	12.9	—	—100.0—		50.0	50.0	—	—	St. Helena
25.0	—75.0—		24	...	5.8	59[5]	29	47.3	68.5	—31.5—		57.9	10.2	26.4	5.5	St. Lucia
...	...	...	...	...	...	...										St. Pierre and Miquelon
...	...	...	44	...	4.4[26]	229[5]	11	28.8	75.0	—25.0—		82.1	17.9	—	—	St. Vincent
...	...	...	...	...	...	...	4.7	76.5	60.9	6.5	32.6	69.2	6.2	8.2	16.4	San Marino
...	...	...	34	...	6.2[26]	...	96	100.0	99.4	—0.6—		38.3	—	59.7	2.0	São Tomé and Príncipe
...	...	...	0.4	...	79.2	60[5]	1,213	0.6	15.8	62.1	22.1	41.8	—58.2—			Saudi Arabia
...	...	...	...	...	5.9[26]	5.0[5]	11,338	59.1	0.1	—99.9—		22.4	77.6	—	—	Senegal
1.8	32.4	65.8	64	...	...	...	7.5	27.8	89.6	—10.4—		100.0	—	—	—	Seychelles
50.3	—49.7—		...	...	0.4[26]	2.0[5]	2,732	38.1	20.7	—79.3—		19.3	80.7	—	—	Sierra Leone
12.5	6.2	81.3	1.4	...	100.0	671[5]	12	20.8	75.0	25.0	—	66.7	—	33.3	—	Singapore
43.4	—56.6—		...	...	...	...	93	3.4	40.0	45.2	14.8	100.0	—	—	—	Solomon Islands
...	...	...	24	...	...	1.0[5]	...	...	...	...	...	...	...	...	...	Somalia
...	...	...	13[4]	...	12.4	90[5]	85,447	70.2	5.9	—94.1—		11.9	79.7	1.3	7.1	South Africa
...	...	...	...	...	1.1[26]	...	3,839	94.8	...	87.1	...	2.4	97.6	—	—	Bophuthatswana
...	...	...	...	...	0.3[26]	...	598	63.5	...	51.3	...	12.6	87.4	—	—	Ciskei
...	...	...	...	...	2.8[26]	...	622	14.9	...	...	...	100.0	—	—	—	Transkei
...	...	...	0.3	...	0.5[26]	4.8	500	64.9	25.4	63.6	11.0	9.2	90.8	—	—	Venda
...	...	...	4.0[4]	...	0.2[26]	...	662	0.8	0.3	—99.7—		100.0	...	...	...	S.W. Africa/Namibia
...	...	...	27[4]	...	15[2]	67[5]	45,702	91.5	23.4	48.5	28.1	42.7	30.9	23.3	3.1	Spain
...	...	...	12[4]	...	24[2]	77[5]	2,036	31.4	62.4	37.6	—	88.3	0.4	2.1	9.2	Sri Lanka
...	...	...	14	...	15[2]	6[5]	31,500	13.3	0.8	88.7	10.5	23.8	76.2	—	—	Sudan, The
33.0	12.5	54.5	26[4]	...	71[2]	109[5]	94	0.6	20.6	79.4	—	40.7	9.4	—49.9—		Surinam
39.7	—60.3—		14[4]	...	16[2]	103[5]	766,775	44.6	2.0	81.1	16.9	19.7	60.6	12.0	7.7	Swaziland
43.9	—56.1—		64[4]	...	1.8[26]	164[5]	8,678	21.1	0.2	95.7	4.1	33.9	4.0	50.6	11.5	Sweden
35.5	—64.5—		234[4]	...	4.3[26]	412[5]	1,363	34.3	49.6	3.1	47.3	42.7	57.3	—	—	Switzerland
...	...	...	0.3	...	14.8[65]	23[5]	6,169[65]	33.3[65]	9.6[65]	56.4[65]	34.0[65]	91.7[65]	—8.3[65]—			Syria
...	...	...	...	...	37.6[26]	400	1,334	37.1	8.6	91.4	—	67.0	—33.0—			Taiwan
56.2	—43.8—		0.3	...	0.8[26]	6.0[5]	7,545	8.5	19.1	72.5	8.4	49.8	10.2	24.7	15.3	Tanzania
...	...	...	44	...	17.6[26]	18[5]	19,774	38.5	10.0	86.7	3.3	96.0	0.6	—3.4—		Thailand
...	...	...	...	...	0.4[26]	2[5]	692[11]	12.7[11]	17.3[11]	—82.7[11]—		71.0[11]	29.0[11]	—	—	Togo
...	...	...	...	...	...	...										Tokelau
8.4	—	91.6	14	...	...	...	58	83.6	57.0	—43.0—		93.1	6.9	—	—	Tonga
63.7	—36.3—		15[4]	...	0.6[26, 68]	42[5]	166[69]	31.6[69]	51.6[69]	43.0[69]	5.4[69]	95.4[69]	4.7[69]	—	—	Trinidad and Tobago
...	...	...	84	...	2.3[26]	18[5]	8,726	56.2	40.9	41.3	17.8	56.2	43.8	—	—	Tunisia
11.5	2.5	86.0	16[4]	...	46.9	45[5]	22,765	29.5	7.2	65.1	27.7	90.4	5.2	1.1	3.3	Turkey
...	...	...	...	...	...	...										Turks and Caicos Is.
...	...	...	...	...	...	...										Tuvalu
...	...	100.0	...	...	2.2[26, 68]	83[5]	2,262	11.3	29.8	70.2	—	100.0	—	—	—	Uganda
...	...	...	...	...	3.1[26]	281[5]	605,700	27.2	—91.6—		8.4	37.5	61.6	—0.9—		U.S.S.R.
...	...	...	...	...	28.6[26]	...	17.5[33]	0.2[33]	64.8[33]	18.2[33]	17.1[33]	97.6[33]	...	1.3[33]	1.1[33]	United Arab Emirates
...	...	...	76[4]	...	0.8[26]	330[5]	18,735	77.5	0.9	71.2	27.9	37.2	60.0	1.6	1.2	United Kingdom
43.4	52.6	4.0	85.7	66.2	12.4	102[5]	399,357	43.6	1.5	86.4	12.1	45.1	42.4	8.8	3.7	United States
11.0	46.7	42.3	23[4]	...	0.5[26]	44[5]	16,518[3]	95.1[3]	2.6[3]	81.6[3]	15.8[3]	11.2[3]	82.5[3]	3.7[3]	2.6[3]	Uruguay
82.6	13.7	3.7	14	...	...	...	219	14.8	40.7	—59.3—		86.3	13.7	...	...	Vanuatu
39.8	12.1	48.1	10[4]	...	1.2[26, 68]	39[5]	26,470	30.0	19.0	59.0	22.0	13.2	57.0	22.8	7.0	Venezuela
...	...	...	6.0[4]	...	22.8[26]	41[5]	7,857	24.1	8.4	—91.6—		65.4	34.6	—	—	Vietnam
53.4	—46.6—		12.2	...	...	157[5]	9.9	29.1	63.7	5.9	30.4	7.0	77.6	9.9	5.5	Virgin Islands (U.S.)
...	...	...	...	...	...	...	5.0	25.0	80.0	—20.0—		100.0	—	—	—	Wallis and Futuna Is.
...	...	...	...	...	...	...										West Bank
...	...	...	...	...	...	...	5,002	18.8	—	—	—	—	100.0	...	...	Western Sahara
...	...	...	...	...	...	45	70	24.8	71.2	28.8	—	93.8	6.2	—	—	Western Samoa
...	...	...	64	...	53.8[26]	9[5]	108	0.3	3.9	85.1	11.0	95.7	4.3	—	—	Yemen (Aden)
35.5[8]	56.9[8]	7.6[8]	14	...	15.2[26]	4[5]	3,515	17.6	0.8	81.5	17.7	43.1	56.9	—	—	Yemen (Ṣan'ā')
12.7	—87.3—		1.5	4.8[37]	12.3	128[5]	12,462	48.8	8.5	84.7	6.8	52.8	26.4	16.2	4.6	Yugoslavia
92.3	—9.7—		0.4	...	...	1.0[5]	5,897	2.6	7.7	—92.3—		70.6	20.1	2.0	7.3	Zaire
15.8	9.7	74.5	14	...	0.3[26]	20[5]	938	1.3	4.5	—95.5—		14.2	38.1	4.0	47.7	Zambia
1.8[8, 33]	26.7[8, 33]	71.5[8, 33]	84	...	1.5[33]	68[5]	29,620	75.6	2.5	—97.5—		34.5	65.7	...	...	Zimbabwe

[1]1967. [2]Irrigated land as percentage of area of arable land, not percentage of number of farms; 1981. [3]1970. [4]Tractors per 1,000 hectares of arable land, 1981. [5]Kilograms per hectare of arable land, 1981. [6]Less than 1.2 hectares. [7]1.2 to 5.0 hectares. [8]Based on area, not ownership. [9]1971. [10]1979. [11]1977. [12]Belgium includes Luxembourg. [13]1.2 to 4.0 hectares. [14]More than 4.0 hectares. [15]Family farms only. [16]Government agro-industrial complexes. [17]Less than 2.0 hectares. [18]More than 2.0 hectares. [19]1976. [20]1981. [21]1.2 to 10.0 hectares. [22]Irrigated land only. [23]1968. [24]State farms and communes only. [25]1975. [26]Irrigated land as percentage of all farmland. [27]1974. [28]1980. [29]1972. [30]1964. [31]Does not include estates, collective farms, or traditional farms. [32]1982. [33]1978. [34]Farms producing mainly for cash sales. [35]3,217 large farms only occupying 2,673,000 hectares, 1981. [36]1969. [37]Percent of farms having electric motors. [38]Excludes temporary bushland available for agricultural use to subsistence farms. [39]Western Libya only. [40]10 to 100 hectares. [41]More than 100 hectares. [42]Peninsular Malaysia excluding shifting cultivators. [43]Smallholder farms only. [44]Average size of estate farm is 400 hectares. [45]Based on total number of households on estates. [46]All Malaysia. [47]Includes rented farms. [48]Excludes part-time farmers. [49]In area, privately owned lands constitute 49.7% of Mexico's farmland, communal land (ejidos) 49.8%. [50]In area, state lands constitute 79.1% of Mongolia's farmland, agricultural cooperatives 20.9%. [51]3 hectares or less. [52]3 to 50 hectares. [53]Almost all squatters. [54]7 hectares or less. [55]More than 7 hectares. [56]Less than 0.4 hectare. [57]0.4 to 4.0 hectares. [58]4 to 10 hectares. [59]20 to 40 hectares. [60]40 to 81 hectares. [61]81 hectares or more. [62]7.1 to 25 hectares. [63]25 to 300 hectares. [64]300 hectares or more. [65]1984. [66]3 hectares or more. [67]2 to 4 hectares. [68]1983. [69]1973. [70]24,600,000 farm households with small plots comprise 8% of total farmland. [71]Abu Dhabi only. [72]2 to 5 hectares. [73]4 to 20 hectares. [74]20 to 72 hectares. [75]72 to 202 hectares. [76]202 hectares or more. [77]Individual holdings only. [78]Less than 8 hectares. [79]8 to 16 hectares. [80]16 to 100 hectares.

Crops and livestock

This table provides comparative data for selected categories of agricultural production for the countries of the world. The data are taken mainly from the United Nations Food and Agricultural Organization's (FAO) annual *Production Yearbook*.

Although the FAO provides standardized guidelines upon which many nations have organized their data collection systems and methods, persistent variations in standards of coverage and reporting periods limit the value of country to country comparisons. The FAO depends largely on questionnaires supplied to each country, but where no official or semiofficial responses are returned the FAO makes estimates, using unofficial or other data. Statistics are based on calendar year periods; that is, data for any particular crop refer to the calendar year in which the harvest (or the bulk of the harvest) occurred. In countries where intensive intercropping and multiple cropping are practiced, the broader parameter of food supply availability (see *Household budgets and consumption* table) may be a better indicator by which to make intercountry comparisons of agricultural production than the more specific components of agriculture presented in this table. In spite of the oftentimes tragic food shortages in several countries in recent years, worldwide agricultural production is probably more

often under-reported than over-reported. Most countries do not report total production; for example, the Soviet bloc, excepting Czechoslovakia, publishes, initially at least, statistics only for collective or cooperative production and excludes the production of privately held plots of land that in some instances represent a significant part of total agricultural production. Some countries report only crops that are sold commercially and ignore crops produced for family or communal subsistence.

Individual categories of crop production also display some peculiarities that may cause statistical discrepancies. The FAO's cereals statistics relate to crops harvested for grain. Some countries, however, report sown or cultivated areas instead, with production statistics calculated from estimates of yield. Millet and sorghum, which in many countries are used as livestock or poultry feed, are excluded by the FAO from the cereals category, while many African nations that use them for grain report them as cereals. Fruit statistics, especially for tropical fruits, are frequently unavailable, and coverage is not uniform, with some countries reporting both commercial fruits and those consumed for subsistence. Figures on wild fruits and berries tend not to be included in national reports at all. Statistical variances also occur among data for individual varieties of fruit. Some

Crops and livestock

country	crops													
	grains				roots and tubers[a]				pulses[b]				fruits[c]		vegetables[d]	
	production ('000 metric tons)		yield (kg/hectare)		production ('000 metric tons)		yield (kg/hectare)		production ('000 metric tons)		yield (kg/hectare)		production ('000 metric tons)		production ('000 metric tons)	
	1974–76 average	1983	1974–76 average	1983	1974–76 average	1983	1974–76 average	1983	1974–76 average	1983	1974–76 average	1983	1974–76 average	1983	1974–76 average	1983
Afghanistan	4,358	5,900	1,298	1,346	246	320	13,727	12,800	32	43	1,570	1,727	808	838	627	990
Albania	713	1,067	2,112	3,046	109	136	7,032	8,774	16	21	305	348	136	162	159	184
Algeria	2,158	1,236	682	549	448	610	7,340	7,625	67	58	695	461	1,515	1,107	676	1,126
American Samoa	...	...	...	...	13	19	18,895	24,063	...	...	...	...	3	2	...	...
Andorra	...	...	...	...	...	...	...	...	...	...	...	...	...	...	...	...
Angola	547	357	756	499	1,907	2,170	13,178	14,045	71	40	589	364	429	425	203	227
Anguilla	...	...	...	...	...	...	...	...	...	...	...	...	...	...	...	...
Antigua and Barbuda	...	...	1,885	1,571	...	1	3,871	8,340	...	...	...	...	7	9	1	1
Argentina	23,653	30,212	1,971	2,265	2,311	2,541	13,278	15,582	176	250	1,092	1,109	6,472	6,471	2,417	2,561
Australia	17,202	30,919	1,384	1,631	699	831	19,785	21,675	106	355	776	930	1,982	2,048	926	1,038
Austria	4,001	5,061	4,000	4,744	1,774	1,015	23,679	24,905	5	2	2,386	2,272	991	1,179	552	679
Bahamas, The	1	1	1,010	1,172	...	...	3,500	4,070	1	1	1,392	1,407	11	12	12	17
Bahrain	...	...	...	...	...	...	29,000	18,000	...	...	...	...	25	46	14	24
Bangladesh	18,112	22,847	1,771	2,042	1,553	1,801	9,945	10,348	223	211	732	691	1,293	1,331	1,045	1,132
Barbados	2	2	2,614	2,500	10	11	10,659	13,464	1	1	1,183	1,246	2	3	6	10
Belgium[2]	1,919	2,070	4,203	4,895	1,325	1,245	33,463	29,021	13	6	2,788	3,899	387	391	1,128	1,025
Belize	20	27	1,276	1,926	2	3	21,170	20,000	1	2	576	592	64	92	2	3
Benin	305	335	721	563	1,143	1,323	7,654	7,218	24	33	387	430	132	151	82	121
Bermuda	...	...	...	...	1	1	18,077	10,250	...	...	...	...	1	1	2	2
Bhutan	141	171	1,424	1,409	36	43	6,602	6,777	2	3	540	602	37	47	9	10
Bolivia	580	490	1,150	1,073	1,157	523	6,975	3,536	16	20	915	1,026	579	490	348	187
Botswana	100	14	599	102	6	7	4,641	5,523	13	15	459	500	8	11	14	16
Brazil	27,873	29,299	1,420	1,614	28,868	24,844	12,006	10,739	2,193	1,652	503	389	13,704	20,328	3,396	4,537
British Virgin Islands	...	...	...	...	...	...	...	...	...	...	...	...	1	1	...	...
Brunei	9	10	2,517	3,384	4	5	4,880	5,918	...	...	...	...	6	13	3	5
Bulgaria	7,602	7,899	3,460	3,700	338	428	11,201	10,486	77	67	681	805	2,052	2,030	1,978	1,690
Burkina Faso	1,139	1,008	532	490	110	119	4,688	4,457	166	176	362	371	41	65	56	82
Burma	9,210	15,103	1,716	2,902	87	206	5,348	8,254	269	552	448	833	1,031	1,044	1,690	1,933
Burundi	305	434	1,134	1,174	1,014	1,144	6,988	7,624	333	327	974	991	944	1,043	126	180
Cameroon	962	793	1,017	768	2,272	1,970	3,516	2,432	90	112	591	542	1,112	903	391	409
Canada	37,568	48,206	2,027	2,230	2,354	2,520	21,501	22,352	138	202	1,439	1,469	663	724	1,444	1,892
Cape Verde	4	3	448	300	17	16	5,360	5,575	1	2	647	1,111	9	11	5	5
Cayman Islands	...	...	...	...	...	...	4,444	4,700	...	...	...	...	1	1	...	...
Central African Republic	97	94	518	504	1,097	1,054	3,231	2,729	5	6	500	500	150	174	38	47
Chad	592	500	573	412	327	501	4,048	4,669	52	56	382	406	87	114	45	74
Chile	1,577	1,642	1,679	2,124	771	691	9,793	8,389	99	119	853	907	1,267	1,736	1,107	1,243
China	243,234	343,729	2,479	3,636	144,211	151,004	12,938	15,716	6,277	6,045	1,076	1,239	6,286	10,461	69,618	85,938
Christmas Island	...	...	...	...	...	...	...	...	...	...	...	...	...	...	...	...
Cocos (Keeling) Islands	...	...	...	...	...	...	...	...	...	...	...	...	...	...	...	...
Colombia	2,882	3,337	2,367	2,473	3,364	4,352	9,243	11,304	127	140	612	651	3,172	4,335	1,111	1,469
Comoros	15	21	1,108	1,120	93	105	3,451	3,376	2	2	548	575	30	38	2	3
Congo	20	9	665	567	588	651	5,668	6,363	7	7	603	628	186	237	27	36
Cook Islands	...	...	...	...	11	12	27,805	31,418	...	...	...	...	15	15	2	2
Costa Rica	252	376	1,735	2,201	36	62	8,360	6,505	15	20	452	511	1,380	1,237	50	65
Cuba	540	587	2,034	2,693	645	969	5,435	6,212	24	27	695	771	494	1,064	399	503
Cyprus	169	98	1,396	1,635	161	233	19,842	21,923	10	6	767	1,016	403	515	106	120
Czechoslovakia	9,619	11,061	3,578	4,512	4,100	3,105	16,026	15,845	101	156	1,342	1,843	614	939	1,008	1,194
Denmark	6,472	6,438	3,705	3,778	743	870	22,497	24,857	11	16	3,025	3,404	144	148	203	230
Djibouti	...	...	...	...	...	...	...	...	...	...	...	...	...	...	...	10
Dominica	...	...	1,293	1,389	23	26	9,742	9,611	1	1	561	593	61	56	4	5
Dominican Republic	335	573	2,696	3,537	365	190	6,073	5,971	70	80	1,071	910	1,262	1,396	188	243
Ecuador	722	539	1,352	1,707	910	659	10,749	10,475	54	48	530	588	3,691	3,699	307	296
Egypt	8,001	8,691	3,921	4,459	909	1,360	17,805	16,979	346	366	2,058	2,181	2,042	2,705	6,357	7,557
El Salvador	575	590	1,543	1,429	22	31	11,724	12,803	38	42	708	771	211	272	99	105
Equatorial Guinea	...	...	...	...	77	88	2,736	2,439	...	...	...	...	13	17	...	...
Ethiopia	4,364	6,763	966	1,334	1,138	1,574	3,259	3,317	635	1,053	727	1,134	183	209	423	507
Faeroe Islands	...	...	...	...	1	1	14,275	13,701	...	...	...	...	...	...	...	...
Falkland Islands	...	...	...	...	...	...	...	...	...	...	...	...	...	...	...	...
Fiji	26	29	2,184	2,284	142	150	9,463	9,511	2	2	879	868	12	14	13	15
Finland	3,436	3,865	2,592	3,177	718	804	14,477	17,748	13	30	2,291	3,202	99	105	96	143

banana and plantain growers, for example, report production in terms of bunches, including the weight of the stalk; others do not. Vegetable statistics include vegetables and melons grown for human consumption only. Some countries do not make this distinction in their reports, and some exclude the production of kitchen gardens and small family plots. In Austria, France, West Germany, and Italy, such small-scale production accounts for 20 to 40 percent of total ouput.

Livestock statistics may be distorted by the timing of country reports. Ireland, for example, takes a livestock enumeration in December that is reported the following year and that appears low against data for otherwise comparable countries because of the slaughter and export of animals at the close of the grazing season. It balances this, however, with a June enumeration, when numbers tend to be high. Milk production as defined by the FAO includes whole fresh milk, excluding milk sucked by young animals but including amounts fed by farmers or ranchers to livestock. Some countries—notably Czechoslovakia, France, Hungary, Italy, and West Germany—include milk sucked by young animals in their reports. Certain countries do not distinguish between milk cows and other cattle, so that yield per cow must be estimated. Some countries do not supply

egg statistics, and estimates must be generated based on the numbers of chickens and reported or assumed egg-laying rates. Some other countries report egg production by number, and this must be converted to weight, using official conversion factors; but, as eggs vary in size and weight, discrepancies may be introduced.

Metric system units used in the table may be converted to English system units as follows:

metric tons × 1.1023 = short tons
kilograms × 2.2046 = pounds
kilograms per hectare × 0.8922 = pounds per acre.

The notes that follow, keyed by references in the table headings, provide further definitional information.

a. Includes such crops as potatoes and cassava.
b. Includes beans and peas harvested for dry grain only. Does not include green beans and green peas.
c. Excludes melons.
d. Includes melons, green beans, and green peas.
e. From milk cows only.
f. From chickens only.

cattle stock ('000 head)		sheep stock ('000 head)		hogs stock ('000 head)		chickens stock ('000 head)		milk[e] production ('000 metric tons)		yield (kg/animal)		eggs[f] production (metric tons)		country
1974–76 average	1983	1974–76 average	1983	1974–76 average	1983	1974–76 average	1983	1974–76 average	1983	1974–76 average	1983	1974–76 average	1983	
3,602	3,800	19,872	20,000	…	…	6,000	7,000	588	556	543	505	13,297	14,200	Afghanistan
463	600	1,163	1,200	127	200	3,000	5,000	231	347	1,547	1,769	6,430	12,000	Albania
976	1,400	9,265	13,750	4	5	16,000	20,000	417	540	926	964	15,633	21,000	Algeria
…	…	…	…	8	8	…	…	…	…	…	…	32	35	American Samoa
…	11	…	91	…	…	…	…	…	…	…	…	…	…	Andorra
2,850	3,300	200	240	355	450	5,000	6,000	138	148	500	502	3,400	3,800	Angola
														Anguilla
8	16	11	12	5	7	—	—	7	6	1,305	1,000	125	150	Antigua and Barbuda
56,745	53,670	34,622	30,000	4,151	3,800	34,000	43,000	5,580	5,700	1,892	1,900	199,879	300,000	Argentina
32,355	22,764	148,491	133,186	2,292	2,498	43,000	44,000	6,688	5,525	2,837	3,141	194,333	205,000	Australia
2,569	2,546	153	199	3,497	3,981	12,000	15,000	3,181	3,760	3,094	3,893	85,830	93,000	Austria
4	4	30	38	16	19	1,000	1,000	2	3	1,000	1,000	317	368	Bahamas, The
5	6	3	7	…	…	…	1,000	6	6	2,769	2,870	1,153	4,300	Bahrain
25,505	36,000	1,067	1,090	…	…	51,000	75,000	727	1,030	250	250	32,954	48,000	Bangladesh
19	19	48	54	38	66	—	1,000	6	8	1,088	1,293	1,417	1,400	Barbados
3,072	3,115	102	115	4,782	5,210	32,000	27,000	3,891	4,170	3,659	4,035	238,639	185,000	Belgium[2]
47	51	3	3	18	17	1,000	1,000	4	4	1,014	1,013	560	680	Belize
706	880	831	1,080	363	500	3,000	5,000	10	13	117	120	2,232	3,420	Benin
…	1	…	…	1	2	…	…	1	2	3,045	3,071	332	480	Bermuda
266	312	39	43	60	74	—	—	9	11	257	257	93	189	Bhutan
3,246	4,200	7,729	9,200	1,164	1,700	6,000	10,000	53	78	1,393	1,418	16,117	25,500	Bolivia
2,578	3,050	290	160	16	7	1,000	1,000	71	98	350	350	477	702	Botswana
91,644	93,000	17,743	17,500	34,866	33,500	308,000	450,000	9,886	10,700	824	728	491,022	835,000	Brazil
2	2	7	8	2	3	…	…	…	…	…	…	…	…	British Virgin Islands
3	4	…	…	13	15	1,000	1,000	…	…	…	…	1,347	2,082	Brunei
1,555	1,783	9,857	10,761	3,247	3,810	34,000	41,000	1,434	2,080	2,278	2,994	99,863	145,761	Bulgaria
2,495	2,950	1,517	2,000	137	195	10,000	14,000	39	47	78	80	5,423	9,500	Burkina Faso
7,410	9,400	187	260	1,596	2,900	16,000	30,000	210	239	245	245	21,906	40,000	Burma
774	560	309	310	35	36	3,000	3,000	49	58	350	350	1,976	2,565	Burundi
2,583	3,000	2,050	2,190	800	1,200	9,000	12,000	34	45	500	500	6,933	9,400	Cameroon
13,936	11,618	515	564	6,065	9,922	81,000	76,000	7,692	7,975	3,738	4,644	314,611	343,000	Canada
11	13	2	1	22	22	—	—	1	2	600	600	116	128	Cape Verde
4	5	…	…	…	1	—	—	…	…	…	…	81	86	Cayman Islands
878	1,500	67	80	111	140	1,000	2,000	3	4	110	110	875	1,066	Central African Republic
3,207	3,600	2,335	2,300	6	6	3,000	3,000	87	97	270	270	2,370	2,970	Chad
3,484	3,865	5,639	6,434	877	1,260	16,000	21,000	991	900	1,344	1,286	61,922	61,200	Chile
56,376	57,450	94,403	106,568	269,884	305,580	698,000	1,144,000	3,438	6,052	487	695	2,283,124	3,614,321	China
…	…	…	…	…	…	…	…	…	…	…	…	…	…	Christmas Island
…	…	…	…	…	…	…	…	…	…	…	…	…	…	Cocos (Keeling) Islands
23,185	24,275	1,945	2,898	1,852	2,244	23,000	34,000	2,133	2,677	941	991	106,990	164,250	Colombia
73	83	7	9	…	…	—	—	3	3	500	500	505	580	Comoros
52	68	48	60	40	25	1,000	1,000	2	3	1,500	1,500	587	937	Congo
…	…	…	…	12	17	…	…	…	…	…	…	80	100	Cook Islands
1,791	2,280	2	3	220	236	5,000	6,000	262	353	1,046	1,261	15,674	17,900	Costa Rica
5,442	6,300	330	370	1,453	2,100	18,000	24,000	886	1,250	1,364	1,645	81,738	112,500	Cuba
32	43	442	500	126	200	3,000	4,000	25	53	3,378	3,118	5,267	8,000	Cyprus
4,559	5,131	819	990	6,556	7,126	39,000	47,000	5,455	6,496	2,894	3,297	224,313	261,000	Czechoslovakia
3,085	2,900	60	59	7,715	9,289	15,000	15,000	4,927	5,425	4,485	5,414	73,033	81,000	Denmark
27	43	283	380	…	…	…	…	1	2	1,067	1,000	225	270	Djibouti
4	4	3	4	8	9	…	…	…	…	…	…	…	…	Dominica
1,896	1,951	50	56	700	143	7,000	9,000	333	460	1,449	2,009	21,500	17,286	Dominican Republic
2,476	3,000	2,104	2,350	2,547	3,600	13,000	42,000	786	970	1,332	1,386	20,603	50,000	Ecuador
2,100	1,826	1,923	1,394	15	15	26,000	28,000	626	650	674	684	69,128	121,900	Egypt
1,059	954	4	4	442	450	3,000	6,000	243	310	960	984	27,223	31,250	El Salvador
4	4	31	34	4	5	—	—	…	…	…	…	95	141	Equatorial Guinea
26,086	26,300	23,201	23,400	17	19	51,000	55,000	542	610	199	221	69,221	75,210	Ethiopia
2	2	69	72	…	…	…	…	…	…	…	…	…	…	Faeroe Islands
9	8	639	669	…	…	—	—	1	1	1,000	1,000	…	…	Falkland Islands
158	157	…	…	16	28	1,000	1,000	45	54	1,605	1,602	1,750	2,552	Fiji
1,854	1,800	127	100	1,091	1,500	9,000	8,000	3,196	3,173	4,141	4,725	81,067	82,600	Finland

Crops and livestock (continued)

country	grains production ('000 metric tons) 1974–76 average	grains production 1983	grains yield (kg/hectare) 1974–76 average	grains yield 1983	roots and tubers[a] production ('000 metric tons) 1974–76 average	roots production 1983	roots yield (kg/hectare) 1974–76 average	roots yield 1983	pulses[b] production ('000 metric tons) 1974–76 average	pulses production 1983	pulses yield (kg/hectare) 1974–76 average	pulses yield 1983	fruits[c] production ('000 metric tons) 1974–76 average	fruits production 1983	vegetables[d] production ('000 metric tons) 1974–76 average	vegetables production 1983
France	36,510	46,260	3,776	4,953	6,156	5,325	20,906	26,141	124	603	1,803	3,369	15,898	11,914	6,413	7,104
French Guiana	1	3	1,635	2,462	15	12	12,295	10,696	...	...	...	...	5	4	1	3
French Polynesia	...	...	...	...	17	12	12,577	8,425	...	...	...	...	4	3	6	7
Gabon	8	11	1,459	1,554	208	237	3,422	3,884	...	...	397	536	82	81	18	25
Gambia, The	83	60	936	853	9	6	3,274	3,000	4	4	250	267	3	4	6	8
Gaza Strip	...	4	...	2,643	...	5	...	16,667	...	...	...	...	244	207	48	56
Germany, East	8,935	10,035	3,575	3,949	9,298	7,500	15,419	17,647	73	83	1,511	1,666	561	755	923	1,278
Germany, West	21,014	23,011	3,973	4,562	11,737	6,088	27,133	24,482	78	29	2,785	2,313	3,879	4,386	1,800	1,998
Ghana	750	480	873	727	3,612	2,450	6,136	5,269	17	11	110	88	1,376	721	445	496
Gibraltar	...	...	...	...	...	...	...	...	...	...	...	...	...	...	...	...
Greece	3,859	4,365	2,492	2,791	894	813	15,003	24,473	113	83	1,186	1,322	3,241	3,636	3,225	3,849
Greenland	...	...	...	...	...	...	...	...	...	...	...	...	...	...	...	...
Grenada	...	...	851	1,005	3	4	5,076	4,707	1	1	1,164	1,990	26	29	2	1
Guadeloupe	...	...	1,628	1,200	41	22	12,450	8,816	...	...	767	433	170	147	23	23
Guam	...	...	1,500	1,500	1	1	13,939	13,214	...	...	...	...	1	1	1	...
Guatemala	989	1,213	1,459	1,198	53	39	3,851	4,083	81	99	651	833	735	936	216	267
Guernsey	...	...	...	...	...	...	...	...	...	...	...	...	...	...	...	...
Guinea	569	412	832	882	765	834	7,115	7,229	27	25	543	455	502	553	347	377
Guinea-Bissau	85	53	1,000	688	32	40	4,872	6,154	2	2	533	567	41	40	22	20
Guyana	252	222	2,139	2,989	22	17	6,604	6,735	1	1	667	571	33	41	7	9
Haiti	442	390	1,176	963	678	718	4,320	3,697	85	89	497	487	898	1,038	249	301
Honduras	441	565	1,093	1,394	19	22	3,468	4,500	32	44	459	629	1,280	1,568	65	105
Hong Kong	3	...	1,764	1,333	1	...	12,870	26,667	...	...	...	...	3	6	179	185
Hungary	12,014	13,713	3,806	4,714	1,585	1,508	12,416	17,806	143	142	1,788	1,709	2,160	2,581	1,788	1,766
Iceland	...	...	...	...	9	12	10,660	11,500	...	...	...	...	...	...	1	1
India	118,742	164,165	1,179	1,554	14,266	16,778	12,063	13,041	10,938	11,791	474	512	15,079	18,939	34,277	43,147
Indonesia	25,598	38,306	2,338	3,112	15,861	16,420	8,360	9,340	295	316	501	499	2,904	3,500	2,422	2,276
Iran	8,221	9,573	1,057	1,224	530	800	9,458	8,519	200	219	1,028	1,033	2,232	2,687	3,281	3,900
Iraq	1,814	1,997	854	954	48	110	8,289	15,714	38	43	769	806	982	1,310	1,631	2,520
Ireland	1,358	1,891	3,929	4,901	1,094	800	25,666	24,768	13	11	4,043	3,929	24	21	246	277
Isle of Man	...	...	...	...	...	...	...	...	...	...	...	...	...	...	...	...
Israel	305	424	2,112	3,014	164	212	30,599	43,905	9	9	1,445	1,196	1,924	2,025	702	911
Italy	17,001	18,084	3,282	3,537	2,964	2,846	16,551	18,958	405	275	1,259	1,330	19,784	21,277	12,165	13,503
Ivory Coast	771	822	813	664	2,865	3,484	4,145	3,991	7	8	607	667	1,296	1,443	251	317
Jamaica	12	4	1,763	1,510	206	192	10,207	11,408	5	9	687	901	306	281	76	97
Japan	16,636	14,113	5,620	5,320	5,313	5,735	21,297	23,738	177	98	1,349	957	6,477	6,700	14,672	15,651
Jersey	...	...	...	...	...	...	...	...	...	...	...	...	...	...	...	...
Jordan	143	177	660	1,032	6	11	11,743	17,748	23	13	716	817	46	118	317	530
Kampuchea	1,382	1,760	1,306	983	81	108	8,403	7,826	17	29	562	763	178	168	457	420
Kenya	3,052	2,666	1,564	1,236	1,152	1,275	7,807	7,822	292	230	476	404	435	637	369	451
Kiribati	...	...	...	...	10	13	8,496	8,873	...	...	...	...	4	5	4	4
Korea, North	6,826	9,488	3,590	4,093	1,532	2,050	12,191	12,424	250	270	765	818	577	1,020	1,891	2,545
Korea, South	8,441	8,653	4,140	5,336	2,297	1,485	16,953	20,385	48	63	806	1,029	595	1,413	5,948	8,869
Kuwait	...	...	2,000	3,279	...	...	10,500	15,000	...	...	...	...	1	1	27	31
Laos	920	1,040	1,312	1,481	55	153	9,939	11,769	13	21	1,494	2,100	73	115	148	205
Lebanon	77	31	1,222	1,278	54	137	6,979	16,279	12	10	840	971	679	762	283	418
Lesotho	180	132	772	996	5	6	12,951	15,409	20	15	617	682	12	15	18	26
Liberia	241	250	1,220	1,190	302	350	3,886	3,867	3	3	494	508	110	127	58	71
Libya	263	195	449	346	82	116	5,071	7,871	7	10	1,131	1,117	134	183	475	609
Liechtenstein	...	...	...	...	10	11	18,679	18,869	...	...	...	...	...	...	...	...
Luxembourg[2]	...	...	...	...	...	...	...	...	...	...	...	...	...	...	...	...
Macau	...	...	...	...	1	2	10,211	10,301	...	...	...	...	3	4	1	2
Madagascar	2,135	2,264	1,805	1,658	1,867	2,614	6,118	5,979	71	54	875	743	953	775	273	285
Malawi	1,268	1,674	1,057	1,220	152	210	3,892	4,000	188	218	612	612	202	230	181	212
Malaysia	2,050	2,009	2,724	2,838	505	555	10,233	9,568	...	...	...	...	853	883	433	513
Maldives	1	...	905	783	6	8	5,155	5,171	...	...	600	600	6	8	14	17
Mali	1,215	880	779	511	86	134	9,041	9,437	33	55	1,088	1,038	9	13	101	235
Malta	4	6	2,089	2,739	20	22	8,784	9,263	2	1	2,117	2,535	9	8	46	45
Martinique	...	...	...	...	35	21	10,018	9,304	...	...	...	...	262	194	28	29
Mauritania	51	38	414	337	5	5	1,119	1,885	16	15	340	259	13	13	3	8
Mauritius	2	1	2,589	2,722	11	15	15,686	22,167	1	1	463	650	8	8	24	28
Mayotte	...	...	...	...	...	...	...	...	...	...	...	...	...	...	...	...
Mexico	15,908	25,256	1,698	2,137	837	1,063	12,070	13,602	1,129	1,706	633	727	5,891	7,208	2,819	3,494
Monaco	...	...	...	...	...	...	...	...	...	...	...	...	...	...	...	...
Mongolia	391	800	900	1,473	33	55	7,655	6,875	2	1	480	550	3	5	23	40
Montserrat	...	...	1,000	1,800	...	...	2,500	2,500	...	...	...	...	2	1	...	...
Morocco	4,748	3,587	1,049	762	213	450	11,449	11,250	543	284	953	682	1,351	1,487	1,220	1,417
Mozambique	700	340	719	380	2,534	2,010	4,617	3,899	73	40	611	320	318	310	184	185
Nauru	...	...	...	...	...	...	...	...	...	...	...	...	...	...	...	...
Nepal	3,780	4,302	1,755	1,867	376	457	5,651	5,821	54	67	397	419	124	145	210	250
Netherlands, The	1,185	1,309	4,771	6,347	5,319	5,457	35,141	33,130	32	46	2,883	3,857	551	523	2,323	2,835
Netherlands Antilles	1	1	653	711	...	...	...	...	...	...	...	...	...	...	...	...
New Caledonia	1	3	2,538	2,672	18	24	5,861	6,305	...	...	688	1,000	8	9	4	4
New Zealand	720	864	3,494	4,507	235	230	25,365	26,455	52	60	2,533	3,000	267	416	315	440
Nicaragua	331	488	1,045	1,595	24	29	4,069	4,030	48	47	768	684	325	348	43	49
Niger	1,119	1,749	395	408	216	211	6,620	7,038	199	284	222	180	28	39	97	148
Nigeria	8,237	7,642	662	611	27,662	28,477	10,062	9,483	845	840	205	204	1,968	2,470	2,434	3,600
Niue	...	...	...	...	2	2	2,186	2,552	...	...	...	...	1	2	...	...
Norfolk Island	...	...	...	...	...	...	...	...	...	...	...	...	...	...	...	...
Norway	904	1,081	3,052	3,379	601	470	22,958	22,387	...	...	...	...	118	128	164	198
Oman	5	3	1,628	3,002	...	...	...	...	...	...	...	...	76	128	8	170
Pacific Is., Trust Territory of the	...	...	1,073	1,133	11	13	8,390	8,250	...	...	600	500	3	2	3	3
Pakistan	13,302	19,314	1,389	1,693	297	578	10,768	10,931	781	709	522	519	2,106	2,455	2,018	2,224
Panama	232	237	1,194	1,580	76	70	8,230	7,250	5	4	320	489	1,186	1,285	37	51
Papua New Guinea	3	3	1,871	1,487	1,027	1,149	6,873	6,820	1	2	500	500	964	1,110	225	262

livestock														country
cattle		sheep		hogs		chickens		milk[e]				eggs[f]		
stock ('000 head)		stock ('000 head)		stock ('000 head)		stock ('000 head)		production ('000 metric tons)		yield (kg/animal)		production (metric tons)		
1974–76 average	1983	1974–76 average	1983	1974–76 average	1983	1974–76 average	1983	1974–76 average	1983	1974–76 average	1983	1974–76 average	1983	
23,939	23,656	10,582	12,103	11,681	11,709	164,000	187,000	29,571	35,150	2,897	3,413	752,667	900,000	France
2	12	...	...	5	10	...	...	...	...	...	...	219	305	French Guiana
6	9	3	2	19	30	...	...	2	2	2,805	1,800	552	900	French Polynesia
3	7	58	80	124	145	1,000	2,000	...	...	250	250	470	1,000	Gabon
284	300	130	185	9	12	—	—	5	5	175	175	355	576	Gambia, The
2	5	20	18	...	...	...	...	13	12	3,205	4,880	1,583	2,778	Gaza Strip
5,533	5,690	1,824	2,198	11,290	12,107	47,000	51,000	8,087	8,208	3,794	3,632	298,652	336,000	Germany, East
14,429	15,098	1,048	1,172	20,164	22,478	92,000	80,000	21,759	26,927	4,017	4,869	878,835	775,000	Germany, West
929	800	1,655	2,000	367	375	11,000	13,000	8	7	55	55	9,907	15,860	Ghana
														Gibraltar
1,219	850	8,334	8,400	765	1,400	29,000	36,000	695	690	1,434	1,980	109,305	125,100	Greece
...	...	20	24	...	...	...	...	...	...	...	...	...	...	Greenland
6	6	8	16	11	11	—	—	1	2	800	800	950	1,000	Grenada
80	90	3	3	32	51	1,000	1,000	11	13	499	500	429	720	Guadeloupe
2	2	...	...	10	14	—	—	...	...	...	...	1,250	1,300	Guam
1,515	2,300	518	550	609	870	11,000	15,000	301	340	911	919	30,893	40,050	Guatemala
														Guernsey
1,493	1,900	400	450	32	44	5,000	9,000	35	44	185	185	5,242	9.765	Guinea
155	225	28	65	81	130	—	—	6	7	170	170	240	336	Guinea-Bissau
275	310	106	117	118	142	10,000	14,000	12	15	783	759	3,417	4,100	Guyana
858	1,300	79	92	1,650	800	4,000	5,000	22	21	223	228	1,780	3,250	Haiti
1,817	2,418	5	5	514	409	4,000	5,000	232	281	650	652	15,240	21,090	Honduras
10	4	...	...	387	510	4,000	7,000	5	4	2,069	2,752	5,800	1,960	Hong Kong
1,950	1,922	1,979	3,180	7,752	9,035	53,000	63,000	1,866	2,800	2,607	3,728	215,438	215,000	Hungary
65	64	857	748	7	12	—	—	128	131	3,483	3,729	2,705	3,650	Iceland
179,462	182,000	40,000	41,700	7,233	8,600	141,000	150,000	10,867	14,000	500	538	463,333	775,000	India
6,211	6,600	3,253	4,300	2,724	3,600	93,000	170,000	62	135	836	844	66,713	235,000	Indonesia
7,238	8,600	34,833	34,500	55	30	58,000	74,000	1,210	1,786	769	787	176,667	200,000	Iran
2,528	3,000	11,626	12,000	...	...	15,000	20,000	675	1,125	750	750	16,050	22,000	Iraq
7,179	6,771	3,706	3,480	881	1,145	9,000	8,000	4,279	5,490	3,031	3,629	39,731	34,000	Ireland
...	...	...	...	...	...	...	...	...	...	...	...	...	...	Isle of Man
291	330	200	240	78	95	19,000	26,000	616	765	6,011	6,955	90,275	100,800	Israel
8,336	9,127	7,985	9,256	8,634	9,132	107,000	110,000	9,475	10,650	3,208	3,499	663,967	640,000	Italy
550	780	997	1,380	232	400	7,000	17,000	23	43	261	344	4,333	18,200	Ivory Coast
277	315	5	6	229	270	4,000	5,000	47	53	1,000	1,000	12,833	17,000	Jamaica
3,672	4,590	13	21	7,720	10,273	244,000	297,000	5,031	7,036	4,051	4,790	1,820,333	2,085,000	Japan
														Jersey
40	40	710	1,000	...	...	23,000	30,000	13	9	813	1,023	7,050	11,070	Jordan
1,150	1,148	2	1	600	717	4,000	4,000	18	16	170	170	2,910	3,500	Kampuchea
9,609	11,500	3,068	6,500	61	100	16,000	19,000	897	1,300	463	480	16,920	26,400	Kenya
...	...	...	...	10	10	—	—	...	...	...	...	100	112	Kiribati
827	1,000	256	330	1,607	2,500	17,000	18,000	27	68	2,000	2,267	71,140	115,000	Korea, North
1,682	1,754	5	4	1,663	2,183	23,000	47,000	163	604	4,321	5,119	173,980	295,000	Korea, South
8	18	114	550	...	...	6,000	8,000	11	30	2,248	2,556	2,102	10,000	Kuwait
326	490	...	...	609	1,300	5,000	6,000	5	7	200	200	13,333	26,000	Laos
60	50	197	140	19	19	5,000	8,000	54	94	1,876	5,000	22,483	31,695	Lebanon
500	600	1,411	1,400	78	65	1,000	1,000	17	21	290	290	765	826	Lesotho
34	42	172	232	90	115	2,000	3,000	1	1	100	100	1,872	2,880	Liberia
178	200	4,039	4,800	...	...	4,000	7,000	53	65	1,194	2,177	6,840	20,558	Libya
8	9	1	2	8	9	—	—	15	18	3,196	3,325	250	250	Liechtenstein
...	...	...	...	...	...	...	...	...	...	...	...	...	...	Luxembourg[2]
...	...	...	...	10	5	—	—	...	...	...	...	525	605	Macau
8,543	10,322	632	630	607	1,300	13,000	18,000	30	41	700	700	9,808	14,164	Madagascar
658	900	82	87	173	210	8,000	8,000	26	39	368	460	9,667	11,050	Malawi
425	600	46	66	1,343	2,100	80,000	78,000	19	24	637	688	90,300	106,000	Malaysia
...	...	...	...	...	...	...	...	...	...	...	...	...	...	Maldives
3,889	5,400	4,867	6,450	25	46	13,000	14,000	78	108	200	200	6,810	7,380	Mali
12	15	8	5	22	5	1,000	1,000	26	40	3,533	4,736	6,059	7,537	Malta
48	58	36	54	35	40	1,000	2,000	4	5	635	738	953	1,600	Martinique
1,121	1,500	3,837	5,000	...	...	3,000	3,000	61	88	350	350	2,388	3,060	Mauritania
52	58	3	4	5	10	1,000	2,000	23	25	2,304	2,500	2,281	3,400	Mauritius
...	...	...	...	...	...	...	...	...	...	...	...	...	...	Mayotte
28,636	33,873	7,432	6,500	13,196	18,900	141,000	203,000	4,949	7,300	620	802	423,777	660,000	Mexico
...	...	...	...	...	...	...	...	...	...	...	...	...	...	Monaco
2,342	2,396	14,346	14,955	14	39	—	—	150	170	299	306	415	1,000	Mongolia
8	9	3	4	2	1	—	—	1	2	750	750	44	48	Montserrat
3,547	3,000	15,023	15,000	11	11	19,000	25,000	479	800	555	630	55,067	80,000	Morocco
1,384	1,440	114	112	143	135	14,000	19,000	58	68	170	170	7,800	11,500	Mozambique
...	...	...	...	2	2	—	—	...	...	...	...	8	9	Nauru
6,583	6,980	2,303	2,480	315	365	20,000	24,000	207	235	500	500	13,000	15,500	Nepal
4,662	5,390	763	750	7,168	10,590	66,000	90,000	10,209	13,200	4,612	5,333	284,103	650,000	Netherlands, The
8	9	8	8	6	8	—	—	4	4	1,296	1,250	457	555	Netherlands Antilles
113	100	5	2	24	20	...	...	3	4	600	600	453	1,000	New Caledonia
9,207	7,800	55,868	70,400	439	425	7,000	8,000	6,116	6,800	2,989	3,400	55,669	57,000	New Zealand
2,560	2,200	2	3	640	520	4,000	5,000	441	124	1,185	687	22,778	31,676	Nicaragua
2,497	3,521	2,216	3,448	26	33	8,000	11,000	65	106	163	200	5,168	7,480	Niger
11,073	12,300	10,124	12,850	882	1,300	85,000	150,000	299	357	270	290	114,983	235,000	Nigeria
1	1	...	...	1	1	—	—	...	...	825	714	34	36	Niue
...	...	...	...	...	...	...	...	...	...	...	...	...	...	Norfolk Island
930	975	1,646	2,272	705	705	4,000	4,000	1,831	2,017	4,667	5,300	38,816	51,000	Norway
126	150	48	140	...	...	1,000	1,000	26	28	700	700	483	743	Oman
9	8	...	...	19	27	...	...	...	...	...	...	131	149	Pacific Is., Trust Territory of the
14,810	16,157	17,493	23,531	...	...	27,000	72,000	2,156	2,353	888	888	43,533	153,000	Pakistan
1,347	1,459	...	...	173	197	4,000	6,000	71	93	949	979	12,233	17,500	Panama
126	134	...	2	1,253	1,450	1,000	1,000	1	...	217	194	1,563	1,818	Papua New Guinea

Crops and livestock (continued)

country	grains production ('000 metric tons) 1974–76 average	1983	grains yield (kg/hectare) 1974–76 average	1983	roots and tubers[a] production ('000 metric tons) 1974–76 average	1983	roots and tubers yield (kg/hectare) 1974–76 average	1983	pulses[b] production ('000 metric tons) 1974–76 average	1983	pulses yield (kg/hectare) 1974–76 average	1983	fruits[c] production ('000 metric tons) 1974–76 average	1983	vegetables[d] production ('000 metric tons) 1974–76 average	1983
Paraguay	401	770	1,400	1,492	1,575	2,334	14,144	14,452	60	84	800	829	607	790	206	222
Peru	1,510	1,519	1,830	2,172	2,425	1,849	7,007	7,400	105	92	824	839	1,593	1,160	744	719
Philippines	8,818	11,535	1,303	1,722	1,890	3,587	5,293	7,556	42	45	711	726	3,213	7,189	1,409	2,114
Pitcairn Island	...	...	...	...	...	...	...	...			...	...	...	...	...	...
Poland	21,133	22,099	2,673	2,726	48,300	34,473	18,743	15,529	271	297	1,223	1,349	1,479	2,572	3,872	4,373
Portugal	1,595	1,087	1,118	870	1,165	1,022	8,764	7,644	89	67	232	215	2,104	1,615	1,697	1,551
Puerto Rico	3	3	747	743	40	35	5,975	5,648	6	7	653	762	286	289	24	33
Qatar	...	1	3,568	3,699	...	...	10,600	10,000	...	...			...	...	...	16
Réunion	13	14	4,641	5,600	11	11	14,651	13,452	1	1	2,787	2,037	23	30	9	11
Romania	16,202	17,695	2,628	2,909	3,874	6,100	12,685	21,371	112	108	124	214	2,419	3,677	3,600	5,130
Rwanda	215	279	1,037	1,142	1,217	2,096	8,299	9,971	199	232	747	823	1,754	2,202	143	181
St. Christopher and Nevis	...	...	...	...	4	4	3,201	3,382	...	...	1,000	1,000	3	3	2	2
St. Helena and Ascension	...	...	...	...	...	...	...	...			...	...	...	...	...	...
St. Lucia	...	...	700	692	9	11	4,500	4,254	...	...	2,000	2,000	101	109	1	...
St. Pierre and Miquelon	...	...	...	...	...	...	...	...			...	...	...	...	...	...
St. Vincent and the Grenadines	...	1	3,193	3,351	23	23	7,340	7,674	...	...	790	962	28	36	2	1
San Marino	...	...	...	...	...	...	...	...			...	...	...	...	...	...
São Tomé and Principe	1	1	1,514	1,556	13	15	12,015	13,393	...	...	...	...	3	4	2	3
Saudi Arabia	291	805	737	1,730	1	3	5,045	7,500	5	7	1,741	1,959	392	561	657	1,047
Senegal	826	486	720	512	110	33	3,049	3,487	20	25	322	386	56	82	66	92
Seychelles	...	...	...	...	...	...	6,250	5,000	...	...	...	...	2	2	1	2
Sierra Leone	584	652	1,428	1,504	122	139	4,306	3,354	28	32	550	588	112	142	147	173
Singapore	...	...	...	...	8	5	6,217	5,770	...	...	...	...	16	8	39	42
Solomon Islands	2	10	1,995	3,333	74	87	13,146	15,016	1	2	777	1,000	10	12	4	5
Somalia	233	244	636	759	31	39	10,800	10,840	8	6	330	333	259	244	25	29
South Africa[3]	11,701	6,134	1,403	944	722	945	12,039	11,386	100	50	764	788	2,570	3,076	1,447	1,679
Bophuthatswana[3]	...	...	...	...	...	...	...	...	...	...	...	...	...	...	...	...
Ciskei[3]	...	...	...	...	...	...	...	...	...	...	...	...	...	...	...	...
Transkei[3]	...	...	...	...	...	...	...	...	...	...	...	...	...	...	...	...
Venda[3]	...	...	...	...	...	...	...	...	...	...	...	...	...	...	...	...
South West Africa/Namibia	61	64	382	386	138	140	8,737	8,750	3	4	1,020	1,143	23	25	21	20
Spain	13,418	13,716	1,834	1,868	5,611	5,155	14,088	15,096	477	325	699	700	10,955	11,998	8,032	8,566
Sri Lanka	1,391	2,240	1,825	2,295	950	810	4,435	9,496	12	29	519	626	956	1,156	218	245
Sudan, The	2,474	2,375	645	495	288	311	3,604	3,503	74	91	1,067	1,169	698	802	760	869
Suriname	170	280	3,630	3,994	3	4	5,860	4,938	...	...	847	880	59	55	3	8
Swaziland	110	53	1,484	980	14	17	3,777	3,488	3	4	634	592	106	113	11	13
Sweden	5,697	5,421	3,665	3,652	1,051	958	23,499	24,251	19	26	1,853	2,040	201	189	237	247
Switzerland	803	888	4,521	5,068	869	711	35,544	30,000	3	1	3,248	3,667	699	751	261	215
Syria	2,480	2,747	950	961	121	300	13,047	16,667	212	178	800	884	520	984	2,044	3,675
Taiwan	...	...	...	...	...	...	...	...	...	...	...	...	...	...	...	...
Tanzania	1,961	2,805	1,003	1,098	5,459	7,266	4,961	5,257	190	227	439	433	1,515	2,139	889	1,014
Thailand	17,478	22,418	1,882	1,974	8,511	17,364	13,598	12,956	196	353	758	650	2,484	3,884	2,771	3,040
Togo	254	286	939	911	870	979	13,024	12,361	23	30	285	379	36	45	56	76
Tokelau	...	...	...	...	...	...	18,615	17,667	...	...	...	...	...	...	...	...
Tonga	...	...	...	...	89	96	10,946	10,977	...	...	...	...	10	11	6	6
Trinidad and Tobago	24	33	2,859	2,977	21	19	11,812	11,759	3	4	1,454	1,671	71	64	32	31
Tunisia	1,153	956	824	585	95	140	9,500	12,727	81	100	557	756	461	487	881	1,163
Turkey	21,239	24,637	1,579	1,918	2,538	3,080	13,871	17,171	697	1,056	1,163	1,153	6,366	8,067	10,437	13,556
Turks and Caicos Islands	...	...	...	...	...	...	...	...	...	...	...	...	...	...	...	...
Tuvalu	...	...	...	...	...	...	...	...			...	...	...	...	...	...
Uganda	1,603	1,562	1,214	1,630	1,982	2,610	3,749	3,805	337	421	635	856	3,303	3,890	244	290
U.S.S.R.	178,965	185,488	1,466	1,596	84,942	83,000	11,088	12,053	7,562	6,600	1,366	1,055	13,926	17,513	27,509	33,189
United Arab Emirates	...	1	...	...	...	1	15,533	15,152	...	...	...	...	29	68	34	130
United Kingdom	14,531	21,504	3,930	5,424	5,578	5,849	25,664	29,995	210	195	2,644	2,624	579	575	3,483	3,559
United States	237,507	208,903	3,339	3,552	16,054	15,312	27,227	28,252	1,050	885	1,425	1,617	24,319	24,918	24,075	26,437
Uruguay	1,099	1,123	1,280	1,709	211	220	5,250	5,946	5	6	878	963	305	314	144	184
Vanuatu	1	1	500	520	30	30	20,108	20,000	...	...	...	...	4	6	5	7
Venezuela	907	1,219	1,548	2,094	539	708	7,647	8,219	39	34	427	519	1,788	2,171	291	405
Vietnam	11,550	14,962	2,127	2,371	2,734	4,900	6,461	5,344	88	137	479	741	1,967	3,083	2,194	2,839
Virgin Islands (U.S.)	...	...	...	...	...	...	...	...	...	...	...	...	...	...	...	...
Wallis and Futuna	...	...	...	...	6	6	10,290	10,258	...	...	...	...	...	1	8	9
West Bank	...	...	...	...	...	...	...	...	...	...	...	...	...	...	...	...
Western Sahara	1	2	696	708	...	...	...	...	...	...	...	...	...	...	...	...
Western Samoa	...	...	...	...	33	41	6,873	6,989	...	...	...	...	53	56	...	...
Yemen (Aden)	107	114	1,651	1,550	1	1	5,030	4,792	...	...	...	...	72	83	103	115
Yemen (Şan'ā')	1,045	317	817	434	71	140	11,042	12,069	70	15	995	219	136	183	167	285
Yugoslavia	15,627	17,268	3,292	3,929	2,783	2,580	8,859	9,416	234	216	1,190	1,122	2,635	3,797	2,506	2,935
Zaire	754	987	745	810	12,385	15,359	6,882	6,902	144	151	609	543	2,423	2,473	452	524
Zambia	1,532	988	1,217	1,669	189	235	3,378	3,710	10	7	595	350	59	85	176	228
Zimbabwe	2,337	1,332	1,446	735	74	94	3,985	4,495	28	52	602	797	88	116	124	139

livestock														country
cattle		sheep		hogs		chickens		milk[e]				eggs[f]		
stock ('000 head)		stock ('000 head)		stock ('000 head)		stock ('000 head)		production ('000 metric tons)		yield (kg/animal)		production (metric tons)		
1974–76 average	1983	1974–76 average	1983	1974–76 average	1983	1974–76 average	1983	1974–76 average	1983	1974–76 average	1983	1974–76 average	1983	
5,152	5,600	364	440	973	1,350	9,000	14,000	119	175	1,906	1,902	17,467	26,300	Paraguay
4,152	3,204	15,227	14,500	2,120	1,890	33,000	40,000	816	757	1,269	1,113	49,978	68,000	Peru
1,716	1,938	30	30	7,096	7,980	47,000	62,000	14	10	1,067	909	165,070	222,000	Philippines
...	...	...	...	...	...	...	...	...	...	...	...	...	...	Pitcairn Island
13,052	11,269	3,209	4,103	20,552	15,587	85,000	61,000	16,521	16,496	2,709	2,901	445,022	422,600	Poland
1,193	990	3,924	5,220	1,899	3,480	16,000	18,000	677	800	2,276	2,373	44,065	72,000	Portugal
549	585	6	6	246	206	5,000	6,000	387	384	2,081	2,302	18,309	19,728	Puerto Rico
7	10	38	53	...	...	—	—	5	6	1,531	1,523	...	...	Qatar
20	19	2	3	93	71	2,000	4,000	4	6	491	577	2,133	2,400	Réunion
5,792	6,010	14,032	16,921	8,789	12,000	63,000	111,000	3,557	3,134	1,726	1,753	251,350	347,500	Romania
677	652	236	312	71	150	1,000	1,000	23	24	296	300	602	1,100	Rwanda
8	8	21	24	17	20	—	—	...	...	...	...	248	325	St. Christopher and Nevis
1	1	1	2	1	1	—	—	...	...	...	...	...	...	St. Helena and Ascension
8	12	10	14	8	11	—	—	1	1	1,272	1,408	445	510	St. Lucia
...	...	...	...	...	...	...	...	...	...	...	...	...	...	St. Pierre and Miquelon
7	8	9	13	5	7	—	—	1	1	1,343	1,217	423	560	St. Vincent and the Grenadines
...	...	...	...	...	...	...	...	...	...	...	...	...	...	San Marino
2	3	1	2	4	3	—	—	...	...	170	170	128	160	São Tomé and Príncipe
284	500	2,064	3,500	...	...	4,000	15,000	142	266	1,000	1,004	11,825	60,000	Saudi Arabia
2,316	2,250	1,679	2,100	182	150	6,000	9,000	80	81	344	360	4,875	7,200	Senegal
2	2	...	...	11	13	—	—	1	1	500	500	347	560	Seychelles
318	351	220	320	26	42	3,000	4,000	17	18	350	350	3,729	5,002	Sierra Leone
5	4	...	...	1,106	1,300	12,000	14,000	1	1	1,000	1,000	23,433	26,945	Singapore
23	23	...	...	40	48	—	—	1	1	600	600	263	280	Solomon Islands
3,665	4,050	9,246	10,400	8	10	2,000	3,000	144	163	345	350	1,920	2,560	Somalia
12,591	13,086	30,762	31,750	1,324	1,450	25,000	32,000	2,498	2,600	2,551	2,826	144,129	180,000	South Africa[3]
...	...	...	...	...	...	...	...	...	...	...	...	...	...	Bophuthatswana[3]
...	...	...	...	...	...	...	...	...	...	...	...	...	...	Ciskei[3]
...	...	...	...	...	...	...	...	...	...	...	...	...	...	Transkei[3]
...	...	...	...	...	...	...	...	...	...	...	...	...	...	Venda[3]
2,783	1,900	5,000	5,500	32	42	—	1,000	62	68	388	412	115	165	South West Africa/Namibia
4,412	5,070	16,103	17,000	8,252	11,700	49,000	54,000	5,199	6,250	2,843	3,371	557,210	719,000	Spain
1,724	1,700	29	28	39	80	6,000	6,000	148	198	408	466	17,164	20,000	Sri Lanka
14,718	19,550	13,880	19,500	...	...	22,000	30,000	840	1,000	500	500	20,310	40,000	Sudan, The
27	53	4	4	18	18	1,000	1,000	8	8	1,552	1,238	2,868	2,750	Suriname
621	700	33	40	18	23	1,000	1,000	32	38	244	253	263	285	Swaziland
1,884	1,932	377	435	2,509	2,620	12,000	13,000	3,175	3,766	4,698	5,680	107,000	115,400	Sweden
1,981	1,919	367	349	2,011	2,166	6,000	6,000	3,389	3,725	3,816	4,461	41,868	44,839	Switzerland
552	800	5,865	11,000			7,000	15,000	260	629	1,093	1,546	29,250	105,000	Syria
...	128[1,4]	...	1771[1,5]	...	4,826[1]	...	44,000[1]	...	501[1,6]	...	...	...	...	Taiwan
11,335	13,446	3,428	4,020	137	175	14,000	19,000	322	387	160	160	23,048	40,300	Tanzania
4,205	4,600	49	22	3,599	3,800	54,000	65,000	4	5	1,250	1,316	82,667	117,500	Thailand
211	260	792	840	257	380	2,000	3,000	3	4	100	100	1,612	4,158	Togo
...	...	...	...	1	1	—	—	...	...	...	...	5	4	Tokelau
6	11	...	...	47	79	—	—	...	...	1,494	1,497	279	384	Tonga
72	76	9	12	54	62	6,000	8,000	7	8	1,733	1,640	7,353	7,700	Trinidad and Tobago
880	560	5,726	5,100	3	4	13,000	15,000	204	230	851	1,150	16,333	42,000	Tunisia
14,490	17,100	40,666	49,636	15	14	39,000	59,000	2,941	3,700	589	587	137,487	250,000	Turkey
...	...	...	...	...	...	...	...	...	...	...	...	...	...	Turks and Caicos Islands
...	...	...	...	...	6	—	—	...	...	...	...	...	13	Tuvalu
4,745	5,100	973	1,080	167	270	11,000	14,000	276	385	350	350	11,860	14,000	Uganda
108,807	117,186	143,125	142,182	66,735	76,671	727,000	1,044,000	90,086	96,000	2,158	2,192	3,096,433	4,116,000	U.S.S.R.
27	30	97	140	...	...	—	3,000	11	5	790	500	947	3,800	United Arab Emirates
14,694	13,331	28,411	34,022	8,013	8,189	133,000	118,000	14,115	17,252	4,227	5,139	798,784	736,483	United Kingdom
129,265	115,199	14,712	12,026	54,858	53,935	391,000	379,000	53,095	63,488	4,769	5,709	3,830,221	4,004,000	United States
10,959	10,308	15,274	20,070	454	440	6,000	6,000	741	818	1,669	1,543	13,069	18,500	Uruguay
105	100	...	...	63	70	—	—	2	2	197	200	203	240	Vanuatu
9,112	12,092	238	412	1,682	3,200	27,000	42,000	1,185	1,552	1,103	1,287	92,756	152,335	Venezuela
1,523	2,000	11	18	8,975	10,785	56,000	50,000	16	30	800	800	109,000	140,000	Vietnam
7	8	...	...	...	...	—	—	3	3	3,732	3,434	170	206	Virgin Islands (U.S.)
...	...	...	...	9	22	—	—	...	...	1,500	1,500	28	40	Wallis and Futuna
...	...	...	...	...	...	...	...	...	...	...	...	...	...	West Bank
...	...	16	22	...	...	...	...	...	...	...	...	...	...	Western Sahara
22	26	...	...	47	60	—	1,000	1	1	1,047	1,000	123	176	Western Samoa
80	120	843	1,000	...	...	1,000	2,000	7	8	400	400	1,423	1,852	Yemen (Aden)
883	950	3,050	3,150	...	...	3,000	4,000	59	65	200	200	9,801	11,495	Yemen (San'ā')
5,769	5,351	7,953	7,452	7,540	8,370	52,000	68,000	3,662	4,550	1,405	1,658	184,917	239,308	Yugoslavia
1,132	1,300	719	760	673	750	11,000	16,000	6	6	786	854	6,465	7,360	Zaire
1,791	2,380	28	40	164	250	18,000	18,000	50	64	300	300	26,947	27,360	Zambia
6,060	5,350	731	455	201	192	8,000	9,000	194	160	1,529	1,553	9,003	11,550	Zimbabwe

[1]1981.   [2]Belgium includes Luxembourg.   [3]South Africa includes Bophuthatswana, Ciskei, Transkei, and Venda.   [4]Includes buffalo.   [5]Includes goats.   [6]Includes goat and sheep milk.

Extractive industries

Extractive industries are generally defined as those activities involved in the exploitation of natural resources and include such industries as mining, forestry, fisheries, and agriculture; the definition is sometimes confined to nonrenewable resources. For the purposes of this table agriculture is excluded; it is covered in tables elsewhere in *Britannica World Data*.

Extractive industries are here divided into three parts: mining, forestry, and fisheries. These major headings are each divided into two main subheadings, one that treats production and one that treats foreign trade. The production sections are presented in terms of volume except for mining, and the trade sections are presented in terms of U.S. dollars. The formulation of the sections was determined by the systems of classification used in standard international sources. "Extractive," for example, may imply the production of primary raw materials only, but because of the way national statistical information is reported the table may also include some processed and manufactured materials as well, since these are often indistinguishably associated with the extractive process (sulfur from petroleum extraction, cured or treated lumber, or "processed" fish). This is also the case in the trade sections, where individual national trade nomenclatures may not distinguish some processed and manufactured goods from unprocessed raw materials.

Mining. In the absence of a single international standard of practice for calculating or reporting value of mineral production, single-country sources have been used to compile mining production figures. Each country has its own methods of classifying mining data, which do not always accord with the principal mineral production categories adopted in this table; namely, "metals," "nonmetals," and "energy." The available data have therefore been adjusted to make them accord better with the definition of each category. Included in the "metal" category are all ferrous and nonferrous metallic ores, concentrates, and scrap; the "nonmetal" group includes all nonmetallic minerals (stone, clay, precious gems, etc.) except the mineral fuels; the last group, "energy," is composed predominantly of the natural hydrocarbon fuels, though it may also include manufactured gas.

Although the contribution (value) of each national mineral sector to its country's gross domestic product is given, statistics regarding the value of mineral production are less readily available in country sources than those regarding the volume of minerals produced. The volume figures, in addition, cannot be aggregated to provide any useful measure of absolute or relative economic importance. This is because the units of production such as tons, barrels, carats, cubic metres, etc., are not economically equivalent, owing to wide differences between countries in terms of the sales or export value of the commodity and of costs for manpower, transportation, capital investment, and so on. Figures for value of production (usually value added by mineral output), though not always available, were sought first, as they provide a relatively consistent standard to compare the importance of minerals both within a particular national economy and among the largest number of national mineral sectors worldwide. Where value added to the gross domestic product was not available, gross value of production or value of sales was substituted. Figures for total value of production are reported here in millions of U.S. dollars to

Extractive industries

country	% of GDP, 1983	mineral production (value added) year	total ('000,000 U.S.$)	metals[a]	nonmetals[b]	energy[c]	trade (value) year	exports total ('000,000 U.S.$)	metals[a]	nonmetals[b]	energy[c]	imports total ('000,000 U.S.$)	metals[a]	nonmetals[b]	energy[c]
Afghanistan	...	1980–81	233.9[1]	—	0.4[1]	99.6[1]	1979	103.0	—	0.1	99.9	—	—	—	—
Albania	...	...	...	...	...	...	...	...	...	...	...	...	...	...	...
Algeria	26.4	1983	9,341.0	—	1.3[2]	98.7[2]	1981	12,574.4	0.3	0.2	99.5	157.6	12.1	27.1	60.8
American Samoa	...	...	...	...	...	...	1984	...	—	—	—	0.1[4]	—	100.0[4]	—
Andorra	...	...	...	...	...	...	...	...	...	...	...	...	...	...	...
Angola	16.1	1983	549.0	...	...	...	1982	807.8	—	15.7	84.3	0.1	100.0	—	—
Anguilla	...	1981		...	...	...	1981	[7]	...	...	...				
Antigua and Barbuda	0.6	1983	0.7	—	100.0		1981	...	...	...	...				
Argentina	2.8	1980	2,988.6	2.9	12.8	84.3	1982	43.5	30.4	24.2	45.4	737.5	12.5	5.0	82.5
Australia	4.5	1980	9,617.4	46.6[9]	8.4[9]	45.0[9]	1982	7,049.3	57.0	2.0	41.0	2,445.7	0.8	10.0	89.2
Austria	0.4	1983	228.2	5.8[4,9]	16.1[4,9]	78.1[4,9]	1982	172.3	36.4	51.8	11.8	2,812.5	12.9	5.8	81.3
Bahamas, The	9.2	1983	153.2[11]				1982	28.7	—	95.4	4.6	3,444.5	—	—	99.9
Bahrain	31.8[4]	1980	1,152.2	—	—	100.0	1982	3,311.1	5.0	—	95.0	1,855.2	0.4	0.1	99.5
Bangladesh	...	...	...	—	5.7[12]	94.3[12]	1980	...	—	—	—	106.2	4.9	28.6	66.5
Barbados	0.3	1983	8.4	—	—100.0—		1982	—	—	—	—	4.9	—	—	100.0
Belgium	0.5	1982	448.8[13]	...	...	...	1982[14]	3,674.7[14]	6.7[14]	87.8[14]	5.5[14]	12,734.2[14]	10.5[14]	26.0[14]	63.5[14]
Belize	0.2	1983	0.5				1980	—	—	—	—	1.4	—	41.4	58.6
Benin	0.2	1983	2.0	—	—100.0[15]—		1983	...	—	—100.0[15]—		—	—	—	—
Bermuda	...	1978–79	2.0	...	...	...	1984	0.1	100.0	—	—	1.6[16]	—	31.6	68.4[16]
Bhutan	0.8[8]	1981	1.0[18]	...	...	...						...	...	...	
Bolivia	6.6	1983	437.0	55.8	—	44.2	1983	767.4	45.3	—	54.7	0.6[19]	100.0[19]	—	—
Botswana	28.7	1983	181.0	12.5[6,9]	86.6[6,9]	0.9[6,9]	[20]	[20]	[20]	[20]	[20]	[20]	[20]	[20]	[20]
Brazil	1.2	1983	2,162.7	25.3[9]	22.1[9]	52.6[9]	1982	2,295.7	84.3	3.5	12.2	11,040.9	0.5	1.5	98.0
British Virgin Islands	...	1980		—	100.0		1980	[21]	—	100.0		0.1	—	100.0	—
Brunei	62.1	1982	2,553.9	...	...	...	1982	3,665.9	—	—	100.0	3.6	17.4	82.6	—
Bulgaria	...	...	...	...	...	...	...	...	...	...	...	...	...	...	...
Burkina Faso	0.1	1983	1.0	—	100.0										
Burma	1.2	1982	71.9[23]	...	...	...	1982	57.3	56.5	21.2	22.3	31.3[24]	—	0.9[24]	99.1[24]
Burundi	...						1982	0.4[4]	100.0[4]	—	—	4.4	—	100.0	—
Cameroon	8.3	1983	509.0[15]	...	...	...	1982	482.3	0.1	—	99.9	29.9	66.6	33.4	—
Canada	5.6	1982	15,441.4	32.0	12.9	55.1	1982	11,717.0	22.1	10.0	67.9	6,451.6	18.8	4.1	77.1
Cape Verde	1.0	1983	1.0	—	100.0		1980	0.4	4.2	95.8	—	0.8	—	—	100.0
Cayman Islands	...						1980	0.3	—	100.0	—	0.4	—	—	100.0
Central African Republic	3.2	1982	20.0[25]	—100.0[25]—			1982	26.8	—	98.3	1.7	1.4[4]	—	100.0[4]	—
Chad	0.5	1983	3.0	—	100.0		1975	0.3	—	100.0	—	0.7	—	100.0	—
Chile	8.9	1982	1,474.8	...	...	...	1982	552.0[4]	90.3[4]	8.8[4]	0.9[4]	352.2	2.0	3.0	95.0
China	...	1982	...	...	...	...	1982	3,923.9	4.1	4.2	91.7	773.4	76.4	15.7	7.9
Christmas Island	...	1982		—	100.0		1982	...	—	100.0		...	...	...	...
Cocos (Keeling) Islands	...						1982								
Colombia	2.9	1982	1,064.9	...	...	...	1982	52.4	0.6	78.0	21.4	290.7	4.8	15.1	80.1
Comoros	—	1983					1976					—	—	—	—
Congo	24.8[6]	1982	668.0[15]	...	...	...	1980	895.8	0.2	4.3	95.5	8.5[2]	—	14.0[2]	86.0[2]
Cook Islands	—	1982					1980					0.1	—	42.1	57.9
Costa Rica	1.9	1979	75.9	—100.0—			1982	1.3[8]	96.7[8]	3.3[8]	—	110.2	—	3.9	96.1
Cuba	...						1982	271.1	100.0	—	—	386.0	0.1	4.6	95.3
Cyprus	0.7	1982	18.3	13.8	86.2	—	1982	16.8	27.4	72.6	—	144.3	—	2.5	97.5
Czechoslovakia	...	1981	4,408.0[9]	10.0[9]	12.5[9]	77.5[9]	1981	448.9[16]	2.5	11.0	86.5[16]	2,993.6[16,19]	15.2[19]	7.1[19]	77.7[16,19]
Denmark	0.8	1982	355.3	—	12.5	87.5	1982	82.9	57.0	37.9	5.1	1,871.6	1.7	4.8	93.5
Djibouti	—	1983		—	100.0		1982	...	—	—	—	22.9[27]	—6.8—		93.2[27]
Dominica	0.9	1983	0.7	—	100.0		1978	0.1	—	100.0	—	0.3	—	24.5	75.5
Dominican Republic	3.9	1981	272.4	95.9[3,9]	4.1[3,9]		1982	195.6	98.8	1.2	—	327.8	0.1	—	99.9
Ecuador	14.4	1982	1,705.7[11]	—2.3[28]—		97.7[11,28]	1982	736.3	0.1	—	99.9	11.0	—	100.0	—
Egypt	23.3	1983	6,917.0	—4.1[3,12]—		95.9[3,12]	1982	1,734.9	—	0.2	99.8	194.0	2.4	14.4	83.2
El Salvador	0.2	1982	5.6	—100.0—			1981	4.0[4]	25.6[4]	74.4[4]	—	214.3	0.5	2.0	97.5
Equatorial Guinea	—	1983					...	...	...	...	...	...	...	...	...

permit comparisons to be made from country to country. Comparisons can also be made as to the relative importance of each sector within a given country.

Since the data for value of mineral production are obtained mostly from country sources, there is some variation in the time periods to which the data refer. In addition, the time period for which production data are available does not always correspond with the year for which mineral trade data are available.

The Standard International Trade Classification (SITC), Revision 2, was used to determine the commodity groupings for foreign trade statistics. The actual trade data for these groups is taken largely from the United Nations annual *Yearbook of International Trade Statistics* and national sources.

Forestry. Data for the production and trade sections of forestry are based on the United Nations annual *Yearbook of Forest Products*. Production of roundwood (all wood obtained in removals from forests) is the principal indicator of the volume of each country's forestry sector; this total is broken down further (as percentages of the roundwood total) into its principal components: fuelwood and charcoal, and industrial roundwood. The latter group was further divided to show its principal component, sawlogs and veneer; lesser categories of industrial roundwood could not be shown for reasons of space. These included pitprops (used in mining, a principal consumer of wood) and pulpwood (used in papermaking and plastics). Value of trade in forest products is given for both imports and exports, although exports alone tend to be the significant indicator for producing countries, while imports of wood are rarely a significant fraction of the trade of most importing countries.

Fisheries. Data for nominal (live weight) catches of fish, crustaceans, mollusks, etc., in all fishing areas (inland waters and marine areas) are taken from the United Nations annual *Yearbook of Fishery Statistics (Catches and Landings)*. Total catch figures are given in metric tons; the catches in inland waters and marine areas are given as percentages of the total catch, as are the main kinds of catch—fish, crustaceans, and mollusks.

Figures for trade in fishery products (including processed products and preparations like oils, meals, and animal feeding stuffs) are taken from the United Nations annual *Yearbook of Fishery Statistics (Fishery Commodities)*. Value figures for trade in fish products are given for both imports and exports.

The following notes further define the column headings:
a. Includes ferrous and nonferrous metallic ores and scraps, such as bauxite, copper, gold (except unwrought or semimanufactured), iron ore, lead, uranium, or zinc.
b. Includes natural fertilizers; stone, sand, and aggregate; and pearls, precious and semiprecious stones, worked and unworked.
c. Includes hydrocarbon solids, liquids, and gases.
... Not available.
— None, less than half the unit indicated, or not applicable.
1 cubic metre = 35.3147 cubic feet
1 metric ton = 1.1023 short tons

forestry, 1983						fisheries, 1983								country
production of roundwood				trade (value '000 U.S.$)		catch (nominal)						trade (value, '000 U.S.$)		
total ('000 cubic metres)	fuelwood, charcoal (%)	industrial roundwood (%)		exports	imports	total ('000 metric tons)	by source (%)		by kind of catch (%)			exports	imports	
		total	sawlogs, veneer				marine	fresh-water	fish	crusta-ceans	mollusks			
6,681	76.6	23.4	12.8	...	28,496	1.5	—	100.0	100.0	—	—	...	...	Afghanistan
2,330	69.0	31.0	31.0	730	3,900	4.0	100.0	—	100.0	—	—	...	...	Albania
1,685	86.7	13.3	1.2	1,502[3]	372,354	70.0	100.0	—	95.5	4.5	—	163	19,545	Algeria
...	...	...	...	...	1,426[5]	0.4	100.0	—	76.0	0.9	—	171,659	1,265	American Samoa
...	...	...	...	...	...	—	—	—	—	—	—	...	...	Andorra
9,003	85.1	14.9	6.2	98[6]	517	112.4	92.9	7.1	99.9	0.1	0.1	...	19,506	Angola
...	...	...	...	...	...	—	100.0	—	100.0	—	—	49	...	Anguilla
...	...	...	...	...	2,596[8]	2.2	100.0	—	99.2	0.8	—	720	1,493[8]	Antigua and Barbuda
10,520	63.3	36.7	16.2	11,092	214,340	416.3	96.5	3.5	87.7	4.7	7.6	171,600	12,400	Argentina
16,015	15.4	84.6	43.6	218,404	615,452	168.6[10]	...	...	42.2[10]	26.1[10]	31.6[10]	319,166	197,779	Australia
13,647	10.4	89.6	58.5	1,282,141	562,903	4.7	—	100.0	100.0	—	—	2,401	76,131	Austria
115	—	100.0	13.0	1,207[3]	5,358	5.2	100.0	—	35.8	53.9	9.8	13,723	1,032	Bahamas, The
...	...	...	...	...	27,348	6.8	100.0	—	84.7	14.5	0.8	...	2,010	Bahrain
32,051	97.1	2.9	1.8	5,695	2,328	728.5	19.8	80.2	100.0	—	—	67,962	...	Bangladesh
...	...	...	...	...	24,258	6.5	100.0	—	100.0	—	—	...	1,840	Barbados
3,041[14]	17.7[14]	82.3[14]	52.0[14]	851,349[14]	1,353,499[14]	48.6	100.0	—	93.3	3.9	2.8	87,012[14]	318,804[14]	Belgium
113	69.9	30.1	30.1	1,408	2,538	1.5	96.7	3.3	40.7	27.3	32.0	5,003	200	Belize
4,210	94.8	5.2	5.2	...	5,643	21.0	19.2	80.8	95.8	4.2	—	860	2,060	Benin
...	...	...	...	...	2,460[17]	0.5	100.0	—	95.8	4.2	—	—	6,208	Bermuda
3,224	91.4	8.6	7.4	501	143[8]	1.0	—	100.0	100.0	—	—	—	—	Bhutan
1,272	88.3	11.7	10.7	5,923	12,400	5.6	—	100.0	100.0	—	—	—	4,860	Bolivia
788	92.5	7.5	—	...	1,640	1.2	—	100.0	100.0	—	—	—	1,230	Botswana
220,248	73.8	26.2	14.4	822,539	149,913	844.5	76.5	23.5	88.8	10.3	0.9	137,177	43,162	Brazil
...	...	...	...	10[4, 22]	1814, 17	0.3	100.0	—	92.1	7.9	—	216[4]	145[4]	British Virgin Islands
296	27.0	73.0	69.6	90	7,182	3.1	96.6	3.4	83.4	16.6	—	—	2,880	Brunei
4,756	35.8	64.2	26.9	16,316	157,570	121.1	88.7	11.3	99.8	0.2	—	16,125	16,525	Bulgaria
7,261	95.7	4.3	0.1	...	4,458	7.0	—	100.0	100.0	—	—	...	1,100	Burkina Faso
19,254	84.2	15.8	9.9	126,000	11,080	585.8	75.6	24.4	100.0	—	—	10,990	—	Burma
3,522	98.9	1.1	0.1	...	179	12.0	—	100.0	100.0	—	—	—	—	Burundi
9,904	80.7	19.3	13.1	104,853	11,544	84.3	52.5	47.5	98.9	1.1	—	2,280	7,430	Cameroon
141,502	3.9	96.1	61.8	10,239,884	840,528	1,337.3	96.3	3.7	89.0	6.2	4.8	1,279,165	335,853	Canada
...	...	...	...	...	904	13.2	100.0	—	99.7	0.3	—	2,261	—	Cape Verde
...	...	...	...	...	...	0.5	100.0	—	—	100.0	—	3,940	68	Cayman Islands
3,049	83.4	16.6	9.5	23,005	2,206	13.0	—	100.0	100.0	—	—	—	—	Central African Republic
8,112	94.1	5.9	—	...	1,352	110.0	—	100.0	100.0	—	—	—	...	Chad
12,849	45.9	54.1	25.7	312,108	43,300	3,978.1	100.0	—	96.8	1.0	1.8	419,049	—	Chile
231,650[26]	66.8[26]	33.2[26]	17.6[26]	519,072[26]	1,564,553[26]	5,213.3	64.7	35.3	80.3	10.5	8.7	281,790	—	China
...	...	...	...	...	...	100.0	—	100.0	—	—	...	...	Christmas Island
...	...	...	...	...	...	—	—	—	100.0	—	—	...	...	Cocos (Keeling) Islands
16,553	83.9	16.1	11.8	46,544	114,644	57.5	21.2	78.8	89.1	10.5	0.4	32,400	66,770	Colombia
...	...	...	...	...	...	4.0	100.0	—	98.7	1.3	—	—	390	Comoros
2,238	67.4	32.6	23.0	49,861	1,980	31.9	62.4	37.6	99.9	0.1	—	600	14,500	Congo
...	...	...	...	...	...	0.8	100.0	—	68.4	0.7	28.4	—	170	Cook Islands
2,631	56.3	43.7	37.4	19,331	70,118	10.9	95.8	4.2	77.1	20.8	0.4	7,750	1,320	Costa Rica
3,193	87.9	12.1	1.1	...	171,451	198.5	92.9	6.2	88.2	8.8	2.3	157,523	36,372	Cuba
74	25.7	74.3	44.6	258	42,433	2.0	97.8	2.2	85.9	0.2	13.9	—	7,538	Cyprus
19,206	9.0	91.0	54.3	401,950	96,505	19.4	—	100.0	100.0	—	—	3,126	77,250	Czechoslovakia
2,953	12.5	87.5	51.5	227,361	749,357	1,862.1	98.7	1.3	95.6	0.8	3.6	928,363	309,211	Denmark
...	...	...	...	...	57	0.4	100.0	—	97.9	2.1	—	—	—	Djibouti
...	...	...	...	...	880	1.5	100.0	—	100.0	—	—	—	540	Dominica
579	98.4	1.6	1.0	17	63,561	13.2	86.9	13.1	82.5	6.6	10.5	3,150	11,300	Dominican Republic
7,795	72.4	27.6	27.3	33,401	79,940	307.3	100.0	—	87.1	11.9	1.0	239,400	—	Ecuador
1,935	95.3	4.7	—	...	534,124	140.0	17.9	82.1	97.5	1.9	0.6	780	68,790	Egypt
4,494	98.0	2.0	1.3	6,587	31,052	7.6	89.5	10.5	26.2	73.8	—	11,934	1,300	El Salvador
465	89.2	10.8	10.8	3,760	...	2.5	100.0	—	76.0	16.0	4.0	—	2,250	Equatorial Guinea

Extractive industries (continued)

country	mining % of GDP, 1983	mineral production (value added) year	total ('000,000 U.S.$)	by kind (%) metals[a]	non-metals[b]	energy[c]	trade (value) year	exports total ('000,000 U.S.$)	by kind (%) metals[a]	non-metals[b]	energy[c]	imports total ('000,000 U.S.$)	by kind (%) metals[a]	non-metals[b]	energy[c]
Ethiopia	0.1	1983	5.0	—100.0—		—	1982	—	—	—	—	173.3	0.2	—	99.8
Faeroe Islands	—	1983	...	...	...	...	1983	—	—	—	—	2.1[16]	1.3	87.2	11.5[16]
Falkland Islands	—	...	...	...	...	...	1975	...	...	...	...	...	...	...	...
Fiji	0.1	1981	1.2[29]	...—100.0[29]—		...	1980	15.3	100.0	—	—	3.8[16]	—	34.4	65.6[16]
Finland	0.3	1981	215.7	57.0	43.0	—	1982	81.2[8]	50.6[8]	42.4[8]	7.0[8]	3,079.6	5.8	4.8	89.4
France	0.8	1981	4,978.5	3.6	32.0	64.4	1982	1,529.8	46.6	31.9	21.5	27,108.1	4.0	3.5	92.5
French Guiana	...	1981	...	—100.0—		...	1982	1.4	—	—	100.0				
French Polynesia	...	1983	...	...	...	...	1982	1.1	21.9	78.1	—	5.1[4, 16]	—[4]	36.7[4]	69.3[4, 16]
Gabon	47.2	1983	1,272.0	8.9	0.1	91.0	1980	2,189.3	12.1	—	87.9	4.9	10.5	89.5	—
Gambia, The	0.1	1983	—	—	100.0	—	1982	—	—	100.0	—				
Gaza Strip	...	...	...	...	...	...	[32]	[32]	...	...	...	...	...	...	...
Germany, East	...	...	...	...	...	...	...	...	...	...	...	...	...	...	...
Germany, West	...	1981	6,070.8[33]	—9.7[33, 34]—		90.3[35]	1982	4,083.2	16.3	16.1	67.6	29,823.1	9.6	3.7	86.7
Ghana	0.3	1983	13.0	96.4[2, 9, 36]	3.6[2, 9, 37]	...	1982	48.9	54.4	23.1	22.5	239.8[19]	41.4[19]	1.5[19]	57.1[19]
Gibraltar	...	...	...	...	...	...	1982	0.7	100.0	—	—				
Greece	1.7	1982	655.0	17.5[8, 9]	49.0[8, 9]	33.5[8, 9]	1982	209.7	48.8	44.4	6.8	2,881.9	2.3	2.8	94.9
Greenland	...	...	...	...	...	...	1983	50.2	96.0	4.0	—	1.1[16]	0.4	75.9	23.7[16]
Grenada	1.0	1983	0.7	—	100.0	—	1984	—	—	—	—	0.1[4]	2.7[4]	—	97.3[4]
Guadeloupe	...	1980	...	—	100.0	—	1982	0.2	100.0	—	—	4.6	—	46.6	53.4
Guam	...	...	...	...	...	...	...	...	...	...	...	...	...	...	...
Guatemala	0.4	1982	28.4	...	...	...	1981	23.1	0.7	5.9	93.4	119.8	—	6.2	93.8
Guernsey	...	...	...	...	...	...	...	...	...	...	...	...	...	...	...
Guinea	15.0	1983	299.0[39]	—100.0[39]—		—	...	...	...	...	...	...	...	...	...
Guinea-Bissau	...	1983	—	—	100.0	—	1980	0.1	24.5	75.5	—	1.2	—	100.0	...
Guyana	5.8	1983	28.1[40]	—100.0[40]—		—	1982	106.7	100.0	—	—	3.5[19]	—	47.2[19]	52.8[19]
Haiti	0.1	1982	102.2	—	100.0[41]	—	1979	18.1	100.0	—	—	0.9	—	100.0	—
Honduras	1.9	1982	21.0	—100.0—		—	1981	36.7	100.0	—	—	72.3	—	4.6	95.4
Hong Kong	0.2	1982	48.8	—	100.0	—	1982	521.8	25.0	74.5	0.5	922.1	3.0	81.7	15.4
Hungary	...	1981	1,982.7[9]	—8.6[9]—		91.4[9]	...	...	...	...	...	1,569.0[42]	...	...	...
Iceland	...	1982	...	—	100.0	—	1984	146.9	96.1	3.9	—	44.9	75.8	14.0	10.2
India	3.3	1982	4,713.9	5.1	6.1	88.8	1980	1,129.9	41.2	58.5	0.3	4,780.0	2.5	15.3	82.2
Indonesia	19.4	1982	17,701.0	...	...	...	1982	18,030.9	1.6	0.1	98.3	1,259.3	4.3	5.7	90.0
Iran	17.9[6]	1981	13,003.0	—8.2[9, 43]—		91.8[9, 43]	1977	23,946.5	0.2	—	99.8	71.6	8.0	81.8	10.2
Iraq	23.9[8]	1980	22,192.8	—	0.1	99.9	1982	10,113.5	—	0.1	99.9	18.7[2]	4.1[2]	95.9[2]	—
Ireland	...	1979	228.7	28.7[2, 9]	70.3[2, 9]	1.0[2, 9]	1982	166.1	64.5	25.4	10.1	343.0	3.2	10.5	86.3
Isle of Man	...	...	...	...	...	...	...	...	...	...	...	...	...	...	...
Israel	...	1981–82	198.2	...	...	...	1982	1,285.9	0.4	99.6	—	2,504.8	0.2	28.3	71.5
Italy	3.2	1980	2,989.0[9]	5.0[9]	28.8[9]	66.1[9]	1982	461.2	28.7	56.3	14.9	24,539.8	5.8	2.5	91.7
Ivory Coast	2.1	1983	110.0	—100.0—		—	1982	57.6	3.5	—	96.5	398.0	—	4.1	95.9
Jamaica	4.1	1983	237.6	97.7[6]	2.3[6]	—	1981	761.2	99.9	0.1	—	7.7	1.1	—	98.9
Japan	0.4	1982	4,922.1	11.7[4, 9]	23.1[4, 9]	65.2[4, 9]	1982	278.6	37.1	61.5	1.4	68,125.9	10.0	2.5	87.5
Jersey	...	...	...	...	...	...	...	...	...	...	...	...	...	...	...
Jordan	3.6	1982	131.4	—	100.0	—	1982	168.5	—	100.0	—	670.8	0.1	2.4	97.5
Kampuchea	...	...	...	...	...	...	...	...	...	...	...	...	...	...	...
Kenya	0.2	1983	10.0	—	100.0	—	1982	49.8	10.6	46.3	43.1	771.4[4]	0.1[4]	0.9[4]	99.0[4]
Kiribati	—	1978	19.2	...	...	...	1981	2.4	—	100.0	—	—	—	—	—
Korea, North	...	...	...	...	...	...	...	...	...	...	...	...	...	...	...
Korea, South	1.6	1982	961.9	4.8	42.6	52.6	1981	110.5	33.6	64.5	1.9	8,206.2	9.6	2.8	87.6
Kuwait	49.8	1982	9.677.7	—	0.3	99.7	1982	8,503.5	0.2	0.1	99.7	51.0	1.8	70.9	27.3
Laos	...	...	...	...	...	...	1974	1.3	100.0	—	—	0.1	—	100.0	—
Lebanon	...	...	...	...	...	...	1982	37.9	54.2	39.7	6.1	562.8	0.1	10.8	89.1
Lesotho	0.7	1983	2.0	—	100.0	—	[20]	[20]	[20]	[20]	[20]	[20]	[20]	[20]	[20]
Liberia	15.0	1983	151.0	93.4[8, 9]	6.6[8, 9]	—	1982	292.1	96.3	3.7	—	106.5[8]	—	3.8[8]	96.2[8]
Libya	50.6	1983	15,471.0	—	0.9[19]	99.1[19]	1982	13,366.5	—	—	100.0	30.9	40.9	59.1	—
Liechtenstein	...	...	...	...	...	...	...	...	...	...	...	...	...	...	...
Luxembourg	...	1982	9.2[9]	—	100.0[9]	—	[14]	[14]	[14]	[14]	[14]	[14]	[14]	[14]	[14]
Macau	...	1979	2.7[1]	—	100.0[1]	—	1981	1.2	—	97.5	2.5	8.6	44.5	28.3	27.2
Madagascar	0.3	1993	6.0	—100.0—		—	1981	16.2[4]	39.0[4]	46.3[4]	14.7[4]	28.3	2.9	—	97.1
Malawi	—	1983	—	—100.0—		—	1980	—	—	—	—	8.6	—	54.3	45.7
Malaysia	4.4	1978	1,689.1	...	...	...	1981	4,075.8	26.1	0.2	73.7	1,174.4	13.7	7.8	78.5
Maldives	1.3	1981	0.8	—	100.0	—	1978	—	—	—	—	—	—	—	—
Mali	...	1983	—	—100.0—		—	1982	4.2	—	100.0	—	1.1	0.1	99.9	—
Malta	...	1982	57.2[47]	—	100.0	—	1981	3.8	39.7	60.3	—	11.4	—	100.0	—
Martinique	...	1983	—	—	100.0	—	1982	1.0	31.0	—	69.0	41.7	—	—	100.0
Mauritania	15.4	1983	110.0	—100.0—		—	1982	149.0	99.9	0.1	—	—	—	—	—
Mauritius	0.1	1983	2.0	—	100.0	—	1978	8.2	—	100.0	—	9.7	—	100.0	—
Mayotte	...	1984	—	—	—	—	...	...	...	...	...	...	...	...	...
Mexico	9.9[6, 11]	1982	16,481.3[11]	5.1[9]	6.4[9]	88.5[9]	1982	16,606.3	2.0	1.1	96.9	387.3	34.1	29.7	36.2
Monaco	...	...	...	...	...	...	...	...	...	...	...	...	...	...	...
Mongolia	...	...	...	...	...	...	...	...	...	...	...	...	...	...	...
Montserrat	0.7	1983	0.2	...	...	...	1982	...	...	...	...	0.1[2]	—	21.7[2]	78.3[2]
Morocco	4.8	1983	541.0	—97.1[8, 9]—		2.9[8, 9]	1982	686.4	11.2	88.1	0.7	1,286.9	—	11.7	88.3
Mozambique	0.4	1983	18.0	—	100.0	—	1982	8.0	11.3	60.4	28.3	11.1	—	100.0	—
Nauru	...	1984	—	—	100.0	—	1984	125.0	—	100.0	—	...	...	...	...
Nepal	0.2	1983	4.7	...	...	...	1983	...	...	...	...	...	...	...	...
Netherlands, The	7.2[8]	1980	9,632.3	—	2.6	97.4	1982	6,430.4	7.6	6.1	86.3	12,488.7	5.9	5.0	89.1
Netherlands Antilles	...	1983	...	—	100.0	—	1982[48]	162.8	—	13.3	86.7	3,265.5	0.2	0.1	99.7
New Caledonia	12.5[6]	1982	113.5	100.0	—	—	1982	54.5	100.0	—	—	8.2	—	6.8	93.2
New Zealand	1.3	1982	318.8	...	...	...	1982	27.6	99.9	0.1	—	615.3	14.3	18.9	66.8
Nicaragua	1.0	1978	6.5[50]	—100.0—		—	1982	...	...	...	...	152.1	—	1.5	98.5
Niger	9.3	1983	169.0	...	...	...	1981	362.4	99.6	0.4	—	9.6	—	100.0	—
Nigeria	20.4	1983	12,739.0	0.2[6]	7.6[6]	92.2[6]	1982	15,646.5	—	—	100.0	135.9	1.0	99.0	—
Niue	—	1983	—	—	100.0	—	1983	—	—	100.0	—	...	...	...	...
Norfolk Island	...	...	...	...	...	...	1983	...	...	...	...	...	...	...	...
Norway	17.0	1982	8,875.6	0.7	1.3	98.0	1982	8,577.9	1.9	0.8	97.3	1,580.5	31.4	7.5	61.1

forestry, 1983						fisheries, 1983								country
production of roundwood				trade (value '000 U.S.$)		catch (nominal)						trade (value, '000 U.S.$)		
total ('000 cubic metres)	fuelwood, charcoal (%)	industrial roundwood (%)		exports	imports	total ('000 metric tons)	by source (%)		by kind of catch (%)			exports	imports	
		total	sawlogs, veneer				marine	freshwater	fish	crustaceans	mollusks			
29,784	93.9	6.1	0.4	...	10,403	3.9	10.3	89.7	100.0	—	—	—	—	Ethiopia
...	...	...	...	...	...	329.9	100.0	—	96.8	2.3	0.9	165,914	2,752	Faeroe Islands
...	...	...	...	...	...	100.0	100.0	—	100.0	—	—	—	—	Falkland Islands
224	6.3	93.7	92.9	4,300	11,159	29.1	89.6	10.4	86.5	1.2	10.8	14,590	7,741	Fiji
38,439	8.3	91.7	42.6	4,160,481	304,667	157.1	78.6	21.4	100.0	—	—	7,857	94,613	Finland
39,839	26.2	73.8	50.2	1,262,795	2,532,332	784.0[10, 30]	...	...	68.7[10, 30]	3.9[10, 30]	27.4[10, 30]	315,621[30]	1,049,658[30]	France
254	26.0	74.0	70.5	3,380	665	1.4	100.0	—	90.9	9.1	—	28,711	26,216	French Guiana
...	...	...	...	...	18,132	3.0	100.0	—	99.9	0.1	—	28	4,968	French Polynesia
2,608	46.9	53.1	53.1	155,255	3,969	52.6	95.0	5.0	96.4	3.5	0.1	—	10,100[4]	Gabon
783	97.3	2.7	1.8	...	164	9.6[31]	93.3[31]	6.7[31]	96.7[31]	3.3[31]	...	2,103[3]	84[3]	Gambia, The
...	...	...	...	...	...	0.8	100.0	—	99.1	0.9	—	...	...	Gaza Strip
10,908	6.9	93.1	38.3	89,900	430,500	239.9	90.7	9.3	99.4	0.3	0.3	...	31,850	Germany, East
29,485	14.2	85.8	44.3	2,226,994	4,880,722	305.6	92.5	7.5	82.6	4.4	13.0	306,444	831,422	Germany, West
9,803	74.3	25.7	21.8	13,707	2,889	228.0	81.1	18.9	99.2	0.2	0.6	22,690	10,560	Ghana
...	...	...	...	...	...	—	—	—	—	—	—	—	—	Gibraltar
2,824	70.5	29.5	24.1	30,761	285,002	100.0	90.0	10.0	92.3	2.7	5.0	22,997	76,705	Greece
—	—	—	—	—	—	107.7	100.0	—	61.7	38.3	—	115,237	830	Greenland
...	...	...	...	...	...	1.8	100.0	—	95.6	1.7	1.7	—	720	Grenada
17	88.2	11.8	11.8	4,143[3]	14,202	8.7	100.0	—	95.3	1.2	3.2	66	8,190	Guadeloupe
...	...	...	...	77	1,935	0.2	73.8	26.2	98.4	1.6	—	1,039	6,613	Guam
6,806	97.7	2.3	2.2	14,141	63,070	4.3	83.2	16.8	41.7	58.3	—	10,860	1,815	Guatemala
...	...	...	...	...	...	[38]	[38]	[38]	[38]	[38]	[38]	...	...	Guernsey
3,644	84.7	15.3	4.9	3,649[19]	...	18.5	94.6	5.4	100.0	—	—	...	4,084	Guinea
528	79.9	20.1	7.6	130	98	2.6	100.0	—	81.1	18.7	0.2	1,580	—	Guinea-Bissau
201	6.0	94.0	89.1	6,260	6,009	27.6	97.1	2.9	84.3	15.7	—	23,000	—	Guyana
5,624	95.8	4.2	4.0	...	4,955	4.0	92.5	7.5	97.5	2.5	—	...	3,650	Haiti
5,211	81.5	18.5	18.2	31,140	30,895	8.4	99.2	0.8	4.2	94.1	1.7	38,760	1,560	Honduras
180	100.0	—	—	40,595	456,166	188.8	96.2	3.8	87.1	6.3	6.6	210,273	439,506	Hong Kong
6,396	44.3	55.7	29.5	103,919	279,910	43.9	—	100.0	100.0	—	—	5,873	41,789	Hungary
—	—	—	—	...	39,661	839.2	99.9	0.1	96.3	1.9	1.8	527,165	1,996	Iceland
232,537	91.4	8.6	6.3	26,558	178,359	2,520.0	61.8	38.2	90.2	9.3	0.5	349,091	—	India
122,249	93.4	6.6	4.4	976,007	209,491	2,112.2	75.4	24.6	90.4	7.2	2.1	267,250	57,885	Indonesia
6,721	34.9	65.1	5.5	38	265,633	34.5	87.0	13.0	94.2	5.8	—	21,600	21,170	Iran
131	61.8	38.2	15.3	...	110,921	26.2	33.3	66.7	100.0	—	—	...	...	Iraq
1,026	4.5	95.5	46.1	35,006	289,296	203.4	100.0	—	92.0	3.9	4.1	97,821	37,208	Ireland
...	...	...	...	...	...	8.4	100.0	—	15.6	0.7	83.7	...	...	Isle of Man
118	9.3	90.7	22.0	12,179	244,909	22.4	42.4	57.6	99.3	0.6	0.1	4,201	34,280	Israel
8,658	47.3	52.7	28.5	518,859	2,913,904	478.4	91.4	8.6	73.0	5.0	22.0	104,522[44]	735,373[44]	Italy
11,839	60.7	39.3	34.5	359,008	18,273	94.0	84.4	15.6	...	...	...	68,301	44,768	Ivory Coast
39	33.3	66.7	64.1	2,435	91,695	8.7	97.4	2.6	100.0	—	—	90	22,420	Jamaica
32,813	1.8	98.2	62.2	733,733	6,063,714	11,250.0	98.0	2.0	85.8	1.8	12.1	787,634	3,946,568	Japan
...	...	...	...	...	...	3.5[38]	100.0[38]	—	7.4[38]	91.9[38]	0.7[38]	...	...	Jersey
9	55.6	44.4	—	8,056	71,149	—	100.0	—	100.0	—	—	...	9,980	Jordan
5,239	89.2	10.8	2.1	173	1,885	63.8	8.0	92.0	99.4	0.6	—	...	...	Kampuchea
29,330	95.0	5.0	1.5	5,279	21,393	97.5	6.6	93.4	99.3	0.6	—	2,582	887	Kenya
...	...	...	...	...	...	24.2	100.0	—	88.9	—	11.0	...	150	Kiribati
6,200	90.3	9.7	9.7	...	1,879	1,600.0	94.4	5.6	100.0	—	—	31,190	...	Korea, North
10,189	68.5	31.5	20.4	188,658	826,387	2,400.4	98.0	2.0	72.7	2.7	23.7	734,602	55,459	Korea, South
—	—	—	—	28,058	143,092	4.1	100.0	—	85.4	14.6	—	19,700	16,240	Kuwait
3,920	94.1	5.9	3.3	8,706	816	20.0	—	100.0	100.0	—	—	—	...	Laos
252	90.1	9.9	9.9	3,239	64,476	1.4	92.9	7.1	100.0	—	—	...	...	Lebanon
293	100.0	—	—	[45]	[45]	—	—	100.0	100.0	—	—	...	1,820	Lesotho
4,580	88.6	11.4	8.4	41,589	5,707	13.6	70.5	29.5	99.4	0.5	0.1	3,395	6,350	Liberia
631	84.9	15.1	10.0	...	120,311	7.5	100.0	—	100.0	—	—	1,480	20,580	Libya
...	...	...	...	...	...	—	—	100.0	100.0	—	—	[46]	[46]	Liechtenstein
[14]	[14]	[14]	[14]	[14]	[14]	—	—	—	—	—	—	[14]	[14]	Luxembourg
...	...	...	...	28	12,435	7.0	100.0	—	42.9	57.1	—	4,230	7,850	Macau
6,262	87.1	12.9	7.5	166	7,989	54.5	22.6	77.4	89.2	10.6	0.1	21,450	—	Madagascar
6,468	94.1	5.9	2.0	600	16,720	58.4	—	100.0	100.0	—	—	940	400	Malawi
41,877	17.6	82.4	79.5	2,174,731	212,918	741.1	98.0	2.0	77.2	12.5	7.9	104,428	88,126	Malaysia
...	...	...	...	...	...	38.5	100.0	—	100.0	—	—	5,150	—	Maldives
4,583	93.7	6.3	0.2	...	1,174	33.0	—	100.0	100.0	—	—	400	—	Mali
...	...	...	...	...	30,850	1.0	99.0	1.0	96.9	0.7	2.4	254	4,564	Malta
11	90.9	9.1	9.1	...	14,096	4.7	100.0	—	96.9	2.1	—	102	12,725	Martinique
53	11.3	88.7	1.9	...	...	53.8	79.6	20.4	...	...	...	159,582	—	Mauritania
30	73.3	26.7	20.0	...	8,792	9.5	99.7	0.3	95.7	0.6	3.7	5,400	6,790	Mauritius
...	...	...	...	...	...	0.7[41]	...	...	...	...	...	...	...	Mayotte
19,805	67.3	32.7	19.5	18,234	367,388	1,070.0	98.1	1.9	86.0	7.5	6.2	393,661	17,226	Mexico
...	...	...	...	...	...	—	100.0	—	100.0	—	—	[30]	[30]	Monaco
2,390	56.5	43.5	43.5	9,300	6,800	0.5	—	100.0	100.0	—	—	...	1,040	Mongolia
...	...	...	...	...	367[5, 8]	0.1	100.0	—	100.0	—	—	—	124[8]	Montserrat
1,697	66.6	33.4	4.0	19,858	160,030	439.9	99.7	0.3	89.3	0.4	10.3	198,929	—	Morocco
14,685	94.5	5.5	0.8	2,744	13,680	42.4	88.2	11.8	78.6	20.7	0.7	40,810	6,445	Mozambique
...	...	...	...	...	...	—	—	100.0	100.0	—	—	...	...	Nauru
14,684	96.2	3.8	3.8	12,000	...	2.1	—	100.0	100.0	—	—	...	...	Nepal
906	11.3	88.7	30.4	427,979	2,037,765	503.3	99.2	0.8	74.5	1.6	23.9	511,401	272,858	Netherlands, The
...	...	...	...	...	6,452	1.8	100.0	—	100.0	—	—	...	...	Netherlands Antilles
12	—	100.0	91.7	...	5,716	2.4	100.0	—	76.6	1.3	1.2	558	2,461	New Caledonia
10,021	0.5	99.5	56.0	338,175	82,903	141.5	100.0	—	79.4	3.5	16.8	206,971[49]	15,974[49]	New Zealand
3,370	73.9	26.1	24.6	4,270	13,321	4.5	91.7	8.3	30.8	67.9	1.3	12,660	760	Nicaragua
3,731	93.8	6.2	—	...	285	6.8	—	100.0	100.0	—	—	90	230	Niger
85,760	91.4	8.6	5.9	707	211,717	515.2	75.8	24.2	99.2	0.8	—	4,651	234,842	Nigeria
...	...	...	...	...	...	...	100.0	—	100.0	—	—	...	...	Niue
...	...	...	...	...	...	...	100.0	—	100.0	—	—	...	...	Norfolk Island
9,553	8.4	91.6	49.3	727,077	373,305	2,822.3	99.2	0.8	96.7	2.7	0.6	977,932	47,804	Norway

Extractive industries (continued)

country	mining % of GDP, 1983	mineral production (value added) year	total ('000,000 U.S.$)	by kind (%) metals[a]	non-metals[b]	energy[c]	trade (value) year	exports total ('000,000 U.S.$)	by kind (%) metals[a]	non-metals[b]	energy[c]	imports total ('000,000 U.S.$)	by kind (%) metals[a]	non-metals[b]	energy[c]
Oman	50.5	1981	4,251.9	...	...	...	1982	4,088.0	—	—	100.0	13.3	—	40.4	59.6
Pacific Is., Trust Terr. of the	...	...	...	...	...	...	...	...	...	...	...	...	...	...	...
Pakistan	1.3	1983	416.1	0.1[9]	18.5[9]	78.9[9]	1982	10.2	—	100.0	—	1,151.3	4.2	2.4	93.4
Panama	0.2	1983	10.0	—100.0—			1982	0.9	100.0	—	—	394.4	—	—	100.0
Papua New Guinea	13.2[4]	1978	208.4	100.0	—	—	1984	333.6	100.0	—	—	3.8[6]	7.2[6]	92.8[6]	—
Paraguay	0.4	1983	24.9	—	100.0	—	1981	...	...	...	...	74.7[19]	—	2.9[19]	97.1[19]
Peru	11.1	1981	2,118.0	38.3	10.9[28]	50.8[28]	1982	906.1	46.4	1.2	52.4	14.9	23.0	66.4	10.6
Philippines	1.8	1982	715.0[53]	72.6	27.4[28]	[28]	1982	796.3	99.6	0.2	0.2	1,603.4	3.5	1.8	94.7
Pitcairn Island	—	...	...	...	...	...	...	...	...	...	...	...	...	...	...
Poland	...	...	...	...	...	...	1981	1,448.7[16]	3.4	27.0	69.6[16]	2,942.8[16]	13.7	8.6	77.7[16]
Portugal	...	1976	83.5	21.9[6,9]	73.2[6,9]	4.9[6,9]	1982	101.2	22.0	77.3	0.7	2,146.6	1.4	5.2	93.4
Puerto Rico	0.1	1982	9.2	...	...	...	...	...	...	...	...	...	...	...	...
Qatar	45.9	1983	2,943.5	...	...	—	1981	5,060.0	—	—	100.0	30.2	98.4	—	1.6
Réunion	...	1983	...	...	...	...	1982	...	...	...	...	20.9	—	—	100.0
Romania	...	1983	...	...	...	...	...	...	...	...	...	...	...	...	...
Rwanda	0.5	1983	27.0	...	...	...	1980	7.7	100.0	—	—	3.4	—	100.0	—
St. Christopher and Nevis	0.2	1983	0.1	—	100.0	—	1981	—	—	—	—	0.4	19.7	0.1	80.2
St. Helena and Ascension	...	1983	—	...	...	...	...	...	...	...	...	...	...	...	...
St. Lucia	1.3	1984	1.3	—	100.0	—	1980	—	—	—	—	...	...	...	...
St. Pierre and Miquelon	...	1983	...	...	...	...	1981	—	—	—	—	0.8	87.0	—	13.0
St. Vincent	0.4	1983	0.4	—	100.0	—	1980	—	—	—	—	0.5[52]	—	65.2[52]	34.8[52]
San Marino	...	...	...	...	...	...	...	...	...	...	...	...	...	...	...
São Tomé and Príncipe	...	1983	...	...	...	...	1983	...	...	...	...	...	...	...	...
Saudi Arabia	39.0	1982	56,794.9	...	...	...	1982	75,989.6	—	—	100.0	151.9	9.1	90.3	0.6
Senegal	1.5	1983	30.0	...	...	...	1981	79.1	2.0	98.0	—	208.0	—	—	100.0
Seychelles	...	1983	...	—	100.0	—	1982	...	98.6	1.4	—	0.3	—	38.7	61.3
Sierra Leone	7.5	1983	114.0	—100.0—		—	1982	90.2	14.5	85.5	—	20.9[52]	—	—	100.0[52]
Singapore	0.4	1983	68.5	...	...	...	1982	299.7	26.2	23.1	50.7	7,777.8	1.0	1.6	97.4
Solomon Islands	0.3	1984	...	...	...	...	1984	0.6[29]	100.0[29]	—	—	...	...	...	...
Somalia	5.3	1983	57.0	—	100.0	—	1980	...	—	100.0	—	0.8	—	74.8	25.2
South Africa	15.3[57]	1983[57]	11,194.7[57]	76.8[9,19]	10.3[9,19]	12.9[9,19]	1981[20]	3,308.6[20]	23.2[20]	41.0[20]	35.8[20]	620.5[20]	12.9[20]	29.5[20]	57.6[20]
Bophuthatswana	52.6[4]	...	...	...	...	...	...	...	...	...	...	...	...	...	...
Ciskei	—	...	...	...	...	...	...	...	...	...	...	...	...	...	...
Transkei	0.6[58]	...	...	...	...	...	...	...	...	...	...	...	...	...	...
Venda	1.7[58]	...	...	...	...	...	...	...	...	...	...	...	...	...	...
Southwest Africa/Namibia	27.5	1984	354.9	—100.0—		—	1983	593.0	64.0	36.0	—	20	20	20	20
Spain	1.4[41]	1977	2,026.1	—35.5—		64.5	1982	267.7	36.8	47.4	15.8	12,664.1	7.7	2.7	89.6
Sri Lanka	1.2	1982	55.7	—100.0—		—	1982	41.2	8.1	91.9	—	506.3	—	3.5	96.5
Sudan, The	0.8	1983	48.0	—100.0—		—	1981	2.1	97.4	2.6	—	162.5	—	—	100.0
Suriname	9.1	1980	152.9	99.9	0.1	—	1981	327.8	100.0	—	—	...	...	...	...
Swaziland	3.2	1983	9.6	9.4[4]	77.3[4]	13.3[4]	1984	17.2	—	86.9	13.1	20	20	20	20
Sweden	0.5	1983	438.5	86.0	14.0	—	1982	554.5	78.3	14.9	6.8	3,928.8	8.7	4.8	86.5
Switzerland	...	...	...	...	...	...	1982	1,086.8	6.4	93.2	0.4	2,353.9	2.4	49.0	48.6
Syria	10.4[8]	1981	1,769.2	...	...	...	1980	1,358.1	—	1.8	98.2	839.4	0.1	1.4	98.5
Taiwan	0.7	1983[9]	434.4	—14.7—		85.3	1984	...	...	...	...	4,680.6	19.5	—	80.5
Tanzania	0.3	1983	12.0	—100.0—		—	1980	49.9	15.4	84.6	—	118.9	1.0	2.4	96.6
Thailand	1.8	1982	643.8	32.8	66.2	1.0	1982	304.7	20.2	79.7	0.1	2,272.0	3.5	5.5	91.0
Togo	6.6	1983	41.0	—	100.0[61]	—	1981	105.3	—	100.0	—	83.2[4]	—	1.4[4]	98.6[4]
Tokelau	—	1981	...	...	...	...	1981	—	...	...	...	...	...	...	...
Tonga	0.5	1983	0.4	—	100.0	—	1982	—	...	...	...	0.4	—	73.2	26.8
Trinidad and Tobago	19.6	1984	2,064.4	—	2.0[4,62]	98.0[4]	1982	1,128.4	—	—	100.0	937.9	1.7	0.8	97.5
Tunisia	11.9	1983	768.0	2.6[9,19]	16.0[9,19]	81.4[9,19]	1981	1,318.9	—	3.9	96.1	576.4	2.2	24.2	73.6
Turkey	2.1	1982	1,035.7	14.5[9]	13.9[9]	71.6[9]	1982	236.1	10.7	62.9	26.4	3,947.7	3.5	1.9	94.6
Turks and Caicos Is.	3.6	1983	1.0	—	100.0	—	...	...	...	...	...	...	...	...	...
Tuvalu	—	1981	...	...	...	...	1981	—	...	...	...	...	...	...	...
Uganda	0.6[6]	1983	—	—	—	—	...	...	...	...	...	...	...	...	...
U.S.S.R.	...	1980	49,039.9	—36.6[9]—		63.4[9]	...	...	...	...	...	...	...	...	...
United Arab Emirates	44.8	1982	15,312.7	...	...	...	1982	15,770.5	0.2	0.1	99.7	41.5	0.6	99.4	—
United Kingdom	6.7	1982	31,280.0	0.1[8,9]	4.2[8,9]	95.6[8,9]	1982	18,437.7	3.3	11.3	85.4	12,785.3	13.4	17.5	69.1
United States	3.4	1982	116,861.0	3.2	5.2	91.6	1982	11,385.3	19.3	17.7	63.0	59,535.8	4.9	5.5	89.6
Uruguay	1.1	1982	120.1	...	...	...	1981	5.6	—	100.0	—	463.2	—	2.0	98.0
Vanuatu	...	1981	...	100.0	—	—	1982	8.[63]	100.0[8]	—	—	2.2	—	75.6	24.4
Venezuela	16.3	1982	12,670.7	—2.1[28]—		97.9[28]	1981	14,437.8	2.3	0.1	97.6	209.0	76.9	21.9	1.2
Vietnam	...	...	...	...	...	...	...	...	...	...	...	...	...	...	...
Virgin Islands (U.S.)	...	...	...	...	...	...	1982	1,195.2	99.8	0.2	—	1,889.9[64]	...	...	...
Wallis and Futuna Is.	...	...	...	...	...	...	...	...	...	...	...	...	...	...	...
West Bank	...	...	...	...	...	...	1982[32]	18.3[32,65]	...	...	...	...	...	...	...
Western Sahara	...	...	—	...	...	...	...	...	...	...	...	...	...	...	...
Western Samoa	...	1984	—	—	—	—	1984	—	...	...	...	...	...	...	...
Yemen (Aden)	0.1[4]	1980	0.9	—	100.0	—	1982	59.0	—	—	100.0	1,089.7	—	—	100.0
Yemen (Şan'ā')	1.2[8]	1981	34.2	—	100.0	—	1982	3.6	—	100.0	—	...	100.0	—	—
Yugoslavia	2.3[6]	1980	3,035.8[9]	28.9[9]	21.0[9]	50.1[9]	1982	66.9	75.3	24.7	—	3,565.2	5.3	6.5	88.2
Zaire	13.4	1983	215.0	...	...	...	1982	89.0	25.9	29.9	44.2	...	...	...	...
Zambia	15.5	1983	517.0	93.0[8]	7.0[8]	—	1982	41.7	12.4	87.6	—	117.1[19]	—	2.5[19]	97.5[19]
Zimbabwe	4.8	1983	254.0	65.5[6,9]	25.1[6,9]	9.4[6,9]	1982	80.4	—	97.6	2.4	10.3	98.5	1.5	—

forestry, 1983						fisheries, 1983								country
production of roundwood				trade (value '000 U.S.$)		catch (nominal)						trade (value, '000 U.S.$)		
total ('000 cubic metres)	fuelwood, charcoal (%)	industrial roundwood (%)		exports	imports	total ('000 metric tons)	by source (%)		by kind of catch (%)			exports	imports	
		total	sawlogs, veneer				marine	fresh-water	fish	crusta-ceans	mollusks			
				352[6,17]	55,035	108.8	100.0	—	100.0	—	—	12,703	2,421	Oman
...	...	...	...			5.5	100.0	—	100.0	—	—	650	1,340	Pacific Is., Trust Terr. of the
19,095	96.9	3.1	1.6	...	82,340	343.4	82.4	17.6	91.8	8.2	—	68,700		Pakistan
2,047	83.4	16.6	13.6	815	28,589	166.1	100.0	—	91.8	8.2	—	72,569[51]	7,984[51]	Panama
6,910	80.1	19.9	16.8	74,025	1,474[52]	1.4	100.0	—	15.7	84.3	—	10,882	22,620	Papua New Guinea
6,822	64.6	35.4	30.4	65,159	7,878	3.5	—	100.0	100.0	—	—			Paraguay
7,775	83.8	16.2	15.0	7,112	67,176	1,486.8	98.3	1.7	95.4	0.9	3.1	172,489	20,251	Peru
35,787	79.6	20.4	12.4	340,182	79,200	1,836.9	69.2	30.8	81.0	4.2	14.7	131,700	12,300	Philippines
...	...	...	...	...	...	...	...	...	100.0	—	—			Pitcairn Island
24,681	11.3	88.7	46.4	139,300	156,422	735.1	95.9	4.1	85.0	—	15.0	83,699	53,993	Poland
8,278	6.0	94.0	46.9	380,422	120,136	246.5	100.0	—	96.0	0.5	3.5	90,689	140,984	Portugal
...	...	...	...	...	...	2.2	100.0	—	80.0	6.6	13.4	54	54	Puerto Rico
—	—	—	—	...	2,505	2.1	100.0	—	96.0	3.7	0.3		1,540	Qatar
33	93.9	6.1	—	...	21,862	3.0	100.0	—	93.3	6.7	—	2,857	14,534	Réunion
22,953	19.9	80.1	37.9	437,710	90,660	242.5	78.8	21.2	100.0	—	—		29,000	Romania
5,157	94.2	5.8	0.3	...	2,605	1.2	—	100.0	100.0	—	—			Rwanda
...	...	...	...	11[8]	857[8]	1.1	100.0	—	100.0	—	—	—	390	St. Christopher and Nevis
...	...	...	...	...	...	0.2	100.0	—	100.0	—	—	126		St. Helena and Ascension
...	...	...	...	5,227[6,55]	6,385	2.6	100.0	—	92.0	8.0	—		570	St. Lucia
...	...	...	...	...	...	10.1	100.0	—	100.0	—	—	5,867	—	St. Pierre and Miquelon
...	...	...	...	...	2,254[5,8]	0.5	100.0	—	100.0	—	—	44	277[8,56]	St. Vincent
...	...	...	...	...	...	—	...	...	...	...	...	44	44	San Marino
6	—	100.0	100.0	...	...	4.0	100.0	—	98.2	0.3	1.5	277		São Tomé and Príncipe
...	...	...	...	...	703,854	2.6	100.0	—	61.7	38.0	0.3	5,730	78,550	Saudi Arabia
3,894	86.6	13.4	0.5	...	27,750	212.9	100.0	—	94.1	2.7	3.2	138,474	21,110	Senegal
...	...	...	...	...	...	3.9	100.0	—	97.3	—	1.3	1,406	82	Seychelles
8,142	98.3	1.7	0.2	...	1,130	53.0	68.9	31.1	96.8	1.3	1.9	8,120	2,236	Sierra Leone
...	...	...	...	463,578	525,730	19.5	97.7	2.3	84.7	11.0	4.3	150,461	196,963	Singapore
512	41.0	59.0	59.0	21,580	592	47.2	100.0	—	99.2	—	—	21,156		Solomon Islands
5,051	98.6	1.4	0.6	6[4]	5,505	15.5	100.0	—	87.1	12.9	—	3,816	214[4]	Somalia
20,524[45]	34.1[45]	65.9[45]	19.3[45]	227,633[45]	247,576[45]	599.9	99.9	0.1	97.8	0.8	0.5	103,121[20]	72,512[20]	South Africa
...	...	...	...	...	...							...	...	Bophuthatswana
...	...	...	...	...	...							...	...	Ciskei
...	...	...	...	...	...							...	...	Transkei
...	...	...	...	...	...							...	...	Venda
45	45	45	45	45	45	341.0	100.0	—	99.5	0.5	—	20	20	South West Africa/Namibia
14,823	10.1	89.9	32.2	381,328	577,471	1,250.0	98.2	1.8	79.1	1.3	19.6	280,978	395,673	Spain
8,363	91.5	8.5	2.2	3,188	29,358	220.0	84.6	15.4	95.0	4.6	0.4	21,200	12,000	Sri Lanka
38,157	95.5	4.5	0.1	...	17,549	29.5	15.1	84.9	100.0	—	—	380	1,146	Sudan, The
266	7.1	92.9	86.1	11,510	13,020	3.6	94.0	6.0	79.2	20.8	—	22,500	3,000	Suriname
2,223	25.2	74.8	14.3	70,220	1,539	—	—	100.0	100.0	—	—	20	20	Swaziland
53,294	8.3	91.7	46.8	4,713,215	432,557	265.5	96.2	3.8	99.3	0.7	—	90,477	261,840	Sweden
4,295	22.2	77.8	58.7	334,799	670,999	3.9	—	100.0	100.0	—	—	3,625[46]	194,265[46]	Switzerland
44	25.0	75.0	34.1	251	103,616	3.8	24.4	75.6	100.0	—	—		13,230	Syria
695	11.4	88.6		125,214[59]	279,958[60]	930.6	74.1	25.9	...	...	...	248,171		Taiwan
39,770	97.3	2.7	0.3	1,028	16,900	272.5	13.0	87.0	99.9	—	0.1	500	517	Tanzania
40,416	89.7	10.3	4.5	29,493	274,870	2,250.0	93.3	6.7	70.9	9.1	12.3	544,941	42,820	Thailand
745	78.5	21.5	2.4	14[19]	483	14.6	95.2	4.8	100.0	—	—	16	4,825	Togo
...	...	...	...	...	...	...	...	...	100.0	—	—			Tokelau
3	—	100.0	100.0	...	1,577	2.0	100.0	—	100.0	—	—		780	Tonga
67	32.8	67.2	64.2	361	132,098	4.5	100.0	—	89.9	10.1	—	844	15,444	Trinidad and Tobago
2,673	96.4	3.6	0.1	81[4]	85,644	67.1	100.0	—	84.1	5.6	10.2	36,556	—	Tunisia
19,193	78.2	21.8	12.9	43,263	57,882	567.3	92.9	7.1	97.6	2.1	0.3	45,574	—	Turkey
...	...	...	...	...	...	1.0	100.0	—	—	38.1	61.9	2,239	—	Turks and Caicos Is.
...	...	...	...	...	...	0.8	100.0	—	100.0	—	—		57[8]	Tuvalu
26,255	94.1	5.9	0.4	38	3,499	172.0	—	100.0	100.0	—	—			Uganda
355,900	23.4	76.6	42.0	2,556,773	964,592	9,756.8	91.8	8.2	96.8	2.4	0.8	324,037	133,389	U.S.S.R.
...	...	...	...	...	...	73.1	100.0	—	99.4	0.6	—	3,220	16,110	United Arab Emirates
3,950	3.5	96.5	62.8	585,895	5,162,626	834.7	99.2	0.8	91.3	4.5	4.2	311,881	908,606	United Kingdom
437,762	23.3	76.7	46.0	5,650,690	8,986,249	4,142.5	98.2	1.8	71.5	6.9	21.4	996,651[54]	3,621,380[54]	United States
2,975	92.8	7.2	0.9	6,646	13,656	144.1	100.0	—	97.3	—	2.7	45,694	412	Uruguay
38	63.2	36.8	36.8	677	451	2.5	100.0	—	91.1	0.8	8.1	5,810	6,300	Vanuatu
1,300	51.1	48.9	46.9	...	275,240	226.9	91.2	8.8	91.0	3.5	5.5	19,755	20,180	Venezuela
23,676	87.9	12.1	5.5	...	8,669	710.0	71.1	28.9	87.3	8.8	3.9	44,530		Vietnam
...	...	...	...	...	...	0.6	100.0	—	94.7	4.6	0.7		3,053[2]	Virgin Islands (U.S.)
...	...	...	...	...	—	—	100.0	—	100.0	—	—			Wallis and Futuna Is.
														West Bank
...	...	...	...	...	...	—	100.0	—	...	...	...			Western Sahara
131	53.4	46.6	44.3	1,270	1,962	3.8	100.0	—	97.4	1.3	1.3		1,190	Western Samoa
270	100.0	—	—	29	11,294	74.1	100.0	—	97.8	—	2.2	5,300	700	Yemen (Aden)
...	...	...	...	...	...	12.2	100.0	—	100.0	—	—		4,160	Yemen (Şan'ā')
15,381	26.5	73.5	34.4	524,347	352,550	79.8	66.7	33.3	97.6	0.5	1.8	23,302	74,298	Yugoslavia
31,265	92.1	7.9	1.1	17,810	5,179	102.0	1.0	99.0	100.0	—	—		31,990[2]	Zaire
9,171	94.6	5.4	1.5	...	21,894	67.2	—	100.0	100.0	—	—		2,220	Zambia
6,696	81.7	18.3	4.5	6,704	18,427	17.7	—	100.0	100.0	—	—		1,838	Zimbabwe

[1]Based on value of sales. [2]1978. [3]1977. [4]1980. [5]Lumber only. [6]1982. [7]Salt exports were valued at U.S.$33,000. [8]1981. [9]Based on value of production. [10]Marine catch only. [11]Includes petroleum refining. [12]Based on value of production of limestone, china clay, and natural gas only; 1975–76. [13]Coal, crude petroleum, and natural gas only. [14]Belgium includes Luxembourg. [15]Mostly crude petroleum. [16]Includes coke and briquettes. [17]Crude wood, lumber, and cork only. [18]Mostly slate, limestone, and coal. [19]1979. [20]South Africa includes Botswana, Lesotho, South West Africa/Namibia, and Swaziland. [21]Sand and gravel exports were valued at U.S.$34,000. [22]Charcoal only. [23]Mostly crude petroleum and natural gas. [24]1974. [25]Mostly diamonds; some gold. [26]China includes Taiwan. [27]Includes petroleum products. [28]Nonmetals includes coal mining. [29]Mostly gold. [30]France includes Monaco. [31]Excludes mollusks. [32]West Bank includes Gaza Strip. [33]Excludes quarrying. [34]Includes crude petroleum and natural gas. [35]Coal mining only. [36]Gold, manganese and bauxite only. [37]Diamonds only. [38]Jersey includes Guernsey. [39]Mostly bauxite and diamonds. [40]Mostly bauxite and gold. [41]1984. [42]Crude petroleum, natural gas, coal, iron ore, and copper ore only. [43]1982–83. [44]Italy includes San Marino. [45]South Africa includes Lesotho and South West Africa/Namibia. [46]Switzerland includes Liechtenstein. [47]Includes construction. [48]Curaçao and Aruba only. [49]Excludes trade with the Cook Is., Niue, and Tokelau. [50]Metal ore only. [51]Excludes the free zone of Colón and the Canal Zone. [52]1976. [53]Excludes crude petroleum. [54]United States includes Puerto Rico. [55]Paper and paperboard only. [56]Cod only. [57]South Africa includes South West Africa/Namibia. [58]1975. [59]Plywood only. [60]Paper and pulp only. [61]1972. [62]Includes agricultural chemicals. [63]Manganese exports were valued at U.S.$11,000. [64]Excludes bauxite imports. [65]Exports of stone and marble to Jordan only.

Manufacturing industries

This table summarizes the activity of the manufacturing sectors of the countries of the world, providing figures for value added, number of establishments, and the distribution of value added by size of establishment (as reckoned by number of employees). The data are organized to show the relative importance of six principal sectors for each country and the concentration of activity within each sector. Although the principal intent is to provide data on the manufacturing sectors of each country individually, the data may also be compared from country to country. Here, however, some caution is advised, as some countries do not classify manufacturing activity according to the scheme outlined in the International Standard Industrial Classification (ISIC) or in accord with the UN statistical paper *International Recommendations for Industrial Statistics,* rev. 1 (1983), the principal bases for the classification of data used in this table. Similarly, they may not define "business enterprise," "establishment," or "employee" in the same way. In addition, each country may use different size classes in categorizing establishments—those employing more than 10 employees, say, or more than 50—skewing the reported distribution by size of establishment.

The sectors for which data have been provided include: food, beverages, and tobacco; textiles, apparel, and leather; wood, paper, chemicals, and related products; primary and fabricated metals and processed minerals; machinery (except electrical) and transport equipment; electrical and electronic machinery. For each of these sectors (for which ISIC definitions are provided below), data are given for value added (or, occasionally, some other measure of value, when value added was not reported), for the number of establishments with fewer than and more than 100 employees (though it sometimes proved impossible to identify the actual distribution in a particular national survey because of its summarization in a national or international source), and, where it was known, for the proportion of the sectoral value added represented by these two groups of establishments.

The collection and publication of national manufacturing data is usually carried out by one of three methods: a full census of manufacturing (usually done every five to ten years for a given country), a periodic survey of manufacturing (usually taken at regular intervals between censuses), and the onetime sample survey (often limited in geographical, sectoral, or size-of-enterprise coverage). The full census is, naturally, the most complete, but since up to ten years may elapse between such censuses, it has often been necessary to substitute a survey of more recent date, but less complete coverage, in order to provide more timely data. For each country the initial date indicates the year of the survey.

The total value added of each national manufacturing sector in U.S. dollars is provided so that the relative importance of that country's overall national manufacturing activity may be compared internationally. The percentage of that total contributed by each sector is also given, and for each sector, the value added is broken down by size of enterprise wherever possible. The dollar figures for value added should be used only with caution, because of inherent uncertainties with respect to accounting methods, purchasing power, national price structures and preferments, exchange rates, and so on.

The figures for numbers of establishments generally refer to each separate physical facility, regardless of the number of separately incorporated

Manufacturing industries

country	year	food, beverages, and tobacco (group 1)					textiles, apparel, and leather (group 2)					wood, paper, chemicals, and related products (group 3)				
		percent of total value added	enterprises				percent of total value added	enterprises				percent of total value added	enterprises			
			1–99 employees		100 or more emp.			1–99 employees		100 or more emp.			1–99 employees		100 or more emp.	
			number	percent of value added	number	percent of value added		number	percent of value added	number	percent of value added		number	percent of value added	number	percent of value added
Afghanistan[1]	1982	48.1	...	...	69	...	24.4	...	...	70	...	20.9	...	...	58	...
Albania	...	...	...	...	...	...	...	...	...	...	...	...	...	...	...	...
Algeria[3,4]	1978	26.4	535	...	...	...	21.6	752	...	...	...	15.5	433	...	...	...
American Samoa																
Andorra	1972	...	142	...	...	...	...	104	...	...	...	...	49	...	...	...
Angola	1973	50.2	...	...	...	...	6.9	...	...	...	...	28.0	...	...	...	...
Anguilla																
Antigua and Barbuda	1980	...	14	100.0	—	—	...	12	100.0	—	—	...	15	100.0	—	—
Argentina	1981	26.8	1,188	...	92	...	9.2	1,059	...	75	...	29.6	1,394	...	101	...
Australia[6]	1980	17.6	3,889	...	460	...	9.1	4,071	...	363	...	19.0	10,412	...	610	...
Austria[7]	1983	16.6	453	...	132	...	10.1	857	...	220	...	35.4	4,270	...	300	...
Bahamas, The[8]	1978	27.6	...	...	...	...	0.3	...	...	...	...	57.9	...	...	...	...
Bahrain	...	...	...	...	...	...	...	...	...	...	...	...	...	...	...	...
Bangladesh[9]	1979	24.8	440	...	...	...	35.9	...	...	1,160	...	19.4	605	...	...	...
Barbados[10]	1979	34.5[11]	38[11]	...	...	...	18.3	...	...	22	...	19.1	50	...	...	...
Belgium[6]	1982	19.6	6,973	...	...	...	12.5[12]	3,824[12]	...	...	...	25.9[13]	6,028[13]	...	...	...
Belize	...	...	...	...	...	...	...	...	...	...	...	...	...	...	...	...
Benin	1978	59.7	...	...	...	...	12.0	...	...	...	...	11.7	...	...	...	...
Bermuda	...	...	...	...	...	...	...	...	...	...	...	...	...	...	...	...
Bhutan	1980	...	...	...	...	...	...	...	...	...	...	...	...	...	...	...
Bolivia[3]	1981	37.0	322	...	...	...	5.6	253	...	...	...	40.8	474	...	...	...
Botswana[6]	1981	44.2	22[16]	...	...	...	15.7	16[16]	...	...	...	5.3	11[16]	...	...	...
Brazil[10]	1980	17.0	26,226	38.6	1,272	61.4	10.9	14,325	23.8	1,913	76.2	30.8	27,752	30.5	1,925	69.5
British Virgin Islands	1978	...	1	100.0	—	—	—	...	...	...	...	...	2	100.0	—	—
Brunei[18]	1980	...	29	100.0	—	—	...	76	100.0	—	—	...	60	100.0	—	—
Bulgaria[8]	1982	21.6	...	...	278	...	13.5	...	...	210	...	5.4	...	...	257	...
Burkina Faso	1979	54.7	14	...	2	...	8.0	4	...	2	...	33.6	27	...	...	...
Burma	...	...	...	...	...	...	...	...	...	...	...	...	...	...	...	...
Burundi	...	...	...	...	...	...	...	...	...	...	...	...	...	...	...	...
Cameroon[10]	1979	52.4	30[19]	...	...	...	13.0	...	...	35[19]	...	12.6	66[19]	...	...	...
Canada	1982	18.4	4,152[20]	44.9[20]	244	55.1	7.1	3,281	37.2	489	62.8	31.3	12,111[20]	31.4[20]	1,381	69.6
Cape Verde	...	...	...	...	...	...	...	...	...	...	...	...	...	...	...	...
Cayman Islands	...	...	...	...	...	...	—	...	...	...	...	...	...	...	...	...
Central African Republic[6]	1980	55.8	12	...	...	...	3.3	3	...	...	...	21.8	8	...	...	...
Chad	1975	44.9	...	...	...	...	39.7	...	...	...	...	3.9	...	...	...	...
Chile[10,16,21]	1980	26.8	6,860	...	160	...	9.0	4,549	...	93	...	26.8	5,959	...	175	...
China[1,22]	1981	14.1	60,107	...	...	...	17.2	...	...	24,607	...	19.7	...	...	42,942	...
Christmas Island	...	...	...	...	...	...	...	...	...	...	...	—	...	...	—	...
Cocos (Keeling) Islands	...	...	...	...	...	...	...	...	...	...	...	...	...	...	...	...
Colombia[9,10]	1981	30.5	1,365	...	...	...	14.5	1,876	...	...	...	32.0	1,165	...	...	...
Comoros	...	...	...	...	...	...	...	...	...	...	...	...	...	...	...	...
Congo	1982	37.0	...	...	...	...	5.0	...	...	...	...	58.0[23]	...	...	...	...
Cook Islands[24]	1978	100.0	15	...	2	...	—	—	...	—	...	—	—	...	—	...
Costa Rica[10,25]	1980	47.6	...	...	44	...	10.1	...	...	50	...	27.5	119	...	...	...
Cuba[1,26]	1982	58.0	...	...	341	...	5.5	...	...	54	...	9.9	...	...	87	...
Cyprus[10,27]	1982	22.6	689	...	...	...	25.4	1,736	...	...	...	27.1	1,855	...	...	...
Czechoslovakia	1982	8.5	...	...	119	...	11.5	...	...	85	...	19.3	...	...	138	...
Denmark[6,28]	1982	24.7	913	...	...	...	5.6	725	...	...	...	27.0	1,802	...	...	...
Djibouti	...	...	...	...	...	...	...	...	...	...	...	...	...	...	...	...
Dominica	...	...	...	...	...	...	...	...	...	...	...	...	...	...	...	...
Dominican Republic[10,22,26,29]	1981	68.6	...	...	860	...	6.0	207	...	...	...	19.3	296	...	...	...
Ecuador[10,30]	1980	32.3	536	...	...	...	15.3	755	...	...	...	26.7	916	...	...	...
Egypt[9,10]	1976	16.0	2,072	...	...	...	31.5	...	...	1,189	...	23.3	...	...	584	...
El Salvador[10]	1981	35.8	...	...	97	...	20.8	...	...	106	...	30.6	112	...	...	...
Equatorial Guinea	...	...	...	...	...	...	...	...	...	...	...	...	...	...	...	...

legal entities (companies, partnerships, parastatal organizations), any of which may operate more than one facility. It was often impossible to establish from the published source material what the actual distribution of establishments by size was. A single total for a particular sector was often the only datum available. In such instances, the *average* size of these establishments was calculated (since the total number of employees in the sector was known), and the figure for number of establishments was placed in the table above or below the 100-employee cutoff accordingly. Such figures are given in italics.

One impediment to international comparability in terms of size of establishment is the size limit the country itself establishes as the minimum reporting unit for such surveys. For a small country it may be both feasible and desirable to survey all establishments, however small, on the grounds that they are few enough to constitute a manageable body of data for analysis, and also that if the country's manufacturers are mostly small operations, then it is precisely this group on which national planners need the most information. For larger countries, the cost to collect and analyze data for all establishments may be prohibitively high, and, moreover, interest from a development point of view may be exclusively in middle and large-scale industry, that needed to permit replacement of imported goods with domestic manufactures. In such a case the country may survey only those establishments with 50 employees or more. Thus, when the distributions of number of establishments are examined, it should be noted (and has been footnoted wherever possible) when such limits in coverage may be applicable.

In terms of the industrial groups implied by the names of the manufac-turing sectors used here, the content of each sector is usually defined by the two- or three-digit level of classification in the ISIC system:

group	EB category	ISIC code (-s)	remarks
1.	Food, beverages, and tobacco	31	
2.	Textiles, apparel, and leather	32	
3.	Wood, paper, chemicals, and related products	33	wood and furniture
		34	paper and products; printing and publishing
		35	industrial chemicals, pharmaceuticals, petroleum and products, rubber, plastics
4.	Primary and fabricated metals and processed minerals	36	pottery, china, glass
		37	iron and steel; nonferrous metals
		381	metal products
5.	Machinery (except electrical) and transport equipment	382 + 384 minus 3825	machinery and transport equipment minus office equipment and computers
6.	Electrical and electronic machinery	383 + 3825	electrical and electronic equipment, plus office equipment and computers

It should be noted that these groups do not account for ISIC groups 385 and 390 (professional goods and other industries, respectively).

primary and fabricated metals; proc. minerals (group 4)					machinery (except elec.) and transport equip. (group 5)					electrical and electronic machinery (group 6)					total manufacturing value added (U.S.$'000,-000)	country
percent of total value added	enterprises				percent of total value added	enterprises				percent of total value added	enterprises					
	1–99 employees		100 or more emp.			1–99 employees		100 or more emp.			1–99 employees		100 or more emp.			
	number	percent of value added	number	percent of value added		number	percent of value added	number	percent of value added		number	percent of value added	number	percent of value added		
2.8	...	...	10	...	3.7[2]	...	...	16[2]	...	2	...	...	2	...	...	Afghanistan
...	...	...	...	...	...	...	...	...	...	...	...	...	...	...	...	Albania
36.5[5]	337[5]	...	5	...	...	5	...	...	...	5	5	...	...	...	2,674	Algeria
...	...	...	...	...	...	25	...	...	...	...	83	...	...	...	...	American Samoa
...	38	...	...	...	...	...	...	...	...	...	...	...	...	...	...	Andorra
10.9	...	...	...	...	3.0	...	...	...	...	1.1	...	...	...	...	593	Angola
...	...	...	...	...	...	...	...	...	...	...	...	...	...	...	...	Anguilla
...	10	100.0	—	—	...	...	...	—	—	...	...	...	—	—	...	Antigua and Barbuda
11.0	206	...	21	...	12.1	...	...	151	...	3.0	...	...	29	...	15,883	Argentina
19.9	2,245	...	323	...	22.5	12,484[2]	...	866[2]	...	6.0	2	...	2	...	33,687	Australia
11.9	759	...	155	...	17.3	965	...	202	...	8.8	300	...	114	...	25,906	Austria
13.5	...	...	...	...	0.7	...	...	...	...	—	—	—	—	—	30	Bahamas, The
...	...	...	...	...	...	...	...	...	...	...	...	...	...	...	...	Bahrain
14.6	332	...	...	...	2.4	...	...	89	...	2.9	83	...	...	...	660	Bangladesh
7.6	25	...	...	...	16.2[2]	...	...	16[2]	...	2	...	...	2	...	48	Barbados
10.1	4,724	...	...	...	31.0[2, 14]	...	...	1,973[2, 14]	...	2	...	...	2	...	18,691	Belgium
...	...	...	...	...	...	...	...	...	...	—	...	...	...	...	...	Belize
4.8	...	...	...	...	11.8[2]	...	...	...	...	2	...	...	...	...	46	Benin
...	...	...	...	...	...	...	...	...	...	...	...	...	...	...	...	Bermuda
...	...	...	...	...	...	...	...	...	...	...	...	...	...	...	...	Bhutan
12.8	181	...	...	...	2.7[15]	36	...	...	...	0.5[15]	14	...	...	...	694	Bolivia
...	39[16, 17]	...	...	...	...	17	...	...	...	...	17	...	...	...	54	Botswana
17.9	25,084	25.3	1,641	74.7	15.6	9,268	18.0	1,651	82.0	5.3	2,245	48.7	558	51.3	77,648	Brazil
...	4	100.0	—	—	...	...	...	—	—	...	...	...	—	—	...	British Virgin Islands
...	70[17]	100.0[17]	—	—	...	17	17	—	—	...	17	17	—	—	...	Brunei
49.4[17]	...	...	239	...	17	...	...	373[16]	...	17	...	...	119	...	...	Bulgaria
3.7	9	...	...	...	...	...	...	...	...	...	...	...	...	...	68	Burkina Faso
...	...	...	...	...	...	...	...	...	...	...	...	...	...	...	564	Burma
...	...	...	...	...	...	...	...	...	...	...	...	...	...	...	...	Burundi
10.1	...	...	9[19]	...	4.7	...	...	8[19]	...	1.7	...	...	9[19]	...	340	Cameroon
21.2	6,379[21]	52.1[21]	458	47.9	15.2	2,489	18.2	392	82.8	6.6	993[21]	29.9[21]	123	70.1	51,037	Canada
...	...	...	...	...	...	...	...	...	...	...	...	...	...	...	...	Cape Verde
...	...	...	—	—	—	—	—	—	—	...	...	...	—	—	...	Cayman Islands
16.2[17]	8[17]	...	...	...	17	17	...	...	...	17	17	...	...	...	16	Central African Republic
11.5	...	...	...	...	—	...	...	...	...	—	...	...	...	...	77	Chad
30.8	3,173	...	100	...	4.4	1,577	...	49	...	1.9	117	...	20	...	6,392	Chile
15.1	...	...	49,567	...	22.8[2]	...	...	102,286[2]	...	2	...	...	2	...	...	China
—	—	—	—	—	—	—	—	—	—	—	—	—	—	—	...	Christmas Island
—	—	—	—	—	—	—	—	—	—	—	—	—	—	—	...	Cocos (Keeling) Islands
12.4	1,126	...	...	...	5.3	539	...	...	...	3.5	210	...	...	...	7,509	Colombia
...	...	...	...	...	...	...	...	...	...	...	...	...	...	...	...	Comoros
23	...	...	...	...	23	...	...	...	...	23	...	...	...	...	217	Congo
—	...	...	—	—	—	...	...	—	—	—	...	...	—	—	...	Cook Islands
6.9	42	...	...	...	4.9[15]	14	...	...	...	2.7[15]	19	...	...	...	663	Costa Rica
8.4	...	...	80	...	6.9	...	...	136	...	0.9	...	...	18	...	...	Cuba
17.0	817	...	...	...	5.4	243	...	...	...	2.0	38	...	...	...	362	Cyprus
20.7	...	...	151	...	32.0	...	...	209	...	6.0	...	...	47	...	...	Czechoslovakia
13.4	1,365	...	...	...	19.0[15]	1,033	...	...	...	6.0[15]	274	...	...	...	9,749	Denmark
...	...	...	...	...	...	...	...	...	...	—	...	...	...	...	...	Djibouti
...	...	...	...	...	...	...	...	...	...	...	...	...	...	...	...	Dominica
3.2	134	...	...	...	2.8[2]	5	...	...	...	2	16	...	...	...	1,113	Dominican Republic
18.0	533	...	...	...	2.1	121	...	...	...	4.4	58	...	...	...	1,355	Ecuador
14.9	...	...	838	...	9.8	...	...	126	...	4.3	...	...	49	...	1,767	Egypt
7.4	47	...	...	...	1.5	14	...	...	...	3.0	10	...	...	...	484	El Salvador
...	...	...	...	...	...	...	...	...	...	...	...	...	...	...	...	Equatorial Guinea

Manufacturing industries (continued)

country	year	food, beverages, and tobacco (group 1) percent of total value added	1–99 employees number	1–99 employees percent of value added	100 or more emp. number	100 or more emp. percent of value added	textiles, apparel, and leather (group 2) percent of total value added	1–99 employees number	1–99 employees percent of value added	100 or more emp. number	100 or more emp. percent of value added	wood, paper, chemicals, and related products (group 3) percent of total value added	1–99 employees number	1–99 employees percent of value added	100 or more emp. number	100 or more emp. percent of value added
Ethiopia[10]	1981	53.0	...	...	153	...	27.3	...	...	77	...	12.8	...	...	127	...
Faeroe Islands		...	...	...	...	...	...	...	...	...	...	...	...	...	...	...
Falkland Islands		...	...	...	...	...	...	...	...	...	...	...	...	...	...	...
Fiji[10, 18]	1980	65.9	62	...	11	...	1.9	78	...	2	...	18.4	136	...	7	...
Finland[8]	1981	11.8	1,007	...	141	...	8.2	752	...	186	...	44.5	2,015	...	432	...
France	1982	17.2	...	...	...	...	7.3	...	...	...	...	24.3	...	...	...	...
French Guiana		...	...	...	...	...	...	...	...	...	...	...	...	...	...	...
French Polynesia		...	...	...	...	...	...	...	...	...	...	...	...	...	...	...
Gabon	1978	17.5	145	...	...	...	2.8	1,482[31]	...	...	...	41.9	64	...	...	...
Gambia, The[10, 29]	1981	46.7	20	...	...	...	1.3	2	...	...	...	6.0	6	...	...	...
Gaza Strip[32]	1982	12.2	202	...	...	...	33.4	523	...	...	...	11.5	212	...	...	...
Germany, East[1]	1983	15.8	...	...	572	...	6.6	...	...	186	...	25.0	...	...	448	...
Germany, West[33]	1983	10.4	3,439	...	1,157	...	4.6	3,886	...	1,323	...	22.8	9,001	...	2,865	...
Ghana[10, 16, 34]	1981	50.2	...	...	61	...	8.7	...	...	85	...	24.9	...	...	164	...
Gibraltar		...	...	...	...	...	...	...	...	...	...	...	...	...	...	...
Greece[10]	1978	19.4	21,202	...	143	...	26.7	30,491	...	254	...	21.4	29,689	...	148	...
Greenland		...	...	...	...	...	...	...	...	...	...	...	...	...	...	...
Grenada		...	...	...	...	...	...	...	...	...	...	...	...	...	...	...
Guadeloupe		...	...	...	...	...	...	...	...	...	...	...	...	...	...	...
Guam		...	...	...	...	...	...	...	...	...	...	...	...	...	...	...
Guatemala[10, 29]	1978	38.2	626	...	...	...	9.9	436	...	...	...	32.4	671	...	...	...
Guernsey		...	...	...	...	...	...	...	...	...	...	...	...	...	...	...
Guinea		...	...	...	...	...	...	...	...	...	...	...	...	...	...	...
Guinea-Bissau		...	...	...	...	...	...	...	...	...	...	...	...	...	...	...
Guyana	1979	...	31	...	...	...	...	8	...	...	...	...	20	...	...	...
Haiti[10]	1982	33.1	425	...	...	...	15.5	135	...	...	...	7.7	94	...	...	...
Honduras	1975	56.1	233	...	...	...	9.9	198	...	...	...	23.0	280	...	...	...
Hong Kong[8, 10]	1980	5.2	906	...	28	...	43.8	8,225	...	644	...	18.5	7,199	...	206	...
Hungary[8]	1980	13.2	1,977	...	194	...	13.4	14,483	...	258	...	25.3	5,229	...	225	...
Iceland[6, 25]	1980	14.6	170	...	...	...	13.5	242	...	...	...	29.8	816	...	...	...
India[6, 35]	1979	10.1	26,469	...	...	...	22.9	...	...	14,700	...	24.5	17,351	...	...	...
Indonesia[6, 36, 37]	1981	31.4	...	...	2,341	...	11.7	...	...	2,153	...	26.7	...	...	1,864	...
Iran[9, 10]	1981	13.0	896	...	...	...	19.9	1,406	...	...	...	33.6	1,150	...	...	...
Iraq[6, 38]	1981	27.9	3,775	...	...	...	15.1	7,797	...	...	...	17.2	4,769	...	...	...
Ireland[6, 38]	1978	29.8	965	...	...	...	9.7	729	...	...	...	26.9	1,275	...	...	...
Isle of Man		...	...	...	...	...	...	...	...	...	...	...	...	...	...	...
Israel[10, 25, 29, 39]	1982	12.0	1,019	...	...	...	10.9	2,071	...	...	...	25.7	3,492	...	...	...
Italy[37]	1981	8.8	...	...	2,011	...	12.2	6,278	...	...	...	24.8	...	...	5,927	...
Ivory Coast[10, 40, 41]	1982	40.6	281	...	...	...	17.2	...	...	75	...	18.7	272	...	...	...
Jamaica[10, 19, 42]	1980	45.9	308	...	...	...	6.9	157	...	...	...	31.3	333	...	...	...
Japan	1982	9.6	49,593	50.1	1,824	49.9	6.3	73,918	70.1	1,610	29.9	23.2	92,706	54.3	2,366	45.7
Jersey		...	...	...	...	...	...	...	...	...	...	...	...	...	...	...
Jordan[6]	1981	20.5	572	...	...	...	6.2	536	...	...	...	34.2	884	...	...	...
Kampuchea		...	...	...	...	...	...	...	...	...	...	...	...	...	...	...
Kenya[6, 21]	1982	38.3	...	...	126	...	12.5	...	...	121	...	26.7	...	...	178	...
Kiribati		...	...	...	...	...	...	...	...	...	...	...	...	...	...	...
Korea, North		...	...	...	...	...	...	...	...	...	...	...	...	...	...	...
Korea, South[10, 44]	1981	15.8	31,884	...	206	...	19.8	26,525	...	721	...	25.6	11,619	...	352	...
Kuwait[10]	1980	5.4	440	...	...	...	5.0	1,867	...	...	...	68.1	552	...	...	...
Laos		...	...	...	...	...	...	...	...	...	...	...	...	...	...	...
Lebanon		...	...	...	...	...	...	...	...	...	...	...	...	...	...	...
Lesotho	1981	...	...	...	...	...	...	...	...	...	...	...	...	...	...	...
Liberia	1982	...	...	...	...	...	...	...	...	...	...	...	...	...	...	...
Libya[45]	1979	15.8	102	...	...	...	4.1	27	...	...	...	80.1[23]	51	...	...	...
Liechtenstein	1975	...	43	...	1	...	...	22	...	2	...	...	69	...	2	...
Luxembourg[6, 37]	1980	6.4	33	...	...	...	2.0	11	...	...	...	18.6	...	...	42	...
Macau[10, 44]	1981	1.5	108	...	...	...	76.2	522	...	...	...	10.2	254	...	...	...
Madagascar[10]	1980	28.2	144	...	...	...	46.7	...	...	51	...	12.4	120	...	...	...
Malawi[8, 46]	1979	40.8	35	...	...	...	10.7	19	...	...	...	48.5[23]	31	...	...	...
Malaysia[6, 8]	1979	25.9	1,255	...	...	...	7.0	489	...	...	...	36.0	2,412	...	...	...
Maldives		...	...	...	...	...	...	...	...	...	...	...	...	...	...	...
Mali	1981	30.0	...	...	...	...	53.0	...	...	...	...	17.0[23]	...	...	...	...
Malta[6]	1981	18.2	393	...	...	...	35.5	250	...	...	...	19.8	630	...	...	...
Martinique		...	...	...	...	...	...	...	...	...	...	...	...	...	...	...
Mauritania		...	...	...	...	...	...	...	...	...	...	...	...	...	...	...
Mauritius[9, 10, 47]	1982	36.9	155	...	...	...	33.5	...	...	136	...	12.0	90	...	...	...
Mayotte		...	...	...	...	...	...	...	...	...	...	...	...	...	...	...
Mexico	1982	24.9	...	...	476	...	12.5	...	...	136	...	28.8	...	...	341	...
Monaco		...	...	...	...	...	...	...	...	...	...	...	...	...	...	...
Mongolia[8]	1980	5.0	...	...	...	...	29.2	...	...	...	...	29.3	...	...	...	...
Montserrat		...	...	...	...	...	...	...	...	...	...	...	...	...	...	...
Morocco[8]	1980	32.1	...	...	...	...	14.9	...	...	...	...	18.7	...	...	...	...
Mozambique	1972	48.1	769	...	93	...	14.9	5	...	62	...	21.4	194	...	110	...
Nauru		...	...	...	...	...	...	...	...	...	...	...	...	...	...	...
Nepal[8]	1977	85.6	2,770	...	35	...	1.9	109	...	10	...	3.9	339	...	12	...
Netherlands, The[6]	1979	14.7	1,242	...	313	...	3.8	1,039	...	265	...	46.4	1,444	...	322	...
Netherlands Antilles		...	...	...	...	...	...	...	...	...	...	...	...	...	...	...
New Caledonia		...	...	...	...	...	...	...	...	...	...	...	...	...	...	...
New Zealand	1981	26.2	933	...	106	...	10.4	1,091	...	89	...	28.7	2,347	...	129	...
Nicaragua[10, 34]	1980	55.9	...	...	102	...	10.9	...	...	65	...	25.3	...	...	103	...
Niger	1982	...	...	...	...	...	...	...	...	...	...	...	...	...	...	...
Nigeria[9, 10]	1980	30.6	...	...	315	...	10.4	...	...	117	...	25.1	...	...	468	...
Niue		...	...	...	...	...	...	...	...	...	...	...	...	...	...	...
Norfolk Island		...	...	...	...	...	...	...	...	...	...	...	...	...	...	...
Norway[10, 29]	1982	13.7	2,369	58.2	94	41.8	3.3	845	73.3	33	26.7	31.9	4,217	65.3	217	34.7

primary and fabricated metals; proc. minerals (group 4)					machinery (except elec.) and transport equip. (group 5)					electrical and electronic machinery (group 6)					total manufacturing value added (U.S.$'000,000)	country
percent of total value added	enterprises 1–99 employees		enterprises 100 or more emp.		percent of total value added	enterprises 1–99 employees		enterprises 100 or more emp.		percent of total value added	enterprises 1–99 employees		enterprises 100 or more emp.			
	number	percent of value added	number	percent of value added		number	percent of value added	number	percent of value added		number	percent of value added	number	percent of value added		
6.8	...	...	48	...	—	—	—	—	—	0.1	3	...	...	...	445	Ethiopia
—	...	...	...	...	...	...	...	...	...	...	...	...	...	...	...	Faeroe Islands
...	...	...	...	...	...	...	...	...	...	...	...	...	...	...	...	Falkland Islands
10.6	8	...	1	...	2.6[2]	80[2]	...	3[2]	...	0.3[2]	2	...	2	...	120	Fiji
14.3	1,024	...	145	...	16.2	896	...	203	...	4.9	139	...	55	...	...	Finland
14.9	...	...	...	...	26.2[15]	...	...	...	...	7.5[15]	...	...	...	...	133,148	France
...	...	...	...	...	...	...	...	...	...	...	...	...	...	...	...	French Guiana
...	...	...	...	...	...	...	...	...	...	...	...	...	...	...	...	French Polynesia
37.8[17]	444	...	...	...	[17]	...	...	...	...	[17]	...	...	...	...	175	Gabon
2.6	3	...	...	...	...	...	...	...	...	—	...	...	...	...	10	Gambia, The
27.5	261	...	...	...	15.6[2]	223[2]	...	...	...	[2]	2	...	...	...	34	Gaza Strip
19.6	...	...	918	...	22.9	...	...	1,299	...	10.1	...	...	347	...	...	Germany, East
17.5	5,340	...	1,044	...	27.1	5,750	...	2,590	...	15.4	3,562	...	2,063	...	230,904	Germany, West
14.1	...	...	54	...	1.0	...	...	14	...	0.6	...	...	6	...	2,387	Ghana
...	...	...	...	...	...	...	...	...	...	...	...	...	...	...	...	Gibraltar
13.1	19,921	...	103	...	19.4[2]	21,662	...	67	...	[2]	5,272	...	36	...	5,161	Greece
...	...	...	...	...	...	...	...	...	...	...	...	...	...	...	2	Greenland
...	...	...	...	...	...	...	...	...	...	...	...	...	...	...	...	Grenada
—	—	—	—	—	—	—	—	—	—	—	—	—	—	—	...	Guadeloupe
...	...	...	...	...	...	...	...	...	...	...	...	...	...	...	...	Guam
12.7	366	...	...	...	1.3	64	...	...	...	2.8	33	...	...	...	781	Guatemala
...	...	...	...	...	...	...	...	...	...	...	...	...	...	...	...	Guernsey
...	...	...	...	...	...	...	...	...	...	...	...	...	...	...	...	Guinea
...	...	...	...	...	...	...	...	...	...	...	...	...	...	...	...	Guinea-Bissau
...	...	...	...	...	...	...	...	...	...	...	1	...	...	...	...	Guyana
43.7[17]	58	...	...	...	[17]	36[2]	...	...	...	[17]	2	...	...	...	178	Haiti
9.0	98	...	...	...	0.6	11	...	...	...	1.1	9	...	...	...	112	Honduras
11.8	363	...	10	...	4.8	7,092[2]	...	278[2]	...	15.9	2	...	2	...	6,552	Hong Kong
22.5	300	...	64	...	12.6	9,418[2]	...	312[2]	...	13.0	2	...	2	...	...	Hungary
39.4[17]	542[17]	...	...	...	[17]	17	...	...	...	[17]	17	...	...	...	308	Iceland
18.0	17,851	...	...	...	15.6	9,603	...	...	...	7.5	3,367	...	...	...	11,584	India
13.5	1,042	...	...	...	11.8	...	...	316	...	4.6	...	...	115	...	4,309	Indonesia
19.1	3,325	...	...	...	9.4[15]	...	...	222[15]	...	4.6[15]	...	...	111[15]	...	9,793	Iran
17.3	3,534	...	...	...	8.7	98	...	...	...	4.6	17	...	...	...	6,055	Iraq
14.7	934	...	...	...	6.3	354	...	...	...	8.5	181	...	...	...	4,915	Ireland
...	...	...	...	...	...	...	...	...	...	...	...	...	...	...	...	Isle of Man
24.5	3,027	...	...	...	12.7[15]	436[15]	...	...	...	12.1[15]	548[15]	...	...	...	5,695	Israel
21.4	...	...	6,140	...	21.1[15]	...	...	3,214[15]	...	8.6[15]	...	...	1,145[15]	...	83,943	Italy
21.6[17]	80[17]	...	...	...	[17]	17	...	...	...	[17]	17	...	...	...	1,092	Ivory Coast
15.0[17]	361[17]	...	...	...	[17]	17	...	...	...	[17]	17	...	...	...	405	Jamaica
19.3	79,249	43.9	2,190	56.1	21.1	51,447	27.3	2,555	62.7	13.9	27,510	19.1	2,406	80.9	288,560	Japan
...	...	...	...	...	...	...	...	...	...	...	...	...	...	...	...	Jersey
32.6[43]	1,366[43]	...	...	...	43, 15	43, 15	...	...	...	0.4[15]	5[15]	...	...	...	501	Jordan
...	...	...	...	...	...	...	...	...	...	...	...	...	...	...	...	Kampuchea
8.5	...	...	76	...	5.9[15]	...	...	33[15]	...	7.6[15]	...	...	16[15]	...	31	Kenya
—	—	—	—	—	—	—	—	—	—	—	—	—	—	—	...	Kiribati
...	...	...	...	...	...	...	...	...	...	...	...	...	...	...	...	Korea, North
17.0	5,401	...	153	...	10.2	10,215[2]	19.8[2]	469[2]	80.2[2]	8.7	2	2	2	2	22,630	Korea, South
16.9	811	...	...	...	3.0[15]	57[15]	...	...	...	1.2	31[15]	...	...	...	1,817	Kuwait
...	...	...	...	...	...	...	...	...	...	...	...	...	...	...	...	Laos
...	...	...	...	...	...	...	...	...	...	...	...	...	...	...	...	Lebanon
...	...	...	...	...	...	...	...	...	...	...	...	...	...	...	21	Lesotho
...	...	...	...	...	...	...	...	...	...	...	...	...	...	...	70	Liberia
[23]	85	...	...	...	[23]	6[2]	...	2	...	[23]	2	...	...	...	628	Libya
...	96	...	1	...	...	4	...	2	...	...	29	...	2	...	...	Liechtenstein
61.0	...	...	42	...	10.4[15]	...	...	26[15]	...	1.6[15]	8[15]	...	...	...	1,181	Luxembourg
0.8	86	...	...	...	1.0[15]	24[15]	...	...	...	2.0[15]	27[15]	...	...	...	135	Macau
5.4	...	...	19	...	3.4	22	...	...	...	1.5	15	...	...	...	206	Madagascar
[23]	18	...	...	...	[23]	3	...	...	...	[23]	2	...	...	...	56	Malawi
11.7	820	...	...	...	7.7	559	...	...	...	11.9	209	...	...	...	3,288	Malaysia
...	...	...	...	...	...	...	...	...	...	...	...	...	...	...	...	Maldives
[23]	...	...	...	...	[23]	...	...	...	...	[23]	...	...	...	...	102	Mali
8.5	244	...	...	...	5.0[15]	58[15]	...	...	...	6.8[15]	38[15]	...	...	...	278	Malta
...	...	...	...	...	...	...	...	...	...	...	...	...	...	...	...	Martinique
...	...	...	...	...	...	...	...	...	...	...	...	...	...	...	...	Mauritania
10.0	77	...	...	...	2.8[15]	19[15]	...	...	...	1.1[15]	12[15]	...	...	...	137	Mauritius
...	...	...	...	...	...	...	...	...	...	...	...	...	...	...	...	Mayotte
15.8	...	...	230	...	11.0	...	...	39	...	4.5	...	...	74	...	35,559	Mexico
...	...	...	...	...	...	...	...	...	...	...	...	...	...	...	...	Monaco
21.7	...	...	...	...	14.7[2]	...	...	...	...	[2]	...	...	...	...	...	Mongolia
...	...	...	...	...	...	...	...	...	...	...	...	...	...	...	...	Montserrat
9.7	...	...	...	...	17.8	...	...	...	...	6.7	...	...	...	...	2,250	Morocco
12.2	113	...	50	...	2.1	15	...	16	...	1.3	9	...	6	...	457	Mozambique
...	...	...	...	...	...	...	...	...	...	...	...	...	...	...	...	Nauru
1.5	106	...	20	...	7.1[2]	113[2]	...	12[2]	...	[2]	2	...	2	...	315	Nepal
13.4	552	...	134	...	11.5	2,513[2]	...	441[2]	...	10.1	2	...	2	...	35,673	Netherlands, The
...	...	...	...	...	...	...	...	...	...	...	...	...	...	...	...	Netherlands Antilles
...	...	...	...	...	...	...	...	...	...	...	...	...	...	...	...	New Caledonia
15.1	476	...	29	...	11.6	2,728	...	125	...	5.1	...	...	...	...	5,068	New Zealand
5.9	43	...	...	...	0.7	8	...	...	...	0.9	9	...	...	...	717	Nicaragua
...	...	...	...	...	...	...	...	...	...	...	...	...	...	...	283	Niger
10.8	...	...	272	...	21.1	...	...	39	...	1.7	...	...	17	...	6,460	Nigeria
...	...	...	...	...	...	...	...	...	...	...	...	...	...	...	...	Niue
...	...	...	...	...	...	...	...	...	...	...	...	...	...	...	...	Norfolk Island
18.9	2,140	37.6	118	62.4	24.1[15]	1,974	15.8	154	84.2	7.1[15]	342	29.1	48	70.9	10,028	Norway

Manufacturing industries (continued)

country	year	food, beverages, and tobacco (group 1)					textiles, apparel, and leather (group 2)					wood, paper, chemicals, and related products (group 3)				
		percent of total value added	enterprises 1–99 employees number	percent of value added	100 or more emp. number	percent of value added	percent of total value added	enterprises 1–99 employees number	percent of value added	100 or more emp. number	percent of value added	percent of total value added	enterprises 1–99 employees number	percent of value added	100 or more emp. number	percent of value added
Oman	...	...	...	...	...	...	...	...	...	...	...	...	...	...	...	...
Pacific Is., Trust Terr. of the	...	...	...	...	...	...	...	...	...	...	...	...	...	...	...	...
Pakistan	1977	36.7	332[20]	10.0	90	90.0	24.6	844[20]	13.8	211	86.2	20.8	522[20]	12.6	115	87.4
Panama[10,29]	1979	48.2	199	...	25	...	10.4	88	...	16	...	22.2	172	...	12	...
Papua New Guinea	1983	56.8	150	...	...	...	0.5	12	...	...	...	24.1	148	...	...	...
Paraguay	1982	36.0	...	...	...	...	12.0	...	...	...	...	52.0[23]	...	...	...	...
Peru[10]	1980	24.7	6,236	...	82	...	12.5	8,613	...	106	...	22.1	7,476	...	148	...
Philippines[16]	1981	42.8	30,605	...	...	...	10.1	34,253	...	...	...	26.8	8,950	...	...	...
Pitcairn Island	...	...	...	...	...	...	...	...	...	...	...	...	...	...	...	...
Poland[48]	1982	19.7	10,841	...	...	...	13.3	9,063	...	...	...	19.6	...	...	5,172	...
Portugal[10,22]	1981	20.4	10,825	...	212	...	24.2	10,387	...	439	...	21.7	11,067	...	270	...
Puerto Rico	1982	11.2	296	22.7	37	77.3	8.4	286	25.6	131	74.4	47.5	578	25.2	68	74.8
Qatar	1984	...	...	...	...	...	...	...	...	...	...	...	...	...	...	...
Réunion	1978	...	35	...	...	...	...	5	...	...	...	...	16	...	...	...
Romania[48]	1982	11.0	...	...	291	...	15.0	...	...	225	...	74.0[23]	...	...	200	...
Rwanda[8,16]	1981	75.7	...	...	17	...	10.1	...	...	3	...	5.8	...	...	17	...
St. Christopher and Nevis	...	...	...	...	...	...	...	...	...	...	...	...	...	...	...	...
St. Helena and Ascension	...	...	...	...	...	...	...	...	...	...	...	...	...	...	...	...
St. Lucia	...	...	...	...	...	...	...	...	...	...	...	...	...	...	...	...
St. Pierre and Miquelon	...	...	...	...	...	...	...	...	...	...	...	...	...	...	...	...
St. Vincent	...	...	...	...	...	...	...	...	...	...	...	...	...	...	...	...
San Marino	1984	...	34	...	...	...	...	65	...	...	...	...	64	...	...	...
São Tomé and Príncipe	...	...	...	...	...	...	...	...	...	...	...	...	...	...	...	...
Saudi Arabia	1977	...	...	...	...	...	...	...	...	...	...	...	...	...	...	...
Senegal[8]	1975	49.7	49	...	...	...	19.8	28	...	...	...	17.5	59	...	...	...
Seychelles	1981	75.4	12	...	...	...	2.3	3	...	...	...	10.8	14	...	...	...
Sierra Leone[8]	1973–74	80.3	...	...	...	...	2.7	...	...	...	...	10.8	...	...	...	...
Singapore[6,9]	1982	5.9	305	...	...	...	4.9	597	...	...	...	33.1	1,057	...	...	...
Solomon Islands	...	...	...	...	...	...	...	...	...	...	...	...	...	...	...	...
Somalia[8,10]	1977	44.5	68	...	...	...	24.4	75	...	...	...	24.8	37	...	...	...
South Africa[8,10]	1976	14.1	1,713	19.4	451	80.6	10.5	1,543	15.7	570	84.3	25.6	3,639	25.6	625	74.4
Bophuthatswana	...	...	...	...	...	...	...	...	...	...	...	...	...	...	...	...
Ciskei	...	...	...	...	...	...	...	...	...	...	...	...	...	...	...	...
Transkei	...	...	...	...	...	...	...	...	...	...	...	...	...	...	...	...
Venda	...	...	...	...	...	...	...	...	...	...	...	...	...	...	...	...
South West Africa/Namibia	...	...	...	...	...	...	...	...	...	...	...	...	...	...	...	...
Spain[6,8]	1977	12.7	15,503	...	...	...	13.5	12,160	...	...	...	29.2	45,502	...	...	...
Sri Lanka[6]	1980	32.9	...	...	217	...	13.7	628	...	...	...	34.8	573	...	...	...
Sudan, The	1982	...	...	...	...	...	...	...	...	...	...	...	...	...	...	...
Suriname	...	...	...	...	...	...	...	...	...	...	...	...	...	...	...	...
Swaziland[6]	1981	47.6	...	...	15	...	2.7	35	...	...	...	40.6	...	...	37	...
Sweden[8]	1981	10.6	766	...	152	...	2.9	707	...	84	...	31.8	2,938	...	466	...
Switzerland	1975	17.3	12,680	...	152	...	9.0	4,750	...	198	...	33.7	17,255	...	311	...
Syria[10,50]	1982	28.7	7,974	...	...	...	25.9	15,116	...	...	...	34.4	12,376	...	...	...
Taiwan	...	...	...	...	...	...	...	...	...	...	...	...	...	...	...	...
Tanzania	1975	42.6	...	...	...	...	16.3	...	...	...	...	17.7	...	...	...	...
Thailand[9,10]	1980	19.5	2,152	...	...	...	26.0	...	...	1,462	...	22.8	2,118	...	...	...
Togo[10]	1979	62.1	...	...	12	...	7.4	3	...	...	...	13.6	26	...	...	...
Tokelau	...	...	...	...	...	...	...	...	...	...	...	...	...	...	...	...
Tonga	1981	73.8	33	100.0	—	—	1.1	11	100.0	—	—	11.7	23	100.0	—	—
Trinidad and Tobago[8,51]	1980	13.0	...	...	97	...	4.0	83	...	...	...	82.8[23]	225	...	...	...
Tunisia	1981	14.1	283	35.9	35	64.1	16.9	276	26.4	124	73.6	22.2	253	26.8	49	73.2
Turkey[10]	1981	21.1	18,692	...	175	...	16.4	65,114	...	195	...	25.7	28,193	...	150	...
Turks and Caicos Islands	...	...	...	...	...	...	...	...	...	...	...	...	...	...	...	...
Tuvalu	...	...	...	...	...	...	...	...	...	...	...	...	...	...	...	...
Uganda[6,8]	1971	43.3	148	19.7	24	39.0	22.8	48	8.7	9	34.1	13.2	113	61.8	21	38.0
U.S.S.R.[3]	1982	20.0	...	...	9,352	...	18.1	...	...	7,786	...	15.6	...	...	3,768	...
United Arab Emirates[9,27]	1978	8.0	73	...	...	...	1.7	67	...	...	...	25.3	209	...	...	...
United Kingdom[6,22]	1981	14.5	4,909	...	514	...	6.2	12,134	...	1,062	...	28.6	27,488	...	1,555	...
United States[6,52]	1981	10.5	22,994	24.1	3,890	75.9	6.1	30,578	24.8	6,204	75.2	28.6	120,525	29.7	9,646	70.3
Uruguay[10,19,29]	1981	33.9	2,789	...	...	...	14.4	1,995	...	...	...	33.0	2,897	...	...	...
Vanuatu	...	...	...	...	...	...	...	...	...	...	...	...	...	...	...	...
Venezuela[29,52]	1979	16.8	2,138	25.2	161	74.8	7.4	1,778	44.1	132	55.9	46.3	2,085	34.7	191	65.3
Vietnam	...	...	...	...	...	...	...	...	...	...	...	...	...	...	...	...
Virgin Islands (U.S.)	...	...	...	...	...	...	...	...	...	...	...	...	...	...	...	...
Wallis and Futuna	...	...	...	...	...	...	...	...	...	...	...	...	...	...	...	...
West Bank	1982	55.0	228	...	...	...	10.0	658	...	...	...	18.7	494	...	...	...
Western Sahara	...	...	...	...	...	...	...	...	...	...	...	...	...	...	...	...
Western Samoa	...	...	...	...	...	...	...	...	...	...	...	...	...	...	...	...
Yemen (Aden)	...	...	...	...	...	...	...	...	...	...	...	...	...	...	...	...
Yemen (Ṣan'ā')	1975	...	6,884	...	...	...	...	2,601	...	...	...	...	147	...	...	...
Yugoslavia	1981	11.5	...	...	1,398	...	16.2	...	...	1,576	...	25.7	...	...	2,942	...
Zaire[8]	1980	44.0	...	...	...	...	20.0	...	...	...	...	36.0[23]	...	...	...	...
Zambia[8,10]	1974	34.5	172	...	...	...	8.3	156	...	...	...	22.0	179	...	...	...
Zimbabwe[6]	1981	22.3	...	...	...	...	18.7	...	...	...	...	25.2	...	...	...	...

[1]Data in value added columns refer to gross output in value of sales. [2]Group 5 includes group 6. [3]Data in value added columns refer to gross output in producer's prices. [4]Enterprise data are for 1969. [5]Group 4 includes groups 5 and 6 and mining and public utilities. [6]Data in value added columns calculated in factor values. [7]Data in value added columns refer to value of production. [8]Total value and percentages calculated on sum of figures directly referable to groups 1–6; may exclude data withheld for confidentiality and minor or ambiguously classified manufacturing. [9]Establishments with 10 or more workers. [10]Value added calculated in producer's prices. [11]Excludes sugar factories and refineries. [12]Excludes leather and leather products. [13]Excludes synthetic fibre industry. [14]Includes professional goods. [15]Group 5 includes and group 6 excludes ISIC 3825 (office machinery and computing equipment). [16]Enterprise data are for 1979. [17]Group 4 includes groups 5 and 6. [18]Enterprise data are incomplete. [19]Enterprise data are for 1978. [20]Includes some enterprises of more than 100 workers. [21]Establishments of 50 or more workers. [22]Enterprise data are for 1980. [23]Group 3 includes groups 4, 5, and 6. [24]Enterprise data are for 1973. [25]Value added data refer to 1979. [26]Includes sugarcane cropping.

primary and fabricated metals; proc. minerals (group 4)					machinery (except elec.) and transport equip. (group 5)					electrical and electronic machinery (group 6)					total manufacturing value added (U.S.$'000,000)	country
percent of total value added	enterprises 1–99 employees number	percent of value added	100 or more emp. number	percent of value added	percent of total value added	enterprises 1–99 employees number	percent of value added	100 or more emp. number	percent of value added	percent of total value added	enterprises 1–99 employees number	percent of value added	100 or more emp. number	percent of value added		
...	...	...	...	...	...	...	...	...	...	...	...	...	...	...	...	Oman
																Pacific Is., Trust Terr. of the
8.7	531[20]	25.3	65	74.7	4.6	379[20]	15.4	34	84.6	3.2	155[20]	31.1	19	68.9	14,142	Pakistan
12.7	58	...	7	...	0.8	912	...	6[2]	...	0.8	2	...	2	...	374	Panama
18.6[17]	142[17]	...	...	...	17	...	...	17	...	17	...	...	17	...	267	Papua New Guinea
...[25]	...	...	...	...	...[23]	...	...	...	...	...[23]	...	...	...	...	816	Paraguay
22.1	98	...	11	...	8.0[15]	1,774	...	83	...	3.1[15]	524	...	5	...	5,204	Peru
8.2	7,454	...	...	...	6.9	2,092	...	—	...	5.2	...	...	268	...	6,123	Philippines
																Pitcairn Island
15.4	...	...	3,144	...	22.3	...	...	1,828	...	7.4	...	...	761	...	...	Poland
33.7[17]	7,938	...	226	...	17	1,351	...	112	...	17	155	...	38	...	7,153	Portugal
3.1	351	53.0	16	47.0	6.7[15]	104	13.9	12	86.1	13.2[15]	112	18.5	69	81.5	8,606	Puerto Rico
...	9	...	...	...	...	187	...	...	...	...	...	...	...	...	30	Qatar
...	...	...	...	...	...	...	...	...	...	7	...	...	...	...	...	Réunion
23	...	...	471[17]	...	23	...	...	17	...	23	...	...	17	...	...	Romania
3.8	...	...	10[17]	...	4.4	...	...	17	...	0.1	...	...	17	...	134	Rwanda
																St. Christopher and Nevis
																St. Helena and Ascension
																St. Lucia
																St. Pierre and Miquelon
...	44	...	...	...	...	241[2]	...	...	...	...	2	...	...	...	...	St. Vincent
																San Marino
																São Tomé and Príncipe
...	...	...	...	...	...	...	...	...	...	...	...	...	...	...	2,829	Saudi Arabia
13.1	34[17]	...	...	...	17	...	...	...	...	17	...	...	17	...	...	Senegal
11.5	5	...	...	...	...	...	...	...	...	...	...	...	...	...	12	Seychelles
6.2	...	...	...	...	—	—	—	—	—	—	...	...	...	...	31	Sierra Leone
12.1	533	...	...	...	21.5	...	...	609[15]	...	20.0	...	...	300[15]	...	4,385	Singapore
																Solomon Islands
6.3[17]	77[17]	...	...	...	17	...	...	17	...	17	...	...	17	...	40	Somalia
27.8	3,195	17.7	559	82.3	16.1	2,450	28.6	344	71.6	5.9	486	16.2	129	83.8	9,070	South Africa
																Bophuthatswana
																Ciskei
																Transkei
																Venda
																South West Africa/Namibia
25.2	22,997	...	...	...	12.8	4,955	...	...	...	6.7	...	...	1,171	...	18,726	Spain
12.1	356	...	...	...	2.4	95	...	...	...	3.5	62	...	...	...	301	Sri Lanka
...	...	...	...	...	...	...	...	...	...	...	...	...	...	...	776	Sudan, The
																Suriname
7.2	35	...	...	...	1.6[2]	...	...	3[2]	...	2	...	...	2	...	103	Swaziland
9.7	509	...	124	...	45.1[2,49]	3,470[2,49]	...	605[2,49]	...	2	2	...	2	...	25,570	Sweden
25.4	16,233	...	301	...	43.3	10,268	...	590	...	...	...	...	...	...	12,800	Switzerland
12.0[17]	17,216[17]	...	...	...	17	17	...	...	...	17	17	...	...	...	1,845	Syria
																Taiwan
23.4[17]	...	...	...	...	17	...	...	...	...	17	...	...	...	...	239	Tanzania
24.9	1,208	...	...	...	3.7	765	...	...	...	0.5	153	...	...	...	5,159	Thailand
16.5	...	...	9	...	—	—	...	...	...	—	—	...	...	...	52	Togo
																Tokelau
12.8[17]	19	100.0	—	—	17	7	100.0	—	—	17	2	100.0	—	—	4	Tonga
23	82	...	...	...	23	27[2]	...	...	...	23	2	...	...	...	735	Trinidad and Tobago
46.8	30	50.3	29	49.7	...	...	...	...	...	...	...	...	...	...	840	Tunisia
21.1	4,992	...	106	...	11.6	57,503	...	199	...	4.0	...	...	...	...	9,590	Turkey
																Turks and Caicos
—	—	—	—	—	—	—	—	—	—	—	—	—	—	—	—	Tuvalu
20.7	20	7.9	8	92.1	...	64	77.0	5	23.0	...	17	...	...	...	73	Uganda
46.3[14,17]	...	...	12,155[14,17]	...	17	...	...	...	...	17	...	...	...	...	...	U.S.S.R.
63.9	285	...	...	...	9.0	5	...	...	...	-8.3	9	...	...	...	266	United Arab Emirates
15.9	15,703	...	1,114	...	22.0	23,098	...	1,675	...	10.5	4,423	...	481	...	146,780	United Kingdom
15.4	52,544	23.4	6,287	76.6	21.8	76,365	20.1	6,751	79.9	12.3	12,103	9.9	2,870	90.1	834,200	United States
9.7	1,538	...	...	...	5.5[15]	761	...	...	...	3.2[15]	410	...	...	...	2,617	Uruguay
																Vanuatu
17.2	2,063	35.0	126	65.0	9.4[15]	408	26.1	65	73.9	2.1[15]	163	30.5	40	69.5	12,869	Venezuela
																Vietnam
																Virgin Islands (U.S.)
																Wallis and Futuna
11.1	610	...	...	...	—	...	...	...	...	...	...	...	...	...	82	West Bank
—	...	...	...	...	...	...	...	...	...	...	...	...	...	...	...	Western Sahara
																Western Samoa
																Yemen (Aden)
...	646	...	...	...	...	782[2]	...	...	...	2	...	...	...	...	...	Yemen (Şan'ā)
22.8	...	...	2,021	...	15.3[15]	...	...	1,150[15]	...	7.4[15]	...	...	512[15]	...	...	Yugoslavia
23	...	...	...	...	23	...	...	...	...	23	...	...	...	...	256	Zaire
12.8	152	...	...	...	19.4	217	...	...	...	2.9	21	...	...	...	520	Zambia
32.1[17]	...	...	...	...	17	...	...	...	...	17	...	...	...	...	1,739	Zimbabwe

[27]Enterprise data are for 1981. [28]Value added data refer to establishments of 20 or more workers; enterprise data refer to establishments of 6 or more. [29]Establishments of 5 or more workers. [30]Establishments of 7 or more workers. [31]Includes petrochemical, rubber, and plastics industries. [32]Value added data are "revenue." [33]Value added data refer to 1982. [34]Establishments of 30 or more workers. [35]Establishment data refer to enterprises of 10 or more workers with electric power and 20 or more without power. [36]Excludes petroleum manufacturing and manufacturing on tea, tobacco, and rubber estates. [37]Establishments of 20 or more workers. [38]Establishments of 3 or more workers. [39]Excludes the diamond industry. [40]Value added data refer to 1980. [41]Enterprise data refer to establishments with a turnover of CFAF12,000,000 or more; value added data exclude petroleum industry. [42]Excludes petroleum industry. [43]Group 4 includes group 5. [44]Value added data refer to establishments of 5 or more workers. [45]Enterprise data refer to 1976. [46]Enterprise data refer to establishments with annual sales of 100,000 kwachas or more. [47]Privately owned establishments only. [48]Socialized sector only. [49]Includes fabricated metal products. [50]Value added data refer to 1981. [51]Enterprise data refer to 1975. [52]Percent of value added by enterprise size and number of enterprises data refer to 1977.

Energy

This table provides data about the commercial energy supplies (reserves, production, consumption, and trade), of the various countries of the world, together with data about their oil pipeline networks and traffic. Many of the data and concepts used in this table are adopted from the United Nations' *Yearbook of World Energy Statistics*.

Electricity. Total installed electrical power capacity comprises the sum of the rated power capacities of all main and auxiliary generators in a country. 'Total installed capacity' (kW) is multiplied by 8,760 hours per year to yield 'Total production capacity' (kW-hr).

Production of electricity comprises the total gross production of electricity by publicly or privately owned enterprises and also that generated by industrial establishments for their own use, but usually excludes consumption by the utility itself. Measured in 1,000,000s of kilowatt-hours (kW-hr), annual production of electricity ranges generally between 30 and 40% of total production capacity. The data are further analyzed by type of generation: fossil fuels, hydroelectric power, and nuclear fuel.

The great majority of the world's electrical and other energy needs are met by the burning of hydrocarbon (fossil) solids, liquids, and gases, either for thermal generation of electricity or in internal combustion engines. Many renewable and nontraditional sources of energy are being developed worldwide (wood, biogenic gases and liquids, tidal, wave, and wind power, geothermal and photothermal [solar] energy, and so on), but collectively these sources are still negligible in the world's total energy consumption. For this reason only hydroelectric and nuclear generation are considered here separately after fossil fuels.

Though hydroelectric power accounts for only a small proportion of the world's primary production, the leading producers were some of the world's principal energy-consuming nations: Canada, the United States,

the U.S.S.R., Brazil, Japan, and Norway, which together accounted for about 60% of the world's production of hydroelectricity.

Nuclear generation is being utilized by more than a score of countries for commercial production. The major producers, the United States and France, accounted for about two-fifths of the nuclear generation of electricity.

Trade in electrical energy refers to the transfer of generated electrical output via an international grid. Total electricity consumption (residential and nonresidential) is equal to total electricity requirements less transformation and distribution losses.

Coal. The term coal, as used in the table, comprises all grades of anthracite, bituminous, subbituminous, and lignite that have acquired or may in the future, by reason of new technology or changed market prices, acquire an economic value. These types of coal may be differentiated according to heat content (density) and content of impurities. Most coal reserve data are based on proved recoverable reserves only, of all grades of coal. Exceptions are footnoted, with proved in-place reserves reported only when recoverable reserves are unknown. Production figures include deposits removed from both surface and underground workings as well as quantities used by the producers themselves or issued to the miners. Wastes recovered from mines or nearby preparation plants are excluded from production figures.

Natural gas. This term refers to any combustible gas (usually chiefly methane) of natural origin from underground sources. The natural gas reserves of Eastern Europe, the U.S.S.R., and the Middle East account for about two-thirds of the world total. The countries with the largest proved reserves were the U.S.S.R., Iran, Iraq, the United States, Algeria, Qatar, and Saudi Arabia. The data for production cover, to the extent

Energy

country	electricity													coal		
	installed capacity, 1983 ('000 kW)	production, 1983		power source, 1983			trade, 1983		consumption				reserves, latest ('000,000 metric tons)	production, 1983 ('000 metric tons)	consumption, 1983 ('000 metric tons)
		capacity ('000,000 kW-hr)	amount ('000,000 kW-hr)	fossil fuel (%)	hydropower (%)	nuclear fuel (%)	exports ('000,000 kW-hr)	imports ('000,000 kW-hr)	amount, 1983 ('000,000 kW-hr)	per capita, 1983 (kW-hr)	residential, 1982 (%)	nonresidential, 1982 (%)			
Afghanistan	394	3,451	1,025	32.3	67.7	—	—	—	1,025	72	...	...	66	165	165
Albania	...	...	2,885	20.3	79.7	—	600	—	2,285	783	...	...	151	1,700	1,900
Algeria	2,397	20,998	8,520	95.8	4.2	—	—	...	8,520	414	24.1[3]	75.9[3]	43	7	907
American Samoa	34	298	70	100.0	—	—	—	—	70	2,059	...	...	—	—	...
Andorra	...	...	...	...	...	...	...	...	...	...	...	...	—	—	...
Angola	600	5,256	1,740	26.1	73.9	—	—	—	1,740	209	27.5[4]	72.5[4]	...	...	...
Anguilla	—	—	—	...	...	...	—	—	—	—	...	...	...	...	...
Antigua and Barbuda	29	254	63	100.0	—	—	—	—	63	808	42.4[5]	57.6[5]	...	...	...
Argentina	14,872	130,279	42,998	49.2	42.8	7.9	6	—	42,992	1,451	28.2	71.8	150	486	978
Australia	30,212	264,657	106,287	87.9	12.1	—	—	—	106,287	6,936	30.1[4]	69.9[4]	59,340	132,440	70,262
Austria	14,555	127,502	42,625	28.2	71.8	—	7,893	4,396	39,128	5,223	23.1[4]	83.4[4]	65	3,041	6,194
Bahamas, The	275	2,409	920	100.0	—	—	—	—	920	4,220	34.2[2]	65.8[2]	...	...	...
Bahrain	588	5,151	2,026	100.0	—	—	—	—	2,026	5,103	...	...	...	—	—
Bangladesh	1,087	9,522	3,758	82.4	17.6	—	—	—	3,758	39	16.5[4]	83.5[4]	242	—	163
Barbados	94	823	370	100.0	—	—	—	—	370	1,423	25.1[5]	74.9[5]	...	—	—
Belgium	12,566	110,078	52,706	52.0	2.2	45.7	4,356	4,038	52,388	5,306	26.9[2]	73.1[2]	440	7,512	14,246
Belize	21	184	58	100.0	—	—	—	—	58	379	...	...	...	—	—
Benin	15	131	5	100.0	—	—	—	110	115	30	...	...	...	—	—
Bermuda	118	1,034	368	100.0	—	—	—	—	368	4,842	40.8[2]	59.2[2]	...	—	—
Bhutan	11	96	26	11.5	88.5	—	—	—	26	19	...	...	...	—	—
Bolivia	517	4,529	1,698	28.2	71.8	—	—	3	1,701	282	33.4[2]	66.6[2]	...	—	1
Botswana	8	8	522[9]	8	8	8	8	829	8	8	...	...	3,500	400	8
Brazil	40,097	351,250	161,970	6.5	93.5	—	244	2	161,728	1,246	21.0	79.0	13,000	6,737	11,485
British Virgin Islands	5	44	21	100.0	—	—	—	—	21	1,615	...	...	...	—	—
Brunei	240	2,102	728	100.0	—	—	—	—	728	2,800	55.3	44.7	...	—	—
Bulgaria	13,288	116,403	42,534	63.2	7.9	29.0	2,221	4,582	44,895	4,910	...	...	3,730	32,390	39,254
Burkina Faso	40	350	115	100.0	—	—	—	—	115	17	...	...	...	—	—
Burma	741	6,491	1,872	39.9	60.1	—	—	—	1,872	50	...	59.1[4,10]	2	54	234
Burundi	9	79	2	100.0	—	—	—	140	142	32	...	...	...	—	—
Cameroon	570	4,993	1,804	5.5	94.5	—	—	—	1,804	195	...	...	...	—	—
Canada	89,800	786,648	408,443	22.9	65.1	12.0	38,835	2,750	372,358	14,896	24.5[4]	75.5[4]	5,906	44,787	43,950
Cape Verde	8	70	12	100.0	—	—	—	—	12	38	...	...	...	...	...
Cayman Islands	14	123	44	100.0	—	—	—	—	44	2,444	53.8[5]	46.2[5]	...	...	...
Central African Republic	30	263	68	4.4	95.6	—	—	—	68	28	17.5[11]	82.5[11]	4	...	...
Chad	38	333	65	100.0	—	—	—	—	65	14	...	...	...	...	...
Chile	3,344	29,293	12,624	29.6	70.4	—	—	—	12,624	1,081	19.5	80.5	1,177	1,030	1,563
China	84,000	735,840	351,440	75.4	24.6	—	—	250	351,690	344	6.1	93.9	99,000	714,530	710,114
Christmas Island	12	105	33	100.0	—	—	—	—	33	11,000	...	...	...	...	...
Cocos (Keeling) Islands	...	...	...	...	...	...	...	...	...	...	...	...	...	...	...
Colombia	6,150	53,874	27,100	27.7	72.3	—	30	—	27,070	984	34.7[4]	65.3[4]	1,035	6,000	5,400
Comoros	4	35	10	100.0	—	—	—	—	10	23	...	...	...	...	...
Congo	149	1,305	185	8.1	91.9	—	—	27	212	128	...	...	...	...	...
Cook Islands	4	35	10	100.0	—	—	—	—	10	526	...	...	...	...	...
Costa Rica	657	5,755	2,700	2.8	97.2	—	—	—	2,700	1,093	43.3[6]	56.7[6]	...	...	...
Cuba	3,000	26,280	11,551	99.5	0.5	—	—	—	11,551	1,166	28.5[2]	71.5[2]	...	...	90
Cyprus	393	3,443	1,221	100.0	—	—	—	—	1,221	1,876	26.6	73.4	...	...	...
Czechoslovakia	18,314	160,431	76,275	86.9	5.1	8.1	6,924	9,296	78,647	5,065	15.9[12]	84.1[12]	5,560	127,385	125,548
Denmark	7,780	68,153	22,186	99.8	0.2	—	3,928	8,135	26,393	5,136	32.5[2]	67.5[2]	...	—	8,666
Djibouti	38	333	126	100.0	—	—	—	—	126	365	...	...	...	...	...
Dominica	7	61	18	11.1	88.9	—	—	—	18	237	53.5[5]	46.5[5]	...	...	...

possible, gas obtained from gas fields, petroleum fields, or coal mines that is actually collected and marketed. (Much natural gas in Middle Eastern oil fields is flared [burned] because it is often not economical to capture and market it.) Manufactured gas is generally a by-product of industrial operations such as gasworks, coke ovens, and blast furnaces. It is usually burned at the point of production and rarely enters the marketplace. Production of manufactured gas is, therefore, only reported as a percentage of domestic gas consumption. Natural gas is not generally a major energy source in less developed countries unless they have extensive reserves of their own, as do Bangladesh, China, and Mexico.

Crude petroleum. Crude petroleum is the liquid product obtained from oil wells; the term also includes shale oil, tar sand extract, and field or lease condensate. Production and consumption data in the table refer, so far as possible, to the same year so that the relationship between national production and consumption patterns can be clearly seen; both are given in barrels.

Proved reserves are that oil remaining underground in known fields whose existence has been "proved" by the evaluation of nearby producing wells or by seismic tests in sedimentary strata known to contain crude petroleum, and that is judged recoverable within the limits of present technology and economic conditions (prices). Proved reserves of crude petroleum are heavily concentrated in the Middle East, North America including Mexico, and the U.S.S.R. The published proved reserve figures do not necessarily reflect the true reserves of a country, because government authorities or corporations often have political or economic motives for withholding or altering such data.

The estimated exhaustion rate of petroleum reserves is an extrapolated ratio of published proved reserves to the current rate of withdrawal/pro-

duction. Present world published proved reserves will last about 30 years at the present rate of withdrawal, but there are large country-to-country variations above or below the average.

Data on petroleum and product pipelines are provided because of the great importance to both domestic and international energy markets of this means of bringing these energy sources from their production or transportation points to refineries, intermediate consumption and distribution points, and final consumers. Their traffic may represent a very significant fraction of the total movement of goods within a country. International data tend to be incomplete, both for the petroleum pipelines (the category for which the most complete data are available) and, still more so, for natural gas, coal, and other types of pipeline systems. Available data for petroleum pipelines vary internationally, some countries reporting only international shipments, others reporting domestic shipments of 50 kilometres or more, and so on.

For data in the hydrocarbons portions of the table (coal, natural gas, and petroleum), extensive use has been made of a variety of international sources, such as those of the United Nations, the International Energy Agency (of the Organization for Economic Cooperation and Development), and the World Energy Conference; of the resources of the U.S. Department of Energy; and of various industry surveys, such as those published by British Petroleum (BP *Statistical Review of World Energy*), the *International Petroleum Encyclopedia,* the *Oil and Gas Journal,* the *Petroleum Economist,* and *World Oil.*

a. Includes refined petroleum products pipelines.

natural gas						crude petroleum							country
published proved reserves, 1985 ('000,000,000 cu m)	production		consumption			reserves, 1985		production, 1984 ('000,000 barrels)	consumption, 1984 ('000,000 barrels)	refining capacity, 1985 ('000 barrels per day)	pipelines (latest)a		
	natural gas, 1984 ('000,000 cu m)	manufactured gas, 1983 (% of total gas consumption)	amount, 1983 ('000,000 cu m)	residential, 1982 (%)	nonresidential, 1982 (%)	published proved ('000,000 barrels)	years to exhaust proved reserves				length (km)	traffic ('000,000 metric ton-km)	
...	2,888	...	179	...	...	...	...	...	...	—	68	...	Afghanistan
4	300	...	397	...	...	211	11	20	26[2]	40	182	...	Albania
3,030	35,679	40.1	3,606	26.8[4]	73.2[4]	7,082	31	226	147[2]	464	6,910	...	Algeria
...	...	...	...	...	...	...	...	...	...	—	—	—	American Samoa
...	...	...	...	...	...	...	...	...	...	—	—	—	Andorra
110	340	13.9	103	...	...	2,147	30	72	11[2]	32	179	...	Angola
...	...	...	...	...	...	...	...	...	...	—	—	—	Anguilla
...	...	...	...	...	...	...	...	...	—	—	—	—	Antigua and Barbuda
668	14,323	13.3	13,683	30.9	69.1	2,348	13	175	183[2]	678	6,290	...	Argentina
516	12,584	34.4	11,874	...	...	1,446	8	182	202[2]	699	2,900	...	Australia
11	1,157	22.2	4,147	25.7[4]	74.3[4]	116	14	8	73	273	725	4,652	Austria
...	—	139.9	...	...	...	...	...	...	62[2]	350	—	—	Bahamas, The
204	5,502	7.5	3,225	...	...	173	11	15	64[2]	250	72	...	Bahrain
368	2,042	0.2	2,020	4.7[4]	95.3[4]	...	...	—	8[2]	31	—	—	Bangladesh
...	12[2]	...	12	...	...	1	1	1	1[2]	3	—	—	Barbados
...	16	22.9	8,489	43.4[2]	56.6[2]	...	...	...	156[7]	693	1,276	866	Belgium
...	...	...	...	...	...	...	...	...	...	—	—	—	Belize
...	...	...	...	...	...	100	40	3	...	—	—	—	Benin
...	...	...	...	...	...	...	...	...	...	—	—	—	Bermuda
...	...	...	...	...	...	...	...	...	...	—	—	—	Bhutan
125	2,540	40.5	284	...	...	157	21	8	7[2]	47	3,165	...	Bolivia
...	...	...	...	...	...	...	...	...	8	—	—	—	Botswana
84	1,912	72.9	1,659	23.4	76.6	2,030	12	169	390[2]	1,305	2,465	...	Brazil
...	...	...	...	...	...	...	...	...	...	—	...	...	British Virgin Islands
145	8,835	2.4	1,211	...	...	1,470	26	57	−2[2]	10	553	...	Brunei
0.8	100	10.2	4,726	...	...	4	7	1	94[2]	300	611	...	Bulgaria
...	...	...	...	...	...	...	...	...	...	—	—	—	Burkina Faso
322	476	0.7	476	—	100.0	733	77	10	11[2]	26	530	...	Burma
...	...	...	...	...	...	...	...	...	...	—	—	—	Burundi
118	—	94.4	...	...	...	531	10	55	23[2]	43	—	—	Cameroon
2,633	77,965	23.5	51,453	20.6[4]	79.4[4]	6,538	12	531	531	1,869	23,564	91,300	Canada
...	...	...	...	...	...	...	...	...	...	—	—	—	Cape Verde
...	...	...	...	...	...	...	...	...	...	—	...	...	Cayman Islands
...	...	...	...	...	...	...	...	...	...	—	—	—	Central African Republic
...	...	...	...	...	...	...	...	...	...	—	—	—	Chad
147	5,091	49.0	940	84.2[6]	15.8[6]	224	16	14	27[2]	141	1,540	...	Chile
425	12,247	...	12,177	...	...	19,500	23	837	630	2,150	7,100	...	China
...	...	...	...	...	...	...	...	...	...	—	...	...	Christmas Island
...	...	...	...	...	...	...	...	...	...	—	...	...	Cocos (Keeling) Islands
117	5,343	10.3	4,636	...	90.0[4,10]	1,200	20	60	68[2]	211	4,935	...	Colombia
...	...	...	...	...	...	...	...	...	...	—	—	—	Comoros
75	20	...	—	...	...	798	17	48	—	21	25	—	Congo
...	...	...	...	...	...	...	...	...	...	—	...	...	Cook Islands
...	—	66.6	...	...	...	...	...	...	42	16	176	—	Costa Rica
...	8	91.5	8	...	...	...	...	...	51[2]	160	—	—	Cuba
...	—	60.7	...	...	...	...	...	...	42	16	—	—	Cyprus
10	736	36.5	8,588	...	...	6	10	1	123[2]	455	2,948	9,104	Czechoslovakia
105	510	67.1	...	...	...	533	31	17	79	176	528	27	Denmark
...	...	...	...	...	...	...	...	...	...	—	—	—	Djibouti
...	...	...	...	...	...	...	...	...	...	—	—	—	Dominica

Energy (continued)

country	installed capacity, 1983 ('000 kW)	production, 1983 capacity ('000,000 kW-hr)	production, 1983 amount ('000,000 kW-hr)	fossil fuel (%)	hydro-power (%)	nuclear fuel (%)	exports ('000,000 kW-hr)	imports ('000,000 kW-hr)	consumption amount, 1983 ('000,000 kW-hr)	per capita, 1983 (kW-hr)	residential, 1982 (%)	non-residential, 1982 (%)	coal reserves, latest ('000,000 metric tons)	coal production, 1983 ('000 metric tons)	coal consumption, 1983 ('000 metric tons)
Dominican Republic	960	8,410	3,400	77.1	22.9	—	—	—	3,400	570			...	—	19
Ecuador	1,833	16,057	4,289	59.7	40.3	—	—	15	4,304	489	40.2[13]	59.8[13]	...	—	...
Egypt	5,610	49,144	23,520	49.8	50.2	—	—	—	23,520	528	9.8[13]	90.2[13]	13	—	1,460
El Salvador	500	4,380	1,610	6.8	52.8	40.4[14]	—	—	1,610	308	29.8[6]	70.1[6]	...	...	...
Equatorial Guinea	7	61	15	86.7	13.3	—	—	—	15	40	...	...	...	...	...
Ethiopia	337	2,952	753	25.0	75.0	—	—	—	753	22	...	...	—	—	—
Faeroe Islands	48	420	170	70.6	29.4	—	—	—	170	4,048	...	...	—	—	—
Falkland Islands	1	9	3	100.0	—	—	—	—	3	1,500	...	...	—	—	—
Fiji	197	1,726	330	84.8	15.2	—	—	—	330	498	22.6	77.4	—	—	18
Finland	11,223	98,313	40,236	25.2	33.2	41.5	679	5,441	44,998	9,293	18.6[4]	81.3[4]	—	—	3,168
France	78,200[15]	685,032[15]	283,400[15]	26.7[15]	24.9[15]	48.3[15]	20,900[15]	7,500[15]	270,000[15]	4,971[15]	30.3[2]	69.7[2]	610	21,255[15]	42,574[15]
French Guiana	38	333	150	100.0	—	—	—	—	150	2,143		58.7[4,10]	—	—	—
French Polynesia	74	648	205	92.2	7.8	—	—	—	205	1,306	...	...	—	—	—
Gabon	175	1,533	535	51.8	48.2	—	—	—	535	475	42.1[6]	57.9[6]	—	—	—
Gambia, The	11	96	40	100.0	—	—	—	—	40	65	...	...	—	—	—
Gaza Strip	...	...	...	...	...	...	...	...	...	...	...	...	...	...	...
Germany, East	21,180	185,537	104,928	86.7	1.6	11.7	3,251	4,605	106,282	6,373	...	...	25,000	277,968	282,094
Germany, West	86,564	758,301	373,813	77.3	5.1	17.6	13,292	23,687	384,208	6,265	26.3[2]	73.7[2]	59,141	213,955	215,824
Ghana	1,060	9,286	2,589	1.6	98.4	—	400	—	2,189	173	...	...	—	—	2
Gibraltar	23	201	61	100.0	—	—	—	—	61	2,033	...	...	—	—	—
Greece	5,888	51,579	22,262	89.5	10.5	—	32	1,915	24,145	2,454	30.6[2]	69.4[2]	1,550	30,594	32,699
Greenland	80	701	174	100.0	—	—	—	—	174	3,283	...	...	—	—	1
Grenada	8	70	25	100.0	—	—	—	—	25	227	46.8[5]	53.2[5]	—	—	...
Guadeloupe	103	902	395	100.0	—	—	—	—	395	1,242		32.9[10]	—	—	...
Guam	302	2,646	1,150	100.0	—	—	—	—	1,150	10,360	36.9[2]	63.1[2]	...	...	...
Guatemala	491	4,301	1,700	79.4	20.6	—	—	—	1,700	214	27.0[4]	73.0[4]	...	...	...
Guernsey	...	...	...	...	...	...	...	...	...	...	...	...	...	...	...
Guinea	175	1,533	499	84.0	16.0	—	—	—	499	96	...	...	—	—	...
Guinea-Bissau	7	61	13	100.0	—	—	—	—	13	15	...	...	—	—	...
Guyana	168	1,472	435	98.9	1.1	—	—	—	435	474	32.5[6]	67.5[6]	—	—	...
Haiti	126	1,104	373	30.3	69.7	—	—	—	373	60	...	...	13[1]	—	...
Honduras	240	2,102	1,150	21.7	78.3	—	12	8	1,146	280	30.6[2]	69.4[2]	21[1]	—	...
Hong Kong	4,230	37,055	14,504	100.0	—	—	368	—	16,114	2,990	20.3	79.7	—	—	3,218
Hungary	5,403	47,330	25,775	89.6	0.6	9.6	1,741	10,817	34,851	3,235	20.8[2]	79.2[2]	4,225	25,213	27,066
Iceland	935	8,191	3,781	0.2	95.0	4.8[14]	—	—	3,781	15,954	20.9[4]	79.1[4]	—	—	33
India	42,180	369,497	147,952	63.7	34.9	1.5	8.5	6	147,873	202	11.1	88.9	1,579	140,696	144,054
Indonesia	5,090	44,588	15,294	90.2	9.8	—	—	—	15,294	96	30.6[4]	69.4[4]	539	486	325
Iran	12,004	105,155	29,900	78.3	21.7	—	—	—	29,900	703	21.1	78.9	193	800	860
Iraq	1,750	15,330	13,700	95.6	4.4	—	—	—	13,700	935	28.9[13]	71.1[13]	...	...	...
Ireland	3,391	29,705	11,178	89.5	10.5	—	—	—	11,178	3,179	41.4[2]	58.6[2]	55	75	1,493
Isle of Man	...	...	188	100.0	—	—	—	—	172	2,530	48.1[2]	51.9[2]	...	...	...
Israel	3,787	33,174	14,578	100.0	—	—	190	—	14,388	3,482	26.7[2]	73.3[2]	31	—	1,684
Italy	51,498[16]	451,122[16]	182,880[16]	71.2[16]	24.2[16]	3.2[16]	2,886[16]	13,968[16]	193,962[16]	3,428[16]	25.0[2]	75.0[2]	31	1,702[16]	18,922[16]
Ivory Coast	1,163	10,188	1,932	10.5	89.5	—	—	—	1,932	211	17.2[6]	82.8[6]	...	...	...
Jamaica	740	6,482	2,350	93.6	6.4	—	—	—	2,350	1,041	29.2[4]	70.8[4]	...	...	...
Japan	159,390	1,396,256	602,357	67.7	14.5	17.6	—	—	602,357	5,067	20.8[4]	79.2[4]	1,068	17,077	91,712
Jersey	...	...	337	...	...	...	...	...	303	3,940	...	...	...	...	...
Jordan	642	5,624	1,918	100.0	—	—	—	—	1,918	591	34.3[5]	65.7[5]	...	...	...
Kampuchea	40	350	140	58.6	41.4	—	—	—	140	20	...	...	...	...	...
Kenya	544	4,765	2,166	19.7	68.2	12.1[14]	—	179	2,345	124	16.8	83.2	—	—	76
Kiribati	2	18	6	100.0	—	—	—	—	6	98	...	...	...	...	...
Korea, North	7,000	61,320	41,000	36.6	63.4	—	—	—	41,000	2,137	...	...	600	49,000	49,350
Korea, South	14,385	126,013	53,047	78.0	5.1	16.9	—	—	53,047	1,334	17.9	82.1	116	18,945	29,666
Kuwait	4,030	35,303	12,830	100.0	—	—	—	—	12,830	7,925	86.5[2]	13.5[2]	...	...	...
Laos	260	2,278	1,250	4.8	95.2	—	765	17	502	119	...	...	...	...	...
Lebanon	668	5,852	1,220	54.1	45.9	—	—	40	1,260	478	...	...	...	...	—
Lesotho	[8]	[8]	[8]	[8]	[8]	[8]	[8]	[8]	[8]	[8]	...	...	...	[8]	[8]
Liberia	305	2,672	1,100	72.7	27.3	—	—	—	1,100	535	...	...	—	—	1
Libya	1,260	11,038	7,150	100.0	—	—	—	—	7,150	2,139	...	...	—	—	1
Liechtenstein	[17]	[17]	[17]	[17]	[17]	[17]	[17]	[17]	[17]	[17]	...	...	...	—	17
Luxembourg	1,315	11,519	797	44.9	55.1	—	360	3,665	4,102	11,269	15.3[2]	84.7[2]	...	—	167
Macau	108	946	385	100.0	—	—	—	—	385	1,266	75.0	25.0	...	—	1
Madagascar	100	876	450	44.9	55.1	—	—	—	450	48	...	...	1,075[1]	—	13
Malawi	147	1,288	486	5.6	94.4	—	1	—	485	74	13.8[6]	86.2[6]	12	—	45
Malaysia	2,610	22,864	12,135	88.8	11.2	—	—	55	12,190	820	19.0	81.0	—	—	110
Maldives	3	26	10	100.0	—	—	—	—	10	60	...	...	...	...	...
Mali	42	368	110	54.5	45.5	—	—	—	110	14	...	...	—	—	...
Malta	177	1,551	675	100.0	—	—	—	—	675	1,790	25.1	74.9	...	...	52
Martinique	65	569	272	100.0	—	—	—	—	272	875		40.9[10]	...	...	...
Mauritania	55	482	103	100.0	—	—	—	—	103	58	...	...	—	—	7
Mauritius	244	2,137	427	78.5	21.5	—	—	—	427	422	...	...	—	—	1
Mayotte	...	...	...	...	...	...	...	...	...	...	...	...	...	...	...
Mexico	22,218	194,630	82,343	73.2	25.2	1.6[14]	88	16	82,271	1,095	17.4	82.6	1,584	7,800	8,350
Monaco	[15]	[15]	[15]	[15]	[15]	[15]	[15]	[15]	[15]	[15]	...	...	...	15	15
Mongolia	460	4,030	1,975	100.0	—	—	—	400	2,375	1,317	...	...	24,000[1]	4,600	4,600
Montserrat	4	35	12	100.0	—	—	—	—	12	923	38.6[5]	61.4[5]	...	...	...
Morocco	1,786	15,645	6,010	90.5	9.5	—	—	—	6,010	272	26.7[4]	73.3[4]	50	817	745
Mozambique	1,803	15,794	6,426	6.4	93.6	—	5,026	100	1,500	113	...	...	240	380	420
Nauru	11	96	27	100.0	—	—	—	—	27	3,375	...	...	...	...	...
Nepal	139	1,218	257	20.2	79.8	—	6	85	336	21	36.9[13]	63.1[13]	...	—	70
Netherlands, The	16,255	142,394	59,639	94.0	—	6.0	1,487	6,131	64,283	4,463	25.9[2]	74.1[2]	240[1]	—	6,994
Netherlands Antilles	400	3,504	2,350	100.0	—	—	—	—	2,350	9,180	...	...	...	...	...
New Caledonia	367	3,215	737	61.9	38.1	—	—	—	737		...	...	2	—	97
New Zealand	6,410	56,152	25,527	19.0	76.6	4.4[14]	—	—	25,527	7,886	35.7[4]	64.3[4]	211	2,418	2,218
Nicaragua	400	3,504	1,080	48.1	49.1	5.8[14]	6	10	1,084	355	...	...	...	...	...

natural gas						crude petroleum							country
published proved reserves, 1985 ('000,000,000 cu m)	production natural gas, 1984 ('000,000 cu m)	manufactured gas, 1983 (% of total gas consumption)	consumption amount, 1983 ('000,000 cu m)	residential, 1982 (%)	non-residential, 1982 (%)	reserves published proved ('000,000 barrels)	years to exhaust proved reserves	production, 1984 ('000,000 barrels)	consumption, 1984 ('000,000 barrels)	refining capacity, 1985 ('000 barrels per day)	pipelines length (km)	pipelines traffic ('000,000 metric ton-km)	
...	31	88.8	37	...	...	...	...	...	12[2]	44	69	...	Dominican Republic
84	476	35.6	...	...	...	831	9	95	35[2]	82	2,158	...	Ecuador
287	3,058	14.7	1,520	0.4	99.6	4,026	14	296	137[2]	369	1,526	...	Egypt
...	—	89.3	...	...	...	...	...	...	4[2]	16	—	—	El Salvador
...	...	...	...	...	...	...	...	...	...	—	—	—	Equatorial Guinea
...	—	100.0	—	...	...	...	...	...	5[2]	14	—	—	Ethiopia
...	...	...	...	...	...	...	...	...	...	—	—	—	Faeroe Islands
...	...	...	...	...	...	...	...	...	...	—	—	—	Falkland Islands
...	...	...	...	...	...	...	...	...	...	—	—	—	Fiji
...	—	44.0	668	0.6[2]	99.4[2]	...	...	...	79	299	—	—	Finland
41	10,574	24.3[15]	25,972[15]	32.4[2]	67.6[2]	221	14	16	666	2,386	7,802	25,999	France
...	...	...	...	...	...	...	...	...	...	—	—	—	French Guiana
...	...	...	...	...	...	...	...	...	...	—	—	—	French Polynesia
17	136	3.7	154	—	100.0[6]	623	10	65	9[2]	20	270	...	Gabon
...	...	...	...	...	...	...	...	...	...	—	—	—	Gambia, The
...	...	...	...	...	...	...	...	...	...	—	...	—	Gaza Strip
10	12,370	31.3	9,154	...	...	2	6	—	166[2]	470	1,700	4,300	Germany, East
182	16,696	26.0	47,231	36.6[2]	63.4[2]	289	10	29	856	2,172	5,732	8,820	Germany, West
—	...	100.0	...	...	...	4	17	—	8[2]	28	3	—	Ghana
...	...	...	...	...	...	...	...	...	...	—	...	—	Gibraltar
0.6	48	106.0	82	...	...	35	4	10	86	390	573	...	Greece
...	...	...	...	...	...	...	...	...	...	—	—	—	Greenland
...	...	...	...	...	...	...	...	...	...	—	—	—	Grenada
...	—	100.0	...	...	...	...	...	...	12[2]	44	—	—	Guadeloupe
...	...	...	...	...	...	...	...	...	...	—	...	...	Guam
1	34	6.3	...	...	...	500	263	2	6[2]	16	48	...	Guatemala
...	...	...	...	...	...	...	...	...	...	—	—	—	Guernsey
...	...	...	...	...	...	...	...	...	...	...	—	—	Guinea
...	...	...	...	...	...	...	...	...	...	...	—	—	Guinea-Bissau
...	...	...	...	...	...	...	...	...	...	...	...	...	Guyana
...	...	...	...	...	...	...	...	...	...	—	—	—	Haiti
...	—	28.5	...	...	...	...	...	...	2[2]	14	—	—	Honduras
...	...	50.0	...	53.9	46.1	...	...	...	...	—	—	—	Hong Kong
78	6,591	11.6	9,688	14.0[2]	86.0[2]	213	14	15	66[2]	242	1,900	2,595	Hungary
...	...	...	...	...	...	...	...	...	4	—	—	—	Iceland
478	3,238	36.1	2,731	...	62.5[10]	3,760	19	198	253[2]	705	5,325	...	India
1,699	20,728	7.1	3,772	0.8	99.2	9,125	19	468	183[2]	631	2,906	...	Indonesia
10,477	10,194	17.1	6,766	—	100.0	37,500	47	800	215[2]	530	9,800	...	Iran
702	510	45.4	436	...	...	38,500	87	440	61[2]	319	4,546	...	Iraq
32	2,300	5.2	2,117	13.9[2]	86.1[2]	...	...	...	31	56	—	—	Ireland
...	...	...	...	...	...	...	...	...	...	—	—	—	Isle of Man
1	68	89.4	59	...	100.0[6]	1	20	—	56[2]	170	998	—	Israel
186	13,904	23.9[16]	26,571[16]	45.6[2]	54.4[2]	598	39	15	635	3,095	3,851	9,310	Italy
90	—	49.9	...	...	...	108	13	8	13[2]	90	...	...	Ivory Coast
...	—	87.5	...	...	...	...	...	...	7[2]	36	10	...	Jamaica
20	2,365	54.7	27,832	61.3[6]	38.7[6]	26	9	3	1,665	4,966	406	...	Japan
...	...	...	...	...	...	...	...	...	...	—	—	—	Jersey
...	—	97.4	...	...	...	...	...	...	19[2]	100	209	...	Jordan
...	...	...	...	...	...	...	...	...	...	—	—	—	Kampuchea
...	—	105.3	—	...	...	...	...	...	14[2]	95	483	...	Kenya
...	...	...	...	...	...	...	...	...	...	—	—	—	Kiribati
...	...	...	...	...	...	...	...	...	15[2]	42	37	—	Korea, North
...	—	68.5	...	100.0	—	...	...	...	198[2]	776	294	...	Korea, South
1,737	4,078	75.3	2,306	...	...	82,714	202	409	183[2]	669	917	...	Kuwait
...	...	...	...	...	...	...	...	...	...	—	...	...	Laos
...	—	20.0	...	...	...	...	...	...	4[2]	17	72	...	Lebanon
—	—	...	—	...	...	...	...	...	8	—	—	—	Lesotho
...	—	100.0	...	...	...	...	...	...	5[2]	15	—	—	Liberia
623	4,248	6.5	8,316[17]	...	...	22,800	57	403	43[2]	330	4,336	—	Libya
—	—	17	...	...	...	...	...	...	...	—	—	—	Liechtenstein
...	—	54.2	310	48.0[2]	52.0[2]	...	...	...	7	—	48	...	Luxembourg
...	—	100.0	—	...	...	...	...	...	...	—	—	—	Macau
...	—	...	...	...	...	...	...	...	2[2]	16	—	—	Madagascar
...	...	...	...	...	...	...	...	...	...	—	—	—	Malawi
1,388	3,398	29.3	341	—	100.0	2,900	18	161	43[2]	205	707	...	Malaysia
...	...	...	...	...	...	...	...	...	...	—	—	—	Maldives
...	...	...	...	...	...	...	...	...	...	—	—	—	Mali
...	...	228.5	...	...	...	...	...	...	...	—	—	—	Malta
...	...	...	...	...	...	...	...	...	3[2]	13	—	...	Martinique
...	...	...	...	...	...	...	...	...	...	—	—	—	Mauritania
...	...	...	...	...	...	...	...	...	...	—	—	—	Mauritius
...	...	...	...	...	...	...	...	...	...	...	...	...	Mayotte
2,172	29,386	25.2[15]	24,721[15]	3.9	96.1	49,260	50	983	425[2]	1,269	12,009	...	Mexico
...	...	...	...	...	...	...	...	...	...	—	—	—	Monaco
—	...	...	...	...	...	...	...	...	...	—	—	—	Mongolia
...	...	...	...	...	64.6[4,10]	...	...	...	...	—	—	—	Montserrat
18	102	41.3	80	...	...	1	8	—	32[2]	78	362	...	Morocco
65	—	100.0	...	...	...	...	...	...	4[2]	17	280	—	Mozambique
...	...	...	...	...	...	...	...	...	...	—	—	—	Nauru
...	...	...	...	...	...	...	...	...	...	—	—	—	Nepal
1,900	68,988	11.9	35,968	46.4[2]	53.6[2]	170	8	21	232	1,499	1,383	—	Netherlands, The
...	...	143.7	...	...	...	...	...	...	176[2]	740	—	—	Netherlands Antilles
...	...	...	...	...	...	...	...	...	...	—	—	—	New Caledonia
148	3,826	2.0	2,186	12.8[4]	87.2[4]	187	27	7	18[2]	53	310	...	New Zealand
...	—	100.0	—	...	...	...	...	...	4[2]	15	56	...	Nicaragua

Energy (continued)

country	electricity installed capacity, 1983 ('000 kW)	production, 1983 capacity ('000,000 kW-hr)	production, 1983 amount ('000,000 kW-hr)	power source, 1983 fossil fuel (%)	power source, 1983 hydro-power (%)	power source, 1983 nuclear fuel (%)	trade, 1983 exports ('000,000 kW-hr)	trade, 1983 imports ('000,000 kW-hr)	consumption amount, 1983 ('000,000 kW-hr)	consumption per capita, 1983 (kW-hr)	consumption residential, 1982 (%)	consumption non-residential, 1982 (%)	coal reserves, latest ('000,000 metric tons)	coal production, 1983 ('000 metric tons)	coal consumption, 1983 ('000 metric tons)
Niger	65	569	252	100.0	—	—	—	128	380	66	...	...	5[1]	43	43
Nigeria	4,020	35,215	8,500	70.6	29.4	—	128	—	8,372	94	45.5	54.5	169	40	40
Niue	1	9	3	100.0	—	...	...	...	3	750			...	...	...
Norfolk Island	...	...	...	...	...	...	...	...	...	...			...	...	...
Norway	22,765	199,421	106,243	0.3	99.7	—	13,817	437	92,863	22,485	27.0[4]	73.0[4]	18	478	885
Oman	611	5,352	1,402	100.0	—	—	—	—	1,402	1,240	...	...	...	...	...
Pacific Is., Trust Territory of the	48	420	148	100.0	—	—	—	—	148	1,021	...	...	...	...	...
Pakistan	4,627	40,533	19,636	46.2	52.9	0.9	—	—	19,636	204	15.9[4]	84.1[4]	645	1,855	2,375
Panama	744	6,517	2,239	61.3	38.7	—	—	—	2,239	1,072	...	19.3[4,10]	...	...	3
Papua New Guinea	323	2,829	1,425	75.4	24.6	—	—	—	1,425	406	...	...	...	...	...
Paraguay	240	2,102	848	15.3	84.7	—	2	—	846	244	17.9	82.1	125[5]	.80	110
Peru	3,167	27,743	9,328	22.1	77.9	—	—	—	9,328	499	...	...	82	1,024	1,233
Philippines	5,634	49,354	20,761	66.1	19.6	14.3[14]	—	—	20,761	399	22.7[6]	77.3[6]			
Pitcairn Island	...	...	...	...	...	...	...	...	...	...	...	...	...	...	...
Poland	26,833	235,057	125,821	97.4	2.6	—	7,183	4,079	122,717	3,327	9.2[2]	90.8[2]	39,000	233,624	194,523
Portugal	5,635	49,363	18,161	55.2	44.8	—	1,057	2,373	19,477	1,960	36.4[4]	63.6[4]	38	190	544
Puerto Rico	4,100	35,916	12,066	98.9	1.1	—	—	—	12,066	3,602	31.0	69.0	...	—	171
Qatar	765	6,701	3,105	100.0	—	—	—	—	3,105	11,050	...	...	...	...	...
Réunion	159	1,393	430	1.2	98.8	—	—	—	430	785	...	...	...	...	...
Romania	17,988	157,575	70,260	85.7	14.3	—	—	2,138	72,398	3,185	...	...	1,150	44,523	48,023
Rwanda	39	342	157	5.1	94.9	—	—	31	188	33	...	...	...	...	...
St. Christopher and Nevis	15	131	35	100.0	—	—	—	—	35	660	...	...	...	...	...
St. Helena and Ascension	2	18	2	100.0	—	—	—	—	2	400	...	...	...	...	...
St. Lucia	16	140	68	100.0	—	—	—	—	68	544	32.5[5]	67.5[5]	...	...	...
St. Pierre and Miquelon	17	149	35	100.0	—	—	—	—	35	5,833	...	...	...	—	—
St. Vincent and the Grenadines	10	88	29	41.4	58.6	—	—	—	29	284	45.3[5]	54.7[5]	...	...	...
San Marino	16	16	16	16	16	16	16	16	16	16	...	...	...	16	16
São Tomé and Príncipe	4	35	11	72.7	27.3	—	—	—	11	120	...	...	...	...	...
Saudi Arabia	9,200	80,592	32,000	100.0	—	—	—	—	32,000	3,071	95.1[6]	4.9[6]	...	...	...
Senegal	165	1,445	631	100.0	—	—	—	—	631	102	...	...	...	...	...
Seychelles	19	166	53	100.0	—	—	—	—	53	746	...	...	...	...	...
Sierra Leone	95	832	292	100.0	—	—	—	—	292	84	...	...	...	—	...
Singapore	2,206	19,325	8,626	100.0	—	—	55	—	8,571	3,417	17.7	82.3	...	—	2
Solomon Islands	13	114	25	100.0	—	—	—	—	25	97	...	...	...	...	...
Somalia	30	263	75	100.0	—	—	—	—	75	14	...	...	...	...	...
South Africa	25,037[8]	219,324[8]	109,185[8]	99.3[8]	0.7[8]	—	150[8]	5,026[8]	114,061[8]	3,299[8]	...	...	51,737	139,557[8]	109,944[8]
Bophuthatswana	...	...	...	...	...	...	...	...	...	...	...	...	...	...	...
Ciskei	...	...	...	...	...	...	...	...	...	...	...	...	...	...	...
Transkei	...	...	...	...	...	...	...	...	...	...	...	...	...	...	...
Venda	...	...	...	...	...	...	...	...	...	...	...	...	...	...	...
South West Africa/Namibia	8	8	8	8	8	8	8	8	8	8	...	...	...	8	8
Spain	31,650	277,254	115,450	68.3	23.9	7.8	4,700	2,000	112,750	2,935	16.7[4]	83.2[4]	951	39,650	44,496
Sri Lanka	952	5,186	2,114	42.4	57.6	—	—	—	2,114	134	14.2[2]	85.8[2]	...	—	28
Sudan, The	313	2,742	1,010	49.5	50.5	—	—	—	1,010	50	...	...	...	—	...
Suriname	415	3,635	1,300	44.2	55.8	—	—	—	1,300	3,704	...	...	...	—	1
Swaziland	8	8	8	8	8	8	8	8	8	8	18.7[6]	81.3[6]	1,820	8	8
Sweden	30,710	269,020	109,635	3.9	58.7	37.4	5,448	10,397	114,584	13,829	26.4[4]	73.6[4]	1	13	2,968
Switzerland	14,110[17]	123,604[17]	51,819[17]	1.9[17]	69.5[17]	28.6[17]	20,267[17]	11,021[17]	42,573[17]	6,701[17]	26.6[2]	73.4[2]	...	—	641[17]
Syria	1,808	15,838	6,175	46.5	53.5	—	137	...	6,038	615	21.2[2]	78.8[2]	...	...	3
Taiwan	12,413	108,734	45,517	49.2	10.9	39.8	—	—			26.3	73.7	140	...	...
Tanzania	258	2,260	705	23.4	76.6	—	—	—	705	34	...	...	200	1	1
Thailand	5,557	48,679	18,875	78.0	22.0	—	17	765	19,623	396	19.5	80.5	103	2,252	2,301
Togo	37	324	173	83.8	16.2	—	—	160	333	121	...	...	...	...	...
Tokelau	...	...	...	...	...	...	...	...	...	...	...	...	...	...	...
Tonga	6	53	12	100.0	—	—	—	—	12	115	...	...	...	...	...
Trinidad and Tobago	760	6,658	2,300	100.0	—	—	—	—	2,300	2,106	25.2[6]	74.8[6]	...	—	...
Tunisia	978	8,567	3,531	99.0	1.0	—	—	—	3,531	513	26.4[6]	73.6[6]	...	—	28
Turkey	6,935	60,751	27,321	58.5	41.5	—	—	2,223	29,544	620	14.2	85.8	1,914	21,110	22,149
Turks and Caicos Islands	9	79	11	100.0	—	—	—	—	11	1,375	...	...	...	...	...
Tuvalu	...	...	...	...	...	...	...	...	...	...	...	...	...	...	...
Uganda	163	1,428	650	1.4	98.6	—	210	—	440	30	...	...	...	...	...
U.S.S.R.	293,558	2,571,568	1,408,100	81.2	12.8	6.0	23,000	300	1,385,400	5,072	...	67.2[2,10]	233,000	674,922	661,501
United Arab Emirates	2,800	24,528	7,900	100.0	—	—	—	—	7,900	6,605	...	...	...	...	...
United Kingdom	66,431	581,936	276,227	79.6	2.3	18.1	—	—	276,227	4,949	35.4[2]	64.6[2]	4,590	119,254	111,687
United States	674,937	5,912,448	2,367,634	73.3	14.1	12.4	3,464	38,668	2,402,838	10,280	34.9[2]	65.1[2]	223,259	712,018	670,545
Uruguay	1,339	11,730	7,343	2.1	97.9	—	3,613	16	3,746	1,262	46.6[2]	53.4[2]	...	...	...
Vanuatu	13	114	23	100.0	—	—	—	—	23	176	...	...	...	...	...
Venezuela	9,812	85,953	41,700	59.2	40.8	—	—	15	41,715	2,417	20.3	79.7	140	39	79
Vietnam	900[18]	7,884[18]	4,200	61.9	38.1	—	—	—	4,200	73	...	...	150	6,000	5,000
Virgin Islands (U.S.)	275	2,409	775	100.0	—	—	—	—	775	7,673	...	...	...	...	...
Wallis and Futuna	...	...	...	...	...	...	...	...	...	...	...	...	...	...	...
West Bank	...	...	...	...	...	...	...	...	...	...	...	...	...	...	...
Western Sahara	56	491	78	100.0	—	—	—	—	78	531	...	...	...	...	...
Western Samoa	13	114	40	82.5	17.5	—	—	—	40	248	...	...	...	...	...
Yemen (Aden)	150	1,314	280	100.0	—	—	—	—	280	139	...	...	...	...	...
Yemen (Şan'ā')	104	911	285	100.0	—	—	—	—	285	46	...	...	1[11]	...	...
Yugoslavia	15,250	133,590	71,571	54.6	30.5	5.5	1,626	2,681	72,626	3,177	26.1[4]	73.9[4]	16,570	59,392	62,022
Zaire	1,716	15,032	4,213	1.5	98.5	—	70	—	4,143	133	...	89.1[4,10]	600	130	165
Zambia	1,728	15,137	10,071	0.3	99.7	—	3,200	20	6,891	1,106	...	84.6[4,10]	24	452	452
Zimbabwe	1,192	10,442	4,426	15.6	84.4	—	10	3,022	7,438	911	...	67.6[10]	734	2,391	2,295

natural gas: published proved reserves, 1985 ('000,000,000 cu m)	production: natural gas, 1984 ('000,000 cu m)	production: manufactured gas, 1983 (% of total gas consumption)	consumption: amount, 1983 ('000,000 cu m)	consumption: residential, 1982 (%)	consumption: non-residential, 1982 (%)	crude petroleum reserves, 1985: published proved ('000,000 barrels)	reserves, 1985: years to exhaust proved reserves	production, 1984 ('000,000 barrels)	consumption, 1984 ('000,000 barrels)	refining capacity, 1985 ('000 barrels per day)	pipelines (latest)[a]: length (km)	pipelines (latest)[a]: traffic ('000,000 metric ton-km)	country
...	...	...	...	...	...	...	...	...	...	...	...	...	Niger
1,332	2,039	0.6	5,638	—	100.0	16,850	34	501	55[2]	250	5,042	...	Nigeria
...	...	...	...	...	...	...	...	...	...	—	—	—	Niue
...	...	...	...	...	...	...	...	...	...	...	...	...	Norfolk Island
2,781	27,457	47.5	−208	...	...	10,843	43	254	66	244	81	4,837	Norway
178	4,143	...	...	...	...	4,500	29	153	—	48	1,300	...	Oman
...	...	...	...	...	...	...	...	...	—	...	...	...	Pacific Is., Trust Territory of the
436	10,116	0.5	8,175	21.3	78.7	102	16	7	36[2]	129	1,000	...	Pakistan
...	—	42.1	...	...	...	50	...	...	14[2]	100	226	...	Panama
14	...	...	...	...	...	...	...	...	...	...	...	...	Papua New Guinea
...	—	25.3	...	...	...	...	...	...	1[2]	8	—	—	Paraguay
28	1,257	19.5	1,032	...	...	670	10	67	55[2]	176	800	...	Peru
1	—	73.5	...	...	...	31	8	4	64[2]	286	357	...	Philippines
...	...	...	...	...	...	...	...	...	...	...	...	...	Pitcairn Island
38	6,069	35.6	9,538	...	...	12	8	1	98[2]	385	1,922	17,473	Poland
...	...	58.6	...	...	...	...	...	...	68	290	11	...	Portugal
...	...	78.9	...	...	...	...	...	...	37[2]	121	...	...	Puerto Rico
4,436	4,417	10.6	5,392	...	...	4,500	31	146	3[2]	56	235	...	Qatar
...	...	...	...	...	...	...	...	...	...	...	—	—	Réunion
35	35,113	7.6	41,939	...	...	1,511	17	89	176[2]	617	4,164	3,705	Romania
40	1[2]	—	1	...	...	...	...	...	...	—	—	—	Rwanda
...	...	...	...	...	...	...	...	...	...	—	—	—	St. Christopher and Nevis
...	...	...	...	...	...	...	...	...	...	—	—	—	St. Helena and Ascension
...	...	...	...	...	...	...	...	...	...	—	—	—	St. Lucia
...	...	...	...	...	...	...	...	...	...	...	...	...	St. Pierre and Miquelon
...	...	...	...	...	...	...	...	...	...	—	—	—	St. Vincent and the Grenadines
...	...	16	16	...	...	...	...	...	...	—	—	—	San Marino
...	...	...	...	...	...	...	...	...	...	—	—	—	São Tomé and Príncipe
3,612	6,796	502.9	1,281	...	83.6[10]	167,088	98	1,702	267[2]	840	6,150	...	Saudi Arabia
...	...	14.3	...	...	...	...	...	...	2[2]	30	...	...	Senegal
...	...	...	...	...	...	...	...	...	...	—	—	—	Seychelles
...	...	...	...	...	...	...	...	...	2[2]	10	—	—	Sierra Leone
...	—	432.0	...	56.8[6]	43.2[6]	...	...	...	273[2]	1,072	—	—	Singapore
...	...	...	...	...	...	...	...	...	...	...	...	...	Solomon Islands
6	...	...	...	...	...	...	...	...	3[2]	10	15	...	Somalia
11	—	100.0	—	...	...	115	...	...	882[2,8]	389	2,679	...	South Africa
...	...	...	...	...	...	...	...	...	...	...	...	...	Bophuthatswana
...	...	...	...	...	...	...	...	...	...	...	...	...	Ciskei
...	...	...	...	...	...	...	...	...	...	...	...	...	Transkei
...	...	...	...	...	...	...	...	...	...	...	...	...	Venda
...	...	...	...	...	...	...	...	...	8	—	—	—	South West Africa/Namibia
18	193	53.7	2,550	...	...	74	4	17	346	1,493	1,984	3,240	Spain
—	—	100.0	—	...	...	...	...	...	11[2]	50	69	...	Sri Lanka
—	—	75.0	...	...	...	300	...	...	8[2]	24	815	...	Sudan, The
...	2[4]	...	...	...	...	...	...	—	...	—	—	—	Suriname
...	—	77.6	...	...	...	...	...	—	...	8	—	—	Swaziland
...	—	...	...	...	...	...	...	...	130	439	—	—	Sweden
35	238	20.1[17]	1,294[17]	38.3[2]	61.7[2]	...	...	...	92	127	314	1,189	Switzerland
23	1,699	54.4	76	...	...	1,398	22	62	68[2]	228	1,819	...	Syria
...	...	...	1,389	...	...	11	12	1	...	543	615	...	Taiwan
115	—	100.0	—	...	...	...	...	...	4[2]	14	982	...	Tanzania
99	2,200	5.9	1,460	...	...	58	7	8	57[2]	176	—	—	Thailand
...	...	...	...	...	...	...	...	...	2[2]	20	—	—	Togo
...	...	...	...	...	...	...	...	...	...	...	...	...	Tokelau
...	...	...	...	...	...	...	...	...	...	...	...	...	Tonga
292	3,452	10.8	3,065	...	...	538	9	62	60[2]	320	1,051	...	Trinidad and Tobago
112	510	8.1	450	3.7[6]	96.3[6]	1,815	45	40	11[2]	34	883	...	Tunisia
29	1,124	75.2	2	...	...	312	21	15	128	460	3,433	—	Turkey
...	...	...	...	...	...	...	...	...	...	—	—	—	Turks and Caicos Islands
...	...	...	...	...	...	...	...	...	...	—	—	—	Tuvalu
...	...	...	...	...	...	...	...	...	...	—	—	—	Uganda
36,529	586,898	12.8	422,099	...	...	81,000	18	4,477	3,309	12,200	75,000	1,353,100	U.S.S.R.
2,812	7,476	11.3	11,333	...	...	36,322	80	456	10[2]	185	830	...	United Arab Emirates
725	40,064	13.4	53,205	52.7[2]	47.3[2]	5,823	7	882	672	2,007	3,840	9,307	United Kingdom
5,860	487,486	18.8	444,312	33.4	66.6	27,170	8	3,197	5,545	15,400	278,035	832,926	United States
...	—	88.5	...	...	11.1[4,10]	...	...	...	10[2]	45	...	...	Uruguay
...	...	...	...	...	...	...	...	...	...	...	...	...	Vanuatu
1,665	17,262	14.6	16,517	9.7	90.3	28,034	42	668	325[2]	1,224	6,850	...	Venezuela
...	...	...	...	...	...	...	...	...	...	—	100	...	Vietnam
...	...	97.6	...	...	...	...	...	...	123[2]	545	—	—	Virgin Islands (U.S.)
...	...	...	...	...	...	...	...	...	...	—	—	—	Wallis and Futuna
...	...	...	...	...	...	...	...	...	...	—	—	—	West Bank
...	...	...	...	...	...	...	...	...	...	—	—	—	Western Sahara
...	...	...	...	...	...	...	...	...	...	—	—	—	Western Samoa
...	—	100.0	—	...	...	...	...	...	16[2]	178	32	...	Yemen (Aden)
...	...	...	...	...	...	...	...	...	...	...	...	...	Yemen (Şan'ā')
80	2,050	24.5	5,139	...	...	273	9	30	106	297	1,523	2,477	Yugoslavia
2	—	100.0	—	...	...	125	9	13	3[2]	17	390	...	Zaire
...	...	100.0	—	...	...	...	...	...	5[2]	25	1,724	...	Zambia
...	—	91.7	...	...	...	...	...	...	...	...	8	...	Zimbabwe

[1]Estimated reserves in place. [2]1983. [3]1972. [4]1981. [5]1984. [6]1980. [7]Belgium includes Luxembourg. [8]South Africa includes Botswana, Lesotho, South West Africa/Namibia, and Swaziland. [9]1982. [10]Transportation and industry only; excludes agricultural, commercial, and public service sectors. [11]1978. [12]1979. [13]1977. [14]Geothermally generated electricity. [15]France includes Monaco. [16]Italy includes San Marino. [17]Switzerland includes Liechtenstein. [18]1975.

Transportation

This table presents data on the transportation infrastructure of the various countries and dependencies of the world and on their commercial passenger and cargo traffic. Most states have roads and airports, with services corresponding to their traffic levels and to the prevailing level of economic development. A number of states, however, lack railroads or inland waterways, because of either geographic constraints or lack of development capital and technical expertise. Pipelines, one of the oldest means of bulk transport if aqueducts are considered, is today the least developed transportation mode worldwide for shipment of bulk materials. Because the principal contemporary application of pipeline technology is to facilitate the shipment of hydrocarbon liquids and gases, coverage of pipelines will be found in the "Energy" table. However, it is also true that pipelines now find increasing application for slurries of coal or other raw materials.

While the United Nations' *Statistical Yearbook* and *Monthly Bulletin of Statistics* provide much data on infrastructure and traffic and have established basic categories and classifications for transportation statistics, the number of countries covered is limited. Several commercial publications maintain substantial data bases and publishing programs for their particular areas of interest: Highway and vehicle statistics are provided by the International Road Federation's annual *Road and Motor Vehicle Statistics* and *World Road Statistics;* the International Union of Rail-

ways' *International Railway Statistics* and Jane's *World Railways* provide similar data for railways; Lloyd's *Register of Shipping Statistical Tables* summarizes the world's merchant marine; the *Official Airline Guide* and the International Civil Aviation Organization's *Digest of Statistics* have also been used to supplement and update data collected by the UN. Because several of these agencies are commercially or insurance-oriented, their data tend to be more complete, accurate, and timely than those of intergovernmental organizations, which depend on periodic responses to questionnaires or publication of results in official sources. All of these international sources are supplemented by national statistical sources to provide additional data. Such diversity of sources, however, imposes limitations on the comparability of the statistics from country to country because the basis and completeness of data collection and the frequency and timeliness of analysis and publication may vary greatly. Data more than five years old are shown in italic.

The categories adopted in the table also have special problems of comparability. Total road length is subject to wide international variation of interpretation, as "roads" can mean anything from mere tracks to highly developed highways. Each country also has individual classifications that differ according to climate, availability of road-building materials, traffic patterns, administrative responsibility, and so on. "Paved roads," by contrast, is a much more tightly definable category, but the proportion of

Transportation

country	roads and motor vehicles (latest)								railroads (latest)					
	roads			motor vehicles			cargo		track length		traffic			
	length		paved (per-cent)	auto-mobiles	trucks and buses	persons per vehicle	short ton-mi ('000,000)	metric ton-km ('000,000)	mi	km	passengers		cargo	
	mi	km									passen-ger-mi ('000,000)	passen-ger-km ('000,000)	short ton-mi ('000,000)	metric ton-km ('000,000)
Afghanistan	11,789	18,974	42	31,754	30,997	268	*1,993*	*2,910*	6	10	...	...	87	127
Albania	13,049	21,000	14	3,500	11,200	146	...	...	253	408	181	291	...	...
Algeria	44,795	72,091	54	573,573	265,577	23	*2,148*	*3,136*	2,576[1]	4,146[1]	936	1,506	*1,381*	*2,016*
American Samoa	186	300	90	2,781	373	10	...	...	—	—	—	—	—	—
Andorra	137	220	55	26,000	...	...	...	...	—	—	—	—	—	—
Angola	44,900	72,300	12	75,000	25,000	81	...	...	1,834[1]	2,952[1]	...	...	...	...
Anguilla	55	88	80	973	239	5.4	...	...	—	—	—	—	—	—
Antigua and Barbuda	237	380	63	7,120	1,209	9.4	...	...	—	—	—	—	—	—
Argentina	136,759	220,093	26	3,540,000	1,360,000	6.0	...	...	22,484	36,185	6,539	10,524	7,702	11,244
Australia	495,208	796,960	39	7,322,500	789,000	1.9	32,964	48,127	4,776	7,687	*1,359*	*2,187*	23,622	34,488
Austria	66,618	107,212	100	2,414,466	222,433	2.9	6,473	9,451	4,174	6,718	4,365	7,025	7,003	10,224
Bahamas, The	2,548	4,100	43	52,341	8,678	3.6	...	...	—	—	—	—	—	—
Bahrain	96	155	100	67,240	21,288	4.3	...	...	—	—	—	—	—	—
Bangladesh	98,522	158,551	12	35,488	21,401	1,628	...	...	1,791[1]	2,883[1]	3,994	6,428	498	727
Barbados	965	1,553	95	24,600	5,100	8.4	...	...	—	—	—	—	—	—
Belgium	79,390	127,766	95	3,263,713	307,276	2.8	11,593	17,451	2,442	3,930	4,007	6,448	5,391	7,871
Belize	1,620	2,607	15	3,098	4,916	19	...	...	—	—	—	—	—	—
Benin	5,220	8,400	10	9,592	7,025	209	...	...	359	578	117	188	121	176
Bermuda	249	400	100	15,840	3,690	2.9	...	...	—	—	—	—	—	—
Bhutan	1,270	2,050	50	1,363	706	644	...	...	—	—	—	—	—	—
Bolivia	25,461	40,975	4	40,638	36,951	78	1,133	1,654	2,320	3,733	345	555	1,160	1,693
Botswana	4,987	8,026	22	11,039	20,739	32	...	...	444	714	...	...	944	1,379
Brazil	709,360	1,141,605	7	10,076,745	1,118,123	12	147,400	215,200	14,346[1]	23,087[1]	8,243	13,266	53,528	77,815
British Virgin Islands	66	107	...	2,100	...	...	...	...	—	—	—	—	—	—
Brunei	766	1,233	35	63,177	9,603	2.9	...	...	12	19	...	...	...	...
Bulgaria	23,384	37,633	91	*815,549*	*130,000*	*9.1*	7,245	10,577	4,379	7,626	5,116	8,233	12,419	18,132
Burkina Faso	5,396	8,684	23	21,182	6,647	238	...	...	321	517	...	...	...	...
Burma	14,206	22,863	17	*43,300*	*44,700*	*386*	...	...	1,949[1]	3,137[1]	1,802	2,900	305	445
Burundi	3,196	5,144	7	7,016	5,700	348	...	...	—	—	—	—	—	—
Cameroon	40,741	65,567	4	59,000	16,500	118	2,029	2,963	729	1,173	200	322	537	784
Canada	243,448	391,792	42	10,530,355	3,293,406	1.8	29,033	42,388	74,600	120,000	1,359	2,187	150,724	220,053
Cape Verde	1,398	2,250	29	4,000	1,343	54	...	...	—	—	—	—	—	—
Cayman Islands	110	177	68	7,354	1,757	2.1	...	...	—	—	—	—	—	—
Central African Republic	14,018	22,560	1	43,121	3,861	52	...	...	—	—	—	—	—	—
Chad	19,092	30,725	1	7,000	5,000	390	...	...	—	—	—	—	—	—
Chile	54,761	88,129	11	620,000	257,000	13	...	...	5,300	8,500	887	1,428	1,578	2,304
China	563,600	907,000	...	265,000	1,768,000	496	53,400	78,000	32,600	52,500	110,191	177,336	454,421	663,444
Christmas Island	20	32	...	759	383	2.9	...	...	12	20	...	...	...	...
Cocos (Keeling) Islands	15	24	...	...	...	...	...	...	—	—	—	—	—	—
Colombia	65,369	105,201	28	672,385	168,096	32	11,115	16,227	2,115	3,403	119	192	493	720
Comoros	278[3]	448[3]	...	—1,800—		199	...	...	—	—	—	—	—	—
Congo	5,124	8,246	10	30,500	78,600	15	*46*	*67*	498	802	242	390	350	511
Cook Islands	213	342	15	168	35	86	...	...	—	—	—	—	—	—
Costa Rica	18,384	29,586	8	101,251	76,485	13	...	...	435	700	...	...	...	...
Cuba	12,400	20,000	44	18,657	28,098	208	...	...	3,058[4]	4,922[4]	1,332[4]	2,144[4]	1,792[4]	2,617[4]
Cyprus	7,016	11,292	48	110,230	38,919	4.4	...	...	—	—	—	—	—	—
Czechoslovakia	46,043	74,100	100	2,221,379	358,736	6.0	13,956	20,376	8,165	13,141	11,734	18,884	46,785	68,309
Denmark	43,388	69,827	100	1,390,339	242,883	3.1	6,000	8,800	1,529	2,461	2,747	4,421	1,036	1,668
Djibouti	1,806	2,906	11	9,000	1,500	32	...	...	66	106	...	...	...	...
Dominica	463	745	50	*3,044*	*1,240*	*19*	...	...	—	—	—	—	—	—
Dominican Republic	10,788	17,362	29	102,127	66,570	35	...	...	881[1,4]	1421[1,4]	—	—	20	29
Ecuador	22,159	35,662	15	230,432	28,127	30	...	...	600[1]	965[1]	43	69	20	29
Egypt	18,684[6]	30,069[6]	47[6]	597,869	227,224	56	*1,079*	*1,575*	2,725	4,385	11,660	18,765	1,577	2,302
El Salvador	7,624	12,269	14	72,547	69,755	34	...	...	374	602	8	12	25	36
Equatorial Guinea	1,715	2,760	12	4,000	3,000	40	...	...	—	—	—	—	—	—

paved to total roads may be distorted by the less comparable total road statistics. Automobile, truck, and bus fleet statistics, which are usually based upon registration, are relatively accurate, though some countries round off figures, and unregistered vehicles may cause substantial undercount. There is also inconsistent classification of vehicle types; in some countries a vehicle may serve variously as an automobile, a truck, or a bus, or even as all three on certain occasions. Relatively few countries collect and maintain commercial road traffic statistics.

Data on national railway systems are generally given for railway track length rather than the length of routes, which may be multitracked. Siding tracks usually are not included, but some countries fail to distinguish them. The United States data include only class 1 railways, which account for about 94 percent of total track length. Passenger traffic is usually calculated from tickets sold to fare-paying passengers. Such statistics are subject to distortion if there are large numbers of nonpaying passengers, such as military personnel, or if season tickets are sold and not all the allowed journeys are utilized. Railway cargo traffic is calculated by weight hauled multiplied by the length of the journey. Changes in freight load during the journey should be accounted for but sometimes are not, leading to discrepancies.

Merchant fleet and tonnage statistics collected by Lloyd's registry service for vessels over 100 gross tons are quite accurate. Cargo statistics, however, reflect the port and customs requirements of each country and the reporting rules of each country's merchant marine authority, and often they are estimates based on customs declarations and the count of vessels entered and cleared. Even when these elements are reported consistently, further discrepancies may be introduced because of ballast, bunkers, ships' stores, or transshipped goods included in the data.

Airport data are based on scheduled flights reported in the commercial *Official Airline Guide* and are both reliable and current. The comparability of civil air traffic statistics suffers from differing characteristics of the air transportation systems of different countries; data for an entire country may be two to three years behind those for a single airport.

Outside of Europe, where standardization of data on inland waterways is necessitated by the volume of international traffic, comparability of national data declines markedly. Calculations as to both the length of a country's waterway system (or route length of lake and coastal traffic) and the makeup of its stock of commercially significant vessels (those for which data will be collected) are largely determined by the nature and use of the country's hydrographic net—its seasonality, relief profile, depth, access to potential markets—and inevitably differ widely from country to country. Data for coastal or island states may refer to scheduled coastwise or interisland traffic.

merchant marine		international cargo (latest)		air						canals and inland waterways (latest)				country
fleet, 1984 (vessels over 100 gross tons)	total dead-weight tonnage, 1984 ('000)			airports with scheduled flights, 1985	traffic (latest)							cargo		
		loaded metric tons ('000)	off-loaded metric tons ('000)		passengers		cargo		mi	km	short ton-mi ('000,000)	metric ton-km ('000,000)	
					passenger-mi ('000,000)	passenger-km ('000,000)	short ton-mi ('000,000)	metric ton-km ('000,000)					
—	—	—	—	3	118	190	14.5	21.2	665	1,070	—	—	Afghanistan
20	79.9	510	360	1	...	...	...	...	...	...	...	...	Albania
147	1,984.6	44,824	13,299	26	1,561	2,512	9.1	13.2	—	—	—	—	Algeria
—	—	84	329	3	...	...	...	...	—	—	—	—	American Samoa
—	—	—	—	—	...	...	...	...	—	—	—	—	Andorra
87	138.6	5,590	1,608	19	570	917	17.2	25.1	727	1,170	...	...	Angola
14	5.5	...	18	1	...	...	...	...	—	—	—	—	Anguilla
3	0.4	33	113	1	68	109	14.8	21.6	—	—	—	—	Antigua and Barbuda
530	3,498.2	35,184	5,568	65	3,765	6,059	131.0	191.3	6,800	11,000	19,326	28,215	Argentina
622	3,227.0	209,832	22,572	443	16,233	26,124	543.9	794.1	5,200	8,368	—	—	Australia
26	215.4	...	...	6	872	1,404	16.1	23.5	222	358	4,910	7,168	Austria
163	5,681.9	22,798	19,906	21	72	116	6.3	9.3	—	—	—	—	Bahamas, The
72	59.2	8,500	2,000	1	553	890	16.3	23.8	—	—	—	—	Bahrain
248	496.9	1,056	6,948	8	813	1,308	15.6	22.8	5,238	8,430	...	...	Bangladesh
35	9.5	211	559	1	205	330	0.3	0.5	—	—	—	—	Barbados
338	3,890.4	38,760	65,316	4	3,510	5,648	371.0	541.7	1,215	1,956	3,405	4,971	Belgium
3	0.8	170	211	7	...	...	...	...	500	800	...	...	Belize
13	4.9	110	749	5	138	222	15.4	22.5	300	500	...	...	Benin
76	1,307.3	181	525	1	...	...	...	...	—	—	—	—	Bermuda
—	—	—	—	1	...	...	...	...	—	—	—	—	Bhutan
2	18.9	...	...	16	544	876	27.3	39.9	6,200	10,000	90	132	Bolivia
—	—	—	—	4	355	570	24.2	35.3	...	...	...	...	Botswana
706	9,420.4	141,732	53,856	126	10,706	17,229	503.2	734.7	27,000	43,000	36,731	53,627	Brazil
32	8.6	7	44	3	...	...	...	...	—	—	—	—	British Virgin Islands
2	1.0	19,158	697	1	...	...	...	...	130	209	...	...	Brunei
197	1,840.8	5,550	24,670	13	1,783	2,870	35.5	51.8	293	471	1,610	2,351	Bulgaria
—	—	—	—	9	112	180	12.3	18.0	—	—	—	—	Burkina Faso
105	128.3	1,248	528	32	139	224	1.7	2.5	5,000	8,000	...	...	Burma
1	0.4[5]	—	—	2	...	...	...	...	—	—	—	—	Burundi
48	87.8	996	3,000	10	346	548	34.3	50.1	1,300	2,100	...	...	Cameroon
1,310	4,209.8	125,000	49,000	60	19,971	32,140	511.4	746.6	2,342	3,769	...	...	Canada
24	21.7	119	388	9	...	...	...	...	—	—	—	—	Cape Verde
252	510.5	4,005	4,131	3	...	...	...	...	—	—	—	—	Cayman Islands
—	—	—	—	1	106	170	20.7	30.2	1,296	2,085	—	—	Central African Republic
—	—	—	—	1	142	229	14.8	21.6	1,400	2,300	—	—	Chad
219	731.5	11,832	5,268	13	969	1,560	77.4	113.0	1,360	2,189	5,629	8,218	Chile
1,262	20,301.8[2]	47,268	57,192	73	3,573	5,750	126.2	184.2	67,000	108,000	51,000	74,000	China
—	—	1,300	53	1	...	...	...	...	—	—	—	—	Christmas Island
—	—	—	—	1	...	...	...	...	—	—	—	—	Cocos (Keeling) Islands
82	480.6	7,128	6,636	79	2,558	4,116	155.3	226.7	8,900	14,300	...	...	Colombia
2	1.8	15	39	3	...	...	...	...	—	—	—	—	Comoros
21	10.8	2,844	552	17	129	208	26.2	38.3	2,312	3,721	—	—	Congo
—	—	7	12	6	...	...	...	...	—	—	—	—	Cook Islands
27	19.3	1,121	1,059	8	336	540	16.6	24.3	475	764	...	...	Costa Rica
418	1,230.1	2,208	2,712	13	1,337	2,151	22.9	33.4	149	240	—	—	Cuba
737	11,801.2	1,812	3,168	2	577	929	70.3	102.7	—	—	—	—	Cyprus
19	276.6	...	...	14	1,198	1,928	35.2	51.4	300	483	2,301	3,360	Czechoslovakia
1,101	7,973.4	11,784	31,020	12	1,944[5]	3,128[5]	86.8[5]	126.7[5]	120	190	1,164	1,700	Denmark
7	2.9	550	815	3	...	...	...	...	—	—	—	—	Djibouti
3	1.2	120	64	2	...	...	...	...	—	—	—	—	Dominica
37	58.0	1,940	2,612	3	299	481	6.2	9.0	—	—	—	—	Dominican Republic
135	578.8	5,319	2,451	13	455	732	20.8	30.4	900	1,500	—	—	Ecuador
390	1,032.1	10,944	33,084	10	2,725	4,386	60.4	88.2	1,900	3,000	1,709	2,495	Egypt
11	3.3	420	1,488	1	208	335	7.1	10.4	—	—	—	—	El Salvador
2	6.7	85	52	1	4	7	0.7	1.0	104	167	...	...	Equatorial Guinea

Transportation (continued)

country	roads length mi	roads length km	paved (percent)	motor vehicles automobiles	motor vehicles trucks and buses	persons per vehicle	cargo short ton-mi ('000,000)	cargo metric ton-km ('000,000)	track length mi	track length km	passengers passenger-mi ('000,000)	passengers passenger-km ('000,000)	cargo short ton-mi ('000,000)	cargo metric ton-km ('000,000)
Ethiopia	22,612	36,391	34	43,107	17,222	663	...	...	485[7]	781[7]	193	310	90	131
Faeroe Islands	124	200	...	10,099	2,277	3.6	...	...	—	—	—	—	—	—
Falkland Islands	24	38	44	720	177	2.2	...	...	—	—	—	—	—	—
Fiji	2,792	4,494	13	29,304	20,211	14	...	...	660	1,062	...	...	...	...
Finland	47,015	75,663	52	1,410,458	190,200	3.0	12,100	17,700	5,644	9,115	2,036	3,276	5,466	7,980
France	499,946	804,585	92	20,600,000	3,230,000	2.3	66,400	97,000	21,493[1]	34,590[1]	37,469	60,300	41,179	60,120
French Guiana	422	680	75	16,789	2,013	3.8	...	...	—	—	—	—	—	—
French Polynesia	460	741	33	16,500	8,500	5.3	...	...	—	—	—	—	—	—
Gabon	4,594	7,393	7	16,043	10,695	41	...	...	210	338	...	...	...	...
Gambia, The	1,916	3,083	15	6,100	1,030	98	...	...	—	—	—	—	—	—
Gaza Strip	...	...	...	11,940	3,748	29	...	...	—	—	—	—	—	—
Germany, East	29,440	47,380	100	3,019,875	276,364	5.1	10,533	15,378	8,840	14,226	14,046	22,605	37,590	54,884
Germany, West	302,764	487,251	99	25,217,800	1,348,200	2.3	86,000	126,000	42,992	69,190	23,997	38,619	40,986	59,839
Ghana	13,535	21,783	3	52,864	24,312	158	...	...	592	953	236	380	41	61
Gibraltar	31	50	100	8,825	894	3.1	—	—	—	—	—	—	—	—
Greece	66,047	106,292	83	1,042,840	574,782	6.1	...	...	1,540[1]	2,479[1]	958	1,541	527	769
Greenland	96	154	41	1,346	897	24	...	...	—	—	—	—	—	—
Grenada	534	860	60	4,784	981	16	...	...	—	—	—	—	—	—
Guadeloupe	1,279	2,059	70	82,652	24,590	3.1	...	...	—	—	—	—	—	—
Guam	419	674	100	39,002	14,653	2.0	...	...	—	—	—	—	—	—
Guatemala	16,422	26,429	11	166,900	81,500	29	...	...	467[1]	751[1]	...	...	80	117
Guernsey	...	...	...	...	...	...	...	...	—	—	—	—	—	—
Guinea	17,600	28,400	5	9,948	9,992	254	...	...	573[1]	922[1]	...	...	...	...
Guinea-Bissau	3,143	5,058	15	—3,807—		211	...	...	—	—	—	—	—	—
Guyana	3,426	5,513	9	20,000	4,610	37	...	...	80[8]	130[8]	—	—	...	...
Haiti	2,292	3,688	18	34,025	4,257	133	...	...	...	...	...	...	...	...
Honduras	5,618	9,042	22	58,920	24,385	49	...	...	624[1]	1,004[1]	524	843	52	77
Hong Kong	769	1,238	100	198,969	84,678	19	...	...	21	34	...	...	...	...
Hungary	18,445	29,684	87	1,258,498	153,992	7.6	7,223	10,546	8,106	13,045	7,006	11,274	15,648	22,845
Iceland	7,867	12,661	12	97,307	12,272	2.2	318	464	—	—	—	—	—	—
India	1,077,000	1,734,000	42	1,171,900	807,500	371	55,500	81,000	37,862	60,933	129,592	208,558	119,000	173,700
Indonesia	83,300	134,000	41	912,997	962,026	88	...	...	4,317	6,947	3,463	5,573	379	553
Iran	67,711	108,970	31	1,532,269	313,006	21	...	...	2,837	4,567	1,560	2,526	2,645	3,861
Iraq	15,699	25,265	65	229,530	152,768	36	...	...	1,264[1]	2,035[1]	543	874	1,977	2,887
Ireland	57,349	92,294	94	718,555	73,832	4.5	...	...	1,236[1]	1,989[1]	509	819	370	540
Isle of Man	357	574	58	—32,473—		2.0	...	...	37[1]	59[1]	...	...	...	...
Israel	2,878	4,631	100	459,178	105,079	7.0	...	...	514	827	151	242	552	806
Italy	184,539	296,986	79	19,616,106	1,671,706	2.7	93,986	137,071	12,292[1]	19,782[1]	23,070	37,128	11,960	17,461
Ivory Coast	28,900	46,500	8	166,920	54,226	41	...	...	761	1,225	620	998	361	527
Jamaica	7,442	11,977	40	40,271	20,167	38	...	...	205[1]	330[1]	49	79	89	129
Japan	697,985	1,123,300	53	25,075,000	8,674,000	3.5	128,213	187,188	16,720	26,908	201,954	325,014	16,045	23,425
Jersey	...	...	...	...	...	...	...	...	—	—	...	...	...	...
Jordan	3,935	6,332	74	118,852	48,884	14	19,133	27,934	384[1]	618[1]	...	...	...	...
Kampuchea	8,296	13,351	20	...	...	...	...	...	403[1]	649[1]	...	...	...	...
Kenya	33,900	54,500	12	114,710	39,584	117	...	...	1,647	2,650	452	728	1,432	2,091
Kiribati	398	640	...	—163—		344	...	...	—	—	—	—	—	—
Korea, North	12,600	20,280	2	...	...	...	...	...	2,720	4,380	...	...	...	...
Korea, South	33,926	54,599	39	380,993	404,323	51	8,793	12,838	3,808	6,129	13,477	21,689	7,965	11,630
Kuwait	1,066	1,715	100	519,626	178,592	2.4	...	...	—	—	—	—	—	—
Laos	6,340	10,200	13	15,000	3,000	217	...	...	—	—	—	—	—	—
Lebanon	4,350	7,000	80	460,400	35,000	5.3	...	...	258	415	5	9	29	42
Lesotho	2,363	3,803	11	5,129	11,962	82	...	...	1	2	...	...	...	...
Liberia	6,268	10,087	5	1,632	1,088	721	...	...	304[1]	490[1]	4[10]	6[10]	1,422[10]	2,076[10]
Libya	12,000	19,300	56	415,509	334,405	4.3	...	...	—	—	—	—	—	—
Liechtenstein	200	323	...	13,498	1,488	1.8	...	...	12	19	...	...	...	...
Luxembourg	1,412	2,272	99	141,081	13,021	2.4	180	263	168	270	178	286	401	586
Macau	56	90	100	16,882	4,324	14	...	...	—	—	—	—	—	—
Madagascar	9,703	15,615	30	26,300	14,245	221	...	...	644[1]	1,036[1]	174	280	153	223
Malawi	7,172	11,542	19	14,102	17,247	199	...	—	490[1]	789[1]	45	72	82	120
Malaysia	24,084	38,759	65	974,170	288,362	12	...	...	1,666	2,681	932[11]	1,500[11]	723[11]	1,056[11]
Maldives	...	...	...	310	107	415	...	...	—	—	—	—	—	—
Mali	8,080	13,004	14	20,000	5,000	294	...	...	401	646	195	314	94	136
Malta	808	1,300	94	74,773	17,871	3.5	...	...	—	—	—	—	—	—
Martinique	1,130	1,819	82	134,923	3,726	2.4	...	...	—	—	—	—	—	—
Mauritania	4,685	7,540	18	11,262	8,437	76	...	...	428[1]	689[1]	...	...	11,000	16,000
Mauritius	1,110	1,787	92	26,082	17,929	23	...	...	—	—	—	—	—	—
Mayotte	134	215	40	—1,300—		41	...	...	—	—	—	—	—	—
Mexico	133,265	214,470	50	5,221,159	1,978,327	10	...	...	16,031	25,799	3,654	5,880	28,957	42,276
Monaco	29	46	100	14,528	3,164	1.5	...	...	1	2	...	...	...	...
Mongolia	29,000	46,700	2	...	...	...	1,047	1,529	1,062	1,710	240	386	3,081	4,498
Montserrat	176	283	74	1,323	114	19	...	...	—	—	—	—	—	—
Morocco	35,777	57,577	45	470,239	232,857	31	655	956	1,105[1]	1,779[1]	872	1,404	2,869	4,188
Mozambique	16,200	26,000	30	49,500	...	...	...	...	2,388	3,843	377	606	3,532	5,156
Nauru	12	19	100	—1,761—		4.0	...	...	—	—	—	—	—	—
Nepal	3,485	5,608	46	14,201	12,638	500	984	1,437	32	52	...	...	...	...
Netherlands, The	68,554	110,327	86	4,770,000	358,700	2.8	11,901	17,375	1,837	2,956	5,555	8,940	2,137	3,120
Netherlands Antilles	750	1,200	100	55,000	8,000	3.8	...	...	—	—	—	—	—	—
New Caledonia	4,427	7,125	72	34,100	1,730	4.1	...	...	—	—	—	—	—	—
New Zealand	57,870	93,133	53	1,400,624	287,731	1.9	...	...	2,754	4,433	267	429	2,227	3,252
Nicaragua	15,500	25,000	16	24,887	9,789	77	...	...	232	373	13	20	10	14
Niger	11,886	19,129	17	34,240	8,761	138	...	...	—	—	—	—	—	—
Nigeria	67,102	107,990	78	262,550	90,731	241	...	...	2,189	3,523	488	785	666	972
Niue	142	229	54	264	64	12	...	...	—	—	—	—	—	—
Norfolk Island	50	80	66	1,802	90	1.1	...	...	—	—	—	—	—	—
Norway	52,202	84,012	62	1,383,367	194,633	2.6	3,715	5,424	2,636	4,242	1,357	2,184	1,816	2,652

merchant marine				air					canals and inland waterways (latest)				country
fleet, 1984 (vessels over 100 gross tons)	total dead-weight tonnage, 1984 ('000)	international cargo (latest)		airports with sched-uled flights, 1985	traffic (latest)				length		cargo		
		loaded metric tons ('000)	off-loaded metric tons ('000)		passengers		cargo		mi	km	short ton-mi ('000,000)	metric ton-km ('000,000)	
					passenger-mi ('000,000)	passenger-km ('000,000)	short ton-mi ('000,000)	metric ton-km ('000,000)					
21	46.8	547	1,753	37	474	762	18.6	27.1	70	113	...	...	Ethiopia
182	67.5	150	300	1	...	...	...	...	—	—	—	—	Faeroe Islands
5	4.1	4	9	1	...	...	...	...	—	—	—	—	Falkland Islands
56	27.8	552	660	16	255	410	4.5	6.6	...	...	...	...	Fiji
332	3,209.2	20,724	29,412	21	1,663	2,676	54.4	79.4	3,764	6,057	3,425	5,000	Finland
1,174	15,093.2	52,284	172,332	60	23,426	37,701	3,880.7	5,665.7	5,324	8,568	4,932	7,200	France
—		30	276	5	...	...	...	...	2,336	3,760	...	...	French Guiana
...	...	13	387	32	...	...	...	...	—	—	—	—	French Polynesia
20	169.2	8,040	631	25	267	430	18.7	27.3	199	320	...	...	Gabon
7	4.2	130	181	1	...	...	...	...	...	...	...	...	Gambia, The
				—									Gaza Strip
409	1,791.0	4,000	15,500	4	1,434	2,307	49.4	72.1	1,441	2,319	1,660	2,424	Germany, East
1,813	9,519.3	43,596	84,984	26	15,083	24,274	1,606.4	2,345.3	2,673	4,302	33,631	49,100	Germany, West
124	208.9	1,471	2,493	4	181	291	21.2	31.0	200	320	...	...	Ghana
54	448.9	7	270	1	...	...	...	...	—	—	—	—	Gibraltar
2,904	62,236.6	20,328	28,224	29	3,794	6,106	54.6	78.2	50	80	585	854	Greece
45	...	176	291	3	9	14	0.16	0.24	—	—	—	—	Greenland
3	0.6	160	63	2	...	...	...	...	—	—	—	—	Grenada
...	...	636	1,104	6	...	...	...	...	—	—	—	—	Guadeloupe
...	...	725	2,315	1	...	...	...	...	—	—	—	—	Guam
8	24.1	926	2,057	2	104	168	5.5	8.1	...	...	...	...	Guatemala
				2									Guernsey
18	2.9	10,000	545	1	90	144	9.6	14.0	805	1,295	...	...	Guinea
15	2.5	25	219	1	5	8	0.7	1.0	...	...	...	...	Guinea-Bissau
104	22.4	2,400	910	18	...	...	...	...	3,700	6,000	...	...	Guyana
6	0.9	723	561	2	...	...	1.3	1.9	60	100	...	...	Haiti
238	390.3	1,450	1,143	4	216	348	1.6	2.4	700	1,200	...	...	Honduras
340	9,586.1	13,980[9]	36,360[9]	1	...	...	...	...	—	—	—	—	Hong Kong
21	112.5			4	770	1,239	15.7	22.9	1,008	1,622	302	441	Hungary
395	165.9	502	1,358	23	1,306	2,101	19.6	28.6	...	...	58	84	Iceland
710	10,368.3	38,900	40,380	70	8,843	14,232	341.2	498.1	12,310	19,811	...	...	India
1,484	2,627.3	102,624	21,120	94	4,884	7,860	136.7	199.6	13,409	21,579	...	...	Indonesia
306	3,410.6	80,000	6,000	10	2,394	3,852	67.6	98.7	626	1,008	...	...	Iran
153	1,790.5	95,750	4,004	1	917	1,476	37.5	54.7	631	1,015	...	...	Iraq
154	270.5	5,000	14,500	7	1,320	2,124	62.5	91.3	454	731	...	...	Ireland
—		3	170	1	...	...	...	...	...	...	...	...	Isle of Man
64	677.5	7,080	9,576	6	3,795	6,108	366.0	534.4	—	—	—	—	Israel
1,590	14,938.9	34,512	187,584	36	8,474	13,638	486.3	710.0	849	1,366	134	195	Italy
64	173.7	4,536	4,848	15	179	288	37.6	54.9	460	740	...	...	Ivory Coast
13	12.9	8,335	4,018	2	764	1,230	7.9	11.6	—	—	—	—	Jamaica
10,495	64,624.3	94,320	602,664	72	39,318	63,267	1,834.4	2,678.2	1,100	1,770	136,655	198,052	Japan
—				1	...	...	...	...	...	...	...	...	Jersey
8	75.5	5,064	6,096	2	2,243	3,610	95.8	139.9	—	—	19,202	28,035	Jordan
3	3.8	10	22	1	...	...	...	...	2,474	3,982	...	...	Kampuchea
25	3.7	1,512	3,792	9	634	1,021	21.5	31.5	...	...	...	...	Kenya
4	1.8	300	69	17	...	...	...	...	3	5	...	...	Kiribati
61	739.9	1,600	4,000	1	52	84	1.4	2.0	1,400	2,250	...	...	Korea, North
1,799	11,211.5	30,612	95,052	3	7,494	12,060	813.6	1,187.9	...	...	6,917	10,099	Korea, South
250	3,879.9	33,300	6,500	1	2,354	3,788	338.8	494.6	—	—	—	—	Kuwait
—		—	—	7	5	8	0.07	0.10	2,900	4,600	...	...	Laos
251	696.7	200	2,500	1	516	831	13.5	19.8	—	—	—	—	Lebanon
—				15	8	13	0.07	0.10	—	—	—	—	Lesotho
1,934	121,394.6	19,000	1,051	8	11	17	0.07	0.10	230	370	...	...	Liberia
105	1,514.1	53,530	12,680	8	915	1,473	3.7	5.4	...	...	...	...	Libya
													Liechtenstein
—	—	—	—	1	57	92	0.2	0.3	23	37	186	272	Luxembourg
311	...	550	570	—	—	...	...	...	...	...	...	...	Macau
60	106.8	312	756	35	239	384	14.4	21.1	727	1,170	...	...	Madagascar
2	0.4			4	45	72	0.8	1.2	891	1,434	—	—	Malawi
429	2,409.6	30,108	22,140	39	3,706	5,964	137.0	200.0	4,534	7,296	...	...	Malaysia
32	204.1	6	45	1	...	...	...	...	—	—	—	—	Maldives
—				9	68	110	0.4	0.6	1,107	1,782	18	27	Mali
195	2,102.0	360	1,536	1	350	564	2.7	3.9	—	—	—	—	Malta
—		373	1,053	1	...	...	...	...	—	—	—	—	Martinique
40	7.1	7,546	508	8	156	251	14.9	21.8	500	800	...	...	Mauritania
18	57.5	879	779	2	276	444	5.7	8.3	—	—	—	—	Mauritius
—				1	...	...	...	...	—	—	—	—	Mayotte
624	2,146.3	77,508	11,148	72	10,633[12]	17,112[12]	102.2[12]	149.2[12]	1,900	3,000	...	...	Mexico
1	5.0	...	—	1	...	...	...	...	—	—	—	—	Monaco
—	—	—	—	1	162	261	3.4	5.0	295	474	3	4	Mongolia
1	1.0	66	46	1	...	...	...	...	—	—	—	—	Montserrat
261	641.2	19,428	11,244	14	1,081	1,739	26.1	38.1	600	1,000	—	—	Morocco
98	45.8	2,613	1,260	7	418	672	9.1	13.3	2,330	3,750	...	...	Mozambique
8	93.4	2,300	68	1	148	238	1.1	1.6	—	—	—	—	Nauru
—		—	—	6	155	250	2.1	3.1	—	—	—	—	Nepal
1,337	6,653.5	80,676	244,056	9	10,566[13]	17,004[13]	997.2[13]	1,455.9[13]	2,718	4,374	4,509	6,583	Netherlands, The
—		46,500	50,600	6	104	167	0.4	0.6	—	—	—	—	Netherlands Antilles
				18					—	—	—	—	New Caledonia
118	305.9	9,012	7,464	36	4,422	7,116	204.9	299.1	1,000	1,600	1,503	2,195	New Zealand
21	27.3	366	1,000	1	47	76	3.8	5.5	1,182	1,902	...	...	Nicaragua
—				6	140	225	14.6	21.3	370	600	...	...	Niger
178	609.7	58,088	15,497	15	1,505	2,422	20.4	29.9	5,328	8,575	...	...	Nigeria
—		—	—	1	...	...	...	...	—	—	—	—	Niue
—		—	—	1	...	...	...	...	—	—	—	—	Norfolk Island
2,271	30,604.8	47,088	17,616	41	2,331	3,752	91.1	133.1	190	306	5,829	8,510	Norway

Transportation (continued)

country	roads and motor vehicles (latest)								railroads (latest)					
	roads			motor vehicles			cargo		track length		traffic			
	length		paved (per-cent)	auto-mobiles	trucks and buses	persons per vehicle	short ton-mi ('000,000)	metric ton-km ('000,000)	mi	km	passengers		cargo	
	mi	km									passen-ger-mi ('000,000)	passen-ger-km ('000,000)	short ton-mi ('000,000)	metric ton-km ('000,000)
Oman	13,050	21,000	14	——26,752——		35	...	...	—	—	—	—	—	—
Pacific Is., Trust Terr. of the	1,000	1,600	25	4,206	2,311	20	...	...	—	—	—	—	—	—
Pakistan	58,955	94,879	65	197,633	82,709	338	...	...	5,473	8,808	11,364	18,288	5,047	7,368
Panama	5,864	9,437	31	113,960	37,051	14	...	...	171	275	...	...	...	...
Papua New Guinea	11,523	18,545	6	18,481	27,938	65	...	...	—	—	—	—	—	—
Paraguay	7,034	11,320	19	35,000	26,000	50	...	...	274	441	14	22	24	34
Peru	19,999	32,185	19	359,700	196,013	33	...	...	1,039[1]	1,672[1]	264	425	355	519
Philippines	96,750	155,700	13	894,927	128,083	51	...	...	711	1,144	142	228	8	12
Pitcairn Island	4	6	—	3		18	...	...	—	—	—	—	—	—
Poland	158,000	254,000	62	3,181,300	733,314	9.3	24,296	35,472	16,886	27,176	34,807	56,016	80,847	118,034
Portugal	32,188	51,802	86	1,268,969	79,427	7.3	...	...	2,933	4,720	3,229	5,196	715	1,044
Puerto Rico	5,802	9,337	86	995,067	153,215	2.8	...	...	57	92	...	...	...	...
Qatar	565	909	55	...	...	...	...	...	—	—	—	—	—	—
Réunion	1,684	2,710	81	118,854	39,046	3.3	...	...	382[17]	614[17]	...	...	...	...
Romania	45,586	73,364	63	250,000	130,000	58	8,077	11,792	6,913	11,125	15,893	25,578	43,030	62,822
Rwanda	4,900	7,900	...	——20,607——		277	...	...	—	—	—	—	—	—
St. Christopher and Nevis	190	305	42	2,593	299	16	...	...	—	—	—	—	—	—
St. Helena and Ascension	109	175	74	——1,124[18]——		5[18]	...	...	—	—	—	—	—	—
St. Lucia	792	1,275	90	4,479	1,171	22	...	...	—	—	—	—	—	—
St. Pierre and Miquelon	67	108	42	1,732	607	2.6	...	...	—	—	—	—	—	—
St. Vincent and the Grenadines	633	1,019	34	4,482	1,306	17	...	...	—	—	—	—	—	—
San Marino	137	220	...	14,749	1,699	1.4	...	...	—	—	—	—	—	—
São Tomé and Príncipe	178	287	69	1,774	265	41	...	...	—	—	—	—	—	—
Saudi Arabia	43,144	69,434	40	1,856,398	1,704,300	2.9	...	...	359[1]	578[1]	65	105	269	393
Senegal	9,134	14,700	25	50,875	27,767	72	375	547	737	1,186	265	426	108	158
Seychelles	160	257	60	3,524	1,086	14	...	...	—	—	—	—	—	—
Sierra Leone	4,635	7,459	16	16,009	4,826	151	36	53	52	84	...	...	...	...
Singapore	1,585	2,551	89	232,340	119,542	7.1	...	...	16	26	...	...	—	—
Solomon Islands	1,305	2,100	12	1,122	1,323	99	...	...	—	—	—	—	—	—
Somalia	12,169	19,584	13	17,754	9,533	191	...	...	—	—	—	—	—	—
South Africa	114,831	184,802	26	2,727,202	1,153,657	8.1	...	...	14,653	23,581	13,049	21,000	71,156	103,886
Bophuthatswana	5,474	8,810	...	...	...	...	...	...	142	228	...	...	...	...
Ciskei	2,322	3,737	...	...	...	...	...	...	87	140	...	...	...	...
Transkei	5,468	8,800	...	...	...	...	...	...	130	209	...	...	...	...
Venda	739	1,189	11	...	...	...	...	...	8	13	...	...	...	...
South West Africa/Namibia	26,011	41,860	10	——71,272——		16	...	...	1,453	2,338	...	...	...	...
Spain	200,170	322,143	56	8,714,076	1,604,038	3.7	63,300	92,400	8,421	13,553	9,678	15,576	7,973	11,640
Sri Lanka	46,487	74,813	40	131,657	101,627	65	...	...	903[1]	1,453[1]	1,505	2,421	155	226
Sudan, The	5,604	9,018	33	150,000	22,000	123	...	...	2,974	4,786	714	1,149	1,096	1,600
Suriname	5,523	8,889	26	31,170	12,850	8.2	...	...	104	167	...	...	...	...
Swaziland	1,692	2,723	19	21,338	8,376	20	...	...	283[1]	455[1]	...	...	...	...
Sweden	80,591	129,698	67	3,006,760	215,260	2.6	14,456	21,105	7,688	12,373	3,956	6,367	11,628	16,977
Switzerland	42,740	68,784	96	2,520,610	201,175	2.4	4,336	6,330	1,777	2,860	5,570	8,964	4,718	6,888
Syria	12,614	20,300	71	79,141	113,440	48	2,569	3,751	1,296	2,086	298	480	510	744
Taiwan	10,919	17,572	72	592,154	333,736	20	4,146	6,053	3,045	4,900	5,302	8,533	1,768	2,581
Tanzania	33,314	53,613	6	48,752	31,930	245	...	...	2,218	3,569	577[21]	929[21]	475[21]	694[21]
Thailand	44,833	72,151	35	451,001	535,735	49	...	...	2,321[1]	3,735[1]	6,003	9,661	1,713	2,501
Togo	4,638	7,464	20	26,067	13,422	68	...	...	321	516	65	104	9	13
Tokelau	...	...	...	...	...	...	...	...	—	—	—	—	—	—
Tonga	269	433	60	662	1,185	53	...	...	—	—	—	—	—	—
Trinidad and Tobago	5,174	8,327	46	200,100	54,620	4.5	...	...	—	—	—	—	—	—
Tunisia	15,766	25,373	52	141,185	147,571	23	572	835	1,251[1]	2,013[1]	462	744	1,159	1,692
Turkey	144,697	232,867	76	812,122	392,927	37	26,980	39,390	5,067[1]	8,156[1]	3,359	5,728	9,177	13,398
Turks and Caicos Islands	75	121	20	...	...	...	...	...	—	—	—	—	—	—
Tuvalu	5	8	...	...	...	...	...	...	—	—	—	—	—	—
Uganda	16,981	27,329	11	10,633	11,245	618	...	...	799[1]	1,286[1]	...	...	...	...
U.S.S.R.	605,000	973,000	79	8,255,000	7,254,000	17	339,500	495,600	89,229	143,600	225,000	362,000	2,470,000	3,600,000
United Arab Emirates	800	1,300	61	130,700	77,600	5.2	...	...	—	—	—	—	—	—
United Kingdom	213,556	343,685	97	15,854,000	1,815,000	3.2	68,500	100,000	14,408	23,187	18,693[23]	30,084[23]	8,532[23]	12,456[23]
United States	3,866,296	6,222,200	85	124,800,000	35,600,000	1.5	526,000	768,000	184,235	296,497	10,998	17,700	919,004	1,341,720
Uruguay	30,952	49,813	20	281,275	49,813	8.8	500	730	1,867[1]	3,004[1]	170	274	123	180
Vanuatu	551	887	4	3,087[25]	242[25]	14[25]	...	...	—	—	—	—	—	—
Venezuela	38,803	62,448	38	1,501,382	795,856	6.9	...	...	278	448	12	19	20	29
Vietnam	37,300	60,000	16	100,000	200,000	163	...	...	1,568	2,523	1,870	3,010	519	758
Virgin Islands (U.S.)	532	856	...	26,500	4,200	3.3	...	...	—	—	—	—	—	—
Wallis and Futuna	62	100	...	...	...	...	...	...	—	—	—	—	—	—
West Bank	...	...	...	18,600	9,826	25	...	...	...	...	...	...	...	..
Western Sahara	3,790	6,100	8	6,284	424	20	...	...	—	—	—	—	—	—
Western Samoa	116	187	68	2,940	385	48	...	...	—	—	—	—	—	—
Yemen (Aden)	1,150	1,850	...	16,500	16,300	57	...	...	—	—	—	—	—	—
Yemen (Şan'ā')	20,541	33,057	6	99,666	140,114	26	...	...	—	—	—	—	—	—
Yugoslavia	71,566	115,174	53	2,770,739	244,770	7.6	13,193	19,262	5,834	9,389	7,208	11,600	19,109	27,900
Zaire	28,379	45,671	18	89,471	16,807	268	...	...	3,576	5,755	242	389	1,214	1,772
Zambia	23,135	37,232	15	105,783	94,780	30	...	...	1,360	2,188	...	...	...	...
Zimbabwe	105,900	170,400	7	224,453	24,246	30	...	...	2,109[1]	3,394[1]	...	...	3,984	6,411

merchant marine		international cargo (latest)		air — airports with scheduled flights, 1985	traffic (latest) — passengers		traffic (latest) — cargo		canals and inland waterways (latest) — length		canals and inland waterways (latest) — cargo		country
fleet, 1984 (vessels over 100 gross tons)	total deadweight tonnage, 1984 ('000)	loaded metric tons ('000)	off-loaded metric tons ('000)		passenger-mi ('000,000)	passenger-km ('000,000)	short ton-mi ('000,000)	metric ton-km ('000,000)	mi	km	short ton-mi ('000,000)	metric ton-km ('000,000)	
26	12.1	16,160	2,800	2	553	890	16.3	23.8	—	—	—	—	Oman
—	—	25	143	9	188	302	3.9	5.6	—	—	—	—	Pacific Is., Trust Terr. of the
82	733.5	2,352	12,408	18	4,265	6,864	190.0	277.4	...	...	...	...	Pakistan
5,499	62,068.9	778	2,698	6	249	400	9.9	14.4	548	882	...	...	Panama
82	29.9	1,950	1,646	134	358	576	8.6	12.5	...	...	...	...	Papua New Guinea
39	44.3	...	...	1	298	479	1.8	2.7	1,900	3,100	...	...	Paraguay
670	1,045.9	6,292	3,199	22	1,059[14]	1,704[14]	29.3[14]	42.8[14]	5,473	8,808	...	...	Peru
946	5,525.6	12,672	18,972	41	5,199	8,368	167.4	244.5	2,000	3,219	—	—	Philippines
—	—	—	—	—	—	—	—	—	—	—	—	—	Pitcairn Island
783	4,304.1	30,600	14,800	12	1,090	1,755	110.1	160.8	1,876	3,019	995	1,452	Poland
359	2,684.9	4,100	19,000	12	2,461[15]	3,960[15]	73.1[15]	106.7[15]	77	124	...	...	Portugal
—	—	16[16]	16[16]	11	...	...	...	...	—	—	—	—	Puerto Rico
61	482.2	16,420	1,700	1	...	...	...	...	—	—	—	—	Qatar
—	—	336	1,104	1	...	...	...	...	—	—	—	—	Réunion
393	3,931.5	10,000	22,000	15	1,351	2,174	46.6	68.0	1,031	1,659	1,745	2,548	Romania
—	—	—	—	2	...	...	...	...	—	—	—	—	Rwanda
2	0.5	36	63	2	...	...	...	...	—	—	—	—	St. Christopher and Nevis
1	2.3	1	12	1	...	...	...	...	—	—	—	—	St. Helena and Ascension
7	3.7	100	188	2	...	...	...	...	—	—	—	—	St. Lucia
—	—	7	64	1	...	...	...	...	—	—	—	—	St. Pierre and Miquelon
49	154.8	16	45	4	...	...	...	...	—	—	—	—	St. Vincent and the Grenadines
—	—	—	—	—									San Marino
2	1.0	12	15	1	...	...	...	...	—	—	—	—	São Tomé and Príncipe
422	6,475.1	299,257	30,000	18	9,309	14,982	1,253.6	1,830.3	—	—	—	—	Saudi Arabia
135	33.6	2,256	2,424	11	142	229	14.5	21.2	935	1,505	...	...	Senegal
3	0.3	6	100	1	...	...	...	...	—	—	—	—	Seychelles
23	1.3	48[9]	228[9]	7	53	86	6.2	9.0	500	800	447	652	Sierra Leone
825	11,038.3	40,344	63,852	1	11,551	18,590	579.6	846.1	—	—	—	—	Singapore
26	4.6	299	95	27	7	11	0.02	0.04	—	—	—	—	Solomon Islands
26	29.3	250	814	9	177	284	3.4	4.9	—	—	—	—	Somalia
278	790.7	69,276	26,758	36	5,906[19]	9,504[19]	317.9[19]	464.1[19]	...	...	...	...	South Africa
—	—	—	—	—	...	...	...	...	...	...	...	...	Bophuthatswana
—	—	—	—	—	—	—	—	—	...	...	...	...	Ciskei
—	—	—	—	1	...	...	...	...	...	...	...	...	Transkei
—	—	—	—	—	...	...	...	...	...	...	...	...	Venda
—	—	—	—	10	...								South West Africa/Namibia
2,529	12,122.1	44,652	88,752	29	10,850	17,462	351.7	513.5	649	1,045	21,836[20]	31,880[20]	Spain
93	1,203.1	1,932	3,588	6	1,543	2,484	42.9	62.6	267	430	...	...	Sri Lanka
23	128.2	916	2,642	13	408	657	4.1	6.0	3,300	5,310	...	...	Sudan, The
25	19.2	6,079	1,518	5	152	245	2.5	3.6	2,800	4,500	...	...	Suriname
—	—	—	—	1	19	30	0.7	1.0	—	—	—	—	Swaziland
679	5,196.0	42,720	48,732	35	3,166	5,096	131.2	191.6	724	1,165	6,200	9,000	Sweden
32	487.4	...	...	5	7,494	12,060	465.9	680.2	13	21	106	155	Switzerland
53	81.9	1,824	3,360	7	588	947	8.8	12.9	418	672	...	...	Syria
543	[2]			9	5,676	9,135	1,080.8	1,578.0	...	...	...	...	Taiwan
39	71.0	1,118	2,040	53	130	210	0.8	1.2	726	1,168	...	...	Tanzania
225	759.1	15,582[22]	19,032[22]	10	5,633	9,065	225.0	328.5	2,500	4,000	...	...	Thailand
8	43.2	704	995	1	121	194	14.4	21.0	30	50	...	...	Togo
—	—	—	—	—	—	—	—	—	—	—	—	—	Tokelau
20	21.2	23	74	1	...	...	...	...	—	—	—	—	Tonga
49	12.4	12,798	11,094	1	957	1,540	3.4	4.9	—	—	—	—	Trinidad and Tobago
63	449.5	4,452	8,700	5	999	1,607	12.9	18.9	—	—	—	—	Tunisia
776	5,174.0	45,144	36,312	16	1,468	2,362	18.0	26.3	1,000	1,600	35	51	Turkey
10	3.3	3	5	5	...	...	...	...	—	—	—	—	Turks and Caicos Islands
2	0.5	—	—	1	...	...	...	...	—	—	—	—	Tuvalu
—	—	—	—	7	89	143	26.3	38.4	—	—	—	—	Uganda
7,095	27,928.3	162,000	63,000	52	110,000	177,000	2,181.0	3,185.0	85,687	137,900	129,800	189,500	U.S.S.R.
225	1,349.7	64,788	8,500	2	2,213	3,562	65.3	95.3	—	—	...	...	United Arab Emirates
2,468	24,140.4	136,140	136,128	128	28,102	45,226	1,119.7	1,634.8	1,461	2,351	30,100	44,000	United Kingdom
6,441	29,139.8	327,768[16]	332,424[16]	824	252,707	406,692	7,279.3	10,627.6	25,727	41,403	387,000	565,000	United States
89	288.4	570[24]	454[24]	7	182	293	0.7	1.0	1,000	1,600	...	...	Uruguay
21	161.4	67	105	9	...	...	...	...	—	—	—	—	Vanuatu
250	1,460.5	60,821	12,093	42	1,737	2,796	72.3	105.6	4,400	7,100	—	—	Venezuela
119	411.0	680	5,000	3	181	291	2.7	4.0	11,000	17,702	—	—	Vietnam
—	—	9,500	12,600	3	...	...	...	...	—	—	—	—	Virgin Islands (U.S.)
—	—	—	—	2	...	...	...	...	—	—	—	—	Wallis and Futuna
—	—	—	—	—	—	—	—	—	...	...	...	...	West Bank
—	—	...	60	1	...	...	...	...	—	—	—	—	Western Sahara
6	35.3	34	89	3	...	...	...	...	—	—	—	—	Western Samoa
28	13.5	3,575	4,834	1	62	100	1.2	1.7	—	—	—	—	Yemen (Aden)
10	1.8	40	2,000	3	420	675	44.6	65.1	—	—	—	—	Yemen (Şan'ā')
480	4,130.7	6,312	22,080	16	3,045	4,901	58.5	85.4	1,243	2,001	2,868	4,187	Yugoslavia
33	121.4	845	1,513	33	424	683	21.0	30.7	8,500	13,700	678	990	Zaire
—	—	—	—	14	343	552	50.6	73.9	1,398	2,250	...	...	Zambia
—	—	—	—	8	344	554	6.4	9.3	...	...	...	...	Zimbabwe

[1]Route length. [2]China includes Taiwan. [3]Paved roads only. [4]Excludes railroads serving the sugar industry. [5]SAS only. [6]National roads only. [7]Includes 100 km of the Chemin de Fer Djibouti–Ethiopien (CDE) in Djibouti. [8]Railroads serve mines only. [9]Includes transshipments. [10]Lamco Railroad only. [11]Peninsular Malaysia and Singapore. [12]Aeronaves de Mexico and Mexicana only. [13]KLM and NLM only. [14]Aeroperu and Faucett only. [15]TAP only. [16]United States includes Puerto Rico. [17]Railroads serve sugarcane plantations only. [18]St. Helena only. [19]SAA only. [20]Coastal shipping. [21]Tanzania Railways Corporation only. [22]Port of Bangkok only. [23]British Railways only; excluding Northern Ireland. [24]Port of Montevideo only. [25]Espirito Santo and Efate only.

Communications

Virtually all the states of the world have a variety of communications media available to their citizens: newspapers (although only daily papers are included in this table), radio broadcast systems, and telephone, post office, and telegraph facilities; most also have television and telex. The focus of this table, therefore, is on the relative density and distribution of communications services. Unfortunately, the availability of information about the infrastructure and traffic volume of these national systems runs far behind the capabilities of the systems themselves. Certain countries publish no information about themselves; others publish data analyzed according to a variety of fiscal, calendar, religious, or other years; still others, while they possess such data almost simultaneously with the end of the business year, may not publish them except in company reports of limited distribution or in national statistical summaries, and only after a delay of up to several years.

The date given for each category of information is that of the majority of the data in the columns indicated, but within each column as much as one-quarter of the data may refer to other years. The data also originate in sources of varying completeness and reliability. Data for some kinds of communications apparatus and traffic are relatively easy to track; telephones, for example, must be installed, and service is recorded so that

it may be charged. But in most countries radios may be purchased by anyone and turned on whenever desired. As a result, data on distribution and use of radio and television apparatus may be collected in a variety of ways—on the basis of numbers of subscribers, licenses issued, periodic sample surveys, census or housing surveys, or private consumer surveys. In some cases the figures have been rounded, and the population data used in calculating the distribution statistics are based on midyear estimates for the relevant years.

The United Nations Educational, Scientific and Cultural Organization (Unesco) publishes in its *Yearbook* extensive data on newspapers, radio, and television that have been collected from standardized questionnaires. The completeness and recency of its data, however, depend on the timely return of each questionnaire, and response rates depend on a variety of factors. In general, however, response rates for inquiries by international organizations in communications are better than in other fields because these organizations and the responsible authorities in each country must conduct day-to-day business and, hence, have a better on-going relationship.

Newspaper statistics are especially difficult to collect and compare. Newspapers continually are founded, cease publication, merge, or change

Communications

country	daily newspapers (latest) number	total circulation ('000)	circulation per 1,000 population	radio, 1984 transmitters (latest)	receivers (all types) ('000)	persons per receiver	television, 1984 transmitters (latest)	receivers (all types) ('000)	persons per receiver	telephone, 1983 receivers ('000)	persons per receiver	traffic, 1982 ('000 calls) local	long-distance	international
Afghanistan	4	92	5	14	135	130.9	1	12.6	1,402	31.7[1]	516.1[1]	——110[2]——		18[2]
Albania	2	145	51	14	210	13.9	166	46	63.3	4.8[4]	579.2[4]	——1,587,500[5]——		118,640[5]
Algeria	4	448	22	55	3,500	6.0	44	1,440	14.7	606.9	33.8			
American Samoa	2	7	200	1	15	2.3	3	7.5	4.6	6.0[4]	5.5[4]			
Andorra	1	...	...	4	8	5.2	...	4.0	10.4	17.7[4]	2.1[4]	...	...	...[1]
Angola	1	50	7	55	130	65.6	...	23	371.3	40.3[4]	202.0[4]	66,080[1]	260[1]	320[1]
Anguilla	—	—	—	2	2.2	2.9	—	—	—	0.58	11.2	424		144[6]
Antigua and Barbuda	1	6	80	5	20	3.9	...	16.6	4.7	10.5	7.5	13[5]	3[5]	359[5]
Argentina	159	...	...	202	10,500	2.8	75	5,915	5.0	2,717.1	10.9	13,196,728[5]	42,936	2,901
Australia	63	4,851	337	284	20,000	0.8	386	5,904	2.6	8,251.1	1.9	5,570,000	821,600	16,500
Austria	30	...	...	498	4,000	1.9	799	3,035	2.5	3,330.2	2.3	——24,631,340[6]——		241,992[6]
Bahamas, The	3	34	154	5	115	2.0	...	50.5	4.5	67.5	3.3	——126,040[1]——		1,571
Bahrain	3	26	59	3	140	3.0	1	122	3.4	87.6	4.5	122,572		22,209[6]
Bangladesh	30	542	6	23	800	120.9	6	255	379.1	122.2[4]	758.0[4]	——347,600[14]——		846. 14
Barbados	2	39	145	1	192	1.3	2	55	4.6	72.8	3.4	——483,000[15]——		1,100[15]
Belgium	26	2,204	224	59	4,607	2.1	49	5,128	1.9	3,984.3	2.5	1,510,166	1,913,887	69,516
Belize	2	6	41	6	72	2.2	...	—	—	8.6	18.0		28,382[5]	90
Benin	1	1	0.3	7	68	57.2	2	17.2	225.5	18.0[1]	198.3[1]	...	548[14]	812[14]
Bermuda	1	14	247	5	100	0.6	...	66[15]	0.8[15]	51.4	1.1	43,805	...	2,081
Bhutan	—	—	—	1	12.5	111.5	...	...	...	14.6[4]	91.1[4]			
Bolivia	12	275	46	184	482	13.0	...	387	16.2	204.7	29.7	...	——1,147——	2,435. 15
Botswana	1	19	22	4	75.8	13.9	...	—	—	16.6	60.9	...		3,903
Brazil	328	5,094	44	962	25,000	5.3	...	23,000	5.8	9,309.0	13.9	12,736,000	1,395,800	7,144
British Virgin Islands	—	—	—	1	12.5	0.9	...	6.8	1.7	2.9[1]	3.8[1]	...	...	133[1]
Brunei	—	—	—	13	52	4.2	2	31	7.0	21.9[4]	9.2[4]	...	22,720[1, 6]	3,760[1, 6]
Bulgaria	12	2,094	230	35	2,150	4.2	339	2,000	4.5	1,513.9	5.9	25,000	344	5,732
Burkina Faso	6	...	...	9	116	57.9	1	20	335.9	13.9[18]	484.8[18]	...	...	42[3]
Burma	6	502	14	7	800	46.2	...	32	1,155	54.0	671.5	——65,000[14]——		5[14]
Burundi	2	20	4	5	160	28.4	...	—	—	6.0[18]	756.2[18]	1,205[15]	553[15]	538[15]
Cameroon	1	35	4	19	785	12.0	...	...	...	47.2[18]	199.1[18]	...	...	1,600. 15
Canada	120	5,570	226	1,226	21,800	1.2	1,163	13,960	1.8	13,656.2	1.8	27,554,131	1,475,376	110,638
Cape Verde	—	—	—	3	47	6.6	...	—	—	1.7	176.2	——15,200[1]——		638[1]
Cayman Islands	...	...	...	4	18	1.1	...	—	—	9.4	2.0	...	...	236[1]
Central African Republic	—	—	—	4	85	29.5	...	1[1]	2,341[1]	5.0[4]	477.2[4]	2,142	538	43
Chad	3	...	...	3	75	65.3	...	...	...	6.5[3]	659.7[3]	...	...	...
Chile	37	945	87	109	17,000	0.7	...	2,645	4.5	608.2	19.2	1,144,925	44,042	1,103
China	53	33,654	33	...	15,000	68.8	...	9,900	104.2	4,712.0	216.5	——667,000——		3,000
Christmas Island	—	—	—	...	2.5	1.2	...	...	...	0.18	3.3	...	...	...
Cocos (Keeling) Islands	—	—	—	...	0.75	0.8	...	...	...	0.18	3.3	...	...	...
Colombia	27	1,222	4.4	...	2,800	10.1	71	1,801	15.7	2,547.2	10.9	1,004,000[15]	168,600[15]	3,500[15]
Comoros	—	—	—	7	40	9.8	...	...	...	0.50	766.1	——940,000[3]——		14[3]
Congo	5	23	14	10	97	17.5	...	4.8	353.1	18.1[18]	93.7[18]	47,582[15]	31,722[15]	1,979[15]
Cook Islands	1	2	118	2	10	1.7	...	—	—	2.1	8.5	...	...	48
Costa Rica	4	180	77	123	190	13.0	...	450	5.5	281.0	8.5	492,569	196,338	1,753
Cuba	17	1,150	118	143	2,135	4.7	58	1,500	6.6	406.4[4]	24.1[4]	——54,000[14]——		453[14]
Cyprus	17	75	116	6	300	2.2	25	167	3.9	164.0	4.0	——524,270[5]——		791,892[5]
Czechoslovakia	30	4,892	318	120	4,202.8	3.7	72	4,350	3.6	3,306.2	4.7	3,785,000	311,000	4,900
Denmark	47	1,821	356	49	2,018.4	2.5	32	1,900.0	2.7	3,633.8	1.4	2,138,992	1,232,469	32,768
Djibouti	—	—	—	3	17.5	19.1	...	11.2	29.9	6.4	51.6	3,688[15]	373[15]	2,522. 15
Dominica	—	—	—	3	20	3.7	...	—	—	4.5	14.4	4,670	...	108
Dominican Republic	7	177	29	188	226	27.0	...	390	15.6	175.1	34.1	2,017,011	8,460	2,933
Ecuador	18	570	64	...	1,875	4.5	...	450	18.7	311.7	26.3	...	...	7,468[6]
Egypt	10	3,484	78	82	12,000	3.9	36	3,860	12.2	521.6[4]	85.6[4]	747,000	16,000	2,070
El Salvador	6	...	...	75	900	5.7	...	300	17.2	100.0	50.0	289,378[5]	124,019[5]	15,209[6]
Equatorial Guinea	2	...	...	3	90	3.5	...	2.1	148.1	1.4[4]	217.4[4]	...	...	...
Ethiopia	3	40	1	9	2,000	21.2	2	45	940	100.8	408.1	304,120[5]	3,338	179
Faeroe Islands	—	—	—	4	16.8	2.7	...	9	5.0	20.4[18]	2.2[18]	...	...	...
Falkland Islands	—	—	—	2	1	2.0	...	9	0.2	0.44[18]	4.6[18]	——4——		12
Fiji	3	67	102	12	300	2.3	...	—	—	49.5	13.6	——6,395[6]——		2,057[6]
Finland	64	2,484	515	100	2,515	1.9	143	1,738.4	2.8	2,643.6	1.8	1,453,405	339,904	13,955

frequency of publication. Data on circulation, sales, and readership are often incomplete, slow to be aggregated at the national level, or regarded as proprietary for either private or governmental publications. In some countries circulation data are virtually nonexistent. In others no daily newspaper exists.

The commercially published annual *World Radio TV Handbook* (J.M. Frost, editor) is a valuable source of information on broadcast media and has complete and timely coverage. It depends on data received from broadcasters, but because some do not respond, local correspondents and monitors are used in many countries, and some unconfirmed or unofficial data are included as estimates.

Telephone data are obtained from the American Telephone and Telegraph Communications' annual, *The World's Telephones,* and a variety of national and secondary sources. A.T.&T. collects its data by sending questionnaires to the telephone agencies of each country, and their statistics tend to be accurate and timely, but some countries, again, fail to supply current data. More than one-quarter of the data are for other than the base year. Several countries also report incomplete data: the national total may exclude figures for some telephone companies, or some portion of the national territory; some countries supply statistics only on telephone exchange lines; some island states report only radio telephones. A number of countries omit data on public coin-box telephones; their statistics, thus, reflect an undercount. The figures for calls under telephone traffic sometimes represent a measure of mechanical activity rather than an enumeration of actual conversations between individuals. Depending on a country's metering system, multiple counting of a single call may occur.

Post office statistics are collected mainly from the Universal Postal Union's annual summary *Statistique des services postaux.*

The statistics on telegraph and telex are derived mainly from the UN-affiliated International Telecommunication Union's *Yearbook of Common Carrier Telecommunication Statistics* with additional statistics from country sources.

Unesco surveys, the diverse industry sources cited above, and scores of national statistical sources have all been used in the compilation of this table because no one source is complete.

... Not available.

—None, nil, or not applicable.

post offices, 1983			telegraph, 1983			telex, 1983				country
num- ber	per- sons per office	pieces of mail handled ('000)	total traffic ('000)	na- tional traffic ('000)	inter- national outgoing traffic ('000)	sub- scriber lines	traffic ('000 minutes)			
							total	national	international outgoing	
349[3]	36,447[3]	11,218[3]	183[2]	95[2]	88[2]	73[2]	...	...	25[2]	Afghanistan
292[3]	7,328[3]	...	...	...	...	...	...	...	...	Albania
1,826	11,856	351,410	3,223	2,882	341	5,895	30,192	21,664	8,528	Algeria
...	...	...	...	...	...	...	...	...	...	American Samoa
...	...	...	...	...	...	...	...	...	...	Andorra
133	53,263	6,177	198[1]	154[1]	44[1]	587[1]	...	...	1,599[1]	Angola
22	272	200	0.9	—	0.9	30	...	...	20	Anguilla
15[3]	5,333[3]	2,262[7, 8, 9, 10]	174	...	174	64[1]	...	...	110[1]	Antigua and Barbuda
5,554	5,016	74,095[11]	11,357	11,141	216	8,816	...	135,982[2]	9,190	Argentina
4,790	2,938	2,995,711	4,866	4,051	815	40,000	58,114[12]	45,492[12]	12,622[12]	Australia
2,644[13]	2,858[13]	2,658,650	1,352	1,096	256	22,928	105,324	71,669	33,655	Austria
127	1,649	34,559	50	20	30	396	1,157	91	1,066	Bahamas, The
10	35,079	76,800	138	17	122	1,946	12,281	2,208	10,073	Bahrain
7,192[3]	12,047[3]	333,133[3]	3,998[14]	3,470[14]	528[14]	461[1]	...	...	855[1]	Bangladesh
16	15,875	17,009[10]	...	...	43	281	...	...	595	Barbados
1,858[13]	5,309[13]	2,910,141	1,353	1,073	280	23,970	110,385	46,753	63,631	Belgium
105	1,385	4,052[8, 9, 10]	...	...	20[1]	51[1]	...	...	72[1]	Belize
106[3]	26,321[3]	11,856[7]	...	422[14]	...	153[14]	...	...	244[1]	Benin
15[3]	3,333[3]	...	...	...	25[4]	453[1]	...	...	1,460[1]	Bermuda
81[3]	16,728[3]	2,266[16]	...	...	...	...	...	...	...	Bhutan
458[3]	11,572[3]	54,609[3]	244	210	34	930[1]	2,087	1,152	935	Bolivia
138	6,786	35,876[8]	...	209[3]	43	407	2,493	722	1,770	Botswana
7,428	17,455	4,257,333[17]	...	15,327[2]	219	56,040	276,571	260,415	16,156	Brazil
5[3]	2,407[3]	...	8[4]	—	8[4]	39[1]	...	...	49[1]	British Virgin Islands
14	14,307	8,014	...	...	...	231[1]	...	...	419[1]	Brunei
2,857[3]	3,101[3]	...	7,593	7,393	199	6,030	30,733	27,463	3,270	Bulgaria
66[3]	90,000[3]	2,128[7]	114[7]	65[7]	49[7]	223	...	...	117[12]	Burkina Faso
1,107	31,900	93,916	1,358[14]	1,280[14]	78[14]	47[14]	...	...	209[14]	Burma
38	120,943	12,558	9	4	5	100	...	...	224	Burundi
150[3]	50,207[3]	64,248[16]	534	417	117	1,035	...	...	2,700	Cameroon
8,295	3,025	6,533,274[19]	...	1,423[2, 20]	720[20]	50,336	...	...	14,550	Canada
...	...	3,522[21]	111[4]	98[4]	13[4]	40[4]	190[4]	58[4]	132[4]	Cape Verde
...	...	2,262[21]	10[4]	—	10[4]	164[1]	...	...	286[1]	Cayman Islands
76	32,310	34,525[22]	47[1]	37[1]	10[1]	134[1]	...	...	353[1]	Central African Republic
24	203,000	938[23]	320[7]	300[7]	20[7]	607[1]	...	127. [12]	188[7]	Chad
764	14,758	164,518[10]	2,800	2,730	70	3,768	...	47,741[5]	4,103	Chile
48,745	21,026	3,540,100[9, 10, 17]	173,762	172,353	1,409	1,373	...	...	4,414	China
2	1,600	...	...	...	...	...	...	...	...	Christmas Island
4	154	...	...	...	...	...	...	...	...	Cocos (Keeling) Islands
...	...	209,461[22]	21,134	21,000	134	5,310	29,298	103,007[5]	6,559	Colombia
9[3]	38,889[3]	1,732[21]	...	17[3]	25[24]	37[4]	...	...	53[4]	Comoros
131	11,450	14,612	260	116	144	329	...	...	798	Congo
...	...	...	...	...	240	41	66	11	55	Cook Islands
342	7,028	74,825	...	223[4]	54	1,439	3,271	1,670	1,601	Costa Rica
700[3]	13,271[3]	86,991[1, 10]	15,986[14]	15,592[14]	394[14]	2,352[1]	20,519[1]	19,338[1]	1,181[1]	Cuba
650	1,007	31,303	151	97	53	2,581	5,449	1,734	3,715	Cyprus
6,101	2,526	71,967[11]	9,946	9,618	328	1,017	...	71,793[5]	5,997	Czechoslovakia
1,298[13]	3,938[13]	1,468,154	401	263	138	11,414	45,463	16,318	29,145	Denmark
5	60,000	1,623	27	—	27	168	507	15	491	Djibouti
63	1,274	2,051	12	—	12	28[1]	...	...	31[1]	Dominica
154[3]	25,807[3]	21,741[23]	...	...	...	...	...	...	...	Dominican Republic
480	18,635	37,260	2,134	2,021	113	1,900	6,971	3,882	3,089	Ecuador
6,870[13]	6,696[13]	441,890	9,302[4]	8,332[4]	970[4]	3,476[4]	13,511[4]	4,584[4]	8,927[4]	Egypt
367	13,484	32,762[8]	1,151	1,106	45	683	896	31	865	El Salvador
19	20,473	51[8, 9, 10]	...	...	...	...	...	...	...	Equatorial Guinea
462	89,029	26,945[9, 10]	225	202	23	631	1,439	514	925	Ethiopia
...	...	233[25]	...	...	4	8	42	—	42	Faeroe Islands
...	...	...	...	...	...	...	...	...	...	Falkland Islands
200	2,940	28,272[10]	118	110	8	448	...	1,530[5]	847	Fiji
3,632	1,340	1,098,005	725	634	91	7,500	25,808	11,858	13,950	Finland

Communications (continued)

country	daily newspapers (latest)			radio, 1984			television, 1984			telephone, 1983		traffic, 1982 ('000 calls)		
	number	total circulation ('000)	circulation per 1,000 population	transmitters (latest)	receivers (all types) ('000)	persons per receiver	transmitters (latest)	receivers (all types) ('000)	persons per receiver	receivers ('000)	persons per receiver	local	long-distance	international
France	90	10,322	191	610	20,000	2.7	2,821	17,290	3.2	29,373.7	1.9		72,655,150[5]	
French Guiana	1	16	230	13	42.5	1.9	8	6.3	12.7	22.1	3.5		90,977[5]	
French Polynesia	2	13	89	6	80	2.1	10	25.6	6.7	27.6	6.0		22,200[5]	2,450[6]
Gabon	1	15	27	16	100	11.5	...	21	54.6	12.1	93.0	13,560[5, 15]	34,800[5, 15]	1,609
Gambia, The	—	—	—	3	100	7.2	...	...	...	3.5[2]	182.0[2]		3,012[14]	41[14]
Gaza Strip														
Germany, East	39	8,936	530	120	6,425	2.6	505	5,970	2.8	3,344.2	5.0	1,296,036	707,841	10,929
Germany, West	368	25,103	408	431	24,598.7	2.5	3,424	22,127.1	2.8	31,370.1	2.0	15,387,180	8,477,510	308,140
Ghana	5	...	...	4	2,020	6.2	7	62	201.5	70.7[4]	168.1[4]		1,800[14]	130[14]
Gibraltar	1	2	80	3	10	3.0	2	7.1	4.2	10.4	2.9	9,330[4]	...	505
Greece	131	...	...	55	4,000	2.5	84	1,710	5.8	3,113.0	3.2	3,044,840	516,480	21,680
Greenland	—	—	—	18	13.5	3.9	...	10	5.3	11.6[18]	4.6[18]			
Grenada	—	—	—	3	50	1.8	...	...	...	5.6[18]	16.2[18]		148[15]	640[15]
Guadeloupe	1	32	98	5	55	6.0	8	46	7.2	68.5	4.8		292,355[5]	
Guam	1	18	171	5	300	0.4	2	78.5	1.4	29.0	3.9	...	...	...
Guatemala	8	224	30	115	320	23.7	...	205	37.1	161.5	46.6	...	...	...
Guernsey	1	16	215	...	...	...	...	...	...	40.0	1.4		28,743	184
Guinea	1	20	4	8	125	42.4	...	7.6	698	10.0[1]	494.3[1]	...	96[6, 15]	98[6, 15]
Guinea-Bissau	1	6	10	4	25	34.2	...	...	...	5.0[1]	160.6[1]	...	...	...
Guyana	2	78	85	8	300	3.1	...	...	...	28.5[4]	31.6[4]	...	...	...
Haiti	4	20	4	48	120	43.2	...	65	79.7	38.4	133.2	...	452	818
Honduras	6	240	61	153	500	8.5	...	136	31.1	37.3	109.8	151,150[6, 15]	112,180[6, 15]	9,090[6, 15]
Hong Kong	62	...	...	24	2,700	2.0	12	1,278	4.2	1,947.5	2.7			12,703
Hungary	27	2,665	249	51	5,500	1.9	42	2,845	3.7	1,338.4	8.0	1,051,120[5]	649,894[5]	305,500[5]
Iceland	6	99	420	26	73.5	3.3	83	71.6	3.4	116.9	2.0		490,571[4, 15]	795[15]
India	1,087	13,033	20	160	22,500	33.4	14	2,100	357.7	3,215.4	228.5	10,335,074	179,220	2,548
Indonesia	94	...	...	301	6,800	24.1	201	3,005	54.6	669.3	238.3	4,949,040[5]	10,632	2,867
Iran	14	...	...	120	8,000	5.4	418	2,000	21.7	2,118.1	19.6	7,371,358	283,997	3,676
Iraq	6	324	23	26	2,200	6.9	21	635	23.9	514.9	28.5		1,518,817[5]	1,506
Ireland	7	771	229	21	2,036.1	1.8	21	721.1	5.0	779.6	4.5		1,662,060[5]	2,920
Isle of Man	—	—	—	...	21.8[1]	3.0[1]	...	21.8[15]	3.0[15]	...	...	...	...	...
Israel	26	825	205	52	1,055	4.0	48	605	7.0	1,410.0	2.9	1,000,000[5]	2,000,000[5]	30,000[6]
Italy	79	4,632	82	1,989	14,010	4.1	1,867	13,831.3	4.1	21,670.0	2.6	10,700,964	4,292,300	95,965
Ivory Coast	1	70	8	24	900	10.8	12	340	28.7	87.7[1]	98.0[1]	...	...	...
Jamaica	3	104	46	19	858.0	2.5	...	200.5	10.8	125.7[4]	16.7[4]	...	1,888	3,667
Japan	154	68,142	575	1,008	94,000	1.3	11,439	30,210	4.0	62,804.1	1.9	...	...	23,535
Jersey	1	23	311	...	...	...	...	...	...	58.3	1.3	40,612[15]	7,119[15]	480[15]
Jordan	5	176	68	13	550	4.6	13	280	9.0	70.8[1]	32.8[1]	...	...	...
Kampuchea	16	...	...	6	200	35.5	...	51	139.2	7.3[1]	886.3[1]	...	...	...
Kenya	2	220	12	22	600	32.6	...	76	257.1	216.7	86.7	7,895	6,857	5,317[6]
Kiribati	—	—	—	1	10	6.4	...	11[13]	5.5[13]	0.82	74.3	6[6]	18[6, 15]	32[6, 15]
Korea, North	10	...	...	...	4,100	4.8	...	1,050	18.7	...	...	...	...	...
Korea, South	25	6,748	171	118	10,255	4.0	126	7,650	5.3	5,158.4	7.7	22,990,368[5]	335,074[5]	3,591
Kuwait	7	391	250	14	750	2.4	10	580	3.1	243.0	6.9	...	...	5,862
Laos	2	12	3	4	225	17.9	...	30	134.2	4.3	920.9		619[7]	22[7]
Lebanon	39	603	228	10	1,500	1.8	5	450	5.9	150.4[4]	17.5[4]	...	...	...
Lesotho	4	47	33	4	42	34.9	...	...	...	5.9[1]	331.3[1]	...	...	...
Liberia	2	...	...	9	760	2.8	...	25	86.4	7.7[4]	262.9[4]	...	...	...
Libya	1	40	12	20	166	21.0	13	171	20.4	102.0[4]	31.6[4]	...	...	...
Liechtenstein	2	15	558	...	8.1[4]	3.3[4]	...	7.6[4]	3.4[4]	22.2	1.2	7,266	12,727[6]	5,242[6]
Luxembourg	5	130	358	7	227	1.6	3	91.2	4.0	232.0	1.6		127,393	62,779[6]
Macau	10	...	...	5	80	3.9	...	59[14]	4.8[14]	23.2	13.1	...	...	9,130[6, 15]
Madagascar	6	55	6	21	1,100	8.9	14	15	649	38.2[4]	241.2[4]		46,000[1]	85[1]
Malawi	2	31	5	10	550	12.4	...	...	...	36.8[18]	185.8[18]	...	...	1,723[15]
Malaysia	42	...	...	82	1,660	9.2	38	1,164.4	13.1	836.6	17.8	...	...	...
Maldives	2	1	6	3	12	14.4	2	1.5	115.5	1.5[4]	105.4[4]		3,192[14]	15[14]
Mali	2	...	...	14	110	70.1	...	...	...	9.5	788.7	...	90	97
Malta	5	...	...	3	150	2.2	4	90	3.7	98.1	3.3	117,491	...	1,111
Martinique	1	32	99	6	46	7.2	8	42.5	7.8	83.6	3.9		237,138[5]	
Mauritania	1	...	...	4	95	17.1	...	0.5	3,246	4.4	362.6	6,722[5]	153[6]	34[6]
Mauritius	7	67	68	3	118	8.5	...	87.5	11.5	47.2	21.0		60,059[15]	1,468[6, 15]
Mayotte	—	—	—	...	6	9.4	...	...	...	0.45	122.4	...	...	...
Mexico	374	...	...	680	22,000	3.5	115	7,550	10.2	5,845.4	12.8	10,888,813	529,827	32,203
Monaco	2	11	408	12	9.6	2.9	5	17.2	1.6	31.0	0.9		11,800[5]	151,000[5]
Mongolia	2	177	100	...	175	10.6	...	57	32.6	42.9	42.0	...	...	...
Montserrat	—	—	—	3	4	2.9	...	1.1	10.7	2.7	4.3		2,723	509[6]
Morocco	8	...	...	36	2,500	9.1	20	1,033.0	22.1	265.7	83.2	...	...	...
Mozambique	3	46	4	39	280	48.9	...	5	2,737	57.4	232.0	54,711	2,635	239
Nauru	—	—	—	1	4	2.0	...	...	...	1.6[4]	5.0[4]	1,304[14]	...	130[14]
Nepal	51	...	...	7	310	52.1	...	...	...	17.4	904.6		3,291[6, 15]	509[6, 15]
Netherlands, The	82	4,610	322	39	4,750	3.0	26	4,453.8	3.2	8,023.0	1.8	2,949,600	2,279,900	98,037
Netherlands Antilles	6	49	208	16	160	1.5	...	57	4.3	65.2	3.7	681,113[6]	8,848[6]	11,671[6]
New Caledonia	2	23	158	3	80	1.8	20	31	4.5	32.6	4.5	13,855	66	408
New Zealand	31	1,025	325	65	2,785	1.2	...	943.5	3.4	1,939.5	1.7	...	110,162	3,653
Nicaragua	3	147	50	87	200	14.7	...	140	21.0	51.2[18]	57.5[18]		175,605[1, 5]	7,860[1, 6]
Niger	1	5	1	19	160	38.0	...	11	553	9.8	604.9		57,366[5]	1,695[6]
Nigeria	15	510	6	111	5,800	16.2	41	460	203.6	708.4	129.0	...	...	2,265
Niue	—	—	—	1	0.9	3.2	...	...	...	0.38	7.9	...	...	...
Norfolk Island	—	—	—	1	1.2	1.8	...	0.4	5.3	0.99	2.1	...	...	26
Norway	85	1,986	483	764	1,500	2.8	1,389	1,326.0	3.1	2,203.6	1.9		4,621,850[5]	117,427[6]
Oman	2	16	17	6	800	1.3	...	46	21.9	31.4	31.2		126,640[5]	4,534[6]
Pacific Is., Trust Terr. of the	—	—	—	11	25.9	5.6	5	5.95	24.5	9.2[4]	15.1[4]	...	...	...
Pakistan	109	1,580	18	28	5,200	18.8	18	1,005	97.2	405.0	234.0		117,240	970
Panama	5	124	61	97	295	7.2	12	240	8.9	202.6	10.3	545,906[15]	637,841[15]	3,382[15]
Papua New Guinea	1	29	9	26	220	14.8	...	...	...	50.5	63.1	35,506[15]	19,013[15]	2,655[15]
Paraguay	5	158	51	56	200	16.4	...	82	40.0	78.0	39.9	174,943[15]	16,849[15]	755[15]
Peru	68	...	...	189	2,225	8.6	...	875	21.9	519.7	36.0	298,559[15]	16,399[15]	506[15]
Philippines	12	974	19	295	2,190	24.4	43	1,000	53.4	658.4	79.1		15,647	3,528
Pitcairn Island	—	—	—	—	...	...	...	...	...	0.02[4]	2.2[4]	...	...	...
Poland	42	7,902	218	...	9,049	4.1	118	8,544	4.3	3,647.6	10.0		893,201	665

post offices, 1983			telegraph, 1983			telex, 1983				country
num-ber	per-sons per office	pieces of mail handled ('000)	total traffic ('000)	na-tional traffic ('000)	inter-national outgoing traffic ('000)	sub-scriber lines	traffic ('000 minutes)			
							total	national	international outgoing	
17,357[26]	3,202[26]	14,687,400[26]	8,422[4]	6,690[4]	1,732[4]	95,383[4]	371,841[4]	249,218[4]	122,623[4]	France
...	...	...	15[4]	13[4]	2[4]	175[4]	422[4]	341[4]	81[4]	French Guiana
89	1,865	11,862	108	74	24	164	421	7	414	French Polynesia
...	...	13,435[3]	272	146	126	640	2,721	876	1,845	Gabon
...	...	...	28[14]	5[14]	23[14]	67[1]	...	...	100[1]	Gambia, The
...	...	...	...	...	...	...	...	...	...	Gaza Strip
11,956	1,396	1,448,220	12,645	10,487	2,158	15,957	—262,087[5]—		...	Germany, East
18,282	3,359	14,898,389	5,990	3,727	2,263	152,826	2,100,677	1,912,169	188,508	Germany, West
237[3]	41,645[3]	103,900[3]	1,760[14]	1,630[14]	130[14]	172[14]	...	...	298[14]	Ghana
3	9,666	3,146	14	5	9	155	333	5	328	Gibraltar
...	...	439,174[3]	3,438	3,153	285	15,178	48,540	29,061	19,479	Greece
...	...	...	...	...	...	...	...	...	...	Greenland
51[3]	2,157[3]	...	...	...	14	44	...	...	108	Grenada
44[3]	7,500[3]	...	50[4]	46[4]	4[4]	427[4]	894[4]	751[4]	143[4]	Guadeloupe
...	...	...	...	...	...	...	...	...	...	Guam
...	...	54,301[24]	...	...	...	...	...	...	...	Guatemala
21	2,666	18,510[8,9,10]	2	1	1	244	...	...	...	Guernsey
...	...	30,809[7]	50	21	29	195	...	...	415	Guinea
...	...	...	...	...	...	...	...	...	...	Guinea-Bissau
129	6,165	23,356	237[24]	149[24]	88[24]	64[24]	197[24]	19[24]	178[24]	Guyana
132[3]	33,106[3]	1,046,472[7]	...	...	...	...	...	...	...	Haiti
508[3]	7,264[3]	60,689[3]	836	815	21	1,092	...	...	848	Honduras
137	39,124	489,184	1,198	9	1,189	20,868	60,134	23,739	36,395	Hong Kong
3,214	3,322	1,697,921	11,861	11,422	439	9,761	...	69,746	8,595	Hungary
150	1,586	38,823	587	566	21	320	...	...	1,048	Iceland
142,296	4,815	10,963,596	60,552	58,307	2,245	21,502	...	192,264[5]	17,039	India
12,978	12,115	350,572	7,281[4]	7,142[4]	139[4]	8,105[4]	...	440,683[4,5]	3,366[4,12]	Indonesia
3,624	11,608	232,286[10]	26,805[18]	26,726[18]	80[18]	3,125	...	...	4,339	Iran
288	48,995	193,996	...	844[4]	...	1,648	5,675	319	5,356	Iraq
2,096[3]	1,662[3]	482,153[7,10]	298	232	66	7,000	18,305	6,407	11,898	Ireland
37	1,748	20,467	...	405	284[1]	4,250	...	22,100[5]	5,850	Isle of Man
615[3]	5,870[3]	448,900[7]	...	...	...	...	...	...	...	Israel
14,204	3,993	6,802,378	24,875[27]	23,353[27]	1,522[27]	55,746[27]	278,338[27]	171,031[27]	107,307[27]	Italy
342	26,023	77,383	581[2]	508[2]	73[2]	1,181[1]	...	...	3,149[1]	Ivory Coast
318[4]	7,063[4]	100,409[4]	772[14]	659[14]	113[14]	312[1]	...	...	630[1]	Jamaica
23,368	5,113	16,230,861	44,696	43,306	1,390	57,000	...	111,103[4]	59,053	Japan
24	3,166	34,031	...	...	...	401	661[2]	460[2]	201[2]	Jersey
738	3,380	91,241	...	...	...	...	...	...	...	Jordan
...	...	10,320[21]	...	...	...	...	...	...	...	Kampuchea
756	24,833	214,761[8,9,10]	...	1,034	3,452[28]	1,750	...	...	3,065	Kenya
5[3]	10,800[3]	374[25,29]	34	27	7	21	44	35	9	Kiribati
...	...	...	...	...	...	...	...	...	...	Korea, North
2,180[13]	18,470[13]	1,103,340[17]	10,443	10,289	154	8,000	10,974	3,079	7,895	Korea, South
50	30,320	151,195[8,9,10]	621	86	535	3,692	12,513	3,324	9,189	Kuwait
...	...	4,496[3]	22[7]	15[7]	7[7]	15[2]	...	...	40[2]	Laos
...	...	...	...	...	...	...	...	...	...	Lebanon
130	10,707	...	...	...	...	138[1]	...	...	35[1]	Lesotho
38	54,078	6,416[17]	...	...	...	...	...	...	...	Liberia
315	10,609	102,121	...	...	...	...	...	...	...	Libya
12	2,209	13,712[17]	30	30	30	30	30	30	30	Liechtenstein
105	3,483	128,404	46[4]	13[4]	33[4]	1,952[4]	9,035[4]	1,789[4]	7,246[4]	Luxembourg
5	70,000	7,924[8]	...	...	36	391	495	34	461	Macau
8,590	1,185	45,033	448[1]	403[1]	45[1]	320[1]	696[1]	162[1]	534[1]	Madagascar
245	25,579	79,959	...	150[3]	1,280[14]	412	...	...	646	Malawi
4,957	2,994	842,149	1,093	820	273	7,980	...	...	9,201[4]	Malaysia
23	6,210	...	29[14]	22[14]	7[14]	75[1]	...	...	53[1]	Maldives
119	53,738	5,466	...	...	...	...	...	...	...	Mali
16[3]	22,500[3]	37,366[3]	75	37	38	747	2,038	175	1,863	Malta
44[3]	7,273[3]	...	49[4]	45[4]	4[4]	371[4]	868[4]	721[4]	147[4]	Martinique
...	...	3,035[3]	42	28	14	214	...	3,560[5]	459	Mauritania
105	9,571	27,130	...	51[1]	46	310	861	61	800	Mauritius
...	...	...	...	...	...	...	...	...	...	Mayotte
13,252[3]	5,087[3]	1,605,316[24]	42,083	41,794	289	23,055	...	171,343[1]	12,715	Mexico
...	...	...	16	8	8	597	...	...	4,254	Monaco
382[3]	3,900[3]	...	...	...	...	...	...	...	...	Mongolia
10[3]	1,000[3]	1,283[7]	4	—	4	26	25	—	25	Montserrat
1,031	19,805	215,170	992	843	149	5,061	3,472[12]	1,910[12]	1,562[12]	Morocco
608	22,989	15,781	...	117[14]	45[4]	558[4]	...	...	1,141[4]	Mozambique
...	...	...	...	...	7[14]	10[14]	...	...	27[14]	Nauru
...	...	...	448	404	83	186	...	...	360	Nepal
2,806	5,129	4,696,500	879	485	394	36,600	...	322,222[5]	82,957	Netherlands, The
...	...	18,733[7]	...	...	978	783	1,784	335	1,450	Netherlands Antilles
269	537	20,397	31	9	23	160	420	16	404	New Caledonia
1,277	2,483	576,010[8,9,10,17]	2,624	2,068	556	4,944	16,932	9,148	7,784	New Zealand
...	...	35,890[21]	25,760[1,28]	4,230[1,28]	1,530[1,28]	391[1]	974[1]	225[1]	749[1]	Nicaragua
159	37,735	5,704	323[1]	278[1]	45[1]	278[4]	...	...	567[4]	Niger
3,167	28,860	1,176,232[8,10]	...	...	...	...	...	...	...	Nigeria
...	...	...	...	...	...	...	...	...	...	Niue
1	2,000	877	...	...	...	...	...	...	...	Norfolk Island
2,794	1,479	1,483,232	584	453	132	9,195	36,034	17,187	18,847	Norway
87	17,241	37,824[8,10]	181	10	171	951	3,807	1,066	2,741	Oman
6[3]	...	...	...	...	...	...	...	...	...	Pacific Is., Trust Terr. of the
11,528	7,652	759,633[17]	5,150	2,650	2,500	3,530	...	30[4,12]	1,810[4]	Pakistan
171	10,671	24,026	620	587	33	1,523	...	...	2,597	Panama
114	29,236	35,521	...	40[28]	27	1,119	3,388	1,762	1,626	Papua New Guinea
400	7,582	5,129	275	239	36	693	...	...	989	Paraguay
2,198	7,749	64,574[9,10]	13,536	13,496	40	2,964	...	84,479[5]	4,818	Peru
2,038[3]	24,303[3]	...	15,732	15,445	287	10,494	14,550	5,211	9,339	Philippines
1	53	...	...	...	...	...	...	...	...	Pitcairn Island
...	...	1,812,347	16,088	15,288	800	27,858	...	...	9,050	Poland

Communications (continued)

country	daily newspapers (latest)			radio, 1984			television, 1984			telephone, 1983		traffic, 1982 ('000 calls)		
	number	total circulation ('000)	circulation per 1,000 population	transmitters (latest)	receivers (all types) ('000)	persons per receiver	transmitters (latest)	receivers (all types) ('000)	persons per receiver	receivers ('000)	persons per receiver	local	long-distance	international
Portugal	22	493	50	80	2,420	4.1	...	1,574	6.3	1,566.9	6.3	1,795,448[5]	2,407,819[5]	649,424[5]
Puerto Rico	4	549	139	90	2,000	1.6	10	815	4.0	693.8	4.7	1,135,406	68,538	1,375
Qatar	3	30	116	11	75	3.9	3	110	2.6	79.6	3.5	...	...	19,992[6]
Réunion	2	51	99	25	120	4.5	...	87	6.2	85.9	6.1	—206,276[5]—		
Romania	36	4,217	186	71	3,223.2	7.0	344	3,900	5.8	2,027.0[1]	11.0[1]	...	...	...
Rwanda	1	0.3	0.1	8	175	33.7	...	...	...	6.6	863.9	7,037	26[1,6]	21[1,6]
St. Christopher and Nevis	2	9	200	2	21	2.1	...	4.5	9.8	2.8	16.1	...	...	76[1]
St. Helena and Ascension	—	—	—	2	3.05	2.3	...	...	...	0.7[4]	6.7[4]	...	...	130
St. Lucia	1	4	33	4	90	1.4	...	...	...	9.6	13.1	...	...	585
St. Pierre and Miquelon	—	—	—	4	1.5	4.0	3	2.95	2.0	3.6	1.7	—1,245[5]—		
St. Vincent and the Grenadines	—	—	—	1	35	3.0	...	...	...	6.1	16.8	—5,980[14]—		120[1]
San Marino	—	—	—	—	8[2]	2.6[2]	...	5[1]	4.3[1]	9.6	2.3	4,048	1,797	...
São Tomé and Príncipe	—	—	—	5	25	4.2	...	...	...	2.2	46.3	1,673[15]	139[15]	13[15]
Saudi Arabia	8	203	24	12	2,800	3.9	6	2,500	4.3	1,274.8	8.2	399,751	124,049	19,297
Senegal	1	45	8	11	321	19.8	1	51	124.5	40.2[2]	141.5[2]	...	...	6,372[14]
Seychelles	1	4	63	1	18.5	3.5	...	0.65	99.6	8.3	7.8	—930—		329[6]
Sierra Leone	1	10	3	3	100	34.9	2	21.7	160.8	16.0[4]	207.3[4]	...	...	540[1,6]
Singapore	12	706	286	21	104.7	24.2	6	471.5	5.4	870.8	2.9	4,013,287	13,321	7,091
Solomon Islands	—	—	—	3	25	10.3	...	...	...	3.0	83.5	...	...	...
Somalia	2	...	...	4	95	59.6	...	...	...	4.8[1]	1,086.4[1]	...	...	...
South Africa	21[31]	1,182[31]	46[31]	...	8,300[31]	3.9[31]	...	2,100[31]	15.3[31]	3,471.5	7.5	—10,267,402[5]—		10,710
Bophuthatswana	[31]	[31]	[31]		[31]	[31]		[31]	[31]	17.0	85.0		716	...
Ciskei	[31]	[31]	[31]		[31]	[31]		[31]	[31]	5.5	133.8	4,344[5]	1,281	...
Transkei	[31]	[31]	[31]		[31]	[31]		[31]	[31]	...	...	...	...	...
Venda	[31]	[31]	[31]		[31]	[31]		[31]	[31]	...	...	...	...	...
South West Africa/Namibia	3	20	19	13	30	35.8	...	15	71.6	62.8	16.7	...	29,146	1,017[6]
Spain	104	2,978	79	442	11,012	3.5	60	10,096	3.8	12,820.2	3.0	...	2,231,021	65,260
Sri Lanka	24	1,681	111	40	3,000	5.3	1	51	310.8	105.8	145.8	2,580[5]	1,020[5]	322
Sudan, The	3	140	7	8	1,450	16.3	3	111	213.0	68.8	318.6	122,460	999	1,654[6]
Suriname	5	...	...	16	187	2.0	...	43	8.7	27.5[18]	13.6[18]	—73,036[5,18]—		1,381[5,18]
Swaziland	1	10	16	7	85	7.5	...	7	91.1	7.5	82.7	39	262	52
Sweden	114	4,363	524	336	3,327.0	2.5	438	3,236.0	2.6	7,410.0	1.1	—20,606,870[5]—		4,275,170[5]
Switzerland	90	2,465	381	215	2,424.3	2.7	825	2,119.8	3.0	4,954.8	1.3	1,285,336	1,057,811	572,088[6]
Syria	9	114	12	9	1,800	5.5	...	500	19.9	468.9	20.5	547,815	13,892	1,720
Taiwan	31	1,750	110	...	6,000	3.1	...	5,235	3.6	4,356.8	4.3	8,665,315	7,987	30,278[6]
Tanzania	3	208	11	19	2,000	10.5	...	10	2,002	99.9	204.0	6,850	3,244	496
Thailand	69	2,580	53	217	7,200	7.0	...	3,000	16.7	576.4	85.4	917,075	41,136	1,413
Togo	3	...	...	11	190	15.3	4	8.5	342.0	11.1	254.7	4,572[5]	142	95[1]
Tokelau	—	—	—	...	...	...	...	...	...	0.003[4]	525.0[4]	...	...	...
Tonga	—	—	—	1	65	1.6	...	...	...	3.5	29.5	10,705[15]	47[15]	146[15]
Trinidad and Tobago	4	168	140	5	375	3.1	6	250	4.7	86.9	13.2	2,700[15]	8,200[15]	550[15]
Tunisia	5	272	40	12	1,150	6.1	10	400	17.5	218.8	31.5	—450,935[5]—		349,037[5]
Turkey	1,115[32]	3,880[32]	89[32]	39	4,310	11.2	153	4,929.7	9.8	2,664.8	17.7	—4,424,601[5,15]—		41,355[6,15]
Turks and Caicos Islands	—	—	—	1	...	...	...	...	...	1.4[18]	5.7[18]	...	...	376[6,15]
Tuvalu				...	7.5[15]	1.1[15]	...	1.1[15]	7.6[15]	0.12[18]	70.6[18]	...	...	...
Uganda	1	25	2	13	280	51.1	...	76	188.4	52.7	264.1	...	...	168
U.S.S.R.	722	85,108	314	...	160,000	1.7	2,882	80,000	3.4	26,667.0	10.2	...	1,454,400	2,130
United Arab Emirates	9	...	...	17	110	11.1	10	110	11.1	319.2	3.7	...	141,403[6,15]	89,397[6,15]
United Kingdom	113	23,472	421	487	41,000	1.4	1,643	18,869.8	3.0	28,733.0	2.0	17,891,000	3,620,000	149,000
United States	1,710	62,415	269	8,359	478,000	0.5	972	141,732	1.7	161,169.8	1.5	297,694,793	36,531,644	237,423
Uruguay	23	555	188	94	1,660	1.8	21	440	6.8	307.6	9.6	586,060	37,896	3,288
Vanuatu	1	1	9	4	15.5	8.8	...	...	...	3.0	43.7	2,200[5]	...	66
Venezuela	69	2,383	176	210	5,250	3.2	42	2,002	8.4	1,021.1	16.1	...	...	69,461[6]
Vietnam	4	...	...	39	6,000	9.7	...	2,250	25.8	102.6[18]	566.2[18]	—7,528[1]—		41[15]
Virgin Islands (U.S.)	3	17	145	9	85	1.2	3	30	3.5	48.2	2.2	96,371	3,670	91
Wallis and Futuna	—	—	—	...	...	...	...	...	...	0.22	56.0	...	15[6,15]	81[6,15]
West Bank	...	...	...	...	...	...	...	...	...	...	...	...	...	...
Western Sahara	—	—	—	...	...	...	...	...	...	1.0[4]	140.0[4]	...	...	...
Western Samoa	—	—	—	6	70[15]	2.3[15]	...	2.5[15]	63.6[15]	7.5	21.2	...	78	208
Yemen (Aden)	3	...	...	6	111	18.6	...	38	54.4	23.4	85.9	40	18	71
Yemen (Şan'ā')	...	...	...	6	110	58.1	...	27	236.5	90.4[4]	67.3[4]	...	...	...
Yugoslavia	27	2,282	103	738	5,849.3	3.9	941	4,650.4	5.0	2,541.5	9.0	—20,788,000[5,15]—		
Zaire	5	45	1.5	22	500	64.2	...	12.5	2,567	31.2	997.3	115	144	228
Zambia	2	113	18	16	1,000	6.4	5	240	26.9	67.2	92.7	...	662	426
Zimbabwe	2	155	21	...	200	39.7	...	99	80.1	236.2	32.8	247,000[5]	22,596	2,060

post offices, 1983			telegraph, 1983			telex, 1983	traffic ('000 minutes)			country
num-ber	per-sons per office	pieces of mail handled ('000)	total traffic ('000)	na-tional traffic ('000)	inter-national outgoing traffic ('000)	sub-scriber lines	total	national	international outgoing	
9,571	1,041	476,514	1,469	1,308	161	14,412	57,024	40,066	16,958	Portugal
124[3]	24,677[3]	...	...	...	...	...	...	...	...	Puerto Rico
25	10,000	30,449	149	8	141	1,040	2,585	720	1,865	Qatar
50[3]	10,340[3]	...	37[4]	30[4]	7[4]	317[4]	789[4]	585[4]	204[4]	Réunion
5,046[3]	4,429[3]	795,199[7]	5,393[14]	5,150[14]	243[14]	6,750[1]	...	...	3,683[1]	Romania
...	...	15,964[3]	35[1]	24[1]	11[1]	79[1]	625[1]	522[1]	103[1]	Rwanda
9[3]	5,000	6,381[3]	16[4]	—	16[4]	34[1]	...	...	47[1]	St. Christopher and Nevis
8	750	155	5[4]	—	5[4]	7[4]	24[4,12]	...	14[4,12]	St. Helena and Ascension
...	...	3,679[7]	19[4]	—	19[4]	76[2]	...	...	105[2]	St. Lucia
...	...	1,714[7,10]	2[4]	1[4]	1[4]	33[4]	42[4]	29[4]	13[4]	St. Pierre and Miquelon
48[3]	2,708[3]	...	14[4]	—	14[4]	53[1]	...	...	44[1]	St. Vincent and the Grenadines
8	2,750	...	27	27	27	27	27	27	27	San Marino
57	1,684	92	3	—	3	35	54	—	53	São Tomé and Principe
437	16,048	495,110	3,219[24]	2,243[24]	976[24]	16,254	...	6,300[12]	23,203	Saudi Arabia
530	11,118	44,391	225[14]	147[14]	78[14]	779	...	...	1,782	Senegal
...	...	1,618[25]	...	—	11	143	251	63	189	Seychelles
113	24,661	27,262	...	20[2]	84[1]	224[1]	373[1]	37[1]	335[1]	Sierra Leone
134	18,780	313,443	377	7	371	14,349	50,111	19,968	30,143	Singapore
99	2,121	5,595	...	...	...	...	...	...	...	Solomon Islands
...	...	...	...	...	...	...	...	...	...	Somalia
2,227[3,31]	13,529[3,31]	1,678,751[3,31]	8,328	8,017	310	27,585	...	261,198[5]	14,829	South Africa
[31]	[31]	[31]								Bophuthatswana
[31]	[31]	[31]	...	...	...	...	...	...	...	Ciskei
[31]	[31]	[31]	...	...	...	...	...	...	...	Transkei
[31]	[31]	[31]	...	...	...	...	...	...	...	Venda
81[3]	12,914[3]	...								South West Africa/Namibia
12,652	3,019	4,350,027	7,329	6,907	422	31,443	94,823	55,352	39,471	Spain
3,618	4,245	834,257	2,095[4]	1,870[4]	225[4]	968	1,572[12]	201[12]	1,371[12]	Sri Lanka
776	26,500	72,095	1,453[7]	1,263[7]	190[7]	416[7]	...	...	1,038[7]	Sudan, The
...	...	...	59	4	56	195	432	48	384	Suriname
72	8,405	17,267	51[1]	45[1]	6[1]	242[1]	1,006[1]	359[1]	647[1]	Swaziland
2,034	4,097	3,011,999[8,10]	298	119	178	16,156	...	...	30,617	Sweden
3,813	1,699	4,124,985	1,568[30]	904[30]	664[30]	35,953[30]	139,426[30]	72,385[30]	67,041[30]	Switzerland
516	18,810	39,914	289	151	138	1,803	...	...	1,903	Syria
11,827[3]	1,533[3]	...								Taiwan
643	31,679	148,696	794	717	78	1,650	...	...	1,253	Tanzania
4,168	11,879	457,307	8,298	8,160	138	3,910	9,394	3,242	6,152	Thailand
388	6,971	...	50	18	32	285	...	...	524	Togo
...	...	...	...	...	...	...	...	...	...	Tokelau
...	...	1,063[11,21]	97	77	20	61	35	1	34	Tonga
229	5,126	27,230	...	217[4]	274[3]	267	...	...	1,053	Trinidad and Tobago
597	11,557	194,934	620	412	208	2,111	5,239	1,522	3,717	Tunisia
48,878	967	851,670	1,187	947	240	8,048	...	51,837[33]	10,946	Turkey
...	...	...	1	—	1	55	...	...	65	Turks and Caicos Islands
...	...	2,313[7]	...	...	...	...	...	...	...	Tuvalu
...	...	28,275[23]	57	52	5	419	262[12]	114[12]	148[12]	Uganda
90,723[3]	2,951[3]	5,925,000[3]	541,012[4]	540,110[4]	902[4]	1,446[4]	...	...	8,458[4]	U.S.S.R.
49	25,008	147,973	647	54	593	6,099	20,123	7,325	12,797	United Arab Emirates
22,058[13]	2,556[13]	12,541,390	1,950	—	1,950	92,600	202,007[12]	104,708[12]	97,399[12]	United Kingdom
39,445	5,743	116,312,705[17]	50,983[4]	45,668[4]	5,315[4]	168,347	...	...	188,699	United States
1,277[3]	2,323[3]	35,356[7]	1,409	1,354	55	1,332	2,123	164	1,959	Uruguay
6	20,833	3,000	...	...	8	70	...	...	199	Vanuatu
809[3]	7,215[3]	347,500[22]	5,148[24]	4,570[24]	578[24]	10,356	...	...	7,970	Venezuela
...	—	...	...	5[1]	672	...	...	10[1,12]	55[12]	Vietnam
5[3]	23,200[3]	...								Virgin Islands (U.S.)
6	2,065	252	9	2	7	3	...	...	7	Wallis and Futuna
...	...	...	...	...	...	...	...	...	...	West Bank
...	...	...	...	...	...	...	...	...	...	Western Sahara
...	...	14,589[3]	...	...	...	...	...	...	...	Western Samoa
109	19,311	17,526	...	17[4]	...	149[4]	371[4]	4[4]	366[4]	Yemen (Aden)
141	60,687	15,682								Yemen (Şan'ä')
3,729	6,140	836,372	13,088	11,864	1,224	12,000	...	...	13,500	Yugoslavia
362	83,592	...	234[4]	167[4]	67[4]	804[4]	...	...	...	Zaire
232	23,578	69,175	20,340[28]	18,383[28]	1,958[28]	1,379	5,378	3,701	1,677	Zambia
232	32,327	179,720	616	562	55	1,584	72,666[5]	19,324[5]	53,341[5]	Zimbabwe

[1]1981. [2]1980. [3]1978. [4]1982. [5]Number of pulses ('000). [6]Number of minutes ('000). [7]1977. [8]Excludes postcards. [9]Excludes printed matter. [10]Excludes small packets. [11]Foreign received and foreign sent only. [12]Number of calls ('000). [13]Permanent post offices only. [14]1979. [15]1983. [16]1972. [17]Domestic and foreign sent only. [18]1984. [19]Domestic only. [20]Telegrams to U.S. are included in national. [21]1973. [22]1974. [23]1975. [24]1976. [25]1971. [26]Includes overseas departments. [27]Italy includes San Marino. [28]Number of words ('000). [29]Includes Tuvalu. [30]Switzerland includes Liechtenstein. [31]South Africa includes Bophuthatswana, Ciskei, Transkei, and Venda. [32]Includes non-daily newspapers. [33]Number of metred units ('000).

Trade: external

The following table presents comparative data on the import and export trade of all the countries of the world. The table analyzes data for both imports and exports in two ways: (1) into several major commodity groups defined in accordance with the United Nations system called the Standard International Trade Classification (SITC) and (2) by direction of trade for each country with major world trading blocs and partners. For purposes of this table, several SITC categories have been aggregated so as to accommodate the commodity groupings indicated by the column headings. These groupings are defined by the use of SITC code numbers placed beneath the column headings. The single digit numbers represent broad SITC categories; the double digit numbers represent subcategories of the single digit categories (27 is a subcategory of 2), the three digit is a subcategory of the double digit (667 is a subcategory of 66). The SITC subdivides these categories to finer degrees of detail, but such distinctions cannot be accommodated here. Where a plus or minus sign is used before one of these SITC numbers, the SITC category or subcategory is being added to or subtracted from the aggregate implied by the total of the preceding sections to form a consistently defined commodity group for all countries. The SITC commodity aggregations used here are listed at the end of this headnote. The full SITC commodity breakdown is presented in the United Nations publication *Standard International Trade Classification Revision 2*.

The SITC was developed by the United Nations through its Statistical Commission as an outgrowth of the need for a standard system of aggregating commodities of external trade to provide international comparability of foreign trade statistics. All member nations of the United Nations are urged to use the SITC system as far as possible in reporting their external trade statistics. The United Nations Statistical Commission has defined external merchandise trade as "all goods whose movement into or out of the customs area of a country compiling the statistics adds to or subtracts from the material resources of the country." Goods passing through the country for transport only are excluded. Statistics in this table refer only to goods and exclude purely financial transactions that are covered in the "Finance" and "National product and accounts" tables.

For purposes of comparability of data, total value of imports and exports is given in this table in U.S. dollars; conversions from foreign currencies are determined according to International Monetary Fund (IMF) average rates for the year for which data are supplied. The commodity categories are given in terms of percentages of the total value of the country's import or export trade (with the exclusions noted above). Value, according to the United Nations Statistical Office, is based on transaction value: for imports, the value at which the goods were purchased by the importer plus the cost of transportation and insurance to the frontier of the importing country (c.i.f. [cost, insurance, and freight] valuation); for exports,

Trade: external

country	year	imports total value U.S.$ (000,000)	food and agricultural raw materials (0 + 1 + 2 − 27 − 28 + 4)	mineral ores and concentrates (27 + 28 + 667)	fuels and other energy (3)	manufactured goods total (5 + 6 − 667 + 7 + 8 + 9)	of which chemicals and related products (5)	of which machinery and transport equipment (7)	of which other (6 − 667 + 8 + 9)	from European Economic Community (EEC)[c]	from United States	from U.S.S.R. and Eastern Europe	from Japan	from all other[d]
			Standard International Trade Classification (SITC) categories (percent)[a, b]			manufactured goods				direction of trade (percent)[a]				
Afghanistan	1982[1]	622.4	16.4	0.5	18.0	65.1	4.5	24.8	35.8	...	1.1	59.7	12.6	26.5
Albania	1980	316.6[2]	...	...	...	...	...	...	...	27.6[2]	2.2[2]	41.0[2]	0.5[2]	28.7[2]
Algeria	1983	10,395.1	24.8	0.5	2.1	72.6	5.9	34.1	32.5	54.6	6.0	4.6	6.0	28.8
American Samoa	1981[3]	115.0	—24.1[4, 5]—		41.3[4]	34.6[4, 6]	1.6[4]	7.2[4]	25.9[4, 6]	...	73.5	...	12.1	14.4
Andorra	1983	233.5[7]	...	...	...	...	...	...	...	...	...	...	...	...
Angola	1979	679.5	—36.9—			63.1	2.9	39.2	21.0	51.3[2]	15.0[2]	...	4.8[2]	28.9[2]
Anguilla	1979	...	...	...	...	...	...	...	...	...	...	...	...	...
Antigua and Barbuda	1978	40.4	35.2	—	1.6	63.2	8.9	23.8	30.5	34.7	34.5	0.5	1.3	29.1
Argentina	1983	4,504.2	9.2	3.5	10.5	76.8	22.9	32.0	21.9	23.8	21.9	1.8	6.8	45.7
Australia	1984[3]	21,814.1	7.9	1.0	9.2	81.9	9.0	38.7	34.2	21.2	21.6	0.3	22.3	34.6
Austria	1984	19,595.9	10.4	2.8	15.1	71.8	10.0	28.0	33.7	60.4	3.5	11.7	3.3	21.2
Bahamas, The	1978	3,149.6	2.2	0.1	92.1	5.6	1.3	1.6	2.7	6.4	6.0	—	0.1	87.5
Bahrain	1983	3,342.1	7.8	0.4	44.6	47.1	4.3	24.3	18.5	22.7	7.0	...	12.7	57.7
Bangladesh	1984[3]	1,710.0	31.9	1.9	9.5	56.7	13.1	19.9	23.7	15.4	11.2	5.3	13.7	54.4
Barbados	1982	549.9	19.0	0.2	16.2	64.6	8.2	28.6	27.8	15.0	38.5	0.3	3.4	42.9
Belgium[8]	1984	55,249.3	15.1	9.1	18.6	57.2	9.9	21.4	25.8	66.8	6.0	4.1	2.1	21.0
Belize	1980	148.2	25.1	0.4	18.4	56.1	6.6	18.9	30.7	23.1	34.7	1.9	5.4	35.0
Benin	1980	331.2	19.0[9]	0.5[9]	9.8[9]	70.6[9]	9.2[9]	26.0[9]	35.4[9]	55.5	4.9	2.0	4.4	33.1
Bermuda	1983	377.3	21.2	0.2	14.3	64.4	7.4	21.2	35.8	14.3	56.3	0.2	4.8	24.4
Bhutan	1983[10]	58.5	...	...	...	...	...	...	...	...	...	...	...	100.0[11]
Bolivia	1983	532.3	—41.1—		0.7	58.2	...	48.4	9.8	16.4	28.1	...	7.3	48.2
Botswana	1982	687.9	16.2	1.7	14.2	67.9	8.2	25.5	34.2	...	1.6	...	0.3	98.0
Brazil	1983	16,783.9	9.6	1.4	55.9	33.2	9.2	16.3	7.7	.12.0	15.6	3.5	3.7	65.3
British Virgin Islands	1982	58.5	28.2	0.4	10.6	60.8	4.3	33.0	23.6	7.8	42.9	—	0.1	49.2
Brunei	1983	725.6	17.3	1.4	1.4	79.9	7.6	38.2	34.0	16.1	19.6	—	19.2	45.1
Bulgaria	1984	12,715.1	—46.9[13]—			44.6[14]	6.1	34.1	4.5[14]	8.1	0.5	76.5	0.6	14.3
Burkina Faso	1983	287.5	27.6	0.8	17.1	54.5	10.0	23.7	20.7	43.6	9.4	0.3	4.3	42.4
Burma	1984[10]	640.7	—19.2—			80.8	...	47.6	...	25.8	...	16.2	33.7	24.3
Burundi	1982	212.9	13.2	2.1	15.3	69.4	7.2	23.6	38.5	45.6	5.4	0.5	7.9	40.6
Cameroon	1982	1,243.2	10.2	2.4	3.7	83.7	13.2	34.8	35.7	65.1	7.6	1.1	6.1	20.1
Canada	1984	73,999.6	8.3	2.5	6.4	82.8	6.1	53.2	23.4	8.6	71.7	0.3	6.0	13.5
Cape Verde	1980	67.8	44.8	—	9.1	46.0	6.6	13.9	25.5	13.9	5.1	0.1	0.4	80.5
Cayman Islands	1981	100.4	21.6	0.2	11.5	66.7	5.1	23.6	37.9	5.3	77.5	—	2.0	15.2
Central African Republic	1980	80.5	21.8	1.7	1.8	74.7	11.8	33.9	29.1	73.5	3.5	0.6	7.2	15.2
Chad	1975	110.0	15.9	0.6	14.2	69.3	16.4	28.8	24.1	58.4	5.7	2.1	1.8	32.0
Chile	1981	6,277.2	13.6	0.9	14.6	70.9	8.5	36.9	25.5	16.8	24.4	0.2	11.7	46.9
China	1984	26,744.3	16.7	1.5[5]	0.5	81.3[6]	15.3	27.1	38.9[6]	11.9	14.8	6.2	31.3	35.9
Christmas Island	...	...	...	...	...	...	...	...	...	...	...	...	...	...
Cocos (Keeling) Islands	...	...	...	...	...	...	...	...	...	...	...	...	...	...
Colombia	1983	4,966.9	13.4	0.8	13.1	72.7	14.4	38.2	20.2	13.9	35.6	2.5	11.1	36.9
Comoros	1976	13.1	—47.1—		13.1	39.8	3.5	17.6	18.8	31.8	—	—	0.5	67.7
Congo	1980	418.2	19.7	0.9	13.9	65.5	10.1	22.5	32.9	63.7	4.4	1.5	3.2	27.2
Cook Islands	1982	20.2	—29.1—		8.4	62.5	6.7	19.1	36.8	5.5[4]	5.0[4]	—[4]	7.6[4]	81.9[4]
Costa Rica	1982	945.2	10.6	0.5	20.0	69.0	20.8	14.6	33.5	9.5	41.0	0.2	4.1	45.2
Cuba	1980	4,708.9	—24.1[15]—		18.1[15]	57.9[15]	4.6[15]	—53.2[15]—		8.0	—	75.1	3.9	13.0
Cyprus	1984	1,357.2	16.5	0.4	18.2	64.9	7.3	26.3	31.3	53.3	5.2	7.9	8.3	25.3
Czechoslovakia	1983	16,324.1	12.0	4.1	30.2	53.6	7.1	31.4	15.1	8.9	0.6	73.1	0.4	16.9
Denmark	1984	16,543.5	15.7	0.7	18.3	65.3	11.2	24.0	30.1	46.1	5.0	4.2	3.9	40.8
Djibouti	1979	97.5	32.8	—	3.7	63.5	4.3	9.2	50.0	64.4	2.4	0.2	7.7	25.4
Dominica	1983	45.1	30.8	0.4	8.3	60.5	12.0	19.0	29.4	23.8	23.1	0.2	7.1	45.8
Dominican Republic	1983	1,279.0	16.6	0.2	36.2	46.9	12.5	16.9	17.5	7.8	36.4	—	4.3	51.4
Ecuador	1982	1,758.4	7.7	0.7	1.6	90.0	19.2	42.9	27.9	18.3	37.4	0.9	13.6	29.9
Egypt	1982	9,077.9	35.4	0.3	4.1	60.2	7.8	29.4	23.0	40.2[16]	16.1[16]	7.7[16]	5.0[16]	30.9[16]
El Salvador	1982	944.8	19.8	0.5	24.6	55.1	19.3	12.0	23.8	10.9	24.7	0.1	2.8	61.6
Equatorial Guinea	1981	43.2	...	...	22.4	...	...	17.4	...	...	...	...	...	100.0[17]

the value at which the goods were sold by the exporter, including the cost of transportation and insurance to bring the goods onto the transporting vehicle at the frontier of the exporting country (f.o.b. [free on board] valuation).

Ideally, the data assembled here should be derived from a single source, thus providing a set of statistics based on a common value system that would permit comparative analysis. It is not possible, however, to gather all such information from a single source; the largest part of the information presented here comes from the United Nations' *Commodity Trade Statistics* (including microfiche format) and the *Yearbook of International Trade Statistics.* These sources, however, do not always provide the most recent data and do not cover some countries listed in this table. Data for such countries as Albania, Botswana, China, Liechtenstein, and many small, nonindependent countries were obtained from other sources. In some cases information was unavailable, as noted.

... Not available.
— None, less than 0.05%, or not applicable.
a. Detail may not add to 100.0 or indicated subtotals because of exclusion of unallocated commodities or because of rounding.
b. SITC category codes:
  0 - food and live animals, chiefly for food.
  1 - beverages and tobacco.

2 - crude materials, inedible, except fuels.
  27 - crude natural fertilizers (organic and inorganic) and nonmetallic minerals (excluding coal, petroleum, and precious stones).
  28 - metalliferous ores and metal scrap.
3 - mineral fuels, lubricants, and related materials (including coal, petroleum, and hydrocarbon products).
4 - animal and vegetable oils, fats, and waxes.
5 - chemicals and related products not specified elsewhere.
6 - manufactured goods classified chiefly by material.
  667 - pearls, precious and semiprecious stones, worked or unworked.
7 - machinery and transport equipment.
8 - miscellaneous manufactured articles.
9 - commodities and transactions not specified elsewhere.
c. EEC of ten countries (Belgium, Denmark, France, West Germany, Greece, Ireland, Italy, Luxembourg, The Netherlands, and the United Kingdom).
d. Percentages in these columns may include value of trade shown as not available (...) in any of the three preceding columns.

exports total value U.S.$ (000,000)	food and agricultural raw materials (0+1+2-27-28+4)	mineral ores and concentrates (27+28+667)	fuels and other energy (3)	manufactured goods total (5+6-667+7+8+9)	of which chemicals and related products (5)	of which machinery and transport equipment (7)	of which other (6-667+8+9)	to EEC[c]	to United States	to U.S.S.R. and Eastern Europe	to Japan	to all other[d]	country
694.3	44.4	—	39.3	16.3	1.7	—	14.6	...	1.4	61.9	0.1	36.6	Afghanistan
342.8[2]	...	...	...	...	...	...	...	22.5[2]	3.6[2]	37.3[2]	—[2]	36.6[2]	Albania
11,158.4	0.3	0.4	98.4	0.9	0.4	—	0.5	59.8	22.7	0.3	3.5	13.7	Algeria
199.1	99.8	—	—	0.2	—	—	0.2	...	99.6	—	0.1	0.3	American Samoa
10.2[7]	...	...	...	...	...	...	...	...	...	...	...	...	Andorra
666.3	14.9	10.7	74.0	0.4	...	...	0.4	19.5[2]	66.3[2]	...	8.2[2]	6.0[2]	Angola
1.6	...	...	...	...	...	...	...	...	10.0	—	...	90.0	Anguilla
12.5	9.4	—	0.3	90.3	4.0	20.1	66.2	7.9	35.1	—	1.8	55.2	Antigua and Barbuda
7,836.1	78.1	0.2	4.5	17.2	4.5	3.4	9.3	21.1	9.9	22.1	4.8	42.1	Argentina
22,453.9	36.1	17.5	21.0	25.4	2.0	5.4	18.0	13.6	10.9	3.4	26.4	45.7	Australia
15,718.1	10.0	1.0	1.5	87.5	9.7	29.9	47.8	53.3	4.1	12.2	1.0	29.4	Austria
3,058.4	0.8	0.3	94.8	4.1	3.6	0.1	0.3	8.8	77.7	—	0.5	13.0	Bahamas, The
3,200.0	0.2	0.1	82.7	17.0	0.2	5.0	11.8	3.6	2.8	...	14.5	79.1	Bahrain
807.1	34.8	—	1.7	63.5	0.7	1.1	61.6	26.0	13.3	4.3	7.7	48.7	Bangladesh
262.8	20.9	—	18.0	61.0	6.8	28.8	25.4	10.2	37.6	—	—	52.2	Barbados
51,701.3	12.6	7.1	7.9	72.3	12.6	21.0	38.8	68.9	6.1	1.8	0.8	22.4	Belgium[8]
82.5	82.2	—	—	17.8	0.4	—	17.4	30.8	61.0	—	0.3	8.0	Belize
39.6	77.2[9]	0.0[9]	4.9[9]	17.9[9]	0.3[9]	5.6[9]	12.1[9]	64.1	0.4	...	10.3	25.2	Benin
22.8	2.0	0.9	0.9	95.8	60.2	11.3	24.2	45.1	24.9	—	0.3	29.8	Bermuda
16.7	...	...	...	...	...	...	...	...	...	...	...	100.0[12]	Bhutan
817.5	...	42.5	51.4	...	...	...	...	16.3	20.8	...	1.9	61.0	Bolivia
456.9	21.7	65.9	0.1	12.3	0.6	2.8	8.9	...	11.9	...	0.1	88.0	Botswana
25,126.8	47.4	8.0	6.3	38.3	5.0	12.1	21.3	27.2	25.9	6.5	6.6	33.7	Brazil
1.2	78.1	2.7	1.5	17.7	0.1	10.2	7.4	4.6	57.4	—	—	38.0	British Virgin Islands
3,385.7	0.1	—	98.9	0.9	—	0.6	0.3	0.7	8.1	—	67.7	23.5	Brunei
12,858.7	22.3	—10.8[13]—		66.9[14]	6.5	47.7	12.7[14]	6.2	0.3	72.4	0.3	20.8	Bulgaria
57.0	89.4	0.1	—	10.5	0.1	4.1	6.3	27.8	0.1	—	4.3	67.8	Burkina Faso
421.5	81.6	14.7	—	3.7	...	...	...	12.3	...	—	6.7	81.1	Burma
87.6	97.5	—	—	2.5	—	—	2.5	32.7	32.0	—	2.7	32.6	Burundi
1,028.9	43.8	—	47.0	9.2	1.3	0.9	7.0	46.1	40.1	0.4	1.2	12.2	Cameroon
86,824.7	19.4	4.7	13.1	62.7	4.8	37.3	20.6	6.1	75.8	2.1	4.8	11.2	Canada
4.2	85.4	9.1	0.3	5.2	1.0	0.6	3.6	11.2	—	—	—	88.8	Cape Verde
0.7	2.1	2.2	—	95.8	94.1	0.5	1.2	—	100.0	—	—	—	Cayman Islands
115.4	71.2	25.0	—	3.8	—	—	3.8	76.6	4.3	0.7	0.1	18.4	Central African Republic
40.0	83.1	0.8	7.9	8.2	0.5	5.4	2.3	6.1	0.3	—	—	93.7	Chad
3,744.8	27.2	17.5	1.8	53.5	2.2	2.6	48.7	33.6	14.4	0.5	10.9	40.5	Chile
25,024.0	21.0	1.6[5]	23.0	54.4[6]	5.2	5.7	43.4[6]	8.7	9.3	5.2	20.6	56.3	China
...	...	...	...	...	...	...	...	...	...	...	...	...	Christmas Island
...	...	...	...	...	...	...	...	...	...	...	...	...	Cocos (Keeling) Islands
3,080.9	65.9	1.2	14.7	18.2	3.4	1.4	13.4	36.5	28.3	3.6	4.4	27.2	Colombia
9.3	64.1	—	5.6	30.3	29.5	—	0.8	71.1	15.2	—	0.1	13.6	Comoros
955.3	—	4.1	89.6	2.7	—	0.2	2.6	54.4	12.7	0.1	0.1	32.7	Congo
3.7	50.5	—	—	49.5	...	...	...	...	1.9	...	2.1	96.0	Cook Islands
876.8	70.6	—	0.9	28.5	7.2	4.2	17.1	25.8	33.7	3.0	0.7	36.8	Costa Rica
5,540.8	89.6	4.6	—	...	...	...	5.8	4.3	—	59.6	2.8	33.3	Cuba
573.9	35.7	1.9	6.3	56.0	3.7	8.6	43.7	27.6	3.4	4.7	0.1	64.3	Cyprus
16,476.6	5.9	0.4	4.8	88.9	6.0	52.0	30.9	9.5	0.3	68.2	0.3	21.6	Czechoslovakia
15,494.5	35.5	0.7	5.2	58.5	8.8	23.0	26.8	42.5	9.6	1.7	2.8	43.5	Denmark
11.4	6.1	—	...	93.9	0.1	1.4	92.5	89.7	—	—	—	10.3	Djibouti
27.5	57.7	0.1	—	42.2	29.8	1.9	10.6	44.1	2.4	—	—	53.5	Dominica
648.3	75.7	0.3	—	24.1	4.0	4.5	15.6	10.4	66.5	6.7	2.3	14.0	Dominican Republic
2,290.8	32.7	—	64.3	3.1	0.3	0.8	2.0	3.8	43.1	1.1	0.7	51.2	Ecuador
3,120.2	21.8	—	66.3	11.9	1.2	—	10.7	38.7[16]	6.6[16]	14.4[16]	2.6[16]	37.7[16]	Egypt
407.6	54.9	0.6	3.1	41.5	6.6	3.0	31.8	19.3	26.4	—	5.3	49.0	El Salvador
13.6	98.7	—	—	1.3	—	—	1.3	...	...	—	...	100.0[18]	Equatorial Guinea

Trade: external (continued)

country	year	imports total value U.S.$ (000,000)	food and agricultural raw materials (0+1+2-27-28+4)	mineral ores and concen-trates (27+28+667)	fuels and other energy (3)	manufactured goods total (5+6-667+7+8+9)	of which chemicals and related products (5)	of which machinery and transport equipment (7)	of which other (6-667+8+9)	from European Economic Community (EEC)[c]	from United States	from U.S.S.R. and Eastern Europe	from Japan	from all other[d]
Ethiopia	1982	784.9	12.9	—	24.6	62.5	10.7	31.6	20.2	37.1	3.9	31.5	9.0	18.5
Faeroe Islands	1984	261.4	11.8	0.7	16.7	70.8	3.4	44.3	23.1	78.2	0.1	—	1.0	20.7
Falkland Islands	1975	3.4	30.9	—	2.6	64.4	5.7	14.4	44.3	88.5	—	0.1	3.3	8.1
Fiji	1983	483.9	18.7	0.3	23.3	57.7	7.9	18.9	30.9	8.1	3.9	0.1	16.8	71.1
Finland	1984	12,442.4	10.1	2.6	25.0	62.3	9.5	29.7	23.1	35.6	5.0	26.2	5.6	27.7
France[19]	1984	103,734.1	14.7	1.8	24.2	59.3	9.6	23.6	26.1	50.3	7.7	3.7	2.6	35.6
French Guiana	1984	248.8	25.3	0.1	14.9	59.8	5.1	27.4	27.3	66.4	7.3	0.2	4.7	21.3
French Polynesia	1983	538.3	21.4	0.3	11.9	66.3	5.3	30.1	30.9	57.7	15.8	0.1	4.3	22.1
Gabon	1983	685.6	18.5	1.0	1.8	78.8	7.5	38.5	32.7	72.0	11.0	0.4	7.4	9.2
Gambia, The	1983[3]	115.4	—34.5[5]—		12.2	53.3[6]	6.9	14.4	32.0[6]	50.3[4]	2.0[4]	4.6[4]	3.4[4]	39.7[4]
Gaza Strip	1983	329.5	13.5	...	...	...	...	...	...	...	...	...	...	100.0[20]
Germany, East	1983	21,524.6	—57.4—			42.6	...	29.9	...	15.9[22]	0.6[22]	61.1[22]	1.5[22]	20.9[22]
Germany, West[23]	1984	152,872.1	15.9	2.7	20.4	60.9	8.6	21.9	30.5	48.0	7.2	5.4	4.2	35.2
Ghana	1980	1,128.6	11.4	0.6	26.7	61.4	15.6	29.7	16.1	41.2	12.1	1.4	3.8	41.6
Gibraltar	1984	88.3	—27.1—		32.0	40.9	...	...	...	69.6[24]	4.4[24]	...	7.3[24]	18.7[24]
Greece	1984	9,628.6	17.0	1.2	27.3	54.5	8.9	25.7	19.9	47.0	2.9	8.5	...	33.9
Greenland	1984	276.0	21.4	0.4	19.5	58.7	3.7	24.0	31.0	85.5	4.9	—	0.6	9.0
Grenada	1980	50.2	36.8	—	12.8	50.4	11.0	14.0	25.5	23.0	20.0	0.6	5.3	51.1
Guadeloupe	1984	598.6	23.9	0.2	17.2	58.7	8.0	22.3	28.4	69.2	2.9	0.2	2.6	25.0
Guam	1979	445.8	17.3	0.1	49.5	33.1	2.2	11.8	19.0	...	32.4	...	7.0	60.6
Guatemala	1981	2,009.3	7.8	0.4	37.8	54.0	15.9	16.0	22.1	10.7	27.4	0.2	5.6	56.1
Guernsey[25]	...													
Guinea	1980	204.4	—10.0—		30.3	59.7	3.0	39.8	16.9	63.8[2]	10.2[2]	5.8[2]	1.7[2]	18.5[2]
Guinea-Bissau	1980	55.5	20.1	2.2	6.2	71.5	5.6	36.4	29.5	25.6	0.5	7.6	0.5	65.8
Guyana	1980	395.9	15.3	0.5	27.6	56.7	7.6	25.9	23.2	28.3	25.3	1.1	2.1	43.1
Haiti	1979[26]	266.1	26.2	0.3	13.0	60.5	9.0	19.9	31.6	13.5	46.1	0.8	8.0	31.7
Honduras	1982	689.9	10.6	0.3	21.8	67.3	18.3	20.3	28.7	10.7	39.6	0.3	6.6	42.8
Hong Kong	1984	28,585.6	14.7	2.4	5.5	77.5	6.9	25.8	44.7	10.9	10.9	0.4	23.5	54.2
Hungary	1983	8,487.6	12.5	1.8[5]	22.8	62.9[6]	13.2	27.2	22.5[6]	19.8	2.6	48.2	1.2	28.1
Iceland	1983	815.4	14.4	5.0	16.3	64.4	7.8	24.2	32.4	47.3[27]	6.8[27]	11.0[27]	4.6[27]	30.3[27]
India	1982[10]	15,239.7	13.1	6.2	38.4	42.3	9.7	14.6	18.0	22.5	10.4	11.1	6.5	49.5
Indonesia	1983	16,351.8	10.4	0.8	25.4	63.5	11.7	34.8	17.0	13.7	15.5	0.6	23.2	47.1
Iran	1977	14,447.6	15.4	0.4	—	83.9	7.2	44.3	32.5	43.3	16.2	5.4	16.1	19.0
Iraq	1978	4,212.6	13.8	0.4	—	85.5	4.7	53.6	27.1	35.8	10.1	8.6	20.9	24.6
Ireland	1984	9,661.9	14.2	1.2	12.4	72.2	11.6	31.2	29.5	64.7	16.5	1.5	3.4	14.0
Isle of Man[25]	...													
Israel	1983	8,587.6	12.1	10.9	17.4	59.5	6.7	31.4	21.4	40.5	19.2	0.6	3.2	36.5
Italy[28]	1984	84,324.3	19.3	2.7	27.6	50.4	9.3	19.1	22.0	43.3	6.1	7.2	1.6	41.8
Ivory Coast	1983	1,813.5	21.1	0.7	18.6	59.6	10.4	24.7	24.5	51.1	4.0	0.8	4.5	39.6
Jamaica	1984	1,183.2	21.7	0.3	30.8	47.3	9.7	16.0	21.5	10.1	45.1	0.4	2.9	41.5
Japan	1984	136,503.0	20.9	6.2	44.3	28.6	5.9	7.5	15.1	6.8	19.8	1.3	—	72.1
Jersey	1980	537.1	23.9	0.4	9.3	66.5	6.5	24.8	35.2	...	...	...	...	100.0[29]
Jordan	1982	3,217.5	19.6	0.5	21.2	58.7	4.8	28.2	25.7	29.8[27]	11.1[27]	4.2[27]	7.4[27]	47.5[27]
Kampuchea	...													
Kenya	1983	1,360.6	11.8	0.6	36.8	50.7	14.0	22.6	14.2	32.1	6.3	0.3	9.5	51.9
Kiribati	1981	22.5	33.1	0.1	18.8	48.0	4.4	22.7	20.9	4.8	5.9	—	13.7	75.6
Korea, North	...													
Korea, South	1984	30,631.5	15.3	3.6	24.0	57.2	8.8	32.0	16.3	8.9	22.4	—	24.9	43.8
Kuwait	1981	6,969.1	15.5	0.4	0.6	83.4	3.9	41.0	38.6	33.7	14.0	1.7	22.7	27.9
Laos	1974	64.8	32.1	0.2	11.2	56.4	6.1	25.7	24.7	17.9	4.7	—	18.8	58.6
Lebanon	1977	1,973.2	21.0	7.0	6.6	65.5	4.6	21.1	39.8	47.6	8.1	7.3	3.0	34.0
Lesotho	1981	504.9	25.1	0.8[5]	9.6	64.5[6]	6.4	17.0	41.1[6]	1.5	0.2	—	—	98.2
Liberia	1981	477.4	22.8	0.8	27.1	49.2	6.9	24.9	17.5	30.3	29.4	0.7	4.7	34.8
Libya	1981	8,381.7	19.4	0.3	1.0	79.3	4.5	38.2	36.7	61.8	6.3	4.6	7.6	19.7
Liechtenstein	1983	187.3	5.5	0.2	0.4	93.9	7.5	28.3	58.1	...	...	...	...	...
Luxembourg	1983	2,501.6	15.4	3.4[5]	15.0	66.3[6]	13.0	22.1	31.1[6]	91.4	2.7	...	0.2	5.7
Macau	1981	712.9	19.5	0.9	6.5	73.1	3.4	9.2	60.6	4.3	5.8	0.1	10.4	79.5
Madagascar	1982	439.0	18.5	0.3	24.4	56.8	11.9	29.5	15.4	48.8	6.2	2.5	5.7	36.8
Malawi	1981	350.1	11.8	0.8	16.9	70.5	17.1	24.3	29.1	33.0	4.3	—	6.3	56.5
Malaysia	1983	13,242.2	12.4	2.1	13.8	71.8	7.9	42.8	21.0	14.0	16.1	0.5	25.3	44.2
Maldives	1983	56.9	34.2	2.5	19.7	43.6	7.1	16.7	19.8	5.6[2]	—[2]	—[2]	13.0[2]	81.4[2]
Mali	1979	304.5	16.5	0.4	16.4	66.7	4.0	44.5	18.1	50.7	2.6	3.4	1.2	42.1
Malta	1983	727.3	18.3	1.1	12.2	68.4	7.0	24.7	36.8	71.5	11.4	2.2	1.4	13.5
Martinique	1984	685.8	20.9	0.1	23.9	55.1	8.6	20.0	26.5	63.3	3.0	0.3	2.0	31.5
Mauritania	1980	285.7	33.6	...	11.9	54.5	...	21.9	32.6	50.6	7.8[2]	...	1.1[2]	40.5[2]
Mauritius	1981	554.0	31.8	1.4	18.1	48.8	7.1	14.8	26.8	27.8	5.4	0.4	5.7	60.8
Mayotte	1984	20.9	23.9	...	19.1	...	...	...	...	...	...	...	...	100.0[32]
Mexico[34]	1982	14,421.6	11.7	1.7	3.3	83.4	8.5	41.0	33.9	15.4	62.5	0.4	5.9	15.8
Monaco[19]	...													
Mongolia	1982	729.8	11.1	—28.7[13]—		60.2[14]	7.1	35.4	17.7[14]	...	...	97.4[35]	...	2.6[35]
Montserrat	1981	18.9	28.5	0.6	11.9	59.0	7.3	18.8	32.9	25.0	26.0	...	5.5	43.4
Morocco	1982	4,315.3	21.6	3.5	27.2	47.7	7.6	23.7	16.5	42.0	6.0	8.0	2.4	41.7
Mozambique	1977	277.7	15.5	13.9[13]	3.7	66.7[14]	8.1	35.6	23.0[14]	31.5	3.8	0.9	5.3	58.5
Nauru	1979[3]	12.0	—34.2[5]—		2.0	63.8[6]	4.4	13.5	45.9[6]	...	...	...	...	...
Nepal	1982[37]	381.0	—17.5[5]—		11.7	70.8[6]	12.1	18.1	40.5[6]	6.3[35]	3.2[35]	10.8[35]	19.2[35]	60.6[35]
Netherlands, The	1984	62,136.1	18.0	2.3	23.9	55.8	9.3	21.8	24.7	53.1	8.9	4.7	2.3	30.9
Netherlands Antilles	1983	4,526.7	—4.0[5]—		84.9	11.1[6]	1.8	4.1	5.2[6]	11.2[2]	13.4[2]	...	1.3[2]	74.1[2]
New Caledonia	1983	303.4	23.7	0.2	23.1	53.0	6.0	20.6	26.4	47.6	10.2	0.1	5.6	36.5
New Zealand	1984	6,197.1	8.0	3.5	13.4	75.1	12.1	32.0	30.9	19.6	15.6	0.5	20.7	43.7
Nicaragua	1982	774.9	12.6	0.3	23.2	63.9	15.8	23.2	24.9	14.1	19.0	7.6	2.4	56.9
Niger	1981	509.7	24.8	1.9	14.8	58.4	6.9	25.7	25.8	47.4	3.7	0.4	2.5	46.0
Nigeria	1981	20,532.1	16.2	1.2	1.2	81.5	9.7	44.0	27.8	52.6	10.7	1.7	13.4	21.7
Niue	1982	2.6	—38.8[5]—		27.8	33.4[6]	6.2	7.2	20.1[6]	...	0.4	...	3.0	96.6[38]
Norfolk Island	1984[3]	14.5	17.1	0.1	11.0	71.8	4.3	12.4	55.2	...	...	...	...	...
Norway	1984	13,890.0	8.9	5.0	10.3	75.8	6.9	36.8	32.1	45.6	9.0	3.6	4.8	37.0

total value U.S.$ (000,000)	food and agricultural raw materials (0+1+2-27-28+4)	mineral ores and concentrates (27+28+667)	fuels and other energy (3)	manufactured goods total (5+6-667+7+8+9)	of which chemicals and related products (5)	of which machinery and transport equipment (7)	of which other (6-667+8+9)	to European Economic Community (EEC)[c]	to United States	to U.S.S.R. and Eastern Europe	to Japan	to all other[d]	country
404.4	91.4	—	7.6	0.9	0.4	—	0.6	31.4	25.8	3.4	7.4	32.0	Ethiopia
158.3	99.1	—	—	0.9	—	0.8	0.1	67.9	18.9	2.4	1.7	9.2	Faeroe Islands
2.6	100.0	—	—	—	—	—	—	100.0	—	—	—	—	Falkland Islands
239.7	62.6	0.1	19.1	18.2	0.8	3.5	13.9	29.4	8.5	—	2.4	59.7	Fiji
13,507.3	17.2	0.5	5.5	76.8	5.4	24.9	46.6	37.4	8.1	20.5	1.3	32.8	Finland
93,310.6	18.7	1.5	3.7	76.0	13.5	33.5	29.1	48.9	8.1	3.2	1.1	38.7	France[19]
37.4	73.8	0.4	—	25.8	0.5	9.3	16.0	25.3	41.5	—	18.1	15.2	French Guiana
41.2	14.4	15.2	—	70.4	2.4	17.2	50.7	70.4	12.6	—	4.9	12.1	French Polynesia
1,475.4	7.5	7.0	79.5	6.0	1.2	0.6	4.1	47.7	25.6	1.8	0.3	24.5	Gabon
48.5	78.0[4]	—[4]	—[4]	22.0[4]	—[4]	—[4]	22.0[4]	63.3[4]	—[4]	0.6[4]	—[4]	36.1[4]	Gambia, The
168.5	24.0	...	...	...	...	...	...	...	...	...	...	100.0[21]	Gaza Strip
23,792.9	———25.6———				74.4	...	47.8	...[22]	...[22]	...[22]	...[22]	...[22]	Germany, East
171,593.4	6.7	0.8	3.3	89.1	13.6	44.8	30.7	47.7	9.6	4.1	1.4	37.1	Germany, West[23]
941.8	82.0	2.4	0.4	15.2	0.2	—	15.0	49.8	9.8	17.9	9.4	13.1	Ghana
33.5	——12.7——		75.0	12.4	2.9	1.3	8.1	...	...	...	...	...	Gibraltar
4,864.5	33.3	4.3	10.1	52.3	4.0	2.5	45.8	54.1	8.3	5.9	1.1	30.6	Greece
172.3	61.1	28.1	—	10.8	—	10.1	0.7	82.1	9.6	—	—	8.3	Greenland
16.9	92.2	—	—	7.7	—	—	7.7	77.2	3.2	1.0	—	18.5	Grenada
86.1	83.8	0.3	1.9	14.0	3.2	7.0	3.7	73.0	1.2	1.6	—	24.2	Guadeloupe
44.4	19.4	2.0	32.7	45.9	2.3	8.3	35.3	...	25.1	...	1.5	73.4	Guam
1,114.8	68.8	—	2.0	29.2	11.1	1.8	16.3	16.7	26.4	0.5	4.5	52.0	Guatemala
													Guernsey[25]
466.7	3.0	96.8	—	0.2	...	...	0.2	31.7[2]	23.5[2]	21.4[2]	—[2]	23.4[2]	Guinea
11.4	87.1	0.3	—	12.6	0.3	—	12.3	5.6	—	—	—	94.4	Guinea-Bissau
389.3	46.8	48.4	—	4.8	1.0	1.7	2.1	35.3	23.9	1.5	2.8	36.5	Guyana
148.4	36.6	12.2	—	51.2	5.0	7.2	39.0	27.2	66.1	—	0.3	6.4	Haiti
655.7	87.2	3.9	0.1	8.8	3.2	0.1	5.5	21.4	52.8	0.1	5.9	19.8	Honduras
28,321.1	5.8	1.7	0.5	92.0	3.5	25.8	62.7	14.0	33.2	0.3	4.4	48.1	Hong Kong
8,721.7	25.4	1.1[5]	9.2	64.3[6]	10.1	30.4	23.8[6]	15.6	2.0	49.4	0.3	32.7	Hungary
748.4	71.6	1.0	—	27.4	0.2	0.7	26.5	38.3[27]	28.4[27]	9.5[27]	3.8[27]	20.1[27]	Iceland
8,742.2	31.9	15.6	2.9	49.6	4.8	7.9	36.8	18.1	11.8	25.3	8.8	36.0	India
21,145.9	12.5	1.4	76.4	9.7	0.6	0.6	8.5	4.5	20.2	0.6	45.8	28.9	Indonesia
25,943.0	1.6	—	97.6	0.8	—	—	0.8	0.6	0.3	0.7	—	98.4	Iran
11,063.9	0.6	—	98.6	0.3	—	—	0.3	48.1[2]	2.2[2]	0.2[2]	6.4[2]	43.0[2]	Iraq
9,628.7	27.8	3.3	1.2	67.7	13.4	28.7	25.6	68.6	9.7	0.5	1.7	19.5	Ireland
													Isle of Man[25]
5,111.7	16.4	26.5	0.3	56.8	14.8	17.1	24.8	34.3	26.1	0.6	3.7	35.3	Israel
73,367.8	8.1	0.5	4.5	86.8	8.5	31.1	47.2	45.4	10.9	3.4	1.1	39.2	Italy[28]
2,067.7	77.0	0.1	11.5	11.4	2.2	2.3	7.0	51.5	12.4	3.0	2.6	30.5	Ivory Coast
745.3	19.4	65.7	2.5	12.5	2.5	2.1	7.9	14.3	48.1	5.1	1.1	31.4	Jamaica
170,113.9	1.6	0.2	0.3	97.9	4.4	66.6	26.9	11.4	35.6	1.8	—	51.2	Japan
209.2	27.6	4.3[30]	—	68.0	1.2	31.1	35.7	...	...	...	—	100.0[31]	Jersey
738.9	27.5	22.8	—	49.7	9.3	16.6	23.8	3.6[27]	—[27]	6.2[27]	1.9[27]	88.3[27]	Jordan
													Kampuchea
984.2	64.1	2.1	20.9	12.9	3.3	1.7	7.9	38.9	6.0	0.7	0.7	53.7	Kenya
3.9	99.3	—	—	0.7	—	—	0.7	...	18.3	...	1.1	80.6	Kiribati
													Korea, North
29,250.9	5.2	0.3	2.9	91.6	2.9	35.7	53.0	11.0	36.0	...	15.8	37.2	Korea, South
16,299.9	——1.3——		83.6	15.1	4.8	4.9	5.4	15.8	0.4	1.1	23.7	59.0	Kuwait
11.3	84.0	11.9	—	4.1	—	—	4.1	0.3	—	—	3.7	96.0	Laos
395.4	20.1	0.5	—	79.2	9.6	11.4	58.2	6.7	3.4	0.5	0.1	89.4	Lebanon
49.6	28.8	42.6	0.1	28.5	0.9	3.3	24.3	10.3	0.1	—	—	89.6	Lesotho
523.6	30.7	66.7	0.1	2.3	0.1	1.0	1.2	64.2	23.0	2.0	1.0	9.8	Liberia
15,571.1	—	—	99.6	0.4	0.4	—	—	46.1	27.4	4.4	2.1	20.0	Libya
454.4	0.3	—	0.2	99.5	6.7	47.1	45.8	37.9	...	...	...	62.1	Liechtenstein
2,179.1	7.9	1.6[5]	0.5	90.0[6]	17.4	13.4	59.2[6]	77.5	4.0	...	0.1	18.4	Luxembourg
678.7	3.2	0.2	—	96.6	1.0	2.4	93.2	40.8	21.0	0.5	1.4	36.3	Macau
329.5	80.8	4.3	7.7	7.1	1.1	1.1	4.9	38.7	14.7	4.2	6.4	35.9	Madagascar
261.6	92.0	—	—	7.9	0.3	—	7.5	41.9	26.0	—	2.3	29.7	Malawi
14,117.6	39.9	1.0	28.4	30.7	0.9	17.2	12.6	14.6	13.2	2.5	19.6	50.0	Malaysia
13.4	51.9	1.4	—	46.7	—	—	46.7	5.8	41.5	0.7	18.8	33.3	Maldives
106.2	76.4	—	—	23.6	0.3	0.5	22.8	57.2	—	—	3.0	39.8	Mali
362.7	6.5	1.7	4.3	87.4	1.4	15.5	70.5	71.3	3.2	5.3	0.1	20.1	Malta
153.6	55.3	0.2	30.5	14.0	4.7	2.7	6.5	56.4	0.2	—	—	43.4	Martinique
194.2	22.0	78.0	—	—	—	—	—	61.0	0.2[2]	...	13.7[2]	25.1[2]	Mauritania
324.0	62.2	1.2	—	36.6	0.4	1.7	34.5	88.5	5.0	0.2	—	6.2	Mauritius
0.9	8.2	...	...	91.7	37.9	...	53.9	...	2.7	...	—	97.3[33]	Mayotte
21,006.1	8.9	2.4	77.6	11.1	3.0	3.7	4.4	12.3	53.5	0.2	6.9	27.1	Mexico[34]
...													Monaco[19]
517.8	48.0	——39.1[13]——		12.9[14]	...	0.1	12.8[14]	...	...	96.7[35]	...	3.3[35]	Mongolia
2.2	13.2	—	0.8	86.0	—	13.0	73.0	15.7[36]	10.5[36]	—[36]	—[36]	73.8[36]	Montserrat
2,058.6	26.4	33.1	4.3	36.2	17.0	0.8	18.4	54.4	1.3	7.1	2.9	34.3	Morocco
129.0	79.7	10.8[13]	4.4	5.0[14]	0.8	0.5	3.7[14]	20.1	26.9	0.2	5.3	47.4	Mozambique
87.9	—	100.0	—	—	—	—	—	...	...	...	4.0	96.0	Nauru
115.3	——80.2[5]——		0.1	19.8[6]	0.1	0.6	19.0[6]	14.3[35]	3.4[35]	7.0[35]	3.0[35]	72.3[35]	Nepal
65,873.9	23.9	1.5	23.0	51.6	16.7	16.5	18.5	71.9	5.0	1.3	0.6	21.2	Netherlands, The
4,409.4	——0.4[5]——		98.4	1.3[6]	0.8	0.3	0.2[6]	10.4	37.8	...	—	51.8	Netherlands Antilles
303.4	1.6	15.9	0.1	82.3	0.3	4.5	77.5	47.1	6.9	—	23.7	22.3	New Caledonia
5,512.7	66.9	0.6	0.4	32.1	4.3	4.5	23.3	19.4	13.5	14.8	14.8	50.7	New Zealand
390.7	90.8	0.1	1.3	7.8	5.0	0.1	2.6	24.3	25.0	7.4	11.5	31.8	Nicaragua
454.8	17.1	79.7	0.9	2.3	—	0.5	1.8	41.5	—	—	17.7	40.8	Niger
17,976.9	2.3	—	96.9	0.8	—	0.2	0.6	33.4	35.6	1.3	1.5	28.2	Nigeria
0.5	——68.4[5]——		—	31.6[6]	—	—	31.6[6]	...	...	...	—	100.0[39]	Niue
2.1	10.2	—	8.6	81.2	0.1	6.2	74.9	...	...	...	...	...	Norfolk Island
18,919.9	7.9	1.5	54.6	36.0	6.1	11.0	18.9	70.0	5.1	0.9	1.4	22.7	Norway

908　Britannica World Data

Trade: external (continued)

country	year	imports total value U.S.$ (000,000)	food and agricultural raw materials (0+1+2-27-28+4)	mineral ores and concentrates (27+28+667)	fuels and other energy (3)	manufactured goods total (5+6-667+7+8+9)	of which chemicals and related products (5)	of which machinery and transport equipment (7)	of which other (6-667+8+9)	from European Economic Community (EEC)[c]	from United States	from U.S.S.R. and Eastern Europe	from Japan	from all other[d]
Oman	1983	2,492.3	15.8	0.3	1.6	82.2	3.7	46.0	32.5	35.5	7.7	0.1	22.0	34.7
Pacific Is., Trust Territory of the	1978[3]	38.9	—46.2[25]—		12.9	40.9[6]	4.8	12.5	23.5[6]	—[41]	—[41]	34.7[41]	25.2[41]	40.1[41]
Pakistan	1983	5,341.0	17.7	1.7	28.4	52.2	10.9	26.2	15.1	21.2	9.5	2.3	14.4	52.6
Panama	1983	1,411.4	11.2	0.2	27.8	60.9	11.8	23.0	26.0	7.7	32.3	0.2	7.8	52.0
Papua New Guinea	1981	1,111.7	19.9	0.3	21.1	58.6	6.0	28.8	23.8	7.2	7.9	—	16.1	68.8
Paraguay	1981	506.1	—13.8—		18.8	67.4	6.1	35.9	25.3	17.3[16]	6.4[16]	—[16]	4.2[16]	72.0[16]
Peru	1982	2,940.3	19.6	0.3	1.7	78.4	12.0	44.2	22.2	16.6	36.8	0.6	12.5	33.5
Philippines	1983	7,978.6	11.0	0.4	27.5	61.1	10.7	21.1	29.3	11.8	23.3	0.5	17.2	47.3
Pitcairn Island	...	...	...	...	...	...	...	...	...	...	...	...	...	...
Poland	1983	10,589.8	15.1	4.2	26.1	54.7	8.7	25.2	20.7	16.8	1.4	59.2	1.1	21.6
Portugal	1984	7,770.7	24.0	1.3	29.2	45.6	10.0	20.4	15.1	35.9	13.6	1.3	2.5	46.7
Puerto Rico	1983[3]	8,506.8	18.9[4]	...	35.4[4]	45.8[4]	3.3[4]	14.4[4]	28.0[4]	...	61.2	...	5.0	33.8
Qatar	1984	1,162.0	22.6	2.4	0.9	74.1	5.8	35.3	32.9	38.4	9.1	0.5	19.2	32.8
Réunion	1984	790.4	25.5	0.2	10.8	63.5	9.1	24.6	29.9	74.3	0.3	—	2.5	22.9
Romania	1983	8,347.8	10.4	—57.0[13]—		32.5[14]	6.8	21.5	4.2[14]	9.7	2.8	43.3	1.1	43.2
Rwanda	1980	243.1	15.7	1.4	12.5	70.4	6.0	25.4	39.0	44.6	4.5	1.3	12.1	37.5
St. Christopher and Nevis	1981	47.7	24.3	0.1	10.9	64.6	8.9	20.5	35.2	21.4	30.1	0.1	3.6	44.7
St. Helena and Ascension	1982[10]	4.8	43.3	...	15.6	41.1	...	12.3	28.8	50.1	—	—	—	49.9
St. Lucia	1982	118.1	26.7	0.4	11.7	61.3	9.8	17.2	34.3	20.5[35]	38.9[35]	0.2[35]	4.9[35]	35.4[35]
St. Pierre and Miquelon	1982	42.0	21.4	—	33.5	45.1	4.3	17.2	23.6	35.6	0.4	—	—	64.0
St. Vincent and the Grenadines	1979	46.3	—39.7—		7.5	52.7	10.5	15.1	27.2	24.9	19.9	—	1.7	53.5
San Marino[28]	...	...	...	...	...	...	...	...	...	...	...	...	...	...
São Tomé and Príncipe	1977	14.8	46.5	3.0[13]	1.9	45.7[14]	10.1	12.8	22.8[14]	...	...	...	...	...
Saudi Arabia	1983	39,198.0	13.1	0.4	0.5	86.0	4.2	41.6	40.2	34.7	19.7	0.6	19.5	25.5
Senegal	1981	1,077.4	28.3	—	30.4	41.3	7.6	17.5	16.2	45.8	4.5	2.6	1.3	45.8
Seychelles	1982	98.0	22.8	—	20.1	57.0	6.4	21.4	29.2	33.4	2.7	3.1	5.8	55.1
Sierra Leone	1981	311.3	—27.1[15]—		17.4	55.5[6]	6.7	22.2	26.6[6]	36.5[41]	8.7[41]	4.5[41]	6.8[41]	43.4[41]
Singapore[42]	1984	28,711.6	13.5	0.7	27.7	58.1	5.1	31.8	21.2	10.0	14.6	0.5	18.3	56.5
Solomon Islands	1982	67.0	20.1	0.3	25.1	54.6	6.6	23.0	25.0	5.1[16]	4.1[16]	—[16]	19.5[16]	71.4[16]
Somalia	1981	512.9	26.6	—	2.3	71.1	2.0	50.0	19.1	65.5	4.3	0.1	1.8	28.3
South Africa[43]	1981	20,828.2	5.7	1.3	0.3[44]	92.7[45]	8.3	41.9	42.5[45]	38.3[27]	15.9[27]	0.1[27]	12.9[27]	32.7[27]
Bophuthatswana[43]	...	...	...	...	...	...	...	...	...	...	...	...	...	...
Ciskei[43]	...	...	...	...	...	...	...	...	...	...	...	...	...	...
Transkei[43]	...	...	...	...	...	...	...	...	...	...	...	...	...	...
Venda[43]	...	...	...	...	...	...	...	...	...	...	...	...	...	...
South West Africa/Namibia[43]	1980	c. 980.0	...	...	...	...	...	...	...	...	...	...	...	...
Spain	1983	29,184.6	16.6	4.1	40.1	39.3	7.7	18.7	12.9	32.3	11.9	3.0	3.4	49.5
Sri Lanka	1983	1,788.4	18.7	0.6	23.9	56.9	6.7	26.2	23.9	17.1	6.4	0.5	17.7	58.3
Sudan, The	1983	1,354.4	18.6	0.3	26.6	54.6	11.0	26.6	17.0	37.3	9.1	1.5	3.2	48.9
Suriname	1976	281.0	11.9	2.3[13]	27.2	57.7[14]	11.5	29.8	16.4[14]	31.1[15]	31.2[15]	0.3[15]	7.4[15]	30.0[15]
Swaziland	1982	520.3	9.9	0.2	14.7	75.2	15.3	21.8	38.0	...	...	...	...	100.0[47]
Sweden	1984	26,339.5	9.3	2.3	19.5	68.9	9.4	31.1	28.4	52.8	8.1	5.7	4.7	28.7
Switzerland	1984	29,779.4	10.7	5.8	10.3	73.3	11.5	24.7	37.1	67.3	6.6	3.1	3.8	19.2
Syria	1983	4,542.3	22.5	0.3	30.2	46.8	7.8	21.9	17.2	32.3	4.4	9.9	6.7	46.7
Taiwan	1984	21,829.6	18.2	2.6	21.6	57.6	11.7	28.4	17.4	8.7	22.9	—	29.4	39.1
Tanzania	1981	867.3	7.6	0.6	30.8	61.0	10.0	35.0	16.1	42.2	1.8	1.1	11.5	43.5
Thailand	1983	10,287.2	8.1	3.0	24.3	64.6	12.9	28.9	22.8	12.7	12.6	1.1	27.4	46.2
Togo	1981	435.8	27.2	0.6	8.4	63.7	6.1	21.3	36.3	64.1	4.2	1.1	5.6	25.0
Tokelau	...	...	...	...	...	...	...	...	...	...	...	...	...	...
Tonga	1982	41.6	34.3	0.7	13.9	51.0	6.4	14.7	29.9	3.2	9.5	—	6.1	81.1
Trinidad and Tobago	1984	1,919.1	25.5	1.5	0.8	72.3	9.1	30.2	33.0	19.3	38.9	0.1	11.1	30.7
Tunisia	1981	3,770.9	17.7	3.7	20.5	58.1	6.7	27.2	24.3	57.4[27]	6.9[27]	3.9[27]	4.2[27]	27.6[27]
Turkey	1984	10,662.8	8.6	2.4	35.6	53.4	14.6	25.3	13.6	27.3	9.9	8.2	3.8	50.8
Turks and Caicos Islands	1984[10]	26.3	—32.1—		11.6	56.3	...	...	...	...	74.7	...	...	25.3
Tuvalu	1982	2.9	26.9	—	16.8	56.3	6.5	16.1	33.7	5.0	...	...	1.1	93.8
Uganda	1976	157.5	8.7	0.7	29.6	61.0	11.1	26.8	23.0	29.1[41]	—[41]	—[41]	1.3[41]	69.6[41]
U.S.S.R.	1984	80,624.0	24.2	...	...	75.5[49]	6.4	36.6	32.5[49]	12.8	4.3	46.7	3.1	33.1
United Arab Emirates	1982	9,439.9	10.3	0.5	6.0	83.1	5.4	40.6	37.1	37.2	13.8	0.4	19.2	29.5
United Kingdom[25, 50]	1984	105,173.7	16.1	4.0	13.0	66.9	8.0	30.1	28.8	44.7	11.9	2.2	4.8	36.4
United States[51]	1984	341,176.8	9.4	2.3	18.5	69.8	4.2	36.1	29.5	17.7	—	0.7	17.7	64.0
Uruguay	1983	787.5	11.3	0.7	36.1	51.9	15.2	24.8	11.9	16.0	7.5	4.2	2.2	70.0
Vanuatu	1982	47.7	29.6	—	14.0	56.4	7.6	16.3	32.5	13.0	1.2	—	12.9	72.9
Venezuela	1981	13,105.9	19.4	0.4	0.8	79.4	10.4	43.4	25.6	18.1	48.3	0.3	8.1	25.1
Vietnam	1982	838.0	...	...	...	...	...	...	...	...	...	...	...	...
Virgin Islands (U.S.)	1978	667.4	11.9	—	58.5	29.6	3.7	8.2	17.6	0.9	58.0	0.1	0.2	40.8
Wallis and Futuna	1981	6.8	24.0	...	16.9	...	...	15.3	...	...	...	...	...	...
West Bank	1983	462.5	12.6	...	...	...	...	...	...	...	...	...	...	100.0[52]
Western Sahara	...	...	...	...	...	...	...	...	...	...	...	...	...	...
Western Samoa	1981	68.3	21.8	—	17.8	60.3	5.6	34.4	20.2	6.3	22.7	—	9.2	61.8
Yemen (Aden)	1977	544.0	—18.1[15]—		46.6	35.2[6]	2.0	22.7	10.6[6]	18.4	—	4.0	11.3	66.4
Yemen (Şan'ā')	1981	1,608.8	32.2	0.1	8.3	59.4	5.6	25.4	28.4	30.8	2.8	1.2	17.7	47.5
Yugoslavia	1983	12,154.5	13.2	3.3	27.2	56.3	14.5	24.0	17.9	30.4	6.4	36.7	0.7	25.8
Zaire	1982	478.4	22.4[15]	1.2[15]	7.6[15]	68.8[15]	10.3[15]	31.7[15]	26.9[15]	63.6	12.7	0.1	1.5	22.0
Zambia	1982	1,001.9	7.5	0.4	20.8	71.4	16.0	34.5	20.8	37.3[4]	7.0[4]	0.6[4]	5.1[4]	49.9[4]
Zimbabwe	1982	1,642.8	4.6	0.7	16.5	78.2	11.6	40.7	26.0	32.8	9.6	—	5.2	51.9

[1]Year ending March 20. [2]Estimated based on trading partners' information. [3]Year ending June 30. [41]1980. [5]Excluding precious stones, etc. (667). [6]Including precious stones, etc. (667). [7]Trade with France and Spain only. [8]Figures for Belgium include Luxembourg (also shown separately). [9]1974. [10]Year ending March 31. [11]Of which 77.3% from India. [12]Of which 97.0% to India. [13]Including metals. [14]Excluding metals. [15]1978. [16]1983. [17]Of which 80.0% from Spain. [18]Of which 86.7% to Spain. [19]Figures for France include Monaco. [20]Of which 91.8% from Israel. [21]Of which 85.8% to Israel. [22]Import figures refer to total trade turnover (figures are not available separately for imports and for exports). [23]Excluding trade with East Germany (1.7% of total imports and 1.3% of total exports). [24]Excluding petroleum products. [25]Figures for United Kingdom include Guernsey, Isle of Man, and Jersey (the latter is also shown separately). [26]Year ending September 30. [27]1984. [28]Figures for Italy include San Marino. [29]Of which 84.9% from United Kingdom. [30]Including coins. [31]Of which 67.3% to United Kingdom. [32]Of which 52.9% from France. [33]Of

total value U.S.$ (000,000)	food and agricultural raw materials (0+1+2-27-28+4)	mineral ores and concentrates (27+28+667)	fuels and other energy (3)	manufactured goods total (5+6-667+7+8+9)	of which chemicals and related products (5)	of which machinery and transport equipment (7)	of which other (6-667+8+9)	to European Economic Community (EEC)c	to United States	to U.S.S.R. and Eastern Europe	to Japan	to all otherd	country
4,382.2	0.9	—	92.0	7.0	0.1	5.7	1.2	18.6[40]	6.6[40]	—[40]	38.5[40]	36.3[40]	Oman
13.7[4]	—94.3[4,5]—			5.7[4,6]	—[4]	—[4]	5.7[4,6]	...	...	...	...	...	Pacific Is., Trust Territory of the
3,074.8	33.7	0.4	1.9	64.0	1.0	1.2	61.9	16.1	6.3	4.2	8.0	65.5	Pakistan
302.6	77.1	0.5	12.1	10.3	2.0	0.2	8.1	14.2	54.2	0.1	0.3	31.2	Panama
874.1	40.7	49.8		9.5	0.1	1.1	8.3	28.4	4.8	1.0	36.0	29.7	Papua New Guinea
295.5	90.6	—		9.4	4.1		5.2	32.6[16]	8.6[16]	—[16]	1.9[16]	56.8[16]	Paraguay
2,812.8	16.2	15.3	26.4	42.1	1.6	1.2	39.3	19.3	35.8	1.6	15.1	28.2	Peru
5,005.3	36.3	8.9	2.3	52.5	1.7	5.1	45.6	17.9	36.0	1.8	20.4	23.9	Philippines
...	...	...	...	...	...	...	...	...	...	...	...	...	Pitcairn Island
11,571.8	9.9	3.3	17.4	69.4	5.5	41.6	22.2	22.7	1.7	50.6	0.5	24.5	Poland
5,210.8	19.2	1.4	3.9	75.6	7.8	17.3	50.6	57.6	8.8	1.6	0.9	31.0	Portugal
8,521.2	13.5		14.5	72.1	31.6	11.9	28.6		83.5	...	0.2	16.2	Puerto Rico
4,512.6	—[35]	—[35]	93.9[35]	6.1[35]	3.9[35]	—[35]	2.2[35]	36.9[35]	0.2[35]	—[35]	33.3[35]	29.6[35]	Qatar
79.6	84.2	0.3	0.5	15.0	5.5	5.2	4.3	79.4	0.4	1.7	0.6	17.9	Réunion
10,089.3	12.6	—29.8[13]—		57.6[14]	10.1	29.1	18.5[14]	23.9	3.9	33.9	1.6	36.8	Romania
73.2	89.4	10.5		0.2	—	—	0.2	14.2	0.8	—	—	85.0	Rwanda
24.3	66.5	—	0.1	33.4	0.4	12.3	20.7	31.3	42.2	—	0.2	26.3	St. Christopher and Nevis
0.1	80.4	—	—	19.6	—	—	19.6	...	...	...	...	...	St. Helena and Ascension
41.6	62.2	0.1	0.4	37.3	1.3	10.4	25.6	37.9[35]	10.6[35]	—[35]	—[35]	51.4[35]	St. Lucia
6.3	99.8	—	—	0.2	—	—	0.2	19.2	79.4	—	—	1.4	St. Pierre and Miquelon
14.8	85.7	—	—	14.3	—	0.5	13.8	49.6	2.6	—	—	47.8	St. Vincent and the Grenadines
...	...	...	...	...	...	...	...	...	...	...	...	...	San Marino[28]
24.1	99.8	...	...	0.2	—	0.1	0.1	...	...	...	...	...	São Tomé and Príncipe
47,813.1	—[40]	—[40]	98.8[40]	1.2[40]	—[40]	0.6[40]	0.6[40]	29.0[40]	7.8[40]	0.1[40]	23.8[40]	39.3[40]	Saudi Arabia
560.8	28.8	14.1	37.4	19.7	6.0	4.0	9.7	30.8	0.2	0.8	1.6	66.6	Senegal
15.2	20.7	0.1	71.9	7.2	—	4.9	2.3	2.4	1.5	—	0.5	95.7	Seychelles
153.0	26.3	66.8	...	6.9	...	...	6.9	63.7[41]	17.8[41]	—[41]	—[41]	18.5[41]	Sierra Leone
24,107.9	14.9	1.0	25.7	58.5	4.8	32.8	20.9	9.7	20.0	1.7	9.4	59.2	Singapore[42]
54.9	96.4			3.6	—		3.6	23.9[16]	0.1[16]	—[16]	43.5[16]	32.6[16]	Solomon Islands
152.0	99.4	—	0.2	0.4	—	0.1	0.2	6.2	—	—	—	93.7	Somalia
20,828.2	12.7	10.2	6.1	71.0	2.3	2.4	66.3	18.0[27]	8.4[27]	0.1[27]	7.7[27]	65.8[27]	South Africa[43]
...	...	...	...	...	...	...	...	...	...	...	...	...	Bophuthatswana[43]
...	...	...	...	...	...	...	...	...	...	...	...	...	Ciskei[43]
...	...	...	...	...	...	...	...	...	...	...	...	...	Transkei[43]
...	...	...	...	...	...	...	...	...	...	...	...	...	Venda[43]
c. 1310	...	...	...	...	...	...	...	...	...	...	...	...	South West Africa/Namibia[43]
19,790.2	17.6	1.0	9.3	72.1	7.6	26.1	38.4	48.0	7.3	2.6	1.5	40.6	Spain
1,066.2	60.1	4.5	10.9	24.4	0.6	1.4	22.4	19.3	17.4	4.9	4.5	53.8	Sri Lanka
623.5	93.9	0.3	2.7	3.1	—	2.2	0.9	24.4	2.0	7.7	5.4	60.6	Sudan, The
274.6	21.6	32.7[13]	—	45.7[14]	43.1	0.5	2.1[14]	27.1[15,46]	39.7[15,46]	0.6[15,46]	6.6[15,46]	26.0[15,46]	Suriname
325.2	63.8	—	0.8	35.3	15.8	4.3	15.2					100.0[48]	Swaziland
29,325.9	12.2	2.1	5.7	79.9	6.2	40.6	33.1	47.9	11.4	2.6	1.4	36.7	Sweden
25,957.8	4.3	5.3	0.4	90.0	21.3	29.9	38.8	50.3	9.8	3.0	3.3	33.6	Switzerland
1,922.9	14.5	1.5	68.8	15.2	1.6	1.1	12.5	30.4	0.1	43.4	—	26.1	Syria
30,409.8	6.9	0.3	1.8	91.0	2.5	28.1	60.3	8.9	48.8	—	10.5	31.8	Taiwan
564.3	82.4	10.1	0.2	7.3	0.7	2.5	4.1	44.4	3.5	2.7	2.8	46.6	Tanzania
6,368.3	61.7	5.4	0.4	32.4	0.9	5.7	25.9	21.2	15.0	1.5	15.1	47.2	Thailand
208.2	32.1	50.6	1.3	16.0	—	1.4	14.6	59.4	—	1.5	0.4	38.6	Togo
...	...	...	...	...	...	...	...	...	...	...	...	...	Tokelau
3.7	86.7	—	—	13.3	—	—	13.3	2.1	9.6	—	—	88.3	Tonga
2,173.4	2.4	0.2	81.2	16.2	10.8	1.5	3.9	15.0	58.2	—	—	26.8	Trinidad and Tobago
2,503.7	10.2	2.0	54.0	33.7	12.8	2.3	18.6	57.2[27]	15.3[27]	0.9[27]	0.1[27]	26.6[27]	Tunisia
7,133.7	44.8[16]	3.3[16]	4.1[16]	47.7[16]	2.7[16]	4.6[16]	40.4[16]	38.3	5.2	3.7	0.5	52.3	Turkey
3.0	100.0								100.0				Turks and Caicos Islands
0.04	81.0[35]	—[35]	—[35]	19.0[35]	—[35]	—[35]	19.0[35]	...	...	...	...	...	Tuvalu
351.7	96.6	0.2	0.8	2.4	—	—	2.4	31.6[41]	48.4[41]	—[41]	—[41]	20.0[41]	Uganda
91,649.0	4.7	2.2[5]	54.4	38.7[6]	3.1	12.5	23.1[6]	20.6	0.4	43.5	1.1	34.4	U.S.S.R.
17,261.0	0.9	—	92.2	6.8[49]	0.2	1.9	4.7[49]	11.6	3.9	—	33.9	50.6	United Arab Emirates
94,224.3	8.3	3.4	21.8	66.5	11.7	30.5	24.4	44.8	14.4	1.9	1.3	37.7	United Kingdom[25,50]
217,888.0	21.1	2.1	4.4	72.4	10.4	42.7	19.3	21.2	—	1.9	10.6	66.2	United States[51]
1,008.4	70.2	0.1	0.1	29.6	3.0	1.1	25.5	19.8	9.8	7.8	2.1	60.5	Uruguay
22.9	98.3[36]	—[36]	—[36]	1.7[36]	—[36]	—[36]	1.7[36]	41.0	25.5	—	2.7	30.8	Vanuatu
20,125.3	0.4	2.0	92.8	4.6	0.7	0.5	3.4	15.0	25.4	0.5	3.9	55.2	Venezuela
430.0	...	...	...	...	...	...	...	...	...	...	...	...	Vietnam
2,512.1			91.3	8.7	6.2		2.5	1.0	96.8	1.3	0.1	0.8	Virgin Islands (U.S.)
—	...	...	...	...	...	...	...	...	...	...	...	...	Wallis and Futuna
206.9	23.3							...	...	...	...	100.0[53]	West Bank
...	...	...	...	...	...	...	...	...	...	...	...	...	Western Sahara
11.2	91.6		0.8	7.6	0.6	2.6	4.4	26.8	10.2	—	7.6	55.4	Western Samoa
180.8	—15.5—		84.0	0.5	—	0.4	0.1	1.8	—	—	9.6	88.6	Yemen (Aden)
47.5	23.8	—	—	76.2	1.6	64.5	10.2	24.6	3.0	0.1	0.1	72.3	Yemen (San'ā')
9,913.5	15.8	0.6	2.5	81.2	9.7	31.2	40.2	23.8	3.5	46.3	0.3	26.2	Yugoslavia
568.0	11.4	70.7	13.5	4.5	...	...	...	85.1	3.5	—	1.1	10.3	Zaire
1,023.9	0.4[54]	0.6[54]	1.2[54]	97.7[54,55]	0.2[54]	0.3[54]	97.2[54,55]	51.1[4]	11.2[4]	1.1[4]	17.0[4]	19.7[4]	Zambia
1,275.7	60.9	1.4	1.6	...	...	...	...	20.3	8.4	0.2	3.4	54.8	Zimbabwe

which 39.7% to France.   34Excludes operations of cosmetics enterprises.   351981.   36Domestic exports only.   37Year ending July 15.   38Of which 71.0% from New Zealand.   39Of which 95.4% to New Zealand.   401982.   411977.   42Excludes fish and marine produce landed directly by Singapore- and peninsular Malaysia-registered fishing boats.   43Figures for South Africa refer to Customs Union of Southern Africa (includes South Africa, Botswana, Lesotho, and Swaziland, also shown separately; also South West Africa/Namibia, Bophuthatswana, Ciskei, Transkei, and Venda).   44Excluding crude oil.   45Including crude oil (including in "special transactions" accounting in total for 25.0%).   46Direction of trade distribution excludes plywood.   47Of which 82.9% from South Africa.   48Of which 34.8% to South Africa.   49Includes unallocated commodities.   50Excludes Norwegian oil imported by pipeline from North Sea oil fields unless sold to U.K. purchaser.   51Figures for United States include Puerto Rico, American Samoa, Guam, and Virgin Islands (U.S.), also shown separately.   52Of which 89.9% from Israel.   53Of which 62.8% to Israel, 36.7% to Jordan.   541979.   55Of which copper 81.8%.

Trade: domestic

The following table presents data relating to domestic wholesale and retail trade for the countries of the world. The section on wholesale trade is based for the most part on establishments engaged primarily in selling goods to retailers and distributors for resale or to purchasers who buy for business and farm uses. The retail trade section is based on businesses engaged in selling merchandise for personal or household consumption; restaurants, when part of the national retail survey, are included, hotels excluded.

The data presented here are based on information received from a variety of direct country and international sources. The direct country sources include such items as correspondence, statistical abstracts, annual reports, and censuses of business and trade. Among the more prominent international sources are various publications of the United Nations dealing with trade and production.

There being no single source or common international methodology for the compilation of data on wholesale and retail trade, nor a single current year on which, by common agreement, the various national reports would be based, allowance must be made for variations in the meaning of the information provided for any single country and for its comparability internationally. Variations occur in part because of the way in which countries define wholesale and retail trade; the conventional capitalist, or free-enterprise, distinction between the wholesale and retail activity (of a single enterprise or an entire national trade sector) may not be clear in some countries, and data may overlap in their final reports. Variations also exist in the kind and level of detail reported. For example, countries may analyze differently the size (number of employees, sales, surface area) of establishments surveyed. The depth of analysis to which the data are subjected may also vary. Trade is affected by the degree of government involvement, which may range from total control of wholesale distribution in some socialist countries, to partial involvement in some strategic sectors, or to complete noninvolvement in fully private trade sectors of capitalist countries. In some smaller countries data may be collected only by inference; for instance, in a country with inadequate resources to survey trade, the number of accounts served by one national tobacco distributor may be the sole datum on the number of that country's retail outlets.

At the extreme left, preceding the year to which the trade data refer, the combined value of the country's wholesale and retail trade as a percentage of gross domestic product or net material product is given.

Both the wholesale and retail sections of the table provide similar detail: establishments or outlets, employees, sales, and derived values for relationships among these measures; the retail section provides an additional breakdown of sales by an end-use classification of retail sales outlets.

Although all sales figures are given in U.S. dollars, the comparability of these dollar figures may differ considerably; for instance, the purchasing power of various national currencies in domestic transactions may bear only a distant relationship to the exchange rate of the same currency in international transactions. The price of goods may also vary, depending on the degree to which they are subject to direct subsidies and artificial cost controls such as tax, investment, or free-trade preferences by a central government seeking to influence social or economic conditions.

Trade: domestic

country	domestic trade as percentage of GDP, 1982	year	wholesale trade					retail trade		
			establishments[a]	employees[b]	sales[c] $'000,000	employees per establishment	sales per establishment $'000	outlets[a]	employees[b]	sales[c] $'000,000
Afghanistan	9.1[1]	...	...	...	...	...	...	...	...	...
Albania	...	1978	...	...	...	...	...	9,254[2]	...	737
Algeria	7.0[3]	1971	2,631[4]	...	749[4]	...	285[4]	3,600	18,000	9,700
American Samoa	...	...								
Andorra	...	1972						592	2,264	
Angola	...	1973	5	...				29,138[5]	...	...
Anguilla										
Antigua and Barbuda	20.9[6]	1980	25	c. 350	...	c. 14.0	...	199	c. 1,000	20[3]
Argentina	17.6[6]	1974	5	5	20,533[7]	5	...	708,421[5]	1,847,290[5]	21,125[7]
Australia	14.0[8]	1982	36,587	343,258[9]	77,040	9.4[9]	739[8]	110,500[8]	737,378[8,9]	43,952[8]
Austria	16.6[6]	1983	11,445[8]	59,370	32,324	5.6[8]	2,958[8]	37,148[8]	60,197	16,225
Bahamas, The[10]	25.6[6,11]	1980	23	1,066	143	46.3	6.235	132	4,059	354
Bahrain	...	...								
Bangladesh	8.1	1981	...	...	...	...	...	...	...	6,300
Barbados	28.9[6]	1982	...	5				1,704[7]	17,600[5,6]	210[3]
Belgium	10.5[12]	1981	55,853	166,900	73,700	3.0	1,321	130,889	197,100	26,098
Belize	15.2[6]	1981						...	...	75[3]
Benin	20.9[6,8]	1980	5	5	...	5	5,13	1535[5,13]	4,455[5,13]	260[13]
Bermuda	...	1980	60[14]	...	...	...	...	300	4,500	400[3]
Bhutan	...	...								
Bolivia	19.9[6]	1981	...	5	...	...	...	...	17,414[5,6,15]	3,265
Botswana	9.6[6]	1979	164	1,600	300	9.8	1,832	1,333	3,600	168
Brazil	15.1[6]	1975	52,722	117,423	49,102	2.2	931	635,812	723,461	42,524
British Virgin Islands	26.7[6,11]	1981	...	...	...	...	...	...	200[16]	5
Brunei	9.5[6]	1982	5	5	...	5	...	654[5]	3,403[5]	
Bulgaria	6.11[6]	1981	...	9,000[8]	...	...	...	38,304[12]	288,588[12]	13,366[12]
Burkina Faso	15.5[6,14]									
Burma	24.3[12]	1981	...	...	...	...	...	...	...	2,030
Burundi	7.5[6]	1981	...	...	...	...	...	...	...	445
Cameroon	11.9[6]	1981	...	...	...	...	...	...	...	2,160
Canada	9.4[6]	1983	30,900[17]	451,665	29,762[17]	10.2[17]	931[17]	156,518[18]	1,058,688[12]	86,201[12]
Cape Verde	...	...								
Cayman Islands	17.0[19]	1972	...	86	...	...	...	...	928	...
Central African Republic	13.3[12,18]									
Chad	30.1[6,20]	1981	...	...	...	...	...	...	...	2,157
Chile	17.5[6]	1981	524	18,900	3,661	36.1	6,987	1,196	28,200	3,344
China	5.41	1982	41,000	762,000[9]	...	18.6	...	2,607,000[12]	8,709,000[9,12]	135,796[12,21]
Christmas Island	...	1981	...	5	—	—	...	5	...	...
Cocos (Keeling) Islands	...	1981	...	5	...	...	...	1	135[5]	
Colombia	13.6[6]	1970[22]	1,363	31,628	931	23.2	683	2,785	72,310	963
Comoros	...	...								
Congo	11.13[6]	...						...	...	...
Cook Islands	24.0[11]	1976	...	5	...	...	...	...	409[5,6]	...
Costa Rica	21.7[6]	1975	332	4,073	35	12.3	104	9,713	26,486	569
Cuba	38.8[6]	1980	...	...	10,369	...	...	51,733	...	8,561
Cyprus	15.2[6]	1982	1,518	9,767[9]	1,227	6.4[9]	808	8,186[12]	15,894[9,12]	997[12]
Czechoslovakia	15.11[6]	1982	...	...	...	...	...	107,861	391,200[8]	22,487
Denmark	11.9[6]	1981	5,515	127,000	29,249	23.0	5,304	52,300[14]	116,000	11,585
Djibouti	16.3[6]	...								
Dominica	10.0[6,11]	1981	...	...	...	...	...	...	...	19
Dominican Republic	16.7[12]	1979	...	...	2,008	...	...	...	24,936[6,23]	827
Ecuador	13.2[6]	1980	2,450	15,591	2,805	6.4	1,145	102,981	179,847	5,922
Egypt	12.8[6,8]	1981	1,766	42,300[9]	3,216	24.09	1,821	2,136	48,200[9]	2,015
El Salvador	24.9[6]	1981	377	4,700	636	12.5	1,688	1,246	7,500	436
Equatorial Guinea	...	...								

The data on distribution of retail sales by kind of consumer goods may have their origin in several different types of data or analysis: One country may aggregate sales data by kind of establishment only (this may be perfectly satisfactory in a country of small, independent outlets); another may aggregate data directly by kind of goods (most easily done in a country with well-developed statistical, tax-reporting, and commercial systems). Other countries may find it impolitic to publish data that reflect the poverty of their distribution network or their supply of consumer goods and may aggregate or publish data for only a few sectors: food or nonfood goods, for example. For countries with only a few trading enterprises in a particular sector, detail must often be withheld to preserve the confidentiality of individual businesses.

The notes that follow further define the various headings.

a. The number of establishments or outlets refers to economic units that operate at a single physical location in one principal kind of activity, whether singly owned or part of a multiunit firm. Such units are not necessarily identical with a company or enterprise.

b. Number of employees refers to full-time and part-time paid workers, including salaried managers and officers; it usually excludes owner-operators.

c. Total sales (also called turnover) includes the value of merchandise sold for cash or credit; amounts received from customers for layaway purchases; receipts from rental or leasing of vehicles, equipment, tools, instruments, etc.; receipts for delivery, installation, maintenance, repair, alteration, storage, and other services.

d. Covers outlets engaged primarily in the sale of food, such as grocery stores, meat and fish markets, and bakeries.

e. Covers outlets engaged primarily in the sale of clothing and shoes; also includes outlets that sell accessory items, such as millinery, furs, umbrellas, wigs, etc.

f. Covers outlets engaged primarily in the sale of home furnishings, including furniture, draperies, floor coverings, household appliances, and home entertainment equipment.

g. Covers outlets that primarily serve food and drink, including restaurants, lunchrooms, cafeterias, social caterers, refreshment places, contract feeders, ice cream parlors, and bars and taverns.

h. Covers outlets engaged primarily in the sale of pharmaceuticals, cosmetics, and perfumes.

i. Covers outlets engaged primarily in the sale of building materials, hardware, garden supplies, paint, glass, and wallpaper.

j. Covers outlets engaged primarily in the sale of motor vehicles, motorcycles, bicycles, and tires, batteries, and other automotive supplies and parts; includes service stations.

k. Covers outlets engaged in the sale of multiple lines of merchandise, such as department stores, variety stores, and country general stores.

l. Covers miscellaneous specialized outlets such as those engaged primarily in the sale of liquors, sporting goods, books, jewelry, photographic equipment, gifts, flowers, cigars, and newspapers.

food[d]	clothing, shoes[e]	home furnishings[f]	eating, drinking[g]	drugs, pharmaceuticals[h]	building materials[i]	automobile parts[j]	general merchandise[k]	other[l]	employees per outlet	sales per outlet $'000	population per outlet	country
...	...	...	...	...	...	...	...	...	...	...	...	Afghanistan
63.2	—			36.8					...	80	277	Albania
...	...	...	...	...	...	...	...	...	5.0	2,700	5,146	Algeria
...	...	...	...	...	...	...	...	...	...	...	...	American Samoa
...	...	...	...	...	...	...	...	...	3.8	...	39	Andorra
...	...	...	...	...	...	...	...	...	...	...	...	Angola
...	...	...	...	...	...	...	...	...	...	...	...	Anguilla
...	...	...	...	...	...	...	...	...	c. 5.0	c. 100	378	Antigua and Barbuda
...	...	...	...	...	...	...	...	...	2.6[5]	...	...	Argentina
49.2	16.5	12.6	—	5.0	4.4	—	...	12.3	6.7[8,9]	398[8]	131[8]	Australia
28.9	14.0	7.9	...	4.6	...	15.0	10.0	19.5	1.6[8]	470[8]	202[8]	Austria
37.0	7.8	4.4	—	2.1	8.8	12.8	4.6	22.5	30.8	2,679	1,591	Bahamas, The[10]
...	...	...	...	...	...	...	...	...	...	...	...	Bahrain
...	...	...	...	...	...	...	...	...	...	...	...	Bangladesh
...	...	...	...	...	...	...	...	...	...	c. 125	144[7]	Barbados
...	...	...	...	...	...	...	...	...	1.5	199	75	Belgium
...	...	...	...	...	...	...	...	...	...	...	...	Belize
...	...	...	...	...	...	...	...	...	29.1[5,13]	...	22,444[5]	Benin
...	...	...	...	...	...	...	...	...	15.0	1,117	182	Bermuda
...	...	...	...	...	...	...	...	...	...	...	...	Bhutan
...	...	...	...	...	...	...	...	...	...	...	...	Bolivia
...	...	...	...	...	...	...	...	...	2.7	126	593	Botswana
...	...	...	...	...	...	...	...	...	1.1	67	165	Brazil
...	...	...	...	...	...	...	...	...	...	...	...	British Virgin Islands
...	...	...	...	...	...	...	...	...	5.2[5]	...	306[5]	Brunei
44.4	14.7	...	...	...	1.4	...	8.4	31.1	7.5[12]	349[12]	232[12]	Bulgaria
...	...	...	...	...	...	...	...	...	...	...	...	Burkina Faso
...	...	...	...	...	...	...	...	...	...	...	...	Burma
...	...	...	...	...	...	...	...	...	...	...	...	Burundi
...	...	...	...	...	...	...	...	...	...	...	...	Cameroon
26.6	5.6	2.5	—	4.0	0.9	28.2	15.3	16.7	4.0[18]	200[8]	138[18]	Canada
...	...	...	...	...	...	...	...	...	...	...	...	Cape Verde
...	...	...	...	...	...	...	...	...	...	...	...	Cayman Islands
...	...	...	...	...	...	...	...	...	...	...	...	Central African Republic
...	...	...	...	...	...	...	...	...	...	...	...	Chad
29.3	9.7	6.0	—	4.5	5.4	22.8	6.8	15.5	23.6	2,796	9,443	Chile
52.9	21.3			25.8					3.3	52	387[12]	China
...	...	...	...	...	...	...	...	...	...	...	662	Christmas Island
...	...	...	...	...	...	...	...	...	...	...	569	Cocos (Keeling) Islands
...	...	...	...	...	...	...	...	...	26.0	346	...	Colombia
...	...	...	...	...	...	...	...	...	...	...	...	Comoros
...	...	...	...	...	...	...	...	...	...	...	...	Congo
...	...	...	...	...	...	...	...	...	...	...	...	Cook Islands
37.7	13.5	6.9	...	8.2	7.0	15.1	5.9	5.7	2.7	59	203	Costa Rica
40.1	14.1	4.3	26.0	2.1	0.6	—	12.8	—	...	166	188	Cuba
21.8	10.8	...	...	3.0	6.9	24.9	...	32.6	1.9[9,12]	122[12]	79[12]	Cyprus
47.8	15.4	5.1	2.1	3.5	2.3	7.4	...	16.4	c. 3.7	352	142	Czechoslovakia
60.9	6.4	5.5	—	1.4	1.9	14.0	3.0	6.9	c. 2.2	c. 222	98[14]	Denmark
...	...	...	...	...	...	...	...	...	...	...	...	Djibouti
...	...	...	...	...	...	...	...	...	...	...	...	Dominica
...	...	...	...	...	...	...	...	...	...	...	...	Dominican Republic
24.2	29.1	8.1	3.0	4.8	4.0	17.8	3.4	5.6	1.7	58	74	Ecuador
...	...	...	...	...	...	...	...	...	22.6[9]	943	20,349	Egypt
7.8[11,24]	2.8[11,24]	12.3[11,24]	...	3.4[11,24]	12.6[11,24]	38.7[11,24]	16.6[11,24]	5.8[11,24]	6.0	350	3,750	El Salvador
...	...	...	...	...	...	...	...	...	...	...	...	Equatorial Guinea

Trade: domestic (continued)

country	domestic trade as percentage of GDP, 1982	year	wholesale trade establishments[a]	employees[b]	sales[c] $'000,000	employees per establishment	sales per establishment $'000	retail trade outlets[a]	employees[b]	sales[c] $'000,000
Ethiopia	9.6[3,12]	1973[25]	375	3,200	...	8.5	...	7,416	17,100	202
Faeroe Islands	11.7[6,8]	1980	...	5	...	...	...	...	1,484[5,6]	...
Falkland Islands	...	1976	2	...	...	...	...	21	...	...
Fiji	17.4[6]	1976	184	2,340	155	12.7	840	2,245	7,620	258
Finland	10.3[6]	1980	8,248	86,164[9]	26,346	10.4[9]	3,194	36,113[12]	158,717[9,12]	25,318[12]
France	12.2[6]	1982	96,900	815,500	200,697	8.4	2,071	413,700	1,134,900	134,493
French Guiana	...	...	...	...	...	...	...	...	...	...
French Polynesia	24.1[6]	...	...	...	...	...	...	...	...	...
Gabon	7.0[14]	...	...	...	...	...	...	...	...	...
Gambia, The	...	1979	...	3,300	...	...	...	...	700	...
Gaza Strip	...	1982	...	5	...	...	...	...	11,000[5]	...
Germany, East	10.0[1,6]	1983	...	...	...	...	...	...	898,500	39,060
Germany, West	10.8[6]	1983	36,318[14]	947,700	288,606	26.3[14]	9,647	249,466[14]	2,004,900	145,805
Ghana	30.1[3,6]	1977[13]	460	1,100	115	2.4	250	2,182	5,700	237
Gibraltar	...	1981	...	595	...	...	...	...	1,354	...
Greece	11.2[12]	1978	25,266	91,341	...	3.6	...	160,599	287,457	...
Greenland	...	1981	...	...	81	...	...	...	...	92
Grenada	16.8[14]	1979	...	5	...	...	...	...	2,262[5]	...
Guadeloupe	17.5[6,8]	1974	...	5	...	...	...	...	11,960[5,6,9]	...
Guam	...	1977	51	546	93[8]	10.7	1,525	531	4,070	353[8]
Guatemala	26.4[12]	1980	...	5	5	...	...	...	51,700[5,9]	844[5]
Guernsey	...	...	...	...	...	...	...	...	...	...
Guinea	...	...	...	...	...	...	...	...	...	...
Guinea-Bissau	...	...	...	...	...	...	...	...	...	...
Guyana	8.6[8]	1980	...	...	...	...	...	147	...	109
Haiti	17.6[6]	1981	...	5	...	...	...	...	3,900[5,9,19]	880
Honduras	11.9[12]	1982	...	5	...	...	...	...	84,541[5,6,9]	800[3]
Hong Kong	18.0[6]	1981	30,887	166,593	38,564	5.4	1,249	47,774	231,163	10,917
Hungary	10.9[1,6]	1981	128	93,000	13,121	726.6	102,511	54,860	353,000	10,879
Iceland	...	1979[27]	970[11]	4,500[9,11]	584[11]	4.6[9,11]	602[11]	1,610	6,830[9]	614
India	14.6[6]	1970	116,000	...	35.2	...	303.4	3,760,000	1,753,000	3,273.7
Indonesia	14.9[12]	1980	5	5	5	...	5	54,632[5]	85,400[5]	3,452[5]
Iran	15.8[6]	1972	18,210	53,522[9]	2,409	2.9[9]	132	218,132	333,106[9]	3,758
Iraq	4.2[6,15]	1976	1,532	2,700	242,675.4	1.8	158,404.3	77,766	106,800	2,471,590.8
Ireland	13.0[6,11]	1977	3,073	40,584	4,593	13.2	1,495	32,332	79,870	4,170
Isle of Man	12.1	1981	...	813	...	...	...	...	2,208	...
Israel	13.0[4]	1977	4,862	33,178	9,037	6.8	1,859	40,000	85,000	1,622[13]
Italy	15.7[6]	1980	120,366[18]	390,000[18]	...	3.2[18]	...	1,013,601	410,000[18]	116,579
Ivory Coast	20.8[6,14]	1978	...	...	...	...	...	50,000	...	3,445[3]
Jamaica	23.5[1]	1979	...	...	...	...	...	...	...	878
Japan	12.3[12]	1982	428,750	4,090,000[9]	1,600,373	9.5[9]	3,733	2,258,494	8,351,000[9]	413,680
Jersey	...	...	...	...	...	...	...	...	...	...
Jordan	16.2[6]	1981	...	...	...	...	...	...	...	1,765
Kampuchea	...	...	...	...	...	...	...	...	...	...
Kenya	8.8[6]	1982[28]	2,161	27,351	...	12.7	...	5,219	29,068	2,877[3]
Kiribati	6.1[6,11]	1976	...	...	...	...	...	35	...	7
Korea, North	...	...	...	...	...	...	...	...	...	...
Korea, South	14.5[6]	1982	45,568	112,400	9,563	2.5	210	749,538	409,300	20,609
Kuwait	9.5[6]	1973	981	6,700	560	6.8	571	11,306	35,300	1,385
Laos	...	...	...	...	...	...	...	...	...	...
Lebanon	28.3[6,20]	1975	...	5	...	...	...	...	130,000[5,6,9]	...
Lesotho	11.1[3,6]	1976	...	5	...	...	...	...	4,649[5,6]	...
Liberia	8.5[3,6]	1974	...	5	...	...	...	...	16,282[5,6]	...
Libya	5.9[6]	1973	1,143	4,776	...	4.2	...	26,908[12]	44,836[12]	...
Liechtenstein	...	1975	67	216	...	3.2	...	228	740	...
Luxembourg	15.7[6,8]	1981	998[14]	7,472[11]	2,285	7.6[11]	2,318[14]	3,970[14]	11,381[11]	1,588
Macau	...	...	...	...	...	...	...	...	...	...
Madagascar	13.0[23]	1976	1,104	...	...	...	...	1,570	...	696[3]
Malawi	12.8[6]	1979[13]	51	17,100	458	335.3	8,988	35	4,200	146
Malaysia	13.3[6]	1980[29]	17,907	102,412	13,430	5.7	750	90,037[12]	66,214[12]	5,562[12]
Maldives	13.4[6]	...	...	...	...	...	...	...	...	...
Mali	16.5[6]	...	...	...	...	...	...	...	...	...
Malta	13.7[12]	1981	5	...	0.932	...	186	4	...	1,994
Martinique	17.1[6,8]	1974	...	5	...	...	...	...	12,799[5,6,9]	...
Mauritania	10.8[6,8]	1971[13]	23	100	22	4.3	939	59	700	22
Mauritius	11.0[6]	1982[13]	5	5	...	5	...	143[5]	5,700[5]	387[3]
Mayotte	...	...	...	...	...	...	...	...	...	...
Mexico	22.8[6]	1975	11,652	130,939	5,051	11.2	434	463,612	987,089	19,121
Monaco	...	...	...	...	...	...	...	...	...	...
Mongolia	33.8	1982[30]	...	...	...	...	...	4,723	37,500	1,061
Montserrat	20.0[6]	1980	...	...	...	...	...	160	200	11[3]
Morocco	14.3[3,6]	1972	...	...	...	...	...	4,000	20,000	5,630[3]
Mozambique	...	1970	...	5	...	...	...	...	64,019[5,6]	...
Nauru	...	...	...	...	...	...	...	...	...	...
Nepal	3.5[12,31]	1976	...	5	...	...	...	...	282,632[5,6]	945[3]
Netherlands, The	13.8[6]	1982	...	564,000	...	...	...	193,077[8]	...	39,824
Netherlands Antilles	26.3[6]	1972	...	5	...	...	...	...	12,764[5]	...
New Caledonia	26.3[6]	...	...	...	...	...	...	...	...	...
New Zealand	22.0[6]	1978	6,183	77,385[9]	9,656	12.5[9]	1,562	32,334	172,851[9]	6,932
Nicaragua	23.6[11,12]	1981	...	5	...	...	...	...	105,053[5,6,8,9]	475
Niger	11.6[6,8]	...	...	...	...	...	...	...	...	...
Nigeria	20.7[6]	1975[13]	255	38,400	3,771	150.6	14,788	181	26,400	1,477
Niue	...	1982	5	...	...	...	...	22[5]	78[20]	...
Norfolk Island	...	1981	...	5	...	...	...	...	271[5]	...
Norway	11.9[6]	1981	11,080	95,671[9]	29,186	8.6[9]	2,634	33,225	127,105[9]	15,729

retail trade									employees per outlet	sales per outlet $'000	population per outlet	country
percent breakdown of sales												
food[d]	clothing, shoes[e]	home furnishings[f]	eating, drinking[g]	drugs, pharma-ceuticals[h]	building materials[i]	automobile parts[j]	general merchandise[k]	other[l]				
...	...	...	...	...	...	...	...	...	2.3	27	...	Ethiopia
												Faeroe Islands
									...	...	95	Falkland Islands
27.8	10.4	1.7	...	1.0	2.6	17.1	22.7	16.7	3.4	115	261	Fiji
39.0	9.1	1.5	...	1.8	11.1	18.1	16.0	3.4	4.4[9,12]	701[12]	132[12]	Finland
39.9	15.9	19.2	—	5.1	—	3.7[26]	...	16.1	2.7	325	132	France
									...	...	...	French Guiana
												French Polynesia
									...	...	...	Gabon
									...	...	...	Gambia, The
												Gaza Strip
51.4	15.1	6.0	—	5.6	6.5	—	15.4	—	...	...	...	Germany, East
28.8	13.5	10.0	—	6.1	—	11.9	—	29.7	8.6[14]	829[14]	246[14]	Germany, West
...	...	...	...	...	...	...	...	...	2.6	108	...	Ghana
									...	...	...	Gibraltar
									1.8	...	59	Greece
									...	...	...	Greenland
									...	...	...	Grenada
									...	...	...	Guadeloupe
7.0[8]	5.9[8]	3.8[8]	20.0[8]	0.6[8]	8.3[8]	14.7[8]	16.8[8]	22.9[8]	7.7	405	183	Guam
									...	...	...	Guatemala
									...	...	...	Guernsey
									...	...	...	Guinea
									...	...	...	Guinea-Bissau
9.7	18.9	13.8	4.5	2.8	10.6	18.6	...	21.1	...	743	5,884	Guyana
									...	...	...	Haiti
									...	...	...	Honduras
18.4	6.8	...	19.9	...	...	8.2	...	55.0	4.8	229	108	Hong Kong
30.5	13.3	6.5	12.0	0.7	13.1	8.2	...	15.6	6.4	198	195	Hungary
33.6	10.7	12.0	—	4.5	—	—	28.6	10.6	4.2[9]	381	152	Iceland
									0.5	0.871	143.4	India
									1.6[5]	63[5]	2,679[5]	Indonesia
									1.5[9]	17	141	Iran
									1.4	31,782.4	148	Iraq
33.7	4.6	8.9	10.5	2.6	3.0	23.9	4.7	8.2	2.5	129	101	Ireland
									...	...	...	Isle of Man
27.3	7.6	8.4	—	—	56.7			...	2.1	...	91	Israel
...	...	...	...	...	...	...	...	...	...	115	56	Italy
									...	...	152	Ivory Coast
80.5	5.8	5.3	...	...	...	...	...	8.4	...	...	...	Jamaica
27.9	9.9	8.0	8.6	2.2	...	8.7	12.3	22.3	3.7[9]	183	52	Japan
									...	...	...	Jersey
									...	...	...	Jordan
									...	...	...	Kampuchea
									5.6	...	3,457	Kenya
									...	189	1,571	Kiribati
									...	...	...	Korea, North
29.4[14]	13.1[14]	8.9[14]	18.9[14]	5.0[14]	...	5.4[14]	1.2[14]	18.0[14]	0.5	33	53	Korea, South
17.0	6.8	13.7	3.4	0.9	7.1	13.2	1.3	36.6	3.1	123	78	Kuwait
									...	...	...	Laos
									...	...	...	Lebanon
									...	...	...	Lesotho
									...	...	...	Liberia
									1.7[12]	...	84[12]	Libya
									3.2	...	105	Liechtenstein
31.0	12.4	12.0	...	3.6	...	32.0	...	8.9	2.9[11]	424[14]	91[14]	Luxembourg
									...	...	...	Macau
									...	c. 450	...	Madagascar
									120.0	4,166	...	Malawi
33.4	7.3	10.8	...	2.5	...	33.3	4.4	8.3	0.7[12]	62[12]	127[12]	Malaysia
									...	...	...	Maldives
									...	...	...	Mali
									...	498	...	Malta
									...	...	...	Martinique
									11.9	368	...	Mauritania
									39.8[5]	...	...	Mauritius
									...	...	...	Mayotte
17.8	7.3	5.8	...	2.8	7.3	24.5	16.6	17.9	2.1	41	130	Mexico
									...	...	...	Monaco
									7.9	225	373	Mongolia
									1.2	c. 70	73	Montserrat
									5.0	c. 4,000	...	Morocco
									...	...	...	Mozambique
									...	...	...	Nauru
									...	...	...	Nepal
									...	333[8]	73[8]	Netherlands, The
									...	...	...	Netherlands Antilles
									...	...	...	New Caledonia
24.3	7.8	7.9	6.7	3.0	2.2	32.8	8.3	7.0	5.3[9]	214	96	New Zealand
									...	...	...	Nicaragua
									...	...	...	Niger
									145.9	816	...	Nigeria
									...	...	...	Niue
									...	...	...	Norfolk Island
35.4	9.9	7.7	...	...	...	28.3	4.6	14.1	3.8[9]	473	123	Norway

Trade: domestic (continued)

country	domestic trade as percentage of GDP, 1982	year	wholesale trade					retail trade		
			establish-ments[a]	employees[b]	sales[c] $'000,000	employees per establishment	sales per establishment $'000	outlets[a]	employees[b]	sales[c] $'000,000
Oman	11.5[12]	1981	...	...	...	...	...	...	...	830
Pacific Is., Trust Terr. of the	...	...	...	...	...	...	...	...	...	...
Pakistan	14.7[12]	1981	...	...	...	...	...	...	...	13,636
Panama	15.9[6]	1971	558	10,028	446	18.0	799	6,611	25,700	434
Papua New Guinea	8.0[15]	1981	...	...	...	...	...	...	...	775
Paraguay	26.6[12]	1981	...	...	...	...	...	...	91,900[20]	1,785
Peru	19.7[6]	1973	4,210	34,100	2,163	8.1	514	103,010	72,200	2,015
Philippines	17.9[6]	1980[13]	20,723	179,300	6,308	8.7	304	280,000	337,000	7,068
Pitcairn Island	...	1982	—	—	—	—	—	1	...	...
Poland	13.8[1,6]	1982[30]	...	117,800	28,297	...	...	245,574	593,700	28,281
Portugal	22.0[3,6]	1980[13]	7,783	161,100[9]	12,375	20.7[9]	1,592	16,547	113,000[9]	4,822
Puerto Rico	15.1[6]	1977	2,208	28,338	4,395	12.8	1,991	36,276	109,654	4,796
Qatar	6.4[6]	1980	...	...	...	...	...	9,996	...	...
Réunion	16.1[6,8]	1982	...	5	...	...	...	...	14,328[5,6]	...
Romania	6.2[1]	1982	...	...	...	...	...	80,082	448,800	16,730
Rwanda	16.1[6]	...	...	...	...	...	...	...	...	...
St. Christopher and Nevis	13.7[6]	...	...	...	...	...	...	...	...	...
St. Helena and Ascension	...	...	...	...	...	...	...	...	...	...
St. Lucia	18.0[6,20]	...	...	...	...	...	...	...	...	...
St. Pierre and Miquelon	...	1982	...	5	...	...	...	...	279[5,6]	...
St. Vincent	10.1[3]	...	...	...	...	...	...	...	...	...
San Marino	...	...	...	...	...	...	...	...	...	...
São Tomé and Príncipe	...	...	...	...	...	...	...	...	...	...
Saudi Arabia	4.3[3,6]	1971[32]	822	2,500	...	3.0	...	35,780	49,500	42,860[3]
Senegal	23.2[6,14]	1979	...	4,600	...	...	...	...	4,400	1,044[3]
Seychelles	22.8[6]	1982	5	5	...	5	...	172	1,300[5]	...
Sierra Leone	13.8[3,6]	1980	...	5	...	...	...	...	7,182[5,6]	555[3]
Singapore	21.8[6]	1981	18,794	107,316	27,260	5.7	1,450	19,298	90,700	4,545
Solomon Islands	7.7[12,19]	1980	...	5	...	...	...	...	1,863[5,12]	...
Somalia	...	...	...	...	...	...	...	...	...	...
South Africa[33]	13.1[6,34]	1977	10,106	232,478	18,983	23.0	1,878	60,774[35]	406,994[35]	14,563
Bophuthatswana[33]	...	...	...	...	...	...	...	...	...	...
Ciskei[33]	...	...	...	...	...	...	...	...	...	...
Transkei[33]	...	...	...	...	...	...	...	...	...	...
Venda[33]	...	...	...	...	...	...	...	...	...	...
South West Africa/Namibia	34	...	...	...	...	...	...	...	...	...
Spain	17.6[6]	1979	40,000	...	...	...	...	710,865	1,400,000	84,839
Sri Lanka	20.2[6]	1979	353	27,600	...	78.2	...	1,583	67,100	1,460[3]
Sudan, The	18.2[11,12]	1981	...	5	...	...	...	...	52,000[5,6,7]	3,278
Suriname	12.2[6]	1981	...	...	...	...	...	...	...	280
Swaziland	7.6[3,6]	1980	35	821	...	23.5	...	385	3,298	...
Sweden	10.4[6]	1982	24,078	162,300	50,934[3]	6.7	2,023[3]	57,960	265,200	32,569
Switzerland	...	1975	13,844	130,600	...	9.4	...	49,972	274,500	27,257[8]
Syria	23.5[6]	1975	2,792	6,200[23]	...	2.3[23]	...	81,167	110,000[9]	4,960[3]
Taiwan	13.4[6]	1982	54,743	153,400	3,700	2.8	68	340,893	148,100	7,492
Tanzania	6.7[6]	1973	...	...	...	...	...	18,300	...	2,404[3]
Thailand	22.7[6]	1980	5,647	187,737	21,532	33.2	3,813	14,622	144,864	4,022
Togo	20.7[3,6]	1972	20	1,200	95	60.0	4,730	96	1,600	28
Tokelau	...	1982	...	...	...	...	...	3	...	...
Tonga	13.7[6]	1976	...	14	...	...	...	...	687	...
Trinidad and Tobago	11.4[6]	1977	124	6,786	509	54.7	4,102	370	15,986	543
Tunisia	...	1973	...	...	...	...	...	2,200	5,000	2,310[3]
Turkey	16.3[12]	1980	22,790	29,607[23]	2,999[23]	1.3[23]	134[23]	284,716	62,308[23]	5,827[14]
Turks and Caicos Islands	...	...	...	...	...	...	...	...	...	...
Tuvalu	...	...	...	...	...	...	...	...	...	...
Uganda	6.4[15]	1977	226	4,100	...	18.1	...	251	3,200	5,285[3]
U.S.S.R.	17.7[1,6]	1983	...	2,375,000[31]	257,700[31]	...	...	1,020,700	7,531,000	436,914
United Arab Emirates	9.7[6]	1981	...	5	5	5	...	13,906[5,6,20]	74,332[5,6,8,9]	2,180
United Kingdom	11.3[6]	1982[32]	100,931[36]	...	217,760[36]	...	2,158[36]	349,659[12,26]	2,264,000[12,26]	122,157[12,26]
United States	16.7[6]	1982	415,829	4,984,880	1,997,895	12.0	4,805	1,923,228	14,467,813	1,065,917
Uruguay	15.6[3,6]	1981	...	...	...	...	...	...	...	4,865
Vanuatu	...	1973	19	109	...	5.7	...	284	1,179	...
Venezuela	8.8[6]	1979	...	...	...	...	...	...	530,978	15,764
Vietnam	...	1977	...	...	...	...	...	...	...	7,894
Virgin Islands (U.S.)	...	1982	104	1,363	197	13.1	1,196	1,191	6,980	489
Wallis and Futuna	...	...	...	...	...	...	...	...	...	...
West Bank	...	1982	...	5	...	...	...	...	17,000	...
Western Sahara	...	...	...	...	...	...	...	...	...	...
Western Samoa	9.5[6,19]	1975	...	11	...	...	...	...	1,708	...
Yemen (Aden)	...	1973	...	5	...	...	...	...	25,509[5,6,9]	...
Yemen (Şan'ā')	17.5[3,6]	...	...	...	...	...	...	...	...	...
Yugoslavia	21.7[3,6,37]	1981	1,215[8]	152,134	25,570	120.9	28,582	80,606	350,649	22,560
Zaire	22.0[12,20]	1971	...	...	...	...	...	1,232	10,800	2,742[3]
Zambia	12.6[6]	1974	494	15,500	977	31.4	1,978	1,636	13,700	587
Zimbabwe	13.1[6]	1982	...	5	...	...	...	...	79,800[5,6]	1,460[3]

food[d]	clothing, shoes[e]	home furnishings[f]	eating, drinking[g]	drugs, pharmaceuticals[h]	building materials[i]	automobile parts[j]	general merchandise[k]	other[l]	employees per outlet	sales per outlet $'000	population per outlet	country
...	...	...	...	...	...	...	...	...	...	...	...	Oman
												Pacific Is., Trust Terr. of the
66.5	13.0	1.1	...	0.4	...	...	...	19.0	...	...	...	Pakistan
33.5	10.9	9.5	...	...	...	...	...	46.1	3.9	66	224	Panama
55.3[15]	8.1[15]	8.7[15]	...	...	...	...	...	27.9[15]	...	...	...	Papua New Guinea
...	...	...	...	...	...	...	...	...	0.7	20	145	Paraguay
24.9[11]	13.9[11]	9.4[11]	...	3.0[11]	11.8[11]	27.9[11]	...	9.1[11]	1.2	25	173	Peru
												Philippines
												Pitcairn Island
43.9[8]				56.1[18]					2.4	115	148	Poland
27.5[15]	13.1[15]	9.1[15]	14.6[15]	6.9[15]	7.8[15]	16.2[15]	...	4.8[15]	6.8[9]	291	593	Portugal
26.8	10.4	5.6	6.4	3.9	4.0	23.9	10.0	9.0	3.0	132	84	Puerto Rico
...	...	...	...	...	...	...	...	...	...	...	25	Qatar
												Réunion
34.6	...	...	18.1	...	...	...	...	47.3	5.6	209	281	Romania
												Rwanda
												St. Christopher and Nevis
												St. Helena and Ascension
												St. Lucia
												St. Pierre and Miquelon
												St. Vincent
												San Marino
												São Tomé and Principe
...	...	...	...	...	...	...	...	...	1.4	...	196	Saudi Arabia
												Senegal
...	...	...	...	...	...	...	...	...	7.6[5]	...	...	Seychelles
												Sierra Leone
1.6	20.8	10.9	9.4	1.6	1.2	20.5	26.8	7.2	4.7	236	127	Singapore
												Solomon Islands
												Somalia
20.5	12.5	8.2	8.9	2.9	1.5	27.5	13.4	4.7	6.7[35]	..	...	South Africa[33]
												Bophuthatswana[33]
												Ciskei[33]
												Transkei[33]
												Venda[33]
												South West Africa/Namibia
...	...	...	...	...	...	...	...	...	2.0	119	52	Spain
...	...	...	...	...	...	...	...	...	42.4	c. 922	9,141	Sri Lanka
												Sudan, The
												Suriname
...	...	...	...	...	...	...	...	...	8.6	...	...	Swaziland
34.8	9.8	12.6	—	...	...	19.3	5.0	18.5	4.6	562	144	Sweden
...	...	...	...	...	...	...	...	...	5.5	...	127	Switzerland
...	...	...	...	...	...	...	...	...	1.4[9]	c. 60	91	Syria
75.8[3]	9.0[3]	10.8[3]	...	...	...	...	...	4.4[3]	0.4	22	54	Taiwan
											825	Tanzania
2.5	2.7	7.1	2.6	1.2	10.5	56.6	5.3	11.5	9.9	275	3,177	Thailand
...	...	...	...	...	...	...	...	...	16.7	297	22,000	Togo
											525	Tokelau
												Tonga
18.6	...	8.5	2.7	...	10.7	28.2	15.3	15.9	43.2	1,467	2,811	Trinidad and Tobago
...	...	...	...	...	...	...	...	...	2.3	...	2,905	Tunisia
13.5[23]	13.5[23]	13.1[23]	...	5.1[23]	9.6[23]	23.5[23]	21.7[23]		0.4[23]	29[14]	158	Turkey
												Turks and Caicos Islands
												Tuvalu
...	...	...	...	...	...	...	...	...	12.7	...	46,673	Uganda
50.3	16.5	5.3	8.8	...	1.0	4.5	6.8	6.8	7.4	428	267	U.S.S.R.
...	...	...	...	...	...	...	...	...	c. 5.3[5,6]	...	50[5,20]	United Arab Emirates
23.1	5.0	6.5	12.7	1.8	2.3	28.1	10.8	9.7	6.5[12,26]	349[12,26]	161[12,26]	United Kingdom
23.1	5.5	9.0	9.8	3.5	4.8	27.5	11.5	5.3	7.5	554	120	United States
												Uruguay
...	...	...	...	...	...	...	...	...	4.2	...	317	Vanuatu
65.1	10.1	7.6	...	...	...	5.0	...	12.2	...	...	...	Venezuela
												Vietnam
26.5	7.1	3.7	8.6	2.2	3.8	13.1	4.6	30.4	5.9	411	97	Virgin Islands (U.S.)
												Wallis and Futuna
												West Bank
												Western Sahara
												Western Samoa
												Yemen (Aden)
...	...	...	...	...	...	...	...	...	...	...	...	Yemen (Ṣan'ā')
26.5	11.3	4.2	...	0.3	5.0	3.8	...	43.5	4.4	280	281	Yugoslavia
...	...	...	...	...	...	...	...	...	8.8	...	22,963	Zaire
...	...	...	...	...	...	...	...	...	8.4	359	901	Zambia
												Zimbabwe

[1]Percent of net material product.   [2]Excludes retail trade network of the agricultural cooperatives.   [3]1981.   [4]1969.   [5]Retail trade data include wholesale trade.   [6]Includes hotels.   [7]1973.   [8]1980.   [9]All persons engaged including proprietors.   [10]Data refer to New Providence island only.   [11]1978.   [12]Excludes restaurants.   [13]Data refer to larger establishments only.   [14]1979.   [15]1976.   [16]1974.   [17]1966.   [18]1971.   [19]1972.   [20]1977.   [21]1983.   [22]12 cities only.   [23]1970.   [24]14 cities only.   [25]Excludes Addis Ababa and Asmera.   [26]Excludes motor vehicles.   [27]Excludes alcohol, petroleum products, construction materials, and automobiles.   [28]Retail trade includes some wholesale trade.   [29]Peninsular Malaysia only.   [30]State- and cooperative-owned establishments only.   [31]1982.   [32]Urban establishments only.   [33]South Africa includes Bophuthatswana, Ciskei, Transkei, and Venda.   [34]South Africa includes South West Africa/Namibia.   [35]Includes hotels, construction, transportation, and communication.   [36]Includes dealing.   [37]Percent of gross material product.

Finance

This table presents major statistical aggregates comprising national financial structure or constituting the basis of certain international economic
comparisons. It includes such data as international reserves, money supply, central banking activity and discount rates, commercial (or "deposit
money") banking activity, and external indebtedness. The country models are broadly similar and permit comparison of internal structure and
external position at a high level of generalization.

One of the principal financial criteria of the relative economic position
of a country is the size of its international reserves. International reserves
as represented in this table comprise the sum of a country's holdings of
Special Drawing Rights (SDRs; an unconditional credit allocation, within
a quota system set by the International Monetary Fund [IMF], of currency
needed by a country to maintain stability of foreign exchange transactions
or markets) and its holdings of foreign exchange vis-à-vis its holdings of
gold With the exception of the developed and a few petroleum-producing
countries, the SDR balances of most countries are minimal, a consequence
of the common practice of using SDRs for payments toward offsetting
adverse balances of trade. The fact that most countries hold the bulk
of their reserves in currencies underlines the scarcity value of gold. The
ratio of external debt to total reserves cannot be interpreted in isolation:
a low ratio, for example, may characterize the situation of a country with
little need to borrow or of one with substantial debt but also the means
to repay it. Much higher ratios, on the other hand, may be manageable,
despite small reserves, if a country's export earnings are also high.

The section on money supply for the country, both as a total and as a per
capita amount, refers to one particular measure of money in circulation:
M1, the sum of money in private sector demand deposit accounts and
outside banks in circulation; it is distinguished from a broader measure of
supply, M2, which is roughly M1 plus "quasi-money" (the time, savings,
and foreign-currency deposits of residents).

The section of the table outlining banking activity and the principal monetary aggregates encompasses both central bank authorities and commercial
(deposit) banks. For both, the principal component aggregates are grouped
under assets and liabilities. For certain countries, the four principal aggregates under assets and liabilities do not comprise the entire total, and the
percentages shown, therefore, may add to less than 100% (or more, when
the net of other liabilities [capital, reserves, undistributed profits, checks,
and other transit items] is negative, reducing the total against which these
percentages are calculated). The items excluded by the choice of categories
are the least significant worldwide but may be important locally; they
include such items as quasi-money, money seasonally adjusted, unused
bank overdrafts, and so on. In the case of the central bank authority, data
are also provided for the central bank discount rate, generally the controlling interest rate for banking and commercial activity in the country.

The largest portion of assets in the case of both central and commercial
banks comprises claims on government and government agencies and
foreign assets and holdings, though some of the latter, such as the large
outstanding loans to socialist and less developed countries of the late

Finance

country	international reserves, 1985[a]			money supply, 1984[b]		central bank authority, 1984[b]								
	total ('000,000 SDRs)	% for-eign ex-change	ratio of external debt to total reserves, 1983[b]	stock ('000,000,000 national currency)	M1 per capita	assets (%)				liabilities (%)				central bank discount rate, 1985
						claims on govern-ment	claims on foreign assets	claims on banks	claims on private sector	reserve money	govern-ment deposits	foreign liabilities	capital accounts	
Afghanistan	285	81.8	4.5[1]	55.7[2]	3,240[2]	57.1[2]	40.7[2]	0.4[2]	0.6[2]	75.2[2]	5.8[2]	0.2[2]	9.8[2]	...
Albania	...	...	...	...	...	...	...	...	...	...	...	...	...	...
Algeria	3,252	85.5	6.2	112.8[1]	5,660[1]	47.2[2]	16.5[2]	35.8[2]	0.5[2]	98.3[2]	0.9[2]	0.4[2]	—	...
American Samoa	...	...	...	...	...	...	...	...	...	...	...	...	...	...
Andorra	...	...	...	...	...	...	...	...	...	...	...	...	...	...
Angola	...	...	...	...	...	...	...	...	...	...	...	...	...	...
Anguilla	...	...	...	...	...	...	...	...	...	...	...	...	...	...
Antigua and Barbuda	16[6]	100.0[6]	8.5	0.062	780	21.1	78.9	—	...	100.0	—	—	—	7.0[7]
Argentina	1,869	91.8	18.5	0.095	3	31.2	33.6	31.7	—	39.2	0.2	21.5	8.8	791.6[8]
Australia	6,426	88.6	...	22.492	1,450	32.3	66.8	—	0.8	64.0	—	—	—	13.5[9]
Austria	4,772	72.1	...	176.4	23,360	3.5	64.6	31.9	—	66.6	1.6	—	32.6	4.5
Bahamas, The	212	94.8	2.0	0.188	830	21.3	78.7	—	—	51.2	20.9	—	25.9	8.5
Bahrain	1,448	97.0	0.5[1]	0.239	580	—	100.0	—	—	21.7	65.3	0.2	18.7	7.0[6]
Bangladesh	288	91.7	7.9	43.748	450	27.4[3]	22.5	38.6	—	51.9	—	32.2	—	11.0
Barbados	131	98.5	2.3	0.306	1,210	25.7	59.1	3.5	11.7	54.6	12.8	37.8	6.9	16.0
Belgium	5,774	64.3	...	933.0	94.630	20.2	79.8	—	—	94.9	—	—	—	9.5
Belize	13	84.6	5.9	0.050	310	82.1	17.9	—	—	68.3	—	18.7	—	12.6[7]
Benin	5	40.0	146.8	94.1	24,190	27.0	2.1	70.9	—	51.5	2.0	41.0	—	10.5
Bermuda	...	...	...	0.036[2]	650[2]	...	...	...	...	...	...	...	...	...
Bhutan	...	...	...	0.050[1, 11]	40[1, 11]	3.9	4.0	2.7	26.5	16.3	6.9	—	0.6	10.0[6, 8]
Bolivia	176	82.4	15.3	3,370.1	538,960	73.2	21.3	3.0	—	18.9	53.4	39.9	—	149.0
Botswana	425	94.8	0.6	0.192	180	—	100.0	—	—	18.0	51.6	—	9.1	9.0
Brazil	10,876	99.1	13.3	23,090.0	174,160	22.1[3]	55.1	5.1	17.1	15.7	22.8	80.8	—	187.36
British Virgin Islands	...	...	...	0.019[13]	1,610[13]	...	...	...	...	...	...	...	...	...
Brunei	...	...	...	0.903[14]	4,650[14]	...	...	...	...	...	...	...	...	7.8[6, 8]
Bulgaria	...	...	...	...	...	...	...	...	...	...	...	...	...	...
Burkina Faso	122	88.5	4.6	66.5	9,900	18.6	68.5	12.9	—	77.0	6.4	12.4	—	10.5
Burma	58	84.5	22.6	12.777	350	−81.0	8.7	172.2	—	126.8	—	15.3	—	...
Burundi	34	70.6	10.4	14.513	1,930	78.5[3]	16.5	2.6	0.7	47.7	8.1	14.9	20.1	7.0
Cameroon	56[6]	87.5[6]	11.8	414.6	44,120	24.6	11.9	63.6	—	60.9	25.8	6.2	—	9.0[6]
Canada	3,137	53.6	...	51.5	2,050	79.1	20.9	—	—	96.4	—	—	—	9.3
Cape Verde	...	...	...	...	...	...	...	...	...	...	...	...	...	...
Cayman Islands	...	...	...	0.020	1,060	...	...	...	...	...	...	...	...	...
Central African Republic	54[6]	94.4[6]	4.6	48.0	19,120	35.4	44.6	20.1	—	62.1	2.0	29.0	—	9.0[6]
Chad	45[6]	97.8[6]	4.6	56.2	11,470	24.4	38.2	37.4	—	78.5	1.1	15.1	—	9.0[6]
Chile	1,705	96.8	3.3	116.2	9,780	15.0	27.0	46.6	11.3	5.9	1.8	37.3	11.7	15.6[8]
China	12,050	90.2	...	212.6	210	...	...	...	...	...	...	...	...	...
Christmas Island	...	...	...	...	...	...	...	...	...	...	...	...	...	...
Cocos (Keeling) Islands	...	...	...	...	...	...	...	...	...	...	...	...	...	...
Colombia	1,025	91.9	3.4	492.4	17,430	39.4	26.5	18.9	2.1	64.3	6.2	6.1	7.6	27.0
Comoros	...	...	...	3.773[5]	10,870[5]	...	...	...	...	...	...	...	...	9.0[6]
Congo	5[6]	40.0[6]	202.9	100.2	59,120	53.5	4.0	42.5	—	50.0	8.7	35.0	—	...
Cook Islands	...	...	...	...	...	...	...	...	...	...	...	...	...	...
Costa Rica	431	99.5	10.6	30.132	12,240	54.7[3]	34.0	9.0	—	38.0	5.7	156.6	3.3	30.0
Cuba	...	...	...	...	...	...	...	...	...	...	...	...	...	...
Cyprus[17]	532	96.1	1.2	0.259	390	18.7	74.7	6.6	—	85.0	4.5	0.5	—	6.0
Czechoslovakia	...	...	...	...	...	...	...	...	...	...	...	...	...	...
Denmark	4,390	90.1	...	153.8	30,110	58.8	25.0	6.3	9.8	12.3	67.3	0.4	—	7.0
Djibouti	...	...	...	19.174	57,240	...	...	...	...	...	...	...	...	...
Dominica	6	100.0	31.5	0.026	350	73.4	26.6	—	—	41.7	—	55.3	—	6.5[7]
Dominican Republic	231	100.0	12.7	1.160	190	47.8	12.4	31.5	—	50.9	—	72.9	6.0	...
Ecuador	533	97.2	9.5	129.058	15,380	29.2[3]	17.0	27.4	8.3	22.8	43.3	52.8	1.9	8.0[1]
Egypt	1,005	91.5	17.7	12.443	260	81.0[3]	10.4	4.9	—	74.6	5.8	17.8	—	13.0
El Salvador	180	91.1	6.0	1.512	300	54.3	9.7	15.1	3.2	36.8	15.3	44.5	10.1	...
Equatorial Guinea	...	...	...	...	...	...	...	...	...	...	...	...	...	...

1970s and early 1980s, have become the chief liabilities. In the case of liabilities for central bank authorities, the chief aggregates are reserve money, foreign payments, and demand and savings deposits. Large claims on government by the central bank authorities usually indicate a government-oriented monetary policy, whereas larger claims on the private sector by commercial banks point to the predominance of the private sector in the economy of the country. Large foreign liabilities under central bank authority often imply an adverse balance of payments position. Similarly, large foreign liabilities among the commercial banking group in the case of a less developed country often represent heavy domestic development expenditure financed by the use of foreign capital.

Because the majority of the world's countries are in the less developed bloc, and because their principal financial concern is external debt and its service, data are given for outstanding external debt rather than for total public debt, which is the major concern in the developed countries. For comparability, the data are given in U.S. dollars. The volume of debt by itself does not create external payment problems. If the country's external debt service (interest payments plus principal repayment) needs can be met by a strong, dependable export market, by export of services, or, occasionally, by direct remittances from abroad (by residents working abroad and sending wages home in foreign currencies, for example), no debt problem need exist. Countries whose debt service ratio (total debt service as a percent of exports of goods and services) is relatively high,

however, must often base their external borrowing policy on maintenance of domestic conditions of strict efficiency and, sometimes, austerity. The failure to adhere to such policies may lead to eventual crises of financial liquidity, deflation, and slower growth.

Ideally, the data presented here should be obtained by utilizing a single international methodology to provide a universally comparable set of international statistics. No international agency, however, can collect such data for all countries because of differences, both overall and in detail, in national definitions of financial aggregates, in accounting methodology, and in the completeness with which it is possible to survey a country's financial activity. The greater part of the data presented in the table comes from the IMF's *International Financial Statistics* and the World Bank's *World Debt Tables*. For certain countries—such as Albania, Angola, Bulgaria, Cuba, the German Democratic Republic, Kampuchea, Poland, and the U.S.S.R.— and many of the smaller nations, these sources are supplemented by other recent data from national, regional, or other international sources. In a few cases the desired data are negligible or unavailable, as noted.

In general, the data refer to the latest available quarter for the year cited. Detailed percentages may not add to 100.0 because of rounding, statistical discrepancy, or nonaccounting of negligible quantities.
— None, less than 0.5 of the last significant figure, or not applicable.
... Not available.
a. Latest month.
b. Year-end.

deposit money banks, 1984[b]										external debt outstanding (disbursed only), 1983[b]							country
assets (%)				liabilities						total ('000,000 U.S.$)	comp. (%)		debt service				
				deposits ('000,000,000 national currency)	composition (%)						public private		total ('000,000 U.S.$)	repayment (%)		debt service ratio (%)	
loans to govern- ment	loans to private sector	re- serves	foreign assets		demand depos.	savings depos.	govt. depos.	foreign liabilities						princi- pal	inter- est		
5.0[2]	40.3[2]	28.3[2]	26.4[2]	14.618[2]	18.2[2]	39.0[2, 4]	—	12.5[2]		1,324[1]	... ...		112[1]	...	...	...	Afghanistan
										100[5]							Albania
5.8[1]	87.1[1]	0.5[1]	6.6[1]	116.723[1]	45.3[1]	11.2[1]	3.1[1]	15.0[1]		12,942	20.8 79.2		4,504	73.1	26.9	33.1	Algeria
...	...	...	...	...	...	...	...	...									American Samoa
...	...	...	...	...	...	...	...	...		4[1]			...			...	Andorra
...	...	...	...	...	...	...	...	...		928[1]	... ...		142[1]	...	...	...	Angola
...	...	...	...	...	...	...	...	...									Anguilla
13.9[3]	62.0	9.9	14.2	0.346	12.0	63.7	—	24.2		80	... ...		1.9	68.4	31.6	2.2	Antigua and Barbuda
17.3	55.0	21.0	6.7	3.431	3.5	34.6[4]	6.1	37.4		24,592	8.2 91.8		2,343	42.7	57.3	24.0	Argentina
24.4[3]	71.4	4.2	—	86.272	16.9	71.1	2.0	0.9		6,232[10]	... ...		...	...	...	...	Australia
27.8[3]	40.5	2.7	29.0	2,015.5	4.6	43.2	2.5	30.8									Austria
21.4	75.6	5.8	−2.8	0.717	19.1	67.4[4]	1.4	—		246	9.7 90.3		52	43.8	56.2	4.3	Bahamas, The
7.3	53.2	3.3	36.2	1.204	13.4	48.9	20.0	8.7		741[1]	... ...		...	...	...	...	Bahrain
34.6[3]	52.9	7.1	5.4	106.5	24.5	54.1	3.8	2.3		4,184	96.5 3.5		143	55.7	44.3	14.7	Bangladesh
21.2	63.5	7.4	7.9	1.169	13.6	59.6	11.8	14.8		278	54.0 46.0		28	41.5	58.5	4.0	Barbados
23.2[3]	15.9	0.3	60.7	7,446.6	6.8	14.8[4]	0.7	73.2		16,011	... ...		...	...	...	...	Belgium
21.7[3]	58.5	10.0	9.8	0.199	11.4	52.7	5.5	26.3		56	79.2 20.8		8.0	65.4	34.6	8.6	Belize
2.3	96.8	0.9	—	133.2	47.5	9.0	5.3	—		615	49.1 50.9		26	50.0	50.0	11.4	Benin
—11.12—			3.5[2]	4,649[2]	20.2[2]	67.02	—	—		279[1]	... ...		113[1]	...	...	...	Bermuda
...	...	...	70.9[1]	0.434[1]	38.9[1]	29.4[1]	—	10.2[1]		6[5, 12]	... ...		...	...	...	...	Bhutan
—	66.6	25.0	8.4	2,696.4	16.0	25.0	—	94.1		2,969	70.2 29.8		267	38.1	61.9	30.5	Bolivia
—	66.6	24.6	8.7	0.358	39.5	50.4	—	3.2		230	86.6 13.4		24	46.4	53.6	2.9	Botswana
40.2[3]	48.5	4.6	6.6	109,665.0	12.4	18.3	7.7	49.3		58,068	17.3 82.7		6,983	28.3	71.7	28.7	Brazil
—22.2—		1.1	74.2	0.206	8.1	52.0	—	36.8		3[14]	... ...		...	...	...	...	British Virgin Islands
...	...	...	...	2.577[14]	...	...	...	...		10[1]	... ...		16[1]	...	...	...	Brunei
										1,400[15]							Bulgaria
11.4	62.8	23.3	2.5	111.1	30.1	23.6	25.2	14.0		398	89.3 10.7		14	47.5	52.5	12.1	Burkina Faso
91.6[3]	5.8	2.6	—	40.849	2.5	13.9[4]	11.3[16]	12.2		2,226	83.1 16.9		150	57.5	42.5	33.5	Burma
43.9	44.6	6.1	5.4	14.661	39.6	37.1	9.3	6.9		284	94.2 5.8		7.8	56.4	43.6	8.1	Burundi
6.5	78.7	1.7	13.1	1,023.9	26.8	31.8	13.5	13.6		1,883	75.6 24.4		219	51.3	48.7	13.9	Cameroon
6.3[3]	72.5	2.1	19.1	275.5	13.8	52.4[4]	1.0	28.5		9,945	... ...		...	...	...	...	Canada
...	...	...	...	...	...	...	...	...		67	100.0 —		2.9	33.3	66.7	38.2[1]	Cape Verde
—	—	—	99.9[2]	108.4[2]	—	—	—	99.9[2]									Cayman Islands
1.9	83.9	1.5	12.7	36.5	29.3	10.6	13.5	3.2		215	80.0 20.0		17	61.5	38.5	11.3	Central African Republic
0.3	82.1	2.7	14.9	56.0	35.8	4.7	4.2	3.0		129	79.1 20.9		0.6	66.7	33.3	0.6	Chad
9.7	81.6	2.6	6.0	1,331.0	3.9	29.1	7.0	64.2		6,828	21.7 78.3		885	37.1	62.9	18.3	Chile
...	...	...	...	...	...	...	...	...									China
...	...	...	...	...	...	...	...	...									Christmas Island
...	...	...	...	...	...	...	...	...									Cocos (Keeling) Islands
6.7	66.1	21.8	5.5	928.7	28.8	33.3[4]	—	14.7		6,899	50.6 49.4		904	42.9	57.1	21.3	Colombia
										83	99.5 0.5		1.5	20.0	80.0	5.6[1]	Comoros
14.4	80.0	1.1	4.4	225.7	23.3	9.3	18.6	21.6		1,487	57.3 42.7		238	67.8	32.2	20.5	Congo
...	...	...	...	...	...	...	...	...		1.0[1]	... ...		—	...	...	...	Cook Islands
10.2[3]	58.1	28.1	3.6	51.940	41.2	63.2[4]	—	8.1		3,315	43.3 56.7		595	15.4	84.6	50.6	Costa Rica
...	...	...	...	...	...	...	...	...		5,103[1]	... ...		736[1]	...	...	...	Cuba
8.6	64.7	21.6	5.1	1.057	13.0	59.7	2.0	17.4		650	39.8 60.2		130	51.8	48.3	10.6	Cyprus[17]
...	...	...	...	...	...	...	...	...		2,700[15]	... ...		...	...	...	...	Czechoslovakia
9.8	61.8	0.8	27.6	379.0	38.3	41.1	—	27.3		11,210	... ...		...	...	...	...	Denmark
...	...	...	...	...	...	...	...	...		33	86.0 14.0		4.2	73.8	28.6	18.4[1]	Djibouti
16.5[3]	62.2	11.9	9.4	0.134	15.6	66.5	—	16.5		33	... ...		1.2	33.3	66.7	3.9	Dominica
22.3[3]	56.9	18.7	2.1	2.821	18.3	35.8	6.1	3.0		2,202	65.8 34.2		231	52.3	47.7	30.2	Dominican Republic
—	83.0	14.7	2.3	214.312	38.4	13.2	—	—		6,239	26.3 73.7		874	58.2	41.8	27.8	Ecuador
30.6[3]	29.1	20.6	19.7	29.781	15.3	45.3[4]	7.9	20.6		15,229	82.3 17.7		1,996	72.9	27.1	27.5	Egypt
4.0	72.3	17.0	6.7	3.846	20.6	56.5[4]	—	2.3		1,065	95.2 4.8		66	44.1	55.9	7.6	El Salvador
...	...	...	...	...	...	...	...	...		103	84.5 15.5		5.0	82.0	18.0	...	Equatorial Guinea

Finance (continued)

country	international reserves, 1985[a]			money supply, 1984[b]		central bank authority, 1984[b]								central bank discount rate, 1985
	total ('000,000 SDRs)	% foreign exchange	ratio of external debt to total reserves, 1983[b]	stock ('000,000 national currency)	M1 per capita	assets (%)				liabilities (%)				
						claims on government	claims on foreign assets	claims on banks	claims on private sector	reserve money	government deposits	foreign liabilities	capital accounts	
Ethiopia	145	94.5	9.1	2.309	50	62.3	4.3	—	—	66.8	6.9	7.1	6.9	3.0[7]
Faeroe Islands	...	...	...	...	...	...	...	...	...	...	...	...	...	...
Falkland Islands	...	...	...	...	...	...	...	...	...	...	...	...	...	...
Fiji	126	88.9	2.5	0.142	210	15.1[3]	84.9	—	—	65.6	6.9	—	23.7	7.5
Finland	3,441	90.1	...	24.945	5,110	5.9	58.3	20.4	15.4	49.5	13.0	2.5	21.1	9.0
France	25,543	81.3	...	1,057.0	19,260	3.8	65.2	31.0	—	44.0	—	4.9	—	9.5
French Guiana	...	...	...	1.091	13,670	...	...	...	...	...	...	...	...	...
French Polynesia	...	...	...	5.492	32,250	...	...	...	...	...	...	...	...	...
Gabon	204[6]	97.1[8]	3.9	167.8	146,470	—	92.4	7.6	—	61.6	34.3	1.4	—	9.0[6]
Gambia, The	1	100.0	51.6	0.100	140	57.0[3]	3.0	40.0	—	35.8	12.5	80.4	9.3	9.5
Gaza Strip	...	...	...	...	...	...	...	...	...	...	...	...	...	...
Germany, East	...	...	...	...	...	...	...	...	...	...	...	...	...	...
Germany, West	48,890	81.1	...	294.8	4,820	10.0	48.3	41.7	—	72.7	0.4	6.6	—	4.5
Ghana	381	94.8	6.9	26.849	2,150	65.1[3]	33.2	3.6	—	36.9	2.4	63.2	—	18.0
Gibraltar	...	...	...	...	...	...	...	...	...	...	...	...	...	...
Greece	1,277	82.6	7.9	631.6	63,750	59.1	13.8	1.4	1.0	72.6	9.4	—	—	20.5
Greenland	...	...	...	...	...	...	...	...	...	...	...	...	...	...
Grenada	23	100.0	3.3	0.077	850	31.6	68.4	—	—	79.0	—	18.3	—	6.5[6, 7]
Guadeloupe	...	...	...	0.915	2,780	...	...	...	...	...	...	...	...	...
Guam	...	...	...	...	...	...	...	...	...	...	...	...	...	...
Guatemala	239	92.5	6.1	0.869	110	76.7[3]	15.5	6.1	—	34.2	12.1	54.1	5.2	9.0[6]
Guernsey	...	...	...	...	...	...	...	...	...	...	...	...	...	...
Guinea	...	...	...	...	...	...	...	...	...	...	...	...	...	...
Guinea-Bissau	...	...	...	...	...	...	...	...	...	...	...	...	...	...
Guyana	2	100.0	105.5	0.619	660	99.1	0.9	—	—	20.3	—	78.2	3.8	14.0
Haiti	12	91.7	46.1	1.400	270	83.6[3]	4.5	0.8	9.7	44.1	6.7	37.1	8.8	...
Honduras	148	100.0	13.8	0.846	200	44.9[3]	20.2	16.0	—	31.8	11.7	58.4	18.3	24.0
Hong Kong	...	...	...	36.791	6,860	...	...	...	...	...	...	...	...	6.2[18]
Hungary	2,351	96.7	4.1	197.2	18,490	4.5	25.2	37.8	—	32.4	6.4	62.2	2.7	13.0[19]
Iceland	198	97.0	...	7.673	31,970	21.5	27.7	50.6	0.2	42.0	19.2	19.4	—	22.5
India	6,645	82.9	4.1	356.0	470	70.0	16.1	3.5	—	64.3	6.5	10.3	8.3	10.0
Indonesia	4,986	95.9	5.7	18,402.0	112,120	7.1	39.4	46.7	6.7	26.8	27.7	3.0	13.4	...
Iran	5,376[1]	89.2[1]	0.8[1]	3,933.4[2]	94,710[2]	78.7[1, 3]	19.6[1]	1.7[1]	—	54.1[1]	13.3[1]	0.4[1]	2.8[1]	9.0[20]
Iraq	...	...	...	...	...	...	...	...	...	...	...	...	...	...
Ireland	3,514	93.5	...	2.020	570	19.2	80.8	—	—	62.5	7.4	—	—	11.5
Isle of Man	...	...	...	...	...	...	...	...	...	...	...	...	...	...
Israel	2,402	98.5	4.1	275.7	65,470	57.7	36.8	5.5	...	5.2	8.8	0.2	—	...
Italy	22,718	81.6	...	279,463.0	4,904,000	51.9	47.4	0.7	—	61.6	—	0.2	—	15.5
Ivory Coast	12	33.3	230.4	574.6	58,950	42.9	0.3	55.7	—	39.7	2.5	61.6	—	10.5
Jamaica	117	95.7	31.0	1.319	570	88.4	10.5	1.1	—	32.2	18.6	128.8	4.5	21.0
Japan	28,404	82.0	...	86,375.0	720,000	57.3	21.6	21.1	—	113.0	5.2	—	—	5.0
Jersey	...	...	...	...	...	...	...	...	...	...	...	...	...	...
Jordan	471	89.2	2.2	0.878	350	39.4	60.6	—	—	147.2	3.8	—	—	6.2
Kampuchea	...	...	...	...	...	...	...	...	...	...	...	...	...	...
Kenya	405	95.8	6.3	13.095	670	52.9	47.1	—	—	46.1	—	48.5	4.5	12.5[6]
Kiribati	...	...	...	...	...	...	...	...	...	...	...	...	...	...
Korea, North	...	...	...	...	...	...	...	...	...	...	...	...	...	...
Korea, South	2,289	98.7	9.1	6,613.0	163,970	22.3[3]	18.9	58.7	—	35.2	9.3	11.1	—	5.0
Kuwait	5,271	83.8	0.2[1]	0.968	540	—	100.0	—	—	52.9	64.1	—	15.0	6.0
Laos	...	...	...	...	...	...	...	...	...	...	...	...	...	...
Lebanon	1,277	73.1	0.1	13.784	5,210	53.0	40.0	4.8	2.2	55.9	34.5	—	—	12.0
Lesotho	50	96.0	2.2	0.103	70	12.1	87.9	—	—	74.9	2.0	9.9	13.8	...
Liberia	2	100.0	35.1	0.092	40	81.3	0.5	0.2	1.0	1.8[21]	2.0	57.1	[21]	9.5[8]
Libya	4,034	87.1	0.1[1]	2.992	860	50.8	47.5	—	1.7	75.8	31.7	—	—	5.0
Liechtenstein	...	...	...	...	...	...	...	...	...	...	...	...	...	...
Luxembourg	...	...	...	49.6[2]	135,540[2]	...	...	...	...	...	...	...	...	9.6[22]
Macau	...	...	...	...	...	...	...	...	...	...	...	...	...	...
Madagascar	35	100.0	50.8	239.9	24,640	91.5	7.2	1.3	—	16.1	25.5	101.0	1.2	5.5[5]
Malawi	36	91.7	45.8	0.154	20	75.9[3]	24.1	—	—	41.3	10.9	51.0	—	11.0
Malaysia	4,139	92.0	2.8	13.357	880	33.2	66.8	—	—	62.5	15.7	4.5	—	4.8
Maldives	5	100.0	11.2	0.114	660	83.5	16.3	0.2	...	70.2	15.4	22.9	2.7	9.0[22]
Mali	50	80.0	52.6	106.2	13,770	65.1	17.6	17.3	—	87.7	—	56.6	—	10.5
Malta	953	91.2	0.1	0.326	990	—	100.0	—	—	77.4	6.7	—	—	6.5
Martinique	...	...	...	1.045	3,170	...	...	...	...	...	...	...	...	...
Mauritania	65	96.9	11.0	9.641	5,940	33.7	33.0	27.0	6.2	27.1	1.1	58.3	22.7	6.0
Mauritius	23	95.7	17.6	2.050	2,030	90.6	8.3	1.1	—	30.5	—	52.8	5.5	11.0
Mayotte	...	...	...	0.114	2,040	...	...	...	...	...	...	...	...	...
Mexico	6,854	98.8	16.7	2,345.6	30,540	71.3	25.7	0.9	—	80.2	—	7.5	—	49.2[6, 7]
Monaco	...	...	...	...	...	...	...	...	...	...	...	...	...	...
Mongolia	...	...	...	...	...	...	...	...	...	...	...	...	...	...
Montserrat	...	...	...	0.009[1, 13]	800[1, 13]	...	...	...	...	...	...	...	...	...
Morocco	126	71.4	71.0	36.779	1,610	72.4	2.4	14.5	7.0	63.0	0.9	41.1	—	7.0
Mozambique	...	...	...	...	...	...	...	...	...	...	...	...	...	...
Nauru	...	...	...	...	...	...	...	...	...	...	...	...	...	...
Nepal	65	83.1	2.5	4.942	310	76.3[3]	19.2	2.8	1.4	56.0	23.3	4.2	—	15.0[2]
Netherlands, The	11,149	73.1	...	83.3	5,770	5.4	86.8	7.8	—	40.2	2.3	—	—	5.5
Netherlands Antilles	80	76.3	3.0[1]	0.467	1,920	32.0	67.8	—	0.2	59.0	11.6	—	17.1	8.0
New Caledonia	...	...	...	3.635	24,630	...	...	...	...	...	...	...	...	...
New Zealand	1,625	99.3	...	3.758	1,160	32.4	50.1	0.2	17.3	16.8	66.5	21.7	—	13.0
Nicaragua	396[6]	99.0[6]	18.1	10.937	3,720	74.3	7.8	17.9	—	34.9	-0.9	84.5	1.3	...
Niger	112	92.0	11.8	78.4	14.740	32.9	45.1	22.0	—	51.6	17.7	28.1	—	10.5
Nigeria	1,186	97.6	11.6	12.204	130	78.8	8.9	2.7	7.4	53.5	12.2	0.8	2.1	8.0[6]
Niue	...	...	...	...	...	...	...	...	...	...	...	...	...	...
Norfolk Island	...	...	...	...	...	...	...	...	...	...	...	...	...	...
Norway	12,641	94.1	...	82.0	19,800	8.0	89.7	2.3	—	30.8	37.1	—	—	8.0

	deposit money banks, 1984[b]								external debt outstanding (disbursed only), 1983[b]							country
assets (%)				liabilities					total ('000,000 U.S.$)	comp. (%)		debt service				
loans to govern-ment	loans to private sector	re-serves	foreign assets	deposits ('000,000,000 national currency)	composition (%)					public	private	total ('000,000 U.S.$)	repayment (%)		debt service ratio (%)	
					demand depos.	savings depos.	govt. depos.	foreign liabilities					princi-pal	inter-est		
52.3[3]	15.9	27.1	4.8	2.796	37.1	40.8	3.2	4.6	1,223	92.6	7.4	66	63.5	36.5	11.5	Ethiopia
																Faeroe Islands
...	...	...	...	...	...	...	...	...	2.0[14]	...	...	...	...	...	...	Falkland Islands
20.6[3]	69.0	8.4	2.0	0.471	17.3	73.9	4.6	1.5	292	78.5	21.5	38	39.0	61.0	7.3	Fiji
1.6	75.6	4.6	18.1	225.457	8.4	50.2	3.0	27.3	3,900[10]	...	...	...	...	...	...	Finland
7.0	75.1	...	...	2,461.0	27.7	38.4	—	...	3,858[10]	...	...	...	...	...	...	France
...	...	...	...	...	...	...	...	...	18[1]	...	...	4.0[1]	...	...	...	French Guiana
...	...	...	...	...	...	...	...	...	114	...	...	15	...	...	...	French Polynesia
22.4	72.0	3.5	2.1	350.0	32.3	30.0	18.7	4.1	729	40.8	59.2	209	75.3	24.7	9.4	Gabon
29.9[3]	44.6	18.5	7.0	0.319	12.7	22.0	—	7.0	162	78.7	21.3	6.7	71.6	28.4	16.4[1]	Gambia, The
																Gaza Strip
...	...	...	...	...	...	...	...	...	9,000[15]	...	...	...	...	...	...	Germany, East
19.9[3]	66.2	3.4	10.5	2,248.2	8.6	31.1	7.9	8.2	27,491[1]	...	...	...	...	...	...	Germany, West
25.7[3]	29.2	42.8	2.3	20.447	42.9	25.0	2.9	3.1	1,095	87.4	12.6	72	58.3	41.7	14.2	Ghana
—24.1[1]—		1.2[1]	—	0.142[1]	—74.5[1]—		—		40[1]	...	...	9.0[1]	...	...	...	Gibraltar
26.3	43.1	22.8	7.8	2,632.4	6.3	60.3	—	24.7	8,194	21.2	78.8	1,318	42.7	57.3	18.3	Greece
																Greenland
21.7[3]	50.3	16.1	11.9	0.166	19.1	58.1	—	15.8	48	...	...	1.9	36.8	63.2	4.7	Grenada
...	...	...	...	...	...	...	...	...	68[1]	...	...	8.0[1]	...	...	...	Guadeloupe
6.2[2]	65.9[2]	...	...	0.439[2]	24.0[2]	76.0[2]	—	—	...	...	...	...	...	...	...	Guam
2.0	80.0	15.6	2.3	2.335	16.3	65.5	—	6.4	1,405	78.7	21.3	141	46.2	53.8	11.7	Guatemala
																Guernsey
...	...	...	...	...	...	...	...	...	1,216	85.5	14.5	70	68.9	31.1	21.4[1]	Guinea
...	...	...	...	...	...	...	...	...	138	80.9	19.1	1.8	88.9	11.1	29.4[1]	Guinea-Bissau
51.6[3]	20.2	26.9	1.3	2.297	12.0	51.2	—	2.8	663	76.7	23.3	56	55.5	44.5	24.6	Guyana
...	59.3	30.7	10.0	1.464	27.1	67.7	—	3.0	434	84.0	16.0	15	53.1	46.9	5.3	Haiti
22.5	70.7	6.5	0.3	2,000.0	22.3	52.7	—	2.3	1,570	73.9	26.1	121	31.2	68.8	14.9	Honduras
—	33.0	1.7	37.3	903.6	—34.1[4]—		—	41.3	224	24.6	75.4	46	61.1	38.9	...	Hong Kong
56.9[3]	30.0	11.7	1.4	653.5	14.2	34.7[4]	—	10.1	6,573	15.3	84.7	1,927	66.0	34.0	18.5	Hungary
2.9	79.5	13.5	4.1	46.724	14.4	39.3	—	24.0	435	...	...	...	...	...	...	Iceland
22.0	68.4	9.6	—	836.5	16.1	68.7	—	—	21,277	92.2	7.8	1,323	58.2	41.8	9.0[1]	India
—	70.4	8.5	21.1	24,183.0	19.9	38.6	5.8	4.0	21,685	55.5	44.5	2,551	50.8	49.2	12.8	Indonesia
17.2	47.7	31.4	3.7	5,387.4	32.8	54.8	—	1.2	5,001[1]	...	...	2,916[1]	...	...	13.1[1]	Iran
...	...	...	...	...	...	...	...	...	2,188[1]	...	...	1,908[1]	...	...	...	Iraq
16.2	46.1	4.2	15.6	17.291	6.3	36.2	0.5	34.3	8,759	...	...	...	...	...	...	Ireland
																Isle of Man
24.7	40.3	1.3	33.8	12,443.5	1.2	71.4	—	53.3	15,149	72.1	27.9	1,949	43.1	56.9	19.6	Israel
22.3	52.6	11.9	13.2	549,188.0	41.5	34.6	—	16.7	...							Italy
1.6	89.2	3.3	5.9	1,191.3	24.4	21.1	7.6	10.0	4,824	33.7	66.3	791	47.7	52.2	30.0	Ivory Coast
22.9[3]	50.7	20.7	5.7	4.901	18.0	58.7	2.1	4.8	1,950	77.4	22.6	205	50.8	49.2	14.6	Jamaica
13.3[3]	79.9	1.8	5.0	359,399.0	17.9	54.3	—	8.4	...							Japan
																Jersey
11.5	62.7	7.5	18.3	1.809	18.6	48.5	6.2	17.4	1,940	83.2	16.8	213	58.6	41.4	11.3	Jordan
...	...	...	...	...	...	...	...	...	241[1]	...	...	—	...	...	...	Kampuchea
19.0[3]	71.7	6.7	2.6	24.417	45.5	40.7	2.5	3.3	2,384	73.0	27.0	305	58.3	41.7	20.6	Kenya
...	...	...	...	...	...	...	...	...	135,[5,12]	...	...	...	...	...	...	Kiribati
...	...	...	...	...	...	...	...	...	627[1]	...	...	...	...	...	...	Korea, North
15.1	73.0	1.8	10.1	46,530.0	8.1	38.4[4]	5.3	25.8	21,472	43.4	56.6	3,743	53.4	46.6	12.3	Korea, South
—	64.0	4.1	31.9	7.866	8.2	44.6	4.9	19.8	1,310[1]	...	...	484[1]	...	...	4.1[1]	Kuwait
...	...	...	...	...	...	...	...	...	60[1]	...	...	2.0[1]	...	...	...	Laos
16.9	48.1	5.9	29.1	90.009	6.8	69.4[4]	0.8	13.7	182	70.5	29.5	50	69.5	30.5	...	Lebanon
26.4[3]	23.8	18.8	31.0	0.287	27.7	51.2	4.3	2.6	145	82.6	17.4	12	47.5	52.5	2.5	Lesotho
1.8	63.0	29.3	6.0	0.196	31.1	27.9	—	18.2	699	76.0	24.0	31	32.7	67.3	6.6	Liberia
—	70.6	21.1	8.3	3.103	61.2	25.7	4.8	1.5	844[1]	...	...	1,060[1]	...	...	7.6[1]	Libya
...	...	...	...	...	...	...	...	...	...	...	...	'				Liechtenstein
—	2.2	—	97.8	6,562.1	0.9	4.2	—	89.1	...							Luxembourg
...	...	...	...	...	...	...	...	...	46[1]	...	...	3.0[1]	...	...	...	Macau
2.9	83.4	4.6	9.1	322.7	46.4	5.1	10.2	6.8	1,490	71.4	28.6	141	54.6	45.4	4.0[5]	Madagascar
26.5[3]	51.0	20.4	2.1	0.449	19.6	52.2	—	11.4	719	76.1	23.9	58	49.2	50.8	31.1	Malawi
14.0	77.1	4.7	4.1	59.331	12.2	54.8	10.3	10.1	10,665	21.7	78.3	954	29.9	70.1	5.8	Malaysia
18.8[3]	53.6	20.4	7.2	0.349	8.4	19.7	4.0	51.6	47	93.6	6.4	4.2	61.9	38.1	5.5	Maldives
3.0	70.8	12.7	13.5	86.3	61.9	11.9	6.9	18.6	881	98.4	1.6	13	49.6	50.4	6.1	Mali
4.9	49.5	30.2	15.4	0.379	8.2	80.2	—	3.4	109	99.7	0.3	9.7	88.7	11.3	1.2	Malta
...	...	...	...	...	...	...	...	...	48[1]	...	...	6.0[1]	...	...	...	Martinique
0.3	94.7	4.3	0.7	14.632	40.3	11.5	0.7	43.0	1,171	89.4	10.6	37	38.4	61.6	10.0	Mauritania
25.0	60.4	9.5	5.0	5.638	19.0	73.5	—	2.3	332	68.8	31.2	84	67.3	32.7	16.4	Mauritius
							—						—	—		Mayotte
20.7[3]	39.8	38.5	0.9	9,863.4	11.2	63.8[4]	—	19.3	66,732	10.1	89.9	9,954	31.2	68.8	35.9	Mexico
																Monaco
...	...	...	...	...	...	...	...	...	6.0[1]	...	...	...	...	...	...	Mongolia
—	71.7[1]	2.9[1]	17.6[1]	0.043[1]	18.8[1]	61.4[1]	—	13.9[1]	2.7	...	...	0.2	—	100.0	2.0	Montserrat
33.5	57.8	2.2	6.5	37.271	52.0	24.2	2.8	0.9	9,445	62.4	37.6	1,120	54.5	45.5	38.2	Morocco
...	...	...	...	...	...	...	...	...	585[1]	...	...	96[1]	...	...	...	Mozambique
...	...	...	...	...	...	...	...	...	25[1]	...	...	8.0[1]	...	...	...	Nauru
34.7[3]	40.8	8.2	16.3	7.923	16.3	74.4	—	3.7	346	99.8	0.2	8.5	54.1	45.9	3.0	Nepal
11.3[3]	46.5	0.4	41.8	482.9	11.4	34.8[4]	—	38.9	...							Netherlands, The
0.4[3]	31.2	1.2	67.3	3.563	7.0	21.2	0.2	65.8	623[1]	...	...	64[1]	...	...	...	Netherlands Antilles
...	...	...	...	...	...	...	...	...	184[1]	...	...	25[1]	...	...	...	New Caledonia
24.9	68.1	0.8	6.2	11.431	25.0	61.9	—	5.2	5,502	...	...	...	...	...	...	New Zealand
—	84.4[2]	13.8[2]	1.8[2]	20.709[2]	26.2[2]	20.5[2,4]	21.6[2]	6.5[2]	3,417	68.3	31.7	83	55.8	44.2	17.6	Nicaragua
16.3	68.2	12.3	3.3	143.8	31.9	15.7	12.1	34.6	631	71.7	28.3	72	49.7	50.3	18.0	Niger
42.5	50.9	4.7	1.9	22.187	27.3	40.7	2.9	0.4	11,757	15.5	84.5	2,040	52.3	47.7	18.6	Nigeria
...	...	...	...	...	...	...	...	...	4.0[5,12]	...	...	...	...	...	...	Niue
																Norfolk Island
26.9[3]	64.2	0.7	8.2	330.2	17.5	56.0	4.6	15.2	1,310	...	...	...	...	...	...	Norway

Finance (continued)

country	international reserves, 1985[a]			money supply, 1984[b]		central bank authority, 1984[b]								central bank discount rate, 1985
	total ('000,000 SDRs)	% foreign exchange change	ratio of external debt to total reserves, 1983[b]	stock ('000,000,000 national currency)	M1 per capita	assets (%)				liabilities (%)				
						claims on government	claims on foreign assets	claims on banks	claims on private sector	reserve money	government deposits	foreign liabilities	capital accounts	
Oman	792	93.7	1.5	0.566	560	1.1	98.9	—	—	45.6	38.5	0.4	16.5	9.5[8]
Pacific Is., Trust Terr. of the	...	...	...	...	...	...	...	...	...	...	...	...	...	...
Pakistan	642	89.6	4.8	107.544	1,100	59.0	22.9	18.1	—	58.2	6.9	23.9	—	10.0
Panama	122	100.0	14.5	0.381	180	57.0[3]	16.8	—	26.2	20.0	17.4	48.6	7.9	...
Papua New Guinea	432	96.8	2.0	0.250	80	3.0	97.0	—	—	30.2	24.5	7.5	21.3	10.0[7]
Paraguay	556	87.4	1.7	96.742	29,490	20.5[3]	55.6	10.9	6.5	63.2	3.4	15.6	9.6	...
Peru	1,345	95.5	5.6	3,491.5	181,900	41.9[3]	41.1	16.0	—	39.7	7.6	27.4	7.4	44.5[2]
Philippines	1,146	94.5	13.7	33.6	630	35.8[3]	17.5	19.1	—	34.6	11.8	89.8	—	11.0[5]
Pitcairn Island	...	...	...	...	...	...	...	...	...	...	...	...	...	...
Poland	...	...	...	...	...	...	...	...	...	...	...	...	...	...
Portugal	1,699	55.9	8.8	801.0	80,160	29.9	65.6	2.2	2.2	38.5	4.2	12.3	7.4	25.0
Puerto Rico	...	...	...	...	...	...	...	...	...	...	...	...	...	...
Qatar	430[6]	77.4[6]	0.8[1]	3.654	12,560	—	98.8	1.2	—	87.0	28.7	—	4.9	5.0[6, 8]
Réunion	...	...	...	2.217	4,120	—	3.0	50.0	47.0	35.6	22.8	5.0	—	...
Romania	547	76.1	11.5	162.3	7,150	—	3.0	50.0	47.0	35.6	22.8	5.0	...	...
Rwanda	109	83.5	2.0	13.454	2,280	22.5[3]	63.7	9.4	1.4	48.9	16.4	17.2	—	9.0[6]
St. Christopher and Nevis	...	...	...	0.023[1, 13]	520[1, 13]	...	...	...	...	...	...	...	...	...
St. Helena and Ascension	...	...	...	...	...	...	...	...	...	...	...	...	...	...
St. Lucia	12	100.0	5.0	0.067	500	38.1	61.9	—	—	86.5	—	9.9	—	7.0[7]
St. Pierre and Miquelon	...	...	...	0.054	9,000	...	...	...	...	...	...	...	...	...
St. Vincent and the Grenadines	16	100.0	4.0	0.050	480	23.7	76.3	—	—	92.5	—	5.6	—	6.5[7]
San Marino	...	...	...	...	...	...	...	...	...	...	...	...	...	...
São Tomé and Príncipe	...	...	...	...	...	...	...	...	...	...	...	...	...	...
Saudi Arabia	26,388	59.2	...	83.0	7,670	—	100.0	—	—	10.2	68.2	—	—	...
Senegal	10	20.0	109.9	191.8	30,200	47.6	0.6	51.8	—	33.6	4.4	65.2	—	10.5
Seychelles	4	100.0	4.0	0.135	2,080	49.2	44.0	6.8	—	67.9	9.7	—	9.8	12.7[7]
Sierra Leone	8	100.0	22.9	0.486	140	99.1	0.9	—	—	47.8	3.4	78.0	—	14.0[6]
Singapore	11,058	98.8	0.1	8.866	3,510	—	100.0	—	—	29.3	12.3	—	—	5.0[18]
Solomon Islands	39	97.4	0.4	0.029	110	4.8	95.2	—	—	46.4	35.8	6.8	29.3	...
Somalia	11	100.0	121.9	5.334	940	72.9[3]	1.7	25.4	—	36.1	20.4	53.9	5.0	8.0[6]
South Africa	590	50.3	...	23.413	730	−1.2	73.4	27.8	—	71.0	18.7	56.8	—	13.5
Bophuthatswana	...	...	...	...	...	...	...	...	...	...	...	...	...	...
Ciskei	...	...	...	...	...	...	...	...	...	...	...	...	...	...
Transkei	...	...	...	...	...	...	...	...	...	...	...	...	...	...
Venda	...	...	...	...	...	...	...	...	...	...	...	...	...	...
South West Africa/Namibia	...	...	...	...	...	...	...	...	...	...	...	...	...	...
Spain	11,292	90.3	...	5,746.0	149,300	46.4	35.7	17.9	—	87.3	5.2	—	8.2	8.0
Sri Lanka	478	98.3	7.4	16.647	1,050	56.7	37.7	5.6	—	38.9	—	30.0	0.4	13.0
Sudan, The	14	100.0	341.8	2.752	120	95.5[3]	0.5	4.0	—	51.8	17.5	33.0	0.4	13.5[5, 8]
Suriname	26	88.5	0.1[1]	0.577	1,550	91.0	9.0	—	—	79.6	2.0	—	6.2	...
Swaziland	82	97.6	2.0	0.068	110	10.8	88.6	0.6	—	57.6	9.9	19.5	8.5	18.0
Sweden	4,427	84.9	...	83.2	9,980	65.8	33.7	0.5	—	49.5	—	0.9	—	10.5
Switzerland	16,503	79.0	...	76.0	11,790	6.0	84.6	9.4	—	70.5	1.8	—	—	4.0
Syria	210[6]	83.3[6]	27.9	34.429[2]	3,580[2]	94.4[2, 3]	2.4[2]	3.2[2]	—	71.3[2]	17.7[2]	10.5[2]	0.4[2]	5.0[2]
Taiwan	...	...	...	616.0[2]	33,140[2]	1.1[3]	83.0	15.6	0.1	43.9	7.3	—	—	7.8[6]
Tanzania	21	100.0	129.9	20.541[2]	1,010[2]	93.9	3.1	3.0	—	79.3	—	17.0	—	4.3[6]
Thailand	1,948	93.9	4.2	93.3	1,860	47.7	36.3	11.9	—	39.7	2.8	12.2	46.4	11.0
Togo	231	98.7	4.6	90.7	31,190	24.5	70.7	4.8	—	71.9	7.7	20.6	—	10.5
Tokelau	...	...	...	...	...	...	...	...	...	...	...	...	...	...
Tonga	...	...	...	...	...	3.4[23]	51.7[23]	24.9[23]	14.5[23]	—89.2[23]—		0.2[23]	10.6[23]	...
Trinidad and Tobago	919	74.4	0.4	2.184	1,870	−6.2	106.2	—	—	73.7	21.5	—	39.9	7.5
Tunisia	90	61.1	6.0	1.814	260	5.2	30.5	64.3	—	62.8	8.5	0.1	18.8	7.0[2]
Turkey	1,202	85.9	10.9	2,292.3	47,490	40.9	45.4	8.1	—	32.2	1.4	65.4	1.1	31.5[1]
Turks and Caicos Islands	...	...	...	...	...	...	...	...	...	...	...	...	...	...
Tuvalu	...	...	...	...	...	...	...	...	...	...	...	...	...	...
Uganda	135	100.0[5]	35.9[5]	72.628	5,070	76.7	23.3	—	—	32.7	29.2	97.9	—	15.5[6]
U.S.S.R.	...	...	...	...	...	...	...	...	...	...	...	...	...	...
United Arab Emirates	2,118[6]	85.1[6]	0.5[1]	8.460	6,910	4.6[2]	83.9	11.5	—	47.1	20.4	0.1	29.6	...
United Kingdom	11,044	68.4	...	51.5	910	72.1	27.4	—	—	70.6	—	22.5	—	11.4[7]
United States	34,366	22.2	...	570.4	2,420	82.2	17.1	—	—	100.0	4.2	0.2	—	7.5
Uruguay	192	50.0	8.3	12.201	4,080	48.1	16.1	10.3	20.6	28.1	17.9	17.3	—	...
Vanuatu	9	88.9	0.6	3.026	22,250	2.1	49.6	48.3	—	58.6	40.0	0.7	10.9	...
Venezuela	9,911	83.8	1.6	82.816	4,910	10.2	86.1	3.7	—	69.8	9.0	—	26.5	13.0[1]
Vietnam	...	...	...	...	...	...	...	...	...	...	...	...	...	...
Virgin Islands (U.S.)	...	...	...	...	...	...	...	...	...	...	...	...	...	...
Wallis and Futuna	...	...	...	...	...	...	...	...	...	...	...	...	...	...
West Bank	...	...	...	...	...	...	...	...	...	...	...	...	...	...
Western Sahara	...	...	...	...	...	...	...	...	...	...	...	...	...	...
Western Samoa	10	90.0	8.2	0.019	120	...	...	...	...	...	...	...	...	12.2[1, 22]
Yemen (Aden)	220	97.7	4.5	0.369	180	81.1	18.9	—	—	94.5	—	8.2	—	...
Yemen (Ṣan'ā')	282	96.8	4.3	16.395	2,570	90.8[3]	8.7	0.4	—	84.7	7.6	1.0	0.8	9.5[8]
Yugoslavia	945	93.0	8.7	1,251.9	54,310	5.6	21.2	66.7	6.5	132.9	1.1	81.4	—	54.0
Zaire	159	89.9	34.3	17.869	560	78.9[2]	19.4[2]	0.4[2]	1.3[2]	62.3[2]	9.7[2]	37.2[2]	6.0[2]	...
Zambia	59	98.3	42.0	0.870	130	89.3	4.6	—	6.1	19.2	—	101.2	—	14.5
Zimbabwe	141	83.0	15.4	0.874	110	29.4	41.5	—	29.1	78.2	—	93.1	—	9.0

deposit money banks, 1984[b]									external debt outstanding (disbursed only), 1983[b]							country
assets (%)				liabilities					total ('000,000 U.S.$)	comp. (%)		debt service				
loans to govern-ment	loans to private sector	re-serves	foreign assets	deposits ('000,000,000 national currency)	composition (%)					public	private	total ('000,000 U.S.$)	repayment (%)		debt service ratio (%)	
					demand depos.	savings depos.	govt. depos.	foreign liabilities					princi-pal	inter-est		
1.7	56.7	10.5	31.2	1.000	13.4	49.0	15.6	9.1	1,125	24.2	75.8	143	63.3	36.7	3.2	Oman
...	...	...	...	...	...	...	...	...	24[1]	...	...	1.0[1]	...	...	...	Pacific Is., Trust Terr. of the
21.5	64.7	8.7	5.1	159.324	34.4	39.7	2.5	4.4	9,755	91.4	8.6	1,069	71.1	28.9	28.1	Pakistan
1.5	8.9	—	89.6	24.807	1.3	5.3	—	90.2	2,986	28.5	71.5	472	39.9	60.1	6.8	Panama
17.2	75.4	5.4	2.0	0.662	23.4	63.1	4.1	7.4	911	37.1	62.9	107	41.4	58.5	11.2	Papua New Guinea
—	55.0	36.9	8.1	212.110	21.1	51.0	—	6.8	1,161	60.6	39.4	85	46.8	53.2	14.9	Paraguay
0.8	54.8	38.5	6.0	8,608.2	12.5	72.0[3]	—	1.3	7,932	43.5	56.5	754	46.1	53.9	19.6	Peru
16.5[3]	62.1	5.2	16.2	224.4	5.3	34.1	3.8	40.9	10,385	46.5	53.5	1,252	48.1	51.9	15.4	Philippines
...	...	...	...	...	...	...	...	...	...	...	...	...	...	...	...	Pitcairn Island
...	...	...	...	...	...	...	...	...	25,350[15]	...	...	...	...	...	...	Poland
6.4	66.7	13.4	13.5	2,313.6	22.7	72.2	5.2	51.3	9,951	24.4	75.6	1,853	54.5	45.5	26.7	Portugal
—49.2[1]—		28.2[1]		13.210[1]	17.5[1]	59.7[1]	5.5[1]	—								Puerto Rico
—	55.5	1.9	42.6	10.545	24.4	50.3	4.5	8.9	352[1]	...	...	241[1]	...	...	...	Qatar
									76[1]	...	...	8.0[1]	...	...	...	Réunion
26.6	63.3	7.2	2.9	601.6	7.9	23.1	—	19.1	7,576	37.1	62.9	1,614	70.7	29.3	13.1	Romania
19.5[3]	56.5	5.4	18.6	17.740	32.4	34.7	10.5	9.3	220	100.0	—	4.2	45.2	54.8	2.6	Rwanda
2.4[1]	60.2[1]	2.8[1]	14.8[1]	0.206[1]	9.5[1]	68.0[1]	1.4[1]	5.5[1]	12	...	...	0.7	—	100.0	2.5	St. Christopher and Nevis
									8.0[5, 12]	100.0[5, 12]—						St. Helena and Ascension
8.0[3]	78.6	4.1	9.3	0.307	10.8	68.8	—	13.4	42	...	...	6.1	—	100.0	2.2	St. Lucia
									4.0[1]	...	...	1.0[1]	...	...	...	St. Pierre and Miquelon
27.1[3]	53.4	9.7	9.9	0.206	12.6	61.3	—	17.8	21	96.2	3.8	1.4	53.8	46.2	2.2	St. Vincent and the Grenadines
...	...	...	...	...	...	...	...	...	...	...	...	...	...	...	...	San Marino
									3.0[1]							São Tomé and Príncipe
—	43.2	8.0	48.8	137.9	34.7	30.3	1.2	5.8	2,732[1]	...	...	2,120[1]	...	...	...	Saudi Arabia
3.6	85.8	5.9	4.7	413.2	26.5	23.1	4.6	15.5	1,496	79.0	21.0	48	35.1	64.9	8.3	Senegal
48.9[3]	37.6	5.1	8.4	0.321	17.2	58.6	6.1	5.6	42	87.1	12.9	2.7	55.6	44.4	3.9	Seychelles
33.9[3]	21.6	36.5	7.9	0.508	43.6	43.8	—	1.9	359	75.6	24.4	9.7	71.1	28.9	7.2	Sierra Leone
6.4	60.8	3.5	29.3	58.554	7.3	31.2	6.0	42.6	1,244	34.2	65.8	394	70.5	29.5	1.3	Singapore
18.0[3]	51.0	27.3	3.6	0.059	27.3	60.5	3.4	6.3	20	100.0	—	0.2	33.3	66.7	0.3	Solomon Islands
13.8[3]	59.7	16.8	9.6	6.239	46.4	25.6	—	—	1,149	85.8	14.2	22	57.0	43.0	13.1	Somalia
4.5	89.7	3.7	2.1	44.075	45.6	39.1	—	5.7	2,090	...	...	...	...	...	...	South Africa
...	...	...	...	...	...	...	...	...	...	...	...	...	...	...	...	Bophuthatswana
...	...	...	...	...	...	...	...	...	...	...	...	...	...	...	...	Ciskei
...	...	...	...	...	...	...	...	...	...	...	...	...	...	...	...	Transkei
...	...	...	...	...	...	...	...	...	...	...	...	...	...	...	...	Venda
0.2	50.5	23.0	—	0.810	—64.7—		24.6	0.4	1.0[1]	...	...	...	...	...	...	South West Africa/Namibia
20.3	56.1	12.7	10.9	27,909.0	12.3	52.9	2.5	13.2	1,787[14]	...	...	...	...	...	...	Spain
6.1	72.3	11.0	10.6	49.151	16.3	56.3	4.7	6.4	2,205	73.3	26.7	167	48.4	51.6	11.9	Sri Lanka
1.8	49.2	28.6	20.4	3.273	40.2	22.1	0.7	5.4	5,726	82.3	17.7	91	59.2	40.8	11.2	Sudan, The
10.2	57.9	29.2	2.8	1.084	24.6	55.2	0.6	4.6	15[1]	...	...	12[1]	...	...	2.4	Suriname
2.8	59.6	33.8	3.8	0.256	19.0	63.0	5.3	3.4	183	95.6	4.5	1S	54.8	45.2	20.4	Swaziland
14.1	74.1	0.9	10.9	586.4	6.4	59.3[4]	—	23.8	10,621	...	...	...	...	...	...	Sweden
2.8	58.0	3.0	36.2	526.3	6.2	37.6	—	24.1	...	...	...	...	...	...	...	Switzerland
59.6[3]	14.4	23.8	2.3	41.314	36.7	12.6	9.3	9.4	2,305	94.5	5.5	304	76.1	23.9	11.2	Syria
15.7[3]	57.8	7.7	10.9	2,363.8	21.2	44.4	5.4	5.8	6,220[1]	...	...	1,340[1]	...	...	...	Taiwan
79.9[2, 3]	7.1[2]	4.1[2]	8.9[2]	24.283[2]	51.7[2]	30.0[2]	3.4[2]	1.7[2]	2,584	81.1	18.9	6.5	45.6	54.4	12.9[1]	Tanzania
15.4[3]	77.1	2.4	5.1	606.5	4.8	74.3	2.5	6.4	7,060	61.1	38.9	949	44.1	55.9	11.3	Thailand
1.5	41.8	41.8	14.9	150.8	34.9	30.1	16.0	16.8	805	80.3	19.7	45	37.2	62.8	16.6	Togo
...	...	...	...	...	...	...	...	...	1.0[5, 12]	...	...	...	...	...	...	Tokelau
									16[1]	...	...	...	...	...	...	Tonga
13.5[3]	68.2	16.8	1.5	8.908	15.6	66.0	5.2	3.8	887	26.8	73.2	225	54.9	45.1	8.5	Trinidad and Tobago
11.0	81.9	1.8	5.3	3.692	30.0	25.7	4.6	9.6	3,427	73.5	26.5	598	67.5	32.5	22.3	Tunisia
15.4[3]	51.8	19.7	13.1	7,052.0	21.1	41.5	5.3	18.7	15,396	69.6	30.4	2,344	50.1	49.9	29.1	Turkey
...	...	...	...	...	...	...	...	...	1.0[1]	...	...	...	...	...	...	Turks and Caicos Islands
...	...	...	...	...	...	...	...	...	4.0[5, 12]	...	...	...	...	...	...	Tuvalu
3.2	50.2	30.8	15.7	65.766	59.7	22.9	0.1	3.7	623	87.1	12.9	82	79.2	20.8	22.3[14]	Uganda
...	...	...	...	...	...	...	...	...	10,900[15]	...	...	...	...	...	...	U.S.S.R.
5.6[3]	40.3	4.0	50.1	88.735	6.7	42.8	5.2	23.4	1,117[1]	...	...	518[1]	...	...	2.7[1]	United Arab Emirates
3.0[3]	24.0	0.5	72.6	602.7	6.6	13.7[4]	—	75.2	...	...	...	...	...	...	...	United Kingdom
14.0[3]	77.0	2.8	6.2	3,045.6	13.3	75.5	0.9	6.1	...	...	...	...	...	...	...	United States
9.9[3]	60.1	14.5	15.5	179.246	2.1	51.1[4]	3.4	15.9	2,523	15.1	84.9	292	32.1	67.8	19.8	Uruguay
0.9[3]	16.2	0.2	82.7	24.643	8.5	32.3[4]	3.3	47.8	3.7	86.5	13.5	0.7	60.0	40.0	...	Vanuatu
6.2[3]	73.8	14.1	5.9	140.459	33.9	55.7[4]	9.5	1.7	12,911	1.8	98.2	2,595	36.1	63.9	15.0	Venezuela
...	...	...	...	...	...	...	...	...	2,760[1]	...	...	75[1]	...	...	...	Vietnam
...	...	...	...	...	...	...	...	...	...	...	...	...	...	...	...	Virgin Islands (U.S.)
...	...	...	...	...	...	...	...	...	2.0[1]	...	...	—	—	—	—	Wallis and Futuna
...	...	...	...	...	...	...	...	...	...	...	...	...	...	...	...	West Bank
...	...	...	...	...	...	...	...	...	...	...	...	...	...	...	...	Western Sahara
...	...	...	...	0.108[24]	...	...	...	...	60	95.0	5.0	3.7	73.0	7.0	18.3[1]	Western Samoa
34.2[3]	5.2	57.3	3.3	0.311	36.3	45.6	10.0	7.4	1,263	100.0	—	46	68.9	31.1	25.1	Yemen (Aden)
3.0[3]	40.4	42.0	14.5	8.821	28.4	43.2	2.4	6.4	1,574	98.8	1.2	42	68.6	31.4	13.9	Yemen (Şan'ā')
0.4	65.5	26.8	7.3	6,610.4	13.9	45.5[4]	—	26.6	9,077	46.9	53.1	1,009	52.1	47.9	7.6	Yugoslavia
1.7[3]	32.2	25.7	40.4	10.517	68.0	10.8	2.1	9.4	4,022	78.4	21.6	127	31.0	69.0	7.0	Zaire
23.6	57.8	15.1	3.5	1.826	31.8	45.7	2.1	6.6	2,638	77.1	22.9	126	38.1	61.9	12.6	Zambia
37.0[3]	53.7	8.4	1.0	2.019	30.1	53.0	—	2.2	1,497	75.8	24.2	435	75.8	24.2	31.6	Zimbabwe

[1]1982. [2]1983. [3]Includes claims on other government agencies and local governments. [4]Includes foreign currency deposits. [5]1980. [6]1984. [7]Treasury bill rate. [8]Time deposit rate. [9]Short-term government bond yield. [10]Foreign currency debts. [11]Excludes Indian rupee currency. [12]Official development assistance only. [13]Cash and demand deposits at local banks. [14]1981. [15]Net hard currency debt to the West. [16]Includes deposits by other government agencies and local banks. [17]Government-controlled area only. [18]Call money (interbank) rate. [19]Short-term credit rate. [20]1979. [21]Reserve money includes capital accounts. [22]Government bond yield. [23]1977. [24]Bank of Western Samoa and Development Bank of Western Samoa only.

Housing and construction

The present table summarizes data about the housing stock and the construction industries of the countries of the world. The principal focus is on the elements that are most comparable internationally: the age of the housing (by decade, so far as possible), the tenure of the householder, construction of exterior walls, the principal physical amenities, the sanitary arrangements, and the amount of space both absolutely (in square metres [10.76 square feet]) and relatively (persons per room). The data on construction characterize the industry in terms of number of units, area, and the portion of the gross domestic product (GDP) represented by each country's construction industry.

Because utilization of housing opportunities, economic development, and patterns of internal migration (favouring, for example, apartments, or temporary, sometimes seasonal, dwellings) differ greatly from country to country, the portion of each country's housing stock for which data are compared is defined as specifically as possible. In general, the numbers refer to permanent, private dwelling units that are usually occupied year-round, whether or not actually occupied on the date of the housing census or survey.

That definition implies the exclusion of certain housing that is often part of national housing censuses: vacation homes, second homes occupied less than half the year, collective or communal dwellings, and so on. The housing unit to which the data on tenure refer may be either the individual dwelling or the household, according to the reporting practice of the country concerned.

The data are collected mostly from national housing censuses and surveys. There has been much activity in recent years under United Nations sponsorship in the field of human settlement. The UN's *Compendium of Housing Statistics* is particularly useful and may be consulted for additional, though older, detail. The UN Centre for Human Settlements in Nairobi, Kenya, collects, analyzes, and publishes data on all aspects of settlement, but a particular focus is the provision of adequate, technologically appropriate housing for the many areas of the world where it is in limited supply.

Many countries conduct a meaningful housing census only in the capital city or in the few largest cities. This choice may result from the lack of ability to collect data for the entire country or from the perception, particularly in a tropical, rural country where adequate dwellings can be

Housing and construction

country	\	housing stock													
	year	dwelling units[a]	median age[b] (years)	decade built (percent)					tenure[c] (percent)			construction of exterior walls (percent)			
				1939 or earlier	1940–49	1950–59	1960–69	1970 or later	owned	rented	collective, vacant, other	traditional materials	sawn/framed wood	masonry or cement	other
Afghanistan	...	...	...	...	...	...	...	...	...	...	...	...	...	...	...
Albania	...	...	...	...	...	...	...	...	...	...	...	...	...	...	...
Algeria	1977	2,208,712[5]	...	...	...	...	23.7	...	56.7	29.4	13.9	...	...	...	...
American Samoa	1980	4,688	13.4	4.2	4.8	7.7	38.4	44.9	71.2	25.1	3.7	4.1	56.3	34.9	4.7
Andorra	...	...	...	...	...	...	...	...	...	...	...	...	...	...	...
Angola	...	...	...	...	...	...	...	...	...	...	...	...	...	...	...
Anguilla	1974	1,588	...	...	...	...	...	...	...	...	...	...	...	...	...
Antigua and Barbuda	1970	15,405[5]	11.1	13.8	9.7	31.4	46.1	—	55.9	40.4	3.7	...	...	...	...
Argentina	1980	7,103,853	21.6	9.1	14.9	17.3	22.0	36.7	67.7	14.8	17.5	6.1	6.7	84.2	3.0
Australia	1981	5,161,163	26.1	—37.9—		10.4	18.6	33.1	61.6	22.6	15.8	...	...	...	...
Austria	1981	3,052,037	63.6	—44.5—		13.3	19.4	22.8	47.7	36.2	16.1	...	...	...	...
Bahamas, The	1980	54,308	30.7	—54.7—			25.6	19.7	51.4	37.4	11.2	4.0[12]	32.3	54.7	9.0
Bahrain	1981	52,810	15.2	41.2	17.1	14.5	—27.2—		60.6[11]	33.6[11]	5.8[11]	2.1[11]	—	95.1[11]	2.8[11]
Bangladesh	1973	13,734,999	...	...	...	...	...	...	92.4	3.8	3.8	...	...	...	...
Barbados	1980	67,138	18.9	—51.3—			20.6	28.1	70.2	21.5	8.3	0.1	68.9[13]	26.3	4.7
Belgium	1981	3,599,977	35.2	48.4[14]	—17.2[15]—		14.2	16.0	59.2	38.1	2.7	...	...	...	...
Belize	1980	27,298	...	—24.6—			30.0	41.0	56.1	27.2	16.7	7.5	73.4	14.0	5.1
Benin	...	644,000[18]	...	...	...	...	...	...	...	...	...	...	...	...	...
Bermuda	1980	20,350	31.2	—67.9—			16.6	15.5	39.4	53.7	6.9	...	1.7[13]	95.1	3.2
Bhutan	...	...	...	...	...	...	...	...	...	...	...	...	...	...	...
Bolivia	1976	989,055[5]	...	...	...	...	47.4	...	69.3	15.1	15.6	...	...	...	...
Botswana	1981	170,262	...	...	...	...	...	...	59.9	17.1	23.0	65.5	—	28.0	2.4
Brazil	1982	27,401,345	...	...	...	...	...	...	61.9	22.3	15.8	...	...	...	...
British Virgin Islands	1980	3,287	21.6	—39.8—		—31.2—		29.0	47.4	48.7	3.6	—	21.6	68.0	10.4
Brunei	1981	28,676	...	...	...	...	...	...	83.8	11.8	4.4	0.2	54.8	36.5	1.7
Bulgaria	1975	2,734,717	17.9	47.0	—34.9—		11.1	7.0	77.3	22.7	—	...	...	...	...
Burkina Faso	...	...	...	...	...	...	...	...	...	...	...	...	...	...	...
Burma	1973	5,587,261	...	...	...	...	...	...	...	...	...	...	...	...	...
Burundi	1979	938,000	...	...	...	...	...	...	98.7[19]	1.1[19]	0.2[19]	...	...	...	...
Cameroon	1976	1,390,896	...	...	...	...	...	...	83.4	11.2	5.4	75.5	13.9	9.5	1.1
Canada	1981	8,281,530[5]	14.6	—41.2—		13.8	17.9	27.1	62.1	37.9	—	...	...	...	...
Cape Verde	...	...	...	...	...	...	...	...	...	...	...	...	...	...	...
Cayman Islands	1979	4,426	16.4[16]	—42.2[16]—		19.6[16]	38.2[16]	—	67.8	32.2	—	1.0	24.0	74.0	1.0
Central African Republic	1975	405,399	...	...	...	...	...	...	...	...	...	82.2	7.1	2.5	8.2
Chad	...	...	...	...	...	...	...	...	...	...	...	...	...	...	...
Chile	1982	2,510,275	20.4	—46.2—			21.1	32.7	53.3[16]	26.3[16]	20.4[16]	...	...	...	...
China	1982	220,100,775	...	...	...	...	...	...	...	...	...	...	...	...	...
Christmas Island	1981	574	14.0[2]	—32.2[2]—			27.2[2]	40.6[2]	—	86.4	13.6	—	1.7	74.7	23.6
Cocos (Keeling) Islands	1981	150	...	...	...	...	33.3	...	—80.7—		19.3	—	6.0	52.0	42.0
Colombia	1973	3,448,164	20.6	46.7	7.9	26.2	19.2	—	53.5	30.7	15.8	36.8	—61.9—		1.3
Comoros	...	...	...	...	...	...	...	...	...	...	...	...	...	...	...
Congo	1979–80[21]	110,000[21]	...	...	...	...	...	...	58.4[21]	40.9[21]	0.7[21]	36.0[22,23]	39.4[22,23]	24.6[22,23]	—
Cook Islands	1981	3,153[5]	14.0	5.9	5.7	16.8	48.6	23.0	85.3[10]	9.4[10]	5.3[10]	...	...	...	...
Costa Rica	1973	330,857	...	...	...	...	36.4	...	60.3	22.9	16.8	2.3	77.5	16.8	3.4
Cuba	1981	2,363,364	24.6	15.0[24]	8.2[25]	21.3[26]	21.6	25.6	...	...	...	1.4	37.1	61.5	...
Cyprus	1982	168,588	22.8	—38.7—			16.0	45.3	60.0	16.5	23.5	11.9	—	87.6	0.5
Czechoslovakia	1980	5,009,771	36.7	—40.0[14]—		15.1[15]	20.3	24.6	44.7	41.7	13.6	—	2.9	93.8	3.3
Denmark	1981	2,161,862	30.8	42.8	6.9	11.0	18.1	21.2	54.9	43.8	1.3	...	...	...	...
Djibouti	1982	25,000	27.6	...	...	...	...	...	...	...	...	—	73.0[28]	22.5	4.5
Dominica	1970	15,148	...	—58.4—			16.9	21.1	3.6	64.7	26.6	8.7	0.2	88.8	10.2	0.8
Dominican Republic	1981	1,114,833[5]	...	—12.4—			—87.6—		70.5[8]	15.6[8]	13.9[8]	31.8[16]	46.2[16]	15.3[16]	6.7[16]
Ecuador	1974	1,251,910	...	...	...	...	31.1	...	63.7	24.0	12.3	63.3	8.9	23.9	3.9
Egypt	1976	7,311,139	...	...	...	...	...	...	...	...	...	...	...	...	...
El Salvador	1971	680,456	...	...	...	...	...	...	48.1	25.5	26.4	37.9	9.6	46.9	5.6
Equatorial Guinea	...	...	...	...	...	...	...	...	...	...	...	...	...	...	...
Ethiopia	1984	9,300,000	...	...	...	...	...	...	...	...	...	...	...	...	...
Faeroe Islands	1977	11,172	32.5	33.7	—26.4—		21.8	15.0	84.5	9.9	5.6	—	43.9	53.5	2.6
Falkland Islands	1972	639	...	...	...	...	1.7	...	...	...	...	...	...	...	...
Fiji	1977[32]	...	8.6	...	...	...	...	...	73.6	16.1	10.3	...	...	...	...
Finland	1980	1,838,058	22.0	19.2	7.8	17.0	20.9	35.1	61.0	20.9	18.1	...	...	...	...

built by hand, that no urgent housing problem exists. This choice may be difficult, however, as planners are usually aware that much housing is physically inadequate to protect dwellers from the elements and that too much of the stock is disadvantageously placed in relation to tainted or disease-infested water supply or to the outfall of unprocessed sewage, or is built of materials (mud, skins, thatch, etc.) that may harbour pests or disease. In the developed countries, median age and the distribution of physical amenities provide strong indicators of the quality and availability of housing.

The data for construction industries in various countries of the world refer to new construction for the most recent year in which a broad range of countries could be surveyed. The data for construction are usually from official documents that authorize construction or that certify after construction that the structure described meets building and fire codes and the like. The figures for completed construction are naturally more reliable but are not available for many countries, necessitating the provision of authorized construction data, which are usually available only for areas regulated by zoning code authorities.

A truer indication of the level of activity in a national construction industry is in the data for its contribution to the national gross domestic product. That figure includes civil engineering projects, such as dams, roads, harbour works and the like, but the relative capacity indicated usually finds its way into the domestic housing (personal, collective, and commercial) industry. The predominance within the "new residential" sector of multiunit housing usually indicates (in a developed country) a particularly mobile society, or (in a developing country) one in which limited development resources obliges planners to concentrate available physical and manpower resources in collective projects.

a. Data refer to permanent, private dwelling units that are usually occupied year-round, whether or not occupied on the census date.
b. Data are estimates unless specifically provided by a country source.
c. Data may be either for dwellings or for households, depending on country reporting practice.
d. Data may be either for construction completed or for construction authorized, depending on country reporting practice.

physical amenities (percent)			sewage disposal (percent)			space[b]			construction industry (1982)						country
									percent of GDP	new residential[d]			new nonresidential[d]		
piped water	electricity	inside toilet or WC	closed public sewer or septic tank	open public sewer	other	average area (sq m)	rooms per dwelling unit	persons per room		1- or 2-unit dwellings	multiunit dwellings	floor area ('000 sq m)	number of units	floor area ('000 sq m)	
...	...	...	...	...	...	...	...	...	3.2[1]	...	...	...	48[2]	65.6[2,3]	Afghanistan
...	...	...	...	...	...	...	...	...	7.2[4]	...	...	...	...	...	Albania
45.8	49.2	...	54.1	—45.9—		...	2.2[6]	2.8[6]	11.7[7]	...	...	...	...	...	Algeria
77.4	96.2	...	83.5	—	16.5	...	3.0	2.3		...	...	...	...	...	American Samoa
...	...	...	...	...	...	...	...	...		—95[2]—		91.3[2]	14[2]	47.5[2]	Andorra
...	...	...	...	...	...	...	...	...	1.7[7]	—1,587[2]—		585.2[2]	210[2]	164.5[2]	Angola
8.1	18.5	30.1	80.0	—	20.0	...	...	...		...	...	...	...	...	Anguilla
85.4	...	...	17.0	—83.0—		...	3.1	...	8.4	...	...	...	...	...	Antigua and Barbuda
72.9	69.2[8]	95.1	77.1	—22.9—		...	3.9	1.3	5.0	—25,716[9]—		3,406[9]	9	9	Argentina
91.1[10]	98.4[11]	89.5	99.0	—1.0—		...	5.1	0.6	6.6[2]	...	...	21,607	18,481	10,980	Australia
95.0	...	85.5	94.3	—	5.7	76.5	2.8	1.0	7.6	18,800	1,400	3,600[9]	300	9	Austria
63.9	77.9	...	63.2	2.2	34.6	...	4.0	1.2	2.8	—677—		...	90	...	Bahamas, The
3.8	94.0[11]	...	29.0[11]		71.0[11]	...	3.0[11]	2.3[11]	11.0[2]	—2,051—		...	1,839	...	Bahrain
...	...	...	1.3	—98.7—		...	2.0	2.9	5.1	...	...	...	...	...	Bangladesh
82.4	83.0	43.6	95.8	0.7	3.5	...	4.2	0.8	6.1	—753[10]—		...	35[10]	...	Barbados
91.9	100.0[16]	79.0	62.5[16]	—37.5[16]—		86.6[17]	5.2	0.5	6.0	23,459	378	16,776[3]	5,257	17,137[3]	Belgium
60.1	59.4	...	21.1	—78.9—		...	2.5[8]	1.9[8]	4.9	...	...	...	...	...	Belize
...	...	...	...	...	...	...	...	...	5.1[7]	...	...	...	...	...	Benin
95.9	...	96.7	96.7	—3.3—		...	3.2	0.7	...	148[4]	12[4]	20.1[4]	15[4]	15.0[4]	Bermuda
...	...	...	...	...	...	...	...	...	1.9[7]	—107—		...	17	...	Bhutan
37.9	33.0	...	12.5	—87.5—		...	...	...	1.9	—2,075[2]—		...	...	...	Bolivia
56.1	5.4	8.6	8.6	20.4	71.0	...	...	...	4.3	—526—		75.4	425	103.3	Botswana
61.3	76.1	28.6	45.1	34.8	20.1	...	5.1[2]	0.9[2]	4.9	—103,469—		20,404	4,121	3,513	Brazil
62.3	90.2	65.1	65.1	25.3	9.6	...	3.9	1.1	11.6[4]	...	...	...	...	...	British Virgin Islands
90.3	85.5	94.2	57.4	—42.6—		...	4.2	1.6	3.0	—12[2]—		...	60[2]	...	Brunei
74.6	99.8	33.2	33.2	—67.8—		...	3.6	1.0	9.7[1]	9,155[7]	1,538[7]	5,540.6[7]	...	...	Bulgaria
...	...	...	...	...	...	...	...	...	4.0	...	...	...	...	...	Burkina Faso
...	...	...	...	...	...	...	...	...	1.8	...	...	...	...	...	Burma
11.0[19]	0.6[19]	...	1.6[19]	—98.4[19]—		...	...	...	5.3	...	...	...	...	...	Burundi
5.2	5.9	2.2	2.2	70.4	27.6	...	4.1	1.2	5.6	—290[2]—		33.8[2]	33[2]	3.3[2]	Cameroon
99.5	100.0	...	98.9	—1.1—		...	5.7	0.5	5.1		1,856	...	9,395	...	Canada
...	...	...	...	...	...	...	...	...	20.3[7]	—242—		30.5	3	0.5	Cape Verde
62.5	79.7	83.7	84.4	9.2	6.4	...	3.7	1.0	...	...	...	...	...	...	Cayman Islands
...	...	...	...	...	...	...	1.1[20]	3.4[20]	4.3	—124[4]—		18.8[4]	57[4]	16.6[4]	Central African Republic
...	...	...	...	...	...	...	...	...	2.1[7]	...	...	...	...	...	Chad
86.5	70.6[8]	...	43.6[16]	—56.4[16]—		...	2.9[16]	1.4[16]	5.6	...	...	25.4	...	161.2	Chile
...	...	...	...	...	...	...	...	...	4.9	...	...	90,200	...	53,370	China
100.0	100.0	100.0[11]	100.0[11]	—	—	...	5.7	1.0	...	...	...	...	...	...	Christmas Island
33.3	100.0	100.0	100.0	—	—	...	6.1	0.6	...	...	...	...	...	...	Cocos (Keeling) Islands
62.7	57.6	...	46.1	—53.9—		...	3.4	1.8	5.2	8,879	5,524	4,929.9	1,172	1,398	Colombia
...	...	...	...	...	...	...	...	...	10.5	...	...	...	...	...	Comoros
37.3[21]	11.4[21]	...	—86.2[21]—		13.8[21]	...	3.7[21]	1.7[21]	4.6[7]	...	...	...	...	...	Congo
88.3[10]	60.6[10]	...	36.7[10]	—63.3[10]—		...	4.0[10]	0.7[10]	4.5[4]	—69—		...	21	...	Cook Islands
81.0	68.8	...	46.1	—53.9—		...	4.0	1.4	3.9	—8,317—		702	3,297	173	Costa Rica
74.1	78.7	45.2	60.9	9.0	30.1	...	4.1	1.0	7.7[1]	—647—		830.3	476	4,445	Cuba
100.0	98.1	74.5	95.6	—4.4—		...	4.6	0.8	11.5	—5,384—		206.1[9]	1,040	9	Cyprus
84.2[27]	100.0	31.7	83.6[27]	0.2[27]	16.2[27]	60.5	3.5	0.9	10.2[1]	26,264		7,702[9]	...	...	Czechoslovakia
100.0	100.0	94.5	98.6	—1.4—		100.8	3.8	0.6	5.4			2,127.9	12,801	3,542.9	Denmark
45.0	58.0	82.0	26.0	23.0	51.0	...	1.9	6.9	7.5	—70—		68.1	40	26.8	Djibouti
91.1[7]	...	12.3	12.3	—87.7—		...	2.8	1.7	9.3	...	...	...	...	...	Dominica
45.4[16]	36.7[16]	11.2[16]	52.1[16]	22.6[16]	25.3[16]	...	2.7[8]	2.0[8]	7.0	9,949	139	727	495	241	Dominican Republic
51.0[29]	41.2	...	28.1	9.9	62.0	...	2.4	2.3	9.6	7,395[30]	2,485[30]	1,659.3[30]	6143[30]	757.1[30]	Ecuador
30.2	45.7	...	...	...	...	...	3.2	1.8	4.7	...	...	...	...	...	Egypt
48.0[29]	34.1	6.3[11]	20.0[29]	—80.0[29]—		...	1.7	3.2	3.4	2,901[30]	72[30]	180.0[30]	33[30]	1.6[30]	El Salvador
...	...	...	...	...	...	...	...	...	4.9[29]	...	...	...	...	...	Equatorial Guinea
...	...	...	...	...	...	...	...	2.7[31]	4.3	—1,637[29]—		122.8[29]	67[29]	20.8[29]	Ethiopia
99.7	99.5	95.0	89.7	8.1	2.2	...	5.5	1.1	10.2[2]	...	...	...	...	...	Faeroe Islands
98.6	...	98.0	98.0	—2.0—		...	7.4	0.4	...	...	...	...	...	...	Falkland Islands
61.1	39.2	...	35.4	—64.6—		...	2.0	...	7.2	—918—		80	159	58	Fiji
89.3	95.6[16]	83.9	90.3	—9.7—		69.0	2.8	0.8	7.3	26,845	771	17,108[3]	31,144	26,630[3]	Finland

Housing and construction (continued)

country	housing stock														
	year	dwelling units[a]	median age[b] (years)	decade built (percent)					tenure[c] (percent)			construction of exterior walls (percent)			
				1939 or earlier	1940–49	1950–59	1960–69	1970 or later	owned	rented	collective, vacant, other	traditional materials	sawn/ framed wood	masonry or cement	other
France	1982	19,590,400	31.0[4]	—71.9[4]—			12.7[4]	15.4[4]	50.7	41.0	8.3	...	...	...	...
French Guiana	1982	21,063	...	...	...	...	23.2[16]		34.5	54.0	11.5	...	...	...	...
French Polynesia	1983	...	13.6	—5.0—		9.0	30.0	56.0	...	...	...	38.0	—62.0—		...
Gabon	1967[22]	15,886	...	...	...	...	...	...	—87.0—		13.0[34]	...	...	...	...
Gambia, The	1973	59,450	...	...	...	...	...	...	...	...	...	...	...	...	...
Gaza Strip	1967	66,819	...	...	...	...	...	...	...	...	...	...	...	...	...
Germany, East	1981	6,562,467	...	—62.4—		6.1	10.1	21.4	23.0[11]	69.3[11]	7.7[11]	...	...	...	...
Germany, West	1982	26,076,000	...	—53.7—			20.5	25.8	33.5[35]	66.5[35]	—	...	...	...	...
Ghana	1970	870,036	...	...	...	...	...	...	...	...	...	...	...	...	...
Gibraltar	1981	6,945	...	...	...	...	...	...	5.2	94.5	0.3	...	...	...	...
Greece	1981	3,999,332	29.2	—30.2[14]—		27.4[15]	20.7	21.5	73.1[23]	26.9[23]	—	...	...	...	...
Greenland	1984	15,066	10.8[10]	—11.9[10]—		18.8[10]	46.5[10]	22.8[10]	39.8	—58.9—		...	...	...	...
Grenada	1970	19,642	18.3	—48.0—		29.0	22.2	0.8	76.5	14.0	9.5	0.4	80.8	17.8	1.0
Guadeloupe	1982	85,629	...	...	...	...	8.1[23]		64.3	29.9	5.8	...	...	...	...
Guam	1980	28,091	...	...	...	...	...	44.6	40.8	47.6	11.6[34]	...	...	...	...
Guatemala	1981	1,259,598	12.5	—62.0—			10.0	28.0	64.7	11.3	24.0	55.6	21.1	19.3	4.0
Guernsey	1976	17,824	...	...	...	...	...	...	63.5	33.5	3.0	...	...	...	...
Guinea	...	...	...	...	...	...	...	...	...	...	...	...	...	...	...
Guinea-Bissau	1979	123,936	...	...	...	...	...	...	...	...	...	95.7	0.1	2.3	1.9
Guyana	1970	129,722	...	—45.8—			31.6	.1.0	56.8	29.8	13.4	3.1	87.2	7.1	2.6
Haiti	1982	1,130,795	...	...	...	...	...	24.1	82.9[10]	4.8[10]	12.3[10]	...	...	...	...
Honduras	1974	526,566	...	—43.1—			37.9	14.2	71.8	16.5	12.7	61.0	26.4	11.7	0.9
Hong Kong	1981	1,061,086	...	...	...	...	13.6	38.3	27.7	70.4	1.9	...	...	...	...
Hungary	1980	3,540,000	38.4	—43.3[14]—		13.6[26]	18.0	25.1	71.4	28.4	0.2	30.8	14.3	54.8	0.1
Iceland	1984	70,777	25.6	18.5	—27.5—		—54.1—		70.3[8]	—29.7[8]—		...	...	71.9[8]	...
India	1981	142,954,921	...	...	...	...	...	...	84.6[11]	15.4[11]	—	...	...	...	...
Indonesia	1980	30,263,273	...	...	...	...	...	...	87.0[11]	5.0[11]	8.0[11]	...	...	...	...
Iran	1976	5,331,220	...	—82.5—				17.5	71.6[6]	16.2[6]	12.2[6]	...	...	...	...
Iraq	1956	741,000	...	...	...	...	...	...	83.0	12.8	4.2	...	...	...	...
Ireland	1971	705,180[5]	47.2	64.5	—20.1—		15.4		68.8	28.9	2.3	...	...	...	...
Isle of Man	1981[32]	24,348	...	...	...	...	...	...	52.5	36.5	1.0	...	...	...	...
Israel	1978	925,000	...	...	...	...	...	...	70.6	26.5	2.9	...	...	...	...
Italy	1981	21,852,717	19.4	—30.8[14]—		19.7[15]	27.5[37]	22.0	50.9[11]	44.1[11]	5.0[11]	...	...	...	...
Ivory Coast	1958[38]	...	...	...	...	...	...	...	...	...	...	...	...	...	...
Jamaica	1982	517,297	...	—33.6—			26.8	39.6	46.7	29.5	23.8	7.1	28.4	54.4	10.1
Japan	1983	34,704,500	13.0	—13.5—		9.7	24.0	52.1	62.4	37.3	0.3	—	77.4	21.5	1.1
Jersey	1981[32]	26,674	...	...	...	...	...	...	48.8	49.2	2.0	...	...	...	...
Jordan	1979	378,815[39]	...	...	...	...	...	...	62.6	30.8	6.6	...	...	...	...
Kampuchea	...	...	...	...	...	...	...	...	...	...	...	...	...	...	...
Kenya	1962[21]	137,000[5]	...	...	...	...	...	...	...	...	...	...	...	...	...
Kiribati	1978	10,802	...	...	...	...	...	...	68.2	17.9	13.9	64.4	—35.6—		
Korea, North	...	...	...	...	...	...	...	...	...	...	...	...	...	...	...
Korea, South	1980	7,969,201	19.0	—26.1—		15.8	18.2	39.9	58.7	39.3	2.0	—	38.8	37.5	23.8
Kuwait	1980	180,400	14.5	—12.2—			38.8	34.5	29.9[18]	53.0[18]	17.1[18]	46.5[40]	—	36.5[40]	17.0[40]
Laos	...	...	...	...	...	...	...	...	...	...	...	...	...	...	...
Lebanon	1970	483,908[5]	...	—30.1[41]—		40.2[42]	29.4	—	...	...	...	...	...	...	...
Lesotho	...	...	...	...	...	...	...	...	...	...	...	...	...	...	...
Liberia	1956[22]	11,000	...	...	...	...	...	...	...	...	...	...	...	...	...
Libya	1973	345,836	...	...	...	...	...	...	62.5	28.0	9.5	...	...	...	...
Liechtenstein	1980	8,421	29.4	—27.1[41]—		15.0[42]	27.1	30.8	53.6	41.7	4.7	...	...	...	...
Luxembourg	1981	128,281[5]	...	—62.1[43]—		11.8[44]	7.8	18.3	54.5	45.5	—	...	...	...	...
Macau	1970	19,306	...	...	...	...	...	...	71.8	28.2	—	—	0.5	99.3	0.2
Madagascar	...	...	...	...	...	...	...	...	...	...	...	...	...	...	...
Malawi	1977[45]	46,110[5]	...	...	...	...	...	...	39.6	—60.4—		...	...	...	...
Malaysia	1980	2,516,295	...	...	...	...	...	...	64.0	23.0	13.0	...	...	...	...
Maldives	1985	29,818	...	...	...	...	...	...	...	...	...	...	...	...	...
Mali	...	...	...	...	...	...	...	...	...	...	...	...	...	...	...
Malta	1967	87,049	...	—81.8[48]—			18.2[49]	—	32.4	63.9	3.7	93.0	...	92.9	0.21
Martinique	1982	85,265	...	...	...	...	...	...	64.1	31.3	7.3	...	...	...	...
Mauritania	...	...	...	...	...	...	...	...	...	...	...	...	...	...	...
Mauritius	1972	146,569	...	—37.0—			55.7	7.3	52.5	31.9	15.6	2.5	6.8	39.3	51.4
Mayotte	1978	10,053	...	...	...	...	...	...	88.1	6.2	5.7	83.6	—7.7—		8.7
Mexico	1980	12,216,462	...	—51.4—			15.4	33.2	66.8	—33.2—		28.2	9.6	56.2	6.0
Monaco	1975	12,625	28.5	—51.4—		22.7	—25.8—		...	...	...	...	...	...	...
Mongolia	1969	242,000	...	...	...	...	...	...	100.0	...	...	...	...	...	...
Montserrat	1980	3,706	...	—47.4—			24.5	28.1	69.2	21.9	8.8	—	60.9	39.0	0.1
Morocco	1971[32]	2,819,213	...	...	...	...	...	...	...	...	...	10.9[21]	—	88.8[21]	0.3[21]
Mozambique	...	...	...	...	...	...	...	...	...	...	...	...	...	...	...
Nauru	1977	508[50]	...	—88.6[50]—				11.4[50]	11.0[31]	80.6[31]	8.4[31]	...	...	...	...
Nepal	1961[51]	37,122	...	...	...	...	...	...	75.3	10.7	14.0	...	...	...	...
Netherlands, The	1977	4,573,000[5]	20.0	22.0[52]	—29.0[53]—		24.6	24.4	...	...	...	...	...	...	...
Netherlands Antilles	1972	46,489	24.0	29.2	—38.6—		—32.2—		58.6	31.0	10.4	—	22.7	66.9	10.4
New Caledonia	1983	35,107	15.8	—9.8—		11.2	32.1	46.9	53.0	31.1	15.9	6.3	21.0	58.1	14.6
New Zealand	1981	1,048,035	...	—64.6—			19.2	16.2	70.8	25.3	3.9	...	...	...	...
Nicaragua	1971	330,422	...	...	...	...	...	...	...	...	...	...	...	...	...
Niger	...	...	...	...	...	...	...	...	...	...	...	...	...	...	...
Nigeria	1961[22]	92,900	...	...	...	...	...	...	8.0	80.9	11.1	...	...	...	...
Niue	1981	673	...	...	...	...	...	...	89.2	7.4	3.4	...	...	...	...
Norfolk Island	1981	845	14.8	—32.8—			32.5	34.7	53.0	35.3	11.7	—	49.8	3.6	46.6
Norway	1980	1,523,512	25.3	35.1	6.9	16.8	18.7	22.5	66.6	23.5	9.9	...	...	...	...
Oman	1982	2,469	...	...	...	...	...	...	...	...	...	...	...	...	...
Pacific Is., Trust Terr. of the	1980	21,363	10.6	2.0	2.7	7.6	24.1	63.6	56.4	34.6	9.0	5.4	41.6	19.4	33.6
Pakistan	1980	12,587,648	17.2[54]	...	17.1[41, 54]	36.7[54, 55]	24.9[54, 56]	21.3[54, 57]	78.4	7.7	13.9	49.2[54]	2.4[54]	41.4[54]	7.1[54]
Panama	1980	364,325[5]	18.0	—47.4—		12.8	18.1	21.7	70.0	21.0	9.0	20.1	—77.3—		2.6
Papua New Guinea	1975[21]	42,860	...	...	...	...	...	...	40.0	—60.0—		...	...	...	...
Paraguay	1982	580,810[5]	21.1	—56.0—			17.0	27.0	80.4	10.5	9.1	21.5	29.7	47.6	1.2
Peru	1981	3,563,643	...	...	...	...	27.0[35]		69.5[35]	16.6[35]	13.9[35]	...	...	...	...
Philippines	1980	8,607,187	...	...	...	...	21.5[16]		80.2	12.4	7.4	36.3	33.6	23.8	6.3
Pitcairn Island	1981	22	...	...	...	...	...	...	...	...	...	...	...	...	...
Poland	1983	10,513,000	...	...	...	...	...	...	...	...	...	...	...	...	...

piped water	electricity	inside toilet or WC	closed public sewer or septic tank	open public sewer	other	average area (sq m)	rooms per dwelling unit	persons per room	percent of GDP	1- or 2-unit dwellings	multiunit dwellings	floor area ('000 sq m)	number of units	floor area ('000 sq m)	country
99.2	98.8[33]	85.0	73.8[18]	—26.2[18]—		77.0[4]	3.7	0.8	6.3	218,452	...	...	...	16,090	France
67.7	80.4	59.1	34.3	—65.7—		...	2.8	1.3	...				...	...	French Guiana
86.0	76.0	76.0	2.0	67.0	31.0	...	3.4		9.4	—7249—		...	9	...	French Polynesia
...	50.5	...	...	...	...	...	3.0	1.3	4.7[30]	—445[18]—		216.1[18]	75[18]	119.4[18]	Gabon
...	...	...	...	...	...	...	...	...	8.1	120[18]	76[18]	...	14[18]	...	Gambia, The
56.3	17.7	42.0	...	...	...	...	...	...	...	...	...	305.0	...	57.6	Gaza Strip
93.9	100.0	60.1	56.6[11]	—43.4[11]—		62.7	2.8	0.9	5.8[1]	...	...	7,452	...	...	Germany, East
99.2[35]	99.7[35]	95.6	94.2[35]	—5.8[35]—		...	4.2	0.6	6.5	145,258	14,612	184,821[3]	35,259	160,532[3]	Germany, West
34.0[29]	...	...	...	...	...	...	...	...	2.7	...	...	...	...	...	Ghana
87.0[23]	...	98.8	73.0[23]	—27.0[23]—		...	3.2	1.2	...	...	...	...	...	...	Gibraltar
81.3[11]	89.0[11]	93.0[11]	39.1[10]	—60.9[10]—		...	3.5[11]	0.9[11]	6.6	37,808	5,044	29,636[3]	13,712	12,874[3]	Greece
62.7[10]	84.2[10]	39.1[10]	23.0	—77.0—		...	2.6	1.3	14.6[10]	...	...	36.6[30]	...	15.3	Greenland
86.5	...	23.0	24.6	—75.4—		...	2.9	1.6	7.0	...	...	...	...	...	Grenada
69.4	77.2	55.4	97.5	—2.5—		...	3.5	1.1	6.4[2]	460[30]	10[30]	91.9[30]	31[30]	40.9[30]	Guadeloupe
99.5	...	96.5	...	...	...	...	4.7	0.7	7.2[2]	...	...	...	...	...	Guam
52.0	37.0	14.3	20.1	3.4	76.5	...	2.4	2.2	3.4	—851[19]—		170.2[9]	...	...	Guatemala
96.5	...	88.8	49.3	—50.7—		...	5.5	0.5							Guernsey
...	...	...	...	...	...	...	...	...	3.8[2]	...					Guinea
3.7	3.9	25.6	25.8	—74.2—		...	1.4	4.5	2.5[29]	...					Guinea-Bissau
81.0	...	26.3	13.0	—87.0—		...	2.7	2.1	6.6	—1,259[2]—		...	56[2]	...	Guyana
12.0[29]	1.1[11]	...	2.0[29]	—98.0[29]—		...	2.2[11]	2.1[11]	5.2	—597[9]—		...	9	...	Haiti
55.0[29]	25.0	13.0	14.4	—85.6—		...	2.4	2.3	5.4	—4,795—		254.1	106	59.5	Honduras
85.7	...	69.2[36]	65.4[36]	—34.6[36]—		53.2[11]	3.1[36]	2.8[36]	7.0	—766—		977	327	2,244	Hong Kong
65.0	98.0	53.3	57.7	—42.3—		60.0	2.0	1.5	10.2[1]	31,032	1,650	25,082[3]	4,168	22,236[3]	Hungary
99.1[8]	94.6[8]	93.6[8]	86.5[8]	—13.5[8]—		...	4.8[8]	0.9[8]	8.7	...	...	917[3]	...	1,276.7[3]	Iceland
...	...	...	...	...	...	...	2.0[11,32]	2.6[11]	4.3	—66,207—		1,445.4[17]	12,145	3,768.5[17]	India
7.2	13.9	...	22.8[11]	—77.2[11]—		59.0	3.3	1.7[11]	5.9	—94,940—		16,654	6,706	2,155	Indonesia
11.0	14.2	26.7	...	...	...	60.0	3.2	2.3[6]	6.4	—63,031[30]—		7,032[30]	29,167[30]	...	Iran
20.8	17.1	...	...	...	...	...	...	...	17.3[30]	...	...	...	...	...	Iraq
73.2	94.7	70.0	72.3	—27.7—		...	4.7	0.9	8.8[29]	...	...	...	...	...	Ireland
...	...	96.8	...	...	...	...	...	0.4	...	...	...	...	...	...	Isle of Man
96.5[11]	96.5[11]	95.0	99.0[23]	—1.0[23]—		...	2.9	1.2	7.9	495	1,765	3,680	...	1,040	Israel
86.1[11]	99.0[11]	82.2[11]	95.7[11]	—4.3[11]—		75.0[11]	3.7[11]	0.8[11]	7.8	22,607[29]	9,047[29]	62,800[3,29]	6,372[29]	34,300[3,29]	Italy
...	0.7	...	...	...	...	...	1.9	1.8	8.0[30]	...	...	...	...	...	Ivory Coast
76.9	54.0	31.3[16]	...	...	...	...	2.4[16]	1.9[8]	8.2	—1,947[18]—		...	235[18]	...	Jamaica
94.0	...	58.2	34.5	—65.5—		85.9	4.7	0.7	8.3	744,800	205,400	119,604	213,700	76,038	Japan
...	...	93.0	...	...	...	...	...	0.5	...	...	...	...	...	...	Jersey
66.7	77.3	55.4[31]	15.7	—84.3—		...	...	...	9.1	—7,500[9]—		1,907.6[9]	9	9	Jordan
...	...	...	...	...	...	...	...	...	...	...	...	...	...	...	Kampuchea
...	...	...	...	...	...	...	1.9	2.5	5.8	—1,592—		252	107	91	Kenya
21.3	23.7	15.5	...	...	...	...	...	...	7.9[4]	...	...	...	...	...	Kiribati
...	...	...	...	...	...	...	...	...	...	...	...	...	...	...	Korea, North
56.1	49.9[16]	94.8[16]	...	...	...	...	3.0[16]	2.3[16]	8.0	—71,506—		16,651	23,380[30]	10,537[30]	Korea, South
17.6[18]	83.3[18]	...	...	...	...	...	3.5[16]	2.1[16]	4.9	—1,757—		2,929	232	1,370	Kuwait
...	...	...	...	...	...	...	...	...	...	...	...	...	...	...	Laos
...	93.4	82.9	...	...	...	...	...	...	3.4[17]	...	...	...	...	...	Lebanon
...	...	...	...	...	...	...	...	...	9.1[30]	...	...	...	...	...	Lesotho
...	...	...	...	...	...	...	2.3[32]	1.7	2.9[30]	...	...	...	...	...	Liberia
62.0	72.1	...	40.6	—59.4—		...	3.3	1.8	11.9	...	...	...	...	...	Libya
96.5	96.6	86.7	90.2	—9.8—		102.0	3.0	1.4	...	...	...	164.5[3]	...	169.5[3]	Liechtenstein
99.4[16]	...	97.0	93.0[16]	—7.0[16]—		86.4[16]	5.3[16]	0.6[16]	6.3	1,221	108	417.6	58	105.5	Luxembourg
80.3	97.3	55.1	...	...	...	...	3.2	2.5		—145—		214.9	12	74.1	Macau
...	...	...	...	...	...	...	...	...	2.5[10]		282[9]	21.4	9	7.8	Madagascar
21.6[46]	15.7[46]	33.0[46]	33.0[46]	—67.0[46]—		...	2.1	1.7	4.1	—93—		...	57	...	Malawi
34.6[16,47]	39.7[16,47]	18.1[16,47]	18.6[16,47]	—81.1[16,47]—		...	2.3[16,47]	2.6[16,47]	5.1	...	...	...	...	...	Malaysia
...	9.8[17]	...	2.5[17]	—97.5[17]—		...	2.3[17]	2.7[17]	7.6	...	...	...	...	...	Maldives
...	...	...	...	...	...	...	...	...	5.7	...	...	...	...	...	Mali
...	...	...	78.5	15.4	6.1	...	3.2	1.3	3.0[2]	—2,162—		...	1,289	...	Malta
77.7	72.3	62.5	22.5	—77.5—		...	3.4	1.1	3.0[30]	...	...	...	...	...	Martinique
...	...	...	...	...	...	...	...	...	6.3[30]	...	...	...	...	...	Mauritania
89.2	70.1	34.1	33.9	—66.1—		...	...	...	5.3	—3,812—		410	393	62	Mauritius
27.4	...	3.9	54.7	—45.3—		...	2.0	2.4	...	...	...	...	...	...	Mayotte
71.2	74.6	...	49.2	—50.8—		...	2.3	2.5	6.3	—7,341[11]—		...	684[11]	...	Mexico
...	100.0	94.1	98.4	—1.6—		...	4.6	0.4	...	...	...	...	...	...	Monaco
0.3	47.5	...	...	...	...	...	...	...	5.1	...	...	183.4[2]	...	113.3[2]	Mongolia
100.0	72.1	...	...	...	...	...	3.5	0.9	10.2	...	...	...	...	...	Montserrat
51.8[21]	68.4[21]	82.3[21]	...	...	...	...	2.1	2.4	7.1[30]	—22,758[9]—		5,591[9]	9	9	Morocco
...	...	...	...	...	...	...	...	...	5.6[30]	—145[18]—		51.7[18]	20[18]	25.0[18]	Mozambique
...	49.2	...	...	...	...	...	3.6[31]	1.6[31]	...	...	...	...	...	...	Nauru
47.7	30.2	6.1	...	...	...	...	3.7	2.0	8.4	...	...	...	...	...	Nepal
...	...	...	...	...	...	...	...	...	7.2	—17,740—		58,947[3]	18,013	51,620[3]	Netherlands, The
88.9	87.4	80.5	...	...	...	...	3.8	1.2		—427—		...	326	...	Netherlands Antilles
85.1	...	68.3	69.2	—30.8—		...	3.3	1.3	6.3	—291—		...	9	...	New Caledonia
92.7[11]	...	97.1[11]	...	...	...	...	5.6	0.5	4.8	...	...	2,014	8,024	2,274	New Zealand
27.9	40.9	19.3	...	...	...	...	2.2	...	3.2	—987[30]—		45.4[30]	30[30]	9.2[30]	Nicaragua
...	...	...	...	...	...	...	...	...	7.6[30]	...	...	...	...	...	Niger
...	81.3	7.0	...	...	...	...	1.4	3.0	8.4	—6,761[10]—		...	3,481[10]	...	Nigeria
18.9	93.0	28.4	14.1	—85.9—		...	4.0	1.2		10	...	...	...	...	Niue
8.6	49.2	...	93.0	—	7.0	...	6.2	0.4	...	...	...	...	...	...	Norfolk Island
97.5[16]	...	81.2	...	...	...	83.5	3.9	0.9	6.0	23,681	508	3,664	3,630	2,776	Norway
...	...	...	...	...	...	...	...	...	6.2	...	...	...	...	...	Oman
...	...	...	...	...	...	...	...	...		—273—		...	...	...	Pacific Is., Trust Terr. of the
43.0	47.7	...	20.6	—79.4—		...	...	...	4.7	...	...	...	...	...	Pakistan
20.7[54]	30.0[54]	73.4[21,54]	...	...	...	...	1.9[54]	3.3[54]	8.8[2]	879	85	304.4	130	270	Panama
80.8	65.8	67.0	90.1	—9.9—		...	2.5	4.6	3.6	—2,102[30]—		...	...	...	Papua New Guinea
...	...	26.4	...	...	...	...	2.2[35]	2.4[35]	6.7	418	33	116.8	1,114	210.6	Paraguay
73.4	89.5	78.0	58.1	—41.9—		42.4	2.5	1.9	3.7	...	...	...	...	...	Peru
41.4	46.0	35.0	44.1	—55.9—		...	2.4[35]	2.3[35]	8.6	—26,352—		2,748	4,203	2,159	Philippines
...	...	85.2	...	...	...	...	5.0	0.6	...	...	...	...	...	...	Pitcairn Island
70.1	96.2	56.6	...	...	...	54.2	3.2	1.1	10.7[1]	54,669	3,457	68,849[3]	63,792	64,004[3]	Poland

Housing and construction (continued)

country	housing stock			decade built (percent)					tenure[c] (percent)			construction of exterior walls (percent)			
	year	dwelling units[a]	median age[b] (years)	1939 or earlier	1940–49	1950–59	1960–69	1970 or later	owned	rented	collective, vacant, other	traditional materials	sawn/ framed wood	masonry or cement	other
Portugal	1981	3,235,630	33.7	—————53.3—————			17.5	29.2	56.7	38.8	4.6	—	0.7	61.0	38.3
Puerto Rico	1980	969,611	15.8	5.7	6.5	15.0	31.6	41.2	65.7	23.8	10.5	—	19.7	77.4	2.9
Qatar	...	...	...	...	...	...	...	...	...	...	...	...	...	...	...
Réunion	1982	141,123	...	...	...	...	21.2[23]	...	54.6	34.5	10.9	...	...	...	...
Romania	1966	5,380,299	...	...	...	...	...	...	...	...	...	...	...	...	...
Rwanda															
St. Christopher and Nevis	1970	11,236	24.2	—60.7——		20.7	18.6	—	52.7	32.7	14.6	—	85.9	11.5	2.6
St. Helena and Ascension	1976	1,147	23.4	...	...	...	...	...	57.7	30.1	12.2	...	...	...	...
St. Lucia	1970	21,753	...	...	...	...	7.1	...	63.8	27.4	8.8	0.6	89.3	8.3	1.8
St. Pierre and Miquelon	1982	1,760	11.3	—————69.0—————			13.8	17.2	77.3	17.8	4.9	...	...	...	...
St. Vincent and the Grenadines	1970	16,940	...	—	...	...	...	...	74.7	16.5	7.9	8.9	64.1	26.1	0.8
San Marino	1979	7,000	...	...	...	...	...	...	73.5	21.9	4.6	...	...	...	...
São Tomé and Príncipe	...	...	...	...	...	...	...	...	...	...	...	...	...	...	...
Saudi Arabia	...	...	...	...	...	...	...	...	...	...	...	...	...	...	...
Senegal	1955[22, 58]	13,000	...	...	...	...	...	...	—84.6—		15.4	...	...	...	...
Seychelles	1977	12,315	...	...	...	...	...	...	46.6	—53.4—		4.1	57.2	38.7	—
Sierra Leone	...	...	...	...	...	...	...	...	...	...	...	...	...	...	...
Singapore	1980	513,224	...	—————63.2—————				36.8	55.0	39.6	5.4	4.7	—————95.3—————		
Solomon Islands	1976[22]	3,423	...	...	...	...	...	...	27.4[10]	43.0[10]	29.6[10]	...	...	...	...
Somalia	...	...	...	...	...	...	...	...	...	...	...	...	...	...	...
South Africa	1970	1,354,520	18.6	24.6	16.0	24.2	35.2	—	...	...	...	...	...	...	...
Bophuthatswana	...	...	...	...	...	...	...	...	...	...	...	...	...	...	...
Ciskei	...	...	...	...	...	...	...	...	...	...	...	...	...	...	...
Transkei	...	...	...	...	...	...	...	...	...	...	...	...	...	...	...
Venda	...	...	...	...	...	...	...	...	...	...	...	...	...	...	...
South West Africa/Namibia	...	...	...	...	...	...	...	...	...	...	...	...	...	...	...
Spain	1980[40]	6,516,589	39.4	39.2	—23.4—		18.5	18.9	57.2[16]	24.4[16]	18.3[16]	...	...	...	...
Sri Lanka	1981	2,811,406	...	...	...	...	11.1[11]	...	69.4	10.1	20.5	...	...	...	...
Sudan, The	1966[21]	253,060	...	...	...	...	...	...	59.2	28.3	12.6	76.5	4.4	16.7	2.4
Suriname	1964	64,434	...	...	...	...	...	...	...	...	...	38.9	...	...	...
Swaziland	1976	86,847	...	...	...	...	...	...	...	...	...	39.9	—————60.1—————		
Sweden	1980	3,669,512	25.2	26.8	10.9	15.5	23.9	19.1	38.9	56.0	5.1	98.7			
Switzerland	1980	2,415,003	...	—————58.1—————			22.6	19.3	29.9	67.1	3.0	...	...	...	...
Syria	1983	1,642,809	...	...	...	...	8.7[16]	—	81.6[16]	15.5[16]	2.8[16]	...	...	...	...
Taiwan	1980	3,171,876[5]	15.3	—13.8[14]—		14.0[15]	42.4[59]	29.8[60]	79.1	11.8	9.1	...	...	...	...
Tanzania	1978	3,554,793	...	—————17.0—————			—83.0——		75.4	19.4	5.2	83.0	—	16.3	0.7
Thailand	1980	8,414,648	...	—22.0[16]—		25.0[16]	53.0[16]	—	83.4	9.1	7.5	15.1	70.0	6.3	8.6
Togo	1958–60	22,274	...	...	...	...	...	...	...	...	...	...	...	...	...
Tokelau	1972	263	...	...	...	...	11.1[61]	...	97.7	2.3	—	...	...	...	...
Tonga	1976	13,908	22.5	52.7	—6.7[62]—		20.3[63]	20.3[64]	85.1	2.5	12.4	35.1	45.4	15.3	4.2
Trinidad and Tobago	1975	193,186[16]	18.7	—49.2[16]—		16.4[16]	33.6[16]	0.8[16]	66.2	24.1	9.7	...	...	...	...
Tunisia	1984	1,313,200	...	...	...	...	...	...	78.9	12.6	8.5	...	...	...	...
Turkey	1975	7,123,085[32]	...	...	...	...	...	...	81.4[16]	18.5[16]	0.1[16]	...	...	...	...
Turks and Caicos Islands	1980	1,644	20.0	—————45.1—————			15.5	39.4	68.6	22.8	8.6	—	36.8	59.9	3.3
Tuvalu	1979	1,079	...	...	...	...	...	...	81.6	12.1	6.6	64.9	4.2	31.0	—
Uganda	...	...	...	...	...	...	...	...	...	...	...	...	...	...	...
U.S.S.R.	1965	61,658,000	...	...	...	...	...	...	...	...	...	...	...	...	...
United Arab Emirates	1968	38,820	...	...	...	...	...	...	...	...	...	...	...	...	...
United Kingdom	1981[65]	21,321,894[66]	32.6	—54.0—		13.0	16.6	16.4	51.1	40.3	8.6	...	...	...	...
United States	1980	86,758,717	22.7	26.1	11.3	17.3	19.4	25.9	59.7	33.0	7.3	...	...	...	...
Uruguay	1975	848,000	...	...	...	...	...	...	52.1	32.1	15.8	...	...	...	...
Vanuatu	1979	22,513	...	...	...	...	...	...	40.9[22]	25.7[22]	33.4[22]	61.4	7.7	13.6	17.2
Venezuela	1981	3,148,199	...	...	...	...	...	...	75.9	17.2	6.9	...	...	...	...
Vietnam	1962[68]	204,000[5]	...	...	...	...	...	...	68.4	28.0	3.6	...	...	...	...
Virgin Islands (U.S.)	1980	32,650	14.7	6.5	3.5	8.9	42.7	38.4	34.6	52.2	13.2	...	...	...	...
Wallis and Futuna	1983	1,389	14.4	—8.0—		11.0	24.0	57.0	94.4[10]	0.6[10]	5.0[10]	67.0	—31.0——		2.0
West Bank	1967	119,165	...	...	...	...	...	...	...	...	...	...	...	...	...
Western Sahara	1974	4,000	...	...	...	...	...	...	32.2[33]	62.3[33]	5.5[33]	...	...	...	...
Western Samoa	1976	32,938	...	...	...	...	...	...	93.4	2.1	4.5	75.6	—24.4—		
Yemen (Aden)	...	...	...	...	...	...	...	...	...	...	...	...	...	...	...
Yemen (Ṣan'ā')	1975[69]	856,059	...	...	...	...	...	...	85.3	7.0	7.7	...	...	...	...
Yugoslavia	1981	6,130,000	...	...	...	...	...	...	70.7[11]	29.3[11]	...	...	...	...	...
Zaire	1967[22]	168,000	...	...	...	...	...	...	47.4	38.3	14.3	...	...	...	...
Zambia	1969	879,000	...	...	...	...	...	...	78.8	21.1	...	...	...	...	...
Zimbabwe	1969	925,581	...	...	...	...	...	...	65.1[70]	32.6[70]	2.3[70]	55.9[71]	—44.1[71]—		

physical amenities (percent)			sewage disposal (percent)			space[b]			construction industry (1982)						country
									percent of GDP	new residential[d]			new nonresidential[d]		
piped water	electricity	inside toilet or WC	closed public sewer or septic tank	open public sewer	other	average area (sq m)	rooms per dwelling unit	persons per room		1- or 2-unit dwellings	multiunit dwellings	floor area ('000 sq m)	number of units	floor area ('000 sq m)	
73.4	89.5	78.0	58.1	—41.9—		...	3.6	1.0	7.6[30]	18,074[30]	1,746[30]	5,290[30]	6,006[30]	1,600[30]	Portugal
95.2	97.4	89.7	89.6	—10.4—		...	4.8	0.8	1.8	3,651	38	2,103.6	996	36.2	Puerto Rico
									6.6	—1,606—			681	...	Qatar
70.6	81.6	50.7	52.4	—47.6—		...	3.5	1.2	4.7[2]	...	...	...	...	...	Réunion
	48.6		12.2	—87.8—		...	2.6	1.4	7.7[1]						Romania
									4.3	—297[30]—		59.6[30]	58[30]	34.4[30]	Rwanda
95.0	...	...	31.8	—68.2—		...	3.0	1.3	7.1						St. Christopher and Nevis
82.7	62.6	46.9				...	4.4	1.1							St. Helena and Ascension
70.0[30]	36.1	...	11.0	—89.0—		...	2.7	1.7	8.3	—339[17]—			46[17]	...	St. Lucia
99.7	99.8	99.2	97.6	—2.4—		...	4.6	0.7	...						St. Pierre and Miquelon
95.0[7]			22.0[7]	—78.0[7]—		...	2.8	1.8	12.5[30]						St. Vincent and the Grenadines
99.8	100.0	98.3	...	...		...	4.5	0.8	...	—120[30]—			52	...	San Marino
									2.0[30]						São Tomé and Príncipe
									13.2	—50,773[9, 30]—			9	...	Saudi Arabia
87.7	95.9	...	...	...		...	2.3	1.5	6.5[30]	—918—		203.6	32	44.5	Senegal
77.5	46.8	35.9	33.1	—66.9—		...	3.6	1.4	5.7	—4,802[9, 17]—			9	...	Seychelles
									4.2[30]						Sierra Leone
90.6[16]	91.8[16]	...	63.6[16]	—36.4[16]—		...	1.8[16]	2.5[16]	9.1	...	...	2,886	2,015	2,627	Singapore
92.7[10]	79.6[10]	89.2	89.2[10]	—10.8[10]—		41.8[10]	2.3[10]	2.0[10]	...	1,174[2]			...	...	Solomon Islands
									2.9[29]						Somalia
...	...	...	...	...		...	3.4	...	4.1	25,390	484	...	...	...	South Africa
															Bophuthatswana
															Ciskei
															Transkei
															Venda
									4.4[30]						South West Africa/Namibia
90.5	94.7	...	87.9	—12.1—		...	4.4[16]		7.2	7,400[10]	15,700[10]	...			Spain
18.2	14.9	4.7	6.7	—93.3—		18.6[16]	2.5	2.1	8.9	—2,626—		338			Sri Lanka
63.9	26.4	70.2	2.6	—97.4—		...	2.2	2.5	5.2[30]	...	...	...	...	...	Sudan, The
...	...	...	19.6	—80.4—		...	2.1	1.9	2.9	—1,123—		381.8[3]	190	...	Suriname
33.4	...	20.0	...			...	...	...	3.9[30]	—100—			36	...	Swaziland
...	...	96.2	96.3	—3.7—		...	4.1	0.6	7.1	26,770	1,193	...			Sweden
...	...	...	92.2	—	7.8	88.0	4.6	0.7	...	13,212	4,466	...	9,058	...	Switzerland
40.2	41.7	...	36.0	—64.0—		90.6	3.0	2.0	6.4	...	...	4,759[30]		612[30]	Syria
79.4	...	94.2	69.3	...		85.9	3.7	1.5	6.9	...					Taiwan
37.2	6.3	...				...	2.5	1.9	3.5	...					Tanzania
17.3	43.0	40.9				...	...	...	5.1	...	...	4,040[30]		4,796[30]	Thailand
4.1	10.3	...	—	—100.0—		...	1.8	3.4	4.3[30]	—153[2]—		43.2[2]	122	...	Togo
2.3	...	2.3				...	...	...							Tokelau
61.3	20.9	42.3	11.2	—88.8—		...	...	...	4.7	—738[9, 30]—		668[9, 30]	9	9	Tonga
71.5[2]	77.0	...	53.7[2]	—46.3[2]—		...	2.9[8]	1.7[8]	17.0	—3,280[30]—		491.9[30]	143[30]	168.3[30]	Trinidad and Tobago
49.4	63.4	...	51.8	—41.2—		...	2.2	2.4	6.4	—17,208—		2,679	...	...	Tunisia
35.9[16]	56.8	73.8[16]				...	2.7[16]	2.2[16]	4.2	22,127	28,134	12,160	3,895	3,785	Turkey
19.9	47.6	...	70.5	—29.5—		...	3.5	1.1	...						Turks and Caicos Islands
65.4	7.4	37.3				...	...	...	13.0[29]						Tuvalu
...	...	...				...	...	...	0.4[30]	—179[35]—		37.3[35]	65[35]	26.8[35]	Uganda
...	...	...				...	3.0	1.3	9.9[1]	...	...	107,976			U.S.S.R.
30.9	24.2	...				...	1.9	1.9	9.0	—792[2]—			315[2]	...	United Arab Emirates
...	...	97.3				...	4.9[66]	0.6	5.2	...					United Kingdom
83.8	52.1[67]	...	98.1	—1.9—		...	5.1	0.6	4.1	...	...	136,000		87,500	United States
63.1	60.7	62.7				...	1.7	2.1	4.5	...	...	620.4		305.9	Uruguay
13.7	11.7	19.1				...	...	...		...	...	10.8			Vanuatu
72.4[11]	76.8[11]	23.9[11]	53.5	—46.5—		...	3.9[11]	1.5[11]	5.4	2,375	500	5,083.1	803	1,389.9	Venezuela
23.7	71.0	...				...	...	...		—400[36]—		212.3[36]	53[36]	59.3[36]	Vietnam
96.3	98.1	86.0	93.6	—6.4—		...	4.2	0.8		833[29]	75[29]	...	262[29]	...	Virgin Islands (U.S.)
23.0	...	9.0	24.0	—	7.6	...	1.8[10]	4.0[10]							Wallis and Futuna
24.5	22.9	58.2				...	4.5	1.2		...	...	574.0		82.5	West Bank
78.5	95.3	...				...									Western Sahara
9.2[58]	18.8[58]	...				...	3.9[58]	1.5[58]	13.2	—156—			128	...	Western Samoa
...															Yemen (Aden)
...	...	...				...	2.0	...	8.8[30]	—5,147—		1,167.4	...	...	Yemen (Ṣan'ā')
67.8	95.7	...				60.7	2.8[11]	1.4[11]	9.5	61,030	1,864	14,872	21,596	10,355	Yugoslavia
...	...	...				...			6.0	—407—		1,105	95	45	Zaire
12.4	27.5[8]	15.1			82.3	...	1.9	2.6	3.5	...					Zambia
	9.3[71]					...	2.8	1.9	3.0	—3,321—					Zimbabwe

[1]Percent of net material product. [2]1980. [3]Volume ('000 cubic metres). [4]1978. [5]Occupied dwellings only; may include seasonal and temporary housing. [6]1966. [7]1983. [8]1960. [9]Residential includes nonresidential. [10]1976. [11]1971. [12]Stucco. [13]Includes wood and brick or wood and concrete. [14]1945 and earlier. [15]1946-60. [16]1970. [17]1977. [18]1975. [19]Data refer to rugos, which usually contain two or three houses each. [20]1959-60; data refer to households and are based on results of a demographic survey of the African population, excluding Bangui town, East Dubangi, and the nomad population. [21]Urban areas only. [22]Capital city only. [23]1974. [24]1933 and earlier. [25]1934-45. [26]1946-59. [27]Housing in the socialist sector only. [28]Includes corrugated steel. [29]1979. [30]1981. [31]1961. [32]Data refer to households. [33]1968. [34]Vacant dwellings only. [35]1972. [36]1973. [37]1961-71. [38]African households in the city of Bouake only. [39]Includes nonconventional housing units. [40]Data are for buildings, not dwelling units. [41]1946 and earlier. [42]1947-60. [43]1947 and earlier. [44]1948-60. [45]Blantyre only. [46]1967. [47]Peninsular Malaysia only. [48]1957 and earlier. [49]1958-67. [50]Nauruan dwellings only. [51]Data are for the cities of Kāthmāndu, Lalitpur, Bhaktapur, Birātnagar, Nepālganj, and Birganj only. [52]1930 and earlier. [53]1931-59. [54]Excludes Islāmābād, North-West Frontier, and Federally Administered Tribal Areas. [55]1947-65. [56]1966-75. [57]1966-80. [58]European-type dwellings only. [59]1961-75. [60]1976 and later. [61]1965 and later. [62]1939-56. [63]1956-66. [64]1966-70. [65]Data exclude Northern Ireland. [66]Data refer to "household spaces." [67]Used for cooking only. [68]Data refer to Saigon (Ho Chi Minh City) only. [69]Data refer to living quarters. [70]Dwellings occupied by Europeans, Asians, and coloureds only. [71]Dwellings occupied by Africans only.

Household budgets and consumption

This table provides data on disposable income of households for both sovereign states and dependencies—how it is obtained and how it is spent. For purposes of this compilation, income comprises pretax monetary payments and payment in kind. The first part of the table provides data on distribution and source of income; the second part analyzes the largest portion of income use—consumption expenditure. Such expenditure is defined as the purchase of goods and services to satisfy current wants and needs. This definition excludes income allocated for taxes, debts, savings and investments, and insurance policies. The last part of the table focuses on food, which (along with housing, examined in the Housing and construction table) is the most important object of consumer spending. The data provided include consumption by major food groups and daily available calories per capita.

For both source of income and consumption expenditure, the primary basis of analysis for most countries is the household, an economic unit that can be as small as a single person or as large as an extended family. For some of the countries that do not compile information by household, the table provides data on personal income and personal expenditure; i.e., the income and expenditure of all the individuals composing a society's households. When no expenditure data at all is available, the table reports the weights of each major category of goods and services comprising a given country's consumer (or retail) price index (CPI). The weighting of the components of the CPI usually reflects the household spending patterns within the country, its principal urban or rural areas, though sometimes only in the country's major city.

The table's income and expenditure data furnish the reader with a general view of the levels of economic development and affluence in most countries. The data on distribution of income show, collectively for an entire country, the proportion of total income earned by households comprising the lowest quintile and highest decile (poorest 20% and wealthiest 10%) within the country. These figures show the degree to which either group represents a disproportionate share of poverty or wealth. A country in which the poorest 20% of households earned only 6% of the nation's income, while the highest 10% disposed of 40% of the same total, would have to be regarded as fertile ground for a campaign to share the wealth.

The data on source of income illuminate aspects of personal condition in the gaining of an income. They indicate, for example, that in poor, agrarian countries income derives largely from self-employment (usually farming) and that in industrial countries, with well-developed systems of salaried employment and social welfare, income derives mainly from wages and salaries and transfer payments (see headnote a). The figures on consumption expenditure reveal the patterns of personal and family use of disposable income and indicate, inter alia, that in developing countries food sometimes absorbs 50 percent or more of disposable income. By contrast, in the larger household budgets of the developed countries, food purchases may account for only 20–30 percent of spending. Each category of expenditure betrays similar complexities of local habit, necessity, and aspiration.

The reader should nevertheless exercise caution when using the data to make intercountry comparisons. Most of the information comes from national surveys, which often differ markedly in the use of definitions, in the coverage of economic or population groups, and in the methods of collection, classification, and tabulation of data. Further, the reference period of the data varies greatly; while a significant portion of the data is from 1979 or later, information for some countries dates from the late 1960s and the early 1970s. This older information is typeset in italic. Finally, intercountry comparisons of annual personal consumption expenditure can be especially misleading because of the

Household budgets and consumption

country	income (latest)						consumption expenditure						
	percent received by		by source (percent)				per capita private final, 1983	by kind or end use (percent of household or personal budget; latest)					
	lowest 20% of households	highest 10% of households	wages, salaries	self-employment	transfer payments[a]	other[b]		food[c]	housing	clothing[d]	health care	energy	education
Afghanistan	...	...	...	...	...	...		...	...	...	...	...	...
Albania	...	...	...	...	...	...		...	...	...	...	...	...
Algeria	...	...	...	...	...	...	1,070	45.6[1]	13.1[1]	14.8[1]	2.5[1]	—	—
American Samoa	...	...	...	...	...	...	...	44.3	23.4	5.8	—	...	...
Andorra	...	...	...	...	...	...	...	...	...	...	...	...	...
Angola	...	...	...	...	...	...	...	...	...	...	...	...	...
Anguilla	...	...	...	...	...	...	...	...	...	...	...	...	...
Antigua and Barbuda	...	...	...	...	...	...	1,100[2]	46.5	28.8[3]	7.5	...	...	3
Argentina	4.4	35.2	...	...	...	...	1,380[2]	...	...	...	...	...	...
Australia	5.4	30.5	64.6	12.0	12.8	10.6	6,370	22.4	19.3	6.8	6.8	2.5	0.4
Austria	...	...	60.0	15.7	16.9	7.4	5,140	20.9	12.1	10.7	4.3	5.3	0.2
Bahamas, The	3.4	...	...	...	...	...	3,940[2]	20.5	14.1	4.0	3.2	3.6	0.1
Bahrain	...	...	...	...	...	...	...	...	...	...	...	...	...
Bangladesh	6.2	32.0	26.9	65.2	0.4	7.5	120	74.5	5.8	5.3	—	9.1	...
Barbados	6.8	...	...	...	...	...	2.820	51.6[4]	13.1	5.1	...	6.2	...
Belgium	7.9	21.5	53.0	24.2	21.5	1.3	5,440	24.1	10.1	7.0	9.2	5.6	0.2
Belize	...	...	84.1	—	—	15.9	900	...	...	...	...	...	...
Benin	8.0	39.0	...	...	...	...	240	...	...	...	...	...	...
Bermuda	...	...	72.2	6.7	2.4	18.7	...	17.3	20.8	5.3	4.1	4.0	2.8
Bhutan	...	...	...	...	...	...	...	...	...	...	...	...	...
Bolivia	4.0	...	...	...	...	...	1,020	41.7	12.6	9.8	4.6	0.7	1.2
Botswana	1.6	...	71.1	23.3	5.5	—	510	48.2	12.6	—	—	—	—
Brazil	2.0	50.6	...	...	...	...	1,140	46.8[5]	4.2[5]	7.5[5]	4.4[5]	5.0[5]	1.9[5]
British Virgin Islands	...	...	...	...	...	...	910[6]	40.3	22.6	9.1	—	...	...
Brunei	...	...	...	...	...	...	...	45.1	5.0[3]	6.1	...	3	7
Bulgaria	...	...	62.9	—	20.0	17.1	870[8]	49.8	8.4	10.7	2.0	—	...
Burkina Faso	...	...	...	...	...	...	160	47.7[1]	5.2[1]	—	5.2[1]	13.7[1]	—
Burma	8.0	...	...	...	...	...	140	49.1[1]	10.4[1]	15.3[1]	2.4[1]	4.0[1]	5.9[1]
Burundi	...	...	...	...	...	...	190	59.6[1]	4.4[1]	11.1[1]	—	5.8[1]	...
Cameroon	...	...	...	...	...	...	500	33.6[1]	14.6[1]	16.3[1]	5.0[1]	—	10
Canada	5.3	23.8	64.9	6.6	15.4	13.1	7,470	18.0	17.1	6.3	3.4	4.2	2.8
Cape Verde	...	...	...	...	...	...	...	...	...	...	...	...	...
Cayman Islands	...	...	...	...	...	...	...	...	...	...	...	...	...
Central African Republic	...	...	...	...	...	...	80[11]	70.5[1]	0.6[1]	9.5[1]	1.0[1]	6.5[1]	—
Chad	8.0	30.0	...	...	...	...	130[12]	45.3[1]	—	3.5[1]	11.9[1]	5.8[1]	...
Chile	4.4	34.8	40.8	51.1	8.1	—	1,210	41.9	13.3	7.6	—	—	7
China	8.5[13]	37.7[13, 14]	...	...	...	...	...	59.3[13]	11.1[13]	11.2[13]	...	...	...
Christmas Island	...	...	...	...	...	...	...	...	...	...	...	...	...
Cocos (Keeling) Islands	...	...	...	...	...	...	...	...	...	...	...	...	...
Colombia	4.0	43.5	49.6	44.8	5.6	—	1,000	36.8	10.7	6.8	5.8	2.2	—
Comoros	...	...	25.6	64.5	8.7	1.2	...	67.9[15]	6.1[15]	11.6[15]	—	—	—
Congo	7.0	43.5	...	...	...	...	520[16]	...	...	...	...	...	...
Cook Islands	...	...	...	...	...	...	340[17]	65.2[1, 4]	3.1[1]	12.4[1]	—	—	—
Costa Rica	3.3	39.5	...	...	...	...	790	40.8	12.3	10.0	—	6.6	7
Cuba	...	...	...	...	...	...	1,180	...	...	...	...	...	...
Cyprus	7.9[15]	...	...	...	...	...	2,140	26.0	5.8	10.8	1.9	2.6	1.1
Czechoslovakia	...	...	75.6	0.3	10.7	13.4	3,480	44.8	9.9	14.9	0.3	—	0.3
Denmark	5.4	22.3	59.1	14.3	—26.6——		6,000	21.8	18.9	5.6	1.9	8.6	1.7
Djibouti	...	...	51.6	36.0	10.5	1.9	780[16]	...	...	...	...	...	...
Dominica	...	...	...	...	...	...	720[2]	65.2	8.9	9.5	—	5.4	—

distortions introduced when converting national currency units into U.S. dollars.

The table's food consumption information includes each country's daily available calories per capita (food supply), which amounts to domestic production and imports minus exports, animal feed, and nonfood uses. For each country the table furnishes a percentage breakdown of all the major food groups that comprise food supply.

The data for daily available calories per capita provide a general view of the nutritional adequacy of each nation's food supply. The following list, based on estimates from the United Nations Food and Agriculture Organization, indicates the regional variation in recommended daily minimum nutritional requirements defined by factors such as climatic ambience and average body weight:

Developing area	Daily nutritional requirement
Africa	2,334 calories
Centrally Planned Asia	2,353 calories
Far East	2,216 calories
Latin America	2,380 calories
Near East	2,455 calories

The breakdown of diet by food groups describes the composition of a nation's diet. A typical breakdown for a low-income country shows an imbalanced diet with heavy intake of cereals, potatoes, or cassava. In the high-income countries, a relatively larger portion of total calories derives from animal products (meat, eggs, and milk).

The reader should always be aware of certain limits on the utility of this food consumption data. First, the data compiled here do not reflect the dietary differences that often exist between socioeconomic groups within a single country. Second, the data, which come from national surveys, often vary in completeness of coverage and degree of accuracy, limiting somewhat the validity of intercountry comparisons.

In compiling this table, Britannica editors rely on both numerous national reports and principal secondary sources such as the International Bank for Reconstruction and Development's *World Development Report* (annual), the International Labour Organisation's *Household Income and Expenditure Statistics 1968–1976* and *Statistical Sources and Methods, vol. 1 Consumer Price Indices*; the 1977 *U.N. Compendium of Social Statistics,* the *U.N. Yearbook of National Accounts Statistics* (annual), the *European Marketing Data and Statistics* (annual), and the Food and Agriculture Organization's *Food Balance Sheets 1979–81* and *1975–77.*

The following terms further define the column headings:
a. Includes pensions, family allowances, unemployment payments, and social security and related benefits.
b. Includes interest and dividends, rents and royalties, and all other income not reported under the three preceding categories.
c. Includes alcoholic and nonalcoholic beverages. Does not include tobacco except where noted.
d. Includes footwear.
e. Usually includes expenditure on household operation.
f. Includes expenditure on cultural activities.
g. May include data not shown separately in preceding categories, including meals away from home.
h. Includes peas, beans, and lentils.
i. Represents pure fats and oils only.
j. Consists mainly of spices, stimulants, sugars and honey, and nuts and oilseeds.

transportation, communication	furniture, utensils[e]	recreation[f]	personal effects, other[g]	daily available calories per capita	cereals	potatoes, cassava	meat, poultry	fish	eggs, milk	fruits, vegetables[h]	fats, oils[i]	other[j]	country
...	...	...	...	1,896	81.5	1.4	3.3	—	3.6	3.7	3.1	3.4	Afghanistan
...	...	...	...	2,657	66.4	2.6	5.2	0.1	6.2	6.5	6.4	6.6	Albania
7.3[1]	6.9[1]	4.3[1]	5.5[1]	2,586	56.8	2.2	2.0	0.2	6.4	6.7	13.1	12.3	Algeria
14.9	—	—	11.6										American Samoa
...	...	...	...	...	...	...	...	...	...	...	...	...	Andorra
...	...	...	...	2,141	35.3	33.8	3.2	0.9	1.9	7.7	7.2	10.0	Angola
...	...	...	...										Anguilla
10.0	...	...	7.2	1,979	34.3	1.4	7.6	2.0	13.6	7.2	12.8	21.2	Antigua and Barbuda
...	...	...	...	3,308	29.8	4.5	22.6	0.3	8.3	5.2	9.7	19.5	Argentina
15.4	7.4	6.2	12.9	3,055	26.1	3.3	19.5	0.7	9.7	5.5	9.6	25.6	Australia
16.3	7.1	5.4	17.7	3,575	19.6	4.0	13.7	0.4	10.5	5.5	23.8	22.5	Austria
15.1	6.0	6.5	26.9	2,200	29.1	1.2	18.3	0.8	7.1	8.0	9.7	25.8	Bahamas, The
...	...	...	...										Bahrain
—	—	—	5.3	1,837	85.4	2.0	0.9	0.8	1.4	2.6	2.8	4.2	Bangladesh
4.6	9.6	...	9.8	3,020	28.8	4.5	14.8	2.0	6.1	4.9	11.6	27.2	Barbados
11.3	15.3	8.9	8.3	3,639	19.2	5.5	19.6	0.8	9.9	5.2	20.7	19.3	Belgium
...	...	...	...	2,714	35.3	7.1	7.3	0.4	9.7	9.3	9.2	21.8	Belize
...	...	...	...	2,174	34.6	37.2	2.2	0.7	0.6	5.6	10.9	8.3	Benin
10.6	11.9	5.4	17.8	2,799	22.5	2.0	19.1	2.8	12.1	8.6	11.2	21.7	Bermuda
...	...	...	...	2,028	85.2	2.4	0.4	0.1	0.6	2.1	5.3	3.9	Bhutan
12.6	8.9	3.1	4.8	2,082	42.1	11.6	8.3	0.3	2.9	8.2	7.8	18.7	Bolivia
—	—	—	39.2	2,352	53.1	1.0	6.0	0.1	9.0	9.6	9.2	12.0	Botswana
6.4[5]	8.6[5]	5.7[5]	6.4[5]	2,578	38.0	8.4	6.9	0.5	5.2	10.4	8.2	22.5	Brazil
10.9	7.7	—	9.4										British Virgin Islands
17.2	8.3	8.9[7]	9.4	2,594	50.0	2.7	6.1	2.0	6.7	4.9	8.8	18.7	Brunei
6.7	5.1	3.1	14.3	3,619	43.7	1.6	9.0	0.3	7.5	6.4	13.8	17.6	Bulgaria
18.6[1]	—	—	—	2,010	70.5	2.1	2.2	0.1	1.5	10.1	3.5	10.0	Burkina Faso
3.8[1]	0.5[1]	1.7[1]	7.5[1]	2,420	81.2	0.3	1.7	1.0	0.7	5.3	5.7	4.0	Burma
—	6.0[1]	—	13.7[1,9]	2,353	25.2	35.4	1.1	0.3	1.3	22.5	3.2	10.8	Burundi
10.5[1]	—	5.1[1]	14.9[1,10]	2,295	32.8	21.1	3.3	0.8	0.8	14.2	3.7	18.2	Cameroon
14.4	8.2	7.2	18.4	3,340	19.8	4.6	19.7	0.9	11.4	6.3	17.2	20.0	Canada
...	...	...	...	2,704	58.5	5.1	1.7	1.8	2.6	8.1	8.7	13.6	Cape Verde
...	...	...	...										Cayman Islands
4.1[1]	0.8[1]	1.3[1]	5.7[1]	2,117	15.9	52.0	4.1	0.5	0.3	6.4	6.1	14.7	Central African Republic
—	—	—	33.5[1]	1,762	57.2	11.2	3.2	1.6	2.6	8.2	3.3	12.7	Chad
11.8	7.8	8.2[7]	9.4	2,759	48.7	3.4	6.7	1.4	6.4	6.8	8.0	18.6	Chile
—	—	18.4[13]		2,426	66.4	12.1	7.6	0.4	1.1	4.1	3.6	4.6	China
...	...	...	...										Christmas Island
...	...	...	...										Cocos (Keeling) Islands
14.4	5.6	5.0	12.7	2,494	33.2	9.6	7.4	0.4	5.3	11.9	7.1	25.2	Colombia
2.3[15]	—	6.6[15]	5.6[15]	2,219	38.4	33.3	2.3	1.2	1.2	9.0	3.3	11.3	Comoros
...	...	...	...	2,433	15.2	49.8	2.0	2.3	0.9	9.0	10.2	10.5	Congo
5.7[1]	9.6[1]	—	4.0[1]										Cook Islands
6.5	8.2	9.2[7]	6.4	2,653	34.3	1.0	5.9	0.5	9.7	9.5	11.0	28.2	Costa Rica
...	...	...	...	2,796	37.6	6.7	7.0	1.2	9.9	7.5	8.8	21.2	Cuba
23.2	11.8	6.4	10.4	3,054	40.0	2.5	13.7	0.4	7.9	9.5	10.1	15.9	Cyprus
8.9	9.5	5.8	5.6	3,393	30.5	4.7	14.8	0.5	10.3	3.3	14.2	21.8	Czechoslovakia
14.8	7.0	7.6	12.1	3,548	18.5	4.3	19.5	2.9	11.3	3.4	18.9	21.1	Denmark
...	...	...	...										Djibouti
—	—	—	11.0	2,018	30.1	17.0	7.4	1.9	5.8	13.8	8.2	15.9	Dominica

Household budgets and consumption (continued)

country	income (latest) percent received by lowest 20% of households	highest 10% of households	by source (percent) wages, salaries	self-employment	transfer payments[a]	other[b]	consumption expenditure per capita private final, 1983	by kind or end use (percent of household or personal budget; latest) food[c]	housing	clothing[d]	health care	energy	education
Dominican Republic	6.3	...	41.7	31.8	1.5	25.0	1,010[2]	31.9[1]	32.4[1]	7.5[1]	—	—	—
Ecuador	2.9	51.5	38.0	53.6	5.4	2.9	1,020	32.2	7.5	10.7	3.8	1.7	—
Egypt	5.8	33.2	...	...	...	...	480[2]	49.7[15]	8.8[15]	14.2[15]	1.8[15]	3.6[15]	2.1[15]
El Salvador	5.5	29.5	...	...	...	...	610	40.9	6.0	9.8	4.1	2.1	1.2
Equatorial Guinea	...	...	...	...	...	...	...	...	...	...	...	...	...
Ethiopia	...	...	...	...	...	...	90	57.4[1]	18	7.8[1]	2.1[1]	—	—
Faeroe Islands	...	...	...	...	...	...	...	...	...	...	...	...	...
Falkland Islands	...	...	...	...	...	...	...	46.0[1]	10.0[1]	13.0[1]	—	5.0[1]	7
Fiji	3.7	37.8	81.5	9.1	—	9.4	1,040	32.0	13.1[3]	5.8	2.3	3	7
Finland	6.3	21.7	62.0	15.5	19.1	3.3	5,520	25.2	17.3	4.9	2.5	3.4	7
France	5.3	30.5	54.7	10.7	26.5	8.1	6,120	20.0	17.0[3]	6.5	13.1	3	0.3
French Guiana	...	...	...	...	...	...	...	50.0[1]	20.0[1]	7.0[1]	9.0[1]	—	—
French Polynesia	...	...	50.7	38.5	9.1	1.6	4,660[2]	36.5	5.9	9.0	1.0	8.6	7
Gabon	3.3	54.4	...	...	...	...	950	54.7[1,4]	13.0[1]	17.5[1]	1.9[1]	—	—
Gambia, The	...	...	...	...	...	...	...	58.0[19]	5.1[19]	17.5[19]	—	5.4[19]	—
Gaza Strip	...	...	...	...	...	...	790[16]	...	...	...	...	...	...
Germany, East	...	...	69.7	—	21.9	8.4	...	29.6	10.9[3,20]	10.8	5.8	3	...
Germany, West	7.9	24.0	84.1	7.1	—	8.8	6,040	26.0	18.4	8.1	—	6.6	7
Ghana	...	...	41.6[21]	47.1[21]	—	11.3[21]	2,140[16]	57.4	11.5[3]	14.3	1.3	3	7
Gibraltar	...	...	...	...	...	...	...	39.0[4]	12.6	11.0	—	—	—
Greece	...	...	41.9	42.4	15.7	—	2,330	32.7	14.1	8.8	3.3	3.0	0.6
Greenland	...	...	...	...	...	...	...	31.5	8.9	9.2	—	7.8	—
Grenada	...	...	...	...	...	...	960[2]	61.5[4]	6.5	8.0	—	6.0	—
Guadeloupe	...	...	—76.8—		—23.2—		...	34.4	12.2	9.2	—	5.7	7
Guam	...	...	...	...	...	...	...	24.1	28.6	10.6	4.8	—	—
Guatemala	5.0	...	...	...	...	...	3,270[2]	43.9[15]	12.8[3,15]	12.6[15]	—	3	—
Guernsey	...	...	...	...	...	...	...	...	...	...	...	...	...
Guinea	...	...	...	...	...	...	...	...	...	...	...	...	...
Guinea-Bissau	...	...	...	...	...	...	...	...	...	...	...	...	...
Guyana	...	...	73.0	—	6.3	20.7	300	42.5[4]	21.4	8.6	—	5.2	7
Haiti	...	...	...	...	...	...	310	48.9	7.9	3.5	8.6	7.0	2.2
Honduras	3.2	50.6	52.6	45.9	1.6	—	552	44.3	22.3[3]	9.1	7.0	3	7
Hong Kong	5.4	31.3	...	...	...	...	3,150	22.1	15.6[3]	18.6	6.0	3	1.2
Hungary	6.9	20.5	79.9	1.9	10.8	7.4	1,210	41.6	3.8	8.8	6.4	3.7	7
Iceland	...	...	—80.0—		—20.0—		6,020	23.8	11.0	8.5	1.7	5.5	0.4
India	7.0	33.6	38.7	44.9	—16.4—		180	55.7	3.3	9.2	2.1	5.0	2.8
Indonesia	6.6	34.0	42.1	41.5	2.5	13.9	340	69.3	12.2[3]	5.1	—	3	—
Iran	3.8	41.7	40.8	28.2	3.7	27.3	2,020	43.8[4]	22.3[3]	9.4	3.9	3	7
Iraq	2.1	...	...	...	...	...	...	55.4	7.9	10.3	2.4	4.1	—
Ireland	7.2	25.1	58.4	25.0	12.3	4.3	3,020	37.9	5.0	6.6	2.6	6.4	2.4
Isle of Man	...	...	...	...	...	...	...	29.1	8.3	6.3	—	11.2	—
Israel	6.0	22.6	89.0	1.4	—9.6—		4,020	26.2	20.0	6.8	3.7	3.0	1.9
Italy	6.2	28.1	49.2	21.5	19.8	9.6	3,990	27.7	9.4	8.2	4.8	4.5	0.4
Ivory Coast	4.0	41.1	44.9	49.9	—5.2—		470	51.7[23]	11.6[23]	8.4[23]	—	8.1[23]	—
Jamaica	2.2	...	70.9	27.3	1.8	—	1,090	35.8	7.7	2.6	2.3	4.8	0.2
Japan	8.7	22.4	—96.0—			4.0	5,770	26.1	4.8	6.8	2.4	6.0	4.1
Jersey	...	...	...	...	...	...	...	...	...	...	...	...	...
Jordan	...	...	...	...	...	...	1,410	53.4	8.2[3]	8.2	3.9	3	2.2
Kampuchea	...	...	...	...	...	...	100[24]	53.0	23.0	9.0	—	—	—
Kenya	2.6	45.8	22.4	—	—	77.6	190	46.5	10.0	7.7	2.2	2.6	1.0
Kiribati	...	...	69.8	21.4	6.0	2.8	4,150[6]	64.0[4]	1.0	8.0	—	3.6	—
Korea, North	...	...	...	...	...	...	...	46.5[25]	0.6[25]	29.9[25]	15.9[25,26]	3.3[25]	—
Korea, South	5.7	27.5	51.9	24.5	4.6	18.9	1,200	46.9	9.4[3]	7.1	5.9	3	3.6
Kuwait	...	...	53.8	20.8	—25.4—		560	37.0[4]	18.7[3]	10.0	1.0	3	—
Laos	...	...	...	...	...	...	...	...	...	...	...	...	...
Lebanon	5.0	45.0	27.9	—	3.0	69.1	...	42.8[1]	16.8[1]	8.6[1]	7.2[1]	4.5[1]	3.9[1]
Lesotho	...	...	42.0	51.6	—6.4—		520	34.0[15]	9.7[15]	19.3[15]	1.8[15]	4.8[15]	4.1[15]
Liberia	5.3	...	...	...	...	...	190[2]	40.1[1,4]	14.9[1]	13.8[1]	—	5.0[1]	—
Libya	10.1	...	...	...	...	...	3,550[2]	37.2	32.2[3]	6.9	3.3	3	7
Liechtenstein	...	...	91.2	8.8	—	—	...	...	...	...	...	...	...
Luxembourg	...	...	—79.1—		—20.9—		6,390[16]	18.6	12.1	7.0	7.3	8.1	7
Macau	...	...	...	...	...	...	...	...	...	...	...	...	...
Madagascar	5.2	...	58.8[1,27]	14.1[1,27]	...	27.1[1,27]	270[27]	35.8	...	12.0	—	—	—
Malawi	10.4	40.1	83.3	6.0	—	11.7	120	39.3[4,28]	13.3[28]	10.7[28]	—	—	—
Malaysia	3.5	39.8	...	...	...	...	1,040	41.1[4,29]	18.2[3,29]	4.7[29]	1.3[29]	3	7
Maldives	...	...	...	...	...	...	320	...	...	...	...	...	...
Mali	...	...	...	...	...	...	240[2]	...	...	...	...	...	...
Malta	...	...	53.7	16.9	17.4	11.9	2,160	33.9	4.3	7.2	3.6	2.0	7
Martinique	...	...	...	...	...	...	3,580	26.4	20.9	24.0	7.2	—	—
Mauritania	...	...	...	...	...	...	330[27]	61.0[1]	24.0[1]	5.2[1]	—	—	—
Mauritius	4.5	...	50.0	45.0	5.0	—	760	50.4[4]	4.0	10.5	3.0	6.4	2.9
Mayotte	...	...	...	...	...	...	...	...	...	...	...	...	...
Mexico	2.9	40.6	58.8	25.4	—15.8—		1,150	34.7[4]	8.5[3]	11.1	4.7	3	7
Monaco	...	...	...	...	...	...	...	...	...	...	...	...	...
Mongolia	...	...	...	...	...	...	...	...	...	...	...	...	...
Montserrat	...	...	...	...	...	...	2,560	54.1[4]	0.7	17.9	—	1.8	—
Morocco	4.0	...	...	...	...	...	410	54.0	7.0	8.5	—	3.0	—
Mozambique	...	...	...	...	...	...	...	...	...	...	...	...	...
Nauru	...	...	...	...	...	...	...	...	...	...	...	...	...
Nepal	4.6	46.5	39.2	—60.8—			120[16]	57.4[1]	11.4[1,3]	10.5[1]	4.2[1]	3	7
Netherlands, The	8.3	21.5	42.3	17.4	28.2	12.1	5,560	17.9	12.3	7.3	12.9	5.9	0.3
Netherlands Antilles	...	...	...	...	...	...	1,130[30]	24.4[31]	18.8[31]	8.7[31]	2.2[31]	—	7,31
New Caledonia	...	...	63.1	23.9	13.0	—	3,580[2]	28.4	13.3	5.6	2.6	8.3	1.3
New Zealand	5.1	28.7	...	...	...	...	4,270	22.5	18.5	6.8	1.4	2.8	7
Nicaragua	3.1[13]	...	70.8	27.6	1.6	—	820	38.5[1,4]	26.7[1]	7.3[1]	—	—	—

| transportation, communication | furniture utensils[e] | recreation[f] | personal effects, other[g] | food consumption | | | | | | | | | country |
| | | | | daily available calories per capita | percent of total calories derived from | | | | | | | | |
					cereals	potatoes, cassava	meat, poultry	fish	eggs, milk	fruits, vegetables[h]	fats, oils[i]	other[j]	
—	—	—	28.2[1]	2,130	33.0	3.4	4.8	0.7	6.6	20.7	11.1	19.7	Dominican Republic
13.0	—	—	31.1	2,114	31.0	4.9	6.2	1.7	8.0	12.4	11.4	24.5	Ecuador
5.2[15]	3.6[15]	1.3[15]	9.7[15]	3,175	64.0	1.5	2.3	0.3	1.7	7.6	11.5	11.1	Egypt
11.2	13.2	3.4	8.1	2,048	56.9	0.9	2.4	0.2	5.3	8.8	8.4	17.1	El Salvador
...	...	...	...	...									Equatorial Guinea
5.3[1]	17.1[1]	3.0[1]	7.3[1]	1,793	68.8	3.9	4.2	—	2.9	9.3	2.2	8.7	Ethiopia
...	...	...	...	3,135	29.3	5.5	15.8	3.9	7.0	3.3	18.0	17.2	Faeroe Islands
—	5.0[1]	—	21.0[1]										Falkland Islands
14.0	9.5	4.3[7]	19.0	3,103	31.2	15.1	3.7	2.7	2.9	4.3	11.5	28.5	Fiji
15.7	7.7	9.2[7]	14.1	3,079	23.9	5.3	15.7	1.8	17.0	3.9	14.1	18.3	Finland
13.9	9.3	6.2	13.7	3,529	22.2	4.4	17.7	1.0	11.0	4.8	18.3	20.7	France
8.0[1]	—	6.0[1]	—	2,718	34.1	5.2	16.9	2.0	7.1	8.0	7.1	19.6	French Guiana
13.1	9.2	8.6[7]	8.1	2,898	36.0	9.0	10.0	2.3	4.9	4.7	13.8	19.2	French Polynesia
6.3[1]	—	—	6.6[1]	2,428	24.2	24.3	6.2	1.9	2.8	14.0	8.3	18.3	Gabon
—	—	—	14.0[19]	2,251	58.9	1.3	3.0	2.1	1.7	2.1	15.0	14.9	Gambia, The
...	...	...	...										Gaza Strip
...	23.3	15.2	4.4	3,689	24.6	7.7	14.2	0.7	8.7	4.0	18.4	21.8	Germany, East
16.3	8.4	8.3[7]	7.9	3,351	20.8	4.7	15.2	0.7	10.2	5.6	18.7	24.1	Germany, West
3.3	3.8	3.9[7]	4.5	1,769	32.8	36.7	2.2	2.8	0.5	9.8	6.8	8.4	Ghana
13.3	10.0	—	14.1										Gibraltar
13.5	7.8	3.2	13.0	3,668	31.8	3.5	10.8	0.8	9.4	9.5	17.6	16.6	Greece
7.8	5.9	11.8[22]	17.1										Greenland
4.0	6.5	—	7.5	2,166	29.9	3.4	6.9	3.2	9.8	12.3	9.8	24.5	Grenada
16.3	6.0	6.6[7]	9.6	2,491	37.9	4.2	9.9	3.5	7.2	10.1	9.3	17.9	Guadeloupe
18.0	—	5.1	8.8	...	...	...	...	...	...	...	...	...	Guam
5.2[15]	4.7[15]	—	20.9[15]	2,138	58.0	0.5	3.5	0.1	4.5	8.5	6.8	18.2	Guatemala
...	...	...	...										Guernsey
...	...	...	...	1,880	41.0	20.4	1.8	0.6	1.1	15.0	14.6	5.4	Guinea
...	...	...	...	2,326	57.7	8.2	3.9	0.3	2.3	6.4	12.6	8.6	Guinea-Bissau
4.8	2.9	6.4[7]	8.2	2,360	53.2	1.4	4.4	1.8	6.0	4.9	7.5	20.8	Guyana
2.8	4.9	2.7	11.5	1,905	40.2	11.4	3.5	0.3	1.5	16.4	3.7	23.1	Haiti
3.0	8.3	2.9[7]	3.1	2,135	54.0	0.6	2.3	0.1	4.8	13.0	8.4	16.7	Honduras
8.3	11.2	7.8	9.2	2,771	34.5	1.2	18.0	3.2	4.4	6.2	17.1	15.4	Hong Kong
7.7	8.0	13.1[7]	6.9	3,484	32.5	3.3	12.7	0.2	9.6	4.7	16.4	20.6	Hungary
18.8	8.8	9.7	11.8	3,087	19.6	4.0	16.4	6.0	19.5	3.2	9.7		Iceland
10.3	4.3	0.9	6.3	2,056	66.5	2.0	0.2	0.2	3.4	9.0	7.4	11.1	India
—	3.8	—	9.6	2,118	68.4	8.3	0.8	1.0	0.4	2.2	6.2	12.7	Indonesia
6.8	7.7	1.4[7]	4.5	2,986	64.1	1.2	3.8	—	2.8	6.4	8.4	13.3	Iran
5.3	6.2	1.2	7.2	2,155	60.6	0.5	3.9	0.2	3.6	8.8	5.9	16.5	Iraq
13.6	6.5	7.9	11.0	3,699	26.0	6.2	15.7	0.7	12.1	5.3	13.8	20.2	Ireland
15.0	6.7	—	23.3										Isle of Man
12.6	11.7	4.2	9.9	3,060	35.4	2.7	10.1	0.8	11.3	8.0	15.1	16.7	Israel
13.7	6.7	7.1	17.4	3,688	34.8	2.3	12.0	0.7	8.6	7.3	16.9	17.4	Italy
—	7.3[23]	—	13.5[23]	2,613	37.8	27.4	3.2	1.5	2.0	9.7	9.5	9.1	Ivory Coast
13.7	5.6	3.2	24.0	2,544	34.7	8.3	6.1	1.5	5.1	7.0	11.5	25.8	Jamaica
9.6	4.1	8.7	27.3	2,852	43.4	2.5	6.3	6.8	5.6	5.3	11.5	18.6	Japan
...	...	...	...										Jersey
5.7	5.9	2.9	9.6	2,107	61.8	1.6	3.7	0.3	5.2	4.1	9.1	14.2	Jordan
—	—	—	15.0	1,925	80.5	1.1	3.7	1.2	0.4	5.0	1.9	6.2	Kampuchea
8.4	9.4	3.1	9.1	2,011	52.6	9.1	4.7	0.3	5.3	8.3	5.8	13.9	Kenya
8.0	2.9	—	12.5	2,718	28.3	17.5	3.6	5.4	1.3	6.2	9.4	28.2	Kiribati
—	3.8[25]	—	—	2,996	68.9	5.6	2.7	2.3	0.9	8.1	2.5	9.1	Korea, North
9.2	2.5	2.8	12.6	3,056	67.7	2.1	3.6	2.2	1.3	6.2	3.8	13.1	Korea, South
15.3	11.0	—	19.3	3,344	37.8	1.0	11.5	0.6	10.5	9.0	11.0	18.6	Kuwait
...	...	...	...	1,929	83.4	1.4	5.5	0.6	1.3	4.3	1.1	2.4	Laos
5.4[1]	2.6[1]	1.9[1]	6.3[1]	2,495	52.7	2.0	3.6	0.2	3.9	8.7	8.0	20.9	Lebanon
9.5[15]	6.9[15]	3.1[15]	6.8[15]	2,424	76.8	0.6	3.8	0.2	2.4	4.6	2.5	9.2	Lesotho
—	6.1[1]	—	20.1[1]	2,276	48.0	22.9	2.5	1.4	0.9	6.0	12.3	6.0	Liberia
9.4	4.6	8.5[7]	2.5	3,812	40.3	1.5	6.0	0.5	6.6	10.3	20.3	14.5	Libya
...	...	...	...										Liechtenstein
18.5	9.1	3.6[7]	15.7	3,639	19.2	5.5	19.6	0.8	9.9	5.2	20.7	19.3	Luxembourg
...	...	...	...	2,418	46.0	0.7	16.9	3.2	3.1	6.3	12.2	11.7	Macau
9.7	—	—	42.5	2,491	60.3	17.2	5.6	0.4	0.5	5.9	3.2	6.9	Madagascar
17.6[28]	9.6[28]	—	9.5[28]	2,208	69.3	2.4	1.4	0.3	0.8	10.8	3.1	11.4	Malawi
16.6[29]	5.9[29]	6.7[7,29]	5.5[29]	2,518	51.2	2.7	4.0	3.1	5.2	4.0	10.4	18.6	Malaysia
...	...	...	...	1,765	42.5	6.4	0.8	12.4	—	12.5	7.7	17.7	Maldives
...	...	...	...	1,893	73.5	2.5	4.2	0.8	2.4	2.9	5.5	8.2	Mali
14.4	10.0	6.0[7]	18.7	2,843	34.5	1.6	12.5	1.4	11.6	5.8	13.7	19.0	Malta
13.7	—	7.8	—	2,673	33.0	4.8	10.0	3.1	5.1	11.3	7.2	25.4	Martinique
—	—	—	9.8[1]	2,074	50.7	0.6	6.1	1.7	16.1	7.9	7.4	9.6	Mauritania
10.0	6.4	—	6.4	2,766	50.0	1.1	2.6	1.4	6.5	4.2	16.6	17.6	Mauritius
...	...	...	...										Mayotte
10.9	13.0	5.5[7]	11.7	2,890	49.9	0.9	5.1	0.7	6.9	9.7	9.1	17.7	Mexico
...	...	...	...										Monaco
...	...	...	...	2,774	52.2	1.5	25.7	0.1	5.3	0.6	5.4	9.1	Mongolia
...	10.2	—	15.3										Montserrat
6.9	3.6	—	17.0	2,606	63.0	1.3	2.6	0.5	2.1	5.0	11.0	14.5	Morocco
...	...	...	...	1,881	34.0	39.5	1.9	0.3	0.9	4.3	10.2	9.0	Mozambique
...	...	...	...										Nauru
2.1[1]	—	7.9[1,7]	6.5[1]	1,933	83.0	1.9	1.1	—	5.0	0.2	4.9	1.9	Nepal
10.7	8.1	9.2	15.3	3,617	17.4	4.6	16.9	0.5	13.5	4.4	21.6	21.0	Netherlands, The
19.4[31]	10.0[31]	6.0[7,31]	10.6[31]	2,712	29.8	2.3	15.4	1.3	9.6	6.3	11.8	23.5	Netherlands Antilles
15.1	3.7	6.4	15.2	2,842	36.9	7.9	10.6	0.4	5.6	5.7	11.7	21.3	New Caledonia
19.3	13.7	2.2[7]	12.8	3,573	21.3	3.3	19.9	0.4	15.8	5.4	16.0	17.8	New Zealand
—	—	—	27.5[1]	2,446	40.5	1.2	6.1	—	7.7	5.1	9.7	29.7	Nicaragua

Household budgets and consumption (continued)

country	income (latest)						consumption expenditure						
	percent received by		by source (percent)				per capita private final, 1983	by kind or end use (percent of household or personal budget; latest)					
	lowest 20% of households	highest 10% of households	wages, salaries	self-employment	transfer payments[a]	other[b]		food[c]	housing	clothing[d]	health care	energy	education
Niger	...	...	...	...	...	...	250	50.5	19.1[32]	7.3	—	—	—
Nigeria	...	...	...	...	...	...	510						
Niue	...	...	...	...	...	...	...	54.5[4]	5.0	5.0	...	...	...
Norfolk Island													
Norway	6.0	22.8	63.0	12.3	19.9	4.7	6,380	25.3	11.2	7.7	4.5	6.3	0.4
Oman							2,550						
Pacific Is., Trust Territory of the	...	...	...	...	...	...		...	...	...	...	...	...
Pakistan	8.0	...	17.9	66.9	0.5	14.7	260	53.3	7.8	9.7	2.0	5.1	1.3
Panama	2.0	44.2	85.3	—	9.2	5.5	1,140	47.3	12.7[3]	4.8	4.9	[3]	[7]
Papua New Guinea	...	...	72.7	2.5	...	24.8	470	60.9[4]	7.2[3]	6.2	—	[3]	—
Paraguay			40.8	56.0[33]	3.1	—	1,640	48.7	16.4	9.7	3.4	—	1.5
Peru	1.9	42.9					580	38.1[4]	15.6[3]	7.3	2.6	[3]	—
Philippines	5.2	38.5	44.8	40.3	2.1	12.8	460	52.4	12.0[3]	6.2	2.9	[3]	2.7
Pitcairn Island	...	...											
Poland	...	...	82.9	—	—	17.1	1,070	50.2	—	7.5	5.6	2.2	[7]
Portugal	5.2	33.4	44.8	21.6	21.1	12.5	1,440	33.8	5.6[3]	11.6	4.4	[3]	0.9
Puerto Rico	3.2	34.7	...	...	...	...	4,240	28.0	16.1[3]	9.0	4.8	[3]	2.2
Qatar							5,970[2]	...	...	...	...	...	...
Réunion	...	...	27.9	8.5	63.6	—	3,440[27]	41.1	21.6[3,32]	9.1	4.8	[3]	[7]
Romania	...	...					1,140	45.6	10.8	17.5	0.9	—	5.4
Rwanda			16.5	71.0	9.5	3.0	210	...	...	...	...	...	...
St. Christopher and Nevis	...	...					580	55.6[4]	7.6	7.5	—	6.6	—
St. Helena and Ascension	...	...						77.0	—	10.0	—	5.0	—
St. Lucia	...	...					700	63.4	10.1	8.1	—	5.6	—
St. Pierre and Miquelon	...	...						...	...	...	...	...	...
St. Vincent and the Grenadines	...	...	...	...	...	...	610	60.5	11.1	6.9	—	6.4	—
San Marino	...	...						45.6	12.2[3]	10.6		[3]	
São Tomé and Príncipe													
Saudi Arabia	...	...	...	...	...	...	3,810	52.2[15,34]	17.2[15,34]	6.6[15,34]	2.1[15,34]	1.8[15,34]	1.1[15,34]
Senegal	5.5	45.4					320	56.0[1]	8.7[1]	11.9[1]	—	5.8[1]	—
Seychelles	...	...				...	1,550	58.0[4]	11.4	9.0	—	4.4	—
Sierra Leone	5.6	37.8	27.9	61.6	—	10.5	340	55.1[4]	7.4[3]	12.9	1.3	[3]	[7]
Singapore	...	...					3,140	25.3	8.8[3]	8.7	2.7	[3]	[7]
Solomon Islands	...	...	98.8	0.6	—	0.5		56.5[1,4]	15.5[1,3]	5.0[1]	—	[3]	—
Somalia	...	...						62.3[1,4]	15.3[1,20]	5.6[1]	—	4.3[1]	—
South Africa	1.9	39.4	82.7	—	4.9	12.4	1,470[35]	31.7	9.9[3]	8.6	3.9	[3]	—
Bophuthatswana	...	...	...	...	...	...	560[27]	...	...	...	...	...	...
Ciskei	...	...						...	...	...	...	...	...
Transkei	...	...						...	...	...	...	...	...
Venda	...	...	56.2	4.8	32.9	6.1		51.2	4.3	11.2	0.5	4.5	1.9
South West Africa/Namibia			78.6	—	2.8	18.6	[35]						
Spain	6.9	24.5	53.9	46.1			2,870	30.6	16.1	8.5	2.3	2.7	2.1
Sri Lanka	7.5	28.2	49.0	51.0			270	52.2	3.4	6.2	1.7	2.9	0.8
Sudan, The	4.0	34.6	35.8	53.0	—	11.2	320[4]	66.5[4]	12.4	5.9	—	—	—
Suriname	9.3		...	...	...	...	2,000[27]	40.0[1]	9.5[1]	11.0[1]	3.6[1]	6.9[1]	2.6[1]
Swaziland	2.8	54.5					740	39.3[4,37]	—	10.0[37]	8.0[37]	6.5[37]	
Sweden	7.4	28.1	62.1	11.0	21.1	5.8	5,680	22.8	20.8	7.3	2.3	6.0	0.2
Switzerland	6.6	23.7	64.7	35.3			9,430	29.1[4]	20.7[3]	5.3	10.9	[3]	[7]
Syria	6.0		...	...	...	...	1,420	48.8[4]	17.7	9.1	—	4.6	[7]
Taiwan	...	...	62.7	24.1	—	13.2	1,380	32.8	28.9[3]	6.8	—	[3]	[7]
Tanzania	5.8	35.6	33.8	59.8	—	6.4	170	54.3[4]	8.6[20]	10.8	4.5	6.6	0.8
Thailand	5.6	34.1	32.6	53.4	0.3	13.7	550	45.7	2.9	10.2	4.7	3.4	0.5
Togo	8.0	30.5					210	56.1	13.7[3]	8.5	2.2	[3]	0.7
Tokelau	...	...						...	...	...	...	...	...
Tonga	...	...					790	55.1	3.8	6.2	—	—	...
Trinidad and Tobago	4.2	31.8	...	...	...	...	3,800[2]	31.4	18.0	16.1	2.5	1.9	1.7
Tunisia	4.1	37.6					5,860	41.8	29.0	8.5	—	—	[7]
Turkey	3.5	40.7	38.9[15]	46.8[15]	9.4[15]	4.9[15]	890[16]	41.2[15]	25.2[15]	14.8[15]	3.3[15]	—	—
Turks and Caicos Islands								...	...	...	...	...	...
Tuvalu	...	...	17.9	76.1	—	6.0		56.0[4]	11.5	7.5	—	—	—
Uganda	6.2		88.3[1,38]	1.8[1,38]	9.9[1,38]		670[6]	63.8[1,38]	9.2[1,38]	7.8[1,38]	1.0[1,38]	—	2.1[1,38]
U.S.S.R.			72.5	27.5				47.2	2.7	15.4	—	—	[7]
United Arab Emirates	...	...					6,310	...	...	...	...	...	...
United Kingdom	7.0	23.4	63.9	10.2	15.3	10.7	4,910	22.6	15.2	6.8	1.1	5.2	0.8
United States	5.3	23.3	66.5	3.8	13.4	16.3	9,210	14.5	16.9	6.2	13.3	4.8	2.0
Uruguay	3.8	33.5	...	...	...	...	1,350	41.3	25.3	12.9	—	—	—
Vanuatu								55.9[4,39]	2.2[3,39]	14.1[39]	—	[3]	—
Venezuela	3.0	35.7					2,600	50.4[4]	9.4[3]	4.9	3.4	[3]	[7]
Vietnam	...	...						...	...	...	...	...	...
Virgin Islands (U.S.)	...	...						25.3[40]	24.9[40]	5.4[40]	...	6.5[40]	—
Wallis and Futuna	...	...						...	...	...	...	...	...
West Bank	...	...					1,210[16]	...	...	...	...	...	...
Western Sahara								...	...	...	...	...	...
Western Samoa	...	...	71.7[15]	8.7[15]	—	19.6[15]		58.8	12.0[32]	4.2	—	—	—
Yemen (Aden)	...	...						...	...	...	...	...	...
Yemen (San'ā')	...	...	12.2	74.1	13.4	0.3	500[2]						
Yugoslavia	6.6	22.9	69.7	30.3			990	47.5	2.5	10.5	2.0	5.4	...
Zaire			...	...	...	...	90	60.6	17.1[3,32]	9.5	2.5	[3]	0.8
Zambia	3.4	46.3	94.0	6.0			340	37.7[4]	11.0	8.3	1.0	—	2.1
Zimbabwe	3.0	55.5	...	...	...	...	520[2]	32.6[4]	6.7	8.4	1.8	4.5	3.5

transportation, communication	furniture utensils[e]	recreation[f]	personal effects, other[g]	daily available calories per capita	cereals	potatoes, cassava	meat, poultry	fish	eggs, milk	fruits, vegetables[h]	fats, oils[i]	other[j]	country
—	[32]	—	23.1	2,440	68.7	4.1	3.5	0.1	2.9	12.0	4.5	4.2	Niger
...	...	...	...	2,378	42.2	25.4	1.9	1.2	1.1	6.3	11.7	10.2	Nigeria
17.5	13.0	...	5.0	...	...	...	...	...	...	...	...	...	Niue
...	...	...	...	...	...	...	...	...	...	...	...	...	Norfolk Island
15.8	8.3	8.1	12.5	3,391	24.5	4.8	11.4	2.4	16.1	4.2	17.4	19.1	Norway
...	...	...	...	...	...	...	...	...	...	...	...	...	Oman
...	...	...	...	...	...	...	...	...	...	...	...	...	Pacific Is., Trust Territory of the
2.5	3.8	0.7	13.8	2,180	63.1	0.6	1.8	0.1	5.9	4.6	10.5	13.5	Pakistan
6.8	8.5	5.8[7]	9.2	2,338	38.9	3.4	7.8	0.6	5.6	9.2	10.9	23.6	Panama
13.0	5.3	—	7.5	2,269	15.4	34.5	6.3	1.9	0.6	26.0	4.4	10.9	Papua New Guinea
4.5	6.2	2.3	7.3	2,839	30.0	15.7	14.6	0.1	4.1	14.7	7.9	12.9	Paraguay
9.8	7.0	7.4	12.2	2,195	43.7	9.6	4.5	2.2	4.6	8.2	8.0	19.1	Peru
3.3	7.0	1.6	11.9	2,405	59.5	7.2	4.5	2.7	1.6	7.6	4.2	12.6	Philippines
...	...	...	...	...	...	...	...	...	...	...	...	...	Pitcairn Island
7.3	11.1	10.7[7]	5.4	3,479	35.2	6.8	10.4	1.0	12.6	3.8	13.9	16.1	Poland
15.2	10.0	4.3	14.2	3,204	39.3	6.1	10.5	1.5	4.3	6.8	15.5	16.1	Portugal
16.3	6.3	4.8	12.5										Puerto Rico
...	...	...	...	3,050	48.8	0.8	10.1	0.5	7.1	11.6	7.8	13.3	Qatar
10.8	[32]	12.6[7]	...	2,782	48.2	1.7	8.9	1.7	4.6	7.0	13.4	14.6	Réunion
8.6	7.8	...	3.4	3,346	43.5	4.2	8.9	0.4	10.0	5.8	12.2	14.9	Romania
...	...	...	...	2,274	10.4	41.9	1.1	—	0.8	28.1	1.3	16.4	Rwanda
4.3	9.4	—	9.0	2,038	26.3	6.4	10.5	2.7	8.5	5.9	9.8	29.8	St. Christopher and Nevis
...	8.0	—	—										St. Helena and Ascension
—	5.1	—	7.7	2,390	27.7	8.5	11.6	2.2	6.5	13.4	11.0	19.0	St. Lucia
...	...	...	...	...	...	...	...	...	...	...	...	...	St. Pierre and Miquelon
—	5.4	—	9.7	2,234	28.7	12.8	6.4	1.0	5.1	7.3	10.7	28.0	St. Vincent and the Grenadines
9.5	...	...	22.1										San Marino
...	...	...	...	2,376	36.2	14.1	1.8	1.5	2.0	8.3	10.9	25.3	São Tomé and Príncipe
4.5[15, 34]	5.9[15, 34]	—	8.6[15, 34]	2,940	44.7	0.7	7.7	0.6	7.7	13.8	10.4	14.4	Saudi Arabia
5.4[1]	1.7[1]	—	10.5[1]	2,346	65.1	0.7	2.9	1.8	2.3	2.6	13.0	11.6	Senegal
4.1	5.4	—	7.7										Seychelles
9.2	8.0	3.8[7]	2.3	1,938	55.0	5.3	1.3	2.0	1.2	7.0	19.6	8.7	Sierra Leone
13.9	8.3	11.9[7]	20.4	3,165	45.6	2.9	12.6	2.0	4.7	7.3	8.5	16.4	Singapore
11.0[1]	—	—	12.0[1]	2,039	20.5	41.1	3.7	4.4	1.2	6.7	8.4	13.9	Solomon Islands
...	...	...	12.1[1]	1,986	50.9	1.1	10.5	0.2	16.8	4.0	8.6	8.0	Somalia
17.4	11.7	5.8	10.9	2,861	53.2	1.3	7.9	0.8	5.5	3.5	7.6	20.2	South Africa
...	...	...	...	...	...	...	...	...	...	...	...	...	Bophuthatswana
...	...	...	...	...	...	...	...	...	...	...	...	...	Ciskei
5.4	11.9	0.9	8.2	...	...	...	...	...	...	...	...	...	Transkei
...	...	...	...	...	...	...	...	...	...	...	...	...	Venda
...	...	...	...	2,183	47.7	14.5	13.8	...	4.8	1.8	10.0	7.4	South West Africa/Namibia
13.6	7.5	4.6	12.0	3,294	25.9	6.3	13.6	1.6	8.9	8.8	16.3	18.1	Spain
14.5	4.6	3.8	9.9	2,251	56.6	4.1	0.4	1.4	2.4	8.4	3.6	23.1	Sri Lanka
...	...	...	15.2	2,314	51.7	1.8	5.2	0.1	5.8	5.3	15.5	14.6	Sudan, The
9.5[1]	6.8[1]	5.8[1]	4.3[1]	2,529	51.6	1.6	6.2	1.8	4.1	3.7	11.5	19.5	Suriname
15.3[37]	9.0[37]	—	11.9[37]	2,553	55.0	2.2	7.3	—	4.7	3.8	6.9	20.2	Swaziland
15.7	6.7	9.8	8.3	3,146	20.1	4.7	17.0	2.2	14.8	4.1	16.7	20.3	Sweden
11.8	5.5	9.8[7]	6.9	3,449	20.9	2.7	18.6	0.5	13.5	6.0	15.8	22.0	Switzerland
3.8	5.1	3.1[7]	7.8	3,005	50.4	1.6	4.0	0.1	5.5	11.8	13.1	13.6	Syria
6.7	—	10.2[7]	14.6	2,749	...	...	...	...	...	...	...	...	Taiwan
6.4	6.3	1.6	0.1	1,955	33.5	31.1	2.9	1.1	2.4	13.7	6.0	9.3	Tanzania
11.7	5.9	3.8	11.2	2,330	66.1	2.7	3.7	1.6	0.7	6.2	2.5	16.5	Thailand
8.6	3.1	0.6	6.5	2,126	39.7	36.5	2.1	1.0	0.3	4.2	6.1	10.2	Togo
...	...	...	...	...	...	...	...	...	...	...	...	...	Tokelau
6.1[1]	12.4	—	16.5	3,200	13.2	42.5	10.9	2.3	1.3	3.3	8.2	18.3	Tonga
10.9	7.9	1.3	8.3	2,837	40.2	3.0	6.7	0.8	7.2	7.4	12.0	22.7	Trinidad and Tobago
4.9	—	7.6[7]	8.2	2,763	55.8	1.3	2.7	0.5	4.3	8.6	14.7	12.1	Tunisia
5.5[15]	—	6.1[15]	3.9[15]	2,937	53.7	3.3	3.5	0.5	4.3	10.8	11.5	12.4	Turkey
...	...	...	...	...	...	...	...	...	...	...	...	...	Turks and Caicos Islands
10.5	...	—	14.5										Tuvalu
2.2[1, 38]	5.4[1, 38]	0.2[1, 38]	8.3[1, 38]	1,784	30.0	18.5	3.3	1.3	2.6	30.3	1.6	12.3	Uganda
—	—	15.0[7]	19.7	3,360	38.4	6.3	9.3	1.8	9.9	4.3	10.9	19.2	U.S.S.R.
...	...	...	...	3,224	31.2	0.9	9.6	1.6	9.5	13.8	16.5	16.9	United Arab Emirates
17.6	6.8	8.4	15.4	3,249	21.1	6.3	15.8	0.7	12.0	4.5	18.1	21.5	United Kingdom
15.9	5.7	6.1	14.5	3,641	18.2	2.9	20.6	0.6	11.7	5.5	16.6	24.0	United States
—	—	—	20.5	2,886	32.5	3.8	20.0	0.4	11.3	4.2	9.7	18.0	Uruguay
9.8[39]	8.0[39]	—	10.0[39]	2,134	24.0	17.9	12.9	3.3	3.2	4.1	5.4	23.8	Vanuatu
12.5	5.9	7.7[7]	5.7	2,646	36.7	2.5	9.5	0.8	9.3	10.4	10.0	20.9	Venezuela
...	...	...	...	2,135	72.9	8.6	4.8	2.2	0.1	3.4	2.0	6.0	Vietnam
11.7[40]	4.3[40]	—	21.8[40]										Virgin Islands (U.S.)
...	...	...	...	...	...	...	...	...	...	...	...	...	Wallis and Futuna
...	...	...	...	...	...	...	...	...	...	...	...	...	West Bank
...	...	...	...	...	...	...	...	...	...	...	...	...	Western Sahara
9.0	[32]	—	16.0	2,234	28.7	12.8	6.4	1.0	5.1	7.3	10.7	28.0	Western Samoa
...	...	...	...	2,273	60.3	0.2	2.9	1.5	4.8	8.6	9.4	12.4	Yemen (Aden)
11.7	8.9	3.9	7.6	2,475	67.3	1.4	4.3	0.4	4.5	10.3	4.9	6.9	Yemen (Şan'ā')
5.7	[32]	2.0	1.7	3,550	47.0	3.3	7.4	0.2	7.8	6.2	14.1	14.0	Yugoslavia
4.3	—	—	35.6	2,130	14.5	58.4	1.8	0.6	0.2	9.4	7.7	7.5	Zaire
6.3	16.4	—	19.8	2,146	70.0	4.7	2.9	0.8	1.5	2.3	4.3	13.4	Zambia
				2,109	63.5	1.2	3.3	0.1	1.8	2.4	8.6	19.1	Zimbabwe

[1]Capital city only. [2]1982. [3]Housing includes energy. [4]Includes tobacco. [5]Urban households in the Federal District only. [6]1978. [7]Recreation includes education. [8]1972. [9]Includes wage taxes. [10]Personal effects and other includes education. [11]1971. [12]1977. [13]Rural only. [14]Highest 20%. [15]Urban areas only. [16]1981. [17]1970. [18]Consumer price index excludes rent. [19]Low-income population in Banjul and Kombo St. Mary only. [20]Housing includes water. [21]Urban areas of eastern region only. [22]Includes shooting, hunting, and fishing. [23]African population only. [24]1966. [25]Workers and clerical workers only. [26]Includes cultural activities. [27]Malagasy households only. [28]Balantyre and Lilongwe only. [29]Peninsular Malaysia only. [30]1973. [31]Curaçao and Bonaire. [32]Housing includes furniture, utensils, and household supplies. [33]Includes property income. [34]Middle-income population only. [35]South Africa includes South West Africa/Namibia. [36]1979. [37]Middle- to high-income families only. [38]Unskilled African workers only. [39]Urban, low-income households only. [40]St. Thomas only.

Health services

The provision of health services in most countries is a large and growing sector of the national economy as well as one of the principal determinants of the quality of life.

This table summarizes the basic indicators of health manpower, hospitals and health-care utilization, mortality rates that are most indicative of general health services, external controls on health (adequacy of food supply and availability of safe drinking water), and sources and amounts of expenditure on health care. Each datum refers more or less directly to the availability or use of a particular health service in a country, and, while each may be accurate as an overall measure, each may also conceal considerable differences in availability of the particular service to different segments of population or regions of the country. In the United States, for example, the availability of physicians ranges from about one per 935 persons in the least well-served state to one per 362 in the best-served, with a rate of one per 188 in the national capital. These disparities are even more pronounced in most other countries, unless the government has made some special effort to achieve a more even distribution of manpower and facilities. In addition, even when trained manpower exists and facilities have been created, the country may lose health professionals via the "brain drain" to foreign countries in which they were trained; or low levels of financial support at the national level may leave facilities underserved; or lack of good transportation may prevent those most in need from reaching the clinic or hospital that could help them.

Definitions and limits of data have been made as specific as possible in the compilation of this table. For example, despite wide variation worldwide in the nature of the qualifying or certifying process that permits an individual to represent himself as a physician, organizations such as the World Health Organization (WHO) try to institute international standards for training and qualification. International statistics presented here for "physicians" refer to persons qualified according to the WHO standards and exclude traditional health practitioners, whatever the local custom with regard to the designation "doctor." Statistics for health manpower in this table uniformly include all those actually working in the health service field, whether in the actual provision of services or in teaching, administration, research, or other tasks. One group of practitioners for whom this type of guideline works less well is that of midwives, whose training and qualifications vary enormously from country to country but who must be included, as they represent, after nurses, perhaps the largest and most important category of health auxiliary worldwide. The statistics here refer to those midwives working in some kind of institutional setting (a hospital, clinic, community health-care centre, or the like) and exclude rural noninstitutional midwives and traditional birth attendants.

Hospitals also differ considerably worldwide in terms of staffing and services. In this tabulation, the term hospital refers generally to a permanent facility offering inpatient services and/or nursing care and staffed by at least one physician. Establishments offering only outpatient or custodial care are excluded. These statistics are broken down into data for general hospitals (those providing care in more than one specialty), specialized facilities (with care in only one specialty), local medical centres, and rural health-care centres; the last two generally refer to institutions that provide a more limited range of medical or nursing care, often less than full-time. Hospital data are further analyzed into three categories of administrative classification: public, private nonprofit, and private for profit. Statistics on number of beds refer to beds that are maintained and staffed on a full-time basis for a succession of inpatients to whom care is provided.

Data on hospital utilization refer to institutions defined as above. Ad-

Health services

country	health personnel							hospitals									
	year	physicians	dentists	nurses	pharmacists	midwives	population per physician	year	number	kinds (%)				ownership (%)			hospital beds per 10,000 pop.
										general	specialized	clinics	rural	government	private nonprofit	private for profit	
Afghanistan	1982[1]	1,160	8	1,054	206	529	14,474	1982	68	66.2	16.2	—	17.6	86.8	13.2	—	3
Albania	1982	3,861	900[4]	6,801[5]	532[5]	5,098[5]	720	1977	928	5.2	3.1	82.4	9.3	100.0	—	—	66
Algeria	1982	6,508	1,920	17,989[1,7]	1,006	2,786[1,7]	3,002	1982	424	—46.2—		53.8	—	85.3[7]	4.4[7]	10.3[7]	23
American Samoa	1982[1]	20	7	141	1	1	1,682	1982	1	100.0	—	—	—	100.0	—	—	43
Andorra	1981	42	...	...	...	...	852	1981	...	...	...	...	...	...	...	...	31
Angola	1980	436	...	3,115[10]	87[10]	284[10]	17,500	1980	347[11]	15.6[11]	12.7[11]	30.5[11]	41.2[11]	66.9[11]	29.1[11]	4.0[11]	27
Anguilla	1982	2	1[13]	16	1[13]	11[13]	3,250	1982	1	—	—	—	100.0	100.0	—	—	37
Antigua and Barbuda	1983	31	4	154	18	160[5]	2,523	1983	1	100.0	—	—	—	100.0	—	—	29
Argentina	1979	79,216	...	...	...	...	351	1980	3,189	84.2	15.8	—	—	41.9	3.6	54.5	53
Australia	1982	27,500	6,200[9]	119,900[9]	5,400[9]	5,930[9]	552	1984	1,036[15]	...	...	...	...	68.9[15]	—31.1[15]—		59
Austria	1984	20,390	956	84,039	1,896	1,056	370	1984	321[9]	...	...	...	...	...	...	...	111
Bahamas, The	1983	218	31[9]	952	37[9]	104[9]	1,018	1983	3	66.7	33.3	—	—	100.0	—	—	43
Bahrain	1982	397	35	2,098	68	276	964	1982	12	42.7	58.3	—	—	75.0	16.7	8.3	35
Bangladesh	1982	12,306	248[1,16]	3,769[16]	...	2,239[16]	7,526	1981	504	19.8	6.2	18.4	55.6	92.1	7.9	—	2[19]
Barbados	1982	221	30	1,050	...	36	1,133	1982	11	27.3	18.2	—	54.5	81.8	—	18.2	86
Belgium	1982	26,593[22]	4,964	91,263	10,177	4,920	371	1982	531	53.3	46.7	—	—	36.3	—63.7—		94
Belize	1984	78	12	209	17	179[16]	2,078	1984	12[7]	58.3[7]	25.0[7]	—	16.7[7]	100.0[7]	—	—	35
Benin	1980	204	13	1,294	55	312	17,020	1980	131	4.6	9.9	80.9	4.6	87.8	12.2	—	11[16]
Bermuda	1983	77	24	436	24	...	726	1983	3	33.3	66.7	—	—	...	...	...	43[15]
Bhutan	1982	64	...	129	...	17	18,100	1982	19	...	...	...	...	...	...	...	5
Bolivia	1978	3,410	1,182[26]	1,552[26]	1,902[26]	...	1,555	1975	345	20.6	13.6	27.5	38.3	76.5	3.2	20.3	22
Botswana	1980	111	20	574	10	714	7,378	1980	53	24.5	62.3	13.2	—	84.9	15.1	—	24
Brazil	1980	97,100	56,015	306,411	5,129	2,526	1,246	1982	23,341	22.6	13.3	—64.1—		64.0	—36.0—		42
British Virgin Islands	1980	6	1	46	2[4]	14	1,859	1980	1	100.0	—	—	—	100.0	—	—	30
Brunei	1982	107	17	627	5	133	1,879	1982	5	80.0	—	—	20.0	80.0	20.0	—	31
Bulgaria	1984	24,000	5,201[9]	47,369[9]	3,965[9]	7,996[9]	373	1984	...	...	...	...	...	...	...	...	91
Burkina Faso	1981[1]	127	14	1,927	46	281	49,820	1977	44	4.5	—	88.7	6.8	100.0	—	—	6
Burma	1984	8,931	410[16]	6,978[1,16]	80[1,16]	15,543[1,16]	4,099	1982	614	49.7	2.4	—	47.9	100.0	—	—	9
Burundi	1983	216	6	1,126	24	73[7]	20,942	1983	33	...	...	...	...	...	...	...	13
Cameroon	1981	640	75[7]	4,320[7]	107[7]	2,266[7]	13,527	1977	1,003	5.8	0.5	87.5	6.2	70.1	23.5	6.4	28[9]
Canada	1980	44,000	10,000[4]	140,000[4]	16,052[4]	...	547	1978	1,226	65.8	26.9	7.3	—	93.4	—	6.6	78
Cape Verde	1980	51[1]	3	187[1]	7[1]	232[1]	5,664[1]	1980	21	9.5	4.8	61.9	23.8	100.0	—	—	22
Cayman Islands	1984	24	6	55	3[7]	14	800	1984	2	50.0	—	—	50.0	100.0	—	—	87
Central African Republic	1980	108	3	900	18	367	21,204	1979	85	7.1	5.9	69.4	17.6	72.9	—	27.1	16[9]
Chad	1980	94	4[1,4]	933[1,4]	9[1,4]	96[1,4]	47,640	1978	4	100.0	—	—	—	—	—	100.0	8
Chile	1982	5,416	1,664	25,889	201	1,930	2,081	1982	247	51.4	19.0	—	29.6	82.2	—	17.8	34
China	1983	587,564[22]	...	849,652	177,721	75,792[16]	1,736	1983	66,662	12.6	4.1	83.3	—	100.0	—	—	21
Christmas Island	1981	2	1	5	1	...	1,500	1982	1	1	—	—	—	—	100.0	—	133
Cocos (Keeling) Islands	1981	1[1]	—	4	—	...	569[1]	1981	1	1	—	—	—	100.0	—	—	73
Colombia	1982	15,261	5,648[5]	26,415[5]	...	...	1,776	1980	849	84.7[7]	15.3[7]	—	—	79.7[4]	—20.3[4]—		18
Comoros	1980	—28—		108	2[4]	13	16,900[4]	1980	17	17.7	—	23.5	58.8	100.0	—	—	22
Congo	1980	278	2[4]	1,915[4]	28[4]	413[4]	5,500	1978	473	0.6	0.2	97.3	1.9	94.9	5.1	—	47
Cook Islands	1982	18	8[1]	65[1]	2[1,16]	8[1,16]	967	1981	8	12.5	—	—	87.5	100.0	—	—	87
Costa Rica	1980	1,506	239	1,192	123[1,5]	...	1,491	1980	39	48.7	28.2	—23.1—		92.3	—	7.7	34
Cuba	1984	19,200	4,134[19]	31,855[19]	700[19]	...	518	1982	375	24.5	56.0	5.6	13.9	100.0	—	—	50[21]
Cyprus	1983	741	222	2,185	189[19]	189[19]	876	1982	124	3.2	—89.5—		7.3	12.1	0.8	87.1	55[14]
Czechoslovakia	1983	53,734	7,911[19]	103,080	7,015[19]	6,792[19]	339	1983	634	36.0	63.5	0.5	—	100.0	—	—	125
Denmark	1983	12,463	2,351[19]	20,979	1,091[19]	708	410	1982	127	87.4	12.6	—	—	91.3	8.7	—	77[21]
Djibouti	1984	46	3	288[16,30]	4	191[16,30]	8,804	1984	29	6.9	3.5	75.8	13.8	100.0	—	—	29
Dominica	1983	26	7	153	10	47[4]	2,846	1983	48	2.1	2.1	91.6	4.2	100.0	—	—	31

mission and discharge, the two principal points at which statistics are normally collected, are the basis for the data on the amount and distribution of care by kind of facility. These data on numbers of patients exclude babies born during a maternal confinement but include persons who die before being discharged. The bed-occupancy and average length-of-stay statistics depend on the concept of a "patient-day," which is the annual total of daily censuses of inpatients. The bed-occupancy rate is the ratio of total patient-days to potential days based on the number of beds; the average length-of-stay rate is the ratio of total patient-days to total admissions.

Two measures that give an excellent indication of the level of ordinary health care in a country are those for infant mortality and for maternal mortality. The former refers to infants who die within a year of birth, the latter to deaths directly attributable to delivery or complications of pregnancy, childbirth, or puerperium (the period immediately following birth). Levels of nutrition and access to safe drinking water are two of the most basic limitations imposed by the physical environment in which health-care activities take place. The nutritional data are based on recommendations of the United Nations' Food and Agriculture Organization for the necessary daily intake (in calories) for a moderately active person of average size in a climate of a particular kind (fewer calories are needed in a hot climate) to remain in average *good* health. Excess intake in the most developed countries ranges to more than 150% of what is required to maintain health (the excess usually being construed to diminish, rather than raise, health). The range of deficiency is less dramatic numerically but far more critical to the countries in which deficiencies are chronic, because the deficiencies lead to overall poor health (raising health service needs and costs), to decreased productivity in nearly every area of

national economic life, and to the loss of social and economic potential through early mortality. By "safe" water is meant only water that has no substantial quantities of chemical or biological pollutants, *i.e.*, quantities sufficient to cause "immediate" health problems.

Two principal kinds of public health-care finance data are given: health insurance and central government budgetary expenditure. The data on insurance refer to public programs only and identify the mandated basis or extent of responsibility for costs or funding required under the relevant law of the principal participants (individuals, employers, and government). Data on public health-care expenditure refer to a consolidated statement of expenditure by all elements of the central government but exclude expenditure by other levels (state, city, etc.). In a number of countries significant governmental expenditures for health-care services are made at these other levels, amounting to 2, 10, and sometimes 20 times the level of central government expenditure. These expenditures may include costs for national health insurance, family-planning programs, and workmen's compensation. Expenditures at the national level for social security are excluded.

The following notes further define the column headings:
... Not available.
— None, nil, or not applicable.
a. Bed-occupancy rates may exceed 100% because stays of partial days are counted as full days.
b. It has been assumed that 100% of the population in countries with developed market and centrally planned economies has access to safe water.
c. Figures larger than 20% include cost of medical benefits and exclude cost of insurance.

| admissions or discharges | | | | | bed occu-pancy rate[a] (%) | aver-age length of stay (days) | mortality | | popu-lation with access to safe water[b] 1980 (%) | food supply (% of FAO require-ment) 1981 | financing of public health care, latest year | | | | | country |
| rate per 10,000 pop. | by kinds of hospital (%) | | | | | | infant mortality per 1,000 live births 1982–83 | maternal mortality per 100,000 live births 1980–81 | | | health-care insurance[c] | | | public health expendi-tures (% of natl. budget) | public health expendi-tures per capita (U.S.$) | |
	general	special-ized	clinics	rural							indiv. (% of earn-ings)	em-ployer (% of payroll)	govt. (% of covered earnings)			
76[2]	52.8[2]	46.7[2]	—	0.5[2]	58.0[2]	8[2]	203.0	...	10	85	—	8.0[6]	100.0	...	1.40[3]	Afghanistan
							44.0	...	...	129	—	8.0[6]	100.0	...	26.20[3]	Albania
577	...	...	...	...	64.1[7,8]	10[7,8]	92.2	...	78	109	4.5[6]	5.5[6]	—	5.6[3]	20.90[3]	Algeria
1,547	100.0	—	—	...	37.8	4	6.8	...	...	...	...	...	...	...	...	American Samoa
...	...	...	...	...	...	...	16.0[9]	...	100	...	...	...	...	...	...	Andorra
296[12]	58.5[12]	...	...	41.5[12]	44.5[12]	16[12]	148.0	113.4[11]	17	97	...	...	...	...	9.00[3]	Angola
1,097	—	—	—	100.0	52.3[4]	6[4]	82.4	...	...	...	...	...	...	10.8	62.00	Anguilla
480	100.0	—	—	...	89.5	13	32.0	170.4[14]	100[14]	82	3.0[6]	5.0[6]	—	9.0	33.20	Antigua and Barbuda
...	...	...	...	...	...	...	35.3	78.1[7]	60	129	3.0	4.5	—	1.1	4.30	Argentina
...	...	...	...	...	...	...	10.4	9.8	97	115	—	—	100.0	10.0	275.90	Australia
2,148[9]	...	...	...	...	82.5[9]	15[9]	11.9	13.8	88	130	3.2	3.2	50.0	12.2	423.60	Austria
999	100.0	—	—	—	88.4[16]	13[16]	25.3	37.0[7]	98[13]	89	1.7[6,17]	7.3[6,18]	—	17.5	207.50	Bahamas, The
1,104	74.0	26.0	—	—	72.6[15]	9[15]	51.8[16]	...	98[16]	...	—	—	—	6.5	231.80	Bahrain
...	...	...	...	...	...	...	133.0	...	68	84	...	...	...	8.5	1.30	Bangladesh
84[2]	93.9	4.6	—	1.5	89.8[20]	34[20]	10.9[21]	23.8	100[19]	127	1.0	1.0	—	10.8	125.40	Barbados
1,552	91.0	9.0	—	—	85.3	19	10.7[21]	13.1[4]	89	142	1.8	3.8	80.0	1.7	103.00	Belgium
...	...	...	...	...	...	...	23.4[21]	48.8[21]	63[16]	119	3.0[6]	4.1[6]	—	9.3	30.70	Belize
...	...	...	...	...	...	...	148.0	...	17	94	—	0.2[23]	—	5.6	3.30[3]	Benin
1,280[15]	...	...	...	...	78.0[15]	10[15]	8.7	...	...	...	24	24	80.0	13.4	0.40	Bermuda
...	...	...	...	...	...	...	144.0	...	8	90[9]	...	...	...	4.3[25]	13.60[25]	Bhutan
...	...	...	...	...	...	...	213.0[21]	...	39	89	2.0	8.0	—	2.0	4.50	Bolivia
691	89.1	6.7	4.2	—	90.0[15]	10[15]	68.4[16]	...	29[16]	105	—	—	—	4.9	18.40	Botswana
...	...	...	...	...	...	...	71.0	...	63	109	8.5[17,27]	10.0[17,27]	—	7.8	36.30	Brazil
868	100.0	—	—	—	75.0	8	42.6	...	90[19]	117	—	—	—	4.0	42.80	British Virgin Islands
1,069	98.5	—	—	1.5	38.0	4	11.5	...	72	117	—	—	—	3.6	0.50	Brunei
2,118[19]	...	...	...	...	84.4[19]	16[19]	16.8[21]	24.1	...	147	—	30.0[6]	100.0[6]	...	84.60[3]	Bulgaria
66[8]	...	...	...	...	63.7[8]	12[8]	149.0[8]	...	14	87	—	11.5[23]	—	6.8	1.50	Burkina Faso
289	75.7	10.1	—	14.2	78.1	9	94.0	...	23	117	1.0	2.0	1.0	7.0	2.00	Burma
...	...	...	...	...	...	...	137.0	...	2[16]	103	—	—	—	8.0[3]	2.10[3]	Burundi
...	...	...	...	...	...	...	116.0	...	49	98	—	7.0[23,28]	—	2.7	4.30	Cameroon
1,677	93.9	6.0	0.1	—	110.4	19	9.3[21]	6.4[4]	99	128	0.8[29]	3.0[29]	50.0[29]	5.2	152.00	Canada
279[12]	...	...	...	...	71.7[14]	11[12]	30.0	134.0[13]	...	120	8.0	15.0	—	...	...	Cape Verde
1,084	90.8	—	—	9.2	65.5[15]	4[7]	2.4[21]	...	99[7]	...	—	—	—	...	...	Cayman Islands
412	43.9	1.0	37.9	17.2	50.7	8	142.0	...	18	93	—	12.0[23,28]	—	5.1	3.30	Central African Republic
...	...	...	...	...	...	...	142.0	...	26	74	—	6.0[28]	—	4.2	1.00	Chad
962[9]	84.9[9]	9.3[9]	—	5.8[9]	73.9	10[9]	20.1[21]	73.1	76	113	6.0	—	—	6.8	49.10	Chile
...	...	...	...	...	...	...	38.0	...	...	104	—	100.0	—	...	3.90	China
...	...	...	...	...	...	...	...	...	100	...	...	...	...	...	...	Christmas Island
256	100.0	—	—	—	...	...	...	...	100	...	...	...	...	...	...	Cocos (Keeling) Islands
613[19]	88.9[4]	11.1[4]	—	—	57.7[4]	7[4]	39.5	133.5[5]	64	112	2.3	4.7	—	4.0	12.30	Colombia
510[4]	63.7[4]	—	—	36.3[4]	67.9[4]	11[4]	107.0	...	...	97	...	...	...	3.1[25]	0.80[25]	Comoros
...	...	...	...	...	...	...	134.5	...	13	110	—	0.2	—	4.9[3]	26.40[3]	Congo
1,352	70.7	—	—	29.3	43.6[15]	9[15]	29.6	...	...	...	...	...	...	...	...	Cook Islands
1,192	77.8	16.7	—5.5—		75.7	8	18.9	22.9	81	117	5.5	9.3	1.3	32.8	67.70	Costa Rica
1,462	49.7	45.7	1.9	2.7	74.4	11	15.0	45.2[4]	62	123	—	10.0	100.0	...	49.70[3]	Cuba
567[15]	...	...	...	...	72.1	8	17.0	...	92[16]	135	6.0[6]	6.0[6]	100.0[6]	6.8	68.40	Cyprus
2,141	81.3	18.4	0.3	—	65.7	14	15.6[21]	12.9[7]	74.5[14]	137	—	20.0[6]	100.0[6]	...	175.70[3]	Czechoslovakia
1,871	97.6	2.4	—	—	79.6	12	7.7	3.8	99	132	—	—	100.0	1.6	78.70	Denmark
...	...	...	...	...	...	...	c. 175	...	...	...	...	...	...	5.8	19.50	Djibouti
729	...	...	...	...	...	...	11.4	117.6[4]	91[14]	86	3.0[6]	5.0[6]	—	8.8	20.80	Dominica

Health services (continued)

country	year	physicians	dentists	nurses	pharma-cists	midwives	population per physician	year	number	general	specialized	clinics	rural	government	private non-profit	private for profit	hospital beds per 10,000 pop.
										kinds (%)				ownership (%)			
Dominican Republic	1980[1]	2,142	...	2,431[31]	...	...	2,575	1973	339	80.5	6.8	—	12.7	40.7	0.3	59.0	16[9,20]
Ecuador	1979	5,720	795	1,531	505	...	1,297	1979	261	18.4	9.2	43.7	28.7	53.7	1.9	44.4	18
Egypt	1982	58,761	8,218	34,371[16]	18,860	9,004[1]	760	1982	1,521	32.3	13.2	15.9	38.6	83.1	3.8	13.1	20
El Salvador	1981	1,793	600	1,734	597[7]	...	2,606	1979	82	15.8	17.1	15.9	51.2	69.5	1.2	29.3	18
Equatorial Guinea	1975	5	...	248	...	2	62,000	1982	65[5]	...	...	...	...	...	...	...	108
Ethiopia	1982	504	16[9]	7,547[9,33]	93[9]	33	79,310	1980	86	32.6	18.6	—	48.8	88.4	9.3	2.3	3
Faeroe Islands	1985	75	34	235	8	13	600	1983	3	33.3	—	—	66.7	100.0	—	—	78
Falkland Islands	1984	3	1	11	—	6	667	1984	1	100.0	—	—	—	100.0	—	—	65
Fiji	1982	325	54	1,342[33]	44[9]	33	2,024	1983	27	11.1	33.3	—	55.6	92.6	7.4	—	26
Finland	1983	9,793	3,712	46,612[19]	5,131	828[19]	496	1983	...	...	...	...	...	...	...	...	131
France	1982	113,000	31,790	407,602	42,498	8,610	480	1982	4,464[35]	—85.4[16,35]—			14.6[16,35]	45.5	—54.5—		114
French Guiana	1982	80	18	309	18	16	885	1982	6	16.7	—	66.7	16.7	33.3	—66.7—		123
French Polynesia	1982	170	51	424[1]	24	10[1]	914	1981	34	8.8	5.9	52.9	32.4	94.1	—	5.9	68
Gabon	1980	265	20[5]	823[5]	28[5]	99[36]	4,053	1981	103	—15.5—		—	84.5	100.0	—	—	44
Gambia, The	1980	66	6[4]	179[4]	2[4]	90[4]	9,587	1978	16	18.8	12.5	—	68.7	87.5	12.5	...	12
Gaza Strip	1982	...	...	...	...	...	...	1982	7	...	...	...	...	100.0	—	—	19
Germany, East	1983	36,181	10,903	...	3,602	...	463	1983	541	...	...	...	...	84.8	—15.2—		102
Germany, West	1984	147,467	33,713	278,716	29,536	5,726	415	1983	3,119	44.7[9]	55.3[9]	...	...	36.3	34.3	29.4	111
Ghana	1981	1,665	95	17,758	611	6,728	6,956	1979	329	2.7	4.9	54.7	37.7	78.4	13.1	8.5	18
Gibraltar	1983	22	5[19]	246	13[19]	14[19]	1,364	1983	3	100.0	—	—	—	100.0	—	—	87
Greece	1983	27,607	8,286	9,255[16,38]	5,082[19]	1,888[19]	357	1982	664	54.8[39]	45.2	[39]	[39]	29.9[16]	3.9[16]	66.2[16]	60
Greenland	1983	58	26	510	...	12	897	1983	17	5.9	—	—	94.1	100.0	—	—	112
Grenada	1981	38	7	337	1[4]	107[4]	2,391	1982	39	7.7	7.7	69.2	15.4	100.0	—	—	67
Guadeloupe	1983	418	101	1,230	135	101	787	1982	27	60.0[4]	30.0[4]	—	10.0[4]	40.7	—59.3—		129
Guam	1982	83	23	396	30	...	1,363	1982	4	25.0	25.0	50.0	—	50.0	—50.0—		217[7]
Guatemala	1981	1,250	275	4,345[1,7]	7[31]	...	5,880	1981	159[10]	38.4[10]	25.8[10]	32.7[10]	3.1[10]	76.7[10]	—	23.3[10]	14
Guernsey	1982	53	21	592	15	31	1,094	1982	5	20.0	80.0	—	—	100.0	—	—	91
Guinea	1981	301[9]	5[1]	570[1]	3[1]	329[1]	16,053[9]	1976	314	1.9	—	87.9	10.1	100.0	—	—	17
Guinea-Bissau	1980[1]	108	3	553	3	163	7,287	1981	17[8]	11.8[8]	—	—	88.2[8]	100.0	—	—	19
Guyana	1980[1]	100	12[7]	881[7]	32[7]	546[7]	8,650	1979	55	20.0	12.7	27.3	40.0	87.3	3.6	9.1	47
Haiti	1980	900	73[1,7]	1,899[1]	6[1,7]	100[7]	5,469	1981	72	—77.8—		22.2	—	61.1	—38.9—		6
Honduras	1982	1,440	183[7]	3,545[9]	392[7]	...	2,748	1982	44	59.1	11.4	—	29.5	43.2	—	56.8	14
Hong Kong	1984[30]	4,609	949	14,029	501	981	1,164	1982	71	43.7	15.5	39.4	1.4	50.7	26.8	22.5	42
Hungary	1984	33,035	3,421[19]	92,518[19]	4,427[19]	2,574[19]	323	1984	...	...	...	...	...	...	...	...	93
Iceland	1982	532	180	2,495[33]	160	33	440	1982	46[9]	54.3[9]	41.4[9]	4.3[9]	—	...	...	...	111
India	1981[30]	268,712	8,648	150,339	155,621	217,981	2,615	1981	25,452	26.7	0.3	65.8	7.2	71.6	—28.4—		8
Indonesia	1981	15,400	2,500[7]	62,200[7]	1,800[7]	76,499[7]	9,774	1978	1,169	14.7	8.3	39.4	37.6	30.2	23.0	46.8	7
Iran	1983	15,945	2,340	29,486	2,650	2,202	2,605	1982	581	71.1	15.5	9.8	3.6	66.4	13.9	19.7	16
Iraq	1981	7,634	1,387	6,082	2,132	2,267	1,791	1982	234	48.3	33.8	2.1	15.8	95.7	—	4.3	17
Ireland	1981	4,443	1,029	24,390[1,33]	2,068	33	775	1980	209	33.5	37.8	1.4	27.3	63.2	21.5	15.3	97
Isle of Man	1982	90	19[1]	750[1]	30	61[1]	747	1981	3	33.3	33.3	—	33.3	100.0	—	—	108
Israel	1982	10,700	2,200	27,300	2,800	115[1]	376	1983	150	28.7	71.3	—	—	34.7	28.7	36.7	64
Italy	1981	97,003	...	186,335[33]	43,500[9]	33	586	1981	1,826	73.7	26.3	—	—	62.8	—37.2—		94
Ivory Coast	1980	500	21[1,13]	2,859[13]	45[1,13]	453[13]	16,494	1975	61	13.1	3.3	—	83.6	98.4	—1.6—		13
Jamaica	1982	319	67	2,279	124	485[9]	7,033	1982	33	78.8	21.2	—	—	90.9	—9.1—		30
Japan	1982	167,952	58,362	546,597	99,326	25,416	705	1983	9,515	93.0	7.0	—	—	20.5	—79.5—		121
Jersey	1982	148	41	646	22	27[16]	517	1983	7	14.3	85.7	—	—	100.0	—	—	109
Jordan	1984	2,310	486	830	800	266	1,091	1982	45	80.0	20.0	—	—	46.7	8.9	44.4	14[21]
Kampuchea	1971	438	71	3,639	79	1,426	15,297	1971	94	35.1	36.2	—	28.7	57.4	2.2	40.4	11[9]
Kenya	1983[30]	2,366	289	18,715	113	...	7,935	1983	504	—42.9—		57.1	—	...	...	...	16
Kiribati	1982[1]	19	2	125	1	213	3,158	1982	34	2.9	—	97.1	—	100.0	—	—	45
Korea, North	1982	45,000	...	...	...	...	417	1982	...	...	...	...	...	...	...	...	130
Korea, South	1983	26,473	4,611	49,587	27,395	5,681	1,509	1983	7,701	—5.8—		94.2	—	...	...	...	15[42]
Kuwait	1983	2,596	238	8,293[19]	714	128	644	1982	30	40.0	36.7	23.3	—	73.3	—	26.7	37
Laos	1983	1,654	15[31]	1,028[31]	16[31]	352[31]	2,394	1983	38[13]	...	...	...	...	...	...	...	24
Lebanon	1982	3,000	730[7]	3,681[7]	1,002[7]	614[7]	1,000	1982	130[10]	...	...	...	...	...	...	...	38
Lesotho	1982	114	6	452	7	...	12,265	1982	113	—17.7—		—82.3—		40.9[5]	59.1[5]	—	16
Liberia	1981	236	21[9]	567[9]	4[9]	114[9]	8,305	1981	85[9]	...	...	...	...	60.0[9]	—40.0[9]—		15
Libya	1982[1]	5,210	384	9,495	514	1,218	637	1982	64	68.8	31.2	—	—	100.0	—	—	48
Liechtenstein	1983	20	7	...	2	...	1,325	...	...	...	...	...	...	...	...	...	...
Luxembourg	1983	627	147	1,098[16]	127[16]	100	604	1983	33	60.6	39.4	—	—	...	...	...	132
Macau	1981	293	105	605	5	1,357	1,000	1977	4	50.0	50.0	—	—	...	...	...	63
Madagascar	1981	901	94	3,779	87	1,423	9,943	1978	749	0.8	1.1	75.7	22.4	100.0	—	—	20
Malawi	1981	121	6	1,695[33]	11	35	51,461	1981	340	13.5	1.8	—84.7—		58.2	—41.8—		19
Malaysia	1982[44]	4,234	863	28,780	626	12,409	3,510	1981[44]	163	20.2	50.4	—	29.4	39.9	—	60.1	27
Maldives	1983	17	...	113	2[1,16]	159[16]	9,882	1983	2	100.0	—	—	—	100.0	—	—	6
Mali	1980	319	15[1]	715[1]	22[1]	272[1]	21,890	1977	192	0.5	81.3	—	18.2	100.0	—	—	6[9]
Malta	1982	413	57	2,962	369	225	786	1983	7	28.6	71.4	—	—	...	...	...	101
Martinique	1982	394	107	1,871	146	106	834	1979	17	17.6	11.9	17.6	52.9	82.3	—	17.7	121[19]
Mauritania	1980	103	4[5]	560[31]	6[5]	19[5]	14,500	1977	12	8.3	—	—	91.7	100.0	—	—	4[7]
Mauritius	1984	642	89	1,467[1]	85	569[1]	1,571	1984	17	41.2	23.5	23.5	11.8	88.2	—11.8—		28[20]
Mayotte	1980	9	1	51	1	2	5,567	1981	2	...	...	...	...	...	...	...	17
Mexico	1980	53,053	1,879[26]	40,998[26]	112[26]	634[26]	1,260	1974	1,575	47.3	10.6	26.2	15.9	...	...	...	10[4]
Monaco	1982	59	32	391	56	6	458	1982	1	100.0	—	—	—	100.0	—	—	134
Mongolia	1982[1]	4,405	180	7,595	290	963	400	1981	1,659	2.1	5.4	71.9	20.6	100.0	—	—	111
Montserrat	1982	5	1	73[16]	2[4]	32[4]	2,335	1981	1	100.0	—	—	—	100.0	—	—	58
Morocco	1981	2,214	182	22,147	135[1]	74	9,056	1982	141	20.6	24.8	44.0	10.6	100.0	—	—	12
Mozambique	1980	309	96[1]	2,156	8[1]	457[1]	39,126	1980	325	3.1	1.2	87.7	8.0	100.0	—	—	13
Nauru	1980	11	2[36]	61[33,36]	1[36]	33	700	1971	2	100.0	—	—	—	50.0	50.0	—	300
Nepal	1984	571	171[1,9]	1,986	11[1,9]	...	28,270	1980	68	88.2	11.8	—	—	82.4	17.6	—	2[21]
Netherlands, The	1984	29,951	6,586	34,500[4]	1,728	1,022	481	1983	810	27.4	72.6	—	—	...	...	...	123
Netherlands Antilles	1975	164	34	...	17	21	1,393	1975	11	—100.0—		—	—	...	...	...	101[14]
New Caledonia	1981	168	49	283	...	23	846	1981	38	10.5	7.9	39.5	42.1	92.1	—	7.9	108
New Zealand	1982	5,210	1,160	22,000	2,300	2,600	615	1982	268[15]	...	...	...	...	38.8[15]	—	61.2[15]	100[14,15]
Nicaragua	1981	1,570	190[1,9]	4,687[9]	...	...	1,800	1976	67	34.3	9.1	41.7	14.9	46.2	—	53.8	20[9]

rate per 10,000 pop.	general	special-ized	clinics	rural	bed occu-pancy rate[a] (%)	aver-age length of stay (days)	infant mortality per 1,000 live births 1982-83	maternal mortality per 100,000 live births 1980-81	popu-lation with access to safe water[b] 1980 (%)	food supply (% of FAO require-ment) 1981	indiv. (% of earn-ings)	em-ployer (% of payroll)	govt. (% of covered earnings)	public health expendi-tures (% of natl. budget)	public health expendi-tures per capita (U.S.$)	country
...	73.1[20]	16.7[20]	—	10.2[20]	59.8[20]	7[20]	28.3	55.3[4]	57	95	2.5[6]	7.0[6]	2.5[6]	10.7	20.00	Dominican Republic
470	—85.0[32]—		15.0	[32]	58.0	8	78.0	216.3[4]	51	93	5.0[6]	1.0	—	7.7	18.40	Ecuador
...	...	...	...	...	...	...	74.2	77.9[7]	84	134	1.0	4.0	—	2.8	10.00	Egypt
378[15]	...	...	...	...	77.1[15]	7[15]	42.2	70.6	48	93	2.5	6.3	...	8.4	11.50	El Salvador
...	...	...	...	...	...	...	137.0	...	...	...	...	...	...	...	...	Equatorial Guinea
1,780	75.7	—	—	24.3	33.2[34]	11[34]	143.0	...	13	93	—	—	—	3.7	1.10	Ethiopia
1,790[16]	100.0[16]				99.3	16	14.9	...	—	...	—	—	—	...	...	Faeroe Islands
...	...	...	...	...	41.7[16]	8[16]	...	...	...	...	...	...	...	...	...	Falkland Islands
997[16]	59.4[16]	10.2[16]	—	30.4[16]	77.1[16]	8[16]	22.0	52.4[4]	69	117	—	—	—	8.2	36.80	Fiji
2,088	58.9[9]	40.8[9]	—0.3[9]—		81.7	19	6.2	6.3[7]	84	113	1.0	1.4	100.0	10.9	340.10	Finland
1,917[35]	...	...	...	...	81.9[35]	14[35]	8.2[21]	12.9	97	141	5.5	8.0	...	14.7	658.50	France
1,666[20]	82.2[20]	...	...	17.8[20]	77.7[20]	17[20]	22.6[21]	...	...	...	...	...	...	...	...	French Guiana
1,472	70.9	...	3.2	25.9	51.7	8	19.5[21]	...	...	109	...	...	...	...	...	French Polynesia
258	...	...	...	...	23.6	13	121.6	...	1[16]	126	—	10.0[28]	—	...	68.20[3]	Gabon
437[15]	...	...	...	...	...	...	203.5	...	12[16]	95	...	...	...	6.3	6.90	Gambia, The
1,134	...	...	...	...	63.4	4	...	...	...	...	...	...	...	...	...	Gaza Strip
1,383	42.8[4]	57.2[4]	—	—	74.0	21	11.4	14.7	82	141	10.0	12.5[37]	100.0	...	340.60[3]	Germany, East
1,812	80.5	19.5	—	—	83.1	19	9.6[21]	20.0	99	125	3.5[17]	3.5[17]	—	19.3	653.50	Germany, West
1,514	100.0	...	...	...	63.2[19]	11[19]	98.0	...	50	83	5.0[6]	11.5[6]	—	5.8	16.30	Ghana
...	...	...	...	...	...	...	—	...	—	...	...	...	...	...	292.30	Gibraltar
1,179	69.4[39]	30.6	[39]	[39]	70.4	13	14.9	11.4	97	149	3.7	3.7	...	10.5	160.80	Greece
2,682	22.2	...	...	77.8	66.7	10	39.6	...	...	...	...	...	...	...	...	Greenland
749[9]	...	...	...	...	...	...	21.2	...	85	91	4.0[6]	4.0[6]	—	15.6	18.70	Grenada
1,478[20]	58.1[20]	41.9[20]	—	—	92.3[20]	20[20]	23.0	106.4[4]	...	105	...	...	...	...	...	Guadeloupe
738[7]	97.6[7]	2.4[7]	—	—	78.8[7]	8[7]	7.5	...	...	...	...	...	...	2.7	32.90	Guam
310	...	...	...	...	...	...	64.1	96.3	42	98	2.0	4.0	25.0	10.9	15.30	Guatemala
977	89.0	11.0	...	...	83.9	28	...	...	...	...	...	...	...	...	...	Guernsey
...	...	...	...	...	...	...	159.0	...	10	84	...	3.2	...	...	3.40[3]	Guinea
326[12]	59.8	—	—	40.2	57.5[12]	11[12]	143.0	...	...	95	...	...	...	...	...	Guinea-Bissau
...	...	...	...	...	...	...	45.0	104.3[5]	93	104	4.9[6]	7.4[6]	—	5.7	14.40	Guyana
123	...	...	...	...	...	...	124.0	...	12	85	2.0[17]	4.0[18]	1.2	9.8[25]	2.00[25]	Haiti
429[9]	75.6[9]	16.7[9]	—	7.7[9]	70.2[9]	8[9]	87.0	82.0[7]	55	94	2.5	5.0	2.5	8.0	9.80	Honduras
1,494	93.6	3.2	3.2	—	82.4	8	9.9[21]	8.0	...	119	—	100.0	...	...	...	Hong Kong
1,961	...	...	...	...	80.5	14	20.0[21]	17.5	44	134	3.0[17]	24.0	100.0	...	127.00[3]	Hungary
2,024	84.0[9]	14.2[9]	1.8[9]	—	95.2	19	7.7	22.8	99	124	2.0	—	100.0	21.0	757.00	Iceland
...	...	...	...	...	...	...	117.0[16]	...	41	94	2.2	4.4	25.0	2.1	0.10	India
66[15]	...	...	...	...	55.1[15]	9[15]	90.3	...	19	113	2.0	5.0	—	2.5	3.30	Indonesia
...	...	...	...	...	...	...	101.0	...	51	122	7.0[6]	20.0[6]	3.0[6]	5.5	54.10	Iran
592	65.5	26.4	7.0	1.1	60.3	6	31.0[16]	...	76	119	5.0[6]	12.0[6,40]	—	...	22.30[3]	Iraq
1,295[15]	...	...	...	...	...	...	9.8	9.7[7]	73	149	1.0	1.0	100.0	15.2[25]	340.40[25]	Ireland
1,274	83.9	7.0	—	9.1	81.2	25	...	...	...	...	...	...	...	22.3	426.40	Isle of Man
1,556	95.8	4.2	—	—	93.1	14	6.6[21]	5.4	99	121	0.8	5.7	—	4.3	197.10	Israel
1,740	90.6	9.4	—	—	69.1	13	11.6[21]	17.1[4]	86	145	1.2	11.9[17]	...	11.5	398.30	Italy
171	...	...	...	...	74.9[15,41]	11[15,41]	121.0	...	14	114	—	5.5[28]	—	3.9	15.40	Ivory Coast
696	82.5	17.5	—	—	72.6[7,15]	9[7,15]	9.2	135.7	82	117	2.5[6]	2.5[6]	...	5.4	26.70	Jamaica
619[16]	97.8[16]	2.2[16]	—	—	82.2[16]	56[16]	6.0[21]	19.2	98	122	4.3	4.3	16.4	...	393.90[3]	Japan
1,721	83.2	16.8	—	—	86.8	24	...	...	...	...	...	...	...	18.4	422.30	Jersey
880	93.6	6.4	—	—	41.0	3	67.0[16]	...	66	106	—	—	—	3.8	21.60	Jordan
...	...	...	...	...	...	...	151.0[21]	...	45	96	—	—	—	...	...	Kampuchea
...	...	...	...	...	...	...	81.0	...	24	87	...	...	...	7.3	7.20	Kenya
633	47.6	—	52.4	—	58.0	15	8.7[4]	...	...	...	...	...	...	...	...	Kiribati
...	...	...	...	...	...	...	32.0	...	...	128	...	...	...	...	2.80[3]	Korea, North
279[42]	97.8[42]	2.2[42]	...	...	60.4[42]	12[42]	37.0	...	79	131	1.5[17]	1.5[17]	100.0	1.6	5.60	Korea, South
1,231	66.4	28.5	5.1	—	71.7	8	22.8	7.8	89	...	...	...	...	6.2	396.50	Kuwait
96[13]	...	...	...	...	19.7[13]	7[13]	121.0	...	48[16]	93	—	—	—	...	0.90[3]	Laos
...	...	...	...	...	...	...	40.2[16]	...	92[16]	119	1.5	5.5	25.0	...	12.80[3]	Lebanon
410[5]	20.8[5]	0.4[5]	6.2[5]	72.6[5]	79.6[5,15]	10[5,15]	110.0	...	23	106	...	...	...	5.4	3.60	Lesotho
...	...	...	...	...	...	...	151.5[16]	...	10	97	—	...	—	7.3	11.80	Liberia
719	...	...	...	...	52.7	13	97.5[16]	...	87	161	1.0	1.4	1.6	...	131.50[3]	Libya
...	...	...	...	...	...	...	7.4[21]	...	...	...	...	...	...	...	...	Liechtenstein
1,807	...	...	...	...	78.8	21	11.2	25.0[7]	98	142	4.1	4.1	50.0	2.2	108.40	Luxembourg
...	...	...	...	...	...	...	12.0[21]	...	...	102	...	...	...	5.7[25,43]	17.30[25,43]	Macau
699[15]	...	...	...	...	57.9[15]	2[15]	67.0	...	26	110	...	8.3[28]	—	...	8.10[3]	Madagascar
361	...	...	...	...	77.8	9	164.0	...	44	96	...	...	...	5.2	2.80	Malawi
635[20]	...	...	...	...	...	...	19.3	50.6[19]	64	114	—	—	100.0	4.4	29.70	Malaysia
272	100.0	—	—	—	62.1[45]	5[45]	77.0	...	...	92	...	...	...	4.6	6.30	Maldives
178	54.9	37.5	—	7.6	58.8	7	149.0	...	23	76	—	2.0	—	2.5	1.20	Mali
1,569[19]	...	...	...	...	83.7[19]	19[19]	11.6[21]	17.5[5]	100	106	8.3[6]	8.3[6]	8.3[6]	10.4	135.80	Malta
1,841	69.0	6.0	11.3	13.7	84.2	23	8.7[21]	27.4[13]	...	112	...	...	...	...	...	Martinique
115	...	...	...	...	97.8	5	136.0	...	17[16]	94	—	2.0	—	2.8	4.30	Mauritania
1,087[20]	...	...	...	...	84.5[9,20]	8[9,20]	24.7[21]	108.4	60	122	—	—	100.0	7.4	22.90	Mauritius
...	...	...	...	...	...	...	53.0	103.4[4]	59	126	2.3	5.6	20.0[46]	1.3	8.90	Mayotte
2,630	100.0	—	—	—	77.6	14	...	...	...	...	...	...	...	...	...	Mexico
...	...	...	...	...	...	...	...	...	...	...	...	...	...	...	...	Monaco
2,508	25.9	33.0	1.1	40.0	89.1	14	49.0	...	21[13]	113	...	...	...	...	12.00[3]	Mongolia
728[9]	100.0	—	—	—	...	...	7.7	—	100	...	...	...	...	...	...	Montserrat
225	57.1	25.1	8.2	9.6	63.5	12	114.4	...	53	105	0.2	0.4	—	2.8	7.80	Morocco
92[15]	...	...	...	...	70.2[15]	9[15]	105.0	...	7	79	...	...	...	...	...	Mozambique
2,660	100.0	...	...	...	...	...	31.2[16]	...	...	...	...	...	100.0	...	...	Nauru
46[15]	...	...	...	...	61.5[15]	7[15]	140.0[21]	...	11	85	—	...	—	4.5	1.10	Nepal
1,181	95.3	4.7	—	—	83.0[15]	13[15]	8.3	7.8	97	134	5.9	14.1	...	11.6	643.30	Netherlands, The
...	...	...	...	...	...	...	14.0[9]	...	...	111	...	...	...	7.9	45.00	Netherlands Antilles
1,468	77.9	3.0	3.2	15.9	57.6	16	11.2	...	...	106	...	...	...	...	...	New Caledonia
...	...	...	...	...	78.7[14,20]	12[20]	9.5[47]	13.9	93	135	—	—	100.0	12.6	372.90	New Zealand
...	...	...	...	...	...	...	75.2	65.2[4]	46	94	4.0	11.0	0.5	14.6	33.70	Nicaragua

Health services (continued)

country	year	physicians	dentists	nurses	pharmacists	midwives	population per physician	year	number	kinds (%) general	kinds (%) specialized	kinds (%) clinics	kinds (%) rural	ownership (%) government	ownership (%) private non-profit	ownership (%) private for profit	hospital beds per 10,000 pop.
Niger	1980	136	10[4]	1,080[4]	12[4]	2,006[4]	40,209	1978	212	1.9	0.5	94.8	2.8	97.2	2.8	—	6[7]
Nigeria	1980	8,037	285	37,370	2,816	27,983	10,800	1980	2,374[48]	25.2	—	74.8	—	...	...	...	7[48]
Niue	1980[1]	2	3	34	...	21	1,600	1983	1	100.0				100.0	...	...	131
Norfolk Island	1981[1]	2	...	8	1	1	1,067	1983	1	...				...	...	...	100
Norway	1982	8,630	3,562	58,525	2,761[49]	694	477	1982	929	8.7	84.5	3.0	3.8	...	...	...	148
Oman	1984	949	63	2,104	148	231[1,19]	1,063	1984	40	—37.5—		—62.5—		100.0	...	...	26
Pacific Is., Trust Terr. of the	1981[1]	55	20	426	2	1	2,465	1981[20]	9	...				...	...	...	46
Pakistan	1983	33,584[30]	1,103[19,30]	11,070[30]	1,770[19]	9,947[19]	2,822[30]	1982	895[8]	62.3	6.1	...	31.6	82.2	1.1	16.7	5
Panama	1983	2,149	409	1,962	157[4]	...	972	1983	50					88.45[1]	—11.65[51]—		36
Papua New Guinea	1984	280	16[9]	3,228[9,33]	9[9]	33	11,635	1980	390	5.1	—	53.6	41.2	46.2	53.8	—	45[21]
Paraguay	1980	1,800	855[7]	2,636[7]	860[7]	783[7]	1,623	1975	143	63.6	4.9	—	31.5	91.6	8.4	—	10[16]
Peru	1982	14,751	3,687[9]	10,065[9]	3,457[9]	2,171[9]	1,236	1977	437	66.4	9.1	24.5	—	60.4	15.6	24.0	16[19]
Philippines	1982	46,579	1,090[1,16]	9,644[1,16]	539[1,16]	9,470[1,16]	1,090	1981	1,711	...				29.9	—70.1—		18
Pitcairn Island	1982	—	—	1[1]	...	...	...	1982	...	...				...	...	...	...
Poland	1984	69,295	17,344	168,107	15,958	18,470	530	1984	782	87.9	12.1	—	—	...	...	...	70
Portugal	1983	22,078	600[19]	23,714[19]	5,061[19]	1,132[19]	453	1982	491	81.5	18.5	—	—	78.8	21.2	—	51[14]
Puerto Rico	1983	7,146	741[9]	14,392[9]	1,436[9]	199[9]	457	1980	111	72.1	27.9	—	—	48.6	19.8	31.5	38[21]
Qatar	1983[1]	419	43	1,029	56	70[16]	671	1983	4	25.0	75.0	—	—	100.0	—	—	32
Réunion	1985	704	193	1,791	174	102	770	1977	11	36.4	18.1	—	45.5	74.2[21,51]—25.8[21,51]—			72[21]
Romania	1984[1]	46,300	7,285[19]	81,031[19]	6,588[19]	12,248[19]	489	1984	437[16]	56.8[16]	32.5[16]	—	10.8[16]	...	...	...	94
Rwanda	1983[1]	258	1[16]	901	6	616[16]	22,093	1983	170	—16.5—		—83.5—		50.0	—50.0—		16
St. Christopher and Nevis	1981	17	5	252	1[9]	123[9]	2,615	1982	3	...				100.0	—	—	55
St. Helena and Ascension	1982	3	1	30[7]	...	77	1,667	1982	8	12.5	12.5	75.0	—	...	...	...	110
St. Lucia	1983	36	5	246	16	66[5]	3,628	1983	5	20.0	20.0	—	60.0	...	...	...	44
St. Pierre and Miquelon	1983	11	2	20[5]	...	1[5]	545	1983	1	100.0	—	—	—	100.0	—	—	167
St. Vincent	1984	24	1	290	...	...	4,300	1984	9	11.1	33.3	22.2	33.3	100.0	—	—	35[19]
San Marino	1979	11	...	...	...	...	2,030	1980	...	...				...	...	...	30
São Tomé and Príncipe	1981	38	—	157	1	13	2,537	1978	16	12.5	—	87.5	—	...	...	...	78
Saudi Arabia	1983[1]	6,453	269[16]	7,040[16]	499[16]	3,273[16]	1,615	1985	157	...		79.5		76.4	—	23.6	26
Senegal	1981	449	70	2,360[1]	139	401	13,000	1977	44	11.4	—	79.5	9.1	100.0	—	—	13[4]
Seychelles	1984	34	7	237	4	131[7]	1,900	1984	6	16.7	16.7	66.7	—	100.0	—	—	56
Sierra Leone	1981	220	30[9]	1,758[9,33]	8[9]	33	16,232	1980	112	0.9	7.2	58.9	33.0	76.8	15.2	8.0	11[16]
Singapore	1984	2,504	475	7,830	409	652	1,010	1984	22	...				50.0	—50.0—		38
Solomon Islands	1983	38	...	599	...	...	6,605	1983	132	6.1	—	93.9	—	72.7	—27.3—		56
Somalia	1981	292	2[9]	1,834[9]	...	556[9]	18,353	1978	...								11
South Africa	1983[30]	21,143	2,994	116,112	6,854	...	1,219	1980	595	...				40.7	—59.3—		41
Bophuthatswana	1982	91	...	3,342	...	...	14,800	1982	156	—6.4—		—93.6—		...	...	...	36
Ciskei	1984	...	...	2,763	...	...	...	1984	25	...				...	...	...	35
Transkei	1978	230	...	4,112	...	...	12,200	1978	31	...				...	...	...	27
Venda	1984	13	...	712	...	...	30,800	1984	52	—9.6—		—90.4—		...	...	...	39
South West Africa/Namibia	1983	199	40	3,293	...	...	5,271	1983	75	...				...	...	...	70
Spain	1983	115,251	4,458	136,992[19]	27,646	4,893[19]	332	1981	1,054	71.2	28.8	—	—	38.8	14.8	46.4	50
Sri Lanka	1983[1]	1,939	275[19]	7,173[19]	441[19]	3,808[19]	7,953	1982	493	5.9	31.4	20.7	42.0	100.0	—	—	28[14]
Sudan, The	1981[1]	2,169	334	13,693	58	376	8,870	1981	160	21.9	5.6	—	72.5	...	...	...	9
Suriname	1979	224	21[4]	660[4]	13[4]	88[4]	1,612	1980	17	29.4	17.6	47.1	5.9	58.8	29.4	11.8	89
Swaziland	1984	80	13	844[4]	10[4]	731[4]	7,971	1978	33	9.1	9.1	48.5	33.3	21.2	57.6	21.2	25[21]
Sweden	1983	19,300	9,000	67,900	822	370	432	1983	1,000	10.3	89.7	—	—	...	...	...	162
Switzerland	1982	17,067[16]	2,927	40,000[7]	1,251	1,650[7]	379[16]	1981	409	47.2	52.8	—	—	...	...	...	105
Syria	1984	5,543	2,045	7,923	2,367	2,071	1,792	1984	182	75.3	24.7	—	—	23.6	—76.4—		12
Taiwan	1983	14,669	2,834	16,778	14,480	2,820	1,268	1983	995	4.8	6.0	89.2	—	...	...	...	31
Tanzania	1982	950[16]	18[4]	8,291	25[5]	2,887	20,168[16]	1982	3,032	4.9	—	87.2	7.9	...	...	...	18
Thailand	1982	7,658	1,142	43,337	3,097	8,851	6,332	1982	1,117	62.0	2.8	—35.2—		...	...	...	17
Togo	1980	139	4	1,575	23	559	18,715	1979	65	10.8	4.6	61.5	23.1	96.9	3.1	—	13[19]
Tokelau	1984[1]	4	1	18[19,33]	...	33	393	1984	3	...		—	100.0	100.0	—	—	248[19]
Tonga	1982[1]	41	19	253	3	161	2,460	1982	9	44.4	—	55.6	—	100.0	—	—	33
Trinidad and Tobago	1980	786	69	2,837	...	...	1,382	1982	25[7]	8.0[7]	16.0[7]	40.0[7]	36.0[7]	60.0[7]	—	40.0[7]	38
Tunisia	1982	1,732	402	12,380[32]	869	33	3,683	1982	119	23.5	20.2	—	56.3	100.0	—	—	21
Turkey	1983	32,263	6,896	29,216	11,428[19]	12,470	1,465	1983	646	74.3	11.3	—	14.4	83.9	—16.1—		21
Turks and Caicos Islands	1983[1]	4	1	12[7]	...	11[7]	2,000	1983	12	8.3	—	91.7	—	100.0	—	—	70[7]
Tuvalu	1984[1]	4	2[19]	18	1[19]	3[19]	1,750	1984	9	11.1	—	88.9	—	100.0	—	—	43
Uganda	1981	611	17	6,778[33]	27	33	21,523	1981	485	15.5	1.2	83.3	—	84.5	15.5	—	15[14]
U.S.S.R.	1984	1,104,300[22]	17	2,880,000[19,33]	86,000	33	258	1984	23,100	...				100.0	—	—	127[21]
United Arab Emirates	1982[1]	1,290	95	2,814	89	...	884	1982	22[16]	50.0[16]	27.3[16]	4.5[16]	18.2[16]	95.5[16]	4.5[16]	—	28
United Kingdom	1983	28,663	15,181	207,400[16]	15,108[19]	20,135[16]	1,967	1982	2,501[16]	...				100.0	—	—	81
United States	1985	527,900	126,000[14]	1,372,000[14]	158,000[14]	2,500	450	1983	6,353	88.4	8.0	3.6[52]	—	34.1	53.6	12.3	51
Uruguay	1984	5,756	2,535	15,200[7]	584	300	523	1983	61	—63.9—			36.1	100.0	—	—	79
Vanuatu	1984	19	2[19]	266[19]	3[19]	5[19]	7,158	1980	21	14.3	—	52.4	33.3	47.6	52.4	—	33[14]
Venezuela	1979	15,359	4,645	38,061[4]	4,063	...	888	1979	446	...				42.1	4.3	53.6	30
Vietnam	1984	16,100	803[1,16]	44,080[16]	4,977[1,16]	13,752[16]	3,602	1981	11,550	1.3	7.9	86.8	4.0	100.0	—	—	35[21]
Virgin Islands (U.S.)	1974	96	...	241	...	...	833	...	...								...
Wallis and Futuna	1981[1]	4	1	27	1	5	2,859	1982	3	33.3	—	—	66.7	100.0	—	—	77
West Bank	1982	...	...	...	...	...	...	1982	17	...				52.9	—47.1—		109
Western Sahara	...	...	...	...	...	...	...										...
Western Samoa	1981	63	7	344	4	42[1]	2,508	1984	30	3.3	—	—	96.7	100.0	—	—	47[19]
Yemen (Aden)	1980	264	9	2,250	16	329	7,390	1980	49	12.2	16.4	34.7	36.7	98.0	2.0	—	16
Yemen (Şan'ā')	1981[1]	896	26	1,665	95	87	6,629	1982	30	63.3	3.3	—	33.3	86.7	13.3	—	5[14]
Yugoslavia	1982	35,245	7,581	67,468	4,923	7,747	642	1982	425[9]	32.5[9]	30.3[9]	37.2[9]	—	...	...	...	61
Zaire	1980	1,900	58[7]	14,661[7]	414[7]	3,043[7]	15,065	1979	942	37.3	38.9	23.8	—	40.9	44.6	14.5	28
Zambia	1982	839	52[16]	3,550[16]	35[16]	1,620[16]	7,186	1981	636	1.9	0.4	87.3	10.4	83.8	14.5	1.7	34[19]
Zimbabwe	1980	1,148	158	5,258	354	2,351	6,411	1980	...					...	...	...	29

Group headers: **admissions or discharges** (rate per 10,000 pop.; by kinds of hospital (%): general, specialized, clinics, rural) · **mortality** (bed occupancy rate[a] (%); average length of stay (days); infant mortality per 1,000 live births 1982–83; maternal mortality per 100,000 live births 1980–81) · population with access to safe water[b] 1980 (%) · food supply (% of FAO requirement) 1981 · **financing of public health care, latest year** (health-care insurance[c]: indiv. (% of earnings), employer (% of payroll), govt. (% of covered earnings); public health expenditures (% of natl. budget); public health expenditures per capita (U.S.$)) · country

rate per 10,000 pop.	general	special-ized	clinics	rural	bed occu-pancy rate[a] (%)	aver-age length of stay (days)	infant mortality per 1,000 live births 1982–83	maternal mortality per 100,000 live births 1980–81	pop. with access to safe water[b] 1980 (%)	food supply (% of FAO require-ment) 1981	indiv. (% of earn-ings)	em-ployer (% of payroll)	govt. (% of covered earnings)	public health expendi-tures (% of natl. budget)	public health expendi-tures per capita (U.S.$)	country
83[15]	...	...	...	...	62.0[15]	9[15]	140.0	...	49	101	...	11.0[23,28]	—	4.1	3.60	Niger
							113.0	...	28	103	6.0[6]	6.0[6]	—	2.5	2.80	Nigeria
2,144	100.0	—	—	—	56.7[9]	14[9]	—	...	...	...	...	...	...	9.6	136.10	Niue
					49.7		...	...						6.5	104.10	Norfolk Island
1,550	88.3	11.5	0.1	0.1	87.2	30	8.1	2.0	98	127	4.4[6]	16.8[6]	4.9[6]	10.6	555.10	Norway
1,542	...	...	...	...	93.8[15,19]	5[15,19]	135.2[50]	...	52	...	...	...	...	3.5	134.10	Oman
1,123	...	...	...	...	46.4	7	22.1	...	...	...	—	7.0	—	11.6[25]	96.60[25]	Pacific Is., Trust Terr. of the
							116.0[21]	...	29	95				1.1	0.60	Pakistan
1,162	...	...	...	...	64.5	7	20.5	73.1	63	104	1.0	8.0	0.8[6]	13.1	103.80	Panama
253[15]	...	...	...	...	...	...	103.0[21]	...	16	78				9.2	26.60	Papua New Guinea
416	90.9	7.8	1.3	—	88.2	14	51.2	468.6	28	125	9.5[6]	16.5[6]	1.5[6]	3.7	7.50	Paraguay
							96.9	103.4[4]	49	94	2.5	5.0	—	5.3	13.00	Peru
							49.0	125.0	55	107	1.3	1.3	100.0	4.1	5.00	Philippines
														15.4	303.00	Pitcairn Island
1,273	...	...	...	...	80.5[19]	17[19]	19.3	11.7	55	129	—	33.0[6]	100.0	9.5	163.90[3]	Poland
902	86.8	13.4	—	—	...	...	19.3	30.6[7]	92	129	8.0[6]	21.0[6]	...	4.4	22.70	Portugal
1,227	95.0	5.0	—	—	64.8	8	16.0	8.2	...	...	...	...	...	24.0[25,43]	148.10[25,43]	Puerto Rico
1,328[16]	54.3[16]	45.7[16]	—	—	...	...	45.0	...	97	...	...	...	...	...	...	Qatar
836[15]	...	...	...	...	82.0[15]	12[15]	11.6	...	...	123	...	...	...	...	...	Réunion
							23.9	139.9	...	124	—	7.0[17]	100.0	0.8	5.90	Romania
428	...	...	...	...	51.4	7	125.0	...	38	97				4.5	1.50	Rwanda
1,328[16]	...	...	...	...	57.4[15]	10[15]	42.8	90.9	95	...				...	...	St. Christopher and Nevis
							16.3	...	...	...				...	...	St. Helena and Ascension
916[9]	...	...	...	...	...	...	17.6[21]	...	70[16]	102	5.0[6]	5.0[6]		...	...	St. Lucia
							9.2[16]	...	...	...				...	...	St. Pierre and Miquelon
772[24]	...	...	...	...	68.3[11,15]	9[11,15]	46.8[16]	...	95[14]	94	—	—	—	10.4	28.60	St. Vincent
1,435	...	...	...	...	69.5	11	4.5[21]	...	...	...				...	...	San Marino
1,733	76.1	—	23.9	—	68.7	12	69.5	...	...	100				...	...	São Tomé and Príncipe
							106.5	...	64	123	—	—	—	1.4[25]	132.70[25]	Saudi Arabia
324	34.2	—	54.8	11.0	77.2	10	141.0	...	35	104	3.0[18]	3.0[18]	—	3.6	4.60	Senegal
1,285[15]	...	...	...	...	60.6[15]	5.9[15]	13.8[21]	...	...	94	5.0[6]	10.0[6]		13.1	48.90	Seychelles
13[15]	...	...	...	...	77.1[15]	18[15]	190.0	...	12[16]	83				6.2	4.50	Sierra Leone
910[20]	73.0[20]	27.0[20]	—	—	73.0[16]	10[16]	8.8[21]	4.7	100	139	—	—	100.0	6.4	84.90	Singapore
							46.0	...	...	76				11.2	14.00	Solomon Islands
							142.0	...	38	90				3.2	2.60	Somalia
							70.7[9]	...	...	117		—–	100.0[6]	3.5[25]	4.40[25]	South Africa
																Bophuthatswana
																Ciskei
																Transkei
																Venda
							115.0	...	...	96				...	...	South West Africa/Namibia
914	91.7	8.3	—	—	73.0	15	7.2	10.4[7]	78	137	4.8[6]	25.8[6]	...	0.6	8.80	Spain
1,623	39.9	15.0	0.8	44.3	88.3	6	37.1	...	22	98	—	—	100.0	3.3	3.60	Sri Lanka
91[15]	...	...	...	...	...	...	121.8	...	46	102	—	—	—	1.3	0.90	Sudan, The
820	93.6	2.4	8.0	6.0	41.6	15	34.9[9]	...	...	113				8.6	58.10	Suriname
456[15]	...	...	...	...	...	...	129.0	...	37	114	—	—	—	5.4	18.10	Swaziland
1,966	90.7	9.3	—	—	79.7	24	6.3[21]	8.2	99	116	—	9.5	—	1.5	75.50	Sweden
1,268	85.8	14.2	—	—	80.1	24	7.7	6.8	96	128	73			12.8	386.00	Switzerland
433	...	...	...	...	39.6	4	57.0	...	71	127				1.1	1.50	Syria
							8.3	...	...	...	1.4[6]	5.6[6]	3.2[6]	...	58.40[3]	Taiwan
706	66.5	—	13.1	20.4	...	...	97.0	...	48	82	5.0[6]	5.0[6]	—	5.5	5.10	Tanzania
...	...	...	...	...	...	...	56.0[21]	...	23	104	—	—	—	5.1	8.00	Thailand
							113.0	...	11	93	—	2.0[23]	—	5.7	4.80	Togo
965[19]	—	—	—	100.0[19]	12.0[19]	11[19]								...	...	Tokelau
718	97.6	—	2.4	—	56.8	10	6.4	...	...	119				...	...	Tonga
980	...	...	...	...	88.6[7,12]	5[7,12]	26.0	81.5[5]	89	113	2.8[6]	5.6[6]	100.0[6]	5.9	104.70	Trinidad and Tobago
634	...	...	...	...	68.7	8	85.0	...	62	121	5.0	15.0	—	6.7	30.10	Tunisia
462	78.3[16]	19.1[16]	—	2.6[16]	44.1[16]	9[16]	110.0	...	69	119	5.0	6.0	—	2.1	6.20	Turkey
							26.0	...	...	...				...	...	Turks and Caicos Islands
628[19]	63.7[19]	—	36.3[19]	—	42.4[15,19]	14[15,19]	42.0	...	...	...				...	...	Tuvalu
							125.0	...	10	74	—	—	—	4.7	1.20	Uganda
							16.3	...	...	129	—	4.4[17]	50.0	2.5	113.00[3]	U.S.S.R.
1,032	78.4[16]	15.4[16]	0.8[16]	5.4[16]	69.6	7	49.6	...	88	...				7.1	491.40	United Arab Emirates
1,216	...	...	...	...	75.8	10	9.6[21]	9.0	99	128	9.0	11.45	85.0	12.5	343.90	United Kingdom
1,555	...	...	...	...	76.4	9	10.5[47]	9.6[7]	99	137	1.3	1.3	—	10.7	383.50	United States
309	...	...	...	...	50.8	8	32.0	48.8[4]	78	109	3.0	4.0	...	3.4	15.30	Uruguay
912	40.5	—	14.0	45.5	33.6	8	94.0[21]	...	...	79			1.5[6]	...	...	Vanuatu
							44.8[9]	64.4[4]	81	107	2.0	4.25[17]	1.5[17]	8.1	94.10	Venezuela
1,587	12.4	8.1	56.6	22.9	80.7	7	73.0[21]	...	24	95				...	1.30[3]	Vietnam
							22.5[4]	280.0	...	...				...	...	Virgin Islands (U.S.)
1,100	76.0	—	—	24.0	49.4	13								...	...	Wallis and Futuna
905	...	...	...	...	78.8	6								...	...	West Bank
																Western Sahara
823	62.0	—	—	38.0	25.4	7	42.0	...	...	90	—	—	—	...	...	Western Samoa
277	...	...	...	...	...	...	142.9[16]	...	37	96				5.1[25]	2.10[25]	Yemen (Aden)
95	89.0	0.4	—	10.6	73.4	18	154.0	...	4	104				5.0	14.40	Yemen (San'ā)
993	81.0[48]	19.0	48	—	77.4	11	31.7	17.8	58	143	8.7	24	...	—	137.60[3]	Yugoslavia
474[15]	...	...	...	...	71.6[15]	12[15]	107.0	...	16	96				3.0[25]	1.20[25]	Zaire
391[15]	...	...	...	...	76.0[15]	7[15]	110.6	...	42	96	5.0[18]	5.0[17]	—	8.4	20.60	Zambia
1,043	40.1	6.1	53.8	—	67.5	7	69.0	...	...	...				6.4	21.20	Zimbabwe

[1]Government-employed health personnel only. [2]Excludes four specialized hospitals. [3]May include expenditures at the intermediate and local levels of government and/or the costs of additional services such as national health insurance and family-planning programs. [4]1978. [5]1977. [6]Includes funds for old-age retirement, incapacitating disability, work injury, and death insurance. [7]1979. [8]Excludes clinics. [9]1980. [10]1973. [11]1972. [12]Excludes specialized hospitals and clinics. [13]1975. [14]1983. [15]General hospitals only. [16]1981. [17]Minimum on a graduated scale. [18]Maximum on a graduated scale. [19]1982. [20]Government hospitals only. [21]1984. [22]Includes physicians practicing dentistry. [23]Employed women only. [24]Graduated rate. [25]Includes expenditures at the intermediate and local levels of government. [26]1974. [27]Excludes rural workers. [28]Includes family allowances. [29]Amounts vary internally. [30]Registered personnel; not all are resident and working in the country. [31]1976. [32]General hospitals includes specialized and rural hospitals. [33]Nurses includes midwives. [34]Rural hospitals only. [35]Excludes hospices and sanatoriums. [36]1971. [37]Excludes hazardous occupations such as mining. [38]Professional nurses only. [39]General hospitals includes clinics and rural hospitals. [40]Excludes oilfield operations. [41]1970. [42]General and specialized hospitals only. [43]Includes welfare. [44]Peninsular Malaysia only. [45]Central Hospital only. [46]Percent of employer contributions. [47]1985. [48]General hospitals includes clinics. [49]Includes pharmaceutical assistants. [50]1975–80 estimate. [51]Based on bed ownership. [52]Health maintenance organizations.

Social protection

This table summarizes the principal social protective activities of the countries of the world. Because the administrative structure, financing, manning, and scope of programmed tasks vary so greatly from country to country, the basis of the comparisons is most often either manpower or finance. The principal impediment to comparison on other bases is the great variety of administrative structures that exist for the conduct of these activities.

Because of the complexity of national programs in terms of eligibility, coverage, term, age limits, financing, payments, and so on, the provision of social security programs for specific social needs is summarized simply in terms of the existence or nonexistence of a specific benefit program. As in the United States, activities connected with a particular benefit may take place at more than one governmental level or through more than one agency at the same level. The data shown here are summarized from the U.S. Social Security Administration's *Social Security Programs Throughout the World.* A bullet symbol (●) indicates that a country has at least one program within the defined area; in some cases it may have several.

Data given for social security expenditure as a percentage of total central governmental budgetary expenditure are from the International Monetary Fund's *Government Finance Statistics Yearbook,* which provides the best and most comparable analytical series on the consolidated accounts of the central governments of the world.

Data on the financing of social security programs are taken in large part from the International Labour Office's *The Cost of Social Security* (triennial), supplemented by national data sources.

Figures for manpower in police and fire services are from a variety of national sources, principally census and manpower surveys, from the 1980–81 census period. The relative scarcity of international sources and data on these topics is in part a reflection of the fact that in many countries these functions are viewed as matters of merely local concern and, as they are not conducted or directly funded by the central government, tend to be ignored in the data collection and publication programs of the central government. The manpower figures refer, for the most part, to full-time, paid professional staff, excluding clerical support and volunteer staff. Fire fighters employed by private companies are included. Personnel in military service who perform either police or fire functions

Social protection

country	social security																
	programs available, 1983					expenditures, 1982 (% of national budget)	finances									
	old-age invalidity, death	sickness and maternity	work injury	unemployment	family allowances		year	receipts					expenditures			
								total ('000,000 natl. cur.)	insured persons (%)	employers (%)	government (%)	other (%)	total ('000,000 natl. cur.)	benefits (%)	administration (%)	other (%)
Afghanistan			●			...	...	...	...	...	...	...	...	...	...	...
Albania	●	●	●		●	...	...	...	...	...	...	...	...	...	...	...
Algeria	●	●	●		●	...	1983	9,462.0	...	...	...	...	7,696.0	...	...	...
American Samoa	...	...	...	...	...	...	1980	2.3	29.3	40.9	...	29.7	0.6	100.0	—	—
Andorra	...	...	...	...	...	...		...	...	...	...	...	...	...	...	...
Angola	...	...	...	...	...	...		...	...	...	...	...	...	...	...	...
Anguilla	...	...	...	...	...	...	1981	...	...	...	...	...	1.0	...	...	...
Antigua and Barbuda	●	●			●	...		...	...	...	...	...	...	...	...	...
Argentina	●	●	●	●	●	28.8	1980	27,318,424.2	38.4	49.4	10.2	2.1	26,433,082.7	94.8	4.4	0.8
Australia	●	●	●	●	●	29.0	1980	17,235.3	13.0	12.3	70.4	4.3	15,807.3	96.0	3.5	0.4
Austria	●	●	●	●	●	45.5	1980	224,889.0	31.3	48.5	16.8	3.4	223,466.0	95.2	2.7	2.1
Bahamas, The	●	●	●			7.4[4]	1979	25.1	...	...	...	...	9.6	...	...	...
Bahrain	●		●			2.1	1980	24,596.0	12.5	43.6	21.1	22.8	3,626.0	70.7	20.2	9.2
Bangladesh	...	...	...	...	...	2.2[4]	1977	466.7	2.2	2.2	93.7	1.9	445.3	99.6	0.4	—
Barbados	●	●	●			17.8	1980	66.1	22.7	28.8	31.0	17.5	37.7	93.6	6.4	—
Belgium	●	●	●	●	●	42.3[2]	1980	884,343.7	18.3	43.3	35.3	3.2	903,666.6	94.3	4.1	1.5
Belize	●		●			1.6	1980	...	...	...	...	...	1.5	...	...	...
Benin	●	●	●		●	8.7[4]	1977	3,654.7	7.4	49.4	41.9	1.3	3,165.6	91.0	8.3	0.7
Bermuda	●					3.1	1981	...	...	...	...	...	2.3[8]	...	...	...
Bhutan	...	...	...	...	...	...		...	...	...	...	...	...	...	...	...
Bolivia	●	●	●		●	0.4	1980	3,628.4	28.8	53.6	6.2	11.5	3,673.3	80.4	19.3	0.4
Botswana						1.8	1981	...	...	...	...	...	0.8	...	...	...
Brazil	●	●	●		●	35.3	1982	6,781,000.0	...	...	...	...	6,900,000.0	...	...	...
British Virgin Islands	...	...	...	...	...	...		...	...	...	...	...	...	...	...	...
Brunei	●					...	1981	...	...	...	...	...	2.5[9, 10]	...	...	...
Bulgaria	●	●	●	●	●	...	1977	2,609.7	—	53.7	40.2	6.1	2,506.0	94.9	0.1	5.0
Burkina Faso	●	●	●		●	5.8	1977	3,727.5	10.1	61.4	24.8	3.7	2,635.7	90.5	9.5	—
Burma	●	●	●			5.9	1977	340.1	1.4	40.9	57.7	—	333.1	99.2	0.8	—
Burundi	●		●		●	3.4[2]	1980	475.0	21.1	39.3	25.7	13.9	266.7	73.5	26.2	0.3
Cameroon	●		●		●	3.9[12]	1982	33.0	...	...	...	...	18.8	...	...	...
Canada	●	●	●	●	●	34.9	1980	41,921.7	7.4	12.8	71.2	8.6	35,523.4	97.5	2.5	—
Cape Verde	...	...	...	...	...	...		...	...	...	...	...	...	...	...	...
Cayman Islands	...	...	...	...	...	...		...	...	...	...	...	...	...	...	...
Central African Republic	●	●	●		●	6.2[1]	1981	2,009.0	...	...	...	...	1,675.0	...	...	...
Chad	●		●		●	1.9[2]	1976	...	...	...	...	...	1,675.0	...	...	...
Chile	●	●	●		●	41.8	1980	139,950.3	20.5	38.3	34.2	7.0	115,545.9	92.5	7.5	—
China	●	●	●			...		...	...	...	...	...	...	...	...	...
Christmas Island	...	...	...	...	...	...		...	...	...	...	...	...	...	...	...
Cocos (Keeling) Islands	...	...	...	...	...	...		...	...	...	...	...	...	...	...	...
Colombia	●	●	●		●	...	1980	52,412.9	16.0	49.8	16.2	18.0	44,180.6	77.6	12.4	10.1
Comoros	...	...	...	...	...	...		...	...	...	...	...	...	...	...	...
Congo	●	●	●		●	...	1980	5,682.0	...	...	...	...	3,957.0	...	...	...
Cook Islands	...	...	...	...	...	...		...	...	...	...	...	...	...	...	...
Costa Rica	●	●	●		●	11.2	1980	3,408.3	27.6	45.9	20.4	6.1	2,927.4	88.8	6.9	4.4
Cuba	●	●	●			...		...	...	...	...	...	...	...	...	...
Cyprus[17]	●	●	●	●		16.7	1980	34.0	30.0	36.3	29.2	4.5	27.6	98.1	1.9	—
Czechoslovakia	●	●	●		●	...	1980	91,367.0	—	3.7	94.6	1.7	91,367.0	99.6	0.4	—
Denmark	●	●	●	●	●	41.3[4]	1980	103,269.1	1.8	5.9	90.2	2.1	100,587.5	97.3	2.7	—
Djibouti	...	...	...	...	...	9.2[4]	1982	1,252.0	...	...	...	...	1,138.0	...	...	...
Dominica	●	●	●			1.5[4]	1979	2.5	...	...	...	...	0.8	...	...	...
Dominican Republic	●	●	●			8.4	1980	136.8	...	...	43.6	4.4	123,852	87.2	8.0	4.8
Ecuador	●	●	●			...	1980	13,643.0	36.9	43.0	0.1	19.9	8,585.0	72.0	28.0	—
Egypt	●	●	●	●		11.1	1983	2,292.5	...	...	...	...	1,197.1	...	...	...
El Salvador	●	●	●			3.8	1980	169.7	23.4	63.0	0.9	3.4	134.1	85.9	14.1	—
Equatorial Guinea	...	...	...	...	...	...		...	...	...	...	...	...	...	...	...
Ethiopia	●		●			4.0[4]	1980	117.7	21.8	70.7	4.5	3.0	79.8	98.2	1.8	—
Faeroe Islands	...	...	...	...	...	...		...	...	...	...	...	...	...	...	...
Falkland Islands	...	●	...	...	...	...		...	...	...	...	...	...	...	...	...
Fiji	●		●			3.0	1980	57.8	28.7	30.8	9.5	31.1	20.5	56.4	43.6	—
Finland	●	●	●	●	●	28.0	1980	40,435.2	7.9	44.9	41.4	5.8	34,646.2	96.5	3.5	—

are presumed to be employed in their principal activity, military service. Figures for criminal offenses known to police, usually excluding civil offenses and minor traffic violations, are taken in part from Interpol's *International Crime Statistics* (biennial) and a variety of national sources. Data for certain countries refer to cases disposed of in court, rather than to complaints. Virtually all data on fire alarms and on expenditure for police and fire services are taken from national statistical sources. Data for fire alarms usually exclude nonemergency calls, medical emergencies, and fire code inspection visits but may include false fire alarms to which a normal response with personnel and equipment was made.

The figures for military manpower refer to full-time, active-duty military service and exclude reserve, militia, paramilitary, and similar organizations. Because of the difficulties attached to the analysis of data on military manpower and budgets (including problems such as data withheld on national security grounds, or the publication of budgetary data specifically intended to hide actual expenditure, or the complexity of long-term financing of purchases of military matériel [how much was actually spent as opposed to what was committed, offset by nonmilitary transfers, etc.]),

extensive use is made of the principal international analytical tools: publications such as those of the International Institute for Strategic Studies (*The Military Balance* and *Strategic Survey*), the Stockholm International Peace Research Institute (*World Armaments and Disarmament*, SIPRI *Yearbook*), World Priorities (*World Military and Social Expenditures*), and the U.S. Arms Control and Disarmament Agency (*World Military Expenditures and Arms Transfers*).

The data on military expenditures are from the sources identified above, as well as from the IMF's *Government Finance Statistical Yearbook* and country statistical publications.

a. A police officer is a full-time, paid professional, including administrative staff, performing internal security functions. Clerical employees, volunteers, and members of paramilitary groups are excluded.

b. A fire fighter is a full-time, paid, professional staff member, including administrative staff. Clerical employees and volunteers are excluded.

c. Includes all active-duty personnel, regular and conscript, performing national security functions. Excludes reserves, paramilitary forces, border patrols, and gendarmeries.

police protection, 1980–81			fire protection, 1980–81			military protection, 1983									country
						manpower[c]		expenditure					arms trade ('000,000 U.S.$)		
offenses (reported to police) per 100,000 population	population per police officer[a]	government expenditure per 1,000 population (U.S.$)	fire alarms per 100,000 population	population per fire fighter[b]	government expenditure per 1,000 population	total ('000)	per 1,000 population	total '000,000 U.S.$	per capita	% of national budget	% of GDP or GNP	imports	exports	
...	...	...	...	...	...	75	5.3	198	13	35.7	5.0	150	0	Afghanistan
1,673.4	...	...	...	...	...	42	15.0	188[1]	74[1]	11.5	7.8[2]	0	0	Albania
4,901.2	464.0	17,676	180	852.6	8,126	130	6.3	1,334	61	6.2	2.7	350	0	Algeria
...	1,125.0	...	...	...	...	—	[3]	—	—	—	—	...	...	American Samoa
...	...	...	...	...	...	...	...	...	...	...	...	...	...	Andorra
2,102.1	...	24,233	...	...	...	54	7.2	1,558	199	62.5	23.2	625	0	Angola
4,166.7	...	25,133	...	...	...	—	[3]	—	—	—	—	...	...	Anguilla
1,101.7	...	...	...	...	...	...	...	...	...	...	...	...	...	Antigua and Barbuda
8,045.0	461.9	16,132	...	...	...	175	5.9	1,523	49	...	2.7	1,000	20	Argentina
						73	4.8	4,637	290	10.2	2.8	370	40	Australia
4,624.8	466.3	...	...	...	...	50	6.7	937	119	3.2	1.3	60	180	Austria
5,799.4	164.8	...	...	...	...	...	...	...	...	1.3[4]	...	...	...	Bahamas, The
1,207.1	183.3	...	...	...	...	2	5.0	168	403	10.8	4.0	20	0	Bahrain
...	...	...	...	...	...	81	0.8	290	2	12.9	2.3	60	0	Bangladesh
2,968.0	...	...	...	...	...	1	3.3	8[5]	275	2.5[5]	0.8[5]	0	0	Barbados
3,955.2[6]	585.5	...	...	...	...	109	11.0	2,911	282	5.7	3.3	340	280	Belgium
...	...	...	...	...	...	7	1.8	20	5	4.1[2]	...	...	...	Belize
1,233.8[7]	...	1,138	...	...	...	...	...	...	...	14.6[1]	2.6	20	0	Benin
8,201.9	182.9	...	...	1,031.5	471	—	[3]	—	—	2.1[2]	—	...	...	Bermuda
...	...	...	...	...	...	...	3.0	...	...	...	...	...	...	Bhutan
...	...	...	...	21,295.5	...	27	4.6	100[5]	17[5]	7.4[5]	1.9[5]	0	0	Bolivia
...	476.9	...	...	3,450.5	...	3	3.0	26	25	7.1	3.0	0	0	Botswana
...	...	...	13	...	...	460	3.5	1,769	12	2.1	0.7	40	110	Brazil
1,865.1	...	...	...	...	...	—	[3]	—	—	—	—	...	...	British Virgin Islands
1,097.8	117.3	126,103	279[9]	...	33,195	4[2]	...	195	837	12.8[11]	2.9[2]	...	...	Brunei
...	...	...	...	...	...	177	19.9	4,282	461	19.6	8.1	140	260	Bulgaria
...	...	...	...	...	...	9	1.4	33	4	20.2	2.8	0	0	Burkina Faso
...	645.3	...	...	...	...	210	5.9	209	5	19.5	3.3	20	0	Burma
...	...	...	...	...	...	7	1.6	41	8	16.1	3.2	0	0	Burundi
...	1,173.1	...	...	...	...	15	1.6	160	16	8.2	2.1	80	0	Cameroon
11,534.6	358.0	...	...	...	...	81	3.3	6,439	248	7.8	2.2	500	180	Canada
...	...	...	...	...	...	4	13.3	13[1]	48[1]	13.5[1]	14.9[1]	0	0	Cape Verde
11,576.8[13]	110.3	33,287	16	550.9	...	—	[3]	—	—	—	—	...	...	Cayman Islands
...	...	...	...	...	...	4	1.6	13	5	10.8	2.0	0	0	Central African Republic
...	...	...	...	...	...	4	0.8	6	1	20.5	2.4	5	0	Chad
3,753.6[13]	375.8	6,459	...	...	...	126	11.0	1,021	85	12.3	4.5	80	0	Chile
...	1,363.5[14]	...	...	...	...	4,100	4.0	34,500	32	30.8	8.6	0	1,500	China
790.4[13]	186.1	...	...	...	...	—	[3]	—	—	—	—	...	...	Christmas Island
...	...	...	...	...	...	—	[3]	—	—	—	—	...	...	Cocos (Keeling) Islands
1,308.5	418.2	...	...	...	...	70	2.5	456	15	9.4	1.2	10	0	Colombia
...	...[15]	...	...	...	...	...	2.5	2	5	15.0	...	...	...	Comoros
...	...[15]	...	...	...	...	11	6.5	79	44	7.4	3.6	10	0	Congo
...	...	...	...	...	...	—	[3]	—	—	—	—	...	...	Cook Islands
558.1	969.1[16]	...	...	952,669[16]	...	4	1.6	17	6	3.5	0.7	0	0	Costa Rica
...	150.0	2,503	...	...	...	250	25.3	1,306	126	...	5.0[5]	700	30	Cuba
489.2	177.7	35,383	...	...	...	10	14.3	83	115	11.2	3.6	20	0	Cyprus[17]
...	...	...	...	...	...	214	13.9	7,157	445	18.3	5.9	100	775	Czechoslovakia
7,941.7	594.1	67,601	...	...	13,548	30	5.9	1,482	278	4.5	2.5	150	5	Denmark
...	...	...	...	...	...	3	8.7	3	10	21.7[11]	...	...	...	Djibouti
...	446.1[18]	3,924[18]	...	18	18	...	...	...	3[4]	1.2[4]	...	...	...	Dominica
...	464.4	...	...	...	...	23	3.7	122	19	9.8[5]	1.5	0	0	Dominican Republic
...	...	...	...	...	...	39	4.6	184	21	11.0	1.6	170	0	Ecuador
4,603.0	446.7	...	...	...	...	447	9.8	2,679	56	17.4	8.3	1,700	50	Egypt
...	...	...	...	...	...	28	5.8	150	30	22.2	4.0	40	0	El Salvador
...	135.0	...	...	...	...	2	6.7	2[1]	11[1]	21.0[1]	3.4[1]	10	0	Equatorial Guinea
417.6[13]	956.4	...	...	...	...	199	6.4	381[5]	12[5]	16.8	8.6	525	0	Ethiopia
...	...	...	...	...	...	—	[3]	—	—	—	—	...	...	Faeroe Islands
...	326.2[19]	38,723	...	—[19]	—	—	[3]	—	—	—	—	...	...	Falkland Islands
1,980.8	408.9[7]	3,629	...	2,602.1[7]	...	2[5]	2.9[5]	14[5]	21[5]	4.4[5]	1.2[5]	0	0	Fiji
10,045.7	643.0	44,927	10.0	1,296.5	4,478	40	8.2	785	153	5.1	1.5	50	350	Finland

Social protection (continued)

country	social security															
	programs available, 1983					expendi-tures, 1982 (% of national budget)	finances									
	old-age invalid-ity, death	sickness and matern-ity	work injury	unem-ploy-ment	family allow-ances		year	receipts					expenditures			
								total ('000,000 natl. cur.)	insured persons (%)	em-ployers (%)	govern-ment (%)	other (%)	total ('000,000 natl. cur.)	benefits (%)	admin-istration (%)	other (%)
France	●	●	●	●	●	44.0[1]	1980	761,712.2	21.0	53.4	24.1	1.5	738,971.1	95.2	3.9	1.0
French Guiana	...	...	...	...	...	...		...	...	...	...	...	...	...	...	...
French Polynesia						...	1975									
Gabon	●	●	●		●	...	1975	6,770.0	...	...	...	...	3,670.0	...	...	...
Gambia, The			●			2.0[20]	1978						2.6	...	...	...
Gaza Strip	...	...	...	...	...	...		...	...	...	...	...	...	...	...	...
Germany, East	●	●	●		●	...	1980	29,627.0	21.9	28.3	49.7	0.1	29,627.0	99.6	0.4	—
Germany, West	●	●	●	●	●	49.7	1980	357,712.0	34.0	34.2	28.9	2.9	355,052.0	96.4	3.1	0.5
Ghana	●	●	●			5.4	1982						511.7	...	...	...
Gibraltar	●	●	...			...		...	...	...	...	...	...	...	...	...
Greece	●	●	●		●	30.6[1]	1980	242,714.0	29.7	47.3	17.0	5.9	209,443.0	95.2	4.5	0.4
Greenland	...	...	...		...	...		...	...	...	...	...	...	...	...	...
Grenada	●	●				5.0[9]	1977						1.8	...	...	...
Guadeloupe	...	...	...	...	...	...		...	...	...	...	...	...	...	...	...
Guam	...	...				...		...	...	...	...	...	...	...	...	...
Guatemala	●	●	●			3.3[2]	1980	133.4	31.6	53.1	8.2	7.1	90.9	88.3	11.7	—
Guernsey	●	●	●		●	...		...	...	...	...	...	...	...	...	...
Guinea	●	●	●			...		...	...	...	...	...	...	...	...	...
Guinea-Bissau	...	...	...		...	...		...	...	...	...	...	...	...	...	...
Guyana	●	●	●			5.5[20]	1980	85,692.0	29.4	43.0	—	27.5	18,591.0	68.9	31.1	—
Haiti	●	●	●			...	1977	60.5	—26.6—		69.9	3.5	52.4	92.7	7.3	—
Honduras	●	●	●			4.5[4]		...	...	...	...	...	...	...	...	...
Hong Kong	●			●	●	...	1982						374.0	...	...	...
Hungary	●	●	●		●	...	1980	106,644.0	14.6	41.1	43.6	0.7	106,646.0	99.5	0.5	—
Iceland	●	●	●	●	●	16.3	1981	932.0	—	14.8	85.2	—				
India	●	●	●			...	1976	30,870.4	—66.1—		22.8	11.1	17,842.9	98.4	0.9	0.7
Indonesia	●	●	●			—		...	...	...	...	...	...	...	...	...
Iran	●	●	●		●	9.2	1982	194,500.0	...	...	...	...	194,500.0	...	...	...
Iraq	●	●	●			...	1977	107.8	9.9	55.6	21.9	12.6	71.0	94.0	2.4	3.6
Ireland	●	●	●	●	●	...	1980	1,896.7	11.6	26.3	61.0	1.0	1,881.3	95.0	4.7	0.2
Isle of Man	...	...	...	...	...	...		...	...	...	...	...	...	...	...	...
Israel	●	●	●	●	●	20.9	1980	7,237.6	16.8	37.0	36.9	9.2	6,409.9	84.2	6.8	9.0
Italy	●	●	●	●	●	33.0	1980	61,563,000.0	10.8	54.8	31.9	2.6	61,318,000.0	89.8	4.3	5.9
Ivory Coast	●	●	●		●	3.1[2]	1980	34,427.0	...	...	...	...	18,864.0	...	...	...
Jamaica	●		●			3.3[9]	1980	115.9	17.2	20.7	36.8	25.3	58.3	91.0	8.9	—
Japan	●	●	●	●	●	...	1980	30,372,556.0	25.9	28.4	31.3	14.5	23,871,420.0	89.8	2.0	8.2
Jersey	...	...	...	...	...	...		...	...	...	...	...	...	...	...	...
Jordan	●		●			16.4	1982						99.2	...	...	...
Kampuchea	●	...	●			...		...	...	...	...	...	...	...	...	...
Kenya	●		●			0.2	1977	55.9	19.6	26.5	38.1	15.8	30.9	97.2	2.8	—
Kiribati	●					...		...	...	...	...	...	...	...	...	...
Korea, North	...	●	●		...	...		...	...	...	...	...	...	...	...	...
Korea, South	●	●	●			9.6	1983						535,200.0	...	...	...
Kuwait	●					8.3	1983	—					—	...	...	...
Laos	...	...	...			...		...	...	...	...	...	...	...	...	...
Lebanon	●	●	●		●	1.2[9]	1977	—					0.9	...	...	...
Lesotho	●					0.5	1983	—					4.2	...	...	...
Liberia	●	●	●			...	1977	192.9	9.1	28.7	58.7	3.5	128.2	96.2	3.2	0.5
Libya	●	●	●			...		...	...	...	...	...	...	...	...	...
Liechtenstein	●		●			...		...	...	...	...	...	...	...	...	...	...
Luxembourg	●	●	●	●	●	49.5	1980	35,758.5	23.8	37.2	25.2	13.7	32,560.9	95.9	3.3	0.8
Macau						...	1981	...	...	...	...	...	...	...	...	...
Madagascar	●	●	●		●	...	1982	19,534.0	...	...	...	...	...	...	...	...
Malawi						1.3	1982	4,690.0	...	...	...	...	...	...	...	...
Malaysia	●	●	●			4.0[1]	1980	2,130.3	—63.6—		0.3	36.0	512.7	85.3	3.4	11.3
Maldives	...	...	...	...	...	19.3	1982						2.0	...	...	...
Mali	●	●	●		●	6.8[4]	1980	4,541.0	8.5	79.4	10.7	1.4	4,837.0	58.4	32.9	8.7
Malta	●	●	●	●	●	35.5	1980	52.6	28.1	33.9	38.1	—	43.6	99.2	0.8	—
Martinique	●	...	...		●	...		...	...	...	...	...	...	...	...	...
Mauritania	●	●	●		●	3.8[4]	1979	441.0	...	...	...	...	382.0	...	...	...
Mauritius	●		●		●	18.2	1977	344.6	6.6	25.3	64.9	3.2	301.8	99.0	0.5	0.5
Mayotte	...	...	...		...	...		...	...	...	...	...	...	...	...	...
Mexico	●	●	●			10.6	1982	253,830.0	...	...	...	...	307,660.0	...	...	...
Monaco	●					...		...	...	...	...	...	...	...	...	...
Mongolia	...	...	...			...		...	...	...	...	...	...	...	...	...
Montserrat						...		...	...	...	...	...	...	...	...	...
Morocco	●	●	●		●	5.9	1980	1,446.7	—89.8—		0.2	10.0	807.6	89.3	10.7	0.1
Mozambique	...	...	...		...	...		...	...	...	...	...	...	...	...	...
Nauru	●					...		...	...	...	...	...	...	...	...	...
Nepal	●		●			0.4	1982						21.7	...	...	...
Netherlands, The	●	●	●	●	●	37.9	1980	113,621.6	33.2	33.2	24.7	8.9	95,237.9	96.5	3.4	0.1
Netherlands Antilles	●	...	●	...	...	11.4[7]	1979						29.1	...	...	...
New Caledonia						...		...	...	...	...	...	...	...	...	...
New Zealand	●	●	●	●	●	29.4	1980	3,898.6	3.1	4.7	89.7	2.4	3,469.8	98.0	1.8	0.3
Nicaragua	●	●	●		●	4.4[1]	1980	711.2	21.2	58.1	16.3	4.5	497.8	88.4	11.6	—
Niger	●	●	●		●	1.7[2]	1980	3,823.5	8.4	80.4	—	11.2	1,594.6	84.1	15.9	—
Nigeria	●	●	●			2.5[9]	1978	—					126.7	...	...	...
Niue	...	...	...			...		...	...	...	...	...	...	...	...	...
Norfolk Island						...		...	...	...	...	...	...	...	...	...
Norway	●	●	●	●	●	34.3	1980	59,512.6	21.0	34.6	42.9	1.5	57,467.2	97.9	2.1	—
Oman						—	1983						—	...	...	...
Pacific Is., Trust Territory of the	●					...		...	...	...	...	...	...	...	...	...
Pakistan	●	●	●			5.0	1982						95.0	...	...	...
Panama	●	●	●			8.3	1977	213.3	23.8	49.7	18.3	8.2	169.4	89.1	10.9	—
Papua New Guinea	●					0.5	1982	—					3.1	...	...	...

police protection, 1980–81			fire protection, 1980–81			military protection, 1983								country
						manpower[c]		expenditure				arms trade ('000,000 U.S.$)		
offenses (reported to police) per 100,000 population	population per police officer[a]	government expenditure per 1,000 population (U.S.$)	fire alarms per 100,000 population	population per fire fighter[b]	government expenditure per 1,000 population	total ('000)	per 1,000 population	total '000,000 U.S.$	per capita	% of national budget	% of GDP or GNP	imports	exports	
4,903.1	632.0	...	...	2,838.6	...	578	10.6	23,793	417	9.3	4.2	60	4,300	France
...	...	...	...	...	...	—	3	108	706	...	...	...	...	French Guiana
...	...	...	...	...	...	—	3	—	—	...	...	...	...	French Polynesia
...	812.0	...	...	...	...	7	7.8	79	84	5.0	2.7	10	0	Gabon
...	...	...	...	...	...	—	0.0	—	—	...	—	0	0	Gambia, The
														Gaza Strip
730.0	...	...	...	...	...	240	14.4	9,806	563	11.9	6.4	760	130	Germany, East
6,603.0	...	...	...	4,328.2	...	496	8.1	23,565	367	10.7	3.4	430	1,800	Germany, West
...	624.0	...	...	...	...	8	0.6	213[5]	16[5]	6.1[5]	0.7[5]	10	0	Ghana
5,759.3	167.2	...	776.4	224.4	...	—	3	—	—	...	—	...	...	Gibraltar
3,787.0	303.3	...	...	...	...	177	17.9	2,526	244	15.0	6.2	470	0	Greece
12,460.5	339.6[21]	109,098	...	3,579.4[21]	...	—	3	...	...	—	—	...	...	Greenland
1,457.2	218.4	15,202	...	...	...	...	...	...	...	13.9[4]	...	...	...	Grenada
...	...	...	...	...	...	—	3	—	—	—	—	...	...	Guadeloupe
...	...	...	...	...	...	—	3	—	—	—	—	...	...	Guam
...	673.1	...	...	...	...	19	2.4	209	25	16.4	2.4	5	0	Guatemala
...	...	...	...	...	...	...	...	...	...	...	...	...	...	Guernsey
...	1,143.9	...	...	...	...	52	9.6	51[1]	10[1]	10.2	4.9	0	0	Guinea
...	...	...	...	...	...	9	11.3	9[5]	11[5]	8.4[5]	4.5[5]	0	0	Guinea-Bissau
5,287.0	...	...	...	...	...	7	8.8	23	29	6.5	5.4	10	0	Guyana
700.6	...	...	...	...	...	8	1.5	24	4	8.9	1.4	0	0	Haiti
...	1,040.0	...	...	...	...	14	3.4	47[4]	16[4]	11.8[4]	2.4[4]	0	0	Honduras
1,600.0	219.3	...	288.3	900.5	9,589	...	2.0[3]	...	...	4.4[3,12]	1.3[2,3]	...	...	Hong Kong
1,219.4	...[15]	...	88.5	...	...	105	9.8	3,134	281	7.6	4.3	30	190	Hungary
1,549.8	...	...	...	...	...	—	3	—	—	—	—	0	0	Iceland
206.2	820.0	...	...	...	...	1,120[5]	1.6[5]	6,546	8	17.6	3.5	950	0	India
192.6	1,319.3	766	...	...	...	280	1.7	2,649	15	13.7	2.8	140	...	Indonesia
...	...[22]	21,088	...	...	...	470	11.1	5,520	124	14.9	5.0	750	0	Iran
518.0	193.5	...	...	...	...	500	34.5	11,900	787	24.9[4]	47.2	5,100	0	Iraq
2,143.8	489.1	58,654	...	...	...	18	5.1	303	83	2.7	1.8	0	0	Ireland
...	...	...	...	...	...	...	...	...	...	...	...	...	...	Isle of Man
6,333.7	191.1	23,099	425.0	...	...	180	45.0	6,229	1,494	24.2	29.0	370	220	Israel
3,453.7	285.7	...	...	...	...	498	8.8	9,609	162	4.7	2.7	170	1,000	Italy
942.3[4]	...	...	...	...	...	14	1.5	85	8	4.1	1.3	30	0	Ivory Coast
2,281.1	659.7	24,259	...	...	2,915	3	1.3	37	15	2.6	1.3	0	0	Jamaica
1,293.6	555.5	55,594	61.0	956.8	25,990	241	2.0	11,500	92	5.5	1.0	750	200	Japan
...	...	...	...	...	...	...	...	...	...	...	...	...	...	Jersey
1,040.6	277.8	27,536	...	...	...	68	26.2	645	238	29.5	14.9	1,100	10	Jordan
...	1,976.6	...	...	...	...	20	3.3	67[23]	10[23]	...	11.0[23]	60	0	Kampuchea
402.9	...	...	...	...	...	18	1.0	138	7	6.9	2.1	50	0	Kenya
2,471.5	425.1	...	...	...	...									Kiribati
...	...	...	...	...	...	784	40.8	3,600	179	29.7[5]	16.7	110	300	Korea, North
1,657.5	441.4	...	15.1	5,653.0	...	602	14.5	4,717	109	27.9	5.8	290	370	Korea, South
617.3	...	...	...	...	...	13	7.6	1,173	662	9.2	4.0	100	0	Kuwait
...	275.2	...	...	...	...	46	12.8	50[4]	18[4]	29.1[23]	...	40	0	Laos
517.3	...	...	...	...	...	25	9.6	437	161	20.0	8.2	240	0	Lebanon
2,640.2	...	...	...	...	...	2	1.4	23	16	10.7	3.7	5	0	Lesotho
...	1,570.0	...	...	...	...	5	2.4	27	12	7.3	2.8	10	0	Liberia
1,092.1[4]	...[15]	26,667	...	...	...	68	19.4	4,223	1,157	26.6	17.5	1,900	70	Libya
...	...	...	...	...	...	...	24	—	—	—	—	...	...	Liechtenstein
2,863.8	434.6	15,067	299.2	3,215.8	...	1	2.5	414	106	2.6	1.0	0	0	Luxembourg
...	...	...	17.2	1,384.6	...	...	...	16	61	16.9	...	...	...	Macau
...	2,904.7	...	...	...	...	29	3.1	61	6	10.2	2.1	10	0	Madagascar
993.4	1,666.7	...	...	...	...	6	0.9	23	3	6.0	1.7	0	0	Malawi
554.7	292.9	...	...	...	...	105	7.0	1,432	91	11.8	5.2	230	0	Malaysia
713.5[13]	35,708.0[9]	2,003	...	—[9]	...	...	6.4[15]	...	—	—	—	...	...	Maldives
...	157.0[15,18]	...	...	...[18]	...	11	1.5	30	3	7.9	2.7	0	0	Mali
1,355.6	276.9	34,223	...	...	...	1	2.5	15	36	2.5	1.1	0	0	Malta
...	1,170.0	...	...	...	...	—	3	—	—	—	—	...	...	Martinique
...	...	...	...	...	...	16	10.0	40	24	17.1	5.8	0	0	Mauritania
...	243.6	...	...	...	...	1	1.0	2	2	0.8	0.2	0	0	Mauritius
...	...	...	...	...	...	—	3	—	—	—	—	...	...	Mayotte
314.6	...	...	23.7	...	...	131	1.7	872	11	1.4	0.6	50	0	Mexico
4,600.0	...	...	...	...	...	...	...	...	...	...	...	...	...	Monaco
...	116.7[25]	...	...	...	...	38	21.1	135[9]	133[9]	15.9	...	30	0	Mongolia
5,625.7[13]	153.6	16,901	...	...	...	...	3	...	...	...	...	...	...	Montserrat
589.1	...[15]	...	...	...	...	135	5.9	1,318	55	17.2	8.2	320	0	Morocco
...	...	...	...	...	...	32	2.5	172[5]	13[5]	29.1	3.5	260	5	Mozambique
...	106.2	...	...	...	...	...	...	...	...	...	...	...	...	Nauru
...	1,000.0	497	...	...	...	25	1.5	27	1	5.5	1.1	5	0	Nepal
4,939.3	552.7	100,727	203.9	...	...	104	7.2	4,673	311	5.5	3.2	670	120	Netherlands, The
3,802.2[26]	...	...	...	...	...	—	3	—	—	0.4[3,4]	...	...	...	Netherlands Antilles
...	...	...	...	...	...	—	3	—	—	—	—	...	...	New Caledonia
11,090.8	642.1	38,418	652.2	1,262.6	...	13	4.1	519	155	4.7	2.2	40	0	New Zealand
...	93.0[27]	...	...	...	...	46	16.4	272	93	16.5	10.2	130	0	Nicaragua
...	2,352.9[28]	...	...	...	...	5	0.8	12	2	3.7	0.9	0	0	Niger
383.5	1,142.1	...	...	...	...	222	2.6	1,723	19	11.7	2.5	300	0	Nigeria
...	274.7	22,816	...	...	...	—	3	—	—	—	—	...	...	Niue
...	620.7	37,420	...	—	...	—	3	—	—	—	—	...	...	Norfolk Island
2,980.3	661.2	78,262	...	1,659.0	27,931	41	10.0	1,844	431	10.1	3.2	240	40	Norway
161.8[4]	131.7	...	...	...	...	20	18.2	1,944	1,695	49.1	27.9	290	0	Oman
...	324.2[29]	...	...	...	...	—	3	—	—	—	—	...	...	Pacific Is., Trust. Territory of the
205.7	722.2	1,954	...	...	...	584	6.2	1,984	20	27.9	5.4	410	300	Pakistan
448.3	...[15]	...	...	...	...	11	5.5	60[5]	31	4.7	1.5	0	0	Panama
1,395.7	721.4	...	...	...	...	3	0.9	30	9	3.0	1.2	0	0	Papua New Guinea

Social protection (continued)

country	social security programs available, 1983 — old-age invalidity, death	sickness and maternity	work injury	unemployment	family allowances	expenditures, 1982 (% of national budget)	year	receipts total ('000,000 natl. cur.)	insured persons (%)	employers (%)	government (%)	other (%)	expenditures total ('000,000 natl. cur.)	benefits (%)	administration (%)	other (%)
Paraguay	●	●	●		●	29.7	1982	14,669.0	...	...	...	...	13,366.0	...	...	...
Peru	●	●	●			0.2[1]	1981		...	...	...	...	2,770.0	...	...	...
Philippines	●	●	●			0.9	1980	4,487.5	30.3	42.2	—	27.5	1,725.9	81.2	18.8	—
Pitcairn Island	...	...	...	...	...	...										
Poland	●	...	...	●	●	...	1980	325,454.0	2.1	52.2	44.2	1.5	304,600.0	98.8	0.5	0.7
Portugal	●	●	●	●	●	26.8[23]	1980	126,998.7	26.2	64.2	9.3	0.4	121,222.9	90.1	9.9	—
Puerto Rico	●	●	●	●	●	...	1980		...	...	...	...	1,041.3	100.0	—	—
Qatar	...	...	...	...	...	...			...	...	...	...		...	...	...
Réunion	...	...	...	...	●	...			...	...	...	...		...	...	...
Romania	●	●	●		●	10.4[4]	1980	59,386.7	...	54.4	45.6	—	51,743.8	100.0	—	—
Rwanda	●		●			2.9[2]	1977	593.9	24.9	41.4	25.1	8.6	191.5	88.2	11.4	0.4
St. Christopher and Nevis	...	...	...	...	...	...			...	...	...	...		...	...	...
St. Helena and Ascension	...	...	...	...	...	...			...	...	...	...		...	...	...
St. Lucia	●	●	●			...	1983	7.9	...	...	...	...	2.0	...	...	...
St. Pierre and Miquelon	...	...	...	...	...	...			...	...	...	...		...	...	...
St. Vincent and the Grenadines	●		●			2.9	1981	—	...	...	...	...	—	...	...	...
San Marino	...	...	...	...	...	...			...	...	...	...		...	...	...
São Tomé and Príncipe	...	...	...	...	...	...			...	...	...	...		...	...	...
Saudi Arabia	●		●			...			...	...	...	...		...	...	...
Senegal	●	●	●		●	4.4	1980	13,903.2	18.1	67.0	5.5	9.5	11,223.9	78.8	8.6	12.6
Seychelles	●	●	●			6.8[9]	1977	—	...	...	...	...	8.2	...	...	...
Sierra Leone	●		●			1.2[12]	1977	10.5	—26.7—		73.3	...	10.0	100.0	...	...
Singapore	●		●			1.4	1980	2,244.8	36.7	44.4	0.2	18.7	786.7	89.0	1.4	9.6
Solomon Islands	●					1.2[20]			...	...	...	...		...	...	...
Somalia			●			1.7[2]	1978	—	...	...	...	...	34.2	...	...	...
South Africa	●	●	●	●	●	...	1981	236.0	...	...	...	...	238.0	...	...	...
Bophuthatswana	...	...	...	...	...	...		...	...	...	...	...	...	...	...	...
Ciskei	...	...	...	...	...	...		...	...	...	...	...	...	...	...	...
Transkei	...	...	...	...	...	...		...	...	...	...	...	...	...	...	...
Venda	...	...	...	...	...	...		...	...	...	...	...	...	...	...	...
South West Africa/Namibia	...	...	...	...	...	...			...	...	...	...		...	...	...
Spain	●	●	●	●	●	61.0[1]	1980	2,400,940.9	12.4	70.7	15.8	1.1	2,426,506.1	95.7	2.7	1.6
Sri Lanka	●		●			12.3	1980	2,092.8	—38.8—		43.6	17.6	1,141.8	95.0	4.1	0.1
Sudan, The	●		●			2.2	1982		...	...	...	...	26.0	...	...	...
Suriname	...	...	...	...	...	6.9[7]	1980	46.0	25.4	32.0	42.6	—	37.1	99.5	0.5	—
Swaziland	●		●			...	1981		...	...	...	...		...	...	...
Sweden	●	●	●	●	●	46.9	1980	183,851.7	1.0	45.9	45.3	7.8	167,315.8	97.5	2.5	—
Switzerland	●	●	●	●	●	49.5	1980	25,571.1	41.2	25.5	25.5	7.8	23,415.8	93.2	2.8	4.0
Syria	●	●	●			8.2[1]	1981	—	...	...	...	...	2,086.0	...	...	...
Taiwan	●	●	●			...			...	...	...	...		...	...	...
Tanzania	●	●	●			1.1[4]	1981	—	...	...	...	...	163.0	...	...	...
Thailand		●	●			2.8	1983		...	...	...	...	4,734	...	...	...
Togo	●	●	●		●	8.9	1980	4,814.0	10.4	77.8	—	11.9	2,350.0	78.1	21.3	0.6
Tokelau	...	...	...	...	...	...			...	...	...	...		...	...	...
Tonga	...	...	...	...	...	...			...	...	...	...		...	...	...
Trinidad and Tobago	●	●	●			6.0[1]	1980	196.1	18.2	36.0	26.9	18.9	110.3	85.4	13.8	0.9
Tunisia	●	●	●	●	●	9.7	1977	124.5	25.6	53.9	3.7	16.8	67.8	90.0	6.1	3.9
Turkey	●	●	●			0.5[1]	1980	218,265.1	27.9	49.9	11.3	10.8	183,922.7	95.5	4.1	0.5
Turks and Caicos Islands	...	...	...	...	...	...			...	...	...	...		...	...	...
Tuvalu	...	...	...	...	...	...	1981		...	...	...	...	0.1	67.6	32.4	—
Uganda	●	●	●			1.5	1983		...	...	...	...	804.0	...	...	...
U.S.S.R.	●	●	●		●	...	1977	54,271.0	—	—	96.4	3.6	54,271.0	100.0	—	—
United Arab Emirates	...	...	...	...	...	2.4	1982		...	...	...	...	482.4	...	...	...
United Kingdom	●	●	●	●	●	25.6[4]	1980	35,698.0	15.8	26.5	54.9	2.9	34,004.0	95.2	2.8	2.0
United States	●	●	●	●	●	33.5	1980	370,597.0	23.4	40.4	29.8	6.4	329,582.0	96.1	3.1	0.8
Uruguay	●	●	●	●	●	54.2	1980	9,779.5	25.1	34.0	38.3	2.6	7,550.5	91.5	7.7	0.8
Vanuatu	...	...	...	...	...	...			...	...	...	...		...	...	...
Venezuela	●	●	●			7.0	1980	4,259.3	26.8	53.5	6.8	12.9	3,336.6	86.0	14.0	—
Vietnam	●	●	●			...			...	...	...	...		...	...	...
Virgin Islands (U.S.)	●	●	●			...			...	...	...	...		...	...	...
Wallis and Futuna	...	...	...	...	...	...			...	...	...	...		...	...	...
West Bank	...	...	...	...	...	...			...	...	...	...		...	...	...
Western Sahara	...	...	...	...	...	...			...	...	...	...		...	...	...
Western Samoa	●		...	...	...	...			...	...	...	...		...	...	...
Yemen (Aden)	...	...	...	...	...	...			...	...	...	...		...	...	...
Yemen (Şan'ā')	...	...	...	...	...	—	1983	—	...	...	...	...		...	...	...
Yugoslavia	●	●	●	●	●	7.2[1]	1981		...	...	...	...	14,450.0	...	...	...
Zaire	●		●			...	1982	98.6	...	...	...	...	108.4	...	...	...
Zambia	●		●	●		0.4	1977	119.8	—40.7—		47.9	11.4	89.4	95.4	4.6	—
Zimbabwe	●		●		...	5.1	1980	9.4	—	48.8	26.0	25.2	6.8	64.5	30.6	4.8

offenses (reported to police) per 100,000 population	population per police officer[a]	government expenditure per 1,000 population (U.S.$)	fire alarms per 100,000 population	population per fire fighter[b]	government expenditure per 1,000 population	manpower[c] total ('000)	per 1,000 population	expenditure total '000,000 U.S.$	per capita	% of national budget	% of GDP or GNP	arms trade imports	arms trade exports	country
...	312.5	...	...	...	...	16	4.6	89	24	19.3	1.9	0	0	Paraguay
424.4	508.6	...	...	...	...	167	9.0	1,065	54	26.2	5.6	180	0	Peru
134	1,158.0	2,423	...	9,094.1	...	157	2.9	771	13	15.1	1.9	40	20	Philippines
...	...	...	...	...	...	—	[3]	—	—	—	—	...	...	Pitcairn Island
1,292.2	350.0[30]	...	55.5	...	...	430	11.7	12,282	321	23.1	5.8	410	650	Poland
7,467.4	624.0[31]	...	...	...	...	93	9.3	814	78	9.9	3.5	50	60	Portugal
5,484.0	380.6	...	229.4	2,869.4	...	—	[3]	—	—	—	—	50	0	Puerto Rico
1,538.7	[15]	...	...	...	...	6	20.0	604[2]	3,020[2]	20.1[2]	9.1[2]	230	0	Qatar
...	216.7	...	...	...	...	—	4.6[3]	—	—	—	—	...	...	Réunion
...	...	...	...	...	...	244	10.8	5,159	219	21.2	4.7	50	450	Romania
358.9	...	...	...	...	...	5	0.9	21	3	10.1	1.4	0	0	Rwanda
...	[18]	...	...	...	...	...	...	...	...	...	...	...	...	St. Christopher and Nevis
...	321.7[7,32]	8,368	...	5,147.0[7,32]	—	—	[3]	—	—	—	—	...	...	St. Helena and Ascension
...	240.3	...	...	...	...	...	...	...	...	...	...	...	...	St. Lucia
...	...	...	...	...	...	—	[3]	—	—	—	—	...	...	St. Pierre and Miquelon
...	204.5[18]	13,198[18]	...	...[18]	...[18]	...	...	...	...	...	6.1[3]	...	...	St. Vincent and the Grenadines
...	...	...	...	...	...	...	...	...	...	...	...	...	...	San Marino
...	500.0	...	...	...	...	...	0.0	...	...	2.5[2]	1.8[2]	0	0	São Tomé and Príncipe
...	280.0	131,140	...	...	...	55	5.3	27,192	2,508	29.6	24.3	3,300	0	Saudi Arabia
...	732.7	...	...	...	...	18	2.9	60	9	9.1	2.3	0	0	Senegal
8,515.2	142.9	...	...	2,416.7	...	1	14.7	8	119	...	...	5	...	Seychelles
...	782.1	...	...	...	...	6	1.6	11	3	6.2	0.9	5	0	Sierra Leone
1,030.8	234.8	...	367.5	2,841.0	...	60	24.0	955	366	17.1	5.8	170	20	Singapore
...	614.3	5,112	...	...	...	...	...	...	...	...	...	...	...	Solomon Islands
...	537.5[18]	...	...	...[18]	...	48	7.7	114	17	22.7	9.1	60	0	Somalia
1,451.0[6]	867.1	28,460	...	...	...	77	2.5	3,132	97	17.8	4.3	0	0	South Africa
...	...	...	...	...	...	...	...	...	...	...	...	...	...	Bophuthatswana
...	...	...	...	...	...	...	...	...	...	...	...	...	...	Ciskei
...	...	...	...	...	...	...	...	...	...	...	...	...	...	Transkei
...	...	...	...	...	...	...	...	...	...	...	...	...	...	Venda
...	...	...	...	...	...	...	[3]	...	...	...	...	...	...	South West Africa/Namibia
1,131.4	362.0[33]	...	...	...	...	340	8.9[3]	4,070	102	9.0	2.1	200	340	Spain
...	861.6	...	...	...	...	19	1.2	76	4	3.9	1.5	0	0	Sri Lanka
2,843.6	740.7	12,049	...	...	...	86	4.3	180	8	9.0	1.7	80	0	Sudan, The
...	...	...	...	...	...	2	5.0	28	68	...	2.2	0	0	Suriname
...	609.8	21,249	...	...	...	3	5.0	18	29	11.5	3.1	0	0	Swaziland
11,159.9	327.7	176,110	189.0	1,234.8	...	68	8.2	3,332	385	6.5	3.3	110	40	Sweden
...	...	135,820	...	...	...	28	4.3	1,961	289	10.2[5]	1.9	290	330	Switzerland
394.6	1,150.0	...	...	...	...	222	22.7	2,138	209	29.8	13.0	1,700	30	Syria
296.8	...	...	...	1,036.3	...	454	24.1	3,925	200	40.2	7.5	460	5	Taiwan
656.6	1,333.3	1,953	...	...	...	43	2.1	122	5	6.3	2.5	30	0	Tanzania
1,279.2	527.8	4,262	...	...	...	250	4.9	1,539	29	19.9	3.9	320	0	Thailand
...	...	...	...	...	...	6	2.1	17	6	6.8	2.4	0	0	Togo
...	214.3	...	...	...	...	—	[3]	—	—	—	—	...	...	Tokelau
...	409.5	7,139	...	...	...	...	[34]	—	5[1]	...	2.7[2]	—	...	Tonga
1,033.7	284.2	...	...	...	...	2	1.8	232	203	5.3	3.2	0	0	Trinidad and Tobago
...	337.8	...	...	...	...	28	4.0	256	35	9.0	2.9	40	0	Tunisia
86.7[13]	1,571.4	...	...	...	...	824	16.7	2,840	55	21.4	4.9	600	230	Turkey
...	113.1[9,18]	20,611	...	...[18]	—	—	[3]	—	—	—	—	...	...	Turks and Caicos Islands
...	294.0	13,069	...	—	...	—	0.0	—	—	—	—	...	...	Tuvalu
...	1,093.3	1,173	...	...	...	13	0.9	102	8	19.6	1.7[20]	30	0	Uganda
...	1,045.4[35]	...	...	...	...	4,400	16.1	258,000	908	40.8	14.0	1,150	9,800	U.S.S.R.
1,500.7	136.0	...	...	...	...	49	40.8	1,867	1,492	36.4	7.9	40	10	United Arab Emirates
5,459.0[36]	400.0	79,281[36]	...	1,427.6	18,439[36]	333	5.9	27,444	470	13.2	5.4	650	1,600	United Kingdom
5,900.0	458.5	73,687	...	1,062.1	27,469	2,222	9.5	217,154	888	25.4	6.6	500	10,600	United States
...	176.5	...	...	...	...	30	10.3	283	93	12.4	3.3	10	0	Uruguay
...	445.0	...	...	...	...	...	...	...	...	...	...	...	...	Vanuatu
923.7	324.3	...	...	...	...	56	3.3	920	52	5.0	1.3	80	0	Venezuela
...	...	...	...	...	...	1,200	20.8	...	...	...	10.5[2]	775	0	Vietnam
3,798[7]	315.0	201,193	980	676.2	...	—	[3]	—	—	—	—	...	...	Virgin Islands (U.S.)
...	...	...	...	...	...	—	[3]	—	—	—	—	...	...	Wallis and Futuna
...	...	...	...	...	...	...	...	...	...	...	...	...	...	West Bank
...	...	...	...	...	...	—	[3]	—	—	—	—	...	...	Western Sahara
...	...	6,997	...	...	...	...	...	...	...	...	...	...	...	Western Samoa
...	1,440.0	...	...	...	...	25	11.9	179	82	21.0	17.4	310	0	Yemen (Aden)
...	500.0	1,905	...	...	...	22	3.9	599	100	32.0	15.4	260	0	Yemen (Ṣan'ā)
1,116.1	...	...	...	...	...	259	11.4	2,309	97	43.7[1]	3.7	130	320	Yugoslavia
...	1,409.1	...	...	...	...	42	1.3	82	2	4.3	1.5	30	0	Zaire
2,714.1	538.1	7,141	...	...	...	16	2.5	451[2]	92[2]	30.6[2]	15.1[2]	0	0	Zambia
...	750.0	12,457	...	...	...	46	5.7	403	47	11.9	6.4	20	0	Zimbabwe

[1]1981. [2]1980. [3]Political dependency; defense is the responsibility of the administering power. [4]1979. [5]1982. [6]Incomplete total. [7]1976. [8]All social services. [9]1977. [10]Pensions only. [11]1984. [12]1983. [13]Offenses disposed of in court. [14]Local officers only. [15]Armed forces perform police functions. [16]1973. [17]Excludes Turkish-occupied Cyprus. [18]Police function includes fire services. [19]1972. [20]1978. [21]1970. [22]340 in urban areas; 272 in rural. [23]1975. [24]Military defense is the responsibility of Switzerland. [25]Includes frontier guards. [26]Aruba and Curaçao only. [27]Includes civilian militia. [28]Includes paramilitary forces. [29]Marshall Islands and Palau only. [30]Militia only. [31]Public security police only. [32]Excludes Ascension. [33]Paramilitary forces. [34]Military defense is the responsibility of New Zealand. [35]MVD (internal security) only. [36]England and Wales only.

Education

This table presents international data on education arranged to provide comparability among the different types of educational systems in the nations of the world. The principal data are, naturally, numbers of students, teachers, and schools, arranged by four principal levels of education—the first, or primary; the general second-level (secondary); vocational second-level; and third level (higher). These data are supplemented by an indicator of each country's capability to educate children who are potentially educable in the age group usually represented at each level. At the first and second level this is given as a net enrollment ratio and at the third level as a gross enrollment ratio. Two additional comparative measures are given at the third level: students per 100,000 population and proportion (percent) of adults over age 25 who have achieved some level of higher or postsecondary education. Data are confined as far as possible to those who have completed their educations and are no longer in school. No enrollment ratio is provided for vocational training at the second level because of the great variation worldwide in what constitutes vocational training (electronics training in a developed country such as West Germany, for example, might be at a level that would qualify as higher education in a less developed country), in the need of countries to promote and direct students into vocational programs (to support national development), and, most particularly, in the age range of students that normally constitute a national vocational system (some will be as young as 14, having just completed a primary cycle; others will be in their mid-50s, either learning a skill for the first time or retraining to acquire a new skill). For such reasons, it is not possible to construct a good comparative measure of overall national vocational programs.

At each level of education, differences in national statistical practice, in national educational structure, and in the kind and extent of public-private institutional mix, training and deployment of teachers, and tim-ing of cycles of enrollment or completion of particular levels of grades all contribute to the problems of comparability between national educational systems.

Even something as basic as reporting the number of schools is not simply a matter of counting red-brick buildings with classrooms in them. Often the resources of a less developed country are such that temporary or outdoor facilities are all that can be afforded, while in a developed but sparsely settled country students might have to travel 80 km (50 mi) a day to find a classroom with 20 students of the same age, leading to the institution of measures such as traveling teachers, radio instruction at home under the supervision of parents, or similar systems.

Such difficulties also limit the comparability of statistics on numbers of teachers, and there may be the further complications that many at any level must work part-time, or that the institutions in which they work may perform a mixture of functions that do not break down into the tidy categories a table of this sort requires (a business school training secretaries must teach language skills as well as typing skills; a general secondary school may have a number of educators dedicated full- or part-time to the teaching of industrial arts or athletics). Separating data for students and teachers in teacher-training programs is particularly difficult, since in certain countries teacher training is defined as higher education, in others as a vocational form of secondary training, and so on. For purposes of this table, teacher training at the secondary level has been treated as vocational education. At the higher level, teacher training is assumed to be one more variety of specialization in higher education itself.

The number of students may conceal great variation in what each country defines as a particular educational "level." Many countries do, indeed, have a primary system comprised of grades 1 through 6 that passes its students on to some kind of post-primary education. But the age of intake,

Education

country	year	first level (primary)					general second level (secondary)					vocational second level[a]	
		schools	teachers[c]	students[d]	student/ teacher ratio	net enrollment ratio	schools	teachers[c]	students[d]	student/ teacher ratio	net enrollment ratio	schools	teachers[c]
Afghanistan	1982	3,820	35,364	1,115,993	31.6	30[1]	447	6,170	124,488	20.2	...	45	1,314
Albania	1983	1,617	26,440	532,300	20.1	...	23[2]	1,250	21,900	10.2	...	242[2]	3,750
Algeria	1983	9,864	99,648	3,241,924	32.5	81[2]	1,429	53,261	1,280,719	24.0	28[4]	713	2,292[3]
American Samoa	1984	32	328[1,5]	7,525	18.0[1,5]	...	8	132[1,5]	3,319[1]	21.2[1,5]	...	1[2]	4[2]
Andorra	1980	12	305	4,711	15.4	...	1	120[6]	2,134	...	...	8	...
Angola	1982	7,026	40,027	1,258,858	31.5	...	182[7]	3,870	132,205	34.2	...	68[7]	410
Anguilla	1982	6	61	1,487	24.4	...	1	20	473	23.7	...	...	...
Antigua and Barbuda	1983	48	426	9,933	23.3	...	16	331	4,197	12.7	...	1	18[8]
Argentina[e]	1984	20,619	218,520	4,430,513	20.3	...	1,987	86,874	656,521	7.6	...	3,117	119,309
Australia	1983	8,336	94,224	1,809,035	19.2	100[3]	1,572	93,273	1,206,771	12.9	82[3]	373	44,776
Austria	1985	3,770	32,492	352,369	10.8	87[2]	1,715	50,613	515,012	10.2	68[9]	1,241	22,157
Bahamas, The	1983	187	1,972	37,097	18.8	...	38	1,334	23,202	17.4	...	...	92[6]
Bahrain	1981	114	2,963	48,406	16.3	78[2]	21	951	23,727	24.9	49[2]	5	233
Bangladesh	1984	43,865	183,793	9,643,000	50.1	61[1]	7,894	81,284	2,191,000	27.0	...	657	13,991
Barbados	1983	139	1,492[5]	34,848	52.5	100[3]	36	1,281[5]	26,552	...	85[3]	6[3]	...
Belgium	1983	2,261	24,106	814,089	33.8	94[3]	759	56,719	848,590	15.0	83[1]	209	6,364
Belize	1984	225	1,515	37,753	24.9	...	24	491	6,532	13.3	...	5[11]	58[11]
Benin	1982	2,480	10,381	404,297	38.9	...	...	1,215[12]	83,207[1]	...	...	...	...
Bermuda	1985	22	312	5,413	17.3	...	13	350	4,134	11.8	...	1	52
Bhutan	1983	136	1,167	41,372	35.5	8[4]	32	251	3,109	12.4	...	4	143
Bolivia	1983	8,514	50,703	1,154,819	22.8	77[2]	845	8,091	174,982	21.6	16[2]	...	...
Botswana	1984	512	6,794	209,772	30.9	84[1]	58	1,216	27,364	22.5	17[1]	26	69
Brazil	1983	190,917	967,975	24,555,789	25.4	76[4]	8,853	180,354	2,944,097	16.3	13[12]	...	...
British Virgin Islands	1984	24	104[5]	2,325	17.9[5]	...	4	74	1,013	13.7	...	—	—
Brunei	1984	178	2,131	34,373	16.1	...	28	1,526	18,565	12.2	...	7[11]	275[11]
Bulgaria	1984	750	5,037	68,314	13.6	98[3]	2,741	65,158	1,129,248	17.3	70[3]	30	13,205
Burkina Faso	1984	1,037	4,796	276,732	57.7	18[3]	79	1,553	43,001	27.7	2[3]	27	484
Burma	1984	27,499	104,754	4,696,289	44.8	65[9]	2,338	41,668	1,210,329	29.0	16[9]	53	1,314
Burundi	1984	875	6,164	302,611	49.1	22[1]	25	475	7,854	16.5	2[1]	36	594
Cameroon	1984	5,582	31,030	1,563,852	50.4	75[4]	365	6,795	218,057	32.1	16[2]	199	2,974
Canada	1986	15,459[13]	269,775[13]	4,948,110[13]	18.3[13]	95[3]	13	13	13	13	85[1]	...	...
Cape Verde	1983	436	1,459	50,000	34.3	...	16	603	10,454	17.3	...	4	76
Cayman Islands	1986	15	145	2,077	14.3	...	8	120[5]	2,265	16.4[5]	...	1	9
Central African Republic	1984	853	4,263	291,444	68.4	56[1]	...	616	52,417	85.1	...	...	90
Chad	1976	783	2,610	210,882	77.0	25	...	590	18,382	31.2	...	...	...
Chile	1983	8,858	62,746[3]	2,139,155	...	...	1,282	...	541,739	...	...	347	...
China	1982	880,516	5,505,000	139,720,000	25.4	...	101,649	2,871,000	45,285,000	15.8	...	3,076	127,300
Christmas Island	1985	2	30	261	8.7	...	1	12	114	9.5	...	1	7
Cocos (Keeling) Islands	1984	2	8	125	15.6	...	1	3	22	7.3	...	...	...
Colombia	1983	33,974	132,210	4,065,540	30.8	...	4,369	91,646	1,846,458	20.1	...	...	...
Comoros	1981	236	1,292	59,709	46.2	...	32	434	13,528	31.2	...	4	27
Congo	1981	1,310	7,186	390,676	54.4	...	122	3,649	168,718	46.2	...	36	1,468
Cook Islands	1984	28	163	2,695	16.5	...	8	169	2,551	15.1	...	...	...
Costa Rica	1983	3,511	11,615	343,800	29.6	91[3]	242	8,213	153,971	18.7	41[3]	...	...
Cuba	1983	11,213	83,358	1,363,078	16.4	98[3]	1,319	65,101	774,410	11.9	61[12]	431	23,098
Cyprus	1985	396	2,193	47,381	21.6	...	93	2,644	43,511	16.5	...	16	492
Czechoslovakia	1985	6,398	94,404	2,037,121	21.6	...	342	9,302	138,436	14.9	...	565	16,748
Denmark	1984	2,892	66,008	735,188	11.2	...	165	7,897	82,583	10.5	...	271[14]	...
Djibouti	1984	52	496	21,847	44.0	...	9	211	4,791	22.7	...	10	123
Dominica	1983	58	635	18,370	28.9	...	8	145	3,234	22.3	...	1	13

the willingness (or economic ability) of parents to send their children or to permit them to finish that level, or the need to withdraw the children seasonally for agricultural work all make even a simple enrollment figure difficult to assess in isolation. All of these difficulties are compounded when a country has instruction in more than one language, or when its educational establishment is so small that higher, sometimes even secondary, education cannot take place within the country, as is the case with a number of the less developed countries or among the smaller island nations of the Pacific. Enrollment figures in this table may, therefore, include students enrolled outside the country.

With all of the limitations to the comparability of the statistics referred to above, the student-teacher ratio does, nevertheless, provide a fairly representative measure of the true ratio of trained educators to the enrolled educable. In general, at each level of education both students and teachers have been counted on the basis of full-time enrollment or employment, or full-time equivalent when country statistics permit. At the primary and secondary levels, net enrollment ratio is the ratio of the number of children within the usual age group for a particular level who are actually enrolled to the total number of children in that age group ($\times$ 100). This ratio is usually less than (occasionally, equal to) 100 and is the most accurate measure of the completeness of enrollment at that particular level. It is not always, however, the best indication of utilization of that particular level. Utilization is best seen in a gross enrollment ratio, which compares total enrollment (of all ages) to the population within the normal age limits for that level. For a country with substantial adult literacy or general educational programs for which both kinds of data are available, the difference may be striking: typically, for a less developed country, even one with a good net enrollment ratio of 90 to 95, the gross enrollment ratio may be 20, 25, even 30% higher, indicating the heavy

use made by the country of facilities and teachers at that level. In this table, however, gross enrollment ratio is provided only at the third level because of the wide range of ages that are typically represented in higher educational enrollment in any particular country.

Literacy data provided here have been compiled as far as possible from data for the population age 15 and over for the best comparability internationally, even though many countries work from quite different assumptions about the best way to measure literacy for their purposes. The age cutoffs may be much different—as low as 6 or 8 years or as high as legal majority in the country concerned. The standards of what constitutes literacy may also differ markedly; sometimes completion of a certain number of years of school is taken to constitute literacy; elsewhere it may mean only the ability to read or write at a minimal level testable by a census taker; in other countries quite sophisticated sample studies have been undertaken to distinguish between those who have completed a good deal of school and are literate and those who have done so but may still be functionally illiterate.

Finally, the data provided for public expenditure on education are generally complete in the sense that they include data for all levels of public expenditure (national, state, local) but are incomplete for certain countries in that they do not include data for private expenditure; in some countries this fraction of the educational establishment may be of significant size. Data, however, are often not available. Occasionally data for external aid to education may be included in addition to domestic expenditure.
a. May include teacher training at the second level.
b. Latest.
c. Full-time.
d. Full-time; may include students registered in foreign schools.
e. General second level includes teacher training at the second level.

		third level (higher)							literacy[b]				public expenditure on education (percent of GNP; latest)	country
students[d]	student/ teacher ratio	institutions	teachers[c]	students[d]	student/ teacher ratio	gross enroll-ment ratio	students per 100,000 popula-tion[b]	percent of population aged 25 and over with post-secondary education[b]	over age	total (%)	male (%)	female (%)		
14,431	11.0	19	1,569	17,542	11.2	1.3	117	3.2	15	20.0	33.2	5.8	2.0	Afghanistan
64,800	17.3	17[2]	1,240	17,500	14.1	6.0[3]	612	...	15	71.5	79.9	63.1	...	Albania
26,216[3]	11.4[3]	15[3]	8,573[3]	100,000[3]	11.7[3]	4.6[1]	398	0.3	15	41.8	55.6	29.1	8.2	Algeria
45[2]	11.2[2]	1	48	1,713	35.7	...	...	12.6	...	...	...	...	6.2	American Samoa
...														Andorra
5,206	12.7	1	300	3,150	10.5	0.4[1]	37	...	15	28.0	36.2	19.3	4.7	Angola
	...	...	...	...	...	...	...	...	14	98.0	98.2	97.9	...	Anguilla
153[9]	...	...						1.3	...	88.7	89.7	88.0	4.0	Antigua and Barbuda
905,755	7.6	1,251	64,230	677,535	10.5	24.5[3]	1,988	6.9	14	94.9	95.5	94.4	3.7	Argentina[e]
729,291	16.3	64	21,866	349,243	16.0	26.3[3]	2,280	21.5	15	99.5	...	...	5.8	Australia
381,261	17.2	52	9,644	162,705	16.9	24.3[3]	2,154	3.3	15	99.0	...	...	5.9	Austria
1,823[6]	19.8[6]	1[1]	127[1]	4,093[1]	32.2[1]	...	...	...	15	89.0	90.6	89.6	9.8	Bahamas, The
2,846	12.2	2	159	3,650	22.9	5.3[2]	581	3.8	14	63.4	74.8	51.9	3.0	Bahrain
416,777	29.8	45	3,842	59,775	15.6	3.5[3]	62	0.9	14	29.2	39.7	18.0	1.7	Bangladesh
2,343[3]	...	2[10]	216[10]	2,954[10]	13.7[10]	13.6[2]	1,536	1.2	15	98.0	98.3	97.7	6.9	Barbados
218,717	31.9	...	...	108,689	...	27.8[3]	2,233	7.5	...	99.0	...	...	6.2	Belgium
737[11]	12.7[11]	11	11	11	11	...	...	1.4	15	91.2	...	...	...	Belize
4,441[1]	...	1	304	4,730	15.6	2.0[3]	168	...	15	27.9	39.8	16.6	5.3	Benin
502	9.7	1	13	105	8.1	...	...	7.4	15	96.9	96.7	97.0	3.1	Bermuda
2,189	15.3	2	16	204	12.8	0.3[2]	25	...	15	18.0	31.0	9.0	...	Bhutan
...	...	25	1,487	13,388	9.0	16.4[3]	1,428	5.0	15	63.2	75.8	51.4	3.1	Bolivia
3,538	21.3	1	104	1,249	12.0	1.4[1]	153	0.5	15	52.4	47.7	56.2	7.7	Botswana
...	...	868	122,697	1,438,992	11.7	12.0[2]	1,126	4.3	14	78.1	79.6	76.6	3.8	Brazil
—	—	—	—	—	—	...	...	5.4	15	98.3	98.1	98.5	4.7	British Virgin Islands
1,362[11]	5.0[11]	11	11	11	11	...	...	9.4	14	80.3	86.5	62.9	1.7	Brunei
66,761	5.1	16	567	7,130	12.6	15.1[3]	1,055	5.2	15	95.5	...	...	6.7	Bulgaria
4,492	9.3	1	216	3,870	17.9	0.5[3]	42	...	15	9.0	14.7	3.3	2.9	Burkina Faso
15,554	11.8	35	5,622	171,245	30.5	4.2[12]	180	...	15	65.9	75.9	56.3	1.6	Burma
6,033	10.2	6	372	2,479	6.7	0.5[1]	48	...	15	32.0	42.3	22.8	3.0	Burundi
70,671	23.8	13[3]	557[3]	11,407[3]	20.5[3]	1.7[1]	143	0.3	15	55.2	70.2	41.0	3.5	Cameroon
...	...	266	59,250	781,270	10.7	39.0[3]	3,931	30.9	14	95.6	95.6	95.7	8.2	Canada
923	12.1	3	199	36	5.5	...	...	7.5	15	49.3	55.3	43.4	7.5	Cape Verde
71	7.9	1	35	762	21.8	...	...	2.9	15	97.5	97.5	97.6	...	Cayman Islands
1,712	19.0	...	297	4,571	15.4	1.3[1]	108	...	15	38.5	58.8	20.4	4.9	Central African Republic
1,198	...	1[3]	85[3]	550[3]	6.5[3]	0.2	14	...	15	17.8	35.6	0.5	2.3	Chad
143,689	...	24	10,372[3]	125,363	...	12.2[3]	1,055	3.8	12	95.6	95.0	93.8	5.8	Chile
1,039,000	9.0	715	287,000	1,154,000	4.0	1.2	115	1.0	11	68.0	...	...	5.7	China
60	8.6	—	—	—	—	...	...	...	15	40.0	35.7	50.0	...	Christmas Island
														Cocos (Keeling) Islands
...	...	216	39,238	365,772	9.3	12.2[3]	1,246	3.3	15	86.3	87.0	85.7	2.6	Colombia
327	12.1	—		430	—	...	...	...	...	59.0	66.1	51.7	5.4	Comoros
18,867	12.9	1[2]	681	6,848	10.1	5.6[2]	472	...	15	56.4	69.5	44.0	6.8	Congo
...	...	...	41.2[3]	360[3]	8.8[3]	...	...	2.1	15	91.8	92.1	91.4	...	Cook Islands
...	...	14	58,942	...	...	27.3[3]	2,975	-5.8	15	93.0	93.2	92.8	5.2	Costa Rica
243,146	10.5	32	12,222	173,403	14.2	19.2[3]	1,753	...	15	91.1	91.1	91.1	6.3	Cuba
5,375	10.9	15	250	2,580	10.3	...	289	7.7	10	89.0	93.5	84.5	3.8	Cyprus
271,234	16.2	36	19,135	174,304	9.1	17.2[3]	1,124	6.0	15	99.6	99.6	99.5	5.2	Czechoslovakia
140,621	...	96[14]	10,411[14]	122,535	...	28.4[1]	2,080	...	14	99.5	...	...	5.2	Denmark
1,540	12.5	—	—	161	...	...	...	...	14	11.9	...	...	3.9	Djibouti
121	9.3	...	59	284	4.8	...	...	1.1	15	70.0	...	...	...	Dominica

Education (continued)

country	year	first level (primary)					general second level (secondary)					vocational second level[a]	
		schools	teachers[c]	students[d]	student/ teacher ratio	net enrollment ratio	schools	teachers[c]	students[d]	student/ teacher ratio	net enrollment ratio	schools	teachers[c]
Dominican Republic	1983	6,009	23,578	1,092,838	46.3	...	...	...	353,729[3]	...	...	...	...
Ecuador	1984	13,011	50,347	1,677,364	33.3	87[4]	582	5,579	69,945	12.5	...	1,199	34,330
Egypt	1981	11,761[3]	140,146	4,748,414[3]	27.8	...	2,715	78,086	2,060,100	26.4	...	519	38,635
El Salvador	1982	2,390	18,182	810,827	44.6	56[1]	233	5,123	74,258	14.6	...	23	...
Equatorial Guinea	1981	511	647	40,110	62.0	...	14[15]	288[15]	3,013[15]	10.5[15]	...	15	15
Ethiopia	1981	6,208	37,844	2,374,362	62.7	...	...	11,184	487,179	43.6	...	...	...
Faeroe Islands	1983	75[13]	...	5,628	...	...	13	...	3,202	...	...	3	...
Falkland Islands	1980	...	15	223	14.9	...	...	11	90	8.2	...	—	—
Fiji	1983	660	4,256[3]	120,244	...	100[1]	140	2,467[3]	44,415	...	...	40	314[3]
Finland	1984	4,238	25,139	369,047	14.7	...	1,082	22,356	316,740	14.2	...	550	15,000
France	1982	67,291	290,933[1]	6,909,559	...	99[1]	11,209[15]	256,284[1,15]	5,052,452[15]	...	79[1]	15	15
French Guiana	1982	66	598[1]	13,675	...	...	14	365[1]	6,339	...	...	5	149[1]
French Polynesia	1984	231	...	39,200	...	...	24	...	12,426	...	...	18	...
Gabon	1983	901	3,781	165,559	43.8	...	47	1,161	22,350	19.3	...	29	582
Gambia, The	1984	180	2,445	60,630	24.8	53[3]	16	605	9,981	16.5	12[3]	16	457
Gaza Strip	1984	291[13]	3,684[13]	99,363	...	...	13	...	48,998	...	...	13	13
Germany, East	1984	5,666	54,971	766,745	13.9	...	5,711	112,172	1,265,349	11.3	...	4,500	56,577
Germany, West	1984	21,453	307,851	4,773,336	15.5	80[1]	5,374	191,730	3,216,542	16.8	...	7,816	87,975
Ghana	1984	8,214[3]	51,631	1,643,455	31.8	...	4,758[1]	32,795	811,865	24.8	...	62[1]	1,727[1]
Gibraltar	1985	14	91	1,904	20.9	...	2	122	1,749	14.3	...	1	25
Greece	1982	9,400	37,947	891,488	23.5	99[2]	2,291	33,613	669,812	19.9	74[4]	766	5,828
Greenland	1983	92[13]	1,092[13]	10,613[13]	9.7[13]	...	13	13	13	13	...	5[10]	1,537[10]
Grenada	1982	67	781	22,066	28.3	...	20	293	6,249	21.3	...	1	21
Guadeloupe	1982	284	2,744[2]	55,751	...	...	59	2,602[4]	49,606	...	...	22[4]	...
Guam	1982	37	772	17,784	23.0	...	19	512	11,997	23.4	...	1	75
Guatemala	1980	6,959	23,770	803,404	33.8	56[3]	...	9,613	156,612	16.3	13[3]	...	...
Guernsey	1984	23	224	4,260	19.0	...	9	297	4,095	13.8	...	1	47
Guinea	1981	2,555	7,165	257,547	35.9	...	...	3,520	89,900	25.5	...	...	425[17]
Guinea-Bissau	1983	719	3,363	74,359	22.1	76[3]	8[3]	543	7,667	14.1	5[1]	4[3]	96[3]
Guyana	1980	424	6,021	164,830	27.4	87[1]	87	2,513	46,595	18.5	...	15	348
Haiti	1983	3,241	16,986	723,041	42.6	40[1]	290	5,367	117,081	21.8	...	2	49
Honduras	1983	6,422	19,300	802,915	41.6	85[3]	356	5,853[15]	540,406	...	...	11	15
Hong Kong	1985	757	19,824	537,345	27.1	95[3]	436[15]	18,119[15]	444,380[15]	24.5[15]	63[3]	15	15
Hungary	1985	3,539	86,367	1,286,648	14.9	98[3]	175	7,709	104,534	13.6	39[4]	72.9	21,801
Iceland	1983	187	2,600	25,000	9.6	...	157	...	21,800	...	...	44	...
India	1983	503,741	1,389,356	55,220,443	39.7	...	175,702	1,849,504	57,398,203	31.0	...	4,878	...
Indonesia	1983	120,162	841,833	24,700,075	29.3	100[3]	16,028	336,336	5,697,231	16.9	17[6]	2,752[3]	65,528[3]
Iran	1985	48,955	268,417	6,336,016	23.6	...	14,534	185,593	3,097,467	16.7	...	472	...
Iraq	1983	10,223	107,364	2,614,927	24.4	94[3]	1,977	32,556	971,827	29.8	49[1]	200	5,974
Ireland	1982	3,475	19,926	571,385	28.7	90[1]	823	18,186	309,598	17.1	81[1]	47[1]	8,255
Isle of Man	1975	38	214	3,647	17.0	...	6	251	4,329	17.2	...	1	32
Israel	1984[19]	1,831	45,607	616,852	13.5	...	519	...	220,596	...	...	369	...
Italy	1984	28,786	276,716[14]	4,068,324	...	98[6]	13,135	333,062[14]	3,708,960	...	66[6]	4,430	199,268[14]
Ivory Coast	1980	4,419	24,441	963,246	39.4	...	113[5]	4,569	172,408	37.7	...	38	...
Jamaica	1984	819	10,630	455,486	42.8	93[2]	694[5]	...	233,723[1]	...	56[2]	12	8,904[1]
Japan	1984	25,064	468,675	11,465,108	24.5	100[1]	16,474	537,557	10,721,217	19.9	92[1]	...	...
Jersey	1983	38	306	5,686	18.6	...	6	73	534	7.3	...	...	...
Jordan	1982	1,129	14,873	473,027	31.8	92[1]	1,038	8,520	181,432	21.3	68[2]	487	6,476
Kampuchea	1982	3,629	38,600	1,548,419	40.1	...	5	78	1,521	19.5	...	6	...
Kenya	1983	11,497	115,094	4,184,602	36.4	72[1]	2,131	16,848	438,424	26.0	9[6]	39	1,255
Kiribati	1983	106	450	13,836	30.7	...	5	65	950	14.6	...	2	14
Korea, North	1982	4,700[8]	...	2,561,674[8]	...	...	...	...	...	...	...	...	...
Korea, South	1984	6,500	126,163	5,257,104	41.7	100[3]	3,893	128,950	4,752,097	36.9	79[3]	643	29,328
Kuwait	1985	257	8,062	140,202	17.4	76[3]	133	7,601	...	...	70[3]	6	654[10]
Laos	1983	6,525	16,454	480,871	29.2	...	1	3,666[1]	78,925[1]	21.5[1]	...	1	939[1]
Lebanon	1982	1,116	21	398,977	...	...	1,405	53,450[21]	250,028	...	...	181	3,563
Lesotho	1982	1,103	5,295	277,945	52.5	72	108	1,368	27,799	20.3	12	12	196[1]
Liberia	1980	1,151	227,431	9,099	25.0	...	275	1,146	52,301	45.8	...	6	63
Libya	1982	2,679	39,214	718,124	18.3	...	1,429	23,891	288,414	12.0	...	184	3,298
Liechtenstein	1986	14	100	1,732	17.3	...	9	108	1,774	16.4	...	1	35[22]
Luxembourg	1982	541	1,734	27,927	16.1	88	53[15]	2,407[15,27]	21,783[15]	...	64	15	15
Macau	1984	77	1,043	31,481	30.2	...	28	664	11,594	17.5	...	1	25
Madagascar	1978	8,002	23,937	1,311,000	54.8	...	...	5,086[6]	131,836[6]	25.9[6]	25.9[6]	126[7]	759[7]
Malawi	1983	2,411	13,714	868,849	63.4	43[2]	60	825	17,232	20.9	...	10	155
Malaysia	1984	6,557	83,760	2,149,014	25.6	...	1,101	54,156	1,227,500	22.7	...	90	3,173
Maldives	1984	65	590	42,598	72.2	...	4	93	841	9.0	...	3	27
Mali	1983	1,558	10,912	65,551	6.0	...	20	890	13,227	14.9	...	11	...
Malta	1985	122	1,648	33,987	20.6	94[1]	66	1,589	22,664	14.3	72[1]	21	443
Martinique	1983	297	3,222[23]	57,532	...	...	271	3,556[15]	93,711	...	...	12	15
Mauritania	1981	599	2,183	90,530	41.5	...	...	646	20,248	31.3	...	...	...
Mauritius	1984	281	6,460	135,391	21.0	89	128	3,563	73,961	20.8	33[6]	7	69[3]
Mayotte	1985	73	447	15,100	33.8	...	1	66	1,418	21.5	...	2[10]	61[10]
Mexico	1984	76,183	437,408	15,219,245	34.8	...	17,620	230,656	4,396,087	19.1	...	4,815	126,705
Monaco	1981	6	1,347	...	...	...	2	1,314	...	...	...	1	751
Mongolia	1984	21	21	21	21	98[3]	674[21]	15,900[21]	410,000[21]	25.8[21]	84[4]	37	1,100
Montserrat	1981	15	1,725	86	20.0	...	...	871	32[2]	...	...	...	59
Morocco	1982	2,498	63,157	2,418,385	38.3	55[1]	644	39,035	900,694	23.1	18[2]	...	...
Mozambique	1983	8,528	29,634	1,402,541	47.3	56[3]	136	2,523	106,975	42.4	5[1]	62	1,228
Nauru	1980	9	102	1,704	16.7	...	2	339	36	9.5	...	2	80
Nepal	1985	11,660	46,484	1,747,857	37.6	...	4,631	17,069	454,511	26.6	...	...	16,815[8]
Netherlands, The	1984	9,606	63,058	1,237,422	19.6	90[3]	1,471	53,770	832,990	15.5	84[3]	1,892	56,963
Netherlands Antilles	1981	125	1,543	32,832	21.3	...	6[8]	669	10,931	16.3	...	44[8]	734
New Caledonia	1985	263	1,529	31,589	20.3	...	45	976[10]	11,445	...	...	28	309[10]
New Zealand	1983	2,585	18,504	469,735	25.4	96[3]	331	12,101	227,831[24]	18.8	...	27	2,920
Nicaragua	1982	4,976	14,105	509,240	36.1	75[1]	323	...	114,868	...	23[2]	62	...

students[d]	student/teacher ratio	third level (higher) institutions	teachers[c]	students[d]	student/teacher ratio	gross enroll-ment ratio	students per 100,000 population[b]	percent of population aged 25 and over with post-secondary education[b]	literacy[b] over age	total (%)	male (%)	female (%)	public expenditure on education (percent of GNP; latest)	country
25,648[3]	...	5		91,115			851	1.9	15	73.6	73.4	73.8	2.1	Dominican Republic
580,351	16.9	17	11,186	267,900	23.9	35.3[1]	3,192	3.2	14	85.2	87.9	82.6	5.6	Ecuador
672,362	17.4	12[3]	11,910	594,597[3]		14.7	1,350	3.4	10	41.9	56.3	27.5	4.5	Egypt
8,684		18	1,414	23,418	16.6	5.7[1]	521	1.9	15	64.2	68.8	60.1	3.8	El Salvador
15	15	...	68	1,140	16.8	3.6	306		...	55.0				Equatorial Guinea
		...	1,137	11,822	10.4	0.6[3]	49		15	4.8	9.3	0.5	4.1	Ethiopia
607	...	6		949					15	100.0	100.0	100.0	...	Faeroe Islands
—		—	—	—					15	98.0				Falkland Islands
2,629	...	5	...	3,947	...	3.2[3]	352	3.3	15	79.0	84.0	74.0	5.8	Fiji
116,906	7.8	21	5,191	119,902	23.1	32.2[3]	2,456	11.9	15	100.0	100.0	100.0	5.8	Finland
15	...	1,094[1]	40,585[1]	1,017,775[1]	25.1[1]	26.9	2,123		...	98.8	98.9	98.7	5.1	France
1,802	...	1	...	236	...			1.1	16	82.0	82.5	81.3	...	French Guiana
3,880	...		10[2]	124[2]	12.4[2]				14	95.0	94.9	95.0	...	French Polynesia
10,545	18.1	1	297	2,651	8.9	3.7[4]	195		15	77.0			3.0	Gabon
8,923	19.5	1[3]	291[3]	38[3]	7.7[3]			0.2	15	20.1	29.1	11.6	5.9	Gambia, The
696	...	1[14]	30[3]	2,387[14]									...	Gaza Strip
414,044	7.3	54	29,700	434,326	14.6	29.7[3]	2,401	8.5	15	100.0	100.0	100.0	5.5	Germany, East
2,718,404	30.3	...	311,460	1,267,263	4.1	30.2[3]	2,325	4.3	15	99.0			4.7	Germany, West
32,288[1]	19.3[1]	3	1,041[1]	7,971[14]		1.3[1]	111	0.4	15	44.8	53.7	36.2	1.8	Ghana
353	14.1	—	—	—					10	99.0	99.0	99.0	7.7	Gibraltar
108,212	18.6	166	11,310	124,694	11.0	16.9[4]	1,296	3.9	14	92.6	96.2	88.4	2.2	Greece
		—	—	—					15	100.0	100.0	100.0		Greenland
213	10.1	...	71	926	13.0			1.0	14	85.0			5.7	Grenada
10,059[2]		1	80	1,719[14]				0.8	15	91.5	92.7	90.3	...	Guadeloupe
1,186	15.8	2[14]	162	3,499	21.6			21.5	...				7.6	Guam
...	...	5[3]	4,490[3]	51,556[3]	11.4[3]	6.8[3]	629	1.2	15	51.1	58.6	43.5	1.8	Guatemala
134	2.9	—							15	100.0	100.0	100.0	...	Guernsey
3,491[17]	8.2[17]	...	1,373[3]	13,182[3]	9.6[3]	3.0[3]	249		...	18.7	33.5	4.4	4.2	Guinea
765	...	...	...	...	...			0.1	7	26.8			5.0	Guinea-Bissau
4,647	13.4	1	...	1,889	...	2.8[5]	304	1.0	15	95.5	97.1	94.0	7.6	Guyana
156	3.2	1	582	3,464	6.0	1.1[2]	96	0.3	15	34.7	37.1	32.5	1.1	Haiti
56,277	...	2	2,153	30,096	14.0	9.7[3]	842	1.0	15	68.6	71.1	66.2	4.3	Honduras
15	15	21	3,169	36,316	11.5	11.1[3]	1,340	7.1	15	77.9	84.3	70.9	3.3	Hong Kong
315,570[15]	14.5[15]	58	14,545	99,986	6.9	13.6[1]	932	7.0	15	98.9	99.3	98.5	5.0	Hungary
4,280	...	4	280	4,780	17.1	19.3[1]	1,878	3.7	15	100.0	100.0	100.0	4.1	Iceland
468,993	...	9,056[2]	259,745[2]	4,924,794[2]	19.0[2]	8.7[4]	746	1.1	15	40.8	54.8	25.7	3.0	India
853,000	...	50[3]	56,322[3]	692,700		4[13]	401	0.8	10	72.0	80.5	63.8	2.2	Indonesia
80,952	17.6[18]	119	13,698	145,809	10.6	3.7[3]	335	...	15	42.7	54.7	29.9	8.5	Iran
94,057	15.7	25	6,674	116,260	17.4	10.1[3]	877	...	15	43.4	62.9	23.3	3.2	Iraq
206[18]	...	58[1]	36,286	3,983[1]	...	22.4[1]	1,779	4.6	15	100.0	100.0	100.0	7.0	Ireland
133	4.2	...	...	...	...	...	...	...	...	...	...	...	...	Isle of Man
89,646	...	7	8,347[3]	92,572	...	30.4[3]	2,519	23.1	14	93.3	96.2	90.5	8.5	Israel
1,620,859	...	71[14]	47,844[14]	1,022,282[14]	21.4[14]	25.4[3]	1,905	2.6	15	93.9	95.3	92.7	5.0	Italy
44,481	...	1	475[4]	10,772	...	2.8[1]	226		15	35.0	44.8	24.0	7.6	Ivory Coast
4,651		11[1]	13,999[1]	837[1,5]		6.4[2]	640	1.1	14	88.6	88.2	89.1	6.9	Jamaica
...	...	1,059	131,923	2,431,708	18.4	30.0[3]	2,029	14.3	15	100.0	100.0	100.0	6.0	Japan
														Jersey
86,269	13.3	46	2,075	50,210	24.2	31.6[1]	1,602	0.8	15	67.6	81.0	54.3	4.9	Jordan
2,754	...	...	...	...					15	48.0				Kampuchea
20,604	16.4	2	900[20]	8,772[20]	9.7[20]	1.0[1]	78		15	47.1	60.0	34.8	6.5	Kenya
122	8.7	1	17	113	6.6				15	90.0			13.5	Kiribati
		175	9,244	200,000	21.6				15	90.0			3.4	Korea, North
897,637	30.6	428	30,049	1,075,969	35.8	21.0[3]	2,392	8.9	15	92.7	97.5	87.9	4.3	Korea, South
5,962[10]	9.1[10]	1	763[10]	14,650[10]	19.2[10]	15.4[3]	1,209	10.1	15	67.5	72.8	60.3	4.2	Kuwait
11,510[1]	12.2[1]	1[1]	140[1]	1,408[1]	10.1[1]	0.4[2]	371		15	45.2	52.8	37.6		Laos
39,045	11.0	18		70,314		28.3[1]	2,587	3.1	10	73.4	82.6	64.2	3.0	Lebanon
2,054	...	14	149[4]	1,091[4]	7.3[4]	1.5[12]		0.1	15	69.9	57.5	80.0	5.7	Lesotho
2,322	36.9	3	190	3,789	19.9	2.3[4]	145	1.0	15	45.6	66.3	25.1	6.3	Liberia
44,789	11.4	8	1,340[2]	25,700		6.4[4]	553	1.0	10	74.4	85.0	62.0	3.7	Libya
75	2.1	—		—				5.4	15	100.0	100.0	100.0		Liechtenstein
15	...	2	181[22]	384		2.6[1]	196		15	98.0			6.0	Luxembourg
480	19.2	4	56	3,968	70.8			1.4	10	61.3	76.4	46.2	...	Macau
9,213[7]	12.1[7]	3[10]	557	32,599[3]		4.1[3]	353		15	53.0			4.9	Madagascar
2,322	15.0	4	305	1,849	6.1	0.3[1]	29	0.2	15	49.9	64.3	37.2	3.5	Malawi
36,543	11.5	9	5,452	55,186	10.2	4.6[1]	467		10	75.0	83.0	66.9	7.6	Malaysia
206	7.6	...	...	...	...	...	...	0.4	15	81.1	80.2	82.0	0.6	Maldives
12,615	...	7	491	5,792	11.8	0.3[2]	24	0.2	15	9.6	13.5	5.9	4.6	Mali
5,237	11.8	1	156	1,337	8.6	3.2[3]	290	2.4	15	84.7	87.4	82.3	3.1	Malta
2,144	...	1	40	1,220	30.5			0.8	16	92.5	91.8	93.2	...	Martinique
1,854	...	3	25	1,374					6	17.4			5.0	Mauritania
444	...	2	184[3]	610		0.8[3]	93	1.2	15	84.6	90.5	78.8	4.7	Mauritius
1,206	19.8	—		33[10]					16	75.0			...	Mayotte
1,841,633	14.5	1,305	92,338	1,121,252	12.1	14.8[3]	1,460	2.6	15	83.0	86.2	79.9	3.4	Mexico
...	...	...	...	...	...	...	...	6.8						Monaco
23,600	21.4	8	1,400	26,000	18.6	25.5[1]	2,227		15	89.5	93.4	85.5	7.0	Mongolia
5	11.8	...	...	...	...	...	...	2.7	15				...	Montserrat
10,300	...	19	2,558	98,513	38.5	6.2[1]	581		15	70.7	82.4	58.7	7.3	Morocco
19,267	16.0	1	352	1,106		0.2[3]	20	0.1	15	33.2	44.4	22.7	0.6	Mozambique
5	16.0	—	—	—	—				...	99.0			...	Nauru
513[8]	32.8[8]	69	3,654	48,229		3.1[2]	292	0.1	6	23.3	34.0	12.0	2.5	Nepal
633,966	11.1	402	29,952	306,416	10.2	31.1[3]	2,670	7.2	15	100.0	100.0	100.0	7.9	Netherlands, The
10,318	14.1	1	20[3]	500[3]	25.0			4.4	...				10.1	Netherlands Antilles
6,906	...	6	63	761	12.1			2.0	15	89.4	90.1	88.7	11.1	New Caledonia
148,448[24]	50.8	7	3,079	56,513[24]	18.3	26.3[3]	2,472	20.1	15	100.0	100.0	100.0	5.3	New Zealand
21,761	...	4	1,369	32,838	24.0	12.9[14]	1,124		15	87.0			4.2	Nicaragua

Education (continued)

country	year	first level (primary)					general second level (secondary)					vocational second level[a]	
		schools	teachers[c]	students[d]	student/ teacher ratio	net enrollment ratio	schools	teachers[c]	students[d]	student/ teacher ratio	net enrollment ratio	schools	teachers[c]
Niger	1981	1,686	5,518	228,855	41.5	...	64	1,371	32,892	24.0	3[12]	8	120
Nigeria	1981	36,683	384,201	14,022,164	36.5	...	4,495	69,005	2,024,024	29.3	...	470	12,156
Niue	1985	7	29	503	17.3	...	1	31	321	10.4	...	—	—
Norfolk Island	1984	2	16	309	19.3	...	...	...	...	...	...	...	...
Norway	1984	3,539	29,992	565,497	18.9	99[1]	918[15]	16,292[15]	188,040[14,15]	...	84[1]	15	15
Oman	1985	308	5,369	155,389	28.9	61[3]	235	2,735	37,906	13.8	14[1]	25	571
Pacific Is., Trust Territory of the	1981	245	1,374	31,099	22.6	...	32[9]	445	6,872	15.4	...	...	39[4]
Pakistan	1984	72,053	206,000	6,412,000	31.1	...	10,433	142,000	2,287,000	16.1	...	266	3,798
Panama	1983	2,376	12,613	335,950	26.6	92[3]	321[15]	9,249[15]	177,987[15]	19.2[15]	49[3]	15	15
Papua New Guinea	1983	2,224	10,130	322,254	31.8	...	111	1,629	41,702	25.6	...	92	548
Paraguay	1983	3,690	21,524	549,637	25.5	90[3]	658[15]	8,356[15]	142,436[15]	17.0[15]	...	15	15
Peru	1982	25,748	116,550	3,692,273	31.7	92[1]	3,289	66,874	1,429,219	21.4	...	768	8,744
Philippines	1982	33,972	264,653	8,670,544	32.8	90	5,023	85,465	2,935,732	34.4	45	331	...
Pitcairn Island	1985	1[13]	1[13]	15	15.0	...	13	13	2	...	...	—	—
Poland	1984	15,020	260,000	4,530,000	17.4	99[3]	879	22,000	326,000	14.8	69[3]	7,479	88,000
Portugal	1983	13,069	76,141	1,305,724	17.1	...	629	38,809	582,495	15.0	...	368	...
Puerto Rico	1985	1,283	23,154[1]	417,540	...	...	605	13,297[1]	337,153[1]	25.4[1]	...	78	2,600[1]
Qatar	1983	106	2,508	34,805	13.9	91[3]	56[3]	2,053	18,346	8.9	59[3]	3[3]	86
Réunion	1985	508	5,087	113,330	22.3	...	85[15]	3,947[15]	69,417[15]	17.6[15]	...	15	15
Romania	1984	14,213	150,539	3,067,446	20.4	...	1,882[15]	51,431[15]	1,453,769[15]	28.3[15]	...	15	15
Rwanda	1982	1,558	13,043	743,067	57.0	66	...	844	12,505	12.7	2	...	36
St. Christopher and Nevis	1985	32	339	7,655	22.6	...	7	286	4,436	15.5	...	2	29
St. Helena and Ascension	1982	8	35	647	18.5	...	4	32	604	18.9	...	2	6
St. Lucia	1985	85	1,139	33,534	29.4	...	11	280	5,321	19.0	...	4	48
St. Pierre and Miquelon	1983	5	59	661	11.2	...	3	56	531	9.5	...	2	40
St. Vincent and the Grenadines	1983	62	1,251	24,551	19.6	...	19	292	5,170	17.7	...	5	39
San Marino	1985	13	151	1,440	9.5	...	3	123	965	7.8	...	...	...
São Tomé and Príncipe	1985	63	517	19,086	36.9	...	10	274	5,656	20.6	...	2	35
Saudi Arabia	1984	7,269	76,615	1,161,096	15.2	52[1]	3,085	35,947	496,778	13.8	23[1]	26	881
Senegal	1981	1,795	10,586	452,679	42.8	39	...	3,574[4]	93,001	...	...	...	...
Seychelles	1984	26	695	14,333	20.6	...	3[15]	147[15]	2,605[15]	17.7[15]	...	15	15
Sierra Leone	1983	1,196	9,519	290,756	30.5	...	174	3,060	69,787	22.8	...	10	320
Singapore	1984	210	10,657	288,623	27.1	97[3]	150	8,236	187,764	22.8	58[4]	88	1,675
Solomon Islands	1984	423	1,536	37,522	24.4	...	20	267	5,118	19.2	...	2	63
Somalia	1981	1,408	8,122	271,704	33.5	22[2]	51	1,350	33,212	24.6	6[2]	26	654
South Africa	1985	17,430[13]	199,949[13]	4,722,832	...	...	13	13	1,539,213	...	...	132	3,733
Bophuthatswana	1982	802	7,221	373,653	51.7	...	310	4,391	115,737	26.4	...	18	360
Ciskei	1982	608	4,646	189,713	40.8	...	152	1,651	53,330	32.3	...	4	66
Transkei	...	...	...	...	...	...	...	...	...	...	...	...	...
Venda	...	...	...	...	...	...	...	...	...	...	...	...	...
South West Africa/Namibia	1983	1,069	7,120	232,306	32.6	...	78	1,864	40,359	21.6	...	6	81
Spain	1984	23,105	232,173	6,870,057	29.6	100[2]	2,547	71,256	1,142,308	16.0	74[2]	2,397	45,339
Sri Lanka	1983	9,612[13]	133,658[13]	2,153,595	...	...	13	13	1,367,754	...	...	25	466
Sudan, The	1981	6,176	46,437	1,524,381	32.8	...	1,477[2]	17,105	403,236	23.6	...	60[2]	1,584
Suriname	1983	294	2,944	74,805	25.4	...	91	1,602	23,401	14.0	...	19	556
Swaziland	1981	467	4,039	134,528	33.3	86[3]	89	1,569	28,833	18.4	...	4	121
Sweden	1985	5,399[13,14]	123,801[13,14]	630,505	...	97[1]	13	13	459,519	...	80[1]	13	13
Switzerland	1985	...	...	418,000	...	...	...	...	396,000	...	...	...	...
Syria	1984	8,393	62,042	1,683,802	27.1	90[3]	1,553	38,149	685,692	18.0	46[3]	156	6,410[14]
Taiwan	1985	2,447	71,057	2,264,518	31.9	...	845[10]	59,871[10]	1,263,810	...	...	202[10]	15,002[10]
Tanzania	1982	9,980[1,26]	88,370[14,26]	3,512,799[14,26]	39.3[14,26]	72[1]	170[2]	3,262	67,602	20.7	...	40	744
Thailand	1980	33,712	346,508	8,068,252	23.3	...	3,761	117,256	2,454,663	20.9	...	1,528	27,484
Togo	1982	2,251	9,619	498,639	51.8	73	248	3,982	122,925	30.9	...	22	348[2]
Tokelau	1983	3[2]	39	482	15.8	...	3[2]	6[2]	80[2]	13.3[2]	...	...	12[2]
Tonga	1983	111	832	16,755	20.1	...	47	767	16,212	21.1	...	12	...
Trinidad and Tobago	1984	465[2,13]	6,443[2]	167,950[14]	...	77[4]	13	1,631[5]	82,482[2]	...	...	8[8]	114[8]
Tunisia	1984	3,066	33,026	1,191,408	36.1	89[3]	335[15]	17,943[15]	364,492[15]	20.3[15]	29[3]	13	13
Turkey	1984	47,324	208,393	6,495,916	31.1	...	5,450	90,078	1,980,523	22.0	...	1,994	40,418
Turks and Caicos Islands	1985	17	1,540	74	20.8	...	3	51	707	13.9	...	—	—
Tuvalu	1983	9	41	966	23.6	100[3]	1	15	250	16.7	...	8	16
Uganda	1982	5,300	44,426	1,616,791	36.4	42	257	6,287	132,051	21.0	...	23	735
U.S.S.R.	1984	71,200	2,360,000[13]	35,700,000	...	...	59,000	...	4,714,000	...	...	4,438	247,418
United Arab Emirates	1983	244[2]	6,599[5]	115,411	...	100[3]	68[2]	4,081[5]	45,442	...	...	4[2]	344
United Kingdom	1983	25,755	211,100	4,302,000	20.4	95[1]	5,473	277,000	4,967,000	17.9	79[1]	786	...
United States	1984	102,699[3,13]	1,359,000	30,780,000	22.6	...	13	1,035,000[15]	13,495,000[15]	13.0[15]	...	13	...
Uruguay	1982	2,291	16,821	343,957	20.4	...	263	...	125,366	...	...	86	...
Vanuatu	1982	286	1,063	23,595	22.2	...	9	126	2,067	16.4	...	2	40
Venezuela	1983	12,816[13]	130,505[13]	2,998,803[13]	23.0[13]	83[1]	13	...	...	...	33[1]	13	...
Vietnam	1984	11,751[13]	427,000[13]	11,779,000[13]	27.6[13]	98[2]	13	...	...	...	...	280	10,200
Virgin Islands (U.S.)	1985	41	981[5]	18,356	...	...	29	799[5]	14,684	...	...	3[22]	27
Wallis and Futuna	1978	...	171	5,348	31.2	...	...	9	277	30.8	...	—	—
West Bank	1984[27]	1,080[13]	8,185[13]	172,787	...	...	13	13	92,500	...	...	13	13
Western Sahara	...	...	...	...	...	...	...	...	...	...	...	...	...
Western Samoa	1984	160	1,502	40,090	26.7	...	39	520	11,761	22.6	...	4	42
Yemen (Aden)	1982	890	10,915	228,893	21.0	...	46	1,271	27,776	21.9	...	13	173
Yemen (Şan'ā')	1981	2,985	9,826	412,573	39.0	22[6]	314	2,023	28,852	14.3	3[6]	29	196
Yugoslavia	1983	12,413	133,661	2,807,220	21.0	79[1]	...	64,783	987,481	15.2	70[6]	...	...
Zaire	1978	7,909	132,759	3,919,395	...	...	2,511	42,212[15]	611,349[4]	...	...	20	15
Zambia	1982	2,894	23,870	1,121,769	47.0	82[2]	142	4,602	104,859	22.8	...	28	406[1]
Zimbabwe	1983	3,962	52,502	2,046,123	39.0	100[3]	790	11,191	316,438	28.3	...	14	953

students[d]	student/ teacher ratio	third level (higher) institutions	teachers[c]	students[d]	student/ teacher ratio	gross enroll-ment ratio	students per 100,000 popula-tion[b]	percent of population aged 25 and over with post-secondary education[b]	literacy[b] over age	total (%)	male (%)	female (%)	public expenditure on education (percent of GNP; latest)	country
2,351	19.6	1	189	1,825	9.7	0.4	34	...	15	9.8	14.0	5.8	4.3	Niger
359,817	29.6	77	...	153,300	...	2.6	222	...	15	30.0	40.5	14.0	3.9	Nigeria
—	—	—	...	...	...	...	...	1.9	15	97.0	...	...	...	Niue
...	...	...	...	...	...	...	...	...	15	100.0	100.0	100.0	...	Norfolk Island
15	...	225	6,883	88,008[14]	11.0[14]	26.6[1]	2,018	9.1	15	100.0	100.0	100.0	8.8	Norway
3,476	6.1	5	72	475	6.6	—	46	...	...	38.0	55.0	20.0	2.3	Oman
...	...	1[2]	158[2]	2,129[2]	13.5[2]	...	...	6.4	15	92.2	93.6	90.8	20.5	Pacific Is., Trust Territory of the
52,000	13.7	122	9,371	137,216	14.6	2.0[4]	169	1.7	15	25.6	36.0	15.2	1.9	Pakistan
15	15	3	2,578	45,824	17.8	22.6[3]	2,140	4.2	15	88.9	88.7	89.1	5.1	Panama
7,392	13.5	3	644	3,954	6.1	1.9[3]	165	...	15	42.3	52.4	31.3	4.7	Papua New Guinea
15	15	2	2,448	31,317	12.8	...	649	2.0	14	85.7	89.6	81.9	1.3	Paraguay
142,154	16.3	35	23,435	277,304	11.8	21.3	1,957	4.5	15	78.7	84.3	73.1	3.4	Peru
...	...	1,038	45,893	1,226,365	26.7	26.6[1]	2,642	11.9	15	88.7	89.9	87.5	2.0	Philippines
...	...	...	...	...	...	...	...	...	15	100.0	100.0	100.0	...	Pitcairn Island
1,313,000	14.9	91	55,769	274,200	4.9	15.6[3]	1,362	5.7	15	98.5	98.9	98.1	3.4	Poland
26,003	...	21	10,578	89,964	8.5	11.2[2]	937	1.6	15	78.2	84.0	72.7	4.7	Portugal
60,045[1]	23.1[1]	22	9,531	155,726	16.3	...	4,703	18.4	15	90.8	91.8	89.8	8.2	Puerto Rico
518	6.0	1[3]	215	4,015	18.7	16.5[3]	1,587	11.6	10	51.1	51.2	50.1	3.1	Qatar
15	15	1	82	3,000	36.6	...	...	...	15	78.7	...	...	...	Réunion
15	15	44	13,344	174,042	13.0	11.4[3]	802	4.6	15	95.8	97.3	94.3	2.7	Romania
640	17.8	...	184	1,213	6.6	...	30	...	15	49.4	62.2	37.2	4.6	Rwanda
240	8.3	1[1]	9[1]	671	7.4[1]	...	151	1.1	15	97.6	97.6	97.7	6.5	St. Christopher and Nevis
38	6.3	—	—	—	—	...	...	...	15	97.1	96.8	97.5	...	St. Helena and Ascension
358	7.5	—	—	—	—	...	...	1.0	15	81.7	80.8	82.4	7.8	St. Lucia
217	5.4	—	—	—	—	...	...	7.5	15	99.5	99.5	99.5	...	St. Pierre and Miquelon
275	7.1	1	19	105	5.5	...	...	0.8	15	85.0	...	...	5.8	St. Vincent and the Grenadines
431	...	—	...	456[25]	—	...	...	2.4	15	97.2	97.8	96.7	5.9	San Marino
405	11.6	...	...	700[25]	—	...	...	0.3	15	50.0	...	...	7.0	São Tomé and Príncipe
2,371	2.7	73	8,631	82,369	9.5	8.7[1]	763	...	15	24.6	34.5	12.2	5.8	Saudi Arabia
10,820	...	...	684	13,560	19.8	2.5	215	0.1	6	47.7	60.4	32.3	3.8	Senegal
15	15	1	143	1,284	9.0	...	...	2.6	15	62.0	...	...	7.0	Seychelles
3,302	10.3	2	303	1,919	6.3	0.6[2]	52	...	5	18.7	23.7	13.7	3.9	Sierra Leone
14,771	8.8	5	3,396	35,783	10.6	10.7[3]	1,261	3.4	10	85.6	92.3	78.6	4.5	Singapore
1,142	18.1	—	...	...	—	...	...	1.6	15	54.1	62.4	44.9	3.6	Solomon Islands
10,629	16.3	1	262	2,332	8.9	0.9[4]	65	...	15	5.2	10.0	0.5	1.8	Somalia
35,394	9.5	96	15,245	204,546	13.4	...	...	3.7[16]	15	79.3	80.6	78.0	4.3	South Africa
6,053	16.8	1	36[2]	816	...	...	...	...	15	75.0	...	...	...	Bophuthatswana
525	8.0	2	40	338	8.4	...	...	...	...	...	...	...	...	Ciskei
...	...	...	...	...	...	...	...	...	...	...	...	...	...	Transkei
...	...	...	...	...	...	...	...	...	...	...	...	...	...	Venda
1,200	14.8	4	137	537	3.9	...	...	...	15	...	...	...	1.9	South West Africa/Namibia
695,180	15.3	33	43,037	692,152	16.1	23.2[2]	1,867	3.7	14	92.8	96.3	89.6	2.6	Spain
8,382	18.0	8	4,120	57,352	13.9	3.6[3]	371	2.3	15	86.1	90.8	81.2	3.0	Sri Lanka
23,696	15.0	17[2]	1,934[2]	32,784	...	2.0[1]	173	...	15	21.6	36.5	6.5	4.7	Sudan, The
9,853	17.7	2	167	734	4.4	2.7[4]	255	...	15	77.8	81.7	74.0	8.3	Suriname
1,473	12.2	1	131	1,063	8.1	...	287	...	15	56.0	57.9	54.5	5.2	Swaziland
179,733	...	...	216,000	...	...	38.2[3]	2,620	15.4	15	100.0	100.0	100.0	9.0	Sweden
251,200	...	...	...	105,900	...	18.6[3]	1,400	2.9	15	99.9	...	...	4.9	Switzerland
63,537	...	60	1,440	134,586	...	16.1[1]	1,489	1.3	10	65.7	80.1	50.8	6.0	Syria
406,365	...	105	20,061	412,381	20.6	...	2,158	...	15	88.9	94.9	82.5	3.4	Taiwan
17,914	24.1	1	893	3,780	4.2	0.4[1]	33	0.2	10	73.5	77.7	69.6	5.9	Tanzania
594,243	21.6	62	23,808	257,353	10.8	22.3[3]	2,146	3.1	15	81.8	88.9	74.9	3.9	Thailand
7,306	...	1	285	4,131	14.5	1.7	145	0.1	15	35.2	46.1	25.1	5.8	Togo
197[2]	16.4[2]	—	—	—	—	...	...	...	15	99.8	99.8	99.8	...	Tokelau
554	...	—	—	—	—	...	...	...	15	92.8	92.9	92.8	3.4	Tonga
7,881[2]	...	1	272	2,923	10.7	4.6[2]	500	1.2	...	92.3	94.8	89.9	5.9	Trinidad and Tobago
...	...	...	4,397	35,426	8.1	5.1[3]	510	1.8	15	47.4	61.2	33.7	5.4	Tunisia
560,415	13.9	288	20,441	323,375	15.8	5.9[3]	593	2.2	6	67.4	79.9	54.6	2.9	Turkey
—	—	—	—	—	—	...	...	4.9	15	86.7	85.0	88.0	...	Turks and Caicos Islands
354	22.1	—	—	100[1,25]	—	...	...	...	15	95.5	95.5	95.5	...	Tuvalu
13,338	18.1	4	640	7,312	11.4	0.6	52	0.1	...	52.5	64.6	40.5	1.3	Uganda
4,502,800	18.2	890	374,000	5,310,300	14.2	21.2[3]	1,971	8.3	15	99.8	...	...	6.7	U.S.S.R.
2,652	7.7	318[2]	8,343[2]	125,209[2]	15.0[2]	6.8[3]	549	6.0	15	68.6	71.0	61.0	1.5	United Arab Emirates
264,813[1]	...	46	31,642	801,000	25.3	19.4[3]	1,520	11.0	15	99.9	...	...	5.7	United Kingdom
...	...	...	870,000	12,400,000	14.2	58.0[1]	5,492	32.2	15	95.5	95.7	95.3	6.8	United States
51,697	...	11	4,149[1]	36,458[1]	8.8	20.4[3]	1,623	6.3	15	96.3	93.5[6]	94.4[6]	2.4	Uruguay
351	8.8	—	—	—	—	...	...	...	...	...	...	...	...	Vanuatu
...	...	106	25,268	282,274	11.2	21.5[3]	2,100	2.6	15	84.9	87.2	82.6	5.8	Venezuela
99,200	9.7	93	18,100	92,500	5.1	2.5[2]	213	...	15	94.0	...	...	3.5	Vietnam
775	28.7	1	84	765	9.1	...	...	17.6	...	...	...	...	7.6	Virgin Islands (U.S.)
—	—	—	—	—	—	...	...	...	14	34.2	35.4	33.0	...	Wallis and Futuna
1,583	...	4[14]	483[4]	7,066[14]	...	...	...	...	...	...	...	...	...	West Bank
...	...	...	...	...	...	...	...	...	...	...	...	...	...	Western Sahara
295	7.0	6	27	356	13.1	...	...	2.2	10	98.3	98.5	98.1	5.9	Western Samoa
1,556	9.0	...	386[2]	3,469[1]	...	2.3[1]	191	...	15	38.9	66.6	10.9	7.2	Yemen (Aden)
4,023	20.5	...	157[2]	4,220	...	1.2[2]	78	...	15	8.3	15.9	0.5	4.8	Yemen (Şan'ā')
612,457[1]	...	357	24,905	386,356	15.5	20.7[3]	1,712	3.9	15	90.5	95.9	85.3	4.4	Yugoslavia
192,329[4]	...	36	2,782	26,430	...	1.2[3]	106	...	15	54.5	73.6	36.7	5.8	Zaire
9,711	...	1	334[1]	3,648	...	1.8[1]	152	0.6	15	68.6	79.3	58.3	5.1	Zambia
14,272	15.0	1	325	4,130[10]	...	0.5[3]	39	0.6	15	70.8	78.0	63.8	6.4	Zimbabwe

[1]1981. [2]1980. [3]1982. [4]1979. [5]Public schools only. [6]1975. [7]1972. [8]1976. [9]1977. [10]1984. [11]Vocational includes third level. [12]1978. [13]First level includes second level. [14]1983. [15]General second level includes vocational. [16]Universities only. [17]1970. [18]Vocational only. [19]Includes East Jerusalem. [20]University of Nairobi only. [21]General second level includes first level. [22]Includes part-time teachers. [23]Public school teachers only. [24]Includes part-time students. [25]Students registered abroad. [26]Tanzania mainland only. [27]Excludes East Jerusalem.

Cultural institutions

This table supplies worldwide statistics for the principal and most comparable elements of cultural activity: publishing, libraries, cinema, performing arts, museums, and nature preservation. For the most part, the data that can be compiled and compared are those measures produced as a result of governmental activity or expenditure, such as copyright and deposit, public funding, taxation, and land-use policy. But the level of activity implied by the figures reflects the degree of interest the people of a particular country have in cultural matters, the financial capacity of their public institutions to support activities often deemed nonessential, such as theatre or music, or, in some cases, their government's emphasis on strengthening and regenerating a national culture, language, and folk tradition that have been lost or attenuated as a result of colonialism or modernization.

Nevertheless, international comparisons of such data should be approached with caution. In older, more prosperous nations, where the physical necessities of life are in secure supply, more money is available for cultural activities—and, indeed, for collecting data on them—than in poor, less developed countries. This will be reflected in the numbers. Yet a poor country with an embryonic statistical system may have a flourishing cultural life that includes theatrical performance, live music, or the practice of arts no longer central to the Western experience, such as oral storytelling, dance, traditional community rituals, and puppetry. Such activities may be more fully integrated into the life of the people than the more measurable cultural pursuits of a developed society.

The statistics actually reported may include books published (copyrighted), cultural facilities, library holdings, seating capacities of theatres and cinemas, attendance (tickets sold), and so on. Even when these figures are recalculated on a per capita basis, apparent differences among countries may be more a function of each country's statistical reporting system than of differences among the cultural habits and preferences of the people.

Furthermore, some kinds of data cannot be given meaningfully. For example, available data on government expenditures for cultural activities represent a wide variety of government policies. Some governments provide no support for cultural activities at any level; others subsidize or support them directly. Some offer tax incentives; others employ artists as teachers, performers, scholars, or archivists. Most national data on manpower engaged in cultural activities are collected on the basis of the individual's main source of income, without regard for his or her aspirations or avocations, part-time paid or unpaid activities, or other less convenient measures. In sum, comparisons of the data provided on national cultural activities should be made with due consideration of their inherent limitations.

A substantial part of the data presented were obtained from periodic surveys by Unesco, and they refer to a wide range of years. Throughout the table, data given in roman type are from 1981 or later; those in italic are from before 1981.

Figures for book production generally include all works published in separate bindings except advertising works, timetables, telephone directories, price lists, catalogs of businesses or exhibitions, musical scores, maps, atlases, and the like. The figures include government publications, school texts, theses, offprints, series works, and illustrated works, even those consisting principally of illustrations. Figures refer to works actually published during the year of survey, usually by a registered publisher, and deposited for copyright. A book is defined as a work of 49 or more pages, a pamphlet as a work of from 5 to 48 pages. A work published

Cultural institutions

country	book publishing								public libraries			
	number of titles				number of copies ('000)				number	volumes ('000)	registered borrowers ('000)	loans per 1,000 population
	books		periodicals	pamphlets	books		periodicals	pamphlets				
	total	of which school textbooks			total	of which school textbooks						
Afghanistan	415[3]	108[3]	51	...	5,981[3]	...	1,094	...	38	230	...	...
Albania	1,037	504	8	112	4,288	3,325	2,894	319	45	5,712	...	...
Algeria	234	...	27	41	...	...	476	...	6	165	...	...
American Samoa	983	24[3]	16	1	33[3]	...	8	1	1	251	...	5,400
Andorra	...	...	...	...	...	...	...	...	...	...	...	...
Angola	33[3]	...	...	24[3]	239[3]	...	...	191[3]	1	15	...	...
Anguilla	...	...	...	...	...	...	...	...	1	...	...	...
Antigua and Barbuda	...	...	...	...	...	...	...	...	...	...	...	...
Argentina	4,962[6]	466[6]	...	...	14,763[6]	4,259[6]	...	...	1,528	9,532	4,201	360
Australia	1,759	...	3,534	599	...	...	...	...	...	...	...	...
Austria	5,821	99	2,108	915	...	...	...	...	2,321[11]	5,531	718	...
Bahamas, The	...	...	...	...	...	...	...	...	...	...	...	...
Bahrain	78	78	...	...	843	843	...	...	1	140	50	78
Bangladesh	857[6]	43	388	6	...	...	657	...	...	...	...	...
Barbados	29	...	120	110	...	...	...	...	1	174	62	1,900
Belgium	9,736[6]	979[6]	10,808	6	...	...	...	...	2,351	24,140	1,731	4,300
Belize	...	...	...	...	...	...	...	...	...	...	...	...
Benin	13	...	...	—	18	...	...	—	...	...	...	...
Bermuda	...	...	...	...	...	...	...	...	1	140	3	...
Bhutan	...	...	...	...	...	...	...	...	...	...	...	...
Bolivia	274	4[3]	106	27	...	...	...	...	...	...	...	...
Botswana	70[3]	...	...	27[3]	35	...	...	33	1	108	30	48
Brazil	12,880	1,911	1,761	5,222	186,750	42,220	...	132,586	...	...	...	...
British Virgin Islands	3[15]	...	2	—[15]	0.5[15]	...	2	—[15]	1	29	...	1,800
Brunei	60	16	3	1	222	95	70	3	1	106	6	230
Bulgaria	4,183	878	1,117	887	52,822	11,143	8,813	6,840	5,758	50,700	2,282	5,700
Burkina Faso	4	...	...	—	...	...	...	—	...	...	...	...
Burma	1,400	...	24	...	...	...	773	...	...	...	...	...
Burundi	...	...	...	...	...	...	...	...	2	34	...	...
Cameroon	22[3]	7[3]	41	...	94[3]	7[3]	...	...	1	6	...	...
Canada	13,954	496	1,384	429	...	...	56,159	...	883	49,874	...	5,800
Cape Verde	...	...	4	...	...	...	...	...	...	...	...	...
Cayman Islands	5	...	...	—	...	...	...	—	1	6	2	2,400
Central African Republic	...	...	...	...	...	...	...	...	...	...	...	...
Chad	...	...	4	...	...	...	...	...	...	...	...	...
Chile	640	340	89	278	3,660	...	...	435	161	581	...	380
China	31,784[6]	4,144[6]	3,100	6	5,880,000[6]	...	1,510,000	6	1,889	...	...	...
Christmas Island	...	...	...	...	...	...	...	...	1	12	3	8,000
Cocos (Keeling) Islands	...	...	...	...	...	...	...	...	1	...	...	...
Colombia	5,877	670	1,034	1,794	27,160	10,003	...	5,577	...	...	...	...
Comoros	...	...	...	...	...	...	...	...	2	8	...	...
Congo	9	...	...	118	285	...	...	1,471	7	55	34	62
Cook Islands	...	...	...	...	...	...	...	...	1	15	3	1,060
Costa Rica	...	70[3]	274	...	121	110[3,23]	163	...	18	...	...	...
Cuba	1,387	874	50	253	42,329	28,273	2,121	2,108	243	3,031	...	440
Cyprus	180[24]	12[24]	105	957[24]	290[24]	120[24]	272	1,936[24]	...	236	...	230
Czechoslovakia	7,202	3,375	1,071	1,415	79,523	20,942	2,455	12,931	9,760	52,821	2,765	5,800
Denmark	6,807	1,016[25]	...	3,382	...	...	...	...	247	30,739	...	15,000
Djibouti	...	...	2	...	...	...	1	...	1	11	...	54
Dominica	...	...	...	...	...	...	...	...	1	15	4	600

simultaneously in more than one country is counted as having been published in each. Data for newspapers are given in the Communications table beginning on page 898.

Data on libraries are for public libraries and exclude other types of collections, such as national, school and university, private, professional, business, and government libraries, even though these may play a significant role locally or nationally. Public libraries were thought to provide the most representative set of figures. Data for "volumes" may reflect either actual holdings or an estimate based on length of occupied shelving.

Statistics on commercial cinema attendance may originate from a variety of screening facilities, including fixed, mobile, or drive-in facilities. Seating capacity is given for fixed facilities only. The data on long (or feature) films may refer to prints with a length of from 1,000 to 3,000 metres, depending on the reporting practices of the individual country. However, there is some consensus among reporting countries on a standard length (for classification purposes) of 2,000 metres.

In the performing arts, many countries (if they report such data at all) include not only the familiar Western performance modes—music, theatre, opera, musical theatre, dance—but also other types of live performance, such as traditional, ceremonial, seasonal, festival, or holiday observances and such entertainments as circuses and puppet and shadow theatre. Data on number of performances and attendance refer to both amateur and professional performances unless footnoted. Statistics on the number of theatres refer to theatre buildings and open-air theatres intended mainly for theatrical and other dramatic performances. Premises only occasionally or partly used for performances of this type, such as cultural centres, cultural houses, youth centres, sports establishments, concert halls, cine-

mas, university and school premises, open-air grounds, antique theatres, historic buildings, and ancient sites, are excluded.

Museum data are derived in large part from surveys by Unesco and the International Council of Museums (ICOM). The number of museums and museum attendance refer to public and private institutions whose exhibits and collections are devoted primarily to art, archaeology and history, natural history and natural science and technology, or ethnology and anthropology; they may be specialized (single theme), regional, or general. National parks and nature reserves, zoos, aquariums, and botanical gardens have not been counted with museums since they are included in the nature conservation section of the table.

Data on nature conservation facilities generally refer to those operated by the national conservation authority (though in many countries, particularly those with federal systems, authority may be lodged with other governmental levels). The data on number of facilities cover all types of facilities operated by the relevant authority, including national parks and monuments, scientific reserves, game reserves, protected landscapes, resource and anthropological reserves,. and multiple-use management areas. Data on surface extent usually include only those facilities with an area of more than 10 sq km (4 sq mi).

The data on national parks and nature reserves are derived from information compiled by the International Union for Conservation of Nature and Natural Resources (IUCN) and from Britannica's holdings of published and unpublished national data. The data on zoos, aquariums, and botanical gardens are mainly from the International Species Inventory System (zoos and aquariums) and the International Association of Botanical Gardens.

cinema					performing arts				museums			nature preservation			country
annual attendance (all cinemas)		fixed cinemas		number of long films produced	number of facilities	number of performances	annual attendance		number	annual attendance		national parks and nature reserves		zoos, botanical gardens etc. (number[2])	
number ('000,000)	per 1,000 population	number	seating capacity ('000)				number ('000)	per 1,000 population		number ('000)	per 1,000 population	number	square metres per capita[1]		
4.9	300	34	19	5	...	...	...	...	7	7	0.5	6	120	1	Afghanistan
...	...	95	29	14	28	2,913[4]	1,650	640	c. 200	...	...	4	39	...	Albania
22.6[5]	1,200[5]	272	138	2	...	...	...	...	32	260	14	1	150	3	Algeria
0.2	7,400	6	6	...	...	...	...	...	1	52	1,700	...	...	...	American Samoa
0.2	6,900	5	2	...	...	14	6	190	2	9	300	—	—	...	Andorra
6.4	900	55	34	1	...	...	...	...	10	...	...	13	12,000	1	Angola
...	...	...	...	...	...	...	...	...	...	...	...	...	...	...	Anguilla
...	...	3	...	...	...	...	...	...	3	...	...	2	320	...	Antigua and Barbuda
43.9[5,7]	1,600[5,7]	1,010[7]	530[7]	27	399	330	4,136[8]	160[8]	318	5,215[9]	200[9]	30	1,200	16	Argentina
...	...	564[7]	...	23	...	1,419[8]	...	...	15	5,279[10]	360[10]	411	21,000	41	Australia
18.0[5]	2,400[5]	481	146	16	...	...	...	...	99	6,177	820	16	1,600	21	Austria
...	...	13	6	...	...	...	...	...	7	...	...	6	5,200	1	Bahamas, The
1.3	3,800	313	...	...	...	...	...	...	3	4	14	...	...	...	Bahrain
...	...	257	161	49	...	...	...	...	38	...	...	3	4	1	Bangladesh
1.2	5,200	6	5	...	1	8	...	...	1	12	47	1	10	...	Barbados
21.6[5]	2,200[5]	500	...	9	...	...	...	...	132[12]	3,454[12]	350[12]	17	8	12	Belgium
...	...	...	...	...	...	...	...	...	5	9	64	—	—	...	Belize
1.1[5]	300[5]	47	4	...	...	...	...	...	3[13]	10[13]	3[13]	5	3,800	...	Benin
0.3	4,200	2	1	...	3	64	17	320	14	...	...	10	5	1	Bermuda
...	...	12	5	...	...	...	...	...	1	16	13	1	4,500	...	Bhutan
31.1[5]	5,700[5]	209	160	1	13	500[8]	123[8]	22[8]	28	...	...	18	7,800	4	Bolivia
0.1[7]	200[7]	1[7]	0.8[7]	...	...	29	...	...	2	52	66	9	111,000	...	Botswana
138.9	...	2,221	906	84	267	1,563	...	...	400	8,838[14]	82[14]	43	880	31	Brazil
40.0[16]	3,300	1	0.4	...	...	3	4	330	1	1	77	7	800	...	British Virgin Islands
2.6	14,700	7	8	...	...	78	9	41	2	107	500	...	...	1	Brunei
93.6	10,500	3,266	742	33	63	17,139	6,200	700	201	17,860	2,000	12	62	4	Bulgaria
4.0	600	12	14	...	...	...	...	...	1	...	...	12	4,500	...	Burkina Faso
...	...	175[7]	136	47	...	...	...	...	12	...	...	5	87	2	Burma
0.1	20	7	2	...	44	...	77	19	2	110	24	7	210	...	Burundi
...	...	52	29	...	...	44[17]	39[17]	5	12	4,641	560	19	2,800	2	Cameroon
87.8	3,700	1,016[7]	604	32	476	14,882[8,18]	5,307[8,18]	220[8,18]	879	26,338[19]	1,100[19]	76	8,900	104	Canada
...	...	...	...	...	...	...	...	...	...	...	...	...	...	...	Cape Verde
0.2[5]	...	4	1	...	...	...	...	...	...	...	...	...	...	...	Cayman Islands
...	...	...	...	...	...	...	...	...	2	...	...	12	26,000	...	Central African Republic
25.4	6,000	13	12	...	4	120[20]	...	...	...	...	...	3	18,000	...	Chad
14.6[5]	1,300[5]	172	110	2	...	811[8]	299[8]	—	69	...	...	26	2,600	10	Chile
18,250	18,100	143,650[21]	...	114	...	...	...	...	409	...	...	49	18	47	China
...	...	...	...	...	...	...	...	...	...	...	...	1	4,800	...	Christmas Island
...	...	...	...	...	...	...	...	...	...	...	...	...	...	...	Cocos (Keeling) Islands
68.0[5]	2,400[5]	391	...	...	14	159[8]	90[8]	3[8]	73	1,442[22]	57[22]	31	1,500	8	Colombia
...	...	...	...	...	...	...	...	...	...	...	...	...	...	...	Comoros
...	...	...	...	1	1	74	...	...	4	...	...	10	8,600	1	Congo
...	...	...	...	...	...	...	...	...	1	6	320	...	...	...	Cook Islands
...	...	...	...	...	9	347[8]	50[8]	24[8]	9	...	...	20	2,500	1	Costa Rica
88.9	9,100	1,363	...	7	47	51,638	...	...	186	5,349	540	4	25	6	Cuba
...	...	...	...	...	12	793	206	330	26	95	150	—	—	1	Cyprus
78.6	5,100	2,882	825	66	83	24,163[8]	9,858[8]	640[8]	231	13,762	920	25	710	42	Czechoslovakia
16.2[5]	3,200[5]	471	103	8	16[26]	4,203[8,26]	1,654[8,26]	330[8,26]	277	7,828[27]	1,530[27]	12	51	19	Denmark
0.6	5,200	4	6	...	...	...	...	...	...	...	...	—	—	...	Djibouti
...	...	3	...	...	...	...	...	...	...	...	...	1	810	1	Dominica

Cultural institutions (continued)

country	book publishing								public libraries			
	number of titles				number of copies ('000)				number	volumes ('000)	registered borrowers ('000)	loans per 1,000 population
	books		periodicals	pamphlets	books		periodicals	pamphlets				
	total	of which school textbooks			total	of which school textbooks						
Dominican Republic	1,504	...	...	715	3,017	...	...	1,320	68	...	...	120
Ecuador	...	...	284	...	...	...	...	...	...	...	...	...
Egypt	1,503	...	194	177	46,620	...	1,516	6,380	223	1,329	31	10
El Salvador	59	6[3]	...	85	...	...	...	...	...	...	...	...
Equatorial Guinea	...	...	...	...	...	...	...	...	...	...	...	...
Ethiopia	150	...	1	...	993	...	2	66	2	20	...	...
Faeroe Islands	...	...	3	...	...	...	2	...	11	108	7	2,850
Falkland Islands	...	...	3	...	...	...	...	...	...	...	...	...
Fiji	84	...	13	26	229	...	...	44	9	91	33	520
Finland	5,562	418	...	1,874	...	...	...	...	1,594[11]	24,876	...	...
France	27,152	...	13,716	15,034	...	...	...	...	1,028	50,470	4,917	1,700
French Guiana	1[3]	—	9	—	2[3]	—	5	1	1	19	0.7	230
French Polynesia	56	8	17	16	92	40	25	10	1	17	1	55
Gabon	...	...	...	...	...	...	...	...	...	...	...	...
Gambia, The	21	20	3	60	9	4	...	...	1	67	...	...
Gaza Strip												
Germany, East	5,600	165	1,178	785	113,782	17,604	22,948	27,606	7,146	41,165	3,854	5,000
Germany, West	48,900	2,747	...	9,692	...	...	...	...	14,211[11]	...	...	2,700
Ghana	78	20[3]	74	67	163	...	254	91	7	929	70	77
Gibraltar	...	...	...	...	...	...	...	...	2	19	6	2,700
Greece	3,618	114	868	430	...	...	...	...	...	...	...	...
Greenland	...	...	...	...	...	...	...	...	1	93	...	...
Grenada	2[3]	...	...	8[3]	2[3]	...	...	9[3]	1	15	1	...
Guadeloupe	...	...	45	...	...	...	142	...	1	90	15	410
Guam	12[3]	...	28	...	0.3[3]	...	...	...	1	189	...	1,600
Guatemala	350	...	...	224	68	...	...	...	1	27	...	...
Guernsey	...	...	...	...	...	...	...	...	...	...	...	...
Guinea	...	...	1	...	...	...	...	...	...	...	...	...
Guinea-Bissau												
Guyana	24	3	65	68	...	...	53	...	...	...	...	...
Haiti	...	...	...	...	...	...	...	...	...	...	...	...
Honduras	...	...	...	...	...	...	...	...	1	...	...	5
Hong Kong	2,934	204	413	626	25,014	1,969	...	4,203	1	1,030	851	810
Hungary	7,600	1,367	1,009	900	99,400	30,200	498,300	8,622	10,272[36]	44,610[36]	2,215[36]	3,600[36]
Iceland	575	...	...	226	...	...	...	...	...	...	...	...
India	10,391	543	17,880	258	...	...	...	...	...	...	...	...
Indonesia	1,617	399	...	705	...	...	...	...	30	460	2,768	...
Iran	2,994[6]	213[6]	180	6	...	...	...	...	385	2,161	...	8
Iraq	182	...	...	...	1,274	...	...	...	...	...	...	...
Ireland	522	38	258	184	...	...	2,987	...	31	7,399	719	4,900
Isle of Man	...	...	...	...	...	...	...	...	...	...	...	...
Israel	4,892[3]	2,908	1,100	313	17,122[6]	9,305	...	6	750	...	...	...
Italy[39]	11,140	1,245	8,265	1,516	145,119	47,286	...	10,624	...	...	...	...
Ivory Coast	23	...	...	6	945	...	...	620	1	25	2	3
Jamaica	81	38	...	18	...	...	...	380	1	1,108	615	1,100
Japan	42,217	1,778[3]	2,353	...	664,254	231,585[3]	...	...	891	58,786	6,521	1,000
Jersey												
Jordan	...	...	40	...	...	...	100	...	1	17	0.4	...
Kampuchea	...	...	3	...	...	...	...	...	...	...	...	...
Kenya	189	40	...	19	...	...	...	...	2	511	98	34
Kiribati												
Korea, North												
Korea, South	33,321	2,722	870	1,008	144,000	36,845	...	3,692	147	1,743	12,819	120
Kuwait	22	...	45	3	325	...	982	34	1	281	...	55
Laos	...	...	...	...								
Lebanon												
Lesotho	...	...	2	...	...	...	10	...	...	...	...	...
Liberia	...	...	...	...	...	...	...	...	1	17	...	...
Libya	481[6]	...	...	6	2,405[6]	...	...	6	5	100	...	...
Liechtenstein	...	...	...	...	...	...	...	...	1	...	9	1,000
Luxembourg	229	9[3]	337	76	...	...	...	...	...	...	...	...
Macau	...	...	...	...	...	...	...	...	4	250	120	...
Madagascar	196	51	...	88	216	83	...	230	28	49	69	...
Malawi	18[3]	...	121	19	...	...	...	...	1	91	20	51
Malaysia	2,133	394	...	2,801	4,689	1,814	...	3,514	18	2,419	400	...
Maldives	3[3]	...	...	...	...	...	...	...	1	8	...	...
Mali	4[3]	...	...	2[3]	4[3]	...	...	4[3]	2	...	...	...
Malta	221	3[3]	248	26	...	...	...	...	1	159	35	1,600
Martinique	3[3]	...	8	18[3]	10[3]	...	14	33[3]	...	...	...	...
Mauritania	21	21	...	20	...	...	...	...	1	26	...	...
Mauritius	47	3[3]	...	33	44	5,000[3]	...	131	4	210	...	...
Mayotte												
Mexico	2,818	...	1,964	...	...	...	...	...	485	2,102	3,574	...
Monaco	105[6]	...	105	6	453[6]	...	792	6	1	130	...	...
Mongolia	6,241[6]	...	35	6	6,100[6]	...	5,500	6	386	8,000	...	...
Montserrat	...	...	...	...	...	...	...	...	1	...	...	...
Morocco	...	...	63	...	...	...	145	...	8	448	...	...
Mozambique	76[3]	29	...	...	2,789[3]	2,300	...	...	1	8	...	...
Nauru												
Nepal	4[3]	...	...	—	70	...	...	—	...	...	...	...
Netherlands, The	13,324	2,321	...	...	...	...	...	...	475	30,722	4,008	11,000
Netherlands Antilles	28	...	...	24	...	...	...	...	1	100	10	930
New Caledonia	40	...	16	1	4	...	38	2	1	34	...	...
New Zealand	1,240	45	...	1,259	...	...	...	...	209	6,077	1,161	9,500
Nicaragua	...	...	...	...	...	...	...	...	...	...	...	...

cinema — annual attendance (all cinemas) number ('000,000)	per 1,000 population	fixed cinemas number	seating capacity ('000)	number of long films produced	performing arts number of facilities	number of performances	annual attendance number ('000)	per 1,000 population	museums number	annual attendance number ('000)	per 1,000 population	nature preservation national parks and nature reserves number	square metres per capita[1]	zoos, botanical gardens etc. (number[2])	country
7.0[5,7]	1,500[5,7]	837[7]	46[7]	...	2	41	74	14	6	...	...	5	390	1	Dominican Republic
...	...	330	...	...	75	148	...	...	23	...	...	9	150	1	Ecuador
46.2	1,200	229	200	...	...	...	...	...	45	1,613	44	...	...	9	Egypt
15.9[5]	...	...	...	...	...	...	...	...	4	388	87	—	—	1	El Salvador
0.5	1,600	10	4	...	...	21[8]	16[8]	47[8]	1	...	...	...	...	...	Equatorial Guinea
...	...	40	36	...	...	253	224	7	12	...	...	10	400	3	Ethiopia
0.3	7,100	9	1	...	...	...	...	...	1	...	...	...	...	...	Faeroe Islands
21.0[16]	10,500	2	0.5	...	...	...	...	...	1	...	...	...	...	...	Falkland Islands
0.3	500	50	40	...	3	255	57	90	1	25	40	2	84	1	Fiji
9.8[5]	2,000[5]	363	95	17	59	10,378[8]	2,658[8]	560[8]	583	...	...	15	2,000	7	Finland
188.2	3,500	4,695	1,363	164	...	19,300[8,28]	10,700[8,28]	200[8,28]	1,434[29]	11,000[13]	210[13]	33[30]	980[30]	79	France
...	...	...	...	...	...	...	...	...	1	12	190	—	—	...	French Guiana
0.5	4,000	6	3	...	2	33[8]	14[8]	99[8]	3	...	...	5	...	...	French Polynesia
1.1	2,100	...	...	...	...	...	...	...	1	...	...	6	14,000	...	Gabon
...	...	...	...	...	...	...	...	...	...	...	...	1	32	...	Gambia, The
...	...	...	...	...	...	...	...	...	...	...	...	...	...	...	Gaza Strip
72.8	4,400	824	255	20	195	75,380	27,128	1,600	664	31,484	1,900	...	...	39	Germany, East
141.8	2,300	3,530	892	90	325	51,300[8]	21,400[8]	350[8]	805[31]	35,300[31]	570[31]	31	59	126	Germany, West
4.4	400	7	16	1	11	3,672	653	61	4	69	6	6	890	3	Ghana
0.2	7,500	4	2	...	3	39	15	450	1	16	500	...	...	...	Gibraltar
55.2	5,900	...	...	33	91	14,760	5,230	560	169	3,373[32]	360[32]	13	88	3	Greece
...	...	...	...	...	...	...	...	...	...	...	...	1	33	...	Greenland
1.2	12,500	6	4	...	28	...	...	...	1	11	120	1	140	2	Grenada
0.8	2,650	...	...	...	...	92	44	130	4	...	...	1	680	...	Guadeloupe
...	...	...	...	...	1	...	...	...	4	...	...	...	...	...	Guam
10.1[5]	1,400[5]	126	85	...	...	206[34]	50[34]	7[34]	13	853	120	6	160	2	Guatemala
...	...	...	...	...	...	...	...	...	9	...	...	...	...	1	Guernsey
...	...	4	...	...	...	...	...	...	16	...	...	1	25	...	Guinea
...	...	...	...	...	...	...	...	...	...	...	...	...	...	...	Guinea-Bissau
13.3[5]	14,700[5]	50	40	...	3	...	...	...	2	235	300	1	130	2	Guyana
6.2[5]	1,300[5]	19[7]	37	...	...	...	...	...	4	73[35]	16[35]	4	8	...	Haiti
...	...	...	...	...	...	...	...	...	3	22	7	6	1,100	3	Honduras
66.0	12,900	89	100	129	8	424[8]	362[8]	93[8]	5	565	130	...	...	3	Hong Kong
70.0	6,500	3,700	547	31	45	15,390[8]	7,206[8]	670[8]	113	7,920	740	7	120	14	Hungary
2.6[5]	11,400[5]	477	...	4	...	...	...	...	24	...	...	24	36,000	2	Iceland
4,600.0[5]	6,800[5]	6,991[7]	4,195	741	...	...	...	...	422	...	...	206	130	42	India
144.9[5]	1,000[5]	1,320	852	90	34	4,600	2,800	19	110	...	...	81	58	12	Indonesia
165.0[5]	4,200[5]	410[7]	264	...	19	848[8]	...	...	44	...	...	60	1,300	3	Iran
...	...	84	65	3	36	743[8]	228[8]	19[8]	15	664	52	...	...	1	Iraq
18.0	5,800	142	...	2	34	10,260[8]	...	...	49	...	...	4	60	5	Ireland
...	...	...	...	...	...	...	...	...	4	...	...	...	...	2	Isle of Man
24.2	6,600	214	152	14	5	275[8,37]	...	...	76	7,151	1,900	27	25	13	Israel
216.2[5]	3,800[5]	7,726	...	c. 100	313	64,238[8]	18,055[8]	320[8]	1,122	22,912[39]	410[39]	12	54	57	Italy[39]
7.0	900	72	42	2	...	...	...	...	1	...	...	10	2,400	2	Ivory Coast
...	...	...	...	...	16	839	1,143	540	5	44[35]	22[35]	2[41]	2	5	Jamaica
149.5	1,300	2,298	918	498	140	39,768[8]	...	...	405	41,468[41]	360[41]	78	270	109	Japan
...	...	...	...	...	...	...	...	...	5	...	...	...	...	1	Jersey
15.0	...	41	20	...	5	64	180	84	1	9	4	2	150	...	Jordan
...	...	...	...	...	...	...	...	...	2	...	...	1	19	...	Kampuchea
9.2	600	40	20	...	...	...	...	...	3	165	11	39	2,600	5	Kenya
...	...	...	...	...	—	23[42]	...	...	...	...	...	...	...	...	Kiribati
...	...	...	...	...	...	...	...	...	17	...	...	...	...	2	Korea, North
44.3	1,100	423	244	85	16	3,449	402	10	56	...	...	14	120	4	Korea, South
3.7[5]	2,500[5]	127	15	...	4	196	...	...	3	259	200	...	...	1	Kuwait
...	...	...	...	...	...	...	...	...	...	...	...	...	...	...	Laos
...	...	...	...	...	...	...	...	...	7	...	...	...	...	1	Lebanon
...	...	...	...	...	...	...	...	...	1	...	...	1	47	...	Lesotho
1.5	800	13	9	...	...	...	...	...	7	...	...	...	...	1	Liberia
11.3	3,600	49	22	...	14	439	160	51	26	50	16	4	500	2	Libya
...	...	...	...	...	...	...	...	...	4	...	...	6	410	...	Liechtenstein
1.1	3,000	...	...	...	4	46	...	...	14	225	630	1	980	...	Luxembourg
3.0	11,700	7	8	...	4	84	...	...	1	24	92	...	...	...	Macau
...	...	...	...	...	70	140	60	7	8	135	16	13	750	3	Madagascar
1.5	300	4	2	...	2	...	...	...	2	10	2	9	1,700	...	Malawi
34.0	2,700	425	...	12	12	1,303	312	25	16	...	...	18	530	6	Malaysia
...	...	...	...	1	11	...	...	...	1	1,194	8,200	...	...	...	Maldives
...	...	...	...	...	...	...	...	...	...	...	...	8	5,400	1	Mali
2.1	5,700	31	21	...	...	...	...	...	14	...	...	2	1.1	2	Malta
1.1	3,450	...	...	...	...	...	...	...	5	...	...	1	17	...	Martinique
...	...	19	8	...	...	...	...	...	...	...	...	2	7,200	...	Mauritania
6.0	6,200	47	47	...	6	136	36	38	2	210	220	22	47	1	Mauritius
...	...	...	...	...	...	...	...	...	...	...	...	...	...	...	Mayotte
264.0[5]	3,700[5]	2,701	...	80	94	17,069[43]	6,549[43]	97[43]	105[44]	7,875[44,45]	120[45]	27	77	11	Mexico
0.1	3,800	3	1	...	3	31	13	500	2	154	6,200	...	...	4	Monaco
16.7	9,400	57	...	3	17	...	3,000	1,700	4	7,400	4,400	3	27,000	...	Mongolia
...	...	1	...	...	1	16	4	360	...	...	...	...	...	...	Montserrat
35.8[5]	2,000[5]	227	147	...	...	...	...	12	...	...	...	9	200	5	Morocco
...	...	...	...	...	...	...	...	9	...	...	...	10	2,600	4	Mozambique
...	...	...	...	...	...	...	...	...	...	...	...	...	...	...	Nauru
...	...	...	...	1	16	65	...	5	...	...	...	7	300	1	Nepal
31.8	2,200	551	154	11	155	17,957[8]	4,106[8]	290[8]	410	12,794	920	21	52	36	Netherlands, The
...	...	...	...	...	...	...	...	...	1	...	...	4	400	2	Netherlands Antilles
1.0	6,900	17	4	...	1	46	...	...	1	30	220	4	2,900	1	New Caledonia
...	...	172	103	9	...	2,287[8]	515[8]	120[8]	110	...	...	100	8,300	15	New Zealand
5.2	1,900	127	74	1	...	...	...	...	9	...	...	2	70	1	Nicaragua

Cultural institutions (continued)

country	book publishing								public libraries			
	number of titles				number of copies ('000)				number	volumes ('000)	registered borrowers ('000)	loans per 1,000 population
	books		periodicals	pamphlets	books		periodicals	pamphlets				
	total	of which school textbooks			total	of which school textbooks						
Niger	4	4	...	1	8	8	...	0.1	...	...	...	...
Nigeria	1,172	290[3]	...	494	...	...	...	...	18	481	206	2
Niue	...	...	...	...	...	...	...	...	1	6	...	...
Norfolk Island	—	—	...	1	—	—	...	1	1	5	0.2	6,000
Norway	3,973	...	4,010	1,202	...	...	...	...	454	14,037	1,059	4,000
Oman												
Pacific Is., Trust Terr. of the	93	26	...	40	47	11	...	80	5[11]	16	...	...
Pakistan	1,279	...	1,262	...	...	...	...	...	...	...	...	...
Panama	114	9[3]	...	57	38[3]	...	...	5[3]	18	26	...	32
Papua New Guinea	...	...	72	...	...	...	...	...	...	...	...	...
Paraguay												
Peru	655	67[3]	507	112	...	...	...	...	520	4,102	...	110
Philippines	421	212	...	10	2,087[49]	...	...	1,031[49]	498[11]	...	182	...
Pitcairn Island												
Poland	8,789	1,643	2,215	2,299	194,900	45,300	27,175	...	9,500	107,700	7,219	4,000
Portugal	6,714[6]	359[25]	1,123	6	32,393[6]	7,709[25]	...	6	118	6,284	2,304	630
Puerto Rico	...	...	...	...	...	...	...	...	5	822	...	...
Qatar	316	219	12	21	2,100	1,533	191	105	6	...	1	26
Réunion	503	13	53	16[3]	...	...	110	...	2	205	...	...
Romania	6,762	...	425	1,659	79,752	...	210,000	8,907	6,348	63,083	4,082	2,100
Rwanda	...	...	16	...	...	...	...	...	5	...	...	...
St. Christopher and Nevis	2[3]	—	...	33[3]	—	—	...	1[3]	1	...	...	...
St. Helena and Ascension	...	...	2	...	...	...	0.5	...	...	...	...	...
St. Lucia	5	—	...	11	15	...	...	18	4	...	...	...
St. Pierre and Miquelon	...	...	...	...	...	...	...	...	3	15	...	...
St. Vincent	...	...	...	...	...	...	...	...	1	...	...	...
San Marino	14	...	...	1	...	...	...	...	...	...	...	...
São Tomé and Príncipe	...	...	...	...	...	...	...	...	1	...	...	...
Saudi Arabia	207	—	80	11	...	—	...	—	8	...	...	...
Senegal	64[3]	...	...	—	287[3]	...	...	—	1	3	...	...
Seychelles	2[3]	...	22	31[3]	...	...	10	...	1	25	9	1,700
Sierra Leone	17[3]	...	...	44[3]	9[3]	4[3]	...	12[3]	11	392	...	...
Singapore	1,088[54]	212	1,506	442[54]	6,044[54]	1,547	...	2,352[54]	1	800	...	...
Solomon Islands	...	...	2	...	...	...	4	...	...	...	...	...
Somalia	...	...	...	...	...	...	...	...	...	...	...	...
South Africa	...	...	...	...	...	...	...	...	85	7,857	...	...
Bophuthatswana	...	...	...	...	...	...	...	...	...	...	...	...
Ciskei	...	...	...	...	...	...	...	...	...	...	...	...
Transkei	...	...	...	...	...	...	...	...	...	...	...	...
Venda	...	...	...	...	...	...	...	...	1	9	2	14
South West Africa/Namibia	...	...	3	...	...	...	18	...	8	157	...	...
Spain	26,964	2,723	5,508	5,174	226,334	46,724	55,352	47,057	c. 1,550	11,730	1,308	170
Sri Lanka	825	51	405	1,527	5,628	2,722	1,565	6,725	650	...	197	...
Sudan, The	...	138[23]	...	—	...	12,905[23]	...	—	2	23	...	...
Suriname	...	...	24	...	...	...	39	...	2	268	54	2,000
Swaziland												
Sweden	5,396[6]	...	3,690	6	...	...	...	...	408	39,031	...	9,300
Switzerland	11,405[6]	149[6]	1,533	6	...	...	31,773	...	...	3,690	...	1,400
Syria	95	...	48	—	310	...	454	—	...	...	...	...
Taiwan	...	...	...	...	...	...	...	...	...	...	...	...
Tanzania	148	5[3]	69	98	...	...	646	...	1	404	10	9
Thailand	4,950	184	990	695	...	...	...	...	1	...	...	...
Togo	...	...	...	...	...	...	...	...	...	...	...	...
Tokelau	...	...	...	...	...	...	...	...	1	0.2	...	...
Tonga	33	5	...	287	0.4	0.1	...	...	...	...	...	...
Trinidad and Tobago	101	7	...	85	...	...	...	...	1	68	1	120
Tunisia	...	172	230	—	...	6,000	...	—	75	875	53	180
Turkey	4,793[6]	...	...	6	...	...	...	...	363	5,044	502	47
Turks and Caicos Islands	...	...	...	...	...	...	...	...	1	7	...	1,000
Tuvalu	...	...	...	...	...	...	...	...	...	...	...	...
Uganda	...	...	...	...	...	...	...	...	1	73	157	32
U.S.S.R.	58,372	3,022	5,308	33,564	1,969,000[6]	...	3,306,000	6	133,462	2,000,660	148,000	12,000
United Arab Emirates	57	35	8	7	646	578	25	163	...	...	...	...
United Kingdom	44,482	1,399	6,408	3,547	...	...	...	...	160	131,338	...	11,000
United States	72,382[65]	...	59,609	4,594[65]	...	...	...	...	10,154	509,332	...	4,300
Uruguay	415	106	396	422	...	...	...	...	...	...	...	...
Vanuatu	...	...	...	...	...	...	...	...	1	12	1	...
Venezuela	3,596	...	...	604	1,194	...	...	...	23	977	66	170
Vietnam	2,176[6]	...	173	6	61,300[6]	...	323	6	316	4,879	...	...
Virgin Islands (U.S)	...	...	...	...	...	...	...	...	6	224	...	...
Wallis and Futuna												
West Bank												
Western Sahara												
Western Samoa	79	...	...	156	39	...	...	43	1	36	...	...
Yemen (Aden)												
Yemen (San'ā')												
Yugoslavia	8,184	1,338	1,408	2,351	46,586	20,480	9,122	11,739	2,101	24,123	4,368	...
Zaire	194[3]	53	...	37[3]	...	...	...	...	11	177	...	...
Zambia	86[7]	4[3]	...	—	235[67]	225[3]	...	—	11	240	...	...
Zimbabwe	323,[67]	22[3]	...	—	263[3, 67]	213[3]	...	—	20	523	...	...

[1]Calculations based on statutory areas, whether of land or water. [2]Excludes zoological and aquatic collections in museums. [3]First editions only. [4]For opera and ballet, drama, and variety only. [5]Excludes attendance at drive-ins, at mobile units, or both. [6]Books includes pamphlets. [7]16-millimetre data not available. [8]Professional only. [9]214 reporting. [10]14 reporting. [11]Library service points. [12]Ministry of Flemish Culture museums only. [13]National museums only. [14]370 reporting. [15]Government publications only. [16]Attendance in 1,000s. [17]Drama, ballet, and dance only. [18]Drama, opera, ballet, and dance only. [19]818 reporting. [20]Amateur ballet, dance, and drama only. [21]Film-projection units. [22]57 reporting. [23]Includes children's books. [24]Excludes some Turkish publications. [25]Includes school pamphlets. [26]Royal theatre and regional theatres only. [27]263 reporting. [28]Drama and opera only. [29]National and public museums only. [30]Includes one nature reserve in the French Southern and Antarctic Lands. [31]Museums with a yearly attendance of 20,000 or more only. [32]83 reporting. [33]13,700,000 square metres per capita; the single national park comprises about one-third of the total area of Greenland. [34]Drama only. [35]3 reporting. [36]Public educational libraries include service points and trade-union libraries. [37]Opera and ballet only.

cinema annual attendance (all cinemas) number ('000,000)	cinema annual attendance per 1,000 population	fixed cinemas number	fixed cinemas seating capacity ('000)	number of long films produced	performing arts number of facilities	performing arts number of performances	performing arts annual attendance number ('000)	performing arts annual attendance per 1,000 population	museums number	museums annual attendance number ('000)	museums annual attendance per 1,000 population	national parks and nature reserves number	national parks and nature reserves square metres per capita[1]	zoos, botanical gardens etc. (number[2])	country
...	...	...	...	...	...	...	...	...	1	600	110	3	1,000	...	Niger
22.7	300	120	...	15	23	...	...	...	18	...	...	19	240	8	Nigeria
...	...	...	...	...	...	...	...	...	2	...	...	...	...	...	Niue
10[16]	5,000	1	0.1	...	1	7	2	1,000	1	...	...	...	...	...	Norfolk Island
16.4	4,000	456	134	9	13	4,357[8]	1,147[8]	280[8]	195	4,573[46]	1,100[46]	31[47]	9,900[47]	7	Norway
0.9	1,100	12	1	...	...	...	...	...	1	...	...	2	11,000	...	Oman
...	...	52	...	...	...	...	...	...	5	...	...	...	...	...	Pacific Is., Trust Terr. of the
176.3	2,200	630	305	79	12	...	48[8]	0.6[8]	10	561	7	5	50	6	Pakistan
7.1	4,800	...	...	...	1	55	...	...	10	...	...	6	3,400	2	Panama
...	...	...	...	...	7	122	265	91	2	100	32	5	39	3	Papua New Guinea
...	...	...	...	...	...	...	...	...	18	...	...	6	3,900	1	Paraguay
33.0	1,900	425[7]	...	2	35	2,388	...	...	9	221	13	18	2,300	2	Peru
...	...	...	...	136	6[50]	121[50]	29[50]	0.6[50]	63	...	...	55	77	5	Philippines
...	...	...	...	...	...	...	...	...	...	...	...	...	...	...	Pitcairn Island
108.1	3,000	1,814	490	35	96	120,000[8]	33,557[8]	920[8]	511	18,131	500	14	35	26	Poland
30.3[5]	3,100[5]	420	230	10	76	3,707	1,126	120	146	1,910[51]	200[51]	15[52]	1,300[52]	10	Portugal
...	...	165	...	...	...	...	...	...	24	...	...	5	49	8	Puerto Rico
0.8[5]	3,200[5]	4	4	1	1	4	1	5	1	60	300	1	...	1	Qatar
...	...	...	...	...	...	...	...	...	3	111	230	...	...	...	Réunion
217.5	9,700	5,665	942	30	149	36,583[8]	15,783[8]	700[8]	465	15,303	680	460[53]	89	9	Romania
0.3	60	12	4	1	9	31	58	12	4	...	...	2	520	...	Rwanda
...	...	...	...	...	...	...	...	...	...	...	...	...	...	...	St. Christopher and Nevis
53.0[16]	8,800	2	1	...	...	1	1	170	1	...	...	...	...	...	St. Helena and Ascension
...	...	6	...	...	...	...	...	...	1	1	8	6	340	...	St. Lucia
...	...	...	...	...	...	...	...	...	1	4	640	...	...	...	St. Pierre and Miquelon
...	...	2	...	...	...	...	...	...	...	...	...	...	...	1	St. Vincent
0.1	4,500	6	3	...	1	26[8]	108	460[8]	11	741	35,000	...	...	...	San Marino
...	...	...	...	...	...	...	...	...	...	...	...	...	...	...	São Tomé and Príncipe
...	...	...	...	...	94	89[42]	90[42]	11[42]	1	37	5	1	480	2	Saudi Arabia
3.8[5]	700[5]	60[7]	...	...	1	122[8]	52[8]	9[8]	3	22	4	9	3,700	4	Senegal
...	...	...	...	...	2	6[42]	3[42]	40[42]	1	8	130	1	3,000	...	Seychelles
...	...	...	...	...	...	...	...	...	1	178	55	...	...	1	Sierra Leone
37.1	15,200	73	36.5	...	3	523	645	270	3	940	390	2	0.3	4	Singapore
0.1[5]	300[5]	2	1	...	...	3	1	5	1	29	150	1	46	...	Solomon Islands
...	...	...	...	...	...	...	...	...	1	...	...	1	890	...	Somalia
31.2	1,200	340	...	12	51	3,597[55]	1,348[55]	54[55]	16[56]	1,501[56]	60[56]	49	1,400	35	South Africa
...	...	...	...	...	...	...	...	...	...	...	...	2	370	...	Bophuthatswana
...	...	...	...	...	...	...	...	...	...	...	...	2	...	...	Ciskei
...	...	...	...	...	...	...	...	...	...	...	...	3	...	...	Transkei
...	...	...	...	...	...	...	...	...	1	...	...	1	...	...	Venda
...	...	...	...	...	...	...	...	...	9	...	...	11	61,000	1	South West Africa/Namibia
173.7[5]	4,600[5]	3,970	2,608	99	366	18,862	6,702	180	554	11,697	320	17	120	22	Spain
63.9	4,300	357	202	42	22	1,002[42]	600[42]	41[42]	9	466	34	33	400	4	Sri Lanka
2.8[5]	200[5]	567	1087	1	...	...	...	...	5	157	9	15	3,100	2	Sudan, The
...	...	...	...	...	...	...	...	...	3	...	...	9	15,000	1	Suriname
...	...	...	...	...	...	...	...	...	1	...	...	6	1,600	...	Swaziland
22.1	2,700	1,239[7]	...	19	45	20,684	3,957	480	218	11,383[57]	1,400[57]	40	1,400	18	Sweden
20.4	3,200	477	160	17	147	25,735	5,811	920	585	...	...	19	130	32	Switzerland
14.5	1,600	92	53	2	5	411	165	20	16	321[58]	42[58]	...	...	...	Syria
140.0	7,900	...	...	...	...	...	...	...	10	...	...	28	84	3	Taiwan
4.0	200	34	15	12	5	21	15	1	6	119[59]	7[59]	15	5,900	...	Tanzania
...	...	376[7]	2677	c. 100	...	...	...	...	64	48	21	57	760	3	Thailand
...	...	...	...	...	...	...	...	...	1	...	...	7	1,500	...	Togo
...	...	...	...	...	...	...	...	...	...	...	...	...	...	...	Tokelau
0.1	1,000	3	2	...	...	...	...	...	...	...	...	5	320	...	Tonga
...	...	72	57	...	...	49[42]	...	...	1	8	7	12	140	1	Trinidad and Tobago
8.8	1,500	82	41	...	12	598	164	26	19	563[60]	90[60]	4	49	3	Tunisia
62.5	1,400	938	506	65	12[61]	1,952[8,61]	604[8,61]	14[8,61]	93	5,196	120	17	59	7	Turkey
...	...	3	1	...	...	3	0.6	100	...	...	...	...	...	...	Turks and Caicos Islands
...	...	...	...	...	...	...	...	...	...	...	...	...	...	...	Tuvalu
1.9[5]	200[5]	177	10	...	...	...	...	...	16	...	...	3	1,300	2	Uganda
4,051.0	14,900	141,641	25,387	259	772	281,800[8]	145,900[8]	540[8]	1,832	174,800	640	142	510	144	U.S.S.R.
6.9	10,300	74	29	...	1	12[34]	36[34]	40[35]	...	...	...	...	...	2	United Arab Emirates
86.0	1,500	1,541	622	41	404	...	40,242[8,18]	720[8,18]	1,768[62]	c. 52,000[63]	920	59[64]	260[64]	155	United Kingdom
1,197.0	5,100	16,000	6,900	226	...	21,596	40,200	170	4,440	329,083	1,500	241	2,300	652	United States
6.2	2,100	120	80	2	25	3,097	...	...	59	...	...	7	100	4	Uruguay
0.1	1,000	3	1	...	...	...	...	...	...	...	...	...	...	...	Vanuatu
67.6[5]	4,700[5]	535	...	7	9	372	206	16	133	...	...	42	5,300	12	Venezuela
324.0	5,800	210	178	15	68	...	42,600[8]	770[8]	9	1,918[66]	37[66]	...	...	2	Vietnam
...	...	...	...	...	...	...	...	...	5	811	7,700	3	750	1	Virgin Islands (U.S.)
...	...	...	...	...	...	...	...	...	...	...	...	...	...	...	Wallis and Futuna
...	...	...	...	...	...	...	...	...	...	...	...	4	...	...	West Bank
...	...	...	...	...	...	...	...	...	...	...	...	...	...	...	Western Sahara
0.5	3,200	6	6	...	...	9	2	11	...	...	...	2	180	1	Western Samoa
5.6[5]	3,100[5]	21	21	...	...	...	...	...	5	...	...	...	...	...	Yemen (Aden)
15.0[5]	2,500[5]	35	28	...	...	...	...	...	...	...	...	...	...	...	Yemen (San'ā')
76.5	3,407	1,189	427	31	149	18,506	4,906	220	387	11,661	520	21	150	19	Yugoslavia
...	...	...	...	...	4	...	...	...	4	...	...	7	2,800	4	Zaire
1.6	300	12	4	...	...	...	...	...	4	163[35]	30[35]	18	10,000	1	Zambia
...	...	...	...	...	...	...	...	...	13	...	...	27	3,600	4	Zimbabwe

[38]Excludes data for the Vatican City. Publishing: (titles) 148 books, 2 pamphlets, 42 periodicals; (copies) 165,000 books, 2,000 pamphlets, 38,000 periodicals. Museums: 1 with annual attendance of 1,718,000. [39]1,083 reporting. [40]Marine parks only. Reserves or sanctuaries thought to be multiple-use management areas are excluded. [41]400 reporting. [42]Amateur only. [43]Excludes amateur opera and musical comedy. [44]National and public museums only. [45]77 reporting. [46]139 reporting. [47]Six of which are associated with Svalbard, Jan Mayen, or Bouvet Island. [48]2,400 sq m per capita excluding Svalbard, Jan Mayen, and Bouvet Island. [49]Books received by the national library only. [50]Metropolitan Manila only. [51]117 reporting. [52]Excludes the Azores and Madeira. [53]Includes botanical, geological, speleological, paleontological, ornithological, and other reserves. [54]Excludes government publications. [55]Performances of state-subsidized regional performing arts councils only. [56]Museums designated "declared cultural institutions" only. [57]213 reporting. [58]13 reporting. [59]5 reporting. [60]15 reporting. [61]Public theatres only. [62]1980. [63]1982 estimate. [64]Excludes areas of "outstanding natural beauty." [65]Books or pamphlets intended for sale to the general public only. [66]8 reporting. [67]School textbooks and government publications only.

BIBLIOGRAPHY AND SOURCES

The following list indicates the principal sources used in the compilation of *Britannica World Data*. It is by no means a complete list, either for international or for national sources, but is indicative only of the range of materials to which reference has been made in preparing this compilation. For example, in addition to the kinds of works cited below, reference has also been made to the constitutions of each country, to the publications of its central or commercial banks, to unpublished information received in correspondence from the countries, and to other more specialized sources.

International Statistical Sources

Africana Publishing Co. *Africa Contemporary Record* (annual).

AT&T. *The World's Telephones* (annual).

Billboard Ltd. *World Radio TV Handbook* (annual).

British Petroleum. *BP Statistical Review of World Energy* (annual).

Council for Mutual Economic Assistance (Comecon). *Statistichesky Yezhegodnik Stran-Chlenov Soveta Economicheskoy Vzaimopomoshchi* (Statistical Yearbook of the Council for Mutual Economic Assistance [annual]).

Europa Publications Ltd. *Africa South of the Sahara* (annual); *The Europa Year Book* (2 vol.); *The Far East and Australasia* (annual); *The Middle East and North Africa* (annual).

European Communities. *ACP: Statistical Yearbook; Basic Statistics* (annual).

Food and Agriculture Organization. *Food Balance Sheets* (irreg.); *Production Yearbook; Trade Yearbook; World Census of Agriculture* (decennial); *Yearbook of Fishery Statistics; Yearbook of Forest Products.*

Gulf Publishing Co. *World Pipelines* (1983).

Her Majesty's Stationery Office. *Yearbook of the Commonwealth.*

Holmes & Meier Publishers. *Latin America and Caribbean Contemporary Record* (annual); *Middle East Contemporary Survey* (annual).

Inter-American Development Bank. *Economic and Social Progress in Latin America* (2 vol.; annual).

Inter-Parliamentary Union. *World Directory of Parliaments* (annual).

International Air Transport Association. *World Air Transport Statistics* (annual).

International Bank for Reconstruction and Development/The World Bank. *World Bank Atlas* (annual); *World Debt Tables* (annual); *World Development Report* (annual); *World Tables* (2 vol. [irreg.]).

International Civil Aviation Organization. *Civil Aviation Statistics of the World* (annual); *Digest of Statistics.*

International Institute for Strategic Studies. *The Military Balance* (annual).

International Labour Organisation. *Household Income and Expenditure Statistics* (irreg.); *Year Book of Labour Statistics.*

International Monetary Fund. *Exchange Arrangements and Exchange Restrictions* (annual); *Government Finance Statistics Yearbook; International Financial Statistics* (monthly, with supplements and yearbook).

International Road Federation. *Road and Motor Vehicle Statistics* (annual); *World Road Statistics* (annual).

Jane's Publishing Co. *Jane's World Railways* (annual).

Lloyd's Register of Shipping. *Lloyd's Register of Shipping: Statistical Tables* (annual).

Longman Group Ltd. *Keesing's Contemporary Archives* (monthly).

Macmillan Press Ltd. *The Statesman's Year-Book.*

Middle East Economic Digest Ltd. *Africa Economic*

Digest (semimonthly); *Middle East Economic Digest* (semimonthly).

Mining Journal. *Mining Annual Review.*

Nordic Council. *Yearbook of Nordic Statistics.*

Official Airline Guides, Inc. *Official Airline Guide* (monthly).

Organization for Economic Cooperation and Development. *Economic Surveys* (annual); *External Debt of Developing Countries* (annual); *National Accounts of Developing Countries* (irreg.).

Oxford University Press. *World Christian Encyclopedia* (David B. Barrett, ed. [1982]).

Pacific Publications. *Pacific Islands Year Book* (irreg.).

PennWell Publishing Co. *International Petroleum Encyclopedia* (annual).

René Moreux et Cie. *Marchés tropicaux & Méditerranéens* (semimonthly).

South Pacific Commission. *Key Economic Indicators* (occasional); *South Pacific Economies: Statistical Summary* (biennial).

Tokyo Metropolitan Government. *Statistics of World Large Cities* (annual).

United Nations (UN). *Compendium of Social Statistics* (irreg.); *Construction Statistics Yearbook; Demographic Indicators of Countries, 1980 Assessment; Demographic Yearbook; Energy Balances 1977–1980 and Electricity Profiles 1976–1981 for Selected Developing Countries and Areas; Energy Statistics Yearbook; Industrial Statistics Yearbook* (2 vol.); *Monthly Bulletin of Statistics; Population Studies* (irreg.); *National Accounts Statistics* (3 vol.; annual); *Population and Vital Statistics Report* (quarterly); *Statistical Yearbook; Supplement to the Statistical Yearbook and the Monthly Bulletin of Statistics* (quinquennial); *Yearbook of International Trade Statistics* (2vol.); *World Housing Survey* (1974).

UN: Conference on Trade and Development. *Handbook of International Trade and Development Statistics* (annual).

UN: Economic Commission for Africa. *African Statistical Yearbook; Demographic and Related Socio-Economic Data Sheets for ECA Member States* (1982); *Survey of Economic and Social Conditions in Africa* (irreg.).

UN: Economic Commission for Europe. *Annual Bulletin of Housing and Building Statistics for Europe; Annual Bulletin of Transport Statistics for Europe.*

UN: Economic Commission for Latin America. *Economic Survey of Latin America* (2 vol.; annual); *Statistical Yearbook for Latin America.*

UN: Economic Commission for Western Asia. *Population Bulletin* (irreg.); *The Population Situation in the ECWA Region* (irreg.).

UN: Economic and Social Commission for Asia and the Pacific. *Foreign Trade Statistics of Asia and the Pacific* (annual); *Statistical Indicators for Asia and the Pacific* (quarterly); *Statistical Yearbook for Asia and the Pacific.*

UN: Educational, Scientific, and Cultural Organization. *Statistical Yearbook; Estimates and Projections of Illiteracy* (1978).

United States: Central Intelligence Agency, *The World Factbook* (annual); Dept. of Commerce, *Foreign Economic Trends* (irreg.), *Overseas Business Reports* (annual), *World Population* (annual); Dept. of Energy, *International Energy Annual;* Dept. of Health and Human Services, *Social Security Programs Throughout the World* (biennial); Dept. of Interior, *Minerals Yearbook* (3 vol.); Dept. of State, *Background Notes* (irreg.).

Vatican (Central Statistics Office of the Church). *Statistical Yearbook of the Church.*

West India Committee and FT International. *The Caribbean Handbook* (annual).

World Health Organization. *World Health Statistics Annual.*

World Priorities. *World Military and Social Expenditures* (Ruth Leger Sivard, ed. [annual]).

World Tourism Organization. *World Tourism Statistics* (annual).

National Statistical Sources

Afghanistan. *Area Handbook for Afghanistan* (1973); *Economic and Social Indicators* (triennial); *First Seven-Year Economic and Social Development Plan, 1355–1361 (March 1976–March 1983); Preliminary Results of the First Afghan Population Census, 1979; Review of the General Socio-economic Situation in the Democratic Republic of Afghanistan During 1358 (21 March 1979–20 March 1980); Statistical Year Book.*

Albania. *Area Handbook for Albania* (1971); *Directives of the 8th Congress of the PLA for the 7th Five-Year Plan (1981–85) of Economic and Cultural Development of the PSR of Albania; An Outline of the People's Socialist Republic of Albania* (1978); *Portrait of Albania* (1982); *Vjetari statistikor R P SH* (Statistical Yearbook of the People's Republic of Albania [annual]); *35 Years of Socialist Albania* (1981).

Algeria. *Algeria: A Country Study* (1979); *Annuaire statistique; Recensement général de la population et de l'habitat, 1977.*

American Samoa. *Annual Report of the Governor of American Samoa to the Secretary of the Department of the Interior; Population of American Samoa* (ESCAP; Country Monograph Series No. 7.1 [1979]); *1980 Census of Population and Housing* (U.S.); *Statistical Bulletin* (annual).

Angola. *Angola: A Country Study* (1979); *Anuário Estatístico; Recenseamento Geral da População, 1960; Situação Economica e Financeira de Angola* (annual).

Anguilla. *Abstract of Statistics, 1960–1982.*

Antigua. *Statistical Yearbook.*

Argentina. *Anuario estadístico de la República Argentina; Area Handbook for Argentina* (1974); *Boletín estadístico trimestral* (quarterly); *Censo nacional de población y vivienda, 1980; Comercio exterior* (annual); *Encuesta permanente de hogares* (irreg.); *Estadistica Mensual* (monthly); *Indicadores industriales* (annual); *Relevamiento estadístico de la economía Argentina, 1900–1980* (1982).

Australia. *Integrated Economic Censuses and Surveys* (1980–81); *Manufacturing Establishments: Details of Operations by Industry Class* (annual); *Monthly Summary of Statistics, Australia; National Income and Expenditure* (annual); *Overseas Trade* (annual); *Social Indicators* (irreg.); *Yearbook of the Commonwealth of Australia; 1981 Census of Population and Housing.*

Austria. *Area Handbook for Austria* (1976); *Der Aussenhandel Österreichs* (Austrian Foreign Trade [quarterly]); *Österreichisches Jahrbuch* (annual); *Österreichs Volkseinkommen* (Austrian National Income); *Sozialstatistische Daten 1970–1980; Statistisches Handbuch* (annual); *Volkserzählung, 1981.*

Bahamas, The. *External Trade Statistics, Report* (annual); *Industrial Production Statistics* (annual); *National Accounts of The Bahamas, 1973–1979; Quarterly Statistical Summary; Social Statistics Report* (annual); *Statistical Abstract* (annual); *Vital Statistics Report* (annual); *Wholesale and Retail Trade Report* (annual); *1980 Census of Population and Housing.*

Bahrain. *Statistical Abstract* (annual); *1981 Census of Bahrain.*

Bangladesh. *Area Handbook for Bangladesh* (1975); *Bangladesh Population Census, 1981; Monthly Statistical Bulletin of Bangladesh; Population of Bangladesh* (ESCAP; Country Monograph Series No. 8 [1981]); *Statistical Pocketbook of Bangladesh* (annual); *Statistical Yearbook of Bangladesh.*

Barbados. *Barbados Economic Report* (annual); *Monthly Digest of Statistics; Report on the Census of Production, 1981.*

Belgium. *Annuaire statistique de la Belgique; Bulletin du commerce extérieur* (annual); *Bulletin de statistique* (monthly); *Chiffres officiels de la population de droit, par commune* (annual); *Recensement général de l'agriculture, 1970; Recensement*

de la population et des logements au 1er mars 1981; Statistiques demographiques (quarterly).
Belize. *Abstract of Statistics* (annual); *Belize Economic Report* (1984); *Development plan (1977–1979).*
Benin. *Annuaire statistique; Recensement des Entreprises 1980* (2 parts); *Recensement général de la population et de l'habitation* (1979).
Bermuda. *Bermuda Digest of Statistics* (annual); *The Economic Structure and National Accounts of Bermuda* (annual); *Report of the Customs Imports and Exports* (annual); *Report of the Population Census, 1980; Report of the Registrar General* (annual).
Bhutan. *Development in a Himalayan Kingdom* (A World Bank Country Study [1983]).
Bolivia. *Area Handbook for Bolivia* (1974); *Bolivia en cifras, 1980; Censo Nacional de población y vivienda de 1976; Resumen estadístico* (annual).
Botswana. *1981 Population and Housing Census; Statistical Abstract* (annual).
Brazil. *Anuário Econômico-Fiscal; Anuário Estatístico do Brasil; Brazil: A Country Study* (1983); *Foreign Trade of Brazil* (annual); *Indicadores Sociais* (1979); *IX Recenseamento Geral do Brasil, 1980.*
British Virgin Islands. *Census of the British Virgin Islands, 12th May 1980 (Provisional); Statistical Abstract* (irreg.); *Trade Report* (1978–80).
Brunei. *Annual Report; Brunei Statistical Yearbook; Report on the Census of Population, 1971.*
Bulgaria. *Area Handbook for Bulgaria* (1974); *Prebroyavane—1975; resultati, perspektivi* (Census of Population—1975: Results, Perspectives); *Statisticheskii yezhgodnik* (Statistical Yearbook).
Burkina Faso (Upper Volta). *La Population de la Haute-Volta au recensement de décembre 1975.*
Burma. *Burma: A Country Study* (1983); 1983 *Population Census (Advance Release); Statistical Abstract, 1976.*
Burundi. *Annuaire statistique; Recensement général de la population, 16–30 août 1979.*
Cameroon. *Area Handbook for the United Republic of Cameroon* (1974); *Note annuelle de statistique; Recensement général de la population et de l'habitat d'avril 1976; Tableaux économiques du Cameroun* (1983).
Canada. *Canada Year Book* (biennial); *Canadian Statistical Review* (monthly); *Census of Agriculture, 1981; National Income and Expenditure Accounts* (quarterly); *1981 Census of Canada.*
Cape Verde. *Boletím Trimestral de Estatística* (quarterly).
Central African Republic. *Annuaire statistique; Recensement général de la population de décembre 1975.*
Chad. *Annuaire statistique.*
Chile. *Agricultura y pesca* (annual); *Anuario de minería; Chile: A Country Study* (1982); *Chile XV censo nacional de población y de vivienda, 21 de abril 1982; Compendio estadístico* (annual); *Cuentas nacionales de Chile, 1960–1980; Informativo estadístico* (quarterly); *Informe social* (quarterly); *Plan nacional indicativo de desarrollo* (quinquennial).
China, People's Republic of. *Almanac of China's Economy, 1983* (irreg.); *China: A Country Study* (1981); *China Official Yearbook; People's Republic of China Year-Book; China Socialist Development* (A World Bank Country Study; 3 vol. [1983]); *Major Figures by 10 Percent Sampling on the 1982 Census of the People's Republic of China; Statistical Yearbook of China; Yearbook of the Encyclopedia of China.*
Christmas Island. *Annual Report; Census of Population and Housing, 30 June 1981.*
Cocos (Keeling) Islands. *Annual Report; Census of Population and Housing, 30 June 1981.*
Colombia. *Boletín mensual de estadística* (monthly); *The Colombian Economy* (1982); *Colombia estadística* (annual); *Cuentas nacionales de Colombia, 1970–1981; Industria manufacturera* (annual); *XIV Censo nacional de población y III de vivienda, octubre 24 de 1973.*
Comoros. *The Comoros: Current Economic Situation and Prospects* (A World Bank Country Study [1983]); *Recensement de la population des Comores, 1966.*
Congo, People's Republic of the. *Annuaire statistique; Area Handbook for the People's Republic of the Congo (Brazzaville)* (1971); *Recensement général de la population de 1974.*
Cook Islands. *Cook Islands Census of Population and Dwellings, 1981; Cook Islands Quarterly Statistical Bulletin.*
Costa Rica. *Anuario estadístico; Censos Nacionales de 1973; Costa Rica: A Country Study* (1984); *Evolución socioeconómica de Costa Rica, 1950–1980; Plan nacional de desarrollo 1979–1982; "Gregorio José Ramírez"; IV Censo de manufactura, 1975.*
Cuba. *Anuario estadístico; Area Handbook for Cuba* (1976); *Censo de población y viviendas, 1981; Compendio estadístico de Cuba* (annual).
Cyprus. *Census of Industrial Production* (annual); *Economic Report* (annual); *Statistical Abstract* (annual); *Statistics of Imports and Exports* (annual).
Czechoslovakia. *Czechoslovakia: A Country Study* (1981); *Statistická ročenka Československé Socialistické Republiky* (Statistical Yearbook of the Czechoslovak Socialist Republic); *Sčítání lidu, domů a bytů 1980* (Census of Population).
Denmark. *Denmarks vareindførsel og-udførsel, 1982* (External Trade of Denmark by Commodities and Countries); *Folke- og boligtaellingen, 1981* (Population and Housing Census); *Statistisk årbog* (Statistical Yearbook).
Djibouti. *Annuaire statistique de Djibouti.*
Dominican Republic. *Area Handbook for the Dominican Republic* (1973); *República Dominicana en cifras* (annual); *VI Censo nacional de población y vivienda, 1981.*
Ecuador. *Censo agropecuario, 1974; Encuesta anual de manufactura y minería; Serie estadística* (quinquennial); *IV Censo de población: III de vivienda resultados anticipados por muestreo* (1982).
Egypt. *Census of Population and Housing, 1976; Egypt: A Country Study* (1982).
El Salvador. *Anuario estadístico; Area Handbook for El Salvador* (1971); *Censos económicos, 1979 (Manufactura diversa; Agroindustrias; Comercio y servicios; Electricidad, construcción, transporte comercial); El Salvador en cifras* (annual).
Ethiopia. *Ethiopia: A Country Study* (1980); *Statistical Abstract* (annual).
Fiji. *Census of Industrial Production* (annual); *Current Economic Statistics* (quarterly); *Overseas Trade of Fiji* (annual); *Report on the Census of the Population, 1976.*
Finland. *Annual Statistics of Agriculture; Economic Survey* (annual); *Population and Housing Census, 1980; Statistical Yearbook of Finland.*
France. *Annuaire statistique de la France; Les Comptes de l'industrie* (1981); *Données sociales* (irreg.); *Le Mouvement économique en France, 1949–1979; Recensement général de la population de 1982; Métropole.*
French Guiana. *Annuaire statistique de la Guyane; Bulletin trimestriel de statistique; Recensement général de la population dans les Départements d'outre-mer en 9 mars 1982, Guyane.*
French Polynesia. *Annuaire statistique; Bilan statistique de l'année; Comptes économiques* (quadrennial); *Résultats du recensement de la population de la Polynésie Française, 29 avril 1977; Te avei'a: Bulletin d'information statistique* (quarterly).
Gabon. *Situation économique, financière et sociale de la République Gabonaise* (annual).
Gaza Strip. *Judaea, Samaria, and Gaza Area Statistics Quarterly; Palestinian Statistical Abstract* (annual).
Germany, East. *Statistisches Jahrbuch der Deutschen Demokratischen Republik.*
Germany, West. *Area Handbook for Germany* (1981); *Statistisches Jahrbuch für die Bundesrepublik Deutschland; Volkszählung vom 27 Mai 1970* (Census of Population).
Ghana. *Economic Survey* (biennial); *Ghana: An Official Handbook* (1977); *Industrial Statistics* (biennial); *Population Census of Ghana, 1984.*
Gibraltar. *Abstract of Statistics* (annual); *Census of Gibraltar, 1981.*
Greece. *Recensement des industries manufacturières: Artisanat, du commerce et autres services* (1978); *Recensement de la population et des habitations, 1981; Statistical Yearbook of Greece.*
Greenland. *Grønland* (annual); *Grønlands befolkning* (Greenland Population [annual]).
Grenada. *Abstract of Statistics* (annual); *Annual Digest of Trade Statistics.*
Guadeloupe. *Annuaire statistique de la Guadeloupe; Comptes économiques* (quinquennial); *Recensement général de la population dans les Departements d'Outre-mer en 9 mars 1982, Guadeloupe.*
Guam. *Annual Economic Review; Annual Report to the Secretary of the Interior; Census of Agriculture* (quinquennial); *1980 Census of Population and Housing.*
Guatemala. *Anuario estadístico; Censos nacionales, 1981: IX de población—IV de habitación; Guatemala: A Country Study* (1983).
Guernsey. *Guernsey Census 1976.*
Guinea, Republic of. *Area Handbook for Guinea* (1975); *Population et développement en République Populaire Revolutionnaire de Guinée* (1980).
Guinea-Bissau. *Boletim Trimestral de Estatística; Recenseamento Geral da População e da Habitação, 16 de Abril de 1979.*
Guyana. *Annual Statistical Abstract; Area Handbook for Guyana* (1969).
Haiti. *Bulletin trimestriel de statistique; Guide économique de la République d'Haiti* (1977); *Haiti: A Country Profile* (1981); *Résultats préliminaires du recensement général (Septembre 1982).*
Honduras. *Anuario estadístico; Censo nacional agropecuario, 1974; Comercio externo* (annual); *Honduras: A Country Profile* (1981); *Honduras en cifras, 1980–1982.*
Hong Kong. *Annual Digest of Statistics; Hong Kong* (annual); *Hong Kong 1981 Census; Hong Kong in Figures* (annual); *Hong Kong Social and Economic Trends* (irreg.); *1978 Survey of Industrial Production.*
Hungary. *Statisztikai évkönyv* (Statistical Yearbook); *1980, Évi népszámlálás* (Census of Population).
Iceland. *Tölfraedihandbók* (Statistical Abstract of Iceland [irreg.]); *Verslunarskýrslur* (External Trade [annual]).
India. *Census of India, 1981; Economic Survey* (annual); *India: A Reference Annual; National Accounts Statistics, 1970–1971, 1978–79; Statistical Abstract* (annual).
Indonesia. *Agricultural Census, 1973; Indikator ekonomi* (monthly); *Indonesia: An Official Handbook* (1984); *Sensus penduduk Indonesia, 1980* (Census of Population); *Statistical Yearbook of Indonesia.*
Iran. *General Census of Population and Housing, November 1976; Iran: A Country Study* (1978); *Statistical Yearbook of Iran.*
Iraq. *Iraq: A Country Study* (1979); *Statistical Abstract* (annual).
Ireland. *Census of Population of Ireland, 1981; National Income and Expenditure* (annual); *Statistical Abstract* (annual).
Isle of Man. *Isle of Man 1981 Census Report; Isle of Man Digest of Economic and Social Statistics* (annual).
Israel. *Foreign Trade Statistics* (quarterly); *Israel: A Country Study* (1979); *Statistical Abstract* (annual).
Italy. *Annuario di statistica agraria: Annuario di statistica forestale; Annuario di statistiche demografiche; Annuario di statistiche industriali; Annuario statistico dell'istruzione; Annuario statistico Italiano; Statistiche sociali* (1981); *12 Censimento general della popolazione, 1981.*
Ivory Coast. *Annuaire statistique; La Côte d'Ivoire en chiffres* (annual); *L'Économie Ivoirienne* (annual).
Jamaica. *Area Handbook of Jamaica* (1976); *Economic and Social Survey* (annual); *Statistical Abstract* (annual); *Statistical Yearbook of Jamaica.*
Japan. *Establishment Census of Japan, 1981; Japan: A Country Study* (1983); *Japan Statistical Yearbook; Statistical Indicators on Social Life* (annual); *Statistics on Japanese Industries, 1980; 1980 Population Census of Japan.*
Jersey. *Report of the Census for 1981; Statistical Digest* (annual).
Jordan. *Census 1979; Family Expenditure Survey* (1980); *Jordan: A Country Study* (1979); *National Accounts* (irreg.); *Statistical Yearbook.*
Kenya. *Economic Survey* (annual); *Kenya Statistical Digest* (quarterly); *Statistical Abstract* (annual).
Kiribati. *National Development Plan, 1979–1982; Report on the 1978 Census of Population and Housing.*
Korea, North. *North Korea: A Country Study* (1981).
Korea, South. *Korea Statistical Yearbook; Social Indicators in Korea* (1981); *South Korea: A Country Study* (1982); *The 5th Five-Year Economic and Development Plan, 1982–1986; 1980 Population and Housing Census.*
Kuwait. *Economic Report* (annual); *General Census of Population and Housing, 1980; Statistical Abstract* (annual).
Lesotho. *Annual Statistical Bulletin; 1976 Population Census Report.*
Liberia. *Area Handbook for Liberia* (1972); *Economic Survey* (annual); *1974 Census of Population and Housing.*
Libya. *External Trade Statistics* (annual); *The Five-Year Development Plan 1981–85; Libya Population Census, 1973; Statistical Abstract for Libya* (annual).
Liechtenstein. *Statistisches Jahrbuch; Volkszählung, 2 Dezember 1980* (Census of Population).
Luxembourg. *Annuaire statistique; Bulletin du STATEC* (monthly); *Recensement général de la population du 31 mars 1981.*

Macau. *Anuário Estatístico; Comercio Externo* (annual); *Inquerito Industrial* (annual).
Madagascar. *Recensement général de la population et des habitats, 1975; Situation économique* (annual).
Malawi. *Area Handbook for Malawi* (1975); *Malawi Population Census, 1977; Malawi Statistical Yearbook; Malawi Yearbook.*
Malaysia. *Fourth Malaysia Plan, 1981–1985; Malaysia: A Country Profile* (1979); *Malaysian Annual Statistical Bulletin; 1980 Population and Housing Census.*
Maldives. *Population and Housing Census, 1985, Preliminary Results; Statistical Yearbook.*
Mali. *Annuaire statistique du Mali; Recensement de la population, 1–16 décembre 1976.*
Malta. *Annual Abstract of Statistics; Census of Agriculture* (annual); *Census of Industrial Production* (annual); *Census of Production* (annual); *Malta Trade Statistics* (quarterly).
Martinique. *Annuaire statistique de la Martinique; Bulletin de statistique* (quarterly); *Comptes économiques de la Martinique* (irreg.); *Recensement de la population dans les départements d'outre-mer, 9 mars 1982—Martinique.*
Mauritania. *Area Handbook for Mauritania* (1972).
Mauritius. *Bi-annual Digest of Statistics; 1980–1982 Two-Year Plan for Economic and Social Development.*
Mayotte. *Recensement général de la population, 1978.*
Mexico. *Anuario estadístico; X Censo general de población y vivienda, 1980.*
Mongolia. *Mongolia in Figures, 1981* (irreg.); *National Economy of the MPR, 1921–81* (1981).
Montserrat. *Caribbean Population Census, May 12, 1980; Statistical Digest* (annual).
Morocco. *Annuaire statistique du Maroc; Economic and Social Development Report, 1981; Morocco: A Country Study* (1978); *Recensement général de la population et de l'habitat de 1982.*
Mozambique. *Anuário Estatístico; Informação Estatística* (1980); *Moçambique Informação Estatística* (annual); *Mozambique: A Country Study* (1985); *1º Recenseamento Geral da População, 1980.*
Nepal. *Census of Manufacturing Establishments, 1976–1977; Population of Nepal* (ESCAP; Country Monograph Series No. 6 [1980]); *The Sixth Plan (1980–85); Statistical Pocket Book* (irreg.).
Netherlands, The. *Landbouwcijfers* (Agricultural Data [annual]); *Maandstatistiek van de buitenlandse handel per goederensoort* (Foreign Trade by Goods [annual]); *Statistical Yearbook of the Netherlands; 14e Algemene volkstelling, 28 februari 1971* (14th General Population Census).
Netherlands Antilles. *Eerste Algemene Volks- en Woningtelling Nederlandse Antillen* (1972); *Statistisch jaarboek* (Statistical Yearbook).
New Caledonia. *Annuaire statistique; Enquête socio-économique, 1980–1981; Recensement général de la population, 1976; La Situation démographique en 1980.*
New Zealand. *New Zealand Census of Population and Dwellings, 1981; New Zealand Official Yearbook.*
Nicaragua. *Anuario estadístico; Censos nacionales, 1971; Nicaragua: A Country Study* (1982).
Niger. *Annuaire statistique; Données de base* (1979).
Nigeria. *Annual Abstract of Statistics; Fourth National Development Plan* (1981); *Nigeria: A Country Study* (1981).
Niue. *Abstract of Statistics* (annual); *Census of Population and Housing, 1976; Niue National Development Plan, 1980–1985.*
Norfolk Island. *Annual Report; Census of Population and Housing, 30 June 1981.*
Norway. *Folke- og boligtelling 1980* (Population and Housing Census); *Industristatistikk* (annual); *Statistisk årsbok* (Statistical Yearbook).
Oman. *Statistical Year Book; The Second Five-Year Plan of Development, 1981–1985.*
Pacific Islands, Trust Territory of the. *Report of the Trusteeship Council to the Security Council on the Trust Territory of the Pacific Islands* (annual); *Report to the United Nations* (annual).
Pakistan. *Economic Survey* (annual); *Pakistan Year Book; Pakistan Statistical Yearbook; Population Census of Pakistan, 1981; Some Socio-Economic Trends* (annual); *10 Years of Pakistan in Statistics, 1972–1982* (1983).
Panama. *Indicadores económicos y sociales* (annual); *Octavo censo de población: Cuarto censo de vivienda, 11 de mayo de 1980; Panama en cifras* (annual); *Situacion económica: Comercio exterior* (annual); *Situacion económica: Cuentas nacionales* (annual); *Situacion económica: Industria* (annual).
Papua New Guinea. *Abstract of Statistics* (quarterly); *National Accounts Statistics—Statistical Bulletin* (quarterly); *Papua New Guinea: Selected Development Issues* (A World Bank Country Study [1982]); *Population of Papua New Guinea* (ESCAP; Country Monograph Series No. 7.2 [1982]); *Rural Industries* (annual); *Summary of Statistics* (annual); *1980 National Population Census.*
Paraguay. *Anuario estadístico del Paraguay; Censo nacional de población y viviendo, 1982.*
Peru. *Censos nacionales; VIII de población: III de vivienda, 12 de julio de 1981; Compendio estadístico* (1982); *Informe estadístico* (annual); *Peru: A Country Study* (1980).
Philippines. *Philippine Statistical Yearbook; Philippine Yearbook; 1980 Census of Population.*
Poland. *Narodowy spis powszechny z dnia 7 XII 1978 r.* (Census of Population); *Poland: A Country Study* (1984); *Rocznik statystyczny* (Statistical Yearbook).
Portugal. *Anuário Estatístico; Estatística Agricolas* (annual); *Estatísticas do Comercio Externo* (annual); *Estatísticas Demograficas* (annual); *Estatísticas Industriais* (annual); *Estatísticas Monetarias e Financeiras* (annual); *Recenseamento Agricola, 1979; XII Recenseamento Geral da População: II Recenseamento Geral da Habitação, 1981.*
Puerto Rico. *Anuario estadístico; Compendio estadísticas sociales* (annual); *Informe económico al gobernador* (Economic Report to the Governor [annual]); *1980 Census of Population* (U.S.).
Qatar. *Economic Survey of Qatar* (annual); *Qatar Year Book.*
Réunion. *Annuaire statistique de la Réunion; Comptes économiques de la Réunion* (irreg.); *Recensement général de la population en 1974: Départements d'outre-mer—Réunion.*
Romania. *Anuarul statistic al Republicii Socialiste România; Recensămîntul populaţiei şi al locuinţelor, din 5 ianuarie 1977; Romania Yearbook.*
St. Christopher and Nevis. *Annual Digest of Statistics.*
St. Lucia. *Annual Statistical Digest.*
St. Pierre and Miquelon. *Résultats du recensement de la population dans les départements d'outre-mer, 9 mars 1982.*
St. Vincent and the Grenadines. *Digest of Statistics* (annual).
San Marino. *Annuario statistico, 1972–1980* (4 vol.); *3 Censimento generale dell agricoltura* (1977); *5 Censimento generale della popolazione* (1979).
Saudi Arabia. *Saudi Arabia: A Country Study* (1985); *The Statistical Indicator* (annual); *Statistical Summary* (Saudi Arabian Monetary Agency [annual]); Statistical Year Book.
Senegal. *Le Sénégal en chiffres* (annual); *Situation économique* (annual).
Seychelles. *National Development Plan, 1982–86; Statistical Abstract* (annual); *1977 Census Report.*
Singapore. *Census of Population, 1980; Economic and Social Statistics, 1960–1982; Economic Survey of Singapore* (annual); *Report on the Census of Industrial Production, 1981; Report on the Survey of Services, 1980; Singapore Yearbook; Yearbook of Statistics Singapore.*
Solomon Islands. *Statistical Yearbook.*
Somalia. *Statistical Abstract* (annual).
South Africa. *South Africa: Official Yearbook of the Republic of South Africa; South African Statistics* (biennial).
Spain. *Anuario estadístico; Censo de población de 1981.*
Sri Lanka. *Census of Population and Housing, 1981; Report on the Survey on Manufacturing Industries, 1979; Sri Lanka Year Book; Statistical Pocketbook of the Democratic Socialist Republic of Sri Lanka* (annual).
Swaziland. *Annual Statistical Bulletin; Report on the 1976 Swaziland Population Census.*
Sweden. *Folk- och bostadsräkningen, 1980* (Population and Housing Census); *Jorbruks-statistisk årsbok* (Yearbook of Agricultural Statistics); *Statistisk årsbok för Sverige* (Statistical Abstract of Sweden [annual]).
Switzerland. *Recensement fédéral de la population, 1980; Statistisches Jahrbuch* (Statistical Yearbook).
Syria. *Census of Agriculture, 1981; General Census of Housing and Inhabitants, 1981; Statistical Abstract* (annual).
Taiwan. *Industry of Free China* (monthly); *Social Indicators of the Republic of China* (1981); *Statistical Abstract* (annual); *Statistical Yearbook of the Republic of China; Taiwan Statistical Data Book* (annual); *Yearbook of Labor Statistics; 1980 Census of Population and Housing.*
Tanzania. *Tanzania Statistical Abstract* (annual); *1978 Population Census.*
Thailand. *Report of the Census of Business Trade and Services, 1981; Foreign Trade Statistics* (monthly); *Report of the 1978 Industrial Census; Report of the Labor Force Survey: Whole Kingdom* (quarterly); *Statistical Handbook of Thailand* (annual); *Statistical Yearbook; 1980 Population and Housing Census.*
Togo. *Annuaire statistique; Plan de développement économique & social, 1981–1985; Recensement général de la population, 1970.*
Tokelau. *Census of Population, 1981; Report of the Administrator of Tokelau for the Year Ended: 31 March 19*** (annual).
Trinidad and Tobago. *Population Census, 1980; Trinidad and Tobago Statistical Pocket Digest* (annual).
Tunisia. *Annuaire statistique de la Tunisie; Recensement général de la population et des logements, 30 mars 1984.*
Turkey. *Diş Ticaret İstatistikleri* (Annual Foreign Trade Statistics); *Genel Sanayi ve İşyerleri Sayımı* (Census of Industry and Business Establishments [1980]); *Genel Nüfus Sayımı, 12. 10. 1980* (Census of Population); *Genel Tarım Sayımı, 1980* (Census of Agriculture); *İnşaat İstatistikleni* (Construction Statistics [annual]); *Türkiye İstatistik Yilliği* (Statistical Yearbook of Turkey); *Tarımsal Yapi ve Üretim* (Agricultural Structure and Production [annual]).
Tuvalu. *Abstract of Statistics* (annual); *Census of the Population, 1979.*
Union of Soviet Socialist Republics. *Narodnoye Khozyaystvo SSSR* (National Economy of the U.S.S.R. [annual]).
United Arab Emirates. *Statistical Yearbook.*
United Kingdom. *Agricultural Statistics United Kingdom* (annual); *Annual Abstract of Statistics; Britain: An Official Handbook* (annual); *National Income and Expenditure* (annual); *Census 1981; Overseas Trade Statistics of the United Kingdom* (annual); *Report on the Census of Production: Summary Tables* (annual).
United States. *Agricultural Statistics* (annual); *Annual Energy Review; Current Population Reports* (Series P-20, P-23, P-25, P-26, P-27, P-28, P-60); *Digest of Education Statistics* (annual); *Minerals Yearbook* (3 vol.; annual); *National Transportation Statistics* (annual); *Statistical Abstract* (annual); *U.S. Exports: SIC-Based Products* (annual); *U.S. Imports: SIC-Based Products* (annual); *Vital and Health Statistics* (series 1–20); *1982 Census of Construction Industries; 1982 Census of Manufacturing; 1982 Census of Mineral Industries; 1982 Census of Retail Trade; 1982 Census of Wholesale Trade; 1982 Census of Agriculture; 1980 Census of Population and Housing.*
Vanuatu. *Overseas Trade* (annual); *Recensement de la population, 1979; Statistical Indicators* (quarterly).
Venezuela. *Anuario estadístico; Censo agropecuario, 1971; Encuesta de hogares por muestreo* (annual); *Encuesta industrial* (annual); *IX Censo general de población y vivienda, 20 de octubre 1981.*
Virgin Islands of the United States. *Annual Report; 1980 Census of Population* (U.S.).
West Bank. *Judaea, Samaria, and Gaza Area Statistics Quarterly; Palestinian Statistical Abstract* (annual).
Western Samoa. *Annual Statistical Abstract; Census of Population and Housing, 1976.*
Yemen Arab Republic. *The Housing and Population Census, February 1975; Statistical Year Book.*
Yugoslavia. *Popis stanovištva i stanova od 31. marta 1981* (Census of Population and Housing as of March 31, 1981); *Statistički godišnjak Jugoslavije* (Statistical Yearbook of Yugoslavia); *Yugoslavia: A Country Study* (1982).
Zaire. *Annuaire statistique; Plan Mobutu: Programme de relance économique, 1979–1981 (Fiches des projects; Transport; Education et santé)* (3 vol.).
Zambia. *Census of Industrial Production, 1974; Household Budget Survey, 1974–1975; Monthly Digest of Statistics; Third National Development Plan, 1979–83; Zambia in Figures* (1980); *1980 Census of Population and Housing.*
Zimbabwe. *Quarterly Digest of Statistics; Zimbabwe: A Country Study* (1983).

A. H. Robins / Anders 961

Index

This index covers both *Britannica Book of the Year* (cumulative for ten years) and *Britannica World Data.*

Entries in black type are titles of articles in the *Book of the Year;* an accompanying page number in light type shows where the article appears in this volume. Numbers in black type indicate the years in which such an article appears. For example, "Archaeology 164; 85:165. *See* Archaeology 84–77" indicates that the article "Archaeology" appeared every year from 1977 through 1984, and may be found in alphabetical order in each of those editions. The reference for 1985 is followed by a page number.

Indented entries in light type that follow black type article titles refer by page number to other places in the text where the subject of the article is discussed. Light type entries that are not indented refer by page number to subjects which are not themselves article titles. Names of people covered in biographies and obituaries are listed as references to the sections **"Biographies"** and **"Obituaries"** within the article "People of the Year"; in those sections the names appear in alphabetical order. References to illustrations are by page number, and are preceded by the abbreviation "il."

The index uses word-by-word alphabetization (treating a word as one or more characters separated by a space from the next word). Names beginning with "Mc" and "Mac" are alphabetized as "Mac"; "St." is treated as "Saint."

A

A. H. Robins (U.S. Co.)
Dalkon Shield settlement 183
Aalto, Hugo Alvar Henrik: *see* **Obituaries 77**
Abbado, Claudio: *see* **Biographies 80**
Abbas, Abul
Italy 529
Abbey Theatre (Ire.)
Irish drama 437
Abboud, Albert Robert: *see* **Biographies 81**
ABC: *see* American Broadcasting Cos.
"Abdallah" (ballet)
dance 189, il.
Abdallah, Ahmed
government reshuffle 458
Abdul-Jabbar, Kareem
basketball 386, il.
Abdullah, Sheikh Muhammad: *see* **Obituaries 83**
Abe, Shintaro
Japanese politics 498
Abelin, Pierre: *see* **Obituaries 78**
Aborigine
nuclear tests 591
special education 230
abortion
religious views 362
Spanish controversy 535
Abraham, Michael
catalysis studies 179
Abrahams, Harold Maurice: *see* **Obituaries 79**
Abramsky, Yehezkiel: *see* **Obituaries 77**
Abrasimov, Petr
Soviet-Japanese relations 499
Abruzzo, Anderson, and Newman: *see* **Biographies 79**
Abruzzo, Ben: *see* **Obituaries 86**
ABT: *see* American Ballet Theatre
Abu Nidal (Pal. leader)
EgyptAir hijacking 479
"Accidental Tourist, The" (Tyler)
literature 306
Acción Democrática, *or* AD (Venez. party)
Venezuela 588
Acción Popular, *or* AP (Peruvian party)
politics 585
Ace, Goodman: *see* **Obituaries 83**
ACGB: *see* Arts Council of Great Britain
Acheampong, Ignatius Kutu: *see* **Obituaries 80**
"Achille Lauro" (It. ship)
Egypt's involvement 482
hijacking 184; 479
international law 291
Italian politics 529
acid rain
environmental issue 242, 243
Acland, Sir Hugh John Dyke: *see* **Obituaries 82**
ACM: *see* Anti-Cult Movement
acquired immune deficiency syndrome, *or* AIDS
clinical trials 179
feline leukemia 259
prisons 188
statistics 254
U.S.
education controversy 228
statistics 562
Action Groups to Halt Advertising and Sponsorship of Tobacco, *or* AGHAST
campaign strategy 180
Acton, Loren il. 376
ACTU: *see* Australian Council of Trade Unions
AD (Venez. party): *see* Acción Democrática
Adair, Paul Neal: *see* **Biographies 78**
Adams, Ansel Easton: *see* **Obituaries 85**
Adams, Harriet Stratemeyer: *see* **Obituaries 83**
Adams, Sir John Bertram: *see* **Obituaries 85**
Adams, John Michael Geoffrey Manningham: *see* **Obituaries 86**
Adams, Lynn
racquetball 415
Adamson, Joy (Joy-Friederike Victoria Gessner): *see* **Obituaries 81**
Adelsohn, Ulf
political policies 535
adenosine diphosphate, *or* ADP
hemorrhagic shock 300
adenosine monophosphate, *or* AMP
hemorrhagic shock 300
adenosine triphosphate, *or* ATP
hemorrhagic shock 299
Admiral's Cup
sailing 418
adolescence
pregnancy rates 348
"Adoration of the Magi, The" (painting)
art sales 173
Adoula, Cyrille: *see* **Obituaries 79**
ADP: *see* adenosine diphosphate
ADRA: *see* Adventist Development and Relief Agency
Adrian, Edgar Douglas Adrian, 1st Baron, of Cambridge: *see* **Obituaries 78**
ADS: *see* Senegalese Democratic Alliance
advanced gas-cooled reactor, *or* AGR
improvements 234
Advanced Tactical Fighter, *or* ATF
progress 266
Adventist Development and Relief Agency, *or* ADRA
foreign aid 365
advertising 265
art sales 173
"Advertising Age" (mag.)
advertising 265
AEG-Telefunken AG, *or* AEG (W.Ger. Co.)
corporate strategy 272
aerial sports 380; **85**:374. *See* **Aerial Sports 84–77**
aerospace 265
Air India explosion 504
fire blocking materials 283
transportation 442
travel safety 183
Aethelwold, St.
art exhibitions 172
AFCO: *see* Australian Federation of Consumer Organizations
Afghanistan 502; **85**:506. *See* **Afghanistan 84–77**
Soviet Union 26; 550
United Nations 448
see also WORLD DATA
African affairs 453; **85**:456. *See* **African Affairs 84–77**
agriculture 150
birth and death statistics 348
dependent states 598
entomology 297
famine aid 363
human rights 261
hydrology 199
Live Aid concert 342
military affairs 329
refugees 351
United Nations 449
world affairs 446
see also individual countries by name
"African Muse, The" (Moore) **82**
African National Congress, *or* ANC
Botswana 456
race relations 360
South Africa 468, 472
African Unity, Organization of, *or* OAU
Moroccan withdrawal 488
summit meeting 453
"Africa's Awakening Giant" (Arnold) **83**
"Africa's Hungry Millions" (Legum) **85**
Afro-Asian Conference
commemoration 510
"After Hours" (film) 334
"Aftermath of Angola, The" (Davidson) **77**
"Again the Summer Agony" (Griffiths) **84**
Agca, Mehmet Ali: *see* **Biographies 84**
trial 185; 530
"Age of Caravaggio, The"
art exhibitions 171
Ager, Milton: *see* **Obituaries 80**
Aggett, Neil Hutchin: *see* **Obituaries 83**
AGHAST: *see* Action Groups to Halt Advertising and Sponsorship of Tobacco
AGR: *see* advanced gas-cooled reactor
Agriculture and Food Supplies 150; **85**:150. *See* **Agriculture and Food Supplies 84–77.** *See* **Fisheries 84–77.** *See* **Food Processing 84–77**
plant growth regulators 298
see also WORLD DATA *and* individual countries by name
Agriculture, Fisheries, and Food, Ministry of (U.K.)
sewage treatment 245
Agt, Andreas Antonius Maria van: *see* **Biographies 79**
Aguilar v. Felton (law case)
decision 290
Ahlers, Conrad: *see* **Obituaries 81**
Ahmed, Fakhruddin Ali: *see* **Obituaries 78**
Ahmed Salah
marathon running 427
Ahn, Philip: *see* **Obituaries 79**
Ahrens, T. J.
geological experiments 197
Ahrweiler, Hélène: *see* **Biographies 77**
AIDS: *see* acquired immune deficiency syndrome
AIDS-related complex, *or* ARC
statistics 254
Aiken, George David: *see* **Obituaries 85**
Ailey, Alvin
modern dance 190
Ailuropoda melanoleuca: *see* giant panda
Air India
disaster 442
air pollution
environment 246
air transportation: *see* aerospace
Airbus 266
Aitken, Sir John William Maxwell: *see* **Obituaries 86**
Akali Dal (Sikh org.)
India 368
negotiations 504
Akhromeyev, Sergey: *see* **Biographies 85**
Akuffo, Fred W. K.: *see* **Obituaries 80.** *See* **Biographies 79**
ALA: *see* American Library Association
Alaska (state, U.S.) 602
"Alaska" (U.S. submarine) il. 329
Alaska National Interests Lands Conservation Act of 1980
petroleum exploration 602
Alaska Native Review Commission
native rights 602
Albania 541; **85**:547. *See* **Albania 84–77**
Yugoslavia 551
see also WORLD DATA
Albers, Josef: *see* **Obituaries 77**
Alberta (prov., Can.)
provincial politics 555
Albertson, Jack: *see* **Obituaries 82**
Alboreto, Michele
automobile racing 381
Albright, Ivan Le Lorraine: *see* **Obituaries 84**
Alburt, Lev
chess 393
alcoholism
mental health studies 257
"Alcyone" (ship)
fisheries 161
Alda, Alan: *see* **Biographies 80**
Aldrich, Robert: *see* **Obituaries 84**
Aleixandre, Vicente: *see* **Obituaries 85**
Alekseyef, Aleksandr: *see* **Obituaries 83**
Alemán, Miguel: *see* **Obituaries 84**
Alexander, Eben Roy: *see* **Obituaries 79**
Alexander, Kelly Miller Sr.: *see* **Obituaries 86**
Alexander, Lincoln: *see* **Biographies 86**
Alexandrovitch, Prince Andrew: *see* **Obituaries 82**
Alfonsín, Raúl: *see* **Biographies 84**
Argentina 569
Latin-American affairs 566
Algeria 479; **85**:483. *See* **Algeria 84–77**
dam projects 239
human rights 261
natural gas 235
petroleum 237
Tunisia 479
see also WORLD DATA
Ali, Kamal Hassan
resignation 481
Ali, Muhammad: *see* **Biographies 79**
Alia, Queen of Jordan (Alia Baha Eddin Toukan): *see* **Obituaries 78**
Alia, Ramiz: *see* **Biographies 86**
Albanian politics 541
Alianza Popular Revolucionaria Americana, *or* APRA (Peruvian party)
politics 585
Alice, Princess (Alice Mary Victoria Augusta Pauline), Countess of Aliyev, Geidar A.
Soviet Union 27
All-America Roses (U.S. org.)
awards 253
All People's Congress, *or* APC (S.L. party)
convention 467
Allan of Kilmahew, Robert Alexander Allan, Baron: *see* **Obituaries 80**
Allen, James Browning: *see* **Obituaries 79**
Allen, Marcus
football 402
Allen, William Ernest Chesney: *see* **Obituaries 83**
Allen, Woody: *see* **Biographies 79**
Allen of Fallowfield, Alfred Walter Henry Allen: *see* **Obituaries 86**
Allen-Williams, David
sailing 417
Allon, Yigal: *see* **Obituaries 81**
allopurinol
hemorrhagic shock 300
"Along with Youth: Hemingway, the Early Years" (Griffin)
study 308
ALP: *see* Australian Labor Party
alpine racing
skiing 419
Alpine World Cup
skiing 419
Alston, Walter Emmons: *see* **Obituaries 85**
aluminum 331
Alusuisse (Swiss Co.)
Icelandic dispute 527
Alvarado, Naty
handball 405
Alvarez Armelino, Gregorio Conrado: *see* **Biographies 82**
Alvin, Juliette: *see* **Obituaries 83**
"Amadeus" (film)
motion pictures 334
amateur radio 436
Amal (Shi'ah militia)
hijack incident 486
Amalrik, Andrey Alekseyevich: *see* **Obituaries 81.** *See* **Biographies 77**
Amaral, Diogo Freitas
Portuguese elections 533
"Amateur Gardening" (Br. mag.)
gardening 253
Amaury, Emilien: *see* **Obituaries 78**
Amba-Bishoi (monastery, Egy.)
Coptic Church 367
Amdahl Corp. (Japan)
information systems 287
Amendola, Giorgio: *see* **Obituaries 81**
"America Enters the World: A People's History of the Progressive Era and World War I" (Smith)
critical decades 307
American Association of Nurserymen
market growth 253
American Ballet Theatre, *or* ABT
new productions 189
American Baptist Churches
meeting 363
American Broadcasting Cos., *or* ABC
Capital Cities Communications Inc. 432; 560
takeovers (special report) 263
American Federation of Jazz Societies
jazz 342
American Florists, Society of
greenery survey 253
"American Ingenuity—Does It Still Thrive?" (Ruzic) **81**
American League
baseball 384
American Library Association, *or* ALA
membership 294
American Motors Corp.
declining sales 267
American Samoa
progress 600
American Stock Exchange, *or* AMEX
trading volume 222
American Telephone and Telegraph Company, *or* AT&T
deregulation problems 281
Information Systems group 285
"American Violence and Public Policy" (study)
crime rates 185
America's Cup
sailing 418
"America's Litigious Society" (Beckwith) **78**
Amersham General Hospital (Bucks., U.K.)
mental health study 257
AMEX: *see* American Stock Exchange
Amiga
information systems 287
Amman (Jor.)
arms deal 485
Amnesty International
execution statistics 187
human rights campaigns 261
Peru 585
Uganda 474
Amon Carter Museum (U.S.)
photography exhibit 345
Amoroso, Emmanuel Ciprian: *see* **Obituaries 83**
Amory, Derick Heathcoat Amory, 1st Viscount: *see* **Obituaries 82**
Amouzegar, Jamshid: *see* **Biographies 78**
AMP: *see* adenosine monophosphate
Amphipithecus mogaungensis
discovery 296, il.
analytical chemistry 179
ANC: *see* African National Congress
anchoveta
El Niño disaster 160
Anda, Geza: *see* **Obituaries 77**
Andean Group (Lat.Am.)
economics 566
Anders, Edward
geological studies 197

G

H

Ouagadougou / Pincay 981

Ouagadougou (Burkina Faso)
arrests 456
Oudin, Jacques: *see* **Obituaries 86**
Oueddei, Goukouni: *see* **Biographies 80**
Chadian politics 457
Libya 488
Ouko, Robert
Kenya 462
Ould Salek, Mustafa: *see* **Biographies 79**
"Our Changing Cities" (Whittingham) **82**
"Our Far Out Neighbours" (Stone) **80**
"Out of Africa" (film)
motion pictures 334
"Outlook for Primary Commodities, 1984 to 1995, The" (study)
mining forecast 330
Ovando, Candía, Alfredo: *see* **Obituaries 83**
"Overstuffed Cellblocks" (Whittingham) **84**
Ovett, Steve: *see* **Biographies 81**
Owen, David Anthony Llewellyn: *see* **Biographies 78**
Owen, Johnny: *see* **Obituaries 81**
Owens, Jesse (James Cleveland Owens): *see* **Obituaries 81**
Owings, Nathaniel Alexander: *see* **Obituaries 85**
Oxford University (U.K.)
β-thalassemia identification 256
rowing championship 417
oxidative phosphorylation
hemorrhagic shock 300
oxygen
hemorrhagic shock 299
Oxyura leucocephala: *see* white-headed duck
Ozal, Turgut: *see* **Biographies 85**
Saudi Arabia visit 490
Turkish affairs 492
Ozawa, Seiji: *see* **Biographies 79**
ozone layer
chlorofluorocarbon threat 242, 244
Ozyornaya (cave, U.S.S.R.)
spelunking 420

P

PA Technology (U.S. Co.)
laboratory design 238
Paasio, Rafael: *see* **Obituaries 81**
Pacific Economic and Cultural Enclave, *or* PEACE
internationalism 15
Pacific Economic Cooperation Conference
Pacific collaboration 15
Pacific Fleet (U.S.S.R.)
defense buildup 16
Packer, Joy: *see* **Obituaries 78**
Packer, Kerry Francis Bullmore: *see* **Biographies 78**
"PAC's-The New Force in Politics" (Beckwith) **83**
Page, Sir Denys Lionel: *see* **Obituaries 79**
Page, George: *see* **Biographies 82**
Pagnani, Andreina: *see* **Obituaries 82**
Paharpur (Bangla.)
historic preservation campaign 259
Paige, Leroy Robert: *see* **Obituaries 83**
Paige, Stephone
U.S. football 402
Painshill (Surrey, U.K.)
garden restoration 253
Paintmakers Association of Great Britain (U.K.)
lead use ban 248
paints and varnishes 278
Pairin Kitingan, Joseph
Malaysian politics 512
"Paix et la folie, La" (Péloquin)
provocative style 310
Pakistan 506; **85**:512. *See* **Pakistan 84–77**
India 505
Islamic principles 369
military affairs 325
see also WORLD DATA
Pakistan People's Party, *or* PPP
politics 506
Paklin, Igor
track 426
Pal, George: *see* **Obituaries 81**
Palar, Lambertus Nicodemus: *see* **Obituaries 82**
Palau, Republic of, *or* Republic of Belau
policies 600
Palazzo dello Sport stadium (Milan, It.)
damage 239
Paleckis, Justas: *see* **Obituaries 81**
Palestine Liberation Front, *or* PLF
"Achille Lauro" hijack 479, 529
Palestine Liberation Organization, *or* PLO
Egypt's position 482
Israel 447, 484
Jordanian partnership 485
peace efforts 477
Palewski, Gaston: *see* **Obituaries 85**
Palme, Sven Olof Joachim: *see* **Biographies 83**
labour mediation 289
political policies 535
Palmer, Leonard Robert: *see* **Obituaries 85**
Pálsson, Thorsteinn
Iceland 527
Palumbo, Peter
architectural project 167
PAN (Mex.): *see* Partido de Acción Nacional
Pan-American Championship
baseball 385
Pan Pacific meet (Japan)
swimming 421
Panagoulis, Alexandros: *see* **Obituaries 77**
Panama 584; **85**:579. *See* **Panama 84–77**
see also WORLD DATA
pancasila
Indonesia's domestic affairs 510
Panhellenic Socialist Movement, *or* Pasok (Gr. party)
policies 526
Pani Panchayat (Indian party)
strategy 248
PAP (Sing.): *see* People's Action Party
Papandreou, Andreas: *see* **Biographies 82**
political policies 526
Papua New Guinea 595; **85**:601. *See* **Papua New Guinea 84–77**
Oceanian affairs 589
see also WORLD DATA
Papuan python, *or* Liasis papuanus
captive breeding 178
Paradox data base management system
processing advances 288
Paraguay 585; **85**:588. *See* **Paraguay 84–77**
West German relations 526
see also WORLD DATA
Paray, Paul: *see* **Obituaries 80**
"Parfüm, Das" (Süskind)
success 311
Paringaux, Bernard
dioxin waste trial 248
Paris Bourse
trading volume 223
Park Chung Hee: *see* **Obituaries 80**
Park Joo Bong
badminton 383
Park Tong Sun: *see* **Biographies 78**
Parker, Alan: *see* **Biographies 77**
Parker, Dave
baseball 385
Parker, Sir Roger Jocelyn (Mr. Justice Parker): *see* **Biographies 79**
Parkfield (Calif., U.S.)
earthquake prediction 198
Parma, Prince Xavier of Bourbon, duke of: *see* **Obituaries 78**
Parodi, Alexandre: *see* **Obituaries 80**
Parrington, Francis Rex: *see* **Obituaries 82**
Parrot, André: *see* **Obituaries 81**
Parrott, Sir Cecil Cuthbert: *see* **Obituaries 85**
Parry, Clive: *see* **Obituaries 83**
Parry, Sir Thomas: *see* **Obituaries 86**
Parsons, Talcott: *see* **Obituaries 80**
Partai Bersatu Sabah (Mal.): *see* Sabah United Party
Partai Islam, *or* PAS (Mal.)
Malaysian politics 512
Parti Québecois, *or* PQ (Can.)
Quebec politics 554
Partido Comunista Español, *or* PCE (Sp.)
Spanish politics 534
Partido de Acción Nacional, *or* PAN (Mex.)
political status 582
Partido Movimento Democratico Brasileiro: *see* Brazilian Democratic Movement Party
Partido Revolucionario Institucional, *or* PRI (Mex.)
political status 582
Parton, Dolly: *see* **Biographies 79**
Partridge, Eric Honeywood: *see* **Obituaries 80**
Party of God: *see* Hizbollah
PAS (Mal.): *see* Partai Islam
Pascal, Pierre: *see* **Obituaries 84**
Pasok (Gr.): *see* Panhellenic Socialist Movement
"Passage to India, The" (film)
fashion influence 251
Pastora Gómez, Edén: *see* **Biographies 85**
Pathfinders (rel. org.)
Seventh-day Adventist Church 365
Patman, John William Wright: *see* **Obituaries 77**
Patocka, Jan: *see* **Obituaries 78**
Patria Libre (El Sal. party)
establishment 579
Patrick, Nigel: *see* **Obituaries 82**
Patriotic Movement for National Renaissance, *or* PRON (Pol.)
election list 545
Patterson, William Allan: *see* **Obituaries 81**
Paul, Alice: *see* **Obituaries 78**
Paul VI (Giovanni Battista Montini): *see* **Obituaries 79**
Paul Francis Webster collection
art sale 173
Paul of Yugoslavia, Prince: *see* **Obituaries 77**
Paull, C. K.
vent community discovery 295
Pavarotti, Luciano: *see* **Biographies 81**
Pawley, Howard: *see* **Biographies 83**
provincial politics 555
Payne, the Rev. Ernest Alexander: *see* **Obituaries 81**
Paynter, Thomas William: *see* **Obituaries 85**
Payton, Walter: *see* **Biographies 77**
football record 402
Paz, Alberto Gainza: *see* **Obituaries 78**
Paz Estenssoro, Víctor: *see* **Biographies 86**
election 572
PBS: *see* Public Broadcasting Service
PBS (Mal.): *see* Sabah United Party
PC: *see* personal computer
PC (Fr.): *see* Communist Party
PCB: *see* polychlorinated biphenyl
PCE (Sp.): *see* Partido Comunista Español
PDS (Braz.): *see* Social Democratic Party
PEACE: *see* Pacific Economic and Cultural Enclave
Peacock, Andrew Sharp: *see* **Biographies 82**
Australian politics 591
Peak Cavern (cave, U.K.)
spelunking 420
peanut
PGRs effects 298
Pebbles (horse) 405
Peccei, Aurelio: *see* **Obituaries 85**
Peck, Gregg il. 415
Peckford, Alfred Brian: *see* **Biographies 80**
Newfoundland policies 552
Peckinpah, Sam (David Samuel Peckinpah): *see* **Obituaries 85**
"Pee-Wee's Big Adventure" (film)
motion pictures 334
Peer, Lyndon Arthur: *see* **Obituaries 78**
Peerce, Jan (Jacob Pincus Perlemuth): *see* **Obituaries 85**
Peete, Calvin
golf 403
"Pegasus Bridge: June 6, 1944" (Ambrose)
World War II study 307
Pei, I. M.: *see* **Biographies 79**
Pei, Mario Andrew: *see* **Obituaries 79**
Pekala, Leszek
Popieluszko trial 546
Peking (China): *see* Beijing
Pelczynski, Tadeusz: *see* **Obituaries 86**
Pelletier, Monique: *see* **Biographies 79**
Pellicer, Camara Carlos: *see* **Obituaries 78**
Pelshe, Arvid Yanovich: *see* **Obituaries 84**
Pelton, Ronald
U.S. security 561
Pendleton, Clarence: *see* **Biographies 86**
Pène du Bois, Raoul, *or* Raoul-Henri-Charles Pène du Bois: *see* **Obituaries 86**
Penfield, Wilder Graves: *see* **Obituaries 77**
Peng Zhen, *or* P'eng Chen: *see* **Biographies 84**
Penikett, Tony
Yukon Territory politics 555
Penn Nouth, Samdech: *see* **Obituaries 86**
Pennsylvania Ballet
new productions 189
Pennsylvania State University Medical Center (U.S.)
artificial heart research 255
penology: *see* prisons and penology
Penrose, Sir Roland Algernon: *see* **Obituaries 85**
Penske, Roger
automobile racing 382
Pentecostal Churches
religious affairs 364
People of 1985:89; **85**:89. *See* **People of the Year 84–77**
People's Action Party, *or* PAP (Sing. party)
Singapore politics 514
People's Temple
cults (special report) 371
Pepper, Art: *see* **Obituaries 83**
Pepper, Claude Denson: *see* **Biographies 84**
Pepsi Cola Co. (U.S.)
ad campaign 265
Percival, Edgar Wikner: *see* **Obituaries 85**
Père David's deer, *or* Elaphurus davidianus
reintroduction projects 177
Pereira, Aristide
Cape Verde politics 457
Pereira, William Leonard: *see* **Obituaries 86**
Perelman, Sidney Joseph: *see* **Obituaries 80**
Peres, Shimon: *see* **Biographies 85**
economic program 289
Israel 483
Middle Eastern affairs 478, 447
Peretz, Yitzhak
Israel 484
Pérez, Alan García
Peruvian politics 585, il. 586
Pérez, Carlos Andrés
Venezuela 588
Pérez Alfonso, Juan Pablo: *see* **Obituaries 80**
Pérez de Cuéllar, Javier: *see* **Biographies 83**
United Nations 447, il. 448
Perham, Dame Margery: *see* **Obituaries 83**
Perkins, Carl Dewey: *see* **Obituaries 85**
Peronists (Arg. party)
Argentina elections 570
Perrealt, Jean-Pierre
modern dance 191
Perriand, Charlotte
art exhibition 170
Perry, William: *see* **Biographies 86**
personal computer, *or* PC
use and market (special report) 286
Pertini, Alessandro: *see* **Biographies 79**
retirement 529
Peru 585; **85**:500. *See* **Peru 84–77**
archaeology 166
democracy (special report) 567
human rights 260
motion pictures 336
see also WORLD DATA
Pesho, Terry
archery 381
Pessoa, Fernando
commemoration 314
pest
entomological studies 296
pesticide
consumer concerns (special report) 182
PET: *see* polyethylene terephthalate
Petersen, William il. 438
Peterson, David: *see* **Biographies 86**
Ontario politics 554
Peterson, Roger Tory: *see* **Biographies 83**
Peterson, Ronnie: *see* **Obituaries 79**
Petit, Roland
ballet 190
Petrehn, John 381
Petri, Elio: *see* **Obituaries 83**
Petrillo, James Caesar: *see* **Obituaries 85**
Petro-Canada
acquisition 553
"Petrodollars and Social Change" (Mansfield) **78**
"Petrodollars on the Prairie" (Ward) **79**
Petroica traversi: *see* black robin
Petroleum Exporting Countries, Organization of, *or* OPEC 236
internal problems 231
Saudi Arabian policy 479, 489
petroleum industry 236
Arctic resources 602
emissions standards 242
production 231
takeover trends (special report) 263
world economy 213
see also individual countries by name
Petrosian, Tigran Vartanovich: *see* **Obituaries 85**
Pettersson, Allan Gustaf: *see* **Obituaries 81**
Peurala, Alice: *see* **Biographies 80**
Pevsner, Sir Nikolaus Bernard Leon: *see* **Obituaries 84**
PFP (S.Af.): *see* Progressive Federal Party
PGI: *see* General Information Program
PGR: *see* plant growth regulator
pharmaceuticals
consumer protection 180
manufacture and marketing 279
Phellinus pomaceus: *see* common wood-rotting fungus
Phelps, Willard
Yukon Territory politics 555
Philadelphia (U.S.)
police firebomb tragedy 187
Philatelic Organizations, Council of (U.S.)
stamp collecting promotion 343
Philately and Numismatics 343; **85**:342. *See* **Philately and Numismatics 84–77**
Philippine crocodile, *or* Crocodylus mindorensis
reintroduction projects 178
Philippines 513; **85**:518. *See* **Philippines 84–77**
global economic role 14
human rights 261
see also WORLD DATA
Phillips, Marjorie Acker: *see* **Obituaries 86**
Phnom Penh regime (Kamp.)
peace negotiations 508
Phoenix (Ariz., U.S.)
architectural designs 169
phosphate rock
production 332
Photography 344; **85**:343. *See* **Photography 84–77**
Phoumi Nosavan: *see* **Obituaries 86**
physical chemistry
research 179
Physics 346; **85**:345. *See* **Physics 84–77**
Piaget, Jean: *see* **Obituaries 81**
Piasecki, Lech
cycling 396
Piatigorsky, Gregor: *see* **Obituaries 77**
Picasso Museum (Paris, Fr.)
opening 338
Piccard, the Rev. Jeanette Ridlon: *see* **Obituaries 82**
Pickens, Slim (Louis Bert Lindley, Jr.): *see* **Obituaries 84**
Pickens, T. Boone, Jr. (Thomas Boone Pickens, Jr.): *see* **Biographies 86**
corporate takeovers (special report) 262
Pickford, Mary: *see* **Obituaries 80**
Pickles, Wilfred: *see* **Obituaries 79**
picoplankton
light absorption 297
"Pictures of the Year" (U.S. phot.)
awards 345
Pidgeon, Walter: *see* **Obituaries 85**
Piedras Negras (Mex.)
political violence 582
Pierce, Samuel R.
urban poverty views (special report) 374
Pierre Saint-Martin (cave, Eur.)
spelunking 420
Pietrasinski, Leszek
Popieluszko trial 546
Pietruszka, Adam
Popieluszko trial 546
Piggott, Lester: *see* **Biographies 78**
horse racing 407
Pignedoli, Sergio Cardinal: *see* **Obituaries 81**
Pilinszky, Janos: *see* **Obituaries 82**
Pilkington, William Henry Pilkington, Baron: *see* **Obituaries 84**
Pillsbury Co. (U.S.)
microwave packaging 162
Pilyugin, Nikolay Alekseyevich: *see* **Obituaries 83**
Pincay, Laffit, Jr.
horse racing 405

Now there's a way to identify all your fine books with flair and style. As part of our continuing service to you, Britannica Home Library Service, Inc. is proud to be able to offer you the fine quality item shown on the next page.

Booklovers will love the heavy-duty personalized embosser. Now you can personalize all your fine books with the mark of distinction, just the way all the fine libraries of the world do.

To order this item, please type or print your name, address and zip code on a plain sheet of paper. (Note special instructions for ordering the embosser). Please send a check or money order only (your money will be refunded in full if you are not delighted) for the full amount of purchase, including postage and handling, to:

Britannica Home Library Service, Inc.
Attn: Yearbook Department
Post Office Box 6137
Chicago, Illinois 60680

IN THE BRITANNICA TRADITION OF QUALITY...

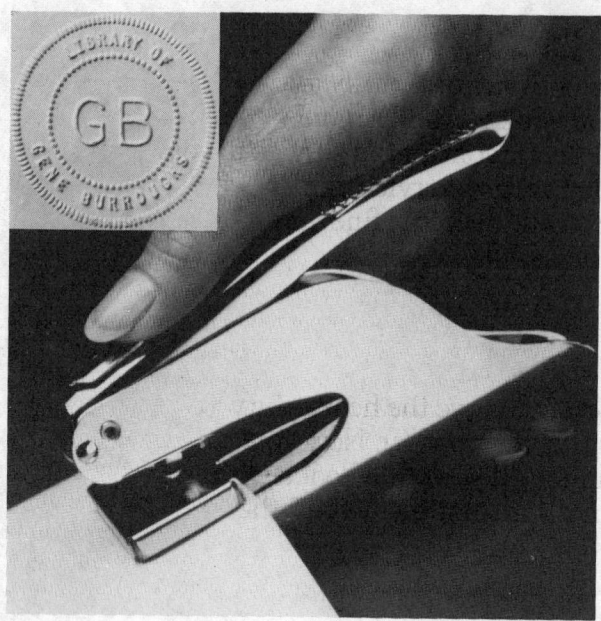

PERSONAL EMBOSSER

A mark of distinction for your fine books. A book embosser just like the ones used in libraries. The 1½″ seal imprints "Library of _____" (with the name of your choice) and up to three centered initials. Please type or print clearly BOTH full name (up to 26 letters including spaces between names) and up to three initials.
Please allow six weeks for delivery.

Just **$20.00**

plus $2.00 shipping and handling

This offer available only in the United States.
Illinois residents please add sales tax

 **Britannica Home Library Service, Inc.**